THE PUBLISHER'S PAGE

Every year we interview a greater number of clients – principal buyers of legal services (usually heads of legal, but often finance directors or chief executives). This year the number exceeds 2000. As a result, more new names have been recommended to us. In particular, we've been told of 'up-and-coming' partners we had not heard of, and we've identified 'associates-to-watch' who have not yet made their mark in the wider legal profession. Other law firms may not have noticed them, but their clients certainly have.

This greater reliance on client interviews has strengthened our research and improved the directory. We shall continue with this approach next year. It has the support of our research auditors, the British Market Research Bureau.

This year we introduce a new category: 'Eminence grise'. It comes at the top of the rankings in sections such as banking and corporate, and provides a niche for those star performers who continue to practise as valuable members of their firms but have cut back on fee-earning. Previously, we didn't know where to put them when they were no longer so visible on deals. We couldn't move them down, and they didn't deserve to be dropped entirely. Some may find the label 'eminence grise' unpalatable, but it was the best we could think of.

Michael Chambers

INTRODUCTION

The research audit and Chambers research team	6	Top UK law firms	14
Best Business Lawyer 2002	10	Law firm overviews	17
Solicitors' charges and remuneration	12	Law firms by size	30

THE LAW FIRMS

SOLICITORS: SPECIALIST AREAS

Administrative & Public Law	41	Crime	250
Advertising & Marketing	50	Debt Recovery	260
Agriculture	53	Defamation	266
Alternative Dispute Resolution	65	E-commerce	276
Arbitration (International)	73	Education	282
Asset Finance	77	Employee Share Schemes	291
including Consumer Finance		Employment	297
Aviation	85	Energy & Natural Resources	334
Banking & Finance	90	Environment	346
Capital Markets	110	EU/Competition	see under Competition/Anti-Trust
including International Debt & Equity,		Family/Matrimonial	364
Securitisation & Repackaging, Derivatives		Financial Services	385
Charities	122	Food	see under Product Liability
Church Law	134	Franchising	391
Civil Liberties	see under Human Rights	Fraud (Criminal)	393
Clinical Negligence	140	Health & Safety	400
Commodities	157	HealthCare	404
Competition/Anti-Trust	163	Housing Associations	see under Social Housing
Construction	175	Human Rights	410
Corporate Finance	202	Immigration	415
Customs & Excise	see under Tax	Information Technology	426
		Insolvency/Corporate Recovery	440
		Insurance	465

THE BAR

Stars at the Bar	1243	Church	1268
Barristers' charges and remuneration	1248	Civil Liberties	see under Human Rights
Set overviews	1249	Clinical Negligence	1269
		Commercial Litigation	1272
		Company	1276

THE BAR: SPECIALIST AREAS

		Competition/European Law	1278
Administrative & Public Law	1253	Construction	1279
Agriculture	1256	Consumer Law	1282
Alternative Dispute Resoluton	see under Solicitors specialist areas	Crime	1284
Arbitration (International)	1257	Defamation	1290
Aviation	1259	Education	1291
Banking	1260	Employment	1293
Chancery	1262	Energy & Natural Resources	1297
Charities	1267	Environment	1298

Chambers & Partners Legal Recruitment 0207 606 8844

Published by **Chambers & Partners Publishing**
(a division of Orbach & Chambers Ltd)
Saville House, 23 Long Lane, London EC1A 9HL
Tel 0207 606 1300
Fax 0207 600 3191

Publisher Michael Chambers
Editor Rieta Ghosh
Deputy Editor Ross Cogan
Assistant Editor Catherine Willberg
Editorial Assistant Joanne Grote
Profiles Editors Richard Pettet, Alex Ballantine
Profiles Assistants Carly Jeffrey
Charlotte Rankin, Hayley Whiting

Production Team Paul Cummings, Jasper John, Laurie Griggs
Business Development Manager Brad Sirott
Distribution Marli Enslin
Orders to: Chambers & Partners Publishing
Printed in England by Polestar Wheatons Ltd

ISBN 0-85514-112-3

Copyright © 2002 Michael Chambers and Orbach & Chambers Ltd

CONTENTS

CHAMBERS UK 2002–2003

Intellectual Property	477
Investment Funds	496
Licensing	504
Litigation (General)	517
Litigation (Banking)	537
Litigation (Civil Fraud)	540
Litigation (Pensions)	542
Litigation (Real Estate)	544
Local Government	572
Media & Entertainment	579
Medical Negligence	see under Clinical Negligence
Offshore (Corporate/Commercial)	831
Parliamentary & Public Affairs	593
Partnership	696
Pensions	603
Personal Injury	617
Planning	639
Private Equity	657
including Buyouts & Investment, Debt, Fund Formation	
Product Liability	665
including Food Law	
Professional Negligence	674
Projects/PFI	685

Property	see under Real Estate
Real Estate	701
Shipping	740
Social Housing	753
Sport	766
Tax (Corporate)	775
Telecommunications	791
Transport	796
Travel	805
Trusts & Personal Tax	812
Offshore (Corporate/Commercial)	831

SOLICITORS: A-Z OF LAW FIRMS

Profiles of firms	835

IN-HOUSE LAWYERS & COMPANY SECRETARIES

Profiles of in-house legal departments for the FTSE 350	1201

SUPPORT SERVICES

A-Z of accountants, consultants and investigators	1225

EU/Competition	see under Competition/European Law
Family/Matrimonial	1301
Financial Services	1306
Fraud	1307
Health & Safety	1310
Human Rights	1312
Immigration	1314
Information Technology	1316
Insolvency/Corporate Recovery	1317
Insurance	1321
Intellectual Property	1323
Licensing	1325
Local Government	1327
Media & Entertainment	1329
Medical Negligence	see under Clinical Negligence
Partnership	1330
Pensions	1331
Personal Injury	1332

Planning	1336
Product Liability	1339
Professional Negligence	1341
Property Litigation	1344
Public International Law	1346
Shipping & Commodities	1348
Sport	1350
Tax	1351

LEADERS AT THE BAR

Barristers' profiles	1353

A-Z OF BARRISTERS' CHAMBERS

London	1507
The Regions	1617

INDEXES

INDEX OF PRACTISING BARRISTERS	1663
INDEX OF LEADING LAWYERS	1693

www.ChambersandPartners.com

INTRODUCTION

CHAMBERS
UK
2002–2003

THE RESEARCH AUDIT
by the British Market Research Bureau

Audit conducted by Trevor Wilkinson (Consultant) and Warren Linsdell (Project Director), BMRB International, August 2002. Their report is quoted here.

"The research methodology employed in the compilation of *Chambers Guide to the Legal Profession* has been independently audited by BMRB International.

The audit covers all elements of the process from researcher training through to data gathering, analysis and reporting. In addition to auditing the process employed by Chambers in compiling the directory, BMRB re-contacted a number of participants in the research programme (both legal practitioners and client-side personnel) to verify their contribution and to obtain their perspective on the research process.

In the audit we found the methodology employed by Chambers to be thorough and robust. The basic methodology used has been successfully employed for a number of years, ensuring consistency over time. This is the fifth year that BMRB has conducted an independent audit of Chambers' research method, and in that time the methodology has been refined and improved in line with BMRB's recommendations.

A further increase in the number of end-client interviews conducted to ensure that the Guide benefits from both the practitioner and client-side perspectives. Ongoing development of the data collection and analysis process to ensure that the research is thoroughly validated and based on a robust methodology. The independent auditing of the research process and willingness to act on recommendations of the auditors. In the following sections we discuss the research methodology in more detail.

RESEARCH METHODOLOGY

The focus of *Chambers Guide to the Legal Profession* is to provide an objective list of recommended legal practitioners (law firms and individual practitioners). This is based on a research programme conducted by a full-time research team in the first half of 2002.

Chambers concentrates on corporate law, rather than high street practice, and this is reflected in the type of firms included in the universe for this study, coverage being of firms with five or more practitioners plus established individual practitioners in the commercial sector.

Chambers draws its sample of solicitors and clients from a number of sources including the Law Society online directory, the online Bar Directory, the Law Society of Scotland and the Law Society of Northern Ireland. Chambers' own database of client contacts includes 50,000 records and is subject to ongoing development by a dedicated team. Data on top legal firms and practitioners is compiled in consultation with practitioners and with client-side personnel (purchasers of legal services). Consultation takes the form of interviews with practitioners and clients, supported and validated by submissions from the main legal firms in each market and by reference to other independent sources of data, such as legal journals, trade press and business press. The 2002-2003 Guide is based on a total of 6,582 interviews, which is 30 more than the total interviews for the 2001-2002 Guide. This represents an extremely robust sample, yielding findings with a high degree of reliability. In accordance with BMRB's recommendations, Chambers have increased the proportion of interviews conducted with client-side personnel, or purchasers of legal services, from 24% of the sample in the 2001-2002 Guide to 33% of the sample for the latest Guide.

Although there is a slight reduction in the number of interviews conducted with solicitors and barristers, the number of legal practitioners interviewed remains above 4,000, which again represents a robust and reliable sample. Interviews were conducted by telephone. This form of data collection has the advantage of reducing bias and avoids respondent self-selection, thereby enhancing objectivity of findings. Within each region and each area of law, the number of interviews varies according to the universe, but in all cases sample sizes were sufficient for the purpose. In some areas, particularly where there are relatively few practitioners, a full census was attempted. For other regions and areas of law the interviews were conducted with a representative sample. The editors and senior researchers have made an effort to visit the leading law firms, following requests from the market, so that the methodology can be fully explained, feedback from leading practitioners obtained and the co-operation of legal practitioners ensured.

THE RESEARCH AUDIT

CHAMBERS RESEARCH TEAM

Chambers researchers work full-time for six months researching the legal profession. They conduct thousands of telephone interviews discussing the strengths of leading specialists and their rankings. This research is audited by the British Market Research Bureau and provides an objective survey of the profession's leading practitioners.

Ross Cogan
(Deputy Editor) Read Philosophy at Nottingham University. M.Phil at St. John's College, Cambridge. PhD in Logic from Bristol in 1998. Has taught at several universities and previously worked in underwriting.

Sheena Lee
(Senior Researcher) Solicitor. Read Chemistry at University of York. Trained with leading niche City practice specialising in environmental law and personal injury. Qualified in 1997 and practised personal injury at legal aid firm.

Michael Leigh
Gained a First in Philosophy from Bristol University, where he also completed a doctorate in modern social contract theory. Has taught ethics and political philosophy and undertaken freelance satire for local newspapers.

Baron Armah-Kwantreng
Read History at University College London. Research consultant at RSG Consulting. Senior researcher Chambers and Partners 1999–2001. Project manager on aid-funded projects in former Soviet Union, India and Nigeria for procurement consultancy.

James Cowdell
Barrister. Read Modern History at The Queen's College, Oxford. Practised at the criminal Bar for five years and was a fee-earner in the family department of a leading London law firm.

Paula Wasley
Read English at Princeton University and took a Diploma in French at the Sorbonne. Subsequently a bilingual assistant at a top Paris hotel and a research assistant to a correspondent at the Paris office of a major news agency.

Adele Caffrey
Read English Literature at the University of Sussex. Previously worked as a researcher for a criminologist at the University of Greenwich and as a paralegal for leading City law firms. Bilingual.

Barbara Gruber
Read Law at University of Munich, Germany. In-house lawyer at a German regional television station and then at an IT company. Last worked for a personal injury law firm in Miami, Florida.

Rob Sears
Read Philosophy at the University of Cambridge. Gained experience in copywriting and freelance journalism before joining the Chambers research team.

Pippa Grèze
Solicitor. Read law at UCW Aberystwyth. LL.M in European and International Trade Law from Leicester University. Trained with a major law firm, subsequently qualifying into commercial property law. Previously worked as a translator and guide in Poitiers, France.

Ben Tendler
Graduated from the University of Bristol with a First in English Literature. Previously worked as a freelance market researcher.

Richard James
Read English Literature at the University of Wales, Cardiff. Former paralegal and recently published author.

Sophie Roberts-Powell
Read French and German at the University of Bristol. Has recently worked in the techsolutions division of a leading American internet advertising solutions company.

Edward Bannell
Read Law at London School of Economics. Worked as a Legal Executive for a leading Australian law firm. Has worked in legal publishing and legal recruitment.

Sarah Thompson
Read English Literature at the University of Cambridge and travelled extensively before becoming a researcher.

Olivia Gordon
Read English Literature at the University of Cambridge. Previously worked as a TEFL teacher and in editorial for a major publisher.

Philippa Nuttall
Read French and German at the University of Cambridge (New Hall College) followed by a maitrise in French literature at the Sorbonne and a postgraduate diploma in journalism. Previous experience includes teaching English in Paris.

James Plummer
Graduated in 2001 with a First in Philosophy and Spanish from King's College, London. Previously freelanced for a national newspaper. Also has written for Chambers' Student Guide.

www.ChambersandPartners.com

THE RESEARCH AUDIT

INTERVIEWS CONDUCTED FOR THE GUIDE

	2001-2002 Guide		2002-2003 Guide	
Solicitors	4,419	(67%)	3,900	(59%)
Barristers	554	(9%)	511	(8%)
Purchasers of legal services	1,579	(24%)	2,171	(33%)
TOTAL	6,552	(100%)	6,582	(100%)

VALIDATION OF FINDINGS

A number of checks have been implemented to validate the findings and ensure that they are not biased by individual responses. Quality is ensured by a number of means. Findings are validated through preparatory research before and during the interviewing period, with legal journals, press releases, professional, trade and business press and submissions from legal firms all referenced to alert the research team to possible changes in the market. The sheer number of interviews conducted ensures that bias is reduced. Comparison of clients' views with those of practitioners allows Chambers to check for consistency. Checking against former years allows Chambers to identify trends and variations over time. The research methods employed and quality control measures implemented serve to ensure that the findings can be reported with confidence.

FEEDBACK FROM PARTICIPANTS

As part of the audit we re-contacted a number of the participants in the research, both within legal practitioners and client-side personnel. Audit interviews were conducted with randomly selected participants, representing a 'spot-check' that interviews did actually take place and to gauge the quality and professionalism of the research process from the respondents' perspective. We are able to confirm that the selected personnel had taken part in the research and that they were the most appropriate personnel to take part in the research. Responses were positive, with the research process and Chambers interviews considered thorough, objective and professional. All audit respondents had a high regard for the publication and were happy to participate in the information gathering process. There was a general sense that the Chambers Guide was the most reliable legal guide and that the research process was the most thorough of all conducted.

CONCLUSIONS

Based on an examination of the research methodology and consultation with participants in the research, it is our conclusion that Chambers Guide to the Legal Profession is based on thorough research practices. Chambers is committed to ongoing improvement of the research process through increasing the number of interviews conducted (particularly with client-side personnel), a commitment to researcher training, continuous improvement of the data gathering process and the application of stringent quality control measures.

THE AUDITOR

BMRB International carried out the audit of the research methodology employed by Chambers and Partners in August 2002. BMRB International is the longest-established UK market research company, one of the top five research agencies in the UK and part of the international marketing services group WPP.

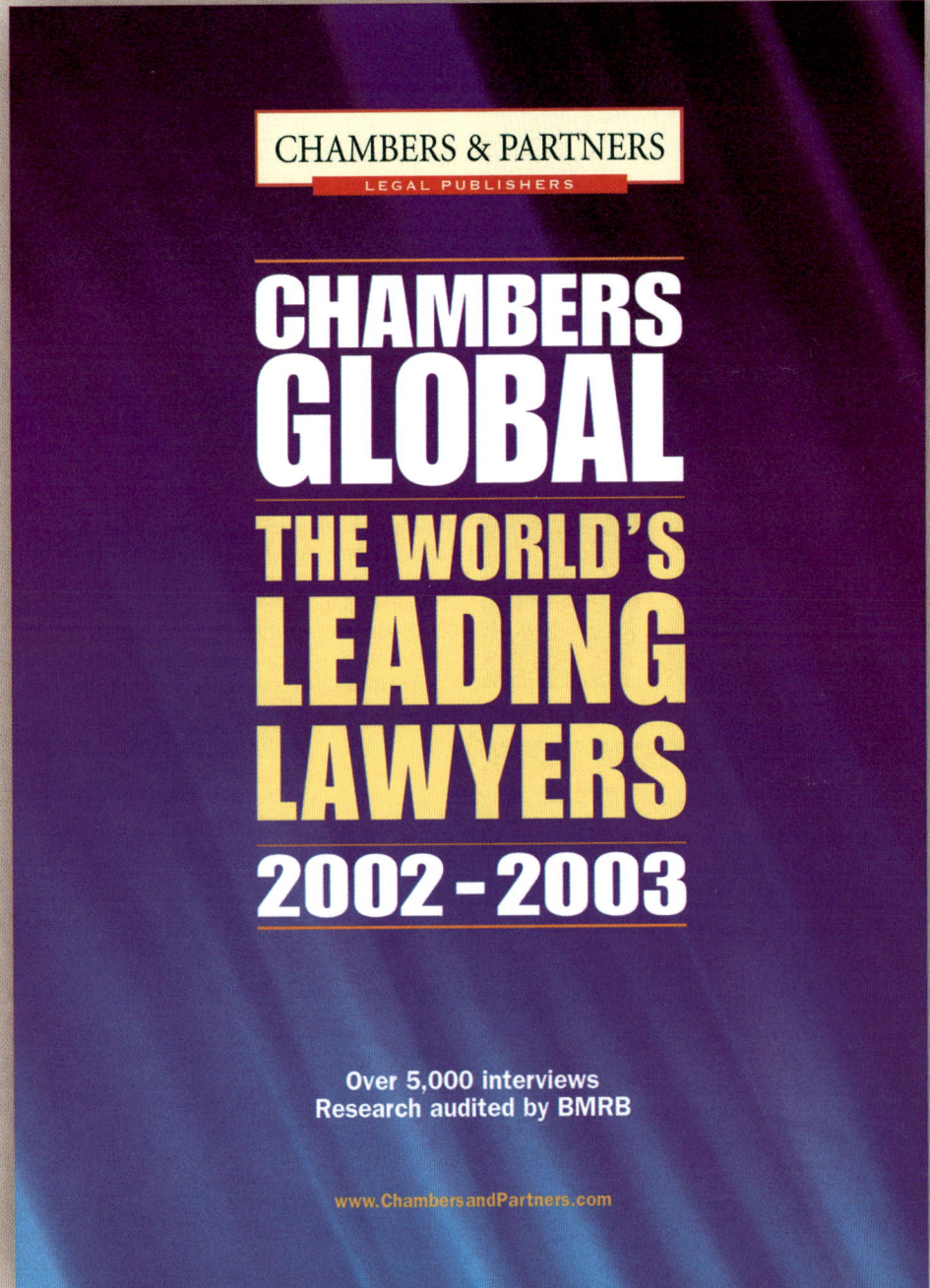

BEST BUSINESS LAWYER 2002

Nigel Boardman
Slaughter and May

By a margin of over three to one, clients have restored Nigel Boardman as Best Business Lawyer. The Slaughter and May stalwart was narrowly beaten last year by his colleague William Underhill. Clients were asked to nominate the lawyer who had contributed most to their business over the past year. A succession of FTSE All-Share clients cited Nigel Boardman as a "trusted business advisor" and praised him as a "creative problem solver," willing to roll up his sleeves and "get on top of the issues."

This year there is no differentiation amongst the runners-up. However, there are some significant changes of personnel. Most striking is the appearance of Linklaters' David Cheyne. For some, he is simply "the best all-round commercial lawyer." He is noted for his stamina, for a "direct and commercial style admired by the chief executive" and for his "unparalleled knowledge of the law." Last year's winner, William Underhill, maintains a strong showing. Identified as amongst the "leading businessmen masquerading as lawyers in the City," he consistently offers a "decisive and pragmatic judgement." Will Lawes of Freshfields Bruckhaus Deringer was singled out, not only for his ability to deal with complex matters but also for his skills in communicating sensitive issues at board level.

The remaining individuals are all new to Best Business Lawyer. The inclusion of Jeff Twentyman from Slaughter and May underlines the firm's continuing depth. Clients describe him as "having a fantastic manner" and being "effective and pleasant in negotia-

BEST BUSINESS LAWYERS

1	Nigel Boardman	Slaughter and May
2	David Cheyne	Linklaters
	Matthew Middleditch	Linklaters
	Nigel Farr	Herbert Smith
	Will Lawes	Freshfields Bruckhaus Deringer
	Jeff Twentyman	Slaughter and May
	William Underhill	Slaughter and May

David Cheyne
Linklaters

Matthew Middleditch
Linklaters

Nigel Farr
Herbert Smith

tions." Matthew Middleditch of Linklaters drew recommendations for his twin competencies of corporate finance and investment funds, where he is characterised as "technically first rate." He was praised for his "attention to detail and common sense" and his obvious "client dedication." Nigel Farr of Herbert Smith is an investment funds expert admired at in-house and board level for providing unprompted commercially focused advice.

Slaughter and May repeats its ascendancy in the firm recommendations, followed by Linklaters, positions unchanged from last year's results. Highlighting a strong showing by national firms, Eversheds, Hammond Suddards Edge and Addleshaw Booth & Co have breached the upper echelons of the table, while Clifford Chance has leapfrogged Allen & Overy to secure sixth place.

Some clients suggested that the smaller and regional firms offer "better value for money" and that "the differential in the quality of the service provided by the magic circle is not worth the extra fees that are paid." However, several interviewees spoke of the pressure from the City to use the big-name firms in order to be viewed as serious players. A silent minority of clients declined to recommend their lawyers for this category. Their reason was a simple one: that while they considered their lawyers to be doing a good job, there was nothing outstanding in their performances. For these clients, lawyers have yet to go the extra step and clearly align technical legal advice with clients' business objectives. ■

TOP TWENTY LAW FIRMS WITH BEST BUSINESS LAWYERS

	Firm	
1	Slaughter and May	35
2	Linklaters	25
3	Freshfields Bruckhaus Deringer	14
4	Herbert Smith	12
5	Eversheds	10
6	Clifford Chance	9
7	Hammond Suddards Edge	8
	Allen & Overy	8
9	Ashurst Morris Crisp	6
	Taylor Joynson Garrett	6
11	DLA	5
	Lovells	5
	Masons	5
14	Berwin Leighton Paisner	4
	Lewis Silkin	4
	Mayer, Brown, Rowe & Maw	4
	Nabarro Nathanson	4
	Norton Rose	4
	Pinsent Curtis Biddle	4
	Wragge & Co	4

Showing number of recommendations received by respondents

Will Lawes
Freshfields Bruckhaus Deringer

Jeff Twentyman
Slaughter and May

William Underhill
Slaughter and May

www.ChambersandPartners.com

SOLICITORS' CHARGES

Our tables are based on comprehensive reports provided by Chambers' recruitment consultants. The figures are for guidance only. Much depends on the relationship a firm has with its clients – some clients are in a position to negotiate fees based on the volume of work they bring. Some firms vary fees from region to region, while others impose a uniform charge. A figure can be agreed based on the complexity, urgency and resource-intensity of a particular matter, rather than a charge by the hour.

PARTNERS' Hourly rates

Area of Practice		Corporate Low	Corporate Average	Corporate High	Commercial Litigation Low	Commercial Litigation Average	Commercial Litigation High	Commercial Property Low	Commercial Property Average	Commercial Property High
London	large	380	450	550	375	430	550	380	430	550
	medium	250	350	425	250	350	425	250	350	400
	small	220	300	400	210	300	400	200	310	385
Bristol	large	130	175	270	120	170	250	140	170	215
	medium	130	160	175	120	170	185	130	150	175
Birmingham	large	220	260	375	220	250	340	220	260	300
	medium	195	210	220	195	210	220	195	210	220
Manchester	large	160	235	300	145	200	300	145	215	300
	medium	140	165	190	140	165	200	140	165	190
Leeds	large	160	220	260	150	220	260	150	220	260
	medium	125	150	165	125	150	200	125	150	165
Edinburgh	large	160	180	200	150	165	200	150	180	200
	medium	140	155	180	125	140	165	140	155	175
Glasgow	large	165	190	215	165	190	215	150	170	200
	medium	130	155	200	150	160	200	150	165	200

ASSISTANT SOLICITORS' Hourly rates

Area of Practice		Corporate Low	Corporate Average	Corporate High	Commercial Litigation Low	Commercial Litigation Average	Commercial Litigation High	Commercial Property Low	Commercial Property Average	Commercial Property High
London	large	185	280	390	175	265	355	175	270	375
	medium	180	250	290	130	240	295	150	225	350
	small	130	220	300	125	220	265	130	215	275
Bristol	large	100	135	185	100	135	175	95	140	170
	medium	75	110	150	75	100	120	75	105	140
Birmingham	large	160	200	250	150	195	200	150	170	200
	medium	160	170	180	150	170	180	150	170	180
Manchester	large	110	160	240	110	150	240	110	155	240
	medium	100	120	140	100	120	140	100	120	140
Leeds	large	120	170	200	120	170	200	120	170	200
	medium	85	105	120	85	105	120	85	105	120
Edinburgh	large	120	145	165	120	135	150	120	140	155
	medium	100	110	145	100	110	145	100	110	145
Glasgow	large	120	145	165	120	135	150	120	140	155
	medium	100	120	150	100	120	150	100	125	150

SOLICITORS' REMUNERATION

Oour quick guide to solicitors' remuneration gives an indication of the range of salaries for newly qualified solicitors and solicitors with five years' post-qualification experience. It will come as no surprise that there is no great difference between 2001 and 2002 private practice salaries. While competition remains stiff between the US firms in London and the major City firms, increases across the board have remained slight – a reflection of the economic slowdown and a more cautious recruitment market. However, the US firms paying mid-Atlantic rather than New York rates are closing the gap between magic circle and New York firm salaries.

In some cases, salary bands have been tightened or abandoned in favour of merit-based remuneration schemes. In the regions, there has been little, if any, movement in salaries, and the broad ranges remain the same. In a range of firms (City-type and high-street firms), newly qualified salaries have increased by up to 5%.

REMUNERATION (March 2002)		Newly Qualified	5 Years PQE
London	large	£52-55,000	£75-85,000
	medium	£48-52,000	£65-80,000
	small	£40-45,000	£50-70,000
South		£20-35,000	£32-55,000
Midlands		£19-34,000	£30-60,000
North		£19-32,500	£30-55,000
Scotland		£18-28,000	£25-50,000
US Firms (NewYork Rates)		£80-90,000	£120-130,000
US Firms (Mid-Atlantic Rates)		£55-65,000	£90-115,000

BY APPOINTMENT
Recruitment consultants to the legal profession

By appointment to the top law firms By appointment to the leading in-house legal departments By appointment to the investment banks By appointment to the US law firms By appointment to the top law firms By appointment to the leading in-house legal departments By appointment to the investment banks By appointment to the US law firms By appointment to the top law firms By appointment to the leading in-house legal departments By appointment to the investment banks By appointment to the US law firms By appointment to the top law firms By appointment to the leading in-house legal departments By appointment to the investment banks By appointment to the US law firms By appointment to the top law firms By appointment to the leading in-house legal departments By appointment to the invest-

23, Long Lane, London EC1A 9HL   Tel: 0207 606 8844   Email: info@chambersandpartners.co.uk
www.chambersandpartners.com

TOP UK LAW FIRMS

Firms with the most recommended lawyers in Chambers tables

Table 'A' shows, for each firm, the total number of lawyers ranked in our lists, whether in band one or band six. It provides an excellent measure of a firm's prominence overall, although it will favour those firms which offer a broad range of specialisms and which have offices spread across a number of regions.

TABLE A: ALL RECOMMENDED LAWYERS

Firm	Individuals ranked in Chambers UK	UK Offices	UK-based partners	UK-based assistants
Eversheds	133	10	328	875
Clifford Chance	114	1	231	854
Linklaters	93	1	189	716
Allen & Overy	90	1	172	697
Freshfields Bruckhaus Deringer	84	1	162	575
Herbert Smith	71	1	140	417
DLA	70	14	342	660
Hammond Suddards Edge	70	6	187	454
Lovells	61	1	147	393
Pinsent Curtis Biddle	59	7	169	297
Addleshaw Booth & Co	54	4	127	262
Wragge & Co	54	2	109	180
Slaughter and May	52	1	105	372
Denton Wilde Sapte	49	4	154	316
Osborne Clarke	48	3	101	227
CMS Cameron McKenna	46	3	135	354
Norton Rose	45	1	121	359
Ashurst Morris Crisp	41	1	98	306
Burges Salmon	36	1	49	121
Mills & Reeve	36	4	59	112
Nabarro Nathanson	36	3	102	288
Simmons & Simmons	35	1	113	273
SJ Berwin	35	1	86	202
Berwin Leighton Paisner	34	2	120	223
Bond Pearce	30	10	62	141
Macfarlanes	30	1	56	151
Olswang	30	2	64	114
Dickinson Dees	29	2	62	103
Dundas & Wilson CS	29	3	59	163
Maclay Murray & Spens	29	3	63	141
Masons	28	6	87	177
Beachcroft Wansbroughs	26	10	128	79
Mayer, Brown, Rowe & Maw	26	3	91	168
Baker & McKenzie	25	1	73	221
Morgan Cole	24	8	83	162
Shepherd+ Wedderburn	24	3	44	97
Taylor Wessing	23	2	93	161
Barlow Lyde & Gilbert	22	3	70	169
McGrigor Donald	21	3	42	97
Richards Butler	21	1	72	110
Stephenson Harwood	21	1	84	126
Charles Russell	19	3	76	94
Field Fisher Waterhouse	19	1	77	108
Clyde & Co	18	3	91	99
Lawrence Graham	18	2	85	105
Travers Smith Braithwaite	18	1	51	111
Bevan Ashford	17	8	85	182
Blake Lapthorn	17	4	59	83
Cobbetts	17	2	73	70
MacRoberts	17	2	31	103
Martineau Johnson	17	2	46	63
Theodore Goddard	17	1	69	116
Walker Morris	17	1	40	86

INDEX TO LEADING LAWYERS: PAGE 1693 ■ IN-HOUSE LAWYERS' PROFILES: PAGE 1201

Unlike Table 'A', Table 'B' ranks firms by the number of lawyers recommended as 'stars' or in band one. Like Table 'A', however, it still favours those firms which offer a range of specialisms and which have offices across the regions.

Again, the magic circle and national firms dominate, but it is notable that the big regional players are coming through, with Wragge & Co, Bond Pearce, Mills & Reeve and Burges Salmon all in the top ten.

TABLE B: LAWYERS RECOMMENDED AS 'STARS' OR IN BAND ONE

Firm	Individuals ranked in '*' or band one	Number of UK offices	Number of UK partners	Number of UK assistants
Eversheds	51	10	328	875
Clifford Chance	30	1	231	854
Linklaters	26	1	189	716
Allen & Overy	23	1	172	697
Burges Salmon	19	1	49	121
Wragge & Co	19	2	109	180
DLA	18	14	342	660
Bond Pearce	17	10	62	141
Freshfields Bruckhaus Deringer	17	1	162	575
Pinsent Curtis Biddle	16	7	169	297
Addleshaw Booth & Co	15	4	127	262
Herbert Smith	14	1	140	417
Osborne Clarke	14	3	101	227
Hammond Suddards Edge	12	6	187	452
Slaughter and May	12	1	105	372
Blake Lapthorn	10	4	59	83
CMS Cameron McKenna	10	3	135	354
Dickinson Dees	10	2	62	103
Lovells	10	1	147	393
Maclay Murray & Spens	10	3	63	141
Morgan Cole	10	8	83	162
Norton Rose	10	1	121	359
Denton Wilde Sapte	9	4	154	316
SJ Berwin	9	1	86	202
Dundas & Wilson CS	8	3	59	163
MacRoberts	8	2	31	103
Shepherd+ Wedderburn	8	3	44	97
Beachcroft Wansbroughs	7	10	128	79
Nabarro Nathanson	7	3	102	288
Olswang	7	2	64	114
Berwin Leighton Paisner	6	2	120	223
Clarke Willmott & Clarke	6	3	52	74
Hempsons	6	3	32	85
Hugh James	6	8	44	53
Manches	6	2	53	71
Martineau Johnson	6	2	46	63
Masons	6	6	87	177
Pannone & Partners	6	1	63	71
Ashurst Morris Crisp	5	1	98	306
Clarks	5	1	16	38
Field Fisher Waterhouse	5	1	77	108
Hill Dickinson	5	4	85	82
Irwin Mitchell	5	4	84	151
Leigh Day & Co	5	2	17	23
McGrigor Donald	5	3	42	97
Richards Butler	5	1	72	110
Tods Murray WS	5	2	37	50
Veale Wasbrough	5	1	24	52

www.ChambersandPartners.com

TOP UK LAW FIRMS

This table ranks firms according to the number of recommended lawyers as a proportion of their size. Naturally, it favours the smaller firms, and it is the high-quality regional players who are prominent.

In the more competitive London market, any rating around 10% is good. Comparing firms within regions makes for interesting reading. Martineau Johnson, for example, has done well to achieve a top ten ranking in a region dominated by Wragge & Co, while in London Olswang and Macfarlanes stand out.

TABLE C: FIRMS PUNCHING ABOVE THEIR WEIGHT
Recommended lawyers as a proportion of firm size

Firm	Number of ranked individuals (total)	UK based partners	UK-based assistants	% of UK lawyers ranked
Burges Salmon	36	49	121	21.18%
Mills & Reeve	36	59	112	21.05%
Wragge & Co	54	109	180	18.68%
Dickinson Dees	29	62	103	17.58%
Shepherd+ Wedderburn	24	44	97	17.02%
Olswang	30	64	114	16.85%
Martineau Johnson	17	46	63	15.60%
McGrigor Donald	21	42	97	15.11%
Bond Pearce	30	62	141	14.78%
Osborne Clarke	48	101	227	14.63%
Macfarlanes	30	56	151	14.49%
Maclay Murray & Spens	29	63	141	14.22%
Addleshaw Booth & Co	54	127	262	13.88%
Walker Morris	17	40	86	13.49%
Dundas & Wilson CS	29	59	163	13.06%
Herbert Smith	71	140	417	12.75%
MacRoberts	17	31	103	12.69%
Pinsent Curtis Biddle	59	169	297	12.66%
SJ Berwin	35	86	202	12.15%
Blake Lapthorn	17	59	83	11.97%
Cobbetts	17	73	70	11.89%
Richards Butler	21	72	110	11.54%
Freshfields Bruckhaus Deringer	84	162	575	11.40%
Lovells	61	147	393	11.30%
Charles Russell	19	76	94	11.18%
Travers Smith Braithwaite	18	51	111	11.11%
Eversheds	133	328	875	11.06%
Hammond Suddards Edge	70	187	454	10.92%
Slaughter and May	52	105	372	10.90%
Masons	28	87	177	10.61%
Clifford Chance	114	231	854	10.51%
Denton Wilde Sapte	49	154	316	10.43%
Allen & Overy	90	172	697	10.36%
Linklaters	93	189	716	10.28%
Field Fisher Waterhouse	19	77	108	10.27%
Ashurst Morris Crisp	41	98	306	10.15%
Mayer, Brown, Rowe & Maw	26	91	168	10.04%
Stephenson Harwood	21	84	126	10.00%
Berwin Leighton Paisner	34	120	223	9.91%
Morgan Cole	24	83	162	9.80%
Clyde & Co	18	91	99	9.47%
Lawrence Graham	18	85	105	9.47%
CMS Cameron McKenna	46	135	354	9.41%
Norton Rose	45	121	359	9.38%
Nabarro Nathanson	36	102	288	9.23%

LAW FIRM OVERVIEWS

In alphabetical order

ADDLESHAW BOOTH & CO
A firm now truly working along national lines, with three flourishing bases in Leeds, Manchester and London.

The London branch moved into profit this year, following three years of investment. This may have been aided by the merger of banking litigation into the commercial litigation practice, which is now run from London.

The hugely successful corporate finance practice remains the jewel in the firm's crown. The teams in Leeds and Manchester continue to notch up leading positions in the Chambers' tables. Competitors and peers consistently point to a blue-chip client list as the reason for this pre-eminence. This has been bolstered by its appointment to the British Airways panel, fending off competition from four regional firms. The corporate finance team advised US-based Goodrich on the UK elements of its £153 million acquisition of the polymer bearings business of Dana Corporation.

The firm now operates in three divisions: transactions; property; and commercial. The property practice continues to be a prominent force in the marketplace, with the real estate and PFI teams in Leeds and Manchester both retaining leading positions in the Chambers' league tables.

About a dozen partners were removed from equity partnership in order to improve profits-per-partner. With the average value of transactions increasing, the firm has cause to be optimistic about the future.

ALLEN & OVERY
A vein of quality runs throughout this firm. Clients describe the lawyers as resourceful and approachable. A network of 26 offices worldwide affords it great international prominence.

The firm's Asian practice is flourishing, while the US practice has gained prominence through the efforts of ISDA specialist Dan Cunningham, formerly of Cravath, Swaine & Moore. David Morley's banking team continues to set the benchmark for major jumbo financings such as the £1.9 billion financing of Le Méridien Hotels. The group has been joined by four leveraged finance partners from Norton Rose, which should also assist the growth of A&O's respected asset finance group. The projects group enjoys a reputation as the default choice for banks. It has also encouraged an active sponsor client base.

But this is not just a banking firm. The corporate group has carved a name for itself as a credible alternative to its largest rivals. Alan Paul is a key figures in the group's expansion, and its diverse client base includes 23 of the Global 100 companies. Privy to big-ticket transactions, the firm has advised Seagram on the $8.15 billion disposal of its worldwide wine and spirits business to Pernod Ricard and Diageo.

The employment practice has performed well through strategic recruitment and effective management. A&O's commercial practice is also serviced by a first-rate private client team, a rare beast among the large City firms.

ASB LAW
This South East giant, already a major force across Kent, Surrey and Sussex, recently made its City debut following its merger with niche London property firm Keene Marsland.

The firm's comprehensive commercial division handles commercial litigation, corporate, property, employment and insolvency advice for a range of clients. National corporates, local authorities, insurance, airline and brewery clients have all been attracted to this firm.

Areas of particular strength include litigation, licensing and insolvency, and the firm was recently awarded a place on the DTI London Disqualification panel. The firm has established dedicated sector teams focusing on new and expanding areas, which include travel & aviation, and TeC (technology, e-commerce and computers).

ASHURST MORRIS CRISP
The firm's global network continues to strengthen, and it has recently added a property practice to the Paris office. Singapore and Tokyo-based lawyers have helped the firm to develop its expertise in structured and leveraged finance transactions.

In London, the capital markets team goes from strength to strength, boosted by the recruitment of lawyers from Weil, Gotshal & Manges. The team has advised Toronto Dominion Bank on its $8 billion EMTN programme, typical of its involvement in large transactions. They also excel in CDOs and the securitisation market, advising investment banks such as Chase and NM Rothschild.

The success in the pan-European private equity sector has fuelled the firm's expansion into Europe, as many transactions have French or German elements to them. The firm recently advised Cinven on its proposed €2 billion acquisition of Vivendi Universal Publishing in France.

Ed Sparrow's litigation team has also scored well this year with its continued involvement in the Sumitomo and Barings affairs.

BAKER & MCKENZIE
Having 63 offices in 35 jurisdictions is key to much of the firm's success. It attracts clients of the calibre of Cisco, DaimlerChrysler and Sony by offering cohesive, multi-jurisdictional teams of specialists. The firm is considered an obvious choice for clients who need advice on local law across the world. As we focus on the London office – the hub for Western European activities – we should bear in mind the office's global reach and the extent of resources available to it.

The corporate team in London has performed well this year with advice offered to Spherion on the IPO of Michael Page, and work with key client Sony on its joint ventures.

The firm excels in the technology and telecoms sectors. It has ridden the wave of convergence with experience in both IP and IT. One highlight has seen IT legend Harry Small act on a trademarks case for Levi Strauss in the European Courts of Justice, successfully arguing against the 'grey goods' importing of Tesco and Costco. E-commerce is a field in which these creative lawyers have displayed their innovation on the design of b2b exchanges and electronic platforms for the trading of derivatives.

Such expertise enhances the firm's profile in capital markets, where its lawyers are recognised for their proficiency in debt and equity issues and derivatives.

Although the litigation team here is smaller when compared with its magic circle rivals, the Grupo Torras fraud litigation has proved it can battle with the best of them.

BARLOW LYDE & GILBERT
Barlow Lyde & Gilbert has been quietly but successfully building its practice in a range of areas. Several years ago its finance expertise received a boost when the firm won a place on Barclay's business lending panel. Recently its competition capabilities were highlighted when a regular client, the Lloyd's Aviation Underwriters' Association (LAUA), selected it to assist in a potentially damaging cartel investigation. Its corporate team is said to be the fastest growing part of the firm.

And the firm's growth isn't limited to the London office. This year it has boosted the capacity of its Hong Kong office with a number of recruitments, and strengthened its small Oxford outpost. The mar-

OVERVIEWS A-Z

ket has yet to acknowledge all this expansion. However, sources do recognise a more dynamic, enthusiastic atmosphere at the firm, which we reflect in this year's tables. Seven new names have been added to its already large number of ranked practitioners. Of course, many of these are in the firm's core areas: insurance and reinsurance; aviation; and professional negligence – specialisms for which it is celebrated. In fact, its position in these areas is becoming more secure. For example, it has cemented its position on the NHSLA panel, and has appeared in cutting-edge cases like Callery v Gray and Sarwar v Alam. This determination not to lose track of its core strengths as it diversifies is something that clients appreciate and competitors consider a wise move.

BEACHCROFT WANSBROUGHS

Insurance, healthcare and negligence remain at the heart of Beachcroft Wansbrough's practice.

Building steadily on this foundation, its national network currently includes London, Bristol, Birmingham, Manchester, Leeds and Winchester. Advisors to the UK's key insurers, the firm's vast expertise across the spectrum of insurance and reinsurance extends to specialist areas such as fire-related fraud and complex policy coverage issues. With its mature practice in personal injury, clinical negligence and professional negligence matters, Beachcroft Wansbrough handles high-end work for clients such as AXA, Norwich Union, Zurich and the Ministry of Defence.

This year sees the firm making significant hires in real estate, commercial litigation, corporate services, employment, projects, IT and construction.

Moving with the times, it launched both a 'fast track' claims division, Mutual Law, and a financial services regulatory consultancy for its institutional clients.

BERWIN LEIGHTON PAISNER

Plans to move to a single site indicate that the year-old merger with Paisner has settled down well. The union has achieved the aim of broadening out the firm's client base. In corporate finance matters the diversity apparent. It has advised European Telecom on its open offer and admission to AIM, and assisted Lex Service on its acquisition of Auto Windscreens.

Real estate and its related specialisms continue to be the areas in which this firm excels. It has advised on the regeneration of the Elephant & Castle in London and continued its work on regeneration issues that have arisen from the Dome project.

Links to the property market have also ensured a profile for its hotels and leisure team. It is in this field that the firm has impressed many with its ability to draw upon cross-departmental teams experienced in construction, financing and development issues. The planning department maintains its traditional spot at the head of the market, with clients such as Tesco. Property finance has fuelled much of the development of this firm's banking practice, and the team has a niche in consumer finance.

The firm has grown since the merger, and clients were keen to stress that it has retained its partner-led approach.

BEVAN ASHFORD

Bevan Ashford continues to develop its network of offices in Bristol, London, Birmingham and the West Country – Exeter, Taunton, Tiverton and Plymouth.

The firm has appointed Ann Conway-Hughes as its first non-legal chief executive. Among other high-profile lateral hires, commercial property partners Lance Conway and Mark Calverley have joined the Bristol and London offices; former head of employment at Shoosmiths, Sara Woffenden, joins the Birmingham team; and former director of corporate services for South Gloucestershire Council, Bethan Evans, heads the regulatory division of the public law department.

The firm has represented the NHSLA and several London and regional trusts and been appointed to Headway's panel of lawyers handling claims on behalf of brain-injured accident victims. It continues to consolidate its impressive experience in its recognised core practice areas of healthcare, clinical negligence, projects/PFI and employment.

This year's ratings indicate the areas in which the firm nips on the heels of the market leaders: namely, corporate finance, commercial litigation, real estate, construction and social housing.

BIGGART BAILLIE

It has been an eventful year for this mid-sized firm. They acquired the highly regarded pension practice of Morison Bishop, a coup for the pensions team that surprised the legal world and raised the firm's profile.

This was followed by a merger with property boutique Steedman Ramage, which brings important retail clients to the firm, such as Sainsbury's, Marks & Spencer and McDonald's. The team can now claim to be one of the most important forces in real estate in Scotland.

The energy team gained the number two spot in the Chambers' league tables. It is a strong suit of the practice, attracting clients such as BP. The corporate department, also an important part of the practice, has witnessed a growth in corporate finance instructions and enjoys a niche in investment work.

BIRD & BIRD

It is probably fair to call Bird & Bird, in the best sense of the word, a boutique. A quick analysis of *Chambers*' rankings shows that it appears in just eight tables. However, what is also striking is how many of those rankings are in the top band – six out of the eight. A similar pattern emerges amongst the partners. Only 12 individuals are ranked, but half of those are in bands one or two. It is hard to think of a better indicator of quality: when this firm plays, it clearly plays to win.

Its focus is on the hi-tech aspects of TMT, boasting top class skill and experience in IT, telecoms and all aspects of intellectual property. Its media expertise is largely confined to sports law. Not surprisingly, the firm has had a slow year following the slump in technology stocks, and profits have dropped. However, the firm has won a stream of solid, mid-sized corporate work from its excellent blue-chip client base, as well as new work from the likes of Californian semiconductor business IXYS, which it assisted on its first European acquisition. Some of this corporate work is pretty big, such as assisting BT in its exit from Concert (the joint venture with AT&T).

Internationally the firm has been on something of a hiring spree. In July it took eight partners and nine assistants from crumbling Andersen Luther to open an office in Germany's IP capital, Düsseldorf. This is just the latest in a series of recruitments, which has also seen the firm boosting its French, Dutch, UK and Swedish offices. The speed with which this has been accomplished bodes well for the firm as it transforms itself from domestic TMT boutique into a global technology player.

BLAKE LAPTHORN

Exciting developments have been afoot at this regional heavyweight firm. In October 2001 it merged with Portsmouth-based Sherwin Oliver, a move that boosted its partner complement by a fifth. The merged outfit planted a specialist insolvency and business recovery team in London, extending its reach beyond Portsmouth, Fareham and Southampton. Headed by former Moon Beever insolvency litigation expert Nick Oliver (son of the firm's head of insolvency, David Oliver), the team launched a joint initiative with the insolvency service to take civil recovery proceedings against company directors on a conditional fee basis.

In addition to boasting one of the largest insolvency departments in the South, Blake Lapthorn has strengthened its leading profile in litigation, corporate finance, clinical negligence and licensing. This is seen in its appointment to several high-profile corporate and government panels, including SEEDA, the NHSLA claimant panel and Whitbread. The merger has also boosted numbers within private client, property and general corporate teams, while extending the firm's commercial breadth in IP and IT.

BOND PEARCE
This firm has developed impressive national coverage with offices in Southampton, Bristol, Plymouth and Exeter and an emerging presence in London and Leeds. Southampton remains its flagship, featuring corporate finance, banking, IT, energy & natural resources, and professional negligence among its highest ranked sectors. The Plymouth office rates highly in environment, employment, health & safety, and claimant personal injury. The expanding Bristol office achieved top ranks in banking, insolvency and licensing.

This year the corporate finance team was joined by Richard Cobb of Virtual Internet, the web hosting company on whose disposal the firm advised. The firm has noticeably shifted up a gear particularly in corporate finance, licensing and IT. Averaging values of £9 million per transaction, it has been involved in high-profile matters such as acting for SDA in the sale of Morrells of Oxford to Greene King for £67 million.

Its work has gained an increasingly international element with deals such as Chicago-based Andrew Corporation's acquisition of Quasar Microwave Technology and significant assets acquisition from Wireless Systems International. Moreover, Bond Pearce took the lead over its rivals outside London by launching an online domain name protection and management service.

BROWNE JACOBSON
This firm has established itself as an important player in the corporate field, taking the top spot in the Chambers corporate finance tables in the East Midlands. Corporate deals have reached an aggregate value of £1 billion. A highlight has been its appointment as lead advisors to Securitas on its creation of Securitas Cash Management, a joint venture combining the sterling cash management operations of Securitas UK, HSBC and Barclays.

Combining its core practice areas of public sector and health work, the team is to expand following its appointment to the NHSLA's 16-firm panel for high-value clinical negligence work. An 11% increase in turnover demonstrates the firm's weight in a diverse set of practice areas, from environment to global M&A.

BURGES SALMON
Burges Salmon enjoys a prominent role as one of the obvious choices for commercial instructions outside London. Few others in the region rival its depth and breadth of expertise in its core practice areas – company commercial, litigation, property, tax and trusts.

Blue-chip industry clients express considerable regard for its specialist sector knowledge, which covers agriculture, transport, charities, employment, pensions, planning and environment.

The firm demonstrated its capabilities in regulatory and competition work in its successful tender for one of the five coveted places on the Ofgem panel (Office of Gas and Electricity Markets). Other prestigious panel appointments include The Crown Estate and Nationwide Building Society. Its client roster is the envy of regional competitors, comprising national and international businesses as well as larger regional corporates such as the Avon Pension Fund, which it recently represented in the sale of a £40 million property portfolio.

Among its raft of star partners, Christopher Godfrey continues to receive praise from leading industry players for his knowledgeable handling of corporate/commercial, funds and financial services matters, while Tim Illston is still recognised as the leading specialist in pensions and investment matters. New lateral hires will enhance the capability of his team as part of the employment, pensions and incentives unit. They will also benefit the firm's environmental law practice.

CMS CAMERON MCKENNA
The CMS network – with offices in 37 countries – has assisted the firm in focusing on the emerging markets. The network has also attracted firms such as the esteemed tax practice Bureau Francis Lefebvre to its membership.

In the London office, energy and natural resources are undoubted areas of strength. Here the Eastern European offices have come to the fore, pooling resources, for instance, to advise on the first coal-fired independent power project in Poland. The department's leading light, Fiona Woolf, has been busy advising on the deregulation of the US electricity supply markets. The projects department has had particular success in transferring its knowledge of transport financing models to Western Europe.

A greater emphasis has been placed on the development of the banking and corporate teams, which both win market approval for their healthy client relationships. A cross-departmental approach serves the firm's clients well, for example in utilising its acknowledged real estate expertise in advising Nomura International on its billion pound acquisition of Le Méridien Hotels.

The one loss of the year has been the departure of product liability expert Ian Dodds-Smith and his pharmaceutical team to Arnold & Porter.

CHARLES RUSSELL
This firm has carved an unusual niche for itself. A respected City practice, it also has offices in Cheltenham and Guildford, while membership of two overseas law associations affords it a prominence on cross-border issues. The firm caters for household name corporates such as Select Appointments, SMEs and entrepreneurs.

The private client group is skilled in the creation of offshore trusts. A strong family department is also on hand to offer assistance.

The corporate team has performed well, attracting instructions from financial institutions and brokers as well as its existing hi-tech client base. It has advised on the first ever joint IPO on AIM and the Toronto Stock Exchange, acting for Canaccord Capital as broker for the Canadian drug company YM BioSciences.

The firm has set up a new media and entertainment practice, having lured a media lawyer from Peter Carter-Ruck & Partners. This fits in well with the firm's acknowledged expertise in defamation. Duncan Lamont's defamation team has defended two Channel Four journalists and ITN against allegations of contempt of court over their refusal to disclose sources to the Bloody Sunday Inquiry. The sports group continues to develop its relationship with the Jockey Club, ensuring its prominence in regulatory matters.

CLARKE WILLMOTT & CLARKE
The South West firm celebrated a record year of growth in the wake of office reorganisation and significant hires. Following its merger with Southampton's Ensor Byfield, the firm consolidated 13 offices into two large purpose-built centres in Taunton.

Among key appointments, its Bristol office gained top UK sports lawyer Ian Smith, whose client roster includes the Professional Cricketers' Association (PCA) and the Professional Rugby Players Association (PRPA). Bristol is also highly in planning, with regional stars Nick Engert and Stephen Pasterfield advising heavyweight clients such as Laing and Westbury Homes.

OVERVIEWS A-Z

Its reputation in claimant-led personal injury and clinical negligence continues to grow. In addition to its appointment as one of 20 specialist firms on the Legal Services Commission's panel for multiparty actions, the firm's high-profile cases include the judicial review against the Government's handling of the foot-and-mouth crisis, the investigation of health damage to veterans of Britain's nuclear testing in the Pacific islands, and the national organ retention scandal.

CLIFFORD CHANCE

The reach of this global practice is matched by its international client roster. Thirty-two offices in 19 countries come together to provide what clients describe as a seamless service.

This finance powerhouse occupies the frontline in the development of cutting-edge structured products. It remains the favourite of many investment banks for jumbo financings such as the €15 billion refinancing of France Telecom. Respected figures such as Michael Bray and Stuart Popham work behind the scenes to ensure that high standards are met.

The corporate team too has carved out a healthy slice of the public M&A market, and has this year entered the top 10 M&A advisors deal list, thanks to the efforts of Clifford Chance Rogers & Wells in New York. A transatlantic team is advising CSN on its proposed merger with Corus Group.

Its US presence has been further bolstered by the acquisition of partners from West Coast-based Brobeck, Phleger & Harrison, many of them securities litigators. These lawyers reinforce the international nature of the commercial litigation team. Jeremy Sandelson has recently returned from his stint on the Thyssen case in Bermuda, and the team has also acted for Philip Morris in a successful action against Rothmans.

Other core practice groups have performed particularly well. The property team under Robert MacGregor has pulled together the twin strands of development and financing. Its work on Canary Wharf remains the envy of many commentators. The insolvency team has risen to the challenge of market conditions and secured itself big-ticket matters, such as Marconi's restructuring.

CLYDE & CO

The firm boosted its international credentials in May 2002 when it announced its merger with 30-lawyer Paris insurance practice Honig Preel Mettetal Buffat Coulon (HPMBC). This makes it the largest insurance and reinsurance practice in France, a good position to be in as the market consolidates.

Insurance lies at the heart of the firm. Its client base reads like an A to Z of the insurance world: ACE; Commercial Union; Equitas; Gard; Hiscox; Skandia; Swiss Re; Winterthur Life; and XL Capital, to name a few. And it is at the forefront of important work, from the conclusion of the Piper Alpha litigation in the House of Lords to issues arising out of the attack on the World Trade Center.

Clyde & Co has offices in Hong Kong, Singapore, Caracas, Dubai, Piraeus and St Petersburg, and 40% of its business now comes from non-UK clients. This year, it recruited two partners and two assistants from rival shipping firm Sinclair, Roche & Temperley, including highly rated trade finance expert Robert Parson.

The firm's Guildford office offers a similar range of services as the London office, but its position close to the M4 corridor makes it a natural choice to service the area's hi-tech companies.

COBBETTS

A cross-Pennine merger with Read Hind Stewart brings the firm to a combined turnover of just over £20 million. The move is expected to strengthen an already flourishing property division.

The firm continues to reap top rankings in three areas of property: real estate; real estate litigation; and social housing. The group has secured instructions from Whitbread on the sale of its entire public house portfolio – 3,000 pubs were involved at a total value of £1.625 billion.

The firm's corporate division forms the other half of the practice, covering a diverse set of disciplines from corporate finance to IP. The IP team is newly ranked this year, following its involvement in high-profile trademark actions.

Read Hind Stewart's focus on owner-managed businesses will complement the long-standing Cobbetts client base of multinational corporations and public and private sector clients. The Cobbetts brand is clearly a regional force to be reckoned with.

CRIPPS HARRIES HALL

A long-established player in Kent, Cripps Harries Hall had good reason to celebrate its 150th anniversary this year. Turnover is up 12% and profits per partner up 23%.

Client recommendations have given the firm respectable rankings in charities, commercial litigation and property, construction, corporate and commercial, employment, insolvency, private client, personal tax, and trusts and probate.

This year, the firm unveiled its extranet system that enables clients to access key documents securely over the internet.

As a commercial practice that caters for listed companies, start-ups and family businesses, the firm is setting its stall as a cost-effective alternative to City firms. In a busy year, the private client department experienced a 40% increase in capacity with specialist lateral hires hailing from Amery-Parkes, Withers, DMH, Coutts & Co and Freshfields.

DECHERT

The merger, more than two years ago, of Dechert Price & Rhoads with Titmuss Sainer Dechert seems to be working well. The firm can boast a great deal of US expertise based in London which makes its claim to levels of experience rarely seen outside top-tier UK firms so plausible – at least in some sectors.

One sector where it has impressed this year is investment funds. The vogue for hedge funds suits the expertise of the London team perfectly. What's more, it can draw upon the retail funds experience of its US operation. Its burgeoning profile in financial services work has seen the firm newly ranked in our financial services tables.

Nor is this a one-off. It is improving or holding its own across the board. The firm makes it into two new tables this year, improving its position in a further five but dropping in none. Its litigation profile, in particular, is rising, allowing it to win some impressive instructions, such as the Abache litigation where it played a leading role.

Real estate is another area of improvement. Although it has since had to cut some staff from the property team, it was able to begin the year by announcing that it had won the tender to advise Land Securities on its £825 million retail warehouse portfolio – further evidence that this is now a genuine candidate for top-tier work.

DENTON WILDE SAPTE

Just over two years ago the firm pulled off a merger of complementary practices. The finance-orientated practice of Wilde Sapte has consolidated well with Denton Hall's expertise in media and entertainment.

A number of key sectors flourish at this firm. Energy and natural resources is one area of specialism, driven by chairman James Dallas. Like Dallas, many of these energy lawyers have in-house experience from both utility companies and Government posts, and they typify the firm's ability to understand their clients' business.

The banking practice thrives under strong relationships with investment banks involved in asset and property finance, and international projects.

On the international front, the firm's far-reaching network has hit a double setback with the departure of its Moscow head to Chadbourne & Parke, and its Beijing managing partner's move to Sidley Austin Brown & Wood. A healthy relationship with US firm Pillsbury Winthrop has ensured a steady flow of transatlantic deals, but suggestions of a merger have been denied.

The corporate team has the capacity to handle big-ticket transactions, which it proved with its advice to Nomura International on its £1.9 billion acquisition of Le Méridien Hotels. The media and sports teams have had a good year, advising The FA Premier League on the exploitation of its rights.

Its real estate experience is also respected, largely thanks to its ability to run cross-departmental teams smoothly, drawing on PFI and finance partners when the need arises. Many of the developments the firm has undertaken are client-driven. It has entered into a formal alliance with Wilbraham & Co, the niche specialist planning firm based in Leeds. This had followed concerns over its capacity to handle large matters for a client base that includes Virgin, Sainsbury's and English Partnerships.

DICKINSON DEES

A firm committed to servicing a national and international client base from the North East. Its lean, focused approach has produced a sizeable 19% profit increase this year.

The established strengths of the firm – corporate finance, banking, and property – have all been confirmed as leading practice areas in the Chambers' tables. The firm can now lay claim to a national presence within projects and transport. Combining these two areas of expertise, the team acted for Govia on the £1.5 billion investment in the New Southern Railway franchise.

A growth area has been work for Government departments and public bodies. The team recently won a tender for appointment to The National Trust panel. Dubbed "the only serious commercial firm in the North East," it appears to have discovered the formula for sustained growth.

DJ FREEMAN

A year of modest growth for the firm, reaching a respectable £34.3 million turnover. The property team is singled out for its expertise and this remains one of the firm's core practice areas. It has acquired Hammond Suddards Edge partner Simon Killick to advise on the corporate elements of property work.

A three-pronged sector focus appears to have served the firm well, with corporate and commercial litigation expertise straddling three areas: insurance; technology and media; and property. Corporate finance also holds its own, with a Chambers' ranking in the second band for smaller deals.

The litigators are recognised for the breadth of their expertise, achieving a ranking in the general commercial litigation tables. An example of this is the firm's representation of AXA in recent film financing litigation, thereby spanning two of the firm's core practice areas and flexing its litigious muscles in the process.

DLA

DLA has aimed its sights on the capability to offer a Europe-wide service to clients. It has a network of associated offices under the D&P brand but so far has secured a merger in Belgium alone, with Price & Partners.

On the home front, it has had a profitable year. Gradually sloughing off its aggressive image, the London office now boasts over 100 partners.

DLA appears to be upholding its assertion that its Yorkshire practices are a vital part of the business. Providing the second largest turnover, the Leeds office acquired Garretts' practice and moved to new premises at Princes Exchange.

DUNDAS & WILSON

A successful exit from its Andersen Legal links leaves this Scottish giant unscathed. The firm has expanded its London capability by taking five partners and nine other fee-earners from the former Garretts. The London branch focuses on two of the firm's specialist areas, financial services and real estate. With an anticipated turnover of £37 million, the firm looks set to hit all financial targets for the year.

The Edinburgh and Glasgow offices concentrate upon five core areas of expertise: financial services; real estate; technology; energy; and public sector work. The Edinburgh office gains top rankings in financial services, real estate and projects/PFI.

EDWARDS GELDARD

This firm started the year by being appointed advisors on the restructured legal panel of Cardiff University, advising on property, IP and employment matters. This comes as no surprise since the firm has recognised expertise in IP and IT matters.

Its property and planning practices are also respected. There are four teams specialising in company-commercial, property, dispute resolution and private client work. The firm has also built up a strong market profile for corporate finance, insolvency and local government work.

EVERSHEDS

The seventh biggest UK law firm in terms of revenue, and the largest grossing national firm, Eversheds focuses on higher value corporate and commercial work for listed company clients.

Two years ago it created a national executive and integrated its seven profit centres into a single pool. Since then, Eversheds' regional presence has gone from strength to strength. The firm gains strong recognition for its glittering client list that include RBS/NatWest, KPMG and PwC. The firm is making strong headway against its rivals in the North, and retains an established presence as one of the 'big four' firms alongside Wragge & Co, Pinsent Curtis Biddle and Hammond Suddards Edge in Birmingham.

To boost the London office, several high-profile partners have relocated there. Among the latest additions are national head of insolvency Jeff Drew and national head of e-commerce Rex Parry. The London banking department is making its name with the likes of David Boyd (ex-Allens Arthur Robinson partner) and former BAE Systems legal director Philip Perotta.

Over the past three years, Eversheds has taken steps to build a legal network across Europe's major centres. It currently has offices in France, Belgium and Monaco, associated firms in Italy, Denmark and Bulgaria, and UK-based Anglo-German and Anglo-Spanish teams. It has bolstered its French and Belgian practices with new hires, and forged alliances with Italian firms, business law specialists Piergrossi Villa Bianchini Riccardi and Milan-based labour and employment law boutique Benvenuto Barozzi Scherini (BBS). But it suffered a setback with the withdrawal from its alliance of intended future merger partner, top 10 Dutch firm Boekel De Nerée. It appears undaunted in its European strategic objective, although notably to date has failed to secure local law capability in Germany.

FIELD FISHER WATERHOUSE

This technology-focused firm has united with other European firms to form the European Legal Alliance which links the firm to Harper Macleod in Scotland, Beauchamps in Ireland, Dubarry le Douarin Veil in France, and Buse Heberer Fromm in Germany. The hope is that a merger will be effected within three years, as the notion of continual convergence lies at the heart of the alliance. This should bring the firm in line with other technology practices, such as Bird & Bird, which have moved towards a greater international reach.

The telecommunications practice – celebrated for its niche in

OVERVIEWS A-Z

telecoms-based property work – has moved up in our rankings. Moira Gilmour is the team's rising star, appointed to assist Hutchison 3G on large-scale property projects.

An important presence in corporate finance work, the firm gains second place in our smaller deals tables. The team fought off competition from magic circle firms to win a tender to act for Overture Services. They advised Overture on its long-term strategic partnership with T-Online. Here, the team was able to demonstrate its growing European legal prowess, as Overture has decided to instruct the group on most of its German law matters. Not only was this a coup for the corporate team, but also it represents the direction in which the practice as a whole is heading.

FRESHFIELDS BRUCKHAUS DERINGER

Clients like the firm's tradition of team-focused collegiality. It takes pains to ensure that its teams, drawn from the 29 global offices, work well together.

The corporate group is one that has impressed clients with its cross-border capacity. Barry O'Brien and the group – favourites for the tricky contested bid – have advised Wolverhampton & Dudley Breweries on Pubmaster's hostile bid, one of the longest battles in recent years. At the cutting edge of company law, Mark Rawlison's team has worked on the dual-listed company structure for the merger of P&O Princess and Royal Caribbean.

Private equity is another strong suit, and here the firm is aiming for the large-scale transactions such as Morgan Grenfell Private Equity's acquisition of Whitbread's 3,000-strong pub estate. The litigation group is known for the dynamic reputations of its relatively young partners. As well as generalists, the team draws upon specialists such as environment expert Paul Bowden. Recent headline cases include the representation of Lloyd's in the Jaffray litigation. The London and Paris arbitration groups form an influential force across Europe. The competition group has excelled this year with its advice to the likes of mmO2 and Hewlett-Packard. Existing corporate clients have long been attracted to the banking group. Its lawyers have also been successful in improving its relationships with financial institutions such as Goldman Sachs.

GOULDENS

"Small, highly focused and highly profitable" is how one source described the firm's corporate finance team. The description is equally applicable to the firm as a whole. It is cautious about growth and, contrary to popular wisdom, has shown little interest in foreign expansion, but it regularly hits almost magic circle level profits, which have hardly been dented by this year's economic downturn.

The key to its success is the high quality of its lawyers. It adopts a hands-off management style, according a great deal of liberty to individual practitioners. The firm is never one to over-lawyer deals, and clients regularly report that their transactions are quickly and efficiently handled.

The heart of the firm is its sleek and efficient corporate practice. "A force to be reckoned with," it is currently developing a private equity profile.

The property department also deserves attention. It has built up an impressive client base and a reputation for development funding techniques.

Both practice groups were shown off to their best effect this year in one of the firm's highlights – its advice to Delancey Estates on the £264 million take private by Tribeca UK.

HALLIWELL LANDAU

A record turnover for 2001-2002 overshoots the £30 million mark. It is reflected in the firm's organic growth which has produced four new equity partners and 11 new partners in the Manchester and London offices. Rapidly becoming the leading advisors for AIM-listed clients, the firm acted on almost 10% of all AIM floats over the past year. Particularly favoured by the entrepreneurial Manchester client base, the team has advised Cardpoint from its inception to its £2.5 million placing and admission to AIM.

A new development in Halliwell's brand has been the establishment of Halliwell Consulting, specialising in executive compensation and share schemes. The firm can now lay claim to being one of the top-tier firms in Manchester.

HAMMOND SUDDARDS EDGE

It has been a roller coaster ride for this regional heavyweight, following its merger with Birmingham and London firm Edge Ellison two years ago. The firm also merged with niche sports law practice Townleys and factoring specialist Wilde & Partners. It also announced its name rebranding to drop the 'Suddards Edge' suffix in late autumn 2002. These investments appear to have been achieved at considerable cost, which will hopefully produce results in time to come.

There have been some partner losses this year, including Manchester-based insolvency partner Duncan Haymes. Former senior partner John Heller became CEO of Hammonds Direct, the demerged, bulk conveyancing arm that he co-founded in 1989. Notable hires in London include Enron Europe's former head of legal and VP Mark Evans, Andersen Legal's head of banking Douglas Colliver, and Baker & McKenzie's Singapore-based finance and projects partner William Abraham. The Lattice Group's general counsel Patrick Somers joins Leeds' corporate finance practice. These additions herald the firm's growing focus on the TMT, utilities, energy, property, construction and chemicals/bioscience sectors within the context of consolidation and continued focus on its regional practices.

HERBERT SMITH

Associations formed with the German firm Gleiss Lutz and the Dutch and Belgian firm Stibbe have ensured that this firm has a greater involvement in pan-European matters. Although talk of mergers is neatly sidestepped, there is evidence of a strengthening of ties amongst these firms. They are doing more transactions together, for instance, and fielding pan-European teams.

Herbert Smith's office in Paris has achieved fast growth over the last year, doubling its fee income to €21.6 million.

The London office has excelled in the twin disciplines of corporate advice and litigation. A quick look at the our rankings shows that the firm has no difficulties in promoting its individual stars. David Gold and Harry Anderson lead a raft of litigation lawyers who have impressed with their breadth of experience. Arbitration specialist Julian Lew has been awarded the honour of silk this year.

Herbert Smith has allocated resources to the development of its banking and finance team, which at present is best known for its work in cutting-edge structured financing and securitisation. Here it welcomes Jane Borrows, formerly of Sidley Austin Brown & Wood.

HILL DICKINSON

A firm traditionally known for its insurance and marine prowess is now showing a greater breadth of expertise. General commercial instructions form the lion's share of work. Real estate has been particularly buoyant following the merger with niche commercial property practice Gorna & Co.

Corporate deals represent a significant share of the firm's £25.5 million turnover. One deal that combined the firm's transport and corporate expertise was the representation of FLS Aerospace in its joint venture with MyTravel Airways. Insurance work continues to attract the attention of the market, with the team securing a position as one of the UK advisors to insurance giant Thomas Miller.

OVERVIEWS A-Z

IRWIN MITCHELL
A litigation powerhouse, whose key clients are banks, insurance companies and other institutional clients. Personal injury litigation is at the helm of the practice, with the firm achieving a top ranking in its Sheffield, Birmingham and London offices. Commercial litigation is achieving a higher profile within the firm. The professional negligence team are tackling the Equitable Life scandal on behalf of former investors, bringing over 140 new clients to the firm in less than a week.

The London branch boasts a notable business crime capability, which is now expanding to offer regulatory advice in light of the new powers conferred upon the FSA. A Chambers' ranking has been achieved in all of the four offices, a feat not matched by all regional firms who have spread their wings. Turnover has increased by 20%, now reaching £71 million.

KENNEDYS
Kennedys has had a good 12 months. It rises this year in five of our ten tables, and we also rank three new practitioners.

The firm's strength lies in insurance litigation. Competitors detect a youthful energy within the firm, and praise its "talented staff giving high-quality advice". The firm has done well in the post-SIF commercial market. It was not on the SIF panel, but is on the panels of ACE, Royal & SunAlliance and Hiscox. Consequently its share of legal professional negligence work is increasing. It recently underlined its growing expertise in this sector, taking a lawyer from Pinsent Curtis Biddle.

A growing area for the firm is construction, where the team has a sound reputation and a broadening practice. The firm boasts a Belfast office, which also has a good reputation for construction. At Brentwood it engages mainly in motor insurance personal injury claims, while its Newmarket office, only opened in May 2001, enjoys a top-class reputation for clinical negligence.

LATHAM & WATKINS
This firm has impressed people with its determined push into Europe. This energy and drive helped it to win the Chambers Global award, *International Law Firm of the Year*. Over the past 18 months it has opened offices in Germany, France, Belgium and Italy, and appointed the first non-American – German managing partner Christoph von Teichman – to its main executive committee.

The "well-run" London office gained a new managing partner this year in UK-qualified finance lawyer David Miles. It has now grown to 19 partners, and is starting to make an impression on the domestic market. Commentators feel that it has become the "first port of call" for a number of US clients, especially on high yield bond and bank debt restructuring. It also enjoys a good name for representing lenders in telecoms financings. Consequently, and for the first time, it enters two tables – banking and finance, and private equity: debt. Finance expert James Chesterman rises in the rankings.

The firm has a little way to go before its roots reach as deeply into the domestic market as more established firms like White & Case. However, its reputation for aggressive growth makes it a firm to watch.

LAWRENCE GRAHAM
An important property player, the firm has recorded a sizeable turnover of £50.5 million. The team is at the helm of classic property deals, managing retail portfolios for clients such as Legal & General and AXA. It ranks in the top band of our medium deals table.

A steady flow of corporate instructions means that the firm stands up well to rival City firms. It has recently received its first major corporate instruction from BT, acting on a £170 million contract to run service provider Redstone's national voice network.

Conversely, a formidable private client practice remains one of the best-known areas of the firm, driven by international expansion. An established presence within private client work at the high end of the market, the firm acts for a swathe of multimillionaires. While the firm has been noted for diversifying outside its traditional practice areas, it nevertheless remains committed to the consolidation of its core strengths.

LESTER ALDRIDGE
Restructured into seven core practice areas comprising banking and asset finance, business, commercial property, international, private individuals, corporate claims and marine, the firm has grown dramatically, reaping the benefits in record turnover and profits this year.

Its second Bournemouth office at Aviation Park near the International Airport bears witness to its successful strategy. Housing the firm's residential property and lenders' remortgage service and its debt recovery division, Fast Track, the office looks set to expand further. In addition to servicing its regional client base, the Fast Track team continues to attract national 'household name' clients such as Xerox, Sony UK, Hanson, Tarmac, British Gas and BP.

LINKLATERS
This corporate and finance giant is underpinned by practices straddling Europe, the US and Asia. Even in a depressed market the corporate team managed to maintain its lead in European transactions. Here David Cheyne's direct, commercial style has gained him some of the best transactions in the market. He has advised Anglo American on the proposed £12.8 billion privatisation of De Beers, while the group has acted for Billiton on its merger with BHP and Lattice Group on its £15 billion merger with National Grid. The corporate group has also focused its attention on the top end of the private equity market.

Haydn Puleston Jones and John Tucker have succeeded in strengthening the firm's banking client relationships. Clients are attracted to their rigorous documentation and quick response times. The capital markets team pushes back the boundaries in its development of structured finance products. The securitisation team has acted on the landmark financing for Welsh Water by Glas Cymru, which involved a $6.2 billion bond programme.

In the insolvency field, Robert Elliott's efforts have been rewarded with headline cases. Enron and the Railtrack administration are just two of the key matters the group has been engaged in. Chris Millard, an e-commerce expert, has arrived from Clifford Chance technology, providing a clear impetus to the firm's capacity in this sector. Christopher Style has driven the litigation and arbitration group on to greater international prominence, while the tax group remains in pole position for innovative advice on cross-border transactions.

LOVELLS
Winner of the Chambers Global award Western European Law Firm of the Year, Lovells has made great strides in its overseas expansion, establishing 26 offices in 19 countries.

This broad church practice is no stranger to intricate cases. The litigation team here has been acting on BCCI v Bank of England for nearly a decade.

The real estate litigation unit is also respected for its activities in large-scale disputes arising from developments in the West End and the City of London. On the non-contentious side, Bob Kidby's real estate group has been involved in cutting-edge development work, such as the regeneration of King's Cross.

The corporate department can act as testament to the success of the firm's European expansion. It has attracted instructions from Corus in connection with its £900 million aluminium business sell-off. The deal was run from Germany with corporate and competition partners in London taking a large role. The corporate tax team has carved a name for itself as the specialists in indirect taxation, thanks in part to the efforts of Greg Sinfield.

Managing partner Lesley MacDonagh has recently announced a streamlining of the management committee, in which an international executive will be created to oversee business strategy. One thing is certain: this firm has risen to the challenge of globalisation, without losing sight of its London roots.

MACFARLANES

Macfarlanes has, according to recent figures, recorded extremely high profits-per-partner. Its powerful corporate finance and private equity practice drives the firm and helps account for its success. It explains how it keeps clients of the quality of Cordiant, Pernod Ricard, Carlton, Kingfisher, Virgin, Legal & General, 3i and Alchemy.

But it is wrong to think of the firm as a corporate boutique. Its property and litigation departments play a full part. The real estate team, for example, has been involved in the massive London Gateway project at Thurrock, advising Shell and P&O. Unlike other City firms, it also maintains a top private client department. Its trusts and personal tax team was so heavily recommended this year that we had to double the number of ranked practitioners.

The firm emphasises quality and accords partners a high degree of freedom to build up their practices. Clients are enthusiastic about this "quality, rather than quantity," approach, which sees it involved in "fantastic deals" despite its size. They also appreciate the high degree of partner involvement compared to some City firms. This perhaps explains why so many Macfarlanes partners appear in Chambers' tables. Lacking international offices, the firm does not lack international work, something that is also blossoming as it develops a 'best friends' style network with leading European players in key jurisdictions.

MACLAY MURRAY & SPENS

The firm has resisted mergers with the big five accountants, unlike its regional counterparts. Nevertheless, it maintains its performance in the corporate finance field, with another year in the top band of the Chambers' league tables. The team acted on the £56 million sale of Inver House Distillers to Thailand's Pacific Spirits Group. Capital projects and PFI are also key areas of expertise, with a niche in refinancing work.

A recent development for the practice has been the joint venture with Edinburgh and Belfast-based planning consultants, Farningham & Co, to form Planning First. This is the first combined legal and planning service in the UK, and will extend the firm's planning capability across the Irish Sea. This is a firm committed to pursuing its own individual path towards growth.

MACROBERTS

The year has been characterised by some important hires for the firm. Top employment lawyer Stephen Miller of Harper Macleod has joined the expanding employment practice, which continues to win the leading position in our league tables. David Davidson of SJ Berwin has been an important addition to the corporate team, injecting dynamism into the private equity division.

This should not obscure the considerable expertise of the construction team, which spends another year at the top spot. The practice also possesses a niche in the educational side of projects work. The firm acted on one of the country's largest PPP deals in education, the £100 million Edinburgh schools project. While not ruling out the possibility of a geographical move into the UK, the firm is currently able to service clients from all areas of the UK from its Scottish base.

MARTINEAU JOHNSON

The proposed move into larger offices in Birmingham has highlighted the firm's ongoing commitment to its Birmingham stronghold.

The education practice continues to thrive as a focal point of the practice, maintaining a leading position in our league tables. The firm has won a competitive tender to advise on the merger between London Guildhall University and the University of North London. Other core areas of expertise lie within corporate and commercial, commercial property and litigation work. The London office is primarily focused on the education and banking sectors. However, the firm is looking to offer a more rounded practice via a merger.

Despite a 7.5% increase in turnover, the firm has seen a drop in profits per equity partner.

MASONS

With a solid pedigree in construction and an established reputation in IT, Masons remains the firm of choice on big-ticket construction and IT matters. It was selected, for example, to advise Wembley National Stadium Limited on the construction and property aspects of the rebuilding of Wembley Stadium. It beat Wragge & Co in winning the George Wimpey group's £17 million outsourcing of its IT function, the second deal of its kind in the construction industry.

The firm has bagged some impressive work in a wider range of sectors, most notably projects/PFI, health & safety and commercial property litigation. Ahead of magic circle City firms, it won a tender to act as lead advisor on the Irish Railway Procurement Agency's construction of Dublin's new metro system, Ireland's largest ever PPP and infrastructure project. It also advised on Dublin's new tram project and gained its first appointment to the litigation panel of global construction and engineering giant AMEC.

As the first major English firm to launch a practice in Scotland three years ago, the firm has bedded down successfully and is actively recruiting. The most notable hire to date is that of high-profile litigation lawyer Eddie MacKechnie, the Lockerbie bombing trial's defence team leader, who joins former colleagues from McGrigor Donald as a consultant.

Masons has experienced more testing times with regard to its global coverage, most notably in Asia, one of its key markets. Following key personnel losses from the Hong Kong and China offices, in Singapore it replaced the dissolved alliance with Cooma Lau & Loh by 'best friends' alliances with construction boutique Chan Tan & Partners and Lim Ang & Partners which focuses on IT, dispute resolution and insolvency.

In addition to its UK network, Masons now operates offices in Brussels, Hong Kong, Singapore and Guangzhou (PRC), with associated offices across the US, Eastern Europe, Scandinavia and Egypt.

MAYER BROWN ROWE & MAW

Before February 2002 Rowe & Maw was a medium-sized, high-quality commercial firm, which, partly through the efforts of head of corporate, Paul Maher, was building a reputation for dynamism. Now it is part of the tenth largest firm in the world, with 1,300 lawyers at 13 offices worldwide.

The firm's strategy of developing the position of secondary advisor to FTSE companies – offering "City service but at a discounted rate" in the words of one client – helped it to build a strong client roster, including companies like Reuters, ICI, Cable & Wireless, Unilever & AstraZeneca. This was attractive to an international player like Mayer, Brown & Platt. In return, Mayer Brown offered the Rowe & Maw lawyers access to considerable expertise, major deals and a ready-made international network.

The union looks a good fit in several ways. The two firms already enjoyed a number of clients in common, and their London offices complemented each other. The early signs are that the integration of

Mayer Brown's small London office into Rowe & Maw has been smooth and that it brings with it high-quality banking, finance and private equity expertise. The Rowe & Maw side offers high-profile teams in areas like pensions, partnership, employment and construction, particularly construction-related professional negligence. Questions have been raised as to whether the combination will appeal to its large corporate clients, but as one of the biggest UK/US mergers to date, its future will be followed with interest.

McGRIGOR DONALD

This year has seen the completion of the firm's link-up with KLegal. The combined firm is expected to reap an annual turnover of £45 million. The London office will join forces with KLegal. However, the Scottish practice will be a separate member of the KLegal International network. This is expected to give the firm the platform for big-ticket corporate and banking deals, and increased exposure to a globalised market.

The firm scored a top ranking in our banking and finance table, and is now working for various London banks. The combined firm fought off competition to act in its first deal together, advising the Scottish Executive on the procurement of broadband for Scotland's public services. Finance work is also integral to key areas such as IP, where the firm acts for investors such as Apax Partners. The link-up is expected to strengthen the firm's position in the Scottish market and propel it into a global arena.

MILLS & REEVE

year of growth for this regional player. It has combined its traditional prowess in educational work with property expertise to act on some of the most significant deals in the PFI sector. The team advised the University of Hertfordshire on a PFI project to redevelop 1,600 student residences and to build sports and leisure centres.

Its Cambridge and Norwich offices maintain top rankings in the real estate and education league tables. The team seals its status as one of the top advisors to higher education institutions, recently winning the University of Leicester and the LSE in competitive tenders.

Banking work is another key strength of the practice, enhanced by the recent establishment of a dedicated banking and finance department in the Cambridge office. The professional indemnity team in London has increased its profile, making its debut in our tables for professional negligence. By building on traditional strengths to embrace new areas, the team can lay claim to a progressive strategy.

MORGAN COLE

Following a strategy review last year, the firm has refocused – in its desire to become a major national practice – on the core sectors of energy, health, insurance and technology. It has restructured its management and invested in the latest technology, including case management software.

Contentious work increased by 13%, with the gain of several key panel appointments including one of five coveted places on Lex Service's new legal panel. The Cardiff office, its traditional stronghold, remains top of the tree for corporate finance and commercial litigation. Extending from London through the Thames Valley to Wales, the firm gains recognition for its expertise in a range of other sectors that include banking & finance, employment, environment, litigation and professional negligence.

NABARRO NATHANSON

Nabarro Nathanson often gets labelled with the 'property-led, public sector' tag. And, of course, it possesses a fine property department. It is making efforts to develop greater financing expertise and more cutting-edge products while retaining its share of traditional work. Competitors applaud the way that it has raised its game.

Inevitably, the property sector also provides many of its highlight deals. These include the massive £2.4 billion acquisition of BT's property portfolio, where the firm represented Land Securities Trillium. Similarly, in the local government sector it boasts "the biggest team and the best clients," according to peers.

However, it is wrong to focus too narrowly on property and the public sector. Nabarro Nathanson offers a broad range of services to its clients. The BT acquisition also gave its "thoroughly commercial" corporate department a chance to show its expertise, advising on the joint venture agreement with the William Pears Group. It is also nurturing a growing reputation for AIM listings and has a good name for private equity and a list of top clients like Cazenove, Alchemy and HSBC Ventures.

Its employment department has taken huge strides forward in the wake of Sue Ashtiany's recruitment (as reflected in this year's tables).

Another department doing well in Chambers' rankings is energy. The practice is split between the London and Sheffield offices and has a particular name for coal and mining work. In Sheffield the firm offers an all-round service to its largely public sector and industrial client base. Its other UK outpost, in Reading, also offers an all-round service but to a client base more tilted towards the hi-tech sector.

NORTON ROSE

It hasn't all been plain sailing this year. The firm lost four 'high yield and acquisition finance' partners to Allen & Overy. Tim Polglase and Andrew Bamber were among the high-profile departures. However, the firm retains its respected asset finance practice under the stewardship of Peter Thorne. It continues to be involved in PFI and international project finance, while shipping finance has yet to lose any of its lustre. The firm has its roots in the shipping market, which accounts in part for its network of 16 offices across Asia and Europe.

The corporate team has secured its place on large transactions. It hit the headlines with its advice to easyJet on the acquisition of low-cost airline Go Fly and its option to acquire Deutsche BA, the German subsidiary of British Airways.

The capital markets team has also had a mixed year. The US group in London successfully advised HSBC Securities (USA) on a Nasdaq flotation, a testament to capital markets team's growing strength in international equities. However, the firm bids farewell to derivatives legend Schuyler Henderson, who has announced his retirement.

The litigation team also gets referrals from finance customers. The civil fraud team, for instance, handles cross-border asset tracing. Interestingly, the post of London managing partner has gone to one of the firm's litigators: Deirdre Walker. At the end of 2002, shipping head Peter Martyr will replace Roger Birkby as chief executive. Continued global expansion will be at the top of Martyr's agenda.

OLSWANG

For a firm of its size, Olswang has an impressive presence in *Chambers*. Thirty-four individual rankings in 17 sections is more than many larger firms manage, a real sign of an firm that can punch above its weight.

It is a genuine TMT firm, with the emphasis on the 'M'. Its media practice is top-ranked for film & TV production and broadcasting, and boasts lawyers of the quality of David Zeffman and Lisbeth Savill. Telecoms and e-commerce are also areas of strength, and the firm has been involved in cutting-edge work, for example advising Boeing in its move to bring high-speed, broadband access to airline passengers.

With the economic slowdown hitting technology firms particularly hard, Olswang has not escaped unscathed. It has lost staff and its recent move to abandon the assistant 'lockstep' was seen by many as a way of saving money. However it has survived some of the worst of the slump by having diversified its practice.

As its rankings show, its technology clients, established or not, can rely upon expertise in areas from employment to tax, defamation to planning. The real estate group deserves a mention. An expanding department, it includes three ranked practitioners and is winning solid middle-range work like the purchase of an £83 million property portfolio for new client Alburn Investments.

Its domestic coverage improved this year with the acquisition of Garretts' Reading office. This eight-partner, 22 fee-earner unit, including ranked practitioners Tim Clark and Alison Harrington, should add strength in the fields of IT, IP, employment, litigation, corporate and property.

OSBORNE CLARKE

Osborne Clarke has met with success in elevating its profile beyond top regional status. The Bristol and Reading offices continue to offer a solid spectrum of expertise across corporate finance, banking, real estate and litigation. Clients report that these offices provide City quality at a reasonable cost.

Its London office achieved a coup in May by gaining Olswang's former head of corporate Adrian Bott, which will enhance its transactional corporate and TMT capability.

Since the formation of the Osborne Clarke Alliance of law firms throughout 15 European cities in 1998, the firm has experienced exponential growth. In addition to mergers with London property boutique McGuinness Finch and Danish firm Pedersen & Jantzen, it reinforced its presence in Frankfurt and opened new offices in Cologne and California's Silicon Valley. The resulting flow of work bears testament to the firm's mounting credibility abroad. Examples include advising US telecoms software producer Bytemobile on licensing matters with Vodafone and Torex's $30 million acquisition of Hiscom, on which it advised in conjunction with Dutch partner Ploum Lodder Princen. Its growing institutional and corporate client base boasts household names such as Microsoft, CompuServe, Vodafone, Hewlett-Packard and Cable & Wireless. Clients attribute Osborne Clarke's success to its consistent team quality and client-facing mentality.

With the marked slowdown in this area of practice, the firm will no doubt be forced, in due course, to make adjustments.

PANNONE & PARTNERS

The decision to consolidate its position in Manchester appears to have reaped dividends for the firm. It has reported a £21.3 million turnover and gained new instructions from Sharp and The AA. Litigation is a core expertise. The team represented Cotton Traders in its significant win against Nike and the RFU in the Court of Appeal. Personal injury and clinical negligence are the twin strengths of the litigation practice. Top rankings were achieved in both practice areas. This should not obscure a fine reputation for corporate work, a department that has greatly contributed to the overall turnover. The firm is one of the few in Manchester to offer a full service, ranging from commercial to private client instructions.

PINSENT CURTIS BIDDLE

A year filled with strategic moves for this successful national firm. They opened an office in Manchester, and acquired the four-partner private equity team of the former Chaffe Street. The Manchester branch should build on the traditional strengths of the firm within private equity, financial institutions and corporate recovery.

The firm now boasts a corporate presence in three focal European jurisdictions following the alliances in France with Granrut Vatier Baudelot, in Germany with Hoffmann Liebs Fritsch Ruhe, and in Sweden with Magnusson Wahlin.

The banking and finance practice is now a national team to be reckoned with, and advised an international syndicate of banks on a £60 million facility for Devro. The corporate finance team has risen from our smaller deals tables to achieve a ranking in the medium deals tables. Much of this strength derives from its work for significant UK corporates and foreign controlled companies. A rise in turnover of 6.5% to reach £84 million is due in part to key mergers and a commitment to its core strengths.

REYNOLDS PORTER CHAMBERLAIN

Together with Barlow Lyde & Gilbert, this firm dominates the professional negligence field. Competitors and clients praise the "outstanding quality" of the team, which includes three top band practitioners. Paul Nicholas, who some sources consider "*the* leading professional negligence solicitor in the country," was especially singled out.

The firm is enjoying a wave of good quality insurance work. Its growing profile for reinsurance sees it rise in this year's rankings. Our tables paint a healthy picture. Like many firms built around a strong insurance practice, it has had a successful year.

There is more to the firm than insurance litigation, though. It has been diversifying its practice steadily, enjoying its most obvious success in the contentious fields. Its partnership team, for example, has a contentious bias, while its improving defamation team boasts an excellent client list, including Associated Newspapers, which it assisted recently in the Angus Deayton affair.

RICHARDS BUTLER

Richards Butler is a cosmopolitan place. Its international network includes offices in Hong Kong, Abu Dhabi, Beijing, Brussels, Piraeus and São Paulo. Many of its lawyers are dual-qualified, 60% of its annual revenue comes from overseas, and in April 2002 it won a Queen's Award for Enterprise for its contribution to international trade.

Commodities – where it reaffirmed its status this year as the country's leading player – and shipping continue to form major strands of its practice. It also has an impressive media and entertainment practice, boasting one of the UK's top film finance practices under Richard Philipps and a client base that includes MTV, the BBC and key client Rank.

Another area that deserves attention is litigation, where the firm enjoys a solid reputation. Its recent, well-publicised decision to advise the Co-op's pension fund on a potential claim against Merrill Lynch points the way to a potentially lucrative future for the practice now that top-tier firms are shunning work against investment banks.

As for its attempt to expand its corporate department, that has yet to bear fruit in terms of an increased profile. However, the firm has only to look as far as its Hong Kong office for an example of how to handle mega-deals.

SHEARMAN & STERLING

Some commentators consider this firm to be the US's most successful legal export, and the London office forms an important link in a major international chain. This year's rankings confirm the London team's improvement. Ranked in six sections, it betters its position in four of them, and sees two more partners ranked.

The tables also reveal the depth of the firm's finance expertise. Clients consider it "number one in the City" for cross-border high yield debt and leveraged acquisition finance. Its deal list certainly adds weight to this claim. The firm represented France Telecom in arranging €15 billion of loan facilities to refinance loans taken out for the acquisition of Orange, and acted in the financing of the £2.14 billion purchase of Yell, including senior and bridge debt.

It enjoyed an excellent year in private equity where its "fantastic multi-jurisdictional capacity," especially in the US and Germany, gives it an edge. In projects too, its "dynamic, enthusiastic" team has a good share of top-end transactions.

The downturn on Wall Street has had an effect, as the firm was forced to cut 13 associates in London and Frankfurt. This does not mean that Shearman & Sterling has stood still. It has begun building a financial regulatory practice, at the request of its international investment bank clients. This happened too late in the year to consider including the firm in Chambers' rankings; however it does illustrate the firm's determination to keep broadening its practice.

SHEPHERD+ WEDDERBURN

This year, the firm opened a London office, capably headed by Stephen Hubner, a former partner at Bird & Bird. The technology sector provides a healthy stream of instructions. Energy is another strong suit, and the firm was chosen in preference to City firms to complete the restructuring of ScottishPower into separate limited liability companies.

The firm enjoys a niche in parliamentary expertise in the form of its public law and policy arm, Saltire. This remains the only team in Scotland to combine policy advice with legal advice, and now advises the Scottish Parliament. The firm's impressive client roster spans limited companies to public sector organisations, with new client wins such as Cap Gemini Ernst & Young. An innovative team, it has a commitment to strengthening its client relationships.

SHOOSMITHS

Following a strategic review, Shoosmiths adopted a programme of internal restructuring with the aim of expanding the practice nationally. A round of partner promotions has been combined with the addition of 13 assistant solicitors, and a qualified accountant Paul Stothard has been appointed as its CEO.

The commercial and financial institutions practices have been reorganised to create four practice sectors, namely, commercial property, corporate/commercial, dispute resolution and Property Direct (the largest solicitors' conveyancing operation in the UK). The firm has closed its Banbury office and doubled the size of its latest office in Milton Keynes. The Northampton office remains the firm's powerhouse, with key strengths in the food, health & safety, planning and corporate finance sectors. Reading is also noted for corporate finance and commercial litigation, whilst real estate expertise is the key to Fareham's profile.

Well regarded for its specialist sector knowledge, the firm's property and retail expertise were sanctioned by its appointment to WHSmith's property panel for acquisitions, disposals, litigation and management, together with existing provider, Manches. Accredited for ISO 9001 and as 'Investors in People', the firm prides itself on delivering City-quality advice to a client roster that includes blue-chip UK companies, emerging technology private companies, European and US-owned corporates, financial institutions, developers and public sector organisations.

SIMMONS & SIMMONS

The firm has recorded a 5.5% increase in turnover, similar to a number of its direct rivals, but following a year of remarkable growth.

Employment star Janet Gaymer has spent the first year of her role as senior partner with her eye on developments overseas. A successful merger was concluded with Nolst Trenité, to the envy of many City practices eager to break into the mature Dutch market. A number of London partners have moved to the offices in Düsseldorf and Milan.

The employment group without Gaymer at its helm continues to thrive. The IP group is respected across Europe for its work on trademarks and branding. The firm is also home to one of London's most successful repackaging and structured finance groups which constitutes a credible alternative to the largest City firms. It has the resources, commerciality and technical know-how to attract clients such as Gallaher and Cadbury Schweppes.

SJ BERWIN

Property is a cornerstone of the practice, and has serviced such household name clients as British Land on leasings and the use of property in structured finance transactions.

Its prowess in the property field has assisted the development of its corporate presence. Complex M&A and pan-European private equity are now handled on a daily basis. Its work in the AIM market is typical of the diversity of its client base.

The firm is respected for its technology, media and telecoms focus. The film finance team has once again proved popular amongst clients. It has worked on sale and leasebacks, and pre-sales for films such as Woody Allen's 2002 project.

The investment funds practice rates as one of the best in the UK, bolstered by its skill in fund formation. Jonathan Blake, for instance, has been credited with the development of key tax-driven structures, and won the respect of lawyers in the US and across Europe. He enjoys the support of a practice that spans German, France, Belgium and Spain.

SLAUGHTER AND MAY

Quality rather than quantity is the mantra here. The firm is skilled in arranging cross-departmental teams that are clearly client-focused. Some observers conclude that the firm fields generalist lawyers. This is true, but there is a deep well of specialist knowledge on tap.

At the heart of the firm lies its world-class corporate department. Justly famed as the M&A firm of choice, it is home to three of the client-nominated Best Business Lawyers (see page 10), including the winner, Nigel Boardman. Client comments indicate that they choose this corporate team for its lack of ego and its 'sleeves rolled up' mentality. Its headline-grabbing transactions include Shell's £4.3 billion acquisition of Enterprise Oil.

Not surprisingly, the firm leads in related areas such as tax and competition. Steve Edge is one of the most sought-after corporate tax specialists. He has used his expertise on Diageo's £9 billion joint acquisition with Pernod Ricard of Seagram's drinks business.

The litigation group has also come to the fore in its work on the Barings saga, Railtrack's administration and claims arising from the mishandling of Unilever's pension fund.

No discussion of Slaughter and May would be complete without a review of its attitude to cross-border expansion. It does have offices in Paris, Hong Kong, Brussels, New York and Singapore. But it has eschewed overseas expansion, instead formulating 'best friends' relationships with key counterparts across the globe. The quality of its relationships is not in doubt. Hengeler Mueller in Germany, and Davis Polk & Wardwell and Cravath, Swaine & Moore in the US, are among the firms that provide transactional assistance. There is a considerable number of clients who prefer the flexibility of choice. Although its strategy is not followed by many, the high standards set by this firm ensure its continued success.

STEPHENSON HARWOOD

The firm grew substantially this year, merging with fellow shipping firm Sinclair Roche & Temperley in May 2002. It was not entirely plain sailing, with some ex-Sinclair's partners leaving for, amongst other places, Clyde & Co. However, it certainly increases the firm's capacity, especially in shipping: something that is reflected in our tables as it moves up to the second band for ship finance. It is also reflected in the number of ranked individuals at the firm – 23 this year compared with last year's 19.

As befits an international shipping firm, a large slice of its revenue comes from foreign clients or from its overseas offices in places like

OVERVIEWS A-Z

Hong Kong, Piraeus, Singapore, Madrid and Guangzhou. For example, it was chosen by the Fieldstone Private Capital Group to assist the Serbian government in the privatisation of three metal processing companies, one of the first instructions in Serbia since the war.

The firm has a name for more than just shipping. It has a solid reputation for litigation, largely thanks to "redoubtable fighter" John Fordham, while Kate Brearley's employment team is widely respected.

TAYLOR WESSING

Taylor Joynson Garrett began trading as Taylor Wessing on 1 September, having pulled off the most talked-about European merger of the year with a minimum of fuss. Despite speculation about the difference in partner profits between the two firms, the merger is one between equals, symbolised by the fact that it will have no single headquarters.

Wessing, one of the last large, independent German practices, was known for its technology focus. With Taylor Joynson's renowned strength in IT, IP, telecoms and e-commerce, the union creates an Anglo-German TMT giant which will be well placed to capitalise on any hi-tech recovery.

But the practice's expansion this year wasn't all international. It swooped in to take over Garretts' Cambridge office, as the Andersen Legal network imploded. Though the timing was fortunate, this move into 'Silicon Fen' makes good sense for the firm and fulfils a long-standing aim. So strong is its technology profile, however, that it's possible to forget that this is a genuine, full service operation. It has a respected profile in banking and corporate finance and an impressive construction department. Real estate is a success story too, with the firm achieving its first ranking having attracted some impressive clients. Taking on the bulk of Garretts' London property team will undoubtedly boost it further.

THEODORE GODDARD

Theodore Goddard hasn't always made the right sort of headlines this year. September 2001 saw the break-up of its merger talks with Salans, Hertzfeld & Heilbronn. This was followed by the loss of eight partners – from corporate, employment and ADR – although the firm recruited some impressive replacements.

More recently, after undergoing a management shake-up, it has employed consultants to assist with an expansion strategy, and a merger is on the cards. Despite being jilted at the altar in the past, the firm does not suffer from a lack of suitors. In the year after the end of its talks with Salans, it apparently received 15 invitations to merger discussions, including one from rivals Olswang. It is easy to see why. The jewel in the firm's crown is its media practice. Its client list reads like a who's who of major media players, including Sony, Universal, Warner, News Group and Times Newspapers. It has an enviable record of innovative work, such as its high-profile database rights litigation for BHB against William Hill. And, in senior partner Paddy Grafton Green, it has the media world's favourite taxman.

Add to this the all-round expertise you would hope for from a medium-sized City firm and you have an attractive merger partner – it achieves solid rankings in our tables for corporate finance, banking, asset finance, litigation, PFI, tax and competition. Few people will be betting against next year being a year of change for the firm.

THOMAS EGGAR

Operating from five offices in London, Chichester, Horsham, Reigate and Worthing, the firm prides itself on its traditional values and history. Earlier this year, it launched an advertising campaign themed on lifestyle planning and targeted towards its private clients.

The largest firm in the South East to gain the Law Society's Lexcel quality mark, it has made 14 key appointments and lateral hires across commercial, IP, property, private client, international work, and litigation and employment sectors.

The pensions trustee practice gained pensions specialist Graham Chrystie and his team from Vizards Wyeth to boost its pensions litigation and trusteeship expertise, following the appointment as its director of Vernon Holgate, former manager of the Government-sponsored Stakeholder Helpline at OPAS. The firm's strategy appears to be bearing fruit: end-of-year figures saw profits per partner increase by 7% and turnover by 18%.

TODS MURRAY WS

The firm has placed itself at the forefront of legal technology with the installation of new operating and application techniques. These allow lawyers remote access to documents, enabling key areas of practice such as PFI and commercial property to have a truly national approach. This is demonstrated by the team's ability to close two major PFI projects at opposite ends of the country in a month: the £42 million refurbishment of Cornwall Schools and the £20 million Aberdeenshire Schools Project.

Corporate, commercial, and media work are also focal areas of practice. The media and entertainment team scores a top ranking in the Chambers' tables following the launch of T2M, which joins the traditional media industries with new media sectors such as e-commerce and IP. The Glasgow office continues to expand, offering expertise in a wide range of corporate and commercial areas.

TRAVERS SMITH BRAITHWAITE

Travers Smith Braithwaite surprised the legal world late in 2001 by opening an office in Berlin with a team of lawyers taken from Coudert Brothers. This office is only small; however its launch held significance for commentators. The firm has built an enviable reputation based on offering a corporate-driven, partner-led service, which places a premium on quality. Inherent in this is a belief in slow, organic growth, a primarily domestic focus and a collegiate, single office ethos. European expansion does not imply a weakening of this stance. Local law capacity of some sort is increasingly necessary.

The size of deals the firm is winning is increasing, as more companies come to recognise it as a credible alternative to the magic circle. The work is becoming increasingly cross-border. This includes big-value international transactions, such as the $20 billion debt recapitalisation it undertook for ntl. Its corporate and private equity teams remain the jewels in the firm's crown, and if anything, are gaining in strength. It rises this year in Chambers' private equity buyouts table while Spencer Summerfield joins Christopher Bell in the top band of corporate finance (medium deals) practitioners.

Other areas, too, have performed well, such as Paul Stannard's excellent pensions team, and financial services, where Margaret Chamberlain has represented CRESTCo for some time. The firm combined its financial services and corporate expertise this year in the large and complex merger of CRESTCo with Euroclear, creating the largest securities settlement provider in Europe.

WALKER MORRIS

One of the most profitable regional firms, fielding a turnover of £31 million. A 20% rise in turnover has been attributed to its commitment to a single site strategy. Nevertheless, it is viewed by clients and competitors as a national law firm. The property team has performed particularly well this year, not only gaining a top ranking in the Chambers' tables, but becoming a national presence in retail and regeneration work. It has also won the tender for Yorkshire Forward, and will oversee the disposal of 160,000 sq m of property.

Litigation and insolvency are two of the core strengths of the practice. The insolvency team recently acted on the high-profile administration of Bradford City FC. The firm has produced another set of figures and rankings to silence their severest critics.

WARD HADAWAY

An important presence in the North East, offering a multi-disciplinary approach. The eclectic healthcare team has won a place on the slimmed-down NHSLA panel. Since gaining its place, the firm has fought off competition from other panel firms to become legal advisor to the North Tyneside Primary Care Trust. It has added to this array of achievements by gaining the number two spot for clinical negligence in the Chambers' league tables.

Commercial litigation is another core practice area, which possesses many trained mediators. While committed to dispute resolution, the team also pursue valid claims with an energy to which rivals aspire. The formidable duo of Ian Collinson and Bob Elliott continue to lead the pack in the region. A progressive outlook inches this firm ever closer to rivalling regional giant, Dickinson Dees.

WATSON FARLEY & WILLIAMS

It has been a busy year at Watson, Farley & Williams. In early 2002, the firm entered merger talks with Simmons & Simmons. Commentators pointed out that its high-class asset finance practice would fit well with Simmons' financing strength, but in the end it was not to be. Ship finance remains one of the firm's great strengths, and it has been involved in some impressive recent deals, including representing Citibank on $175 million and $350 million facilities for CP Ships. It has, however, expertise across the range of asset classes and a sound banking practice with some good clients.

Its litigation practice has clearly impressed the market as it is ranked in Chambers for the first time, and the firm retains an international network with offices in places like Singapore and Piraeus. It is also boosting its energy practice with some new recruitment. This combination of an international focus and mixed finance and energy expertise is bearing fruit in some interesting transactional work, such as advising leading Brazilian engineering company Odebrecht on the $153 million sale of its oil and gas subsidiary to Enterprise Oil.

WEIL GOTSHAL & MANGES

The firm is among the largest of the US-based, international law firms in London. Private equity, corporate finance, and structured finance are the order of the day here. The capital markets team stands out as the hub for Weil Gotshal's European efforts, and it derives benefit from having offices in Frankfurt and Warsaw. Jacky Kelly's team is at the forefront of the drive for whole business securitisation. She has advised Nikko Principal Investments in the securitisation of Powell Duffryn ports business.

Clients told us that the firm has made the best attempt of any in building up its team of UK lawyers. Mike Francies heads the office and leads the group's charge on the corporate market. He is a TMT specialist with a lively personality, and his responsive approach has attracted clients of the calibre of Hicks, Muse, Tate & Furst.

Multi-jurisdictional matters are the clear attraction for this firm, which can draw upon 13 offices worldwide. And yes, the London office does have one eye on transatlantic business, but it is the second largest office in the network, after New York. As such, it enjoys critical mass and a growing prominence for European matters.

WHITE & CASE

Though most major law firms claim to be global, this can often mean the opening of a few satellite offices or a high-profile merger. For some, however, like White & Case, it means something rather more ambitious. People are often surprised that it now boasts more lawyers in its EMEA (Europe, Middle East and Africa) area than in the US. In recognition of this, it has devolved power to the EMEA board, and these international offices now enjoy a considerable degree of autonomy. Despite the downturn, it has been vigorously expanding across Europe. A glance at the recent legal press shows it bolstering its offices in, amongst other places, Paris, Hamburg, Helsinki, London and Prague.

The energetic London office, which has been open since 1971, enjoys a growing profile. This is reflected in this year's Chambers directory. The firm wins new rankings in the private equity and energy tables, and gains four new ranked practitioners, including highly regarded Dan Hamilton from CMS Cameron McKenna, who boosts its insolvency presence. Finance remains at the core of its UK practice. It is "excellent around the world" for projects and asset finance. Banking also deserves a close look. With the office's star, Maurice Allen, at the helm, it is getting involved in some enormous deals, such as assisting Chase and Morgan Stanley in arranging a £1.3 billion working capital facility and a £2.5 billion senior facility for ntl.

WITHERS

Withers' surprise merger with New York firm Bergman, Horowitz & Reynolds in January 2002 raised a few eyebrows. Accomplished quietly and with little fuss, the merger has established the firm at the forefront of international trusts work, though competitors query how it will affect its referral network. The firm now boasts offices in New York, Milan and New Haven, and professes plans to expand into the West Coast of America, Switzerland and the Far East. In the process of merging, it coincidentally became the first UK top 100 law firm to take advantage of the Limited Liability Partnership Act 2000.

The firm remains high-quality, focused private client outfit with an impressive roster of clients. It represents at least 15% of the *Sunday Times* 'Rich List', including politicians, pop stars, newspaper editors and members of the aristocracy, as well as wealthy families from mainland Europe, the Middle East and the US.

Its three strongest practices are agriculture, family and matrimonial, and trusts and personal tax, in all of which it attains a top band ranking. Its charities practice, under the highly respected Alison Paines, is also forging ahead. The firm offers a range of other services, and enters our civil fraud tables for the first time, no doubt on the back of high-profile work such as the Grupo Torras litigation where it has represented Sheikh Fahad Al-Sabah resisting enforcement of the $800 million judgment.

WRAGGE & CO

A move away from their Birmingham-first strategy has led the firm to increase the capability of its London office. The appointment of Herbert Smith property partner Gerald Bland heralds the birth of a London-based property team, with Bland as the national head.

The Midlands giant has proved its continuing muscle in corporate finance deals, advising on a disposal for Preussag for £375 million. Technology is another key practice area, comprising one of the largest groups in the UK, with an increasingly international focus. Not content with fielding a large number of FTSE 100 companies, the firm has lured several Fortune 500 clients into the fold, including Ford.

The firm also prides itself on a supportive working culture, and it ranked as the highest placed law firm in *The Sunday Times*' Best 100 Companies To Work For survey. A slower year than previous years in terms of turnover for this regional powerhouse; nevertheless, the firm still raked in an impressive figure of £78 million. It is gearing itself up to tackle the London market in the same way that has resulted in its mastery of the Birmingham market.

LAW FIRMS BY SIZE

The following pages show tables listing the 50 largest firms in the UK, followed by a region by region analysis.

NATIONWIDE The 50 largest firms

		Partners	Asst Solrs	Other Fee Earners	Total Solrs
1	Eversheds	328	875	612	1203
2	Clifford Chance	231	854	264	1085
3	Linklaters	189	716	37	905
4	Allen & Overy	172	697	312	869
5	Freshfields Bruckhaus Deringer	162	575	354	737
6	DLA	286	n/a	n/a	723
7	Hammond Suddards Edge	187	454	315	641
8	Herbert Smith	140	417	215	557
9	Lovells	147	393	210	540
10	CMS Cameron McKenna	135	354	122	489
11	Norton Rose	121	359	176	480
12	Slaughter and May	105	372	132	477
13	Denton Wilde Sapte	154	316	189	470
14	Pinsent Curtis Biddle	169	297	120	466
15	Ashurst Morris Crisp	98	306	168	404
16	Nabarro Nathanson	102	288	73	390
17	Addleshaw Booth & Co	127	262	388	389
18	Simmons & Simmons	113	273	144	386
19	Berwin Leighton Paisner	120	223	101	343
20	Osborne Clarke	101	227	111	328
21	Baker & McKenzie	73	221	98	294
22	Wragge & Co	109	180	275	289
23	SJ Berwin	86	202	79	288
24	Bevan Ashford	85	182	104	267
25	Masons	87	177	72	264
26	Mayer, Brown, Rowe & Maw	91	168	82	259
27	Taylor Wessing	93	161	59	254
28	Barlow Lyde & Gilbert	70	169	71	239
29	Irwin Mitchell	84	151	458	235
30	Weightman Vizards	76	152	44	228

The rankings in this table are determined by the number of solicitors working in the region. They are based on partner and assistant solicitor figures only: all other fee-earners are excluded.

NATIONWIDE The 50 largest firms – continued

		Partners	Asst Solrs	Other Fee Earners	Total Solrs
31	Dundas & Wilson CS	59	163	54	222
32	Morgan Cole	73	144	123	217
33	Stephenson Harwood	84	126	66	210
34	Beachcroft Wansbroughs	128	79	757	207
35	Bird & Bird	59	148	43	207
36	Macfarlanes	56	151	33	207
37	Maclay Murray & Spens	63	141	70	204
38	Bond Pearce	62	141	93	203
39	Thompsons	61	136	162	197
40	Clyde & Co	91	99	92	190
41	Lawrence Graham	85	105	67	190
42	Halliwell Landau	66	122	87	188
43	Field Fisher Waterhouse	77	108	61	185
44	Theodore Goddard	69	116	25	185
45	Berrymans Lace Mawer	73	110	97	183
46	Richards Butler	72	110	83	182
47	Olswang	64	114	53	178
48	Shoosmiths	58	116	207	174
49	Mills & Reeve	59	112	85	171
50	Charles Russell	76	94	98	170

TABLES — LAW FIRMS BY SIZE

LONDON The 150 largest firms

#	Firm	Ptnrs	Asst Solrs	'02	'01	'00	'99
1	Clifford Chance	231	854	1085	1086	924	932
2	Linklaters	189	716	905	900	696	721
3	Allen & Overy	172	697	869	808	691	614
4	Freshfields Bruckhaus Deringer	162	575	737	699	781	577
5	Herbert Smith	140	417	557	532	470	456
6	Lovells	147	393	540	498	473	473
7	Norton Rose	121	359	480	452	424	380
8	Slaughter and May	105	372	477	442	513	400
9	CMS Cameron McKenna	128	328	456	455	471	432
10	Denton Wilde Sapte	149	304	453	438	448	n/a
11	Ashurst Morris Crisp	98	306	404	402	357	356
12	Simmons & Simmons	113	273	386	390	378	404
13	Berwin Leighton Paisner	120	223	343	313	n/a	n/a
14	Baker & McKenzie	73	221	294	275	234	177
15	SJ Berwin	86	202	288	279	264	198
16	Nabarro Nathanson	81	206	287	249	227	255
17	Mayer, Brown, Rowe & Maw	90	167	257	n/a	n/a	n/a
18	Eversheds	76	174	250	202	196	184
19	Taylor Wessing	90	156	246	n/a	n/a	n/a
20	Barlow Lyde & Gilbert	68	164	232	208	219	190
21	DLA	112	n/a	225	n/a	210	194
22	Hammond Suddards Edge	72	139	211	180	180	n/a
23	Stephenson Harwood	84	126	210	165	166	161
24	Bird & Bird	59	148	207	212	210	125
25	Macfarlanes	56	151	207	172	166	145
26	Lawrence Graham	85	105	190	195	171	168
27	Field Fisher Waterhouse	77	108	185	178	156	134
28	Theodore Goddard	69	116	185	163	179	147
29	Richards Butler	72	110	182	164	160	149
30	Travers Smith Braithwaite	51	111	162	154	128	125
31	Dechert	49	110	159	139	136	127
32	Masons	55	102	157	189	150	132
33	Olswang	56	97	153	181	141	109
34	Reynolds Porter Chamberlain	56	94	150	133	118	117
35	D J Freeman	49	84	133	114	114	114
36	Clyde & Co	66	65	131	131	130	128
37	KLegal	30	100	130	83	46	n/a
38	Pinsent Curtis Biddle	53	74	127	121	n/a	n/a
39	Charles Russell	57	68	125	125	112	109
40	Shearman & Sterling	22	103	125	105	103	68
41	Osborne Clarke	45	75	120	107	76	45
42	Holman Fenwick & Willan	57	62	119	105	114	100
43	Davies Arnold Cooper	40	78	118	103	113	150
44	Trowers & Hamlins	47	65	112	104	96	96
45	Weil, Gotshal & Manges LLP	28	83	111	113	100	97
46	Withers LLP	49	61	110	111	105	101
47	Ince & Co	49	60	109	90	123	90
48	Gouldens	42	67	109	100	138	114
49	Nicholson Graham & Jones	52	54	106	103	102	101
50	White & Case LLP	32	74	106	99	70	42
51	Farrer & Co	52	52	104	89	91	88
52	Speechly Bircham	39	62	101	86	81	71
53	Watson, Farley & Williams	31	66	97	91	98	91
54	Kennedys	44	51	95	96	89	86
55	Howard Kennedy	42	48	90	80	72	64
56	Mishcon de Reya	38	51	89	74	62	58
57	Lewis Silkin	38	48	86	74	59	58
58	Sidley Austin Brown & Wood	28	58	86	125	n/a	n/a
59	RadcliffesLeBrasseur	50	35	85	n/a	n/a	n/a
60	Manches	35	48	83	70	79	79
61	Beachcroft Wansbroughs	54	28	82	164	195	187
62	Berrymans Lace Mawer	26	51	77	79	83	135
63	Bristows	28	46	74	81	75	60
64	Tite & Lewis	17	58	75	62	n/a	n/a
65	Russell Jones & Walker	30	41	71	58	58	48
66	Jones, Day, Reavis & Pogue	11	60	71	53	36	n/a
67	Harbottle & Lewis	17	53	70	68	68	68
68	Kingsley Napley	36	33	69	69	58	56
69	Latham & Watkins	19	50	69	68	41	22
70	Davenport Lyons	28	40	68	66	51	41
71	Bircham Dyson Bell	37	30	67	64	70	49
72	McDermott, Will & Emery	21	45	66	62	55	n/a
73	Sullivan & Cromwell	14	51	65	43	33	33
74	Fladgate Fielder	34	30	64	64	58	54
75	Landwell	20	44	64	63	56	85
76	Finers Stephens Innocent	36	27	63	79	77	57
77	Wedlake Bell	32	31	63	61	57	51
78	Penningtons	24	36	60	59	41	36
79	Forsters	22	38	60	53	50	47
80	Capsticks	27	32	59	52	57	55
81	Tarlo Lyons	28	27	55	51	43	40
82	Russell-Cooke	23	32	55	53	47	40
83	Morgan Cole	22	32	54	n/a	n/a	n/a
84	Hodge Jones & Allen	20	34	54	53	44	42
85	Addleshaw Booth & Co	20	33	53	39	n/a	n/a
86	Boodle Hatfield	25	27	52	52	46	43
87	Fox Williams	14	36	50	48	41	37
88	LeBoeuf, Lamb, Greene & MacRae, LLP	12	37	49	50	50	44
89	Cleary Gottlieb Steen & Hamilton	11	38	49	41	40	38
90	Collyer-Bristow	26	20	46	37	32	28
91	Cadwalader, Wickersham & Taft	8	38	46	32	n/a	n/a
92	Davis Polk & Wardwell	13	33	46	47	33	33
93	Winckworth Sherwood	18	27	45	45	40	43
94	Payne Hicks Beach	26	18	44	38	29	20
95	Salans	17	26	43	37	42	43
96	Skadden, Arps, Slate, Meagher & Flom LLP	9	34	43	34	43	32
97	Reed Smith Warner Cranston	21	21	42	45	34	34
98	Debevoise & Plimpton	10	32	42	33	n/a	n/a
99	Vizard Oldham Brooke Blain	26	15	41	n/a	n/a	n/a
100	Beaumont and Son	20	21	41	40	42	37

Headquarters of the Greater London Authority

The rankings in this table are determined by the number of solicitors working in the region. They are based on partner and assistant solicitor figures only: all other fee-earners are excluded.

www.ChambersandPartners.com

TABLES — LAW FIRMS BY SIZE

LONDON The 150 largest firms – continued

		Ptnrs	Asst Solrs	'02	'01	'00	'99
101	Devonshires	15	26	41	40	37	19
102	Dewey Ballantine LLP	11	30	41	38	28	n/a
103	Pritchard Englefield	25	16	41	36	40	39
104	Hill Taylor Dickinson	22	18	40	43	43	23
105	Jeffrey Green Russell	22	18	40	41	44	45
106	Sacker & Partners	20	20	40	35	33	31
107	Dawsons	21	18	39	34	34	31
108	Covington & Burling	9	29	38	n/a	n/a	24
109	Rosling King	10	27	37	37	37	50
110	Bates, Wells & Braithwaite	18	18	36	36	32	42
111	Teacher Stern Selby	17	19	36	34	34	30
112	Hobson Audley	14	22	36	35	33	37
113	Hempsons	13	23	36	33	32	29
114	Milbank, Tweed, Hadley & McCloy	7	29	36	42	29	20
115	Campbell Hooper	20	15	35	32	32	35
116	Weightman Vizards	16	19	35	n/a	n/a	n/a
117	Thomas Cooper & Stibbard	19	15	34	30	26	25
118	Shook, Hardy & Bacon	17	17	34	n/a	n/a	n/a
119	Leigh, Day & Co	14	20	34	27	n/a	n/a
120	Arnold & Porter	12	22	34	n/a	n/a	n/a
121	Fisher Meredith	10	24	34	33	38	36
122	Prince Evans	6	28	34	30	31	31
123	Hamlins	18	14	32	30	27	30
124	Rooks Rider	13	19	32	34	27	32
125	Fishburn Morgan Cole	11	21	32	29	30	30
126	Squire, Sanders & Dempsey LLP	11	21	32	32	n/a	n/a
127	TV Edwards	8	24	32	31	34	34
128	Edwin Coe	21	10	31	33	32	33
129	KSB Law	19	12	31	34	36	35
130	Clintons	17	14	31	31	27	22
131	Steptoe & Johnson LLP	14	17	31	n/a	n/a	n/a
132	Bindman & Partners	12	19	31	30	30	26
133	Thompsons	12	19	31	31	n/a	21
134	Hale and Dorr	9	22	31	46	38	n/a
135	Levenes	9	22	31	n/a	37	34
136	Edwards Duthie	6	25	31	88	n/a	15
137	Goodman Derrick	21	9	30	29	29	25
138	The Simkins Partnership	20	10	30	30	25	27
139	Coudert Brothers	8	22	30	n/a	30	31
140	William Sturges & Co	17	12	29	29	29	25
141	Hextalls	16	13	29	31	36	35
142	Memery Crystal	15	14	29	30	26	25
143	Irwin Mitchell	11	18	29	n/a	n/a	16
144	Kirkland & Ellis	9	20	29	n/a	n/a	n/a
145	Vinson & Elkins LLP	9	20	29	n/a	n/a	n/a
146	Wilmer, Cutler & Pickering	9	20	29	n/a	n/a	n/a
147	Bevan Ashford	6	23	29	n/a	n/a	n/a
148	Constant & Constant	16	12	28	34	34	29
149	Tuckers	1	27	28	28	32	n/a
150	Sheridans	17	10	27	n/a	n/a	n/a

The rankings in this table are determined by the number of solicitors working in the region. They are based on partner and assistant solicitor figures only: all other fee-earners are excluded.

THE SOUTH The 20 largest firms

		Ptnrs	Asst Solrs	'02	'01	'00
1	Blake Lapthorn — Fareham, Portsmouth, Southampton	53	77	130	102	120
2	asb law — Brighton, Chatham, Crawley (2), Croydon, Horsham, Maidstone, Mitcham	45	37	82	114	82
3	Thomas Eggar — Chichester, Horsham, Reigate, Worthing	39	38	77	70	75
4	Cripps Harries Hall — Tunbridge Wells	35	41	76	70	71
5	Penningtons — Basingstoke, Godalming, Newbury	30	44	74	69	55
6	Lester Aldridge — Bournemouth, Christchurch, Southampton	34	36	70	62	55
7	Bond Pearce — Southampton (3)	18	41	59	65	59
8	Clyde & Co — Guildford	24	34	58	58	58
9	Thomson Snell & Passmore — Tonbridge, Tunbridge Wells	31	24	55	55	55
10	DMH — Brighton, Crawley, Worthing	30	22	52	53	52
11	Hart Brown — Cobham, Cranleigh, Farnham, Godalming, Guildford (2), Woking	16	34	50	48	51
12	Shoosmiths — Basingstoke, Fareham	12	38	50	64	46
13	Stevens & Bolton — Guildford	20	29	49	47	46
14	Warner Goodman & Streat — Fareham, Portsmouth (2), Southampton, Waterlooville	18	30	48	36	34
15	Paris Smith & Randall — Southampton	15	28	43	39	36
16	Brachers — Maidstone	20	22	42	44	39
17	Coffin Mew & Clover — Cosham, Fareham, Gosport, Havant, Portsmouth, Southampton	20	27	47	41	41
18	Moore & Blatch — Lymington (2), Southampton (2)	13	26	39	44	42
19	Barlows — Chertsey, Godalming, Guildford	13	25	38	38	34
20	White & Bowker — Eastleigh, Winchester (2)	15	13	28	n/a	n/a

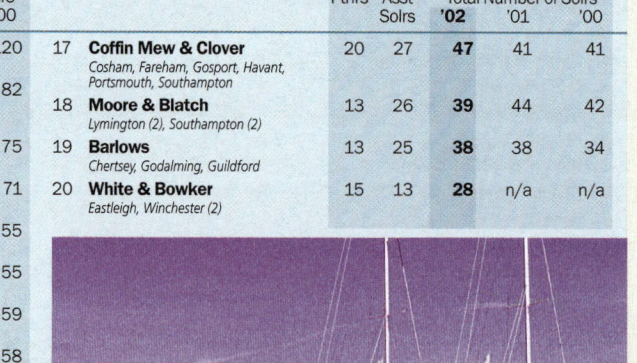

Gun Wharf, Portsmouth

The rankings in this table are determined by the number of solicitors working in the region. They are based on partner and assistant solicitor figures only: all other fee-earners are excluded.

TABLES — LAW FIRMS BY SIZE

THAMES VALLEY The 20 largest firms

		Ptnrs	Asst Solrs	Total '02	'01	'00
1	Morgan Cole — Oxford, Reading (2)	24	57	81	81	79
2	Iliffes Booth Bennett (IBB) — Chesham, Slough, Uxbridge (3)	20	44	64	57	47
3	Pitmans — Reading	15	46	61	60	39
4	Pictons — Bedford, Central Milton Keynes, Hemel Hempstead, Luton, St Albans, Stevenage, Watford	30	30	60	58	69
5	Taylor Walton — Harpenden, Hemel Hempstead (2), Luton, St Albans	24	34	58	54	54
6	Clarks — Reading	16	38	54	41	49
7	Henmans — Oxford, Woodstock	21	30	51	49	42
8	Linnells — Oxford	21	20	41	30	34
9	Manches — Oxford	18	23	41	37	31
10	Osborne Clarke — Reading	10	30	40	33	n/a
11	Matthew Arnold & Baldwin — Watford	16	22	38	34	32
12	Boyes Turner — Reading	18	19	37	34	32
13	B P Collins — Beaconsfield (2), Gerrards Cross, Marlow	17	20	37	31	30
14	Blaser Mills Winter Taylors — Aylesbury, Chesham, Harrow, High Wycombe (3), Rickmansworth	17	19	36	36	41
15	Darbys — Oxford	18	17	35	34	30
16	Shoosmiths — Milton Keynes, Reading	13	22	35	42	44
17	Kidd Rapinet — Aylesbury, Beaconsfield, High Wycombe, Maidenhead, Reading, Slough	20	10	30	30	n/a
18	Nabarro Nathanson — Reading	7	23	30	n/a	n/a
19	Bower & Bailey — Banbury, Oxford, Witney	14	15	29	36	56
20	Blandy & Blandy — Reading	12	17	29	27	n/a

The rankings in this table are determined by the number of solicitors working in the region. They are based on partner and assistant solicitor figures only: all other fee-earners are excluded.

Radcliffe Camera, Oxford

SOUTH WEST The 20 largest firms

		Ptnrs	Asst Solrs	Total '02	'01	'00	'99
1	Bevan Ashford — Bristol, Exeter, Plymouth, Taunton, Tiverton	75	150	225	191	175	160
2	Burges Salmon — Bristol	49	121	170	175	168	148
3	Osborne Clarke — Bristol	46	122	168	160	123	137
4	Bond Pearce — Bristol (2), Exeter, Plymouth	44	100	144	135	34	94
5	Clarke Willmott & Clarke — Bristol, Taunton	47	66	113	95	91	93
6	TLT Solicitors — Bristol	32	50	82	77	78	n/a
7	Veale Wasbrough — Bristol	24	52	76	68	55	49
8	Foot Anstey Sargent — Exeter (2), Plymouth	26	47	73	76	70	n/a
9	Lyons Davidson — Bristol (2), Plymouth	19	51	70	59	54	47
10	Thring Townsend — Bath, Swindon	36	26	62	57	n/a	n/a
11	Stephens & Scown — Exeter, Liskeard, Plymouth, St Austell, Truro	33	20	53	58	61	64
12	Davies and Partners — Bristol, Gloucester	16	34	50	39	39	42
13	Beachcroft Wansbroughs — Bristol (2)	25	22	47	84	70	63
14	Stones — Exeter, Okehampton, Sidmouth, Taunton, Tiverton, Torrington	23	23	46	39	35	32
15	Michelmores — Exeter, Sidmouth	20	25	45	41	33	23
16	Wolferstans — Plymouth (2), Plymstock, Taunton	26	13	39	40	48	42
17	Wilsons — Salisbury	19	16	35	36	36	29
18	Rickerbys — Cheltenham	17	18	35	n/a	32	34
19	Woollcombe Beer Watts — Bovey Tracey, Chagford, Exeter, Newton Abbot, Torquay	26	8	34	35	35	36
20	Porter Dodson — Bridgewater, Taunton, Wellington, Yeovil	19	15	34	n/a	n/a	33

The Cathedral, Salisbury

The rankings in this table are determined by the number of solicitors working in the region. They are based on partner and assistant solicitor figures only: all other fee-earners are excluded.

www.ChambersandPartners.com

TABLES ■ LAW FIRMS BY SIZE

WALES The 10 largest firms

		Ptnrs	Asst Solrs	Total Number of Solrs '02	'01	'00	'99
1	**Eversheds** Cardiff	35	68	**103**	81	85	86
2	**Morgan Cole** Cardiff, Swansea	33	66	**99**	103	105	112
3	**Hugh James** Bargoed, Blackwood, Cardiff, Merthyr Tydfil, Pontlottyn, Talbot Green, Treharris	42	50	**92**	83	78	66
4	**Leo Abse & Cohen** Cardiff, Swansea	11	47	**58**	58	51	51
5	**Edwards Geldard** Cardiff	21	33	**54**	61	56	66
6	**John Collins & Partners** Swansea	15	19	**34**	43	40	n/a
7	**Palser Grossman** Cardiff Bay, Swansea	15	18	**33**	33	33	27
8	**Dolmans** Cardiff (2)	12	20	**32**	32	32	26
9	**Gamlins** Colwyn Bay, Conwy, Holywell, Llandudno, Rhos-on-Sea, Rhyl	11	16	**27**	21	27	27
10	**Douglas-Jones Mercer** Swansea	12	13	**25**	23	25	23

Cardiff Bay

The rankings in this table are determined by the number of solicitors working in the region. They are based on partner and assistant solicitor figures only: all other fee-earners are excluded.

MIDLANDS The 30 largest firms

		Ptnrs	Asst Solrs	Total Number of Solrs '02	'01	'00	'99
1	**Eversheds** Birmingham, Nottingham	62	234	**296**	259	245	167
2	**Wragge & Co** Birmingham	103	169	**272**	396	340	275
3	**Pinsent Curtis Biddle** Birmingham	59	133	**192**	146	n/a	n/a
4	**freethcartwright** Derby, Leicester, Nottingham	50	72	**122**	104	100	104
5	**Browne Jacobson** Birmingham, Nottingham	39	82	**121**	113	102	95
6	**Hammond Suddards Edge** Birmingham	42	71	**113**	127	127	n/a
7	**Nelsons** Derby, Leicester, Nottingham	51	52	**103**	108	72	72
8	**Martineau Johnson** Birmingham	43	60	**103**	100	94	64
9	**Shoosmiths** Northampton (2), Nottingham	33	56	**89**	102	95	108
10	**DLA** Birmingham	28	53	**81**	81	81	75
11	**Gateley Wareing** Birmingham, Leicester, Nottingham	19	51	**70**	68	49	36
12	**Lee Crowder** Birmingham	20	39	**59**	60	51	38
13	**The Smith Partnership** Burton-Upon-Trent, Derby (2), Leicester (2), Longton, Newcastle-under-Lyme, Swadlincote	21	36	**57**	57	45	39
14	**Anthony Collins Solicitors** Birmingham	17	35	**52**	50	45	41
15	**Irwin Mitchell** Birmingham	16	36	**52**	48	46	35
16	**Challinors Lyon Clark** Birmingham, Edgbaston, West Bromwich	25	26	**51**	46	45	44
17	**The Wilkes Partnership** Birmingham (2)	18	31	**49**	42	42	41
18	**Thompsons** Birmingham, Nottingham, Stoke-on-Trent	9	40	**49**	49	42	41
19	**Harvey Ingram Owston** Leicester	21	27	**48**	50	52	54
20	**Edwards Geldard** Derby, Nottingham	19	27	**46**	44	n/a	n/a
21	**Higgs & Sons** Brierley Hill, Dudley, Kingswinford, Stourbridge	25	19	**44**	42	40	36
22	**Weightman Vizards** Birmingham, Leicester	19	21	**40**	31	34	34
23	**Wright Hassall** Leamington Spa	22	16	**38**	37	32	30
24	**Hewitson Becke + Shaw** Northampton	15	21	**36**	32	32	33
25	**Morton Fisher** Bewdley, Bromsgrove, Halesowen, Kidderminster, Stourport-on-Severn, Worcester	24	11	**35**	35	43	43
26	**Toller Hales & Collcutt** Corby, Kettering, Northampton, Wellingborough	20	15	**35**	33	37	35
27	**Shakespeares** Birmingham	20	14	**34**	45	50	52
28	**Garretts** Birmingham	8	25	**33**	33	31	27
29	**Flint, Bishop & Barnett** Ashbourne, Belper, Derby (4), Matlock	19	12	**31**	n/a	n/a	31
30	**Tinsdills** Leek, Newcastle-under-Lyme, Stoke-on-Trent (2)	16	15	**31**	n/a	31	32

Birmingham

The rankings in this table are determined by the number of solicitors working in the region. They are based on partner and assistant solicitor figures only: all other fee-earners are excluded.

TABLES — LAW FIRMS BY SIZE

EAST ANGLIA The 10 largest firms

		Ptnrs	Asst Solrs	Total Number of Solrs '02	'01	'00	'99
1	Eversheds Cambridge, Ipswich, Norwich	42	96	**138**	128	123	99
2	Mills & Reeve Cambridge, Norwich	49	87	**136**	137	139	129
3	Taylor Vinters Cambridge	27	35	**62**	70	55	47
4	Hewitson Becke + Shaw Cambridge, Saffron Walden	32	27	**59**	59	59	50
5	Ashton Graham Bury St Edmunds, Felixstowe, Ipswich	22	17	**39**	37	37	43
6	Prettys Ipswich	16	20	**36**	36	36	34
7	Fosters Bungay, Norwich, Wymondham	15	15	**30**	27	n/a	20
8	Greenwoods Peterborough	14	16	**30**	33	31	33
9	Birkett Long Chelmsford, Colchester, Halstead	17	12	**29**	25	n/a	n/a
10	Birketts Ipswich	19	8	**27**	n/a	29	29

King's College and chapel, Cambridge

The rankings in this table are determined by the number of solicitors working in the region. They are based on partner and assistant solicitor figures only: all other fee-earners are excluded.

NORTH WEST The 12 largest firms

		Ptnrs	Asst Solrs	Total Number of Solrs '02	'01	'00	'99
1	DLA Liverpool, Manchester	57	113	**170**	170	170	145
2	Halliwell Landau Manchester	58	106	**164**	146	126	132
3	DWF Liverpool, Manchester, Warrington	55	107	**162**	116	91	119
4	Addleshaw Booth & Co Manchester	52	107	**159**	162	148	122
5	Weightman Vizards Liverpool, Manchester	41	112	**153**	91	93	93
6	Hill Dickinson Chester, Liverpool, Manchester	76	70	**146**	119	110	110
7	Eversheds Manchester	31	113	**144**	123	77	114
8	Pannone & Partners Manchester	63	71	**134**	121	93	82
9	Cobbetts Manchester	55	60	**115**	104	87	87
10	Hammond Suddards Edge Manchester	31	68	**99**	94	94	n/a
11	Berrymans Lace Mawer Liverpool, Manchester	36	49	**85**	91	114	101
12	Brabners Chaffe Street Liverpool, Manchester, Preston	39	44	**83**	n/a	43	44

Pier Head, Liverpool

The rankings in this table are determined by the number of solicitors working in the region. They are based on partner and assistant solicitor figures only: all other fee-earners are excluded.

www.ChambersandPartners.com

TABLES — LAW FIRMS BY SIZE

YORKSHIRE The 30 largest firms

		Ptnrs	Asst Solrs	Total Number of Solrs '02	'01	'00
1	**Hammond Suddards Edge** Bradford, Leeds	42	176	**218**	127	127
2	**DLA** Bradford, Leeds (2), Sheffield	68	143	**211**	211	188
3	**Addleshaw Booth & Co** Leeds (2)	55	122	**177**	171	159
4	**Eversheds** Leeds	48	115	**163**	149	139
5	**Irwin Mitchell** Leeds, Sheffield	57	97	**154**	150	141
6	**Pinsent Curtis Biddle** Leeds	49	87	**136**	134	n/a
7	**Walker Morris** Leeds	40	86	**126**	123	121
8	**Nabarro Nathanson** Sheffield	14	59	**73**	62	62
9	**Lupton Fawcett** Leeds	30	32	**62**	55	50
10	**Andrew M. Jackson** Hull	23	32	**55**	54	53
11	**Ford & Warren** Leeds	19	33	**52**	60	47
12	**Gordons Cranswick Solicitors** Bradford, Keighley, Leeds	30	18	**48**	53	49
13	**Rollits** Hull, York	30	18	**48**	48	47
14	**Gosschalks** Hull	26	20	**46**	52	46
15	**Keeble Hawson** Leeds (2), Sheffield	26	19	**45**	45	46
16	**Ison Harrison** Garforth, Leeds (3), York	15	26	**41**	57	34
17	**Howells** Sheffield (3)	13	28	**41**	34	27
18	**Hempsons** Harrogate	8	30	**38**	37	37
19	**Hamers** Doncaster, Hull, Leeds, Sheffield	6	28	**34**	26	34
20	**Harrowell Shaftoe** Haxby, York (2)	15	18	**33**	27	29
21	**Attey Dibb and Clegg** Barnsley, Doncaster (2), Goldthorpe, Mexborough, Rotherham, Thorne, Wath-upon-Dearne	23	9	**32**	34	32
22	**Beachcroft Wansbroughs** Leeds (2)	18	12	**30**	58	77
23	**Last Cawthra Feather** Bradford, Ilkley, Shipley	14	15	**29**	24	23
24	**Morrish & Co** Leeds (2)	11	18	**29**	n/a	n/a
25	**Praxis Partners** Leeds	7	22	**29**	29	n/a
26	**Cobbetts** Leeds	18	10	**28**	n/a	n/a
27	**Wrigleys** Leeds, Sheffield	12	16	**28**	24	25
28	**McCormicks** Harrogate, Leeds	14	13	**27**	24	n/a
29	**Brooke North** Leeds	17	9	**26**	26	26
30	**Denison Till** York	15	10	**25**	24	24

The rankings in this issue are determined by the number of solicitors working in the region. They are based on partner and assistant solicitor figures only: all other fee-earners are excluded.

Civic Hall, Leeds

NORTH EAST The 10 largest firms

		Ptnrs	Asst Solrs	Total Number of Solrs '02	'01	'00
1	**Dickinson Dees** Newcastle upon Tyne, Stockton on Tees	62	103	**165**	140	120
2	**Eversheds** Newcastle upon Tyne	34	75	**109**	108	110
3	**Ward Hadaway** Newcastle upon Tyne, South Shields	44	51	**95**	85	77
4	**Watson Burton** Newcastle upon Tyne	20	29	**49**	45	41
5	**Hay & Kilner** Newcastle on Tyne (2), Wallsend	21	17	**38**	33	32
6	**Blackett Hart & Pratt** Darlington, Darlington, Durham (3), Newcastle upon Tyne (2), Newton Aycliffe	23	11	**34**	34	n/a
7	**Robert Muckle** Newcastle upon Tyne	11	22	**33**	33	33
8	**Crutes Law Firm** Middlesbrough, Newcastle upon Tyne	16	16	**32**	35	38
9	**Tilly Bailey & Irvine** Barnard Castle, Darlington, Hartlepool, Stockton on Tees	14	17	**31**	28	42
10	**Browell Smith & Co** Ashington, Cramlington, Forest Hall, Newcastle upon Tyne	4	24	**28**	n/a	n/a

The rankings in this issue are determined by the number of solicitors working in the region. They are based on partner and assistant solicitor figures only: all other fee-earners are excluded.

Tyne Bridge, Newcastle

INDEX TO LEADING LAWYERS: PAGE 1693 IN-HOUSE LAWYERS' PROFILES: PAGE 1201

SCOTLAND The 30 largest firms

	Firm	Ptnrs	Asst Solrs	'02	'01	'00	'99
1	Dundas & Wilson CS Edinburgh, Glasgow	51	157	208	213	193	168
2	Maclay Murray & Spens Edinburgh, Glasgow	54	124	178	163	94	95
3	Shepherd+ Wedderburn Edinburgh, Glasgow	42	93	135	120	97	90
4	MacRoberts Edinburgh, Glasgow	31	103	134	111	102	87
5	McGrigor Donald Edinburgh, Glasgow	40	93	133	140	129	129
6	Brodies Edinburgh	34	63	97	85	82	73
7	Biggart Baillie Edinburgh, Glasgow	36	56	92	63	60	53
8	Tods Murray WS Edinburgh, Glasgow	37	50	87	85	82	69
9	Burness Edinburgh, Glasgow	33	48	81	71	65	67
10	Paull & Williamsons Aberdeen (2), Edinburgh	30	42	72	63	77	70
11	Anderson Strathern WS Edinburgh (2), Haddington	26	45	71	68	52	53
12	Ledingham Chalmers Aberdeen, Edinburgh, Inverness	36	28	64	59	62	51
13	Henderson Boyd Jackson WS Edinburgh, Glasgow	22	38	60	54	61	61
14	McClure Naismith Edinburgh, Glasgow	20	38	58	55	54	52
15	Bishops Solicitors (formerly Morison Bishop) Edinburgh, Glasgow, Hamilton, Livingston	25	30	55	58	65	65
16	Thorntons WS Arbroath, Dundee, Forfar, Perth	25	27	52	48	42	41
17	Morton Fraser, Solicitors Edinburgh	24	28	52	51	48	49
18	Semple Fraser Edinburgh, Glasgow	21	27	48	44	45	32
19	Turcan Connell Edinburgh	15	30	45	39	35	37
20	Brechin Tindal Oatts Edinburgh, Glasgow	16	28	44	38	33	31
21	Simpson & Marwick Aberdeen, Dundee, Edinburgh, Glasgow	16	28	44	42	41	39
22	Harper Macleod Edinburgh, Glasgow (2)	20	20	40	33	30	29
23	DLA Edinburgh, Glasgow	15	21	36	36	36	n/a
24	Balfour & Manson Edinburgh	18	15	33	38	32	32
25	Stronachs Aberdeen, Inverness	16	17	33	36	37	34
26	Wright, Johnston & Mackenzie Edinburgh, Glasgow	17	15	32	32	n/a	32
27	Drummond Miller WS Bathgate, Dalkeith, Dunfermline, Edinburgh (2), Glasgow, Livingston, Musselburgh	18	13	31	31	34	34
28	Lindsays WS Edinburgh (3), North Berwick	17	13	30	n/a	n/a	22
29	Archibald Campbell & Harley WS Edinburgh	15	14	29	n/a	n/a	23
30	Fyfe Ireland WS Edinburgh	13	16	29	n/a	34	35

Scottish Parliament Foyer, Edinburgh

The rankings in this issue are determined by the number of solicitors working in the region. They are based on partner and assistant solicitor figures only: all other fee-earners are excluded.

THE LAW FIRMS

CHAMBERS
UK
2002–2003

ADMINISTRATIVE & PUBLIC LAW

London (Traditional): 41; London (Commercial): 42; The Regions: 44; Scotland: 47; Profiles: 48

Research approved by BMRB For this edition, **Chambers'** researchers conducted 6,582 interviews – 3,900 with law firms, 511 with barristers and 2,171 with clients. The validity of the research was scrutinised by BMRB International, who audited both the methodology and the results at our offices in London. They interviewed **Chambers'** researchers and cross-checked sample interviews. Details of the audit appear on page 7.

LONDON — TRADITIONAL

ADMINISTRATIVE & PUBLIC LAW: TRADITIONAL — LONDON

1
- Bindman & Partners

2
- Leigh, Day & Co

3
- Mayer, Brown, Rowe & Maw
- Nabarro Nathanson

4
- Bates, Wells & Braithwaite
- Levenes
- Mackintosh Duncan
- Sharpe Pritchard
- Teacher Stern Selby
- Winstanley-Burgess

5
- Bhatt Murphy
- Fisher Meredith
- Hickman & Rose
- Winckworth Sherwood

LEADING INDIVIDUALS

1
- **CHILD Tony** Mayer, Brown, Rowe & Maw
- **GROSZ Stephen** Bindman & Partners
- **STEIN Richard** Leigh, Day & Co

2
- **BURGESS David** Winstanley-Burgess
- **MACKINTOSH Nicola** Mackintosh Duncan
- **RABINOWICZ Jack** Teacher Stern Selby
- **RUEBAIN David** Levenes

3
- **DAY Martyn** Leigh, Day & Co
- **GRIFFITHS Trevor** Sharpe Pritchard
- **ILEY Malcolm** Nabarro Nathanson
- **TROTTER John** Bates, Wells & Braithwaite

This book is the product of 6,582 1/2 hour interviews. See p.7 for BMRB audit. Within each band, firms are listed alphabetically. See individuals' profiles p.48

BINDMAN & PARTNERS (see firm details p.872) Peers were "*constantly impressed by the way in which it pushes the boundaries.*" The firm's exclusive top-tier status did not go undisputed, and in the opinion of many interviewees the gap between it and the rest of the field is narrowing, but it retains the edge on the basis of its superior resources and volume, as well as the high profile of the work undertaken. In some people's opinion the "*best human rights lawyer in the country,*" **Stephen Grosz** (see p.413) has become the mainstay of the practice. Recent highlights for his team include cases involving press intrusion, licensing, the monitoring of patients' telephone calls, professional regulation and the rights of people with learning difficulties to state protection from abuse. Other areas of expertise include advising groups and individuals on new anti-terrorism legislation, and the representation of transsexuals seeking recognition of their new identity. **Clients** War on Want; Mencap; The Law Society; The Soho Society.

LEIGH, DAY & CO (see firm details p.1036) Attracting instructions on some "*hugely challenging judicial reviews,*" barristers admire the team's ability to "*structure its cases well,*" and claim that it is building on and increasing its already considerable presence. **Richard Stein** (see p.49) ("*proactive and cutting edge*") was leading solicitor recently in the Oliveri case, a judicial review taken to the ECJ on behalf of Canadian doctor, Nancy Oliveri. It concerned the licensing by the European Medicines Evaluation Agency and the EU Commission of deferiprone, a treatment for thalassemia. The group is particularly strong in planning and environment, community care and social security, with the caseload often involving challenges to government policy on behalf of individuals or groups. Much of its recent work has been medical in flavour following the firm's involvement in 'Miss B,' and other potential challenges to health policy. It also acted for the FPA in response to the challenge by the Society for the Protection of the Unborn Child as to the legality of the morning after pill. "*An astute campaigning lawyer,*" **Martyn Day** (see p.670) continues to be seen as a key player. **Clients** Individual applicants; human rights organisations.

MAYER, BROWN, ROWE & MAW (see firm details p.1060) An "*outstanding, dedicated practice,*" the firm has comfortably sustained its high profile through involvement in cases like Magill v Porter, the Westminster 'Homes for Votes' case, in which it represented the external auditor, John Magill. A lead solicitor in this case, **Tony Child** (see p.577) possesses "*a fantastically expansive array of knowledge*" according to peers. His strengths lie in audit and local government, areas for which the firm is well known, though interviewees enthusiastically emphasised his adaptability. Indeed, under Child's leadership, the practice has made inroads into the commercial sphere, from where an increasing number of its public law cases originate. Other highlights include advice to East Lindsey District Council on public law issues surrounding the redevelopment of land for a major superstore. Areas of expertise, in which the team advises local authorities, include the Human Rights Act, provision of care for the elderly, local government finance and the establishment of companies. **Clients** Local authorities; Northern Ireland Audit Office; public and private community care and health service providers.

NABARRO NATHANSON (see firm details p.1080) "*Big competitors on a national scale,*" the firm convincingly retains its market share, with clients remarking favourably on its expertise in procurement and related public sector partnership work, as well as corporate governance of public bodies. In this context it covers judicial reviews, particularly in the health and education sectors. **Malcolm Iley** (see p.48) is praised for "*working closely with his clients and building constructive relationships,*" particularly in public-private enterprises. However, commentators wait to see whether the move of Ray Ambrose to a consultancy role will affect the practice. Recent highlights have included advising local authorities on innovative outsourcing projects in the education sector, e-governance and data protection matters. **Clients** Local authorities; further education colleges; London boroughs; health trusts.

BATES, WELLS & BRAITHWAITE (see firm details p.859) Charity and immigration-related work continues to be the mainstay for the firm in this area. Described as striking "*a fine balance between academic rigour and a practical approach,* " **John Trotter** fronts its operation. He has been increasingly involved in giving non-contentious, pre-emptive advice to the firm's traditional clients, which include a range of regulatory and professional membership bodies, successfully decreasing the number of judicial reviews reaching court. The practice also acts on behalf of applicants. **Clients** Regulatory and professional bodies; individual applicants.

LEVENES (see firm details p.1040) Best known for its "*excellent education profile,*" the practice also undertakes administrative law activity in relation to disability and community care matters. One competitor commented that "*you cannot talk about public law without mentioning,*" **David Ruebain** (see p.290) who is regarded as a key player in this sector. Highlights for the team include a challenge to a health authority, on behalf of a disabled client, in relation to the provision of residential care. **Clients** Public Concern at Work; Independent Panel for Special Educational Advice; Network 81.

MACKINTOSH DUNCAN Held in particularly high regard for its community care work and

ADMINISTRATIVE & PUBLIC LAW — LONDON

associated healthcare matters, the firm retains its market profile in this field. Characterised by peers as a "*dedicated campaigner,*" **Nicola Mackintosh** is respected for having "*a high level of expertise and a work rate to match.*" The firm's involvement in high-profile judicial reviews also extends to the fields of employment and mental health. **Clients** Applicants.

SHARPE PRITCHARD (see firm details p.1127) Considered by clients a "*switched-on firm,*" it "*stands out as a considerable local authority practice.*" Recent highlights include acting for a local authority in a House of Lords case testing the compatibility of the Human Rights Act with section 187B of the Town and Country Planning Act, concerning powers in dealing with gypsies. The team also acted for West Yorkshire Police in the Khan case, involving the refusal by a chief constable to give a reference for a police officer who had brought racial discrimination proceedings against him. Said to have "*an amazing grip on procedural issues,*" **Trevor Griffiths** (see p.48) has an established stature in the field. **Clients** Local authorities; public bodies.

TEACHER STERN SELBY (see firm details p.1157) The team has grown recently, consolidating its widely recognised education expertise. Acting mainly for individual applicants, it covers a range of judicial reviews and statutory appeals, including one recent Court of Appeal case on the sale of undervalued land by a local authority. A major educational establishment has consulted the team on the potential judicial review of a qualitative rating given by an external agency. Described by some commentators as "*a hero in terms of education law,*" **Jack Rabinowicz** (see p.290) continues to shine as the firm's standout partner. Health, community care and social security are also areas where the firm is active. **Clients** Individual applicants.

WINSTANLEY-BURGESS (see firm details p.1193) "*Absolutely dedicated to getting the best results for his clients,*" **David Burgess** is considered a "*towering giant in the midst of a top immigration practice.*" It is in this sector that the firm receives a considerable number of its instructions, which are supplemented by advice on a range of associated community-based matters. The practice also covers public law matters relating to various civil liberties cases. **Clients** Individual applicants.

BHATT MURPHY Mounting challenges against the Criminal Cases Review Commission, the Director of Public Prosecutions, the Police Complaints Authority and the Metropolitan Police has earned the firm a high profile for prisoners' rights work and police actions. It has a challenge pending in the Administrative Court, on behalf of the applicants, to determine whether the state failed to safeguard detainees at Yarl's Wood immigration centre in Bedfordshire. The practice is overseen by Raju Bhatt. **Clients** Applicants.

FISHER MEREDITH (see firm details p.956) New to the tables this year, peers remarked upon its impressive level of involvement in public law challenges. These are frequently to the Home Office on behalf of asylum seekers, or to local authorities on behalf of disabled clients, and it has also represented a pressure group in relation to the reconfiguration of health services. Led by Pat Wilkins, other areas of recent activity have included infringement of privacy by the press. **Clients** Individual applicants.

HICKMAN & ROSE (see firm details p.995) Specialising in administrative law within the criminal justice system, the practice continues to be praised by peers for its work in this context. It acted in the second Hirst case, concerning the right of prisoners to hold telephone interviews with journalists under Article 10. Other areas of recent activity include the rights of suspects at the police station, and the categorisation of prisoners. The firm also attracts instructions relating to mental health matters. Daniel Machover oversees the practice. **Clients** Individual applicants.

WINCKWORTH SHERWOOD (see firm details p.1192) Known for the strong ecclesiastical bent to its practice, the firm continues to attract the admiration of practitioners in the field, chiefly for its work in the charity and education sectors. Other areas covered by this knowledgeable and skilled team include health and housing. **Clients** Charity and education sector clients.

LONDON — COMMERCIAL

HERBERT SMITH (see firm details p.992) Considered to "*have the edge*" in terms of breadth of practice, peers and clients applaud this "*highly commercial outfit.*" An inter-departmental team of specialist practitioners regularly acts for applicants, respondents and intervening third parties. It covers wide-ranging regulatory and statutory powers as well as investigations by the DTI and FSA. Governmental and other public bodies feature prominently in its client roster. Commentators "*could not speak highly enough*" of **Andrew Lidbetter** (see p.48), who they admire for being "*down-to-earth and exceptionally committed to his clients.*" He acted for British Sugar in judicial review challenges to the decision by the Intervention Board for Agricultural Produce to impose penalties in connection with the operation of the Common Agricultural Policy. He also featured in a team advising the executive of the Panel on Takeovers and Mergers on WPP Group's attempt to allow its bid for Tempus to lapse, invoking the material adverse change condition. Other highlights for the firm include advising the British Aggregates Association on a potential judicial review challenge to the Aggregates Levy, based on EU law and the European Convention on Human Rights. This case has been stayed at the Court of Appeal pending proceedings at the ECJ. **Clients** The Law Society; IMRO; Horserace Betting Levy Board; Severn Trent Water.

CLIFFORD CHANCE (see firm details p.911) This firm stands out for many interviewees because of the "*unrivalled resources of its dedicated team,*" which, as part of its international network, has the capacity to advise on public and administrative law in most jurisdictions. Advising public bodies and corporations on a range of matters including statutory construction, the team is experienced in tribunal hearings and public inquiries as well as regulatory matters. Praised by clients for his "*highly focused commercial approach,*" **Michael Smyth** (see p.49) possesses a "*commanding presence,*" as well as an "*excellent grasp of political issues and an ability to work round them.*" He recently assisted GE on the procedural and corporate human rights elements of its challenge to the European Commission's decision to block its $46 billion merger with Honeywell. He also acted for Consignia in its attempt to prevent Hays from allegedly infringing the licence regime established under the Postal Services Act 2000. Other highlights for the team include acting for the Emirates Cricket Board on its Commission of Inquiry into match-fixing allegations. New client wins include the Audit Commission, WDA and the MS Society. **Clients** Post Office; University of Cambridge; Public Health Laboratory Service; London Electricity.

LOVELLS (see firm details p.1045) One client told researchers he was "*delighted by the experience of working with the firm,*" while peers noted that its position near the top of the table is "*well deserved.*" As part of its European network, a team of "*consistently high performers*" is able to act on multi-jurisdictional issues. Typical clients are drawn from sectors including manufacturing, retail, financial services, telecommunications and broadcasting. Rated for its human rights expertise, the team acted for BAT and Imperial Tobacco in JR proceedings against the Secretary of State for Health, challenging the Tobacco Control Directive on EU law and human rights grounds. This directive would

LONDON ■ ADMINISTRATIVE & PUBLIC LAW

ADMINISTRATIVE & PUBLIC LAW: COMMERCIAL
■ LONDON

1 Herbert Smith

2 Clifford Chance
Lovells

3 Allen & Overy
Freshfields Bruckhaus Deringer
Simmons & Simmons

4 Beachcroft Wansbroughs
CMS Cameron McKenna
Denton Wilde Sapte
SJ Berwin
Slaughter and May
Theodore Goddard
Travers Smith Braithwaite

LEADING INDIVIDUALS

1 LIDBETTER Andrew *Herbert Smith*
SMYTH Michael *Clifford Chance*

2 MCDERMOTT Jennifer *Lovells*

3 BOWDEN Paul *Freshfields Bruckhaus Deringer*
WATSON Peter *Allen & Overy*

ASSOCIATES TO WATCH
MONEY-KYRIE Rebecca *SJ Berwin*

This book is the product of 6,582 1/2 hour interviews. See p.7 for BMRB audit. Within each band, firms are listed alphabetically. See individuals' profiles p.48

---

place strict new obligations on tobacco manufacturers relating to tar and nicotine yields, health warnings and labelling. It also intervened successfully for Waitrose and Kimberley Developments in a judicial review challenging the proposed redevelopment of land at Chandler's Ford. **Jennifer McDermott** (see p.48) maintains her "*tremendous reputation*" as the "*focus point for the practice.*" The firm's regulatory work has been boosted recently by winning new instructions from the Rail Regulator and the FSA Complaints Commissioner. **Clients** Radio Communications Agency; Sport England; BAT; NATS.

ALLEN & OVERY (see firm details p.841) "*Leading the chasing group*," this was described by clients as a "*high-powered practice*," providing "*partner support of the highest calibre.*" Commercial litigator **Peter Watson** (see p.570) continues to be a "*serious player*" in the field, according to peers. Recent highlights include acting for the SFA (now the FSA) in connection with the Fleurose matter, a landmark decision establishing that the disciplinary proceedings of the financial regulators are civil not criminal in nature. While the case clarified a number of Human Rights Act issues, it may yet be referred to the European Court of Human Rights. The team also advised the Arts Council on reorganising the structure of arts funding in England, including the amalgamation of the Arts Council and the operations of the Regional Arts Boards. Other areas of expertise include advice on the restructuring of utilities companies, and involvement in high profile public inquiries. **Clients** Film Council; Radiocommunications Agency; Countryside Alliance; Radio Authority; Treasury Solicitor.

FRESHFIELDS BRUCKHAUS DERINGER (see firm details p.964) Receiving market accolades for its "*true breadth of talent,*" the practice provides a wide range of regulatory advice, and is well known for its environmental expertise. In this respect, the team have advised BNFL on the JR challenges brought by Greenpeace and Friends of the Earth to the authorisations granted for its new MOX plant at Sellafield. Busy in the financial services sector, it is defending Lloyd's in the ongoing Jaffray litigation at the Court of Appeal. This has involved attempts by Names to raise human rights issues following the judgement against them in The Society of Lloyd's v Sir William Jaffray and others. It also advised JT International in its challenge to the EU's proposed Tobacco Control Directive. **Paul Bowden** (see p.357) has established a "*big reputation*" as head of the international environmental planning and regulatory group. The team is active within a number of other market sectors, including energy, insurance, EU/anti-trust, pharmaceuticals and sport. **Clients** Bank of England; Lloyd's of London; National Pharmaceutical Association; Football Association; One2One.

SIMMONS & SIMMONS (see firm details p.1136) With "*loyal clients and valuable work,*" the firm convincingly retains its market share, which is especially strong in the media, telecoms and energy sectors. Its impressive caseload includes a recent high-profile judicial review for Interbrew. This caused the Secretary of State to reconsider a decision, based on the recommendation of the Competition Commission, not to permit Interbrew to merge the brewing interests of Whitbread and Bass, which it had recently acquired. Head of litigation, Philip Vaughan, oversees the firm's work in this area, which includes defending decisions by regulators and challenging decisions taken. **Clients** ITC; Railtrack; One2One; Interbrew; WorldCom; BP Amoco; Shell; OFGEM.

BEACHCROFT WANSBROUGHS (see firm details p.860) Core areas for this firm include education, health and local government, in which the practice is increasingly "*making its presence felt,*" through advisory and preventative measures. The London team, led by Julian Gizzi, recently acted for NICE on its appraisal process and the redrafting of its appeal procedure. It also advised the Improvement & Development Agency on the Local Authority Modernisation Programme. The group acts on matters relating to central government, including public law issues surrounding the £600 million disposal of assets by the Secretary of State for Health and NHS Estates. It also boasts experience of regulatory matters in the finance, insurance and sports sectors. **Clients** NICE; English Cricket Board; Association of British Insurers; Higher Education Funding Council for England; CIPFA.

CMS CAMERON MCKENNA (see firm details p.914) The firm continues to be considered a "*serious force,*" though interviewees regard the departure of Ian Dodd Smith and his pharmaceuticals team to Arnold & Porter as big news. The group is particularly firmly established in one of the discipline's expanding sectors, utilities regulation, while it retains an impressive reputation for its expertise in the public law aspects of planning and environment, PPP and PFI and financial services. It also continues to service pharmaceuticals companies. The firm is currently acting for a Russian oligarch against the Russian government at the European Court of Human Rights. Commercial litigator Tony Marks is active in this field. **Clients** National Grid; pharmaceutical companies.

DENTON WILDE SAPTE (see firm details p.935) The team delivers high levels of regulatory advice to the energy industry and is reinforcing its credentials in the property and regeneration, sports, technology, media and telecommunications sectors. Recent highlights have included acting for the Central London Partnership and the Circle Initiative on public law issues relating to public-private partnership companies. This concerned the regeneration of sites at Coventry Street, Lower Marsh, Bankside, Holborn and Paddington. The group is also advising the European Commission, in conjunction with PwC, on the legal and regulatory framework for the €3 billion Galileo global satellite navigation project, and assisting the RFU on the creation of England Rugby Limited. The team, including Sandra Banks, has recently won appointment to OFTEL's panel of external legal advisors. **Clients** OFGEM; MoD; University College London.

SJ BERWIN (see firm details p.867) Best known for its high planning and environment profile, it is seen by competitors as "*raising its game,*" with the firm's public law and human rights group now firmly established under the leadership of Michael Rose. Its stated aim is to offer specialist capability in commercial judicial review. Currently involved in a potential class action relating to compensation for breach of property and human rights, other areas of expertise for the team include utilities and energy, in which it has recently received new instructions, as well as media and telecommunications. The group is felt to benefit from the support of specialist litigators and the ability to put together multidisciplinary teams. **Clients** Planit Events; AES Electricity Act License Holders; MEP Green Group.

SLAUGHTER AND MAY (see firm details p.1140) Although competitors do not consider

ADMINISTRATIVE & PUBLIC LAW ■ THE SOUTH/SOUTH WEST

the firm to enjoy high visibility in this area, they acknowledge that the "*quality of its partners and work*" are "*second to none.*" Its advice to Ernst & Young in relation to its role as special administrator of Railtrack, and associated public law obligations, is a case in point. It has also successfully defended Deutsche Bank in the House of Lords against the Inland Revenue. This case established whether an Inspector of Taxes is authorised to issue a notice requiring disclosure by a tax payer of material which is subject to a claim for legal professional privilege. Commercial litigator Nick Gray is active in this field. **Clients** Deutsche Bank; Ernst & Young; Oxford Centre for Islamic Studies.

THEODORE GODDARD (see firm details p.1158) It is "*often used as a touchstone*" by clients, who say that the firm has a proven track record of "*achieving results in challenging situations.*" Core areas of judicial review expertise lie in advertising, sport and education. Recent highlights include advising OFTEL on the terms of the ANF Agreement to be offered by BT to all network operators wishing to take advantage of local loop unbundling, most recently setting the contractual service levels which BT must offer. The team has also acted on behalf of Hampshire Waste Services, in successfully resisting an application for JR. Other areas of expertise include acting for applicants and for overseas governments challenging or resisting challenges to decisions of the UK government. Areas of growth for the firm include food, pharmaceuticals and healthcare. Martin Kramer and Guy Leigh share overall responsibility for its work. **Clients** Advertising Standards Authority; Airport Coordination; OFTEL.

TRAVERS SMITH BRAITHWAITE (see firm details p.1166) "*No list of this kind would be complete without it,*" according to interviewees. The firm has enjoyed less of a profile in this area of late, though it continues to provide a high volume of advisory services. Focusing on telecoms (particularly licensing matters,) property and banking issues, it is also experienced in revenue inquiries and powers of investigation. Notable work this year has included advising the Equitable Life Late Joiners Action Group against Equitable Life, a case involving complex regulatory matters. Dispute resolution partner Jonathan Leslie features in this sector. **Clients** Ulster Bank; Channel 5 Broadcasting; Redland Aggregates.

THE SOUTH

ADMINISTRATIVE & PUBLIC LAW: GENERAL
■ THE SOUTH

1. **Knights** Tunbridge Wells

LEADING INDIVIDUALS

1. **KNIGHT Matthew** Knights

This book is the product of 6,582 1/2 hour interviews. See p.7 for BMRB audit. Within each band, firms are listed alphabetically. See individuals' profiles p.48

KNIGHTS The firm retains its unique standing in the South, thanks to the efforts of lead partner **Matthew Knight** (see p.48). The team acts for both individuals and companies, and is particularly involved with judicial reviews in relation to planning appeals. Advice to existing clients on the Political Parties Elections and Referendums Act 2000, and on issues arising out of the Local Government Finance Act, form the bulk of its remaining workload. Other areas of expertise include advising countryside, farming and sports clients on the implications of administrative decisions. In a new departure for the firm, it has advised a join venture in relation to an innovative PFI scheme. **Clients** Countryside Alliance; National Smallbore Rifle Association; National Farmers Union.

SOUTH WEST

ADMINISTRATIVE & PUBLIC LAW: GENERAL
■ SOUTH WEST

1. **Bevan Ashford** Bristol
2. **Bobbetts Mackan** Bristol
   Clarke Willmott & Clarke Bristol, Taunton

This book is the product of 6,582 1/2 hour interviews. See p.7 for BMRB audit. Within each band, firms are listed alphabetically.

BEVAN ASHFORD (see firm details p.869) Possessing a "*huge knowledge bank for all things health authority-related,*" it is this sector in which the firm is best known. At the forefront of advising on the development of health services, the practice has been busy with the structuring of section 31 agreements and associated governance and accountability issues. It has also seen an increase in the defence of human rights-related challenges in connection with mental health and community care matters. Education highlights include advising OFSTED on the regulation of day-care and early years education in six regions, involving enforcement action against providers. Bethan Evans has joined the firm to head up a new regulatory division, while Richard Annandale, head of the health and social care department, is active in the field. Planning and local authority issues are also catered for by the firm. **Clients** National Clinical Assessment Authority; OFTED; Wiltshire Health Authority; North & East Devon Health Authority.

BOBBETTS MACKAN (see firm details p.879) Sustaining its profile for judicial review challenges on behalf of individuals, the team enjoys a particularly high reputation for expertise in relation to mental health matters. Defendant solicitors commend the firm for "*doing an excellent job for its clients.*" **Clients** Individual applicants.

CLARKE WILLMOTT & CLARKE (see firm details p.907) Operating in the local government, education, social services, planning and farming sectors, barristers admired its "*economical approach.*" Acting from its Bristol and Taunton offices, the group appears for and against local authorities in roughly equal measure, and was recently visible on a foot and mouth-related judicial review. William Whiteley oversees the public law content of the commercial litigation department, which recently assisted Gloucestershire County Council planning department in a successful judicial review against the Secretary of State. This concerned whether the development of certain property could be regarded as reconstruction for the purposes of highway planning control. **Clients** Local authorities; farming interests; individuals.

WALES/MIDLANDS ■ **ADMINISTRATIVE & PUBLIC LAW**

WALES

ADMINISTRATIVE & PUBLIC LAW: GENERAL
■ WALES

1 Eversheds Cardiff
2 Edwards Geldard Cardiff
Morgan Cole Cardiff

LEADING INDIVIDUALS
1 COLE Alun Morgan Cole
EVANS Eric Eversheds
WILLIAMS Huw Edwards Geldard

This book is the product of 6,582 1/2 hour interviews. See p.7 for BMRB audit. Within each band, firms are listed alphabetically. See individuals' profiles p.48

EVERSHEDS (see firm details p.689) Continuing to "*dominate in Wales,*" the firm is praised by clients for being "*fully conversant with the public sector,*" and benefits from its national network. The team provides advice to an expansive client base of public bodies on, inter alia, procurement, statutory interpretation, JR and rule changes. Highlights include advising the National Assembly for Wales on the public law elements of the financing of the Wales Millennium Centre. It also assisted Stroud College in JR proceedings against DEFRA, contesting the refusal of planning permission for the development of college land. With his "*long experience of the sector,*" **Eric Evans** (see p.577) is widely admired by peers. **Clients** Estyn (Her Majesty's Inspectorate for Education and Training in Wales); Wales & West Housing Association; Elim Housing Association.

EDWARDS GELDARD (see firm details p.944) With strong environment and planning expertise, the practice also undertakes advice to local authorities. Known for its innovative approach, it recently assisted Finnforest BBH in the first statutory challenge of its kind in the Administrative Court for Wales and Chester. This concerned CPOs for the Newport (Gwent) Southern distributor road scheme. Head of department **Huw Williams** (see p.49) continues to build on a well-established reputation. He has been busy providing advice to public bodies on development and redevelopment schemes, highway closures and land transactions. **Clients** Welsh Development Agency; Arts Council of Wales; Derbyshire County Council; Wrexham County Borough Council.

MORGAN COLE (see firm details p.296) A leading practice in the area, it has sustained its competitive edge, according to interviewees, and is particularly well regarded for acting for health authorities. The practice embraces both public and private sector work, alongside traditional advice to public authorities. Its national reach gives it the capacity to win instructions from major clients, such as the Human Fertilisation and Embryology Authority, for whom it is the sole legal advisor. "*Widely recognised in the public sector,*" **Alun Cole** has long-standing experience in the field. **Clients** Local authorities; health authorities; NHS trusts; Cardiff Bay Development Corporation.

MIDLANDS

ADMINISTRATIVE & PUBLIC LAW: GENERAL
■ MIDLANDS

1 Pinsent Curtis Biddle Birmingham
Tyndallwoods Birmingham
Wragge & Co Birmingham
2 Browne Jacobson Nottingham
Martineau Johnson Birmingham

LEADING INDIVIDUALS
1 GOULD Jean Tyndallwoods
KEITH-LUCAS Peter Wragge & Co
SHINER Philip Public Interest Lawyers
2 WALLACE Alastair Tyndallwoods
WHITE Martin Pinsent Curtis Biddle

This book is the product of 6,582 1/2 hour interviews. See p.7 for BMRB audit. Within each band, firms are listed alphabetically. See individuals' profiles p.48

PINSENT CURTIS BIDDLE (see firm details p.1102) "*Well renowned for anything institutional in Birmingham,*" the firm is said by competitors to be consolidating its already strong presence. Having been appointed to Birmingham City Council's planning and property panel, recent highlights have included advising it on the administrative law elements of regeneration projects. Involvement in service delivery mechanisms in areas as diverse as health, schools, and street lighting, as well as sizeable housing transfers and advice to central government on strategic partnering and pathfinder projects, all contribute to its workload. Planning and compulsory purchase specialist **Martin White** (see p.49) remains well-regarded by market sources for his skill and dedication. **Clients** County councils; health trusts; London Boroughs of Islington, and Newham.

TYNDALLWOODS (see firm details p.1172) This "*impressive public law team*" covers community care, asylum support, education, planning and environment. Interviewees were particularly impressed by its "*astute management of challenges,*" often brought on human rights grounds, in which its practitioners have a "*considerable depth of knowledge.*" The expanding department includes "*thoughtful and hardworking,*" **Jean Gould** (see p.48) who has a national reputation in the field. She recently acted in litigation concerning community care service policies, including the application of Article 6 to appeals against charging levels and the availability of restitution. **Alastair Wallace** (see p.49) was commended to researchers for his "*tenacious approach.*" He recently acted for applicants challenging the closure of services for the elderly in Solihull, and brought a successful challenge on health grounds against the granting of planning permission for a mobile telephone mast. Acting for individuals seeking gender reassignment treatment, and advising on village green matters, also feature as niche areas of expertise, while the development of a prisoners' rights practice has bolstered its profile. **Clients** Residents Action Group for the Elderly; individual applicants.

WRAGGE & CO (see firm details p.1197) Its "*depth of experience*" in advising local authorities guarantees the firm top-tier status in the view of peers. Its practice covers advice to major corporate and public clients on JR, human rights, constitutional and regulatory law. Highlights include advising the Electricity Association on the implementation of the Utilities Act 2000 in relation to electricity supply and distribution. This included advice on the drafting of new licences and on negotiations with Ofgem and the DTI on the form of licence conditions. Admired for "*successfully making the transition from a local authority background to private practice,*" **Peter Keith-Lucas** is among the most highly respected practitioners in the field. The team also offers extensive administrative experience as well as expertise in public law property and planning matters. **Clients** Prison Service; English Heritage; Maritime Agency; 75 local authorities; Guidance Accreditation Board; Consumer Council for Postal Services.

BROWNE JACOBSON (see firm details p.891) The firm continues to be held in high regard by market sources. Areas of expertise include advising local authorities on PPP and corporate governance matters, as well as acting on prosecutions. Bringing its environmental experience to bear, it acted recently on a human rights-based injunction and JR actions for English Nature concerning sites in Hampshire and Norfolk. Newly appointed by Birmingham City Council for public law and property work, the team is headed up by Nick Parsons. Recent successes include conducting advocacy for the Countryside Council for Wales at the Tir Mostyn Wind Farm Inquiry. **Clients** English

ADMINISTRATIVE & PUBLIC LAW ■ EAST ANGLIA/THE NORTH

Nature; DTI; Countryside Council for Wales; local authorities.

MARTINEAU JOHNSON (see firm details p.1056) Its "*strong reputation in the education sector*" is unrivalled in the region and extends nationwide. It is this sector which sees the team's highest profile involvement in JR proceedings, which have recently included defending Coventry University against a challenge by a student disputing the application of disciplinary procedures. Head of education, Nicola Hart oversees much of the firm's public law work. **Clients** Birmingham University; Aston University; other educational institutions and funding bodies.

OTHER NOTABLE PRACTITIONERS A "*force to be reckoned with,*" **Phil Shiner** wins market applause for his success in establishing Public Interest Lawyers as a player in the region. His most recent high profile project has been acting for a group of Gurkhas against the MoD for discrimination and violation of their human rights.

EAST ANGLIA

ADMINISTRATIVE & PUBLIC LAW: GENERAL
■ EAST ANGLIA

1. **Mills & Reeve** Norwich
1. **Richard Buxton** Cambridge

LEADING INDIVIDUALS

1. **BUXTON Richard** Richard Buxton

This book is the product of 6,582 1/2 hour interviews. See p.7 for BMRB audit. Within each band, firms are listed alphabetically. See individuals' profiles p.48

MILLS & REEVE (see firm details p.864) The team benefits from a "*deep understanding of local government*" according to clients. Though an increasing amount of work is being carried out from its Birmingham-based public law unit, under Nicholas Hancox, the East Anglian offices remain best known in the market for the firm's local government, health, planning and education-related work. Through the efforts of its Birmingham office, the firm has also been appointed to the Birmingham City Council panel to undertake adult social services litigation, public law and property work. **Clients** Local authorities; NHS trusts.

RICHARD BUXTON The firm is perceived by some interviewees to be "*in a league of its own,*" due to the exertions of **Richard Buxton**, who barristers claim is capable of achieving "*astonishing successes*" in court. A recent example is that of Burkett at the House of Lords, concerning the time limits for judicial reviews. Residents and action groups continue to provide him with the bulk of his instructions, which often lead to appearances at the High Court and Court of Appeal, with some cases going as far as the European Court of Human Rights. **Clients** Individual applicants; wildlife trusts; CPRE.

THE NORTH

ADMINISTRATIVE & PUBLIC LAW: GENERAL
■ THE NORTH

1. **Eversheds** Leeds, Manchester
2. **Irwin Mitchell** Sheffield
3. **Addleshaw Booth & Co** Manchester
3. **Pinsent Curtis Biddle** Leeds
4. **Beachcroft Wansbroughs** Leeds
5. **Howells** Sheffield

LEADING INDIVIDUALS

1. **CIRELL Stephen** Eversheds
2. **DOBSON Nicholas** Pinsent Curtis Biddle

This book is the product of 6,582 1/2 hour interviews. See p.7 for BMRB audit. Within each band, firms are listed alphabetically. See individuals' profiles p.48

EVERSHEDS (see firm details p.949) The firm's Northern stronghold commands great respect from interviewees, who acknowledge it as being at the hub of "*an altogether switched-on national operation.*" Advice to public authorities, in areas as diverse as strategic partnerships, PFI, constitutional matters and waste management, has featured among the year's highlights. "*Well-versed in public sector matters,*" head of local government **Stephen Cirell** (see p.577) is said to be "*as strong a lawyer as you are likely to come across in the field.*" He has been heavily involved in e-government initiatives, including advice to South Norfolk District Council on connection to the National Land Information Service. Other matters include the preparation of new political constitutions for Southend-on-Sea Unitary Council, Walsall Metropolitan Council and Lichfield Council. Its proactive advice on JR-related issues is valued by clients. **Clients** Local authorities; regional development agencies.

IRWIN MITCHELL (see firm details p.1009) Renowned for its "*imaginative and well-thought through challenges,*" often on behalf of individuals against the government, the firm has had an unusually high number of important cases this year even by its own standards. These have included mounting a successful challenge in the European Court of Human Rights, leading to a wider definition of cases meriting exceptional funding. Education, health, social services, prisons, criminal due process and regulatory work are all areas in which the team offers expertise. Viewed by rivals as having a top-class applicant practice, it also acts for local authorities, institutions and businesses. In the field of PPP, clients praise the team for its "*excellent understanding of legislation and politics, as well as the operational aspects involved.*" Growth in planning public inquiries has also been a feature of recent work. Andrew Lockley heads the public law department. **Clients** Individual applicants; companies; institutions; local authorities.

ADDLESHAW BOOTH & CO (see firm details p.838) Though not as visible as in past years, the litigation and dispute resolution team continues to advise on judicial review actions, as well as to develop its human rights expertise, and wins respect from clients and competitors alike. Recent highlights for the team include acting for an examination board on a challenge to its malpractice appeals system, raising issues of fair trial and the right to education. The team also advises existing public authority clients on the development of policy in line with convention rights, as well as covering planning and project-related matters. Susan Garrett is active in this practice area. **Clients** Public authorities.

PINSENT CURTIS BIDDLE (see firm details p.1102) Perceived by interviewees to derive its public law profile from its strength in public sector projects, the firm is well supplied with instructions from a considerable client base of public authorities, including government departments, educational institutions and NHS bodies. Indeed, it has recently won instructions on four new hospital projects, including Birmingham and Leicester, two of the largest. National head of local government **Nicholas Dobson** (see p.577) enters the tables for the first time having received warm praise from peers. He particularly impressed in his role as advisor to the Welland Partnership, a new appointment for the firm, on a government-sponsored community pathfinder project. **Clients** DfES; NHS Estates; Secretary of State for Health; Department of Health; Crown Prosecution Service; local authorities; universities.

BEACHCROFT WANSBROUGHS (see firm details p.860) Drawing on its considerable health and education capacity, the firm has successfully defended two recent human rights challenges. It acted for Lincolnshire Health Authority and County Council at the Court of Appeal in a 'home for life case,' concerning the right of authorities to relocate patients from one hospital unit to another. Acting for a hospital trust, it won a case determining whether a mental health patient had the right to influence treatment decisions. The public law team, headed by Melanie Print, has also completed advice on the establishment of Lincolnshire Partnership Trust. **Clients** NHS bodies; GP practices; private health care providers.

HOWELLS (see firm details p.1002) Police actions, prisoners' rights and community care are the core strengths of this "*robust practice.*" Through co-operation with the firm's immigration and education teams, it sustains a wide range of work, often with a civil liberties slant. It has acted in judicial reviews in relation to council tax committal, community care, and taxi licence appeals. Landmark cases have included that of Green, which determined that the Police Complaints Authority must disclose documents and invite comments before deciding whether an officer should face disciplinary charges. The team is led by assistant solicitors Richard Price and Peter Mahy. **Clients** Individual applicants.

SCOTLAND

ADMINISTRATIVE & PUBLIC LAW: GENERAL
■ SCOTLAND

1
- **Brodies** Edinburgh
- **Dundas & Wilson CS** Edinburgh
- **McGrigor Donald** Glasgow
- **Shepherd+ Wedderburn** Edinburgh

2
- **Biggart Baillie** Edinburgh
- **Simpson & Marwick** Edinburgh

3
- **Burness** Edinburgh
- **Tods Murray WS** Edinburgh

LEADING INDIVIDUALS
1 **SHAW Kate** Simpson & Marwick

This book is the product of 6,582 1/2 hour interviews. See p.7 for BMRB audit. Within each band, firms are listed alphabetically. See individuals' profiles p.48

BRODIES (see firm details p.889) Despite William Holligan's departure to take up an appointment on the Sheriff Court bench, interviewees believe that the firm has sustained a "*quality operation.*" The public law group, continuing its business under Neil Collar, has planned ahead, recruiting Robin Macpherson from Robson McLean. Recent highlights have included acting in human rights-based mental health appeals at the Privy Council and Inner House of the Court of Session. The team also advised the DTI on the public law aspects of separating the transmission, distribution, generation and supply businesses of the Scottish electricity companies. It has been appointed as the sole external lawyers to Aberdeen City Council, and reappointed to advise the SRA on new franchising agreements. **Clients** Local Authorities and other government bodies.

DUNDAS & WILSON CS (see firm details p.943) Possessing, in the opinion of interviewees, "*true strength and depth, with ability across the board,*" this is deemed an accomplished operation with expertise in a range of sectors. Drawing on its energy client base, the firm has been particularly busy in negotiating with SEPA on administrative law issues. Court cases on behalf of clients in, *inter alia*, licensed gaming, sports and construction have featured as recent highlights. It also sustains a big profile in the fields of health, education and local authority work. As head of the local government department, Michael McAuley is active in public law. **Clients** Scottish and Southern Energy; Scottish Water; Medical Defence Union.

MCGRIGOR DONALD (see firm details p.1065) Perceived by clients to possess "*talented public sector lawyers,*" the firm retains its position in the top-tier. It services a top class local government and utilities client base, on matters covering local authority powers, public procurement, and European structural funding issues. Alan Boyd, an expert on Scottish parliamentary and public affairs, is head of public law. His team has successfully completed advice to the Department for Regional Development (Northern Ireland) on the drafting of new legislation for Belfast, Londonderry and Warrenpoint ports. The firm's ground-breaking PPP work also often incorporates a public law dimension. **Clients** Local Authorities; Aberdeenshire Housing Department; Department for Regional Development (Northern Ireland).

SHEPHERD+ WEDDERBURN (see firm details p.1130) The firm boasts a "*highly impressive client base,*" according to rivals, and has a core of local government work. It enjoys particular strength in vires issues and the contracting out of services, and handles a steady flow of PFI work. In the past year it has acted in around half of Scotland's major local authority projects. Following the retirement of Ian McLeod, the firm's public law work is spearheaded by the Saltire team which includes Hazel Moffar, led by Gordon Downie. The group recently represented Angus and City of Dundee Councils in the A92 road PFI project Public Inquiry. **Clients** East Dunbartonshire Council; North Lanarkshire Council; Highland Council; Aberdeenshire Council; West Lothian Council; Midlothian Council; City of Edinburgh Council.

BIGGART BAILLIE (see firm details p.871) Clients and practitioners alike agree that the firm maintains a strong profile in the sector through its impressive catalogue of recent cases. It continues to act for the Meat and Livestock Commission in an ongoing JR challenge to the MLC levy on certain cattle, which now has wider implications following the involvement of Scottish ministers on behalf of the intervention board. Other highlights include advising Scotnursing on a challenge to a hospital trust over its tendering process for the provision of nurses. David Kidd and Murray Shaw are both active in the field. **Clients** Meat and Livestock Commission; Highland Council; British Railways Board.

SIMPSON & MARWICK (see firm details p.1138) Operating from offices in Edinburgh, Glasgow, Aberdeen and Dundee, the practice is a great favourite of local authorities. Its stated aim is to prevent JR challenges to its impressive raft of clients, but is also more than capable of negotiating matters once they have gone to court. Commentators praised Kate Shaw (see p.49) for her breadth of knowledge and understanding of all JR and local government issues. **Clients** Local authorities.

BURNESS Located within the firm's corporate department, the public law team, led by Stephen Phillips, has had a busy year. Highlights include acting for the City of Edinburgh and Midlothian Councils, developing the corporate structures and land option arrangements for the joint venture driving the South East Wedge project. It has also assisted the Scottish Executive on the transfer, to Scottish Enterprise and Highlands & Islands Enterprise, of the Careers Service operations throughout Scotland. **Clients** Scottish Borders Council; Scottish Enterprise; Developing North Ayrshire; East Lothian Council; Gorbals Initiative.

TODS MURRAY WS (see firm details p.1164) This "*knowledgeable, responsive team*" is well regarded for its public law work in the interesting, busy sectors of education, environment, housing and planning. In the last year the team, which includes Elaine Brailsford, has advised SEPA in relation to the possibility of pollution from the Doonray nuclear reconditioning facility. It is also advising a major council in an ongoing dispute. The firm was praised by clients for the "*robust*" way it defends public bodies in JRs. **Clients** Angus Council; Dundee City Council; Forestry Commission; SEPA; Scottish Screen.

ADMINISTRATIVE & PUBLIC LAW ■ NORTHERN IRELAND

NORTHERN IRELAND

ADMINISTRATIVE & PUBLIC LAW: GENERAL
■ NORTHERN IRELAND

1. **Cleaver Fulton Rankin** Belfast
   Madden & Finucane Belfast

LEADING INDIVIDUALS

1. **FARIS Neil** Cleaver Fulton Rankin
   RITCHIE Angela Madden & Finucane

This book is the product of 6,582 1/2 hour interviews. See p.7 for BMRB audit. Within each band, firms are listed alphabetically. See individuals' profiles p.48

CLEAVER FULTON RANKIN (see firm details p.910) Advising individuals, local authorities and NGOs, the firm continues its involvement in a broad spectrum of public law work. Recent activity has included advising local authorities on the impact of the Human Rights Act. Judicial reviews on planning permission decisions also contribute to its workload. **Neil Faris** (see p.359 & p.729) continues to be well received by the market. **Clients** Sentence Review Commission; BT; Sports Council; local authorities.

MADDEN & FINUCANE (see firm details p.1050) A "*politically important*" firm, appeals on behalf of prisoners continue to be its forte. Its most high-profile recent work has included judicial review challenges to the Parades Commission and activity on behalf of the families in the Bloody Sunday Inquiry. According to interviewees, **Angela Ritchie** shows "*commitment to making the case for her clients heard.*" **Clients** Individual applicants.

THE LEADERS IN ADMINISTRATIVE & PUBLIC LAW

BOWDEN, Paul
Freshfields Bruckhaus Deringer, London
(020) 7936 4000
paul.bowden@freshfields.com
See under Environment, p.357

BURGESS, David
Winstanley-Burgess, London
(020) 7278 7911

BUXTON, Richard
Richard Buxton, Cambridge
(01223) 328933

CHILD, Tony
Mayer, Brown, Rowe & Maw, London
(020) 7782 8686
tchild@ev.mayerbrownrowe.com
See under Local Government, p.577

CIRELL, Stephen
Eversheds, Leeds
(0113) 243 0391
stephencirell@eversheds.com
See under Local Government, p.577

COLE, Alun
Morgan Cole, Cardiff
(029) 2038 5385

DAY, Martyn
Leigh, Day & Co, London
(020) 7650 1200
See under Product Liability, p.670

DOBSON, Nicholas
Pinsent Curtis Biddle, Leeds
(0113) 244 5000
nicholas.dobson@pinsents.com
See under Local Government, p.577

EVANS, Eric
Eversheds, Cardiff
(029) 2047 1147
See under Local Government, p.577

FARIS, Neil
Cleaver Fulton Rankin, Belfast
(028) 9024 3141
n.faris@cfrlaw.co.uk
See under Environment, p.359, Real Estate, p.729

GOULD, Jean
Tyndallwoods, Birmingham
(0121) 624 1111
jgould@tyndallwoods.co.uk
Specialisation: Particularly interested in social welfare and human rights applications of public law and in public interest litigation. Cases include R v Sefton MBC ex parte Help the Aged and others, and R v North Lancashire Health Authority ex parte A, D & G.
Career: Formerly project solicitor at the public law project and now a partner at *Tyndallwoods* and trainer in community care law for Carers National Association. Member of the Legal Services Commission Public Interest Advisory Panel.
Publications: Contributes articles to 'Legal Action' and other journals.
Personal: BA Hons. Taught in Inner London before qualifying in 1990.

GRIFFITHS, Trevor
Sharpe Pritchard, London
(020) 7405 4600
Specialisation: Partner specialising in judicial review, statutory and planning appeals, in the Administrative Court, conducts appeals to Court of Appeal and House of Lords. In addition deals with assessment of costs and environmental and planning injunction work.
Career: Joined *Sharpe Pritchard* in 1982, qualified in 1984 and became a partner in 1987.
Personal: Born 6 December 1957. Educated at Bishop Wordsworth School 1969-76 and U.W.I.S.T 1976-79. Recreations include golf and cricket. Lives in London.

GROSZ, Stephen
Bindman & Partners, London
(020) 7833 4433
s.grosz@bindmans.com
See under Human Rights, p.413

ILEY, Malcolm
Nabarro Nathanson, London
(020) 7524 6909
m.iley@nabarro.com
Specialisation: Main practice area is public law relating to local government, government departments and public sector powers generally. Experience in local authority outsourcings, asset transfer, regeneration, compulsory purchase, planning, education, competition and PFI, including the consideration of wider European involvement. Advisor to The Audit Commission; ethical standards, public sector governance, Treasury Rules on public sector governance and finance. Clients have included London boroughs, district and county councils, government departments, local authority-related companies, higher and further education, LAWDAC, and urban development corporations. Media advisor and broadcaster on public sector legal issues. Contributor to the public sector regional press.
Career: Qualified in 1976. Began career in the private sector, transferred to local government and later became a senior lawyer with Leeds City Council. Appointed City Solicitor and Deputy Chief Executive for Plymouth City Council. Held other senior posts in Lancashire, Sussex and Norfolk. Joined *Nabarro Nathanson* in 1997 as a partner and Head of Public Sector Group.
Personal: Born 12 April 1950. College Governor. F.E. Governor, company director, policy advisor to government (eg PPPs/DTLR).

KEITH-LUCAS, Peter
Wragge & Co, Birmingham
(0870) 903 1000

KNIGHT, Matthew
Knights, Tunbridge Wells
(01892) 537311
knights@atlas.co.uk
Specialisation: Senior partner. Main area of practice is judicial review. Also handles defamation, crime, trespass, compulsory purchase compensation, commercial litigation and advising on and drafting legislation. Acted in Sawrij & Swalesmoor Mink Farm Ltd v Lynx & Others; in R v Somerset County Council ex parte Fewings, Leyland & Down and in British Field Sports Society ats Commissioners of HM Customs & Excise. Author of various articles.
Prof. Memberships: Law Society.
Career: Qualified in 1982 after joining *Farrer & Co* in 1980. Worked at *Sinclair Roche & Temperley* 1982-84, then at *Cripps Harries Hall* 1984-94, from 1986 as a partner. Established *Knights* in 1994.
Personal: Born 2 April 1957. Attended Eltham College 1970-76, Newcastle University 1976-79 and College of Law 1979-80. Leisure interests include hunting and shooting.

LIDBETTER, Andrew
Herbert Smith, London
(020) 7374 8000
andrew.lidbetter@herbertsmith.com
Specialisation: Solicitor Advocate with considerable experience of dealing with a wide range of commercial disputes. Has a specialist public law practice including judicial review, statutory appeals, ECHR issues, professional regulation, DTI investigations, other inquiries, disciplinary proceedings, local government and environmental cases. Clients include both claimants and regulators. On the advisory board of 'JR' (Judicial Review).
Prof. Memberships: Administrative Law Bar Association.
Career: Qualified 1990. Partner 1998.
Publications: Author of 'Company Investigations and Public Law - A Practical Guide to Government Investigations' (1999); 'Judicial Review' and 'Human Rights' chapters in 'Blackstone's Civil Practice' (2002).
Personal: Educated at Worcester College, Oxford (First class law degree and BCL).

MACKINTOSH, Nicola
Mackintosh Duncan, London
(020) 7357 6464

MCDERMOTT, Jennifer
Lovells, London
(020) 7296 2000
jennifer.mcdermott@lovells.com
Specialisation: Media litigation, particu-

THE LEADERS ■ ADMINISTRATIVE & PUBLIC LAW

larly including defamation, privacy, confidentiality and print and broadcasting regulatory matters. Advises many newspapers and corporate clients. Extensive expertise also in commercial judicial review, having been involved in several high profile applications against and in conjunction with many regulatory authorities; speaks at conferences and on radio and television on both judicial review and media law.
Prof. Memberships: Member of the Media Society, the Royal Television Society, Society of Editors, Executive Board of JUSTICE; Amnesty International; Administrative Law Bar Association.
Career: Qualified 1981 with *Lovells*; partner 1989.
Publications: On the editorial board of 'Communications Law'; contributes to publications such as the 'Press Gazette' and 'PLC'.

MONEY-KYRIE, Rebecca
SJ Berwin, London
(020) 7533 2222

RABINOWICZ, Jack
Teacher Stern Selby, London
(020) 7242 3191
j.rabinowicz@tsslaw.com
See under Education, p.290

RITCHIE, Angela
Madden & Finucane, Belfast
(028) 9023 8007

RUEBAIN, David
Levenes, London
(020) 8881 7777
druebain@levenes.co.uk
See under Education, p.290

SHAW, Kate
Simpson & Marwick, Edinburgh
(0131) 557 1545
kate.shaw@simpmar.com
Specialisation: Acts for a number of Scottish local authorities and other government departments in EL and PL claims and administrative law. Expertise in judicial review actions, Inner House appeals and licensing appeals. Has a particularly detailed knowledge of the unique pressures and difficulties faced by clients in the public sector, both economic and political.
Prof. Memberships: Law Society of Scotland
Career: Qualified 1978, Partner in litigation department since 1982.

SHINER, Philip
Public Interest Lawyers, Birmingham
(0121) 702 2110

SMYTH, Michael
Clifford Chance, London
(020) 7600 1000
michael.smyth@cliffordchance.com
Specialisation: Litigation and Dispute Resolution Department. Partner specialising in commercial litigation and dispute avoidance, media litigation and public law.
Career: Qualified 1982; Partner since 1990.
Personal: Royal Belfast Academical Institution; Clare College, Cambridge (MA Law).

STEIN, Richard
Leigh, Day & Co, London
(020) 7650 1200
Specialisation: Practice covers administrative and public law particularly with a human rights emphasis including health, town planning and community care matters. Acts principally for campaigning and community groups and individuals in judicial reviews of local authorities and public authorities. Acted in R v HFEA exp Diane Blood, forced caesarian re S, ex parte Belgium Pinochet case, Ms B v an NHS Trust (right to die) case.
Prof. Memberships: Administrative Law Bar Association; Public Law Project Management Committee; Member of the Law Society Mental Health and Disability Committee.
Career: Called to the Bar 1982. Admitted solicitor 1994. Joined *Leigh Day & Co* 1993.

TROTTER, John
Bates, Wells & Braithwaite, London
(020) 7551 7777

WALLACE, Alastair
Tyndallwoods, Birmingham
(0121) 624 1111
Specialisation: Partner. Head of public law department. Specialises in administrative and public law on behalf of applicants in a range of, mainly, local government related issues, in particular community care, education, planning and health law. Considerable experience in judicial review on behalf of individuals and campaigning groups in public interest cases. Has particular interest in asylum support, village greens mobile phone masts and care home closures. Has contributed articles to 'Legal Action' and 'Mineral Planning'.
Career: Joined *Tyndallwoods* in 1991
Personal: Film, music and cycling.

WATSON, Peter
Allen & Overy, London
(020) 7330 3000
peter.watson@allenovery.com
See under Litigation, p.570

WHITE, Martin
Pinsent Curtis Biddle, Birmingham
(0121) 200 1050
martin.white@pinsents.com
Specialisation: Handles planning and related areas, including highways and environmental issues, with emphasis on major projects, planning appeal work, development plans, issues of planning gain, Section 106 agreements, regeneration and compulsory purchase. Has acted in appeals relating to major inward investment, airports and business parks, for local Planning Authorities and private sector clients. Also handles local government and public law generally. Author of articles, speaker at conferences and seminars on planning gain and general planning issues.
Prof. Memberships: Law Society (Member of Planning Panel), Legal Associate of Royal Town Planning Institute.
Career: Qualified in 1979. Articled at Solihull Council 1977-79. Joined *Pinsent & Co* in 1981. Partner in 1987.
Personal: Born 1953. Attended Cambridge University 1972-76; Newcastle Polytechnic 1976-77. Interests include drama and music.

WILLIAMS, Huw
Edwards Geldard, Cardiff
(029) 2023 8239
huw.williams@geldards.co.uk
Specialisation: Partner, Public Law. Principal area of practice encompasses public, planning and environmental law. Has worked extensively since 1987 on major urban renewal projects for the Welsh Development Agency, Cardiff Bay Development Corporation and local authorities, including numerous compulsory purchase orders, Parliamentary procedures relating to the Cardiff Bay Barrage project and joint ventures. Advice to both public and private interests on planning law and related matters including highways and utilities. Environmental experience includes cases relating to water pollution and contaminated land. Retained on a number of Millennium projects including Wales Millennium Centre and National Botanic Garden of Wales. Other public bodies advised include Cardiff University, National Library of Wales and the Arts Council of Wales.
Prof. Memberships: Law Society.
Career: Qualified 1978. Assistant Solicitor, Mid Glamorgan County Council 1978-80, Senior Assistant Solicitor 1980-84 and Principal Assistant Solicitor (Environmental Services) 1984-87. Joined *Edwards Geldard* in 1987 and became Partner in charge of public law in 1988.
Personal: Born 4 January 1954. Attended Llanelli Grammar School 1965-72, then Jesus College, Oxford 1972-75 (MA). Member of Council and Chairman, Cardiff and South East Wales branch, The Oxford University Society; Treasurer, Wales Public Law and Human Rights Association; Member, Law Society Welsh Affairs Working Party. Member of the Advisory Committee, Centre for Professional Legal Studies. Cardiff University. Leisure pursuits include scuba diving, skiing, occasional sailing, naval history, art and architecture.

ADVERTISING & MARKETING

London: 50; Profiles: 52

Research approved by BMRB For this edition, **Chambers'** researchers conducted 6,582 interviews – 3,900 with law firms, 511 with barristers and 2,171 with clients. The validity of the research was scrutinised by BMRB International, who audited both the methodology and the results at our offices in London. They interviewed **Chambers'** researchers and cross-checked sample interviews. Details of the audit appear on page 7.

OVERVIEW These remain gloomy times for the advertising industry, with 2002 so far seeing little loosening of purse strings. Britain's biggest companies are continuing to keep a tight rein on their advertising budgets and it is the large international agencies that are feeling the pinch most keenly. Advertising campaigns are being scaled down in favour of more easily measured direct marketing and sales promotions, although online campaigns appear to be faring slightly better than their traditional counterparts. Although our tables focus on the traditional mainstream advertising sector, one should not ignore the developments in e-commerce and the use of technology as a marketing stream, such as work spearheaded by e-commerce specialist Rafi Azim-Khan of McDermott, Will & Emery. *Chambers* refers you to the E-commerce Section of this guide for a further review of developments in this sector.

LONDON

ADVERTISING & MARKETING — LONDON

1
- Lewis Silkin
- Macfarlanes
- Osborne Clarke

2
- The Simkins Partnership

3
- Hammond Suddards Edge
- Theodore Goddard

4
- Lawrence Graham
- Olswang
- Taylor Wessing

5
- Clifford Chance
- Mayer, Brown, Rowe & Maw

6
- Baker & McKenzie
- CMS Cameron McKenna
- Harrison Curtis
- Lovells

LEADING INDIVIDUALS

1
- ALEXANDER Roger — Lewis Silkin
- GROOM Stephen — Osborne Clarke

2
- BIRT Tim — Osborne Clarke
- DRESDEN Brinsley — Lewis Silkin
- HALL-SMITH Vanessa — Harrison Curtis
- SWAN Charles — The Simkins Partnership

3
- BRAFMAN Guilherme — Kaye Scholer LLP
- COURTENAY-STAMP Jeremy — Macfarlanes
- EARLE Rupert — Theodore Goddard
- THOMAS Richard — Clifford Chance

4
- BYRT Sarah — Mayer, Brown, Rowe & Maw
- WEGENEK Robert — Hammond Suddards Edge

UP AND COMING
- CROWN Giles — Lewis Silkin
- RAYMAN Alice — The Simkins Partnership

This book is the product of 6,582 1/2 hour interviews. See p.7 for BMRB audit. Within each band, firms are listed alphabetically. See individuals' profiles p.52

LEWIS SILKIN (see firm details p.1041) The firm continues to sustain its "*enviable reputation*" within the area. In addition to a raft of leading lights and an unmatched client roster, it possesses recognised strength across the spectrum of corporate, pure advertising and marketing work, and is applauded for its relentless efforts to "*drive the practice forward*." Clients include many of the top advertising and marketing services agencies, as well as PR agencies, blue-chip advertisers and industry bodies. Presided over by "*leading industry figure and spokesman*" **Roger Alexander** (see p.52), the team benefits from the presence of "*extremely knowledgeable*" **Brinsley Dresden** (see p.52), who was strongly endorsed for his contractual, copy and sales promotion expertise. It received a boost recently with the arrival of "*star in the making*" **Giles Crown** (see p.52), former head of legal at TBWA UK, who rivals say "*is charming as well as extremely intelligent*." The team continues to assist Havas and its UK subsidiaries with work including the purchase of The Maitland Consultancy. It also represented a consortium of AMV Group companies on its appointment to provide the BBC with above-the-line advertising, direct marketing, PR, media buying and planning advice in connection with the collection and administration of the TV licence. **Clients** Havas; ehsrealtime; Abbot Mead Vickers Group; Mother; Laura Ashley; Dentsu.

MACFARLANES (see firm details p.1047) This "*quality firm*" is built around the respected figure of **Jeremy Courtenay-Stamp**. Recommended for its "*wide coverage*" of advertising issues, its ability to draw on the firm's strong corporate practice makes it arguably the leading player in the corporate side of the sector. Rivals told researchers that the team has "*continued its progress.*" In addition to many of the major advertising and marketing agencies, including Saatchi & Saatchi, the group advises a growing number of brand-owning clients such as Pret A Manger, Anheuser-Busch, Ford, Pepsi and KFC. Recent highlights include advising Cordiant on the acquisition of MicroArts, a leading US e-business consultancy, negotiating contracts for the services of Bruce Willis and Salma Hayek for Saatchi & Saatchi, and advising Bates UK on arrangements for Elton John to feature in Consignia's Christmas TV commercial. **Clients** Cordiant; Saatchi & Saatchi; Bates UK; Viacom Outdoor; Zenith Media; WPP; Omnicom; BMP DDB Needham.

OSBORNE CLARKE (see firm details p.1090) Felt to have "*invested heavily*" in the area, the team is now seen to be reaping the rewards. It has cemented its reputation as a leading player, commanding the respect of rivals and clients through its "*great knowledge of the people and the industry*," and in particular its marketing and corporate law expertise. Clients applauded the group's "*excellent network*," "*experience with market leaders*" and "*genuine interest in the industry.*" "*Clever and technical*" **Stephen Groom** is credited by peers with boosting the team's profile, while corporate star **Tim Birt** is also warmly recommended for his "*industry knowledge.*" The team recently advised Leo Burnett on content work and rights contracts, and advised the shareholders of Wolff Olins on the company's acquisition by Omnicom Group. **Clients** Bartle Bogle Hegarty; Leo Burnett; Lowe Lintas; BDH\TBWA; Magellan; Aegis; Greenline Communications; Wolff Olins; Yahoo!

THE SIMKINS PARTNERSHIP (see firm details p.1136) The quintessential West End advertising and media firm, it is praised by rivals for its "*commitment*" to the area. The "*small but focused*" team has built up expertise over a long period and regularly advises on clearance, IP, corporate/commercial, internet and digital media issues. **Charles Swan**'s (see p.52) reputation as one of the area's gurus precedes him. He has recently spent several months advising the IPA while it looked for an in-house lawyer. "*Able and enthusiastic*" **Alice Rayman** (see p.52) recently advised J Walter Thompson on the contract between Coty and Kate Moss for television and print ads for Rimmel cosmetics. She also advised OMD on its contract with DoubleClick for the provision of ad-serving software. **Clients** IPA; Abbot Mead Vickers BBDO; BMP DDB; J Walter Thompson; Lowe Lintas; Tribal DDB; OMD International.

LONDON ■ ADVERTISING & MARKETING

> **TOP IN-HOUSE LAWYERS**
>
> **Juliet ASHLEY**, Group Solicitor, Omnicom
> **Philip CIRCUS**, Director of Legal Affairs, Institute of Sales Promotion
> **Kate FULTON**, Chief Counsel, Young & Rubicam Ltd
> **Larissa JOY**, Vice-Chairman, Ogilvy UK
> **Fiona POOL**, Omnicom General Counsel, Omnicom Europe
>
> The Omnicom team is well represented on this years list after an outstanding year. **Juliet Ashley** and **Fiona Pool** are recognized for their "excellent" work. The "seasoned" **Philip Circus** is another new addition with numerous recommendations. **Kate Fulton**, is "one of the most experienced lawyers around" and **Larissa Joy** has a long track record in this field.
>
> In-house lawyers profiles p.1201

HAMMOND SUDDARDS EDGE It has been a good year for the team that, following its merger, now benefits from former sports boutique Townley's sponsorship and marketing expertise. Clients strongly recommended the group for its "*speedy, comprehensive advice*" as well as its "*commercial, collaborative*" style. Researchers were told that **Robert Wegenek** "*speaks plain English*" and is carving out an enviable profile for himself within the community. The team recently advised J Walter Thompson on its global appointment to provide advertising services to Vodafone. It also provided advice on the Johnnie Walker advertisements featuring Martin Scorsese, and on Levi's 'Freedom to Move' pan-European campaign. **Clients** Ogilvy & Mather; J Walter Thompson; Young & Rubicam; Bartle Bogle Hegarty; Hill & Knowlton; Starcom Motive Partnership; Mindshare; Outrider; Virgin Mobile.

THEODORE GODDARD (see firm details p.1158) Though most often associated by rivals with ASA and judicial review work, the firm boasts a range of clients and advises on a large volume of promotion, advertising, data protection and sponsorship matters. Clients were impressed by its "*quality investigation of issues or potential issues*" and "*efficient, proactive*" approach, singling out "*top class*" **Rupert Earle** (see p.52). The team recently advised the ASA on several disputes with French Connection over the advertising of its FCUK brand. It also advised News Group on the 'Music 4 You' national promotion with Coca-Cola in newspapers, packaging, and online. **Clients** ASA; Direct Marketing Association; Signet Group; World Sports Network; QinetiQ.

LAWRENCE GRAHAM (see firm details p.1031) A well-known name in the industry, the team advises on a range of regulatory, sales, marketing, promotion and below-the-line advertising issues. Other instructions have concerned direct distribution and e-commerce marketing. A recent highlight for the group, which includes Mike Smyth, was advising the Body Shop on multichannel distribution. It also assisted the National Lottery Commissioners on the award of a new licence, and on the advertising and promotion of the lottery. On the e-commerce side, it has acted for ValueClick on contractual matters. **Clients** Body Shop; ValueClick.

OLSWANG (see firm details p.1087) Researchers found the team, including Jonathan Goldstein, to be gaining a firm foothold in the area. Though not well known for agency work, it draws on the firm's large TMT client base, advising on a range of advertising and marketing issues. Commended by clients for its "*commerciality and hard work,*" it is felt to possess many "*excellent negotiators.*" The team advised Channel 4 on bringing interactive advertising to customers receiving Sky Digital. It also advised M&C Saatchi on campaigns for Nestlé All Stars, Currys, NatWest, Expo 02 and Swisscom. **Clients** Channel 4; M&C Saatchi; Shine.

TAYLOR WESSING (see firm details p.1156) The firm advises a clutch of leading international advertising and marketing clients on IP, litigation and commercial matters. Admired for its sound commercial advice, the team, including Tim Eyles, is acknowledged by clients to be "*good across the board.*" Recent work has included advising advertisers in connection with their agency contracts, and acting for DACS and the Association of Photographers in litigation against agencies. **Clients** AGENCY.COM; CIA Media; Omnicom; TBWA; Visa; Wella; Zenith Media; Saatchi & Saatchi; DACS; Association of Photographers.

CLIFFORD CHANCE (see firm details p.911) This "*quick and helpful*" group pools IP, e-commerce and litigation expertise, advising major brand-owning clients on a range of marketing and advertising issues. Sales promotions, price competition, direct marketing, e-commerce and data protection issues form much of the workload. In addition, it advises on combating phenomena such as 'brand bashing'. A former director of consumer affairs at the OFT, **Richard Thomas** (see p.595) is singled out by peers and clients for his public policy knowledge. **Clients** ONdigital; Reuters; Safeway; Mars; Intel; Coca-Cola; Eurostar.

MAYER, BROWN, ROWE & MAW (see firm details p.1060) Copy clearance work for advertising agencies comprises the bulk of the team's workload, though it also regularly handles contracts, IP and sponsorship matters. Its recent transatlantic merger provides extra multi-jurisdictional clout. **Sarah Byrt** (see p.52) maintains a strong profile in the area, winning plaudits from clients and competitors. **Clients** Publicis Groupe; McCann-Erickson.

BAKER & MCKENZIE (see firm details p.855) The team benefits from the firm's strong international network and is known for advising agencies on copy clearance, and advertisers on agency contracts and advertisements across the media. With Ilana Saltzman at the helm, additional fields of expertise for the group include e-commerce, data protection, marketing and sales promotions. **Clients** Advertising agencies.

CMS CAMERON MCKENNA (see firm details p.914) Despite a waning profile, according to competitors, in the wake of Guilherme Brafman's departure to Kaye Scholer LLP, the team, with IP expert Stephen Whybrow, continues to handle advertising issues on both the agency and advertiser side. **Clients** Advertising agencies; advertisers.

HARRISON CURTIS (see firm details p.987) A popular choice for an impressive list of clients, this "*small, but quality*" niche player specialises in media, communications and entertainment. It handles a mixture of agency and client contracts, copy advice, artist deals, data protection and internet-related matters. "*Bright, thoughtful and patient*" **Vanessa Hall-Smith** is one of the sector's leading lights and has built up a core of loyal and enthusiastic clients. The team recently acted for BMP DDB on a number of talent deals for major campaigns including Terry's chocolates, with Dawn French, and British Gas, with Paul Whitehouse. **Clients** BMP DDB; Burkitt DDB; WWAV Rapp Collins Scotland; Spaced UK; Visa International.

LOVELLS (see firm details p.1045) Advising many of the leading brand-owners and agencies, the firm's reputation is strongest in ancillary areas such as corporate and employment. Nevertheless, it has expertise across the range of advertising, marketing and sponsorship issues, and has recently advised on marketing campaign strategies. Operating from within the commercial and trading law practice, Peter Watts spearheads the team. **Clients** Interpublic.

OTHER NOTABLE PRACTITIONERS Guilherme Brafman (see p.52) of Kaye Scholer is highly regarded for his corporate work. "*Genuinely steeped in the industry,*" he is admired by peers for his experience and knowledge, particularly on the corporate side of the field.

ADVERTISING & MARKETING ■ THE LEADERS

THE LEADERS IN ADVERTISING & MARKETING

ALEXANDER, Roger
Lewis Silkin, London
(020) 7074 8001
roger.alexander@lewissilkin.com
Specialisation: Partner in Corporate Department. Advising companies in the Marketing Services Industry in relation to corporate finance, mergers, acquisitions, flotations and high level employment issues. Acts for a raft of companies in the sector, both public and private, including some of the largest agency groups; also advises industry bodies. Lectures in the UK and overseas on issues and trends in the industry.
Prof. Memberships: Law Society, Solicitors European Group, Society of Share Scheme Practitioners.
Career: Qualified 1965. Partner at *Lewis Silkin* 1965. Head of Marketing Services Law Group. Lead Partner 1989-98. Senior Partner 1999.

BIRT, Tim
Osborne Clarke, London
(020) 7809 1000

BRAFMAN, Guilherme
Kaye Scholer LLP, London
(020) 7014 0550
gbrafman@kayescholer.com
Specialisation: Corporate, M&A, Advertising & Marketing, IT, e-commerce, media, copyright, Financial Services and sitting as arbitrator. All aspects of advertising, client contracts, artists' agreements, campaign clearance, and especially the buying and selling of agencies, PR companies and financial services businesses. Advertising disputes and high-level hiring and firing.
Prof. Memberships: MCI Arb; City of London Solicitors Company; The Law Society.
Career: Qualified 1979 with *Slaughter and May*. 1983 founded *Brafmans* which (as *Brafman Morris*) merged in 1989 with *Cameron Markby Hewitt* (now *CMS Cameron McKenna*). Managing Partner, London office of *Kaye Scholer LLP* February 2001.
Publications: Various articles and chapter in an encyclopaedia of International Joint Ventures.
Personal: Educated at Downing College, Cambridge. Lives in London and Norfolk. Married, 2 sons. Interests: Family, tennis, swimming, food, etc. Fluent in Portuguese and French.

BYRT, Sarah
Mayer, Brown, Rowe & Maw, London
(020) 7782 8832
sbyrt@eu.mayerbrownrowe.com
Specialisation: Intellectual property with a particular emphasis on advertising, publishing and media matters. Acts for several agencies including McCann-Erickson, CDP, Camp Chipperfield Hill Murray and Maher Bird Associates. UK contributor to a major French advertising law textbook.
Career: LLB (Law with French) Birmingham and Limoges Universities. Joined *Rowe & Maw* as trainee in 1986. Has specialised in IP since qualifying in 1988. Made Partner in 1995.
Personal: Food, travel, friends.

COURTENAY-STAMP, Jeremy
Macfarlanes, London
(020) 7831 9222

CROWN, Giles
Lewis Silkin, London
(020) 7074 8090
giles.crown@lewissilkin.com
Specialisation: Advertising, marketing and communications law, including contentious and non-contentious matters.
Prof. Memberships: Member of the Bar, Advertising Lawyers Group.
Career: Barrister, Chambers of Richard Rampton QC, 1 Brick Court (1995-2000). Head of Legal and Business Affairs, TBWA UK Group (2000-01).
Publications: 'Advertising Law and Regulation', Butterworths, 1998.
Personal: St Paul's School, Barnes, Jesus College, Cambridge and UCL. Triathlon, Adventure races, theatre and films.

DRESDEN, Brinsley
Lewis Silkin, London
(020) 7074 8069
brinsley.dresden@lewissilkin.com
Specialisation: Head of Advertising Law and Partner in the Intellectual Property Unit specialising in non-contentious IP law. Advises advertising agencies, advertisers, and clients on clearance issues such as parodies of feature films, unauthorised references to living individuals, incorporation of third party IP rights; negotiating contracts between advertisers and agencies, and for talent appearing in advertising campaigns. Also advises on making and defending complaints to the ITC, the BACC and the ASA. Participated in negotiating and drafting standard form client/agency agreements for both the above-the-line and below-the-line sectors of the industry. Increasingly involved with new media advertising, including clearances for internet advertising and sales promotion and drafting web site design and hosting contracts. Regularly lectures on a wide range of legal issues concerning advertising and marketing.
Prof. Memberships: European Advertising Lawyers Association; Global Advertising Lawyers Alliance; Advertising Law Group.
Career: Born 25 February 1966; Educated King's College School, Wimbledon; University of Bristol (LLB Hons 1987); College of Law, Guildford; King's College London (LLM 1999). Trained *Nabarro Nathanson* and qualified 1991. *BT Group Legal Services* 1993-96; *Lewis Silkin* 1996; Partner 1999.
Personal: Interests include sailing, swimming and the arts.

EARLE, Rupert
Theodore Goddard, London
(020) 7606 8855
rupertearle@theodoregoddard.co.uk
Specialisation: Media and public law with particular emphasis on advertising and marketing law. Has acted for the Advertising Standards Authority for many years (including in the defence of many judicial review challenges to their decision), and provides copy and trading standards advice to many commercial organisations, including the airline, high street retail and telecoms businesses.
Prof. Memberships: Law Society.
Career: Qualified at *Theodore Goddard* in 1988, partner 1997.
Personal: Educated at Winchester and Cambridge University. Interests include pots and strange places.

GROOM, Stephen
Osborne Clarke, London
(020) 7809 1000

HALL-SMITH, Vanessa
Harrison Curtis, London
(020) 7611 1720

RAYMAN, Alice
The Simkins Partnership, London
(020) 7907 3029
alice.rayman@simkins.com
Specialisation: Partner in Advertising and Marketing Group advising advertisers, agencies, media companies, production companies and others in the sector on the full range of corporate and commercial issues. Particular experience in corporate work such as company and business acquisitions, joint ventures and shareholder arrangements for agencies; commercial agreements such as client/agency agreements, talent contracts, merchandising and rights contracts; internet related work such as software contracts, web design agreements and website terms and conditions; employment and freelancer contracts, as well as other general commercial contracts.
Career: Training *Richards Butler* 1991-93; *Harbottle & Lewis* 1994-2000; *The Simkins Partnership* 2000-date, partner 2001.

SWAN, Charles
The Simkins Partnership, London
(020) 7907 3060
charles.swan@simkins.com
Specialisation: Head of Advertising and Marketing Group. Main area of practice is advertising law, advising advertisers, their agencies and trade associations. Also advises generally on intellectual property law, especially in relation to photography. Co-author of Butterworth's 'Encyclopaedia of Forms and Precedents' (Advertising title), co-author of 'The ABC of UK Photographic Copyright', and author of the Advertising Industry section in 'Copinger and Skone James on Copyright', 14th edition.
Career: Qualified 1983. Articled at *Woodham Smith* 1981-83 before moving to *Speechly Bircham*. Joined *The Simkins Partnership* in 1985 and became a partner in 1990. General Secretary of Advertising Law International.
Personal: Born 1956. Attended Cambridge University 1975-78.

THOMAS, Richard
Clifford Chance, London
(020) 7600 1000
richard.thomas@cliffordchance.com
See under Parliamentary & Public Affairs, p.595

WEGENEK, Robert
Hammond Suddards Edge, London
(020) 7655 1000

AGRICULTURE

London: 53; The Regions: 54; Scotland: 59; Profiles: 60

Research approved by BMRB For this edition, **Chambers'** researchers conducted 6,582 interviews – 3,900 with law firms, 511 with barristers and 2,171 with clients. The validity of the research was scrutinised by BMRB International, who audited both the methodology and the results at our offices in London. They interviewed **Chambers'** researchers and cross-checked sample interviews. Details of the audit appear on page 7.

OVERVIEW The agricultural sector remained in flux this year, as it struggled to come to terms with the repercussions of last year's foot-and-mouth disease (FMD) crisis. Abetted by hostile global market conditions, the crisis forced or prompted many farmers to make substantial changes or to bow out altogether. Restructuring, diversification, amalgamation and commercial land letting kept many firms busy, while land transfer was more common in the badly hit Western regions than in the wealthier East. On the contentious side, the fallout from FMD dominated more directly – in the form of actions against DEFRA over compensation or clean-up. The NFU's limiting of its panel to just nine firms has not diminished those big players which do not feature on it, with Burges Salmon retaining easily the highest profile nationwide. At the other end of the spectrum, however, a consensus view is emerging that, as the legal demands of farmers become more complex, the days of those firms merely dabbling are numbered.

LONDON

AGRICULTURE — LONDON

1
- Farrer & Co
- Macfarlanes
- Withers LLP

2
- Currey & Co
- Dawsons
- Lee & Pembertons

3
- Boodle Hatfield
- Payne Hicks Beach

LEADING INDIVIDUALS

1
- JESSEL Christopher Farrer & Co
- LANE Andrew Withers LLP

2
- FINDLEY Christopher Bircham Dyson Bell
- FURBER James Farrer & Co
- HORNBY John Macfarlanes
- MOORE John Macfarlanes
- PRING Simon Farrer & Co

3
- ELLIOTT Penelope Withers LLP
- JACKSON Andrew Macfarlanes
- KEDDIE Joanne Dawsons
- SYMINGTON Anita Lee & Pembertons

This book is the product of 6,552 1/2 hour interviews. See p.7 for BMRB audit. Within each band, firms are listed alphabetically. See individuals' profiles p.60

FARRER & CO (see firm details p.952) In its 301st year, this "*bastion of tradition in the best sense*" continued to expand its agricultural team and its client base. The core business remains sales and acquisitions for landed estates, with further expertise in heritage, manorial rights and farm business tenancies. **Christopher Jessel** (see p.62), portrayed by peers as a "*guru*," is respected both as an academic and a practitioner. **Simon Pring** (see p.63) and **James Furber** (see p.61) are well known as solicitors to the Duchy of Lancaster and the Duchy of Cornwall respectively.

MACFARLANES (see firm details p.1047) Despite a commercial realignment over recent years, the firm provides a "*princely service*" to a client base that includes large institutions, greenfield developers and wealthy international investors. The team, headed by the "*sensible, measured*" **John Hornby**, has particular expertise in mineral work, land transactions and complex estate management. **John Moore** commands wide respect among peers, while **Andrew Jackson** was applauded by clients for his "*first-rate guidance.*" The team provided commercial and environmental advice this year to an institutional client on a proposed gravel pit in East Anglia.

WITHERS LLP (see firm details p.1194) While the core of its work remains conveyancing, this "*wunderfirm*" also has specialist expertise in insolvency, taxation and agricultural holdings issues. **Penelope Elliott** (see p.61) is lauded for her tax work and **Andrew Lane** (see p.61) was described typically by one client as "*top dog in London.*" A highlight of last year was the high-profile acquisition of the Ashcombe Estate for Madonna and Guy Ritchie.

CURREY & CO Retaining its position this year, the firm is praised for the advice it gives to a "*highly impressive*" roster of clients. Led by Nicholas Powell, the team is skilled in every aspect of agricultural land transfer.

DAWSONS (see firm details p.932) This respected team is known principally for its superb contentious practice, and continues to handle a raft of complex cases from landlord and tenant disputes to professional negligence claims. "*Litigator and a half*" **Joanne Keddie** (see p.62) was singled out for her expertise in EC quotas and employment issues. The team also provides the full range of tax and property services to its private client base.

LEE & PEMBERTONS (see firm details p.1036) Representing individual farmers as well as large estates, this burgeoning non-contentious practice was the unreserved top choice of some clients. Led by **Anita Symington** ("*the legal equivalent of green-fingered*"), the team is thought to proffer "*massive expertise*" in landlord and tenant matters, diversification and conveyancing.

BOODLE HATFIELD (see firm details p.881) This firm acts for landed estates and the rural holdings of urban estates and institutions. The team's taxation work under Kate Howe won particular praise from rivals, while other prominent features of the workload include partnership reorganisations and landlord and tenant matters.

PAYNE HICKS BEACH (see firm details p.1097) This venerable London firm has a desirable private client list, which is dominated by large landed estates. The agricultural department, which includes partner Alastair Murdie, provides a comprehensive service from agricultural holdings advice and disposals to complex tax planning. Clients include Lands Improvement Holdings.

OTHER NOTABLE PRACTITIONERS Christopher Findley (see p.60) continues to develop his reputation as a "*supreme expert*" at Bircham Dyson Bell in Westminster.

www.ChambersandPartners.com

AGRICULTURE ■ THE SOUTH/THAMES VALLEY/SOUTH WEST

THE SOUTH

AGRICULTURE
■ THE SOUTH

1. **Brachers** Maidstone
   White & Bowker Winchester
2. **Cripps Harries Hall** Tunbridge Wells
   Thomas Eggar Chichester, Horsham
3. **Knights** Tunbridge Wells

LEADING INDIVIDUALS
1. **FELLINGHAM Michael** Penningtons
   KNIGHT Matthew Knights
   KYRKE Richard Thomas Eggar
   STEEL John White & Bowker

This book is the product of 6,552 1/2 hour interviews. See p.7 for BMRB audit.
Within each band, firms are listed alphabetically. See individuals' profiles p.60

BRACHERS (see firm details p.886) This "*well-organised firm*" opted out of the NFU panel system this year, but continues to represent a range of estates. Highlights included a complex succession arrangement for a 1,000-acre holding and trust/tax advisory work on a £10 million option agreement. The team, led by Simon Palmer, has additional experience in landlord and tenant work, quota disputes and environmental/planning work. This year also marks the retirement of the celebrated Douglas Horner.

WHITE & BOWKER This well-honed practice has been active this year in the fields of mineral rights, quota issues and farm sales and purchases. Team leader **John Steel**'s (see p.63) name was one of the first to spring to the lips of both solicitors and clients ("*always innovative and inventive*"), and his strong team was recommended for its contentious and non-contentious work on rights of way, tax planning and landlord and tenant issues.

CRIPPS HARRIES HALL (see firm details p.922) This robust team was appointed to the NFU legal panel in place of Brachers this year. As well as expertise in every aspect of rural property matters, from farm selling to telecoms masts, Andrew Fermor's team was seen by market commentators as being an authority on equine law.

THOMAS EGGAR (see firm details p.1160) Operating with a finely struck balance between contentious and non-contentious work, this firm boasts a healthy private client base. This year, the workload was dominated by several high-value land transactions. Interviewees endorsed **Richard Kyrke** (see p.62) as "*always thorough.*" He heads a team whose other specialities include complex tax planning and diversification. Clients include BG Transco, Exbury Estate and Knepp Castle Estate.

KNIGHTS Often winning referrals from the NFU when panel firms are overstretched or suffer conflicts of interests, this contentious practice specialises in disputes over property, animal welfare and sporting and environmental issues. **Matthew Knight** (see p.48), a "*leader in his field,*" won plaudits from rivals and clients, while, according to one source, the firm's work overall "*could not be faulted.*"

OTHER NOTABLE PRACTITIONERS Michael Fellingham (see p.61) of Penningtons continues to elicit market commendation for his "*clear, measured advisory work.*"

THAMES VALLEY

AGRICULTURE
■ THAMES VALLEY

1. **Henmans** Oxford, Woodstock
2. **Pryce Collard Chamberlain** Abingdon, Wantage
   Stanley Tee Bishop's Stortford

LEADING INDIVIDUALS
1. **CAPEL Stuart** Pryce Collard Chamberlain

This book is the product of 6,552 1/2 hour interviews. See p.7 for BMRB audit.
Within each band, firms are listed alphabetically. See individuals' profiles p.60

HENMANS (see firm details p.990) Fronted by Roger Henman, this expanding firm represents estates in Oxfordshire, Wales and beyond. Last year saw a number of acquisitions and disposals, of land and quotas, as well as instructions in partnership restructuring and the commercial letting of farm buildings. The firm continues to act for the Royal Agricultural Benevolent Institution.

PRYCE COLLARD CHAMBERLAIN Endorsed for its expertise in acquisitions and tenancy matters, this firm has also been active in the fields of farm finance reorganisation and succession. Headed by notary **Stuart Capel** (see p.60), the team has a client base respected throughout the region.

STANLEY TEE (see firm details p.1145) This active firm can boast the full range of rural property expertise alongside specialist knowledge of mineral rights, environmental issues and employment law. The team, whose advice was described by clients as being "*dependable and realistic,*" is steered by Richard Tee.

SOUTH WEST

BURGES SALMON (see firm details p.894) With its "*unique and fertile bedrock of contentious expertise,*" this star agricultural firm retains its pole position, drawing strong recommendations from across the UK. The "*ruthless, capable and businesslike*" **Peter Williams** (see p.64) has impressed clients with his knowledge of banking disputes and farm receiverships, while **James Buxton** (see p.60) was widely praised for his milk quota work. **William Neville** (see p.63) was singled out to researchers for his robust litigating style: "*he knows how close to the bone to put the knife,*" said one client. Other clients were keen to recommend **Della Evans** (see p.61) ("*a terrier with an exceptional mind*") as well as the "*exceptionally capable*" **Alastair Morrison** (see p.62). Senior associate **Miles Farren** (see p.61) was also held in high regard. Work stemming from the foot-and-mouth crisis has kept the firm busy, and it continues to advise on land development, disposals and acquisitions. This year also saw the retirement from full-time practice of Andrew Densham, this sector's elder statesman, and the return of William Batstone to the Bar.

WILSONS (see firm details p.1191) Rivals expressed envy at this firm's "*outstanding private client list.*" The mainly non-contentious practice, led by the "*instinctive and sensible*" **Robert Swift** (see p.64), was particularly active this year in restructuring and conveyancing. **Peter Fitzgerald** (see p.61), rated for his specialist knowledge of heritage law, is also included in this strong and diverse team.

CLARKE WILLMOTT & CLARKE (see firm details p.907) This energetic firm has this year won the NFU contract in place of Bond Pearce. Highly proficient in planning, environmental law, quota litigation and judicial reviews, the group was judged to have "*the perfect balance between contentious and non-contentious work.*"

SOUTH WEST/WALES ■ AGRICULTURE

AGRICULTURE
■ SOUTH WEST

1. Burges Salmon Bristol
2. Wilsons Salisbury
3. Clarke Willmott & Clarke Bristol, Taunton
   Thring Townsend Bath
4. Bevan Ashford Bristol
   Stephens & Scown Exeter
5. Battens (with Poole & Co) Yeovil
   Charles Russell Cheltenham
   Osborne Clarke Bristol
6. Pardoes Bridgwater
   Porter Dodson Yeovil

LEADING INDIVIDUALS

1. BUXTON James Burges Salmon
   NEVILLE William Burges Salmon
   WILLIAMS Peter Burges Salmon
2. EVANS Della Burges Salmon
   MORRISON Alastair Burges Salmon
   RUSS Tim Clarke Willmott & Clarke
   SWIFT Robert Wilsons
3. CHEAL Jonathan Thring Townsend
   FARREN Miles Burges Salmon
   FITZGERALD Peter Wilsons

This book is the product of 6,552 1/2 hour interviews. See p.7 for BMRB audit.
Within each band, firms are listed alphabetically. See individuals' profiles p.60

"*Bold litigator*" **Tim Russ** (see p.63) has been heavily involved in actions against government bodies over FMD.

THRING TOWNSEND (see firm details p.1162) Representing a broad spread of farmers and landowners, this NFU panel firm continues to receive instructions in conveyancing and farm tenancies, as well as in livestock, quota and employment matters. "*Flamboyant*" Jonathan Cheal (see p.60) leads this committed team. Highlights of the year included a successful public rights of way appeal and several appeals against DEFRA.

BEVAN ASHFORD (see firm details p.869) This firm boasts an impressive regional client base. It is experienced in partnership arrangements and contentious work involving quota disputes, European court litigation and arbitrations. The "*busy and well-organised*" team includes John Bosworth.

STEPHENS & SCOWN Adjudged to have "*substantial repute in the region,*" the practice acts for a number of large Cornish estates, in addition to individual farmers. The team, which includes Martin Clayden, was active this year advising farmers on their rights with respect to the FMD contiguous cull. Further expertise is on offer concerning the range of agricultural property activities.

BATTENS (WITH POOLE & CO) Although this traditional firm was felt to be less visible than in recent years, it has maintained a client base, which includes landed estates and some sizeable farms. Robert Unwin's "*pragmatic*" team was exercised in the past 12 months by exit planning work as well as farm business tenancies and farm refinancing.

CHARLES RUSSELL (see firm details p.904) Pronounced "*rising stars*" by interviewees, this firm acts mainly for traditional landed estates and institutions in the South West and beyond. Adept at the full gamut of rural property work, including heritage law and succession planning, Christopher Page's team was summed up by one client as "*smooth, smooth operators.*"

OSBORNE CLARKE (see firm details p.1090) This "*efficient*" firm is perceived by peers to approach agricultural law from a highly commercial angle. It represents a broad range of wealthy landed estates in the South West region. Best known for its expertise in farm sales and purchases, Robert Drewett's team also has experience in the legal issues surrounding mobile telephone masts.

PARDOES This solid firm applied its property expertise to a steady flow of farm sales and purchases this year. Representing large estates and small farmers, it has particular knowledge of tax planning and subsidy issues. Jeremy Orchard is head of department.

PORTER DODSON (see firm details p.1105) "*Adept generalists*" with a strong local reputation. The team offers services in matters ranging from landlord and tenant work to partnership structures and employment issues. Brian Maxwell leads the team.

WALES

AGRICULTURE
■ WALES

1. John Collins & Partners Swansea
   Margraves Llandrindod Wells
2. Gabb & Co Abergavenny
   Morgan Cole Cardiff

LEADING INDIVIDUALS

1. HARRIS Edward John Collins & Partners
   MARGRAVE-JONES Clive Margraves
2. RODGERS Christopher Margraves
   STEPHENS Jonathan Jonathan Stephens & Co

This book is the product of 6,552 1/2 hour interviews. See p.7 for BMRB audit.
Within each band, firms are listed alphabetically. See individuals' profiles p.60

JOHN COLLINS & PARTNERS This multi-talented, dynamic practice undertakes a largely contentious workload for a client base that is slanted towards local farmers and farming businesses. **Edward Harris** ("*unbeatable*") continues to win marketplace acclaim for his role at the helm of a team that includes Rory Hutchings. The department's profile has been boosted by a recent rights of common case taken to the House of Lords, and by cases relating to pollution caused by the burial of FMD-infected carcasses.

MARGRAVES This esteemed firm focuses on agricultural property, taxation and trust issues, with a client roster comprising estates, individual farmers and agribusinesses. **Clive Margrave-Jones** is warmly recommended by interviewees who also single out the "*academically excellent*" Professor **Christopher Parker Rodgers**.

GABB & CO (see firm details p.966) Over 240 years old, this firm has a "*solid bedrock of agricultural knowledge*" from which to advise its local clientele. Led by David Vaughan, the team's particular specialist areas are property, taxation and trust work.

MORGAN COLE (see firm details p.1075) The firm is endorsed as a commercially astute practice on the NFU panel for Wales and Herefordshire. Phillip Howell-Richardson runs a team offering a spread of services from contentious property work to tax planning and quotas.

OTHER NOTABLE PRACTITIONERS
Jonathan Stephens (see p.60) maintains his reputation as a "*charming, details-oriented solicitor*" at Usk firm Jonathan Stephens & Co.

AGRICULTURE ■ MIDLANDS/EAST ANGLIA

MIDLANDS

AGRICULTURE
■ MIDLANDS

1 **Arnold Thomson** Towcester
2 **Hewitson Becke + Shaw** Northampton
Martineau Johnson Birmingham
Wright Hassall Leamington Spa
3 **Knight & Sons** Newcastle-under-Lyme
Lodders Stratford-upon-Avon
4 **Gwynnes** Wellington
Lanyon Bowdler Shrewsbury
Manby & Steward Bridgnorth, Wolverhampton
Morton Fisher Worcester

LEADING INDIVIDUALS

1 **DAVIS Nigel** Nigel Davis Solicitors
LODDER David Lodders
THOMSON Michael Arnold Thomson
2 **BARNETT Ian** Hewitson Becke + Shaw
QUINN James Morton Fisher

This book is the product of 6,552 1/2 hour interviews. See p.7 for BMRB audit. Within each band, firms are listed alphabetically. See individuals' profiles p.60

ARNOLD THOMSON (see firm details p.850) The practice has carved out a niche representing owner-occupiers under the leadership of "*hard-working, illustrious*" **Michael Thomson** (see p.993). The team continues to be active in practice areas such as partnership arrangements and machine sharing, as well as the full spectrum of property work and diversification to alternate forms of income.

HEWITSON BECKE + SHAW (see firm details p.762) This growing, "*forward-looking*" practice has a substantial client base with the emphasis on landed estates. Alongside its track record in conveyancing and landlord and tenant matters, the team is well known for its far-reaching activities, which include quota work and disputes over set-aside. Group leader **Ian Barnett** (see p.60) was praised by rivals as "*a premier league player.*"

MARTINEAU JOHNSON (see firm details p.1056) This "*highly proficient outfit*" is unrivalled in Birmingham for its clout and expertise in agricultural work. Representing some 20 large landed estates during the last 12 months, the practice is commended for its work in conveyancing, tenancy matters and succession planning. The team includes Hugh Carslake and Ian Flavell.

WRIGHT HASSALL (see firm details p.1197) Acting principally for farmers, this highly regarded firm was said by peers to take a "*calm and intelligent approach*" to its agricultural workload. The team has special knowledge of conveyancing, farm business tenancies, quota work and option agreements. Graham Davies takes the helm this year following top-rated Robin Ogg's retirement from partnership. The firm continues to represent the Royal Agricultural Society of England.

KNIGHT & SONS Described by interviewees as "*pretty major players,*" the firm has retained its status as NFU panel firm for the area, and continues to receive instructions from farmers in contentious matters ranging from criminal offences to contractual disputes. The team, which includes Bob Hoyle and Richard Jones, is also active in advising landed estates and tenants on non-contentious property matters.

LODDERS (see firm details p.1044) "*A practice carved by a craftsman,*" brimmed one client. The firm is accomplished in all aspects of agricultural law, and has recently been active in estate partitioning, farm business tenancies and milk quota work. Head of department David Lodder (see p.62) was commended as a "*dedicated agricultural enthusiast.*"

GWYNNES Representing wealthy farmers and landed estates, this niche practice concentrates on property and tax matters. It has secured an increasing number of landlord and tenant instructions. The team, led by Michael Gwynne, also handles work ranging from tenancy disputes to sporting and mineral rights.

LANYON BOWDLER The department provides non-contentious advice to landowning clients that "*makes good legal sense,*" according to peers. The team, led by Andrew Evans, is capable of dealing with work relating to quotas, tax planning and diversification issues.

MANBY & STEWARD (see firm details p.1052) Enjoying a mixed client roster of landed estates and tenant farmers, this "*level-headed outfit*" has undertaken work in conveyancing, succession and diversification this year. The team includes Steve Corfield.

MORTON FISHER (see firm details p.880) Peers commend the firm as "*super troubleshooters.*" Its main figure, **Jim Quinn** (see p.63), draws particular commendations for his expertise in tenancy and partnership disputes. Although the practice has a litigious bent, it also handles a healthy spread of non-contentious work for landowning clients.

OTHER NOTABLE PRACTITIONERS Nigel Davis (see p.60) (Nigel Davis Solicitors) has been occupied this year with a variety of contentious cases in the areas of landlord and tenant work, animal welfare and partnership. Peers acknowledge that he has a "*unique understanding of the issues facing working farmers.*"

EAST ANGLIA

MILLS & REEVE (see firm details p.1071) Widely held to fall within agricultural law's own magic circle, this substantive practice acts for wealthier landed estates, farms and institutions. Head of department **William Barr** (see p.60) provides "*crystal clear*" and professional advice, while researchers were impressed by the level of commendation for **Matthew Arrowsmith-Brown** (see p.60). The team, which takes on the full gamut of non-contentious work, is rounded off by the respected **Michael Aubrey** (see p.60). Highlights of last year include acting for a consortium to purchase the Albury Hall Estate.

ROYTHORNE & CO This "*handsome, traditional firm*" continues to be a major presence in the Lincolnshire region. Representing clients from 500 to 5,000 acres, the group has been active this year in the buying and selling of farms and the establishment of joint ventures and machinery co-operatives. **Graham Smith** (see p.63), described by one rival as a "*font of wisdom,*" is supported by the "*conscientious and heavyweight*" **Alan Plummer** (see p.63). The team, which currently holds the NFU panel place for the area, is also known for its expertise in business structuring and capital tax advice.

BARKER GOTELEE "*The toast of Brussels*", this specialist practice continues to focus its energies on European agriculture issues. Team head Richard Barker (see p.60), a "*major player on the Continent,*" was heavily involved in the legal complexities surrounding food quality assurance standards. The group also offers a range of services to domestic clients, and received praise for its expertise in landlord and tenant and quota matters. The Highly respected Geoff Whittaker has now joined the ALA. Clients include ADAS and the Meat & Livestock Commission.

TAYLOR VINTERS (see firm details p.1156) This expansive practice boasts an eclectic client roster, including institutions, agribusinesses and charities, as well as landed estates and family farms. The team includes **Jeanette Dennis** (see p.61), who was widely admired for her client-

EAST ANGLIA/NORTH WEST — AGRICULTURE

AGRICULTURE
EAST ANGLIA

1 Mills & Reeve Cambridge, Norwich
Roythorne & Co Spalding
2 Barker Gotelee Ipswich
Taylor Vinters Cambridge
3 Birketts Ipswich
Hewitson Becke + Shaw Cambridge, Saffron Walden
Howes Percival Norwich
4 Ashton Graham Bury St Edmunds, Ipswich
Prettys Ipswich
5 Greene & Greene Bury St Edmunds
Wilkin Chapman Louth

LEADING INDIVIDUALS

1 BARR William Mills & Reeve
SMITH Graham Roythorne & Co
2 ARROWSMITH-BROWN Matthew Mills & Reeve
BARKER Richard Barker Gotelee
HEAL Jeremy Howes Percival
HORWOOD-SMART Adrian Taylor Vinters
PLUMMER Alan Roythorne & Co
3 AUBREY Michael Mills & Reeve
DENNIS Jeanette Taylor Vinters
HARBOTTLE James Birketts
POUND Toby Prettys

This book is the product of 6,552 1/2 hour interviews. See p.7 for BMRB audit.
Within each band, firms are listed alphabetically. See individuals' profiles p.60

friendly manner, and **Adrian Horwood-Smart** (see p.61), regarded by the marketplace as a "*terrific operator.*"

BIRKETTS (see firm details p.875) The team represents clients ranging from large landed estates to owner-occupiers. It has been particularly visible in the field of conveyancing this year, with **James Harbottle** (see p.62) securing the respect of client interviewees. Consultant Angela Sydenham is a valuable resource for the department.

HEWITSON BECKE + SHAW (see firm details p.993) In addition to its client base of landed estates and farmers, this firm acts for landowning and conservation charities. The team, which includes Denise Wilkinson, has seen a further increase in the number of sales, acquisitions and diversifications over the past 12 months. Interviewees singled out the firm's "*vigorous*" presence in the market.

HOWES PERCIVAL (see firm details p.1003) This firm's reputation certainly benefits from that of team leader **Jeremy Heal** (see p.825); interviewees singled him out as "*first rate to deal with in any aspect of rural property law.*" Skills on offer at this firm range from conveyancing to complex consortium agreements.

ASHTON GRAHAM The team, which includes David Wybar, acts for a rural client base that comprises commercial owner-occupiers, larger farmers and landed estates. Landlord and tenant and general estate management matters are a key feature of the workload, as well as diversification issues and employment law.

PRETTYS (see firm details p.1106) This firm, described by other solicitors in the market as "*a pleasure to work with,*" holds the NFU panel contract for the area. Representing many working farmers, the practice has received instructions in diversification, retail co-operatives and partnership rearrangements in the last 12 months. Head of team **Toby Pound** (see p.63) is held out by many as an "*ambassador for the industry.*"

GREENE & GREENE The Bury St Edmunds firm is recognised for its long-standing client base of local farmers and landowners. The team, led by Michael Batt, is skilled in land sales and purchases and capital tax/estate planning. It has been heavily involved in farm business tenancy advice.

WILKIN CHAPMAN This local practice has been active in conveyancing this year, with instructions also received in farm business tenancies and tax planning. The team, which includes senior partner Philip Day, acts for a client list featuring several local farm businesses that each farm in excess of 4,000 acres.

NORTH WEST

AGRICULTURE
NORTH WEST

1 Cartmell Shepherd Carlisle
2 Hibbert Durrad Moxon Nantwich
Oglethorpe Sturton & Gillibrand Lancaster
Walker Smith & Way Chester
3 Birch Cullimore Chester
Mason & Moore Dutton Chester
Napthens Preston

LEADING INDIVIDUALS

1 CARTMELL Timothy Cartmell Shepherd
COLLINS Peter Walker Smith & Way
GILLIBRAND Martin Oglethorpe Sturton & Gillibrand
YOUNG David Hibbert Durrad Moxon
2 TOMLINSON Geoffrey Napthens

This book is the product of 6,552 1/2 hour interviews. See p.7 for BMRB audit.
Within each band, firms are listed alphabetically. See individuals' profiles p.60

CARTMELL SHEPHERD Robust and single-minded firm with a strong reputation countrywide. The team provides both non-contentious and contentious services. It has attracted attention this year for its FMD work, including judicial reviews against DEFRA. "*Leading light*" **Timothy Cartmell** fronts the department and remains the first port of call for many clients.

HIBBERT DURRAD MOXON (see firm details p.995) Offering "*watertight advice,*" the firm has been active with instructions from farmers with family and financial difficulties. Further skills exercised this year include tax planning and partnership restructuring for the mainly tenant/owner-occupier client base. **David Young**'s team is also experienced at agricultural conveyancing.

OGLETHORPE STURTON & GILLIBRAND (see firm details p.1086) Acting for owner-occupiers and landowners, this robust practice deals with agricultural issues from tenancy disputes to milk quotas. The team also won plaudits for its knowledge of sporting and rights of way issues. Clients appreciated the "*silver tongue*" of department head Martin Gillibrand .

WALKER SMITH & WAY This well-regarded Cheshire firm has been exercised this year by diversification work, farm reorganisations and succession management. The practice is also endorsed for its knowledge of landlord and tenant matters. Head of department **Peter Collins** (see p.60) was adjudged "*pragmatic, quick and clear.*"

BIRCH CULLIMORE Interviewees pointed to the firm's "*strong Cheshire presence.*" David Mason's team advises large estates on work ranging from conveyancing and quotas to tax planning and diversification.

MASON & MOORE DUTTON Rory Lea's team acts mainly for working farmers in the Cheshire and North Wales areas. It is involved in tax and succession planning, milk quotas and property transfer.

NAPTHENS (see firm details p.1081) A "*sharp act,*" this firm has retained its place on the NFU panel. It has been kept busy advising its working farmer-dominated client base on FMD settlements. Further expertise in conveyancing, tax work and partnership restructuring has been on display. **Geoffrey Tomlinson**, head of department, was admired by rival solicitors.

AGRICULTURE ■ YORKSHIRE/NORTH EAST

YORKSHIRE

AGRICULTURE
■ YORKSHIRE

1
- Addleshaw Booth & Co Leeds
- Grays York
- Rollits Hull
- Stamp Jackson and Procter Hull
- Wrigleys Leeds

LEADING INDIVIDUALS

1 STONE James Addleshaw Booth & Co
2 GITTINGS Simon Stamp Jackson and Procter

This book is the product of 6,552 1/2 hour interviews. See p.7 for BMRB audit. Within each band, firms are listed alphabetically. See individuals' profiles p.60

ADDLESHAW BOOTH & CO (see firm details p.838) "*Highly experienced*" **James Stone** (see p.63) heads a team known in the marketplace for its work in succession planning and contract agreements. The firm represents private clients and large estate owners on property investment, tenancy issues, quotas and VAT issues.

GRAYS (see firm details p.977) This smaller firm has an enviable roster of landowning clientele. The team, led by Lyn Rickatson, is respected for its knowledge of landlord and tenant issues. Other prominent elements in the workload this year include advising on quotas, contracts and refinancing.

ROLLITS (see firm details p.1115) Representing both large landowners and small farmers, this firm has a strong presence in East Yorkshire and Lincolnshire. Despite its lower profile in this field, the practice has been active across the full spectrum of property issues. The team, which includes Neil Franklin, can draw upon the expertise of litigation and tax specialists in other departments.

STAMP JACKSON AND PROCTER 150 years old this year, the practice is respected throughout the Yorkshire marketplace. Acting for farmers and estates in the Holderness area and beyond, the team has received instructions in management agreements, whole farm transactions and diversification arrangements. An increasing level of referrals from English Nature enables it to deploy its nature conservation and horticultural expertise. It is fronted by the "*thorough*" **Simon Gittings** (see p.62).

WRIGLEYS (see firm details p.1199) Described as a "*trustworthy*" team, it boasts an impressive roster of estates. The team has a reputation for dealing with property work for private trusts, while further areas of experience include rights of way and diversification matters.

NORTH EAST

AGRICULTURE
■ NORTH EAST

1 Dickinson Dees Newcastle upon Tyne
2 Ward Hadaway Newcastle upon Tyne
3 Latimer Hinks Darlington
4 Jacksons Stockton on Tees

LEADING INDIVIDUALS

1 HARGREAVE Hume Dickinson Dees
2 HEWITT Christopher Ward Hadaway
   KIRKUP Simon Dickinson Dees

This book is the product of 6,552 1/2 hour interviews. See p.7 for BMRB audit. Within each band, firms are listed alphabetically. See individuals' profiles p.60

DICKINSON DEES (see firm details p.938) The firm retains its top position in the area by a clear margin. "*Doyen – the expert*" **Hume Hargreave** (see p.62) is the first name to be recommended by many interviewees, while head of department **Simon Kirkup** (see p.62) was said to "*know the job inside out – from placing telephone masts to selling portions of farms.*" The firm represents a broad spread of clients from across the country, with an emphasis on landed estates in the North. Work this year has included joint venture arrangements, farm/partnership restructuring and tax planning. In the past year, the team has advised on the transfer of approximately 40,000 acres of agricultural and sporting estates.

WARD HADAWAY (see firm details p.1180) The team represents a varied client list of agribusinesses, charities, mineral operators, public bodies, landlords and tenants. **Christopher Hewitt** (see p.62) ("*able and reliable*") is active across the spectrum of rural legal provision.

LATIMER HINKS Anne Elliott leads the agricultural department at this firm, which is viewed by peers as "*eminently sensible.*" Advising local landowners and farmers, the practice receives instructions in tax planning, partnership agreements and the range of agricultural property matters.

JACKSONS (see firm details p.1011) Interviewees agreed that the firm is developing a "*strong commercial agriculture reputation*" off the back of its NFU panel membership. The department, led by Phil Corbett, acts primarily for smaller farmers in matters including conveyancing, landlord and tenant work and commercial disputes.

SCOTLAND

AGRICULTURE
■ SCOTLAND

1
- **Anderson Strathern WS** Edinburgh
- **Brodies** Edinburgh
- **Turcan Connell** Edinburgh

2
- **Thorntons WS** Dundee, Forfar
- **Tods Murray WS** Edinburgh

3
- **Burnett & Reid** Aberdeen
- **Gillespie Macandrew WS** Edinburgh
- **Lindsays WS** Edinburgh
- **Turnbull, Simson & Sturrock WS** Jedburgh

4
- **McLean & Stewart** Dunblane
- **Murray Beith Murray W S** Edinburgh
- **Paull & Williamsons** Aberdeen

LEADING INDIVIDUALS

1
- **FOX Alasdair** Anderson Strathern WS
- **STRANG STEEL Malcolm** Turcan Connell

2
- **BLAIR Michael** Thorntons WS
- **DALRYMPLE Hew** Brodies
- **RENNIE Donald** Donald Rennie WS
- **ROBERTSON Jonathan** Turcan Connell
- **SHEARER Roy** Lindsays WS
- **STURROCK David** Turnbull, Simson & Sturrock WS

3
- **DRYSDALE James** Anderson Strathern WS
- **HOULDSWORTH David** Brodies
- **TURCAN Robert** Turcan Connell

4
- **ANDERSON Alastair** Anderson Beaton Lamond
- **GILLINGHAM Adam** Turcan Connell

This book is the product of 6,552 1/2 hour interviews. See p.7 for BMRB audit.
Within each band, firms are listed alphabetically. See individuals' profiles p.60

ANDERSON STRATHERN WS (see firm details p.844) This "*nimble giant*" of a firm wins acclaim from both clients and rivals. The "*responsible and phenomenally knowledgeable*" **Alasdair Fox** (see p.61) heads up the team, which includes high-profile **James Drysdale** (see p.61) ("*a cracking lawyer*"). Instructions this year have included matters connecting to FMD, opencast mining and alternative energy sources, as well as the usual agricultural conveyancing. Clients include The National Trust for Scotland, The Crown Estate and The Buccleuch Estates.

BRODIES (see firm details p.889) This "*heavyweight*" practice boasts a long and enviable list of landed estate clients, for which it provides the full range of rural property services. The team also has extensive experience and specialist knowledge of forestry, mineral rights and renewable energy sources. **Hew Dalrymple** (see p.60) won plaudits for his agricultural property and tax expertise, while **David Houldsworth** (see p.60) "*deals effectively with titled landowners.*"

TURCAN CONNELL (see firm details p.1170) A balance of contentious and non-contentious work for a range of landowning clients is undertaken. The team boasts four Law Society-accredited specialists in agricultural law: **Malcolm Strang Steel** (see p.61) is dubbed "*the leading player in Scotland;*" **Jon Robertson** (see p.61) is "*someone who gets things done quickly and sensibly;*" **Robert Turcan** (see p.61) ("*a quality practitioner*") and new to the tables this year and **Adam Gillingham** (see p.61) ("*pinpoints problems and solves them*"). The team has this year received instructions on diversification, wind farming and land sales/purchases.

THORNTONS WS (see firm details p.1162) This big player in the Angus and Perthshire regions undertakes diverse agricultural work for a broad range of clients. Last year, the team played a significant role in the break-up of the Panmure Estate in Angus. Team head **Mike Blair** (see p.60) is a "*hard-working, clear communicator.*"

TODS MURRAY WS (see firm details p.1164) Marked out as a "*blossoming presence in the market,*" this standout firm's client base features public bodies, charities and private landowners, old and new. John Fulton's "*talented*" team has been involved in the full gamut of agricultural legal work, including joint venture partnerships and large-scale property transfer. The client base here features the Forestry Commission and the RSPB.

BURNETT & REID An "*affable, sensible, practical*" Aberdeen-based firm, its client base contains an increasing number of tenants as well as landlords. The team, headed by Alastair Robertson, handles the full gamut of contentious and non-contentious work, including acquisitions and sales, landlord and tenant work, quota work and tax planning. Unusually, the firm also offers an estate management role for its landed clients.

GILLESPIE MACANDREW WS (see firm details p.971) Timothy Myles' team represents both large estates and agribusinesses, as well as owner-occupiers. Its expertise in buying and selling land, sporting law and renewable energy sources is recognised by the market.

LINDSAYS WS (see firm details p.1042) "*A top-notch department*" proclaimed peers. The team deals with a broad range of estate work for its landowning clients, including tax planning, tenancy disputes, property transfers and sporting and mineral rights issues. Lead partner **Roy Shearer** (see p.63) is the backbone of the practice, winning special acclaim for his "*unique expertise*" in crofting law.

TURNBULL, SIMSON & STURROCK WS (see firm details p.1171) This local firm owes much of its strength to "*experienced all-rounder*" **David Sturrock** (see p.64). It undertakes conveyancing, quota work, landlord and tenant work and partnership arrangements for a range of agricultural clients.

MCLEAN & STEWART Endorsed as a "*strong local firm,*" its client base is dominated by working farmers. The department, led by James McIldowie, is active across the board, although particular commendation was afforded to its knowledge of landlord and tenant-related issues.

MURRAY BEITH MURRAY W S (see firm details p.1079) A "*solid, traditional outfit,*" it acts for a large number of agricultural landowners in Scotland. The team receives primarily non-contentious instructions in matters from succession planning and conveyancing to forestry and conservation.

PAULL & WILLIAMSONS (see firm details p.1096) This "*sturdy*" operation has a client base of landed estates, commercial farmers and agribusinesses. Clive Phillips' team has been active in landlord and tenant work, succession planning and tax advice.

OTHER NOTABLE PRACTITIONERS Donald Rennie (see p.60) was easily the highest profile sole practitioner in Scotland according to our interviewees; he was commended for his "*extraordinary depth of knowledge.*" **Alastair Anderson** (see p.60) of Perth firm Anderson Beaton Lamond was described typically as a "*highly competent troubleshooter.*"

AGRICULTURE ■ THE LEADERS

THE LEADERS IN AGRICULTURE

ANDERSON, Alastair H
Anderson Beaton Lamond, Perth
(01738) 639999
aha@abl-law.co.uk
Specialisation: Dealing with all aspects of agricultural law with particular emphasis on farm and estate purchase and sale, forestry, windfarms and landlord and tenant. Also related general business - wills, trusts, tax planning, arbitrations, quotas, corporate and employment law. Involved in farm diversification, steading and housing developments.
Prof. Memberships: Accredited by the Law Society of Scotland as a Specialist in Agricultural Law; Notary Public; Scottish Landowners Federation Law & Parliamentary Committee; past Chairman Perthshire Agricultural Society.
Career: Edinburgh and Amsterdam Universities: qualified 1975.
Personal: Family man, Rotarian, enjoys golf, shooting and outdoor pursuits.

ARROWSMITH-BROWN, Matthew
Mills & Reeve, Norwich
(01603) 693215
matthew.arrowsmith-brown@mills-reeve.com
Specialisation: Advising farming businesses and families. Examples of particular issues covered are FBTs for diversification; cooperative arrangements; irrigation schemes; family business disputes.
Prof. Memberships: Law Society; Agricultural Law Association; Royal Agricultural Society of England; Royal Norfolk Agricultural Association; Farmers' Club.
Career: Clifton College; University of York; articles and 2.5 years post qualification with *Slaughter and May* 1974-79; *Mills & Reeve* 1979 to date; partner since 1981.
Personal: Brought up on Dartmoor farm; married; two daughters (21 and 23); driving fast cars.

AUBREY, Michael J
Mills & Reeve, Cambridge
(01223) 222397
michael.aubrey@mills-reeve.com
Specialisation: Partner in Agriculture Department. Practice covers all areas of agricultural property work and in particular corporate and institutional agriculture. Main areas of work include acquisition and disposal of agricultural and development land and estates, the imposition of reserving future development value, agricultural tenancies, minerals, share farming, contract farming and partnerships.
Prof. Memberships: Royal Forestry Society; Law Society; Agricultural Law Association.
Career: BSc (Hons) in Agricultural Economics from University of Newcastle Upon Tyne. Joined *Mills & Reeve* in 1989 and became a partner in 1997.
Personal: Leisure interests include rugby, cricket and morris dancing.

BARKER, Richard
Barker Gotelee, Ipswich
(01473) 611211
Specialisation: Acting for landowners, farmers, the food industry and government agencies throughout the UK. Head of Agricultural team dealing with all aspects of agricultural law both UK and EC Community legislation. His particular expertise is EC legislation and lobbying the EC Institutions on matters including state aids, competition, food quality standards and food health issues. Has an office in Brussels. Council member Suffolk Agricultural Association. Chairman Suffolk Professional European Committee. CLA branch member. Member of the EU Team Europe Panel of specialist speakers. Speaks nationally at seminars on agricultural and EU matters and writes regularly for specialist publications and newspapers and broadcasts on agricultural and EU matters. Is now forging links with law firms in Poland and Hungary advising upon representation before the Commission and the EU Parliament.
Prof. Memberships: Qualified 1969. Now Senior Partner of *Barker Gotelee, Solicitors* and Managing Director of Stanyer Consulting Limited dealing with the non-legal aspects of lobbying and EU and UK policy.

BARNETT, Ian
Hewitson Becke + Shaw, Northampton
(01604) 233233
ianbarnett@hewitsons.com
Specialisation: Senior Partner. Agricultural Property Division. Main area of practice is agriculture. Also deals with commercial property and charities.
Prof. Memberships: Northants Committee CLA.
Career: Qualified in 1965. Joined *Hewitson Becke + Shaw* in 1967, becoming a Partner in 1968 and Senior Partner in 1994.
Personal: Born in 1940. Educated at Repton School and Oxford University 1958-61 (MA). Undersheriff of Northamptonshire since 1973. Leisure interests include field sports, antiques, food and wine.

BARR, William
Mills & Reeve, Cambridge
(01223) 222480
william.barr@mills-reeve.com
Specialisation: Partner in Agriculture Department. Work covers farm tenancies and partnerships, share farming, quotas and farm taxation. Most recently he has been involved in food chain issues and reviewing the structures of farm businesses and co-operatives. Co-author of 'Farm Tenancies'. Lectures frequently and contributes the share farming section to 'Agricultural Law Tax & Finance' and agricultural articles to 'Solicitors' Journal'.
Prof. Memberships: Law Society, Agricultural Law Association, USA Agricultural Law Association.

BLAIR, J Michael G
Thorntons WS, Forfar
(01307) 466886
jmgblair@thorntonsws.co.uk
Specialisation: Partner in Private Client and Head of Agricultural Division. Handles agriculture and environmental matters, including the purchase and sale of estates and large farm properties and succession planning. Also acts in capital tax matters. Has contributed to Greens Guide to Environmental Law in Scotland. Frequent speaker at conferences. Accredited by The Law Society of Scotland as a specialist in Agricultural Law (one of three agricultural specialists in the division).
Career: Joined *Thorntons WS* in 1984; has been a Partner since 1986.
Personal: Attended Edinburgh University, graduating in 1976. Lives in Perthshire.

BUXTON, James
Burges Salmon, Bristol
(0117) 902 2758
james.buxton@burges-salmon.com
Specialisation: All aspects of the law relating to agricultural holdings including disputes relating to security of tenure, succession cases, rent reviews and end of tenancy compensation claims together with all aspects of milk and other commodity quotas.
Prof. Memberships: Agricultural Law Association, Law Society, Solicitors' Association of Higher Court Advocates.
Career: Called to the Bar in 1971, joined *Burges Salmon* in 1982 and became a partner in 1984. Granted rights of audience in the High Courts in 1997. Contributor to 'Halsbury's Laws of England' (Agriculture Volume) and 'Butterworth's Encyclopaedia of Forms and Precedents'.
Personal: Born 1948, read law and economics at Trinity College, Cambridge.

CAPEL, Stuart
Pryce Collard Chamberlain, Wantage
(01235) 763338
spbcapel.notary@virgin.net
Specialisation: Advising all aspects of farming and rural commercial property work including equestrian establishments. Particular work dealing with restructuring of rural businesses, partnerships and financial rearrangements. Diversification of agriculture work, including extensive work in option agreements. Acquisitions and disposals of farm, agricultural and equestrian establishments. Planning agreements, wills, trusts and tax planning.
Prof. Memberships: CLA; Agricultural Law Association; NFU; TFA.
Career: Articled to *Beachcrofts* (clerk to the Governors of Christ's Hospital). Joined *Pryce & Co* as Partner 1970. Notary Public 5 February 1976.
Personal: Born 27 October 1942. Attended Stowe 1956-61, followed by Kings College, London. Leisure interests: music, country matters, education, snooker and trains. Lives in the environs of Oxford.

CARTMELL, Timothy H
Cartmell Shepherd, Carlisle
(01228) 516666

CHEAL, Jonathan
Thring Townsend, Bath
(01225) 340 000
Specialisation: Partner in Agriculture Department. Main areas of practice are agricultural law and real property law. Work includes farm sales and purchases, landlord and tenant, partnerships, succession and wills, tax, quotas, town and country planning and farm buildings, rights of way, easements and housing of farm workers and has wide experience of public speaking, lectures and seminars.
Prof. Memberships: Previously Legal Advisor at Country Landowners Association Head Office in London, 1983-87. Currently a professional member of CLA, NFU and TFA. Sits on CLA Somerset Committee; approved panel AMC solicitors, Agricultural Law Association.
Career: Qualified in 1976. Articled in London and Sussex. Worked in Hong Kong 1976-82; CLA 1983-87. Joined *Thrings & Long* in 1987, becoming a Partner in 1989.
Personal: Born 30 June 1950.

COLLINS, Peter
Walker Smith & Way, Chester
(01244) 357 400
petercollins@wsw-law.com
Specialisation: Agriculture and Head of Company/Commercial Department. Handles cases before the Agricultural Land Tribunals and Agricultural Arbitrators and conducts advocacy personally. Also deals with milk quota disputes and farming partnership disputes.
Prof. Memberships: Agricultural Law Association, Member of the Chartered Institute of Arbitrators.
Career: Qualified in 1968. Joined *Walker Smith & Way* in 1971 and became a Partner in 1973.
Personal: St. Peter's School, York 1956-61 and St. John's College, Cambridge 1962-65.

DALRYMPLE, Hew
Brodies, Edinburgh
(0131) 228 3777
hew.dalrymple@brodies.co.uk
Specialisation: He specialises in all aspects of Rural Property Law, Country Estate work and Private Client practice. He has a special interest in farming, asset protection, and capital taxation and minerals and acts for a number of prominent landowners and their families and other high net worth individuals and commercial concerns with rural interests.
Prof. Memberships: Society of Her

60   INDEX TO LEADING LAWYERS: PAGE 1693 ■ IN-HOUSE LAWYERS PROFILES: PAGE 1201

THE LEADERS — AGRICULTURE

Majesty's Writers to the Signet.
Career: Edinburgh Academy; Edinburgh University; *Brodies WS* from 1975 to date.
Personal: Leisure interests include shooting, fishing, painting and sketching and travel.

DAVIS, Nigel R
Nigel Davis Solicitors, Belper
(01335) 372889

DENNIS, Jeanette
Taylor Vinters, Cambridge
(01223) 225211
jad@taylorvinters.com
Specialisation: Partner in agriculture department. Principal area of practice is agriculture. Work includes sales and purchases of farms and land, tenancies (including Agricultural Holdings Act 1986, Agricultural Tenancies Act 1995 and short term business leases), crop loss claims and financial arrangements for farmers.
Prof. Memberships: Cambridge Young Solicitors; Cambridge Law Society; Agricultural Law Association; Vice Chairman of the Game Conservancy Trust; Cambridgeshire Committee.
Career: Joined *Taylor Vinters* in 1988 and qualified in 1990. Has specialised in agricultural law since qualification. National AgriLaw Lecturer and BBC Radio contributor.
Personal: Graduated from Hull University in 1987(LL.B).

DRYSDALE, James
Anderson Strathern WS, Edinburgh
(0131) 220 2345
Specialisation: All aspects of agricultural and rural law covering business structures, purchases, sales and leasing, forestry, salmon fisheries, sporting rights, land use and management including diversification, development and minerals. Head of the firm's Environmental Unit dealing with environmental legislation relating to land, wildlife, pollution or otherwise.
Prof. Memberships: Society of Writers to HM Signet, Agricultural Law Association, National Society for Clean Air and Environmental Protection and UKELA.
Career: Qualified in 1982. Partner at *Anderson Strathern* since 1986. Accredited as a specialist in Agricultural Law by the Law Society of Scotland (accreditation renewed 2001). Certificate in Environmental Law.
Personal: Educated Brancote School, Scarborough 1964-69; Winchester College 1969-74; Aberdeen University 1975-78. Leisure pursuits include field sports. Born 30 April 1956. Lives in Kinross-shire.

ELLIOTT, Penelope
Withers LLP, London
(020) 7597 6000
penny.elliott@withersworldwide.com
Specialisation: Head of *Withers*' Landed Estate Group. Principal specialising in buying and selling of agricultural land and estates; advice on landlord and tenant issues; farming partnership; share farming and contract farming; agricultural insolvency; capital taxation; heritage property.
Prof. Memberships: Agricultural Law Association; Country Landowners Association (Cambridge and Bedfordshire branch committee); Legal and Parliamentary Committee.
Career: Trained at *Taylors*, Newmarket; qualified in 1985; partner at *Mills & Reeves* 1988-1998. Partner *Withers* 1998. Directorships - Fitzwilliam Museum Trust.
Personal: Educated at Girton College, Cambridge.

EVANS, Della
Burges Salmon, Bristol
(0117) 902 2781
della.evans@burges-salmon.com
Specialisation: Agriculture, primarily agricultural business advice; farming partnerships - advice and disputes; agricultural landlord and tenant - advice and disputes.
Prof. Memberships: Law Society, Agricultural Law Association.
Career: Qualified at *Burges Salmon* in 1991 and became a partner in 1995. Author of Sweet & Maxwell's 'Legislation Handbook on the Agricultural Tenancies Act 1995' and a contributor to 'Butterworths Encyclopaedia of Forms and Precedents on Agriculture'. Also co-author of Scammell & Densham's 'Law of Agricultural Holdings'.
Personal: University of West of England and LLM at University of Bristol.

FARREN, Miles
Burges Salmon, Bristol
(0117) 902 2785
miles.farren@burges-salmon.com
Specialisation: Agricultural law particularly contentious landlord and tenant matters; claims for possession of land; milk and other agri-commodity quotas; contentious probate and inheritance claims; partnership creation and dissolution. Speaker at lectures and seminars on agricultural law.
Career: Former NFU Local Secretary in Shropshire; strong links with NFU. LLB (Hons) part time Staffordshire University; qualified 1994.
Personal: Shropshire born and bred. Member of the Agricultural Law Association.

FELLINGHAM, Michael
Penningtons, Godalming
(01483) 791800
fellinghammb@penningtons.co.uk
Specialisation: Tax planning strategies for rural businesses. Preserving the taxation benefits of farmers after diversification of farming businesses.
Prof. Memberships: STEP.
Career: Lecturer, College of Law, Guildford. Partner of *Penningtons*, formerly head of private client department, now finance partner.
Personal: St Catharine's College, Cambridge in mathematics and law. Married with one daughter. Golf, bridge.

FINDLEY, Christopher
Bircham Dyson Bell, London
(020) 7227 7000
christopherfindley@bdb-law.co.uk
Specialisation: All aspects of law including agricultural holdings and arbitrations and farm business tenancy legislation, advising agricultural estates on land and tax issues. Town and country planning, experience includes options and sales of farm land and buildings for development, representation at Planning Appeals, Local Plan Inquiries and Judicial Review proceedings. Milk quota and subsidy law CAP reform. Extensive experience in creation and dissolution of farming partnerships and companies. Advising on mineral extraction and waste disposal sites.
Prof. Memberships: Country Landowners Association (Oxfordshire Committee) and Legal & Parliamentary Sub-Committee member, Agricultural Law Association (Committee), National Farmers Union, Tenant Farmers Association.
Career: Qualified in 1979 Head of Agricultural Law Department at *Thomas Mallam* Oxford 1983-93. Joined *Cole & Cole* as Partner and Head of Agricultural Law Department 1994. Joined *Bircham Dyson Bell* as a partner in 2001.

FITZGERALD, Peter R
Wilsons, Salisbury
(01722) 412412
Specialisation: Partner in Farms and Estates Department. Specialises in agricultural estates including stately homes, chattels, heritage law, agricultural law and tax. Firm represents some 280,000 acres of agricultural land. Author of occasional articles on heritage and taxation matters and occasional speaker at conferences and seminars.
Prof. Memberships: CLA, HHA.
Career: Qualified in 1969. Partner at *Fladgate Fielder* 1975-95. Joined *Wilsons* as a Partner in 1995.
Personal: Educated at Canford School and Trinity College, Oxford (MA). Lives near Wincanton, Somerset.

FOX, Alasdair
Anderson Strathern WS, Edinburgh
(0131) 220 2345
Specialisation: Head of Rural Department and Land Ventures Unit with over 30 years experience of all aspects of rural property law. Particular expertise in the area of agricultural landlord and tenant law and agricultural arbitrations (acting principally for arbiters but also for parties). Practice also covers advice to major estate proprietors, purchase and sale of rural properties and land ventures including Diversification Agreements, opencast mining options and licences.
Prof. Memberships: Society of Writers to HM Signet; Law Society of Scotland's Rural Affairs Committee, Agricultural Law Association. Member of Scottish Office Consultative Panel on Land Reform (landlord and tenant); consultant to Scottish Law Commission on agricultural dispute resolution and irritancies in leases.
Career: Qualified in 1969. Partner at *Anderson Strathern WS* since 1972. Accredited by the Law Society of Scotland as a specialist in agricultural law 1993. Renewed 1998.
Personal: Educated at Lime House School, Carlisle 1954-59, Fettes College, Edinburgh 1959-64 and at the University of Edinburgh 1964-67. Leisure pursuits include sailing, skiing, shooting and fishing. Born 1 January 1946. Lives in Edinburgh.

FURBER, James
Farrer & Co, London
(020) 7242 2022
wjf@farrer.co.uk
Specialisation: Agricultural estates, property and institutional investment and most other aspects of property law. Solicitor to the Duchy of Cornwall. Partner in and head of estates and private property team.
Prof. Memberships: Law Society, Holborn Law Society (President 1996-97).
Career: Joined *Farrer & Co* in 1976. Qualified in 1979. Became an associate in 1981 and a partner in 1985.
Publications: 'Encyclopaedia of Forms & Precedents, Volume 36, Sale of Land - Trusts for Sale and Requisitions on Title.' Contributor to Television Education Network 1991-96.
Personal: Born 1 September 1954. Attended Westminster School and Gonville & Caius College, Cambridge. Married with three children. Lives in Blackheath. Leisure interests include golf.

GILLIBRAND, Martin
Oglethorpe Sturton & Gillibrand, Lancaster
(01524) 67171

GILLINGHAM, Adam
Turcan Connell, Edinburgh
(0131) 228 8111
arg@turcanconnell.com
Specialisation: Partner specialising in all aspects of rural property and practice, including agricultural law; quota matters; commercial development of estate properties (eg purchase, break up and sale on) quarrying; forestry; fish and shell fish farming; conservation and environment; fishing and sporting estates; also acts for a number of private individuals, including landowners, their families and trusts.
Prof. Memberships: Writer to the Signet. Accredited as a specialist in agricultural law by the Law Society of Scotland.
Career: Trainee *Brodies WS*; qualified 1983; assistant solicitor 1983-85; assistant solicitor *W & J Burness* 1985-89; partner 1989-97; partner *Turcan Connell* 1997 to date; directorship: Trustee John Muir Birthplace Trust.
Personal: Born 1958; resides Edinburgh; married, three children. Sailing, gardening, cycling, member New Club, Edinburgh; Club Nautico, Javea.

AGRICULTURE ■ THE LEADERS

GITTINGS, Simon
Stamp Jackson and Procter, Hull
(01482) 324591
srg@sjplaw.co.uk
Specialisation: Conservation and environmental issues (advisor to English Nature). Land management and development.

HARBOTTLE, James
Birketts, Ipswich
(01473) 406278
james-harbottle@birketts.co.uk
Specialisation: Agricultural and equestrian property law specialist with clients across East Anglia, the South of England and overseas.
Prof. Memberships: ALA, CLA.
Career: 1992-96 *Allen & Overy*; 1996-2000 *Burges Salmon*; 2000-date *Birketts*.
Publications: 'Law Society Conveyancing Handbook 2002' - Agricultural Land Section.
Personal: Married with one child.

HARGREAVE, R Hume M
Dickinson Dees, Newcastle upon Tyne
(0191) 279 9234
Specialisation: Partner in Agriculture Group. Main area of practice agriculture, encompassing all aspects of land ownership and management, partnerships, agricultural tenancies and European Law. Speaks frequently at RICS/CAAV conferences and seminars; writes regularly for the press.
Prof. Memberships: Agricultural Law Association.
Career: Qualified in 1971. Partner in *Dickinson Dees* since 1974.
Personal: Born 24th September 1940. Shrewsbury School 1954-59, Merton College, Oxford 1959-63.

HARRIS, Edward
John Collins & Partners, Swansea
(01792) 773773

HEAL, Jeremy
Howes Percival, Norwich
(01603) 762103
jpwh@howes-percival.co.uk
See under Trusts & Personal Tax, p.825

HEWITT, Christopher
Ward Hadaway, Newcastle upon Tyne
(0191) 204 4000
Specialisation: Head of Countryside Law Group, specialising in agricultural holdings, quotas, partnerships, business and property law, land use, minerals and planning. Wide ranging cases for farmers, landowners and rural institutions. Spoken at CLA, RICS, CAAV and many other conferences on agricultural law. Regular contributor to local press.
Prof. Memberships: Law Society, Country Land and Business Association, Agricultural Law Association.
Career: Qualified in 1971, Partner in 1987 upon joining *Ward Hadaway*.
Personal: Born 16th September 1947. Attended Sedbergh School and the University of Newcastle upon Tyne.

HORNBY, John
Macfarlanes, London
(020) 7831 9222

HORWOOD-SMART, Adrian
Taylor Vinters, Cambridge
(01223) 225209
adrian.horwood-smart@taylorvinters.com
Specialisation: Partner in agriculture department. Principal area of practice is agriculture. Work includes landlord and tenant, contracting and management agreements, other joint farming operations, partnership arrangements, quota and set-aside transactions and the land law aspects of landed estates and farms. Regularly lectures at seminars and conferences.
Prof. Memberships: Law Society, Agricultural Law Association, Notaries Society.
Career: Qualified in 1977. At *Waltons & Morse* 1977-79 before joining *Taylor Vinters*. Became a partner in 1983.

HOULDSWORTH, David
Brodies, Edinburgh
(0131) 228 3777
david.houldsworth@brodies.co.uk
Specialisation: David Houldsworth is Head of the Private Business Department specialising in agricultural and related matters, including landlord/tenant issues, farming contracts, acquisition of farms and estates, nature conservation, diversification, land reform and all other matters relating to rural businesses; he acts for a number of large estates and advises on every aspect of their business affairs; David has overall responsibility for the clients' tax and succession planning.
Prof. Memberships: Director: North Atlantic Salmon Fund (UK) Limited; Member of the Cairngorm Recreation Trust; Member Scottish Landowners Federation Law & Parliamentary Committee.
Personal: David received an LLB from the University of Edinburgh in 1974 and qualified in 1977. He has been a Partner with *Brodies* since 1981. He is married with one daughter and his interests include family farming and forestry businesses and the future of the countryside. When time allows he plays golf at Muirfield and Nairn, he fishes and shoots throughout Scotland; he is an avid gardener and enjoys contemporary art.

JACKSON, Andrew
Macfarlanes, London
(020) 7831 9222

JESSEL, Christopher
Farrer & Co, London
(020) 7242 2022
Specialisation: Partner in estates and private property team. Main area of practice covers rural estates, agriculture and manors. Acts on farms, common land and rural estate work generally including development sales with trust and personal advice. Also covers charity and constitutional work, establishing and advising charities on parliamentary and administrative law. Author of 'The Law of the Manor 1998, Farms and Estates - A Conveyancing Handbook', 1999, 'Development Land Overage and Clawback' (2001) and numerous articles in professional and investment magazines. Lectures extensively in London and elsewhere.
Prof. Memberships: Law Society.
Career: Joined *Farrer & Co* in 1967. Qualified in 1970. Became a partner in 1979.
Personal: Born 16 March 1945. Attended Bryanston School 1958-63, Balliol College, Oxford 1964-67. Leisure interests include archaeology. Lives in Guildford.

KEDDIE, Joanne
Dawsons, London
(020) 7421 4872
j.keddie@dawsons-legal.com
Specialisation: Practice covers advising landed estates, farming companies and partnerships regarding all aspects of agricultural business, in particular, negligence and compensation claims, contentious and non-contentious employment issues and quota claims.
Prof. Memberships: Law Society, Agricultural Law Association, Employment Lawyers Association, London Solicitors Litigation Association, CLA and NFU.
Career: Joined *Dawsons* in 1988 and qualified in 1990, became a Partner in 1995 and Head of the Litigation and Employment Departments in 1998.

KIRKUP, Simon
Dickinson Dees, Newcastle upon Tyne
(0191) 279 9374
simon.kirkup@dickinson-dees.com
Specialisation: Handles all aspects of agricultural law. Particular expertise in landlord and tenant issues, quotas and livestock premiums, agricultural land tribunal matters, arbitrations, farming partnerships and farm sales and purchases. Regularly lectures at seminars and conferences.
Prof. Memberships: Agricultural Law Association.
Career: Attended Sedbergh School 1979-84 and Exeter University 1985-88. Joined *Dickinson Dees* in 1990 and qualified in 1992. Is a partner in and head of the firm's agriculture group.
Personal: Born 31 August 1966. Leisure interests including fishing, shooting and golf.

KNIGHT, Matthew
Knights, Tunbridge Wells
(01892) 537311
knights@atlas.co.uk
See under Administrative & Public Law, p.48

KYRKE, Richard
Thomas Eggar, Horsham
(01403) 214500
richard.kyrke@thomaseggar.com
Specialisation: Partner and head of agricultural law unit. Handles all aspects of agricultural law, particularly landlord and tenant issues, and advises on commercial property matters, including sales and purchases and diversification.
Prof. Memberships: Agricultural Law Association, CLA, NFU.
Career: 1951. Educated Marlborough College. Qualified 1976. Partner in *Thomas Eggar* since 1979.

LANE, Andrew
Withers LLP, London
(020) 7597 6000
andrew.lane@withersworldwide.com
Specialisation: Principal in Property Department. Practice covers all types of agricultural property work including agricultural holdings law, estate management and sales and acquisitions of farms and estates. Also advises on tax implications of property transactions; particularly Capital Gains Tax and VAT. Clients range from private individuals through family trusts and institutions to major plcs.
Prof. Memberships: Agricultural Law Association, Royal Agricultural Society of England.
Career: Was a full-time farmer between 1978 and 1987. Joined *Withers* in 1987 qualifying in 1992 and becoming a partner in 1994.
Personal: Born 22 January 1957. Educated Malvern College 1970-74 Christ's College Cambridge 1975-78. Lives near Salisbury, Wiltshire.

LODDER, David
Lodders, Stratford-upon-Avon
(01789) 293259
david.lodder@lodders.co.uk
Specialisation: The law relating to agricultural holdings and rural estates, landlord and agricultural tenant matters, partnerships, succession and tax issues, diversification schemes, EEC quotas, acquisitions and disposals.
Career: Educated at Uppingham School/Sheffield University. Articled in Sheffield. Joined family firm (then *G F Lodder & Sons*) 1974, became partner in 1978. Head of large agricultural department.
Personal: Country Landowners Association. Legal Parliamentary Committee Member. National Farmers Union. Agricultural Law Association.

MARGRAVE-JONES, Clive
Margraves, Llandrindod Wells
(01597) 825565

MOORE, John
Macfarlanes, London
(020) 7831 9222

MORRISON, Alastair
Burges Salmon, Bristol
(0117) 939 2258
alastair.morrison@burges-salmon.com
Specialisation: Is in the complexities of sale and purchase of large estates, country houses and farms, and commercial farm investment and development. Also advises on agricultural tenancies and agricultural mortgages.
Prof. Memberships: Law Society; member of the Agricultural Law Association, member of Legal and Parliamentary sub-

committee of the Country Land and Business Association.
Career: Trained and practised for five years with *Macfarlanes* before moving to practise in the North East for five years. Joined *Burges Salmon* as a partner in 1997.

NEVILLE, William
Burges Salmon, Bristol
(0117) 939 2202
william.neville@burges-salmon.com
Specialisation: Works exclusively for the agricultural industry doing both litigation and general advisory work. He works for clients across the whole industry and has specialised in a wide range of CAP related issues including: cereals, milk, beef, sugar, oilseeds, flax/hemp, poultry, pigs, trade in live animals, agri-chemicals and fertilizers, plant breeder rights, and food safety.
Prof. Memberships: Agricultural Law Association, Law Society Food Law Group, British Institute of Agricultural Consultants, Royal Association of British Dairy Farmers, National Farmers Union Professional, National Institute of Agriculture and Botany, Countryside Alliance and Royal Agricultural Society.
Career: Joined *Burges Salmon* after eight years at the Bar, re-qualified as a solicitor in 1987 and became a partner in 1989. Author of 'A Guide to the Reformed Common Agricultural Policy', and contributing author to Halsbury's Laws of England Agriculture volume.
Publications: Contributing author to Halsbur's 'Laws on Agriculture', and has published 'A Guide to the Reformed Common Agricultural Policy'.
Personal: Leisure interests include fly fishing and mountain biking.

PLUMMER, Alan J
Roythorne & Co, Spalding
(01775) 724141
alanplummer@roythorne.co.uk
Specialisation: Partner in Litigation Department. Main areas of practice are landlord and tenant litigation, particularly relating to agricultural holdings, contentious trust matters, employment law and professional indemnity litigation. Speaker at seminars and other professional conferences.
Prof. Memberships: ALA and Law Society Negligence Panel member.
Career: After gaining a degree in Bacteriology he joined *Roythorne & Co* in 1976 and qualified in 1979.

POUND, Toby
Prettys, Ipswich
(01473) 232121
tpound@prettys.co.uk
Specialisation: Agricultural property and landlord and tenant law.
Prof. Memberships: Member of Agricultural Law Association.
Career: Articled at *Prettys* 1978-80; admitted 1980; became partner at *Prettys* 1982; managing partner 1992-95.
Personal: Educated Highgate School and University of Nottingham. Married with three children. Hon. Secretary of Suffolk County Cricket Club since 1991; member of Ipswich Golf Club.

PRING, Simon
Farrer & Co, London
(020) 7242 2022
Specialisation: Partner in the estates and private property team. All aspects of property law with an emphasis on agricultural estates, charity land holding and VAT. Assistant solicitor to the Duchy of Lancaster.
Prof. Memberships: Holborn Law Society.
Career: Blundell's School, Devon; Robinson College, Cambridge. Joined *Farrer & Co* 1986, partner 1995.
Personal: Born 24 March 1964. Married. Lives in London. Leisure: country pursuits and golf.

QUINN, JS
Morton Fisher, Worcester
(01905) 610410
jim.quinn@mortonfisher.com
Specialisation: Partner in business division. Principal field of activity relates to agricultural matters, including landlord and tenant issues, agreements and disputes, tribunal and arbitration work, general estate advice and quota work. Also advises on commercial property matters, including sales and purchases and commercial and agricultural estate development.
Prof. Memberships: Member Law Society; Agricultural Law Association.
Career: Qualified in 1964. Joined *Morton Fisher* and became a partner in 1964.
Personal: Born 11th July 1939. LL.B Birmingham University 1960. Leisure interests include golf, computing, caravanning and family. Lives in Malvern.

RENNIE OBE, Donald G
Donald Rennie WS, Edinburgh
(0131) 476 7007

ROBERTSON, Jonathan
Turcan Connell, Edinburgh
(0131) 228 8111
jmr@turcanconnell.com
Specialisation: Partner in rural property section; specialist in agricultural law, crofting, forestry, aquaculture, conservation, diversification, rural finance, sporting and fishing, rural conveyancing, waste disposal, mining and development work, planning and environmental law. Considerable experience in hotel and leisure and general commercial property.
Prof. Memberships: Member Agricultural Law Association. Accredited as a specialist in agricultural law by the Law Society of Scotland. Writer to the Signet. Notary Public.
Career: Attended University of Aberdeen (LLB (Hons), DipLP). Articled *Dundas & Wilson CS* 1984-86; qualified 1986; assistant solicitor 1986-90; associate 1990; partner 1990-97. Partner *Turcan Connell* 1997.
Personal: Born 1960. Resides East Lothian. Leisure interests include walking.

RODGERS, Christopher
Margraves, Llandrindod Wells
(01597) 825565

RUSS, Tim
Clarke Willmott & Clarke, Taunton
(01823) 445218
truss@cw-c.co.uk
Specialisation: Partner specialising in agricultural and property litigation. This includes landlord and tenant disputes, partnership disputes, banking issues involving farmers probate and chancery work relating to rural land owners, professional negligence and EU quotas. He regularly deals with judicial review and related administrative work. He is a mediator qualified with ADR Group and CEDR, and is experienced in arbitration law. He regularly acts as advocate or advisor in agricultural arbitrations. Recent highlights include Reakes v DEFRA on the DEFRA implementation of the Organic Conversion scheme and Persey v DEFRA which sought a public enquiry into Foot and Mouth Disease. Numerous cases concerning compensation to farmers and payments due to contractors for cleaning and disinfection after FMD.
Prof. Memberships: Agricultural Law Association, Country Landowners Association, Fellow of the Chartered Institute of Arbitrators, The Food Law Group Society of Contentious Trust Practitioners, Property Law Association.
Career: Bristol Polytechnic (LLB); articled with *McFarlane Guy*; joined *Clarke Willmott & Clarke* in October 1987; admitted November 1988; made partner in 1994.

SHEARER, Roy
Lindsays WS, Edinburgh
(0131) 477 8706
rgs@lindsays.co.uk
Specialisation: All aspects of landed estate work including; agricultural law, crofting law, minerals, salmon fishings, shootings, right of way.
Prof. Memberships: The Law Society of Scotland, The WS Society, Notary Public.
Career: Over 30 years' experience in landed estate work Partner at *Lindsays WS* since 1970.

SMITH, Graham C H
Roythorne & Co, Spalding
(01775) 724141
grahamsmith@roythorne.co.uk
Specialisation: Partner in private client/agriculture department. Diverse workload includes tax planning and trusts, pensions, partnership and company affairs, succession planning, contracting and management agreements.
Career: Joined *Roythorne & Co* in 1972 and qualified in 1974. Author of practice texts such as 'Agricultural Law' and 'Agricultural Precedents Handbook' and editor of EMIS Professional Publishing's newsletter on Agricultural Law. Speaker at seminars, various accountants' and surveyors' conferences and for Central Law Training on Agricultural Law.

STEEL, John
White & Bowker, Winchester
(01962) 844440
Specialisation: Partner in agricultural and environmental law group. Main areas of practice are environmental and agricultural, including agricultural tenancy successions, public rights of way, mineral abstraction and landfill, and water pollution cases. Also handles charity and education work, including formation of charities, advice to school governors and work for higher and further education colleges. Has written on pollution for the Agricultural Law Association Journal and the Royal Institution of Chartered Surveyors Technical Bulletin. Lectures on farm pollution, rights of way, acted on winning side in Court of Appeal case McGowan v Jewell. Holds Masters degree in Environmental Law from De Montfort University.
Prof. Memberships: Country Landowners Association, Agricultural Law Association.
Career: Qualified 1975, having joined *White & Bowker* in 1973. Became a partner in 1977. Member of the Country Landowners Association Legal and Parliamentary Committee 1988-92 and of its Hampshire Branch Committee 1981-86 and 1987-92. Agricultural Law Association Treasurer 1990-94.
Personal: Born 9 May 1949. School Governor. Leisure interests include woodland management. Lives in Winchester.

STEPHENS, Jonathan
Jonathan Stephens & Co, Usk
(01291) 673344

STONE, James
Addleshaw Booth & Co, Leeds
(0113) 209 2000
james.stone@addleshawbooth.com
Specialisation: Partner in property and projects group. Main areas of practice are PF/PPP, agriculture, commercial property and property tax. Work includes property investment, tenancy issues (including termination, compensation and succession rights), quotas, property finance, capital taxation and VAT.
Prof. Memberships: Law Society, Agricultural Law Association.
Career: Qualified in 1981. Joined the firm in 1981, becoming a partner in 1988.
Personal: Attended Bristol Grammar School 1964-75 and Exeter University 1975-78. Leisure interests include mountaineering, photography and travel. Lives in Harrogate.

STRANG STEEL, Malcolm
Turcan Connell, Edinburgh
(0131) 228 8111
mgss@turcanconnell.com
Specialisation: Handles mainly rural property matters, including landlord and tenant, acting for proprietors of a number of landed estates with let farms and fishing interests as well as for tenants; and in purchase and sale of landed

AGRICULTURE ■ THE LEADERS

estates. Handles related taxation issues, and timeshare matters including fishings. Has lectured on numerous occasions to the Law Society of Scotland and other seminars on agricultural law and sporting law.
Prof. Memberships: Convener of Law Society of Scotland's Rural Affairs Committee; Convener of Legal and Parliamentary Committee of Scottish Landowners' Federation; Secretary of Scottish Agricultural Arbiters Association; Member, Agricultural Law Association; Member, Securities Institute.
Career: Partner *W & J Burness* 1973-97; partner *Turcan Connell* 1997-date.
Personal: Eton College; Trinity College, Cambridge; Edinburgh University.

STURROCK, David
Turnbull, Simson & Sturrock WS, Jedburgh
(01835) 862391
dps@tssjed.co.uk
Specialisation: Managing Partner. Main area of practice is agricultural law. Handles all aspects of land ownership, Agricultural Holdings (Scotland) Acts, quotas and arbitrations. Also handles wills, succession and inheritance tax planning. Has addressed a variety of Conferences and Seminars.
Prof. Memberships: Law Society of Scotland; Accredited by Law Society of Scotland as a Specialist in Agricultural Law; Writer to the Signet; Notary Public.
Career: Qualified in 1966. Joined *Turnbull, Simson & Sturrock* in 1966, becoming a partner in 1968 and managing partner in 1990.
Personal: Born 16 March 1943. Attended Rugby School 1956-61 and Edinburgh University 1961-65. Lives in Jedburgh.

SWIFT, Robert
Wilsons, Salisbury
(01722) 412 412
rs@wilsonslaw.com
Specialisation: Head of Farms and Estates department. Advises farmers and landowners on Agricultural Law, business restructuring, farm tenancies (including successions) and in connection with the sale and purchase of farms and estates. Firm represents some 280,000 acres of agricultural land.
Prof. Memberships: Agricultural Law Association, Country Landowners Association and the Farmers Club.
Career: Spent a number of years in industry before qualifying as a solicitor. Qualified in 1989. Partner since 1994. Head of Farms and Estates Department since 1998. A member of the Agrilaw Committee and a regular speaker at agricultural conferences. Contributor to 'Farmers Weekly' and the farming press.
Personal: Born 1959. Lives in Warminster, Wiltshire. Interests include walking, Spanish and South America.

SYMINGTON, Anita
Lee & Pembertons, London
(020) 7824 9111

THOMSON, Michael
Arnold Thomson, Towcester
(01327) 350266
miket@arnoldthomson.com
Specialisation: Partner specialising in agriculture. Main area of work covers agricultural property, development work, tenancies, quotas livestock premia and sporting rights. Regularly addresses farming and professional audiences.
Prof. Memberships: Agricultural Law Association, Country Land and Business Association, National Farmers Union.
Career: Qualified 1981. Co-founder of *Arnold Thomson* in 1990.
Personal: Born July 1954. Attended Wrekin College 1967-71, then University College, London 1972-76. Leisure pursuits include shooting, golf and cricket. Lives in Northants.

TOMLINSON, Geoffrey
Napthens, Preston
(01772) 883883

TURCAN, Robert
Turcan Connell, Edinburgh
(0131) 228 8111
rct@turcanconnell.com
Specialisation: Joint Senior Partner specialising in land law, trusts and tax planning, advisor to a substantial number of landowners and farmers.
Prof. Memberships: The Law Society of Scotland, Society of Writers to HM Signet. Accredited as a specialist in agricultural law by the Law Society of Scotland.
Career: Trinity College, Oxford (MA) and University of Edinburgh (LLB). Articled *Shepherd & Wedderburn WS*; qualified 1972; Partner at *Dundas & Wilson CS* 1973-97. Member of Law and Parliamentary Taxation Committee, Scottish Landowners Federation; director of the Abercairny Estates Limited and others.
Personal: Born 1947. Resides Fife. Married with four children. Leisure interests include fox hunting, gardening, shooting and fishing.

WILLIAMS, Peter Rhys
Burges Salmon, Bristol
(0117) 939 2000
peter.williams@burges-salmon.com
Specialisation: National leader in agricultural banking disputes. Continues to advise in relation to disputes in respect of agricultural property and quotas.
Prof. Memberships: Fellow of the Chartered Institute of Arbitrators, member of Agricultural Law Association, Non-Administration Receivers Association and the British Institute of Agricultural Consultants.
Career: Joined *Burges Salmon* in 1980, qualified in 1982 and became a Partner in 1987.
Publications: Joint author of the 'Encyclopaedia of Forms and Precedents on Agriculture'; 'Halsbury's Laws on Agriculture' and Sweet & Maxwell's 'Agricultural Law, Tax and Finance'. Also author of (with Richard Bedford) the RICS publication 'Farm Receiverships' and (with Michael Johnstone) the *Burges Salmon* publication 'Farm Cottages'. He is a contributor to 'Scammell & Densham's Law of Agricultural Holdings', the CAAV publication 'Dispute Resolution' and the forthcoming RICS electronic textbook 'Dispute Resolution and Avoidance'. Blundell Memorial lecturer in 1992.

YOUNG, David
Hibbert Durrad Moxon, Nantwich
(01270) 624225

ALTERNATIVE DISPUTE RESOLUTION

London: 65; The Regions: 67; Profiles: 68

Research approved by BMRB For this edition, **Chambers'** researchers conducted 6,582 interviews – 3,900 with law firms, 511 with barristers and 2,171 with clients. The validity of the research was scrutinised by BMRB International, who audited both the methodology and the results at our offices in London. They interviewed **Chambers'** researchers and cross-checked sample interviews. Details of the audit appear on page 7.

OVERVIEW Mediations are down on the year, despite Government policy and some notable and costly rebukes from the courts. Nevertheless, the conditions continue to mature and commentators are all optimistic that there will be a meteoric rise in cases over the next few years. One factor that may affect the general perception of the market is that many small regional mediations remain invisible, although it is this arena that has received a considerable boost, as local businesses discover the process and local lawyers gain in experience. Following discussions with practitioners, *Chambers* has this year merged the solicitor and barrister tables.

LONDON

LEADING INDIVIDUALS

+ **NAUGHTON Philip** 3 Serjeants' Inn
WILLIS Tony Panel of Independent Mediators

1
ANDREWARTHA Jane Clyde & Co
PRYOR Nicholas Panel of Independent Mediators
RUTTLE Stephen Brick Court Chambers
SHAPIRO David SJ Berwin

2
ALLEN Anthony CEDR Solve
BROWN Henry Penningtons
FINCHAM Anthony CMS Cameron McKenna
MACKIE Karl CEDR Solve
MARSH William Sole Practitioner
MILES David Glovers

3
CORNES David Winward Fearon
CURTIS Tony CEDR Solve
DODSON Charles Sole Practitioner
GAITSKELL Robert Keating Chambers
KALLIPETIS Michel Littleton Chambers
KERSHEN Lawrence Tooks Court Chambers
NEWMARK Chris Baker & McKenzie
ROGERS Beverly-Ann Serle Court
SIBLEY Edward Sibley & Co

4
BAXENDALE Presiley Blackstone Chambers
BIRCH Elizabeth 3 Verulam Buildings
BISHOP John Masons
MIDDLETON-SMITH Charles Hammond Suddards Edge
NEILL Robert Herbert Smith
RIVERS Elizabeth Sole Practitioner

5
ABRAMSON John LeBoeuf, Lamb, Greene & MacRae
AEBERLI Peter 46 Essex Street
ALLEN Heather CEDR Solve
BRODIE Bruce 39 Essex Street
HOLLOWAY Julian Berwin Leighton Paisner
MANNING Colin Littleton Chambers
TESTER Stephen CMS Cameron McKenna

See individuals' profiles p.68

PHILIP NAUGHTON QC (see p.1453), **3 Serjeant's Inn** Known as "*Mister Mediation*," Naughton has an "*impish*" style, which is nevertheless "*tough and tenacious.*" An "*extremely intelligent*" man, he towers as the "*grand old man of the Bar*," specialising in construction, engineering litigation, plant contracts and professional negligence. Peers agree that he always delivers in mediations and continues to use his skills to great effect in arbitrations.

TONY WILLIS (see p.71), **Panel of Independent Mediators** An "*utterly fantastic mediating machine*" who achieves the respect and trust of both clients and lawyers thanks to "*gravitas, wisdom and authority.*" "*The divinity of the mediation profession,*" he inspires confidence thanks to the "*depth and clarity of his understanding*" and his "*astonishing*" level of experience. For sheer volume of mediations Willis cannot be beaten; he has conducted somewhere in the region of 90 mediations over the last year. He is a generalist who works well with lawyers who have spent decades in the trenches.

JANE ANDREWARTHA (see p.68), **Clyde & Co** A "*tough but wonderfully warm*" and "*straight-talking*" lawyer of "*great talent and charm,*" she is "*vastly experienced*" as both mediator and representative. Specialist in reinsurance and insurance, both marine and non-marine as well as aviation, she has handled a wide range of complex disputes frequently of a cross-border or multi-party nature. Clients credit her with a "*clearer picture and fuller understanding than most*" and an "*almost instinctive awareness*" of the distinction between ADR and mainline litigation and arbitration.

NICHOLAS PRYOR (see p.70), **Panel of Independent Mediators** This "*popular*" practitioner takes an approach that is "*adaptable*" and very much in demand. Clients feel that he "*makes a positive difference to any process*" and value his hands-on approach. Peers acknowledge him as "*charming,*" one who is "*relaxed but capable of appropriate toughness.*" Originally a commercial litigator specialising in the banking, insurance and financial fields, he has built a fine reputation handling single and multi-party mediations across a wide and varied range of practice areas.

STEPHEN RUTTLE QC (see p.1472), **Brick Court Chambers** A "*talented and charismatic*" mediator "*so well regarded it's untrue.*" Interviewees claim that he is "*so charming that the clients want to make the process work for him.*" Combining "*great technical ability*" with "*a good sense of humour in a first class mind,*" he "*builds rapport at the door.*" His mediations practice has blossomed and now makes up well over half of his workload, with a focus on insurance, reinsurance and banking. Unlike dyed-in-the-wool barristers, Ruttle is "*not overly confrontational or barristerial,*" but all the same he "*sniffs the settlement, latches onto it and is unbelievably tenacious.*"

DAVID SHAPIRO (see p.71), **SJ Berwin** This very senior and respected figure is "*unsurpassable for the right case and the right client.*" He is in huge demand and has worked in an array of different areas, favouring complex, cross-border multi-party challenges. Clients regard him as "*eccentric and impressive*" and commentators argue that he is "*not everybody's cup of tea.*" His "*radical and unique skill set*" bespeaks a "*wonderful character.*" He is admired as a "*tough straight-shooter.*"

ANTHONY ALLEN (see p.68), **CEDR Solve** Considered "*the absolute star in his clinical negligence sector,*" he commands great respect for his "*sensitivity*" and experience. He is a pioneer of mediation training for the legal profession and NHS clinical negligence managers. Contributions to the field include helping to develop and implement schemes for time-limited mediation and strategic mediations for catastrophic injury cases.

HENRY BROWN (see p.69), **Penningtons** Regarded by many as one of its founding

ALTERNATIVE DISPUTE RESOLUTION ■ LONDON

fathers, Brown "*wrote the book*" on ADR. Originally trained with John Haynes in New York, he is admired for his "*presence and authority*" and commands respect from all quarters. "*Decency and infinite patience*" combine to make him a "*discreet conjuror of settlements.*" An experienced commercial and family mediator and trainer, he now has a broad range that focuses on civil-commercial disputes.

ANTHONY FINCHAM (see p.69), **CMS Cameron McKenna** As a partner in the employment department of a leading City firm, Fincham's practice is less busy in this field than some of the dedicated practitioners. He is, all the same, highly sought after for his "*calm, quiet and fatherly bedside manner,*" and commentators value him as "*the listening, non-interfering type.*" He advises on all areas of employment law and his "*down to earth*" manner sets him apart from other City lawyers. "*Patient and unflustered,*" he has a reassuring effect on clients.

KARL MACKIE (see p.70), **CEDR Solve** One of the best known names in the business, the "*incredibly relaxed*" Mackie was a pioneer of the field and is regarded as a "*font of wisdom.*" A non-practising barrister, he has had an active year and handles high-value mediations across a range of sectors. His "*conciliatory style makes it all seem effortless.*" He is considered effective because "*he knows when to get proactive*" and "*judges things to a nicety.*"

WILLIAM MARSH (see p.70), **Sole Practitioner** Seen in some quarters as "*one of the greats,*" Marsh is deemed an experienced player known for his "*great and gentle style.*" Sources agree that he "*knows how to deal with the non-legal issues as well.*" Rated for his "*excellent reality-checking in risk analysis,*" he is considered "*charming, sensible and realistic.*" He handles high-value commercial matters and medical negligence. Clients are particularly impressed by his ability to handle high emotions. His "*deep commitment*" to ADR has seen him active in developing ADR systems overseas in countries like Slovakia.

DAVID MILES (see p.70), **Glovers** One of the ADR trailblazers, Miles is increasingly seen as "*a grandee*" who promotes the field. Long regarded as a "*fantastic construction mediator,*" he has a distinctive, non-invasive style that ensures he will always be in demand. He is part of CEDR's mediator training faculty and a member of the Panel of Independent Mediators, and is associated with the development of ADR systems in Commonwealth countries.

DAVID CORNES (see p.194), **Winward Fearon** This "*classic*" mediator is "*equally at home in mediation and engineering.*" His "*huge industry experience,*" "*prolific*" writing and "*excellent complex-matter practice*" make him "*unbeatable for this niche.*" His style is "*flexible*" and "*gentle,*" and peers and clients regard him as "*first class.*"

TONY CURTIS (see p.69), **CEDR Solve** "*Unfailingly courteous,*" he is regarded as an "*amazing man*" and a "*fabulous facilitative mediator.*" He is a "*brilliant communicator,*" "*skilful*" at involving clients in the search for solutions and, in the words of one commentator, "*he certainly does have teeth, though he won't bang heads.*" Old hands note that his "*sound basic skills*" carry him through the "*increasing diversity*" of his practice.

CHARLES DODSON (see p.69), **Sole Practitioner** To many, he is a byword for "*sheer excellence*" with a reputation for highly skilled risk-analysis and "*superb for highbrow cases.*" His "*charming and humorous*" manner is not suited to all situations, and commentators agree that he would be a "*fish out of water in a streetfight.*" In his element he is "*focused and tight*" and impresses clients with his "*relaxed and professional*" style. One of his great strengths, warn peers, is that "*he is all too easily underestimated.*"

ROBERT GAITSKELL QC (see p.1402), **Keating Chambers** With his "*nicely persuasive*" manner, "*awesome engineering skills*" and "*honed legal mind,*" this construction specialist is "*impressive in all sorts of ways.*" Sought after for complex engineering projects, especially in the energy/power sector, he has no shortage of referrals. Commentators remark that he is "*terrifyingly clever and calm.*"

MICHEL KALLIPETIS QC (see p.1426), **Littleton Chambers** A "*delightful people-person*" with a "*huge personality*" and an "*absolutely terrific way with mediations,*" Kallipetis is sometimes seen by peers as "*a bit of a lone wolf.*" His practice combines employment law with professional negligence and general commercial work. He has also advised and acted on several occasions in disputes in the entertainment, music and film industries. Commentators report that he can be a little "*brusque,*" but that this is a good thing: "*he turns up the heat as needed, and applies pressure masterfully.*"

LAWRENCE KERSHEN QC (see p.1428), **Tooks Court Chambers** A "*smooth and energetic*" operator who garners approval for his "*superb interpersonal skills.*" Deeply involved on the training side, Kershen has been somewhat less visible on the mediations scene recently. He has the ability to "*set people at their ease through the effective use of humour*" and is "*respected for both his skill and his seniority.*"

CHRIS NEWMARK (see p.70), **Baker & McKenzie** Known as "*a real gentleman,*" he specialises in commercial disputes and has a track record in the telecoms industry; he was recently involved in a $11 million dispute over the completion of a fibre-optic network. His "*confident bedside manner*" coupled with rich experience in complex matters "*set him up well for big-ticket mediations.*" He has established a reputation as an "*amenable and pragmatic*" mediator, often handling CEDR referrals.

BEVERLY-ANN ROGERS (see p.1470), **Serle Court** Mediates both privately and through CEDR, and is valued for her "*unpompous*" approach and her "*patience and stamina.*" Her mediation practice is growing across a spectrum of sectors, and she is a specialist in property and probate. Clients report that she "*handles difficult situations and difficult people well*" and "*stands out as exceptional among the juniors for her ability to bring about settlement.*" She "*has her fingers on the crux of the issues.*"

EDWARD SIBLEY (see p.71), **Sibley & Co** With an "*idiosyncratic style*" that is "*very personal,*" Sibley "*tells it like it is.*" He sticks with "*a formula that works well*" and is "*prepared to step in and be forthright.*" He "*likes to take a leading role,*" which, under the right conditions, is effective. Clients are impressed by his "*commanding presence and grey hairs,*" and these help to dispel fears of partiality.

PRESILEY BAXENDALE QC (see p.1363), **Blackstone Chambers** Though new to the scene, Baxendale enters the tables this year on the basis of "*great strength in public sector work*" and a good record in multi-handed work, often for central and local government. She "*leads by example and others follow.*" Peers regard her move upwards through the ranks as "*a matter of course, should she continue in this.*" She accepts CEDR referrals and has a reputation for commercial generalism. She has handled mediations in a range of sectors including construction, education, employment and housing. Commentators feel that "*her personality suits this business,*" and that she is "*intellectually immensely able yet easy-mannered.*"

ELIZABETH BIRCH QC (see p.1365), **3 Verulam Buildings** A "*notoriously gifted mediator*" who "*inspires confidence*" and "*gets results.*" Birch specialises in commercial law including banking and financial services, commodities, and insurance and reinsurance. She is known for her ability to "*get past the mini-trial mindset*" and for her "*tenacity.*" To be found on high-value, technical and multiparty disputes, her name is often connected with shipping.

JOHN BISHOP (see p.69), **Masons** Senior partner at his firm, Bishop is considered "*unparalleled in all things construction.*" He is a "*thoughtful and intelligent*" mediator, "*good at pressurising people in a subtle way.*"

CHARLES MIDDLETON-SMITH **Hammond Suddards Edge** In contrast to the non-interven-

LONDON/THE REGIONS ■ ALTERNATIVE DISPUTE RESOLUTION

tionists, this "*marvellously understated and fair*" practitioner is "*decidedly proactive.*" He "*puts people at ease*" and is "*highly sought after*" for his "*commercial flair.*" Considered able across widely differing sectors, he handles matters of great complexity in a "*calm and contained*" fashion. He is particularly admired for his work in entertainment, publishing, IP and defamation.

ROBERT NEILL (see p.70), **Herbert Smith** Thanks to his considerable commitments at Herbert Smith this "*bright, gentle and affable*" lawyer is "*asked for more often than he is available.*" Credited with "*considerable cerebral charm,*" he is a "*sensible and user-friendly chap*" who "*comes over well.*" Clients are reassured by his "*pleasant, straightforward and genuine*" style, which inspires confidence. His practice covers areas such as banking, business sale agreements and professional negligence.

ELIZABETH RIVERS (see p.71), **Sole Practitioner** Generally associated with environmental and employment law. An "*interesting character,*" she has broad-based experience, focusing on disputes involving interpersonal aspects within boardrooms and partnerships. Her career spans over 60 mediations, with experience in multi million pound disputes. She is also a senior member of CEDR's training faculty.

JOHN ABRAMSON LeBoeuf, Lamb, Greene & MacRae "*Try him, you'll like him*" insisted one peer. This is a lower volume but top-quality practitioner with a reputation for aviation and insurance. Observers expect that the "*technically adept*" Abramson will achieve greater exposure as he gains a deeper experience. An active member of the American Bar Association, researchers were told that things are "*ticking over nicely,*" and his "*full, impressive potential will one day be realised.*"

PETER AEBERLI (see p.1355), **46 Essex Street** Associated more with arbitrations than ADR these days, this "*quietly effective*" practitioner is kept busy with a variety of activities focusing on his construction/architecture specialism. He lectures and writes and sits on numerous panels.

HEATHER ALLEN (see p.68), **CEDR Solve** An "*accomplished*" mediator and facilitator who has a "*good understanding of what makes people tick.*" Particularly at home in conflict prevention and management, inside and across organisations, she is "*able to build relationships and handle highly charged situations.*" An "*energetic and persistent*" character, Allen has built a reputation for a "*practical and problem-solving approach,*" especially in the areas of employment and voluntary organisations. She is a member of the CEDR faculty and known as a "*skilled trainer.*" She is new to our tables this year and has about 12 disputes under her belt in the past 12 months.

BRUCE BRODIE (see p.1372), **39 Essex Street** Mediation is a distinct sub practice that complements his main focus on commercial arbitrations. Business disputes, professional negligence and insurance disputes all form part of his expertise.

JULIAN HOLLOWAY (see p.196), **Berwin Leighton Paisner** A CEDR-trained mediator, Holloway has long been involved in ADR. This "*enthusiastic*" practitioner is a specialist in construction and civil engineering.

COLIN MANNING (see p.1441), **Littleton Chambers** Regarded as "*something of a wit,*" Manning is regarded by peers and clients alike as "*really good fun.*" A specialist in commercial contract disputes, Manning has a name in the areas of computers, entertainment and media law, professional negligence and product liability.

STEPHEN TESTER (see p.683), **CMS Cameron McKenna** The firm as a whole received acclaim for "*really making mediation a central plank of their litigation practice.*" The "*committed and resolute*" Tester is in the vanguard of that process, and specialises in professional indemnity, construction and directors' and officers' insurance.

THE REGIONS

LEADING INDIVIDUALS

★ **HOWELL-RICHARDSON Phillip** Morgan Cole
  PATON Andrew Pinsent Curtis Biddle
1 **LLOYD-JONES Jonathan** Linnells
2 **BRADBEER Ronald** Eversheds
  GATENBY John Addleshaw Booth & Co
  GLAISTER Anthony Keeble Hawson
  GOYDER Bill Sole Practitioner
  SMITH Quentin Addleshaw Booth & Co
  WINKWORTH-SMITH John Sole Practitioner
3 **DAVIES Mike** Veale Wasbrough
  HOUGHTON Paul Lupton Fawcett
  KENDALL John John Kendall
  TEMPLE Euan Toller Hales & Collcutt

See individuals' profiles p.68

PHILLIP HOWELL-RICHARDSON Morgan Cole One of the legendary figures in the area, the "*incredibly focused*" Howell-Richardson is an operator with "*tremendous presence*" who pioneered the use of ADR and arbitration in the regions. His is nevertheless a truly national name in commercial disputes. Observers applaud his "*subtle way with people,*" and remark that "*he's got it where it counts.*" He is a member of the panel of the Court of Appeal Mediators and chairman of ADR Net.

ANDREW PATON (see p.70), **Pinsent Curtis Biddle** The cream of the provincial crop and accredited by both ADR Net and CEDR, Paton has been "*influential*" in the area for about a decade and has mediated across a broad range of subjects. He is credited with "*great initiative on moving cases into mediation*" and his "*terrier*" qualities "*keep the process going until settlement.*" "*Intuitive and instinctive,*" he "*comes across as natural and quietly tenacious.*"

JONATHAN LLOYD-JONES Linnells Rated as "*absolutely superb*" by his peers, he was recently appointed to the Law Society's working party on ADR and is vice-chairman of ADR Net. Even as senior partner he finds time to do a healthy number of mediations, mostly in construction and professional negligence and often against architects. Most of his referrals are from ADR Net and direct from law firms. Peers praise his ability to "*establish the trust of all parties.*"

RONALD BRADBEER (see p.69), **Eversheds** Combining "*approachability and gravitas in a smooth package,*" his is a well-known name in commercial disputes. He specialises in commercial contracts, employment tribunal cases and construction matters. Though based in Newcastle, he travels extensively around the country, and is a member of the CEDR Training Faculty and the CEDR Lawyers Role Faculty. "*Unflappable,*" he receives the plaudits of his peers.

JOHN GATENBY (see p.558), **Addleshaw Booth & Co** The senior partner here, he handles high-value contractual disputes and specialises in cross-border work. He is credited with "*great commercial nous*" and "*strikes an imposing figure.*" "*Meticulous and particular,*" he "*dots every I and crosses every T.*" He is also well known on the lecture circuit.

ANTHONY GLAISTER (see p.69), Keeble Hawson The "*gentlemanly*" chairman of the Association of Northern Mediators, peers regard him as "*a complete one-off.*" Those who have worked with him report that he has "*an effective and light touch.*" With ten or so mediations under his belt this year, his primary focus is on construction, but he covers a broad range that includes breach of contract, employment and property.

www.ChambersandPartners.com 67

ALTERNATIVE DISPUTE RESOLUTION ■ THE LEADERS

BILL GOYDER (see p.69), **Sole Practitioner** Praised for his "*commercial but human touch,*" he is a "*warm and sensible individual.*" Ex-managing partner at Jackson's, his practice covers construction engineering, with a bias towards North Sea and offshore oil industry disputes. He is also endorsed for his involvement in professional negligence matters. This year saw him involved in more than five cases.

QUENTIN SMITH (see p.71), **Addleshaw Booth & Co** "*Energetic and persuasive,*" he has a useful ability to "*tune into what people want.*" A career spanning over 30 mediations establishes his reputation in personal injury, professional negligence, commercial contracts, defamation and property. Commentators say that "*he thoroughly deserves the hype*" and consider him a "*growing player and future star.*"

JOHN WINKWORTH-SMITH (see p.71), **Sole Practitioner** Known for his "*tenacity and patience,*" this Northern mediator "*has the bearing*" to go with his broad and admired practice in general commercial disputes. He has niche experience in construction and mechanical engineering.

MIKE DAVIES (see p.69), **Veale Wasbrough** Leading the ADR group at the firm, he is said to have "*great familiarity with the themes and principles*" of the field. He specialises in mediating employment-related disputes in the workplace.

PAUL HOUGHTON **Lupton Fawcett** Possessing a "*forceful touch*" that "*works well for a certain type,*" he is a Leeds-based mediator with commercial contract and professional negligence experience. Capable of "*guiding the process,*" he is sought after for a good volume of disputes.

JOHN KENDALL **Sole Practitioner** "*The man for expert determination,*" he has over seven years experience in construction disputes, and has also handled a range of matters including private banking, landlord and tenant matters and outsourcing. A consultant on expert determination for CEDR, he "*literally wrote the book.*"

EUAN TEMPLE (see p.71), **Toller Hales & Collcutt** With "*oodles of experience*" in corporate/commercial matters, he has a "*canny ability to see the commercial basis of a dispute.*" A founder-director of ADR Net, he has acted in over 50 mediations covering areas like partnership disputes, banking security claims, professional negligence and libel.

NON-LEGALLY TRAINED PRACTITIONERS

LEADING INDIVIDUALS
[1] **JACKSON-STOPS Mark** In Place of Strife
RICHBELL David Sole Practitioner
TABAKIN Roger Sole Practitioner

See individuals' profiles p.68

MARK JACKSON-STOPS (see p.70), **In Place of Strife** An "*inventive*" mediator of "*enormous skill*" who is "*not afraid to try things out.*" He spent 20 years as a qualified surveyor before founding In Place of Strife as a specialist mediation practice. The firm is known mainly for construction and time-limited matters, especially property development and finance. His "*carefully judged*" style means he is also sought for a sweeping range that includes IP, defamation, insurance, taxation and accountancy.

DAVID RICHBELL (see p.70), **Sole Practitioner** A "*superb communicator*" who "*really engages the parties*" and achieves "*a remarkable settlement record.*" A chartered surveyor, his busy practice has expanded considerably beyond the construction sphere. Known as a "*supreme people-manager,*" he is also "*numerate in a lateral way, devising novel and agreeable solutions.*" Clients respond well to his "*forceful and credible*" style, and he "*remains calm in multi-handed mediation,*" "*knocking heads together only as necessary.*"

ROGER TABAKIN (see p.71), **Sole Practitioner** "*The most senior accountant in the business,*" he is very involved with CEDR. Focusing almost exclusively on mediation, he is "*calm, rational and polite.*" Peers applaud his "*gentlemanly approach*" claiming he is "*always well received.*"

THE LEADERS IN ALTERNATIVE DISPUTE RESOLUTION

ABRAMSON, John
LeBoeuf, Lamb, Greene & MacRae, London
(020) 7459 5000

ALLEN, Anthony
CEDR Solve, London
(020) 7645 1450
tallen@cedr-solve.com
Specialisation: Has mediated personal injury, clinical negligence, professional indemnity, contract, multi-party holiday illness, construction, housing and banking disputes. Particularly involved in developing mediation for personal injury and clinical negligence. Involved in mediating several major multi-party disputes between claimants and public bodies.
Prof. Memberships: *CEDR Solve* mediator; *CEDR* Director since 2000, responsible for personal injury and clinical negligence claims mediation; *CEDR* Training Faculty Member.
Career: MA Cambridge. Formerly partner with *Bunkers, Brighton & Hove* (from 1972), now consultant.
Publications: Co-author of 'The ADR Practice Guide: Commercial Dispute Resolution' (Butterworths 2000).

ALLEN, Heather
CEDR Solve, London
(020) 7536 6060
h_t_allen@msn.com
Specialisation: Mediator: contractual disputes; complex employment claims including discrimination; media; regulatory and professional negligence; property; NHS disputes. Facilitator: assisted negotiation and decision-making; strategic planning; team and leadership issues; conflict management and prevention.
Prof. Memberships: *CEDR Solve* mediator (accredited 1995); barrister (non-practising Inner Temple); CEDR Mediator Training Faculty; Assessor for Law Society Civil and Commercial mediation Panel; FRSA.
Career: Full-time mediator and facilitator. Business experience in oil industry, advertising and publishing. Trained as a barrister.
Publications: Editor and contributor, 'CEDR Mediator Handbook'.
Personal: English degree, University of London. Leisure interests include theatre; saxophone; sport; travel; languages; family.

ANDREWARTHA, Jane
Clyde & Co, London
(020) 7623 1244
jane.andrewartha@clyde.co.uk
Specialisation: Specialist in dispute resolution. Practice involves major insurance and reinsurance litigation, claims and liability work. Is an accredited and very experienced CEDR mediator (about 85 mediations) and also sits as arbitrator and early neutral evaluator. Represented underwriters in the Swazi Airline hijack, involved in personal injury aspects of Piper Alpha, claims settlement and reinsurance aspects of Eastern European Newbuildings. Aviation practice consists of representing insurers and aviation interests in defence and policy matters including TAM, Brazil, Rutaca Venezuelan crash and other similar accidents. Most recently involved in issues arising out of the September 11th World Trade Centre losses. Also involved in general aviation - light aircraft and helicopters. Clients include most major London and foreign market insurance and reinsurance companies and many Lloyd's syndicates. Is a regular lecturer, conference speaker and contributor to insurance industry publications.
Prof. Memberships: Law Society, CEDR accredited mediator, MCI Arb, update author of the international publication 'Journal of Maritime Law & Commerce', Association of Average Adjusters (associate member), Lloyds (associate member), member of Air Law Group of the Royal Aeronautical Society.
Career: Qualified in 1976, having joined *Clyde & Co* in 1974. Became a Partner in 1980. London Head of the firm's Latin American offices from 1989-97. Former Head of Aviation and member of Board of Management (Finance Partner from 1993).
Personal: Born 20 December 1952. Attended Exeter University 1970-73 (LLB Hons). Leisure activities include skiing, powerboat racing (now spectator only) and swimming. Lives in London.

THE LEADERS ■ ALTERNATIVE DISPUTE RESOLUTION

BISHOP, John
Masons, London
(020) 7490 4000
john.bishop@masons.com
Specialisation: Specialises in UK and International Construction and Engineering matters since qualifying, more recently also in Professional Negligence disputes. Major matters include LTRS, MTR, SSDS and Second Harbour Crossing in Hong Kong, Falklands Airfield, Tiffany Oil Platform, Channel Tunnel, Eurostar, Cairo Plaza, Jubilee Line, Keadby Power Station, LNG facilities (Brunei), Lloyds Building, M25, A27, several arbitrations from Indonesian Geothermic programme; conducted disputes at all levels of the English Courts, domestic arbitrations and international arbitrations under ICC, UNCITRAL and Stockholm Chamber rules as well as ADR processes. Also acts as mediator, adjudicator and arbitrator.
Prof. Memberships: Dean of the Faculty of Mediation & ADR, Chairman of the Joint Consultative Committee of the London Court of International Arbitration, Vice Chairman of the Academy of Experts, President of the Technology and Construction Solicitors Association (TeCSA), Chairman of TeCSA IT Committee. Past Chairman of TeCSA, Past Member of TCC (Technology and Construction Court) Users Committee, TCC's Rules Committee, IT Committee, ADR Committee, Law Society Civil Litigation Committee, ISE Committees on Expert Evidence and Woolf Reforms, Founder Member of CEDR, Chartered Institute of Arbitrators' Committees on new forms of arbitration and ADR, British Academy of Experts Sub Committee on Expert Evidence. Editorial board of Construction Law Journal. Lectures include Blundell Memorial lecture, Bar Conference, Judicial Studies Board, National Contractors Group annual lecture, Chartered Institute of Arbitrators, Kings College (Univ. of London).
Career: Qualified 1971, partner 1972, admitted Hong Kong 1983, managing partner 1986-1990, senior partner 1990 to date. Qualified adjudicator (TeCSA), mediator (CEDR).
Personal: Sherborne School. LLB Hons Queen Mary College, University of London. Leisure interests include golf, fishing, cooking and tomatoes.

BRADBEER, Ronald
Eversheds, Newcastle upon Tyne
(0191) 241 6345
ronaldbradbeer@eversheds.com
Specialisation: Principal areas of expertise are clinical negligence, industrial disease and professional negligence. Principal legal advisor to area health authorities and trusts for many years. Specialised in negligence for over 30 years. Also handles commercial disputes specialising in commercial contracts, employment tribunal cases and construction matters. Head of *Eversheds'* ADR Group.
Prof. Memberships: Accredited Mediator with Centre for Dispute Resolution (1993), a member of the CEDR Training Faculty. CEDR Lawyers' Role Faculty, Law Society.
Career: Joined *Wilkinson Maughan* in 1960. Qualified in 1963. Partner in 1967, managing partner in 1993 and senior partner in 1996. Consultant 2002.

BROWN, Henry
Penningtons, London
(020) 7457 3000
mediate@brownadr.com
Specialisation: ADR (mediation), intellectual property, partnerships, shareholder disputes, professional negligence and contractual disputes. Extensive training experience.
Prof. Memberships: Law Society, CEDR, Panel of Independent Mediators, Chartered Institute of Arbitrators, Mediation UK. Association for Conflict Resolution. On CPR Institute's International Panel of Distinguished Neutrals (New York) and practitioner member, Law Society's Mediation Panel.
Career: Qualified South Africa, 1962 and England & Wales 1975. Established *Simanowitz & Brown* 1975. Partner *Birkbeck Montagu's* 1980-91, *Penningtons* 1991-94. Consultant from 1994.
Publications: Author of 'Law Society's ADR Report' (1991), co-author of 'ADR Principles and Practice' (1993/1999).
Personal: Born 29 May 1939. Educated at University of Cape Town, University of South Africa, College of Law. Certificate in Fundamentals of Psychotherapy and Counselling (Regents College, 1994).

CORNES, David
Winward Fearon, London
(020) 7420 2800
david.cornes@winwardfearon.co.uk
See under Construction, p.194

CURTIS, Tony
CEDR Solve, London
(020) 7536 6060
Specialisation: IT and telecom sectors; distribution, agency and franchise; aviation; multi-party disputes. Over the last nine years has mediated in almost all areas of commercial disputes, plus PI and professional negligence. Cases range in value from £100,000 to £60 million.
Prof. Memberships: *CEDR Solve* mediator - accredited in 1991; member of *CEDR's* Training Faculty; Law Society; various other appointments over the years.
Career: Managing partner of a medium-sized firm of solicitors until left practice to concentrate on mediation. Now has a busy mediation practice (mediated 22 cases last year, with 77% settlement rate). Regularly leads and co-facilitates training courses in mediation and legal representation.
Personal: Married, two children. Keen private pilot. Amateur musician. Interests include theatre, languages and meeting people.

DAVIES, Mike
Veale Wasbrough, Bristol
(0117) 925 2020
mdavies@vwl.co.uk
Specialisation: Founder member of ADR Group. Involved in ADR since 1991. Background in all aspects of litigation with particular mediation experience in employment issues, contract disputes, professional negligence claims, and financial services litigation. Specialist in employment related mediation.
Career: Qualified in 1978. MA, PhD. Partner *Veale Wasbrough*, since 1981. Head of Employment Law Team. Two cases successfully taken to the Court of Appeal in 1999. Advisor to University of West of England Bar Training Course for ADR. Lecturer on ADR for the UWE Professional Skills Course for training solicitors.
Personal: Born 1945. Educated at Cardiff University.

DODSON, Charles
Charles Dodson - Sole Practitioner, Alresford
(07802) 389 127
cpdodson@candovermediation.com
Specialisation: Mediator on broad range of UK and international commercial disputes including professional negligence, insurance/reinsurance, pensions, rail industry, partnership/board disputes, commodity trading, government contracts. Total value of disputes mediated, 2000-2001, over £200m. Became involved in ADR when resident partner in *Lovell White & King's* New York office in mid 80's. Subsequently involved in setting up *CEDR*. One of *CEDR's* original directors, five month secondment 1995, accredited mediator 1996 and member of *CEDR* mediator and lawyer training faculties.
Career: Partner *Lovell White & King/Lovell White Durrant* 1981-98; managing partner 1991-1995. Insead AMP 1991. Dispute resolution advisor including the Russian Government on DFID funded project.

FINCHAM, Anthony
CMS Cameron McKenna, London
(020) 7367 3000
anthony.fincham@cmck.com
Specialisation: Employment and Commercial Litigation.
Career: Degree in Modern History (Oriel College, Oxford). Qualified 1980. Partner *Cameron McKenna* from 1984. Member of City of London Solicitors Company Employment Law Sub-Committee. Non-executive director of ADR Net Limited. Editor of employment section of Sweet & Maxwell 'Practical Commercial Precedents'.
Personal: Married with three children.

GATENBY, John
Addleshaw Booth & Co, Manchester
(0161) 934 6548
john.gatenby@addleshawbooth.com
See under Litigation, p.558

GLAISTER, Anthony
Keeble Hawson, Leeds
(0113) 244 3121
anthonyglaister@keeblehawson.co.uk
Specialisation: Anthony has a wide experience of resolving disputes including contractual, partnership, property and general commercial disputes and has acted as advocate and representative in all levels of courts and in arbitration and adjudications both here and abroad. Appointed as adjudicator in construction disputes, as an arbitrator in domestic disputes and as a mediator in a wide range of areas.
Prof. Memberships: A member of the Chartered Institute of Arbitrators and the International Bar Association as well as being Chairman of the Association of Northern Mediators and member of the Technology and Construction Solicitors Association. TECSA Adjudicator, CEDR, Law Society and CIArb Mediator.
Career: Qualified in 1980. Partner in *Fox & Gibbons*, London from 1985 to 1989, *Denison Till* Leeds from 1989 to 2001 and *Keeble Hawson* Leeds since. Reader in Construction Law and Arbitration at Leeds Metropolitan University.

GOYDER, Bill
Bill Goyder - Sole Practitioner
Darlington
(01325) 730234
Bill@wgoyder.freeserve.co.uk
Specialisation: Experience in civil and mechanical engineering contractual disputes, construction, oil and gas, insolvency, partnership, professional negligence claims and mental health representation. Extensive mediation experience having mediated over thirty disputes and acted as a solicitor in a further fifteen cases.
Prof. Memberships: Director ADR Net Limited, former Member of Law Society's Mental Health Panel.
Career: International Paper Company, New York, USA, qualified 1968. Assistant Solicitor Berkshire County Council. Contracts Manager *Head Wrightson & Co*, 1970-73, partner *Hewitt Brown-Humes & Hare* 1973-83, partner *Jowett & Goyder* 1983-90, partner *Jacksons* 1990-2000.
Personal: Born 12.5.42. Educ Mill Hill, Trinity College Cambridge. Chairman of Governors, Polam Hall School, Darlington. Part time jazz musician.

HOLLOWAY, Julian
Berwin Leighton Paisner, London
(020) 7427 1373
julian.holloway@blplaw.com
See under Construction, p.196

HOUGHTON, Paul
Lupton Fawcett, Leeds
(0113) 280 2000

HOWELL-RICHARDSON, Phillip
Morgan Cole, Cardiff
(029) 2038 5385

ALTERNATIVE DISPUTE RESOLUTION ■ THE LEADERS

JACKSON-STOPS, Mark
In Place of Strife, London
(020) 7917 9449
stops@mediate.co.uk
Specialisation: Professional negligence, insurance, commercial contract and property disputes among many others. Especially multi-party disputes working alone or with experts in specialist subject areas as co-mediators.
Prof. Memberships: Chartered surveyor (FRICS), CEDR-accredited mediator, Associate of the Chartered Institute of Arbitrators.
Career: As a professional in property in 1970s and 1980s, now as full time mediator, having trained in UK and USA. Alumnus of the Program for the Instruction of Lawyers at Harvard Law School 2001 under Professor Roger Fisher. Founder in 1995 of mediation service provider, *In Place of Strife*, operating a panel of experienced mediators. Has mediated over 250 matters. On Mediation Panel of the Court of Appeal.
Personal: Born 1950. Educated Christ Church, Oxford (MA).

KENDALL, John
John Kendall, Presteigne
(01544) 260019

LLOYD-JONES, Jonathan
Linnells, Oxford
(01865) 248607

MACKIE, Karl
CEDR Solve, London
(020) 7536 6060
kjmackie@cedr-solve.com
Specialisation: Major UK and international commercial, employment and public sector disputes. Mediated first substantial Court of Appeal case (NRG), facilitated resolution of British & Commonwealth Holdings and other major litigation cases.
Prof. Memberships: IBA; British Psychological Society; Chartered Institute of Arbitrators; Barrister (Gray's Inn); PhD and MBA.
Career: University of Nottingham; Honorary Professor in ADR - University of Birmingham; Partner in business strategy consultancy; Arbitrator and Mediator with ACAS; founding Chief Executive of *CEDR*; former director of studies, Management Programmes, Commerce and Industry Group of the Law Society.
Publications: Co-author - 'International Mediation: the Art of Business Diplomacy'; co-author - 'The ADR Practice Guide'; Editor - 'The Handbook of Dispute Resolution'; co-author - 'Learning Lawyers Skills'; 'Lawyers in Business'.
Personal: Films, writing, skiing, Fellow of RSA.

MARSH, William
William Marsh - Sole Practitioner, London
(020) 7917 6040
wramarsh@aol.com
Specialisation: Mediates a broad range of cases (UK and internationally), particularly multi-party actions, including commercial contract, insurance/reinsurance, professional negligence, shareholder, medical negligence/PI, pensions, IT and others. Formerly an executive director of CEDR since shortly after its launch. Currently advising UK, Slovakian and Russian governments on (unrelated) dispute resolution issues, as well as some major corporates. Recent cases include international energy case, nine-party commercial fraud case, multi-party pensions dispute, and shareholder group actions. Mediated the disputed takeover of Brighton & Hove FC at the request of the English Football Association.
Prof. Memberships: Member of UNCITRAL Experts Group on international commercial conciliation, Law Society, *CEDR Solve* Mediator, Mediator for the CMAP (Centre de Mediation et d'Arbitrage de Paris), Advisory Council Member of Coventry Centre for International Reconciliation.
Career: Solicitor in Paris (*Linklaters*) and UK (*Osborne Clarke*). Full time in mediation since 1991.
Publications: Co-author of 'The ADR Practice Guide: Commercial Dispute Resolution' (Butterworths, 1995 & 2000), and numerous articles on ADR.
Personal: Educated at Durham University (1981-84). Married with three children. Lives in Sussex. Speaks French.

MIDDLETON-SMITH, Charles
Hammond Suddards Edge, London
(020) 7655 1000

MILES, David
Glovers, London
(020) 629 5121
dmiles@glovers.co.uk
Specialisation: Partner in Construction Department. Has specialised in construction since 1978. Deals with contract negotiations, joint venture agreements, claims involving both arbitration and litigation acting both for employers and contractors in the UK and overseas. Acted in the cases Rees Hough, Viking Grain and St Martins. Member of CEDR and TeCSA training faculty and lecturer on ADR. Mediator (CEDR/CIA & B AE). Adjudicator TeCSA and CEDR.
Prof. Memberships: F.C.I.Arb, TeCSA, Society of Construction Law.
Career: Commission Regular Army (1966-1971). Joined *Alan Wilson & Co* in 1978, Partner 1979. Merged with *Glovers* in 1986.
Publications: Contributing Author 'Construction Conflict Management and Resolution'. Co-Author 'The ADR Practice Guide'.
Personal: Born 22nd June 1946. Haileybury 1960-64. Leisure interests: tennis, cricket, shooting, opera. Lives in North Moreton, Oxon.

NEILL, Robert
Herbert Smith, London
(020) 7374 8000
robert.neill@herbertsmith.com
Specialisation: Partner with a broad experience in major commercial and banking related litigation, often with an international element, including breach of warranty claims, fraud, misrepresentation, breach of fiduciary duty and insurance regulatory investigations. Is also a practising mediator who is on the *CEDR Solve* panel and has also mediated for the CPR Institute for Dispute Resolution in the US.
Prof. Memberships: Solicitor of Supreme Court of Hong Kong; City of London Solicitors Company.
Career: Qualified with *Herbert Smith* in 1976; became a Partner in 1984; spent 3 years in the firm's Hong Kong office (1987-1990).

NEWMARK, Chris
Baker & McKenzie, London
(020) 7919 1000
chris.newmark@bakernet.com
Specialisation: Partner. Practices commercial international arbitration and litigation as well as alternative dispute resolution techniques (including mediation and expert determination). Has advised clients in mediation in both England and the United States and practices as mediator for commercial disputes. Has particular experience as both mediator and counsel in disputes related to the telecoms industry.
Prof. Memberships: The Law Society, LCIA, MClarb.
Career: Qualified 1990. At *Baker & McKenzie* since 1988. Elected partner in 1997. Spent 1993-94 working in the firm's Chicago office. Trained as mediator with CPR, New York in 1994. Accredited CEDR mediator since 1995. Member of the ICC Commission on International Arbitration and CPR International Panel of Distinguished Neutrals.
Personal: Born 16 January 1964. Educated at Abingdon School, Birmingham University and the University of Limoges, France. Interests include golf and photography. Lives in Greenwich.

PATON, Andrew
Pinsent Curtis Biddle, Birmingham
(0121) 200 1050
andrew.paton@pinsents.com
Specialisation: Partner and head of insurance litigation in Birmingham. Defending claims against professionals on instructions of their insurers. Uses mediation extensively to resolve claims. Acts as mediator in wide range of cases.
Prof. Memberships: Training faculty of CEDR. Director of ADR Net Limited. Founder member of the Panel of Independent Mediators. Chairman of the Association of Midlands Mediators. Associate of the Chartered Institute of Arbitrators; member of the Policy Committee.
Career: Articled *Cripps Harries Hall & Co*, Tunbridge Wells. Qualified 1981. Joined *Pinsent Curtis Biddle* 1981. Partner 1985.
Personal: Born 1957. Educated at Bishop Vesey's Grammar School, Sutton Coldfield and Exeter University (LLB). Interests include yacht and dinghy racing, cycling and tennis.

PRYOR, Nicholas
Nicholas Pryor - Panel of Independent Mediators, London
(020) 7359 2819
nicholaspryor@sotheby-road.co.uk
Specialisation: ADR and mediation. Has been mediating since 1986. Now acting full time as an independent mediator, and in representing parties at mediation and/or advising on the use of mediation. Specialises in large scale, multi-party commercial mediations, particularly insurance, reinsurance and professional indemnity matters. Has completed over 350 successful mediations.
Prof. Memberships: Founder member, Panel of Independent Mediators; Registered Mediator, CEDR; Accredited Mediator, ADR Group; Member, CPR Institute for Dispute Resolution (New York); Member, Mediation Panel, London Court of International Arbitration; Member, British Association of Lawyer Mediators; Member Chartered Institute of Arbitrators.
Career: Called to Bar (Middle Temple) 1970. Admitted solicitor 1980. Assistant *Rowe & Maw* (1980-82); assistant *Coward Chance/Clifford Chance* (1982-89); partner *Manches* (1990-95); company solicitor KWELM Management Services Ltd (1995-96).
Personal: Born 1946. Lives Highbury, London.

RICHBELL, David
David Richbell - Sole Practitioner, Melchbourne
(01234) 709907
david@richbell.org
Specialisation: One of the busiest UK commercial mediators, imposes maximum two mediations per week. Once profiled as the 'most experienced construction mediator in Europe' but now offers a broader portfolio including employment, professional negligence, heavy engineering, sports, partnership, franchise and personal injury disputes. Is the leading Co-Mediation pairing with Presiley Baxendale QC, specialising in large multi-party civil and commercial disputes. Formed MATA (Mediation and Training Alternatives) in 2001 and in past year trained lawyers in UK, Italy, Switzerland, Netherlands, Finland, Ireland, Kenya and Bermuda. Runs annual Advanced Mediator Training course in Rome each September.
Prof. Memberships: Former FRICS and MCIOB, currently MCIArb and Registered CEDR Mediator.
Career: Own chartered surveying practice 1977-96. CEDR Executive Director 1993-2001 (full time from 1996). Now full time independent commercial mediator and trainer.
Publications: Wrote/compiled 'CEDR Mediator Handbook'.
Personal: Ordained lay preacher. Working, with others, to form Christian Mediator network. Married, five children, two

THE LEADERS ■ ALTERNATIVE DISPUTE RESOLUTION

cats, one peacock. Visit websites for more details (www.richbell.org and www.mata.org.uk).

RIVERS, Elizabeth
Elizabeth Rivers - Sole Practitioner, London
(020) 8527 8654
mediate@elizabethrivers.co.uk
Specialisation: Commercial mediator dealing with a broad range of UK and international disputes. Particular interests in disputes involving an interpersonal dimension such as employment, boardroom, partnership and organisational disputes. Recently mediated a £1m race discrimination claim against a Japanese bank. Other subject areas mediated include environmental, professional negligence, banking, contract and intellectual property.
Prof. Memberships: *CEDR Solve* Mediator - accredited 1992; Member of CEDR training faculty since 1993; Facilitator for the Environment Council.
Career: *Eversheds* (London) 1986-96: litigator dealing with a broad range of commercial matters. Pioneered awareness and development of ADR across the firm. 1997-present: independent mediator.
Personal: Currently studying humanistic psychology. Interests: wilderness trekking, a capella singing, dance.

SHAPIRO, David
SJ Berwin, London
(020) 7533 2421
d.shapiro@sjberwin.com
Specialisation: Alternative Dispute Resolution: accredited as a mediator by CEDR (Britain's Centre for Dispute Resolution), is on numerous mediation panels, was Director and Chief Mediator of JAMS Endispute Europe, and is currently Visiting Professor of Law, Nottingham Law School and Visiting Fellow, Department of Law, London School of Economics and Political Science, where he teaches mediation and mediation advocacy. Consultant to *SJ Berwin* where he serves as Director of that firm's ADR Services Unit.
Prof. Memberships: Centre for Dispute Resolution; CPR Institute for Dispute Resolution (Panel of Distinguished Mediators); British Assn. Of Lawyer Mediators; City Disputes Panel; Int. Bar Assn.; American Bar Assn.; The Chartered Inst. Of Arbitrators; Soc. of Professionals in Dispute Resolution (SPIDR); International Academy of Mediators (IAM).
Career: Formerly senior founding partner and Head of Litigation, *Dickstein, Shapiro & Morin,* New York and Washington DC. Since arriving in the UK in 1996, has successfully mediated more than 100 major disputes in this country and Europe. He was organiser of and lead-off speaker on 'Introduction to ADR', part of the Judicial Studies Board's Stage 1 seminars for UK judges and is a lecturer and writer on mediation issues.
Publications: Publications include 'Consumer Participation in Antitrust Class Actions,' 41 ABA Antitrust I.J. 257 (1972); 'Management of Consumer Class Actions after Eissen', 26 Mercer I.Rev. 851 (1975) (with James vanR. Springer); 'Trained Neutrals', New Law Journal (March 1997); 'Expert Mediators Not Experts as Mediators', 16 CEDR Resolutions (Spring 1997); 'ADR in the Commercial Court - One Year Later', 17 CEDR Resolutions (Summer 1997); 'ADR Under the New Civil Procedure Rules', Durham Univ. I.Rev. (Summer 1999); 'Pushing the Envelope - Selective Techniques in Tough Mediations', [2000] ADRLJ 89,117, 'Tough Talking', Solicitors Journal (9 November 2001).

SIBLEY, Edward
Sibley & Co, London
(020) 7395 9790
Specialisation: Senior partner. Principal area of practice is international and domestic civil litigation, arbitration and mediation, including insurance and reinsurance disputes, professional negligence, product liability and civil fraud. Has acted as a mediator and advocate in over 100 commercial mediations. He has addressed conferences worldwide on issues relating to the conflict of laws and comparative law.
Prof. Memberships: Member of the Union Internationale des Avocats; American Bar Association; International Bar Association; The Law Society and the New York State Bar.
Career: Qualified in 1965. Articled with *Clifford Turner* 1961-64 and joined *Berwin & Co.* upon qualification. Became a partner in 1968. Thereafter became a founder partner *Berwin Leighton* in 1970 and managing partner 1984-86. Also admitted New York State Bar 1985 and founder member and director of the Centre for Dispute Resolution (CEDR) 1989; CEDR appointed mediator 1992; Solicitor Advocate Higher Courts (Civil) 1995; Fellow of the Chartered Institute of Arbitrators 1999.
Publications: Publications include 'The European Community 1992 and Beyond'.
Personal: Born 21 July 1935. Educated at Rhymney Grammar School and University of Wales, Aberystwyth 1958-61 (First Class Honours and Sir Samuel Evans Prize for the best student of the year). Member of Reform Club and MCC.

SMITH, Quentin
Addleshaw Booth & Co, Manchester
(0161) 934 6566
quentin.smith@addleshawbooth.com
Specialisation: Partner in Litigation & Dispute Resolution Group specialising in insurance litigation, personal injury, professional negligence, policy issues and product liability. Head of Health & Safety Unit and Media & Sports Unit. Has mediated over 40 disputes around the country, with a success rate of around 95%. These have included personal injury, business contracts, professional negligence, clinical negligence, partnership, defamation, insurance, discrimination, employment and property. Specific examples include: employer's liability personal injury action with a scheduled value of £2.4million, liability, causation and quantum in dispute: clinical negligence claim scheduled at over £2million following brain surgery; defamation and child abuse; claim against solicitors over alleged negligent commercial property transactions and business collapse; subrogated claim brought by insurers against accountants following fraud prosecution; and dispute involving PFI contract and building management systems.
Career: Articled Clerk, Solicitor and Partner with *James Chapman & Co,* in Manchester, 1985-96; Partner in *Addleshaw Sons & Latham* then *Addleshaw Booth & Co.* 1996 to date. Frequent speaker at events; in the last 12 months, he has made presentations at meetings with insurers, Association of Personal Injury Lawyers (APIL), Commercial Bar, Law Society (Dublin) Association of Local Authority Solicitors, corporate and commercial bodies, CEDR's forum and conference.
Publications: As a member of CEDR's teaching faculty, he frequently writes, and presents, on Mediation.
Personal: Extensive experience in arts, media and sport including sale of fine art, theatre management and music. Chair of Sale Rugby Football Club ('Sale Sharks').

TABAKIN, Roger
Roger Tabakin - Sole Practitioner
London
(020) 8374 2562
tabakin@pobox.com
Specialisation: One of the first accountants to undertake commercial mediations in the UK, having mediated since 1991. Member CEDR Training Faculty 1993. On number of specialist mediation panels. Mediated disputes involving professional negligence; acquisition and mergers; intellectual property; partnership, shareholder disagreements; consequential loss, loss of profit claims; insurance and pension; generally issues where professional accountancy background is of value. Undertaken number commercial mediations and achieved significant record of settled outcomes.
Prof. Memberships: Institute of Chartered Accountants of Scotland: Society of Chartered Accountants, South Africa: Chartered Institute of Arbitrators; CEDR Accredited Mediator 1991.
Career: Provides consultancy service as facilitator, negotiator, mediator. Actively assists training commercial mediators; development of facilitative techniques for commercial dispute resolution; participating with establishment of dispute resolution processes in Russian Federation and Slovakia. Possesses skills and awareness essential for multinational and cross-cultural business disputes.
Personal: Married. Two children. Theatre; mountain walking; skiing; cooking;
African tribal art; limited edition graphics; attempting to learn Japanese.

TEMPLE, Euan
Toller Hales & Collcutt, Northampton
(01604) 258558
eft@tollers.co.uk
Specialisation: European law, M&A work, competition law, MBOs, joint ventures, e-commerce, partnerships, intellectual property licensing, R&D contracts, commercial mediation.
Prof. Memberships: Accredited mediator 1990 with ADR group; Law Society's European Group.
Career: Graduated Cambridge. Qualified 1970. Has lectured on mediation at home and abroad, and contributed articles on the subject. A regular speaker at conferences on e-commerce, competition and commercial law.
Personal: Western and central European history. Hockey (player and umpire).

TESTER, Stephen
CMS Cameron McKenna, London
(020) 7367 2894
skt@cmck.com
See under Professional Negligence, p.683

WILLIS, Tony
Panel of Independent Mediators, London
(020) 7221 5893
tonywillis@notwo.co.uk
Specialisation: Independent mediator in business, financial and regulatory matters. Appointed direct and also by institutions such as CEDR, ADR Group, *In Place of Strife,* Chartered Institute of Arbitrators, InterMediation, CPR (NY) and others. Mediating since the early 1990s and full time mediator since 1998. More than 300 mediations conducted on a wide variety of subjects including oil and gas, insolvency, banking, construction and engineering, IT, insurance, shareholder disputes, partnership disputes, professional negligence, employment, pharmaceuticals, tax, charities and many others. Also appointed as settlement counsel.
Career: LLB (New Zealand) 1966, Barrister and Solicitor High Court of New Zealand, Solicitor England and Wales, 1971, partner *Clifford Chance* 1973, joint managing partner 1987-89, head of litigation practice 1989-96, consultant 1998-2001, CEDR accredited mediator, Fellow Chartered Institute of Arbitrators, Fellow International Academy of Mediators (US), International Panelist CPR Institute for Dispute Resolution (NY), Advanced Panel LEADR (Australia and New Zealand), founding member Panel of Independent Mediators (PIM).
Personal: Born 1941. Lives in central London. Founding Chairman Solicitors Pro Bono Group, now Chairman of SPBG Advisory Council. Chairman of Council Wycombe Abbey School.

WINKWORTH-SMITH, John
John Winkworth-Smith, Bakewell
(01629) 640269

ALTERNATIVE DISPUTE RESOLUTION ■ THE LEADERS

Specialisation: Practising commercial mediator. Solicitor and former Regional Managing Partner of DLA. Founder Director of CEDR and a Board member until 1999. Very experienced mediator in a wide range of disputes up to £10m in value including defence contracts, manufacturing industry, construction industry, telecoms, private company disputes, railway industry and employment. Formerly litigation lawyer specialising in large commercial cases with a foreign element, particularly in USA, Italy and Japan.

Prof. Memberships: Registered and Accredited with CEDR and Academy of Experts. Law Society Member. Member of Association of Northern Mediators.

Career: Partner and then Regional Managing Partner of DLA 1970-99. Former Chairman and Director of a number of charitable companies. Farmer.

ARBITRATION (INTERNATIONAL)

London: 73; Profiles: 75

Research approved by BMRB For this edition, **Chambers'** researchers conducted 6,582 interviews – 3,900 with law firms, 511 with barristers and 2,171 with clients. The validity of the research was scrutinised by BMRB International, who audited both the methodology and the results at our offices in London. They interviewed **Chambers'** researchers and cross-checked sample interviews. Details of the audit appear on page 7.

OVERVIEW *Chambers* again emphasises that these tables reflect arbitration practices based in London. Because of the nature of international arbitrations, firms call more widely on their global resources than can be shown here. These additional resources are properly a subject for our *Global Guide* and we refer the reader to that for more information. A select group of international arbitration practices dominates the arena, but we have also included practices that do in fact conduct arbitrations in their specialist fields, globally and under different rules and jurisdictions. Joint ventures, especially in telecoms and technology, have generated a healthy flow of work through the triggering of arbitration clauses. At the same time, increasing numbers of US firms, such as Vinson & Elkins and White & Case are *"at the door,"* though not, in all cases, via London offices. Our researchers report an increase in the number of *ad hoc* arbitrations as opposed to institutional referrals.

LONDON

ARBITRATION (INTERNATIONAL)
■ LONDON

1
- Clifford Chance

2
- Freshfields Bruckhaus Deringer
- Herbert Smith

3
- Allen & Overy

4
- Linklaters
- Lovells
- Wilmer, Cutler & Pickering

5
- Baker & McKenzie
- Debevoise & Plimpton
- Masons
- Norton Rose
- Shearman & Sterling
- Simmons & Simmons

6
- Ashurst Morris Crisp
- Clyde & Co
- Holman Fenwick & Willan
- Ince & Co

This book is the product of 6,552 1/2 hour interviews. See p.7 for BMRB audit. Within each band, firms are listed alphabetically.

CLIFFORD CHANCE (see firm details p.911) Unlike its principal opposition, London really is the firm's *"power base"* for international arbitrations, and here it is acknowledged that it has *"colossal strength in depth"* and a *"seamlessly integrated practice"* that *"makes the most of a great international network."* Competitors admit that *"it's the one to chase,"* especially on the finance side. Undisputed king here is the *"tough but perfectly constructive"* **John Beechey** (see p.75), whose increasing experience as a sitter marks him out as *"one of the greats."* He continues to secure a following for his *"sensitive"* treatment of a case and possesses an *"unerring feel for clients."* **Audley Sheppard** (see p.76) is *"emerging into his own"* and commentators describe him as *"unflappable, ever polite and conscientious."* For hostile situations, respondents recommend the *"seriously clever"* **Robert Lambert** (see p.75). Recent matters include acting for the Czech Republic under UNCITRAL rules and a US-Czech bilateral investment treaty in a dispute over investment in the Czech Republic's first private television company.

FRESHFIELDS BRUCKHAUS DERINGER (see firm details p.964) *"Still the blue-blooded City aristocracy,"* commentators agree that this practice is *"easily the top in Europe,"* with *"unique strength in depth"* across the region, and globally. There is less consensus on the role that London plays in the firm's *"superb international network,"* with practitioners based in the Paris office continuing to take the greater share of plaudits. All the same, a *"fabulous client base"* generates a healthy volume of interesting work, often ad hoc, and always handled *"professionally and efficiently"* to an acknowledged standard of *"tremendous quality."* The London team is *"straight and formidable,"* and can be *"like having a tiger by the tail."* The team has particular experience in investor-state arbitration under investment protection treaties. Competitors proclaimed, *"you have to get up early to take on"* **Nigel Rawding** (see p.76), *"a bloody good litigator, forthright and experienced,"* who impresses with his *"serious charisma."* **Philip Croall** (see p.75) is a *"no-nonsense hard-worker"* who is *"thorough and personable."* Amongst recent matters was an action for a multinational chemical concern against various Indian joint venture partners in Mumbai.

HERBERT SMITH (see firm details p.992) A good-sized team, which has grown out of a highly respected litigation outfit. The *"polished"* arbitration group conducts much of its own advocacy. It is *"genuinely international in outlook"* and *"less likely to lapse into the litigator's mindset"* than some rivals. The practice has a strong presence in the CIS and former Eastern Bloc, and is best known for investment disputes, energy and IP and life sciences. It is increasingly involved in ICSID. *"The heart of the team"* is the *"truly remarkable"* **Julian Lew QC** (see p.75), who was recently made silk after 30 years in the business. *"Learned and senior,"* he is *"pleasantly lacking in arrogance,"* and respected for his conduct in international tribunals. The construction sphere is dominated by the *"knowledgeable"* **Michael Davis** (see p.194) and the *"articulate"* **David Brynmor Thomas** (see p.75). The latter impresses with his *"patina of easiness, coupled with huge ambition,"* which means that *"he has what it takes to go all the way to the top."* Observers agreed that *"clever and plausible"* **Larry Shore** (see p.76) *"always delivers."* Highlights of the past year include advising a foreign investor in a claim against the government of a CIS country, and acting for a US multinational in ICC arbitrations.

ALLEN & OVERY (see firm details p.841) *"Always and dependably well organised,"* this is a *"thoughtful and considered"* team that is *"heading for the big time."* Commentators note with approval the *"superb professionalism"* of a *"stately and patrician"* team of *"growing depth."* Its main strength lies in the banking and finance sphere, and the London arbitration group works closely with offices worldwide, with a dedicated presence in the Far and Middle East and throughout Europe. *"Quietly doing the work and building the practice,"* there are plans to expand in France, the Czech Republic and Hungary. *"Absolutely formidable"* **Judith Gill** (see p.558) is judged *"easily equal to the challenge of growing the practice."* She impresses observers with her *"true class"* and *"a down-to-earth attitude and preparedness to get stuck in."* The team receives a welcome fillip in the arrival from Freshfields' Paris office of *"bright and astute"* **Stephen Jagusch** (see p.75). *"Young, but oft-appointed,"* he is regarded as a *"well-grounded, intelligent"* practitioner of the best calibre. The team has acted on enforcement proceedings for South American companies against a CIS state and various entities arising out of oil and gas ventures, and advised a private power company on claims against an Eastern European state in an ICSID arbitration following investments made during the privatisation of the power industry.

www.ChambersandPartners.com

73

ARBITRATION (INTERNATIONAL) ■ LONDON

LEADING INDIVIDUALS

1
- **BEECHEY John** Clifford Chance
- **BORN Gary** Wilmer, Cutler & Pickering
- **LEW QC Julian** Herbert Smith
- **MARRIOTT QC Arthur** Debevoise & Plimpton

2
- **CAPPER Phillip** Lovells
- **GILL Judith** Allen & Overy
- **RAWDING Nigel** Freshfields Bruckhaus Deringer
- **SHEPPARD Audley** Clifford Chance
- **STYLE Christopher** Linklaters

3
- **BRYNMOR THOMAS David** Herbert Smith
- **CROALL Philip** Freshfields Bruckhaus Deringer
- **LAMBERT Robert** Clifford Chance
- **MITCHARD Paul** Skadden, Arps, Slate, Meagher & Flom

4
- **COLBRIDGE Christopher** Shearman & Sterling
- **DAVIS Michael** Herbert Smith
- **KING Ronnie** Ashurst Morris Crisp
- **NAIRN Karyl** Simmons & Simmons
- **SHACKLETON Stewart** Baker & McKenzie
- **WINTER Jeremy** Baker & McKenzie

5
- **FRASER David** Baker & McKenzie
- **SHORE Larry** Herbert Smith
- **YORK Stephen** Vinson & Elkins LLP

UP AND COMING
- **JAGUSCH Stephen** Allen & Overy

See individuals' profiles p.75

LINKLATERS (see firm details p.1043) The team is said to "*have made a great push*" in the field of international arbitration, "*biting smartly at the heels of the big boys.*" The broad commercial and projects-driven practice is characterised by a "*traditional approach*" that has secured "*great results.*" Observers applaud the "*smart and switched-on*" **Christopher Style** (see p.76), who has "*all the requisite authority,*" although his duties as head of litigation have resulted in reduced visibility. Greg Reid has joined from the Paris office, and is expected to bolster London's operations. The team has acted for the Dabhol Power Company on its multi-jurisdictional dispute with the Maharashtra State Electricity Board, and advised EOG Resources in a dispute under UNCITRAL rules with a Caribbean government over royalties.

LOVELLS (see firm details p.1045) A team with its "*shirtsleeves rolled all the way up,*" observers point to its "*admirable drive*" and suggest that it has, perhaps, "*a lower profile than its quality merits.*" Best known in the field of construction, the practice is "*broadening nicely*" and making "*optimal use of its Continental connections.*" "*Quick-thinking*" **Phillip Capper** (see p.75) is "*tremendously impressive and speaks with authority,*" and has, through experiences like acting for ALSTOM on rail-related matters, added to his acknowledged expertise in construction. The "*prolific and effective*" team has advised a major Japanese corporation in an ICC arbitration sparked by a joint venture, and acted for a European engineering company against a communications company.

WILMER, CUTLER & PICKERING (see firm details p.1190) An "*astute boutique*" that "*always looks good in a beauty parade.*" This "*busy and focused*" international arbitration practice's main areas of expertise cover joint ventures, construction and engineering, trade, securities and oil and gas. The London office does "*punch above its weight,*" although commentators ascribe much of its profile to the "*awesome*" Gary Born (see p.75), rather than his team of dedicated experts. Born is regarded as "*up with the great and good,*" and his "*towering personality*" and "*inimitable*" style has ensured a "*class client base.*" Paul Mitchard has left the firm to take up an invitation by Skadden, Arps, Slate, Meagher & Flom to start its London arbitration practice. The team has acted in some of the largest arbitrations, such as an ICC matter in Brussels, under German, French and Belgian law, in which the break-up of a joint venture between European telecommunications majors was resolved.

BAKER & McKENZIE (see firm details p.855) A "*truly international*" arbitrations practice specialising in construction and engineering projects, particularly power, and notably active in Eastern Europe and Central Asia. An international client base provides a "*regular diet of highly respectable work.*" Commentators note that the team is "*ever more visible in London.*" Jeremy Winter (see p.201) is an "*astute all-rounder,*" joined this year by **Stewart Shackleton** (see p.76) from Simmons & Simmons. The latter is a prolific writer, regarded as "*intelligent and determined.*" David Fraser (see p.75) receives plaudits from his peers, and represents the firm at the LCIA. A recent highlight case for the firm involved acting for a Japanese electronics company and its Indian distributor on the termination of a distribution agreement.

DEBEVOISE & PLIMPTON (see firm details p.933) Lacking the corporate strength of some rivals in London, this is nevertheless "*a strong if enigmatic*" firm with "*great worldwide breadth.*" Sources acknowledged the firm as the "*real champion of international arbitration.*" Arthur Marriott QC is the "*grand old man of this game.*" He is credited with "*great presence*" and an ability to "*focus on the bigger picture.*" Arrived from the "*powerful*" New York office, David Rivkin is spending more time in London to boost the practice here.

MASONS (see firm details p.1057) The "*pre-eminent construction and technology*" firm, it is inevitable peers judged this "*focused*" team to be "*exceptionally good at arbitrations in its specialist fields.*" Here it "*sets the standard,*" and it boasts a sound track record in power-related matters, and has experience of arbitrations under UNICITRAL. Robert Knutson has left to join Corbett & Co.

NORTON ROSE (see firm details p.1084) This "*prolific*" team, headed by Juliet Blanch, comprises "*stylish operators,*" and is part of an international group that has a presence in Europe, and extends as far as Bahrain, China, Russia and Singapore. Its experience in arbitration covers such areas as shipping, energy, commodities and mining, construction, engineering and insurance. Recent matters include acting for a North American public company in a Stockholm chamber of commerce arbitration, subject to Russian law, in a dispute with a Russian company triggered from a joint venture agreement for mineral exploration.

SHEARMAN & STERLING (see firm details p.1129) This firm is principally thought of for its Paris and Singapore offices, and while a volume of good work is generated out of the US, the London team is "*really starting to buzz.*" A substantial ICSID practice and a "*dynamic*" team are "*maturing well,*" acknowledge interviewees. The team is headed by the "*calm and collected*" Christopher Colbridge. Commentators remark that he "*has a difficult task ahead of him,*" but that "*he has the requisite skills, and will get there.*" The team was involved in a high-value ICC dispute by a multinational corporation with mining interests in Australia.

SIMMONS & SIMMONS (see firm details p.1136) This firm is "*cropping up more and more*" for a raft of quality clients across sectors including construction, finance, pharmaceuticals and publishing. Commentators regard the team as "*a classy, professional group,*" which has recently been tightened up across Europe. The recruitment drive continues and several lawyers have been added to capacity over the past year. Amongst the firm's recent setbacks, however, must be counted the departure of Stewart Shackleton to Baker & McKenzie. The practice is still dominated by Karyl Nairn (see p.76), a "*popular and energetic performer,*" focusing full-time in this area. Known as "*a fine proceduralist,*" it is said that "*she really understands the field's law and lore.*" The team acted in an UNCITRAL matter involving various European finance houses in relation to investments in the former USSR.

ASHURST MORRIS CRISP (see firm details p.852) This "*efficient and charming*" team has handled matters for large Japanese corporates, and the likes of Siemens and TotalFinaElf. The key name here is Ronnie King (see p.561), "*a go-to-person, positive and extremely bright.*" He receives admiration for his skills as an advocate, and is particularly associated with energy matters. The team acted for a major Japanese trading house in an LCIA dispute with its Russ-

THE LEADERS ■ ARBITRATION (INTERNATIONAL)

ian joint venture partner concerning a Russian oilfield.

CLYDE & CO (see firm details p.913) A "*quality outfit*" commended for its work on "*interesting, complex and high-value matters*," most often in shipping, insurance and commodities. It has carved out a niche acting for insurers in many of the Bermuda excess liability claims, a market in which they dominate. A wide reach sees the team active all over the world and particularly in Hong Kong.

HOLMAN FENWICK & WILLAN (see firm details p.999) Interviewees commend the team for its "*quality case-handling*" in the areas of shipping and commodities. The team also has expertise in energy, reinsurance and technology matters under a variety of jurisdictions.

INCE & CO (see firm details p.1008) The firm has increased its capacity in the core area of LMAA shipping arbitrations over the past year with the opening of offices in Paris, Hamburg and Le Havre. Well versed in ICC matters, the team consists of "*fine litigators across the board*," with experience in insurance, commodities, energy and international trade. The team is headed by a group comprising Steven Fox, Ben Horn, Chris Jefferis and Nick Shepherd.

OTHER NOTABLE PRACTITIONERS The "*measured*" Paul Mitchard's (see p.76) evolution from litigator to arbitrator continues to attract interest. He has been recruited by Skadden, Arps, Slate, Meagher & Flom from Wilmer, Cutler & Pickering, and over half of his practice is now arbitrations-related. Peers agree that Vinson & Elkins is "*making a lot of noise*," which is ascribed to the success of "*focused and knowledgeable*" Stephen York (see p.76). Reputed to be "*really skilful at seeing and seizing an opportunity*," he has a vibrant practice in ADR and IT, which is now focusing more on arbitrations, especially in the oil and gas arena.

THE LEADERS IN ARBITRATION (INTERNATIONAL)

BEECHEY, John
Clifford Chance, London
(020) 7600 1000
john.beechey@cliffordchance.com
Specialisation: Litigation and Dispute Resolution Department. Partner and head of International Commercial Arbitration and Construction Group dealing with all arbitration, ADR; contentious construction; commercial litigation
Career: Partner since 1983.
Personal: MA (Oxon) French and German.

BORN, Gary
Wilmer, Cutler & Pickering, London
(020) 7872 1000
gborn@wilmer.com
Specialisation: Managing partner in international arbitration/litigation department. Principal area of practice is international arbitration. Represents European, US, Asian and other corporate clients in international commercial arbitration under all major institutional rules (ICC, LCIA, AAA, Stockholm, IACAC) and ad hoc (UNCITRAL) in all leading fora. Other main area of practice is international litigation (US) including advice on issues of jurisdiction, foreign sovereign immunity, international judicial assistance, conflict of laws. Particular expertise in joint ventures, telecommunications, M&A, construction, sales and agency disputes.
Prof. Memberships: American Law Institute, International Bar Association, American Bar Association, British Institute of International and Comparative Law, American Society of International Law.
Career: Joined *Wilmer, Cutler & Pickering* in 1984. Became a partner in 1988 and managing partner in London office in 1991.
Publications: Author of 'International Commercial Arbitration' (2nd edition, Kluwer 2000), 'International Civil Litigation in US Courts' (3rd edition, Kluwer 1996) and 'International Arbitration and Foreign Selection Agreements' (Kluwer 1999). Has undertaken numerous speaking engagements.
Personal: Educated at Haverford College, Haverford, Pennsylvania 1973-78 (BA, summa cum laude) and University of Pennsylvania Law School 1978-81 (J.D., summa cum laude); law clerk to Chief Justice William H Rehnquist and Judge Henry J Friendly. Proficient in German.

BRYNMOR THOMAS, David
Herbert Smith, London
(020) 7374 8000
david.brynmor.thomas@herbertsmith.com
Specialisation: Partner specialising in international commercial arbitration and litigation, particularly in disputes arising from major infrastructure and engineering projects. Solicitor Advocate, with higher rights of audience before the English High Court. Acts as counsel in all forms of international arbitration, whether ad hoc, using the UNCITRAL Arbitration Rules or subject to institutional rules, including those of the ICC and the LCIA. Also sits as an arbitrator.
Prof. Memberships: City of London Solicitors' Company; London Court of International Arbitration; Chartered Institute of Arbitrators; on the panel of arbitrators of the GCC Commercial Arbitration Association.
Career: The University of Edinburgh (MB, ChB 1987); Admission, 1993; Partnership, 2000.

CAPPER, Phillip
Lovells, London
(020) 7296 2000
phillip.capper@lovells.com
See under Construction, p.xxx

COLBRIDGE, Christopher
Shearman & Sterling, London
(020) 7655 5000

CROALL, Philip
Freshfields Bruckhaus Deringer, London
(020) 7936 4000
philip.croall@freshfields.com
Specialisation: Partner specialising in arbitration, ADR and commercial litigation. Handles all aspects of international commercial arbitration work. Has appeared on Counsel in arbitrations under rules of the major arbitration institutions including the ICC, the LCIA as well as in ad hoc arbitration under the UNCITRAL Rules. Speaks regularly at seminars and writes articles on arbitration and international dispute resolution techniques. Also involved in all kinds of commercial litigation including cases relating to banking and financial services regulation.
Prof. Memberships: Associate of the Chartered Institute of Arbitrators.
Career: Qualified at *Freshfields* in 1985. Partner at *Freshfields* 1992.
Personal: Born 22 August 1959.

DAVIS, Michael
Herbert Smith, London
(020) 7374 8000
michael.davis@herbertsmith.com
See under Construction, p.194

FRASER, David
Baker & McKenzie, London
(020) 7919 1000
david.fraser@bakernet.com

GILL, Judith A E
Allen & Overy, London
(020) 7330 3000
judith.gill@allenovery.com
See under Litigation, p.558

JAGUSCH, Stephen
Allen & Overy, London
(020) 7330 3000
stephen.jagusch@allenovery.com
Specialisation: Partner specialising in international commercial arbitration. Has qualified as a solicitor advocate and enjoys rights of audience in all higher courts. Has acted as advisor and advocate to dozens of international companies and many governments across the world and subject to a wide variety of governing substantive and procedural rules and laws. He has been appointed as arbitrator in several international arbitrations.
Prof. Memberships: Fellow of the Chartered Institute of Arbitrators; alternate member of the ICC's Commission on Arbitration; Swiss Arbitration Association; International Arbitration Institute; LCIA.
Career: Articled *Simpson Grierson*, Auckland; admitted as solicitor New Zealand 1990; admitted England and Wales 1995; associate *Freshfields*, London and Paris 1995-2000; associate *Allen & Overy* 2000; partner 2002.
Personal: Education: University of Auckland (1989 BCom and LLB; 1994 Mcom Law).

KING, Ronnie
Ashurst Morris Crisp, London
(020) 7638 1111
ronnie.king@ashursts.com
See under Litigation, p.561

LAMBERT, Robert
Clifford Chance, London
(020) 7600 1000
robert.lambert@cliffordchance.com
Specialisation: Litigation and Dispute Resolution Department. Partner specialising in the law and practice of international arbitration, conflicts of law and jurisdiction particularly in disputes involving international engineering, construction and infrastructure projects.
Career: Trained *Clifford Chance*; qualified 1989; Partner 1997.
Personal: Oxford University (St Edmund Hall), BA (Hons) Law (1st Class).

LEW QC, Julian
Herbert Smith, London
(020) 7374 8000
julian.lew@herbertsmith.com
Specialisation: Head of International Commercial Arbitration Practice Group. Partner specialising in international commercial arbitration. Advises and represents clients as counsel in international arbitration arising out of all kinds of international commercial transactions. Has been involved with arbitrations under the rules of all the major arbitrations institutions, including in particular International Chamber of Commerce,

www.ChambersandPartners.com

75

ARBITRATION (INTERNATIONAL) ■ THE LEADERS

International Centre for the Settlement of Investment Disputes, Stockholm Institute, Zurich Chamber of Commerce, American Arbitration Association and ad hoc under the UNCITRAL Arbitration Rules. He is also regularly appointed as an arbitrator.
Career: Date of admission (Bar) 1970; New York State Bar 1985; appointed QC 2002. Visiting Professor and Head of the School of International Arbitration, Centre for Commercial Law Studies, Queen Mary, University of London. Has written extensively and lectured on all aspects of international commercial arbitration.
Personal: LLB (Hons) (London) 1969; Doc-Juris Catholic University of Louvain, Belgium (magna cum laude) 1977.

MARRIOTT QC, Arthur
Debevoise & Plimpton, London
(020) 7786 9000

MITCHARD, Paul
Skadden, Arps, Slate, Meagher & Flom LLP, London
(020) 7519 7050
pmitchard@skadden.com
Specialisation: Main areas of practice are international commercial arbitration and litigation, including ICC, LCIA, ICSID, insurance, engineering and construction arbitrations, commercial, financial and administrative and public law disputes and regulatory investigations. A Solicitor-Advocate. Admitted as a Solicitor in England and Hong Kong. Accredited CEDR mediator, member of CPR's panel of distinguished neutrals and a Fellow of the Chartered Institute of Arbitrators. Has represented domestic and international companies and State organisations in many major disputes. Has given seminars in London, Moscow, the USA and the Middle and Far East on international arbitration.
Prof. Memberships: Law Society, American Bar Association, International Bar Association, City of London Solicitors' Company.
Career: Qualified in 1977. Worked at *Slaughter and May* 1977-84 in London and Hong Kong. Joined *Simmons & Simmons* in 1984, becoming a partner in 1985 and was head of litigation 1994-98; in January 1999 became a partner based in the London office of *Wilmer, Cutler & Pickering* before leaving to become Head of European Litigation and Arbitration at *Skadden, Arps, Slate, Meagher & Flom LLP* in October 2001.
Personal: Born 2 January 1952. Attended Taunton School 1960-70 and Lincoln College, Oxford 1971-74. Leisure interests include travel, reading and walking. Lives in Chalfont St Giles, Buckinghamshire, England.

NAIRN, Karyl
Simmons & Simmons, London
(020) 7628 2020
karyl.nairn@simmons-simmons.com
Specialisation: Major cases in 2001-2 include institutional and ad hoc arbitrations for a major oil company, various European trading companies, an international sporting organisation, a worldwide banking consortium, a government agency and a British telecommunications company.
Prof. Memberships: Member LCIA. Fellow, CIA. Member for Australia (alternate), International Court of Arbitration of the ICC.
Career: Qualified as barrister and solicitor, Supreme Court of Western Australia, 1988; admitted as a solicitor in England and Wales in 1991. Joined *Simmons & Simmons* 1991; Partner in 1996; Head of International Arbitration Group.
Personal: University of Western Australia (B.Juris [Hons], LLB [Hons]) and LSE, University of London (LLM).

RAWDING, Nigel
Freshfields Bruckhaus Deringer, London
(020) 7936 4000
nigel.rawding@freshfields.com
Specialisation: Partner in litigation department and London head of *Freshfields'* London/Paris International Arbitration Group. International dispute resolution specialist representing clients in major commercial disputes involving litigation, international arbitration and ADR procedures. International arbitration experience includes ICC, LCIA, UNCITRAL and ad hoc cases. Litigation experience comprises a wide variety of High Court commercial cases. Co-author of 'The Freshfields Guide to Arbitration and ADR' (Second revised edition Kluwer, 1999). Member of ICC Commission on International Arbitration and director of the LCIA. Regular contributor to arbitration journals and conference speaker on subjects relating to the resolution of international disputes.

SHACKLETON, Stewart
Baker & McKenzie, London
(020) 7919 1943
stewart.shackleton@bakernet.com
Specialisation: Paris +33 1 53 053 131 International Arbitration Group. Has acted in over 100 international commercial and construction arbitrations. Counsel and arbitrator in public international law disputes, including arbitration involving States, State entities and public international organisations. Advises on jurisdiction and conflicts of law disputes. Practice also includes advising on challenges to arbitral awards in France and England; acting in multijurisdictional banking and commercial litigation; advocacy before courts in France and before international arbitral tribunals in French and English; acting in CEDR administered international mediation proceedings. Sitting as party-appointed arbitrator. Chairman and sole arbitrator in ICC and LCIA proceedings.
Prof. Memberships: Member for Canada, ICC Commission on International Commercial Arbitration; London Court of International Arbitration; Fellow, Chartered Institute of Arbitrators; Swiss Arbitration Association; French Arbitration Association; French Arbitration Committee; Indian Council of Arbitration; British Institute of International and Comparative Law; British Columbia International Commercial Arbitration Centre; Vice-President of the European Lawyer's Association; Member for Canada of the International Arbitration Committee, International Law Association.
Career: Has practised in Canada, Hong Kong, Paris and London. Avocat au Barreau de Paris (1994) (conseil juridique stagiaire 1991-94); Solicitor of the Supreme Court of England and Wales (1994); Solicitor of the Supreme Court of Hong Kong (1995); Barrister and Solicitor, Ontario (1993).
Personal: MSc in Construction Law and Arbitration (University of London); DEA in Public International Law (University of Paris I); DSU in Private International Law (University of Paris II); Maîtrise en Droit Civil - mention droit des affaires (University of Paris II); DEA in African Law (University of Paris I); Diplome in Comparative Law (University of Paris II); LLB (University of Western Ontario). Working languages: French, English and Scandinavian languages, knowledge of German and Spanish.

SHEPPARD, Audley W
Clifford Chance, London
(020) 7600 1000
audley.sheppard@cliffordchance.com
Specialisation: Litigation and Dispute Resolution Department. Partner specialises in the resolution of disputes, in particular arising out of infrastructure projects (including investment, engineering and construction disputes).
Career: Qualified New Zealand 1985, England 1990; joined *Coward Chance* 1986; *Clifford Chance* Dubai 1994; Partner since 1995.
Personal: Victoria University of Wellington, NZ (LLB Hons 1983, Bcommerce 1984); Cambridge University, UK (LLM 1986).

SHORE, Larry
Herbert Smith, London
(020) 7374 8000
laurence.shore@herbertsmith.com
Specialisation: Partner specialising in international commercial arbitration and litigation.
Prof. Memberships: London Court of International Arbitration; Research Advisory Committee of the Global Center for Dispute Resolution Research.
Career: Joined *Herbert Smith* in 1995. Became a partner in 1999. 1995: Attorney Adviser International, Office of the Legal Adviser, U.S. State Department. 1989-95: associate, *Williams & Connolly* (Washington, DC). 1983-86: Assistant Professor of History, Queen's University (Canada).
Publications: Disclosure and Impartiality, 'Dispute Resolution Journal' (Feb 2002); The Advantages of Arbitration for Banking Institutions, 'Journal of International Banking Law' (Nov 1999).
Personal: J.D. with distinction, Emory Univ. School of Law; PhD (History) The Johns Hopkins University; BA with highest honours, The University of North Carolina at Chapel Hill.

STYLE, Christopher
Linklaters, London
(020) 7456 4286
christopher.style@linklaters.com
Specialisation: Specialises in commercial litigation and arbitration. Has practised in proceedings before the High Court of Justice and Commercial Court, and has advised on questions of international public law before international tribunals. Has conducted numerous arbitrations, both ad hoc and institutional (ICC, LMAA, LCIA etc). Also advised on multijurisdictional disputes, financial services disputes, professional negligence, corporate litigation, oil and gas disputes and shipping disputes.
Career: Partner and Head of Litigation and Arbitration, 1985 to date. 1979-85: Assistant Solicitor, *Linklaters* London; 1983: six months with the Litigation Department of *Sullivan & Cromwell* New York; 1977-79: Articled Clerk, *Linklaters*. 1978: MA Law; 1976-77: City of London Polytechnic, Law Society Part II; 1973-76: Trinity Hall, Cambridge, BA Law (Cantab).

WINTER, Jeremy
Baker & McKenzie, London
(020) 7919 1000
jeremy.winter@bakernet.com
See under Construction, p.201

YORK, Stephen
Vinson & Elkins LLP, London
(020) 7065 6033
syork@velaw.com
Specialisation: Co-chair, International Dispute Resolution Practice of *Vinson & Elkins*. Main areas of practice involve representing corporations in international arbitration and commercial litigation, principally in the projects, construction, energy and IT/telecoms sectors, and in Investor-State disputes. Particularly experienced in work involving complicated engineering or technology where there has been a project or risk management failure. Well known in the field of ADR, both as counsel and as mediator. Appointed as Arbitrator by ICC, LCIA and in Ad hoc (UNCITRAL) arbitrations.
Prof. Memberships: Fellow Chartered Institute of Arbitrators and Chartered Arbitrator; LCIA; International Arbitration Club; Law Societies of England & Wales and Hong Kong. Board Member CEDR.
Career: St Catharine's College, Cambridge (1979, BA, MA). Admitted solicitor England & Wales 1982; Hong Kong 1984.
Publications: 'Practical ADR' (Sweet & Maxwell); 'A Guide to the Law of Electronic Commerce' (Butterworths).
Personal: Born 1958. Married with four children. A resident of Cambridge.

ASSET FINANCE

London: 77; The Regions: 80; Consumer Finance: 80; Profiles: 81

Research approved by BMRB For this edition, **Chambers'** researchers conducted 6,582 interviews – 3,900 with law firms, 511 with barristers and 2,171 with clients. The validity of the research was scrutinised by BMRB International, who audited both the methodology and the results at our offices in London. They interviewed **Chambers'** researchers and cross-checked sample interviews. Details of the audit appear on page 7.

OVERVIEW The aviation sector is facing a period of intensified pressure in the face of a weakened market and the aftermath of September 11th. Issues such as liability coverage and restructuring have risen to the fore. Airlines that did not previously lease out aircraft are now doing so in a bid to generate much needed cash, whilst borrowers and lenders are renegotiating existing deals. Deal-flow is sluggish and the balance of power has shifted towards the banks, whose credit committees are more circumspect than previously. At the same time, borrowers are tapping into a wider market, extending their reach beyond banks to institutional lenders. The trend towards the use of capital markets structures has continued, and receivables financing is increasingly preponderant. Railtrack's demise has dealt a further blow to the asset finance market, with many related deals collapsing. However, the recent £1 billion procurement of 785 new trains by Stagecoach Holdings is seen as encouraging, and it is predicted that the re-franchising process will generate more transactions in the future. The shipping sector has remained comparatively stable, with an upturn in the financing of costly assets such as LNG carriers.

LONDON

ASSET FINANCE — LONDON

1
- Clifford Chance
- Freshfields Bruckhaus Deringer
- Norton Rose

2
- Slaughter and May

3
- Allen & Overy
- Denton Wilde Sapte

4
- Linklaters
- Lovells
- Watson, Farley & Williams
- White & Case

5
- CMS Cameron McKenna
- Harbottle & Lewis
- Simmons & Simmons
- Theodore Goddard

6
- Beaumont and Son
- Herbert Smith

This book is the product of 6,552 1/2 hour interviews. See p.7 for BMRB audit. Within each band, firms are listed alphabetically.

CLIFFORD CHANCE (see firm details p.911) "*Able to turn a hand to most things,*" the team's reputation for top quality work endures, weathering a series of recent departures. Competitors see aviation as its strongest suit, although the team also boasts high profile rail clients, including Railtrack. "*Excellent partners*" and a loyal core of financial clients keep it at the cutting edge, though some opine, "*you sometimes have to thump the desk to get someone senior.*"

"*Technically gifted*" **Geoffrey White** (see p.84) remains the pillar of the practice. Dubbed "*the great white*" of cross-border aircraft deals, he exercises a formidable knowledge of the field. He is supported by "*able youngster*" **William Glaister** (see p.82) who has developed a niche in restructurings, and "*star*" **Simon Lew** (see p.83), a securitisation specialist recently active in US cross-border lease work, whose profile among rivals has soared this year. **Clive Carpenter** (see p.81) has a long-standing reputation for aircraft finance, and has been prominent acting for the arranger in a number of big-ticket transactions. **Clients** BAE Systems; GATX Financial Corporation; WestLB.

FRESHFIELDS BRUCKHAUS DERINGER (see firm details p.964) "*Incontrovertibly at the top*" is a typical response to this team, which is distinguished by its wealth of leading lights, international capability and sheer volume of transactions. A classic practice covering all areas of asset finance and leasing, the team is most visible on aviation deals.

Enormously popular and a "*delight*" to work with, **Bob Charlton** (see p.81) remains extremely busy with a foot in both the rail and aviation camps. All concur, "*if you get Bob, you're laughing.*" Receding from the limelight due to managerial duties, **Simon Hall** (see p.82) is nevertheless "*outstandingly competent*" for aircraft finance. Head of asset finance, **Tim Lintott** (see p.83) is rated for his aircraft expertise, whilst **Andrew Littlejohns** (see p.83) is increasingly visible, often for banks and lessors on a range of aviation and rail transactions. According to one rail client; "*Andrew's incredible speed makes him invaluable.*" **Mark Freeman** (see p.82) brings impressive finance expertise to the table, and **Robert Murphy** (see p.83) rises in Chambers' rankings following extensive market recommendation for his work on behalf of airlines, lessors, arrangers and lenders. **Clients** ABN Amro; AerFi; Bank of America; Barclays; Bayerische Landesbank; Credit Agricole Indosuez; Crédit Lyonnais; Dresdner Kleinwort; Iberia; Deutsche Bank; Société Générale; Xinjiang Airlines.

NORTON ROSE (see firm details p.1084) This has been an exceptional year for the team, which so far appears unaffected by the partner losses from its banking department. Peers told Chambers researchers that the firm possesses "*unrivalled specialist knowledge*" of asset finance, with strength on both the industry and banking sides. Clients are reassured by the "*spread of great partners*" and impressed by the "*efficient service.*" Shipping and aviation lie at the heart of the practice, although rail is also a sector of expertise.

Regularly referred to as "*the best aviation lawyer in the City,*" **Peter Thorne** (see p.84) spearheads the team. Interviewees warmly commended his "*sensible and commercial*" approach. **Jeremy Gibb** (see p.748) received accolades for his "*professionalism*" and experience in complex shipping matters, whilst head of aviation **Jeremy Edwards** (see p.82) adds further weight to the team. "*Co-operative*" **Gordon Hall** (see p.82) has been visible on shipping transactions, and interviewees also endorsed transport specialist **Alan Crookes** (see p.82) who has recently advised the Airline Group in its successful bid to become the Government's strategic partner in the PPP for National Air Traffic Services. "*Thoughtful and hardworking*" **Simon Hartley** (see p.748) is building up a powerful following for ship leasing, and peers and clients consistently recommended "*immensely thorough*" senior associate **Keith Sandilands** (see p.84), who enters the rankings this year.

The team recently advised European airlines, operating lessors and debt providers on Japanese Operating Leases for more than 50 aircraft. It advised DVB Nedship on a structured loan for $102 million, including revolving credit facility and substantial lease financing, and also advised a major European flag carrier in relation to a $1 billion ECA-backed flexible financing facility. The group continues its negotiation of provision by Porterbrook Leasing of Mark 1 replacement rolling stock (up to 700 vehicles). **Clients** Scandinavian Airlines System; Lloyds TSB Leasing; KLM Financial Services; HSBC Rail; Halifax Asset Finance; Crédit Lyonnais; ANZ Investment Bank.

SLAUGHTER AND MAY (see firm details p.1140) A small, high quality, niche practice with a strong domestic manufacturer and air-

ASSET FINANCE ■ LONDON

TOP IN-HOUSE LAWYERS

Alan BUCHANAN, Company Secretary, British Airways

Stephen GARRATT-FROST, Head of Legal Services, HSBC Holdings

Janet GREGORY, UK Legal Director, GE Capital Equipment

Robin ISAACS, Head of Legal Services, Strategic Asset Finance, Lloyds TSB Corporate

Mike KILBEE, Legal Director, Lloyds TSB

Mike McCLENAN, Senior Director, Bank of Scotland Business Banking

Ian WOODCOCK, Group Legal, Royal Bank of Scotland

Alan Buchanan is the only new addition to the list this year with numerous recommendations for not only his own "*excellent reputation,*" but also that of the British Airways team as a whole. The "*experienced*" **Stephen Garratt-Frost** and the "*efficient*" **Janet Gregory** are again deserving of inclusion. Similarly **Mike Kilbee**, **Mike McClenan** and **Ian Woodcock** all continue to receive very positive feedback, while **Robin Isaacs** completes the list as the most recommended in-house lawyer in this sector.

In-house lawyers profiles p.1201

---

line client base. Researchers were told that the firm is "*technically the best of the bunch*" with "*impressive finance and tax knowledge,*" although its practice is less broad than some competitors'. Presiding over the team, twin "*Rolls-Royces of the asset finance firmament*" **Peter Jolliffe** (see p.83) and **Tom Kinnersley** (see p.83) enjoy widespread recognition in the market. Clients claim that they are "*expensive, and good value!*" whilst peers agree that "*both partners are pragmatic and sensible on deals.*" The team has recently acted for international banks, UK lessors, lessees and equipment manufacturers. **Clients** Abbey National; Boeing; Bombardier; British Airways.

ALLEN & OVERY (see firm details p.841) Recognised for its "*extensive involvement*" in the area, the firm has a broad reach of expertise across the spectrum of industry sectors and jurisdictions, and this is reflected in its expanding client base. Chambers researchers found its most visible following amongst aircraft lessors, although the firm's distinguished client roster features a raft of lenders.

Among the many partners recommended at the firm, interviewees singled out asset finance veteran **Julia Salt** (see p.84) as "*charming and bright – a real force in the marketplace.*" Popular with peers and respected by clients, head of finance **Graham Smith** (see p.84) is noted for his co-operative and friendly manner, whilst **Mario Jacovides** (see p.83) has built up, inter alia, extensive experience in satellite financing. **Andrew Joyce** (see p.83) was endorsed for his aircraft leasing expertise, and "*brainy*" **David Smith** (see p.84) has experience in domestic and cross-border structured transactions across a range of industries.

Supported by the firm's securitisation and tax departments as well as its international network, the team has been involved in advising Barclays Structured Asset Finance on a $350 million UK tax lease financing of 12 Boeing aircraft for DHL. In shipping, the team has acted for JP Morgan Chase on two major syndicated financings involving LNG carriers (aggregate value over $350 million), whilst for rail the team advised Stagecoach on its £1 billion rolling stock and service provision order. **Clients** ABM AMRO; AerFi; Barclays Structured Asset Finance; CIBC; Japanese Bank of International Cooperation; Deutsche Bank; GE Capital; HBOS; JP Morgan Chase; Kreditanstalt für Wiederaufbau; Lloyds TSB Leasing; Lombard Global Finance.

DENTON WILDE SAPTE (see firm details p.935) The "*large and dynamic*" team has bounced back following the defections it suffered a few years ago. Researchers found that its reputation, particularly for aviation and UK tax-based leasing, is flourishing. The team has also consolidated its rail practice and has recently advised on financing rolling stock manufacturing contracts and Railtrack assets. Whilst not known for its cross-border expertise, domestic asset finance is seen as a particular strength of the firm.

With "*admirable stamina*" **Adrian Miles**, one of asset finance's éminences grises, maintains a high level of involvement in the area. Interviewees endorsed "*terribly able*" **Gregory Kahn** for his aircraft work. He recently led the team acting for Airtours on the $100 million sale and leaseback of four used A320 aircraft. Head of general asset finance **Lisa Marks** has cemented her reputation in the area, especially for tax-based leasing. She recently advised Lombard and Barclays on separate fixtures lease financings of track, signalling and related railways assets for Railtrack.

Approaching the area from a different angle, **Andrew Collins** is known to be "*terrific*" at property. Head of aviation **Colin Thaine** recently spearheaded the team advising a syndicate of banks led by Crédit Lyonnais on the $1.3 billion export credit supported financing of 27 new Airbus aircraft for Lan Chile, some combined with Japanese operating lease structures. "*Stand-out name*" **Nick Chandler** advised the Spanish regional airline, Air Nostrum, in a series of financing and operating lease transactions for the delivery of 16 Bombardier aircraft. **Clients** GE Capital; ABN AMRO; Citibank; IBJ; Lloyds TSB Leasing; Qatar Airways; Air Nostrum; easyJet; Sabena; KBC; Sovereign; SEB Finans; NIB Capital; Hapag-Lloyd.

LINKLATERS (see firm details p.1043) Operating in tandem with the firm's New York office and supported by a formidable European network, the London team possesses enviable resources for big-ticket work. Although increasingly visible on rail transactions, its profile has dipped on the aircraft side.

Ron Gibbs (see p.82) remains at the helm, his "*knowledge and experience*" of the field undisputed. He led the team advising Petroleo Brasileiro on the insurance settlement and the termination of financing arrangements following the loss of the P-36 production platform off the coast of Brazil, which involved several tranches of creditors and complicated intercreditor arrangements governed by English and US laws.

The firm advised the SRA on the procurement of 785 units for the South West Trains franchise. The deal was worth £1 billion and constitutes one of the largest rolling stock procurements since UK rail privatisation.

The team also advised Emirates on the financing of five Airbus A330-200 aircraft, worth in aggregate approximately $500 million, financed through Japanese Operating Leases. **Clients** Flightlease; Emirates; Lloyds TSB Leasing; First Asset Finance; SNCF; SRA.

LOVELLS (see firm details p.1045) The team is continuing to forge ahead, its aircraft, leasing and finance work impressing both peers and clients. On the rail side, the firm acted for ALSTOM Tranport and ALSTOM Transport Service on the lease financing of 14 Coradia Class 180 trains by Angel Trains. On the aviation side, it advised Bank Gesellschaft Berlin as senior debt providers on the JOL of two A320's for Condor. With a focus on aviation, **Robin Hallam** (see p.82) spearheads the team. His leasing experience is broad and covers leveraged and operating leasing as well as tax-based and defeased leases. A "*young guy who knows what he's doing,*" **Keith Wilson** (see p.84) has built up a loyal core of industry lessee and financial institution clients. **Clients** Lombard Aviation Capital; Bank Gesellschaft Berlin; Tubelines; ALSTOM Transport; Xerox; National Air Traffic Services

WATSON, FARLEY & WILLIAMS (see firm details p.1181) "*Deeply rooted in the industry,*" the firm specialises in shipping and offshore-related matters, with expertise in oil and gas. Unanimously acclaimed for its unrivalled practice on the side of ship lessees, its team is felt to be strong, albeit specialised. It also handles a large number of aircraft deals, often for the lessor. Clients praise the firm's "*straightforward commercial approach*" and note that it is "*good value for money.*"

"*Hardworking and dedicated*" **David Osborne** (see p.83) is rated for his aircraft and shipping finance work, whilst clients singled out "*commercial and inventive*" **James Watters** (see p.84) for his "*excellent industry knowledge*" and financing expertise. Recent work has involved structured asset finance transactions including the sale and purchase of leasing companies and leasing portfolios, as well as a substantial amount of middle ticket leasing. More specifically, the firm has acted for the lessee on the

LONDON ■ ASSET FINANCE

LEADING INDIVIDUALS

1
- CHARLTON Bob *Freshfields Bruckhaus Deringer*
- HALL Simon *Freshfields Bruckhaus Deringer*
- JOLLIFFE Peter *Slaughter and May*
- KINNERSLEY Tom *Slaughter and May*
- THORNE Peter *Norton Rose*
- WHITE Geoffrey *Clifford Chance*

2
- CARPENTER Clive *Clifford Chance*
- LINTOTT Tim *Freshfields Bruckhaus Deringer*
- LITTLEJOHNS Andrew *Freshfields Bruckhaus Deringer*
- MILES Adrian *Denton Wilde Sapte*
- SALT Julia *Allen & Overy*

3
- EDWARDS Jeremy *Norton Rose*
- GIBB Jeremy *Norton Rose*
- GIBBS Ronald *Linklaters*
- HALLAM Robin *Lovells*
- KAHN Gregory *Denton Wilde Sapte*
- OSBORNE David *Watson, Farley & Williams*

4
- JACOVIDES Mario *Allen & Overy*
- JOYCE Andrew *Allen & Overy*
- SMITH Graham *Allen & Overy*
- WALKLING Kim *Simmons & Simmons*
- WATTERS James *Watson, Farley & Williams*

5
- COLLINS Andrew *Denton Wilde Sapte*
- GLAISTER William *Clifford Chance*
- HALL Gordon *Norton Rose*
- LEW Simon *Clifford Chance*
- THAINE Colin *Denton Wilde Sapte*
- TOTT Nick *Herbert Smith*

6
- BENSON Justin *White & Case*
- CHANDLER Nick *Denton Wilde Sapte*
- CROOKES Alan *Norton Rose*
- FREEMAN Mark *Freshfields Bruckhaus Deringer*
- HARTLEY Simon *Norton Rose*
- MACCARTHY Rory *Theodore Goddard*
- MARKS Lisa *Denton Wilde Sapte*
- MURPHY Robert *Freshfields Bruckhaus Deringer*
- SMITH David *Allen & Overy*
- WESTERN Mark *White & Case*
- WILSON Keith *Lovells*

UP AND COMING
- SANDILANDS Keith *Norton Rose*

ASSOCIATES TO WATCH
- BEASLEY Adrian *White & Case*

This book is the product of 6,552 1/2 hour interviews. See p.7 for BMRB audit.
See individuals' profiles p.81

lease of an LNG newbuilding vessel on time charter to Enron, with support for the lease obligations provided by way of a letter of credit. The firm also advised Ozrail Leasing on the $35 million finance lease out/operating leaseback of 100 in-service railways. **Clients** Exmar (UK) Shipping; Ozrail Leasing; Dresdner Kleinwort Wasserstein; Leif Høegh & Co; Atlas Lease Management.

WHITE & CASE (see firm details p.1185) A medium-sized practice which capitalises on its cross-border strength. Much of its activity is centred on aviation deals, which have recently included several multi-jurisdictional leasing transactions for international airlines and lenders. Justin Benson (see p.81) in particular is known for his aircraft-related expertise, while co-head of the firm's EMEA asset finance group, Mark Western (see p.84), has a reputation for being "*pleasant to deal with*" and acts for lenders, lessees, lessors and arrangers.

The team recently assisted the Royal Bank of Canada on the €200 million refinancing of two Airbus A340-300 on lease to Olympic Airways, which involved the restructuring of the debt from a euro-denominated export credit lease financing into two tranches: a senior secured tranche with first ranking security over the aircraft and a tranche benefiting from a Greek government guarantee. **Clients** Airtours; Babcock & Brown; Bank of Tokyo-Mitsubishi; Royal Bank of Canada; Tyco Capital; WestLB.

CMS CAMERON MCKENNA (see firm details p.914) The firm has been developing its medium ticket aircraft and rail practices, and is considered an improving outfit, especially on the rail side. There, the team acted for Angel Trains on the leasing of new rolling stock to First Great Western and First North Western. It has also recently acted for Metronet regarding its bid for London Underground franchises. On the aircraft side, it has recently been visible advising operator lessors. Clients informed researchers that the team, including Paul Richardson, is "*strong, with an impressive focus*." **Clients** GATX; BAE Systems; Angel Trains; Société Générale; Metronet; Lloyds TSB Leasing.

HARBOTTLE & LEWIS (see firm details p.983) This niche aviation practice is treasured by several airline heavyweights for its "*commercial view*" and attentive service. According to larger rivals the team possesses the "*necessary intellectual oomph,*" whilst clients enthuse "*they give you maximum attention and are cost-effective.*" Dermot Scully oversees the team. Recent work has included advising Virgin on unwinding the leasing and financing transactions for the sale of its Boeing 747 (G-VIRG) to a Nigerian operator, as well as on other subleasing and leasing agreement matters. It has also advised British Midland on numerous aircraft lease novations. **Clients** Virgin Atlantic; British Midland; TNT Worldwide Express.

SIMMONS & SIMMONS (see firm details p.1136) Best known amongst competitors for its work on behalf of the British government, the team's caseload straddles PFI and non-PFI matters, securitisations and project finance. Operating in tandem with the firm's capital markets, banking and tax divisions, it acts for a broad range of clients including European governments, aircraft lessors, and banks, and much of the work has an international flavour.

Kim Walkling (see p.84) ("*lovely to deal with*") is well respected by the market. The aviation industry is increasingly a source of work for the team. Recent examples of business include acting on the DERA PPP and assisting the MoD on the future strategic tanker aircraft project. **Clients** MoD; Railtrack; Kanematsu; Nissho Iwai; European Investment Bank; Barclays Capital; American Express Bank.

THEODORE GODDARD (see firm details p.1158) Market commentators consider this a "*fine*" broad-based practice covering aviation financing and leasing, rolling stock and general equipment leasing. Led by the banking and projects division, the team fields aviation specialists, tax-based asset and structured finance specialists, and a significant proportion of the caseload is cross-border.

"*Immensely thorough*" Rory MacCarthy (see p.83) has developed a niche for aircraft work. Recent work has included advising British Airways and its subsidiary, CityFlyer Express, in relation to the Japanese Operating Lease-based financing of six new Avro RJ100 aircraft. It has also advised Mitsubishi in relation to the purchase and financing of five new Boeing 767-300 aircraft leased to Japan Airlines. On the rail side, its has acted for Anglia Railways on an innovative lease and hire arrangement with HSBC Rail. **Clients** British Airways; Lan Chile; Anglia Railways; Aviation Capital; Iran Air; Christiania Bank.

BEAUMONT AND SON Another niche aviation practice, this firm also boasts strength in insurance and litigation. Said to "*punch above its weight,*" the team, led by James Edmunds, acts for financiers and bank subsidiaries advising on documentation and medium ticket transactions. Recent work has included advising start-up airlines as operating lessees, advising on acquisitions of portfolios and leasing companies and on receivables financing. **Clients** Western Industrial Finance; Lombard; British Airways; ING.

HERBERT SMITH (see firm details p.992) Connected with the firm's PFI and projects practice, the team, which features well known and respected figure Nick Tott (see p.699), covers rail work and fixtures leasing. Recent instructions include advising Fasttrax (a Halliburton-led consortium) on the provision of heavy equipment transporters on a PFI basis. **Clients** HSBC Rail; Eurotunnel; South West Trains; EIB; Philippine Airlines.

ASSET FINANCE ■ THE REGIONS

THE REGIONS

ASSET FINANCE
■ THE REGIONS

1
- **DWF** Manchester
- **Lester Aldridge** Bournemouth
- **McClure Naismith** Glasgow
- **Morton Fraser, Solicitors** Edinburgh

2
- **Burges Salmon** Bristol
- **Hammond Suddards Edge** Birmingham
- **Osborne Clarke** Bristol

LEADING INDIVIDUALS

1
- **BOCHENSKI Tony** DWF
- **MASKILL Andrew** DWF
- **WOOD Bruce** Morton Fraser, Solicitors

2
- **CAMPBELL Morag** McClure Naismith
- **HEATH Kevin** Lester Aldridge
- **LUMSDEN Christopher** Pinsent Curtis Biddle

UP AND COMING
- **DALY James** Lester Aldridge

This book is the product of 6,552 1/2 hour interviews. See p.7 for BMRB audit.
Within each band, firms are listed alphabetically. See individuals' profiles p.81

DWF (see firm details p.943) This has been a quieter year for the team after last year's flurry of new arrivals. Tightly interwoven with the firm's banking practice, its caseload is evenly split between contentious and non-contentious work, with a core client base consisting of finance houses and leasing companies. Peers continue to praise **Andrew Maskill**'s (see p.83) "*vast experience,*" whilst **Tony Bochenski** (see p.81), formerly in-house at the Bank of Scotland, appears to have seamlessly meshed his practice with that of the firm. The team has continued to be active on receivables financing transactions. **Clients** Bank of Scotland; ING Lease (UK); Sovereign Finance.

LESTER ALDRIDGE (see firm details p.1038) The firm is deemed by peers to be "*keeping a handle*" on its asset finance practice despite the loss of Pip Giddins. The team includes high profile players **James Daly** (see p.82) and **Kevin Heath** (see p.82). It is particularly active within the FLA and maintains its profile for small to medium ticket work, both contentious and non-contentious. Handling a wide range of equipment and vehicle finance and leasing work, it advises financiers and leasing companies. **Clients** DaimlerChrysler Financial Services.

McCLURE NAISMITH (see firm details p.1062) "*The firm for mainstream work in Scotland,*" according to market sources, it has established itself firmly in the field. Featuring many "*well known players*" amongst its clients, the team, spearheaded by **Morag Campbell** (see p.81), is developing a niche in the marine sector. This year it has been involved in securitisation transactions and receivables acquisitions as well as sale and leaseback advice, invoice discounting, factoring, security and documentation issues. Instructions have included actions for delivery of vehicles and other goods financed by hire purchase, conditional sale and lease agreements, and advising on title disputes in relation to hire purchase, conditional sale and lease agreements. **Clients** Bank of Scotland; Barclays Mercantile; Lombard; First National; Close Asset Finance; Singer & Friedlander Commercial Finance; Kreditfinance Corporation; Nissan Finance (GB).

MORTON FRASER, SOLICITORS (see firm details p.1077) Described to *Chambers'* researchers as "*pre-eminent in Scotland,*" head of corporate **Bruce Wood** (see p.84) was warmly recommended by both peers and clients. Active on both sides of the Scottish border, he and his team have recently advised Clydesdale Bank Asset Finance on funding for Asset Investment Capital's £40 million acquisition of a portfolio of operating lease agreements from Newcourt Financial. Regular work includes advice on receivables financing and equipment financing. The team is also involved on employer car loan scheme agreement funding for vehicle sourcing and maintenance companies and several of the UK's largest employers. **Clients** Clydesdale Bank Asset Finance; Royal Bank Leasing; Dresdner Kleinwort Benson; National Astoria Group.

BURGES SALMON (see firm details p.894) The "*respected*" team focuses on rail transactions and achieves particular renown for its work on behalf of First Great Western, First North Western and First Great Eastern. Recent instructions include leasing and financial arrangements surrounding the acquisition of new train fleets (total value £400 million). The team, with Patrick Boumphrey, also acted for the MoD in relation to its recent procurement of future offshore patrol vessels on a leasing transaction (value approximately £76 million). **Clients** First Great Western; First North Western; First Great Eastern; Standard Chartered Bank.

HAMMOND SUDDARDS EDGE A "*well-established*" practice with a loyal following of impressive clients. Led by Audrey Robertson, the team has recently been involved in the provision of credit facilities and equipment leasing agreements. **Clients** GE Capital; Barclays Mercantile Business Finance; Bank of Scotland; First National Bank.

OSBORNE CLARKE (see firm details p.1090) "*Cost-conscious and approachable,*" the team, including Jeremy Cross, is a popular choice with clients. Active predominantly on small to medium ticket deals, recent work has included advising GATX on a series of leasing and venture leasing transactions and on general lease finance and security issues, cross-border leasing and kit recovery. The firm also assisted ALD Automotive as lessor on a wide range of leasing, hire purchase, finance and security issues, including a £13 million vehicle lease and supply transaction. **Clients** ALD Automotive; GATX; John Deere Bank; Newcourt/Dell.

OTHER NOTABLE PRACTITIONERS Christopher Lumsden (see p.83) recently moved with several colleagues from Chaffe Street to establish Pinsent Curtis Biddle's Manchester office where he advises on asset finance, leasing, property finance and debt issues both for banks and borrowers.

CONSUMER FINANCE   NATIONWIDE

BERWIN LEIGHTON PAISNER (see firm details p.866) The firm achieves its profile in this area thanks largely to the presence of consumer finance guru **Dennis Rosenthal** (see p.83). He is well known as a consultant to the DTI and OFT, and advisor to the Consumer Credit Trade Association and CIFAS. He also assists an array of banks, building societies and credit card issuers on matters such as credit and hire agreements, terms of trading, savings account terms, security documentation and ancillary agreements. Recent instructions include drafting a range of new credit products for Creation Financial Services, and settling a range of new agreements for the financing of insurance premiums on behalf of various finance companies. **Clients** Creation Financial Services; HFC Bank; Mitel Telecom; Northern Rock; Norwich & Peterborough Building Society; Portman Building Society; Premium Credit.

LESTER ALDRIDGE (see firm details p.1038) This firm boasts a "*young and dynamic*" team, which was praised by clients for its "*proactive approach.*" Covering transactional and contentious work, it has a cross-section of large and small clients including general finance houses, banks, specialist lenders, public bodies and retailers, with particular experience in motor finance. Formerly in-house at VW Financing, James Daly specializes in non-contentious matters including consumer credit law, commercial document drafting and financing arrangements for financial services products. **Clients** Singer & Friedlander; Dixons; Lombard; DaimlerChrysler Financial Services.

THE LEADERS ■ ASSET FINANCE

ASSET FINANCE
CONSUMER FINANCE ■ NATIONWIDE

1
- Berwin Leighton Paisner London
- Lester Aldridge Bournemouth
- McClure Naismith Glasgow

2
- Addleshaw Booth & Co Leeds
- Eversheds Cardiff, Leeds
- Salans London

LEADING INDIVIDUALS

1
- JOHNSTONE Frank McClure Naismith
- ROSENTHAL Dennis Berwin Leighton Paisner

2
- FINCH Stephen Salans Hertzfeld & Heilbronn
- GUEST Jonathan Eversheds
- TOWERS Lennox Addleshaw Booth & Co

3
- COHEN Howard Salans Hertzfeld & Heilbronn
- GAINES Alison Salans Hertzfeld & Heilbronn

This book is the product of 6,552 1/2 hour interviews. See p.7 for BMRB audit.
Within each band, firms are listed alphabetically. See individuals' profiles p.81

McCLURE NAISMITH (see firm details p.1062) *"Particularly familiar with the Scottish marketplace,"* although by no means confined to it, the team elicits a warm response from peers and clients. *Chambers* researchers were informed that **Frank Johnstone** (see p.83) has *"excellent knowledge"* of data protection issues and the Consumer Credit Act. The team has recently advised the Consumer Credit Trade Association and the FLA on Scottish legal matters, and has represented a joint venture bank on the legal and regulatory issues arising from the creation of its website. It has also defended a major finance house on a substantial damages claim arising from the alleged wrongful repossession of goods. **Clients** Bank of Scotland; Fleetline Finance; Close Consumer Finance.

ADDLESHAW BOOTH & CO (see firm details p.838) Known for its close ties with banking clients, peers regard the firm as *"strong and active"* in the area, and researchers found that clients are impressed by its *"efficiency, promptness and commerciality."* The team combines expertise in asset and consumer finance, and focuses on small to medium ticket work. **Lennox Towers** (see p.84) spearheads the team, which has recently been involved in the preparation of standard documentation for consumer credit transactions and advising on related issues such as advertising, prize competitions, data protection and the purchase and sale of receivables. Work has also included advising on the advertising and delivery of products via the internet and internet payment systems. **Clients** National Australia Group; Woolwich; Skipton Building Society; Hitachi Credit; Co-operative Insurance Society; Airtours; Argos.

EVERSHEDS (see firm details p.949) This is widely regarded as a high quality practice, with strength in both Cardiff and Leeds. Clients claim that *"excellent all-rounder"* **Jonathan Guest** (see p.82) gives *"spot-on"* advice, and peers agree that he is *"pleasant and efficient."* The team acts for banks, finance houses and retailers on matters such as the provision of serviced and unserviced credit card products, loan and card account documentation, compliance, and advertising issues. Recent matters have included advice on equity release schemes for mortgage holders. **Clients** Virgin; Legal & General; GE Capital Fleet Services; Bank of Scotland.

SALANS (see firm details p.1121) *"One of the best firms,"* according to numerous sources, it boasts a handful of leading lights. **Stephen Finch** (see p.82) was praised to *Chambers'* researchers for his *"good sense."* His knowledge covers the broad sweep of consumer issues and he is a well known face within the FLA. Insolvency specialist **Alison Gaines** (see p.82) was strongly endorsed by peers for her consumer finance work, whilst **Howard Cohen** (see p.81) has extensive experience in car leasing. **Clients** FCE Bank; Nissan Finance; Bank of Ireland; Barclays; Daewoo; Guinness Mahon; Saab; Jaguar Financial Services; Volkswagen Financial Services.

THE LEADERS IN ASSET FINANCE

BEASLEY, Adrian
White & Case, London
(020) 7600 7300

BENSON, Justin
White & Case, London
(020) 7397 3820
jbenson@whitecase.com
Specialisation: Partner in the bank finance department. Main area of practice is asset finance and leasing with particular experience in advising banks, financial institutions, lessors and arrangers in the aviation industry. Also has a broad background in international bank finance and has advised major financial institutions on a broad range of cross-border transactions.
Prof. Memberships: Law Society of England and Wales.
Career: Qualified 1992 at *Sinclair Roche & Temperley*; also worked at *Freshfields* and *Weil Gotshal & Manges*. Joined *White & Case* in 2000.
Personal: Born 1968. Educated at Dulwich College 1978-85, Southampton University 1986-89 (LLB) and College of Law, Guildford, 1989-90 (Solicitors Finals). Married with three children.

BOCHENSKI, Tony
DWF, Manchester
(0161) 228 3702
tony.bochenski@dwf.co.uk
Specialisation: Asset finance and banking including structured finance, equipment leasing, acquisition finance, receivables funding.
Prof. Memberships: Manchester Law Society. Previously member of Law Society Commerce and Industry Group, North West Committee; ex-member of Finance and Leasing Association Legal Sub-committee.
Career: Kenning Motor Group Plc 1974-76; admitted as solicitor 1976; solicitor BL (UK) Limited 1976-82; Group Solicitor TNT (UK) Limited 1982-84; Bank of Scotland Group 1984-2000; appointed Director and Group Solicitor Capital Bank Plc 1996; joined *Davies Wallis Foyster* as Head of Banking and Asset Finance Group 2000.
Personal: Marple Hall Grammar 1966-70; University of Sheffield 1970-73; College of Law, Chester 1973-74. Interests include home, family, skiing, bridge, rugby and cricket (as observer), travel and holidays (when time permits).

CAMPBELL, Morag
McClure Naismith, Glasgow
(0141) 204 2700
mcampbell@mcclurenaismith.com
Specialisation: Asset Finance: sale and leaseback; securing property and assets generally including heritable (real) property, vehicles, receivables, income streams; block and invoice discounting; tailoring English financial products for effective use in Scotland; advising on differences between English and Scots law in specialist area.
Prof. Memberships: Admitted as a solicitor in Scotland: 1981.
Career: Hillhead High School, Glasgow; University of Glasgow: LLB (Hons) 1979; *Anderson & Gardiner*: Apprentice 1979-81; Assistant Solicitor 1981-83: Partner 1983-84; *McClure Naismith*: Partner 1984-date.
Personal: Singing (choral); music; theatre.

CARPENTER, Clive
Clifford Chance, London
(020) 7600 1000
clive.carpenter@cliffordchance.com
Specialisation: Banking and finance. Partner specialising in asset finance, leasing and banking in relation to heavy transportation assets (aircraft, ships, rolling stock), satellites and plant and machinery, the securitisation of transportation assets and tax driven structures employed in such financings.

CHANDLER, Nick
Denton Wilde Sapte, London
(020) 7246 7000

CHARLTON, Bob
Freshfields Bruckhaus Deringer, London
(020) 7936 4000
bob.charlton@freshfields.com
Specialisation: Partner specialising in asset finance and leasing (in particular, aircraft and rolling stock), cross-border financings, structured finance, export credit finance and project finance.
Career: Educated Trinity Hall, Cambridge (1975-78). Qualified England 1981; Hong Kong 1986; Brunei 1987; partner with *Freshfields* since November 1999; partner in another leading international law firm since 1987.
Personal: Born 1957.

COHEN, Howard
Salans, London
(020) 7509 6000
hcohen@salans.com
Specialisation: Partner in the banking and finance department specialising in asset finance and leasing (notably consumer credit law) and retail banking. Advises finance houses, leasing companies and banks on all aspects of their activities, including procedures, documentation and marketing. Has particular expertise in motor vehicle financing, having spent a total of three years on secondment in the legal department of a leading motor manufacturer's captive finance company. Experience includes the securitisation of motor finance and other trade receivables. Lectures on consumer credit law and related issues.
Prof. Memberships: Law Society.
Career: Formerly a partner at *Harris Rosenblatt and Kramer*, London.
Personal: Education: London School of

www.ChambersandPartners.com

ASSET FINANCE ■ THE LEADERS

Economics (1983 LLB Hons). Interests include: opera and aviation.

COLLINS, Andrew
Denton Wilde Sapte, London
(020) 7246 7000

CROOKES, Alan
Norton Rose, London
(020) 7283 6000
crookesam@nortonrose.com
Specialisation: Partner whose practice ranges from asset finance (particularly equipment leasing) to corporate acquisitions and disposals (including private equity transactions). He has acted on two major acquistions of rail rolling stock companies: Angel Train Contracts (for Royal Bank of Scotland); Eversholt Leasing (for Forward Trust). He acted for AES on its acquisition of Drax Power Station and also for the Finalrealm Consortium on its bid for United Biscuits. He led the *Norton Rose* team which acted for The Airline Group on the NATS PPP.
Prof. Memberships: City of London Solicitors' Company.
Career: Qualified in 1981 while at *Norton Rose*. Became a partner in 1988.
Personal: Born 27 May 1957. Educated at Durham University 1975-78. Enjoys music (particularly opera). Lives in Shenfield.

DALY, James
Lester Aldridge, Bournemouth
(01202) 786173
james.daly@lester-aldridge.co.uk
Specialisation: Asset finance, consumer finance, leasing, HP, funding and security documents, data protection, e-commerce, financial services law, consumer credit law. Moved to *LA* in December 2000 from Head of Legal and Member of Board at Volkswagen Financial Services.
Prof. Memberships: Law Society; Finance and Leasing Association.
Career: Business degree from Heriot-Watt University, followed by first career in marketing, switched to law and 13 years 'in house' before joining *LA* in December 2000 as head of non-contentious asset finance and banking.
Publications: Features from time to time in legal commentaries of legal magazines.
Personal: Educated in Scotland, qualified as an English lawyer. Interested in theatre, writing and horse racing.

EDWARDS, Jeremy
Norton Rose, London
(020) 7283 6000
edwardsjp@nortonrose.com
Specialisation: Partner in banking department. Head of international aviation business group. Specialises in structured and asset finance, particularly of aircraft and rolling stock. Expertise includes all aspects of operating and finance leases, sales and purchases of aircraft and rolling stock, cross-border leases and export credit financing. Recent transactions include advising various airlines and banks on numerous Japanese operating leases, some export credit backed; advising on multi-option aircraft financing facilities; advising on Brazilian export credit back financing of Embraer aircraft; advising UK Lessor on purchase and leasing of new and used rolling stock.
Career: Joined *Norton Rose* in 1987. Qualified 1989. Spent three years in the firm's Paris office. Elected to partnership May 1997. Speaks fluent French.

FINCH, Stephen
Salans, London
(020) 7509 6000
sfinch@salans.com
Specialisation: Partner and head of the banking and finance department. Advises lending institutions on all aspects of their activities, both consumer and commercial lending. Current work includes providing advice on asset finance and leasing arrangements, including off-shore and tax-based leasing and securitisations, factoring project finance, repo facilities, syndicated loans, finance house management and service contracts as well as providing advice on retail banking law. Writes and lectures regularly on consumer finance and retail banking law.
Prof. Memberships: Law Society of England & Wales. Serves on E-banking and Non Prime Financial Committees of the Finance and Leasing Association.
Career: Qualified in 1975.
Personal: Education: University of London (1973 LLB Hons).

FREEMAN, Mark
Freshfields Bruckhaus Deringer, London
(020) 7936 4000
mark.freeman@freshfields.com
Specialisation: Finance, in particular asset finance, leasing and structured finance. Main specialisation is aircraft financing.
Prof. Memberships: Law Society; admitted in UK and Hong Kong.
Career: Qualified 1969. Partner 1974.
Personal: Educated at Emmanuel College Cambridge. Leisure interests include motor racing, skiing, scuba.

GAINES, Alison
Salans, London
(020) 7509 6000
againes@salans.com
Specialisation: Partner in the banking and finance department specialising in asset finance, consumer finance and non-contentious insolvency. Alison has extensive experience advising clients in the finance industry on all aspects of loan finance, asset finance and consumer finance and on insolvency issues affecting her clients. Alison has particular knowledge of the motor finance industry and consumer credit law. She has written various articles on insolvency law and on consumer credit law.
Prof. Memberships: Law Society, International Bar Association, R3.
Career: Qualified 1980. In-house counsel with Lloyds Bowmaker (now part of the Lloyds TSB group), London 1980-84. Community Law Centre, New York City 1984-86. Partner *Hill Bailey* London 1986-89. Formerly partner at *Harris Rosenblatt and Kramer*. Alison is also admitted to practice in New York.
Personal: Education: Birmingham University 1977 (LLB Hons). Leisure interests include hill walking, climbing and football.

GIBB, Jeremy
Norton Rose, London
(020) 7283 6000
gibbjsp@nortonrose.com
See under Shipping, p.748

GIBBS, Ronald
Linklaters, London
(020) 7456 5984
ron.gibbs@linklaters.com
Specialisation: Principal areas of practice include financing and commercial transactions involving all aspects of aviation. Involvement in major domestic and international asset financings, shipping and related transactions.
Career: 1989 to date: Partner and Head of International Aviation and Asset Finance Groups, *Linklaters*; 1982-89: Assistant Solicitor, *Linklaters*; 1982: admitted as a solicitor. 1982: University College, London, Diploma in Air and Space Law; 1980: College of Law, Guildford, Solicitors Finals; Leicester, BA (Hons) Law 1979.

GLAISTER, William
Clifford Chance, London
(020) 7600 1000
william.glaister@cliffordchance.com
Specialisation: Banking and finance. Partner specialising in advising financiers and lessors on all aspects of asset finance and leading.
Career: Qualified 1993; Partner since 2000.
Personal: Warwick School, Warwick, Warwickshire; University College, London (BA Hons 2:1) 1989; College of Law, York 1989-91.

GUEST, Jonathan
Eversheds, Leeds
(0113) 243 0391
jonathanguest@eversheds.com
Specialisation: Consumer credit – acting for banks, building societies, finance houses and retailers in the provision of credit card products, fixed term loan documentation and compliance and advertising issues. Experience includes selling credit card receivable and debt transfer arrangements, data protection compliance, data warehousing arrangements and joint ventures in the credit sector. Lectures and provides seminars on the consumer credit legislation and provides input on proposals to deregulate the legislation.
Prof. Memberships: Consumer credit - trade association and data protection forum.
Career: Qualified 1982, partner 1986.
Personal: Interests include walking, trying to keep classic cars on the road and skiing.

HALL, Gordon
Norton Rose, London
(020) 7283 6000
hallgcc@nortonrose.com
Specialisation: Partner specialising in asset finance: ships; aircraft; rolling stock. Emphasis on structured financing involving tax and operating leases.
Prof. Memberships: City of London Solicitor's Company; International Bar Association; Baltic Exchange.
Career: Admitted 1980. Partner at *Norton Rose* 1988. 1985-88, resident in Singapore office. 1988-89, resident in Bahrain office.

HALL, Simon
Freshfields Bruckhaus Deringer, London
(020) 7936 4000
simon.hall@freshfields.com
Specialisation: Global Head of Finance Practice. Main areas of practice are asset and aircraft finance, and banking and structured finance.
Prof. Memberships: Law Society; City of London Solicitors Company.
Career: Qualified 1979 after joining *Freshfields* in 1977. Became a partner in 1985.
Publications: Co-author of 'Aircraft Financing' (Euromoney 3rd edition, 1998); co-author of 'Leasing Finance' (Euromoney 3rd edition, 1997).
Personal: Born 6th February 1955.

HALLAM, Robin
Lovells, London
(020) 7296 2000
robin.hallam@lovells.com
Specialisation: Aviation, rail and asset finance; secured lending, leveraged and operating leasing, tax based and defeased leases, securitisation, export credit and vendor sales finance, engine and equipment leasing principally in aviation but also in ships, containers, rolling stock and other forms of large assets. Substantial experience in aircraft securitisations and other aircraft finance transactions involving capital markets.
Prof. Memberships: City of London Law Society, Aviation Club – Associate Member, ISTAT.
Career: Qualified 1980. Hong Kong 1981-82; Singapore 1982-83; Partner *Lovells* 1995. Has written and lectured on a variety of subjects involving aircraft and rail finance.

HARTLEY, Simon
Norton Rose, London
(020) 7283 6000
hartleysr@nortonrose.com
See under Shipping, p.748

HEATH, Kevin
Lester Aldridge, Bournemouth
(01202) 786134
kevin.heath@lester-aldridge.co.uk
Specialisation: Asset finance and leasing (small to middle ticket), insolvency and commercial lending litigation. Particular emphasis on title disputes, fraud and urgent injunctive work. Associate member of the Finance & Leasing Association – sits on the litigation

forum.
Career: Qualified in 1988 with *Norton Rose*, joined *Lester Aldridge* in 1992, became a partner in 1996 and is now Head of the Asset Finance and Banking Team.
Personal: Education: Southampton University (1986). Leisure: reformed Spurs fan. Family: Catherine (13), Jessica (13) and Elizabeth (9).

JACOVIDES, Mario
Allen & Overy, London
(020) 7330 3000
mario.jacovides@allenovery.com
Specialisation: Partner in the International Asset Finance Group specialising in asset finance and leasing, he particularly focuses on structured and large-scale tax-based and cross border lease financings, export credit supported transactions, Polish leveraged leases, Japanese leases and US leases. He represents financiers, operators, and manufacturers in aircraft, ship and satellite financings as well as financiers in the acquisition and disposal of portfolios of assets.
Career: Qualified *Wilde Sapte*, (1989), Partner (1996); Partner *Allen & Overy* 1998.
Personal: Interests include golf, squash and ornithology.

JOHNSTONE, Frank
McClure Naismith, Glasgow
(0141) 204 2700
fjohnstone@McClureNaismith.com
Specialisation: Partner specialising in consumer credit law, asset recovery and data protection. Consumer credit law. Represents a number of finance houses, leasing companies, banks and credit card companies, with particular emphasis on litigation/debt recovery, sale and supply of goods and data protection. Convener of the Consumer Law committee of the Law Society of Scotland, convener of the Privacy committee of the Law Society of Scotland, member of the Legal Advisory group of the Scottish Consumer council, member of the Consumer Law committee of the International Bar association, chairman of Money Advice Liaison group (Scotland) and a frequent lecturer on consumer/credit law, data protection and debt recovery.
Career: Qualified 1982, joined present firm in 1985. Became a partner in 1988.
Personal: Born 12 October, 1957. Graduated MA, LLB, Glasgow University, British Universities Lightweight Boxing Champion 1979 – Runner up 1980.

JOLLIFFE, Peter
Slaughter and May, London
(020) 7600 1200
peter.jolliffe@slaughterandmay.com
Specialisation: Aircraft and asset financing.
Prof. Memberships: The Law Society.
Career: Qualified in 1981 after joining *Slaughter and May* in 1979. Became a partner in 1989.
Personal: Born 6 June 1957. Educated Downing College, Cambridge. Lives in London.

JOYCE, Andrew
Allen & Overy, London
(020) 7330 3000
andrew.joyce@allenovery.com
Specialisation: Asset finance and leasing.
Career: Partner in the International Asset Finance Group. His work has involved advising on a variety of secured and unsecured financings, including acting for financiers, lessors and manufacturers in the aircraft, rail and project finance areas. He spent nearly a year on secondment with GPA negotiating and documenting operating leases and aircraft acquisitions and disposals.

KAHN, Gregory
Denton Wilde Sapte, London
(020) 7246 7000

KINNERSLEY, Tom
Slaughter and May, London
(020) 7600 1200
tom.kinnersley@slaughterandmay.com
Specialisation: General banking, in particular structured finance and asset finance.
Prof. Memberships: The Law Society.
Career: Qualified 1972. Partner 1980.
Personal: Born 28 May 1947. Educated Hertford College, Oxford. Lives in London.

LEW, Simon
Clifford Chance, London
(020) 7600 1000
Simon.Lew@cliffordchance.com
Specialisation: Banking and finance. Partner specialising in banking, asset finance, leasing and securitisation.
Career: Articled *Clifford Chance*; qualified 1989; Partner since 1996.
Personal: Carmel College, Wallingford; Churchill College, Cambridge (BA 1986).

LINTOTT, Tim
Freshfields Bruckhaus Deringer, London
(020) 7936 4000
timothy.lintott@freshfields.com
Specialisation: Asset and project finance, including power stations and transmission, aviation, airports.
Prof. Memberships: Admitted in UK, Hong Kong.
Career: 1976-94 *Freshfields*, London and New York; 1984-92 *Baker & McKenzie*, Hong Kong; 1992 to date *Freshfields*, London.
Personal: Married, three daughters.

LITTLEJOHNS, Andrew
Freshfields Bruckhaus Deringer, London
(020) 7936 4000
andrew.littlejohns@freshfields.com
Specialisation: Specialises in aircraft and rail finance, and procurement and related products (including insurance, asset value support, securitisations and joint ventures).
Career: Education: Lincoln College, Oxford. Became partner in 1987.

LUMSDEN, Christopher
Pinsent Curtis Biddle, Manchester
(0161) 247 8270
chris.lumsden@pinsents.com
Specialisation: Partner in banking department, specialising in ship, aircraft and equipment finance but practice includes debt/equity swaps, documentary credits, management buyins and buyouts, invoice discounting, reconstructions and refinancings. Also experienced in corporate acquisitions and disposals.
Prof. Memberships: Law Society.
Career: *Chaffe Street*, partner 1990. Partner *Pinsent Curtis Biddle* 2002.

MACCARTHY, Rory
Theodore Goddard, London
(020) 7606 8855
rorymaccarthy@theodoregoddard.co.uk
Specialisation: Head of *Theodore Goddard's* Aviation Group. Advises airlines, leasing companies and banks on a range of aviation matters, mainly involving aircraft financing.
Prof. Memberships: Member of the Law Faculty of the IATA Aviation Training and Development Institute, Law Society, International Bar Association.
Career: Solicitor. LLB (London). MA (Business Law). Diploma in Air and Space Law.
Publications: Contributing author to the 'Handbook of Airline Finance' (published by McGraw-Hill). Author of various articles on aviation law.
Personal: Pilot (UK and US licences).

MARKS, Lisa
Denton Wilde Sapte, London
(020) 7246 7000

MASKILL, Andrew
DWF, Manchester
(0161) 228 3702
asm@dwf-law.com
Specialisation: Middle and big ticket asset finance including receivables funding, tax based structures and equipment leasing.
Prof. Memberships: Law Society.
Career: Articled *Wilde Sapte*; qualified 1990; *Eversheds*; *Alsop Wilkinson*; partner *Davies Wallis Foyster* 1998.
Personal: Leeds Grammar School; Manchester University (LLB Hons); guitar (blues and rock); golf; running; languages (French and German); resides Manchester.

MILES, Adrian
Denton Wilde Sapte, London
(020) 7246 7000

MURPHY, Robert
Freshfields Bruckhaus Deringer, London
(020) 7936 4000
robert.murphy@freshfields.com
Specialisation: Partner in asset finance group, specialising in aviation finance, including the use of cross-border tax-based leasing structures, export credit agency supported financing and aircraft-based capital markets transactions. He advises a wide range of clients on aircraft financing transactions including banks, airlines, leasing companies, manufacturers and arrangers.
Career: Qualified Ireland, England and Wales. Joined *Freshfields* in 1993, having worked as an in-house lawyer with the Irish aircraft leasing company GPA. Partner 1998.
Personal: Educated Trinity College, Dublin; University College, Dublin. Born 1961.

OSBORNE, David
Watson, Farley & Williams, London
(020) 7814 8000
dosborne@wfw.com
Specialisation: Partner in international finance group. Practice encompasses asset finance, leasing, secured lending, securitisation and structured finance; clients include lessors, lessees, originators, lenders and other credit providers.
Prof. Memberships: Law Society; New York Bar (admitted 1993).
Career: Ipswich School; Downing College, Cambridge; *Linklaters & Paines* 1979-82; *Watson, Farley & Williams* 1982 to date; *Watson, Farley & Williams* New York office 1990-95.
Personal: Married, three children.

ROSENTHAL, Dennis
Berwin Leighton Paisner, London
(020) 7427 113
dennis.rosenthal@blp.com
Specialisation: Partner in Company and Commercial Department. Advises banks, finance and leasing companies, building societies and trade associations on all aspects of their commercial activities. Deals with transactions; drafts agreements including standard form agreements; structures and advises on equipment and vehicle and receivables financing, retail credit schemes, sales and purchases of receivables, joint ventures and innovative products, including in relation to credit cards, personal loans, point of sale agreements, mortgages and bank savings products. Advises on commercial law, retail banking law, consumer credit law, advertising and marketing law, financial services law, insurance, fraud prevention, money laundering and data protection.
Prof. Memberships: Member of The Law Society, IBA, British South Africa Law Association.
Publications: Assistant Editor of 'Goode: Consumer Credit Law and Practice' and 'Goode: Consumer Credit Reports'; author of 'Guide to Consumer Credit Law & Practice' (Butterworths) and 'Financial Advertising and Marketing Law' (Sweet & Maxwell); contributor to 'Consumer Credit' in Halsbury's Laws of England.

ASSET FINANCE ■ THE LEADERS

SALT, Julia
Allen & Overy, London
(020) 7330 2553
saltj@allenovery.com
Specialisation: Partner specialising in asset based finance. Has extensive experience in aircraft and other asset financing including finance and operating leasing, cross-border transactions, securitisations and structured loans. Experience also includes project financing, telecommunications financing and securitisation.
Career: Articled *Allen & Overy*, qualified 1980, partner 1985.
Personal: Oxford University (1977 MA). Born 1955. Enjoys sailing, golf, opera, literature.

SANDILANDS, Keith
Norton Rose, London
(020) 7 444 3031
sandilandsak@nortonrose.com
Specialisation: Partner in banking department. Specialises in asset and structured finance focusing in particular on the shipping and aviation sectors. Expertise includes all aspects of domestic and cross border finance and operating leasing (including taxed based structures) and the sale and purchase of aircraft and ships
Prof. Memberships: Law Society.
Career: Edinburgh University LLB (Hons.) Dip. LP.

SMITH, David
Allen & Overy, London
(020) 7330 3000
david.smith@allenovery.com
Specialisation: Partner in the International Asset Finance Group, he represents all parties in domestic and cross-border structured transactions, both leasing and debt-based. Extensive experience of financing assets in many industries including telecoms and transportation (ships, aircraft, railways and containers). Experience includes export credit backed and government-guaranteed debt facilities, tax-based lease structures (including UK tax leases and US Lease-In-Lease-Outs and QTEs), off-balance sheet structures, vendor financing type structures and non tax-based leases including operating leases with and without residual value support, as well as combining these structures.
Career: Solicitor *Richards Butler*, 1984, Partner 1989; Partner *Wilde Sapte*, 1991; Partner *Allen & Overy*, 1999.
Personal: Born 1960, married with two children, enjoys family, motor cars, golf, cricket, eating out and theatre. BA Jurisprudence, Brasenose College, Oxford, 1981.

SMITH, Graham
Allen & Overy, London
(020) 7330 3000
graham.smith@allenovery.com
Specialisation: Asset Finance and Leasing partner and global practice leader of the International Asset Finance Group. A specialist in asset finance for over 18 years, his experience included numerous large value lease financings of both fixed and movable assets in transport, power and telecommunications. He has advised at all levels of the industry from the purchase and sale of leasing companies and portfolios, to retail finance documentation, setting up cross-border sales aid schemes and the integration of lease finance into infrastructure projects.
Career: Royal Grammar School Guildford; Nottingham University (1979 BA Hons Law); Guildford College of Law (1980). Trained *Wilde Sapte*; qualified 1982; assistant solicitor 1982, partner asset finance group 1987, head of leasing 1993; partner *Allen & Overy* asset finance group,1999.
Personal: Born 1958; resides London. Enjoys modern art, golf, classic cars, food and wine.

THAINE, Colin
Denton Wilde Sapte, London
(020) 7246 7000

THORNE, Peter
Norton Rose, London
(020) 7283 6000
thornepg@nortonrose.com
Specialisation: Partner in banking department. Asset finance. Clients include airlines, financial institutions and arrangers. Major transactions in 01/02 included advising lessors on restructuring leases on Welsh Water and Anglian Water financial restructurings, advising banks and ECAs on Garuda restructuring and advising lenders on various JOL financings for aircraft.
Prof. Memberships: International Bar Association, Royal Aeronautical Society.
Career: Qualified 1971. Joined *Norton Rose* that year. Partner since 1977.
Publications: Author of Aircraft Mortgages chapter in 'Interest in Goods' (2nd edn Lloyds of London Press 1998).
Personal: Born 2 June 1948. Attended Clifton College 1962-65.

TOTT, Nick
Herbert Smith, London
(020) 7374 8000
nicholas.tott@herbertsmith.com
See under Projects/PFI, p.699

TOWERS, Lennox
Addleshaw Booth & Co, Leeds
(0113) 209 2026
lennox.trowers@addleshawbooth.com
Specialisation: Consumer finance - advises banks, building societies, finance companies and retailers on secured and unsecured lending, leasing and hiring, standard documentation, joint ventures, purchase and sale of receivables, credit cards, regulatory and compliance matters, data protection, advertising and sales promotion and general consumer credit issues.
Prof. Memberships: Finance and Leasing Association, Consumer Credit Trade Association, Building Societies Association, Council of Mortgage Lenders.
Career: Qualified in 1971. Partner 1974.
Personal: Graduate of Exeter University. Leisure activities include family pursuits, walking and sailing.

WALKLING, Kim
Simmons & Simmons, London
(020) 7628 2020
kim.walkling@simmons-simmons.com
Specialisation: Big ticket asset finance and leasing, predominantly aviation; 2000/2001 Highlights: Acts for MOD on the Future Strategic Tanker Airlift Project and the Strategic Sealift Project and the financing of a fleet of aircraft for a Japanese lessor.
Prof. Memberships: European Air Law Association.
Career: Qualified 1982. LLB (Hons) London (UCL).
Publications: Various contributions to magazines.
Personal: Married, two children.

WATTERS, James
Watson, Farley & Williams, London
(020) 7814 8000
jwatters@wfw.com
Specialisation: Partner in international finance group. Principal areas of practice are banking, asset and trade finance. Work includes the provision of asset finance in the UK and elsewhere by leasing, loan, receivable discounting and other facilities, and the sale and purchase of leasing companies and lease portfolios and conventional and structured trade finance facilities. Frequent lecturer and editor of section on Equipment Leasing in 'Asset and Project Finance: Law & Precedents' (Sweet & Maxwell).
Career: Qualified in September 1972. Partner at *Watson Farley & Williams* since May 1992.
Personal: Educated at KCS Wimbledon and Pembroke College, Oxford. Lives in London.

WESTERN, Mark
White & Case, London
(020) 7397 3709
mwestern@whitecase.com
Specialisation: Partner in Banking Department. Regularly represents major financial institutions on all aspects of banking law. Has particular expertise in the fields of asset and acquisition finance. Has worked extensively in the aircraft finance sector representing lessors, financial institutions, lessees and arrangers on operating leases, bank facilities and tax driven structures.
Prof. Memberships: Law Society of England and Wales.
Career: Qualified 1998. Partner at *Weil Gotshal & Manges* before joining *White & Case* in 2000.

WHITE, Geoffrey
Clifford Chance, London
(020) 7600 1000
geoffrey.white@cliffordchance.com
Specialisation: Banking and finance. Partner specialising in asset financing, banking and leasing.
Career: Articled *Freehill Hollingdale and Page*, Melbourne, Australia; qualified 1972 Melbourne Victoria, 1977 England, 1987 Japan; *Nakagawa Godo Law Office*, Tokyo 1977-80, 1983-85, 1986-87; Partner *Clifford Chance* since 1978.
Personal: The Hutchins School, Hobart, Tasmania; University of Melbourne (LLB Hons and B Comm) 1966-71; Southern Methodist University, Dallas, Texas (LLM 1972-73).

WILSON, Keith
Lovells, London
(020) 7296 2000
keith.wilson@lovells.com
Specialisation: Partner specialising in asset finance. Transactions include debt financings, tax leases, operating leases, defeasance arrangements and restructuring. Major clients include Xerox, NATS, Chevron Texaco, Granada, Bank of Nova Scotia, British Regional Airlines, BTM Capital Corporation and Erste Bank.
Prof. Memberships: Law Society. Society of Scottish Lawyers in London.
Career: Trained *J & A Hastie SSC*; qualified Scotland 1986; Hong Kong 1989; England and Wales 1991; Partner *Lovells* 1998.
Personal: Born 1963. Resides Harpenden. Married with one daughter. Interests include curling, running, supporting Scottish rugby and football. Member Rust Nail Curling Club; Supporter Hearts FC.

WOOD, Bruce
Morton Fraser, Solicitors, Edinburgh
(0131) 247 1000
rbw@morton-fraser.com
Specialisation: Partner and Head of Corporate Division. Main areas of practice are asset and project finance and leasing, banking and debt factoring. Acts for Scottish finance companies throughout the UK and for English-based (and foreign-based) finance companies in Scotland: large, medium and small ticket work. Also handles general corporate work. Author of 'Location: Leasing and Hire of Moveables' in the Laws of Scotland; Scottish section of Davies, 'Security Interests in Mobile Equipment', Scottish section of Salinger; 'Factoring Law and Practice', section on Moveables in 'Green's Practice Styles'; 'Die Floating Charge Als Kreditsichereit Im Schottischen Recht'. Has lectured widely at legal seminars on leasing of moveables, joint ventures, Consumer Credit Act, banking practices in Scotland, corporate law in Scotland, the globalisation of law firms and of the practice of law.
Prof. Memberships: Law Society of Scotland, WS Society, Finance and Leasing Association.
Career: Qualified 1976. Joined *Morton Fraser Milligan WS* in 1974, becoming a Partner in 1977 and Head of Corporate Division in 1991. Lecturer in Conveyancing at Edinburgh University 1979-89; Convenor of Conveyancing Teachers of the Scottish Universities in the Diploma in Legal Practice 1986-89. World Chairman of Interlaw 1988-91.
Personal: Born 2 October 1951. Holds an LLB (1st class Hons, Edinburgh 1973) and an LLM (UC Berkeley, 1974). Leisure interests include medieval history and golf. Lives near Penicuik.

AVIATION

London: 85; Scotland: 87; Profiles: 87

Research approved by BMRB For this edition, **Chambers'** researchers conducted 6,582 interviews – 3,900 with law firms, 511 with barristers and 2,171 with clients. The validity of the research was scrutinised by BMRB International, who audited both the methodology and the results at our offices in London. They interviewed **Chambers'** researchers and cross-checked sample interviews. Details of the audit appear on page 7.

LONDON

AVIATION: REGULATORY
■ LONDON

1
- Beaumont and Son
- Denton Wilde Sapte

2
- Lane & Partners
- Norton Rose

3
- Barlow Lyde & Gilbert
- Slaughter and May

4
- Clark Ricketts
- Harbottle & Lewis

5
- Theodore Goddard

LEADING INDIVIDUALS

1
- BALFOUR John Beaumont and Son
- O'DONOVAN Hugh Denton Wilde Sapte

2
- FARRELL Patrick Norton Rose
- GIMBLETT Richard Barlow Lyde & Gilbert

3
- CHAPPATTE Philippe Slaughter and May
- HOWES Colin Harbottle & Lewis
- RICKETTS Robert Clark Ricketts
- SCULLY Dermot Harbottle & Lewis

This book is the product of 6,552 1/2 hour interviews. See p.7 for BMRB audit. Within each band, firms are listed alphabetically. See individuals' profiles p.87

BEAUMONT AND SON The practice has loyal admirers who maintain that it "*remains head and shoulders above the rest.*" Its overall reputation as a "*serious heavyweight*" owes much to the "*quiet and formidable*" John Balfour (see p.88), ("*king around these parts*"). "*A real class act*," he has "*a great academic touch.*" The team has acted for the EC Commission on a review of the third package of aviation legislation, and has been pursuing a complaint to the EC Commission against an airline and a government for alleged infringement of EC law. It has also been advising airlines on issues arising from the events of September 11th, particularly in connection with insurance, leasing and ticket surcharges. **Clients** Major airlines and their insurers, including ACE; AIG; AMLIN; GAUM; WAIG.

DENTON WILDE SAPTE (see firm details p.935) Observers commended this "*outstanding general regulatory practice*" for its acknowledged "*specialist aero-political expertise*". The practice comprises EU competition law, and offers advice to carriers, chief among them easyJet. Clients enthuse that "*their knowledge of our business is extensive*," and describe a team of "*leading-edge lawyers.*" Key figure here is the "*charming, effective and compelling*" Hugh O'Donovan (see p.89), regarded by many sources as "*the best general aviation lawyer around*" and an "*excellent communicator.*" The team has acted for Delta on the proposed alliance between American Airlines and British Airways, and acted for Opodo, an online travel agency owned by nine major European airlines. **Clients** easyJet; Opodo; Delta; United Airlines; British Airways; FedEx; National Jet Italia; GB Airways; Airfreight Express; TAG Group.

LANE & PARTNERS (see firm details p.1028) A smaller outfit, but one with a history of "*great aviation law*", it was especially commended for air transport licensing. European competition law, airport and tour operator regulation, aviation finance and leasing feature in the workload, and the team is involved in the broader aspects of commercial law as it relates to airlines, airports and tour operators. Richard Venables remains active as a consultant, and is the lead figure at this firm. The team continued to represent a foreign airline in a dispute about leasing arrangements in the English High Court, and it advised a British airline about alleged state-aided funding of a European airline. The team continues to advise clients about European law relating to the ownership and control of airlines, and about slots and other airport-related issues. **Clients** KLM (UK); Bristow Helicopters.

NORTON ROSE (see firm details p.1084) Often encountered on the other side of financings, competitors have a "*healthy respect*" for this "*top-drawer practice.*" The team is regarded as skilled "*especially on the corporate side*," and observers await its development now that competition specialist Trevor Soames has joined Howrey Simon Arnold & White. The "*delightful*" Patrick Farrell (see p.88) is highly valued as a litigator. The team acted for easyJet on the £374 million conditional purchase of Go. **Clients** Star Alliance; United Airlines; easyJet; the airline consortium running NATS; Olympic Airlines; FlexJet.

BARLOW LYDE & GILBERT (see firm details p.858) The regulatory team here is "*making great inroads into this market*" and contributes to the perception of the firm as "*a good all-rounder*." "*Highly respected*" Richard Gimblett (see p.88) has a reputation for regulatory work, which is "*established, and carries weight.*" He acted for the CAA on the fatal accident inquiry concerning a Cessna Titan at Glasgow Airport. **Clients** CAA; Rolls-Royce; Messier Services; Lithuanian Airways; IATA.

SLAUGHTER AND MAY (see firm details p.1140) "*Pragmatic and unstuffy*," this team has a reputation for "*awesome*" competition work for British Airways, and aircraft finance. It also has extensive experience in multiple regulatory matters. Occupying the upper echelons of the market, the practice is certainly known for its "*exceptionally bright lawyers.*" The "*sharp*" Philippe Chappatte (see p.169) comes highly recommended by clients and peers. The team acted for the government in the privatisation of NATS, and represented Airtours in a competition case before the European Court. **Clients** Airtours; BA; SAS.

REGULATORY

TOP IN-HOUSE LAWYERS

REGULATORY

Rupert BRITTON, Head of Legal, Civil Aviation Authority

Tim BYE, Legal Director & Company Secretary, British Midland

Richard CHURCHILL-COLEMAN, Group General Counsel, TUI (UK) Ltd

Maria DA CUNHA, Legal Director, British Airways

Owen HIGHLY, Commercial Lawyer, British Airways

Robert WEBB, General Counsel, British Airways

Rupert Britton is "*extremely well respected,*" and has impressed with his depth of experience, being "*one who has been around the block a few times.*" **Tim Bye** brings a "*good commercial overview of the sector*" to the table, while **Richard Churchill-Coleman** has secured the admiration of specialists in the field. **Owen Highly** has carved out a name for himself at British Airways. He is joined in the list by the competition specialist **Maria da Cunha**, who has taken over following Stephen Walsh's departure to Associated British Ports. Commentators contend that **Robert Webb** "*knows more about regulatory matters*" than any other in-house counsel.

INSURANCE & LITIGATION

James HEALY-PRATT, Director of Claims and Legal Operations, Amlin Aviation

Ken WALDER, Director of Operations, BAIG

Specialist solicitors admire the technical expertise of **James Healy-Pratt**, while **Ken Walder** has attracted commendation as "*a major force*" in the field, and one who applies his "*vast experience*" to each case.

In-house lawyers profiles p.1201

www.ChambersandPartners.com

AVIATION — LONDON

CLARK RICKETTS (see firm details p.907) The firm enjoys good contacts with regulatory authorities and correspondent lawyers. It was singled out to researchers as a *"100% niche"* team that *"knows its way around."* Robert Ricketts (see p.89) has *"deep experience,"* and is recognised as *"a canny operator."*

HARBOTTLE & LEWIS (see firm details p.983) Recognised as *"players of note"* in the aviation sector, this team undertakes regulatory matters generated by corporate deals. It has experience of airline start-ups, EU licensing requirements, operating and service agreements, service and route licensing. The firm has also advised on the lobbying of UK and EU regulators. Colin Howes (see p.88) offers specialist corporate finance and strategic advice, whilst Dermot Scully (see p.89) is *"expert"* in aircraft finance/regulatory law. **Clients** Aerobrokers; British Midland; British World Airlines; Caribjet; Fairflight Corporate Jets; Sky Service Belgium; TBJ Airways; TNT; Virgin Atlantic Airways; World Courier; UNI Airways.

THEODORE GODDARD (see firm details p.1158) *"Acclaimed for leasing work,"* this practice has strength in aircraft financing and operating leases. Regulatory capability has *"improved recognisably,"* and commentators praise the team's niche strengths in this area. The team services an impressive range of international clients, and advised Airport Coordination Limited (ACL) on competition and regulatory compliance issues regarding airport slot arrangements. **Clients** ACL; Atlas Air; Aviation Capital Group; British Airways/CityFlyer Express; Cessna Aircraft Company; Iran Air; LOT; Mitsubishi; Nissho Iwai; Qatar Airways; Ryanair; Sumitomo; US Airways.

LONDON

AVIATION: INSURANCE & LITIGATION — LONDON

1. Beaumont and Son
2. Barlow Lyde & Gilbert
3. CMS Cameron McKenna
   DLA
4. Clark Ricketts
5. Clyde & Co
   Ince & Co
   Linklaters

LEADING INDIVIDUALS

1. **GATES Sean** Beaumont and Son
2. **BRYMER Tim** CMS Cameron McKenna
   HUGHES Nicholas Barlow Lyde & Gilbert
   KAVANAGH Giles Barlow Lyde & Gilbert
3. **ANDREWARTHA Jane** Clyde & Co
   CLARK David Beaumont and Son
   CLARK Ian Clark Ricketts
   FRANKLIN Mark DLA
   GIMBLETT Richard Barlow Lyde & Gilbert
   MCGILCHRIST Neil Beaumont and Son
   SCORER Tim Thomas Cooper & Stibbard
   WILLCOX David Beaumont and Son
4. **CETTA Maria** Beaumont and Son
   FARRELL Patrick Norton Rose
   FITZSIMMONS Anthony Ince & Co
   PHIPPARD Simon Barlow Lyde & Gilbert
   SHEBSON Jeremy Barlow Lyde & Gilbert

UP AND COMING
COPPINGER Vincent DLA

This book is the product of 6,552 1/2 hour interviews. See p.7 for BMRB audit. Within each band, firms are listed alphabetically. See individuals' profiles p.87

BEAUMONT AND SON The first into the aviation insurance market, and some sources claim it remains *"undoubtedly the biggest and the best."* This *"technically great, experienced and efficient"* team secures a *"lion's share of instructions"* and enjoys strong ties to airline insurers. The workload is primarily aviation liability insurance. Clients and peers endorse the team's big names: *"practical"* Sean Gates (see p.88) is *"enormously experienced"* and regarded as a *"key"* figure in the marketplace. Clients also value David Willcox (see p.89) for his *"user-friendly style"* and great experience in accident work, whilst *"charming and courteous"* David Clark (see p.88) retains the respect of peers. *"Figurehead"* Neil McGilchrist (see p.89) has a *"great profile with clients"* and a *"good academic grasp"* of the field. Maria Cetta's (see p.88) *"sharp mind"* makes her prime choice for many clients. The team acted for Air New Zealand in its successful action against Ringway Handling Services for damage to an aircraft. It also successfully defended Embraer and BF Goodrich in the claim brought by Knight Air arising out of a fatal aircraft accident. **Clients** Major airlines and their insurers, including ACE; AIG; AMLIN; GAUM; WAIG.

BARLOW LYDE & GILBERT (see firm details p.858) *"What they lack in senior stars, they make up for in impressive and promising younger lawyers,"* claim interviewees. This *"well-organised and managed"* team is active on financial and liability matters. The core of the practice is aviation insurance-funded liability work both at home and overseas. It acts for underwriters, brokers and insureds, and the team has acknowledged strength in litigation. Ian Awford has left for Australia, as scheduled, but there is no shortage of admired lawyers at the firm. *"Fastidious"* Nicholas Hughes (see p.88) is respected for his leasing work, while Giles Kavanagh (see p.89) is *"settling into the industry well,"* and *"may well come to outshine them all."* Richard Gimblett (see p.88) remains respected by commentators, who also enthused about the *"capable and clever"* Jeremy Shebson (see p.89). The *"talented"* Simon Phippard (see p.89) makes it into our table for the first time this year. The team acted for BAE Systems in defending court proceedings brought by the Abu Dhabi Government, and acted for SAAB in arbitration proceedings brought by SAS Commuter regarding an incident at Stockholm airport. **Clients** BAE Systems; IATA; CAA; FTO; SAAB; ACE Aviation; Amlin Aviation; Global Aerospace Underwriting Managers; Swiss RE; WAIG; FLS Aerospace; Qantas Airways.

INSURANCE & LITIGATION

CMS CAMERON MCKENNA (see firm details p.914) This *"first-rate"* team is known for its complex insurance instructions derived from the French, US and German markets. At the *"core"* of this practice is the *"highly effective"* Tim Brymer (see p.88), who is credited with *"a good pedigree in this field,"* particularly in product liability issues. He led a team acting for a major European aircraft manufacturer to defend product liability claims brought by international airlines. The firm also acted for a South African airline in proceedings in Italy arising out of an accident at Pristina associated with UN/WPF flights (mercy/aid - related operations). **Clients** RJ Kiln & Co; LG Cox & Co; ACE/Sturge; Limit Underwriting; Hill Aviation; Airbus Industries; AIG Europe (UK); The Gerling Insurance Service Company; Heritage Group; Global Aerospace; Pilatus; British Aerospace Airbus.

DLA (The practice has grown across the aviation sector, despite the loss of Tim Scorer to Thomas Cooper & Stibbard. Mark Franklin drives this entrepreneurial and well-trained practice, and Vince Coppinger from Beaumont & Son has joined the team.

CLARK RICKETTS (see firm details p.907) The firm is commended by market commentators as a *"reasonable and respectable operation,"* admired especially for plaintiff work. The *"lean"* team is respected as a *"decent bunch"* with *"a unique aviation niche"* in contracts and disputes. It benefits from a healthy relationship with the CAA. The team also advises companies on the use of their corporate jets, and assists start-ups in a range of issues. Peers have *"no hesitation in referring"* their clients to Ian Clark (see p.88) for actions against the market, and acknowledge that he is *"a far better lawyer than his discreet profile would suggest."* **Clients** GAMTA; BHAB.

CLYDE & CO (see firm details p.913) The firm has been tested by the departure of Jeremy Shebson to Barlow Lyde & Gilbert, but it remains endorsed for its healthy insurance and reinsurance workflow. This is complemented by

SCOTLAND ■ AVIATION

expertise in cargo issues and *"fine war-risk work."* Clients are drawn from the insurance market itself, and include Lloyd's syndicates and companies. Lead figure here is the *"sensible, practical and down-to-earth"* **Jane Andrewartha** (see p.87), applauded for *"great insurance work in all its guises,"* and for a *"polished, effective and sometimes tough"* style. She also has a fine reputation in mediations. The team continues to represent various interests in the accident investigation into the crash of a MD11 at the Chek Lap Kok airport in Hong Kong, which has now extended to liability issues. It also represents London underwriters in the multimillion dollar satellite coverage arbitration dispute. **Clients** Insurance companies and brokers; airlines and aviation ancillary companies (fuel supply companies, repair facilities).

INCE & CO (see firm details p.1008) The core of this practice is in the insurance market, and *"its skill set is increasingly in demand post-September 11th."* The practice has a reputation for running international litigation and contract issues, with an especially *"long reach"* in Asia. The team has been engaged for IATA, the Lloyd's Aviation Underwriters' Association and the Aviation Insurance Offices Association in separate, ongoing insurance issues arising out of September 11th. Practice head **Anthony Fitzsimmons** (see p.88) is *"not afraid to put noses out of joint,"* and has *"made a name for himself"* with IATA. He is an insurance specialist, handling liability and reinsurance claims. The team has represented a brakes manufacturer in a matter arising out of the crash-landing of an A340 Airbus at Heathrow. **Clients** Insurers; IATA; airlines; aircraft owners; regulators; manufacturers; airports.

LINKLATERS (see firm details p.1043) The decline in BA work notwithstanding, the team handles a healthy level of instruction from BAE Systems. It is recognised for its work in large disputes, acting in complex and sensitive cases for major players, often in an international context. Litigation partner James Gardner is a key contact in this aviation group, which represented KLM in arbitration proceedings against Alitalia, heard by an international tribunal in The Hague. It also acted for BAE Systems in High Court proceedings against Euroair, a Portuguese airline. **Clients** BAE Systems; Honeywell; KLM; Sabena; Swissair.

OTHER NOTABLE PRACTITIONERS Tim Scorer (see p.89) has left DLA for Thomas Cooper & Stibbard, a firm that *"understands insurance properly."* Affectionately regarded, peers concur that clients *"follow him wherever he goes."* Admired as a litigator, and for his *"commercial style,"* **Patrick Farrell** (see p.88) at Norton Rose is recommended for his insurance knowledge.

SCOTLAND

AVIATION
■ SCOTLAND

1. **Maclay Murray & Spens** Glasgow
   Shepherd+ Wedderburn Edinburgh
   Simpson & Marwick Edinburgh

LEADING INDIVIDUALS
1. **ANDERSON Peter** Simpson & Marwick
   CLARK Richard Maclay Murray & Spens
   DONALD Hugh Shepherd+ Wedderburn

This book is the product of 6,552 1/2 hour interviews. See p.7 for BMRB audit. Within each band, firms are listed alphabetically. See individuals' profiles p.87

MACLAY MURRAY & SPENS (see firm details p.1048) **Richard Clark** (see p.88) is *"the first and obvious port of call"* for his clients. He led the team acting for British Airports Authority in a dispute relating to the arrestment of aircraft in Edinburgh and Aberdeen. The team was also instructed by the underwriters of an aircraft servicing company regarding an aircraft crash. **Clients** Cessna Aircraft Company; PTG Helicopters; British Airports Authority; British Aerospace; underwriters.

SHEPHERD+ WEDDERBURN (see firm details p.1130) The team is involved in most of the landmark decisions in Scotland surrounding the interpretation of the Warsaw Convention, and it is a leader in the field in terms of volume and quality of work. It generally acts for insurers' interests, and has a good working relationship with London aviation specialists Beaumont & Son. *"Mightily experienced"* **Hugh Donald** (see p.151) heads the team, which was instructed by Global Aerospace in regard to an accident involving a Cessna aircraft, that crashed after take-off from Glasgow Airport. It also recently acted together with Beaumont's for Bristow Helicopters v King in the House of Lords. **Clients** Bristow Helicopters; Edinburgh Air Charter; Global Aerospace; KLM.

SIMPSON & MARWICK (see firm details p.1138) This is a specialist professional indemnity and civil litigation firm with expertise in defender reparation. The team acts for clients (largely from the insurance industry) in claims arising from personal injury, professional negligence, public and employers' liability and major accidents. **Peter Anderson** (see p.552) is *"an accomplished solicitor advocate"* with expertise in professional indemnity, personal injury, and major accident claims. The team is involved in ongoing litigation against British Aerospace Flying College in a matter regarding a trainee fatality. **Clients** BA; CAA; Air UK; Boeing; British Aerospace.

THE LEADERS IN AVIATION

ANDERSON, Peter
Simpson & Marwick, Edinburgh
(0131) 557 1545
peter.anderson@simpmar.com
See under Litigation, p.552

ANDREWARTHA, Jane
Clyde & Co, London
(020) 7623 1244
jane.andrewartha@clyde.co.uk
Specialisation: Specialist in dispute resolution. Practice involves major insurance and reinsurance litigation, claims and liability work. Is an accredited and very experienced CEDR mediator (about 85 mediations) and also sits as arbitrator and early neutral evaluator. Represented underwriters in the Swazi Airline hijack, involved in personal injury aspects of Piper Alpha, claims settlement and reinsurance aspects of Eastern European Newbuildings. Aviation practice consists of representing insurers and aviation interests in defence and policy matters including TAM, Brazil, Rutaca Venezuelan crash and other similar accidents. Most recently involved in issues arising out of the September 11th World Trade Centre losses. Also involved in general aviation – light aircraft and helicopters. Clients include most major London and foreign market insurance and reinsurance companies and many Lloyd's syndicates. Is a regular lecturer, conference speaker and contributor to insurance industry publications.
Prof. Memberships: Law Society, CEDR accredited mediator, MCI Arb, update author of the international publication 'Journal of Maritime Law & Commerce', Association of Average Adjusters (associate member), Lloyd's (associate member), member of Air Law Group of the Royal Aeronautical Society.
Career: Qualified in 1976, having joined Clyde & Co in 1974. Became a Partner in 1980. London head of the firm's Latin American offices from 1989-97. Former Head of Aviation and member of Board of Management (Finance Partner from 1993).
Personal: Born 20 December 1952. Attended Exeter University 1970-73 (LLB Hons). Leisure activities include skiing, powerboat racing (now spectator only) and swimming. Lives in London.

AVIATION ■ THE LEADERS

BALFOUR, John
Beaumont and Son, London
(020) 7709 5000
jbalfour@beaumont.co.uk
Specialisation: Partner in Aviation Department. Practice includes regulation, EC and CAA work; accidents, liability and insurance; sale, purchase and leasing and other commercial arrangements; international issues. Author of 'European Community Air Law' and of many articles on aviation in the professional press. Lectures extremely widely; recent engagements include conferences and courses organised by the Royal Aeronautical Society, IFURTA Aix-en-Provence, ENAC Toulouse, Cranfield University, European Aviation Club and European Air Law Association.
Prof. Memberships: Royal Aeronautical Society (Past Chairman, Air Law Group); European Air Law Association (Secretary); European Aviation Club (Board Member). Board Member of the International Institute of Air and Space Law, Leiden University.
Career: Qualified 1979, having joined *Frere Cholmeley Bischoff* in 1977. Became a Partner in 1986 and Head of the Aviation Group in 1993. Joined *Beaumont and Son* as a Partner in 1997.

BRYMER, Tim
CMS Cameron McKenna, London
(020) 7367 3000
trb@cmck.com
Specialisation: Partner – aviation group specialising in aviation and aerospace law and claims. Represents aviation insurers, airlines and manufacturers worldwide. Responsible for pioneering use of common law injunction in restraining forum shopping following aviation disasters.
Prof. Memberships: Founder member of Lawyers' Flying Association. Member of Guild of Pilots and Air Navigators. Elected member of Royal Aeronautical Society Air Law Discussion Group and Insurance Institute of London Aviation Committee. Holder of current pilot's licence.
Career: Dulwich College; College of Air Training, Hamble; College of Law, Lancaster Gate. Qualified 1977.
Personal: Art, music, tennis, cycling and flying.

CETTA, Maria
Beaumont and Son, London
(020) 7709 5220
mcetta@beaumont.co.uk
Specialisation: Partner in aviation department. Practice includes all types of aviation liability and insurance law.
Prof. Memberships: Law Society; former member Lloyds of London Law Reform Committee, International Union of Aviation Insurers Legal and Claims Study Group.
Career: Qualified 1989; partner *Beaumont and Son* 1993; Lloyds of London 1995-2000; partner *Beaumont and Son* 2000.
Personal: Born 18 September 1960.

CHAPPATTE, Philippe
Slaughter and May, London
(020) 7600 1200
philippe.chappatte@slaughterandmay.com
See under Competition/Anti-trust, p.169

CLARK, David
Beaumont and Son, London
(020) 7709 5140
dclark@beaumont.co.uk
Specialisation: Partner in aviation department. Main areas of practice are all aspects of aviation liability work; also handles personal injury work for defendants. Extensive experience of dealing with claims in UK, France and Francophone countries, South America, India, European and Scandinavian countries. Matters handled include Swiss Bank Corporation v Brinks-MAT, Randolph Fields v Watts and others, Swissair-SR.111 Nova Scotia accident and securing awards for British Airways and their insurers from the United Nations Compensation Commission for Iraq/Kuwait war losses.
Prof. Memberships: Law Society; British, Brazilian and Portuguese Law Association; Anglo/Brazilian Society. Faculty member of IATA Learning Centre Management Development programme
Career: Qualified 1980. Partner 1986.
Personal: Born 8 March 1952. Attended University of Southampton and College of Law.

CLARK, Ian
Clark Ricketts, London
(020) 7404 1551
ianclark@clarkricketts.com
Specialisation: Partner specialising in all aspects of aviation law, including regulatory matters and litigation. Legal advisor to the General Aviation and Manufacturer's Association and the British Helicopter Advisory Board. Advises airlines, aircraft manufacturers and distributors, maintenance organisations, aircraft lessors and financiers, and corporate aircraft owners.
Career: Pilot and flying instructor RAF 1966-82. London University LLB. Qualified as a solicitor 1985. Established the firm of *Clark Ricketts* 1995. Speaks frequently at international aviation conferences.
Personal: Born in Northumberland. Flies aircraft of various types. Lives in Hampshire.

CLARK, Richard
Maclay Murray & Spens, Glasgow
(0141) 248 5011
rafc@maclaymurrayspens.co.uk
Specialisation: Senior litigation partner specialising in aviation, fraud and financial services and shipping litigation. Recent cases include Silkair crash in Indonesia, Landcatch v The Braer Corporation and IOPCF. Co-author of the Scottish section of Butterworths 'Aircraft Finance'.
Career: Edinburgh University (LLB 1973).
Personal: Born 1949.

COPPINGER, Vincent
DLA, London
(08700) 111 111

DONALD, Hugh
Shepherd+ Wedderburn, Edinburgh
(0131) 473 5159
hugh.donald@shepwedd.co.uk
See under Clinical Negligence, p.151

FARRELL, Patrick
Norton Rose, London
(020) 7283 6000
farrellpa@nortonrose.com
Specialisation: (for aviation: insurance and litigation) Advises airlines, brokers, banks, financiers and underwriters on aviation insurance matters including liability claims world-wide, coverage disputes, advice on wordings and insurance claims generally. Acts for underwriters in political risk matters arising out of aircraft finance transactions and for airlines in regulatory matters.
Prof. Memberships: MRAeS; chairman of the Royal Aeronautical Society Air Law Group; chairman of the UK ICC Commission on Air Transport. Member of Institute of Travel and Tourism, IBA, LSLA, CLLS.

FITZSIMMONS, Anthony
Ince & Co, London
(020) 7623 2011
anthony.fitzsimmons@ince.co.uk
Specialisation: Partner, leader of aviation team; specialises in handling aviation, insurance and reinsurance problems of all types, including investigations and reputation, brand, regulatory and competition problems; enjoys devising practical solutions to problems in these markets, including creating new insurance products.
Prof. Memberships: Royal Aeronautical Society and its Air Law committee; Associate Member of the Institute of Electrical Engineers.
Career: Qualified as solicitor 1980; partner *Ince & Co.*
Publications: 'European Insurance Competition Law' (1994 Graham and Trotman); Editor of 'Pollution Law and Insurance' (1997 Klower International); Associate Editor of 'Geneva Papers on Risk and Insurance'.
Personal: Education: Cambridge (MA Engineering); requalified as a lawyer, Cambridge and London. Leisure: family, walking, gardens. Personal: resides London.

FRANKLIN, Mark
DLA, London
(08700) 111 111

GATES, Sean
Beaumont and Son, London
(020) 7709 5000
sgates@beaumont.co.uk
Specialisation: Joint senior partner and head of aviation claims department. Main area of practice is aviation insurance and liability. Represents insurers and airlines in respect of claims made against them, and insurers in respect of policy decisions with airlines and reinsurers. Also handles libel and slander work, representing both plaintiffs and defendants in defamation actions. Author of articles in numerous journals, frequent speaker on aviation issues. Legal adviser International Union of Aviation Insurers. Former Chairman Air Law Committee, Royal Aeronautical Society.
Career: Qualified in 1972. Joined *Beaumont and Son* in 1973, becoming a partner in 1978 and head of aviation claims department in 1991. Senior partner 1 November 1997. Arbitrator with Cour Internationale d'Arbitrage Aerien et Special.
Personal: Born 4 February 1949. Leisure pursuits include collecting 19th Century illustrated books. Lives in London.

GIMBLETT, Richard
Barlow Lyde & Gilbert, London
(020) 7247 2277
rgimblett@blg.co.uk
Specialisation: Aviation and travel law; commercial litigation.
Prof. Memberships: Member of the IATA International Law Faculty; member of the European Centre for Space Law.
Career: Called to Bar 1982. Legal adviser, UK Civil Aviation Authority 1985-1988. Admitted as a solicitor in 1990; Partner *Barlow Lyde & Gilbert*, 1996.
Personal: BA Hons (Oxon) (1981). Director of FTO Trust Fund Ltd; private pilot.

HOWES, Colin
Harbottle & Lewis, London
(020) 7667 5000
colin.howes@harbottle.com
Specialisation: Partner. Handles corporate, commercial and regulatory work for a variety of clients, most of whom are in the entertainment, leisure and travel industries.
Prof. Memberships: Law Society; European Air Law Association.
Career: Qualified in 1981. Joined *Harbottle & Lewis* in 1979, became a Partner in 1984.
Publications: Author of 'Slot Allocation at Heathrow Airport: The Legal Framework'.
Personal: Born 1956. Attended Ipswich School 1967-74; Oriel College, Oxford 1975-78. Lives in London.

HUGHES, Nicholas
Barlow Lyde & Gilbert, London
(020) 7247 2277
nhughes@blg.co.uk
Specialisation: Head of aerospace department. Main area of practice is aviation law, covering aviation insurance and reinsurance, liability law, carriage of goods and aviation regulatory law. Also space insurance.
Prof. Memberships: Royal Aeronautical Society, Law Society, International Bar Association, American Bar Association.
Career: Qualified in 1981. Joined *Barlow Lyde & Gilbert* in 1979, partner 1984. Director of Association of Insurance and

THE LEADERS — AVIATION

Risk Managers (AIRMIC) 1992 to date.
Publications: General editor (aviation) of 'Contracts for the Carriage of Goods by Land, Sea and Air' (LLP); editorial consultant of 'Transport Law and Policy'.
Personal: Born 10th October 1955. Attended Sheffield University, BA Law (Hons). Lives in London.

KAVANAGH, Giles
Barlow Lyde & Gilbert, London
(020) 7247 2277
gkavanagh@blg.co.uk
Specialisation: Partner specialising in all aspects of aviation law, including insurance disputes (claims and coverage), product liability, regulatory and contractual advice. Work in the last 12 months includes: advising major British and French manufacturers on commercial/contractual claims; Swedish arbitration proceedings (SAS Commuters v SAAB); Danish arbitration proceedings (Premiair v FLS Aerospace); Air Law Group.
Prof. Memberships: Royal Aeronautical Society; Air Law Group.
Career: Before joining *BLG* in 1999, Giles was recommended as a leading aviation barrister in the 'Chambers and Partners Directory'. He appeared for the regulator in the reported cases of Philcox v CAA (CA) and in Perrett v Popular Flying Association (CA) and for insurers in mass disaster litigation, including the Kegworth crash. As a barrister he also appeared in a number of substantial arbitrations.
Publications: Regular contributor to aviation legal periodicals and conference speaker.
Personal: Education: St John's College, Cambridge; MA, LLM, President of Cambridge Union Society, Michaelmas 1981. Recreation: swimming, golf, tennis, deep sleep. Lives Kingston Hill with wife, Anna and three children, Tierney, Conall and Erin.

MCGILCHRIST, Neil
Beaumont and Son, London
(020) 7709 5000
nmcgilchrist@beaumont.co.uk
Specialisation: Joint Senior Partner. Work comprises aerospace and insurance litigation.
Prof. Memberships: Law Society.
Career: Qualified in 1969 as a Barrister of the Middle Temple, becoming a Partner in *Beaumont and Son* in 1981.
Personal: Born 8 December 1946. Attended Wadham College, Oxford, then Inns of Court School of Law. President of University of Oxford Law Society, 1966.

O'DONOVAN, Hugh
Denton Wilde Sapte, London
(020) 7246 7000
hod@dentonwildesapte.com
Specialisation: Partner in Corporate Department and Aviation Industry Group. Main area of practice is aviation, covering air transport regulation, commercial agreements in aviation, EC and competition law, airline and airport operations, aircraft leasing and airport financing. Also covers travel agents and tour operators. Regular speaker at various conferences and seminars on aviation-related topics.
Prof. Memberships: Law Society, International Bar Association, Royal Aeronautical Society, Aviation Committee of the UK International Chambers of Commerce, member of Council of the Airport Operators' Association.
Career: Called to the Bar in 1975. Practised as a barrister before joining *Knapp Fishers* in 1985. Left for *Richards Butler* in 1987 (Partner 1989). Became a solicitor in 1988. Joined *Wilde Sapte* as a Partner in 1991.
Personal: Born 19 August 1952. Attended Royal Grammar School, Guildford 1963-69 then Balliol College, Oxford 1970-73. Leisure pursuits include music, golf, skiing and rugby refereeing. Lives in Witley, Surrey.

PHIPPARD, Simon
Barlow Lyde & Gilbert, London
(020) 7247 2277
sphippard@blg.co.uk
Specialisation: Specialising in aviation; air carriers' liability and claims handling, major disasters and accident investigations; product liability; regulators' liability, goods in transit claims; aviation insurance, regulatory and transactional advice and representation; space insurance.
Prof. Memberships: The Law Society of England and Wales; Royal Aeronautical Society.
Career: Articled *Clifford Turner/Clifford Chance*, admitted 1989; assistant solicitor *Barlow Lyde & Gilbert* 1995; partner 1998.
Publications: Contributor to 'Aircraft Finance' and 'Aircraft Liens and Detention Rights' (both Sweet & Maxwell).
Personal: King's College, London (LLB); Associate of King's College; University College, London (1988 Certificate in Air and Space Law). Holds a private pilot's licence. Married with two children aged eight and six; resides in London. Speaks modest French.

RICKETTS, Robert
Clark Ricketts, London
(020) 7404 1551
robertricketts@clarkricketts.com
Specialisation: Partner specialising in all aspects of aviation law, with particular emphasis on aircraft finance and leasing and regulatory work for airlines, leasing companies, aircraft operators, aircraft distributors, maintenance organisations and banks and who works closely with a wide network of law firms in many jurisdictions.
Prof. Memberships: The Royal Aeronautical Society and The Law Society.
Career: Qualified 1987, with *Norton Rose*, then went to *Frere Cholmeley* in 1989 and set up *Clark Ricketts* in 1995. Partner since 1995.
Publications: Author of the 'Aircraft Financing and Leasing' section of the Butterworths 'Encyclopaedia of Forms and Precedents'.
Personal: Born 1962, educated at University College, London. Married with children and lives in London.

SCORER, Tim
Thomas Cooper & Stibbard, London
(020) 7390 2224
tim.scorer@tcssol.com
Specialisation: Partner in Aviation Department. Practice deals principally with aviation claims and aviation insurance disputes, litigation and arbitration. Handles a wide range of aviation interests including airlines, aircraft operators, airports and aerodromes, helicopters, gliders and parachuting, and contractual documents relative to those interests. Author and lecturer on a wide range of legal issues affecting the aviation industry, such as airworthiness, airport operations, carriage by air and aviation legal liabilities generally.
Prof. Memberships: Member of the Royal Aeronautical Society, Lawyers Flying Association (Chairman), Lawyers Pilots Bar Association (International Vice-President), City of London Law Society, Guild of Air Pilots and Air Navigators (Liveryman).
Career: Qualified in 1966. 10 years with provincial firm as litigation partner followed by two years in the Public Relations Department of the Law Society. Partner in *Barlow Lyde & Gilbert* 1980-92. Aviation Partner in *Jarvis & Bannister* 1992-97. Aviation Partner in *DLA* 1997-2001.
Personal: Born 25 June 1941. Attended Repton School, Derbyshire, followed by College of Law. Leisure interests include flying as a private pilot, photography and music. Lives in Essex.

SCULLY, Dermot
Harbottle & Lewis, London
(020) 7667 5170
dermot.scully@harbottle.com
Specialisation: Head of the Aviation Group at *Harbottle & Lewis*. Acts for airlines and other aviation businesses advising on all legal aspects of their operations, particularly aircraft acquisition and regulatory issues. Clients include Virgin Atlantic, TNT, Uni Airways and British Midland. Holds an air law qualification from University College, London. Other specialism is employment law and also has an extensive employment law practice.
Prof. Memberships: Member of the Air Law Committee of the Royal Aeronautical Society.
Publications: Has written articles for many industry publications and is a speaker at industry conferences.

SHEBSON, Jeremy
Barlow Lyde & Gilbert, London
(020) 7643 8831
jshebson@blg.co.uk
Specialisation: Passenger and cargo legal liability; aviation product liability; accident litigation. Has acted for aviation insurance market on claims in various jurisdictions, including providing advice on policy wordings and standard terms and conditions in the aviation industry. Also involved in disputes arising out of aircraft leases including repossessions.
Prof. Memberships: Royal Aeronautical Society.
Career: Joined *Clyde & Co* in 1989, became a Partner in 1998; joined *BLG* as a Partner in 2001. Aviation-related cases of note include Malca Amit v British Airways (1999), acted for the successful insurers in London arbitration (2002) concerning the 1999 disappearance of a Bell 206 helicopter in Columbia and handling claims arising in Ecuador from January 2002 crash of Fairchild Aircraft with loss of 26 lives.
Publications: Contributes articles in aviation/insurance press and speaks on aviation-related topics at conferences.
Personal: Graduated in law from London School of Economics in 1988. Married to Ruth with four sons. Enjoys football, being a keen Arsenal fan, and has also run three London marathons for charity.

WILLCOX, David
Beaumont and Son, London
(020) 7709 5314
dwillcox@beaumont.co.uk
Specialisation: Partner in aviation department. Main areas of practice are aerospace, commercial litigation and insurance litigation. His practice in aviation law covers handling of passenger and hull claims in respect of major accidents involving fixed and rotary wing operations including a large number of accidents in Africa, passenger cargo and baggage liability claims, advising on rights and liabilities of aviation engineering and maintenance organisations, and commercial litigation.
Prof. Memberships: Law Society.
Career: Qualified in 1981. Became a partner in 1987.
Personal: Born 25 March 1957. Attended Sheffield University. Past examiner aviation law and claims – Chartered Insurance Institute.

BANKING & FINANCE

London: 90; The Regions: 96; Scotland: 102; Profiles: 103

Research approved by BMRB For this edition, **Chambers'** researchers conducted 6,582 interviews – 3,900 with law firms, 511 with barristers and 2,171 with clients. The validity of the research was scrutinised by BMRB International, who audited both the methodology and the results at our offices in London. They interviewed **Chambers'** researchers and cross-checked sample interviews. Details of the audit appear on page 7.

OVERVIEW As anticipated, the slowdown in public M&A work has led to a proportional effect in financings. Jumbo transactions and new deals have been fewer and far between, although the mid-market has stood up pretty well with "*propitious*" conditions prevailing in sectors such as property finance. In contrast, the new plethora of creditors has upped the levels of restructuring, refinancing, corporate recovery and scheduling work. Overall, banking transactions are becoming increasingly complex, with euro-linked deals inevitably involving a cross-border dimension and a greater integration of securitisation and bonds. The syndicated loans market is becoming more conservative as the increasing diligence of credit committees results in more labour-intensive transactions concerned with credit standing and underwriting risk. Banks are moving away from rigid full-service panel systems, preferring a "*non-prescriptive*" attitude with emphasis on specific skills sets and product expertise. Practitioners perceive these trends as an advantage for smaller firms, for whom "*genuine specialism*" and diversity of work "*is the key*," while concurring that there is "*clear blue water between the top three firms and the rest*." In the regions banking expertise is important but so is "*building strong relationships*" – a view confirmed by recent panellisations that have "*carved up the market*." Reflecting market conditions in London, the slack in acquisition finance has been taken up primarily by restructuring and property finance, while asset finance, once regarded as London's sole preserve, is an expanding sector. In Scotland and Northern Ireland, project and PFI financing is the booming sector that has been instrumental in raising the profile of many firms such as Maclay Murray & Spens and John McKee & Son.

LONDON

BANKING & FINANCE: LARGER DEALS
■ LONDON

1
- Allen & Overy
- Clifford Chance

2
- Linklaters

3
- Freshfields Bruckhaus Deringer

4
- Norton Rose

5
- Ashurst Morris Crisp
- Lovells
- Shearman & Sterling
- Slaughter and May

6
- Denton Wilde Sapte
- Herbert Smith
- White & Case

BANKING & FINANCE: MEDIUM DEALS
■ LONDON

1
- Berwin Leighton Paisner
- CMS Cameron McKenna
- DLA
- Simmons & Simmons

2
- Baker & McKenzie
- Macfarlanes
- Travers Smith Braithwaite

3
- Gouldens
- Latham & Watkins
- SJ Berwin
- Taylor Wessing
- Watson, Farley & Williams

4
- Dickson Minto WS
- Eversheds
- Theodore Goddard

This book is the product of 6,582 1/2 hour interviews. See p.7 for BMRB audit. Within each band, firms are listed alphabetically.

ALLEN & OVERY (see firm details p.841) "*Still the ones to beat – these lawyers set the benchmark in terms of quality;*" the team attracts a plethora of superlatives from key industry figures. The team's "*IBM factor for highly visible transactions*" remains highly prized: "*There is never a major challenge – it's an easy decision for bankers to instruct this group.*" Clients rate its "*deep quality bench*" in acquisition finance, projects and property finance and capital markets issues, while some opine: "*They keep top - level syndicated loans to themselves.*" Its competitors eulogise about a "*cohesive, crafted practice with talented individuals from top to bottom,*" while clients say that they are "*consistently impressed by anyone we get across different areas.*"

Described by one of his peers as "*a Krug claret from an excellent vintage,*" **David Morley**'s (see p.107) abiding reputation in jumbo investment grade work imbues him with "*an aura that is bigger than the firm.*" Praised by clients as a "*great strategic thinker*" who transacts in an "*extremely efficient, good-humoured*" style, he advised on the £1.9 billion jumbo financing of Le Méridien Hotels by CIBC World Markets and Merrill Lynch. His peers view **Stephen Gillespie** (see p.105) as "*undoubtedly good news*" on the other side. "*Tough but not too aggressive,*" he "*fights his corner extremely well for his clients.*" He advised on the €5.5 billion WIND Telecomunicazioni refinancing, one of Europe's largest sub-investment grade deals of the year. Dubbed by clients "*the elder statesman*" in leveraged and acquisition finance matters, **Tony Keal** (see p.106) is a "*direct communicator*" who gives an "*efficient, thorough and brisk*" service. He advised WestLB on the £885 million total facilities supporting the bid for Wolverhampton & Dudley Breweries by Silverhoney, and advised Rabobank as arranger of the £79 million senior and mezzanine facilities for the financing of the £128.5 million leveraged acquisition by WT Tiger Three of the WT Foods Group. "*A class act*" in syndicated loans, **Mike Duncan** (see p.105) does "*a stalwart job of protecting his clients.*" He advised BNP Paribas on two highlight matters: firstly as co-arrangers with HSBC on the $1.1 billion acquisition financing for Allied Domecq; and secondly, with Citibank/SSSB, JPMorgan and Lehman Brothers on the $3 billion acquisition financing for Schlumberger's acquisition of Sema. **Tony Humphrey** (see p.106) is "*insanely good*" and "*the lawyer of choice*" for clients on acquisition and project finance matters, while former Norton Rose acquisition finance specialist **Tim Polglase** (see p.664) continues to impress both his peers and clients with his "*high-quality, rigorous*" style. "*Absolute star*" **Trevor Borthwick** (see p.104) also "*does great investment work*" for clients such for the Royal Bank of Scotland/NatWest, which he advised on the £1 billion financing of ScottishPower. "*Refreshingly committed to moving transactions forward,*" telecoms expert **Stephen Kensell** (see p.106) deals in an "*intelligent, calm*" manner that "*clients love.*" He advised on the £3.5 billion revolving credit facility for mmO2 (formerly BT Wireless), and the £2.4 billion UMTS financing for Hutchison 3G UK for the establishment of a 3G mobile network in the UK. "*Intelligent and innovative*" **Peter Schulz** (see p.108) is "*extremely reliable for getting deals done.*" He advised Dresdner Kleinwort Wasserstein (DKW) in a €650 million loan to the German-incorporated subsidiaries of Sasolin on its acquisition of the businesses of RWE-DEA, and acted on a €600 million syndicated facility for Swiss company Xstrata in its bid for Spanish-based Asturiana de Zinc. A "*class operator*" on the mezzanine side, **Euan Gorrie** (see p.663)

LONDON ■ BANKING & FINANCE

TOP IN-HOUSE LAWYERS

Laurie ADAMS, Head of Legal and Compliance, ABN AMRO

Richard BENNETT, Group General Manager, Legal and Compliance, HSBC Holdings

Mitchell CALLER, Senior Vice President and Associate General Counsel, JP Morgan Chase

Alex CAMERON, Head of Legal for London and Europe, Barclays Capital

Paul CHELSOM, Director of Legal and Compliance, Credit Suisse First Boston

John COLLINS, Global Products Legal Head, ABN AMRO

Simon DODDS, General Counsel, Deutsche Bank

William ELLIOT, Executive Legal Director, Goldman Sachs

James GLEDHILL, Senior Vice President and Co Head of Corporate Finance Legal, Citibank

Clare JONES, Senior Vice President and Co Head of Corporate Finance Legal, Citibank

Ian JAMESON, European Corporate Counsel, Lehman Brothers

Geoffrey JOHNSON, General Counsel, Lloyds TSB

Terry MILLER, Managing Director and General Counsel, Goldman Sachs International

Jeremy OGDEN, Deputy General Counsel & General Counsel for Barclays Private Equity & Regional Counsel for Europe, Barclays Private Clients

Richard ROSENTHAL, Morgan Stanley

Howard TRUST, General Counsel and Company Secretary, Barclays

Stuart WILLEY, Chief Counsel – Investment Business, Financial Services Authority

Andrew WHITTAKER, Deputy General Counsel, Financial Services Authority

Mitch Caller is "definitely a great name" in the sector, and "extremely able," **Clare Jones** remains respected for her transaction management. Commended for their "absolutely excellent" technical skills and knowledge of the sector are **Geoffrey Johnson** and **Laurie Adams**. **Alex Cameron** and **William Elliot** feature; their "high level of intelligence" is cited as a key attribute. Recommendations flowed for **James Gledhill**, **Howard Trust** and **Simon Dodds**, all of whom were complimented as "highly personable" and "easy to work with" by private practitioners. **Richard Bennett** and **Paul Chelsom** have a "good commercial knowledge," a trait shared by **Ian Jameson**, who is also likened for his "efficiency." **John Collins** was described as "quite simply a superb banking lawyer." **Jeremy Ogden**, who is always "one step ahead of the game," and Stuart Willey who represents the Financial Services Authority and is "one of the best lawyers around – fully deserving of a mention." At the same institution is **Andrew Whittaker**, described as "on the ball." **Howard Trust**'s key attribute is that he "always thinks ahead rather than just reacting." **Richard Rosenthal** was praised for his commercial awareness, while **Terry Miller** was dubbed "highly impressive."

In-house lawyers profiles p.1201

"uses his knowledge well without being pedantic." He advised WestLB on the £188 million senior debt financing to support the £208 million MBO of Jim Beam Brands (Greater Europe) by Kyndal International. Also recommended were "experienced" **Andrew Bamber** (see p.662) (ex-Norton Rose), "thorough" global lending partner **David Murray** (see p.107) and "constructive" **Simon Roberts** (see p.108). Further team highlights include the $3.4 billion Brambles/GKN merger and advising Barclays Capital in a $2.5 billion corporate facility for BHP Billiton. **Clients** Barclays Capital; JPMorgan Chase; Morgan Stanley; Royal KPN; United Business Media ; ABN AMRO; Goldman Sachs; Citigroup; Dresdner Bank; Deutsche Bank; RBS; HSBC; CIBC; UBS Warburg.

CLIFFORD CHANCE (see firm details p.911) The team is jointly ensconced at the top with a "megadeal ethos" that is underpinned by its bedrock of expertise in securitisation and debt. Its "superb global strategy" sanctions its rating by some leading industry players as a significant presence in Germany and across Europe. Admired by its competitors for being "great at being able to institutionalise a client relationship," premier finance houses elucidate that they "save the time needed to explain the in-house perspective." The team includes some "hands-on, pragmatic" partners; it "engages massive organisation to execute matters with regimented precision" and "can solve problems from scratch with top marks. Interviewees still recognise "seasoned practitioners" Michael Bray and Stuart Popham as "key figures that advise on a whole range of issues" at management level.

His peers comment that **Mark Campbell** (see p.104) "looks too young to carry his gargantuan workload." The team's "fronting veteran" in acquisition finance and rescheduling, he is judged by sources to be "big in the Legal Marketing Association [LMA]" and a "consummate draughtsman and negotiator." He acted for Barclays Capital and Deutsche Bank on the €1.855 billion acquisition of AssiDomän by Kappa Packaging. Popular among his peers and clients, **James Johnson** (see p.106) has an "extrovert, decisive and unfazeable" style. He advised France Telecom on its €15 billion refinancing. "Suave and urbane" **Malcolm Sweeting** (see p.109) can "smooth over rough spots and pull everyone together," while clients revere him as "a heavyweight, whose opinion counts for a lot." He has advised on the €1.65 billion senior debt financing for the Messer Griesheim LBO, and acted for the lead arrangers, UBS Warburg and DKW, providing $4.55 billion facilities for the $18.7 billion public-to-private acquisition of De Beers. Peers rate "top-dog bruiser" **Mark Stewart** (see p.664) for his "well-rounded understanding" of the debt and equity market and his "sterling" work for sponsors. He advised Yell on its £2.14 billion LBO. **Alan Inglis** (see p.663) "talks the client's language," and is "innately numerate and superb on detail." Together with colleagues in 11 other jurisdictions, he advised the lead arrangers on the €1.60 billion senior debt financing for the acquisition of the Cognis Group from Henkel, the second largest European industrial LBO of the year. Noted for having cemented the firm's links with Chase, media and telecoms specialist **Lee Cullinane** (see p.104) advised on the €30 billion senior facilities for Olivetti's acquisition of Telecom Italia. Clients also recommend **Peter Kilner** (see p.106) as an "exceptionally bright partner rising into the league – he can relate to anyone." **Robert Lee** (see p.106) "bears all the hallmarks of a well-trained partner," while **Robert Smith** (see p.108) specialises in housing associations work. "Phenomenonally able" **Michael Bates** (see p.104) and "realistic all-rounder" **Suzy Stewart** (see p.109) both received endorsement during research. Together with offices in seven jurisdictions, the team advised Nomura and the Grand Hotels Group on the £1.9 billion leveraged acquisition of Le Méridien Hotels from Compass. The team advised on several other major acquisitions including Rhaig, Lit2.2 billion senior facilities for Seat, and €240 million senior facilities for Necta Vending from Electrolux. It also advised the London branches of The Dai-Ichi Kangyo Bank, the Fuji Bank and Industrial Bank of Japan, in relation to their corporate reorganisation that involved working with a large range of sectors within the firm. **Clients** Citigroup; Barclays; JPMorgan; Deutsche; HSBC; ABN AMRO; Goldman Sachs; Morgan Stanley; BNP Paribas; Dresdner; CSFB; UBS Warburg; BankAmerica; RBS; WestLB; ING Barings; Mediobanca; Lloyds TSB Capital Markets; LMA.

LINKLATERS (see firm details p.1043) Its competitors concede that the "highly visible" team has been "building up its market share intelligently" across investment grade, mid-market and new deals sectors, by leveraging off the firm's blue-chip corporate finance brand and nurturing corporate finance relationships with the investment banks. "Its broad experience adds value," claim clients. Interviewees identified its key strengths in capital markets and securitisation. Clients report that these lawyers "do the most fantastic, rigorous job to a first-class standard in an incredibly short time."

His peers pay homage to "guru-like figure," **Haydn Puleston Jones** (see p.108): "one of the City's finest draughtsmen with about the biggest intellect of them all." One client recounted that he "did a bloody good job turning around extremely complex documentation and agreed it in two days flat without breaking into a sweat or apparently going to bed." He advised Pirelli on the €1.8 billion secured syndicated facility for Olimpia's acquisition of Olivetti. **John Tucker** (see p.109) is credited by his peers as a "five-star team leader" and one who enjoys a "good rapport with the banks." He advised JPMorgan as joint co-ordinator and lead arranger of a syndicated debt facility for $1.4 billion to Xstrata, the newly London-listed natural resources company, and advised BHP Billiton on the $2.5 billion syndicated facility for its dual listed company structure. **Gideon Moore** (see p.107) "listens to

BANKING & FINANCE ■ LONDON

LEADING INDIVIDUALS

EMINENCES GRISES

★ **Bray Michael** Clifford Chance
★ **Popham Stuart** Clifford Chance

MORLEY David Allen & Overy

[1]
CAMPBELL Mark Clifford Chance	**EREIRA David** Freshfields Bruckhaus Deringer
GILLESPIE Stephen Allen & Overy	**JOHNSON James** Clifford Chance
KEAL Anthony Allen & Overy	**PULESTON JONES Haydn** Linklaters
SWEETING Malcom Clifford Chance	

[2]
ALLEN Maurice White & Case	**BALFOUR Andrew** Slaughter and May
DUNCAN Michael Allen & Overy	**HUMPHREY Tony** Allen & Overy
STEWART Mark Clifford Chance	**TUCKER John** Linklaters

[3]
COTTIS Matthew Lovells	**EVANS Edward** Freshfields Bruckhaus Deringer
PIERCE Sean Freshfields Bruckhaus Deringer	**POLGLASE Timothy** Allen & Overy
SLATER Richard Slaughter and May	**VICKERS Mark** Ashurst Morris Crisp

[4]
BORTHWICK Trevor Allen & Overy	**CHESTERMAN James** Latham & Watkins
INGLIS Alan Clifford Chance	**KENSELL Stephen** Allen & Overy
MOORE Gideon Linklaters	**SCHULZ Peter** Allen & Overy
WARD Anthony Shearman & Sterling	**WARD Nigel** Ashurst Morris Crisp
WHITE Giles Linklaters	

[5]
CULLINANE Lee Clifford Chance	**ELLIOTT Robert** Linklaters
FURMAN Mark Macfarlanes	**GORRIE Euan** Allen & Overy
MURRAY Neil Travers Smith Braithwaite	**SHORT Stephen** Ashurst Morris Crisp

[6]
BAMBER Andrew Allen & Overy	**CARSLAW Debbie** Sidley Austin Brown & Wood
DISS Paul SJ Berwin	**DUKES Rodney** Taylor Wessing
KILNER Peter Clifford Chance	**LEE Robert** Clifford Chance
LONG Peter Herbert Smith	**MURRAY David** Allen & Overy
SMITH Robert Clifford Chance	**WAGHORN Mark** Berwin Leighton Paisner
WILSON Dave Theodore Goddard	

UP AND COMING

BATES Michael Clifford Chance	**FREEMAN Adam** Lovells
JAMES Benedict Linklaters	**NACCARATO John** CMS Cameron McKenna
ROBERTS Simon Allen & Overy	**STEWART Suzy** Clifford Chance

ASSOCIATES TO WATCH

COCHRANE Charles Clifford Chance

See individuals' profiles p.103

---

what to expect" when dealing with the team, appreciating that its "*can-do attitude helps deals happen.*" Expressing confidence that they can "*stand back and let the team get on with it*," its clients endorsed the practice's "*strong geographical diversity*" and "*well-managed European network.*" These lawyers are "*professional, transaction-focused, and solutions-oriented.*" Among its leading lights, clients single out "*extremely savvy, technically minded*" David Ereira (see p.105) and Edward Evans (see p.105), who is "*laid-back but highly effective*" on regulatory aspects of "*any type of transaction*." Also commended by clients for "*doing a great job*," Sean Pierce (see p.108) advised Deutsche Bank as underwriter and arranger of £1.1 billion acquisition facilities to Etex for the acquisition of Glynwed Pipe Systems businesses in the UK and worldwide. The team has advised Permira (formerly Schroder Ventures) and Goldman Sachs PIA as private equity buyers of the worldwide Cognis businesses out of Henkel on their €1.6 billion facilities, and advised mmO2 on its £3.5 billion demerger facilities. It also represented Central Holdings on the $1.9 billion facilities to DB Investments for the take private acquisition of De Beers, and advised Schlumberger on its $3 billion facility for the acquisition of Sema. **Clients** ABN AMRO; Citigroup; JPMorgan; CIBC World Markets; Deutsche Bank; RBS; UBS Warburg; Compass; Kingfisher; mmO2; Schlumberger; Cinven; Goldman Sachs; Permira; MGPE; Whitehall Street Real Estate.

NORTON ROSE (see firm details p.1084) Market sources are "*waiting to see*" what impact will follow the loss of key players from the team's acquisition finance practice. The majority concur, however, that it "*will remain strong*" in its broad base of telecoms, project finance and asset finance, while retaining a "*solid practice*" in mid-market acquisition finance work. Industry players on both sides express respect for the "*receptive, well-integrated and practical*" team, led by Stephen Parish, although currently, "*no names stand out.*" The team advised the lead arrangers JPMorgan, CIBC World Markets, The Bank of New York and TD Bank Europe in the £2.25 billion financing of Telewest Communications Networks and Telewest Finance. It also acted for Banc of America Securities and Bank of America providing SEK1.1 billion facilities for the acquisition of Sapa Autoplastics Group, and assisted Bank of Scotland in providing more than £50 million facilities for the acquisition of two hotels from SAS Radisson Group by two overseas-based companies. **Clients** HSBC; ANZ Bank; Bank of New York; CIBC Wood Grundy; Toronto-Dominion Bank; RBS; ABN AMRO; Société Générale; Deutsche Bank.

ASHURST MORRIS CRISP (see firm details p.852) "*Long and strong in the leveraged arena,*" the team enjoys a market reputation as "*prime choice*" for blue-chip finance houses in non-

---

the other side's perspective." He advised on the €2.1 billion syndicated facility with which Telelnvest acquired 10% of TPSA from the Polish Government. Former banker Giles White (see p.109) "*leads brilliantly at the forefront of the house*" with a loyal client following attracted by his industry knowledge. He advised Barclays in the financing of the acquisition by Ferroatlantica and Energie Baden-Württemberg (EnBW) of Hidroelectrica del Cantábrico (Hidroelectrica). "*Personable*" Robert Elliott (see p.458) leads the restructuring and insolvency practice, with a key role in new lendings. He advised the creditor banks on the restructuring of the John Laing Group's banking facilities. "*Aggressive*" homegrown partner Benedict James (see p.106) enjoys a rising reputation with high profile project financings such as assisting DB Investments, the consortium formed by Central Holdings, Anglo American and Debswana Diamond Company, in the $4.55 billion financing of its take private of the De Beers group.

Together with the Paris office, the team advised CSFB on the launch of a bid by Groupe Partouche for all the shares and convertible bonds of Compagnie Européenne de Casinos (offer value €294 million). It also advised Barclays Capital as global co-ordinator and sole bookrunner in the senior and subordinated debt financing of the public takeoveie. **Clients** ABN AMRO; Barclays Capital/ Barclays Bank; CSFB; Deutsche Bank; Dresdner; HBOS; HSBC; HVB Europe; Lloyds TSB; JPMorgan Chase; Merrill Lynch; Morgan Stanley; RBS/NatWest; Standard Chartered; UBS Warburg.

FRESHFIELDS BRUCKHAUS DERINGER (see firm details p.964) The team's "*fantastic corporate client list*" protracts its image as a leading borrower's counsel across the full sector range, although observers consider it a "*pukka player in the debt market*" for top global finance houses that include Goldman Sachs. Interviewees lauded its key sector strengths in project finance, PFI, asset finance and securitisations. Competitors vouch that they "*always know*

LONDON ■ BANKING & FINANCE

investment grade and mid-market work. According to its competitors, it is *"building sensibly and strategically"* on the back of an excellent corporate and private equity practice and *"extremely professional"* French and German capability. Clients value its *"in-depth market knowledge"* across acquisition, leveraged finance, property and PFI finance sectors. They endorse the team as a *"smart, versatile group"* that produces *"impressive documents within a 24-hour turnaround time"* and *"works hard to allow time to consider the options."* Among its *"charismatic, commercial"* partners, *"ebullient"* **Mark Vickers** (see p.664 enjoys a high profile in UK mid-market leveraged and acquisition finance, while some attribute him with *"the greatest city expertise on public-private issues."* Clients commend *"quietly spoken"* **Nigel Ward** (see p.664) for his *"traditional, solutions-oriented yet flexible"* deal approach. The *"forthright"* **Stephen Short** (see p.108) is *"making an impression"* on deals with Ineos, Merrill Lynch and Barclays. He acted for Lehman Brothers on a €200 million complex cross-border leveraged refinancing and new acquisition by CFS Holding, and also advised it in the £144 million bid for Britax International by Seton House Acquisition. The team's principal European LBO highlights include Ineos Chemicals (€1.1 billion) for Barclays Bank/Barclays Capital, and RHM Finance (£745 million) for RBS. **Clients** Bank of Scotland; Barclays Bank/Barclays Capital; ING Barings; Lehman Brothers; Merrill Lynch; RBS.

LOVELLS (see firm details p.1045) Market sources commend this *"broad, mature"* general banking practice that is *"justly famed"* for its long-standing links with Barclays. The team garners plaudits for its domestic acquisition finance and LBO capability and *"upward profile"* in project finance. There exists also a *"solid underpinning"* in capital markets and turn-around work that includes insolvency and corporate recovery. Clients commend *"strong motivator"* **Matthew Cottis** (see p.663) who *"engenders the team's constructive spirit"* and *"makes a valuable contribution"* on acquisitions. He represented RBS on the MBO of Milbury Community, and also advised on the acquisition by Kappa Packaging of AssiDomän. Singled out by clients as *"good to have on one's side"* **Adam Freeman** (see p.663) advised CIBC World Markets on the £220 million buyout of Dignity Caring Funeral Services.

Team highlights include the London Underground financing, acquisition financings for Bank of Scotland (£400 million) and CIBC (£800 million), and advising the latter together with its co-arrangers Allied Irish Bank and Bank of Ireland in the €27 million LBO of BWG Group. Further afield, the team has been heavily involved in major projects such as Rome Airport. **Clients** EIB; Deutsche Bank; CSFB; Crédit Agricole Indosuez; CIBC; DKW; Bank of Scotland; Banque Indosuez; Barclays; Crédit Lyonnais; ING; Lloyds TSB; Standard Chartered.

SHEARMAN & STERLING (see firm details p.1129) Considered by premier finance houses to be *"number one in the City"* for cross-border high-yield debt and leveraged finance, the team also attracts strong market endorsement for its expertise on complex US tax issues and telecoms-related project finance work. Competitors acknowledge its *"powerful connections"* in the US market, also rating its *"significant presence in Germany."* Clients commend its *"outstanding securitisations and capital markets expertise"* while noting that it outsources heavily in related areas such as tax, environment and property on the domestic front. Clients distinguish *"industrious technician"* **Anthony Ward** who retains his *"superb"* reputation in high-yield acquisition finance. He heads a team of *"top-calibre lawyers"* that acted for Merrill Lynch and CIBC as underwriters of the £1.45 billion senior and high-yield bridge

Top Ten Loans (June 2001 to June 2002)

	Borrower	Lawyers to Borrower	Mandated Arranger	Lawyers to Lead Arrangers	Value (millions)	Loan Type
1	Network Rail	Linklaters	Barclays, Citibank NA, Dresdner Kleinwort Wasserstein, HSBC, Merrill Lynch International Ltd, Royal Bank of Canada, Royal Bank of Scotland plc, WestLB, UBS Warburg	Allen & Overy	£9,000.000	Term Loan
2	Vodafone AirTouch plc	In-house team	UBS Warburg, ABN-AMRO Bank NV, Banca di Roma SpA, Banc of America Securities Ltd, Bank of New York, Bank of Tokyo-Mitsubishi Ltd, Barclays, Bayerische Landesbank, BNP Paribas, Citibank NA, Commerzbank AG, Deutsche Bank AG, Fuji Bank Ltd, HSBC, ING Barings, IntesaBci SpA, Lehman Brothers International, Lloyds TSB Capital Markets, National Australia Bank Ltd, Royal Bank of Scotland plc, Sumitomo Mitsui Banking Corp, Toronto-Dominion Bank, WestLB	Allen & Overy	$13,275.000	Revolving Credit
3	France Telecom	N/a	ABN-AMRO Bank NV, Bank of Tokyo-Mitsubishi Ltd, Barclays, BNP Paribas, Citibank NA, Credit Agricole Indosuez, Credit Lyonnais SA, Credit Suisse First Boston, Deutsche Bank AG, Dresdner Kleinwort Wasserstein, HSBC, ING Barings, JP Morgan plc, Mizuho, Royal Bank of Scotland plc, SG, Sumitomo Mitsui Banking Corp, WestLB	Clifford Chance	$15,000.000	Revolving Credit
4	Vodafone AirTouch plc	In-house team	Bank of America, Bank of Tokyo-Mitsubishi Ltd, Barclays, BayernLB, BNP Paribas, Citibank NA, Commerzbank AG, Deutsche Bank AG, HSBC, ING Barings, JP Morgan plc, Landesbank Schleswig-Holstein Girozentrale, Lehman Brothers International, Lloyds TSB Capital Markets, Mizuho, National Australia Bank Ltd, Nomura International plc, Sumitomo Mitsui Banking Corp, Royal Bank of Scotland plc, Toronto-Dominion Bank, UBS Warburg, WestLB	Allen & Overy	$10650.000	Revolving Credit
5	British Telecommunications plc (BT)	Linklaters	ABN-AMRO Bank NV, Bank of Tokyo-Mitsubishi Ltd, Barclays, BayernLB, Citibank NA, Deutsche Bank AG, HSBC, Lloyds TSB Bank plc, Industrial Bank of Japan Ltd, Royal Bank of Scotland plc, SG	Clifford Chance	£5,500.000	Revolving Credit
6	SOFTEL	N/a	JP Morgan plc, Mediobanca SpA	Allen & Overy	€8,000.000	Revolving Credit
7	DaimlerChrysler AG	N/a	Deutsche Bank AG, JP Morgan plc	In-house team	$7,000.000	Revolving Credit
8	Imperial Tobacco	Allen & Overy	ABN-AMRO Bank NV, BNP Paribas, Deutsche Bank AG, JP Morgan plc, Morgan Stanley Dean Witter, Royal Bank of Scotland plc	Clifford Chance	$6615.878	Revolving Credit
9	Railtrack plc	N/a	Barclays, Dresdner Kleinwort Wasserstein, Merrill Lynch International, Royal Bank of Scotland plc	Allen & Overy	£4,400.000	Revolving Credit
10	BAe Systems plc	N/a	Dresdner Kleinwort Wasserstein, JP Morgan plc	Linklaters	$6,100.000	Term Loan

Source: Dealogic

BANKING & FINANCE ■ LONDON

financing of the acquisition of Yell by Hicks, Muse Tate & Furst and Apax Partners, and subsequently acted on the high-yield bond issue. The team also acted for France Telecom in its €15 billion loan facilities arranged to refinance facilities for the acquisition of Orange. For Barclays Capital and Citibank (joint bookrunners), Abu Dhabi Investment, KfW, Bank of Tokyo-Mitsubishi and RBS, it assisted in the $1.6 billion financing of the Shuweihat Independent Water and Power project in Abu Dhabi. **Clients** Morgan Stanley; Merrill Lynch; Deutsche Bank; UBS Warburg; Goldman Sachs; Bear Stearns; Barclays Bank; BNP Paribas; Société Générale; RBS; ABN AMRO; CIBC; Citigroup.

SLAUGHTER AND MAY (see firm details p.1140) "*Prime borrowers' counsel*" with its "*supreme corporate client base,*" competitors declare that the team "*commands respect by virtue of its undoubted quality.*" Observers highlighted its activities in the eurobonds market and strengthened stance with lead arrangers following the JPMorgan/Chase merger. Endorsing the team as "*a strong contender*" in conflict situations, several clients rated "*amazingly calm yet dogged*" **Andrew Balfour** (see p.104) as their "*top choice*" for his championing of 'plain English' drafting. He advised on several revolving loan facilities that included Corus Group and Corus UK (€2.4 billion), Eureko (€1.5 billion) and Telecom Italia (€8 billion). Clients also commend "*user-friendly*" **Richard Slater** (see p.108), who advised JPMorgan as arranger of syndicated loan facilities (€1.7 billion) for Sampo of Finland for its acquisition of Storebrand of Norway. The team advised on syndicated loans to refinance existing debt for Charter (£175 million) and Slovnaft ($165 million), and represented Prudential Banking in the renewal of the 364-day tranche of its £1.1 billion loan facility. **Clients** AIG; Goldman Sachs; Lehman Brothers; JPMorgan; Société Générale; Emap; Telecom Italia; South African Reserve Board and the Republic of South Africa; Corus Group.

DENTON WILDE SAPTE (see firm details p.935) Interviewees commended this "*well-developed finance practice*" as "*a solid player with a great track record*" in mid-market asset, property and trade finance, restructuring, project finance, social housing and leveraged insolvency work. Despite having lost some of its key players, the team still gains considerable respect in the market for its practitioners and the "*large throughput of work that flows from its long client list.*" Clients list the team's strengths as being "*good value for money, commercial, able to meet tight deadlines and extremely pleasant to work with.*" The team represented a syndicate of banks led by Crédit Lyonnais on the $1.3 billion export credit supported financing of 27 new Airbus aircraft for LanChile, and advised on a $3 billion secured limited recourse and transferable term loan programme in Asia for Fleet National Bank in Singapore. Japan Bank for International Co-operation instructed the firm on a $3 billion oil pre-export facility provided through a special purpose company to a finance company of National Iranian Company. **Clients** Morgan Stanley; GE Capital; Nokia; Fleet National Bank; RBS; DKW; Citibank; Standard Bank; Abbey National Treasury Services; Bayerische Landesbank; WestLB.

HERBERT SMITH (see firm details p.992) Market sources concur that the team is "*enhancing its reputation*" by leveraging work off its corporate practice, as exemplified by its inclusion on the panels of Lloyds TSB and RBS. Typically seen acting for borrowers and large property companies such as Greycoat, the team is respected for its advice on the securitisation aspects of the Eurotunnel project. Clients commend the group's capability on documentation aspects and heavy transactional structuring issues. Clients report that property finance partner **Peter Long** (see p.107) is "*focused on problem-solving, clued-up about what is required, and delivers.*" He advised on several bilateral property financings with Barclays as lender, and acted on the financing of Kruidvat Beheer's acquisition of Superdrug from Kingfisher involving facilities of €560 million. The finance team advised the Brunner Mond Bondholder Committee on the restructuring of soda ash producer Brunner Mond Group's £50 million and $125 million high-yield bonds, and assisted Kajima Cambridge on the successful PFI project for serviced accommodation at the Department for Environment, Food & Rural Affairs (DEFRA). Norwich Union Mortgage Finance instructed the firm in the joint provision of £320 million financing with Bayerische Landesbank for the acquisition of a property portfolio by an offshore vehicle from Royal London. The team advised BNP Paribas as sole lead arranger, bookrunner, facility agent and technical bank on $100 million secured financings for Addax Petroleum's Nigerian oil and gas interests. **Clients** Bank of Scotland; JPMorgan Chase; Time Warner; Barclays Bank; Norwich Union; Greycoat; First Choice; Stagecoach; Eurotunnel; BSkyB.

WHITE & CASE (see firm details p.1185) Industry players are seeing more of the team that is perceived to be "*building on its formidable US reputation*" and "*gaining profile on the back of some good deals,*" most notably for Deutsche Bank. Against the perception that there is room to increase its critical mass, some opine that it is "*acquiring the right people and moving in the right direction.*" The team gains widespread commendation for "*holding its own in prime-quality project finance*" with a "*diverse geographical coverage*" that includes Central and Eastern Europe. Deemed a "*solid alternative*" on conflicts, clients "*take comfort in its capable individuals and global reputation.*" Head of finance **Maurice Allen** (see p.103) still eclipses his colleagues' profiles with his "*effective marketing*" and "*pleasant, consensual*" approach. He acted for Barclays Capital, DKW and Industrial Bank of Japan on a $900 million receivables financing in Saudi Arabia. The team assisted Chase and Morgan Stanley on the provision of a £1.3 billion working capital facility and a £2.5 billion senior facility to ntl for the purchase of the residential cable business of Cable & Wireless. It acted for BNP Paribas as arranger and underwriter of a £250 million term loan facility for Euronext UK to finance its acquisition of LIFFE, one of the world's leading derivatives exchanges. **Clients** ABN AMRO; BNP Paribas; Barclays Capital; CSFB; Deutsche Bank; DKW; Morgan Stanley; Industrial Bank of Japan; WestLB.

BERWIN LEIGHTON PAISNER (see firm details p.866) The firm continues to attract market recognition that primarily attaches to its "*sophisticated and highly effective*" property finance and PFI work. The property-driven practice tends to eclipse its general banking capacity, which can be demonstrated by its representation of both borrowers and lenders, and formal appointments to the panels of RBS, Barclays and National Australian Bank for work that includes refinancing and securitisation work. Clients attest that it "*comes through every time*" with an "*excellent degree of service and professionalism.*" Property finance expert **Mark Waghorn** (see p.109) features highly within the team of "*fine practitioners.*" It advised RBS on several major financings, which included the principal financing of 12 hotels as part of the acquisition of Le Méridien Hotels by Nomura International's Principal Finance Group for a total consideration of £1.9 billion, and an £821.6 million National Car Parks (NCP) buy-out. The team also advised RBS International on the £220 million acquisition of 280 Bishopsgate. **Clients** RBS; Barclays; Abbey National Treasury Services; Société Générale; Rheinhyp Rheinische Hypothekenbank; Marylebone Warwick Balfour Group; Millennium Commission; Haslemere Estates.

CMS CAMERON MCKENNA (see firm details p.914) Its competitors respect the team that "*delivers a good product*" in projects and PFI work. It boasts niche expertise in energy and rail sector work that flows naturally from the firm's core client base, handling equity and outsourcing work for banks. Despite some erosion of its long-standing links with Lloyds TSB, the team still garners recognition for its "*strong client depth overall.*" Commending the "*pleasant, cohesive team atmosphere,*" clients report that it is "*efficient, good value and does extremely well on sticky issues.*" They single out "*responsive*" **John Naccarato** (see p.107), who can "*pick out the key issues on a transaction*" and "*be relied upon to carry the file himself.*" He acted for Enterprise Inns in negotiating a £73 million term and revolving facility for three acquisitions of pub estates from Scottish & Newcastle,

LONDON — BANKING & FINANCE

Wolverhampton & Dudley and Morgan Grenfell. The team advised on the pioneering public-to-private deal for the UK's National Air Traffic Services, and has assisted the Department for Transport Local Government and the Regions (DTLR) on the Railway Administration of Railtrack. **Clients** DTLR ; Lloyds TSB; RBS; National Australia Bank; First Union.

DLA Market sources identify the team as steady players leveraging uniquely and successfully off its regional presence. The team is well-versed in domestic acquisition finance , and the debt side of private equity stands out here.

SIMMONS & SIMMONS (see firm details p.1136) Eschewing corporate 'plain vanilla' work, the team (headed by Harvey Chalmers) boasts "*considerable expertise*" in capital markets, securitisation and structured finance. It continues to expand its transactional focus and integration across Europe via its network, and is increasing its volume of work with a cross-border element. Key matters in this regard include acting for the EIB on a €740 million loan to Wind Telecomunicazioni, a joint venture between Italy's Enel and France Telecom, as part of a €5.5 billion refinancing. The team also advised the Gallaher Group in the €2 billion and £900 million revolving credit facilities for its £1.14 billion acquisition of Austria Tabak, and represented Pacific Century CyberWorks (PCCW) on the refinancing of its US$12 billion bridge facility, which included a bond issue and joint venture funded in US and Hong Kong dollars. **Clients** Barclays Bank/Barclays Capital; EIB; Gallaher; Interbanca; Interbrew; Pacific Century CyberWorks; Société Générale.

BAKER & MCKENZIE (see firm details p.855) Adjudged by interviewees to have "*a good all-round presence internationally,*" it represents a solid corporate borrower base of clients across a diverse global playing field. Its key focus remains in multi-jurisdictional acquisition and asset finance, derivatives and capital markets. Clients opine that the team is "*excellent in structuring work,*" producing "*consistently high-quality documentation across many jurisdictions.*" One reported that it "*hones in on complex problems and adds good value.*" Its "*huge experience and great know-how from handling numerous deals*" enables the team to "*distinguish market practice boundaries and find the right balance.*" Advising with 22 other offices worldwide, the team, led by Christopher Hogan, acted for Allianz Capital Partners in the joint acquisition with Goldman Sachs of Aventis' interest in Messer Griesheim. It also acted for France Telecom in a €400 million structured financing for its joint acquisition of a stakeholding in TPSA, a Polish telecoms company. Vendor financiers have instructed the firm in 3G financings throughout several European jurisdictions, totalling over £3.5 billion. **Clients** Apax; Hewlett-Packard; Industrial Bank of Japan; Standard Bank London; Allianz Capital Partners; France Telecom; Nortel Networks.

MACFARLANES (see firm details p.1047) Its competitors are impressed by the team's middle-market finance expertise across the structured finance, acquisition, property and trade sectors. It is often seen handling work primarily for borrowers within the context of the firm's formidable private equity practice. Clients commend the "*slightly stretched but experienced and well-focused*" team that is led by "*likeable*" **Mark Furman** who is "*knowledgeable*" on acquisition finance matters. He advised Alchemy on the public-to-private bids for Novara and Anglian Windows, and acted on the private acquisition of Totectors. The team advised Pernod Ricard on its $5 billion facilities for its joint bid with Diageo for Seagram's spirits and wines business. It also represented RBS Leveraged Finance on its acquisition facilities for the buyouts of The Mill and Hillarys Blinds, and advised Royal Bank Private Equity on the buyout of Queensborough and the public-to-private bids for Expamet and Britax International. **Clients** RBS; 3i; Alchemy; Bank of Scotland; Pernod Ricard; WestLB; Royal Bank Private Equity; GSC Partners Europe.

TRAVERS SMITH BRAITHWAITE (see firm details p.1166) Observed by market sources to have been "*doing some pretty good deals*" of late, the team continues to "*successfully leverage*" work that includes acquisition and property finance off its corporate and funds client base. Clients recommend the team's "*service quality, speed and attention to detail*" on inter-lender documentation and securities facilities documentation for commercial investment and development work. "*Reasonable*" property finance partner **Neil Murray** (see p.107) heads a "*user-friendly*" team of strong partners and assistants, who all possess a "*good base of technical knowledge.*" He advised RBS on bilateral and syndicated secured property finance loan facilities including the Arts Hotel project, and assisted RBS International on loan facilities to offshore property investment vehicles. The team has advised ntl in a £200 million term facility made available to GE Capital, and vendor financing made available by Export Development Corporation and Cisco to ntl Investment Holdings. **Clients** Allgemeine Hypothekenbank Rheinboden; Bank of Scotland; Berlin-Hannoversche Hypothekenbank; Export Finance & Insurance Corporation of Australia; Fortis; NM Rothschild & Sons; RBS; RBS International.

GOULDENS (see firm details p.976) Best known for its borrower-led practice in property finance, the team operates within the context of its "*sterling corporate practice.*" Tom Budd leads the team with "*high-profile individuals*" that focuses on complex work, such as acting for Pillar Property and The Hercules Unit Trust in a £375 million credit facility funded through an innovative commercial paper structure allowing the borrower access to the CP market, arranged by HVB Real Estate Capital. It also acted for Ashtenne Holdings and The Ashtenne Industrial Fund on a £180 million loan facility for the acquisition of properties. **Clients** Pillar Property; Ashtenne Holdings; Standard Bank London; Arlington Securities; The Hercules Unit Trust; Lloyds TSB Commercial Finance; Mothercare; Oversea-Chinese Banking Corporation; HypoVereinsbank; City of London Office Unit Trust.

LATHAM & WATKINS (see firm details p.1030) Observers feel that the team is "*making an impact*" as a "*one-stop shop*" for US high-yield bond and bank debt restructuring. Its competitors commend the "*well-run outfit*" for its "*excellent knowledge and good people,*" while clients express awareness that it is "*making a strong push.*" Characterised as having an "*off-the-wall*" style, **James Chesterman** (see p.104) continues to enjoy a strong market reputation in acting for lenders in telecoms financings. **Clients** Bank of America; CSFB; Deutsche Bank; ING Capital.

SJ BERWIN (see firm details p.867) Interviewees perceive that the team is "*set to make quite an impact*" within its remit of property and structured finance for corporate and fund clients. Clients rate its expertise on loan recovery and anti-trust law aspects. "*Thorough and reliable*" **Paul Diss** (see p.105) acted for Standard Bank London and others on a €118 million facility for the acquisition of a publicly listed Czech telecoms company. It also advised on a £94 million facility provided by Bayerische Landesbank for the acquisition of a mid-town landmark building, and acted for Gullane Entertainment on the £85 million financing for the acquisition of Guinness World Records. **Clients** AMP Group; HBOS; RBS; Standard Bank London; Standard Chartered Bank; Banco Santander Central Hispano; Lloyds TSB; Dresdner Kleinwort Benson; Deutsche Hypothekenbank; British Land; BNP; Société Générale.

TAYLOR WESSING (see firm details p.1156) Commended by interviewees as "*solid property finance specialists,*" the team is perceived to have been making "*big efforts in the sector*" for key clients such as Anglo Irish Bank. It is also widening its focus to encompass projects and overseas work, primarily in China. Practitioners "*like the way it handles the law,*" distinguishing **Rodney Dukes** (see p.105) as the best-known personality within the finance projects group. He advised BHF-Bank as underwriters of a £140 million facility for the development finance of a new Marriott hotel and residential units in Docklands. He and the team represented Bank of Scotland and RBS on their agreement to fund Crown Dilmun in connection with Harrods

BANKING & FINANCE ■ LONDON/THE SOUTH & SOUTH WEST

depository in a £72 million club deal. It also advised GMAC on a pilot scheme to test a US-styled 'through lending' structure for the UK mortgage market. **Clients** Anglo Irish Bank; Bank of Scotland; BHF-Bank; GMAC; Halifax.

WATSON, FARLEY & WILLIAMS (see firm details p.1181) Its competitors acknowledged that the team's *"extremely high-quality"* asset finance practice, particularly in shipping, trade and aircraft matters, ensures a respectable market profile. The team, led by Michael Kenny, advised Petroleum Geo-Services on the securitisation of a portion of its multi-client seismic data library. It also advised Crédit Lyonnais on a $250 million syndicated loan for Coflexip. As a testament to its broader reach, the team represented Bluewater on a $600 million secured revolving credit facility for general corporate and project finance purposes. **Clients** BG Bank; JPMorgan Chase; Citibank; Close Brothers; Fortis; HBOS; Nordea; RBS; Société Générale; Westdeutsche Landesbank Girozentrale.

DICKSON MINTO WS (see firm details p.938) Its competitors *"come across the team a lot,"* typically acting for Scottish banks or private equity houses on leveraged structures. Clients *"recognise its high-quality individuals with well-honed skills in the LBO market."* The team (led by Michael Barron) *"does an outstanding job."* The team advised RBS in its financing package for the £180 million secondary buyout of Wightlink from Cinven, and advised Leisure Link Holdings on the financing of its £230 million purchase of the Leisure Link group of companies by way of a secondary buyout, with debt finance provided by NIB Capital Bank. BC Partners instructed the team in its financing of the €1.1 billion LBO of Galbani, involving European cross-border aspects. **Clients** BC Partners; Henderson Private Capital; Charterhouse Development Capital.

EVERSHEDS (see firm details p.949) Leading practitioners credit the team as having *"broken into transactional work in a serious way"* by employing a *"successful strategy."* Led by Philip Perrotta, the team handled a range of key matters that include advising Capita IRG on an issue of depositary interests listed on AIM and settled through Crest, and advising Al Rajhi Investment on several leasing matters. **Clients** HSBC; Lombard Corporate Finance; Jarvis.

THEODORE GODDARD (see firm details p.1158) The team gains market commendation for its *"first-class"* general and structured property finance work, representing lenders such as RBS. It also handles financing matters in a range of other sectors that include film receivables. Clients approve its *"lateral-thinking, technical advice,"* identifying **Dave Wilson** (see p.109) as an *"efficient lawyer who has his head screwed on and gets the deal done."* He acted for RBS as arranger and underwriter of a £215 million facility for the London & Regional Group to assist in its building interest acquisition from JPMorgan Chase, and the refinancing of other property. The team advised Bayerische Landesbank on the £270 million financing provided to the purchaser of Woolgate Exchange, and advised Abbey National Treasury Services in the £156 million facility provided to the purchaser of a prime freehold site in central London for RBS' new headquarters. **Clients** Abbey National Treasury Services; Anglo Irish; Bank Austria; Burdale Financial; The Law Debenture Trust; RBS.

OTHER NOTABLE PRACTITIONERS Clients rate the *"realistic"* approach of property finance expert **Debbie Carslaw** who *"will help achieve a practical compromise."* She has recently joined Sidley Austin Brown & Wood from Denton Wilde Sapte.

THE SOUTH & SOUTH WEST

BANKING & FINANCE
■ THE SOUTH & SOUTH WEST

1. **Burges Salmon** Bristol
   Osborne Clarke Bristol
2. **Bond Pearce** Bristol, Southampton
3. **CMS Cameron McKenna** Bristol
4. **Blake Lapthorn** Southampton

LEADING INDIVIDUALS
1. **FORBES** Sandra Burges Salmon
   JEFFRIES Graham Bond Pearce
   KINSEY Julian Bond Pearce
2. **AL-NUAIMI** Omar Osborne Clarke
   LEEMING Richard Burges Salmon
3. **CROSS** Jeremy Osborne Clarke
   WILTSHIRE Peter CMS Cameron McKenna

This book is the product of 6,582 1/2 hour interviews. See p.7 for BMRB audit.
Within each band, firms are listed alphabetically. See individuals' profiles p.103

BURGES SALMON (see firm details p.894) Market sources endorse the team's *"robust"* general banking capability in structured, property and asset finance, particularly in the rail sector. Its competitors describe it as *"sensible, commercial and pleasant to deal with,"* while clients report that it is *"practical at finding solutions."* Clients commend City-trained team leader **Sandra Forbes** (see p.105) as one *"often aware of a problem in advance"* because she *"knows the business inside out."* She advised FirstGroup on new bilateral facilities (aggregate value exceeding £200 million), and on banking aspects of its £300 million bond. She is ably assisted by *"affable, pragmatic"* **Richard Leeming** (see p.107), who advised Nationwide Syndications in its £250 million of participations in syndicated property finance facilities. The team advised AIB Capital Markets on a £25 million facility to an entertainment company. **Clients** AIB Capital Markets; Bank of Scotland; FirstGroup; HSBC; Lloyds TSB; Nationwide.

OSBORNE CLARKE (see firm details p.1090) The consensus among interviewees was that the practice enjoys the *"highest market profile"* in the region for its corporate banking expertise. Clients are impressed by its *"dedicated"* standards of teamwork, with one commenting: *"I can go straight through to completion with the assistants."* Clients vouch that **Omar Al-Nuaimi** gives them *"a degree of confidence,"* while his peers attest to his *"pragmatic"* approach to dealdoing. He acted for Bank of Scotland in Tribal Group's acquisition of GWT Group (value £6 million), and advised Lloyds TSB on Charterhouse's £8.3 million acquisition of the issued share capital of HS Publishing. Despite a lower profile on account of his involvement in Californian asset finance work, **Jeremy Cross** attracts market recommendation as an *"extremely competent technician."* He acted for Bank of Scotland in a £3.5 million MBO of the CPG Group, and advised RBS jointly with the London office on the £35 million acquisition of Reylon Group by Steinhoff. The team advised Bank of Scotland on its provision of an integrated acquisition and asset finance package to plant and rental group Hydrex. **Clients** Bank of Scotland; Barclays; Fortis Bank; GATX Financial; HSBC; Lloyds TSB; RBS.

BOND PEARCE (see firm details p.879) The team is *"making a good job of it"* in Bristol, according to industry players, who opine that *"what they do, they do extremely well."* Banks perceive it as *"a great alternative"* to the established players for the *"red carpet treatment."* The team has benefited from its appointments to national panels of Bank of Scotland for client banking work, and to Barclays Bank for acquisition finance and corporate lending work. Clients report that Bristol-based **Julian Kinsey** (see p.106) delivers an *"excellent service"* on acquisition and structured finance matters, while **Graham Jeffries** (see p.106) in Southampton impresses his peers with his knowledge of *"fine technical detail."* The Bristol team acted for Barclays on its financing of a high-profile MBO of A-Gas and other acquisition finance transactions. It also acted for RBS on its provision of £13 million development finance facilities to Deeley Freed Group for the redevelopment of its flagship site in central Bristol. The Southampton team acted for Bank of Scotland on various

WALES/ MIDLANDS ■ BANKING & FINANCE

acquisition finance and corporate banking transactions, including the acquisition of Stanrew Electronics and Jefco Services. **Clients** Bank of Scotland; Fortis; Lloyds TSB; RBS; Barclays.

CMS CAMERON MCKENNA (see firm details p.1090) Market sources deem that the firm is thriving within its unique placing in the local market. Its competitors perceive its main strength as "*virtually acting as in-house counsel*" to Lloyds TSB on litigation and recovery matters, which comprise the bulk of its workload. The team also handles Bristol-based general commercial and domestic transactional work with support from the London office. **Peter Wiltshire** (see p.109) heads a team that competitors find "*pragmatic and easy to deal with*," and he also gains strong recognition for his insolvency expertise. Following its success in the Court of Appeal, the team was also successful in taking the high-profile Shanning case to the House of Lords. **Clients** AIB; Lloyds TSB; RBS/NatWest.

BLAKE LAPTHORN (see firm details p.877) Some interviewees opined that the team, led by Kathryn Shimmin, has "*sewn up banking in Southampton.*" Firms perceived it as an active presence in corporate-driven banking work. The team acted for Bank of Scotland as lender in a £49 million term debt refinancing, and advised on its £12.5 million term debt facility to Basepoint for the construction of enterprise centres and refinancing of existing property portfolio. It also advised the borrower in a £23 million term debt facility for the MBI of ICS Industrial Cooling Systems. **Clients** Bank of Scotland; HSBC; RBS/NatWest; Lloyds TSB; Capital Bank.

WALES

BANKING & FINANCE
■ WALES

1. **Eversheds** Cardiff
2. **Edwards Geldard** Cardiff
3. **Morgan Cole** Cardiff

LEADING INDIVIDUALS
1. **VAUGHAN Philip** Eversheds
2. **MORGAN Meryl** Morgan Cole

This book is the product of 6,582 1/2 hour interviews. See p.7 for BMRB audit.
Within each band, firms are listed alphabetically. See individuals' profiles p.103

EVERSHEDS (see firm details p.949) "*Indisputably*" distinguished as a "*pure banking outfit,*" interviewees rate it as the team with "*the greatest resource and quality of delivery*" in the region. It handles a broad range of banking work from high-volume consumer finance matters such as credit card agency debt collection, to complex project financings and PFI. Its diverse client base includes blue-chip financial institutions, VCs and housing associations. **Philip Vaughan** (see p.109) continues to garner market plaudits as the region's leading banking lawyer in company, commercial and insolvency-related banking matters. Noted by his peers for his "*excellent draughting technique,*" he advised Bank of Scotland on the restructuring of the Bank of Wales, involving transfer of loans and deposits exceeding £600 million. He also advised Investec Bank on its provision of facilities to a Guernsey-based investment company ($105 million) and an offshore investment company ($200 million). The team also advised the Welsh Development Agency on a project for the establishment of a new company to utilise European Objective One funding and putting in place financing arrangements with Barclays Bank. **Clients** Bank of Scotland; Lloyds TSB; ABN AMRO; Legal & General; Barclays; Investec Bank; Principality Building Society; Deutsche Hypo Bank.

EDWARDS GELDARD (see firm details p.944) "*Well respected*" by local clearing banks, the team, led by Karl Baranski, handles a general mix of corporate, acquisition finance and property work. Clients can rely on the team to provide a "*personable, responsive, detailed service,*" while its competitors report on its "*professional*" approach in transactions. The team acted for several clearing banks on their loan provisions for infrastructure and environmental development, sporting facilities development, and for a major rugby football club. It also advised on several privately funded partnership film deals backed by bank guarantees. **Clients** Barclays; RBS/NatWest; Bank of Wales; HSBC; Bank of Scotland.

MORGAN COLE (see firm details p.1075) "*A good quality outfit,*" according to clients, who appreciate the team's ability to deliver "*sound, commercial judgement*" on a broad range of work. The team handles secured lending work that covers projects and PFI, working capital, multicurrency syndicated loan facilities and asset finance. Consumer Credit Act lending is also a feature of the workload. Clients comprise an even mix of lenders and borrowers, including housing associations, finance companies, and public and private corporations. "*Unassuming*" **Meryl Morgan** is commended as a "*sound pair of hands*" on banking finance matters. The team acted for Bank of Wales in a range of secured lending transactions including facilities of £14.75 million for a commercial retail park development. It continues to advise on loan and consumer credit-related matters for Swansea Building Society, and the Finance Wales Investments loan fund for Welsh SMEs (a subsidiary of the Welsh Development Agency). **Clients** HSBC; RBS; Bank of Wales; Finance Wales Investments; Julian Hodge Bank; Principality Building Society; Swansea Building Society.

MIDLANDS

PINSENT CURTIS BIDDLE (see firm details p.1102) The team garners widespread plaudits for the "*excellent quality*" attained by its broad banking practice. Competitors observe that it typically "*bags the bigger transactions*" within the region's acquisition finance sector. They applaud the team's "*refreshing*" approach, singling out **Stephen Miles** (see p.107) as a "*deal-focused, solutions-driven*" practitioner who "*sees things quickly resolved.*" He advised IMI on the issue of $100 million guaranteed unsecured notes to PRICOA, and advised HSBC and Allied Irish Bank on their £73.5 million joint funding of The BSS Group. Her peers commend "*promising and technically gifted*" Alice Broadfield (see p.104), who has joined from Eversheds, as "*hands-on and extremely good to deal with.*" Patrick Twist is also on hand to provide advice on PFI financings. The team also advised IM Properties on the £38.5 million financing by Nationwide Building Society of a mixed portfolio of properties. **Clients** HSBC; IMI; RBS; Barclays; Bank of Scotland; Doncasters; IM Properties.

EVERSHEDS (see firm details p.949) "*Still making good strides*" despite some defections, the team has maintained its image as one that "*the banks want to use.*" In addition to advising on top-level acquisition finance work, the Birmingham office has expertise in asset finance and invoice discounting. Peers admire "*feisty*" **Pat Johnstone** (see p.106) as an "*excellent, no-nonsense technician.*" She advised MGR Capital on the negotiation of £320 million funding from HBOS for the acquisition of finance leases from Rover Financial Services, and advised Lloyds TSB on its provision of £20 million facilities for Powerhouse Retail's acquisition of ScottishPower's retail business. Nottingham's property finance focus remains undiminished. "*Pleasant and practical,*" **Stephen Kitts** (see p.240) "*gets the deal sorted,*" according to his clients. He acted for RBS in the public company takeover by Cosalt of SEET (£20 million facilities) and in

www.ChambersandPartners.com 97

BANKING & FINANCE ■ MIDLANDS

BANKING & FINANCE
■ MIDLANDS

1. **Pinsent Curtis Biddle** Birmingham
2. **Eversheds** Birmingham, Nottingham
3. **Wragge & Co** Birmingham
4. **DLA** Birmingham
   Gateley Wareing Birmingham
   Martineau Johnson Birmingham
5. **Browne Jacobson** Nottingham
6. **Hammond Suddards Edge** Birmingham

LEADING INDIVIDUALS

1. **BAKER Ian** Martineau Johnson
   JOHNSTONE Pat Eversheds
   MADDEN Andrew Gateley Wareing
   MILES Stephen Pinsent Curtis Biddle
   PALLETT Julian Wragge & Co
2. **BROADFIELD Alice** Pinsent Curtis Biddle
   WOOLCOCK Brian DLA
3. **ALLTON Ashley** Hammond Suddards Edge
   ALTON Philip Gateley Wareing
   BRIERLEY Chris Wragge & Co
   KITTS Stephen Eversheds
   MURRAY Duncan Browne Jacobson
   UP AND COMING
   WALKER Gary Wragge & Co

This book is the product of 6,582 1/2 hour interviews. See p.7 for BMRB audit.
Within each band, firms are listed alphabetically. See individuals' profiles p.103

---

the £20 million buyout of New Pimpernel by 3i. The team advised amelca on a £9.6 million development funding facility from Bank of Scotland for a dairy plant, and represented Fortis Bank in a £10 million loan facility to Brantano UK for warehouse acquisition and development. **Clients** RBS/NatWest; Bank of Scotland; Fortis; HSBC; Lloyds TSB; Barclays.

WRAGGE & CO (see firm details p.1197) Still overwhelmingly viewed as "*a powerful presence*" on the corporate and private equity side of its banking practice, the team's profile in representing lenders remains somewhat obscured. It does, however, enjoy a "*superb reputation*" among its competitors for property finance and recovery-related work. His peers commend "*top-notch analyst*" **Julian Pallett**, who "*gets issues sorted rapidly with minimum fuss*." He acted for Hampshire Centre LP on its £108 million maximum borrowing from a syndicate of banks for a property development in Bournemouth. He also acted for Royal Bank Private Equity on the buyout of Vickers Turbine Components (and other groups) involving facilities of £53 million senior debt, £30 million junior debt and £21 million mezzanine from Bank of Scotland. Clients also singled out **Chris Brierley** and **Gary Walker** as "*capable technicians*." The team acted for RBS on the provision of a £37 million secured loan facility to IM Properties (RBS) for the refinancing of a commercial property portfolio. It also acted for Hypothekenbank on refinancings for Essen totalling £110 million. **Clients** Chelsea Building Society; HSBC; Lloyds TSB; Skipton Building Society; West Bromwich Building Society; Castlemore Securities.

DLA It is viewed by market sources as a force in Birmingham, bolstered also by its London office. The team acts for lenders in the acquisition finance market. Property finance specialist **Brian Woolcock** was warmly commended by clients for his effort and enthusiasm. **Clients** Bank of Scotland; RBS; Barclays; GM AC; Fortis.

GATELEY WAREING (see firm details p.967) Viewed by its competitors as "*sterling dealdoers*" in mid-market work, the team acts for a spread of local lenders within the context of its focus on corporate transactions. Sources credit the team's "*technically strong, hands-on*" leader **Andrew Madden** for having developed its acquisition finance practice "*particularly well.*" He acted for Barclays Bank providing acquisition finance facilities totalling £16 million to Rainbow Corporatewear. Benefiting from the addition of "*quality practitioner*" **Philip Alton** from Garretts, the team advised Bank of Scotland on providing acquisition finance and other facilities to Pertemps Group, and to United Brands for £8 million worth of US acquisitions. It also advised Lloyds TSB and its commercial finance arm on the £7 million MBO of Silvertown Holdings. **Clients** Bank of Scotland; HSBC; Barclays; Lloyds TSB.

MARTINEAU JOHNSON (see firm details p.1056) Enjoying an increasing profile, the team garners impressive plaudits for its quality and "*efficient client service.*" Typical work includes medium-sized property and acquisition finance deals and invoice discounting. The team also advises on facilities, letters of credit, swaps and other documentation issues.

At the "*centre of the team,*" **Ian Baker** (see p.455) gains market respect as a "*good all-round banking lawyer.*" His peers report that he is "*on the ball and doesn't indulge in point-scoring.*" As one client explained: "*He can advise in an instant and makes it easy for you to take the advice.*" He advised Lloyds TSB on providing facilities of €41.6 million to a Dutch company for the development of a shopping centre in Holland, that featured cross-border work in Holland, Luxembourg and the US. The team advised RBS on providing facilities to the Welsh Industrial Partnership of up to £32 million for the development of industrial properties in Wales. **Clients** Lloyds TSB Bank; RBS; Bank of Scotland; Fortis; HSBC; Handelsbanken; Allied Irish Bank; Nationwide; Bank of Ireland.

BROWNE JACOBSON (see firm details p.891) "*Strong in the East,*" the team is said to provide "*high-quality advice*" on syndicated loans and securities work. Representing an even mix of client lenders and borrowers, its practice covers acquisition and development finance. Housing and education sector and charities on a national and international basis are all sources of instruction. His peers commend Nottingham-based **Duncan Murray** (see p.107) as "*technically sound and commercial.*" He acted for RBS on a £23 million development financing of a limited company, and advised NatWest on a £6 million acquisition of French group SEFAC. The team advised RBS and Dresdner Bank on £60 million funding and refinancing of Menzies Hotels. It also advised The Governor and Company of Bank of Scotland on the provision of acquisition finance for the MBO of SER Systems. **Clients** RBS; HSBC; Fortis.

HAMMOND SUDDARDS EDGE Its competitors "*watch with interest*" the team that is "*steadily building*" its profile in the region, while clients express that they "*seek an opportunity*" to instruct it. Specialising in invoice discounting work, the team focuses on larger deals (debt size £10 million plus), and also advises on cross-border aspects in conjunction with the firm's offices in France and Germany. It is widely acknowledged to have succeeded in "*plugging gaps*" following internal reorganisation with the key addition of ex-Lovells leveraged finance specialist, **Ashley Allton**, who peers rate as "*a welcome addition*" to the banking market. The team advised Bank of Scotland, HSBC and RBS on cross-border debt facilities of £80 million for Icelandic-listed company Bakkavör Group's acquisition of an English company, and advised PwC on debt facilities of £348 million for the take private of Britax. Further team highlights included advising Bank of Scotland in connection with its £45 million facilities to a joint venture with St Modwen for the acquisition of various former Marconi properties and the Elephant and Castle shopping centre, and advising Lattice Energy Services in connection with a substantial project finance facility for a power plant in the north of England. **Clients** Bank of Scotland; RBS; Lloyds TSB Bank; HSBC; Barclays Bank; Lloyds TSB Commercial Finance; Royal Bank Commercial Services; NM Rothschild.

EAST ANGLIA

BANKING & FINANCE
EAST ANGLIA

1
- Eversheds Cambridge, Norwich
- Mills & Reeve Cambridge, Norwich

2
- Taylor Vinters Cambridge

LEADING INDIVIDUALS

1
- CROOME Andrew Eversheds

UP AND COMING
- CLARKE Claire Mills & Reeve

ASSOCIATES TO WATCH
- SEED Sarah Mills & Reeve

This book is the product of 6,582 1/2 hour interviews. See p.7 for BMRB audit. Within each band, firms are listed alphabetically. See individuals' profiles p.103

EVERSHEDS (see firm details p.949) The team that "*banks expect to use*" for its "*deep resources and reliable standards.*" "*Sensible, commercial* **Andrew Croome** (see p.104) leads the Norwich team that continues to represent all of the region's key clearing banks on a local, national and international basis. Primarily advising on corporate and property-based work, the team also handles asset-backed commercial paper conduits. It is key adviser to NHP as borrower and provider of sale and leaseback finance, and has acted on the renegotiation of a £113 million facility from a syndicate of banks. The team has also advised RBS/NatWest in the £3 million mixed loan facilities to demerge companies from FSL Group. **Clients** NHP; HBOS; RBS/NatWest; Barclays; HSBC; Norwich & Peterborough Building Society.

MILLS & REEVE (see firm details p.1071) A "*significant East of England presence,*" clients seek out the team for its "*considerable depth of local experience*" and "*full range of specialist expertise.*" The banking and finance group advises on acquisition finance, property-related finance, PFI, asset finance and insolvency matters on behalf of major clearing banks, building societies and existing corporate clients. According to users, "*there is always someone to take the baton,*" and it "*comes across as competent and powerful*" in deals. Heading a "*seamlessly professional*" team, Cambridge-based **Claire Clarke** (see p.104) acted for Ashwell on banking aspects of the PFI for DHE Wattisham. The team completed a string of high-value work for Bank of Scotland (that recently set up a local regional office in Cambridge), such as the £2.5 million MBO of Cambridge Vacuum Engineering. Other highlights include acting for Spearhead International on a €7.6 million cross-border financing loan from EBRD that involved taking security in Poland and the Czech Republic. **Clients** Nationwide; HBOS; RBS; Lloyds TSB; Bank of Scotland.

TAYLOR VINTERS (see firm details p.1156) An "*able, clever*" small team (jointly led by Matt Collen and James Allen) that clients consider to be "*equal to the rest in quality.*" It handles MBOs, acquisitions, structuring and property-based work within an integrated banking and corporate finance practice. In addition to advising Lloyds TSB, the team was appointed as regional adviser to RBS and as panel solicitor for Weatherbys Bank and Royal Underwriting Agency. The team advised pension trustees and independent directors on banking arrangements on the sale of the May Gurney Group. It also advised on discounting arrangements in respect of a £5 million confidential invoice and a £200 million full recourse trade bill. **Clients** Lloyds TSB; Royal Underwriting Agency; Weatherbys Bank.

NORTH WEST

BANKING & FINANCE
NORTH WEST

1
- DLA Liverpool, Manchester

2
- Eversheds Manchester

3
- Addleshaw Booth & Co Manchester
- Halliwell Landau Manchester

4
- Cobbetts Manchester
- DWF Liverpool, Manchester
- Hammond Suddards Edge Manchester

5
- Kuit Steinart Levy Manchester

LEADING INDIVIDUALS

★
- WOOLLEY Simon DLA

1
- DALE Nigel Eversheds
- WHATNALL John Halliwell Landau

2
- MOLLOY Susan Halliwell Landau
- REARDEN Shaun Cobbetts

3
- EDWARDS Jonathan Hammond Suddards Edge
- GOSNAY Andrew Pinsent Curtis Biddle
- SHEPHERD Claire Hammond Suddards Edge

UP AND COMING
- GRAY Amanda Addleshaw Booth & Co
- MORGAN Matthew DLA

ASSOCIATES TO WATCH
- FAWKE Derek Addleshaw Booth & Co

This book is the product of 6,582 1/2 hour interviews. See p.7 for BMRB audit. Within each band, firms are listed alphabetically. See individuals' profiles p.103

DLA Interviewees agreed that the firm has won the most dominant profile in the market this year, with a great run in acquisition finance. Clients vouched for a responsive and commercial team that includes the region's leading light, Manchester-based **Simon Woolley** and his number two **Matthew Morgan**.

EVERSHEDS (see firm details p.949) An "*established*" practice, it has a "*mature*" client base of institutional lenders and corporate borrowers. Interviewees characterised the team's style as "*sensible and direct.*" Opining that his "*forceful image is mellowing,*" his peers rate **Nigel Dale** (see p.104) as an "*incisive technician and a good team-gatherer.*" He advised Caradon Plumbing Holdings on £130 million of new debt facilities by HSBC Private Equity, following completion of its disposal programme, and advised Ultraframe on a £60 million syndicated facility agreement to fund its US acquisition. A key highlight for the team was advising NM Rothschild on its provision of £48 million of senior and mezzanine debt to Parkdean, the UK's second largest operator of caravan parks. **Clients** RBS/NatWest; Yorkshire Bank; HSBC Private Equity; Barclays; Co-operative Bank; BBA Group; Bank of Scotland.

ADDLESHAW BOOTH & CO (see firm details p.838) Judged to have "*done extremely well*" in property finance, the team is endorsed for its "*robust*" assistant-level resources and "*key relationships*" with leading banks and top-level corporates. Clients reported that it takes a "*flexible approach and understands our needs well.*" They expressed "*great confidence*" in **Amanda Gray**'s (see p.105) "*technically solid documentation*" skills. She led the team that advised RBS in its £10.38 million MBO financing of Cross Services Group, one of Manchester's largest acquisition finance transactions. The team also advised Clydesdale Bank on facilities extended to the Harbour Group for commercial property investment purposes, and advised Lamont Holdings and L Gardner Group in the restructuring of their existing banking facilities. **Clients** Barclays Bank; Britannia Building Society; National Australia Group; RBS/NatWest.

HALLIWELL LANDAU (see firm details p.982) Interviewees opined that the team's "*long-standing*" market presence and "*strong grasp*" on the SME sector bolstered its lowered profile on major panels. Clients vouched that "*unflappable, meticulous*" team head **John Whatnall** (see p.109) is "*easy to deal with*" on banking and corporate finance matters. He advised on the £50 million revolving credit facility provided by Bank of Scotland to Sterling Capitol, and acted on Zurich Insurance's provision of a performance bond facility for a Cambridge-based PFI project to develop the Ministry of Agriculture's new offices. **Sue Molloy** (see p.107) also received client endorsement for her "*commercial, pragmatic*" approach. She advised Barclays on its £7 million joint venture provision to Chestergate Seddon for construction of a distri-

BANKING & FINANCE ■ NORTH WEST/YORKSHIRE

bution warehouse. **Clients** First National Bank; Bank of Scotland; RBS; Co-operative Bank; Lloyds TSB; Barclays; AIG; Zurich Insurance.

COBBETTS (see firm details p.914) Adjudged by clients "*the reliable, cost-effective alternative*," the team is best known for its property finance expertise on small-to mid-sized deals. The addition of former Chaffe Street partner **Shaun Rearden** (see p.108) ("*a traditional generalist*") will strengthen the team with his "*tight*" HBOS links. He led the team advising RBS Strategic Investment Group on the mezzanine-funded buyouts of Mentor and Artel Rubber. The team also advised the Bank of Scotland on its provision of £18.5 million funding to Figurevalue, to go towards the redevelopment of a West Midlands shopping centre, and acted on the provision of senior debt facilities for the development capital funding of the Living Venture Group. A further highlight included acting for Progress Housing Group on a new £135 million funding package provided by Nationwide Building Society. **Clients** Bank of Scotland; RBS; Anglo Irish Bank; Cheshire Building Society; West Bromwich Building Society.

DWF (see firm details p.943) Competitors concede that it boasts the "*strongest asset finance practice in town*," with clients such as Capital Bank, Lloyds TSB and Bank of Scotland. Primarily advisors to medium-sized corporations and private investment funds, the team was also appointed to Bank of Scotland's corporate banking panel of advisors. Tony Bochenski leads the Manchester team that advised the bank in relation to its £76 million refinancing of the MG Rover vehicle fleet, and the £29.5 million MBO of Perrys Motor Sales from Perry Group. It also advised Bank of Scotland on a £56 million retail investment properties joint venture purchase with an investment syndicate. The team has acted for Merseyside Special Investment Fund on its establishment of two investment facilities for SME business and mezzanine finance. **Clients** Bank of Scotland; Lloyds TSB; Co-operative Bank; Girobank; RBS/NatWest; Five Arrows Commercial Finance; city invoice finance; Alliance & Leicester Invoice Finance.

HAMMOND SUDDARDS EDGE It has provided "*active competition*" in corporate funding transactions, despite holding a lower profile this year. In addition to its primary focus in acquisition finance, the team handles a broad spread of work that includes PFI and property finance, while developing its presence in the asset-based lender market. Peers "*have a lot of time for*" **Jonathan Edwards** and **Claire Shepherd**. The team acted for Riverland on the development of a free trade hall funded by HBOS, and acted for NatWest on its funding of several healthcare portfolios. It also advised GMAC on three MBIs (totalling £10 million) and represented GE Capital on debt-related work. **Clients** Bank of Ireland; GE Capital; RBS; Barclays; Lloyds TSB; Co-operative Bank; GMAC Commercial Credit.

KUIT STEINART LEVY (see firm details p.1026) Adjudged by competitors a "*solid, quality firm*," the team, led by Steve Eccleston, retains its reputation as "*well-known advisors*" to Lloyds. Interviewees also noted its links to Allied Irish and Anglo Irish Banks and locally-based owner-managed businesses. A member of the Nationwide's specialist panel on offshore syndicated loans, the team acted for Anglo Irish Bank in its £10 million financing of a UK industrial portfolio, and advised the RBS corporate lending unit on the £10 million financing for the purchase of investment property. Further highlights included acting for Allied Irish Bank in its £10 million purchase of an office unit at Lincoln's Inn Fields. **Clients** Lloyds TSB; Bank of Ireland; Britannia Building Society; Girobank; RBS; AIB; Anglo Irish Bank; Nationwide.

OTHER NOTABLE PRACTITIONERS Interviewees on both sides of the Pennines viewed **Andrew Gosnay**'s (see p.105) move from Pinsent Curtis Biddle's Leeds office to Manchester as "*interesting news.*" He now heads the team that includes former Chaffe Street partners, said by market sources to benefit from a "*solid*" client base and reputation among banks.

YORKSHIRE

BANKING & FINANCE
■ YORKSHIRE

1. **Addleshaw Booth & Co** Leeds
2. **DLA** Leeds
   Hammond Suddards Edge Leeds
3. **Eversheds** Leeds
   Pinsent Curtis Biddle Leeds
   Walker Morris Leeds

LEADING INDIVIDUALS

1. **DAY Sarah** DLA
   MITCHELL Patrick Hammond Suddards Edge
   PAPWORTH Richard Addleshaw Booth & Co
2. **CLELAND John** Pinsent Curtis Biddle
   SMITH Mark DLA
3. **AKITT Ian** Walker Morris
   TAYLOR Michael Walker Morris

UP AND COMING
   HANDY David Addleshaw Booth & Co
   OWEN Simon Hammond Suddards Edge
   WALTERS Kathryn Hammond Suddards Edge
   WURZAL Jason Eversheds

This book is the product of 6,582 1/2 hour interviews. See p.7 for BMRB audit.
Within each band, firms are listed alphabetically. See individuals' profiles p.103

ADDLESHAW BOOTH & CO (see firm details p.838) It is "*an institutional giant*" who competitors continue to view as "*extremely effective players that still get the lion's share*" despite the loss of its leader Mark Chidley to the Royal Bank of Scotland, and banking panel reorganisations. "*Bright technician*" **Richard Papworth** (see p.108) is renowned for his big-ticket housing association funds work, such as the transfers of local authority housing and the creation of special purpose vehicles. He acted for Bradford & Bingley on the £111.5 million facilities provided to Pennine Housing 2000 to fund the Calderdale LSVT. "*A favourite*" with key national banks, former 3i lawyer **David Handy** (see p.105) gives "*clear, experienced advice*" on leveraged finance and Treasury-related capital markets matters. He acted for Kirkgate Group on the public to private of Dewhirst Group, involving bank facilities of £98 million from HSBC and IBJ. The team has also advised Bank of Scotland on the MBO of the Bon Marché Group, involving syndicated loan facilities of £41.5 million. **Clients** 3i Group; Bank of Scotland; Bradford & Bingley; Britannia Building Society; Clydesdale Bank; Co-operative Bank; HSBC; NM Rothschild & Sons; National Australia Group; NatWest; Nationwide Building Society; RBS; Yorkshire Bank.

DLA Interviewees praised the highly focused team for its strong complementary skill set in real estate and leveraged finance. The Leeds-based office also covers acquisition and structured finance, including projects, PFI and insurance, securitisation and asset-based lending. **Sarah Day** and **Mark Smith** enjoy a loyal following among lenders. They acted for Bradford & Bingley as agent and arranger in relation to a £200 million term loan facility to the Workspace Group, and acted for Leeds United as issuer in the £60 million securitisation of the club's gate and season ticket receipts.

HAMMOND SUDDARDS EDGE Its competitors admire the team's "*great strength*" in leveraged and acquisition finance matters, having "*beefed up*" in terms of partner strength. Clients praise its "*enormous input,*" pointing to "*exceptional ringmaster*" **Patrick Mitchell** for his "*clear commercial guidance.*" Key members of the "*sensible, industrious*" team include **Simon Owen**, who advised HSBC on the take private of Dewhirst Group, and **Kathryn Walters**, who advised Bank of Scotland on the MBO of Ellis Fairbank Holdings. Highlight matters for Barclays included advice on its joint financing of general facilities for Appleyard

YORKSHIRE/NORTH EAST ■ BANKING & FINANCE

Finance Holdings, and provision of property development facilities to Birmingham University. **Clients** RBS/NatWest; Bank of Scotland; Barclays; Lloyds TSB; GMAC; HSBC.

EVERSHEDS (see firm details p.949) "*Still up there*" despite partner losses, the team retains its image as "*lawyer's lawyers*" and a "*panel player for quality work.*" His peers opine that City-trained banker Jason Wurzal (see p.109) is "*more than competent*" on retail matters. He advised Bank of Scotland on its £10 million property development facility to Teesmac for a Yorkshire retail development, and Rutland Fund Managers on the £50 million acquisition of Edinburgh Woollen Mills. The team advised Spectrasite Transco Communication on the £65 million syndicated loan facility made available by CIBC World Markets, and represented Leeds City Council on all funding aspects of a high-profile PFI project for seven schools, involving senior debt of £42.5 million. **Clients** Bank of Scotland; Co-operative Bank; HSBC; Fortis; NatWest; Heywood Williams Group; Peter Black Holdings.

PINSENT CURTIS BIDDLE (see firm details p.1102) An "*experienced*" team continued to enjoy a leading reputation in mortgage banking and acquisition matters, such as mortgage sale agreements. Clients value its "*speed and sheer ability*" on related areas of expertise such as tax, singling out "*down-to-earth*" team leader John Cleland (see p.104) for his "*thorough, honest and commercial view*" on securitisations matters. His highlights included advising RBS on three separate PFI facilities with a total debt of £45 million, and acting for Amber Homeloans (a subsidiary of Skipton Building Society) on a £130 million mortgage book acquisition. The team acted for York St John College on a £15.5 million refinancing, and advised on all UK aspects of the $675 million acquisition of Masonite by Premdor. **Clients** Fleet National Bank; Skipton Mortgages; RBS; HBOS; Barclays; HSBC.

WALKER MORRIS (see firm details p.1178) The firm is viewed by market sources as a "*first-rate independent*" team with a cross-Pennines reach. It has "*a good following*" for its leveraged finance expertise in small- to mid-sized deals, and enjoys a "*healthy profile*" acting for borrowers on property development funding deals. An "*unfazeable*" team, its competitors praise its "*likeable individuals,*" while clients note its "*practical understanding*" of their businesses. "*Highly commercial*" Ian Akitt (see p.103) advised Cattles on the arrangement of £400 million multicurrency working capital facilities, and "*technically astute*" Michael Taylor (see p.109) advised Bank of Scotland on its £100 million committed working capital facilities to a national construction company. Team highlights included acting for Aquarius on the double demerger of Collins and Hayes Group and Airbath Group, which involved negotiating the simultaneous conclusion of three separate senior debt facilities from three separate funders. The team also acted for Fortis in the £20 million MBO from Kelda of White Rose Environmental Group. **Clients** Bank of Scotland; Fortis; Lloyds TSB Commercial Finance; RBS/NatWest.

NORTH EAST

BANKING & FINANCE
■ NORTH EAST

1. **Dickinson Dees** Newcastle upon Tyne
2. **Eversheds** Newcastle upon Tyne
   Ward Hadaway Newcastle upon Tyne
3. **Robert Muckle** Newcastle upon Tyne

LEADING INDIVIDUALS
1. **HARKER Chris** Dickinson Dees
2. **HARRISON Julie** Ward Hadaway
   KIRTLEY Deborah Dickinson Dees
   ON Nicholas Eversheds
3. **MCNICOL Stephen** Robert Muckle

This book is the product of 6,582 1/2 hour interviews. See p.7 for BMRB audit. Within each band, firms are listed alphabetically. See individuals' profiles p.103

DICKINSON DEES (see firm details p.938) The "*well-organised*" team shares the firm's "*long-established cachet*" in the market. Clients seek it out for "*large, complex deals*" because they have "*the utmost confidence*" in its resources. One reported: "*I go to them if I have a tricky problem.*" His peers praise "*urbane*" Chris Harker (see p.105) for his venture capital-related expertise, while clients find him "*supportive and well in control*" of their business. He advised Allied Irish Bank on its £50 million syndicated loan facility to finance a leisure club portfolio, and acted on an £8 million development loan facility to finance construction of a new campus for Stockton & Billingham College. Clients also endorsed Deborah Kirtley's (see p.106) "*cool, calm*" dealing style. An "*eminently capable*" practitioner, she "*gets the job done with no feathers ruffled.*" She advised Barclays Bank on the £13 million refinancing of existing facilities belonging to a property development company. The team also advised Barclays on a £28 million securitisation of Leicester City Football Club, and on a £42 million acquisition facility to Premier Dawn to fund a £17 million acquisition and refinance existing facilities. **Clients** Nationwide Building Society; Barclays; Bank of Scotland; Northern Rock; Newcastle Building Society; RBS; Allied Irish Bank.

EVERSHEDS (see firm details p.949) Interviewees praised the "*amply connected*" team ("*a great choice for conflicts*") as a "*prime work winner*" in the local, national and international arenas. Commended by clients for its "*broad-ranging legal expertise,*" the team is typically seen acting for both borrowers and lenders on transactional funding work such as property-backed commercial mortgages. Widely acknowledged as "*an incisive, commercial technician,*" Nick On (see p.107) is one who clients instruct when they want to "*go for the jugular.*" He advised Bank of Scotland as lead bank and arranger of facilities to Matrix Moorgate to acquire and develop office premises in the City of London (£82 million), and to Matrix Carlton Square to acquire and develop office/retail premises in Edinburgh (£55 million). The team also advised the bank on its provision of £58 million acquisition and development facilities to Matrix Bunhill Row. **Clients** Barclays; RBS/NatWest; Yorkshire Bank; Co-operative Bank; Clydesdale Bank; Northern Rock; HSBC; Dunbar Bank; Bank of Scotland.

WARD HADAWAY (see firm details p.1180) "*Making great inroads,*" the team is "*readily available and well-resourced,*" according to observers. Recent appointees to the panels of National Australia Group and Barclays Lending and Finance, competitors also note its equal strength in acting for borrowers. Clients commend its commercial investment expertise, singling out "*steady, trustworthy*" head of banking Julie Harrison (see p.106). The team acted for Bank of Scotland in a complex £5 million MBO of JCM, and acted for Circatex in its acquisition of Viasystems. **Clients** Barclays; Bank of Scotland; Handelsbanken; Newcastle Building Society.

ROBERT MUCKLE This team of "*intelligent lawyers*" enjoys a "*respectable*" reputation advising owner-managed businesses and other borrowers on property and commercial finance matters. It also acts for banks and building societies on MBO and property development funding and other commercial lending matters. Its competitors praise the team's "*competent delivery of client-led services,*" while clients appreciate its "*clear explanation of the issues.*" They commend "*proactive, professional*" team leader Stephen McNicol (see p.107) for being "*prepared to go the extra mile*" on banking and insolvency issues. The team was involved in the North East regional investment fund scheme run by Barclays for loan financing for SMEs. **Clients** Bank of Scotland; Newcastle Building Society; Lloyds TSB; Co-operative Bank; Dunbar Bank; Yorkshire Bank; Svenska Handelsbanken; Clydesdale Bank.

BANKING & FINANCE ■ SCOTLAND

SCOTLAND

BANKING & FINANCE ■ SCOTLAND

1
- **Dickson Minto WS** Edinburgh
- **Dundas & Wilson CS** Glasgow
- **Maclay Murray & Spens** Edinburgh, Glasgow
- **McGrigor Donald** Edinburgh, Glasgow

2
- **Burness** Edinburgh
- **Shepherd+ Wedderburn** Edinburgh
- **Tods Murray WS** Edinburgh

3
- **MacRoberts** Edinburgh, Glasgow

4
- **McClure Naismith** Glasgow

LEADING INDIVIDUALS

1
- **KELLY Susan** Maclay Murray & Spens
- **MCHALE Colin** Dickson Minto WS

2
- **MCKAY Colin** McGrigor Donald
- **STONEHAM Michael** Dundas & Wilson CS

3
- **BURNSIDE Graham** Tods Murray WS
- **LAING Robert** Maclay Murray & Spens
- **PATRICK Hamish** Tods Murray WS
- **WILSON Scott** Burness

4
- **MACAULAY Iain** McGrigor Donald
- **MORTON David** Dundas & Wilson CS
- **PHILLIPS Stephen** Dundas & Wilson CS
- **SANDERS Shona** Shepherd+ Wedderburn
- **SCOTT Christopher** Burness
- **SOPPITT Alan** Burness

UP AND COMING
- **WATSON Michael** McGrigor Donald

This book is the product of 6,582 1/2 hour interviews. See p.7 for BMRB audit.
Within each band, firms are listed alphabetically. See individuals' profiles p.103

DICKSON MINTO WS (see firm details p.938) Adjudged by its competitors "*a delight to deal with*," it is "*without doubt a leading presence*" in acquisition finance. Clients affirm that the team's "*huge depth of resources*" enables it to do "*a splendid job within tight deadlines*" on MBOs and acquisition and structured finance matters. Among those who bolster the team's leading image, **Colin McHale** (see p.107) is "*absolutely excellent*" on private equity and acquisition finance. His peers declare: "*It goes without saying, there is no one at his level*" as regards deal flow, experience and client contacts. He advised Bank of Scotland as lead bank and arranger of £50 million of senior facilities in the £80 million public to private of Expamet International led by Royal Bank Private Equity, and on its funding of significant acquisitions by Grampian Country Food Group in the UK, Thailand and Germany. On the corporate side, the team advised The Miller Group in the provision of £220 million of bilateral facilities provided to it by a number of banks. **Clients** Bank of Scotland; RBS.

DUNDAS & WILSON CS (see firm details p.943) The firm is historically regarded as "*the firm to catch*" on account of its "*top-level, broad-ranging*" work and the high-quality standards set by its assistants. Widely respected as a team of "*scholarly technicians*," it continues to enjoy "*considerable success*" in property finance and PFI, and retains its image as "*the one to choose for closing large projects*" despite recent departures. Clients maintain that the team's "*efficient, reliable performance*" will persist despite the firm's split from the Andersen's network. According to some sources, Edinburgh-based **Michael Stoneham**, head of PFI infrastructure finance, and asset finance supremo, is "*the best team leader of the decade*" and "*streets ahead*" of his peers in terms of technical ability. He advised Newcourt Capital in its innovative financing of an education sector project, involving £44.5 million of senior and junior debt financing. His peers commend "*bright*" head of banking **Stephen Phillips** for his expertise in derivatives and specialist financial products. He advised Bank of Scotland as agent and arranger of £614 million senior, junior and mezzanine financing of the sale and leaseback of the Woolworths property portfolio. The transaction involved a cross-border team of legal advisors. Seen acting for both lenders and borrowers, **David Morton** in Glasgow is described as an "*incredibly personable and pragmatic*" practitioner. He advised Bank of Scotland in the £130 million integrated cross-border financing of Abbot Group's acquisition of German-listed companies Deutsche Tiefbohr from Preussag. **Clients** Abbey National; CGNU; Lloyds TSB; National Australia Group; RBS; Bank of Scotland; Scottish Widows Bank.

MACLAY MURRAY & SPENS (see firm details p.1048) "*Well-focused commercially, it provides an excellent service*," according to clients. This "*model*" team of "*bright, personable*" lawyers has grown with the addition of two property finance partners from Dundas & Wilson. "*Sharp, businesslike*" Edinburgh team leader **Susan Kelly** (see p.106) enjoys a high market profile in acquisition and related structured finance. She is supported by "*civilised*" **Robert Laing** (see p.106), who peers note for his corporate banking expertise. The team advised key client Bank of Scotland on its joint venture with Macdonald Hotels to acquire the Heritage portfolio of hotels from Compass, and on its joint venture with Manor Kingdoms to acquire St Andrews Homes. The team also advised Bank of Scotland on the acquisition of the Sauchiehall Street Centre by Capital & Regional and Stannifer. **Clients** Lloyds TSB; Bank of Scotland; RBS; Bank of Ireland; Deutsche Bank; Den Norske Bank; Hypobank; Clydesdale Bank; Prudential; CGNU; Halifax; Abbey National.

MCGRIGOR DONALD (see firm details p.1065) "*A forward-thinking firm that is doing well*," agreed interviewees. An "*established presence*" in PFI and PPP, the team also advises on project finance that covers the energy and power sectors, and on capital markets and joint ventures transactions. It boasts cross-border capacity in conjunction with the London office, and has recently merged with multidisciplinary practice, KLegal. Clients include London-based banks, funders and guarantee bond finance project lenders. They commend its "*competitive, commercial, thorough*" approach, while its competitors consider the team "*highly efficient.*" Regarded as the team's "*key figure*," **Colin McKay** (see p.107) in Edinburgh impresses peers with his "*practical*" management skills. "*Professional and gentlemanly*" Glasgow-based **Iain Macaulay** (see p.697) is "*measured and technically able*" on retail banking and integrated finance work. Edinburgh-based projects partner **Michael Watson** (see p.700) "*can think from the client's perspective and make the right commercial decisions*" on infrastructure and PFI matters. The team advised Bank of Scotland and EIB on the Edinburgh Schools PPP Project, and advised RBS on its multimillion pound funding to Vale Retail to purchase a shopping centre. **Clients** Bank of Scotland; Intelligent Finance; MBIA; RBS.

BURNESS Market sources opine that the firm shines in project and property-based finance, the latter backed by a large property department. Clients commend "*successful*" team leader **Scott Wilson** for his constructive approach to acquisition finance matters. He acted for Bank of Scotland Joint Ventures in its provision of £230 million debt and equity facilities to Sapphire Retail Fund, a joint venture with Stannifer Group. The "*responsive*" team also features "*details lawyer*" **Christopher Scott** and "*superb*" head of corporate **Alan Soppitt**. He acted for GE Capital in its £450 million committed facility to Fiat Auto Financial Services. The team acted for RBS in its £260 million acquisition from Scottish & Newcastle and forward management of 456 public houses located across the UK. **Clients** Bank of Scotland; RBS; GE Capital Woodchester; Standard Life Bank; Anglo Irish Bank; Barclays.

SHEPHERD+ WEDDERBURN (see firm details p.1130) Its competitors describe the team as "*sparky and fun to deal with,*" while clients vouch for its "*consistent, safe service*" and "*accurate, partner-led*" approach. Typically seen on borrower-led property and securitisation work, it also boasts cross-border capability. "*Technically strong*" **Shona Sanders** (see p.108) gained peer commendation as one who has "*moved the practice forward.*" She advised Pinnacle Schools on the provision of £48 million of facilities and loan stock for construction and refurbishment of three schools in Fife. The team acted as Scottish agents on behalf of RHM

NORTHERN IRELAND/THE LEADERS — BANKING & FINANCE

Finance on the £650 million whole business securitisation of RHM Food Group. It also acted for Bank of Scotland on its provision of development finance (aggregate value in excess of £15 million) to joint venture companies that included a major UK developer. **Clients** HSBC; Bank of Scotland; Preferred Mortgages; Clydesdale; RBS.

TODS MURRAY WS (see firm details p.1164) Interviewees admire the practice for its specialist securitisations and structured finance expertise. Competitors perceive that the "*compact*" team is broadening its scope towards corporate banking and projects. They specifically noted its acquisition finance work for London 'magic circle' firms on securitisations with Scottish SPVs. "*Blue-blooded, Edinburgh-based*" clients rely on the team, rating **Hamish Patrick** (see p.108) as a "*strong technician*" in securitisation. He acted for Bank of Scotland, then the merged HBOS, in a series of capital markets issues including a $2.175 billion corporate loan securitisation and €500 million fixed-to-floating rate subordinated notes. **Graham Burnside** (see p.104) has "*built up an excellent reputation*" on trust-related securitisations and City referral work. He acted for Kyndal International on the £200 million MBO of Kyndal Spirits, and advised JPMorgan Securities as lead manager in Scottish aspects of securitisation of RHM Foodbrands, involving the issue of £650 million floating and fixed rate notes by RHM Finance. **Clients** JPMorgan Chase; Morgan Stanley; CSFB; Bank of Scotland; Britannia Group; Barclays; RBS; Deutsche; Skipton Building Society; First National Bank.

MACROBERTS (see firm details p.1049) Having featured among its competitors "*from the very beginning*," the team typically acts for borrowers in property development, acquisition finance and projects/PFI financings. Perceived by market sources as "*growing aggressively*," the team, led by Norman Martin in Edinburgh, acted for Anglo Irish Bank on two large property portfolio deals with Western Heritable and Belgrave Properties. It also advised RBS in the £89 million public to private of Regalian Properties, a London-based property development group. **Clients** Anglo Irish Bank; Clydesdale Bank; Bank of Scotland; RBS; 3i Group; Halifax; Bank of Ireland; Railtrack; GE Capital.

MCCLURE NAISMITH (see firm details p.1062) Its competitors recognise the team's niche strengths in asset and consumer finance, particularly leasing and HP work. In a testament to its increasing focus on corporate banking, the team, led by John Blackwood, acted for Bank of Scotland on a number of high-value commercial property and tax-driven syndicates in both Scotland and England. Further highlights for the bank include numerous Scottish-based structured transactions for its structured finance arm. The team is also the sole Scottish firm to undertake security and facility documentation work on a UK-wide basis for its commercial banking services arm. **Clients** Bank of Scotland; Lloyds TSB; Sainsbury's Bank; Chase Manhattan.

NORTHERN IRELAND

BANKING & FINANCE
■ NORTHERN IRELAND

1
- Arthur Cox Belfast
- John McKee & Son Belfast
- L'Estrange & Brett Belfast

LEADING INDIVIDUALS
1
- **CREED Angus** Arthur Cox
- **HENDERSON Brian** L'Estrange & Brett

2
- **ROSS Lex** John McKee & Son

ASSOCIATES TO WATCH
- **MCCAMMON Avril** John McKee & Son

This book is the product of 6,582 1/2 hour interviews. See p.7 for BMRB audit. Within each band, firms are listed alphabetically. See individuals' profiles p.103

ARTHUR COX (see firm details p.850) Market sources acknowledge that the team "*does a good deal for its clients*" that typically derive from the blue-chip banking community. "*Thorough*" **Angus Creed** (see p.104) leads the team that competitors admire for its solid links with the Bank of Ireland and Ulster Bank. Property finance, syndicated loans and MBOs all feature in the team's workload. **Clients** Anglo Irish; Ulster Bank; Allied Irish; Bank of Ireland; Barclays; Bank of Scotland (Ireland); Irish Intercontinental.

JOHN MCKEE & SON (see firm details p.1015) Clients report that these lawyers "*give a strong service on chunky, complex commercial work*." Jointly headed by "*pragmatic, creative*" **Lex Ross** (see p.108) and Avril McCammon, competitors typically see the "*technically competent*" team acting as borrowers' counsel on PFI fundings, and involved in new projects with a strong emphasis on property-related matters. The only Northern Irish legal firm to be an associate member of the LMA, it also handles MBOs, property acquisitions, M&As and syndicated loans. Team highlights included advising funder Northern Bank on the £130 million MBO of Clinical Trial Services from Galen, representing AIB and Bank of Ireland in a syndicate facility for the acquisition of a shopping centre and associated investment portfolio (£28 million), and advising Bank of Ireland on a PFI contract for upgrading vehicle test centres (£57 million). **Clients** Ulster Bank Group; Bank of Ireland; Bank of Scotland (Ireland); AIB Group (UK); Nationwide Building Society.

L'ESTRANGE & BRETT (see firm details p.1039) "*They have the Rolls-Royce solution to everything.*" Clients that include corporate borrowers and major banks use the "*professional, capable*" team for larger transactional property, corporate and restructuring work. Its association with Dublin firm McCann FitzGerald reinforces its cross-border expertise. His peers think highly of "*seasoned*" property finance specialist **Brian Henderson** (see p.106), while clients report that he "*keeps us on the right track.*" He advised long-standing client Ulster Bank on the reorganisation of its business banking in Northern Ireland and the Republic of Ireland. The team acted as lead adviser to Ulster Bank and Bank of Ireland in a substantial senior debt club facility to part-finance the construction of a cement plant owned by a subsidiary of one of Northern Ireland's leading companies, Lagan Holdings. **Clients** Ulster Bank; Bank of Scotland; RBS/NatWest; Bank of Ireland; Abbey National; First Trust.

THE LEADERS IN BANKING AND FINANCE

AKITT, Ian
Walker Morris, Leeds
(0113) 283 2500
iaa@walkermorris.co.uk
Specialisation: Acquisition finance, MBO/MBI finance, project finance and property development and investment funding. Highlights this year include acting for banks and borrowers on over 12 leveraged buyouts including the double demerger of Aquarius Group plc; £400 million+ multicurrency financing for Cattles plc, £140 million US/UK private placing; £120 million property financing; a number of PFI projects.
Career: Qualified 1988 – Norton Rose; Pinsent Curtis (Leeds) 1989-94; Garretts (Leeds) 1994-99; Walker Morris 1999.
Personal: Educated Wetherby High School and University of Sheffield. Leisure interests include golf, tennis, skiing. Married with four children. Resides Bardsey.

ALLEN, Maurice
White & Case, London
(020) 7397 3690
mallen@whitecase.com
Specialisation: Leading international finance lawyer with particular expertise in banking and acquisition finance.
Prof. Memberships: Law Society of Eng-

BANKING & FINANCE ■ THE LEADERS

land & Wales.
Career: Head of Finance, *White & Case*, London and member of European Executive Committee. Former head of *Weil, Gotshal & Manges'* London office. Former *Clifford Chance* banking partner.

ALLTON, Ashley
Hammond Suddards Edge, Birmingham
(0121) 222 3000

AL-NUAIMI, Omar
Osborne Clarke, Bristol
(0117) 917 3000

ALTON, Philip
Gateley Wareing, Birmingham
(0121) 234 0000

BAKER, Ian
Martineau Johnson, Birmingham
(0121) 678 1575
ian.baker@martjohn.com
See under Insolvency, p.455

BALFOUR, Andrew
Slaughter and May, London
(020) 7600 1200
andrew.balfour@slaughterandmay.com
Specialisation: Works mainly on banking and capital markets transactions. Particular experience in syndicated loans, structured finance, project finance, acquisition finance, international equity issues, bonds, commercial paper and medium term notes. Also advises banks and corporate clients on general banking and treasury matters.
Prof. Memberships: The Law Society; Honorary Fellow of The Association of Corporate Treasurers.
Career: Qualified 1981 and became a partner of *Slaughter and May* in 1988. Resident partner in New York office 1991-93.
Personal: Educated at Nailsea School (1968-75) and Manchester University (1975-78).

BAMBER, Andrew
Allen & Overy, London
(020) 7330 3000
andrew.bamber@allenovery.com
See under Private Equity, p.662

BATES, Michael
Clifford Chance, London
(020) 7600 1000
Specialisation: Banking and finance. Partner specialising in domestic and cross-border banking and structured finance, in particular: acquisition finance, MBOs, corporate restructurings and tax, regulatory and accounting enhanced structured finance.
Career: Articled *Clifford Chance*; qualified 1993; admitted to the Law Society of Hong Kong 1995.
Personal: Leeds Grammar School and Berkhamsted School; Exeter University (LLB); College of Law.

BORTHWICK, Trevor
Allen & Overy, London
(020) 7330 3000
trevor.borthwick@allenovery.com
Specialisation: Trevor is a partner in the banking department with experience in all forms of bank finance. He specialises in particular, in syndicated loans, securitisations and acquisition finance, project finance, structured trade finance and workouts and reschedulings.
Career: Tonbridge School; Magdalene College, Cambridge (BA, 1984; LLM, 1985). Trained *Allen & Overy*, qualified 1989; partner 1997.
Personal: Born 1962, resides Wimbledon, enjoys golf and rugby.

BRIERLEY, Chris
Wragge & Co, Birmingham
(0870) 903 1000

BROADFIELD, Alice
Pinsent Curtis Biddle, Birmingham
(0121) 200 1050
alice.broadfield@pinsents.com
Specialisation: Corporate banking, acquisition finance, lending and security arrangements. Also acts for corporate borrowers.
Career: Trained at *Watson, Farley & Williams*. Qualified and joined *Eversheds* in 1997. Joined *Pinsent Curtis Biddle* in 2002.
Personal: Born 1973. Educated Bablake School, Coventry; Selwyn College, Cambridge (MA Law). Interests include horse riding, theatre and reading. Lives in Leamington Spa, Warwickshire.

BURNSIDE, Graham
Tods Murray WS, Edinburgh
(0131) 226 4771
graham.burnside@todsmurray.com
Specialisation: Partner in banking department. Asset and corporate finance, including securitisation, banking and refinancing. Developed, with partner Hamish Patrick, structures used in securitisation of Scottish assets. Has presented papers on securitisation of Scottish assets.
Prof. Memberships: Writer to the Signet.
Career: Qualified in 1978 *Dundas & Wilson CS*. Coal Industry Pension Fund 1979. Joined *Tods Murray WS* in 1983. Partner in 1984.
Personal: Born 1954. Educated at George Heriot's School, Edinburgh University (LLB Hons 1976). Governor of St. Columba's Hospice. Leisure: music, hill walking.

CAMPBELL, Mark
Clifford Chance, London
(020) 7600 1000
mark.campbell@cliffordchance.com
Specialisation: Banking and finance. Partner specialising in banking work including leveraged transactions, syndicated lending, structured finance and corporate reconstruction.
Career: Articled *Coward Chance*; qualified 1984; Partner since 1991; Joint Managing Partner of Finance Practice 1998 onwards.
Personal: 1981 Oriel College, Oxford (BA).

CARSLAW, Debbie
Sidley Austin Brown & Wood, London
(020) 7778 1800

CHESTERMAN, James
Latham & Watkins, London
(020) 7710 1004
james.chesterman@lw.com
Specialisation: Partner with expertise in financial matters, including leveraged finance, media and telecommunications finance, workouts and restructurings. Experienced in all forms of senior and mezzanine finance, public to private transactions, leveraged buyouts and cross-border acquisition financing.
Career: Qualified as a solicitor in 1987, *Clifford Chance* 1985-94; *Freshfields* 1994-95; Partner *Weil Gotshal & Manges* in London 1995-2000; Partner *Latham & Watkins* 2000.
Personal: Born 1963. Resides London. Education: Sidney Sussex College, Cambridge University BA (1984).

CLARKE, Claire
Mills & Reeve, Cambridge
(01223) 222403
claire.clarke@mills-reeve.com
Specialisation: Corporate Finance Partner, specialising in corporate finance and banking. Recent deals have included setting up a US $100m venture capital fund and AIM float of MMI Group Plc acting on the financing aspects of a £60m Norfolk and Norwich millennium project and acting on a £18m refinancing of the Pelcome Group.
Career: Trained *Allen & Overy*, qualified 1993; 1993-96, assistant solicitor at *Allen & Overy* in the banking department specialising in reconstruction and insolvency; 1996-99, assistant solicitor at *Mills & Reeve* in the corporate services group specialising in corporate finance and banking; 1999 to date, partner at *Mills & Reeve*.
Personal: Born 1968, resides Suffolk.

CLELAND, John
Pinsent Curtis Biddle, Leeds
(0113) 244 5000
john.cleland@pinsents.com
Specialisation: Partner and Head of Banking, Leeds, with a particular expertise in Project Finance and PFI. Acted for RBS in £46 million facility for Bradford & Northern HA. Secured and unsecured funding, asset financing and mortgage book acquisitions and disposals.
Career: Qualified 1990. Solicitor *Simmons & Simmons* 1990-96; Partner *Simmons & Simmons* 1996-97; Partner *Pinsent Curtis Biddle* 1997-date.
Publications: Various articles on legal implications of EMU.
Personal: Belmont Academy, Ayr; Cambridge University 1983-87; London University 1989-91. Principal interest – family; other interests reading and football.

COCHRANE, Charles
Clifford Chance, London
(020) 7600 1000

COTTIS, Matthew
Lovells, London
(020) 7296 2000
matthew.cottis@lovells.com
See under Private Equity, p.663

CREED, Angus
Arthur Cox - Northern Ireland, Belfast
(028) 9023 0007
acreed@arthurcox.ie
Specialisation: Partner and Head of Banking Group. Banking security and advisory work.
Prof. Memberships: Law Society of Northern Ireland. Law Society of England and Wales.
Career: Qualified 1976. In-house lawyer with Bank of Ireland from 1976 to 1987. Joined *Norman Wilson & Co* 1987. Became partner in *Arthur Cox – Northern Ireland* in May 1996.
Personal: Born: 10 June 1951. Educated at Campbell College, Belfast and Pembroke College, Cambridge.

CROOME, Andrew
Eversheds, Norwich
(01603) 272727
andrewcroome@eversheds.com
Specialisation: Non-contentious company and banking work, handling a wide variety of matters for lenders and borrowers.
Career: Qualified in 1978 with *Allen & Overy*. Joined *Eversheds* in 1979 becoming a partner in 1982.
Personal: Born in Essex in 1954. Educated in Essex, Suffolk and at Trinity Hall, Cambridge. Lives in North Norfolk.

CROSS, Jeremy
Osborne Clarke, Bristol
(0117) 917 3000

CULLINANE, Lee
Clifford Chance, London
(020) 7600 1000
lee.cullinane@cliffordchance.com
Specialisation: Banking and finance. Partner specialising in general banking with emphasis on acquisition, telecoms and project finance.
Career: Qualified 1988; Partner since 1995.
Personal: 1985 London University (LLB); 1986 (SFC).

DALE, Nigel A
Eversheds, Manchester
(0161) 831 8000
nigeldale@eversheds.com
Specialisation: Partner and Head of Banking Department, *Eversheds* Manchester. Advises on all aspects of banking related matters, acting for banks and other financial institutions as well as borrowers. Main areas of practice include acquisition finance transactions, the full range of bilateral and syndicated facilities of all types, property finance, refinancings and restructurings, and advising on security. Regularly acts for a large number of banks and other financial institutions including The Bank of Scotland, The Royal Bank of Scotland plc, Barclays Bank PLC, HSBC Bank PLC, The Co-operative Bank PLC, NM Rothschild & Sons Limited and Lloyds Bank Plc. Significant practice in advising large corporates on major banking transactions. Key deals in 2001 include £130m new debt facilities for Caradon Plumbing Holdings (HSBC Private Equity) following

successful disposal programme, £60m facilities for Ultraframe plc to fund US acquisition and advising NM Rothschild & Sons Limited on the sole underwrite of £50m facilities to Parkdean Holidays. 2001 also saw a significant number of reconstructions and refinancings acting for Banks, Borrowers and Equity Investors.
Career: Qualified in 1986 whilst at *Eversheds Hepworth & Chadwick*. Joined *Hammond Suddards* in 1990 and became partner at *Hammond Suddards* in 1993. Became Partner at *Eversheds* in 1996.
Personal: Born 1962. Leisure pursuits include motor sports and cars generally, supporting Halifax Town, gardening and walking.

DAY, Sarah
DLA, Leeds
(08700) 111111

DISS, Paul
SJ Berwin, London
(020) 75332834
paul.diss@sjberwin.com
Specialisation: Partner advising banks, other financial institutions and corporate clients on a wide variety of financing issues. Specialises in (1) commercial lending (bilateral and syndicated) in the fields of acquisition, project, trade and property finance; (2) derivatives and other treasury products; (3) banking regulation and compliance; (4) payment transmission services and (5) debt restructuring and insolvencies. A number of those transactions are in acquisition and structured finance for borrowers in emerging jurisdictions. Spends an increasing amount of time preparing and advising banks and corporate clients on derivative transactions including credit and equity derivatives and repurchase agreements. Has recently been appointed external legal advisor to the Association for Payment Clearing Services (APACS).
Prof. Memberships: Hong Kong Society, City of London Solicitors Company, International Bar Association
Career: Trained *Linklaters & Paines*, qualified 1976; joined *Stephenson Harwood* 1977; partner 1982-99; *Stephenson Harwood* Hong Kong office 1980-84; Partner *SJ Berwin* since November 1999.
Personal: St Joseph's College, Stoke on Trent; St Mary's College, Toddington; St Catharine's College, Cambridge (1973 BA). Married to Jan (née Fletcher); 1 daughter (Nicola) and 2 sons (Jonathan and Matthew). Leisure: cricket coaching, cycling, cinema and book collecting.

DUKES, Rodney
Taylor Wessing, London
(020) 7300 7000
r.dukes@taylorwessing.com
Specialisation: Debt finance, particular specialisations include acquisition, telecom and property finance. In the last five/six years acting for BHF-Bank, Bank of Scotland/Halifax in relation to a variety of projects and property investment and development financings.
Prof. Memberships: Law Society
Career: *Taylor Garrett/Taylor Joynson Garrett* (now *Taylor Wessing*) 1982-date.
Personal: Bryanston School, Keele University, Law and Economics. Reside - Northwood. Two children Max and Charlotte.

DUNCAN, Michael G
Allen & Overy, London
(020) 7330 3000
michael.duncan@allenovery.com
Specialisation: Partner dealing in areas of practice comprising all types of banking and corporate finance, including in particular syndicated loans (acting for a variety of banks and borrowers), acquisition finance, asset financing, property finance, workouts/reschedulings.
Career: Articled *Allen & Overy*; qualified 1981; partner 1987.
Personal: Cambridge University (1978 MA). Born 1957.

EDWARDS, Jonathan
Hammond Suddards Edge, Manchester
(0161) 830 5000

ELLIOTT, Robert
Linklaters, London
(020) 7456 4478
robert.elliott@linklaters.com
See under Insolvency, p.458

EREIRA, David
Freshfields Bruckhaus Deringer, London
(020) 7936 4000
david.ereira@freshfields.com
Specialisation: Partner in finance department. Responsible for co-ordination of banking and property finance practices. Acts for banks, international institutions, investors and borrowers on banking leveraged and finance related work. Acts for banks, corporations and investors on property related investments.
Prof. Memberships: Law Society, City of London Solicitors Company sub-committee on Banking Law; International Bar Association, sub-committees B and E; Justice.
Career: Qualified in 1981 Banker. Worked at *Wilde Sapte* 1981-90, from 1984 as a partner. Joined *Freshfields* in 1990, becoming a partner in 1991. Lives in London.

EVANS, Edward
Freshfields Bruckhaus Deringer, London
(020) 7936 4000
edward.evans@freshfields.com
Specialisation: Partner in finance department. Main areas of practice are banking and project and asset finance. Also handles energy law work. Has addressed numerous conferences and seminars on these subjects.
Career: Qualified 1980, having joined *Freshfields* in 1978. Became a partner in 1986.
Personal: Born 12 December 1954. Attended RGS High Wycombe 1964-72, then Trinity College Cambridge 1973-77. Leisure interests include rugby, fishing and racing. Lives in London.

FAWKE, Derek
Addleshaw Booth & Co, Manchester
(0161) 934 6000

FORBES, Sandra
Burges Salmon, Bristol
(0117) 902 2707
sandra.forbes@burges-salmon.com
Specialisation: Head of the finance group specialising in corporate banking (including acquisition finance) and asset finance. Important transactions in the last 12 months have included: acting for FirstGroup plc on aggregate new facilities in excess of £500 million; acting for HBOS on the provision of £7.65 million of facilities on the buyout of Allen & Heath and on three other facilities for the provision of structured finance, including the buyout of the Hatch Group banking facilities of circa £83,500,000 for the acquisition of assets from Express Diaries; advising a train company operating in the leaving aspect of the procurement of new rolling stock in connection with a franchise bid.
Prof. Memberships: Law Society.
Career: Trained with *Frere Cholmeley*, qualified in 1989, joined *Burges Salmon* in 1991, becoming a partner in 1996.
Personal: Manchester University 1983-86. 1st Class Honours in Law Society Finals.

FREEMAN, Adam
Lovells, London
(020) 7296 2000
adam.freeman@lovells.com
See under Private Equity, p.663

FURMAN, Mark
Macfarlanes, London
(020) 7831 9222

GILLESPIE, Stephen
Allen & Overy, London
(020) 7330 3000
stephen.gillespie@allenovery.com
Specialisation: Stephen Gillespie is a partner in the banking department, specialising in international finance with an emphasis on acquisition finance (particularly management buyouts, leveraged buyouts and leveraged acquisitions; acting for senior and mezzanine lenders and for venture capitalists and equity providers); secured cross-border financings; structured finance; mainstream syndicated lending; complex restructuring; reconstructions and workouts; stocks, bond and securities financings; corporate rescues and insolvencies.
Prof. Memberships: Law Society. City of London Solicitors Company.
Career: Articled *Stephenson Harwood* 1985-87, associate *Freshfields* 1987-91, associate *Allen & Overy* 1991-95, Partner 1995.
Personal: Born 1962. Educated at Foyle and Londonderry College and Trinity College, Oxford (MA (Hons) Jurisprudence 1984). Interests include family, reading, outdoor pursuits and music. Lives in St. Albans.

GORRIE, Euan
Allen & Overy, London
(020) 7330 3000
euan.gorrie@allenovery.com
See under Private Equity, p.663

GOSNAY, Andrew
Pinsent Curtis Biddle, Manchester
(0161) 247 8282
andrew.gosnay@pinsents.com
Specialisation: Banking partner. Mainstream banking, asset finance, leasing, property project finance and debt issues. Deals include acting for Speedy Hire plc on their £28 million syndicated loan facilities and SIG plc on US$120 million US and UK private placements. Has also advised BPT plc on their £75 million Eurobond and US$120 million debt private placement and HSBC on the £100 million public to private of Allied Textiles plc.
Career: Qualified 1985. *Cameron Markby Hewitt* 1983-86. Joined *Simpson Curtis* (now *Pinsent Curtis Biddle*) in 1986, becoming a partner in 1990.
Personal: Born 1961. Uppingham School 1974-79; Newcastle University 1979-82 and College of Law 1982-83. Interests include walking, skiing, travel and theatre.

GRAY, Amanda
Addleshaw Booth & Co, Manchester
(0161) 934 6344
amanda.gray@addleshawbooth.com
Specialisation: All aspects of corporate banking with emphasis on property finance (including social housing) and acquisition finance.
Career: Qualified 1993; Partner 2000.

HANDY, David
Addleshaw Booth & Co, Leeds
(0113) 209 2432
david.handy@addleshawbooth.com
Specialisation: In all aspects of banking and finance, with principal focus on acquisition finance and corporate treasury and capital markets. Highlights of the past year include advising HSBC Bank plc in the provision of facilities to Humber Growers Limited to fund an acquisition; advising MyTravel Group plc on the renewal of its principal bonding facility; advising various financial institutions in the establishment of equity release mortgage products; and advising Skipton Building Society with regard to its medium term note programme.
Career: Qualified October 1993; joined *Addleshaw Booth & Co* January 1995. Became a Partner at *Addleshaw Booth & Co* in February 2000.
Personal: Graduated from University of Sheffield in 1990 and spent 1990-91 at Chester College of Law. Married with two sons, living in Leeds. Leisure interests include rugby union, motoring and Everton FC.

HARKER, Chris
Dickinson Dees, Newcastle upon Tyne
(0191) 279 9254
chris.harker@dickinson-dees.com
Specialisation: Main areas of practice are banking and commercial lending includ-

BANKING & FINANCE ■ THE LEADERS

ing acquisition, development and project finance. Works for banks and building societies as well as quoted and unquoted companies as borrowers. Major transactions in the last year have been for Newcastle Building Society (9 facilities aggregating approx £55m), Bank of Scotland, Allied Irish Bank (including £50 million syndicated loan facility for national chain of health clubs, Barclays, Co-operative Bank and a quoted company (£150 million syndicated loan facility).

HARRISON, Julie
Ward Hadaway, Newcastle upon Tyne
(0191) 204 4000
Specialisation: Head of banking unit. Acts for clearing banks, financial institutions, and borrowers in relation to secured and unsecured loans, acquisition finance, property development and project finance, refinancing and security issues, debt restructuring and invoice discount.
Prof. Memberships: Law Society.
Career: Qualified January 1984; articled at *Norton Rose*; joined *Ward Hadaway* in 1997 as a partner having worked for *Middleton Potts* and *Robert Muckle*.

HENDERSON, Brian
L'Estrange & Brett, Belfast
(028) 9023 0426
Specialisation: Partner and head of banking unit. All types of banking and finance work.
Prof. Memberships: The Law Society of Northern Ireland. Member of Non-contentious Business committee; Solicitors European Group (NI)
Career: Qualified 1976. Administrative Trainee European Commission; Partner in *L'Estrange & Brett* since 1979.
Personal: Born 1951. Education: Trinity College Dublin, BA (Mod) LLB.

HUMPHREY, Tony
Allen & Overy, London
(020) 7330 3000
tony.humphrey@allenovery.com
Specialisation: Partner specialising in structured finance with substantial experience in a wide range of corporate and financing transactions. Has extensive experience in all aspects of financing, particularly tiered or structured debt/equity financings including international project financings, acquisition financings and other complex multi-sourced financings. He has advised on transactions worldwide including the North Sea, North America, the Gulf, the Far East and Australia. He has given numerous public lectures on various aspects of financing, including 'The Bankability of Project Agreements', 'Project Finance - The Security Package', 'Sponsor Support' and 'Comparative Offtake Arrangements'.
Prof. Memberships: Member, Section on Energy and Natural Resources Law of the International Bar Association.
Career: Articled *Allen & Overy*, qualified 1975, Partner 1981.
Personal: Durham University (1972 BA). Born 1951.

INGLIS, Alan
Clifford Chance, London
(020) 7600 1000
alan.inglis@cliffordchance.com
See under Private Equity, p.663

JAMES, Benedict
Linklaters, London
(020) 7456 2000
benedict.james@linklaters.com
Specialisation: Has broad banking and finance experience, acting particularly for lenders but also for major corporates. His main areas of specialism include syndicated lending, acquisition financings and infrastructure finance.
Career: 2000 Partner *Linklaters*; 1995 joined Banking Department *Linklaters*; 1993 articles at *Linklaters*.
Personal: Education: Jesus College, Cambridge University (First Class Hons in Classics).

JEFFRIES, Graham
Bond Pearce, Southampton
(023) 8082 8868
gjeffries@bondpearce.com
Specialisation: Partner in the specialist Banking and Insolvency Group and Head of Southampton Banking Team. Advises clearing and secondary banks, finance houses, invoice discounters and other financial institutions specialising in structured and acquisition finance, MBOs, project and property finance, asset finance, regulatory matters, engineering of new products, and bank related restructurings. Also acts for borrowers on acquisition finance transactions.
Prof. Memberships: Member of the Association of Business Recovery Professionals (R3) and the Society of Computers and Law.
Career: Articled with *McKenna & Co*, qualified in Banking Group, 1989. Joined *Bond Pearce* 1999 as Partner in Banking and Insolvency Group.

JOHNSON, James
Clifford Chance, London
(020) 7600 1000
james.johnson@cliffordchance.com

JOHNSTONE, Pat
Eversheds, Birmingham
(0121) 232 1083
patjohnstone@eversheds.com
Specialisation: Corporate banking, lending and security arrangements.
Career: Qualified 1986. Joined *Evershed & Tomkinson* in 1984.
Personal: Born 1955. Educated Dumfries Academy, Glasgow University (MA), Grenoble University. Interests include ballet and horse riding. Lives near Stratford upon Avon.

KEAL, Anthony
Allen & Overy, London
(020) 7330 3000
anthony.keal@allenovery.com
Specialisation: Tony Keal became a partner at *Allen & Overy* in 1982. He specialises in domestic and cross-border acquisition finance (including LBOs, public bids and trade purchases) and other structured finance products. He leads the Leveraged Finance Group.
Prof. Memberships: Law Society and City of London Solicitors Company.
Career: Articled *Allen & Overy*, qualified 1976; Legal advisor and Company Secretary, Libra Bank plc 1976-78; Assistant Solicitor *Allen & Overy* 1979-81; Partner 1981.
Personal: Born 1951; Educated Stowe School and New College, Oxford University (1973, BA Jurisprudence).

KELLY, Susan
Maclay Murray & Spens, Edinburgh
(0131) 226 5196
smk@maclaymurrayspens.co.uk
Specialisation: Advises lenders and borrowers alike on all aspects of banking and finance work including structured finance, property finance, leasing and opinion work.
Career: Strathclyde University (1987-91); trainee, *Maclay Murray & Spens* (1991-93); assistant solicitor *Maclay Murray & Spens* (1993-96); Bank of Scotland secondment (1994); associate, *Maclay Murray & Spens* (1996-98); partner, *Maclay Murray & Spens* (1998-date); Head of Banking and Finance Department, *Maclay Murray Spens* (2001-date).
Personal: Theatre, opera, antiques, travelling.

KENSELL, Stephen
Allen & Overy, London
(020) 7330 3000
stephen.kensell@allenovery.com
Specialisation: He practises in all areas of banking and finance, with a particular emphasis on syndicated lending, acquisition finance, telecommunications financing, international collateral, repo and structured finance generally.
Career: Associate *Blake Dawson Waldron*, Sydney (1990-94); Associate *Allen & Overy* (1994-98), Partner (1998). Admitted as a solicitor (NSW and High Court of Australia) 1990; admitted as a solicitor (England and Wales) 1996.
Personal: Macquarie University, Sydney (BA 1987, LLB 1990).

KILNER, Peter
Clifford Chance, London
(020) 7600 1000
peter.kilner@cliffordchance.com
Specialisation: Banking and finance. Partner specialising in banking, structured finance and securities.
Career: Trainee and assistant *Clifford Chance* 1989-98; Partner since 1998.
Personal: Royal Grammar School, Newcastle upon Tyne; Cambridge University (BA Natural Sciences 1985); Newcastle Polytechnic.

KINSEY, Julian
Bond Pearce, Bristol
(0117) 929 9197
jkinsey@bondpearce.com
Specialisation: Partner in the specialist Banking and Insolvency Group. Specialises in banking and asset finance work for banks, building societies and other financial institutions. Deals with all aspects of lending, refinancing and security issues particularly in connection with acquisition finance for clients based in Bristol, London and the South. Particular experience of issues relating to the financing of the motor sector.
Career: Qualified 1984, joined *Bond Pearce* 1988 having worked for City firm *Linklaters and Paines*, becoming Partner 1993.
Publications: Regular contributor to 'Corporate Briefing' published by Monitor Press.

KIRTLEY, Deborah
Dickinson Dees, Newcastle upon Tyne
(0191) 279 9000
law@dickinson-dees.com
Specialisation: Specialises in mainstream banking, corporate and acquisition, development and project finance work. Works for banks as well as quoted and unquoted companies as borrowers. Major transactions in the last year have been for Bank of Scotland (including the £110m refinancing of Malmaison Hotels, Barclays and Royal Bank of Scotland).
Career: Partner, banking group April 1999. Qualified 1991.
Personal: Travel and Sunderland AFC.

KITTS, Stephen
Eversheds, Nottingham
(0115) 9507000
stephenkitts@eversheds.com
See under Corporate Finance, p.240

LAING, Robert J
Maclay Murray & Spens, Edinburgh
(0131) 226 5196
rjl@maclaymurrayspens.co.uk
Specialisation: Partner and member of banking and finance department. Acts for major clearing banks and other financial institutions as well as for borrowers in the provision of debt finance, including term loans, secured and unsecured lending, MBO/MBI finance and PFI finance. Also general corporate law.
Prof. Memberships: Law Society, Law Society of Scotland, International Bar Association.
Career: Qualified in 1977 (England) and 1985 (Scotland). University of Cambridge (MA 1974). At *Slaughter and May* 1975-83.
Personal: Born 1953.

LEE, Robert
Clifford Chance, London
(020) 7600 1000
robert.lee@cliffordchance.com
Specialisation: Banking and finance. Partner specialising in structured finance (both domestic and cross-border), syndicated loans, MBOs, acquisition financing and corporate restructurings, also specialises in advising Spanish banks and corporations on financing matters generally.
Career: Trained with *Clifford Chance*; qualified 1990; Partner since 1997.
Personal: Exeter University, LLB Law Degree.

106　INDEX TO LEADING LAWYERS: PAGE 1693 ■ IN-HOUSE LAWYERS PROFILES: PAGE 1201

THE LEADERS ■ BANKING & FINANCE

LEEMING, Richard
Burges Salmon, Bristol
(0117) 939 2216
richard.leeming@burges-salmon.com
Specialisation: Banking partner - specialising in securitisations and structured finance (including both acquisition finance and property finance). Special work includes advising issuers and originators on securitisations totalling over £350 million and advising lenders on bilateral and syndicated acquisition and property finance transactions of up to £250 million. Clients include Bank of Scotland, Bayerische landesbank and Nationwide Property Finance.
Career: Trained at *Ashurst Morris Crisp* 1991-93, secondment to Bankers' Trust 1994. Joined *Burges Salmon* later that year. Partner from 1 May 2000.

LONG, Peter
Herbert Smith, London
(020) 7374 8000
peter.long@herbertsmith.com
Specialisation: Deputy head of the finance division. Has experience in acting for banks and borrowers in a wide range of domestic and international financial transactions, both secured and unsecured. This experience includes advising lenders on property and project financings. Also provides advice to insolvency practitioners upon issues of insolvency law.
Prof. Memberships: International Bar Association; City of London Law Society.
Career: Joined *Herbert Smith* as trainee in 1982; qualified 1985; became Partner in 1991.
Personal: St. Catharine's College, Cambridge.

MACAULAY, Iain
McGrigor Donald, Glasgow
(0141) 248 6677
iain.macaulay@mcgrigors.com
See under Projects/PFI, p.697

MADDEN, Andrew
Gateley Wareing, Birmingham
(0121) 234 0000

MCCAMMON, Avril
John McKee & Son, Belfast
(028) 9023 2303

MCHALE, Colin
Dickson Minto WS, Edinburgh
(0131) 225 4455
colin.mchale@dmws.com
Specialisation: Partner 1997. Banking

MCKAY, Colin
McGrigor Donald, Edinburgh
(0131) 777 7000
colin.mckay@mcgrigors.com
Specialisation: Head of Infrastructure for *KLegal* and *McGrigor Donald* as well as Head of Banking Group, UK. Banking and debt finance generally; more particularly acquisition finance and property finance.
Prof. Memberships: Law Society of Scotland. The Law Society (England and Wales).
Career: *Biggart Baillie & Gifford* 1986-88; *Freshfields* (London and Tokyo) 1988-93; *Biggart Baillie & Gifford* (Glasgow) 1993-March 1999; *McGrigor Donald* April 1999 to date.

MCNICOL, Stephen
Robert Muckle, Newcastle upon Tyne
(0191) 244 2904
smcnicol@robertmuckle.co.uk
Specialisation: Partner and Head of the Banking and Business Recovery Units. Specialises in corporate banking and commercial lending including all forms of acquisition and structured finance, business turnaround and all aspects of corporate insolvency. Clients include major clearing banks, buyin/buyout teams, insolvency practitioners and company directors.
Prof. Memberships: Law Society, Association of Business Recovery Professionals, Insolvency Lawyers Association.
Career: Qualified 1995 with *Robert Muckle*. Joined *Lovells* in 1997. Rejoined *Robert Muckle* as a Partner in September 2000.

MILES, Stephen
Pinsent Curtis Biddle, Birmingham
(0121) 626 5709
stephen.miles@pinsents.com
Specialisation: Non-contentious banking and finance work. Acts for both financial institutions and corporates – including, in particular, the national acquisition finance teams of the major clearing banks. Has considerable experience of cross-border transactions and of advising UK corporates on US private placements.
Prof. Memberships: Law Society and Birmingham Law Society
Career: Joined *Pinsent Curtis Biddle* 1989. Qualified 1991; partner 1997.

MITCHELL, Patrick
Hammond Suddards Edge, Leeds
(0113) 284 7000

MOLLOY, Susan
Halliwell Landau, Manchester
(0161) 831 2693
smolloy@halliwells.co.uk
Specialisation: Practice covers loan and other credit/facilities letters/agreements, single bank, syndicated single/multi-borrower, multi-option facilities, tender panel agreements and working capital facilities, acting for senior mezzanine lenders and borrowers. Dealing with property development and investment finance, leasing and hire purchase facilities, guarantees, loan notes, standstills, intercreditors, providing a full range of banking services. Acts for clearing banks, specialised finance banks, merchant and foreign banks as well as borrowers.
Career: Qualified in 1981 at *Addleshaw Sons & Latham*. Partner at *Alsop Wilkinson* 1989-95. Joined *Garretts* as a partner in June 1995. Joined *Halliwell Landau* in January 2000.
Personal: Interests include theatre, walking, reading, cinema and wine.

MOORE, Gideon
Linklaters, London
(020) 7456 4458
gideon.moore@linklaters.com
Specialisation: Acquisition finance (both leveraged and investment grade), receivables finance, structured finance, project finance and PFI workouts.
Career: 1999 to date: Partner, *Linklaters*; 1995-99: *Dibb Lupton Alsop*; 1987-95: *Clifford Chance*. 1990; University of London, LLM; 1981-84: University of London, LLB.

MORGAN, Matthew
DLA, Manchester
(08700) 111111

MORGAN, Meryl
Morgan Cole, Cardiff
(029) 2038 5385

MORLEY, David
Allen & Overy, London
(020) 7330 3000
david.morley@allenovery.com
Specialisation: Banking and Corporate Finance: Debt. Acts for banks and financial institutions, as well as borrowers, on all types of debt and structured finance transactions with particular emphasis on syndicated loans, project finance, telecommunications finance, public bid and other acquisition finance, property and asset finance.
Career: Articled *Allen & Overy*, qualified 1982, trainee solicitor Brussels 1981, assistant solicitor 1982-88. One year on secondment at Chase Investment Bank Limited 1985, partner 1988. Managing Partner, Banking Department 1998.
Personal: St John's College, Cambridge (1979 MA). Born 1956.

MORTON, David
Dundas & Wilson CS, Glasgow
(0141) 222 2200

MURRAY, David
Allen & Overy, London
(020) 7330 3000
david.murray@allenovery.com
Specialisation: Partner involved in a wide range of international and domestic financing transactions including workouts and restructurings, structured finance, acquisition finance, property and development finance, North Sea oil financings and syndicated facilities.
Career: Articled *Allen & Overy*; qualified 1983; partner 1993.
Personal: Born 1957. Educated Bedford School; St Catherine's College, Cambridge (1980 BA, 1983 MA).

MURRAY, Duncan
Browne Jacobson, Nottingham
(0115) 976 6538
dmurray@brownej.co.uk
Specialisation: Banking and insolvency. Advising banks and other institutional lenders, corporates and insolvency office holders on a wide range of lending and recovery solutions. Work areas include acquisition and structured finance, property and development finance, security issues, restructuring and workouts.

Particular experience of transactional work, especially for MBO/MBI/IBO funding including public to private and cross-border acquisition finance.
Prof. Memberships: Law Society of England and Wales, Association of Business Recovery Professionals (R3).
Career: Trained *Hammond Suddards*. Qualified 1988. Solicitor *Hammond Suddards* 1988-90. Solicitor *Simpson Curtis* starting 1990, associate 1992 and partner 1995. Deputy head of banking and finance – *Pinsent Curtis*1997-1999. Partner and head of banking and insolvency – *Browne Jacobson* 1999.
Personal: Education: Bexhill-on-Sea High School, Whitley Bay High School, University of Huddersfield (LLB Hons), Southampton University (LLM).
Leisure: golf, photography, hill walking, films.

MURRAY, Neil
Travers Smith Braithwaite, London
(020) 7248 9133
neil.murray@traverssmith.com
Specialisation: Banking – principally acquisition finance and property finance. Also general banking, securitisation, project finance, structured finance. Principal transactions over the last year include Arts Hotel Complex, Barcelona; €150m investment property portfolio loan in Italy; Cleveland Centre, Middlesborough £90m loan; Fairview New Homes investor refinancing – various transactions including leveraging of European property funds and limited partnerships (onshore and offshore).
Prof. Memberships: City of London Law Society; FIABCI; Investment Property Forum.
Publications: Various articles in the 'Estates Gazette' and 'Law Society Gazette' concerning property finance.
Personal: LLB (Soton), MA (Lond).

NACCARATO, J
CMS Cameron McKenna, London
(020) 7367 3000
john.naccarato@cmck.com
Specialisation: Banking and international finance *CMS Cameron McKenna*, London. Partner dealing with banking and finance, and general corporate insolvency.
Career: Articled *Pritchard Englefield & Tobin*; qualified 1984; Assistant Solicitor *Pritchard Englefield & Tobin* 1984-85; Assistant Solicitor *Wilde Sapte* 1985-87; Assistant Solicitor *McKenna & Co* 1988-91, Partner 1991.
Personal: Born 1958; resides London. Educated at Hazelwick School, Crawley, Southampton University (1980 LLB).

ON, Nicholas
Eversheds, Newcastle upon Tyne
(0191) 241 6082
nicholason@eversheds.com
Specialisation: Partner. All aspects of non-contentious banking and finance work including transactional lending and finance, regulatory work and restructuring. Regularly acts for a large

BANKING & FINANCE ■ THE LEADERS

number of banks and other financial institutions as well as large corporate borrowers. Particular expertise in property development finance on a national basis and acquisition finance.
Career: Qualified 1991 at *Robert Muckle*. Secondment with *Bank of Scotland Legal Services* in Edinburgh in 1993. Partner at *Robert Muckle* 1995. Joined *Eversheds* as partner August 1999.
Personal: Born 1963. Educated Cheltenham Grammar School, St. Catherine's College, Oxford (BA) and University of Northumbria. Married with two children. Plays the piano, golf and football.

OWEN, Simon
Hammond Suddards Edge, Leeds
(0113) 284 7000

PALLETT, Julian
Wragge & Co, Birmingham
(0870) 903 1000

PAPWORTH, Richard
Addleshaw Booth & Co, Leeds
(0113) 209 2310
richard.papworth@addleshawbooth.com
Specialisation: Heads the firm's National Banking Unit. Specialist in banking, acquisition finance, property finance, social housing finance, project finance, education sector finance, building society treasury work, capital markets and derivatives. Particular responsibility for the firm's social housing finance practice. Worked extensively for funders on LSVT financings and refinancings and mainstream RSL funding. Acted for the funders on around half of the LSVTs to complete in the last two years including the £240m funding for the Coventry LSVT arranged by Nationwide and RBS. Has led social housing finance transactions aggregating in excess of £8.5 billion. Acted for Bradley & Bingley on the only Scottish LSVT to date (Berwickshire). Involved in the Pathfinder Local Authority Housing PFI projects.
Prof. Memberships: Law Society, Leeds Law Society.
Career: Qualified 1989 with *Travers Smith Braithwaite*. Joined the firm 1991. Appointed partner 1995.
Personal: Educated at Christ Church, Oxford. Interests include golf, cricket and football. Lives in Knaresborough. Married with two sons.

PATRICK, Hamish
Tods Murray WS, Edinburgh
(0131) 226 4771
hamish.patrick@todsmurray.com
Specialisation: Partner in banking department. Debt finance and recovery, including conventional banking, asset finance, PFI/project finance, innovative funding structures and funding reorganisation. Developed, with partner Graham Burnside, structures for securitisation of Scottish assets. Author, speaker and university examiner in field.
Career: Qualified 1989. Partner 1992.
Personal: Born 1962. Attended Dollar Academy, Edinburgh University (LLB 1st Class Hons 1984; DipLP 1985; PhD 1994: Cross-border securities and insolvency). Leisure: family, music, sports.

PHILLIPS, Stephen
Dundas & Wilson CS, Edinburgh
(0131) 228 8000

PIERCE, Sean
Freshfields Bruckhaus Deringer, London
(020) 7936 4000
sean.pierce@freshfields.com
Specialisation: Partner in the London office. Practice encompasses all aspects of banking work. Sean specialises in representing lenders but his clients also include corporates and other borrowers. In terms of products Sean has recently focused on cross-border leveraged buy-outs, acquisition financings, and restructurings. Sean has practised in New York and Hong Kong as well as London.

POLGLASE, Timothy
Allen & Overy, London
(020) 7330 3000
timothy.polglase@allenovery.com
See under Private Equity, p.664

PULESTON JONES, Haydn
Linklaters, London
(020) 7456 4454
haydn.puleston-jones@linklaters.com
Specialisation: Specialist in banking, including acting for arrangers, lenders and borrowers on syndicated and structured financings, with particular expertise in merger and acquisition financing and telecommunications financing. Extensive experience of advising steering committees, syndicates and distressed corporates on domestic and international defaults and reschedulings.
Prof. Memberships: Since 1998: Member of Loan Market Association Working Party on Primary Documentation; Since 1996 Member of the Single Currency Liaison Group of the Financial Law Panel.
Career: 1967-70, King's College, London University, LL.B (Hons). 1970-71, College of Law, Law Society Part 2 Examination (Honours). Qualified 1973. 1973-79, Assistant Solicitor, *Linklaters*. Since 1979, Partner, *Linklaters* in Banking Group. 1995-99, Head of Banking, *Linklaters*. Since 1998, Head of Banking Management Team, *Linklaters*.

REARDEN, Shaun
Cobbetts, Manchester
(0161) 833 7020
shaun.rearden@cobbetts.co.uk
Specialisation: Acquisition finance, property finance, restructuring, receivables finance and asset finance. Other area of work is consumer credit.
Prof. Memberships: Law Society.
Career: Qualified in 1979 while at Rutherfords in Liverpool. In-house solicitor at Littlewoods 1980-82, then manager of legal department North West Securities to 1986. Legal Advisor Co-operative Bank to 1989 then partner and head of banking at *Addleshaw Sons & Latham*. Joined *Chaffe Street* in 1999 and then *Cobbetts* in 2002.

ROBERTS, Simon C
Allen & Overy, London
(020) 7330 3000
simon.roberts@allenovery.com
Specialisation: Partner specialising in domestic and international banking transactions with particular emphasis on syndicated loans, acquisition finance, property finance and securitisations.
Career: Trained *Allen & Overy*; qualified 1993; Partner 2000.
Personal: Bishop Vesey's School, Sutton Coldfield; University of Bristol (1989) LLB. Born 1968, resides Chislehurst.

ROSS, Lex
John McKee & Son, Belfast
(028) 9023 2303
lex_ross@jmckee.co.uk
Specialisation: Advises banks and financial institutions on lending and security matters and has particular expertise in acting for funders in private finance initiative work. Also advises insolvency practitioners, particularly administrative receivers, on all legal matters arising from corporate recovery and insolvency including sales of businesses and assets and claims by creditors.
Prof. Memberships: Law Society of Northern Ireland.
Career: Qualified 1967; Partner in *John McKee & Son* from 1972.
Personal: Born 23 December 1942. Educated at Strathallan School, Perthshire and Queens University, Belfast.

SANDERS, Shona
Shepherd+ Wedderburn, Edinburgh
(0131) 473 5260
shona.sanders@shepwedd.co.uk
Specialisation: Acquisition and Project Finance.
Prof. Memberships: Law Society of Scotland. Law Society (England and Wales).
Career: 1987-91/1993-98 *Dundas & Wilson* Banking Team (Partner 1997); 1993 sabbatical including time at *Allen, Allen & Hemsley*, Sydney. 1998-99 *Mallesons Stephen Jaques*, Sydney; Senior Associate, Project Finance Team. 1999 to date *Shepherd+ Wedderburn*; Partner in and Head of Banking Group.
Personal: Born 1966. University of Edinburgh: LLB (1986), DIP LP (1987). Qualified in English Law 1998.

SCHULZ, Peter F
Allen & Overy, London
(020) 7330 3000
peter.schulz@allenovery.com
Specialisation: A broad practice in banking and international finance, encompassing syndicated and structured lending, acquisition financing, the banking aspects of CDO issues and workouts and restructurings. Recent transactions he has led include multijurisdictional acquisition and bid financings including Sasol/Condea and Xstrata/Asturiana de Zinc, a variety of emerging market loans and several jumbo corporate credits including for Anglo American and Bombardier.
Career: Articled *Allen & Overy*, qualified 1983, Partner 1989.

Personal: Educated at Haberdashers' Aske's School, Elstree; Downing College, Cambridge (MA Law).

SCOTT, Christopher
Burness, Edinburgh
(0131) 473 6000

SEED, Sarah
Mills & Reeve, Cambridge
(01223) 364422

SHEPHERD, Claire
Hammond Suddards Edge, Manchester
(0161) 830 5000

SHORT, Stephen
Ashurst Morris Crisp, London
(020) 7638 1111
stephen.short@ashurst.com
Specialisation: Partner specialising in domestic and cross-border structured finance (leveraged and other acquisition finance); recent transactions include (for Lehman Brothers) finance for a vehicle sponsored by PBPE to fund the public bid of Britese plc; (for CSFB, Lehman Brothers and RBS) finance for a vehicle sponsored by a consortium led by K&R to acquire Legrand SA; (for Cinven and RBPE) finance for the acquisition of NCP from Cendant.
Career: Qualified 1989; partner 1998.
Personal: Education: LLB, LLM. Born 1964. Resides London.

SLATER, Richard
Slaughter and May, London
(020) 7600 1200
richard.slater@slaughterandmay.com
Specialisation: Partner in financial/commercial department. Head of financing stream. Principal area of practice is debt financing of all types, including syndicated loan facilities, structured financings, securitisations, project financings and bond and note issues. Has also acted on international equity offerings, flotations, privatisations and corporate and commercial work of a general nature.
Prof. Memberships: The Law Society.
Career: With *Slaughter and May* throughout. Articles 1970; qualified 1972; partner 1979. Hong Kong office 1981-86.
Personal: Born 18 August 1948. Educated at University College School, Hampstead (1956-65), Lycée Michelet, Paris (1965-66) and Pembroke College, Cambridge (1966-69). Lives in London.

SMITH, Mark
DLA, Leeds
(08700) 111111

SMITH, Robert
Clifford Chance, London
(020) 7600 1000
robert.smith@cliffordchance.com
Specialisation: Banking and finance. Partner specialising in banking, housing associations and public sector work.
Career: Partner since 1987.

SOPPITT, Alan
Burness, Edinburgh
(0131) 473 6000

108   INDEX TO LEADING LAWYERS: PAGE 1693 ■ IN-HOUSE LAWYERS PROFILES: PAGE 1201

THE LEADERS — BANKING & FINANCE

STEWART, Mark
Clifford Chance, London
(020) 7600 1000
mark.stewart@cliffordchance.com
See under Private Equity, p.664

STEWART, Suzy
Clifford Chance, London
(020) 7600 1000
Specialisation: Real estate. Partner specialising in finance including real estate investment and development finance, secured and structured finance, corporate financings and restructurings.
Career: Articled *Williams & Williams*, Brisbane, Australia; admitted in Queensland 1988 and in England 1991; *Theodore Goddard*, London 1989-90; joined *Clifford Chance* 1990; Partner since 2001.
Personal: Wycombe Abbey School; University of Queensland, Australia (LLB (Hons)).

STONEHAM, Michael
Dundas & Wilson CS, Edinburgh
(0131) 228 8000

SWEETING, Malcom
Clifford Chance, London
(020) 7600 1000
malcom.sweeting@cliffordchance.com
Specialisation: Banking and finance. Partner specialising in global finance.
Career: Partner since 1990.
Personal: BA Business Law 1978; Law Finals 1979.

TAYLOR, Michael
Walker Morris, Leeds
(0113) 283 2500
Specialisation: Work includes acquisition finance, MBO/MBI finance and general banking, lending and security advice, restructuring and workouts.
Career: Qualified 1986; partner *Walker Morris* 1991.
Personal: Attended King Edward VI School, Lichfield and University of Bristol 1980-83. Leisure interests include hockey and fly-fishing. Lives in Leeds.

TUCKER, John C
Linklaters, London
(020) 7456 4496
john.tucker@linklaters.com
Specialisation: Areas of specialisation include syndicated lending, secured and structured financings, acquisition, trade and project finance and reorganisation work. Represents banks, bank syndicates and other creditors as well as companies and sponsors in international financing transactions. Responsible for numerous multi-sourced and leveraged financings for acquisitions, telecoms and projects. In Australia: experience of corporate and commercial work with particular emphasis on takeovers, flotations, acquisitions and disposals, joint ventures, reorganisations and related financings.
Career: Since 1999: Head of Banking Department; 1990 to date: Partner, *Linklaters*; 1989-90: Assistant Solicitor, *Linklaters*; 1988: admitted as a Solicitor in England and Wales; 1984-89: Partner, *Finlaysons*, South Australia; 1980: admitted as a Barrister and Solicitor in South Australia. 1982: South African Institute of Technology, BA (Accountancy); 1979: University of Adelaide, LLB (Hons).

VAUGHAN, Philip
Eversheds, Cardiff
(029) 2047 1147
Specialisation: Practice covers a wide range of non-contentious banking and finance work and includes transactional work (including project and acquisition finance), regulatory advice and drafting of standard documentation for banks, building societies and finance companies. Has a particular expertise in consumer credit work. Also involved in a wide range of non-contentious insolvency work acting for receivers, administrators and liquidators and advising lenders on enforcement of security and restructuring/refinancings.
Career: Qualified 1984. Formerly with *Clifford Chance* and National Westminster Bank Legal Department. Joined current firm in 1987 and became partner in 1988.
Personal: Born 14 December 1958. Educated at Haverfordwest Grammar School, St. Edmund Hall, Oxford (M.A.) and Emmanuel College, Cambridge (LL.M.).

VICKERS, Mark
Ashurst Morris Crisp, London
(020) 7638 1111
mark.vickers@ashursts.com
See under Private Equity, p.664

WAGHORN, Mark
Berwin Leighton Paisner, London
(020) 7760 1000
mark.waghorn@blplaw.com
Specialisation: Partner, and head of property finance group, specialising in property finance (including investment and development funding) and property related insolvency and turnaround work. Wide range of clients including banks, institutions, finance houses, senior and mezzanine funders and borrowers. Work includes lead partner for RBS/NatWest. Recent transactions include highly structured £1.9bn hotels sale and leaseback with Nomura and Compass Hotels; advising on the £470 million development financing of more London Bridge (GLA, Ernst & Young and Bacon & Woodrow London HQs); advising on the financing of the redevelopment of Battersea Power Station; advising on the £144m financing of the Nike Town/Top Shop (Arcadia Group) building at Oxford Street. Lead partner for KBC Bank NV acting recently on the sale of a secured commercial property loan portfolio to First National Bank. Acting on the £100m+ refinancing of the MWB Leisure Fund I limited liability partnership. Advising Marylebone Warwick Balfour on the £90m syndicated financing to acquire Liberty's (including the flagship store). A member of the team advising the Millennium Commission Capital Projects team having now dealt with more than £1.75bn of funding in relation to over £2.5bn of developments.
Prof. Memberships: Member of Law Society; Association of Business Recovery Professionals; Non Administrative Receivers Association; Society for Computers & Law.
Career: Trained at *Berwin Leighton*, qualified January 1992 and became a partner in 1997 and head of property finance in 1999.
Publications: Writes for Sweet & Maxwell Commercial Transaction Checklists on property development and insolvency and contributes occasional articles elsewhere.
Personal: Education: Bristol Grammar School, Exeter University, University of the West of England. Plays football. Car nut. Life member of CAMRA.

WALKER, Gary
Wragge & Co, Birmingham
(0870) 903 1000

WALTERS, Kathryn
Hammond Suddards Edge, Leeds
(0113) 284 7000

WARD, Anthony
Shearman & Sterling, London
(020) 7655 5000

WARD, Nigel
Ashurst Morris Crisp, London
(020) 7859 1236
nigel.ward@ashursts.com
See under Private Equity, p.664

WATSON, Michael
McGrigor Donald, Edinburgh
(0131) 777 7071
michael.watson@mcgrigors.com
See under Projects/PFI, p.700

WHATNALL, John
Halliwell Landau, Manchester
(0161) 835 2673
jwhatnall@halliwells.co.uk
Specialisation: Partner and Head of Corporate Department. Main areas of practice are banking and corporate finance.
Prof. Memberships: Law Society, Securities Institute.
Career: Qualified in 1981. Worked at *Herbert Oppenheimer Nathan & Vandyk* 1982-86. Joined *Halliwell Landau* in 1986, becoming a partner in 1987.
Personal: Born 22 June 1957. Attended The Queen's College, Oxford 1975-78. Leisure interests include opera. Lives in Wilmslow, Cheshire.

WHITE, Giles
Linklaters, London
(020) 7456 4494
giles.white@linklaters.com
Specialisation: Head of Global Finance and Projects. Areas of specialisation include syndicated lending, merger and acquisition finance, structured products (such as tax enhanced financings) and South African based financings. Represents arrangers and banks as well as companies in both UK and international transactions.
Career: Since 1991: Partner, *Linklaters*, London; 1995-96: Head of International Finance, *Linklaters*, Hong Kong; 1992-96: Partner, *Linklaters*, Hong Kong; 1991-92: Partner *Linklaters* London; 1988-91: Assistant solicitor, *Linklaters* London; 1985-88: *Credit Suisse First Boston Limited*, London; 1982-85: *Sonnenberg, Hoffmann & Galombik*, Cape Town, South Africa.
Personal: 1980-81: University of Cape Town, LL.B; 1979: Admitted as barrister, Inner Temple, London; 1976-78: Oxford, MA (Law), Rhodes Scholar.

WILSON, Dave
Theodore Goddard, London
(020) 7880 5760
davewilson@theodoregoddard.co.uk
Specialisation: Partner in the Banking and Projects Group at *Theodore Goddard*. He is a graduate of Edinburgh University and has worked in the banking sector in London and New York since 1984. He is the account partner for National Westminster Bank with *Theodore Goddard* and has worked with NatWest (and now RBS) on a large number of structured property financings, including large development projects undertaken by limited partnerships.

WILSON, Scott
Burness, Glasgow
(0141) 248 4933

WILTSHIRE, Peter
CMS Cameron McKenna, Bristol
(0117) 934 9300
prw@cmck.com
Specialisation: Non-contentious banking, including rescue and workouts.
Career: Articled *Cameron Markby/Cameron Markby Hewitt* 1988-90. Qualified *Cameron Markby Hewitt*, London, 1990. Bristol *Cameron Markby Hewitt* 1991-date (now *CMS Cameron McKenna*). Partner 1999.
Personal: Church. Armchair sports critic. Singing. Married, five children.

WOOLCOCK, Brian
DLA, Birmingham
(08700) 111111

WOOLLEY, Simon
DLA, Manchester
(08700) 111111

WURZAL, Jason
Eversheds, Leeds
(0113) 243 0391
jasonwurzal@eversheds.com
Specialisation: Work covers all areas of banking related matters, including acquisition finance, property finance, project finance and PFI. Transactions include acting for Peter Black on £304m take private funded by RBS and Swinton Group on the £27m acquisition of Collinade Insurance Brokers.
Career: Qualified at *Lovell White Durrant* in 1994; joined *Ashurst Morris Crisp* in 1996 (including one year's secondment to Bankers Trust); joined *Eversheds* in 1999, partner in 2000.
Personal: Leeds Grammar School and Nottingham University. Walking and gardening.

CAPITAL MARKETS

London – International Debt & Equity: 110; Securitisation & Repackaging: 113; Derivatives 115; Profiles: 117

Research approved by BMRB For this edition, **Chambers'** researchers conducted 6,582 interviews – 3,900 with law firms, 511 with barristers and 2,171 with clients. The validity of the research was scrutinised by BMRB International, who audited both the methodology and the results at our offices in London. They interviewed **Chambers'** researchers and cross-checked sample interviews. Details of the audit appear on page 7.

LONDON

INTERNATIONAL DEBT & EQUITY

CAPITAL MARKETS: INTERNATIONAL DEBT & EQUITY
■ LONDON

1
- Allen & Overy
- Clifford Chance
- Linklaters

2
- Freshfields Bruckhaus Deringer

3
- Ashurst Morris Crisp
- Cleary Gottlieb Steen & Hamilton
- Shearman & Sterling
- Simmons & Simmons
- Slaughter and May

4
- Baker & McKenzie
- Herbert Smith
- Lovells
- Norton Rose
- Weil, Gotshal & Manges

LEADING INDIVIDUALS

1
- CANBY Michael Linklaters
- EASTWELL Nicholas Linklaters
- WELLS Boyan Allen & Overy

2
- BURN Lachlan Linklaters
- DUNNIGAN David Clifford Chance
- EDLMANN Stephen Linklaters
- MILLER Stephen Allen & Overy

3
- CLARK Charles Linklaters
- FRANK David Slaughter and May
- PITKIN Jeremy Freshfields Bruckhaus Deringer
- THOMSON Keith Linklaters
- WEDDERBURN-DAY Roger Allen & Overy

4
- BICKERTON David Clifford Chance
- BROWN Jane Linklaters
- DUNLOP Stewart Clifford Chance
- GREENE Edward Cleary Gottlieb Steen & Hamilton
- MACVICAR Robert Clifford Chance
- PRIDMORE Nigel Linklaters

5
- EATOUGH David Clifford Chance
- MCFADZEAN Christopher Linklaters
- OVENDEN Simon Linklaters
- QURESHI Ashar Cleary Gottlieb Steen & Hamilton
- SHURMAN Daniel Allen & Overy

UP AND COMING
- JACKAMAN Jake White & Case
- MORRIS Tim Clifford Chance

This book is the product of 6,582 1/2 hour interviews. See p.7 for BMRB audit. Within each band, firms are listed alphabetically. See individuals' profiles p.117.

ALLEN & OVERY (see firm details p.841) The firm enjoys a long-standing reputation in capital markets transactions, and fields one of the biggest teams. Industry commentators recognise that it controls the largest share of the MTN programme field, and has a subsequent weighting towards a "*tightly focused*" debt capital markets practice, which is backed by "*quality lawyers.*" The outstanding practice provides the advantage of formidable client relationships and a high volume of work. The group has made a major impression on the market with 154 standalone bond issues, 149 MTN programmes and 627 MTN drawdowns. Equity is catered for, and despite the slow market conditions, the firm has acted on one of the few high-profile offerings: Royal KPN's latest €5 billion equity offering. High yield transactions continue to feature.

The team is headed by **Boyan Wells** (see p.121), a "*prominent personality with an incisive mind,*" who proffers "*confident leadership.*" His capital markets work sits alongside his international management commitments, while he continues to act on innovative tier one issues, lately for Lloyds Bank in its retail product listed on Frankfurt, Euronext and Madrid. Teamed with him is **Stephen Miller** (see p.119), adjudged a "*transactional strength,*" who consulted on the first Dutch direct tier one issue for ING Groep. "*Commercially minded*" **Roger Wedderburn-Day** (see p.120) is a "*great client pleaser,*" and has built up strong relationships with the investment banks. **Daniel Shurman** (see p.119) is known for his development of specialist products and is described as "*straightforward and energetic.*" Peers agree that he acted "*extremely effectively*" on the first eurobond issue for a Russian entity, advising ING Barings and UBS Warburg (*inter alia*) on a €300 million eurobond for the City of Moscow.

Further highlights for the team include advising Salomon Brothers as arrangers on a £5 billion EMTN Programme for GlaxoSmithKline and the subsequent £1 billion issue, the largest ever single tranche sterling corporate bond. Combining its US and UK expertise, the equity team advised The Hellenic Republic and Public Power Corporation (PPC), Greece's state-owned electricity utility on a privatisation, which included offerings outside the US under Regulation S and in the US under Rule 144A. **Clients** ABN AMRO; Bank of America; Barclays Capital; Bear Stearns; Citigroup; Commerzbank; CSFB; Deutsche Bank; Goldman Sachs; JPMorgan; Lehman Brothers; Merrill Lynch; Morgan Stanley; Nomura; UBS Warburg.

CLIFFORD CHANCE (see firm details p.911) Commended for its international network - particularly in Europe - the firm's strength is founded in the debt side of capital markets. Clients agree that the group offers "*fantastic capacity and depth,*" and has a handful of partners, "*second to none in quality,*" who handle a volume of MTN programmes. On the equity side, the firm is felt to benefit from the additional support of its Rogers & Wells partners, and is also complemented by the strength of its US partners based in the London office. IPOs originating from continental Europe have been the main feature of the equities group.

"*Dynamic*" **David Dunnigan** (see p.117) was endorsed by peers for his smooth team management skills and his "*superb rapport with clients.*" He has acted on a number of sovereign transactions over the past year in Eastern and Central Europe, Turkey and Brazil. Debut debt transactions included acting for Friuli, an Italian region, the Bank of Cyprus and Novartis. "*Personable*" **Stewart Dunlop** (see p.117) has established a number of global EMTN programmes for major names such as Sony, Finmeccanica, Storeband and SAS. "*Commercial in his approach and always busy,*" **Robert MacVicar** (see p.119) and his colleague, the "*client savvy*" **David Eatough** (see p.117), are on the team covering a wide range of debt issues, from MTN programmes to the tier one and tier two transactions for clients such as Standard Chartered. Our interviewees pointed to the "*practical and deal-focused*" **Tim Morris** (see p.119) as one who has been "*actively making a name for himself in the sector;*" he advised UBS Warburg in its issuance of $310 million of UBS AG bonds, exchangeable into shares of YUKOS, Russia's second largest oil company. "*Approachable and reasonable*" **David Bickerton** (see p.694) "*knows what's going on*" in the project bond financings market.

In a key deal of the year, the firm advised MBIA as monoline insurer and SSSB and the Royal Bank of Scotland, as joint lead arrangers, on the £2 billion securitisation used by Glas to finance the management-led buyout of the Welsh Water-regulated water business from Hyder. The US group has been acting on most of the European equity highlights such as the advice rendered to the Kingdom of Norway, acting through the Ministry of Petroleum and

LONDON ■ CAPITAL MARKETS

TOP IN-HOUSE LAWYERS

INTERNATIONAL DEBT & EQUITY

Kate CRAVEN, Director, Debt Capital Markets, Law & Compliance, Merrill Lynch International

Tim GRAYSON, Managing Director, Goldman Sachs

Carol MOIR, Executive Director of Transactions Legal, UBS Warburg

Roger MUNGER, Global Head of GFM Legal, ABN AMRO

Julia PEARCE, Director, Head of Transaction Management Group, Debt Capital Markets Group, Credit Suisse First Boston (Europe).

Roger SCOTTS, Executive Director, Goldman Sachs International

Kevin SOWERBUTTS, Head of Global Legal Transaction Management Group, BNP Paribas

Harry STANLEY, Executive Director, Morgan Stanley

An "aura of seniority" now surrounds **Kate Craven**; she is "good at guiding her colleagues to get results" and has "handled the difficult new areas created by FSMA with aplomb." "Unflappable" **Tim Grayson** "has a broad base of knowledge and experience." "Fabulous" **Carol Moir** impresses as one "not prepared to mince her words;" hard-working, she is "100% committed to the transaction." **Roger Munger** "keeps his eye firmly on the bigger picture," while "efficient" **Julia Pearce** employs a "constructive approach – she has a good combination of commercial and technical nous." Practitioners rate **Roger Scotts'** "great attitude to deals – he has a good understanding of what is important and knows how to manage the personalities." The "fine global co-ordination skills" of **Kevin Sowerbutts** were singled out; he enjoys a "huge standing" in the eyes of private practitioners. **Harry Stanley** is a "fantastic decision-maker" and an "experienced operator" in the debt markets.

In-house lawyers profiles p.1201

Energy, on the partial privatisation and IPO of Statoil, a $2 billion deal. **Clients** BNP Paribas; Barclays Capital; CableEuropa; Citigroup; CSFB; Deutsche Bank; Goldman Sachs International; HSBC Markets; JPMorgan; Merrill Lynch International; Morgan Stanley Dean Witter; SSSB; UBS Warburg.

LINKLATERS (see firm details p.1043) Industry commentators claim the firm stands astride the market with its balanced debt and equity capacity, although conditions have driven the group to pull on its well-established debt capital markets expertise. It enjoys a "*diverse international practice*" with emphasis on pan-European exchangeables and convertible bonds, and structured deals, areas in which our interviewees noted its "*fantastic depth of experience.*" Although some voiced reservations over distractions caused by the firm's European merger programme, many clients described the group as "*our sensible and commercial lifeline.*" The firm maintains its interest in the emerging markets. One of the notable exchangeable bond deals involved advising Prada Holding in the issue of €700 million notes with conditional exchange rights into shares of Prada Holding issued by Deutsche Bank.

Team head **Michael Canby** (see p.117) is a "*pragmatic strategist*" whose wealth of experience provides the group with an envied advisory resource. "*Senior statesman*" **Lachlan Burn** (see p.117) is still considered "*one of the leading lights of the sector.*" Leading the firm's Central and Eastern European work, **Nicholas Eastwell** (see p.117) manages to "*get stuck in,*" while clients admire "*his energy and focus.*" **Stephen Edlmann** (see p.117) is respected by clients not only for his "*excellent response time*" but also for his ability to "*present issues clearly.*" "*Focused and feisty all-rounder*" **Nigel Pridmore** (see p.119) was dubbed "*quick on the uptake.*" He and **Christopher McFadzean** (see p.119) advised SSSB on the structuring and issue by Bank of Scotland of £300 million perpetual regulatory tier 1 securities; McFadzean was particularly endorsed to our researchers for his convertible bond work.

Having built a reputation in Asia, **Keith Thomson** (see p.120) is the first port of call for clients seeking his "*technical brilliance,*" while the "*highly intelligent*" **Charles Clark** (see p.117) complements his general securities work with a niche in derivatives. "*Unique and technically astute*" **Jane Brown** (see p.117) is an "*effective operator,*" who has developed a following for her MTN programmes, and "*gentlemanly*" **Simon Ovenden** (see p.283772) has "*smoothly*" established his presence in the market following a posting in the Moscow office. On the equity side, the firm has advised Capio on its £85 million equity offering by way of private placement into Sweden, the UK, US, Finland, France, Germany and Switzerland. **Clients** Barclays Capital; BNP Paribas; Citigroup; CSFB; Deutsche Bank; JPMorgan Chase; Lehman Brothers; Merrill Lynch; Morgan Stanley; UBS Warburg.

FRESHFIELDS BRUCKHAUS DERINGER (see firm details p.964) Clients commend the equity team as "*user-friendly and pragmatic with young partners that are driving the practice forward.*" Although the firm is judged to have avoided the route of mainstream debt capital markets, our researchers were impressed by the level of backing amongst clients for its bespoke convertible, exchangeable and equity-linked transactional work. Much of the group's profile has an equity weighting, drawing on a strong issuer client base.

"*Reliable and charming*" **Jeremy Pitkin** (see p.119) has advised the joint global co-ordinators on the partial privatisation of Public Power Corporation, the state electricity company in Greece, in which 15% of the company was sold in the IPO, to both Greek retail and institutional investors and included a 144A tranche. Supported by its respected US partners in London, the team underlined its cross-border capabilities by handling BT's transfer of its mobile communications businesses and assets to mmO2 and subsequent demerger and listing on the LSE and NYSE.

Renowned for its close relationship to US investment banks, the firm advised Goldman Sachs on the placing of equity certificates by Deutsche Bank (representing an entitlement to one BSkyB ordinary share), allowing Vivendi Universal to monetise part of its stake. The team acted for Morgan Stanley in the offering by Iberdrola International of €740 million zero-coupon exchangeable bonds. In the past year, the firm has handled nine SEC-registered equity offerings and 38 144A equity offerings. **Clients** ABN AMRO Rothschild; Banca IMI; BNP Paribas; Commerzbank; Deutsche Bank; Euronext; Goldman Sachs; Merrill Lynch; Morgan Stanley; Nomura International; SSSB; UBS Warburg.

ASHURST MORRIS CRISP (see firm details p.852) The firm's "*successful corporate practice*" and its strength in securitisation has helped build the profile of the debt and equity practice; it is a tight ship "*on the rise.*" The potential of the former Weil, Gotshal & Manges structured finance partners is judged to have been realised. Though known more for its CDO practice, the team lead by Richard Kendall covers structured products, project bonds, European high yield and equity offerings. Debt highlights of the past year included a future receivable cross-over project bond deal for Ipswich Town FC. It has also advised Toronto Dominion Bank on its $8 billion EMTN programme, and acted for NM Rothschild in establishing its £300 million EMTN programme. On the equity side, the firm has particularly been involved in stand-alone European equity offerings - advising banks and corporates alike. US registered offerings such as Galen's US registered £300 million global offering, are examples of the team's breadth. It also advised Deutsche Bank on the acquisition of Varta by way of IPO (DM800 million). **Clients** Credito Italiano; Bank of Scotland; ING Baring; JPMorgan Chase Bank; Morgan Stanley; NM Rothschild; Salomon Brothers International.

CLEARY GOTTLIEB STEEN & HAMILTON (see firm details p.910) One of the few US law firms that covers the UK and US markets, interviewees attest to its "*broader-angled approach*" in comparison to its direct competitors. "*Consistently visible all product spheres,*" the firm is commended for its work in sovereign and high yield debt. **Ashar Qureshi** (see p.119) impresses with his "*ferocious intelligence;*" he is not only "*someone to bounce questions off*" but also "*inspires confidence*" in his clients. In the past year he has counselled the brokers on BT's £5.9 billion rights offering. His senior colleague and "*figurehead,*" **Edward Greene** (see p.118), is considered the "*guru of US international securities law.*" He applies a "*robust and pragmatic approach*" to his London-generated and US-related work. The team advised Lazard Capital Markets/Lazard Frères in the €300 million private placement of shares of IRP Holdings. It also represented the managers, led by Goldman

www.ChambersandPartners.com

111

CAPITAL MARKETS ■ LONDON

Sachs and Morgan Stanley, in the Dixon Group offering of bonds exchangeable into shares of Wanadoo (€260 million). **Clients** Abbey National; Cable & Wireless; Deutsche Bank; Deutsche Telekom; Goldman Sachs; HSBC; Morgan Stanley Dean Witter; Nortel; SSSB.

SHEARMAN & STERLING (see firm details p.1129) One of the few US firms to provide international equity offerings advice on a multi-jurisdictional level, it fields both US and UK-qualified partners and has a strong track record in US-registered offerings and 144A placements. Beyond this, the breadth of the practice includes high yield and investment grade debt as well as asset-backed, hybrid and derivative debt financing. Head of practice Pamela Gibson led the team (together with the support of the European offices) in the reflotation of Orange following its acquisition by France Telecom - this included institutional offerings and retail offers in Europe, together with an employee share offer in 12 countries. Advising Merrill Lynch and joint lead arrangers CIBC and Deutsche Bank, the team was involved in the financing of the £2.14 billion purchase of Yell; the debt package consisted of senior and bridge debt, the latter being refinanced through the issuance of high yield debt. **Clients** AngloGold; BT; Deutsche Bank; France Telecom; Goldman Sachs; Merrill Lynch; Morgan Stanley; Nokia; UBS Warburg.

SIMMONS & SIMMONS (see firm details p.1136) Better known for its repackaging practice, this "*hard-working outfit,*" headed by Tony Smith, also caters for the debt and equity markets. On the debt side, the firm advises investment banks and corporate clients on transactions including bond issues, high yield debt issues and MTN programmes. The structured finance team has this year welcomed the arrival of a US-qualified, former Simpson Thacher & Bartlett partner. On the equity side, Ian Sideris has led the team in advising the Spanish Government on the IPO of Iberia. Further highlights included advising BNP Paribas and Abaxbank on the international aspects of and the underwriting arrangements for Graniti-Fiandre's global offering raising €110 million. The firm also acted for Gallaher Group on a placing to raise £150 million. **Clients** Deutsche Bank AG London; Lehman Brothers; UBS Warburg; Barclays Capital; Bank of America; CSFB.

SLAUGHTER AND MAY (see firm details p.1140) Unsurprisingly, considering its "*powerful corporate client base,*" market commentators perceive the firm's capital markets practice to be weighted towards equities. Work produced is "*always of high quality,*" and interviewees attested to the team's peformance on "*the more complex and massive equity deals.*" An impressive international transactions list belies peer comment that ascribes the firm with a more domestic focus.

"*Commercial and technically bright*" **David Frank** (see p.118) leads the way here. The team's recent work includes acting for Orange in its €48.1 billion listing in Paris and London, through a global share offer. Also on the equity front was advice to Goldman Sachs and UBS Warburg on the £3 billion placing of new Vodafone shares, raising funds to part-finance the acquisition of BT's interest in Japan Telecom, The J-Phone Group and Airtel. Debt transactions have included work for Banco Santander and HypoVereinsbank on the €126.5 million 6.4% guaranteed bonds issued by Algarve International (a toll road project). Examples of the team's skilful handling of "*the most intricate work*" include advising CGNU on the issuance of £700 million subordinated notes due in 2036 and €800 million due in 2021. It has also worked with key client Abbey National on its new euro commercial paper programme. **Clients** Abbey National; British Airways; COLT Telecom; CGNU; Goldman Sachs; Marks & Spencer; Orange; UBS Warburg; Unilever.

BAKER & MCKENZIE (see firm details p.855) Market commentators commend this equity-weighted firm, particularly for its track record in the emerging Eastern European market. The firm's strength in tax-structured financing is also seen as a major asset. Corporate partner Peter Magyar and the team acted for Spherion in the £560 million IPO of shares of Michael Page International. Further work included the team's representation of the issuer Macquarie Infrastructure Group, owner of private toll roads, in an $800 million offering of stapled securities pursuant to Rule 144A and Regulation S. The firm has acted on several high yield offerings in Western Europe and emerging Eastern Europe, most recently having represented Kamps on a €300 million offering of high yield notes led by JPMorgan. **Clients** CA IB Investmentbank; CSFB; Dresdner Kleinwort Benson; SSSB.

HERBERT SMITH (see firm details p.992) Market sources commend the firm's strong equities showing, securing instruction from its already prominent corporate client base. The team has also been spotted in the debt market this past year, with its work for Bank of Scotland drawing accolades. This team of young partners is making its impact on the market, acting for underwriters and issuers alike, on UK IPOs and a range of debt structures. CSFB provides the marquee relationship that affords the firm significant deals. Clients informed our researchers of the team's responsiveness, commending its ability to react quickly on the most complex of matters.

Martina Asmar has returned after a short secondment to the Frankfurt office of German counterpart Gleiss Lutz. She was part of a team that acted for British Airports Authority on its exchange offer of bonds. For Bank of Scotland, the team advised on the listed issue of £300 million fixed rate perpetual regulatory tier one securities. Despite the slow market, the firm has handled IPOs this year, including Michael Page (£650 million), Friends Provident (£4 billion) and Real Estate Opportunities (£800 million). Triple listing advice was offered to Sinopec on its $3.4 billion IPO in Hong Kong, New York and London. **Clients** Bank of Scotland; CSFB; Carnival; Deutsche Bank; Goldman Sachs; Lazard Capital Markets; Merrill Lynch.

LOVELLS (see firm details p.1045) Active in the debt sphere, the firm focuses on the issuers' side in the emerging markets, often including high yield transactions. It also has a healthy track record in exchangeable and convertible bonds. David Hudd has led the team in deals such as the €100 million 12.5% subordinated notes offering by Kappa Beheer of bonds, featuring attached warrants and ranking *pari passu* with its outstanding high yield bonds. A further highlight saw the firm instructed by Barclays Bank on its $750 million reserve capital instruments, qualifying as tier 1 capital offered in the US under 144A. Active in the emerging markets, the team acted for FCE Bank Polska and FCE Credit Polska on the issue of a PLN1 billion debt programme. **Clients** ALSTROM; Bank Austria; BNP Paribas; Crédit Agricole Indosuez; CSFB; Electricité de France; Ford Motor Credit; Kappa Beheer; Lehman Brothers, Merrill Lynch; Suez Lyonnaise des Eaux.

NORTON ROSE (see firm details p.1084) Market commentators endorsed this team's "*strong, young partners*" for their efforts in "*building a healthy practice.*" In light of the slow equity market, the firm has concentrated on private debt deals, many of which are tax-driven. The caseload has featured structured investment vehicles such as tier one note programmes and upper tier two hybrids. Christian Parker covers both the debt and equity markets, acting on a number of securities tax and regulatory arbitrage issues for large multinationals. On the debt side the team has advised the Bank of Ireland on an issue of €600 million innovative tier 1 capital notes. Recent equity-linked work has involved the advice rendered to easyJet on its follow-on equity offering, after having acted on the company's IPO in the UK and US last year. The firm also acted for SSSB on The Wellcome Trust's sale of £1.8 billion of shares in GlaxoSmithKline. The team's activities in catastrophe bonds is enhanced by its strong cross-fertilisation with the corporate insurance group. **Clients** ABN AMRO; BMW; Carlsberg; Citibank; CSFB; Deutsche Bank; easyJet; HSBC; Royal Bank of Scotland; Stemar; TXU; WestLB Panmure.

WEIL, GOTSHAL & MANGES (see firm details p.1183) Interviewees pointed to the firm's US-focused equities practice, which has made attempts at regrowth following the departure last year of key team members. "*One to watch,*"

LONDON ■ CAPITAL MARKETS

rivals claim it also benefits from offices in Frankfurt and Warsaw. It advises on both debt and equity offerings, including high yield, bond offerings and public and private placements for issuers. The team advised Merrill Lynch on the €463.5 million share offering of Fortum, made by the Republic of Finland. Paul Claydon and the team have also advised Yell on its proposed, but delayed, IPO.

OTHER NOTABLE PRACTITIONERS Interviewees endorsed **Jake Jackaman** (see p.118) of White & Case as a "*client-focused, hard-working*" lawyer. UK and US-qualified, he is thought to compete "*head-on with the big names,*" particularly in the emerging Eastern European markets.

LONDON

ALLEN & OVERY (see firm details p.841) This respected practice has scored well with its concentration on whole business securitisations. Its raft of "*top-quality work*" has included some of the highest profile UK deals, and rivals conclude that "*working with them leaves no room for mistakes.*" These talented partners are the envy of competing firms ("*we'd like to poach from them*") and the range of work sees property and automotive industries catered for alongside complex conduit work. Heading the group is "*exuberant and effective*" **David Krischer** (see p.118), who "*delights clients*" with his creative thinking. He has led his team in advice to SSSB as lead manager in the £1.8 billion asset-backed securitisation by Telereal of leasehold properties acquired from and leased back to British Telecom. "*Exceptionally hard-working - a lively enthusiast*" is how clients view **Julian Tucker** (see p.120), while peers point to him as "*the property expert with loyal clients.*" He handled the Canary Wharf financing, advising on the £875 million innovative securitisation of further properties on the Canary Wharf estate.

"*Superb draftsman*" **Paul Bedford** (see p.117) brings his expertise in synthetic structures to the deal table. He is "*wise and calm*" and "*sensitively understands the needs of his clients.*" The team has acted on the award-winning Welsh Water securitisation, advising Western Water Distribution in a unique landmark £2 billion structured financing, making this heavily regulated sector more attractive to investors. Judged to have "*established herself in interesting work,*" **Angela Clist** (see p.117) has attracted a following with her "*sound pragmatic approach.*" She and colleague **Christian Lambie** (see p.119) ("*bright and charming*") have helped to develop the whole business securitisation technology.

One of the highlights which the repackaging expert **Geoff Fuller** (see p.118) acted on was advising Goldman Sachs International as arranger of a €350 million funded arbitrage CDO, through Copernicus Euro CDO-I, with respect to a portfolio composed of 75% in loans and 25% in bonds. Clients further praised the younger members of the team as "*technically superb,*" displaying "*academic prowess.*" Clients Barclays Capital; Bear Stearns; CICB; Citigroup; Deutsche Bank; Development Bank of Singapore; Goldman Sachs; JPMorgan; Merrill Lynch International; Morgan Stanley; Nomura; Rabobank; Westdeutsche Landesbank Girozentrale.

CLIFFORD CHANCE (see firm details p.911) The sheer size of the practice remains one of its outstanding features, while peers view it as the market leader in the development of new products encompassing the UK, US and European markets. Leading the field in credit card and mortgage-backed deals, the team is said to be "*moving into new areas,*" and focusing on the "*huge transactions.*"

Heading the London securitisation group is **Chris Oakley** (see p.119), whose "*detailed knowledge can be trusted*" especially as "*there is nothing he hasn't seen before.*" One of the main highlights the team has worked on this year was the advice rendered to SSSB and the Royal Bank of Scotland as joint lead arrangers on the £2 billion securitisation used by Glas to finance the management-led buyout of the Welsh Water-regulated business from Western Power Distribution.

"*At the cutting edge,*" **Kevin Ingram** (see p.118) is an "*energetic and creative lawyer, driven by his clients' objectives.*" Heading the international group is technically experienced **John Woodhall** (see p.121), while "*strong all-rounder*" **Peter Voisey** (see p.120) has carved out his niche in consumer asset work. His colleague **Andrew Forryan** (see p.118) places an emphasis on real estate transactions. "*Committed hard-worker*" **Stephen Curtis** (see p.117) is deemed "*securitisation through and through,*" having handled numerous deals, particularly credit card-related transactions.

The team has been advising Dresdner Kleinwort Wasserstein and Merrill Lynch as deal managers in a complex whole business financing, involving the purchase of over £1.1 billion of Eurotunnel junior debt, funded solely by the issue of £900 million notes (both Reg S and 144A), which were secured on the repurchased junior debt. Further, the team advised WestLB, BNP Paribas and Finanzaria Internazionale as joint lead arrangers and the Bank of New York as trustee on the first European public communications securitisation for Telecom Italia, a €2 billion asset-backed note programme.

FRESHFIELDS BRUCKHAUS DERINGER (see firm details p.964) Clients are convinced of the high levels of service and commitment of this team. They also commend the level of multi-jurisdictional support, with the firm deploying its high-profile lawyers throughout the overseas offices. Ian Falconer's move to Paris

SECURITISATON & REPACKAGING

and Stuart Axford to Frankfurt are recent departures that strengthen the network, while Alan Newton has returned from Italy to lead the securitisation group in London. Covering a spread of asset classes, the firm manages its workload expertly and is an international brand name, which "*scores well overseas.*" Whole business securitisations, warehouse financings, cash and synthetic CLOs, CBOs, CDOs, complex tax-driven products and derivative-based (credit and equity-linked) transactions are catered for here. A broad exposure of work is afforded to the team, with additional skill in insurance derivatives, repos and stock-lending, project bonds and the convergence between insurance and capital market transactions. **David Trott** (see p.120) is respected as one who brings a "*stamp of quality*" to any product, while his colleague **Marcus Mackenzie** (see p.119) "*doesn't try to score points.*" He recently acted on the Telereal/BT outsourcing, advising Telereal on its acquisition of BT's property portfolio, funded in part by a £1.8 billion note issue by Telereal Securitisation. "*Technically skilled*" **James McKeand** (see p.119) has also secured the endorsement of his peers. In the past year, he acted on the Atlas securitisation, a sovereign securitisation by the Greek Government, in which he and the team advised BNP Paribas, Deutsche Bank, EFG Eurobank Ergasias and NBG International as arrangers.

LINKLATERS (see firm details p.1043) The firm is commended by clients for its "*proven reliability and helpful partnership approach,*" which also benefits from the backing of its worldwide network. Its strong mainstream capital markets, finance and corporate practice gives added weight and the firm covers the full range of securitisation and repackaging matters, involving actual asset transfer transactions, synthetic securitisations and actual and synthetic repackagings. Julian Davies heads the team, which acted on the landmark structured financing for the Welsh Water business ('Glas') involving a $6.2 billion bond programme and £2 billion initial bond issue, advising Glas Cymru Cyfyngedig. Part of his team is the "*impressive*" **Jim Rice** (see p.119), who clients agree "*manages projects well: on schedule and with a commercial sense - high marks allround.*" In a recent highlight, he represented Financial Security Assurance (guarantor), Royal Bank of Scotland (lead manager) and the Bank of New York

113

CAPITAL MARKETS ■ LONDON

CAPITAL MARKETS: SECURITISATION & REPACKAGING
■ LONDON

1
- Allen & Overy
- Clifford Chance

2 Freshfields Bruckhaus Deringer

3 Linklaters

4
- Ashurst Morris Crisp
- Sidley Austin Brown & Wood
- Simmons & Simmons

5
- Slaughter and May
- Weil, Gotshal & Manges

6
- Lovells
- Norton Rose

LEADING INDIVIDUALS

1
- INGRAM Kevin *Clifford Chance*
- KRISCHER David *Allen & Overy*

2
- BEDFORD Paul *Allen & Overy*
- OAKLEY Chris *Clifford Chance*
- TROTT David *Freshfields Bruckhaus Deringer*

3
- FORRYAN Andrew *Clifford Chance*
- FULLER Geoff *Allen & Overy*
- HANDLING Erica *Ashurst Morris Crisp*
- HUGHES Richard *Linklaters*
- KELLY Jacky *Weil, Gotshal & Manges*
- MACKENZIE Marcus *Freshfields Bruckhaus*
- RAINES Marke *Shearman & Sterling*
- RICE Jim *Linklaters*
- TUCKER Julian *Allen & Overy*
- VOISEY Peter *Clifford Chance*
- WOODHALL John *Clifford Chance*

4
- BRESSLAW James *Simmons & Simmons*
- CLIST Angela *Allen & Overy*
- PENN Graham *Sidley Austin Brown & Wood*
- SMITH Christopher *Slaughter and May*

5
- BORROWS Jane *Herbert Smith*
- HUDD David *Lovells*
- MCKEAND James *Freshfields Bruckhaus Deringer*
- SMITH Christian *Weil, Gotshal & Manges*
- SMITH Sarah *Sidley Austin Brown & Wood*
- VOISIN Michael *Linklaters*
- WALKER John *Milbank, Tweed, Hadley & McCloy*
- WALSH Jonathan *Norton Rose*

UP AND COMING
- CURTIS Stephen *Clifford Chance*
- LAMBIE Christian *Allen & Overy*

ASSOCIATES TO WATCH
- SKUTER John *Allen & Overy*

This book is the product of 6,582 1/2 hour interviews. See p.7 for BMRB audit. Within each band, firms are listed alphabetically. See individuals' profiles p.117

"*runs his team well*" in deals involving investment fund repackagings, convertible bond repackagings and credit-linked notes.

ASHURST MORRIS CRISP (see firm details p.852) Particularly known for its CDO/CLO practice, the strong corporate base of this firm further enhances its securitisation and structured finance capacity. The team's client base in this field consists mainly of lenders and underwriters - often Japanese - and the firm has also been seen to act for clients on project finance securitisations. Since the arrival of "*CDO expert*" **Erica Handling** (see p.118), the firm's potential in capital markets has been realised, with peers commending its skill in both securitisation and synthetic structuring.

The team has acted on 15 CDOs in 2001, such as a matter for JPMorgan Chase Bank, the Euromax MBS (€198 million). For Promus I, the firm handled a CDO structure that provided an extended ramp up period of up to four years, during which time the purchase of assets can be funded through drawings under a revolving loan facility, with the possibility of refinancing through further note issue at a later date. The firm has also been involved in future receivables cross-over project bond work (Ipswich) and in whole business securitisation.

SIDLEY AUSTIN BROWN & WOOD (see firm details p.1134) Interviewees ascribe "*a lot of potential*" to the firm, especially remarking on its "*healthy*" conduit work. The merged US firm is "*performing well*" in the London market, although it has a concentration on the US-related matters. Its workload encompasses a variety of assets and synthetic structures, and the firm advises originators, arrangers, monoline insurance companies, trustees and a rating agency on the issues relating to the creation of special purpose vehicles.

Clients describe the team as "*intelligent and easy-going.*" "*Successful*" **Graham Penn** (see p.119) is said to be "*one of the founding fathers of the securitisation market;*" he acted for Lehman Brothers on its £467 million securitisation of commercial mortgages, backed by UK loans using a special purpose vehicle, Windermere CMBS. His colleague, the "*committed and technically excellent*" **Sarah Smith** (see p.120), advised on the special purpose vehicle, Granite Mortgages 01-2, established to securitise residential mortgage loans originated by Northern Rock. In a further highlight, the firm represented Morgan Stanley Real Estate and a number of Italian associated entities on a €1 billion securitisation of Italian non-performing loans.

SIMMONS & SIMMONS (see firm details p.1136) Although the market sees the firm traditionally as placed in the repackaging sector, this "*broad-ranging*" team advises on a range of structured financings and asset-backed securities, increasingly developing its presence in the CDO market. Visible on a number of "*complex transactions,*" the team is thought to have a keen eye for the lead managers' perspective.

"*Charming and technically sound*" **James Bresslaw** (see p.117), who "*completely immerses himself in his work,*" has advised The British Land Company on its £875 million securitisation of the Meadowhall Shopping Centre. He and his team have also advised Diners Club Europe, Diners Club Germany and Diners Club Benelux in the acquisition and securitisation of a €600 million portfolio of present and future charge card receivables.

Another highlight over the past year was the advice rendered to the Ministry of Defence in connection with the Short Term Strategic Airlift Programme, a £434 million securitisation of the Government's military aircraft leasing payments.

SLAUGHTER AND MAY (see firm details p.1140) Market commentators acknowledge that the firm is "*taking this sector seriously.*" Commended for its strong client relationship ethos, the firm continues to act for major securers, advising on a raft of transactions ranging from full swaps to synthetic securitisations, often with a German or Italian contingent. Peers respect **Christopher Smith** (see p.120) and clients appreciate his "*technically detailed*" advice. The team has acted on a $5 billion synthetic securitisation of an asset-backed securities portfolio, and remains envied for its ties to mainstay client Abbey National (the Treasury Service branch). The firm further acted for Alliance UniChem on a securitisation of receivables arising from the sale of pharmaceutical products and services. Last year also saw the €2 billion highlight asset-backed note programme for Telecom Italia. For CGNU/Norwich Union, the team securitised its equity release mortgages for £244.5 million.

WEIL, GOTSHAL & MANGES (see firm details p.1183) Clearly aiming to satisfy strong client relationships on both sides of the Atlantic, this relatively small team has made "*the best stab of any*" in building up its team of UK lawyers. It is commended by peers as a "*serious and credible*" practice, with clients emphasising its "*proactive approach.*" The asset-backed conduit side of the practice received particular plaudits, with the team further handling whole business and further asset class securitisations, alongside its CDO coverage. "*Problem-solver*" **Jacky Kelly** (see p.118) combines "*commerciality with a personable approach to deals.*" She leads the team and has acted for Nikko Principal Investments in connection with the acquisition of Powell Duffryn and subsequent securitisation of the ports business - a £305 million whole business securitisation. Her colleague, "*technically minded, user-friendly*" **Christian Smith** (see p.120), specialises in the asset-backed conduit sector. He recently represented JPMorgan Chase as

---

(bond trustee) on the issue of £100 million guaranteed secured index-linked bonds by Sutton and East Surrey Water. Peers value the "*engaging*" **Richard Hughes** (see p.118) as a strong team player and "*one of the most charming guys out there.*" The repackaging sector is in **Michael Voisin**'s (see p.120) skilled hands. He

LONDON — CAPITAL MARKETS

lead manager and arranger in the MTN and CP programme established for the €170 million securitisation of Huntsman's US and European trade receivables. The firm has also acted on the £60 million Chrysalis securitisation of its global music publishing catalogue, representing Royal Bank of Scotland and Barclays Bank.

LOVELLS (see firm details p.1045) Making its presence felt in both the securitisation and the repackaging sectors, the firm's corporate client base is said to "*make all the difference.*" Enjoying a "*strong track record,*" the team handles a great deal of property-backed deals, and also focuses on the CDO market. It has been particularly successful of late on the pan-European front. Clients commend this smaller team as "*a prime choice due to the time devoted to our cause,*" and admired the commitment of its "*talented, bright, young team.*" **David Hudd** (see p.118) led the team on matters such as acting for BNP Paribas on its five synthetic CDOs through Riviera Finance 1 and 2, CDO Master Investments/2 and Serena Finance, involving a mezzanine risk on a portfolio of credit default swaps. Team member Brian Carne assisted on the RHM Finance acquisition through Doughty Hanson by means of a whole business securitisation, backed by income from RHM's businesses and secured on intellectual property, real property and other assets.

In combination with the Paris office, the team further acted for Assurances Generales de France IART as credit enhancer of Citibank's securitisation of part of its project finance loan portfolio.

NORTON ROSE (see firm details p.1084) The workload here features instructions from leading rating agencies and asset-backed conduit transactions for banks and arrangers. Sources endorsed the firm's "*burgeoning practice*" in the securitisation sector. **Jonathan Walsh** (see p.120) heads the team; he was the key partner in advising HSBC as arranger and conduit sponsor in connection with a securitisation financing of a major UK electricity company, including issues regarding both present and future electricity receivables. The past year also saw the team advising on a €1 billion residential mortgage-backed transaction involving the securitisation of Portuguese assets originated by Banco Comercial Português. Another asset-backed transaction for the same originator saw the firm acting for Deutsche Bank as UK and German counsel in the issue of NOVA Finance No. 2 €352.1 million secured floating rate notes due in 2007.

OTHER NOTABLE PRACTITIONERS "*Effective operator*" **Jane Borrows** (see p.117) has joined Herbert Smith from Sidley Austin Brown & Wood. Her arrival is judged to be "*particularly positive for the firm,*" bringing as she does, a "*wide knowledge.*" "*Talented*" **Marke Raines** is busy building the securitisation practice at Shearman & Sterling. "*Pragmatic*" **John Walker** (see p.120) at Milbank, Tweed, Hadley & McCloy has a keen eye on the CDO/CBO market, but also handles residential mortgages and public securitisations.

LONDON — DERIVATIVES

CAPITAL MARKETS: DERIVATIVES
LONDON

1. Allen & Overy
2. Clifford Chance
   Linklaters
3. Freshfields Bruckhaus Deringer
4. Slaughter and May
5. Baker & McKenzie
   Norton Rose

LEADING INDIVIDUALS

1
- BENTON David — Allen & Overy
- FIRTH Simon — Linklaters
- GOLDEN Jeffrey — Allen & Overy
- HADDOCK Simon — Allen & Overy
- MOTANI Habib — Clifford Chance

2
- WARNA-KULA-SURIYA Sanjev — Slaughter and May

3
- BROWN Claude — Clifford Chance
- RUDIN Simeon — Freshfields Bruckhaus Deringer

4
- BATES Chris — Clifford Chance
- BUSH Jane — Clifford Chance

UP AND COMING
- TREDGETT Richard — Allen & Overy

This book is the product of 6,582 1/2 hour interviews. See p.7 for BMRR audit. Within each band, firms are listed alphabetically. See individuals' profiles p.117

ALLEN & OVERY (see firm details p.841) Many clients pronounced this the "*best derivatives practice in London,*" impressed by its "*talented, responsive lawyers.*" The firm's counselling to ISDA in Europe, the US and South East Asia is central to the firm's profile in this arena but belies its broader scope. Peers acknowledge the firm's "*vast range and expertise,*" which encompasses synthetic CBOs, CLOs and securitised derivatives. It is involved in new product development – catastrophe derivatives, hybrid securitisations and exchange-traded products all feature in the workload. The firm has recently assisted ISDA in achieving legislative reform in Eastern and Central Europe and advised on its work with the Central Bank of Brazil in the regulatory implementation of recent Brazilian legislation.

Dubbed the "*frontman of derivatives,*" **Jeff Golden** (see p.118) handles much of the work for ISDA, including policy issues and project drafting. His colleague, **David Benton** (see p.117) ("*sharp and responsive*"), brings a commercial drive to his expertise in credit derivatives. "*Energetic*" **Simon Haddock**'s (see p.118) legal judgement is highly valued, particularly by traders, while interviewees predict a bright future for rising star **Richard Tredgett** (see p.120).

The team advised on the preparation of the industry-standard US law netting opinions for the GMSLA, and has worked with ISDA on the launch of an e-commerce product (netalytics) providing ISDA members with an on-line information resource.

CLIFFORD CHANCE (see firm details p.911) Closing in on A&O, the firm is commended not only for the size of its "*dedicated derivatives practice,*" but also for its "*breadth of its expertise.*" Peers contend: "*if I were a client, I'd go there.*" OTC derivatives, credit and equity-linked transactions, futures and exchange-traded derivatives are major areas of expertise. Crisis-related issues (following September 11th and the collapse of major issuers) feature in the caseload, and the team is applauded for its regulatory knowledge. The firm achieves strong market penetration by means of its international presence. Clearly at the cutting edge, it has also advised on the development of weather derivatives and fund-linked derivatives.

"*Talented diplomat*" **Habib Motani** (see p.119) is particularly known for his concentration on equity-linked transactions. He advised on JPMorgan's use of equity derivatives to facilitate SAI's (Italian insurer) divestment of its stake in La Fondiara. **Claude Brown** (see p.117) focuses on the credit derivatives, and led the team's efforts for Barclays Capital on a €500 million CDO (Barclays Blue Eagle). Interviewees commend **Jane Bush** (see p.117) as an "*effective team player;*" her work covers the range with an OTC derivatives weighting. But both Bush and **Chris Bates** (see p.389) are seen to handle the regulatory and exchange-traded derivatives. The firm has advised on the acquisition of LIFFE by Euronext, as well as handling work for clients and trade associations on the introduction of the Financial Services and Markets Act.

LINKLATERS (see firm details p.1043) Backed by its "*fantastic*" mainstream capital markets practice, the derivatives practice here has moved away from its "*back-burner*" image. Interviewees credit the team with building a

115

CAPITAL MARKETS ■ LONDON

TOP IN-HOUSE LAWYERS

DERIVATIVES

Richard ATKINSON, Director of Law & Compliance and Senior Counsel, Merrill Lynch International

David BLOOM, Senior Legal Adviser, HSBC Holdings

Edmond CURTIN, Managing Director, Credit Suisse First Boston

David GEEN, Executive Director and Senior Counsel, Goldman Sachs International

David LEWIS, Managing Director & Associate General Counsel, JPMorgan Chase

Joan MA, Executive Director, Morgan Stanley

Jon ORMOND, Legal Adviser, Deutsche Bank

Charles ROSS-STEWART, Executive Director, UBS Warburg

Bill Ryan, Director, Deutsche Bank

"*Street savvy*" **Richard Atkinson** can "*deal with the legal issues and cut through them to give commercial advice;*" he is one who "*relishes the complexities.*" **David Bloom** has a "*clear understanding of cross-border issues*" and a "*great depth of experience.*" "*Clever*" **Edmond Curtin** is "*one of the senior figures on the scene,*" while "*articulate and astute*" **David Geen** offers "*an exceptional understanding*" of the derivatives market. **David Lewis** is a "*strong technician*" with a "*wealth of experience,*" and **Joan Ma** is an "*effective deal-doer.*" Observers value **Jon Ormond** as "*a key shield for the private practice lawyer – he can make deals happen.*" "*Approachable*" **Charles Ross-Stewart** is "*immersed in the derivatives market,*" while "*effective senior player*" **Bill Ryan** ensures that "*cutting edge-stuff*" is part of his daily routine

In-house lawyers' profiles p.1201

"*tremendous reputation*" in the OTC and securitised derivatives markets. The emphasis in the past year has been on structured credit derivatives transactions, acting for the originators and investors as well as investment banks. A further increase in instructions has been seen in credit default swaps (achieving synthetic securitisations) and synthetic CLOs. One such highlight included the firm's advice to Deutsche Bank as arranger of the Marylebone Road CBO 3, originated by Abbey National (€8 billion).

"*Good technician and highly intelligent*" **Simon Firth** (see p.118) is a primary figure in this field, and has been instructed by PwC on the restructuring of commodity and credit derivatives issues by the Enron group of companies, and in the provision of advice concerning derivatives entered into by group members.

JPMorgan Chase instructed the team in an equity-linked transaction with Transnet, a government-controlled South African company - raising $500 million for the Republic of South Africa. The firm also advised market participants on disputes about whether exchangeable bonds issued by Railtrack could be delivered under credit default swaps based on the 1999 ISDA Credit Derivatives Definitions.

FRESHFIELDS BRUCKHAUS DERINGER

(see firm details p.964) Clients commend the team's "*high-quality work,*" in particular pointing to its expertise in stock lending securities, repos and tax-driven products. The fully integrated structured finance group covers the full range of derivative-based transactions, including credit derivatives, equity and insurance derivatives, capital raising/arbitrage transactions and project bonds. Beyond its transaction-based work, the group advises the Stock Lending and Repo Committee and ISMA.

"*Technically astute*" **Simeon Rudin** (see p.119) derives a great advantage from his tax background; peers endorse his "*pragmatic approach,*" agreeing he is "*great with clients.*" Lately, he has acted for CIBC World Markets as lead arrangers on the first European CDO to have assets denominated in different currencies held within the special purpose vehicle, the Duchess CDO.

The team also handled the Leonardo CLO, advising Merrill Lynch on this synthetic CLO transaction relating to a portfolio of aircraft financings, and represented Morgan Stanley on the establishment of its European retail warrant and certificate issuance programmes. The latter exemplifies the firm's skill in co-ordinating multi-jurisdictional programmes.

SLAUGHTER AND MAY

(see firm details p.1140) This small team covers derivatives as part of wider transactions, acting for corporates and financial institutions on credit default swaps, equity swaps, structured notes and programmes, synthetic securitisation, interest rate and currency derivatives. It has also been involved in insurance transformer vehicles. **Sanjev Warna-kula-suriya** (see p.120) impresses market sources with his creative drive and intelligence and stands out particularly for his work on behalf of Abbey National. He has also been active for several financial institutions on matters regarding portfolio credit default swaps. In connection with the setting up of a new ISDA Master Agreement for a corporate client, the firm negotiated and prepared confirmations relating to certain swap transactions.

BAKER & MCKENZIE

(see firm details p.855) Instructing clients are happy to retain the firm's services due to its "*highly professional approach, which offers more partner attention.*" While Chris Hogan heads the practice, Matthew Dening is also a key contact for many clients who appreciate his team's grasp of "*making the deal work.*" The team continues to service clients such as end-users and financial institutions, but of most interest has been the firm's work with regard to emissions trading. Here the team has acted for IETA (International Emissions Trading Association) and has advised Natsource-Tullet in relation to its standard form emission trading documentation, involving green gas issues.

Dening and the team advised Nexgen on its derivatives and other structured products. The firm also advised Citicorp in the hedging activities of Beta Finance, one of its structured investment vehicles. An important part of the practice remains the equity-linked derivatives transactions, which often require advice in a variety of jurisdictions.

NORTON ROSE

(see firm details p.1084) This year has seen the retirement of the "*grandfather of derivatives,*" Schuyler Henderson, depriving the team of its most high-profile capital markets figure. Although undoubtedly a loss, the firm has had success in "*boosting its presence*" with Bruce Somer as its key derivatives partner. The team covers a broad range of work from structured finance and dispute resolution to regulatory and tax advice on the establishment of financial institutions and equity-linked transactions. It has also been involved in the enforcement of derivative agreements. In the insurance sector, the team has provided advice on risk transfer products. In the last year, Henderson and the team represented a bank in a €2.2 billion synthetic CDO offering, and the firm has advised Brit Insurance on an insurance product, utilising an offshore protected cell captive structure. Ashanti Goldfields instructed the firm in the restructuring of its gold hedge book as part of its general finance restructuring.

THE LEADERS IN CAPITAL MARKETS

BATES, Chris
Clifford Chance, London
(020) 7600 1000
chris.bates@cliffordchance.com
See under Financial Services, p.389

BEDFORD, Paul
Allen & Overy, London
(020) 7330 3000
paul.bedford@allenovery.com
Specialisation: Partner specialising in securitisation transactions.
Career: Qualified *Allen & Overy* (1982); assistant solicitor (1982-87); partner (1988).
Personal: Born 1956. Educated at Brighton College and Warwick University (1979, LLB).

BENTON, David
Allen & Overy, London
(020) 7330 3000
david.benton@allenovery.com
Specialisation: Partner with the Derivatives Group. He is a regular writer and speaker on the legal and documentation aspects of derivatives, including collateral, credit derivatives and the hedging aspects of structured financings.
Career: Articled *Allen & Overy* (1988); qualified (1990); partner (1997).
Personal: Born 1966. Educated Corpus Christi College, Cambridge (1987, BA Hons Law).

BICKERTON, David
Clifford Chance, London
(020) 7600 1000
david.bickerton@cliffordchance.com
See under Projects/PFI, p.694

BORROWS, Jane
Herbert Smith, London
(020) 7374 8000
jane.borrows@herbertsmith.com
Specialisation: Partner with extensive capital markets experience, both as a banker and a lawyer. Since the first securitisation transactions in the UK in the 1980s, she has focused primarily on securitisation, both domestic and cross-border. Advises lead managers, originators, trustees and other market participants such as monoline insurers, primarily in relation to public issues. Practice covers a wide range of securitised assets, including residential and commercial mortgages, trade receivables, property rentals, equipment leases, hire purchase and conditional sale contracts, bonds, commercial loans and regulatory capital markets.
Career: LLB (Hons), Queen Mary College, University of London. Sloan Fellow of London Business School.
Publications: Edited 'Current issues in Securitisation' (Sweet & Maxwell).

BRESSLAW, James
Simmons & Simmons, London
(020) 7628 2020
james.bresslaw@simmons-simmons.com
Specialisation: Securitisation and structured finance.
Prof. Memberships: Law Society.
Career: *Simmons & Simmons* 1984 to date.

BROWN, Claude
Clifford Chance, London
(020) 7600 1000
claude.brown@cliffordchance.com
Specialisation: Banking and finance. Partner specialising in derivatives and structured products.
Career: Partner since 1998.

BROWN, Jane
Linklaters, London
(020) 7456 4642
jane.brown@linklaters.com
Specialisation: Experience covers a wide range of international securities work, including advising underwriters and issuers in connection with issues of debt, equity and equity-related securities, as well as derivative and structured products.
Career: Qualified 1986. Foreign lawyer programme, *Sullivan & Cromwell* New York 1986-87. Assistant Solicitor *Linklaters* 1987-88 (New York). Assistant solicitor *Linklaters* 1988-92 (London). Partner *Linklaters* London 1992 to date.

BURN, Lachlan
Linklaters, London
(020) 7456 4614
lachlan.burn@linklaters.com
Specialisation: Specialist with over 24 years experience in banking and capital markets issues. Typical matters handled include GDRs, convertible bonds and derivatives of all types.
Prof. Memberships: Legal advisor to the International Primary Market Association. External examiner to the University of London.
Career: Articled at *Linklaters* and qualified in 1976; 1976-82 – Assistant Solicitor, *Linklaters*; Partner in *Linklaters* since 1982. Seconded to the Paris office from 1982-87. 1992-94 Member of the Legal Risk Review Committee. Partner. *Linklaters* London 1987 to date.

BUSH, Jane
Clifford Chance, London
(020) 7600 1000
jane.bush@cliffordchance.com
Specialisation: Banking and finance. Partner specialising in derivatives, repackaging and banking.
Career: Articled *Clifford-Turner/Clifford Chance*, qualified 1983; Partner since 1988.
Personal: Exeter University (Law 2:1).

CANBY, Michael
Linklaters, London
(020) 7456 4624
michael.canby@linklaters.com
Specialisation: Head of Global Securities Group. Specialist in capital markets transactions, including debt and equity financings, derivative products and documentation (having been involved in the drafting of the various stages of industry standard documentation), and advising on structured financings.
Career: Qualified 1980, 1980-86 assistant solicitor, *Linklaters*, seconded to New York 1982-84. Partner *Linklaters* London (International Finance Department) 1986-88. Partner *Linklaters* Paris 1988-95 (and Managing Partner of the Paris office 1992-95). Partner, in charge of the London Global Securities Group, since 1995.

CLARK, Charles
Linklaters, London
(020) 7456 4630
charles.clark@linklaters.com
Specialisation: Extensive experience of international securities issues, derivatives and capital markets transactions.
Career: 1980-82 Trainee Solicitor *Linklaters*; 1982-83 Assistant Solicitor *Linklaters* London; 1983-86 Assistant Solicitor *Linklaters* Paris; 1986-89 Assistant Solicitor *Linklaters* London; 1989 to date, Partner *Linklaters* in the International Finance Department.

CLIST, Angela H
Allen & Overy, London
(020) 7330 3000
angela.clist@allenovery.com
Specialisation: Partner specialising in securitisation.
Prof. Memberships: Registered Foreign Lawyers, English Law Society 2000.
Career: Solicitor in New Zealand before joining *Allen & Overy*. Qualified in 1992; associate *Kensington Swan*, New Zealand (1992-96); associate *Allen & Overy* (1996-2000); partner *Allen & Overy* (2000).

CURTIS, Stephen
Clifford Chance, London
(020) 7600 1000
Specialisation: Capital Market Department. Partner specialising in all types of structured financings, in particular, securitisation of real estate assets, whole businesses, sports receivables, credit cards, corporate loans and trade receivables.
Career: Joined *Clifford Chance* as an articled clerk in 1991; Partner since 2000.
Personal: University College School London; Manchester University (LLB Hons); College of Law Chancery Lane.

DUNLOP, Stewart
Clifford Chance, London
(020) 7600 1000
stewart.dunlop@cliffordchance.com
Specialisation: Partner specialising in advising arrangers/borrowers in connection with EMTN Programmes and bond issues by developed and emerging market borrowers; regulatory capital issues; structured notes and equity-related issues.
Career: Articled, *Allen & Overy*. Qualified 1991. Partner, *Clifford Chance* May 2000.

DUNNIGAN, David
Clifford Chance, London
(020) 7600 1000
david.dunnigan@cliffordchance.com
Specialisation: Capital markets. Partner specialising in European capital markets, all forms of debt and equity-related capital markets products.
Career: Articled *Turner Kenneth Brown*; qualified 1986 *Coward Chance/Clifford Chance*; Partner since 1992.
Personal: 1980-83 Nottingham University (LLB 2:1).

EASTWELL, Nicholas W
Linklaters, London
(020) 7456 4660
nick.eastwell@linklaters.com
Specialisation: Specialises in capital markets transactions including issues/offerings of debt, equity-related debt, equity and depositary receipts in international markets. In addition areas of practice include repackagings of bonds, funds and other financial assets, debt issuance programmes.
Career: Assistant Solicitor, *Linklaters* London, Corporate and International Finance Department 1982-83. Assistant Solicitor Hong Kong, International Finance Department, 1983-86. Assistant Solicitor, *Linklaters* Hong Kong, Head of International Finance Department, 1986-89, Partner *Linklaters* Hong Kong, Head of International Finance Department, 1989-90. Partner *Linklaters* London, International Finance Department, 1990-98. Partner *Linklaters* London Capital Markets Department 1998 to date. Managing Partner *Linklaters* Central and Eastern Europe 1999 to date.

EATOUGH, David
Clifford Chance, London
(020) 7600 1000
david.eatough@cliffordchance.com
Specialisation: Banking and finance and capital markets. Partner specialising in debt and equity, capital markets, including MTN programmes, preference shares, structured and convertible bonds and high-yield and short-term markets.
Career: Called to the English Bar 1986; Solicitor 1993. Joined *Clifford Chance* 1992. Partner since 1997.
Personal: Oxford University.

EDLMANN, Stephen
Linklaters, London
(020) 7456 4512
stephen.edlmann@linklaters.com
Specialisation: Specialist for over 20 years in debt, equity and equity-related issues in the international markets advising both issuers and investment banks. Areas covered include bonds, medium-term note and commercial paper programmes, convertible and exchangeable bonds, share and GDR issues and associated listing and regulatory rules and regulations.
Career: 1973-76 Trinity Hall Cambridge, Open Exhibitioner MA Law; 1977-79 Articled Clerk, *Linklaters*; 1979-85 Assis-

CAPITAL MARKETS ■ THE LEADERS

tant Solicitor, *Linklaters* London and New York; 1985 to date Partner *Linklaters*; 1995 to date Head of International Finance Department. Member of Executive Committee and International Board of *Linklaters & Alliance*.

FIRTH, Simon
Linklaters, London
(020) 7456 3764
simon.firth@linklaters.com
Specialisation: Specialisms include the structuring and documentation of derivatives transactions (with a particular emphasis on regulatory capital analysis) and providing general legal and regulatory advice to participants in the financial markets.
Career: 1998 to date Head of *Linklaters* Derivatives Practice; 1996-98: Partner, *Linklaters* London, Financial Markets Group; 1993-96: Assistant Solicitor, *Linklaters* London, Financial Markets Group; 1992-93: Assistant Solicitor, *Linklaters* New York; 1990-92: Assistant Solicitor, *Linklaters* London, Corporate Department; 1986: Christ Church, Oxford University (MA Jurisprudence).

FORRYAN, Andrew
Clifford Chance, London
(020) 7600 1000
andrew.forryan@cliffordchance.com
Specialisation: Capital markets. Partner specialising in real estate, whole business and consumer loan securitisation.
Career: Trainee with *Slaughter and May*, qualified 1985; *Slaughter and May* 1985-93; *Clifford Chance* 1993-95 and 1997-date; *Sidley & Austin* 1995-97.
Personal: University of Cambridge, Jesus College (1982).

FRANK, David
Slaughter and May, London
(020) 7600 1200
david.frank@slaughterandmay.com
Specialisation: Extensive eurobond and international equity experience with issuers in the UK and around the world. Also handles corporate and banking work with a number of listed plc clients and is active in the venture capital and project financing areas.
Prof. Memberships: The Law Society; International Bar Association.
Career: Qualified 1979. Assistant Solicitor, *Slaughter and May*, 1979-86. Partner *Slaughter and May*, 1986. Head of Capital Markets, 1993. Practice Partner 2001.
Personal: Born 29 April 1954. Educated Shrewsbury School 1967-72. University of Bristol 1973-76. Interests include cars and lawn tennis. Lives in Surrey.

FULLER, Geoff
Allen & Overy, London
(020) 7330 3000
geoff.fuller@allenovery.com
Specialisation: Partner specialising in international and domestic capital markets matters, with particular experience in repackagings and other structured finance transactions, debenture stocks and advising corporate trustees. Head of *Allen & Overy's* Repackaging Group.

Prof. Memberships: Fellow, Society for Advanced Legal Studies; City of London Solicitors' Company
Career: Articled *Allen & Overy*, qualified (1986), partner (1994).
Publications: Author 'Corporate Borrowing, Law and Practice', (1st edition 1995, 2nd edition 1999). Contributor to 'Gore Browne on Companies' – loan capital chapter.
Personal: Educated Borden Grammar School and Mansfield College, Oxford University (1983 MA).

GOLDEN, Jeffrey
Allen & Overy, London
(020) 7330 3000
jeffrey.golden@allenovery.com
Specialisation: Partner responsible for US law practice consisting of over 100 lawyers worldwide. Areas of practice include a wide range of international capital markets matters, including swaps and derivatives, international equity and debt offerings and US private placements and listings; advises the International Swaps and Derivatives Association and a broad range of commercial and investment banks, borrowers, arrangers, underwriters and issuers.
Prof. Memberships: American Bar Association (Chairman US Lawyers Practising Abroad Committee (1990-96); Council, Section of International Law and Practice (1996-). New Jersey State Bar Association, New York State Bar Association, American Society of International Law, International Bar Association, The Law Society.
Career: Admitted New York Bar 1979, New Jersey 1978, and the Supreme Court of the United States 1983. *Cravath, Swaine & Moore*, New York 1978-83; *Cravath, Swaine & Moore*, London 1983-94; Partner *Allen & Overy* since 1994.
Personal: Education Duke University, USA (1972, BA); The London School of Economics and Political Science (1970-1971); Columbia University School of Law, USA (1972-75, JD).

GREENE, Edward
Cleary Gottlieb Steen & Hamilton, London
(020) 7614 2254
egreene@cgsh.com
Specialisation: All matters relating to US regulation of capital markets and financial institutions. Involved in the counselling and representation of corporate issuers, investment banks, merchant banks and commercial banks principally in connection with mergers and acquisitions, securitisation of assets, distributions of securities in domestic and international financings, and enforcement proceedings before the US Securities and Exchange Commission.
Career: 1983 to date, Partner, *Cleary Gottlieb*; 1981-82, General Counsel of the Securities and Exchange Commission; 1979-81, Director of the Division of Corporate Finance of the Securities and Exchange Commission.

HADDOCK, Simon A
Allen & Overy, London
(020) 7330 3000
simon.haddock@allenovery.com
Specialisation: Partner specialising in structured finance and derivatives. Founder member of the firm's derivative products group in London prior to spending five years in Hong Kong. Since returning to London in the summer of 1997, he has concentrated on developing the firm's structured products expertise and has been extensively involved in the whole range of derivative products. He is a regular speaker at conferences and seminars on swaps, derivatives and international securities offerings.
Career: Articled *Allen & Overy*, qualified England and Wales 1986, Hong Kong 1992, assistant solicitor 1986-92, partner 1992, Hong Kong office (1992-97). London office since 1997.
Personal: Leeds University (1982 LLB). Born 1960. Resides in the UK.

HANDLING, Erica
Ashurst Morris Crisp, London
(020) 7859 2485
erica.handling@ashursts.com
Specialisation: She advises on the full spectrum of capital market transactions, concentrating on structured products including credit derivatives, repackagings and collateral debt obligations. She and her team advised on Eurocredit I, the first wholly Euro dominated CDO, and also worked on more recent innovative transactions, such as the long ramp up Promus CDO and the hybrid funded/synthetic CDO Jazz.
Career: Joined *Ashursts* in May 2001 from *Weil, Gotshal & Manges*, where she was made a partner in 1998. She completed her legal education at Exeter University and Guildford Law School and qualified as a solicitor at *Allen & Overy*.

HUDD, David
Lovells, London
(020) 7296 2000
david.hudd@lovells.com
Specialisation: Head of *Lovells'* capital markets and securitisation practice. Extensive experience of securitisations and repackagings, debt issues (including high yield bonds), international equity and equity-linked offerings and derivatives.
Prof. Memberships: The City of London Solicitors' Company, The Law Society.
Career: Christ Church, Oxford University 1977-80 (MA Jurisprudence). Qualified 1983. *Linklaters* 1981-85; Paribas 1985-90; Sanwa International 1990-93; Indosuez 1993-94; joined *Lovells* as a partner in 1994.

HUGHES, Richard
Linklaters, London
(020) 7456 4508
richard.hughes@linklaters.com
Specialisation: Structured finance Partner specialising in securitisation, asset finance, syndicated loans and property finance. Involved in a number of market

leading deals across the spectrum of structured finance.
Career: 1998 to date; Partner, *Linklaters*. Qualified 1987.

INGRAM, Kevin
Clifford Chance, London
(020) 7600 1000
kevin.ingram@cliffordchance.com
Specialisation: Capital markets. Partner specialising in debt securitisation, principal finance, asset-backed commercial paper conduits, structured repackagings, secured lending and all types of structured finance transactions.
Career: Trainee and Assistant *Clifford Chance* 1989-98; Partner since 1998.
Personal: St Cyres Comprehensive School, Penorth; University College, Oxford University (1987 BA Jurisprudence – 1st Class Hons, 1989 Bachelor of Civil Law – 1st Class Hons).

JACKAMAN, Jake
White & Case, London
(020) 7600 7300
jjackaman@whitecase.com
Specialisation: Partner in capital markets and structured finance. Represents major financial institutions in relation to debt capital markets, securitisation, funded and synthetic collateralised debt obligations and future flow transactions.
Prof. Memberships: Member of Law Society of England and Wales.
Career: Qualified 1994 (UK) and 1991 (New York). Joined *White & Case* in 2000 as a Partner, from *Clifford Chance*.

KELLY, Jacky
Weil, Gotshal & Manges, London
(020) 7903 1000
jacky.kelly@weil.com
Specialisation: Heads up the firm's securitisation practice in London. She has been closely involved in the UK securitisation market since its inception in the mid-eighties. Her securitisation experience spans a number of asset types, including residential and commercial mortgages, commercial property, trade receivables, chargecards, equipment leases, autoloans and leases, corporate loans, aerospace assets and intellectual property assets in Europe, Asia and the US. Jacky has advised a number of clients in connection with the establishment of rated asset-backed conduits, structured investment vehicles and CDO's. She is also active in the principal finance market, most recently completing a deal in the transport and infrastructure sector.
Career: *Clifford Chance* 1986-96; *Weil, Gotshal & Manges* 1996-date.

KRISCHER, David
Allen & Overy, London
(020) 7330 3000
david.krischer@allenovery.com
Specialisation: Qualified in the US. Worked within *Allen & Overy* international capital markets department 1986; requalified as solicitor. Head of Securitisation Practice Group. Extensive experience in international capital markets transactions; advised on a wide range of

118   INDEX TO LEADING LAWYERS: PAGE 1693 ■ IN-HOUSE LAWYERS PROFILES: PAGE 1201

THE LEADERS — CAPITAL MARKETS

asset-backed finance transactions for banks and originators in the UK and across Europe, including Trafford Centre, Broadgate, Madame Tussauds, Canary Wharf, the married service housing, commercial and consumer loans, future assets and infrastructure projects. Advised on the establishment of leading structured programmes.
Prof. Memberships: Law Society's City of London Solicitors' Company; American Bar Association.
Career: Admitted to the Bar, State of Illinois (1982). Associate *Hoffman & Davis* Chicago, USA (1982-85). Associate *Allen & Overy* (1985-92), Partner (1992).
Personal: Born 1956. Oberlin College (1978, BA); Northwestern University, (1982, JD cum laude); BCL Oxford University, (1986, BCL).

LAMBIE, Christian
Allen & Overy, London
(020) 7330 3000
christian.lambie@allenovery.com
Specialisation: Partner specialising in securitisation.
Career: Admitted as solicitor, Scotland 1994, England and Wales 1997; associate Allen & Overy, 1996; partner 2001.
Personal: University of Glasgow (1991, LLB Hons). Born 1969.

MACKENZIE, Marcus
Freshfields Bruckhaus Deringer, London
(020) 7936 4000
marcus.mackenzie@freshfields.com
Specialisation: Partner in finance department specialising in whole business and other asset securitisations and other capital markets/derivatives and banking transactions acting for investment banks, originators and issuers.
Prof. Memberships: Law Society.
Career: 1988: joined *Freshfields*. 1993: worked in *Freshfields* New York office. 1994: seconded to *Salomon Brothers International* in London. 1998: joined partnership.
Personal: Educated at Bristol University and Guildford Law School. Speaks French, German and Spanish.

MACVICAR, Robert
Clifford Chance, London
(020) 7600 1000
robert.macvicar@cliffordchance.com
Specialisation: Capital markets. Partner specialising in banking and capital markets, especially in commercial paper, medium term notes, debt securitisation.
Career: Articled *Freshfields*: qualified 1979; solicitor *Freshfields* 1979-82; solicitor *Freshfields*, Singapore 1983-84; solicitor *McKenna & Co* 1984-85; solicitor *Coward Chance* 1985-87; Partner since 1988.
Personal: Rugby School; Keble College, Oxford (BA Hons 2nd class Jurisprudence 1973-76).

MCFADZEAN, Christopher
Linklaters, London
(020) 7456 4626
chris.mcfadzean@linklaters.com
Specialisation: Specialist with over 15 years experience in capital market, privatisation and banking transactions, advising issuers, borrowers and managers internationally. As a member of *Linklaters* Asia Business Group, advises international clients on investments in Asia and Asian clients on European investments. Areas of practice include equity, equity-linked and debt capital markets, securitisations and structured finance, privatisations, corporate rescue and financial restructurings.
Career: 1989 to date Partner, *Linklaters*; 1991-97 Partner and Head of *Linklaters*, Singapore; 1986-89 Assistant Solicitor, *Linklaters*, London; 1984-86 Assistant Solicitor, *Linklaters*, Hong Kong; 1982-84 Assistant Solicitor, *Linklaters* London; 1980-82 Articled Clerk, *Linklaters*.

MCKEAND, James
Freshfields Bruckhaus Deringer, London
(020) 7936 4000
james.mckeand@freshfields.com
Specialisation: Partner specialising in banking, capital market, securitisation and aviation finance.
Career: Qualified 1978; Partner *Freshfields* 1984; *Freshfields* Singapore 1981-85; Managing Partner Tokyo 1991-97 (admitted as gaikokuho-jimu-bengoshi).
Personal: Liverpool University (1976 LLB Hons).

MILLER, Stephen M
Allen & Overy, London
(020) 7330 3000
stephen.miller@allenovery.com
Specialisation: Partner in International Capital Markets Department.
Career: Qualified 1992. Partner 1998.

MORRIS, Tim
Clifford Chance, London
(020) 7600 1000
tim.morris@cliffordchance.com
Specialisation: Capital markets. Partner specialising in capital markets and derivatives.
Career: Articled *Burges Salmon*; qualified 1982; Partner *Clifford Chance* since 1996.
Personal: Hereford Cathedral School; Brasenose College, Oxford (MA 1977).

MOTANI, Habib
Clifford Chance, London
(020) 7600 1000
habib.motani@cliffordchance.com
Specialisation: Banking and finance. Partner specialising in derivatives, capital markets and financial markets.
Career: Partner since 1986.

OAKLEY, Chris
Clifford Chance, London
(020) 7600 1000
chris.oakley@cliffordchance.com
Specialisation: Capital markets. Partner specialising in international asset securitisation, structured repackagings and all types of structured finance transactions.
Career: Articled *Coward Chance*; qualified 1983; Partner since 1990.
Personal: Redborne School, Ampthill, Beds; Worcester College, Oxford (BA Hons Jurisprudence).

OVENDEN, F Simon
Linklaters, London
(020) 7456 2560
simon.ovenden@linklaters.com
Specialisation: International capital markets including issues of debt and equity securities in both UK domestic and international markets including Russia, India, South East Asia and the Middle East. Recent experience includes advising on international equity offerings and private placements, and advising on restructurings of loans and other debt obligations in Russia.
Career: 2000 to date: Partner, *Linklaters* London, International Finance Department; 1997-2000: Partner, *Linklaters* Moscow; 1993-96: Assistant Solicitor, *Linklaters* London; 1991-93; Assistant Solicitor, *Linklaters* Hong Kong; 1987-91: Assistant Solicitor, *Linklaters* London. 1986-87: College of Law, Law Society Finals; 1983-86: Cambridge University, Faculty of Law.

PENN, Graham
Sidley Austin Brown & Wood, London
(020) 7360 3600
gpenn@sidley.com
Specialisation: Securitisation, structured finance, banking and bank regulation.
Career: Partner *Cameron Markley Hewitt* 1988-94. Partner *Sidley & Austin* 1994. Following merger of *Sidley & Austin* and *Brown & Wood* on 1 May 2001, partner *Sidley Austin Brown & Wood*.

PITKIN, Jeremy
Freshfields Bruckhaus Deringer, London
(020) 7936 4000
jeremy.pitkin@freshfields.com
Specialisation: Partner. Specialises in all aspects of international debt and equity capital markets offerings and privatisations. His work has included acting for the arrangers on the MTN programmes of the Hellenic Republic and Bank Austria, for issuers (such as the United Kingdom, the Republic of Lebanon, Rolls-Royce, Kingfisher, Repsol and Banco Espirito Santo), and for managers of international equity offers by BSkyB, Alpha Credit Banks, Elcoteq, Erste Bank, Gazprom and Mobistar. He has worked on privatisation transactions in Croatia, Greece, Latvia, Poland, Russia and the United Kingdom.
Career: Partner 1993.
Personal: Jeremy was born 1955 and educated at King's College, London.

PRIDMORE, Nigel
Linklaters, London
(020) 7456 4634
nigel.pridmore@linklaters.com
Specialisation: Specialist in capital markets, advising investment banks and issuers. Main areas of practice include UK corporate issues, equity linked products, regulatory capital issues, medium-term note programmes, emerging market debt and equity offerings and structured and derivative products.
Career: 1998 to date: Partner in the International Finance Department, *Linklaters* London; 1994-98: Assistant Solicitor, *Linklaters* London; 1992-94: Assistant Solicitor, *Linklaters* New York 1990-92: Assistant Solicitor, *Linklaters* London; 1988-90: Articled Clerk, *Linklaters*. 1986-88: College of Law; 1983-86: Emmanuel College, Cambridge, MA History.

QURESHI, Ashar
Cleary Gottlieb Steen & Hamilton, London
(020) 7614 2226
aqureshi@cgsh.com
Specialisation: Partner specialising in international corporate finance and in particular capital markets transactions.
Career: Joined *Cleary Gottlieb* in 1990, becoming a partner in 1999.

RAINES, Marke
Shearman & Sterling, London
(020) 7655 5000

RICE, Jim
Linklaters, London
(020) 7456 4525
jim.rice@linklaters.com
Specialisation: Finance and international capital markets, particularly structured finance, securitisations, project bonds and repackagings.
Career: Partner *Linklaters*, London 1999 to date; 1997-98: Partner, *Linklaters* Hong Kong; 1989-97: Partner, *Linklaters* London; 1986-89: Assistant Solicitor, *Linklaters* London; 1984-86: Assistant Solicitor, *Linklaters*, New York; 1982-84: Assistant Solicitor, *Linklaters* London; 1980-82: Articled Clerk, *Linklaters*. 1979: Christ Church, Oxford University, Jurisprudence (First Class).

RUDIN, Simeon
Freshfields Bruckhaus Deringer, London
(020) 7936 4000
simeon.rudin@freshfields.com
Specialisation: Partner in the finance department advising on all aspects of capital markets work, including private and public debt, including equity, credit and commodity linked debt issues, tax structured financings, securitisations, CLOs, CBOs, CDOs, repackagings and all aspects of derivatives transactions (both exchange trade and over the counter), including repo and stocklending. Advises on alternative risk transfer and structured insurance products and transactions. Advises extensively on product development. Head of *Freshfields* Derivatives Unit.
Prof. Memberships: Law Society; City of London Solicitors Company.
Career: Qualified 1983. Partner 1995.
Personal: Born 1961. Attended St. Catharines College, Cambridge.

SHURMAN, Daniel J
Allen & Overy, London
(020) 7330 3000
daniel.shurman@allenovery.com
Specialisation: Partner in *Allen & Overy's* capital markets department since 1999, specialising in international equity

CAPITAL MARKETS ■ THE LEADERS

offerings.
Career: Assistant solicitor, *Theodore Goddard* (1990-96), Seconded to *Dewey Ballantine*, New York (1994-95). Associate, *Allen & Overy* (1996-99), Partner (1999).
Personal: Born 1965, Highgate School, Nottingham University (LLB). Leisure interests include sailing and walking. Resides in London.

SKUTER, John
Allen & Overy, London
(020) 7330 3000

SMITH, Christian
Weil, Gotshal & Manges, London
(020) 7903 1049
christiansmith@weil.com
Specialisation: Securitisation partner specialising in UK and European asset-backed structured finance. Has wide experience of advising both arrangers and originators in respect of diverse asset classes and, in particular, of advising sponsors in the establishment of commercial paper conduits and their subsequent use in funding arrangements for UK and European borrowers.
Career: Qualified in 1990. *Clifford Chance* 1988-96; *Morgan Stanley* 1996-97; *Weil, Gotshal & Manges* 1997, partner 1999.
Personal: LLB (London School of Economics, 1978).

SMITH, Christopher
Slaughter and May, London
(020) 7600 1200
christopher.smith@slaughterandmay.com
Specialisation: Main areas of practice include securitisations, structured financings and the full range of capital markets and banking transactions.
Career: Qualified 1980; Partner 1987.

SMITH, Sarah
Sidley Austin Brown & Wood, London
(020) 7360 3600
sarah.smith@sidley.com
Specialisation: Securitisation; structured finance; banking and financial services regulation.
Career: Qualified 1990. Partner *Sidley & Austin* 1995. Following merger of *Sidley & Austin* and *Brown & Wood* on 1 May 2001, partner *Sidley Austin Brown & Wood*.

THOMSON, Keith
Linklaters, London
(020) 7456 4584
keith.thomson@linklaters.com
Specialisation: Specialist in securities transactions; advising lead managers and issuers in respect of issues of debt, equity-related debt, equity and depositary receipts in international capital markets. Advises clients in medium-term note programmes, commercial paper programmes and derivative transactions. Has acted in securities transactions in Australia, Scandinavia, Switzerland, Holland, Spain, South Africa, the UK and in Turkey, Greece, Russia, Zimbabwe, Indonesia, India, Pakistan, Thailand and Kazakhstan.
Career: Since 1986: Partner, Global Securities Group, *Linklaters*; 1983-86: Solicitor, International Finance Department, *Linklaters*; 1981-83 Assistant Solicitor, *Linklaters* Hong Kong; 1979-81 Assistant Solicitor, *Linklaters* Corporate Department. 1975-76: Cambridge University, LLB (Law). 1975 Durham University (BA Law).

TREDGETT, Richard P
Allen & Overy, London
(020) 7330 3000
richard.tredgett@allenovery.com
Specialisation: Richard Tredgett is a partner who joined *Allen & Overy* in 1993. He has experience in advising on international transactions, and in particular OTC derivatives. He has worked on many documentation projects for the International Swaps and Derivatives Association, including the 1997 ISDA Government Bond Option Definitions, ISDA's EMU Protocol, the 1998 ISDA Euro Definitions and the 2000 ISDA Definitions. He was also extensively involved in ISDA's European economic and monetary union working groups and is a frequent speaker on derivatives documentation, collateral and the legal aspects of monetary union.

TROTT, David
Freshfields Bruckhaus Deringer, London
(020) 7936 4000
david.trott@freshfields.com
Specialisation: He has worked extensively in the banking and capital markets field acting for lenders, borrowers and arrangers on secured and unsecured transactions. He has particular experience of, and expertise in, asset-backed and structured transactions. He has been involved in securitisations since 1988, working on a number of the early mortgage backed deals to take place in the UK. More recently he has worked on a number of operating company securitisations in the UK (Welcome Break, Punch Taverns and WightLink) and several pan-European multi-seller trade receivables programmes for corporate and asset-backed conduit issuers.
Career: Qualified 1988; partner 1997.
Personal: Born 1963. Educated Durham University.

TUCKER, Julian A
Allen & Overy, London
(020) 7330 3000
julian.tucker@allenovery.com
Specialisation: A Partner in the International Capital Markets Department, Julian has an extensive range of securitisation experience, particularly in property based financings.
Prof. Memberships: Law Society.
Career: *Lovell White Durrant*, 1987-92; *Cameron Markby Hewett*, 1993-94; Associate *Allen & Overy*, 1994; Partner 1998.
Publications: Articles published in ISR, IFR, IFLR.
Personal: University College London (LLB 1985). London University (LLM 1986). Cooking, music, theatre and family.

VOISEY, Peter G
Clifford Chance, London
(020) 7600 1000
peter.voisey@cliffordchance.com
Specialisation: Capital markets. Partner specialising in international asset securitisation and structured finance transactions.
Career: Articled at *Lovells*; qualified 1987; Partner 1994; joined *Clifford Chance* as a Partner in 2000
Personal: Brentwood School, Brentwood, Essex; Trinity Hall College, Cambridge (MA (Hons) Modern Languages).

VOISIN, Michael
Linklaters, London
(020) 7456 4606
michael.voisin@linklaters.com
Specialisation: Specialises in capital markets securities work with particular emphasis on sophisticated financial products, note programmes and regulatory capital raising for financial institutions; responsible for the development of *Linklaters*' medium-term note programme practice and one of the core partners in *Linklaters*' derivatives practice.
Career: Since 1996: Partner *Linklaters*; 1991-96: Assistant Solicitor, *Linklaters*; 1991: Admitted as a Solicitor of the Supreme Court of England and Wales; 1988-91: Legal Assistant, *Linklaters*; 1987-88: Pupil Barrister; 1987: Called to the Bar of England and Wales. 1986-87: Inns of Courts School of Law, London; 1983-86: Worcester College, Oxford University.

WALKER, John
Milbank, Tweed, Hadley & McCloy, London
(020) 7448 3059
jwalker@milbank.com
Specialisation: John Walker is a partner in the firm's capital markets group. His practice encompasses the full range of capital markets instruments, including fixed and floating rate, convertible, exchangeable and capital bonds and bonds with warrants. He has significant experience in relation to securitisation and receivables financings in respect of a diverse range of domestic and overseas receivables and was instrumental in applying capital markets instruments and derivative products to meet the alternative risk transfer requirements of a major European reinsurer. He acted for HM government on the sale of a significant receivables portfolio. Having acted for issuers, arrangers and investors on numerous financing transactions, he is entirely familiar with customary and synthetic financing techniques to secure tax, balance sheet or regulatory capital advantage. He has extensive experience of customary swap, equity and credit-linked products, and related documentation, as well as more bespoke derivatives used for specific transactions. He has acted for a number of leading edge financial institutions in developing their product portfolios and executing related transactions. In relation to the nascent European CDO (collateralised debt obligation) market, John has acted as transaction counsel on numerous balance sheet, arbitrage and synthetic transactions.
Career: Trained *Masons*, qualified 1987; solicitor *Freshfields* 1987-94; partner *Wilde Sapte* 1994-98; partner *Cadwalader, Wickersham & Taft* 1998; partner *Milbank, Tweed, Hadley & McCloy* 2000.
Personal: Born 1961. Desborough School; Southampton University (1984 LLB); Law School, Lancaster Gate. Resides London. Leisure interests include theatre, music and travel.

WALSH, Jonathan
Norton Rose, London
(020) 7283 6000
walshjgf@nortonrose.com
Specialisation: Securitisation/repackaging. Acts for investment banks, corporates, arrangers and sponsors on a variety of UK and international securitisation and repackaging transactions, including synthetic structures, asset backed securities issues and asset-backed commercial paper conduits.
Prof. Memberships: Law Society. The Oriental Club.
Career: Kings College London, LLB, called to the bar 1984, requalified as a solicitor 1988. Secuitisation partner, *Norton Rose* international securities group 1997, Head of International Securities Group 2000.
Publications: Editor of the 'International Securities Quarterly' and author of articles for other various publications.
Personal: Obscure rock music (pop trivia bore), cooking and mixing cocktails, swimming, skiing and surfing (very badly).

WARNA-KULA-SURIYA, Sanjev
Slaughter and May, London
(020) 7600 1200
sanjevwks@slaughterandmay.com
Specialisation: Partner specialising in capital markets, derivatives, securitisation and structured finance.
Career: Articled *Slaughter and May*; qualified 1990; Partner 1997.
Personal: Born 1964. Educated at King's College, London University (1986 LLB First Class Hons). Resides London. Leisure: cricket, theatre.

WEDDERBURN-DAY, Roger
Allen & Overy, London
(020) 7330 3000
roger.wedderburn-day@allenovery
Specialisation: Partner specialising in all aspects of international debt and equity capital markets work. Eurobonds, medium term note programmes, privatisations and other international equity offerings and different types of equity linked debt, including convertible and exchangeable bonds, particularly in relation to emerging markets.
Career: Articled *Allen & Overy*, qualified (1987), Associate (1987-1995), Partner

---

120   INDEX TO LEADING LAWYERS: PAGE 1693 ■ IN-HOUSE LAWYERS PROFILES: PAGE 1201

(1995).
Personal: Born 1962. Bishop Wordsworth Grammar school. University College, London (LLB Hons, 1985).

WELLS, Boyan
Allen & Overy, London
(020) 7330 3000
boyan.wells@allenovery.com
Specialisation: Managing Partner of the International Capital Markets Department. Areas of practice include advising managers and issuers on all aspects of international capital markets work, high yield issues and derivative transactions; particular specialisations include medium term note programmes, listed and unlisted warrant issues and programmes and building societies.

Career: Articled *Allen & Overy*, qualified (1981), Partner (1987).
Personal: Educated Colston's School and Wadham College, Oxford (1978 MA). Born 1956. Resides Dulwich.

WOODHALL, John
Clifford Chance, London
(020) 7600 1000
john.woodhall@cliffordchance.com
Specialisation: Banking and finance. Partner specialising in securitisation.
Career: Partner *Clifford Chance*, Hong Kong 1988.

CHARITIES

London: 122; The Regions: 124; Scotland: 128; Profiles: 129

Research approved by BMRB For this edition, Chambers' researchers conducted 6,582 interviews – 3,900 with law firms, 511 with barristers and 2,171 with clients. The validity of the research was scrutinised by BMRB International, who audited both the methodology and the results at our offices in London. They interviewed Chambers' researchers and cross-checked sample interviews. Details of the audit appear on page 7.

OVERVIEW The role of lawyers in this sector has never been so crucial: the Charity Commission has stepped up its activities, and a reform of regulatory procedures will soon take effect in Scotland. Additionally, charities are increasingly run along business lines, requiring greater commerciality in their advisors.

LONDON

CHARITIES — LONDON

1
- Bates, Wells & Braithwaite

2
- Farrer & Co

3
- Nabarro Nathanson
- Withers LLP

4
- Berwin Leighton Paisner
- Bircham Dyson Bell
- Charles Russell
- Sinclair Taylor & Martin

5
- Allen & Overy
- Claricoat Phillips
- Harbottle & Lewis
- Macfarlanes
- RadcliffesLeBrasseur
- Stone King

6
- Herbert Smith
- Lawrence Graham
- Lee Bolton & Lee
- Linklaters
- Trowers & Hamlins
- Winckworth Sherwood

This book is the product of 6,582 1/2 hour interviews. See p.7 for BMRB audit. Within each band, firms are listed alphabetically.

BATES, WELLS & BRAITHWAITE (see firm details p.859) The top-rated charities firm nationwide, it is universally praised for its "*superb advice and breath-taking scale of work.*" At the hub remains a trio of key individuals: **Andrew Phillips** (see p.131) is regarded by clients and competitors alike as "*an utter legend,*" who maintains his presence despite attending sessions in the House of Lords; "*leading light*" **Stephen Lloyd** (see p.130) "*truly understands the dynamics of charities,*" while **Fiona Middleton** (see p.131) exhibits an "*excellent, practical approach.*" Over the past year the firm has been active in the merger of the Royal Opera House and Friends of Covent Garden, as well as the reorganisation of the Wordsworth Trust and the setting up of the Booker Prize Foundation. New to this year's rankings, **Rosamund Smith** (see p.132) is recommended for her knowledge of fund-raising law and for being "*a new and integral part of a truly impressive team.*" **Clients** Charities Aid Foundation; The British Red Cross Society; Tate; Shelter; YMCA England; The Prince's Trust; ChildLine; RNIB; The Save the Children Fund; Amnesty International.

FARRER & CO (see firm details p.952) While there were some initial concerns about how well "*truly impressive performer*" **Anne-Marie Piper** (see p.132) would fit into the Farrer & Co set-up, any doubts have now been truly allayed. With "*wonderful, high-powered*" **Judith Hill** (see p.130), she forms a dynamic duo that one barrister described as "*the Batman & Robin of charity law.*" Although still felt by the market to be tailing Bates, Wells & Braithwaite, our researchers were told that the firm is narrowing the gap. A successful year was capped by the merger of the Imperial Cancer Research Fund and The Cancer Research Campaign into a new charitable company called Cancer Research UK, a deal worth £300 million. It also advised the Coram family on their controversial proposals for a new museum. **Clients** Academy of Medical Sciences; National Association of Air Ambulance Services; The Stephen Lawrence Trust; The Prince's Trust; Women's Royal Voluntary Service.

NABARRO NATHANSON (see firm details p.1080) Competitors and clients are unstinting in their praise for this "*respected and admired*" firm, which is seen as reaping the fruit of its energetic cultivation of the charities market. Highlights of the last year include winning a favourable judgment on behalf of the RSPCA in its ongoing and ground-breaking membership case, and advising the Royal National Lifeboat Institute on the review of its royal charter, one of the main objects of which was to enable them to operate on inland waters. The firm's star player remains the "*enthusiastic, personable*" **Jonathan Burchfield** (see p.129) who peers say "*knows his stuff and runs a good game.*" Since publication of last year's book the firm's charity lawyers have moved to the London office, while support staff remain in its Reading outpost. **Clients** RSPCA; RNLI; The National Trust; The Save the Children Fund; Diabetes UK; The Guide Dogs for the Blind Association; Great Ormond Street Hospital Children's Charity.

WITHERS LLP (see firm details p.1194) Although still respected for its "*considerable charity expertise,*" the firm is felt by some commentators to have been less visible in the marketplace over the last year. Clients and competitors wait to see what effect its merger with New York private client outfit Bergman, Horowitz & Reynolds will have. An experienced department is founded upon the skills and reputation of "*standout practitioner*" **Alison Paines** (see p.131), "*a great asset for any firm.*" Over the last year it has been involved in the merger of Macmillan Cancer Relief and Cancerlink, as well as the restructuring of the Fire Services National Benevolent Fund. It also undertakes contentious work for charities. **Clients** Guy's & St Thomas' Charitable Foundation; Macmillan Cancer Relief; The Salvation Army; RSPB; British Heart Foundation; Marie Curie Cancer Care; Barristers' Benevolent Association; Thalidomide Trust.

BERWIN LEIGHTON PAISNER (see firm details p.866) Our researchers were told that, while some within the industry still consider the loss of Anne-Marie Piper to have set the practice back, most now believe that it is making a swift recovery. It boasts the "*excellent*" **Moira Protani** (see p.132) who competitors acknowledge is "*becoming a strong player; definitely very smart,*" while the team's bulwark remains **Martin Paisner** (see p.131), "*one of the top practitioners in the country.*" It recently advised the Millennium Commission on an innovative £100 million project to enable charities to provide grants for individuals to carry out community initiatives. **Clients** BAFTA; Church of God United Kingdom; The Holocaust Educational Trust; Macfarlane Trust; Millennium Commission; Royal Academy of Music; Tesco Charity Trust; Wellcome Trust.

BIRCHAM DYSON BELL (see firm details p.873) This well-regarded charities firm is praised by clients for being "*expert in the more exotic side of charities; useful in the bigger cases.*" It has been involved in some high-profile charities work over the last year, including the reorganisation of BBC Children in Need, as well as offering advice to a leading charity in relation to data protection. **Simon Weil** (see p.133) remains a key performer, praised for "*taking excellent care of clients.*" **Clients** World Association of Girl Guides & Girl Scouts; The Hospital Management Trust; BBC Children in Need; The Draper's Company; Blue Cross.

LONDON ■ CHARITIES

LEADING INDIVIDUALS

[1]
- HILL Judith *Farrer & Co*
- LLOYD Stephen *Bates, Wells & Braithwaite*
- PAINES Alison *Withers LLP*
- PIPER Anne-Marie *Farrer & Co*

[2]
- BURCHFIELD Jonathan *Nabarro Nathanson*
- MIDDLETON Fiona *Bates, Wells & Braithwaite*
- PHILLIPS Andrew *Bates, Wells & Braithwaite*
- PHILLIPS Ann *Stone King*
- PROTANI Moira *Berwin Leighton Paisner*
- TAYLOR James Sinclair *Sinclair Taylor & Martin*

[3]
- CLARICOAT John *Claricoat Phillips*
- DOLLIMORE Jean *RadcliffesLeBrasseur*
- PAISNER Martin *Berwin Leighton Paisner*
- PORTRAIT Judith *Portrait Solicitors*

[4]
- MEAKIN Robert *Stone King*
- PHILLIPS Hilary *Claricoat Phillips*
- SCOTT Michael *Charles Russell*
- SMITH Rosamund *Bates, Wells & Braithwaite*
- SYED Catriona *Charles Russell*
- WALSH Brian *Campbell Hooper*
- WEIL Simon *Bircham Dyson Bell*

See individuals' profiles p.129

CHARLES RUSSELL (see firm details p.904) This "*good-sized, knowledgeable*" practice is gaining an increasing visibility in the market. It has been busy over the last year on various aspects of charities work including set-ups, constitutional issues, joint ventures and mergers, and it assisted in the acquisition of a science centre by a large charitable foundation. **Michael Scott** (see p.132) is described as "*a fine leader for charity work*," and receives good support from "*class act*" **Catriona Syed** (see p.133). **Clients** Marie Curie Cancer Care; RADA; Royal Airforce Benevolent Fund; London Philharmonic Orchestra.

SINCLAIR TAYLOR & MARTIN This niche firm is seen to be consolidating its position at "*the clever end of the market.*" Highlights of the last year include the establishment of the Damilola Taylor Trust and the merger of London Lighthouse with the Terrence Higgins Trust – the largest consolidation so far in the HIV sector. Although still active, Lindsay Driscoll has now settled into the role of consultant; however **James Sinclair Taylor** (see p.133) boasts a burgeoning reputation. **Clients** The United Kingdom Committee for UNICEF; MS Society; Royal Blind Society; Down's Syndrome Association.

ALLEN & OVERY (see firm details p.841) The retirement of Peter Mimpriss in October 2002 means that the department is left without its best-known personality. As such, say peers, the jury is still out until a new leading presence emerges. With its superb client base, however, it has been involved in some impressive work over the last year. This includes setting up the World Trade Centre Disaster Fund as a registered charity in one day – the fastest time in which a charity has ever been established. **Clients** The Arts Council of England; Royal Botanic Gardens, Kew; Royal Shakespeare Company; The Prince's Trust; Wellcome Trust; College of Law; Leeds Castle Foundation.

CLARICOAT PHILLIPS This focused firm, described to *Chambers'* researchers as "*tiny but effective,*" is praised throughout the industry. The highly respected duo of **John Claricoat** (see p.129) and **Hilary Phillips** (see p.131) are considered to be "*excellent at the areas they're interested in.*" They advise charities in registration and dealings with the Charity Commission, as well as undertaking advisory work for a number of bodies. **Clients** Educational foundations.

HARBOTTLE & LEWIS (see firm details p.983) This experienced team is recommended for its work for large public charities, although market commentators felt that it was less visible in this sector than in previous years. With the firm's well-known media expertise, much of its work has a media flavour. For example, Robert Porter's team recently advised NetAid (UK) on preparations for an awareness-raising concert and multimedia web cast designed to combat poverty. The team is also still involved in ongoing work with Comic Relief and The Diana, Princess Of Wales Memorial Fund. **Clients** Central School of Speech and Drama; English National Opera; London Lighthouse; New Shakespeare Company.

MACFARLANES (see firm details p.1047) Although not a core area for this corporate powerhouse, it has been admired by competitors for its steady progress over the last 12 months, with clients saying that its "*skills are in the details.*" Owen Clutton's team has been active in various constitutional matters, where it has particular experience of the issues facing royal charter charities. It was recently involved in establishing a charity raising funds through events linked to a number of universities. The team also boasts particular skills relating to trustee remuneration and tax. **Clients** Royal Academy; National Missing Persons Helpline; The Trusthouse Charitable Foundation; The Lister Institute.

RADCLIFFESLEBRASSEUR (see firm details p.1107) Opinions remain divided about how much progress this practice has made since the arrival of highly rated authority **Jean Dollimore** (see p.130), with many feeling that the next 12 months could prove crucial. Nevertheless, early signs are positive with the firm boasting a wide variety of clients, and acting on high-profile work like the merger of The Cancer Research Campaign with the Imperial Cancer Research Fund. **Clients** The Children's Society; Animal Health Trust; Combat Stress.

STONE KING (see firm details p.1151) The provinces' best-known firm is now flexing its muscle in the capital, and gaining an increasing share of the national limelight. It boasts a "*superb specialist team*" (including West Country star Michael King a couple of days a week) and offers a wide range of skills. Last year it was active in numerous investigations by the Charity Commission and consequential reorganisations. Lead partner **Ann Phillips** (see p.131) is described as "*one of the most efficient practitioners in the country.*" **Robert Meakin** (see p.131) is also recommended. **Clients** Battersea Dogs Home; Spectrum; National Catholic Fund; Scope.

HERBERT SMITH (see firm details p.992) Recommended to our researchers as "*a bright, experienced team on the corporate side of charities,*" John Wood's group has experience of the spectrum of charity law, including the commercial, litigation, tax, IP and property aspects. Recent highlights have included a high-profile merger and the setting up of a large charitable trust. **Clients** Sporting, educational and artistic charities.

LAWRENCE GRAHAM (see firm details p.1031) Noted across the marketplace for its expertise in all aspects of charities law, it is recommended by clients as a firm that "*inspires a wonderful sense of trust.*" Martyn Gowar's team has been active in a number of high-profile undertakings including the setting up of the Jubilee Bridge project. **Clients** Motability; Marie Curie; Friends of the Earth; Action Against Hunger; RNIB.

LEE BOLTON & LEE (see firm details p.1034) Some competitors consider that this Westminster firm has arrived at its charities expertise through its strength in educational and ecclesiastical work. Certainly it has key skills in those fields that make it an "*absolute authority*" on church law. However, it is also recommended for its work for housing associations and social landlords, as well as possessing deep expertise in setting up a diverse group of new charities. **Clients** Educational, ecclesiastical and housing charities.

LINKLATERS (see firm details p.1043) While not perhaps the most visible firm on the charities map, this small team continues to be treasured by its clients. They describe it as "*solution-driven*" and "*offering a common sense and practical approach.*" Led by Nigel Reid, its key work recently included the establishment of an endowment fund for the Royal Opera House and a number of high-profile set-ups. **Clients** Royal Opera House; CAFOD; Tate Gallery; SANE.

TROWERS & HAMLINS (see firm details p.1168) Although some market sources consider the firm less visible since the loss of Jean Dollimore, it still has a well-respected niche in housing matters, while its wide client base testifies to its breadth of skill. Ian Davis' team was busy over the last year in a high-profile, ongoing

CHARITIES ■ THE SOUTH/THAMES VALLEY

dispute concerning a decision by a charitable trust to close one of its care homes. The case has been referred to the Court of Appeal. **Clients** The Enabling Partnership; Nuffield Hospitals Trust; Methodist Homes; Arthritis Care; National Childbirth Trust.

WINCKWORTH SHERWOOD (see firm details p.1192) "*Doing some impressive work,*" the firm acts for a wide range of charities, but is most visible within the charitable housing sector where its highly respected social housing expertise comes into play. It has recently been involved in a number of important charitable set-ups of theatre and sporting bodies. Paul Morris' group also has a good reputation for its educational work. **Clients** Marshall's Charity; Greycoat Foundation; National Energy Foundation; The United Westminster Schools Foundation.

OTHER NOTABLE PRACTITIONERS The "*dazzlingly good*" Judith Portrait (see p.132), of Portrait Solicitors in Association with Denton Wilde Sapte, remains highly recommended for her Sainsbury's Charitable Trust work, where she has "*a reputation to knock the spots off a Dalmatian.*" Brian Walsh (see p.133) of Campbell Hooper joins the rankings this year. He is praised for his skill in legacies work and recommended as "*knowledgeable in the most friendly fashion.*"

THE SOUTH

CHARITIES ■ THE SOUTH

1
- Blake Lapthorn Portsmouth
- Thomas Eggar Chichester

2
- Barlows Guildford
- Cripps Harries Hall Tunbridge Wells
- Griffith Smith Brighton
- Lester Aldridge Bournemouth
- Thomson Snell & Passmore Tunbridge Wells

LEADING INDIVIDUALS

1
- CAIRNS Elizabeth Sole Practitioner
- DAVIS Elizabeth Blake Lapthorn

This book is the product of 6,582 1/2 hour interviews. See p.7 for BMRB audit. Within each band, firms are listed alphabetically. See individuals' profiles p.129

BLAKE LAPTHORN (see firm details p.877) This strong charities firm was recommended to researchers by clients and competitors alike. Clients particularly appreciate the team's knack of "*understanding and advising in a practical, applicable way,*" while lead partner Elizabeth Davis was said to have "*a huge volume of information at her fingertips.*" The firm has been busy over the last year in various constitutional and commercial issues, including high-level negotiations concerning a large merger in the region. **Clients** The Mary Rose Trust; Hampshire Autistic Society; Connaught Drill Halls Trust; RYA Sailability.

THOMAS EGGAR (see firm details p.1160) This well-regarded firm is recommended by clients for "*always taking a keen and understanding interest.*" Active in all the key areas of charity work, it handles governance, regulatory, commercial, property and employment matters. Christopher Butcher's team has recently assisted a major local independent school in turning from a charitable trust into a company limited by guarantee. **Clients** Diocese of Chichester; Pallant Charitable Trust.

BARLOWS Christine Goodyear's team can lay claim to considerable skill in the corporate funding side of charities work, and was recommended to researchers for its business sense. To this it adds expertise in all the day-to-day aspects of charities law. Recent experience includes involvement in a number of important set-ups and mergers. The firm also offers a niche in training charities staff in contract matters. **Clients** WWF; The National Trust.

CRIPPS HARRIES HALL (see firm details p.922) Peter Scott's forward-looking team has been busy over the last year assisting charities in developing and redeveloping their constitutions, and helping them adapt to the new culture of risk management. The firm also profits from its expertise in the more traditional charitable areas and has been active in setting up several new charitable trusts. **Clients** Great Britain Sasakawa Foundation; Royal Historic Society.

GRIFFITH SMITH (see firm details p.979) Managing to hold a tight grip on a wide range of work, this Brighton-based firm continues to impress. Tim Smith's team enjoys a key niche in advising on community initiatives and is active on new deal work, constitutional issues, property deals and the setting up of limited companies for charities. Much of its work is for service providers, and it represents charities far beyond its South coast home. **Clients** Schools; elderly and disabled charities.

LESTER ALDRIDGE (see firm details p.1038) The firm maintains a strong reputation in this sector, receiving numerous recommendations from its peers. This year its non-contentious workload enjoyed steady growth while contentious work for charities blossomed. Its key clients remain large charitable bodies, for whom it acts in a great deal of probate work both in the UK and inter nationally. Barry Glazier's team has recently been involved in setting up a number of charitable trusts. **Clients** Bournemouth Orchestras; Army Air Corps Fund; Western Association of Ballet Schools; SCOPE.

THOMSON SNELL & PASSMORE (see firm details p.1161) Although market sources consider this to be a relatively low-profile outfit, the firm has witnessed a growth in new instructions from educational and arts charities. Jeremy Passmore's team has been busy assisting clients in various commercial schemes across the region, and has worked on a number of foundations and conversions. **Clients** Royal British Legion Industries.

OTHER NOTABLE PRACTITIONERS Sole practitioner Elizabeth Cairns (see p.129) continues to have a glowing reputation within the charities sector, particularly for her academic work.

THAMES VALLEY

BROOKSTREET DES ROCHES (see firm details p.890) This firm's reputation is based largely on the bright impression made by partner Ken Brooks (see p.129), who was described by one source as the "*quickest, nicest and plain best*" lawyer in the region. It has been involved in the formation of new charities, and boasts expertise in setting up quasi-profit arms. A highlight of the last year was its work assisting educational charities with their pre-school work in deprived areas. **Clients** Educational charities.

MANCHES (see firm details p.1052) This busy firm is regarded by commentators as firmly established in the local and national markets. It possesses renowned expertise in constitutional work, which has seen it help to rewrite the statutes of a number of educational bodies. It has also recently taken on the Charity Commission in a high-profile case. Alan Poulter (see p.132) "*always gives expert advice*" and leads a small team, which can rely on the support of other departments within the group when the need arises. **Clients** Islamic Trust; The National Trust;

THAMES VALLEY/THE SOUTH WEST ■ CHARITIES

CHARITIES
■ THAMES VALLEY

1
- BrookStreet Des Roches Witney
- Manches Oxford
- Winckworth Sherwood Oxford

2
- Henmans Oxford
- Linnells Oxford

LEADING INDIVIDUALS

1
- BROOKS Ken BrookStreet Des Roches
- JEFFREYS Peter Henmans
- POULTER Alan Manches
- REES John Winckworth Sherwood
- SAUNDERS Joss Linnells

This book is the product of 6,582 1/2 hour interviews. See p.7 for BMRB audit. Within each band, firms are listed alphabetically. See individuals' profiles p.129

Royal Opera House Benevolent Fund; Oxford Colleges.

WINCKWORTH SHERWOOD (see firm details p.1192) Lead partner **John Rees** (see p.139) is recommended as a frank, authoritative presence by both clients and competitors. The firm's key client base remains on the ecclesiastical side of charity work. Over the last year it has conducted property transactions and set-ups for charities, as well as reorganisations of bodies hoping to attain limited liability status. It has also been involved in a number of constitutional issues for the Church of England. **Clients** Ecclesiastical charities.

HENMANS (see firm details p.990) This "*impressive team full of common sense ideas*" was rated highly by clients this year. Known for its skills in legacy work – which are seen as among the best outside London – the firm is also growing stronger in pure constitutional work. Active in a number of set-ups, including the creation of an important new medical charity in the region, the firm is also taking instructions concerning regulatory work. Lead partner **Peter Jeffreys** (see p.130) is described by clients as "*excellent and responsive – the reliable top man.*" **Clients** RNIB; The Guide Dogs for the Blind Association; RSPCA; Imperial Cancer Research Fund; The Royal British Legion; Oxfam.

LINNELLS (see firm details p.1044) **Joss Saunders** (see p.132) remains the key name in this firm, where he combines his role with that of company secretary and in-house lawyer for Oxfam. He is felt to be so well-suited to his work that one source described him as "*always destined to make a name for himself in charities.*" With a client base that includes local and national charities, and governmental organisations affiliated to charities, he has recently advised World Vision in an attempt to appeal to young people through the use of text messages. **Clients** Oxfam; Opportunity International; World Vision; Water Aid.

THE SOUTH WEST

CHARITIES
■ THE SOUTH WEST

1
- Stone King Bath

2
- Bond Pearce Exeter
- Burges Salmon Bristol
- Osborne Clarke Bristol
- Veale Wasbrough Bristol
- Wilsons Salisbury

3
- Rickerbys Cheltenham
- Thring Townsend Bath
- Tozers Exeter

LEADING INDIVIDUALS

★
- KING Michael Stone King

1
- WOODWARD Mark Osborne Clarke

2
- DE'ATH Gary Veale Wasbrough
- NICHOLSON Jonathan Bond Pearce
- WYLD Charles Burges Salmon

This book is the product of 6,582 1/2 hour interviews. See p.7 for BMRB audit. Within each band, firms are listed alphabetically. See individuals' profiles p.129

STONE KING (see firm details p.1151) This is considered by many to be amongst the country's leading charities firms. It boasts the hugely respected **Michael King** (see p.130) who many regard as "*the best charities lawyer in the land – even including London,*" for his "*excellent track record and absolutely wonderful contacts.*" He has recently been appointed receiver and manager of a charity by the Charity Commission. Below him is a "*brilliant team which makes the firm one of the best in the country.*" Over the last year it has been involved in a number of high-profile mergers, transfers and joint ventures. **Clients** Moorfields Eye Hospital; Jewish Care; Scope; Spectrum.

BOND PEARCE (see firm details p.897) This well-known practice is seen as increasing its profile over the last year, with particular skills and services in the areas of property and employment. It has been offering IT and patent advice to large charities, as well as guiding charity managers through the changing constitutional requirements. Lead partner **Jonathan Nicholson** (see p.131) was described to researchers as "*combining a tax background with a keen charities brain.*" **Clients** Theatre Royal Plymouth; The National Trust; Cluewin Trust; Robert Owen Foundation; Cornwall College; English Heritage; Rose Road Association.

BURGES SALMON (see firm details p.894) Many clients and competitors praised **Charles Wyld** (see p.830) as "*a man who immediately springs to mind for his charities expertise.*" His highly competent team is busy on the formation of new trusts and charities, compliance, management and tax issues. With strong leanings towards health, housing and education work, it has over the last year advised a number of charities on taking advantage of income relief on share schemes. **Clients** At-Bristol; Bath Spa Trust; The National Trust.

OSBORNE CLARKE (see firm details p.1090) This busy practice is continuing to impress, and boasts skills in charity formation, regulatory matters, and property and employment advice to charities. **Mark Woodward** is praised for his "*clear and prompt advice.*" Highlights over the last year include handling a successful multimillion pound Heritage Lottery Fund bid, as well as a property dispute for a major wildlife charity. **Clients** Merchants' Colston Trust; Shaw Trust; Sue Ryder Care; Macmillan Cancer Relief; The Theatre Royal Bath.

VEALE WASBROUGH (see firm details p.1174) The combination of this firm's nationally renowned education skills and well-regarded charity specialist **Gary De'Ath** (see p.130) has given it a great profile within this sector. Seen as leading the way in its work for private schools, the firm acted recently on the incorporation of a major independent school established by royal charter. It also assisted in the establishment of an international charity. **Clients** Harry Crook Foundation; The Arthritic Association; Wakefield Grammar School Foundation; The Muscular Dystrophy Group.

WILSONS (see firm details p.1191) The appointment of Alison McKenna, barrister and former assistant commissioner at the Charity Commission is thought likely to boost this Salisbury team. Praised as being "*fast, efficient and able to speak plain English,*" the group acts in the establishment and registration of charities, fund-raising and advises on charitable subsidies. It has a strong focus on constitutional and regulatory work. **Clients** The National Motor Museum; Royal Commonwealth Society; Wiltshire Wildlife Trust.

RICKERBYS (see firm details p.1113) This "*booming*" firm continues to receive good notices for its work and is felt by some market commentators to have a virtual monopoly in Gloucestershire. Led by John Clarke, the group has a good feel for educational charities. Its knowledge of church law also gives it the skills to amend articles for religious charities. The firm has been involved in a number of sizeable mergers recently, across various sectors. **Clients** UCAS; The Cheltenham Ladies' College; Cheltenham College; Cheltenham & Gloucester College of Higher Education.

CHARITIES ■ WALES/MIDLANDS/EAST ANGLIA

THRING TOWNSEND (see firm details p.1162) This effective firm is active in all areas of charity law, with a particularly strong practice in land issues relating to charities. Quentin Elston's team has recently acted in the winding-down of a charity and a multimillion pound transfer of property assets, as well as various planning and licensing matters. Although still highly recommended, some commentators believe that the firm is less visible in the market than in previous years. **Clients** St John's Hospital; R J H Trust; Mr Willats' Charity.

TOZERS (see firm details p.1165) Holding a long and established reputation for assisting church charities, Richard King's team has now developed acknowledged skills in the areas of disabled and public benefit bodies. The last year has seen them carry out a number of set-ups, and the firm also enjoys a steady stream of work in amalgamations and reconstitutions of large organisations. **Clients** Plymouth Roman Catholic Diocese; Prior Park College; Forward Living; IRSE.

WALES

CHARITIES ■ WALES

1 Edwards Geldard Cardiff

This book is the product of 6,582 1/2 hour interviews. See p.7 for BMRB audit. Within each band, firms are listed alphabetically.

EDWARDS GELDARD (see firm details p.944) The only firm within the principality to receive sustained recommendations, it acts for a client base that includes large and emerging charities, as well as a number of important set-ups. It recently advised a large local charity over the details of a trading subsidiary, and saved a charitable legacy for a large youth charity. Giselle Davis' team offers a bilingual service for charities that need their articles in both Welsh and English. **Clients** The National Botanic Garden of Wales; The National Library of Wales; Wales Millennium Centre; The English Speaking Union.

MIDLANDS

CHARITIES ■ MIDLANDS

1 Anthony Collins Solicitors Birmingham
  Martineau Johnson Birmingham
  Wragge & Co Birmingham
2 Hewitson Becke + Shaw Northampton
  Lee Crowder Birmingham

LEADING INDIVIDUALS

1 THOMPSON Romaine Anthony Collins Solicitors
2 FEA Michael Martineau Johnson
  FOX Julie Wragge & Co

This book is the product of 6,58 1/2 hour interviews. See p.7 for BMRB audit. Within each band, firms are listed alphabetically. See individuals' profiles p.129.

ANTHONY COLLINS SOLICITORS (see firm details p.845) This highly regarded firm retains the respect and recommendations of its competitors. With an impressive client base, which includes Christian, regeneration and housing charities, the firm has been active in constitutional work, property and employment matters. It has recently assisted in the reorganisation of a royal charter charity. **Romaine Thompson** (see p.133) remains the key figure, and was described to researchers as "*so plugged into the world of charities that she truly feels the flow.*" **Clients** The Shaftesbury Society; Spring Harvest; Parkinson's Disease Society; United Kingdom Evangelization Trust.

MARTINEAU JOHNSON (see firm details p.1056) This established team is praised for the size of its client base and the focus it brings to its work. The highly rated **Michael Fea** (see p.130) leads a team that can draw upon many skills from across the firm. It administers a number of charitable trust funds worth in total over £200 million. The firm's acknowledged skills in education mean that it also has strong relationships with the educational trusts in the region. **Clients** The Foundation for Conductive Education; Christian Vision; City of Birmingham Symphony Orchestra.

WRAGGE & CO (see firm details p.1197) This charity department was described by one competitor as "*a big fish in a small pond,*" so it's no surprise that it is expanding its work nationwide. Although Louise Woodhead is no longer visible in the market following her elevation to deputy managing partner, **Julie Fox** was described by peers as "*competent, efficient and highly focused on client service.*" The team assisted the Talyllyn Railway in mid-Wales on its registration as a charity, and advised the West Midlands Arts Board on the Arts Council's reorganisation proposals. **Clients** English Heritage; Talyllyn Railway; Sutton Coldfield College; William A Cadbury Charitable Trust.

HEWITSON BECKE + SHAW (see firm details p.993) This "*really solid charities group*" has been building a strong reputation in the East Midlands. Clare Colacicchi runs a team that handles mainly small private charities and the local branches of national charities. It is active in incorporations, investment management, mergers and consolidations and has strong connections with independent schools and hospitals, for which it handles the whole range of charities law. The team advised last year on the incorporation of an historic educational foundation. **Clients** St Andrew's Hospital; Harbour Trust; RSPB.

LEE CROWDER (see firm details p.1035) Martin Woodward runs a team that handles "*an excellent client base of old, established charities,*" with a particular specialism in religious, educational and grant-making charities. Its expertise in employment work is well known, while property skills have come into play with the selling off of a number of redundant churches. Over the last year it has sealed a multimillion pound deal within the education sector. **Clients** King Edward's School Foundation; The United Reform Church (West Midlands Province); Birmingham College of Food, Tourism & Creative Studies.

EAST ANGLIA

MILLS & REEVE (see firm details p.1071) The team won praise this year from many sources, leaving our researchers in no doubt about how strong it remains in the region. It has enjoyed a busy year establishing charitable trusts, registering charities, setting up trading subsidiaries and giving asset advice, particularly for educational and public sector charities. **John Herring** (see p.130) was highly recommended by peers for his expertise and enthusiasm. **Clients** Major landowning bodies; ecclesiastical charities.

TAYLOR VINTERS (see firm details p.1156) With a fine team which includes the "*charmingly pragmatic*" **Jennifer Warren** (see p.738), the firm is known for the skill and quantity of its work across the region. It is active for various Cambridge colleges and has an impressive repu-

NORTH WEST/NORTH EAST ■ CHARITIES

CHARITIES
■ EAST ANGLIA

1. Mills & Reeve Norwich
   Taylor Vinters Cambridge
2. Cozens-Hardy & Jewson Norwich
   Greenwoods Peterborough
   Hewitson Becke + Shaw Cambridge
   Leathes Prior Norwich

LEADING INDIVIDUALS

1. HERRING John Mills & Reeve
   WARREN Jennifer Taylor Vinters
2. MARTIN Matthew Cozens-Hardy & Jewson
   NORTON Philip Hansells

This book is the product of 6,582 1/2 hour interviews. See p.7 for BMRB audit.
Within each band, firms are listed alphabetically. See individuals' profiles p.129

tation in constitutional work, with a specialisation in the leasing, acquisition and developing of properties for charitable trusts. **Clients** Cambridge colleges.

COZENS-HARDY & JEWSON Although Matthew Martin (see p.131) remains the "real McCoy" in charities work, the firm itself is believed by some sources to have kept a low profile over the last year. With an active interest in a number of Norwich trusts, the team handles a lot of work in the educational, welfare and health sectors, while the tightening of Charity Commission regulations means that it is witnessing an increase in constitutional work. **Clients** Norwich Consolidated Charities; Norwich Town Close Estate Charity; Anguish's Educational Foundation; Memorial Trust of the Second Air Division.

GREENWOODS (see firm details p.978) "Always ready with a good spread of professional, prompt advice" was the verdict of one commentator on this busy firm. Shelagh Smith's team has developed a clear focus on the corporate side of charities work. It is active on a number of reorganisations of large charities and endowment funds. The firm has also set up subsidiary trading companies, as well as looking at codes of practice for professional institutes. **Clients** Institute of Credit Management; Wyggeston & Queen Elizabeth I College; Peterborough Environment City Trust.

HEWITSON BECKE + SHAW (see firm details p.993) Flowing along with a steady stream of work, Peter Ewart's team maintains a healthy profile. It acts for large national and local charities and has recently been busy in creations and conversions. With a client base that includes a number of colleges, the group has recently finished a large job for a scientific charity. **Clients** RSPB; Fund for Addenbrooke's.

LEATHES PRIOR This small Norwich firm continues to be a player in the market, and is said by competitors to "*actually out-punch its weight.*" It enjoys a long history of work for the church and large national bodies, advising both the charities and their trustees on, among other things, the setting up and registration of trusts or companies limited by guarantee. **Clients** Local and national charities.

OTHER NOTABLE PRACTITIONERS Philip Norton of Hansells also comes recommended.

NORTH WEST

CHARITIES
■ NORTH WEST

1. Birch Cullimore Chester
   Brabners Chaffe Street Liverpool
2. Halliwell Landau Manchester
   Oswald Goodier & Co Preston
   Pannone & Partners Manchester

This book is the product of 6,582 1/2 hour interviews. See p.7 for BMRB audit.
Within each band, firms are listed alphabetically.

BIRCH CULLIMORE This "*old, respected firm*" draws on an impressive client base of religious, educational and health charities, and won considerable praise from the market for its straightforward and dependable advice. The team, which includes Nick Cummings, offers advice on formations, property, employment, incorporations and corporate services. **Clients** Local and national charities.

BRABNERS CHAFFE STREET (see firm details p.885) "*By far the best firm in Liverpool*" in the view of some competitors, this practice is seen as having strengthened its position over the last year. Drawing on a wide range of skills from across the firm, it offers advice to charities on constitutional matters, employment, property and litigation. Stephen Brodie's team has been involved in the establishment of a drug abuse charity for the Greater Manchester Police Authority, as well as dealing with governance matters for the Liverpool Muslim School. **Clients** Merseyside Youth Association; Huyton Community Partnership; Let's Get Serious; Liverpool College; International Harp Centre.

HALLIWELL LANDAU (see firm details p.982) This strong team handles a wide range of work across the charities sector. It has been involved in the formation, administration, reconstitution and wind-up of charitable clients. With a particular focus in education and health, the firm has received a number of instructions from medical research bodies. Geoffrey Shindler's team is currently advising various charities on their new responsibilities to the Charity Commission. **Clients** Royal Schools for the Deaf Manchester; Radiology History & Heritage Charitable Trust.

OSWALD GOODIER & CO (see firm details p.1091) Mark Belderbos' team handles a wide range of charities work for its large and impressive client base. Best known for its work advising the Catholic Diocese of Lancaster, the firm also handles grant-making and educational charities. It advises on commercial agreements, share agreements and transfers, as well as the more bread-and-butter work of property and employment. **Clients** RC Diocese of Lancaster; Montfort Missionary Society; Congregation of the Daughters of Wisdom; Nazereth House.

PANNONE & PARTNERS (see firm details p.1092) Although not as large and visible as some of its competitors, the firm is praised for the efficiency of its advice. Katharine Peterson's team has great expertise in working for public sector-associated charities. It has recently dealt with a reorganisation for a large charity, as well as setting up companies limited by guarantee. **Clients** Manchester Care; Working Class Movement Library; National Museum of Labour History; Tameside Sports Trust.

NORTH EAST

WRIGLEYS (see firm details p.1199) One London source described this as being - alongside Stone King - "*the only firm in the regions of note.*" It boasts a nationally renowned set of individuals, including Matthew Wrigley (see p.830), who is "*so established he's like the York Minster of charities law*" and Malcolm Lynch (see p.130), who is "*a prize draw to any firm; a human magnet for charity clients*." Highlights of the last year include acting on the merger of two horticultural societies and the purchase of one Christian media company by another. The team also advised on a coupon bond issue designed to make £50 million available towards regeneration in London. **Clients** Major heritage, educational and religious charities.

ADDLESHAW BOOTH & CO (see firm details p.838) Seen by its rivals to be "*moving along at a brisk pace,*" this charities department maintains a strong presence in Leeds, with supplementary

CHARITIES ■ NORTH EAST/SCOTLAND

work being carried out at the Manchester office. The team - which includes Pervinder Kaur - has great expertise in giving commercial advice to charities, and has recently assisted a national charity with commercial and constitutional issues. It has also advised universities on questions relating to PPP projects and helped to set up not-for-profit organisations. **Clients** Large national and local charities.

GRAYS (see firm details p.977) Competitors and clients praised the "*talented bunch of people*" at this firm and, in particular, the highly rated **Tony Lawton** (see p.130). The team has been busy over the last year with an increasing number of registrations, as well as constitutional matters. It also handles risk assessment advice for a number of large organisations, and boasts well-known expertise in the fields of trust and tax. **Clients** Roman Catholic Diocese of Middlesborough; Dean and Chapter of York; Lady Elizabeth Hastings Charity.

DICKINSON DEES (see firm details p.938) This large firm is highly praised by local clients, who are impressed by its responsiveness on small jobs ("*perfect for the two-minute query*") as well as large, innovative deals. The team - which includes Sean Nicolson - has experience of complex health and education work, and won positive notices for its work with museums and public attractions. This includes advising on funding arrangements for the Bowes Museum. The firm's in-house forensic accountant has led a number of investigations into charitable organisations. **Clients** Northern Arts; Tyneside Charitable Trust; Newcastle upon Tyne Hospitals NHS Trust; Newcastle upon Tyne University Development Trust; Netherton Park; Newcastle upon Tyne Royal Grammar School; The National Trust.

IRWIN MITCHELL (see firm details p.1009) This high-profile firm is forging a strong reputation for itself in the charities field. Andrew Uprichard's team focuses on service providers, and has a niche in advising medical charities (which complements the firm's well-regarded personal injury work). Over the last year it has advised the University of Sheffield on the creation of the Trust for Research into Freemasonry. **Clients** Sheffield City Trust; Sheffcare; Sheffield Galleries & Museums Trust.

ROLLITS (see firm details p.1115) Having taken the decision to boost its charity department with the hiring of high-flyer **Ros Harwood** (see p.130) (described by competitors as a "*well-connected, intelligent self-starter*") the firm is now reaping the dividends. It assists a wide spectrum of clients, which include diocese, higher education institutions and national and international charities. The team has been busy over the last year on a £50 million joint venture to set up a large conservation centre. It was also recently involved in the setting up of Charity Bank, which lends money and gives mortgages to charities at a preferential rate. **Clients** Scope; Peabody Trust; Joseph Rowntree Foundation; A Sporting Chance Clinic; St Edmund's School, Canterbury; University of Hull.

MCCORMICKS (see firm details p.1063) Although it is better known for its considerable sports practice, Peter McCormick's team has continued to quietly impress. Heavily involved with a number of large Catholic charities in the region, it carries out a range of constitutional and tax work. It has also been involved in a number of high-profile set-ups and registrations, including establishing a new charity designed to provide support for young musicians. **Clients** The Duke of Edinburgh's Award; The Outward Bound Trust; The Order of the Holy Paraclete; The Northern Ballet Company; Age Concern.

SCOTLAND

ANDERSON STRATHERN WS (see firm details p.844) This traditionally sound firm is described by rivals as "*one of the prime movers in the country.*" A strong team is kept active on a raft of charity issues, including set-ups, reorganisations and trading matters. Last year it advised the National Trust for Scotland on a number of high-profile transactions, as well as playing a big part in the ongoing Iona Cathedral Trust case. Its leading individual remains the "*top-notch*" **George Russell** (see p.132), described by clients as "*well-versed and charming.*" **Clients** The National Trust for Scotland; Iona Cathedral Trust; Youth Clubs Scotland; Royal College of Art; Fettes College.

TURCAN CONNELL (see firm details p.1170) Described to researchers as "*racing away in poll position,*" this practice enjoys a celebrated reputation in the country. Boasting two big hitters, the team has been involved in the Scottish aspects of the UK-wide reorganisation of the YMCA, and also acted in the merger of four MacRobert trusts into one. **Simon Mackintosh** (see p.131) is described by competitors as "*having a massive brain for charities work,*" while **Douglas Connell** (see p.129) was praised as "*influential, energetic and bright.*" **Clients** The Art Galleries of Scotland Foundation; National Museums of Scotland; National Galleries of Scotland; The Save the Children Fund.

BIGGART BAiLLIE (see firm details p.871) This busy department's reputation is founded upon the presence of **Gordon Wyllie**, described by market sources as "*brilliantly skilled and keenly focused.*" The team carries out work across Scotland, and has particular expertise in heritage and grant-making trusts. It was involved last year in advising a trust that manages charitable funds of £20 million. **Clients** Charitable trusts.

TODS MURRAY WS (see firm details p.1164) Well-regarded for its skills and the scale of its practice, this team can "*rightly boast having fingers in most pies.*" It is particularly known for its work with entertainment and arts charities, and has a niche in serving charities from Scotland's gay community. Active in formations, incorporation, constitutional matters and commercial and property work, the "*knowledgeable*" **Peter Ryden** (see p.132) receives high praise from clients and competitors. **Clients** RSPB; The Guide

THE LEADERS — CHARITIES

LEADING INDIVIDUALS

1
- CONNELL Douglas Turcan Connell
- MACKINTOSH Simon Turcan Connell
- RUSSELL George Anderson Strathern WS

2
- RENNIE Brenda Balfour & Manson
- WYLLIE Gordon Biggart Baillie

3
- REITH David Lindsays WS
- RYDEN Peter Tods Murray WS

See individuals' profiles p.129

Association in Scotland; St Columba's Hospice; Federation of Scottish Theatre.

BALFOUR & MANSON (see firm details p.856) With "*charity queen*" **Brenda Rennie** (see p.132) at the helm, the practice retains a strong position. Its client base includes a number of large social and medical charities for which it acts on a range of work including formations. The team has recently been busy in a large incorporation. **Clients** Age Concern Scotland; Rock Trust.

LINDSAYS WS (see firm details p.1042) This prominent firm has been active over the last year in commercial work, mergers and consolidations, and has witnessed a particular rise in incorporations. The "*superb*" **David Reith** (see p.132) presides over a team that is well-known for its work in the education sector. Over the last year it handled a large number of set-ups, including those of several building preservation trusts. **Clients** University of Edinburgh; Stevenson College.

BURNESS (see firm details p.1041) Handling general advice and commercial contracts, Paul Pia's team has a strong niche in representing arts and housing charities. It advises on, *inter alia*, property, employment, corporate governance and joint ventures. The firm has helped set up a number of non-charitable subsidiaries, and is known for its strong skills in charity tax law. **Clients** Scottish Arts Council; The Big Issue Foundation; The Millennium Commission; Scottish Federation of Housing Associations.

GILLESPIE MACANDREW WS (see firm details p.971) Seen as having a rising profile in the sector, competitors note that the firm is doing an impressive job and "*making use of its historic connections.*" Tom Murray's team has recently advised on the restructuring of a large charity, and assisted a national charity on resolving the question of a disputed estate. It also handles commercial and licensing work, as well as helping with accounts and regulation. **Clients** Scottish Goldsmiths Trust; Royal British Legion Scotland; Scottish Countryside Trust; Scottish SPINA BIFIDA Association.

MACROBERTS (see firm details p.1049) David MacRobert's team has been involved over the last year in, among st other things, the setting up of charitable trusts and the conversion of a listed building into a museum. With a client base that includes a number of important public charities as well as substantial private clients, the firm also handles cross-border issues. **Clients** KIND (Scotland); SENSE (Scotland).

MORTON FRASER, SOLICITORS (see firm details p.1077) Having been involved in the formation of a number of charities that have grown into large national bodies, Scott Rae's team offers a broad range of advice and experience to the modern organisation. Handling a great deal of employment, property and tax work, the firm's cross-departmental team boasts a breadth and depth of resources. **Clients** George Watson's College; RYA Scotland; Scottish Wildlife Trust; Scottish Agricultural College.

SHEPHERD+ WEDDERBURN (see firm details p.1130) Andrew Holehouse's department has strong experience of advising charities on tax and regulatory issues. It has recently established a medical charity to research into intestinal disorders, as well as advising Scottish-Power in its consultations on funding issues with national charities. **Clients** Barnardos; Royal Air Force Benevolent Fund; Royal College of Surgeons; Dunblane Help Fund.

TC YOUNG (see firm details p.1199) Thought by industry insiders to be on the up, this firm's main charity work remains in social housing. Mark Ewing's team has been busy over the last year converting housing providers to charities, even holding public seminars on the subject. It has also been involved in a number of set ups. **Clients** Erskine Hospital; The Princess Royal Trust for Carers; Turning Point Scotland; The Charities Aid Foundation.

THE LEADERS IN CHARITIES

BROOKS, Ken
BrookStreet Des Roches, Witney
(01993) 771616
Specialisation: Company and Commercial Partner. All types of commercial property transaction including, in particular, work for national retail chains, site acquisitions and disposals, development work, joint ventures, general estate work, statutory agreements, retail parks, building schemes, security work, funding, planning, taxation and environmental matters. Also specialises in charity work including the establishment and administration of charities and their property work. Clients include a number of publicly quoted companies and banks, charities such as Oxfam and Merton College, Oxford; Co-operative Societies like Oxford, Swindon and Gloucester Co-operative Society Limited and substantial UK and international retailers like Blockbuster Entertainment Ltd, Game Stores Group Ltd and McDonald's Restaurants Ltd.
Prof. Memberships: Law Society, Association of Charity Lawyers, European Law Group, Thames Valley Commercial Lawyers Association, Berks Bucks and Oxon Law Society, Oxford & District Solicitors Association.
Career: Qualified in 1982. With *Linnells* from 1980 to 1994; as a partner from 1985. Co-founder of *BrookStreet des Roches* in April 1994.
Personal: Born 23 January 1956. Educated at King Edward VI, Guildford. Leisure interests include things historical and archaeological; reading music and walking; dining out and good company. Lives in South Leigh outside Witney.

BURCHFIELD, Jonathan
Nabarro Nathanson, London
(020) 7524 6700
j.burchfield@nabarro.com
Specialisation: Partner and head of charity group. Work covers constitutions of charities and the impact of charity law on all areas of charities' activities; Trustee of a significant grant-making charity. Contributed to 'Charity Appeals: the Complete Guide to Success'.
Prof. Memberships: Deputy Chairman of the Charity Law Association, Chartered Institute of Taxation, Society of Trust and Estate Practitioners.
Career: Qualified in 1978, having joined *Turner Kenneth Brown* in 1976. Became a Partner in 1983.
Personal: Born 22 February 1954. Leisure interests include family and cricket. Lives in Guildford.

CAIRNS, Elizabeth
Elizabeth Cairns, Maidstone
(01622) 858191
Specialisation: Specialist charity law practice established since 1990. Areas of particular interest include charitable status, constitutional issues, incorporation of charities and dispute resolution. She aims to give a high quality and sophisticated service to a wide range of charities and voluntary organisations.
Career: Charity Commission 1972-79; *Jaques & Lewis* 1979-90 (partner 1984).
Publications: 'Charities: Law & Practice' (Sweet & Maxwell) 3rd edn 1996; 'Fundraising for Charity' (Tolley) 1996.

CLARICOAT, John
Claricoat Phillips, London
(020) 7226 7000
philcoat@aol.com
Specialisation: Specialist in charity law. Fellow of the Society for Advanced Legal Studies. Consultant to several large national charities and city solicitors. Joint author with Hilary Phillips of 'Charity Law A-Z Key Questions Answered' published by Jordans.
Career: In private practice before joining the Government Service. Joined the charity commission in 1966. Served for 28 years reaching grade 5.

CONNELL, Douglas
Turcan Connell, Edinburgh
(0131) 228 8111
dac@turcanconnell.com
Specialisation: Joint Senior Partner. Specialist in trusts, tax planning, asset protection, charities and heritage property; acts as principal advisor to many chairmen and chief executives regarding their personal business and to the trustees of a number of major national charities, as well as private charitable foundations.
Prof. Memberships: President Scottish Young Lawyers Association 1975-76; member of Revenue Committee the Law Society of Scotland 1979-92; chairman Edinburgh Book Festival 1991-95; member Scottish Arts Council and chairman Lottery Committee, Scottish Arts Council 1994-97.
Career: Attended University of Edinburgh (LLB). Articled *Dundas & Wilson CS*; qualified 1976; Partner 1979-97.
Personal: Born 1954. Resides Edinburgh. Leisure interests include books, travel and good food.

CHARITIES ■ THE LEADERS

DAVIS, Elizabeth
Blake Lapthorn, Portsmouth
(023) 9222 1122

DE'ATH, Gary
Veale Wasbrough, Bristol
(0117) 925 2020
gde-ath@vwl.co.uk
Specialisation: Associate, Charities Group. Main areas of practice are charities formation and constitutional issues, (including consortia and joint working arrangements), strategic development, fundraising agreements and general commercial contractual issues.
Prof. Memberships: West Midlands Charitable Trusts Group, West Midlands Charity Trustees Forum, The Institute of Charity Fund-Raising Managers, The Charity Law Association, The Society of Trust and Estate Practitioners.
Career: Qualified, 1976. Joined *Shakespeares* in 1986 and became a Partner in 1989, *Wragge & Co*, 2000. Joined *Veale Wasbrough* in 2001.
Personal: Born 1951. Kings College, University of London 1970-73, West Midlands Honorary Consul to Cote d'Ivoire.

DOLLIMORE, Jean
RadcliffesLeBrasseur, London
(020) 7227 7453
jean.dollimore@rlb-law.com
Specialisation: Partner and Head of Charities Group. Advises a broad range of charities on all aspects of charity law with an emphasis on constitutional structures and the powers and duties of trustees. Particularly experienced in the charity law aspects of the work of charitable housing associations. Also experienced in wills, trusts and the administration of estates. Experienced speaker and contributor to charity publications.
Prof. Memberships: Law Society; Member of the Executive Committee of the Charity Law Association; Charities Correspondent for Private Client Business; Society of Trust and Estate Practitioners.
Career: Trained *Boodle Hatfield*. Qualified 1972. Partner *Trowers & Hamlins* 1984-2001, Head of Charities Group. Joined *RadcliffesLeBrasseur* as a partner in September 2001.
Personal: Educated Hitchin Girls Grammar School and Lady Margaret Hall, Oxford. Lives in London.

FEA, Michael
Martineau Johnson, Birmingham
(0121) 678 1480
michael.fea@martjohn.com
Specialisation: Thirty years estate planning, all aspects of charity law, wills, trusts, succession and probate. Trustee/clerk to a number of charities.
Prof. Memberships: STEP; Charity Law Association; Law Society.
Career: Partner 1971. Notary Public. Member West Midlands Mental Health Tribunal. Deputy Registrar Birmingham Diocese.
Personal: Born 1939. Winchester College (1954-58). Married with four children. Recreations include: tennis, shooting, fishing, concerts, opera and gardening. Lives in Worcestershire.

FOX, Julie
Wragge & Co, Birmingham
(0870) 903 1000

HARWOOD, Ros
Rollits, York
(01904) 625790
ros.harwood@rollits.com
Specialisation: Charity law exclusively. Acting for a wide range of charities on all aspects of charity law. Has written numerous articles for national newspapers and charity sector periodicals. Also frequent speaker at seminars.
Prof. Memberships: Secretary of the Charity Law Association. Law Society. ACEVO – Association of Chief Executives for Voluntary Organisations.
Career: Head of Charity Group at *Rollits*. First joined *Lee Bolton & Lee* as trainee in 1987. Partner at *Speechly Bircham* 1998-2000. Joined *Rollits* as Partner in January 2001.
Personal: Educated at Bath High School for Girls, GDST and Churchers College, Petersfield; Birmingham University LLB. Enjoys hockey, cycling, walking, gardening. Lives in North Yorkshire.

HERRING, John
Mills & Reeve, Norwich
(01603) 693209
john.herring@mills-reeve.com
Specialisation: All aspects of charity law with particular emphasis on ecclesiastical charities and charity property. Also Registrar of Diocese of Norwich and legal secretary to the Bishop of Norwich.
Prof. Memberships: Law Society, Ecclesiastical Law Association (former Executive Committee Member), Ecclesiastical Law Society.

HILL, Judith
Farrer & Co, London
(020) 7242 2022
Specialisation: Partner and Head of the Charity Team. Main area of practice is charity law, including the establishment of charities, constitutional issues and trading companies. Also experienced in art and heritage law, general private client work, covering trusts, wills, capital taxation. Contributor to 'Trust Law International', 'The Charity Law and Practice Review', 'NGO Finance' and assistant editor of 'Art, Antiquity & Law', on advisory editorial board of 'The Charity Law & Practice Review' and the editorial board of 'Trust Law International'. Consultant editor of Peter Luxton's 'The Law of Charities' published by OUP. Regularly addresses conferences on charity law topics. Member of the Advisory Group to the Performance and Innovation Unit's Review of the legal and regulatory framework of the voluntary sector.
Prof. Memberships: Law Society, Holborn Law Society, International Bar Association (Co-Chairman Committee 20 1997-2001), Charity Law Association (Chairman).
Career: Joined *Farrer & Co* in 1973, qualifying in 1975. Moved to *Shoosmiths & Harrison* in Northampton in 1979, until 1981. Re-joined *Farrer & Co* in 1985. Partner 1986.
Personal: Born 8 October 1949. Attended Brighton & Hove High School 1956-69, Newnham College, Cambridge 1969-72. Appointed Lieutenant of the Victorian Order in 1995. Leisure pursuits include gardening and reading. Lives in London.

JEFFREYS, Peter
Henmans, Woodstock
(01993) 811396
peter.jeffreys@henmans.co.uk
Specialisation: Charity law, charity legacy administration. Acts for a growing number of national charities including BSPCA, RNIB, and Guide Dogs. Regular lecturer to the legal profession and the charity sector.
Prof. Memberships: Charity Law Association; STEP.
Career: Articled *Meade-King*, Bristol (1989-91). Qualified and joined *Henmans* 1991. Associate 1995. Partner 1996.
Publications: Recognising and dealing with fraud ('Trusts & Estates Law Journal', Jan 2000). 'Uncovering Probate Fraud' (Quarterly Journal, 'The Association of Corporate Trustees', October 2000).
Personal: Educated: Uppingham School; Exeter University. Interests include music and singing generally. Member of The National Trust, Friends of Peterborough Cathedral. Liveryman, Worshipful Company of Glass Sellers. Resides Chipping Norton.

KING, Michael
Stone King, Bath
(020) 7796 1007
michaelking@stoneking.co.uk
Specialisation: Charity and education law. Head of Charity Unit at *Stone King*, Bath and London.
Prof. Memberships: Law Society, Charity Law Association, Education Law Association.
Career: Articled: *Stone King & Wardle*, and *Charles Russell & Co*. 1969-74. Qualified 1974; Partner *Stone King* 1975 (Chairman: 1996); opened London Office 1990. Chairman, Catholic Charity Conference since 1991. Chairman, Charity Law Association 1997-2000; President, Bath Law Society 2001-02.
Publications: 'The Charities Acts Explained' (stationery office 2000) ISBN 0 11 702384 1.
Personal: Born 9 February 1949. Trustee of several charities. Leisure interests include tennis, sailing, shooting and watching rugby. Married with three children; lives in Bath.

LAWTON, F A (Tony)
Grays, York
(01904) 634771
Specialisation: Partner in 1967. Main area of practice is charity law, conveyancing in relation to charity property, formation of charities and negotiating with Charity Commissioners. Also experienced in work relating to education (especially statutory interpretation of the Education Acts), unincorporated associations, non-Companies Act companies and housing associations.
Prof. Memberships: Law Society, Yorkshire Law Society, Charity Law Association, Education Law Association.
Career: Qualified 1966. Joined *Grays* in 1967. Partner 1967. Board Member, Trustee Savings Bank of Yorkshire & Lincoln 1976-89. Committee Member, Conference of Solicitors for Catholic Charities 1967-date. (Chairman 1998-date).
Personal: Born 9 July 1940. Attended Bordeaux University 1958-59, then Corpus Christi College, Cambridge 1959-62. Leisure pursuits include history, gardening and foreign travel. Lives in York.

LLOYD, Stephen
Bates, Wells & Braithwaite, London
(020) 7551 7777
s.lloyd@bateswells.co.uk
Specialisation: Partner in charity and company commercial department. Acts for a large number of leading charitable organisations on a wide range of matters, including constitutional, contract, intellectual property and charity law. Also provides advice to small and medium sized businesses. Author of 'Barclays Guide to the Law for the Small Business' and 'Charities, Trading and the Law' and of numerous articles. Co-author with Fiona Middleton of 'The Charities Acts Handbook'. Contributor to 'The Charities Administration Handbook' and 'The Fundraisers Guide to the Law'. Gave at least 20 lectures in 1999.
Prof. Memberships: Charity Law Association, Law Society.
Career: With *Freshfields* 1975-78. Qualified in 1977. Joined *Bates, Wells & Braithwaite* in 1980 and became a partner in 1984.
Personal: Educated at Bristol University 1969-72 (History) and Cambridge University 1973 (Law). Trustee of three charities and of executive committee of Charity Law Association. Recreations include reading, cycling, theatre and music.

LYNCH, Malcolm
Wrigleys, Leeds
(0113) 244 6100
law@malcolmlynch.com
Specialisation: A solicitor who specialises in charity law and financial services, particularly relating to socially responsible investment. Has been involved in several studies for the European Commission on banking and financing of micro-firms and for the DTI on the financing of renewable energy.
Prof. Memberships: Member of Charity Law Association, Co-operative Law Association.
Career: Qualified in 1983 while with *Booth & Co* in Leeds. Joined *Titmuss Sainer & Webb* in 1983, then economic development solicitor to Kirklees Metropolitan Council, West Yorkshire, 1984-

87. Became solicitor to Industrial Common Ownership Movement Limited, 1987-89 and then principal of *Malcolm Lynch* in 1989 until joining *Wrigleys* as a Partner in 2000.
Personal: Born 29 April 1955. Attended Colchester Royal Grammar School 1996-73. University of Birmingham 1974-77. Postgraduate School of Yugoslav Studies, University of Bradford and Skopje University, Yugoslavia 1977-79. Fellow of RSA. Director of Ecology Building Society. Lives in Leeds.

MACKINTOSH, Simon
Turcan Connell, Edinburgh
(0131) 228 8111
sam@turcanconnell.com
Specialisation: Main areas of practice are tax, trusts and charities. Work includes tax planning, heritage property (often with an international element), charity law and practice and trust establishment, variation and practice. Lead Partner for a number of the firm's major charity clients. Joint Head of the firm's charity unit. Member of the Law Society of Scotland Tax Law Committee and of its panel on Trust Law and Charity Law Accreditation.
Prof. Memberships: Society of Trust and Estate Practitioners, International Academy of Estate and Trust Law.
Career: Partner *Turcan Connell* 1997; Partner *W & J Burness WS* 1985-97; non-executive director of Macphie of Glenbervie Ltd and past board member of the Edinburgh International Book Festival. Member of the Scottish Executive Commission on reform of charity law.
Publications: Co-author of 'Revenue Law of Scotland', 1987. Contributor to Butterworths' 'Scottish Older Client Law Service'.

MARTIN, Matthew T
Cozens-Hardy & Jewson, Norwich
(01603) 625231
Specialisation: Consultant in Private Client Department. Main areas of practice are charity law and administration. Solicitor and clerk to Trustees of a number of charities, including Norwich Consolidated Charities, Norwich Town Close Estate Charity, Anguish's Educational Foundation, The Memorial Trust of the 2nd Air Division USAAF and Laura Elizabeth Stuart Memorial Trust. Chairman of the Norfolk Archaeological Trust.
Prof. Memberships: Law Society, Charity Law Association.
Career: Joined *Cozens-Hardy & Jewson* in 1962. Qualified in 1967. Became Partner in 1969. Consultant in 1996.
Personal: Born 28 June 1943. Attended Bradfield College, Berkshire 1957-61. Under Sheriff of City of Norwich 1987-94. Leisure pursuits include golf and gardening.

MEAKIN, Robert
Stone King, London
(020) 7628 2020 ext: 4432
robertmeakin@stoneking.co.uk
Specialisation: Practice covers the full range of Charity Law advice including Charitable Status and applications for registration as a charity, applications for Schemes and Orders from the Charity Commissioners and representing charity trustees subject to investigation by the Charity Commissioners. In addition specialises in investment (has advised on the creation of four CIF's), trading and fundraising, Commercial Sponsorship, lottery, and partnership funding. Regularly writes articles on charity law and gives seminars to charity officers and trustees. Particular expertise in environmental charities and landfill tax funding.
Prof. Memberships: Charity Law Association, Charities' Tax Reform Group, Advisory Board Member of The European Association for Planned Giving.
Career: Legal Advisor to the Charity Commissioners 1988-93. *Lovell White Durrant* Charity Group 1993-95. *Speechly Bircham* 1995-97; *Simmons & Simmons* 1997-2000.
Publications: 'Charity in the NHS: Policy and Practice' (Jordans 1998).

MIDDLETON, Fiona
Bates, Wells & Braithwaite, London
(020) 7551 7777
f.middleton@bateswells.co.uk
Specialisation: Charity Commission 1979-88. Partner in Charity Department 1990-2002 and now a consultant. Deals with all aspects of law relating to charities and other voluntary organisations. Operates the Charity Law Advisory Service for Solicitors. Co-author of 'Charity Investment, Law & Practice', 'The Charities Acts Handbook' and Jordans Charities Administration Service. Member of the NCVO/Charity Commission working party on trustee training which produced the report 'On Trust: Increasing the Effectiveness of Charity Trustees and Management Committees'.
Prof. Memberships: Charity Law Association. Law Society.
Career: Lecturer in Law, Kings College, London University 1972-79. Legal Advisor to the Charity Commission 1979-87. Joined *Bates, Wells & Braithwaite* in 1988 and became a partner in 1990 and consultant in 2002.
Personal: Born 18 January 1948. Trustee of Barnardos. Recreations include gardening, bee keeping and opera.

NICHOLSON, Jonathan
Bond Pearce, Plymouth
(01752) 266633
jnicholson@bondpearce.com
Specialisation: Partner and Head of the Private Client Group. Almost 40 years experience in wills, trusts and personal tax. Specialist in charity law and Solicitor to several major charities.
Prof. Memberships: Member of the Society of Trust and Estate Practitioners (former Chairman of West of England branch) and the Association of Charity Lawyers.
Career: Graduate of Trinity College, Dublin, qualified in 1968 and joined the University of Zambia as lecturer in law, returning to the UK in 1971. Joined *Meade King* in Bristol and was Solicitor to the Bristol Municipal Charities. Moved to *Bond Pearce* in 1983, becoming Partner 1985.

NORTON, Philip
Hansells, Norwich
(01603) 615731

PAINES, Alison
Withers LLP, London
(020) 7597 6000
Specialisation: Head of charities practice. Charity law and related tax and trust advice for not-for-profit organisations and their donors. Advises on structure, status, operations (including trading issues) and funding. Particular expertise in charitable issues relating to the NHS and government related charities. On editorial board and contributor to Kluwer's 'International Charitable Giving: Law and Taxation' and contributor to Tolley's 'Charities Manual' and FT Law and Tax's 'Practical Trust Precedents'.
Prof. Memberships: Charity Law Association (Executive Committee member); Society of Trusts and Estates Practitioners.
Career: Qualified 1981. Solicitor with *Crossman, Block & Keith* 1981-87; joined *Withers* 1988 and became a partner in 1991.
Personal: Educated Notting Hill and Ealing High School GPDST 1966-73; Girton College Cambridge 1974-78 (classics and law); trustee of two grant-making foundations.

PAISNER, Martin
Berwin Leighton Paisner, London
(020) 7760 1000
martin.paisner@berwinleightonpaisner.com
Specialisation: Practice embraces tax and estate planning advice with particular emphasis on the high net worth entrepreneur, including trust structures both for the UK based (whether domiciled or not) and an international clientele. In addition, he advises widely on all aspects of charity law involving both grant-making and functional charities and serves as trustee of, and Solicitor to numerous charitable bodies.
Prof. Memberships: Law Society, Society of Trust and Estate Practitioners, Charity Law Association.
Career: Born 1 September 1943. Attended St Paul's School, London 1956-61, Sorbonne University, Paris 1961-62, Worcester College, Oxford 1962-65 and Ann Arbor, Michigan 1966-67. Honorary Fellow of Queen Mary and Westfield College, University of London. Qualified 1970. Partner at *Paisner & Co* (now *Berwin Leighton Paisner*) in 1972.
Personal: Leisure pursuits include antiquarian book-collecting (18th and 19th Century English and American literature), inter-war travel posters, music, reading, communal interests and learning from his children all the things he never knew! Currently Chairman of The Jerusalem Foundation (UK). Member of The Reform Club.

PHILLIPS, Andrew
Bates, Wells & Braithwaite, London
(020) 7551 7777
Specialisation: Founding partner. Main area of practice is charities, and secondarily business law and defamation. Author of 'Charitable Status: A practical handbook', now in its fourth edition; 'Charity Investment: Law and Practice'; and 'The Living Law', a guide to the law for young people. Occasional freelance journalist, regular broadcaster, particularly as Legal Eagle on BBC 2's Jimmy Young Show.
Prof. Memberships: Law Society.
Career: Qualified 1964. Founded *Bates Well & Braithwaite*, London in 1970. Co-founder in 1971 and first Chairman of the Legal Action Group. Founder and first Chairman of the Citizenship Foundation in 1989 (continuing). Initiated the Lawyers in the Community scheme and Solicitors Pro Bono Group (of which first President, continuing). Founder in 1971 of PARLEX Group of European Lawyers. Lib Dem Life Peer 1998.
Personal: Born 15 March 1939. Attended Uppingham school, then Trinity Hall, Cambridge. Trustee of Guardian/Observer newspapers and various charities. Non-Executive Director of four commercial companies. Leisure pursuits include politics, golf, cricket, history and the arts. Born, bred and lives in Sudbury, Suffolk.

PHILLIPS, Ann
Stone King, London
(020) 7796 1007
annphillips@stoneking.co.uk
Specialisation: Partner. All aspects of charity law and related tax issues. Work ranges from charity formation and advice to charities on constitutional, taxation and governance issues, to variation, mergers and dissolution. Articles in 'Charities Finance', 'Charities Management', 'Trusts and Estates Law Journal' and others.
Prof. Memberships: Law Society, Charity Law Association, Society of Trust and Estate Practitioners.
Career: Qualified in 1979. *Stephenson Harwood* 1977-2001. *Stone King* 2001-date.
Personal: Educated at St Hugh's College, Oxford (MA). Married with two children. Vice-Chairman of the Research Ethics Committee of Great Ormond Street Hospital/Institute of Child Health.

PHILLIPS, Hilary
Claricoat Phillips, London
(020) 7226 7000
philcoat@aol.com
Specialisation: Specialist in charity law. Fellow of the Society of Advanced Legal Studies. Consultant to several large national charities and city solicitors. Joint author with John Claricoat of numerous articles on charity law topics.
Career: In private practice before joining DES in 1970. Joined the Charity Commission in 1973. Served for 21 years reaching Grade 6.

CHARITIES ■ THE LEADERS

PIPER, Anne-Marie
Farrer & Co, London
(020) 7242 2022
amp@farrer.co.uk
Specialisation: Partner in the charity team. Practice encompasses charity law ranging from the formation and registration of new charities, advice to charity trustees on various matters including permissible activities, trading and commercial activities and tax-efficient fundraising through to the restructuring, variation and dissolution of charities. Also encompasses Charity Commission investigations and receiver and managerships. Acts for sponsors of new charities; directors, trustees and organisers of existing charities; and companies making charitable gifts or having dealings with charities. Frequent contributor of articles to professional publications on charity law subjects.
Prof. Memberships: Founder and Member of Executive Committee of Charity Law Association.
Career: Called to the Bar in 1980. Noble Lowndes Personal Financial Services 1980-83. Joined private client department at *Richards Butler* in 1983. Admitted as a solicitor in 1988 and became a Partner in 1989. Headed Charity Team at *Paisner & Co* where she was a Partner from 1994 to 2001 when she joined *Farrer & Co* as a Partner.
Personal: Born 27 January 1958. Attended North Walsham Secondary School 1969-74, then Norfolk College of Arts & Technology 1974-76. Went on to University College, London, 1976-79 and the Council of Legal Education 1979-80. Charity trustee. Leisure pursuits include family life and reading. Lives in London.

PORTRAIT, Judith
Portrait Solicitors in Association with Denton Wilde Sapte, London
(020) 7320 3888
Specialisation: All aspects of charity law, advising both grant-making and service-providing charities. Also advising on private trusts, estate and tax planning for individuals and trustees.
Career: Treasurer of The Henry Smith Charity; Trustee and Legal Advisor to the Sainsbury Family Charitable Trusts.
Personal: Educated St Paul's Girls' School and St Hugh's College Oxford. Married; resides in Cambridge.

POULTER, Alan
Manches, Oxford
(01865) 722106
alan.poulter@manches.co.uk
Specialisation: Principal areas of practice include advice to charitable and educational institutions, including universities and the colleges of Oxford University, formation of new charities, private trusts, tax-planning and related work for private clients.
Prof. Memberships: Charity Law Association; Society of Trust and Estate Practitioners.
Career: Qualified 1971 while at *Biddle & Co*. Joined *Morrell Peel & Gamlen* 1974 and became a Partner in 1975. Became Partner in *Manches* on the merger of *Morrell Peel and Gamlen* in 1997.
Personal: Born 4 November 1945. School Governor and Trustee of various charities.

PROTANI, Moira
Berwin Leighton Paisner, London
(020) 7427 1198
moira.protani@berwinleightonpaisner.com
Specialisation: Head of the Charities Group. Advises on all aspects of the law as it affects charities, donors and businesses which deal with charities. Encompasses a whole range of matters including establishment of charities, trustee powers and duties, taxation, grant-making, fundraising, mergers, constitutional and good governance issues. Acted for the Millennium Commission in establishing a permanent endowment fund for the benefit of the individuals within the community. Frequently lectures on charity law issues.
Prof. Memberships: Charity Law Association, the Law Society and the Royal Society of Arts.
Career: Trained at and employed by *SJ Berwin*. Qualified in 1990. Became a Partner of *SJ Berwin* in 1998. Became a Partner of *Berwin Leighton Paisner* in September 2000.
Publications: Has written numerous articles on charity law. Most recently 'Singing for Your Supper?', 'Dresdner RCN Global Investors – Top 3000 Charities' (2002); 'Dealing with Founder Syndrome', NGO Finance April 2000.
Personal: Born 1 October 1957; interests include international travel; food and wine and tapestry. Sits on the boards of four charities.

REES, John
Winckworth Sherwood, Oxford
(01865) 297 200
jrees@ws-oxford.co.uk
See under Church, p.139

REITH, David
Lindsays WS, Edinburgh
(0131) 477 8708
Specialisation: Partner in and Head of Commercial Department. Main area of practice is commercial property, but specialises in charities, including building preservation and other conservation work. Acted for Lothian Building Preservation Trust in successful campaign to save Mavisbank House, near Edinburgh, from demolition. Legal advisor to the Scottish Seabird Centre millennium founded project and the Scottish Association of Citizens Advice Bureaux. Has spoken at various seminars on charity law.
Prof. Memberships: Law Society of Scotland, WS Society.
Career: Qualified in 1974, having joined *Lindsays WS* in 1972. Became a Partner in 1976. Director of Scottish Historic Buildings Trust, Cockburn Conservation Trust, Scottish Sculpture Trust, Boilerhouse Theatre Company and other charitable companies. Secretary of Scottish Seabird Centre and Queensberry House Trust. Treasurer of the Cockburn Association and Fet-Lor Youth Club.
Personal: Born 15 April 1951. Educated at Fettes College 1965-69 and Aberdeen University 1969-72. Leisure interests include winemaking, gardening and architectural heritage. Lives in East Lothian.

RENNIE, Brenda
Balfour & Manson, Edinburgh
(0131) 200 1275
brenda.rennie@balfour-manson.co.uk
Specialisation: Head of Private Client Department. As part of a general private client practice, has developed a particular interest in charities and in the elderly and disabled. Has considerable experience in setting up charities and giving ongoing advice. The administration of private charitable trusts is a specialty. Is the Solicitor to Age Concern Scotland.
Prof. Memberships: WS; Member of the WS Society Legal Education Committee; Member of Society of Trust and Estate Practitioners; Trustee and chairman – High Blood Pressure Foundation.
Career: Qualified in 1971, having joined *Balfour & Manson* in 1969. Became a Partner in 1976.
Publications: Editor of Butterworths 'Scottish Older Client Law Service'.
Personal: Born 21 December 1947. Educated in Aberdeen and graduated University of Aberdeen LLB Hons 1969. Enjoys reading, walking and looking at buildings. Lives in Edinburgh.

RUSSELL, George
Anderson Strathern WS, Edinburgh
(0131) 220 2345
george.russell@andersonstrathern.co.uk
Specialisation: Main areas of practice are charities, trusts and tax planning and financial services. Charity work includes setting up charities and ongoing advice for a number of charitable trusts and large charities; clients include Napier University.
Career: Edinburgh University, qualified 1973, Partner 1976; Chairman Scottish Solicitors' Staff Pension Fund; Member Executive of Queen's Nurses Institute of Scotland; Member Scottish Council for National Parks; Fiscal of WS Society; Council Member National Trust for Scotland 1991-96; awarded MBE in 1995.
Personal: Born 1946; resides Linlithgow, West Lothian. Enjoys hill walking, skiing, music and golf.

RYDEN, Peter
Tods Murray WS, Edinburgh
(0131) 226 4771
maildesk@todsmurray.com
Specialisation: Charities, Succession, Trusts, and Estate Planning.
Prof. Memberships: STEP.
Career: Articled at *Biggart Baillie Gifford*; qualified 1980; *Tods Murray* 1980, Partner 1987.
Personal: Born 1956; resides Edinburgh.

SAUNDERS, Joss
Linnells, Oxford
(01865) 248 607
jss@linnells.co.uk
Specialisation: Partner and head of charity unit. Company secretary at Oxfam. Acts for educational, medical, development, children's and church charities, and grant-making trusts. Also active in e-business, intellectual property and publishing.
Prof. Memberships: Charity Law Association, Society for Computers and Law, Oxford Publishing Society.
Career: Qualified 1988. *Theodore Goddard* 1986-92. Eastern Europe 1992-95. Ran Polish branch of Prince of Wales Business Leaders' Forum. Lecturer, Warsaw University. Joined *Linnells* 1995.
Publications: NCVO's 'Guide to Contracts with Public Bodies' (1998); 'Business Law and Practice' (Cambridge Board of Continuing Education); contributor to 'Higher Education and the Law' (Open University).
Personal: Born 1962. Educated Trinity College, Oxford. LLM London. Trustee of charities working in education, in Africa, and a grant-making Trust. Also trustee of Helen House, the country's first children's hospice. Advisory Council Oxford University Law Foundation. Advisory board of Hugh Pilkington Charitable Trust.

SCOTT, Michael
Charles Russell, London
(020) 7203 5069
mikes@cr-law.co.uk
Specialisation: Charity, company and commercial law. Constitutional and commercial advice to the Royal Air Force Benevolent Fund, the Royal College of Nursing of the United Kingdom, The British Computer Society and others. Various transactions over the past year for other charities and institutions.
Prof. Memberships: The Charity Law Association, The Law Society.
Career: Joined *Charles Russell* as a trainee 1975. Qualified 1978 (and in Hong Kong 1979). Hong Kong Office 1979-85. Became a partner in 1985. Head of the Charities Group.
Publications: 'Butterworths Charity Law Handbook'. Various articles.
Personal: Wellington College, The Queen's College, Oxford. Married, three children. Leisure interests: Various outdoor sports.

SMITH, Rosamund
Bates, Wells & Braithwaite, London
(020) 7551 7777
r.smith@batewells.co.uk
Specialisation: Charity lawyer with particular emphasis on trading and fundraising issues and intellectual property. Major cases last year included establishment of the Booker Prize charity and Agreements with Booker Plc, Big Food Group Plc and the new sponsor The Man Group Plc.
Prof. Memberships: Steering Committee member of NCVO Voluntary Sector

THE LEADERS — CHARITIES

Publishers' Forum; Company Secretary Booker Prize Foundation and Booker Prize Trading Limited; Member of the Charity Law Association and the Lotteries Council; Lectures on charity law for Directory of Social Change (DSC) and Institute of Charity Fundraising Managers (ICFM). Secretary to the Committee on the Penalty for Homicide Chaired by Lord Lane.
Career: Trained *Bates, Wells & Braithwaite*, qualified 1994; Partner 1999.
Publications: Contributing author to 'The Non-Profit Sector in the UK' published by CAF and DSC; contributing author to 'Jordans Charities Manual'; co-author of 'The Fundraiser's Guide to the Law' published by DSC.
Personal: Born 1966; resides in London; Bristol University (2:1 Political Science); Leisure interests – the Arts (Chair of Poet in the City); Community, Tai Chi, Travel and Walking.

SYED, Catriona
Charles Russell, London
(020) 7203 5000
catrions@cr-law.co.uk
Specialisation: International and domestic private client work, including tax and estate planning for UK and non-UK domiciliaries; trusts; charity law and practice; trust aspects of commercial transactions.
Prof. Memberships: STEP Technical Committee member; Charity Law Association; City of London Solicitors Company; Law Society; Fellow of the Society of Advanced Legal Studies.
Career: Practised at the Chancery Bar 1983-86. *Norton Rose* 1986-97. Joined *Charles Russell* (partner 1997).
Personal: Leisure interests include family, opera, fine wine, walking, travel and reading.

TAYLOR, James Sinclair
Sinclair Taylor & Martin, London
(020) 8969 3667
jst@sinclairtaylor.co.uk
Specialisation: Partner specialising in charity law. Main area of practice is charity law. His work includes charity formation and mergers, company law, property transactions, internal structure and employment law, trading VAT and contracts with funders. Also deals with not for profit organisations, housing associations, schools and local authorities, advising on property, employment, corporate and charity law. Has substantial involvement in the urban regeneration development trust, learned societies, pressure groups, third world charities and housing. Much of his work is with organisations providing care accommodation and treatment. Author of numerous articles and of the 'Voluntary Sector Legal Handbook' and of the 'Company Handbook and Registers for Voluntary Organizations'. Involved in training for charities with A.C.E.V.O. Directory for Social Change, Charity Finance Directors Group and other organisations.
Prof. Memberships: Charity Law Association.
Career: Qualified in 1975. Founded *Sinclair Taylor & Martin* in 1981.
Personal: Charity trustee of a wide variety of organisations.

THOMPSON, Romaine
Anthony Collins Solicitors, Birmingham
(0121) 212 7401
romaine.thompson@anthonycollinssolicitors.com
Specialisation: Heads up the constitution and charities department within the regeneration team providing specialist legal services to numerous charities, churches, RSLs, Community Associations and not for profit organisations throughout the UK. The department advises charities on all legal aspects of their activities such as formation and registration, compliance with the Charity Commission requirements, restructuring, fund-raising, trustee training, advice on employment law, copyright and property management issues. The department publishes free briefings for clients updating them on legal issues and also offers a fixed fee legal audit.
Prof. Memberships: Romaine is a member of the Charity Law Association, the Ecclesiastical Law Society.
Career: Educated at Trinity Hall, Cambridge. Qualified 1988. Romaine joined *Anthony Collins Solicitors* in 1989 and became a partner in 1993. She has written articles for professional journals and lectures on charity law issues.

WALSH, Brian
Campbell Hooper, London
(020) 7222 9070
brianwalsh@campbellhooper.com
Specialisation: Both domestic and international probate and trust litigation. Represents a number of leading charities in all aspects of financial and ancillary matters. Appointed to the Panel of Professional Receivers, representing many individuals, who are either elderly or infirm, in their day to day affairs and before the Court of Protection. Cases: Richardson v RSPCA (Hong Kong) and Benham/Ratcliffe, a leading Inheritance Tax decision in favour of charities' continuing exemption from tax.
Prof. Memberships: The Association of Contentious Trust and Probate Specialists; the Society of Trust and Estate Practitioners; Solicitors for the Elderly.
Career: Joined *Campbell Hooper* in 1997 from *Messrs Hempsons* (joined 1970).
Publications: Contributor to Tolleys 'Tax Encyclopaedia of Forms and Precedents'; 'Law Society's Probate Handbook'. Also gives seminars both internally and externally to charities and banks.
Personal: Fly fishing and golf.

WARREN, Jennifer
Taylor Vinters, Cambridge
(01223) 423444
jennifer.warren@taylorvinters.com
See under Real Estate, p.738

WEIL, Simon
Bircham Dyson Bell, London
(020) 7227 7000
simonweil@bdb-law.co.uk
Specialisation: Specialist areas comprise charities, tax planning, commercial property for institutional investment clients (frequently with charitable status) and the resolution of potentially contentious issues for charities and others, arising out of wills, trusts and co-ownership of property. Important cases have included advising a substantial corporate charity with a turnover running into ten figures on governance and trustee duties; converting an educational trust from an unincorporated charity to a company limited by guarantee; arranging the reorganisation of a livery company's charitable trust with a view to protecting individual members of the company who had previously been personally liable to third parties; the disposal by legally binding tender to companies invited to bid, of a major commercial site in High Holborn; the establishment of a comprehensive divestment programme for a group of charities with a common trustee, involving the setting up of real property and securities investment pooling schemes; creating a corporate vehicle for the service provider aspects of a group of almshouse charities.
Prof. Memberships: CLA. EAPG. ACTAPS. Law Society.
Career: Served on the firm's Premises and General Purposes Committee and Staff Committee, becoming the Partner responsible for the firm's practice development in 1988. Continued in the latter role until 1992 and was Head of the Private Client Department between 1991 and 1995. Financial Services Act Compliance Officer between 1991 and 1997 and took a leading role in establishing Bircham Dyson Bell Investment Management. Head of the Charities Group since 1996.
Personal: Opera, singing and music generally; drawing; wine; reading history and novels (normally pre-1900); member of Chatham House (RIIA) with a particular focus on central Europe; tennis; swimming; riding; member of Oxford and Cambridge Club. Also active within St. Mary's Church Islington.

WOODWARD, Mark
Osborne Clarke, Bristol
(0117) 917 3000

WRIGLEY, Matthew
Wrigleys, Leeds
(0113) 244 6100
See under Trusts & Personal Tax, p.830

WYLD, Charles
Burges Salmon, Bristol
(0117) 902 2773
charles.wyld@burges-salmon.com
See under Trusts & Personal Tax, p.830

WYLLIE, Gordon
Biggart Baillie, Glasgow
(0141) 228 8000

CHURCH LAW

London: 134; The Regions: 135; Profiles: 137

Research approved by BMRB For this edition, **Chambers'** researchers conducted 6,582 interviews – 3,900 with law firms, 511 with barristers and 2,171 with clients. The validity of the research was scrutinised by BMRB International, who audited both the methodology and the results at our offices in London. They interviewed **Chambers'** researchers and cross-checked sample interviews. Details of the audit appear on page 7.

OVERVIEW Although the Clergy Discipline Measure has yet to come into force, disciplinary work is on the increase, with a number of abuse cases making news. Church bodies are also increasingly seeking advice on the potential effects of other major legislation, such as the implications of the Disability Discrimination Act for church buildings, or of the Human Rights Act on, for example, employment policies at church schools. Apart from this, the usual faculty legislation, education and charity work continue to form the staple diet of ecclesiastical lawyers. This section is divided into firms working primarily or exclusively for the Church of England, which tend to possess diocesan registrars, and firms dealing with other denominations and religions. In keeping with the structure of the Church of England and the Roman Catholic Church, many of the most respected solicitors can be found in the regions.

LONDON — CHURCH OF ENGLAND

CHURCH: CHURCH OF ENGLAND — LONDON

1. Lee Bolton & Lee
   Winckworth Sherwood

LEADING INDIVIDUALS

1. BEESLEY Peter Lee Bolton & Lee
   MORRIS Paul Winckworth Sherwood
   RICHENS Nicholas Lee Bolton & Lee

This book is the product of 6,582 1/2 hour interviews. See p.7 for BMRB audit.
Within each band, firms are listed alphabetically. See individuals' profiles p.137

LEE BOLTON & LEE (see firm details p.1034) "*The obvious people – a first-class firm, which hardly needs any recommendation,*" it is involved in matters ranging from advising on the legality of putting aerials on churches to running the faculty office of the Archbishopric of Canterbury. **Peter Beesley** (see p.137) is the chairman of the Ecclesiastical Law Association as well as registrar for both the Guildford and Ely Dioceses and joint registrar for the Diocese of Hereford. Well known for his church education work, interviewees were full of praise for his "*excellent*" knowledge and experience. **Nicholas Richens** (see p.139) is equally well respected. One source described him as "*frighteningly good – a walking encyclopaedia.*"

WINCKWORTH SHERWOOD (see firm details p.1192) Acting both for the Church of England and the Roman Catholic Church, this is a consummate, "*platinum card*" ecclesiastical law practice. "*Nobody knows more*" than "*incredibly knowledgeable and charming*" **Paul Morris** (see p.139), the registrar for the Dioceses of London and Southwark, who is considered one of the best church lawyers in the country. The firm is well regarded for its church schools work, and handles intricate property matters for the Roman Catholic Diocese of Brentwood and Archdiocese of Westminster as well as its Church of England dioceses. It has recently witnessed an increase in work advising church authorities on the potential implications for them of the Human Rights Act, the Data Protection Act, the Disability Discrimination Act and the Clergy Discipline Measure.

LONDON — OTHER DENOMINATIONS

CHURCH: OTHER DENOMINATIONS — LONDON

1. Carter Lemon Camerons
   Ellis Wood
   Pothecary & Barratt

This book is the product of 6,582 1/2 hour interviews. See p.7 for BMRB audit.
Within each band, firms are listed alphabetically.

CARTER LEMON CAMERONS The firm acts for the Baptist Union, and Baptist trust corporations and bodies, as well as other independent churches, church bodies and church-related charities. Peers find the team, led by Duncan Tuft, "*pleasant and knowledgeable.*"

ELLIS WOOD Although not high profile, this firm continues to be involved in this area for a client base that includes Catholic bodies. The team includes Simon Howell.

POTHECARY & BARRATT This firm is best known for its work for the Methodist Church and Methodist bodies. It also represents other church bodies such as the London Bible College and the Scripture Union.

THE SOUTH & SOUTH WEST

CHURCH OF ENGLAND

CHURCH: CHURCH OF ENGLAND
THE SOUTH & SOUTH WEST

1. **White & Bowker** Winchester
2. **Brutton & Co** Fareham
   Follett Stock Truro
   Harris & Harris Wells
   Michelmores Exeter
   Thomas Eggar Chichester
3. **Batt Broadbent** Salisbury
   Madge Lloyd & Gibson Gloucester

LEADING INDIVIDUALS

1. **WHITE Peter** White & Bowker
2. **BERRY Timothy** Harris & Harris
   BUTCHER Christopher Thomas Eggar
   FOLLETT Martin Follett Stock
   TYLER Hilary Brutton & Co
3. **JOHNSON Andrew** Batt Broadbent
   PEAK Chris Madge Lloyd & Gibson
   WHEELER Richard Michelmores

This book is the product of 6,582 1/2 hour interviews. See p.7 for BMRB audit.
Within each band, firms are listed alphabetically. See individuals' profiles p.137

WHITE & BOWKER The profile of this firm has risen above others in the area this year, largely due to **Peter White**'s (see p.139) outstanding reputation. He has been registrar for the Diocese of Winchester for over 20 years and is extremely widely acclaimed as "*pastoral, sensible, thorough and bright, with all-round knowledge.*"

BRUTTON & CO Another firm to rise in *Chambers*' tables this year, peers attribute its growing profile to **Hilary Tyler**, registrar for the Diocese of Portsmouth, who was described to researchers as "*a persuasive advocate and a robust litigator*" as well as "*very good to deal with.*"

FOLLETT STOCK The principal name here is **Martin Follett** (see p.138), registrar for the Diocese of Truro, who is "*excellent, hands-on and really involved in the diocese.*"

HARRIS & HARRIS (see firm details p.987) **Timothy Berry** (see p.138) is diocesan registrar for both Bristol and Bath & Wells. He is respected by knowledgeable sources as "*switched on and up-to-date.*"

MICHELMORES (see firm details p.1068) **Richard Wheeler**, diocesan registrar for Exeter, has a successful practice at this thriving firm.

THOMAS EGGAR (see firm details p.1160) **Christopher Butcher** (see p.138) is registrar for the Diocese of Chichester. Recent work has included acting in Consistory Court disputes between clergy and parishioners. Others in the field rate him highly as "*thorough and painstaking.*"

BATT BROADBENT The "*knowledgeable*" **Andrew Johnson** is registrar for the Diocese of Salisbury.

MADGE LLOYD & GIBSON Chris Peak continues to win recognition as registrar for the Diocese of Gloucester.

THE SOUTH & SOUTH WEST

OTHER DENOMINATIONS

CHURCH: OTHER DENOMINATIONS
THE SOUTH & SOUTH WEST

1. **Stone King** Bath
2. **Larcomes** Portsmouth
   Tozers Exeter

LEADING INDIVIDUALS

1. **KING Michael** Stone King
   KING Richard Tozers
   TISDALL Miles Larcomes

This book is the product of 6,582 1/2 hour interviews. See p.7 for BMRB audit.
Within each band, firms are listed alphabetically. See individuals' profiles p.137

STONE KING (see firm details p.1151) This "*proactive*" practice enjoys a high standing in ecclesiastical law. Church matters are dealt with by its "*pre-eminent*" charity and education groups. The Catholic Church is a major client, with work including collaborations, hive-offs and mergers among its different organisations. The firm also acts for the Representative Body of the Church in Wales and Anglican bodies on matters ranging from data protection to governance. Charity expert **Michael King** (see p.138) is the lead partner.

LARCOMES This firm acts for the Roman Catholic Diocese of Portsmouth. **Miles Tisdall** (see p.139) was acknowledged by interviewees to have a solid profile.

TOZERS (see firm details p.1165) Acting for the Roman Catholic Diocese of Plymouth, under the leadership of **Richard King**, its notable recent work includes setting up a deed of trust for a joint-denominational school.

WALES

OTHER DENOMINATIONS

CHURCH: OTHER DENOMINATIONS
WALES

1. **Allington Hughes** Wrexham
   LG Williams & Prichard Cardiff

This book is the product of 6,582 1/2 hour interviews. See p.7 for BMRB audit.
Within each band, firms are listed alphabetically.

ALLINGTON HUGHES Although not well known outside its area, this firm is felt to retain a profile representing Roman Catholic clients.

LG WILLIAMS & PRICHARD The firm continues to act for the Roman Catholic Archdiocese of Cardiff. Typical work includes dealing with churches, schools and presbyteries. The firm has recently organised a review of child protection procedures, and has acted on behalf of the Archdiocese in disciplinary matters. Susan Lyons is the contact partner.

CHURCH LAW ■ THAMES VALLEY, MIDLANDS & EAST ANGLIA/THE NORTH

THAMES VALLEY, MIDLANDS & EAST ANGLIA

CHURCH OF ENGLAND

CHURCH: CHURCH OF ENGLAND
■ THAMES VALLEY, MIDLANDS & EAST ANGLIA

1 Winckworth Sherwood Oxford, Chelmsford
2 Claytons Luton
   Martineau Johnson Birmingham
   Wellman & Brown Lincoln
3 Birketts Ipswich
   Latham & Co Melton Mowbray
   Manby & Steward Wolverhampton
   Rothera Dowson Nottingham

LEADING INDIVIDUALS
1 REES John Winckworth Sherwood
2 CARSLAKE Hugh Martineau Johnson
   CHEETHAM David Claytons
   WELLMAN Derek Wellman & Brown
3 HALL James Birketts
   HEMINGWAY Ray Sole Practitioner
   HODSON Christopher Rothera Dowson
   HOOD Brian Winckworth Sherwood
   KIRKMAN Trevor Latham & Co
   THORNEYCROFT John Manby & Steward

This book is the product of 6,582 1/2 hour interviews. See p.7 for BMRB audit. Within each band, firms are listed alphabetically. See individuals' profiles p.137

WINCKWORTH SHERWOOD (see firm details p.1192) In Oxford, the Reverend Canon **John Rees** (see p.139) is registrar for the Southern Province of Canterbury, acting directly for the Archbishop of Canterbury. He is widely regarded by lawyers in the field as the national "*star and number one guy.*" Sources praise his "*charming, approachable and helpful*" manner and admire his "*firm and far-reaching grasp of everything with which he is addressed.*" His office is seen by many as "*very efficient; the obvious choice.*" In Chelmsford, **Brian Hood** (see p.138) continues to earn respect in his role as the registrar for the Diocese of Chelmsford. Overall, say peers, "*the Winckworth crowd is absolutely excellent.*"

CLAYTONS Registrar for the Diocese of St Albans for 24 years, **David Cheetham** (see p.138) has "*considerable experience*" and is seen as one of the best ecclesiastical lawyers in the country. He performs a high proportion of disciplinary work and his litigation skills are especially recommended.

MARTINEAU JOHNSON (see firm details p.1056) The registrar for the Diocese of Birmingham, **Hugh Carslake** (see p.138), is well liked by clients and peers and has an especially commended knowledge of ecclesiastical charity law.

WELLMAN & BROWN Derek Wellman, registrar for the Diocese of Lincoln, is said to be "*an extremely sound and experienced lawyer*" who draws wide acclaim.

BIRKETTS (see firm details p.875) **James Hall**, registrar for the Diocese of St Edmundsbury and Ipswich for the last four years, is perceived by others in the field to be "*someone who clearly knows his stuff.*"

LATHAM & CO **Trevor Kirkman** is the new diocesan registrar for Leicester. Impressed peers note that, because he is also a minister, he "*really understands the issues from both sides.*"

MANBY & STEWARD (see firm details p.1052) **John Thorneycroft** (see p.139) is the registrar for the Diocese of Lichfield and is known for having "*a terrific amount of experience on a wide range of issues.*" One source claimed that "*he would be the first person I would call if I had a problem.*" He has been involved in ongoing litigation and enjoys the support of "*a strong team.*"

ROTHERA DOWSON (see firm details p.1118) As diocesan registrar for Southwell, **Chris Hodson** (see p.138) is said to be "*good news; sensible and down-to-earth.*" Peers particularly rate his advice on church school admission appeals.

OTHER NOTABLE PRACTITIONERS **Ray Hemingway** is the diocesan registrar for Peterborough and is able to be instructed as a sole practitioner. He is highly rated as "*knowledgeable*" and someone who "*works closely with clergy and diocese.*"

THAMES VALLEY, MIDLANDS & EAST ANGLIA

OTHER DENOMINATIONS

CHURCH: OTHER DENOMINATIONS
■ THAMES VALLEY, MIDLANDS & EAST ANGLIA

1 Anthony Collins Solicitors Birmingham

This book is the product of 6,582 1/2 hour interviews. See p.7 for BMRB audit. Within each band, firms are listed alphabetically.

ANTHONY COLLINS SOLICITORS (see firm details p.845) This firm wins respect in the market for its work with Roman Catholic, Anglican and Free Church clients. Romaine Thompson is the contact partner.

THE NORTH

CHURCH OF ENGLAND

DENISON TILL "*Serious-minded*" **Lionel Lennox** (see p.138), registrar for the Northern Province of York and personal advisor to the Archbishop of York, continues to win "*great respect.*" He advises frequently on matters of clergy discipline and has special expertise in faculty jurisdiction and its relationship with listed buildings and planning laws.

GAMON ARDEN & CO **Roger Arden**, diocesan registrar for Liverpool and vice-chair of the Ecclesiastical Law Association, is "*a man of vast experience who knows ecclesiastical law backwards.*" He rises in this year's rankings after winning considerable plaudits from fellow practitioners.

MC DARLINGTON Registrar for the Diocese of Manchester, **Michael Darlington** "*stands head and shoulders above many others*" according to one interviewee. He was roundly praised as "*experienced, quietly efficient and good at representing clergy in trouble and explaining the law.*"

BELL & BUXTON The "*quietly competent*" **Miranda Myers**, registrar for the Diocese of Sheffield, has a growing reputation. Peers claim that she has "*developed her expertise well.*"

BIRCH CULLIMORE **Alan McAllester** is registrar for the Diocese of Chester and enjoys a very strong academic reputation. Recent work has included a case involving safety in churchyards.

DIXON, COLES & GILL (see firm details p.939) **Linda Box** (see p.138) is registrar for the Dio-

THE NORTH/THE LEADERS ■ CHURCH LAW

CHURCH: CHURCH OF ENGLAND
■ THE NORTH

1 Denison Till York

2 Gamon Arden & Co Liverpool
MC Darlington Manchester

3 Bell & Buxton Sheffield
Birch Cullimore Chester
Dixon, Coles & Gill Wakefield
Roebucks Blackburn
Tunnard & Co Ripon

4 Gordons Cranswick Solicitors Leeds
Sinton & Co Newcastle upon Tyne

LEADING INDIVIDUALS

1 ARDEN Roger Gamon Arden & Co
DARLINGTON Michael MC Darlington
LENNOX Lionel Denison Till

2 BOX Linda Dixon, Coles & Gill
HARDING Nicola Tunnard & Co
HOYLE Thomas Roebucks
MCALLESTER Alan Birch Cullimore
MYERS Miranda Bell & Buxton

3 FAIRCLOUGH Neville Smith Roddam
HOLMES Susan Sole Practitioner
LOWDON Jane Sinton & Co
TUNNARD Chris Tunnard & Co

This book is the product of 6,582 1/2 hour interviews. See p.7 for BMRB audit.
Within each band, firms are listed alphabetically. See individuals' profiles p.137

cese of Wakefield and is rated by peers as "*approachable and practical, with common sense when it comes to getting down to work.*"

ROEBUCKS "*Lively and outgoing*" Tom Hoyle, registrar for the Diocese of Blackburn, is especially well regarded for his work as an advocate at Consistory Court hearings.

TUNNARD & CO The only diocese in the North to have two registrars, Ripon and Leeds is served by both Nicola Harding and Chris Tunnard. Harding specialises in faculty work and child protection matters and has a fast-growing reputation as "*something of a dynamo*" who displays "*a down-to-earth, practical, common-sense approach.*" Tunnard does property work for the diocese and is said to be "*a good draughtsman.*"

GORDONS CRANSWICK SOLICITORS Stuart Robertson is the registrar for the Bradford Diocese. He is known to have considerable experience in secular law, but competitors say that he has still to build up a profile in the ecclesiastical field.

SINTON & CO (see firm details p.1139) Jane Lowdon (see p.138), together with two others at the firm, acts for the Newcastle Diocesan Board. Sources say that she is visible in property and education-related issues, and note her growing experience.

OTHER NOTABLE PRACTITIONERS At Smith Roddam, Neville Fairclough is the registrar for the Diocese of Durham. This is considered a lower-profile and less involved role than most other registry posts, but still one that includes Consistory Court work, conveyancing and formalities relating to ordination. Sole practitioner Susan Holmes is diocesan registrar for Carlisle, in which role she demonstrates experience and "*a steady hand.*"

THE NORTH

CHURCH: OTHER DENOMINATIONS
■ THE NORTH

1 Grays York

2 Fieldings Porter Bolton
Hill Dickinson Liverpool
Oswald Goodier & Co Preston

LEADING INDIVIDUALS

1 LAWTON Tony Grays

2 BELDERBOS Mark Oswald Goodier & Co

This book is the product of 6,582 1/2 hour interviews. See p.7 for BMRB audit.
Within each band, firms are listed alphabetically. See individuals' profiles p.137

GRAYS (see firm details p.977) This York-based firm boasts a national reputation for ecclesiastical law. It advises a number of Roman Catholic dioceses, charities and religious orders, and also retains some long-standing Church of England work. High-flier Tony Lawton (see p.138) is said by peers to "*do a huge amount for the Roman Catholic Church*" and is valued for his "*sound and able*" advice.

FIELDINGS PORTER This Bolton-based firm was described by market sources as having a "*traditional*" profile. It acts for the Salford Roman Catholic Diocese.

OTHER DENOMINATIONS

HILL DICKINSON (see firm details p.995) This cross-departmental, four-partner team advises Jewish and Catholic charitable trusts, as well as Methodist and Church of England clients, on a range of matters including litigation relating to the rights of clergy. Paul Walton heads the team and is a member of the Catholic Office for the Protection of Children and Vulnerable Adults.

OSWALD GOODIER & CO (see firm details p.1091) "*Sound*" Mark Belderbos (see p.137) is the leading light at this firm for ecclesiastical matters. The team acts for Roman Catholic charities, religious orders and the Roman Catholic Diocese of Lancaster.

THE LEADERS IN CHURCH LAW

ARDEN, Roger
Gamon Arden & Co, Liverpool
(0151) 709 2222

BEESLEY, PF
Lee Bolton & Lee, London
(020) 7222 5381
Specialisation: Particular expertise in Church of England work. Registrar of the Diocese of Ely; registrar of the Diocese of Guildford; joint registrar of the Diocese of Hereford; registrar of the Faculty Office of the Archbishop of Canterbury; a member of the Legal Advisory Commission of the General Synod of the Church of England. Also handles education and charity work. Solicitor to the National Society and to the Board of Education of the General Synod; registrar of the Woodard Corporation. Joint contributor to Volume 13 (2) 'Encyclopaedia of Forms and Precedents-Ecclesiastical Law'. Speaker at and promoter of several conferences and seminars on ecclesiastical charity and education matters.
Prof. Memberships: Law Society, City of Westminster Law Society (ex-President), Ecclesiastical Law Association (Chairman), Ecclesiastical Law Society (Secretary), Charity Law Association.
Career: Qualified 1967. Joined *Lee Bolton & Lee* in 1968, becoming a partner in 1969.
Personal: Born 30 April 1943. Attended Kings School Worcester, then Exeter University 1961-64 and College of Law 1964-65. Lives in London.

BELDERBOS, Mark
Oswald Goodier & Co, Preston
(01772) 253841
OswGoodier@aol.com
Specialisation: All aspects of Charity Law, acting for many charitable organisations, both religious and secular. Ecclesiastical and Education. Commercial Property, particularly on behalf of chari-

www.ChambersandPartners.com

137

CHURCH LAW — THE LEADERS

table organisations. Substantial amounts of General Trust work.
Career: Qualified 1967. Partner 1968.
Personal: Born 9 November 1942. Educated at Stonyhurst College and University of Liverpool (LLB).

BERRY, Timothy
Harris & Harris, Wells
(01749) 674747
Specialisation: Ecclesiastical and charity law. Registrar, Diocese of Bath and Wells and Diocese of Bristol. Secretary to the Bath & Wells Diocesan Advisory Committee. Has expertise in Trust and Inheritance Tax Law.
Prof. Memberships: Ecclesiastical Law Association, Ecclesiastical Law Society.
Career: Qualified in 1970. Joined *Harris & Harris* as a partner in 1970. Now senior partner.
Personal: Born 5 January 1945. Holds an LLB (Liverpool 1966). Leisure interests include gardening, walking and music. Lives at West Cranmore near Shepton Mallet, Somerset.

BOX, Linda M
Dixon, Coles & Gill, Wakefield
(01924) 373467
box@dixon-coles-gill.co.uk
Specialisation: Ecclesastical law, charity law.
Prof. Memberships: Law Society, Ecclesiastical Law Association, Ecclesiastical Law Society.
Career: LLB 1970; qualified solicitor December 1973; Deputy Diocesan Registrar 1979-93; Diocesan Registrar 1994 to date.
Personal: Married with two sons. Interests include walking in the Lake District, theatre and the opera.

BUTCHER, Christopher
Thomas Eggar, Chichester
(01243) 786111
christopher.butcher@thomaseggar.com
Specialisation: Partner and Head of Charities Unit. Main area of work is probate, wills, powers of attorney and ecclesiastical law.
Prof. Memberships: Law Society, Chichester & District Law Society (President 1996-97), Society of Trust and Estate Practitioners, Ecclesiastical Law Association, Charity Law Association and Ecclesiastical Law Society.
Career: Qualified as a solicitor 1973, Partner in *Thomas Eggar* 1977, Notary Public 1995, Chichester Diocesan Registrar 1999.
Publications: Co-author of 'Probate Practice Manual' (Sweet & Maxwell).
Personal: Mill Hill School 1961-67, Southampton University 1967-70. Married with three children. Involved in local community and family life, walking and riding.

CARSLAKE, Hugh
Martineau Johnson, Birmingham
(0121) 678 1486
hugh.carslake@martjohn.com
Specialisation: Main area of practice covers tax planning, trusts and estate planning and ecclesiastical law. Acts for the owners of landed estates and private individuals in their personal and trustee capacities. Registrar for and legal advisor to the Diocese of Birmingham.
Prof. Memberships: Law Society, STEP. Ecclesiastical Law Association (ELA).
Career: Qualified in 1973, having joined *Martineau Johnson* in 1972. Became a Partner in 1974, Notary Public in 1981, Head of Private Client Department in 1991 and Diocesan Registrar in 1992.
Personal: Born 15 November 1946. Attended Rugby School, 1960-65, then Trinity College, Dublin, 1966-70. Chairman of the Barber Institute of Fine Arts (University of Birmingham); Trustee of the Worcester Cathedral Appeal Trust. Leisure interests include family, music and gardening. Lives in Warwickshire.

CHEETHAM, David
Claytons, St Albans
(01727) 865765
Specialisation: Partner in Ecclesiastical, Charity and General Property Department. Principal areas of practice are ecclesiastical and charity law. Acts as legal advisor to the Church of England in the Diocese of St. Albans and Registrar of the Consistory Court. Has some experience of advocacy in other Consistory Courts. Deals with general work in relation to charity owned property and over 130 church schools. Has handled cases involving access through churchyards and sale of church treasures. Panel member at various Ecclesiastical Law conferences. Has been involved in the establishment of two hospices.
Prof. Memberships: Law Society, Ecclesiastical Law Society, Ecclesiastical Law Association (Chairman 1996-98), SBA.
Career: Joined *Claytons* as a clerk in 1962. Qualified in 1971. Became a Partner in 1972. Senior Partner from 1985. Registrar of St. Albans Diocese from 1978.
Personal: Born 3 August 1941. Educated at Merchant Taylors School, Crosby, and Dunstable Grammar School. School governor, local charity trustee. Leisure pursuits include exploring old churches and some sporting interests. Lives in St. Albans.

DARLINGTON, Michael C
MC Darlington, Manchester
(0161) 834 7545

FAIRCLOUGH, Neville
Smith Roddam, Durham
(01388) 603073

FOLLETT, Martin
Follett Stock, Truro
(01872) 260744
martin.follett@follettstock.co.uk
Specialisation: Full range of ecclesiastical work including property, charity, education and contentious faculty work.
Career: Sidney Sussex College, Cambridge. Qualified 1977. Deputy Registrar 1983. Registrar of the Diocese of Truro 1987.

HALL, James
Birketts, Ipswich
(01473) 232300

HARDING, Nicola
Tunnard & Co, Ripon
(01765) 600421

HEMINGWAY, Ray
Ray Hemingway – Sole Practitioner, Peterborough
(01733) 262523

HODSON, Christopher
Rothera Dowson (Incorporating German and Soar), Nottingham
(0115) 9100 600
Specialisation: As Diocesan Registrar for the Diocese of Southwell involved in all aspects of ecclesiastical law including advice to bishops, archdeacons, clergy, parochial church councils and any persons requiring ecclesiastical legal advice. The extent of the work includes property matters, clergy discipline matters, advice as to qualifications and rights of marriage, ecclesiastical planning law, i.e. faculty jurisdiction and even extends to having advised other dioceses in connection with ecclesiastical matters. In addition works for the Southwell Diocesan Board of Finance and in this context is required to give advice in all areas of work affecting Church of England including commercial matters, property matters and employment matters.
Prof. Memberships: Member of the Ecclesiastical Lawyers Association, the Ecclesiastical Law Society and the Notaries Society.

HOLMES, Susan
Susan Holmes – Sole Practitioner, Carlisle
(01228) 560617

HOOD, Brian
Winckworth Sherwood, Chelmsford
(01245) 262212
bjhood@winckworths.co.uk
Specialisation: Partner in Ecclesiastical Department (Chelmsford). Specialises in ecclesiastical law. Deputy Registrar to Bishop of Chelmsford 1976-89. Registrar and Bishop's Legal Secretary since 1989. Also handles property and charities law, private and commercial matters.
Prof. Memberships: Ecclesiastical Law Association, Ecclesiastical Law Society.
Career: Qualified as a solicitor in New Zealand in 1966. Qualified in the UK in 1976. Joined *Winckworth Sherwood* as a partner in 1977.
Personal: Born 8 February 1943. Educated at Marlborough College, New Zealand 1956-62 and the University of Canterbury, New Zealand 1963-67 (LLM Hons). Leisure interests include golf, tennis, music and theatre. Lives in Terling, Essex.

HOYLE, Thomas
Roebucks, Blackburn
(01254) 274000

JOHNSON, Andrew
Batt Broadbent, Salisbury
(01722) 411141

KING, Michael
Stone King, Bath
(020) 7796 1007
michaelking@stoneking.co.uk
See under Charities, p.130

KING, Richard
Tozers, Exeter
(01392) 207020

KIRKMAN, Trevor
Latham & Co, Melton Mowbray
(01664) 563012

LAWTON, F A (Tony)
Grays, York
(01904) 634771
See under Charities, p.130

LENNOX, Lionel
Denison Till, York
York (01904) 611411
Specialisation: Partner. Main area of practice is ecclesiastical law. Registrar of the Province and Diocese of York; Registrar of the Convocation of York; Legal Secretary to the Archbishop of York; Member of the Legal Advisory Commission of the General Synod. Expanding areas of practice are town and country planning and charity law. Advanced Professional Diploma in Planning and Environmental Law from Leeds Metropolitan University 1994. Legal advisor to various charities. Notary Public 1992.
Prof. Memberships: Yorkshire Law Society, Ecclesiastical Law Society.
Career: Qualified in 1973. Worked at *Denison Suddards* as a partner 1976-80; assistant legal advisor to the General Synod of the Church of England 1981-87. Joined *Denison Till* as a partner in 1987.
Personal: Attended St John's School Leatherhead 1962-67 and University of Birmingham 1967-70. Notary Public 1992. Lives in York. Trustee: St. Leonard's Hospice, York and Yorkshire Historic Churches Trust.

LOWDON, Jane
Sinton & Co, Newcastle upon Tyne
(0191) 212 7800
j.lowdon@sinton.co.uk
Specialisation: Diocesan Registrar and legal advisor to the Bishop. Day to day knowledge of ecclesiastical law. Commercial and residential property and conveyancing; charity law; conveyancing and commercial matters; wills.
Career: BA (Law) Trent Polytechnic. Qualified 1979. 20 years in private practice. Joined *Sinton & Co* 2000.

MCALLESTER, Alan K
Birch Cullimore, Chester
(01244) 321066

THE LEADERS — CHURCH LAW

MORRIS, Paul
Winckworth Sherwood, London
(020) 7593 5000
pcemorris@winckworths.co.uk
Specialisation: Partner and head of ecclesiastical and education law department. Head of department since 1987; previously Joint Head of Institutional Property Department 1984-87, with expertise in commercial property law. Has acted in controversial cases involving clergy discipline, re-ordering of church buildings and re-development of redundant churches and church land.
Prof. Memberships: Law Society, City of Westminster Law Society, Ecclesiastical Law Society, Ecclesiastical Law Association.
Career: Qualified in 1978. Joined *Winckworth & Pemberton* in 1978, becoming a Partner in 1981. Registrar and Bishop's Legal Secretary, Diocese of London. Registrar and Bishop's Legal Secretary, Diocese of Southwark. Joint Registrar, Diocese of Leicester. Solicitor to Southwark Diocesan Board of Finance. Solicitor to the London Diocesan Fund. Chapter Clerk of Southwark Cathedral.
Personal: Born 21 September 1950. Attended Westminster Abbey Choir School 1960-64, Westminster School 1964-68 and UCNW Bangor 1968-72. Leisure interests include music and the family. Lives in West London and Charlbury, Oxfordshire.

MYERS, Miranda
Bell & Buxton, Sheffield
(0114) 249 5969

PEAK, Chris
Madge Lloyd & Gibson, Gloucester
(01452) 520224

REES, John
Winckworth Sherwood, Oxford
(01865) 297200
jrees@ws-oxford.co.uk
Specialisation: Partner in ecclesiastical, education and charities department. Main area of practice is ecclesiastical law. Registrar, Province of Canterbury. Registrar, Diocese of Oxford. Legal Advisor to the Anglican Consultative Council (the international liaison body for the Anglican Communion worldwide). Extensive experience in contested faculty cases, including Court of Arches Judgment in Re St. Luke, Maidstone: wide acquaintance with education law issues on behalf of governors and trustees.
Prof. Memberships: Ecclesiastical Law Association, Ecclesiastical Law Society (Treasurer).
Career: Qualified 1975. Joined *Winckworth Sherwood* 1986. Partner 1988.
Personal: Born 21 April 1951. Holds LLB (Southampton 1972), MA (Oxon 1984) and MPhil (Leeds 1984). Leisure interests include photography and cycling. Lives in Oxford.

RICHENS, NJ
Lee Bolton & Lee, London
(020) 7222 5381
Specialisation: Education law and charity law, particularly with reference to church schools and school sites. Advised the Church of England Board of Education on the School Standards and Framework Act 1998 and the Education Act 2002. Joint contributor to Volume 13(2) 'Encyclopaedia of Forms and Precedents – Ecclesiastical Law'. Joint author of 'Charity Land and Premises' (Jordans 1996). Deputy registrar, Diocese of Guildford.
Prof. Memberships: Ecclesiastical Law Society (Deputy Secretary); Ecclesiastical Law Association (Secretary); Charity Law Association.
Career: Admitted 1985. Joined *Lee Bolton & Lee* in 1991.
Personal: Born 1960; Educated Marple Hall High School, Stockport and Downing College Cambridge. Lives in East London.

THORNEYCROFT, John
Manby & Steward, Bridgnorth
(01746) 761436
j.thorneycroft@manbys.co.uk
Specialisation: Main area of practice cover ecclesiastical law, charity law, trusts and asset protection. As Registrar of Lichfield Diocese has experience in all areas of ecclesiastical law and his firm has particular experience in conduct matters and contested faculty matters.
Prof. Memberships: STEP Ecclesiastical Law Association and Ecclesiastical Law Society.
Career: Admitted 1966. With *Manby & Steward* since 1966.
Personal: Born 1939. Educated Pembroke College Cambridge. Lives near Shifnal in Shropshire. Married with four children.

TISDALL, Miles
Larcomes, Portsmouth
(023) 9266 1531
enquiries@larcomes.co.uk
Specialisation: Charity law. Acts for Roman Catholic Diocese of Portsmouth.
Prof. Memberships: Law Society.

TUNNARD, Chris
Tunnard & Co, Ripon
(01765) 600421

TYLER, Hilary A G
Brutton & Co, Fareham
(01329) 236171

WELLMAN, Derek
Wellman & Brown, Lincoln
(01522) 525463

WHEELER, Richard
Michelmores, Exeter
(01392) 436244

WHITE, Peter
White & Bowker, Winchester
(01962) 844440
peter.white@wandb.co.uk
Specialisation: Consultant in ecclesiastical and residential property department. Principal area of practice covers all aspects of ecclesiastical law. Appointed Diocesan Registrar for the Diocese of Winchester and Bishop's Legal Secretary 1981. Other main area of work is residential property.
Prof. Memberships: Current Secretary of Hampshire Law Society, member of Ecclesiastical Law Association, Ecclesiastical Law Society, Notaries Society, Law Society.
Career: Qualified in 1970 while at *White & Bowker* and became a partner in 1974.
Personal: Born 28 August 1945. Attended Winchester College 1958-63, then New College, Oxford 1964-67. Leisure pursuits include golf, cricket and fives. Lives in Romsey.

CLINICAL NEGLIGENCE

London: 140; The Regions: 142; Scotland: 148; Profiles: 149

Research approved by BMRB For this edition, Chambers' researchers conducted 6,582 interviews – 3,900 with law firms, 511 with barristers and 2,171 with clients. The validity of the research was scrutinised by BMRB International, who audited both the methodology and the results at our offices in London. They interviewed Chambers' researchers and cross-checked sample interviews. Details of the audit appear on page 7.

OVERVIEW This year has seen the creation of a government panel to investigate how clinical negligence claims are handled, with the aim of reducing the cost of claims to the state. At the lowest end of the scale, the new 'resolve' scheme is being implemented by a number of firms to deal with claims below £15,000. Firms are placing increasing emphasis on mediation initiatives, aiming to keep cases out of court whenever possible. There are also increased efforts on the part of law firms to employ staff to assist victims with the problems they may encounter during and after claims, which includes counselling to relatives.

LONDON

MAINLY CLAIMANT

CLINICAL NEGLIGENCE: MAINLY CLAIMANT — LONDON

1. Leigh, Day & Co
2. Alexander Harris
   Bindman & Partners
   Charles Russell
   Kingsley Napley
3. Evill and Coleman
   Field Fisher Waterhouse
   Parlett Kent
4. Irwin Mitchell
   Russell Jones & Walker
   Stewarts

LEADING INDIVIDUALS

1. BARTON Grainne *Alexander Harris*
   FAZAN Claire *Bindman & Partners*
   LEVY Russell *Leigh, Day & Co*
   MCNEIL Paul *Field Fisher Waterhouse*
   VALLANCE Richard *Charles Russell*
   WINYARD Anne *Leigh, Day & Co*
2. BATTEN Elizabeth *Parlett Kent*
   CAHILL Julia *Kingsley Napley*
3. BLYTHE Deborah *Evill and Coleman*
   DONOVAN Terry *Bindman & Partners*
   DYSON Henry *Leigh, Day & Co*
   EDDY Alison *Irwin Mitchell*
   LEE Terry *Evill and Coleman*
   LEWIN Olive *Leigh, Day & Co*
   MARTINEZ Liz *Evill and Coleman*
   ROHDE Kate *Kingsley Napley*

This book is the product of 6,582 1/2 hour interviews. See p.7 for BMRB audit. Within each band, firms are listed alphabetically. See individuals' profiles p.149

LEIGH, DAY & CO (see firm details p.1036) "*Always a strong player,*" this outfit continues to lead the field in London. Endorsed by interviewees as "*the most organised and proactive*" operation, defendant solicitors see it as "*formidable opposition*" whose lawyers "*obviously know what they're doing.*" Size, resources and contacts enable it to cover the full range of clinical negligence claims, and each of its partners has developed an area of specialist interest. The firm loses a leading practitioner in Sarah Leigh, who has retired, but a stable raft of talented practitioners remain. **Russell Levy** (see p.153) is a "*lateral thinker,*" who impresses with his willingness to "*be innovative about the way he conducts litigation.*" He has a strong focus on infectious disease and heart valve cases. **Anne Winyard** (see p.156) is a birth injuries and blood specialist, and is described as "*in a league of her own.*" Adjudged "*tremendous with clients,*" she also enjoys a "*great aptitude for and interest in medicine.*" "*Thoughtful*" **Henry Dyson** (see p.151) undertakes orthopaedic and genetics claims, while **Olive Lewin** (see p.153) is a "*personable*" practitioner. The firm is also home to a doctor and two part-time forensic accountants. High-value cases of recent times include the retrieval of £2.43 million on behalf of a catastrophically injured baby, and a £3 million cerebal palsy claim.

ALEXANDER HARRIS (see firm details p.839) The firm has successfully secured a definite presence in London with a team that displays an "*understanding of medicine and an ability to relate to lay clients.*" The opening of a new office in Solihull further strengthens its national presence. Typical claims handled include high-value cerebal palsy, orthopaedic and psychiatric matters. Involvement in the Touche case has heralded the team's increasing workload in private hospital-related matters. Inquests and judicial reviews are other growth areas. The "*extraordinarily hard-working*" **Grainne Barton** (see p.149) received plaudits from all quarters. Defendants call her "*substantial opposition,*" while her "*high-quality litigation*" and "*fantastic client care*" are often singled out.

BINDMAN & PARTNERS (see firm details p.872) "*Extremely strong legal and advocacy skills*" are some of the firm's best assets. It handles a wide variety of cases, including wrongful birth claims, and matters arising from GPs, A&E, obstetrics, anaesthetics, orthopaedic care, plastic and abdominal surgery. It also appears in claims for failure to diagnose cancer, brain haemorrhage and cardiac conditions. Head of the group, **Claire Fazan** (see p.151) draws the highest praise from competitors, defendant solicitors and barristers alike. An "*absolute professional,*" with a "*pragmatic approach,*" she is a popular choice for litigation. "*Superb*" **Terry Donovan** (see p.151) is a new addition to the rankings, following endorsement from peers. It has recently appeared in several brain-injured children cases and a misdiagnosis of breast cancer claim.

CHARLES RUSSELL (see firm details p.904) The team is commended for its "*thorough awareness of medical issues.*" Its typical workload involves birth injury cases, neurological and orthopaedic claims. Of late, it has been acting on behalf of trustees responsible for administering the government compensation fund for CJD victims. The team is headed up by the "*superb*" **Richard Vallance** (see p.155). He is described by contemporaries as "*utterly reliable, sensible and realistic*" and is currently working as part of a government committee reviewing clinical negligence claims in the UK. The team has this year obtained £1.35 million on behalf of a boy misdiagnosed by a hospital for a neurological disease.

KINGSLEY NAPLEY (see firm details p.1023) A "*well-structured and practical*" team, it undertakes a broad spectrum of matters, with particular focus on fatal claims. Brain injury, obstetrics, delayed diagnosis and mis-management of diabetes all feature on the work roster. The firm has obtained interim payments following admissions of liability on behalf of a number of clients, enabling the purchase of several properties in which brain-damaged children can be cared for. The team is led by **Julia Cahill** (see p.150) ("*extremely capable*") and has been strengthened by the appointment of Alison Moore as a new partner. **Kate Rohde** (see p.155) is praised by market commentators as "*charming and conscientious.*"

EVILL AND COLEMAN (see firm details p.950) Sources feel that the team has "*done a lot this year*" and it is widely regarded as a quality operation, handling catastrophic cases, mismanagement and cerebral palsy. **Terry Lee** (see p.634) is a highly esteemed lawyer who also has a substantial personal injury practice, and **Liz Martinez** (see p.154) "*deals co-operatively, putting her clients' interest very much at the fore.*" **Deborah Blythe** (see p.149) received commendation for her ability to simultaneously apply a "*soothing balm,*" while her approach is "*sensible – hard when needs be.*" Recent cases handled by the team include the retrieval of around £3 million on behalf of a quadriplaegic child and £4 million on behalf of a little girl seriously injured during birth.

FIELD FISHER WATERHOUSE (see firm details p.954) "*Committed*" **Paul McNeil** (see p.154) heads this growing clinical negligence outfit. Recent cases include obtaining £2.25 million damages on behalf of the child victim of paediatric negligence. The team handles a broad range of claims relating to areas such as anaesthetics, cerebral palsy, dentistry, obstetrics, orthopaedic surgery and GP claims.

PARLETT KENT (see firm details p.1095) Leading light, **Elizabeth Batten** (see p.149) handles a significant number of psychiatric claims, while head of department Caroline Jenkins specialises in gynaecology and cervical cancer matters. The group recently retrieved £5 million on behalf of a brain-damaged baby and has appeared in several learning disability and abuse cases.

IRWIN MITCHELL (see firm details p.1009) "*Always a strong contender,*" with its national presence, the firm has secured its presence in London with a "*focused and commercial*" approach. **Alison Eddy** (see p.151) heads the department and has particular interest in obstetrics and in cases of women injured during childbirth. In recent times the firm has acted in a psychiatric negligence claim and failure to diagnose breast cancer.

RUSSELL JONES & WALKER (see firm details p.1120) It is predominantly trade union-related claims that make up the caseload and the firm deals with maximum severity matters involving brain and spinal injury. It has also witnessed an increase in plastic surgery claims. Child-related matters, particularly cerebral palsy are an area of focus. The team also appears in claims relating to infertility treatment and unplanned pregnancy, inquests, negligent dental treatment and those involving elderly patients in hospitals and nursing homes. Clients have spoken of the team's "*good bedside manner and interpersonal skills.*" Rosamund Rhodes-Kemp is head of department.

STEWARTS (see firm details p.1150) The majority of the firm's caseload involves spinal injury and it is instructed by spinal units throughout the UK. It also undertakes brain injury claims. Team leader Kevin Grealis has expertise in child injury including cerebal palsy. Clients praise the team's "*fantastically helpful service.*" It handles a number of claims around the £1-4 million mark at any one time, and has recently obtained damages for failure to diagnose cancer, failure to deliver a full-term baby and failure to treat head injury.

LONDON — MAINLY DEFENDANT

CLINICAL NEGLIGENCE: MAINLY DEFENDANT — LONDON

1. Capsticks
2. Hempsons
3. Weightman Vizards
4. Bevan Ashford
   RadcliffesLeBrasseur

LEADING INDIVIDUALS

1. **HOLMES John** Hempsons
   LEIGH Bertie Hempsons
   MASON David Capsticks
2. **DINGWALL Christian** Bevan Ashford
   FIELD Rena Weightman Vizards
   SMITH Janice Capsticks
3. **HAY Katie** Capsticks
   SWANTON Vicki Berrymans Lace Mawer

This book is the product of 6,582 1/2 hour interviews. See p.7 for BMRB audit. Within each band, firms are listed alphabetically. See individuals' profiles p.149

CAPSTICKS (see firm details p.900) Claimant solicitors perceive that this outfit has "*gone from strength to strength,*" with partners appreciated as "*tough opponents*" in litigation. After a successful year, the department has taken on seven new assistants. It recently published the results of a study of 57,000 births to assist in the adjudication of brain-damaged baby claims, and acts for around 150 NHS Trusts, PCTs and health authorities in London and the South East. **David Mason** (see p.154) is a highly respected practitioner, who represented the health service in the Climbie case. Peers endorsed both **Janice Smith** (see p.155) ("*impressive*") and **Katie Hay** (see p.152).

HEMPSONS (see firm details p.989) "*Big players,*" the group fields some of the sector's best known names. The team is headed by the "*entertaining*" and ubiquitous **Bertie Leigh** (see p.408). "*An obvious leader in his field,*" his knowledge of medicine is deemed by some "*unrivalled.*" **John Holmes** (see p.152) is widely considered a "*top-notch*" practitioner. The team acts for the MDU, general medical and dental practitioners in private practice, as well as trusts and health authorities in London and the South East. It is strengthened by sister offices in Yorkshire and the North West.

WEIGHTMAN VIZARDS (see firm details p.1183) The team has established itself following the merger, and is now perceived by peers as "*a powerful force*" in the defendant market. It retained its place on the NHSLA, and is currently involved in a number of group actions including representing all the babies in the Bristol inquiry. It appeared in the sodium valporate investigation (a drug given to pregnant mothers) and recently represented Great Ormond Street in the conjoined twins case. **Rena Field** (see p.151) is a highly esteemed partner in the team, who "*places her clients' interests first and foremost.*"

BEVAN ASHFORD (see firm details p.869) Overseen by the respected **Christian Dingwall** (see p.150), the London branch of the national operation has recently acquired extra office space to accommodate its growing team. A "*professional*" outfit, it acts for the NHSLA and several London and regional trusts. Recent cases have involved a high-value neuro surgical case, cerebral palsy and spinal claims.

RADCLIFFESLEBRASSEUR (see firm details p.1107) Possessed of "*some highly talented people,*" this operation is deemed by peers to be "*one of the most experienced firms in England*" for clinical negligence defence. Although the team has lost its place on the NHSLA panel, clients continue to endorse its "*expertise, quality and quick reaction time.*" Simon Dinnick and Andrew Parsons head the group.

OTHER NOTABLE PRACTITIONERS The "*absolutely excellent*" **Vicki Swanton** (see p.155) has moved from Browne Jacobson to strengthen Berryman Lace Mawer's clinical negligence capacity.

CLINICAL NEGLIGENCE ■ THE SOUTH/THAMES VALLEY

THE SOUTH — MAINLY CLAIMANT

CLINICAL NEGLIGENCE: MAINLY CLAIMANT — THE SOUTH

1. **Blake Lapthorn** Portsmouth, Southampton
2. **Thomson Snell & Passmore** Tunbridge Wells
3. **Penningtons** Basingstoke, Godalming
   Wynne Baxter Brighton

LEADING INDIVIDUALS

1. **MCCLURE Alison** Blake Lapthorn
   WATSON Andrew Thomson Snell & Passmore
2. **HOOPER John** Wynne Baxter
   MINTER Melanie Wynne Baxter

This book is the product of 6,582 1/2 hour interviews. See p.7 for BMRB audit.
Within each band, firms are listed alphabetically. See individuals' profiles p.149

BLAKE LAPTHORN (see firm details p.877) Able to handle a wide range, much of the firm's work lies in claims relating to general surgery and oncology, urology, gynaecology and obstetrics. It has witnessed an increasing amount of investigation into GPs' conduct and recently settled a birth brain injury case for £1 million. It is a member of the 'Resolve' scheme, which exists to handle claims of under £15,000. **Alison McClure** is widely regarded as "*a leading light*" in her field.

THOMSON SNELL & PASSMORE (see firm details p.1161) An "*extremely respected*" operation headed by the "*high-profile*" **Andrew Watson** (see p.156). Peers applaud his sound judgement and agree that he heads "*a strong team indeed.*" A broad range of claims are handled including fatal accident, orthopaedic, cancer, gynaecology, paediatric and cerebral palsy. The group is taking on an increased level of instructions on a conditional fee basis.

PENNINGTONS (see firm details p.1098) Tim Palmer has taken over as head of this Basingstoke and Godalming-based practice and the recruitment of cerebral palsy specialist Philip Lea from George Ide Philips further strengthens the team. It has represented 70 couples in their claims for damages against an embryologist accused of falsifying records in the Hampshire Clinic. Neurosurgery and cerebral palsy are areas of specialism, although the team is able to handle a broad range of claims.

WYNNE BAXTER Contemporaries call this the "*top firm in Brighton,*" and agree that it is a prime choice for referrals. The group's profile is reinforced by the highly esteemed duo of **Melanie Minter** (see p.154) and **John Hooper** (see p.153). The practice encompasses claims arising from obstetrics and gynaecology, orthopaedics, anaesthetics, general surgery, general practice and dentistry. The unit has particular skill in brain injury matters.

THE SOUTH — MAINLY DEFENDANT

CLINICAL NEGLIGENCE: MAINLY DEFENDANT — THE SOUTH

1. **Beachcroft Wansbroughs** Winchester
2. **Brachers** Maidstone

LEADING INDIVIDUALS

1. **MCGRATH Matthew** Beachcroft Wansbroughs
   SHEATH John Brachers

This book is the product of 6,582 1/2 hour interviews. See p.7 for BMRB audit.
Within each band, firms are listed alphabetically. See individuals' profiles p.149

BEACHCROFT WANSBROUGHS (see firm details p.860) A highly visible operator in the region, it acts for the majority of local trusts. The "*highly experienced*" **Matthew McGrath** (see p.154) is widely rated by his peers and his team is bolstered by newly made-up partner Cheryl Blundell. Much of the caseload relates to obstetrics, while cerebral palsy and neurosurgery remain areas of strength. It advises on mental health sectioning, consent and confidentiality. **Clients** NHSLA.

BRACHERS (see firm details p.886) **John Sheath** (see p.155) leads this "*highly professional offering.*" It is receiving a growing number of claims from the NHSLA, and gained new trust clients. It covers a full range of negligence matters but has particular skill in cerebral palsy cases and mental health consent cases. **Clients** NHSLA.

THAMES VALLEY — MAINLY CLAIMANT

CLINICAL NEGLIGENCE: MAINLY CLAIMANT — THAMES VALLEY

1. **Boyes Turner** Reading
2. **Osborne Morris & Morgan** Leighton Buzzard
3. **Harris Cartwright** Slough

LEADING INDIVIDUALS

1. **DESMOND Adrian** Boyes Turner
2. **BROWN Susan** Boyes Turner
   OSBORNE Tom Osborne Morris & Morgan

This book is the product of 6,582 1/2 hour interviews. See p.7 for BMRB audit.
Within each band, firms are listed alphabetically. See individuals' profiles p.149

BOYES TURNER (see firm details p.883) Widely acclaimed for its "*personable and professional*" approach to clients, the team recovered over £10 million in damages during the past 12 months, and has initiated a brain injury support group. The group is headed up by **Adrian Desmond** (see p.150) who is widely rated by interviewees for his "*care in looking after clients.*" He is also admired as one who "*gets to grips with the economics of a case.*" **Susan Brown** (see p.150), described to researchers as "*particularly impressive,*" typifies the firm's pool of talent. The team has been active in neurological, cerebral palsy and birth injury claims.

OSBORNE MORRIS & MORGAN Adjudged a high-quality operation, many sources singled out the group's niche strength in brain injury claims, supplied by the "*wonderful*" **Tom Osborne**. The firm is also respected for its work on cerebral palsy, Erb's Palsy, spinal injury and anaesthetics claims.

HARRIS CARTWRIGHT (see firm details p.986) Peers point to the "*sound advice*" offered by this outfit, which has a good track record in obstetrics and birth trauma cases. The team is led by Christopher Gooderidge, and has recently been involved in awareness-raising days about the drug Baclofen. It undertakes matters ranging from £15,000 to claims running into millions, and its presence in this field is bolstered by a registered nurse.

SOUTH WEST — CLINICAL NEGLIGENCE

SOUTH WEST — MAINLY CLAIMANT

CLINICAL NEGLIGENCE: MAINLY CLAIMANT — SOUTH WEST

1
- Barcan Woodward — Bristol
- Preston Goldburn — Falmouth

2
- Clarke Willmott & Clarke — Bristol, Taunton
- John Hodge & Co — Weston-super-Mare
- Withy King — Bath

3
- Over Taylor Biggs — Exeter
- Russell Jones & Walker — Bristol
- Wolferstans — Plymouth
- Woollcombe Beer Watts — Newton Abbot

LEADING INDIVIDUALS

1
- BARCAN Richard — Barcan Woodward

2
- ENGLAND Richard — John Hodge & Co
- FERGUSON Gerry — Withy King
- GOLDBURN Tim — Preston Goldburn
- HANNAM Andrew — Clarke Willmott & Clarke
- YOUNG Magi — Parlett Kent

3
- OVER Christopher — Over Taylor Biggs
- PARFORD Simon — Wolferstans
- SOLLY Gillian — Russell Jones & Walker
- VICK Laurence — Michelmores
- VOISIN Maria — Bond Pearce

This book is the product of 6,582 1/2 hour interviews. See p.7 for BMRB audit. Within each band, firms are listed alphabetically. See individuals' profiles p.149

BARCAN WOODWARD "*Definitely at the top,*" the firm has a particular focus on orthopaedic, bowel, gynaecological and fatal claims. It owes much of its reputation to **Richard Barcan**. "*Still out there at No.1,*" peers concur that his "*reputation is deserved*" not only for the high levels of client care, but also for his practical approach to cases. Client rehabilitation remains a key aspect of the firm's work.

PRESTON GOLDBURN Widely regarded throughout the regions, the firm is busy on a variety of matters including the development of a local mediation initiative with Plymouth and Cornwall NHS trusts. Alongside its work, which covers a broad spectrum, the team has seen a dramatic increase in opthalmology and dental cases. "*Energetic and enthusiastic*" **Tim Goldburn** is respected throughout the region.

CLARKE WILLMOTT & CLARKE (see firm details p.907) Market sources attest to the "*significant section of the market*" that this firm has captured and agree that they are "*happily referring clients*" here. It is best known for its involvement in national organ retention litigation relating to the Bristol Royal Infirmary children's heart inquiry and Alder Hey hospital in Liverpool. New partner recruit Mervyn Fudge is lead solicitor in these matters. Cerebral palsy claims constitute the majority of the firm's caseload, and it also undertakes a significant number of ENT matters. **Andrew Hannam** (see p.152) is a "*big player*" in this region, endorsed for his effective mediations, as well as for being "*an aggressive litigator when he needs to be.*"

JOHN HODGE & CO This firm handles a large number of birth injury claims, including a recent cerebral palsy settlement for £2.4 million. Gynaecology, GP, A&E and cardiological claims are other areas of focus, and the team has seen a growth in the number of private hospital matters it is receiving. **Richard England** (see p.151) is a "*perfectly sensible*" practitioner, often advising in combination with his colleague, Frances Wright.

WITHY KING (see firm details p.1195) Interviewees consistently praised the quality of this team. It has a dedicated cerebral palsy unit, and is also involved in a range of claims such as negligent kidney transplantation, failure to diagnose TB and negligent use of unlicensed drugs. **Gerry Ferguson** (see p.151) is a well-respected member of the team.

OVER TAYLOR BIGGS The group is strengthened by the presence of "*clever operator*" **Christopher Over**. The firm has been active of late in a spate of breast screening claims. It covers all aspects of clinical negligence, recently settling a cerebral palsy claim for £2.3 million.

RUSSELL JONES & WALKER (see firm details p.1120) Paul Rumley has taken over as head of department in the Bristol office of this national firm, which is able to field the talented **Gillian Soley** (see p.636). The team covers a wide range of claims from low-value, such as incorrect vaccination, to higher value cerebral palsy matters. It is participating in the small claims management 'Resolve' scheme. The group has recently been involved in a misdiagnosis of cancer claim, and the matter of a patient seriously injured during an operation.

WOLFERSTANS (see firm details p.1195) The "*competent and experienced*" **Simon Parford** (see p.154) heads up this Plymouth and Taunton-based group. Although his focus remains brain injury matters, his practice also includes cerebral palsy, undiagnosed meningitis, anaesthetic injury and wrongful prescription claims. The rest of the team undertakes congenital dislocated hip claims, and matters relating to cosmetic surgery, spinal pathology, psychiatry and orthopaedics.

WOOLLCOMBE BEER WATTS Derek Reed's well regarded team has impressed peers with its skill in handling the range and volume of its caseload. It advises on the spectrum of clinical negligence matters and has settled a cerebral palsy claim for £1.4 million. It is currently involved in an ongoing high-value psychiatric case.

OTHER NOTABLE PRACTITIONERS **Magi Young** (see p.156) of Parlett Kent is commended both locally but also on the London circuit; peers describe her as a "*fantastic, approachable*" lawyer. At Michelmores, **Laurence Vick** (see p.155) is known particularly for his heart work, while **Maria Voisin** of Bond Pearce is endorsed as "*sensible; she does a fine job for her clients' best interests.*"

SOUTH WEST — MAINLY DEFENDANT

CLINICAL NEGLIGENCE: MAINLY DEFENDANT — SOUTH WEST

1
- Bevan Ashford — Bristol

2
- Beachcroft Wansbroughs — Bristol

This book is the product of 6,582 1/2 hour interviews. See p.7 for BMRB audit. Within each band, firms are listed alphabetically.

BEVAN ASHFORD (see firm details p.869) Still clearly the largest and most highly regarded defendant practice in the region, it fields lawyers who are "*good at seeing the bigger picture.*" Clients indicated their appreciation of its partners' "*impressive experience*" and "*personalised service*" on offer. Joanna Lloyd has a special interest in obstetrics and gynaecology, cerebral palsy and neurosurgery. Others in the team focus on mental health, educational indemnity and group actions. **Clients** NHSLA.

BEACHCROFT WANSBROUGHS (see firm details p.860) Peers admire the team's "*sharp and productive*" approach to litigation, while its lawyers continue to be endorsed as "*reasonable and helpful.*" The acquisition of new clients in the local vicinity and across the Midlands is

CLINICAL NEGLIGENCE ■ SOUTH WEST/WALES/MIDLANDS

LEADING INDIVIDUALS
1 MONTGOMERY Nigel *Beachcroft Wansbroughs*

See individuals' profiles p.149

anticipated to generate an increasing level of instructions. Areas of focus are obstetrics, renal and neurology claims. "*Sensible*" Nigel Montgomery (see p.154) is the group's standout practitioner and "*obviously a serious player*" in the field. **Clients** NHSLA.

WALES

MAINLY CLAIMANT

CLINICAL NEGLIGENCE: MAINLY CLAIMANT
■ WALES

1 Huttons *Cardiff*
2 Hugh James *Cardiff*
   John Collins & Partners *Swansea*
3 Edwards Geldard *Cardiff*
   Russell Jones & Walker *Cardiff*

LEADING INDIVIDUALS
1 MUSGRAVE Tim *Huttons*
2 DAVIES Andrew *Hugh James*
   ROSSER Mari *Hugh James*
   THOMAS Keith *John Collins & Partners*

This book is the product of 6,582 1/2 hour interviews. See p.7 for BMRB audit. Within each band, firms are listed alphabetically. See individuals' profiles p.149

HUTTONS (see firm details p.1007) The "*incredibly thorough and experienced*" Tim Musgrave leads this small, focused team. Sources from across the region agree that this team is "*rightly placed at the top*," for the high quality of advice and wide coverage. It focuses on cases with a human rights element and has recently settled birth injury claims and taken a case regarding consent to spinal surgery to trial.

HUGH JAMES (see firm details p.1004) This "*high-profile*" team is headed by "*widely respected*" Andrew Davies (see p.150) and can call upon the "*terrier-like*" litigation skills of Mari Rosser (see p.155). It covers a wide range of claimant work. The firm has committed resources to catastrophic claims, particularly head and spinal injuries and here rehabilitation remains an important part of its advice. The firm is also one of the few to have been awarded a Legal Services Commission franchise for its work in this field.

JOHN COLLINS & PARTNERS This "*capable and efficient*" operation has witnessed an increase in the number of claims it handles. It has expertise in cerebral palsy cases and other birth injury matters and also undertakes fatal cases and brain tumors. The team includes a qualified doctor. Keith Thomas is head of department.

EDWARDS GELDARD (see firm details p.944) Tom Beech sits at the helm of this "*competent*" team, which advises on a range of claims including, brain injury and breast implant-related matters. Its highest value success of late was a claim for £2.5 million.

RUSSELL JONES & WALKER (see firm details p.1120) Welsh language speaker Sonia McGarrigle is head of this department. A variety of work is handled, and the firm has strength in cerebral palsy matters (particularly for children), orthopaedic, amputations, obstetric and gynaecological claims. It has been involved in a number of inquests, including one into the negative side effects of anti-depressants. Other work highlights are its success in obtaining over £2.5 million of compensation for a widow and her children following a GP's negligence in diagnosing cancer.

MIDLANDS

MAINLY CLAIMANT

CLINICAL NEGLIGENCE: MAINLY CLAIMANT
■ MIDLANDS

1 freethcartwright *Nottingham*
   Irwin Mitchell *Birmingham*
2 Anthony Collins Solicitors *Birmingham*
   Challinors Lyon Clark *Birmingham*

LEADING INDIVIDUALS
1 BALEN Paul *freethcartwright*
   FOLLIS Richard *Alexander Harris*
   HALL Antony *Anthony Collins Solicitors*
2 BANNISTER Richard *Challinors Lyon Clark*

This book is the product of 6,582 1/2 hour interviews. See p.7 for BMRB audit. Within each band, firms are listed alphabetically. See individuals' profiles p.149

FREETHCARTWRIGHT (see firm details p.963) One of the region's "*big players*," this operation accrues wide commendation from competitors. Head of department Paul Balen (see p.149) is praised as a "*bright chap*" and many feel he has "*the highest profile in the Midlands*." Along with colleague Jane Williams, he led the settlement protocol for the Leicester cervical smear cases and is currently representing over 100 children wrongly diagnosed with epilepsy by a paediatrician in Leicester Royal Infirmary. Other areas of focus for the team include cosmetic surgery and group actions regarding the MMR vaccine and hepatitis-related claims.

IRWIN MITCHELL (see firm details p.1009) "*Always strong contenders*," the team is felt by clients to have "*a huge amount of experience and capability in this area.*" Peers commented on the departure of key player Richard Follis, but the general consensus pointed to a depth of talent that will easily bear the loss. Lisa Jordan, who recently settled the Parkes V New Cross hospital claim for £2.65 million, takes over as head of department. Cases handled include brain injury and inquest cases and it has noticed a recent flurry of multimillion pound wrongful birth claims.

ANTHONY COLLINS SOLICITORS (see firm details p.845) "*Sensible operators,*" the Birmingham team is held in high esteem by peers. Amongst the claims recently taken on: it obtained £3.4 million on behalf of a child injured during birth. It has acted in cosmetic surgery, cancer misdiagnosis and spinal injury matters. Tony Hall (see p.152) is "*thoroughly knowledgeable on his subject,*" and contemporaries profess that they "*have a lot of time for him.*"

CHALLINORS LYON CLARK Peers singled out Richard Bannister (see p.149) as a "*dependable and thorough*" lawyer. He is supported by a strong team that includes a nurse and which undertakes the full range of claims including neurological, obstetric and oncology.

OTHER NOTABLE PRACTITIONERS Richard Follis (see p.151) ("*superb*") now heads up Alexander Harris's new Solihull operation.

144   INDEX TO LEADING LAWYERS: PAGE 1693 ■ IN-HOUSE LAWYERS PROFILES: PAGE 1201

MIDLANDS

CLINICAL NEGLIGENCE: MAINLY DEFENDANT
■ MIDLANDS

1. **Bevan Ashford** Birmingham
2. **Browne Jacobson** Birmingham, Nottingham
2. **Weightman Vizards** Birmingham

LEADING INDIVIDUALS

1. **AYRE Carole** Browne Jacobson
1. **BARBER Paul** Bevan Ashford

ASSOCIATES TO WATCH

HODGETTS Tim Weightman Vizards

This book is the product of 6,582 1/2 hour interviews. See p.7 for BMRB audit. Within each band, firms are listed alphabetically. See individuals' profiles p.149

MAINLY DEFENDANT

BEVAN ASHFORD (see firm details p.869) Operating in conjunction with its offices in London and Bristol, the firm is establishing its presence in Birmingham. It has been handling claims relating to brain-injured babies, gynaecology and breast surgery. **Paul Barber** (see p.149) has a focus on mental health and psychiatric claims, while Katrina McCrory specialises in clinical dispute resolution. **Clients** NHSLA.

BROWNE JACOBSON (see firm details p.891) Best known for its group action work for the NHSLA, the team "*gets to the issues quickly and deals with them effectively.*" Peers portray the team as "*constructive*" and "*keen to get on with the early investigation of cases.*" **Carol Ayre** (see p.149) was recommended to researchers as a "*sensible and positive*" practitioner. She has recently been involved in four high-profile multi party actions. The team is currently handling claims over the million pound mark, and has recruited as a partner Richard Slack from Eversheds. **Clients** NHSLA.

WEIGHTMAN VIZARDS (see firm details p.1183) The third NHSLA panel firm in the Midlands, this team was rated as a "*highly focused*" outfit. Tim Hodgetts is part of the team that has a "*a real grasp*" of relevant issues and is always "*on the ball.*" **Clients** NHSLA.

EAST ANGLIA

CLINICAL NEGLIGENCE: MAINLY CLAIMANT
■ EAST ANGLIA

1. **Cunningham John** Thetford
2. **Gadsby Wicks** Chelmsford
3. **Attwater & Liell** Harlow
3. **Morgan Jones & Pett** Great Yarmouth
3. **Scrivenger Seabrook** St Neots
4. **Prettys** Ipswich

LEADING INDIVIDUALS

1. **JOHN Simon** Cunningham John
2. **GADSBY Gillian** Gadsby Wicks
2. **JONES David** Morgan Jones & Pett
2. **WICKS Roger** Gadsby Wicks
3. **KERRY David** Attwater & Liell
3. **SCRIVENGER Mark** Scrivenger Seabrook
3. **SEABROOK Vicki** Scrivenger Seabrook

This book is the product of 6,582 1/2 hour interviews. See p.7 for BMRB audit. Within each band, firms are listed alphabetically. See individuals' profiles p.149

MAINLY CLAIMANT

CUNNINGHAM JOHN (see firm details p.925) Adjudged an "*excellent*" team of lawyers, it is led by **Simon John** (see p.153), whose "*experience and long-standing reputation*" are nationally well-known. The team undertakes a substantial number of high-value brain injury claims and has recovered £14 million in the last 12 months. It has been involved with cases spanning the Atlantic; it has advised on claims against US Air Hospitals and a matter in which a boy was maltreated in hospitals in both the UK and US. Other areas of focus are cancer misdiagnosis, keyhole surgery and fatal cases.

GADSBY WICKS (see firm details p.967) This niche clinical negligence has a reputation that extends beyond its immediate region. Amongst an "*experienced*" team of lawyers are the well known **Gillian Gadsby** (see p.152) and **Roger Wicks** (see p.156). The team also includes a qualified nurse. Brain injury, misdiagnosis and general surgery claims are just part of this firm's broad caseload.

ATTWATER & LIELL The "*sound*" advice of this outfit is widely respected by peers, who also commend the efforts and dedication of its lead lawyer **David Kerry** (see p.153). The team has the capability to cover a wide range of clinical negligence claims relating to orthopaedic surgery, gynaecology and cerebral palsy. It recently acted on behalf of a woman mis-diagnosed in hospital and subsequently killed by water on the brain.

MORGAN JONES & PETT "*Easy to deal with,*" commented peers of this team, which is also said to "*fight its clients' cases hard.*" **David Jones** (see p.153) is renowned for his "*sensible approach*" and concentrates on high-value claims, while the rest of the firm handles the full range of cases. Areas of expertise include failure to diagnose cancer and A&E claims. It recently undertook a claim on behalf of a patient given an overdose of antibiotics and left with permanent damage.

SCRIVENGER SEABROOK (see firm details p.1124) This "*experienced*" outfit fields practitioners who "*definitely know their way around a case.*" The team continues to adapt to a change of focus from defendant to claimant and is now handling a significant amount of clinical negligence claims, particularly linked to brain damage. It also covers dental negligence and eye-related claims. **Vicki Seabrook** (see p.155) and **Mark Scrivenger** (see p.155) are widely rated by peers.

PRETTYS (see firm details p.1106) Stephen Skinner and this "*focused team*" undertake cases on a no-win, no-fee basis. Peers commend the firm's broad coverage, which includes paediatric, gynaecology, orthopaedic and failure to diagnose claims. Recently, it has appeared in a small class action on behalf of patients that suffered from misuse of anaesthetic by a surgeon. It also obtained damages for a woman experiencing serious PTSD after the still-born birth of her child.

EAST ANGLIA

CLINICAL NEGLIGENCE: MAINLY DEFENDANT
■ EAST ANGLIA

1. **Kennedys** Newmarket

This book is the product of 6,582 1/2 hour interviews. See p.7 for BMRB audit. Within each band, firms are listed alphabetically.

LEADING INDIVIDUALS

1. **CHAPMAN John** Kennedys

See individuals' profiles p.149

MAINLY DEFENDANT

KENNEDYS (see firm details p.1019) Still the only viable defendant presence in this region, peers appreciate the "*sensible*" approach of **John Chapman** (see p.150). This respected team handles claims on behalf of the NHSLA as well as advising trusts directly and recently settled a high-value cerebral palsy case. **Clients** NHSLA.

CLINICAL NEGLIGENCE ■ NORTH WEST

NORTH WEST — MAINLY CLAIMANT

CLINICAL NEGLIGENCE: MAINLY CLAIMANT ■ NORTH WEST

1. **Pannone & Partners** Manchester
2. **Alexander Harris** Altrincham
3. **Jones Maidment Wilson** Manchester
   Leigh, Day & Co Manchester
   Linder Myers Manchester

LEADING INDIVIDUALS

1. JONES Stephen Pannone & Partners
   KITCHINGMAN John Pannone & Partners
2. ALEXANDER Ann Alexander Harris
   SCATES Olivia Jones Maidment Wilson
3. JONES Eddie Jones Maidment Wilson
   WARD Trevor Linder Myers
   UP AND COMING
   HERBERTSON Lesley Alexander Harris

This book is the product of 6,582 1/2 hour interviews. See p.7 for BMRB audit. Within each band, firms are listed alphabetically. See individuals' profiles p.149

PANNONE & PARTNERS (see firm details p.1092) Although interviewees attest to the fact that "*everyone there is top class*," much of the firm's profile lies with **Stephen Jones** (see p.153) and **John Kitchingman** (see p.153). These two highly respected members of a "*consistently good*" team advise on the most complex of cases. The team has increased its partner size recently by making up Laura Morgan. The most significant trend within this group has been to handle a smaller number of higher value claims, including cerebral palsy, anaesthetic misuse and cosmetic surgery. Smaller claims remain keenly catered for. Some high-value results in the past year include £3.9 million for a negligence at birth claim, £2.9 million for an undiagnosed cerebral haemorrhage and £3.4 million for brain injury sustained at birth due to mismanagement of labour.

ALEXANDER HARRIS (see firm details p.839) "*Main operators*" in the North-West, this firm is generally felt to enjoy both volume and variety of cases and the expertise to match. Soon to be strengthened by a new office in Solihull, the group handles cerebral palsy, orthopaedic and misdiagnosis of cancer claims, and has noted an increase in claims against private hospitals. It has also been involved in an increasing number of human rights-related matters and judicial reviews. **Ann Alexander** (see p.149) continues to be a highly rated practitioner with particular focus on birth trauma, cerebral palsy and anaesthetic awareness. Her peers find **Lesley Herbertson** (see p.152) "*sensible to deal with.*"

JONES MAIDMENT WILSON **Olivia Scates** (see p.155) and **Eddie Jones** (see p.153) are highly rated practitioners at this respected firm. It has handled high-value cases, including retrieving £2.4 million on behalf of a woman with cerebral palsy and a case revolving around the failure to diagnose paraplegia after spinal surgery. The firm also handles matters across the board with a caseload comprising fatal accidents, orthopaedics and cancer claims.

LEIGH, DAY & CO (see firm details p.1036) Although the Manchester branch of this firm does not possess quite the reputation and stature of its London counterpart, this team is still considered "*a major player*" in the North West. Headed up by Frank Patterson, it is committed to handling high-value cases, which include head injury, cancer, misdiagnosis and referrals from the Spinal Injuries Association. It undertakes a number of claims on behalf of the Royal British Legion, which tend to have an orthopaedic element.

LINDER MYERS (see firm details p.1042) Clients appreciate the "*standard of documentation*" at this firm and "*the effective way it manages claims.*" Peers admire the "*excellent job*" that **Trevor Ward** (see p.156) does in the clinical negligence sphere. The team is well versed in the use of conditional fees and other funding methods.

NORTH WEST — MAINLY DEFENDANT

CLINICAL NEGLIGENCE: MAINLY DEFENDANT ■ NORTH WEST

1. **Hempsons** Manchester
2. **Hill Dickinson** Liverpool
3. **George Davies** Manchester

LEADING INDIVIDUALS

1. GIBBONS Anthony Hill Dickinson
   HARRISON Frances Hempsons
2. BALL Anne Hempsons
   BATCHELOR Claire George Davies
   MOWAT Allan Hill Dickinson

This book is the product of 6,582 1/2 hour interviews. See p.7 for BMRB audit. Within each band, firms are listed alphabetically. See individuals' profiles p.149

HEMPSONS (see firm details p.989) Deemed an "*exemplary firm*," this outfit of "*big-hitters*" is respected by competitors across the country. These lawyers are "*sensible and serious*" in their approach, and the well-managed unit offers a "*uniformity of quality advice and high-calibre staff across the board.*" Peers commend its "*excellent client support skills.*" The team includes the "*outstanding*" **Frances Harrison** (see p.408) and **Anne Ball** (see p.149), the latter deemed "*understated but first rate*" by peers. Over the past year the group has represented 10 health authorities, 29 NHS Trusts and 12 Primary Care bodies as well as the Manchester Mental Health Partnership, NHS Executive (NW region), NHS Estates and the National Blood Service.

HILL DICKINSON (see firm details p.995) The team has successfully attained a balance between being "*tough operators*" and "*nice people to work with*" claim its peers. The consensus is that "*these lawyers certainly know what they are doing.*" **Anthony Gibbons** (see p.152) and **Allan Mowat** (see p.408) ("*hands-on*") are leading lights in the clinical negligence sector.

GEORGE DAVIES (see firm details p.968) "*Key players*" on the defendant scene, this team is felt to be "*constructive*" in its approach. Clients rate its "*prompt response and good general support.*" In the aftermath of the NHSLA panel cuts, the firm has garnered more work from a wider range of trusts and has been involved in a number of high-profile group actions. It is acting on claims arising from the misuse of spinal injections across the UK, and is involved in nationwide litigation regarding claims about the ventilation of babies. The team also receives a number of neurological claims from a major teaching hospital. **Claire Batchelor** (see p.407) is the team's respected leader. **Clients** NHSLA.

YORKSHIRE/NORTH EAST — CLINICAL NEGLIGENCE

YORKSHIRE — MAINLY CLAIMANT

CLINICAL NEGLIGENCE: MAINLY CLAIMANT — YORKSHIRE

1. **Irwin Mitchell** Sheffield
2. **Heptonstalls** Goole
3. **Lester Morrill** Leeds

LEADING INDIVIDUALS

1. **BODY David** Irwin Mitchell
   PICKERING John Irwin Mitchell

This book is the product of 6,582 1/2 hour interviews. See p.7 for BMRB audit. Within each band, firms are listed alphabetically. See individuals' profiles p.149

IRWIN MITCHELL (see firm details p.1009) Market sources were clear in their commendation of this, the "*pre-eminent*" firm in this sphere. Its presence cuts a swathe across the UK, and peers characterise the approach of its "*dedicated team*" as "*quick to get to the heart of the case.*" David Body (see p.149) continues to be something of a national icon in this field, described by his contemporaries as "*a class act.*" John Pickering (see p.154) is commended as "*efficient*" in his approach to cases, which he treats with the "*utmost compassion.*" Amongst the range of claims undertaken, the team has recently handled a large number of birth injury and neurosurgical cases. It appeared in a case relating to failure to prescribe beta interferon, a drug for multiple sclerosis and continues to appear in investigations into the claims of children injured by their mother's use of anti convulsive drugs during pregnancy. The team works in tandem with its national network of offices.

HEPTONSTALLS (see firm details p.991) The firm continues its "*long-standing reputation*" for quality. It handles cases from the highest to lowest value including cerebral palsy, brain damage caused at birth and delay in the diagnosis of cancer. The team fields five specialists in clinical negligence, including John Burman and Sarah Johnson, both members of AVMA and the Law Society Medical Negligence Panel.

LESTER MORRILL The Leeds-based operation was valued by interviewees who agree it "*runs big cases sensibly,*" while defendant solicitors opine "*it gives you confidence when they are on the other side.*" The "*hands-on*" approach of its partners is also respected by peers. The team is headed by Julia Morrill, and has expertise in cases related to brain-damaged infants.

YORKSHIRE — MAINLY DEFENDANT

CLINICAL NEGLIGENCE: MAINLY DEFENDANT — YORKSHIRE

1. **Hempsons** Harrogate

LEADING INDIVIDUALS

1. **LOVEL John** Hempsons
2. **D'ARCY Adrienne** Hempsons
   EVANS Stephen Hempsons

This book is the product of 6,582 1/2 hour interviews. See p.7 for BMRB audit. Within each band, firms are listed alphabetically. See individuals' profiles p.149

HEMPSONS (see firm details p.989) Clients reported to researchers that "*the firm's team structure facilitates close, regular contact with us.*" Its prompt response time and a flexible approach were also complimented. Operating with the benefit of a national network, the group has secured a steady flow of instruction from its main client, the NHSLA. It is also developing regulatory work, and its involvement with mental health trusts. Other areas of focus are brain-damaged babies and failure to diagnose claims. "*Practical litigator*" Stephen Evans (see p.151), John Lovel (see p.153) ("*sensible*") and Adrienne D'Arcy (see p.150) ("*responsive*") all received warm recommendations during our research. Clients NHSLA; health authorities; Primary Care Trusts; The National Blood Service.

NORTH EAST — MAINLY CLAIMANT

CLINICAL NEGLIGENCE: MAINLY CLAIMANT — NORTH EAST

1. **Hay & Kilner** Newcastle upon Tyne
   Peter Maughan & Co Gateshead
   Samuel Phillips & Co Newcastle upon Tyne
2. **Ben Hoare Bell** Sunderland
   Freemans Newcastle upon Tyne
   Watson Burton Newcastle upon Tyne

LEADING INDIVIDUALS

1. **MAUGHAN Peter** Peter Maughan & Co
   SPEKER Barry Samuel Phillips & Co
2. **CURRAN Angela** Watson Burton

This book is the product of 6,582 1/2 hour interviews. See p.7 for BMRB audit. Within each band, firms are listed alphabetically. See individuals' profiles p.149

HAY & KILNER A "*visible*" presence in the marketplace, the team includes a qualified doctor (an obstetrician) and is headed by AVMA panel and Spinal Injuries Association member David Bradshaw. Recent claims have involved mismanagement of life long eczema and burning caused by UVB radiation, breast cancer, negligent surgery and late meningitis diagnosis. It handles a substantial number of cerebral palsy claims, including one recently settled for £1.35 million.

PETER MAUGHAN & CO The firm has this year closed its Sunderland office in order to consolidate its Gateshead operation. The group undertakes several high-value cerebral palsy claims at any one time. Peter Maughan (see p.154) leads the team, which advises on failure to diagnose meningitis, general claims and catastrophic injuries among its broad caseload.

SAMUEL PHILLIPS & CO (see firm details p.1122) "*Going out for clinical negligence in a big way,*" the team has a long track record in advising this region. High-profile Barry Speker (see p.155) is supported by a high calibre team that includes Rod Findlay. The group acts for a number of local trusts and has a strong training programme.

BEN HOARE BELL Simon Garlick heads this well-regarded claimant outfit, which is expanding in light of its increasing workload. The group generally acts against trusts, GPs and private practices in the North East. It takes on the full range of claims, which includes a steady flow of high value birth injury cases. The group employs a nurse to assist in the screening process.

FREEMANS Contemporaries warmly endorsed this small team, saying "*they're doing an awful lot, to a consistently high standard.*" Helen Thompson heads the group that covers a wide spectrum of claimant work, with particular expertise in cerebral palsy and birth injury cases. Other areas of focus include pharmaceutical dispensing errors and failure to diagnose orthopaedic fracture.

CLINICAL NEGLIGENCE ■ NORTH EAST/SCOTLAND

WATSON BURTON The team is led by "*alert, experienced mediator*" **Angela Curran** (see p.150), whom interviewees portray as "*a thorough lawyer, particularly client-friendly.*" Peers avow that they "*wouldn't hesitate to refer to her.*" She specialises in birth trauma, although as a unit, the firm covers every aspect of clinical negligence. A recent highlight for the team was achieving a £2.85 million settlement on behalf of a child rendered quadriplaegic during the neo natal period.

NORTH EAST   MAINLY DEFENDANT

CLINICAL NEGLIGENCE: MAINLY DEFENDANT
■ NORTH EAST

1. **Eversheds** Newcastle upon Tyne
2. **Ward Hadaway** Newcastle upon Tyne

LEADING INDIVIDUALS
1. **KEEBLE Jeffrey** Ward Hadaway
   WEATHERBURN David Eversheds

This book is the product of 6,582 1/2 hour interviews. See p.7 for BMRB audit. Within each band, firms are listed alphabetically. See individuals' profiles p.149

EVERSHEDS (see firm details p.949) "*Shining stars*" for defendant work in the North East, the firm takes the lion's share of NHSLA work in this region. Contemporaries acknowledge that it is "*undoubtedly head and shoulders above the rest.*" It has a core caseload of birth injury claims and a steady flow of mental health instructions. Clients include the NHS Trusts, PCTs and an amalgamated North-Eastern mental health trust. The team is headed by "*major player*" **David Weatherburn** (see p.156). **Clients** NHSLA; City Hospitals Sunderland NHS Trust; Tyne Tees & Hartlepool NHS Trust; South Durham NHS Trust; Newcastle, North Tyneside & Northumberland NHS Trust; Harrogate NHS Trust; Rotherham General Hospitals NHS Trust.

WARD HADAWAY (see firm details p.1180) Market sources judged this team to be "*good opponents,*" who have had had a successful year; it has acquired several new trusts clients, giving it a current total of 22 on its roster. Claims relate to a wide variety of negligence claims and the team continues to act in a number of cerebral palsy and opthalmology cases. **Jeffrey Keeble** (see p.153) maintains a distinguished reputation.

SCOTLAND   MAINLY CLAIMANT

CLINICAL NEGLIGENCE: MAINLY CLAIMANT
■ SCOTLAND

1. **Anderson Strathern WS** Edinburgh
   Balfour & Manson Edinburgh
   Drummond Miller WS Edinburgh

LEADING INDIVIDUALS
1. **CARR Robert** Anderson Strathern WS
   TYLER Alfred Balfour & Manson

This book is the product of 6,582 1/2 hour interviews. See p.7 for BMRB audit. Within each band, firms are listed alphabetically. See individuals' profiles p.149

ANDERSON STRATHERN WS (see firm details p.844) Rated for its client service, the team has been heavily involved of late in fatal claims. It focuses on cases involving children and is currently handling several cases of severe brain damage. It also represents children adversely affected by epileptic drugs taken by their mothers during pregnancy. **Robert Carr** (see p.150) is considered by many to be "*friendly and reassuring to clients.*"

BALFOUR & MANSON (see firm details p.856) Of **Alfred Tyler** (see p.637) it is said, "*the overall quality of service he provides is second to none.*" Underneath him exists a team of talented lawyers, which maintains its profile for group actions and high-value claims.

DRUMMOND MILLER WS (see firm details p.942) Peers regard this as a "*substantial practice,*" which fields two Law Society of Scotland-accredited specialists, Grant McCulloch and Liesa Spiller. It has recently been involved in complex obstetrics and paediatric cases.

SCOTLAND   MAINLY DEFENDANT

CLINICAL NEGLIGENCE: MAINLY DEFENDANT
■ SCOTLAND

1. **Shepherd+ Wedderburn** Edinburgh

LEADING INDIVIDUALS
1. **DONALD Hugh** Shepherd+ Wedderburn
   GRIFFITHS John Shepherd+ Wedderburn

This book is the product of 6,582 1/2 hour interviews. See p.7 for BMRB audit. Within each band, firms are listed alphabetically. See individuals' profiles p.149

SHEPHERD+ WEDDERBURN (see firm details p.1130) Clients value this group for the "*superb service*" it provides; it "*reacts quickly and keeps you informed.*" **Hugh Donald** (see p.151) ("*approachable, personable and knowledgeable*") and the "*experienced*" **John Griffiths** (see p.152) are the department's two partners. It acts regularly for the MDDUS and recently defended it against a woman who had suffered compartment syndrome after treatment for a knife wound. It also represented the Ambulance Service at a fatal accident inquiry into the circumstances of the death of a farm labourer, regarding alleged delay in attendance. **Clients** MDDUS; Medical Protection Society; Scottish Ambulance Service.

THE LEADERS IN CLINICAL NEGLIGENCE

ALEXANDER, Ann
Alexander Harris, Altrincham
(0161) 925 5555
ann@alexharris.co.uk
Specialisation: Managing partner specialising in all areas of clinical negligence and concomitant issues of public and legal policy. The treatment of children has become a centre of excellence, with a long history of cerebral palsy and anaesthetics cases. To this expertise has been added work with criminal law aspects (representing families of Beverly Allitt's victims), and more recently is acting for in excess of 200 families representing 100 victims and alleged victims of Harold Shipman. Ann campaigned for their rights in overturning decisions made by authorities, particularly the government's decision to hold the Shipman inquiry in private. Acting on behalf of the Leicester Epilepsy Concern Parents and Carers Group and individual cases alleging misdiagnosis of epilepsy in children over a number of years. Ann contributes regularly to television news and current affairs programmes, is an expert frequently consulted by radio reporters and producers, and has been extensively quoted in the press. Lectures on medical negligence issues to legal and medical audiences, and is a visiting Fellow at the Department of Journalism Studies, University of Sheffield.
Prof. Memberships: Law Society, AVMA, ATLA (Member of Executive Committee Birth Trauma Litigation Group), assessor to Law Society Specialist Medical Negligence Panel. Member of Editorial Board of Health Care Risk Report.
Career: Qualified in 1978 and then became co-founder of *Alexander Harris* in May 1989. First practice in this country specialising exclusively in clinical negligence and pharmaceutical product liability. The practice also has a specialist personal injury department.
Personal: Born 5 November 1954. Attended University College, London (LL.B 1974), Nottingham Law School 1997 (MBA). Lives in Hale, Cheshire.

AYRE, Carole
Browne Jacobson, Nottingham
(0115) 976 6223
cayre@brownej.co.uk
Specialisation: Head of Medical Negligence Practice Group and Deputy Head of Insurance and Public Risk Department. Acts exclusively for the NHS, building up the firm's medical negligence teams in Nottingham and Birmingham from scratch following the firm's appointment to the NHSLA Panel of solicitors. Has handled high profile multi-party claims, including 200 claims made in connection with diagnoses of epilepsy by Dr Holton in Leicester. Also acts for NHS Trusts on a wide range of policy and patient related issues, and is involved in the forthcoming DOH Inquiry into the activities of Richard Neale, Consultant Obstetrician and Gynaecologist, struck off by the GMC two years ago. Has substantial past experience of representing claimants in personal injury actions, which gives her an insight and understanding of the claimants' perspective.
Prof. Memberships: FOIL; Nottingham Medico Legal Society.
Career: Qualified in 1981. Began her career at *Browne Jacobson* dealing with public authority work and returned to become a partner there after 10 years in partnership at *Keeble Hawson* in Sheffield.
Personal: Born 14 February 1956. Graduated in law from Durham University in 1977. Lives in Nottingham.

BALEN, Paul
freethcartwright, Nottingham
(0115) 936 9369
paul.balen@freethcartwright.co.uk
Specialisation: Offices also at Derby and Leicester. Head of personal litigation. Main areas of practice are clinical negligence and product liability claims and the co-ordination of group actions and clinical negligence claims. Is co-ordinating the Trilucent soya breast implants claims; Leicester cervical smear; MMR, 3M hip and silicone breast implant claims. Editorial board member of Health Care Risk Bulletin. Lecturer on medico-legal matters to doctors and lawyers. Is a Radio Nottingham phone-in 'Legal Eagle'. Co-author of 'Multi-Party Actions' (LAG 1995).
Prof. Memberships: Law Society (Personal Injury Specialist Panel and Clinical Negligence Specialist Panel assessor) National Secretary of APIL 1998-2000; Referral Solicitor for AVMA. Member of ATLA, APILA. Senior Fellow CPIL.
Career: Joined *Freeth Cartwright* in 1975. Qualified in 1977. Partner 1980.
Personal: Born 25 February 1952. Attended Nottingham High School 1960-71, then Cambridge University 1971-74.

BALL, Anne
Hempsons, Manchester
(0161) 228 0011
apb@hempsons.co.uk
Specialisation: Partner in Healthcare Litigation Department. Principal area of practice is medical negligence acting for health service bodies and individual doctors and dentists in defence of high value claims. Successfully defended two brain damage baby cases at trial in 2001. Other main area of practice is defending doctors and dentists accused of committing criminal offences. Cases include defending allegations of murder (R v Shipman), manslaughter (R v Lane), rape, indecent assault and fraud. Also advises doctors and dentists facing disciplinary action before the General Medical Council and General Dental Council.
Prof. Memberships: Law Society.
Career: Graduate of Kings College London. Articled with *Hempsons*. Admitted in 1987 and became a partner in 1991.

BANNISTER, Richard
Challinors Lyon Clark, Birmingham
(0121) 212 9393
rlb@challinors.co.uk
Specialisation: Handles all types of clinical negligence claims including obstetric, oncology, orthopaedic, neurosurgery, GP liability and general surgery. Legal Aid, CFA and privately funded cases. Representation at inquests.
Prof. Memberships: AVMA and Law Society specialist referral panels; APIL; Birmingham Medico Legal Society.
Career: Qualified 1990, became a partner in 1993.
Personal: Married, three sons. Leisure pursuits include football and cricket.

BARBER, Paul
Bevan Ashford, Birmingham
(0121) 634 5006
paul.barber@bevanashford.co.uk
Specialisation: Partner in the firm's Public Sector and Insurance and Recovery Divisions. Has over 25 years focused experience of all levels of medical and other litigation within the NHS. Has acquired an understanding of medical issues and complexities which has enabled him to win the confidence of clinicians in the firing line - essential to the successful defence of claims and to their early settlement in appropriate cases. Has worked across the full range of claims, specialising in top level clinical negligence claims and many psychiatric claims. Has a particular interest in mental health law and the Human Rights Act and has lectured many times on these issues. Also had a prominent role in a number of high profile mental health inquests. Has addressed an International Symposium on Perinatal Asphyxia.
Prof. Memberships: Law Society.
Career: Trained with *Bevan Ashford*. Admitted 1976; Partner 1979.

BARCAN, Richard A
Barcan Woodward, Bristol
(0117) 925 8080

BARTON, Grainne
Alexander Harris, London
(020) 7430 5555
grainnebarton@alexharris.co.uk
Specialisation: Partner and head of clinical negligence department, London. Exclusively handles claimant clinical negligence matters and is renowned for her commitment, energy and enthusiasm in this area of the law. Main areas of practice are cerebral palsy, anaesthetic awareness, cancer, keyhole surgery and dental matters. Acted in R v H.M Coroner for Inner North London District, Ex parte Touche (successfully Judicially Reviewed the decision by the Coroner not to hold an inquest into the death of the client's wife), Tredget v. Bexley Health Authority (nervous shock) in 1994 and Smyth v. Riverside Health Authority (malaria case) in 1993.
Prof. Memberships: APIL, AVMA, Law Society, Clinical Negligence Panel.
Career: With *Boyes Turner & Burrows* 1987-90. Qualified in 1989. Joined *Pritchard Englefield* in 1990 and became a partner in 1993. Joined *Alexander Harris* as partner April 1999.
Personal: Born 8 October 1963. Educated at Brunel University 1982-86. Past Honorary Secretary of TSG. Lives in Epsom, Surrey.

BATCHELOR, Claire
George Davies, Manchester
(0161) 236 8992
See under Healthcare, p.407

BATTEN, Elizabeth
Parlett Kent, London
(020) 7430 0712
Specialisation: Clinical negligence specialist since 1991. Particular interest in oncology, brain injury, accident and emergency cases and in psychiatric negligence, also negligence and abuse of people with learning disabilities. Reported case of Mahmood v Siggins. Lectures to lawyers and health professionals on clinical negligence and related topics.
Prof. Memberships: Law Society. Law Society Medical Negligence panel. AVMA referral panel member. APIL member.
Career: Admitted 1977. Partner in *Parlett Kent* from 1993. BA (Cantab) in Economics.

BLYTHE, Deborah
Evill and Coleman, London
(020) 8789 9221
Specialisation: Partner. Main areas of practice are clinical negligence, including brain damage at birth, head injuries, gynaecology, cancer cases, dental cases, fatal accident claims and Court of Protection work.
Prof. Memberships: APIL, Law Society Clinical Negligence Panel, Law Society Personal Injury Panel.
Career: Qualified in 1984. *G.L. Hockfield and Co* 1984-92 (Partner from 1987); *Evill and Coleman* 1992 (Partner from 1993).
Personal: Keen yachtswoman. Sailed 3,000 miles across the Atlantic in a 38 foot yacht raising money for the charity Headway in 1999.

BODY, David
Irwin Mitchell, Sheffield
(0870) 1500 100
Bodyd@irwinmitchell.co.uk
Specialisation: Partner in personal injury department. Head of national clinical negligence team. Main area of practice is clinical negligence on behalf of plaintiffs. Acted in Maynard v West Midlands RHA, Davis v City and Hackney Health Authority, Aboul-Hosn v Governors of National Hospital for Nervous Diseases, Bolitho v City and Hackney Health Authority, Hopkins v McKenzie,

CLINICAL NEGLIGENCE ■ THE LEADERS

Fisher v North Derbyshire Health Authority and the Creutzfeldt-Jacob Disease Litigation. Represented the variant CJD victims' families at the BSE Inquiry 1998-2000. 2000-1, negotiated No Fault Compensation Scheme for BSE Claims, now implementing this scheme for clients through vCJD Compensation Trust. Lectures regularly to both doctors and lawyers. Chair of Medical Negligence Special Interest Group of APIL (1992-95).
Prof. Memberships: APIL, AVMA, ATLA (ATLA Birth Trauma Litigation Group).
Career: Qualified in 1981. Worked at *Halls* 1981-91, from 1984 as a partner. Joined *Irwin Mitchell* in 1991 as a partner.
Publications: Author of chapters on 'The Conduct of Proceedings' in Powers & Harris 'Medical Negligence' (all editions), and on 'Creutzfeld Jacob Disease Litigation for Multi-party Action' (Ed. Christopher Hodges).
Personal: Born 1 August 1955. Attended Hereford High School and Corpus Christi College, Oxford (BA Hons, 1976). Leisure interests include despairing about Welsh rugby. Lives in Sheffield.

BROWN, Susan
Boyes Turner, Reading
(0118) 959 7711
sbrown@boyesturnerlegal.co.uk
Specialisation: Partner handling clinical negligence cases on behalf of claimants. Experienced in dealing with claims involving all of the medical disciplines. Has particular experience of cases involving severe and permanent disability, especially brain injury. Special interest in cases involving maternal injury during child birth, gynaecology and cases involving bowel surgery. Founder and organiser of 'Special Lives' a support group for families with disabled children.
Prof. Memberships: Law Society Clinical Negligence Panel Member; AVMA Referral Panel of Solicitors; APIL; CPIL.
Career: Qualified in 1992 and joined *Boyes Turner* the same year. Partner since 1998.

CAHILL, Julia
Kingsley Napley, London
(020) 7814 1200
jcahill@kingsleynapley.co.uk
Specialisation: Partner and head of clinical negligence department. Specialist in clinical and professional negligence claims. Cases mainly involve serious disability or death. Advises on complaints procedures. Advises on inquests into death during medical care. Particular expertise in obstetric negligence claims on behalf of mother and child. Special interest in delayed diagnosis of meningitis in children and delayed diagnosis/mismanagement in adults of cervical cancer, bowel cancer, breast cancer and mismanagement of diabetes. Practice also covers legal negligence involving the pursuit of claims against legal advisors in medical negligence cases. Interesting recent cases include McAllister v Lewisham and North Southwark Health Authority, Davis v Jacobs, Camden & Islington Health Authority, Novartis Pharmaceuticals (UK) Ltd.
Prof. Memberships: Law Society Panel of Specialist Medical Negligence Solicitors; AVMA Lawyers Referral Panel; Member APIL, APLA, ATLA. Secretary to the APIL Medical Negligence Special Interest Group 1998-99. CEDR Accredited Mediator.
Career: DIP Physiotherapy 1976. Qualified LLB 1980. Assistant Director, Action for Victims of Medical Accidents 1984-88. Partner *Parlett Kent & Co* 1992-94. Joined *Kingsley Napley* as partner in September 1994.
Personal: Two children. Lives in Islington, London.

CARR, Robert
Anderson Strathern WS, Edinburgh
(0131) 220 2345
robert.carr@andersonstrathern.co.uk
Specialisation: Partner in litigation department. Accredited by the Law Society of Scotland as a medical negligence specialist and admitted as a solicitor/advocate with extended rights of audience in the highest Scottish civil courts. Almost 20 years of practice in civil litigation covering all areas of court and tribunal work. One of a team involved in advising insurers, particularly in personal injuries and related actions, and in advising the Royal College of Nursing as their appointed Scottish agents. The RCN instructions cover the full spectrum of criminal and civil court work and employment law matters, including frequent advice on medical negligence issues and regular appearance at fatal accident enquiries. Also speaks and lectures to insurers, nurses and doctors on many aspects of civil law and court procedure and practice. Head of the firm's Parliamentary Unit; assisted the RCN in its evidence before the Scottish Parliament on the Adults with an Incapacity Bill. Represented the Denholm family at the much publicised recent fatal accident enquiry in relation to the death of Darren Denholm who died whilst undergoing dental surgery under general anaesthetic; the case resulted in a finding that dental surgery under general anaesthetic should no longer be conducted outside a hospital setting. *Anderson Strathern* also dealt with the case of Richard Adamson, one of the first medical negligence actions in Scotland to proceed before a jury for almost 50 years, which resulted in an award for pain and suffering of £100,000 for a young man whose only testicle was negligently removed by doctors at a hospital in West Lothian. Has also been pioneering in Scotland damages for children who have suffered disability as a consequence of their mothers undergoing anticonvulsant therapy whilst pregnant. Also acts for the Parole Board for Scotland and the Mental Welfare Commission for Scotland.

CHAPMAN, John
Kennedys, Newmarket
(01603) 693 380
Specialisation: Partner specialising in medical negligence defence.
Career: Articled *Daynes Chittock & Back*; qualified 1976; partner *Eversheds Daynes Hill & Perks* 1979; member of *Eversheds'* board of management; Head of Litigation Department 1996; joined *Mills & Reeve* April 1999 as partner in medical negligence team.
Personal: Amateur dramatics, vintage farm machinery, gardening, classic cars.

CURRAN, Angela
Watson Burton, Newcastle upon Tyne
(0191) 244 4444
Specialisation: Acts for claimants in all types of medical negligence cases. Special interest in obstetric cases. Accredited and experienced mediator; involved in the NHSLA clinical negligence mediation pilot scheme.
Prof. Memberships: Member of the Law Society Personal Injury and Medical Negligence Panels. AVMA, APIL and ADR Net.
Career: Joined *Watson Burton* 1992 as articled clerk. Associate 1998. Head of Medical Negligence Unit.
Personal: Educated at Newcastle University (BSC 1983) and College of Law, York. Native of Newcastle. Leisure time devoted to family, gardening and wine.

D'ARCY, Adrienne
Hempsons, Harrogate
(01423) 522331
aed@hempsons.co.uk
Specialisation: Partner and team leader in the Clinical Negligence Department. Work includes medico-legal advice to and representation of NHS Trusts, Health Authorities and their staff in medical negligence actions and Inquests. Frequently involved in high values and high profile cases.
Prof. Memberships: Law Society.
Career: Qualified in 1984. Trained at *Jacksons*, Middlesborough. Partner 1985-87. *Hepworth and Chadwick* (*Eversheds*), Leeds 1987-88. Admitted as a solicitor in Hong Kong 1988. *Johnson, Stokes and Master*, Hong Kong 1988-94. *Le Brasseur J Tickle* 1994-96. Joined *Hempsons* 1996.
Personal: Born 23 April 1959. Educated at Queen Margaret's, York and City of London Polytechnic (LLB Hons. Business Law). Lives in North Yorkshire. Married with two children.

DAVIES, Andrew
Hugh James, Bargoed
(01443) 822022
andrew.davies@hughjames.co.uk
Specialisation: Partner and Head of 18 strong Clinical Negligence Department. Has wide experience in clinical negligence work from obstetric negligence involving brain injury and Erb's Palsy through to maternal injuries. Whilst his work has a broad spectrum over the last 12 months he has handled an increasing number of claims involving paediatric negligence as well as orthopaedic claims for professional sports men. Has delivered seminars to Community Health Council's and to general practitioners.
Prof. Memberships: Law Society's Medical Negligence Panel and Personal Injury Panel as well as AVMA Referral Panel. Member of APIL.

DESMOND, Adrian
Boyes Turner, Reading
(0118) 952 7219
adesmond@boyesturnerlegal.co.uk
Specialisation: Head of clinical negligence and personal injury. Acts for claimants in all types of clinical accident and personal injury cases with special interest in cases of maximum severity, brain, spinal, obstetric and paediatric injury. Has acted in many high profile and reported cases. AVMA referral solicitor since 1984. Assessor to and member of Law Society specialist medical negligence panel since formed in 1995 and personal injury panel. Secretary then co-ordinator of medical negligence special interest group of the Association of Personal Injury Lawyers. Author of legal and medical articles on issues related to medical negligence. Deputy Taxing Master Supreme Court Taxing Office 1994-98. Spinal Injuries Association and Headway Panel Solicitor.
Prof. Memberships: AVMA, APIL, SIA, Headway, ATLA, European Brain Injury Society, Richard Grand Society.
Career: Qualified and joined *Boyes Turner* in 1980.

DINGWALL, Christian
Bevan Ashford, London
(020) 7822 7901
christia.dingwall@bevanashford.co.uk
Specialisation: Head of *Bevan Ashford's* NHS Claims Department whose clients include the NHS Litigation Authority and insurers. Is experienced in handling all types of clinical negligence cases including multi-party actions, cerebral palsy claims and other complex medical cases. Also has experience in mediation and has used this alternative form of dispute resolution to the NHS's advantage. Important cases include Poynter v Hillington HA and Jenkins v Lambeth Southwark and Lewisham HA. Other past cases include R v Brent & Harrow HA ex p London Borough of Harrow; R v South Western Hospital ex p M and R v North West London ex p Stewart. Has presented lectures and seminars on clinical negligence litigation and healthcare law to clients and at national conferences.
Prof. Memberships: Law Society.
Career: Qualified in 1986. Partner at *Le Brasseur J Tickle* 1988-2000 and *Bevan Ashford* from April 2000.
Personal: Born 28 December 1959. Educated at Bristol University 1979-82 and the College of Law 1982-84. Leisure activities include gardening. Lives in New Malden, London.

THE LEADERS ■ CLINICAL NEGLIGENCE

DONALD, Hugh
Shepherd+ Wedderburn, Edinburgh
(0131) 473 5159
hugh.donald@shepwedd.co.uk
Specialisation: Partner. Specialist in clinical negligence, representing doctors and dentists in civil claims, inquiries and disciplinary proceedings. Also aviation representing airline and helicopter operators in both civil claims and accident inquiries. On the panel appointed to handle claims against solicitors under Law Society of Scotland Master Policy.
Career: Qualified in 1975, having joined *Shepherd+ Wedderburn* in 1973. Became a partner in 1977. Administrative Head of Litigation Department 1990-94. Appointed Managing Partner in April 1994, and Chief Executive from April 1995 - April 1999.
Personal: Born 5 November 1951. Educated at Edinburgh University. Family Mediator. Chairman, Family Mediation Scotland. Leisure interests include gardening, walking and church. Lives in Edinburgh. Awarded OBE for services to family mediation in Scotland.

DONOVAN, Terry
Bindman & Partners, London
(020) 7833 4333
Specialisation: Personal Injury and Clinical Negligence Department. Main areas of work are catastrophic and fatal injuries caused by clinical negligence and personal injury, stress and bullying in the workplace; professional negligence (solicitors and in education).
Prof. Memberships: Law Society Specialist Panels: Personal Injury and Clinical Negligence; AVMA Specialist Panel – Clinical Negligence.
Career: Partner *Bindman & Partners*; Qualified 1988; Articles, *Boyd & Hutchinson*; Assistant Solicitor, *Richards Butler* (shipping and commercial litigation); Assistant Solicitor, *Compton Carr*, began specialisation in clinical negligence; Partner; *Bolt Burdon*, Clinical Negligence; Joined present firm 1996.
Publications: Contribution to Inns of Court Bar Finals Training Material 'Dealing with the Professional Client'; contributed chapter to 'Advising Clients with HV and Aids', Butterworth.
Personal: Born 1958. Resides London. Education: Reading University B.S. Hons 1980. Main leisure activities, clubs: Parenthood, walking, reading, gardening and DIY.

DYSON, Henry
Leigh, Day & Co, London
(020) 7650 1200
Specialisation: Claimant Clinical Negligence and arranging representation for families at inquests following deaths after medical intervention.
Prof. Memberships: APIL and the Medico-Legal Society. Law Society Clinical Negligence Panel Member. Legal Services Commission Funding Review Committee member.
Career: Joined *Leigh Day & Co* in 1991. Partner in 1998.

Personal: Born 1963. Degree in Biochemistry followed by CPE and LPC. Qualified 1989.

EDDY, Alison
Irwin Mitchell, London
(0870) 1500 100
eddya@irwinmitchell.co.uk
Specialisation: Partner specialising in clinical negligence and catastrophic injury. Particular interest in birth trauma, maternal injury, consent and neurosurgery. Recent settlements include cases of cerebral palsy, erbs palsy, spinal injury, delay in diagnosis of cancer and failure to adequately asses psychiatric patients resulting in suicide or severe injury. Recent reported cases include Groom v Selby. The Court of Appeal upheld a finding that damages were recoverable by the claimant for the cost of bringing up a disabled child in a wrongful birth claim where the child had been apparently healthy but exposed to bacteria at birth, resulting in the development of meningitis. Settlement in the last year of a number of head injury cases in excess of £1 million, the highest being £3.5 million for a 17 year old after a discount had been given for contributory negligence. Regularly lectures on various aspects of medical law to lawyers and clinicans. Author of a number of legal and medical articles, most recently on 'Consent in Obstetrics' in 'The Obstetrician and Gynaecologist', April 2002.
Prof. Memberships: AVMA; APIL; ATLA; Member of Law Society Clinical Negligence and Personal Injury Panel.
Career: Qualified in 1978. Partner with *Robin Thompson and Partners* 1983. Joined *Irwin Mitchell* as a Partner November 1995, to open the London office.
Personal: Born 1954. Educated at Manchester University 1973-76. Five children. Interests include skiing, opera and travel.

ENGLAND, Richard
John Hodge & Co, Bristol
(0117) 9292281
richard.england@johnhodge.co.uk
Specialisation: Partner in charge of litigation based at the firm's Bristol office. Specialises in Medical Negligence and Personal Injury Cases. Undertaken Cases Nationwide, including multi-party actions, Paediatric heart operations, cerebral palsy and brain damage cases.
Prof. Memberships: Member of the Law Society Medical Negligence and Personal Injury panels and the Association of Personal Injury Lawyers.
Career: Born 14 February 1951. LLB (Hons) Leeds University 1973. Qualified 1978. Partner *John Hodge* since 1980.

EVANS, Stephen
Hempsons, Harrogate
(01423) 842780
s.evans@hempsons.co.uk
Specialisation: Partner in healthcare litigation in the firm's Harrogate office. Principal area of practice is clinical negligence. Special interest in mental health issues. Regularly represents NHS Trusts at inquests. Also gives general advice on patient related issues including consent and confidentiality. Lectures regularly to doctors, healthcare managers and claims handlers.
Prof. Memberships: Law Society.
Career: Qualified in 1989. Joined *Hempsons* in 1996 and became a Partner in 2002.
Personal: Educated at Manchester University.

FAZAN, Claire
Bindman & Partners, London
(020) 7833 4433
Specialisation: Partner in charge of the personal injury and clinical negligence department at *Bindman & Partners* since 1989. She has a national reputation as one of the leading solicitors in the field of claimant clinical negligence litigation. Her experience covers claims ranging from those of maximum severity to those that are less severe. Particular area of expertise and specialisation is in claims for children and adults who have suffered permanent brain injury and associated disability as a consequence of failings in medical care. Her experience in these types of claims is extensive and includes claims arising from obstetric, neo-natal, anaesthetic, neurological and accident and emergency care.
Prof. Memberships: Law Society Clinical Negligence Panel; AWMA Panel; Association of Personal Injury Lawyers; Accredited CEDR Mediator.
Career: Qualified 1985; *Bindman & Partners* 1987 to date, Partner 1989.
Publications: Co-author of 'Medical Negligence Litigation: A Practitioner's Guide' by Irwin, Fazan and Allfrey, published by LAG; contributing author to 'The Medical Accidents Handbook - a Practical Guide for Patients and their Advisors'.

FERGUSON, Gerry M
Withy King, Bath
(01225) 425 731
gerry.ferguson@withyking.co.uk
Specialisation: Partner specialising in clinical negligence and product liability claims for claimants, including benzodiazepine/breast implant multi-party litigation. Experience of high value claims, cerebral palsy, paraplegia, and psychiatric negligence cases.
Prof. Memberships: Law Society (Clinical Negligence Specialist Panel), APIL, ATLA, APLA and AVMA (panel member). Legal Services Commission Funding Review Committee. Bath and North East Somerset and Swindon Community Legal Service Partnerships, Clinical Society of Bath, MIND Legal Network.
Career: Involved in medical negligence litigation since 1981. Joined *Withy King* in 1989 as the only fee earner handling medical negligence work. Since then the clinical negligence department has grown to four part-time and five full-time fee-earners with a strong regional reputation.
Personal: Born 23 July 1953. Education: Epsom College; Birmingham University. Married with two sons. Lives in Bath. Leisure interests: Motor sport photography.

FIELD, Rena
Weightman Vizards, London
(020) 7663 2222
rena.field@weightmanvizards.com
Specialisation: Principal area of practice is clinical negligence, acting for defendant NHS Trusts, Health Authorities and NHSLA with particular emphasis on larger cases, especially birth injury cases. She has considerable experience of health service law, covering general advisory issues, consent, mental health and inquests. Leading cases include Re L (1996: use of force to carry out caesarean section on incompetent patient); Re MB (1997: Court of Appeal decision on capacity test for caesarean section).
Prof. Memberships: Law Societies of England, Wales and Ireland; CEDR accredited mediator.
Career: Qualified Ireland 1979; partner *Hughes & MacEuilly* until 1985; joined *Le Brasseur J. Tickle* 1989, partner 1990-2001; joined *Weightman Vizards* as a partner in April 2001.
Publications: Lectures regularly to health service bodies on topical medico-legal issues.
Personal: B.C.L National University of Ireland. Lives in Surrey, two children.

FOLLIS, Richard
Alexander Harris, Solihull
(0121) 711 5111
richard.follis@alexanderharris.co.uk
Specialisation: Partner with over 20 years experience of clinical negligence work. Particular expertise in birth injury, orthopaedic and fatal accident cases. Wide experience of claims arising in other medical and surgical specialties. Acted for successful claimants in a number of > £2M awards including cerebral palsy arising from birth trauma and failure to diagnose hydrocephalus. Acted for parents' support group and individual claimants in organ retention claims arising from Birmingham Children's Hospital and elsewhere. Previously, member of steering committee with generic work responsible for Nationwide Organ Retention Group litigation. Now acting for support group and families in claims arising from misdiagnosis and treatment of epilepsy at Leicester. Frequent advocate including particularly at Inquests.
Prof. Memberships: Law Society, Council Birmingham Law Society, Council Birmingham Medico-Legal Society, AVMA Lawyers Support Group. Chairman AVMA Midlands LSG. Hon. Part-time tutor Department of Bio-medical ethics, University of Birmingham. Member of Law Society and AVMA referral clinical negligence panels. Legal Services Commission Funding Review Committee.
Career: Qualified in 1981. Partner, *Irwin*

CLINICAL NEGLIGENCE ■ THE LEADERS

Mitchell 1999. Partner, *Alexander Harris*, 2002.
Personal: Educated Halesowen Grammar School 1968-74. University College, Cardiff 1976-79.

GADSBY, Gillian
Gadsby Wicks, Chelmsford
(01245) 494929
gmg@gadsbywicks.co.uk
Specialisation: Partner dealing with medical negligence. Acts exclusively for plaintiffs and has specialised in medical negligence since qualification. Particular specialisation in women's health issues. Other main area of practice is medical product liability. Has handled a number of cases involving products affecting women, including the oral contraceptive pill, copper 7 IUD and tampon induced toxic shock syndrome, both here and in the USA. Article 'Special issues facing women in medical negligence' published in AVMA Journal in 1992. Extensive radio and broadcasting experience on national and local TV and radio, including Radio 1 and GMTV.
Prof. Memberships: Association of Personal Injury Lawyers (APIL), Association of Trial Lawyers of America.
Career: Qualified in 1989. Established *Gadsby Wicks* in 1993.
Personal: Born 15 November 1965. Educated at the University of East Anglia 1983-86 (LLB Hons).

GIBBONS, Anthony
Hill Dickinson, Liverpool
(0151) 236 5400
Specialisation: Partner in health department. Principal areas of practice are medical negligence, employment law and NHS advisory work. Handles a large volume of medical negligence cases, particularly brain damage cases of high value. Another significant element of work involves NHS property transactions acting on behalf of major NHS clients in the disposal of surplus property and in particular redundant hospitals. Important cases handled include Booth v Warrington Health Authority (disclosure of witness statements referred to in experts reports), Ashcroft v Mersey Regional Health Authority (standard of care of consultants in medical negligence cases) and O'Toole v Liverpool Health Authority (first self-funded structural settlement case in the medical negligence field). Major clients include North West Regional Health Authority and all NHS trusts in Cheshire and Merseyside. Has given lectures to various NHS clients. Participated as a presenter in Liverpool Law Society course on medical negligence.
Prof. Memberships: Law Society.
Career: Qualified in 1972. Former in-house legal advisor with Mersey RHA 1980-90. Joined *Hill Dickinson* as a partner in 1990. Presently a partner *Hill Dickinson*.
Personal: Born 10 October 1947. Educated at Xaverian College, Manchester 1959-66 and Nottingham University 1966-69 (Nottingham Co-operative Society Prize 1968, Hill Prize 1969). Leisure pursuits include food, wine and watching sport. Lives in Chester.

GOLDBURN, Tim
Preston Goldburn, Falmouth
(01326) 318900

GRIFFITHS, John
Shepherd+ Wedderburn, Edinburgh
(0131) 473 5445
john.griffiths@shepwedd.co.uk
Specialisation: Partner. Main area of practice is medical negligence: previously Solicitor at the Central Legal Office for the Scottish Hospital Service, advising and acting for the 15 Scottish Health Boards. With present firm, acts for a leading medical defence organisation. Chairman of Law Society Panel to accredit solicitors with specialist experience in medical negligence work. Has been responsible for the conduct of litigation in the Scottish Supreme Court, the Court of Session, House of Lords and Sheriff Courts all over Scotland. Has specialist interest in representing parties at Fatal Accident Inquires and advising generally on all aspects of work relating to medical negligence and the National Health Service. Is engaged at any one time in an average of 300 claims, litigations or contentious matters relating to medical or dental negligence. Also advises on employment law with a particular emphasis on disciplinary cases against doctors and dentists with regular appearances before the GMC and GDC. Accredited a specialist in employment law by the Law Society of Scotland. Has spoken and chaired conferences on medical negligence frequently. Author of a number of chapters in a textbook edited by Sir Michael Drury 'Clinical Negligence in General Practice' Radcliff Medical Press Ltd. Since July 2000 appointed a Part-time Chairman of Employment Tribunal.
Prof. Memberships: Law Society of Scotland.
Career: Qualified in 1971. Trainee at *Shepherd+ Wedderburn* and *MacAndrew Wright and Murray WS* 1969-71. Joined Central Legal Office for National Health Service in Scotland in 1972, becoming Chief Assistant Solicitor in 1984 and Acting Legal Adviser 1988-89. Joined *Simpson & Marwick WS* as Partner in 1989. *Shepherd+ Wedderburn* May 2000.
Personal: Born 16 September 1944. Attended Edinburgh Academy; Wadham College, Oxford 1962-65 and Edinburgh University 1967-69. Lives in Edinburgh.

HALL, Antony
Anthony Collins Solicitors, Birmingham
(0121) 212 7406
tony.hall@anthonycollinssolicitors.com
Specialisation: Acts for both legally aided and privately funded claimants or under conditional fee agreements in all aspects of medical and personal injury litigation, but especially obstetric, GP, cancer misdiagnosis, orthopaedic and brain damage claims. Expertise in medical ethics claims including those involving refusal of consent to treatment. Recent case awards include £4.5 million, £3.4 million and £2.4 million.
Prof. Memberships: Law Society Medical Negligence Panel, Referral Panel solicitor for Action for Victims of Medical Accidents (AVMA), Law Society Personal Injury Panel, member of Medical Negligence Special Interest Group of Association of Personal Injury Lawyers, Clinical Negligence Specialist Member of Legal Aid Board Committee, member of Birmingham Medico-Legal Society.
Career: Qualified 1986. Assistant solicitor with *Anthony Collins* 1986-89. Associate with a Worcestershire law firm 1989-90. West Midlands Regional Health Authority 1990-92. *Anthony Collins* 1992 onwards (partner since 1994).

HANNAM, Andrew
Clarke Willmott & Clarke, Bristol
(01823) 445407
ahannam@cw-c.co.uk
Specialisation: Partner with wide experience of investigating and litigating clinical negligence cases with a particular interest in cerebral palsy cases as well as being involved in several multi-party actions. Regular speaker to organisations such as SCOPE and Mencap on medico-legal issues. Particular highlight from last year included Davis v Taunton and Somerset NHS Trust £2.5m cerebral palsy claim.
Prof. Memberships: Law Society's Panel of Medical Negligence Lawyers, Action for Victims of Medical Negligence referral panel, Bristol Medico-Legal Society.
Career: Guildford Law School; Exeter University (LLB); articled with *CW&C* in October 1980; admitted in October 1982; made partner in 1989.
Publications: A number of his cases have been reported in Clinical Risk and Health Care Risk Report.

HARRISON, Frances
Hempsons, Manchester
(0161) 228 0011
fah@hempsons.co.uk
See under Healthcare, p.408

HAY, Katie
Capsticks, London
(020) 8780 2211
Specialisation: Partner in Clinical Law Department. Handles all types of medical negligence litigation for NHS clients. Has a particular interest in larger cases, especially birth injury baby cases. She helped to pioneer structures in the health service. She has advised on the drafting of the NHS Executives Guidance on the subject and has had articles published on this and other medico-legal issues. She manages a team of lawyers and has significant departmental management responsibilities.
Prof. Memberships: Law Society, Association of Women Solicitors.
Career: Qualified in 1988 following articles at *Howard Kennedy*. With *Cole & Cole*, Oxford 1988-90. Joined *Capsticks* in 1990. Became a partner in November 1992. Member of firm's Management Committee.
Personal: Born 24 January 1964. Educated at Reading Abbey School 1976-82, Oxford Polytechnic (BA Hons in Law with History) 1982-85. Interests include running, reading and cinema. Lives in London.

HERBERTSON, Lesley
Alexander Harris, Altrincham
(0161) 925 5555
Specialisation: Partner and head of department specialising in clinical negligence for claimants. Expert in cerebral palsy and catastrophic injury work, maintaining a keen interest in gynaecological, urological, surgical and ENT cases and works closely with PTSD and radiation damaged claimants. Acted in the much publicised Down's Syndrome discrimination cases. Has settled a number of cerebral palsy cases for £2m, recently recovered £40,000 for an infant facial palsy case and settled a wrongful birth claim two days into trial, where quantum took account of the child's disability. Regularly lectures to legal and medical audiences on topics such as conditional fee agreements and the CPR.
Prof. Memberships: President Trafford Law Society, member Law Society Clinical Negligence, Law Society Personal Injury Panel, Association of Personal Injury Lawyers, Manchester Law Society, Legal Services Commission Funding Review Panel.
Career: Trained *Pannone & Partners*; qualified 1990; Partner *Alexander Harris* 1995. John Mackrell prize, Howard and Innes Watson prize and the Stephen Heelis prize.

HODGETTS, Tim
Weightman Vizards, Birmingham
(0121) 233 2601

HOLMES, John
Hempsons, London
(020) 7839 0278
j.holmes@hempsons.co.uk
Specialisation: Partner in healthcare litigation department. Principal area of practice is medical negligence acting for health service bodies in defence claims. Also gives general advice in clinical issues and mental health (including human rights). Reported claims include Sion v Hampstead Health Authority, Clunis v Camden & Islington Health Authority, R v Bournewood NHS Trust and D v NHS Trust. The Firm is on the panel for the NHS Litigation Authority (NHSLA).
Prof. Memberships: Law Society.
Career: Qualified in 1984. Joined *Beachcroft Stanleys* in 1986 and became a Partner in 1992. Joined Hempsons in 2001.
Personal: Educated at Bristol University 1978-81.

THE LEADERS ■ CLINICAL NEGLIGENCE

HOOPER, John
Wynne Baxter, Brighton
(01273) 775533
jhooper@wynnebaxter.com
Specialisation: Senior partner and leading member of Clinical Negligence Department at the firm's Head Office in Brighton. Wynne Baxter was among the first in the country to receive a Legal Aid Franchise in Clinical Negligence, recognition of their undoubted expertise and professionalism in the field. With more than 20 years' clinical negligence experience, he has recovered millions of pounds' compensation for clients who have suffered injury in all fields including obstetrics and gynaecology, having particular experience in brain damage cases. Represented the Claimant in the landmark case of Cassel v Riverside HA.
Prof. Memberships: Law Society Clinical Negligence and Children Panels; AVMA Referral Panel.
Career: Admitted 1962; Partner in Selwood Leathes Hooper 1963-97 merged with Wynne Baxter in 1997.
Personal: Educated Worthing High School; London University Law Degree.

JOHN, Simon
Cunningham John, Thetford
(01842) 752401
Specialisation: Main area of practice is catastrophic injuries. Leads a team of 19 PI/clinical negligence (CN) lawyers and paralegals. Has particular expertise in head, spinal injuries and CN. Notable and landmark cases: Farrant v Thanet DC (diving/tidal pool); Webb (a child) v Darbon (1st Judgement for identifying 30mph too fast); Edwards v Ogg (largest CN award for child £3.9 million); Mullings v Norfolk CC (Judgement for Councils failure to grit); first NHS mediation; first structured settlement in East Anglia; first order for evidence by satellite link; largest award for amputee; many awards in excess of £1 million. Experience in litigation in Canada and many US states. Recent awards: £3.5 million CN and £2.5 million brain injury. Lectures widely.
Prof. Memberships: AVMA, Headway and SIA Solicitor panels; Law Society CN and PI panels; sustaining member of ATLA (Brain and Birth Litigation groups); Richard Grand Society; APIL (Co-ordinator Clinical Negligence SIG); UKABIF Treasurer. Fellow of the Society for Advanced Legal Studies; European Brain Injury Society.
Career: Qualified 1969, partner 1971, formed Cunningham John 1973.
Publications: Editor of BPILS chapter 'PI Litigation in the USA'. Author of papers: 'Split Trial'; 'Plaintiff's Offer to Settle - resulting in PART 36 CPR. Editor of 'ATLA Intnl Newsletter'

JONES, David
Morgan Jones & Pett, Great Yarmouth
(01493) 334700
david.jones@m-j-p.co.uk
Specialisation: Clinical negligence since 1981. Member of Law Society Clinical Negligence Panel since 1995. Special interest in cerebral palsy cases, most recent settlement £2.3 million. Founder member of Norfolk & Norwich Medico-Legal Society.
Prof. Memberships: APIL, AVMA, Law Society Clinical Negligence and Personal Injury Panels.
Career: Qualified in 1981, became Partner in 1984 and Senior Partner in 1997.

JONES, Eddie
Jones Maidment Wilson, Manchester
(0161) 828 1934
eddiej@jmw.co.uk
Specialisation: Partner in clinical negligence department specialising in claimant clinical negligence and mental health law. Deals with all aspects of clinical negligence litigation with a particular interest in psychiatric negligence. Co-ordinated the Maden litigation group action on behalf of patients indecently assaulted by their psychiatrist.
Prof. Memberships: Referral Panel Solicitor for Action for Victims of Medical Accidents, Member of the Law Society Clinical Negligence panel and Mental Health Review Tribunal Panel. Member of Association of Personal Injury Lawyers. Member of a local NHS Trusts Clinical Ethics Committee.
Career: Qualified 1992. Previously with Hempsons. Joined Jones Maidment Wilson in 1998; Partner from 1999.
Publications: Publications include 'Violence from Patients in the Community: Will the Courts Impose a Duty of Care on Mental Health Professionals,' with M Kennedy in 'Criminal Behaviour and Mental Health' 5 1995.

JONES, Stephen
Pannone & Partners, Manchester
(0161) 909 3000
stephen.jones@pannone.co.uk
Specialisation: Partner in clinical negligence department. Specialised in clinical negligence work since qualification. Also covers mental health and has a specific interest in psychiatric negligence, represented patients at Ashworth Hospital in the Fallon Inquiry which reported in January 1999. In August 1999 represented VC, a 16 year old anorexic in proceedings brought by local Trust to force feed. In February 2000 appointed solicitor to the Royal Liverpool Children's Inquiry into the retention of organs following postmortems at Alder Hey Hospital which reported in January 2001. Previously a member of Birmingham Royal Orthopaedic Hospital Cancer Cases Co-ordinating Committee. Presently acting for Denise Hendry, wife of former Scotland football captain Colin Hendry and for the family of England footballer Robbie Fowler. Biggest settlements: £3.4m for seven year old with cerebral palsy (2002), £3.25m for 19 year old with cerebral palsy (1999).
Prof. Memberships: Member of Law Society Clinical Negligence Panel, AVMA Solicitors Referral Panel, MIND Legal Network.
Career: Joined Pannone & Partners in 1984, qualified in 1986 and became a partner in 1992.
Personal: Educated at Manchester Grammar School and Queens College, Cambridge. Leisure interests include football.

KEEBLE, Jeffrey
Ward Hadaway, Newcastle upon Tyne
(0191) 204 4312
jeffrey.keeble@wardhadaway.com
Specialisation: Head of litigation department and healthcare unit. Nominated partner to NHS Litigation Authority. Specialist in all aspects of health law including injuries of utmost severity. Regular lecturer in medico-legal topics and clinical risk management. Major clients include Newcastle upon Tyne Hospitals NHS Trust and North Durham Healthcare NHS Trust.
Prof. Memberships: Law Society; Medico-Legal Society.
Career: Qualified in London in 1978. Joined Ward Hadaway in 1991 and became partner specialising in health law in 1993.
Personal: Born 24 June 1954 in Hackney. Attended Hackney Downs Grammar School and Leeds University. Enjoys rugby union, cricket and exotic holidays. Lives in Tyne Valley.

KERRY, David G
Attwater & Liell, Harlow
(01279) 638823
david.kerry@attwaterliell.co.uk
Specialisation: All areas of clinical negligence including cerebral palsy, deaths in hospitals, failure to diagnose. Dealt with the leading case of Wilsher v Essex Area Health Authority. Now spends all his time dealing with clinical negligence cases.
Prof. Memberships: Member of Law Society and AVMA Clinical Negligence Panels. Fellow of the College of Personal Injury Law, member of the Legal Services Commission's Funding Review Panel.
Career: Qualified as a solicitor in 1979, becoming a Partner in Attwater & Liell in 1981. Since then has dealt with clinical negligence claims. Also lectures to other solicitors on clinical negligence for the College of Personal Injury Law.
Publications: Occasional articles and case reports in Clinical Risk and other professional publications.
Personal: LLB (Hons) London University. Married with three sons. Increasing interest in keeping fit and sailing.

KITCHINGMAN, John
Pannone & Partners, Manchester
(0161) 909 3000
john.kitchingman@pannone.co.uk
Specialisation: Partner in Clinical Negligence Department. Head of department dealing with all aspects of medical law and claims for clinical negligence with emphasis on cases of maximum severity.
Prof. Memberships: Law Society Medical Negligence panel, AVMA referral panel, APIL Medical Negligence Special Interest Group, ATLA, Justice.
Career: Qualified in 1975, became partner in Pannone & Partners 1978.
Personal: Fellow of RSA. Leisure pursuits include walking, birdwatching, and travel. Lives in Altrincham.

LEE, Terry
Evill and Coleman, London
(020) 8789 9221
Terry.Lee@evillandcoleman.co.uk
See under Personal Injury, p.634

LEIGH, Bertie
Hempsons, London
(020) 7839 0278
mamsl@hempsons.co.uk
See under Healthcare, p.408

LEVY, Russell
Leigh, Day & Co, London
(020) 7650 1200
russ@leighday.co.uk
Specialisation: Joint head of clinical negligence department. Principal area of practice is claimant clinical negligence and medical devices (product liability) litigation. Is a regular commentator on clinical negligence and related topics.
Prof. Memberships: AVMA. Secretary and then Co-ordinator of APIL Medical Negligence Special Interest Group 1992-96. Member of APIL Executive Committee 1996-99. Member Lord Chancellor's Departments Medical Negligence Working Party and Minors' Funds Working Group, Council member of Campaign for Freedom of Information, member Steering Group UK Collaborative Network of Cerebral Palsy Registers. ATLA.
Career: Qualified 1984. Joined Leigh Day & Co as a partner in 1991.
Personal: Born 15 March 1956.

LEWIN, Olive
Leigh, Day & Co, London
(020) 7650 1200
Specialisation: Partner in the clinical negligence department. Handles mainly clinical negligence cases involving severe injury and death. Also handles a multi-party product liability claim. Has advised the British Cardiology Society on Human Rights for the 5th UK cardiology review.
Prof. Memberships: AVMA, Liberty, APIL.
Career: Qualified as a registered General Nurse (RGN) in 1982. Qualified as a solicitor in 1990.
Personal: Enjoys travel, films, food, wine, and reading.

LOVEL, John
Hempsons, Harrogate
(01423) 522331
wjml@hempsons.co.uk
Specialisation: Medical negligence. National Health Service law. Project leader (Northern and Yorkshire) Department of Health, clinical negligence mediation pilot.
Prof. Memberships: Law Society.
Career: Shrewsbury School; University College London - LLB Hons 1971; CEDR accredited mediator 1996.

CLINICAL NEGLIGENCE ■ THE LEADERS

Trained at *Sintons*; qualified 1974; partner at *Maughan & Hall* 1975; solicitor with Yorkshire Regional Health Authority 1976; legal advisor to Yorkshire Regional Health Authority 1989; head of Yorkshire Health Legal Services 1990; partner *Hempsons* 1996.
Personal: Squash, cycling, skiing.

MARTINEZ, Liz
Evill and Coleman, London
(020) 8789 9221
liz.martinez@evillandcoleman.co.uk
Specialisation: Partner. Specialist in clinical negligence. Mediator. Interests include anaesthetic brain damage, cerebral palsy and birth trauma, obstetrics, gynaecology, cardiology, general surgery and fatal cases. Recent cases include Webster v Hammersmith Hospital NHS Trust 2002.
Prof. Memberships: APIL, Law Society Personal Injury panel. CEDR Accredited Mediator.
Career: Qualified 1990. *Osborne Morris & Morgan* 1988-93 (partner from 1991). Yorkshire Health Legal Services 1993-94. *Evill and Coleman* 1994 (partner from 1995).

MASON, David
Capsticks, London
(020) 8780 4701
dmason@capsticks.co.uk
Specialisation: Now concentrating on healthcare litigation and advisory work specialising in public law, mental health and inquiries after many years of mainly defending clinical negligence claims. Recent cases include acting as advocate for all four NHS bodies involved in the Victoria Climbie Inquiry; successfully defending two different judicial reviews arising as advocate in a successful benefits appeal tribunal following the withdrawal of benefits from 80 residents in a learning disability scheme: the successful appeal saved the NHS £1.7 million per annum. Was the only defence lawyer on Lord Woolf's Steering Group for Medical Negligence and was the defence Solicitor on the Clinical Disputes Forum from 1996-2001. Also lectures to senior health service managers and clinicians and appears on radio and television on a variety of medico-legal topics. He is Honorary Legal Advisor to the College of Health.
Career: Called to the Bar 1984. Employed barrister with *Thomas Watts & Co* 1986-88. Joined *Capsticks* in 1988 as employed Barrister. Requalified as Solicitor and became a Partner in 1990. Elected Fellow of the Society for Advanced Legal Studies 1998.
Publications: Co-author of 'Litigation - A risk management guide for midwives', published by the Royal College of Midwives. He was also co-author of the Clinical Disputes forum 'Pre-Action Protocol for the Resolution of Clinical Disputes' and the CDF 'Guidelines on experts' discussions in the context of clinical disputes'.
Personal: Born 1955. Attended Winchester College 1969-73, then Oriel College, Oxford 1974-77 (MA in experimental psychology). Dip L (City University) 1983. Lives in Wimbledon.

MAUGHAN, Peter J
Peter Maughan & Co, Gateshead
(0191) 477 9779
mailroom@gatlaw.demon.co.uk
Specialisation: Claimant medical negligence and personal injury claims. Visiting lecturer in nursing law to the University of Northumbria at Newcastle.
Prof. Memberships: FCIArb, FSALS, ADR Group, ATLA, APIL, APLA, AVMA.
Career: Principal and senior partner of *Peter Maughan & Co* since 1981. Arbitrator and Mediator.
Personal: Liberal Democrat Councillor and Parliamentary and Euro-Parliamentary Candidate. Rotarian. RSPCA Chairman Newcastle. Married, three sons. Highlands of Scotland - history and language.

MCCLURE, Alison
Blake Lapthorn, Portsmouth
(023) 9222 1122

MCGRATH, Matthew
Beachcroft Wansbroughs, Winchester
(01962) 705500
mmcgrath@bwlaw.co.uk
Specialisation: Partner specialising in all aspects of clinical negligence and Health Service Law. Is the firm's liaison partner to the NHSLA. Regularly advises clients on issues of consent, confidentiality and access to records. Lectures on risk management issues to clinicians as well as advising on clinical governance. Deals with high-value obstetric claims. Has obtained Court orders for emergency treatment and is responsible for quality of service of the clinical negligence department in the office. Sits on the Sub-committees of the Clinical Disputes Forum dealing with mediation and delays in litigation. Previously had wide experience in insurance litigation before joining the firm both in England and Australia.

MCNEIL, Paul
Field Fisher Waterhouse, London
(020) 7861 4000
Specialisation: Partner in the Medical Litigation Department of *Field Fisher Waterhouse* specialising in Clinical Negligence, Personal Injury and Product Liability, acting mainly for claimants. Has particular experience in cases involving head and other serious injuries. Publications include 'International Product Liability' (1993) co-author and 'The Medical Accidents Handbook' (1998) co-editor and contributor. Also lectures on various aspects of medical law.
Prof. Memberships: Law Society Medical Negligence Panel; Association of Personal Injury Lawyers; AVMA; Fellow Society for Advanced Legal Studies.
Career: Qualified 1983. *Field Fisher Waterhouse* 1992. Partner since 1994.
Personal: Educated at All Saints' Comprehensive, Huddersfield 1975-77 and Sheffield University 1977-80. Leisure pursuits include tennis, running and skiing. Born 26 July 1958. Lives in Putney, London.

MINTER, Melanie
Wynne Baxter, Brighton
(01273) 775533
mminter@wynnebaxter.com
Specialisation: Clinical negligence claims on behalf of Claimants. Experience in claims involving all types of injury. Interests include cardiac surgery, cardiology, severe injury claims, brain damage, cervical cancer and breast cancer, obstetrics and gynaecology, fatal cases, claims for children. Acts for publicly funded and private clients. Involved in Trilucent breast implant litigation.
Prof. Memberships: APIL, Law Society Clinical Negligence Panel.
Career: 1984 qualified as RGN at St Bartholomew's Hospital. Qualified in 1990. Assistant Solicitor at *Norton Rose* 1990-92. Moved to *Capsticks* in 1992 and became a Partner in 1994. Joined *Wynne Baxter* in 1999. Appointed Partner in 2002.
Personal: Born 3 September 1962. LLB University of Wales 1987.

MONTGOMERY, Nigel
Beachcroft Wansbroughs, Bristol
(0117) 918 2321
nmontgomery@bwlaw.co.uk
Specialisation: Partner and head of clinical negligence litigation in Bristol. Specialises in Defendant clinical negligence and legal issues arising from the day to day provision of health care. Joined the Bristol office in May 1999 to lead its growing Health team. Has 17 years experience of medico-legal advisory and litigation work. In addition to dealing with medico legal claims of the utmost complexity, has substantial experience in defending group actions and specialises in obstetric, renal and neurology claims. Is a regular contributor to health publications and lectures widely at conferences on medico legal issues.
Career: Qualified 1985; partner, *Lyons Davidson* 1990-99, joined *Beachcroft Wansbroughs* May 1999.

MOWAT, Allan
Hill Dickinson, Liverpool
(0151) 236 5400
See under Healthcare, p.408

MUSGRAVE, Tim
Huttons, Cardiff
(029) 2037 8621

OSBORNE, Tom
Osborne Morris & Morgan, Leighton Buzzard
(01525) 378177

OVER, Christopher
Over Taylor Biggs, Exeter
(01392) 823811

PARFORD, Simon
Wolferstans, Plymouth
(01752) 663295
sparford@wolferstans.com
Specialisation: Partner and Head of the Clinical Negligence Department. Acts exclusively for claimants in clinical negligence claims with a specialist interest in claims involving head and brain injury, in particular those involving injuries sustained at birth.
Prof. Memberships: Law Society Clinical Negligence Panel Assessor. Law Society Clinical Negligence Panel. AVMA Referral Panel. APIL.
Career: Qualified with *Wolferstans* in 1983 and became a partner in 1988.
Personal: Born 12 November 1958. Educated Plymouth College and Birmingham Polytechnic. Leisure pursuits include rugby (watching), tennis and photography.

PICKERING, John
Irwin Mitchell, Sheffield
(0114) 276 7777
pickeringj@irwinmitchell.co.uk
Specialisation: Partner and Head of Personal Injury Department with specialist interest in clinical negligence, product liability, catastrophic injury cases and cases with an international element. Currently involved in the Hatfield and Selby train crash cases; dealt with the two cerebral palsy cases involved in the Heil v Rankin landmark judgment in the Court of Appeal, namely Warren (£3.1m damages) and Annable. Subsequent separate Court of Appeal hearing on Warren dealt with the question of multiplier; Van Oudenhoven v Griffen Inns Ltd (£950,000 damages for head injury as a result of pub blackboard accident); Hodgson & others v Imperial Tobacco Ltd & Gallaher & Hergall (acting on behalf of smoking-related lung cancer victims against major UK tobacco manufacturers – case included a Court of Appeal decision on Conditional Fee agreements); Ward v Newalls Insulations and Cape Contractors (the then highest damages award in this country of £750,000 for an asbestos disease case); Thomas v Cgarkes (head injury sustained abroad; damages of £750,0000 a record award for the Canary Islands); Bird v Hussain (a record award for chronic pain suffered as a result of a road traffic accident). Important cases include Hepworth v Kerr (medical negligence case in which a patient suffered paralysis after a routine ear operation); other actions include acting in test cases for industrial deafness and Vibration White Finger, the latter leading to *Irwin Mitchell's* involvement in the VWF Solicitors Steering Group and the subsequent £500m settlement scheme with Bristol Coal.
Prof. Memberships: Claimant Solicitors Representative on the Clinical Disputes Forum. Member of and Assessor for the Law Society's Personal Injury Panel. Member of The Law Society's Medical

THE LEADERS — CLINICAL NEGLIGENCE

Negligence Panel and the AVMA Medical Negligence Panel. Former Executive Committee Member and a Secretary of APIL. Member of The Board of Governors of The Association of Trial Lawyers of America (ATLA). Past co-chair of International Practice Section and Member of the Board of the Birth Trauma Litigation Group, England and Wales Representative of the Pan European Organisation of Personal Injury Lawyers (PEOPIL).
Career: Articled *Irwin Mitchell*; qualified 1979; Partner 1980; National Head of Personal Injury Department of *Irwin Mitchell* and Member of the Management Board.
Publications: Co-author of the Clinical Negligence Pre-Litigation Protocol. Regularly lectures in the UK and abroad on the subjects of Medical Negligence and Personal Injury. Co-author of Jordan's Civil Court Service and contributor to Clinical Negligence in General Practice.
Personal: Born 1955, resides Sheffield. Married with two children. Interests include theatre, squash, golf and motor racing.

ROHDE, Kate
Kingsley Napley, London
(020) 7814 1200
krohde@kingsleynapley.co.uk
Specialisation: Majority of practice is medical negligence and clinical negligence litigation on behalf of plaintiffs. Experienced in claims involving all types of injury. Particular interest in obstetric claims and claims on behalf of children.
Prof. Memberships: AVMA, APIL.
Career: Qualified in 1989. With *Compton Carr* 1987 to December 1995, as a partner from 1993. Joined *Teacher Stern Selby* as partner in 1996. Moved to *Kingsley Napley* as a partner in March 1997.
Personal: Born 3 November 1963, educated at University College London, lives in London.

ROSSER, Mari
Hugh James, Merthyr Tydfil
(01685) 371 122
Specialisation: Acts for claimants in all types of medical accidents with special interest in claims of maximum severity, brain, spinal, obstetrics and paediatric injury as well as fatal accident cases.
Prof. Memberships: AVMA, APIL member of the Law Society's Clinical Negligence Panel and member of the AVMA Solicitors Referral Panel, Member of the Legal Services Commission Appeals Committee.
Career: Qualified 1991. *Edwards Geldard* to 2001. *Hugh James* – Partner May 2001.
Personal: Born 6 June 1966. University College of Wales Aberystwyth 1986-89. Lives in Cardiff.

SCATES, Olivia
Jones Maidment Wilson, Manchester
(0161) 832 8087
olivias@jmw.co.uk
Specialisation: Partner and Head of Clinical Negligence Department. Firm has had a clinical negligence franchise since its introduction in February 1999. Wide experience of advising in all types of clinical negligence litigation for claimants, including cases of maximum severity. Recent settlements include cases of cerebral palsy, spinal injuries, anaesthetic awareness, orthopaedic injuries and several cases of delay in diagnosis of cancer as well as gynaecological cases.
Prof. Memberships: Referral Panel Solicitor for Action for Victims of Medical Accidents and The Spinal Injuries Association. Member of Law Society Negligence Panel, Member of Association for Personal Injury Lawyers (special interest groups: clinical negligence and spinal injuries). Legal Services Commission Funding Committee Member.
Career: Qualified 1989. Partner 1993.

SCRIVENGER, Mark
Scrivenger Seabrook, St Neots
(01480) 225700
markscrivenger@sslaw.co.uk
Specialisation: Founding partner specialising in medical negligence. Firm was founded to act in clinical negligence and personal injury cases. Individual specialism was defendant medical negligence but now claimant clinical negligence. Acted in Royal College of Nursing v DHSS.
Career: Qualified LLB, Melb (1967) Barrister and Solicitor Supreme Court of Victoria 1968 and High Court of Australia 1976. Qualified in England and Wales 1977. Principal solicitor, Royal College of Nursing 1977-87. Founded *Scrivenger Seabrook* in 1988.

SEABROOK, Vicki
Scrivenger Seabrook, St Neots
(01480) 225701
vickiseabrook@sslaw.co.uk
Specialisation: Founding partner in litigation firm. Has specialised in personal injury since qualification. Later expanded into defendant medical negligence but now acts on behalf of claimants in clinical negligence. Acted in Davis v Barking Havering and Brentwood Health Authority. Member of Law Society Clinical Negligence Panel.
Career: Qualified in 1979. At the Royal College of Nursing 1979-85, *Merriman & White* 1985-86, *Beachcroft Stanley* 1986-88 and *Le Brasseurs* 1988-89 before establishing *Scrivenger Seabrook*.
Personal: Educated at Barnet College 1970-72 and Central London Polytechnic 1973-76 (LLB Hons).

SHEATH, John
Brachers, Maidstone
(01622) 680 401
johnsheath@brachers.co.uk
Specialisation: Deals principally with clinical negligence and health service law. Has had the conduct of successful defence in many high profile decisions including Dobbie v Medway Health Authority, PVS and mental health consent cases.
Prof. Memberships: Chairman of the West Kent and East Kent GP Performance Review Panels.
Career: Educated at Sir Joseph Williamson's Mathematical School, Rochester. 1963-69. Southampton University 1970-73. *Norton, Rose, Botterell & Roche* 1974-81. Joined *Brachers* in 1981. Partner 1983. Head of the firms Healthcare Team. Firm appointed to NHSLA panel in April 1998, re-appointed April 2001. Head of Litigation Department. Regularly lectures on selected health topics and tutor in Advanced Litigation Practice Diploma. Accredited mediator with ADR Group.

SMITH, Janice
Capsticks, London
(020) 8780 2211
Specialisation: Partner in clinical law department specialising in clinical negligence claims with a particular interest in cases involving obstetrics, orthopaedics and A&E, also deals with a variety of NHS advisory matters. Co-ordinates *Capsticks*' clinical governance programme including running training for Trust Boards. Advises Trusts on their risk management arrangements, particularly helping to identify high risk specialities and develop incident reporting schemes. Regular lecturer on *Capsticks*' Diploma in Risk Management and also lectures on various aspects of medical law.
Prof. Memberships: Law Society and its committees concerning issues of clinical negligence.
Career: Qualified in 1985. Assistant Solicitor with *Herbert Smith* 1985-86. Assistant solicitor at *Beckman & Beckman* 1987-90. Joined *Capsticks* in 1990 and became a partner in 1991, member of Firm's Management Committee.
Personal: Born 24 March 1960. Attended Tunbridge Wells Grammar School for Girls 1971-78, then Leeds University 1978-81 before taking a year out to work for the Boys Brigade. Vice President of London District Boys' Brigade and Director of Oasis Trust. Lives in Bicester.

SOLLY, Gillian
Russell Jones & Walker, Bristol
(0117) 927 3098
g.c.solly@rjw.co.uk
See under Personal Injury, p.636

SPEKER, Barry
Samuel Phillips & Co,
Newcastle upon Tyne
(0191) 232 8451
barryspeker@samuelphillips.co.uk
See under Family, p.155

SWANTON, Vicki
Berrymans Lace Mawer, London
(020) 7865 3378
Specialisation: Senior Assistant in the Clinical Negligence Department. Taking on negligence work for the MPS, insurers and disciplinary actions.
Career: Qualified in 1994, moved from *Browne Jacobson* (Birmingham) to *Berrymans Lace Mawer* in July 2002.

THOMAS, Keith
John Collins & Partners, Swansea
(01792) 773773

TYLER, Alfred
Balfour & Manson, Edinburgh
(0131) 200 1210
fred.tyler@balfour-manson.co.uk
See under Personal Injury, p.637

VALLANCE, Richard
Charles Russell, London
(020) 7203 5000
richardv@cr-law.co.uk
Specialisation: Partner in Litigation Department. Acted for claimants in the leading cases of Naylor v Preston Area Health Authority, 1987 2 All ER 353 and Thomas v Brighton HA 1998 3 All ER 481. Has lectured on medical negligence to lawyers, doctors and nurses since 1984. Contributed to Powers and Harris's 'Clinical Negligence' (Butterworths) and has written numerous articles.
Prof. Memberships: Assessor of Law Society Clinical Negligence Specialist Panel, Member of AVMA Specialist Panel, Mediator in Court of Appeal, Member of the Medico-Legal Society.
Career: Qualified in 1970. Partner in *Compton Carr* 1972 and, following merger, in *Charles Russell* 1996.
Personal: Born 1947. Squash, gardening and theatre. Lives near Saffron Walden.

VICK, Laurence
Michelmores, Exeter
(01392) 436244
lnv@michelmores.com
Specialisation: Partner/Head of Clinical Negligence Department. Claimant. Specialisms: paediatric/adult cardiac surgery, birth injuries - cerebral & Erb's palsy, gynaecology, spinal and plastic/cosmetic surgery, neurological injury. Lead solicitor to Bristol Heart Children Action Group at Bristol Royal Infirmary Public Inquiry, also handling related fatal and brain damage claims with significant PTSD, consent, exemplary/aggravated damages, 'corporate failure', increased risk issues. Legal Advisor to Constructive Dialogue for Clinical Accountability.
Prof. Memberships: AVMA referral panel, member and assessor Law Society's Clinical Negligence Panel, ATLA, APIL, Associate of Chartered Insurance Institute and Chartered Insurance Practitioner.
Career: Qualified 1981. Joined *Michelmores* 1999.
Personal: Born 14 December 1952. Attended King Edward VI Camp Hill, Birmingham and Lanchester Polytechnic. Married - 4 children. Lives Sidmouth.

VOISIN, Maria
Bond Pearce, Plymouth
(01752) 266633

CLINICAL NEGLIGENCE ■ THE LEADERS

WARD, Trevor
Linder Myers, Manchester
(0161) 837 6806
trevor.ward@lindermyers.co.uk
Specialisation: Obstetrics; oncology; general surgery: Jones v Central Manchester HA: CP - 2.15M (190 PSL2A). Involved in MoD Group action cases re failure to diagnose and treat.
Prof. Memberships: AVMA, APIL, Law Society, ATLA, Greystoke.
Career: 1984 - *Linder Myers*, Manchester. Predominantly claimant clinical negligence and personal injury.
Publications: Book chapter – 'Funding of Claimant Injury Claims' – published 2000.
Personal: Manchester Metropolitan University 1981 (Maxwell Law Prize) Qualified October 1986. Married with two daughters. Interests include shooting. Lives in Adlington, Macclesfield.

WATSON, Andrew
Thomson Snell & Passmore, Tunbridge Wells
(01892) 510000
awatson@ts-p.co.uk
Specialisation: Partner and head of clinical negligence department. Deals exclusively with clinical negligence claims. Special areas of expertise are head and spinal injuries. Acted in Dobbie v Medway Health Authority, Bova v Spring, Harris v Bromley Health Authority and Taylor v West Kent Health Authority.
Prof. Memberships: APIL.
Career: Qualified in 1975, having joined *Thomson Snell & Passmore* in 1973. Became a partner in 1981. Panel solicitor for AVMA. Member of the Law Society's Clinical Negligence Panel.
Personal: Born 29 March 1950. Educated at Oxford (MA 1st Class Honours) 1968-71. Recreations include literature, music, running and cuisine. Lives in Tunbridge Wells.

WEATHERBURN, David
Eversheds, Newcastle upon Tyne
(0191) 241 6040
davidweatherburn@eversheds.com
Specialisation: Clinical negligence defence and major trauma work for insurers.
Career: Articled *Ingledew Boterell*; qualified 1987; partner *Eversheds* 1996.
Personal: Born 1962. Family, rugby, Morpeth RFC.

WICKS, Roger
Gadsby Wicks, Chelmsford
(01245) 494929
rrw@gadsbywicks.co.uk
Specialisation: Since the early 1980s he has specialised increasingly in clinical negligence and medical product liability litigation solely on behalf of claimants. He was Chief Assessor of the Law Society's Clinical Negligence Panel from 1994 to 2000. He has lectured extensively to lawyers on civil litigation and clinical negligence issues, and has contributed to numerous legal and other publications.
Prof. Memberships: Law Society; Association of Personal Injury Lawyers; Association of Trial Lawyers of America. Fellow of the Royal Society of Medicine.
Career: Founding partner of *Gadsby Wicks* in 1993.

WINYARD, Anne
Leigh, Day & Co, London
(020) 7650 1200
Specialisation: Partner and specialist in clinical negligence. Acts for claimants. Cases mainly involve serious disablities or death, including both adults and children who have suffered brain damage as a result of medical treatment. Publications include chapters in both 'Medical Negligence' (Powers & Harris) and 'Safe Practice in Obstetrics and Gynaecology' (Clements). Regular speaker at medico-legal conferences and seminars.
Prof. Memberships: AVMA, APIL, ATLA.
Career: Qualified 1977. Partner, *Fisher Meredith* 1983-92. Joined *Leigh Day & Co* as partner in 1992.

YOUNG, Magi
Parlett Kent, Exeter
(01392) 494455
myoung@exeter.parlettkent.co.uk
Specialisation: Clinical Negligence Specialist with particular expertise in cases of maximum severity (eg recent awards in excess of £2 million). Specialises in acting for children injured at or around birth (eg cerebral palsy and Erbs Palsy), for people injured as a result of psychiatric negligence, handles brain injury and spinal injury cases and has particular expertise in obstetric and gynaecology cases and cancer cases. Acts for many people with learning difficulties and has an interest in education and community care provision. Has particular specialism in cases of sexual abuse of patients by health care workers. Also handles personal injury claims including claims against local authorities. Interested in issues of accountability and regularly trains nurses, social workers, doctors and clinical risk managers and lawyers. Also interested in psychological effects of litigation. Undertook research on 'Why patients sue doctors' (Lancet 1994) and has trained solicitors on dealing with distressed clients. Acts for clients nationwide particularly in the South East and South West of England and heads *Parlett Kent*'s Exeter office.
Prof. Memberships: AVMA referral solicitor, member of and assessor for Law Society Medical Negligence Panel. ATLA.
Career: Qualified in 1987 with *Pannone Napier* and *Pannone Blackburn* from 1987-92. Partner from 1991. Joined *Parlett Kent* in 1992 and became a partner in 1993.
Personal: Born 8 December 1960. Bristol University (B.Soc. Sci. 1982).

COMMODITIES

London (Physicals): 157; London (Futures): 159; Profiles: 160

Research approved by BMRB For this edition, **Chambers'** researchers conducted 6,582 interviews – 3,900 with law firms, 511 with barristers and 2,171 with clients. The validity of the research was scrutinised by BMRB International, who audited both the methodology and the results at our offices in London. They interviewed **Chambers'** researchers and cross-checked sample interviews. Details of the audit appear on page 7.

OVERVIEW The commodities sector continues to consolidate, with this year seeing the collapse of Andre & Cie and the takeover by Cargill International of Continental Grain Company, while soft commodities' prices – notably cotton, coffee and some metals – remain depressed. Big disputes have traditionally been driven by market price, but sophisticated clients are increasingly hedging their margins to restrict potential losses. Lawyers are looking instead to the frontier areas, particularly the CIS, where the disbanding of governmental and quasi-governmental trade organisations has spawned a raft of new trading houses, which frequently lack sophisticated risk-management techniques. Energy trading is expanding with the liberalisation of the European markets. In terms of value it now dwarfs the traditional physical commodities. It has attracted a different type of firm – principally those with strong energy and finance capabilities rather than a shipping background. It would heavily distort the tables to include these firms; therefore, we have excluded energy trading from this section. Some, like Ince & Co, will have strength in oil and gas trading, but they also have traditional commodities strength. Energy trading will be dealt with, for the time being, within our Energy section. Those firms with a strong name for it – for example, Denton Wilde Sapte, Herbert Smith, Allen & Overy, Linklaters, Lovells and Slaughter and May – are covered there. Commodity futures remains a small, highly specialised area, with the tendency of practitioners to work across financial services and derivatives making it hard to categorise. Commentators warn that commodity derivatives are being sucked into the regulatory framework – notably by the Investment Services Directive – with implications for the cost base.

PHYSICALS

COMMODITIES: PHYSICALS
LONDON

1. Richards Butler
2. Middleton Potts
3. Hill Taylor Dickinson
4. Clifford Chance
   Clyde & Co
   Holman Fenwick & Willan
   Ince & Co
5. Holmes Hardingham
   RD Black & Co
   Stephenson Harwood
   Thomas Cooper & Stibbard

RICHARDS BUTLER (see firm details p.1112) Experience, resources and a great client base have contributed to the perception amongst competitors that "*Richards Butler now has to be the number one in this area.*" Traditionally one of the leading commodities specialists, rivals attribute its premier position to the strength of its team: "*in terms of the overall size and calibre of the partner core, it leads the field.*" Clients, meanwhile, appreciate the quality service: "*its lawyers are reasonably priced, knowledgeable and listen to us.*" At the pinnacle of the profession is **David Pullen** (see p.161). One of the great names of the sector, "*with a wealth of knowledge and a positive, unequivocal style,*" clients agree: "*he doesn't talk in code.*" Beneath him, "*commercial and dynamic*" **Richard Swinburn** (see p.161) is "*plainly the leader in waiting,*" while **Diane Galloway** (see p.160) is "*intellectually sharp and a tough litigator,*" who is well known for her work with Glencore. **Kyri Evagora** (see p.160) is "*an energetic, 'gunning for it' lawyer,*" building an enviable reputation. John Emmott has left to become consultant to the firm in Kazakhstan. The firm is seeing its workload diversify, with more trade finance disputes, credit risks, confiscations and misappropriations. Traditional trade arbitrations still form the bulk of its work, and, like many firms, it is involved in unwinding the fallout from Enron. It recently represented Tradigrain in Tradigrain SA v SIAT SpA and Others, a complex, multi-jurisdictional case against 30 insurers involving the theft of commodities in India. **Clients** Glencore International; Tradigrain; Louis Dreyfus Trading.

MIDDLETON POTTS (see firm details p.1069) In the view of one barrister this is "*a cracking good outfit covering the gamut of foodstuffs.*" It enjoys a long tradition at the top of the commodities world and "*enjoys a pretty good share of the traditional market*" which it carves up with Richards Butler. Since stepping down as senior partner, **Christopher Potts** (see p.161) has been busy fee-earning. One of the grand old men of the sector, he is "*hugely experienced and knowledgeable*" and, according to sources, has a "*feel for trading as well as being a good lawyer.*" The firm's younger lawyers, like **Petra Leseberg** (see p.161), have inherited this trait: "*They are thorough, you don't read nonsense in their submissions and they understand how the trade operates.*" The department's leading figure is "*shrewd and effective operator*" **David Lucas** (see p.161), the new senior partner and, in the opinion of some, "*one of the best commodities lawyers around.*"
The team frequently appears in the Commercial Court and before numerous trade arbitration tribunals. While classic GAFTA work may currently be down, other commodities are busy providing instruction, especially cotton. Middle Eastern clients have been especially active and, as with many firms, trade finance is an expanding area. The firm has recently represented a Far Eastern trading house in two high-profile GAFTA cases, one of which has gone on to the High Court. **Clients** Several leading commodities houses; trade finance banks; traders and insurers.

HILL TAYLOR DICKINSON (see firm details p.996) Like Middleton Potts, the market considers this "*a traditional physical dispute resolution firm*" with strength in soft commodities. However, some rivals believe that its "*younger, more energetic*" approach is allowing it to pull away from the chasing pack: "*It's made a lot of headway and picked new clients.*" Its standout practitioner is "*intelligent, effective and personable*" **Jeff Isaacs** (see p.160), who is well known for advising the two sugar associations, while the recruitment in 2000 of "*tenacious*" **Brian Perrott** (see p.161), with his "*coalface experience at Cargill,*" is felt to have benefited the firm. A growing team, it is visible advising trade association arbitrators as well as appearing as counsel. Its work is expanding towards the futures side, and it is increasingly involved earlier in the contractual process, health-checking contracts. Over the last year the department has been busy in disputes arising from the Enron collapse, including freight forward agreements with Enron and the disputed ownership of cargoes at sea. **Clients** International commodities houses.

CLIFFORD CHANCE (see firm details p.911) The corporate and finance giant enjoys a unique position in this sector as it is by far the largest firm with a genuine, top-flight commodities practice. Market opinion pointed to

www.ChambersandPartners.com 157

COMMODITIES ■ LONDON

LEADING INDIVIDUALS

[★]
- **PULLEN David** Richards Butler

[1]
- **GALLOWAY Diane** Richards Butler
- **ISAACS Jeffrey** Hill Taylor Dickinson
- **LUCAS David** Middleton Potts
- **SWINBURN Richard** Richards Butler

[2]
- **BLACK Richard** RD Black & Co.
- **MARTIN Patricia** Altheimer & Gray
- **PARSON Robert** Clyde & Co
- **POTTS Christopher** Middleton Potts
- **TURNER Paul** Clyde & Co

[3]
- **EVAGORA Kyri** Richards Butler
- **LEACH Ben** Stephenson Harwood

[4]
- **BEST David** Clyde & Co
- **HICKEY Denys** Ince & Co
- **PERROTT Brian** Hill Taylor Dickinson
- **PRIOR Judith** Clifford Chance
- **SHEPHERD Stuart** Ince & Co

[5]
- **ASPINALL Mark** Shaw and Croft
- **SWART Chris** Holman Fenwick & Willan
- **WALSER Nicholas** Holmes Hardingham
- **WILLIAMS Charles** Thomas Cooper & Stibbard

UP AND COMING
- **LESEBERG Petra** Middleton Potts

ASSOCIATES TO WATCH
- **KONYNENBURG Frederick** Middleton Potts

This book is the product of 6,552 1/2 hour interviews. See p.7 for BMRB audit. Within each band, firms are listed alphabetically. See individuals' profiles p.160

---

the firm's strong reputation in advising the associations, but its work appearing as counsel in arbitrations and its trade finance expertise is also noted. Not as visible in traditional physicals arbitrations, the team has nevertheless been involved in some interesting contentious work. Sugar cases, in particular, are increasing, and the firm also enjoys a healthy share of oil and metals-related work. This year has seen the retirement as partner of the hugely respected Ed Patton. His mantle is being picked up by Mark Morrison; however, competitors believe that he has yet to stamp his name on the sector. They mention, instead, **Judith Prior** (see p.161), who "*does a lot of oil and has a sensible, commercial attitude,*" as well as being an advisor to the sugar associations. The firm recently represented Veba Oil Supply and Trading in the Court of Appeal on the effect of a particular provision in a sales contract relating to the decision of the independent inspector. **Clients** LIFFE; sugar associations.

CLYDE & CO (see firm details p.913) "*A few years ago I wouldn't have mentioned Clydes,*" said one competitor, "*but one has to recognise its expansion.*" The recruitment two years ago of **Paul Turner** (see p.162) ("*a tough opponent*") is considered to have been the catalyst for the firm's commodities growth. He brought with him a first-rate sugar practice and has diversified into liquids. The recruitment this year, from Sinclair Roche & Temperley, of "*user-friendly, bright and thorough*" **Robert Parson** (see p.161), only reinforces the sense of a firm on the way up. He brings with him an "*interesting and lucrative*" trade finance practice and, although it is too early to judge market reaction, commentators consider this a firm to watch. Market sources also recognise that it has a strong oil and metals practice, and some rivals claim that "*it is increasingly visible in non-traditional work.*" At present, much of its work involves countries of the former Soviet Union, and it has also been active in Algeria and Iraq under the oil-for-food programme. It also boasts niche expertise in advising commodities clients on the effect of WTO matters. **David Best** (see p.160) has been less visible recently on commodities work but is still active in the sector. Clients rate him "*extremely talented with the ear of QCs.*" The firm recently represented CR Sugar in a dispute involving parties in China. **Clients** Glencore; Tate & Lyle; Gill & Duffus; ED&F Man; Sucre Export London Ltd.

HOLMAN FENWICK & WILLAN (see firm details p.999) Although the team is better known for shipping, commentators acknowledge that it "*has good contacts with the commodities world and is always prepared and knowledgeable.*" According to commentators the loss this year of leading light Patricia Martin, to Altheimer & Gray, is still too recent for its consequences to be assessed. However, they note that, although she was thought by many to be central to the practice, the firm still boasts a sizeable department in London, plus the support of its offices abroad. Its highest profile practitioner now is "*pleasant and reasonable*" **Chris Swart** (see p.161). This year has seen a big increase in metals and oil and gas-related work, with the firm assisting a number of parties in disputes following the collapse of Enron. Derivatives disputes and structured trade finance are also growing parts of its workload. A commanding position amongst Eastern European trading houses has seen the firm enjoy recent success representing Russian traders in sugar disputes. **Clients** Vitol.

INCE & CO (see firm details p.1008) Founded on its top class shipping reputation, the commodities team is developing a strong profile in its own right, as competitors endorse its "*tremendously good lawyers and litigators.*" Its highest profile partners are **Stuart Shepherd** (see p.161) ("*efficient with good judgement*") and **Denys Hickey** (see p.160), who clients say is "*pragmatic, responds quickly and consistently follows through.*" Shepherd led in one of the firm's recent highlights, representing Agrosin, Singapore in a 13-day trial against the owners of the 'David Agmashenebeli' over alleged wrongful clausing in bills of lading. Oil and gas is the department's speciality, though it has other commodities work, particularly sugar. It typically represents trading houses and clients resourcing crude and refined products, often trading on into the US market. The team successfully represented Ferrell International in a dispute with Sonatrach Petroleum concerning the validity of a floating law clause in a charter party. **Clients** Ferrell International; Vitol Services; Tate & Lyle; Ronly Holdings; Glencore.

HOLMES HARDINGHAM (see firm details p.1000) A respected shipping firm, it is principally known in the commodities field as advisor to FOSFA, though it also takes part in grain and edible oils arbitrations and some oil trading. One market source noted that "*the firm has run some cases successfully, and it acts for big French consumers as well.*" It recently conducted an appeal to the Commercial Court for just such a French client, arising out of a GAFTA award. The team also acts a lot on behalf of cargo inspection companies, which throws up a quantity of related professional negligence work. **Nicholas Walser** (see p.162) retains his respected reputation in the sector. **Clients** FOSFA; international grain houses; foreign oil traders.

RD BLACK & CO (see firm details p.1108) A small but specialist commodities outfit, it represents trading houses and buyers of all sizes, principally on contentious work. The pillar of the practice is "*real street fighter*" **Richard Black** (see p.160) ("*extremely argumentative, but he does a great job for his clients*"), who is praised for his "*dynamic, individualistic style*" and hard work. Competitors note his expertise in FOSFA work and strong links to America and the Far East; however, he is also active in grain, petroleum, crude and metal disputes, and is seeing an increase in trade finance working for the banks. A highlight of the year has been the firm's continuing involvement in the Sumitomo litigation. **Clients** International trading houses.

STEPHENSON HARWOOD (see firm details p.1138) The department has undergone two large changes this year. The merger of Sinclair Roche & Temperley with Stephenson Harwood may lend its highly rated commodities team increased international trade and finance strength and a greater overseas reach. However, it coincides with the loss of respected figure Robert Parson to Clyde & Co. Market sources are waiting for the dust to clear before assessing the results. The firm is still heavily involved in major commodities dispute resolution and acts for trading houses as well as banks. It benefits from the experience of "*sensible and down-to-earth*" **Ben Leach** (see p.160). Although perhaps less visible than in the past, competitors say that "*his knowledge goes a long way back,*" and he is always reliable. The firm has recently been kept busy advising on the creative use of trade finance in developing markets. **Clients** International commodities trading houses; trade finance banks.

THOMAS COOPER & STIBBARD (see firm details p.1159) A compact team with consider-

LONDON ■ COMMODITIES

able experience and a global spread, some competitors rate it "*more visible than most small firms.*" Its best-known figure is **Charles Williams** (see p.162), praised for his "*methodical and thorough*" approach. The market is watching to see the effects of the collapse of client Andre & Cie, although the firm has been active in the run-off. There is a strong Chinese side to the practice, which it has been developing over the last year, recently representing Chinese interests in two arbitrations before The Sugar Association of London. **Clients** Andre & Cie; European Grain and Shipping Ltd; ITOCHU; Chinese interests.

OTHER NOTABLE PRACTITIONERS "*Tough, gregarious and commercial,*" **Patricia Martin** is popular with clients, who rave "*she's amongst the best for GAFTA, FOSFA and sugar: she's good on submissions, persuasive and really knows how to communicate with arbitrators.*" Her recent move from Holman Fenwick & Willan to Altheimer & Gray was met with interest by the market, who note that the American firm's strong Eastern European presence will assist her in developing her emerging markets practice. "*Tenacious and aggressive*" **Mark Aspinall** (see p.160) at Shaw and Croft is felt to be building a commodities practice. Competitors note that he is "*focused on the oil side,*" especially the Italian tanker market, while clients praise the firm as good for a tough case – "*sometimes you need someone who will fight back.*"

FUTURES

COMMODITIES: FUTURES
■ LONDON

1. Clifford Chance
2. Denton Wilde Sapte
   Linklaters
   Simmons & Simmons
3. Richards Butler

LEADING INDIVIDUALS

1. **FINNEY Robert** Denton Wilde Sapte
   HARDING Mark Clifford Chance
   JOHANSEN Lynn Clifford Chance
   PLEWS Tim Clifford Chance
2. **FIRTH Simon** Linklaters
   MELROSE Jonathan Simmons & Simmons
3. **TURING Dermot** Clifford Chance

This book is the product of 6,552 1/2 hour interviews. See p.7 for BMRB audit.
Within each band, firms are listed alphabetically. See individuals' profiles p.160

CLIFFORD CHANCE (see firm details p.911) The team is universally acknowledged to be "*a cut above*" the opposition. "*Known for market share and quality,*" its hegemony is based on its unrivalled client base: "*there are four exchanges, it acts for three of them and that is where the quality work comes from,*" admit competitors. Additionally, it represents trade associations, banks, and underlines the gulf with its admirable number of recognised practitioners. At the top of the tree is **Tim Plews** (see p.161), considered by some rivals to be the "*strongest and highest profile lawyer in the industry.*" **Lynn Johansen** (see p.160) represents banks, securities houses and investment firms, as well as exchanges, and retains a particularly high profile for energy-related derivatives, while **Mark Harding** (see p.160) "*has been in the industry a long time,*" bringing valuable in-house experience from his time at UBS Warburg. New to the rankings this year, **Dermot Turing** (see p.162) was praised by clients as a "*sharp new partner, definitely on the potential A-list.*" The group acted in three of the most important deals of the year. It represented the International Petroleum Exchange (IPE) on its takeover by ICE, acted for LIFFE on its takeover by Euronext and advised Jiway on the transfer of ownership from Morgan Stanley to the OM Group. **Clients** LIFFE; London Clearing House; IPE; OM; LBMA; ICE; Morgan Stanley; UBS Warburg; Lehman Brothers; Deutsche Bank; CSFB.

DENTON WILDE SAPTE (see firm details p.935) The firm is "*hugely active on the energy trading side*" according to competitors. The firm is home to a top class energy practice, and much of the work of the futures team is related to energy trading. For example, it advised Ofgem on the settlement netting and other issues relating to the implementation of NETA. Valued for his futures expertise, **Robert Finney** brought his impressive knowledge to bear advising on this. He was praised by market sources for his "*pleasant and completely straightforward*" approach. The firm's banking practice also bolsters the offering with futures playing a part in commodity financing. The decision of respected practitioner Edward Black to leave the firm has diminished its market profile somewhat. The team has assisted The Futures and Options Association in adapting its documentation for energy and oil market participants. **Clients** Ofgem; WestLB; KBC Bank; Transco; Man Financial; Glencore.

LINKLATERS (see firm details p.1043) The department has improved its position in commodity derivatives over the last year and rises in our rankings. Some commentators even consider it the closest rival to Clifford Chance, claiming that it has "*a stronger regulatory practice*" than the other contenders and firmer links to financial institutions. But it is its position as exclusive advisor to the LME to which competitors inevitably refer. This produces interesting work and affords the firm an enviable position. Operating from a group that conducts a range of derivatives and regulatory work, the team has recently assisted BNP Paribas in setting up a new associate broker member business from scratch. Its best-known figure is **Simon Firth** (see p.160). **Clients** LME.

SIMMONS & SIMMONS (see firm details p.1136) Competitors claim that the firm has been less visible over the last year, believing that its profile is higher in energy trading. They acknowledge, however, that it remains "*one of the main contenders*" amongst the chasing pack. A lot of the team's work is energy-related, although it also has a large market share of metals work. Strong regulatory expertise and experience of liaising with the FSA has led to large amounts of investigations and disciplinary work. It is also gaining a greater knowledge of weather derivatives, in line with a drive in the market towards greater understanding of weather risk. The firm has been assisting Sempra Energy Trading on its proposed purchase of Enron Metals Ltd following Enron's collapse. The commodities and futures advice on that transaction was led by **Jonathan Melrose** (see p.161), who is praised by clients for his "*great store of experience acquired over years.*" **Clients** AIG Trading Group; Prudential-Bache International; Sempra Energy Trading; Medway Power; WeatherXchange.

RICHARDS BUTLER (see firm details p.1112) Not as well known for its derivatives work as it is on the physicals side, the firm is nonetheless recognised as a player in the futures market. Richard Parlour heads a growing team, which has recently enjoyed success in winning derivatives work from new commodities houses. It now represents two European exchanges and, over the last year, represented three of the six leading commodities brokers. For these, the firm has assisted in developing several commodities derivatives trading platforms, enabling them to trade easily between themselves. **Clients** Several leading commodities brokers.

COMMODITIES ■ THE LEADERS

THE LEADERS IN COMMODITIES

ASPINALL, Mark
Shaw and Croft, London
(020) 7645 9000
mark.aspinall@shawandcroft.com
Specialisation: Main areas of practice are split between all aspects of shipping litigation/arbitration but predominantly in Tanker operations (oil, LPG and chemical) covering unseaworthiness actions, cargo claims, charterparty disputes; and oil trading disputes for the Independents, covering crude and products sale contracts (physical and paper), processing and netback agreements and related problems concerning letters of credit and trade finance. Also experienced in shipping fraud, asset tracing and joint venture agreements (oil biased).
Prof. Memberships: Baltic Exchange, Institute of Petroleum.
Career: Articled *Shaw & Croft*. Qualified 1994. Partner 1998.
Personal: Born 1962. Lives in London. Leisure interests: football, golf, tennis, travel and occasional surfing.

BEST, David
Clyde & Co, London
(020) 7623 1244
David.Best@clyde.co.uk
Specialisation: Litigation disputes concerning oil and gas, metal, sugar and other international commodity contracts, both in arbitration and court, and related charterparty and bill of lading disputes. Client base is worldwide with current disputes in the London High Court and arbitration and in foreign courts eg. Dubai, Paris and Hong Kong, working with *Clyde & Co*'s regional offices. Acts principally for commodity traders and charterers. Part of the team acting for Glencore following the collapse of Metro Trading International Inc.

BLACK, Richard
RD Black & Co., London
(020) 7600 8282
Specialisation: Partner specialising in shipping and commodities litigation and arbitration. Wide experience since 1978 of maritime and commodity arbitrations (both physical and futures) and Commercial Court hearings relating to shipping, trading, trade finance, insurance and commercial litigation disputes and regulatory work with a particular emphasis on charterparty and cargo claims and commodity disputes including GAFTA, FOSFA, crude oil and petroleum and LME. Clients include international trading houses, commodity and derivatives traders, banks, oil majors and traders, shipowners, charterers and marine insurers. Major cases include Deutsche Schachtbau v Raknoc & Shell International; Kloeckner v Gatoil; the M.V. 'P', The 'Taria', Comdel v Siporex.
Prof. Memberships: Law Society, GAFTA and FOSFA, supporting member LMAA.
Career: Qualified in 1977. Joined *Middleton Potts* from *Coward Chance* in 1984, becoming a Partner in 1985. In December 1996, resigned from *Middleton Potts* to set up *RD Black & Co.*
Personal: Born 22 March 1951. Holds an LLB from Manchester, 1969-72. Leisure interests include tennis, chess and history. Lives in Oxshott.

EVAGORA, Kyri
Richards Butler, London
(020) 7772 5896
ke@richardsbutler.com
Specialisation: International trade and commodities: his experience covers the related disciplines of international trade, trade finance, shipping and insurance. Recent high profile cases include 'Spiros C' (Court of Appeal); Agrokor AG v Tradigrain SA; Vinprom Rousse v Bulgarian Vinters (Court of Appeal); Tradigrain S.A v SIAT and others; and Tradigrain S.A v Al Hadha Trading Corporation. He has extensive experience of advising in a number of significant trade finance-related matters. Has lectured for GAFTA and the IGPA.
Prof. Memberships: Law Society.
Career: Articled with *Sinclair Roche & Temperley*; solicitor 1994-99; solicitor with *Richards Butler* 1997; partner at *Richards Butler* 2000.
Personal: Born 1 November 1968; educated at The Latymer School, Edmonton and Bristol University. Lives in London.

FINNEY, Robert
Denton Wilde Sapte, London
(020) 7242 1212

FIRTH, Simon
Linklaters, London
(020) 7456 3764
simon.firth@linklaters.com
Specialisation: Specialisms include the structuring and documentation of derivatives transactions (with a particular emphasis on regulatory capital analysis) and providing general legal and regulatory advice to participants in the financial markets.
Career: 1998 to date Head of *Linklaters* Derivatives Practice; 1996-98: Partner, *Linklaters* London, Financial Markets Group; 1993-96: Assistant Solicitor, *Linklaters* London, Financial Markets Group; 1992-93: Assistant Solicitor, *Linklaters* New York; 1990-92: Assistant Solicitor, *Linklaters* London, Corporate Department; 1986: Christ Church, Oxford University (MA Jurisprudence).

GALLOWAY, Diane
Richards Butler, London
(020) 7772 5884
dg@richardsbutler.com
Specialisation: Principal areas of practice are commodities arbitrations and litigation, including in Grain and Feed Trade Association, Liverpool Cotton Association, Refined Sugar Association and FOSFA. Recent experience also includes Chinese Trade Arbitration (CIETAC). Has lectured for GAFTA and Sugar Association of London. Also specialises in sanctions related litigation.
Career: LLB Trinity College, Cambridge, then Masters in International Law, Harvard Law School, USA. Joined *Richards Butler* in 1984 after internship with New York firm.

HARDING, Mark
Clifford Chance, London
(020) 7600 1000
mark.harding@cliffordchance.com
Specialisation: Banking and finance. Partner specialising in financial services, markets and institutions work, including regulatory advice and derivatives, both OTC and exchange-traded.
Career: Joined *Clifford Chance* 1980; qualified 1982; Partner 1987-96; General Counsel of UBS Warburg 1996-2000; rejoined *Clifford Chance* November 2000.
Personal: 1976-79 Jesus College, Cambridge (MA degree in French, German and Law); 1979-80 College of Law (Law Society Finals).

HICKEY, Denys
Ince & Co, London
(020) 7623 2011
Specialisation: Partner. A major part of his practice involves oil and gas trading disputes. Has acted in disputes involving many of the oil majors and independent oil traders in connection with contracts for the sale of crude, products and gas. Also involved in metals trading including LME disputes, tolling contracts, offtake agreements and other aspects of metals trading with particular reference to the FSU. Involved in disputes relating to time and voyage charters, long term contracts of affreightment, storage contracts, and shortage and contamination claims. Has advised on short and long term contracts and problems arising out of letters of credit and trade finance and the application of EU and UK competition law. Has spoken at numerous conferences on the legal aspects of transport, trading, letters of credit and EC competition law, and is a regular speaker at the Centre for Petroleum and Mineral Law at the University of Dundee.
Career: Post-graduate studies in Public International and EC Law, then qualified as a barrister. Joined *Ince & Co.*, requalified as a solicitor and became a partner in 1986.
Personal: Born 1952. Lives Saffron Walden. Leisure interests include golf, cycling and skiing.

ISAACS, Jeffrey
Hill Taylor Dickinson, London
(020) 7283 9033
jeff.isaacs@htd-london.com
Specialisation: Partner. Practice covers the full range of maritime and Sale of Goods law, but with a specialisation in 'dry' shipping and Commodities disputes including both High Court litigation and arbitration at the various Trade Associations, including GAFTA, FOSFA, The Refined Sugar Association, The Sugar Association of London, LME and IGPA. Regularly sits as legal assessor to arbitration panels at the Sugar Associations and GAFTA. Author of articles on Shipping and Commodities matters. Speaks at seminars and on the GAFTA Trade Education Course. Shipping Editor of 'Law and Transport Policy'.
Prof. Memberships: Law Society, and through *Hill Taylor Dickinson* GAFTA, FOSFA and Refined Sugar Association.
Career: Qualified in 1983 having joined *Hill Taylor Dickinson* in 1981. Associate in 1987. Partner in 1989.
Personal: Born 11 April 1959. Attended Dulwich College then Christ's College, Cambridge (BA 1980). Leisure interests include tennis, badminton, horse riding, wine making and tasting and skiing. Lives in Putney.

JOHANSEN, Lynn
Clifford Chance, London
(020) 7600 1000
lynn.johansen@cliffordchance.com
Specialisation: Banking and finance. Partner specialising in derivatives and financial regulation with a particular focus on exchange-traded derivatives issues and commodity derivatives with a focus on energy products.
Career: Qualified 1985; Partner since 1995.
Personal: MA (CANTAB) in History.

KONYNENBURG, Frederick
Middleton Potts, London
(020) 7600 2333

LEACH, Ben
Stephenson Harwood (incorporating Sinclair Roche & Temperley), London
(020) 7329 4422
ben.leach@shlegal.com
Specialisation: Consultant. Main area of specialisation is commodity trades, from litigation and arbitration to drafting and advising on commodity sales, contracts and associated documentation. Conducted over 100 arbitrations before GAFTA, FOSFA, Refined Sugar Association, London Metal Exchange, London Rice Brokers' Association and various other hard and soft commodity trade associations in London and abroad. Contributed to the Law Commission Working Group on title to goods forming part of a bulk. Also a specialist in shipping and oil trade litigation.
Prof. Memberships: Law Society
Career: Articled to *Richards Butler* in 1969, qualified as a solicitor in 1971, joined *Sinclair Roche & Temperley* in 1975 and became a partner in 1978. Joined *Stephenson Harwood* in May 2002, when *Sinclair Roche & Temperley* and *Stephenson Harwood* combined to form an enlarged firm.
Personal: Born 24 October 1945. Attended Leeds University 1965-68. Accredited CEDR mediator.

THE LEADERS ■ COMMODITIES

LESEBERG, Petra
Middleton Potts, London
(020) 7600 2333
pvl@middletonpotts.co.uk
Specialisation: Partner specialising in international trade and commodities. Advises a worldwide client base on the financing, trading and transportation of commodities with disputes both in arbitration (GAFTA, FOSFA, LME, CAL and RSA) and court. Also well known as an advisor to banks on trade finance related matters as well as disputes arising from the collapse of Enron and its numerous subsidiaries. Lectures regularly to the trade, associations and financial institutions. Fluent in French and German, having studied both languages and worked in Paris and Hamburg.
Prof. Memberships: Law Society.
Career: Qualified 1992 *Richards Butler*; joined *Middleton Potts* 1998; Partner *Middleton Potts* 1999.
Personal: Born 27 April 1966. Lives in London. Enjoys fine wine and swimming.

LUCAS, David
Middleton Potts, London
(020) 7600 2333
dl@middletonpotts.co.uk
Specialisation: Partner in Commercial Litigation Department. Main area of practice is commodities, trade finance and shipping. Extensive experience of arbitration and litigation, acting for commodity trading houses (including the majors), oil companies and traders, shipowners, leading trade finance banks, insurers and P&I Clubs. Also acts extensively as legal advisor to Trade Association arbitrators. Major cases handled include Bremer v Vanden-Avenne, The Montone, The Caspian Sea, The Pegase, The Afovos, The Golden Bear, The Future Express, Czarnikow-Rionda v Standard Bank and The Elpa.
Prof. Memberships: Law Society.
Career: Qualified in 1972. Associate, *Crawley & de Reya* 1974-76. Founding Partner at *Middleton Potts* in 1976. Senior Partner since May 2001.
Personal: Born 15 December 1947. Attended St Paul's School 1960-65, then Bristol University 1966-69.

MARTIN, Patricia
Altheimer & Gray, London
(020) 7786 5700

MELROSE, Jonathan
Simmons & Simmons, London
(020) 7628 2020
jonathan.melrose@simmons-simmons.com
Specialisation: Partner in Financial Markets Department. Handles all types of work relating to financial services and markets, including commodities/derivatives, securities, collective investment vehicles and asset management. Regular speaker at conferences and seminars.
Prof. Memberships: Union Internationale des Avocats, Law Society, The Securities Institute, Member of Commodities Committee of the Futures and Options Association.
Career: Qualified 1985, having joined *Simmons & Simmons* in 1983. Became a Partner in 1991.
Personal: Born 21 April 1959. Holds an MA (Hons) Oxon, 1981.

PARSON, Robert
Clyde & Co, London
(020) 7623 1244
robert.parson@clyde.co.uk
Specialisation: Partner in Commodity and Trade Finance Group. Specialises in trade, structured and transactional trade finance facilities and enforcing trade finance obligations in letters of credit and other instruments. He also advises on commodity contracts and disputes and internet-based trading and finance.
Prof. Memberships: Law Society.
Career: Qualified 1986. Partner *Middleton Potts* 1995-2001; Partner *Sinclair Roche & Temperley* 2001. Partner *Clyde & Co* 2002.
Personal: Born 7 February 1961. Sheffield University LLB 1979-82.

PERROTT, Brian
Hill Taylor Dickinson, London
(020) 7280 9131
brian.perrott@htd-london.com
Specialisation: Specialist areas include: dispute resolution involving all forms of dry shipping work and all aspects of international physical commodity trading (grain, rice, oil, sugar, coffee, crude oil, rubber, metals) and paper trading (derivatives and exchange related disciplinary proceedings). Other specialist areas include environmental and protest group injunctive work, documentary credit problems, exchange proceedings and e-trading. Reported cases include: Cargill Investor Services v Monrovia; Ceval Alimentos SA v Agrimpex Trading Co. Ltd; Ceval International Limited v Cefetra and Cefetra v Soules; Cargill Inc v Tate & Lyle; Evergos Naftiki Eteria v Cargill Plc; Sun Valley Foods v Fusion; Cargill France v Toepfer; Cargill International v Stone & Rolls; Cargill Plc v Greenpeace. Clients include: Cargill, Al Khaleej Sugar Co, Shell, Bhp Billiton, Sinochem, Swiss Marine.
Prof. Memberships: Law Society.
Career: Trained *Holman Fenwick Willan*; former head of litigation group at Cargill; partner *Hill Taylor Dickinson* 2000.
Publications: A regular contributor to 'Lloyd's List' 'Public Ledger' and 'Commodities Now' and regular speaker at International Trade Seminars.
Personal: Born 1966. Resides Sevenoaks. Attended Mt St Joseph's College, Ireland; University College Cardiff (LLB); College of Law, Guildford.

PLEWS, Tim
Clifford Chance, London
(020) 7600 1000
tim.plews@cliffordchance.com
Specialisation: Banking and finance. Partner specialising in law and regulation of, and trading in, international financial markets the structuring of innovative investment products including funds.
Career: Articled *Coward Chance*, qualified 1988; Partner since 1994.
Personal: Durham School; Trinity College, Cambridge (MA 1984).

POTTS, Christopher
Middleton Potts, London
(020) 7600 2333
crp@middletonpotts.co.uk
Specialisation: Former Senior Partner of *Middleton Potts*. Over 35 years experience of law and practice relating to commodities, carriage of goods, insurance (marine and non-marine) and international trade. Many major cases handled relate to leading authorities. Clientele includes major trading houses, carriers, insurers and banks. Regularly lectures to trade audiences.
Prof. Memberships: Law Society.
Career: Qualified in 1965. Partner at *Crawley & de Reya* 1967-76. Founding Partner of *Middleton Potts* in 1976.
Personal: Born 1 July 1939. Read law at University of London 1958-61. Lives in London.

PRIOR, Judith
Clifford Chance, London
(020) 7600 1000
Specialisation: Shipping. Senior solicitor, Shipping and International Trade Group.
Career: Admitted as a solicitor in England and Wales 1982; *Coward Chance* 1983-87; *Clifford Chance* 1987-date.
Personal: Sidney Sussex College, University of Cambridge (MA (Law)).

PULLEN, David
Richards Butler, London
(020) 7772 5886
dmp@richardsbutler.com
Specialisation: Partner in International Trade and Commodities. Main area of practice is commodity trading disputes, including arbitration and advice work in grain (GAFTA), vegetable oil (FOSFA), sugar (RSA and SAOL), metals and oil trading (ICC). Also handles documentary credits advice work, and advises on litigation disputes in customs and EU matters. Cases have included the 1973 US Prohibition cases, Naxos, Panchaud Freres and Toepfer v Continental Grain. Instructor at the University of Pennsylvania Law School 1963-64. Regular speaker at trade related conferences.
Prof. Memberships: Supporting Member of London Maritime Arbitration Association; Associate Member Chartered Institute of Arbitrators.
Career: Qualified 1967. At *Richards Butler* since 1964.
Personal: Born 1941. Taunton School 1954-59, then University College Oxford 1960-63.

SHEPHERD, Stuart
Ince & Co, London
(020) 7623 2011
Specialisation: Main areas of practice are commodities and shipping. Is involved in advising those trading in various commodities, in particular oil, oil products and commodities traded on GAFTA terms, and handles all aspects of dry shipping work, with particular emphasis on carriage of goods by sea and charterparty disputes with particular emphasis on litigation. Leading reported cases have included 'Mathraki' (1989), 'Lefthero' (1992), 'Boucraa' (1993) and 'Kriti Rex' (1996). Author of articles on a number of commodity matters. Speaks at Informa shipping seminars and on the GAFTA's CPDP programme.
Prof. Memberships: Member of IBA, LMAA, and through *Ince & Co.*, GAFTA, FOSFA and Refined Sugar Association.
Career: Qualified in 1984, having joined *Ince & Co.* in 1982. Became a partner in 1990.
Personal: Born 17 October 1959. Attended Bexhill Grammar 1971-78, then University College, Cardiff 1978-81. Leisure interests include golf and skiing. Lives in Mayfield, East Sussex.

SWART, Chris
Holman Fenwick & Willan, London
(020) 7264 8211
chris.swart@hfw.co.uk
Specialisation: Shipping and international trade. LG Caltex v CNPC & CPTDC series of arbitrations. Court of Appeal Ref 2001 2All ER97.
Career: Partner at *Holman Fenwick & Willan* since 1995; Qualified England and Wales 1991; *Lovell White Durrant* 1988-95 (incl. articles); Attorney, South Africa Admitted 1987. Articles Syret Godlonton-Fuller Moore Inc, Cape Town.
Personal: Rhodes Scholar (Natal & Magdalen); Magdalen College, Oxford 1985 (Jurisprudence); University of South Africa 1986 (LLB); University of Cape Town 1982 (BA Hons); University of Natal 1979-80 (BA, BA Hons). Born 1959. Resides Latimer, Buckinghamshire. Married with 4 children. Leisure: tennis, golf, chess.

SWINBURN, Richard
Richards Butler, London
(020) 7247 6555
rgs@richardsbutler.com
Specialisation: Advises trading companies, trade associations, banks and governments on all aspects of the buying, selling, financing and transporting of commodities.
Career: Qualified in 1988. Partner at *Richards Butler* 1994.
Personal: Born 1963. Educated at Sedbergh School, Cumbria and Robinson College, Cambridge.

161

COMMODITIES ■ THE LEADERS

TURING, Dermot
Clifford Chance, London
(020) 7600 1000
Specialisation: Banking and finance. Partner specialising in risk management for financial institutions, regulation and derivatives.
Career: Joined *Clifford Chance* as trainee 1990; qualified 1991; Partner since 1999.
Personal: Sherborne School; King's College, Cambridge (BA1982); New College, Oxford (DPhil 1986).

TURNER, Paul
Clyde & Co, London
(020) 7623 1244
Paul.Turner@clyde.co.uk
Specialisation: Partner handling commodities. Work includes trade arbitrations before the Sugar Associations, GAFTA, FOSFA, Cocoa Association, Coffee Trade Federation and Rice Association. Also handles oil disputes, bills of lading and charter party disputes, largely before commercial courts or the London Maritime Arbitrators Association.
Prof. Memberships: Law Society, Associate Member of the Sugar Association of London.
Career: Qualified 1973. Partner with *Thomas Cooper & Stibbard* from 1977-85. Founder partner of *Turner & Co.* in 1985. *Turner & Co* merged with *Clyde & Co* in January 2000.
Personal: Born 16 September 1948. Attended Skegness Grammar School 1960-67, then University College, London, 1967-70. Leisure interests include walking, travelling and eating. Lives in Esher, Surrey.

WALSER, Nicholas
Holmes Hardingham, London
(020) 7280 3200
Nicholas.Walser@HHlaw.co.uk
Specialisation: Partner specialising in 'dry' shipping law, including commodity trade disputes. Work covers charterparty disputes, cargo loss/damage claims, and international sale contracts including agricultural commodities (GAFTA and FOSFA contracts) and oil trading. Major cases include the 'TFL Prosperity' (H.L.) (1984) Soules v Intertradex (1991) and Soules v P.T. Transap (1998). Associate member of French Maritime Law Association. Fluent French. Working knowledge of German.
Career: Qualified in 1977. Partner in *Ingledew Brown Bennison & Garrett* 1979-89. A founding Partner of *Holmes Hardingham* in 1989.
Personal: Born 31 December 1952. Attended Cambridge University (MA 1975). Lives in London.

WILLIAMS, Charles
Thomas Cooper & Stibbard, London
(020) 7481 8851
charles.williams@tcssol.com
Specialisation: International trade: sale of goods, commodities, shipping; trade and commodity finance; credit and political risk insurance; counter trade; electronic trade. Major cases include Feedex v Warde; Argo Hellas; C Joyce; Dominique; Woodhouse Drake & Carey; Jeffrey S Levitt Limited (in receivership); Laconian Confidence; Metro. Lectures regularly on various subjects including electronic commerce, sale of goods, trade finance, charterparties and bills of lading. Lectures on the Carriage of Goods by Sea at the University of Cardiff.
Prof. Memberships: Chairman of the British Maritime Law Association Committee on Arbitration and ADR (1993-99). Member of the Bolero Consortium and advisor on shipping law (1994-95); director of the Bolero Association (1998-99); member of the Legal Working Party of the Electronic Commerce Association (1995-96).
Career: Qualified at *Thomas Cooper & Stibbard* in 1979. Joined *Lovell White & King* in 1979 as an assistant, moved to *Richards Butler* in 1982 as an assistant. In 1998 moved to *Wilde Sapte* as an Assistant Solicitor, becoming a Partner the following year. Moved to *Thomas Cooper & Stibbard* in 1994 as a Partner.
Publications: 'Bills of Lading in Trade Finance'.
Personal: University of Birmingham 1972-75, LLB (Hons).

COMPETITION/ANTI-TRUST

London: 163; The Regions: 166; Scotland: 168; Profiles: 169

Research approved by BMRB For this edition, **Chambers'** researchers conducted 6,582 interviews – 3,900 with law firms, 511 with barristers and 2,171 with clients. The validity of the research was scrutinised by BMRB International, who audited both the methodology and the results at our offices in London. They interviewed **Chambers'** researchers and cross-checked sample interviews. Details of the audit appear on page 7.

OVERVIEW In the past, merger control work has tended to dominate this area of the law. However, the emphasis has swung towards the behavioural side with the effects of encroaching recession and the introduction of the Competition Act. Armed with new powers under the Act, the OFT has been flexing its muscles, leading to a marked increase in investigatory and cartel cases. Digesting the implications of this, commercial concerns are seeking legal advice on compliance, while at the same time attempting to use the Act as a stick with which to beat their competitors. The result has been a growth in instructions for law firms, a trend set to continue with the potential criminalisation of cartel behaviour and push towards the decentralisation of enforcement from Brussels to European nation states.

LONDON

COMPETITION/ANTI-TRUST
■ LONDON

1
- Freshfields Bruckhaus Deringer
- Herbert Smith
- Linklaters
- Slaughter and May

2
- Lovells
- Simmons & Simmons

3
- Allen & Overy
- Ashurst Morris Crisp
- Denton Wilde Sapte
- SJ Berwin

4
- Baker & McKenzie
- Clifford Chance
- Norton Rose

5
- Bristows
- CMS Cameron McKenna
- Eversheds
- Richards Butler
- Theodore Goddard

This book is the product of 6,582 1/2 hour interviews. See p.7 for BMRB audit. Within each band, firms are listed alphabetically.

FRESHFIELDS BRUCKHAUS DERINGER (see firm details p.964) This high quality operation was universally described by clients and other practitioners as "*fully deserving of its pre-eminence in the market,*" with much commendation for the group's commercially effective approach. A stand-alone practice, it combines a traditional strength in merger clearance work with expertise in all other major sectors including compliance, state aid, public procurement and cartel investigations. Fully integrated within the firm's pan-European competition group, its "*core individuals are at the very top of the profession*" and include regulatory expert **David Aitman** (see p.169), who has recently advised mmO2 in relation to the Oftel referral to the Competition Commission of fixed-to-mobile licence modifications for all MNOs. The diffuse mix further contains "*sober and assured*" **Nicholas Spearing** (see p.173) and **Deirdre Trapp** (see p.173), "*a lively, dynamic extrovert,*" who was praised by clients for "*always meeting deadlines and producing polished written work.*"

The team has advised Hewlett-Packard on the non-US merger control aspects of its proposed global merger with Compaq; a case in which newcomer to the tables **Rod Carlton** (see p.169) had a key role. It has also advised LVMH on its joint venture project with De Beers to create flagship retail jewellery stores. An example of the firm's presence at the cutting edge of the market was provided by its securing of only the second ever 100% exemption from fines under the EC leniency arrangements on behalf of Sappi. **Clients** ABN AMRO; Airtours; BNFL; BT; English Welsh and Scottish Railway; Hewlett-Packard; ICI; London Underground; P&O Princess Cruises; Rank; Sony Pictures; Tesco; UK COAL; Visa International.

HERBERT SMITH (see firm details p.992) Top rated despite the lower market profile of its merger practice, this firm is recognised by our interviewees as "*a giant on the contentious side.*" It has enjoyed particular public exposure following the introduction of the UK Competition Act, appearing on behalf of Napp and Aberdeen Journals in the earliest infringement cases and acting for Robert Wiseman Dairies in the first case in which the OFT sought to impose an interim injunction. Its practice reaches well beyond this, however, encompassing Article 81 and 82 EC cases, state aid, monopoly references, public procurement and regulatory matters.

"*Dedicated and intellectually sharp,*" **Dorothy Livingston** (see p.172) has handled major client BSkyB for a number of years and is felt to dovetail well with **Elizabeth McKnight** (see p.172), "*a smart practitioner*" who is strong on the economics side and "*never intimidated by other people's ideas.*" Also in the team are **Jonathan Scott** (see p.173), described by rivals as "*pragmatic and fun to work with,*" and the "*pugnacious*" **Richard Fleck** (see p.170). Our interviewees pointed to the more junior **Stephen Wisking** (see p.174), one of the first to become a solicitor advocate, who is felt to be an asset in an increasingly contentious competition landscape.

Recent transactional highlights include acting for FIA in a case relating to Formula One and other professional motor sport, and appearing on behalf of Virgin Atlantic in fighting the renewed proposed alliance between British Airways and American Airlines. The group also appeared for Vodafone in relation to the Competition Commission's investigation into Oftel's proposals to regulate the price of interconnection to mobile networks and the ensuing Competition inquiry. **Clients** Associated British Foods; BAT; BSkyB; Coca-Cola; Eurotunnel; Freeserve; Pilkington; Vodafone; Yorkshire Water.

LINKLATERS (see firm details p.1043) Part of a Europe-wide team of a hundred plus lawyers, the London base of this international leader was much praised for "*its dream client base*" and "*commercial understanding.*" It has particular expertise in merger control, state aid regulation, anti-dumping, and international trade matters. Lead individual **Bill Allan** (see p.169) is highly esteemed amongst both peers and clients as "*one of the cleverest brains in the City*" who melds "*great industry with a relaxed style.*" He has been heavily involved in advice to De Beers on issues raised by Articles 81 and 82, and merger control rules.

Younger, but similarly recommended, were **Michael Cutting** (see p.169), who "*fizzes with ideas,*" and **Gavin Robert** (see p.173), known for his "*detailed knowledge of the law and healthy contacts with the Commission.*" The latter led the team advising on the competition aspects of BP's acquisition of 51% of Veba Oel, alongside colleagues from the Cologne and Brussels offices. Cutting and the group acted for the Six Continents acquisition of Posthouse Hotel Chain. The firm has further advised Scottish & Newcastle on the Article 81 implications of a major UK competitor's purchase of a continental brewer. **Clients** De Beers; Reed Elsevier; Hutchison Netherlands; Rotterdam and Municipal Port Management; Lloyds TSB; Scottish & Newcastle.

SLAUGHTER AND MAY (see firm details p.1140) This "*tremendous practice*" was praised by rivals and clients alike as "*quality through and through.*" Its top-drawer client base feeds work

COMPETITION/ANTI-TRUST ■ LONDON

LEADING INDIVIDUALS

★ **NICHOLSON Malcolm** Slaughter and May
WHISH Richard Sole Practitioner

1
AITMAN David Freshfields Bruckhaus
ALLAN Bill Linklaters
BRIGHT Christopher Shearman & Sterling
CARSTENSEN Laura Slaughter and May
FREEMAN Peter Simmons & Simmons
KON Stephen SJ Berwin
LIVINGSTON Dorothy Herbert Smith
MCKNIGHT Elizabeth Herbert Smith
POLITO Simon Lovells
TRAPP Deirdre Freshfields Bruckhaus

2
CHAPPATTE Philippe Slaughter and May
MARTIN ALEGI Lynda Baker & McKenzie
PARR Nigel Ashurst Morris Crisp
SCOTT Jonathan Herbert Smith
SMITH Martin Simmons & Simmons
SPEARING Nicholas Freshfields Bruckhaus

3
AINSWORTH Lesley Lovells
FINBOW Roger Ashurst Morris Crisp
FRIEND Mark Allen & Overy
HOLMES Katherine Richards Butler
SIBREE William Slaughter and May
WEITZMAN Polly Denton Wilde Sapte

4
PHEASANT John Lovells
ROBERT Gavin Linklaters
WOTTON John Allen & Overy

5
COHEN Ralph SJ Berwin
COLEMAN Martin Norton Rose
CUTTING Michael Linklaters
FLECK Richard Herbert Smith
HOLMES Simon SJ Berwin
HUTCHINGS Michael Michael Hutchings
KELLAWAY Rosalind Eversheds
KIM Suyong Denton Wilde Sapte
LEIGH Guy Theodore Goddard
LINDSAY Alistair Allen & Overy
LOUVEAUX Bertrand Slaughter and May
OSBORNE John Clifford Chance
ROSE Stephen Eversheds
USHER Tom SJ Berwin

UP AND COMING
CARLTON Roderick Freshfields Bruckhaus
GIBSON-BOLTON Elaine SJ Berwin
MOBLEY Samantha Baker & McKenzie
WISKING Stephen Herbert Smith

See individuals' profiles p.169

through to a team particularly noted for mergers, acquisitions and joint venture work, but which also has a key role in the regulatory sphere. **William Sibree** (see p.173), "*a man of fierce intellect and deadly purpose,*" has recently returned from Brussels to join an established group of talented individuals led by "*legendary merger specialist*" **Malcolm Nicholson** (see p.172). The latter advised Consignia on its joint ventures and UK and EU liberalisation issues, and represented Airtours on its appeal to the European Court against the Commission's decision to block its acquisition of First Choice.

Also present are the "*robust*" **Philippe Chappatte** (see p.169), who, along with "*bright young thing*" **Bertrand Louveaux** (see p.172), acted for BA regarding its proposed alliance with American Airlines. **Laura Carstensen** (see p.169) garnered praise for "*her effective, commercial approach;*" she advised Orange on the EC's Article 81 inquiry into mobile international roaming charges, and assisted Hilton Group (Ladbroke) in its complaint to the OFT against the trading practices of the British Horseracing Board.

ECMR work at the firm includes acting for Laporte on its acquisition by Degussa, and advising Cadbury Schweppes in its acquisition of Pernod Ricard's soft drinks business. Regulatory highlights include acting as United Utilities' standing counsel on competition issues and advising BNFL on restructuring in advance of proposed part privatisation. **Clients** Abbey National; Airtours; BNFL; Boots; British Airways; Cadbury Schweppes; GlaxoSmithKline; JCB; Orange; Thames Water; United Utilities.

LOVELLS (see firm details p.1045) "*Excellent on the litigation side*" agree clients, this practice is, in addition, now enjoying an increased proportion of merger throughput activity. Recent notable moves on this front have included advising Autologic on multi-jurisdictional merger control issues and securing Phase 1 merger clearance for a joint venture between the two bidders for the contract to build Berlin Airport. The practice remains well balanced, also embracing investigatory, state aid, public procurement, regulatory and European Court proceedings work.

Its lead lawyer, **Simon Polito** (see p.172), is "*a calm, collected figure who always presents clear and trenchant advice.*" He presides over a talented team which includes "*intellectual top-notcher*" **John Pheasant** (see p.172) (also the firm's International Practice Manager) and the "*dynamic and diplomatic*" **Lesley Ainsworth** (see p.169). She advised Kappa on its proposed acquisition of AssiDomän's packaging business securing approval under EU merger regulations, which included four authorities outside the EU.

Key matters undertaken of late include acting on the Mars/Royal Canin merger, representing Novell in the EC's proceedings against Microsoft for abuse of dominance, and advising Shimano of Japan on a controversial anti-dumping case. The firm also represented ONdigital in the OFT investigation into BSkyB. **Clients** Equitable Life; Mars; Granada; Texaco; Kappa; ONdigital; Nintendo; BT Cellnet.

SIMMONS & SIMMONS (see firm details p.1136) This practice rises in the tables this year in recognition of the "*uniformly high standard*" of its practitioners. Its core strengths lie in international cartel and regulatory work but merger and general litigation matters also feature highly. **Peter Freeman** (see p.170) is the engine of the practice, "*a mild-mannered but tremendously capable*" practitioner who generated fulsome praise from clients. Heading a strong group, he has an able foil in **Martin Smith** (see p.173) whose "*manner sits well in negotiations.*"

Together the two have continued to work on the long-running Interbrew case, attempting to overturn the Secretary of State's prohibition of the acquisition of Bass Brewers. The team has also assisted Barclays in the 19-month monopoly inquiry into SME banking and acted for one of the defendants in the vitamins cartel case. **Clients** AOL; Barclays; Cadbury Schweppes; Gallaher; Interbrew; ITC; Ofgem; Railtrack; Six Continents; Wal-Mart.

ALLEN & OVERY (see firm details p.841) Praised by our interviewees as being "*constructive, sensible and helpful,*" this firm allies traditional merger notification duties with an increasing amount of regulatory and behavioural work under the Competition Act. Its team, although perceived as being composed of fewer star individuals than its main rivals, is nevertheless felt to provide excellent advice. **Mark Friend** (see p.170) is seen as "*cautious but cerebral,*" while **John Wotton** (see p.174) "*commands respect, especially on regulatory matters,*" where he has particular expertise in the media, telecoms and water regulation sectors. Former barrister **Alistair Lindsay** (see p.171), meanwhile, gives an edge on the litigation front, being highly rated for his court work.

The group has had a major role in the ongoing British Racing inquiry into the terms set by the British Horseracing Board for licences to bookmakers of rights to broadcast British races. It has further acted in the Mastercard/Europay and Scottish Milk inquiries, and has advised One 2 One on the reference to the Competition Commission on call termination charges. **Clients** Accenture; Alliance & Leicester; BT; Coral; Imperial Tobacco; Marconi; News Corporation; One 2 One; Twentieth Century Fox; Vivendi; William Hill.

ASHURST MORRIS CRISP (see firm details p.852) Unusual in having in-house economists to advise, this firm has succeeded in creating a stand-alone practice of some repute. Covering mergers and related transactions, competition inquiries and investigations, state aid and procurement, and regulatory matters, it possesses individuals who are, according to clients, "*quick to grasp the point and expeditious in the turnaround of paperwork.*" **Nigel Parr** (see p.172) is "*diligent and incisive, bringing a deeply intellectual approach*" to his cases, while **Roger Finbow** (see p.170) is celebrated especially in the mergers sphere.

The team acted for Finmeccanica on EC merger control issues in connection with the formation of a guided weapons joint venture. It

LONDON ■ COMPETITION/ANTI-TRUST

also advised Johnston Press in the Competition Commission Inquiry into its proposed acquisition of the East Midlands newspaper titles of Trinity Mirror. A busy year on the investigation front has also seen the group acting for BT in relation to a number of investigations by Oftel into alleged anti-competitive practices. **Clients** Allied Domecq; BT; British Midland; Dairy Industry Federation; Ford Motor Company; IBM; Motorola; Northern Foods; QVC; United Business Media.

DENTON WILDE SAPTE (see firm details p.935) A consensus exists amongst our interviewees that this young team has done well to steady the ship following the departure of David Aitman to Freshfields Bruckhaus Deringer in 2001. The caseload remains substantial with the firm enjoying a strong client base in the pharmaceutical and retail sectors to complement its existing niche strengths in sport, media, banking and transport. Tackling both behavioural and merger control matters, **Polly Weitzman** (see p.174) received particular praise from clients for being "*always sharp and on top of her game,*" and is supported by **Suyong Kim** (see p.171), "*a clear communicator and a calming influence.*" The latter appeared to good effect on the Mastercard/Europay case advising MEPUK on the OFT's investigation following a notification for exemption under the Competition Act.

Other cases handled by the team include acting for Liberty Media on competition issues arising from a number of transactions, and appearing for the World Professional Billiards and Snooker Association over allegations of breach of Article 81 and 82 prohibitions. **Clients** Barclaycard; Film Distributors' Association; Hasbro; Liberty Media International; Premier League; Twentieth Century Fox Home Entertainment.

SJ BERWIN (see firm details p.867) Adjudged by our interviewees to be a firm at home before both the national and EU courts, this is "*a thriving trade and regulatory practice.*" The firm has offices in Madrid, Paris and Munich, and accordingly is known for the international flavour of its work, which includes merger notification, and trade and regulation matters. Its dominant figure is **Stephen Kon** (see p.171) who has successfully built the practice from a litigation base. "*Energetic and intellectual,*" he is known for the "*sophisticated and courteous manner*" in which he conducts his cases. Other members of this respected team include the "*precise*" **Simon Holmes** (see p.171) and the "*sparky*" **Elaine Gibson-Bolton** (see p.170). Within this broad framework lies a further capacity for specialism with the "*switched-on*" **Tom Usher** (see p.173) impressing in the media sphere and **Ralph Cohen** (see p.169) bringing expertise in the trade sector.

Recent highlights include acting for Dixons in resisting a challenge initiated by John Lewis and Tempo before the OFT to two exclusive distribution agreements entered into by Dixons with Compaq and Packard Bell. The group has also advised four AES electricity generators in the UK on regulatory matters. **Clients** Dixons; Marks & Spencer; Morgan Stanley Dean Witter; AES; Coca-Cola Enterprises; Diageo; Ladbroke Group; Universal Music Group.

BAKER & MCKENZIE (see firm details p.855) Undertaking merger, regulatory and compliance work in equal proportions, this international player trades off its global connections to secure a notable slice of the competition market. The practice remains ineluctably linked to the name of **Lynda Martin Alegi** (see p.172), who was commended by clients and peers for her "*ability to keep up with developments in the legal field*" twinned with "*a comprehensive understanding of the client's commercial needs.*" In previous years, reservations have existed as to whether she enjoys the necessary support to drive the practice, however these are now met with the inclusion in our tables this year of the "*direct and persuasive*" **Samantha Mobley** (see p.172).

Recent notable cases include representing Shell on the acquisition from RWE/DEA of its downstream oil and petrochemical business and advising Sony on the notification of its 3G mobile communications joint venture with Ericsson. The team has also acted for Christie's former chief executive in the Christie's/Sotheby's Auction Houses case and, drawing on its IP talents, represented Levi's before the UK courts in its action to prevent unauthorised grey imports of US goods. **Clients** Avis Europe; Camelot; Canon (UK); Kellogg Company of Great Britain; Seiko; Shell; Sony; Tetra Pak.

CLIFFORD CHANCE (see firm details p.911) Operating as part of a wider European Union team, this firm's London partners enjoy a diverse diet of work. Merger control, investigatory, state aid, public procurement, regulatory and all general behavioural work is undertaken. The firm represented EMI on the Commission and OFT investigations into CDs and represented Quaker Oats on its merger with Pepsi. Its regulatory experts have further advised a range of financial institutions in relation to the energy and water industries, whilst specialist behavioural advice is provided to a number of leading corporate clients. Yet the belief persists that the team lacks the array of high-flying practitioners necessary to challenge for top honours. The recent retirement of Jim Wheaton now leaves **John Osborne** (see p.172) as the sole entrant in our tables. **Clients** Accenture; Aventis; BNP; CGNU; Consignia; EMI; Eurostar; LIFFE (Holdings); MusicNet; Philip Morris; Safeway; TV3; Wessex Water.

NORTON ROSE (see firm details p.1084) This practice continues to garner plaudits from our interviewees despite the loss of the respected Trevor Soames to Howrey Simon Arnold & White and the reassignment to Brussels duties of John Cook. Sustained largely by merger control work but also covering general behavioural matters, the practice has an enviable client base, giving the firm considerable inroads into the banking, rail and energy sectors.

Lead partner **Martin Coleman** (see p.169) is known for his "*fighting qualities*" and "*skill in translating complex legalese into comprehensible commercial language.*" He recently acted for HSBC in the MEPUK (Mastercard/Europay) case and advised P&O on the establishment of a joint venture with, and sale of 50% of, Associated Bulk Carriers to Eurotower. The team as a whole also secured merger clearance for the leading French and UK internet service providers Wanadoo and Freeserve. **Clients** AXA; BMW; France Telecom; Hallmark Entertainment Network; HSBC; Mars; P&O Stena Line; SAS; Scottish Power; Xerox.

BRISTOWS (see firm details p.888) Operating within a firm solidly focused on IP rights, this department is endorsed by our interviewees for its "*high quality expertise and long track record in running competition cases.*" Inevitably, the emphasis is on the interface between IP and competition law with advice being given on European mergers and filings, compliance work and commercial agreements. Under the stewardship of Pat Treacy the team has advised Bayer on the competition aspects of commercial arrangements for its pharmaceutical, crop protection and animal health divisions. The group also advised Schering-Plough Animal Health Care in an OFT investigation under the Fair Trading Act, and acted for Chiron on the competition aspects of certain provisions of its European-wide technology licensing agreements. **Clients** AstraZeneca; Bayer; Chiron; Guinness; ICI Paints; Kodak; ntl; Siemens; Tetley; VIA Technologies.

CMS CAMERON MCKENNA (see firm details p.914) "*A big firm with a broad capability,*" this practice's profile overall is diminished only by its inability to field a major leading individual in the area. The group operates at both UK and EC levels and has a strong presence in Brussels, securing a varied caseload which incorporates merger control notification, state aid submissions and advice on Articles 81 and 82. The pharmaceutical and financial services areas remain strong, although transport has featured particularly highly over the past year with the team working on the reorganisation of Railtrack and the related refinancing of the Channel Tunnel Rail Link. It also advised Metronet on its bid for the London Underground Public Private Partnership and represented American Home Products on the Competition Commission inquiry into veterinary medicines. **Clients** American Home Products; Amazon.co.uk; Barclays Capital; Camelot; Channel Tunnel Rail Link; Consignia; Hutchison; Metronet; Railtrack.

COMPETITION/ANTI-TRUST ■ LONDON/SOUTH WEST/WALES

EVERSHEDS (see firm details p.949) In a market traditionally dominated by firms handling large-scale merger work, this department has successfully concentrated on behavioural and investigatory work. Taking advantage of the changing landscape following the introduction of the 1998 Competition Act it has been involved in a number of dawn raids and Section 26 investigations, often serviced by cross-office teams. **Ros Kellaway** (see p.171) ("*bright and with a strong commercial practice*") has worked on securing the first ever full immunity from fines for a company involved in a UK price fixing cartel, and successfully defended a multi-national sports goods manufacturer over allegations of price fixing. She is joined by **Stephen Rose** (see p.173), who "*gives the group an extra dimension*" through his merger control expertise. **Clients** ASDA Stores; BPI; Huntsman (Europe) BVBA; Novartis UK; Volkswagen Group (UK).

RICHARDS BUTLER (see firm details p.1112) A straight regulatory/anti-trust practice which also incorporates public procurement and state aid work. Its reputation lies mainly in its efforts in the media and transport sectors where Katherine Holmes (see p.171) has proved "*an effective presence for many years.*" Chairman of the Joint Working Party of the UK Bars and Law Societies on Competition Law, interviewees informed our researchers that she has "*a brilliant mind and always presents well in meetings.*" Her department acted for DaimlerChrysler UK on the reorganisation of its dealer network and in defending the group action brought on behalf of some dealers. Its media clients include the BBC which it has advised, inter alia, on potential changes to media regulations in the lead-up to the publication of the new Communications Bill. The firm also advised Direct Line on acquisitions of insurance businesses in Germany. **Clients** BBC; DaimlerChrysler UK; GNER; The Portman Group; Rank; Universal.

THEODORE GODDARD (see firm details p.1158) Active, for the most part, in non-merger related matters, the department is endorsed by clients for its "*business-oriented approach.*" Its core areas lie in the media, sports, telecoms, airline and healthcare sectors, where it can rely on a team that includes three lawyers who have worked for the Commission. Regulatory, and most obviously anti-dumping, issues are a speciality with **Guy Leigh** (see p.171), who brings his "*huge depth of experience*" to bear leading a team that provides ongoing competition advice to the British Horseracing Board. The firm has recently advised the Director General of Telecommunications on the process needed to introduce more competition into the local loop through local loop unbundling. **Clients** Associated British Foods; British Horseracing Board; Buena Vista International; Delta; Director General of Telecommunications; National Audit Office; Ryanair.

OTHER NOTABLE PRACTITIONERS "*Guru figure*" **Chris Bright** continues to busy himself with the task of establishing a competition platform at Shearman & Sterling. Often sought out by the financial press for his views in this field, his is a name much respected amongst his peers. **Richard Whish** maintains his position as "*up with the very best cerebrally*" in this most academic of legal disciplines. Also recommended is sole practitioner **Michael Hutchings** (see p.171) who is seen by his peers as "*a leading light on law reform.*"

SOUTH WEST

COMPETITION/ANTI-TRUST
■ SOUTH WEST

1. **Burges Salmon** Bristol
2. **Bond Pearce** Plymouth

LEADING INDIVIDUALS
1. **CLAYDON Laura** Burges Salmon
   COPPEN Simon Burges Salmon

This book is the product of 6,582 1/2 hour interviews. See p.7 for BMRB audit. Within each band, firms are listed alphabetically. See individuals' profiles p.169

BURGES SALMON (see firm details p.894) Although well capable of handling merger and regulatory work, this practice is increasingly aligning itself to behavioural cases. It has developed expertise in Competition Act issues through overseeing compliance audits, devising compliance programmes and setting up a dawn raid support group. Our researchers were impressed by the level of commendation for a team containing "*sensible lawyers one can deal with*" of the likes of **Laura Claydon** (see p.169), who is particularly adept in the investigatory and regulatory markets. Her colleague, **Simon Coppen** (see p.169), provides a "*more front-end role,*" exercising his "*substantial brainpower*" on the competition aspects of joint ventures. The team acted on the first OFT dawn raids, a number of investigations under Chapters I and II of the Act, and provided a broad range of advice on the application of EU and UK competition law to trading practices and policies. It further advised FirstGroup on the negotiation of undertakings to be given to the Secretary of State concerning the acquisition of SB Holdings. **Clients** FirstGroup; Racecourse Association; CHC Helicopter; Great Western Trains.

BOND PEARCE (see firm details p.879) Nick Page, although not a specialist practitioner in this field, handles competition work in a "*thoroughly decent*" manner. Unlike many others, the practice is not merger-driven, tending to concentrate more on compliance advice, dawn raids, state aid, and general Competition Act matters. With a strong retail client base, the group has advised on a number of high value commercial agreements and has acted on a variety of market conduct and compliance issues. It has also been appointed to the dawn raid panels for Hapag-Lloyd and Transco. **Clients** B&Q; Crown Estate Commissioners; Royal Yachting Association; Vosper Thorneycroft.

WALES

EDWARDS GELDARD (see firm details p.944) Ceri Delemore leads a team that acts for a client base largely constituted of manufacturers, academic organisations and the service sector. Accordingly, much of the work is for private clients, although some work is undertaken in the public sector for the likes of the Welsh Development Agency. The focus lies on merger notification, public procurement and general advice on commercial agreements. However, the last couple of years have witnessed an upsurge in pure competition inquiries from utility clients in the regulatory sphere and the team has also increasingly been working on internal compliance policies for major plc clients. **Clients** Public bodies; private corporates.

EVERSHEDS (see firm details p.949) The two part-time competition partners in Cardiff have now been joined by a specialist assistant (Tim London) to take advantage of the new Competition Act climate. Formerly known for its state aid and procurement work, the practice now has an additional capacity to handle work relating to compliance, dawn raid attendance and trading agreements. The team attended at one of the first Commission dawn raids and advised Anacomp on its response to a Section 26 notice, whilst also providing ongoing advice to Tarmac in relation to various trading agreements. The firm has also kept up its fine tradition on state aid work by advising the Welsh Development Agency on the implications of many of its different publicly funded activities. **Clients** Welsh Development Agency; MCCB; Dow Corning.

WALES/MIDLANDS/THE NORTH — COMPETITION/ANTI-TRUST

COMPETITION/ANTI-TRUST — WALES

1 Edwards Geldard Cardiff
Eversheds Cardiff
Morgan Cole Cardiff

This book is the product of 6,582 1/2 hour interviews. See p.7 for BMRB audit. Within each band, firms are listed alphabetically.

MORGAN COLE (see firm details p.1075) A firm which takes a national approach led out of Oxford by David Whibley. The Welsh arm, in common with the Thames Valley and London offices, handles state aid, public procurement and merger control work and further enjoys a sizeable public sector client base. Recent highlights for the national team include acting for a substantial multi-national company in an investigation into alleged price fixing, and representing a major petrol producer in respect of its network of reseller agreements. **Clients** Numerous clients in the energy, insurance and technology sectors.

MIDLANDS

COMPETITION/ANTI-TRUST — MIDLANDS

1 Pinsent Curtis Biddle Birmingham
Wragge & Co Birmingham
2 Eversheds Birmingham

LEADING INDIVIDUALS

1 LOUGHER Guy Wragge & Co
REES Kate Pinsent Curtis Biddle

This book is the product of 6,582 1/2 hour interviews. See p.7 for BMRB audit. Within each band, firms are listed alphabetically. See individuals' profiles p.169

PINSENT CURTIS BIDDLE (see firm details p.1102) Built up on the back of public procurement work, an area in which it is still regarded by our interviewees as strong, this practice has evolved into a much more multi-faceted beast. Operating as part of a national network it is now "*formidable on the contentious side,*" acting on dawn raids and other Competition Act-related issues. Cartel work is increasingly a speciality, with the firm having represented one client being pursued by both the Commission and US authorities. Main partner **Kate Rees** (see p.173) was commended to our researchers for her "*likeable personality and keen analytical mind.*" She continues to be expert on public procurement and has handled all such issues arising from the £45 million joint purchase of agency nursing services by all of the London NHS Trusts. **Clients** ARRIVA; Lattice; Glanbia; Iceland; BBC; Federal-Mogul.

WRAGGE & CO (see firm details p.1197) The biggest specialist competition team in the Midlands, which draws much of its vitality from an excellent corporate base. This feeds through a constant stream of high-level merger work, although the reputation of the practice is such that it effortlessly generates work of its own accord. M&A, state aid, public procurement, trade law and investigatory matters are all handled by a team consistently described by clients as "*responsive to a tight deadline.*" Now consolidated into a 16-strong Competition, Public Law and Regulation Team, the group is headed by **Guy Lougher**, celebrated for his "*swift and incisive advice.*" The firm acted for the British Betting Outlets Association on making a formal complaint under the Competition Act against the British Horseracing Board and has advised a range of public and private sector clients on public procurement issues. **Clients** British Betting Outlets Association; British Airways; Castrol; HJ Heinz; Ordnance Survey; Postwatch.

EVERSHEDS (see firm details p.949) This practice clearly benefits from being part of a national whole that includes sister offices in London, Nottingham, Cardiff and Leeds. The Midlands arm does, however, generate its own work largely in response to the needs of its corporate clients. Although active on the merger front where it has, for example, advised Britax International on its £441 million public to private merger filing, it is especially concerned with the behavioural side. Here, the group has advised and attended on three dawn raids, assisted Birmingham International Airport on various aspects of its pricing policy, and counselled Diageo on the competition implications of the disposal of Guinness World Records. The team is led by Richard Prowse. **Clients** Britax International; Birmingham International Airport; DSM UK; Granada Compass; Volvo Truck and Bus.

THE NORTH

COMPETITION/ANTI-TRUST — THE NORTH

1 Eversheds Leeds
2 Addleshaw Booth & Co Leeds
3 Pinsent Curtis Biddle Leeds
4 Dickinson Dees Newcastle upon Tyne

LEADING INDIVIDUALS

1 COLLINSON Adam Eversheds
2 DAVEY Jonathan Addleshaw Booth & Co
JURKIW Andrij Pinsent Curtis Biddle
LINDRUP Garth Addleshaw Booth & Co
3 WARWICK Neil Dickinson Dees
4 MCDONNELL Phil Addleshaw Booth & Co
SCHOLES Jeremy Walker Morris

This book is the product of 6,582 1/2 hour interviews. See p.7 for BMRB audit. Within each band, firms are listed alphabetically. See individuals' profiles p.169

EVERSHEDS (see firm details p.949) In common with the rest of the offices in its national network, this firm's Northern presence concentrates heavily on behavioural/investigatory matters. Ruth Connorton drives the Newcastle department along effectively but the jewel in the crown remains the Leeds branch under **Adam Collinson** (see p.169). "*Combative, but a well-rounded, full-service competition lawyer,*" his status is such that peers agree he is "*everybody's major competitor.*" His recent highlights include a submission on behalf of Stanley Leisure to the OFT regarding abuse of dominance by the British Horseracing Board, and advising Kuwait Petroleum (GB) on the competition issues arising out of Kuwait's participation in the Oil Industry Memorandum of Understanding. Cases handled in the Newcastle office include advising six major brewers on obtaining positive guidance for non-notification of an agreement relating to the use of drinks dispensing equipment. **Clients** BPI; Stanley Leisure; Huntsman Europe; ASDA; Guinness.

ADDLESHAW BOOTH & CO (see firm details p.838) Geographically split between Manchester and Leeds, although cohesive in its approach, this is a team housing "*some of the best academic brains*" in the region. The workload tends heavily towards trade and regulatory matters while public procurement remains a key area and the occasional dawn raid, merger control and investigatory case is handled. Its key individuals endorsed by our interviewees are **Jonathan Davey** (see p.170), "*a man of many talents who is academically ahead of the game,*" and **Garth Lindrup** (see p.171), "*a careful, thoughtful lawyer with a real feel for the subject.*" Now joined by two recent additions, the team has offered state aid advice to the Northwest Development Agency, and represented Oystertec on merger control in eight EU and non-EU jurisdictions arising from its acquisition of plumbings fittings business Delta. It is also on standby for dawn raid support for a number of clients, including some multi-national companies with offices in the region. The group has been joined by former Garretts man **Phil McDonnell** (see p.172), a veteran of a number of interesting utility and regulation cases. **Clients** adidas (UK); Airtours; ASDA; BAT; Eddie Stobart; Invensys; Lancaster University.

COMPETITION/ANTI-TRUST ■ THE NORTH/SCOTLAND

PINSENT CURTIS BIDDLE (see firm details p.1102) An eclectic portfolio sees this practice handling merger clearance, public procurement, parallel imports, compliance issues, Commission investigations and complaints under the Competition Act. It has come to particular prominence recently for its cartel work and involvement with dawn raids, where it is a particular leader in the field. The prop of the practice is **Andrij Jurkiw** (see p.171), a merger and behavioural expert who "*comes across with the clients very well.*" Often working in close co-operation with other of the firm's offices, he has defended a client accused of participation in a major international cartel and defended a retail client accused of being involved in an anti-competitive agreement. He also obtained merger clearance for Abbot's £136 million acquisition of Deutsche Tiefbohr. **Clients** Abbot; Arla Foods; Pace Micro Technology; SIG; Smith & Nephew.

DICKINSON DEES (see firm details p.938) With a strong reputation, particularly in the transport sector, this team has carved a reputation amongst our interviewees as "*the premier full-service competition practice in Newcastle.*" Its non-contentious capability covers state aid, anti-dumping, compliance programmes and regulatory notifications whilst it also wins plaudits for its merger clearance activities. As a mark of distinction it handled the first ever dawn raid under the Competition Act and has followed this up with three further cases, all of which are allegations of cartel behaviour under Chapter I. The engine of the practice is **Neil Warwick** (see p.173), who "*has really earned his spurs*" and obtained a name outside the region. Other cases he has handled include an EC merger clearance on behalf of Govia/Go-Ahead, and the securing of clearance from the OFT for ARRIVA to acquire a High Wycombe bus company. The firm has also set up group-wide compliance programmes for Go-Ahead and ARRIVA. **Clients** ARRIVA; Go-Ahead; Nike UK.

OTHER NOTABLE PRACTITIONERS Jeremy Scholes (see p.173) of Walker Morris, although largely preoccupied with matters academic, is further recognised as having amassed a wealth of experience on merger control.

SCOTLAND

COMPETITION/ANTI-TRUST ■ SCOTLAND

1
- Maclay Murray & Spens Edinburgh, Glasgow
- Shepherd+ Wedderburn WS Edinburgh

2
- Biggart Baillie Glasgow
- Burness Edinburgh
- Dundas & Wilson CS Edinburgh
- MacRoberts Glasgow

LEADING INDIVIDUALS

1
- DEAN Michael Maclay Murray & Spens

2
- DOWNIE Gordon Shepherd+ Wedderburn WS
- MILLER Colin Biggart Baillie

3
- MCLEAN James Burness

This book is the product of 6,582 1/2 hour interviews. See p.7 for BMRB audit. Within each band, firms are listed alphabetically. See individuals' profiles p.169

MACLAY MURRAY & SPENS (see firm details p.1048) Now fully independent from the firm's corporate department, this competition team has increased its visibility amongst its competitors. A sound client base produces a welter of merger work amidst a general diet of procurement, state aid, and behavioural work. Lead partner **Michael Dean** (see p.170) is described as a "*gregarious empire builder*" much appreciated by his clients and credited with having improved turnover significantly. Ever looking to expansion he has secured a position for the team on the panel of legal advisors to Ofgem, advising on a range of regulatory and competition matters. Examples of his general work include advising on an EC investigation into alleged cartel activity and assisting clients on both EC and OFT dawn raids. He has further advised Scottish Enterprise on a range of EC-related issues and counselled a major trade association on the competition implications of Scottish Parliament proposals to regulate lobbyists. **Clients** British Polythene Industries; Grampian Holdings; Ofgem; Scottish Enterprise; Pringle.

SHEPHERD+ WEDDERBURN WS (see firm details p.1130) Public procurement, state aid, compliance and behavioural work are all handled along with merger control activity. Fronted by **Gordon Downie** (see p.170), the team has a healthy relationship with Scottish Power and has recently outstripped its rivals to become principal advisor to Scottish Enterprise. Fundamentally a corporate finance lawyer, Downie has successfully remoulded himself and is judge by our interviewees as "*highly confident and technically superb*" in this area. Supported by an assistant who is a pure competition specialist, he acted for Lothian Buses in a complaint to the OFT concerning a rival's abuse of dominance and advised John Wood Group on a major joint venture to serve Shell in the North Sea. The firm has also acted as consultant to the Scottish Executive in examining the options for restructuring the Western Isles Ferry Services and has given procurement advice to the Scottish Parliament. **Clients** Lothian Buses; Royal & Ancient Golf Club; Scottish Newcastle; Scottish Enterprise; Scottish Parliament; Scottish Rugby Union.

BIGGART BAILLIE (see firm details p.871) A firm with "*a definite presence*" claim our interviewees; its caseload comprises substantial public procurement work fused with general competition advice on commercial agreements. **Colin Miller** "*knows what he's about,*" having previously gained valuable experience in the larger English firms and has seen his compliance and cartel practice burgeon with the introduction of the Competition Act. He has, for example, advised Graham's Dairies on an OFT investigation into an alleged cartel in the Scottish dairy market and continues to advise The Drambuie Liqueur Company on the competition law implications of its distribution arrangements. **Clients** Global Video; The Drambuie Liqueur Company; Graham's Dairies.

BURNESS Despite the lack of dedicated specialists in this area "*perfectly competent competition advice*" is available here. Servicing its corporate clients, assistance is provided on acquisitions, disposals, procurement and the impact of the Competition Act on individual businesses generally. The majority of the work is negotiated, within a broader practice, by **Jim McLean**, who is noted for his "*great mind and up-to-the-minute knowledge of the law.*" **Clients** Corporates.

DUNDAS & WILSON CS (see firm details p.943) The bulk of this practice is taken up with assisting existing corporate clients on EU and UK competition issues. For the most part, merger advice is provided for clients looking to embark on joint ventures, with the public procurement side of affairs being handled by a separate department. Christian Hook heads a team which has advised East of Scotland Water on competition issues, including the reviewing of business practices, the putting in place of compliance programmes and the redrafting of agreements. The group also advised the Royal Bank of Scotland on the buyout of a 50% stake in Virgin Direct Personal Finance. **Clients** Macfarlane; Scottish Media; Rangers Football Club; Royal Bank of Scotland.

MACROBERTS (see firm details p.1049) David Flint handles competition matters within the framework of a broader practice. Dealing with competition issues where they impact upon his general caseload, he concerns himself with merger notifications, compliance and third-party interventions. Flint is a member of the CBI Competition Panel, and also represents British Energy on all its competition issues. **Clients** British Energy; Coca-Cola Schweppes; Johnston Press; Campbell Distillers.

THE LEADERS IN COMPETITION/ANTI-TRUST

AINSWORTH, Lesley
Lovells, London
(020) 7296 2000
lesley.ainsworth@lovells.com
Specialisation: Specialist work includes UK and EC competition law (advisory work, investigations by the Office of Fair Trading, the Competition Commission and the EC Commission and proceedings before the European Court of Justice and national courts; state aids; free movement of goods and services; advice on proposed EU legislation and the implementation of EU legislation in Member States.
Prof. Memberships: Member, Solicitors' European Group.
Career: Articled *Lovells*; qualified 1981; London 1979-83; Brussels office 1983-85; secondment to *LeBoeuf, Lamb, Leiby & McRae* 1985-86; London since 1986; Partner 1988.

AITMAN, David
Freshfields Bruckhaus Deringer, London
(020) 7936 4000
david.aitman@freshfields.com
Specialisation: Partner. Advising on all areas of EC and domestic competition law, particularly in the energy, transport, manufacturing, retail, communications and media sectors, and on regulation, in connection with privatised utilities.
Prof. Memberships: Competition Law Association; International Bar Association.
Career: Qualified 1982. Partner *Denton Hall* 1988. Joined *Freshfields Bruckhaus Deringer* 2001.
Publications: Editor of intellectual property licensing in Butterworths' 'Encyclopedia of Competition Law', of competition law in 'Practical Intellectual Property' and in the 'Yearbook of Media Law' and author of telecoms chapter in 'Bellamy & Child'.
Personal: Born 1956. Educated at the Royal Academy of Music.

ALLAN, Bill
Linklaters, London
(020) 7456 3574
bill.allan@linklaters.com
Specialisation: Specialises in EC and UK anti-trust law, mergers and acquisitions, and other competition and trade-related areas of the law. He has extensive experience in the UK and EC context, representing clients from diverse industries including the utilities, food, transport, brewing, leisure, chemicals and computer industries.
Prof. Memberships: Member of the Advisory Board of the Centre of European Legal Studies, Cambridge University.
Career: Head of the EU and Competition Law Group since 1999. Partner, *Linklaters* London since 1982. 1989-92, Partner, Head of *Linklaters* Brussels. 1982-89, Partner, *Linklaters* London. 1976-82, Assistant Solicitor, *Linklaters* London.

BRIGHT, Christopher
Shearman & Sterling, London
(020) 7655 5000

CARLTON, Roderick
Freshfields Bruckhaus Deringer, London
(020) 7936 4000
roderick.carlton@freshfields.com
Specialisation: Partner in competition and trade group advising on EU and UK competition laws, including merger control, joint ventures, monopolies, distribution, licensing and state aids.
Prof. Memberships: Joint Competition Law Working Party of the Bars and Law Societies of the UK
Career: Assistant solicitor at *Freshfields* 1990-99; year spent on secondment to Reuters' in-house legal department 1994-95; partner 1999.

CARSTENSEN, Laura
Slaughter and May, London
(020) 7600 1200
laura.carstensen@slaughterandmay.com
Specialisation: Partner, Competition Department. Practice in UK and EU competition law, predominantly in relation to strategic corporate events (M&A; key changes in business policy and practice) and contentious situations (cartel/abuse of dominance inquiries). Extensive experience before the European Commission, Office of Fair Trading, Competition Commission and European Courts.
Career: Qualified 1987 with *Slaughter and May* and became a Partner in 1994.
Personal: Born 11 November 1960. Educated Withington Girls School, Manchester, then St. Hilda's College, Oxford (English Lang. & Lit.). Lives in Hampstead, London.

CHAPPATTE, Philippe
Slaughter and May, London
(020) 7600 1200
philippe.chappatte@slaughterandmay.com
Specialisation: Provides a wide range of UK and EU competition law advice (including on state aid) in connection with transactions, litigation and regulatory investigations. Recent EU cases include the proposed dual listed company merger between BHP and Billiton, the proposed merger of British Airways and KLM, the mobile joint venture between Ericsson and Sony, Telia/Telenor and Carnival's acquisition of P&O. Involvement in European Court cases and Competition Commission investigations both in monopoly and in merger cases. Recent UK cases include acting for Punch in its contested acquisition of the Allied pub estate, the Carlton/United/Granada and Anglo/Tarmac mergers, British Airways' acquisition of British Regional Air Lines and the Royal Caribbean/P&O merger.
Prof. Memberships: Co-founder of European Competition Lawyers Forum.
Career: Bryanston School. Oxford University (BA Law, First Class). Université Libre de Bruxelles (Lic.Sp.Dr. Eur., Highest Distinction). Qualified *Slaughter and May* 1982. Partner 1989. Responsible for running and development of Brussels office between April 1991 and August 1996.
Personal: Three children.

CLAYDON, Laura
Burges Salmon, Bristol
(0117) 939 2273
laura.claydon@burges-salmon.com
Specialisation: Main area of practice is competition and regulatory law; advised on and attended the first dawn raids in the UK under the 1998 Act; has conducted many merger cases and competition investigations before the OFT acting particularly for clients in the transport, food, sports and media and oil and gas industries. Recent cases include: the MMC inquiry into the acquisition by FirstBus plc (now FirstGroup plc) of SB Holdings Limited and subsequent review by the DTI/OFT which reduced divestment to behavioural undertakings; the Competition Commission inquiry into the acquisition by CHC Helicopter Corporation of Helicopter Services Group (referred September 1999); advised on and attended the first dawn raids in the UK under the 1998 Act; many cases involving allegations of price-fixing, market sharing, predatory behaviour, predatory pricing and refusal to supply. Advises on competition audits and compliance procedures in view of the new Competition Act 1998.
Prof. Memberships: Solicitors European Group, Law Society
Career: Joined *Burges Salmon* in 1988 and became a partner in 1996. Until 1990 she worked in the corporate service group gaining general experience in all types of company and commercial work dealing mostly with private companies.

COHEN, Ralph
SJ Berwin, London
(020) 7533 2701
ralph.cohen@sjberwin.com
Specialisation: Partner specialising in EU and UK competition law and EU trade and customs law. Has extensive experience representing clients before the OFT, Competition Commission and European Commission across a wide range of industries. Practice areas include EU and UK merger clearances and co-ordinating multijurisdictional filings, advising on compatibility of commercial agreements with competition law compliance, cartel leniency applications, anti-dumping investigations, WTO and general customs related issues.
Prof. Memberships: Solicitors European Group.
Career: Qualified 1983. Partner at *SJ Berwin* 1991.
Personal: Born 10 May 1959. Attended Clifton College, and University of Southampton. Married with three sons.

COLEMAN, Martin
Norton Rose, London
(020) 7444 3347
colemanmay@nortonrose.com
Specialisation: Martin Coleman is Head of the Competition and EC Department at *Norton Rose*. He has led many cases before the European Commission, the Office of Fair Trading, The Competition Commission and UK sectoral regulators. Martin specialises in merger control (including contested bids), advising complainants and respondents in relation to investigations by competition authorities and advising businesses on antitrust compliance and competition law strategic planning. Martin has extensive experience in the application of UK and EC regulations in areas such as energy, transport, banking and financial services.
Career: Qualified 1978; Degree BA, BCL Oxford; Languages – French.
Publications: Martin is a regular speaker at conferences on EC and competition law topics and has written a number of articles for both specialist and more general publications. He is also co-author (with Michael Grenfell) of 'The Competition Act 1998' (OUP, 1999).

COLLINSON, Adam G
Eversheds, Leeds
(0113) 243 0391
adamcollinson@eversheds.com
Specialisation: Partner in Commercial Department and Head of EU/Competition Practice for Leeds/Manchester. EU and UK competition and related commercial law. Significant exposure to automotive and chemical industries. Particular experience in advising on competition law compliance, merger control and pricing and distribution strategies. Advised Asda in its campaigns to end resale price maintenance for books and OTC medicines.
Prof. Memberships: Law Society's European Group (Committee Member – Yorkshire Branch).
Career: Qualified in 1990 (*McKenna & Co*). Joined *Eversheds* in 1994. Became a Partner in 1998. Educated at Oundle School and Durham University (Hatfield College).
Publications: Co-authored 'CBI Business Guide to Competition Act' (July 2001).
Personal: Married with two daughters. Lives in Wetherby.

COPPEN, Simon
Burges Salmon, Bristol
(0117) 939 2291
simon.coppen@burges-salmon.com
See under Transport, p.801

CUTTING, Michael
Linklaters, London
(020) 7456 3514
michael.cutting@linklaters.com
Specialisation: Specialist in EU and UK competition and utility law and practice.

COMPETITION/ANTI-TRUST ■ THE LEADERS

Considerable experience of the application of competition law in the telecommunications, leisure and transport sectors.
Career: 1984 Trinity Hall, Cambridge University, MA. 1995 to date Partner Competition and Regulatory Law Group *Linklaters*. 1988-95 Assistant Solicitor *Linklaters*. 1986-88 articled clerk *Linklaters*.

DAVEY, Jonathan
Addleshaw Booth & Co, Manchester
(0161) 934 6349
jonathan.davey@addleshawbooth.com
Specialisation: Partner in Trade & Regulatory Department, Commercial Services Division. Main areas of work in this field are UK and EC competition law (including mergers and anti-competitive behaviour), public procurement law and state aids. Has been involved in the recent past in a number of significant notifications and complaints to the EC Commission and has considerable experience of UK Merger Control and of advising on UK competition law generally.
Prof. Memberships: Association Internationale des Jeunes Avocats, CBI National Consumer Law Advisory Panel, North West Law Society's European Group.
Career: Joined the firm in 1986 and qualified in 1988. Became an Associate in 1992 and a Partner in 1994.
Personal: Educated at Manchester University 1982-85 (LLB Hons) and the College of Law, Chester 1985-86 (1st Class Hons in Law Society Final Examination). Enjoys hill walking, travel and good food.

DEAN, Michael
Maclay Murray & Spens, Glasgow
(0141) 248 5011
mjd@maclaymurrayspens.co.uk
Specialisation: Brussels +32 2 282 8415 Head of EU and Competition Law Department. Practice covers agency, distribution, EC, UK and multi-state merger clearances, advising on general competition law issues, general European law issues; Competition Commission proceedings; public procurement issues, procedures and notices. Also Scottish Parliament issues. Recent cases involved European Commission and OFT cartel investigations following dawn raids. Implementation of compliance programmes across six European jurisdictions. Advice on dominance and pricing. Re-appointed to the panel of law firms advising the UK electricity and gas regulator. Advised extensively on the Utilities Act and Licensing Schemes. Frequently presents to business lawyers on export issues, competition and European law. Recent presentation included 'European Distribution' at ALI-ABA Conference in San Francisco.
Prof. Memberships: Law Society of Scotland; Scottish Lawyers European Group. Competition Law Association.
Career: Qualified 1986. Assistant Solicitor, *Lovell White Durrant*, London 1988-90. Assistant Solicitor and Partner *McGrigor Donald* 1991-97. Recruited by *Maclays* as Partner. Former external examiner, Europa Institute, Edinburgh.
Personal: Educated at St. Aloysius' College, Glasgow 1968-78, University of Glasgow (LLB Hons and Diploma in Legal Practice) 1978-83, and at the College of Europe, Bruges, (Diploma in Advanced European Studies) 1983-84. Interests include golf. Born 15 January 1960. Lives in Glasgow.

DOWNIE, Gordon
Shepherd+ Wedderburn, Edinburgh
(0131) 473 5162
gordon.downie@shepwedd.co.uk
Specialisation: Head of the firm's Competition and Regulation Group, which deals with the full range of UK and EC competition law work, ranging from merger and anti-trust clearances, to contentious proceedings and complaints to the OFT and European Commission. Experienced in assisting clients in setting up and maintaining compliance programmes to minimise their exposure to the legal consequences of breach of competition laws. Also advises clients across a variety of regulated sectors in their dealings with sectoral regulators, such as OFGEM, OFWAT, and OFTEL, and on compliance with their regulatory obligations.
Prof. Memberships: Law Society of Scotland, WS Society, Scottish Lawyers European Group, member of LSS Competition Law Sub-committee.
Career: Qualified 1992 with *Shepherd+ Wedderburn*. Assumed as partner in 1998.
Personal: Born 7 May 1966. University of Edinburgh, graduated LLB (Hons) 1988. European University Institute, graduated LLM 1990. Lives in Edinburgh.

FINBOW, Roger
Ashurst Morris Crisp, London
(020) 7638 1111
roger.finbow@ashursts.com
Specialisation: Partner in company department. Member of competition group. Head of sports law group. Handles all aspects of corporate and commercial law, and competition law, especially mergers regulation. Recent matters include: Competition Commission inquiries into the merger of United News & Media and Carlton Communications; the acquisition by Air Canada of Canadian Airways; the joint venture between Pentre and Askern; the merger between Exel and Ocean Group; the joint ventures between Smith & Nephew and Beiersdorf. Joint author of 'UK Merger Control: Law and Practice'.
Career: Qualified in 1977. Joined *Ashurst Morris Crisp* in 1975, becoming a partner in 1984.
Personal: Born 13 May 1952. Attended Woodbridge School 1963-70 and Mansfield College Oxford 1971-74 (MA 1977). Leisure interests include classic cars, collecting model cars, motor biking, keeping fit, ballet. Director of Ipswich Town Football Club Co. Limited; governor of The Seckford Foundation. Lives in the Suffolk/Essex borders.

FLECK, Richard
Herbert Smith, London
(020) 7374 8000
richard.fleck@herbertsmith.com
Specialisation: Worldwide Practice Partner. Has built up a wide-ranging practice embracing competition and regulation, corporate, insolvency, dispute resolution and accountancy work and has been involved in many high-profile transactions and disputes.
Prof. Memberships: Member of the Auditing Practices Board since 1986. Inspector appointed by the Bank of England under the Banking Act 1986.
Career: Qualified 1973. Partner at *Herbert Smith* since 1979.
Personal: Educated at Southampton University.

FREEMAN, Peter
Simmons & Simmons, London
(020) 7628 2020
peter.freeman@simmons-simmons.com
Specialisation: Head of EC and competition law. Area of practice is EC and UK competition and regulatory law, including mergers. Sector specialisations include broadcasting, energy and utilities and consumer products. Recent cases include the Competition Commission SME Banking Inquiry (for Barclays).
Prof. Memberships: IBA, UIA, Law Society, Competition Law Association. Chairman of the Regulatory Policy Institute, Oxford.
Career: Barrister 1972. Joined *Simmons & Simmons* in 1973. Solicitor 1977. Partner 1978.
Publications: Joint General Editor (with Richard Whish) of 'Butterworths Competition Law'. Author (with Richard Whish) of 'A Guide to the Competition Act 1998'. (Butterworths, 1999).
Personal: Born 2 October 1948. Attended Kingswood School, Bath; Goethe Institut, Berlin; Trinity College, Cambridge and Université Libre de Bruxelles. Leisure interests include naval history and music.

FRIEND, Mark
Allen & Overy, London
(020) 7330 3000
mark.friend@allenovery.com.
Specialisation: Partner specialising in UK and EC competition law and utilities regulation. Has wide experience of dealing with the OFT, competition commission, sectoral regulators and the EC Commission.
Prof. Memberships: Member of City of London Law Society Competition Law Sub-committee, Solicitors European Group, IBA.
Career: Qualified 1982, Partner 1990. Numerous contributions to legal journals on competition law.
Personal: Gonville and Caius College, Cambridge University (1979 BA Law) Université Libre de Bruxelles (Lic Spec en Droit Eur 1983).

GIBSON-BOLTON, Elaine
SJ Berwin, London
(020) 7533 2463
elaine.gibson-bolton@sjberwin.com
Specialisation: EU, competition and regulatory law with a particular expertise in 'regulated industries' such as energy, transport, media and communications. Regularly represents clients before the European Commission, Competition Commission, Office of Fair Trading, DTI and utility regulators. Team Leader of 'Legal Business Competition Team of the Year 2000', for successfully challenging Ofgem on behalf of US electricity generators AES before the Competition Commission in their wholesale electricity pricing investigation. She advises on a wide range of energy related matters including gas and electricity liberalisation. She is also heavily involved with advising on the application of EU and UK competition law and regulation to the air transport sector. She also has extensive experience advising on proactive and reactive behavioural matters under the UK Competition Act and EC Treaty. Also known for experience in EU and UK mergers and joint ventures. Has developed a particular expertise in the application of the EC Merger Regulation and domestic merger provisions to complex private equity transactions, advising a range of private equity houses, funds and industry trade associations and investors in close conjunction with the firm's private equity group. She continues to divide her working week between London and Brussels. Elaine writes and lectures widely on EU and competition law.
Prof. Memberships: Member of the Institute for Advanced Legal Studies; Law Society's European Group; Freeman of the City of London Solicitors' Livery Company; member European Aviation Association; founder Women in Media; member Regulatory Policy Institute.
Career: University of Reading LLB (Hons) 1980-83; University of Amsterdam, Postgraduate Diploma in European Integration 1983-84; Trained *Clifford Harris & Co* 1985-87; qualified 1987; *Holman, Fenwick and Willan* 1987-89; *Freshfields*, London and Brussels 1989-93; *SJ Berwin*, London and Brussels 1993 to date; Partner 1997.
Publications: 'Subsidiarity' – National Courts and EC Competition Matters; 'The Times' – GATT – The Perspective from Brussels; 'News Brief' – Kellogg's Cornflakes as Loss Leaders; 'Briefing Note' – The Double Whammy for Recording Artists' Contracts; 'PLC – The Sony Dispute' Failed bid for Freedom; 'Water Bulletin' – Gas Lights the Way; 'WA Rothnie Book Review' – Parallel Imports; 'Dealmaker' – How does the EC Merger Regulation Influence Private Equity.
Personal: Foreign travel; sports; film and music.

THE LEADERS — COMPETITION/ANTI-TRUST

HOLMES, Katherine
Richards Butler, London
(020) 7772 5945
kmh@richardsbutler.com
Specialisation: Partner in EU and competition group; specialises in EC and UK competition law and EC law generally. Advises clients from a wide variety of industries, including transport, media and entertainment, leisure, food and drink, construction, pharmaceuticals, telecommunications and computer software.
Prof. Memberships: Chairman of Joint Working Party of the UK Bars and Law Societies on Competition Law; Solicitors European Group; former Chairman and Vice-President of the Bar Association for Commerce, Finance and Industry (BACFI).
Career: Qualified as a barrister (1973). Joined *CBI* in 1976 becoming head of commercial law; from 1981 senior legal advisor to two major public companies; in 1989, joined *Richards Butler*, became partner in 1991.

HOLMES, Simon
SJ Berwin, London
(020) 7533 2222
simon.holmes@sjberwin.com
Specialisation: A wide range of work including extensive range of merger work acting for the parties, complainants or third parties; advising on dominance issues (pricing/discounts/parallel imports etc); a wide range of commercial arrangements both on and off-line.
Prof. Memberships: Recent chairman, Law Society's European group.
Career: 1st Class Hons, Law and Economics from Cambridge. Grande Distinction, Licence Spéciale en Droit Européen, Brussels University.
Personal: Married, two daughters. Walking, cycling, film.

HUTCHINGS, Michael
Michael Hutchings, Warminster
(07768) 105777
mbh@dircon.co.uk
Specialisation: Advice on all aspects of EU law, especially internal market, competition and regulation; UK implementation of EU law; UK competition law.
Prof. Memberships: British Institute of International and Comparative Law (Chairman of Executive Committee). Solicitors European Group (Former Chairman). European Competition Law Review (Editorial Board).
Career: Qualified 1973; articled with *McKenna & Co* ; partner *Lovell White Durrant* 1981-96; established independent sole practice 1996.
Personal: Born 8 November 1948.

JURKIW, Andrij
Pinsent Curtis Biddle, Leeds
(0113) 294 5180
andrij.jurkiw@pinsents.com
Specialisation: Head of competition, Leeds. Specialises in merger clearances, OFT, EC Commission and Competition Commission investigations; notifications and complaints to EC Commission; competition law litigation; competition law compliance programmes; parallel imports and public procurement. Important cases: advising Whitbread and Punch Retail on the merger implications of the £250m sale of First Quench to Nomura; advising Arriva plc in relation to the first dawn raids by the OFT under the Competition Act 1998; acting in one of the few concluded Early Guidance Applications under the Competition Act and in what is believed to be the first interim measures application under the Competition Act. Currently acting in a major concurrent cartel investigation by the EC Commission and US Department of Justice and defending two cartels being investigated by the OFT following dawn raids (which we also attended).
Prof. Memberships: Law Society. Solicitors' European Group.
Career: Articled *Slater Heelis* 1987-89; *Hammond Suddards* EC Unit 1989-91; *Eversheds* (Manchester) 1991-94, setting up EC Practice. *Pinsent Curtis Biddle* 1994 to date. Partner 1999. Law degree – Leeds Metropolitan University.
Personal: Travel, choral singing, fine wines, classic cars, photography.

KELLAWAY, Rosalind
Eversheds, London
(020) 7919 4500
kellawr@eversheds.com
Specialisation: Rosalind Kellaway chairs the Eversheds national EU and Competition Group. Her practice covers all aspects of EU and competition law practice with particular expertise in motor industry, financial services, insurance industries and utilities work. She handles all types of related commercial work including distributive and licensing systems and complex contractual work generally.
Prof. Memberships: Solicitors European Group, CBI Competition Law Committee, Joint Bar Council and Law Society Working Party on Competition Law.
Career: Qualified in 1984. Joined *Jaques & Lewis* (now *Eversheds*) in 1981, becoming a partner in 1989.
Publications: 'Competition Act 1988: A Practical Guide' (Tolleys).
Personal: Born 10th June 1957. Attended Lewes Priory School and the University of Sussex 1979 (BA Law with French). Leisure interests include riding. Lives in Lewes.

KIM, Suyong
Denton Wilde Sapte, London
(020) 7246 7000
sk@dentonwildesapte.com
Specialisation: Practises UK EC competition law. Advises on transactions (mergers, joint ventures and other commercial arrangements) and contentious matters (cartels and abuse of market power inquiries). Also advises on competition and regulatory issues in relation to the regulated utilities. Particular experience of the media, telecommunications, energy and transport sectors. Extensive experience before the European Commission, Office of Fair Trading, Competition Commission and European Courts.
Prof. Memberships: Regulatory Policy Institute, Oxford; Law Society's European Group.
Career: Qualified *Richards Butler* 1988; joined *Lovells* Brussels 1990; Partner *Denton Wilde Sapte* 1999.
Personal: Born 1962. Educated Wellington College, Berkshire; St Anne's College, Oxford (English Language & Literature); and London Business School (MBA).

KON, Stephen
SJ Berwin, London
(020) 7533 2237
stephen.kon@sjberwin.com
Specialisation: Head of the EU and Competition Department at *SJ Berwin*. Extensive experience in representing clients in contentious and non-contentious EU and domestic competition work, as well as general EU law. Regularly represents clients in proceedings before the Office of Fair Trading, the Monopolies and Mergers Commission, the European Commission and the Court of First Instance and the European Court of Justice in Luxembourg. Represented the European Commission in a number of competition cases before the CFI and the ECJ and has acted in a number of significant merger clearance enquiries; for example for Guinness in the EU clearance of its merger with Grand Metropolitan, for which the team won the Legal Business Competition Team of the Year award, and most recently for Diageo in the phase one clearance of its joint acquisition of the Seagram spirits and wines business with Pernod Ricard.
Prof. Memberships: 1986 Chairman of the Law Society's Solicitors' European Group; International Bar Association; Law Society's Solicitors' European Group.
Career: With *SJ Berwin* since formation in 1982, previously with a major City law firm; subsequently taught European Community and Competition Law at the Universities of Sussex and Reading. Most recently visiting lecturer at University of Oxford.
Publications: Has written and lectured extensively on various subjects relating to EU and competition law and numerous articles in most of the leading European law reviews, and most recently *SJ Berwin's* major looseleaf publication, 'The Competition Law of the UK'.

LEIGH, Guy
Theodore Goddard, London
(020) 7606 8855
guyleigh@theodoregoddard.co.uk
Specialisation: Mergers and acquisitions (domestic and international), public takeovers, board removal proxy battles, flotations, rights issues, secondary issues, public placings, venture capital, private placings, management buy-outs, public to private transactions, joint ventures, shareholders' agreements, investment consortia, corporate reconstructions, listing rules and corporate governance advice, directors' duties, shareholder actions, the law relating to shareholder meetings, insolvency advice to directors, share options and executive service agreements.
Prof. Memberships: Law Society.
Career: Career:*Sacker & Partners* (1978-80), Articled Clerk; *Forsyte Kerman* (1980-82), Assistant; *Speechly Bircham* (1982-89), Assistant/Partner; *Mishcon de Reya* (1989-95), Partner; *Theodore Goddard* (1995-to date), Partner.
Publications: Co-author with Diana Guy of 'The EEC and Intellectual Property'. The author of various articles on EC law and a frequent speaker at the competition law conferences.
Personal: Education: Gravesend School for Boys (1969-74); University College, London (1974-77); College of Law, Lancaster Gate (1977-78). Born 10 May 1956 (Gillingham, Kent). Married (Jane) – two children (Anna 7 and Alex 5). Interests: eating out, cinema, seeing friends, playing with my children, gardening and DIY (under duress), golf (very badly), IT (my wife says I am a computer nerd and my son is turning into one), walking (everywhere), following Gillingham FC (who else would?).

LINDRUP, Garth
Addleshaw Booth & Co, Manchester
(0161) 934 6242
garth.lindrup@addleshawbooth.com
Specialisation: Partner in Trade and Regulatory Department, Commercial Group. Work includes UK and EU competition law, especially merger control, articles 81 and 82, public procurement, joint ventures, distribution, agency and franchising, state aid. Editor, 'Butterworths Competition Law Handbook' and various other publications; Chairman, Law Society's European Group 1994-95.
Prof. Memberships: IBA, LIDC, CBI Competition Panel, ICC Competition Committee.
Career: Qualified 1975. Joined firm in 1979 and became Partner in 1984.
Personal: Holds BA, LLM (Cantab).

LINDSAY, Alistair
Allen & Overy, London
(020) 7330 3000
alistair.lindsay@allenovery.com
Specialisation: Partner in the European Antitrust Group. Called to the Bar in 1993 and practised extensively in EU, competition and public law. Whilst at the Bar, acted in the Factortame (Spanish fishermen) damages claim and taught EU law part-time at LSE. Since joining *Allen & Overy*, has requalified as a solicitor and has practised extensively in EU and competition law including mergers and restrictive agreements at both EU and UK level, utilities and litigation.
Career: Associate *Allen & Overy* (1997-2001), Partner (2001).
Publications: 'Practitioners Handbook of EC Law', Free Movement of Goods

COMPETITION/ANTI-TRUST — THE LEADERS

chapter (jointly with Paul Lasok QC and Peter Roth QC). Numerous articles in legal journals.
Personal: Born 1971. Girton College, Cambridge University (BA 1992).

LIVINGSTON, Dorothy
Herbert Smith, London
(020) 7374 8000
dorothy.livingston@herbertsmith.com
Specialisation: Specialises in all aspects of EU and UK competition law. Practice includes work on restrictive agreements, monopolies, anti-competitive practices, abuse of dominant position, mergers, state aids and procurement. Works extensively on matters involving regulatory law and has considerable experience spanning several fields including the utilities, broadcasting and other media.
Prof. Memberships: Competition Law sub-committee and Chairman Banking Law sub-committee of the City of London Law Society, Financial Law Panel Working Party on State Aid, Advisory board Centre of European Law at King's College, London. Bank of England Financial Markets Law Committee.
Publications: 'The Competition Act 1998: a Practical Guide' (2001); 'Competition Law and Practice' (1995); Contributor of three new chapters on competition law to 'Finance Leasing' (Euromoney, 1997).

LOUGHER, Guy
Wragge & Co, Birmingham
0870 903 1000

LOUVEAUX, Bertrand
Slaughter and May, London
(020) 7600 1200
bertrand.louveaux@slaughterandmay.com
Specialisation: A broad range of UK and EC competition law. Has wide experience before the European Commission, the Office of Fair Trading and the Competition Commission (including both merger and monopoly enquiries). Recent merger cases have included British Steel/Hoogovens, BAT/Rothmans, Carlton/United/Granada, Lincoln/Charter and Lloyds TSB/Abbey National. He acted for Nomura/GPC in obtaining the landmark Article 81 'pubco' decision and for British Airways on its alliance with American Airlines. He regularly advises clients on Articles 81 and 82 of the EC Treaty and the 1998 Competition Act.
Career: Qualified 1994 with *Slaughter and May* and became a Partner in 2001.
Personal: Born 28 April 1967. Educated London School of Economics (MSc Economics).

MARTIN ALEGI, Lynda
Baker & McKenzie, London
(020) 7919 1000
lynda.martin.alegi@bakernet.com
Specialisation: Partner and Head of Department dealing with EC competition law – appeal against Article 85 decisions – lysine cartel (ADM), cement cartel (The Rugby Group plc); UK competition law – MMC Investigations – brown goods (Sony), photocopiers (Canon), fine fragrances (Guerlain), condoms (Mates); merger control – EC – Shell/DEA (for Shell), de Havilland Case (for Aerospatiale/Alenia), Glaxo Smith Kline/Block Drug (for Block Drug), Gillette/Parker Pen (for Parker Pen), - UK, Rockwool/Owens Corning (for Rockwool); advisory work (including Canon, Camelot, Levi Strauss, Sony, Tetra-Pak).
Prof. Memberships: CBI Competition Panel; ICC UK Committee on Law and Practices Relating to Competition.
Career: Articled *Baker & McKenzie*, qualified 1977, Partner 1981.
Publications: Editor of Sweet & Maxwell's 'Encyclopaedia of Information Technology Law' (Competition Law chapter).
Personal: Woodford County High School; Newnham College, Cambridge (1973 MA); Institute of European Studies - Free University of Brussels (1975 Licence Speciale). Languages: French, Italian. Born 1952; resides London.

MCDONNELL, Phil
Addleshaw Booth & Co, Manchester
(0161) 934 6700
phil.mcdonnell@addleshawbooth.com
Specialisation: Advises on EC and UK competition law and merger control including all aspects of business practices, pricing, distribution and sales strategies, corporate acquisition, joint ventures and alliances. Deals with complaints, investigations and compliances matters.
Prof. Memberships: Law Society, Solicitors European Group.
Career: Articled *Lovell White Durrant* (London and Hong Kong); *Lovell White Durrant* (London, New York and Brussels) 1988-93; commercial manager North West Water International Ltd 1994-5; *Garretts* 1995 (partner 1999) Head of EU & Competition.
Personal: Educated St Ambrose College Hale Barns; Wadham College Oxford.

MCKNIGHT, Elizabeth
Herbert Smith, London
(020) 7374 8000
elizabeth.mcknight@herbertsmith.com
Specialisation: Partner specialising in all aspects of EU Law with particular expertise in competition law (both EU and UK), intellectual property and the law relating to regulated utilities.
Prof. Memberships: Law Society, International Bar Association.
Career: Qualified in 1988 and became a partner in 1994.
Personal: BA Jesus College, Oxford, LLM (EC Law) London School of Economics, 1990.

MCLEAN, James
Burness, Edinburgh
(0131) 473 6000

MILLER, Colin
Biggart Baillie, Glasgow
(0141) 228 8000

MOBLEY, Samantha
Baker & McKenzie, London
(020) 7919 1000
samantha.mobley@bakernet.com
Specialisation: Partner specialising in competition law (both UK and EC). Experienced in defending companies involved in international cartel investigations.
Prof. Memberships: ICC UK Competition Law Committee; Law Society European Group Committee; American Bar Association.
Career: Trained *Baker & McKenzie*, qualified 1993; spent a year in *Baker & McKenzie's* Washington DC office on anti-trust cases 1995-96.
Publications: Joint editor of 'Global Merger Notification Handbook' (Cameron May); Chapter on Collaboration Agreements for 'PLC Competition Manual'.
Personal: Born 1967; resides London; one daughter and one son; qualified PADI rescue diver (scuba diving).

NICHOLSON, Malcolm
Slaughter and May, London
(020) 7600 1200
malcolm.nicholson@slaughterandmay.com
Specialisation: EU, competition and regulatory law. Head of *Slaughter and May's* competition group. His practice covers the full range of UK and EU antitrust work for a number of blue chip clients (including RECs and other utilities), governments and regulatory authorities. On the UK competition front, he has extensive experience before the Competition Commission, including both merger and monopoly enquiries, and he deals regularly with the OFT. On the European front, he has been engaged in a number of competition cases before the Commission and the Court of Justice and in obtaining regulatory clearances from the Merger Task Force. He was heavily involved in the regulatory and competition aspects of the major UK privatisations and currently advises a number of electricity and water utilities with regard to price controls and other regulatory matters.
Career: Qualified in 1974 with *Slaughter and May* and became a partner in 1982.
Personal: Born March 1949. Educated Haileybury, Cambridge University, Brussels University. Married with six children.

OSBORNE, John
Clifford Chance, London
(020) 7006 8005
john.osborne@cliffordchance.com
Specialisation: Corporate and anti-trust. Partner specialising in competition and EU law.
Career: Partner since 1980.

PARR, Nigel
Ashurst Morris Crisp, London
(020) 7638 1111
nigel.parr@ashursts.com
Specialisation: Advises in relation to all aspects of UK and EC competition law and utilities regulation, particularly merger control. Has acted in relation to more than 40 UK Competition Commission inquiries including monopoly investigations, mergers and anti-competitive practices and in relation to a number of investigations under the Competition Act 1998. He regularly acts for clients in relation to notifications to and investigations by the EC Commission, and has drafted many competition law compliance programmes.
Career: LLB, LLM, PhD. Partner, head of the competition group, co-author (with Roger Finbow) of 'UK Merger Control Law & Practice' (Sweet & Maxwell, 1995), and author of the competition section of PLC's 'Asset and Share Purchases' manuals, as well as numerous articles on EC law and competition-related matters. Tutor in EC law and intellectual property law at Exeter University 1984-86.

PHEASANT, John
Lovells, London
(020) 7296 2000
john.pheasant@lovells.com
Specialisation: EC and UK competition law in all its aspects, but particularly contentious proceedings and competition policy/regulation. Significant experience as an advocate before the Commission in administrative proceedings, and before the Court of First Instance and European Court of Justice on appeals (including interim measures). Co-author of 'Competition Law' (Butterworths) and Editor of division on prohibited horizontal agreements.
Prof. Memberships: Member of the Advisory Board of the Regulatory Policy Institute, Oxford.
Career: Articled *Lovells*. Qualified 1979; partner since 1985. Brussels office: 1980-1983 and 1986 - present.

POLITO, Simon
Lovells, London
(020) 7296 2000
simon.polito@lovells.com
Specialisation: Principally EC and UK competition law. Expertise acquired since late 1970s in numerous Commission cases under Articles 81 and 82 and the Merger Regulation as well as UK merger and monopoly inquiries. Advises UK, European and US multinationals on competition issues affecting manufacturing and service industries. Also advises on regulatory aspects of privatised industries, utilities and broadcasting.
Prof. Memberships: Member Joint Working Party on Competition Law of UK and Irish Bars and Law Societies; also of UK Committee of ICC on Competition Law and European Lawyers Forum.
Career: Called to Bar (Middle Temple) 1972. Qualified as solicitor with *Lovells* in 1976, partner 1982. Worked in Brussels 1977-81 (including 1990 'stage' with the Commission) and as a resident Brussels partner from 1988. Now based primarily in London.

THE LEADERS — COMPETITION/ANTI-TRUST

REES, Kate
Pinsent Curtis Biddle, Birmingham
(0121) 200 1050
kate.rees@pinsents.com
Specialisation: EU and UK competition law including UK and EU merger clearances and OFT, Competition Commission and European Commission enquiries. Very extensive public procurement practice.
Career: LLB Hons 1st class. *Pinsent Curtis Biddle* 1986. Qualified in 1988. Partner in 1993.

ROBERT, Gavin
Linklaters, London
(020) 7456 3364
gavin.robert@linklaters.com
Specialisation: Specialist in EU trade law and particularly in the areas of anti-trust, merger control, public procurement and state aid. Sectors of specialist expertise include healthcare, telecoms/media, transport and energy.
Prof. Memberships: Legal consultant to the European Commission High Level working group on public-private partnership financing of trans-European transport projects (sub-group 4 on legal and administrative issues). Member of Liberalisation of Trade in Services (LOTIS) Committee of British Invisibles.
Career: Since 1999: Partner, *Linklaters* London; 1994-99: Assistant Solicitor, *Linklaters* Brussels; 1993-94: Assistant Solicitor, *Linklaters* London (EC and Anti-trust Department); 1992-93: Secondment to European Commission Legal Service; 1990-92: Trainee Solicitor, *Linklaters* London. 1989-90: Licence Spéciale en Droit Européen, Université Libre de Bruxelles; 1988-89: Law Society Finals, College of Law, Chancery Lane, London; 1985-88: Emmanuel College, Cambridge, BA (Hons) in Law.

ROSE, Stephen
Eversheds, London
(020) 7919 4785
roses@eversheds.com
Specialisation: All aspects of EC and UK competition law with a focus on the Competition Act 1998 and mergers, acquisitions and joint ventures.
Career: Qualified 1991; articled with *Slaughter and May*; partner at *Eversheds* 1997.
Personal: Born 27 May 1965; educated at St Edmund Hall, Oxford (1984-87); lives in Great Shelford, Cambridge.

SCHOLES, Jeremy
Walker Morris, Leeds
(0113) 283 2500
jas@walkermorris.co.uk
Specialisation: 20 years' experience of applying competition and EU law (the main areas of his practice) in a wide range of commercial contexts (transactions, litigation, dealing with regulatory authorities, compliance/advisory work). Recent work of note has included R v The Law Society, ex p Dalton (the 'test case' litigation against the former Solicitors' Indemnity Fund monopoly); representing one of the large grocery supermarket chains in the Competition Commission enquiry; application of the Competition Act 1998 to local authorities; defence of an EC cartel investigation; currently advising a European Commission experts' group on competition aspects of R&D co-operation.
Prof. Memberships: Law Society's European Group (former chairman of the East Midlands branch); Competition Law Association; LIDC (International Competition Law Association) (a national reporter for 1997/98).
Career: Law degrees from Cambridge and the Collège d'Europe, Brugge, Belgium. Qualified 1981. *Freshfields; Waltons & Morse; Wells & Hind/Eversheds,* Nottingham (partner till 1993; set up and led the *Eversheds* competition law practice group nationally); then several years a sole practitioner; now head of *Walker Morris*'s competition and EU law practice. Part-time law lecturer at Sheffield University and a visiting lecturer at the Université de Nancy II in eastern France.
Publications: Various, including the commercial agency chapter in the PLC Commercial Contracts manual.
Personal: Works in French; also speaks good German and Dutch.

SCOTT, Jonathan
Herbert Smith, London
(020) 7374 8000
jonathan.scott@herbertsmith.com
Specialisation: Head of EU/Competition Department. Partner specialising in commercial and anti-trust litigation, merger control and regulatory work involving the Office of Fair Trading, the Competition Commission and the EC.
Prof. Memberships: IBA. American Bar Association.
Career: Worked at the Council of Europe Human Rights Directorate 1979. Joined *Herbert Smith* in 1979, Qualified in 1981, becoming a Partner in 1988.
Publications: Contributor to 'EC Merger Control Reporter'. Editor, merger chapters of Longman's 'Competition Law and Practice'.

SIBREE, William
Slaughter and May, London
(020) 7600 1200
william.sibree@slaughterandmay.com
Specialisation: All areas of EU and UK competition law both contentious and non-contentious, including mergers, monopoly and Competition Act references, cartel investigations, Article 82 proceedings, state aid and litigation before the Court of Justice and Court of First Instance.
Career: Admitted to the Bar (Inner Temple) 1984. Pupillage at Monckton Chambers (1984-85). Joined *Slaughter and May* 1986. Partner 1993.
Personal: Born 19 March 1961. Educated at Eton College and Queens' College, Cambridge (MA). Fluent in French and German. Interests include bridge, opera and skiing.

SMITH, Martin
Simmons & Simmons, London
(020) 7628 2020
martin.smith@simmons-simmons.com
Specialisation: Partner. Main area of practice is competition and regulatory work (both EC and UK). Has experience of dealing with all the main EC and UK competition law authorities. Advises on EC and UK merger control and regularly co-ordinates multiple merger filings. In 2001 he advised Interbrew on its successful High Court challenge to a decision by the UK Secretary of State (the first such success in a merger case).
Prof. Memberships: Law Society, City of London Solicitors' Company Competition Law Sub-committee, CBI Competition Panel, Solicitors European Group, International Bar Association.
Career: Qualified in 1981. Joined *Simmons & Simmons* in 1977, becoming a Partner in 1986, having worked at *Dechert Price & Rhoads* (Philadelphia) 1978 and *Linklaters & Paines* 1983-85.
Publications: Author of two major divisions of 'Butterworths Competition Law' and of 'Competition Law: Enforcement and Procedure' (2000). Frequently speaks at conferences and seminars.
Personal: Born 27 August 1955. Attended St Catharine's College, Cambridge 1974-77 (MA) and University of Pennsylvania (LLM) 1978-79. Leisure interests include sport, music and walking.

SPEARING, Nicholas
Freshfields Bruckhaus Deringer, London
(020) 7936 4000
nicholas.spearing@freshfields.com
Specialisation: Partner in Competition and Trade Group. Main area of practice is EC/Competition law. Extensive experience in monopolies, mergers and restrictive practices cases at both UK and EC levels. Acted for leading companies on inquiries, including the motor industry, banking services, brewing, and electrical goods and underwriting fees. Merger control work for a wide range of clients.
Prof. Memberships: Law Society, City of London Solicitors Company, Former Chairman Solicitors' European Group.
Career: Qualified 1978. Partner 1984.
Publications: Co-author of Mergers section of Butterworths' 'Competition Law'.
Personal: Born 1954. Educated Hertford College, Oxford 1972-75. Leisure pursuits include family, travel and golf.

TRAPP, Deirdre
Freshfields Bruckhaus Deringer, London
(020) 7936 4000
deirdre.trapp@freshfields.com
Specialisation: Joint head of Competition and Trade group. Main area of practice is competition and regulatory law. Has conducted monopolies, mergers and restrictive practices cases under both EU and UK jurisdictions. Extensive experience in utility, transport and media regulation.
Prof. Memberships: Solicitors' European Group; ABA anti-trust section, structural review task force; EC Commission, ICN mergers working group on notification and procedures.
Career: Joined *Freshfields* in 1987. Partner 1995.
Personal: Born 1961. Attended St Hilda's College, Oxford 1980-1983 reading Philosophy, Politics and Economics.

USHER, Tom
SJ Berwin, London
(020) 7533 2728
tom.usher@sjberwin.com
Specialisation: All aspects of EC law; expertise in competition/IP rights matters, also sports and broadcasting, collective selling and e-commerce. Litigation of EU issues in Europe and in the National Courts.
Prof. Memberships: Current chairman of the Law Society's European Group.
Career: Trained at *SJ Berwin*, qualified 1993, Partner 1999.
Publications: 'This monopoly of music' (Ent Law Rev). 'The UK Competition Act 1998' (*SJ Berwin*). Advisory Board of Jordan's 'Competition Law Journal'.
Personal: Fettes College, Edinburgh; University of Saarbrucken, Germany; King's College London. Leisure: music, cricket, golf, rugby and cooking. Married with two children.

WARWICK, Neil
Dickinson Dees, Newcastle upon Tyne
(0191) 279 9375
neil.warwick@dickinson-dees.com
Specialisation: Competition law (both UK and EU) and EU law including European funding, anti-dumping and state aid. Major cases include Leeds Cartel case (the first ever dawn raid in the UK) acting for Arriva, Merger Task Force reference for the acquisition of Connex South Central by Govia Ltd, the OFT investigation into replica football kits, and the OFT investigation into the building supply market. Highlights of the last 12 months include full compliance programmes for a number of clients (in particular Arriva and Go-Ahead), work with Nike, Stagecoach, Coca Cola and Transco. Successful ERDF regional funding application for the North East Investment Funds I, II and III and the European state work in connection with the creation of Capital North East (one of the first two RVC funds in the UK). Successful defence of C3D's hostile bid for Go-Ahead.
Prof. Memberships: Law Society.
Career: Joined *Dickinson Dees* as a trainee in 1991, qualified in 1993, Partner in 2001.
Publications: 'Croner Risk Management'.
Personal: Dame Allan's School, Newcastle University. Hobbies – football (five-a-side and eleven-a-side and watching Newcastle United), hockey, gym and running. Leisure – cooking, reading, DIY. Married with two young sons.

COMPETITION/ANTI-TRUST ■ THE LEADERS

WEITZMAN, Polly
Denton Wilde Sapte, London
(020) 7246 7000
fmaw@dentonwildesapte.com
Specialisation: Practises UK and EC competition law in relation to both non-contentious matters (mergers, joint ventures, restrictive agreements) and contentious matters (cartels and abuse of market power inquiries). Particular experience in the media and energy sectors. Extensive experience before the European Commission, Office of Fair Trading and Competition Commission.
Prof. Memberships: Competition Law Society; The Law Society.
Career: Qualified in 1988 with *Denton Hall*. Became a Partner in 1995.
Publications: Editor of section on gas in Butterworths 'Encyclopaedia of Competition Law'.
Personal: Born 1961. Educated Godolphin & Latymer School, London; then Edinburgh University (Modern History).

WHISH, Richard
Richard Whish – Sole Practitioner, London
(020) 7848 2237

WISKING, Stephen
Herbert Smith, London
(020) 7374 8000
stephen.wisking@herbertsmith.com
Specialisation: Practices in all areas of competition law both in the EU and UK. Has particular experience in relation to mergers, regulatory investigations, competition litigation and broadcasting regulation. Advises clients in the areas of media, life sciences, the internet and IT.
Prof. Memberships: The Law Society.
Career: Qualified as barrister and solicitor (Australia) in 1988, as solicitor (England and Wales) in 1998 and as solicitor advocate in 1999. Joined *Herbert Smith* in 1997, becoming partner in 2000.
Personal: LLB (1988) and BEc (1988) at the University of Adelaide, LLM (1991) at Jesus College, University of Cambridge.

WOTTON, John
Allen & Overy, London
(020) 7330 3000
john.wotton@allenovery.com
Specialisation: Partner specialising in UK, EU and international competition and trade law and in broadcasting and communications law. Has represented major public and private sector UK and international clients in numerous merger proceedings in the UK, EU and internationally, and on many other anti-trust investigations and proceedings. Also advises on distribution and licensing, public procurement and government regulation in the utilities sector. Lectures on competition and broadcasting law and is an office holder in the Law Society's European Group. Active member of the firm's Communications Group, Public Procurement Group and Bioscience Group.
Prof. Memberships: Treasurer, Law Society's European Group.
Career: Qualified 1978; Partner 1984.
Personal: Born 1954. Jesus College, Cambridge University (1975, MA).

CONSTRUCTION

London: 175; The Regions: 181; Scotland: 189; Profiles: 191

Research approved by BMRB For this edition, **Chambers'** researchers conducted 6,582 interviews – 3,900 with law firms, 511 with barristers and 2,171 with clients. The validity of the research was scrutinised by BMRB International, who audited both the methodology and the results at our offices in London. They interviewed **Chambers'** researchers and cross-checked sample interviews. Details of the audit appear on page 7.

OVERVIEW Research has found that clients are demanding that their legal advisors have the capacity to handle international projects, PFI and other finance-related elements, which increasingly make up construction work. Other cross-over areas, such as facilities and service management, are frequently considered as part of the overall construction package. Commercial considerations continue to muscle in on the traditional litigious approach of the sector. Adjudication is also now to the fore, with the majority of observers concurring that it is far more prevalent than envisaged on its introduction. Many firms that were focused primarily on litigation have had to adjust accordingly; those with an established niche practice remain, although even here some are beginning to show signs that they, too, are looking to broaden their horizons.

LONDON

CONSTRUCTION — LONDON

1. Masons
2. CMS Cameron McKenna
   Shadbolt & Co
3. Berwin Leighton Paisner
   Fenwick Elliott
   Linklaters
   Mayer, Brown, Rowe & Maw
4. Allen & Overy
   Clifford Chance
   Freshfields Bruckhaus Deringer
   Herbert Smith
   Lovells
   Norton Rose
   Taylor Wessing
5. Ashurst Morris Crisp
   Denton Wilde Sapte
   Hammond Suddards Edge
   Kennedys
   Macfarlanes
   Nicholson Graham & Jones
   SJ Berwin
   Trowers & Hamlins
   Winward Fearon
6. Baker & McKenzie
   Beale and Company
   Berrymans Lace Mawer
   Campbell Hooper
   Davies Arnold Cooper
   Glovers
   Simmons & Simmons

This book is the product of 6,582 1/2 hour interviews. See p.7 for BMRB audit. Within each band, firms are listed alphabetically.

MASONS (see firm details p.1057) "*The sheer breadth of its domestic litigation practice is fantastic,*" acknowledged one peer, and it is widely agreed that the size of this team and its long-standing commitment to the construction sector secures its pre-eminence. It acts on behalf of 18 out of the top 20 contractors in the UK. "*By far and away the most focused team,*" the respected "*professional*" group has "*a good mix of specialisms.*" Although some commentators found its approach to be aggressive, many clients endorsed a "*system that delivers on time and on price.*"

Despite his managerial responsibilities, **John Bishop** (see p.192) is still regarded as "*a leader and a focal point*" around which the rest of the department turns. A "*depth of knowledge that is unique*" and an "*ability to get to grips with a huge brief quickly*" ensure that he remains at the head of our table on merit. **Tony Bunch** (see p.192) continues to be praised for his adversarial strength, while **Martin Harman** (see p.196) was recommended for his "*civility and good humour; yet he remains no-one's soft touch.*" Experienced **Mark Roe**'s (see p.199) "*sharp*" commercial sensibilities were underlined, while **Martin Roberts** (see p.199) ("*sound to deal with*") and **Mark Lane** (see p.197) ("*a motivated individual with a clear, balanced view, especially for e-procurement*") also garnered praise within the largest construction team in the UK.

On the non-contentious side, the firm has seen growth in infrastructure and projects work. The roads sector has flourished this year; it acted for the short-listed bidders on the Irish National Roads Programme. In India, the team has advised the contractor on the first two annuity-based roads projects to close, and is assisting an international joint venture as preferred bidder on the Jaipur-Kishengangh national highways project. Known for its expertise in light rail schemes, it has represented short-listed bidders for Manchester Metrolink Phase 3 and the DLR London City Airport Extension.

Over the last year, the firm has increased its focus on the financial side of non-contentious construction work and now acts for funders and numerous consortia. The increased use of procurement in the market as a whole has enabled the firm to use its client base to take a leading role in prime contracting issues; it has advised on both the Ministry of Defence's prime contracting project and NHS ProCure 21. The firm conducts a third of its work overseas, acting on an arbitration on behalf of the Government of Lebanon concerning the rehabilitation and extension of Beirut International Airport. It has also represented an international consortium in an ICC arbitration concerning a dispute with a South American contractor over the design and construction of a pipeline and marine terminal facility in East Africa. **Clients** Sir Robert McAlpine; Amey; Birse Construction; Bovis-Lend Lease; Crown House Engineering; Durkan Pudelek; Hyder Consulting; Interserve; Jarvis; John Mowlem & Company; Kier Build; Mansell Construction Services; Rolls-Royce Power Engineering; Wates Construction.

CMS CAMERON MCKENNA (see firm details p.914) Traditionally associated with the contentious side of construction work, the department has seen an increase in the number of non-contentious matters in which it is involved. Split into construction, related insurance and property teams, the "*always straightforward*" department services a genuinely broad client base. **Trevor Butcher**'s (see p.193) project-related work ensures that he remains the firm's leading name, while **Caroline Cummins**' (see p.194) profile is in the ascendant. Leading clients referred to her as being "*genuinely impressive – she has made enormous strides in the sector.*" Considered "*clever and tactically aware,*" she has represented Panatown (and its sister company, the Unex Group) in its series of claims and subsequent appeals against Alfred McAlpine. Although he has now retired and taken up a post as a consultant, Peter Long remains a great source of technical advice, while contentious specialist **Henry Sherman** (see p.200) maintains "*an excellent reputation*" through his focused work on property-related matters. **Marc Hanson** (see p.195) has continued to act for a subsidiary of Chelsfield on its ongoing redevelopment of Paddington basin, under a two-stage tender contract procurement pioneered by the firm. The firm has also continued work on behalf of Prudential Assurance at the Green Park office development in the Thames Valley.

www.ChambersandPartners.com

CONSTRUCTION ■ LONDON

TOP IN-HOUSE LAWYERS

Michael BLACKER, Head of Legal Services, Amec Capital Projects

Peter BRINLEY-CODD, Solicitor and Legal Services Manager, Sir Robert MacAlpine Ltd

Peter CHADWICK, Company Secretary, Bovis Lend Lease Ltd

Patricia Dryden, Head of Litigation, London Underground

Graham GIBSON, Head of Group Legal Services, John Laing plc

Martin LENIHAN, Legal Advisor, Skanska Construction Ltd

Frank MCCORMACK, Head of Legal Services, Balfour Beatty plc

Phillip MORRIS, Solicitor, Balfour Beatty plc

Simon Williams, Chief Solicitor, Taylor Woodrow

Hilary WILSON, Legal Adviser, Skanska Construction Ltd

Respected for having "*brought the organisation's legal functioning into a consolidated, organised unit*," **Michael Blacker** has a strategic profile that is "*good for putting across the important points for the industry.*" **Peter Chadwick** was described as "*quiet, efficient and switched on.*" Focusing on PFI-related work, **Peter Brinley-Codd** was considered "*extremely professional and perceptive.*" **Patricia Dryden** was lauded as a "*tough litigator and clear in her thinking*" and "*extremely streetwise.*" **Graham Gibson** impresses with a style that is "*relaxed and assured*" and for "*using outside lawyers sensibly.*" Private practitioners continued to recommend the respected **Frank McCormack** above all others – "*a strategic lawyer, thoughtful and effective at separating out the issues that count.*" Although he is not as directly involved in day to day work as in previous years, his knowledge of the industry and the approach he brings to deals is "*a marvellous demonstration*" to the industry. **Phillip Morris** "*has a deserved reputation*" Combining "*excellent construction skills with public procurement knowledge,*" **Hilary Wilson** is a "*bright, tenacious opponent,*" while and her colleague **Martin Lenihan** remains highly regarded. The experienced **Simon Williams** "*can really pull all the required strands of a deal together*" with "*sound, strong, effective and commercial advice.*"

In-house lawyers' profiles p.1201

PFI-related drafting and dispute resolution for clients in the oil and gas sectors has fed additional work. It has been involved in two TCC actions concerning floating production storage and off take vessels in the North Sea, representing both Norwegian company Aker and Brazilian contractor Odebrecht. Closer to home, it has advised John Laing on disputes arising out of the PFI National Physical Laboratories project at Teddington . **Clients** AES; Aker; AMEC; Balfour Beatty Major Projects; Baxter Healthcare; BI Group; Canary Wharf Group; Carillion; Controlled Demolition; Cubic Corporation; Daniel Contractors; DTLR; Gillette; Graphwide; Hilton Hotel Group; Interior; J Murphy & Sons; John Laing; Kier Group; Kobe Steel; Metro n et; Morrison Construction; Odebrecht; Panatown; Pfizer; Rolls-Royce Power Ventures; Sony; Taylor Woodrow; Tractebel; Wellcome Trust.

SHADBOLT & CO (see firm details p.1126) The firm has made a strong showing this year, with the market acknowledging a gradual broadening of the practice, achieved without a diminution in the depth of its experience. The firm operates from its closely tied Reigate and London branches. Client feedback has been universally positive and confirms the firm's involvement in broader instructions – it has "*consolidated this year and made a name for itself, particularly in the field of adjudication.*" Frequently singled out, **Dick Shadbolt** (see p.200) is now recognised as being backed by an experienced and committed team, which is "*commercial without being difficult, providing high-calibre advice.*" Interviewees agreed that Shadbolt himself is "*superb at getting the work in*" and "*an ambassador for the construction industry.*"

Domestically, the firm has acted for a major contractor on the construction of an airport terminal building in the UK. **Dominic Helps** (see p.196) has impressed with his tenacity and "*energetic and realistic*" approach. An "*enormous presence,*" he has aided a UIC contractor in a multimillion pound dispute arising out of a hospital development. International and foreign work continues to be a major focus, supported by overseas offices; it has acted for a German contractor in the construction of a large oil refinery in India. Qualified engineer **Simon Delves** (see p.194), recommended to Chambers for his non-contentious skills, has also acted for a Japanese contractor in an ICC arbitration concerning a gas turbine station in Bangladesh and has been involved in disputes relating to a hydroelectric project in Uganda. **Liam O'Hanlon** (see p.198) is best known for being "*a combative litigator,*" especially for construction engineering disputes. One rival admitted: "*I would use him for a serious dispute if I needed my corner fought.*" He has worked for an international property developer in a successful ICC arbitration relating to a complex of luxury apartments and retail units. **Clients** Amey; Galliard Homes; Galliford Try; Taylor Woodrow; WS Atkins.

BERWIN LEIGHTON PAISNER (see firm details p.866) Interviewees felt that the firm is now reaping the tangible rewards of its merger with Paisner & Co, uniting the non-contentious strength of Berwin Leighton with Paisner's respected dispute resolution team. The property development, PFI and construction teams of the merged firm are thought to be combining well, resulting in a sizeable unit with real breadth. Peers point to a firm that is going "*from strength to strength and mounting a serious challenge,*" while clients spoke of the "*time spent understanding our concerns and finding ways to resolve problems with serious attention to the detailed work.*" Leading light **Terry Fleet** (see p.195) has advised HOK Sport on its engagement as lead designers for the proposed sports stadium complex for Benfica in Lisbon. Respected for "*facilitating the client's perspective,*" he has also assisted The Hospital Group for the construction of a recording studio, club and restaurant on the site of an old hospital in Covent Garden. **Michael Gibson** (see p.195) remains "*one of the top in his field through pure expertise,*" and is appreciated for his lack of airs and graces and a tough negotiating style. He is associated with the PFI side of the firm's construction work, having aided various government departments and NHS Trusts on the construction of hospitals and schools. Contentious specialist and "*lateral thinker*" **Julian Holloway** (see p.196) has acted for Ballast on a dispute over the roof of a leisure centre development, built over an existing Sea Life Centre, and also represented London Electricity on a variety of cable damage and associated claims. Clients endorsed **Caroline Pope** (see p.199) as "*extremely bright*", she has been instructed by the UK Atomic Energy Authority on its claims against a consortium of companies engaged to decommission the fire-affected nuclear production plant at Sellafield. **John Wright** (see p.201) ("*knowledgeable and with a lot of common sense*") has represented one of the parties in the substantial litigation involving the Braehead Shopping Centre. **Bob Maynard** (see p.197) is deemed an expert with "*a real knack for delivering issues for non-lawyers.*" He has led on advice to US corporation Chief Industries in a dispute with a Middle Eastern company over its construction of grain handling and storage facilities. Yorkshire Water has instructed the firm in the prosecution of an approximately £10 million claim against Taylor Woodrow and other parties connected to the construction of a sewage treatment plant in Yorkshire. It has also aided the Wales Millennium Centre on the construction procurement aspects of its £104 million performing arts centre in Cardiff Bay, the new home of Welsh National Opera. **Clients** AMEC; Arcadia; Balfour Beatty; Ballast; Bouygues; Carillion; Chief Industries; Costain; Gap; Higgins Group; Highways Agency; HOK Sport; Home Office; London Electricity; Ocsports; Royal Bank of Scotland; SAK Investment Management ; Skanska; Snamprogetti; Tesco; The Hospital Group; Wales Millennium Centre; Wellhouse NHS Trust; West Sussex CC; Yorkshire Water.

FENWICK ELLIOTT (see firm details p.953) Post-Woolf, the firm has "*continued to impress with its skill and dominance in the adjudication market*," partly as a result of a solid base in sub-contractor clients, and a focus on the oil and gas, and international sectors. The non-contentious element of its work has also witnessed growth. Recent hires have swelled the team's ranks, although it continues to operate with a high ratio of partners to other fee-earning staff.

A leading ambassador for construction law and an undoubted star, Robert Fenwick Elliott retired in March 2002 to take up a post as a con-

LONDON ■ CONSTRUCTION

LEADING INDIVIDUALS

1
- **BISHOP John** Masons
- **CAPPER Phillip** Lovells
- **RUSHTON John** Mayer, Brown, Rowe & Maw

2
- **BUNCH Anthony** Masons
- **DAVIS Michael** Herbert Smith
- **LEVINE Marshall** Linklaters
- **ROE Sally** Freshfields Bruckhaus Deringer

3
- **BIRKBY Gillian** Mayer, Brown, Rowe & Maw
- **CRITCHLOW Julian** Fenwick Elliott
- **GOULD Nicholas** Lovells
- **HUDSON James** Nicholson Graham & Jones
- **REES Peter** Norton Rose
- **ROBERTS Martin** Masons
- **WINTER Jeremy** Baker & McKenzie

4
- **BURCH Simon** Linklaters
- **GIBSON Michael** Berwin Leighton Paisner
- **MOSEY David** Trowers & Hamlins
- **SHERMAN Henry** CMS Cameron McKenna

5
- **BRIDGEWATER Martin** Norton Rose
- **HOLLOWAY Julian** Berwin Leighton Paisner
- **WHITE Neil** Taylor Wessing

6
- **BOURGEOIS Christopher** Taylor Wessing
- **GARTHWAITE Helen** Taylor Wessing
- **HOUGH Christopher** Fenwick Elliott
- **MAYNARD Robert** Berwin Leighton Paisner
- **O'HANLON Liam** Shadbolt & Co
- **THOMAS Nick** Kennedys

UP AND COMING
- **HANSON Marc** CMS Cameron McKenna

ASSOCIATES TO WATCH
- **HENCHIE Nicholas** Mayer, Brown, Rowe & Maw

- **BLACKLER Tony** Macfarlanes
- **MINOGUE Ann** Linklaters
- **SHADBOLT Richard** Shadbolt & Co

- **BUTCHER Trevor** CMS Cameron McKenna
- **HARMAN Martin** Masons
- **ROE Mark** Masons
- **STEADMAN Tim** Clifford Chance

- **CORNES David** Winward Fearon
- **FLEET Terry** Berwin Leighton Paisner
- **HOSIE Jonathan** Hammond Suddards Edge
- **JONES David** Hammond Suddards Edge
- **REGAN Michael** Mayer, Brown, Rowe & Maw
- **RUSSELL Victoria** Fenwick Elliott

- **CUMMINS Caroline** CMS Cameron McKenna
- **LANE Mark** Masons
- **SHAW Peter** Taylor Wessing

- **GOWAN Daniel** Davies Arnold Cooper
- **RACE David** Nicholson Graham & Jones
- **WRIGHT John** Berwin Leighton Paisner

- **CANHAM Stephanie** Trowers & Hamlins
- **HOLMES Patrick** Macfarlanes
- **JENKINS Jane** Freshfields Bruckhaus Deringer
- **NURNEY Simon** Macfarlanes
- **POPE Caroline** Berwin Leighton Paisner

See individuals' profiles p.191

sultant to the firm. **Julian Critchlow**'s (see p.194) "*intellectual ability and broader vision*" has helped to offset this move, while clients consider **Victoria Russell** (see p.200) "*authoritative – an acknowledged expert*." Dual-qualified engineer **Christopher Hough**'s (see p.196) down-to-earth approach was also noted, particularly for adjudications.

Appreciated by clients as "*small enough to be flexible, but still big enough for the work*," the firm has represented an Argentinian oil and gas contractor in its action against a consortium, successfully sued over its disclosure of documents. The large team has also assisted a contractor concerning defects on a building owned by Unilever Bestfoods, and has represented a FTSE 250 developer on a dispute over the development of a nightclub. Non-contentious advice has included the drafting of contracts for a major contractor in the computer telehousing industry, and involvement on a £300 million project in Knightsbridge. **Clients:** Ballast; Barkers; Bellwater; Benson; John Doyle; Government of Pakistan; Henry Boot; Kier Construction; Kvaerner; Morgan Lovell; Natural History Museum; Norwest Holst; O'Keefe; Overbury; Sindall; University of Brighton.

LINKLATERS (see firm details p.1043) The firm is well known for its projects-related expertise and as a non-contentious heavyweight, although on the contentious side it has a lower profile. Market feedback indicates that the property, projects and construction focus of the firm exemplify its clear, cohesive team approach. The firm has increased its international construction capacity in response to the increasing globalisation of the construction market. It has assisted the Dabhol Power Company in multi-jurisdictional litigation and arbitration arising out of the $3 billion Dabhol power station project, and has advised the lead arrangers on a 30-year concession to design, build and operate the 'Interior Norte' Portuguese highway.

The firm's profile was considerably bolstered by the arrival of non-contentious expert **Ann Minogue** (see p.198) from CMS Cameron McKenna just over a year ago, with her clients such as Stanhope and Lottery-funded arts projects. "*The optimum construction lawyer,*" she continues to receive plaudits for her expertise and ability to attract new business, while rivals acknowledge that in opposition "*you know you'll have a battle.*" She has assisted Stanhope on the construction of buildings at Paternoster Square, involving three deals and lettings for the development adjacent to St Paul's Cathedral to create a new City square.

Despite a quieter year in the sector generally, the firm's leading project practice has influenced its construction work. Advice to BBC Property Partnerships is typical of this, as is assistance to the Strategic Rail Authority over the extension of the East London Line, building five new stations and enhanced infrastructure links to the national rail network. Clients appreciated the team's "*universally good people*" and professional support. **Marshall Levine** (see p.197) brings "*decades of efficiency and understanding*" to his main areas of focus, adjudication and PFI. **Simon Burch**'s (see p.193) practice includes power and infrastructure projects as well as international petrochemical developments. Highlights include the completion of the new £250 million GlaxoSmithKline headquarters building, and assistance on various high-profile arts projects, including the English National Opera, Tate Gallery, Royal Albert Hall and the Victoria & Albert Museum. **Clients** Amey; BBC Property Partnerships; BP; Carillion; Dabhol Power Company; EMCOR Drake & Scull Engineering; Enron; Heron International; Hub Power Company; Impregilo; Lend Lease; Nepco; Royal Albert Hall; Stanhope; Strategic Rail Authority; Tate Gallery.

MAYER, BROWN, ROWE & MAW (see firm details p.1060) Part of the firm's commercial dispute resolution group, it is too early to say what shape the department will have following the transatlantic merger with Mayer, Brown & Platt. It seems certain that oil and gas, and power projects will continue to be at the forefront of the firm's contentious construction practice. It has drafted and negotiated contracts for power projects in several countries on behalf of a major international turbine supplier. The team has acted for the Metropolitan Police South East London 's design and build contractor in relation to PFI projects. A consistency of professionalism enables the team to "*get to the core issues.*" **John Rushton** ("*commercial and as tough as old boots when he needs to be*") remains a key figure in the market. **Michael Regan**'s insurance-linked practice is still a force of some repute, while the "*wise and focused*" non-contentious expertise of **Gillian Birkby** (see p.192) again scored highly in our research. Of highest profile in the last year has been the team's work on claims relating to the explosion at the Corus steel works at Port Talbot. It has also been involved in claims relating to the design and build of three major hotel complexes and those relating to a crane collapse at Canary Wharf. International work has increased dramatically. The department has seen a number of claims on behalf of reinsurers and professionals, and it continues to represent an American company over claims arising out of its manufacture and

CONSTRUCTION ■ LONDON

supply of a process plant for an Asian cement plant facility. It has advised clients on bespoke amendments to the new FIDIC contracts for use on a variety of international projects. **Clients** Alfred McAlpine; Amey; Axima Building Services; Carillion; Costain; GE Power Systems; Haden Young; John Sisk & Sons; Kajima; Lever Fabergé ; Laing; John Mowle m & Company ; Nationwide; Nippon Steel Corporation; Persimmon; RJ Wallace; Southern Water; Staveley; St George; The Grocers' Company; Unilever; Wimpey Homes; WS Atkins.

ALLEN & OVERY (see firm details p.841) Weighted towards the non-contentious side, the construction group's work is a combination of domestic property development work, PFI and international projects. Interviewees reflected on the "*cohesive and sensible*" nature of a group that understands the market. Led by head of department John Scriven, the team possesses a good mix of skills and "*provides extremely clear documentation, and both broad-ranging and specialised advice.*" The property development side of the firm's construction work includes advice to the lenders on the Heron Quays and St Martin's Court developments at Canary Wharf and Paternoster Square respectively. Assistance to Union Fenosa on the construction aspects of the first LNG project in Egypt typifies the manner in which the firm's leading projects practice combines with its construction team. The firm is also involved in advice to Barts & The London NHS Trust on PPP/PFI-related construction issues. **Clients** Barts & The London NHS Trust; Union Fenosa.

CLIFFORD CHANCE (see firm details p.911) Such is the obvious power of the firm's real estate practice and its related international projects and PFI skills that it has long been able to provide a large combined team with a good line in construction work. Clients consider these lawyers "*the sort of people who get the job done.*" Acting for developers or their funders, a balance is maintained between support work and stand-alone instructions, and it is well-placed to capitalise on the increasing internationalisation of the construction industry and the prominence of financing issues.

"*Completely on top of what he's doing,*" **Tim Steadman** (see p.699) leads a non-contentious team that has "*impressed with its quality and attention to detail.*" It has worked alongside Multiplex Construction on the financing and construction of the new national football stadium at Wembley. Client Electricité de France typifies the firm's international leanings, and the team has continued to represent the group on documentation for the Altamira power plant in Mexico, and procurement assistance for additional plants in Rio de Janeiro and Laos. Closer to home, it has assisted Canary Wharf's in-house construction team on the documentation for the redevelopment of its remaining land. The contentious side of the business, led by international arbitration star John Beechey, has continued to act for a theme park in one of the Gulf states on a dispute, and has aided Edison Mission on a matter arising out of the construction of a power plant in Sicily. A considerable list of other international projects includes acting on a dispute over the construction of a plasterboard plant in Brazil, and assisting Siemens in connection with separate disputes over the construction of power stations overseas. **Clients** Bechtel; Bombardiert; Canary Wharf; China Petroleum Pipeline Bureau; Corporation of London; Daewoo; Derwent Cogeneration; Edison Mission; Electricité de France; Farnborough Airport; Grantchester; Haden Drysys International; Helical Bar; Minerva; Multiplex Constructions (UK); Rolex.

FRESHFIELDS BRUCKHAUS DERINGER (see firm details p.964) Respected for its work on behalf of developers, the firm is one of several in our table that can call on an established broad client base and international contacts for much of its construction work. "*Organised and perceptive, hard but honest,*" the department's two principal areas of focus are complex, international disputes and high-value projects work.

The undoubted figurehead for the practice is the "*determined and tenacious*" **Sally Roe** (see p.199). "*She makes all the points that you hope you would have made,*" said one competitor. Some interviewees pointed to the lack of partners with a comparable profile, although that belies the reputation of "*down-to-earth*" **Jane Jenkins** (see p.197), who many dub "*impressive.*" The firm has continued to advise on major premises' development at Canary Wharf, and has assisted London Transport on the proposed London Underground PPP. The firm's activities on behalf of Telereal on its telephone exchange property outsourcing contract with BT is just one transaction that the firm is currently pushing across Europe. Internationally, the firm has been working for Jawa Power in mediation of claims by its EPC contractor, for extensions of time in the construction of a thermal power station in Indonesia. The firm has also acted for KEDO on the construction of two 1,000-MW light water reactors in North Korea, and has aided ENEL on the erection of two large wood-burning power stations in Italy. **Clients** BNFL; ENEL; Jones Lang LaSalle; KEDO; London Transport; Powergen; Jawa Power; Telereal.

HERBERT SMITH (see firm details p.992) The firm's construction practice is weighted towards the contentious side, acting predominantly for funders on UK and international arbitrations. "*Pragmatic, realistic and developer-focused,*" much of the firm's work is linked to its corporate, energy and PFI teams. The moderately sized team under "*real professional*" **Michael Davis** (see p.194) has aided Halliburton in engineering disputes both nationally and internationally, and has been instructed by General Electric and Lockheed Martin on separate disputes. Non-contentious assistance for London & Continental Railways on the project for the Channel Tunnel Rail Link, and advice to National Air Traffic Services on the construction of the new Scottish Centre for air traffic control add projects-related breadth to the firm's noted contentious side. It has also aided Land Securities on the BBC outsourcing development at White City. **Clients** BAT; British Airports Authority; General Electric; Halliburton; Land Securities; Lockheed Martin; London & Continental Railways; London Stock Exchange; National Air Traffic Services ; Vodafone.

LOVELLS (see firm details p.1045) Considered by the market to have its focus in the non-contentious and related PFI and projects arenas, much of the firm's success in this area can be attributed to its international engineering practice. According to clients, the department "*approaches complex projects in a way that others would do well to follow.*" Group head **Phillip Capper** (see p.193) is best known for his "*measured and constructive*" work on international mechanical and engineering projects. Considered to have intellectual as well as practical leanings, he is judged "*a real asset to the firm in terms of market awareness.*" His large team has advised Deutag on the design, build and operate contract of a large drilling rig for the OKIOC oil companies consortium, a project that utilised several of the firm's overseas offices. **Nicholas Gould** (see p.195) is lauded for his work on arbitration and dispute management, especially in Japan and the US. He "*cuts through to the key points and tries to get a good deal*" and has assisted Mitsubishi on an ICC arbitration relating to a dispute with a Korean joint venture over a cement plant in Saudi Arabia. On the Channel Tunnel Rail Link, the firm has advised the project manager, and has also assisted on the NEC contracts for construction of the railway and infrastructure issues with Railtrack and others. The firm has strong parallel abilities in facilities management and outsourcing, enabling it to answer the related service elements of many construction deals. **Clients** A LSTOM Power; BAA Lynton; Barclays; Carillion; Deutag; Haslemere; Land Securities; Mars; Mitsubishi; Prudential.

NORTON ROSE (see firm details p.1084) Dispute resolution, in the form of arbitrations and adjudications, make up much of the firm's work in construction and engineering. The team has a broad, strongly international and employer-led client base, and can draw from its project finance and property development arms. Clients we spoke to described construction as "*an important aspect of work for the firm.*" Contentious work has seen leading partner **Peter Rees** (see p.199) advising Braehead in its successful defence against Bovis-Lend Lease concerning the design and construction of a shopping and leisure centre in Glasgow. Head of department Christopher Hill has acted for

LONDON ■ CONSTRUCTION

Siemens in an ICC arbitration arising out of the construction of a combined cycle power station in Asia. The firm's resources have united in its advice to project companies and lenders relating to the construction and operation aspects of potential defects in new technology gas-fired power stations. **Martin Bridgewater** (see p.192) is an "*excellent disputes man,*" and our research showed that more individuals in the department are beginning to cultivate a market profile. New client Bechtel has benefited from the firm's advice on the infrastructure renewal element of the South Central rail franchise, and the team continues to represent the lenders to the Tubelines Group. **Clients** AES; Bechtel; Bouygues; Braehead; Capital Shopping Centres; Depfa; Edison Gas ; Enelpower; Helical Bar; Scottish-Power; Siemens; Sir Robert McAlpine; Snamprogetti; Workspace Group.

TAYLOR WESSING (see firm details p.1156) One of a number of firms making efforts to dedicate additional resources in this area, the firm's main revenue generator remains its contentious practice. Clients have been "*impressed, particularly for arbitration matters.*" **Peter Shaw** (see p.200) was commended to *Chambers* for his knowledgeable advice. Accredited mediators **Neil White** (see p.201) ("*a fine practitioner with a rare combination of legal ability and commercial acumen*") and **Christopher Bourgeois** (see p.192) have been instructed on a variety of disputes arising from major projects. The latter has continued to advise Mitsubishi Heavy Industries on claims connected to the construction of a power plant, arising from US Chapter 11 proceedings. The firm also successfully represented Toyota (GB) on four adjudications arising out of a £25 million contract. **Helen Garthwaite** (see p.195) is a non-contentious specialist, brought into the firm a year ago on the development side, for heavyweight work with international consortiums. The non-contentious unit has had success on infrastructure work, advising Westminster City Council on the Paddington LVTA for the construction of a major road bridge affecting rail, canal and telecommunications links. The department has provided construction advice for the funding of a £150 million Docklands development of a hotel and apartments for BHF-Bank. It has also delivered consortium documentation to contractor Jackson Civil Engineering for an £80 million electricity distribution network. **Clients** Bank of Scotland; BHF-Bank; Eve Group (including Jackson Civil Engineering); Fortis Bank; Gracechurch Leisure; LPL Electrical Services; Merlin Entertainment Group; Mitsubishi Heavy Industries; Toyota (GB); Westminster City Council.

ASHURST MORRIS CRISP (see firm details p.852) New partner Logan Mair is part of a team of "*talented individuals*" applauded by peers for its projects-related work and "*a positive approach – straightforward and pleasant to deal with.*" Its contentious work has included the successful mediation of a claim by the owners of a North Sea offshore platform. The group has also advised engineers on a claim by contractors for both an additional $50 million and a 12 -month extension arising from the construction of a power station in Asia. The international theme has continued with successes for the group's Asia practice. These have included advice to Japanese consortia on the construction of a petrochemical complex in Saudi Arabia, and a similar project for sponsors in Germany. Domestically, the group has been involved in drafting framework agreements for capital maintenance contracts for BT, as well as advi sing the British Racing Drivers' Club over the construction of new access roads and infrastructure for Silverstone. Ipswich Town FC has also employed the firm on the construction of two new stands. **Clients** British Racing Drivers ' Club; BT; Centrica; Chelsfield; Citibank; Exchequer Partnership; Hitachi; IBM; Ipswich Town FC; Marubeni Corporation ; Mitsubishi Heavy Industries; Partnerships UK; PiCKO; Royal Bank of Scotland; Stanhope; Sumitomo; Summit Healthcare.

DENTON WILDE SAPTE (see firm details p.935) The firm has shifted the emphasis of its construction group towards the non-contentious project-related side. The team advised Thames Water as shareholder in, and contractor to, Metronet, the preferred bidder for the London Underground PPP, over the terms of two principal subcontractor contracts for modernisation, refurbishment and civil engineering works. Under head of department Julian Pope, the "*responsive*" and professional group has also advised on the drafting of turnkey construction, operation and maintenance, and power-purchase contracts in support of a bid for the development of two gas-fired power stations in Nigeria. Additionally, the firm has been working with the Highways Agency to update their contract documentation for its DBFO roads programme, including the A1 Darrington to Dishforth project. **Clients** BAA; Daifuku Europe; Highways Agency; M OD ; Shell International; Thames Water.

HAMMOND SUDDARDS EDGE The "*proactive unit*" is recognised by many interviewees to be growing, although some await its response to the increasing internationalism of the construction market. The recent opening of a new, predominantly construction-based office in Hong Kong is the first step, and the firm has already seen instructions from several Chinese contractors. Clients said that they "*clearly have the strength and depth to deal with major issues .*" Procurement specialist **Jonathan Hosie** ("*a great mind*") is a key part of a broadly based and independent department weighted towards employers and public sector work. One of "*the biggest hitters around,*" **David Jones** has assisted London Underground on the Piccadilly Line extension to Terminal 5. Peers agree he has "*gravitas, expertise and good client-handling skills.*" Work for contractors and facilities management are also features of his work. Highlights for the firm include the non-contentious drafting of the prime contracts for Defence Estates, particularly in Scotland for single unit a ccommodation, which involved cutting down Defence Estates work from thousands of contracts to only a few. PFI and associated construction work has also been at the fore, including framework-driven due diligence on behalf of the purchaser of PFI subcontracts for five education schemes. Renewable energy projects have occupied the team, such as drafting the EPC contracts for the Blaen Bowi and Parc Cynog wind farms for TXU and M & N. Pipeline work in the Middle East and a considerable amount of work in Japan (for the likes of Mitsubishi Heavy Industries) rounds off the firm's portfolio. **Clients** Bovis-Lend Lease; Infraco JNP; Infraco SSL; Interserve; London Underground; M OD ; States of Jersey; Staveley Industries; Taylor Woodrow; TXU; Wates Construction.

KENNEDYS (see firm details p.1019) Historically an out-and-out contentious specialist in architects' insurance and associated professional work, the firm was considered by many interviewees to be making significant moves into other areas of construction. The appointment of a chief executive at the firm has freed up much of senior partner **Nick Thomas**' (see p.683) time, and the effect is a greater recognition both of his own contribution to the sector ("*excellent ability and a formidable opponent*") and that of the firm.

Adjudged to have "*a good grasp of the issues,*" the firm has acted for a large group of insurers on the damage to the works used in the construction of the Cardiff Bay Barrage. It has assisted quantity surveyors in an adjudication among the Welsh Assembly, the Richard Rogers Partnership and Hanscomb, and has also worked for an international contractor on a domestic power generation project in England and Ireland. Overseas instructions illustrative of the firm's specialist expertise have included representations on behalf of the insurers on a Peruvian claim arising from El Niño damage to a canal and dam, as well as assistance to the Kingdom of Saudi Arabia on a construction insurance dispute. Most recently, the team has been instructed by AXA over the £100 million fire at a Centre Parcs holiday resort. **Clients** Allianz Cornhill; AXA RE Insurance; Coca-Cola; Gerling Insurance; Kingdom of Saudi Arabia; Norwich Union; Royal & SunAlliance; Trenwick International.

MACFARLANES (see firm details p.1047) "In the ascendant," say peers; there is "*a momentum effect and they are obviously investing in this area.*" The firm has been associated for some time with its bright star, **Tony Blackler**, a

CONSTRUCTION ■ LONDON

"*smooth contentious operator – tactically switched-on.*" The firm's programme of consolidation and deliberate, gradual growth appears to be paying dividends. Highlighted for his workload and down-to-earth approach, **Patrick Holmes** led a team negotiating the construction documentation and infrastructure issues for the CIT Group development at London Bridge, the More London project, which includes the new GLA building. **Simon Nurney** has successfully concluded an arbitration defence on behalf of developer Alstadtbau against a UK contractor. The group remains predominantly a domestic construction practice, with both contentious and non-contentious work for Associated British Ports, including the Humber International Terminal at Immingham. Projects-related work has afforded the team a greater international profile, with new instructions via projects in St Lucia, South America and Abu Dhabi in the last year reflecting this trend. **Clients** Altstadtbau; Associated British Ports; Canary Wharf Contractors; Christ's Hospital; CIT Group; Kajima Construction Europe; OCCI; Universal Music; WS Atkins.

NICHOLSON GRAHAM & JONES (see firm details p.1083) The firm was praised for its co-operative approach with clients, who reflected on its "*serious attention to the detail work*" and an ability to "*find the extra dimension.*" High-profile partner **James Hudson** (see p.197) ("*a polished operator*") acted for O'Rourke on the acquisition of John Laing Construction, inheriting a substantial flow of UK and international contracts and claims that should assist the firm in growing this area in the future. The team has also acted for Henderson Global Investors on the construction aspects of the Moor House redevelopment. Head of department **David Race** (see p.199) has acted for the West African Portland Cement Company on the construction of a new 3,000 tonne per day clinker line at Ewekoro in Lagos, and in connection with the installation of a new captive power station adjacent to the site. Contentious work has included acting for Phillips Petroleum on its claim against Snamprogetti over the defective design of a compressor on a gas platform in the North Sea, and advice to the Merchant Retail Group on a claim relating to the £13 million fitting-out contract at the House of Fraser store at Bluewater in Kent. **Clients** DTI; Eurostar (UK); Greenwich Council; Henderson Global Investors; HSBC; Infraco Sub Surface Systems; London REMADE; Lorne Stewart; O'Rourke; Phillips Petroleum; West African Portland Cement Company.

SJ BERWIN (see firm details p.867) The firm's sizeable property team and considerable resources have played a key role in raising its construction profile. Its small construction team is applauded as "*good at getting to know their clients – they go out of their way to do that.*" Domestic work for developers makes up the largest tranche of its caseload. Head of the practice Ian Insley has led on advice to British Land on the non-contentious construction aspects for the pre-let of 375,000 square feet of the Plantation Place development to Accenture. The team also advised AXA REIM on the sale of Premier Place for £166 million, which took place mid-development. This was augmented by instructions from Colas on its dispute with Morrison Construction over water ingress problems at Rockingham Speedway. **Clients** Axa REIM; British Land; Brixton Estates; Colas; Gazeley; Marks & Spencer; Pinacl; J Sainsbury's.

TROWERS & HAMLINS (see firm details p.1168) Traditionally known for its experience in the social housing market, the firm has recently focused on work connected to the PPC (Project Partnering Contract) 2000 scheme that **David Mosey** (see p.198) developed. "*Innovative – it gets used and delivers results and has made a real difference,*" agree peers. Notwithstanding the relative youth of the scheme, it has contributed greatly to the firm's profile, with construction now its fastest growing department. Non-contentious assignments remain its major strength. The team has aided a large number of commercial developer clients, including The Berkeley Group on its various schemes at Kings Cross, Chelsea Bridge Wharf, Paddington basin and the Royal Arsenal at Woolwich. It also continues to advise housing associations and regulatory bodies. Partner **Stephanie Canham** (see p.193) personifies the firm's "*down-to-earth and realistic*" approach to transactions. The group has assisted British Aerospace on a £200 million partnering contract involving three contractors, and has been assisting Surrey County Council on a ten-year, £340 million programme for highways infrastructure repair and maintenance. Work has also included a £270 million long-term maintenance and long-term repair deal for Sheffield County Council. **Clients** BAE Systems; The Berkeley Group; BBC; Sheffield CC; Surrey County Council.

WINWARD FEARON (see firm details p.1193) Interviewees endorsed this niche contentious practice, which is modelled in the more traditional style. The unit is structured around the figure of lawyer and mediator **David Cornes** (see p.194), judged "*a tower of strength for the firm.*" The firm currently occupies a valuable slot in the sector for those seeking litigation.

BAKER & MCKENZIE (see firm details p.855) Its international network and the presence of litigator and solicitor advocate **Jeremy Winter** (see p.201) are the firm's two main assets. Linking with its projects teams, the non-contentious side of this practice has been specifically targeted in recent times, affording it success with international, privately financed infrastructure schemes. Winter leads from the front, and is said to be "*an experienced and considered litigator who understands dispute resolutions and mediation.*" Contractors and sponsors make up much of the firm's client base. The small London team has continued to advise the National Petroleum Industrialisation Company on its planned $533 million joint venture with Baswell for a polypropylene plant in Saudi Arabia. The firm has also concluded an action against Balfour Beatty on behalf of Kelston Sparkes concerning a road project in South West England. Winter also headed the group that prepared the Society of Construction Law's 'best practice' protocols for disputes on projects and cost overruns. **Clients** Kelston Sparkes; National Petroleum Industrialisation Company.

BEALE AND COMPANY (see firm details p.862) Predominantly concerned with professional indemnity and construction-related insurance work for engineers (which makes up around half of the firm's turnover), it can nevertheless field a strong construction-related team. Contractors and professional consultants make up much of the client roster. Representations continued on behalf of the engineers on the restructuring and eventual reopening of the Millennium Bridge in London. Clients speak of a proactive firm "*in a class of its own*" that "*thinks of positive ideas to get things moving.*" First and foremost a contentious practice, the team has also seen non-contentious work increase in the last twelve months under the experienced eye of managing partner John Ward. This is a result from both the increase in demand for professional indemnity advice on professional contracts and the rising premiums now evident throughout the insurance and related markets. **Clients** Millennium Bridge Trust.

BERRYMANS LACE MAWER (see firm details p.865) The main focus of the non-contentious practice lies in claims against professionals and contractors. The team, located in London, Dubai and other international offices, has successfully defended a claim on behalf of Davy McKee arising out of an explosion at a methanol plant in India. Interviewees noted an increase in the amount of insurance-related work on which the firm is involved. Senior Partner Paul Taylor, in particular, leads by example with a fine international reputation, particularly in the Middle East. The firm has acted for surveyors Austen Associates in a successful defence of a claim, and has assisted Arup in defence of a claim for breach of copyright. **Clients** Carillion; Cunninghams; Griffiths & Armour; Norwich Union; Oscar Faber; Arup; Waterman Partnership; Whitby Bird & Partners.

CAMPBELL HOOPER (see firm details p.899) The influx of a team from Taylor Woodrow a year ago has brought with it a widening of the firm's focus, adding those developers carrying out large-scale construction work to the firm's traditional, contractor client base. Large regeneration schemes have been a source of instruction in the last year. This has included contractual advice for Countryside Properties (Commercial) on the ongoing Chatham Maritime regeneration of the former Royal Navy Dockyards into a new marina. Under group head Duncan Salmon, the small team has advised on the procurement and construction of a large desalination plant. Reading Borough Council instructed the firm on the negotiation of a joint venture and profit-sharing agreement with Thames Water, concerning the relocation of an existing sewerage plant onto derelict and contaminated land owned by the Council, with a view to redeveloping the existing site.

On the contentious side, the firm has continued to defend a claim arising out of the construction of the Greenwich Millennium Village for alleged non-payment of fees, and has successfully resisted an attempt by a works contractor to improperly 'borrow' the main contractor's name in order to sue the employer directly. It has defended Geoconsult on its prosecution by the Health & Safety Executive over the collapse of the Heathrow Express Tunnel and has acted for an overseas client against a household insurer in respect of a multimillion pound claim arising from a latent defects policy. **Clients** Carillion Construction; Conran Group; Countryside Properties (Commercial); David Wilson Homes; Geoconsult; Greenwich Millennium Village; Northacre; Phillimore Hill; Reading Borough Council; Taylor Woodrow Construction.

DAVIES ARNOLD COOPER (see firm details p.930) The firm has been refocusing on work of an international nature, although it remains recognised more readily for its contentious construction work. A large team has represented Ghazi Barotha Contractors in Pakistan in connection with a $500 million dispute. The non-contentious side has been buoyed by a closer integration with the firm's property group. Daniel Gowan (see p.195) is a "*realist – he cuts to the chase and can see where the deal is.*" He has been instructed by Jacobs Gibb in Jordan over a civil engineering dispute, and has recently been involved in an ICC arbitration for the Victorian Channels Authority arising from a capital dredging contract in Melbourne Harbour. Additional mileage is made from the firm's construction insurance practice, dealing with associated professional indemnity and similar claims. The mid-sized team has acted for the public liability insurers of Matthew Hall in the flooding of the NatWest headquarters. Allianz and Gerling also instructed it over the collapse of a crane at Canary Wharf in May 2000. **Clients** Alfred McAlpine Construction; Allianz; Balfour Beatty; Gerling; Jacobs Gibb; Independent; John Mowlem; RJ Wallace; Royal & SunAlliance; Walter Llewellyn & Sons; Victorian Channels Authority.

GLOVERS This niche practice is primarily centred on construction head David Miles, although the group has also recently taken on dual-qualified quantity surveyor Philip Eyre. The firm's construction client base is contractor-oriented and primarily domestic, and its resources are focused towards the contentious side. The firm continues to represent Sir Robert McAlpine on payment disputes adjudications regarding a Blackfriars hotel development and a Northampton day centre. Non-contentious assistance for London & Paris Estates at the Royal Exchange was a further significant transaction. For a small firm, it has a significant international focus, advising on an arbitration concerning a waste water treatment works in Bangkok. It has also resolved a claim brought by a professional client in the Privy Council against a Trinidad-based insurance company. **Clients** Croydon Park Hotel; Hurley, Robertson & Associates; Laserbore; Sir Robert McAlpine.

SIMMONS & SIMMONS (see firm details p.1136) In common with many of its peers, the firm has experienced a rise in non-contentious work this year. Increased adjudication has resulted in more advice to a broad church of clients on the management of risk before entering into contracts. A part of a growing PFI/PPP element to its construction work has been advice to the Greek Government on financing structures, procurement policy and contract drafting on the construction of six new motorways into Athens for the 2004 Olympics, at a cost of €4.9 billion. The firm has also acted for the regional authority on the extension of the Athens Metro. Railway infrastructure has been to the fore in recent times, assisting London Underground company Infraco JNP, and continuing to aid Railtrack on the construction and related aspects of its various Channel Tunnel Rail Link, Thameslink and West Coast Line upgrade projects. The Nationwide Building Society has instructed the firm on both contentious and non-contentious work, including matters relating to its branch refurbishment programme. The team has further aided a contracting consortium with a $200 million claim for delay and defective work on a trans-continental submarine fibre-optic cable. It has also been instructed by BP on the redevelopment programme at its Sunbury-on-Thames centre. **Clients** Abu Dhabi Investment Company; BP; Infraco JNP; Government of Greece; Nationwide Building Society; Railtrack.

THE SOUTH

CONSTRUCTION
■ THE SOUTH

[1] **Shadbolt & Co** Reigate
[2] **Blake Lapthorn** Portsmouth
Cripps Harries Hall Tunbridge Wells

LEADING INDIVIDUALS
[3] **HELPS Dominic** Shadbolt & Co
[6] **DELVES Simon** Shadbolt & Co

This book is the product of 6,582 1/2 hour interviews. See p.7 for BMRB audit. Within each band, firms are listed alphabetically. See individuals' profiles p.191

SHADBOLT & CO (see firm details p.1126) See London editorial p.176.

BLAKE LAPTHORN (see firm details p.877) The firm retains a high proportion of non-contentious domestic work, with a gradual increase in the number of contractors and consultants in its client base. On the non-contentious side, Peter Barber's team has advised McCarthy & Stone on contracts and subcontracts. It has also given public procurement and contract advice to West Sussex County Council for the redevelopment of Chichester High School for Girls. Clients endorsed the firm's positive approach. It has been involved in dispute resolution and ICC arbitration for Alcatel on a number of issues, including the installation of a Pacific Ocean cable network. The small group has assisted Christchurch Borough Council on disputes concerning drain replacement and associated highway works, and it represents David Lloyd Leisure on disputes arising from its expansion programme. **Clients** Christchurch Borough Council; David Lloyd Leisure; McCarthy & Stone; West Sussex County Council.

CRIPPS HARRIES HALL (see firm details p.922) Traditionally a strong commercial property firm, it has a bias towards employers in local authorities and house building. Since leaving Laytons in 2001, Jane Ryland has been building up the contentious side of the practice, which has seen an increase in the number of main contractors and larger subcontractors clients. The firm's construction lawyers work closely with the property team, and additional expertise is gained from the former head of legal at Wates Construction, partner Bill Mackie. Work for government authorities is an area of concentration for the firm. It also assisted a national main contractor in a successful defence of a money claim for works, losses and expense by a subcontractor. The firm continues to assist with ongoing advice to Gravesham Borough Council over the redevelopment of the town centre. The CPS and Customs & Excise are also sources of instruction on non-contentious issues. **Clients** Berkeley Homes (Eastern); Crown Prosecution Service; GLN Developments; HM Customs & Excise; Wates Construction.

CONSTRUCTION ■ THAMES VALLEY/SOUTH WEST

THAMES VALLEY

CONSTRUCTION
■ THAMES VALLEY

1. **Clarks** Reading
   Linnells Oxford
   Morgan Cole Oxford, Reading
6. **Corbett & Co** Teddington

LEADING INDIVIDUALS

1. **RINTOUL David** Clarks
4. **CORBETT Edward** Corbett & Co

This book is the product of 6,582 1/2 hour interviews. See p.7 for BMRB audit.
Within each band, firms are listed alphabetically. See individuals' profiles p.191

CLARKS (see firm details p.908) This is a predominantly contentious group focusing on the domestic market. It has moved to increase its client base on the non-contentious side with additional work for both contractors and sub-contractors. The firm has followed the market trend, focusing on adjudications and arbitration. Considered a good negotiator, **David Rintoul** (see p.199) has acted for a number of clients, either bringing or defending claims using the adjudication process under the 1996 Construction Act. He led a successful defence on behalf of a NHS Trust to a £2 million adjudication claim, and helped BOC defend a £1 million arbitration against it. **Clients** BOC; Thames Water; various NHS Trusts.

LINNELLS (see firm details p.1044) Weighted on the contentious side, the firm has seen almost a doubling of the amount of adjudication work in which it is involved, as well as a corresponding increase in the number of subsequent enforcement cases dealing with adjudication decisions. Richard Wade is a member of this small team, which conducts contentious work for small to medium-sized contractors and deals with non-contentious issues for contractors and local developers.

MORGAN COLE (see firm details p.1075) The highly experienced arbitration specialist Andrew Campbell heads the firm's small team. It has advised the Council for the Central Laboratory of the Research Councils (CCLRC) on the construction of the £50 million building required for the new synchrotron light source. The firm has also assisted on many construction-related matters, providing specialist advice to NHS Trusts and other public sector bodies, and working with Barclays Bank in the extension of its major facilities management contracts with national contractors. **Clients** Barclays Bank; CCLRC; TotalFinaElf; NHS Trusts; developers ; consultants ; contractors.

CORBETT & CO (see firm details p.919) The practice is primarily contentious, with a significant international aspect. It has been instructed by a Japanese consulting engineer in relation to a leaking hydroelectric power station in Indonesia, and has been involved in ICC arbitrations for Van Oord ACZ concerning unforeseen boulders at a site in Geelong, Australia. **Edward Corbett** (see p.194) makes good use of his "*proven expertise in FIDIC contractual disputes*" for the International Federation of Consulting Engineers. A recent arrival from Masons has strengthened the team's capacity. Further demonstrating the international leanings of the practice, Corbett's "*co-operative approach to problem-solving*" has been utilised by a South African contractor against a Kuwaiti company concerning sums due for multimillion dollar work done at Addis Ababa airport. **Clients** Hinkins & Frewin; Hyundai; Kasese Cobalt Company; Nippon Koei; Van Oord ACZ.

SOUTH WEST

CONSTRUCTION
■ SOUTH WEST

1. **Masons** Bristol
2. **Bevan Ashford** Bristol, Exeter
3. **Beachcroft Wansbroughs** Bristol
   Burges Salmon Bristol
4. **Laytons** Bristol
   Osborne Clarke Bristol
5. **Bond Pearce** Plymouth
   Veale Wasbrough Bristol

LEADING INDIVIDUALS

1. **COLLINGWOOD Mark** Masons
   HARLING Marcus Burges Salmon
   REDMOND John Osborne Clarke
2. **HARRIS Adam** Masons
   VASEY John Beachcroft Wansbroughs
3. **BIRCH John** Bevan Ashford
   GUPPY Nicholas Laytons
   HALL Priscilla Osborne Clarke
   HANLEY Christine Bond Pearce
   HOWE Martin Bevan Ashford

This book is the product of 6,582 1/2 hour interviews. See p.7 for BMRB audit.
Within each band, firms are listed alphabetically. See individuals' profiles p.191

MASONS (see firm details p.1057) This team benefits from being part of the powerful Masons national construction network, with many regional divisions of national contractors counted among its clients. Local and regional contractors also make up a significant proportion of its client base, with work for employers a small but notable regional focus. Competitors spoke of its "*competence and efficiency*," while clients were pleased with the firm's "*speed of response and level of input*." Although the firm's workload is split evenly between contentious and non-contentious matters, the former has had the higher profile this year. Partner **Mark Collingwood** (see p.193) acted successfully for Crown House Engineering against a national contractor in four linked adjudications concerning mechanical and electrical engineering issues. The office also assisted a joint venture of international contractors against a property developer on a claim in excess of £6.5 million that was processed and achieved within eight weeks. **Adam Harris** (see p.196) remains respected for his non-contentious and contentious work for contractor clients. The firm was also instructed by AMEC in tripartite adjudication proceedings, and by AEA Technology over contractual issues concerning the decommissioning of a works in Dounreay. **Clients** AEA Technology; AMEC: Carillion; Cowlin Construction; Crown House Engineering; Lorne Stewart; Macob; Miller Construction; M O D; Pearce Group.

BEVAN ASHFORD (see firm details p.869) Starting from a position of some strength locally, the firm has expanded its involvement in partnering and collaborative forms of procurement within construction. This has been particularly evident in the firm's traditional client base of public client and health-related groups. The team has advised on the drafting of construction documentation for the NHS Pro-Cure 21 initiative, to introduce supply chain management and collaborative working. The MOD has also benefited from the preparation by the firm of replacement procurement contracts. **John Birch** (see p.192) is the standout figure in the Exeter office, while **Martin Howe** (see p.197) in Bristol used his experience of PFI and PPP projects to assist a major contractor on the drafting of a subcontract to fit with the ACA Project Partnering Agreement. Private sector clients now make up more than half of the group's work, with increasing forays into the specialist and main contractor markets often tied in with the firm's projects work. The team has represented European supermarket group Lidl UK in adjudication and arbitration proceedings concerning a design and build project in North Wales. Further adjudications for the firm's traditional client base of NHS Trusts and partnering advice to four housing associations have featured in its caseload. **Clients** Bovis-Lend Lease; Cardiff & Vale NHS Trust; Gwent NHS Trust;

182 INDEX TO LEADING LAWYERS: PAGE 1693 ■ IN-HOUSE LAWYERS PROFILES: PAGE 1201

SOUTH WEST ■ CONSTRUCTION

Invicta Leisure; John Mowlem & Company; Knightstone Housing Association; Lidl UK; Lorne Stewart; MOD; MT Højgaard; National Federation of Builders; Phi Group; Places for People Group; Sarsen Housing Association; University of Bristol.

BEACHCROFT WANSBROUGHS (see firm details p.860)
Respected for its insurance-related expertise, the group has this year concentrated on work for new clients in the Lloyd's market. Although this aspect does make up the majority of the firm's construction-related work, non-contentious support in tandem with the firm's property department is its other main tranche. The latter has included development work for Railtrack on the re-opening of the Portishead Branch Line. The firm has also seen a rise in instructions from the public sector. The group has produced construction contracts on the major redevelopment of Georges Square in Bristol. More traditionally for the firm, it has successfully defended a £2.5 million claim against architects in the case of Unigate v Turner. Based in Bristol, **John Vasey** (see p.201) (an "*efficient litigator*") co-ordinates the firm's "*responsive and cost-effective*" construction practice nationwide. **Clients** NHS Trusts; Lloyd's; Railtrack.

BURGES SALMON (see firm details p.894)
The firm is considered strongest for its non-contentious expertise on behalf of public and institutional clients. Under group head ("*easy to deal with*") **Marcus Harling** (see p.196), the department has worked with the Arts Council of Wales on various projects, including the Wales Millennium Centre at Cardiff. Much of the firm's construction work is often linked with its leading projects practice. It has assisted the MOD on a new project to provide a Defence Sixth Form College and has been involved on a new PPP fire station project at Canary Wharf. The team has advised United Milk on a £42 million turnkey contract for a new dairy processing facility, and has been instructed on new train depots for First Great Western. Its reach also extends out of the region, where it has assisted Orange PCS on the construction aspects of its new Paddington basin site. **Clients** Arts Council of Wales; FirstGroup; Gloucester College of Arts & Technology; London Fire & Emergency Planning Authority; London Fire Brigade; MOD; The National Trust; Optical Micro Devices; Orange PCS; Royal Botanic Gardens, Kew; United Milk.

LAYTONS (see firm details p.1032)
The firm has seen its non-contentious arm take centre stage for the first time. The Bristol office has focused this year on contentious and subcontractor work, a group with whom it already has strong links, while the firm's Guildford branch has concentrated on the building contractor side. Non-contentious documentation and drafting has included advice on the regeneration of Gravesend town centre for Barratt, and on the construction of a new depot for David Hathaway Transport. National head of construction **Nick Guppy** (see p.195) leads the small team, which has represented Staveley Industries on adjudications relating to claims under £3 million over a contract for mechanical and engineering works at Nuffield Hospital, Cheltenham. It has also aided DE Stamp Felt Roofing Contractors on an insurance policy construction case involving £1.2 million contingent claims. **Clients** Barratt Homes; Britannia Construction; Cowlin Construction; Fencing Contractors Association; Landscape Institute; National Federation of Roofing Contractors; St James Homes; Staveley Industries.

OSBORNE CLARKE (see firm details p.1090)
The firm is best known for its employer-related work, with a keen focus on the contentious side. **John Redmond** led the team on behalf of Birse Construction in a dispute with St David Ltd on a partnering contract. The team assisted Redstone Communications on a variety of matters, including a £1 million adjudication against Cable & Wireless. Although non-contentious cases form the minority in terms of volume, the firm is involved in significant non-contentious deals. The department was instructed by the Nishimatsu Construction Company to advise on the contractual aspects of the Dublin Port Tunnel project, as well as the tunnel contract for the Channel Tunnel Rail Link. It continues to act for Transco on a large number of contentious matters, and has provided advice internationally to Skyspan regarding a contract for the roof of the Asian Games Stadium in Busan, Korea. **Priscilla Hall** enters our tables this year on the basis of commendations for her non-contentious experience. Her work has included advice to QinetiQ on framework agreements and PFI-related matters. **Clients** Argos; Birse Construction; Drake & Scull; Freightliner; Nishimatsu Construction Company; QinetiQ; Redstone Communications; Skyspan; Transco.

BOND PEARCE (see firm details p.879)
Having taken on the non-insurance business interests of the now defunct Cartwrights, the expanded team remains primarily associated with development work for national retailers and funded project work. The group operates between the Plymouth and Southampton offices and is headed by **Christine Hanley** (see p.195). It has advised on Phase II of the National Marine Aquarium in Plymouth and on the major Portland Square development for the University of Plymouth. This has been complemented by assistance on several potential waste to energy projects, and advice to a major retailer on redevelopments and the associated contract outsourcing work. **Clients** Devonport Royal Dockyard; H Mason (Falmouth); IET Energy; Midas Construction; National Marine Aquarium; Plymouth & South West Co-operative Society; University of Plymouth; University of Southampton.

VEALE WASBROUGH (see firm details p.1174)
Head of construction Roger Hoyle has led the compact but growing team on a complete review of all contract documentation for BNFL/Magnox. It has also acted on similar non-contentious drafting for a new manufacturing facility on behalf of Airbus UK. The group also successfully defeated an adjudication ambush on behalf of Cowlin Construction. **Clients** Airbus UK; BNFL/Magnox; Cowlin Construction; Isotemp Ductwork; MOD; Parsons Brinckerhoff Constructors.

CONSTRUCTION ■ WALES/MIDLANDS

WALES

CONSTRUCTION
■ WALES
1. **Eversheds** Cardiff
1. **Hugh James** Cardiff
1. **Morgan Cole** Cardiff, Swansea

LEADING INDIVIDUALS
1. **HERBERT Mary** Eversheds
1. **NEWMAN Paul** Hugh James

This book is the product of 6,582 1/2 hour interviews. See p.7 for BMRB audit. Within each band, firms are listed alphabetically. See individuals' profiles p.191

EVERSHEDS (see firm details p.949) The "*extremely capable*" Mary Herbert (see p.196) led the small team advising John Mowlem on construction documentation for a new shopping centre in Newport, and has also assisted elinia on the construction aspects of a new £90 million offices and data centre development for British Telecommunications. Although the firm was most recognised in our research for its non-contentious work, Sir Robert McAlpine has instructed the group on two adjudication and enforcement proceedings relating to the Caspian Point Development in Cardiff Bay. BG Foods also benefited from the firm's help on a £3 million arbitration concerning a new food factory in Devon. **Clients** BG Foods; Blaenau Gwent; elinia; John Mowlem & Company; National Assembly of Wales; Sir Robert McAlpine.

HUGH JAMES (see firm details p.1004) Although the former Hugh James Ford Simey has now demerged, the bulk of the construction practice remains with the Hugh James arm. The firm makes good use of its long-standing connections with the Welsh Rugby League, with partner Michael Jefferies providing ongoing advice to the Millennium Stadium company regarding roof difficulties and failures. Contentious work has led the way this year, and the team has been commended for its tough litigating style. It has assisted a major water utility group on a number of adjudications for sewage replacement pipes, as well as on indemnity issues arising from pipework damage. The experienced Paul Newman (see p.198), a practicing barrister, assisted contractors David McLean on a £1 million adjudication concerning extensions of time and money in a refurbishment in South Wales. His work, coupled with that of another barrister at the firm, enables the department to deal with more advocacy matters in-house than some of its competition. **Clients** Barratts; David McLean; Hyder; Lorne Stewart; Millennium Stadium; Watkin Jones; Welsh Rugby Union.

MORGAN COLE (see firm details p.1075) A recent firm-wide restructuring programme, combined with the departure of property partners to form Morgan La Roche, has weakened the profile of construction work at this firm. Nevertheless, contentious work continues for a broad client base and comprises the majority of instructions. Through its advice to Norwich Union on the Association of Chartered Engineers' insurance scheme, the team has also overseen a large increase in construction-related professional indemnity work, tying in with core areas at the firm overall. Away from litigious matters, group leader for Cardiff, Paul Millar, has lobbied the construction industry on behalf of Rockwool in relation to deleterious materials clauses. **Clients** AMEC; Babtie; Castleoak; David McLean Developments; Impregilo; Independent Insurance (through Aurora Corporate Services); Norwich Union; Arup; Rockwool; Royal Bank of Scotland; Welsh Development Agency; Welsh Health Estates.

MIDLANDS

CONSTRUCTION
■ MIDLANDS
1. **Wragge & Co** Birmingham
2. **Hammond Suddards Edge** Birmingham
3. **Gateley Wareing** Birmingham
4. **DLA** Birmingham
   freethcartwright Nottingham
   Pinsent Curtis Biddle Birmingham
5. **Browne Jacobson** Nottingham
   Eversheds Birmingham, Nottingham
   Lee Crowder Birmingham
   Shoosmiths Northampton

LEADING INDIVIDUALS
1. **BAYLIS Simon** Wragge & Co
2. **BARRETT Kevin** Wragge & Co
   LLOYD JONES David Gateley Wareing
3. **BERWICK Guy** freethcartwright
   BESSY James Hammond Suddards Edge
   BRADLEY Graeme DLA
   BROWN Jeffrey Lee Crowder
   DAVIES Peter Gateley Wareing
   PIGOTT Ashley Wragge & Co
   WILCOCK Christopher Hammond Suddards Edge
   YULE Ian Wragge & Co

ASSOCIATES TO WATCH
BIRD Christina Wragge & Co

This book is the product of 6,582 1/2 hour interviews. See p.7 for BMRB audit. Within each band, firms are listed alphabetically. See individuals' profiles p.191

WRAGGE & CO (see firm details p.1197) The pre-eminent construction outfit in the Midlands, interviewees commented in particular on its nationwide penetration. National clients speak positively of the firm's resources: "*Well-organised and acquainted with the procedures involved, they have got it down to a fine art.*" Work is predominantly domestic and contentious, on behalf of both contractors and some subcontractors. The firm is considered to "*catch the eye most, with talented people who you know will consistently do a good job – no weak links.*"

This, by far the largest construction team in the region, is lead by dual-qualified quantity surveyor Simon Baylis. "*Quietly efficient and on the ball,*" he was commended to *Chambers* for his commercial approach. He successfully acted on the dispute between Balfour Beatty-AMEC (Jubilee Line) Joint Venture and Railtrack concerning the London Underground extension, a case that highlighted the firm's ability to poach work from the City. Kevin Barrett was considered by peers to be "*an astute performer, who fights his corner hard, yet remains level-headed.*" Ashley Pigott ("*an impressive lawyer and mediator*") advised a Swiss contractor on a £70 million flour mill project, while the respected Ian Yule has been busy with instructions relating to his specialism of construction PFI and PPP projects. The firm has also pursued a dispute for Carillion over the Norfolk & Norwich Hospital PFI project. In conjunction with its property team, the group prepared contract documentation for the £50 million Hampshire Centre for Castlemore Securities, and alongside the projects group, it advised British Energy on its £65 million design and build Eggborough Flue Gas Desulphurisation Plant. **Clients** AMEC Capital Projects; Balfour Beatty Civil Engineering; Birse Construction; Bowmer & Kirkland; British Airways; British Energy; Cadbury Schweppes; Carillion; Clugston Construction; Kier; MEPC; Miller; M OD; Morgan Estates; John Mowlem & Company; Transco.

HAMMOND SUDDARDS EDGE The effects of losing leading light David Lloyd Jones to Gateley Wareing will take time to ascertain. The group as a whole is known for its contentious and contractor-based work. Although the market commented that partner Chris Wilcock had been relatively low profile since his relocation from the firm's Manchester office, he has recently secured contentious instructions from Interserve. New to our tables this year, James Bessy has impressed with his inventive approach and is known for fighting his clients' corner. Non-contentious work for Lattice Energy Services on the construction of its first CHP plant project in the UK is illustrative of the practice's breadth. The firm also drafted major subcontracts for the £35 million Dudley Hospitals' PFI Project, and advised Leicester City on all construction aspects of its new 32,000-seat stadium at Freeman's Wharf. **Clients** Galliford Try; Interserve; Lattice Energy Services ; Leicester City FC ; Millennium Point; M O D; ProLogis; Richardson Barberry Properties; Wilson Bowden.

GATELEY WAREING (see firm details p.967) The arrival of **David Lloyd Jones** from regional rival Hammonds at the beginning of 2002 seems sure to consolidate the profile of this fair-sized practice. Contentious work, particularly adjudications, has taken up the lion's share of recent instructions. It has assisted a developer on a £10 million dispute arising out of significant land settlement problems at a site in the north west. The firm has recently been active on work for domestic contractors and subcontractors. Possessing a strong contentious practice, **Peter Davies** is considered *"proactive,"* with a personable style offering *"sensible and commercial advice."* The firm has also aided a major water utility on a review of all its standard form contracts, and advised on procurement methods. Advice on the construction aspects of educational PFI schemes has also been at the fore, acting for the Birmingham Roman Catholic Diocese Schools Commission PFI project relating to Willenhall School and a number of schools in Stoke-on-Trent. The non-contentious caseload has generally increased as the firm secures a healthy level of instruction from developers and funding institutions. **Clients** AIB; Black Country Housing Association; Carillion Construction; Deloitte & Touche; Dunbar Bank; George Wimpey; Institute of Electrical Engineers; KPMG; Royal Bank of Scotland; Thames Water Utilities.

DLA A strong national practice that acts most often for major contractors and mid-range developers alongside its advice to consortia and banks and funders on PFI-related construction projects. Adjudication and litigation, as well as ICC international arbitration, predominate on the contentious side. Real estate and construction partner **Graeme Bradley** was endorsed during our research.

FREETHCARTWRIGHT (see firm details p.963) The group enjoys a wide-ranging client base, with the emphasis on developers. It received publicity in landing MANSELL as a client through the efforts of **Guy Berwick** (see p.192), *"one of the best we've come across in the way he approaches and analyses a problem,"* according to clients. Partner Ian Tempest heads a moderately sized unit that has continued to grow this year. As well as the majority of MANSELL's work, the firm advised Gleeds on the project management of a sports stadium redevelopment. The team acted for Experian on the construction of a £20 million data processing facility in Nottingham. It also has a strong presence in the regional university sector, assisting Monk Estates in the development of student accommodation in Nottingham, and working with the developer of a similar £19 million scheme in Leicester. It represented Loughborough University on a £15 million construction and facilities management outsourcing project. **Clients** Anglo Irish Bank; Bellway Homes; Brydon Developments; Derwent Housing Association; East Midlands Development Agency; Experian; Gleeds; Henry Davidson Developments; Loughborough University; MANSELL; Millennium Commission; Monk Estates; NatWest; Pickering Properties; Severn Trent Properties; Sladen Estates; Stannifer Hotels; Thomas Fish & Sons; University of Nottingham.

PINSENT CURTIS BIDDLE (see firm details p.1102) In an effort to benefit from the firm's leading projects practice, the construction team has been relocated from property to the projects department. The group represented ABB Power Construction in an adjudication against Norwest Holst Engineering, a matter that created new law on the definition of the term 'construction operations' under the Construction Act. Under Birmingham construction head Chris Kelly, the firm has assisted on a dispute for works on a new part of the London Underground network, and was further appointed by the Property Advisers to the Civil Estate (PACE) to draft contracts to be used throughout Government. This followed on from the firm's prior appointment to revise the Government's standard forms of contract. **Clients** ABB Power Construction; ALSTOM; Carillion Construction; Castlemore Securities; HM Prison Service; PACE; various NHS Trusts.

BROWNE JACOBSON (see firm details p.891) The firm's modest unit was augmented by the arrival of three construction lawyers from Nelsons at the start of 2002. The group deals with contentious matters for contractors and sub-contractors, and secures non-contentious instructions from banks and funders. Head of department Peter Westlake was instructed by Stevin Rock JV on a dispute in the United Arab Emirates concerning alleged faulty crushing equipment at a quarry. The team advised ROL Gibson Lea in a landmark case concerning the applicability of construction legislation to shop-fitting activities. It also aided Worcester City Council in an action against Carillion concerning the alleged removal of asbestos, on which the team won indemnity costs. **Clients** NatWest; RG Carter; ROL Gibson Lea; Royal Bank of Scotland; Shaw Group UK; Stevin Rock JV; Worcester County Council.

EVERSHEDS (see firm details p.949) The Midlands offices have had a low market profile in the last year, although this may in part be due to those outside the firm being unaware of several weighty but confidential matters currently being handled. Birmingham-based energy expert Malcolm Titcomb oversees the Midlands team. It has been involved in an increased number of adjudications, and the team retains its healthy level of instruction from developers and contractors. It has assisted a contractor in a £44 million claim against the Government in relation to extensions of time, loss and expense. **Clients** Jarvis; Terra Nitrogen; Worcester County Council ; Herefordshire County Council.

LEE CROWDER (see firm details p.1035) Non-contentious matters handled by this team have increased, but the keystone to this practice remains its contentious side. Head of department **Jeffrey Brown** (see p.192) leads a small but experienced team, comprising lawyers and engineers, that has a particular following among contractors. *"Aware of the issues and polished at putting them across,"* the firm has acted for Ballast in three major disputes, including one against a national firm of claims consultants. It assisted Marley Davenport in a multimillion pound dispute relating to the alleged defective performance of cooling towers and was appointed to advise c/PLEX on a £35 million project in West Bromwich. The firm has also targeted work for utility and engineering companies. **Clients** Ballast; Bombardier Transportation; c/PLEX; Marley Davenport.

SHOOSMITHS (see firm details p.1133) Work for developers and specialist subcontractors as well as advice on issues relating to property finance are the key sectors at this construction department. Now a united, standalone department, it has emerged from the firm's dispute resolution and property groups. ADR expert Chris Cox leads the team, which is respected for its negotiation and mediation skills; the firm is noted by interviewees for its particular expertise in comparative dispute resolution advice. This was demonstrated in its work on a five-party mediation involving an NHS trust, architects and both contractor and subcontractor against a project manager. The team was instructed on a £250,000 adjudication concerning variation, delay and subsequent costs relating to a NHS Trust PFI hospital. It also successfully opposed the siting of a telecommunications mast within the grounds of a school. **Clients** NHS Trusts; contractors; subcontractors.

CONSTRUCTION ■ EAST ANGLIA/NORTH WEST

EAST ANGLIA

CONSTRUCTION
■ EAST ANGLIA

1. **Eversheds** Cambridge, Ipswich, Norwich
   Mills & Reeve Cambridge
2. **Hewitson Becke + Shaw** Cambridge
3. **Greenwoods** Peterborough

LEADING INDIVIDUALS
1. **OATS Simon** Eversheds
   PLASCOW Ronald Mills & Reeve
   WOOD Martin Greenwoods

This book is the product of 6,582 1/2 hour interviews. See p.7 for BMRB audit. Within each band, firms are listed alphabetically. See individuals' profiles p.191

EVERSHEDS (see firm details p.949) Ipswich-based partner **Simon Oats** (see p.198) is the office's most prominent figure. The small team can call on the wider national resource provided by the firm. It has advised Wilcon Homes on several multimillion pound mixed-use urban regeneration schemes, both within and outside the region, and was instructed by the RMC Group on disputes arising out of a £150 million cement plant. The branch has also assisted TXU Europe on the development of its new European headquarters, and represented the Lea Valley Regional Park Authority on the construction aspects of a proposed new national athletics stadium. **Clients** Lea Valley Regional Park Authority; RMC Group; TXU Europe; Wilcon Homes.

MILLS & REEVE (see firm details p.1071) There is a strong tie-in with the firm's property department, on matters such as development and PFI projects. Interviewees portrayed the service as "*value-added,*" and the firm is well known for its non-contentious work on behalf of employers in the education and health sectors. **Ron Plascow** (see p.198) has aided Anglia Polytechnic University on a number of key projects to expand its campuses on several sites, including the creation of new business schools. He has also assisted the East of England Development Agency on a variety of new developments. The team advised Thames Waste Management on the construction aspects of its bid for the £400 million plus waste regeneration scheme for East London. Other work has included representations for a national client on a multimillion pound office refurbishment project in Birmingham, and ongoing advice to a NHS Trust over defective flooring at one of its hospitals. **Clients** Anglia Polytechnic University; East of England Development Agency; Thames Waste Management; contractors; banks.

HEWITSON BECKE + SHAW (see firm details p.993) Lead partner Tim Richards has advised the University of Cambridge on a profusion of different projects, including the development of its West Cambridge site. He and the team have also assisted on the documentation of Cancer Research UK's new research facility at its Addenbrooke's site. The small team has advised Turnstone Estates on the complex construction documentation required for its Cambridge Leisure and Homerton Street redevelopment schemes, and has been assisting in the relocation of a number of companies to the region. It attracts a good proportion of work from the East Midlands, such as Scottish & Newcastle's new headquarters building in Northampton. On the contentious side, a highlight has been its advice to a group of subcontractors involved in the Panatown v McAlpine case. **Clients** Accelerys; David Webster; Gemini; i2; Li DCO; Medical Research Council; Millennium Pharmaceuticals; Perry Group; Scottish & Newcastle; Semitool; Silvarco; St Andrew's Hospital; Turnstone Estates; University of Cambridge; VKR Holding.

GREENWOODS (see firm details p.978) Contentious work is the construction department's main pillar. Partner **Martin Wood** heads a group that has assisted a contractor on a dispute with a subcontractor concerning a millennium project in Norwich, and has represented a major water utility on a £4 million arbitration concerning costs and the efficiency of the construction of a sewage plant. In the non-contentious sphere, the team has prepared bespoke forms of contract for a large food manufacturer, and is assisting Peterborough Hospitals NHS Trust on the building of an acute healthcare facility. **Clients** NHS Trusts; contractors; manufacturers; utilities companies.

NORTH WEST

CONSTRUCTION
■ NORTH WEST

1. **Masons** Manchester
2. **Hammond Suddards Edge** Manchester
3. **Mace & Jones** Liverpool
4. **Addleshaw Booth & Co** Manchester
   DLA Liverpool, Manchester
5. **Halliwell Landau** Manchester
   Hill Dickinson Liverpool
6. **Elliotts** Manchester
   Pannone & Partners Manchester

LEADING INDIVIDUALS
1. **DAVIES Edward** Masons
   SALMON Ken Mace & Jones
2. **BAKER Huw** Masons
   CHINN David Hill Dickinson
   MOSS David Hammond Suddards Edge
3. **PINSENT Jim** DLA
   ROUT Peter DLA

This book is the product of 6,582 1/2 hour interviews. See p.7 for BMRB audit. Within each band, firms are listed alphabetically. See individuals' profiles p.191

MASONS (see firm details p.1057) The "*pole position*" belongs to the Manchester office of this national template, predominantly representing contractors on contentious matters. **Edward Davies** (see p.194) ("*sensible, pragmatic – someone you can do business with*") and **Huw Baker** (see p.191) (*a "hands-on bright chap who gets his head down"*) lead the team. Spreading the construction net wide, the firm has aided Carillion on the construction aspects of a student residences and sports and leisure facility PFI project at the University of Hertfordshire. Clients: Alfred McAlpine Construction; AMEC; Bovis-Lend Lease; HBG Construction; Kier Build; MJ Gleeson Group; Shepherd Construction; Totty Construction Group; University of Hertfordshire; Wates Construction.

HAMMOND SUDDARDS EDGE Unusually, the firm's PFI/PPP and projects group is located within its construction department and the two interact extensively on the majority of transactions. Activities have included advising United Utilities on its £800 million framework agreement, and advice to a major contractor on the NHS ProCure 21 pilot scheme. In a similar vein, the firm also advised the Greater Manchester Tramways Ltd (GMTL) consortium bidding for Phase 3 of the Manchester Metrolink development, and is aiding Manchester City Council in its social housing PFI. The last year has seen a gradual development of the firm's employer and contractor client base, with non-contentious work in the slight ascendant. National head of construction **David Moss** was commended by peers for his "*extremely thorough*" approach. The team has assisted BNFL on the group-wide generic review of its construction and engineering contracts, and has assisted TXU with contractual issues connected to a new power station. On the contentious front, it has been instructed by the Port of Mostyn on a dispute concerning a dredging contract at a new roll-on/roll-off ferry terminal, and by United Utilities on a dispute relating to the design and construction of a waste water plant in Liverpool. **Clients** Balfour Beatty Construction; Birse Construction; BNFL; CNIM; GMTL; Manchester Airport; Manchester CC; North Consulting; Shaw Group; TXU Europe; United Utilities Water.

NORTH WEST/YORKSHIRE ■ CONSTRUCTION

MACE & JONES (see firm details p.1047) Following his move with a colleague from Manchester's Kirk Jackson, **Ken Salmon**'s (see p.200) new firm has leapt into the tables this year. Lauded from all quarters, Salmon is "*knowledgeable, calm and has a way with people.*" Clients consider him "*a true construction specialist*," contending that "*there is no-one better for complex, small-value issues.*" The bolstered construction group brings with it specialisms in work for subcontractors and employers. Salmon and his two colleagues have assisted Halton College on the construction of a new sixth form college in Widnes, and advised Ashfield Healthcare concerning a new headquarters building in Leicestershire. The team has also advised on lengthy negotiations for a complex multimillion pound contract in the railways sector. These lawyers are also much involved in adjudications relating to issues of time and loss, expenses and enforcement proceedings. **Clients** Artisan Regeneration; Ashfield Healthcare; Balfour Beatty; Co-op erative Bank; Eric Wright Group; Poppleton & Appleby; Thomas Barnes & Sons; Halton College.

ADDLESHAW BOOTH & CO (see firm details p.838) The firm is best known regionally for its non-contentious side. Interviewees agree it has "*a positive approach, and an informal way of dealing with things, developing working relationships.*" It has continued to assist AMEC with contract advice at the Sportscity development at Eastlands, Manchester, and has acted for Birchwood Park Estates concerning procurement strategy and document negotiation at a development in Warrington. **Clients** AMEC; Birchwood Park Estates; City of Bradford MDC; Evans of Leeds; Halifax; Jarvis; John Mowlem & Company ; Kelda Group; Marshall Construction; Royal Exchange Theatre; SBG Group; Tibbett & Britten.

DLA The practice follows the national approach with assistance to contractors and developers on a range of issues. **Jim Pinsent** in Liverpool and Manchester-based commercial and projects partner **Peter Rout** stood out in particular from our interviews.

HALLIWELL LANDAU (see firm details p.982) The firm is heavily indebted to its insurance clientele, and as such is widely respected in the market for its performance bond work on behalf of institutional clients. Karen Spencer leads a good-sized team with streams of expertise in development and project-related construction work. The group has acted for New Hampshire Insurance Company on an action commenced by Bovis against Braehead, concerning a performance bond issue connected to the Braehead Park Retail Centre in Glasgow. It has also acted on a large number of construction-related prosecutions, including work on behalf of the directors of Balfour Beatty, and has assisted Time Computers on the construction of a £4 million call centre for use by Trillium. There is also a good track record in matters related to the nuclear industry. **Clients** AIG Europe (UK) ; Costain; John Mowlem & Company ; New Hampshire Insurance Company; Time Computers.

HILL DICKINSON (see firm details p.995) An accredited mediator and adjudicator, **David Chinn** (see p.193) commands a small and "*professional*" team. Chinn's analytical approach is said to "*pare the problem down to the bone so that you don't waste time.*" The firm can draw from a broad client base regarding both contentious and non-contentious work.

ELLIOTTS (see firm details p.947) Head of department Michael Woolley leads a team that acts in the main for contractors and employers, developers and their financiers. He acted for the successful defendant in Baxall & Norbain v Sheard Walshaw on a matter that demonstrated there was no duty to the subsequent occupier of a property from the contractor who built it. The firm is also representing Norwest Holst Soil Engineering in the long-running Panatown v Alfred McAlpine case. **Clients:** Birse Construction; Henry Boot; Hyder Consulting; Norwest Holst Soil Engineering; insurers.

PANNONE & PARTNERS (see firm details p.1092) Researchers were impressed by the department's good clientele and its involvement in some significant transactions, yet the firm maintains a low profile in the market. Head of department Tom Ellis is involved on behalf of the Greater Manchester Passenger Transport Executive (GMPTE) in the construction of Phase 3 of the £650 million Metrolink tram system. The firm is negotiating and drafting agreements for infrastructure works for the Commonwealth Games, and has advised Manchester Airport on all the ongoing construction and infrastructure projects that its two recently purchased regional airports have underway. In contentious matters, the small team has aided Austrian Energy on a £7 million dispute arising from the installation of a boiler in a Cypriot power plant. It has further represented the National Computing Centre on a claim against the architects and engineers for the construction of its new site without the requisite radio waves and radiation proofing. **Clients** Galliford Try; GMPTE; Granada Entertainment; Larsen & Toubro; Manchester Airport; Salford University; Southampton FC; Tyco; University of Manchester; Urban Splash.

YORKSHIRE

ADDLESHAW BOOTH & CO (see firm details p.838) In common with its offices in the north west, the firm is better known for its non-contentious work and transactions related to projects and property. National head of non-contentious work **Richard Cockram** (see p.193) led the team on the relocation of The Met Office from Berkshire to Exeter, working with the Ministry of Defence on strategy, procurement and contractual issues. His reputation for commerciality runs parallel with his skill as "*a subtle draughtsman.*" The small team has prepared bespoke contracts for the Halifax on the redevelopment of its former Leeds headquarters into mixed-use facilities, and has also given general strategic advice to a regional development authority. In contentious matters, the group has acted for a national hotel chain in a multimillion pound dispute regarding the development of a new hotel and advised a nightclub on a negligence claim relating to a purpose-built venue. **Clients** Halifax; The Met Office; MITIE Group; MOD; SGB Group; St James Securities; Thornfield Properties; professional indemnity insurers.

HAMMOND SUDDARDS EDGE This growing team is renowned for its robust contentious practice that has won a following for its quick response times and increased international work, particularly in the Far East. Recent examples include advising a Japanese contractor on a $45 million ICC arbitration concerning the construction of a power station. Closer to home, the firm advised a services subcontractor on a £70 million dispute concerning the National Physical Laboratory in Teddington. Partners **Mark Hilton** and **Simon Palmer** are known for their construction litigation experience, including both adjudication and mediation. On the non-contentious front, the firm has advised Allied London on the procurement and construction aspects of the £500 million redevelopment of Spinningfields, Manchester. Making good use of the firm's national reach, the team is assisting English Partnerships and the Regional Development Agencies in a review of the project documents used for procuring and executing construction works. **Clients** Allied London; AMEC; Birse Construction; John Mowlem & Company ; Mitsubishi Heavy Industries; NG Bailey; Nippon Koie; Shepherd.

MASONS (see firm details p.1057) Enjoying strong ties with national contractors, the Leeds office has also seen an increase in the number of local and smaller contractors among its client base. Its caseload remains predominantly contentious. The group of three partners, backed up by considerable support, is considered by some peers to be "*larger and stronger than many*

187

www.ChambersandPartners.com

CONSTRUCTION ■ YORKSHIRE

CONSTRUCTION
■ YORKSHIRE

1. **Addleshaw Booth & Co** Leeds
   Hammond Suddards Edge Leeds
2. **Masons** Leeds
3. **DLA** Leeds, Sheffield
4. **Walker Morris** Leeds
5. **Eversheds** Leeds
   Irwin Mitchell Leeds
   Nabarro Nathanson Sheffield
   Pinsent Curtis Biddle Leeds

LEADING INDIVIDUALS

1. **BENTLEY Bruce** DLA
2. **COCKRAM Richard** Addleshaw Booth & Co
   HILTON Mark Hammond Suddards Edge
   PALMER Simon Hammond Suddards Edge
3. **ROBSON Nigel** Eversheds
4. **HARTLEY Keith** Masons
   SCOTT Martin Walker Morris
   STANIFORTH Alison Eversheds

This book is the product of 6,582 1/2 hour interviews. See p.7 for BMRB audit. Within each band, firms are listed alphabetically. See individuals' profiles p.191

---

representations for specialist subcontractors, most notably in the steel sector. For example, lead partner **Martin Scott** (see p.200) has assisted Cleveland Bridge on issues arising from the collapse of a crane at Canary Wharf, and the group continues to assist Dew Pitchmastic on litigious matters. The non-contentious side has also grown. Advice to education authorities and colleges has included acting for Warrington College on a new £12 million campus development, and a similar project for Loretto Sixth Form College, Lancashire. The team has also worked with the Manor Group on the £20 million BBC studio development in Hull, and advised Rushbond on a new auditorium at Quarry Hill in Leeds, also for the BBC and the Leeds College of Music. **Clients** Cleveland Bridge Group; Dew Pitchmastic; Manor Group; Royal Bank of Scotland; Rushbond; Warrington College Institute.

EVERSHEDS (see firm details p.949) Working in tandem with the Manchester office, the Leeds branch has made progress in the expansion of its contractor client base. The international market is also an area of renewed focus, in particular Malaysia and Singapore. Head of department **Nigel Robson** (see p.199) advised the Hull Millennium aquarium project, 'The Deep', on a variety of disputes, and has acted for Rolls-Royce Power Engineering Group on disputes arising from a power project in India. On non-contentious matters, **Alison Staniforth** (see p.200) has assisted Leeds City Council on the construction aspects of its £250 million grouped-schools PFI project. The team has this year been augmented by the arrivals of a dual-qualified engineer and a surveyor, and it has secured a position on the panel of MJ Gleeson. **Clients** Leeds City Council; MJ Gleeson Group; NG Bailey; Rolls-Royce Power Engineering Group.

IRWIN MITCHELL (see firm details p.1009) Despite a rise in the number of adjudications, the firm still maintains a balance between its contentious and non-contentious offering. Developers make up much of the client base, alongside subcontractors and main contractors. The departure of construction head David Kilvington to set up his own practice is sure to necessitate a refocusing, although clients were quick to commend the whole team as "*reliable, thorough and good value for money*." Now under the auspices of property head Kevin Docherty, the group advised developers and funders on construction projects around the country, and acted for contractors and employers on building contract claims, arbitrations and adjudications. It has acted on the drafting of JCT documents, and acted on behalf of defendants in major High Court construction litigation arising from disputes in the construction project which gave rise to the Panatown/McAlpine arbitrations. **Clients** Henry Boot; development companies; specialist subcontractors and contractors.

NABARRO NATHANSON (see firm details p.1080) Department head Mark Rocca has led the firm's well-supported team on advice to Ballast on the enforcement of an adjudication award in its favour. On the non-contentious side, the firm's work is dominated by its involvement in major projects. It has assisted the Mill Group/Norwich Union PPP Fund on its Newham Schools PFI scheme and has worked with DEFRA on engineering and contractual disputes concerning the foot and mouth crisis. **Clients** Ballast; Calderdale, Denbighshire and Kent local authorities; DEFRA; Mill Group/Norwich Union PPP Fund; UK Coal Mining; Wates Construction.

PINSENT CURTIS BIDDLE (see firm details p.1102) The group, which clients endorsed as "*thorough and commercial,*" is strongly allied to the firm's PFI and projects practice, and has been further augmented by an increase in property-related matters.

Partner Jonathan Hawkswell has now left to set up a practice with David Kilvington of Irwin Mitchell, and the market awaits the impact of his departure. Partner Dean Larder is now in charge of the Leeds team. Domestic employers make up the majority of its client base, although banks, funders and contractors have also recently been added to the portfolio. It has advised funders on the construction aspects of a £19 million schools PFI project in Sunderland. On the contentious side, the team represented a development company on a ground-breaking adjudication case where the High Court ruled that adjudication was a legal process requiring leave of the court. Mediation on behalf of a contractor resulted in the resolution of its contractual disputes with a national utilities company. The group's "*common-sense advice*" has also been in evidence on behalf of a large engineering contractor in striking out a claim by subcontractors for variations and loss and expense. It has also represented a Premiership football club in resisting a final account claim by a main contractor following the construction of a stadium. **Clients** Close Brothers Investment; Clugston; Drivers Jonas; John Mowlem & Company; Leeds Bradford International Airport; Sunderland AFC; Teesland; University of Huddersfield; University of Leeds.

---

have credited." It has worked on an adjudication against a specialist contractor concerning plate bonding, as well as in defence of a claim relating to a rail refurbishment project. Regional office head **Keith Hartley** (see p.196) and partner Mark Harris successfully concluded a substantial dispute concerning a floating, production, storage and offloading (FPSO) vessel. The latter is also currently advising an international contractor on disputes over two combined heat and power stations in the north of England, valued in excess of £50 million. The firm is advising Galliford on a substantial design-related dispute at a hotel conversion project in Leeds City Centre. **Clients** Alandale Construction; AMEC; Ballast ; Birse; Bowmer & Kirkland; Britcon; Churchfield; Dorman Long Construction; EnergieKontor; Galliford Northern; Holroyd; Mowlem Construction; National Grid; Pipeline Constructors; SDC Builders; Snape Roberts; Timber Frame Solutions.

DLA Leading partner **Bruce Bentley** continues to dominate the regional market and this Sheffield team as a user-friendly expert called upon by contractors, developers and funders.

WALKER MORRIS (see firm details p.1178) Contentious work for contractors remains the firm's staple, securing an increasing number of

NORTH EAST/SCOTLAND ■ CONSTRUCTION

NORTH EAST

CONSTRUCTION
■ NORTH EAST

1 **Dickinson Dees** Newcastle upon Tyne
Eversheds Newcastle upon Tyne
Watson Burton Newcastle upon Tyne

LEADING INDIVIDUALS

1 **LANGLEY Robert** Watson Burton
WRIGHTON Ralph Eversheds
2 **LEWIS Simon** Dickinson Dees
ROWLAND Simon Dickinson Dees
UP AND COMING
HENDERSON Nick Dickinson Dees

This book is the product of 6,582 1/2 hour interviews. See p.7 for BMRB audit.
Within each band, firms are listed alphabetically. See individuals' profiles p.191

DICKINSON DEES (see firm details p.938) The firm's large, non-contentious caseload is made up predominantly of referrals from its property development and PFI projects teams. The firm has provided advice to privatised public utilities, pharmaceutical companies and universities. It was involved in the £1.5 billion infrastructure upgrade on the South Central railway network, and assisted Northern Electric on the construction of wind farms and the related reinforcement work for its distribution network. Among this sizeable team, **Simon Lewis** (see p.197) is best known for his non-contentious and PFI work, and receives strong support from **Simon Rowland** (see p.200) and **Nick Henderson** (see p.196). The contentious arm of the practice is more standalone in nature, and has advised a major contractor in a potential action against an NHS Trust concerning the scope of its obligations under a PFI scheme for the construction of a new hospital. It also defended a major utility company in a multimillion pound claim brought by one of its service contractors, and successfully advised a housing association in connection with a claim against its architects for professional negligence. **Clients** EHV; Northern Electric; pharmaceutical and utilities companies; public sector partners

EVERSHEDS (see firm details p.949) The firm, with a client base personified by main contractors, public sector bodies and commercial developers, has seen marked increases in international activities and construction work relating to oil and gas. Department head **Ralph Wrighton** (see p.201) has led on non-contentious matters, such as due diligence exercises on several major transactions for the Bank of Scotland, and work for Derwentside College on a new campus. He has also led a small team on international contracts advice for Pipeline Integrity International, and has advised AMEC on several adjudications. **Clients** AMEC; Bank of Scotland; Derwentside College; Northumbrian Water; Pipeline Integrity International; University of Northumbria at Newcastle.

WATSON BURTON Traditionally a contentious specialist, this department is one of the mainstays of the firm. Under the stewardship of **Robert Langley** (see p.197), it acts for local developers and specialist subcontractors, as well as design professionals and London-based underwriters. On the non-contentious side, work for developers has included instructions from Collingwood Developments on the £28 million south bank of the Tyne Bridge Hilton International hotel project. It has also provided construction documentation for the University of Sunderland on the development of its £80 million St Peters Phase III multimedia centre. Contentious work has included assistance for the subcontractors in an action concerning fire protection works on the two new Canary Wharf towers in London, and a dvice to Skanska concerning its relations with subcontractors over the Hull Waste Water Treatment works. The department has been appointed to the legal panel of the National Federation of Builders. **Clients** Collingwood Developments; Northern Land; Skanska; University of Sunderland; Whessoe.

SCOTLAND

MACROBERTS (see firm details p.1049) Contentious matters form the bedrock of this practice, acting on behalf of main contractors, developers and their consultants. "*On the radar a lot,*" this expanding team has been involved with the Channel Tunnel Rail Link and the new Scottish Parliament building. It has also acted for Railtrack in an ECC adjudication concerning the Forth Rail Bridge. Head of the construction group **Lindy Patterson** (see p.198) has an established reputation that is second to none. A solicitor advocate and litigator, "*her profile is indeed untouchable – she has ability and personality, and doesn't like losing.*" Clients appreciate that **Neil Kelly** (see p.197) is "*a first-class technical lawyer, hard-working and with close attention to our needs*." Also respected for his general commercial litigation skills, **David Arnott** (see p.191) "*has built up a great area of expertise and has driven his practice forward.*" Based in the Glasgow office, **Craig Turnbull** (see p.200) was commended for his organised and efficient service.
  The experienced team has represented Carillion in defence of a claim by engineers' insurers concerning the effect of a transfer of existing contracts between parties in a design and build contract. It also represented Karl Construction in an action against Palisade Properties, which threw out protective measures in construction by confirming that the uniquely Scottish order of inhibition (preventing the sale of real property) was contrary to the European Convention on Human Rights. **Clients** AMEC; Amey; British Energy; Carillion; Ford; Karl Construction; Miller Group; Railtrack; Royal Scottish Academy of Music & Drama; Taylor Woodrow.

MASONS (see firm details p.1057) Market sources agreed that the firm has achieved success in consolidating its expansion of the last few years. Contentious work is the firm's forte, consisting largely of adjudications on behalf of main contractors, with instructions from employers and specialist contractors and consultants also a feature of the caseload. Leading p artner **Vincent Connor** (see p.193) is "*a high-energy lawyer and networker*" and has led the team on a number of high-level disputes. His transactional work includes advice on contractual issues surrounding a £20 million high-profile light rail project. He is partnered by **Alastair Morrison** (see p.198), viewed by interviewees as "*a strategic thinker*" with good "*commercial judgement.*" The sizeable group has also been heavily involved in contract procurement issues, advising clients on the Ministry of Defence's prime contracting project and the NHS ProCure 21 scheme. **Clients** Ballast; Jarvis; John Mowlem & Company.

MCGRIGOR DONALD (see firm details p.1065) Considered by some interviewees as the best firm for non-contentious construction work in Scotland, its integration with the KLegal network will be watched closely. The firm enters the association as an established player with a strong contractor and employer client base and enjoying a healthy track record in construction procurement and disputes. A number of internal promotions have strengthened the team, which is acknowledged "*to understand the clients' priorities.*" The procurement team has aided Henry Boot Scotland on its Anniesland development, and has been involved in the £42 million development of a drug manufacturing facility. **Brandon Nolan** (see p.198) is the head of dispute resolution across the firm, entailing greater management duties. "*Absolutely intimidating in the nicest possible way,*" his "*even-handed*" approach has assisted Morrison Construction on a multimillion pound claim at adjudication and in court. He also led the team defending Sir Robert McAlpine against claims by a works package contractor on a hospital PFI project. **Clients** AWG Morrison; Babcock Support Services; BP Energy; City Inn; Edmund Nuttall; Forth

www.ChambersandPartners.com

189

CONSTRUCTION ■ SCOTLAND

CONSTRUCTION
■ SCOTLAND

[1] **MacRoberts** Edinburgh, Glasgow
Masons Edinburgh, Glasgow
[2] **McGrigor Donald** Edinburgh, Glasgow
[3] **Dundas & Wilson CS** Edinburgh, Glasgow
[4] **Maclay Murray & Spens** Glasgow
Shepherd+ Wedderburn Edinburgh
[5] **Biggart Baillie** Glasgow
Bishops Solicitors (Formerly Morison Bishop) Glasgow
Burness Edinburgh
Ledingham Chalmers Aberdeen

LEADING INDIVIDUALS

[1] **CONNOR Vincent** Masons
MORRISON Alastair Masons
PATTERSON Lindy MacRoberts
[2] **KELLY Neil** MacRoberts
MCLEAN Alistair Dundas & Wilson CS
NOLAN Brandon McGrigor Donald
SHAW Murray Biggart Baillie
[3] **ARNOTT David** MacRoberts
TURNBULL Craig MacRoberts
WELSH John Bishops Solicitors
UP AND COMING
TAYLOR Kevin Shepherd+ Wedderburn

This book is the product of 6,582 1/2 hour interviews. See p.7 for BMRB audit.
Within each band, firms are listed alphabetically. See individuals' profiles p.191

Ports; Henry Boot Scotland; Morrison Construction; Royal Bank of Scotland; Sir Robert McAlpine.

DUNDAS & WILSON CS (see firm details p.943) Traditionally one of Scotland's leading firms, it has recently extricated itself from the AndersonLegal alliance. The firm has maintained both its market profile and the respect of its peers for a practice that is increasingly being asked to advise on contentious construction issues relating either to PFI/PPP schemes or energy projects. Construction-related advice to banks has also been prominent and the team works closely with the firm's real estate department. Pure construction work makes up about half of the firm's work in the field, with the emphasis on high-end transactions in the engineering sector. Miller Construction successfully instructed **Alistair McLean** on an arbitration concerning limitations relating to loss and expense claims. "*Diligent – he gets the deal done,*" McLean has also advised on construction procurement issues surrounding a project in central Edinburgh for the National Galleries of Scotland. The Falklands Islands Government was represented by the firm in two multimillion pound claims made by a civil engineering company, and the firm advised Blyth & Blyth on its action against Carillion concerning the effect of a novation in design and build contracts. Additionally, the team provides wider construction and engineering advice on a variety of major projects for West of Scotland Water. **Clients** Blyth & Blyth; Falkland Islands Government; John Mowlem & Company; Miller Construction; MJ Gleeson; National Galleries of Scotland; Norwich Union; West of Scotland Water Authority.

MACLAY MURRAY & SPENS (see firm details p.1048) Much of the developer-led firm's work is property-related and, while it is traditionally considered a non-contentious specialist, it has taken advantage of the sector-wide rise in adjudications to add to its contentious workload. Head of department Mark Macaulay has led the team on the drafting of various contracts for a £70 million campus and R&D space for biomanufacturing companies in Midlothian. Clients say that the firm's commercial approach "*makes life easy, as we are not deluged with paperwork that we don't need to see.*" The team has also assisted on the documentation for a mixed-use tourist development at Loch Lomond, and acted for a major retail organisation in a dispute with a contractor concerning the refurbishment of one of its stores. **Clients** Bank of Scotland; BBC; Kilmartin Developments; Lloyds TSB ; McDermott Marine Construction; Miller Developments; Motherwell Bridge Engineering; Robertson Construction; Scottish Enterprise; Stannifer Developments; Wilson Bowden Developments.

SHEPHERD+ WEDDERBURN (see firm details p.1130) A proportion of its construction work is driven from its powerful commercial property and banking arms, accounting for the larger number of developers in its client base than contractors. Interviewees agreed that the firm's non-contentious side takes centre stage, with a particular focus on energy projects. Partner **Kevin Taylor** (see p.200) was instructed by ScottishPower in both its offshore and onshore wind farm projects, making specific use of the firm's abilities in construction and procurement. The team also assisted the Scottish Parliamentary Corporate Body on similar matters relating to the construction of the Parliament building. Clients cite commerciality and attention to detail as its key skills, and they appreciate the firm's pragmatism and efforts to simplify issues. The team has acted on contentious matters, representing a subcontractor in a dispute with the main contractor at a water treatment works over a wide range of contractual issues, including concurrent delay and tests for completion. The unit has further aided Delancey in a long-running dispute concerning a city centre development in Glasgow. **Clients** Amey; Craigforth Services; CRE Energy; Delancey (Glasgow); Ellerman Investments; Miller Developments; Parlison Properties; Royal London Mutual Assurance; Scottish Amicable; Scottish Parliamentary Corporate Body; ScottishPower; Sir Robert McAlpine; Waterfront Edinburgh; White Young Green.

BIGGART BAILLIE (see firm details p.871) The firm has recently concentrated on work for developers and contractors, assisting the Glasgow 1999 Festival Company on an arbitration concerning a publicly funded project. Some recent arrivals from the merger with Steedman Ramage have bolstered the practice. Head of department **Murray Shaw** is a respected and experienced figure; peers consider him "*pleasant to deal with – when he's on the other side, things run smoothly.*" His partner-led offering has further acted on a range of adjudications for contractors and subcontractors. **Clients** Broderick Structures; Glasgow 1999 Festival Company; Lilley Construction; Masondryden.com; ScottishPower.

BISHOPS SOLICITORS (see firm details p.1076) The team has continued to grow, undertaking an increasing number of contract procurement matters and referral work for house builders, property developers and local authorities on civil engineering and PPP projects. The firm's traditional base in contentious construction litigation remains to the fore, acting for insured engineers and other professionals in connection with indemnity claims. Highlight of the year was the firm's advice to SL Timber Systems on its action against Carillion concerning the insolvency of the parties following a previous judgment. Under professional indemnity leader **John Welsh** (see p.683), the team continues to be involved in a number of Court of Session's cases. These have included instructions from engineers and insurers over indemnity claims and on adjudications such as a matter concerning environmental issues on the west coast of Scotland. **Clients** SL Timber Systems; engineers and professionals; insurers.

BURNESS A small team with access to a wide client base, the group is located within John Miller's projects department. The unit, under partner Chris Mackay, has continued to focus on contentious construction work for a broad church of clients, including an increasing number of property developers. This has prompted the firm to set up a unit to provide advice to this sector. The firm also has a solid presence in the education arena. **Clients** AMA Consulting; Ballast (Scotland); Bank of Scotland; Barclays Bank; Bison Properties; City of Edinburgh Council; Grosvenor Development; Hart Builders; Jarvis; JB Bennett (Contracts); Lothian NHS Trust; Old Course; Onyx Land Technologies; Scottish Media Group; Summers & Partners; West Lothian Council.

LEDINGHAM CHALMERS (see firm details p.1034) Considered by observers to be one of the dominant firms in the Aberdeen area, its all-round construction practice links together with its property team and a strong base in energy, and oil and gas. Furthermore, the small team continues to advise Medical Centres (Scotland) on the development and lease agreements for the construction of medical centres for NHS Trusts and GP practices throughout Scotland. Department head Jennifer Howitt advised Trett

SCOTLAND/NORTHERN IRELAND/THE LEADERS ■ CONSTRUCTION

Consulting on its appointment by joint venture company Morrison Bachy Soletanche, in a dispute against the British Waterways Board. She has concentrated on adjudications work, both representing clients and advising adjudicators. The team has continued its advice to Morrison Properties on the construction issues of a 60,000 sq ft office development at Riverside House, Aberdeen, and also has advised the University of Aberdeen on construction matters concerning the development and sale of student accommodation. **Clients** Baxter, Dunn & Gray; Cala Properties (Scotland) ; David Adamson & Partners; Highlands & Islands Enterprise; Kenmore Residential; MacDonalds Hotels; Medical Centres (Scotland); Richard Irvin Group; Rigblast Energy Services; Trett Consulting; University of Aberdeen.

NORTHERN IRELAND

CONSTRUCTION
■ NORTHERN IRELAND

[1]
- **Carson McDowell** Belfast
- **Elliott Duffy Garrett** Belfast
- **Johns Elliot** Belfast
- **L'Estrange & Brett** Belfast

[2]
- **Cleaver Fulton Rankin** Belfast
- **Kennedys** Belfast
- **Tughans** Belfast

LEADING INDIVIDUALS
[1]
- **BECKETT Sam** L'Estrange & Brett
- **CRAIG Seán** Kennedys

[2]
- **DAVISON Peter** Carson McDowell
- **FOX Brendan** Cleaver Fulton Rankin

This book is the product of 6,582 1/2 hour interviews. See p.7 for BMRB audit.
Within each band, firms are listed alphabetically. See individuals' profiles p.191

CARSON MCDOWELL (see firm details p.901) Interviewees commended this *"professional outfit"* with a robust client base, consisting primarily of contractors and professionals. Partner **Peter Davison** (see p.194) is able to draw upon an experienced group with a broad practice. He was particularly recommended for his thorough handling of contracts and disputes. On the contentious side, the small and focused team has also advised employers in both the public and private sectors.

ELLIOTT DUFFY GARRETT (see firm details p.947) Michael Lynch oversees the firm's construction unit, which is located within the firm's litigation practice, and is commended for its commercial approach to litigious matters.

JOHNS ELLIOT (see firm details p.1016) The firm will no doubt undergo a period of adjustment following the retirement of managing partner Maurice Butler. One of the firm's leading lights, he will remain as a consultant, and has overseen the growth of a talented team. Its workload remains predominantly contentious, handling contract disputes and arbitrations.

L'ESTRANGE & BRETT (see firm details p.1039) Sourced from the firm's property and litigation teams, much of the dedicated construction unit's work is PFI/PPP-related, with the bulk being non-contentious assistance for developers in Northern Ireland. The other main client stream comes from contractors seeking commercial advice on matters before they run into potential problems, a process facilitated by the firm's cross-border alliance with a Dublin firm. Litigation partner **Sam Beckett** (see p.192) is well respected for his construction disputes work, with a practical and down-to-earth style that prompted competitors to reflect that *"you know that the case won't have any problems if you are against him."* The partner-led team has assisted Morrison Homes on various developments and has advised private property company Cusp on construction issues related to its Lisburn Square and Diamond Centre developments. Jarvis continues to use the firm as its sole Northern Irish construction advisor, and the team has also acted on the construction aspects of a wide range of projects, including education-related PFIs. **Clients** AWG Morrisons; Cusp; Jarvis; Northwin Consortium; O'Hare & McGovern; Queen's University Belfast.

CLEAVER FULTON RANKIN (see firm details p.910) The firm remains a contentious specialist, with the vast majority of its work in this area comprising building claims for loss or expense and large, one-off arbitrations. Its broad client base contains many local councils and house building associations. **Brendan Fox** (see p.195) mixes his construction expertise with work in intellectual property. The small team has acted on an arbitration for developers City Hotel Group in Derry concerning a licensing issue, and has aided the Finn Engineering Company in a £300,000 claim against a Scottish company concerning works in Germany. The firm has also represented a contractor in a £700,000 claim against Belfast City Council for loss, expense and works due. **Clients** City Hotel Group; Finn Engineering Company.

KENNEDYS (see firm details p.1019) This small satellite to the London practice is run locally by contentious partner **Seán Craig** (see p.194). Market sources consider him *"thorough and good to deal with."* The firm has advised McNicholas on various contentious matters and provides professional indemnity assistance to surveyors and other professionals. **Clients** McNicholas; insurers; surveyors.

TUGHANS (see firm details p.1169) Located in its litigation and arbitration group, the team has assisted the Northern Ireland Housing Executive on an arbitration concerning the recovery of money overpaid to a contractor. Splitting his time between construction and other litigious matters, associate Michael McCord has also aided Tesco Stores in a dispute over the practical completion of a building contract, and was instructed by Mivan over a local school whose new gymnasium roof was alleged to have been defective. **Clients** Mivan; Northern Ireland Housing Executive; Tesco Stores.

THE LEADERS IN CONSTRUCTION

ARNOTT, David
MacRoberts, Edinburgh
(0131) 229 5046
david.arnott@macroberts.com
Specialisation: Resolution of commercial disputes and in particular property, construction and engineering disputes by means of negotiation, adjudication, arbitration and litigation at all levels including the conduct of cases before the Court of Session and the House of Lords. Also involved in advising clients at the stage of drafting and concluding contracts and lectures on construction law both to clients and the wider construction industry. Accredited by the Law Society of Scotland as a specialist in construction law.
Prof. Memberships: Member of the Society of Construction Law. Member of the Property Litigation Association.
Career: Joined *MacRoberts* in 1991. Qualified in 1993. Became a Partner in 2000.
Personal: Born 1968. Graduated LLB (Hons) Edinburgh University in 1990. Lives in Edinburgh. Leisure interests include running, golf and has two young children.

BAKER, Huw
Masons, Manchester
(0161) 234 8357
huw.baker@masons.com
Specialisation: Partner specialising in non-contentious transactional construction and major project work. Considerable experience in dealing with the procurement aspects of a diverse range of construction projects including residen-

CONSTRUCTION ■ THE LEADERS

tial, retail, leisure, commercial and industrial schemes, large scale urban renewal and infrastructure projects and several major PFI/PPP projects.
Prof. Memberships: Society of Construction Lawyers. Member of TECSA. TECSA accredited adjudicator.
Career: Qualified in 1987. In September 1998 moved from *Addleshaw Booth & Co* where he had been partner in charge of the Manchester construction team to head up PFI and major project work in *Masons*' Manchester office.
Personal: Born 22 September 1962. Graduated from Cambridge University in 1984 with 1st Class Honours in Law. Leisure pursuits include gardening, walking and reading. Lives in Hebden Bridge, West Yorkshire.

BARRETT, Kevin
Wragge & Co, Birmingham
(0870) 903 1000

BAYLIS, Simon
Wragge & Co, Birmingham
(0870) 903 1000

BECKETT, Sam
L'Estrange & Brett, Belfast
(028) 9023 0426
sam.beckett@lestrangeandbrett.com
Specialisation: Partner. Main area of work: civil litigation, including construction, planning law and professional negligence.
Prof. Memberships: Law Society of Northern Ireland. Member Contentious Business committee, Chancery Division Liaison committee; Commercial Division Liaison committee; Society of Construction Law.
Career: Qualified 1980. Partner in *L'Estrange & Brett* since 1986.
Personal: Born 1957. Education: Queen's University, Belfast (LLB).

BENTLEY, Bruce
DLA, Sheffield
(08700) 111111

BERWICK, Guy
freethcartwright, Nottingham
(0115) 6936 9369
guy.berwick@freethcartwright.co.uk
Specialisation: Solving problems and winning cases. Wide experience of all commercial disputes, now working solely in his firm's Construction Group.
Prof. Memberships: Fellow of the Chartered Institute of Arbitrators.
Career: 1979, LLB Nottingham University. 1994, FCIArb. 1996, LLM Advanced Litigation (with Distinction), Nottingham Law School. External examiner Nottingham Law School 2001. Qualified 1982. Joined present firm 1983. Partner, construction group.
Personal: Interests include football and Blackburn Rovers. Married to Kate, two daughters, Katrina and Stephanie.

BESSY, James
Hammond Suddards Edge, Birmingham
(0121) 222 3000

BIRCH, John
Bevan Ashford, Exeter
(01392) 663388
j.birch@bevan-ashford.com
Specialisation: Works from both the firm's London and Exeter offices. Specialist construction lawyer having extensive experience of dispute resolution in the construction industry. Acts for and advises international and national contractors in mediations, adjudications, arbitrations and litigation. Recent reported cases – Midland Veneers Ltd v Unilock, Hescorp Italia Spa v Morrison, Impresa Castelli Spa v Cola Holdings Ltd. Heads up the *Bevan Ashford* construction law team based in the Westcountry. Recently spoke at conferences on adjudication and current construction issues. Former quantity surveyor having wide and varied experience of construction industry.
Prof. Memberships: Society of Construction Law, Law Society.
Career: Quantity surveyor for 17 years prior to entering legal profession. Chief Quantity Surveyor for international contractor in Middle East. Qualified 1986, *Townsends* 1984-99. Joined *Bevan Ashford* as partner 1999.
Personal: Resides South Hams, Devon. Leisure interests include, walking and reading.

BIRD, Christina
Wragge & Co, Birmingham
(0870) 903 1000

BIRKBY, Gillian
Mayer, Brown, Rowe & Maw, London
(020) 7782 8772
gbirkby@eu.mayerbrownrowe.com
Specialisation: Construction and engineering law, both contentious and non-contentious. Involved in innovative forms of contracting leading to reduced confrontation. Expert in the application of the CDM Regulations (Health and Safety).
Prof. Memberships: ACIArb. Honorary Member of the Association of Planning Supervisors. Chairman of the Construction Industry Council's Task Force on Health and Safety.
Career: Qualified in 1981 and Partner *Rowe & Maw* 1988. Co-author, construction companion to 'Extension of Time' ((RIBA) Enterprises Ltd 2002).
Personal: Dundee University (1975 MA Hons). Walking and archaeology.

BISHOP, John
Masons, London
(020) 7490 4000
john.bishop@masons.com
Specialisation: Specialises in UK and international construction and engineering matters since qualifying, more recently also in professional negligence disputes. Major matters include LTRS, MTR, SSDS and Second Harbour Crossing in Hong Kong, Falklands Airfield, Tiffany Oil Platform, Channel Tunnel, Eurostar, Cairo Plaza, Jubilee Line, Keadby Power Station, LNG facilities (Brunei), Lloyds Building, M25, A27, several arbitrations from Indonesian Geothermic programme; conducted disputes at all levels of the English Courts, domestic arbitrations and international arbitrations under ICC, UNCITRAL and Stockholm Chamber rules as well as ADR processes. Also acts as mediator, adjudicator and arbitrator.
Prof. Memberships: Dean of the Faculty of Mediation and ADR, Chairman of the Joint Consultative Committee of the London Court of International Arbitration, Vice Chairman of the Academy of Experts, President of the Technology and Construction Solicitors Association (TeCSA), Chairman of TeCSA IT Committee. Past Chairman of TeCSA, Past Member of TCC (Technology and Construction Court) Users Committee, TCC's Rules Committee, IT Committee, ADR Committee, Law Society Civil Litigation Committee, ISE Committees on Expert Evidence and Woolf Reforms, Founder Member of CEDR, Chartered Institute of Arbitrators' Committees on new forms of arbitration and ADR, British Academy of Experts Sub Committee on Expert Evidence. Editorial board of 'Construction Law Journal'. Lectures include Blundell Memorial lecture, Bar Conference, Judicial Studies Board, National Contractors Group annual lecture, Chartered Institute of Arbitrators, Kings College (Univ. of London).
Career: Qualified 1971, partner 1972, admitted Hong Kong 1983, managing partner 1986-90, senior partner 1990 to date. Qualified adjudicator (TeCSA), mediator (CEDR).
Personal: Sherborne School. LLB Hons Queen Mary College, University of London. Leisure interests include golf, fishing, cooking and tomatoes.

BLACKLER, Tony
Macfarlanes, London
(020) 7831 9222

BOURGEOIS, Christopher
Taylor Wessing, London
(020) 7300 7000
c.bourgeois@taylorwessing.com
Specialisation: Head of the Construction and Engineering Group and an accredited mediator, with in-depth experience of construction and engineering disputes from earlier stage risk management and resolution in negotiation and through adjudication, arbitration, expert determination and litigation proceedings. As a result of his risk management expertise, he is often consulted by clients at the feasibility and planning stage of major projects. Clients include UK and foreign construction and engineering companies engaged in on and offshore (including in the North Sea) projects, process engineering, water treatment, rail and the manufacture of plant for power projects, electrical and other technical components as well as UK and foreign government agencies, and authorities.
Prof. Memberships: Society of Construction Law; Worshipful Company of Arbitrators; Fellow, Chartered Institute of Arbitrators; Member, City of London Law Society Construction Law Practice Sub-Committee.
Career: Qualified 1975, Solicitor *Freedmans* 1977-79 Partner *Freedmans* 1979-96, Admitted Hong Kong 1983, Partner *Taylor Joynson Garrett* 1996.
Personal: Interests include shooting, vintage/classic car restoration and driving, property restoration and theatre. Lives in Bookham, Surrey.

BRADLEY, Graeme
DLA, Birmingham
(08700) 111111

BRIDGEWATER, Martin
Norton Rose, London
(020) 7444 2834
bridgewaterm@nortonrose.com
Specialisation: Partner in construction and engineering group. Main area of practice covers non-contentious construction and engineering contracts, both UK and international, and PFI/PPP projects. Generally advises developers or contractors on major UK building projects, bidders or funders on PPP/PFI projects and banks or sponsors on infrastructure, process plant and independent power projects.
Prof. Memberships: International Bar Association, Society of Construction Lawyers.
Career: Qualified in England and Wales in 1976, and in Hong Kong in 1978. Joined *Nabarro Nathanson* in 1980, became a partner in 1984 and headed the firm's construction department from 1986-97. Joined *Norton Rose* in 1997.

BROWN, Jeffrey
Lee Crowder, Birmingham
(0121) 236 4477
Specialisation: Contentious and non-contentious work on behalf of developers, main contractors, sub-contractors and their insurers.
Prof. Memberships: Technology and Construction Solicitors Association, Chartered Institute of Arbitrators, Chartered Insurance Institute.
Career: Assistant Solicitor *Pinsent & Co* 1981-82 (now *Pinsent Curtis Biddle*); Assistant Solicitor *Johnson & Co* 1982-84 (now *Martineau Johnson*); *Neil F Jones* 1984-99 (Partner 1986, Senior Partner 1993-99); Partner and Head of Construction and Engineering Department *Lee Crowder* 1999-date.
Publications: Co-author 'Professional Negligence in the Construction Industry' (published in 1998 by LLP).
Personal: Resident Nant-Y-Deri, Gwent. Married with one son. Interests – sailing, windsurfing, swimming.

BUNCH, Anthony
Masons, London
(020) 7490 6216
anthony.bunch@masons.com
Specialisation: Partner and Chairman of Energy Sector. Member of Partnership

192

Board. Has experience in all aspects of contentious and non-contentious matters relating to construction and energy law. Has drafted a full range of contracts for major projects in the UK and Far East on behalf of employers, major contractors and international consultants. Has conducted proceedings to all levels, including the House of Lords, and in other countries including Hong Kong, Singapore and China. His primary experience concerns all forms of arbitration proceedings and in particular proceedings which concern the energy sector. The majority of his dispute resolution work now relates to major disputes concerning the oil and gas industry. Author of numerous articles on dispute resolution and in particular ADR. Joint author on the chapter on Hong Kong in the 'International Handbook on Commercial Arbitration' and the specialist chapter on construction in the 'Handbook of Arbitration Practice'. Speaks widely on construction and energy issues.
Prof. Memberships: Member of the Chartered Institute of Arbitrators, Former Council Member of Chartered Institute of Arbitrators, Member of TECSA, Member of the Departmental Advisory Committee responsible for the Arbitration Act 1996, Member of the International Advisory Board to the Arbitration Institute of the Stockholm Chamber of Commerce; CEDR Accredited Mediator.
Career: Qualified in 1978, having joined *Masons* in 1976. Became a Partner in 1980 and Equity Partner in 1982. Admitted as a Solicitor in Hong Kong in 1985; Senior resident Partner in Hong Kong office 1985-90. Managing Partner 1991-96. Worldwide Managing Partner 1996-2002.
Personal: Born 8 February 1953. Holds a BA (Hons) from Nottingham. Leisure interests include cycling, music and theatre. Lives in Radlett, Herts. Four children.

BURCH, Simon
Linklaters, London
(020) 7456 3582
simon.burch@linklaters.com
Specialisation: Construction Group, Commercial Property Department. Specialist in construction and engineering law and contracts advising owners, contractors and funders. Main areas of practice include UK property development/construction projects, private finance initiative developments and project financing of power, infrastructure and petrochemical developments internationally. Prior to *Linklaters*, 10 years experience in contract formulation, negotiation and commercial management of construction contracts associated with major offshore platform developments in the North Sea and 5 years experience managing the construction phase of a major hospital redevelopment on behalf of the client.
Career: Partner at *Linklaters* since 1994. 1989-94 – assistant solicitor, *Linklaters*;

1984-89 – Conoco (UK) Limited; 1980-84 – Bechtel Great Britain Ltd; 1979-80 – Bovis Construction Ltd; 1974-78 – Wellington Hospital Board (NZ); qualified 1974 (New Zealand), 1991 (UK).

BUTCHER, Trevor
CMS Cameron McKenna, London
(020) 7363 3000
trevor.butcher@cmck.com
Specialisation: Partner in projects group. Main area of practice is in major infrastructure projects, particularly private finance work in the UK and internationally including central and eastern Europe. Particular specialisation in transport infrastructure projects, especially roads, light rail and heavy rail. Acted for DETR on the BNRR project and part of team on CTRL. Also acted on numerous DBFO road projects leading teams on the M40, A55 and A130 deals and acting on similar projects overseas including road and rail projects in Poland. Author of various articles and speaker at a number of conferences on PFI and PPP projects. Drafted the Association for Project Management standard form appointment.
Career: Qualified in 1986, having joined *McKenna & Co.* in 1984. Became a Partner in 1992.
Personal: Born 10 February 1960. Graduated from Leicester University in 1983.

CANHAM, Stephanie
Trowers & Hamlins, London
(020) 7423 8000
scanham@trowers.com
Specialisation: A Senior Partner in *Trowers and Hamlins* Projects and Construction Group. Has specialised in construction law for the past 14 years and is a well known and highly respected commercial construction specialist, particularly among developers. Has considerable experience in construction related matters, having advised in negotiations on major projects across the private and public sectors with substantial involvement in PFI, joint ventures, major commercial developments, partnering and Egan compliant procurement.
Prof. Memberships: Member of the Construction Law Practice Sub-Committee of the City of London Solicitors' Company, the Chartered Institute of Arbitrators and the Society of Construction Law.
Career: Member of the Construction Clients Forum/JCT Working Party and a regular contributor of articles to journals. Lectures widely on construction and development issues and is a well known IBC/SBIM speaker by invitation for developers.
Publications: Has contributed to several construction-based publications including Butterworths' 'Encyclopedia of Construction Forms and Precedents', co-authoring a guide to design and build.
Personal: Two children and a house husband (previously a lawyer).

CAPPER, Phillip
Lovells, London
(020) 7296 2000
phillip.capper@lovells.com
Specialisation: Partner, specialising in International Arbitration, Engineering and Construction. Recognised authority on engineering and construction risks and contracts. Substantial experience of international arbitration; as advisor, advocate and arbitrator. Worked on projects for highways, rail, power, defence, and process plant, building and construction in many countries worldwide. Lead counsel for TML, the Channel Tunnel contract consortium, under English and French law – keynote speaker on this at US AAA DART conference. Advised foreign state electricity generator/distributors, national gas distributors, high-speed rail authorities and suppliers, metro and light rail projects and privately financed infrastructure projects. Has sat as Arbitrator in ICC and LCIA arbitrations. Drafted the disputes clauses in standard forms NEC 2nd edition and ICE 7th. Engaged as expert by French Association of International Contractors (SEFI) to evaluate FIDIC's EPC Silver Book.
Prof. Memberships: UK member of the ICC Commission on International Arbitration in Paris. He directs the International Diploma of the Chartered Institute of Arbitrators.
Career: Formerly partner in construction and engineering and Head of International Arbitration at *Masons*. He is a visiting Professor in Construction Law and Arbitration at King's College London, and before moving to London in 1988 he was Chairman of the Faculty of Law at the University of Oxford. He has been a Fellow of Keble College Oxford for 23 years.
Publications: For CIRIA's 'Client's Guide to Risk in Construction' wrote legal risk management. Founding Editor of 'Construction Industry Law Letter' from 1983 to 1990. Recent publications include 'Construction Industry Arbitrations' in Sweet & Maxwell's 'Handbook of Arbitration Practice' 3rd ed, and former General Editor of 'Emden's Construction Law'.
Personal: Born 1952. French language.

CHINN, David
Hill Dickinson, Liverpool
(0151) 236 5400
Specialisation: All types of construction and engineering matters. Acts for insurers, developers, employers, local authorities, NHS trusts, main contractors, sub contractors and members of the professional team.
Prof. Memberships: Member of TeCSA, Society of Construction Law, Chartered Institute of Arbitrators, Law Society, Secretary of the Liverpool Branch of the Society for Computers and Law.
Career: 1982-87 *Mace & Jones* (incorporating Latin & Masheder); 1988-date *Hill Dickinson* (became partner in 1992). Fellow of Chartered Institute of Arbitrators (January 1996); TeCSA Adjudicator (September 1996); Accredited Mediator (June 1997).
Publications: Various articles on arbitration, ADR and adjudication.
Personal: Lives in Southport, loves include family, Liverpool F.C., most sports and vintage fountain pen collection.

COCKRAM, Richard
Addleshaw Booth & Co, Leeds
(0113) 209 2000
richard.cockram@addleshawbooth.com
Specialisation: Partner, Head of Non-Contentious Construction. Construction drafting and PFI projects.
Prof. Memberships: Fellow, Chartered Institute of Arbitrators. Member, Society of Construction Lawyers.
Career: Qualified 1973. Partner, *McKenna & Co.*, 1986-89. Joined the firm in 1989.
Publications: 'Manual of Construction Agreements' (Jordans, 1998, 2nd edition 2001).
Personal: Educated: Cambridge University 1967-70: MA in Law. Interests include books and walking.

COLLINGWOOD, Mark
Masons, Bristol
(0117) 924 5678
mark.collingwood@masons.com
Specialisation: Partner in Construction and Engineering Group. Heads *Masons'* 30 lawyer Bristol office and the firm's Construction and Engineering team in Bristol. Specialist construction lawyer since qualification. Particular specialisms include litigation, arbitration, adjudication and dispute resolution generally, contract and project documentation negotiation and drafting. Has acted in many 'heavyweight' construction cases – civil engineering and building in the UK and abroad. Drafted project documentation for £350m Devonport dockyard redevelopment scheme. Lectures frequently on the law relating to the construction industry.
Prof. Memberships: Law Society, Faculty of Building.
Career: Qualified in 1980. Articled at *Crossman Block and Keith* 1978-80, before joining *Masons*. Became a Partner in 1985.
Personal: Born 19 December 1954. Attended Durham University, taking a BA in law and politics. Leisure interests include tennis. Has four young children.

CONNOR, Vincent
Masons, Glasgow
(0141) 248 4858
vincent.connor@masons.com
Specialisation: Partner specialising in contentious construction law, including tactical and strategic advice and the pursuit and defence of claims in a variety of forms of dispute resolution.
Prof. Memberships: Law Society of Scotland and Technology and Construction Solicitors Association.

CONSTRUCTION ■ THE LEADERS

Career: Educated at Glasgow University 1982-87 (LLB 1st class honours. 1986, DipLP 1987). Assistant Solicitor *Hughes Dowdall* 1987-90. Qualified as Notary Public in 1989. Joined *McGrigor Donald* in 1990, became an Associate in 1993 and assumed as a Partner in 1995. Accredited as a Solicitor Mediator in 1994. Jointly established *Masons*' Scottish practice in 1998.
Personal: Born 1964. Leisure interests include music, cinema and running. Married. Resides in Glasgow.

CORBETT, Edward
Corbett & Co, Teddington
(020) 8943 9885
ecorbett@corbett.co.uk
Specialisation: Active in the UK and all over the world advising contractors, clients, consultants and others on building and civil engineering procurement, contract preparation and negotiation, on dispute avoidance, management and resolution including mediation, adjudication and, if unavoidable, arbitration. Author of 'FIDIC 4th – A Practical Legal Guide'. Regular seminar speaker.
Prof. Memberships: FCIArb, SCL, IBA Committee T, FIDIC Sub-committee, TeCSA, Affiliate Member of FIDIC, FIDIC Mediator and Adjudicator, AAA Panellist. Former partner at *Masons*.
Personal: Born 10 September 1957. MSc in Construction Law and Arbitration, King's College. MA Jurisprudence, Oxford; Accredited Adjudicator and Mediator. Keen sailor and windsurfer.

CORNES, David
Winward Fearon, London
(020) 7420 2800
david.cornes@winwardfearon.co.uk
Specialisation: Founding Partner. Gives advice to those involved in building, civil engineering and the construction professions (architects, engineers and quantity surveyors) and their insurers. Handles High Court and arbitration work, including international. Involved in major non-contentious projects including private finance. CEDR accredited Mediator (80 mediations completed). Arbitrator (UK and overseas). Regular speaker at conferences in the UK and occasionally abroad.
Prof. Memberships: Fellow of the Institution of Civil Engineers, Fellow of the Chartered Institute of Arbitrators, Law Society, Society of Construction Law, Technology and Construction Court Solicitors Association, International Bar Association.
Publications: Author of 'Design Liability in the Construction Industry', contributor to 'Construction Contract Policy'. Joint author of 'Collateral Warranties' Second Edition 2002.
Personal: Born 31 August 1944. Attended King's College, University of London. Member of Electoral Reform Society and Charter 88. Leisure interests include walking, travelling, opera. Lives Winslow, Bucks.

CRAIG, Seán
Kennedys, Belfast
(028) 90 240067
s.craig@kennedys-law.com
Specialisation: Construction related litigation. Disputes against professionals: architects, engineers, surveyors, geophysicists etc. Also claims against brokers and financial advisors. Acted for Lewis and Tucker on the BBL case. Also deals with commercial disputes.
Prof. Memberships: English Bar 1985; Law Society (England) 1988; Law Society (Northern Ireland) 1994; Law Society (Republic of Ireland) 1998.
Career: Joined *Kennedys*' City office in June 1987, becoming a Partner in January 1993. Helped establish *Kennedys*' Belfast office which opened in March 1996.

CRITCHLOW, Julian
Fenwick Elliott, London
(020) 7956 9354
jcritchlow@fenickelliott.co.uk
Specialisation: Partner specialising in both non-contentious and contentious construction matters and arbitration.
Prof. Memberships: Fellow of the Chartered Institute of Arbitrators; CEDR accredited mediator; TeCSA registered adjudicator; Associate Fellow of the Society for Advanced Legal Studies; member of TeCSA; member of the Construction Contracts Mediators Group; member of the Arbitration Club, member of the American Judicature Society; member of King's College Construction Law Association; Commissioner of the Foundation for International Commercial Arbitration; Liveryman of the Worshipful Company of Arbitrators.
Career: Qualified 1984. University College London (LLB 1981). King's College London (MSc 1993). King's College London (PhD 2000). Articled *Field Fisher and Martineau*.
Publications: Author of 'Making Partnering Work in the Construction Industry' (Chandos 1998), joint author of 'Arbitration Forms and Precedents' (LLP 2000), contributor to the 'Construction Law Handbook' (Thomas Telford 2000), Arbitration Editor of 'Amicus Curiae', Construction Law Editor of the 'Journal of ADR, Mediation and Negotiation'.
Personal: Born 1958. Married, two children. Leisure interests include shooting and English poetry.

CUMMINS, Caroline
CMS Cameron McKenna, London
(020) 7367 2914
cxc.cmck.com
Specialisation: Concentrates on disputes resolution work for the construction industry. Clients are generally main contractors and employers. Cases have involved a wide range of issues and projects. Has also advised on non-contentious matters including PFI projects. CEDR accredited mediator and TeCSA accredited adjudicator.
Prof. Memberships: Law Society; Society of Construction Law; TeCSA (committee member).
Personal: Attended St George's School, Ascot 1972-78 then Jesus College Oxford 1979-82. Qualified in 1989 after spending some years working for *United Biscuits plc*. Joined *CMS Cameron McKenna* in 1992 and became a partner in the construction group in 1996.

DAVIES, Edward
Masons, Manchester
(0161) 234 8234
edward.davies@masons.com
Specialisation: Construction and engineering work, particularly energy and infrastructure projects, together with technology expertise. Litigation, arbitration and ADR (trained as mediator by American Arbitration Association in San Francisco) and CEDR accredited mediator.
Prof. Memberships: Law Society, Manchester Law Society, Society of Construction Law, American Arbitration Association. Joint co-ordinator of CIB International Research Group on conflict management. Visiting research fellow UMIST (University of Manchester Institute of Science and Technology).
Career: Qualified 1982. Joined *Masons* 1986 in London. Became partner and established Manchester office in 1989.
Publications: Joint editor – 'Dispute Resolution and Conflict Management in Construction (An International Review).'
Personal: Born 1958. Manchester University (LLB); College of Law Guildford then Kings College London MSc. Lives in Manchester.

DAVIES, Peter
Gateley Wareing, Birmingham
(0121) 234 0000

DAVIS, Michael
Herbert Smith, London
(020) 7374 8000
michael.davis@herbertsmith.com
Specialisation: Head of Construction and Engineering Group. Involved with major national and international construction and civil engineering projects, advising and conducting construction and civil engineering disputes both within the English jurisdiction and in international arbitration worldwide. These arbitrations include references under the ICC, LCIA, UNCITRAL, UNECE and Stockholm Arbitration Institute Rules. Has advised on numerous projects both nationally and internationally, including a number of independent power, process and aerospace projects. Also has long experience of conducting litigation in the High Court, as well as adjudications, expert determination and alternative forms of dispute resolution.
Career: Qualified 1977. Partnership 1986. Lectured extensively in respect of construction, civil engineering and arbitration.

DAVISON, Peter
Carson McDowell, Belfast
(01232) 244951
peter.davison@carson-mcdowell.com
Specialisation: Over 20 years of practical experience in general commercial litigation, arbitration, adjudication and mediation with particular reference to construction matters, working for both private and public sector under ICE/JCT/GC and other forms of contract. Advising on drafting and negotiation of building agreements and ancillary documentation (warranties, bonds etc). Established links with leading construction counsel in Belfast and London and experienced expert witnesses if required. Law Society ADR training course completed.
Prof. Memberships: Law Society of Northern Ireland. Society of Construction Law.
Career: 1974 MA Trinity College, Dublin (Legal Science), joined *Carson & McDowell* and admitted solicitor 1977. Partner 1979.

DELVES, Simon
Shadbolt & Co, Reigate
(01737) 226277
simon_delves@shadboltlaw.com
Specialisation: Partner in Construction Group. Advises clients in respect of a wide variety of building, construction and engineering projects both domestically and internationally including power stations of various types, dams, hotels, harbour works, roads, commercial buildings, refineries, infrastructure works, cabling systems, street works, bridge works, process facilities, water treatment facilities, reservoirs, land reclamation projects, tunnels and residential developments. Has worked extensively on UK domestic forms of contract, ad hoc contracts and FIDIC contracts in various jurisdictions including Hong Kong, China, Nigeria, Uganda, Tanzania, Bangladesh, Lesotho, Taiwan, Thailand, Denmark and Egypt. Is experienced in various forms of dispute resolution including litigation, international arbitration, domestic arbitration, adjudication and other alternative dispute resolution procedures including conciliation and dispute adjudication and dispute review boards procedures.
Prof. Memberships: Technology and Construction Solicitors Association, Institution of Civil Engineers, Member of the Law Society.
Career: 1975-81 Gleeson Civil Engineering; 1979-81 Biwater Limited; 1981-82 Wade Adams Construction Ltd (based in Tanzania); 1985-87 articles at *DMH*; 1987-93 *Lovells*; 1993-date *Shadbolt & Co* (Partner since 1994).
Personal: Born 1953. Leisure interests include sailing and family.

THE LEADERS ■ CONSTRUCTION

FLEET, Terry
Berwin Leighton Paisner, London
(020) 7760 1000
terry.fleet@blplaw.com
Specialisation: Partner and Head of Construction and Engineering Department. Principal area of practice is construction law advising on building and civil engineering projects in the UK and internationally, including procurement strategy, contract drafting and negotiation, bonds, warranties, insurance, contract advice and dispute resolution. Has advised in connection with major projects in the UK, the Caribbean, Europe (including Eastern Europe), Africa, the Middle East and the Far East. Currently involved in major office, retail, road, power, leisure and PFI projects in the UK, and overseas most recently in Bahrain, the Congo, Hungary, Norway, Poland and Russia. Clients include institutions, government departments, funders, developers, major construction and engineering companies and professional architectural and civil engineering consultants. Has written articles in 'Construction Law', 'Building', 'Property Week', 'Estates Gazette' and 'Chartered Surveyor Weekly'. Co-author of 'Tolleys Guide to Construction Contracts'. Speaks at conferences on construction law matters.
Prof. Memberships: The Law Society, International Bar Association and Society of Construction Law.
Career: Qualified in 1980. Articled at *Heald & Nickinson* 1977-79 and moved to *Speechly Bircham* 1979-80. Legal Advisor to Costain Group 1980-82, Babcock International 1982-84 and Cementation International (Trafalgar House), 1984-87. Joined *Berwin Leighton* in 1987 before becoming a Partner in 1988, now *Berwin Leighton Paisner*.
Personal: Born 1954. Attended Southampton University (graduated 1976 LLB Hons). Leisure interests include flying, travel and family. Lives in Twickenham.

FOX, Brendan
Cleaver Fulton Rankin, Belfast
(028) 9027 1325
b.fox@cfrlaw.co.uk
Specialisation: Construction and property litigation, intellectual property and competition law.
Prof. Memberships: The Law Society of Northern Ireland.
Career: Educated at St Patrick's College, Knock, Belfast and The Queen's University of Belfast (LLB). Qualified in 1991. Became a partner in *Cleaver Fulton Rankin* 1 April 1998.
Personal: Born 7 December 1966. Hobbies include music and sport.

GARTHWAITE, Helen
Taylor Wessing, London
(020) 7300 7000
h.garthwaite@taylorwessing.com
Specialisation: Provides construction advice and documentation for a wide range of corporations and institutions owning, occupying, financing, investing in and designing development projects in the office, retail, industrial and leisure sectors as well as significant civil engineering and infrastructure projects. Experienced in public and privately funded schemes, including partnering and PFI arrangements; due diligence and development support for corporate and property deals; construction e-procurement and technology. Writes and lectures regularly and is often asked for comment by the specialist construction industry media, featured in Building magazine's '40 under Forty' as one of the top 40 personalities in the construction industry under 40 years of age.
Prof. Memberships: Secretary and Member of Council of the Society of Construction Law; Member, Chartered Institute of Arbitrators.
Career: Qualified 1990, Solicitor *Nabarro Nathanson* 1990-96, Partner and Head of Construction and Engineering, *Lewis Silkin* 1996-2001, Partner *Taylor Joynson Garrett* 2001.
Personal: MSc Construction Law and Arbitration (1992). Interests include yachting and woodland management. Lives in Westminster.

GIBSON, Michael
Berwin Leighton Paisner, London
(020) 7760 1000
mike.gibson@blp.com
Specialisation: Partner. All aspects of law and practice relating to construction and engineering procurement in the UK and internationally, advising authorities, developers, funds, government agencies, health trusts, contractors and designers on contracts for design, construction, financing and facilities management of major building and engineering projects and resolution of disputes arising from them. Principally involved with projects assembled under PPP.
Prof. Memberships: Society of Construction Law.
Career: Admitted in 1977. Legal Department of Costain Group 1975-78. Head of Legal Department, Construction Division, Trafalgar House plc, 1981-87. Joined *Berwin Leighton* (now *Berwin Leighton Paisner*) in 1987 as co-founder of its Construction and Engineering Group. Head of Construction and Engineering Group until 1998.
Personal: Born 1952. Educated at St. Edward's School, Oxford 1965-70 and Southampton University 1970-74. Lives in Oxshott, Surrey.

GOULD, Nicholas
Lovells, London
(020) 7296 2000
nicholas.gould@lovells.com
Specialisation: Principal area of practice is construction, with particular emphasis on engineering and international projects and energy. Has drafted, advised on, and helped resolve disputes on a wide range of construction, project, engineering and energy contracts over 30 years in the UK and many overseas countries. Has experience of project finance and of all forms of dispute resolution. Co-authored the book 'International Commercial Arbitration' (LLP 1996).
Prof. Memberships: Law Society, International Bar Association, (Member of the Council of the Section on Business Law and past Co-Chairman of the International Contruction Projects Committee), Fellow of the Chartered Institute of Arbitrators and Associate of the Chartered Institute of Patent Agents.
Career: Qualified in 1967 with *Lovells*, became a partner in 1971. Established construction and engineering practice in the late 1960s.

GOWAN, Daniel
Davies Arnold Cooper, London
(020) 7936 2222
dgowan@dac.co.uk
Specialisation: Executive Partner, Head of Construction Group. Handles all aspects of contentious and non-contentious construction work, contract drafting and reviewing, joint ventures, arbitration and litigation. Experienced in mechanical and civil engineering and building. Also handles construction insurance, including professional indemnity, contractors all risks and public liability claims. Acted for Petrotrin (Trinidad) in dispute with SNC Lavalin; PI insurers in Heathrow Tunnel collapse and Eurotunnel disputes; Victorian Channels Authority in dredging dispute with Van Oord and Jacob GIBB in dispute with Arab Polash Company. Has spoken on many publicly-paid-for seminars for Hawkesmere, and for a number of in-house seminars and presentations to the construction industry.
Prof. Memberships: Fellow, Chartered Institute of Arbitrators;
Career: Qualified in New Zealand in 1976, and in England in 1983. Worked at *Meredith Connell & Co.*, New Zealand, 1975-78, then *Freedman & Co.*, London, 1980-83. Joined *Davies Arnold Cooper* in 1983, becoming a Partner in 1987.
Personal: Born 2 October 1951. Leisure interests include cricket, tennis, golf, theatre, opera, music and reading. Lives in Rotherwick, Hampshire.

GUPPY, W Nicholas
Laytons, Bristol
(0117) 930 9530
nick.guppy@laytons.com
Specialisation: Head of Construction Law and Editor of quarterly publication, 'Laytons Building'. Qualified in 1976 and worked in London until 1990 with ever increasing specialisation in construction law. Acts for a wide range of employers, contractors and sub-contractors on both contentious matters (now mainly adjudication, but litigation and arbitration not dead yet!) and non-contentious. Regularly speaks at seminars.
Prof. Memberships: Law Society.
Career: Qualified in 1976. Joined *Laytons* in 1990 and became a Partner in 1992.
Personal: Born in 1951. Leisure interests include family life, squash and golf. Lives in London.

HALL, Priscilla
Osborne Clarke, Bristol
(0117) 917 3000

HANLEY, Christine
Bond Pearce, Plymouth
(01752) 677602
chanley@bondpearce.com
Specialisation: Partner and Head of the Construction and Engineering Group. Specialises in funded project work, waste to energy projects, construction dispute avoidance and resolution including adjudication, TCC litigation and arbitration.
Prof. Memberships: Fellow of the Chartered Institute of Arbitrators and member of the Society of Construction Lawyers. Committee member of the South West Construction Network. Chairperson of South West Women in Construction.
Career: Qualified 1989, becoming Associate 1997 and Partner 1998.
Publications: A contributor to 'The Construction Act-Time for Review', published by Kings College London, and regularly invited to lecture on construction law and project work. Paper presented at Kings College University of London. Speaker at CIOB/CIC Objective One Conferences and CIOB seminars on partnering in various counties.

HANSON, Marc
CMS Cameron McKenna, London
(020) 7367 2366
marc.hanson@cmck.com
Specialisation: Principally provides construction procurement advice and drafts construction and facilities management contracts for major construction and outsourcing projects. Recent projects include the redevelopment of Paddington Basin for Chelsfield, Prudential's development of Green Park, the development of Legoland 4, Munich, and the construction of the National Football Centre for the Football Association Subsidiary England Football Enterprises.
Prof. Memberships: The Society of Construction Law; Editorial Board of Facilities Management Legal Update; BIFM.
Career: Joined *McKenna & Co* as articled clerk 1992; qualified 1994 and became a partner in *CMS Cameron McKenna* in 2001.
Publications: Author of The Chartered Institute of Building Standard Form of Facilities Management Contract, The PACE GC/Works/10 Standard Form of Facilities Management Contract and 'Guide to Facilities Management Contracts', 2nd edition, published 2002.
Personal: Born 1968, read Politics at the University of East Anglia (1986-89). Leisure interests: motorsport and Arsenal FC. Married with a daughter and residing in Surrey.

195

CONSTRUCTION ■ THE LEADERS

HARLING, Marcus
Burges Salmon, Bristol
(0117) 939 2206
marcus.harling@burges-salmon.com
Specialisation: Head of construction unit advising on all aspects of construction and engineering projects, insurance and risk and related liability and claim issues. Specialises in PPP, PFI and project structures procurement and implementation. Current projects include a series of waste to energy projects, chp projects, a £40m process plant and advising London Fire Brigade on its Corporate Property Project.
Prof. Memberships: Society of Construction Law, Committee of the Technology and Construction Solicitors' Association (TeCSA). Specialist practice consultant to RIBA.
Career: Qualified in 1985, joined *Burges Salmon* in 1986 and became a partner in 1992.
Publications: Author, 'TeCSA Protocol on Expert Evidence', Contributing Editor to Tolley's 'Knights Best Value and Public Procurement', RICS training video, 'Copyright in the Construction Industry'.

HARMAN, Martin
Masons, London
(020) 7490 4000
martin.harman@masons.com
Specialisation: Partner and Head of Infrastructure Group worldwide. Main area of practice major infrastructure projects covering both contentious and transactional work. Advising various international entities, both governmental and private, upon the procurement of major infrastructure projects in collaboration with the private sector, and in that capacity, advising upon contract procurement strategy and drafting of project documentation. Substantial experience of Light Rail Transit Systems and Airport Projects Worldwide. Has undertaken international arbitrations in Hong Kong, Lebanon, Singapore, Kuwait, Yemen, Pakistan and India. Lectures widely for various international conference organisers.
Prof. Memberships: Faculty of Building, International Bar Association, Law Society of Hong Kong. Member of editorial team of the International Arbitration Law Review; member of Chartered Institute of Logistics and Transport; Chairman British Consultants Bureau's East Asia and Pacific Group, committee member of British Trade International's Asia Pacific Advisory Group.
Career: Qualified in 1971. Joined *Masons* in 1975, becoming a Partner in 1976. Admitted in Hong Kong 1983; first resident Partner at *Masons* in Hong Kong 1983. Head of Infrastructure Group of *Masons* worldwide.
Personal: Born 24 December 1946. Attended Brighton College, Brighton 1960-65, then Bristol University 1966-69. Leisure interests include wooden toy making, walking, reading and music. Lives in London.

HARRIS, Adam
Masons, Bristol
(0117) 924 5678
adam.harris@masons.com
Specialisation: Partner in Infrastructure Group. Contentious and non-contentious work with a particular interest in PFI. A specialist in the building, civil engineering, process plant and electricity industries. Acts for both contractors and employers.
Career: Qualified 1981. *Lovell White Durrant* 1982-88 (Hong Kong 1983-87). Admitted Hong Kong 1984. Partner at *Masons* 1990.
Personal: Born 3 January 1956. Educated Wellington School and Birmingham University (LLB).

HARTLEY, Keith
Masons, Leeds
(0113) 233 8905
keith.hartley@masons.com
Specialisation: Partner in Construction and Engineering Group. Leads 17-lawyer Construction and Engineering team in Leeds. Dispute resolution including High Court, arbitration and ADR and major project work, including many PFI and BOT schemes. Particular interests are transport systems and infrastructure and offshore process installations. Worked in UK and several Asian countries.
Prof. Memberships: Law Society, Chartered Institute of Arbitrators, Pacific Lawyers Association.
Career: Joined *Masons* in 1980. Admitted as solicitor in England (1982) and in Hong Kong (1984) and became a partner in 1986. Resident in Hong Kong for 10 years before becoming Managing Partner of Leeds office in 1995.
Personal: Born 11 October 1957. Educated at King's College, London. Lives at Adel near Leeds.

HELPS, Dominic
Shadbolt & Co, Reigate
(01737) 226277
dominic_helps@shadboltlaw.com
Specialisation: Specialises in the handling of all sorts of building and civil engineering disputes, both domestic and international. Cases on which he has worked include the Tsing Ma Bridge, Heathrow Tunnel Collapse, the Broadgate development and MEPAS tunnel dispute. Also acted for a major German contractor on a number of substantial ICC arbitrations. Acted for parties involved in adjudication and in enforcement of adjudicators' decisions. Involved in many of the reported enforcement decisions. Non-contentious experience includes drafting documentation for a major project finance project and acting for funds, developers, contractors and consultants on a wide variety of drafting work. Regular contributor to the construction and legal press and speaker on construction law. Accredited adjudicator (TeCSA).
Prof. Memberships: Technology and Construction Solicitors Association (Secretary); Society of Construction Law; Law Society; Arbitration Club (Chairman, Law Courts Branch).
Career: Articled and qualified with *Linklaters & Paines* 1983. Joined *Lovell White & King* (later *Lovell White Durrant*) in Hong Kong in 1985, returning to London office in 1986. Became a partner with *Shadbolt & Co* in 1996.
Personal: Born 8 July 1956. Attended Radley College, Oxon, then Cambridge University 1975-78 and 1979-80. In between was staff writer for Management Today. Leisure interests include playing cricket, Arsenal FC, scuba diving, reading novels/history and cinema. Lives in Reigate.

HENCHIE, Nicholas
Mayer, Brown, Rowe & Maw, London
(020) 7248 4282

HENDERSON, Nick
Dickinson Dees, Newcastle upon Tyne
(0191) 279 9281
nick.henderson@dickinson-dees.com
Specialisation: Partner in the construction and engineering group, specialising in dispute resolution. He has had experience in all forms of dispute resolution including arbitration and High Court litigation. Increasingly involved in adjudication having acted for employers, contractors, sub-contractors and professionals in the adjudication process. Has experience of enforcing adjudicator's decisions in the courts, both in London and the regions. Also has extensive experience of mediations. Has most recently become increasingly involved in the prosecution of professional negligence claims.
Prof. Memberships: Member of Chartered Institute of Arbitrators, ADR Net.
Career: Qualified while at *Dickinson Dees* in 1993. Partner 2000.
Personal: Nottingham University 1986-89 LLB Hons. Interests include cricket; golf; football; rugby; reading; history.

HERBERT, Mary
Eversheds, Cardiff
(029) 2047 1147
maryherbert@eversheds.com
Specialisation: Contractual claims, both defects claims and loss and expense claims. Extensive experience in arbitration, mediation, and adjudication in the health, energy, offshore and process plant sectors as well as in general building and engineering. Also very experienced in PFI, contract drafting, amending and professional appointments and warranties.
Prof. Memberships: Law Society.
Career: Qualified in 1988 and joined *Eversheds*, becoming a partner in 1993.
Personal: Theatre, art and gardening. Lives in Cardiff.

HILTON, Mark W
Hammond Suddards Edge, Leeds
(0113) 284 7000

HOLLOWAY, Julian
Berwin Leighton Paisner, London
(020) 7427 1373
julian.holloway@blplaw.com
Specialisation: Partner. Construction and commercial litigation/arbitration and alternative dispute resolution. Former director of Centre for Dispute Resolution Limited ('CEDR') and Vice Chairman of CEDR's Construction Industry Working Party. Member of Drafting Committee of CEDR's Model Rules for Adjudication. Case Notes Editor of 'Construction Law Journal'. CEDR accredited mediator (1993). Acts as mediator and for parties engaged in the mediation process. On CEDR's and RIBA's panel of adjudicators and is actively engaged in numerous adjudications. Member of the Construction Contacts Mediators Group. Has also been involved in setting up 'e-mediation' services.
Prof. Memberships: Law Society. Technology and Construction Court Solicitors Association.
Career: Articles with *Denton Hall & Burgin* 1979-81. Qualified Solicitor since 1981. Assistant Solicitor *Brecher & Co* 1981-83. Assistant Solicitor with *McKenna & Co* 1984-88. Partner *McKenna & Co* 1988-92. Partner *Greenwoods* 1993 to 2000. Partner *Paisner & Co*, now *Berwin Leighton Paisner* 2001 to date.
Personal: Born 1954.

HOLMES, Patrick
Macfarlanes, London
(020) 7831 9222

HOSIE, Jonathan
Hammond Suddards Edge, London
(020) 7655 1000

HOUGH, Christopher
Fenwick Elliott, London
(020) 7956 9354
chough@fenwickelliott.co.uk
Specialisation: Partner and Chartered Civil Engineer. Contentious and non-contentious construction and engineering law. Adjudicator Panel Member for TeCSA, RICS, RIBA, ICE, CIOB CIC and CIArb. Founder member of adjudication.co.uk. UK – substantial adjudication, arbitration, litigation and ADR proceedings concerning offices, hospitals, residential buildings, oil platforms, motorways, lifting equipment and tunnels. International – power stations and steelworks in South Africa, onshore oil facilities, ports and dry docks in the Middle East, oil pumping and export facilities in Sudan and transportation infrastructure in Malaysia.
Prof. Memberships: Fellow of the Institution of Civil Engineers, Fellow of the Chartered Institute of Arbitrators, Chairman of the TeCSA Adjudication Sub-Committee, Member of the Law Society, the ICE Conciliation and Adjudication Advisory Panel, the Society of Construction Law and the British Tunnelling Society.
Career: BSC (Civil & Structural Engineering) 1980 MSc (Construction Law &

Arbitration) 1997. Chartered Engineer 1984. Contractors and consultants UK, South Africa, Qatar. Solicitor 1990. *Masons*, *Allen & Overy* (Dubai), *Speechly Bircham*. Partner *Ralph Hume Garry* (1997) and *Fenwick Elliott*.
Personal: Born 8 August 1959. Married with four children.

HOWE, Martin
Bevan Ashford, Bristol
(0117) 918 8975
martin.howe@bevanashford.co.uk
Specialisation: Partner. Construction law with particular experience of drafting and interpretation of construction-related documentation. Principal draftsman of suite of construction documents for the MOD (DEFCON 2000) and of construction documentation for NHS Estates 'Procure 21' initiative. Joint author of leading construction forum 'Collaborative Construction Contract' and author of chapters on Construction and Dispute Resolution in Sweet & Maxwells 'Public Private Partnerships and PFI'. Also experienced in the resolution of construction disputes.
Prof. Memberships: Regional co-ordinator for the Society of Construction Law in Bristol. Member of the Reading Construction Forum. Fellow Member of the Faculty of Building. Member of 'Teamwork 2001'.
Career: Qualified 1983. Joined *Bevan Ashford* as a partner in May 2000.
Personal: Born 1958. Educated King's College, London.

HUDSON, James
Nicholson Graham & Jones, London
(020) 7360 8150
james.hudson@ngj.co.uk
Specialisation: Partner in Construction and Engineering Department. Principal area of practice is construction and engineering law. Has extensive experience of litigation, arbitration and other forms of ADR including mediation and adjudication. Important cases have included 'Minter v WHTSO' and 'ICI v Bovis' and others.
Prof. Memberships: Past Chairman (now Vice President) of Technology and Construction Solicitors Association (TeCSA), Chairman TeCSA Civil Litigation Committee, Member of TCC Users Committee, Society of Construction Law, International Bar Association and was a member of the Official Referees Working Group to the Woolf Enquiry.
Career: Called to the Bar in 1972. Qualified as a Solicitor in 1977. Joined *Bristows Cooke & Carpmael* in 1979 and became a Partner in 1984. Joined *Nicholson Graham & Jones* as a Partner in 1998. Accredited TeCSA adjudicator. Accredited CEDR adjudicator and mediator.
Personal: Born 13 May 1949. Educated at Winchester College 1962-66 and King's College, London (LLB Hons, 1971). Leisure activities include golf, tennis and cricket.

JENKINS, Jane
Freshfields Bruckhaus Deringer, London
(020) 7936 4000
jane.jenkins@freshfields.com
Specialisation: Has broad experience of dispute resolution on major construction and engineering projects. Contentious work covers ADR, arbitration and litigation in construction and energy sectors including public procurement bid challenge advice. Non-contentious work covers PFI (including road, rail and prisons projects,) process plant and power projects and institutional development.
Prof. Memberships: City of London Solicitors Company; CEDR accredited mediator.
Career: Qualified 1988, partner 1996.
Publications: Contributor to Sweet & Maxwell's 'Construction Law: Themes and Practice' and LLP's 'Privity of Contracts: Impact of the Contract: (Rights of Third Parties) Act 1999.'
Personal: Born 1963, educated at Lincoln College, Oxford.

JONES, David
Hammond Suddards Edge, London
(020) 7655 1000

KELLY, Neil J
MacRoberts, Edinburgh
(0131) 229 5046
neil.kelly@macroberts.com
Specialisation: Practice covers full range of advice to commercial clients in connection with dispute avoidance and resolution (Adjudication, Arbitration, Court, ADR) with particular reference to the construction and civil engineering industries acting for related professions, employers, contractors, sub-contractors and suppliers. Contributor to 'Mac-Roberts on Scottish Building Projects' and regular lecturer on construction and civil engineering matters.
Prof. Memberships: Notary Public, Associate of the Chartered Institute of Arbitrators, Commissioner of the Scottish Council for International Arbitration, Member of International Bar Association, Convenor of the Scottish Branch of the Adjudication Society.
Career: Aberdeen University (LLB with Distinction and Dip. LP). Trainee *MacRoberts*; qualified 1984; Partner 1990.
Personal: Born 28 June 1961. Interests include opera and classical music. Lives in Edinburgh.

LANE, Mark
Masons, London
(020) 7490 6214
mark.lane@masons.com
Specialisation: Principally contract drafting and dispute resolution. Includes ICC arbitrations (Ghana, Gambia, Greece, Maldives), domestic litigation and contract drafting for international and UK infrastructure projects. Also handles EU public procurement advising contracting authorities (including government departments, agencies and utilities) on tendering and structuring tendering procedures under PFI schemes. Acted on Harbour City litigation in Hong Kong; Channel Tunnel and Canary Wharf projects. Also acted on PFI and international BOT projects including roads and water and waste water treatment works (project agreements and construction issues). Contract drafting on other water related projects includes projects in India, the Philippines, Australasia and Scotland. Editor-in-chief of *Masons*' 'Water Yearbook'. Has extensive African experience (much of it FIDIC related) including matters in Nigeria, Gambia, Ghana, Mozambique, Kenya and Mali. In 1998, led *Masons*' team acting for the Government of Ukraine in negotiations to establish the Project Management Unit to manage the project to render the Chernobyl Nuclear Reactor No. 4 safe. (ongoing.) Experienced conference speaker nationally and internationally.
Prof. Memberships: Society of Construction Law; IBA (Committee T) Past Chairman of Sub-committee on International Procurement in Construction Projects; European Construction Institute (Member of Executive Committee).
Career: Qualified in 1975. Partner at *Masons* since 1988.
Personal: Born 18 March 1950. Educated at Cranleigh School 1962-67 and Trinity College, Cambridge 1968-72. Lives in London.

LANGLEY, Robert
Watson Burton, Newcastle upon Tyne
(0191) 244 4444
Specialisation: Partner in Commercial Litigation Department. Head of Construction Unit (5 Partners, 10 Solicitors, 9 Graduate Assistants). Practising Mediator and Adjudicator. Specialises in construction law and professional indemnity. Head of Commercial Litigation. Handles contractual disputes in construction, engineering and fabrication. Also undertakes professional indemnity and professional negligence work, both tortious and contractual. Has acted in a wide range of disputes including those in the construction process, injunctive work and particularly in the context of off-shore fabrication and engineering and a number of major arbitrations. Clients include fundholders, major contractors, public utilities, developers, further education institutions, design consultants, estate surveyors and valuers, foreign lawyers and Underwriters. Regular speaker at conferences and seminars including degree courses and CPD.
Prof. Memberships: Law Society, Chartered Institute of Arbitrators, ADR Net, Technology and Construction Solicitors Association, Fellow of the Society of Advanced Legal Studies.
Career: Called to the Bar in 1975. Re-qualified as a Solicitor in 1979. Partner in 1981 at *Watson Burton*, Newcastle upon Tyne.
Personal: Educated at Oxford University (BA Jurisprudence 1974). Leisure interests include yachting, skiing, the hills and history. Lives in Newcastle upon Tyne.

LEVINE, Marshall
Linklaters, London
(020) 7456 3580
marshall.levine@linklaters.com
Specialisation: Significant experience in construction and engineering advising both employers, contractors and banks associated with construction and engineering projects.
Prof. Memberships: 1995 to date: Member of British Consultants Bureau.
Career: Partner and Head of *Linklaters* Construction and Engineering Group and Partner in *Linklaters* Private Finance Initiative Practice Group. 1989 to date: Partner, *Linklaters*, 1982-89: Assistant Solicitor, *Linklaters*. 1987-89: Reading University, MSc (Construction Management); 1985: ACIArb Institute of Chartered Arbitrators; 1980-84: Reading University, BSc (Estate Management); 1975-78: UCL University, LLB.

LEWIS, Simon
Dickinson Dees, Newcastle upon Tyne
(0191) 279 9552
simon.lewis@dickinson-dees.com
Specialisation: Covers full range of construction law, including offshore and minerals industries. In particular deals with dispute resolution, particularly arbitration, ADR and adjudication. Also extensively involved in PFI work. Acts for all sectors of the construction industry. Writes and lectures extensively on construction law and PFI issues. Has a regular column in Building magazine. General editor of and contributor to 'Tolley's Guide to Construction Contracts.'
Prof. Memberships: Member of the Chartered Institute of Arbitrators, member of TECSA (accredited adjudicator) and ARCOM.
Career: Qualified 1986. Joined *Lovell White Durrant* 1988. Joined *Dickinson Dees* 1992 (Partner from 1995).
Personal: Born 20 November 1960. Bristol University 1979-83 : LLB, LLM. Interests include: cinema, hill walking and American Football. Lives in Newcastle upon Tyne.

LLOYD JONES, David
Gateley Wareing, Birmingham
(0121) 234 0000

MAYNARD, Robert
Berwin Leighton Paisner, London
(020) 7760 4009
bob.maynard@blplaw.com
Specialisation: Partner in the Construction and Engineering Group at *Berwin Leighton Paisner* specialising in litigation, arbitration, adjudication, ADR processes, project and advisory work for clients from all sides of the construction industry. Has acted in recent years for Balfour Beatty, Carillion, TML, Wimpey, HBG-HAM, Yorkshire Water, Erick Van Egeraat Associated Architects, Chief Industries Inc., Tesco, Decoma, Hy-ten and the Environment agency. Major matters in the last year include: successfully settling Chief Industries' dispute

CONSTRUCTION ■ THE LEADERS

over grain handling in Egypt and leading the teams representing Yorkshire Water in very large multi-party proceedings concerning the enhancement of one of its largest sewage treatment works and representing Carillion on a number of disputes arising from a very large mixed-use commercial development.
Prof. Memberships: Society of Construction Law.
Career: Assistant Solicitor, *Rowe & Mawe*, 1987-90; *Mackenzie Mills*, 1990-93; *Barlow Lyde & Gilbert*, 1994-97. Partner, *Barlow Lyde & Gilbert*, 1997-2001.
Personal: Born 1962. Educated Latymer Upper School, Hammersmith, London; and Bristol University, LLB (Hons) 1984. Married with two children. Interests include golf, skiing, cinema and theatre. Languages: Italian and French. Resides London.

MCLEAN, Alistair
Dundas & Wilson CS, Edinburgh
(0131) 228 8000

MINOGUE, Ann
Linklaters, London
(020) 7367 2505
ann.minogue@linklaters.com
Specialisation: Construction law specialist with 22 years' experience in drafting and disputes work on building and construction related contracts for a number of major developments and projects. She has advised developers, occupiers, lenders and government and industry bodies.
Prof. Memberships: BPF Construction Committee, 'Justice' Committee (legal remedies for home-owners), Latham Working Group 10, JCT Drafting Sub-Committee, Governor London Contemporary Banco Trust, Member City University Council.
Career: 2001 to date: Partner, *Linklaters*; 1997-2001: Partner, *CMS Cameron McKenna*; 1985-97: Partner, *McKenna & Co*; 1980-85: Assistant, *McKenna & Co*; 1978-80: Articles, *McKenna & Co*. 1974-77: Clare College, Cambridge, Law Tripos Parts I and II; 1966-73: Aylesbury Girls' High School.

MORRISON, Alastair
Masons, Glasgow
(0141) 248 4858
alastair.morrison@masons.com
Specialisation: Partner providing legal and strategic advice on all aspects of construction projects, drafting of bespoke contracts and construction arbitration and litigation. Specialising in construction and engineering law and has a depth of experience in major projects.
Prof. Memberships: Law Society of Scotland, International Bar Association Construction Division and Technology and Construction Solicitors Association.
Career: Attended University of Cape Town, University of Glasgow (LLB Hons, DipLP). Assistant solicitor *Digby Brown* 1986-89; assistant solicitor *McGrigor Donald* 1989-93; associate partner *Dundas & Wilson CS* 1993-94; Partner and Head of Construction and Engineering Group 1994-98; Jointly established *Masons'* Scottish practice in 1998.
Personal: Born 1962. Resides Glasgow. Leisure interests include running and rugby.

MOSEY, David
Trowers & Hamlins, London
(020) 7423 8000
dmosey@trowers.com
Specialisation: Partner, Commercial. Head of Projects and Construction Group. Has advised for more than 20 years on UK and international construction law, including major projects in the commercial, industrial, housing, urban regeneration, health and education sectors. Substantial involvement in PFI and leading advisor on partnering and Egan-compliant procurement. Particular expertise in procurement strategies, risk analysis, standard and bespoke contracts and professional appointments. Author of 'PPC2000' (the first standard form of Project Partnering Contract) and of 'Design and Build in Action' (Chandos 1998).
Prof. Memberships: Member of working groups of CIC, Local Government Task Force and Housing Forum and member of the Society of Construction Law, also a highly experienced conference/seminar speaker.

MOSS, David J
Hammond Suddards Edge, Manchester
(0161) 830 5000

NEWMAN, Paul
Hugh James, Cardiff
(029) 2039 1171
paul.newman@hughjames.com
Specialisation: Barrister in Construction and Civil Engineering Department. Member of *Hugh James'* specialist advocacy section. Has a full practising certificate and rights of audience in all the courts of England and Wales. Member of *Hugh James'* specialist advocacy section. Deals with contentious and non-contentious construction law. Regularly appears as advocate in arbitration and court hearings and sits as an adjudicator. Has provided seminars on construction law to many organisations, including the College of Law and professional bodies. Author and/or co-author of 10 books as well as papers on construction law and dispute resolution.
Prof. Memberships: Called to the Bar by Gray's Inn November 1982, Fellow of the Chartered Institute of Arbitrators, accredited Adjudicator for the Royal Institute of British Architects. ADR Group accredited mediator.
Career: Called to the Bar in November 1982 and joined the firm in August 1999.
Personal: Born 5 March 1958. Educated at Clare College, Cambridge (1976-80), City University, London (1980-81) and the Inns of Court School of Law (1981-82).

NOLAN, Brandon
McGrigor Donald, Glasgow
(0141) 248 6677
brandon.nolan@mcgrigors.com
Specialisation: Head of Construction and Engineering Unit. All aspects of construction law including contract drafting, appointment documentation, contract advice, disputes and mediation work. Currently involved in procurement and dispute work in all parts of the UK as well as internationally. Has conducted the advocacy in a number of substantial arbitrations. Sits from time to time as an arbitrator. A frequent speaker at commercially organised seminars.
Prof. Memberships: Member of the Chartered Institute of Arbitrators; Society of Construction Law; International Bar Association; Technology and Construction Solicitors Association.
Career: Qualified 1980 with *McGrigor Donald & Co* (as it was then). Became a Partner in 1987. Head of the Construction and Engineering Unit at *McGrigor Donald*. Head of the Dispute Resolution Business Group within *McGrigor Donald* and *KLegal*.
Personal: Born 4 November 1955. Educated at Glasgow University 1974-78. Leisure interests include visiting a gym and films.

NURNEY, Simon
Macfarlanes, London
(020) 7831 9222

OATS, Simon
Eversheds, Ipswich
(01473) 284546
simonoats@eversheds.com
Specialisation: Construction and engineering related law encompassing contractual advice and disputes resolution. Acts for a number of substantial construction clients including employers, developers, contractors and professionals. Particular experience in engineering contracts, arbitration, adjudication and projects.
Prof. Memberships: Law Society, Society of Construction Law, Interact.

O'HANLON, Liam
Shadbolt & Co, London
(020) 7332 5750
liam_ohanlon@shadboltlaw.com
Specialisation: Heavyweight construction specialist with extensive experience in conducting major dispute resolution by negotiation, mediation, litigation and arbitration, both in the UK and internationally.
Prof. Memberships: Law Society, Society of Construction Law.
Career: Trained at London Borough of Camden; qualified 1977; local government 1974-86; private practice *McKenna & Co/Cameron McKenna* 1986-99; Partner at *Shadbolt & Co* 1999-date.
Personal: Gunnersbury Grammar School, London W3; Bristol University LLB; golf, football, hill walking, modern history; five children, resides Winchmore Hill, London.

PALMER, Simon
Hammond Suddards Edge, Leeds
(0113) 284 7000

PATTERSON, Lindy A
MacRoberts, Edinburgh
(0131) 229 5046
lindy.patterson@macroberts.com
Specialisation: Specialises in contentious building and civil engineering matters. Widely regarded as one of Scotland's leading construction and civil engineering law experts. Acts for employers, construction and engineering companies, architects and engineers, regularly handling disputes in arbitration and litigation covering all aspects of building and civil engineering disputes. Acts for a number of Professional Indemnity Insurers covering negligence of professionals in the construction industry. Represents clients in the Commercial Court and the Court of Session, as one of Scotland's first Solicitor Advocates and the first female Solicitor Advocate. Speaks regularly at industry seminars and contributes to building and civil engineering publications.
Prof. Memberships: Obligations Committee of the Law Society; Industrial and Professional Liaison Body of Napier University in connection with the Department of Building and Surveying; Writer to the Signet; Commercial Court Consultative Committee set up to monitor the workings of the Commercial Court; Law Commission Contract Law Advisory Group; lay member of RICS Chairman's Advisory Group; associate, Chartered Institute of Arbitrators.
Career: Trainee Solicitor *W & J Burness* 1980-82. Solicitor *Biggart Billie & Gifford* and *Menzies Dougal* 1982-85. Joined *Bird Semple* 1985, became Partner 1988; Solicitor Advocate 1993. Head of Construction Group at *MacRoberts* (Partner 1997). Contributes regularly to publications and seminars.
Personal: Graduated LLB (Hons) Edinburgh University 1980. Skiing, hill walking and watersports.

PIGOTT, Ashley
Wragge & Co, Birmingham
(0870) 903 1000

PINSENT, Jim
DLA, Liverpool
(08700) 111111

PLASCOW, Ronald H
Mills & Reeve, Cambridge
(01223) 222 261
ron.plascow@mills-reeve.com
Specialisation: Partner in Construction and Projects Department. Has practised exclusively in construction and civil engineering since 1982 beginning in industry at Trafalgar House plc and subsequently at *Lovell White Durrant* in London. Regularly advises on the JCT, ICE, ECC and most other forms of standard contracts including partnering forms, used in the UK and on FIDIC Contracts used abroad. Prepares and drafts construction contracts, consul-

tants' appointments and bonds and warranties. Represents employers and contractors involved in litigation in the Courts, or in arbitration. A trained mediator familiar with the use of other ADR techniques to resolve disputes and has represented clients in mediations and conciliations. Editor of 'Arbitration Practice and Procedure, Interlocutory and Hearing Problems' (Lloyd's of London Press Ltd) first edition, contributing author to 'Tolleys Guide to Construction Contracts', regular speaker at conferences arranged by the RICS, RIBA, ICE and CIArb. Past Secretary to the East Anglia Branch of the CIArb.

POPE, Caroline
Berwin Leighton Paisner, London
(020) 7760 1000
carolinepope@blplaw.com
Specialisation: Partner specialising in contentious construction and civil engineering. Represents clients from all sides of the construction and engineering industry in project advice and a wide range of dispute resolution including mediation and adjudication. Has particular experience of tunnelling, power and nuclear projects, defects claims in prestigious office buildings and shopping centres. Has been involved in expert determinations under the IChemE form of contract.
Prof. Memberships: Society of Construction Law; The Law Society of England and Wales; the British Tunnelling Society and the Technology and Construction Solicitors' Association.
Career: Articled *Stilgoes*; qualified 1985; Solicitor *Rowe & Maw* 1985-93; Solicitor *Barlow Lyde & Gilbert* 1993, Partner 1997. Partner, *Berwin Leighton Paisner* 2001.
Personal: Born 1958; Sherborne School for Girls; London School of Economics (BSc Economics). Resides in Berkshire.

RACE, David
Nicholson Graham & Jones, London
(020) 7360 8106
david.race@ngj.co.uk
Specialisation: Head of Construction and Engineering Department. Main areas of practice are construction and engineering law. Handles major infrastructure projects, particularly in transport, and international project work in process engineering and related fields. Also undertakes general commercial work including project finance, joint ventures, procurement, tendering and contracting in the private and public sectors. Major clients include Lafarge Cement UK, West African Portland Cement plc, YANBU Cement Company, Essex County Council, Eurostar (UK) Limited and London REMADE. Author of various articles for professional journals. A TeCSA accredited adjudicator. Honorary Solicitor to the Samaritans.
Prof. Memberships: Institute of Arbitrators, Society of Construction Law. Technology and Commercial Construction Solicitors Association.
Career: Qualified in 1974. Joined *Nicholson Graham & Jones* as Partner in 1987. Before qualifying worked in overseas banking 1969-71. Legal Advisor to Mass Transit Railway Corp., Hong Kong 1978-82 and Chief Solicitor to Blue Circle Industries PLC 1985-87.

REDMOND, John
Osborne Clarke, Bristol
(0117) 917 3000

REES, Peter
Norton Rose, London
(020) 7283 6000
reespj@nortonrose.com
Specialisation: Head of *Norton Rose* Litigation Department and Senior Partner in the Construction and Engineering Law Group. All aspects of contentious and non-contentious construction and engineering law. Particular expertise in international arbitration (especially ICC and LCIA). Has advised government departments, multilateral agencies, international organisations and international contractors. Sits as an arbitrator.
Prof. Memberships: Chairman International Construction Projects Committee of IBA; Chairman Technology and Construction Solicitors Association; solicitor representative on Technology and Construction Court User's Committee; Fellow Chartered Institute of Arbitrators; accredited TECSA adjudicator; Board of Advisers, Centre for International Legal Studies, Member Institute of Petroleum.
Career: Qualified 1981 with *Norton Rose*. Partner 1987.
Personal: Born 21 April 1957. MA from Downing College, Cambridge University. MBA from Nottingham Trent University. Leisure interests include football (still crazy enough to be playing), golf and scuba diving.

REGAN, Michael
Mayer, Brown, Rowe & Maw, London
(020) 7248 4282

RINTOUL, David
Clarks, Reading
(0118) 960 4675
davidrintoul@clarks-solicitors.co.uk
Specialisation: Partner specialising in construction and heads the firm's specialist construction law group; represents employers, end users, contractors and sub-contractors with substantial experience in bringing and defending adjudication, arbitration and litigation claims relating to contractual disputes, professional negligence and defects; also advises on and represents clients in alternative dispute resolution processes including expert determination; regularly advises employers, design team consultants and contractors and specialist sub-contractors on standard form and bespoke contracts and terms of appointments, joint venture agreements and surety documentation; has spoken at several internal and external seminars on specialist construction law issues; also Co-Chair of TAGLaw network construction/real estate Speciality Group.
Prof. Memberships: Chartered Institute of Arbitrators; Society of Construction Law; Adjudication Society.
Career: Trained *Clarks*; qualified 1989; partner 1995.
Personal: Born 1965; married with two children.

ROBERTS, Martin
Masons, London
(020) 7490 4000
martin.roberts@masons.com
Specialisation: Partner and Manager of Construction and Engineering Group. Specialises in dispute resolution and non-contentious advice on construction and engineering matters. Leads team of lawyers advising contractors, employers, professionals and insurers on wide range of issues and projects. Recently involved in advising on Croydon Tramlink, issues arising from various FM Contracts for MOD establishments, major adjudication resulting from construction contract for refurbishment of a central London hotel, international arbitration proceedings relating to the construction of a hospital in Jordan, Navotas Power Station (Philippines) where advised successful Plaintiff in Hopewell Project Management Ltd v Ewbank Preece Ltd 1998 1 LLR and subsequent dispute resolution process, major refurbishment of holiday centres for UK leisure group, construction of CHP Plant in UK and claims arising from major road project in South East. Currently advising on various issues relating to HGCR Act, Arbitration Act and on several adjudications and mediations. Accredited CEDR Mediator and Panel Adjudicator.
Prof. Memberships: Law Society, elected committee member of City of London Law Society, member of Litigation Sub-Committee of City of London Law Society, Society of Construction Law, ORSA, CEDR.
Career: Qualified 1979, Partner with *Masons* 1983, member of *Masons*' Partnership Strategy Board 1992-97, Manager of Construction and Engineering Group 2000 onwards.
Personal: Born 11 April 1955. Attended City of London Freeman's School, Kingston University (BA Hons) Law. Leisure interests include theatre, cinema, pop music, tennis, swimming and two children. Lives in Sussex.

ROBSON, Nigel R
Eversheds, Leeds
(0113) 243 0391
nigelrobson@eversheds.com
Specialisation: Partner in Construction and Engineering Unit. Principal area of practice involves handling contractual disputes arising from construction or engineering projects on JCT, ICE, GC Works and FIDIC forms of contract or bespoke contracts with particular emphasis on contractual claims and defects claims. Both in the UK and internationally has considerable experience in relation to hospitals, process engineering, power stations, offshore, waste incinerators, major civil engineering and defence related projects. Other main area of work involves drafting and amending commercial agreements for construction and engineering projects.
Prof. Memberships: Law Society; Fellow, Chartered Institute of Arbitrators.
Career: Qualified in 1977 and went on to join *Eversheds*, becoming a Partner in 1980. Managing Partner of *Eversheds* North East 1992-2000. Head of Construction International 2000.
Personal: Born 23 May 1951.

ROE, Mark
Masons, London
(020) 7490 6545
mark.roe@masons.com
Specialisation: Partner specialising in major projects and international dispute resolution in the Construction Industry. Expert in advising on major projects in the engineering construction and related industries. Has advised and acted extensively in the resolution of disputes by mediation and mini-trial/structured settlement procedures, adjudication arbitration (both UK and international), expert determination and litigation. Sits as a mediator. Drafted several construction specific sets of mediation rules. Advises on transactional matters, partnering and PFI. Has advised on a number of major PFI deals. Currently advising on a major partnering initiative. Lectures on ADR, partnering, project management and construction law matters. Described previously in 'Chambers' as a "flamboyant streetfighter with a good grasp of the issues" – a description which his clients seemed to recognise.
Prof. Memberships: TECSA Committee Member, Former Director of CEDR 1989-99, Accredited Mediator.
Career: Qualified in 1981. Joined *Masons* in 1981. Partner of *Masons* since 1985.
Personal: Born 30 May 1955. Attended the John Fisher School 1965-73, educated at Balliol College, Oxford 1974-77. Leisure interests include rugby, tennis, cycling, skiing, theatre and the arts and crafts movement. Lives in Central London.

ROE, Sally
Freshfields Bruckhaus Deringer, London
(020) 7936 4000
sallyroe@freshfields.com
Specialisation: Partner in Litigation Department. Authorised to exercise rights of audience in the Higher Courts (Civil Proceedings), July '95. Head of Construction and Engineering Group. Extensive experience of litigation and arbitration in these fields, acting for employers and contractors. Also handles non-contentious projects including property developments and infrastructure projects. Other areas of practice include advising on the application of the EC Procurement Regime.
Prof. Memberships: City of London Solicitors Company.
Career: Qualified in 1981. Joined *Freshfields* in 1988, becoming a Partner in 1990.

CONSTRUCTION ■ THE LEADERS

Personal: Born 1956. Attended Wakefield Girls' High School 1965-74 and St Hilda's College, Oxford 1974-77.

ROUT, Peter
DLA, Manchester
(08700) 111111

ROWLAND, Simon
Dickinson Dees, Newcastle upon Tyne
(0191) 279 9000
Specialisation: Non-contentious work. Acts for clients from all disciplines of the construction industry including developers, funders, main and sub-contractors and designers. Particular emphasis on development work but also experienced in partnering heavy civil engineering, process engineering and offshore work. Regularly speaks on such topics as building contracts, appointments, warranties and development.
Prof. Memberships: Law Society.
Career: Educated at University of Newcastle Upon Tyne (LLB Hons). Articled at *Watson Burton*. Qualified September 1992. Joined *Dickinson Dees* November 2001.
Personal: Born 5 December 1967. Enjoys playing football and golf, listening to music and socialising.

RUSHTON, John Michael
Mayer, Brown, Rowe & Maw, London
(020) 7248 4282

RUSSELL, Victoria E
Fenwick Elliott, London
(020) 7956 9354
vrussell@fenwickelliott.co.uk
Specialisation: Partner. Handles contentious and non-contentious construction and engineering matters with a special emphasis on litigation, adjudication, arbitration and ADR. Advises employers, main contractors, specialist subcontractors and members of the professional team on a variety of points of law, practice and procedure. Has dealt with a number of complex construction disputes, some arising from the various JCT and ICE standard forms of contract and others from bespoke contractual arrangements. German speaker. Experienced arbitrator, CEDR accredited mediator and TECSA and CIOB adjudicator.
Prof. Memberships: TECSA, IBA (Business Section), LCIA, Society of Construction Law (Council Member since 1990, Chairman 2000-02), European Society of Construction Law (President 2001-); Chartered Institute of Arbitrators – Fellow (1991). Member of the Diploma in Arbitration Advisory Board of the College of Estate Management in Reading (1991-97). Liveryman of the Worshipful Company of Constructors. Master of the Worshipful Company of Arbitrators (2001-). Fellow of the Chartered Institute of Building (2001).
Career: Qualified and joined *Freedmans* in 1981. Became a Partner in 1985. Joined *Berrymans* in 1996. Joined *Fenwick Elliot* 2000.
Personal: Born 12 October 1956. Educated at Benenden School, Kent 1968-73 and Exeter University 1974-77 (LLB Hons). Former member of Benenden School Trust and Alumni Board of Exeter University. Lives in West London. Two sons born 1991 and 1993.

SALMON, Ken
Mace & Jones, Manchester
(0161) 236 2244
kenneth.salmon@maceandjones.co.uk
Specialisation: Partner, Head of Construction Unit. Main area of work is building and civil engineering disputes, in court adjudication and arbitration, and advising on contract documentation. Conducts in-house seminars for clients.
Prof. Memberships: Law Society, TECSA, A.C.I. Arb.
Career: Qualified 1973.
Personal: Born 16 April 1946. Leisure pursuits include cycling, five-a-side soccer, hill walking, music and reading. Lives in Warrington.

SCOTT, Martin
Walker Morris, Leeds
(0113) 283 2500
mls@walkermorris.co.uk
Specialisation: Partner and Head of Construction Group. Practice covers the full range of construction and engineering law, both contentious and non-contentious. Particularly active in the field of disputes where defects whether by design or in construction are the central issue. Acts mainly for Employers/Developers and specialist sub-contractors but also undertakes work for main contractors within the region.
Career: Qualified 1985. At *Scott Turnbull & Kendall*, now *Walker Morris*, since 1984. Became a Partner in 1992.
Personal: Born 13 August 1959. Educated at Ashville College, Harrogate and Leicester Polytechnic BA Law. Interests include flying, farming and family. Lives in Harrogate.

SHADBOLT, Richard
Shadbolt & Co, London
(020) 7332 5750
Dick_Shadbolt@shadboltlaw.com
Specialisation: Senior Partner. Main area of practice is construction law, including work on engineering and major projects, with experience in UK and internationally since 1967. Particular experience of structuring and drafting of contracts for major projects and construction. Litigation and arbitration work covered as well as environmental, trade and other commercial matters. Author of articles in professional and other periodicals and occasional lecturer on International Construction Contracts. Regular speaker at professional conventions and international conferences on construction contract and other legal topics. Arbitrator and Mediator.
Prof. Memberships: Law Society, Law Society of Hong Kong, American Bar Association (Associate Member), International Bar Association, Inter-Pacific Bar Association, British Consultants Bureau.
Personal: Born 18 December 1942. Attended Okehampton Grammar School 1954-60; King's College, London 1961-64 then College of Law, Guildford 1967. Leisure pursuits include family life.

SHAW, Murray
Biggart Baillie, Glasgow
(0141) 228 8000

SHAW, Peter
Taylor Wessing, London
(020) 7300 7000
pshaw@taylorwessing.com
Specialisation: Former senior partner of niche construction practice *Freedman Church*, with over 25 years experience of construction and engineering law. Acts for clients from all sectors of the construction industry. Head of the International Arbitration Group advising on contentious and non-contentious international construction matters including heavy and light rail projects and power and process facilities in the UK and overseas.
Prof. Memberships: Society of Construction Law; Fellow, Chartered Institute of Arbitrators; Council Member, Technology and Construction Court Solicitors Association responsible for the Annual Symposium; Reading Construction Forum, IBA Business Section.
Career: Qualified 1980, Solicitor *Freedmans* 1973-80 Partner *Freedmans* 1990-96, Senior Partner *Freedman Church* 1991, Partner *Taylor Joynson Garrett* 1996.
Personal: Interests include golf, sailing, skiing, gardening, walking and good food and wine. Lives in London.

SHERMAN, Henry
CMS Cameron McKenna, London
(020) 7367 2526
hcs@cmck.com
Specialisation: Partner in domestic and international construction advice for all sectors of the construction industry and, in particular, international arbitration and litigation and disputes resolution by mediation, adjudication and other informal routes. Regularly addresses seminars and workshops and writes on legal subjects in the construction and legal press.
Prof. Memberships: Society of Construction Law. Board member, Design and Build Foundation.
Career: Qualified in 1977. Joined *McKenna & Co* in 1983. Partner with *CMS Cameron McKenna* in Hong Kong and London.
Personal: Born 1952. Leisure interests include idling whenever possible with his family on the Isle of Wight.

STANIFORTH, Alison J
Eversheds, Leeds
(0113) 243 0391
alisonstaniforth@eversheds.com
Specialisation: Partner, construction and engineering. Principal area of practice is construction/engineering. Drafting and negotiating contracts, professional appointments and ancillary documents. Important matters handled include PFI/PPP, particularly hospitals and schools; facilities management agreements; power generation projects; projects in China, mainland Europe and Poland; railway track and maintenance. Clients include British Waterways Board, Weir Pumps Limited, Morrison Construction & Kier. Visiting lecturer at Leeds Metropolitan University (MSc in Arbitration and Construction Law). Conference speaker for RICS, CIOB, the Institute of Structural Engineers and IRR.
Prof. Memberships: CIArb, TeCSA, Common Purpose Graduate, Network.
Career: Qualified 1985 with *Herbert Smith* 1983-86. Joined *Hepworth & Chadwick* 1986; became a Partner at *Eversheds Hepworth & Chadwick* in 1991.
Personal: Born 13 December 1957. Leeds University 1976-79 (LLB), Trinity Hall, Cambridge 1980-83 (MLitt), Nottingham Trent 1999 (MBA). Interests include golf, malt whiskey and gardening.

STEADMAN, Tim
Clifford Chance, London
(020) 7600 1000
tim.steadman@cliffordchance.com
See under Projects/PFI, p.699

TAYLOR, Kevin
Shepherd+ Wedderburn, Edinburgh
(0131) 473 5299
kevin.taylor@shepwedd.co.uk
Specialisation: Non-contentious construction, projects and PFI/PPP across all sectors including property development; engineering, infrastructure, process plant, energy, outsourcing/facilities management; corporate PFI.
Prof. Memberships: Law Society of Scotland, Writer to the Signet.
Career: Articled *Steedman Ramage*; *Shepherd+ Wedderburn* 1994 to date; secondment to The Scottish Office M6 DBF0 Project (1997-98); Partner and Head of Construction and Special Projects Group 1998 to date.
Personal: Perth High School; Edinburgh University. Sport, travel, reading and music.

THOMAS, Nick
Kennedys, London
(020) 7614 3674
n.thomas@kennedys-law.com
See under Professional Negligence, p.683

TURNBULL, Craig
MacRoberts, Glasgow
(0141) 332 9988
craig.turnbull@macroberts.com
Specialisation: Partner in Construction Group representing employers, contractors, sub-contractors and consultants in litigation, adjudication and arbitration. Regularly acts as arbiter's clerk and as legal advisor to adjudicators. In addition represents construction clients in health and safety and environmental prosecutions and advises generally on those matters. Acts for AMEC, Safeway, Carillion,

Railtrack, Henry Boot, Smith Kline Beecham and British Energy amongst others.
Prof. Memberships: Society of Construction Law, Member of the Chartered Institute of Arbitrators.
Publications: Co-author of 'MacRoberts on Scottish Building Contracts'.
Personal: Born 1966. Lives Glasgow. Married, one son. Leisure interests include golf and football.

VASEY, John
Beachcroft Wansbroughs, Bristol
(0117) 918 2000
jvasey@bwlaw.co.uk
Specialisation: Well known for construction-related claims for insurers but increasingly acting also on contentious and non-contentious issues for developers and contractors. Has detailed knowledge and experience of the insurance provisions of construction and development contracts. Typically handles the contract aspects of major property damage and contractors' 'all risks' claims. Also deals with professional indemnity claims on behalf of architects and engineers and is involved in defending construction-related health and safety precautions. In addition to work for insurers, acts for major contractors, public authorities and developers. A keen exponent of cheaper and quicker methods of resolving disputes. Team works closely with the firm's expanding property group on a range of major developments across the country. Major new clients include Railtrack and the ACE Engineers Insurance scheme.
Career: Qualified in 1980. *McKenna & Co* 1984-87. Joined *Beachcroft Wansbroughs* in 1988. Partner in 1993.

WELSH, John
Bishops Solicitors (formerly Morison Bishop), Glasgow
(0141) 248 4672
john.welsh@bishopslaw.biz
See under Professional Negligence, p.683

WHITE, Neil
Taylor Wessing, London
(020) 7300 7000
n.white@taylorwessing.com
Specialisation: Provides non-contentious and contentious construction and civil engineering advice with particular expertise in the construction aspects of financing and procuring developments and infrastructure projects. Major project experience extends to the energy sector (major generating plants, wind power projects, incineration and combined heat and power plant projects) airport infrastructure including BOT projects in South Africa and Egypt, docks and roads. Advised on the procurement and structuring of construction operations for the regeneration of Chatham Royal Naval Dockyard for English Partnerships, the GLA Building, reconstruction of a Grade 1 listed office in St James and a four star hotel in Prague. Head of *Taylor Joynson Garrett*'s Dispute Resolution Department and a CEDR mediator with extensive experience of dispute resolution in the construction industry, including handling a dispute arising from the first PFI project and copyright and design liability disputes. A regular contributor to 'Building' magazine.
Prof. Memberships: Society of Construction Law.
Career: Qualified 1975, Solicitor *Parker Garrett* 1975-80, Partner *Taylor Garrett* 1980-89, Partner *Taylor Joynson Garrett* (now *Taylor Wessing*) 1989.
Personal: Interests include cricket, tennis, squash, cinema and theatre. Lives in East Sussex.

WILCOCK, Christopher
Hammond Suddards Edge, Birmingham
(0121) 222 3000

WINTER, Jeremy
Baker & McKenzie, London
(020) 7919 1000
jeremy.winter@bakernet.com
Specialisation: Resolution of construction and projects disputes by arbitration, litigation and ADR. Particular expertise in civil engineering matters. 20 years' experience of construction law in a total of 30 countries around the world (particularly Europe, Africa and the Middle East). Conducts own advocacy in arbitration and in High Court. Frequent speaker and writer on construction and arbitration topics. Chairman of Society of Construction Law Working Group on delay analysis.
Prof. Memberships: Hon Fellow of Institution of Civil Engineering Surveyors, Society of Construction Law, Technology and Construction Solicitors Association (Member of Committee). Member of Association for Project Management, Fellow of the Geological Society, Member of LCIA.
Career: Qualified 1979. Joined *Baker & McKenzie* London 1980. Worked in *Baker & McKenzie*'s Sydney Office 1982-84. Partner 1987.
Personal: Born 26 December 1953. Warwick University (LLB Hons 1975). Lives in Toys Hill, Kent.

WOOD, Martin
Greenwoods, Peterborough
(01733) 887700

WRIGHT, John
Berwin Leighton Paisner, London
(020) 7760 1000
john.wright@blplaw.com
Specialisation: Member of *BLP*'s Construction and Engineering Group. Acts for contractors, sub-contractors, professional indemnity insurers and employers and frequently sits as an adjudicator and mediator. Is an Accredited Mediator with CEDR (Centre for Dispute Resolution) and an Accredited Adjudicator with TeCSA (Technology and Construction Solicitors' Association). Is a TeCSA committee member, a Fellow of the Chartered Institute of Arbitrators, a member of the Society of Construction Arbitrators and a Freeman of the Worshipful Company of Arbitrators.
Career: Qualified in 1976. Head of the *Warner Cranston* Construction Department from 1984-98. Joined *BLP* in 1999.
Personal: Born 2 May 1952. Educated Hereford Cathedral School 1963-69 and St John's College, Cambridge 1970-73 (BA 1973, MA 1977). Leisure interests include golf, cricket, wine and theatre. Lives in Richmond, Surrey.

WRIGHTON, Ralph
Eversheds, Newcastle upon Tyne
(0191) 261 1661
ralphwrighton@eversheds.com
Specialisation: Partner. Head of Construction and Engineering Group in North East. Specialising exclusively in construction law since 1979 in connection with civil engineering, power generation, offshore engineering, environmental and process engineering and building projects in the public and private sectors both in the UK and overseas. Over 10 years' involvement in international arbitration conducted in the main European arbitration centres. Regularly advising on major infrastructure contracts including education, health and local government projects and major dispute management and resolution.
Prof. Memberships: Law Society. The Society of Construction Law. Northern Dispute Resolutions.
Career: Articled *Berwin Leighton*. Qualified 1976. Partner *Eversheds* 1990.
Personal: Born 1951. Educated at University College London. Interests include music and history.

YULE, Ian
Wragge & Co, Birmingham
(0870) 903 1000

CORPORATE FINANCE

London: 202; The Regions: 214; Scotland: 228; Profiles: 232

Research approved by BMRB For this edition, Chambers' researchers conducted 6,582 interviews – 3,900 with law firms, 511 with barristers and 2,171 with clients. The validity of the research was scrutinised by BMRB International, who audited both the methodology and the results at our offices in London. They interviewed **Chambers'** researchers and cross-checked sample interviews. Details of the audit appear on page 7.

Corporate Finance Survey

Position	Firm	No. of Client Recommendations
1	Linklaters	72
2	Freshfields	67
2	Slaughter and May	67
4	Allen & Overy	52
5	Clifford Chance	50
6	Herbert Smith	48
7	Eversheds	41
8	Ashurst Morris Crisp	34
9	DLA	31
10	Wragge & Co	27
11	Lovells	25
12	Pinsent Curtis Biddle	23
13	CMS Cameron McKenna	22
13	Norton Rose	22
15	Addleshaw Booth & Co	19
16	Hammonds	17
17	Berwin Leighton Paisner	15
18	Nabarro Nathanson	12
19	Mayer, Brown, Rowe & Maw	11
20	Field Fisher Waterhouse	10
20	Shepherd & Wedderburn	10
20	Simmons & Simmons	10

THE SURVEY
Each year we survey FTSE All Share company clients - speaking to the key buyers of legal services. We ask them which corporate finance teams they rate. This year the results are based on 350 responses. The results show that the larger City firms are still performing well. However, the real winners this year are the national and regional firms, such as Eversheds and Wragge & Co.

OVERVIEW That 2001 was a difficult market for M&A has been widely reported. The sharp downwards course that followed the dot.com-fuelled delirium of 1999 and 2000 was exacerbated by the events of September 11th and was further shaken by the Enron scandal in early 2002. With the larger deals hardest hit, corporate departments reacted by switching to restructuring, as clients focused increasingly on core business. Opinion remains divided on how the market will develop during 2002/2003. Lawyers report that, while deals are still in the pipeline, fewer are coming to fruition. The number of IPOs that were proposed has greatly outweighed those achieved. However, many have been cheered by the ECJ's ruling on the illegality of restrictions by some European governments on foreign ownership of privatised companies, which, together with the planned overhaul of EU takeover law, may pave the way for an increase in cross-border deals.

LONDON

LARGER DEALS

CORPORATE FINANCE: LARGER DEALS
■ LONDON

1
Freshfields Bruckhaus Deringer
Linklaters
Slaughter and May

2
Allen & Overy
Clifford Chance
Herbert Smith

3
Ashurst Morris Crisp

4
Lovells
Macfarlanes
Norton Rose

5
Simmons & Simmons

This book is the product of 6,582 1/2 hour interviews. See p.7 for BMRB audit. Within each band, firms are listed alphabetically.

FRESHFIELDS BRUCKHAUS DERINGER (see firm details p.964) "*An all-round star,*" the firm continues to set high standards, advising on many of the most prestigious European cross-border transactions. Its "*impressive resources*" and deep pool of "*extremely able lawyers*" have secured instructions of the billion pound mark, a remarkable achievement in what has been a quiet transactional market. Clients profess that they are drawn by its "*seamlessly co-ordinated service*" across Europe and the Far East, whilst competitors acknowledge that its offering of "*quality specialists across a range of industries is excellent, whether buying or selling.*" The corporate group is supported by recognised experts in fields such as competition, tax and real estate, and benefits from the firm's highly ambitious and successful pan-European structure. In line with the market, it has recently handled a greater proportion of private M&A, restructurings and disposals, although its relationships with international corporate and investment banking clients ensure its presence when high-profile public deals take place. Viewed by many as "*a brilliant lawyer with deep business understanding,*" senior partner Anthony Salz has shifted his focus onto management matters. Still keeping a hand in at the high end, clients remain awed by his "*ability to always see the bigger picture*" and the "*energy and interest he unfailingly gives to his work.*"

Though many clients singled out the firm for its emphasis on teamwork, valuing its "*rare ability to listen and to comprehend our needs,*" it continues to generate some of the sector's brightest and most dynamic stars. "*A robust heavyweight with commanding presence,*" **Barry O'Brien** (see p.243) co-led the team advising The Wolverhampton & Dudley Breweries on Pubmaster's hostile bid, one of the longest hostile battles in recent years, whose defence included a special dividend coupled with share capital consolidation. The transaction is typical in its use of the firm's deep resources, pulling as it did on tax partners in London and New York. Head of the corporate department, O'Brien was consistently praised to researchers as "*a great negotiator with enormous experience;*" he also advised on Schlumberger's £3.6 billion acquisition of Sema. Deemed by many observers to be "*among the best there is,*" **Mark Rawlinson** (see p.245) recently led the team acting for P&O Princess on its proposed merger with Royal Caribbean, bringing together London- and New York-listed entities under a dual listed company structure (DLC). He and **Ed Braham** (see p.234) co-led the team advising Valentia Consortium on its acquisition of eircom, in a take private of the former monopoly incumbent fixed line network provider. The transaction tested the mettle of the team, which faced a bidding war with Denis O'Brien's e-Island consortium, in what proved to be one of the most high-profile private equity deals of the year. "*Creative and solutions-oriented,*" Braham "*just gets better and better every year*" and remains active for key client Kingfisher. **Will Lawes** (see p.240) continues to impress the market with his "*agile mind;*" he brings a "*pragmatic and quietly effective*" approach to the deal table.

LONDON — CORPORATE FINANCE

LEADING INDIVIDUALS

EMINENCES GRISES

★ BERINGER Guy *Allen & Overy*
★ CANN Anthony *Linklaters*
★ SALZ Anthony *Freshfields Bruckhaus Deringer*

[*]
BOARDMAN Nigel *Slaughter and May*

[1]
COOKE Stephen *Slaughter and May*
MIDDLEDITCH Matthew *Linklaters*
PAUL Alan *Allen & Overy*
UNDERHILL William *Slaughter and May*

[2]
BRAHAM Edward *Freshfields Bruckhaus Deringer*
EMMERSON Tim *Freshfields Bruckhaus Deringer*
HATTRELL Martin *Slaughter and May*
PALMER James *Herbert Smith*
SIGNY Adam *Clifford Chance*

[3]
ASHWORTH Chris *Ashurst Morris Crisp*
LONG Julian *Freshfields Bruckhaus Deringer*
RANDELL Charles *Slaughter and May*
WOOTTON David *Allen & Overy*

[4]
BARNARD Stephen *Herbert Smith*
CHILDS David *Clifford Chance*
CRANFIELD Richard *Allen & Overy*
MURPHY Frances *Slaughter and May*
RYDE Andy *Slaughter and May*
SUTTON Robert *Macfarlanes*
WIPPELL Mark *Allen & Overy*

[5]
BEARDSLEY Alison *Allen & Overy*
CHARNLEY William *McDermott, Will & Emery*
DAVIDSON John *Lovells*
ELLARD John *Linklaters*
GOODALL Caroline *Herbert Smith*
KING Peter *Linklaters*
MARCHANT Simon *Freshfields Bruckhaus Deringer*
NICHOLSON Graham *Freshfields Bruckhaus Deringer*
STERN Robert *Slaughter and May*
VON BISMARCK Nilufer *Slaughter and May*

UP AND COMING
BEASTALL Jonathan *Clifford Chance*
JACOBS Charles *Linklaters*

CHEYNE David *Linklaters*

LAWES William *Freshfields Bruckhaus Deringer*
O'BRIEN Barry *Freshfields Bruckhaus Deringer*
RAWLINSON Mark *Freshfields Bruckhaus Deringer*

CLARKE Timothy *Linklaters*
GODDEN Richard *Linklaters*
MACAULAY Anthony *Herbert Smith*
PECK Andrew *Linklaters*

CLARK Adrian *Ashurst Morris Crisp*
PEARSON David *Clifford Chance*
SACKMAN Simon *Norton Rose*

BOND Richard *Herbert Smith*
CLARK Tim *Slaughter and May*
HATCHARD Michael *Skadden, Arps, Slate, Meagher & Flom LLP*
PEARSON Chris *Norton Rose*
STEPHENSON Barbara *Norton Rose*
TWENTYMAN Jeff *Slaughter and May*

BELLIS Tim *Herbert Smith*
COPPIN Jonathan *Norton Rose*
DAVIS James *Freshfields Bruckhaus Deringer*
EVANS Stuart *Simmons & Simmons*
JAMES Glen *Slaughter and May*
LETH Mary *Macfarlanes*
MARTIN Charles *Macfarlanes*
NORMAN Guy *Clifford Chance*
SULLIVAN Michael *Linklaters*

HOWLES Kate *Clifford Chance*
JOHNSON David *Slaughter and May*

See individuals' profiles p.232

He recently advised BT on the £4.8 billion disposal of its Japanese and Spanish interests and the demerger of its wireless operations. Clients valued **Tim Emmerson** (see p.236) as an "*extremely knowledgeable transactional operator.*" He has forged a niche in transactions with a French element and has built up a loyal following amongst investment banks, who appreciate his clear understanding of how to structure deals. "*Unassuming, practical and effective*" **Julian Long** (see p.241) is respected for his work with Marconi, having advised on its UK and US listings and the demerger of its defence interests. **James Davis** (see p.235) impresses clients through his ability to "*smoothly co-ordinate and lead*" transactions. He advised Compass Group on the £3.26 billion sale of the Forte hotel estate, which involved negotiations for each of the brands (such as Posthouse and Meridien) and drew upon advice from the real estate team based in Paris. The firm has a healthy track record in the media and telecoms sectors, the latter including both carriers and hardware. Its efforts here and in the utilities sector are spearheaded by "*thorough*" **Simon Marchant** (see p.242). He has secured a new client in DSP, the US-Israeli chip manufacturer, after advising on the merger between Parthus Technologies and Ceva, a subsidiary of the DSP group. **Graham Nicholson** (see p.243) has acted for the London Stock Exchange in the £390 million bid to acquire the London International Financial Futures and Options Exchange (LIFFE), and has been advising Prudential on its £17.4 billion offer for American General. A further key highlight for the firm this year is its advice to Tempus Group on its acquisition by WPP Group: a £435 million public takeover forced to complete by a UK Takeover Panel ruling in Tempus' favour, following WPP's attempt to pull out after the material adverse change brought on by the events of September 11th. **Clients** Air Liquide; Bass; BT; Compass Group; Hewlett-Packard; ICI; Marconi; P&O; Powergen; Prudential; Rolls-Royce; Telewest; mmO2; Royal Bank of Scotland; JPMorgan Chase; CSFB; Société Générale; UBS Warburg; SSSB; Nomura; Deutsche Bank.

LINKLATERS (see firm details p.1043) Widely commended as a "*fantastically polished outfit,*" it continues to display expertise across the board. The team handles high-profile cross-border public M&A as well as a substantial volume of domestic work, restructurings and private M&A in an array of sectors from telecoms and technology to utilities, pharmaceuticals, rail and insurance. Despite the downturn, the team has been visible on a number of impressive high-value deals, and regularly sits at the top of European transactional deal surveys. It has this year advised Billiton on its merger with BHP, the Halifax Group on its merger with Bank of Scotland and DB Investments on its merger with De Beers. The firm's acclaimed mining strength was demonstrated by its recent advice on the BHP/Billiton merger, with the group also involved in pioneering work relating to the use of DLC structures.

Clients agree that the team is equally proficient when acting as the driving force behind a deal, as when called upon as an adjunct to a large in-house team; "*they pitch the advice just right, opting for a good working relationship over egos.*" Rivals pointed to the firm's success in creating a "*balanced corporate and financing strength*" and this is perceived to have bolstered its already buoyant core of investment banking clients. Recent transactions have included acting for Dresdner Kleinwort Wasserstein (DrKW) on the recommended offer by Dow for Ascot, and the disposal by Ascot of property companies to an MBO team. Although observers believe that Anthony Cann's commitments as senior partner keep him away from the transactional front line, clients report that his guidance is most valuable: "*affable, modest and extremely able, he makes deals happen.*"

Clients repeatedly commented on the team's "*extraordinarily talented lawyers*" and the "*high level of co-operation and dedication*" on offer. The "*undisputed star*" remains **David Cheyne** (see p.234). Recognised by peers for his "*unparalleled knowledge of the law*" as well as his "*direct and commercial style,*" he is commended by clients as a "*whole business advisor, not just there for the battles.*" He recently advised Anglo American on the proposed £12.8 billion privatisation of De Beers by DB Investments (the consortium formed by Anglo American, Central Holdings and Debswana). He also represented Network

CORPORATE FINANCE ■ LONDON

Rail (formerly CLG) on its £6.9 billion acquisition of all shares in Railtrack. Researchers found that **Matthew Middleditch**'s (see p.243) profile is continuing to soar. Described by peers as "*agreeable, straightforward, unassuming and clear,*" he recently advised DrKW on the public tender offer by UniCredito Italiano and Allianz for 55% of the issued share capital of Zagrebacka Banka (431 million). He was also present on the recommended acquisition by Lafarge of Blue Circle Industries for £3.1 billion, and acted for Scottish & Newcastle on its £1.2 billion takeover of the Finnish drinks company Oyj Hartwall Abp. **Andrew Peck** (see p.244) is prime choice for "*innovative solutions*" in highly regulated industries; he "*combines practicality with a deep understanding of the technicalities*" and remains "*fair-minded*" in his approach. He has acted on the merger of Halifax Group and the Bank of Scotland for £28 billion.

"*An intellectual giant with a creative mind,*" **Richard Godden** (see p.238) advised CSFB on the recommended takeover offer for Sema by Schlumberger (value £3.6 billion). A details man, he continues to hold a loyal client roster packed with leading institutional names. "*Extremely courteous*" **Tim Clarke** (see p.235) takes the lead in both domestic and international privatisations. "*Utterly professional and incredibly knowledgeable about the rail industry,*" **John Ellard** (see p.801) is also known for his privatisation expertise. **Michael Sullivan** (see p.247)'s experience covers M&A and equity offerings. He advised on DB Investments' proposed privatisation of De Beers alongside Cheyne, and has acted for BP on its £260.9 million acquisition of an additional 15% stake in OAO SIDANCO, the Russian-based oil and gas company. **Peter King** (see p.240) received plaudits for his "*keen intellect*" and "*good commercial approach.*" Often commended for his track record in equities issues, he has advised the underwriters Merrill Lynch, Deutsche Bank, Morgan Stanley and SSSB on the proposed flotation of Punch Taverns.

New to *Chambers*' ranking this year, **Charlie Jacobs** (see p.239) has been described as a "*superb lawyer with considerable elan.*" He has achieved widespread recognition for his work on Billiton's DLC merger with BHP, and also advised Innogy, the UK's largest electricity supplier, on its acquisition by RWE, by way of a £3.1 billion cash offer.

Although the firm's expansion in Europe has not met with unilateral success, it has a presence on the ground across the Continent, prompting a cohesive team approach to transactions. Examples include the takeover by EDS of Systematics, under German law, involving teams in Germany and Belgium, and the acquisition by Lafarge of Blue Circle, drawing on its French, English, US and German law capabilities. **Clients** AXA; SRA; BT; Six Continents; Vodafone Group; Dixons; Innogy; Capio; CSFB; DrKW; SSSB; Merrill Lynch; HSBC.

SLAUGHTER AND MAY (see firm details p.1140) The "*thoroughbred*" team continues to flourish, winning clients and impressing competitors with its "*lean, responsive teams, which deliver succinct advice,*" and its unflagging visibility on headline transactions. Considered to have a "*broader spread of knowledge and experience throughout the ranks*" than many competitors, clients feel confident that they can rely upon any team member put before them: "*you know before they come to a deal that they have seen and solved every possible angle in every variety of transaction.*" The group is also felt to have developed its own distinctive "*pugilistic*" style, where "*big-name partners roll their sleeves up and perform with no trace of ego.*" Though it continues to be best known for its advice to leading corporates on high-value domestic deals, the firm's links with some of the most prestigious European firms in key financial centres mean that it is at little disadvantage on cross-border deals. The team recently co-advised Aceralia Corporación Siderúrgica, Arbed and Usinor in conjunction with Elvinger, Hoss & Prüssen (Luxembourg), Cuatrecasas (Spain) and Bredin Prat (France) on their three-way merger. Strong ties also exist with Hengeler Mueller in Germany and both Davis Polk & Wardwell and Cravath, Swaine & Moore in the US.

Resident corporate guru **Nigel Boardman** (see p.233) retains his star status. "*Easy to get on with and effective in everything he does,*" claim peers, while clients value his "*broad vision*" and "*clarity of thought - he knows how to make a deal work.*" He recently advised BHP on the DLC merger between BHP and Billiton, and has advised oil giant Shell on its £4.3 billion acquisition of Enterprise Oil. Boardman was also instructed by Orange in its listing in Paris and London through a global offer of shares. **Stephen Cooke** (see p.235) is felt to be growing in stature following his appointment as head of the M&A group, cementing his reputation as "*one of the finest technical lawyers in the City.*" His ease and charm have won him a raft of supporters, and he recently advised Diageo on its and Pernod Ricard's acquisition of Seagram's spirits and wine business for $8.15 billion. "*An authoritative presence and ferociously bright,*" **William Underhill** (see p.248) is joint head of the firm's e-commerce and TMT groups. He recently advised American General on the agreement between American General and Prudential on terms of a merger (£18.1 billion). One of the firm's most prolific stars, he also advised Blue Circle Industries on its recommended acquisition by Lafarge, and assisted Goldman Sachs and UBS Warburg in Vodafone's share issue to the value of £3 billion.

Martin Hattrell (see p.239) remains a popular choice, lauded for his "*awareness of issues that extends far beyond the corporate finance department.*" He advised Wittington Investments on the take private of Fortnum & Mason, and represented D. Carnegie & Co in its disposal by Singer & Friedlander. M&A expert **Charles Randell** (see p.245) approaches transactions with a "*calm and confident manner.*" He specialises in energy-related matters, and has advised E.ON on its proposed recommended pre-conditional cash offer for Powergen. Alongside Fried, Frank, Harris, Shriver & Jacobson, he advised Invensys on its sale of its Invensys Flow Control Business to Flowserve for $535 million. Senior partner **Tim Clark** (see p.235) has a "*razor-sharp intellect,*" which he brings to bear in both M&A and flotation work, although his management commitments lead him to be less visible in the marketplace. Described by clients as an "*extremely clever chap,*" **Glen James** (see p.475)' experience covers M&A and corporate restructurings, especially within the insurance sector. He advised Old Mutual in the release of lock-up arrangements it had entered into with St. Paul, allowing the placing of its ordinary shares, and provided corporate advice to CGNU on the issue of a subordinate bond worth £1.2 billion.

Rivals envy **Robert Stern** (see p.247) his "*wide client base,*" and, though undoubtedly skilled in M&A, he is commended for his work in equity and debt offerings. He advised the underwriters (Investec Henderson Crosthwaite and DrKW) on the placing and open offer of health club operator, Fitness First, and has advised Thames Water Utilities Finance on the issuance of a series of £175 million index-linked guaranteed notes. "*Constructive and technically spot on*" **Frances Murphy** (see p.243) acted with **Jeff Twentyman** (see p.248) in advice to Abbott Laboratories in its £164.7 million acquisition of the cardiovascular stent business of Biocompatibles International. Twentyman's reputation continues to soar (he advised on the Lafarge/Blue Circle transaction with Underhill), and many interviewees were won over by his "*extremely sound judgement and thoroughly charming manner.*" That is not to say he cannot "*turn up the heat*" when circumstances dictate. He advised STAR Capital Partners in its acquisition of two UK gas distribution affiliates of TotalFinaElf Midstream by way of a SPV called Inexus. These instructions form a significant new client gain for the firm's private equity ambitions. Peers described M&A and equity offerings expert **Andy Ryde** (see p.245) as a "*cracking lawyer*" who typifies the "*entirely reasonable face of Slaughters.*" He is leading the team advising Corus Group on its proposed £3 billion merger with Brazilian steel producer Companhia Siderúrgica Nacional (CSN). **Nilufer von Bismarck** (see p.248) and **David Johnson** (see p.240) both received substantial peer approval as "*promising young lawyers.*" Johnson has this year handled advice to Punch Tavern on its aborted flotation, and continues to enjoy a strong relationship with GlaxoSmithKline. **Clients** Diageo; Blue Circle; BHP Billiton; E.ON; American General; Orange; Enskilda Securities; Old Mutual; Emap; Carlton Communications; Goldman Sachs; SSSB; UBS Warburg; Cazenove; DrKW.

LONDON ■ CORPORATE FINANCE

ALLEN & OVERY (see firm details p.841) All observers agreed that the "*steady and sensible*" team has enjoyed a successful year with visibility on an enviable volume of complex transactions. An array of "*real stars,*" particularly at partner level, should not distract from the team's "*deep pool of talented youngsters,*" which has developed over recent years. Having "*ridden the steepest of learning curves,*" the team is gradually overcoming its traditional characterisation as "*a corporate offering built out of a finance firm.*" An expansive corporate client base bears testament to this fact. Recent highlights include advising Cable & Wireless on its £3.9 billion disposal of Cable & Wireless Optus, and acting for BT on its £2.14 billion sale of the Yell group. Naturally, the firm maintains its powerful investment banking relationships, and it acts as corporate advisor to 23 of the Global 100 companies and 62 of the Fortune 500. It is often to be seen advising on cross-border transactions, such as advising Seagram on the $8.15 billion disposal of its worldwide wine and spirits business to Pernod Ricard and Diageo. The group also fields a substantial US team from at home and in Germany, while the New York office has a budding securities team.

Now senior partner and less visible on the front line, Guy Beringer's reputation continues to precede him. He remains a valuable store of market knowledge and tactical skill. The headline figure here is undoubtedly **Alan Paul** (see p.244), who has carved out a niche for UK and international public bids. Clients appreciate that he is "*extremely easy on the ear when explaining complicated issues.*" He recently advised AEP and Xcel Energy on the £1.84 billion sale of Yorkshire Power Group. Paul is also head of the private equity group. Advisor to a loyal core of FTSE 100 clients, **David Wootton**'s (see p.249) expertise incorporates M&A, JVs and equity capital markets. Deemed a "*heavyweight player*" blessed with a keen eye for the smooth passage of a transaction, he recently advised Smiths Group on the £940 million demerger of its automotive systems division. M&A specialist **Mark Wippell** (see p.249) has built up solid relationships with a range of financial institution clients, and is respected as advisor to US companies targeting European entities. Head of corporate, the "*intellectually agile*" **Richard Cranfield** (see p.235) has gained recognition for his "*interesting combination of capital markets and corporate knowledge,*" as well as his role as "*client gatherer and minder.*" He recently advised Cazenove and Merrill Lynch on BT's £5.9 billion rights issue. **Alison Beardsley** (see p.233) enters *Chambers*' tables this year, following extensive recommendations from both peers and clients as an "*effective lawyer and delightful to deal with.*" She recently advised The William Pears Group on its £2.2 billion joint venture with Land Securities Trillium. Media, telecoms and IT continue to be key strands to this practice, particularly in the light of its ties of a transatlantic transaction, it advised SunGard Data Systems, a US software provider, on its £167 million acquisition of UK-based Guardian iT. It represented the sponsors on the £7.5 billion demerger of mm02 from BT, and has advised communication services group WPP on its contested £454 million takeover bid for Tempus, also advising on material adverse change issues following the events of September 11th. Also involving a contested bid, the firm has represented a £700 million hostile bid for airport operator TBI. **Clients** Alliance & Leicester; BAE Systems; BT; Cable & Wireless; Coral; Emap; Ericsson; Heineken; ICI; KLM; Montedison; Nestlé; Pfizer; SAP; Royal & SunAlliance; Sage Group; TNT; UPC; Virgin Group; Seagram; Shell International; Six Continents.

CLIFFORD CHANCE (see firm details p.911) A triumphant year for the "*substantial and consistently reliable*" team, which is seen to have done deals at a "*rattling pace.*" Though often eclipsed by the firm's high-profile financial institutions and private equity relationships, the corporate client base is undoubtedly strong, and the team has succeeded in capturing a healthy share of what have proven to be thinly scattered public company deals. In the private equity field, the firm has acted for Candover in the CHF580 million MBO of Swissport International from bankrupt carrier Swissair, in a transaction that drew upon offices in the US, Luxembourg, Germany, France and the Netherlands. Instructing clients point to the group's "*long-standing knowledge of a wide number of sectors and a seemingly endless depth of resources.*" This global corporate practice now comprises some 160 partners, with 45 based in London. Its US offering has scored well in recent US M&A tables, and looks set to attract technology clients on the West Coast with its recent recruitment of former Brobeck, Phleger & Harrison securities partners. European and international cross-border transactions remain at the forefront of this firm's sights. In addition to the firm's powerful network, clients admit to benefiting from "*competitive prices*" and an "*impressively broad technical expertise,*" with many commenting on the team's "*deep understanding of drafting nuances.*"

"*Extremely personable*" **Adam Signy** (see p.246) reels in the clients; he has a constructive negotiating style and attracts commendation for his "*clear and regular communications.*" A private equity and M&A specialist, he recently

Top Ten M&A Deals involving a UK Company (Jan 1st – Jul 17th 2002)

	Target Name	Lawyers to Target	Bidder Name	Lawyers to Bidder	Value (US$m)
1	Lattice Group Plc	Linklaters, Shearman & Sterling	National Grid Group Plc	Lattice Group Plc, CMS Cameron McKenna, LeBoeuf, Lamb, Greene & MacRae	18,140.371
2	Railtrack Plc (in receivership)	Ashurst Morris Crisp, Slaughter and May, Simmons & Simmons	Network Rail Ltd	Linklaters	11,590.666
3	Innogy Holdings Plc	Linklaters	RWE AG	Cravath, Swaine & Moore, Allen & Overy, Hengeler Mueller	7,374.519
4	Enterprise Oil Plc	Herbert Smith, Davis, Polk & Wardwell	Royal Dutch/Shell Group,	Slaughter and May, Cravath, Swaine & Moore, Allens Arthur Robinson	6,199.328
5	Miller Brewing Co	Clifford Chance, Wachtell, Lipton, Rosen & Katz, Webber Wentzel Bowens	South African Breweries Plc	Lovells, Cleary, Gottlieb, Steen & Hamilton	5,527.670
6	Reemtsma Cigarettenfabriken GmbH (90.01%)	Slaughter and May Hengeler Mueller	Imperial Tobacco Group Plc	Weil, Gotshal & Manges, Allen & Overy, Ashurst Morris Crisp	4,577.416
7	Castorama Dubois Investissements SCA (45%)	Ginestié Paley-Vincent & Associés	Kingfisher Plc	Freshfields Bruckhaus Deringer	4,294.573
8	Southern Water Plc	Clifford Chance	Vivendi Universal	Simmons & Simmons	3,010.279
9	Southern Water Plc	Freshfields Bruckhaus Deringer	First Aqua Ltd (IBO)	Clifford Chance	2,927.735
10	The Unique Pub Company Plc, Voyager Pub Group Ltd	Clifford Chance, Macfarlanes	Investor Group	Allen & Overy, CMS Cameron McKenna, Ashurst Morris Crisp, Davis, Polk & Wardwell	2,865.888

Source: Dealogic

Excludes withdrawn deals, share buy-backs; deal value includes debt; target or bidder nationality is UK

CORPORATE FINANCE ■ LONDON

co-advised the Yell management team on the £2.2 billion sale of Yell to a consortium of private equity firms. "*Thorough, detailed and on occasion cautious,*" **David Pearson**'s (see p.244) broad experience covers private equity, flotations and secondary issues, as well as M&A. He recently advised Guy Hands and Terra Firma Capital Partners on the acquisition of the £2 billion investment portfolio of Nomura's Principal Finance Group by a newly formed limited partnership. The firm has also advised Merrill Lynch, Bank of Scotland and Rodinheights (the bidder) on the €1.8 billion public-to-private takeover offer for Green Property, the Irish property investment company, in one of the largest European public to privates in 2002. Head of corporate **David Childs** (see p.235) continues to inspire confidence with what clients describe as his "*proactive, technical and available*" approach. He co-advised Barclays Bank on the merger of its Caribbean banking interests with those of CIBC to create First-Caribbean International Bank. He also acted alongside projects partners in London and M&A partners in New York in advice to Missouri-based Aquila on the $264 million acquisition of an ownership interest in the holding company of Midlands Electricity. A recent secondee to The Takeover Panel, **Guy Norman** (see p.243) co-advised the London futures and options exchange on its sale. He remains best known for his key ties to investment banks. **Jonathan Beastall** (see p.233) has made a splash advising GKN on the demerger of its support services activities and their combination with Brambles, in a DLC structure encompassing 25 jurisdictions. "*Clear, efficient and to the point*" **Kate Howles** (see p.239) enters the rankings this year following considerable market endorsement. She is one of a raft of younger Clifford Chance partners starting to carve a name for themselves in this field; she has strong ties to key client EADS. In the consumer goods sector, the firm has advised Philip Morris on the $5.6 billion merger of Miller Brewing with South African Breweries; the firm's client holds a 36% interest in the new SABMiller group. Property also remains a core strength; the firm advised Thistle Hotels on its £600 million sale of 37 hotel businesses to a subsidiary of Euro & UK Property Ltd, a private venture capital company. **Clients** Accenture; Arcadia; Carrefour; Coca-Cola; CSFB; CVC Capital Partners; EADS; France Telecom; Goldman Sachs; Intel; Merrill Lynch; Morgan Stanley; Philip Morris; Siemens; Volvo; UBS Warburg.

HERBERT SMITH (see firm details p.992) "*Flavour of the month,*" the corporate team here is currently the name on everybody's lips, its profile having rocketed following involvement on a steady stream of "*complex one-off deals*." One client acknowledged that over the years the group has "*changed out of all recognition, but I'd hesitate from placing it in the top tier just yet.*" The team has expertise in many sectors, with dedicated specialists covering media, pharmaceuticals and e-commerce, as well as insurance/financial institutions and energy. The firm has been particularly occupied in the latter two fields, having recently advised Bank of Scotland on its merger with Halifax, and Northern Electric on its asset swap with Innogy. Peers admit to being impressed by the firm's "*edge and focus,*" while clients maintain that the team is "*bright and diligent.*" Yet to follow the European merger charge of its rivals, the firm maintains its respected Paris offering alongside its exclusive alliance with Germany's Gleiss Lutz and Benelux firm Stibbe. Although the retirement of Marian Pell is seen as a blow for the firm's prominence in the insurance sector, the corporate team retains a number of stars boasting a broad base of knowledge. "*Pleasant to deal with*" **Anthony Macaulay** (see p.242) recently led the team advising Carnival on its £3.2 billion takeover offer for P&O Princess Cruises. He also advised The Takeover Panel's Executive on WPP's invoking of the material adverse change condition to lapse its bid for Tempus. An "*outstanding negotiator,*" **James Palmer** (see p.243) has impressed clients with his drafting of complex agreements and his project management skills. He advised Interactive Investor in its recommended takeover by AMP, the Australian financial services group. He was also part of the team advising Time on its £1.15 billion acquisition of IPC Media. **Stephen Barnard** (see p.232) has built up a loyal following amongst the professional partnerships community, and he enjoys a powerful reputation for his work with investment banks. Senior partner **Richard Bond** (see p.341) is less visible at the front line, focusing instead on management duties, although he remains a valuable resource, attracting clients, being as he is "*a great starting point if you want to construct the right team.*" Head of department **Caroline Goodall** (see p.238) advises on a wide range of corporate work, including M&A and corporate governance issues. "*Dynamic*" **Tim Bellis** (see p.233) is widely tipped as a "*star in the making;*" he is thought to typify the firm's entrepreneurial spirit and the commitment encouraged during a transaction. Further highlights for the team include advising De Beers on the $19.6 billion takeover by DB Investments, and assisting Bank of Scotland on the purchase of the motor finance business of Rover Financial Services for £330 million. **Clients** GE Capital; Northernf Scotland; Securicor; Interactive Investor; Petrobras; BAT; BAA; BT; Bradford & Bingley; Chevron; Eurotunnel; Freeserve; Stagecoach; Time Warner; Lazard; Merrill Lynch; PwC; Publicis; Zurich Financial Services.

ASHURST MORRIS CRISP (see firm details p.852) The team has steadfastly held its ground with sustained involvement on a large range of deals, and performed well in the year's global M&A deal tables. Observers singled out the firm for its user-friendly style, where transactions are completed with "*good humour*" and a "*strong technical expertise*" is consistently on hand to ensure the smooth running of deals. Clients appreciate the group's "*constructive approach,*" which they feel is "*engineered to get things done, rather than point score.*" A thriving Paris office belies competitor claims of a greater domestic focus here; the Paris team has this year been involved in the £740 million LBO of Vivendi's publishing interests. Budding teams can also be found in Frankfurt, Munich, Milan and Madrid, although they have yet to reach the high standards attained in the French market. Alongside big-ticket M&A sits a powerful profile in private equity and investment. The key client here is Cinven, and the group has advised the private equity house on the proposed £2 billion acquisition of Nomura's Unique and Voyager UK pub estates. Charlie Geffen and the team also advised 3i and the Go Fly management team on its acquisition by easyJet. A burgeoning capital markets team has afforded a growing presence in the investment community, although much of the big-ticket M&A is derived from its enviable corporate client roster.

Chris Ashworth (see p.232) is distinguished in the market by his frequent appearance on complex large-value acquisitions. He recently co-advised Alfred McAlpine on the proposed £461 million disposal of McAlpine Homes to George Wimpey. He also represented Railtrack in the £6.9 billion acquisition of all its shares by Network Rail (formerly CLG), which also involved the bridge financing to refinance Railtrack's debt. "*Measured, efficient and highly skilful*" **Adrian Clark** (see p.235) achieves recognition as a "*legal intellect.*" Rated in particular for his listed company work, he advised SSSB as one of the financial advisors to Schlumberger Investments on its recommended cash offer for Sema. Clark also acted for Johnston Press in its proposed acquisition of Regional Independent Media Holdings for £560 million together with an associated £220 million rights issue. The firm continues to advise key client Royal & SunAlliance, most recently acting on the £133 million cash disposal of its Isle of Man-based life assurance operation to Friends Provident. The firm has also advised Taylor & Francis Group on its proposed £300 million bid for Blackwell Publishing. **Clients** Debswana Diamond Company; SSSB; Danisco; Finmeccanica; AMS; Continental Holdings; eircom ESOP Trustee; Imperial Tobacco Group; BT; ABN AMRO Corporate Finance; National Express; Dewhirst Group; Go Fly; British Midland.

LOVELLS (see firm details p.1045) 18 offices in Europe, three in the US and five in Asia are a testament to the global ambitions of this firm. Mergers on the Continent - France, the Netherlands and German in particular - have ensured that the firm is a prime choice for cross-border transactions. The corporate groups in Germany and London have recently won the mandate from Corus to act on the £900 million disposal

LONDON ■ CORPORATE FINANCE

of its aluminium business. It is, perhaps then, its success in channelling resources overseas that has led some peers to opine that the London offering has had a lower profile. Nevertheless, the team continues to handle a substantial volume of work for its high-quality financial institution clients, consolidating its relationships with the likes of UBS Warburg and Merrill Lynch, which it advised on the hostile takeover bid by Carnival for P&O Princess Cruises. It has also advised JPMorgan Chase on the Billiton/BHP merger. Insurance remains a clear forte of the practice; it has recently advised The Equitable Life Assurance Society on the sale of its subsidiary Permanent Insurance Company to Liverpool Victoria for £150 million. **John Davidson** (see p.473) has impressed the market with his knowledge of the equity capital markets and M&A: he was commended to researchers as one of the area's "*heavyweights.*" He recently advised US corporate SEQUENOM on its share-for-share merger with Gemini Genomics ($238 million). He also led the team advising LSE-listed South African Breweries on its £3.84 billion acquisition of US-based Miller Brewing Company, in a transaction that saw Lovells supply lawyers from ten of its offices. **Clients** Granada; Exxon; Barclays; Lazard; TI Automotive.

MACFARLANES (see firm details p.1047) The firm continues to gain ground. Researchers were impressed by the growing respect afforded to it by enthusiastic competitors and clients, and by the team's constant high quality of service. A different stamp of firm when compared to many in this list, the relatively small team is felt to attract "*quality, rather than quantity,*" with M&A and private equity seen as pillars of the practice. Clients praised in particular its "*consistency,*" though due to its focused approach, commentators noted a "*lack of breadth*" compared with other more sectorally focused City rivals. A distinctly Slaughter and May approach to the question of expansion overseas is adopted here, although peers continue to commend its presence on "*fantastic international deals.*" Among the firm's many "*able performers*," **Robert Sutton** ("*a great deals man*") and "*incredibly bright*" **Mary Leth** were described as "*a class act.*" Senior partner Sutton co-led the team advising Pernod Ricard on its £5.5 billion acquisition of the wine and spirits business of Seagram. He and Leth advised Gleacher & Co as a financial advisor to Bank of Scotland in the £28 billion Bank of Scotland/Halifax merger. Although better known for his expertise in private equity transactions, **Charles Martin** also received widespread market endorsement for a broader scope. He recently led the team advising Register.com on its offer for Virtual Internet, and acted for the Candover-led consortium on the sale of Regional Independent Media to Johnston Press. Other highlights for the team include advising JPMorgan and Merrill Lynch as financial advisors to Lloyds TSB Group on its £19.8 billion offer for Abbey National. Also in the financial services sector, the team advised Legal & General in its disposal of Legal & General Bank and Legal & General Mortgage Services to Northern Rock (value £131 million). It also advised Cazenove as sponsor and financial advisor to Autologic Holdings on its acquisition of 40% of GAL for £366 million, funded through a rights issue. **Clients** Carlton Communications; Kingfisher; Omnicom; Cordiant Communications; Pernod Ricard; JPMorgan; Merrill Lynch; Kingspan Group.

NORTON ROSE (see firm details p.1084) "*Great to work with,*" a "*highly commercial and friendly team*" claim instructing clients, who appreciate the firm "*understands the right gearing of a deal, and, most importantly, the chemistry of individuals that make it work.*" Competitors point to a "*good combination of corporate and finance prowess*" that has ensured it a balanced base of experience. Investment banking relationships with HSBC, Lehman Brothers and WestLB are thought to generate a healthy deal flow, although the market is awaiting the impact caused by the loss of key LBO/acquisition finance partners to Allen & Overy. Often to be found on "*the complex end of M&A*" transactions across a range of sectors, it is in the fields of insurance, financial services, transport and telecoms that the team stands out. Home to a number of well-known figures in the corporate sphere, some sources perceived that the quiet market has not afforded the limelight to its more junior, but equally competent, members.

Spearheading the team, **Barbara Stephenson** (see p.247) "*has bags of personality - bright and quick.*" Able to "*control deals well,*" she recently led the team advising Taylor Woodrow in its £525 million hostile bid for Bryant Group. "*Pleasant and professional*" **Simon Sackman** (see p.245) "*does a good job in making deals run smoothly,*" although his duties as senior partner have resulted in a reduced transactional visibility. One client believed that he was a "*businessman masquerading as a lawyer,*" such is his commerciality. He advised Benchmark Group in the transfer of its entire interest in the Jersey limited partnership Benchmark. Clients endorsed **Chris Pearson** (see p.244) as a "*down-to-earth, practical lawyer, utterly flexible and responsive to our needs.*" He advised Siemens on the UK aspects of its acquisition from Mannesmann of a controlling stake in Atecs Mannesmann, the holding company of the engineering and automotive business, and acted on its subsequent reorganisation. "*A bright chap with a smashing institutional practice,*" **Jonathan Coppin** (see p.235) co-led the team advising Eni on the £2.7 billion recommended cash offer by Lazard and JPMorgan on behalf of Agip Investments for Lasmo. Despite its merger with parts of German firm Gaedertz, the firm's pan-European expansion has not had the profile of some of its rivals. It has scored some success in its efforts to promote the US securities group based in London, which has recently advised HSBC USA on the Nasdaq listing of shares and ADS of Randgold Resources. The team also assisted on the Eni transaction and assisted the corporate group in its advice to SSSB on Eureko's public offer for the share capital in Interamerican Hellenic Life Assurance, one of the largest public company takeovers in Greece. In the insurance sector, the firm advised Friends Provident on its acquisition of the Isle of Man-based life assurance operation of Royal & SunAlliance (£133 million). **Clients** Bank of Scotland; Barclays Bank; BMW; Carlsberg; Harvey Nichols; ING Bank; easyJet; JPMorgan; P&O; SSSB; United Airlines.

SIMMONS & SIMMONS (see firm details p.1136) Although some observers believe that this is "*a fine firm, currently lacking a strong identity,*" there is a consensus among interviewees that it has been a year of consolidation. The first half of 2002 saw the firm engaged in ultimately futile merger talks with Watson, Farley & Williams, a proposed move that had more synergy in the banking sphere than corporate finance. A "*highly motivated*" corporate team has concentrated on "*revamping*" its department, placing the international stage firmly at the head of the agenda. The firm continues to expand its international reach and has recently established offices in Tokyo and Düsseldorf, as well as merging in Rotterdam with Nolst Trenité. The corporate practice now comprises a network of 15 offices, and is making inroads into the investment banking markets, while large mandates (such as from key client Interbrew) ensure it a respectable presence. Over 30% of the Fortune Global 500 are active clients and new client wins include Duke Street Capital, Deutsche Bank and YUKOS Oil. Energy, technology, financial services, rail and biotech are all sectors of expertise. It has recently secured instruction from Vivendi Environnement on its acquisition of Southern Water from First Aqua Holdings in a transaction valued at £2.05 billion. The private equity arena has seen the group benefit from its relationship with Hawkpoint to advise on the £448 million creation of Wellington Re, a reinsurance operator.

Although the group's raft of talented younger partners remains low profile, sources were quick to recommend the group head of corporate finance, **Stuart Evans** (see p.236). A "*thoroughly personable lawyer,*" he has impressed with *his "astonishing breadth of skills used on a complicated deal.*" The team recently advised Interbrew on the £1.2 billion sale of Carling Brewers to Adolph Coors Company, which included pre-sale reorganisation, during which the retained businesses were separated. It advised Gallaher Group on its acquisition for £469 million of the 41.13% stake held by the Austrian Government in Austria Tabak, a transaction supported by offices in Paris and Tokyo. Involving its lawyers in New York, the firm advised the shareholders

207

CORPORATE FINANCE ■ LONDON

of Geneva Technology on the $692 million merger with Ohio-based Convergys. **Clients** Gallaher Group; CDC Capital Partners; Interbrew; Prudential Insurance; Cadbury Schweppes; Telegraph Group; WorldCom; KPMG Corporate Finance.

OTHER NOTABLE PRACTITIONERS Michael Hatchard (see p.239) of Skadden, Arps, Slate, Meagher & Flom is respected for his involvement in "*heavyweight deals with a US element.*" He has advised Azurix on the £1.24 billion sale of Wessex Water to YTL Utilities. Clients commended **William Charnley** (see p.234) of McDermott, Will & Emery as a "*true business lawyer,*" singling out his ability to "*cut through the morass of detail.*"

LONDON — MEDIUM DEALS

CORPORATE FINANCE: MEDIUM DEALS ■ LONDON

1. **CMS Cameron McKenna**
   Travers Smith Braithwaite
2. **Gouldens**
   Mayer, Brown, Rowe & Maw
   SJ Berwin
   Weil, Gotshal & Manges
3. **Baker & McKenzie**
   Denton Wilde Sapte
4. **Berwin Leighton Paisner**
   Hammond Suddards Edge
   Taylor Wessing
   Theodore Goddard
5. **Dechert**
   DLA
   Eversheds
   Nabarro Nathanson
   Olswang
   Osborne Clarke
   Pinsent Curtis Biddle

LEADING INDIVIDUALS

1. BELL Christopher Travers Smith Braithwaite
   FRANCIES Michael Weil, Gotshal & Manges
   SUMMERFIELD Spencer Travers Smith Braithwaite
2. BARNES Oliver Travers Smith Braithwaite
   BENNETT John Berwin Leighton Paisner
   BIRT Tim Osborne Clarke
   BURROW Robert SJ Berwin
   CHESTER Martin Theodore Goddard
   MAHER Paul Mayer, Brown, Rowe & Maw
   STELLA Keith Berwin Leighton Paisner
   WATSON Sean CMS Cameron McKenna
3. BOTT Adrian Osborne Clarke
   CARMEDY Russell Gouldens
   LEVY Graeme Olswang
   MORGAN Simon Olswang
   STEDMAN Graham Theodore Goddard
   STEINFELD Michael Dechert
   THORNEYCROFT Max Gouldens
   WAYTE Peter DLA
4. BATES Stephanie Mayer, Brown, Rowe & Maw
   GEE Tim Baker & McKenzie
   HAMILL Robert Hammond Suddards Edge
   NEWMAN Iain Nabarro Nathanson
   ROSENBERG Daniel Taylor Wessing
   WINTER Hilary Gouldens

This book is the product of 6,582 1/2 hour interviews. See p.7 for BMRB audit. Within each band, firms are listed alphabetically. See individuals' profiles p.232

CMS CAMERON MCKENNA (see firm details p.914) This sizeable, "*straightforward and efficient*" team, with **Sean Watson** (see p.249) at its helm, was commended for its clear focus on the international corporate market. It attracts medium- to large-sized deals from a host of corporate clients, who value the group's "*all-round knowledge and dependability*" and told researchers that it is "*at times excellent*" in advising on both the technical complexities of a transaction and the big picture issues. Rivals appreciate its "*commercial, co-operative and sensible*" approach and highlighted its specialist sector expertise: the team scores well with high-profile activity within the energy and utilities sectors and on matters relating to construction, hotels and leisure, hi-tech and the emerging biotech markets. In line with conditions, the firm has been less active in IPOs, but continues to be involved in open offers and the secondary markets. Best known for its work with corporates, the firm is also building a following among banking institutions; it has recently advised Investec and ABN AMRO on corporate finance matters. On the international front, the firm has added M&A teams in France and Italy to the CMS network. Further recent highlights for the team include acting for Nomura International on its successful acquisition of the Le Méridien Hotel chain for £1.9 billion, and advising The Wellcome Trust in connection with the sale of 100 million shares in GlaxoSmithKline (transaction value £1.8 billion). Renowned for its utilities expertise, the team was instructed by National Grid Group on the acquisition of the US electricity and gas utility, Niagara Mohawk Holdings. **Clients** BAE Systems; Billiton; BP; Consignia; Energis; HSBC; Nestlé UK; Sara Lee UK Holdings.

TRAVERS SMITH BRAITHWAITE (see firm details p.1166) The "*rock solid*" team continues to handle high-calibre M&A including an array of public takeovers, and equity offerings. It is characterised by competitors as a "*high-quality firm that hasn't and doesn't want to reach the critical mass of the magic circle,*" but one that has successfully built up a "*great client base with able people at all levels.*" Easily pigeon-holed as a private equity firm, this tag belies an active client base, stretching across both domestic and cross-border transactions, which pulls on the firm's traditional corporate finance strength. Clearly one of the field's luminaries, senior partner **Christopher Bell** (see p.233) stands out in the market as a "*gifted lawyer and a true gent.*" He recently advised on the disposal of two trading divisions by FCX International for £86.7 million. **Spencer Summerfield**'s (see p.247) soaring reputation does not appear to have been affected by his close ties to troubled cable giant ntl. He was acclaimed to *Chambers* as a "*star*" and warmly commended for his "*constructive*" approach when at the deal table. He recently advised ntl on the sale of its broadcast division and the restructuring of its £12 billion debt. Clients appreciate that head of corporate **Oliver Barnes** (see p.232) is a "*straight-talker who gets things done.*" He recently advised on the public to private of Heal's, in a transaction worth £33.1 million. An established Paris office has generated a healthy flow of cross-border instructions and the firm has this year initiated a fledgling practice in Berlin. Although not the broadest of European offerings, the firm has proved itself capable of complex project management. Typical of this cohesive service is the instruction by Apax Partners on the €418.5 million buyout of the Italian fund management group Azimut from Bipop-Caire, in which the firm was responsible for lawyers in Italy, Luxembourg and the US. The TMT group has also continued to grow, with transactions handled for Pace Micro Technology, Channel 5 and London Bridge Software. **Clients** ntl; FCX International; Pace Micro Technology; Deloitte & Touche Corporate Finance.

GOULDENS (see firm details p.976) "*A force to be reckoned with,*" according to competitors, the group is achieving increasing renown as a "*small, highly focused and highly profitable*" outfit. It is comfortable advising both institutions and corporates; recent work includes public-to-private transactions, general M&A, IPOs and secondary placings. The mid-tier financial institutions focus has once again paid dividends, with the team receiving instructions from the likes of WestLB Panmure, Investec Henderson Crosthwaite and Teather & Greenwood. It advised the latter on the AIM flotation of LiDCO Group, a manufacturer of cardiac monitoring devices. The work here is often cross-border in nature; it has advised long-standing client Standard Bank London on its acquisition of Jardine Fleming Bank from JPMorgan Chase for £84 million. This was led by the "*ebullient*" **Russell Carmedy** (see p.234), who also recently advised new client Gyrus Group on the dual acquisition of the US Ear, Nose and Throat division of Smith & Nephew and cash tender offer for Somnus Medical Tech-

LONDON ■ CORPORATE FINANCE

nologies for a combined consideration of £103.8 million. Head of department **Max Thorneycroft** (see p.248) is admired by many observers for his "*natural, easy manner;*" he recently led the team advising on the public to private of Mid Kent Holdings for £106 million. Intellectual property, life sciences and hi-tech transactions are thriving at this firm, which is able to exert its cross-departmental clout. One of the group's younger partners who has a keen eye on this sector is the "*highly dependable*" **Hilary Winter** (see p.249). She recently advised Tissue Science Laboratories on a bridge finance facility and subsequent flotation on AIM, valued at £32.5 million. A respected property expertise has also seen the firm advising Delancey Estates on its take private by Tribeca UK for £264 million. Private equity is a growing focus at the firm and the charge is led by the highly respected Adam Greaves; *Chambers* also refers you to this section of the *Guide*. **Clients** Standard Bank London; Gyrus Group; Tissue Science Laboratories; WestLB Panmure; Delancey Estates; Investec Henderson Crosthwaite.

MAYER, BROWN, ROWE & MAW (see firm details p.1060) Described to *Chambers* as "*a collection of strong individuals with a flourishing practice,*" the team is widely predicted to be enjoying an enhanced deal flow following the firm's successful merger with US-based Mayer, Brown & Platt. The recent workload has encompassed a range of M&A, restructuring and JVs. Commentators pointed to the growth of the equities practice, which is underpinned by solid expertise across a broad spectrum of sectors, most notably in telecoms and pharmaceuticals. The group's client roster features a litany of impressive plcs, often drawn from the FTSE 250, and private equity firms. "*High-flyer*" **Paul Maher** (see p.242) recently advised AIM-listed telecoms company Zipcom on a fund-raising through two placings of 133,460,000 new shares, and acted for Marconi on its joint venture with Oxford GlycoSciences to form Confirmant. "*Enthusiastic corporate finance expert*" **Stephanie Bates** (see p.232) recently advised Syngenta on the sale of its sulcotrione herbicide Mikado to Bayer for $50 million. **Clients** AstraZeneca; Bayer; Cable & Wireless; Deutsche Telekom; Doughty Hanson; GE Power Systems; HMV; Kingfisher; Marconi; Novartis; Rhodia; Unilever.

SJ BERWIN (see firm details p.867) Powered by "*traditional M&A and private equity,*" the team is regularly seen on medium-sized acquisitions. Commentators attribute its sound performance to the group's attitude: "*fleet of foot and aggressive, they have the edge in a tough marketplace.*" At the helm, sought-after **Robert Burrow**'s (see p.234) "*feet rarely touch the ground.*" The AIM market has been a thriving arena for the firm, which derives a great advantage from the diversity of its client base. The property sector continues to be a lucrative source of instructions and the team has acted for its mainstay client British Land by advising BL Davidson (formed for the purpose by British Land) on its recommended cash offer for the shares in Asda Property Holdings, valued at £231.7 million. In a further highlight, the team advised Gullane Entertainment on its £45.4 million acquisition of the Guinness World Records business from Diageo. IPOs and share placings have been a source of work, and the team has been active on UK equity market deals; it advised The Future Network on its £33 million rights issue and acted for alphyra group, which is dual-listed on the London and Irish Stock Exchanges, on its €35 million placing and open offer. It also advised First Artist on its admission to AIM. Offices in France, Germany and Spain are a testament to the firm's commitment towards cross-border transactions, and it continues to have a renowned presence in the TMT and financial services sectors. **Clients** Gullane Entertainment; Diageo; The Future Network; Northern Ventures; First Artist.

WEIL, GOTSHAL & MANGES (see firm details p.1183) Recent staff movements within the firm do not seem to have ruffled the feathers of this "*ambitious*" corporate department, which offers an integrated US/UK law capability. Market sources agree that it maintains a strong profile for medium- to large-sized deals with a private equity flavour. The group offers US and UK expertise to an assortment of clients in sectors such as TMT, real estate, biotech and pharmaceuticals. Spearheading the group is **Mike Francies** (see p.237), head of the London office, who is said to "*work like a Trojan for his clients, utterly responsive;*" he wins many fans with his "*larger than life personality and astute intelligence.*" A TMT expert, Francies is renowned for his close relationship with private equity firm Hicks, Muse, Tate & Furst, which the team advised alongside Apax Partners on their £2.14 billion acquisition of Yell. The team subsequently advised Yell on its £414 million purchase of US publishing house McLeod USA phone directories unit in January 2002. Other highlights included advising Nikko Securities on the $800 million public-to-private acquisition of Powell Duffryn, and representing the management team and bidder on the public-to-private takeover bid for listed target, Burford Holdings. **Clients** Hicks, Muse, Tate & Furst; Apax Partners; Nikko Securities Co; Burford Holdings; GE Capital Global Consumer Finance; WestLB; The Derby Cycle Corporation; Dresdner Kleinwort Capital.

BAKER & MCKENZIE (see firm details p.855) A successful year for the rapidly evolving team, which was praised to researchers for its "*range of skills across the disciplines.*" Although smaller in size, the firm is likened in terms of approach to its larger City rivals. The team in London remains a key player on the international scene and the hub for European transactions, but is also seen to be handling increasing volumes of domestic work for UK corporates, such as safety product manufacturer Kidde. Possessed of "*user-friendly lawyers,*" interviewees commented on the strong team ethos, perhaps borne from the efforts dedicated to producing an integrated, cohesive international group. Head of global M&A **Tim Gee** (see p.237) specialises in domestic and cross-border M&A, equity capital markets and privatisations. He recently acted for Spherion on the £560 million IPO of shares of Michael Page International. He remains the most high-profile member of this respected team. The corporate group operates in three teams, whose focus is TMT, financial institutions and the energy, manufacturing and chemicals sectors. Key instructions for the firm include advising Sony on its JV with Telefonaktiebolaget LM Ericsson, to merge their mobile phone businesses worldwide, and advising Macquarie European Infrastructure on its €816 million acquisition of a 40% interest in Grupo Ferrovial's subsidiary. The firm also acted for Management Consulting Group on its placing and open offer and acquisition of Parson Group for $55 million. **Clients** Sony; BP Amoco; Calpine; Nortel Networks; Macquarie Infrastructure Group; Allianz Capital Partners; United Business Media; PepsiCo; Deutsche Bank; Compaq; CSFB; SSSB.

DENTON WILDE SAPTE (see firm details p.935) Peers applauded the firm's prowess in banking, TMT, energy and project financing, which has led to an increased concentration on cross-border transactions. This large team has a sector-focused approach and a substantial track record in cross-border complexities that has secured its appointment on a range of high-value deals. Head of the corporate department Philip Goodwin led the group that advised key client Liberty Media on the $15 billion spin-off from AT&T, and on the acquisition of six regional cable operating companies from Deutsche Telekom for £3.198 billion. It also advised on Liberty Media's role as the largest corporate investor in Vivendi, in relation to Vivendi's $10.3 billion purchase of the film and television interests of USA Networks. A small number of staff have been moved to overseas offices in the Far and Middle East, a result most notably of former head Steven Goodman's efforts to develop the practice in Hong Kong. In the utilities sector, the firm has advised London Electricity on its purchase of the Eastern Electricity energy distribution group from TXU (value £1.45 billion) and its acquisition of West Burton power station for £306 million.

Highlights in terms of AIM-related work included acting for Orchard Furniture in its acquisition of World Sport Group and Parallel Media Group International for £65.7 million. It also acted for MotionPoster in a placing of 14 million shares on the AIM market, and advised a European airline on its reverse takeover of an

CORPORATE FINANCE ■ LONDON

undisclosed AIM-listed company. Neil Vickers leads the firm's efforts in the AIM sector. **Clients** Liberty Media; London Electricity; TotalFinaElf; PETRONAS; Virgin; Marks & Spencer; MBNA; Pearson Television; Sony Pictures; Microsoft.

BERWIN LEIGHTON PAISNER (see firm details p.866) The "*flourishing*" team has enjoyed a buoyant year following its successful merger in May 2001. It handles medium-ticket M&A for an array of national and international corporates, including many plcs, as well as a significant volume of AIM work. Drawing on specialist expertise in an array of sectors, the team boasts clients such as Burberry, Alba, European Telecom and Courts. The property and finance sectors continue to supply a healthy deal flow, and the firm has maintained its focus on hi-tech, media and leisure companies. It has this year advised European Telecom on its open offer and placing and move to AIM, and acted for Chorion on its acquisition of the literary works of Georges Simenon. Led by "*guiding star*" **John Bennett** (see p.233), the firm advised Numerica Group in the admission of Numerica's shares to AIM and a placing of its shares by Collins Stewart raising £30 million. **Keith Stella** (see p.247) led the team advising TripleArc on its acquisition of print management company gl2 and its admission to AIM with a market capitalisation of £23 million. An additional highlight for the team was acting for Lex Service on its £112 million acquisition of Auto Windscreens. **Clients** Lex Service; Static 2358; LINPAC Group; Chorion; TripleArc; Stagecoach Theatre Arts; European Telecom.

HAMMOND SUDDARDS EDGE "*Going great guns,*" the team maintains its "*good quality*" image among a range of corporate, private equity and institutional clients for small to mid cap work. Interviewees singled out "*brilliant*" **Robert Hamill** for his ability to "*discern the real issues and find practical solutions.*" Recently present on an impressive volume of European M&A for UK and international corporate clients, the group has advised SurfControl on its $100 million acquisition of Cyber Patrol and its $17.3 million acquisition of CSM Security Management. It also acted for Yule Catto & Co on its £54 million acquisition of 50% of the issued share capital of Harlow Chemicals Company from Clariant. The team continues to foster its reputation as a leading force in advertising and media services, with its sports expertise receiving a huge boost following the firm's merger with Townleys, specialists in this field. Recent work includes advising The Football League on its £105 million new media joint venture with ntl, and acting for Sports Internet Group on its £300 million acquisition by BSkyB. **Clients** BP Amoco; WPP Group; Compass Group; Clear Channel Communications; Apax Partners; Royal Bank Private Equity; Collins Stewart; Williams de Broë.

TAYLOR WESSING (see firm details p.1156) Targeting cross-border work, the firm has recently pulled off a merger with German-based Wessing, and confirmed that further European expansion in key jurisdictions is on the agenda. In the UK, the firm remains best known for its AIM IPO work, and can draw upon an integrated corporate and IP expertise. It demonstrated its long-term commitment to the TMT, pharmaceutical and life sciences sectors with the opening of a Cambridge office in early 2002, pooling the talents of the respected former Garretts team. Both rivals and clients agreed that this "*savvy*" group is "*particularly straightforward to deal with,*" understanding, as it does, the complexities of a transaction and the greater commercial issues. **Daniel Rosenberg** (see p.245) led the team advising Merloni Elettrodomestici on the acquisition of 50% of GDA (General Domestic Appliances) from Marconi for €195.5 million. The firm also advised Huon Holdings on the £181.75 million reverse takeover of The Innovation Group, and represented OMG on its AIM admission and placing arrangements, raising £6.9 million (the market capitalisation on admission was £36.7 million). **Clients** 365 Corporate; Amgen; Landis; L'Oreal Golden; Macmillan; Nomura International; South Bank University; TDK; Touchstone Group; Visa; TBWA; Quadrant Group; Synergy Healthcare.

THEODORE GODDARD (see firm details p.1158) It has been a testing year for the firm. In addition to the collapse of merger talks with Salans Hertzfeld & Heilbronn in September 2001, March 2002 saw several departures from the corporate department. Nevertheless, the group's market profile remains buoyant. Described by rivals as "*a straightforward bunch who know how to handle complex transactions in a speedy manner,*" the team's solid foundation is reckoned to ensure recovery. Clients agree, "*technically strong, they understand our business - these are the lawyers we trust.*" "*Extremely experienced*" **Martin Chester** and "*hands-on*" **Graham Stedman** (see p.247) (head of department) were singled out as leading lights by interviewees. The group advised South Africa's AngloGold on the UK aspects of the hostile takeover offer for Normandy Mining, Australia's largest gold miner. Other highlights included acting on Innovision Research & Technology's £40 million AIM flotation for Peel Hunt, the placing agent and broker. Communications, media and IT are spheres of strength for the firm, and it has advised Kirch-Gruppe, the German media group, on its acquisition of the Formula One World Championship group. **Clients** Delta; Diageo; Wyevale garden centres; ABN AMRO; ARM Corporate Finance; Peel Hunt; Cathay International Holdings.

DECHERT (see firm details p.934) Distinguished by its work for US clients on UK and European acquisitions and joint ventures, the team remains a prime choice for transatlantic instructions. Its insurance sector experience is admired, and the firm has had success acting for owner-managed businesses and entrepreneurs. Media and technology has proved to be a source of instruction; the firm has advised NewMedia SPARK on its $30 million US merger with GlobalNet Financial.com, in a public share for share agreement, and acted for Hachette Livre on its £40 million acquisition of Octopus Publishing. "*Easy to work with, intelligent and commercial*" **Michael Steinfeld** (see p.247) led an international team advising Travelex on the corporate, regulatory and competition aspects of its £440 million acquisition of the Thomas Cook Global & Financial Services division. Further highlights for the team included advising US-based Pitney Bowes on the UK aspects of acquisitions including the document management and outsourcing business of Danka Business Systems for $290 million, the acquisition of Secap for €220 million and the purchase of the international mail and messaging business of Bell & Howell for $51 million. **Clients** BRIT Insurance Holdings; Fairview New Homes; Rhodia; Madisons Coffee.

DLA **Peter Wayte** remains at the helm of this sizeable group. Observers perceive the firm to be developing its presence in private equity-related deals, although the corporate team is felt to operate under the shadow of the banking department.

EVERSHEDS (see firm details p.949) Recognised for its "*enthusiastic*" approach to deals on a national level, the London team has had a successful year advising high-profile clients on M&A and IPO transactions. Its client roster features a range of FTSE 100 and overseas corporates, a significant number of which are active within the financial services sector. Researchers have been impressed with the growth in value of the team's transactions and its increasing focus on the European cross-border markets. Martin Issitt and the team recently acted for DuPont on the European aspects of the $7.8 billion sale of pharmaceuticals business to Bristol-Myers Squibb, and advised Thales on the sale of Thales Instruments to RIG Holding Ltd Partnership for £85 million. The team also advised on the IPO of Caffè Nero. Highlights within the financial services arena included advising Legal & General on its strategic alliance with Barclays, under which Barclays is to sell the Legal & General pensions and investment products. It has also advised M&G, Threadneedle, Jupiter and Gartmore on a funds supermarket joint venture and subsequent purchase of M&G's business. **Clients** Thales; AMP; Dow Chemical; DuPont; Time Products; Legal & General; Diageo.

NABARRO NATHANSON (see firm details p.1080) Observers rate this as a "*thoroughly commercial*" team, and it continues to make inroads into the mid cap market, achieving sub-

LONDON ■ CORPORATE FINANCE

stantial endorsement for its property finance and projects sector focus. It has acted on several headline transactions, boasts a number of impressive UK corporate clients and has a growing expertise in cross-border M&A. Private equity activities continue: the firm has acted for the management in the £65 million MBO of Shepperton Studios, and advised Cazenove Private Equity on the third-round financing of crocus.co.uk. Also in the technology sector, the firm has advised long-standing client NewMedia SPARK on its contested merger with GlobalNet Financial.com and its takeover of Spütz. "*Pragmatic*" **Iain Newman** (see p.243) "*keeps a cool head and gets things done.*" Property remains part of the foundations of this group and Newman and his team advised Land Securities Trillium on the 50:50 Telereal joint venture with The William Pears Group for the acquisition of BT's property portfolio (£2.4 billion). In the leisure sector, the firm advised Silverhoney on its hostile £453 million cash offer for the shares in The Wolverhampton & Dudley Breweries. Other recent highlights included advising Investec Henderson Crosthwaite in a £16.3 million fund-raising by Hercules Property Services and acting for Dwyka Diamonds on its £20 million flotation on AIM. **Clients** NewMedia SPARK; Collins Stewart; Oracle; The Body Shop International.

OLSWANG (see firm details p.1087) Following a phase characterised by a string of impressive deals and a soaring market profile, the recent slump within the TMT sector and struggling IPO market has resulted in a quieter year for the "*tremendously enthusiastic*" team. While peers view the defection in February 2002 of former head of corporate Adrian Bott to Osborne Clarke as a blow, the group retains its appeal for clients, who praised its "*friendly, confident and relaxed*" attitude. It boasts expertise in all aspects of corporate work from M&A and private equity to domestic flotations, although its reputation in the area remains strongly associated with its widely acknowledged media, communications and technology strength. "*Talented*" **Simon Morgan** (see p.243) recently advised New Star Asset Management Group on two fund-raisings, raising £50 million in total, and acted on its planned acquisition of Artemis Capital Management. Admired by peers as "*incredibly smart, one of the most technically proficient,*" **Graeme Levy** (see p.241) heads the finance team and specialises in banking and insolvency matters. The firm's recent activity within the TMT sector includes acting for Anite Group on a series of acquisitions in the IT consultancy and software fields, and on the disposal of a number of its existing business streams. In the property sector, the firm has acted for the management team of Delancey Estates on the agreed £256 million offer though its SPV, Tribeca UK, for Delancey Estates. **Clients** Anite Group; BBC Worldwide; Bloomberg; Delancey Estates; Freeserve; HIT Entertainment; Moneybox; Motorola; UUNET; The Maiden Group.

OSBORNE CLARKE (see firm details p.1090) The team continues to gain ground, impressing all quarters with its "*outward-facing mentality, where the client always comes first.*" This broadly based, deal-driven department has a marketing services and digital games niche. Its varied client base comprises a mix of institutions, listed and private companies. In a bid to bolster its international capability, the firm merged with Danish firm Pedersen & Jantzen at the beginning of 2002, has recently strengthened its presence in Frankfurt and has opened an office in Cologne. It already benefits from a European network of alliance firms, and, in conjunction with its Dutch partner Ploum Lodder Princen, it recently advised Torex on the acquisition of Hiscom for $30 million. Among the firm's big-hitters, **Tim Birt** was frequently described to researchers as a "*truly excellent tactician, a real star.*" He has built up the firm's strength in stock exchange-related matters. **Adrian Bott** (see p.233) joins the team from Olswang, where he was formerly head of corporate. He has carved out a name for himself in public company work within the TMT sector. His arrival is set to boost an already respected hi-tech, telecoms and media strength. The team advised Marlborough Stirling on its IPO on the London Stock Exchange (£248 million) and acted for Tribal Group on its admission to AIM, raising £14 million. M&A highlights included advising Wolff Olins' shareholders on the acquisition of the company by the Diversified Agency Services divison of Omnicom Group, and advising 3i on the sale of shares of Serviceteam Holdings for £56.5 million. **Clients** StepStone; Torex; Marlborough Stirling; Vanco; Redstone Telecom; Majestic Wine; NRX Global; 3i; Rowan Dartington; Altium Capital.

PINSENT CURTIS BIDDLE (see firm details p.1102) It has been a positive year for what some describe as a "*high-level corporate operation.*" The "*well-staffed department*" led by Alan Greenough has managed to offset the current dip in IPOs by an increase in M&A activity for its mostly midcap clients. Other areas of activity for the team have included restructurings and public-to-private work. Recent AIM-related transactions included the return of funds of J2C, which was delisted in December, while M&A highlights included acting for the international energy services company Abbot Group on a series of transactions culminating in the £135 million acquisition of Deutag. The team also represented US drugs manufacturer Perrigo Company (quoted on NASDAQ) in its acquisition of Wrafton Laboratories from McBride. Domestic flotation work includes advising Parkman Group on its placing on the Official List (£44 million). **Clients** Fulcrum Pharma; e-xentric; J2C; Abbot Group; Powerhouse; Powell Duffryn; PizzaExpress; Brewin Dolphin Securities.

LONDON — SMALLER DEALS

BIRD & BIRD (see firm details p.874) The team's promising emergence in this area has been arrested by the TMT slump. Industry focus remains key to its strategy however, and it has recently handled a range of acquisitions, JVs and stock exchange work for a mix of domestic and international clients in the communications, IT, e-commerce and pharmaceutical sectors. Highlights included advising academic research internet portal ingenta on its acquisition of Catchword for £11.2 million, and assisting Daisytek International (listed on NASDAQ) on its £10 million investment in ISA International and ISA's associated delisting from the Official List of the LSE and its admission to AIM. Other work included advising BT on the unwinding of its global joint venture with AT&T. **Clients** ingenta; Daisytek International; Orchid BioSciences; Tularik; BT; Expocentric; Sega Japan.

MEMERY CRYSTAL (see firm details p.1067) Unanimously regarded as one of the premier firms for AIM work, the "*unflagging*" department continues to elicit an enthusiastic commendation from rivals and clients. Acting for NOMADS and FTSE 500 companies, it handles a wide array of equity issuing, M&A, MBOs and public-to-private deals, and has carved out a niche for itself within the sports community. "*Tough and commercial*" **Lesley Gregory** (see p.238) is a long-standing figure in the market. She leads the "*ambitious*" team that recently advised Collins Stewart in a placing and open offer of new ordinary shares for Oystertec to raise £30.6 million to fund the acquisition of IBP from Delta. Other highlights for the team included advising Seymour Pierce on First Artist's acquisition of FIMO Sports Promotion, the placing of 10 million new ordinary shares and admission to AIM, and advising Wembley and 24dogs.com on the launch of a new global tote betting service, 24dogstote.

STEPHENSON HARWOOD (see firm details p.1147) Market commentators judged the team to be composed of some "*quality people*" and having a strong name in the financial services

www.ChambersandPartners.com

CORPORATE FINANCE ■ LONDON

CORPORATE FINANCE: SMALLER DEALS
■ LONDON

1
- Bird & Bird
- Memery Crystal
- Stephenson Harwood

2
- DJ Freeman
- Field Fisher Waterhouse
- Lawrence Graham
- Reed Smith Warner Cranston
- Richards Butler

3
- Harbottle & Lewis
- Lewis Silkin
- Nicholson Graham & Jones

4
- Fox Williams
- Hobson Audley
- Howard Kennedy
- Marriott Harrison

5
- Beachcroft Wansbroughs
- Charles Russell
- Coudert Brothers
- Manches
- Middleton Potts
- Steptoe & Johnson LLP
- Watson, Farley & Williams
- Wedlake Bell

LEADING INDIVIDUALS

1
- **AUDLEY Max** Hobson Audley
- **GREGORY Lesley** Memery Crystal

2
- **GRAYSTON Clare** Lewis Silkin
- **JOHNS Michael** Nicholson Graham & Jones
- **STORAR Michael** Lawrence Graham
- **WILLIAMS Christine** Fox Williams

3
- **BAKER Andrew** Wedlake Bell
- **BROCKBANK Anthony** Field Fisher Waterhouse
- **DEAN Kevin** Stephenson Harwood
- **FAGELSON Ian** Reed Smith Warner Cranston
- **SWEET Jon** Marriott Harrison

This book is the product of 6,582 1/2 hour interviews. See p.7 for BMRB audit. Within each band, firms are listed alphabetically. See individuals' profiles p.232

---

sector. Boosted by its fusion with the respected Sinclair Roche & Temperley team, it continues to focus on core business sectors such as maritime services, property, new economy and the financial industry. It is underpinned by strong regulatory and tax expertise, and has recently been visible advising on a range of deals for well-known financial and hotel clients. Interviewees described **Kevin Dean** (see p.236) as "*a good chap who knows how the business world works.*"

The group advised Macdonald Hotels on both its £235 million acquisition of Heritage Hotels and its unsuccessful bid to acquire the Posthouse chain from Forte. It also represented HSBC on the outsourcing of its cheque and credit clearing business. **Clients** Accor; Macdonald Hotels; Minit; Royal Canin; Six Continents; PA Consulting; Barclays Bank; Bayerische Landesbank Girozentrale; KPMG; Standard Bank London.

DJ FREEMAN (see firm details p.939) The "*sharp*" team handles AIM listings, partnership and M&A transactions, though peers continue to perceive that its main strength lies in property-driven corporate deals. Led by Richard Spiller, it continues to build on the firm's expertise within the property, insurance, media and communication sectors, representing private and public companies, institutions and individuals. Recent AIM highlights included advising on the demerger of Pilat Technologies into two AIM-listed companies, and involvement in the £14 million AIM flotation of Symphony Plastic Technologies. M&A work included acting for Glenchewton on the £75 million reverse takeover and buyback by i-spire. **Clients** Capital & Regional; Reed Elsevier; Tenon; Fulham FC; RBS; GfK.

FIELD FISHER WATERHOUSE (see firm details p.954) Rivals warmly endorsed the team for its dot.com and hi-tech know-how, pointing to its involvement in M&A, capital raisings and joint ventures. The group, which includes **Anthony Brockbank** (see p.234) ("*an excellent lawyer who gets on with the transaction*"), covers a broad sweep of work with a number of instructions taken from the public sector and retail. Its lengthening client roster features brokers such as Seymour Pierce and Investec as well as smaller AIM- and OFEX-listed companies. The team recently advised interactive marketing company Overture on contract negotiations relating to its long-term strategic partnership with T-Online. This client also turns to the firm for German law advice, a testament to the success of the firm's international ambitions.

LAWRENCE GRAHAM (see firm details p.1031) The firm holds court to a range of small- to medium-sized deals, often derived from its brewing, leisure and hotel client base. Commended to researchers as a "*steady, sensible*" lawyer, head of the company and commercial department, **Michael Storar** remains the star individual here. He presides over the M&A team, which advised Scottish & Newcastle (S & N) on its sale of 456 pubs to the Royal Bank of Scotland for £260 million. The team also acted on S & N's sale of 432 pubs to Enterprise Inns and 214 outlets to Noble House Leisure for £361 million. Further highlights included advising Topland on its acquisition of a property holding company from Marks & Spencer for £348 million. On the flotation side, the team advised Stream Group on its AIM debut, raising £3.4 million, which valued the company at £15 million. **Clients** BT; Coffee Republic; Brancote Holdings; Investec Henderson Crosthwaite; Lion Technologies; Legal & General; Scottish & Newcastle.

REED SMITH WARNER CRANSTON (see firm details p.1109) According to some rivals, the team is "*motoring ahead*" on account of the increased level of transatlantic work, which has resulted from its merger. The integrated group provides M&A advice with a specialist slant in sectors such as financial services, insurance, e-commerce and banking to French, US and UK corporate clients. "*Friendly and incisive,*" **Ian Fagelson** (see p.236) has won the respect of clients and competitors for his "*quality advice.*" The corporate team has recently assisted new client Eurostar Group on a £35 million relaunch of its train service including the refurbishment of the fleet and lounges. This transaction called upon the strong French team based in the London office.

RICHARDS BUTLER (see firm details p.1112) Visible from time to time on larger deals, the "*solid and trustworthy*" team has experience advising an array of UK and international public companies on multi-jurisdictional transactions. The team is often called upon to advise on regulatory and takeover issues. Demonstrating the firm's cross-border capability, David Boutcher and his team recently advised Cordiant in the merger of its media-buying business, Zenith, with the media-buying business of Publicis - the value of the assets was approximately £300 million. Other recent highlights for the department included acting for Salton (listed on the NYSE) on its £50.1 million recommended cash offer for Pifco Holdings. Christopher Jackson led the team, which advised Direct Line via its Italian subsidiary AllState Diretto Assicurazioni Danni on its acquisition of R oyal Insurance, the Italian direct motor insurance operation of Royal & SunAlliance. **Clients** BBC Worldwide; MTV; Close Brothers Private Equity; Direct Line; France Telecom; Hemscott; Skanska.

HARBOTTLE & LEWIS (see firm details p.983) It has been a busy year for this "*spirited, dynamic*" team, seen by sources to be advising its "*active*" client base on a broad sweep of M&A, private equity and stock exchange-related transactions. The firm is widely recognised for its TMT and leisure industry expertise, and *Chambers* found that clients are drawn both by its "*confidence-inspiring knowledge*" of their businesses and its corporate finance expertise. The firm's most high-profile client, Virgin, instructed the team on the £27.5 million sale of its interest in Le Manoir aux Quat' Saisons and La Residencia to Orient-Express Hotels. Other highlights for the team led by Colin Howes included advising on the start-up of Digital Network News (a joint venture among Chrysalis Holdings, Capital Radio, UBC Media Group, GMG Radio Holdings and Trafficlink) that will provide information bulletins and a rolling local news service for MXR Digital. AIM-related work included advising Chrysalis Books on its takeover of AIM-quoted C&B Publishing (£2 million with an additional £5 million to be

LONDON — CORPORATE FINANCE

invested by way of working capital). **Clients** Virgin; Telstar; First Property Online; SCi Entertainment.

LEWIS SILKIN (see firm details p.1041) A steady flow of cross-border disposals and acquisitions attests to the team's skill in the corporate market; its transactions have an increasingly European flavour. Clients endorse the team as "*hands-on and constructive,*" and it maintains its profile despite the quiet flotation market. Researchers also found that "*swift turnaround*" and a "*can-do mentality*" ensure its popularity with clients. "*Excellent on AIM floats,*" **Clare Grayston** (see p.238) continues to be warmly commended by the market. The team advised on the multi-jurisdictional sale of Twynstra Holdings, an architecture consultancy, to its 23-strong management team. It also advised Careline Services on its sale to D interactive (listed on Euronext) for £10 million with further payments based on future performance. **Clients** Havas Advertising; Accord Holdings; Abbott Mead Vickers Group; Haymarket Publishing; House of Fraser; Groupe Chez Gerard.

NICHOLSON GRAHAM & JONES (see firm details p.1083) Peers and clients regard the department as a "*user-friendly, solid operation,*" with strength in the core areas of M&A, AIM, private equity and partnership law. Managing partner **Michael Johns** (see p.240) is esteemed for his expertise in all aspects of corporate work including venture capital, MBOs and equity issues. Clients are drawn from diverse sectors, ranging from manufacturing, property and financial services to entertainment and publishing. Recent highlights for the team included advising NASDAQ-listed Oshkosh Truck Corporation on its acquisition of Geesink-Norba Group, the European market leader in refuse collection vehicles and waste compactors, for €150 million in a transaction that saw the acquisition of three main corporate groups in the Netherlands, Sweden and the UK. The team also advised Hercules Property Services on its £30.5 million acquisition of the entire issued share capital of Cadogan Insurance Services, and the goodwill and assets of Baker Lorenz and Kounnis Brokers. The transaction was funded by a placing and open offer to raise £15.5 million and a further £15 million banking facility. **Clients** GWR Group; Middlesex Holdings; Kleeneze; Henderson Global Investors; Oshkosh Truck; Peregrine Systems.

FOX WILLIAMS (see firm details p.962) It has been a rewarding year for the "*doughty and industrious*" team, which has been increasingly visible on the gamut of domestic and international acquisitions, disposals, joint ventures and fund-raisings. Described by rivals as a "*leading figure within the community*" **Tina Williams** (see p.602) spearheads an "*excellent, tight-knit team.*" An international M&A, corporate finance, restructurings and share schemes expert, she led the team advising Xchanging on the setting up of Ins-sure, a JV with Lloyd's of London and International Underwriters Association, which has an estimated £20 billion annual turnover of premiums and claims settlements. Other recent highlights for the department included advising Simply Hub on its pre-IPO fund-raising, and Karen Millen Holdings on the sale of a minority shareholding to a syndicate led by Icelandic company, Kaupthing. **Clients** Xchanging; Simply Hub; General Atlantic; Karen Millen.

HOBSON AUDLEY (see firm details p.997) The "*focused*" corporate finance group concentrates primarily on smaller international and AIM transactions. Bucking the market trend, it has recently been visible on a larger volume of AIM-related deals than many of its competitors and continues to benefit from alliances with firms in the US and Germany. Respected **Max Audley** (see p.232) "*certainly knows his stuff;*" peers portray his expertise and client-handling skills as the main reasons that the firm "*punches well above its weight.*" His team recently advised US-based company Clean Diesel Technologies on its AIM listing in late 2001, and represented Nabarro Wells in the introduction to AIM of Portman, an Australian-based iron ore group (£84 million). HFP Holdings instructed the firm on its acquisition by Millfield for £10 million. **Clients** Halliburton; Electronic Data Systems; Amway; Investec Henderson Crosthwaite; Viacom/Simon & Schuster.

HOWARD KENNEDY (see firm details p.1001) According to interviewees, the group has recently experienced "*tremendous growth,*" especially in M&A and the property sector, though it remains best known for its presence within the AIM market and for tax-related transactions. Alan Banes sits at the helm of this company and commercial team, which regularly handles M&A, stock exchange, AIM and OFEX flotations, VCT work, rights issues and unquoted public share offerings. Clients applaud the group's "*personalised, dedicated*" service. In 2001, the team entered into a JV with accountants Levy Gee to promote a NOMAD service for AIM clients. Recent highlights for the team include advising The Wigmore Group on its £1.67 million placing, underwritten open offer and flotation on AIM. It acted for ProVen Media VCT on its £30 million flotation on the LSE, and advised Vinci Park Holdings UK on its £15.6 million purchase of the car parks at University Hospital of Wales, Cardiff and at Ninewells Hospital, Dundee. **Clients** Beeson Gregory; Public Network s; The Sport Entertainment & Media Group; Venture Technologies Academic Research Partners VCT; Sydney & London Properties.

MARRIOTT HARRISON (see firm details p.1054) Researchers were left in no doubt about the quality of this "*focused*" team. Its work for high-profile media clients has captured the attention of all quarters of the market, and many consider the budding department to be "*moving up the scales.*" The client roster features a range of media companies, private equity houses and VC institutions. The team is home to the "*dynamic and totally capable*" **Jon Sweet** (see p.248), who has been present on a number of high-value deals such as advising Albion Chemicals on the purchase of Hays Chemicals (value £107 million). He and the team also advised Eagle Rock Entertainment on a £34 million transaction resulting in the transfer of the controlling interest in Eagle Rock from edel music, and acted for Robertson Research Holdings on its disposal for £59 million. **Clients** Albion Chemicals; Beaufort Group; Eagle Rock Entertainment; eTechnology VCT; Eurostar Group; Online Travel Corporation.

BEACHCROFT WANSBROUGHS (see firm details p.860) Simon Hodson and the team handle corporate regulatory, advisory and transactional work, mainly for private clients and an array of water and insurance companies. Recently active on a high volume of acquisitions, share sales and JV agreements, the team is deemed by peers to be a "*helpful, bright bunch who get on with the job.*" It has recently advised Historic Collections Group on the acquisition of Past Times, and East Surrey Holdings on the purchase of 24.5% of Northern Ireland's Phoenix Natural Gas from BG Energy Holdings. **Clients** AssiDomän Packaging UK; Balfour Beatty; Norwich Union Insurance; Vivendi Water UK.

CHARLES RUSSELL (see firm details p.904) This is a broad practice that spans AIM, OFEX and M&A for a high-profile client base comprising new economy and hi-tech companies and, increasingly, financial advisors and brokers. Spearheaded by Simon Gilbert, M&A highlights included acting for the management of Ericsson Enterprise Solutions on its sale to Apax Partners for €480 million, and advising Scoot.com on the sale of *Loot* to the Daily Mail General Trust for £45 million. In the AIM arena, the team acted for Cora Group on its placing to raise approximately £10 million and its listing on AIM. **Clients** Scoot.com; Damovo UK; CDC Group; Collins Stewart; Williams de Broe; Select Appointments Group; Sirrus Group.

COUDERT BROTHERS (see firm details p.920) Although market sources commented on the firm's low profile this year, it remains well respected for a workload that comprises M&A transactions for European and US-based multinationals. It is the team's presence in the international arena, rather than domestic transactions, which provides the department in London with its staple diet. Led by Dean Poster, it recently acted for Telelogic AB's wholly owned subsidiary Telelogic Acquisition Company on the acquisition of, and merger with, QSS for $115 million.

CORPORATE FINANCE ■ LONDON/THE SOUTH

Clients Ascom Holdings; Caboto Securities; MTS; EuroMTS; Coredeal MTS; Telenor; Merck KGaA.

MANCHES (see firm details p.1052) As well as expertise within the publishing field, the team is well known for its loyal core of retail, property, technology and entrepreneurial clients. Its mainstay remains mid-cap and international M&A, although it does handle smaller volumes of fund-raising. Housed within the corporate and technology group, the corporate finance team, which includes Melvin Pedro, recently acted for Condé Nast Publications on the acquisition of Johansens Independent Hotel Guides. It also acted for Ultrasis (listed on the London Stock Exchange and admitted to techMARK) on its offer to acquire the ordinary shares in Ultrasis North America that it did not already own, in a one-for-one fully underwritten rights issue raising approximately £6.8 million. **Clients** Blackwells; Canon UK; Bally Group; Bouygues; Moss Bros Group; Woolwich; Syngenta.

MIDDLETON POTTS (see firm details p.1069) The firm operates an integrated corporate and commercial practice, drawing on expertise in diverse areas such as shipping, PFI, asset finance, energy and banking. Many clients are overseas public companies or state-owned institutions, which David Godfrey's team advises on acquisitions, joint ventures and restructurings as well as related employment and regulatory issues. The firm recently advised ABX Logistics UK on its acquisition of the European Freight Forwarding division of Nightfreight International Logistics. **Clients** ABX Logistics; Belgrave Properties; Assicurazioni Generali; Global Direct Dealing.

STEPTOE & JOHNSON LLP (see firm details p.1148) Bedding down following its US merger, this small London team caters for UK, EU and international clients. Jonathan Polin leads a group that has its primary focus in small - to medium-sized M&A work for a niche clientele composed of hi-tech, gaming and internet gaming companies. The team has advised Stratos in its $240 million acquisition of BT's Aeronautical & Marine Division, and acted for GFInet in its acquisition of Fenics. In the hi-tech sphere, the firm acted for Business Objects in the acquisition by its subsidiary of Blue Edge Software for $6 million. The property sector has also proved to be a fruitful source of corporate instruction.

WATSON, FARLEY & WILLIAMS (see firm details p.1181) AIM-related work is the cornerstone of the firm's corporate practice, with clients including public and private domestic companies alongside a growing number of NOMADS. Though often achieving renown on account of its shipping expertise, the corporate team is bolstered by a broad sweep of experience in areas ranging from energy, natural resources and transport to TMT, travel and leisure. The team recently advised Black Rock Oil & Gas on its recommended takeover offer for Black Rock Petroleum (an Australian company listed on OFEX) and its placing and admission to AIM to raise around £1 million. It also advised Charles Stanley as nominated advisor/broker to Capcon Holdings regarding the latter's application for admission to AIM and related placing. **Clients** Charles Stanley; Black Rock Oil & Gas; The Sports Café Group; Beaumont Cornish; Voss Net; Citadel Holdings.

WEDLAKE BELL (see firm details p.1182) The team has recently handled a host of domestic and cross-border transactions, ranging from £1-27 million. Its experience spans M&A for public, private, overseas and domestic companies in a range of sectors. AIM listings and advising NOMADS such as Hoodless Brennan are a regular source of instructions and the firm has increasingly secured investment management work. **Andrew Baker** (see p.232) has built up a significant following in the community for "*quality work with a European dimension.*" The team advised the shareholders of Ely Fund Managers on the sale of the business to Dexia Banque Internationale a Luxembourg (£26 million). It also acted for Europacom.net on the acquisition of European ISP LCR Telecom, and advised Hoodless Brennan and Nabarro Wells on Meridien Group's admission to AIM. **Clients** The Global Group; Stanhope Communications; Eurotel Systems; Intrepid Energy; Nestor Healthcare Group.

THE SOUTH

BLAKE LAPTHORN (see firm details p.877) Distinguished by its "*high-calibre*" advice and sizeable presence, this firm retains its high market approval. The team has been bolstered by its recent merger with niche Portsmouth practice, Sherwin Oliver, adding further expertise in insolvency, M&A, IP/IT and franchising to an existing full-service operation. MBOs, MBIs and share acquisitions remain a real strength here; it recently advised a management team on a £22 million MBI. The team has acted for Brockhampton Holdings in the £77 million MBO of Portsmouth Water, and advised Cobham on the £40 million acquisition of Omnipless. Both **Sean Wright** and **Kathryn Shimmin** have impressed our interviewees with their commercial nous. **Clients** Bank of Scotland; Beales; HSBC; Lloyds TSB; NatWest; Royal Bank of Scotland (RBS) ; Pratt & Whitney.

BOND PEARCE (see firm details p.879) "*Consistently good,*" this firm has an impressive brand name for corporate work that benefits from a strong network of southern offices. Clients appreciate the proactive commercial understanding of these lawyers, who have an ability to stay "*one step ahead of what you require.*" The group features the highly regarded **Graham Jeffries** (see p.106), who has a track record in both corporate finance and banking. The transactional work often has a private equity flavour, for a client base that includes local companies and larger plcs. **Clients** Chilworth Manor; Computer Associates.

SHADBOLT & CO (see firm details p.1126) Transactional matters here included big-ticket M&A, and this growing department profits from its strong construction client base. It also has a healthy following among an increasing number of local businesses. Key figure in this team is **Andrew Trotter** (see p.248), described to researchers as "*personable – a deal-doer and not a point-scorer.*" The group acted for Galliford Try on its acquisition of the issued share capital of Gerald Wood Homes, and advised on the acquisition by Caffyns of the issued share capital of Skinners Eastbourne. It also acted for Microscience on the £25.5 million investment by Advent and JPMorgan. **Clients** Microscience; Schoolsnet; Edmund Nuttall.

STEVENS & BOLTON (see firm details p.1149) The firm has an enviable reputation in the market, endorsing the high technical standards it attains. The client roster features major corporates and owner-managed businesses with typical deals falling in the £5-60 million range. Head of corporate **Richard Baxter** (see p.232) was commended by clients as "*fully transparent, sensible and realistic.*" He is ably aided and abetted by "*highly experienced*" **Keith Syson** (see p.248). Highlights for the team included advising Delphis Holdings on its sale to Morse for up to £40 million, and acting for Procter & Gamble on its sale of the Milton brand in the UK and Eire to Laboratoire Rivadis. They also advised the management team of royalblue technologies on the MBO for £24 million from royalblue group. **Clients** Morse; Procter & Gamble; Berkeley Morgan Group; Chas A Blatchford & Sons; ENER.G; GDS Group; Hays.

ASB LAW (see firm details p.851) This "*professional and prompt*" team was praised by clients for its "*ability to get under the skin of things.*" Sources feel the merged firm has "*come a long way*" in promoting the cohesiveness of the group. The full-service department deals with M&A, disposals and restructuring; in the banking sector the team has secured a place on five regional panels. Practice development partner Russell Bell is a key partner in the group. The team has acted on the sale of C-side, a chain of 26 public houses and clubs for £15 million, and advised on the purchase by First Choice of Virgin Sun for £5.9 million. It also acted on the

THE SOUTH ■ CORPORATE FINANCE

CORPORATE FINANCE
■ THE SOUTH

1
- **Blake Lapthorn** Fareham, Portsmouth, Southampton
- **Bond Pearce** Southampton

2
- **Shadbolt & Co** Reigate
- **Stevens & Bolton** Guildford

3
- **asb law** Crawley
- **Brachers** Maidstone
- **Clyde & Co** Guildford
- **Cripps Harries Hall** Tunbridge Wells
- **Lester Aldridge** Bournemouth, Southampton
- **Mundays** Cobham
- **Paris Smith & Randall** Southampton
- **Rawlison Butler** Crawley
- **Thomas Eggar** Chichester, Horsham, Reigate, Worthing

4
- **DMH** Brighton, Crawley
- **Shoosmiths** Fareham
- **Thomson Snell & Passmore** Tunbridge Wells

5
- **Coffin Mew & Clover** Southampton

LEADING INDIVIDUALS

1
- **BUTLER-GALLIE Stuart** Brachers
- **TROTTER Andrew** Shadbolt & Co

2
- **BAXTER Richard** Stevens & Bolton
- **JEFFRIES Graham** Bond Pearce
- **WRIGHT Sean** Blake Lapthorn

3
- **CHATFIELD James** Rawlison Butler
- **HEATHCOCK Andrew** Paris Smith & Randall
- **MUNDAY Peter** Mundays
- **SADKA Tim** Rawlison Butler
- **SHIMMIN Kathryn** Blake Lapthorn
- **SYSON Keith** Stevens & Bolton

This book is the product of 6,582 1/2 hour interviews. See p.7 for BMRB audit.
Within each band, firms are listed alphabetically. See individuals' profiles p.232

---

high-value cross-border sale of Practical Print Solutions to OCE (UK). **Clients** First Choice Holidays; Caspian Publishing; RBS/NatWest; Bank of Scotland; Practical Print Solutions; The Book People.

BRACHERS (see firm details p.886) Dominant within its locale, this expanding young team has made great inroads into the wider southern marketplace. A specialisation in the insurance sector is also reaping dividends. Clients of a rival firm praised the team, which had rescued a deal: "*If it wasn't for them, the deal would not have happened.*" **Stuart Butler-Gallie** (see p.234) was endorsed by peers, who credited him with "*recruiting a strong team that has gelled well.*" His "*quick turnround*" and professional manner have won him many fans. In the commercial waste sector, Butler-Gallie acted for Verdant Capital on the acquisition of Ecovert, the municipal waste collection and recycling division of SAUR UK. Further highlights for the team included advice to Towergate Underwriting Group on the acquisition of Stafford Knight Holdings and the businesses of John R Poel & Company and Dentists Insurance Committee. The team also handled the £2.5 million MBO of Letraset from Esselte UK. **Clients** Charlton Athletic FC; Towergate Underwriting Group; Planit Holdings; Letraset; Brookes & Bentley; Ecovert; Kent Pharmaceuticals; General Dynamics United Kingdom.

CLYDE & CO (see firm details p.913) Clients applauded the team for delivering "*timely and efficient advice*," while competitors acknowledged them as "*serious competitors*," with a strong local presence and the resources of an international firm. The client base ranges from multinationals, plcs and large limited companies to family-owned businesses. Key client Dairy Crest has provided a constant stream of work throughout the year. The head of department is Andrew Holderness. Highlight deals included advising Schlumberger Evaluation & Production Services (UK) on its acquisition of Baker Jardine and Associates. The team also advised Biochemie, the generics drugs subsidiary of Novartis Pharma on all matters relating to the acquisition of Lagap Pharmaceuticals. **Clients** Johnson & Johnson; Cathedral Capital; BRIT Insurance Holdings; Dairy Crest; Bass; William Reed Holdings; Novartis Pharma; Securico.

CRIPPS HARRIES HALL (see firm details p.922) "*Pure heavyweights*," this firm fields lawyers, who rivals claim are "*the sort who will work with you, not against you.*" The dedicated team of corporate specialists, headed by Trevor Carney, has enjoyed a year packed with a number of big-ticket transactions. A major highlight was acting for the vendors on the £30 million disposal of Just Learning. The group subsequently acted for one of the vendors on the acquisition of a continuing interest of the company. It also acted for Croudace Homes on the acquisition of the entire issued share capital of Portland Homes, and advised Feedback on the acquisition from the University of Lincoln of its shares in Teknical, a joint venture company providing solutions for internet-based educational programmes. **Clients** Dencare Management Group; JSC Ispat Karmet; Paydens; Swiss Life; Croudace; Elifar.

LESTER ALDRIDGE (see firm details p.1038) This "*high-quality*" offering acts for local, national and international clients on the gamut of corporate issues. Head of department David Ashplant leads a team that has "*an intelligent approach to problem-solving and great attention to detail.*" It acted for a subsidiary of Cobham in the establishment of a joint venture regarding civil airliner maintenance in Europe, with Singapore Aerospace Technologies. The team also acted for Hugh Symons on the disposal of part of its interest in Elata and advised on the share sale of a subsidiary for Biffa. Experienced in cross-border transactions, the team also advised Navision Damgaard, a Danish-listed company, on the reorganisation of its UK business interests. **Clients** Bath Travel; Biffa; CDI-Anders Elite; Cobham; Hugh Symons; Newday Group.

MUNDAYS (see firm details p.1078) A growing team acclaimed by peers as "*deal-doers who are technically proficient.*" The retail pharmaceutical sector is an area of strength, and the team advised Allied Unichem on the expansion of its subsidiary, E Moss. Information technology and related hi-tech matters are a growing specialism at the firm. Popular **Peter Munday** (see p.243) heads the team; "*he does not waste time.*" He led the team on the acquisition of the Taylor Pharmacy chain for £68 million. The team also advised Biwater on its disposal of Spectrascan, and acted for Portfern in its acquisition of The Ultimate Event Company (UK) from Availeon. A further highlight for the team was its advice to the Octagon group of companies and the management team on their acquisition of Octagon Developments, with an associated MBI of Octagon Group. **Clients** SHL Group; B i water.

PARIS SMITH & RANDALL (see firm details p.1093) "*Technically strong and always sensible*," this firm can boast a department that "*knows how to look after its clients.*" Firm ties within the manufacturing sector remain in existence, while a focus on core specialisms in banking, corporate and insolvency has reaped rewards. Department head **Andrew Heathcock** is "*good on the detail.*" He has led on several matters for Vosper Thornycroft including disposals, acquisitions and a joint venture. The team also acted on the £8 million MBO for MAP80 Systems, and the disposal and acquisition of a manufacturing business from Photobition. **Clients** Vosper Thornycroft; Southampton Leisure Holdings; Millbrook Furnishing Industries; Kenwood.

RAWLISON BUTLER A team that is small by design, it was the subject of client approbation as "*on the ball, always fair and value for money.*" Peers viewed the firm as one of the traditional quality players in this market. Two specialist partners handled a range of corporate work encompassing M&As, MBOs, shareholder structures, joint ventures and corporate governance. Advice to US companies is also a feature for the department. **Tim Sadka** is "*responsive – he stands his ground and makes his point.*" He advised the management team of C-side on its £17 million MBO. The "*smooth*" **James Chatfield** advised Century Dynamics and its UK subsidiary on the acquisition of a business division from WS Atkins, and represented a US investor on the disposal of Regal Securities to ADT Fire & Security. **Clients** Suzuki GB; Dragon Health Clubs; TBC Group; California Software.

THOMAS EGGAR (see firm details p.1160) The team, led by Tony Edwards, is perceived by market commentators as a traditional firm with a "*strong private client reputation.*" The team has enjoyed strong growth this year and undertakes instructions from City institutions to local businesses. Offices from Horsham to Worthing have handled an array of corporate matters. These

CORPORATE FINANCE ■ THE SOUTH/THAMES VALLEY

range from the completion within two weeks of the multimillion pound purchase of the spare parts business of BAE Systems, to acting for the shareholders of Parklands Group in the sale of the entire issued share capital to Thyssen Aufzuge. The team has also advised on the disposal of the entire issued share capital of Henlow Leisure for a consideration over £4 million, including the Café Med chain of restaurants. **Clients** Wyndeham Press Group; Britannia Pharmaceuticals; Charleston Trust; NCH Marketing Services; RF Saywell; Wimpy International.

DMH (see firm details p.940) Since the arrival of entrepreneur and corporate lawyer Ian Wilson, the team has reorganised, recruited several ex-City players and consolidated its Crawley office. Clients applauded a team that "*comes up with solutions rather than avoiding the issue.*" A long history with banking clients is attested to by a steady stream of work from the RBS. Highlights included acting for Tesla Magnetic on its restructuring, including a £5 million repurchase of shares and a special dividend. The team also acted for South Devon Railway on a public share issue of up to £2 million. **Clients** HSBC Enterprise Fund; Bank of Scotland; RBS/NatWest; Venture Finance.

SHOOSMITHS (see firm details p.1133) "*Personable lawyers and a good local practice,*" the firm also enjoys the resources of a network of offices. Based at the Fareham Business Park, the team, led by Louise Finlayson, acts for national and local clients, and boasts a strong IT capability. Working jointly with its Nottingham office, the team acted for Abbey National in the creation of a joint venture company valued at £400 million. It also acted for the management of Edes in a £10 million MBI. **Clients** HJ Heinz; Tandberg Television; Royal Bank of Scotland; Abbey National; KBC Advanced Technologies

THOMSON SNELL & PASSMORE (see firm details p.1161) James Partridge heads a team that handles the full range of corporate advice. Clients based in the South and referrals from other regions provide a steady flow of instruction, while food production and road maintenance are areas of specialism. Turnover continues to increase, while disposals and acquistions have formed the backbone of the work. The team has also recently carried out a private placing. **Clients** Pura; Colas; Dean & Wood; William Ransom & Son.

COFFIN MEW & CLOVER Clients endorsed the firm for its "*efficiency and ability to get the deal done.*" It handles a mixture of funding and transactional work; of late the team has acted on MBOs, corporate restructuring, acquisitions and disposals. Highlights included acting on the sale of an electronics company to Chalton Group for £4 million and the sale of Siddalls Financial Services Group to the Slater Group for £3 million. **Clients** Owner-managed businesses; banks.

THAMES VALLEY

CORPORATE FINANCE
■ THAMES VALLEY

1. **Osborne Clarke** Reading
2. **Manches** Oxford
3. **Brobeck Hale and Dorr** Oxford
   Clarks Reading
   Kimbells Milton Keynes
   Nabarro Nathanson Reading
   Pitmans Reading
   Shoosmiths Reading

LEADING INDIVIDUALS

1. ANGEL Peter Manches
   GOWANS Andrew Osborne Clarke
2. HUTCHINSON John Pitmans
   JONES Hugh Osborne Clarke
   LEE Richard Clarks
3. DREW Dean Shoosmiths
   HAMBLETON Jonathan Kimbells
   LEYSHON Greg Osborne Clarke
   LOAKE Jonathan Brobeck Hale and Dorr
   PILLMAN Joe Brobeck Hale and Dorr
   TAYLOR Glyn Nabarro Nathanson

This book is the product of 6,582 1/2 hour interviews. See p.7 for BMRB audit. Within each band, firms are listed alphabetically. See individuals' profiles p.232

OSBORNE CLARKE (see firm details p.1090) The firm boasts a team that has "*established a big presence*" in the Reading market and beyond. The group has completed 87 deals worth over £1 billion for its institutional and corporate client base, displaying its expertise in the M&A, private equity and banking arenas. Perceived by peers to be "*easy to deal with,*" the team includes **Andrew Gowans**. Overwhelmingly approved of by the marketplace, he is "*impressive with clients and eminently sensible.*" A major highlight for the firm this year is its advice to Vanco on the disposal of its network repair businesses and the subsequent IPO that comprised a £14 million placing of shares to institutions and admission to the Official List at a £55 million market cap. "*Technical*" **Greg Leyshon** led the MBO of the Early Learning Centre from John Menzies for £29.6 million on behalf of 3i Group. **Hugh Jones** was praised for his finance capabilities. He acted for Parc Technologies on the investment by CSFB, Cisco BV, Advent International and Soros for £15 million. The team also acted for npower Communications on the acquisition of approximately 230,000 indirect access telephony customers from ntl for £17 million. Richard Smerdon has retired from the practice. **Clients** 3i Group; Lloyds TSB Development Capital; Vanco; British Gas; Fortis; Bank of Scotland; Royal Bank of Scotland.

MANCHES (see firm details p.1052) Clients endorsed a "*superb, responsive and commercial,*" team that has proved itself to have "*multifaceted expertise.*" The firm enjoys a good lock on the hi-tech market, with a client base that leans towards publishing, IT and biotech. "*Impressive*" head of department **Peter Angel** (see p.232) led the team acting for Oxford University Press on its acquisition of Blackstone Press for approximately £14.5 million, in a deal that involved both a purchase of assets and shares. The team also acted for Oxford Gene Technology (OGT) on the acquisition by Arrow Therapeutics of OGT's DNA microarray business. The deal included a licence of OGT's patented technology and was largely funded using Arrow shares. The team also acted on the demerger of the MCS Group under Section 213 of ICTA 1988. **Clients** British Salt; Hogg Robinson; DAF Trucks; Mayflower Corporation; Oxford Gene Technology; Oxford University Press.

BROBECK HALE AND DORR (see firm details p.888) The firm received mixed reactions in the marketplace, including those who questioned the viability of its niche focus on the national and international technology markets. Most agreed that it is home to "*serious players, a most particular kind of lawyer.*" **Jonathan Loake** (see p.241) is "*commercial and pragmatic,*" while head of the Oxford office **Joe Pillman** (see p.244) continues to impress all quarters with his hard-working attitude and deep knowledge of the hi-tech sector. The year has seen spinouts from Oxford University and increasingly international work. Key transactions have included the flotation of Akers Laboratories on AIM. The group also acted for Ask Jeeves on the purchase of Carlton and Granada Internet, and advised Screen in its hat-trick of acquisitions, acquiring BAe Civil Systems, Pentyre and Joyce-Loebl. **Clients** Akers Laboratories; CRC Group; Screen; BMG Entertainment; Oxonica.

CLARKS (see firm details p.908) The "*respectable, decent firm,*" which rivals would refer work to, is led by chairman and head of corporate **Richard Lee** (see p.241). Acclaimed as "*personable and highly intelligent,*" he brings an expertise in MBOs and employee share schemes to the deal table. The team has been further bolstered by the recruitment of Simon Thorne, ex-head of legal at SITA, who brings specialist knowledge of waste management and renew-

THAMES VALLEY/SOUTH WEST — CORPORATE FINANCE

able energy. The team acts for a broad range of clients including multinationals, mid-sized corporates and local owner-managed businesses. Trade sales, second- and third-round funding and start-ups have been a feature of the past year. Highlight deals included acting for Buckingham Research on its £6 million sale to a listed company, and advising on the MBO of Imotion. **Clients** SITA; Norsk Hydro; Bunzl; Fazer Group; CfBT Education Services; Dynes Semiconductor; Axiom Systems; Highcroft Investment Trust.

KIMBELLS (see firm details p.1023) An ability to "*understand the complexities of a business*" set this team apart from its competitors. M&A and financing matters are at the forefront of this practice that has a niche in the waste industry. Clients value corporate partner **Jonathan Hambleton** (see p.239): "*Every time we use him, we feel we have won the battle; he can make things easy and talk in layman's terms.*" He acted for the shareholders in Lavelle & Sons and Hodgejoy Recycling on their sale to Viridor Waste Management for a consideration in excess of £6 million. A further highlight was the firm's involvement in the sale of Fire Protection Services and five subsidiaries, turning over in excess of £22 million, to Kidde. The team has been dealing with work of an increasingly international flavour; it acted on the sale of a railway and safety consultancy group with offices in Ireland, Hong Kong and Singapore to Lloyd's Register of Shipping. **Clients** Dawsongroup; Minolta UK; Nationwide Access; MHA Systems; South West Saab; MidCo Waste Management.

NABARRO NATHANSON (see firm details p.1080) This busy office is headed by the "*extremely capable*" **Glyn Taylor** (see p.248). The team remains focused on technology and has advised on a number of AIM flotations, fundraising, joint ventures and other TMT-driven corporate work. It advised Premier Management Holdings on the first issue by an AIM-listed company of eurobonds listed on the London Stock Exchange. The team also advised Oracle on the disposal of its Energy Downstream Division, and acted for Keith Prowse on its £6 million MBO. In a major highlight, it advised London Scottish Bank on its entry into the credit card market through a joint venture that related to a £75 million securitisation facility. **Clients** Bank of Scotland; Costco; ET Capital; HSBC; London Scottish Bank; MTI Partners; Oracle; Really Useful Group; Ninth Floor Group; Sun Microsystems; The Met Office.

PITMANS (see firm details p.1103) Clients commended a team that "*responds quickly and provides a proactive service*," while rivals recognised it as a firm that "*punches above its weight.*" The traditional client base is now juxtaposed against an increasing number of private equity and start-up companies experiencing growth. MBOs and seed financings have been a feature this year. **John Hutchinson** (see p.239) was singled out for his "*user-friendly approach.*" The team advised Madford Developments on its acquisition and back-to-back sale of three companies owning retail parks as part of a £70 million transaction. Further key transactions included advising the MBO team for the £5 million purchase of Lexis PR, and acting for the Bank of Scotland in the restructuring of its funding to Associated Facilities Holdings. **Clients** Bank of Scotland; Biocompatibles; De Beers; Royal Bank of Scotland.

SHOOSMITHS (see firm details p.1133) A strategic review of the firm's organisation means that corporate matters for the Thames Valley region are now handled across the Reading and Milton Keynes offices. The firm's client base ranges from plcs and American-parented companies to smaller private companies. The team has recently advised the management team of Expamet International on its £69 million buyout offer. M&A and corporate finance specialist **Dean Drew** (see p.236) retains commendation from the marketplace. The group also acquired Datarome for Aspective, which included the drafting of bespoke retention arrangements and a consideration payable in cash and shares. A further highlight has seen it advising the management team of Rohan Group and the company on a secondary buyout. **Clients** ComponentSource; Black Box; SGI; The Open University; Thames Water Utilities; Aspective; South East of England Regional Development Agency (SEEDA).

SOUTH WEST

BURGES SALMON (see firm details p.894) Displaying "*technical brilliance,*" the firm is thought by clients to be leaving its more conservative image behind. Less aggressive and overtly expansionist than its main rivals, the team sets the high standard of quality by which the market judges itself. M&A, takeovers, flotations and equity financings form just part of this firm's experience. Among a group of strong individuals, head of corporate finance **Chris Godfrey** (see p.238) is a "*smooth operator who inspires confidence*" and "*a good commercial driver of transactions who won't score points off you.*" Recognised for his investment trust work, he led the team on the £16 million MBO of A-Gas. Head of company commercial **Roger Hawes** (see p.239) is a "*no-nonsense, collaborative and pragmatic*" lawyer. He advised The Eurostore Group on the £13.25 million MBO of Eurostore Holdings. Several clients commended the "*first-class and technically excellent*" **Alan Barr** (see p.232); he led a £12.5 million acquisition for Tyco Holdings (UK) and advised FirstGroup on a multimillion pound joint venture to bid for the new trans Pennine passenger rail franchise. **Richard Spink** (see p.246) has been spearheading the firm's private equity work. He acted for TDG on its IR£15 million acquisition of INT. The "*senior and commercially astute*" **David Marsh** (see p.601) advised Exeter Investment Group on the raising of £102 million through two placings of Guernsey closed-end funds listed in London. **Clients** Science Systems Group; Systems Union; Orange; Bristol & West; Gooch & Housego; Exeter Investment Group; Motion Media; Surface Technology Systems; ECI Ventures.

OSBORNE CLARKE (see firm details p.1090) "*Effective, if aggressive,*" the group boasts "*an impressive team who work well together.*" Secondary issues and private placements as well as MBO, MBI and IBO deals have been a feature over the past year. Simon Beswick continues to act out of the firm's Palo Alto office, while head of corporate and commercial **Bruce Roxburgh** has impressed with his "*genial and constructive*" bedside manner. He advised Marlborough Stirling on its IPO on the London Stock Exchange, valuing the company at £248 million. **Patrick Graves** is "*a patrician and a first-class documentation lawyer.*" He advised Tribal Group on its admission to AIM. **Paul Cooper** provoked strong endorsement from the marketplace; "*businesslike and to the point,*" he advised the management team of Bede Leisure Retail on the £625 million purchase of that company from Bass Leisure Retail. Observers described head of private equity **Alisdair Livingstone** as "*highly competent and personable.*" As client care partner for 3i, he advised the company on the MBO of tour operator Allez France Group by Holiday Places Group and acted on the syndicated IBO of Allen & Heath. **Clive Watts** was commended by peers as "*always a pleasure to deal with.*" He acted for Western Power Distribution on the £20 million MBO of Hyder Consulting Group and Wallace Evans and subsidiaries. **Clients** 3i Group; MITE Group; Bank of Scotland; Dresdner Kleinwort Benson Private Equity; Invensys; Pubmaster Group; Western Power Distribution Group.

BEVAN ASHFORD (see firm details p.869) Clients applauded a firm that "*provides quality representation to local businesses at a lower cost than City firms,*" while "*giving a balanced commercial and legal view.*" Renowned for its strong public sector practice, the team is thought to "*talk a hard game*" and benefit from expertise in the healthcare sector. Based in the Exeter office, practice area head **Simon Rous** (see p.245) is "*exceptionally talented,*" advising a number of key clients. Acquisitions and disposals are a fea-

CORPORATE FINANCE ■ SOUTH WEST

CORPORATE FINANCE
■ SOUTH WEST

1
- **Burges Salmon** Bristol
- **Osborne Clarke** Bristol

2
- **Bevan Ashford** Bristol, Exeter
- **Bond Pearce** Exeter, Plymouth
- **TLT Solicitors** Bristol

3
- **Foot Anstey Sargent** Exeter, Plymouth
- **Michelmores** Exeter

4
- **BPE** Cheltenham
- **Charles Russell** Cheltenham
- **Clark Holt** Swindon
- **Laytons** Bristol
- **Lyons Davidson** Bristol
- **Stephens & Scown** Exeter, St Austell, Truro
- **Veale Wasbrough** Bristol

LEADING INDIVIDUALS

1
- **COOPER Paul** Osborne Clarke
- **GODFREY Christopher** Burges Salmon

2
- **BARR Alan** Burges Salmon
- **GRAVES Patrick** Osborne Clarke
- **PESTER David** TLT Solicitors
- **ROUS Simon** Bevan Ashford
- **ROXBURGH Bruce** Osborne Clarke

3
- **COOMBS Richard** Foot Anstey Sargent
- **HAWES Roger** Burges Salmon
- **HEWES Simon** Bond Pearce
- **JONES Michael** CMS Cameron McKenna
- **MORSE Stephen** Michelmores

4
- **ACOCK Roger** Lyons Davidson
- **LEWIS Mark** Foot Anstey Sargent
- **LIVINGSTONE Alisdair** Osborne Clarke
- **RUNDALL Francis** Charles Russell
- **SPINK Richard** Burges Salmon

5
- **BELLEW Derek** Veale Wasbrough
- **KELIHER James** Stephens & Scown
- **MARSH David** Burges Salmon
- **WATTS Clive** Osborne Clarke

This book is the product of 6,582 1/2 hour interviews. See p.7 for BMRB audit. Within each band, firms are listed alphabetically. See individuals' profiles p.232

---

ture, while highlights include d the firm's advice on the multimillion pound joint venture between the Architen and Llandrell Group of Companies. **Clients** Schlumberger Industries; Grey Matter Holdings; Global Investment House of Kuwait; ABS Hovercraft, Germany; Bank of Scotland; HSBC; Medical Industrial Equipment.

BOND PEARCE (see firm details p.879) Although continuing to act on an integrated office basis, this firm is perceived to be investing heavily in the Bristol office. The merger with Cartwrights is also a significant boost, providing excellent links to the leisure, licensing and IT markets. Head of corporate in the South and South West is **Simon Hewes** (see p.239), who has established a corporate team to complement the firm's banking capability. Clients range from small companies and mid-sized corporates to multinationals. Highlights include acquisitions for Newsquest Media Group of both the Dimbleby Group of newspapers and the companies publishing the Gatwick and Horley Life titles. The team also acquired LSC Group for Devonport for over £13 million. Buyouts have proved a fruitful source of instruction, and the team has this year advised on the MBO of Allen & Heath for £9 million. **Clients** Computer Associates; Two Four Productions; Momentum Financial Services; Friends Provident Life Office.

TLT SOLICITORS (see firm details p.1163) The group, perceived by clients as "*young, keen and responsive*" is "*making a mark for itself*," while peers commended it as "*a breath of fresh air*." Handling M&A and mainstream corporate work, the department boasts a specialist niche in OFEX projects. Managing partner **David Pester** (see p.244) received the lion's share of praise directed towards the group, impressing sources as a "*commercial, organised deal-doer.*" The team acted on a number of corporate transactions for Alfred McAlpine, including the acquisition of Ryan Utility Services from Speedy Hire for £12.7 million. The team also acted on the transfer of the NMGW accountancy practice into Numerica Group on its AIM float, and advised on the acquisition of County Bookshops, a 60-branch chain. **Clients** Aardman Animations; University of Bath; Advanced Technology (UK); Avon Rubber; Alfred McAlpine; Barclays Bank; Hanson.

FOOT ANSTEY SARGENT (see firm details p.1958) Observers felt that this team had rationalised "*and looks more commercial as a result.*" Working across the Plymouth and Exeter offices, the group enjoys a strong client base, and specialist sectors include e-commerce, hi-tech, financial services and media. **Richard Coombs** (see p.235) is "*commercially minded; you can reach a solution with him, no matter what the problem.*" He led the team on the restructuring of Plymouth Marine Laboratory, and on the Civil Servants' Annuities Assurance Society's £18 million transfer of engagements to Royal Liver Assurance. The more technical **Mark Lewis** (see p.241) is highly regarded for his work in the competition sector. He acted for Northcliffe Newspapers Group on the Fish4 online advertising joint venture. The team also advised on the purchase by SIFAM Instruments of the nano positioning components division of SDL Queensgate. **Clients** UKRD Group; Northcliffe Newspapers Group; Bank of Scotland; David & Charles.

MICHELMORES (see firm details p.1068) Respected by the local market, this is a thriving practice perceived to have "*progressed considerably.*" Possessed of a "*high-quality*" workload, the group is led by Malcolm Dickinson. "*Sensible and hard-working*" **Stephen Morse** specialises in M&A, buyouts and private equity matters. The firm has advised on the sale of Claremont Capital Group to Rix Europe (Spinnaker), and completed a £45 million joint venture for the University of Cornwall. **Clients** ROC; TJ Brent; Claremont Capital; Interlube.

BPE (see firm details p.884) Peers acknowledged that the team has "*upped its game.*" The department has expanded, and the firm has established a corporate team in Birmingham, as well as an association with Estonian law firm, Law Firm Heta. The group "*enjoys a high profile with mid-cap and AIM companies.*" Specialising in raising money, floating and selling owner-managed businesses, the "*pragmatic*" team is led by John Workman. Highlights included acting for Summit Medical on a £17 million MBO, and advising Quickmove Properties on the £16 million refinance and purchase of minority shareholders' interests. A further highlight was the acquisition of six target companies (AIM reverse takeover) for £1.4 million. **Clients** Mears Group; DCS Europe; Ultronics Group; Barclays Bank; Royal Bank of Scotland.

CHARLES RUSSELL (see firm details p.904) Providing "*a better service than many top City firms,*" clients praised the team for its "*accessibility to partners and outstanding quality work.*" Richard Norton heads a group commended by peers as "*clever, experienced and pragmatic in its dealings.*" A major highlight was acting for Trifast on its acquisition of Special Fasteners Engineering in Taiwan for approximately £15 million. "*Top-class*" Francis Rundall (see p.245) acted for Browallia International, a Dutch investment holding company, in its successful bid for British Mohair Holdings. The team acted for the US-based LawGibb Group on the sale of its European and African operations (value $25 million), and advised Montpellier Group on its successful £10 million bid for VHE Holdings. **Clients** Trifast; Howle Holdings; Eagle Star; Pennant International; Healthcare Service Group; Matcon; Travail Group.

CLARK HOLT (see firm details p.907) Clients praised a "*business-focused practice*" that provides "*a wonderful service,*" proffering "*the scope and experience we require.*" The team, led by Richard Clark, is gaining a reputation for its skill in the IT sector. It advised the vendors of Symetris on its sale to AIM-listed Mettoni for £4.4 million, and advised Blick on its acquisition of Alpha Services. It also acted for Equiinet on the purchase of the Equiinet business from the receiver of DICA Technologies and on the subsequent cash injection. **Clients** AIT Group; Blick; DICA Technologies; e-xentric (UK); genetix gx; Isotron; Transense Technologies.

LAYTONS (see firm details p.1032) The team has of late acted on acquisitions, disposals, joint ventures and investment arrangements. Rival firms were particularly impressed with the healthy client roster, the star of which is the rela-

SOUTH WEST/WALES ■ CORPORATE FINANCE

tionship with key client Somerfield Stores. The team advised Somerfield Stores on the sale of its 24/7 internet shopping business. Head of department Richard Brown is "*extremely well respected.*" Further highlights have seen the team acting on the MBO of the Duke of Cornwall Hotel in Plymouth for over £4 million, and advising on several acquisitions and joint ventures for the EH Bennett Group. **Clients** Somerfield Stores; David S Smith Group; Anglo-Welsh Group; EH Bennett Group; Zuken Group; National Packaging Council.

LYONS DAVIDSON (see firm details p.1045) Boasting a broad mix of work, the experience here includes co-purchases, disposals and high value reorganisations. Much of the profile of this group rests on the shoulders of **Roger Acock** (see p.232) ("*a great guy*"). The client base ranges from clearing banks to private sector clients, some plcs and owner-managed businesses. The firm has this year advised on a refinancing for a client. **Clients** Grafton Group; Momentum Financial Services; Knapp New Homes; SITA Environmental Trust.

STEPHENS & SCOWN The firm has a strong Devon and Cornwall presence acting for local industries such as leisure, agriculture, nursing homes and the property sector. Quarrying and waste disposal are niche specialisms offered by the team. It has played a key role in establishing Finance South West, a non-profit making company charged with promoting Finance Cornwall, a major venture capital and loan fund, with the aid of Objective 1 ERDF funds for business in Cornwall. **James Keliher** advised a management team on its MBO of ARCOL. The team also acted for IMERYS in the sale and respective purchase of its two house building companies to Wainhomes (North West).

VEALE WASBROUGH (see firm details p.1174) The group handles corporate work for owner-managed businesses, funding, acquisitions and disposals. David Worthington heads the team, which has expanded with the recruitment of David Emanuel, formerly of Clarke Willmott & Clarke, and Nick Smith of Thring Townsend. **Derek Bellew** (see p.600) retains the respect of the market, although he has been less visible of late. The MOD remains a major client for the firm, and it recently instructed the team on all matters for the digitisation of defence communications – the UK's biggest defence communications contract, worth £1.8 billion. Further highlights included advising Greenoak Marketing Group on a £1.3 million private placing of shares in the financial services group. It also advised the shareholders of Toracomm on its sale to Powerwave Technologies, a NASDAQ-listed US telecoms business for a multimillion dollar consideration. **Clients** MOD; Ironside Technologies Europe; Fire Service College; UK Hydrographic Office; IOP Publishing; University of Bristol; Hobbs Properties.

OTHER NOTABLE PRACTITIONERS Rivals know **Michael Jones** (see p.240) of CMS Cameron McKenna as "*a sensible but robust negotiator,*" while clients appreciate that "*he takes the trouble to know a business, and his availability is excellent.*" At the time of going to press, he has relocated to the firm's London office, although he continues to serve his South West client base.

WALES

CORPORATE FINANCE
■ WALES

[1] **Morgan Cole** Cardiff
[2] **Berry Smith** Cardiff
Edwards Geldard Cardiff
Eversheds Cardiff
M and A Solicitors Cardiff

LEADING INDIVIDUALS

[1] **MACINTOSH Duncan** Morgan Cole
[2] **BOUND Andrew** Berry Smith
LOWE Paul Eversheds
MORRIS Andrew Edwards Geldard
[3] **BERRY Stephen** M and A Solicitors
CHERRY Robert Morgan Cole
PEARSON Jeffrey Edwards Geldard
[4] **FERNANDEZ LEWIS Jon** MLM
THOMAS Michelle Eversheds

This book is the product of 6,582 1/2 hour interviews. See p.7 for BMRB audit.
Within each band, firms are listed alphabetically. See individuals' profiles p.232

MORGAN COLE (see firm details p.1075) Major corporates provide a steady stream of work for this high-profile team. Listings, public takeovers and sales and acquisitions in transactional and investment matters all feature in its workload. **Duncan Macintosh** was perceived by peers as the firm's top rainmaker. He handles buyouts and M&A, and has acted on behalf of the management team of TotalFinaElf Connect on their IBO. **Robert Cherry** is head of the team's plc work. As client care partner for the PHS Group, he led on its flotation onto the Official List, and has this year handled 27 acquisitions for the firm aggregating in excess of £27 million. A further highlight for the team was its advice to Mitel on the sale of its systems-related business worldwide. **Clients** BP Amoco; HSBC; Zarlink Semiconductors; PHS Group; British Energy; Focus Do It All.

BERRY SMITH Competitors find the firm "*pleasant to deal with and non-aggressive,*" agreeing that this is a "*highly professional team handling quality work in a friendly environment.*" The team has a long track record of handling large transactions and continues to cater for small- to medium-sized owner-managed businesses on acquisitions, disposals and MBOs. Head of department **Andrew Bound** (see p.234) was commended by peers as prime choice for referrals. The firm acts for parts of Finance Wales, including The Wales Innovation Fund, and for companies obtaining financing from the fund. Highlights for the team included acting for the 36 shareholders of Jones Chromatography and its two subsidiaries in connection with its $18 million purchase by Argonaut Technologies. The team also acted on the disposal of Premier Manufacturing (PVCu) and has acted on a series of small-end MBOs. **Clients** Image Metrics; N ODOR International; The Wales Innovation Fund; Bank of Wales.

EDWARDS GELDARD (see firm details p.944) A team resoundingly praised by clients as "*friendly, rapid and thorough*" was commended by rivals for its ability to be "*precise without being pedantic.*" The group is envied for its client base, which has recently seen the additions of Kidde and United Utilities. Observers pointed to **Andrew Morris** (see p.243) as a "*helpful, commercial*" player, while **Jeffrey Pearson** (see p.244) was applauded by clients as "*amenable, approachable and able.*" Among a multitude of acquisitions and disposals over the past 12 months, the team has acted for M4 Data on its sale to Quantum for £60 million. It also advised on the disposal of Hyder Services to Logica on behalf of WPD, and acted in the acquisition by Spectrum Technologies of RTMC. The team has advised Kidde on its UK reorganisation. **Clients** WPD; United Utilities; Pendragon; S4C; Barclays Bank; Kidde.

EVERSHEDS (see firm details p.949) This "*slick operation*" benefits from the resources of a nationwide operation. The group has acted on a number of reorganisations, and acquisitions for a number of Welsh SMEs, as well as national and international clients. **Paul Lowe** (see p.241) was lauded as "*a good operator and deal manager,*" while **Michelle Thomas** (see p.248) is recommended for her focus on private sector work. A major highlight for the team was the establishment of Finance Wales, which involved all the documentation associated with the £80 million loan, together with the equity and mezzanine facilities to be invested. The team also acted on the secondary £17.5 million MBO for the vendors and management of Hydrex Group,

CORPORATE FINANCE ■ WALES/WEST MIDLANDS

and advised the multimillion pound sale of Griffin Windows to MASCO. **Clients** Caledonia Investments; Hawtin; IQE; Solectron (California); Ben Sherman; WDA.

M AND A SOLICITORS (see firm details p.1053) This small firm has won the respect of its competitors while clients commended an "*impressive, prompt and professional service.*" It specialises in mergers and acquisitions, disposals and fund-raisings, although a commercial and property service exists. Managing partner **Stephen Berry** (see p.233) is a "*cordial lawyer*" whose techical prowess is not in doubt. The firm has advised IQE on its £40 million commercial alliance with Motorola and its public fund-raising, and it also acted on the £35 million funding and purchase of Glasgow Prestwick International Airport in January 2001 by an international consortium of investors led by Omniport. A further highlight was advising on the £40 million financing and subsequent series of acquisitions by Dr JD Hull & Associates dental group. **Clients** IQE; Biotrace International; Peter's Food Service; Omniport; Gamma Projects; Macob Projects.

OTHER NOTABLE PRACTITIONERS Jon Fernandez Lewis (see p.237) of MLM retains commendation from the marketplace for his "*eye for detail.*"

WEST MIDLANDS

CORPORATE FINANCE
■ WEST MIDLANDS

1 Wragge & Co *Birmingham*
2 Eversheds *Birmingham*
3 Hammond Suddards Edge *Birmingham*
   Pinsent Curtis Biddle *Birmingham*
4 DLA *Birmingham*
   Gateley Wareing *Birmingham*
   Lee Crowder *Birmingham*
   Martineau Johnson *Birmingham*

LEADING INDIVIDUALS

1
DWYER Maurice *Wragge & Co*
METCALFE Ian *Wragge & Co*
PSYLLIDES Milton *Eversheds*

2
EASTGATE Andrew *Pinsent Curtis Biddle*
LEWIS Susan *Eversheds*
MILLINGTON Jeremy *Wragge & Co*
STILTON Andrew *Martineau Johnson*

3
GARNETT Chris J *Eversheds*
GREEN Guy *Eversheds*
GRONOW Simon *Pinsent Curtis Biddle*
HAYWARD Paul *Gateley Wareing*
HAYWOOD Richard *Wragge & Co*
HULL David *Hammond Suddards Edge*
LAVERY James *DLA*
MCHUGH Peter *Eversheds*
RAWSTRON Chris *DLA*
VAUGHAN David *Wragge & Co*

4
ALLEN Amanda *Hammond Suddards Edge*
BIRCHALL Roger *Hammond Suddards Edge*
BRAITHWAITE Stephen *Wragge & Co*
DAWES Edward *Wragge & Co*
HUGHES David *Pinsent Curtis Biddle*
LAWTON SMITH Andrew *Wragge & Co*
SEABROOK Michael *Eversheds*
WARD Michael *Gateley Wareing*
WRIGLEY Richard *Martineau Johnson*

This book is the product of 6,582 1/2 hour interviews. See p.7 for BMRB audit. Within each band, firms are listed alphabetically. See individuals' profiles p.232

WRAGGE & CO (see firm details p.1197) Competing in the national and international arena, the firm drew praise across the board for its "*professionalism*" and its "*core of outstanding quality.*" Well-known among City rivals, the firm has had great success in its strategy of using the lower Birmingham cost base to attract big-ticket transactions, handled with the "*utmost ease and skill.*" The client base here includes FTSE 100 clients and large multinationals, while a recent reorganisation of the team ensures clients are serviced on a sectoral basis. Names such as Rank Hovis MacDougall, Cadbury Schweppes and Powergen appear on the roster, which keeps expanding; the firm this year secured its place on the corporate panel of aggregates giant RMC Group. **Jeremy Millington** is the new department head; he advised on a £128.8 million acquisition by Wilson Connolly. "*Practical*" **Maurice Dwyer** is head of private equity, and led the team on the buyout of Smartstream Group, Hymatic Group and Initial Personal Services. A leading figure in the market, he is thought to be a valuable tactical resource in deal negotiations. Technology partner **Ian Metcalfe** advised Focus on its acquisition of US software company MPO. Observers agreed that the firm's managing partner, **Richard Haywood**, is "*a pleasure to deal with because he is such a gent.*" He specialises in joint ventures and M&As. Head of the firm's technology group **David Vaughan** acted for AT&T on the sale of AT&T Communications (UK) to Viatel. **Stephen Braithwaite** specialises in public company work, while **Edward Dawes** is well-liked by both clients and peers. He acted on the Folkes Group's £38.7 million recommended public-to-private takeover by Folkes Holdings. "*Sensible and down-to-earth*" **Andrew Lawton Smith** is head of the enterprise team and acted on the MBO of A-Gas for 3i. **Clients** Powergen; Severn Trent; Cadbury Schweppes; McDonald's; AT&T; HJ Heinz; Lattice Group; William Hill; Lloyds TSB Development Capital.

EVERSHEDS (see firm details p.949) '*Possessing a fine commercial approach,*" the firm is perceived by peers to have secured "*a high number of quality deals*" that ensure its "*prominent position*" both in the Birmingham marketplace and beyond. It fields teams in both Birmingham and Nottingham, which act as a strongly cohesive offering on transactions, while observers agree that it derives an advantage from its national network and respected brand name. It remains best known for its work with its respected old economy client base in the industry, leisure and automotive sectors. Among this group of "*talented lawyers*" is the "*charming, consummate all-round lawyer*" **Milton Psyllides** (see p.244). Admired as "*good with clients,*" he acted for Novara on the contested £25 million takeover by Findel. **Sue Lewis** (see p.241) is "*technically one of the most capable corporate lawyers around,*" while clients commended her as "*commercially astute – you know you will wrap up a deal quickly with her on your side.*" She advised MG Rover Holdings on the £340 million purchase of Rover Financial Services (GB) from BMW (UK) Holdings (the team had previously acted for the Phoenix consortium in its high-profile purchase of Rover). **Chris Garnett** (see p.237) specialises in mergers and acquisitions for private-to-public companies, while **Guy Green** (see p.238) has this year acted for Bakkavor on the purchase of Katsouris (Fresh Foods) and Fillo Pastry for £100 million, in a transaction funded by way of a share offering on the Icelandic Stock Exchange. Head of department **Peter McHugh** (see p.242) acted for Diageo on the sale of Guinness World Records to Gullane. **Michael Seabrook** (see p.246) ("*a deal-doer*") retains the endorsement of the market in a year that has seen him act on high-value MBOs. **Clients** MG Rover; Rolls-Royce; Britax; Unipart; Mothercare; Fujitsu; Carlsberg-Tetley.

HAMMOND SUDDARDS EDGE The development of the firm's European operations in France, Italy, Germany, Spain and Holland has afforded it some success in capturing the cross border market. Team leader **David Hull** acted on the $4.4 billion outsourcing deal, forming part of the acquisition by Jabil Circuit of Marconi Communications businesses across four jurisdictions. The group has been bolstered by the recruitment of **Amanda Allen** from Pinsent Curtis Biddle. Peers were impressed with her negotiation skills: "*She is tough and takes no prisoners.*" A major highlight for the team has been acting for PwC on the Britax public-to-private deal by way of a £441 million MBO – PwC represented the MBO vehicle, Seton House Group. **Roger Birchall** specialises in

WEST MIDLANDS/EAST MIDLANDS ■ CORPORATE FINANCE

MBOs, MBIs, acquisitions and disposals. The team also advised Jabil Circuit on its acquisition of the printed circuit board assembly and build business of Compaq Computer Manufacturing, and on the specialist manufacturing arm of Alcatel. **Clients** Jabil Circuit; Focus Solutions Group, Aston Villa FC ; Leicester City FC; Galliford Try.

PINSENT CURTIS BIDDLE (see firm details p.1102) Clients spoke of a "*straight-up and practical team that pitches the right level of service – they don't overlawyer a deal.*" These practitioners have won a following with their "*good commercial acumen.*" Peers perceived that the loss of Jim Lavery to DLA and Amanda Allen to Hammond Suddards Edge may impact on the team, but acknowledged that the depth of talent and long-established presence in the market will ultimately see it undiminished. M&A for larger public and private companies dominates, while clients are of an increasingly international flavour. Head of department **Andrew Eastgate** (see p.236) is a "*personable lawyer*" and one of the key figures in the market. **Simon Gronow** (see p.238) acted for IMI on the disposal of its businesses in the energy control sector in the UK, US and France for £55 million. Clients "*would recommend*" **David Hughes** (see p.239) "*any day.*" He acted for Babcock International Group and Siemens on the sale of their respective interests in Railcare to ALSTOM. A further highlight was advising IM Group on an investment in The Funding Corporation, believed to be one of the largest start-ups in the past five years at £115 million. The group also represented the management team on the £441 million MBO of Britax, in a public-to-private transaction. **Clients** IMI; Glanbia; isoft Group; Babcock International Group.

DLA A small team bolstered by the addition of "*top rainmaker*" **Jim Lavery** from Pinsent Curtis Biddle. **Chris Rawstron** retains commendation from the marketplace although he is deemed less high profile recently.

GATELEY WAREING (see firm details p.967) The team, which is recommended for its "*entrepreneurial approach,*" acts for owner-managed businesses and smaller companies, venture capital providers and clearing banks. **Michael Ward** is senior partner and head of corporate services, and, although less visible on the transactional front, he is a strong client winner and valuable source of knowledge. **Paul Hayward** was acclaimed by clients as one who "*cuts through the nonsense.*" He led the team advising the management buyout team on the £100 million institution-led acquisition of the Vickers Turbine Components Division (renamed Ross Catherall), and the subsequent acquisition by Ross Catherall Group of Doncasters. The team also acted on the £15 million BIMBO of CAP Aluminium for Aberdeen Murray Johnstone, and advised the management team on the £25 million MBO of MiniBusPlus. **Clients** Institutions; owner-managed businesses.

LEE CROWDER (see firm details p.1035) The team is securing a reputation for representing institutional clients, alongside its base of SMEs, while Gresham Trust and Alfred McAlpine Special Projects are recent additions to the client roster. The team advises on the whole gamut of corporate finance, and has been particularly involved in the structuring of joint ventures. The team, led by Graham Muth, has advised on the sale of Sabre Supply & Electronics to Tyco and acted in the MBO of John Hickton & Sons. It also advised on the purchase by People's Choice Rentals of Colour Scene (Televisions). **Clients** Airflow Streamlines; Royal Bank of Scotland; 10 Group; C SFM (Holdings); Alfred McAlpine Special Projects; Bank of Scotland; Utopia Group.

MARTINEAU JOHNSON (see firm details p.1056) "*Smartly focused on their speed and clear delivery of advice,*" claim clients; the group possesses "*genuine VCT expertise.*" Deal values now average at £14.5 million. The client base ranges from large manufacturers and corporates through to entrepreneurs and smaller companies that have grown up with the firm throughout their financing rounds. **Andrew Stilton** (see p.247) leads the team, and was praised for his ability to handle deals in a "*straightforward and professional way; there is no point-scoring with him.*" He acted for the management of Beazer Partnerships and Torwood in the £20 million MBO of these companies. **Richard Wrigley** (see p.249) acted for Newco and management on the £16 million Rainbow Corporatewear buy and build. Further highlights for the group included acting for ALSTOM UK in the purchase of Railcare for £10 million, and acting for the Taylor family on the reorganisation and sale of the Dudley Taylor Group for £120 million. **Clients** South Staffordshire Group; Foresight Technology VCT; Enterprise VCT; ALSTOM UK; Trivest VCT; Matrix e-Ventures Fund VCT; Claverley Group; Manganese Bronze Holdings.

EAST MIDLANDS

BROWNE JACOBSON (see firm details p.891) A "*respected and well-liked team,*" it consistently performs a "*professional job.*" The team has enjoyed a strong year with a transactions roll call that features M&A and private equity, valuing in excess of £1 billion. "*Highly respected*" department head **Rob Metcalfe** (see p.243) is "*personable, sensible – he just gets on with it.*" He led the team on the £25 million acquisition of Pimpernel International by its management team. Work is of an increasingly international flavour. "*Dynamic*" **Gavin Cummings** (see p.235) acted for the Greek-listed company M J Maillis on the UK acquisitions of United Packaging from TT Electronics and Samuel Strapping Systems from a Canadian vendor. **Nigel Blackwell** (see p.233) was endorsed for his "*practical approach to problem solving.*" An additional highlight for the team was acting for the French company D interactive on its £10 million acquisition of Craline. **Clients** UtiliTec; Saint-Gobain/Stanton; Securitas UK.

EVERSHEDS (see firm details p.949) Clients are attracted to this group due to its "*deep resources - they can do it all for you.*" M&A work for large corporate clients has been a feature this year, although all aspects of corporate finance work are handled. "*Hard but fair*" head of department **Stephen Kitts** (see p.240) gained extensive market recommendation. "*Technically proficient and well-liked by clients,*" rivals stated that they would refer work to him when conflicted out. He acted for Amelca on its admission to OFEX and advised Rolls-Royce Power Engineering on the sale of the Allen Steam Turbines business. The recruitment of **David West** (see p.249) from Edwards Geldard was seen as a coup for the team. He acted for Advantica Technologies on the acquisition of RISX Environmental. Team "*mentor*" **David Wild** (see p.249) is "*a good operator who is not afraid to muck in on a deal.*" He acted for the management of Paragon Labels on its multimillion pound MBO. Lauded as "*a great deal-doer,*" **Ben Johnson** (see p.240) led the team acting for NBGI Private Equity on the IBO of Hamworthy Heating out of Powell Duffryn for £12 million. **Crispin Bridges Webb** (see p.234) makes an entry into our tables this year on the back of strong client recommendation. A "*first-class operator,*" he acted for Allied Healthcare (UK) on the £35 million acquisition of Staffing Enterprises. **Clients** Britax International; Jessops; Rolls-Royce; Weetabix.

EDWARDS GELDARD (see firm details p.944) This firm has "*cracking clients who supply good quality work.*" The rapidly expanding team was seen to be building on its strong foundation and growing in stature. It has a strong base of owner-managed businesses and is thought to dominate the Derby market. Peers have "*a lot of time for*" department head **Andrew Borkowski** (see p.233); he led the team acting for the UK advisors on the flotation of Ennex International on AIM. The team also acted for Pendragon on the purchase from the Ford Motor Company of a 49% interest in 28 Ford dealerships, in a trans-

CORPORATE FINANCE ■ EAST MIDLANDS

CORPORATE FINANCE
■ EAST MIDLANDS

1 Browne Jacobson Nottingham
Eversheds Nottingham
2 Edwards Geldard Derby, Nottingham
freethcartwright Nottingham
Gateley Wareing Leicester, Nottingham
Howes Percival Northampton
Shoosmiths Northampton, Nottingham
3 Harvey Ingram Owston Leicester
Hewitson Becke + Shaw Northampton

LEADING INDIVIDUALS

1 KITTS Stephen Eversheds
METCALFE Rob Browne Jacobson
2 JANSEN Karl freethcartwright
MOORE Austin Gateley Wareing
3 BLACKWELL Nigel Browne Jacobson
BORKOWSKI Andrew Edwards Geldard
BRIDGES WEBB Crispin Eversheds
BROOKSHAW Oliver Shoosmiths
CUMMINGS Gavin Browne Jacobson
JOHNSON Ben Eversheds
ROWLEY Robert Freethcartwright
SEARY Peter Shoosmiths
SINGH Jit Howes Percival
WEST David Eversheds
WILD David Eversheds

This book is the product of 6,582 1/2 hour interviews. See p.7 for BMRB audit.
Within each band, firms are listed alphabetically. See individuals' profiles p.232

action for cash and assumed debt in excess of £23 million. A further highlight was acting for CITEL Technologies in raising over £9 million of development capital over a 12-month period. **Clients** Chubb; Pendragon; Norcross; Newell Rubbermaid; Yale; Baxi.

FREETHCARTWRIGHT (see firm details p.963) A "*focused team of thorough and tenacious practitioners*" was deemed to a have greater depth at the junior level than was perhaps perceived historically. The group has this year handled deals with a total value of over £250 million. Corporate finance matters ranged from private company work to acquisitions and disposals. "*Pragmatic and commercial*" Karl Jansen (see p.240) led the team on an AIM flotation, which was completed in 5 weeks. A new entry to our tables this year, Robert Rowley (see p.245) was lauded by clients for his "*low-key and balanced style*," while his patience and "*ability to explain things in layman's terms*" are seen as key attributes in completing a transaction. The team acted for the vendor shareholders in the sale of Benson McGarvey to an AIM-listed company, and acted for the vendor shareholders of the Elmsteel Group on its sale to Rotec. **Clients** Paul Fabrications; Flow Industries; Inditherm; Elmsteel; Bodycare.

GATELEY WAREING (see firm details p.967) Rivals pointed to "*a great organisation that has pushed its presence as a definite market player*," and agreed that it derives a great advantage from its "*popular team who work well together.*" Researchers were overwhelmed with feedback for Austin Moore, perceived as the group's key personality. His commitment was noted as his strong point : " *He will fight for his clients, and possesses an enthusiasm that means he will work through the night.*" He acted for the management on the $8 million MBO of Serif (Europe). Although the Leicester office has recently lost a partner to Irwin Mitchell, the base in Nottingham remains strong with clients taken from local and national plcs and owner-managed businesses. Highlights for the group include acting for DCC on the £10 million acquisition of the assets and undertaking of Alta Gas. The team also acted on two public offers for e-gosystems raising £7 million. **Clients** Plcs, owner-managed businesses and institutions.

HOWES PERCIVAL (see firm details p.1003) The team is lauded by peers for its "*ease of dealing with people – they do not blind you with science.*" Such standards are maintained by the "*straightforward and commercial*" Jit Singh (see p.246), whom clients feel is a prime choice "*if you have a tough negotiation on your hands.*" He led the team acting for Ricardo in the sale of non-core subsidiaries to, and a worldwide joint venture with, Schenck Pegasus, in a transaction that involved numerous questions of competition law. The client base comprises plcs, financial institutions and multinationals, while the team has completed 75 deals with an aggregate value of over £1 billion. The team has also acted for Nampak in the disposal to different purchasers of its housewares and garden products businesses, and advised the board of Dunsterville Allen in the context of a contested/hostile takeover bid by a fully listed company. **Clients** Groupe Norbert Dentressangle; Ricardo Group; Shanks Group; Renault; Nampak.

SHOOSMITHS (see firm details p.1133) Competitors envy the team its "*large plc clients that they look after well,*" while clients commended a "*sound and commercial team*" that impresses as "*slick and polished*" on transactions. National head of corporate and commercial Oliver Brookshaw leads the team from the Nottingham office, while Peter Seary (see p.246) was singled out as a "*hard-working, experienced*" member of the team. A strong local and national player, over 50% of the deals handled by the Midlands-based offices were from outside the immediate region. M&A, reorganisations and joint ventures are part of the corporate service offered by the firm. A highlight for the team was advising Northampton Saints rugby club on its admission to OFEX. A further key deal was the refinancing of, and share and business acquisitions for, the Casella Group, with a total deal value of over £20 million. **Clients** Games Workshop Group; British Gypsum; Gala Leisure; Tomkins; Northampton Saints RC.

HARVEY INGRAM OWSTON (see firm details p.988) One of the biggest corporate teams in Leicester, it has a healthy client base largely focused on private clients, owner-managed businesses and a smaller proportion of listed companies. Head of corporate law John Stobart and Simon Astill are the key contacts here. The team is active in private equity, restructuring, acquisitions and disposals. **Clients** Shoe Zone; Midlands Co-operative Society; Walkers Midshires Foods; Bland Bankart; Bank of Scotland.

HEWITSON BECKE + SHAW (see firm details p.993) "*First-rate individuals who provide sensible advice*" and offer "*an excellent range of experience*" according to clients. The team works in close correlation with the Cambridge office, and Richard Ingram heads up the Northampton offering. The team has enjoyed a strong year with 36 deals worth over £100 million. Clients range from plcs and owner-managed businesses to international corporations such as Pittway International and Demco. Highlights included acting on the £26 million MBO of the Perry Group's national motor division, and advising Church & Co on the sale of A Jones & Sons to a consortium of investors. **Clients** Pittway International; Vartech Telecommunications.

EAST ANGLIA

CORPORATE FINANCE
EAST ANGLIA

[1]
- **Eversheds** Norwich
- **Mills & Reeve** Cambridge, Norwich

[2]
- **Hewitson Becke + Shaw** Cambridge
- **Taylor Vinters** Cambridge
- **Taylor Wessing** Cambridge

[3]
- **Birketts** Ipswich
- **Prettys** Ipswich

[4]
- **Greene & Greene** Bury St Edmunds
- **Greenwoods** Peterborough

LEADING INDIVIDUALS

[1]
- **FISCHL Nicolas** Mills & Reeve
- **GOULD Terry** Eversheds
- **SHORT John** Taylor Vinters

[2]
- **DIX John** Hewitson Becke + Shaw
- **HUNTER James** Mills & Reeve
- **STANFIELD Glynne** Eversheds

[3]
- **CROOME Andrew** Eversheds
- **FALKUS Bryony** Mills & Reeve
- **MARDLE David** Taylor Wessing
- **THOMSON Chris** Greene & Greene
- **WAINE Ian** Prettys
- **WHYBROW Annette** Birketts

UP AND COMING
- **AUSTIN James** Birketts

This book is the product of 6,582 1/2 hour interviews. See p.7 for BMRB audit. Within each band, firms are listed alphabetically. See individuals' profiles p.232

EVERSHEDS (see firm details p.949) A firm that "*takes the initiative, smooths out problems and meets tight deadlines*" was applauded by clients. The team benefits from a triumvirate of offices across the region that operate as a "*well-honed*" single unit. Norwich retains its strong corporate focus, while a budding presence in Cambridge has been bolstered by the recruitment of "*top rainmaker*" **Glynne Stanfield** (see p.247) from Mills & Reeve. Based in the Norwich office, **Terry Gould** (see p.238) has a national reputation for his constructive approach to deals, and he is often found advising in the publishing sector. The corporate financing activities of **Andrew Croome** (see p.104) are supported by his banking prowess. A team perceived as "*sensible and pragmatic*" by peers has acted for Cambridge University on a number of spin-outs, while MBOs and MBIs continue to form a substantial measure of the portfolio. Key highlights included the May Gurney acquisition and MBO for £20 million, and the placing and acquisition of 30 separate dental practices within the last 12 months for Oasis Healthcare. The team has also advised on the spin-out and investment from Toshiba Research Europe for TeraView. **Clients** Southern Cross Healthcare; Celsis International; NHP; May Gurney.

MILLS & REEVE (see firm details p.1071) "*A totally professional outfit,*" the team was commended by clients as "*prompt and commercial.*" It enjoys a broad client base ranging from overseas entities to substantial local businesses. The Cambridge office has exhibited an expertise in biotech fundings. In line with market conditions, the group has this year undertaken a number of restructurings and reverse takeovers. Although some observers felt the team's profile would diminish with the departure of Glynne Stanfield, a number of strong individuals and big-ticket transactions have proved its resilience. **Nic Fischl** (see p.237) is "*bright and technically minded;*" he advised Foundation Systems on its restructure and demerger into three separate entities, and assisted in new venture capital funding for those entities. New partner **James Hunter** (see p.239) has impressed on pharmaceutical deals as "*an intelligent deal-doer – straightforward and responsive.*" He advised the shareholders of Radiophone on the sale of the entire share capital of the company to A Novo. The "*detailed and thorough*" approach of **Bryony Falkus** (see p.237) has won client approval; she acted for Anglian Group on its £160 million public-to-private buyout. **Clients** Porex; University of Cambridge.

HEWITSON BECKE + SHAW (see firm details p.993) Envied by rivals for its "*excellent clients,*" this respected team is led by "*the technically capable*" **John Dix** (see p.236). Dealing exclusively with venture capital work, he acted for Iceni BioDiscovery in its £3 million funding from three VC funds, and advised Cambridge Training and Development on its purchase by the AIM-listed Tribal Group. The team works across offices, drawing on resources in Northampton as required. M&A and venture capital-financed transactions are a strong feature here. The group also acted on the acquisition by Domino Printing Science of Alpha Dot, and advised on the sale by the Daily Mail Group of Johansens to Condé Nast Publications. **Clients:** Plastic Logic; Kamelian; Cambridge Research & Innovation.

TAYLOR VINTERS (see firm details p.1156) This busy practice, which has seen a flurry of activity in the technology sector, has been heavily involved in MBOs and MBIs of late. Led by the highly respected **John Short** (see p.246), the team's major transactions over the past year have included the sale of a transatlantic hi-tech Cambridge company, BioRobotics to US firm Apogent for over $20 million. The team also acted on the sale of construction giant May Gurney to a management buyout team and assisted in the first-round funding for existing hi-tech start-up sm-spatial (3G technology), Smart Bead Technologies and Cambridge Meditech. **Clients** Artisan (UK); May Gurney; The Automation Partnership; Analysys.

TAYLOR WESSING (see firm details p.1156) Observers reacted to the opening of the firm's new office in Cambridge (January 2002) with optimism, claiming themselves "*fascinated to see how this one will develop.*" It has made a positive start by incorporating the old Garretts team, excluding Gerry Fitzgerald who now has a role as a venture capitalist. Clients applauded a team which "*takes the initiative and provides a friendly and personal service.*" Mirroring the London office's TMT focus, the added depth of resource and brand loyalty afforded to the new group is anticipated to garner a greater level of instruction. "*Commercial, pragmatic and responsive*" **David Mardle** (see p.242) retains the commendation of the marketplace, while the team is now headed by an original Taylor Joynson Garrett practitioner in the form of Simon Walker. Acting largely on behalf of funders, the team's recent highlights have included acting for Gilde IT Fund on the $15 million funding of Cambridge Broadband. It also advised Technomark Ventures in its investments in biotech companies Matrix Therapeutics (£2 million), Biotex (£9 million) and Syngenix (£5 million). **Clients** Amadeus Capital Partners; Cambridge Silicon Radio; De Novo Pharmaceuticals; Cambridge Gateway Fund; Generics Group; TTP Communications.

BIRKETTS (see firm details p.875) "*The leading practice in Suffolk,*" acknowledge market commentators. Headed by "*senior and well-respected*" **Annette Whybrow** (see p.249), the team has seen its traditional client base expand from transport, distribution and brewing to encompass the hotel and leisure sectors. Sales, acquisitions and MBOs have been a source of instruction throughout the year while a steady flow of work has come from the banking sector. A healthy base of local clients has also seen the development of the firm's TMT offering. **James Austin** (see p.232) is a talented member of this team. **Clients** Local and international corporates.

PRETTYS (see firm details p.1106) Peers commended "*charismatic*" **Ian Waine**'s (see p.248) ability to be "*commercial and pragmatic.*" He typifies the team's constructive approach to the deal table; "*incredibly experienced – he won't score points off you.*" The team acts for companies and owner-managed businesses, enjoying niche strengths in IT and transport. Deal flow this year has stretched beyond the local region and consisted of sales, acquisitions and MBOs. **Clients** Owner-managed businesses.

GREENE & GREENE An eclectic client base of plcs and institutionally backed private companies provides company acquisitions, disposals and funding work for the team. "*Bright and confident*" **Chris Thomson** was endorsed for his "*quick-witted*" assessment of transactions. High-

CORPORATE FINANCE ■ EAST ANGLIA/NORTH WEST

lights for the team included advice to the Western Medical Group on its collaborations with Abbott Laboratories of the USA and Chugai Pharmaceutical Company of Japan. The team also acted for UBS Warburg and others on the sale of the entire issued share capital of Litho-Tech to the Carlton Barclay Group, and advised BLR Trust on the acquisition of asset leasing business Heggart & Co. **Clients** Western Medical Group; private clients.

GREENWOODS (see firm details p.978) The firm enjoys "*considerable dominance in the Peterborough market*," and has been bolstered by the recruitment of David Woods from Eversheds. Handling a range of corporate matters from M&A to joint ventures, the group's forte lies in the media, IT, biotech and food industry arenas. **Clients** Media groups; aviation and transport companies.

NORTH WEST

CORPORATE FINANCE ■ NORTH WEST

1. **Addleshaw Booth & Co** Manchester
   Eversheds Manchester
2. **DLA** Liverpool, Manchester
3. **Halliwell Landau** Manchester
4. **Brabners Chaffe Street** Liverpool, Manchester
   Hammond Suddards Edge Manchester
5. **Cobbetts** Manchester
   DWF Liverpool, Manchester
   Pannone & Partners Manchester
6. **Kuit Steinart Levy** Manchester
   Wacks Caller Manchester

This book is the product of 6,582 1/2 hour interviews. See p.7 for BMRB audit. Within each band, firms are listed alphabetically.

ADDLESHAW BOOTH & CO (see firm details p.838) "*Major players locally and nationally*," the size and depth of the firm's powerhouse department is enabling it to survive the downturn unharmed. As the number of IPOs has decreased, it has instead concentrated on takeovers and take privates, as well as assisting financial institutions on more conventional corporate work. Private equity-related deals have also risen to fill the gap.

Although Mark Warburton has left for an in-house position, the department boasts such a wealth of talent that peers believe this is unlikely to affect it. An "*extremely able and effective negotiator*," Keith Johnston (see p.240) is said by clients to have a "*quiet, determined and constructive manner – he doesn't miss anything*." Interviewees praised Paul Devitt (see p.236) for offering "*a polished service*" and "*a good understanding of business*." He acted recently for long-term client Airtours on the £350 million international placing of Carnival's stake in the company, a deal in which Richard Lee (see p.241) ("*straightforward and commercial*") also assisted. Darryl Cooke (see p.235) won plaudits from the market, particularly for buyout expertise, while Paul Lee (see p.241) was especially respected for his client skills.

Considered by clients to offer "*quality service and extremely good project management skills*," the team assisted Trafficmaster on the £31 million acquisition of California-based Teletrac, a reverse triangular merger not possible in the UK. It also represented Aberdeen Murray Johnstone on the sale of John Kennedy Holdings to Balfour Beatty for £43 million. **Clients** 3i Investments; Aberdeen Murray Johnstone; Airtours; Barclays Private Equity; Kingfisher; Oystertec; Trafficmaster.

EVERSHEDS (see firm details p.949) In common with other leading firms, it can call on strong resources locally and nationwide. A potent, effective and "*personable*" unit, it has picked up a lot of new clients over the past 12 months and, despite the market conditions, has been involved in a number of IPOs. Following the success of last year's Caradon Plumbing IBO, the "*absolutely first-rate*" Edward Pysden (see p.244) has acted on the £310 million sale of Mira Showers to US-based Kohler. "*So bright you can't get anything past him*," according to competitors, Pysden's combination of extensive legal expertise and "*perceptive, intelligent and clear commercial thinking*" was also invaluable on the £210 million take private of Lynx Group by a subsidiary of Skandia Insurance Company.

Clients praised the firm for its competitive rates and responsive service. Daniel Hall (see p.238), who was instructed by Coats on its recent £300 million disposal programme, heads "*a good team with some outstanding people*." His "*particularly high profile*" is said to have "*helped shape the perception of the practice*." Although some interviewees thought that he hid his light under a bushel, Geoffrey Blower (see p.233) draws on a deep well of corporate experience, while M&A expert Peter Halpin (see p.238) was visible this year working with the shareholders of Peter Black on its £300 million take private. **Clients** Berry Birch Noble; Caradon Plumbing; Coats; Eurocall Limited; Manchester Airport; Ultraframe.

DLA Peers acknowledge that this "*well-organised business*" has retained its market position in the teeth of the slowdown, and remains highly visible acting on bigger deals for its broad base of larger clients. M&A remains an important corporate area for the firm at both the regional and national level. Andrew Holt and Michael Prince, both of whom have maintained strong profiles, lead the charge. Holt was particularly recommended for private equity-related work, and has a matter-of-fact approach that clients and competitors appreciate, while Prince is a "*good, strong operator*," who sources say dominates the market in Liverpool. **Clients** Local and national corporates.

HALLIWELL LANDAU (see firm details p.982) Well-known for servicing entrepreneurial clients, the team is said to rival its local competitors for size and quality. Viewed by market sources as a hungry firm that has grown aggressively, it acted on almost 10% of all AIM floats last year. However, in a year when the market for primary and secondary fund-raising has been poor, some interviewees felt that its profile had dipped.

Senior partner Alec Craig (see p.235) has particular experience in the hi-tech and biotech sectors and was admired for his ability to bring in new business. His colleague John Whatnall (see p.109) ("*technically superb*") combines corporate with financial expertise, while competitors praise M&A specialist Clive Garston (see p.237) for his "*good, commercial approach to transactions.*" Well-respected Rebecca Grisewood (see p.238) was part of a team acting on the £35 million acquisition of filtration specialists Madison Filter Group for Gamma Holdings, and the £53.5 million disposal of Swinton Holdings by Royal & SunAlliance. **Clients** Altium Capital; Gamma Holdings; Royal & SunAlliance; RWE NUKEM; Tomkins; Umbro International.

BRABNERS CHAFFE STREET (see firm details p.885) The newly merged firm can now claim a larger team with increased resources and support. Focused on mid-sized corporate work, it acts predominantly for professional partnerships and owner-managed companies on a range of general corporate transactions. Clients appreciate the team's "*thorough understanding*" of their businesses, although interviewees claim that it is still too early to assess the full effects of the merger.

Senior partner of the Manchester office, Robert Street (see p.247), led the team's advice to Coats Viyella on its £12 million MBO, while managing partner Michael Brabner (see p.234) assisted Rage Software, one of the firm's stable of computer games sector clients, in arranging equity credit line and banking facilities to the value of £20 million. The team also worked on the reorganisation of The Riverside Group, involving £550 million of assets, and acquired Heysham Port on behalf of The Mersey Docks and Harbour Company. **Clients** A NOVO Digicom; Cariad; Coats Viyella; Limpia; Pin Croft Dyeing & Printing Co; Rage Software; The Riverside Group; SK Electronics; Trainstation; Zap.

NORTH WEST ■ CORPORATE FINANCE

LEADING INDIVIDUALS

★ PYSDEN Edward Eversheds

1
HOLT Andrew DLA
PRINCE Michael DLA

2
CRAIG Alec Halliwell Landau
DEVITT Paul Addleshaw Booth & Co
HALL Daniel Eversheds
JOHNSTON Keith Addleshaw Booth & Co
LEE Richard Addleshaw Booth & Co

3
BLOWER Geoffrey Eversheds
COOKE Darryl Addleshaw Booth & Co
GARSTON Clive Halliwell Landau
HALPIN Peter Eversheds
LEE Paul Addleshaw Booth & Co
STREET Robert Brabners Chaffe Street
WHATNALL John Halliwell Landau

4
BRABNER Michael Brabners Chaffe Street
DOWNS William Hammond Suddards Edge
GRISEWOOD Rebecca Halliwell Landau
LEVY Robert Kuit Steinart Levy
NEEDHAM Andrew DWF
O'CONNOR Mark DWF
TURNBULL Robert Cobbetts

See individuals' profiles p.232

HAMMOND SUDDARDS EDGE Although the firm boasts a strong reputation for listings work, like many in the North the team has spent the last year working on more mainstream M&A deals. Competitors acknowledge that it remains "*a major presence*" in the region, particularly in the utilities, technology, biosciences and engineering sectors.

Head of the Manchester office **William Downs** specialises in M&A and commercial contracts work. He has advised SSL International on its £13.5 million disposal of non-core businesses and on the £20.8 million MBI of CSC Division. The team flexed its burgeoning international muscles this year, advising Greif Brothers on the UK aspects of its $900 million purchase of the Van Leer Group, and assisting petroleum group Octel on the acquisition of a manufacturing business across Holland, Greece, the British Virgin Islands and Singapore. **Clients** Coats; Co-operative Group; Findel; Gresham Trust; HSBC Private Equity; Innogy; Kodak Company; Lattice Group; Lorien; Octel; Royal Bank Development Capital; SSL International; SurfControl; TXU Europe Power.

COBBETTS (see firm details p.914) Clients and competitors alike praised this team for its steady, assured and consistently good performances. Having merged with Read Hind Stewart, it has doubled in size within five years and can now boast a trans-Pennine capacity. Building upon its strong profile amongst medium-sized local corporates, it now boasts an enviable client list, including national and US companies. It also assists venture capitalists on start-up funding, exits and refinancings. Well respected for his technical skill and experience, **Robert Turnbull** (see p.248) has assisted Kids of Wilmslow, a chain of pre-school nursery care providers, on its £7 million MBI and refinancing. His department was instructed by Electra Fleming and its management shareholders in the sale of Motorcycle City to Dixon Motors, and also assisted Kingsland Wines and Spirits on its £11 million MBO, achieved without recourse to venture capital. **Clients** Aberdeen Murray Johnstone; GMAP; Kingsland Wines and Spirits; Messenger Leisure; Sonoco Products Company; Transgenomic; Tyco International; York Trust; UNCL.

DWF (see firm details p.943) This expanding corporate finance and M&A team boasts specialisms in the food and financial services sectors. Arguably the strongest corporate group in Liverpool, renewed attention to investment funds work has led to some top-class instructions, such as assisting the Merseyside Special Investment Fund on a two-year round of fund-raising, carried out by **Mark O'Connor** (see p.243). The arrival of the well-regarded **Andrew Needham** (see p.243) from Addleshaw Booth & Co to head the Manchester office is now beginning to have an effect. "*Strong, experienced and putting together a good team,*" he advised Brewin Dolphin Securities on all aspects of the £8 million placing of Synergy Healthcare. The firm also acted for the Princes Group on the purchase of the UK Napolina business from Unilever, and assisted Barloworld on the £24 million cross-border acquisitions of a group of eight overseas companies. **Clients** Altium Capital; Barloworld; Brewin Dolphin Securities; Inter Link Foods; Merseyside Special Investment Fund; Monstermob; Princes Group; Westbury.

PANNONE & PARTNERS (see firm details p.1092) The firm has seen an increase this year in risk management and commercial contracts work. Able to draw on the firm's impressive litigation and property expertise, Søren Tattam's team has the expertise to handle complex corporate matters and enjoys particular strength in transport-related work and large-scale outsourcing contracts. "*Always available and responsive,*" according to clients, it has completed the £241 million acquisition by Manchester Airport of the East Midlands and Bournemouth Airports. The "*forthright and commercially sensitive*" department has also assisted on the disposal of the business and assets of Freshbake Foods, and has acted on Sleepmaster's £8 million share capital disposal to Homestyle Group. **Clients** British Tourist Authority; Compal Electronics; Cotton Traders; G&J Seddon; Hay Management Consultants; Kellogg Company; Manchester Airport; Milliken & Company; Prestolite Electric; Texaco; Urban Splash Group.

KUIT STEINART LEVY (see firm details p.1026) Founded upon the respected figure of corporate and commercial head **Robert Levy** (see p.241), the firm has grown this year through lateral hires. Involved in AIM listings, the majority of the team's work has been small- to medium-sized transactions and joint ventures for mid-range clients. Increasingly, this extends beyond the immediate region. It handled the £12 million AIM flotation of asSeenonScreen Holdings and the £8 million acquisition of World Sports Solutions on behalf of Mottram Holdings. The firm also advised ASC Computer Software over development capital funding worth £2.25 million to enable it to take its electronic patient record and subscribing software to the mass market. **Clients** ASC Computer Software; Karrimor International; Mottram Holdings; Stirling Group; Thomsons Group; Lloyds TSB Development Capital.

WACKS CALLER (see firm details p.1177) The firm has responded to the downturn in some sections of the corporate market by building up its client base of entrepreneurial owner-managed businesses. Martin Caller's team recently assisted Axiomlab in a £12 million placing, and represented internet incubator Oxygen Holdings in the acquisition of Tera Goup. It also acted for Portland Ceramics in its sale to Boots Chemist, and has worked on a number of acquisitions and investments for marketing and online recruitment groups. **Clients** Altium Capital; Axiomlab; Cheshire Life; city invoice finance; ITM Communications; Manpower; Media Square; Morson Projects; Oxygen Holdings; Portland Ceramics; Rexonline.

CORPORATE FINANCE ■ YORKSHIRE

YORKSHIRE

CORPORATE FINANCE
■ YORKSHIRE

1 **Addleshaw Booth & Co** Leeds
2 **Eversheds** Leeds
   Hammond Suddards Edge Leeds
3 **DLA** Leeds, Sheffield
4 **Pinsent Curtis Biddle** Leeds
   Walker Morris Leeds
5 **Lupton Fawcett** Leeds
   Rollits Hull, York
6 **Andrew M Jackson** Hull
   Cobbetts Leeds
   Gosschalks Hull
   Irwin Mitchell Leeds, Sheffield

LEADING INDIVIDUALS

1 **DA COSTA Alastair** DLA
   DARWIN Andrew DLA
   GILBERT Ian Walker Morris
2 **EMMETT Paul** Walker Morris
   JOHNSON Robin Eversheds
   LIPPELL Sean Addleshaw Booth & Co
   MCINTOSH Ian Addleshaw Booth & Co
   SHAW Martin Pinsent Curtis Biddle
3 **ARMITAGE David** Hammond Suddards Edge
   CUNNINGHAM Kevin Irwin Mitchell
   GREENFIELD Ian Hammond Suddards Edge
   HARRISON Wendy DLA
   HOPKINS Stephen Eversheds
   JONES Jonathan Hammond Suddards Edge
   SMART Peter Walker Morris
   ASSOCIATES TO WATCH
   CAULDWELL Helen Eversheds

This book is the product of 6,582 1/2 hour interviews. See p.7 for BMRB audit. Within each band, firms are listed alphabetically. See individuals' profiles p.232

ADDLESHAW BOOTH & CO (see firm details p.838) In terms of volume of cases and size of team, the firm continues to lead the region and is a presence nationally. With the IPO sector remaining relatively flat, it has targeted traditional M&A work for national clients, assisting on mid-market work and private equity-related matters. An institutional client base, including 3i and a number of banks, ensures that it maintains high visibility and a "*strong presence*" in the marketplace. However, Tim Wheldon's departure for an in-house position prompted some interviewees to question whether the firm could maintain its current profile without big-name replacements.

Corporate finance head **Sean Lippell** (see p.241) is described by peers as "*a good operator and a charismatic leader.*" His department represented Nobia AB on its £134 million acquisition of the Magnet group from Enodis. Also well respected, **Ian McIntosh** (see p.242) led a team on behalf of bidding vehicle Kirkgate Group in the £112 million take private of the Dewhirst Group. He also led on a rare acquisition of a regulated bank, that of Sun Bank by the Portman Building Society for £95 million. Clients praised the "*good commercial and legal balance*" of a group that works closely with its Manchester office, most recently on the £149 million sale by Kingfisher of its financial services division to GE Capital Bank. **Clients** 3i Group; Kingfisher; Kirkgate Group; Magnet; NM Rothschild & Sons; Nobia AB; Portman Building Society.

EVERSHEDS (see firm details p.949) Benefiting from the respected national brand, the firm impressed many interviewees with its large, growing team, commitment to the region and strong client base. It has increased the volume of its general M&A instructions over the past year, and enjoys a particularly loyal following within the financial services, TMT, food and retail markets, while its burgeoning international profile has led to European and US transactions now accounting for a quarter of the work of the Yorkshire office.

"*Pragmatic*" **Robin Johnson** (see p.240) is said by clients to "*come up with great ideas.*" He has acted on several of the team's largest transactions, assisting Dayco Products on the £106 million acquisition of LLC Pneumatics and AEA Technology on the £75 million disposal of its Nuclear Consulting Division. Heading up both the Leeds and Manchester offices, "*user-friendly*" **Stephen Hopkins** (see p.239) led on Anglo American's £30 million disposal of Cleveland Potash. Another highlight of the past year was its appointment to the panel of the National Australia Bank group, which includes Yorkshire Bank. **Clients** AEA Technology; Anglo American; ASDA Stores; Dayco Products; Greencore Group; Marmon; Next; Peterhouse Group; Rutland Trust; Wolseley Group.

HAMMOND SUDDARDS EDGE The Leeds corporate group has enjoyed a steady stream of work in M&A and other areas of corporate activity. Also head of the firm's engineering group, **David Armitage** advised Curtiss-Wright on its £42 million acquisition of Spirent's non-core aerospace component business. **Ian Greenfield** was instructed by Bon Marché Group on its £40 million partial refinancing and equity release, and its subsequent £75 million sale to Peacocks. He also assisted Europower on its recommended takeover by Oystertec. Well-respected **Jonathan Jones** has been busy with ECI Ventures' £10 million MBO of Gregory Pennington. Clients; Amber Doors Holdings; Bon Marché Group; Curtiss-Wright; ECI Ventures; Europower; FKI; Jewson; PM Group; Qpark; Royal Bank Development Capital; Yule Catto.

DLA This small team is built around two "*energetic*" stars, who service the firm's top-notch client base of companies ranging from household names to mid-sized local corporates. Competitors admire the group's "*aggressive*" approach, acknowledging that its lawyers "*fight hard and are good at retaining clients.*" The arrival of several new staff members from Garretts "*has helped in terms of substance,*" according to peers. Lead partners **Alastair Da Costa** and **Andrew Darwin** are a major presence in Leeds and Sheffield respectively. Da Costa's "*technical skills*" and "*proven judgement*" were much praised, while Darwin's "*tenacious*" style was also appreciated. **Wendy Harrison** also won plaudits, in particular for her work in private equity-related transactions. **Clients** Local and national corporates.

PINSENT CURTIS BIDDLE (see firm details p.1102) Highly reputed both regionally and nationally, the corporate team, headed by "*professional and knowledgeable*" **Martin Shaw** (see p.246), has consolidated over the past 12 months, receiving a steady stream of M&A and debt restructuring transactions for existing clients. The departure of Michael Robinson to an in-house position, however, has led to some suggestion in the market that the team's visibility has dropped.

Clients remain full of praise for the group's "*excellent service*" and "*timely advice.*" It recently worked for ten months on behalf of BPT and its financial advisor on its successful £477 million public to private auction sale. "*Commercial and with no messing about,*" the group possesses an impressive roster of clients, including CGNU, for which it acted, along with a group of other insurers, on the acquisition of a 40% stake in IFA portal AssureSoft from software provider Misys. **Clients** Abbeycrest; BPT; Barclays Private Equity; Brown, Shipley & Co.; CGNU; Cosalt; DfES; Pace Micro Technology; SIG; Speedy Hire.

WALKER MORRIS (see firm details p.1178) "*Sensible and with a hands-on approach,*" this highly profitable regional heavyweight impressed clients and competitors alike with its genuine and consistent commercial attitude. Recently winning places on both the StrataGas and Yates Group legal panels for corporate and related advice, it has spent the past year focusing on disposals and increasing its business share outside of the Yorkshire region.

A "*good operator, technically proficient and reasonable to deal with,*" **Ian Gilbert** (see p.237) acted for Evans of Leeds on its acquisition of White Rose Development Enterprises from the Kelda Group. **Paul Emmett** (see p.236) "*continues to fly the flag*" for the firm, advising on the triple demerger of Collins and Hayes Group and Airbath Group from Aquarius, and on their subsequent AIM listings. Head of department **Peter Smart** (see p.246) was recommended to researchers for his experience and client skills. He advised Homestyle Group on its £12 million

YORKSHIRE/NORTH EAST ■ CORPORATE FINANCE

acquisition of Sleepmaster. **Clients** Aquarius Group; Butler Group; Evans of Leeds; Homestyle Group; Lloyds TSB Development Capital; Persimmon; Tay Homes.

LUPTON FAWCETT This expanded and strengthened team is experienced in a range of M&A transactions, AIM flotations and fundraising, much of it up to a value of around £25 million. Led by Bob Harrap, the department has "*good contacts and a cost-effective service for a certain type of deal,*" according to market sources. It has advised on a wide range of large, complex transactions, including AIM listings for marketing communications group Real Affinity and software company MOS International, as well as on a number of sales and acquisitions for listed companies. **Clients** Federal-Mogul; ICM Computer Group; Jarvis Porter; MOS International; Musedia; Real Affinity; TEAMtalk Media Group.

ROLLITS (see firm details p.1115) This traditional firm more than holds its own in the local marketplace. With its dedicated, regional focus, it is active on purchases, disposals and transactions in the debt buyout market, mostly up to a value of around £20 million, on behalf of its client base of owner-managed businesses. Head of company commercial Richard Field, who also runs the firm's banking group, leads a team that includes experienced financial advisers. It has acted on a diverse range of matters including supply agreements, credit facilities, joint ventures, sales and acquisitions and funding arrangements. **Clients** Corporates.

ANDREW M JACKSON (see firm details p.845) Amongst the leading players in Hull, the team under Mark Warburton has focused on mainstream M&A work and disposals for owner-managed businesses, and has particular expertise in the food sector. The firm is currently expanding its commercial capacity, and benefits from regular referrals and instructions from the accountancy market. **Clients** Local corporates.

COBBETTS (see firm details p.914) In taking over the former Read Hind Stewart, Manchester-based Cobbetts is seizing the opportunity to expand across the Pennines, reaching new clients and offering enhanced services to its existing base of mid-sized corporates. Although the merger was too recent to ascertain its effects on the market, observers note that the firm, which has already recruited extra staff, looks to be making steady progress. **Clients** Local and national corporates.

GOSSCHALKS Best known in the market for its commercial property and licensing expertise, the firm's corporate finance team assists local private companies on M&A and MBO work, and enjoys some work for plcs and quoted groups. Company commercial head Simon Lunt leads a team that has assisted Humber Growers on its multimillion pound acquisition of tomato growers Van Heyningen Brothers. Strong on partner involvement, the group has also assisted Dixon Motors on a Super Class 1 stock exchange transaction, and on the sale and leaseback of its operating premiums and SPVs. The firm has become directly authorised by the FSA and acts as corporate advisor to several OFEX members. **Clients** Dixon Motors; Fidelity Systems; HPI Group; Humber Growers; MSI Software Technology; Newlands Scientific.

IRWIN MITCHELL (see firm details p.1009) The firm has adapted to the market downturn with an increase in disposal mandates and debt-funded buyouts. Department head **Kevin Cunningham** (see p.235) acted for the shareholders of Cestrum Group in its £10.3 million disposal to Heywood Williams Group, and assisted ZOO Media on its £7 million reverse takeover by Kazoo3d. The compact team also advised the Bank of Scotland on its £14.6 million facility for the redevelopment of the County Stand at York Racecourse. **Clients** Aberdeen Murray Johnstone; Adfil; ELDON Electric; John Mowlem & Company; Matthews Foods; Pan-Credit Systems; Salzgitter; Severfield-Rowen; Wilton Investments; ZOO Media Corporation.

NORTH EAST

CORPORATE FINANCE
■ NORTH EAST

1. **Dickinson Dees** Newcastle upon Tyne, Stockton on Tees
2. **Ward Hadaway** Newcastle upon Tyne
3. **Eversheds** Newcastle upon Tyne
4. **Robert Muckle** Newcastle upon Tyne
5. **Watson Burton** Newcastle upon Tyne

LEADING INDIVIDUALS

1. **BELLIS Nigel** Dickinson Dees
   HULLS Martin Ward Hadaway
2. **DAVISON Andrew** Eversheds
   FLYNN John Dickinson Dees
   PASS Jamie Dickinson Dees
   PHILLIPS Robert Robert Muckle
3. **GILTHORPE Ian** Robert Muckle
   HARKER Chris Dickinson Dees
   HOYLE Andrew Watson Burton
   SPETCH Mike Eversheds
   WILLIAMS Nigel Dickinson Dees

This book is the product of 6,582 1/2 hour interviews. See p.7 for BMRB audit. Within each band, firms are listed alphabetically. See individuals' profiles p.232

DICKINSON DEES (see firm details p.938) "*On top since the year dot,*" according to competitors, with a large and expanding practice, the department has undertaken a considerable amount of transactional work in the last year. This includes advice to the management team of East Midlands and Bournemouth Airports on the £234 million sale to Manchester Airport.

The group can offer a number of name partners with recent experience of major deals. Department head **Nigel Bellis** (see p.233), a "*constructive, sensible, decent individual*" according to competitors, assisted Grainger Trust on its joint venture with Deutsche Bank and £477 million joint bid for BPT. **John Flynn** (see p.237) ("*pragmatic and prepared to listen*") was instructed by the Go-Ahead Group on its £72 million acquisition of British Midland's ground handling business, while **Jamie Pass** (see p.244) assisted Lloyds TSB Development Capital on the demerger and AIM flotation of software group Comeleon. Finance expert **Chris Harker** (see p.105) has advised Northern Venture Managers on a variety of private equity-related matters, including the IBO of Stainton Metal Company. The year-old Tees Valley office, led by experienced and respected **Nigel Williams** (see p.249), has focused primarily on matters relating to the sale of substantial owner-managed businesses. **Clients** ARRIVA; BPT; CN Group; Comeleon; East Midlands and Bournemouth Airports; Go-Ahead Group; GOVIA; Lloyds TSB Development Capital; Northern Rock; Northern Venture Managers.

WARD HADAWAY (see firm details p.1180) Though not on the same scale as the regional leader, the firm's large team was felt by market sources to have closed the gap between it and the top tier. Despite market conditions, it has been involved in a number of AIM flotations, including that of software group Comeleon (£21 million) and optical filter manufacturer Zytronic (£15.5 million). It also assisted in the reverse takeover of the AIM-listed Names.co Internet company and on the £84 million IBO of Mi Services from Motherwell Bridge. Corporate head **Martin Hulls** (see p.239) was said by rivals to be "*pragmatic but no pushover.*" He has assisted on the £55 million techMARK flotation of X-ray equipment company Bede, and was extolled by rivals for his understanding of the financial services sector. **Clients** Bede; Comeleon; Zytronic.

EVERSHEDS (see firm details p.949) Acquisitions and disposals have kept the firm busy of

CORPORATE FINANCE ■ NORTH EAST/SCOTLAND

late, most notably its assistance to the seven local authority owners of Newcastle International Airport on the £300 million sale of a 49% stake. Highly respected **Andrew Davison** (see p.236) was involved in the Newcastle Airport deal, while head of department **Mike Spetch** (see p.246), respected for his experience and determination, has worked with Northern Enterprise on nine recent private equity investments in North East-based companies. Highly respected Michael Spriggs has left for an in-house position: peers comment it is too early to say what effect this will have on the department. **Clients** Invensys; Newcastle International Airport; Northern Enterprise; Reg Vardy; Simpsons Malt; UK Land Estates.

ROBERT MUCKLE With the slump in the venture capital market, the firm has witnessed an upsurge in rescue-type transactions and bank-supported M&A deals. The mid-sized team recently assisted the management on the £5 million MBO of Valeo Transmission from its French motor components parent, and also advised software group Atlantic EC on its reverse takeover by AIM-listed company Atlantic Global. **Robert Phillips** (see p.244) acted on the acquisition of media company Dr Otter from joint administrative receivers, while **Ian Gilthorpe** (see p.237), who has left his managing partner role for a more hands-on senior partner position, worked for the Stainton Metal Company on its £9 million MBO. **Clients** Atlantic EC; Bank of Scotland; Barclays Bank; Derwent Systems; Hedley Purvis; Kenmore Technical Services; McLean; Valeo Transmission; Yorkshire Bank.

WATSON BURTON While still a notable presence in the region, the firm was not felt by interviewees to command quite the profile of the top four. That said, the group has grown over the last year, and is developing a reputation amongst private companies outside of the immediate area. Senior partner **Andrew Hoyle** (see p.239) was instructed by AIM-listed company Lady In Leisure on the placing of £250,000 worth of shares, while the team acted for Canadian group Extreme CCTV on its acquisition of Derwent Systems. Further highlights included the unit's advice to Associated Co-operative Creameries on the complex purchase of Express Dairies' milk supply business in the north of England. **Clients** Albany Group Holdings; Associated Co-operative Creameries; CWS Group; Lady In Leisure; Lloyds TSB Bank; Premier Direct Group; Saint-Gobain Quartz.

SCOTLAND

CORPORATE FINANCE
■ SCOTLAND

1
- **Dickson Minto WS** Edinburgh, Glasgow
- **Maclay Murray & Spens** Edinburgh, Glasgow

2
- **Dundas & Wilson CS** Edinburgh
- **McGrigor Donald** Edinburgh, Glasgow
- **Shepherd+ Wedderburn** Edinburgh

3
- **Burness** Edinburgh, Glasgow
- **MacRoberts** Edinburgh, Glasgow
- **Paull & Williamsons** Aberdeen
- **Tods Murray WS** Edinburgh

4
- **Biggart Baillie** Edinburgh, Glasgow
- **Ledingham Chalmers** Aberdeen, Edinburgh

5
- **Brodies** Edinburgh
- **McClure Naismith** Edinburgh, Glasgow
- **Semple Fraser** Glasgow
- **Thorntons WS** Dundee

6
- **Fyfe Ireland WS** Edinburgh
- **Henderson Boyd Jackson WS** Edinburgh
- **Iain Smith & Company** Aberdeen
- **Stronachs** Aberdeen

This book is the product of 6,582 1/2 hour interviews. See p.7 for BMRB audit. Within each band, firms are listed alphabetically.

DICKSON MINTO WS (see firm details p.938) The firm has established a unique position in Scotland, and an unmatched profile for high-value corporate finance transactions. Such is its reputation, it can draw on a client base that reaches far outside Scotland. It is the firm of choice for many banks and financial institutions based in London, where it also has an office. It also remains the preferred team for many UK corporations involved in European deals. The firm is respected for its "*energetic and hard-working ethos*" and its ability to "*imaginatively interpret the unusual angle to achieve a commercial and legal solution.*"

Bruce Minto (see p.243) was said by peers to "*epitomise the commercial, sensible approach of the firm.*" Considered "*a superb networker and very likeable,*" he "*will compromise in unimportant areas to get the deal done*" according to clients. **Roderick Bruce** (see p.234) was also praised for his transactional ability, with competitors commenting that "*you know the transaction will go smoothly if he is on the other side.*" Experienced **Kevan McDonald** (see p.242) was also praised for his commercial nous, while **Keith Anderson** (see p.232) was described as "*helpful in taking the transaction forward.*" Sample highlights from a considerable list of major deals include advice to General Hospitals Group on its £1.1 billion securitisation.

Exhibiting its "*uniform commerciality,*" the team aided Wood Mackenzie on its £26 million buyout from Deutsche Bank, and advised Weatherford on its £175 million acquisition of Orwell Group. "*Enthusiastic and committed to giving a timely and informed response,*" it has also worked on the US IPO of Inveresk Research International. The firm's investment funds unit has this year received its first instructions from Scottish Widows, and, on the private equity side, it has assisted Henderson Private Equity on the £230 million IBO of Leisure Link. **Clients** Aon Risk Services; Artemis; Belhaven Brewery Group; Christian Salvesen; Havelock Europa; Henderson Private Equity; Intelli; McLaren Global Systems; Schlumberger; Scott Oswald; Weatherford; Wood Mackenzie.

MACLAY MURRAY & SPENS (see firm details p.1048) Respected by peers for its "*straightforward culture,*" many interviewees believe that it and Dickson Minto are putting some distance between themselves and the chasing pack. Its depth of resources and wealth of experience are brought to bear on both large, single transactions and on regular volume work for clients such as 3i and Scottish Equity Partners. According to clients and competitors, the firm boasts a host of "*uniformly good lawyers with the right approach,*" who regularly appear on headline deals. One such is **Magnus Swanson** (see p.247) who oversaw the £56 million sale of Inver House Distillers to Thailand's Pacific Spirits Group. "*Quite charming, with steel underneath,*" according to rivals, he gives clients "*a service they want in a manner they desire.*" **Ian Lumsden** (see p.241) has "*a great legal brain,*" which has been put to good use advising on a number of disposals, including Motherwell Bridge's sale of its Welding Systems and MB Composites divisions. Senior partner **Bruce Patrick** (see p.244) also continues to be warmly recommended, although he has had a lower profile this year.

"*Approachable and friendly*" **Graeme Sloan** (see p.246) was instructed by Scottish Widows on the outsourcing of various functions to international group State Street, and on the establishment of several limited partnership investment vehicles. Long-term client BPI worked with **Hilary Kane** (see p.240) on the sale of its retail carrier bag business to Bunzl. Her "*positive attitude*" would also have assisted Stagecoach on the £33 million sale of Glasgow Prestwick International Airport to a New Zealand-led consortium. New to our tables this year and recommended for especially complex transactions, **Michael Livingston** (see p.241) assisted Grampian Holdings on its £49 million disposal of The Edinburgh Woollen Mill and was involved in the demutualisation of Scottish Life. The firm's strength in refinancing and reorganisation is exemplified by **Kenneth Shand** (see p.246) ("*extremely easy to work with*") and his restructuring work with Semple Cochrane. The team has also assisted on top-quality fundraising work, such as the capital reorganisation and placing and open offer by the Gartmore

SCOTLAND ■ CORPORATE FINANCE

LEADING INDIVIDUALS

1
- MCNEILL Morag *McGrigor Donald*
- MINTO Bruce *Dickson Minto WS*
- SWANSON Magnus *Maclay Murray & Spens*

2
- BRUCE Roderick *Dickson Minto WS*
- GRAY Colin *McGrigor Donald*
- LUMSDEN Ian *Maclay Murray & Spens*
- MCDONALD Kevan *Dickson Minto WS*
- RAFFERTY John *Burness*
- WILL James *Shepherd+ Wedderburn*

3
- ALLAN David *Biggart Baillie*
- ANDERSON Keith *Dickson Minto WS*
- BARRIE Sidney *Paull & Williamsons*
- CUNNINGHAM Neil *MacRoberts*
- DICKSON Ian *MacRoberts*
- GIBB Stephen *Shepherd+ Wedderburn*
- GLEN Marian *Shepherd+ Wedderburn*
- HARDIE David *Dundas & Wilson CS*
- PATRICK Bruce *Maclay Murray & Spens*
- SLEIGH Andrew *Burness*
- SLOAN Graeme *Maclay Murray & Spens*

4
- BUCHAN Gordon *Paull & Williamsons*
- FRIER George *McClure Naismith*
- KANE Hilary *Maclay Murray & Spens*
- LIVINGSTON Michael *Maclay Murray & Spens*
- MASTERS Richard *McGrigor Donald*
- MCGINN James *MacRoberts*
- MEIKLEJOHN Iain *Shepherd+ Wedderburn*
- ROSE Kenneth *Dundas & Wilson CS*
- RUSSELL Stuart *Semple Fraser*
- SHAND Kenneth *Maclay Murray & Spens*
- SIMMONS William *Tods Murray WS*
- SMITH Campbell *Biggart Baillie*
- STARK Jamie *Paull & Williamsons*

See individuals' profiles p.232

Monthly Income Trust to raise up to £79 million. **Clients** 3i; Allied Distillers; Bank of Scotland; BPI; Compaq; Deutsche Bank; Grampian Holdings; John Menzies; LTG; Motherwell Bridge; Robert Wiseman Dairies; Scottish Enterprise; Scottish Radio Holdings; Scottish Widows; Semple Cochrane; Stagecoach.

DUNDAS & WILSON CS (see firm details p.943) Despite the firm's withdrawal from the Andersen Legal network, it retains a highly respected name throughout the UK, with admired strength and depth in its corporate team and a superb blue-chip client base. One of the largest corporate teams in Scotland, as IPOs and public issues have decreased, it has refocused on M&A and transactions involving real estate, including investment schemes involving limited partnerships and tax-efficient vehicles.

Group leader **David Hardie** continues to be recommended to researchers, though he was felt to have been less visible during the past year. Also well respected, **Kenneth Rose** led a team acting for long-term client the Royal Bank of Scotland on its £100 million buyout of a 50% stake in Virgin Direct Personal Finance. Already boasting a strong reputation in the financial services sector, the hi-tech and biotech industries are now growing sources of instruction. The team assisted optical software group Kymata on its £89 million sale to Alcatel and has also worked with the University of Glasgow's spin-out optoelectronics company, Intense Photonics, on a successful first round of fund-raising. **Clients** Ardana Bioscience; Intense Photonics; Kymata (now Alcatel Optronics UK); The Miller Group; National Australia Group Europe; Royal Bank of Scotland; Scottish Radio Holdings; Viragen.

MCGRIGOR DONALD (see firm details p.1065) Although interviewees are waiting to see what direction the firm will take following its link-up with KPMG, the retention of the McGrigor Donald name in Scotland is an indication of the firm's high profile and commercial weight. The corporate team utilises the firm's property strength and banking expertise well, working outside Scotland for domestic companies like HBOS. It also boasts niche expertise in refinancing for technology businesses. Highlights of the last year include assisting ScottishPower on the disposal of a retail chain and acting for Halladale on its AIM flotation.

"*Extremely talented and tenacious,*" according to rivals, **Morag McNeill** (see p.242) has worked on Brewin Dolphin's reverse takeover of Berry Birch & Noble via a share offer for Berkeley Financial Services Group. She remains the "*first choice on complicated matters*" for a number of clients. **Colin Gray** (see p.238) heads the UK corporate practice group and spends a few days each week in the London office. A talented, personable lawyer, he acted for West Coast Capital on a series of joint ventures, including a £200 million scheme with Grantchester to develop retail warehouses. Sharing his time between the firm's Glasgow and Belfast offices, **Richard Masters** (see p.242) has "*a no-nonsense approach that gets the job done.*" He advised Pacific Spirits (UK) on the £56 million acquisition of the issued share capital of Blair Mhor. **Clients** Bank of Scotland; Brewin Dolphin Securities; Celtic; Direct Line Life Insurance Company; Pacific Spirits (UK); ScottishPower; Wainhomes; West Coast Capital.

SHEPHERD+ WEDDERBURN (see firm details p.1130) Regarded by many in the market as a "*progressive, go-ahead firm,*" the team has historic strength in financial services work. This was put to good use recently in its work on several Eurobond programmes, including ScottishPower's issue of instruments valued at $7 billion. The last year has also seen a concerted effort to assist fund-managing companies, culminating in its work with The Scottish Provident Institution on the massive demutualisation and £2 billion sale of its business to Abbey National.

The group has increased its workload in the TMT and life sciences sectors, with practiced corporate finance head **James Will** (see p.249) advising biotech group Strakan Group on its £45 million private equity fund-raising, a deal in which the team also played a crucial project management role. Clients praised it for "*pulling out all the stops for you,*" while maintaining a "*friendly and cheerful, practical and commercial*" attitude. "*Capable and organised*" **Stephen Gibb** (see p.237) continues to be well received by the market. **Marian Glen** (see p.237) is considered to have particular expertise on the financial services side, as is **Iain Meiklejohn** (see p.242). The team assisted Friends Ivory & Sime in its £128.9 million acquisition of the retail investment and managed pension businesses of FPLO. **Clients** Bank of Scotland; Cairn Energy; Edinburgh Fund Managers; Friends Ivory & Sime; NMT Group; ScottishPower; The Scottish Provident Institution; Stagecoach Group.

BURNESS A well-respected name in this area, the firm has focused on its core activity of MBOs for large, predominantly private, companies. For example, the team aided the management of Bett Inns in the £13 million purchase of 15 pubs, three hotels and a nightclub from Bett Brothers. Peers consider it to be "*consolidating and progressing well.*" Other recent highlights include advising Acuid on an $8 million investment by Mercury Asset Management, and representing Highland Spring on its acquisition of The Gleneagles Spring Water Company. "*Practical, sharp and with a hands-on approach,*" **John Rafferty** acted for Toronto-based Hummingbird on its £13.5 million acquisition of Scottish software company PeopleDoc, a transaction carried out wholly online. **Andrew Sleigh** was recommended by clients for his ability to overcome difficulties during transactions. **Clients** Acuid; Baxters; Bett Inns; Brewin Dolphin Securities; FairBriar; Highland Spring; Hummingbird; Idesta Group; Scottish Equity Partners; SEET; SMG.

MACROBERTS (see firm details p.1049) Appreciated for its specialism in construction-related corporate issues, the team has focused this year on traditional M&A. Peers considered the firm to be more "*constructively aggressive*" than some and "*a good choice for problem situations,*" while clients appreciated "*a supportive and capable team, which gives us its undivided attention.*" The firm recently assisted the Johnston Press on its acquisition of titles from Trinity Mirror and Best Guides, and worked with the Royal Bank of Scotland on the £89 million public to private of Regalian Properties. "*Experienced and capable*" **Neil Cunningham** (see p.235) has acted for AWG in relation to various joint ventures, while **Ian Dickson** (see p.236) ("*a lot of commercial acumen*") advised British Energy on a deal with Ontario Power Generation to acquire nuclear power stations.

CORPORATE FINANCE ■ SCOTLAND

Qualified in Scotland and England, **James McGinn** (see p.242) was recommended to researchers for his venture capital-related corporate work. **Clients** AWG; Bank of America; Bank of Scotland; Bridgepoint Capital; CIBC World Markets; Curtis Fine Paper; Initiative Software; ISI Group; Johnston Press; Keydata UK; Memex; Royal Bank of Scotland.

PAULL & WILLIAMSONS (see firm details p.1096) Famed for its oil and gas work, the firm remains, in the eyes of most interviewees, the biggest and best in Aberdeen and retains its premier status there. Clients praise its mixture of "*legal knowledge and commercial acumen.*" Unlike much of the Scottish market, the oil and gas sector has enjoyed a contra-cyclical boom, leading to a stream of corporate-related work in this area. Praised by peers as "*exceptionally experienced,*" corporate head **Sidney Barrie** (see p.232) has assisted First Oil on a number of acquisitions, including that of Roots Gas. Described by several interviewees as "*the pre-eminent corporate lawyer in the region,*" he "*doesn't dwell on academic niceties.*" **Gordon Buchan** (see p.234) has been involved in a number of matters in the upstream oil and gas sector, where the large, partner-led team has advised BP on the disposal of gas interests in the North Sea. "*Highly rated*" **Jamie Stark** (see p.247) is a new entry to our tables this year, winning praise for his practical approach, especially on cross-border work. **Clients** ASCO; BP; Dana Petroleum; FirstGroup; First Oil; Orwell Group; The PSL Group; Talisman Energy.

TODS MURRAY WS (see firm details p.1164) Buoyed by some huge, high-profile deals, and respected by competitors for striving to strengthen and deepen its corporate abilities, the firm has been active in a range of traditional M&A and corporate deals, often involving property investment elements. The team made all the right impressions as Scottish legal advisors to the Bank of Scotland on its high-profile merger with the Halifax, leading to the establishment of HBOS. It was led by **William Simmons** (see p.699), who went on to assist HBOS in connection with its raising of £6 billion to augment its Tier 1 Capital base. Other highlights for the firm included advising PeopleDoc on its sale to Hummingbird and working on Scotland's largest ever MBO, that of US distiller Jim Beam Brands Worldwide's UK operations. Other recent work includes substantial restructurings and AIM listings. **Clients** Bank of Scotland; HBOS; Jim Beam Brands Worldwide; KeyWorld Investments; Maclay Group; PeopleDoc; Taylor Woodrow.

BIGGART BAILLIE (see firm details p.871) Respected by peers for its quietly competent approach, the corporate team acted for AorTech International on its transfer from AIM to the Official List. Corporate department head **David Allan** is said by clients to understand transactions well and to be reasonable to deal with. Managing partner **Campbell Smith** remains on hand for advice and support. The team has advised Danish AVK Holdings' subsidiary Glenfield Valves on the acquisition of the businesses and assets of engineering group Glenfield & Kennedy. **Clients** Aberdeen Asset Managers; AorTech International; Brewin Dolphin Securities; Glenfield Valves; Scottish Amicable Life; UA Comms.

LEDINGHAM CHALMERS (see firm details p.1034) In common with other Aberdeen firms, the oil and gas side of its corporate business has been busy this year. Included in its long list of recent highlights is the sale of independent oil start-up Highland Energy, with assets in the southern North Sea, to the German-listed company RWE-DEA. The Edinburgh office, too, has experienced some growth, if not to the same extent, and the firm remains one of only two 3i panel firms in Scotland. Under the leadership of Malcolm Laing, the compact team has acted for SPS-AFOS Group on the 3i-funded acquisition of Global Completion Services in Louisiana and Houston. Through its Edinburgh office, it has also aided Macdonald Hotels in its joint venture to acquire Heritage Hotels for £230 million. **Clients** 3i Group; Bank of Scotland; CALA Group; John Wood Group; Macdonald Hotels; Newco; Ramco Energy; Rigblast Group; SPS-AFOS Group.

BRODIES (see firm details p.889) Despite a lower profile this year, according to some interviewees, the firm remains a well known presence in the market, respected in particular for its public sector work. It was recently reappointed by the Strategic Rail Authority (SRA) to deal with its ongoing franchising agreements, and also received work from the DTI concerning the separation of the businesses of Scottish electricity companies. The well-sized team under corporate head John Smith handles volume transactions as well as highly complex work. Property-related corporate work is a particular strength, and the firm assisted Land Securities Trillium on the Scottish aspects of the £2.38 billion acquisition by Telereal of BT's UK property portfolio, one of the largest outsourcing deals in the UK. **Clients** DTI; IFA Portfolio; Joint Stock Company Hotel Tbilisi; Land Securities Trillium; MAB (UK); MOD; Shetland Leasing and Property Developments; SRA.

MCCLURE NAISMITH (see firm details p.1062) The firm has taken on new staff from the industry and has been involved in several major deals. Peter Wilson, the corporate head of the growing Edinburgh office, and his team continued to assist on the Scottish aspects of Pernod Ricard's acquisition of Seagram's wine and spirits business, and advised Norsk Hydro and Sustainable Asset Management (SAM) on a £6 million investment in offshore wave energy group Ocean Power Delivery.

In Glasgow, **George Frier** (see p.237) and the group assisted Hydro Seafood GSP on its sale to Norwegian company Leroy. It was also involved in the corporate reorganisation and AIM flotation of patent attorneys Murgitroyd Group, the only such company so far to be listed. **Clients** Hydro Seafood GSP; Kyndal International; Murgitroyd Group; Norsk Hydro; Sustainable Asset Management.

SEMPLE FRASER (see firm details p.1125) Praised by clients for its commercial acumen and "*solid business advice,*" this corporate team concentrates on work for the upper end of the SME market and for its entrepreneurial clients. Unit head **Stuart Russell** (see p.245), who continues to attract warm recommendation, advised Insensia Group on its public offer and admission of shares to the OFEX market, as well as on its subsequent acquisition of Company Eye. The team has acted on a number of disposals, including the sale of the spring water division of Coffee Express to Watsons Water (Holdings). Praised by clients for its "*competent, efficient and timely*" advice, the team also acted for the vendors on the £13 million sale of Oakwood Foods to Macphie of Glenbervie. **Clients** Aspects Software; The Bed Shed Group; Coffee Express; Insensia Group; Macaskill Haulage; Oakwood Foods; Strathclyde Pharmaceuticals.

THORNTONS WS (see firm details p.1162) This high-profile Dundee firm has a strong presence in the local market and has a solid client base. Well known for assisting academic and educational groups with their corporate requirements, recent work has included establishing biotech spin-outs for Dundee's universities and advising technology and software groups. The team has seen its corporate work increase with additional instructions from banks, and has acted on the MBO of a UK-based transport company and on a number of disposals and acquisitions. **Clients** Universities; technology companies; local corporates.

FYFE IRELAND WS (see firm details p.966) A partner-led team continues to do good work at this efficient, mid-sized firm. Following a mixture of arrivals and departures over the last few years, head of corporate David Lindgren has overseen a reorganisation of the team. Known for strength in the property sector, it has continued to act on behalf of The University of Edinburgh's spin-out companies, and has assisted in some substantial fund-raising activities, including a £100 million joint venture for a hotel company. Clients find its London satellite office an additional benefit. **Clients** Property companies; local corporates.

HENDERSON BOYD JACKSON WS Typical work at the firm includes share issues, such as the recent £10 million share issue for The Capital Pub Company, and MBOs, including the £6 million buyout of textile dyeing and finishing group Langholm Dyeing, where the team represented Royal Bank of Scotland. The firm's experience of corporate insolvency work has also been put to use, acting for the purchaser of Signum Circuits from the receiver. **Clients** BUE Marine; The Capital Pub Company; Heriot-Watt University; Highfield; Jarvis; Peel Hunt; Royal Bank of Scotland; Signum Circuits.

IAIN SMITH & COMPANY A "*small group with good people,*" according to interviewees, this Aberdeen-based practice continues to pursue predominantly mid-range work for a broad sweep of clients, including private companies and start-ups. **Clients** Local corporates.

STRONACHS New to the tables this year, competitors believe that this corporate team is carving out an enviable reputation. Praised for bringing a lot of energy and enthusiasm to the table, the team is particularly active on deals within the energy sector, many of them with an international flavour. The department, led by David Rennie, has recently acted for oil and gas production company, Venture Production, on a £40 million placing and London listing. **Clients** Oil and gas companies.

NORTHERN IRELAND

CORPORATE FINANCE
NORTHERN IRELAND

[1]
- Carson McDowell Belfast
- L'Estrange & Brett Belfast

[2]
- Mills Selig Belfast

[3]
- Arthur Cox Belfast
- Tughans Belfast

[4]
- Cleaver Fulton Rankin Belfast
- Elliott Duffy Garrett Belfast

[5]
- Johns Elliot Belfast
- Johnsons Belfast

LEADING INDIVIDUALS

[1]
- FULTON Richard Mills Selig
- IRVINE John L'Estrange & Brett
- JAMISON David Carson McDowell
- JOHNSTON Michael Carson McDowell

[2]
- GRAY Richard L'Estrange & Brett

[3]
- CANAVAN Kerry Arthur Cox
- MCBRIDE Paul L'Estrange & Brett

[4]
- MARSHALL John Johnsons
- WILLIS John-George Tughans

UP AND COMING
- MCVEIGH Kevin Elliott Duffy Garrett
- STAFFORD Peter Arthur Cox

UP AND COMING
- TAYLOR Alan Carson McDowell

This book is the product of 6,582 1/2 hour interviews. See p.7 for BMRB audit. Within each band, firms are listed alphabetically. See individuals' profiles p.232

CARSON MCDOWELL (see firm details p.901) Researchers were impressed with the level of commendation shown to the team's individuals. "*Pleasant and pragmatic*" **Alan Taylor** (see p.248) was noted for his work in the IT and energy sectors, while **David Jamison** (see p.240) was endorsed as "*easy to work with – a dealdoer.*" Colleague **Michael Johnston** (see p.240) is also "*technically strong and practical.*" The team advised Viridian Group on its sale to a management buyout team of the insurance and consumer finance business of Open + Direct. It also acted for HCL Technologies in the establishment of its Northern Ireland-based call centre operation conducted by its subsidiary company HCL Technologies (Northern Ireland). **Clients** Nigen; Open + Direct; Translink.

L'ESTRANGE & BRETT (see firm details p.1039) The group was acclaimed by peers as "*the front-runners in corporate work.*" A raft of talent at partner level includes head of corporate **John Irvine** (see p.239), ex-City lawyer **Richard Gray** (see p.238) and **Paul McBride** (see p.242), who has a focus on M&A, MBOs and venture capital projects. The team acted for Dr Allen McClay on an acquisition from Galen Holdings of its Clinical Trial Division for £130 million, the largest MBO of its kind in Northern Ireland. It also completed the disposal for JP Corry Group of the timber and builders materials division of the RK Timber Group to Wolseley Centers. **Clients** UTV; Sx3; Viridian.

MILLS SELIG (see firm details p.1072) An "*approachable team,*" it fields the "*capable and commercial*" **Richard Fulton** (see p.237). A good mix of work sees the team carrying out restructuring, fund-raising, acquisitions and disposals for plcs and Northern Ireland-based blue-chip companies. The team advised First Derivatives on its flotation on AIM. Biotechnology is an emerging niche for the team, while funding for venture capital houses remains a forte. **Clients** DCC Energy (N I); First Derivatives; Crescent Capital (NI); Enterprise Equity (NI); Galen Holdings.

ARTHUR COX (see firm details p.850) Local businesses, cross-border work and referrals from London have kept the team occupied on a series of acquisitions, MBOs and MBIs. The team is led by **Kerry Canavan** (see p.234), applauded by peers for being "*reasonable and a good technician.*" She is ably aided by **Peter Stafford** (see p.247). Highlights for the group include a multimillion pound acquisition of a dairy business and a MBO of a supply chain management company for £4.8 million. **Clients** Technology companies; supermarkets.

TUGHANS (see firm details p.1169) An "*aggressive and forthright team*" boasts the presence of **John-George Willis** (see p.249), a lawyer who "*will get on with things.*" The firm acts on M&A, buyouts and disposals. The team acted on the MBO, backed by Alchemy Partners, of the financial services and retail credit businesses of Open + Direct for £111.4 million. It also represented Arogan in the acquisition of three Northern Irish textiles operations. **Clients** Amacis; Kainos Software; Meridio.

CLEAVER FULTON RANKIN (see firm details p.910) The team deals with the whole spectrum of corporate work, covering partnership agreements, refinancing, sales and acquisitions. A growing corporate client base sees major plcs with an interest in Northern Ireland sat alongside local councils and sole traders. An increasing amount of work in the energy sector has also been witnessed. The team, led by head of department Jenny Ebbage, advised on Northern Irish corporate aspects of the sale and leaseback of the BT property portfolio. The team has also advised on the £14 million investment in the Northern Ireland Science Park. **Clients** NI Science Park Foundation; BT; Galleon; William Dowling.

ELLIOTT DUFFY GARRETT (see firm details p.947) The team acts for local and international organisations on the range of corporate matters. Former in-house banking lawyer **Kevin McVeigh** (see p.242) is the notable individual here, offering in particular specialist expertise in European law matters. **Clients** Local corporates.

JOHNS ELLIOT (see firm details p.1016) This well-respected firm acts for public companies and large corporate bodies on company reorganisations, mergers and MBOs, and flotations. Respected Maurice Butler is now acting on a consultancy basis for the firm, while David Leitch is the key contact partner for corporate matters. **Clients** Local corporates.

JOHNSONS (see firm details p.1016) The team continues to act on acquisitions and disposals for its primarily private corporate client base. "*Pragmatic and straightforward,*" **John Marshall** was warmly recommended during our research. **Clients** Local corporates

CORPORATE FINANCE ■ THE LEADERS

THE LEADERS IN CORPORATE FINANCE

ACOCK, Roger
Lyons Davidson, Bristol
(0117) 904 5887
racock@lyonsdavidson.co.uk
Specialisation: Recently moved from *Bond Pearce* to *Lyons Davidson* to continue corporate work, specialising in corporate finance. Whilst at *Bond Pearce* led teams on many high profile MBO, MIB, IBO and other corporate finance transactions across the Southern region, including £35m buyout of British International from CHC Helicopter Corporation, £150m merger of Flagship Foods, MBO of financial services division of Aon Corporation to form Momentum Financial Services and 2 major acquisitions for Flagship Foods. Since joining *Lyons Davidson* in May 2001 has completed a £97m refinancing for a listed PLC and numerous acquisitions and disposals including its sale of a South West based housebuilding company. Special interest and experience in waste mangement and aviation law.
Prof. Memberships: Member of the International Bar Association and Solicitors European Group. Chairman of the Devon and Cornwall Branch of the Institute of Directors. Director of SITA Environmental Trust and PLC Employee Share Trust.
Career: Qualified 1980. Partner at *Bond Pearce* 1985. Previous firm *Durrant Piesse* (now *Lovells*); *Bond Pearce*.

ALLAN, David
Biggart Baillie, Glasgow
(0141) 228 8000

ALLEN, Amanda
Hammond Suddards Edge, Birmingham
(0121) 222 3000

ANDERSON, Keith T
Dickson Minto WS, Glasgow
(0141) 229 4455
keith.anderson@dmws.com
Specialisation: Partner in corporate department, based in Glasgow. Corporate and commercial; mergers and acquisitions, management buyins and outs, institutional buyouts, sale and purchase of companies and businesses, refinancings.
Prof. Memberships: Law Society of Scotland; Society of Writers to the Signet.
Career: Qualified in 1981. Joined *Dickson Minto WS* as senior assistant in 1989 and assumed as a partner in 1994.
Personal: Born 24 January 1957. Attended George Watson's College 1962-75; University of Edinburgh 1975-79 (LLB(Hons)). Leisure interests include rugby, golf, football and music.

ANGEL, Peter
Manches, Oxford
(01865) 722106
peter.angel@manches.co.uk
Specialisation: Head of the Corporate Department of *Manches*, Oxford. Specialises in mergers, acquisitions, management buyouts and buyins and joint ventures with a particular interest in venture capital work. Regular speaker at seminars on corporate finance topics.
Career: Qualified 1970.
Personal: Born 27 July, 1946. Attended Maidstone Grammar School 1959-64 and then University College London. Board member of The College of Estate Management. Lives in Oxford.

ARMITAGE, David W K
Hammond Suddards Edge, Leeds
(0113) 284 7000

ASHWORTH, Chris
Ashurst Morris Crisp, London
(020) 7638 1111
chris.ashworth@ashursts.com
Specialisation: Mergers and acquisitions, corporate finance, insolvency, transactional work and finance. Clients include investment banks and corporates such as United Business Media, Deutsche Telekom, British Telecom, AMVESCAP, Northern Foods plc, Virgin, Royal Sun Alliance, Railtrack Group and Henlys.
Career: LLB graduate of Southampton University. Lectured at Manchester University. Joined *Ashurst Morris Crisp* in 1982 and became a partner in 1986, head of company in 2001.

AUDLEY, Max
Hobson Audley, London
(020) 7450 4500
maudley@hobsonaudley.co.uk
Specialisation: Head of company department. Specialises in corporate finance, IPOs, MBOs, takeovers, mergers and acquisitions.
Prof. Memberships: International Bar Association – Company Law Committee. Associate of American Bar Association - Business Law Section. Association of German-speaking lawyers.
Career: Qualified 1980. Co-founded *Hobson Audley* 1983. Has built up a team of experienced corporate lawyers.

AUSTIN, James
Birketts, Ipswich
(01473) 406212
james-austin@birketts.co.uk
Specialisation: Acts for a significant number of well-known East Anglian clients, as well as some US multinationals. Heads up *Birketts'* Technology Team, which incorporates a thriving trademark practice.
Prof. Memberships: IOD, ITMA, ELTA.
Career: 1984-89 *Lovells*; 1989-date *Birketts*.
Personal: Read civil engineering at Imperial College, London, before qualifying as a Solicitor in the City. Married with three children. Plays the odd game of squash and tennis.

BAKER, Andrew
Wedlake Bell, London
(020) 7395 3031
abaker@wedlakebell.com
Specialisation: Partner. Specialises in corporate law. Acts for a wide range of listed companies, brokers and venture capitalists with regard to mergers and acquisitions, equity issues and flotations. Speaker at seminars and conferences with regard to corporate governance and buying and selling companies.
Career: Articled with *Slaughter and May* in 1970. Qualified 1972, joining the Commercial Department of *Slaughter and May*. Joined *Wedlake Bell* in 1979 becoming a Partner in 1982. Head of Corporate Finance from 1985-2001. President of the international alliance of independent commercial law firms, TELFA (Trans European Law Firms Alliance). Member of committees of European Association of APCIMS-EASD. Member of the Corporate Finance Faculty.
Personal: Born 12 October 1946. LLB (Hons) Birmingham 1969. Lives in Surrey. Also a Director of The Global Group plc, The Egyptian-British Chamber of Commerce and Lambeth Building Society.

BARNARD, Stephen
Herbert Smith, London
(020) 7374 8000
stephen.barnard@herbertsmith.com
Specialisation: Partner handling a wide range of company and commercial work including corporate finance, takeovers, mergers and acquisitions, private equity and leveraged transactions, privatisations and major projects and reorganisations. His work involves listed clients as well as financial intermediaries, institutions and government. Has often been involved in the largest and most complex transactions.
Career: Qualified 1974. Partner at *Herbert Smith* since 1983.
Personal: Educated at Southampton University.

BARNES, Oliver
Travers Smith Braithwaite, London
(020) 7295 3000
Oliver.Barnes@TraversSmith.com
Specialisation: Head of *Travers Smith Braithwaite's* Company Department. Corporate and corporate finance. Public takeovers, mergers and acquisitions, flotations and secondary issues. Corporate governance.
Prof. Memberships: Member of Law Society's Company Law Committee; International Bar Association.
Career: Articled at *Travers Smith Braithwaite*. Qualified 1976. Partner 1980.
Personal: Born 1950. Educated at Eton College and Trinity Hall, Cambridge.

BARR, Alan
Burges Salmon, Bristol
(0117) 939 2255
alan.barr@burges-salmon.com
Specialisation: Company law and corporate finance including business and company acquisitions and disposals, public company flotations and reversals, equity financing and takeovers, corporate restructuring and management buyouts and buyins for clients such as Brandon Hire plc FirstGroup plc, Milk Link, Orange Personal Communications, Rotork plc, Science Systems plc, Surface Technology Systems plc, Tyco Holdings. Alan acts for and is company secretary of Bristol City Football Club.
Prof. Memberships: Law Society's Standing Committee on Company Law.
Career: Trained with *Slaughter and May*, joined *Clifford Chance* for four years, joined *Burges Salmon* in 1986 and became a partner in 1988.
Personal: Brought up in Northern Ireland, graduated in law from University of Wales. Keen hill walker, cyclist and swimmer.

BARRIE, Sidney
Paull & Williamsons, Aberdeen
(01224) 621621
sbarrie@paull-williamsons.co.uk
Specialisation: Partner in the Corporate Department specialising in MBOs and acquisitions and disposals. Also advises on general corporate law, including reconstructions, investment documentation and contractual work.
Prof. Memberships: Law Society of Scotland; Society of Advocates in Aberdeen.
Career: *James & George Collie* 1971-73. Joined *Paul & Williamsons* 1973, partner 1978.
Personal: Educated at Robert Gordon's College, Aberdeen 1962-68 and at Aberdeen University 1968-71. Leisure pursuits include golf and watching football. Lives in Aberdeen. Born 14 June 1950.

BATES, Stephanie
Mayer, Brown, Rowe & Maw, London
(020) 7782 8833
sbates@eu.mayerbrownrowe.com
Specialisation: Mergers, acquisition and disposal, corporate finance, joint ventures.
Prof. Memberships: International Bar association.
Career: Articled *Rowe & Maw*; qualified 1985; seconded to Australian Law firm 1987. Admitted to New South Wales 1989; Partner *Rowe & Maw* 1991.
Personal: North London Collegiate School; Southampton University (LLB). Born 1960; Resides London and Kent. Opera, gardening and travel.

BAXTER, Richard
Stevens & Bolton, Guildford
(01483) 734 213
Specialisation: All aspects of company law, including acquisitions, disposals, MBOs and other venture capital transactions, reorganisations, joint ventures and new issues. Recent transactions include the sale of Delphis Consulting plc to Morse plc for up to £40 million and the purchase by Hays Personnel Services Limited of leading legal recruitment consultants ZMB Limited for a substantial

232 INDEX TO LEADING LAWYERS: PAGE 1693 ■ IN-HOUSE LAWYERS PROFILES: PAGE 1201

THE LEADERS ■ CORPORATE FINANCE

undisclosed sum.
Career: St Paul's School; Exeter University (LLB Hons). 1985 *Clifford-Turner* (now *Clifford Chance*). Specialised in corporate finance before joining *Stevens & Bolton*, becoming Partner in 1990. Head of Company/Commercial Department.
Publications: Contributor to 'Tolley's Company Law'.
Personal: Born 5 May 1962. Married with two children. Leisure interests include golf (Hankley Common Golf Club), fishing, horse riding, other sport, cinema, gardening and family.

BEARDSLEY, Alison
Allen & Overy, London
(020) 7330 3000
alison.beardsley@allenovery.com
Specialisation: Partner specialising in corporate finance work, including private and public company takeovers (including public to private), share issues, cross-border merges and acquisitions and joint ventures. Substantial privatisation experience. Partner responsible for graduate recruitment.
Career: Articled *Allen & Overy*; qualified 1983; secondment with Bowater Plc 1985-87; partner 1990.
Personal: Ecclesbourne School; Jesus College, Oxford (1980, BA Hons).

BEASTALL, Jonathan
Clifford Chance, London
(020) 7600 1000
Jonathan.Beastall@cliffordchance.com
Specialisation: Corporate. Partner specialising in corporate finance, M&A, takeovers and Stock Exchange matters.
Career: Articled *Clifford-Turner*; qualified 1985; Partner since 1993; admitted as a solicitor of the Supreme Court of New South Wales.
Personal: Birmingham University.

BELL, Christopher
Travers Smith Braithwaite, London
(020) 7295 3000
christopher.bell@traversmith.com
Specialisation: Corporate and corporate finance – mergers and acquisitions, equity financings, MBO's and MBI's. Corporate governance issues.
Prof. Memberships: Member of the City of London Solicitors Company.
Career: Articled at *Crossman Block & Keith*, 1969; became an assistant at *Travers Smith Braithwaite* in 1971 and was elected a Partner in 1976. Is now the Senior Partner.

BELLEW, Derek
Veale Wasbrough, Bristol
(0117) 925 2020
dbellew@vwl.co.uk
See under Partnership, p.600

BELLIS, Nigel
Dickinson Dees, Newcastle upon Tyne
(0191) 279 9250
Specialisation: Partner in Company and Commercial Department. Handles flotations, share issues, mergers and acquisitions, IT contracts, e-commerce advice and complex commercial agreements. Clients include public companies, utilities and substantial private companies, as well as public sector organisations.
Prof. Memberships: Law Society.
Career: Qualified in 1977. Joined *Dickinson Dees* in 1980 and became a Partner in 1982.
Personal: Born 1953. Educated at Cambridge University 1971-74. Lives in Newcastle upon Tyne.

BELLIS, Tim
Herbert Smith, London
(020) 7374 8000
tim.bellis@herbertsmith.com
Specialisation: Partner in corporate division. Has concentrated particularly in the areas of mergers and acquisitions, corporate finance, securities offerings and capital markets transactions on international stock exchanges (London, Hong Kong and Luxembourg) and investment and joint venture work. The clients for whom he acts range from international and regional investment and merchant banks, publicly owned and private companies to government organisations and regulatory bodies.
Career: Qualified in 1981 and became partner in 1987.

BENNETT, John
Berwin Leighton Paisner, London
(020) 7760 1000
john.bennett@blplaw.com
Specialisation: Mergers and acquisitions, corporate finance, private equity and general company and securities law specialist.
Prof. Memberships: City of London Law Society Company Laws Sub-committee.
Career: Qualified in 1983 with *Berwin Leighton*. Became a Partner in 1987. Head of Corporate.

BERRY, Stephen
M and A Solicitors, Cardiff
(029) 2066 5793
Specialisation: Corporate and commercial work with an emphasis on mergers, acquisitions, disposals and fund-raisings. Transactions in the last 12 months include advising on the acquisition of Glasgow Prestwick Airport from Stagecoach Group plc and further transactions in the aviation sector; a major fundraising by JDH Holdings Limited together with a series of acquisitions in the dental sector; the acquisition by Cleary Foods Limited of the Mountstevens bakery chain.
Career: 1991-93 *Herbert Smith*; 1993-99 *Eversheds*, appointed partner in 1998; 1999 present *M and A Solicitors*, one of the founding partners.
Personal: Married with two daughters. Lives in Cardiff and is a keen sportsman. He enjoys sailing, skiing, windsurfing, rugby and football.

BIRCHALL, Roger
Hammond Suddards Edge, Birmingham
(0121) 222 3000

BIRT, Tim
Osborne Clarke, London
(020) 7809 1000

BLACKWELL, Nigel
Browne Jacobson, Nottingham
(0115) 976 6210
nblackwell@brownej.co.uk
Specialisation: Private corporate acquisitions and disposals.
Career: *Browne Jacobson* from 1986 to present day.
Personal: Married with twins (11 months) – currently no time for anything else.

BLOWER, Geoffrey
Eversheds, Manchester
(0161) 831 8000
geoffreyblower@eversheds.com
Specialisation: Partner in Corporate Department, *Eversheds*, Manchester. Main area of practice is corporate finance including mergers and acquisitions, flotations, management buyouts, disposals, stock exchange and "Blue Book" work and non-contentious corporate work. Sector experience includes dairy industry, pharmaceuticals, leisure, automotive and engineering. Principal transactions include the Co-operative Wholesale Society's £111m disposal of its Food Manufacturing Group; again for the Co-operative Wholesale Society spearheaded the team which dealt with the complex exchange of assets and businesses with Dale Farm Dairy Group where the total assets involved were £30m; Stanley Leisure plc in its £15m recommended takeover of Gus Carter plc and its subsequent casino and betting shop acquisitions; for Kingspan Group in the acquisition of Kooltherm Holdings Limited and for United Northwest Co-operatives Limited in its acquisition of Hanburys Limited and its chain of 30 convenience stores and in the Society's acquisition of Nevins Limited and its 12 convenience store chain and a chain of 26 'Dawn til Dusk' convenience stores. He acted for Quicks Group plc in its acquisition of the Motor Retail Division of Caverdale Group plc (comprising some 30 companies) for £45.5m with its attendant Rights Issue and Placing and for Granville Private Equity in its £20m MBI of Ora Electronics UK Limited. His more recent deals include acting for Holidaybreak plc (formerly Eurocamp plc) in its £37.5m recommended takeover of Baldwins plc and the subsequent disposal of Baldwins restaurant division; for the United Northwest Co-operatives and West Midlands Co-operative Society in the joint venture with First Choice PLC in relation to the development 'Holiday Hypermarkets'; for Stanley Leisure plc in its attempted £350m acquisition of the Coral betting business and the subsequent disposal of this interest for E4SM; and in its successful £86.4m recommended takeover of Capital Corporation PLC, and the acquisition of two internet casinos; for Holidaybreak in its £30m acquisition of Explore Worldwide Limited and for United Norwest Co-operatives in its acquisition of SCI's Funeral Business in Northern Ireland.
Prof. Memberships: Law Society, Securities Institute.
Career: Qualified in 1972 and became a Partner in 1974.
Personal: Born 14 March 1948. Leisure pursuits include walking, cricket and theatre.

BOARDMAN, Nigel
Slaughter and May, London
(020) 7600 1200
nigel.boardman@slaughterandmay.com
Specialisation: M&A, corporate finance, corporate and commercial. Advises UK and overseas companies and investment banks on the full range of corporate transactions, including acquisitions, disposals, takeovers, joint ventures, financings, flotations, MBOs and general corporate advice.
Career: Qualified in 1975 while with *Slaughter and May*. Joined the Corporate Finance Department of *Kleinwort Benson Limited* before returning to *Slaughter and May*, becoming Partner in 1982 and Head of Corporate in 1996.

BOND, Richard
Herbert Smith, London
(020) 7374 8000
richard.bond@herbertsmith.com
See under Energy, p.341

BORKOWSKI, Andrew
Edwards Geldard, Derby
(01332) 378314
andrew.borkowski@geldards.co.uk
Specialisation: Acquisitions and disposals; MBOs and MBI; equity fund raising; cross-border deals; joint ventures; flotations and regularly advises banks on transactions. Recent work includes a number of transactions for Chubb plc, Pendragon plc, Newell Rubbermaid Inc, HBOS and RBS.
Prof. Memberships: Law Society.
Career: With *Edge & Ellison* prior to joining *Edwards Geldard* in 1991.
Personal: Educated at Queen Elizabeth Grammar School and The Nottingham Trent University. Married with two children.

BOTT, Adrian
Osborne Clarke, London
(020) 7809 1000
Specialisation: Partner in corporate group. Main area of practice is corporate finance. Consistently involved in corporate activities ranging from M&A, MBOs and MBIs, through flotations (including many on AIM), rights issues, placings and other means of financing, to private equity (acting for both providers and consumers), both in domestic and international transactions. Clients are predominantly quoted or subsidiaries of multinationals. Most have a technology, communications or media bias. Also active in significant corporate joint ventures (such as BBC Worldwide/Flextech and Carphone Warehouse/AOL) and a broad spectrum of commercial contracts and employee incentivisation schemes. Has handled numerous consortium arrangements, leading a variety of consortia in bids for various TV and radio

233

CORPORATE FINANCE ■ THE LEADERS

broadcasting licences.
Prof. Memberships: Law Society, British Venture Capital Association.
Career: Qualified in 1980. *Rooks Rider* 1978-87, from 1984 as a partner. Partner at *Olswang* from 1988.
Personal: Born 9 June 1956. Charterhouse School 1969-73, Manchester University 1974-77 and Guildford Law School 1977.

BOUND, Andrew
Berry Smith, Cardiff
(02920) 345511
abound@berrysmith.com
Specialisation: Full range of corporate and commercial work including acquisitions, MBOs, refinancing and joint venture arrangements.
Prof. Memberships: Law Society.
Career: Qualified in 1989. Articled at *Eversheds*, Cardiff. Joined *Berry Smith* in 1984 as a Partner.
Personal: Born 25 March 1965. Educated at Reading University and Guildford College of Law. Interests include travelling and motor sports.

BRABNER, Michael
Brabners Chaffe Street, Liverpool
(0151) 600 3000
michael.brabner@brabnerscs.com
Specialisation: Corporate/corporate finance.
Prof. Memberships: Law Society.
Career: Shrewsbury School; Liverpool University; qualified 1974. Worked in corporate department of *Herbert Oppenheimer Nathan & Van Dyke* 1974-76. Partner *Brabner Holden Banks Wilson* 1976 to date.

BRAHAM, Edward
Freshfields Bruckhaus Deringer, London
(020) 7936 4000
edward.braham@freshfields.com
Specialisation: Partner in *Freshfield Bruckhaus Deringer's* Worldwide Corporate Group; specialising in domestic and cross-border public and private mergers and acquisitions, private equity deals and equity issues. Also a member of the firm's IT strategy committee and co-leads the firm's European public M&A know-how group. He is based in London.
Prof. Memberships: Law Society.
Career: Qualified 1987, Partner 1995.
Personal: Born 1961. Educated at Worcester College, Oxford 1980-84 (BA, BCL).

BRAITHWAITE, Stephen
Wragge & Co, Birmingham
(0870) 903 1000

BRIDGES WEBB, Crispin
Eversheds, Nottingham
(0115) 950 7000
Specialisation: Principal area of practice is UK and international corporate work, corporate finance and mergers and acquisitions, including public takeovers and flotations. Clients are mainly public companies (both in the UK and overseas), large corporates and fast growth companies.
Career: Qualified in 1988. *Freshfields* 1986-95. Joined *Eversheds* 1995. Partner 1996.
Publications: Contributes to various publications and is an editor for 'Tolleys Company Law'.
Personal: Married with 3 children.

BROCKBANK, Anthony
Field Fisher Waterhouse, London
(020) 7861 4000
alb@ffwlaw.com
Specialisation: Corporate finance with specialisation in flotations and public company mergers and acquisitions. Advises UK and overseas companies and brokers, nominated advisors and sponsors on the full range of transactions including flotations and fundraisings, takeovers and general corporate advice.
Career: Trained *Linklaters*; qualified 1986; *Hobson Audley* 1989-93; partner 1993-2000; partner *Field Fisher Waterhouse* 2000.
Personal: Born 1960; MA Modern History; Christ Church, Oxford.

BROOKSHAW, Oliver
Shoosmiths, Nottingham
(0115) 906 5040
oliver.brookshaw@shoosmiths.co.uk
Specialisation: M&A/Corporate finance. Flotation of Northampton Saints Plc (Rugby club) on OFEX establishment and funding of joint venture Stainton Capital Holdings (£20 million); joint venture and outsourcing of facilities management services for Abby National plc; acquisition of Howes & Curtis, Jermyn Street.
Prof. Memberships: Law Society, IoD. The City of London Solicitor Company (livery company).
Career: Trained with *Linklaters & Paines* (now *Linklaters & Alliance*). Qualified 1983. 1983-89: solicitor in corporate department of *Linklaters & Paines*. Joined *Shoosmiths* in 1989, partner 1991. Head of Corporate Department.
Personal: Education: Uppingham School, Oriel College, Oxford. Member of the Honourable Artillery Company.

BRUCE, Roderick
Dickson Minto WS, Edinburgh
(0131) 225 4455
roderick.bruce@dmws.com
Specialisation: General corporate, mergers and acquisitions, venture capital, reorganisation.
Prof. Memberships: Law Society of Scotland; Writer to the Signet.
Career: Boroughmuir Secondary School; Edinburgh University (LLB (Hons 2.1)).
Personal: Wife: Jane; Four children: three girls, one boy. Squash, skiing, golf, rugby (spectating), theatre.

BUCHAN, Gordon
Paull & Williamsons, Aberdeen
(01224) 621621
gabuchan@paull-williamsons.co.uk
Specialisation: General corporate law (particularly acquisitions and disposals) and oil and gas law.
Career: Qualified 1976; Partner in corporate department at *Paull and Williamsons* since 1981. Non-executive director of Aberdeen Football Club plc.
Personal: Born 1952.

BURROW, Robert
SJ Berwin, London
(020) 7533 2777
robert.burrow@sjberwin.com
Specialisation: Partner in corporate finance department. Main area of practice is domestic and international merger and acquisition work.
Prof. Memberships: Law Society.
Career: Qualified in 1975. Joined *SJ Berwin* as a partner in 1985. Managing Director of J Rothschild & Co Ltd 1982-85.
Personal: Born 24 March 1951. Educated at Fitzwilliam College, Cambridge 1969-72. Leisure interests include cars, tennis, and skiing. Lives in Surrey.

BUTLER-GALLIE, Stuart
Brachers, Maidstone
(01622) 776427
sbg@brachers.co.uk
Specialisation: Focuses on M&A work, private equity transactions, AIM company work, joint ventures (UK and international) and general corporate work.
Career: Articled *Denton Hall* 1988-90. Qualified *Denton Hall* 1990. Joined *Brachers* January 96. Partner May 97.
Personal: Born 1 March 1964. St. Dunstan's College Catford. Sheffield University (LLB). Law School Chester. SSVC in Regular Army 1PWO (Prince of Wales's Own Regiment of Yorkshire). Married, five children. Local Borough Councillor. Cross country running, military history.

CANAVAN, Kerry
Arthur Cox–Northern Ireland, Belfast
(028) 9023 0007
kcanavan@arthurcox.ie
Specialisation: Company commercial including M&As, fundraisings, commercial agreements.
Prof. Memberships: Law Society of Northern Ireland.
Career: Trained with *Slaughter and May*, post-qualification experience in this general company and commercial department; joined *Norman Wilson & Company* in Belfast 1993, which merged with *Arthur Cox* Northern Ireland in 1996.
Personal: Educated: Coleraine High School and St Catharine's College Cambridge.

CARMEDY, Russell
Gouldens, London
(020) 7583 7777
Specialisation: Specialist in corporate finance and mergers and acquisitions, with an established following of corporate clients, merchant banks, brokers and other financial institutions. Advises sponsors of and investors in companies on all aspects of corporate transaction, including due diligence investigations, negotiation of contractual documentation, fund raising circulars and takeover bids. Particularly renowned for all aspects of public to private takeover work and advising on corporate and commercial matters relating to the Lloyd's insurance market.

CAULDWELL, Helen
Eversheds, Leeds
(0113) 243 0391

CHARNLEY, William
McDermott, Will & Emery, London
(020) 7577 6910
WCharnley@europe.mwe.com
Specialisation: Head of Corporate and London Senior Partner. Principal area of practice is corporate finance covering public and private mergers and acquisitions, disposals, joint ventures, flotations and other issues, and capital raising for companies acting for underwriters and issuers of securities, private equity transactions and general corporate advice.
Prof. Memberships: Law Society, Institute of Chartered Secretaries and Administrators, The Drapers Company.
Career: Articled at *Slater Heelis* in Manchester 1985-87, then joined *Booth & Co* (now *Addleshaw Booth & Co*) and became a partner in 1990; joined *Simmons & Simmons* as a partner in 1994; joined *McDermott, Will & Emery* in November 1998; Managing Partner, *McDermott, Will & Emery* promoted to Senior Partner in 1998.
Personal: Born 21 August 1960. Attended Rivington and Blackrod Grammar School 1971-78, Bolton Institute 1978-80, Sheffield Hallam University (formerly Sheffield City Polytechnic) 1980-81, Lancaster University 1981-83 and Manchester Metropolitan University (former Manchester Polytechnic) 1984-85. Director CD Bramall Motor Group plc 2000-. Leisure pursuits include country sports, art, opera and wine. Lives in London. Married with son and daughter.

CHATFIELD, James
Rawlison Butler, Crawley
(01293) 527744

CHERRY, Robert
Morgan Cole, Swansea
(01792) 634634

CHESTER, Martin
Theodore Goddard, London
(020) 7606 8855

CHEYNE, David
Linklaters, London
(020) 7456 3164
david.cheyne@linklaters.com
Specialisation: Spent five years in *Linklaters'* Hong Kong office working on corporate, international bond and banking transactions. On returning to *Linklaters'* London office in 1986, rejoined the Corporate Department and has been involved in a wide range of corporate transactions including all types of M&A work, joint ventures, flotations and general corporate finance work.
Career: Qualified 1974. 1974-80 Assistant Solicitor, *Linklaters* London; 1980-81 Partner, *Linklaters* London; 1981-86 Partner, *Linklaters* Hong Kong office;

THE LEADERS ■ CORPORATE FINANCE

1986 to date Partner, *Linklaters* London and Head of *Linklaters* Corporate Department.

CHILDS, David
Clifford Chance, London
(020) 7006 1213
david.childs@cliffordchance.com
Specialisation: Corporate. Partner specialising in corporate finance, particularly M&A.
Career: Articled *Clifford Chance*; qualified 1976; Partner since 1981.
Personal: Sheffield University; University College, London (LLB, LLM).

CLARK, Adrian
Ashurst Morris Crisp, London
(020) 7638 1111
adrian.clark@ashursts.com
Specialisation: Corporate/M&A.
Career: Educated – Peterhouse, Cambridge (MA). Qualified 1983. *Slaughter and May* 1981-86; *Ashurst Morris Crisp* 1986 onwards. Partner 1990. Seconded to Take-over Panel 1988-90.

CLARK, Tim
Slaughter and May, London
(020) 7600 1200
tim.clark@slaughterandmay.com
Specialisation: Senior Partner. Principal area of practice is UK and international corporate work, corporate finance and mergers and acquisitions (including public takeovers, flotations, international equity offerings), advising corporate and investment bank clients. Practice also involves demutualisations (building societies and insurance companies).
Prof. Memberships: The Law Society.
Career: Qualified 1976 with *Slaughter and May*. Became Partner in 1983; Senior Partner 2001.
Personal: Born 9 January 1951. Educated at Sherborne School and Pembroke College, Cambridge. Interests include theatre, sport, Italy and flying. Lives in London.

CLARKE, G Timothy H
Linklaters, London
(020) 7456 3304
tim.clarke@linklaters.com
Specialisation: Specialist in UK corporate finance and company law, with a particular experience of privatisations internationally. Main areas of practice include public and private mergers and acquisitions, issues, joint ventures, general corporate advice and privatisations.
Career: 1971-72: College of Law, Law Society Part 2; 1968-1971, Cambridge University BA, Law. 1972-74 articled clerk, *Linklaters*; 1974-82, Assistant Solicitor *Linklaters*; 1982 to date Partner, *Linklaters*; Head of International Privatisations *Linklaters*;

COOKE, Darryl
Addleshaw Booth & Co, Manchester
(0161) 934 6000
darryl.cooke@addleshawbooth.com
Specialisation: Partner in Corporate Finance Group; Head of ABC Private Equity. Principal areas of practice are venture capital, management buyouts and corporate finance. Author of 'Management Buy-outs' (Sweet and Maxwell); 'Venture Capital: Law and Practice' (Sweet and Maxwell) and 'Due Diligence: A Practical Guide' (Sweet & Maxwell).
Career: Joined firm as a Partner in 1995.
Personal: Educated at Leeds University (LLB, LLM). Plays golf, squash and tennis in his spare time as well as fell and marathon running. Lives in Kerridge, Cheshire.

COOKE, Stephen
Slaughter and May, London
(020) 7600 1200
stephen.cooke@slaughterandmay.com
Specialisation: Partner in Company/Commercial Department. Principal area of practice is company and commercial work with a particular emphasis on M&A.
Prof. Memberships: The Law Society.
Career: Qualified in 1984 while with *Slaughter and May*. Worked in the New York office 1989-90; became a Partner in 1991 and Head of M&A in 2001. Publications include 'Takeovers' (Legal & Commercial Publishing, 1997).
Personal: Born 7 March 1959. Educated Lincoln College, Oxford (1978-81). Lives in London.

COOMBS, Richard
Foot Anstey Sargent, Exeter
(01392) 411221
richard.coombs@foot-ansteys.co.uk
Specialisation: Partner in charge of company commercial team. Corporate finance, mergers, acquisitions, MBOs, MBIs, share schemes, FSA compliance, friendly societies.
Prof. Memberships: IOD, Chamber of Commerce.
Career: Qualified 1979. *Clifford Chance* 1977-80, *Turner Kenneth Brown* 1980-81, *British Coal* 1981-85, *Bond Pearce* 1985-94 (partner from 1988). Joined *Foot Anstey Sargent* as partner in 1994.
Personal: Born 16 March 1954. Attended Kings School Chester, Cardiff High School, Downing College, Cambridge (First in Law). Interests: walking and music.

COOPER, Paul
Osborne Clarke, Bristol
(0117) 917 3000

COPPIN, Jonathan
Norton Rose, London
(020) 7283 6000
coppinjds@nortonrose.com
Specialisation: Main area of practice is corporate finance in particular mergers and acquisitions, flotations and international securities offerings.
Prof. Memberships: Member of the Law Society's Company Law Committee.
Career: Articled at *Norton Rose* 1987-89, Partner Corporate Finance Department *Norton Rose* 1996.
Publications: Author of numerous articles in professional publications.
Personal: Married (Lucy). Hobbies include sailing and running.

CRAIG, Alec
Halliwell Landau, Manchester
(0161) 831 2691
iacraig@halliwells.co.uk
Specialisation: Senior Partner. Specialises in all corporate finance work. Work includes MBO's and MBI's, flotations, mergers, sales and acquisitions. Specialist in institutional fundraising in the technology area. Has spoken at numerous seminars and conferences.
Prof. Memberships: Law Society, Institute of Management, Securities Institute.
Career: Qualified in 1985, joining *Halliwell Landau* in the same year. Became a partner in 1989. Senior Partner in 2000.
Personal: Born 28 September 1957. Attended Sheffield University 1979-82 then London College of Law 1983. Non Executive director of several public and private companies. Leisure interests include football, skiing and fell walking. Lives in Alderley Edge.

CRANFIELD, Richard
Allen & Overy, London
(020) 7330 3000
richard.cranfield@allenovery.com
Specialisation: Head of Corporate Department. Has a wide range of corporate finance experience including domestic and cross-border mergers and acquisitions, privatisations and buyouts and capital markets work for equity and debt financings. He lead the *Allen & Overy* team which advised the DTI on the privatisation of British Energy, the team which advised Cable & Wireless on the formation of Cable & Wireless Communications in 1996 and its division into two in 1999/2000, the sale of their interests in One2One to Deutsche Telekom and the sale of Hong Kong Telecom to PCCW. He is currently advising DFID on the public/private partnership for Commonwealth Development Corporation.
Career: Articled (*Allen & Overy*), qualified 1980, Partner 1985, Head of Corporate Department 1999, (*Allen & Overy*).
Personal: Born 1956. Educated at Winchester College and Fitzwilliam College, Cambridge (1977 MA; Economics part I, Law part II). Married with four children.

CROOME, Andrew
Eversheds, Norwich
(01603) 272727
andrewcroome@eversheds.com
See under Banking & Finance, p.104

CUMMINGS, Gavin
Browne Jacobson, Nottingham
(0115) 976 6157
gcummings@brownej.co.uk
Specialisation: Corporate finance specialising in MBIs, MBOs, IBOs, disposals, mergers and acquisitions and private equity. Recent transactions include the £30m refinancing of Brandons PLC and associated acquisition of Moorland Poultry Ltd.
Prof. Memberships: Law Society.
Career: Articled *Browne Jacobson*. Qualified 1994. Partner 2000.
Personal: Born 1970, Stamford; educated at Stamford School and Nottingham University (BA Hons Law) Interests: football, cricket, golf.

CUNNINGHAM, Kevin
Irwin Mitchell, Leeds
(0113) 234 3333
cunningham@irwinmitchell.co.uk
Specialisation: Corporate finance, mergers and acquisitions, buyouts and venture capital.
Prof. Memberships: The Law Society.
Career: Qualified 1979. Joined *Irwin Mitchell* 1983. Partner 1985 and appointed to Management Board in 1989.
Personal: Born 1956. Interests include tennis and skiing.

CUNNINGHAM, Neil
MacRoberts, Glasgow
(0141) 332 9988
neil.cunningham@macroberts.com
Specialisation: Corporate finance, joint ventures, limited partnerships, reconstructions and general partnership law. Recent deals include acting for Glenvarigill Company Limited in connection with several acquisitions and disposals; acting for Nomura Bank in limited partnership work; acting for AWG plc in relation to various joint ventures and disposals.
Prof. Memberships: Law Society of Scotland, Institute of Chartered Accountants in England & Wales, Institute of Chartered Accountants of Scotland (Investigation Committee).
Career: Price Waterhouse, Chartered Accountants, London and Glasgow 1984-88; *Ledingham Chalmers*, Solicitors, Aberdeen 1989-91; *MacRoberts*, Solicitors, Glasgow 1991 to date (became a partner in 1995), Head of Corporate Group.
Personal: Born August 6, 1964. Married with three daughters. Leisure interests include golf, football and squash.

DA COSTA, Alastair
DLA, Leeds
(08700) 111111

DARWIN, Andrew
DLA, Sheffield
(08700) 111111

DAVIDSON, John
Lovells, London
(020) 7296 2000
john.davidson@lovells.com
See under Insurance, p.473

DAVIS, James
Freshfields Bruckhaus Deringer, London
(020) 7936 4000
james.davis@freshfields.com
Specialisation: Corporate finance, acting for companies and investment bank on M&A and equity issues. Clients include Cinven, Compass, Hays, Logica, Scottish and Southern Energy and Wolseley.
Career: Balliol College, Oxford. Partner since 1976.
Personal: Wife (Sally) and four children. Interests include golf and fishing.

CORPORATE FINANCE ■ THE LEADERS

DAVISON, Andrew J
Eversheds, Newcastle upon Tyne
(0191) 241 6277
andrewdavison@eversheds.com
Specialisation: Partner in corporate department. General company law with particular reference to public company, corporate finance, and mergers and acquisitions work.
Prof. Memberships: Chairman of Law Society Standing Committee on Company Law. Member of DTI Company Law Review Consultative Committee. Member of London Stock Exchange Primary Markets Group.
Career: Qualified in 1985, becoming a partner in 1986.

DAWES, Edward
Wragge & Co, Birmingham
(0870) 903 1000

DEAN, Kevin
Stephenson Harwood (incorporating Sinclair Roche & Temperley), London
(020) 7329 4422
kevin.dean@shlegal.com
Specialisation: Head of M&A. Practice consists principally of acting for corporate clients, investment institutions and government and international bodies. Has considerable experience of UK and international mergers and acquisition work, corporate finance, joint ventures and privatisations. In recent years he has concentrated on contentious UK M&A, advising active fund management groups and clients particularly in the international transportation, property, new technology, financial services and leisure sectors. He has also been widely involved in international restructurings. Is also very involved in shareholder democracy matters and has extensive knowledge of the mid-cap, SME and private equity worlds.
Prof. Memberships: Law Society, IBA.
Career: Qualified in 1979. Joined *Sinclair Roche & Temperley* in 1984, becoming a Partner in 1985. Became a Partner at *Stephenson Harwood* in 2002 when *Sinclair Roche & Temperley* and *Stephenson Harwood* combined to form an enlarged firm. Previously worked at *Nabarro Nathanson* and *Clifford-Turner*.
Personal: Born in 1954. Educated at High Wycombe RGS and Lincoln College, Oxford University (MA, Jurisprudence). Lives in Islington. Leisure interests include defending his castle in Umbria and cricket and rugby.

DEVITT, Paul
Addleshaw Booth & Co, Manchester
(0161) 934 6000
paul.devitt@addleshawbooth.com
Specialisation: Partner in Corporate Finance Group. Company and corporate finance, with particular specialisation in public company and public issue work: flotations; public issues; takeovers; other public company/stock exchange-related advice; acquisitions and disposals of companies and businesses.
Prof. Memberships: Law Society; London Stock Exchange Regional Advisory Group – North West.
Career: Qualified 1988. Joined the firm in 1993. Partner from 1995.
Personal: Educated at University of Bristol (LL.B). Lives in Wilmslow. Trustee of the Lowry Centre.

DICKSON, Ian
MacRoberts, Glasgow
(0141) 332 9988
ian.dickson@macroberts.com
Specialisation: Partner in Corporate Group. Although principal area of practice is corporate law and corporate finance, also practises in electricity (and in particular) nuclear energy law. Acts for British Energy.
Prof. Memberships: Law Society of Scotland, International Bar Association, American Bar Association, Institute of Directors.
Career: Qualified 1971. Joined *MacRoberts* in 1973. Partner in 1977, now its Chairman. Non-executive Director of Johnston Press plc (1987-2000).
Personal: Born 10 April 1950. Attended Hillhead High School, Glasgow 1962-68; then Strathclyde University 1968-71. Chairman of Friends of the Beatson Oncology Centre. Leisure interests include music, golf and football. Lives in Glasgow.

DIX, John
Hewitson Becke + Shaw, Cambridge
(01223) 461155
johndix@hewitsons.com
Specialisation: Main area of practice is corporate finance work: acquisitions, disposals, MBOs/MBIs and venture capital funding. Acts for two venture capital providers and many high technology and biotech companies.
Prof. Memberships: Law Society.
Career: University of Sydney BA(Hons) and LLB. Solicitor New South Wales 1986. Qualified in UK 1991. *Hewitson Becke + Shaw* since 1988. Partner 1996.
Personal: Born 1961. Resides Cambridge.

DOWNS, William N
Hammond Suddards Edge, Manchester
(0161) 830 5000

DREW, Dean
Shoosmiths, Reading
(0118) 965 8765
dean.drew@shoosmiths.co.uk
Specialisation: Mergers and acquisitions, venture and development capital, MBOs and joint ventures, particularly in the technology sector. Clients include major US and UK corporates, technology start-ups and other emerging companies.
Prof. Memberships: Law Society.
Career: Trained in London, qualified in 1990 and joined *Shoosmiths* in 1995 becoming a Partner in 1997 and Head of the Thames Valley Corporate Team in 1998.
Personal: Educated at Leeds University. Leisure interests include music, swimming and tennis. Married with three children. Lives in Newbury.

DWYER, Maurice
Wragge & Co, Birmingham
(0870) 903 1000

EASTGATE, Andrew
Pinsent Curtis Biddle, Birmingham
(0121) 200 1050
andrew.eastgate@pinsents.com
Specialisation: Partner and Head of Corporate in Birmingham. He acts predominantly for UK and overseas quoted companies, being responsible for the firm's relationships with Glanbia, Severn Trent, PPG and ISS. In 2001, he led on transactions for Siemens, Severn Trent, ISS, Tate & Lyle and Federal Mogul.
Prof. Memberships: Law Society.
Career: Qualified in 1980. Assistant Solicitor with *Stephenson Harwood* 1980-83. *Pinsent & Co.* from 1983. Partner in 1985 and Head of Corporate, Birmingham in 1997.
Personal: Born 1956. Attended Uppingham School and Mansfield College, Oxford.

ELLARD, John
Linklaters, London
(020) 7456 3324
john.ellard@linklaters.com
See under Transport, p.801

EMMERSON, Tim
Freshfields Bruckhaus Deringer, London
(020) 7936 4000
tim.emmerson@freshfields.com
Specialisation: Mergers and acquisitions, IPOs, securities and derivatives law. Legal advisor to the Takeover Panel (on Takeover Code issues) and to numerous investment banks and companies on a wide range of commercial matters including numerous takeovers and IPOs.
Career: BA (Hons) Law (First), Sussex University; MA EC Law (First), College of Europe, Bruges.

EMMETT, Paul
Walker Morris, Leeds
(0113) 283 2500
pde@walkermorris.co.uk
Specialisation: Partner in Corporate Department. Principal area of practice is corporate finance, mergers and acquisitions. Work includes flotations, rights issues, other forms of equity financing, acquisitions and disposals. Other main area of practice is general corporate advice. Important transactions have included the £30 million demergers of Collins and Hayes Group Plc and Airbath Group Plc from Aquarius Group Plc, the £300 million demerger of TeamTalk.com from IMS Group plc, £150 million offer by TOTAL for the minority shareholdings in Kalon Group plc, £140 million offer by Homestyle Group plc for Harveys Furnishing plc, £35 million acquisition of Sheffield Forgemasters Group Limited, £41 million acquisition of The Decorative Holding Company Limited by Rosebys Plc, £23 million acquisition of North Shoe Limited by Brown & Jackson Plc and £75 million offer by BUPA for Goldsborough Healthcare plc. Author of several articles in the 'Yorkshire Post' and legal journals. Has spoken at seminars on Stock Exchange listing rules and director's duties.
Prof. Memberships: Law Society.
Career: Qualified in 1987. With *Slaughter and May* 1985-91. Joined *Walker Morris* in 1991 and became a Partner in 1993.
Personal: Born 7 November 1961. Educated at Cheadle Hulme School, Cheshire 1974-80 and King's College, London University 1981-84. Lives in Leeds.

EVANS, Stuart
Simmons & Simmons, London
(020) 7628 2020
stuart.evans@simmons-simmons.com
Specialisation: Head of Corporate Finance at *Simmons & Simmons*. Led teams advising: Lloyd's Members' Agents on the formation of Wellington Re, Interbrew on its acquisition of the beer businesses of Whitbread and Bass; Pacific Century CyberWorks on its acquisition of Cable and Wireless HKT; Wal-Mart on its acquisition of Asda.
Career: Qualified in 1972. With *Slaughter and May* 1972-79. Joined *Simmons & Simmons* in 1979, Partner since 1981.
Publications: Chapter on Transactions in 'A Practitioner's Guide to the FSA Listing Rules'; Chapter on Mergers and Acquisitions in 'A Practitioner's Guide to the FSA Regulation of Investment Banking'. Chair Islington International Festival and Reader St Stephen's, Canonbury.
Personal: Born 31 December 1947. Educated Royal Grammar School, Newcastle-upon-Tyne 1956-66, Leeds University 1966-69.

FAGELSON, Ian
Reed Smith Warner Cranston, London
(020) 7403 2900
ifagelson@reedsmith.co.uk
Specialisation: Partner in Company/Commercial Department. Handles corporate and financial transactions, including corporate finance, mergers and acquisitions and banking. Wide experience of both public and private corporate and financial transactions, including complex international mergers and acquisitions, disposals, financings, restructurings, debt and equity issues (public and private) and joint ventures. Also deals with insurance and reinsurance, including the establishment of innovative structured reinsurance programmes. University lecturer 1977-79. Subsequently regular conference and seminar lecturer on corporate and banking topics.
Prof. Memberships: Law Society, American Bar Association.
Career: Qualified in 1980, having joined *Warner Cranston* in 1979. Became a Partner in 1981 and Senior Partner in 1997.
Personal: Born 22 April 1952. Educated at the University of Southampton 1970-73 (LLB) and Oxford University 1973-75 (BCL). Enjoys theatre, reading and loafing. Lives in London.

THE LEADERS ■ CORPORATE FINANCE

FALKUS, Bryony
Mills & Reeve, Norwich
(01603) 693225
bryony.falkus@mills-reeve.com
Specialisation: Partner in corporate department. Work covers acquisitions and sales, MBOs, MBIs, reconstructions, offers of securities and UKLA work. Also handles corporate insolvency generally and in particular receiverships and administrations, acting for banks, specialised lending institutions and insolvency practitioners.
Prof. Memberships: Law Society.
Career: Qualified 1976; partner *Pickering Kenyon* 1980; partner *Mills & Reeve* 1992.

FERNANDEZ LEWIS, Jon
MLM, Cardiff
(029) 2046 2562
jfl@mlmsolicitors.com
Specialisation: Corporate finance including venture capital and loan funding (both for providers and recipients of such funding), company and business acquisitions and disposals, corporate reorganisation and refinancing. Acts for Wesley Clover Corporation and Celtic House, substantial private equity funds providing seed and development capital to telecoms technology companies.
Prof. Memberships: Law Society.
Career: Articled at *Morgan Bruce*, qualified 1984. Partner in *Eversheds Phillips & Buck* 1988-93. Partner in *Rubin Lewis O'Brien* 1993-98. Partner in *Bevan Ashford* 1998 to 2001. Partner in *MLM* since April 2001.
Personal: Born 1958. Educated at Bushey Meads School, Hertfordshire and University College, Cardiff. Lives in Cardiff. Married with a daughter. Leisure interests include playing golf and tennis, watching football and rugby.

FISCHL, Nicolas
Mills & Reeve, Norwich
(01603) 693223
nick.fischl@mills-reeve.com
Specialisation: MBOs, MBIs, private equity, joint ventures. Also facilities management and other computer/IT agreements.
Prof. Memberships: Law Society, Norfolk and Norwich Law Society.
Career: Qualified with *Clifford Turner* 1979. Joined *Mills & Reeve* in 1984. Partner *Mills & Reeve* 1986.
Personal: MA (Cantab).

FLYNN, John
Dickinson Dees, Newcastle upon Tyne
(0191) 279 9252
john.flynn@dickinson-dees.com
Specialisation: Partner in Corporate Finance Department. Work includes mergers and acquisitions, flotations, rights issues and similar related Stock Exchange work, as well as joint ventures. Acted in the acquisition of Thameslink and Thames Trains rail franchises, the £300 million acquisition by Arriva of British Bus and the £513 million sale by Arriva of AAS. Led the team voted UK Regional Corporate Team of the Year by Legal Business Magazine. Recently led the team which successfully defended the hostile bid by C3D for long-standing client Go-Ahead, believed to be the most comprehensive defeat of a hostile bid and led the team which acted for Go-Ahead on the acquisition of Connex South Central.
Prof. Memberships: Law Society.
Career: Qualified in 1979. Joined *Dickinson Dees* in 1981, becoming a Partner in 1986.

FRANCIES, Michael
Weil, Gotshal & Manges, London
(020) 7903 1000
michael.francies@weil.com
Specialisation: Head of the London office and a member of the firm's 13 member management committee. His practice is in both the UK/US axis and across Europe. He specialises in public and private mergers and acquisitions, equity issues (IPOs and secondary), private equity/venture capital/MBOs and joint ventures. His clients span the telecommunications and new technology sectors, and include major corporates as well as financial advisors and private equity funds.

FRIER, George
McClure Naismith, Glasgow
(0141) 204 2700
gfrier@McClureNaismith.com
Specialisation: Partner, corporate finance and commercial/tax/VAT. Handles complex negotiations for commercial contracts specialising in MBOs/MBIs, mergers, banking, trade acquisitions and sales, insolvency and shareholder disputes. Recent deals include acting for management in the £208m MBO of Kyndal Spirits Ltd; advisor to Murgitroyd Group plc in its AIM flotation; sale of Hydro Seafood GSP Ltd to Levoy TS; advised Caupain International on joint venture with Morrison Bourmore Ltd; MBI of GOALS Soccer Centres Ltd.
Career: Trained *Dorman Jeffrey*, qualified 1987, Assistant *Maclay Murray & Spens* 1987-93, Associate *McClure Naismith* 1993-94, Partner 1994.
Personal: Born 1962, resides Glasgow. Educated at Morrison's Acadamy, Glasgow University (1984 LLB Hons Private Law). Leisure pursuits include hill walking, family, theatre, cycling and bad golf.

FULTON, Richard
Mills Selig, Belfast
(028) 9024 3878
richard.fulton@nilaw.com
Specialisation: Main areas of practice are mergers, acquisitions and disposals, company reorganisations, joint ventures and corporate finance generally. Represents major venture capital houses. Has extensive experience in mergers and acquisitions and joint ventures both locally and internationally.
Prof. Memberships: Law Society of Northern Ireland.
Career: Queens University, Belfast LLB 1976. Qualified England and Wales 1980. Qualified Northern Ireland 1990. Joined *Mills Selig* 1991.
Personal: Windsurfing, countryside, literature. Lives outside Belfast.

GARNETT, Chris J
Eversheds, Birmingham
(0121) 232 1000
Specialisation: Mergers and acquisitions, flotations, public company share issues and takeovers, corporate reconstructions and joint ventures.
Prof. Memberships: Law Society.
Career: Birmingham University. Articled to *Eversheds* (formerly *Evershed & Tomkinson*) 1983-85, Associate 1989, Partner 1992.
Personal: Married to Kathryn; with two children, Daniel (aged nine) and Anna (aged seven). A keen interest in natural history, particularly ornithology, and enjoys playing tennis and watching football and cricket.

GARSTON, Clive R
Halliwell Landau, Manchester
(020) 7256 3627
crg@halliwells.co.uk
Specialisation: Senior Partner of London office. Specialises in all aspects of corporate finance and general corporate work, particularly mergers, acquisitions and flotations.
Prof. Memberships: Law Society, International Bar Association, American Bar Association, Institute of Directors. Member Corporate Law Committee of CBI.
Career: Articled at *Hall Brydon* qualified 1968, Partner 1971, Partner *Halliwell Landau* 1978. Senior Partner (1989-95)
Personal: Education Manchester Grammar School, Leeds University (1965 LLB). Born 1945 resides London and Hale, Cheshire, enjoys cricket and football.

GEE, Tim
Baker & McKenzie, London
(020) 7919 1000
timothy.gee@bakernet.com
Specialisation: Public and private company M&A, privatisation and equity capital markets transactions, acting for underwriters and issuers. Extensive cross-border and emerging markets experience. Identified as one of the UK's leading privatisation lawyers in Euromoney's 'Guide to the World's Leading Privatisation Lawyers' and as one of the UK's leading M&A lawyers in Euromoney's Guide to the World's Leading Mergers and Acquisitions Lawyers. Head of *Baker & McKenzie*'s Global M&A Practice Group.
Prof. Memberships: The Law Society; City of London Solicitors Company.
Career: Educated at Worcester College, Oxford. Qualified in 1986 with *Baker & McKenzie*. 1989-90 *Baker & McKenzie*, Hong Kong. 1991 *Baker & McKenzie*, Budapest. Partner in 1992.
Personal: Married with two sons. Interests include rugby and fly fishing.

GIBB, Stephen
Shepherd+ Wedderburn, Edinburgh
(0131) 473 5211
stephen.gibb@shepwedd.co.uk
Specialisation: Partner in the Corporate Department.
Prof. Memberships: Institute of Directors, Writer to the Signet.
Career: Trained *Bird Fyfe Ireland*, qualified 1988 (Scotland), 1993 (England and Wales), 1995 (WS); assistant *Bird Semple Fyfe Ireland* 1988-91; associate *Bird Semple Fyfe Ireland* 1991-93; associate *Fyfe Ireland* 1994; partner 1994-99; partner *Shepherd+ Wedderburn* 1999.
Personal: Education: King's Park; Glasgow University (1985 LLB Hons). Born: 1964. Resides: Edinburgh. Leisure: Football, guitar, music, children (own).

GILBERT, Ian
Walker Morris, Leeds
(0113) 283 2500
img@walkermorris.co.uk
Specialisation: Partner in Corporate Department. Main area of practice is corporate finance, management buyouts and venture capital. Has been involved in venture capital and development capital for 18 years, acting on both sides. Involved in numerous MBOs of varying size and complexity, including take privates, as well as public and private company acquisitions and disposals, flotations, joint ventures, and share issues.
Career: Qualified in 1981. With 3i Group Plc 1979-85. Joined *Walker Morris* in 1985 and became a Partner in 1986.
Personal: Born 22 July 1957. Educated at Sheffield University 1975-78. Recreations include sport, travel and white water rafting. Lives in Follifoot.

GILTHORPE, Ian
Robert Muckle, Newcastle upon Tyne
(0191) 244 2901
imgilthorpe@robertmuckle.co.uk
Specialisation: Partner in Commercial Department. Senior Partner and Business Development Partner. Main area of practice is corporate finance, including MBOs, acquisitions, disposals, sources of finance, debt restructuring and flotation.
Career: Qualified in 1978. Partner 1979. Current non-executive directorships: Vald Birn (UK) Ltd, Mercantile Building Society.

GLEN, Marian
Shepherd+ Wedderburn, Edinburgh
(0131) 473 5177
marian.glen@shepwedd.co.uk
Specialisation: Partner in corporate finance, specialising in mergers and acquisitions and joint ventures; recent deals include acting for Friends Ivory & Sime plc in the £128.9 million acquisition from Friends Provident of their retail investment business (Friends' Provident Unit Trust Managers Limited), their managed pension fund business (Friends Ivory & Sime Managed Pensions Funds Limited) and as a company engaged in the marketing of investment trusts and other retail investment prod-

CORPORATE FINANCE ■ THE LEADERS

ucts (Ivory & Sime TrustLink Limited); and acting for Scottish Power UK plc in setting up of a joint venture company with United Utilities plc, Northern Electric plc and The Electricity Supply Board to administer competitive tendering processes for the procurement of certain products. Also head of firm's Funds and Financial Services Group.
Prof. Memberships: Institute of Directors; British/German Jurists Association.
Career: Trained at *Dundas & Wilson*, Edinburgh; qualified 1989; solicitor *Linklaters & Paines*, London, 1989-94; joined *Shepherd+ Wedderburn* 1994; partner 1996.
Personal: Education: Notre Dame High School, Glasgow/Glasgow University (1983 MA Hons French and German); Edinburgh University (1987 LLB). Born 1960; resides Edinburgh. Leisure: hill walking, golf and travel. Languages: French and German.

GODDEN, Richard
Linklaters, London
(020) 7456 3610
richard.godden@linklaters.com
Specialisation: Specialist in general corporate advisory work and corporate transactions. Advises a wide range of corporate clients, professional services organisations and investment banks on public mergers and takeovers, joint ventures, private merger and acquisition transactions, reorganisations, flotations, other corporate equity fundraising and equity sales and general corporate advice.
Career: 1990 to date: Partner, Corporate Department, *Linklaters*; 1988-90: Secretary to Takeover Panel; 1987-88: Assistant Solicitor, Corporate Department, *Linklaters* London; 1985-87: Assistant Solicitor, *Linklaters* Hong Kong; 1982-85: Assistant Solicitor, Commercial Department, *Linklaters* London; 1980-82: Trainee Solicitor, *Linklaters* London. 1979-80: College of Law; 1976-79: Trinity Hall, Cambridge University, MA First Class.

GODFREY, Christopher
Burges Salmon, Bristol
(0117) 939 2219
chris.godfrey@burges-salmon.com
Specialisation: Corporate finance and investment funds. Recent deals include £16m MBO of A-Gas International; £28m flotation of Compast Power (for the issue); £44.7m sale of Regency Financial Holdings plc.
Prof. Memberships: Law Society.
Career: Trained with *Linklaters*, qualifying in 1986, and joining *Burges Salmon* later that year, becoming a Partner in 1990.
Personal: Jurisprudence, Hertford College, Oxford 1980-83.

GOODALL, Caroline
Herbert Smith, London
(020) 7374 8000
caroline.goodall@herbertsmith.com
Specialisation: Specialises in corporate work with a particular emphasis on corporate finance and mergers and acquisitions. Has been involved, as an advisor to both companies and to investment banks, in numerous takeovers (hostile and agreed), international mergers and acquisitions, international share issues, IPOs, flotations, rights issues and placings. Has also advised on a number of cross-border transactions and complicated international joint ventures.
Prof. Memberships: City of London Solicitors' Company.
Career: Admitted in 1980 and became a partner in 1987. Head of the Corporate Division.

GOULD, Terry
Eversheds, Norwich
(01603) 272727
terrygould@eversheds.com
Specialisation: Head of corporate finance with particular experience in M&A and private equity. Within last 12 months worked on the acquisitions and disposals for ECNG and CGNU. Has worked increasingly on developing business in North America. Addresses seminars.
Prof. Memberships: Law Society.
Career: Qualified 1977 with *Freshfields*. Joined present firm in 1978 and became a partner in 1981.
Personal: Born 7 March 1952. Attended Downing College, Cambridge 1971-74. Governor Norwich School. Lives in Norwich.

GOWANS, Andrew
Osborne Clarke, Reading
(0118) 925 2000

GRAVES, Patrick
Osborne Clarke, Bristol
(0117) 917 3000

GRAY, Colin
McGrigor Donald, Glasgow
(0141) 248 6677
colin.gray@mcgrigors.com
Specialisation: Head of Corporate Unit. Acquisition and sales of businesses/companies (both listed and non-listed). Acting on Institutional Investments (on both debt and equity sides). General Corporate (including inward investment franchise agreements, etc).
Prof. Memberships: Law Society of Scotland; Law Society of England and Wales; Society of Scottish Lawyers in London.
Career: 1980-84 Glasgow University (LLB, DipLP). 1987 to date, *McGrigor Donald* (Partner, November 1991).
Personal: Married June 1993 to Lee (nee Robertson). Three children, Hannah, Oliver and Scarlett. Leisure interests include golf and trying to keep fit by cycling to and from work.

GRAY, Richard
L'Estrange & Brett, Belfast
(028) 9023 0426
richard.gray@lestrangeandbrett.com
Specialisation: Partner, corporate department. Main areas of practice are corporate, corporate finance and banking work. Also active in project finance and PFI work.
Prof. Memberships: Law Society of Northern Ireland; Law Society of England and Wales.
Career: Called to the Northern Ireland Bar in 1989. Admitted as a solicitor in England and Wales in 1992 and in Northern Ireland in 1992. Assistant solicitor with *Cameron Markby Hewitt* (now *Cameron McKenna*) 1989-92. Partner in *L'Estrange & Brett* since 1996.
Personal: Born 1966. Education: Queen's University of Belfast (LLB). Course advisor (company law): Institute of Professional Legal Studies, Belfast.

GRAYSTON, Clare
Lewis Silkin, London
(020) 7074 8004
clare.grayston@lewissilkin.com
Specialisation: Head of Corporate Department. Practice includes general corporate advisory role plus mergers and acquisitions and corporate finance in the small to mid-cap field.
Prof. Memberships: Active in l'Association International des Jeunes Avocats.
Career: Qualified in 1985. Other interests: Director (Chair of Finance Committee) of Women in Film and Television (UK) Limited (1992-98), Director of Living Earth Foundation (environmental charity) (1995-96). Published author on a number of comparative law texts. French speaker.
Personal: Born 1960. Lives in central London.

GREEN, Guy
Eversheds, Birmingham
(0121) 232 1000
Specialisation: Corporate finance with a private equity bias, mergers and acquisitions for both private and public companies advising buyers, sellers and funders.
Career: Qualified at *Bird & Bird* in 1982. Partner at *George Green & Co* 1989-99. Became Partner at *Eversheds* in January 2000 heading up *Eversheds* Private Equity Team.
Personal: Leisure interests include sailing, hockey, skiing and golf.

GREENFIELD, G N Ian
Hammond Suddards Edge, Leeds
(0113) 284 7000

GREGORY, Lesley
Memery Crystal, London
(020) 7242 5905
lgregory@memerycrystal.com
Specialisation: Corporate and commercial matters including corporate finance, acquisitions and disposals, Official List and AIM, capital raising and joint ventures. Included in The Hot 100 lawyers shaping the Legal Profession in 2001 and has been involved in over 80 AIM transactions since its start in 1995. Work in corporate finance has resulted in the firm being recognised as niche firm of the year for 2001.
Prof. Memberships: The Law Society, Quoted Companies Alliance and the British Association for Sport and Law.
Career: Articled *Courts & Co*. Qualified 1983; Solicitor *Memery Crystal* 1983-88; Partner since 1988.
Personal: Born 1960; resides London.

GRISEWOOD, Rebecca
Halliwell Landau, Manchester
(0161) 831 2686
rgrisewood@halliwells.co.uk
Specialisation: Handles a range of corporate finance work principally mergers, acquisitions, venture and development capital transactions, MBOs and MBIs.
Career: Articled *Halliwell Landau*. Qualified in 1988. Made Partner in 1995, Corporate Department.
Personal: Born 1963. Attended Liverpool University 1981-84 (LLB). Lives in Saddleworth. Enjoys theatre, travel and her three children.

GRONOW, Simon
Pinsent Curtis Biddle, Birmingham
(0121) 625 3072
simon.gronow@pinsents.com
Specialisation: Partner in Corporate Finance Department. Principally engaged in general corporate work for UK and international public companies and investment banks/brokers, including flotations, rights issues, takeover offers, capital reconstructions, acquisitions and disposals, and corporate governance.
Prof. Memberships: Law Society.
Career: Qualified 1986. Joined *Pinsent Curtis Biddle* in 1984, partner in 1991.
Personal: Born 1961. Educated at King's College Cambridge 1979-83.

HALL, Daniel
Eversheds, Manchester
(0161) 831 8000
danielhall@eversheds.com
Specialisation: Head of corporate. Mergers and acquisitions and corporate finance for public and private companies. Expertise in Takeover Code offers. Regular speaker at seminars and conferences.
Prof. Memberships: Law Society. British American Business Group. Committee Member of Institute of Fiscal Studies.
Career: Trainee Solicitor, *Eversheds* (Manchester) 1985-87, Solicitor (Company Dept.) *Clifford Chance* 1987-92. Partner *Eversheds* (Manchester) 1992. Head of Corporate – January 1999.
Personal: Born 29 August 1962. Educated Repton Preparatory School, Repton School, Bristol University and London College of Law. Leisure pursuits include golf, shooting and fishing. Lives in Wilmslow, Cheshire. Married. Son Benjamin and daughter Isabel.

HALPIN, Peter
Eversheds, Manchester
(0161) 831 8000
peterhalpin@eversheds.com
Specialisation: Mergers and Acquisitions with a specialism in private equity and venture capital. National Head of private equity and venture capital. Transactions include listing and global offer of Telecity plc and institutional buyout of Peter Black Group.
Prof. Memberships: Law Society.
Career: Liverpool University (LLB). Partner at *Addleshaw Booth & Co* (1995).

THE LEADERS ■ CORPORATE FINANCE

Joined *Eversheds* as Partner in 1998.
Personal: Born 19 October 1964. Leisure pursuits include following rugby (league and union). Lives in Warrington. Married with three children.

HAMBLETON, Jonathan
Kimbells, Milton Keynes
(01908) 350206
jonathan.hambleton@kimbells.com
Specialisation: All aspects of corporate finance and public/private company mergers and acquisitions.
Prof. Memberships: Law Society.
Career: 1988-92 *Slaughter and May*. 1992-95 Assistant Solicitor, *Kimbells*. 1995, Partner in *Kimbells*. 1998, Head of Corporate, *Kimbells LLP*.
Personal: Educated Rossall School and Mansfield College, Oxford (MA). Member, Northampton RFC. Interests: winter moutaineering (aspiring Monroist). Married, two children.

HAMILL, Robert
Hammond Suddards Edge, London
(020) 7655 1000

HARDIE, David
Dundas & Wilson CS, Edinburgh
(0131) 228 8000

HARKER, Chris
Dickinson Dees, Newcastle upon Tyne
(0191) 279 9254
chris.harker@dickinson-dees.com
See under Banking & Finance, p.105

HARRISON, Wendy
DLA, Leeds
(08700) 111111

HATCHARD, Michael
Skadden, Arps, Slate, Meagher & Flom LLP, London
(020) 7519 7020
mhatchard@skadden.com
Specialisation: Partner specialising in corporate finance and M&A. Principally mergers, acquisitions and joint ventures and the full range of securities distribution transactions, particularly where significant UK/US implications arise.
Career: Qualified 1980 with *Theodore Goddard*, partner 1985. Joined *Skadden, Arps* as a partner in 1994; head of the English practice.
Personal: Born 21 November 1955.

HATTRELL, Martin
Slaughter and May, London
(020) 7600 1200
martin.hattrell@slaughterandmay.com
Specialisation: Corporate Department. Principal area of practice is corporate and commercial law, in particular mergers and acquisitions.
Prof. Memberships: The Law Society.
Career: Qualified in 1987 with *Slaughter and May* and became a Partner in 1994.
Personal: Born 9 August 1961. Educated at Ampleforth College, Yorkshire and The Queen's College, Oxford.

HAWES, Roger
Burges Salmon, Bristol
(0117) 939 2243
roger.hawes@burges-salmon.com
Specialisation: Corporate finance and private equity. Recent deals include the secondary buyout of specialist short run book printer Anthony Rowe Books, the £9m MBO of Surface Inspection Limited, advising Wessex Water Limited on its £360 million joint venture with MWH Harza and advising the vendors of Ruda Holiday Park to Parken Leisure Plc for a multimillion pound consideration.
Prof. Memberships: Law Society.
Career: Qualified in 1984, joined *Burges Salmon* in 1988 from *Linklaters*, became a Partner in 1990 and Head of *Burges Salmon's* Company/Commercial Department.

HAYWARD, Paul
Gateley Wareing, Birmingham
(0121) 234 0000

HAYWOOD, Richard
Wragge & Co, Birmingham
(0870) 903 1000

HEATHCOCK, Andrew
Paris Smith & Randall, Southampton
(023) 8048 2482

HEWES, Simon
Bond Pearce, Bristol
(0117) 929 9197
shewes@bondpearce.com
Specialisation: Partner and Head of Corporate Finance. Specialises in M&A, private equity deals, including MBO's, MBI's and IBO's, corporate reorganisations and reconstructions, shareholder arrangements and general corporate. Recent deals include the management buyout of Allen & Heath Limited and the acquisition for Newsquest of the Dimbleby Newspaper Group.
Career: Qualified in 1987 with *Pinsent & Co*, Birmingham (now *Pinsent Curtis Biddle*). Joined *Hepherd Winstanley & Pugh* in 1992, becoming a Partner in 1994. Joined *Bond Pearce* as a Partner in 1998 on merger.

HOLT, Andrew
DLA, Manchester
(08700) 111111

HOPKINS, Stephen Martyn
Eversheds, Leeds
(0113) 243 0391
stephenhopkins@eversheds.com
Specialisation: Vastly experienced corporate finance partner acting for clients such as Anglo American, Tarmac, Hazelwood Foods, EWS and WRG. Has edited the financial assistance chapter of Tolley's 'Company Law'. Corporate finance practice continues to develop. Became overall head of the corporate group in Leeds and Manchester in 2000. Has significant specialist knowledge of the food sector and has acted on four corporate transactions in that sector in the past 12 months. He leads *Eversheds* extensive food sector team who act for Greencore Group, Nestle, ABF, Richmond Foods and McCains amongst others.
Prof. Memberships: Law Society.
Career: Qualified in 1984. Joined *Eversheds* in 1988. Became a Partner in 1991.
Personal: Born 17 March 1960. Attended Sheffield University 1978-81. Leisure interests include golf, competitive swimming, cricket and rugby. Lives near Wetherby.

HOWLES, Kate
Clifford Chance, London
(020) 7600 1000
Kate.Howles@cliffordchance.com
Specialisation: Corporate. Partner specialising in general company and commercial work, corporate finance, M&A and takeovers.
Career: Partner since 1986.

HOYLE, Andrew
Watson Burton, Newcastle upon Tyne
(0191) 244 4444
Specialisation: Wide range of corporate and insolvency work involving transactional and security issues arising from instructions received from banks and insolvency practitioners.
Prof. Memberships: Law Society.
Career: Qualified as a solicitor in 1985. Joined *Watson Burton* as a partner in March 1992.

HUGHES, David
Pinsent Curtis Biddle, Birmingham
(0121) 625 3066
david.hughes@pinsents.com
Specialisation: Partner in Corporate Department. Corporate finance, including mergers and aquisitions, takeovers and primary and secondary equity issues. He is a senior corporate partner for a number of the firm's major listed clients and also acts for a number of US, German and other multinational companies on UK transactions. Recent transactions include acting for DONCASTERS plc on its US $260 million takeover bid by RCG Holdings and for Babcock International Group on the sale of the Claudius Peters Group. He heads the firm's German desk, frequently advising German companies investing in the UK.
Career: Qualified in 1980. Partner in 1987. Worked at *Nabarro Nathanson* 1978-82, then *Slaughter and May* 1982-85, before joining *Pinsent & Co* in 1985.
Personal: Born 1955. Attended Wolverhampton Grammar School 1966-73, then Jesus College, Oxford 1973-77.

HULL, David
Hammond Suddards Edge, Birmingham
(0121) 222 3000

HULLS, Martin
Ward Hadaway, Newcastle upon Tyne
(0191) 204 4000
Specialisation: Corporate finance; public company work; private equity transactions; MBOs/MBIs.
Prof. Memberships: Law Society.
Career: LLB from Birmingham University. Practised in Birmingham and Nottingham before moving to the North East in 1993. Became Head of Commercial Department in 1994.
Personal: Keeping fit, mountain biking, fast cars, motor racing. Married with three young daughters.

HUNTER, James
Mills & Reeve, Norwich
(01603) 693267
james.hunter@mills-reeve.com
Specialisation: Company sales and acquisitions and general corporate finance matters. Acted on acquisitions worth £45 million over two years for one US client. Recently acted on the sale of Radiophone Limited to the UK subsidiary of a French listed company and the sale of F1 Harness Systems to a German listed company. Acted for a mixture of universities, charities and private companies on the establishment of the Iceni Seedcorn Fund LLP. Also advises on start-ups, fund raising and joint ventures/commercial agreements.
Prof. Memberships: Law Society.
Career: Trainee at *Mills & Reeve* (1993-95). Solicitor at *Mills & Reeve* (1995-2000). Associate at *Mills & Reeve* 2000-01. Partner 2001 to date.
Personal: Married. Cycling, gardening, sailing, fishing. LLB (UEA) – College of Law, York.

HUTCHINSON, John
Pitmans, Reading
(0118) 958 0224
jhutchinson@pitmans.com
Specialisation: Company/commercial specialist whose main areas of work include MBO/MBIs, acquisitions, disposals, private equity and bank funding.
Career: Qualified 1990. Partner 1994.
Personal: Born 7 December 1961. Lives in Oxford. Interests include golf, football and opera.

IRVINE, John
L'Estrange & Brett, Belfast
(028) 9023 0426
john.irvine@lestrangeandbrett.com
Specialisation: Partner and head of corporate department. Main area of work: Corporate and commercial law.
Prof. Memberships: Law Society of Northern Ireland.
Career: Lecturer in law: Queen's University, Kingston, Ontario; University of Central Lancashire. Tutor in law, University of Exeter; course tutor, Institute of Professional Legal Studies, Belfast. Qualified 1986. Partner in *L'Estrange & Brett* since 1988.
Personal: Born 1957. Education: Queen's University, Belfast (LLB), Queen's University, Kingston, Ontario (LLM).

JACOBS, Charles
Linklaters, London
(020) 7456 3332
charles.jacobs@linklaters.com
Specialisation: Primarily engaged in mergers and acquisitions, domestic and international capital raisings, joint ventures, privatisations and other general corporate work, often with an international element.
Career: 1999 to date Partner, *Linklaters*; 1992-99 Solicitor *Linklaters*; 1990-92 Articled Clerk, *Linklaters* (six month secondment to *Linklaters* New York); 1987 Leicester University LLB; St John College, Johannesburg.

CORPORATE FINANCE ■ THE LEADERS

JAMES, Glen
Slaughter and May, London
(020) 7600 1200
glen.james@slaughterandmay.com
See under Insurance, p.475

JAMISON, David
Carson McDowell, Belfast
(028) 9024 4951
david.jamison@carson-mcdowell.com
Specialisation: Emphasis on mergers, acquisitions and disposals, intellectual property and insolvency.
Prof. Memberships: Law Society of Northern Ireland and Law Society of England and Wales.
Career: Born 1964. Qualified 1989. University of Manchester. Articled and practised in London and latterly in North of England prior to returning to Northern Ireland in 1995. Partner 1998.

JANSEN, Karl
freethcartwright, Nottingham
(0115) 935 0363
karl.jansen@freethcartwright.co.uk
Specialisation: Corporate transactional work including mergers and acquisitions, management buyouts/buyins, private equity and refinancing, acting for buyers, sellers and equity/debt funders. Highlights of last year include the sale of Elmsteel Group to Rotec GmbH and acting for management on the MBO of LSUK from Finelist plc and the BIMBO of Chortex from Coats Viyella plc.
Career: Articles with *Davies Arnold Cooper*, London. Joined present firm on qualification in 1990. Appointed partner in 1994. Appointed head of corporate in 1999.
Personal: Educated at Loughbrough Grammar School and the London School of Economics. Season ticket holder at Leicester City FC. Married with two children.

JEFFRIES, Graham
Bond Pearce, Southampton
(023) 8082 8868
gjeffries@bondpearce.com
See under Banking & Finance, p.106

JOHNS, Michael
Nicholson Graham & Jones, London
(020) 7648 9000
michael.johns@ngj.co.uk
Specialisation: Managing Partner and Partner in the Company and Commercial Department. Main area of practice is corporate finance. Work includes acquisitions, mergers, venture capital, buyouts, equity issues, yellow book work and general corporate work for public listed companies. Member of sports group; acts for organisations and individuals in the sports field including sponsors and sports organisers. Has spoken at seminars both in the UK and USA on subjects such as buyouts, international strategic activities, law firm management and sports sponsorship. Non-Executive Director of Merchant Retail Group Plc.
Prof. Memberships: Institute of Directors, Law Society. Chairman of Globalex.

JOHNSON, Ben
Eversheds, Nottingham
(0115) 950 7000
benjohnson@eversheds.com
Specialisation: Corporate finance, predominantly private equity and M&A.
Prof. Memberships: Law Society.
Career: Qualified 1988; *Burges Salmon* 1986-98 (seconded to *Wragge & Co* 1988-89) a partner from 1996. Partner at *Eversheds* 1998 to date.

JOHNSON, David
Slaughter and May, London
(020) 7600 1200
david.johnson@slaughterandmay.com
Specialisation: M&A (including public takeovers), corporate finance, corporate and commercial.
Career: Nottingham High School; Trinity Hall, Cambridge. Qualified in 1993 whilst at *Slaughter and May*. Elected to partnership in 2000.
Personal: Lives in London.

JOHNSON, Robin
Eversheds, Leeds
(0113) 243 0391
robinjohnson@eversheds.com
Specialisation: A corporate finance and commercial partner specialising in M&A, purple book and joint venture work with a strong emphasis on technology. Member of the Regional Advisory Group for the Stock Exchange. Robin is client partner for a number of US corporates including Parker Hannifin Corporation, Marma Gray, SPX Corporation and Geon Corporation as well as leading advisor to UK listed companies such as AEA Technology plc, CD Bramall plc, Chapelthorpe plc Trans EDA plc, Richmond Foods plc and K3 Technology plc. Extensive experience on public takeover bids, having been involved in 27 since March 1998. Voted one of "40 under 40" to watch by the Yorkshire Business Insider in 1999. He appeared as the only London based lawyer in the top 10 European M&A lawyers in 2001.
Career: Qualified 1987, partner 1994.
Publications: A number of articles on corporate governance have been published in publications such as 'International Financial Law Review', 'Company Secretary' and 'Practical Audit and Accounting'.
Personal: Born 1963, resides Leeds, married with two children.

JOHNSTON, Keith
Addleshaw Booth & Co, Manchester
(0161) 934 6000
byj@addleshaw-booth.co.uk
Specialisation: Partner in Corporate Finance Group. Principal area of practice is corporate finance mainly for listed companies including mergers and acquisitions, takeovers and general transaction and corporate advice. Other main areas of work include public/private sector partnerships and project work (see separate entry).
Prof. Memberships: Law Society. Chairman: North West Company Secretaries' Forum. Member of Projects Group at the firm.
Career: Qualified in 1976. Became a Partner in 1981. 1991-94 member of board of *Norton Rose* M5 Group. Board member of *Addleshaw Booth & Co*.
Personal: Educated at London University 1970-73 (External). Governor of The Grange School, Hartford, Cheshire. Company Secretary API Group plc (part-time). Leisure pursuits include Liverpool FC, skiing, chess and tennis. Lives in Hale, Cheshire.

JOHNSTON, Michael
Carson McDowell, Belfast
(028) 9024 4951
michael.johnston@carson-mcdowell.com
Specialisation: Mergers and acquisitions, subscription and shareholders agreements PFI/PPP, MBOs and MBIs and JVs. Advised Andrews in relation to the sale of Ormo Bakery to BBL, Translink in relation to commercial matters generally. Advising the University of Ulster in Springvale Project and Coolkeeragh Group Limited with regard to major corporate restructuring.
Prof. Memberships: Law Society of Northern Ireland.
Career: Joined *Carson McDowell* in 1983; admitted as solicitor in Northern Ireland 1984; became a partner at *Carson McDowell* 1993.

JONES, Hugh
Osborne Clarke, Reading
(0118) 925 2000

JONES, Jonathan
Hammond Suddards Edge, Leeds
(0113) 284 7000

JONES, Michael
CMS Cameron McKenna, Bristol
(0117) 930 0200
mgj@cmck.com
Specialisation: Partner in charge of the Bristol corporate practice. The practice covers all company and corporate finance work with particular emphasis on mergers and acquisitions, private equity and venture capital, flotations, takeovers, financings, joint ventures and general corporate advice.
Career: Qualified with *McKenna & Co* in 1987; *McKenna & Co* 1987-89; Investment Banking Division of Samuel Montagu & Co. Ltd 1989-92; and HSBC Investment Bank (Asia) Limited 1992-97, becoming a Director; Partner *CMS Cameron McKenna* 1997.
Personal: Born 23 November 1960. Educated at Haberdashers' Aske's School, Elstree; Durham University and College of Law, Guildford. Married with three children, lives in Bath.

KANE, Hilary
Maclay Murray & Spens, Glasgow
(0141) 248 5011
hak@maclaymurrayspens.co.uk
Specialisation: Partner specialising in mergers and acquisitions (including cross-border) and corporate finance. Recent transactions include advising HP/Compaq Computer Corporation on the sale and outsourcing of its PCBA operations at Ayr to Jabil Circuit Inc; lead partner advising on the demerger of the non power operations of the Clyde Blowers Group and the sale of its power operations for c £60m; advising Stagecoach Holdings plc in its £33.4m sale of Glasgow Prestwick International Airport, advising British Polythene Industries plc in its successful defence of Macfarlane Group's hostile takeover bid and its tender offer to buy back c 30% of its shares.
Prof. Memberships: Mergers and Acquisitions Committee of AIJA (International Lawyers Association).
Career: Articled *Maclay Murray & Spens*; qualified 1985; partner, *Maclay Murray & Spens*, since 1991; established London office where partner in charge before returning to Glasgow office in 1997.
Personal: Craigholme School; Glasgow University (LLB 2(1) Hons, Dip LP). Born 1962; resides Glasgow. Enjoys good food and wine, spinning, watching football, skiing.

KELIHER, James
Stephens & Scown, Exeter
(01392) 210700

KING, Peter
Linklaters, London
(020) 7456 3448
peter.king@linklaters.com
Specialisation: Specialist in UK corporate finance and company law, advising corporate clients and investment and merchant banks. Main areas of practice include international equity, public and private mergers and acquisitions, joint ventures and general corporate advice.
Career: Co-Head International Equity Practice. 1990 to date: Partner, *Linklaters*. 1977-80: St John's College, Cambridge.

KITTS, Stephen
Eversheds, Nottingham
(0115) 950 7000
stephenkitts@eversheds.com
Specialisation: Corporate finance, private equity and acquisition finance for banks and mezzanine lenders and venture capitalists as well as general mergers and acquisitions.
Prof. Memberships: Law Society.
Career: Joined *Eversheds* in 1987 and became a Partner in 1994. Qualified 1987. Head of corporate at *Eversheds* East Midlands.
Personal: Lives in Nottinghamshire with his wife and two children. Enjoys golf.

LAVERY, James
DLA, Birmingham
(08700) 111111

LAWES, William
Freshfields Bruckhaus Deringer, London
(020) 7936 4000
william.lawes@freshfields.com
Specialisation: Main practice areas are mergers and acquisitions, demergers, joint ventures, restructurings, international offerings and UK domestic issues of all types. Acts for a range of corporate clients (with a media and telecoms bias) and investment banks. His major trans-

actions include the demerger of MMO2 from BT and the mergers of BP and Amoco, SmithKline and Beecham and Lloyds Bank and TSB.
Prof. Memberships: City of London Solicitors Company.
Career: Qualified as barrister and solicitor in New Zealand in 1986. Joined *Freshfields* in 1986. Partner 1994.
Personal: Born 1964. Educated Victoria University, Wellington NZ and Gonville and Caius College, Cambridge.

LAWTON SMITH, Andrew
Wragge & Co, Birmingham
(0870) 903 1000

LEE, Paul
Addleshaw Booth & Co, Manchester
(0161) 934 6000
paul.lee@addleshawbooth.com
Specialisation: Senior Partner of *Addleshaw Booth & Co*, Partner in the corporate finance group. Work covers acquisitions and disposals for both listed and non-listed companies. MBOs and venture capital specialising in strategic advice and business planning. Addresses conferences and seminars.
Career: Qualified 1970. Joined the firm in 1970, becoming a Partner in 1973, Managing Partner in 1991 and Senior Partner in 1997.
Personal: Attended Clare College, Cambridge. Director of several companies, both public and private, including banking and property. Former Chairman of the CBI -North West. Chairman of the Royal Exchange Theatre; Chairman of the Board of Governors of Chetham's School of Music and a member of the board of governors of Royal Northern College of Music. Director of Northern Ballet Theatre. Leisure interests include the arts, sport and wine. Lives in Manchester.

LEE, Richard
Addleshaw Booth & Co, Manchester
(0161) 934 6435
richard.lee@addleshawbooth.com
Specialisation: Partner in corporate finance group. Work covers mergers and acquisitions, City Code takeovers (in particular public to private transactions), flotations and secondary issues. Also deals with general corporate work including UKLA compliance.
Prof. Memberships: Law Society, Manchester Law Society.
Career: Qualified in 1983 before joining the firm in 1986. Became a partner in 1988.
Personal: Educated at Trinity College, Cambridge 1977-80. Leisure interests include sport and family. Lives in Wilmslow.

LEE, Richard
Clarks, Reading
(0118) 960 4638
richardlee@clarks-solicitors.co.uk
Specialisation: Head of corporate. Work covers company law, corporate finance and private equity, public issues, company acquisitions and transaction finance. Advises large corporates, owner/managers, buyin and buyout teams and debt and equity funders. Richard also has a significant practice in employee share schemes.
Prof. Memberships: Thames Valley Commercial Lawyers Association (Co-founder 1987, Chairman 1991-93).
Career: Qualified in 1976. Held various marketing positions with Shell International 1969-72; trained with *Norton Rose* specialising in corporate finance until 1980. A partner at *Simpson Curtis* (now *Pinsent Curtis Biddle*) 1981-86. Head of corporate at *Clarks* since 1986.
Personal: Born 16 June 1947. BSc (Economics and Politics) from Bristol University 1969. Leisure interests include golf, music and theatre. Lives in Reading.

LETH, Mary
Macfarlanes, London
(020) 7831 9222

LEVY, Graeme
Olswang, London
(020) 7208 8754
gdl@olswang.com
Specialisation: Partner and Head of Finance Unit. Specialises in corporate, finance and insolvency matters, acting for corporates, institutions, insolvency practitioners and banks. Work includes mergers and acquisitions, joint ventures and public issues, as well as all aspects of funding and insolvency. Co-author of 'Practical Insolvency Precedents' (Sweet & Maxwell) and formerly a consulting editor to Butterworths 'Encyclopedia of Forms and Precedents'.
Career: Qualified 1985. Previously at *Herbert Oppenheimer, Nathan & Vandyk*, *Richards Butler* and *SJ Berwin & Co* (partner there from 1990). Joined *Olswang* as a partner in 1995.
Personal: Born April 1959. Educated at Trinity Hall, Cambridge. Interests include tennis, theatre (musicals) and playing the guitar.

LEVY, Robert
Kuit Steinart Levy, Manchester
(0161) 832 3434
robertlevy@kuits.com
Specialisation: Corporate finance; corporate and commercial; tax investigation.
Prof. Memberships: Manchester Law Society.
Career: Articled *Kuit Steinart Levy*; qualified 1984; Partner *Kuit Steinart Levy* 1988; Executive Partner 2000.
Personal: Born 1959. Manchester Grammar School & University College London – 1981 LLB Hon. Resides Manchester. Interests – tennis, theatre, amateur dramatics. Member, Royal Exchange Theatre special events committee, active involvement in the Starlight Foundation.

LEWIS, Mark
Foot Anstey Sargent, Exeter
(01392) 411221
mark.lewis@foot-ansteys.co.uk
Specialisation: Partner. Leader of commercial services division. Practice covers a wide range of corporate finance activities including mergers and acquisitions and public and private fund raisings. Also handles company and commercial work, including joint ventures and other strategic commercial agreements and has very substantial experience of public takeovers, flotations and secondary issues on the London Stock Exchange as well as privatisations.
Prof. Memberships: Law Society.
Career: Qualified in 1978. Joined *Foot Anstey Sargent* as a partner in 1995.
Personal: Born 1953. Attended Millfield School 1965-71 and Exeter College, Oxford 1972-75 (Exhibitioner). Lives near Exeter.

LEWIS, Susan
Eversheds, Birmingham
(0121) 232 1063
susanlewis@eversheds.com
Specialisation: Transactional work (including multijurisdictional). Used to heading a large team of lawyers (where the job demands) on substantial matters. Acted for the Phoenix Consortium in the acquisition of Rover Group from BMW.
Career: Oxford University 1976-79. Articled at *Evershed & Tomkinson*, became a partner in 1988. Has been with *Eversheds* throughout career.
Personal: Married with two children. The time for non-work related external interests is almost non-existent, and limited to children and Aston Villa!

LEYSHON, Greg
Osborne Clarke, Reading
(0118) 925 2000

LIPPELL, Sean
Addleshaw Booth & Co, Leeds
(0113) 209 2081
sean.lippell@addleshawbooth.com
Specialisation: Partner and Head of Corporate Finance Group. Principal area of practice is corporate finance. Work includes public issues, takeovers, MBO/MBIs and private equity, mergers and acquisitions (including cross-border/international transactions), demergers and corporate reconstructions and corporate joint ventures.
Prof. Memberships: Law Society.
Career: Qualified in 1979. Joined June 1999.
Personal: Educated at Kelly College, Tavistock and Durham University. Leisure interests include keeping fit, walking, reading, wine and films.

LIVINGSTON, Michael
Maclay Murray & Spens, Glasgow
(0141) 248 5011
mbl@maclaymurrayspens.co.uk
Specialisation: Partner specialising in corporate finance and financial services. Particular experience working with public companies and in the insurance sector. Advises on listings, capital issues and takeovers and financial services regulatory matters. Has also advised on insurance demutualisations.
Career: After qualifying, spent 10 years in industry. Joined *Maclay Murray & Spens* in 1992.
Personal: Born 1958.

LIVINGSTONE, Alisdair
Osborne Clarke, Bristol
(0117) 917 3000

LOAKE, Jonathan
Brobeck Hale and Dorr, Oxford
(01235) 823000
loake@bhd.com
Specialisation: Partner. Company mergers and acquisitions, group reorganisations, MBOs, venture capital subscriptions, corporate transactions in the music industry. Clients include a wide range of technology companies, venture capitalists, publishers and record companies.
Prof. Memberships: IBA; Thames Valley Commercial Lawyers' Association (former Chairman).
Career: Editor with *Hodder & Stoughton*. Qualified with *Denton Hall* in 1979; left after four years to co-found *Dallas Brett*. Partner at *Dallas Brett* from 1983-97. Partner at *Morgan Cole* from 1997-2000.
Personal: Born 21 March 1951. Educated at Rugby School and Trinity College, Oxford. Married with three children. Leisure pursuits include sport, reading and music.

LONG, Julian
Freshfields Bruckhaus Deringer, London
(020) 7936 4000
julian.long@freshfields.com
Specialisation: Is a corporate partner based in London and is a member of *Freshfield's* European M&A Group. Sector experience includes pharmaceuticals, food, publishing and water.
Career: Partner at *Freshfields* since 1995.

LOWE, Paul
Eversheds, Cardiff
(029) 2047 1147
paullowe@eversheds.com
Specialisation: UK and international corporate finance including flotations, public and private company mergers, acquisitions and disposals; joint ventures; MBOs, MBIs, establishment of venture capital funds and limited partnerships, etc, together with general corporate advice.
Prof. Memberships: The Law Society, Institute of Bankers, Cardiff Business Club, Institute of Directors.
Career: Solicitor qualified in Hong Kong. *Phillips & Buck* 1982-87. *Richards Butler* Hong Kong 1988-91. *Eversheds* 1991-date.
Personal: Interested in golf, running and water sports.

LUMSDEN, Ian G
Maclay Murray & Spens, Edinburgh
(0131) 226 5196
igl@maclaymurrayspens.co.uk
Specialisation: Partner in corporate department specialising in corporate finance and mergers and acquisitions. Work includes flotations, rights issues and other fund raising activity for plcs as well as acquisitions and disposals for listed and unlisted companies and invest-

CORPORATE FINANCE ■ THE LEADERS

ment trust reconstructions. Advised Motherwell Bridge Holdings Limited in the £75m disposal of its Information Systems Division; John Menzies plc in its £79m acquisition of Ogden Ground Services and Grampian Holdings plc in its £49m disposal of Edinburgh Woollen Mill.
Career: Qualified in 1976. University of Cambridge (BA 1972), University of Edinburgh (LLB 1974). Spent two years working with *Slaughter and May* in London 1978-80.
Personal: Born 1951.

MACAULAY, Anthony
Herbert Smith, London
(020) 7374 8000
anthony.macaulay@herbertsmith.com
Specialisation: Partner in corporate division. Experienced in company and commercial matters, especially corporate finance work, including takeovers and flotations. Has particular expertise in relation to the Takeover Code (having spent two years as Secretary to the Takeover Panel) and insider dealing.
Career: Qualified in 1974. Became a partner at *Herbert Smith* in 1983.
Personal: Educated Keble College, Oxford.

MACINTOSH, Duncan
Morgan Cole, Cardiff
(029) 2038 5385

MAHER, Paul
Mayer, Brown, Rowe & Maw, London
(020) 7782 8815
pmaher@eu.mayerbrownrowe.com
Specialisation: Head of Corporate Group and a member of the International Policy and Planning Committee which governs the firm. Expertise in mergers and acquisitions, flotations and private equity. Main focus in recent years has been transactional and private equity work in both the telecoms and chemicals sectors.
Prof. Memberships: Law Society.
Career: Articled to *Boodle Hatfield* 1982-84; Solicitor ICI Group Legal Department, 1984-90; Solicitor at *Rowe & Maw* 1990. Partner 1992.
Personal: Born 30 July 1959. London Law Degree, LLB Bristol. Interested mainly in books, politics and travel. Other leisure pursuits include running, football and squash. Lives in Wandsworth Common.

MARCHANT, Simon
Freshfields Bruckhaus Deringer, London
(020) 936 4000
simon.marchant@freshfields.com
Specialisation: Partner specialising in mergers and acquisitions, securities and corporate work. Co-heads the firm's global telecoms, media and technology group.
Career: Articled *Stephenson Harwood*; qualified 1989. Joined *Freshfields* 1989. Spent 1993 on secondment to the New York firm of *Crorath, Swaine & Moore*. Partner *Freshfields* 1997.
Personal: Born 1964. Educated Southampton University.

MARDLE, David
Taylor Wessing, Cambridge
(01273) 355977
d.mardle@taylorwessing.com
Specialisation: Partner, Cambridge office (Corporate Department). Advises on a wide range of corporate transactions, including private equity transactions and mergers and acquisitions. Notable transactions include the shareholders in the Dalehead Group on the £150 million merger with Roach Foods, advising TTP Communications plc on its IPO on the London Stock Exchange (valuing the company at £542 million) and Astron Group on its £92 million merger with e-doc Group plc.
Prof. Memberships: Law Society.
Career: *Denton Hall* 1990-94; *Allen & Overy* 1994-99; *Garretts* 1999-2001; *Taylor Johnson Garrett* 2001 to date.
Personal: Worcester College, Oxford (1985-88) (BA) and Guildford College of Law. Interests include all sports. Married with two children.

MARSH, David
Burges Salmon, Bristol
(0117) 939 2288
david.marsh@burges-salmon.com
See under Partnership, p.601

MARSHALL, John
Johnsons, Belfast
(028) 9024 0183

MARTIN, Charles
Macfarlanes, London
(020) 7831 9222

MASTERS, Richard
McGrigor Donald, Glasgow
(0141) 567 9226
richard.masters@mcgrigors.com
Specialisation: Corporate acquisitions/sales/fund raisings. Successes so far in year 2001: acted for Klick Photopoint on its acquisition of the Max Spielmann photo processing business; Tyco in its acquisition of the Macfarlanes Plastic Division; Pacific Spirits in its acquisition of Inverhouse Distillers; Frazier International in its sale to Mirec B.V. and *McGrigor Donald* in its merger with KLegal.
Prof. Memberships: Law Society of Scotland.
Career: Associate *McGrigor Donald*, 1993. Partner Corporate Finance, 1996. Partner *KLegal* 2002.
Personal: Educated at Wallace High School, Northern Ireland and Strathclyde University. Married with two children, Tom (nine) and Michael (six). Main intrests, hill walking, motor racing, football, fine food and wine.

MCBRIDE, Paul
L'Estrange & Brett, Belfast
(028) 9023 0426
paul.mcbride@lestrangeandbrett.com
Specialisation: Corporate and commercial including mergers and acquisitions, management buyouts, venture capital and project finance.
Prof. Memberships: Law Society of Northern Ireland.
Career: Queens University, Belfast (LLB), Cambridge University (LLM). Called to the Northern Ireland Bar in 1990. Admitted as a solicitor in Northern Ireland in 1993. Partner in *L'Estrange & Brett* since 1998.

MCDONALD, Kevan
Dickson Minto WS, Edinburgh
(0131) 225 4455
kevan.mcdonald@dmws.com
Specialisation: Partner in corporate department. Main areas of practice are corporate and commercial: mergers and acquisitions, management buyins and outs, sales and purchases of companies and businesses, refinancings and corporate finance. Recent deals include the purchase of Filofax for Charles Letts and the buyout of VFG.
Prof. Memberships: Law Society of Scotland, IBA.
Career: Qualified in 1982. Joined *Dickson Minto WS* as senior assistant in 1985 and assumed as a partner in 1987.
Personal: Born 7 July 1958. Attended Aberdeen University 1976-79 (LLB) and Dundee University 1979-80 (Diploma in Petroleum Law). Leisure interests include fishing, swimming and squash. Lives in Edinburgh.

MCGINN, James
MacRoberts, Glasgow
(0141) 332 9988
james.mcginn@macroberts.com
Specialisation: Corporate finance including mergers and acquisitions and private equity. Recent deals include acting for RBDC in further funding of Alpha Telecom; acting for Bridgepoint Capital Partners Ltd in further funding to PSL Group to fund £20m acquisition of AGR Group.
Prof. Memberships: Law Society of Scotland. Law Society (England and Wales).
Career: University of Glasgow 1980-85 (LLB Hons; Dip LP). Qualified 1986 Scotland; 1994 England. Assistant *Levy & McRae*, Glasgow 1987; assistant *Talyor Vinters*, Cambridge 1988-89; assistant *Dickson Minto WS*, London 1990-96, Edinburgh 1997; *MacRoberts* 1997; partner 1988.

MCHUGH, Peter
Eversheds, Birmingham
(0121) 232 1000
petermchugh@eversheds.com
Specialisation: Head of corporate services, Birmingham. Handles mainly M&A and corporate advisory work
Prof. Memberships: Birmingham Law Society.
Career: Qualified in 1982. Became a Partner in 1989
Personal: Born 23 July 1958. Lives in Hartlebury, Worcestershire. Fellow of the RSA.

MCINTOSH, Ian
Addleshaw Booth & Co, Leeds
(0113) 209 2000
ian.mcintosh@addleshawbooth.com
Specialisation: Partner in corporate finance group. Corporate finance and company law including mergers and acquisitions, joint ventures, MBOs and private and public capital raisings. Acts for a range of public and private companies, and financial institutions.
Prof. Memberships: Law Society.
Career: Qualified 1983. Joined the firm in 1988, becoming a Partner in 1989.
Personal: Leisure interests include golf, cinema and playing the drums badly.

MCNEILL, Morag
McGrigor Donald, Glasgow
(0131) 777 7000
morag.mcneill@mcgrigors.com
Specialisation: Corporate finance including mergers, acquisitions, MBOs, MBIs, IBOs and Flotations. Deals: Acted for Orbital Software Holdings plc in the recommended offer by Sopheon plc, acted for Pacific Spirits UK Limited in the £60 million recommended offer for Blaumhor Limited; acted for Brewin Dolphin Securities Limited, financial advisors to Berry Birch & Noble plc in the £70 million reverse takeover by Berkeley Financial Services Group plc.
Prof. Memberships: Member of the RSA.
Career: 1977-83 Edinburgh University (LLB, DipL, LLM). 1983-86 Trainee and Assistant, *Pairman Miller & Murray WS*, Edinburgh. 1986-88 Assistant *Herbert Oppenheimer Nathan & Vandyke*, London. Joined *McGrigor Donald* July 1988, Associate November 1989, Partner May 1991, Head of Corporate Finance 1994-98. Head of Corporate Unit (Scotland) 2002-.
Personal: Married to David P. Sellar, Advocate. One child. Leisure interests include cinema, swimming and the arts.

MCVEIGH, Kevin
Elliott Duffy Garrett, Belfast
(028) 9024 5034
kevin.mcveigh@edglegal.com
Specialisation: Banking and corporate finance; mergers and acquisitions; competition law.
Prof. Memberships: Law Society of N Ireland; Law Society England and Wales.
Publications: EU law sub-editor, Bulletin of Northern Ireland Law.

MEIKLEJOHN, Iain
Shepherd+ Wedderburn, Edinburgh
(0131) 473 5253
iain.meiklejohn@shepwedd.co.uk
Specialisation: Partner in Corporate Department. Main areas of practice are corporate finance, mergers and acquisitions, banking, company law, small and medium businesses and insolvency law. Scottish Editor of 'International Bank Secrecy'.
Prof. Memberships: Law Society of Scotland.
Career: Apprenticed to *Allan Dawson Simpson & Hampton* 1976-78. Qualified in 1976 and joined *Shepherd+ Wedderburn*. Became a Partner in 1982.
Personal: Born 3 November 1954. Educated at Edinburgh Academy 1961-72 and Edinburgh University 1972-76.

THE LEADERS ■ CORPORATE FINANCE

Director of The Scottish Trust for Underwater Archaeology, Stagecoach ESOP Trust Limited and Aggreko QUEST Trustee Limited.

METCALFE, Ian
Wragge & Co, Birmingham
(0870) 903 1000

METCALFE, Rob
Browne Jacobson, Nottingham
(0115) 976 6000
rmetcalfe@brownej.co.uk
Specialisation: Corporate/corporate finance. Wide experience of transaction oriented work heading unit which advises buyers, sellers and funders (equity and debt).
Prof. Memberships: Law Society.
Career: Articled *Eking Manning*. Qualified 1980. Partner *Browne Jacobson* 1985.
Personal: Born 1956; Educated Barnard Castle School, Co. Durham and Nottingham University (LLB Hons). Resides Nottingham. Interests: football, cricket, squash, watersports, climbing and trekking, travel and music.

MIDDLEDITCH, Matthew
Linklaters, London
(020) 7456 3144
matthew.middleditch@linklaters.com
Specialisation: Specialist in UK corporate finance and company law advising both corporate clients and investment banks. Main areas of practice include: public and private mergers and acquisitions, joint ventures and general corporate work.
Career: 1990 to date: Partner, *Linklaters*; 1988-90; Assistant Solicitor, *Linklaters*; 1986-88: Assistant Solicitor, *Mills & Reeve*, Norwich; 1982-86: Assistant Solicitor, *Linklaters*, 1980-82: Articled Clerk, *Linklaters*. 1979-80: College of Law, Law Society Final Examinations; 1976-79: Trinity College, Cambridge, MA Law.

MILLINGTON, Jeremy
Wragge & Co, Birmingham
(0870) 903 1000

MINTO, Bruce
Dickson Minto WS, Edinburgh
(0131) 225 4455
bruce.minto@dmws.com
Specialisation: Work includes Stock Exchange listings, Purple Book work generally, investment funds, mergers and acquisitions and institutional finance.
Prof. Memberships: Law Society of Scotland.
Career: Qualified in 1981. Formed *Dickson Minto WS* in 1985.
Personal: Born 30 October 1957. Attended Edinburgh University 1975-79. Leisure interests include golf, shooting and music.

MOORE, Austin
Gateley Wareing, Nottingham
(0115) 983 8200

MORGAN, Simon
Olswang, London
(020) 7208 8606
sdm@olswang.com
Specialisation: Partner, corporate. Corporate finance. Advises businesses and professional advisors on business start-ups, joint ventures, equity issues, acquisitions, disposals and takeovers. More recent transactions have included the flotations of Jupiter Dividend & Growth Trust plc, New Star Investment Trust plc, Paradigm Media Investments plc and WMRC plc and various private equity financings for Two Way TV, Moneybox Corporation and New Star Asset Management Group.
Career: Qualified in 1987. Joined *Frere Cholmeley Bischoff* in 1985, becoming a Partner in 1994. Joined *Olswang* in August 1998.
Personal: Born 25 June 1963. Attended Oakwood Comprehensive School 1974-79, Thomas Rotherham College 1979-81 and Pembroke College, Cambridge 1981-84. Married with three children.

MORRIS, Andrew
Edwards Geldard, Cardiff
(029) 2023 8239
andrew.morris@geldards.co.uk
Specialisation: Corporate finance, company and business acquisitions and disposals, management buyouts and buyins; joint ventures and reorganisations, advises companies receiving and banks and other organisations providing venture capital.
Prof. Memberships: Law Society.
Career: Assistant Solicitor between 1989 and 1995. Partner in *Edwards Geldard* since 1995.
Personal: Born 1965. Educated at Lady Mary High School, Cardiff and University of Glamorgan. Lives in Cardiff.

MORSE, Stephen
Michelmores, Exeter
(01392) 436244

MUNDAY, Peter
Mundays, Cobham
(01372) 809005
peter.munday@mundays.co.uk
Specialisation: Head of Corporate Department and Senior Partner. Mergers, acquisitions and disposals. Clients include Alliance UniChem Plc, The Vending Corporation Ltd, Waymede Healthcare Plc, Biwater Plc, Service Graphics Ltd, Fullers Logistics Group Holdings Ltd, Sommer Holdings Ltd, HL Group Plc, E. Moss Ltd, Fine Fragrances & Cosmetics Ltd, Morgan Elliott Group Ltd, Kewill Systems Plc. Has undertaken lecture tours of USA under the title 'Building a Bridge To The United States of Europe'.
Personal: Born 31 October 1938. Educated: College of Law Guildford. Leisure interests include umpiring hockey and cricket – member of the MCC. Lives in Oxshott, Surrey.

MURPHY, Frances
Slaughter and May, London
(020) 7600 1200
frances.murphy@slaughterandmay.com
Specialisation: General practice consists principally of acting for corporate clients and investment banks on corporate finance and M&A transactions, both in England and overseas, and generally on corporate matters. Wide experience of acquisitions and disposals (both public and private), joint ventures and of equity and debt financing structures. Also has a significant practice in relation to demutualisation of building societies.
Prof. Memberships: The Law Society.
Career: Qualified in 1983 after articles with *Slaughter and May*. Became a Partner in 1990, after a year in the Hong Kong office.
Personal: Born 24 September 1957.

NEEDHAM, Andrew
DWF, Manchester
(0161) 228 3702
andrew.needham@dwf.co.uk
Specialisation: Partner and head of corporate finance. Specialising in mergers and acquisitions, flotations and stock market issues, venture capital, and management buyouts and buyins.
Prof. Memberships: Law Society.
Career: Qualified in 1975 and became a partner of *Addleshaw Sons & Latham* in 1977 and head of corporate finance in 1991. On the merger of *Addleshaw Sons & Latham* and *Booth & Co*, became head of the corporate finance department of *Addleshaw Booth & Co* until 1998. Andrew then joined Datagroup plc, a holding company of an IT service group. Andrew joined *DWF* in 2000 as head of corporate finance.
Personal: Born 3 September 1950. Educated at Trinity College, Cambridge 1968-72. Holds company directorships and is charity trustee. Leisure pursuits include squash, tennis, golf and skiing. Lives in Knutsford, Cheshire.

NEWMAN, Iain
Nabarro Nathanson, London
(020) 7524 6423
i.newman@nabarro.com
Specialisation: Partner specialising in corporate and corporate finance. Head of Public Equity Group. Diversified practice including flotations, fundraisings, private equity transactions and mergers and acquisitions. Acts for a number of investment banks and public companies.
Prof. Memberships: BVCA.
Career: Qualified in 1990 with *Nabarro Nathanson*. Became a Partner in 1997.
Personal: Born 1966. Attended St. Bees School and Mansfield College, Oxford. Principal leisure interest is spending time with my wife (Vicki) and three children (Anna, Peter and Mark).

NICHOLSON, Graham
Freshfields Bruckhaus Deringer, London
(020) 7936 4000
graham.nicholson@freshfields.com
Specialisation: Partner dealing with corporate and securities law, and mergers and acquisitions, particularly in relation to the financial services industry. Co-head of the firm's Financial Institutions Group and relationship partner for a number of the firm's major clients.
Career: Qualified 1974. Partner 1980.
Personal: Born 1949. Educated at Trinity Hall, Cambridge.

NORMAN, Guy T D
Clifford Chance, London
(020) 7006 1950
guy.norman@cliffordchance.com
Specialisation: Corporate. Partner specialising in corporate finance, M&A and takeovers.
Prof. Memberships: Law Society.
Career: Articled *Clifford Chance*; qualified 1991; seconded to *J. Henry Schroder & Co. Ltd* 1993-94; seconded to Takeover Panel 1997-99; Partner since 1998.
Personal: Sevenoaks School; 1988 Downing College, Cambridge (BA Law) 1991 (upgraded to MA).

O'BRIEN, Barry
Freshfields Bruckhaus Deringer, London
(020) 7936 4000
barry.obrien@freshfields.com
Specialisation: Partner in Corporate Department: Co-head of Global Corporate Department. Specialises in mergers and acquisitions and securities work much of which has an international element. Acts for a number of the firm's key investment banking clients as well as a wide range of corporate clients. In 1996 led a team of 200 lawyers on the implementation of the Reconstruction and Renewal plan for the Lloyds of London insurance market.
Prof. Memberships: Law Society.
Career: Qualified in 1978. Joined *Freshfields* in 1983 and became a partner in 1986.
Personal: Born 1952. Educated at University College, London. Enjoys sport. Lives in London.

O'CONNOR, Mark
DWF, Liverpool
(0151) 236 6226
moc@dwf-law.com
Specialisation: Corporate finance transactions, business structuring, commercial advice, corporate governance, public company work and the establishment of regional investment funds.
Prof. Memberships: Law Society.
Career: Articled *Cuff Roberts North Kirk*; qualified 1980; Partner *Davies Wallis Foyster* 1984; Head of Corporate.

PALMER, James
Herbert Smith, London
(020) 7374 8000
james.palmer@herbertsmith.com
Specialisation: Partner specialising in mergers and acquisitions and corporate finance work, including takeovers (both hostile and agreed), schemes of agreement, joint ventures, demergers and other restructurings, IPOs and other securities offerings.
Prof. Memberships: Chairman of City of London Law Society, Company Law sub-committee.
Career: Joined 1986, qualified 1988, Partner 1994.
Personal: Educated at Winchester College and Queens' College Cambridge 1982-85.

CORPORATE FINANCE ■ THE LEADERS

PASS, Jamie
Dickinson Dees, Newcastle upon Tyne
(0191) 279 9285
jamie.pass@dickinson-dees.com
Specialisation: Mainstream corporate finance, mergers and acquisitions, new issues and private equity work.
Prof. Memberships: Law Society.
Career: Educated Doncaster Grammar School and Jesus College, Cambridge. *Clifford Chance* 1986-92. Joined *Dickinson Dees* in 1992. Partner 1995.
Personal: Born Doncaster, resides Newcastle upon Tyne.

PATRICK, Bruce
Maclay Murray & Spens, Edinburgh
(0131) 226 5196
brp@maclaymurrayspens.co.uk
Specialisation: Senior partner experienced in all areas of corporate law but most notably in venture capital, MBO's/MBI's, receiverships and ship finance. Vice-Convenor of the Company Law Committee of the Law Society of Scotland. Has been a panel solicitor for 3i plc for over 25 years. Head of the firm's Scottish Parliamentary Group.
Career: Qualified 1973. University of Oxford (BA 1967) and University of Edinburgh (LLB 1971). Former managing partner of *Maclay Murray & Spens* (1991-94). Senior partner (2000-).
Personal: Born 1945.

PAUL, Alan
Allen & Overy, London
(020) 7330 3000
alan.paul@allenovery.com
Specialisation: Partner in the Corporate Department. Principal area of work is corporate finance, particularly corporate acquisitions with a specialisation in public takeovers and transactions for financial buyers.
Prof. Memberships: Law Society.
Career: Qualified 1980, Partner 1985. Secretary of Takeover Panel (on secondment) 1985-88.
Personal: Born 19 July 1954. Attended St. Paul's School 1966-72, University College, Oxford University (1977 BA, MA). Lives in London.

PEARSON, Chris
Norton Rose, London
(020) 7283 6000
pearsoncc@nortonrose.com
Specialisation: Main area of practice is public company and stock exchange transactions, including public company takeovers, other mergers and acquisitions, flotations, securities offerings, and company reconstructions and institutional investments. Also international transactions, including cross-border mergers and acquisitions and joint ventures. Important public company transactions include Guinness/Grand Metropolitan (£22 billion); Texas Utilities/The Energy Group (£4.45 billion); Ciba Specialty Chemicals/Allied Colloids (£1.42 billion); Trinity/Mirror Group (£2.1 billion); Mannesmann/Orange (£20 billion) and Airtours/Carnival, a subscription and partial offer involving Carnival acquiring 29.5% of Airtours for some £200 million. Securities transactions include the flotation of Beeson Gregory and the "trombone" rights issue by Trinity International Holdings to raise £182 million in connection with the acquisition of regional newspaper interests of The Thomson Corporation and the HSBC Holdings Enhanced Scrip Dividend Scheme. Other mergers and acquisitions include the linked disposal by Siemens of its shareholding in GPT Holdings to GEC and acquisition of GEC's shareholding in Siemens GEC Communication Systems (£700 million). International transactions include the formation of a cross-border joint venture between Redland and Koramic in respect of brick products in Belgium and Holland (to create the largest facing brick manufacturer in continental Europe) and the establishment of a joint venture, Sun International Investments (owned by Royale Resorts, Caledonia Investments and World Leisure Group) to invest over US$100 million in the billion dollar Paradise Island resort project in the Bahamas.
Prof. Memberships: Member of the Law Society, the City of London Solicitors Company and the Royal Automobile Club; also the Firm's representative on the City of London Law Society Company Law Sub-Committee.
Personal: Family status: married. Hobbies/interests: squash, tennis, rugby, theatre and cinema.

PEARSON, David
Clifford Chance, London
(020) 7006 1429
david.pearson@cliffordchance.com
Specialisation: Corporate. Partner specialising in corporate finance, takeovers, flotations, mergers and acquisition and secondary issues, also venture capital, management buyouts and buyins.
Career: Articled *Clifford Chance*, qualified 1989; Partner since 1996.
Personal: Asheville College, Harrogate; Downing College, Cambridge (MA Law).

PEARSON, Jeffrey
Edwards Geldard, Cardiff
(029) 2023 8239
jeff.pearson@geldards.co.uk
Specialisation: Corporate finance, public takeovers, mergers and acquisitions and multijurisdictional joint ventures. Recent work includes a number of transactions for Barclays Bank plc, United Utilities plc, Hyder Business Services Group Limited, WPD Inc, Pendragon plc, Chevron in the quoted company sector and a wide variety of acquisition and disposal work in the private company sector.
Prof. Memberships: Law Society.
Career: *Slaughter and May* London between 1984 and 1991. Partner in *Edwards Geldard* since 1991.
Personal: Born 1961. Educated at Bishop Gore SC, Swansea and University College of Wales, Aberystwyth. Married with two children. Lives in Cardiff.

PECK, Andrew
Linklaters, London
(020) 7456 3454
andrew.peck@linklaters.com
Specialisation: In charge of one of the Corporate Department's groups. Deals with a wide range of corporate and corporate finance work, including new issues, mergers and acquisitions, and reorganisations, with extensive experience in the financial services sector.
Career: Group leader in the corporate practice. 1984: Seconded to the Council for the Securities Industry to assist in drafting a City response to the Gower Report; 1983 to date: Partner, *Linklaters*; 1981-83: Assistant solicitor, Corporate Department, *Linklaters*; 1976-81: Corporate Finance Department, NM Rothschild & Sons Limited (Assistant Director 1980); 1973-76: Assistant solicitor, Corporate and Tax Departments, *Linklaters*; 1971-73: Articled clerk, *Linklaters*. 1967-71: Cambridge University, MA, LLB.

PESTER, David
TLT Solicitors, Bristol
(0117) 917 7777
dpester@TLTsolicitors.com
Specialisation: Corporate finance. Mergers, acquisitions and disposals, other corporate finance and company law. Particular experience of OFEX, AIM and other listings. Led a series of acquisitions and disposals for Alfred McAlpine including the acquisition of Ryan Utility Services Ltd for £12m (including assumption of debt) and a series of disposals to Numerica plc.
Prof. Memberships: Company Secretary of Bristol Tourism and Conference Bureau. Bristol Chamber of Commerce and Initiative.
Career: Manchester University, BA (1st), Bristol University, LLM (Employment and Corporate Law); articled at *Lawrence Tucketts* (now *TLT Solicitors*, the merged firm of *Trumps* and *Lawrence Tucketts*), admitted 1989.
Personal: Sailing and football.

PHILLIPS, Robert
Robert Muckle, Newcastle upon Tyne
(0191) 244 2906
rjphillips@robertmuckle.co.uk
Specialisation: General Corporate Finance. Partner and Head of Commercial Group – quality commercial work for both public and private companies. Specialisation in corporate sales and acquisitions and investment venture capital.
Career: Articled *Denton Hall*; work in corporate finance sector; two years with *Memery Crystal*. Qualified 1990. Joined *Robert Muckle* as an Associate in 1994; became a Partner in 1997 and Group Head in 2000.

PILLMAN, Joe
Brobeck Hale and Dorr, Oxford
(01235) 823000
pillman@bhd.com
Specialisation: Partner. Handles general company law for technology companies including flotations, mergers and acquisitions, MBOs, MBIs and reconstructions. Important matters handled include several acquisitions by Screen and CRC, various investments in Bookham Technology, including private placements by Intel and CISCO, the dual listings of QXL and Bookham Technology on the LSE and NASDAQ and the listing of Screen and Akers Biosciences on AIM.
Career: Qualified in 1977. Partner with *Cole & Cole* from 1983-2000. Partner with *Brobeck Hale and Dorr* 2000 to date.
Personal: Born 7 July 1952. Educated at Rugby School 1965-69 and Cambridge University 1970-74. Lives in Northumberland.

PRINCE, Michael
DLA, Liverpool
(08700) 111111

PSYLLIDES, Milton
Eversheds, Birmingham
(0121) 232 1067
miltonpsyllides@eversheds.com
Specialisation: Partner. Public company transactions, including flotations, mergers and acquisitions, new issues and funding transactions.
Prof. Memberships: Chairman of the Midlands Stock Exchange Regional Advisory Group. Member of the Law Society and the Birmingham Law Society. Treasurer of the Birmingham Law Society. Member of the Birmingham Law Society Company Law Sub-committee. Council Member West Midlands CBI.
Career: Qualified March 1978 with *Evershed & Tomkinson*. Partner May 1984 with *Evershed & Tomkinson*. Eversheds national firm created May 1989.
Personal: Born 30 October 1953. Brockley County Grammar School and Liverpool University. Married with one daughter and one son.

PYSDEN, Edward
Eversheds, Manchester
(0161) 831 8000
edwardpysden@eversheds.com
Specialisation: Senior Partner specialising in Corporate and Commercial work. Corporate finance covering flotations, acquisitions, MBOs and Yellow Book work, recently with a great deal of international flavour. In the last 18 months he has completed well over £1 billion of deals. These have included acting for HSBC Private Equity on its purchase of Caradon Plumbing for £490 million and divestments of Mira Showers for £301 million and Twyfords for £80 million. Overseas transactions include the acquisition of New York internet company Lindberg for Bodycote International Plc and Four Seasons Sunrooms for Ultra-

THE LEADERS ■ CORPORATE FINANCE

frame Pl, each valued at $100 million. Lectures on Company Law at the Manchester Business School and the Henley and Ashridge Schools of Management. Director of Marketing Manchester.
Prof. Memberships: Chairman of the Hallé Concert Society; past Chairman of pro.manchester.
Career: Articled at *Alexander Tatham* 1970-72 and became a Partner in 1974. Appointed Senior Partner of the firm (now *Eversheds*, Manchester) in 1993.
Personal: Born 6 May 1948. Attended Dulwich College 1959-60, King's School, Macclesfield 1960-66, and Manchester University 1966-69. Leisure pursuits include golf, classical music, food and wine. Lives in Alderley Edge.

RAFFERTY, John
Burness, Edinburgh
(0131) 473 6000

RANDELL, Charles
Slaughter and May, London
(020) 7600 1200
charles.randell@slaughterandmay.com
Specialisation: Company/commercial.
Career: Articled *Slaughter and May*; qualified 1982; partner 1989.
Personal: Educated at Trinity College, Oxford.

RAWLINSON, Mark
Freshfields Bruckhaus Deringer, London
(020) 7936 4000
mark.rawlinson@freshfields.com
Specialisation: Partner in the corporate department specialising in mergers and acquisitions, particularly international and cross-border. Also covers general corporate finance (including IPOs, rights issues and other issues) and joint ventures. Publications include 'A Practitioners Guide to Corporate Finance and the Financial Services Act 1986' (contributor) and 'Rights Issues Practice Manual' (contributor and editor).
Career: Qualified 1984. Assistant solicitor, *Freshfields* 1984-90. Partner since 1990. Listed as one of the top 15 'Best Business Lawyers' in Chambers' 1998 survey.
Personal: Educated at Haberdashers' Aske's School, Elstree and Sidney Sussex College, Cambridge 1976-80. Interests include family and sport. Born 1957. Lives in London.

RAWSTRON, Chris
DLA, Birmingham
(08700) 111111

ROSE, Kenneth
Dundas & Wilson CS, Edinburgh
(0131) 228 8000

ROSENBERG, Daniel
Taylor Wessing, London
(020) 7300 7000
d.rosenberg@taylorwessing.com
Specialisation: Corporate partner with considerable experience in a wide range of corporate issues, including M&A, joint ventures and IPOs, with a particular focus on inward investment from North America. Deals include advising Transamerica Corporation on its £750 million acquisition of Tiphook's container leasing business; advising Harnischfeger Industries Inc on its successful £200 million unilateral takeover offer for Dobson Park Industries plc; advising US Can Corporation on its acquisition of aerosol can making businesses in the UK, Italy, France, Spain and Germany from Crown Cork & Seal for approximately £38 million and advising Merloni Elettrodomestici SpA on its €195m acquisition of Marconi's 50% stake in General Domestic Appliances Limited (Hotpoint).
Prof. Memberships: Law Society's Company Law Committee, CBI's Corporate Law Panel, Negotiated Acquisitions Committee of the ABA's Section of Business Law and North American Taskforce of London First Centre.
Career: Articles with *Slaughter and May* 1985-7; *Berwin Leighton* 1987-2001 (partner from 1992). Joined *Taylor Joynson Garrett* as a partner in 2001.
Publications: General Editor of Sweet & Maxwell's 'Practical Commercial Precedents' and author of 'Public Companies' section of the work.
Personal: Born 1962. Educated at West Hatch High School, Chigwell, and Gonville & Caius College, Cambridge. Leisure interests include family, music (Advisory Council of the London Symphony Orchestra and trustee of Awards for Young Musicians), theatre and cycling.

ROUS, Simon
Bevan Ashford, Exeter
(07977) 471330
s.rous@bevan-ashford.com
Specialisation: Heads *Bevan Ashford's* Corporate & Banking Team. Simon is active in corporate finance, MBO's, mergers and acquisitions and new issue work. He spent 25 years specialising on corporate transactions. Much of his work is London based or international, especially from Germany, the USA and the Middle East. Simon spends part of the week at his flat on Hyde Park and *Bevan Ashford's* London Office, enabling him to deliver on London based and international transactions at regional charge-out rates. Simon's team has grown over the last year to 18 with five recruits from London firms including *Theodore Goddard*. The Department had a record year in 2001 advising on transactions with an aggregate value of over £3.5 billion for clients including Actaris UK Limited, Lloyds TSB Bank Plc, the Bank of Scotland, Travel Alliance Holdings Limited (London), Sprue Aegis Plc (Coventry), Banco Totta & Açores S.A. (Portugal), Dr Foster Limited, (London), Schlumberger (Paris and Houston) and Suffolk County Council. For more details see www.bevan-ashford.com/deals
Prof. Memberships: CBI (Southwest), Devon Community Foundation and Exeter University Business Leaders Forum.
Career: Simon read Law at Trinity College Cambridge and then spent 11 years with *Clifford Chance* in London, Paris, Brussels, the Middle East and New York before joining *Bevan Ashford*.

ROWLEY, Robert
Freethcartwright, Leicester
(0116) 201 4000
Specialisation: Corporate finance: company acquisitions, sales, restructuring, MBOs, MBIs. Recent transactions include acting for the founder shareholders in the Travelsphere Limited £80 million equity release.
Prof. Memberships: Law Society.
Career: Having trained as a corporate lawyer with City of London law firm *Clifford Chance*, he joined niche Leicester commercial law firm *Barradales* where he became Senior Partner four years before that firm's merger with *freeth-cartwright* in 1998.
Personal: Education: Wyggeston Boys School, Leicester and Queen Elizabeth Grammar School, Wakefield. University of London, LLB (Honours), Vollege of Law, Guildford. Leisure interests include rugby union squash and classic cars.

ROXBURGH, Bruce
Osborne Clarke, Bristol
(0117) 917 3000

RUNDALL, Francis R S
Charles Russell, Cheltenham
(01242) 221122
francisr@cr-law.co.uk
Specialisation: Corporate finance, acquisitions and disposals, public and private. Also advises on flotations and other capital raising projects. Recent work includes acting for Montpellier Group PLC on the acquisition of significant assets from the Union Group; acting for Pennant International Group PLC on its placing and open offer.
Career: Marlborough College; University College, Durham. Qualified 1975; Assistant Solicitor at *Slaughter and May* 1975-78; joined *Charles Russell* 1978, becoming a partner in 1981.
Personal: Secretary to Network Gloucestershire Limited. Chairman of the appeal for the Choral Scholarship Fund of the Abbey School, Tewkesbury. Leisure interests include hunting and shooting, opera and church music.

RUSSELL, Stuart
Semple Fraser, Glasgow
(0141) 221 3771
stuart.russell@semplefraser.co.uk
Specialisation: Corporate partner principally involved in corporate law and corporate finance, but with particular interest in joint ventures, IP/IT and technology/e-commerce generally. Recent projects include acting for Miller BoS, a joint venture between Miller Group and Bank of Scotland, in respect of the Alba Campus, Livingston; advising SMG plc on web hosting and web design contracts and advising Insensia Group plc on its admission to OFEX.
Prof. Memberships: Law Society of Scotland; International Bar Association; American Bar Association (Associate); Institute of Directors.
Career: Articled *Browning & Bowes* 1984; legal assistant, *Anderson Fyfe Stewart & Young*, 1984-86; legal assistant, *Bird Semple Fyfe Ireland WS*, 1986-89; *Boyds*, 1989-97, Partner from 1991; Partner, *Semple Fraser WS*, 1997 to date.
Personal: Born 1960. Educated at Eastwood High School and Glasgow University. Graduated LLB (Hons) 1981 and DipLP (1982). Interests include tennis, skiing, music, food and wine. Member of the Wine Society and the Scotch Malt Whisky Society.

RYDE, Andy
Slaughter and May, London
(020) 7600 1200
andy.ryde@slaughterandmay.com
Specialisation: Partner specialising in general corporate and corporate finance; acts for a number of listed companies and investment banks in connection with mergers and acquisitions and corporate finance transactions.
Career: Articled *Slaughter and May*; qualified 1989; Partner 1996.
Publications: Author of 'Share Dealings - Restrictions and Disclosure Requirements', a chapter in the 'Practitioner's Guide to the City Code on Takeovers and Mergers'.
Personal: Born 1964. Educated at the Minster School, Southwell, Nottinghamshire, and Wadham College, Oxford (1986 MA Hons Jurisprudence). Resides Northwood. Interests: sports.

SACKMAN, Simon
Norton Rose, London
(020) 7283 6000
sackmansl@nortonrose.com
Specialisation: Partner and head of corporate finance. Main practice area is mergers and acquisitions, IPOs and other equity issues, demergers and other restructurings. Also experienced in investment trusts, the property/hotel sector and regulatory investigations. Recent transactions include the proposed merger of Deutsche Börse with the London Stock Exchange, the offer for Pifco by Salton, Finalrealm's offer for United Biscuits, the purchase of EM.TV of 50 percent of Formula One and the subsequent restructuring of EM.TV, the sale by Benchmark of a portfolio of West End properties to The West End of London Property Unit Trust, and its joint venture with JE Robert, the enquiry into Lanica's bid for CWS, the DTI enquiry into the flotation of Mirror Group Newspapers, the reconstruction of Henderson EuroTrust and numerous hotel acquisitions, including the Caledonian in Edinburgh and the Landmark and the Kensington in London.
Prof. Memberships: Law Society, City of London Solicitors Company, International Bar Association.

SADKA, Tim
Rawlison Butler, Crawley
(01293) 527744

245

CORPORATE FINANCE ■ THE LEADERS

SEABROOK, Michael
Eversheds, Birmingham
(0121) 232 1084
michaelseabrook@eversheds.com
Specialisation: Partner in Corporate Services Department specialising in private equity. Work includes IBOs, MBOs and MBIs and mergers and acquisitions (both domestic and international).
Prof. Memberships: Law Society, Securities Institute.
Career: Qualified in 1976 with *Lovell White & King*. Assistant solicitor at *Clifford Turner* 1977-79. With *Needham & James* 1980-86 (partner from 1981). Joined *Evershed & Tomkinson* as a partner in 1986. Now deputy senior partner (Birmingham).
Personal: Born 24 March 1952. Educated at King Edward's School, Birmingham 1963-70 and Exeter University (LL.B) 1970-73. Recreations include cricket, golf, soccer, rugby, and horse racing. Lives in Dorridge, Solihull.

SEARY, Peter
Shoosmiths, Nottingham
(0115) 906 5000
Specialisation: Corporate finance, predominantly M&A including RHM – sale of overseas food and BPB plc acquisition of Rawlplug Group.
Career: Qualified with *Shoosmiths* and became a Partner in 1998.
Personal: Interests include rugby, sailing and classic cars.

SHAND, Kenneth
Maclay Murray & Spens, Glasgow
(0141) 248 5011
kds@maclaymurrayspens.co.uk
Specialisation: Head of corporate department. Kenneth handles a range of mainstream corporate transactions, principally for private companies both large and small; his practice covers mergers and acquisitions, MBOs/MBIs/IBOs and institutional finance. Throughout 2001-02 Kenneth worked on the restructuring of Semple Cochrane plc following the discovery of accounting discrepancies at the Group during the period of tenure of the previous board of directors; his team completed Irish listed company DCC plc's acquisition of BP's Scottish distribution business and DuPont's disposal of its DuPont Photomasks UK business; Kenneth continued to advise major clients such as The Edrington Group, Ayrshire Metal Products and Sports Connection and assisted 3i and several local enterprise companies on a variety of investments; Kenneth leads the firm's inward investment team which advises a number of foreign headquartered businesses including Compaq, Mack Technologies and Sally Beauty. Leads the firm's inward investment team which advises a number of foreign headquartered businesses including Compaq, Mack Technologies and Sally Beauty.
Prof. Memberships: Law Society of Scotland.
Career: *Maclay Murray & Spens* 1982-84 (trainee); *Maclay Murray & Spens* 1984-88 (assistant solicitor); *McKenna & Co* 1988-89 (assistant solicitor); *Maclay Murray & Spens* 1989-date (partner).
Personal: Education: Glasgow Academy (1969-77); University of Glasgow (1981 LLB Hons); University of Glasgow (1982 Diploma in Legal Practice). Leisure interests: most sports, especially golf, rugby, tennis and football. Family: married with one son and one daughter.

SHAW, Martin
Pinsent Curtis Biddle, Leeds
(0113) 244 5000
martin.shaw@pinsents.com
Specialisation: Head of Corporate Department, Leeds. Specialises in corporate finance and company law including M&A, stock exchange primary and secondary issues and company reorganisations primarily for public listed companies. Recent transactions include: The SIG plc bid for Roskel plc (£26m), the bid by Baan Company NV for the CODA Group plc (£11.1m), the BPT £75m London Stock Exchange listing of Eurobonds, the Sunderland PLC strategic media alliance with the BskyB Group plc (£13m), the OFEX flotation of SquareSum plc, the disposal by Yule Catto & Co plc of its William Cox Plastics subsidiary (£14.5m), the refinancing of Youngs Bluecrest Seafood Holdings (£53m), an auction sale and recommended takeover bid for BPT plc by Deutsche Bank/Grainger Trust (£477m), the Cosalt plc bid for SEET plc and associated debt facilities (£29m), the SIG plc acquisition of Capco Holdings Limited (IRL £41m) and Newcastle United plc's refinancing and media arrangements with NTL (£30m).
Prof. Memberships: Member of the Solicitors European Group; the American Bar Association and the International Bar Association.
Career: Articled *Simpson Curtis* (now *Pinsent Curtis Biddle*) 1966-69. Qualified 1969. Lecturer in law (part-time) Leeds Metropolitan University. Partner 1971. Former managing partner at *Simpson Curtis*.
Personal: Member of Headingley Rotary Club (past council member and Chairman of International Services Committee); Chairman of Governors of Gateways School. Hon. Secretary of Yorkshire Regional Committee of the Variety Club of Great Britain.

SHIMMIN, Kathryn
Blake Lapthorn, Southampton
(023) 8063 1823

SHORT, John
Taylor Vinters, Cambridge
(01223) 225 158
john.short@taylorvinters.com
Specialisation: Partner in company/commercial department. Work covers acquisitions and sales, reconstructions, venture capital, investment, and MBO/MBIs. Also handles insolvency and banking, advising receivers and liquidators. Advises on taking and enforcing security.
Prof. Memberships: Law Society, Committee Member of Eastern Region Branch of R3.
Career: Qualified 1974. Trainee and solicitor at *Prettys*, Ipswich, 1972-75; assistant solicitor at *Coward Chance*, London, 1976-78. Joined *Taylor Vinters* in 1979, became a partner in 1982. Secretary of Cambridgeshire and District Law Society, 1983-87; Vice President 1999-2000; President 2000-01.
Personal: Born 28 December 1949. Attended Sheffield University 1968-71. Leisure interests include walking, music and photography.

SIGNY, Adam
Clifford Chance, London
(020) 7006 1210
adam.signy@cliffordchance.com
Specialisation: Corporate. Partner specialising in corporate finance, M&A, takeovers and MBOs.
Career: Articled *Clifford Chance*; qualified 1982; Partner since 1987.
Personal: City of London School; Sussex University (Economics).

SIMMONS, William
Tods Murray WS, Edinburgh
(0131) 226 4771
william.simmons@todsmurray.com
See under Projects/PFI, p.699

SINGH, Jit
Howes Percival, Leicester
(0116) 247 3500
jxs@howes-percival.co.uk
Specialisation: Managing Partner and Head of Corporate Department in Leicester. Specialises in corporate finance and other corporate transactions, such as joint ventures. During the last year, the *Howes Percival* corporate team concluded over 75 deals with an aggregate value of over £1 billion; he acted as lead partner on a substantial proportion in number and value of those deals.
Career: Trained *Howes Percival*; qualified 1989; associate *Howes Percival* 1992; Partner 1994; Managing Partner of Leicester office and Head of Corporate Department 1997; elected to management board and Head of HR 1998.
Personal: Education: Educated at Crown Hills Community College, Leicester. Wyggeston and Queen Elizabeth V1 Form College. Leicester University (1986 LLB Hons 2:1). Leisure: Football, cricket. Family Details: Married with three daughters.

SLEIGH, Andrew
Burness, Glasgow
(0141) 248 4933

SLOAN, Graeme
Maclay Murray & Spens, Edinburgh
(0131) 479 2867
gecs@maclaymurrayspens.co.uk
Specialisation: Partner specialising in corporate finance, mergers and acquisitions and private equity. Has extensive experience in public company work, advising both companies and financial advisors. Principal clients include Bank of Scotland, Candover, John Menzies, McDermott International and Scottish Widows.
Career: *Balfour & Manson*, trainee solicitor 1985-87; *Arthur Young*, tax senior 1987-88; *Maclay Murray & Spens*, assistant solicitor 1998-89; *Freshfields*, manager 1990-92; *Maclay Murray & Spens*, partner 1992 to date.

SMART, Peter
Walker Morris, Leeds
(0113) 283 2500
pcs@walkermorris.co.uk
Specialisation: Head of Corporate. Main areas of practice are corporate finance, M&A work, venture capital and (because they're interesting) the resolution of shareholder disputes.
Prof. Memberships: Law Society.
Career: Qualified in 1979, having joined *Walker Morris* in 1977. Became a Partner in 1981, Managing Partner 1993-98 and Chairman in 2001. A director of several public and private companies.

SMITH, Campbell
Biggart Baillie, Glasgow
(0141) 228 8000

SPETCH, Mike
Eversheds, Newcastle upon Tyne
(0191) 241 6070
mikespetch@eversheds.com
Specialisation: Corporate finance, mergers and acquisitions.
Prof. Memberships: Law Society.
Career: Qualified Oct 1988. Three years in corporate department of *Hammond Suddards*. Then (1991) joined *Wilkinson Maughan* and then *Eversheds* in 1997. Head of corporate, *Eversheds* North East.
Personal: University of Leicester – LLB (Hons). Married, two children.

SPINK, Richard
Burges Salmon, Bristol
(0117) 939 2218
richard.spink@burges-salmon.com
Specialisation: Venture capital and corporate finance. Numerous venture capital transactions include acting for Scottish and Southern Energy plc on its £10m e-commerce investment in Simple2, the first web based company to offer virtual employee financial services; Orange Ventures on its £16 million investment in Digital Rum; and ECI Ventures on three transactions including the £10.5 million buyout of MM Group. Other transactions include acting for Motion Media on its admission to the Official List, various acquisitions by Transport Development Group plc and acting for Gooch & Housego plc on its £4.75 m acquisition of US corporation Neo Technologies.
Prof. Memberships: Law Society.
Career: Trained and worked with *Freshfields* including a six month secondment in New York. Qualified in 1989. Joined *Burges Salmon* in 1994 becoming a Partner in 1999. Has had two secondments - one with *Steele Hector & Davis* in Florida and the other with Transport Development Group plc as in-house counsel. Downing College, Cambridge 1984-88,

THE LEADERS ■ CORPORATE FINANCE

Masters in Public International Law.
Personal: Cricket, golf and rowing.

STAFFORD, Peter
Arthur Cox - Northern Ireland, Belfast
(028) 9023 0007
pstafford@arthurcox.ie
Specialisation: General corporate finance including M&A, takeovers, fundraisings, buyouts and shareholders agreements. Also financial services work.
Prof. Memberships: Law Society of Northern Ireland; Law Society of England and Wales.
Career: Assistant Solicitor *Herbert Smith*, London 1995-97. Corporate Finance Executive IBI Corporate Finance, Belfast 1997-99. Assistant Solicitor with *Arthur Cox* Northern Ireland since 1999.
Personal: Educated at Royal Belfast Academical Institution and Jesus College, Cambridge.

STANFIELD, Glynne
Eversheds, Cambridge
(01223) 443666
glynnestanfield@eversheds.com
Specialisation: Joined *Eversheds* as a Corporate Partner in July 2002. Advises on the full range of corporate finance transactions. Recent experience includes dealing with the successful LSE flotation of Bioscience VCT plc and the AIM admissions of Pursuit Dynamics plc and Medical Marketing International Group plc. Advised BoS on its £35m funding of May Gurney's MBO and RBS and Lloyds TSB on a range of matters. Has worked on VC deals for management teams such as ANT Limited and advised VC funds such as Cambridge Technology Management Limited and The University of Cambridge Challenge Fund on investment deals. Particularly interested in the exploitation of technology from the University sector, he has advised a number of Universities on spin-outs and related matters. Continues to advise the Cambridge MIT Insitute on its corporate legal issues.

STARK, Jamie
Paull & Williamsons, Aberdeen
(01224) 621 621
JGCStark@paull-williamsons.co.uk
Specialisation: Partner in Corporate Department specialising in corporate finance including national and international merger and acquisition work, debt and equity funding and MBOs and MBIs.
Career: Educated Merchiston Castle School, Edinburgh, Dundee University (1986 LLB Hons). Qualified 1989. Partner with *Paull & Williamsons* since 1998.

STEDMAN, Graham
Theodore Goddard, London
(020) 7606 8855
grahamstedman@theodoregoddard.co.uk
Specialisation: Mergers and acquisitions (domestic and international), public takeovers, board removal proxy battles, flotations, rights issues, secondary issues, public placings, venture capital, private placings, management buyouts, public to private transactions, joint ventures,
shareholders' agreements, investment consortia, corporate reconstructions, listing rules and corporate governance advice, directors' duties, shareholder actions, the law relating to shareholder meetings, insolvency advice to directors, share options and executive service agreements
Prof. Memberships: Law Society.
Career: *Sacker & Partners* (1978-80): Articled Clerk. *Forsyte Kerman* (1980-82): Assistant *Speechly Bircham* (1982-89): Assistant/Partner. *Mishcon de Reya* (1989-95): Partner. *Theodore Goddard* (1995 to date): Partner.
Personal: Education: Gravesend School for Boys (1969-74). University College, London (1974-77). College of Law, Lancaster Gate (1977-78). Born 10 May 1956 (Gillingham, Kent). Married (Jane) - two children (Anna seven and Alex five). Interests include eating out, cinema, seeing friends, playing with my children, gardening and DIY (under duress), golf (very badly), IT (my wife says I am a computer nerd and my son is turning into one), walking (everywhere), following Gillingham FC (who else would?).

STEINFELD, Michael
Dechert, London
(020) 7583 5353
advice@dechertEU.com
Specialisation: Partner in Corporate Finance Group, Business Law Department. Corporate finance, mergers and acquisitions, and general company and commercial work, involving mainly Stock Exchange listed and overseas companies.
Career: Qualified in 1970, having joined *Titmuss Sainer & Webb* (now *Dechert*) in 1968. Became a Partner in 1972.
Personal: Born in 1943. Educated at Pembroke College, Oxford. Interests include skiing, football, good food and France. Lives in London.

STELLA, Keith G
Berwin Leighton Paisner, London
(020) 7760 1000
keith.stella@blplaw.com
Specialisation: Partner and Head of Corporate Finance. Practice covers the full range of corporate finance activities, including flotations, secondary offerings, bids and takeovers (both public and private). Acts for wide range of listed and private companies, as well as for banks, brokers and other intermediaries.
Career: Qualified 1978. Partner from 1980. Educated at City of London School and University College, London (LLB 1st Class Hons). First Class Hons in Law Society Finals.
Personal: Living in Hertfordshire. Interests include classical music, antiques and wine.

STEPHENSON, Barbara
Norton Rose, London
(020) 7283 6000
stephensonb@nortonrose.com
Specialisation: Main area of practice is corporate finance, including public company takeovers, other mergers and acqui-
sitions, initial public offerings, securities offerings and company reconstructions and institutional investments. Also international transactions, including cross-border, mergers and acquisitions and joint ventures. Important transactions handled include the £2.5 billion takeover of Eastern Group by Hanson, the £1.4 billion acquisition of the investment banking business of Schroders by Citigroup by way of scheme of arrangement and non Code offer and the flotation of Fox Kids Europe on the Amsterdam Stock Exchange. Corporate clients include Taylor Woodrow, Pillar Property, Fox Kids Europe, Old Mutual, QBE, Blacks Leisure Group, Matsushita Electric Europe and TBI. Investment banks include Schroders Salomon Smith Barney, Credit Agricole Indosuez, HSBC, SG Hambros, Credit Lyonnais, West LB and ABN Amro.
Prof. Memberships: Member of the Law Society.
Personal: Married with three daughters.

STERN, Robert
Slaughter and May, London
(020) 7600 1200
robert.stern@slaughterandmay.com
Specialisation: General practice consists principally of acting for corporate and investment bank clients on corporate finance and M&A transactions, both in England and overseas and generally on corporate matters. Wide experience of acquisitions and disposals (both public and private), joint ventures and of equity and debt financing structures.
Career: BA in French and German at The Queen's College, Oxford. Qualified as a solicitor in 1986. Became a partner in 1993.

STILTON, Andrew
Martineau Johnson, Birmingham
(0121) 678 1556
andrew.stilton@martjohn.com
Specialisation: Corporate finance: buyouts, buyins and general merger and acquisition work as well as venture capital and flotation work. Also some banking work.
Prof. Memberships: Law Society, Securities Institute, member of the Law Society's Company Law Committee.
Career: Qualified in 1981. Partner in *Ryland Martineau* in 1985. Partner in *Martineau Johnson* on merger in 1987.
Personal: Born 31 October 1957. Educated at Trinity Hall, Cambridge. Leisure interests include cricket, football, music and travel until parenthood intervened.

STORAR, Michael
Lawrence Graham, London
(020) 7379 0000

STREET, Robert
Brabners Chaffe Street, Manchester
(0161) 236 5800
robert.street@brabnerscs2.com
Specialisation: Corporate Partner. Handles all areas of company commercial work including corporate finance, company and business acquisitions and disposals, intellectual property and com-
mercial contracts.
Prof. Memberships: Law Society.
Career: Qualified in 1975. Articled at *Coward Chance* (now *Clifford Chance*). Became a partner at *Harold Chaffe & Co* in 1978. Partner at *Chaffe Street* 1983-2001 and *Brabners Chaffe Street* from 2002.
Personal: Born 25 May 1951. Involved with North West Kidney Research. Leisure interests include golf, cricket, fell walking and skiing. Lives in Pott Shrigley, Cheshire.

SULLIVAN, Michael
Linklaters, London
(020) 7456 3166
michael.sullivan@linklaters.com
Specialisation: Corporate department. Specialist in corporate law including mergers and acquisitions, initial and secondary public offerings, corporate reorganisations.
Career: 1994 to date: Partner, *Linklaters*, Corporate Department; 1991-94: Assistant Solicitor, *Linklaters*; 1990-91: Foreign Temporary Associate, *Davis Polk & Wardwell* New York; 1987-90: Assistant Solicitor, *Linklaters*; 1985-87: Articled Clerk, *Linklaters*. 1984: King's College, University of London, LLB (Hons).

SUMMERFIELD, Spencer
Travers Smith Braithwaite, London
(020) 7295 3000
Spencer.Summerfield@TraversSmith.com
Specialisation: Corporate finance; company.
Prof. Memberships: Law Society.
Career: Chigwell School; Cambridge University, Gonville & Caius College; College of Law, London; Joined *Travers Smith Braithwaite* as a Trainee Solicitor in 1987; made a Partner in 1997.
Personal: Interests include cinema/theatre, aerobics, rugby. Married to Karen. One son, Louis

SUTTON, Robert
Macfarlanes, London
(020) 7831 9222

SWANSON, Magnus
Maclay Murray & Spens, Glasgow
(0141) 248 5011
mps@maclaymurrayspens.co.uk
Specialisation: Partner in corporate department. Principal areas of work are MBOs/MBIs, mergers and acquisitions and joint ventures. Led the team on the £30m MBI of Phillips International Auctioneers and its subsequent sale to LVMH group; led the team acting for Redwood Group in the taking private of Clyde Blowers Plc, the first significant take private completed in Scotland and in recent times with £61m of funding provided by 3i and the subsequent secondary buyout and reoganisation of the group financed by Sawmill Capital and the Bank of Scotland, and the MBO of Pelikan Hardcopy – a multinational business bought from NuCote, which was then in Chapter II insolvency proceedings. Recent disposals include the £85m disposal of Stiell to Alfred McAlpine plc and the £60m disposal of

CORPORATE FINANCE ■ THE LEADERS

Blairmhor Distillers to Pacific Spirits. Winner of 1998 Legal Dealmaker of the Year Award.
Career: Qualified in 1982. University of Edinburgh (LLB 1980). Spent 18 months working in New York with *Paul Weiss Rifkind Wharton & Garrison* (1986-87).
Personal: Born 1958.

SWEET, Jon
Marriott Harrison, London
(020) 7209 2020
jon.sweet@marriottharrison.co.uk
Specialisation: Partner in Corporate Department. Main area of practice is corporate and commercial, principally venture capital, mergers and acquisitions and general corporate finance. Handles a mix of private and public company work, but primarily private company. Has a broad range of experience in company/business sales and purchases, complex company and group restructurings, financings (debt and equity) and joint ventures as well as more general commercial advice such as agency and distribution. Past experience has included the full range of stock exchange and takeover code work. Also handles banking and insolvency.
Prof. Memberships: Law Society, Associate Member of BVCA.
Career: Qualified in 1982. Worked at *Slaughter and May* 1980-90 (including 1986-88 in the Hong Kong office). Partner at *Iliffes* 1990-93, and at *Marriott Harrison* since 1993.
Personal: Born 7 March 1956. Attended Trinity College Glenalmond 1969-74, Brunel University 1975-79 and Guildford Law College 1979-80. Leisure interests include target rifle shooting, motor sport and classic cars. Lives in Hertfordshire.

SYSON, Keith
Stevens & Bolton, Guildford
(01483) 734 215
keith.syson@stevens-bolton.co.uk
Specialisation: All aspects of company and corporate finance work including acquisitions, disposals, MBOs/MBIs and other venture capital work. Recent deals include the sale of Hays Clinical Support Services (a division of Hays Commercial Services Limited) to Synergy Healthcare plc and the sale of ATM Parts Company Limited to ACAL plc.
Career: Southampton University; articled *Boodle Hatfield*; qualified 1991; joined *Stevens & Bolton* 1991, becoming Partner 1999.
Personal: Born 29 June 1967. Married. Leisure interests include golf and motorsport.

TAYLOR, Alan
Carson McDowell, Belfast
(028) 9024 4951
alan.taylor@carson-mcdowell.com
Specialisation: Specialisation in intellectual property and IT. Advises University of Ulster and its technology arm, UUTECH, in relation to technology spin out companies.
Prof. Memberships: Law Society of Northern Ireland.
Career: Qualified 1995. Joined *Carson McDowell* 1996. Appointed Associate 1999. Appointed Partner 2002.
Publications: 'Recognising Intellectual Property'; collaboration with Murgitroyd & Co, sponsored by the Law Society of Northern Ireland and the Institute of Chartered Accountants in Ireland.
Personal: Education: University of Dundee (LLB (Hons)); Institute of Professional Legal Studies (Queen's University, Belfast). Interests: keen golfer. Family: married with one son.

TAYLOR, Glyn
Nabarro Nathanson, Reading
(0118) 925 4637
g.taylor@nabarro.com
Specialisation: Corporate finance particularly flotations, venture capital, fundraisings, and mergers and acquisitions.
Prof. Memberships: Law Society; Oxford University Business Alumni.
Career: *Nabarro Nathanson* trainee 1985-87, assistant solicitor 1987-94, equity partner 1994 to date.
Publications: Numerous magazine articles.
Personal: Dartford Grammar School pre 1979. Oxford University (Hertford College) 1979-82. MA (English). College of Law 1983-85. Cricket, tennis, football (supports Arsenal F.C.). Theatre and music concerts.

THOMAS, Michelle
Eversheds, Cardiff
(029) 2047 1147
michellethomas@eversheds.com
Specialisation: Partner specialising in corporate and corporate finance. Advises UK and international clients on corporate transactions including mergers and acquisitions, private equity, joint ventures, corporate funding and restructurings. In addition to the UK and United States, she has worked on transactions in South Africa, France, Spain, Italy, Austria, Sweden and The Netherlands.
Prof. Memberships: The Law Society; Member of New York Bar.
Career: Joined *Eversheds* as a Partner in 1999 following eight years practice in London with *Freshfields* and *Baker & McKenzie*.
Personal: Born 3 November 1966. LLB, University College Eversheds. LLM - University College Berkeley. Fulbright and John Rankin Scholar. Admitted to NewYork State Bar 1994.

THOMSON, Chris J
Greene & Greene, Bury St Edmunds
(01284) 762211

THORNEYCROFT, Max
Gouldens, London
(020) 7842 6111
mbt@gouldens.com
Specialisation: Advises a range of public and private companies, banks and brokers on mergers and acquisition transactions and equity and debt financings. Throughout the 1980s and 90s, he has been involved in all of Hanson plc's major acquisitions and disposals including its four way demerger in the mid 90s and its more recent concentration on the building materials sector. In addition, he advises Tomkins, TT Group, the Swan Group (the holding companies for Mid Kent Water, which is owned by West LB), Sibir Energy and Severn Trent Water plc as well as a number of private companies and entrepreneurs from the United Kingdom and abroad such as Kingston Metals Limited, which acquired the stainless steel and aluminium distribution business of Glynwed International plc for £100 million, UK Plant Limited, which disposed of its plant hire business to Ashtead Group plc for £20 million, the shareholders of Eurotel Telecom Holdings Limited which was sold to a 3i backed MBO for £30 million and Integralis Limited which reversed into Neuer Markt quoted Articon Information Systems AG for £171 million and Bonhams which acquired the Phillips UK auction business. On the financing side, he led the corporate aspects of the firm's advice to Bankers Trust on its loan of $2.1 billion to Huntsman to fund the acquisition of part of the business of ICI as well as advising houses such as Investec Henderson Crosthwaite, Campbell Lutyens, Strand Partners and Bulldog Partners.
Prof. Memberships: The Law Society and the CBI Corporate Law Committee.
Career: After reading law at Oxford, he qualified at *Macfarlanes* in 1975 and then spent six years in the Corporate Finance Department of *Norton Rose* before joining *Gouldens* in 1981 and becoming a Partner in 1983. Managing Partner 1987-97. Head of the Company Department 1997 to date.
Personal: Educated King's School Macclesfield, Cheshire. Member of the Fund Raising Committee of Lincoln College, Oxford. Leisure pursuits include skiing, rugby, opera and gardening. Lives Holland Park and Gloucestershire.

TROTTER, Andrew
Shadbolt & Co, Reigate
(01737) 226277
andrew_trotter@shadboltlaw.com
Specialisation: Partner and Head of Corporate Department. Main area of practice is company sales and purchases and corporate finance, including MBOs, MBIs, venture capital, joint ventures and cross-border transactions. Leads a team which also handles general company commercial work, including franchising, IT contracts and intellectual property. Regular lectures on his subject, including a series of seminars 'Buying and Selling Unquoted Companies' and an address to US lawyers on UK and EU competition law. Recent deals include the £25.5 million third round financing of microscience limited and the purchase by Caffyns plc of Skinners Eastbourne.
Career: Qualified in 1981. At *Withers* 1977-83, *Norton Rose* 1983-85, *Donne Mileham & Haddock* 1985-97 and *Shadbolt & Co* from May 1997.
Personal: Born 5 August 1954. Educated at Lancing College and Oxford. Lives in Cuckfield in Sussex. Interests include football and golf.

TURNBULL, Robert
Cobbetts, Manchester
(0161) 833 5201
robert.turnbull@cobbetts.co.uk
Specialisation: Mergers and acquisitions, MBOs & MBIs, venture capital, joint ventures, corporate finance.
Career: Partner with *Cobbetts* since 1992.
Personal: Educated at King Edward VII School, Lytham and Cambridge University.

TWENTYMAN, Jeff
Slaughter and May, London
(020) 7600 1200
jeffrey.twentyman@slaughterandmay.com
Specialisation: Mergers and acquisitions, corporate finance, public and private equity finance, joint ventures and commercial contracts, acting for listed and unlisted companies and investment banks; Partner in Technology, Media and Telecoms Practice Group, acts extensively for companies and investors in the telecommunications and technology sectors, but represents clients in all sectors.
Career: Articled *Slaughter and May*; qualified 1991; *Morgan Grenfell & Co. Limited* (1993-94); *Slaughter and May* 1994; Partner 1998.
Personal: Born 1965. Educated at Sackville School, East Grinstead and the University of Newcastle-upon-Tyne (1987 LLB). Resides London; two daughters.

UNDERHILL, William
Slaughter and May, London
(020) 7600 1200
william.underhill@slaughterandmay.com
Specialisation: Specialises in corporate finance, including acting for underwriters and issuers of securities, M&A, and regulation of securities markets. Joint Head of TMT and IP Group. Editor of 'Weinberg and Blank on Takeovers and Mergers'.
Career: Qualified 1983 with *Slaughter and May*. Partner 1990.

VAUGHAN, David
Wragge & Co, Birmingham
(0870) 903 1000

VON BISMARCK, Nilufer
Slaughter and May, London
(020) 7600 1200
nilufer.vonbismarck@slaughterandmay.com
Specialisation: Partner specialising in corporate finance, general company and commercial work and some banking.
Career: Articled *Norton Rose* 1986-90; qualified 1988; *Slaughter and May* 1990 to date; partner 1994.
Personal: Born 1961. Educated at James Allen's Girls' School and Trinity College, Cambridge (1983 BA Law 2 (1)). Resides London.

WAINE, Ian
Prettys, Ipswich
(01473) 232 121
iwaine@prettys.co.uk
See under Insolvency, p.464

THE LEADERS — CORPORATE FINANCE

WARD, Michael
Gateley Wareing, Birmingham
(0121) 234 0000

WATSON, Sean
CMS Cameron McKenna, London
(020) 7367 2802
sean.watson@cmck.com
Specialisation: Partner in Corporate Department. Advises corporate, investment banking and venture capital clients on all areas of corporate finance including corporate reconstructions, takeovers, mergers and acquisitions, flotations, international equity offerings, placings, secondary equity offerings and venture capital transactions.
Prof. Memberships: Law Society, City of London Solicitors Company.
Career: Qualified in 1972. Joined *McKenna & Co* in 1979, becoming a partner in the same year.
Personal: Born 5 April 1948. Attended The Leys School, Cambridge, 1961-66 and Manchester University 1966-69. Leisure interests include tennis, golf, skiing, gardening and family. Lives in Weybridge, Surrey.

WATTS, Clive
Osborne Clarke, Bristol
(0117) 917 3000

WAYTE, Peter
DLA, London
(08700) 111111

WEST, David E
Eversheds, Nottingham
(0115) 950 7000
westd@eversheds.com
Specialisation: Corporate finance: mergers and acquisitions, MBO/MBIs and general corporate work for range of public and private companies operating in various sectors including aerospace, food, textiles, property and engineering.
Prof. Memberships: Derby Law Society and Law Society.
Career: Qualified: 1977 after LLB Birmingham University. Joined as Partner 1990 from *Hammond Suddards Edge*.
Personal: Resides Kirby Muxloe, Leics. Leisure: rugby, golf, skiing, family.

WHATNALL, John
Halliwell Landau, Manchester
(0161) 835 2673
jwhatnall@halliwells.co.uk
See under Banking & Finance, p.109

WHYBROW, Annette
Birketts, Ipswich
(01473) 406 357
annette-whybrow@birketts.co.uk
Specialisation: Principal areas of practice are mergers and acquisitions and disposals, MBO/MBIs, joint ventures, venture capital and bank funding. Also member of the Copyright Tribunal and Chairman of the Insolvency Practisoners Tribunal.
Prof. Memberships: Law Society.
Career: University College of Wales, Aberystwyth: (1st Class Hons). Articled and trained at *McKenna & Co* (1974-80). Partner *Birketts* 1981.
Personal: Married with two children. Governor: Suffolk College. Main leisure activity: parenthood.

WILD, David
Eversheds, Nottingham
(0115) 950 7000
davidwild@eversheds.com
Specialisation: Corporate finance and MBOs.
Prof. Memberships: Council Member, Derby Law Society.
Career: Articled *Wells & Hind*, Nottingham. Qualified 1981. Partner *Eversheds* 1985.
Personal: Born 1956. Educated Nottingham High School and Jesus College, Cambridge.

WILL, James
Shepherd+ Wedderburn, Edinburgh
(0131) 473 5318
james.will@shepwedd.co.uk
Specialisation: Head of Corporate Finance. Main areas of practice are Stock Exchange work, company law, mergers and acquisitions, major start-ups and development capital.
Prof. Memberships: Law Society of Scotland, Society of Writers to Her Majesty's Signet.
Career: Qualified in 1978. With *Tods Murray WS* 1978-79 and *Clifford Chance* 1980-81. Joined *Shepherd+ Wedderburn* in 1981 and became a partner in 1982.
Personal: Born 30 April 1955. Educated at Merchiston Castle and Aberdeen University.

WILLIAMS, Christine
Fox Williams, London
(020) 7628 2000
cjwilliams@foxwilliams.com
See under Partnership, p.602

WILLIAMS, Nigel
Dickinson Dees, Stockton on Tees
(01642) 631 706
nigel.williams@dickinson-dees.com
Specialisation: M&A work, particularly owner managed business sales and disposals for corporate clients. Tasked with spearheading *Dickinson Dees'* push into the Tees Valley via their brand new offices at Teesdale.
Prof. Memberships: Newcastle upon Tyne Law Society, Durham & North Yorkshire Law Society.
Career: Trained with *Cameron Markby Hewitt* (now *CMS Cameron McKenna*), qualifying in 1991. Spent five years with *Eversheds* before moving to *Dickinson Dees*.
Personal: Newcastle University and Chester College of Law. One psychiatrist wife and two cats. Leisure interests include any form of sport and frequent trips to William Hill and Ibiza.

WILLIS, John-George
Tughans, Belfast
(028) 9055 3344
j-g.willis@tughans.com
Specialisation: Handles all types of company and commercial work including mergers and acquisitions. MBOs/MBAs, joint ventures and public and private share issues. Represents several of Northern Ireland's leading technology companies.
Career: Qualified 1984. Assistant solicitor at *Tughans* 1987-92. Partner since 1992.
Personal: Educated at The Royal School, Dungannon and Queen's University Belfast. Interests include family and sport.

WINTER, Hilary
Gouldens, London
(020) 7842 6181
hw@gouldens.com
Specialisation: Partner of the Company Department. Principal areas of practice: corporate finance and mergers and acquisitions. Extensive experience in UK equity markets, acting for corporate finance houses and companies.
Career: Joined *Gouldens* in 1984, qualified in 1986 and made Partner in 1993.
Personal: Attended Queen Mary College London and Guildford College of Law. Married Martin Winter, partner at *TJG* and has two children. Main interest is water-skiing. Lives in London.

WIPPELL, Mark
Allen & Overy, London
(020) 7330 3000
mark.wippell@allenovery.com
Specialisation: Specialises in corporate finance, mergers and acquisitions and securities offerings, advising investment banks and major international quoted companies. Has particular expertise in transactions involving US companies and transactions in the financial sector. Has acted on numerous public and private transactions throughout Europe.
Prof. Memberships: Member of International Bar Association.
Career: Educated at Oxford University (MA) 1979; Tulane University, USA (LLM 1980); admitted as Solicitor (1983); admitted as attorney in New York (1987); became *Allen & Overy* Partner in 1999. Previously a Partner in *Ashurst Morris Crisp* (1990-98).
Personal: Born 1958.

WOOTTON, David
Allen & Overy, London
(020) 7330 3000
david.wootton@allenovery.com
Specialisation: Partner in Corporate Department since 1979, handling a wide variety of corporate and company legal matters including corporate finance, public and private mergers and acquisitions, IPOs, flotations and joint ventures.
Prof. Memberships: Member of the Worshipful Company of Fletchers and Court of Common Council of the Corporative of London.
Career: Qualified 1975; Associate *Allen & Overy* 1975-79; Partner *Allen & Overy* since 1979.
Personal: Bradford Grammar School; Jesus College, Cambridge University (1972 BA; 1975 MA).

WRIGHT, Sean
Blake Lapthorn, Southampton
(023) 8063 1823

WRIGLEY, Richard
Martineau Johnson, Birmingham
(0121) 678 1586
richard.wrigley@martjohn.com
Specialisation: Corporate finance, particularly private equity, acquisitions, disposals and joint ventures. Recent deals include £15m Rainbow HBI, £68.5m sale of 80 pharmacies and £44.7m acquisition of Regency Warranties and six other acquisitions and joint ventures for South Staffordshire Group plc.
Prof. Memberships: Securities Institute (Chairman of Technical Committee, Midlands Region.)
Career: Partner *Martineau Johnson* 1996; Norwich (King Edward VI) School; Leeds University.
Personal: Golf, wine, family. Lives in Harborne.

CRIME

London: 250; The Regions: 252; Scotland: 255; Profiles: 255

Research approved by BMRB For this edition, **Chambers'** researchers conducted 6,582 interviews – 3,900 with law firms, 511 with barristers and 2,171 with clients. The validity of the research was scrutinised by BMRB International, who audited both the methodology and the results at our offices in London. They interviewed **Chambers'** researchers and cross-checked sample interviews. Details of the audit appear on page 7.

OVERVIEW The replacement of the Legal Aid Board with the Criminal Defence Service has shaken up the criminal law community and many solicitors are still considering their options. The extra administration costs required by the Legal Services Commission are thought to have already contributed to some firms ceasing to practice in this field, and a wave of consolidations is still anticipated. Practitioners are still nervous about the prospect, still only at the ideas stage, of a Salaried Defence Service which may mean clients being deprived of the choice of which solicitor would represent them.

LONDON

CRIME — LONDON

1
- Bindman & Partners
- Birnberg Peirce & Partners
- Edward Fail Bradshaw & Waterson
- Kingsley Napley
- Saunders & Co
- Taylor Nichol

2
- Edwards Duthie
- Hallinan, Blackburn, Gittings & Nott
- Hickman & Rose
- Hodge Jones & Allen
- Powell Spencer & Partners
- Russell Jones & Walker
- Simons Muirhead & Burton
- Thanki Novy Taube

3
- Andrew Keenan & Co
- Fisher Meredith
- Henry Milner & Co
- McCormacks
- Reynolds Dawson
- Russell-Cooke
- Tuckers
- TV Edwards
- Venters Solicitors
- Victor Lissack & Roscoe
- Whitelock & Storr

4
- Burton Copeland
- Christian Fisher Khan
- Claude Hornby & Cox
- Dundons
- Iliffes Booth Bennett (IBB)
- Joy Merriam & Co
- Stokoe Partnership

This book is the product of 6,582 1/2 hour interviews. See p.7 for BMRB audit. Within each band, firms are listed alphabetically.

BINDMAN & PARTNERS (see firm details p.872) The team enjoys "*a great reputation in the field,*" with peers praising its skill, dedication and "*strength and depth.*" Fronted by the "*fantastically good*" **Neil O'May** (see p.258), the team handles the whole range of criminal defence work from terrorism, homicide and public order work to 'race' cases involving police misconduct. One of many recent highlights was representing the journalists of 'MacIntyre Under Cover.'

BIRNBERG PEIRCE & PARTNERS With a "*singularly impressive reputation*" **Gareth Peirce** remains renowned for miscarriage of justice cases and terrorist work. Her stock is rising in the related field of civil liberties and peers praise her enthusiasm and expertise. The firm as a whole was also acknowledged to "*merit a top place.*"

EDWARD FAIL BRADSHAW & WATERSON (see firm details p.944) This firm is especially well known for its practice in "*east end heavyweight crime.*" Armed robberies, murders and police corruption work all feature heavily and peers rate **Edward Preston** "*one of the top*" practitioners in the region.

KINGSLEY NAPLEY (see firm details p.1023) Though the firm remains better known for its expertise in white-collar crime, its reputation for blue-collar work is growing rapidly. Competitors acknowledge that "*for quality, it takes a lot of beating.*" Boasting "*lots of good people,*" the team covers, *inter alia*, child sex abuse cases and money laundering, and it has a niche in representing high-profile footballers.

SAUNDERS & CO (see firm details p.1123) The firm has a strong name in heavyweight crime, and peers expressed a lot of respect for the expertise of leading light **James Saunders** (see p.258). Asset forfeiture is a specialism, as are privy council cases. A major highlight of the past year has been representing Tony Martin at the Court of Appeal.

TAYLOR NICHOL A "*hands on, dedicated team*" who "*all have good reputations,*" it is known for handling quality work. The "*highly committed*" **James Nichol** was acknowledged as "*one of the best*" while **Mark Ashford** was recommended for his Youth Court work, and **Carolyn Taylor** also received strong market commendation. A major recent triumph for the firm was the low-profile but groundbreaking R v Pendleton.

EDWARDS DUTHIE The firm includes "*big hitters*" **Bernard Huber** and **Shaun Murphy** (see p.257). It handles the spectrum of criminal cases, and its criminal team can also draw on the expertise of a specialist group dealing with civil actions against the police.

HALLINAN, BLACKBURN, GITTINGS & NOTT (see firm details p.982) This outfit handles high-profile work smoothly and efficiently with no fuss. Extradition, judicial review and white-collar crime feature in the repertoire while "*thorough*" **Colin Nott** (see p.257) enjoys a strong market reputation. Peers were also impressed by the work of **Sian Williams**.

HICKMAN & ROSE (see firm details p.995) This firm is widely known for its specialism in prison law, but boasts expertise on all areas of high-profile criminal work. Market sources rate **Jane Hickman** (see p.256) highly, as she "*is professional, hardworking and really fights for her clients.*"

HODGE JONES & ALLEN (see firm details p.997) One of the largest practices in London, competitors envy its "*substantial caseload of interesting work.*" Crime remains a major focus for this growing firm, with work ranging from large scale conspiracies and serious assaults to extraditions. Leading practitioner **Mark Studdert** (see p.258) commands respect from peers and is visible in a broad range of work including homicide.

250   INDEX TO LEADING LAWYERS: PAGE 1693 ■ IN-HOUSE LAWYERS PROFILES: PAGE 1201

LONDON ■ CRIME

LEADING INDIVIDUALS

1
- **HASLAM Mark** Burton Copeland
- **NICHOL James** Taylor Nichol
- **PEIRCE Gareth** Birnberg Peirce & Partners

2
- **ASHFORD Mark** Taylor Nichol
- **EDWARDS Anthony** TV Edwards
- **FISHER Michael** Christian Fisher Khan
- **HICKMAN Jane** Hickman & Rose
- **MILNER Henry** Henry Milner & Co
- **NOTT Colin** Hallinan, Blackburn, Gittings & Nott
- **O'MAY Neil** Bindman & Partners
- **PRESTON Edward** Edward Fail Bradshaw & Waterson
- **SAUNDERS James** Saunders & Co
- **THANKI Girish** Thanki Novy Taube

3
- **BIRD Steven** Birds Solicitors
- **BURTON Anthony** Simons Muirhead & Burton
- **HALLAM Richard** Claude Hornby & Cox
- **HEWITT Stephen** Fisher Meredith
- **HUBER Bernard** Edwards Duthie
- **KEENAN Andrew** Andrew Keenan & Co
- **MERRIAM Joy** Joy Merriam & Co
- **MURPHY Shaun** Edwards Duthie
- **POWELL Greg** Powell Spencer & Partners
- **ROSCOE Robert** Victor Lissack & Roscoe
- **RYAN Ian** Russell-Cooke
- **STUDDERT Mark** Hodge Jones & Allen
- **TAUBE Martin** Thanki Novy Taube
- **TAYLOR Carolyn** Taylor Nichol
- **TSIATTALOU Bambos** Stokoe Partnership
- **VENTERS June** Venters Solicitors
- **WILLIAMS Sian** Hallinan, Blackburn, Gittings & Nott

See individuals' profiles p.255

POWELL SPENCER & PARTNERS (see firm details p.1105) This substantial practice is best known for its work in the North London arena. One competitor described **Greg Powell** (see p.258) as the "*doyen of Brent Magistrates Court.*"

RUSSELL JONES & WALKER (see firm details p.1120) Historically known for its police federation work on the disciplinary and regulatory front, the team enjoys a strong market position in a broad range of criminal work including murder, rape and manslaughter. Judicial review and high-profile public inquiries (including Victoria Climbié and Harold Shipman) are also dealt with. Rod Fletcher heads the team.

SIMONS MUIRHEAD & BURTON (see firm details p.1137) A full range of criminal defence work is undertaken by this "*fine team*" led by the charismatic **Anthony Burton** (see p.255). Drugs cases form a particular niche while the team also boasts a dedicated privy council offering.

THANKI NOVY TAUBE (see firm details p.1158) This "*smooth operation*" deals with cutting-edge work alongside a staple diet of police station matters, appellate work, miscarriage of justice cases and prison rights. The team includes **Martin Taube** (see p.258) who competitors say "*will bust a gut for a client,*" while "*thorough and charming*" **Girish Thanki** (see p.259) also wins substantial praise.

ANDREW KEENAN & CO Peers praise this "*wonderful*" operation for its commitment, drive and expertise. **Andrew Keenan** is singled out for particular praise.

FISHER MEREDITH (see firm details p.956) A large team is busy on all areas of defence work including business crime and cross-jurisdictional issues. **Stephen Hewitt** (see p.256) has had a lower profile this year, possibly due to management responsibilities but is still respected by the market.

HENRY MILNER & CO "*Doing heavier end crime, the firm has some of the best work around,*" according to competitors. Its main name remains "*robust*" **Henry Milner** who was said to enjoy "*a strong repeat following.*"

MCCORMACKS (see firm details p.1063) This centrally located team handles an array of criminal matters. Praised as "*leading lights,*" its interesting cases and energetic performance led one competitor to claim "*there's an air of excitement whenever the firm is in court.*"

REYNOLDS DAWSON (see firm details p.1110) A solid, established crime firm, it is known to represent the police federation. Also recently visible on a number of public inquiries, it retains commendation from the marketplace.

RUSSELL-COOKE (see firm details p.1119) Still best known for its work on the Colin Stagg case, this Wandsworth-based practice, headed by **Ian Ryan** (see p.258), was deemed by peers to have a strong and continuing presence.

TUCKERS A traditional heavyweight crime practice is enhanced by a "*progressive*" approach to case management, with an "*efficient*" casework department streamlining paperwork. Its work includes, inter alia, armed robberies and serious drugs conspiracies.

TV EDWARDS (see firm details p.1171) **Anthony Edwards** (see p.256) enjoys a reputation which some commentators consider "*second to none as a criminal practitioner.*" Also well known as a lecturer and writer, some peers believe that he has been less visible recently, but the firm's focus is not thought to have suffered.

VENTERS SOLICITORS (see firm details p.1175) "*Hardworking and capable*" department head **June Venters** (see p.259) has enjoyed a busy year. Among other things, she defended an accused in the Dome Jewel heist and represented a co-accused in the widely reported Euston hit & run murder. The department has also recently acted in the largest drugs conspiracy in the UK.

VICTOR LISSACK & ROSCOE (see firm details p.1175) The "*Attorney General of Bow Street*" **Robert Roscoe** (see p.258) heads a general crime practice which handles a variety of cases from disciplinary work for police forces and the transport police, through to general criminal and motoring offences.

WHITELOCK & STORR (see firm details p.1185) A "*dedicated and stylish group of young lawyers*" form the team here. It has been involved in a number of high-profile cases including representing members of the 'So Solid Crew' in a murder trial and acting in a large case involving alleged prison officer corruption.

BURTON COPELAND (see firm details p.895) The "*first class*" and ever-popular **Mark Haslam** (see p.256) fronts a team which has now established a strong general crime presence in what is traditionally known as a specialist fraud firm. Substantial C&E prosecutions, the runaway army couple and a heavy motoring work load have all played their part in the past year.

CHRISTIAN FISHER KHAN (see firm details p.906) **Mike Fisher** (see p.256) still commands "*a fantastic reputation*" although market sources perceive his profile to have fallen in recent years. The team's workload includes serious offences such as organised crime and terrorism.

CLAUDE HORNBY & COX (see firm details p.909) Although perceived to have had a lower profile this year, peers acknowledge that this "*quietly respectable firm*" is still a first choice for court martial work. **Richard Hallam** (see p.256), who competitors respect as "*solid, with clear ideas,*" remains its leading name.

DUNDONS The firm is best known for its presence in the South London market. It wins respect for its competence and for handling a broad criminal workload which runs from traffic offences through to murders.

ILIFFES BOOTH BENNETT (IBB) (see firm details p.1007) This "*strong and impressive team*" handles criminal work from its Uxbridge office. Peers were impressed by the range and complexity of work handled. The team has recently acted in a case involving a large scale conspiracy to rob and burgle, and 'Operation Draft,' a high-profile super-grass case involving drugs importation and police corruption.

JOY MERRIAM & CO A major practice with a particularly strong reputation in the Stoke Newington area, it undertakes a wide variety of

CRIME ■ LONDON/SOUTH WEST/WALES

criminal cases. **Joy Merriam** (see p.257) commanded respect from peers for both the amount and type of work she handles.

STOKOE PARTNERSHIP A new entrant this year on the strength of heavy market recommendations, this fast growing outfit is headed by a "*big name in heavy duty work,*" **Bambos Tsiattalou**. Organised crime cases form a strong feature of the workload, while the team has also acted in some large cases of alleged police corruption. Its recent work on the Mardi Gras bombings has been especially high profile.

OTHER NOTABLE PRACTITIONERS The "*great*" **Steven Bird**, formerly of Simons Muirhead & Burton, now has his own firm, **Bird & Co**, based in Wandsworth. Peers deemed him "*a good player with a solid general practice.*"

SOUTH WEST

CRIME
■ SOUTH WEST

1
- **Bobbetts Mackan** Bristol
- **Douglas & Partners** Bristol

2
- **Nunn Rickard Solicitor Advocates** Exeter
- **Sansbury Campbell** Bristol
- **St James Solicitors** Exeter
- **Stones** Exeter

3
- **Kelcey & Hall** Bristol
- **Wolferstans** Plymouth

LEADING INDIVIDUALS

1
- **BUTLER Michael** Nunn Rickard Solicitor Advocates
- **FANSON David** Douglas & Partners
- **FRANCIS Vanessa** St James Solicitors
- **MILES Anthony** Bobbetts Mackan
- **NUNN Stephen** Nunn Rickard Solicitor Advocates
- **ROSE Timothy** Douglas & Partners
- **SVENSSON Zara** St James Solicitors

This book is the product of 6,582 1/2 hour interviews. See p.7 for BMRB audit.
Within each band, firms are listed alphabetically. See individuals' profiles p.255

Bobbetts Mackan retains a strong position, albeit, according to some competitors, with a slightly reduced profile. **Tony Miles** (see p.257) is renowned for his specialism in Courts Martial work, an area in which the firm is still felt to top the tree. **Douglas & Partners** are, in the opinion of one commentator, "*the main player in the area.*" A strong team includes trial advocate **Timothy Rose**, and **David Fanson** who handles a general case load. The team has a niche in youth courts work. **Nunn Rickard** is a new offering this year. It boasts highly regarded **Stephen Nunn** (see p.257) and "*talented and steady advocate*" **Michael Butler** (see p.255), both formerly of Stephens & Scown. Another new entrant to the tables is **Sansbury Campbell**. Peers admire its "*high number of good people,*" which includes David Campbell. The team deals with a wide range of criminal work, but is especially well known for heavyweight matters including business crime and drugs importation. It recently acted on the case of a 12 year old who murdered a six month old: the first of its type post-Bulger. **St James Solicitors** is another new offering this year with the "*extremely capable*" **Zara Svensson** from Stones combining with **Vanessa Francis**, formerly of Hugh James Ford Simey ("*the one I would call if I was in trouble.*") **Stones** manages to retain a presence despite this, although the market is following its progress with interest. "*One of the major players,*" Bristol firm **Kelcey & Hall** have won the respect of peers, especially for its record on drugs importation cases, while **Wolferstans** remains a player in the Plymouth area.

WALES

CRIME
■ WALES

1
- **Huttons** Cardiff
- **Martyn Prowel Solicitors** Cardiff

2
- **Colin Jones** Barry
- **Gamlins** Rhyl
- **Graham Evans & Partners** Swansea
- **Robertsons** Cardiff
- **Spiro Grech & Harding-Roberts Solicitors** Cardiff

LEADING INDIVIDUALS

1
- **HUTTON Stuart** Huttons
- **PROWEL Martyn** Martyn Prowel Solicitors

2
- **JONES Gwyn** Gamlins

3
- **PENNINGTON John** Savery Pennington
- **RICHARDS Geraint** Martyn Prowel Solicitors
- **WILLIAMS Ian** Robertsons

This book is the product of 6,582 1/2 hour interviews. See p.7 for BMRB audit.
Within each band, firms are listed alphabetically. See individuals' profiles p.255

Huttons was described by peers as "*large and well-recognised.*" Although **Stuart Hutton** (see p.257) was thought to be less visible around the courts now, peers felt he still merited his top slot for his knowledge and experience. **Martyn Prowel Solicitors** also commanded respect: "*if I were accused of murder, I would go there,*" said one competitor. **Martyn Prowel** (see p.398) himself is felt to have been less visible of late, though his name still carries enormous respect, while **Geraint Richards** (see p.258) has an increasingly impressive reputation. The team at **Colin Jones** has "*the cream of the market in Barry,*" and, sources say, "*deals with things in a proper and straight manner.*" **Gwyn Jones** of **Gamlins** has a busy and thriving practice. His varied workload has included representing the infamous egg-thrower in the John Prescott case. **Graham Evans & Partners** remains the top presence in Swansea while **Robertsons** continues to do the whole gamut of crime with **Ian Williams** remaining a recognised figure. **Spiro Grech & Harding-Roberts** is renowned for its impressive volume of work, and its reputation in the area of juvenile crime. At **Savery Pennington**, **John Pennington** earns respect from the market for his experience.

MIDLANDS

CRIME
MIDLANDS

[1] **Cartwright King** Nottingham
Fletchers Nottingham
The Johnson Partnership Nottingham
The Smith Partnership Derby
[2] **Glaisyers** Birmingham
Nelsons Nottingham
Varley Hadley Siddall Nottingham
[3] **Banners Jones Middleton** Chesterfield
Barrie Ward & Julian Griffiths Nottingham
Bate Edmond Snape Coventry
Bradley & Clarke Chesterfield
Brethertons Rugby
Elliot Mather Chesterfield
Jonas Roy Bloom Birmingham
Kieran Clarke Solicitors Chesterfield
Parker & Grego Birmingham
Purcell Parker Birmingham
Tyndallwoods Birmingham
Woodford-Robinson Northampton

LEADING INDIVIDUALS
[1] **GOULBORN Caroline** Fletchers
[2] **JOHNSON Digby** The Johnson Partnership
MATHER Bertie Elliot Mather
PURCELL Michael Purcell Parker
TOMLINSON Kevin Kieran Clarke Solicitors

This book is the product of 6,582 1/2 hour interviews. See p.7 for BMRB audit.
Within each band, firms are listed alphabetically. See individuals' profiles p.255

"*A strong firm with a big presence,*" **Cartwright King** has enjoyed a busy year including appearing in several murder proceedings and a Criminal Cases Review Commission appeal to the Court of Appeal. Dealing with everything from minor cases through to the Old Bailey, **Fletchers** is bolstered by the presence of **Caroline Goulborn**. According to some sources, she is "*the leading criminal lawyer of her generation*" in the Midlands, respected for her determined and aggressive style. **The Johnson Partnership** handles the gamut of crime. A major presence in the area, the firm was noted as having "*a lot of work, and getting good results,*" while "*charismatic*" **Digby Johnson** was praised for his "*intellectual capacity*." "*Very strong,*" **The Smith Partnership** emerged from our research as the highest profile crime firm in Derbyshire, with an enviable name amongst peers, while **Glaisyers**, "*a sound conventional criminal practice,*" holds a similar position in Birmingham. Renowned for its mixture of white and blue collar work, **Nelsons** was stoutly commended by market sources. Prisoners' rights is an area of expertise for the team. Rapidly expanding **Varley Hadley Siddall** "*has a decent foothold in the market.*" Recent work has included anti-social behaviour orders. **Banners Jones Middleton** undertakes a range of criminal matters from minor offences through to murder, but is especially associated with more serious crime. **Barrie Ward & Julian Griffiths** deals with a range of interesting matters including internet pornography and sex offence cases, though some sources claimed that its profile had been lower of late. **Bate Edmond Snape** retains a presence in Coventy, while **Bradley & Clarke** and Rugby-based **Brethertons** also enjoy a market profile. **Bertie Mather** of **Elliot Mather** was noted by peers as a "*well known and good*" advocate with many years of experience, while his firm was said to be an "*effective presence*" in the Derbyshire market. **Jonas Roy Bloom** is a new firm making a splash in the Birmingham market. Although peers felt it was too early to comment in detail on its performance, they acknowledged it as a player. **Kieran Clarke Solicitors** is the result of a merger between Kieran & Co and Clarke Solicitors. **Kevin Tomlinson** there deals with the gamut of crime but is especially connected with public order and animal rights cases. From its excellent position opposite Birmingham's Victoria Law Courts, **Purcell Parker** has a strong profile, with **Michael Purcell** particularly respected. **Tyndallwoods** and **Woodford-Robinson** also boast strong criminal practices. **Parker & Grego**, has a solid reputation though the market watches with interest what will happen following Kevin Grego's decision to become a barrister.

EAST ANGLIA

CRIME
EAST ANGLIA

[1] **Belmores** Norwich
Overbury Steward Eaton & Woolsey Norwich
TMK Solicitors Southend-on-Sea
[2] **Copleys** Huntingdon
David Charnley & Co Romford
Gepp & Sons Chelmsford
Hatch Brenner Norwich
Hunt & Coombs Peterborough
Lucas & Wyllys Great Yarmouth
Thanki Novy Taube Harlow

LEADING INDIVIDUALS
[1] **BECKFORD Trevor** Beckford & Co
COLE Michael Cole's Solicitors
FISHER Ian Overbury Steward Eaton & Woolsey
NICHOLLS Simon Belmores
[2] **CARR Kenneth** Thanki Novy Taube
KELLY Philip Kelly Solicitors
MASTERS Peter Thomson Webb & Corfield
MUSTERS Patrick TMK Solicitors

This book is the product of 6,582 1/2 hour interviews. See p.7 for BMRB audit.
Within each band, firms are listed alphabetically. See individuals' profiles p.255

Led by "*talented advocate*" **Simon Nicholls**, the team at **Belmores** can handle "*anything that is thrown at them,*" up to and including murder trials. Although it elicited a mixed reaction, competitors conceded that "*it has the lion's-share of the local market.*" **Overbury Steward Eaton & Woolsey** is bolstered by the presence of "*superb*" **Ian Fisher** (see p.256) ("*dedicated, hardworking and thorough.*") Its range of work runs from traffic offences through to murder. **TMK Solicitors** was described to researchers as "*a first rate practice.*" "*For efficiency and quality of work, it can match any London firm*" was the view of one barrister. **Patrick Musters** (see p.257) leads the team, and, according to one interviewee, you would be hard pressed to find a better "*first port of call.*" The team has acted in the largest drugs operation to date in the UK, and gained considerable profile from its role in the Stanstead hijacking. **Michael Cole** of Cole solicitors is widely respected as "*a top notch practitioner*" who is both skilled and pleasant to deal with. **Copleys** remains the main presence in Huntingdon, while "*polished outfit*" **David Charnley & Co** has the highest profile name in Romford despite the departure of **Ken Carr** (see p.256) to **Thanki Novy Taube**, an "*important new presence*" whose newly-established Harlow office is ranked for the first time. It is building a strong reputation and can claim recent involvement in armed robbery and large drugs cases. **Gepp & Sons** was considered by rivals to have been less visible last year, although the Chelmsford office is handling a lot of legal aid work. The mature team at **Hatch Brenner** commanded respect across the board, while **Hunt & Coombs** remains the main player in Peterborough. In Great Yarmouth, **Lucas & Wyllys** retains a strong market reputation and has been involved recently in important drugs cases and armed robberies. **Trevor Beckford** of Beckford & Co was described by peers as "*a busy practitioner with a growing profile*" while **Philip Kelly** (see p.257) of Kelly Solicitors is said to have "*a niche practice dealing with high profile crime.*" Drugs importation cases have been a major feature this year.

www.ChambersandPartners.com

CRIME ■ NORTH WEST/NORTH EAST

NORTH WEST

CRIME
■ NORTH WEST

1 **Betesh Fox & Co** Manchester
Burton Copeland Liverpool, Manchester
Jones Maidment Wilson Manchester
Maidments Manchester
Tuckers Manchester

2 **Brian Koffman & Co** Manchester
Cunninghams Manchester
Draycott Browne Manchester
Forbes Blackburn
RM Broudie & Co Liverpool

3 **Cobleys** Salford
Farleys Blackburn
Garstangs Bolton
Jackson & Canter Liverpool
Kristina Harrison Solicitors Salford
Russell & Russell Bolton
The Berkson Globe Partnership Liverpool

LEADING INDIVIDUALS

1 **GROGAN Peter** Jones Maidment Wilson
MAIDMENT Allan Maidments
SINCLAIR Franklin Tuckers

2 **BROUDIE Robert** RM Broudie & Co
CUTTLE Barry Cuttle & Co
DRAYCOTT Shaun Draycott Browne
FREEMAN Nicholas Freeman & Co
MACKEY Michael Burton Copeland

3 **KOFFMAN Brian** Brian Koffman & Co
PETER Charles The Berkson Globe Partnership

This book is the product of 6,582 1/2 hour interviews. See p.7 for BMRB audit.
Within each band, firms are listed alphabetically. See individuals' profiles p.255

Betesh Fox enjoys a high market standing and is especially renowned for combining an impressive general crime practice with white collar expertise. Another firm well known for its expertise in fraud, **Burton Copeland** is a towering presence across the region. Rivals acknowledge that, under the guidance of **Michael Mackey** (see p.257), it has developed a premier reputation for high quality criminal work. **Jones Maidment Wilson** was described to researchers as "*professional and well regarded,*" with **Peter Grogan** (see p.256) particularly praised as "*skilled, hardworking and able to cope with a large workload.*" **Allan Maidment** (see p.257) also won a lot of praise from peers, while **Maidments** is a "*firm of choice*" for many interviewees. "*Internally well organised and efficient,*" **Tuckers** enjoys the presence of the current chairman of the CLSA, **Franklin Sinclair**, who is liked and admired by peers. The firm was described as a "*substantial player which stands its ground*" dealing with a huge range of cases from minor offences to the truly heavyweight. **Brian Koffman** is the leading light at **Brian Koffman & Co**. A steady defence firm, it is well known for its expertise in prison law and its commitment to client care. "*An excellent firm which is on the way up*" was the consensus amongst rivals about **Cunninghams**. However the market waits to see what effect the retirement of "*extremely able advocate*" Martin Cunningham will have on the practice. **Shaun Draycott** is the standout figure at **Draycott Browne**. The team there handles a large amount of serious crime ranging from drugs offences to professional murders. **Forbes** is, interviewees claim, "*a good firm with a good share of the market*" in Blackburn. The team has separate Crown Court and special casework departments. A highlight has been the acquittal, on an abuse of process argument, of two people charged with murder. **RM Broudie & Co** is a leading player in Liverpool where, although he divides opinion, everyone concedes that **Robert Broudie** is "*exceptionally able.*" **Cobleys** retains a solid presence in the market place, as does Blackburn-based **Farleys** which enjoys a high visibility in police actions and prison rights work. Its high-calibre caseload has recently included acting for seven people accused of involvement in a drugs conspiracy. **Garstangs** was praised by competitors for its high profile work and described as "*enjoying great strength in the region.*" **Jackson & Canter** handles a variety of cases ranging from serious drugs offences to immigration prosecutions. **Kristina Harrison Solicitors** has a number of offices throughout the North West dealing with the spectrum of criminal cases, while **Russell & Russell** is one of the largest players in the region with offices from Chester to Rochdale. Its broad general crime practice is rooted in the Magistrates and Crown Courts. **The Berkson Globe Partnership** also retains its position in the marketplace. Researchers were told that **Barry Cuttle** (see p.256) of **Cuttle & Co**, besides being "*a lovely man,*" is an efficient and dedicated practitioner, while **Nicholas Freeman** of **Freeman & Co** "*is high profile and knows traffic law inside out.*"

NORTH EAST

CRIME
■ NORTH EAST

1 **David Gray Solicitors** Newcastle upon Tyne
Grahame Stowe, Bateson Leeds
Henry Hyams Leeds
Irwin Mitchell Sheffield
Sugaré & Co Leeds

2 **Howells** Sheffield
Levi & Co Leeds
The Max Gold Partnership Hull
Williamsons Solicitors Hull

LEADING INDIVIDUALS

1 **SUGARÉ Anthony** Sugaré & Co

This book is the product of 6,582 1/2 hour interviews. See p.7 for BMRB audit.
Within each band, firms are listed alphabetically. See individuals' profiles p.255

David Gray Solicitors retains its place at the top after sustained plaudits from solicitors and the bar. "*A superb team with a big, high profile caseload,*" it specialises in heavyweight crime. Noted for its "*effectiveness at doing a job,*" **Grahame Stowe, Bateson** is a major criminal practice which has handled some of the most notorious murders in Leeds, including the Leanne Tiernan case. It also acted in the ground-breaking R v Wardle. With offices in Barnsley, Harrogate and Hull, **Henry Hyams** is heavily involved in general criminal work. Active in the Magistrates and Crown Courts, the team has seen an increase in sexual offences and burglary. **Irwin Mitchell** continues to be active in this area, although peers consider it less visible than in the past. **Anthony Sugaré** (see p.258) remains a well known name in the market place, while his firm, **Sugaré & Co**, commands a strong reputation amongst peers for mainstream crime. **Howells** has specialisms in Youth Court work, public order offences and white collar crime, and conducts around half of its own High Court advocacy. It has been visible recently acting on the Whittaker double murder case and has also had the case of Penfold referred to the Criminal Cases Review Commission. **Levi & Co** has less of a profile this year but, interviewees note, continues to do a good body of criminal work. **The Max Gold Partnership** handles a large volume of legally aided work, while **Williamsons** has enjoyed a busy year acting on everything from corporate manslaughter to traffic offences, and achieved an acquittal on a high profile murder charge.

SCOTLAND/NORTHERN IRELAND/THE LEADERS ■ CRIME

SCOTLAND

CRIME — SCOTLAND

1
- **Beltrami & Co** Glasgow
- **McCourts** Edinburgh

2
- **Gilfedder & McInnes** Edinburgh

3
- **Adams Whyte** Edinburgh
- **Blair & Bryden** Greenock
- **Condies** Perth
- **Fleetwood & Robb** Inverness
- **Gallen & Co** Glasgow
- **George Mathers & Co** Aberdeen
- **Gordon & Smyth** Glasgow
- **Hall & Haughey** Glasgow
- **HBM Sayers** Glasgow
- **Levy & McRae** Glasgow
- **Livingstone Browne** Glasgow
- **McKay Norwell WS** Edinburgh
- **More & Co** Edinburgh
- **Ness Gallagher** Wishaw
- **Ross Harper** Glasgow

This book is the product of 6,582 1/2 hour interviews. See p.7 for BMRB audit. Within each band, firms are listed alphabetically.

LEADING INDIVIDUALS

1
- **PRENTICE Alexander** McCourts

2
- **BELTRAMI Joseph** Beltrami & Co
- **DUFF Alistair** McCourts
- **GILFEDDER Brian** Gilfedder & McInnes
- **MACARA Murray** Beltrami & Co
- **MAIN Douglas** McCourts
- **McINNES John** Gilfedder & McInnes
- **MORE George** More & Co

See individuals' profiles p.255

"One of the best in Glasgow," according to peers, highly rated traditional crime practice **Beltrami & Co** is led by "the grand old man" of Scottish criminal law, **Joseph Beltrami**. The team, which includes active and respected **Murray Macara**, deals with heavyweight crime such as the Darren Jenkinson case, and has experience of murders and drugs importation. It boasts four solicitor advocates. **McCourts** has a strong team which includes "young and able" **Alex Prentice**. Competitors admired the way he has built on "the striking progress of his early career," and consider him "one of the best" in the country despite his relative youth. **Alistair Duff** and **Douglas Main** also enjoy strong reputations in their field. Traditionally a big competitor, **Gilfedder & McInnes** was not felt to have been as visible as in previous years, though **John McInnes** still has a commanding presence. From its office in Edinburgh, **Adams Whyte** enjoys a profiled position, while **Blair & Bryden** handles a range of criminal work from its three offices in Greenock, Clydebank and Glasgow. **Condies** and **Fleetwood & Robb** also handle volumes of criminal work, and **Gallen & Co** is well thought of. **Gordon & Smyth** and **George Mathers & Co** were considered by competitors less visible this year than in the past. **McKay & Norwell** was singled out as "good and busy," while the "well respected" team at **More & Co** and the eponymous **George More** also picked up recommendations from competitors. Other firms who were commended to researchers are **Levy & McRae**, **Livingstone Browne**, **Ness Gallagher**, **Ross Harper**, **Hall & Haughey** and **HBM Sayers**.

NORTHERN IRELAND

CRIME — NORTHERN IRELAND

1
- **Bogue and McNulty** Belfast
- **Brendan Kearney Kelly & Co** Derry
- **Donnelly & Wall** Belfast
- **Flynn & McGettrick** Belfast
- **Madden & Finucane** Belfast

2
- **Babington & Croasdaile** Londonderry
- **JJ Rice** Belfast
- **McClenahan Crossey & Co** Coleraine
- **Millar Shearer & Black** Cookstown
- **Richard Monteith** Portadown
- **Trevor Smyth & Co** Belfast

This book is the product of 6,582 1/2 hour interviews. See p.7 for BMRB audit. Within each band, firms are listed alphabetically. See individuals' profiles p.255

The firms featured in in the Northern Ireland chapter all proffer a broad base of expert generalist advice on criminal matters. **Madden & Ficucane** continues to advise on the Saville Inquiry into the events of Bloody Sunday. The firm is based in Belfast and has offices in Downpatrick and Armagh. **Bogue & McNulty**, **Donnelly & Wall** and **Flynn & McGettrick** are all recommended for their depth of resources. **Brendan Kearney Kelly & Co** is based in Derry and respected for its work on miscarriages of justice and judicial review. **Babington & Croasdaile**, **JJ Rice**, **McClenahan Crossey & Co**, **Millar Shearer & Black**, **Richard Monteith** and **Trevor Smyth & Co** were all recommended as broad criminal practices offering a significant level of capacity.

THE LEADERS IN CRIME

ASHFORD, Mark
Taylor Nichol, London
(020) 7272 8336

BECKFORD, Trevor
Beckford & Co, Norwich
(01603) 660000

BELTRAMI, Joseph
Beltrami & Co, Glasgow
(0141) 221 0981

BIRD, Steven
Birds Solicitors, London
(020) 8874 7433

BROUDIE, Robert
RM Broudie & Co, Liverpool
(0151) 227 1429

BURTON, Anthony
Simons Muirhead & Burton, London
(020) 7734 4499
anthony@smab.co.uk
Specialisation: Senior Partner. Main area of practice is white collar crime and enquiries by DTI, SFO, Customs & Excise and Inland Revenue. Also handles other criminal defence work and libel. Has written for law journals and national newspapers, and lectured on criminal law. Is also a regular broadcaster.
Prof. Memberships: Law Society, LCCSA, IBA. Member of the Council of Justice, Recorder of the Crown Court, Higher Courts (Crime) Advocate.
Personal: Vice chairman of the Board of the Royal Court Theatre. Groucho Club.

BUTLER, Michael
Nunn Rickard Solicitor Advocates
Exeter
(01392) 200888
Specialisation: Criminal defence work.

His practice covers all aspects of criminal law, with emphasis on serious crime, including drugs importation and other large-scale drugs-related cases, substantial frauds, paedophile/sexual offences and murder. Has successfully represented defendants in a number of recent high-profile and nationally reported cases. Regularly appears as an advocate in Magistrates Courts, Crown Courts, courts martial, and professional disciplinary proceedings.
Prof. Memberships: Law Society.

www.ChambersandPartners.com

CRIME ■ THE LEADERS

Career: Qualified 1992. Partner 1997.
Personal: Born in 1965. Lives in Exeter.

CARR (HIGHER COURT ADVOCATE), Kenneth
Thanki Novy Taube, Harlow
(020) 7485 5558
kcarr@tntlaw.co.uk
Specialisation: Wide range of criminal defence work preparing many complex cases including R v Ali Ahmed Safi and others (Stansted Hijacking Case). Extensive experience of preparing VHCC cases particularly white collar crime and regulatory work. Qualified to appear as an advocate in war crimes cases at the International Criminal Tribunal for Yugoslavia and currently assisting in the defence of a Moslem charged with war crimes. Also regularly appears as an advocate in substantial Crown Court cases.
Prof. Memberships: Member of law Society, SAHCA, European Criminal Bar Association and Intenational Criminal Defence Attorneys Association, Serious Fraud Panel.
Career: Worked as a freelance advocate for many years prior to becoming a Partner in *TNT* in 2002.

COLE, Michael
Cole's Solicitors, Norwich
(01603) 441111

CUTTLE, Barry M
Cuttle & Co, Manchester
(0161) 835 2050
jerry_cuttles@lineone.net
Specialisation: Criminal Law. Appointed as solicitor in the Strangeways prison riots to negotiate between prisoners and officers towards ending of individual personal disputes in 1990.
Prof. Memberships: Law Society.
Career: Qualified in January 1963. Worked with the Crown Prosecution Service in Manchester. Promoted to new CPS Department in charge of Bolton Borough, thereafter in Lanchashire County Prosecutions. Formed *MB Cuttle & Co* 1972. Deals with crime of all levels, and many fraud conspiracy murders. Now senior partner of *MB Cuttle & Co*.
Personal: Educated at Worksop College in Nottinghamshire. Married with two children and upon leaving school at Worksop, became heavily involved in swimming, particularly long distance and raising money for good causes. Interested in all sports. Officer in the Cheshire RGT. Shena (wife) teacher and past president of Soroptimist International Manchester Club; Louise (daughter) bar clerk; Fraser (son) has joined the practice and is an officer with the Cheshire RGT.

DRAYCOTT, Shaun
Draycott Browne, Manchester
(0161) 833 1333

DUFF, Alistair
McCourts, Edinburgh
(0131) 225 6555

EDWARDS, Anthony
TV Edwards, London
(020) 7790 7000
ate@tvedwards.com
Specialisation: Senior partner. Criminal Department. Lecturer on all aspects of criminal practice, and specialist in criminal costs and professional conduct.
Prof. Memberships: Law Society; London Criminal Courts Solicitors Association; CLSA; LAPG; member of Legal Services Commission; editorial board of Criminal Law Review and Executive Board of Justice.
Career: Qualified in 1974, having joined *TV Edwards* in 1972. Became Senior Partner in 1993.
Publications: 'Advising the Suspect in the Police Station' and 'Criminal Defence: A Guide to Good Practice'. Regular contributor to 'Law Society Gazette'.
Personal: Born 6 December 1949. Attended Bristol University, taking a first class LLB in 1971. Leisure interests include walking, reading and theatre.

FANSON, David
Douglas & Partners, Bristol
(0117) 955 2663

FISHER, Ian
Overbury Steward Eaton & Woolsey Norwich
(01603) 610481
ifisher@overburys.co.uk
Specialisation: All areas of Criminal Defence practice, in particular serious violent crime, major drugs offences and serious fraud.
Career: Qualified in1988; post-qualification experience in general litigation followed by a year with Crown Prosecution Service. With *Overburys* for the past 11 years and currently Head of the Criminal Department.
Personal: Law graduate; married with two children. In limited leisure time enjoys sport, literature, mountaineering and deep-sea diving.

FISHER, Michael
Christian Fisher Khan, London
(020) 7831 1750
Specialisation: Criminal defence work including many serious criminal trials (political cases, fraud cases, murder, miscarriages of justice). Acted in IRA trials and for defendants accused of riot and major fraud. Specialises in civil liberties cases.
Prof. Memberships: Law Society; Member of Central London Duty Solicitor Scheme.
Career: *Vizards* 1970-73; *DJ Freeman* 1973-76; founded *Michael Fisher & Co* (later *Fisher Meredith*) 1976-85. Co-founded *Christian Fisher* with Louise Christian in 1985.

FRANCIS, Vanessa
St James Solicitors, Exeter
(01392) 204205

FREEMAN, Nicholas
Freeman & Co, Manchester
0161 236 7007

GILFEDDER, Brian
Gilfedder & McInnes, Edinburgh
(0131) 553 4333

GOULBORN, Caroline
Fletchers, Nottingham
(0115) 959 9550

GROGAN, Peter
Jones Maidment Wilson, Manchester
(0161) 832 8087
lornab@jmw.co.uk
Specialisation: Crime advocacy – serious fraud work. For further details apply for a copy of interactive CD Rom Video.
Career: Qualified September 1982.

HALLAM, Richard
Claude Hornby & Cox, London
(020) 7437 8873
Specialisation: Partner in Criminal Litigation Department since 1989. Has substantial experience of conducting cases in the Magistrates Courts, Higher Criminal Courts and before Courts Martial in UK and Germany. Normally instructed as a defence advocate, but has experience of prosecuting for the CPS and will prosecute privately for individuals or organisations. Nationwide experience of prosecuting video piracy cases. Defends in professional disciplinary proceedings. Has successfully represented defendants facing allegations of murder, terrorism, large-scale drugs importation and fraud, but equally interested in defending clients charged with less serious offences.
Prof. Memberships: London Criminal Courts Solicitors Association, Legal Aid Practitioners Group.
Personal: Born 24 April 1948. Educated at the King's School, Canterbury and Oxford University. Lives in London.

HASLAM, Mark
Burton Copeland (London), London
(020) 7430 2277
mhaslam@burtoncopeland.co.uk
Specialisation: Partner in Criminal Litigation Department. Practice covers all areas of criminal defence work including white collar, large scale drugs cases, serious public order offences and murder and manslaughter cases. Acted successfully in a number of substantial prosecutions brought by Customs & Excise including Charrington and Others. Has experience of Court Martial Proceedings and defended Christine Dryland, the wife of Major Dryland, in a highly publicised murder trial in Germany. Recently represented Sgt. Jason Arder and Lance Bombardrer Heidi Cochrane in a case of AWOL which attracted a considerable amount of public interest. Also specialises in motoring cases including excess alcohol, careless driving and speeding. Regular broadcaster and lecturer on criminal legal affairs on radio, television and at seminars and conferences.
Prof. Memberships: Immediate Past President of the London Criminal Courts Solicitors Association, member of the Criminal Law Committee of the Law Society, member of the Criminal Law Solicitors Association, Deputy Vice-Chairman of Forces Law and the Law Society nominee on the Legal Services Commission High Costs Cases Appeal Panel and Contract Review Body. Sits as a Solicitor Assessor in High Court taxation matters.
Career: Qualified in 1981, worked at *Claude Hornby & Cox* from 1979-93 and *Magrath & Co* from 1993-97. Partner at *Burton Copeland* from January 1998.
Personal: Born 16 June 1957. Attended Wellington College, Berkshire 1971-76 and Pembroke College, Cambridge, 1976-79 (MA). Leisure interests include cricket, horse racing and the theatre. Married and lives in Cobham in Surrey.

HEWITT, Stephen
Fisher Meredith, London
(020) 7622 4468
stephenh@fishermeredith.co.uk
Specialisation: Managing Partner and Department Head of one of the largest and most successful criminal defence teams in London. Wide experience of criminal defence and associated civil liberties work with long history of dealing with major homicide, sex offences, drug trafficking and business crime cases. Particular experience of acting for mentally disturbed defendants and undertaking complex appeals. Lectured on aspects of criminal practice, legal aid franchising, contracting and law firm practice management. Member of national committee of LAPG; Fellow of Institute of Advanced Legal Studies. Currently completing a part time MBA in Law Firm Management at Nottingham Trent University.
Prof. Memberships: Law Society, London Criminal Courts Solicitors Association, Criminal Law Solicitors Association, Liberty, Justice.
Career: Qualified 1980. Joined *Fisher Meredith* as Partner in 1986.
Publications: 'Legal Aid Practice Manual' Sweet & Maxwell (co-author).
Personal: Born 14 November 1953. Lives in Hove with wife and two children.

HICKMAN, Jane
Hickman & Rose, London
(020) 7700 2211
Specialisation: Heads one of Britain's leading criminal law firms. Vast experience in handling criminal defence work nationwide, particularly murder and serious crime. Creative strategist who fights hard for clients and who 'takes no prisoners'. Has specialist skill in managing complex scientific and medical issues. Particularly capable with cases where lawyer negligence contributes to a miscarriage of justice. Writes and lectures on quality issues in criminal defence firms.
Prof. Memberships: Law Society, LCCSA, Legal Action Group (committee member).
Career: MA (First Class Hons) Edinburgh 1972. Qualified 1977. Founded *Hickman & Rose* in 1991. MBA in law firm management from Nottingham Law School 2000. Special advisor to Lord

Justice Auld in his Criminal Courts Review, 2000-01. Secretary of Criminal Appeal Lawyers Association 2002.

HUBER, Bernard
Edwards Duthie, London
(020) 8472 0138

HUTTON, Stuart
Huttons, Cardiff
(029) 2037 8621
smch@huttons-solicitors.co.uk
Specialisation: Senior partner. Criminal department. Has been primarily involved in criminal work for over 20 years. Also deals with childcare, adoption and fostering. Has been on the Childcare panel for over 10 years. Has handled some notable murder cases, including the high profile Tooze double Farmhouse murder and the acquittal of Jonathan Jones, another the subject of the Bloody Valentine book, and 'vigilante' killing Penrhys, Rhondda, Mid Glamorgan. Has had continuing success in taking miscarriages of justice to the Court of Appeal. Former part-time chairman of Social Security Appeals tribunals. Has special interest in entertainment and media law.
Career: Qualified in 1975. With *Edwards Geldard* 1973-86 (as a partner from 1976). Established own practice, *Huttons*, in August 1986. The practice has a reputation for specialist litigation.
Personal: Born 21 October 1946. Lives in Cardiff.

JOHNSON, Digby
The Johnson Partnership, Nottingham
(0115) 941 9141

JONES, Gwyn
Gamlins, Rhyl
(01745) 343500

KEENAN, Andrew
Andrew Keenan & Co, London
(020) 8659 0332

KELLY, Philip
Kelly Solicitors, Great Dunmow
(01371) 877706
kellysols@btinternet.com
Specialisation: Solicitor Advocate specialising in all areas of criminal litigation with particular emphasis on international drugs importations, white collar fraud, supergrass cases and acting on behalf of police officers. Has travelled to Holland, USA, West Indies and Pakistan to undertake enquires on behalf of defendants. Has represented defendants attracting national and international notoriety.
Prof. Memberships: Law Society, Criminal Law Solicitors Association, Association of Higher Court Advocates, London Criminal Courts Solicitors Association, Serious Fraud Panel.
Career: Admitted January 1980. Higher Court Advocate April 1994. Member of Serious Fraud Panel 2000.
Personal: Born 22 February 1951. Avid supporter of Welsh Rugby.

KOFFMAN, Brian
Brian Koffman & Co, Manchester
(0161) 832 3852

MACARA, J D Murray
Beltrami & Co, Glasgow
(0141) 221 0981

MACKEY, Michael
Burton Copeland (North), Manchester
(0161) 827 9500
mikemackey@burtoncopeland.com
Specialisation: Criminal practitioner with experience in all aspects of criminal prosecutions, including road traffic and prosecutions by HSE and Trading Standards. For the past two decades has primarily been involved in the defence of the most serious criminal cases, including numerous murders, serial robbery and sexual offences. Substantial experience of major drug trafficking cases and criminal confiscation proceedings generally. Particular expertise in forensic aspects of investigations, including challenge of DNA evidence and scrutiny of medical expert statements, especially with reference to 'shaken baby' and child abuse prosecutions. Has been involved in many leading Appeal cases including McGarry (adverse inference) and lately, the case of Sally Clark.
Career: Admitted 1974; West Yorkshire County Prosecuting Solicitors' Office 1976; *Glaisyers*, Manchester 1976-80; *Crossley Mackey*, Manchester 1980-87; *Burton Copeland* 1987 to present.
Personal: De La Salle College, Leeds University. Aged 52, married and lives in Altrincham. Interests include music, astronomy and computers.

MAIDMENT, Allan
Maidments, Manchester
(0161) 834 0008
allan.maidment@maidments.co.uk
Specialisation: Senior Partner of *Maidments*. Works exclusively in crime and commercial fraud. Founded *Maidments* in 1993 as a specialist criminal law practice with particular emphasis on serious crime and commercial fraud. Developed the firm into one of the country's leading criminal law practices with three offices in Manchester and offices in Birmingham, Liverpool, London, Bolton, Leeds, Sale and Salford.
Prof. Memberships: A Member of the Law Society and Local Societies in Manchester and Birmingham. Former Member of the Manchester Duty Solicitor Committee. Member of the Criminal Law Solicitors Association. Member of the Serious Fraud Panel. Chairman of Serious Fraud Association.
Career: Educated in Scotland, LLB Leeds University. Qualified in 1976.

MAIN, Douglas
McCourts, Edinburgh
(0131) 225 6555

MASTERS, Peter
Thomson Webb & Corfield, Cambridge
(01223) 578088

MATHER, B J
Elliot Mather, Matlock
(01629) 584885

MCINNES, John
Gilfedder & McInnes, Edinburgh
(0131) 553 4333

MERRIAM, Joy
Joy Merriam & Co, London
(020) 8980 7171
Specialisation: Senior Partner of an East London Criminal Practice established in 1987. Substantial expertise in all areas of criminal law and attributes her firm's success and large client following to giving equal attention to all cases whether involving major crime or not. Works with a professional and dedicated team of criminal lawyers. The firm is a member of the Serious Fraud Panel.
Prof. Memberships: Member of the Law Society, Committee member of the LCCSA and Thames Duty Solicitor Committee.

MILES, Anthony
Bobbetts Mackan, Bristol
(0117) 311 9202
tmiles@bobbettsmackan.co.uk
Specialisation: Partner responsible for specialist criminal defence team, Higher Court Advocate (crime), member of CDS serious fraud panel. 30 years experience in the conduct of cases before the criminal courts. Has developed an expertise in the defence of cases before courts martial. Handles full range of criminal defence work including serious fraud cases, complex murder and drugs cases, and allegations of sexual abuse. 24 hour helpline: (0117) 929 8987.
Prof. Memberships: Law Society, Bristol Law Society (Former President), CLSA, LAPG.
Career: Qualified in 1972. Joined *Bobbetts Mackan* in 1972, becoming a Partner in 1974.
Personal: Born 12 February 1947. Leisure interests include sailing, walking, skiing and reading.

MILNER, Henry
Henry Milner & Co, London
(020) 7831 9944

MORE, George
More & Co, Edinburgh
(0131) 557 1110

MURPHY, Shaun
Edwards Duthie, London
(020) 8472 0138
Specialisation: Partner in Criminal Litigation Department. Crown Court Recorder. Criminal law specialist. Advocate in criminal proceedings on a regular basis in courts throughout the London area. Qualified as a Higher Courts Advocate. Also a Privy Council Agent. Other areas of practice are care proceedings and civil litigation. Involved in prosecution work on behalf of North East London Probation Service, London Borough of Barking and the Port of London Authority. Member of Duty Solicitor Schemes (Newham and Thames) and Child Care Panel. Member of Legal Services Commission Area Committees.
Prof. Memberships: London Criminal Courts Solicitors Association, Criminal Law Solicitors Association, West Essex Law Society, Academy of Forensic Sciences.
Career: Qualified in 1979 after articles at *Duthie Hart & Duthie*. Became a Partner in 1982.
Personal: Born 10 June 1956. Educated at Warwick University 1974-77 (LLB Hons). School Governor. Enjoys most sports. Lives in Wanstead, London.

MUSTERS, Patrick
TMK Solicitors, Southend-on-Sea
(01702) 339222
pmusters@tmksols.co.uk
Specialisation: Solicitor advocate specialising in all areas of criminal litigation especially serious crime (murder, armed robbery and sexual offences), prison mutiny and escape, large drug importations, serious white collar fraud and international terrorism. Cases have attracted national and international notoriety. Substantial experience on advice on appeal against conviction. Advising foreign lawyers on English criminal procedure.
Prof. Memberships: Law Society, Criminal Law Solicitors Association, Association of Higher Court Advocates, London Criminal Courts Solicitors Association, Serious Fraud Panel, British Academy of Forensic Scientists. Member of Legal Services Commission Funding Committee and Regional Duty Solicitor Committee, Avrio Advocati International Criminal Defence Group, European Criminal Bar Association.
Career: Admitted June 1978. Higher Court advocate April 1994
Personal: Born 20 July 1952. Educated Allhallows School, Lyme Regis. Consultant to both BBC Radio Essex and Essex Radio on criminal law matters.

NICHOL, James
Taylor Nichol, London
(020) 7272 8336

NICHOLLS, Simon
Belmores, Norwich
(01603) 617947

NOTT, Colin
Hallinan, Blackburn, Gittings & Nott London
(020) 7233 3999
Specialisation: Specialist in criminal defence work, extradition and judicial review.
Career: Qualified 1978. Sole practitioner 1979-82. Joined *Hallinan Blackburn Gittings & Nott* as a partner 1982.
Personal: Born 27 June 1952. Educated Weymouth Grammar School, London University. LLB (Hons). Interests: sport, rugby and football in particular, theatre and travel.

NUNN, Stephen
Nunn Rickard Solicitor Advocates Exeter
(01392) 200 888
Specialisation: Criminal defence work with substantial experience of trial advocacy. Caseload ranging from murder to summary charges. Acted in a number of

CRIME ◼ THE LEADERS

high profile matters including large scale importation, MOD land fraud conspiracy and Serious Fraud Office cases. Granted Higher Court Rights in June 1994. Court and Police Station duty solicitor.
Prof. Memberships: Law Society. Devon & Exeter Law Society. Magistrates and Crown Court User Groups, Area Justice Strategy Committee. CLSA.
Career: Qualified 1981. Joint winner Law Society centenary competition 'My Favourite Solicitor' 1995 for work in miscarriage of justice case. Partner *Stephens & Scown* until founding of *Nunn Rickard Solicitor Advocates* April 2002.
Personal: Born 1955. Lives in Exeter.

O'MAY, Neil
Bindman & Partners, London
(020) 7833 4433
info@bindmans.com
Specialisation: Wide-range of criminal defence work from murder and terrorist cases to more general crime with an emphasis on Human Rights. All types of serious fraud (SFO, Customs and DTI cases) – Supervisor status for the Legal Services Commission Serious Fraud Panel of approved solicitors for large-scale fraud cases – particularly those involving professionals (solicitors and accountants) as defendants. Represented accused in SFO prosecution from collapse of Norton plc and the continuing Jubilee Line Extension Fraud. Particular expertise in large-scale public order arrests and multi-defendant trials (from Poll Tax demonstrators to the recent May Day events). Specialist in cases involving complex scientific and expert evidence including computer and internet crime. Extensive experience in defending journalists (the 'AVP Productions' trial in Manchester and recently, journalists on the 'MacIntyre undercover' series in criminal investigations). Regularly instructed by doctors and medical workers (including investigations into manslaughter by gross negligence) and other 'professionals in trouble' (including professional body disciplinary proceedings. Instructed by companies in Corporate Manslaughter enquiries. Defending against top prosecution teams, including the Anti-Terrorist Squad (in the Israeli Embassy bombing case and IRA mortar attack on Heathrow Airport) and Special Branch on Official Secrets Act cases. Experience in the defence of complex drugs cases and sexual abuse cases (R v Reeves). Fresh evidence appeals in the Court of Appeal and investigations of miscarriages of justice (including R v Siôn Jenkins). Inquests including the deaths in police custody and judicial review. Ground-breaking cases in the House of Lords (R v Doody & Others; R v Aziz & Others; R v English). Recent involvement on behalf of Amnesty in the Pinochet case. Human Rights Act specialist (R v Offen & Others). Writer, lecturer and broadcaster. Called to give evidence before the Home Affairs Select Committee on miscarriages of justice in sex abuse cases.
Prof. Memberships: Law Society; London Criminal Courts Solicitors Association; Criminal Law Solicitors Association.
Career: Degree in Biochemistry, BSc (Hons). Londoner Qualified 1985. Joined *Bindman & Partners* as Head of the Criminal Department in 1990.

PEIRCE, Gareth
Birnberg Peirce & Partners, London
(020) 7284 4620

PENNINGTON, John
Savery Pennington, Cardiff
02920 457222

PETER, Charles
The Berkson Globe Partnership Liverpool
(0151) 236 1234

POWELL, Greg
Powell Spencer & Partners, London
(020) 7624 8888
Specialisation: Criminal defence, especially murder, conspiracies to import and supply drugs, armed robbery. Magistrates Court advocacy.
Prof. Memberships: Haldane Society, Liberty.
Career: Qualified 1973. Degrees in Law (LSE) and Psychology (Birkbeck).
Publications: Co-author of a 'Practical Guide to the Police and Criminal Evidence Act'.

PRENTICE, Alexander
McCourts, Edinburgh
(0131) 225 6555

PRESTON, Edward
Edward Fail Bradshaw & Waterson London
(020) 7790 4032
eddiep@efbw.co.uk

PROWEL, Martyn
Martyn Prowel Solicitors, Cardiff
(02920) 470909
mprowel@mped.globalnet.co.uk
See under Fraud, p.398

PURCELL, Michael
Purcell Parker, Birmingham
(0121) 236 9781

RICHARDS, Geraint
Martyn Prowel Solicitors, Cardiff
(02920) 470909
grichards@mped.globalnet.co.uk
Specialisation: General crime, Magistrates and Crown Court advocacy.
Prof. Memberships: Law Society.
Career: LLB Wales 1977-1980. Qualified 1984.
Personal: Married with three children.

ROSCOE, Robert
Victor Lissack & Roscoe, London
(020) 7240 2010
robertroscoe@victorlissack.co.uk
Specialisation: Partner in Crime Department. Main areas of practice are white-collar fraud, serious criminal offences, extradition and general criminal practice.
Prof. Memberships: Law Society; City of Westminster and Holborn Law Society; London Criminal Courts Solicitors' Association; Criminal Law Solicitors' Association, Solicitor's Association of Higher Court Advocates.
Career: Qualified in 1976. Higher Courts (Criminal Proceedings) Qualification 1994. Joined *Victor Lissack & Roscoe* in 1969, becoming a partner in 1978. Law Society council member 1992-98; chairman of Criminal Law Committee 1995-98. LCCSA: President 1996-97; chairman of no 14 Regional Duty Solicitor Committee (1991-97), Deputy District Judge (Magistrates Court) 1997-2002.

ROSE, Timothy
Douglas & Partners, Bristol
(0117) 955 2663

RYAN, Ian
Russell-Cooke, London
(020) 8788 0005
ryani@russell-cooke.co.uk
Specialisation: Head of the Criminal Department leading a team of five fee-earners; deals with the full range of criminal defence work but specialises in larger and more complex cases including murder, armed robbery, sexual offences, drugs cases, extradition, and all types of fraud including VAT fraud and diversion frauds. Has a particular interest in cases involving forensic or medical issues. Successfully defended Colin Stagg and has been involved in a number of other high profile cases that have attracted national attention. More recently has specialised in representing professional people (particularly solicitors) in criminal and disciplinary pro0ceedings. Solicitor Advocate in the Crown Court and regular appearances as an advocate at professional disciplinary tribunals.
Prof. Memberships: Member of the LCCSA.
Career: Qualified 1987. Partner from 1995. Head of department 2000.

SAUNDERS, James
Saunders & Co, London
(020) 7404 2828
james@saunders.co.uk
Specialisation: Senior Partner and Head of Criminal Law. Member LSC Fraud Panel, handling major fraud trials (eg Wickes Plc), asset forfeiture (eg Norris - House of Lords) and directors disqualification. Also undertakes traditional crime trials and appeals (eg Tony Martin appeal – CA). Particularly experienced in forensic science issues, DNA, firearms and medical. Civil Liberties & ECHR issues. Media commentator on criminal law.
Career: Articled at/founder, North Kensington Law Centre. Qualified 1972. Established *Saunders & Co* 1974.
Personal: Born 1948. King Edward VII School, Sheffield. Leicester University.

SINCLAIR, Franklin
Tuckers, Manchester
(0161) 233 4321

STUDDERT, Mark
Hodge Jones & Allen, London
(020) 7482 1974
Specialisation: Partner in large franchised criminal department dealing with wide range of offences. Own specialisation – homicide, drug importation, fraud.
Prof. Memberships: Member Liberty; Haldane Society; Prisoners Advice Service. Organiser and administrator of Highbury and Old Street Duty Solicitor scheme. Member London Criminal Courts Solicitors' Association for whom he lectures.
Career: Qualified 1979. Joined *Hodge Jones & Allen* 1985, partner 1987.
Personal: Lives in Stoke Newington with partner and young son. Interests: film, popular culture, food.

SUGARÉ, Anthony
Sugaré & Co, Leeds
(01132) 446978
Specialisation: Very experienced advocate with over 30 years experience specialising in criminal and road traffic matters. Recommended by leading motoring organisation. Provides representation for defendants in all areas of criminal law, both legal aid and private. Instructed in many high profile cases and acknowledged as a leader in his field. Wide expertise in representing sportsmen and sporting associations in enquiries.
Prof. Memberships: Immediate Past President of the Leeds Law Society.
Career: Qualified in 1970. Founded and became Senior Partner of *Sugare & Co* in 1974.
Personal: Born 16 July 1943. Attended Leeds Grammar School and Manchester University. Leisure pursuits include rugby league, golf and horse racing. Lives in Leeds.

SVENSSON, Zara
St James Solicitors, Exeter
(01392) 204205

TAUBE, Martin
Thanki Novy Taube, London
(020) 7485 5558
Specialisation: Deals with serious and complex cases involving fraud (SFO Prosecution), drugs, money laundering, armed robbery; specialisation in criminal cases with mental health issues including R v Clunis which led to wholesale changes in mental health law and appellate cases; specialisation also in scientific forensic issues.
Prof. Memberships: Member of the LCCSA and the British Academy of Forensic Science.
Career: Has been working in defence practices since 1982 and admitted in 1989; founding member of *Thanki Novi Taube* in 1992; regular appearances for the last four years on BBC Radio 2's Jimmy Young Show.

TAYLOR, Carolyn
Taylor Nichol, London
(020) 7272 8336

THANKI, Girish
Thanki Novy Taube, London
(020) 7833 5800
girishthanki@tntlaw.co.uk
Specialisation: Wide range of criminal defence and appellate work including murder, armed robberies and white collar crime. Considerable experience of handling complex and weighty cases. Specialist knowledge of Forensics and Scientific Issue. Active extradition practice. Appellate work including House of Lords and the Privy Council. Judicial reviews in the criminal context.
Prof. Memberships: Member of Law Society Task Force on the Implementation of the Human Rights Act, Member LCCSA, BAFS, IBA, Liberty, Justice, Prisoner's Advisory Service, Inquest, The Law Society.

TOMLINSON, Kevin
Kieran Clarke Solicitors, Chesterfield
(01246) 211006

TSIATTALOU, Bambos
Stokoe Partnership, London
(020) 8558 8884

VENTERS, June
Venters Solicitors, London
(020) 7277 0110
j.venters@venters.co.uk
Specialisation: Representation in all areas of criminal law with the focus being on the most serious cases including serious fraud and white collar crime. Most notable cases include the 'Dome' Robbery, the 'Euston Handbag' murder, international multimillion pound football fraud (result rigging – floodlights), various high profile sexual offences cases, UK's largest drugs conspiracy, UK's largest armed robbery. Public law childcare: representation of children and adults involved in Children Act and associated proceedings. Most notable cases include shaking baby syndrome, Munchausen by proxy, sexual abuse, neglect. Considerable media involvement which includes BBC1 documentary entitled 'Law Women'; BBC 1 Breakfast Television; BBC2 Newsnight; Channel 4 Richard and Judy Show; BBC1 Kilroy; Channel 4 News at 7; BBC News 24; ITN News; BBC1 News; Radio 5 Live; News Direct Radio; LBC Radio; FLR Radio. Numerous public speaking engagements undertaken in recent years including Child Care Law speech to fellow practitioners and members of the judiciary; LAG Conference 1999 video-linked live to North America; Solicitors Association Higher Courts Advocates 2001.
Prof. Memberships: Solicitor Advocate Higher Courts (all proceedings); Member of the Children Panel; Criminal Duty Solicitor (Police Stations and Courts); President London Criminal Courts Solicitors Association; Law Society Accredited Trainer; Gray's Inn Solicitor Advocacy Trainer; Law Society Children Panel Assessor; Recorder (Crown Court).
Career: Qualified 1984. June Venters founded *Venters Solicitors* (formerly *Venters & Co*) in May 1991. Since then the firm has grown in reputation and status and is now widely regarded with considerable respect both from clients and fellow practitioners alike. June Venters is known for her personal commitment and dedication as well as the thoroughness of her approach.
Publications: Various published articles. Author of 'Standard Letters and Forms for the Criminal Practitioner'.

WILLIAMS, Ian
Robertsons, Cardiff
(029) 20237777

WILLIAMS, Sian
Hallinan, Blackburn, Gittings & Nott
London
(020) 7233 3999

DEBT RECOVERY

London: 260; The Regions: 260; Scotland: 264

Research approved by BMRB For this edition, **Chambers'** researchers conducted 6,582 interviews – 3,900 with law firms, 511 with barristers and 2,171 with clients. The validity of the research was scrutinised by BMRB International, who audited both the methodology and the results at our offices in London. They interviewed **Chambers'** researchers and cross-checked sample interviews. Details of the audit appear on page 7.

OVERVIEW Much debt recovery is a matter of mail merging pre-litigation letters to debtors and following up with enforcement proceedings if payment is not forthcoming. As such, efficiency is the principle differentiator between firms and the key to running an efficient debt recovery outfit is an advanced IT system. Some of these also offer clients online access to progress reports. Defended cases with a high level of complexity must be dealt with by the kind of strong commercial litigation teams boasted by many of the firms in our tables.

LONDON

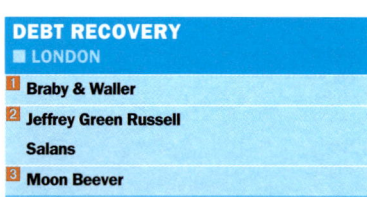

DEBT RECOVERY
■ LONDON
1. Braby & Waller
2. Jeffrey Green Russell
   Salans
3. Moon Beever

This book is the product of 6,582 1/2 hour interviews. See p.7 for BMRB audit. Within each band, firms are listed alphabetically.

BRABY & WALLER (see firm details p.885) "*At the top of the debt recovery tree,*" according to competitors; although part of Irwin Mitchell since 1998, the team retains an independent identity and brand both here and in its Sheffield office. Its fully merged IT system enables the progress of cases to be followed online by clients, while allowing the 25-strong unit to operate coherently across the two sites. The team has experience of a large number of sectors including construction materials, factoring, oil and distribution, as well as finance houses and surveyors. **Clients** Hepworth; Lafarge Aggregates; Paypoint Network; Blue Circle Industries.

JEFFREY GREEN RUSSELL (see firm details p.1013) Occupying a "*batch niche,*" this team of 20 won respect from peers for its bullish determination. The group handles the commercial and consumer debt work of a broad base of clients, with a particular focus on the hire industry and credit card companies. Other clients include banks, IT recruitment firms, local authorities and electrical wholesalers. The group offers a bespoke service and provides advice to clients on credit control procedures. **Clients** Citibank; Diners Club; American Express.

SALANS (see firm details p.1121) This Bromley office undertakes defended and undefended debt recovery work under the supervision of a senior litigator. The team conducts bespoke work on behalf of banks and building societies and has a particular name in the field of motor finance. A full case management service includes initial letters, interest calculations and follow-up actions, such as the repossession of hire-purchase goods. **Clients** Citibank International; Nissan Finance; Ford Credit.

MOON BEEVER New to our tables this year, the firm collects predominantly commercial debt. Known for its efficient handling of volume debt recoveries, the team of 28 can draw on the expertise of partners and associates for contested work. It provides a tailor-made, value-added, end-to-end service featuring full online transparency. **Clients** Financial houses; accountants; companies from the sports industry.

THE SOUTH

DEBT RECOVERY
■ THE SOUTH
1. **Brachers** Maidstone
2. **Blake Lapthorn** Portsmouth
3. **Lester Aldridge** Bournemouth
4. **Cripps Harries Hall** Tunbridge Wells
   Lovetts Guildford
   Trethowans Southampton
5. **DMH** Brighton

This book is the product of 6,582 1/2 hour interviews. See p.7 for BMRB audit. Within each band, firms are listed alphabetically.

BRACHERS (see firm details p.886) 24 executives and 18 support staff constitute this respected and expanding practice. The team has the technology and flexibility to cater to any client requirement, "*from a simple pre-action letter to a bespoke gold service.*" With the focus on high-volume computerised work, the group acts for major companies in the credit card, building, IT, transport, healthcare and employment sectors. **Clients** EDS; Travis Perkins; Amex; Eurotunnel; English, Welsh and Scottish Railways.

BLAKE LAPTHORN (see firm details p.877) This team of nine, including one partner and an assistant, is "*always on the radar screen,*" according to one market source. Although it regularly handles consumer debt, its focus is on high-volume commercial work. Benefiting from the strong insolvency expertise within the firm, the team currently acts for over 300 clients, including one major multinational blue-chip and collects debts for other solicitors and accountants. **Clients** SGB Services.

LESTER ALDRIDGE (see firm details p.1038) Seen as a "*growing force*" in debt recovery, this 21-strong team (19 fee-earners and two partners) is especially well known for its bulk recovery work for finance companies but also has a strong track record across industries as diverse as energy, publishing, accountancy, manufacturing and waste management. Other clients include local authorities, housing associations and building suppliers. The debt recovery division has recently rebranded itself as 'Lester Aldridge Fast Track'. **Clients** Finance companies; corporates; local authorities.

CRIPPS HARRIES HALL (see firm details p.922) "*Unimpeachable quality,*" according to rivals, the assistant-led team of six, which can count on the support of two partners for contested cases, provides a bespoke package to the firm's general commercial client base. Instructions from accountants who are dealing with liquidations and administrations account for a large proportion of the team's time. **Clients** National Provident Institution; Duncan Web Offset.

LOVETTS This "*smart set-up*" is one of the few law firms to deal exclusively with debt recovery and perhaps the only one to deal exclusively with commercial trade debt. Taking on a balance of contested and uncontested cases, the team includes five solicitors and is large enough to ensure each client has a regular contact person. The client base includes a wide spread of sectors, with recruitment and media and pub-

THE SOUTH/THAMES VALLEY/SOUTH WEST ■ DEBT RECOVERY

lishing being especially well represented. **Clients** TMP Worldwide; Capita Group; Volvo Bus and Truck; Kaiser + Kraft.

TRETHOWANS (see firm details p.1105) Rivals set considerable store by this team of four, now based solely in Southampton. The unit provides a comprehensive service to a client base ranging from large plcs to one-man trading outfits. A particular growth area this year has been the recovery of parking fees for car park management companies and local authorities. The team has strong ties to the litigation department, which supports it in difficult contested cases. **Clients** Local authorities; corporates.

DMH (see firm details p.940) Backed up by the commercial litigation department, this team of six won sustained market approval. Having invested in its IT system, it provides services including cash flow consultancy, course tracing and status reports. The factoring industry keeps the group busy, as does one major utilities company. Other regular clients include small- to medium-sized professional services outfits. **Clients** Seaboard; Venture Finance; Atalink.

THAMES VALLEY

DEBT RECOVERY
■ THAMES VALLEY

1
- **Shoosmiths** Reading

2
- **Boyes Turner** Reading
- **Clarks** Reading
- **Denton Wilde Sapte** Milton Keynes
- **Morgan Cole** Reading

3
- **Fennemores** Milton Keynes
- **Matthew Arnold & Baldwin** Watford

This book is the product of 6,582 1/2 hour interviews. See p.7 for BMRB audit. Within each band, firms are listed alphabetically.

SHOOSMITHS (see firm details p.1133) Interviewees expressed admiration for the "*dedicated*" individuals making up this team of 27. "*Really good at what it does,*" according to clients, the group focuses on business-to-business debt and has noticed an increase in foreign instructions this year, with debts recovered as far away as Dubai. The main clients are large businesses, ranging from recruitment agencies and food companies to freight services and publishing outfits. This year, the group launched a new product allowing clients online access to their debt portfolio and the option to instruct their personal account manager over the internet. **Clients** Large businesses.

BOYES TURNER (see firm details p.883) It has been a good year for this "*busy*" debt recovery team of two partners and three fee-earners. The group prides itself on bespoke service and expedience in specialist areas including recruitment, spread betting, internet provision and freight forwarding. Clients have access to the in-house dispute resolution team for the more complex disputed cases. **Clients** Kimberly-Clark.

CLARKS (see firm details p.908) Although keeping a low profile in the debt recovery community, this small team has had an active year doing general invoice debt recovery work for clients ranging from small, local businesses to FTSE 100 companies. A large number of instructions come from educational institutions chasing room fees, IT companies and professional services entities. Manufacturing and construction clients also feature highly on the roster. **Clients** Large corporates; educational institutions.

DENTON WILDE SAPTE (see firm details p.935) Operating out of the commercial litigation department, a team of four receives instructions from an impressive client base including banks, overseas trade debt insurers and a public school. The group, described as being "*set up effectively to handle large clients,*" has substantial experience of collecting overseas debts. **Clients** The Royal Bank of Scotland Group.

MORGAN COLE (see firm details p.1075) This team of eight does mainly large-scale recovery but also collects individual debts for invoice discounters when their clients enter liquidation or administration. A substantial volume of work comes from the factoring industry and the group is currently looking to expand. **Clients** NTL; Oxford Brookes University; Venture Finance; Fortis Commercial Services.

FENNEMORES Having upgraded its computer system and expanded its team, this practice attracted warm comments from the market. The group deals with both trade debt, for which it has a particular reputation within the manufacturing industry, and consumer debt. It undertakes pre-litigation, high-volume recovery work and more complex, low-volume work. A computerised system that schedules calls to debtors at pre-determined stages of the collection process enhances the efficiency of the service. **Clients** Manufacturers; other corporates.

MATTHEW ARNOLD & BALDWIN (see firm details p.1058) This "*thriving*" five-strong team, which can count on the support of a partner, offers a tailor-made recovery service to clients from the professional service sector, the vehicle finance industry, the office supply market and the publishing world. Access to premium insolvency and commercial litigation departments adds muscle to the group, which is also recognised for its expertise in bulk mortgage repossessions. **Clients** Barclays Bank.

SOUTH WEST

DEBT RECOVERY
■ SOUTH WEST

1
- **Bond Pearce** Plymouth

2
- **Beachcroft Wansbroughs** Bristol
- **Burges Salmon** Bristol
- **Clarke Willmott & Clarke** Bristol
- **Osborne Clarke** Bristol
- **TLT Solicitors** Bristol

This book is the product of 6,582 1/2 hour interviews. See p.7 for BMRB audit. Within each band, firms are listed alphabetically.

BOND PEARCE (see firm details p.879) An "*impressive team*" according to competitors, it boasts niche strength in the retail, education and financial services sectors. Five paralegals run a computerised debt recovery system, while two experienced advocates, one with higher rights of audience, step in to deal with contested debts. The unit serves clients nationally as well as in the South West region. **Clients** B&Q; Friends Provident; University of Northumbria; University of Southampton.

BEACHCROFT WANSBROUGHS (see firm details p.860) This practice's high-quality work has won it a strong position, both in the regional and national marketplaces. Praising the team's efficiency, one client noted "*you can trust it to do a good job.*" The department takes on high-volume work for a range of plcs, corporate clients, insurance companies and owner-managed businesses. **Clients** Imperial Tobacco; Spandex; Royal & SunAlliance Insurance.

BURGES SALMON (see firm details p.894) Operating out of the commercial litigation department, the team handles high-volume debt recovery for clients from the horseracing business, as well as for car leasing companies, a major electrical wholesaler and a major international car manufacturer. The team offers a

DEBT RECOVERY ■ SOUTH WEST/WALES/MIDLANDS

complete debt recovery package, from letters before action to advice regarding insolvency proceedings. **Clients** Car industry and wholesaler clients.

CLARKE WILLMOTT & CLARKE (see firm details p.907) This group of 15 fee-earners and one partner undertakes predominantly high-volume debt recovery work using a new computerised system. Having expanded this year, the practice, which is admired by peers, acts for a number of banks, liquidators and receivers, blue-chip companies and local owner-managed businesses. **Clients** ExxonMobil; RAC; Danish Bacon.

OSBORNE CLARKE (see firm details p.1090) One solicitor and six paralegals make up this "*estimable and improving*" debt recovery team. Offering a pre-litigation collections service on a contingency, no recovery-no fee basis, it conducts a large body of work for a major building society, with other instructions coming from power companies and financial houses. **Clients** Financial institutions; other corporates.

TLT SOLICITORS (see firm details p.1163) This large practice is divided into secured and unsecured debt teams. The unsecured department specialises in shortfall recoveries and has taken on an increasing amount of work for the factoring and invoice discounting sectors. The secured department picks up volume and bespoke work from clearing banks and building societies. A reported growth area this year is the sub-prime mortgage market. **Clients** Financial institutions.

WALES

DEBT RECOVERY ■ WALES

1. **Eversheds** Cardiff
2. **Edwards Geldard** Cardiff
   John Collins & Partners Swansea

This book is the product of 6,582 1/2 hour interviews. See p.7 for BMRB audit. Within each band, firms are listed alphabetically.

EVERSHEDS (see firm details p.949) A consensus emerged during our interviews that this mammoth team has the highest profile and the heftiest workload in Wales. The unit specialises in serving financial houses from all corners of the Eversheds network and conducts mortgage enforcements, personal loan/overdraft collections and mortgage shortfalls, for which it is particularly well regarded. The practice has formed a commercial relationship with Bear Stearns & Co Inc, the US investment bank, allowing its clients to participate in debt sales. **Clients** Abbey National; GE Capital Global Consumer Finance; HBOS.

EDWARDS GELDARD (see firm details p.944) This firm, known for its "*proactive*" approach to debt recovery work, handles a mixture of high-volume and larger individual debts for clients ranging from big insurers to small local businesses. Utilities and finance companies also feature highly in its client list. Unusually, the practice buys and sells debt portfolios itself, via its subsidiary 'Go Debt'. **Clients** Halifax; Derbyshire Building Society; Betterware; HSBC.

JOHN COLLINS & PARTNERS Based within the commercial division, five fee-earners and five support staff specialise in the recovery and collection of volume commercial debt. The firm, which prides itself on its commitment to the sector, acts for a client base including housing associations, major plcs, private hospitals and commercial enterprises. **Clients** Corporates; public bodies.

MIDLANDS

DEBT RECOVERY ■ MIDLANDS

1. **Wragge & Co** Birmingham
2. **Eversheds** Nottingham
   Hewitson Becke + Shaw Northampton
   Reed Smith Warner Cranston Coventry
   Shakespeares Birmingham
3. **Browne Jacobson** Nottingham
   freethcartwright Nottingham
   Wright Hassall Leamington Spa

This book is the product of 6,582 1/2 hour interviews. See p.7 for BMRB audit. Within each band, firms are listed alphabetically.

WRAGGE & CO (see firm details p.1197) This popular firm is acknowledged by rivals to dominate the regional market and, with its outstanding reputation preceding it, much of its work is on a national level. Recognised by peers to have strategically developed its IT system, it focuses on volume debt recovery with full case management and automated document production. The substantial team, which includes one partner and an assistant solicitor, acts for clients in a broad range of sectors. **Clients** Local and national corporates.

EVERSHEDS (see firm details p.949) The team in the Midlands collects bulk debts for a client base that includes local authorities, service providers and manufacturing companies. Typical work includes pre-litigation letters and enforcement proceedings and the unit offers clients online access to case files. **Clients** Corporates; public bodies.

HEWITSON BECKE + SHAW (see firm details p.993) A core staff of 11 undertakes mainly commercial debt work for a client base including finance businesses, software houses, steel producers and water companies. The team offers a comprehensive service including external access to debt records via the internet and has the capacity to collect debts in 100 different jurisdictions through its network of legal practices and tracing agents. **Clients** Finance businesses; other corporates.

REED SMITH WARNER CRANSTON (see firm details p.1109) This 14-strong unit, which includes one partner, specialises in commercial trade debt recovery for large plcs. Clients include trade and credit insurance agencies, manufacturers and financial institutions. As well as computerised bulk work, the team spends a proportion of its time on defended debts, from enforcement proceedings to High Court and County Court actions. **Clients** Sara Lee Courtaulds; Anchor Trust.

SHAKESPEARES (see firm details p.1127) This Birmingham-based practice has a staff of seven. The team recovers volume and individual debts for clients ranging from small-rural owner-managed businesses to major plcs. It also continues to provide an overseas recovery service for a large bank. **Clients** Corporates.

BROWNE JACOBSON (see firm details p.891) Five full-time members of staff, including one partner, provide a comprehensive debt recovery service, from pre-legal letters to court actions. Dealing with both volume debts and individual cases, the team serves clients from large corporations to one- or two-person businesses. **Clients** Parceline.

FREETHCARTWRIGHT (see firm details p.963) The team provides a fixed fee service for the recovery of consumer and commercial debt, from pre-litigation letters to winding up petitions. It also offers a service called 'Courtcheck', providing High Court and County Court information on all UK businesses. The unit acts for approximately 275 clients, including housing associations, building suppliers and vehicle rental companies. Debt recovery and credit reference agencies also figure in the roster. **Clients** Bass Brewers; Nottingham Trent University; Paul Smith.

WRIGHT HASSALL (see firm details p.1197) A "*motivated*" team, according to peers, it boasts the capacity to deal with high-value individual debts as well as bulk lower-value debts. The unit, which includes six full-time fee-earners, serves a diverse client base and has recently invested in its IT system. **Clients** W H Smith News; Zenith Windows; Staybright Windows.

EAST ANGLIA

DEBT RECOVERY
■ EAST ANGLIA

1. **Birketts** Ipswich
2. **Ashton Graham** Bury St Edmunds
   Gotelee & Goldsmith Ipswich
   Greenwoods Peterborough
   Prettys Ipswich

This book is the product of 6,582 1/2 hour interviews. See p.7 for BMRB audit. Within each band, firms are listed alphabetically.

BIRKETTS (see firm details p.875) Competitors believe that this Ipswich-based firm remains "*dominant*" in the region. It represents building merchants, a major regional newspaper group and a commercial vehicle parts supplier, recovering mainly high-volume debts from across the country. **Clients** Regional corporates.

ASHTON GRAHAM This steady team of two serves clients ranging from small owner-managed businesses to plcs, with the agricultural sector being particularly well represented. The firm also runs a successful small claims service that helps clients prepare their own cases. **Clients** Corporates; small businesses.

GOTELEE & GOLDSMITH This small team has staked out a particular reputation in the haulage world, with companies from the local freight industry well represented on its client roster. The unit undertakes a range of debt recovery work for a broad base of clients. Advice on credit and debt management procedures is also available. **Clients** P&O Group.

GREENWOODS (see firm details p.978) Operating under the brand name 'Debt Devils', this five-strong unit won applause from the market for its "*sensible approach to debt handling.*" It offers a full recovery service to a client roster ranging from multinationals down to small, local businesses, with varying volume requirements. **Clients** Electrical Contractors Association; Thomas Cook.

PRETTYS (see firm details p.1106) This team of four, plus one partner, recovers large, individual commercial debts as well as some volume commercial debts. The client base is representative of the surrounding economy, and contains a spread of freight, shipping and transport companies. **Clients** Norfolk Line; DFDS Transport.

NORTH WEST

DEBT RECOVERY
■ NORTH WEST

1. **Thomas A Higgins & Co** Wallasey
2. **Bermans** Liverpool
   DWF Warrington
   Halliwell Landau Manchester
   Lees Lloyd Whitley Liverpool
3. **Cuff Roberts** Liverpool

This book is the product of 6,582 1/2 hour interviews. See p.7 for BMRB audit. Within each band, firms are listed alphabetically.

THOMAS A HIGGINS & CO This massive debt recovery firm, focused squarely on uncontested, high-volume debt collection, can claim with some justification to be the most prominent in England. There is no denying the market's perception that this is a "*slick*" and efficient operation. Pre-litigation letters, sent promptly, are the firm's stock in trade, though it does get involved in more complex cases. **Clients** Corporates.

BERMANS This "*snappy,*" 16-strong team offers a full debt recovery package, from letter-before-action to enforcement proceedings. The unit is divided into teams, reflecting the make-up of the client base, which deal with government bodies, the factoring industry, brewing, and media business. The practice also represents a major bank. This year saw the launch of 'Bermans Online', a flexible system granting clients remote access to the information they need. **Clients** Government bodies; corporates.

DWF (see firm details p.943) Acknowledged to be a "*watertight*" outfit, this team serves the debt recovery needs of clients from the financial and commercial sectors. Undertaking mainly volume undefended work, the group is looking to expand and is recognised by the market to have invested in its IT systems. Two partners are available to support the four full time fee-earners over contested debts. **Clients** Lloyds TSB; Commercial Finance Ltd.

HALLIWELL LANDAU (see firm details p.982) Dealing in high-volume commercial debt collection, this "*efficient and professional*" firm has kept its reputation in the area. The varied client base includes finance companies, brewers and computer wholesalers. The team is well known for its expertise in mortgage repossessions and for its work in the brewing industry. **Clients** Waverley Vintners; Arnold Clarke Finance; Logitek Distribution; Lex Multipart.

LEES LLOYD WHITLEY A total of 40 staff, including two partners and one assistant, take on bulk work for clients in the private and public sectors. HM Customs and Excise and the Insolvency Service are two of its most prominent public sector clients, while in the private sector the unit collects business-to-business debt for financial institutions, insolvency practitioners, fuel suppliers, oil companies and vehicle rental companies. **Clients** Royal & SunAlliance; GE Capital.

CUFF ROBERTS This 12-member debt recovery practice is integrated with the firm's insolvency department. This year its focus has continued to swing towards trade debt. It also deals with agricultural debt and insolvency-related book debt and has seen an increasing number of cases defended. Among the unit's clients are accountants, institutions and individual traders. **Clients** Littlewoods; Liverpool and London Trade Protection Society; Nationwide Building Society.

DEBT RECOVERY ■ NORTH EAST/SCOTLAND

NORTH EAST

DEBT RECOVERY
■ NORTH EAST

1 Hammond Suddards Edge Bradford
2 Cobbetts Leeds
   DLA Bradford
   Eversheds Leeds
3 Braby & Waller Sheffield
   Ford & Warren Leeds
   Lupton Fawcett Leeds
   Walker Morris Leeds

This book is the product of 6,582 1/2 hour interviews. See p.7 for BMRB audit. Within each band, firms are listed alphabetically.

HAMMOND SUDDARDS EDGE Rated by practitioners across the country for its handling of volume debts for commercial clients, this unit is *"unquestionably at the forefront of the debt recovery scene."* Operating as a separate business unit under the name 'debtlinedirect', it serves over 600 clients including financial houses, recruitment agencies and building suppliers. The team consists of 85 people in total, including a small group of solicitors who deal with defended cases. Growth areas this year include local authority sundry recoveries, motor car finance work and collections for steel stockholders. **Clients** Large corporates; finance houses; local authorities.

COBBETTS (see firm details p.914) Following its merger with Read Hind Stewart, the firm's debt recovery practice has relocated from Manchester to Leeds and now operates under the brand name 'Incasso'. The team, numbering 30, undertakes telephone collections, trace work and trace enquiries and includes a receivables management team. The lion's share of the work is undefended volume collection for a diverse client roster that features plcs, owner-managed businesses and local authorities. **Clients** Lambeth Borough Council; Fuji Photo Film; VP plc; Chrysalis Radio.

DLA This large department is recognised by rivals across the country to be a *"key volume player,"* with the capacity to collect debts *"swiftly and painlessly."* The unit offers assistance with court actions as well as pre-legal letters and telephone calls, and also provides a full insolvency service. It acts for a wide range of commercial entities, including various major UK lenders. **Clients** Financial services companies; other corporates.

EVERSHEDS (see firm details p.949) With a high number of fee-earners, this *"standout"* team is felt by interviewees to lack neither manpower nor capability. With a client base that includes major plcs and financial services providers from across the region, it can call upon the litigation and insolvency resources of the network. It runs a call centre for the collection of bulk debts for banks and credit card companies. **Clients** Banks; other corporates.

BRABY & WALLER (see firm details p.885) Although the practice has been part of Irwin Mitchell since its acquisition in 1998, Braby & Waller retains an independent identity and brand. Its computer system is fully merged across the Sheffield and London offices, allowing a total team of 25 to co-ordinate its activities. It has particular experience of the construction materials, surveying, finance, factoring, oil and distribution sectors. **Clients** Hepworth; Lafarge Aggregates; Paypoint Network; Blue Circle Industries.

FORD & WARREN (see firm details p.959) This team of eight, including one partner, has doubled in size in the past 12 months. Providing a full service, including pre-litigation letters, doorstep collections and recoveries in Scotland and Ireland, the unit was described as *"impressive"* by rivals. It recovers debts for a client base drawn primarily from brewers, commercial landlords, finance companies, hauliers and local authorities. **Clients** Finance companies; local authorities; other corporates.

LUPTON FAWCETT This team of 24 offers a comprehensive debt recovery service, including insolvency proceedings, handled with online transparency. Clients, which range from plcs and large insurers to private companies and debt collection agencies, benefit from the attention of a specialist partner. **Clients** Hewden Stuart; Polypipe; Ellis & Everard; Sun Microsystems.

WALKER MORRIS (see firm details p.1178) Operating under the brand name 'Walker Morris Collect', this large team acts primarily for financial institutions, with petroleum companies and healthcare providers also featuring in the client list. The majority of the work taken on by the 28 members of staff (including two partners) is uncontested volume work. **Clients** Financial services providers; other corporates.

SCOTLAND

DEBT RECOVERY
■ SCOTLAND

1 McClure Naismith Glasgow
2 Morton Fraser, Solicitors Edinburgh
   Nolan Macleod Glasgow
   Yuill & Kyle Glasgow
3 Blacklock Thorley Edinburgh
   Henderson Boyd Jackson WS Edinburgh
4 Bishops Solicitors (Formerly Morison Bishop) Glasgow
   Bonar Mackenzie WS Edinburgh
   Golds Glasgow
   Macdonalds Glasgow
   Shepherd+ Wedderburn Edinburgh

This book is the product of 6,582 1/2 hour interviews. See p.7 for BMRB audit. Within each band, firms are listed alphabetically.

McCLURE NAISMITH (see firm details p.1062) *"No one in Scotland can touch the firm,"* admitted one peer. Having implemented 'Sol-case', its computer system that allows clients online access to cases, the team is receiving a growing number of instructions from England, Wales and Northern Ireland. A proportion of the debts taken on go to litigation and the 14-strong team benefits from the attentions of two partners. **Clients** General Guarantee; Singer and Friedlander Commercial Finance; Close Asset Finance; Bank of Scotland.

MORTON FRASER, SOLICITORS (see firm details p.1077) Peers applauded this *"effective"* debt recovery practice for both its secured and unsecured work. On the secured side, its clients include building societies and educational institutions. On the unsecured side, the unit specialises in debt recovery for asset finance institutions and invoice discounting companies. The work of this firm is primarily in Scotland's Sheriff Courts. **Clients** Financial institutions; corporates.

NOLAN MACLEOD (see firm details p.1084) This firm's *"active and diligent"* debt recovery practice focuses on volume collections for a list of clients spanning sectors such as banking, finance, vehicle retail, building and leisure. The team offers a complete debt recovery service, from letters to enforcement proceedings, and instructs Sheriff Officers directly at the courts. **Clients** Businesses.

YUILL & KYLE A department of eight collects debts for small traders, international corporations and building societies and provides credit control advice. The firm's website features free debt recovery downloads, including a letter template with interest calculator. **Clients** Bradford and Bingley; Clydesdale Bank; Scottish Widows.

BLACKLOCK THORLEY (see firm details p.876) Recovering high-volume and larger debts for a client base dominated by collection agencies, commercial businesses and wholesale companies, this standalone practice has made a particular name for itself in the field of secured debt retrieval. One partner, four solicitors and five support staff make up the "*industrious*" team. **Clients** Corporates.

HENDERSON BOYD JACKSON WS Operating out of the litigation department, this team of 10 can count on the support of experienced lawyers for its more complex contested debts. Having invested strategically in its IT systems, the team also targets the bulk recovery market. It has set up a pre-legal division to deal with collect out situations for banks, liquidators and receivers. **Clients** Banks; Credit insurers; Regional businesses.

BISHOPS SOLICITORS (see firm details p.1076) Forming part of the Bishops side of this newly de-merged entity, this historically strong commercial debt recovery practice can draw on the firm's insolvency and litigation expertise. It takes on fairly large, low-volume work for a number of clients. **Clients** Alliance & Leicester; BP Fuels; Turner and Company.

BONAR MACKENZIE WS This "*busy*" team of three paralegals and seven support staff continued to develop its online debt recovery case management system this year. The unit's broad client base features creditors from the banking and financial services sector as well as local companies such as hauliers and surveyors. **Clients** Bank of Scotland; Cheltenham & Gloucester; Newcastle Building Society.

GOLDS Known for its hi-tech case management system, this 15-strong department is divided into three units - secure recoveries, motor finance and unsecured debt recoveries. The team prides itself particularly on repossessions for high-street lenders, and also acts for the invoice discounting and factoring industry. **Clients** Financial services providers.

MACDONALDS Well regarded by peers for its work with the factoring industry, this team of three solicitors, one trainee and three paralegals also serves finance leasing clients and handles routine debt in sectors including brewing and subcontracting. Construction is also a growing area. **Clients** Rentokil; Scottish & Newcastle; First National Business Equipment Leasing; City Capital.

SHEPHERD+ WEDDERBURN (see firm details p.1130) Renowned in Scotland for its recovery of VAT, landfill tax and betting and gaming duties on behalf of HM Customs & Excise, this "*illustrious*" firm also has clients in the areas of factoring, invoice discounting, banking and commercial property. Four full-time solicitors and five fee-earners are led by two partners. **Clients** HM Customs & Excise; HSBC Bank; Scottish Environmental Protection Agency; Bank of Scotland; Thomas Cook Retail.

NORTHERN IRELAND

DEBT RECOVERY
■ NORTHERN IRELAND

1	**Comerton & Hill** Belfast
2	**Bigger & Strahan** Belfast
3	**Cleaver Fulton Rankin** Belfast
	Diamond Heron Belfast
	John McKee & Son Belfast
	McManus Kearney Belfast

This book is the product of 6,582 1/2 hour interviews. See p.7 for BMRB audit. Within each band, firms are listed alphabetically.

COMERTON & HILL (see firm details p.918) Felt to have a "*decent share of the market,*" this Belfast practice concentrates on high-volume debt recovery on behalf of clients from the finance, building and motor industries. The team ("*fizzing with good ideas*") is made up of two partners, one assistant solicitor and three paralegals. **Clients** HSBC Bank; NIIB Group.

BIGGER & STRAHAN (see firm details p.871) Enjoying the support of strong commercial litigation and insolvency departments, this small team has a notable presence in the factoring sector. It offers a complete letters to litigation service to banks, English and Irish finance companies and clients on the European mainland. **Clients** Financial services clients; other corporates.

CLEAVER FULTON RANKIN (see firm details p.910) A small team, with the back-up of a solicitor, it takes on debt work for financial institutions, schools and construction companies among others. A substantial volume of its instructions come from England. **Clients** Financial institutions; public bodies.

DIAMOND HERON This team's local profile is sustained by work for Ulster Bank, one of the financial institutions for which it collects outstanding balances. Other clients include debt collection agencies, credit unions, hire companies and newspapers. The unit is experienced in bankruptcy, possessions orders and actions in the High, County and Small Claims Courts. **Clients** Ulster Bank; Halifax.

JOHN MCKEE & SON (see firm details p.1015) The small team takes on bulk work for financial institutions, credit agencies, construction companies and debt recovery agencies. It continues to receive instructions from clients in England and Denmark as well as Northern Ireland.

MCMANUS KEARNEY It acts for major finance houses and trade creditors via debt collection agencies, as well as for traders. The majority of debts collected by this team of two solicitors, one partner and one fee-earner fall into the volume category and are not defended.

DEFAMATION

London: 266; The Regions: 269; Scotland: 270; Profiles: 271

Research approved by BMRB For this edition, **Chambers'** researchers conducted 6,582 interviews – 3,900 with law firms, 511 with barristers and 2,171 with clients. The validity of the research was scrutinised by BMRB International, who audited both the methodology and the results at our offices in London. They interviewed **Chambers'** researchers and cross-checked sample interviews. Details of the audit appear on page 7.

OVERVIEW The Data Protection and Human Rights Acts are playing increasingly important roles in a practice area riddled with privacy, qualified privilege and copyright issues. Against this background, straight-libel appears to be on the decline. A lot more libel work goes on in-house and behind closed doors these days. The development of the CFA (conditional fee arrangement) model continues and is still fluid in its form. Some effort has also been made to give greater recognition to non-print media and non-contentious work.

LONDON

DEFAMATION — LONDON

[1]
- Davenport Lyons
- Farrer & Co
- Olswang
- Peter Carter-Ruck and Partners
- Schillings

[2]
- D J Freeman
- David Price Solicitors & Advocates
- Reynolds Porter Chamberlain
- Theodore Goddard

[3]
- Pinsent Curtis Biddle
- Russell Jones & Walker

[4]
- Bindman & Partners
- Charles Russell
- Clifford Chance
- Goodman Derrick
- H2O
- Lovells
- Simons Muirhead & Burton
- Wiggin & Co

[5]
- Finers Stephens Innocent
- Harbottle & Lewis
- Lee & Thompson
- Lewis Silkin
- Mishcon de Reya

This book is the product of 6,582 1/2 hour interviews. See p.7 for BMRB audit. Within each band, firms are listed alphabetically.

DAVENPORT LYONS (see firm details p.927) A "*sensible*" team comprising "*knockabout, practical lawyers*" who command almost universal respect. It is best known for defendant work, with the advantage of a healthy claimant practice to boot. Peers envy its "*loyal client base and range of interesting work.*" Busy on behalf of the tabloids, the team provides a "*thoroughly effective*" service that is "*technically excellent.*" It pioneered Data Protection Act litigation on behalf of Lord Ashcroft, and is increasingly busy on the privacy matters. The team handled the Naomi Campbell case for The Mirror under the auspices of "*solutions-driven, practical*" **Kevin Bays** (see p.271), ("*no swank — just fantastic judgement.*") He also led the team that successfully defended Pressdram, publishers of Private Eye, against a nine-year-old claim by Stuart Condliffe. Also notable is the "*economic and focused*" **Philip Conway** (see p.271). Clients observe that the team "*gets better and better;*" these lawyers "*do things properly without faffing around.*" **Clients** Daily Mirror; Sunday Mirror; Daily Express; OK! Magazine; Private Eye; The Lawyer; United Business Media; Omnibus Press; Virgin Radio.

FARRER & CO (see firm details p.952) This offering, the result of a merger with Crockers, is respected as "*a pukka defendant*" firm, which boasts some "*great new clients.*" This is a broad, high-volume defendant practice, especially active for the regional papers and for Murdoch. Sources agree that the team "*gives a good fight*" and produces "*fine workmanship.*" Best known is the "*approachable and funny, yet impressively aloof*" **Robert Clinton** (see p.271). He is "*calm in a crisis*" and respected for his "*sure-footed defence of his clients' interests.*" Newspaper man **Richard Shillito** (see p.274) has a "*shrewd and wise head*" for defendant libel matters. "*Colourful*" **Rupert Grey** (see p.272) is an "*acquired taste*" to some, but a "*superb advocate*" to all, with expertise in libel and copyright. New to our tables this year is the "*talented*" **Julian Pike** (see p.273). His "*good brain and excellent organisation,*" and "*a golden touch with witnesses,*" have earned him the approbation of the market. The team acted for the Financial Times and the Independent in their contest, together with other news publishers, with Interbrew. It also handled a test case under the Protection from Harassment Act for The Sun in Thomas v News Group Newspapers. **Clients** Financial Times; IHT; Johnston Press; The Economist; Builder Group; News Group Newspapers; Haymarket Publishing.

OLSWANG (see firm details p.1087) One of the best, the Olswang team is known for its "*clinical efficiency, great drive and a good eye.*" It enjoys a glittering client base, and remains the "*first port of call for newspapers*" and those active in the TMT sector. The team has been quick to grow its offering in privacy work, alongside traditional defendant libel. The departure of Debbie Ashenhurst to the US has not diminished its offering. The team has "*settled after a fantastic run*" of instructions in the newspaper sector. The animus of this team is **Geraldine Proudler** (see p.273) ("*high-class, charming and sensible*") who cannot be beaten for depth of experience in the field. Peers acknowledge her as "*a formidable opponent.*" **Julia Palca** (see p.273) is known also for employment-related work, and one client observed that "*she's the best libel litigator I've ever met.*" The team acted for Sir Christopher Gent in his libel action against the Telegraph Group, and advised the Evening Standard in its defence against Sir Norman Foster in the Portland stone affair at the British Museum. **Clients** Guardian Newspapers; Associated Newspapers; Mirror Group; Grigori Loutchansky; Freeserve; Thus; MTV; Bloomberg; Tom Cruise; M&C Saatchi; RSPCA.

PETER CARTER-RUCK AND PARTNERS (see firm details p.1099) This operation has evolved as an "*efficient predator*" within its niche. Its "*pioneering*" CFA model remains the object of speculative excitement throughout the field. Known principally for its "*hardcore claimant work,*" the team also represents a broad range of defendant clients from the world of print. There is a strong caucus of opinion that values this firm; "*they're easy to knock, but courageous and inventive – they've added real value to clients.*" "*Old trooper*" **Nigel Tait** (see p.275) ("*ruthless*") is widely seen as "*the voice and driver of PC-R.*" He acted for Dr Joe Rahamim in a CFA action against ITN and also against Channel 4. "*Calm and measured*" **Alasdair Pepper** (see p.273) has some notable defendant cases under his belt, and **Andrew Stephenson**'s (see p.274) "*dedication*" inspires a wary respect in his opponents. In what has been hailed as a coup, the team is joined by the "*practical*" **Mark Thomson** (see p.275) from Schillings, who brings "*an eye for detail and great flair.*" The market also awaits the impact of Barton Taylor from Gouldens, the latest recruit to the team. Sources agree that "*aggressive*" **Cameron Doley** (see p.271) is "*pure Carter-Ruck.*" The team acts for a range of publishers and other companies, but remains best known for its high-profile work for celebrated claimants from the worlds of politics, entertainment and sport. It also has a niche in representing Arab princes and dignitaries.

LONDON ■ DEFAMATION

TOP IN-HOUSE LAWYERS

John BATTLE, Head of Compliance, ITN
Nick BRAITHWAITE, Group Legal Advisor, Associated Newspapers
Aliastair BRETT, Legal Manager, The Times
Patricia BURGE, Company Solicitor, The Times
Siobhain BUTTERWORTH, Head of Legal Affairs, Guardian Newspapers Ltd
Paul CHINNERY, Head of Legal & Regulatory Compliance, Channel 5
Charles COLLIER-WRIGHT, Group Legal Manager, Trinity Mirror plc
Tom CRONE, Legal Manager, News International
Sarah JONES, Head of Litigation, BBC
Marcus PARTINGTON, Solicitor, Trinity Mirror plc
Jan TOMALIN, Head of Legal & Compliance, Channel 4
Justin WALFORD, Legal Advisor, Express Newspapers
Arthur WYN-DAVIES, Legal Manager, The Telegraph
Eddie YOUNG, Group Legal Advisor, Associated Newspapers

John Battle *is respected for his technical knowledge and case management. Respected* **Nick Braithwaite** *has recently moved to this in-house role from Bindmans.* **Alastair Brett** *is "certainly not one to shy away from the fray." "Awesome"* **Patricia Burge** *displays "a calm front in the face of battle," while* **Siobhain Butterworth** *is a "robust lawyer who certainly knows the law."* **Paul Chinnery** *is "enormously hard-working and committed," and one not afraid to show his "feisty side."* **Charles Collier-Wright** *received heavy endorsement during the research. Although some find* **Tom Crone**'s *style to be "aggressive," all agree that "he picks his cases well." "Sharp"* **Sarah Jones** *leads one of the largest in-house teams around and drew commendation for her level-headed manner. "Bright and incisive"* **Marcus Partington** *has been involved in the Naomi Campbell case this year and is "clear-headed" in his approach.* **Jan Tomalin** *has been described as "the absolutely best in her field." Heavy endorsement leapt forth for* **Justin Walford**; *typifying "a good combination of academic knowledge and pragmatism," he is a "libel lawyer's libel lawyer" who "quickly gets shot of the no-hoper cases."* **Arthur Wyn-Davies** *is "always commercial and astute," while interviewees singled out* **Eddie Young** *as "an absolute stalwart – a rock."*

In-house lawyers' profiles p.1201

Clients HarperCollins; The Scotsman; Chelsea Football Club; TEG Environmental.

SCHILLINGS (see firm details p.1123) Regarded by many as the leading claimant firm in the business, its ascendance owes much to its "*fantastic celebrity client base*" and its "*hard-hitting*" name partner. Under the domination of "*strong-willed and commercially savvy*" **Keith Schilling** (see p.274), the team is known for its robust operation, which "*specialises in beating-up newspapers.*" Mark Thomson's departure to rival Peter Carter-Ruck and Partners has been followed with the making-up of equity partners. The team has been joined by **Martin Cruddace** (see p.271) from The Mirror, while the arrival from Finers Stephens Innocent of "*knowledgeable and enthusiastic*" Amber Melville-Brown (see p.273) is also likely to bring rewards. **Clients** Naomi Campbell; John Cleese; Angus Deayton; Bernie Ecclestone; Formula One; Foster and Partners; MG Rover; Racehorse Owners Association; Jamie Theakston; Tiger Aspect Productions.

D J FREEMAN (see firm details p.939) Consistently highly recommended, here is a stalwart practice of top calibre that is a major hit with clients; "*a specialist team that makes me feel comfortable and confident*" and popular with the Bar. The team undertakes a range of interesting work and is closely associated with film-makers and broadcasters, especially Channel 4. Adjudged to have "*extensive knowledge and a brilliant manner with producers,*" these lawyers "*really know their way around journalists and programme-makers.*" The absence of flamboyance helps promote "*quick, practical solutions.*" The high standards of the team are set by the "*tenacious, fair and perspicacious*" **Susan Aslan**, who manages to combine "*calm confidence*" with "*dazzling flair.*" The team defended Channel 4 in a libel action brought by police officer David Gregson, in relation to the 'Trial and Error' series. It also gives general advice to the likes of Carlton and Channel 5. **Clients** Channel 4; Channel 5; Carlton Television; Working Title Films; Reed Business Information.

DAVID PRICE SOLICITORS & ADVOCATES
Widely regarded as propagating a genuine alternative to Peter Carter-Rucks' CFA model, this is an "*astutely managed*" operation – "*small and nimble.*" Under its "*indefatigable*" name partner it has "*captured – even created – a market.*" Accusations that it is a "*one-man band*" are belied by the good-sized team that labours well together. The balance between paralegals and lawyers is "*unorthodox, but it works,*" and the team has picked up some high-profile work. **David Price** (see p.273) "*breaks the mould.*" He is "*terrific and unique*", with advocacy skills that form the backbone of a genuine one-stop shop. "*Full of ideas*" and "*prepared to take risks,*" he led the team acting for actor David Soul against The Mirror. The firm's client base is comprised of a wide range of claimants, members of the public as well as celebrities.

REYNOLDS PORTER CHAMBERLAIN (see firm details p.1111) The profile of this "*proactive, calm and resourceful*" group has been raised by involvement in a number of high-profile cases, and its ongoing relationship with Associated Newspapers. Onlookers applaud the creation of a strong media-focused team through the hire of "*tough and determined*" **Liz Hartley** (see p.272). She has made "*real inroads in libel, defence and insurance work.*" Popular with clients, **Keith Mathieson** (see p.273) is a "*serious player*" who acts for newspapers and broadcasters. As well as acting on the high-profile Loutchansky case, the team has acted for Tom Bower in a precedent-setting action against Sir Richard Branson in relation to fair comment, and has advised Associated Newspapers in the Angus Deayton affair. **Clients** Associated Newspapers; Independent Newspapers; Times Newspapers; HTV; The National Magazine Company; CMP Information; The Spectator; Christian Aid; Mencap.

THEODORE GODDARD (see firm details p.1158) Adjudged "*a real Rolls-Royce of a firm,*" it has a long-standing relationship with Times Newspapers. The offering here is a good range of privacy, libel and cyberlibel expertise with an emphasis on defendant work. The "*magnificent*" **Martin Kramer** (see p.272) "*opens doors*" and leads "*an impeccable team*" that possesses "*incredibly bright junior partners.*" He is supported by **Katherine Rimell** (see p.274), who has a "*knockout record in the courts.*" The team acted for Michael Douglas, Catherine Zeta Jones and OK! Magazine in its action against Hello! and advised The Times and The Sunday Times in various defences against libel actions brought by, amongst others, President Taylor of Liberia and Mikhail Khodorkovsky. **Clients** Times Newspapers; Northern & Shell; Western Provident Association; Easyspace; Christopher Little Consultants.

PINSENT CURTIS BIDDLE (see firm details p.1102) The "*wily, experienced and technically astute*" **David Hooper** (see p.272) holds the fort at this "*traditional*" practice. Over time, the focus has shifted from insurance work to encompass a broad business-based practice, largely in the service of "*a fantastic publishing base.*" The team acted for Simon & Schuster in the headline-grabbing Loutchansky matter, and represented Robert Loftus against the tabloid Sundays in claims arising out of allegations by Mohamed Al Fayed. **Clients** Forbes Magazine; Simon & Schuster; Bloomsbury Publishing; Random House; Lord Ashcroft; Little, Brown.

RUSSELL JONES & WALKER (see firm details p.1120) Competitors claim that this firm is "*the reason why you have to be nice to public servants.*" This respected team fields "*assiduous and tough lawyers*" for their chief clients, the Police Federation. Add to that successful work for clients from the unions and politics. The team has been heavily involved in post and pre-publication work, mostly for claimants, but occasionally defendants. The practice is busy enough to have recruited over the last year, and the client base broadened. Acting for an august group of Neil Hamilton's supporters, **Sarah Webb** (see p.275) led a team to victory over Mohamed Al Fayed in the Court of Appeal. **Clients** Lord Carter; Paul Hewitt; Geoffrey Seed; Anya Oyewole; National Autistic Society; Manchester Evening News; The Police Federation; First Division Association; NASUWT; Musicians' Union; IPMS; Equity; MPO.

DEFAMATION ■ LONDON

LEADING INDIVIDUALS

1
- **ASLAN Susan** D J Freeman
- **CLINTON Robert** Farrer & Co
- **PROUDLER Geraldine** Olswang
- **SCHILLING Keith** Schillings

2
- **BAYS Kevin** Davenport Lyons
- **HARTLEY Liz** Reynolds Porter Chamberlain
- **HOOPER David** Pinsent Curtis Biddle
- **KRAMER Martin** Theodore Goddard
- **PRICE David** David Price Solicitors & Advocates
- **SHILLITO Richard** Farrer & Co
- **TAIT Nigel** Peter Carter-Ruck and Partners

3
- **CONWAY Philip** Davenport Lyons
- **GREY Rupert** Farrer & Co
- **MIRESKANDARI Razi** Simons Muirhead & Burton
- **PEPPER Alasdair** Peter Carter-Ruck and Partners
- **STEPHENSON Andrew** Peter Carter-Ruck and Partners

4
- **BINDMAN Geoffrey** Bindman & Partners
- **MATHIESON Keith** Reynolds Porter Chamberlain
- **MCCUE Jason** H2O
- **ROBERTSON Rhory** Kerman & Co
- **SMYTH Michael** Clifford Chance

5
- **ARMSTRONG Nicholas** Goodman Derrick
- **CRUDDACE Martin** Schillings
- **DADAK Roderick** Lewis Silkin
- **FOX Paul** H2O
- **LAMONT Duncan** Charles Russell
- **MCDERMOTT Jennifer** Lovells
- **PALCA Julia** Olswang
- **PIKE Julian** Farrer & Co
- **RIMELL Katherine** Theodore Goddard
- **SKREIN Michael** Richards Butler
- **STEPHENS Mark** Finers Stephens Innocent
- **THOMSON Mark** Peter Carter-Ruck and Partners
- **WEBB Sarah** Russell Jones & Walker

UP AND COMING
- **DOLEY Cameron** Peter Carter-Ruck and Partners
- **MELVILLE-BROWN Amber** Schillings

ASSOCIATES TO WATCH
- **TENCH Dan** Olswang

See individuals' profiles p.271

BINDMAN & PARTNERS (see firm details p.872) The practice is known for high-profile libel work and "*some seriously heavy cases*" arising out of human rights and civil liberties issues. Increasing experience and expertise in the realm of privacy meshes well with the practice's freedom of expression and breach of confidence pedigree. Chief here is the "*venerable*" **Geoffrey Bindman** (see p.412), who has "*excellent political connections.*" The team acted for Anna Ford in her challenge to the Press Complaints Commission, and represented Amnesty International in the extradition proceedings against General Pinochet. **Clients** Amnesty International; Anna Ford; New Statesman.

CHARLES RUSSELL (see firm details p.904) Possessing the capacity to do some "*fantastic media work*" for high-profile client ITN, the practice here rests on the "*strong*" shoulders of **Duncan Lamont** (see p.272). He is respected as a "*talented author*" with a "*good grasp*" of the issues. Lamont led the team defending two Channel 4 journalists and ITN against allegations of contempt of court over their refusal to disclose sources to the Bloody Sunday Inquiry. The team also defended ITN and Channel 4 in the libel case brought by Dr Joe Rahamim. **Clients** ITN; Hello!; Jason Fraser; Lennox Lewis.

CLIFFORD CHANCE (see firm details p.911) A fluent and skilled clearance practice with a 24-hour response unit ready to service the reputations of its corporate clients, often derived from the US. The team provides a global pre-publication service and is most closely identified with its work for main client Reuters, which it represented on the Interbrew case. It also conducts a significant amount of ratings work for Standard & Poor's. Guiding light here is "*man of many parts*" **Michael Smyth** (see p.49), an "*accomplished*" lawyer who is well-equipped to field any media matters that arise. He acted for Multiplex, builders of the new Wembley Stadium, against accusations of corruption by The Guardian and others. **Clients** Reuters; Multiplex; Standard & Poor's; Jupiter International Group; Business Week; Consignia.

GOODMAN DERRICK (see firm details p.973) A broad, "*thoroughly capable*" media practice, where the emphasis lies on television, it is most at home on contentious matters. The practice has achieved a good mix of both defendant and claimant work. The team vets the News at Ten for main client Granada. **Nicholas Armstrong** (see p.271) heads up the practice and has won the respect of his peers. He acted for ITV/Celador on the media and libel aspects of a case in which a winner was accused of cheating. **Clients** ITV; Granada; Chrysalis Television; Scottish Media Group.

H2O (see firm details p.980) The firm has shed its grey-goods practice that was bolted on over a year ago, but its defamation/media practice is still intact. It remains "*the firm of choice for libel in Ireland.*" Historically the team has acted for defendants, and has been involved in the occasional reputation management matter for politicians, such as David Trimble. There is also a good spread of newspaper and magazine work, including a number of big trials for the likes of The Times (in Ireland) and The Express (in London). An increased volume of post-publication work secures its ties with publishing houses. Star name here is "*charming Ireland specialist*" **Jason McCue** (see p.273), who has "*real clout in the celebrity world.*" He has been working on the Omagh bombing matter, which has entailed working closely with The Mail. **Paul Fox** (see p.271), a "*pleasant solicitor advocate with loyal clients,*" focuses 100% of his time in the area of libel.

LOVELLS (see firm details p.1045) The team conducts a varied bag of work on both the claimant and defendant sides, largely for corporate clients, but also for broadcasters and newspapers. There has been a run of cases for The Observer, and also for The Guardian v Interbrew. Sources describe this as a "*detailed and academic*" outfit. "*Unassuming and quiet*" **Jennifer McDermott** (see p.48) "*can handle anything*" and wins heartfelt respect. She led the team acting for The Guardian in its defence against David Irving. **Clients** Guardian Newspapers; Express Newspapers; The Scotsman Publications.

SIMONS MUIRHEAD & BURTON (see firm details p.1137) A "*great-quality outfit*" with a strong reputation for celebrity crime work. Clients liked the team's "*laid-back and flexible*" approach, finding the lawyers particularly good with programme-makers and journalists. Leading light here is the "*smooth and professional*" **Razi Mireskandari**, a "*man you can do business with,*" who is gifted with an "*acute defendant outlook*" and great litigation skills. The team acted for Random House in Random House v Allason. **Clients** Random House; Channel 4; Dennis Publishing; Penguin; Time Out; Greenpeace; Friends of the Earth; specialist trade magazines and local newspapers; prominent individuals.

WIGGIN & CO (see firm details p.1186) This "*discreet but increasingly visible*" practice is regarded by interviewees as "*one of the most sensible out there.*" It has built up a "*great-quality*" defamation practice, mostly for defendants, and boasts an "*impressive media, insurance and private client base.*" Most of the work in this area consists of content-based contentious work for media companies. The practice centres around **Caroline Kean** (see p.272), a "*charming lawyer*" and "*most definitely a player.*" **Clients** print; music and broadcasting clients; insurers.

FINERS STEPHENS INNOCENT (see firm details p.955) Primarily associated with US publishers, broadcasters and the occasional online concern, this practice continues to develop its expertise in cross-border litigation. The departure of Amber Melville-Brown to Schillings is seen as a blow to the firm, though it has succeeded in bringing the "*assiduous and spirited*" **Mark Stephens** (see p.274) back into the fray. A media lawyer, his practice covers a broad front. The team has a niche working for US companies having difficulties in the UK. It acted for Time in defence of a multi-jurisdictional libel action brought by the Reuben brothers and Trans-World Metals. **Clients** Time;

THE REGIONS — DEFAMATION

Turnaround Publisher Services; Pye Dog Productions; CNN International; The Wall Street Journal; Dow Jones; CBS; NBC; Penthouse Magazine (USA); The New York Times.

HARBOTTLE & LEWIS (see firm details p.983) Specialist media lawyers with an "*entirely creditable defamations offshoot,*" this small practice is known as "*the guard dog*" for Richard Branson. The heart of the practice is mostly non-contentious work for a wide celebrity client-base centred on the music and entertainment industries. Gerrard Tyrrell leads a team that acted for 19 Management on the Pop Idol series, and also advised Will Young and Gareth Gates. **Clients** Richard Branson; 19 Management; Will Young; Gareth Gates; Sophie Dahl; Alec Stewart; Annie Lennox; Anthony Hopkins; David Frost; Rowan Atkinson; Gary Rhodes; Bell Pottinger; Henry's House; Atomic Kitten; Duke of Beaufort; The Prince's Trust.

LEE & THOMPSON New to our tables this year, here is a niche media and entertainment firm best known for advising celebrity claimants from the music and film industries. It has a well-deserved reputation as "*a one-stop shop for celebrities,*" taking up their cases against the red-tops and Sunday papers, covering the waterfront of issues, including privacy. The team is led by Gordon Williams, who acted for the Beckhams against the Sunday People's attempts to publish unauthorised photographs of their residence in Hertfordshire. **Clients** Victoria and David Beckham; Nicole Appleton and Liam Gallagher; Trevor Bentham; Mel B.

LEWIS SILKIN (see firm details p.1041) Although at its roots an "*excellent advertising practice,*" turnover in defamation and related work is up on the year. Best-known name here is **Roderick Dadak** (see p.271), a prolific writer who acts for private individuals, newspapers, accountancy and banking clients, amongst others. He led the team acting in Windsor v Express Newspapers, which concerned libel claim brought by Roger Windsor, former CEO of the NUM. The team has recently recruited a barrister with in-house experience at an advertising agency and a niche in clearance matters. There has been an increase in instructions arising out of new media areas, especially the internet. **Clients** Express Newspapers; Newsquest; Harris Lipman; Heritable Bank; Durlacher; Bonhams; Sentinel Ventures.

MISHCON DE REYA (see firm details p.1072) Best remembered for its role in the Irving v Penguin Books case, this team "*crops up here and there on high-profile jobs*". Historically centred on defendants, claimant work is up and the team undertakes reputation management for corporates. Copy clearance is also catered for here. Karen Sanig manages a team that was recently bolstered by the arrival of a new associate, and which is supported by some heavy-hitting consultants. It undertakes no CFA work and is increasing its own experience in advocacy. The team acted for Oryx Natural Resources against the BBC, which accused it of links to Al Qaeda, and advised Roy Philpott against The Sunday Telegraph's allegations that he worked for Mugabe. **Clients** Oryx Natural Resources; Roy Philpott; private individuals; broadcasters, newspapers and publishers.

OTHER NOTABLE PRACTITIONERS After the collapse of Swepstone Walsh, the immensely popular **Rhory Robertson** "*a diamond in the rough*" is now at Kerman & Co. He is considered an "*experienced and reliable*" media man, a robust litigator well regarded for his work on newspaper matters. **Michael Skrein** (see p.274) at Richards Butler retains the regard of the market for his strong standalone libel practice for Hollywood stars in England, and advice on copy compliance.

THE REGIONS

DEFAMATION — THE REGIONS

1. **Foot Anstey Sargent** Exeter
   Wiggin & Co Cheltenham
2. **Brabners Chaffe Street** Liverpool
   Cobbetts Manchester
3. **Pannone & Partners** Manchester
   Wragge & Co Birmingham

LEADING INDIVIDUALS

1. **JAFFA Tony** Foot Anstey Sargent
2. **LEWIS Mark** George Davies
   MANLEY Mark Brabners Chaffe Street
   STONE Peter Cobbetts
3. **KEAN Caroline** Wiggin & Co

This book is the product of 6,582 1/2 hour interviews. See p.7 for BMRB audit. Within each band, firms are listed alphabetically. See individuals' profiles p.271

FOOT ANSTEY SARGENT (see firm details p.958) The firm has established a "*muscular, professional reputation*" for defending its core base of regional newspaper clients. **Tony Jaffa** (see p.272), known in the trade for his "*methodical, informed*" writings, leads a team with broad defendant experience in areas including pre-publication advice and challenges to Secrecy Orders in the courts. This year, the team has taken on a high-profile case for Jamaican newspaper, The Sunday Gleaner. The group also handles online defamation matters for newspaper clients, and represents a small number of book publishers. **Clients** Northcliffe Newspapers Group.

WIGGIN & CO (see firm details p.1186) See London editorial.

BRABNERS CHAFFE STREET (see firm details p.885) This warmly regarded Liverpool practice is led by the "*media savvy*" **Mark Manley** (see p.272). Previously, his "*brisk*" department took on a balance of defendant and claimant work, but two new clients, The Liverpool Daily Post & Echo and the Manchester Evening News, have created a bias towards the defendants. The group also advises radio stations, publishers and individuals in libel, slander and contempt of court claims. This year, the group has been running a popular training programme on claims avoidance for the staff of radio stations. **Clients** Insider Group; Johnson Press (formerly Regional Independent Media); all 20 Emap plc radio stations.

COBBETTS (see firm details p.914) Of lead partner **Peter Stone** (see p.274), one rival said, "*I would hire him if I had made an ill-advised or incendiary comment.*" The team has a tight relationship with the Manchester Evening News, and has been particularly busy this year dealing with allegations of contempt and breach of injunction. The firm's other defamation clients are corporations and individual claimants including local celebrities. Stone divides his time between defamation and his property litigation practice.

PANNONE & PARTNERS (see firm details p.1092) The firm acts mainly for individual claimants including members of the public, sports personalities and politicians. Department head, William Lister, and the team also deal with instances where a company believes its name or business has been defamed. The firm prides itself on its success in resolving cases by apology or retraction.

WRAGGE & CO (see firm details p.1197) Nick Cunningham leads a team of "*adept litigators*" who undertake work for indemnity insurers and existing corporate clients in the Midlands and beyond. The team, which operates out of the IP department, has been tested this year by a lengthy and complex case in defence of a local authority.

OTHER NOTABLE PRACTITIONERS "*Ace litigator*" **Mark Lewis** of George Davies impressed rivals with his 'silky' handling of a high-profile privacy case brought by a professional footballer.

DEFAMATION ■ SCOTLAND/NORTHERN IRELAND

SCOTLAND

DEFAMATION — SCOTLAND
1. **Bannatyne, Kirkwood, France & Co** Glasgow
   Levy & McRae Glasgow
2. **Carruthers Gemmill** Glasgow

LEADING INDIVIDUALS
1. **SMITH Martin** Bannatyne, Kirkwood, France & Co
   WATSON Peter Levy & McRae
2. **GEMMILL Thomas** Carruthers Gemmill

This book is the product of 6,582 1/2 hour interviews. See p.7 for BMRB audit. Within each band, firms are listed alphabetically. See individuals' profiles p.271

BANNATYNE, KIRKWOOD, FRANCE & CO (see firm details p.856) Practice head **Martin Smith** (see p.274), recommended as "*bold but thoughtful,*" commanded respect among interviewees. His team is well known for its defence work for a wide spread of daily and weekly newspapers. It has also received regular instructions from individuals in the political world. Accusations that the practice is aggressive are fended off by acknowledgement of its "*golden track record.*" **Clients** Independent Newspapers; The Scotsman Publications; Associated Newspapers; The Guardian; The Observer.

LEVY & MCRAE (see firm details p.1041) "*Prime movers in Scottish defamation,*" this Glasgow firm has a strong reputation across the country for defendant work. The team, ably headed by "*gregarious, upfront*" **Peter Watson** (see p.275), provides a legal shield for newspaper and TV clients such as The Herald and Channel 4. The smaller pursuer side of the practice is also in rude health, with the team representing Irene Adams MP this year in a claim against The Guardian. The firm has witnessed a general increase in enquiries about online defamation.

CARRUTHERS GEMMILL Primarily a defendant practice for publications owned by Express Newspapers, this "*assiduous*" unit also undertakes occasional pursuer cases. **Thomas Gemmill** is "*multifaceted and amiable*" according to research interviewees. He leads a team held to be particularly well versed in privacy law. **Clients** Express Newspapers.

NORTHERN IRELAND

DEFAMATION — NORTHERN IRELAND
1. **Johnsons** Belfast
   Mills Selig Belfast
2. **Elliott Duffy Garrett** Belfast
   McKinty and Wright Belfast

LEADING INDIVIDUALS
1. **SPRING Paul** Mills Selig
   TWEED Paul Johnsons
2. **DEENY Brian** Elliott Duffy Garrett
   UP AND COMING
   MCDONNELL Paul McKinty and Wright

This book is the product of 6,582 1/2 hour interviews. See p.7 for BMRB audit. Within each band, firms are listed alphabetically. See individuals' profiles p.271

JOHNSONS (see firm details p.1016) Recognised as the leading claimant practice in Northern Ireland, the team has represented a glittering host of celebrities. It has cemented its reputation in the field by winning a number of high-profile settlements on behalf of Van Morrison. Observers commend head of department **Paul Tweed** (see p.275) as a "*prizefighter.*" The group continues to advise on claims arising from Sean McPhilemy's book 'The Committee', the first batch of which comes up for hearing this year, and takes on defendant work for the Belfast and Dublin editions of The Sunday Times. **Clients** Patrick Kielty; The Corrs.

MILLS SELIG (see firm details p.1072) Esteemed lead partner **Paul Spring** (see p.274) is "*not afraid to take the bull by the horns.*" He has been busy this year, for the most part regularly defending newspaper clients, TV stations and publishers. The firm is popular with English clients that have a substantial defamation workload in Northern Ireland. The team receives occasional claimant instructions from celebrities. **Clients** RTE; Irish Independent; Irish Star; News Group Newspapers; Guardian Newspapers; ITN; Channel 4; Hodder & Stoughton.

ELLIOTT DUFFY GARRETT (see firm details p.947) **Brian Deeny** (see p.271) is a "*a reliable backstop*" for a portfolio of defendant clients including the Mirror Group newspapers. Although his "*diplomatic*" group has not been highly visible in the courtroom this year (exceptions include a commercial slander allegation in County Court), it has achieved various settlements, and advised a number of high-profile claimants in libel cases. The team also has experience of representing other solicitors and barristers who are being accused of or alleging libel or slander.

MCKINTY AND WRIGHT (see firm details p.1066) The "*enthusiastic and user-friendly*" **Paul McDonnell** (see p.273) drives this Belfast firm's defamation practice. Principally a defendant outfit, work is undertaken for newspapers and publishing companies and, increasingly, for individuals such as lawyers, architects and engineers, who have professional indemnity insurance. McDonnell also takes on occasional corporate claimant cases, and is well versed in issues relating to contempt and reporting restrictions. **Clients** The Belfast Telegraph; Sunday Life; Telegraph Group.

THE LEADERS IN DEFAMATION

ARMSTRONG, Nicholas
Goodman Derrick, London
(020) 7404 0606
narmstrong@gdlaw.co.uk
Specialisation: Partner in Media Department specialising in media litigation for clients in UK and France, especially defamation and privacy/confidentiality: securing remedies for claimants (especially against tabloid press), defending media organisations against action (including pre-broadcast/publication clearance); also harassment protection, contempt, copyright and passing off, obscenity, public and human rights law, judicial review, French-related litigation matters. Recent activity: acting for BBC undercover journalist Donal MacIntyre in his libel action against Kent Police; for the Countess of Dudley (formerly film star Maureen Swanson) in libel actions against Macmillan and the Mail on Sunday; for French football club FC Bordeaux in an action against Derby County FC; for ITV and Celador in relation to Major Charles Ingram, a contestant on 'Who Wants to be a Millionaire'; and advising the makers and cast members of television programmes including Coronation Street, Emmerdale, EastEnders, Tonight with Trevor MacDonald.
Prof. Memberships: Royal Television Society; Law Society.
Career: Qualified 1986. Trained and qualified with *Theodore Goddard* (London and Paris). Joined *Goodman Derrick* Media Group 1994
Publications: Numerous in-house seminars and related briefing papers and articles for clients and contacts on media law issues.
Personal: Educated Nottingham High School and Jesus College Cambridge. Hobbies include music, cars, French and English literature, cinema, food and drink.

ASLAN, Susan
D J Freeman, London
(020) 7583 4055

BAYS, Kevin
Davenport Lyons, London
(020) 7468 2600
kbays@davenportlyons.com
Specialisation: Defamation, publishing and media law. Principal solicitor for Private Eye for over 15 years. Other publisher clients include Mirror Group, Penguin Books, Express Newspapers, John Brown Publishing and Centaur Communications. Also acts for claimants in defamation cases and media related disputes such as breach of confidence, privacy and data protection. Recently acted for Penguin Books in the major libel action brought by revisionist historian David Irving arising out of a book entitled 'Denying the Holocaust', and for the defendant newspapers in Jamie Theakston's and Naomi Campbell's claims for breach of confidence and under the Data Protection Act.
Prof. Memberships: Law Society.
Career: Qualified 1979, having joined *Wright Webb Syrett* in 1977. Became a partner in 1982.
Personal: Born 24 April 1955. Leisure interests include skiing, golf, cricket, football and travelling. Member of The Media Society and The Groucho Club.

BINDMAN, Geoffrey
Bindman & Partners, London
(020) 7833 4433
info@bindmans.com
See under Human Rights, p.412

CLINTON, Robert
Farrer & Co, London
(020) 7242 2022
rgc@farrer.co.uk
Specialisation: Senior Partner. Head of media. Main areas of practice are defamation and publishing related litigation. Involves extensive range of claimant and defendant work for prominent individuals, institutions and companies, including newspaper and publishing companies. Pre and post-publication advice involving privacy, breach of confidence, contempt etc. Intellectual property work, covering general trademark and passing off work for commercial clients.
Prof. Memberships: Media Society. International Bar Association.
Career: Qualified in 1975. Joined *Farrer & Co* in 1972. Became partner in 1979. Senior Partner 2002.
Personal: Born 1948. Attended Brasenose College, Oxford 1967-71. Lives in London.

CONWAY, Philip
Davenport Lyons, London
(020) 7468 2600
pconway@davenportlyons.com
Specialisation: Partner in litigation department. Main area of practice is defamation, especially with regard to the newspaper and entertainment industries and undertakes a growing amount of pre-publication work. Acts for Private Eye, Mirror Group Newspapers, Express Newspapers, Centaur Communications and Omnibus Press.
Prof. Memberships: Law Society (Member of Privacy and Defamation Working Committees).
Career: Qualified in 1984. Joined *Wright Webb Syrett* in February 1986. Became partner in August 1988. Joined *Davenport Lyons* as a partner on merger with *Wright Webb Syrett* in March 1995.
Personal: Born 15 April 1959. Attended Aldenham School 1972-77. Former director Southend United Football Club. Member of The Media Society, Groucho Club and a barker of The Variety Club of Great Britain.

CRUDDACE, Martin
Schillings, London
(020) 7453 2500
martin@schillings.co.uk
Specialisation: Defamation, breach of confidence. Recent high profile matters: Angus Deayton. Whilst at Mirror Group Newspapers acted in a number of high profile actions: Elton John v MGN Ltd, Graeme Souness v MGN Ltd and HRH Princess of Wales v MGN Ltd.
Prof. Memberships: British Association of Sport and Law.
Career: 1986-88 Articled at *Schilling & Lom*; 1988-90 *Masons*; 1990-2002 Mirror Group Newspapers (Head of Legal Department from 1997).
Publications: Regular contributor to Guardian Media Law Page.
Personal: Squash, golf, rowing and running. Season ticket holder (Arsenal Football Club). Racehorse owner.

DADAK, Roderick
Lewis Silkin, London
(020) 7074 8080
rod.dadak@lewissilkin.com
Specialisation: Partner and Head of Defamation. Main areas of practice in media law are defamation (libel and slander); malicious falsehood; privacy; confidentiality; contempt and data protection issues. Regularly deals with regulatory bodies including the Press Complaints Commission, Broadcasting Standards Commission and the Advertising Standards Authority. Long experience in acting for the media, particularly newspapers and publishers. Undertakes both Plaintiff and Defendant work and pre-publication libel reading. Cases include for Express Newspapers, Roger Windsor; Scott (libel) for Associated Newspapers; Associated Newspapers Limited v Lucas Box; Kiffin; Sethia; Tobias Cash 'n Carry (libel); judicial reviews; Associated Newspapers v Pickering; passing off; Associated Newspapers v Insert Media Limited; contempt on behalf of Express Newspapers in the Geoff Knights and Magee cases; copyright Associated Newspapers v News Group Newspapers Limited; Confidentiality/Privacy Stephens v Avery. Acts for many celebrities and high profile individuals. Advises companies, individuals and ISPs on defamation on the internet. Lectures at seminars and appears on TV and radio on defamation and related matters. Regularly contributes to the 'Solicitors Journal.'
Prof. Memberships: Law Society, Media Society.
Career: Qualified in 1972. Joined *Lewis Silkin* in 1998 as Head of Defamation, formerly with the *Simkins Partnership*.
Personal: Educated Lancing College and King's College, London (LLB (Hons)). Enjoys tennis and the arts and holidaying in Provence (when possible). Married with three sons.

DEENY, Brian
Elliott Duffy Garrett, Belfast
(028) 9024 5034
brian.deeny@edglegal.com
Specialisation: Head of Defamation Unit. Also specialises in commercial litigation and professional negligence. Acts for numerous national newspapers. Also very extensive experience acting for plaintiffs in libel and slander actions. Has been involved in many high profile actions in Northern Ireland.
Prof. Memberships: Law Society of N Ireland.
Career: Graduated University College, Dublin 1982. Admitted solicitor 1985. Admitted partner 1990.
Personal: Born in 1960. Married with three children. Interests include a variety of sports, music, current affairs and travel.

DOLEY, Cameron
Peter Carter-Ruck and Partners, London
(020) 7353 5005
cameron.doley@carter-ruck.com
Specialisation: Claimant and defendant defamation, privacy and human rights work. Broad range of publishing and broadcasting clients including three of the ITV companies and the National Magazine Company (the publishers of 'Esquire', 'Cosmopolitan' and 'Good Housekeeping'); claimant clients include a strong Arab and Middle Eastern component as well as plcs, sportsmen and politicians. Important cases include Esquire ats Reichmann, Skuse v Granada, HTV ats Welsh Rugby Union, Awwad v Geraghty. Undertakes large proportion of claimant work on a 'no win, no fee' basis; recent CFA cases include Horgan v News of the World (libel arising out of newspaper's 'naming and shaming' campaign) and Express v Windsor (claim brought by former NUM Chief Executive following allegations that he worked as an MI5 mole during the miners' strike), both of which resulted in the recovery of substantial sums in damages. Is presently working on a number of cases, both in the UK and elsewhere, arising out of the events of 11 September 2001.
Career: Graduate of The Queen's College, Oxford (MA Hons 1st Class) and The College of Law (CPE Distinction; Law Society Finals Hons); joined *Peter Carter-Ruck and Partners* as trainee solicitor in 1990; qualified 1992; partner 1995; managing partner 2001.

FOX, Paul
H2O, London
(020) 7886 0740
paul.fox@h2o-law.com
Specialisation: Media law, particularly defamation, contempt, confidentiality and privacy, but also soft intellectual property and advertising. A qualified solicitor advocate, provides advice at all

DEFAMATION — THE LEADERS

procedural stages from pre-publication clearance and emergency remedies through to litigation (and relevant publishing/broadcasting codes) and high court advocacy. A mixed claimant and defendant practice of broadcasters, magazines and individuals.
Career: Qualified 1986, Hong Kong 1994, Solicitor Advocate Higher Courts-Civil 2001.
Personal: Cycling, football (QPR supporter) and modern history.

GEMMILL, Thomas
Carruthers Gemmill, Glasgow
(0141) 333 0033

GREY, Rupert
Farrer & Co, London
(020) 7242 2022
rcg@farrer.co.uk
Specialisation: Partner in media team. Principal area of practice is defamation and copyright. Retained by leading magazine and newspaper publishers and their insurers to advise on libel and allied matters prior to publication and post-publication complaints. Also by leading photographic/syndication agencies to handle matters connected with literary and artistic copyright. Lectures, writes and gives seminars. Also retained by high profile individuals in advisory, pre-emptive and plaintiff work. Clients include: The Financial Times, Telegraph Group, Emap, Hello! Limited, Royal Geographical Society, The Liverpool Institute for Performing Arts and Members of Parliament.
Prof. Memberships: Fellow of Royal Geographical Society.
Career: Qualified in 1975, served articles with *Farrer & Co*. Joined *Crockers* in 1981, partner in 1983, head of department in 1989, senior partner in 1997. Rejoined *Farrer & Co* in 2001 when merged with *Crockers Oswald Hickson*.
Personal: Born 1946. Educated Wellington College and UCL. Principal leisure activities are expeditions to wild places and building barns. Married, three daughters; lives in the South Downs.

HARTLEY, Liz
Reynolds Porter Chamberlain, London
(020) 7242 2877
ebh@rpc.co.uk
Specialisation: Partner and Head of Media and Technology Group. A very experienced litigation practitioner with wide knowledge of the media, in particular the newspaper industry. Principal areas of practice are defamation and media related litigation, including contempt of court, breach of confidence, privacy, malicious falsehood, reporting restrictions, content issues, PCC and BSC complaints and copyright infringement. Also provides pre-publication clearance and advice. Acts for several national newspaper groups as well as magazines and insurers. Also experienced in information technology disputes and has represented both users and suppliers of IT products and services. Has advised on IT disputes in banking, manufacturing, publishing, health, aviation and in privatisations.
Prof. Memberships: The Media Society; honorary fellow of the American Bar Association; The Society for Computers and the Law.
Career: Qualified 1982. Chairman of London Young Solicitors Group 1987-88. Partner, *DJ Freeman* 1987, head of commercial litigation from 1996. Joined *RPC* as a partner 1997.
Personal: Born 1957. Education: Royal Masonic School for Girls; University of Sheffield (LLB Hons). Resides Surrey. Leisure: music, reading and walking.

HOOPER, David
Pinsent Curtis Biddle, London
(020) 7418 7000
david.hooper@pinsents.com
Specialisation: Head of Technology and Media in London. Main area of practice is media and defamation, entertainment, copyright matters, publishing and broadcasting and new media. Acted for Peter Wright and the publishers in the Spycatcher case. Successfully involved in defending libel actions brought by Robert Maxwell. Acted for John Major in his libel action and for the Sunday Times against Derbyshire County Council and Forbes magazine against Berezovsky in the House of Lords and for other publishers defending claims brought by Russian businessmen Rakhimov and Loutchansky. Has written many articles on media matters in periodicals and the national press and regularly addresses conferences.
Prof. Memberships: American Bar Association, Libel Defense Resource Center.
Career: Qualified 1971 as a Barrister and in 1977 as a Solicitor. Joined *Biddle* as a Partner in 1986.
Publications: Publications include 'Public Scandal Odium and Contempt', 'Official Secrets: The Use and Abuse of the Act' and 'Reputations Under Fire', (Little, Brown 2001) a survey of the law of libel in the last 10 years.
Personal: MA (Oxon). Lives in London and Wales.

JAFFA, Tony
Foot Anstey Sargent, Exeter
(01392) 203992
arj@foot-ansteys.co.uk
Specialisation: Partner. Head of media team and commercial litigation division. Handles libel, contempt of court, court secrecy orders and related law for media clients. Author of articles and reviews on all aspects of media law. Speaker at conferences for the Newspaper Industry.
Prof. Memberships: Law Society; Society of Notaries.
Career: Qualified in 1980. Articled at *Boyce Hatton & Co*. 1978-80. Worked at *Wilde Sapte* 1980-83, before joining *Foot Anstey Sargent* in 1983. Became a partner in 1987. Chairman of the Devon Young Solicitors Group 1989-90; member of National Committee of Young Solicitors Group 1988-89. Notary Public 1989.
Personal: Born 6 August 1956. Attended St Boniface's College, Plymouth 1967-74 and Oxford University 1974-77. Leisure interests include windsurfing, sailing and cycling. Married with two children. Lives in Torquay.

KEAN, Caroline
Wiggin & Co, Cheltenham
(01242) 224114
caroline.kean@wiggin.co.uk
Specialisation: Partner, head of litigation department. Main areas of practice are defamation and media related commercial litigation. Includes contentious work for plaintiffs, defendants and insurers, advising on copy pre-publication and broadcast, confidence, privacy, data protection act, copyright and passing off. Specialises in private seminars to companies and organisations on issues which include media handling/damage limitation and systems.
Prof. Memberships: Law Society; The Media Society (Council Member). Legal advisor to Women in Journalism.
Career: Articled *Rubinstein Callingham*. Qualified 1985. Partner 1987. Partner *Olswang* 1989-95. Joined *Wiggin & Co* 1995 as a partner and head of litigation.
Personal: Born 1960. Burford School 1971-78, Newnham College, Cambridge 1978-81. College of Law, Lancaster Gate 1981-82.

KRAMER, Martin
Theodore Goddard, London
(020) 7606 8855
martinkramer@theodoregoddard.co.uk
Specialisation: Media-related litigation for corporate and individual clients, both claimants and defendants. Main publishing clients are 'The Sunday Times' and 'The Times' and 'OK!' magazine. Areas of expertise include libel and slander; malicious falsehood; breach of confidence/privacy; contempt of court; human rights cases relating to freedom of expression; official secrets; copyright and passing off. Recent and current cases include successfully defending 'The Times' and book publishers Hurst & Company in a libel action brought by President Charles Taylor of Liberia; acting for Michael Douglas, Catherine Zeta-Jones and Northern & Shell against 'Hello!' in which the Court of Appeal first recognised the right to privacy in English law; acting for The Gleaner of Jamaica in appeal to the Privy Council over the proper level of damages in defamation cases; acting for Jennifer Aniston in privacy/breach of confidence claim against the 'Sport'. Other main area of practice: public law.
Prof. Memberships: The Law Society, Constitutional and Administrative Law Bar Association, The Media Society.
Career: Qualified 1969. Partner 1978.

LAMONT, Duncan
Charles Russell, London
(020) 7203 5000
duncanl@CR-law.co.uk
Specialisation: Media law and reputation management. Representing broadcasters, magazines and newspapers, including before the Broadcasting Standards Commission, providing election coverage, pre-publication advice and protection of confidential information and intellectual property. Also advising individuals and publishers on media issues.
Career: Barrister 1985-87, in-house media lawyer Sunday Mirror 1987-89, qualified as solicitor 1990. Partner at *Biddle* now at *Charles Russell* (since February 2001).
Publications: Articles in 'Press Gazette', 'Guardian', 'Times', Society of Authors. Television media pundit.
Personal: MA in law from Cambridge, Diploma in copyright law from King's College, University of London. West Ham fan, Edinburgh Fringe Festival, Henley Regatta and opera lover!

LEWIS, Mark
George Davies, Manchester
(0161) 236 8992

MANLEY, Mark
Brabners Chaffe Street, Liverpool
(0151) 600 3000
mark.manley@brabnerscs.com
Specialisation: Partner and Head of Commercial Litigation Department. Main area of practice is defamation, acting for radio stations, newspapers, broadcasters and publishers. Also acts for claimants in libel cases. Panel member on Lloyd's Syndicate 702 Libel Panel. Preferred EMAP Radio advisor. Also handles general commercial litigation. Has acted in libel actions against several MPs, the ex-Lord Mayor of Liverpool, and in several commercial libel cases both for and against newspapers. Author of numerous articles on mediation services. Spent two years as Partner in Lawyers Planning Services lecturing on financial services, practice management and defamation. Accredited mediator with both CEDR and ADR Group.
Prof. Memberships: Law Society, British Association for Sport and the Law.
Career: Qualified in 1987, becoming an Assistant Solicitor at *Loosemores*. Partner in Lawyers Planning Services since 1989. Joined *Brabner Holden* in 1991, and appointed Partner in 1992.
Personal: Born 17 August 1962. Attended St Nicholas and De La Salle Schools, then Liverpool University and Christleton College of Law. Leisure interests include his family, Everton FC, sports (golf and snooker) and writing music. Lives in Chester.

THE LEADERS — DEFAMATION

MATHIESON, Keith
Reynolds Porter Chamberlain, London
(020) 7242 2877
kam@rpc.co.uk
Specialisation: Partner in IP and Media Department. Main area of practice is media law, particularly defamation, but including contempt of court, reporting restrictions, copyright and passing off. Has acted for and against numerous national and regional newspaper and magazine groups and their insurers. As well as litigation, advises on copy clearance and pre-broadcast issues, including compliance. Clients include national newspapers, business and consumer magazine publishers, broadcasters and media insurers.
Career: Qualified 1983 with *Lovell White & King*. Joined *Oswald Hickson Collier* 1990. Partner 1992. Partner *Davies Arnold Cooper* 1997-2000. Joined *Reynolds Porter Chamberlain* May 2000.
Personal: Born 1959. Caius College, Cambridge 1977-80. Postgraduate diploma in UK and European law of copyright, King's College, London 1997.

MCCUE, Jason
H2O, London
(020) 7886 0740
jason.mccue@h2o-law.com
Specialisation: Partner specialising in media law (privacy and defamation), human rights, (including international matters), reputation management (including PR and lobbying) and legal campaigns (eg acting for the victims of the Omagh bomb). Expertise in complex investigations (including money laundering, terrorism, organised crime), multijurisdictional legal issues, international human rights issues (violations), political issues, publishing, media management and internet issues. Recent clients include well known politicians, celebrities and authors, as well as newspapers, television companies and publishers.
Career: Qualified in England and Wales, Republic of Ireland and Northern Ireland.
Personal: Queen Mary's College, London. Enjoys travel, folk music and hiking.

MCDERMOTT, Jennifer
Lovells, London
(020) 7296 2000
jennifer.mcdermott@lovells.com
See under Administrative & Public Law, p.48

MCDONNELL, Paul
McKinty and Wright, Belfast
(028) 9024 6751
paulmcdonnell@mckinty-wright.co.uk
Specialisation: Extensive defamation practice both advisory and litigation for local and national media. Also acts for corporate and individual clients in this area. Other main areas of practice are commercial litigation, professional negligence and general insurance defence litigation.
Prof. Memberships: Law Society of Northern Ireland, Society of Editors.
Career: Qualified 1993. Partner in *McKinty & Wright* since 2000.

MELVILLE-BROWN, Amber
Schillings, London
(020) 7453 2500
amber@schillings.co.uk
Specialisation: Specialising in defamation, Amber is experienced in both claimant and defendant work, her practice historically including a number of US heavyweight newspapers, publications and broadcast organisations, UK publishers and distributors, including pre-publication/broadcast advice and litigation. Practice areas include defamation, media management for individuals and corporations, invasion of privacy, breach of confidence, malicious falsehood and other media related matters.
Career: Admitted in 1995. Training contract at *Simons Muirhead & Burton*. Moved to *Stephens Innocent* in April 1996 and with *Finers Stephens Innocent* post merger, December 1999. Formerly Head of Defamation at *Finers Stephens Innocent* until joining *Schillings* as a partner in January 2002. Appointed to the Law Society Civil Litigation Defamation Reference Group. External Examiner for the College of Law LPC Media Course.
Publications: Media Law columnist for the 'Law Society Gazette'. Contributes to other publications on legal and other matters, including 'The Independent' and 'The Times' newspapers, and US publications including the 'American Bar Association' magazine.

MIRESKANDARI, Razi
Simons Muirhead & Burton, London
(020) 7734 4499

PALCA, Julia
Olswang, London
(020) 7208 8888
jcp@olswang.com
Specialisation: Main areas of practice are media and employment litigation. Represents both print and broadcast defendants, and some plaintiffs, in defamation, breaches of copyright and other media and entertainment-related disputes including judicial review of decisions of media regulatory and quasi-regulatory bodies. Also advises mainly employers on all aspects of employment law, including unfair and wrongful dismissal, discrimination and the application of restrictive covenants. Acted as an in-house libel litigator to a major newspaper group 1985-86. Speaks on both media and employment law issues.
Career: Qualified in 1980. Joined *Olswang* in 1986, becoming partner in 1987. Appointed part-time Employment Tribunal Chairman.
Publications: Author of 'Employment Law Checklists' and numerous articles on media and employment issues.

PEPPER, Alasdair
Peter Carter-Ruck and Partners, London
(020) 7353 5005
alasdair.pepper@carter-ruck.com
Specialisation: One of the most experienced media lawyers in the business. He is viewed as having "a no nonsense style, gets things done and clients like him". Alasdair has a busy media practice. His highlight for 2000/2001 was achieving a settlement for Kevin Keegan against 'The News of the World' which included the payment of £150,000 damages. In 2001/2002 he obtained a very substantial settlement from 'The Sunday Telegraph' for another client. He has also acted successfully for many other prominent and well known individuals, companies and organisations. In addition, Alasdair has a thriving defendant practice acting for Express Newspapers, the Scotsman and HarperCollins among other publishers. Alasdair is the architect behind *Carter-Ruck's* groundbreaking and very successful Conditional Fee Agreement ('No win No fee') scheme and also its MediaAlert service through which it helps clients to deal with hostile media interest.
Prof. Memberships: Law Society, IBA.
Career: Qualified in 1984. Has remained with *Peter Carter-Ruck and Partners* since qualification. Became partner in 1986.

PIKE, Julian
Farrer & Co, London
(020) 7242 2022
jcp@farrer.co.uk
Specialisation: Partner in the Media Team, specialising in all aspects of media litigation. Acted for the defendant in Cook/Carlton v New Group Newspapers and Mills v News Group Newspapers. Also advises on sporting disputes.
Prof. Memberships: Media Society; Society of Editors; British Association of Sport and the Law.
Career: Trained *Farrer & Co*; qualified 1992; partner 1999.
Publications: Contributory editor to 'Butterworths Civil Court Practice'.
Personal: Education: Taunton School; Southampton University (LLB). Leisure: Member of MCC and Harlequins; golf; family. Born: 1967; resides Teddington.

PRICE, David
David Price Solicitors & Advocates, London
(020) 7916 9911
enquiries@lawyers-media.com
Specialisation: A solicitor advocate who offers a 'one-stop' service, including representation at trial. Principal area of practice is defamation and media litigation, representing both claimants and a wide range of publishers. Pioneer of a conditional fee scheme for publishers. Has acted in many high profile and landmark cases.
Career: Qualified as a solicitor (1990). Barrister (1991). Principal of *David Price Solicitors & Advocates* since 1993.
Publications: Author of 'Defamation: Law, Procedure and Practice' published by Sweet & Maxwell 2000.
Personal: Born 16 October 1963. Educated at Haberdashers' Aske School (1970-82), Harvard High School, Los Angeles (1982-83) and Manchester University (1983-86).

PROUDLER, Geraldine
Olswang, London
(020) 7208 8888
gap@olswang.com
Specialisation: Head of Defamation. Main area of practice is media law including defamation, contempt of court, breach of confidence, broadcasting complaints and associated matters. She acts for national newspapers, magazine and book publishers, PR agencies, media and other companies, as well as acting for claimants. Geraldine has led the teams in cases that include: acting for 'The Guardian' in its successful defences against former cabinet minister Jonathan Aitken and Neil Hamilton MP; acting for Demon Internet (now Thus plc) in its defence of libel proceedings brought by Laurence Godfrey – the case produced one of the first High Court judgements in relation to alleged internet libel; acting for Marks & Spencer plc in its successful action against Granada Television; acting for Mr George Carman QC (just before his death) against Punch magazine and obtained for him a half page apology in Punch together with damages paid to a cancer charity plus his legal costs; acted for Sir Christopher Gent, Chief Executive of Vodaphone, in his action against the Telegraph Group; acted for Mr Peter Gadsby, vice-chairman of Derby County FC and chairman of Birch plc in a libel action against Mr Stuart Webb, a former director of Derby County FC (*Olswang* recovered a total of £350,000 for Mr Gadsby in damages and costs, including £150 000 damages, which is one of the largest damages figures of the last few years); acted for Associated Newspapers in defending proceedings brought by Lord Foster and his company over Evening Standard articles about the British Museum; acting for The Daily Mirror in proceedings brought by Victor Kiam, chairman of Ronson plc; acted for The Sunday Mirror in defending contempt of Court proceedings over the stoppage of a criminal trial in Leeds against Leeds footballers.
Prof. Memberships: Law Society, Media Society.
Career: Qualified 1980. Became a partner with *Lovell White & King* (now *Lovells*) in 1987. Joined *Olswang* as a partner 1995. Now also a trustee of the Scott Trust, which owns 'The Guardian' and 'The Observer'.
Personal: Born 2 July 1956. BA Law at Nottingham University 1974-77. Lives in London.

DEFAMATION ■ THE LEADERS

RIMELL, Katherine
Theodore Goddard, London
(020) 7606 8855
katherinerimell@theodoregoddard.co.uk
Specialisation: Main practice areas are media-related litigation, particularly defamation, malicious falsehood, confidence, official secrets, rights of free expression and privacy under the Human Rights Act and public law. Advises a wide variety of corporate and individual clients, both plaintiffs and defendants. Represents 'The Times' and 'The Sunday Times' in many libel actions including the Reynolds action which extended the defence of qualified privilege to the media. Involved in the first privacy action on behalf of Michael Douglas, Catherine Zeta-Jones and 'OK!' magazine.
Prof. Memberships: The Law Society, Justice and the Constitutional and Administrative Law Bar Association.
Career: Qualified in 1985. Partner of *Theodore Goddard* in 1997.

ROBERTSON, Rhory
Kerman & Co, London
(020) 7451 9800

SCHILLING, Keith
Schillings, London
(020) 7453 2500
Specialisation: Senior partner. Main areas of practice are media and Internet litigation especially libel, privacy and copyright. Represents many well-known figures including Bernie Ecclestone, Elizabeth Hurley and Naomi Campbell as well as numerous corporate clients. Other areas of practice include divorce.
Career: Articled at *Wright Webb Syrett* before setting up present practice.
Publications: Contributor on libel, privacy and copyright in the 'Entertainment Law Review'.
Personal: Born 25 July 1956. MA in European Business Law. Mountaineering. Member of Groucho's and Chelsea Arts Club.

SHILLITO, Richard
Farrer & Co, London
(020) 7242 2022
ras@farrer.co.uk
Specialisation: Partner in Media Team. Main area of practice is defamation. Acts for a large number of national, regional and trade press clients and their insurers. Other areas of expertise are contempt, reporting restrictions and copyright.
Career: Qualified in 1976, having joined *Oswald Hickson, Collier & Co* in 1973. Became a partner in 1984. Joined *Farrer & Co* in 2001 when merged with *Crockers Oswald Hickson*. Previously a trainee journalist at Yorkshire Weekly Newspaper Group Limited, 1970-72.
Personal: Born 13 March 1948. Attended Westminster School, then Magdalen College, Oxford (1970, PPE (Hons)). Leisure interests include music and sailing. Lives in London. Married, with three daughters.

SKREIN, Michael
Richards Butler, London
(020) 772 5720
spms@richardsbutler.com
Specialisation: Partner. A leading lawyer in intellectual property and media. Work is mainly litigation, but also advisory, particularly in relation to insurance and advertising and media clearance work. Specialist areas of work include administrative law, aviation, competition, contempt of court, defamation, insurance, intellectual property (the law of confidence, copyright, patents and trade marks), international law and judicial review. Has years of experience in the aviation, food and drink, insurance, leisure, (including sports) and media industries as well as many other areas of litigation after over 20 years as a litigation partner in a firm with very broad and notably international scope of practice. His team's media work won 'The Lawyer 2001 Litigation Team of the Year' Award.
Prof. Memberships: Fellow of the Society for Advanced Legal Studies; Law Society; The City of London Solicitors' Company; Copinger Society, the Baltic Exchange.
Career: Articled *Richards, Butler & Co* 1971; qualified 1973; partner since 1976; head of litigation department 1990 to 1996; lectured on advertising law, copyright infringement, intellectual property and defamation implications of the Internet, libel and trade marks; chair of the Protecting the Media series of conferences, the market leader.
Personal: Born 1947. Educated at Oxford University (MA, Modern History) and the University of Southern California (AM *magna cum laude* International Relations). Honor Society of *Phi Kappa Phi*.

SMITH, Martin B
Bannatyne, Kirkwood, France & Co, Glasgow
(0141) 221 6020
martin@b-k-f.demon.co.uk
Website: www.bkf.co.uk/
Specialisation: The practice, which was established in Glasgow in 1785, covers the full range of intellectual property work and includes all aspects of defamation and media law with particular reference to Scotland. The practice numbers amongst its clients major newspaper and publishing companies and also acts for British Actors Equity Association in Scotland.
Prof. Memberships: A former journalist who graduated in Law at The University of Edinburgh and is admitted as a Notary Public in Scotland.
Career: Qualified in 1971 and joined *Bannatyne, Kirkwood, France & Co* in 1973 attaining the position of senior partner in 1995. Also a consultant with Messrs. *Peter Carter-Ruck & Partners* in London, being a registered foreign lawyer.
Personal: Educated at the High School of Glasgow and University of Edinburgh. Interests include writing on media matters and lecturing on the subject. In addition, is a former Chairman of the oldest Scottish Football Club, Queen's Park FC and has represented the Club at Scottish Football League and Scottish Football Association levels.

SMYTH, Michael
Clifford Chance, London
(020) 7600 1000
michael.smyth@cliffordchance.com
See under Administrative & Public Law, p.49

SPRING, Paul
Mills Selig, Belfast
(028) 9024 3878
paul.spring@nilaw.com
Specialisation: Head of litigation department. Main area of practice is libel. Represents national newspapers, broadcasting organisations and book and magazine publishers. Extensive experience of libel litigation for both defendants and plaintiffs. Areas of practice include breach of confidence, contempt of Court, press complaints, copyright and pre-publication work. Other major areas of practice are commercial litigation, product liability litigation (clients include British American Tobacco) and IP.
Prof. Memberships: Law Society of Northern Ireland.
Career: Qualified 1983. Litigation partner since 1988.
Personal: Educated Belfast Royal Academy and London School of Economics (graduating in Law in 1981). Leisure interests include cycling, architecture, the countryside and two young children! Lives near Belfast.

STEPHENS, Mark
Finers Stephens Innocent, London
(020) 7323 4000
Specialisation: Has been described by the 'Law Society Gazette' as '...*the patron solicitor of previously lost causes*'. It is this reputation for creativity with law that leads international publishers and broadcasters to his door. Has created a niche in international comparative media law and regulation. His practice takes him to the Commonwealth, Europe and the USA. He is Chair of the Management Board of the postgraduate Programme in Comparative Media Law & Social Policy at Wolfson College, Oxford University. Groundbreaking human rights work forms the foundation of much of his work. He is regularly asked to litigate privacy, free speech and public interest issues before domestic and international Courts (including the European Court of Human Rights). CNN recently retained Mark who was successful in gaining camera access to the Shipman inquiry. Mark sits on the editorial boards of 'Communications Lawyer', 'Copyright World', and 'EIPR'. As founding Chair (now VC) of the Internet Watch Foundation, he has lectured for the Foreign & Commonwealth Office and the Department of Trade & Industry on internet content control and regulation. Is also regular commentator on legal matters both on television and radio including 'Points of Law' – a BBC radio 4 programme that took a light hearted look at legal affairs.
Career: Qualified in 1982.
Personal: Born 7th April 1957.

STEPHENSON, Andrew
Peter Carter-Ruck and Partners, London
(020) 7353 5005
andrew.stephenson@carter-ruck.com
Specialisation: Partner in litigation department. Early in his career, conducted the successful defence of criminal proceedings brought under the Official Secrets Act. Acted for Martin Packard, who was in awarded £450,000 damages for libel in 1987, a record at the time. Main area of practice since 1982 is defamation, acting for claimants, including government ministers, MPs of all the main political parties and sports and music personalities. Also acted for defendants including book, magazine and newspaper publishers and television companies. Also experienced in media law generally, including the law of contempt, copyright and passing off. Has handled a number of leading defamation cases where jurisdiction has been an issue, including: Papendreou v Time magazine; Bachchan v Dagens Nyheter (Swedish publication); Schapira v Ha'aretz (Israeli publication); Berezovsky v Forbes.
Prof. Memberships: Law Society, Media Society.
Career: Graduate of University College London 1975-78. Council of Stock Exchange 1979-81. Joined *Peter Carter-Ruck and Partners* in 1982; qualified 1983; became partner in 1986.

STONE, Peter
Cobbetts, Manchester
(0161) 833 5246
peter.stone@cobbetts.co.uk
Specialisation: Over 25 years experience in litigation for national and regional blue-chip clients. Particular expertise in commercial property litigation (forfeiture, dilapidations, covenants, contested lease renewals, brewery/licensed retailer work) and in defamation (plaintiff and defendant) for individual and media clients.
Prof. Memberships: Law Society. Notaries Society.
Career: Articled at *Cobbetts*, 1974. Qualified 1976, partner 1979.
Personal: Born 1951. Educated at Rossall School and Liverpool University (LLB Hons 1st class). Leisure interests include fell walking, climbing and mountain biking.

THE LEADERS ■ DEFAMATION

TAIT, Nigel
Peter Carter-Ruck and Partners, London
(020) 7353 5005
nigel.tait@carter-ruck.com

Specialisation: Partner in Media Department. Main area of practice is media law, acting mainly for claimants. Cases of interest include Beta Construction v Channel 4 (award of £568,000 – highest ever libel award paid to a company); Telnikoff v Matusevitch (first libel case to go to the House of Lords for over a decade – award of £240,000); Jack Slipper v BBC (£50,000 damages – leading case on liability for republication); X v Y (settlement of £200,000 plus costs); Jonathan Hunt (aged 6) v The Sun (settlement of £35,000 plus costs to mother and son – youngest ever libel plaintiff); Farargay v Al Hayat (award of £170,000 plus costs); Scholar v Mail (award of £100,000 plus costs); Gorman v Mudd (award £150,000 plus costs); Morelli v Sunday Times (award of £45,000 plus costs – first conditional fee libel action to go to trial); Kirby Harris v Baxter (leading case on trial by jury); Victor Kiam v Sunday Times (£45,000 plus costs – upheld by the Court of Appeal); Shah v Standard Chartered Bank (leading case on resonable grounds to suspect); Kiam v The Mirror (award of £105,000 plus costs – upheld by the Court of Appeal); Walker v Newcastle Chronicle (settlement of £100,000 plus costs); Rahamim v Channel 4 and ors (settlement of £175,000 plus costs and broadcast apology on Channel 4 news); X v Sunday Sport (injunction to restrain publication obtained within 2 hours of receiving instructions); Y v Sunday Sport and anor (the first injunction ever obtained in the new tort of privacy resulting in the pulping of 40,000 copies of a magazine); Rahamim v Dennis Publishing (settlement of 30,000 plus costs during "first offer of amends" trial). Conducts wrongful and unfair dismissal actions (including claims for slander and libel). Head of firm's employment group. Also conducts personal injury work (highest award £755,000). Has spoken at the Oxford Union Debating Society on three occasions on law reform.
Prof. Memberships: Member of Law Society Privacy, Defamation and Pre-Action Protocol Working committees.
Career: Qualified in 1988, having joined *Peter Carter-Ruck and Partners* in 1986. Appointed partner in 1990.
Publications: Contributor to 'Carter-Ruck on Libel and Slander' 4th and 5th editions; contributor to 'McNae's Essential Law for Journalists'. Has presented numerous papers to conferences on media law, defamation, conditional fees and privacy.

TENCH, Dan
Olswang, London
(020) 7208 8888

THOMSON, Mark
Peter Carter-Ruck and Partners, London
(020) 7353 5005
mark.thomson@carter-ruck.com

Specialisation: Member of the Defamation and Media Litigation Department. He specialises in all aspects of media law, including defamation, confidence, human rights and privacy and acts for both claimants and defendants. His other areas of practice in media litigation include human rights, copyright and passing off, and his expertise also covers media regulatory work involving BSC, PCC and ITC. He acts for a wide variety of high profile clients and companies.
Prof. Memberships: Law Society.
Career: MA (Hons), Cambridge. Qualified 1988; articled at *McKenna & Co* before joining *Schilling & Lom* where he became a partner in 1992. In 2002 he joined *Peter Carter-Ruck and Partners* as a partner.
Publications: Articles: Privacy and prior restraint after the Human Rights Act – 'Communications Law' and A new respect for the right to privacy – 'Legal Week'. Co-contributor to 'Privacy and the Media – The Developing Law', Editor Hugh Tomlinson QC.
Personal: Born 22 October 1959. Epsom College, 1972-78; Cambridge University, 1978-81. Leisure interests include films, reading and tennis.

TWEED, Paul
Johnsons, Belfast
(02890) 240183
pt@johnsonslaw.co.uk

Specialisation: Defamation – the most well-known case being for B J Eastwood against the boxer Barry McGuigan, resulting in an award of £450,000. Currently acting for Van Morrison and Patrick Kielty in a number of high profile libel actions. Acted for Robert McCartney QC, the former MP for North Down, who was awarded £80,000 in a high profile case against 'The Irish Times' on the eve of the 1997 General Election, and for the actors Liam Neeson and Natasha Richardson against a number of Irish newspapers in relation to false reports regarding the state of their marriage. Has represented the Irish band The Corrs and is currently involved in multiple defamation actions against UK and US-based internet book distributors, requiring the issue of what is believed to be the largest number of writs in respect of the publication of one book. Acts for a number of other media, political, public, business and legal personalities and also on the defence side for newspapers (including 'The Sunday Times') and other publications, in both Belfast and Dublin. Other areas of media practice include copyright and related entertainment work. Personal injury – has had more than 20 years of experience in acting for a number of major insurance companies in both Northern Ireland and the Republic of Ireland.
Prof. Memberships: Incorporated Law Society of Northern Ireland (1978); Law Society of England and Wales (1993); Law Society of Ireland (1999).

WATSON, Peter
Levy & McRae, Glasgow
(0141) 307 2311
peterwatson@lemac.co.uk

Specialisation: Media; defamation; libel; aviation; international claims and litigation; personal injury litigation; public and fatal accident inquiries; civil and criminal litigation; Inland Revenue and Customs & Excise investigation; employment law; partnership law; Secretary of the Lockerbie Air Disaster Group; Secretary of Braer Disaster Group; Member of the Steering committee of the Piper Alpha Disaster Group; Gecas v Scottish Television plc; Cavendish v The Scotsman Publications & Others; representing the Dunblane Families at the Dunblane public inquiry; involved in litigation in more than 12 countries other than the UK.
Prof. Memberships: Law Society of Scotland; SSC Society; APIL; ATLA; past President of the Society of Solicitor Advocates; Chairman of the Scottish Mediation Bureau; Member of the IBA.
Career: BA in Economics, University of Strathclyde; Bachelor of Law, University of Edinburgh; research at Scandinavian Maritime Institute and thereafter at Dundee University, Centre for Petroleum and Mineral Law Studies; visiting scholar in International Law, Nova University, Florida, USA; on the board of Anglia Sports Law Research Centre.
Publications: Author of 'In Pursuit of Pan Am' and 'The Search for Justice – A Case for Reform to the Civil Justice System in Britain'.
Personal: Horseracing; travel; married with two daughters, Anna and Sophie.

WEBB, Sarah
Russell Jones & Walker, London
(020) 7837 2808
s.l.webb@rjw.co.uk

Specialisation: Acts for a number of lawyers and members of the judiciary and members of parliament in libel claims including recent claims on behalf of Lord Carter, the recently retired Labour chief in the House of Lords, and the prospective Conservative MP Jonathan Bullock in a claim against the Guardian, and continues to advise a number of high profile individuals and commercial organisations on pre-publication issues including privacy and breach of human rights. She has also recently acted for the contributors to Neil Hamilton's libel action who successfully defeated the claim against them by Mr Al Fayed in the Court of Appeal. Also acts for defendants including Manchester Evening News.
Prof. Memberships: Law Society, Equine Lawyers Association.
Career: Articled to *McDonald Stacey*; qualified in 1983; joined *Russell Jones & Walker* in 1983, partner since 1990.
Publications: Published a number of articles in 'Solicitors Journal', 'The Lawyer' and the 'Law Society Gazette' and has a regular column in an equestrian magazine.
Personal: Educated at Malvern Girls College of Law. Resides in Kent. Interests include family and horse riding.

www.ChambersandPartners.com

275

E-COMMERCE

London: 276; The Regions: 278; Profiles: 279

Research approved by BMRB For this edition, **Chambers'** researchers conducted 6,582 interviews – 3,900 with law firms, 511 with barristers and 2,171 with clients. The validity of the research was scrutinised by BMRB International, who audited both the methodology and the results at our offices in London. They interviewed **Chambers'** researchers and cross-checked sample interviews. Details of the audit appear on page 7.

LONDON

TOP IN-HOUSE LAWYERS

Christopher HEATHER, Group Legal Counsel, Vizzavi Europe
Jessica HENDRIE-LIANO, Legal Counsel, Freeserve.com
Marijke REID, Sky Interactive

The only new addition to this year's list is **Jessica Hendrie-Liano**, acclaimed as "clued-up and industry-savvy." **Marijke Reid** and **Christopher Heather** continue to invoke recommendations for their work. Deserving of special mention is the legal team at AOL, which was praised for its "excellent efficiency."

In-house lawyers profiles' p.1201

BIRD & BIRD (see firm details p.874) The firm retains its place at the forefront of the market, according to one client, due to "*fantastic expertise blended with sophisticated commercial advice.*" It is now to be seen more often on deals for its blue-chip clients than for dot.com start-ups. Not only is **Graham Smith** (see p.281) an IT litigator, but he is also "*the authority on e-commerce law,*" and an important figure within the E-Commerce Directive. The loss of Graham Defries to Weil, Gotshal & Manges LLP has been received with mixed reactions by the market, although many acknowledge that the depth of the team remains constant. A highlight for the team has been advising the Government on a series of interactive television pilots, including one that allowed subscribers to make doctors' appointments online. Financial services have provided a wealth of instruction for the team, including advise to PayPal, the US e-cash product provider on the regulatory issues concerning its roll-out in the UK. The group was then instructed on the roll-out in several other jurisdictions. International b2b exchanges have included a joint internet portal for a consortium of operators in the electrical equipment industry. **Clients** Expocentric; Netscalibur; Digital Wellbeing; lastminute.com; Magex.

OLSWANG (see firm details p.1087) The practice is perceived to be able to "*knit the disciplines of e-commerce and IP together well.*" The team is receiving more strategic work from key industry players, who believe the firm possesses "*unparalleled experience on deal flow and rights.*" Upheld by the market as "*a true expert,*" **John Enser** (see p.280) is experienced in all areas of e-commerce work. Head of department **Kim Nicholson** (see p.437) has been described as "*a demon for hard work, really impressive on corporate transactions,*" while **Matthew Cowan** (see p.280) is viewed by sources as a "*sensible operator.*" Infrastructure work has included advice to Freeserve on its complaints to the UK Government about the VAT status of AOL. Despite the e-commerce downturn, the firm represents such success stories as eBay, now its principal advisors. On the corporate side, the team represented the founder shareholders of Peoplesound on the disposal of Peoplesound to Vitaminic, in a transaction worth $40 million. **Clients** MSN; Demon; Granada Media Group; Ladbrokes; Sony.

BAKER & MCKENZIE (see firm details p.855) Long established in the IT sector, this 60-strong e-commerce team, which is derived from all practice areas, is viewed as "*stable, doing well despite the bust, with a refreshing approach to the work.*" The crossover with IT and telecoms is a strength of the team; it has acted on the m-commerce IT platform created by Hutchison 3G. **Harry Small** (see p.438) is widely recognised as an IT expert; however, he is also lauded for "*knowing the e-commerce sector incredibly well; a fantastic all-rounder.*" **Robbie Downing** (see p.280) ascends the tables, singled out for his "*commitment to the area, an expert.*" He has worked on competition issues surrounding the creation and operation of b2b exchanges such as Centradia. A key attribute of the team resides in its global reach. It is involved in high-value finance work, advising State Street on the operation of Global Link, the electronic platform for derivatives, and other investment products. **Clients** Cisco Systems; Compaq; Hewlett-Packard; Pacific Century Cyber Works; agency.com.

CLIFFORD CHANCE (see firm details p.911) The firm is seen to have invested heavily within the area, "*taking it seriously, undertaking the heavyweight projects, reaching for the top of the tables.*" This drive has been impeded somewhat by the loss of Chris Millard to Linklaters. Nevertheless, **David Griffiths** (see p.435) appears to be stepping forward, perceived to be a "*top-flight technical lawyer, particularly hot on e-banking.*" The team, including the up-and-coming **Daniel Sandelson** (see p.591), presents a broad focus, bringing expertise in various disciplines to each case. **Clients** Carrefour; MusicNet.

KEMP LITTLE LLP (see firm details p.1019) A team that "*punches above its weight,*" according to observers. A technology boutique, it is "*a master of its trade.*" Competitors concede the team "*receives consistently good press from its clients.*" **Richard Kemp** (see p.436) has been pronounced "*worthy of his top ranking;*" he is seen "*on the meaty deals; he really understands the industry.*" He has been particularly active in the music sector, advising clients such as PPL on the use of online services both to market and to fulfil sales of its product. The team has also acted for Sports Interactive, the developers of 'Championship Manager', advising it on publishing agreements and WAP-based gaming opportunities. On the financial side, the team has advised QBE Insurance on the development of a bespoke e-commerce system allowing international extended warranty cover to be written by its corporate clients. **Clients** PPL; Expedia; DZ Bank; Thomson Financial; Image.net.

TAYLOR WESSING (see firm details p.1156) The firm is perceived not only to be admirably withstanding the burst of the dot.com bubble, but also to be strengthening its position within the market. The opening of an office in Cambridge is seen as a boon to the team, whose "*excellent all-round technology practice*" has impressed many observers. In addition, the team boasts the role of European general counsel to an impressive roster of US clients. This includes Priceline.com, which the team advised on its 'Name Your Own Price' business model for the sale of flight tickets. The team, led by Glyn Morgan, has experienced a growth in data protection work, advising clients such as Hiscox on the data protection aspects of its insurance portal. Corporate work has included advice to 365 Corporation on the sports internet joint venture with Chrysalis, creating Rivals.com. The market anticipates a greater European flavour following its recent merger with German firm, Wessing. **Clients** Signify Solutions; Citrix Systems; TheGlobalResident.com; Vizzavi; UpMyStreet.com.

DENTON WILDE SAPTE (see firm details p.935) The team's strength is felt to lie in an understanding of the online aspects of media work. Nevertheless, the focus here is upon the convergence of a wide range of disciplines, from defamation to data protection. Work for established corporates has held prominence within the team; it has acted for Opodo on the establishment of the online travel portal joint venture backed by various airlines, from Lufthansa to British Airways. Litigation is another string to the firm's bow; it has acted for Freeserve on a dispute regarding the enforcement of web site

LONDON ■ E-COMMERCE

E-COMMERCE
■ LONDON

[1]
- Bird & Bird
- Olswang

[2]
- Baker & McKenzie
- Clifford Chance
- Kemp Little LLP
- Taylor Wessing

[3]
- Denton Wilde Sapte
- Field Fisher Waterhouse

[4]
- Allen & Overy
- Berwin Leighton Paisner
- Harbottle & Lewis
- Osborne Clarke

[5]
- Ashurst Morris Crisp
- Bristows
- Brobeck Hale and Dorr
- Herbert Smith
- Linklaters
- Lovells
- Masons
- SJ Berwin
- Tarlo Lyons
- The Simkins Partnership
- Theodore Goddard

LEADING INDIVIDUALS

[1]
- ENSER John Olswang
- KEMP Richard Kemp Little LLP
- MCNEIVE Liam McNeive Solicitors
- MILLARD Christopher Linklaters
- SMITH Graham Bird & Bird

[2]
- CHISSICK Michael Field Fisher Waterhouse
- HAFTKE Mark KLegal
- KAYE Laurence Sole Practitioner
- NICHOLSON Kim Olswang
- SMALL Harry Baker & McKenzie

[3]
- DOWNING Robbie Baker & McKenzie
- GRIFFITHS David Clifford Chance
- REES Chris Herbert Smith

[4]
- AZIM-KHAN Rafi McDermott, Will & Emery
- CALOW Duncan Denton Wilde Sapte
- COWAN Matthew Olswang
- PHILLIPS Mark Harbottle & Lewis
- RENDELL Simon Osborne Clarke
- TURNER Mark Herbert Smith
- WILLIAMS Alan Denton Wilde Sapte

UP AND COMING
- GREW Chris Brobeck Hale and Dorr
- MULLOCK James Osborne Clarke
- SANDELSON Daniel Clifford Chance

This book is the product of 6,582 1/2 hour interviews. See p.7 for BMRB audit.
Within each band, firms are listed alphabetically. See individuals' profiles p.279

---

development and shareholders' agreements with the ITC. **Duncan Calow** (see p.280) represents key client Teletext on television, web and mobile projects. **Alan Williams** (see p.592) has been advising Wisden on the launch of the Wisden.co.uk web site. **Clients** Turner; Bertelsmann; Palm; ProQuest; The FA Premier League.

FIELD FISHER WATERHOUSE (see firm details p.954) The firm is perceived by the market to have been structured towards the representation of start-up clients , but has nevertheless "*held its ground within public sector work*" following the downturn. Led by the "*expert*" **Michael Chissick** (see p.280), the team advised Newcastle City Council on its £14 million project to set up a digital city, to make Newcastle the broadband centre of the North East. On the litigation side, the team successfully settled Advantage Europe's proceedings against web site designers Concept NMT over the quality of services rendered. Corporate work has flourished, representing established clients alongside dot.com survivors such as ADVFN.com, which the team advised on the acquisition of financial web site UK-invest.com and related fund-raising. **Clients** Medipurchase; EmdexTrade; Accenture; Quadriga Worldwide; Ordnance Survey.

ALLEN & OVERY (see firm details p.841) Clients and competitors concur that the team does not simply focus upon corporate matters, but "*understands the salient issues*" permeating the industry. Since the practice has historically represented major corporates and financial institutions rather than dot.coms, it has fared better than most in the depressed market. Possessed of the capability to undertake the largest deals, the team, led by Laurence Jacobs, advised UBS on internet web site terms and conditions and the export of encryption technology. The team possesses a niche within financial services b2b work, acting for Iboxx, the brainchild of various financial services companies from Morgan Stanley to BNP Paribas, that publishes and sells financial indices to prepare a standard customer licence agreement. On the contentious side, the team has been appointed by William Hill on various domain name disputes. **Clients** 365 Corporation; ING Barings; News Corporation; Thomson Financial; adidas.

BERWIN LEIGHTON PAISNER (see firm details p.866) A successful merger and an innovative approach to the sector advances the practice in our tables. The team has advised Pearson Broadband on the establishment of a Pearson educational project. "*Important corporate players,*" the team continues in its role as primary advisor to significant e-commerce businesses, Tesco.com and FT.com. Media deals have included work for MCPS-PRS on the development of online management of music rights and royalties. E-government projects have been undertaken for several London boroughs. Quentin Solt specialises in the growing area of corporate finance advice to technology businesses and their funders. **Clients** GUS; Le Méridien Hotels; Learn.co.uk; Experian; Guardian Unlimited.

HARBOTTLE & LEWIS (see firm details p.983) Peers point to "*a smaller outfit, which has embraced the electronic era.*" The team has advised Chrysalis on its joint venture with 365 Corporation, merging the respective internet sports businesses to form Rivals Digital Media. The team also acts for Rivals, advising it on strategy and development. **Mark Phillips** (see p.281) is best known for his work on computer games. On the corporate side, the team has advised Talkcast on the disposal of its wireless marketing applications business to Xtempus. The team represented International Sportsworld Communicators on hosting agreements for the World Rally Championship web site. **Clients** Digital News Network; Amazon.com; First Property Online; Freshwater; MSN.

OSBORNE CLARKE (see firm details p.1090) The firm is a recognised force within the corporate sector of technology. The team advised Citibank in negotiations with Consignia to assist in the overhaul of its benefits payment operation. The opening of an office in Silicon Valley, California has provided an advantage to the team in the acquisition of important technology clients. The practice is headed by **Simon Rendell**, a prime choice for referrals claimed his peers. He has led the team in its work for Stepstone, advising it on pan-European commercial, litigation and restructuring issues. **James Mullock** has demonstrated his commitment to data protection work, in his authorship of a guide to the Data Protection Act. **Clients** Yahoo!; Barclays Bank; Brokat; Vodafone; KPMG.

ASHURST MORRIS CRISP (see firm details p.852) A cross-departmental team, whose strength is felt to lie in its capacity for substantial deals. Online clients include Bush Internet on its procurement of internet portal services from ITV Active. Offline companies include many insurance bodies, the representation of which is a niche strength of the team. One such client is Royal & SunAlliance, which the team advised on the development of an employee benefits web-based platform, including competition and data protection advice. The team, led by Mark Lubbock, has been active in the finance arena, appointed by various investment banks including Nomura, on investments in e-commerce companies. **Clients** AltaVista; Virgin.net; Chase Capital Partners; Thus; United News & Media.

BRISTOWS (see firm details p.888) Although some commentators felt that the firm's profile lies in IP, the e-commerce team actually forms a part of the IT team, with substantial crossover between the two sectors. This technologically adept team, led by Rachel Burnett, has advised Finsoft on software development and joint venture agreements in relation to online betting.

www.ChambersandPartners.com

277

E-COMMERCE ■ LONDON/THE REGIONS

One forte lies in its representation of e-commerce suppliers, such as netdecisions, advising it on hosting terms for the establishment of a new hosting business. **Clients** BIW Technologies; Guinness; British Airways; The Future Network; Institution of Electrical Engineers.

BROBECK HALE AND DORR (see firm details p.888) Interviewees perceived this firm to be one of the harder hit by the US technology downturn. Nevertheless, clients praise the team's M&A and corporate skills. Led by corporate expert **Chris Grew** (see p.280), it acted for Flutter.com in its merger with Betfair to form one of the UK's largest online betting operations, with an annual trading volume in excess of £500 million. On the finance side, the team aided Atriax, the electronic marketplace for foreign exchange products, which commenced trading in June 2001. The technology-focused teams represent a broad range of clients, from venture capitalists to public authorities. **Clients** Cisco Systems; Ask Jeeves; BuildOnline; WeightWatchers.com; Danske Venture Partners.

HERBERT SMITH (see firm details p.992) With a flair for the corporate and competition elements of e-commerce work, the team represents a broad spectrum of clients from blue-chip entities to the public sector. "*Excellent for client care,*" **Mark Turner** (see p.439) has advised internet share-dealing company SELFtrade UK on the launch of new services on the internet. In true Herbert Smith style, the contentious side of the practice is flourishing, acting for Capital One bank in its dispute with DMR Consulting regarding the provision of online credit card application and credit card-related software. **Chris Rees** (see p.438) is noted for his expertise within the crossover between IT and e-commerce. **Clients** Critical Path; Enterprise Oil; ICANN; BAA; Fox International.com.

LINKLATERS (see firm details p.1043) The arrival of "*e-commerce figurehead*" **Chris Millard** (see p.280) has caused ripples throughout the market, anticipating that the team will increase in profile over the coming year. The past year's work has included instructions from established businesses, in particular banks, expanding their e-business capability. The multi-jurisdictional team advised the joint venture Merrill Lynch HSBC on infrastructure and regulatory requirements for setting up an internet bank that was launched in May 2001. On the commercial side, Tiscali UK has been advised on a variety of e-commerce matters, including the acquisition of a number of ISPs. **Clients** JPMorgan; CSFB; Vizzavi; Dresdner Kleinwort Benson; Centrica.

LOVELLS (see firm details p.1045) A corporate-based team, its niche lies within advice to banks regarding online financial products. A highlight for the team has been the establishment of a web-based trading platform for Standard Chartered Bank. This deal has included advice in various jurisdictions on agreements concerning hyperlinking, framing, content provision and co-branding. The team has also advised UMBRO.COM and Sportsio on its acquisition of online sports business, One Sport. **Clients** Barclays Bank; Standard Chartered Bank; Fidelity Investments; Swiss Reinsurance Company; John Lewis.

SJ BERWIN (see firm details p.867) This cross-departmental team has particular expertise in the competition side of e-commerce. Tom Usher has led the team in assisting the International Federation of the Phonographic Industry to create a global licensing structure to facilitate internet delivery of music by simulating and web casting. Contentious and online gambling matters have comprised work for William Hill in its appeal to the ECJ regarding the online database infringement ruling with the British Horseracing Board. **Clients** Hilton; mmO2; ukbetting; Ticketmaster; Coca-Cola.

TARLO LYONS (see firm details p.1155) The team, led by Simon Stokes, has provided cross-border data protection advice to a major electronics company regarding a global e-HR portal and database. On the financial side, the team has advised Atriax on technology and e-commerce aspects of its foreign exchange dealing platform. **Clients** GE Global eXchange Services; SWIFT SCRL; ATSCo; Standard Chartered Bank; BACTA.

THE SIMKINS PARTNERSHIP (see firm details p.1136) Spanning a range of new media work, the focus here is on media clients. The team advised Sony UK on the establishment, development and transfer of a major music portal. Clients outside the scope of media included EPIC, the licensing body for the vast GPRD medical database, widely used by pharmaceutical companies and academic research units. EPIC has been advised on the collection and compilation of anonymous patient data extracted from GP practices for its online database. **Clients** WAP Forum; NewsNow; Mobile Music Forum; AMI; Omnicom Media Division.

THEODORE GODDARD (see firm details p.1158) A cross-departmental group, it is geared towards its media client base. A highlight for the team has been acting for Universal Music following its acquisition of MP3.com; UK and European regulatory and contractual issues were thrown up, such as online music licensing and data protection. Paul Renney is a key member of the team. It also advised the Daily Mail General Trust on its acquisition of the online part of Loot from Scoot UK. **Clients** British Horseracing Board; EMI/Zomba; Easyspace; Leisure Link; News Group Newspapers.

OTHER NOTABLE PRACTITIONERS Liam McNeive (see p.280) of McNeive Solicitors has been described as "*a pure e-commerce lawyer; he has incredible clients and knows the market inside out.*" However, the firm has not yet achieved the profile of the "*expert*" himself. "*Top e-commerce*" lawyer, **KLegal**'s **Mark Haftke** (see p.280) was recommended to our researchers, while **Rafi Azim-Khan** (see p.279) of **McDermott, Will & Emery** has developed expertise across e-commerce and advertising-related matters. Now a sole practitioner following the break up of Garretts, **Laurence Kaye** (see p.280) continues to be active in the field of e-publishing.

THE REGIONS

OSBORNE CLARKE (see firm details p.1090) "*A commercial team, which immediately grasps the key issues,*" claimed clients. The firm is respected for its national reach. The Bristol team has acted for Bristol & West on its online mortgage services and IT infrastructure. **Ashley Winton** remains the prominent practitioner in the Reading office, receiving recommendations from City practitioners. The Reading team has received instructions from various large purchasers of e-commerce technology, working on innovative deals such as barbox, the b2b drinks portal and electronic marketplace owned by Bass Brewers. Another key sector has been the mature e-commerce infrastructure providers, such as Clarus, for which the team has negotiated an online trading exchange solution with Barclays. **Clients** Lloyds TSB; Stepstone; Sift; Amazon.com; Kompass International.

ADDLESHAW BOOTH & CO (see firm details p.838) Pushing for the top spot, the team has been lauded by clients as "*supportive business partners, providing superb strategic advice.*" Members of the technology team devote part of their time to e-commerce work, giving the team its breadth of expertise. Innovative deals have been undertaken, such as e-commerce contracts relating to financial services for @Charcol, which will sell FS products online. Led by Paul

THE REGIONS/THE LEADERS ■ E-COMMERCE

E-COMMERCE
■ THE REGIONS

1
- Osborne Clarke Reading

2
- Addleshaw Booth & Co Manchester
- Halliwell Landau Manchester
- McGrigor Donald Edinburgh
- Nabarro Nathanson Reading
- Shepherd+ Wedderburn Edinburgh
- Wragge & Co Birmingham

3
- Maclay Murray & Spens Edinburgh
- Masons Edinburgh, Glasgow
- The Law Offices of Marcus J O'Leary Wokingham

LEADING INDIVIDUALS

1
- BAILES Tony Nabarro Nathanson
- BOAG-THOMSON Joanna Shepherd+ Wedderburn
- O'LEARY Marcus The Law Offices of Marcus J O'Leary
- SALMON John Masons
- WINTON Ashley Osborne Clarke

This book is the product of 6,582 1/2 hour interviews. See p.7 for BMRB audit. Within each band, firms are listed alphabetically. See individuals' profiles p.279

Bentham, the team has also been advising Guardian Media Group on content for the Sportloco web site. **Clients** Airtours; Argos; Britannia Building Society; 3i; Advance Mortgage Funding.

HALLIWELL LANDAU (see firm details p.982) A commercial team, it is situated within the firm's IT department. The team features Craig Chaplin, who worked on a web site development agreement for Eunite in its design of an online gambling site for a major UK company. Financial work has been prominent, acting for Legal & General on a b2c web-based application for IFAs to sell products to consumers. **Clients** Chamber of Business Enterprises; NettGain Solutions; JD Williams; Live Information Systems.

MCGRIGOR DONALD (see firm details p.1065) Highly regarded by the market for its focus within the sector, the team moves up the tables. One competitor commented: "*It is good to see them on the other side; they know how to get deals done.*" One of the strongest corporate offerings in Scotland, it is no surprise to see the firm advising on joint ventures, content acquisitions or advertising contracts. Strength also lies in contentious disputes.

NABARRO NATHANSON (see firm details p.1080) A key player in Reading, the firm's reputation for corporate e-commerce deals is manifested by the activities of high-profile **Tony Bailes** (see p.279). The arrival of Jeremy Newton from Sun Microsystems to head the non-contentious e-commerce practice has been a boost to the team. This industry-focused team has advised London Scottish Bank on the e-commerce aspects of the online credit card, Accucard. Nikon has been advised on the establishment of its online FotoShare service, and on the roll-out of the product across Europe. **Clients** Oracle; Met Office; British Land; Direct Wines; Coats.

SHEPHERD+ WEDDERBURN (see firm details p.1130) This active firm was singled out by interviewees for its public sector expertise. Glasgow-based **Joanna Boag-Thomson** (see p.434) is recommended by clients for her attention to detail. She led the team on its representation of Scottish University for Industry, negotiating the contracts for its online learning facilities. In a complex project involving new areas of law, the team advised Thus in its appointment as registration authority for Origo Secure Internet Services. This was for a closed community PKI project for the financial services industry. **Clients** Cap Gemini Ernst & Young; Friends Ivory Sime; Scottish Enterprise; Scottish & Newcastle; Scottish Parliamentary Corporate Body.

WRAGGE & CO (see firm details p.1197) "*A big player in the market,*" it is noted for its blue-chip client base. The team's focus lies mainly within the offline market. Bill Jones and the team are advising British Airways on e-commerce joint ventures and portals for business customers. Another highlight has been the representation of Ernst & Young on an e-procurement project with the MOD, allowing it to acquire supplies online. The financial sector has been a source of growth, advising financial services companies on their web sites becoming interactive. **Clients** Britannic Assurance; London Borough of Croydon; BTopenworld; Bulmers; William Hill.

MACLAY MURRAY & SPENS (see firm details p.1048) This IP and technology department is engaged in some high-profile e-commerce work. Led by Fiona Nicholson in Glasgow, the team has been active on contentious instructions, dealing with a number of cybersquatting cases. Mediation work has included the representation of a Singaporean company in dispute with a Scottish web site design company. The team advises the 'e-development engine' joint venture from Sun, Cisco, Oracle and the Royal Bank of Scotland, which is aimed at established business and promotes use of internet technologies. **Clients** EasyGroup; Clipserver.com; PCB Systems.

MASONS (see firm details p.1057) Following acclaim by clients as "*the best for depth of expertise and understanding of the marketplace,*" the practice is newly ranked this year. The team resides within the IT department, and is led by **John Salmon** (see p.281). It advised online learning business, The Mindwarp Pavilion, on securing private equity funding and data protection issues. The team acts for suppliers of e-commerce solutions such as Realise, for which the team provided advice on contracts with a number of financial organisations including Schroders. **Clients** The Mindwarp Pavilion; software providers; financial services companies.

THE LAW OFFICES OF MARCUS J O'LEARY (see firm details p.1030) "*A niche practice,*" it boasts the presence of "*technology whiz*" **Marcus O'Leary** (see p.437). A joint IT and e-commerce team undertakes work for companies specialising in these areas. These range from industry bodies to multinational corporations. **Clients** Leading national and international clients.

THE LEADERS IN E-COMMERCE

AZIM-KHAN, Rafi
McDermott, Will & Emery, London
(020) 7577 3468
razimkhan@europe.mwe.com
Specialisation: Partner heading McDermott, Will & Emery's e-business and marketing groups in Europe and a member of the firm's international e-business group. Specialises in advertising/marketing, entertainment, intellectual property, internet/e-commerce and commercial law. Has considerable experience of advising media, marketing and leading corporate clients on wide range of advertising, sales promotions, sponsorships (eg France '98 World Cup), lotteries, newspaper and television promotions (eg UK's first £1 million prize promotions on TFI Friday and Virgin Radio); protection of intellectual property and on all aspects of e-commerce, including, full 'e-audits' of sites, e-enablement projects and B2B/B2C operations for multi-nationals, major ISPs, B2B exchanges. Experience also of data protection, distance selling, Pan-EU online contracting, PKI, digital TV and interactive media, net shopping, gaming and portals. Lectures regularly and is co-author of 'e-Commerce from Cradle to Grave'; 'A Practitioner's Guide to Regulation of the Internet'; and PLC's 'International Sales and Marketing Practice Manual'. Rafi is the firm's representative to the Advertising Law Group and the e-Commerce Law Group.
Career: Qualified 1993. Previously at Lewis Silkin 1993-95, Cameron McKenna 1995-97, Theodore Goddard 1997-2000.
Personal: Educated at Cranbrook College, Queen Mary College, University of London (LLB Hons), and College of Law, Chancery Lane (LSF). Keen sportsman and enjoys travel, music and motor racing. Resides London.

BAILES, Tony
Nabarro Nathanson, Reading
(0118) 925 4602
a.bailes@nabarro.com
Specialisation: Partner and Head of Technology, Media and Telecommunications Group. Sole area of practice is in IT and e-commerce disputes of all types, acting for a wide range of major US and European owned multinational computer and communication companies, including Sun Microsystems and Siemens. Jointly led the team acting for the major complainant in the landmark Digital case before the EC Commission. Acted with a fast growing specialist team in relation to over 30 substantial high-value disputes arising from systems inte-

279

E-COMMERCE ■ THE LEADERS

gration and software development contracts, outsourcing contracts and PFI based projects.
Personal: Born 15 May 1951. Married with four children. Lives in Oxford.

BOAG-THOMSON, Joanna
Shepherd+ Wedderburn, Glasgow
(0141) 566 8570
joanna.bt@shepwedd.co.uk
See under Information Technology, p.434

CALOW, Duncan
Denton Wilde Sapte, London
(020) 7320 3794
dcc@dentonwildesapte.com
Specialisation: Senior solicitor specialising in publishing and digital media work. Advises content owner, producer and distributor clients on a wide range of projects including Internet, on-line and e-commerce services; print, CD-Rom, DVD and video games publishing; broadband, interactive television and mobile services.
Prof. Memberships: International Association of Entertainment Lawyers and Publishers Association Legal Committee.
Publications: Written and spoken widely on the legal issues of digital media including contributions to specialist and legal press, national newspapers, radio and television. Contributor (with Alan Williams) to 'Halsburys Laws on Internet Publishing', (Butterworths, 1999); author (with Alan Williams and Nicholas Higham) of 'Digital Media: Contracts, Rights and Licensing', (2nd edn, Sweet & Maxwell, 1998).

CHISSICK, Michael
Field Fisher Waterhouse, London
(020) 7861 4000
mpc@ffwlaw.com
Specialisation: Head of IT and e-commerce law group which comprises a team of seven partners and 18 specialist lawyers. Main areas of practice include outsourcing projects, IT programming, data protection, digital mixed media, electronic commerce and m-commerce contracts.
Prof. Memberships: Law Society; Solicitors European Group; FAST Legal Advisory Group; Computer Law Association.
Career: 1st Class Degree in Law (LLB); Law Society Finals 1st Class; Masters Degree in IT and Telecommunications.
Publications: Author of 'Internet Law' published in October 1997 by FT Publications and co-author of 'Electronic Commerce Law and Practice' published in 1999, 2000 and 2001 by Sweet & Maxwell.

COWAN, Matthew
Olswang, London
(020) 7208 8888
mac@olswang.com
Specialisation: Corporate and commercial work in the technology and telecommunications fields. Acted on the establishment of Worldpop.com and flotation of Netstore plc. Practice includes venture capital funding (acting for both companies and investors), joint ventures, acquisitions and commercial arrangements for clients operating in the technology and telecommunications sectors.
Career: Joined *Olswang* in 1993 upon qualification and became a partner in 1999. Attended Bristol Grammar School 1979-86, then Exeter University 1986-90.
Personal: Born 31 March 1967. Lives in Surrey.

DOWNING, Robbie
Baker & McKenzie, London
(020) 7919 1000
robbie.downing@bakernet.com
Specialisation: Partner specialising in IT and telecoms with a particular focus on e-commerce and anti-trust. Key clients include agency.com, Bolero Association, Cisco Systems, COLT, espotting.com, Global Freight Exchange and ntl.
Prof. Memberships: Society of Computers & Law; Computer Law Association.
Career: Articled *Baker & McKenzie*; qualified 1988; Associate 1988-90; Legal Advisor IBM (UK) Limited 1990-92; lecturer in law King's College, London 1992-95; *Baker & McKenzie*, London 1995; Partner 1998 to date.
Publications: 'EC Information Technology Law' (John Wiley 1995); edited 'Baker & McKenzie Guide to IP in the IT Industry' (Sweet & Maxwell 1998); UK section of 'Doing E-Commerce in Europe' (Baker & McKenzie 2001); editor of monthly e-commerce alerts in 'plc' magazine.
Personal: King Edwards VI School, Birmingham; Exeter College, Oxford (1984 BA Jurisprudence [1st Class] Martin Wronker Prize); Law Society Finals (1985); Université Libre de Bruxelles (1986 Licence Spéciale en Droit Européen; la plus grande distinction).

ENSER, John
Olswang, London
(020) 7208 8716
jxe@olswang.com
Specialisation: Principal area of practice: commercial and regulatory advice for Internet, interactive TV, television and music industries. Specialises in all aspects of digital media solutions in business-to-business and consumer markets. Clients include ISPs, leading websites, broadcasters, digital TV platform operators, internet technology providers, major film and record companies, retailers and insurers.
Prof. Memberships: ICC.
Career: Qualified: 1989. *Frere Cholmeley* 1987-94 (Brussels 1993-94). *Olswang* 1994 to date. Partner since 1996. School: Queen Elizabeth's Hospital, Bristol 1975-82. Pembroke College, Oxford 1982-85.
Personal: Born 21 October 1964. Married (one son). Lives in London.

GREW, Chris
Brobeck Hale and Dorr, London
(020) 7645 2400
grew@bhd.com
Specialisation: Principally advises technology companies on venture capital investments, US securities law issues (particularly initial public offerings for non-US companies on Nasdaq and the European new markets), cross-border mergers and acquisitions and general corporate transactions. Advises a wide range of high technology (particularly software and Internet) companies as well as the investment banks, venture capitalists and other financial intermediaries that serve technology companies. Selected as a Top Deal Maker by the 'Wall Street Journal European Edition'. Also named as one of The Digital Dozen - Top Individual Lawyers by 'The Insider's Guide to Legal Services - Digital Media & E-commerce'.
Prof. Memberships: Registered foreign lawyer; Bar of England and Wales (Honourable Society of Middle Temple); American Bar Association; New York State Bar Association.
Career: Partner, registered foreign lawyer, *BHD*, 1997 to present; associate *BHD* 1992-97; associate *Hughes Hubbard & Reed*, 1989-92; barrister, Chambers of Michael West QC (Gray's Inn), 1987-88.

GRIFFITHS, David
Clifford Chance, London
(020) 7600 1000
See under Information Technology, p.435

HAFTKE, Mark
KLegal, London
(020) 7694 2500
mark.haftke@klegal.co.uk
Specialisation: Head of e-business and Digital Media Group. Recent work includes representation of MM02, Sony Music Europe, The Daily Telegraph, Vitaminic, and Global Interactive Gaming.
Prof. Memberships: International Association of Entertainment Lawyers; Society for Computers and Law, Computer Law Association, BLACA, Law Society of England and Wales.
Career: Qualified as Barrister at law 1886; re-qualified as Solicitor 1990. Joined *Russells* 1988; Partner at *Russells* 1992; joined *Bird & Bird* 1995; Partner 1997; Joined *Klegal* as Partner 2000.
Publications: Contributing author to 'Copyright and Design Law'; co-author and consultant editor of 'Practitioner's Guide to regulation of the Internet'.

KAYE, Laurence
Laurence Kaye, Radlett
(07768) 190159
Specialisation: Digital media law, publishing and privacy. Clients range from multinationals to start-ups. Committed to providing creative and cost-effective solutions to clients. Wide ranging experience in handling contracts, joint ventures and transactions in the media, information and online industries. Represents a number of industry bodies, including European Publishers Council, on copyright and e-commerce legal issues. He advised the UK publishing industries on the implementation of the EU directive for the Legal Protection of Databases into UK law.
Prof. Memberships: Law Society, Society for Computers & the Law.
Career: Qualified in 1975. *Brecher & Co* 1975-80. Partner, *Saunders Sobell Leigh & Dobin*, 1980-1994. Partner, Head of New Media, *The Simkins Partnership*, 1994-1998. Partner, *Paisner & Co*, 1998-2000. Partner, Head of Technology, Media and Communications, *Garretts*, 2000-2002.

KEMP, Richard
Kemp Little LLP, London
(020) 7710 1610
See under Information Technology, p.436

MCNEIVE, Liam
McNeive Solicitors, London
(020) 7253 0536
liam@mcneive.com
Specialisation: *McNeive Solicitors* was established in 1998 to provide a cost-effective, informal and responsive service to businesses operating in the media, communications and technology sectors. While the firm is widely recognised for its expertise in addressing myriad e-commerce law issues, it also has discrete specialisms in information technology and telecommunications law, copyright and publishing (books; music; video; multimedia), computer games, fashion goods, betting, gaming, lotteries and auctions. The firm continues to act for a wide variety of clients including Happy Group (providers of FriendsReunited), AOL UK and AOL Europe, QXL Ricardo plc, The National Trust and Good Technology. By maintaining low overheads, and a pragmatic focus on the commercial realities surrounding each piece of work performed, the firm provides a service which is appropriate to the needs of its clients, whether small, medium or large.

MILLARD, Christopher
Linklaters, London
(020) 7456 2676
christopher.millard@linklaters.com
Specialisation: Head of ITC Practice.
Career: Manchester Grammar School; University of Sheffield (LLB Hons 1980); University of Toronto (MA 1982, LLM 1983). Partner *Clifford Chance* since 1992; partner *Linklaters* 2002.

MULLOCK, James
Osborne Clarke, London
(020) 7809 1000

NICHOLSON, Kim
Olswang, London
(020) 7208 8731
See under Information Technology, p.437

O'LEARY, Marcus
The Law Offices of Marcus J. O'Leary, Wokingham
(0118) 989 7110
See under Information Technology, p.437

THE LEADERS ■ E-COMMERCE

PHILLIPS, Mark
Harbottle & Lewis, London
(020) 7667 5000
mark.phillips@harbottle.com
Specialisation: Partner and head of both the Interactive and New Media Group and the Publishing Group specialising in commercial and corporate work for media, leisure and arts industries.
Prof. Memberships: Law Society, Society for Computers and Law.
Career: Qualified in 1986. Worked at *Clifford Chance* 1984-88. Joined *Harbottle & Lewis* in 1988, became a partner in 1990.
Personal: Born 1961. Attended Manchester Grammar School 1972-78, University College, London 1979-82. Trustee of Performing Arts Lab and School Governor.

REES, Chris
Herbert Smith, London
(020) 7374 8000
christopher.rees@herbertsmith.com
See under Information Technology, p.438

RENDELL, Simon
Osborne Clarke, London
(020) 7809 1000

SALMON, John
Masons, Glasgow
(0141) 248 4858
john.salmon@masons.com
Specialisation: Partner and Head of IT in Scotland and Ireland specialising in providing non-contentious IT and e-commerce advice to new economy and traditional businesses throughout the UK and Europe. Particular experience in dealing with e-commerce, new media suppliers and developers and online financial services companies. He was a founding partners of *Masons*' new media and e-commerce service OUT-LAW.COM.
Prof. Memberships: Law Society of Scotland, Scotland IS and Society for Computers and Law.
Career: Attended Edinburgh University 1987-91 LLB Hons and Strathclyde University 1991-92 DipLP. Formerly IT programmer/consultant. *Bird Semple* 1995-99. Joined *Masons* as Partner in 1999, establishing the firm's Information Technology Practice in Scotland.
Personal: Resides Glasgow. Leisure interests include hockey and running.

SANDELSON, Daniel
Clifford Chance, London
(020) 7006 8237
daniel.sandelson@cliffordchance.com
See under Media & Entertainment, p.591

SMALL, Harry
Baker & McKenzie, London
(020) 7919 1000
harry.small@bakernet.com
See under Information Technology, p.438

SMITH, Graham
Bird & Bird, London
(020) 7415 6000
graham.smith@twobirds.com
Specialisation: Computer project disputes, commercial litigation in computer and telecommunications industries. Evidence, document imaging and computer records. Internet law including domain name disputes, website advice, internet/e-mail use policies and regulatory issues. Intellectual property disputes. Gave evidence to the House of Lords Science and Technology Select Committee on Digital Images as Evidence. Advised Guernsey on its electronic transaction legislation.
Prof. Memberships: American Intellectual Property Law Association; Computer Law Association; eCentre Legal Advisory Group; Fellow of the Society for Advanced Legal Studies.
Career: Qualified 1978. Joined *Bird & Bird* 1983. Partner 1985.
Publications: Contributes a section on Non-Contractual Liability to the looseleaf 'Encyclopaedia of Information Technology Law' (Sweet & Maxwell). Editor and a co-author of the book 'Internet Law and Regulation' (Sweet & Maxwell, 3rd edition January 2002). Speaks and writes regularly in the UK and abroad mainly on IT and internet legal issues.
Personal: Born 1953. Educated Bristol University (LLB, 1975). Lives London.

TURNER, Mark
Herbert Smith, London
(020) 7374 8000
mark.turner@herbertsmith.com
See under Information Technology, p.439

WILLIAMS, Alan
Denton Wilde Sapte, London
(020) 7320 6249
apw@dentonwildesapte.com
See under Media & Entertainment, p.592

WINTON, Ashley
Osborne Clarke, Reading
(0118) 925 2000

EDUCATION

London: 282; The Regions: 283; Scotland: 287; Profiles: 288

Research approved by BMRB For this edition, Chambers' researchers conducted 6,582 interviews – 3,900 with law firms, 511 with barristers and 2,171 with clients. The validity of the research was scrutinised by BMRB International, who audited both the methodology and the results at our offices in London. They interviewed Chambers' researchers and cross-checked sample interviews. Details of the audit appear on page 7.

OVERVIEW The practice of education law has snowballed in recent years. Educational negligence litigation has increased dramatically with parents challenging admission procedures and adult dyslexics suing their former schools for failure to recognise or support their needs. Many firms now specialise in niche areas of 'pure' education law such as autism, dyslexia, bullying and exclusions, as opposed to the commercial contracting that once constituted the bulk of the market. With the government's policy of mainstream inclusion, special educational needs issues have come to the fore, especially since new anti-discrimination laws took effect in September 2002. On the commercial side, HE institutions are increasingly taking intellectual property advice on how to exploit research by starting 'spin-out' companies.

LONDON

EDUCATION: INSTITUTIONS
LONDON

1. Eversheds
2. Beachcroft Wansbroughs
3. Lee Bolton & Lee
   Winckworth Sherwood
4. Farrer & Co
   Lawfords
   Reynolds Porter Chamberlain
5. Berrymans Lace Mawer

LEADING INDIVIDUALS

* **HALL John** Eversheds
1. **GIZZI Julian** Beachcroft Wansbroughs
2. **BEESLEY Peter** Lee Bolton & Lee
   CAREW-JONES Owen Winckworth Sherwood
   MCCREATH Rob Eversheds
   THATCHER Michael Winckworth Sherwood
3. **CAPSTICK Charlotte** Berrymans Lace Mawer

This book is the product of 6,582 1/2 hour interviews. See p.7 for BMRB audit. Within each band, firms are listed alphabetically. See individuals' profiles p.288

EVERSHEDS (see firm details p.949) A national team with local delivery, Eversheds remains without doubt the most respected education practice both nationally and within the capital. The firm advises HE and FE institutions, plus some schools, on the spectrum of education law from governance, student issues and policy-making to IP spin-outs, commercial contracts and mergers. **John Hall** (see p.289), the London-based national education chairman, is the most esteemed name on the institutions side. "*Wonderfully pleasant*" with "*an exceptional brain*," he "*knows education inside out*" and is admired by clients and competitors alike. **Rob McCreath** (see p.289), who heads a team working for universities, colleges and national charities, also impresses as "*efficient and conscientious*." **Clients** University of Oxford; Universities UK; The Community College Hackney.

BEACHCROFT WANSBROUGHS (see firm details p.860) Advising HE institutions and high-profile national education bodies, this enormously respected firm has a strong reputation for traditional education work. Head of department **Julian Gizzi** (see p.288) attracts unanimous respect from interviewees for his ability and focus. Recent work for the team has included advising the Qualifications and Curriculum Authority (QCA) regarding the alleged failures of Edexcel. **Clients** University of Cambridge; Jesus College, Oxford; QCA.

LEE BOLTON & LEE (see firm details p.1034) Noted by interviewees for its "*unrivalled*" experience of working for ecclesiastical schools, the firm's admirers point to its traditional atmosphere and long experience. Skilled in a broad range of education law, the team is praised by peers for its professional and solid approach. "*Jolly*" head of department **Peter Beesley** (see p.288) is described as "*a consummate professional who knows his stuff.*" **Clients** Ecclesiastical schools.

WINCKWORTH SHERWOOD (see firm details p.1192) The firm is best known for its religious education work. It has recently been visible at judicial reviews and in the House of Lords representing Catholic and foundation schools on reinstatements following exclusions. It also acts for religious educational charities, HE and FE institutions and non-religious clients on everything from PFI, employment and property to negligence claims. The team was said by interviewees to offer "*an omnibus, cradle-to-grave service with a lot of emphasis on client care.*" Head of department **Michael Thatcher** (see p.290) is considered "*a delightful chap,*" while "*excellent*" **Owen Carew-Jones** (see p.288) follows fast in his footsteps. **Clients** St Mary's College; London and Southwark Diocesan Boards of Education.

FARRER & CO (see firm details p.952) The firm's work has snowballed this year and it rises in our tables as its level of market recognition has grown. Best known for representing high-profile private schools, it also acts for HE institutions and education bodies. Clients praise the team for knowing "*all the ins and outs of litigation and advisory work,*" and offering a dedicated service on everything from constitutional reorganisation, employment and mergers to discrimination claims and special educational needs. Highly respected Henry Boyd-Carpenter has retired and is replaced as head of department by David Smellie. **Clients** Eton College; Westminster School; St Paul's Girls' School.

FIRMS ACTING FOR INSTITUTIONS

LAWFORDS The firm represents both institutions and individuals, but is best known for its work for HE and FE clients. The team, led by Clive Robertson, oversees work ranging from the merger of the Universities of North London and London Guildhall, to dealing with student complaints about courses and discrimination. It has recently been involved in reviewing FE institutions' admission procedures. Its "*personal approach*" is popular with clients. **Clients** London Guildhall University; University of North London; FE colleges.

REYNOLDS PORTER CHAMBERLAIN (see firm details p.1111) Best known for its work for education unions and bodies, the highly regarded team, led by Geraldine Elliott, also acts for schools, FE colleges and local education authorities. Recent work has included representing teachers in a high-profile pensions case, advising school heads on fatalities on school trips and assisting the Learning and Skills Council in the establishment of a new sixth-form college. **Clients** ATL; NASUWT; Amersham and Wycombe College.

BERRYMANS LACE MAWER (see firm details p.865) This department, led by "*pragmatic and robust*" **Charlotte Capstick**, has been recommended both for its expertise in advising educational institutions on insurance matters, and for an approach to litigation which is described by clients as "*extremely solid, sensible and supportive.*" **Clients** Schools; HE institutions.

LONDON/THE SOUTH & SOUTH WEST ■ EDUCATION

LONDON

EDUCATION: INDIVIDUALS
■ LONDON

1
- Levenes
- Teacher Stern Selby

2
- Ashok Patel & Co
- Fisher Meredith

3
- Coningsbys Croydon
- Gills Southall

4
- John Ford Solicitors

LEADING INDIVIDUALS

1
- RABINOWICZ Jack *Teacher Stern Selby*
- RUEBAIN David *Levenes*

2
- CONRATHE Paul *Coningsbys*
- PATEL Anjan *Ashok Patel & Co*
- WILKINS Patricia *Fisher Meredith*

3
- FORD John *John Ford Solicitors*
- GILL Jaswinder *Gills*
- SILAS Douglas *Alexander Harris*

UP AND COMING
- JACKMAN Angela *Fisher Meredith*

This book is the product of 6,582 1/2 hour interviews. See p.7 for BMRB audit.
Within each band, firms are listed alphabetically. See individuals' profiles p.288

LEVENES (see firm details p.1040) Levenes has soared to the top this year, with **David Ruebain** (see p.290) considered practically a household name among solicitors in the field. Described by researchers as "*one of the best solicitors by a long way*" in education, he "*knows it backwards.*" The team specialises in special educational needs, with "*clever, methodical*" Ruebain a "*protagonist for those with disabilities.*" Recently the firm has represented IPSEA challenging the guidance given to schools on special educational needs. It also offers training and consultancy on the changes to disability discrimination law.

TEACHER STERN SELBY (see firm details p.1157) "*The godfather of education,*" **Jack Rabinowicz** (see p.290), has long been renowned as one of the top education lawyers in the country, and is still rated as such by competitors. He is "*a major league brain-box*" who is both "*very approachable*" and "*a tenacious lawyer for the individuals.*" The firm's recent high-profile cases have focused on exclusions and bullying outside the school gates, and the team also has a good reputation in special educational needs work.

ASHOK PATEL & CO This "*aggressive*" firm has a reputation for taking risks and shaking things up, and is popular with clients, one of whom describes its lawyers as "*wonderful – they were the only ones to deal with my case properly.*" The education team, headed by the "*dynamic and persistent*" **Anjan Patel**, fights tooth and nail for its clients and was described by peers as "*developing quite a practice in exclusions*" – notably acting in the Alperton School case – as well as handling racial discrimination and special educational needs claims.

FISHER MEREDITH (see firm details p.956) The education team's main clients are young people with disabilities or special educational needs. Handling a large number of exclusion and discrimination cases and running training courses on education law, the firm was described by peers as "*committed to its clients*" and "*politically aware.*" "*Sensible*" head of department **Patricia Wilkins** (see p.290), who chairs the Education Law Practitioners' Group, continues to be well respected, while **Angela Jackman** (see p.289) is gaining an "*outstanding*" reputation as "*clear, direct and focused.*"

FIRMS ACTING FOR INDIVIDUALS

CONINGSBYS (see firm details p.918) This "*efficient*" team specialises in advising autistic children and has a good name across the field of special educational needs work. Team leader **Paul Conrathe** (see p.413) was described by peers as a "*big player.*" He does tribunal work and lectures, as well as being substantially involved in human rights related work in the High Court.

GILLS (see firm details p.972) The firm, which specialises in education law, is well known for representing students in disputes with college and university authorities. Praised for its commitment and expertise, it recently won a landmark case suing a college for issuing worthless qualifications. **Jaswinder Gill** (see p.288) continues to be highly regarded.

JOHN FORD SOLICITORS A "*sensible*" team that is "*very familiar with the framework*" of education law. **John Ford** is recommended by market commentators as having "*a keen mind for public law issues.*" The firm covers a range of cases including special educational needs, exclusions and admissions, and educational negligence.

OTHER NOTABLE PRACTITIONERS **Douglas Silas** (see p.290) has moved from Levenes to Alexander Harris this year, where he is setting up an education and public law department. Rated by the foremost practitioners in education as "*a bright young man*" and one to watch, his specialism is in representing deaf children, although he also handles other special educational needs and acts for schools contesting local education authorities.

THE SOUTH & SOUTH WEST

EDUCATION: INSTITUTIONS
■ THE SOUTH & SOUTH WEST

1
- Stone King Bath
- Veale Wasbrough Bristol

2
- Rickerbys Cheltenham

3
- Bevan Ashford Bristol
- Bond Pearce Plymouth, Southampton

4
- Beachcroft Wansbroughs Bristol
- DMH Brighton
- Michelmores Exeter
- Thomas Eggar Chichester

5
- Osborne Clarke Bristol
- Steele Raymond Bournemouth
- Tozers Exeter

This book is the product of 6,582 1/2 hour interviews. See p.7 for BMRB audit.
Within each band, firms are listed alphabetically.

STONE KING (see firm details p.1151) This "*highly reputable*" firm also operates from London, but it is to the Bath branch that it owes its massive reputation. It covers a broad range of education law including PFI, property, relocations, employment, governance, admissions and exclusions, and transfers of trusteeship. Most visible representing schools, especially Catholic schools, it also acts for FE colleges and individuals. Head of department **Richard Gold** (see p.289) is a leading light at a national level. Competitors describe him as "*a big hitter*" and "*a pioneer*" in the field with a real depth of knowledge. **Michael King** (see p.130), was also recommended, especially for work related to educational charities. **Clients** St John's College; Royal Grammar School; William Ellis School.

FIRMS ACTING FOR INSTITUTIONS

VEALE WASBROUGH (see firm details p.1174) With over 700, mainly independent, schools as clients and a dedicated schools team comprising 11 full-time fee-earners, this large operation works on a national scale, even advising overseas. Regarded as a "*leader*" in the field, the team's expertise includes fraud recovery, PFI, defending school closures, successful admission appeals, disputes, employment issues, defamation, setting up foundations and advising on discrimination. **Robert Boyd** (see p.288) is highly respected by peers and clients who describe him as "*charismatic*" and "*knowledgeable.*" **Clients** Rugby School, Millfield School, North London Collegiate School.

RICKERBYS (see firm details p.1113) Clients appreciate this smaller, more local firm for its

www.ChambersandPartners.com

EDUCATION ■ THE SOUTH & SOUTH WEST

LEADING INDIVIDUALS

1. **GOLD Richard** Stone King
2. **BOYD Robert** Veale Wasbrough
3. **CLARKE John** Rickerbys
   DICKINSON Malcolm Michelmores
   KING Michael Stone King

See individuals' profiles p.288

high quality of service. The team, which increasingly attracts clients on a national level, mainly advises independent schools, but also acts for some FE colleges and a local university on issues including liaisons and transitions between FE and HE institutions, employment, governance, claims and risk management. Clients praise the firm for "*always being there when you need to talk a problem through*" and having "*a really sensible approach.*" "*Friendly, responsive, humorous and professional*" John Clarke (see p.288) leads the department. **Clients** University of Gloucestershire; FE colleges; independent schools.

BEVAN ASHFORD (see firm details p.869) This well-known and acclaimed department has grown this year. It provides advice at a national level to HE and FE colleges, local authorities and educational bodies like OFSTED, on the "*heavy*" stuff: PFI (for which it has a particularly good reputation), student accommodation schemes, tax, employment, property, construction and rationalisation. This year the "*excellent and straightforward*" department, under the leadership of David Hutton, advised Falmouth College of Art on a joint venture to combine two HE institutions. **Clients** Bristol City Council; Bovis Lend Lease; Falmouth College of Arts.

BOND PEARCE (see firm details p.879) The firm offers a full range of services to universities and FE colleges across the region, advising on issues from educational negligence to IP and technology spin-offs, commercial contracts, tax, constitutional matters and employment. In Plymouth the respected department, headed by Nikki Duncan, has recently supervised the establishment of two new local medical schools. Peers regard it as "*a potential threat – up and coming*" with "*the right skills*" and a growing profile outside the South West. The Southampton branch is also esteemed, with Nick Barwood and Christina Tolvas-Vincent leading a busy practice. **Clients** University of Plymouth; University of Southampton; Cornwall College.

BEACHCROFT WANSBROUGHS (see firm details p.860) Under the leadership of Helen Staines, this "*excellent*" department has been achieving national recognition and praise. It principally handles educational negligence, bullying and harassment claims for public and state schools and universities, coming out of its strong insurance practice. **Clients** University of Bristol; Millfield School; Lincolnshire County Council.

DMH (see firm details p.940) The department, led by Martin Allen, works closely with the University of Sussex, advising principally on IP and building contracts. It has also acted recently in race relations claims made against two schools, and represented a bank in a refinancing deal for an FE college. Enjoying a sound regional reputation, clients rate its "*in-depth knowledge*" and and praise the team's "*keen interest in educational affairs – it is very much in touch with educational developments.*" **Clients** University of Sussex; London Borough of Croydon; Diocese of Arundel & Brighton.

MICHELMORES (see firm details p.1068) This business-focused firm covers the range of education law, including disputes, property matters, employment, funding, contracts and spin-offs. Led by highly respected corporate and funding specialist Malcolm Dickinson, who won respect from peers for his depth of knowledge, the team advises clients ranging from FE and HE institutions to state, independent and specialist schools. **Clients** University of Exeter; Exeter College; West of England School for Children of Little or No Sight.

THOMAS EGGAR (see firm details p.1160) Though experienced in a broad range of education law, much of this firm's work concerns property and employment. Under head of department Peter Stevens, it advises a large number of FE colleges, plus HE institutions and private schools, for which its advice is particularly respected. Recent work has included assisting in the merger of two FE colleges and the closure of a school. **Clients** Chichester College of Arts, Science and Technology; Christ's Hospital; City College Brighton and Hove.

OSBORNE CLARKE (see firm details p.1090) Best known for its specialised work in large-scale commercial projects, funding agreements and technology spin-outs, the firm is most visible advising universities on commercial issues. In the last year the team, with Joachim Steinbach at its head, has advised the University of Bath on banking, tax, corporate and property matters. **Clients** University of Plymouth; University of Bristol; University of Bath.

STEELE RAYMOND (see firm details p.1146) With a dedicated education law department headed by Peter Rolph, the firm provides advice to HE and FE institutions and independent schools on issues including student claims, spin-outs, government funding, employment, redundancies and reorganisations. Though lower profile on the individual side, it also offers assistance to parents, particularly on exclusions and special educational needs. **Clients** Bournemouth University.

TOZERS (see firm details p.1165) Although not considered a high-profile outfit, this firm retains a sound reputation in the education sector, advising both private and state schools. Richard King heads the department. **Clients** Schools; other educational institutions.

THE SOUTH & SOUTH WEST

EDUCATION: INDIVIDUALS
■ THE SOUTH & SOUTH WEST

1. **AE Smith & Son** Stroud
2. **Blake Lapthorn** Fareham

LEADING INDIVIDUALS

1. **LOVE Robert** AE Smith & Son

This book is the product of 6,582 1/2 hour interviews. See p.7 for BMRB audit.
Within each band, firms are listed alphabetically. See individuals' profiles p.288

AE SMITH & SON (see firm details p.1141) This remains one of the most respected firms in the country for representing individuals, and to many in the market it is "*top of the list on special educational needs.*" It has been outstandingly successful in educational negligence, in particular Special Educational Needs Tribunal work, under Robert Love (see p.289), whose phenomenal reputation makes him one of the supreme education lawyers nationwide. Peers note his "*vast amount of experience,*" particularly in dyslexia cases, and "*sensible approach.*" "*I just

FIRMS ACTING FOR INDIVIDUALS

keep hearing about him;*" said one competitor "*he just keeps winning cases.*"

BLAKE LAPTHORN (see firm details p.877) Covering all areas of education litigation, including judicial reviews, tribunal work on special educational needs, exclusions, admissions, bullying and educational negligence, the firm stands out in the South. Head of department Sarah Palmer and her colleagues are described by peers as "*commercial, sensible people.*"

THAMES VALLEY/WALES/MIDLANDS ■ EDUCATION

THAMES VALLEY

EDUCATION: INSTITUTIONS
THAMES VALLEY

1. **Manches** Oxford
   Morgan Cole Oxford
   Winckworth Sherwood Oxford

This book is the product of 6,582 1/2 hour interviews. See p.7 for BMRB audit. Within each band, firms are listed alphabetically.

MANCHES (see firm details p.1052) This esteemed practice acts for HE and FE colleges, independent schools, education charities and other education bodies. It offers advice on a broad range of issues including IP, IT, spin-outs, technology transfer, corporate activity, constitutions, charity law and discrimination. It also supports 25 Oxford colleges on property and employment issues. Daff Richardson leads this "*well-respected*" team. **Clients** University of Sussex; Council for the Central Laboratory of the Research Councils; Natural Environment Research Council.

MORGAN COLE (see firm details p.1075) This firm has experience of advising a range of educational institutions, acting for a number of universities, FE colleges and private schools. The team, under the leadership of Robert Breedon, has a sound reputation for assisting on both the contentious and the commercial aspects of the sector. **Clients** Universities; schools; FE colleges.

FIRMS ACTING FOR INSTITUTIONS

WINCKWORTH SHERWOOD (see firm details p.1192) John Rees heads the Oxford branch of this well-regarded practice, and works closely with the strong London-based team. Focusing on religious and diocesan schools, it enjoys a particularly fine reputation among clients within the religious education sector. Its expertise covers everything from PFI, employment and property issues to educational negligence claims. **Clients** Schools.

WALES

EDUCATION: INSTITUTIONS
WALES

1. **Eversheds** Cardiff
2. **Morgan Cole** Cardiff

This book is the product of 6,582 1/2 hour interviews. See p.7 for BMRB audit. Within each band, firms are listed alphabetically.

EVERSHEDS (see firm details p.949) The department is praised by market sources for its "*wide range of experience*" and constructive attitude. Kim Howell heads a team which clients describe as "*interested, receptive and keen to work in partnership.*" The firm's recent highlights include advising a university on the conduct of students and professional accountability, acting on a merger between two FE colleges and reviewing the workings of the General Teaching Council for Wales. **Clients** University of Glamorgan; Cardiff University; General Teaching Council for Wales.

FIRMS ACTING FOR INSTITUTIONS

MORGAN COLE (see firm details p.296) This sound and sensible team, led from Oxford by Robert Breedon, acts for universities, FE colleges and schools throughout Wales. Its expertise extends across the range of education-related work and it enjoys the support of a loyal client base who find it "*strong and approachable.*" **Clients** FE colleges; schools; universities.

WALES

EDUCATION: INDIVIDUALS
WALES

1. **Russell Jones & Walker** Cardiff
2. **Sinclairs** Penarth

LEADING INDIVIDUALS
1. **IMPERATO Michael** Russell Jones & Walker

This book is the product of 6,582 1/2 hour interviews. See p.7 for BMRB audit. Within each band, firms are listed alphabetically. See individuals' profiles p.288

RUSSELL JONES & WALKER (see firm details p.1120) This team is known well beyond Wales for its active involvement in educational negligence cases. "*A good, user-friendly practice,*" according to clients, its solicitors "*know the sector well.*" The firm has witnessed an increase this year in educational negligence cases relating to dyslexia and racial discrimination and is handling one dyslexia case worth around £250,000. Head of department **Michael Imperato** (see p.289) is well regarded, and enjoys the backing of a team which is said to "*know what parents are talking about.*"

FIRMS ACTING FOR INDIVIDUALS

SINCLAIRS A thriving, busy department, its work ranges from special educational needs and general educational negligence claims to public law applications and judicial review work. The department, headed by Michael Charles, acts exclusively on education and children's law, and attracts substantial recommendations.

MIDLANDS

EDUCATION: INSTITUTIONS
MIDLANDS

1. **Martineau Johnson** Birmingham
2. **Eversheds** Birmingham, Nottingham
3. **Wragge & Co** Birmingham
4. **Browne Jacobson** Nottingham

LEADING INDIVIDUALS
1. **HART Nicola** Martineau Johnson
   PHARAOH Paul Martineau Johnson

This book is the product of 6,582 1/2 hour interviews. See p.7 for BMRB audit. Within each band, firms are listed alphabetically. See individuals' profiles p.288

MARTINEAU JOHNSON (see firm details p.1056) One of the top education firms nationally, according to the market it is "*way out on its own*" in the Midlands. Clients praise work which is "*splendid*" for quality and value, and appreciate the team's "*pleasant and friendly*" approach. Head of department **Nicola Hart** (see p.289) is acclaimed by peers as a "*sharp, experienced, realistic, client-centred person*" who is developing a great team, having recently made some intelligent recruitments. **Paul Pharaoh** (see p.289) also retains his excellent reputation in the market. This year the firm has advised universities and FE colleges on issues including mergers, IP, funding, PFI, litigation and disciplinary procedures. **Clients** London Guildhall University; University of North London; University of Wales, Aberystwyth.

FIRMS ACTING FOR INSTITUTIONS

EVERSHEDS (see firm details p.949) Although the team operates across the Midlands, it is the Birmingham branch that rivals consider the most highly visible. Peers describe it as "*very professional – the sort of people you can do business with.*" The Nottingham branch is also visible and "*well regarded.*" The team, which operates across the region, provides a broad spectrum of services to HE and FE institutions, and is currently expanding and enjoying new resources. Anthony Heath heads the cross-office department. **Clients** De Montfort University; University of Derby; National College for School Leadership.

EDUCATION ■ MIDLANDS/EAST ANGLIA/THE NORTH

WRAGGE & CO (see firm details p.1197) Representing ten local FE colleges and some HE institutions, the firm concentrates on partnership deals with local authorities, employment, property and construction. Philip Clissitt leads a team that competitors regard as "*extremely professional and efficient.*" **Clients** Tameside College; Walsall College of Arts & Technology; Sutton Coldfield College.

BROWNE JACOBSON (see firm details p.891) New to our ranking tables in education this year, the firm is recognised by peers as "*a major player.*" Headed up by commercial law specialist Paul Southby, the team offers advice on matters including fraud, property, IP, biotech and educational negligence for schools, universities and FE colleges. The firm has also been appointed to the OFSTED regulatory panel. **Clients** The Nottingham Trent University; De Montfort University; The University of Nottingham.

EAST ANGLIA

EDUCATION: INSTITUTIONS
■ EAST ANGLIA

1. **Mills & Reeve** Cambridge, Norwich
2. **Eversheds** Cambridge, Norwich
3. **Birkett Long** Colchester
   Wollastons Chelmsford

LEADING INDIVIDUALS

1. **ATTLE Gary** Mills & Reeve
   STANFIELD Glynne Eversheds

This book is the product of 6,582 1/2 hour interviews. See p.7 for BMRB audit. Within each band, firms are listed alphabetically. See individuals' profiles p.288

MILLS & REEVE (see firm details p.1071) Greatly respected by interviewees as one of the best all-round education practices nationally, the firm acts primarily for universities and has many clients outside East Anglia. **Gary Attle** (see p.288), who is rated highly by peers and clients, supervises a team that provides a complete service from IP and spin-outs to advising on student complaint procedures and human rights legislation. Its "*excellent*" client care structure is held in particular esteem by the market as a symbol of the firm's commitment: clients claim that the team "*really wants its relationships to work.*" **Clients** LSE; University of Cambridge; The University of Nottingham.

EVERSHEDS (see firm details p.949) By focusing its operations on its new Cambridge office, Eversheds has thrown down the gauntlet to Mills & Reeve. Although some education work will continue to be done from Norwich, the Cambridge office will take over the bulk of the firm's education work in the region. The team is headed by London-based leading light John Hall, but newly recruited, **Glynne Stanfield** (see p.247), formerly head of HE at Mills & Reeve, boasts a formidable reputation in the region. **Clients** Downing College, Cambridge; Oxford, Cambridge & RSA Examinations; Consortium for Higher Education Energy Purchasing.

FIRMS ACTING FOR INSTITUTIONS

BIRKETT LONG (see firm details p.875) Catering for local schools, HE and FE institutions and other educational bodies, this firm offers advice on the whole range of education law. This year the respected team, headed by Philip George, acted in the merger that created Thurrock and Basildon College. It also assisted in other formations and advised schools on special needs, contractual and institutional matters. **Clients** University of Essex; Colchester Institute; Thurrock & Basildon College.

WOLLASTONS (see firm details p.1196) "*A good commercial practice*" in the view of competitors, it is led by Nicholas Cook. This year the team has advised Anglia Polytechnic University on new property acquisitions, and assisted FE colleges on admissions procedures. It has also been active assisting parents on admissions and overseeing procurement for institutions. **Clients** Anglia Polytechnic University; FE colleges.

THE NORTH

EDUCATION: INSTITUTIONS
■ THE NORTH

1. **Eversheds** Leeds, Manchester, Newcastle upon Tyne
2. **Pinsent Curtis Biddle** Leeds
3. **Addleshaw Booth & Co** Manchester
4. **DLA** Liverpool
   Irwin Mitchell Sheffield
   Robert Muckle Newcastle upon Tyne

LEADING INDIVIDUALS

1. **BOARDMAN John** Eversheds

This book is the product of 6,582 1/2 hour interviews. See p.7 for BMRB audit. Within each band, firms are listed alphabetically. See individuals' profiles p.288

EVERSHEDS (see firm details p.949) Eversheds' education team is as pre-eminent in the North as it is in London. **John Boardman** (see p.288) towers over the area. Described by competitors as "*down to earth and approachable with an unrivalled knowledge of education,*" clients respect his invaluable advice; as one said: "*when I'm in doubt I go to John Boardman.*" He heads the "*absolutely brilliant*" department for Leeds and Manchester, which is seen by peers as "*covering all bases,*" and wins respect across a range of services. Chris Hugill's team in Newcastle is also considered "*on top of the game.*" Across the North this year, Eversheds' education highlights include providing a successful web-based governance system for colleges and advising HE and FE institutions on complex litigation, tax, mergers and construction matters. **Clients** The University of York; University of Northumbria at Newcastle; West Cheshire College.

PINSENT CURTIS BIDDLE (see firm details p.1102) The firm covers a broad range of education work including litigation brought by students, employment issues, constitutional advice, PFI and advice on IP spin-outs. Its impressive client base includes around 25 schools and universities across the country. Competitors acknowledge that the group is on the rise and is biting at Eversheds' heels in the North. John McMullen heads the team. An employment star, his expertise is felt to give the firm "*a real edge*" on employment-related work. Its handling of educational negligence is also respected by peers. **Clients** University of Leeds; The University of Manchester; University of Durham.

ADDLESHAW BOOTH & CO (see firm details p.838) The firm represents a number of education bodies including examination boards, universities, FE colleges and schools. It recently acted for a university on a claim made by a PhD student, and represented a private education group taking over a London borough's education services. Other recent client-centred initiatives include conducting seminars on the implications of human rights legislation for education and drafting an 'off-the-shelf' race relations policy. The well-liked team, led by Jonathan Davey, is considered "*definitely a player*" by peers. **Clients** The University of Sheffield; Lancaster University; Nord Anglia Education Group Companies.

DLA Successful and visible in Merseyside, the team was especially noted by market sources for its work in property development for educational institutions. Recent highlights have included acting for Yale Sixth Form College in the development of a new campus in Wrexham and advising the Department of Education in Northern Ireland on the development of new campuses for FE colleges. Mark Beardwood heads the team. **Clients** Schools; HE and FE institutions.

THE NORTH/SCOTLAND — EDUCATION

IRWIN MITCHELL (see firm details p.1009) Andrew Lockley leads a respected practice concentrating on educational negligence. Rivals admire the team and clients speak highly of it – according to one it "*couldn't be faulted*." The firm has experience in conducting, and avoiding, litigation and has acted in disputes about special educational needs, admissions, exclusions, school closures, bullying and educational negligence. **Clients** Schools; other bodies.

ROBERT MUCKLE This "*responsive, professional*" team focuses on the commercial side of the education market, though it also advises on educational negligence matters. It represents a broad range of educational bodies and institutions, for example acting recently in a joint venture between a college and a training provider. Tony McPhillips heads this department. **Clients** University of Northumbria at Newcastle; Gateshead College; 3F.

THE NORTH

EDUCATION: INDIVIDUALS
THE NORTH

1. Elaine Maxwell & Co Lancaster

LEADING INDIVIDUALS
1. MAXWELL Elaine Elaine Maxwell & Co

This book is the product of 6,582 1/2 hour interviews. See p.7 for BMRB audit.
Within each band, firms are listed alphabetically. See individuals' profiles p.288

FIRMS ACTING FOR INDIVIDUALS

ELAINE MAXWELL & CO (see firm details p.946) Nationally respected as a "*fighter*" with "*gravitas*," clients say that Elaine Maxwell (see p.289) "*knows what she's talking about and understands how oppressive the education system is for those with special needs.*" In addition to regularly appearing at the Special Educational Needs tribunal and being a specialist in autism, she advises on general educational negligence. She was recently involved in a landmark case concerning diabetes discrimination. She also provides advice to schools on issues such as admissions.

SCOTLAND

EDUCATION: INSTITUTIONS
SCOTLAND

1. Dundas & Wilson CS Edinburgh
2. Anderson Strathern WS Edinburgh
   Thorntons WS Dundee
3. Brodies Edinburgh
   Ledingham Chalmers Aberdeen
   Lindsays WS Edinburgh
   Maclay Murray & Spens Glasgow

LEADING INDIVIDUALS
1. BRYMER Stewart Thorntons WS

This book is the product of 6,582 1/2 hour interviews. See p.7 for BMRB audit.
Within each band, firms are listed alphabetically. See individuals' profiles p.288

DUNDAS & WILSON CS (see firm details p.943) The firm's high profile in Scotland keeps it at the number one spot this year. It advises universities and schools, and has recently been busy assisting Edinburgh City Council as procurer in an 18-school PPP scheme. The team has also assisted universities with outsourcing and commercial arrangements, and worked on a property deal for a university research park. The practice, led by Brian Leggat, is admired by peers for its size, superb client list and long-standing prestige. **Clients** University of St Andrews; University of Glasgow; The University of Edinburgh.

ANDERSON STRATHERN WS (see firm details p.844) The practice, headed by Alasdair Fox, has grown in visibility this year and is regarded by market sources as on the way up. It represents all types of educational institution including schools for those with special needs. This year the well-respected team has represented Napier University on all aspects of its development, and acted for schools at the Scottish Parliament, arguing for their exclusion from public right of access land reforms. **Clients** Napier University; Fettes College; Edinburgh College of Artfs.

THORNTONS WS (see firm details p.1162) Entering our rankings this year, this "*extremely good*" and "*very active*" practice has received glowing reports. Its "*strong, long-standing*" relationship with the University of Dundee was particularly noted by interviewees, and it represents a range of HE and FE institutions on matters including IP, property, drafting regulations and student discipline, as well as holding seminars and forums on issues like discrimination and copyright. Head of department Stewart Brymer (see p.288) is described as "*an extremely enthusiastic, very bright fellow,*" well known and respected by peers. **Clients** University of Dundee; Napier University; Dundee and Angus Colleges.

BRODIES (see firm details p.889) This firm's growing practice advising FE colleges is seen as "*important and successful,*" with its work for the Higher Education Funding Council also noted approvingly by peers. The team, under Brenda Scott, offers help on policy, regulations, commerce, employment, property and procurement, and has an ethos of concentrating on pure education law. **Clients** Telford College; Association of Scottish Colleges; Scottish Higher Education and Further Education Funding Councils.

FIRMS ACTING FOR INSTITUTIONS

LEDINGHAM CHALMERS (see firm details p.1034) The firm is a big player in the Aberdeen area for education law, handling employment, property, contractual work, student and academic disputes and asset realisation programmes for its enviable client base of educational institutions. John Rutherford is head of the team, which this year oversaw the merger of Northern College with the University of Aberdeen. **Clients** University of Aberdeen, International School of Aberdeen.

LINDSAYS WS (see firm details p.1042) Enjoying a high degree of respect from the market, this team focuses on commercial, property and technology spin-out projects for a mainly HE and FE client list. Roy Shearer is the lead partner working for Edinburgh University. **Clients** The University of Edinburgh; Stevenson College, Edinburgh; a private school.

MACLAY MURRAY & SPENS (see firm details p.1048) The firm has a commercial focus, advising education clients in matters including co-ordinating spin-outs, PFI, construction, e-commerce, collaborations, acquisitions, contractual work, employment, IP and litigation. Fiona Nicolson, who has particular expertise in commercial and IP projects, heads the well-known and respected department. **Clients** Glasgow School of Art; The Robert Gordon University; Scottish FE Unit.

EDUCATION ■ THE LEADERS

THE LEADERS IN EDUCATION

ATTLE, Gary
Mills & Reeve, Cambridge
(01223) 222394
gary.attle@mills-reeve.com
Specialisation: Lead Partner of firm's University Business Group. Acts for universities and colleges (eg appeals to the Visitor; discrimination claims; judicial review; defamation; injunctions. Advises on governance and liability issues. Clients include University of Cambridge; Imperial College; LSE; Quality Assurance Agency; University of Nottingham; Association of Colleges.
Prof. Memberships: Education Law Association; Universities and Colleges Education Law Network.
Career: Trained *Mills and Reeve*, qualified 1992, partner 1999, trained as mediator 1996.
Personal: Born 1968; resides Cambridge. Education: Lincoln College, Oxford (1st class in law). Leisure: young family, church, sport.

BEESLEY, PF
Lee Bolton & Lee, London
(020) 7222 5381
Specialisation: Particular expertise in Church of England work. Registrar of the Diocese of Ely; registrar of the Diocese of Guildford; joint registrar of the Diocese of Hereford; registrar of the Faculty Office of the Archbishop of Canterbury; a member of the Legal Advisory Commission of the General Synod of the Church of England. Also handles education and charity work. Solicitor to the National Society and to the Board of Education of the General Synod; Registrar of the Woodard Corporation. Joint Contributor to Volume 13 (2) 'Encyclopaedia of Forms and Precedents-Ecclesiastical Law'. Speaker at and promoter of several conferences and seminars on ecclesiastical charity and education matters.
Prof. Memberships: Law Society, City of Westminster Law Society (ex-President), Ecclesiastical Law Association (Chairman), Ecclesiastical Law Society (Secretary), Charity Law Association.
Career: Qualified 1967. Joined *Lee Bolton & Lee* in 1968, becoming a partner in 1969.
Personal: Born 30 April 1943. Attended Kings School Worcester, then Exeter University 1961-64 and College of Law 1964-65. Lives in London.

BOARDMAN, John
Eversheds, Manchester
(0161) 831 8000
johnboardman@eversheds.com
Specialisation: Partner in education law department and Vice Chair of the Education Group, specialising in governance and company/commercial matters. Principal areas of work is education law, advising higher and further education institutions and schools. Also advises other non-profit making bodies.

Prof. Memberships: ELAS, Charity Law Association, Justice, Associate of Institute of Risk Management.
Career: Qualified 1979 while at *Alexander Tatham*, now *Eversheds* and became a partner in 1986.
Publications: Contributes to articles and various specialist education law journals and gives numerous lectures and seminars on these areas. Also an author of the chapter on trading companies in 'Higher Education and the Law'.
Personal: Born 26 July 1955. Attended Manchester Grammar School 1966-73 and Downing College, Cambridge 1973-76. Former Governor of a further education college. Forum Member of an Education Action Zone. Leisure pursuits include pottery, bats, films, books, music and guinea pigs. Lives in Mellor, Derbyshire.

BOYD, Robert
Veale Wasbrough, Bristol
(0117) 925 2020
rboyd@vwl.co.uk
Specialisation: Partner and head of schools team. Partner in charge of the education department which has advised more than 700 independent schools in the UK and abroad and some special and grant maintained schools in the last decade. Advises schools in matters of governance, management, structural change, incorporation, charity and trust issues, the parent contract and many other concerns. An invited speaker at seminars all over the country for HMC, GBA, IAPS, GSA, and SHMIS.
Prof. Memberships: Bristol Law Society; Education Law Association.
Career: Qualified 1972. Joined *Veale Wasbrough* as a partner in 1988. Council of Bristol Law Society 1986-88; Council Member of Academy of Experts 1989; Co-opted to Judicial committee 1992.
Publications: Author of textbook 'Independent Schools: Law, Custom and Practice' (Jordans, 1988) and 'Running a School Boarding House' (BSA, 2000) and of the Parent Contract and numerous other education templates and articles on education issues.
Personal: Born 1946. Stonyhurst College 1960-65 and Birmingham University 1966-69.

BRYMER, Stewart
Thorntons WS, Dundee
(01382) 229111
Specialisation: Partner in Business Law Department. Accredited by The Law Society of Scotland as a specialist in commercial leasing and intellectual property law. Has acted in relation to a number of large out-of-town non-food retail parks, several investment sales and in rent review arbitrations. Chairman of Editorial Review Board of 'The Conveyancing Manual'. Has lectured on conveyancing, leasing and intellectual property at university level and for the Law Society and

IBC legal studies. Honorary Professor of Law at University of Dundee.
Prof. Memberships: The Law Society of Scotland, Association of University Technology Managers. Convenor of the Conveyancing Committee of The Law Society of Scotland.
Career: Qualified and joined *Thorntons WS* in 1979. Became a Partner in 1983. Appointed solicitor to the University of Dundee in 1993.
Personal: Born 30 January 1957. Attended Morgan Academy 1969-75 and University of Dundee 1975-79 (1st Class Hons).

CAPSTICK, Charlotte
Berrymans Lace Mawer, London
(020) 7638 2811

CAREW-JONES, Owen
Winckworth Sherwood, London
(020) 7593 5034
ocarew-jones@winckworths.co.uk
Specialisation: Education and employment, mainly acting for institutions eg Governing Bodies and Diocesan Boards. Acted for Governors in Court of Appeal cases ex p C and ex p L on the meaning of reinstatement after a permanent exclusion, the latter now before the House of Lords.
Prof. Memberships: Law Society, Education Law Association.
Career: Qualified teacher. Trainee, then solicitor, now partner with *Winckworth Sherwood*.
Publications: Various articles eg 'Infant Class Size Prejudice' in 'Education Public Law and the Individual'.
Personal: MA (Cantab). Married with three children.

CLARKE, John
Rickerbys, Cheltenham
(01242) 246425
john.clarke@rickerbys.com
Specialisation: Head of *Rickerbys'* Education and Employment Team and has specialised in education and employment law for 10 years. Advises universities, colleges and schools in both the independent and maintained sector on a wide variety of issues ranging from corporate governance to day to day employment issues. Writes and lectures for a number of educational and professional bodies throughout the UK.
Prof. Memberships: Employment Lawyers' Association, Education Law Association, Charity Law Association.
Career: Qualified 1977, joined *Rickerbys* in 1982 becoming a Partner in 1984 and Senior Partner in 1996.
Personal: University of Kent BA (Hons) Law, Buckingham University Diploma in Education Law. Interests include sailing and Austin Healeys.

CONRATHE, Paul
Coningsbys, Croydon
(020) 8680 5575
paulconrathe@coningsbys.co.uk
See under Human Rights, p.413

DICKINSON, Malcolm
Michelmores, Exeter
(01392) 436244

FORD, John
John Ford Solicitors, London
(020) 8800 6464

GILL, Jaswinder
Gills, Southall
(020) 8893 6869
jgill@gills-solicitors.co.uk
Specialisation: Offers expert legal advice in protecting and promoting students' legal rights in the law of higher education. Has gained a nationwide reputation as the leading lawyer in the country in this area in challenging local authorities and universities, previously being unfamiliar territory. Set up his own firm to offer specialist guidance and advice for students aggrieved by decisions made by the above bodies. Also involved in bringing about a greater sense of awareness of legal remedies available to students within a complex framework of education law. Many cases involve novel issues and will have a strong element of wider public importance issues for all students. Specialises in challenging (a) local authorities' decisions refusing discretionary and mandatory awards in the area of student funding and (b) decisions made by universities/colleges regarding examination results, by way of judicial review proceedings. In respect of the latter, also handles cases involving damages for breach of contract and/or negligence. Also focuses on judicial review proceedings within the education field embracing statements of special educational needs and appeals, exclusion appeals and admissions.
Publications: Co-author of the recent publication 'Universities and Students' (2001) specifically dealing with the growing number of legal actions by students against universities. This book contains live case studies handled by Jaswinder Gill as well as providing an up to date and authoritative guide to student's rights and remedies with regard to the law and procedure in higher education.

GIZZI, Julian
Beachcroft Wansbroughs, London
(020) 7894 6556
jgizzi@bwlaw.co.uk
Specialisation: Partner, head of public law department. All aspects of education law including funding matters, incorporations, mergers, joint ventures, enquiries, judicial reviews and e-learning.
Prof. Memberships: Law Society.
Career: Qualified in 1981, having joined *Beachcroft Stanleys* in 1979. Became a partner in 1986. Member of the Structure and Governance Working Group of the National Committee of Inquiry into Higher Education. Fellow of the Royal Society of Arts. Member of the Admis-

THE LEADERS — EDUCATION

sions and Exclusions Appeals Panel of the Schools' Commission.
Publications: Butterworths' 'Education Law Manual' (General Editor).
Personal: Born 13 February 1957. Educated at Downside School and Cambridge University. Lives in Little Chart, Kent.

GOLD, Richard
Stone King, Bath
(01225) 337599
Specialisation: Partner specialising in education work. Acts for schools, FE colleges, parents and students in all aspects of education law including governor training and PFI projects. Addresses conferences and seminars organised by IBC Jordans and Education Law Association and others. Author of 'Running a School 2002-2003 - Legal Duties and Responsibilities'. Member of Advisory Board 'Education, Public Law and the Individual'. Author of 'The Education Act Explained' (The Stationery Office).
Prof. Memberships: Education Law Association (ELAS) (Member of Executive Committee).
Career: Qualified 1968. Joined *Stone King* in 1999 as a Partner. Head of Education Law.
Personal: Born 21 October 1941. Attended William Ellis School 1953-61, then Trinity College, Cambridge 1961-65. Chair of Governors, William Ellis School 1978-87. Chair of Trustees, William Ellis School 1978-present. Governor, Ravenscroft School 1992-96. Governor, Jews Free School 1994-present. Leisure pursuits include music, theatre, reading and sport.

HALL, John
Eversheds, London
(020) 7919 4500
hallj@eversheds.com
Specialisation: Partner and chairman of *Eversheds* education group. Work includes governance, the Education Acts, employment law, industrial relations, judicial review, the student relationships, commercial law, funding and asset management. Clients include over 94 universities and other higher education institutions and 230 further education colleges.. Also handles company/commercial and employment and constitutional advice for professional and other bodies.
Prof. Memberships: Law Society, Chair of the Further and Higher Education Group of Education Law Association, Fellow of the Royal Society of Arts. Fellow of the Institute of Continuing Professional Development.
Career: Read law at Wadham College, Oxford and qualified in 1975. Partner at *Wedlake Saint* 1978-93. Chair, London Young Solicitors' Group, 1985; Company Secretary, Polytechnics and Colleges Employers' Forum, 1988; Governor, Barnet College of Further Education, 1992; Company Secretary, Colleges' Employers' Forum, 1992; Council Member of the Royal College of Music (1999) governor of Lochinver House School (1999) and a member of the Courts of Middlesex University and University of Surrey, Roehampton. Joined *Eversheds* in 1994 as a partner.
Publications: General Editor 'Purposive Governance - an annotated guidance for further education colleges' (Sweet & Maxwell). Contributor to the 'Times Education Supplement' and education press. Author of further and higher education module in University of Buckingham Postgraduate Diploma in Education Law and contributor on 'Higher Education and the Law' (Open University Press) and The Journal of College and University Law (the National Association of College and University Attorneys).
Personal: Born 23 December 1948. College Governor. Leisure interests include walking, music, history, art and Spain. Lives in Hadley Wood, Barnet, Herts.

HART, Nicola
Martineau Johnson, Birmingham
(0121) 678 1311
nicola.hart@martjohn.com
Specialisation: Partner and Head of *Martineau Johnson*'s Education Practice. Leads specialist education team and the firm's full service to university and college clients. Practice covers a wide range of work, from university mergers, joint ventures and international work, to disputes with students and academic staff and judicial review. A regular speaker at education sector conferences and seminars, and contributes articles to education law and sector publications.
Career: Qualified 1988, *Le Brasseurs*; joined *Martineau Johnson* 1989; Partner since 1995; Head of Education since 1997.
Publications: Introduction and chapters on student issues in 'Higher Education Law' 2nd edition, Jordons 2002; 'Teacher Stress: the Consequences of Harassment and Bullying', Monitor Press, 2000.
Personal: Born 1962. Educated Worcester Girls Grammar School and Jesus College, Oxford. Director, Midlands Arts Centre (MAC).

IMPERATO, Michael
Russell Jones & Walker, Cardiff
(029) 20262 800
Specialisation: Education law and claimant personal injury. Acts particularly for children with special educational needs. Receives referrals from several charities. Acting for several claimants in high value educational negligence claims. Involved in high profile cases such as the North West Teenager, originally prevented from attending Gordonstone School by the Local Authority. Also instructed in exclusion cases and admissions. Undertakes legal aid work with education law franchise. Written articles, presented seminars and lectured on education law at University of Glamorgan. Member of Law Society Personal Injury panel, LSE appeals committee and National Education Forum.
Prof. Memberships: ELAS - Convenor for Wales & West, PEOPIL, ATLA, Law Society, CPIL Secretary of Wales.
Career: Qualified 1990 with *Hugh James*, Cardiff. 1994-97 *Gabb & Co*, Abergavenny. Joined *RJW* 1997. Partner from 1999.
Personal: Born 24 May 1962. Education at Whitchurch High School, Cardiff and Reading University 1980-84. Taught history for two years. School governor. Interests include sport, politics and young family. Lives in Cardiff.

JACKMAN, Angela
Fisher Meredith, London
(020) 7622 4468
Specialisation: Special educational needs, exclusions and judicial review. Earliest reported case was R v Board of Stoke Newington School ex p M (1994) ELR 131. Extensive lecturing including Law Centres Federation National Conferences and Legal Action Group Education Law Course. Has also lectured with Counsel of Goldsmith Building on Special Educational Needs. Member of the Legal Focus Group of the Advisory Centre for Education exclusions project 'Action on Exclusions'. She developed Supervisor Standards in education franchises within the LSC. She convened the Law Centres Federation Education Group between 2000-2001.
Prof. Memberships: Secretary of the Education Law Practitioners Group. Member of the Advisory Centre for Education.
Career: Qualified in 1987 and practised at *Evans Butler Wade Solicitors*. Then practised at Hackney Community Law Centre 1988-2001. Solicitor at *Fisher Meredith* since 2001.
Publications: Co-editor of Legal Action Group Hand Book 'Support for Asylum Seekers'. Legal Action Group Training materials. Special Educational Needs paper for the Education Group of Goldsmith Building.
Personal: Obtained BA Honours in Law from Balliol College, Oxford University in 1984. Has worked extensively with voluntary organisations and on occasions as a Consultant Legal Advisor.

KING, Michael
Stone King, Bath
(020) 7796 1007
michaelking@stoneking.co.uk
See under Charities, p.130

LOVE, Robert
AE Smith & Son, Stroud
(01453) 757444
robertlove@aesmith.co.uk
Specialisation: Partner. Special educational needs.
Prof. Memberships: Law Society, Convenor of Special Needs Interest Group of Education Law Association, member of Advisory Board - Education & Public Law Journal.
Career: Qualified 1975. Partner in *A.E. Smith & Son* since 1988.
Personal: Has been practising in this area for over twelve years.

MAXWELL, Elaine
Elaine Maxwell & Co, Lancaster
(01524) 840810
em@elainemaxwellsolicitors.co.uk
Specialisation: Own specialist firm handling solely education law and community care for children with disabilities. Area of practice covers admissions, exclusions, employment in education, transport cases, with particular expertise in special educational needs and tribunal appeals, disability discrimination in education and claims by students. Provides seminars and advice to parent groups and professional advisors on statementing system, and higher education law. Recent cases include disability discrimination claim for diabetic pupil, challenges on statementing policies of local education authorities, actions by students for breach of contract, and educational negligence.
Prof. Memberships: Education Law Association (Regional Co-ordinator), Employment Lawyers Association.
Career: Called to Bar 1974, has advised on education law since 1990, admitted as Solicitor 1991, Partner *Marsden Huck* 1995-98, set up *Elaine Maxwell & Co* 1998.
Personal: Born 1951, attended Nottingham High School for Girls, then Manchester University.

MCCREATH, Rob
Eversheds, London
(020) 7919 4608
robmccreath@eversheds.com
Specialisation: Employment and HR advice, particularly for employers in the further and higher education sectors and other not-for-profit/special purpose organisations; advice on aligning HR and organisational structures with strategic goals; advice on HR aspects of mergers and transfers; advised the Bett Committee on Higher Education Pay and Conditions.
Career: 1982-85 Thorn EMI (primarily in employee relations and personal management); 1986-92 *Ashurst Morris Crisp*; 1992-93 *Wedlake Saint*; 1994-date *Eversheds* (partner 1998).
Personal: Loretto School, St Edmund Hall, Oxford and City Universities. Interests: skiing, holidays in strange places.

PATEL, Anjan
Ashok Patel & Co, London
(020) 7797 6300

PHARAOH, Paul Grenville
Martineau Johnson, Birmingham
(0121) 678 1314
paul.pharaoh@martjohn.com
Specialisation: Partner in Education Department. Handles contractual, property-related and constitutional issues for higher and further education institutions. Speaker on education law and judicial review at various conferences and seminars.
Prof. Memberships: Law Society, ELAS.
Career: Qualified in 1971. Joined *Bettinsons* in 1969, becoming Partner in 1973.

www.ChambersandPartners.com

EDUCATION ■ THE LEADERS

Partner in *Shakespeares* on merger 1990. Partner in *Martineau Johnson* 1996. Law Society council member 1990-2002. Midlands convenor for Education Law Association. Member of Lakes College West Cumbria Corporation.
Publications: Author of articles in various legal journals, chapters on judicial review in 'Higher Education and the Law' and on due diligence in 'Managing Mergers', and module on law affecting pupils in school for University of Buckingham Diploma in Education Law. Member of editorial advisory board, 'Education Law Journal'.
Personal: Born 1947. Attended Manchester University 1965-68 and Liverpool College of Commerce 1968-69. FRSA.

RABINOWICZ, Jack
Teacher Stern Selby, London
(020) 7242 3191
j.rabinowicz@tsslaw.com
Specialisation: Partner in litigation department. Main areas of practice include education, medical negligence, and personal injury work.
Prof. Memberships: Director of Disability Law Service, Chair of Education Law Association (ELAS), Steering Committee of Whooping Cough Claims, Action for Victims of Medical Accidents (AVMA), American Trial Lawyers Association (ATLA), Medico-Legal Society, Association of Personal Injury Lawyers (APIL), Law Society's Group for the Welfare of People with a Mental Handicap, Council of Registration of Schools teaching Dyslexia (CresTeD).
Career: Qualified in 1977. Currently a partner with *Teacher Stern Selby*.

RUEBAIN, David
Levenes, London
(020) 8881 7777
druebain@levenes.co.uk
Specialisation: Has been a practising solicitor for the last 13 years. He heads the department of Education and Disability law with *Levenes Solicitors*, which specialises in all aspects of public law and human rights law including education law, community care and health law and disability discrimination law. He has published and taught nationally and internationally on education and disability law and is co-author of 'Notes on the Disability Discrimination Act' (the 10th edition of which is soon to be published), co-author of 'Taking Action', a 'Guide for Parents of Children with Special Educational Needs' (now in its 3rd edition), co-author of 'Education Law and Practice' and co-author of the 'Atkin's Court Forms' volume on 'Education Law'.
Prof. Memberships: Trustee of the Disability Discrimination Act Representation and Advice Project; Member of the Law Society's Mental Health and Disability Committee; Member of the Editorial Board of Disability and Society journal; Council Member of the Alliance for Inclusive Education; Vice Chair of Disability Equality in Education (a charitable training organisation); Member of the Board of Advisors of the Disability Law Service; Member of the Education Law Association; member of the Education Law Practitioners Group; Member of the Disability Discrimination Act Advisers Group; Member of the Editorial Board of Community Care Law Reports; Member of the National Autistic Society's Panel of Specialist Education Law Solicitors; a Consultant to the Public Law Project's Research Project on Evaluating the Impact of the Human Rights Act on Judicial Review; Fellow of the British American Project; and Honorary Legal Advisor to the Independent Panel for Special Education Advice (a national charity providing assistance to parents of children with special educational needs).

SILAS, Douglas
Alexander Harris, London
(020) 7430 5555
douglas.silas@alexanderharris.co.uk
Specialisation: Expert in education, disability and public law issues. Acts on behalf of children, disabled people and their families who may be experiencing difficulties with their schools, local education authorities, colleges and other institutions. Focuses on the areas of special educational needs, including appeals to and from the Special Educational Needs Tribunal and judicial reviews of local education authorities or other statutory bodies. Formerly a registered trainee British Sign Language Interpreter. Represented Jeff McWhinney, the first deaf Chief Executive of the British Deaf Association, in a test case challenge against the refusal of deaf people to serve as jurors. Alexander Harris is one of the few firms on all three specialist legal panels of the Disability Rights Commission.
Prof. Memberships: Trustee of the Disability Law Service. Member of Law Society, Education Law Association, Disability Discrimination Act Advisors Group, Deaf Legal Access Group, and British Deaf Association Advisory Panel.
Career: Joined *Levenes* Solicitors in 1995 as trainee solicitor. Admitted 1997. Associate *Alexander Harris* 2002.
Personal: Born on 28 September 1966. Educated: John Lyons, Harrow; South Bank University (LL.B (Hons)); College of Law (LPC).

STANFIELD, Glynne
Eversheds, Cambridge
(01223) 443666
glynnestanfield@eversheds.com
See under Corporate Finance, p.247

THATCHER, Michael
Winckworth Sherwood, London
(020) 7593 5000
mcthatcher@winckworths.co.uk
Specialisation: Partner in education, ecclesiastical and charities department. Acts for voluntary aided schools, foundation schools, voluntary controlled schools, Church of England and Roman Catholic boards of education and finance, further education colleges and local education authorities. Also acts for charities, airlines, and in general commercial and property law. Has acted in Judicial Review of Appeal Committee decisions, all types of disciplinary and appeal hearings, and Commission for Racial Equality proceedings against Governors. Author of various editorials in the specialist press. Has spoken at a wide range of conferences and seminars on various aspects of education and employment law.
Prof. Memberships: Law Society; Ecclesiastical Law Association; Ecclesiastical Law Society; Education Law Association.
Career: Qualified in 1968. From 1969 to 1989 was clerk to the Governors of St Clement Danes School, to St Clement Danes Parochial Charities and to Isaac Ducketts Trustees. Registrar to the Diocese of Rochester, Deputy Registrar to the Diocese of London, Chapter Clerk St Paul's Cathedral.
Personal: Born 19 May 1943. Attended Ardingly College 1956-60, then King's College, London 1961-64, and College of Law 1964-65. Clerk to the Worshipful Company of Cooks, Secretary to the Reunion des Gastronomes.

WILKINS, Patricia
Fisher Meredith, London
(020) 7622 4468
patw@fishermeredith.co.uk
Specialisation: Head of Education and Community Care Department which specialises in education law; health law and all aspects of community care. She has a particular specialisation in special educational needs. Recent cases include R (on the application of C) v Governors of B School, re-instatement of an excluded pupil; R (on the application of A) v L.B. of Lambeth, provision of services to children in need under S17 Children Act 1989. Founder and Chair of Education Law Practitioners Group for lawyers/advocates acting on behalf of applicants. Presents LAG course on Education with other team members and has been commissioned as co-author to produce Law Society book on Education law.
Prof. Memberships: Education Law Practitioners Group; Education Law Association; Legal Action.
Career: Admitted 1992. Developed specialism in education and community care before joining *Fisher Meredith* in 1997.
Personal: School governor.

EMPLOYEE SHARE SCHEMES

London: 291; The Regions: 293; Scotland: 293; Profiles: 294

Research approved by BMRB For this edition, **Chambers'** researchers conducted 6,582 interviews – 3,900 with law firms, 511 with barristers and 2,171 with clients. The validity of the research was scrutinised by BMRB International, who audited both the methodology and the results at our offices in London. They interviewed **Chambers'** researchers and cross-checked sample interviews. Details of the audit appear on page 7.

OVERVIEW The ESS sector continues to bloom. Although the downturn in the markets has depressed transactional activity, a healthy appetite for new schemes has produced work to compensate. Changing legislation and a growing awareness of the benefits of taper tax relief are two of the stimuli for this appetite, but companies competing to provide maximum choice and value for their employees is another. For most small clients, Enterprise Management Incentives (EMIs) are the first choice, and as the £15 million ceiling lifts to £30 million, mid-size companies are getting in on the act too. Share Incentive Plans (SIPs), after a rocky start with the old name AESOPs, are now finding favour, with 279 schemes having been approved by February 2002, (out of 565 applications). Not surprisingly, the international share schemes market continued to grow, putting big firms with global office networks at an even greater advantage. In London, the Linklaters team retains pole position by a small margin, while in the regions, Pinsent Curtis Biddle, who has consolidated its London presence, remains in a class of its own.

LONDON

EMPLOYEE SHARE SCHEMES — LONDON

1. Linklaters
2. Allen & Overy
   Clifford Chance
   Freshfields Bruckhaus Deringer
3. Herbert Smith
   Slaughter and May
4. Ashurst Morris Crisp
   Lovells
   Norton Rose
   Travers Smith Braithwaite
5. Baker & McKenzie
   Field Fisher Waterhouse
   Nicholson Graham & Jones
   Pinsent Curtis Biddle

This book is the product of 6,582 1/2 hour interviews. See p.7 for BMRB audit. Within each band, firms are listed alphabetically.

LINKLATERS (see firm details p.1043) With "*unique clout and breadth of practice*," the Linklaters employee incentives team holds on to its position just ahead of the pack. Figurehead **Janet Cooper** (see p.294) is a "*dynamic leader*" who has worked hard to bolster the firm's name, while **Anne Croft** (see p.294) provides "*formidable technical know-how*." **Graham Rowlands-Hempel** (see p.296) was also endorsed by clients for his practical approach. Although some concern was expressed over the high assistant/partner ratio, clients were overwhelmingly positive about the team's ability to deliver "*innovative, high-grade multi-jurisdictional advice*." The team continues to undertake corporate support as well as standalone work for leading FTSE 250, Euro 300 and Fortune 500 companies, with a particular focus on the e-commerce and telecommunications markets. A highlight last year was the implementation of an innovative 50-country share scheme for BP. The department also developed 'Clients extranet' technology enabling clients to access share plan documentation remotely. **Clients** Freeserve; Halifax; ICI; Lloyds TSB; Reuters; Vodafone.

ALLEN & OVERY (see firm details p.841) A flourishing, forward-looking team, its workload is balanced between stand-alone design work and corporate support. **Stephen Chater** (see p.294) is commended for "*clear and client-led advice*," while the new additions from Garretts, **Paul McCarthy** (see p.295) and **Sylvie Watts** (see p.296), have now had time to make their presence felt. McCarthy brings "*deep knowledge and a direct manner*" to the table, while Watts, who moves up our rankings this year after considerable peer approval, is said to be toiling hard to build up the firm's profile. The integrated global office network facilitates work across international jurisdictions for its top-class client list of public and private companies across the world. This year, the group advised WPP on its acquisition of the Tempus Group, a case that involved various types of plan and eight separate jurisdictions. It advised BT on its corporate re-organisation. **Clients** News International; British Telecom; Serco Group.

CLIFFORD CHANCE (see firm details p.911) This "*approachable, resourceful*" team works out of the integrated employment, pensions and benefits department, advising clients on a corporate support and stand-alone basis. Peers were full of praise for **Robin Tremaine** (see p.296) ("*head honcho, wise and likeable*") while **Kevin Thompson** (see p.296) was commended for his transactional work. "*Luminous spark*" **Daniel Hepburn** (see p.295), previously with Linklaters, joins our tables this year after sustained market praise. Clients benefit from the group's affiliation to remuneration consultancy New Bridge Street Consultants. The practice advises FTSE 100 companies and banks on a global basis, and has been particularly active lately in France and the USA. Memorable recent work includes the launch of three separate plans for Accenture and advising LIFFE on its takeover by Euronext. **Clients** Brambles Industries; Diageo; Debenhams; Unilever, WS Atkins.

FRESHFIELDS BRUCKHAUS DERINGER (see firm details p.964) The team advises FTSE 100 companies and major global plcs from within the combined employment, pensions and benefits department. Headed up by "*tax guru*" **Simon Evans** (see p.294), it was said by clients to excel where lateral thinking is required. Peers also admired "*extremely able*" **Jocelyn Mitchell** (see p.295). The team has devoted more resources this year to new scheme design, and the newly formed European share schemes working group helps in the transfer of intelligence and expertise between offices across the world. Meanwhile, the domestic practice thrives with innovative new schemes for the likes of Pearson, for whom it implemented a novel LTIP. Another highlight was advising on the demerger of mmO2 from British Telecom, a deal that required much innovative thinking. **Clients** ICI; HP; Tempus Group; AMP.

HERBERT SMITH (see firm details p.992) The practice boasts a deep knowledge of the sector, and is led by industry pioneer, **Colin Chamberlain** (see p.294). "*He was a leader then and still is,*" said one admiring client. International companies also benefit from the expertise of "*cosmopolitan*" **Paul Ellerman** (see p.294). The lion's share of the work involves advice in connection with large-scale corporate transactions, from M&A and IPOs to schemes of arrangement and demergers. The team has recent experience of SIP implementation and acted in the extension of a French company's plans to UK subsidiaries. The team has also acted for Time Warner on its £1.1 billion takeover of IPC and implemented SIPs for BG Group, British American Tobacco and Lattice. **Clients** Channel 5; Friends Provident; Kruidvat; LiDCO Group.

EMPLOYEE SHARE SCHEMES ■ LONDON

LEADING INDIVIDUALS

[1]
- **CHAMBERLAIN Colin** Herbert Smith
- **COHEN David** Norton Rose
- **COOPER Janet** Linklaters

[2]
- **CODRINGTON Eddie** Slaughter and May
- **CROFT Anne** Linklaters
- **EVANS Simon** Freshfields Bruckhaus Deringer
- **FENN Jonathan** Slaughter and May
- **MITCHELL Jocelyn** Freshfields Bruckhaus Deringer
- **TREMAINE Robin** Clifford Chance

[3]
- **CHATER Stephen** Allen & Overy
- **NICHOLL Victoria** Travers Smith Braithwaite
- **RANDALL Paul** Ashurst Morris Crisp
- **ROWLANDS-HEMPEL Graham** Linklaters
- **WHITEWRIGHT Louise** Lovells

[4]
- **ALLEN Barbara** Ashurst Morris Crisp
- **ELLERMAN Paul** Herbert Smith
- **INGLE Michael** Baker & McKenzie
- **JACOBS Michael** Nicholson Graham & Jones
- **MCCARTHY Paul** Allen & Overy
- **NUTTALL Graeme** Field Fisher Waterhouse
- **POSTLETHWAITE Robert** Pinsent Curtis Biddle
- **THOMPSON Kevin** Clifford Chance
- **WATTS Sylvie** Allen & Overy

UP AND COMING
- **HEPBURN Daniel** Clifford Chance

See individuals' profiles p.294

SLAUGHTER AND MAY (see firm details p.1140) Predominantly servicing the firm's existing client base of blue-chips and major plcs, the practice is particularly rated for its domestic transactional expertise. Operating from the employment and pensions department, neither partner works exclusively on share schemes, but the quality of work was nonetheless held by interviewees to be "*consistently high class.*" If **Eddie Codrington** (see p.294) doesn't know something, "*it isn't worth knowing,*" said one peer, while **Jonathan Fenn** (see p.294) is "*effervescent and focused.*" This year, the team looked after the share scheme aspects of Blue Circle's acquisition by Lafarge and Hepworth's acquisition by Vaillant. **Clients** Whitbread; Blue Circle; Hepworth; Marks & Spencer.

ASHURST MORRIS CRISP (see firm details p.852) The "*stalwart*" practice is divided roughly equally between transactional work in support of corporate clients and free-standing advisory activity. An increasing level of international work has come the team's way this year and it represented Virgin Group Investments, Skandia UK and the management team of Go-Fly in transactions. The group's highest profile personalities are head of department **Paul Randall** (see p.296) ("*genteel, clued-up, engaging*") and **Barbara Allen** (see p.294) ("*a geyser of common sense*"). **Clients** Virgin Group Investments; Skandia UK.

LOVELLS (see firm details p.1045) This expanding department pivots around lead partner **Louise Whitewright** (see p.296), still highly visible as secretary of the Share Scheme Lawyers Group. Her knowledge of share plans is matched by her "*luminous personal skills.*" The team is the main share plan adviser to Barclays, for whom it implemented one of the first SIPs. It recently advised T1 Automotive on the share scheme aspects of its demerger from Smiths Industries. In addition to design and transaction work, the dedicated share incentives department received various remedial instructions this year. **Clients** Barclays; T1 Automotive.

NORTON ROSE (see firm details p.1084) With "*the share schemes supremo*" **David Cohen** (see p.294) at the wheel, this practice has seen an increasing volume of standalone implementation and maintenance work for employees based all over the world. Cohen, described to researchers as "*a hands-on academic,*" continues to chair the Share Scheme Lawyers Group and work with the Inland Revenue towards streamlining and improving share plan legislation. The group's client base includes FTSE 100 and FTSE 250 corporates and private companies. It acted last year for Eni in its £2.7 billion takeover of Lasmo and for easyJet in its takeover of Go. **Clients** Eni; easyJet.

TRAVERS SMITH BRAITHWAITE (see firm details p.1166) **Victoria Nicholl** (see p.295), "*on top of the EMI game,*" fronts a department focused towards the incentive plans of unlisted companies. The group, working closely with the employment and pensions departments, takes on a mix of standalone and transactional work. Praised by clients and perceived by peers to have a "*growing share of the market,*" it has advised this year on private equity buyouts and corporate finance transactions. It also acted on the share scheme aspects of Nightfreight's public-to-private and established new schemes for Budgens and Pinewood Studios Holdings. **Clients** McCarthy & Stone; Kier Group; Majedie Investments; Universe Group; FCx International.

BAKER & MCKENZIE (see firm details p.855) Recognised by the market as a "*truly global practice,*" with its integrated international network the firm is able to serve the advisory and transactional needs of multinational corporations, including the implementation of foreign schemes in the UK. The UK outfit advised Sony this year on the share schemes terms of its joint venture agreement with Ericsson, and worked with the San Francisco office on Peregrine's acquisition of Remedy Corp. On the domestic front, the firm acts as a consultant to independent share scheme administrating companies. **Michael Ingle** (see p.295) heads the practice and "*knows his business like the palm of his hand.*" **Clients** Sony.

FIELD FISHER WATERHOUSE (see firm details p.954) This self-contained department now has its own brand – 'Equity Incentives Limited' – after acquiring the share schemes practice of Capital Strategies. The group owes much of its success to "*soft-talking heavyweight*" **Graeme Nuttall** (see p.295), who rivals say has an "*awesome knowledge of the tax aspects of employee share schemes.*" Nuttall's profile is boosted by his role in developing share schemes legislation. In addition to a roster of UK plcs and multinationals, the firm has a niche client base of organisations with unusual structures, including co-operatives and employee-owned companies. It recently designed a SIP for Guardian iT, and has undertaken an increasing amount of work for companies committed to employee participation. **Clients** Scott Bader Company; Nationwide Building Society; John Lewis Partnership; BT Exact Technologies; Arriva.

NICHOLSON GRAHAM & JONES (see firm details p.1083) With a client base of quoted and unquoted companies from the financial service sector, the technology industry and the sports and leisure market, this "*dependable*" firm is fronted by the "*venerable*" **Michael Jacobs** (see p.295). The firm is often consulted over problem cases and advised last year on a complex reconstruction of share options for a fund manager. **Clients** FFastFill; Sportech; Merrydown.

PINSENT CURTIS BIDDLE (see firm details p.1102) The practice has long had a strong reputation in the regions. This year, new recruits from Capital Strategies, including "*mover and shaker*" **Robert Postlethwaite** (see p.295), give it a permanent London presence for the first time. Since the offices in Birmingham, Leeds and the capital are fully and seamlessly integrated, clients also benefit from the attentions of David Pett and Judith Greaves. The team represents around 200 international corporations and smaller private companies, providing advice on every aspect of share incentives, including a financial modelling service. It recently advised IMI on the design and implementation of a SIP. **Clients** Misys; Pace Micro Technology; Smith and Nephew; Yorkshire Bank; Abbey National.

---

292 INDEX TO LEADING LAWYERS: PAGE 1693 ■ IN-HOUSE LAWYERS PROFILES: PAGE 1201

THE REGIONS

EMPLOYEE SHARE SCHEMES
THE REGIONS

1. **Pinsent Curtis Biddle** Birmingham, Leeds
2. **Addleshaw Booth & Co** Leeds, Manchester
   Eversheds Birmingham
   Wragge & Co Birmingham
3. **Osborne Clarke** Bristol

LEADING INDIVIDUALS

★ **PETT David** Pinsent Curtis Biddle
1. **GREAVES Judith** Pinsent Curtis Biddle
2. **GREEN Lawrence** Eversheds
   HAYES Richard Addleshaw Booth & Co
3. **POOLE Kevin** Wragge & Co
   WOMERSLEY Mark Osborne Clarke

This book is the product of 6,582 1/2 hour interviews. See p.7 for BMRB audit. Within each band, firms are listed alphabetically. See individuals' profiles p.294

PINSENT CURTIS BIDDLE (see firm details p.1102) The leading firm in the regions by some distance, this year it developed a serious London presence. Star practitioner **David Pett** (see p.295) is based in Birmingham although he spends a large proportion of his time in the capital. If Pett is "*a share schemes prophet,*" as his London rivals admit, then the book he edits, *Employee Share Schemes,* is the industry's Bible. Also enjoying national repute thanks to her "*high-calibre advice*" is head of department **Judith Greaves** (see p.294). The firm, which offers top class tax expertise, represents a large number of blue-chip multinationals and smaller private companies. It advised Smith and Nephew this year on a raft of complex share scheme issues, from an approved CSOP to the granting of discretionary options to employees in Europe and Australasia. The group has also launched a unique product called the EXSOP, an efficient way of ensuring future growth of shares with full taper relief. **Clients** Misys; Pace Micro Technology; IMI; Yorkshire Bank; Abbey National.

ADDLESHAW BOOTH & CO (see firm details p.838) The group has moved out of the tax department into a new dedicated employee benefits department. Taking on a mix of stand-alone and support work, it represents a broad base of clients from small private companies upwards. This year, the team advised on the Dewhirst Group's management buyout, and implemented a SIP for Daniel Thwaites. It also spent a large amount of time producing appraisals of existing schemes on behalf of venture capital houses. Experienced department head **Richard Hayes** (see p.295) was praised for having a mind "*as quick as a computer and inventive with it.*" **Clients** 3i; Airtours; Provalis; Royal Doulton; United Utilities.

EVERSHEDS (see firm details p.949) Acting for a mixture of small emergents and big plcs at home and abroad, the firm has had a "*successful year*" in the eyes of its peers. **Lawrence Green** (see p.295) ("*single-handedly developed the firm's share scheme practice*") leads the team from the firm's business tax group, and can draw on the assistance of the Leeds, Manchester and Norwich offices. It won considerable plaudits this year for its work with MG Rover. A further highlight was advising Dow Chemicals on its takeover of Ascot Group, a case which required expertise in SIPs, executive option schemes, LTIPs and employee trusts. **Clients** Britax International; Madison Filtration.

WRAGGE & CO (see firm details p.1197) Operating out of the tax department, the group receives a flow of instructions from FTSE 250 companies as well as smaller unquoted corporates. It increasingly provides advice on new compliance standards and remedial measures. This year it introduced new schemes in 27 jurisdictions for RMC Group, and advised on the handling of existing incentive schemes during the takeover of Biddle by Carver. Lead partner **Kevin Poole** ("*competent and responsive*") is held in high regard by the marketplace. **Clients** British Airways; Cambridge Antibody Technology Group; Dowding & Mills; Kalamazoo Group.

OSBORNE CLARKE (see firm details p.1090) Working out of the pensions and employee benefits unit, the steadily developing department is fronted by "*adroit*" **Mark Womersley**. It acts for smaller domestic clients in the FTSE 250 or below and is a panel firm for a number of major plcs. Typical work includes transactional support for existing clients in the communications and IT sectors. This year it helped establish a SIP for Allied Domecq and an LTIP for HP Bulmer Holdings. It also advised Marlborough Stirling on offshore employee share ownership trusts following the company's flotation. **Clients** 3i; C&J Clarks.

SCOTLAND

EMPLOYEE SHARE SCHEMES
SCOTLAND

1. **Dundas & Wilson CS** Edinburgh
   Maclay Murray & Spens Glasgow
   MacRoberts Glasgow

LEADING INDIVIDUALS

1. **TROTTER Peter** MacRoberts
   UP AND COMING
   TURLEY Brendan Dundas & Wilson CS

This book is the product of 6,582 1/2 hour interviews. See p.7 for BMRB audit. Within each band, firms are listed alphabetically. See individuals' profiles p.294

DUNDAS & WILSON CS (see firm details p.943) Peer recommendations suggest that the share scheme practice has a strong independent reputation, with "*dedicated*" **Brendan Turley** keeping up his profile. EMIs have kept the team busy following the lifting of the £15 million ceiling, and there has also been an increase in remedial instructions involving options that have gone underwater. Much of the team's advice is for existing technology clients, particularly university spin-outs. This year, it advised on the sale of Kymata to the Alcatel Group, and implemented an SAYE scheme for FTSE 100 company Scottish and Southern Energy. **Clients** Intense Photonics; SMG; Ardana Bioscience.

MACLAY MURRAY & SPENS (see firm details p.1048) Maureen Burnside heads up the employee incentives practice from within the employment, pensions and benefits department. The "*fresh, client-focused*" team advises on all aspects of the design and implementation of approved and unapproved schemes for quoted and unquoted companies. It acted on the crucial share scheme aspects of Blairmhor's £56 million sale, and was one of the firms employed by 3i to deal with the needs of its investment portfolio of companies. **Clients** Stiell.

MACROBERTS (see firm details p.1049) Share scheme instructions are carried out from an integrated pensions and employee benefits group headed by the esteemed and "*detail-oriented*" **Peter Trotter** (see p.296). The practice can draw on the employment, trust and tax expertise within the firm. This year, EMI implementation has been on the up, as has the proportion of private technology companies in the firm's client base. The team advised on a super cash bonus tranched exit scheme for the senior management of a large Scottish hi-tech company. A further highlight was advising on the sale of Business Computer Technology to Anite Group. **Clients** Capable Projects; Omnia Books.

EMPLOYEE SHARE SCHEMES ■ THE LEADERS

THE LEADERS IN EMPLOYEE SHARE SCHEMES

ALLEN, Barbara
Ashurst Morris Crisp, London
(020) 7859 1312
barbara.allen@ashursts.com
Specialisation: Partner in employee benefits and incentives. Advises on all aspects of the design and implementation of employee share schemes, long-term incentive plans and bonus arrangements, including the use of employee benefit trusts. Has considerable experience of the implications of flotations, mergers and acquisitions, management buyouts and demergers on such arrangements. Major clients include Dynacast International Ltd, Galen Holdings plc, ICAP plc, Imperial Tobacco Group plc, The Laird Group plc and Xansa plc.
Prof. Memberships: Share Schemes Lawyers Group; GEO.
Career: Qualified 1983. Joined *Ashursts* 1988; Partner 2001.
Publications: Directors as Trustees chapter in 'Company Directors: Law and Liability' (Sweet & Maxwell).

CHAMBERLAIN, Colin
Herbert Smith, London
(020) 7374 8000
colin.chamberlain.@herbertsmith.com
Specialisation: Partner specialising in employee share schemes and one of the leading experts in this area. Has advised some 225 or more companies, large and small, on employee share schemes in the UK and overseas, employee cash incentives, ESOPs, corporate individual savings account/personal equity plans and profit related pay.
Career: Qualified in 1977. Worked as a director of the former CC&P, now part of Bacon & Woodrow 1985-89. Became a partner at *Herbert Smith* in 1989.
Publications: 'Practical Guide to Employees' Share Schemes', Tolley's, and regular speaker at conferences on share scheme issues.
Personal: Educated at Sussex University.

CHATER, Stephen
Allen & Overy, London
(020) 7330 3000
slephen.chater@allenovery.com
Specialisation: Partner specialising in employee tax and share incentives in an international context including advice on all aspects, particularly employee share schemes, cash-based incentives, senior executives remuneration packages and executive remuneration generally.
Prof. Memberships: Law Society; Share Scheme Lawyers Group (member of training committee); Society of Share Scheme Practitioners.
Career: Joined *Allen & Overy* 1979; qualified 1981; partner 1989.
Personal: Educated at Hartlepool Grammar School and Oxford University (1981 MA). Born 1956. Lives in Surrey.

CODRINGTON, Eddie
Slaughter and May, London
(020) 7600 1200
eddie.codrington@slaughterandmay.com
Specialisation: Main areas of practice are employee benefits, pensions and employment. Deals with the establishment of all types of employee benefit plans, both cash and share based, ESOPs and AESOPs. Also handles pensions work including setting up, merger and termination of pension schemes.
Prof. Memberships: The Law Society, Association of Pensions Lawyers, Share Scheme Lawyer Group.
Career: Joined 1974, qualified 1976, partner 1985.
Personal: Born 12 April 1951. St Benedict's School, Ealing 1957-70. Birmingham University 1970-73. Interests include family and sport (watching).

COHEN, David
Norton Rose, London
(020) 7283 6000
cohendhj@nortonrose.com
Specialisation: Employee share ownership in all its various forms.
Prof. Memberships: Fellow of the Chartered Institute of Taxation; chairman of the Share Scheme Lawyers Group. Member of the advisory group set up by the government in March 1999 to work with the Inland Revenue on the development of the new employee share schemes.
Career: Qualified in 1980. Joined *Norton Rose* as a partner in May 1998. Visiting fellow in Employee Share Ownership Law at London University's Centre for Commercial Law Studies since 1995.
Publications: Author of 'Employee Participation in Flotations' annually since 1987. Contributor to the 'Encyclopaedia of Forms and Precedents'. Regular contributor to the 'Financial Times'. Member of editorial board of Palmer's 'Company Law'. Joint author of 'The New Employee Share Incentives: AESOPs and EMI' published by Sweet & Maxwell.
Personal: Born Cardiff 15 December 1955. Educated Jesus College, Oxford. Governor of Independent Jewish Day School. Vice-president, Glamorgan County Cricket Club. Lives in London.

COOPER, Janet
Linklaters, London
(020) 7456 3662
janet.cooper@linklaters.com
Specialisation: Employee Incentives Group, Head of the Global Employee Incentives Team. Specialises in employee share plans, executive incentives and corporate governance. On qualification was a general corporate lawyer before specialising in employee and executive plans, familiar with how corporate transactions affect employee share plans. Her work includes advising on, designing and drafting documentation for a variety of global and executive plans for multinationals, advising on corporate governance implications for executive plans, advising on related financial products for financial services organisations. Developed online database for global employee share plans.
Prof. Memberships: Director of Employee Share Ownership Centre; founder member of Share Schemes Advanced Studies Group; Committee member of Share Scheme Lawyers Group; Director of Global Equity Organisation (GEO); member of Recruitment Society. Member of Institute of Business Ethics.
Career: Head of the Global Employee Incentives Team. 1991 to date, partner *Linklaters*. 1984-91 Assistant Solicitor *Linklaters*. Leeds University, LLB.

CROFT, Anne
Linklaters, London
(020) 7456 3706
anne.croft@linklaters.com
Specialisation: Joined *Linklaters* Tax Department in 1988 after a career at the Bar and in tax consultancy. Moved to the Pensions, Employment and Shares Schemes Department in 1992, shortly after its formation, as 'local' tax specialist. Now in the Employee Incentives Group. Current specialisations include design and implementation of all types of share schemes, and also cash bonus schemes; tax treatment of all types of share schemes, and also cash bonus schemes, from the point of view of both the employer and the employee; National Insurance contributions and PAYE, and other areas of employee taxation; employee benefit trusts; complex corporate transactions and their impact on share schemes; start-ups and spinoffs.
Prof. Memberships: Fellow of the Chartered Institute of Taxation.
Career: Called to the Bar 1975; LLM, tax and company law (University of London) 1976. Requalified as a solicitor 1990; joined *Linklaters* Tax Department 1988; moved to Employment and Shares Schemes Department 1992; Consultant *Linklaters* 1998.

ELLERMAN, Paul
Herbert Smith, London
(020) 7374 8000
paul.ellerman@herbertsmith.com
Specialisation: Experienced share schemes lawyer, having established a wide range of schemes for a large number of quoted and unquoted companies. Has worked on many takeovers, flotations, demergers and schemes of arrangement. Has also been at the forefront of the development of international share schemes, helping to establish various types of share incentive arrangements in numerous countries worldwide.
Prof. Memberships: Share Scheme Lawyers Group; The Global Equity Organisation.
Career: *Ashurst Morris Crisp* 1990-94; *Clifford Chance* 1994-2000. Joined *Herbert Smith* as a partner in November 2000.
Personal: Girton College, Cambridge.

EVANS, Simon
Freshfields Bruckhaus Deringer, London
(020) 7936 4000
simon.evans@freshfields.com
Specialisation: Partner in employment pensions and benefits department. Specialises in share option, restricted share plan and ESOP arrangements, relating both to establishment of schemes and advice on the impact of corporate transactions on schemes. Also handles employment law, notably executive appointments and dismissals. Devised numerous long term incentive plans and other tailor-made incentive schemes. Regularly lectures on share scheme topics.
Prof. Memberships: Share Scheme Lawyers Group.
Career: Qualified in 1983. Joined *Freshfields* in 1981, becoming a partner in 1991.
Personal: Born 16 June 1957. Attended Rugby School 1970-75; MA from Sidney Sussex College, Cambridge, 1976-79. Lives in Staplehurst, Kent.

FENN, Jonathan
Slaughter and May, London
(020) 7600 1200
jonathan.fenn@slaughterandmay.com
Specialisation: Principal areas of practice are employee share schemes (both Inland Revenue approved and unapproved, including deferred bonus and long-term incentive schemes and ESOPs) and pensions, including in particular the pensions aspects of M&A and corporate transactions, as well as general pensions advice.
Prof. Memberships: The Law Society; Share Scheme Lawyers Group (member of Committee); Society of Share Scheme Practitioners; Association of Pension Lawyers (member of Legislative and Parliamentary Sub-Committee).
Career: Qualified 1986. At *Slaughter and May* 1984 to date. Became a Partner in 1995.
Personal: Born 30 May 1961. Educated at Maidstone Grammar School and King's College, London. Lives in Kent.

GREAVES, Judith
Pinsent Curtis Biddle, Leeds
(0113) 244 5000
judith.greaves@pinsents.com
Specialisation: National Practice Head of Tax. Main areas of practice are employee share schemes: approved and unapproved schemes (including Enterprise Management Incentives and SIPs), long term incentive plans, employee trusts, employee buyouts and international schemes; and corporate tax, covering acquisitions and disposals, group reorganisations and MBOs.
Prof. Memberships: Share Schemes Lawyers Group; the Global Equity Organisation.
Career: Qualified 1986 with *Linklaters & Paines*. Joined *Pinsent Curtis Biddle* in 1988, becoming Partner in 1991.

THE LEADERS ■ EMPLOYEE SHARE SCHEMES

GREEN, Lawrence
Eversheds, Birmingham
(0121) 232 1042
lawrencegreen@eversheds.com
Specialisation: Advises on planning and implementation of all types of employee share incentive arrangements. Acts for a range of quoted and private companies on UK and overseas implications and for overseas companies implementing share schemes in the UK. Charge-out rate is £295 per hour.
Career: Trained with *Evershed & Tomkinson* and qualified in 1988. Originally practised as a corporate tax lawyer before specialising exclusively in employee share incentives. Partner and head of *Evershed's* National Share Incentives group.
Personal: Born 8 March 1964. Educated at Queen Elizabeth Grammar School, Trinity Hall, Cambridge and Chester Law School. Leisure interests include cycling and mountain walking.

HAYES, Richard
Addleshaw Booth & Co, Manchester
(0161) 934 6419
richard.hayes@addleshawbooth.com
Specialisation: Partner in employee benefits department, commercial division. Specialises in employee share schemes including ESOPs, option schemes, EMIs and long term incentive schemes for both public and private companies.
Prof. Memberships: Law Society, Society of Share Scheme Practitioners.
Career: Qualified in 1972. Joined the firm in 1973, becoming a partner in 1975.
Personal: Trinity Hall, Cambridge (MA 1969, LLB 1970). Leisure interests include railways, opera, classical music and sheep.

HEPBURN, Daniel
Clifford Chance, London
(020) 7600 1000
Specialisation: Tax, Pensions and Employment Department. Senior lawyer specialising in employee share schemes both in the UK and internationally including share option schemes, employee trusts, tax approved schemes and executive incentives generally.
Career: Qualified 1992; *Travers Smith Braithwaite* 1992-95; *Linklaters* 1995-2001; joined *Clifford Chance* 2002.
Personal: The King's School, Canterbury; University College, Oxford University.

INGLE, Michael
Baker & McKenzie, London
(020) 7919 1000
michael.ingle@bakernet.com
Specialisation: Practice covers the full range of employee benefits and employment taxation. Co-ordinates the firm's practice in the area of share schemes and incentive plans, including the related transactional issues. Works closely with share schemes colleagues in other *Baker & McKenzie* offices around the world in designing and implementing cross-border schemes. Clients include banks, software and other hi-tech companies and numerous multinational companies.
Prof. Memberships: Share Schemes Lawyers Group; ProShare.
Career: Qualified 1981. At *Dunham Brindley & Linn* 1979-84, Engineering Employers Federation 1984-85; *Baker & McKenzie* from 1985 (Partner from 1990).
Personal: Born 27 April 1951. Lives in London and Sheringham, Norfolk. Educated in Canada and obtained LLB degree from the University of Western Ontario in 1974.

JACOBS, Michael
Nicholson Graham & Jones, London
(020) 7648 9000
michael.jacobs@ngj.co.uk
Specialisation: Tax; employee share schemes; international tax, trusts, charities, and public sector bodies. Author of 'Tax on Take-overs' (7 editions) and 'Rewarding Leadership' (published by Quoted Companies Alliance, February 1998); contributor to 'Tolley's Tax Planning' and 'Tolley's VAT Planning'. Consultant editor of Tolley's 'Trust Law International'.
Prof. Memberships: Trust Law Committee (Founder Member and Secretary, 1994-1997, Executive Committee Member); Share Scheme Lawyers Group (Founder Member and Vice-Chairman); Executive Committee (Member 1999-2002) and Employee Share Schemes Committee (Chairman 1996-2002) Quoted Companies Alliance; Deputy Chairman, The Young Committee on Corporate Governance and Investment of Charities (ACEVO); STEP; IFS; Charity Law Association; FRSA; Academician of (i) the Academy of the Learned Societies for the Social Sciences and (ii) International Academy of Estate & Trust Law; Fellow of The Society for Advanced Legal Studies.
Career: Articled at *Nicholson Graham & Jones* (1970). Partner 1976. Head of Private Client Department 1981.

McCARTHY, Paul
Allen & Overy, London
(020) 7330 3000
paul.mccarthy@allenovery.com
Specialisation: Partner specialising in employee share incentives and executive remuneration. Advises on all aspects of employee share incentives, including design, shareholder communication, corporate governance and best practice and their tax cost implications. Also deals with high-level recruitment and terminations. Wide experience of advising in connection with flotations, mergers and acquisitions.
Prof. Memberships: Share Scheme Lawyers Group.
Career: Educated at Bancroft's School and St Edmund Hall, Oxford. *Freshfields* 1985-93, qualified 1987; *Garretts* 1993-94, Partner 1994-2001. *Allen & Overy*, Partner 2001.
Personal: Born 1961.

MITCHELL, Jocelyn
Freshfields Bruckhaus Deringer, London
(020) 7936 4000
jocelyn.mitchell@freshfields.com
Specialisation: Main areas of practice are share schemes and employee benefits. Deals with the establishment and ongoing advisory work relating to share option schemes, long term incentive plans, ESOPs, QUESTs and international share schemes. Has extensive experience of share schemes and employment issues on mergers and acquisitions and flotations. Also advises on senior executive terminations, employment tax and the law relating to directors and corporate governance.
Prof. Memberships: Share Scheme Lawyers Group.
Career: Qualified in 1985. *Freshfields* 1995 (partner 1997).

NICHOLL, Victoria
Travers Smith Braithwaite, London
(020) 7295 3000
Victoria.Nicholl@TraversSmith.com
Specialisation: Advises on employee taxation and design, implementation and operation of UK and international employee incentives. Specialises in employee share options, enterprise management incentives bonus and long-term incentive plans, employee benefit trusts and QUESTs (including financing), corporate governance and employee benefits both generally and in relation to MBOs, flotations and other corporate transactions.
Prof. Memberships: Share Scheme Lawyers Group; Society of Share Scheme Practitioners; ESOP Centre.
Career: Qualified 1987. Joined *Travers Smith Braithwaite* 1989. Partner 1995. Head of Employee Incentives Group.

NUTTALL, Graeme
Field Fisher Waterhouse, London
(020) 7861 4000
gjn@ffwlaw.com
Specialisation: Partner in the tax department. Particular interest in employee share schemes. Has advised on the employee ownership aspects of privatisations both in the UK and overseas in Bulgaria, Macedonia, Romania and Slovenia. Regularly addresses conferences both in the UK and internationally on tax and employee share schemes. Frequently called on to assist in lobbying government for tax and other changes to encourage employee ownership, and now a member of the HM Treasury advisory group involved in helping the Inland Revenue develop new share schemes. European regional co-ordinator of Global Reward Plan Group.
Prof. Memberships: Associate of the Institute of Taxation since 1985; member of the Share Schemes Lawyers Group since 1989; member of the Taxation committee of the Intellectual Property Institute; member of HM Treasury employee ownership advisory group (1999).
Career: Qualified 1984. Assistant solicitor, *Field Fisher Martineau* 1984-88. Partner since 1988. Spent six months on secondment to *Touche Ross & Co* in 1987. Non-executive director of Job Ownership Ltd. Managing Director *Equity Incentives Limited*.
Publications: Publications include 'Employee Ownership - Legal and Tax Aspects' (co-author) 1987; 'Share Incentives for Employees' (co-author) 1990; 'Butterworths Tax Planning' (looseleaf service) (contributor); 'Butterworths UK Corporate Finance' (2nd edn 1992) (contributor); 'Nelson-Jones and Nuttall's Tax Tables' (5 editions) (co-author); 'Nuttall's Tax Tables 1994-95'; 'Sponsorship Endorsement and Merchandising' (co-author) (2nd edn 1998); 'Electronic commerce-law and practice' (co-author) (3rd edn 2001); 'Essential law for the tax practitioner' (contributor) (3rd edn 2001).
Personal: Educated at Price's Grammar School, Fareham, Hants. and Peterhouse, Cambridge (MA law) 1978-81. Lives in Surrey.

PETT, David
Pinsent Curtis Biddle, Birmingham
(0121) 200 1050
david.pett@pinsents.com
Specialisation: Tax partner and head of the employee share schemes team in Birmingham. Acknowledged specialist in all aspects of employee share schemes and employee trusts. His expertise includes: executive and employee share schemes, Share Incentive Plans/AESOPs and Enterprise Management Incentives, restricted share plans, ESOPs, share options and executive incentive schemes, both UK and international, corporate tax, mergers and acquisitions, demergers, international transactions and VAT. Was a member of the Advisory Group which worked with the Inland Revenue in putting together the legislation governing the AESOPs and EMIs.
Prof. Memberships: The Share Scheme Lawyers Group, the Global Equity Organisation and the Birmingham Share Scheme Practitioners Group.
Career: Qualified 1980, became a partner in 1985.
Publications: Author of 'Employee Share Schemes' Sweet & Maxwell (two volume updated looseleaf) and with David Cohen 'The New Employee Share Incentives: AESOPS and EMI' (Sweet & Maxwell 2000).
Personal: Educated at Lincoln College, Oxford.

POOLE, Kevin
Wragge & Co, Birmingham
(0870) 903 1000

POSTLETHWAITE, Robert
Pinsent Curtis Biddle, London
(020) 7418 7307
robert.postlethwaite@pinsents.com
Specialisation: All forms of share-based incentives for listed and private companies, including SIPs, EMI, LTTPs, other

EMPLOYEE SHARE SCHEMES ■ THE LEADERS

option plans, trusts. Transactions include flotations, bids, other acquisitions, TUPE. Clients include Integrated Dental Holdings and Dawson Holdings.
Prof. Memberships: Share Schemes Lawyers Group, Global Equity Organisation (GEO), Quoted Companies Alliance - Share Schemes Committee.
Career: Qualified 1986 as a corporate lawyer. Corporate Strategies 1995-2001; joined *Pinsent Curtis Biddle* 2001.
Personal: Educated at Trinity School, Croydon and the University of Bristol. Lives in Hertfordshire. Leisure interests include family, photography, cycling and fell walking.

RANDALL, Paul
Ashurst Morris Crisp, London
(020) 7859 1298
paul.randall@ashursts.com
Specialisation: Partner and head of employee benefits and incentives. Advises on the design, implementation and operation of domestic and international employee share option and acquisition schemes, incentives and employee trusts. Transactional experience covers MBOs, flotations, bids, mergers and privatisations. Advises on tax, corporate, stock exchange and governance aspects. Major clients include Albert Fisher, Amvescap, Coca-Cola HBC, Exel, The Laird Group plc, National Express, Royal & Sun Alliance and Taylor Nelson Sofres.
Prof. Memberships: Share Scheme Lawyers Group (member Corporate Governance Committee).
Career: Qualified 1984. Joined *Ashurst Morris Crisp* 1987, partner 1995.

ROWLANDS-HEMPEL, Graham
Linklaters, London
(020) 7456 3680
graham.rowlands-hempel@linklaters.com
Specialisation: Specialises in employee share plans and executive incentives and related matters. On qualification was a corporate tax lawyer before specialising in employee share plans and executive incentives. Main areas of practice include advising on, designing and drafting documentation on employee share plans and executive incentives, including UK revenue approved plans, restricted stock plans, employee share ownership plans (ESOPs) and other executive incentive arrangements.
Career: 1998 to date: Partner, *Linklaters*; 1994-98: Senior Assistant, *Linklaters*; 1987-94: Assistant solicitor, *Simmons & Simmons*. Spent three months with the Inland Revenue as technical advisor advising on the Government's new share plan. University of South Bank, LLB Law.

THOMPSON, Kevin
Clifford Chance, London
(020) 7006 8930
kevin.thompson@cliffordchance.com
Specialisation: Tax, Pensions and Employment Department. Partner specialising in employee share schemes, executive remuneration and all areas of employee taxation.
Career: Qualified as a barrister 1988; joined *Clifford Chance* 1988; requalified as a solicitor in 1992.
Personal: St Cuthbert's Grammar School, Newcastle Upon Tyne; St John's College, Cambridge.

TREMAINE, Robin
Clifford Chance, London
(020) 7600 1000
robin.tremaine@cliffordchance.com
Specialisation: Tax, Pensions and Employment Department. Partner, Head of Employee Share Schemes Unit in the UK and on a global basis. Has more than 20 years experience of devising and implementing employee share incentive arrangements for quoted and unquoted companies.
Career: Qualified as barrister in 1979; requalified as a solicitor in 1986; Partner since 1989.
Personal: Plymouth College; Trinity Hall, Cambridge (MA (Cantab) 1978).

TROTTER, Peter
MacRoberts, Glasgow
(0141) 332 9988
peter.trotter@macroberts.com
Specialisation: Partner and Head of Pensions and Employee Benefits Group. Pensions law (including professional independent trusteeship) and Employee Share and Management Incentive Schemes.
Prof. Memberships: Associate of Pensions Management Institute (NAPF Prize and Scottish Group Prize 1993); member of Society of Share Scheme Practitioners and Association of Pension Lawyers; PMI Scottish Group Committee member; OPAS advisor.
Career: LLB (Birm); LLB (Edin); Dip LP (Strath); APMI; Partner, Pensions and Employee Benefits Group, *MacRoberts* 1998.
Publications: Various newspaper and magazine articles.

TURLEY, Brendan
Dundas & Wilson CS, Glasgow
(0141) 222 2200

WATTS, Sylvie
Allen & Overy, London
(020) 7330 3000
sylvie.watts@allenovery.com
Specialisation: Partner specialising in incentives. Advises on the full range of incentives work, including all-employee share arrangements, executive remuneration issues and global share plans. Advises a broad client base on the design and implementation of incentives plans and on the impact of corporate transactions on such plans.
Prof. Memberships: Share Schemes Lawyers Group.
Career: *Theodore Goddard* 1986-90; *Linklaters* 1990-94; BT legal department 1994-96; *Garretts* 1996-2001 (partner in 1997); *Allen & Overy*, partner 2001.
Personal: Born 1961. Educated at St Paul's Girls' School and Cambridge.

WHITEWRIGHT, Louise
Lovells, London
(020) 7296 2000
louise.whitewright@lovells.com
Specialisation: Principal area of practice is employee share schemes and employee benefits advising on all aspects of the design, structure, establishment and operation of approved and unapproved employee share schemes (including ESOPS, restricted share schemes and international share schemes) for private and public companies. Deals with all aspects of these schemes on flotations, takeovers, privatisations etc.
Prof. Memberships: Law Society; Share Scheme Lawyers Group (Secretary and member of Executive Committee). City of London Lawyers and Global Equity Organisations.
Career: Articled *Rakisons* 1984-86; qualified 1986 with *Lovells* as an assistant solicitor in the tax group. Specialised in employee share schemes from 1987 and became a partner in 1996.

WOMERSLEY, Mark
Osborne Clarke, Bristol
(0117) 917 3000

EMPLOYMENT

London: 297; The Regions: 304; Scotland: 315; Profiles: 319

Research approved by BMRB For this edition, **Chambers'** researchers conducted 6,582 interviews – 3,900 with law firms, 511 with barristers and 2,171 with clients. The validity of the research was scrutinised by BMRB International, who audited both the methodology and the results at our offices in London. They interviewed **Chambers'** researchers and cross-checked sample interviews. Details of the audit appear on page 7.

OVERVIEW Employment law remains a stable area of practice for all firms, and legislative initiatives relating to paternity, maternity and adoption leave, religious discrimination and the National Works Council Directive are expected to provide departments with further scope for work. *Chambers* employment section covers all aspects of labour law from corporate employment policy advice, contentious discrimination and unfair dismissal claims and union recognition matters, to individual and collective redundancy agreements and large scale corporate reorganisations. Many of the larger City firms tend to focus on employment considerations arising out of mergers, acquisitions and other joint ventures, while smaller, more specialised firms handle a volume of tribunal and high court claims as well as executive compensation and severance agreements. Firms such as Thompsons and Pattinson & Brewer are well known for their national applicant representation and are most frequently seen acting for trade unions and their members in a range of employment disputes.

LONDON

MAINLY RESPONDENT

EMPLOYMENT: MAINLY RESPONDENT
■ **LONDON**

[1] Simmons & Simmons
[2] Allen & Overy
   Baker & McKenzie
[3] Eversheds
   Fox Williams
   Herbert Smith
   Lewis Silkin
   Lovells
   Mayer, Brown, Rowe & Maw
[4] Charles Russell
   Clifford Chance
   Dechert
   Denton Wilde Sapte
   Linklaters
   McDermott, Will & Emery
   Nabarro Nathanson
   Olswang
   Slaughter and May
[5] Beachcroft Wansbroughs
   Berwin Leighton Paisner
   Boodle Hatfield
   CMS Cameron McKenna
   Doyle Clayton
   Farrer & Co
   Freshfields Bruckhaus Deringer
   Hammond Suddards Edge
   Macfarlanes
   Norton Rose
   Osborne Clarke
   Salans
   Speechly Bircham
   Stephenson Harwood
   Theodore Goddard
   Travers Smith Braithwaite

This book is the product of 6,582 1/2 hour interviews. See p.7 for BMRB audit. Within each band, firms are listed alphabetically.

SIMMONS & SIMMONS (see firm details p.1136) Historically the leading practice in London, the firm maintains its edge, albeit a narrowing one, over the chasing pack. Recognised for its "*longstanding commitment to the field,*" the group has a national reputation for its "*depth of resources*" and "*lion's share*" of interesting work for major corporations. Newly appointed senior partner, "*employment goddess*" Janet Gaymer remains available for strategic advice and has been assisting on governmental employment initiatives. Her pre-eminent reputation continues to attract prestige and "*headline work*" for the practice; however, commentators believe the group will face a challenge to maintain pole position without Gaymer's daily involvement in the practice. The firm has noted strength in the financial sector, acting for a number of bulge bracket investment banks. Department head, "*gentlemanly*" William Dawson (see p.322) is growing in stature as Gaymer's successor. "*Experienced*" Simon Watson (see p.332) was noted for his "*sound judgement*" and sensible outlook. These two leading practitioners advise CSFB on employment matters, including general labour law obligations in a number of different jurisdictions, such as France, Italy and the Netherlands. On the contentious side, the group has been involved in some high-profile whistleblowing cases and represented Refuge Assurance before the Employment Appeals Tribunal (EAT) in relation to obligations to inform and consult in the context of collective redundancies. In addition, individual practitioners advise a steady base of corporate clients on risk management issues. **Clients** Associated British Ports; Deutsche Bank; Railtrack; Crown Prosecution Service; Swiss Re Financial Products; Barclays; Telegraph; Royal Shakespeare Company; Invesco.

ALLEN & OVERY (see firm details p.841) Seen to be the most serious challenger to Simmons & Simmons' pre-eminent position, the firm has "*come on in leaps and bounds*" through strategic recruitment and "*effective management.*" Benefiting from the firm's outstanding corporate base, practitioners receive a steady stream of high level transactional work. It has, however, also made a concerted effort to strengthen its contentious employment capabilities. Some commentators consider it to be "*the only magic circle firm with a plausible self-standing employment practice.*" The group now ranks amongst the larger employment teams in the city and provides cross-border advice through the firm's global network. Department head, Mark Mansell (see p.327) rates highly for his "*professionalism*" and "*no-nonsense approach.*" Recommended for his "*breadth of vision,*" Mansell is credited as the driving force behind the practice's rapid development. "*Assertive*" Karen Seward (see p.330) brings "*boundless energy and fantastic client skills*" to contentious and non-contentious matters. She is best known for her expertise in discrimination matters, including dignity at work and bullying. Up-and-coming Stefan Martin (see p.327) has recently been visible acting on the Nomura unpaid bonus case. Practitioners advise a large proportion of financial services clients and maintain distinct client-focused departments offering bespoke training services. Recently, the group acted for ACE Insurance Group on interlocutory applications for injunction relief at the High Court. **Clients** KPMG; HSBC Investment Bank; Bank of America; Accenture; GE Capital; Sega Enterprises; Level 3 Communications; Nestlé; Cable & Wireless.

BAKER & MCKENZIE (see firm details p.855) This large, internationally-focused team is said to "*combine youth and energy,*" advising multinational corporates across a variety of industry sectors. Clients believe practitioners' ability to "*link up with lawyers in offices around the world*" to be a substantial advantage in cross-jurisdictional advisory work. The group is reputed for pan-European projects, with individuals noted for their expertise in matters before European

297

www.ChambersandPartners.com

EMPLOYMENT ■ LONDON

LEADING INDIVIDUALS

1
- **AARONS Elaine** Eversheds
- **DAVIES James** Lewis Silkin
- **JEFFREYS Simon** CMS Cameron McKenna
- **YOUNSON Fraser** McDermott, Will & Emery
- **AUERBACH Simon** Pattinson & Brewer
- **FROST Peter** Herbert Smith
- **MANSELL Mark** Allen & Overy

2
- **BURD Michael** Lewis Silkin
- **FARR John** Herbert Smith
- **OSMAN Chris** Clifford Chance
- **ROSKILL Julian** Mayer, Brown, Rowe & Maw
- **DAWSON William** Simmons & Simmons
- **JACOBS Howard** Slaughter and May
- **ROBERTSON Nicholas** Mayer, Brown, Rowe & Maw
- **WYNN-EVANS Charles** Dechert

3
- **ADAMS Elizabeth** Beachcroft Wansbroughs
- **BREARLEY Kate** Stephenson Harwood
- **GREEN David** Charles Russell
- **JEFFERS Raymond** Linklaters
- **MANN Jane** Fox Williams
- **SEWARD Karen** Allen & Overy
- **WHINCUP David** Hammond Suddards Edge
- **ASHTIANY Sue** Nabarro Nathanson
- **DALE Stephanie** Denton Wilde Sapte
- **HARPER David** Lovells
- **JULYAN Alan** Speechly Bircham
- **O'BRIEN Christine** Baker & McKenzie
- **WATSON Simon** Simmons & Simmons

4
- **CAVALIER Stephen** Thompsons
- **FEINSTEIN Naomi** Lovells
- **FOX Ronnie** Fox Williams
- **THOMPSON Tony** Macfarlanes
- **DALGARNO David** McDermott, Will & Emery
- **FLANAGAN Tom** Stephenson Harwood
- **MORDSLEY Barry** Salans

5
- **BREEN Helga** Eversheds
- **COOPER Edward** Russell Jones & Walker
- **DINELEY Rachel** Beachcroft Wansbroughs
- **HOWARD Clive** Russell Jones & Walker
- **LANGLEY Dale** Dale Langley & Co
- **LILLEY Andrew** Travers Smith Braithwaite
- **RUSSELL Timothy** Norton Rose
- **TAYLOR Catherine** Olswang
- **BRIMELOW Russell** Boodle Hatfield
- **DANIELS Paul** Russell Jones & Walker
- **GALLAGHER Yvonne** Lawrence Graham
- **HUNTER Ian** Bird & Bird
- **LEVINSON Stephen** KLegal
- **RALPH Nick** Archon
- **SMELLIE David** Farrer & Co

UP AND COMING
- **DANDRIDGE Nicola** Thompsons
- **GOODWILL Christopher** Clifford Chance
- **MARTIN Stefan** Allen & Overy
- **NESBITT Sean** Taylor Wessing
- **WETHERFIELD Alison** McDermott, Will & Emery
- **EVASON John** Baker & McKenzie
- **KEEBLE Sarah** Olswang
- **MAYHEW Lisa** Lovells
- **TEMPERTON Ellen** Baker & McKenzie

See individuals' profiles p.319

Works Councils. Commended for "*clear advice*" and "*cost effective service*," interviewees report that the practice "*brings a lot of brains to the party.*" Most notably, practice head **Christine O'Brien** (see p.329) is considered a leading figure for her "*understanding of business concerns.*" O'Brien has been advising the executive directors of Railtrack in connection with administration proceedings, service agreements, variation letters and confidentiality issues. Younger partners **John Evason** (see p.323) and **Ellen Temperton** (see p.331) were recommended as up-and-coming practitioners for their respective strengths in TUPE and data protection. On the contentious side, the firm continues to represent JPMorgan on an ongoing sex discrimination claim before the EAT brought by Aisling Sykes. Other areas of expertise include employment tax and collective rights matters. **Clients** JPMorgan; United Business Media; Sony; BP Chemicals; Cisco; Camelot; AOL; Equant; Hewlett-Packard; Nortel; Lloyd's of London; Avis; Airtours.

EVERSHEDS (see firm details p.949) Pre-eminent among the national practices, the firm boasts 130 employment law practitioners spread across 11 offices in England and Wales. In London, department head **Elaine Aarons** (see p.319) is considered the "*lynchpin*" of the practice. Something of a "*rainmaker,*" Aarons has leveraged a high-profile ELA reputation into "*making Eversheds a force to be reckoned with.*" Engaged in both practice development and a variety of contentious and transactional matters, she is said to be "*prepared to take tough strategic decisions.*" She recently advised De Beers on the employment aspects of a joint-venture with Louis Vuitton, providing counsel on senior executive contracts and TUPE. A "*fearsome*" team includes younger partner **Helga Breen** (see p.320). She is said to "*add stability*" to negotiations, but "*can match aggression for aggression when she needs to.*" Breen has experience of large scale collective redundancies and TU recognition claims. The team acts for a number of education and local authority clients and recently advised OFSTED on the transfer of 1,500 care staff from local authorities across the country. The practice offers an HR consultancy and has recently expanded through recruitment to the London office. **Clients** HSBC Investment Bank; FSA; Dow Chemical; Toronto Dominion Bank; Deloitte & Touche; Queen Mary and King's Colleges, University of London.

FOX WILLIAMS (see firm details p.962) This "*boutique*" practice is as well known for its representation of high-profile individuals in employment cases as for its volume of employer-based advisory work. Employment and partnerships form the two core practice areas for the firm and, thanks to the group's "*clear commitment to employment,*" it is a frequent recipient of referral work from larger city firms. The group's "*go-getter*" attitude wins praise from clients who find the team "*responsive and business-minded.*" Consistently attracting top-end work, the group acts for well-known names in the insurance, financial, technology, education, and e-commerce sectors. It boasts a number of highly regarded personalities, including department head, **Jane Mann** (see p.327). An active and visible figure at the employment bar due to her role as ELA co-founder and chairman, she specializes in employment litigation for corporates and individuals, to which she contributes a sound knowledge of immigration matters. Peers commend her as a "*down to earth*" individual with "*real enthusiasm for the subject.*" Mann recently obtained a substantial settlement for Isabelle Terrillon in relation to her well-publicised sex discrimination claim against Nomura International. Founding partner **Ronnie Fox** (see p.323) has an equally high profile for his work on termination agreements. A "*strategic thinker,*" Fox advised John Mayo in his departure from Marconi and continues to win mentions for his representation of individual Law Society employees in their case against vice president Kamlesh Bahl. **Clients** BHP Billiton; Broadview International; Added Value Company; OFTEL; Mellon Bank; Charter; National Instruments; The College of Law; Lawn Tennis Association.

HERBERT SMITH (see firm details p.992) This is a "*top drawer*" contentious practice complemented by a healthy workload of non-contentious employment matters off the back of UK and international dealwork. Upholding the firm's general reputation for quality litigious work, the group receives widespread recommendation for its representation of corporates in discrimination claims and injunction proceedings before the EAT and the High Court. Additionally, it is visible acting for senior executives in contractual disputes and compensation agreements. Practice head, **John Farr** (see p.323), is known to be "*tough but gentlemanly*" in difficult negotiations. He has particular experience in defending financial institutions against discrimination claims, and most recently represented CSFB on two claims of racial discrimination. "*Measured*" partner **Peter Frost** (see p.323) is "*fantastically good*" in tribunals – "*he knows when to press buttons and when to litigate.*" Frost recently advised PwC/Independent Insurance on all employment aspects of Independent Insurance Group's collapse, including defending tribunal claims by ex-employees. On the non-contentious side, the group has expertise in team moves resulting from mergers and restructurings and can advise on works councils and union recognition matters. **Clients** British American Tobacco; Northern Electric; UBS Warburg; Iceland; CSFB; Chevron/Texaco; Credit Lyonnais; Standard & Poor's.

LEWIS SILKIN (see firm details p.1041) Described by interviewees as a "*friendly*" practice, "*alive to developments in employment law*" the team is acknowledged to have considerably raised its market profile. In recent years it has grown through "*savvy recruiting*" and the employment department now comprises close to a quarter of the overall firm. The group focuses on media and advertising clients and acts for a number of law firms in employment disputes and negotiations. It is deemed by peers to be "*uniformly excellent*" and to offer "*extremely good value.*" A well known figure in employment circles, **James Davies** (see p.322) was praised as "*commercial and pragmatic*" and is credited with bringing the firm increasingly into the spotlight. He co-heads the practice with "*shrewd*" partner **Michael Burd** (see p.320) a "*tough cookie*" who "*keeps his head in litigation*" and "*always produces first-rate documents.*" The team advises a share of high-level individual employees and has been involved in training initiatives for corporate clients. It has recently represented the actors' union, Equity, in a dispute with film producers over the amounts its members receive for secondary uses of films in which they appear. **Clients** BAA; Dow Chemical; Bonhams; Pizza Express; AXA Group; Worldcom; Rio Tinto; Odeon Cinemas; FT Knowledge; Royal Albert Hall; The Lowe Group; Hermes Group.

LOVELLS (see firm details p.1045) This "*focused*" practice is reputed to have "*strength at a number of levels.*" The firm has devoted resources to developing its European offices and can now co-ordinate multi-jurisdictional employment advice on cross-border transactions and documentation. "*Accomplished*" practitioner Andrew Williamson is retiring from practice, but leaves a solid group with "*top technical skills*" behind him. Practice head **David Harper** (see p.324) has been described as "*firm but fair*" in his approach to negotiations. He led the team advising Honeywell on a claim for union recognition involving a full-scale ballot under the auspices of the CAC. Partner **Naomi Feinstein** (see p.323) is reported to have

a "*good tactical sense of what will work in litigation*" and was described to researchers as particularly impressive on discrimination matters. She recently acted for 3i in a major UK restructuring. The group maintains strong ties with Barclays and has advised the bank on a range of sensitive tribunal claims relating to race, sex and disability discrimination, equal pay and unfair dismissal. The recent acquisition of two new partners is perceived to deliver a substantial boost to the practice. In particular, **Lisa Mayhew** (see p.328), recently of Charles Russell, is esteemed a "*rising star*" in the field and ranks for the first time this year in the up-and-coming tables. **Clients** Barclays; 3i; Merrill Lynch; Tomkins; Honeywell; IKEA; Ford; Esso; Trinity Mirror; Texaco; Woolwich.

MAYER, BROWN, ROWE & MAW (see firm details p.1060) Commentators look on with interest to see the effects of the firm's recent US-UK merger, speculating on the group's opportunities to increase its international focus. Generally, the team is seen to be "*making great strides*" in employment and rates highly for its "*sound, pragmatic advice.*" Many attribute the group's success to department head, **Julian Roskill** an "*immensely experienced*" practitioner with a "*clear vision*" for his team. Junior partner **Nick Robertson** is both "*supremely bright*" and "*technically excellent.*" Interviewees praise him warmly as a "*star of the future*" who is "*going places quickly.*" The team offers 'behind the scenes' advice on boardroom disputes and senior executive arrivals and departures and supports the corporate department on major acquisitions, restructurings and joint ventures. On the contentious side it acted for Aviation Defence International in the Court of Appeal on the application of TUPE to out-sourcing and whether a transferee's motive for not taking staff can be investigated by a tribunal. Within the past year the practice has also seen an increase in instructions relating to stress and personal injury claims. **Clients** DHL; Kingfisher; Independent News & Media; Reuters; Marsh Corporate Services; Danske Bank; EMI; Watson Wyatt.

CHARLES RUSSELL (see firm details p.904) This "*responsive*" team applies a "*flexible*" approach to a range of contentious and transactional matters. The group is distinguished by its expertise in discrimination claims and success in novel suits in the EAT, Court of Appeal and House of Lords. Head of the employment and pensions unit, **David Green** (see p.324) has "*made a good name for himself*" representing senior executives in severance and compensation agreements. He has recently been acting in the important Harvest Town Circle v Rutherford on whether the upper age limited for unfair dismissal and redundancy payments is discriminatory. The practice has attracted a growing number of clients within the leisure sector and continues to assist a stable base of financial ser-

vices, manufacturing and trade association clients. Individual practitioners have particular knowledge of maternity and paternity issues, while the practice as a whole has been involved in some notable pro-bono work such as race discrimination case Anay v. University of Oxford. **Clients** Royal College of Nursing; London Philharmonic Orchestra; KLM; Scoot; Singer & Friedlander; Interserve; Hoares Bank; The Jockey Club; American Embassy; The Law Society.

CLIFFORD CHANCE (see firm details p.911) Bigger and broader than the group's reputation for high quality support work suggests, the practice benefits from a ready base of household name clients. It provides employment advice in connection with both large corporate transactions and day-to-day problems and planning. **Chris Osman** (see p.329) heads the employment unit and has extensive expertise in merger, reorganisation and redundancy situations. His "*unassuming*" manner and "*measured*" approach are a big hit with clients, particularly among the practice's large base on financial institutions. In addition to an array of transactional work, in the past year Osman has taken the lead for the private sector in working out the government's retention of employment model for health sector PFI work. "*Helpful*" **Chris Goodwill** (see p.324) has experience of collective employment issues and senior executive/director dismissals, and remains rated as an up-and-coming practitioner. Notable work for the group includes advising Accenture as part of their New York IPO and co-ordinating advice to them on employment issues throughout the world. **Clients** Bank of New York; ABN AMRO; Honda; Lego; Volvo; Kvaerner; KKR; Ernst & Young; Intel; HSBC; Dynegy; XL Insurance; JPMorgan Chase; CGNU; Applied Power; Accenture; Rolex.

DECHERT (see firm details p.934) Valued for its client care and commercial advice, this "*small but potent*" practice holds its own against larger competitors. Head of department **Charles Wynn-Evans** (see p.333) is described by clients as "*amenable and easy to deal with*" but is felt by rivals to be a "*clever and fearsome*" opponent. He and his team rate highly for their "*understanding of business concerns*" and "*willingness to listen to all sides.*" An eclectic client base includes heavy concentrations of financial services, insurance, retail and media companies. Additional practices in the US, France, Belgium and Luxembourg allow the group to provide cross-border employment advice to multinationals. The team has been advising on and co-ordinating collective consultations over business transfer and redundancies for Bridge Information Systems and Telerate. It has also recently assisted a number of high-profile individuals in claims, including representing two professional footballers in disputes with their former clubs. **Clients** Lloyds TSB; Travelex; Mellon Bank; Etam; Hercules; JC Decaux United; Saatchi &

EMPLOYMENT ■ LONDON

Saatchi; St. Ives Web; Amlin; South African Airways; Mizuho Capital Markets; Saga.

DENTON WILDE SAPTE (see firm details p.935) This full-service practice has noted strength in the aviation, TMT and energy sectors. "*Understated*" department head **Stephanie Dale** (see p.322) was warmly praised for her leadership abilities. Interviewees report that she "*knows how to get things done.*" In the past year Dale has been instructed by several airlines, including BA, Delta and Swissair/Sabena in relation to post-September 11th employment problems. The team is once again seen to be gathering manpower following some recent additions at both partner and senior assistant level. Expertise ranges from industrial relations to PFI/PPP and executive departures. Benefiting from the firm's overall renown for corporate restructuring work, the group has lately been active in advising on a number of insolvency-related employment matters, including the employment aspects of Federal Moguls administration/Chapter 11 proceedings. On the contentious side, the group acted for Sainsburys and Tibbett & Britten defending a 100+ multi-applicant employment tribunal case for unfair redundancy, TUPE claims and a protective award arising out of the closure of a distribution depot. **Clients** Ford Motor; Old Mutual; British Airways; Universal; Nokia; Interpublic Group of Companies; Paramount Home Entertainment; Capital Radio; Chicago Bridge and Iron.

LINKLATERS (see firm details p.1043) With access to the firm's enormous base of blue-chip corporations, the market perceives this group's major strength to be in corporate support work on large and complex international transactions. It is able to orchestrate cross-border employment advice with specialists in Asia and Europe and is frequently seen on the largest global M&A, joint venture, PFI/PPP and property deals. The group has, however, also devoted resources to building up its employment litigation capabilities and receives a sizeable portion of standalone advisory work in relation to restructurings, pan-European employment law compliance and strategic planning. "*Gentlemanly*" head of employment, **Raymond Jeffers** (see p.325) is said to be "*an extremely nice chap but he doesn't let that get in the way.*" "*Cerebral*" in style, peers and clients report that he is "*well versed in employment law.*" He recently advised AstraZeneca on the outsourcing of its IT infrastructure (£1.7 billion) throughout 26 countries in Europe, Asia, the Americas and Australasia. On contentious matters, the group has been involved in unusual claims relating to sexual orientation discrimination, workplace stress and employee whistle-blowing. **Clients** BHP Billiton; BP; London Electricity; BBC; Innogy; ABN AMRO; Toronto Dominion Bank; Vodaphone; Lloyds TSB; Halifax Group; Uniq; Computacenter; CSFB.

MCDERMOTT, WILL & EMERY (see firm details p.1064) A "*heavyweight*" practice of "*big name employment specialists,*" the team has forged close ties with the HR and legal departments of major international corporations and financial institutions on the strength of its high-profile partners. Best known is "*slick*" **Fraser Younson** (see p.333), a "*larger than life*" character noted for his strategic advice and ability to "*see the big picture.*" Younson is reported to have a "*thorough understanding of EU Works Council issues*" and was particularly recommended for complex pan-European transactions. A "*tough negotiator,*" **David Dalgarno** (see p.322) focuses primarily on high court litigation within the financial sector. His expertise in this area ranges from garden leave injunctions, restrictive covenants, wrongful dismissal claims and employment tribunal discrimination claims. Younger partner **Alison Wetherfield** (see p.333) was described as "*bright and commercial*" and enters the rankings this year. Recent highlights include advising BAE systems on the employment aspects of a joint venture with Xchanging for the provision of HR services to BAE, and representing United Airlines at a tribunal in relation to US-UK cross staffing and hiring. **Clients** Avis Europe; Fuji Bank; Industrial Bank of Japan; EMI; Baden-Wurrtembergische; Emerson Electric; Levi Strauss; United Airlines; Dow Jones; Balfour Beatty; Dai-ichi Kangyo Bank.

NABARRO NATHANSON (see firm details p.1080) The recruitment of high-profile practitioner **Sue Ashtiany** (see p.319) over a year ago has dramatically boosted the firm's standing in the London market. Since her arrival the group has doubled in size, now numbering two partners and ten assistants. Praised as "*down to earth*" and possessing a "*phenomenal knowledge of employment,*" Ashtiany is well known for her expertise in discrimination matters and management changeovers. Her continued presence in London is expected to further revitalise the department. Within the past year the group has defended HSBC in a multiple claim brought by 78 employees concerning bonuses; advised on a restructuring programme for Unipart Group and the Rover Businesses Unit; and defended Oxford University in judicial review proceedings. **Clients** HSBC; Ofgem; Land Securities; The Met Office; Oxford University Press; Unipart; Philips Electronics UK.

OLSWANG (see firm details p.1087) This "*lively*" group offers "*constructive*" advice in both standalone and corporate-driven transactional matters. The team is particularly popular with clients in the TMT sector, who believe it to be "*in tune with market developments.*" Partner **Catherine Taylor** (see p.331) has "*come up quickly in the field.*" She divides her time between High Court litigation and general advisory work and has been seen acting for the likes of Bloomberg, Yahoo! and MC Saatchi. **Sarah Keeble** (see p.326) was described as similarly "*switched on.*" Her practice is more generalist in nature, encompassing TUPE law, trade union recognition matters and discrimination claims within the Employment Tribunal. The group represents high-level individuals in termination arrangements and has seen an increase in redundancy instructions. Additional strength exists in the areas of data protection and restrictive covenant agreements. In the past year the firm has acted for Elizabeth Murdoch's company, Shine Limited, on implementing employment arrangements, and acted in the restructuring of a finance house. **Clients** Warner Music; ITE; Cantor Fitzgerald; Minerva; BBC Worldwide; The Law Society; Tokyo Mitsubishi International; HIT Entertainment; Yahoo!; Channel 4 Television.

SLAUGHTER AND MAY (see firm details p.1140) Fuelled by the massive engine that is the firm's corporate department, the team provides employment support on complex and high-value commercial transactions. This non-contentious practice rates highly both for the consistent technical quality of its practitioners and its access to large multinational clients. Leading figure **Howard Jacobs** (see p.325) was described to researchers as "*pre-eminent for M&A employment matters.*" An employment law generalist, he contributes substantial knowledge of pensions and share schemes issues to transactional due diligence and TUPE advice. Interviewees appreciate his "*straight-talking*" style and can rely on him to "*call a shovel a shovel.*" "*Entirely at ease in the boardroom,*" Jacobs was frequently recommended for senior executive termination agreements and management reorganisations. Major recent work for the group includes advising on the pensions and employment aspects in Japan, Sweden and the UK of a joint venture between the mobile telephone businesses of Ericsson and Sony. **Clients** Schroders; Cadbury Schweppes; Star Capital Partners; E.ON.

BEACHCROFT WANSBROUGHS (see firm details p.860) Traditionally associated with public sector and health work, the firm is increasing its marketshare of commercial clients. Operating at a national level, the firm has employment practitioners based in offices across the country. "*Clear-sighted*" **Elizabeth Adams** (see p.319) heads the national practice and has extensive experience in relation to TUPE and working time issues. In charge of the London practice is **Rachel Dineley** (see p.322), who was roundly commended by interviewees for her knowledge of discrimination issues. The group has notable strength in contentious matters and was instructed by ICI in a leading case dealing with misrepresentation and TUPE transfers, Hagen and Others v ICI Chemicals and Polymers and Others. Additional highlights for the group include representing fire authorities in cases brought by the Fire Brigades Union, on behalf of 14,000 retained fire fighters, to test the Part-time Workers Regulations. The team has also advised the Business Services Association on proposals for changing the way TUPE operates in NHS PFI deals. **Clients** Business Services Association; Kvaerner Oil and Gas; ICI; University Hospital of Coventry & Warwickshire NHS Trust; London Probation Board; Jones Lang LaSalle; Logica.

BERWIN LEIGHTON PAISNER (see firm details p.866) Clients have only positive things to say about the "*quality of service and breadth of expertise*" provided by Berwin Leighton Paisner's team. With greater resources available since last year's merger, the team can provide wide-ranging advice to a stable base of financial and commercial clients and individual senior employees. The three-partner practice is led by Rob Eldridge and has earned a reputation in high-profile discrimination cases. In the past year it advised the private finance unit of the Department of Health concerning an alternative to non-clinical NH trust employees transferring out of the sector on PFI/PPP projects. The team also provided harassment training to Tullett & Tokyo Liberty following adverse publicity arising out of 'Nazi uniform' allegations. The firm is currently representing Schroder Securities in an ECJ appeal regarding a much publicised equal pay claim brought by employee Julie Bower. **Clients** BAFTA; Medisys; The Newspaper Society; KLM; AON; Marriott Ownership Resorts; Little Chef and Travelodge; Universal Music; Whitbread; Time Products; Psion.

BOODLE HATFIELD (see firm details p.881) Key figure Russell Brimelow (see p.320) heads the employment practice from the firm's growing Oxford office and divides his time between the two sites. Said to inspire "*tremendous client loyalty*" the team advise a large body of media, technology and communications clients on contentious work, strategic issues and day-to-day employment problems. Additionally, the team frequently receives referral work in connection with senior executive termination agreements. Practitioners are said by clients to offer "*attentive*" service and "*constructive, business savvy*" advice. The team has been advising Viacom and its subsidiaries on restructuring, EU law changes and the drafting of employment handbooks and policies. At the applicant level, the team has advised the managing director of a PR Agency which took out a High Court injunction to prevent him working with or for any competitor. **Clients** MTV Europe; Viacom; Computacenter; Instinet; Blockbuster; Sky TV; JCB; Thomson Financial; Energis; Nickleodeon UK.

CMS CAMERON MCKENNA (see firm details p.914) In addition to corporate support work on m&a, insolvency and PPP projects, the practice undertakes corporate governance work, tribunal and high court employment litigation and general advisory work. The group is felt by clients to offer "*straightforward*" advice and was commended for its "*efficient use of the firm's CMS network*" in large transactions. At the helm is "*personable*" Simon Jeffreys (see p.325), commonly described to researchers as the "*face of the Cameron McKenna practice.*" His highly praised communication skills serve him well both in the employment law conference circuit and in complex commercial negotiations. He led the group in providing employment due diligence and advice to Nomura on its £1.9 billion acquisition of the Meridien chain of hotels, encompassing around 150 properties in 55 countries. On the contentious side, the practice successfully represented a financial sector client in a £4 million wrongful dismissal claim brought by a former country manager based in South Africa. **Clients** Commerzbank; DERA; Bayer; IGE Medical Systems; Convergys-CBIS; BAE Systems; Aventis; Amazon.com; Eli Lilly; Pfizer; Virgin Atlantic; Wellcome Trust; KPMG; Porsche; CBS.

DOYLE CLAYTON (see firm details p.942) This niche employment firm, with its mixed applicant/respondent practice, is widely praised as "*an incredibly impressive outfit.*" Six specialist employment lawyers, led by founding partners Peter Doyle and Darren Clayton, benefit from their first-class reputation in receiving high levels of individual employee referrals from larger City firms. Big employer-based practices frequently see the team on the other side of senior executive terminations, negotiations and disputes and rate it highly for its "*sensible*" approach. Individual practitioners are said to "*know when to fight their corner and when to compromise.*" Although the firm's market reputation largely rests on its work for individuals, the greater share of the workload actually involves instructions from corporate employers in relation to discrimination claims and large scale redundancies. **Clients** Sara Lee; Dixons; Shanks.

FARRER & CO (see firm details p.952) Said to be "*scooping up*" conflict work from larger city practices, this group is popular with peers and clients and receives a large share of referral work. Department head David Smellie (see p.331) "*knows his stuff*" and is seen to be successfully building up the combined employment and pensions practice. The team was particularly recommended for its representation of high-profile, wealthy individuals and in the past year advised 1,000 investment bankers seeking advice on 'golden hellos' or 'golden handshakes.' An illustrious client list includes a large number of education, arts and research institutions as well as notable charities and media organisations. The firm acted in Ebuzoeme and Anywanwu v South Bank University and Student Union. Other noteworthy cases include Charterhouse School's handling of a school master undergoing a sex change and a reported race discrimination claim against one of the Royal Households. **Clients** RHM Foods; NESTA; Westpac; ANZ Bank; Campanile; Haymarket; Starbucks; Amerada Hess; The National Gallery; Victoria &Albert Museum; Imperial War Museum; Independent Schools Council; Independent Schools' Bursars Association.

FRESHFIELDS BRUCKHAUS DERINGER (see firm details p.964) Employment is handled from within an integrated employment, pensions and benefits team providing multi-disciplinary advice on large commercial transactions, contentious matters and general corporate governance. Nicholas Squire leads a large "*dependable*" team, envied for the quality of its client base and deal lists. The firm recently created a European working group to deliver seamless service to companies operating in multiple jurisdictions. Over the past year, the group has seen an increase in insolvency-related employment matters, trade union and collective issues and workforce rationalisations. The practice advised Andersen on employment issues related to the receivership, administration and liquidation of various members of the Photobition Group, and acted for Hewlett-Packard on the implementation of a worldwide redundancy plan. **Clients** Agilent Technologies; ICI; British Nuclear Fuels; Goldman Sachs; AMP; P&O; Reuters; Logica; Kingfisher; UK Coal; Lafarge; Tyco; Ineos; Novar; Seagram; KPMG; British Telecom.

HAMMOND SUDDARDS EDGE This strong operation is, in the words of one competitor, "*even stronger for its support outside of London.*" The group acts almost exclusively for employers, with a heavy concentration of clients in the financial, media and advertising sectors. A "*feisty character,*" department head David Whincup is, say clients, uniquely distinguished in his ability to "*make employment law fun.*" **Clients** National Australia Bank; Electronics Boutique; Cornhill Insurance; Japan Airlines; Bodyshop; ABN AMRO; Best Foods; Granada Compass.

MACFARLANES (see firm details p.1047) Situated within a broader employment, pensions and benefits group, the three- partner employment practice offers cross-disciplinary advice on a range of employment issues. "*Accomplished*" department head, Tony Thompson is best known for his expertise in employment litigation, but also handles a full load of non-contentious and advisory matters. Noted strength exists in relation to injunction proceedings. The team recently acted on behalf of ICAP in overturning an injunction brought by senior broker Julian Swain in both London and New York. Non-contentious matters include advising on a 300-employee TUPE transfer arising out of Barracuda Group's acquisition of 50 pubs from Wolverhampton and Dudley Breweries. **Clients** 3i; ICAP; Jaguar Racing; Barracuda Group; Cinven; Ian Schrager Hotels; Kentucky Fried Chicken; Credit Suisse Asset Management; Carlton

EMPLOYMENT ■ LONDON

Communications; Regional Independent Media; Pernod Ricard.

NORTON ROSE (see firm details p.1084) The practice offers a full employment law service encompassing a range of contentious and non-contentious issues. With employment specialists located throughout Europe, the group is able to co-ordinate non-UK employment law advice on cross-border matters, and provides additional support on related immigration issues. Practice head **Tim Russell** (see p.330) was commended to researchers for "*driving Norton Rose forward*" and "*coming up with innovative ideas.*" A part time tribunal chairman, he is well known for his expertise in boardroom disputes and employment tribunal claims. He recently successfully defended Mizuho Capital Markets in a six-day sex discrimination case brought by its in-house lawyer. The past year has seen the launch of the practice's employment intranet service, which has met with an enthusiastic response from clients. Transactional work has included advising Airline Group in its successful bid to become the government's strategic partner in the PPP for National Air Traffic Services. **Clients** P&O; France Telecom; Kelda Group; Axon; AXA; HSBC; Burberry; Exxon Mobil; Continental Airlines; English Heritage; Bovis; CGNU; easyGroup; Lancaster Landmark.

OSBORNE CLARKE (see firm details p.1090) The employment practice operates on a national level with four partners in London able to draw on the resources of a large Bristol practice. Clients appreciate the group's "*professionalism and responsive attitude.*" Ralph Nathan leads a London team which was rated for its "*understanding of business demands.*" It has a loyal following of media clients whom it advises on all aspects of employment law, with particular expertise in restraint of trade and business restructures. The team recently advised online bank, Egg, on a rationalisation project across three sites nationally and the associated transfer of staff to a joint-venture company. It has specialists focusing on everything from TUPE transfers and trade union recognition, to restrictive covenants and maternity rights. It also occasionally represents senior executives in termination negotiations. The group notably achieved a settlement for a magic circle law firm against indirect sex discrimination claims brought by a female employee. **Clients** Prudential; Nomura International; Dexia Banque Internationale; Independent Television Commission; Toa Re Underwriting; Zurich Insurance; Cosworth Racing; Nortel Networks UK.

SALANS (see firm details p.1121) The firm's strong reputation in the field is due largely to the profile of highly-rated practitioner, **Barry Mordsley** (see p.328), the "*man behind the Salans practice.*" Well regarded for his expertise in unfair dismissal claims, Mordsley sits as part time employment tribunal chair. He is supported by one additional partner and four assistants covering the gamut from senior executive severance agreements to corporate support and advisory work. Clients report that the team "*always gets right to the issues.*" The group has been advising William Baird on a major redundancy programme involving 4,000 employees. On the contentious side, the firm recently acted for the British Cycling Federation on a case determining whether an athlete is legally an employee of a sports governing body. **Clients** Parity Group; National Grid; Rotch Property; British Cycling Federation; Rotary Watches; Northumbrian Water.

SPEECHLY BIRCHAM (see firm details p.1141) The practice continues to attract high quality recruits, most recently Chris Southam from the Bristol office of Osborne Clarke. Three full-time partners maintain close links with the firm's pensions and employee benefits practices to provide "*complete picture*" advice on claims and remuneration arrangements in redundancy situations. Department head **Alan Julyan** (see p.326) was particularly noted by clients and competitors for his knowledge of TUPE and board level negotiation skills. The firm has been acting for Takenaka UK in a large scale redundancy exercise, and represented a division of Drake International in relation to various employment claims, including unfair dismissal, race and trade union discrimination. It has an emphasis on City financial institutions, but also acts for a broad range of manufacturing, leisure, health care and charity clients. **Clients** EMI Records; The Law Debenture Corp; GWK Group; Dan Technology Holdings; Royal Bank of Scotland; P&O Properties; Thomas Cook; RSPB.

STEPHENSON HARWOOD (see firm details p.1147) The strong reputations of two headline partners keep this team within any list of leading employment practices. Practice head **Kate Brearley** (see p.320) was praised as having "*lots of substance.*" Like the team beneath her, she is known for her "*responsive*" attitude and quick turnaround of work: "*she just gets on and does it*" say clients. Brearley acts for both corporate employers and senior level executives in large team moves and individual redundancies and has particular expertise in restrictive covenants, confidentiality issues and injunction proceedings. Her colleague **Tom Flanagan** (see p.323) has a high profile in the application of TUPE to corporate transactions and outsourcing. The group draws upon practitioners in the related areas of immigration, pensions, tax and employee benefits in advising a range of shipping, merchant banking, telecoms manufacturing and educational clients. In the past year it has acted for Midland Bank (now HSBC) in a major test case relating to part time pensions. It also advised MacDonald Hotels on its bids to purchase Hertigate Hotels and the Posthouse chain from the Forte Hotel division of Compass. **Clients** HSBC; KPMG; Laing Homes; MacDonald Hotels; Credit Suisse Group; EM Production; sports.com; Gibson Dunn & Crutcher; Christie's International; Den norske Bank; Vodafone.

THEODORE GODDARD (see firm details p.1158) This combined employment and employee benefits practice, under the leadership of partner Jane Bullen, has been strengthened by the recent addition of a new partner. Employment specialist Peter Cooke continues as managing partner and is therefore not visible in daily fee-earning work. The group covers the full spectrum of employment matters from executive termination agreements to tribunal claims. Interviewees commented on practitioners' "*attention to detail*" and "*personable*" client manner. Recent highlights include advising a multinational corporation on the implications of a UK downsizing exercise and associated collective consultation issues. The team also represented a dismissed senior financial sector employee in complex high-value claims. **Clients** ABC News; British Exhibition Contractors Association; Le Creuset (UK); Medical Research Council; NCR; Diageo; Bond Technologies; Carr Futures; SAIC; Delta; Chrysalis Group.

TRAVERS SMITH BRAITHWAITE (see firm details p.1166) According to market sources this "*small but practical*" group "*doesn't make a big song and dance over problems.*" Praised as capable and hardworking, this "*civilized*" practice is said to have admirably preserved "*traditional values of courtesy and straightforward dealings.*" Many clients feel the smaller size of the firm to ensure more personal service. Praised for his "*pukka manner*" and "*excellent clarity and thoroughness,*" **Andrew Lilley** (see p.326) is popular with both competitors and clients. He continues to lead his team in advising the Bank of England in relation to the introduction of its flexible benefits programme for all its staff (around 1,900 employees). Additionally, the firm has recently advised Apax Partners on the employment aspects of a management buy-out of the Italian fund management firm, Azimut Holdings. **Clients** 3i; Channel 5; Harvey Nash; AIG Europe; Harland & Wolff Holdings; J Rothschild Assurance Holdings; Digital Vision; Air Partners; Guinness UDV.

OTHER NOTABLE PRACTITIONERS Dale Langley (see p.326) operates a respected "*one man shop*" at niche practice Dale Langley & Co, acting for individual applicants on a referral basis. Also acting for employees, "*trustworthy*" Nick Ralph (see p.329) of Archon was singled out as a "*good strategy man*" who "*doesn't stand on ceremony.*" **Ian Hunter** (see p.325) is seen to be raising the profile of the Bird & Bird practice. Well known both for his "*practical advice*" and writing on employment issues, Hunter recently advised on a 300 partner mass redundancy scheme. "*Confident*" **Yvonne Gallagher** at Lawrence Graham "*gets straight to the point*" in negotiations. At Klegal, **Stephen Levinson** (see p.326) is considered a "*pillar of the employment law community.*" The arrival of "*straightforward*" **Sean Nesbitt** (see p.328) from Garretts heralds good things for the newly merged Taylor Wessing. This up-and-coming practitioner was particularly recommended for international corporate reorganisations and redundancy situations.

LONDON

EMPLOYMENT: MAINLY APPLICANT
LONDON

1 Pattinson & Brewer
   Russell Jones & Walker
2 Thompsons
3 Bindman & Partners
   Rowley Ashworth
4 Lawfords
5 Irwin Mitchell

This book is the product of 6,582 1/2 hour interviews. See p.7 for BMRB audit. Within each band, firms are listed alphabetically.

PATTINSON & BREWER (see firm details p.1095) The departure of highly rated David Cockburn to become a certification officer is felt to be an "*honour*" for the practice. Despite this loss, the firm retains its pre-eminent position in the marketplace as the trade unions' top choice for difficult employment matters. "*Par excellence for collective law practice,*" the group is known for its "*steely*" approach and practitioners' ability to "*cut through the emotion and posing of a situation.*" In addition to a volume of trade union work, the group also undertakes claims for private clients and senior executives. "*Intellectual heavyweight*" **Simon Auerbach** (see p.319) appears regularly in the EAT. "*Academic*" in style, he covers all areas of employment law from union recognition issues to TUPE and discrimination matters. Clients value his ability to "*always come up with a new angle.*" In the past year the group has acted in a European Court of Human Rights appeal on a case concerning the right to representation by trade unions, and appeared in the EAT on a case determining whether the police authority is responsible for acts of alleged discrimination by individual police officers. A sizeable London practice is supported by an additional team of employment specialists in the Bristol office. **Clients** TGWU; RMT.

RUSSELL JONES & WALKER (see firm details p.1120) Frequently associated with major client, the Police Federation, this "*large but focused*" practice undertakes contentious work for trade unions, senior executives and individual applicants. The group is experienced in public law issues and is developing a leading reputation in whistleblowing matters, having fielded a number of new cases involving senior charity employees, hospital doctors and city executives. Department head, **Edward Cooper** (see p.321) is a prominent figure in the market. He and his team were praised for their skill at "*identifying a sensible route early on and sticking to it.*" "*Charming and urbane*" **Clive Howard** (see p.325) and "*feisty*" **Paul Daniels** (see p.322) were also singled out for their work in the field. Major recent highlights include representing four female employees of United Airlines on a breach of maternity rights claim that raised issues surrounding the rights of overseas workers to pursue statutory employment claims in the UK. The team also acted for a BBC weatherman in a case establishing that whistleblowing activities which occurred before the Public Interest Disclosure Act of 1998 came into force are also protected. The firm has recently devoted resources to developing an electronic update service for trade union clients. **Clients** Police Federation; FDA; TUC; Disability Rights Commission; NASUWT; GMB (London Region); UniFI; MSF; CONNECT (formerly STE); Directors Guild of Great Britain; RCN.

THOMPSONS Said by market sources to have an "*impressive franchise*" in collective employment issues, the firm has teams around the country receiving instructions from major trade unions and the Equal Opportunities Commission. Interviewees point to synergies between the employment and personal injury practices and to the team's strength in advising on employment claims with PI and health and safety elements. In the London market, "*everyone knows*" **Stephen Cavalier** (see p.321), a leading trade union solicitor said to be "*at the cutting edge of new legal developments.*" Described to researchers as "*a real ideas man,*" he heads the national practice and covers all areas of trade union law from industrial action to TUPE and European union recognition requirements. In the past year he acted successfully for BECTU in a European Court case concerning paid annual leave under working time regulations. The practice also represented the Equal Opportunities Commission in Julie Bowers' much publicised £1.5 million equal pay case. Up- and-coming practitioner **Nicola Dandridge** (see p.322) is said to be "*making a name for herself in disability discrimination.*" **Clients** Unison; Amicus; GPMU; PCS; ASLEF; FBU; NUJ; BECTU.

BINDMAN & PARTNERS (see firm details p.872) According to market sources, the firm's respected applicant practice operates as an extension of its top flight civil liberties focus. It is less dependent than other ranked applicant firms on trade unions for its workload, receiving instead the bulk of its instructions from individual applicants. Additionally, the group advises the firm's institutional base of not-for-profit sector clients including charities, London Boroughs and the Labour Party. Specialising in "*out of the ordinary*" discrimination cases, practitioners were praised for their "*comprehensive knowledge of human rights law and its applications to employment.*" **Clients** Law Society; Labour Party; Birkbeck College.

ROWLEY ASHWORTH Acting exclusively for trade unions, a sizeable London team is supported by additional practitioners in the firm's Birmingham office. Interviewees praised the group for its consistent quality across partner and associate levels. Paul Evans leads it in advising on all aspects of industrial relations and employment law at the collective and individual level. This extends from the drafting of union rule books and the election of union officials to representing employees on contractual matters and unfair dismissal claims. During the past 12 months the group advised Amicus on its successful CAC application for recognition at Honda, and represented the applicant in an EAT case relating to a sick employee's entitlement to holiday pay under the Working Time Regulations 1998. **Clients** Amicus; GMB; RMT; TGWU; USDAW.

LAWFORDS This growing team, led by Joy Drummond, was warmly recommended as a quality practice, offering "*clear, straightforward advice*" to employees at all levels. Clients appreciate team members' "*rapid turnaround of documents*" and the substantial knowledge of pensions law which they contribute to employment negotiations. Supplementing its stable base of trade unions and legal expense insurers, the firm is handling an increasing amount of work for private clients. The group has expertise in whistleblowing cases and has developed a specialisation in the banking and finance sector particularly in relation to regulatory references under the Financial Services Act. The firm continues to assist UNIFI in test litigation and in achieving settlements in part-time pension rights cases. **Clients** AMICUS; UNIFI; trade unions; legal expense insurers; individuals

IRWIN MITCHELL (see firm details p.1009) The practice concentrates largely on trade union sponsored work, providing advice on constitutional issues, mergers and transfers of engagements, and assisting unions in drafting employment rule books. The London team's profile is bolstered by support from strong applicant practices in Sheffield and Leeds. New

EMPLOYMENT ■ LONDON/THE SOUTH

recruit, Bronwen Jenkins heads the department, acting for individuals and trade unions on discrimination cases. The firm, which includes a dedicated human rights and discrimination law unit, recently represented an applicant against the Post Office in a case alleging serious sexual harassment. It also successfully defended a union against claims that its membership register had not been kept up to date and therefore did not comply with legal requirements, and assisted the MSF in drafting the proposed instrument of transfer and new constitution in relation to its merger with the AEEU to form AMICUS. **Clients** AUT; AMICUS; NATFHE; UNIFI; LMA.

THE SOUTH

EMPLOYMENT ■ THE SOUTH

1. **DMH** Crawley
2. **Blake Lapthorn** Portsmouth
3. **Bond Pearce** Southampton
   Rawlison Butler Crawley
4. **asb law** Crawley
   Brachers Maidstone
   Cripps Harries Hall Tunbridge Wells
   Paris Smith & Randall Southampton
   Thomson Snell & Passmore Tunbridge Wells
5. **Lester Aldridge** Bournemouth, Southampton
   Pattinson & Brewer Chatham
   Stevens & Bolton Guildford

LEADING INDIVIDUALS

1. **DABBS Louise** Rawlison Butler
   SHERRARD Harry Sherrards
2. **CRAWFORD Adrian** DMH
   TATA Rustom DMH
   TOLVAS-VINCENT Christina Bond Pearce
   WHITEMORE Sarah Warner Goodman & Streat
3. **CRAFT Max** Blake Lapthorn
   PARNELL Catherine Bond Pearce

This book is the product of 6,582 1/2 hour interviews. See p.7 for BMRB audit. Within each band, firms are listed alphabetically. See individuals' profiles at p.319

DMH (see firm details p.940) Competitors commend the firm's decision to consolidate the previously dispersed employment team within the Crawley office as a "*sensible strategic move.*" The practice retains its top band position in the South due to the "*enormous combined experience*" of its partners. **Adrian Crawford** (see p.321) is highly regarded for his expertise in TUPE matters while department head **Rustom Tata** (see p.331) was praised to researchers as "*extremely skilled in the jousting of the industrial tribunal world.*" Widely regarded practitioner Quentin Barry continues as a consultant to the practice. The firm is reported to have traditional expertise in trade union matters which gives the employer-focused practice an "*applicanty feel.*" A predominantly public sector client base is complemented by an increasing number of private sector clients, especially in the financial sphere. The team has been involved in a multi-applicant case following the reorganisation of hospital working arrangements, and is currently representing a financial services client in an EAT, TUPE consultation case. In addition, it has recently set up a bespoke training arm to advise clients on a full range of employment and disciplinary issues. **Clients** Thistle Hotels; HFC Bank; FIMAT; NHS trusts; local authorities.

BLAKE LAPTHORN (see firm details p.877) This highly regarded practice prides itself on its advocacy strength, with all eight dedicated specialists undertaking their own advocacy up to the appeals level. The team was widely praised by clients and competitors alike for its "*depth of resources*" and solid base of manufacturing, retail and leisure sector clients. Individual practitioners can draw upon a background in industry when advising large corporations on transactional matters and HR policy. The group also acts for a small proportion of employees at all levels. It recently represented the Hampshire Training and Enterprise Council on its transfer to the Learning Skills Council and Business Link, including related issues of collective consultation, restructuring and TUPE. According to competitors, **Max Craft** "*pops up all the time*" in tribunal. **Clients** Automobile Association; Southampton Cargo Handling; Alcatel; Kerry Foods; Johnson Controls.

BOND PEARCE (see firm details p.879) Best known for its large share of public sector clients, the Southampton team works closely with the firm's other offices in providing contentious and non-contentious advice to educational clients and major corporations. **Christina Tolvas-Vincent** (see p.332) was recommended by peers for her "*good commercial sense*" and expertise in tribunal claims. She is visible representing national retailers and London solicitors in a range of discrimination and unfair dismissal claims. She recently represented several further education colleges in connection with reorganisations, advising on aspects such as redundancy selection and collective consultation. Junior practitioner **Catherine Parnell** (see p.329) continues to receive market commendation for her "*client friendly*" attitude. Notable recent work includes advising the Disability Rights Commission on drafting the sections of the code of practice dealing with further and higher education for post-16 year olds. **Clients** B&Q; Isle of Wight College; Consignia; The National Trust; New Look; Virgin; Kingfisher; Woolworths; English Heritage; Nycomed Amersham; BAT.

RAWLISON BUTLER "*Excellent*" **Louise Dabbs** was commended by competitors for her skill in transactional negotiations. Based in the Crawley office, she heads a team praised by clients for its prompt and "*sensible*" advice. A frequent recipient of referrals, it is expert in a range of employment law including anti-discrimination policies, contractual policies, grievance procedures and related tax matters. **Clients** Local employers.

ASB LAW (see firm details p.851) Servicing businesses of all sizes throughout Kent, Surrey and Sussex this 12 strong team is visible on regional transactions. It boasts specialist expertise on director terminations and the Human Rights Act. Department head Rebecca Thornley-Gibson maintains close ties with clients in the travel and aviation sectors while other individuals specialise in trade union issues and the TUPE implications of receivership and liquidation. The firm advised Virgin Atlantic Airways in connection with its restructuring and redundancy programme introduced following the events of September 11, and successfully represented liquidators in defending 20 protective award applications following the failure of Pearce Securities Systems. **Clients** First Choice Holidays; Dalkia Energy & Technical Services; Etex SA UK Companies; Kent Institute of Art and Design; Church of England/Canterbury Diocesan Board of Finance.

BRACHERS (see firm details p.886) The mixed respondent/applicant practice at Maidstone receives support from a number of London-based specialists including Alan Hannah. The Maidstone group is led by business reorganisation specialist Madeleine Thomson. It represents employers and employees in a range of tribunal cases and disciplinary hearings involving, inter alia, work-related stress and race and sex discrimination claims. Ties with local NHS trusts have brought in advisory work in relation to pension rights claims, changes to the Whitley Council conditions, and the drafting of contracts for a nurse workforce. The group has expertise in collective employment issues and recently negotiated with unions on the TUPE transfer of the Letraset business out of Esselte UK. **Clients** Eurotunnel; General Dynamics UK; Kimberly Clark; Link Insurance; The Tate Gallery; Kent Pharmaceuticals.

CRIPPS HARRIES HALL (see firm details p.922) This employer-based practice provides employment support on a range of transactional work and, according to admiring clients,

THE SOUTH/THAMES VALLEY ■ EMPLOYMENT

"*works towards achieving a quick and practical settlement*" on contentious matters. Additionally, the firm receives a share of work for senior executives within the banking and finance sectors on referral from larger London firms. Under the leadership of Roger Byard, the four person team recently advised a corporate client on the TUPE consequences of an unsuccessful PPP bid. Team members also have experience in trade union recognition matters in the context of business closures. **Clients** Bexley Community Leisure; Dencare Management Group; Swiss Life (UK).

PARIS SMITH & RANDALL (see firm details p.1093) The practice retains its hold on middle market work, attracting favourable comment from small- and medium-sized businesses and legal expense insurer clients. Traditional strength in contentious employment has been expanded to include non-contentious corporate support and advisory functions. The department, headed by Mary Siddall, receives instructions from the Equal Opportunities Commission and recently represented a former RAF officer challenging Joint Defence Council policies on maternity leave and breastfeeding. Other notable work includes representing a number of applicants challenging the legitimacy of the retirement age of 65 under sex discrimination legislation, and providing support on two acquisitions for Vosper Thornycroft. **Clients** Vosper Thornycroft; Glen Dimplex; Southampton Institute; Skandia Life Assurance; Mondial Assistance (UK); Millbrook Furnishing Industries; Wallenius Wilhelmsen Lines UK.

THOMSON SNELL & PASSMORE (see firm details p.1161) A "*client-friendly*" practice, the market waits to see whether it can sustain its position following the loss of leading figure Jill Kelly to Reading-based firm Clarks. The employment team forms part of the firm's commercial division and benefits from a loyal base of small- to medium-sized, family-owned businesses. It undertakes TUPE and staff reorganisations, discrimination claims and union recognition matters, and enjoys a particular name for advising educational institutions on employment regulation. Within the past year the group defended a large High Court breach of contract claim brought by a former director of a construction company, negotiated a termination deal for the Head of SkyOne and advised a national firm of surveyors on the introduction of new employment procedures. **Clients** Colas; Astell Scientific; Advanced Healthcare; Floplast; Crazy Horse 1842; Boots; Shell International; Pura; East Sussex County Council; Royal British Legion Industries.

LESTER ALDRIDGE (see firm details p.1038) A new addition to *Chambers*' rankings, the firm has been building up a specialist employment team operating across its Bournemouth and Southampton offices. Practitioners are said by clients to "*work well as part of a team*" and offer "*commercial advice rather than a legal textbook answer.*" The team, led by Susan Evans, handles a range of matters with specific expertise in relation to employee handbooks and restructuring situations. Individuals have advised employers in relation to disciplinary proceedings involving computer-misuse by an employee, and defended multi-party tribunal cases involving the application of TUPE to national collective agreements. **Clients** Anders Elite; Dorset Healthcare NHS Trust; Kenwood; Kerry Foods; National Care Homes Association; Portman Building Society; North Dorset District Council; Teachers Provident Society.

PATTINSON & BREWER (see firm details p.1095) Widely regarded as the leading applicant practice in the region, the firm acts for trade unions, members and private clients in a large number of contentious claims. Particular strength exists in relation to discrimination and human rights matters. The team has been involved in a number of TUPE cases within the transport industry and advises individual employees on executive severance agreements. Paul Meeham is the contact partner for the group. **Clients** RMT; Communication Workers Union; TGWU.

STEVENS & BOLTON (see firm details p.1149) Demonstrating a "*sound grasp of employment law principles*" the firm handles a mix of transactional TUPE matters, tribunal claims and restrictive covenant and injunction issues. The four fee-earner team, headed by partner Paul Lambdin, is increasingly called upon to advise employers in relation to trade union issues. Additionally, it is experienced in maternity and part time employee rights and handles all manner of unfair dismissal, race, sex and disability claims. **Clients** Local employers and applicants.

OTHER NOTABLE PRACTITIONERS Harry Sherrard (see p.330) of Sherrards is "*well connected*" in the aviation world and acts for a number of airlines in sex, disability and race discrimination claims. He operates a niche employment practice in Haywards Heath, said to "*punch well above its weight*" and has recently opened a branch office in London.

Although Sarah Whitemore at Warner Goodman & Streat was particularly recommended for her "*hard work on behalf of applicants*," she maintains a balanced practice, acting equally for individuals and employers. She recently handled an EAT case involving a working time issue.

THAMES VALLEY

EMPLOYMENT
■ **THAMES VALLEY**

1. **Clarks** Reading
2. **Osborne Clarke** Reading
3. **Henmans** Oxford
   Morgan Cole Oxford, Reading
   Pitmans Reading
   Underwoods Hemel Hempstead

This book is the product of 6,582 1/2 hour interviews. See p.7 for BMRB audit. Within each band, firms are listed alphabetically.

CLARKS (see firm details p.908) A "*leading practice in the Thames Valley,*" the group advises a large base of household name plcs on a full range of employment matters. Although primarily a respondent-based practice, it undertakes unusual applicant work and has had some notable success in novel claims. Interviewees "*have no hesitation in recommending*" department head Michael Sippitt (see p.330). An experienced advocate, he recently acted in a well publicised tribunal case for Times Newspapers against a freelance journalist who claimed employment status. His team is said to apply a "*cross-disciplinary*" approach to employment matters. It was further strengthened this year with the acquisition of "*client-friendly*" Jill Kelly (see p.326) from Thomson Snell & Passmore. Kelly was singled out by interviewees for her skill at "*clearly communicating all the important issues.*" The practice is advising on a case in the EAT on disability discrimination and has noted strength in relation to data protection issues. **Clients** Amey; John Menzies; News International; BMW Financial Services; Sun Microsystems; Blue Circle Industries; Global Crossing; TM Group; Gleesons; Danzas.

OSBORNE CLARKE (see firm details p.1090) The firm is said by competitors to be "*pouring resources into the Thames Valley*" and is becoming increasingly visible on local employment matters. The two-partner Reading practice works closely with larger teams in London and Bristol in co-ordinating work at a national level. Commended as "*progressive,*" commentators were impressed by the team's high level of organisation and professionalism. Department head Danielle Kingdon is a "*significant presence*" in the Reading market. The past year has seen the group advising AOL (UK) on data protection issues, providing HR support to Xerox on restructuring and outsourcing and defending Chesterton in injunction proceedings

www.ChambersandPartners.com   305

EMPLOYMENT ■ THAMES VALLEY/SOUTH WEST

LEADING INDIVIDUALS

[1] KELLY Jill Clarks
SIPPITT Michael Clarks
[2] CATER Sheila Pitmans
HENNEY Colin Henmans
KINGDON Danielle Osborne Clarke
UNDERWOOD Kerry Underwoods

See individuals' profiles p.319

against new recruits in alleged breach of restrictive covenants. **Clients** Innogy; Honda (UK); Informatica; Vanco; Allied Worldwide; International Power; William Sutton Trust; Clarus eMEA; Nationwide Building Society; BG; Hazell Carr; SITA Holding (UK).

HENMANS (see firm details p.990) This "*committed*" practice is distinguished by its high proportion of individual applicant cases, which now comprises almost 40% of the team's workload. Team members were praised for their "*principled*" approach to employment law, and their mixed practice is said to give the group a "*practical view of what the other side is thinking.*" Typical work ranges from tribunal appearances to corporate risk management, with particular strength in the healthcare and pharmaceutical sectors. Lead partner **Colin Henney** (see p.325) was praised by peers for his "*personable*" and "*enthusiastic*" approach. The firm is currently representing the defendant in a multi-applicant case concerning the application of the Equal Treatment Directive to public sector promotion and pay mechanisms. Practitioners undertake advocacy themselves and are active in various pro-bono cases. **Clients** Employers; applicants.

MORGAN COLE (see firm details p.1075) Although market sources claim that the profile of this practice has diminished since the loss of Sue Ashtiany to Nabarro Nathanson over a year ago, employment remains a key area for the firm. The practice operates on a national basis, with seven partners and 25 assistants distributed across five offices and located within a, recently reorganised, combined employment, pensions and benefits group. Wendy Leydon is the contact person for the Thames Valley practice. Significant recent work includes defending UK AEA against a claim brought under the Public Interest Disclosure Act, and advising service provider, Your Communications, on the employment aspects of e-security and e-business applications. **Clients** Alcoa Manufacturing (GB); BP; Fraikin; HSBC; EMI Compact Discs; Cardiff International Airport; RAC; Xerox; Osprey Publishing; ICI Paints; Atlantic Technology (UK).

PITMANS (see firm details p.1103) Interviewees report that, in recent years, the practice has been growing and is becoming an established player in the Reading market. It has attracted a loyal client base with concentration in the property and housebuilding, computer, and pharmaceutical sectors, and acts for an increasing number of US companies with European subsidiaries. While most work is respondent-based, the firm does advise high-profile executives on severance arrangements. **Sheila Cater** (see p.321) was recommended by peers for precisely this sort of work and enters the tables this year. The team recently defended a High Court injunction in relation to restrictive covenants in an agreement for the sale of a travel agency. It has also advised on large-scale redundancy programmes within the construction and IT industries. **Clients** Biogen; Dura Automotive; Berkeley Homes; Chartered Institute of Marketing; Infineum UK; Porsche Great Britain; Vivendi Universal Publishing; Keltech; ICL.

UNDERWOODS (see firm details p.1173) A boutique firm specialising in employment and personal injury claims for both applicants and respondents. Founding partner **Kerry Underwood** (see p.332) is a well known figure in the local market, particularly noted for his representation of senior employees. A diverse client base includes large plcs, small owner-managed businesses, individual directors and the Equal Opportunity Commission. The firm has lately been involved in a large number of cases involving maternity and part-time workers' rights. Highlights of the last year include acting in a disability discrimination and constructive dismissal case concerning alleged failure to make reasonable adjustments for an employee with diabetes. The firm is also notable for its work on behalf of individual solicitors requiring employment advice. **Clients** Circle IMC; Langco; Unitech; Jennings Brothers.

SOUTH WEST

EMPLOYMENT
■ SOUTH WEST

[1] Bevan Ashford Bristol
Bond Pearce Plymouth
Burges Salmon Bristol
Osborne Clarke Bristol
[2] Pattinson & Brewer Bristol
Thompsons Bristol
Thring Townsend Bath
[3] Burroughs Day Bristol
TLT Solicitors Bristol
Veale Wasbrough Bristol
[4] Clarke Willmott & Clarke Taunton
Michelmores Exeter
Stephens & Scown Exeter

This book is the product of 6,582 1/2 hour interviews. See p.7 for BMRB audit. Within each band, firms are listed alphabetically.

BEVAN ASHFORD (see firm details p.869) Competitors have a high regard for this large group of "*able and accomplished*" employment specialists. The firm has traditionally been pre-eminent in the public sector where it advises a large proportion of NHS trusts and local government authorities. However, in recent years, it has broadened its focus to include FTSE 100 and large local employers. Team members are said by clients to "*understand commercial realities*" and were especially praised for the quality of their documentation which "*always does what you want it to.*" **Sarah Lamont** (see p.326) and **Julian Hoskins** (see p.325) are the two leading Bristol-based partners. Lamont's practice emphasises international PFI-type transactions while Hoskins rates highly for his advocacy skills and litigation experience. The team has been instructed by Orange in a group action following large scale dismissals for e-mail abuse, and is representing an NHS trust in the High Court and employment tribunal proceedings brought by a dismissed consultant. **Clients** Orange; HSBC; McArthur Group; St. George's NHS Trust; Parsons Brinkerhoff; Digital Mobility; Rolls-Royce; Allied Domecq; Birmingham Women's Hospital NHS Trust; Audit Commission.

BOND PEARCE (see firm details p.879) The firm's merger with Bristol firm Cartwrights has substantially expanded the practice's capacity in the region. Although the Plymouth group, in the view of the market, remains the stronger practice, many see the firm as "*beefing up its Bristol team*" and the recent additions in the area will prove a big advantage in competing for work with the larger Bristol-based practices. Plymouth partner and national department head, **Nikki Duncan** (see p.322), is "*immensely liked*" by peers and clients. Within the practice, a sub-team concentrates entirely on corporate transactions, advising large employers on consultation requirements and TUPE transfers in relation to mergers and acquisitions. The group also has considerable experience in contentious claims and regularly undertakes tribunal and appellate level advocacy. Over the past year it has advised several national clients on strategic planning and the development of employee consultation schemes, including advice on handling trade union recognition bids. **Clients** University of Plymouth; Consignia; Roach Foods; The Virgin Group; Safeway Stores; Tibbett & Britten; First Western National Bus; Toshiba; The National Trust; Brittany Ferries.

BURGES SALMON (see firm details p.894) This "*well rounded*" practice is said by competitors to strike a balance between corporate support and standalone employment matters. Practitioners are described as "*alert to business*

SOUTH WEST — EMPLOYMENT

LEADING INDIVIDUALS

1
- DUNCAN Nikki Bond Pearce
- HEMMING Julian Osborne Clarke

2
- LAMONT Sarah Bevan Ashford
- SEATON Christopher Burges Salmon

3
- BENSON Nick Michelmores
- HOSKINS Julian Bevan Ashford
- ROBERTS Stephen Thring Townsend

UP AND COMING
- DAVIES Julie Veale Wasbrough
- THOMAS David Burroughs Day

See individuals' profiles p.319

---

concerns" and are appreciated by clients for their ability to "*bring a new perspective to an issue.*" In addition to the standard range of tribunal and advisory work, the firm offers training, seminars and secondment services to clients. "*Down to earth*" practice head, **Christopher Seaton** (see p.330) draws upon substantial knowledge of immigration law in advising multinational corporates on employment policy. In the past year, the practice has seen a growing number of restrictive covenant/injunction cases. Notable recent work includes acting for Standard Chartered Bank on the restructuring of its private banking function and consequent redundancy exercise. It also advised the Posthouse Hotel group in connection with shift working patterns, casual employees and Sunday working. The employment team is located within a combined employment, pensions and incentives unit. **Clients** Bristol Water; Posthouse Hotel Group; Alexandra; Bristol & West; BAE Systems; Standard Chartered Bank; NAAFI; J Rothschild Assurance; United Biscuits (UK).

OSBORNE CLARKE (see firm details p.1090) The loss of Chris Southam to Speechly Bircham is believed by market sources to be only a minor setback to a practice marked by "*overall strength in depth.*" Competitors rate the team highly for "*sheer manpower*" and its large base of household name clients. Subdivided along client lines, it works closely with highly rated teams in London and Reading on complex matters. "*Outstandingly good*" **Julian Hemming** heads the Bristol practice and is highly visible advising on the employment aspects of corporate transactions. The group has noted strength in industrial relations, particularly within the shipping and media sectors. Among the year's highlights are advising Amcor Flexibles Europe in connection with a joint venture across 14 European jurisdictions, and counselling Marlborough Stirling on the employment implications of its £75.7 million IPO. The Bristol practice has recently been strengthened by an additional recruitment at partner level. **Clients** Amcor Europe; The Medical Defence Union; 24seven Utility Services; Marlborough Stirling; Mosaic Group; P&O; Somerfield; PGA; Clarks; United Bristol Healthcare NHS Trust.

PATTINSON & BREWER (see firm details p.1095) Cathy Tailby heads the Bristol practice in its employment work on behalf of trade unions and individual employees. Expertise extends from termination and contract negotiations to advice on disciplinary proceedings and discrimination cases, however the group was particularly recommended to researchers for cases with health and safety or equal pay elements. **Clients** Trade unions; individual applicants.

THOMPSONS The firm acts exclusively for trade unions and their members in employment rights cases including race and sex discrimination, unfair dismissals, equal pay claims and TUPE cases. The employment department, which co-operates closely with the firm's highly regarded personal injury practice has particular experience in dealing with stress at work and occupational injury claims. The firm recently secured a £200,000 compensation award for a female firefighter in a headline sex discrimination case. **Clients** ASLEF; CDNA; AUT; BALPA; FBU; GPMU; AEEU.

THRING TOWNSEND (see firm details p.1162) A dedicated employment team, based in Bath, advises both employers and employees on contentious and non-contentious employment matters. Leading name **Stephen Roberts** (see p.329) has a good reputation amongst fellow practitioners for his knowledge and approach, and regularly receives referral work. The team acts for a number of clients in the agricultural, education and sports sectors and has particular expertise in employment issues relating to European directives and Human Rights legislation. **Clients** Employers and applicants.

BURROUGHS DAY "*Rapidly gaining a profile in the region,*" the firm has made a name for itself in private client applicant work and receives frequent referrals from larger Bristol firms. The group represents directors and senior managers of large plcs, and a growing number of individual solicitors, as well as undertaking a volume of work on a 'no win no fee' basis for employees at all levels. On the employer side, practitioners provide contentious and non-contentious advice to manufacturing and engineering companies and nursing homes. The group is visible on multi-party actions involving protective awards, breach of contract and unfair dismissal. Recent work in this area includes acting for 65 former employees of Viatel Global Communications in a multi-million pound litigation. Younger partner **David Thomas** (see p.331) enters the rankings this year after winning substantial praise from peers. **Clients** 24seven Vending; Avon Residential Care Homes Association; Bristol and Western Engineering and Manufacturing Association; Bristol City Council.

TLT SOLICITORS (see firm details p.1163) The practice has grown substantially at the associate level and is correspondingly thought by interviewees to be strengthening its position in the market. The team, headed by Alana Weeks, is said to take a "*coolheaded, analytical*" approach to employment problems. Firm-wide strength in the insurance and financial services sectors has assisted it in advising on a number of recent redundancy and reorganisation schemes. In-house advocates represent regional and national employers on discrimination claims and trade union disputes. The firm recently acted in a high-profile case following the first striking off of a teacher for incompetence. **Clients** Aardman Animations; Allied Dunbar; Zurich Financial Services; Eagle Star; St Paul International Insurance; United Parcel Service; Helphire; Fortis Insurance.

VEALE WASBROUGH (see firm details p.1174) A compact and "*well managed*" team, under the direction of partner Mike Davies, provides general advice for a large base of small- to mid-sized regional businesses, but is best known for representing local authorities and independent schools. The past year has seen the team active in a number of EAT cases, most notably TUPE case Nixon and Others v The Church Schools Company. On the transactional side, it has advised both Airbus UK and Avon Rubber on major restructuring programmes. Younger partner **Julie Davies** was newly recommended as an up-and-coming practitioner. **Clients** Airbus UK; BNFL; Theatre Royal, Bath; Heritage Hotels; Tower Casino Group; University of Bristol; Direct Line; Fire Service College; St. Johns Ambulance; Fords Design Group; McBraida.

CLARKE WILLMOTT & CLARKE (see firm details p.907) A new addition to the tables, the employer-focused team has a "*strong Taunton power base*" composed of NHS trust, educational and agricultural clients. The practice is also retained to act for the Equal Opportunities Commission and draws upon related expertise in health and safety law. "*Approachable*" team members are reported by market sources to have their "*feet on the ground.*" Practitioners have extensive experience of tribunal advocacy, restrictive covenants, wrongful dismissal and TUPE matters. Kevin Jones heads the practice. **Clients** Equal Opportunities Commission; public/private sector organisations; plcs; senior executives.

MICHELMORES (see firm details p.1068) Highly-rated **Nick Benson** heads a small but busy employment law practice from within the firm's company commercial department. The team acts for employers and employees on a broad range of contentious claims, redundancy exercises, and executive severance agreements. Benson successfully defended Exeter Golf & Country Club against an unfair dismissal claim and acted for Kerry Foods in a TUPE case which settled before a Court of Appeal hearing. **Clients** Kerry Foods; Alamo; Exeter Golf & Country Club; individual employees.

EMPLOYMENT ■ SOUTH WEST/WALES/MIDLANDS

STEPHENS & SCOWN Acting primarily for west country businesses, the practice has a heavy emphasis on contentious work. In Exeter the team, headed by Nigel Moore, has a strong reputation and was singled out by market sources for "*looking out for the client's best interests.*" It has recently been visible representing mid-sized employers in a range of unfair dismissal cases and sex, race and disability discrimination claims. **Clients** Employers and applicants.

WALES

EMPLOYMENT
■ WALES

1. **Eversheds** Cardiff
2. **Morgan Cole** Cardiff, Swansea
3. **Edwards Geldard** Cardiff
   Hugh James Cardiff
4. **Palser Grossman** Cardiff Bay

LEADING INDIVIDUALS

1. **DU-FEU Vivian** Eversheds
   WARREN Martin Eversheds
2. **REES Anthony** Morgan Cole
   WILLIAMS Audrey Eversheds
3. **CLARKE Michael** Morgan Cole
4. **DAVIES Joanne** Morgan Cole
   LOVE Alison Hugh James
   NOTT Christopher Palser Grossman

This book is the product of 6,582 1/2 hour interviews. See p.7 for BMRB audit. Within each band, firms are listed alphabetically. See individuals' profiles p.319

EVERSHEDS (see firm details p.949) A "*centre of excellence*" for the highly reputed national practice, the Cardiff team retains a "*dominant position*" within the Welsh market both for its strong connections to the network and concentration of high profile practitioners. As head of the national practice, leading figure **Viv Du-Feu** (see p.322) plays a largely management role, coordinating matters between Eversheds' numerous UK offices. "*Impressive*" **Martin Warren** (see p.332) heads the Cardiff practice and was particularly noted for his experience in industrial relations. He also devotes time to advising North American clients on UK employment law. "*Highly effective*" **Audrey Williams** (see p.333) specialises in discrimination claims. Interviewees report that the group handles "*more than the lion's share of public sector work in Wales*" as well as providing employment support to large private companies. Amongst last year's highlights was the firm's successful defence of Panasonic against claims of racial discrimination and failure to promote. It also handled advisory work for easyJet on labour relations issues. **Clients** Environment Agency; easyJet; University of the West of England; GE Caledonian; Panasonic; One-2-One; Nycomed Amersham; Robert Bosch.

MORGAN COLE (see firm details p.1075) With teams in both Cardiff and Swansea, the practice is a major force in the Welsh employment market. Particular strength exists in the public sector, where the group maintains close ties with a range of NHS trusts, public authorities and research institutions. In the private sector it boasts a large number of energy companies amongst its clients. "*Straightforward*" **Anthony Rees** heads the national employment, pensions and benefits practice and has a reputation as a "*creative thinker.*" **Michael Clarke** is visible advising health and education clients on redundancies, employment policy and discrimination claims. He recently represented a university in restructuring an academic department. **Joanne Davies** focuses primarily on commercial matters and has expertise in relation to outsourcing and TUPE issues. The team recently advised PHS Group on employment issues arising from its flotation. **Clients** Financial Services Compensation Scheme; GasForce; BP; Scottish and Southern Power; Wireless Systems International; Associated British Ports; Unipart; Amey; Cardiff and Vale NHS trust; Welsh Development Agency.

EDWARDS GELDARD (see firm details p.944) This "*highly responsive*" team of employment specialists is led by Stephen Jenkins. A client base of mainly small- to medium-sized local employers is supplemented by connections with major financial and corporate institutions such as Citibank and Chubb. The group handles a lot of TUPE work in outsourcing situations and advises in-house HR teams on planning and policy preparation. Recent work includes representing the respondent in the high profile TUPE court of appeal case Willer v ADT. It also acted for Amalgamated Cleaning Services in a tribunal defence of a race discrimination claim involving potential liability of customer and contractor. **Clients** Citibank; Welsh Water; Chubb; Yale Security Products; Hyder Business Services; Cardiff University; First Cymru Buses; ASW; NCM Credit Insurance; Amalgamated Cleaning Services.

HUGH JAMES (see firm details p.1004) Recent restructuring has created a centralised employment practice run from Cardiff but servicing clients across Wales. **Alison Love** (see p.327) is credited by competitors with building up an able and "*increasingly visible*" team. The group's focus is gradually shifting from a mainly applicant to a predominantly respondent practice. Situated within the commercial services division, the practice undertakes non-contentious advisory work for mid-sized corporates but has a higher profile for tribunal work. It has been defending a respondent in a long running race discrimination case, N Huggins v Gwent Police and Others, and successfully appealed against a finding of unfair dismissal at the EAT. **Clients** Envirovac 2000; Leekes of Llantrisant; TIB; WRU/ Millennium Stadium; Royal College of Nursing; Swift Credit Services; Yu Sung (UK); Sekisui UK.

PALSER GROSSMAN Acting equally for applicants and respondents, this small team has "*done well for itself*" according to local market sources. Operating from Cardiff Bay, it focuses on commercial employment matters, advising local businesses on transactions and employment policies and representing wealthy individuals and corporate directors in severance agreements. A well known "*character*," **Christopher Nott** was commended for his work in raising the team's profile. The group has recently advised a number of retail clients on the employment aspects of restructuring exercises. **Clients** Dyson; International Greetings; Episode; TRW.

MIDLANDS

EVERSHEDS (see firm details p.949) A year of swings and roundabouts has seen a number of partner and associate exchanges between the Midlands branches of Eversheds and Hammond Suddards Edge. Following last year's acquisition of "*pragmatic*" **Julia Edwards** (see p.323), the firm has lost David Beswick and a group of associates to HSE. Despite this, interviewees felt that the size and strength of the Eversheds' national network keep the practice squarely on top in the region. Onlookers, however, are curious to see how the changes will pan out between the two rivals over the next few years. Department head **Martin Hopkins** (see p.325) is reported to have been "*highly successful at marketing Evershed's Birmingham branch.*" Although perceived by competitors to be increasingly active in business development, he retains his reputation as a "*key player*" in the market. Nottingham-based **Hilary Campion** (see p.320) rates highly as a "*straightforward*" practitioner with a sensible approach to negotiations. The firm co-ordinated employment advice for Diageo on its acquisition of Sea-

MIDLANDS — EMPLOYMENT

EMPLOYMENT
MIDLANDS

1
- **Eversheds** Birmingham, Nottingham
- **Wragge & Co** Birmingham

2
- **Hammond Suddards Edge** Birmingham

3
- **Martineau Johnson** Birmingham
- **Pinsent Curtis Biddle** Birmingham

4
- **DLA** Birmingham
- **Shakespeares** Birmingham

5
- **Browne Jacobson** Nottingham
- **freethcartwright** Nottingham
- **Higgs & Sons** Brierley Hill

LEADING INDIVIDUALS

1
- **BESWICK David** Hammond Suddards Edge
- **CHITTY Martin** Wragge & Co

2
- **CHAMBERLAIN Jonathan** Wragge & Co
- **DEAN Veronica** Hammond Suddards Edge

3
- **BENSON Edward** Browne Jacobson
- **GILLESPIE Michael** Lee Crowder
- **HOPKINS Martin** Eversheds
- **JONES Alan** DLA
- **MARSHALL Ian** Martineau Johnson
- **WOFFENDEN Sara** Bevan Ashford

4
- **CAMPION Hilary** Eversheds
- **EDWARDS Julia** Eversheds
- **HIBBS Michael** Shakespeares
- **JONES Linda** Pinsent Curtis Biddle
- **POTTER David** freethcartwright

5
- **ARMSTRONG Ruth** Gateley Wareing
- **HODGE Andrew** Wragge & Co
- **JAMIESON Andrew** Nelsons
- **MASON Helen** Mason and Co

This book is the product of 6,582 1/2 hour interviews. See p.7 for BMRB audit. Within each band, firms are listed alphabetically. See individuals' profiles p.319

---

grams' Wine & Spirits business in all jurisdictions except North America, and advised on the UK employment law implications of the integration of the businesses of IBM and Lotus Development. **Clients** Associated British Foods; Cap Gemini Ernst & Young UK; Alliance & Leicester; 3M; Hewlett-Packard.; IBM UK; Diageo; British Energy; Yellow Pages; McDonald's.

WRAGGE & CO (see firm details p.1197) Although reckoned by some market sources to be "*the most stable of the Birmingham practices,*" it has not been unaffected by a year of change. Most notably, Jane Ellis has retired from the practice. The firm's employment resources are concentrated in the Birmingham office under the leadership of department head **Martin Chitty** . "*Amiable and pleasant,*" he receives warm recommendations from fellow practitioners and is well regarded for his business protection and re-organisation experience. He has lately been involved in defending a major manufacturer against a large union claim concerning holiday pay and the validity of an industrial action ballot. "*Charming*" **Jonathan Chamberlain** "*makes clients purr*" says one competitor. Known to be "*exceptionally hard-working,*" he recently advised an investment services institution on collective redundancies in the UK. Highly respected **Andrew Hodge** focuses on corporate governance and executive control issues and has been advising a major US investment bank on employment issues arising from 17 outsourcing contracts. **Clients** AT&T; British Airways; Mazda UK; Powergen; BUPA; Viatel; Severn Trent; Taylor Woodrow; English Heritage; Bovis Homes; LloydsTSB; Muller Dairies; BT.

HAMMOND SUDDARDS EDGE The recruitment of highly rated **David Beswick** , one of the biggest names in the region, from Eversheds is thought to go a long way towards filling in the gaps left by the loss of Julia Edwards a year ago and this year's retirement of James Retallack. Commentators feel it is too early to predict the likely effects of Beswick's move, however, and wait to see how the practice will develop under his influence. **Veronica Dean** retains her reputation as an expert in contentious employment matters. With "*considerable experience*" behind her, Dean "*fights hard when she needs to.*" Clients report that she is "*good to have on your side.*" Her practice focuses largely on industrial relations issues and discrimination claims. The team advised Enterprise Inns on the integration of its £900 million acquisition of Laurel Partnership, and represented a football authority on a discrimination claim brought by former football league referees. The firm has recruited an HR director to head the national consultancy from the Birmingham office. **Clients** Unipart; Jewsons; Baer; Prologis; Interserve; Boots; Autoglass; Birmingham International Airport; Aggregate Industries; Compass Group.

MARTINEAU JOHNSON (see firm details p.1056) This "*young, dynamic team,*" headed by **Ian Marshall** (see p.327), is said by interviewees to be building up a profile in the area. "*Cerebral*" Marshall is said to "*speak the client's language*" and give "*sensible, down to earth*" advice. He has recently acted in a High Court application for an injunction to obtain a seven-day stay against a threatened strike. The team boasts a strong reputation in the education sector and has acted for a number of educational institutions in high profile sex, race and disability discrimination cases. Clients appreciate its "*approachability*" and willingness to travel. The group handles increasing amounts of trade union recognition matters and redundancy exercises. Transactional work includes advising on the employment aspects of a £500 million plus deal for Convergys. **Clients** ATS Euromaster; Express & Star; Shipley Europe; Warwick University; Aston University; Bullough; Manganese Bronze Holdings; Staffordshire University; Capio Healthcare.

PINSENT CURTIS BIDDLE (see firm details p.1102) The loss of big name partner Colin Goodier leaves the practice "*short on grey-hairs,*" although many expect that the practice will quickly stabilise under the leadership of "*extremely talented*" **Linda Jones** (see p.326). Goodier's departure has thrust Jones increasingly into the public eye, attracting much positive comment from local practitioners. Describing her as a "*market-facing*" individual, interviewees predict that she will "*drive the team forward.*" She handles a heavy load of TUPE and redundancy cases while other team members focus on discrimination matters for a diverse base of blue chip employers. Strength in collective issues and groundbreaking contentious work is illustrated by the group's defence of Sunderland Housing Group against a claim for protective awards brought by Unison on behalf of 1,400 employees. This alleged a failure to inform and consult in accordance with TUPE following the largest ever voluntary transfer of housing stock by a local authority into the private sector. **Clients** NEC Group; Misys; Glanbia; HSBC; University of Birmingham; Siemens; BG International; Alstom; KPMG; Transco.

DLA Although the firm's Birmingham branch is not felt to possess as strong an employment team as its Yorkshire practices, **Alan Jones** is said by market commentators to lead a small but able group covering the full range of contentious and non-contentious matters for its blue-chip client base. Colleagues like having Jones on the other side because he is "*interested in getting things resolved.*" The practice acts predominantly for employers with individual practitioners particularly noted for their advocacy skills. **Clients** Corporate employers.

SHAKESPEARES (see firm details p.1127) Considered the lynchpin of the practice, **Michael Hibbs** (see p.325) is easily the most visible member of this team. A "*top drawer*" practitioner, he is a visiting employment law professor at the University of Central England. He is said by market sources to lead a "*bright, business oriented*" team handling mainstream commercial employment work. Although the group acts primarily for employers, it is the frequent beneficiary of referrals from local firms for executive level applicant representation. **Clients** Local corporates.

BROWNE JACOBSON (see firm details p.891) A leading Nottingham firm, it has a strong following among health and local authority clients. The practice covers all aspects of employment law from TUPE transfers and tribunal advocacy to executive severance negotiations and the drafting of disciplinary procedures. "*Personable*" department head **Edward Benson** (see p.319) has "*long experience in the field*" and rates highly amongst rivals for his expertise in discrimination matters and ter-

309

EMPLOYMENT ■ MIDLANDS/EAST ANGLIA

mination payments. The team successfully defended the Leicestershire Police in a high-profile race discrimination claim and has acted as ballot scrutineer in relation to various mass redundancy consultations. The Nottingham group is now supported by additional practitioners based in the London and Birmingham offices. **Clients** The Royal Wolverhampton Hospitals NHS Trust; Wilkinson Group; Derbyshire Police Authority.

FREETHCARTWRIGHT (see firm details p.963) This six-solicitor Nottingham team receives support from additional practitioners based in the firm's Leicester office. The team was praised by competitors and clients for its "*high standards of quality*" and "*excellent client service*," with lead partner **David Potter** (see p.329) singled out as an "*employment ace.*" The firm works closely with in-house HR departments in drafting contracts, rule-books and employment procedures and handles a volume of unfair dismissal and discrimination claims in tribunal. Individuals have been advising major players in the textile industry on redundancy programmes and problems arising from changes to shift patterns and remuneration rates. On the contentious side, practitioners have been involved in cases concerning the interpretation of the National Minimum Wage Legislation, and represented a multinational group in a five-figure sexual harassment, unfair dismissal and equal pay claim. **Clients** Powergen UK; Experion.

HIGGS & SONS Interviewees believe that the practice will face a challenge to maintain its profile following the retirement of key figure Roger Field. The team, which is now headed by John Smith, has historically been the central point of referral for high level applicant cases and it remains to be seen whether it can continue to attract the same volume of instructions without Field's leadership. In the past year the group has successfully defended a claim in the employment tribunal for a large NHS Trust and several prominent consultants against allegations of race discrimination, victimisation and unfair dismissal. **Clients** Allied Carpets; Wolverhampton & Dudley Breweries; Magnet; Sandwell Healthcare NHS Trust; HP Bulmer.

OTHER NOTABLE PRACTITIONERS Renowned practitioner **Sara Woffenden** (see p.333) has left Shoosmiths to build up an employment practice at Bevan Ashford, Birmingham. Her recruitment is seen to be a major coup for the practice. "*First rate*" litigation lawyer, **Michael Gillespie** (see p.324) at Lee Crowder is reported to give "*measured advice*" and "*always has his eye on what he wants to achieve.*" He maintains a high profile in the region through his role as Midlands representative to the Employment Lawyers Association. At Nelsons, **Andrew Jamieson** (see p.325) is rated as an "*impressive advocate*" for applicant cases while "*lively*" **Ruth Armstrong** of Gateley Wareing is recommended as a "*pragmatic, service oriented*" lawyer who "*punches well above her weight.*" Rival practices frequently refer interesting cases to "*excellent*" **Helen Mason** (see p.327) who operates a niche employment practice at Mason & Co.

EAST ANGLIA

EMPLOYMENT
■ EAST ANGLIA

1
- Eversheds Cambridge, Norwich
- Hewitson Becke + Shaw Cambridge
- Mills & Reeve Cambridge, Norwich

2
- Greenwoods Peterborough
- Steele & Co Norwich
- Taylor Vinters Cambridge

3
- Prettys Ipswich

LEADING INDIVIDUALS

1
- SAYER Nick Hewitson Becke + Shaw
- WARNOCK Owen Eversheds

2
- HEMMINGS Richard Sole Practitioner

3
- BROWN Nicola Mills & Reeve
- CASSEL Richard Hatch Brenner
- DILLARSTONE Robert Greenwoods
- LYNE Amanda Taylor Vinters
- PRYKE Oliver Taylor Vinters
- TYNDALL Timothy Hewitson Becke + Shaw

4
- BLOOM Martin Hegarty & Co
- MATHER Ian Eversheds
- SCOULAR Gillie Mills & Reeve
- YATES Tracy Eversheds

ASSOCIATES TO WATCH
- ALDRED Hilary Hewitson Becke + Shaw

This book is the product of 6,582 1/2 hour interviews. See p.7 for BMRB audit. Within each band, firms are listed alphabetically. See individuals' profiles p.319

EVERSHEDS (see firm details p.949) The combined manpower of the Cambridge, Ipswich and Norwich offices gives this group enormous strength in the region. At the helm is highly rated **Owen Warnock** (see p.332), widely respected for his "*sterling work on disability discrimination.*" Warnock recently acted for Eastern Counties Newspapers in connection with an application by the GMPU for compulsory trade union recognition. At the Cambridge office, **Ian Mather** (see p.328) advises a large number of hi-tech and education clients on tribunal claims, executive severances and changes in employment policy. He has lately been advising Cambridge Water Company on the outsourcing of a service employing over 100 workers. **Tracy Yates** (see p.333) focuses on equal opportunities work and has experience advising senior level executives on termination negotiations. In-house HR consultants provide additional support on commercial matters. The firm has recently been appointed to the Virgin Group legal panel and is providing Virgin Money and Virgin Direct with on-going advice on a major re-organisation and merger. **Clients** Cambridge Antibody Technology; Dairy Crest; Elan Pharma; Cambridge Water Company; Harlow College; Eastern Counties Newspapers; Manor Bakeries; Virgin.

HEWITSON BECKE + SHAW (see firm details p.993) This growing employment practice is distributed between the Cambridge and Northampton offices. Described by competitors as "*bright and quick witted,*" the team advise on all employment aspects from TUPE matters and employment documentation to trade union consultation and discrimination claims. "*Shrewd*" department head **Nick Sayer** (see p.330) is especially visible on part-time workers' pensions cases. He and partner **Tim Tyndall** (see p.332) were also noted for their expertise in restrictive covenants and injunction work. The team undertakes much of its own advocacy and receives international referral work through membership of a global employment law association. It recently received a boost with the recruitment of three additional assistants. The past year has seen an increase in advisory work on new workplace legislation and regulations, as well as a growing number of instructions relating to large scale business re-organisations and relocations. **Clients** TNT International; Johnson Matthey; Booker Cash and Carry; Travis Perkins; Scottish & Newcastle.

MILLS & REEVE (see firm details p.1071) This full service firm covers the spectrum of employment law matters and continues to hold its own against competitors as one of the "*main players in the area.*" On the advisory side, the team is engaged in drafting employment documents and providing HR support on business transfers, reorganisations and large scale redundancies. It also handles employment disputes and has expertise in discrimination and constructive dismissal claims in tribunal and the High Court. The practice is best known for its connections with local health trusts and educational institutions. Cambridge-based **Nicola Brown** (see p.320) advises a number of colleges and higher education clients on contractual and disciplinary issues. The Cambridge office also acts for a large body of local hi-tech companes in restructuring and collective consultation issues. In Norwich, "*lively*" **Gillie Scoular** (see p.330) draws upon an in-house background in the media and publishing sectors when advising on service agreements, contracts and senior executive dismissals. The firm successfully defended an educational institution in an unfair dismissal claim brought under the Public Interest Disclosure Act. **Clients** Educational and health sector: agricultural clients.

GREENWOODS (see firm details p.978) This Peterborough-based practice focuses on contentious employment matters, with practitioners known for their advocacy skills and frequent tribunal appearances. The team acts exclusively for respondents and has a loyal following among local corporate clients in the construction, retail and pharmaceutical sectors. Employment is a key area for the firm, with two partners and four assistants concentrating on contentious and non-contentious employment and employee benefits work. Highly rated **Robert Dillarstone** heads the group and was widely recommended to researchers for his expertise and client skills. His team regularly advises on race and disability discrimination claims, parental leave, working time regulations, disciplinary procedures and Wages Act cases. **Clients** Railtrack; Emap; Enterprise Oil; Barnados; Willmott Dixon.

STEELE & CO (see firm details p.1145) Norman Lamb's departure to become an MP is considered by competitors to be a blow to the practice's profile, although he remains available as a consultant. However, the reputation Lamb built up through co-ordinating the high-profile armed forces pregnancy dismissal cases lives on and the firm continues to rate as an "*effective unit*" with "*unique experience*" in the field. The current team is headed by Oliver Brabbins, a former barrister, and undertakes a large amount of transaction-related work for an increasingly commercial client base, with a particular concentration in the food industry. The six fee-earner Norwich team can draw upon additional resources located in the London office. The firm has advised Schlumberger on a factory relocation and is handling a large equal pay claim against the MoD. **Clients** George Wimpey; Bowater Windows; Campbell Foods; Bird's Eye Wall's; The Stationery Office; Tulip International; Great Yarmouth College; Start-Rite Shoes.

TAYLOR VINTERS (see firm details p.1156) This expanding team has strong ties to hi-tech, IT and telecoms clients who see it as "*in tune with market developments.*" "*Firey*" **Mandy Lyne** (see p.327) leads the practice and has a strong reputation for multiple redundancy matters. She recently assisted a major horticultural printing industry client in averting industrial action following a pay dispute. Peers are happy to refer matters to her and senior associate **Oliver Pryke** (see p.329), an "*approachable*" practitioner heavily involved in advising pharmaceutical clients. Pryke has been acting in a complex unfair and wrongful dismissal case involving allegations of discrimination against a school teacher. The firm's ability to call upon Richard Hemmings as a consultant is considered a major resource for the practice. **Clients** Educational institutions; hi-tech industries; pharmaceutical companies; high-level managers.

PRETTYS (see firm details p.1106) This Ipswich-based practice benefits from a local concentration of hi-tech and transport companies. The firm acts for many of the large hauliers operating out of Felixstowe port and has an additional niche in sports-related employment work. Richard Stace leads a four-lawyer group which principally advises owner-managed companies based in Suffolk and Essex, though a small percentage of its work involves representing employees on compromise agreements. It combines its employment skills with expertise on executive immigration matters and has recently acted for a local stables and a football club on a range of employment issues. **Clients** NFU; agricultural, technology and transport interests.

OTHER NOTABLE PRACTITIONERS In addition to his work as a consultant to Taylor Vinters, **Richard Hemmings** (see p.324) maintains a thriving independent practice at The Law Offices of Richard Hemmings. Noted as a "*seasoned campaigner in the employment field,*" he advises a mix of public and private sector clients on commercial employment matters and has recently been dealing with a major reorganisation of NHS health authorities. "*Tough but fair,*" **Richard Cassel** (see p.321) of Hatch Brenner is rated by peers as a "*wise and effective individual.*" **Martin Bloom** (see p.319) at Hegarty & Co also receives widespread endorsement from interviewees. He acts for employers and individuals and regularly advises big name corporations GAP and Thomas Cook on employment matters.

NORTH WEST

EMPLOYMENT
NORTH WEST

[1]
- **Addleshaw Booth & Co** Manchester
- **Eversheds** Manchester
- **Hammond Suddards Edge** Manchester

[2]
- **DLA** Liverpool, Manchester
- **Mace & Jones** Liverpool, Manchester
- **Whittles** Manchester

[3]
- **Cobbetts** Manchester
- **Thompsons** Liverpool, Manchester

[4]
- **DWF** Liverpool, Manchester
- **Halliwell Landau** Manchester
- **Pannone & Partners** Manchester

This book is the product of 6,582 1/2 hour interviews. See p.7 for BMRB audit. Within each band, firms are listed alphabetically.

ADDLESHAW BOOTH & CO (see firm details p.838) Competitors rate this a "*well resourced*" department with "*excellent coverage*" throughout the region. Practitioners were described as "*analytical*" and particularly commended for their strategic advice on employment policy and planning. "*Top of the tree*" is **Malcolm Pike** (see p.329). He heads the practice and has built close ties with the airline industry. He has recently been acting for American Airlines in applications for compulsory trade union recognition under the Employment Relations Act 1999. **Andrew Chamberlain** (see p.321) also rates highly with competitors and clients for his "*sheer presence*" and "*intellectual ability.*" Chamberlain has been acting for a management team in a 'management walk-out' and recently advised Airtours in injunctive proceedings against a senior executive upon his departure to a competitor. The team handles increasing amounts of work in connection with PPP and PFI projects for NHS trusts, universities and local bodies. **Clients** American Airlines; United Utilities; Nord Anglia Education Group; Co-operative Bank; British Airways; Manchester Metropolitan University; Central Manchester NHS Trust; API Group; Unilever; Trinity Mirror.

EVERSHEDS (see firm details p.949) Another "*strong link in the Eversheds chain,*" the two-partner 16 associate Manchester practice has a large base of regional corporate clients and acts in tandem with other offices on national work. The team has grown aggressively in recent years and now includes an HR consultant and professional support lawyer to assist on advisory work. Department head **Peter Norbury** (see p.328) takes a "*combative*" approach to employment litigation and, according to market sources, can be relied upon to "*put his best foot forward for the client.*" Younger partner **Michael Thompson** (see p.331) has an established profile in unfair dismissal and discrimination claims. Notable recent work for the group includes advising a plc on a major outsourcing exercise involving TUPE and redundancy issues and acting for a national employment agency

EMPLOYMENT ■ NORTH WEST

LEADING INDIVIDUALS

1
- CHAMBERLAIN Andrew Addleshaw Booth & Co
- HANTOM Charles Whittles
- NICKSON Sue Hammond Suddards Edge
- NORBURY Peter Eversheds
- PIKE Malcolm Addleshaw Booth & Co

2
- EDWARDS Martin Mace & Jones
- WATSON Judith Cobbetts

3
- CLARKE Mary DLA
- MALONE Michael Mace & Jones
- PARKINSON Helen Whittles
- RESTON Vincent DLA
- THOMPSON Michael Eversheds
- TRANTER Ian Hammond Suddards Edge

4
- JACKS David Weightman Vizards

See individuals' profiles p.319

client with regard to a 'springboard' injunction against former employees. **Clients** Football Association; Asda; United Utilities; Surrey Free Inns; UMIST.

HAMMOND SUDDARDS EDGE This large team of "*skilled technicians*" has been successful in establishing a profile as one of the leading practices in the region, according to its competitors. While a large percentage of its work is standalone, the team also benefits from the firm's stable base of manufacturing, finance and leisure industry clients in providing support on corporate transactions. Manchester-based **Sue Nickson** heads up the national employment practice and co-ordinates deal-work across the firm's UK and European offices, while "*accomplished*" **Ian Tranter** is seen by interviewees as a "*real asset to the team*." The group has recently acted for Motorola on a restructuring scheme and advised Manchester Airport in relation to potential industrial action. An employer-based firm, the practice accepts only occasional applicant cases. **Clients** Motorola; Crédit Lyonnais; Air 200; Niceday; First Choice Holidays; Matalan Retail.

DLA "*Well rounded*" practices in Liverpool and Manchester operate within the firm's national 90-lawyer employment team. The group acts in contentious and non-contentious work across a variety of sectors and was praised by interviewees for its expertise and commercial attitude. Department head **Mary Clarke** and "*steady*" **Vincent Reston** were particularly recommended to researchers as leading employment lawyers. Following the firm's merger with consultancy business MCG, DLA has established a specialist HR consultancy advising on trade union relations, discrimination and diversity management. **Clients** Local employers.

MACE & JONES (see firm details p.1047) Employment is a core area for the firm, and it boasts a large team of practitioners "*steeped in the business*." The group advises plcs, local businesses and public bodies on all aspects of employment law. Although it now acts primarily for employers, its historic reputation stems from a volume of discrimination and equal pay cases for the Equal Opportunities Commission in the 1990s, and the firm still receives referral work at all levels. Particular strength exists in public sector work where the practice draws upon related expertise in health and safety, pensions and employee benefits. In Manchester **Michael Malone** (see p.327) was singled out to researchers for his knowledge of discrimination law and ability to "*put clients at ease.*" Liverpool-based **Martin Edwards** (see p.323) is a well-known employment academic who "*appreciates the commerciality of employment issues.*" He recently acted for Alderhay Children's Hospital in relation to the departure of a chief executive. **Clients** Merseyside Police; Emerald Airways Group; Mersey Docks and Harbour Company; Northwest Development Agency; Highways Agency; Littlewoods; Shell.

WHITTLES (see firm details p.1186) "*The leading applicants firm in the North West,*" according to some sources, the team "*crops up all the time*" acting for trade unions and staff associations. Respondent solicitors enjoy "*crossing swords*" with the practice's "*impressive individuals.*" Much of the practice's reputation rests on the individual renown of "*big name player*" **Charles Hantom**. He and "*pragmatic*" **Helen Parkinson** handle increasing amounts of discrimination, unfair dismissal and equal pay disputes. The group has achieved high-value settlements for individuals, including a recent £12,000 award for a union member in a maternity leave rights dispute. Practitioners undertake all aspects of collective employment law, including union recognition applications, ballots and collective bargaining proceedings. While most work is union-based, the group also acts for non-union applicants. **Clients** Trade unions; members; individual applicants.

COBBETTS (see firm details p.914) This "*young and dynamic*" team handles a mix of respondent and applicant work. Department head **Judith Watson** (see p.332) has a "*well deserved reputation*" in the area, especially for representing senior executives in negotiating termination agreements. On the employer side the group acted for Gateway Computers on its European reorganisation and rationalisation, and advised Matalan on the departure of its chief executive and appointment of a replacement. Contentious matters include assisting United Co-operative in a whistle blowing sexual harassment case and acting for Leeds Rhinos in the Sterling Discriminatory claim. **Clients** Disability Rights Commission; Matalan; United Norwest Co-operatives; Gateway Computers; Driver Hire Group Services.

THOMPSONS Practitioners in Liverpool and Manchester have long experience of advising trade unions and union members on a variety of employment claims. The firm handles a volume of contentious matters, with particular expertise in TUPE and equal opportunities. A large personal injury practice complements its employment strength, giving the team an edge in advising on combined employment and PI claims. The firm secured an award of £10 million for North Yorkshire school meals staff in a House of Lords equal pay case. **Clients** FBU; GMB; UNISON; UNIFI.

DWF (see firm details p.943) Recommended to researchers for its "*attentive client service*" and "*hands on*" approach to employment problems, this corporate-driven practice is divided between the firm's Liverpool and Manchester offices. Under the leadership of Andrew Leitherland, the group has experience in union recognition matters and has successfully attracted a number of insurance clients to the practice. It has been active advising senior board members of retail and house-building plcs in executive severance agreements, and recently provided TUPE advice to an MBO team on a bid to acquire a shipbuilding company. **Clients** Liverpool John Moores University; Landround; Telewest Communications.

HALLIWELL LANDAU (see firm details p.982) This "*switched on*" team has been strengthened by the acquisition of a number of practitioners from Weightmans' Manchester practice. Working in tandem with a strong corporate department, it has seen an increase in insolvency-related work and collective redundancy situations. Stephen Hills heads a "*balanced*" team, equipped to handle all manner of contentious and non-contentious employment concerns. The group advised joint venture company KTH on issues arising from the acquisition from receivership, and restructuring of the automotive division of Transtec. It also recently represented a major client in the Northern Ireland Industrial Court and Central Arbitration Committee in London on an application by a trade union for recognition. **Clients** ICL; Kwik-Fit; Wilton Investments; Ladbrokes; Umbro International.

PANNONE & PARTNERS (see firm details p.1092) Although better known for its applicant work, the Manchester practice acts for a growing base of corporate clients ranging from small businesses to multinational corporations. Christine Bradley leads an "*energetic*" team, particularly recommended for its strength in contentious matters. The group successfully defended the Bank of England in connection with a £1.5 million breach of contract and disability discrimination claim brought by a former employee. It also represented a North West football league club in connection with the termination of five players' contracts. The team handles an increasing

NORTH WEST/YORKSHIRE ■ EMPLOYMENT

amount of corporate support work, including advising on the employment aspects on the disposal of Vlasic Foods. **Clients** Bank of England; Reebok UK; MBNA International; International Paper Containers (UK); KPMG; Radisson SAS Hotel; Society of Chiropodists & Podiatrists; Tetrosyl; Emmaus UK.

OTHER NOTABLE PRACTITIONERS David Jacks (see p.325) heads the Liverpool employment practice of the newly merged Weightmans Vizards firm. Ating in TUPE tribunals and director disputes, Jacks has a loyal following among local education clients.

YORKSHIRE

EMPLOYMENT
■ YORKSHIRE

1. **Pinsent Curtis Biddle** Leeds
2. **Hammond Suddards Edge** Leeds
3. **Addleshaw Booth & Co** Leeds
   DLA Leeds, Sheffield
4. **Cobbetts** Leeds
   Eversheds Leeds
   Ford & Warren Leeds
   Walker Morris Leeds
5. **Irwin Mitchell** Sheffield
   Nabarro Nathanson Sheffield
   Rollits Hull

LEADING INDIVIDUALS

★ **MCMULLEN John** Pinsent Curtis Biddle
1. **BOOTH Christopher** Pinsent Curtis Biddle
   SHRIVES Mark Hammond Suddards Edge
2. **BRADLEY David** DLA
3. **EMMOTT Jeremy** DLA
   HILL David DLA
   TWEEDIE Colin Addleshaw Booth & Co
4. **DRAKE Ronald** Cobbetts
   HEARN Keith Ford & Warren
   PUGH Keith Nabarro Nathanson
   ROBERTSON Stuart Gordons Cranswick Solicitors

This book is the product of 6,582 1/2 hour interviews. See p.7 for BMRB audit. Within each band, firms are listed alphabetically. See individuals' profiles p.319

PINSENT CURTIS BIDDLE (see firm details p.1102) Interviewees attribute the firm's historic pre-eminence in the region to the powerful reputation of national head of employment, **John McMullen** (see p.328). An academic by background, he has a leading profile in TUPE matters and is well known for his prolific writing on the subject. Competitors acknowledge that he "*knows the law inside and out*" and "*attracts clients through his enormous reputation.*" He is complemented by "*client-friendly*" **Christopher Booth** (see p.320), a "*personable chap*" who "*takes a commercial view*" of daily employment problems. The practice includes a team specialising in European Works Councils and is able to co-ordinate international matters with the firm's Brussels Office. It has recently been advising companies such as Boots, LloydsTSB and Morgan Stanley on European Works Council Directive compliance. Significant transactional matters for the year include advising Marconi on the employment aspects of its UK restructuring exercise and acting for LEX Service on the acquisition of the RAC. An in-house HR consultancy arm provides ongoing training and advice to clients. **Clients** AstraZeneca; Barclays; Marks & Spencer; University of Leeds; Yorkshire Building Society; Cap Gemini (UK); Carlton Cards; Antalis; GNER; LloydsTSB; English Partnerships.

HAMMOND SUDDARDS EDGE The closest challenger to Pinsent Curtis Biddle's traditional hegemony in the region, the group has earned a reputation for its "*hard nosed, commercial approach*" to employment law. It acts for a sizeable base of medium to large corporates and derives strength from its national network. In addition to two partners and sixteen Leeds-based associates, the team includes two professional support lawyers advising on daily HR issues. Peers have a high regard for practice head **Mark Shrives** (see p.330). A "*safe pair of hands,*" he advises on TUPE, discrimination and board level executive severances. **Martin Brewer** was recommended for his focus on corporate transactional work and has recently been advising a client on the employment aspects of a £1 billion transaction. Highlights for the group include defending ICI against a multi-claimant compensation claim in the high court and representing Consignia in a series of tribunal claims. Catherine Prest has left the practice to return to her former firm, Eversheds. **Clients** ICI; Kelda Group; Consignia; Yates Wine Lodges; McCann Erikson; PPG Industries; Field Packaging Steel Group.

ADDLESHAW BOOTH & CO (see firm details p.838) **Colin Tweedie** (see p.332) heads a two-partner, four associate team in Leeds covering a range of contentious and non-contentious employment matters. "*Adored by clients,*" he is said to be "*direct and to the point*" with his advice. Often representing respondents, he has lately been visible acting in over 70 part-time pensions cases for major clients and defending a large financial institution against sensitive multi-witness constructive dismissal/sex discrimination claims. The Leeds practice works closely with the larger, highly-rated Manchester team. Internal HR consultants offer training and support to a base of manufacturing, leisure, banking, retail and educational clients. The firm also advises the Press Association on matters ranging from disciplinary terminations and immigration to data protection and contractual issues. **Clients** Virgin Express Airlines; Yorkshire Group; CGNU; Leeds Metropolitan University; McIntyre (UK); J Sainsbury; Kettle Foods; Gerber Foods; Dabs.com; Jaycare; Yorkshire Building Society; Royal Doulton.

DLA A "*national presence*" in the employment field, this strong team of "*solid performers*" benefits from a depth of resources and personnel distributed among offices in Leeds and Sheffield. It can also draw on support from across the Pennines in its well-regarded Manchester and Liverpool offices. The Yorkshire practice contains a number of recommended figures. Head of employment **David Bradley** was described by competitors as "*very easy to work with.*" His colleagues **David Hill** and **Jeremy Emmott** were also mentioned to researchers as cutting high-profile figures in the market. **Clients** Employers.

COBBETTS (see firm details p.914) The recent merger of Read Hind Stewart with this large player in the Manchester market is expected to produce a powerful employment practice. In Leeds, the firm retains its traditional base of small, owner-managed businesses and local authority clients but is acquiring an increasingly commercial focus through the influence of the Manchester team. Practice head and part time tribunal chairman **Ron Drake** (see p.322) receives general market commendation. The group was commissioned to act as European counsel to an American textile manufacturer, assisting on UK employment matters. It also recently appeared in EAT case Thompson v SCS & Opentext. **Clients** Contract cleaners; manufacturers; a national blue collar contracting company.

EVERSHEDS (see firm details p.949) Although the Leeds practice is not considered as high profile as its counterparts in other regions, interviewees believe the firm's national reputation and coverage to be of considerable advantage to the group. Department head Peter Norbury adds seniority to a young team which has been growing steadily at junior levels. The past year has seen an increase in high-level redundancy and industrial action matters. The group recently advised CGNU on works council issues and acted for BT Cellnet on a large-scale redundancy exercise. On the contentious side, the team defended Dupont in a four-day race discrimination case. **Clients** CGNU; Freightliner; BT Cellnet; ASDA; Carpets International; Dupont; Grattan; Ventura.

EMPLOYMENT ■ YORKSHIRE/NORTH EAST

FORD & WARREN (see firm details p.959) This active group has a diverse client base including NHS trusts, local industries and large plcs. "*Well connected*" within the transport sector, practitioners have noted expertise relating to employment issues specific to hauliers and rail employers. Under the leadership of **Keith Hearn** (see p.324), who wins warm praise from competitors and clients alike, the group handles a range of equal pay, trade union recognition, and disciplinary matters. **Clients** Local employers.

WALKER MORRIS (see firm details p.1178) Concentrating largely on local markets, the group has a respected profile among Leeds-based clients and practitioners. David Smedley heads a practice seen to be steadily growing through recruitment and internal appointments. Within the past year the group has attracted a number of new housebuilding and construction clients, as well as US-based companies with local subsidiaries such as Redhats (UK). Its strength in public sector projects is demonstrated by its recent work for Education Leeds. Here it assisted in its creation and the subsequent transfer of employees following the reorganisation of the Leeds education function. Additionally, the group takes on HR consultancy work and has recently advised on the legal and HR aspects of several large redundancy programmes. **Clients** Selfridges ; Caterpillar UK; BT Cellnet; United News Shops; Barratt Homes Leeds; IMS Group; Professional Cricketers Association; Thermawear; Intech Solutions.

IRWIN MITCHELL (see firm details p.1009) This mixed respondent and applicant practice has a marked emphasis on contentious work. The firm boasts a strong base in Sheffield under the leadership of Barry Warne and a smaller Leeds practice led by Simon Coates. The group has experience of advising on a range of TUPE, discrimination claims and executive severance matters for transport, education and steel industry clients. Notable recent work includes acting for George Graham in his settlement negotiations with Tottenham Hotspur FC, and advising on the handover of functions by the Sheffield TEC to the Learning and Skills Council and the Small Business Service. The Leeds practice has represented a major finance company in relation to seven injunctions for restraint of trade worth approximately £2 million. **Clients** AES Engineering; CBR Group; Ufi; Sheffield College; Severfield Reeve; Amari Metals; Thorntons; McCain Foods (GB); Smithson Mason.

NABARRO NATHANSON (see firm details p.1080) Particularly recommended for collective matters, individual practitioners have long experience of industrial relations issues. "*Extremely shrewd*" department head **Keith Pugh** (see p.329) reportedly "*knows how to run cases.*" Highly accomplished in contentious tribunal and High Court cases on behalf of local industries, he and his team have been representing the British Coal Corporation on an equal value claim brought by 1,300 claimants. Individual practitioners regularly conduct their own advocacy. The group is currently acting in one of the first cases under the National Minimum Wage Act and regulations, Bellfield and Others v Aviation and Airport Services, and has particular strength in relation to PFI and outsourcing matters. At a national level, it can draw on the strength of its London team and benefits from an impressive corporate client list in providing transactional support on high-value acquisitions and disposals. **Clients** Conoco; Costco Wholesale UK; Action for Employment; HSBC; Siemans; IMG; DTI; Capital Shopping Centres; British Coal Corp; Fenner.

ROLLITS (see firm details p.1115) Competitors regard the departure of Pauline Molyneux to chair employment tribunals full time as a setback to the market profile of the practice. The current group of three partners and two associates under the leadership of Neil Maidment advises a diverse group of hi-tech, charity and public sector clients on a range of employment concerns, and boasts experience of sex, race, and disability discrimination claims. On the applicant side, it is instructed by senior and middle ranking employees on severance agreements and employment disputes. Practitioners recently advised on the HR implications of a housing association merger and acted for a university on TUPE issues arising out of a transfer of a campus site. **Clients** Charities; hi-tech companies; education and public sector clients.

OTHER NOTABLE PRACTITIONERS Stuart Robertson (see p.329) at Gordons Cranswick Solicitors remains highly rated for his "*thorough*" approach to TUPE and working time issues. A part-time tribunal chairman, he has been described as "*impartially judicial*" in his advice.

NORTH EAST

EMPLOYMENT ■ NORTH EAST

1
- **Dickinson Dees** Newcastle upon Tyne
- **Eversheds** Newcastle upon Tyne
- **Short Richardson & Forth** Newcastle upon Tyne
- **Thompsons** Newcastle upon Tyne

2
- **Crutes Law Firm** Newcastle upon Tyne
- **Jacksons** Stockton on Tees
- **Samuel Phillips & Co** Newcastle upon Tyne
- **Ward Hadaway** Newcastle upon Tyne
- **Watson Burton** Newcastle upon Tyne

This book is the product of 6,582 1/2 hour interviews. See p.7 for BMRB audit. Within each band, firms are listed alphabetically.

DICKINSON DEES (see firm details p.938) A large, well-resourced practice is geared towards big commercial transactions and standalone corporate advisory work. The group acts almost exclusively for respondents and, in addition to a large base of corporate clients, advises various NHS trusts, local authorities and private sector clients on employment concerns. On the contentious side, the team handles tribunal advocacy and senior executive terminations and has recently been advising the Environment Agency on equal pay claims. Its best known practitioner is "*steady*" **Robin Bloom** (see p.320). In the past year the firm has acted for Newcastle United on the termination of its chief executive's contract and advised Go Ahead on the acquisition of British Midland's ground holding business, involving 2,500 employees in the UK, Ireland and Jersey. In addition the practice offers clients an HR consultancy package. **Clients** Nike; Black & Decker; Environment Agency; Durham University; British American Tobacco.

EVERSHEDS (see firm details p.949) The Newcastle group continues to attract household name clients through dint of the firm's national reputation as dedicated employment specialists. "*Enthusiastic*" **Simon Loy** (see p.327) offers "*reliable*" advice to education, health and public sector clients. Within the past year, he has acted in a major board level dispute raising jurisdictional issues between English and Scottish employment tribunals, and a test case under the Working Time Regulations. Particular expertise exists in issues of data protection, sex discrimination and injunctions under the Human Rights Act. The team includes dedicated HR consultants providing continued support and training to employers. It also boasts niche experience in novel disability discrimination claims relating to speech impediments and non-facial disfigurements. **Clients** Virgin Trains; BASF; De La Rue; Northern Rock; Akzo Nobel; Sainsbury's; L'Oreal; British Polythene Industries; University of Newcastle; Nissan; Invensys.

SHORT RICHARDSON & FORTH Employment is a core practice area for the firm, and the team is well regarded locally as a successful unit with some major clients. "*Always courteous*," **Michael Short** (see p.330) brings a "*great experience and depth of knowledge*" of both sides of the industry to his employment practice. He handles a volume of compromise agreement terminations, and regularly appears in employ-

NORTH EAST/SCOTLAND ■ EMPLOYMENT

LEADING INDIVIDUALS

1
- CROSS Stefan *Thompsons*
- SHORT Michael *Short Richardson & Forth*

2
- BLOOM Robin *Dickinson Dees*
- GIBSON Robert *Samuel Phillips & Co*
- LOY Simon *Eversheds*
- SMITH Tim *Crutes Law Firm*

3
- FLETCHER Kevin *Jacksons*
- HESSELBERTH David *Ward Hadaway*

UP AND COMING
- TWINEHAM Andrew *Jacksons*

ASSOCIATES TO WATCH
- MCGOWAN Paul *Watson Burton*

See individuals' profiles p.319

ment tribunals around the country. Clients range from individual applicants and owner-managed businesses to plcs. The team also possesses expertise in relation to maternity leave and advocacy in protracted tribunal hearings. **Clients** Benfield Motor Group; Newcastle Building Society; Durham County Council; Redcar & Cleveland Borough Council; Chester-le-Street District Council; Greggs; St Regis Paper Company.

THOMPSONS An applicant practice, acting almost exclusively for trade unions and members in tribunal claims, the Newcastle team functions as part of a national network. Although the firm accepts cases on behalf of individual applicants, private client work comprises only a small portion of the practice. Considered "*by far the best applicant's lawyer*" in the region "*astute*" **Stefan Cross** is widely recommended as the "*guru of Thompsons Northeast.*" A "*hard-working*" lawyer, "*willing to fight his client's corner,*" Cross attracts warm praise from opponents and clients alike. **Clients** UNISON.

CRUTES LAW FIRM (see firm details p.924) Well known for its work for NHS trusts and local authorities, the three-solicitor practice earns commendation from peers as a "*professional*" outfit, "*alive to developments in employment law.*" Team members handle their own advocacy in discrimination and unfair dismissal claims, with highly-rated **Tim Smith** (see p.331) appearing regularly in tribunal on behalf of public bodies and private sector employers. The practice also occasionally undertakes employment matters for the Treasury Solicitor and provides training seminars on disciplinary proceedings, part-time workers' rights and the Human Rights Act. **Clients** Public sector and commercial companies.

JACKSONS (see firm details p.1011) Based in Stockton on Tees, the practice is directing efforts towards building up additional employment capacity in Leeds and Tyneside. It handles a full range of contentious and non-contentious matters, with most of the team undertaking their own advocacy at tribunal level. A "*hard ball player*" by reputation, practice head **Kevin Fletcher** is also a part-time tribunal chairman. He recently won an indirect sex discrimination case for British Bakeries, establishing that changes to indirect sex discrimination legislation could not be applied retrospectively. "*Hardworking*" younger partner **Andrew Twineham** is praised by competitors as a "*pleasure to deal with.*" He recently handled a multiple redundancy application for an engineering company and represented a local authority on a race relations case. **Clients** British Bakeries; Corus; NFU; Black & Decker; Samsung.

SAMUEL PHILLIPS & CO (see firm details p.1122) Tribunal work is a "*strong suit*" of this sizeable Newcastle practice. Although evenly split between applicant and respondent work, the group has a higher profile for its representation of individuals in race, sex and disability discrimination claims. "*Tenacious*" managing partner **Robert Gibson** (see p.324) mixes contentious employment with family and personal injury matters. Notable recent work includes a claim alleging breach of the national minimum wage requirements against a major bus company and a Public Interest Disclosure Act claim against a sitting MP. On the respondent side the firm advised a local NHS trust in connection with alleged breaches of the working time regulations. It also provides in-house training to commercial clients on the Human Rights Act, stress at work and e-mail monitoring. **Clients** Newcastle upon Tyne Hospitals NHS Trust; Alfas Group; Ultimate Leisure; Wessex Taverns; Metnor Galvanising.

WARD HADAWAY (see firm details p.1180) This "*balanced*" practice handles a mix of contentious and non-contentious work for national and North Eastern employers, and was recommended to researchers for its representation of public sector clients, including health authorities and regional funding bodies. Practitioners advise on redundancy issues, disciplinary procedures and tribunal claims. Leading figure **David Hesselberth** (see p.325) was described as an "*able and fair opponent.*" The group advised on the employment aspects of the acquisition of Viasystems. **Clients** Barratts; Warner Lambert; Wilkinson Sword; South Tyneside Healthcare NHS Trust; Northumbrian Environmental Management; Philips Components.

WATSON BURTON This "*committed*" group enters the *Chambers*' rankings following widespread market recommendation. The employer-based practice, headed by Christopher Welch, handles a "*good spread of work*" according to competitors, and has a noted contentious slant. Practitioners are visible representing local industrial clients and a large number of educational institutions against discrimination, unfair dismissal and TUPE claims. Within the past year the team has defended Northumberland College in connection with claims of sex discrimination and charges of unlawful deduction from wages. **Clients** PB Power; Newcastle College; University of Sunderland; Northumberland College; Amco Corporation; American Bureau of Shipping.

SCOTLAND

MACLAY MURRAY & SPENS (see firm details p.1048) The 2001 merger of this corporate heavyweight with employment specialists Mackay Simon combined longstanding employment expertise with a large commercial client base, resulting in a powerful market presence. Despite the recent retirement of leading practitioner Shona Simon, the firm holds on to its pole position. Many ascribe the team's pre-eminent reputation to the knowledge and expertise of department head **Malcolm Mackay** (see p.327). A "*man of vision*" Mackay is widely considered to be one of the few dedicated employment practitioners in the region. He was particularly commended by competitors for his work in the European market and skill in TUPE matters. The firm has advised in relation to a number of plant shutdowns and outsourcing schemes, and recently assisted Blue Arrow in obtaining six interim interdicts against former employees attempting to set up a competing business. On the employee side, the practice represented footballers dismissed by St Johnstone Football Club. "*Commercially minded*" **Jane Fraser** (see p.323) enters the rankings this year following widespread market commendation. **Clients** Allied Distillers; Bank of Bermuda; Compaq; Serco; Guinness UDV; Pilkington Optronics; BBC Scotland; Du Pont Photomasks (UK); Educational Institute of Scotland; BPI.

MACROBERTS (see firm details p.1049) This large commercial practice was praised by market sources for its "*real focus on employment.*" Its corporate client base, heavily concentrated in the energy sector, is complemented by a number of education clients. Particularly recommended for TUPE work, the team handles the full range of advisory and contentious employment matters. "*Veteran*" lawyer **Raymond Williamson** (see p.333) has recently been busy advising on TUPE and redundancies in connection with the largest sale of retail outlets by a utility in Scotland. The team also boasts up-and-coming practitioner **Emma Bell** (see p.319) who was described by competitors as a

EMPLOYMENT ■ SCOTLAND

EMPLOYMENT
■ SCOTLAND

1
- **Maclay Murray & Spens** Glasgow
- **MacRoberts** Edinburgh, Glasgow

2
- **Dundas & Wilson CS** Edinburgh
- **McGrigor Donald** Glasgow

3
- **Burnside Kemp Fraser** Aberdeen
- **Shepherd+ Wedderburn** Edinburgh

4
- **Blackadders** Dundee
- **Brechin Tindal Oatts** Glasgow
- **Brodies** Edinburgh
- **Harper Macleod** Glasgow
- **McClure Naismith** Edinburgh, Glasgow
- **Paull & Williamsons** Aberdeen

5
- **Anderson Strathern WS** Edinburgh
- **Biggart Baillie** Glasgow
- **Kidstons & Co** Glasgow
- **Maxwell MacLaurin** Glasgow
- **Raeburn Christie & Co** Aberdeen
- **Thompsons** Edinburgh

LEADING INDIVIDUALS

1
- **MACKAY Malcolm** Maclay Murray & Spens
- **WILLIAMSON Raymond** MacRoberts

2
- **BURNSIDE David** Burnside Kemp Fraser
- **COCKBURN Alistair** Maxwell MacLaurin
- **CULLEN Joyce** Brodies
- **GUNN Sheila** Shepherd+ Wedderburn
- **KEMP Sandy** Burnside Kemp Fraser
- **MACLEOD Euan** Dundas & Wilson CS
- **MILLER Stephen** MacRoberts
- **SALUJA Sean** Paull & Williamsons

3
- **ATACK Iain** Kidstons & Co
- **BELL Emma** MacRoberts
- **GRIFFITHS John** Shepherd+ Wedderburn
- **MCKENZIE Rod** Harper Macleod
- **NICOL Diane** McGrigor Donald
- **SPEIRS William** Brechin Tindal Oatts
- **THOMAS Alun** Anderson Strathern WS
- **THOMSON Alan** McClure Naismith
- **WALKER David** Dundas & Wilson CS
- **YOUNG Jim** McGrigor Donald

UP AND COMING
- **FRASER Jane** Maclay Murray & Spens

This book is the product of 6,582 1/2 hour interviews. See p.7 for BMRB audit.
Within each band, firms are listed alphabetically. See individuals' profiles p.319

University; British Energy; Intelligent Finance; Scottish Provident.

DUNDAS & WILSON CS (see firm details p.943) This large, specialist team benefits from the firm's reputation for quality and is visible providing support on substantial corporate transactions for financial services, corporate and public sector clients. Despite its formal split from the Andersen network, the group continues to receive Andersen referrals on international projects. It boasts particular strength in employment advice relating to insolvency and restructuring. Partners are also adept in employment advocacy, and handle a large proportion of disability, race and sex discrimination, harassment, stress and unfair dismissal claims in employment tribunals. "*Straightforward*" **Euan MacLeod** was especially rated by competitors for his advocacy skills. He recently acted for Raytheon Systems in resisting a claim of unfair dismissal for alleged whistleblowing under the 1998 Public Disclosure Act. In the Glasgow office, **David Walker** has a good name in the market for general employment advice and recently represented RBS on the employment aspects of its acquisition of a stake in the £100 million Virgin One current account mortgage business. **Clients** University of Glasgow; Interserve; Maxi Haulage; Royal Bank of Scotland; Standard Life; University of Edinburgh; Quantanova.

MCGRIGOR DONALD (see firm details p.1065) The firm's merger with Klegal is expected to provide the practice with a wider reach, extending the Scottish brand name into international markets. Clients appreciate the firm's ability to contribute complementary advice in related aspects of health and safety and media relations, and report that practitioners "*can interpret law and give advice in a business context.*" The current team is split between the Edinburgh and Glasgow offices with a greater emphasis on technology clients within the Edinburgh practice. "*Laid back*" **James Young** (see p.333) has been representing Chivers Brothers in a strike action over pay, including court involvement in picketing issues. His Glasgow-based colleague **Diane Nicol** (see p.328) presents a "*balanced view*" on commercial transactions. The group is currently developing a bespoke training unit. **Clients** Wisdom Information Technologies; Orbital; Chivers Brothers; Rank Group; National Semiconductor; Ladbrooks Casinos; Allhotels.com.

BURNSIDE KEMP FRASER (see firm details p.895) This well-respected Aberdeen firm maintains a niche practice geared towards servicing local offshore oil industry clients. It has expertise in the application of TUPE, union recognition legislation and dismissal and discrimination claims, especially within an energy context. The firm also advises educational clients including local colleges and universities. Founding partners **David Burnside** (see p.320) and **Sandy Kemp** (see p.326) were highly rated by competitors for their litigation expertise and combined knowledge of personal injury and employment law. **Clients** Oil and gas companies; educational establishments.

SHEPHERD+ WEDDERBURN (see firm details p.1130) A strong commercial practice with strength in the public sector, the group was particularly recommended for its work representing doctors and professionals on employment claims. Practice head **Sheila Gunn** (see p.324) is seen to have strengthened its market reputation. She brings a background in litigation to strategic advisory work for large UK institutions, with particular concentration in the financial services and technology sectors. Clients describe her and her team as "*proactive*" and "*forward thinking.*" **John Griffiths** (see p.152) is another widely respected figure among local practitioners. He appears regularly in employment tribunals and has recently been appointed as part-time tribunal chairman. The firm offers HR consultancy services and recently advised a large listed company on the outsourcing of its HR functions. **Clients** HSBC Financial Services; Bausch & Lomb; Scottish Ambulance Services; Health and Safety Executive; Mitsubishi Electronic UK; Scottish Tourist Board; Scottish Life; Stagecoach Holdings.

BLACKADDERS (see firm details p.876) Strongest of the firms in the Tayside and Angus area, this Dundee practice boasts two accredited employment specialists under the leadership of part-time employment tribunal chairman Sandy Meiklejohn. The team handles all aspects of contentious and non-contentious employment law and accepts applicant claims. Recent reported work includes a successful defence of the Dundee Business Support Group against a constructive unfair dismissal claim and representating the applicant in a test case determining whether an executor could institute and proceed with a disability discrimination claim in Scotland. **Clients** NCR Financial Solutions; Travel Dundee; VIS Entertainment; Day International; Madison Cable; Douglas Group.

BRECHIN TINDAL OATTS This insurance-based practice is seen to have expanded its employment capacity, recently recruiting practitioners to advise from the Edinburgh office. Although it represents a number of employees and senior executives, the greater share of work is advising employers within the leisure, pharmaceutical, education and charity sectors. "*First class*" **Bill Speirs** (see p.331) "*has done an excellent job in capitalising on the existing strengths of the firm.*" He recently advised a senior executive within the banking sector in achieving a settlement in connection with disability and sex discrimination, breach of contract and equal pay claims. On the employer side, the firm

"*rising star*" who is "*coming up quickly through the ranks,*" while the recruitment from Harper Macleod of highly respected **Stephen Miller** (see p.328) will further boost its profile. The group undertakes advisory work in connection with PFI projects and has recently been counselling on the employment aspects of the construction of the Channel Tunnel Rail Link. It also provides employment law update training to clients throughout the UK. **Clients** Scottish Power; Southern Water; Motorola; Royal Infirmary of Edinburgh; Safeway Stores; Orkney Council; Glasgow Caledonian

advised a software supplier on consultation issues and planning in relation to a large redundancy scheme. **Clients** Employers and employees.

BRODIES (see firm details p.889) Valued equally for its "*commercial acumen*" and "*sense of humour*" Brodies is reported to offer "*customised, business-focused*" advice to clients in the retail, finance, technology and public sectors. Recently recruiting at the associate and assistant levels, it enjoys a loyal following within Scotland, and was also noted for its ability to handle transactions south of the border. Key figure **Joyce Cullen** (see p.321) is a solicitor advocate and a well known presence on the employment conference circuit. Major recent work for the group includes advising RBS on setting up a 50-consultant HR unit to provide guidance on disciplinary and grievance cases, and on issues relating to a European Works Council following the bank's merger with NatWest. **Clients** RBS/NatWest; Sainsbury's; Scottish National Assurance; Scottish Prison Service; ASA Ltd; Enterprise-Rent-A-Car UK; BAE Systems; Sykes Europe; Edinburgh and Lothian Tourist Board.

HARPER MACLEOD (see firm details p.985) A growing team of four partners and four assistants rates highly among mid-sized to large corporates, education institutions and public authorities. It handles a large body of contentious work for employers but also represents senior executives in tribunal claims. The market waits to see what effect the loss of highly-rated practitioner Stephen Miller to MacRoberts will have on the outfit, however it still boasts senior employment partner, **Rod McKenzie** (see p.328). Concentrating on heavy-duty contentious work, he serves as a part-time employment tribunal chairman and is known for his "*no-nonsense*" approach and "*deep experience in the field.*" The group advised Dumfries & Galloway College on its first major restructuring involving trade union consultation and collective redundancies. At the applicant level, the firm represented a transplant surgeon in race discrimination proceedings against the University of Glasgow. **Clients** Box Clever; East Dunbartonshire Council; J&T Group; LloydsTSB Scotland; Dumfries and Galloway College; Aberdeen City Council; Scotland On Line; Optical Express; Ryden; Tulloch Group.

MCCLURE NAISMITH (see firm details p.1062) This well-respected respondent firm has a bias towards contentious matters. An "*enviable client base*" is drawn from the oil and gas, mining, transport, educational, pharmaceutical and public sectors. The practice includes employment specialists in both Glasgow and Edinburgh, with key figure **Alan Thomson** (see p.332) receiving particularly warm recommendations from peers. The group recently acted for the respondent in Fowlie v Score (Europe) Ltd, an unfair dismissal claim involving supervision and health and safety issues, and successfully defended a major retailer against sexual harassment and discrimination claims in employment tribunals in Northern Ireland. **Clients** Stagecoach Scotland; First Engineering; SCA Packaging; Your More Store; Gist.

PAULL & WILLIAMSONS (see firm details p.1096) Known for its niche in advising oil and gas industry clients, the practice draws upon health and safety expertise in advising on contracts, training procedures and safety documentation. The team is also experienced in trade union issues and has handled a large number of collective bargaining agreements. Department head **Sean Saluja** (see p.330) was praised by competitors for "*growing the practice nicely.*" He and his team are said to "*produce good, well thought out work.*" Saluja's individual practice is weighted towards contentious tribunal work in which he handles much of his own advocacy. However, the team in general undertakes a balance of contentious and non-contentious issues for large- and medium-sized companies and public bodies. **Clients** Aberdeen Asset Management; ABB Vetco Gray; Consafe Engineering; FirstGlasgow; GlobalSantaFe Techserve (NS); Halliburton; Schlumberger Evaluation & Production Services.

ANDERSON STRATHERN WS (see firm details p.844) Noted particularly for his work on disability discrimination, "*professional*" **Alun Thomas** (see p.331) is seen by market sources to be building a good team at Anderson Strathern. Clients praise its "*good service at competitive rates.*" Thomas has considerable experience in the field and represents a range of large- and medium-sized employers in the corporate and educational sectors, as well undertaking applicant work. He has a particular interest in discrimination issues, from both sides of the industrial debate, and recently appeared for the respondent in the high-profile tribunal case Walkingshaw v JMG. **Clients** Royal College of Nursing; Edinburgh College of Art; Scottish Rugby Union; Edinburgh Zoo.

BIGGART BAILLIE (see firm details p.871) This group has been increasing its focus on employment law and has formed close ties with many larger Scottish corporations. Paul Brown heads a growing group that includes two solicitor advocates representing employers in employment tribunals, the EAT and the Scottish Supreme Court. Additionally, the practice offers employment training in the form of client seminars and employment law updates. The group continues to advise Aberdeen Asset Management on general employment matters and Scottish Power Generation and Thus on agency personnel and call centre contracts. The past year has seen an increase in work negotiating termination agreements for senior executives. **Clients** Greater Glasgow; Clyde Valley Tourist Board; Aberdeenshire Council; Scottish Power Generation; Aberdeen Asset Management; Marine Harvest; ScotRail; Thus.

KIDSTONS & CO (see firm details p.1022) This smaller firm is well known for its specialisation in employment. It acts largely for small to medium-sized corporates in West Scotland, advising on contracts, TUPE matters and disability and sex discrimination tribunal claims. Highly regarded **Iain Atack** (see p.319) heads a three-person team and draws general market commendation for his efficiency and "*personable*" manner. Non-contentious work for the group includes drafting service agreements for senior executives, disciplinary rules, grievance procedures, staff handbooks and offering other general advice. **Clients** Dixons Stores Group; 3M; Alliance & Leicester.

MAXWELL MACLAURIN Highly recommended for applicant work, **Alistair Cockburn** (see p.321) is an "*experienced and resourceful street-fighter*" who enjoys an enviable reputation among his peers for his ability to "*get his teeth into employers.*" A litigator by background, this "*tenacious*" advocate maintains a broad practice, focusing largely on contentious employment matters and related commercial and PI litigation. **Clients** Employers and employees.

RAEBURN CHRISTIE & CO Peers and clients have no difficulty in recommending **Reg Christie** for high-quality respondent work. A "*shrewd*" practitioner, Christie and his small team undertake a high proportion of work for employers in the oil industry. This includes the negotiation of termination agreements, preparation of new employment documents, and defence of tribunal applications. Christie, who also undertakes a share of employee work for directors and senior level applicants, has earned a reputation in the market as an able advocate. **Clients** Employers and employees.

THOMPSONS This well-known trade union firm has highly rated offices in Edinburgh and Glasgow. One of the largest applicant practices in Scotland, the group is reported to "*pop up all the time*" acting for unions and union members. Practitioners regularly represent individual employees at tribunals, EAT and civil courts on issues ranging from unfair dismissal and breach of contract to discrimination and victimisation. The firm is currently acting in the EAT in Bald v Capital Press Agency, a novel victimisation case brought under the Working Time Regulations 1998. Margaret Gribbon in Glasgow is the group's contact partner. **Clients** NUJ; trade union members.

NORTHERN IRELAND

EMPLOYMENT
NORTHERN IRELAND

1 Jones & Cassidy Belfast

2 Cleaver Fulton Rankin Belfast
Elliott Duffy Garrett Belfast
L'Estrange & Brett Belfast

3 Carson McDowell Belfast
Culbert and Martin Belfast

4 Napier & Sons Belfast

LEADING INDIVIDUALS

1 JONES Beverley Jones & Cassidy

2 BRETT Adam L'Estrange & Brett
BROCK Adrienne Elliott Duffy Garrett
CASSIDY Fiona Jones & Cassidy
COLL Harry Elliott Duffy Garrett

3 GRAY David Culbert and Martin
PRYTHERCH Rosalie Cleaver Fulton Rankin
TURTLE Brian Carson McDowell

UP AND COMING
O'NEILL Orlagh Napier & Sons

This book is the product of 6,582 1/2 hour interviews. See p.7 for BMRB audit. Within each band, firms are listed alphabetically. See individuals' profiles p.319

JONES & CASSIDY This highly regarded niche firm specialises in discrimination matters. Although originally set up to take on applicant claims, it has succeeded in attracting contentious work for a number of corporate employers and maintains ties with the Equality Commission. Considered by peers to be an "*obvious choice*" for all types of discrimination claims, practitioners command an "*absolute wealth and depth of expertise*" in the area. "*Formidable*" advocate **Beverley Jones** was particularly mentioned in relation to equal pay claims while "*first-class*" partner **Fiona Cassidy** "*looks problems squarely in the eye.*" **Clients** Applicants; Local employers.

CLEAVER FULTON RANKIN (see firm details p.910) A two-partner commercially focused practice, it is seen to be developing in scope under the leadership of "*sunny*" **Rosalie Prytherch** (see p.329). Typical work includes delivering non-contentious advice and supporting the firm's large company/commercial department on transactional matters. Recommended for her ability to "*turn her hand to any employment issue,*" Prytherch has particular experience in transfer of undertakings and restrictive covenant work. On the contentious side, practitioners command notable litigation experience and have recently seen an increase in multi-party and serial victimisation claims. Work for individuals extends to negotiation of severance packages for senior executives. Recent transactional work includes acting for Lindsay Cars on the acquisition of other Ford Dealerships to become one of Northern Ireland's 'Big Three' motor groups. Ties with Dublin firm Matheson Ormsby Prentice assists the group in offering cross-border advice on employment matters. **Clients** Waterways Ireland; Open University; Clinton Cards; Presbyterian Church in Ireland.

ELLIOTT DUFFY GARRETT (see firm details p.947) This commercially-based practice has the capacity to handle all aspects of employment law from industrial relations and unfair dismissal claims to TUPE matters and drafting of documentation and procedures. **Adrienne Brock** is seen by peers advising substantial local manufacturing and industrial interests. A "*consummate businessman,*" **Harry Coll** (see p.321) is now managing partner of the firm. Although less visible on day to day matters, he continues to provide strategic input in business planning and his reputation in the field attracts substantial clients to the employment practice. The group also takes on a small percentage of applicant work and occasionally receives instructions from the Equality Commission. **Clients** Queen's University; Goldenvale; Seagate; public sector clients.

L'ESTRANGE & BRETT (see firm details p.1039) The comprehensive employment practice at this firm covers such diverse areas as data protection, equal pay, unfair dismissal, union activities and internet usage policy. It has particular expertise in discrimination claims within the context of educational institutions, and represents major client Queen's University on a variety of matters. Additionally, the firm's link with Dublin-based McCann Fitzgerald Solicitors allows the group to co-ordinate cross-border employment advice. Key figure **Adam Brett** (see p.320) was praised by peers for his advocacy skills and has lately been active in a number of restrictive covenant proceedings involving substantial costs orders. **Clients** NTL; Queen's University Belfast; Toys 'R' Us; Carphone Warehouse; Coca-Cola; Liberty Information Technology; Cornhill Insurance; Galen; Sainsbury's; Visteon; RMC.

CARSON MCDOWELL (see firm details p.901) This five-practitioner team acts for respondents, many within the healthcare, education or public sectors. In the past year it has been heavily involved in representing health trusts in relation to part-time worker pension claims. **Brian Turtle** (see p.569) maintains a mixed practice in employment, professional indemnity and insurance, focusing on the litigious aspects of each. The practice is gradually building up a share of non-contentious work and recently advised HCL Technologies on TUPE matters arising from its acquisition of a BT call centre. Additionally the group provides advice on immigration and work permits and has experience of trade union recognition matters. **Clients** HCL Technologies; Waterways Ireland; Avalanche Technology; further education establishments; health trusts.

CULBERT AND MARTIN Best known for its work on behalf of the Equality Commission, the practice acts for both applicants and respondents. Sex and disability discrimination claims are considered by market sources to be amongst the team's major strengths. Practice head **David Gray** was praised by competitors for the thoroughness of his advice. The group advises private and business clients on a full range of redundancy, unfair dismissal and discrimination claims. **Clients** Employers; Applicants.

NAPIER & SONS A Belfast respondent practice, it is reported to have an impressive roster of major clients. Although still overshadowed by the firm's insolvency practice, the employment team is gaining renown in the market through the work of "*impressive*" associate **Orlagh O'Neill**. An employment specialist, she has been "*carving a niche*" for herself in racial equality matters. The group also has expertise in disability discrimination matters and proven experience in industrial tribunals. Practitioners are frequently called upon to advise on the employment aspects of restructuring exercises and counsel company directors on voluntary termination agreements. **Clients** Post Office; Equality Commission; BT; Fujitsu Telecom.

THE LEADERS IN EMPLOYMENT

AARONS, Elaine
Eversheds, London
(020) 7919 4500
aaronse@eversheds.com
Specialisation: Partner in employment and pensions group dealing with the full range of contentious and non-contentious employment law matters. Advises employers and senior executives. Specialises in all aspects of employment law, including high level strategic advice, business reorganisations, international projects, service agreements, bonus schemes, restrictive covenants, senior executive severances, board room disputes and high profile discrimination cases. Well known conference speaker, regularly appearing on radio and television.
Prof. Memberships: Employer's Forum on Statute and Practice (Chair), Vice Chair City of London Law Society Employment Law Sub-Committee, Complinet HR online news service (member of editorial board), Employment Lawyers Association (member, having been an officer 1997-2000, Management Committee Member 1992-2000).
Career: Qualified in 1982 with *Norton Rose* specialising in employment law since then. Head of employment at *Eversheds* London (and its predecessor firms) since 1989.
Publications: General editor of Tolley's 'Termination of Employment'.

ADAMS, Elizabeth
Beachcroft Wansbroughs, London
(020) 7242 1011
eadams@bwlaw.co.uk
Specialisation: Partner and national leader of employment; practice covers contentious and non-contentious employment work undertaken for both public and private sector clients and in particular discrimination and the Transfer of Undertakings (Protection of Employment) regulations 1982 (TUPE). Particular interest in EU social policy aspects and working time. Lectures extensively on all aspects of expertise; regular contributor to the firm's Employment Focus and contributor to 'Strategic Procurement for the NHS' (The NHS Confederation).
Prof. Memberships: Member of the City of London Solicitors Employment sub-committee; member of the Employer Lawyers Association and its International Committee. Former Management committee member and chair of the International Committee.
Career: LLB (Hons) Law 1977. Admitted 1980 at *Beachcroft Hyman Isaacs* (now *Beachcroft Wansbroughs*) from 1981. Partner 1986 to date.
Personal: Born 15 April 1955. Interests include reading and travel. Lives in Horsley.

ALDRED, Hilary
Hewitson Becke + Shaw, Cambridge
(01223) 461155

ARMSTRONG, Ruth
Gateley Wareing, Birmingham
(0121) 234 0000

ASHTIANY, Sue
Nabarro Nathanson, London
(020) 7524 6000
s.ashtiany@nabarro.com
Specialisation: Specialist employment and discrimination lawyer and Head of Group. Specialises in project and advisory work, major cases and transactions. Acts principally for employer clients in the public and private sector. These include HSBC Bank plc, University of Oxford, The Office of Gas and Electricity Markets, The Met Office, Unipart Ltd and Philips Electronics (UK) Limited. Writes and lectures extensively on employment and discrimination law and organisational change issues including worker consultation. This includes training for the Cabinet Office and Civil Service as well as project management on cultural change and diversity issues. Contributing Editor to Tolley loose-leaf encyclopaedia on Employment Law – author of chapter on Race Discrimination. Contributing Editor to CCH on line Employment Law Services. Contributing Editor to 'FL Memo Employment Law and Discrimination Law' (forthcoming). Contributing Editor to Sweet & Maxwell's 'Employment Precedents and Company Policy Documents'.
Prof. Memberships: Employment Lawyers Association; Industrial Law Society; Fellow – Institute of Advanced Legal Studies; Law Society.
Career: Worked for the UN High Commissioner for Refugees. Qualified in 1986 with the Oxford firm of *Cole and Cole* and became a Partner in 1989. Joined *Nabarro Nathanson* as a Partner in 2001.
Personal: Educated in Iran and the UK. Commissioner, Equal Opportunities Commission (December 2000-); Member, Court Oxford Brookes University; Acting Chairman, Oxfordshire Ambulance Trust; Honorary Fellow, Harris Manchester College, Oxford. Languages: English, French, Farsi.

ATACK, Iain F
Kidstons & Co, Glasgow
(0141) 221 6551
mail@kidstons.co.uk
Specialisation: Senior partner. Main area of practice is employment law: accredited as a specialist by the Law Society of Scotland. Advises mainly employers on all aspects of employment law. Part-time Chairman of Employment Tribunals. Also handles general civil litigation and factoring law. Advises invoice factors on all commercial matters. Major clients include several large plcs operating both in England and Scotland, banks, financial institutions and many medium-sized companies. Lectures at conferences. Formerly tutor in advocacy and pleading at Glasgow University.
Prof. Memberships: Law Society of Scotland, Royal Faculty of Procurators in Glasgow, Employment Law Group. Member, Law Society of Scotland Employment Law Committee.
Career: Qualified in 1971. Joined *Kidstons & Company* in 1972, becoming a partner in 1975 and senior partner in 1993. Council member of Royal Faculty of Procurators, 1989-92. Committee member of Employment Law Group since 1984. Chairman of NHBC Appeal Tribunal since 1990.
Personal: Born 22 November 1947. Attended Kelvinside Academy, Glasgow, then St Andrew's University. Leisure interests include walking, skiing and sailing.

AUERBACH, Simon
Pattinson & Brewer, London
(020) 7400 5100
sauerbach@pattinsonbrewer.co.uk
Specialisation: Partner in Employment Department. Practises in all areas of labour, employment and discrimination law. Particular interest in transfers of undertakings, industrial conflict and trade union law. Has addressed meetings of the Industrial Law Society, Employment Lawyers' Association and the Institute of Employment Rights. Occasional media commentator.
Prof. Memberships: Industrial Law Society, Institute of Employment Rights, Employment Lawyers' Association.
Career: Qualified in 1985. Partner with *Pattinson & Brewer*. Member of the Council of ACAS since November 2001.
Publications: Co-author of 'A Guide to The Employment Act 1988' author of 'Legislating for Conflict' (OUP, 1990), and 'Derecognition and Personal Contracts' (IER, 1993) and the chapter on statutory recognition in 'Employment Rights at Work' (IER, 2001). Has had articles published in the 'Industrial Law Journal' and 'Political Quarterly'. Regular writer in specialist publications and conference speaker.
Personal: Born in 1961. Educated at Oxford University (BA in Jurisprudence, 1st Class Hons, 1982 and D.Phil, 1988). Lives in London.

BELL, Emma
MacRoberts, Glasgow
(0141) 332 9988
emma.bell@macroberts.com
Specialisation: Partner in Employment Law Group. Accredited by Law Society of Scotland as a specialist in employment law. Significant experience in conducting Employment tribunal and Employment Appeal tribunal hearings and in negotiating exit and entrance packages at senior executive level. Advises on disability, sex and race discrimination issues and the implications of collective redundancies, business transfers and business re-organisations, as well as change management.
Prof. Memberships: Law Society of Scotland.
Career: Trained with *John Wilson & Co.* Qualified 1993. Assistant, Associate and Partner (2000) with *MacRoberts* in employment law group.
Personal: St Josephs College, Dumfries; University of Strathclyde LLB (Hons), Dip LP, NP. Leisure interests include biking, skiing, hockey. Lives in Glasgow.

BENSON, Edward
Browne Jacobson, Nottingham
(0115) 976 6211
ebenson@brownej.co.uk
Specialisation: Practice covers full range of employment law services including drafting contracts of employment, drafting policies and procedures, representation at employment tribunals, unfair dismissal, redundancy pay, discrimination, equal pay, minimum wage, working time, union recognition etc.
Prof. Memberships: Member of Industrial Law Society.
Career: Admitted 1980. *Slaughter and May* 1978-82. Joined *Browne Jacobson* 1989, partner since 1993.
Publications: Contributor and general editor of 'Employment Law Service for IPD', published by Jordans. Assistant editor of handbooks and supplements at IDS (1982-84). Editor of 'Industrial Relations Legal Information Bulletin (1985-89)'. Author of 'A Guide to Redundancy Law' and 'The Law of Industrial Conflict' – both published by MacMillan.

BENSON, Nick
Michelmores, Exeter
(01392) 436244

BESWICK, David
Hammond Suddards Edge, Birmingham
(0121) 222 3000

BLOOM, Martin
Hegarty & Co, Peterborough
(01733) 346333
Specialisation: Partner and head of employment law department. Undertakes a wide range of contentious and non-contentious employment work primarily for business clients, but also for individuals. Undertakes advocacy at Employment Tribunals and regularly presents seminars across the UK to clients and fellow professionals.
Prof. Memberships: Law Society; Employment Lawyers Association; Industrial Law Society.
Career: Joined *Hegarty & Co* in 1979, qualified in 1981 and became partner in 1983. Appointed part-time Employment Tribunal chairman in 1995.
Personal: Born 23 March 1956, educated at King's School Peterborough and Leicester University (LLB). College of Law, Chester. Leisure activities include squash and fly-fishing.

EMPLOYMENT ■ THE LEADERS

BLOOM, Robin
Dickinson Dees, Stockton on Tees
(01642) 631700
law@dickinson-dees.com
Specialisation: Employment law and employment litigation (including use of alternative dispute resolution).
Prof. Memberships: Law Society. Founder Member Newcastle Industrial Tribunal User Group.
Career: Educated: Rugby School, Durham University and Chester College of Law. Career: Articled *Cohen Jackson* and *Addleshaw Sons and Latham*. Admitted October 1982, worked for and subsequently Partner in *Cohen Jackson*, now *Jacksons*. Trained as mediator by ADR Net Ltd.
Personal: Married with two children. Main leisure interests are sport (mainly watching but still play the occasional game of cricket); foreign travel; gardening.

BOOTH, Christopher
Pinsent Curtis Biddle, Leeds
(0113) 244 5000
chris.booth@pinsents.com
Specialisation: Specialises in employment law dealing with high-profile executive terminations, trade union recognition, TUPE, restrictive covenants and discrimination cases.
Prof. Memberships: Employment Lawyers Association (ELA). Leeds Law Society. Affiliate member of CIPD.
Career: Educated at Hull University (LLB 1984). Joined former *Simpson Curtis* (now *Pinsent Curtis Biddle*) in 1987 on qualification. Partner 1993.
Personal: Born 1963. Leisure interests: golf, skiing, cooking, family and personal computer.

BRADLEY, David
DLA, Sheffield
(08700) 111111

BREARLEY, Kate
Stephenson Harwood (incorporating Sinclair Roche & Temperley), London
(020) 7809 2107
kate.brearley@shlegal.com
Specialisation: Partner, Head of Employment, Pensions and Benefits Practice Group. Handles all aspects of contentious and non-contentious employment law acting for public and private sector clients, high profile senior executives/directors and teams of employees seeking to join competitors. Leading expert and co-author of the key textbook on competition in the employment field. Regularly advises on all aspects of employee competition including drafting and enforcement of restrictive covenants. Work includes drafting/negotiating service agreements, and termination packages; Employment Tribunal; County and High Court claims; stress and discrimination claims; boardroom disputes; employment aspects of corporate transactions; TUPE transfers. Cases of note include representing Charing Cross and Westminster Medical School (now Imperial College School of Medicine) in the fixed term contract case Bhatt v Charing Cross and Westminster Medical School and Another. Chairs conferences and lectures for IBC, EuroForum, CLT and TQPC on employment related topics.
Prof. Memberships: City of London Solicitors Company (Member of the Employment Law Sub-Committee); Employment Lawyers Association; Work Foundation; United Kingdom Environmental Law Association.
Career: Called to the Bar 1979 and has specialised predominantly in employment law since qualification. Joined *Stephenson Harwood* in 1986; qualified as a solicitor in 1989; partner 1989.
Publications: Brearley and Bloch, 'Employment Covenants and Confidential Information'; 'Law Practice and Technique' (Butterworths).
Personal: Born 1957. Educated Harrogate Ladies College and Exeter University 1975-78, LLB Hons.

BREEN, Helga
Eversheds, London
(0207) 919 4824
breenh@eversheds.com
Specialisation: Partner in employment, pensions and immigration group. Specialises in all aspects of law for corporates and senior executives in both the private and public sector. Her particular interests are project management, business transfers, mergers and acquisitions, directors, executive recruitment and severances. Has developed high level expertise in the banking and financial sectors, particularly financial services regulation and the employment law aspects of outsourcing. Major clients include the Financial Services Authority, Deloitte & Touche/Deloitte Consulting, Cazenove & Co. Responsible for *Evershed's* Corporate Immigration Services and director/co founder of the Employers' Forum on Statute & Practice. Runs *Eversheds* London client seminar programme and conducts training sessions for clients and external providers. Writes and lectures regularly on employment and HR issues.
Prof. Memberships: Employment Lawyers' Association. Employers' Forum on Statute & Practice (director and co-founder).
Career: BA (Hons) Classics 1981. Qualified 1986 employee benefits group, *Linklaters & Alliance* (then *Linklaters & Paines*). 1991 *PricewaterhouseCoopers* (then *Coopers & Lybrand*). Joined *Eversheds* in 1992 and became a partner in 1994.
Personal: Born 1959. Married with two children. Lives Reigate in Surrey.

BRETT, Adam
L'Estrange & Brett, Belfast
(028) 9023 0426
adam.brett@lestrangeandbrett.com
Specialisation: Partner. Main area of work: employment law, discrimination law and commercial litigation.
Prof. Memberships: Law Society of Northern Ireland.
Career: Qualified 1981. Partner in *L'Estrange & Brett* since 1985.
Personal: Born 1957. Education: Oxford University (MA). Committee Member Employment Lawyers Group in Northern Ireland and Member Employment Lawyers Association. Contributor to two Sweet and Maxwell publications on employment law.

BRIMELOW, Russell
Boodle Hatfield, Oxford
(020) 7318 8135
rbrimelow@boodlehatfield.com
Specialisation: Partner and head of employment group. Covers all aspects of employment law for companies of all sizes, with some work for senior individuals. Areas of expertise include business transfers (TUPE), working time, executive terminations and discrimination law.
Prof. Memberships: Employment Lawyers Association, Industrial Law Society, Law Society, Immigration Law Practitioners Association, Discrimination Law Association.
Career: Qualified 1991. With *Denton Hall* 1988-94. Joined *Boodle Hatfield* in 1994, becoming an associate in 1996 and a partner in 1997.
Publications: Writes a weekly column in 'Personnel Today' as well as a range of articles in 'Employers Law', 'Employment Law Journal', 'The Independent', 'Croner's Employment Law Journal' and others. Co-wrote Tolley's 'Working Time' looseleaf. On editorial board of Croner's Questions and Answers. Bulletin and European Newsletters.
Personal: Born 1963. Oxford graduate. Father of three. Keen traveller, cyclist, piano, guitar and tennis player.

BROCK, Adrienne
Elliott Duffy Garrett, Belfast
(028) 9024 5034

BROWN, Nicola
Mills & Reeve, Cambridge
(01223) 222 282
nicola.brown@mills-reeve.com
Specialisation: Specialises in all aspects of employment law acting mainly for employers both in the public and private sector. Deals with contract drafting, advice on dismissals and industrial tribunal claims. Increasing emphasis on discrimination claims and advice on the Transfer of Undertaking Regulations.
Career: 1983 – LLB University of Southampton; 1987 – qualified as a solicitor; 1987-90 – assistant solicitor *Kennedys*, Chiswell Street, London; 1990-95 – senior solicitor *Mills & Reeve*, Cambridge; 1995 to date – partner *Mills & Reeve*, Cambridge.

BURD, Michael
Lewis Silkin, London
(020) 7074 8000
michael.burd@lewissilkin.com
Specialisation: Partner and joint head of the employment team. Advises in all aspects of employment law. Particular areas of interest include contested dismissals and redundancy, business transfers, Employment Tribunal claims and advice aimed at preventing employment disputes and ensuring compliance with statutory regulations.
Prof. Memberships: Employment Lawyers Association. Committee Member, London Solicitors Litigation Association. President of City of Westminster Law Society (1995/96).
Career: Qualified 1986. Partner at *Lewis Silkin*, 1988.
Publications: Consultant Editor, Croner's 'Managing Termination of Employment'. Section Editor, Employment Section, Gee Publishing, 'Practical Tax Planning and Precedents'.
Personal: Born 07/02/58. BA Columbia University 1980. MPhil Cambridge University 1982.

BURNSIDE, David M
Burnside Kemp Fraser, Aberdeen
(01224) 327500
Specialisation: Senior Partner in Court Department. Main area of practice is employment. Has handled employment tribunal cases since 1967 in the fields of redundancy, unfair dismissal, sexual and racial discrimination and transfer of undertakings. Acts for a number of major clients in these matters. Accredited by the Law Society of Scotland as an Employment Law Specialist since 1990. Also handles personal injury work (Member of Personal Injury Panel). Since 1970 has worked predominantly for claimants. Has substantial experience of offshore cases, although also deals with many cases involving injury at work or in road traffic accidents and medical negligence. Joint lead negotiator in Piper Alpha for claimants. Group spokesman for steering committees involving major helicopter crashes. Gives occasional lectures for the Law Society, IPM and other outside bodies. Has considerable media experience arising from matters of local and national interest.
Prof. Memberships: Law Society of Scotland, Society of Advocates in Aberdeen, Association of Personal Injury Lawyers, Aberdeen Bar Association, Employment Law Group, ATLA.
Career: Qualified in 1966. Established *Messrs Burnside Advocates* as Senior Partner in 1989; firm became *Burnside Kemp Fraser* in 1994. President of Junior Chamber of Commerce, Aberdeen, 1978-79; President of Aberdeen Bar Association 1987-89; Board Member of Legal Defence Union since 1990; Scottish Convenor and Member of National Executive Committee of APIL 1990-96. Treasurer of Employment Law Group. President of Society of Advocates in Aberdeen 2000-01.
Personal: Born 5 March 1943.

CAMPION, Hilary
Eversheds, Nottingham
(0115) 950 7000
hilarycampion@eversheds.com
Specialisation: All areas of employment

law, contentious and non-contentious. Acts principally for employers but also executive severances.
Prof. Memberships: Employment Lawyers' Association; Nottinghamshire Law Society.
Career: Articled at *Ashton Hill and Co*, Nottingham 1976-78; Lecturer, College of Law, Chester 1978-80; *Eversheds*, Nottingham (formerly *Wells & Hind*) 1980- date. Partner since 1983.
Publications: Various articles in professional and local journals. Contributor to 'Workplace Survival Guide'.
Personal: Emmanuel College, Cambridge MA. CAMRA Member. Derby County Football Club supporter. Enjoys skiing and windsurfing.

CASSEL, Richard
Hatch Brenner, Norwich
(01603) 660811
richardcassel@hatchbrenner.co.uk
Specialisation: All aspects of employment and discrimination law. Wide experience of advocacy and tribunal practice and procedure. Advises a substantial number of large and small employers in relation to Employment Law issues both individual and collective.
Career: Qualified as a solicitor in 1980. Partner at *Crotch Brenner and Dunkley* in Norwich. Since 1992 partner and head of employment law department of *Hatch Brenner*. Part-time chairman of the Employment tribunal from 1993.
Personal: Born 1950, educated at Stationers' Company's School, London and University of Warwick. Lives in Norwich, married with three daughters.

CASSIDY, Fiona
Jones & Cassidy, Belfast
(028) 9064 2290

CATER, Sheila
Pitmans, Reading
(0118) 958 0224
scater@pitmans.com
Specialisation: All types of contentious and non-contentious employment law, including discrimination. Wide experience of acting for both public and private sector employers and employees.
Prof. Memberships: ELA, Law Society.
Career: Qualified in 1981; worked in-house at National Coal Board Legal Department prior to spending three years in the City. Joined *Morgan Cole*'s Employment Department in Oxford 1989; Partner 1991. Joined *Pitmans* as a Partner January 2001.

CAVALIER, Stephen
Thompsons, London
(020) 7290 0000
Specialisation: Head of Employment Rights Unit. Partner specialising in employment and trade union law. Practice covers a range of employment and trade union work including transfer of undertakings, European law, dismissals, trade union law, rule books, industrial disputes and all aspects of collective and individual labour law. Involved in a number of significant cases on the application of the TUPE Regulations to competitive tendering, including the leading Court of Appeal case, conducting Francovich claims against UK government under Acquired Rights Directive and Judicial Review challenging the Consultation Regulations, plus first UK reference to the European Court on the Working Time Directive. Expert witness to the European Parliament on Acquired Rights Directive. Frequent speaker at union conferences, fringe meetings and national and international seminars. Author of 'Transfer of Undertakings: Employment Rights' and several articles and publications.
Prof. Memberships: Industrial Law Society (Chair), Institute of Employment Rights, ETUC Legal Experts Network.
Career: Qualified in 1986. Joined *Thompsons* in 1987 and became a Partner in 1989.
Personal: Born 26 February 1962. Educated at St Edmund Hall, Oxford 1980-83. Member of the Labour Party.

CHAMBERLAIN, Andrew
Addleshaw Booth & Co, Manchester
(0161) 934 6444
andrew.chamberlain@addleshaw-booth.com
Specialisation: Partner in Employment Department. All aspects of employment law including the drafting of service agreements, Transfer of Undertakings Regulations, restrictive covenant injunctions, executive terminations and all contentious employment matters (including advocacy at the Employment Tribunals), employment aspects of M&A work, and immigration matters.
Prof. Memberships: Employment Lawyers Association.
Career: Joined the firm in September 1995.
Personal: Educated at the University of Nottingham. Interests: golf, rugby, cricket and squash.

CHAMBERLAIN, Jonathan
Wragge & Co, Birmingham
0870 903 1000

CHITTY, Martin
Wragge & Co, Birmingham
0870 903 1000

CLARKE, Mary
DLA, Manchester
(08700) 111111

CLARKE, Michael
Morgan Cole, Cardiff
(029) 2038 5385

COCKBURN, Alistair
Maxwell MacLaurin, Glasgow
(0141) 332 5666
acockburn@maxwellmaclaurin.co.uk
Specialisation: Partner in Litigation Department. Main area of practice is employment law, primarily the representation of employers in relation to proceedings before employment tribunals throughout the whole of the UK including representation before the Employment Appeal Tribunal. Also represents individual employees before tribunals in Scotland and to both in relation to the formation of service agreements and the implications at termination, particularly with regard to covenants. Also handles litigation generally.
Prof. Memberships: Law Society of Scotland, Royal Faculty of Procurators in Glasgow, Glasgow Bar Association.
Career: Qualified in 1972. Joined *Tilston MacLaurin* in 1970, becoming a Partner in 1974. Accredited as a Specialist in Employment Law by the Law Society of Scotland in 1992.
Personal: Born 8 March 1950. Attended High School of Glasgow 1961-67, then University of Glasgow 1967-70 (LLB). Solicitor member of the Scottish Solicitors Discipline Tribunal. Leisure interests include golf. Lives in Brookfield, Renfrewshire.

COLL, Harry
Elliott Duffy Garrett, Belfast
(028) 9024 5034
harry.coll@edglegal.com
Specialisation: Partner and head of employment and education law unit. Practice covers all aspects of employment and discrimination law including advising on contractual arrangements for senior employees, dispute resolution and representation at tribunals and elsewhere. Clients include public authorities, third level educational institutes and commercial sectors.
Prof. Memberships: Employment Lawyers Association, American Bar Association.
Career: Qualified 1973. Partner in *Elliott Duffy Garrett* since 1975.
Personal: Born 1946. Educated at Queen's University, Belfast. Awarded OBE in 1994 for services to employment.

COOPER, Edward
Russell Jones & Walker, London
(020) 7339 6435
Specialisation: Partner and head of national employment department. Principal area of practice is trade union and employment law. Advises on a wide range of industrial employment and constitutional issues. Also covers administrative and public law. Advises on police terms and conditions of service; acts on union mergers, major privatisations, terms and conditions reviews, new legislation, health and safety, pensions, disputes, discrimination and other employment cases. Clients include the TUC, Police Federation, NASUWT, entertainment unions and trade unions in the public and private sectors. The department (now of over 25 executives and with a national presence) has growing employee private client practice.
Prof. Memberships: Industrial Law Society.
Career: Qualified in 1984. With *Simmons & Simmons* 1982-85. Joined *Russell Jones & Walker* in 1985 and became a Partner in 1988.
Publications: Author of the trade union section of 'CCH Employment Law Service' and trade union section 'Butterworths Encyclopaedia of Forms and Precedent'.
Personal: Born 1959. Educated at Bristol University 1977-80. Leisure interests include jazz, saxophone, cricket, theatre and tennis. Lives with family in London SW15.

CRAFT, Max
Blake Lapthorn, Fareham
(01489) 579990

CRAWFORD, Adrian
DMH, Brighton
(01293) 605 072
adrian.crawford@dmh.co.uk
Specialisation: Partner dealing in all aspects of employment law. He has a particular interest in the Transfer of Undertakings (Protection of Employment) Regulations 1981 and considerable experience in advising on the employment aspects of corporate transactions of all sizes and types. He advises companies, banks, public authorities and senior executives. He regularly appears in employment tribunals and the Employment Appeal Tribunal.
Prof. Memberships: Member of the Employment Lawyers Association.
Career: Trained at *Simmons & Simmons*, qualifying in 1988, made partner in 1995; joined *DMH* as partner 1998.
Personal: Leisure interests include family, walking, cycling, gym and waiting for his children to be old enough to sail.

CROSS, Stefan
Thompsons, Newcastle upon Tyne
(0191) 269 0400

CULLEN, Joyce
Brodies, Edinburgh
(0131) 228 3777
joyce.cullen@brodies.co.uk
Specialisation: Head of Litigation Department and member of the Employment Law Group providing a full range of advice to companies, institutions, partnerships and individuals, including a major Scottish Bank, national retailers, colleges, professional firms and clients in the industrial and manufacturing sectors. Extensive experience as an advocate in Employment Tribunals, EAT and the Court of Session.
Prof. Memberships: Member of the Management Committee of the Employment Lawyers Association, Industrial Law Group, Institute of Directors. Member of the General Teaching Council, Scotland.
Career: Qualified in 1981. With *Brodies*, initially as an Assistant Solicitor, then as a Partner since 1986. Accredited specialist in employment law and Solicitor Advocate with extended rights of audience in the Civil Courts.
Personal: Born in 1958. Educated Leith Academy, Edinburgh and Dundee University. Married with three children. Interests include travel and playing the cello.

EMPLOYMENT ■ THE LEADERS

DABBS, Louise
Rawlison Butler, Crawley
(01293) 527744

DALE, Stephanie
Denton Wilde Sapte, London
(020) 7246 4880
sjd@dentonwildesapte.com
Specialisation: Head of Employment and Immigration Group. Covers the whole range of contentious and non-contentious employment law and industrial relations. Work includes director and senior management packages, discrimination, redundancies, rationalisation of employment practices, transactional work including TUPE and trade union issues. Seconded to British Airways 1990-91 to advise on a wide range of employment issues.
Prof. Memberships: International Bar Association, Industrial Law Society, Institute of Personnel and Development, Devonshire House Management Club, ILPA, Employment Lawyers Association
Career: Qualified 1985. Legal Advisor, A.T.L. (Teachers' Trade Union) 1986-87. Joined *Denton Hall* in 1987 and became a Partner in 1993.
Personal: Educated at the University of Newcastle 1979-82 (LLB).

DALGARNO, David
McDermott, Will & Emery, London
(020) 7577 6945
ddalgarno@europe.mwe.com
Specialisation: Partner in Employment group of 12 specialist lawyers. Undertakes all types of advisory employment work, contractual and statutory, contentious and non-contentious; primarily for employers, but also acts for senior executives. Principal interests include management of integration, employee consultation and organisational change programmes, collective and trade union issues, discrimination, trial advocacy. He also advises on employee benefits and share scheme issues. He frequently speaks on employment law issues; the author of the 'CCH Employment Contracts' manual. Clients include UK and global financial institutions, major industrial concerns, airlines, major retail businesses, inward investors and 'Fortune 500' companies.
Prof. Memberships: Employment Lawyers Association, City of London Law Society Employment Law Sub Committee, Industrial Law Society.
Career: Called to the Bar at Inner Temple 1978; in-house lawyer specialising in employment and labour law at Courtaulds plc 1979-87; Head of Employment Warner Cranston 1987-99. Joined McDermott, Will & Emery 1999.
Personal: Born in 1955. Educated at Hatfield School 1969-74 and Warwick University 1974-77. ICSL 1977-78.

DANDRIDGE, Nicola
Thompsons, London
(020) 7290 0000
Specialisation: Head of Equality, Partner specialising in employment law and sex, race and disability discrimination, and equal pay. Involved in a number of significant cases including the TUC's judicial challenge of the Maternity and Parental Leave Regulations leading to amendment of the regulations; Bower v Schroders, the highest award of compensation made in a sex discrimination case (£1.4m); and numerous other key discrimination decisions. Frequent speaker at union and national meetings and seminars.
Prof. Memberships: Director of Disability Discrimination Act Representation and Advice Project.
Career: Joined *Thompsons* in 1989. Partner in 1992. Qualified as Solicitor in England in 1989 and in Scotland in 1990.
Personal: Educated at St Hilda's College, Oxford and Glasgow University. Member of the Labour Party.

DANIELS, Paul
Russell Jones & Walker, London
(020) 7339 6409
p.a.daniels@rjw.co.uk
Specialisation: Specialises in advising employees and trade unions on all aspects of employment law. Particular expertise in complex discrimination cases (particularly disability), whistleblowers, trade union victimisation and senior executive terminations. Recent cases include Goodwin V Patent Office and Wilding V British Telecom.
Career: Joined *Linklaters* in 1991, qualified in 1993. Joined *Russell Jones and Walker* in 1995, became a Partner in 2000.
Personal: Educated in Swansea and Oxford University (Wadham College). Leisure interests include climbing, travelling, acting, pretentious films and the Welsh rugby team.

DAVIES, James
Lewis Silkin, London
(020) 7074 8035
james.davies@lewissilkin.com
Specialisation: Partner and joint head of employment team. Advises in all areas of employment law. Particular interests include EC employment law, discrimination law, workplace privacy, TUPE and sports law.
Prof. Memberships: Employment Lawyers Association (previously Treasurer, and on Management Committee for seven years, Chair of Working Groups on TUPE, workplace privacy and Age Discrimination); European Employment Lawyers Association; ILS; CIPD; ILPA; and BASL. Management Committee of the AIRE Centre. Member Advisory Group of the Employers Forum on Age.
Career: Qualified in 1988. At *Denton Hall* 1986-90. Joined *Lewis Silkin* in 1992.
Personal: Born 26 February 1962. Educated at Ysgol Gyfun, David Hughes, Menai Bridge; Leicester University (LLB and LLM); and Strasbourg University (Dip Ed Jr Fr). Long-suffering supporter of Glamorgan Cricket and Welsh rugby; most sports and travel.

DAVIES, Joanne
Morgan Cole, Cardiff
(029) 2038 5385

DAVIES, Julie
Veale Wasbrough, Bristol
(0117) 925 2020

DAWSON, William
Simmons & Simmons, London
(020) 7628 2020
william.dawson@simmons-simmons.com
Specialisation: Has advised on numerous acquisitions, disposals and mergers and transfers of undertakings, both UK and internationally, for major corporations and institutions. He has a strong City-based practice acting for insurance, banking and financial services institutions covering a wide range of complex issues associated with 'high flyers' and has a strong focus on cases involving 'reputational risk'. Has handled many interlocutory matters. Has been voted a 'leading expert' in employment law for several years.
Prof. Memberships: Law Society.
Career: He joined the Employment Law Department at *Simmons & Simmons* in 1981 and became a partner in 1986. He is an employment law practitioner and the department's head and Managing Partner. He gained his MA (Hons) law degree from Cambridge University in 1977 and was admitted as a solicitor in England and Wales in 1980.

DEAN, Veronica
Hammond Suddards Edge, Birmingham
(0121) 222 3000

DILLARSTONE, Robert
Greenwoods, Peterborough
(01733) 887700

DINELEY, Rachel
Beachcroft Wansbroughs, London
(020) 7242 1011
rdineley@bwlaw.co.uk
Specialisation: Practice in both contentious and non-contentious employment work on behalf of employers and individuals in the public and private sectors. Regularly deals with commercial transactions and preparation/negotiation of executive service agreements as well as board room disputes, dismissals and executive termination packages. Has developed a particular expertise in the protection of data, confidential information and enforcement of restrictive covenants. Has an in-depth knowledge of discrimination law and is a member of the editorial board of Croner's 'Discrimination Law Briefing' in addition to writing the chapter on race discrimination and contributing to two other chapters of Croner's book 'Discrimination Law'. Also advises on work related stress issues. Regularly lectures on these and other topics and devises and delivers training to corporate clients.
Prof. Memberships: Member of the Employment Law Association; Chartered Institute of Personnel and Development; Industrial Law Society.
Career: University of Exeter Scholar LLB (Hons) 1979. Admitted in 1983. Solicitor and then partner at *Denton Hall* before joining *Beachcroft Stanleys* in December 1994.
Personal: Married and lives in the Chiltern Hills. Interests include theatre, extensive travel, photography, skiing and walking.

DRAKE, Ronald
Cobbetts, Leeds
(0113) 246 8123
ron.drake@cobbetts.co.uk
Specialisation: Unfair/wrongful dismissal, redundancy, equal pay, discrimination and harassment industrial action, TUPE transfer and contracting out. Involved as lead solicitor in Tanks & Drums v T & GWU, Kelman v Care, Janciuk v Winerite, and the Staffordshire Legionnaires' Disease Public Inquiry.
Prof. Memberships: Associate of the Chartered Institute of Arbitrators; affiliate of the Institute of Personnel & Development; member of the Employment Lawyers Association; Industrial Law Society; Competition Law Association; British-Nordic Lawyers Association.
Career: Bradford GS, Manchester University and Chester College of Law. Articles to J Aucott at *Edge & Ellison*, Birmingham. Partner *Last Suddards* (later *Hammond Suddards*) 1981-90. Partner *Read Hind Stewart* 1990 to merger with *Cobbetts* from May 2002. Part-time chairman of Employment Tribunals (Newcastle Region) 1997.
Personal: Married to ex-solicitor teacher, two children. Interests are choral singing, classical music, Scandinavian culture and music. Director of Arts & Business Yorkshire, Kirklees Media Centre Ltd.

DU-FEU, Vivian
Eversheds, Cardiff
(029) 2047 1147
vivdufeu@eversheds.com
Specialisation: Partner. Head of the *Eversheds* national Human Resources Group of over 220 lawyers and business advisors. Has wide experience in providing advice on all aspects of contentious and non-contentious employment law. Lectures and writes regularly on various employment issues and is a member of the editorial advisory board for Croners.
Prof. Memberships: A Fellow of the Chartered Institute of Personnel and Development (CIPD); Director of Principle Training Limited.
Career: Graduate of University of Wales College of Cardiff. Qualified in 1979. Became a Partner in 1984.
Personal: Married and resides in Cardiff.

DUNCAN, Nikki
Bond Pearce, Plymouth
(01752) 677601
nduncan@bondpearce.com
Specialisation: Lead Employment Partner with over 20 years experience in employment law litigation, advocacy and the employment aspects of corporate

THE LEADERS — EMPLOYMENT

transactions and discrimination law issues. Regularly speaks at, or chairs, both regional and national employment law seminars and conferences. Has had published numerous articles and given radio and television interviews on topical employment law issues.
Prof. Memberships: Elected Secretary of the Employment Lawyers Association (the first time anyone outside London has been appointed to this key role), previously their UK Training Co-ordinator. Member of the European Employment Lawyers Association and the Regional IT Users Consultative Committee.
Career: Qualified in 1979. Joined *Bond Pearce* in 1982, becoming Partner 1985. Previous firm *McKenna & Co.*

EDWARDS, Julia
Eversheds, Birmingham
(0121) 232 1000
juliaedwards@eversheds.com
Specialisation: All aspects of employment law including unfair, wrongful and constructive dismissal, sex, race and disability discrimination, corporate reorganisation and executive severance.
Prof. Memberships: Employment Lawyers Association. Association of Women Solicitors.
Career: Articled *Edge & Ellison* (latterly *Edge Ellison* then *Hammond Suddards Edge*). Admitted 1992; associate 1996; Partner 1998.
Personal: Born 1968. Alice Ottley School, Worcester, 1973-86 and Bournemouth University 1986-89. Lives in Worcestershire.

EDWARDS, Martin
Mace & Jones, Liverpool
(0151) 236 8989
Specialisation: Head of Employment Law Department. Employment law specialist with extensive advocacy experience. Advises on all aspects of industrial relations law and acts for major clients in the public and private sectors throughout the UK. Also expert in relation to computer contracts. Major cases include Lavery v Plessey Telecommunications (maternity leave) and Brookes v CLS Care Services (TUPE).
Prof. Memberships: Law Society, Liverpool Law Society, Employment Lawyers Association, Society for Computers and Law, Society of Authors, Crime Writers Association.
Career: Qualified in 1980 while at *Mace & Jones*. Became a Partner in 1984.
Publications: Advised on film 'Letter to Brezhnev'. Author of 'Dismissal Law', 'Managing Redundancies', 'Careers in Law', 'How to get the Best Deal from your Employer', 'Understanding Computer Contracts', 'Know-How for Employment Lawyers', 'Tolley's Equal Opportunities Handbook' and numerous articles.
Personal: Born 7 July 1955. Attended Balliol College, Oxford 1974-77. 1st Class Honours Degree in Law. Leisure pursuits include writing crime novels about Liverpool solicitor Harry Devlin, the first of which was nominated for the award for best first crime novel of 1991. Lives in Lymm, Cheshire.

EMMOTT, Jeremy
DLA, Leeds
(08700) 111111

EVASON, John
Baker & McKenzie, London
(020) 7919 1000
john.evason@bakernet.com
Specialisation: Partner in the Employment Law Department and Head of Collective Rights with particular expertise in collective consultation, union recognition and industrial relations, European Works Councils, TUPE, employment tax, collective redundancies, executive terminations and the protection of confidential information and the enforcement of restrictive covenants. He has clients in the financial, transport, media and manufacturing sectors. He is a regular speaker at conferences and seminars and a regular contributor to various legal and personnel publications.
Prof. Memberships: Member of the Industrial Law Society, the Employment Lawyers Association (ELA) working party on TUPE and will be a member of the ELA working party on the national information and constitution directive.
Career: Trained at *Baker & McKenzie*, qualified 1993, Partner 1999 to date.
Publications: Author of the chapter on Collective Redundancies in the Sweet & Maxwell loose-leaf work 'European Employment Law and the UK' and the author of a chapter and editor for the European section in the Sweet & Maxwell book, 'Transfer of Undertakings'.

FARR, John
Herbert Smith, London
(020) 7374 8000
john.farr@herbertsmith.com
Specialisation: Partner in employment and trusts department. Well known for his representation of companies and senior individuals in contentious matters, including High Court applications in connection with restrictive covenants, confidential information and group defections. Also advises on corporate governance and boardroom disputes; bonus disputes; dismissals and redundancies; pension disputes; discrimination and harassment claims and partnership disputes. Non-contentious work covers, inter alia, business transfers and reorganisations, devising and introduction of new terms of employment and implementation of new UK and European employment and trade union legislation. Covers immigration and work permit matters.
Prof. Memberships: Member of the City of London Solicitors' Company Employment Law Committee.
Career: Qualified in 1974. Partnership 1982.
Personal: LL.B. (London).

FEINSTEIN, Naomi
Lovells, London
(020) 7296 2000
naomi.feinstein@lovells.com
Specialisation: Deals with all aspects of employment law, both contentious and non-contentious, including advice on employment contracts, termination packages, employment tribunal claims, redundancies and reorganisations, general day to day employment advice and the employment aspects of corporate transactions.
Career: Articled *Osborne Clarke* and *Lovell White & King*. Qualified 1987. Partner *Lovell White Durrant* (now *Lovells*) 1997.

FLANAGAN, Tom
Stephenson Harwood (incorporating Sinclair Roche & Temperley), London
(020) 7809 2148
tom.flanagan@shlegal.com
Specialisation: Managing partner, employment, pensions and benefits practice group. Employment law, providing a full range of advice to companies, institutions and partnerships with particular experience in the banking and finance sector. Also has strong experience in acting for high profile individuals, negotiating both employment and termination packages. Tom is one of the country's leading experts on the application of TUPE to corporate transactions and outsourcing, and on the changing law of employee consultation, including both European works councils and the Information and Consultation Directive. Cases of note include representing the UK banking sector, through HSBC, in the part-time pensions cases in the European Court of Justice and House of Lords in Fletcher v Midland Bank, Preston v Wolverhampton Borough Councils.
Prof. Memberships: Employment Lawyers Association; Industrial Law Society; Institute of Personnel and Development; Institute of Directors.
Career: Qualified 1979. *Brian Thompson & Partners*, Manchester 1980-84; *Barlow Lyde & Gilbert* 1984-85; *Speechly Bircham* 1985-92 (partner 1988); partner in *Booth & Co* (then *Addleshaw Booth & Co*) 1992-98; joined *Stephenson Harwood* as partner in July 1998.
Publications: Sections on 'Transfer of Undertakings Regulations' and 'Employment and Self-employment' in 'Tolley's Employment Law'.
Personal: Born 16 January 1954. Educated at Ushaw College, Durham; St Mary's College Middlesborough; University College London. Interests include playing guitar, theatre, blues and jazz. Resides in London.

FLETCHER, Kevin
Jacksons, Stockton on Tees
(01642) 643643

FOX, Ronnie
Fox Williams, London
(020) 7614 2517
rdfox@foxwilliams.com
Specialisation: Main areas of practice are employment and partnership law. Specialises in advising on payments on termination of employment. Frequently instructed by listed companies on the departure of senior executives. Past Master of the City of London Solicitors' Company, past Chairman of the IBA Practice Management Sub-committee; past Member of the Law Society Law Management Section Advisory Group. Frequently broadcasts and is the author of numerous articles on employment, partnership and management.
Prof. Memberships: European Employment Lawyers Association, IBA, Law Society Employment Law Committee, City of London Law Society, Employment Lawyers' Association.
Career: Qualified 1972. Senior Partner at *Fox Williams*.
Publications: Author of 'Payments on Termination of Employment' (now in its 3rd edition).

FRASER, Jane
Maclay Murray & Spens, Glasgow
(0131) 479 2763
jef@maclaymurrayspens.co.uk
Specialisation: Partner in the employment law division. Acts on behalf of a wide range of private and public sector clients with particular expertise in business transfers, reorganisations and redundancies, working time and data protection issues. Extensive experience appearing for employees in employment tribunals throughout the UK and the Employment Appeal Tribunal. Regular conference speaker and lecturer at several Scottish universities.
Career: Trained with employment law specialist firm, *Mackay Simon*. Qualified 1995. Assistant, Associate and Partner (1999) with *Mackay Simon*, now Partner in *Mackay Murray & Spens* since merger with *Mackay Simon* in 2001.
Personal: University of Edinburgh. LLB (Hons)(First Class); Interests: spending time with family, cinema, hill walking, travel. Lives in Edinburgh.

FROST, Peter
Herbert Smith, London
(020) 7374 8000
peter.frost@herbertsmith.com
Specialisation: Partner in employment group. Handles a wide variety of contentious and non-contentious employment issues with a substantial general advisory practice. Non-contentious matters include advice on a wide range of major domestic and cross-border transactions; drafting of all types of employment related documentation, particularly arrangements for directors; implementing large redundancy exercises and dealing with day to day disciplinary matters. His advisory practice includes assessing the impact of recent UK and EU legislation, particularly

EMPLOYMENT ■ THE LEADERS

regarding equal opportunities and trade unions/ works councils.
Prof. Memberships: Member of the Employment Lawyers Association Legislation and Policy Sub-Committee.
Career: Emmanuel College, Cambridge. Qualified 1985. Partnership 1994.

GALLAGHER, Yvonne
Lawrence Graham, London
(020) 7379 0000

GIBSON, Robert
Samuel Phillips & Co, Newcastle upon Tyne
(0191) 232 8451
robertgibson@samuelphillips.co.uk
Specialisation: Applicant and respondent work in unfair dismissal, race, sex and disability claims. Special interest cases this year being claims under the National Minimum Wage, Working Time Regulations, whistleblowing and equal pay. Advice on policies and procedures. In-house training and employment audits.
Prof. Memberships: ELA; ACAS appointed Arbitrator; Deputy District Judge.
Career: Qualified as Assistant Solicitor 1984; Partner at *Samuel Phillips* 1990; Managing Partner 2000.
Personal: Royal Grammar School, Newcastle University, Trustee Talbot House Independent School. Married with two children. Sports: Golf and rugby.

GILLESPIE, Michael
Lee Crowder, Birmingham
(0121) 236 4477
michael.gillespie@leecrowder.co.uk
Specialisation: Acting for employees (especially senior executives) and employers in employment disputes. Clients include Wesylan Assurance Services, Nationwide Accident Repair Services and Airflow Streamlines plc.
Prof. Memberships: Midlands representative of Employment Lawyers Association.
Career: Admitted in 1971.
Publications: Occasional articles.
Personal: Educated in Birmingham and went to Birmingham University. Married with two children. Interested in the theatre and photography.

GOODWILL, Christopher
Clifford Chance, London
(020) 7600 1000
christopher.goodwill@cliffordchance.com
Specialisation: Tax, pensions and employment. Partner specialising in all aspects of employment.
Career: Trainee *Clifford Chance* 1986; qualified in 1988; Partner since 1995.
Personal: Lancaster University (LLB) (Sweet & Maxwell Law Prize); Trinity Hall, Cambridge (LLM).

GRAY, David J
Culbert and Martin, Belfast
(028) 9032 5508

GREEN, David
Charles Russell, London
(020) 7203 5317
davidg@cr-law.co.uk
Specialisation: Partner in Employment, Pensions and Employee Benefits Unit. Handles all aspects of employment law, including individual employment rights, employee benefits, contractual and policy documentation, discrimination, health and safety, equal opportunities, wrongful dismissal, redundancy, protection of confidentiality and goodwill, collective labour law, immigration and employment issues resulting from mergers and acquisitions. Member of editorial board of Croners Employer, Industrial Relations and Discrimination Briefing Notes. Author of various articles in a range of publications, including 'Management Consultancy' and 'Tolleys Employment Law'. Author of 'Business Basics Staff'. Has spoken at and chaired a number of seminars.
Prof. Memberships: Association of Employment Lawyers.
Career: Qualified in 1978. Worked at *Taylors Newmarket* 1976-83 (from 1981 as a Partner); then *McKenna & Co.* 1983-85 and *Clifford Chance* 1985-91. Joined *Charles Russell* in 1991 as a Partner.
Personal: Born 1953. Attended John Lyon School, Forest School and University of London. Committee Member of Downham Town FC. Follows all forms of sports. Leisure interests include gardening. Lives in Downham Market, Norfolk.

GRIFFITHS, John
Shepherd+ Wedderburn, Edinburgh
(0131) 473 5445
john.griffiths@shepwedd.co.uk
See under Clinical Negligence, p.152

GUNN, Sheila
Shepherd+ Wedderburn, Edinburgh
(0131) 473 5181
sheila.gunn@shepwedd.co.uk
Specialisation: Head of Employment Unit at *Shepherd+ Wedderburn*. Accredited as an employment specialist by the Law Society. Advising (i) Scottish Power on the recent joint venture with Alfred McAlpine to set up Core Utility Solutions Limited; (ii) MOD on various projects; (iii) University of St Andrews on a recent high profile sex discrimination case; (iv) Scottish Environmental Protection Agency; (v) Glasgow Service Centre on its current staff reorganisation; (vi) Scottish Enterprise on numerous projects and reorganisations; (vii) Edinburgh Fund Managers plc on the appointment of their new Chief Investment Officer from Merrill Lynch; (viii) advising Friends Ivory & Sime plc on all the employment aspects of the integration of staff following their acquisition of Royal Sun Alliance; (ix) advising Cyril Sweet Limited on employment aspects of a proposed PFI project in respect of Rotherham Schools; (x) advising Edinburgh Woollen Mill, Aberdeenshire Council, Deep-Sea Leisure plc and Allied Domecq on employment issues. Also engaged in delivery of innovative training to managers and HR managers for OKI (UK) Limited, Scottish Life, Friends Ivory & Sime plc, Edinburgh Fund Managers plc, Baillie Gifford, NMT plc and Ethicon/Johnson & Johnson. Speaker each year at Scottish conferences run by IBC and by Whitepaper Conferences (latest IBC 30 October 2001, Whitepaper 21 May 2002). Regular columnist in Scottish national newspapers and regularly asked to contribute comments to articles in Scottish and UK national newspapers on employment issues. Featured as one of only six Scots Lawyers in 'Legal Business' 40 young regional stars under 40. Also featured as 12th in 'Unlimited Magazine's' Top 50 under 50.
Career: Governor of Hutcheson's Grammar School; Glasgow University (1985 LLB Hons; 1986 Dip. LP).
Personal: Born in 1963; resides in Strathaven. Leisure interests include skiing and walking.

HANTOM, Charles
Whittles, Manchester
(0161) 228 2061

HARPER, David
Lovells, London
(020) 7296 2000
david.harper@lovells.com
Specialisation: Deals with all aspects of employment law both collective and individual, including executive contracts and severance packages (plus tax, pension and employee benefits aspects), all tribunal litigation, redundancies, discrimination, restrictive covenants, union recognition claims and employment policies and practices. Handles all employment aspects of transactional work, particularly in relation to PPP/PFI transactions. Regularly appears as an advocate in Employment Tribunals. Substantial experience of collective labour law issues including, recently union recognition claims and injunction proceedings.
Prof. Memberships: Employment Lawyers' Association, City of London Solicitors Employment Law Sub-committee.
Career: Articled with *Lovell White & King* (now *Lovells*); qualified 1978; Partner 1986.
Publications: Principal editor of CCH Employment Manual, member of editorial board of Employment Lawyer and regular writer on employment matters.
Personal: Born 1954. Educated Stowe School and Keble College, Oxford. Lives in Richmond. Married with four children.

HEARN, Keith
Ford & Warren, Leeds
(0113) 243 6601
clientmail@forwarn.com
Specialisation: Managing Partner and Head of Employment Law. Experienced since 1973 in all aspects of employment law. Acted as labour relations advisor on construction of Sullomvoe Oil Terminal and other major projects. Deals with competition issues arising out of human resources matters. Extensive experience in full range of applications before Industrial Tribunals including unfair dismissal and sex and race discrimination. Regularly appeared before the Employment Appeal Tribunal. Practice includes High Court employment based work – injunctions, damages against directors, and restrictive covenants. Recently involved on behalf of a number of train operating companies in injunction proceedings against RMT Union following strike ballots. Wide experience of developing and delivering management training for health service and numerous commercial clients, especially in the area of change management. Received degree of Masters of Laws in European Management and Labour Law in 1995, the subject matter of the dissertation being Fair Competition in the Road Haulage industry. Currently involved in extensive research and advice particularly to the train and passenger transport sector on the effect of and the implications arising from the application of the working time directive to the transport sector.
Principal clients including PSV, train and LGV operators, hospital trusts and other public health bodies.
Prof. Memberships: Industrial Law Society.
Career: Joined *Ford & Warren* in 1974. Became Partner in 1976. Became Managing Partner in 1989. Leeds University LL.B 1967-70. Leicester University LLM 1995.
Personal: Leisure interests include scuba diving instruction and racing cars.

HEMMING, Julian
Osborne Clarke, Bristol
(0117) 917 3000

HEMMINGS, Richard
The Law Offices of Richard Hemmings LLM Solicitor, Ipswich
(01473) 833844
Hemmings@dial.pipex.com
Specialisation: Employment law – predominantly for corporate, NHS and local authority clients. Particularly contentious employment law and TUPE. Management training on all employment law issues.
Prof. Memberships: Member of the Council of Employment Tribunal Chairmen.
Career: LLB (London), LLM (London). Qualified 1974. Partner, 1976-97. Established specialist sole practice employment law, May 1997. Employment Tribunal Chairman (part-time), 1997. Practising in Ipswich, Cambridge and London Docklands. Consultant with Cambridge solicitors, *Taylor Vinters*.
Publications: Author of the Stationery Office 'Point of Law' series on Employment Law Acts.

THE LEADERS — EMPLOYMENT

HENNEY, Colin
Henmans, Oxford
(01865) 722181
colin.henney.henmans.co.uk
Specialisation: Partner and Head of Employment Team. Sole area of practice is employment. Handles the full range of employee and employer work, both contentious and non-contentious. Undertakes advocacy in EAT and employment tribunals. Member of ELAAS advice and representation scheme at EAT. Involved in ACAS training, giving seminars at individual conciliation workshops since 1990. Also provides training to major employer clients and insurers.
Prof. Memberships: Employment Lawyers' Association, Industrial Law Society.
Career: Qualified in 1982. Articled with *Rickerby Watterson* 1980-82; joined *Henmans* in 1983, becoming a Partner in 1987; Managing Partner 1991-93.
Personal: Born 25 November 1957. Attended Daniel Stewart's and Melville College, Edinburgh 1962-75, and Oxford University 1976-79 (Law, BA). Leisure interests include music, golf and Partick Thistle FC. Lives in Eynsham, Oxfordshire.

HESSELBERTH, David
Ward Hadaway, Newcastle upon Tyne
(0191) 204 4322
david.hesselberth@wardhadaway.co.uk
Specialisation: Head of employment unit. Dealing with all aspects of employment law. Conducts own advocacy in Employment tribunals. Part-time chairman of Employment tribunals.
Career: Attended RGS Newcastle then Leeds University. Qualified 1976. Trained at *Ward Hadaway* and became a partner in 1987.
Personal: Golf and sailing.

HIBBS, Michael
Shakespeares, Birmingham
(0121) 631 5367
michael.hibbs@shakespeares.co.uk
Specialisation: All areas of employment law both contentious and non-contentious. Advises mainly employers but also senior employees. Undertakes advocacy in the tribunals. Author of numerous articles. Provides training for a variety of organisations and clients. Speaker at seminars and conferences.
Prof. Memberships: Law Society; Member of Employment Law Committee of Birmingham Law Society; Employment Lawyers Association.
Career: Qualified 1983. Solicitor with *Maurice Putsman & Co* 1983-85; *Bettisons* 1985 (became *Shakespeares* 1990). Partner from 1987. Head of employment law from 1998. Visiting professor of employment law at the University of Central England in Birmingham.
Personal: Born 1958. Leisure pursuits include gardening, walking, watching cricket and rugby.

HILL, David
DLA, Leeds
(08700) 111111

HODGE, Andrew
Wragge & Co, Birmingham
0870 903 1000

HOPKINS, Martin
Eversheds, Birmingham
(0121) 232 1000
Specialisation: Partner and head of employment. Main area of practice is employment and industrial relations law. Has wide experience of handling all types of contentious and non-contentious employment work in both the public and private sector. Has an international practice and advises many US businesses on UK start up issues. Leads team of 32 specialist employment lawyers, trainers and HR professionals.
Prof. Memberships: Member of Institute of Personnel and Development and Employment Lawyers Association.
Career: Joined *Eversheds* 1980, qualified in 1982, and made partner and head of employment in 1989.
Publications: Co-author of 'Health and Safety: Are You at Risk?' (1993), 'The Maternity Manual' (1994), 'The Law of Harassment' (1998) and 'EU and International Employment Law' (2000). Speaks frequently on employment issues and regularly delivers in-house tailored training courses for clients.
Personal: Born 28 October 1957. Attended Warwick School 1971-76 and Coventry University 1976-79. Leisure interests include family and travel. Lives in Lighthorne, near Warwick.

HOSKINS, Julian
Bevan Ashford, Bristol
(0117) 975 1608
julian.hoskins@bevanashford.co.uk
Specialisation: Acts for employers throughout the UK, advising on all aspects of employment and discrimination law, both contentious and non-contentious. South West Representative of Employment Lawyers Association 2002. Has extensive advocacy experience in the higher courts and appears regularly in the EAT and Employment tribunals as advocate for clients of the firm's various offices. Frequent speaker at seminars, both internal and external, and provides tailored training for clients.
Prof. Memberships: Employment Lawyers Association.
Career: Called to the Bar in 1987; practised at 1 Serjeants Inn, Fleet Street, 1987-95. Joined *Bevan Ashford* 1995. Re-qualified as a solicitor and became a partner in 1998.
Publications: Co-author of Butterworths Tolley 'Xpert HR Employment Law Reference Manual'.
Personal: Born 1962.

HOWARD, Clive
Russell Jones & Walker, London
(020) 7339 6432
c.p.howard@rjw.co.uk
Specialisation: Specialises in employment law. From employees' perspective, with particular emphasis on executive disputes and terminations, discrimination and data protection. Recent cases include Turner v Grovit (injunction preventing employer from legal action overseas), Edgar v Met Office (whistleblowing) and Jenvey v ABC (implied terms – redundancy).
Prof. Memberships: ELA
Career: Articled *Gordon Dadds*; qualified 1988. Assistant solicitor *Russell Jones & Walker* 1989-94; Partner 1994.
Personal: Kingston Grammar School, Worcester College, Oxford. Interests: family, tennis, golf, skiing, QPR.

HUNTER, Ian
Bird & Bird, London
(020) 7415 6000
Specialisation: Employment and Immigration Partner. Main area of practice is employment law. Specialises in negotiation of payments on termination of employment, the Transfer of Undertakings Regulations, employment aspects of acquisitions and disputes, immigration and sex, race and disability discrimination. Has handled departures from the boards of listed companies and advised on major outsourcing projects.
Prof. Memberships: Law Society, Employment Lawyers' Association.
Career: Qualified in 1989. Joined *Bird & Bird* in 1996.
Publications: Co-author of 'Britain's Invisible Earnings'. Regular contributor to 'The Financial Times' and professional press. Author of 'The WHICH? Guide to Employment Law'. Appears regularly on BBC TV and radio.
Personal: Born 1961. Educated at Campbell College Belfast and Bristol University. Writing, current affairs. Lives in London.

JACKS, David
Weightman Vizards, Liverpool
(0151) 242 7997
david.jacks@weightmanvizards.com
Specialisation: Practice in both contentious and non-contentious employment work and industrial relations law. Principally acts for employers but also for senior executives to negotiate severance packages. Experienced advocate in the employment tribunals. Strengths also in advising companies on contracts of employment/service agreements, restructuring/redundancy strategies, TUPE and discrimination matters.

JACOBS, Howard
Slaughter and May, London
(020) 7600 1200
howard.jacobs@slaughterandmay.com
Specialisation: Executive engagements and dismissals. TUPE.
Prof. Memberships: City of London Solicitors' Company Employment Law Sub-committee.
Career: *Slaughter and May* since 1975.
Personal: Winchester College. Pembroke College, Cambridge. Married, three children. Interests: family and gardening.

JAMIESON, Andrew P
Nelsons, Nottingham
(0115) 989 5217
andy.jamieson@nelsons-solicitors.co.uk
Specialisation: Employment law with particular emphasis on disability discrimination and TUPE issues. Involved in major case Kirker v British Sugar, which remains the highest disability discrimination award to date. Highlight of recent years has been the 'Emplus' scheme which provides an all-encompassing insurance backed service for employer clients.
Prof. Memberships: Law Society. Member of the Employment Lawyers Association.
Career: Articled with *Notts*. County Council 1980-82. Chief Prosecuting Solicitors Office 1982-85. Joined *Nelsons* 1985. Admitted as Partner 1988.
Publications: Regular contributor to legal and business journals on employment related subjects.
Personal: Educated: Punahou School USA, Keele University and Chester College of Law. Leisure interests include military history and music; plays guitar in a band comprising three other lawyers. Married with 3 children.

JEFFERS, Raymond
Linklaters, London
(020) 7456 3702
raymond.jeffers@linklaters.com
Specialisation: Specialist in employment law while covering all aspects of this area, principal role has been advising public and private sector clients of the firm (national, multinational and foreign) on all aspects of employment law.
Prof. Memberships: Chairman UK Employment Lawyers Association's Legislative and Policy Committee since 1999. Chairman International Bar Association Employment and Industrial Relations Committee since 2001. Chairman, City of London Solicitors' Company Employment Law Sub-Committee since 2002.
Career: 1998 to date: Co-Chair of Labour Practice Group; 1997 to date: Leader of *Linklaters*' Employment Group; 1986 to date: Partner, *Linklaters*; 1980-85: Assistant Solicitor, *Linklaters*; 1978-79: Trainee Solicitor, *Linklaters*. 1975-77: Oxford University BCL.

JEFFREYS, Simon
CMS Cameron McKenna, London
(020) 7367 3000
sbj@cmck.com
Specialisation: Partner Employment Group. Has specialised in employment and labour relations law since qualifying, advising predominantly employer clients in the private and public sectors on all aspects of their legal relationship with employees and trade unions. Work includes employee and trade union aspects of acquisitions, disposals, IPOs and outsourcing deals together with advice on director-level issues, corporate governance and corporate social responsibility. Has conducted litigation for clients up to the Court of Appeal. Has spoken at numerous conferences and seminars. Contributor to 'Commercial

EMPLOYMENT ■ THE LEADERS

Checklists' and joint editor of 'Employment Precedents and Company Policy Documents' and 'Transfer of Undertakings' published by Sweet & Maxwell.
Prof. Memberships: Employment Lawyers Association; European Employment Lawyers Association; Industrial Law Society; City of London Law Society; Member Law Society of England and Wales Employment Law Committee.
Career: Joined *CMS Cameron McKenna* in 1980 and qualified in 1982. Became a Partner in 1988.

JONES, Alan
DLA, Birmingham
(08700) 111111

JONES, Beverley
Jones & Cassidy, Belfast
(028) 9064 2290

JONES, Linda
Pinsent Curtis Biddle, Birmingham
(0121) 623 8655
linda.jones@pinsents.com
Specialisation: Head of employment department, Birmingham. Specialises in all areas of employment law with particular experience of large scale redundancies, outsourcing and TUPE in the public and private sectors, executive termination agreements.
Prof. Memberships: Law Society; Employment Lawyers Association; Birmingham Law Society Employment Law Committee; CIPD.
Career: Educated at Nottingham University 1982-85. Articled to *Pinsent & Co*. Qualified in 1994. Moved to *Wragge & Co* in 1999 as associate. In 2001 rejoined *Pinsent Curtis Biddle* as partner and subsequently head of department. Previously worked in Human Resources for subsidiary of Mobil Oil Company Limited.
Personal: Married with one son. Leisure interests include food, wine, art, jazz music and supporting Newcastle United Football Club.

JULYAN, Alan
Speechly Bircham, London
(020) 7427 6407
alan.julyan@speechlys.com
Specialisation: Practice covers full range of employment and labour law specialising in the employment and corporate governance issues arising on the recruitment, retention and termination of senior executives, TUPE and the management of organisational change.
Prof. Memberships: Law Society. Committee member of the Employment Law Sub-committee of the City of London Law Society. Member of the Industrial Law Society and the Employment Lawyers Association.
Career: Qualified 1974. Joined *Speechly Bircham* and became partner in 1977.
Publications: Author 'Key Employees-Drafting Service Agreements' and joint editor of 'Employment Precedents and Employment Policies' both published by Sweet & Maxwell.
Personal: Born 14 October 1949. Educated at Bristol Grammar School and Lanchester Polytechnic. Interests include tennis, watercolour painting and jazz.

KEEBLE, Sarah
Olswang, London
(020) 7208 8669
sxk@olswang.com
Specialisation: Sarah specialises in all aspects of employment law, both contentious and non-contentious. She is an acknowledged expert on the recently introduced family friendly laws and discrimination issues. In addition, she is very experienced on union law and is an established speaker at seminars on employment issues.
Prof. Memberships: Law Society.
Career: Articles – *Lovell White Durrant* (1987-89); solicitor – *Warner Cranston* (1989-94); solicitor – *Manches* (1994-99, becoming a partner in 1997); joined *Olswang* as a partner, September 1999.
Personal: Education: Nottingham University – 2:1 BA (Hons); Guildford School of Law (All Heads Passed First Attempt). Leisure: two young daughters.

KELLY, Jill
Clarks, Reading
(01189) 953 3918
jillkelly@clarks-solicitors.co.uk
Specialisation: Practical and commercial advice to corporate clients and senior executives on employment contracts, tribunal claims and HR practice. Particular expertise in contractual issues, TUPE and injunctions to enforce post-termination non-competition restrictions.
Prof. Memberships: Employment Lawyers Association; Employment Lawyers Association Training Committee; Committee of the St Hilda's College Law network.
Career: Trained at *Baileys Shaw & Gillett*, London; qualified in 1995; joined *Thomson Snell & Passmore* in 1996. Joined *Clarks*, Reading 2002.
Publications: Regular contributor to Personnel Today Magazine and the Employment Lawyers Association Briefing.
Personal: University St Hilda's College, Oxford. Lives near Abingdon.

KEMP, Sandy
Burnside Kemp Fraser, Aberdeen
(01224) 327500
Specialisation: Has specialised in employment law and personal injury claims throughout career. Accredited as an Employment Law Specialist by the Law Society of Scotland and member of Assessment Committee for Personal Injury panel. Advises employers and individuals on all aspects of employment law, particularly in relation to offshore oil industry. Has lectured for Law Society and others on employment law, negotiation and on personal injury claims, both generally and arising from offshore industry.
Prof. Memberships: Law Society of Scotland, Society of Advocates in Aberdeen, Employment Law Group, European Employment Lawyers Association, Association of Personal Injury Lawyers, Association of Trial Lawyers of America, Pan European Organisation of Personal Injury Lawyers.
Career: Qualified 1983. Partner at *Philip and Kemp* 1986. Joined *Burnside* 1994 and established *Burnside Kemp Fraser*.
Personal: Born 8 February 1959.

KINGDON, Danielle
Osborne Clarke, Reading
(0118) 925 2000

LAMONT, Sarah
Bevan Ashford, Bristol
(0117) 918 8943
sarah.lamont@bevanashford.co.uk
Specialisation: Partner in employment law department dealing with all aspects of contentious and non-contentious employment law including employment aspects of corporate transactions and PFI; TUPE; service agreements; sex, race, disability discrimination; equal pay; restrictive covenants; trade unions/industrial action; redundancy/reorganisations; and employment litigation including tribunals and advocacy.
Prof. Memberships: Law Society; Institute of Personnel and Development; Employment Lawyers Association; Industrial Law Society; Bristol Law Society Equal Opportunities Committee; National Employment Tribunal Users Consultative Committee.
Career: MA Cambridge University, trained *Macfarlanes*, London. Qualified 1992, *Veale Wasbrough*, Bristol 1994-99. Joined *Bevan Ashford* as partner 1999.
Publications: Co-author of Jordan's 'Secretarial Administration', Jordan's/IPD 'Employment Service', Sweet & Maxwell's 'Public and Private Partnerships' and Butterworths Tolley 'Xpert HR Employment Law Reference Manual'. Regularly publishes articles and speaks at employment seminars/courses, including tailored training for clients, and lectures on the Legal Practice Course.
Personal: Astronomy, painting and sketching.

LANGLEY, Dale
Dale Langley & Co, London
(020) 7464 8433
dale.lan@btinternet.com
Specialisation: Handles all aspects of contentious and non-contentious employment law, for both individual and corporate clients, with particular knowledge of company law, tax and stock exchange requirements. Often acts for senior city brokers, analysts and traders, and for top executives, including the main board of FTSE 100 companies.
Prof. Memberships: Employment Lawyers Association, Law Society.
Career: Downer Grammar School. Southampton University LLB 2:1 in 1976 (Maxwell Prizewinner 1977). Articled at *Stephenson Harwood*, qualifying in 1981; in 1986 joined *Ashurst Morris Crisp*, establishing their employment law group in 1988. Left in 1993 to set up *Langley & Co*. His firm (now *Dale Langley & Co*) specialises only in employment law, with particular emphasis on acting for the individual.
Personal: Cycling and tennis. Four children.

LEVINSON, Stephen
KLegal, London
(020) 7694 2500
Specialisation: Partner and Head of *KLegal's* Employment Law Department. Advises on all aspects of employment law including the acquisition and sale of business, discrimination claims, and European law. Also acts for many senior executives when they part company with their employers. Deals with litigation at all levels from the Employment Tribunal to the House of Lords. Has extensive experience as an advocate.
Prof. Memberships: Treasurer of the Employment Lawyers Association and past Chair of the Industrial Law Society and a founder member of the Law Society Employment Law Committee of which he was a member for more than 15 years. Also member of the Editorial Committee for the 'Industrial Law Journal' and the Users' Group of the Employment Tribunal. Fellow of the Chartered Institute of Arbitrators.
Career: Joined *Paisner & Co* in 1974. Qualified as a solicitor in 1976. Appointed Partner in 1978 (Litigation Department). Formed Employment Department in 1988. Moved to *KLegal* in 2000.
Personal: Born 12.2.1947. Educated at Claysmore School, Dorset and Leicester University. Lives in St John's Wood. Interests include tennis, cricket and collecting wood engravings. School Governor.

LILLEY, Andrew
Travers Smith Braithwaite, London
(020) 7295 3253
Andrew.Lilley@TraversSmith.com
Specialisation: Advises on UK/EC employment law and employee relations. Experience includes executive employment contracts; severance arrangements; corporate issues (Transfer of Undertakings Regulations, managing integration etc.); employee consultation (including European works councils), trade union issues, restrictive covenants, redundancy programmes and all aspects of employment litigation and industrial disputes.
Prof. Memberships: Employment Lawyers Association; Industrial Law Society; Law Society.
Career: Qualified at *Freshfields*. Joined *Travers Smith Braithwaite* in 1995, Partner from 1997.
Publications: 'Tolley's Employment Law' (contributing author). Other publications include articles in 'The European Lawyer' and 'Employment Law Journal'.

THE LEADERS ■ EMPLOYMENT

LOVE, Alison
Hugh James, Cardiff
(029) 2039 1075
alison.love@hughjames.com
Specialisation: Employment law, including both contentious and non-contentious work. Particular interest and experience in discrimination claims. Recently defended a lengthy and high profile racial discrimination claim. Regularly conducts training seminars for a variety of organisations including the Chamber of Commerce and the Law Society as well as in-house and external seminars for clients. Regularly speaks at employment law and HR conferences and is currently lecturing on the PGD/MSC human resources management course at the University of Glamorgan.
Prof. Memberships: Employment Lawyers Association. Member of the Chartered Institute of Personnel and Development.
Career: Prior to qualifying as a solicitor, worked for a number of years in personnel within the public and private sector. Since qualifying in 1992, specialised in employment work acting for a broad range of clients. Joined the firm in April 1999 as a Partner and Head of the Employment Law Group.
Publications: Regular contributor to national newspapers and business HR journals including 'Croners', 'Employee Benefits', 'Personnel in Practice' and 'Personnel Management'. BBC Wales Radio commentator.
Personal: Ex-county swimmer. Any spare time now spent with her two young sons.

LOY, Simon
Eversheds, Newcastle upon Tyne
(0191) 241 6149
simonloy@eversheds.com
Specialisation: All aspects of European and domestic employment law including discrimination, TUPE, equal pay and trade union law. Involved in several reported cases on equal pay, collective consultation and trade union discrimination.
Prof. Memberships: Industrial Law Society; Employment Law Association.
Career: Research Assistant, University College, London. Joined *Eversheds* 1992; Partner 1996; Head of Employment Team at Newcastle office.

LYNE, Amanda
Taylor Vinters, Cambridge
(01223) 423444
mandy.lyne@taylorvinters.com
Specialisation: Partner and head of employment department. Work involves all aspects of employment law, national and European, contentious and non-contentious for companies, institutions and individuals. Contracts and benefits, reorganisations and redundancies, dismissals, transfers of undertakings, equal opportunity and human rights, restrictive covenants. In-house training. Tribunal advocacy. Clients include major high tech, biotechnology, telecoms, printing, pharmaceutical, education (including Cambridge University, other Colleges and schools) and national public sector bodies.
Prof. Memberships: Law Society, Employment Lawyers Association, Industrial Law Society.
Career: Called to the bar in 1969. Qualified as a solicitor in 1981. Joined *Vinters* in 1986 (becoming *Taylor Vinters* after merger in 1988). Became partner in 1989.
Personal: Educated in Adelaide, Australia and Cambridge (MA, LLB). Keen sailor, tennis player, theatre, film and concert goer. Member of boards of two diverse Cambridge charitable organisations.

MACKAY, Malcolm
Maclay Murray & Spens, Edinburgh
(0131) 226 5196
mrm@mclaymurrayspens.co.uk
Specialisation: Partner. Practises only in the field of employment law. Lectures in employment law at various universities. Particular interests – industrial relations, transfer of undertakings.
Prof. Memberships: Society to Writers of HM Signet. Member of Institute of Personnel and Development. Law Society of Scotland Employment Law Committee.
Career: Qualified in 1975. Founded *Mackay WS* now *Mackay Simon WS* in 1988 (now the employment law division of *Maclay Murray & Spens*).
Publications: Co-author of Employment Law Update in the 'Journal of the Law Society of Scotland' co-editor of 'Greens Employment Law Bulletin'; co-author of 'Employment Law' published by Greens 1998.
Personal: Born 24 January 1953. Attended Edinburgh University. Lives in Edinburgh.

MACLEOD, Euan
Dundas & Wilson CS, Edinburgh
(0131) 228 8000

MALONE, Michael
Mace & Jones, Manchester
(0161) 236 2244
michael.malone@maceandjones.co.uk
Specialisation: Partner in Employment Department. Extensive advocacy experience notably in complex sex discrimination and equal pay cases. Deals with the whole range of employment work acting mainly for employers.
Prof. Memberships: Law Society; International Bar Association.
Career: Admitted in 1968; Partner at *Henry Fallows & Co* in Bolton from 1968-91; Partner in *Mace & Jones* since 1991.
Publications: Recent publications include 'Your Employment Rights', 'Discrimination Law – A Practical Guide' and the Employment Law section of 'Butterworths Guide on Law for Accountants'. Has also spoken regularly at conferences and seminars.
Personal: Born Bury 1943, educated at Brasenose College, Oxford. Leisure pursuits include tennis, bridge, golf, walking, theatre. Lives in Bolton.

MANN, Jane
Fox Williams, London
(020) 7628 2000
jemann@foxwilliams.co.uk
Specialisation: Advises a number of employers (particularly in the financial services and technology sectors) in relation to employment law issues and business immigration. Works closely with in-house legal and HR to provide an integrated service to line management. Has handled a number of difficult and high profile cases. Also acts for senior executives in relation to the termination of employment. Discrimination law, FSA regulation, data protection, ill health at work and EU employment law are particular interests.
Prof. Memberships: Co-founder of Employment Lawyers Association and former Chairman and currently Life Vice-President of the Association. Former Treasurer of the Immigration Law Practitioners Association. Member of the International Bar Association, Member of the Industrial Law Society, the Employment Law Sub-Committee of the City of London Law Society and The American Immigration Lawyers Association. Associate Member of the Institute of Personnel and Development.
Career: Qualified 1981. Worked at *McKenna & Co* 1979-86, then at *Denton Hall* until 1994, where became a Partner. Joined *Fox Williams* in 1994 as a Partner.
Publications: Legal contributor to 'Exe-Comp', software to calculate executive compensation. Devised and reported on a survey of women's rights at work for the International Bar Association.
Personal: Born 1957. Attended Cambridge University 1975-78.

MANSELL, Mark
Allen & Overy, London
(020) 7330 3000
mark.mansell@allenovery.com
Specialisation: Partner specialising in contentious and non-contentious employment law. Has extensive experience of dealing with all types of employee representative bodies and devising contracts, policies and procedures. Advises on the full range of contentious matters and High Court and tribunal. Has substantial experience in dealing with multijurisdictional employment issues – from mergers and acquisitions to outsourcing and individual and collective dismissals.
Prof. Memberships: Employment Law Sub-Committee of the City of London Solicitors Company; European Employment Lawyers Association; Employment Lawyers Association.
Career: LLB (Hons) London University (1982). Qualified as Solicitor 1985. Legal Advisor, CBI Employment Affairs Directorate (1985-87). Assistant Solicitor *Allen & Overy* 1987-91, Partner (1992).

MARSHALL, Ian
Martineau Johnson, Birmingham
(0121) 678 1377
ian.marshall@martjohn.com
Specialisation: All aspects of employment law, contentious and non-contentious, largely for employers. Trial experience includes actions against trade unions, injunctions, contempt of court, and wrongful dismissal. Advice on TUPE, severance agreements, restrictive covenants and equality issues in the private and educational sectors.
Prof. Memberships: Employment Lawyers Association, Birmingham Law Society, Birmingham Employment Tribunal Users Group.
Career: Articled *Ryland Martineau & Co*; partner in *Ryland Martineau & Co*. 1976; *Martineau Johnson* 1987; Head of Employment Department 1994.
Personal: Born 1947. Rugby School and Magdalene College, Cambridge. Married, four children. Lives in Edgbaston, Birmingham. Chairman of council, Edgbaston High School for Girls. Birmingham and Edgbaston Debating Society. St Paul's Club, Birmingham. Fell Walking.

MARTIN, Stefan
Allen & Overy, London
(020) 7330 3000
stefan.martin@allenovery.com
Specialisation: Stefan became a partner in the employment, pensions and incentives department in 2000. He advises on the full range of employment law matters, both contentious and non-contentious. Increasingly, his work involves providing and co-ordinating advice in relation to Europe as well as the UK. He regularly advises in relation to high level terminations, discrimination issues, drafting executive contracts of employment, drafting and commenting on employment policies and advising in relation to the employment issues which arise in relation to business transfers. His contentious work involves conducting both high court and tribunal proceedings concerning contractual and statutory claims. Stefan is a regular speaker at client seminars and is head of the department's Workplace Representation and Consultation Group (WoRC).
Prof. Memberships: Employment Lawyers' Association; European Employment Lawyers' Association.
Career: Articled *Allen & Overy* 1990; partner since 2000.
Publications: Contributor to various employment law journals.
Personal: Born 1965. Educated University of Hull (LLB 1988).

MASON, Helen
Mason and Co, Bakewell
(01629) 815175
helen@masonandco.co.uk
Specialisation: All aspects of employment law. Acts for both employers and employees, particularly senior executives.
Prof. Memberships: Law Society.
Career: Formerly with *Wragge & Co*,

EMPLOYMENT ■ THE LEADERS

Birmingham and now one of two partners in a niche firm in Bakewell, Derbyshire.
Personal: Graduate of Birmingham University (LLB Hons). Married (and in partnership with) Robin Mason (ex-*Eversheds*, Birmingham). One child. Interests include art, reading and theatre.

MATHER, Ian Philip
Eversheds, Cambridge
(01223) 443 666
ianmather@eversheds.com
Specialisation: Partner in employment department. Heads the employment team in Cambridge. Represents a wide range of employers in various industry sectors including high technology, pharmaceuticals, education, health and the police. His work includes advocacy in the Employment Tribunals dealing with sex, race and disability discrimination as well as unfair dismissal. Ian speaks regularly on employment law topics. In 2002, represented a major company in defeating a High Court claim for stigma damages.
Prof. Memberships: Law Society.
Career: York University (BA Hons Economics, 1979) and Newcastle Polytechnic 1981-82 (CPE and LSF).

MAYHEW, Lisa
Lovells, London
(020) 7296 5702
lisa.mayhew@lovells.com
Specialisation: Specialises in all areas of employment law, primarily acting for employers. She has extensive experience in high profile discrimination cases and regularly advises on employment issues arising out of the Data Protection Act. During the last 18 months, she has worked in-house for the John Lewis Partnership and a well-known investment bank. She is a regular speaker for Butterworths Tolley and co-author of Sweet & Maxwell's 'Discrimination Remedies and Quantum'.
Prof. Memberships: Employment Lawyers' Association; Employers' Forum on Disability.
Career: 1992-2000 employment lawyer at *Charles Russell* (partner for one year). 2000-present employment lawyer at *Lovells*, partner since 1 May 2002.
Publications: Co-author of Sweet & Maxwell's 'Discrimination: Remedies and Quantum'.
Personal: Keen interest in all sports – particularly football. Enjoys going to the theatre and cinema. Attended Southampton University and obtained degree in law.

MCGOWAN, Paul
Watson Burton, Newcastle upon Tyne
(0191) 244 4444

MCKENZIE, Rod
Harper Macleod, Glasgow
(0141) 221 8888
rod.mckenzie@harpremacleod.co.uk
Specialisation: Lead partner in the litigation department specialising in employment and sports law. Involved in the full range of UK and EU employment and sports law work for corporate clients and public and local authorities, sports organisations, clubs and others. Has dealt with many of Scotland's precedent creating cases and is a regular attendee at the Employment Appeal Tribunal. Law Society of Scotland accredited specialist in employment law. Recently listed as one of 'the world's leading employment lawyers'. Regularly lectures and writes on the subject. Chairman of Scottish Rugby Union Disciplinary Appeals Committee and member of International Rugby Football Board Disciplinary Appeals Panel.
Prof. Memberships: Law Society of Scotland; Industrial Law Group.
Career: Qualified 1982. Assistant solicitor, *Harper Macleod* 1982-84. Partner since 1984.
Personal: Educated at High School of Stirling 1970-76, Strathclyde University 1976-79, and Stirling University 1979-80. Leisure pursuits include golf and gardening. Born 1 July 1958. Lives in Hamilton, Lanarkshire.

MCMULLEN, John
Pinsent Curtis Biddle, Leeds
(0113) 244 5000
john.mcmullen@pinsents.com
Specialisation: Partner and national head of employment group. Acts for a wide range of household name plcs, national and multinational, universities and public sector organisations. Leading authority on transfer of undertakings. Expert on European Works Councils. Part-time Professor of Labour Law at University of Leeds.
Prof. Memberships: FCIPD. FRSA. Founder member Law Society's Employment Law Committee. Industrial Law Society Executive Committee; International Bar Association, Member; fellow, Society for Advanced Legal Studies; executive committee member Involvement and Participation Association.
Career: Qualified in 1978. With *Rotheras*, 1978-80. Fellow in Law at Girton College, Cambridge, 1980-86. Bye Fellow 1986-2000. Partner, *Rotheras* 1986-91. Partner and head of employment, *Simpson Curtis*, 1991. National head of employment, *Pinsent Curtis Biddle*, 1995.
Publications: Author 'Business Transfers and Employee Rights', 'Butterworths Employment Law Guide', 'Aspects of Employment Law', 'Acquired Rights of Employees', 'Tolley's Employment Law' (Joint), 'Redundancy: The Law and Practice', 'Jordans/IPD Employment Law Service', 'Working Time: Law and Practice'. Contributes widely to legal, human resources and business journals. Member, editorial board Sweet & Maxwell's 'Encyclopaedia of Employment Law'.
Personal: Born 1954. Educated Emmanuel College, Cambridge (BA 1975, double 1st Class (Hons), MA 1979, PhD 1993).

MILLER, Stephen
MacRoberts, Glasgow
(0141) 332 9988
stephen.miller@macroberts.com
Specialisation: Partner in the Employment Law Group; represents some of Scotland's largest employers and has a large public sector practice.
Prof. Memberships: British Association of Sport and Law; former member Law Society of Scotland Mental Health and Disability Committee; Employment Law Group Committee.
Career: Trained *Ross Harper & Murphy*, qualified 1990; Partner *Harper MacLeod* 1994; Partner *MacRoberts* 2002; Law Society of Scotland accredited specialist in employment law 1996. Has lectured extensively on employment law for a number of years and currently lectures on the Robert Gordon University employment law Masters Course.
Publications: Author of 'Judicial Review of Sporting Bodies' chapter in 'Sport and the Law – The Scots Perspective' (2000).
Personal: Born 1965; resides Glasgow. Graduated LLB (Hons) Aberdeen University (1987). Leisure interests include football, cycling, tennis and literature.

MORDSLEY, Barry
Salans, London
(020) 7509 6000
bmordsley@salans.com
Specialisation: Partner and head of the employment department. All employment law issues covered, contentious and non-contentious, drafting and advising on contracts and handbooks, restrictive covenants, discrimination, transfer of undertakings, executive terminations and collective representation issues. Lectures and writes frequently on employment law.
Prof. Memberships: Founder member of the Management Committee of the Employment Lawyers' Association and a member of numerous sub-committees. Formerly on the Law Society's Employment Law committee for many years and made major contributions on disability and age discrimination reports. Fellow of the Chartered Institute of Personnel and Development and a Fellow of the Institute of Continuing Professional Development.
Career: Qualified in 1972. Formerly a partner at *Harris Rosenblatt and Kramer*, London. Part-time Chairman of Employment Tribunals (England and Wales) since 1984.
Publications: Editorial board member of Croners 'Discrimination Law Briefing' and co-author of 'Butterworths Employment Law Guide' as well as of 'Butterworths Older Clients Service'. A regular contributor to various major HR publications such as 'People Management' and 'Personnel Today'.
Personal: Interests include theatre, music, travel, squash, cricket and football.

NESBITT, Sean
Taylor Wessing, London
(020) 7300 7000
s.nesbitt@taylorwessing.com
Specialisation: All aspects of employment law including executive employment and termination, commercial transactions and TUPE.
Prof. Memberships: Employment Lawyers' Association, Industrial Law Society, Association of Pension Lawyers, Immigration Law Practitioners' Association.
Career: Qualified 1991; *Slaughter and May* 1991-97, *Taylor Wessing* 2002.
Publications: Chapter on TUPE in Sweet & Maxwell's 'Encyclopedia of Employment Law'.
Personal: Born 1966. Educated at Hertford College, Oxford. Married, three children.

NICKSON, Sue
Hammond Suddards Edge, Manchester
(0161) 830 5000

NICOL, Diane
McGrigor Donald, Glasgow
(0141) 248 6677
diane.nicol@mcgrigors.com
Specialisation: Glasgow based Partner in the firm's employment law unit. Advises on all aspects of employment law. Significant experience in advising on high level strategic reorganisations for a number of multinationals. She recently advised on a large scale downsizing and is currently involved in a harmonisation project for a leading UK company. She has considerable experience in defending employers at Employment Tribunal. She successfully defended a major global company in a 12 day bullying case.
Prof. Memberships: Law Society of Scotland; Employment Lawyer's Association; Employment Law Group (Scotland) and European Employment Lawyers Association.
Career: Qualified in 1989. Spent one year with Australian law firm *Blake Dawson Waldron* and two years at *Maclay Murray & Spens* before joining *McGrigor Donald* in 1992. Became a partner in 1997.
Publications: Recent Publications: 'Employment Law Journal', 'The Firm Magazine', 'The Scotsman' and other publications.
Personal: Born 2 September 1965; Educated Shawlands Academy, Glasgow and Glasgow University (LLB (Hons) (First Class)). Married. Interests include running, hillwalking and travel.

NORBURY, Peter
Eversheds, Manchester
(0161) 831 8000
peternorbury@eversheds.com
Specialisation: Head of employment for Leeds and Manchester. Experienced advocate before Employment Tribunals throughout the UK and Employment Appeal Tribunal, together with representation at Joint Industries Board hearings. Particular expertise in trade unions,

executive terminations, TUPE and restructuring. Key work on collective issues including recognition agreements and CAC proceedings. Regular speaker at seminars and conferences and contributor to publications. Reported cases include Monsanto v TGWU, Roevin BP v Gillick, Akzo Coatings v Thompson and others, Rock Refrigeration v Seward, Merchant Ferries v Brown and Atlas Wright v Wright.
Prof. Memberships: Employment Lawyers Association, Industrial Law Society, RSA, EFSP.
Career: Qualified in 1978 and stayed with the firm before being made Partner in 1984.
Personal: Born 12.1.53. Educated at Manchester Grammar School and Sheffield University. Interests include rugby and golf. Lives in Saddleworth.

NOTT, Christopher
Palser Grossman, Cardiff Bay
(029) 2045 2770

O'BRIEN, Christine
Baker & McKenzie, London
(020) 7919 1000
christine.o'brien@bakernet.com
Specialisation: Partner and Head of the London Employment Law Department, and co-chair of the *Baker & McKenzie* European Employment Group. Specialises in contentious and non-contentious employment law, including corporate re-organisations, transnational mergers and acquisitions, advice on European Works Councils and collective issues and EU employment law. Has acted in high profile discrimination cases for public and private sector clients, including investment banks and other financial institutions.
Prof. Memberships: Law Society, Employment Lawyers Association, Industrial Law Society.
Career: Qualified 1987 with *Simmons & Simmons*. Joined *Baker & McKenzie* in 1989 and became a Partner in 1995.
Publications: Frequent speaker at external conferences, contributor to various publications including the new Sweet & Maxwell publication 'European Employment Law and the UK' and television appearances commenting on employment law issues.

O'NEILL, Orlagh
Napier & Sons, Belfast
(028) 90244602

OSMAN, Chris
Clifford Chance, London
(020) 7600 1000
chris.osman@cliffordchance.com
Specialisation: Tax, pensions and employment. Partner and head of employment unit specialising in all aspects of employment law.
Career: Articled *Coward Chance*; qualified 1976; Partner since 1981.
Personal: 1973 Ramsden School; Southampton University (LLB).

PARKINSON, Helen
Whittles, Manchester
(0161) 228 2061

PARNELL, Catherine
Bond Pearce, Southampton
(023) 8063 2211
cparnell@bondpearce.com
Specialisation: Solicitor advising on all aspects of employment work, especially contentious matters, including advocacy at Employment Tribunals. Advises public and private companies in particular on matters relating to sex, race and disability discrimination, contested dismissals, major redundancies and large-scale reorganisations. Particular importance is placed on preventative advice to avoid disputes. Provides in-house training to clients and other HR professionals.
Prof. Memberships: Member of the Employment Lawyers Association.
Career: Articled with *Higgs & Sons*; qualified 1997; joined *Bond Pearce* 2000.

PIKE, Malcolm
Addleshaw Booth & Co, Manchester
(0161) 934 6443
malcolm.pike@addleshawbooth.com
Specialisation: Partner and Head of Employment Department. Main areas of practice are employment and industrial relations law. Includes drafting and advising on terms and conditions of employment, personnel policies and collective agreements, industrial relations and other trade union matters, discrimination and equal pay, board room disputes, defending and prosecuting High Court and Employment Tribunal proceedings and advising on employment aspects of the sale and reorganisation of companies and businesses. Various publications include 'The Lawyers Factbook', 'Essential Facts Employment,' Butterworths' 'Encyclopaedia of Forms and Precedents,' 'Workplace Discrimination' and Jordan's 'IPD Employment Law Service.' Regular speaker at seminars and conferences.
Prof. Memberships: Law Society, Employment Lawyers Association, Industrial Law Society, Manchester Industrial Relations Society, IBA, ABA.
Career: Qualified in 1984. Joined the firm as a Partner in 1992.
Personal: Attended Leicester University 1978-81.

POTTER, David
freethcartwright, Nottingham
(0115) 936 9369
david.potter@freethcartwright.co.uk
Specialisation: Advises on all aspects of employment law, predominantly on instructions from employers, in-house legal teams and senior director/employees. Has recently handled litigation on behalf of employers seeking to protect their confidential information and also a number of race, sex and disability discrimination claims. Has also provided strategic employment advice on a wide range of issues including TUPE, data protection and redundancy. Regularly speaks at seminars and provides in-house training.
Prof. Memberships: Employment Lawyers Association.
Career: Articled at *Freeth Cartwright* (now *freethcartwright*); qualified in 1989; Partner in 1994. Current Head of Employment.
Personal: Born 1964. Educated at Rossall School and Reading University (LLB). LLM (Advanced Litigation) with distinction at Nottingham Trent University 1996. Resides in Nottingham. Interests include hockey and golf.

PRYKE, Oliver
Taylor Vinters, Cambridge
(01223) 423444
oliver.pryke@taylorvinters.com
Specialisation: Specialises in all aspects of employment law, both contentious and non-contentious. Acts for private and public sector organisations and senior employees with a particular emphasis on clients in high-tech, biotechnology and pharmaceutical industries. Provides in-house training to clients and other HR professionals.
Prof. Memberships: Employment Lawyers Association.
Career: Qualified as a solicitor in 1996. Joined *Taylor Vinters* in January 1998. Became a Partner in 2002.
Personal: Born 30 July 1971. Educated at The Judd School, Tonbridge and Oxford University (BA Hons in Law 1989-92). A keen tennis player and pianist. Lives in Suffolk.

PRYTHERCH, Rosalie
Cleaver Fulton Rankin, Belfast
(028) 9027 1322
r.prytherch@cfrlaw.co.uk
Specialisation: Acts for employers in the retail, manufacturing, financial, education and IT sectors and for local councils and public bodies. Deals with the broad spectrum of contentious work and provides corporate support and advice. Has gained an impressive reputation in the area of restrictive covenant disputes where clients have enjoyed considerable success and is also recognised for expertise in dealing with TUPE issues.
Prof. Memberships: Employment Lawyers' Group (NI). Law Society of Northern Ireland.
Career: Qualified 1987. Partner in *Cleaver Fulton Rankin* 1996.

PUGH, Keith
Nabarro Nathanson, Sheffield
(0114) 279 4000
k.pugh@nabarro.com
Specialisation: Employment law specialist for 20 years dealing with both contentious and non-contentious issues ranging from drafting employment contracts policies and procedures; tribunal claims; restrictive covenants and garden leave; trade union recognition and collective issues; industrial action, transfer of undertakings and working time and minimum wage issues. Instructed by BFL in BFL v Meade (House of Lords).
Prof. Memberships: Law Society. Employment Lawyers Association. Industrial Law Society.
Career: Admitted 1980. British Coal Legal Department 1980-90. Joined *Nabarro Nathanson* as a partner in 1990. Head of employment department.
Personal: Music, food, wine and gardening.

RALPH, Nick
Archon, London
(020) 7397 9650
n.ralph@archonlaw.co.uk
Specialisation: Partner. Handles contentious and non-contentious employment matters for both employers and employees.
Prof. Memberships: Employment Lawyers Association.
Career: Qualified as a solicitor at *Ashurst Morris Crisp* in 1988. Moved to *Archon* (formerly *Langley & Co*) in 1997. Partner from 1998.
Publications: Contributor to Sweet & Maxwell's 'Company Directors: Law and Liability'. Editor of Sweet & Maxwell's 'Practical Commercial Precedents'.
Personal: Born 9 December 1963. Attended Exeter University, LLB (Hons). Lives in Hammersmith.

REES, Anthony
Morgan Cole, Swansea
(01792) 634634

RESTON, Vincent
DLA, Liverpool
(08700) 111111

ROBERTS, Stephen
Thring Townsend, Bath
(01225) 340101
sroberts@ttuk.com
Specialisation: Deals with all areas of contentious and non-contentious employment law including dismissals, discrimination, transfers of undertakings and redundancies. Particular experience in education, sport and agriculture sectors.
Prof. Memberships: Employment Lawyers Association; Justice: British Association for Sport and Law.
Career: Qualified 1980. Became a partner with *Thrings and Long* 1988. Head of employment law at *Thring Townsend* 2000.
Personal: BA Law, University of Kent 1977. LLM (Employment and European Law), University of Bristol 2000. Married with two sons. Lives near Bath.

ROBERTSON, Nicholas
Mayer, Brown, Rowe & Maw, London
(020) 7248 4282

ROBERTSON, Stuart
Gordons Cranswick Solicitors, Bradford
(01274) 202190
stuart.robertson@gordonscranswick.co.uk
Specialisation: All aspects of employment law. Extensive experience of Employment Tribunal advocacy. Particular knowledge of sex and race discrimination, restrictive covenants and major

EMPLOYMENT ■ THE LEADERS

redundancy/ reorganisation exercises. Regular presenter of seminars to clients and to outside bodies including Chamber of Commerce and ACAS.
Prof. Memberships: Employment Lawyers Association.
Career: Bradford Grammar School. Trinity Hall, Cambridge. Articled: *Durrant Piesse*. Qualified: October 1982. *Hepworth & Chadwick*, Leeds 1982-86. *Dibb Lupton* 1986-92. Joined *Gordons Wright & Wright* as partner in 1992. Part-time Employment tribunal chairman 1994. Deputy Registrar, Bradford Diocese (Church of England) 1997, Diocesan Registrar 2002.
Personal: Born 1 May 1957. Married with two children. Church activities, hill walking, rugby league.

ROSKILL, Julian
Mayer, Brown, Rowe & Maw, London
(020) 7248 4282

RUSSELL, Timothy
Norton Rose, London
(020) 7444 2468
russellt@nortonrose.com
Specialisation: Partner and Head of Employment Unit of 18 solicitors. Specialising purely in employment law. Has handled many major transfer of undertakings, wrongful dismissal and sex discrimination cases. Part time employment tribunal chairman. Practical approach based on in-house commercial experience.
Prof. Memberships: Law Society, Employment Lawyers Association, CBI Employee Relations Panel, Industrial Law Society, London Chamber of Commerce.
Career: Worked at *Wilde Sapte* 1982-86. Qualified in 1985 and was Ciba Geigy's legal advisor 1986-87. Senior legal advisor at Lloyds Bank 1987-91. Joined *Hammond Suddards* in 1991 and became a Partner in 1992. Joined *Norton Rose* 1999.
Personal: Born 17 June 1960. Educated at Pocklington School and Cambridge University. Enjoys all sports. Lives in West London.

SALUJA, Sean
Paull & Williamsons, Aberdeen
(01224) 621621
sasaluja@paull-williamsons.co.uk
Specialisation: Almost exclusive area of practice is employment. Advises mainly employers on all aspects of employment and collective relations matters both contentious and non-contentious. Appears regularly in tribunals in both Scotland and England. Has dealt with a number cases involving transfer of undertakings and contracting issues in the offshore oil industry. Lectured on employment law from 1991-95 at Aberdeen University. Regularly presents seminars and training programmes for clients.
Prof. Memberships: Law Society of Scotland, Employment Law Group. Accredited by the Law Society of Scotland as a specialist in employment law.
Career: Graduated in 1989, LLB Hons (1st Class); diploma in Legal Practice, 1989. Qualified 1991.
Personal: Born 1967. Interests include golf, walking and travel.

SAYER, Nick
Hewitson Becke + Shaw, Cambridge
(01223) 461155
nicksayer@hewitsons.com
Specialisation: Partner and Head of Employment Law Department. Principal area of practice is contentious employment matters, particularly injunctive relief (trade secret and confidential information matters, non-competition, non-solicitation and non-dealing covenants, search orders, orders for delivery up, etc.). Also deals with all other contentious and non-contentious employment matters, including wrongful dismissal, unfair dismissal, redundancy, discrimination, trade disputes and other collective employment matters, transfers of undertakings, drafting contracts of employment. Has presented seminars to other professionals and clients and written numerous articles.
Prof. Memberships: The Employment Lawyers Association; The Industrial Law Society; the Institute of Employment Rights; Fellow of the Society for Advanced Legal Studies.
Career: Joined *Hewitson Becke + Shaw* in 1985. Qualified in 1987. Became a partner and Head of Employment Law in 1993.
Personal: Born 26 September 1961. Educated at the Cambridgeshire High School for Boys 1973-80 and Leicester University 1981-84. Awarded an LLM in Law and Industrial Relations from Leicester University in 1993. Leisure pursuits include cricket, photography and gardening. Lives in Cambridgeshire.

SCOULAR, Gillie
Mills & Reeve, Norwich
(01603) 693 265
gillie.scoular@mills-reeve.com
Specialisation: Has specialised in employment law for 20 years, 13 of which were in London. Deals with all aspects of contentious and non-contentious employment law, acting mainly for employers but also for senior executives within the public and private sectors. Work includes service agreements; restrictive covenants; review and drafting of documentation (contracts, handbooks, policies); business reorganisations; TUPE; the employment aspects of corporate transactions (mergers, acquisitions, disposals); board room disputes; senior executive severances; redundancies (collective and individual); discrimination; Employment Tribunal claims; collective trade union issues. Conducts external and internal seminars for clients.
Prof. Memberships: Law Society, Employment Lawyers Association.
Career: Qualified in 1980; articled clerk, solicitor and then partner at *Jaques and Co/Jaques & Lewis*, London (1978-89) before joining a major publishing, multi-media, printing and newspaper group based in London as in-house Group Commercial Lawyer (1989-92); with *Mills & Reeve* since 1992.
Personal: Educated at Sherborne School for Girls, then Cambridge University (Girton College) graduating in law (1977); married with three young daughters (triplets); leisure interests currently limited but would include theatre, choral singing, music, travel and entertaining; lives in Norfolk.

SEATON, Christopher
Burges Salmon, Bristol
(0117) 939 2000
chris.seaton@burges-salmon.com
Specialisation: Head of Employment dealing with full range of contentious and non-contentious employment work. Experienced tribunal advocate and frequent user of Bristol Mercantile Court for wrongful dismissal and other contractual claims as well as employment related injunctions. Advisor to a number of multinational companies based in USA and Europe.
Prof. Memberships: Employment Lawyers Association, European Employment Lawyers Association, Bristol Employment Tribunal Users Committee, policy advisor on the Regional Committee of IPD.
Career: Royal Navy Officer 1979-90. Trainee at *Burges Salmon* 1991-93. Specialised in employment law from 1993; associate in 1997; partner in 1999. Appointed head of Employment in July 1999. One of three partners on the firm's International Steering Committee.
Publications: Regular contributor to the 'Employment Law Journal'. Author of a chapter on European Works Councils for 'International Employment Law' published by the Centre for International Legal Studies.
Personal: Married with two daughters. Interests include sailing, skiing, music and squash.

SEWARD, Karen
Allen & Overy, London
(020) 7330 3000
karen.seward@allenovery.com
Specialisation: Specialises in contentious and non-contentious employment law and occupational health and safety.
Prof. Memberships: Employment Lawyers Association: European Employment Lawyers Association.
Career: Trained *Simmons & Simmons*. Qualified 1990. *Stephenson Harwood*, Partner 1996. *Pinsent Curtis*, Partner 1997. *Allen & Overy*, Partner 2000.
Publications: 'Tolley's Maternity and Parental Rights: A Practical Guide to Maternity, Parental and Dependant Care Leave'; 'Tolley's Working Time'; 'Croner's: The International Mobile Worker'.
Personal: LLB (Hons) Bristol 1987. LSF College of Law 1988.

SHERRARD, Harry
Sherrards, Haywards Heath
(01444) 473344
advice@harrysherrard.com
Specialisation: Employment law. Acting for many well-known employers in the South East, with a particular emphasis on aviation and travel related businesses. Clients include KLM, Emirates and Lufthansa. Advised Aer Lingus through its recent extensive redundancy programme. Recent new clients include BASF and the newly merged cancer charity, Cancer Research UK. Active in employment law training with training clients which include GlaxoSmithKline and Novartis.
Prof. Memberships: CIPD, IoD, CBI, ELA.
Career: Previously Head of Employment Law at large regional practice, established *Sherrards* in 1999. The practice is multidisciplinary, and as well as providing core employment law services, the firm offers a range of human resource consultancy skills, as well as its own branded employment/legal expenses insurance policy. Recent expansion has seen recruitment of a solicitor and an employment law paralegal.
Personal: Heavily involved in the motor racing world, a qualified RAC Motor Sports Association instructor, active racer and proprietor of a small motor racing team. Plays bass guitar in a rock band.

SHORT, Michael
Short Richardson & Forth, Newcastle upon Tyne
(0191) 232 0283
mcs@short-richardson-forth.co.uk
Specialisation: Founder Partner in Employment Law Department. Has 25 years' experience in employment law, acting on both sides of industry and dealing with the full range of employment law matters including appearing before employment tribunals regularly throughout the country and lecturing regularly on employment law matters to Companies. Extensive experience in senior executive terminations.
Prof. Memberships: Member of the Law Society's Employment Law Committee, Employment Lawyers Association, Industrial Law Society and is the Secretary of the Newcastle Employment Tribunal Users Group.
Career: Senior Partner and founding Partner of *Short Richardson & Forth* since 1978.
Personal: Leisure interests include theatre. Lives in Newcastle-upon-Tyne.

SHRIVES, Mark
Hammond Suddards Edge, Leeds
0113 284 7000

SIPPITT, Michael
Clarks, Reading
(0118) 958 5321
michael.sippitt@clarks-solicitors.co.uk
Specialisation: *Clarks Solicitors*' manag-

ing partner and head of the firm's employment services team. Specialises in employment work, handling both contentious and non-contentious business and appearing as an advocate in tribunals. Deals with all areas of employment and discrimination law. Leads a specialist team which acts for a wide range of corporate and institutional clients including: News International, Sun Microsystems, Blue Circle Industries, BMW (GB), Global Crossing, John Menzies, Amey, Gleesons, University of Reading and Danzas. Has also been much involved in providing in-house management training for corporate clients on employment and discrimination issues. He has a particular interest in collective employment law issues and employment relations, on which he has spoken frequently. Member of the CBI's Employment Relations Panel and Southern Region Human Resources Forum. Formerly a part-time university lecturer in Labour Law. Also a member of the Advisory Board of the TAGLaw International Legal Network and of the Network Employment Speciality Group.
Prof. Memberships: Employment Lawyers Association.
Career: Trained at Clarks Solicitors, became a Partner in 1978 and Managing Partner in 1997.
Personal: Graduated from Southampton University with a 1st class LLB honours degree and obtained honours in the Law Society Finals. Active in Church membership. Other interests include chairmanship of a charitable trust and golf.

SMELLIE, David
Farrer & Co, London
(020) 9242 2022
dcs@farrer.co.uk
Specialisation: Main area of practice is employment law. Experience with commercial and institutional clients including newspapers, magazines, banks, public bodies and academic establishments, as well as an increasing proportion of high-profile individual work. Has been involved in advising many such clients on restructuring and redundancy programmes and on the transfer of undertakings regulations, as well as handling industrial disputes, team moves and individual cases.
Prof. Memberships: Employment Lawyers Association.
Career: Joined *Farrer & Co* in 1987 as a trainee. Qualified in 1989, became a Partner in 1996. David heads *Farrer & Co's* employment and pension team. Given a four star ranking in the 'Insiders Guide to Employment Law' and runner-up in Employment Lawyer of the Year.
Publications: Published a considerable amount, in various Croners publications, in Butterworths' 'Company Service' (the employment chapter) and in Tolley's 'Employment Policies and Precedents'. Also regularly asked to contribute to various employment law magazines including 'Employment Lawyer'.

Personal: Born 1964. Educated at Glenalmond College and St John's College, Cambridge (MA). Lives in London.

SMITH, Tim
Crutes Law Firm, Newcastle upon Tyne
(0191) 212 5600
tim.smith@crutes.co.uk
Specialisation: Head of Employment Law acting predominantly for NHS, Local Authority and company clients. Particular interest in contentious employment law and TUPE. All advocacy undertaken in-house.
Prof. Memberships: Member of The Employment Lawyers Association. Member of The Employment Tribunals User Group.
Personal: Born 4 April 1959. Educated at Whitby Grammar School. Masters degree in Employment Law.

SPEIRS, William
Brechin Tindal Oatts, Glasgow
(0141) 221 8012
wscs@bto.co.uk
Specialisation: Advises mainly employers – from a number of spheres including retail, insurance, leisure, financial, social housing and the further education sector – on all areas of industrial relations and employment law. Specialist areas: transfer of undertakings; redundancy schemes; race and sex discrimination; and directors' service contracts. Seminar speaker on topical employment issues.
Prof. Memberships: Law Society of Scotland; The Society of Solicitors to the Supreme Court; The Royal Faculty of Procurators in Glasgow.
Career: Graduated in 1972, LLB (Hons) Public Law, Glasgow University, Notary Public. Practised Employment Law since 1978. Partner 1984.
Publications: Author of the employment law section of W Green's 'Scottish Human Rights Service' (published by Sweet & Maxwell).
Personal: Golf and travel.

TATA, Rustom
DMH, Brighton
(01293) 605068
rustom.tata@dmh.co.uk
Specialisation: Partner and Head of Employment Group, deals with all aspects of employment law and specialises in the European influence on UK employment law, education employment contracts and corporate reorganisations; appears regularly as an advocate in the Employment Tribunal and Employment Appeal Tribunal.
Prof. Memberships: Employment Lawyers Association.
Career: University of Sussex, BA Law and French; King's College, London, LLM. Articled *DMH*; qualified 1992; Associate 1994; Partner 1996. Lectures extensively on employment issues, often at the invitation of local CIPD and other business organisations, such as Business Link and the Institute of Chartered Secretaries.
Personal: Born 1965, resides Brighton.

TAYLOR, Catherine
Olswang, London
(020) 7208 8711
cjt@olswang.com
Specialisation: Employment law, specialising in both contentious and non-contentious. Specific experience in enforcing post termination restrictions and High Court litigation generally. Also has extensive experience of advice on pan-European employment law issues.
Prof. Memberships: ELA; ILS; IPD; EELA.
Career: Trained at *Norton Rose*, qualifying in 1993. Moved to *Olswang*, in 1995 and became a partner in 1998.
Publications: 'Employment Law Checklists' – joint author with Julia Palca.

TEMPERTON, Ellen
Baker & McKenzie, London
(020) 7919 1000
ellen.temperton@bakernet.com
Specialisation: A Partner in the Employment Law Department of *Baker & McKenzie*. She specialises in all aspects of employment law with litigation expertise in several leading cases. Has spoken at many external conferences and client workshops and is an expert on the employment law implications of human rights legislation, employee fraud, data protection and privacy issues and collective rights.
Prof. Memberships: Sits on a subcommittee of the Legislative Group of the Employment Lawyers Association which focuses on employee privacy.
Career: Articled *Macfarlanes*, qualified 1991; Partner *Baker & McKenzie* 1998.
Publications: Has contributed articles to various publications and is a regular contributor to 'People Management', 'Commercial Lawyer' and internal *Baker & McKenzie* publications, e.g. 'Sexual Harassment Laws Across Europe'.

THOMAS, Alun
Anderson Strathern WS, Edinburgh
(0131) 220 2345
alun.thomas@andersonstrathern.co.uk
Specialisation: Deals extensively with all aspects of employment law, contentious and non-contentious. Specific interests in the discrimination field and was involved in the first Disability Discrimination Act case in Scotland. Involved in a number of cases advising senior management in both commercial and public sector institutions in relation to internal and external inquiries including disciplinary hearings. Regularly assists other firms in providing specialist employment law advice to them and to their clients at times of crisis including the design of redundancy consultation and selection processes and TUPE acquisitions. Involved in landmark cases testing the boundaries of human rights and other cutting edge issues including disability discrimination, legal aid in Employment Tribunals, and post Seymour Smith cases in Scotland. Regularly appears in Employment and Employment Appeal Tribunals and on the lecture circuit.
Prof. Memberships: Member of the Committee of the Scottish Discrimination Law Association, he is on the combined Panel of Scottish Solicitors for the joint Equality Commissions initiative and is a member of ELA, DLA and DDARap.
Career: Qualified 1983, assumed as Partner 1990. Head of the *Anderson Strathern* Employment Unit. Accredited by the Law Society of Scotland as a specialist in employment law.
Personal: Born 1958, resides East Lothian.

THOMAS, David
Burroughs Day, Bristol
(0117) 930 7559
dt@bd4law.com
Specialisation: Undertakes a wide range of Employment Tribunal work for employers and employees. Non-contentious work includes advising on, drafting and introducing employment documentation. Highlights of the year include representing 66 former employees of Viatel Global Communications against liquidators and NTL. Has particular expertise in representing businesses in the care sector, and SME engineering and manufacturing sector.
Prof. Memberships: Employment Lawyers Association and Bristol Employment Tribunal Users Committee.
Career: Qualified in 1991, became partner in 1999 and Head of Employment Department in 2000.

THOMPSON, Michael
Eversheds, Manchester
(0161) 831 8000
michaelthompson@eversheds.co.uk
Specialisation: Deals with all aspects of employment law work both contentious and non-contentious acting mainly for employers. Extensive experience both in the public and private sectors. Experienced advocate before the Employment Tribunal and the Employment Appeal Tribunal. Particular expertise in executive terminations, TUPE and injunctive relief. Regularly provides training to clients both in-house and on external courses. Reported cases include Atlas Wright v Wright; BBA Friction Ltd v Pointon and others; Mancat v Faulkner.
Prof. Memberships: Employment Lawyers Association, The Law Society and the Industrial Society.
Career: Qualified with the firm in 1992, became senior solicitor in 1997 and was promoted to Partner in May 2000.
Personal: Born 8 October 1965. Educated at Leeds University. Interests, all sports, particularly football and golf. Lives in Manchester.

THOMPSON, Tony
Macfarlanes, London
(020) 7831 9222

EMPLOYMENT ■ THE LEADERS

THOMSON, Alan
McClure Naismith, Glasgow
(0141) 204 2700
athomson@mcclurenaismith.com
Specialisation: Lead partner in employment unit. Almost exclusively engaged in employment law practice. Principally advising employers but has a growing practice in pursuing claims for senior executives and negotiating severance arrangements. Regularly appears before Employment Tribunals. Heads a growing team of lawyers in the firm's Glasgow and Edinburgh offices focusing on employment law matters.
Prof. Memberships: Law Society of Scotland, Employment Law Group (Scotland) and Employment Lawyers Association.
Career: Trained at *McGrigor Donald*, qualifying in 1976. Joined *McClure Naismith* in 1976 and became a partner in 1979.
Personal: Born in 1952 and lives in Glasgow. Educated at The High School of Glasgow (1957-70) and Edinburgh University (1970-74), LLB (Hons). Enjoys skiing, and escaping from employment law to remote croft on west coast of Scotland.

TOLVAS-VINCENT, Christina
Bond Pearce, Southampton
(023) 8082 8881
ctolvas-vincent@bondpearce.com
Specialisation: Partner and Head of Employment at *Bond Pearce*. Specialises in both contentious and non-contentious employment issues, including representing employers at employment tribunal hearings. Advises on discrimination issues, dismissals, termination packages, contracts of employment, employment policies and employment aspects of transfers of undertakings and lectures on employment issues. Has particular experience of the retail and education sectors.
Prof. Memberships: Member of the Employment Lawyers Association and the Law Society's European Group. Also a qualified Finnish lawyer and a member of the Finnish Bar Association.
Career: Joined *Bond Pearce* in May 1998 (Partner with *Hepherd Winstanley & Pugh* 1 April 1997). Qualified March 1989 (Finland).

TRANTER, Ian
Hammond Suddards Edge, Manchester
(0161) 830 5000

TURTLE, Brian
Carson McDowell, Belfast
(028) 9024 4951
See under Litigation, p.569

TWEEDIE, Colin
Addleshaw Booth & Co, Leeds
(0113) 209 2032
colin.tweedie@addleshawbooth.com
Specialisation: Partner in Employment Law Department. Has specialised exclusively in employment law and industrial relations since qualification. Deals with all aspects, mainly for employers, including employment contracts, procedures and policies, restrictive covenants, discrimination, high level terminations, the employment aspects of the sale and reorganisation of companies and businesses and contentious matters including appearing before employment tribunals throughout the country. Conducts seminars for clients, lectures and has appeared on local radio. Author of occasional articles.
Prof. Memberships: Employment Lawyers Association.
Career: Qualified in 1978. Joined firm as Partner in 1998.
Personal: Educated at Fitzwilliam College, Cambridge 1972-75. Leisure interests include sports, railways and Scottish history.

TWINEHAM, Andrew
Jacksons, Stockton on Tees
(01642) 643643

TYNDALL, Timothy
Hewitson Becke + Shaw, Cambridge
(01223) 461155
timtyndall@hewitsons.com
Specialisation: Practises exclusively in employment law, both contentious and non-contentious. Regularly appears as an advocate in Employment Tribunals and has substantial experience in the area of injunctions. Deals with personnel aspects of the firm's merger and acquisition work and corporate restructuring. Presents seminars to other professionals and clients.
Prof. Memberships: Employment Lawyers' Association.
Career: Educated at Liverpool College and Hull University. Qualified in 1988 and became a partner at *Hewitson Becke + Shaw* in 1998 having practised in Liverpool and Leeds.
Personal: Interests include Liverpool FC, family life and three children. Lives in Trumpington, Cambridge.

UNDERWOOD, Kerry
Underwoods, Hemel Hempstead
(01442) 430900
Specialisation: Senior Partner of *Underwoods*. Practice covers full range of employment law acting for employers and employees. Well known for advocacy in employment tribunals and the EAT where he is a member of the Employment Law Advisors Appeal Scheme. Clients include plcs and a number of Directors of plcs. Founded Regan Underwood lecturers, as well as delivering lectures regularly for the University of Cambridge, the Law Society and others. Appears regularly on radio, television and in the national press in relation to legal topics. Conducts in-house training for government departments, local authorities and major companies. Was successful appellant's advocate, pro bono, in leading pregnancy rights case of Day v T Pickles Farms Ltd (1999) IRLR 217. Advocate in other reported cases.
Prof. Memberships: Fellow Chartered Institute of Arbitrators, Association of Trial Lawyers of America, Law Society, Employment Tribunal Chairman 1993-2000, Employment Law Advisors Appeal Scheme, Transport and General Workers Union, Equal Opportunities Commission Panel, Fellow Society for Advanced Legal Studies.
Career: Qualified in 1981. Set up *Underwoods* in 1991. Pioneered contingency fees, fixed fees and menu-pricing in Employment Tribunals. Pioneered television advertising. Pioneered 'Community Law Club' concept. Author of best seller 'No Win No Fee No Worries'. Editor of 'Employment Law and Litigation'. Editorial Board Member of 'Litigation Funding'. Editor Costs Products Section of Butterworths 'Personal Injury Law Service'. Director and Editorial Board Member of 'Independent Lawyer'. Part-time Employment Tribunal Chairman 1993-2000. London Borough Councillor 1978-82. Parliamentary Candidate 1979. Only UK employment lawyer listed in Association of Trial Lawyers of America Directory. Advisor to the Civil Justice Council re costs. Chairman and Director of Victim Support.
Personal: Born in 1956. Leisure interests include cricket, football, literature, especially poetry of TS Eliot, and Elvis Presley. Has travelled extensively around the world.

WALKER, David James
Dundas & Wilson CS, Glasgow
(0141) 222 2200

WARNOCK, Owen
Eversheds, Norwich
(01603) 272727
owenwarnock@eversheds.com
Specialisation: Has specialised in employment law for 21 years and heads the *Eversheds* East of England employment department, consisting of 19 lawyers, two human resources consultants and one employment law trainer. He has considerable Employment Tribunal advocacy experience and has particular strength in discrimination law and collective issues including trade union recognition. He is a regular speaker on employment law issues at events ranging from local IPD groups to CBI and similar national conferences. Employment law is main area of practice, but also advises on food and drink law.
Prof. Memberships: Employment Lawyers Association, Industrial Law Society, The Food Law Group.
Career: Qualified 1982 with *Daynes Hill & Perks* (partner 1985).
Publications: Consultant Legal Editor to the CCH Disability Manual and co-author of 'Employment Law in the NHS' (Cavendish 1995).
Personal: Born 5 April 1957. Graduated in Law from Cambridge University in 1979. Lives in Norwich.

WARREN, Martin
Eversheds, Cardiff
(029) 2047 1147
martinwarren@eversheds.com
Specialisation: Partner and Head of the Employment Department at *Eversheds* Cardiff office. An experienced employment lawyer with particular expertise in strategic and reorganisational issues, trade union recognition, redundancies and business transfers, industrial action, balloting, and in the area of collective labour law generally. Acted successfully for employer clients in reported cases including O'Dea v ISC Chemicals (Court of Appeal 1995) and Alcan Extrusions v Yates (EAT 1996). Advises multinational companies, in particular in the US, on the implications of developments in UK labour and employment law.
Prof. Memberships: Member of the Employment Lawyers Association; Member of the Cardiff Employment Tribunal User Group; Fellow of the Royal Society of Arts; Member of the Reform Club; Member of the American Employment Law Council; Member of the American Bar Association.
Career: Qualified in 1985. Joined *Phillips & Buck* in 1986 (now *Eversheds*). Became a Partner in 1989.
Personal: Resides in Magor, Gwent.

WATSON, Judith
Cobbetts, Manchester
(0161) 833 5205
judith.watson@cobbetts.co.uk
Specialisation: Partner and head of *Cobbetts*' 10-strong employment law team. Handles the whole spectrum of employment law and industrial relations issues. Specialist interest in discrimination and regularly advises on negotiation of senior executive recruitment contracts and severance packages. A regular media spokesperson for the firm who manages training for clients on all issues concerning human resources and employment.
Prof. Memberships: North West representative and a management committee member of the Employment Lawyers Association.
Career: Educated at Sheffield High School for Girls and Sheffield University (1981-84). Articled with *Leak Almond & Parkinson* (later *Cobbetts*). Qualified in 1987. Became a partner in January 1997.

WATSON, Simon
Simmons & Simmons, London
(020) 7628 2020
simon.watson@simmons-simmons.com
Specialisation: Employment law. Simon has a strong City-based employment law practice acting for insurance and major corporations and regularly advises on the employment aspects of acquisitions, disposals and mergers including the Transfer of Undertakings Regulations. In addition, Simon has extensive experience of handling litigation both in the industrial tribunal and the High Court.
Prof. Memberships: Law Society.
Career: St. Catherines's College, Oxford, College of Law, *Simmons & Simmons*.
Personal: Bridge, Opera.

THE LEADERS ■ EMPLOYMENT

WETHERFIELD, Alison
McDermott, Will & Emery, London
(020) 7577 3489
awetherfield@europe.mwe.com
Specialisation: Partner in *McDermott, Will & Emery*'s Employment Department, specialising in labour and employment law; contentious and non-contentious, especially TUPE and other M&A related employment issues.
Prof. Memberships: Employment Lawyers' Association (Management Committee); European Employment Lawyers Association.
Career: Employment lawyer, New York 1987-92; visiting professor of employment law, University of Tokyo 1992-95; pupil barrister at 2 Hare Court (now Blackstone Chambers) 1995-96; associate in employment department of *Warner Cranston* 1996-99; joined *McDermott, Will & Emery* in 1999; made partner in 2001.
Publications: Co-author of Tolley's 'Termination of Employment'. Frequent contributor of articles to employment journals.
Personal: Trinity Hall, Cambridge; Harvard Law School. Speaks Japanese. Married, two sons. Interests include theatre and travel.

WHINCUP, David
Hammond Suddards Edge, London
(020) 7655 1000

WHITEMORE, Sarah
Warner Goodman & Streat, Fareham
(01329) 288121

WILLIAMS, Audrey
Eversheds, Cardiff
(029) 2047 1147
audreywilliams@eversheds.com
Specialisation: Partner in the Employment Law Department at Eversheds Cardiff office. Specialises in employment law. Particular experience of sex discrimination, race discrimination and disability discrimination. Advises on diversity, maternity, parental leave, harassment and bullying policies; providing advice and training for establishing such policies; grievance procedures and counselling. Author of a number of publications.
Prof. Memberships: Member of the Chartered Institute of Personnel and Development.
Career: Graduate of Southampton University; qualified in 1989, joined *Eversheds Phillips and Buck* in 1989 (now *Eversheds* Cardiff); became a Partner in 1993.
Personal: Married and resides in Cardiff.

WILLIAMSON, Raymond
MacRoberts, Glasgow
(0141) 332 9988
raymond.williamson@macroberts.com
Specialisation: Partner in Employment Group. Specialist in employment law since the early 1970s. Advises on the drafting of contracts of employment, on management of staff, on redundancies and disciplinary matters. Also experienced in representing clients' interests before employment and other tribunals. Holder of specialist authorisation from the Law Society of Scotland in employment law. Convenor of the Law Society's Employment Law Committee and Chairman of the Employment Law Specialisation Committee. Lectures extensively on employment matters for various course giving bodies and has been an external examiner on employment law at Glasgow University. Author of the chapter on employment law in Greene & Fletcher's 'The Law and Practice of Receivership in Scotland'.
Prof. Memberships: Law Society of Scotland, Royal Faculty of Procurators in Glasgow.
Career: Joined *MacRoberts* solicitors in 1966 and qualified in 1968. Became a Partner in 1972.
Personal: Born 24 December 1942. Educated at the High School of Glasgow 1949-60 and the University of Glasgow 1960-66. Vice-Chairman of the Royal Scottish Academy of Music and Drama; Governor of The High School of Glasgow; Chairman of the John Currie Singers Ltd; Chairman National Youth Choir of Scotland; Chairman Scottish International Piano Competition. Leisure interests include music and gardening. Lives in Glasgow.

WOFFENDEN, Sara
Bevan Ashford, Birmingham
(0121) 634 5038
sara.woffenden@bevanashford.co.uk
Specialisation: Partner in the Employment Department. Specialises in all aspects of employment law both non-contentious and contentious. Has a special interest in the TUPE regulations, family friendly policies, reorganisations and employee representation and has been part-time Chairman of the Employment Tribunal East Midlands since 1998. Regularly writes and lectures on employment law issues and has been listed in legal directories as a leader in her field.
Prof. Memberships: Part time Chairman of Employment Tribunals (England and Wales); Midlands representative on Management Committee of Employment Lawyers Association 1995-2000; Member of Training Committee of Employment Lawyers Association.
Career: Educated Leeds University. Admitted 1985. 1985-89 *Bettinsons*, Birmingham; 1989-94 *Pinsent & Co*; 1994-98 *Wragge & Co*; 1998 *Shoosmiths* – Partner; 2001 *Bevan Ashford* Birmingham – Partner.
Personal: Born 1959. Leisure interests currently limited to chauffeuring children (nine and five).

WYNN-EVANS, Charles
Dechert, London
(020) 7775 7545
charles.wynnevans@eu.dechert.com
Specialisation: Partner and head of the employment unit. Deals with all aspects of contentious and non-contentious employment law, including discrimination, transfers of undertakings, share option and incentive schemes, senior executive appointments and departures and restrictive covenant matters. Regularly contributes to journals and books on employment law matters.
Prof. Memberships: Industrial Law Society, Employment Lawyers' Association, Law Society.
Career: Joined *Titmuss Sainer & Webb* (now *Dechert*) in 1990. Qualified 1992. Appointed partner 1997.
Personal: Born 1967. Educated at King Henry VIII School Coventry; Bristol University (LLB 1988) and Merton College, Oxford (BCL 1990). Interests include cricket, rugby and current affairs. Married with one daughter and one son. Lives in Dulwich.

YATES, Tracy
Eversheds, Norwich
(01603) 272727
tracyyates@eversheds.com
Specialisation: Employment, handling unfair dismissal and a wide range of other Tribunals claims, including sex, race and disability discrimination, and breach of contract claims for commercial clients, including undertaking advocacy in the Employment Tribunals. Also handles wrongful dismissal claims in the courts. Advises commercial clients and senior employees in respect of compromise agreement/severage packages; and on all aspects of employment law (TUPE, redundancy, dismissals etc). Drafting, and advising on service agreements, consultancy agreements and statements of main terms and conditions of employment. Immigration: Advises on applications for entry clearance, work permits and naturalisation.
Prof. Memberships: Law Society and Employment Lawyers Association.
Career: Qualified October 1986. Trainee solicitor, *Daynes, Chittock & Back* 1984-86; partner *Eversheds* 1992 to date.
Personal: Two daughters – Helena and Sophia.

YOUNG, Jim
McGrigor Donald, Edinburgh
(0131) 777 7000
jim.young@mcgrigors.com
Specialisation: Team Leader of UK Employment. Has been involved in Employment Law since the initiation of UK legislation in the 1970s. Team Leader of UK Employment Law Unit and provides advice on a full range of Employment Law issues. Particular concerns of clients in the past year have included rationalisation issues; the impact of new regulation on working practices (ie part-timers); trade union issues including claims for recognition and legal remedies on possible strike action, and the increase in discrimination claims. Has represented and continues to represent a large number of clients at Employment Tribunals. Member of the Law Society Committee of Employment Law; member of Institute of Personnel and Management; speaker at conferences on various aspects of employment law; Scottish contributor to Employment Precedents and Company Policy documents.
Prof. Memberships: Law Society of Scotland; Institute of Personnel and Management.
Career: Qualified in 1975 at *McGrigor Donald & Co*. After two years as Legal Officer West Lothian District Council and two years as Assistant Solicitor at *Moncrieff Warren Patterson & Co.*, became Partner in 1979 and joined *McGrigor Donald* as Partner in 1985.
Personal: Born 26 February 1950. Educated at Hutchesons' Boys Grammar School and the University of Glasgow. Leisure interests include watching and participating in sport (now mainly golf), Contemporary Scottish Art and Theatre. Lives in Edinburgh.

YOUNSON, Fraser
McDermott, Will & Emery, London
(020) 7577 6992
fyounson@europe.mwe.com
Specialisation: (Bar 1975) Partner and Head of Employment Group. His practice covers all areas of contentious and non-contentious employment law, including executive severance, employment aspects of mergers and acquisitions, sex, race and disability discrimination, employee fraud, breach of fiduciary duties, restrictive covenants, wrongful and unfair dismissal and redundancy, TUPE, union recognition, industrial disputes, worker representation and European Work Councils, EU labour law, Employment Tribunal advocacy and compensation claims, transnational reorganisation and collective redundancies.
Prof. Memberships: Law Society, Industrial Law Society, Former Chairman and now life Vice-president of Employment Lawyers Association.
Career: Qualified for the Bar in 1975, and as a Solicitor in 1987. Previously Employment Law Adviser to British Aerospace Group HQ, and previously Editor of 'IDS Brief'. Joined *Baker & McKenzie* in 1983-99, becoming a Partner in 1990. Joined *McDermott, Will & Emery* 1999.
Publications: Author of 'Employment Law Handbook', 'Employment Law and Business Transfers – A Practical Guide', 'Croner's Industrial Relations Law', and contributor to 'PLC' and the 'Law Society Gazette' on employment law issues. Lectures extensively on labour law; 'Transfers of Undertakings' (Sweet & Maxwell).
Personal: Born 11th November 1952. Attended Oxford University. Lives in Houghton, Cambs.

ENERGY & NATURAL RESOURCES

London: 334; The Regions: 338; Scotland: 340; Profiles: 341

Research approved by BMRB For this edition, **Chambers'** researchers conducted 6,582 interviews – 3,900 with law firms, 511 with barristers and 2,171 with clients. The validity of the research was scrutinised by BMRB International, who audited both the methodology and the results at our offices in London. They interviewed **Chambers'** researchers and cross-checked sample interviews. Details of the audit appear on page 7.

OVERVIEW A moment's silence, please, for Enron. Its collapse caused collateral damage throughout the sector, and most especially to companies that emphasise energy trading over owning/operating plants. Most companies now face a tough market with little new investment and an atmosphere of caution. The market is rich in restructuring and refinancing. The LNG market is maturing nicely and, since it is predominantly governed by English law, generating plenty of work for the London firms. The majors are busy offloading their North Sea assets to smaller, more entrepreneurial companies. Coal mining in the North of England is giving way to low volumes of regeneration and open cast work. State aid to the coal industry is due to run out this year, despite moves to extend it. Price wars in the aggregates market are driving out small operators, and many await the impact of the aggregates tax due this year. M&A is down as the quarrying industry settles, while renewables continue to attract interest if not the volume of committment. New legislation on renewables is hoped for, as the government attempts to resolve difficulties posed by NETA and planning laws. US firms continue to do well in this market, especially those with international oil and gas and trading expertise. The future belongs to the larger firms with genuinely international reach, able to handle the global energy markets and M&A activity. There is an increased sector-wide focus away from projects towards trading and buying and selling assets. NETA has given rise to a steady stream of contracts work. With bilateral market relations now possible, there is a healthy level of instruction as old contracts based on the Pool are renegotiated.

LONDON

DENTON WILDE SAPTE (see firm details p.935) The team is renowned amongst our interviewees for its "*bespoke*" regulatory work on behalf of top-flight clients and its excellence in "*pure energy*" matters. A growing industrial client base includes work for electricity trading companies. "*Part of the industry's fabric*," the team was recently released from the advisory board of Ofgem and is able to act for clients such as ELEXON, the Balancing and Settlement Code company arising out of NETA. Although peers anticipate a break in its "*gamekeeper*" stereotype, with a greater emphasis placed on the breadth of its practice, work continues in the regulatory field for the likes of OFREG in Northern Ireland. Advice to the MOD on Project Aquatrine continues to boost its reputation in the water sector.

The traditional home of "*some of the best heads around,*" particularly at the senior level, the firm has this year seen the retirement of legendary Myles Cave-Browne-Cave. **James Dallas**, though regarded as a "*great lawyer,*" is thought to be less visible since becoming chair of the firm. Undisputed "*regulatory god*" **Charles Wood** is popular with clients and is "*always in the thick of things.*" Together with the respected **David Birchall**, he advised the DTI on whether to approve or modify transfer schemes submitted by electricity companies. The team also acted for TotalFinaElf on restructuring the Humber Power Project and related electricity trading issues, and advised Gazprom on matters relating to the West-East China Pipeline. The market awaits the impact on the firm's profile in minerals now that David Moroney has left to head up the Singapore practice. **Clients** Innogy; Powergen; British Energy; Scottish and Southern Energy; TotalFinaElf; DTI; ELEXON; London Electricity; Newmont Gold Company; OAO Gazprom; Amerada Hess; MOD; Transco.

HERBERT SMITH (see firm details p.992) The team is justly famous for its "*focused*" litigation, which is complemented by great regulatory (especially utilities) and transactional (especially public M&A) strength. It has a glittering client base and a growing reputation for gas and energy trading; and it handled the first financing of a power project under NETA for Centrica. Acknowledged by peers as a "*powerful force*" in heavily structured power deals, researchers heard about "*a genuine all-rounder*" that is "*easily one of the most outstanding practices in the field.*" The firm's environmental capacity is also trusted by prestige clients. The team is rich in stars and clients are reassured by its depth and expertise. "*Larger than life*" **Henry Davey** (see p.342) is "*hard-working and enthusiastic*" and renowned for power deals; he advised Northern Electric on its asset swap with Innogy. The "*superb*" **Paul Griffin** (see p.342) "*pulls the practice into the premier league*" and, alongside his respected power expertise, continues to dominate the field of oil and gas. **Richard Bond** (see p.341) is "*top of the tree*" and admired for his intellect and experience, though managerial duties keep him from the coalface. **Adrian Clough** (see p.341) is noted in electricity matters, and **Elizabeth McKnight** (see p.343) has a strong reputation at the Bar and is sought out for EU competition and regulatory advice. The "*extraordinarily able*" **Ted Greeno** (see p.342) is everywhere on the litigation scene and represented the CATS pipeline owners in a dispute with Enron. The water sector is still ruled by **Trevor Turtle** (see p.344), who handles corporate and regulatory matters for a range of water and sewerage companies, including the British Waterways Board. The team has been active in the development of the gas industry in Israel and the first LNG project in China. Instructed by Enterprise Oil, it advised on the contested takeover by Eni and also on the £4.3 billion bid by Shell Resources. **Clients** BP; Shell; TotalFinaElf; Marathon Oil; Anadarko Petroleum; Burlington Resources; Centrica; RWE; TXU; Goldman Sachs; Petrobras; Anglian Water; Electricité de France; Northern Electric; Enterprise Oil.

ALLEN & OVERY (see firm details p.841) "*Certainly not just bankers,*" the team has real depth and wins a high volume of repeat work from a core of "*élite clients*" on both transactional and regulatory matters. Efforts to build up a comprehensive energy practice have paid off, especially on the electricity side, where the dedicated European energy group shines. Possessing a "*good balance of pragmatism, industry knowledge and corporate prowess,*" the team is admired for its "*sheer quality*" and is a serious contender for the top slot. Clients value its "*commercial and receptive*" service, its European network and the "*peerless*" banking depth. The team retains its reputation for lending to the industry and still has "*the best name in the business for projects.*" "*Sector-striding*" **Ian Elder** (see p.342) heads up the energy group and has been busy with NETA and the £421 million sale of BG's gas storage business to Dynegy. He is assisted by **Mark Walker** (see p.344) ("*innovative – he thinks the issues through*"), a new entry to our tables this year, and one felt to "*cover a broad range of disciplines well.*" **John Scriven** (see p.344) has a construction background and leads a capable water team that advised Vivendi in its bid on Project Aquatrine. Commentators

LONDON ■ ENERGY & NATURAL RESOURCES

ENERGY & NATURAL RESOURCES
■ LONDON

1
- Denton Wilde Sapte
- Herbert Smith

2
- Allen & Overy
- Clifford Chance
- CMS Cameron McKenna
- Freshfields Bruckhaus Deringer
- Linklaters

3
- Ashurst Morris Crisp
- Norton Rose
- Slaughter and May

4
- Lovells
- Nabarro Nathanson
- Simmons & Simmons
- Vinson & Elkins LLP

5
- Dewey Ballantine
- Field Fisher Waterhouse
- Lawrence Graham
- Masons
- Morgan Cole
- Shearman & Sterling

6
- Baker & McKenzie
- Baker Botts
- Coudert Brothers
- Milbank, Tweed, Hadley & McCloy
- Watson, Farley & Williams
- White & Case

LEADING INDIVIDUALS
OIL & GAS

1
- GRIFFIN Paul *Herbert Smith*
- SALT Stuart *Linklaters*
- WOOD Charles *Denton Wilde Sapte*

2
- BOND Richard *Herbert Smith*
- PICTON-TURBERVILL Geoffrey *Ashurst Morris Crisp*
- STANGER Michael *Lovells*

3
- BLAKE Peter *Clifford Chance*
- DALLAS James *Denton Wilde Sapte*
- DAVEY Henry *Herbert Smith*
- ELDER Ian *Allen & Overy*
- GREENO Ted *Herbert Smith*
- HIGGINSON Antony *Baker Botts*
- PUGH Chris *Freshfields Bruckhaus Deringer*
- REES Jonathan *Freshfields Bruckhaus Deringer*
- SAUNDERS Mark *Dewey Ballantine*

4
- BRETTON Linda *Lawrence Graham*
- CARVER Jeremy *Clifford Chance*
- COFFELL Howard *Field Fisher Waterhouse*
- DANN Adam *Dewey Ballantine*
- JONES Gareth *Nabarro Nathanson*
- KING Ronnie *Ashurst Morris Crisp*
- VERRILL John *Lawrence Graham*

This book is the product of 6,582 1/2 hour interviews. See p.7 for BMRB audit. Within each band, firms are listed alphabetically. See individuals' profiles p.341

---

across the industry were sorry to see the retirement of Roger Davies. The team advised Petro-Canada on the $2 billion acquisition of upstream assets of Veba Oil & Gas and acted for BG Group in its $350 million acquisition of Enron's Indian upstream interests. **Clients** BG Group; TXU; ExxonMobil; The National Grid Company (NGC); Shell; AES; Duke Energy; RWE; Barking Power; British Energy; London Electricity.

CLIFFORD CHANCE (see firm details p.911) The firm fields senior figures, judged "*absolutely awesome*" by our interviewees, and the team as a whole is prominent in both upstream and electricity matters. Enjoying a reputation for "*top tier projects,*" the team benefits from the firm's famous banking practice and serves a raft of top banks as well as power, project and petrochemical companies. Experience in regulatory matters and in market reform stands out and the team has advised portfolio generators and IPPs on NETA-related matters. Beyond question is the reputation of "*client-friendly*" Peter Blake (see p.341) ("*bags of common sense – he cuts through complexity*") on whose shoulders the firm's reputation in this sector largely rests. He is especially known for his work on power projects, but his expertise cuts across the sector. On the oil and gas side, Jeremy Carver (see p.341) is a familiar figure on contentious matters and Michael Cuthbert (see p.342) remains highly respected for his mining skills. The team advised International Power on all tolling aspects of the Rugeley deal and continues to be involved with the project company on the Dolphin pipeline project. It also advised Dynegy on its acquisition of BG's storage business. **Clients** UtiliCorp United; Dynegy; Fortum; ABN AMRO; IFC; Electricité de France; HSBC; AES; InterGen; National Power.

CMS CAMERON MCKENNA (see firm details p.914) Competitors envy the prestigious reputation this team has in "*premier*" regulatory and electricity matters. Great experience in restructurings means that the team remains active in the aftermath of NETA's introduction and on the codification of connection arrangements. There are two regulatory stars here. Fiona Woolf (see p.345) is "*unique in the industry*" with her "*extraordinary experience*" in the field of electricity market design. A slightly lower profile this year is due to her temporary removal to the US to help authorities there with their own market restructuring. Robert Lane (see p.343) is the "*systems regulatory guru*" who provided regulatory expertise to the team that advised National Grid on its merger with Lattice. He is also involved in the establishment of the market in Northern Ireland and Interconnects with the Republic. The firm's political contacts and experience in Eastern Europe ensure a thriving water projects practice. Headed by the "*pleasant and approachable*" Richard Temple (see p.344), the team has increased its profile by acting for a major bidder on the Aquatrine deal.

On the oil and gas side, the team is better known for upstream work. Rafique Khan and Sally Tyne have taken on consultant roles within the firm; nevertheless, the practice remains buoyant and has recently acted for BP on the due diligence relating to Veba's sale of upstream assets. **Clients** NGC; NIE; RAO UES of Russia; BP; Enterprise Oil; Cairn Energy; OMV; state agencies; foreign governments; utilities.

FRESHFIELDS BRUCKHAUS DERINGER (see firm details p.964) This "*first-class*" outfit impressed our interviewees for its "*really superb*" M&A transactions and litigation. Dispute resolution is up thanks to market liberalisation and inevitable conflicts on regulatory and competition issues. Leading figure Chris Pugh (see p.343) is valued as a "*thoughtful litigator backed up by good assistants;*" he acted for Rowan and its UK subsidiary BAOL in the Gorilla dispute with Amoco (UK) et al. Our researchers heard great things of the team's work in gas and power regulatory matters. It has been busy on NETA work and contracts, projects and financings, and secured involvement in the post-Pool trading environment. Auctions and M&A in the oil and gas sector feature heavily and its head, Jon Rees (see p.343), acted for E.ON on its disposal of Veba Oel to BP. The team has also been active on behalf of German acquirers. Kent Rowey (see p.343) received warm commendation as a "*fine projects man,*" while Patrick Wallace (see p.344) is "*clearly excellent and knowledgeable.*" **Clients** BC Hydro; BNFL; E.ON; CMS Energy; Electricité de France; NGC; Powergen; Rowan Companies; ScottishPower; USExim; Agip; International Power; Goldman Sachs; Conoco.

LINKLATERS (see firm details p.1043) "*Splendid projects and financial services for banks*" are the signature theme of this top-drawer energy team, which acts for sponsors and lenders, governments and contractors with equal ease. Peers acknowledge the "*real quality*" of advice and high volume of instruction from clients such as BP and Innogy. Admired throughout the industry, Stuart Salt (see p.343) "*brings a combination of energy savvy and corporate professionalism.*" The team will be further enhanced by the return of "*specialist*" Jonathan Inman from Tokyo. Ever popular with trading companies thanks to its financial services expertise, the firm has recently acted as advisor to Innogy on the €8.5 billion acquisition offer by RWE. For combined M&A and mining experience, the "*invaluable*" Christopher Kelly (see p.342) continues to win approval. The team acted for Edison Mission on the £650 million sale of the Fiddler's Ferry and Ferrybridge plants, and advised the project company on the Sakhalin II project developing the Piltun-Astokhskoye and Lunskoye Fields. **Clients** London Electricity; Duke Energy; Dynegy; Edison Mission; El Paso; Innogy; Mirant; NRG; BP; Shell Gas; Sasol; BG Group.

ENERGY & NATURAL RESOURCES ■ LONDON

TOP IN-HOUSE LAWYERS

ELECTRICITY

Yehuda COHEN, Head of Legal, Dynegy Europe Ltd
Nigel FOWKES, Solicitor, Innogy Plc
Robert HIGSON, Group Solicitor & Company Secretary, London Electricity Group Plc
Eldon PETHYBRIDGE, General Counsel, British Gas

Nigel Fowkes and **Eldon Pethybridge** are commended for their "high level of technical ability" and for having a "sound knowledge" of the sector. Private practitioners applaud **Robert Higson**'s "absolutely excellent deal management skills" and claim he is "easy to work with," while **Yehuda Cohen** is respected for his knowledge of this ever developing sector.

OIL & GAS

David BATE, Legal Manager, Enterprise Energy Ireland
Barbara BLUM, Shell
Justin BOYD, Hess Energy
Ian CHITTY, Solicitor, BG Group
Alan DUNLOP, Vice President & General Counsel, Exploration and Production, Amerada Hess

A new addition to this year's list is the "outstanding" **Barbara Blum**, who comes highly recommended by those at the top of the industry. The "experience" and "efficiency" of **Alan Dunlop** and **David Bate** was the subject of much commendation. **Ian Chitty** was praised for his "good commercial understanding." **Justin Boyd** ("excellent abilities") has moved to Hess Energy following the collapse of Enron.

WATER

Keith DONALD, General Counsel, International Water
David Paul HOSKER, Head of Legal Services, United Utilities
Michael KNIGHT, Company Solicitor, Severn Trent Water
Victoria RIGBY, International Counsel, Vivendi Water

The highly reputable **David Paul Hosker** and **Victoria Rigby** are commended for their "efficiency." Sources singled out **Michael Knight** for his "extreme intelligence," while **Keith Donald** was warmly praised for his "commercial understanding."

In-house lawyer's profiles p.1201

ASHURST MORRIS CRISP (see firm details p.852) A healthy client base and good team depth ensure a loyal following in the marketplace, with particular accolades drawn to its M&A and upstream capabilities. An overseas reach is demonstrated by its action for the State of Kuwait in the renegotiation of the Arabian Oil Company's concession over the offshore divided zone, and the team has recently won a beauty contest to advise on petrochemical projects in the Middle East. "*Steady hand*" **Geoffrey Picton-Turbervill** (see p.343) advised KazTransOil on certain pipeline projects, and acted on a project in the recently created joint development zone between Nigeria and São Tomé e Principe. The team has a staunch reputation for dispute resolution domestically and overseas; it handles most of the contentious work for Centrica and is known for its abandonment and construction work. Litigation specialist **Ronnie King** (see p.561) appeared for an electricity supplier to the disputes panel set up under the Balancing and Settlement Code. "*Alone at the top*" on the mining side, **Philip Hurst** (see p.342) heads a mining and minerals practice with a strong overseas presence. It advised the ED Group on explorations in Peru and the Dominican Republic. It also acted for the Petrochemical Industries Company, a wholly owned subsidiary of Kuwait Petroleum Corporation, on two new major petrochemical projects in Kuwait, with a combined value of US$3.4 billion. **Clients** ScottishPower; BritNed; Singapore Power; ABN AMRO; AES; ANZ; BNP Paribas; CIBC; ESB National Grid; ExxonMobil Power; Renewable Energy Systems; Siemens.

SLAUGHTER AND MAY (see firm details p.1140) Although much of the energy practice is spun out of the firm's "*cracking*" corporate practice, it does include many significant one-offs. Most importantly, clients rave about the high quality throughout the team and its "*understanding of our business needs.*" The practice is handled by "*gifted individuals*" who undertake a smaller amount of oil and gas upstream and downstream work, some big projects and electricity trading work including contracts under NETA. About half of the practice is energy-related M&A, such as acting for E.ON in its acquisition of Powergen. This year has seen the retirement of Martin Roberts, whose finance skills have infused the team; he was part of the team that recently acted for Eesti Energia and the Republic of Estonia on the sale of part of the country's main electricity generator. Commentators extolled the "*absolutely stellar*" **Paul Stacey** (see p.344) ("*pleasant and pragmatic*"), who played an important role in the introduction of NETA and continues to advise various utilities on the renegotiation of their power purchase contracts (especially long term). **Clients** E.ON; United Utilities; HM Government; Irish Commission for Electricity Regulation; AES; YTL; Cluff Mining; Blue Circle; BHP; Shell; Star Capital Partners; Premier Oil; Enron; RWE; Thames Water.

LOVELLS (see firm details p.1045) David Moss leads a respected practice, which maintains its reputation for gas work, both regulatory and transactional, and has a name in energy trading. An impressive client base continues to drive a busy practice and the firm's international depth lends a healthy advantage. Dispute resolution is a key feature of the practice, and it has acted on electricity competition matters in Germany and advised oil majors and power companies in matters including arbitrations, ADR and court proceedings in Asia, the Americas and the CIS. The firm's Paris office gives it an edge in francophone Africa. Leading name here is undoubtedly **Michael Stanger** (see p.344) ("*exceptionally talented and highly commercial*") whose practice includes both upstream and power work. He was involved in the team's action for an international oil major's bid to develop upstream and midstream business in the CIS. **Clients** Statoil; Entergy-Koch Trading; Hess Energy Trading Company; Centrica; Amerada Hess Gas; ExxonMobil; BP Gas & Power; Esso UK.

NABARRO NATHANSON (see firm details p.1080) Twin centres in London and Sheffield afford the firm a great national practice with close ties to the North and the coal and mining industries there. A full-service practice with a virtual monopoly on coal work and niche expertise in mining, much of the workload comprises litigation for diverse energy clients. Commercial contracts and property are something of a staple, and the team is particularly well regarded for its work in environmentally compatible energy schemes and PFI/PPP. The team was recently appointed by Slough Heat & Power to advise on the effects of NETA on smaller generators. Head of group **Robert Tudway** (see p.344) is a familiar face in the electricity sector and is highly rated for his knowledge. He has a wide practice that covers generation, supply, gas and regulatory matters and is well known for his academic contributions to the field. "*Heavily used*" **Gareth Jones** (see p.342) has a reputation for straight contractual and regulatory work and is experienced in the gas, coal and mining side. The team acted for London Electricity on a contract for a flue gas desulphurisation plant at a Nottinghamshire power plant, and advised on the Channel Tunnel Rail Link and other private electricity distribution projects. It has also been handling a number of quarry development proposals for Lafarge. **Clients** Bonus Windfarms; BRECSU; BP; British Sugar; Celtic Energy; The Coal Authority; Conoco; EniChem; London Electricity; The London Power Company; RJB Mining; Southampton City Council; UK Nirex; UK Waste Management.

SIMMONS & SIMMONS (see firm details p.1136) Endorsed by our interviewees for its steady workflow from oil majors, the team has a good reputation for upstream, pipelines and regulatory work in Europe and China and, particularly, the Middle East. A "*fine showing in the Caspian*" region is reflected in the firm's work for BP on its involvement in the Caspian Pipeline Consortium. The team inspires respect for its contentious work, as well as for M&A and finance-related matters, and while its work for Enron was largely limited to derivatives-related work, instruction levels should not be affected by the recent collapse. As well as ongoing work on Project Dolphin, the team, including Susan Beck, acted for BG and Amerada Hess on North Sea development. **Clients** Amerada Hess; BG; BP; Beijing Datang; ExxonMobil; Mitsubishi; Northern Ireland Department of Enterprise, Trade and Investment; Ofgem; PETRONAS; Shell; Taiwan National Power; TotalFinaElf; Texaco; UAE Offsets Group; Veba Oil & Gas; Vivendi.

LONDON — ENERGY & NATURAL RESOURCES

LEADING INDIVIDUALS
ELECTRICITY

1. **BLAKE Peter** Clifford Chance
   ELDER Ian Allen & Overy
   WOOLF Fiona CMS Cameron McKenna
2. **DAVEY Henry** Herbert Smith
   LANE Robert CMS Cameron McKenna
   SALT Stuart Linklaters
   STACEY Paul Slaughter and May
3. **BIRCHALL David** Denton Wilde Sapte
   CLOUGH Adrian Herbert Smith
   GRIFFIN Paul Herbert Smith
   MCKNIGHT Elizabeth Herbert Smith
   PICTON-TURBERVILL Geoffrey Ashurst Morris Crisp
   ROWEY Kent Freshfields Bruckhaus Deringer
   TUDWAY Robert Nabarro Nathanson
   WALKER Mark Allen & Overy
   WALLACE Patrick Freshfields Bruckhaus Deringer

ASSOCIATES TO WATCH
TOWNER Chris Herbert Smith

LEADING INDIVIDUALS
MINING

1. **HURST Philip** Ashurst Morris Crisp
2. **CUTHBERT Michael** Clifford Chance

UP AND COMING
KELLY Christopher Linklaters

LEADING INDIVIDUALS
WATER

1. **TURTLE Trevor** Herbert Smith
2. **TEMPLE Richard** CMS Cameron McKenna
3. **LANE Mark** Masons
   SCRIVEN John Allen & Overy

See individuals' profiles p.341

VINSON & ELKINS LLP (see firm details p.1176) Globally, there are few firms able to equal V&E's reputation in the energy sector, and the long-established London branch is regarded as "*by far the best US firm in this market.*" Its roots lie in classic oil and gas business, and with an aggressive and dynamic corporate depth, the team continues to win the support of prestige energy clients and competitors. An absence of top-flight UK lawyers, coupled with the collapse of flagship client Enron, leads some commentators to wonder how the office is set to develop; researchers found, however, that the team grew steadily in 2001. The practice has diversified, adding projects and structured finance depth to its traditional oil, gas, power and regulatory capacity. Also, there is now clear expertise in dispute resolution as the contentious practice is bolstered with fresh blood. A varied workload has included acting for Shell on an LNG port in India and acting for a bidder for a stake in Project Dolphin. John LaMaster led a team acting for Fortum in the €180 million divestiture of interests in Oman to Mitsui. **Clients** First Reserve; Duke Energy; Dynegy; Fortum; FW Oil; Kazakh State Pipeline Company; Government of Lithuania; LUKOIL; Shell.

DEWEY BALLANTINE (see firm details p.937) The consistent quality of this "*genuine energy team*" cannot be overlooked. In addition to a thriving international practice in oil and gas and power projects, the London team, headed by the "*truly outstanding*" Mark Saunders (see p.344) ("*a name to conjure with*"), undertakes highly specialist corporate work for the likes of TotalFinaElf, Powergen and Premier Oil. It is also building a fine reputation for itself in the energy trading markets, and is engaged in the negotiation and finalisation of contracts for American Electric Power (AEP) in the UK and throughout Europe. The team acted for TotalFinaElf in its £100 million disposal of two gas transportation companies. The profile of the London office is set to rise with the recent elevation of the acclaimed and experienced **Adam Dann** (see p.342) to the partnership. **Clients** TotalFinaElf; Premier Oil; Varco; OMV; Oil Spill Response; AEP; Alpha Thames; NRG Energy; Amerada Hess; Agip; Occidental Petroleum; Ruhrgas; Willbros.

FIELD FISHER WATERHOUSE (see firm details p.954) This highly respected team is frequently mentioned by peers, and researchers found that it continues to enjoy an "*unequalled*" reputation in pipeline matters. In this field, "*you can't get any better*" than **Howard Coffell** (see p.342), "*a true specialist*" admired for his expertise and effectiveness.

LAWRENCE GRAHAM (see firm details p.1031) Lower in profile since the takeover of Lasmo, our interviewees felt that the team has yet to reassert itself. However, researchers report a general endorsement of the team's quality and some optimistic speculation on its future development. Clients endorsed the "*vigorous efforts*" of **John Verrill** and **Linda Bretton** remains highly respected by key players.

MASONS (see firm details p.1057) Nationally active, this team gets ten out of ten for "*pushing aggressively in this sector,*" with an increasing international workload and a good profile on the Paris scene. Its construction industry prowess should not obscure a well-rounded energy practice that encompasses oil and gas, power and water. The "*indispensable*" **Mark Lane** (see p.342) remains respected, and researchers were told that the team looks "*increasingly credible*" since its creation two years ago. It is well regarded for its expertise in FPSOs, fixed and floating platforms and nuclear and fossil fuel power stations, and is growing its knowledge in renewables. Business has been brisk in Scotland, where the team recently closed two major PPP projects. An established practice in contentious matters assists the energy group and the firm's profile in the water sector remains buoyant thanks to ongoing work for ONDEO Degrémont. Highlight transactions of the last year include acting for AWG in negotiations for the Beijing No.10 BOT water project and advising the Government of Sri Lanka in the Greater Negombo water privatisation. The team also acted for MJ Gleeson on the £100 million Loch Katrine water project. **Clients** TBV Power; AEA Technology; Innogy Holdings; NGC; National Wind Power; Ogden Group of Companies; Black & Veatch International (USA); Kvaerner Oil & Gas; TXU Europe; Odebrecht Oil & Gas Services; Duke Engineering; OWL Technologies; ONDEO Degrémont.

MORGAN COLE (see firm details p.1075) Clients agree that the "*speed and depth of this firm is fantastic,*" and it is sought after for "*first-rate quality at non-City prices.*" The team also elicits the spontaneous approbation of barristers, especially for oil-related work. The experienced and efficient team is made up of "*personable lawyers of the best calibre*" and provides a good regional network; the latter may be one reason why no individual personalities were singled out during the research. Expertise in oil and gas exploration is kept sharp through involvement in North Sea projects, and the team is also active downstream. Work for Kerr-McGee recently included the integration of a swathe of gas fields and a connecting pipeline with an existing third-party export system. The team is also engaged in arbitration work for TotalFinaElf. **Clients** BP; TotalFinaElf; British Energy; Kerr-McGee; Conoco; Lagos State; Scottish & Southern Energy; International Power.

SHEARMAN & STERLING (see firm details p.1129) Due to market conditions, this team has had a lower profile than some commentators had anticipated. All the same, this "*international projects engine*" crops up in a range of matters and continues to win the respect of peers. Best known for its finance-related work, the team undertakes high-end work, but not volume. The considerable London practice is bound up with offices on the Continent and in the Middle East. In a matter involving both Islamic financing and English law, the team acted for the arrangers on the $1.6 billion Shuweihat independent water and power project in Abu Dhabi. **Clients** BG; Edison Mission; Bechtel; AES Oasis; CMS Energy; AngloGold; InterGen; PSEG Global; Azurix; Wessex Water.

BAKER & MCKENZIE (see firm details p.855) Led by Hugh Stewart and Neil Donoghue, this international firm draws its clients from around the world and a range of sectors. Researchers found a strongly transactional practice with international scope, which has nevertheless been developing its domestic UK/EU business. Globally, the focus is on upstream and downstream oil and gas, and the London office is supported by an impressive network encompassing the world's principal petrochemical centres. The coverage is illustrated by acting for BP Chemicals in its multibillion dollar US and European

ENERGY & NATURAL RESOURCES ■ LONDON/THE SOUTH/MIDLANDS

joint ventures in high density polyethylene. Niche expertise is in multi-jurisdictional M&A and oil and gas pipelines, and the team is rated for its competition advice across the sector. On the electricity side, it has focused on M&A, power projects and trading, and leads the way on climate change issues. The European offices, especially London and Paris, garner special praise for work in the water sector. The team has also acted for the consortium leading the $410 million financing of the Sohar and Salalah pipelines in Oman. **Clients** BP Chemicals; Calpine; Shell International; Arab Banking Corporation; IBJ; EIB; LG International; AES; Siemens; BNP Paribas; Vivendi; ONDEO.

BAKER BOTTS (see firm details p.854) Within this thriving global practice, the London team boasts "*a steady flow of work for some interesting clients*," and the team has swollen to the tune of four associates to handle the workload. It is led by **Tony Higginson** (see p.342) ("*damned good stuff!*") on such matters as acting for Dove Energy on the development of oilfields in Yemen and various North Sea transactions for EDC. Oil and gas occupies much of its market profile, but the firm has also been active on electricity trading and gas for energy generation for the likes of Dynegy and Reliant. **Clients** RWE; Odebrecht Oil & Gas; Veba Oil & Gas; Dynegy; Reliant; Baker Hughes; DNO; Dove Energy; EDC (Europe); Gaz de France;

Sasol; Entergy Power Group; Frontera Resources; LUKOIL.

COUDERT BROTHERS (see firm details p.920) The movement of Steven Beharrell to chair the firm from New York has diminished the London team's profile in this sector. The team continues to be recommended for its work in international dispute resolution, project financing and transactional M&A.

MILBANK, TWEED, HADLEY & MCCLOY (see firm details p.1070) The firm's international projects practice, which is backed by an impeccable banking operation, continues to have a strong following amongst peers. It acts mainly on the sponsor/borrowers' side and was involved for BNP Paribas and WestLB in the financing of the Salalah power project in Oman. It was also appointed by Viridian to advise the sponsors on the €220 million financing of the first independent power project in Eire. **Clients** Tractebel; TotalFinaElf; Shell; International Power; Foster Wheeler; WestLB; Deutsche Bank; Chase; ABN AMRO; BNP Paribas.

WATSON, FARLEY & WILLIAMS (see firm details p.1181) Led by Douglas Wardle, this team is acknowledged to have increased its profile and involvement in the sector. It is respected for its work on power generation projects in Eastern Europe, Spain and the UK. It also has a strong track record in LNG transportation and upstream oil. The firm advised Horizon Energy on an Italian IPP at Montenero di Bisaccia, and acted for AES Sirocco on a €1 billion brownfield coal-fired power plant at Maritsa East 1 in Bulgaria. **Clients** Exmar; Sempra; Gaz de France; DaimlerChrysler; AES; Horizon Energy; Duke Energy International; Bluewater; Odebrecht-SLP Engineering; Petroleum Geo-Services.

WHITE & CASE (see firm details p.1185) Endorsed by peers during our research, the firm's energy profile derives from its strong international projects and power practice. It is particularly noted for work in Eastern and Central Europe, Russia and the CIS. The team has grown over the last year and features expertise in energy-related construction matters, disputes, finance and M&A. Projects man Peter Finlay is the well-known and respected contact here. The team acted for Nordea Bank Finland in the financing of a floating power station in the Dominican Republic for EGE Haina. It also advised MOL on its planned synthetic merger with PKN. **Clients** ABN AMRO; ANZ; Hungarian Privatisation Authority (APV); BNP Paribas; DEPA; EBRD; HypoVereinsbank; International Power; Lasmo; Mission Energy; Newmont Mining Corporation; Shell; Williams Energy.

THE SOUTH

ENERGY & NATURAL RESOURCES — THE SOUTH

1 Bond Pearce — Plymouth, Southampton
2 Veale Wasbrough — Bristol

LEADING INDIVIDUALS

1 SMITHERS Tim — Veale Wasbrough
TRINICK Marcus — Bond Pearce

This book is the product of 6,582 1/2 hour interviews. See p.7 for BMRB audit. Within each band, firms are listed alphabetically. See individuals' profiles p.341

BOND PEARCE (see firm details p.879) The practice here has its roots in environmental law and the firm remains pre-eminent in the renewables sector. The team is acknowledged for its work in acquisitions, planning and financing of both on- and offshore projects, and is busier than ever in Scotland. The firm has recently expanded its expertise to cover energy from waste projects. The increasing acceptance of wind farming has boosted the firm's national profile and the reputation of **Marcus Trinick** (see p.344) in particular; he is especially respected for his work on the financing side. The team acts on the majority of offshore wind farm projects in the country, and is active in the waste and minerals sectors and on tidal and marine current projects. **Clients** United Utilities; Shell; British Energy; ScottishPower; National Wind Power; TXU; Renewable Energy Systems.

VEALE WASBROUGH (see firm details p.1174) **Tim Smithers**' (see p.736) hand is firmly on the tiller and this team maintains its reputation as cross-country UK pipeline specialists. Esso's Jetline aviation fuel pipeline still constitutes the bulk of the workload, with the team offering advice on planning, regulatory and environmental requirements. The firm has recently been instructed on a compulsory purchase project for Transco. **Clients** Esso Petroleum Company; TotalFinaElf; Transco; Huntsman.

MIDLANDS

ENERGY & NATURAL RESOURCES — MIDLANDS

1 Wragge & Co — Birmingham
2 Eversheds — Birmingham
  Knight & Sons — Newcastle-under-Lyme
  Martineau Johnson — Birmingham
3 Edwards Geldard — Derby
  Kent Jones and Done — Stoke-on-Trent

This book is the product of 6,582 1/2 hour interviews. See p.7 for BMRB audit. Within each band, firms are listed alphabetically.

WRAGGE & CO (see firm details p.1197) The practice has grown by a quarter over the last year and there are some impressive new names on the client list. The team is able to field experienced in-housers. In a boost to its international practice, the team has acted on non-revenue water projects in Poland and Malaysia and been appointed the main legal advisor to Severn Trent International. Researchers were told of deep electricity expertise in particular and of high deal volumes, particularly in "*tough M&A.*" Practice head **Neil Upton** is commended for his "*industry knowledge;*" he acted for Powergen on the development of the Scroby Sands offshore wind farm project. Transactionally focused **David Hamlett** "*suits the team's commercial outlook.*" The team acted for RWE Trading UK on its Grid Trade Master agreements. **Clients** AES Energy; Amey Utilities; Aquila Energy; BP; British Energy; East Midlands Electricity; Fortum; Kinetica; Government of Macedonia; London Electricity; Marubeni; MOD; National Grid; Powergen; Severn Trent.

MIDLANDS/THE NORTH ■ ENERGY & NATURAL RESOURCES

ENERGY & NATURAL RESOURCES
■ MIDLANDS

1
- Wragge & Co Birmingham

2
- Eversheds Birmingham
- Knight & Sons Newcastle-under-Lyme
- Martineau Johnson Birmingham

3
- Edwards Geldard Derby
- Kent Jones and Done Stoke-on-Trent

LEADING INDIVIDUALS

1
- HAMLETT David Wragge & Co
- UPTON Neil Wragge & Co
- WHITEHEAD Andrew Martineau Johnson

2
- BRENNAN Paul Martineau Johnson
- CALLADINE Paul Knight & Sons
- REEVES Tony Kent Jones and Done

This book is the product of 6,552 1/2 hour interviews. See p.7 for BMRB audit. Within each band, firms are listed alphabetically. See individuals' profiles p.341

EVERSHEDS (see firm details p.949) Best known for its work on the electricity side, the team also handles gas, mining, water and energy trading, with a national profile that reflects its cohesive team approach. An experienced downstream practice is coupled with the achievement of a creditable reputation in renewables. Its international profile is the highest of any firm in this table. Department head Malcolm Titcomb is highly respected. Highlights of the year include acting for 24 Seven Utility Services in a joint venture with Stadtwerke Kiel to manage and operate electricity, water and gas distribution networks in the Kiel area. The team also advised Cleveland Potash on a combined heat and power tolling agreement for a mining company. **Clients** Cinergy; Midlands Electricity; Ridgewood Power; Energy Power Resources; 24 Seven Utility Services; Eskom; TXU Energy; Trinity Energy.

KNIGHT & SONS "*Outstanding*" minerals specialists, this team is respected by peers for its work with some of the top minerals operators in the country on acquisitions and disposals, ownership and environmental matters. The team acts on options for mineral leases and plant site leases, and offers advice on tax-saving schemes in connection with the aggregates tax. Praised for its depth, clients also feel that the team is "*resource-rich*" and "*able to handle anything.*" Tony Bell remains active in his new role as consultant, while our interviewees were keen to endorse the "*impressive*" Paul Calladine (see p.341). **Clients** Ibstock Brick; Hanson Quarry Products Europe; WBB Minerals.

MARTINEAU JOHNSON (see firm details p.1056) This "*quality bunch, boosted by ex-industry lawyers,*" offers experienced advice on regulatory and contractual issues; it is often brought in to redraft documents whenever there is a modification to the CUSC. Most of the workload is in the electricity sector, with gas work also a feature, and the firm has close ties to the renewables sector. Leading partners **Andrew Whitehead** (see p.345) and **Paul Brennan** (see p.341) have the respect of both peers and clients. The team advised new client Warwick Energy on the purchase of a portfolio of generating assets from the receivers of Independent Energy, and acted for NGC on aspects of the introduction of NETA. **Clients** npower Direct; NGC; East Midlands Pipelines; EnMO.

EDWARDS GELDARD (see firm details p.944) Ongoing work for Powergen occupies much of the time of Roman Surma's utilities-dominated practice. The team has a track record in advising on business separation and a review of connection agreements to comply with NETA and the Utilities Act. Work in renewables sees the team advising a variety of clients on the new renewables regime and the climate levy. **Clients** Powergen; United Utilities Green Energy; BNFL.

KENT JONES AND DONE (see firm details p.1020) This niche minerals specialist practice boasts some top-flight clients, including mineral operators and The Crown Estate. It undertakes both planning and mining work. Tony Reeves has an established reputation in minerals law and is an authority on coal mining subsidence. Recent matters include advising on lease arrangements in Staffordshire, a quarry extension in Cheshire and contested restoration obligations in Derbyshire. **Clients** The Crown Estate; Laporte; landed estates; mineral operators.

THE NORTH

ENERGY & NATURAL RESOURCES
■ THE NORTH

1
- Nabarro Nathanson Sheffield

2
- Addleshaw Booth & Co Leeds
- Dickinson Dees Newcastle upon Tyne
- Wake Dyne Lawton Chester

3
- DLA Leeds
- Hammond Suddards Edge Manchester
- Pinsent Curtis Biddle Leeds
- Wrigleys Leeds

LEADING INDIVIDUALS

1
- LOGAN Niall Nabarro Nathanson
- LYNCH Malcolm Wrigleys
- RENGER Mike Nabarro Nathanson
- WAKE Brian Wake Dyne Lawton
- WHITAKER Neil Pinsent Curtis Biddle

This book is the product of 6,582 1/2 hour interviews. See p.7 for BMRB audit. Within each band, firms are listed alphabetically. See individuals' profiles p.341

NABARRO NATHANSON (see firm details p.1080) "*Top of the heap*" full-service practice, it has a virtual monopoly on coal work. Expertise covers all aspects of minerals, mining and quarrying, as well as litigation for energy clients. The team also handles commercial contracts and the environment and property aspects of a deal. Highlight matters of the last year include acting for London Electricity on a contract for a flue gas desulphurisation plant at a Nottinghamshire power plant and advising Lafarge Aggregates on quarry development proposals. The "*thorough*" Niall Logan (see p.343) is an expert on mineral right issues and the lead partner for The Coal Authority. Mike Renger (see p.343) is courted by clients seeking his litigation and environment expertise in liabilities arising out of the abandonment and restoration of mines and quarries. **Clients** The Coal Authority; UK COAL; Celtic Energy; Hanson Brick; Pioneer Aggregates.

ADDLESHAW BOOTH & CO (see firm details p.838) This "*great energy outfit*" handles both corporate and specialist energy work for an envied client base. Energy trading contracts and renewables work are increasing in volume, and the team also tackles metering and projects/PFI in the utilities sector. Commentators praised the team's work in waste to energy and outsourcing of water treatment. Sandra Humphrey leads the team that continues to act for Brey Utilities on its £800 million bid on the MOD's Aquatrine project. The team advised Yorkshire Water in the negotiation and drafting of its renewables portfolio of contracts. **Clients** Kelda Group; Brey Utilities; Aquila Energy; Innogy; UtiliCorp.

DICKINSON DEES (see firm details p.938) The market acknowledges a "*broad practice of real quality*" with expertise in gas, regulatory issues and power and electricity. The team advises its "*committed client base*" on issues arising out of NETA and associated contracts. Work for major client Northern Electric includes advising on the split of its supply and distribution businesses under the Utilities Act 2000 and a range of regulatory and supply and purchase advice in the electricity and gas markets. The team is also experienced in the Renewables Obligation and the Climate Change Levy. **Clients** Northern Electric; offshore producers and suppliers; generators; PFI sponsors.

WAKE DYNE LAWTON (see firm details p.1177) Interviewees agree that this "*small but perfectly formed*" team has "*recruited well*" and

ENERGY & NATURAL RESOURCES ■ THE NORTH/SCOTLAND

is "*thriving.*" Specialists in coal and wind, with some pipeline work, its workload is also largely concerned with minerals, and on the extraction side, the practice acts for landowners and operators on various schemes. Clients hail from the northern Home Counties, Dorset, East Midlands and Cheshire. There has been notable growth in renewables, and the practice acts for wind farm developers both locally and in Europe. Winning universal acclaim is the experienced former in-house lawyer **Brian Wake** (see p.363). "*Ebullient and highly practical,*" he has the ability to "*talk to the industry in its own language.*" **Clients** Tarmac; Renewable Development Company; Peel Holdings.

DLA The team was boosted by the acquisition of Roger Collier from Hammonds. It has made a concerted bid for dominance in the minerals area, and peers acknowledge its real depth in this respect.

HAMMOND SUDDARDS EDGE The team's profile in the North has diminished with the loss of Roger Collier to DLA and the retirement of Gwyn Williams. The firm continues with its focus on power generation and transmission and waste water facilities. Its client base includes energy and water companies, and power station operators and developers.

PINSENT CURTIS BIDDLE (see firm details p.1102) This "*solid and dependable*" dedicated minerals and landfill unit continues to secure a following for its high-quality minerals work on behalf of operators and landowners. Neil Whitaker (see p.345) ("*bright and effective*") has particular expertise on the property side and acts for a number of landed estates and for Hanson. **Clients** Hanson.

WRIGLEYS (see firm details p.1199) A niche team here acts for landowners on granting options and extraction licenses for opencast coal mining, sand and gravel. A major source of instruction is the nascent wind farming industry, where **Malcolm Lynch** (see p.343) is prominent on projects involving local communities. The team is active in the development of a market in woodchip fuels. **Clients** Baywind Energy Co-operative.

SCOTLAND   OIL & GAS

ENERGY: OIL & GAS
■ SCOTLAND

1. **CMS Cameron McKenna** Aberdeen
   Ledingham Chalmers Aberdeen
   Paull & Williamsons Aberdeen

LEADING INDIVIDUALS

1. **RUDDIMAN Robert** Ledingham Chalmers
   WARNE Penelope CMS Cameron McKenna
   UP AND COMING
   MILLAR Stephen Paull & Williamsons

This book is the product of 6,582 1/2 hour interviews. See p.7 for BMRB audit. Within each band, firms are listed alphabetically. See individuals' profiles p.341

CMS CAMERON MCKENNA (see firm details p.914) The Aberdeen office is focused on the oil and gas industry, with much of the workload centred on service contracts and on licensing and regulatory matters. There is a considerable litigation capacity and fee-earners are qualified in both English and Scots law. This team is rapidly expanding and there is an Edinburgh office that handles Court of Session cases. The practice is led out of London and Aberdeen by **Penelope Warne** (see p.344), who has been actively involved in advising oil companies on oil and gas exploration activities in the Faroe Islands. **Clients** BP; Cairn Energy; Conoco; ExxonMobil; Enterprise Oil; Shell UK.

LEDINGHAM CHALMERS (see firm details p.1034) This "*impressive bunch*" of "*pure oil and gas specialists*" handles a broad range of work for both operators and service providers. The practice ranges across the oil and gas sector and is noted for experience in agreements for bidding and licensing, pipelines, transportation, joint operations and unitisation. It boasts a rich and deep technical expertise and the workload includes a "*truly international*" dimension centred on Eastern Europe, the Middle East and North Africa. The team is led by **Robert Ruddiman** (see p.343) ("*simply the best*"), and acted for Ramco Energy on a joint venture in Poland with German utility RWE and advised the Seven Heads gas development off Ireland. The team also advised TotalFinaElf Exploration UK on the SEAL/SILK pipeline system and its involvement in an international joint venture/acquisition. **Clients** Amalgamated Scottish Oil; Aramark; Centrica; Conoco; Dana Petroleum; Fugro-UDI; George Craig Group/North Star Shipping; Highland Energy; John Wood Group; Ministry of Oil, Bahrain; Ramco Energy; Ruhrgas; Schlumberger; Stolt Offshore; Talisman Energy; TotalFinaElf Exploration UK; Tullow Oil; Turkish Petroleum.

PAULL & WILLIAMSONS (see firm details p.1096) This "*class corporate act*" is increasingly looking to London clients, for whom it provides advice on North Sea gas matters. The staple diet here is the buying and selling of North Sea assets and North Sea developments. A major source of business is the transfer of ownership from the traditional majors to smaller players as the market matures. **Stephen Millar** (see p.343) is regarded by his peers as "*enthusiastic and committed.*" He was part of a team acting for Talisman Energy in a North Sea asset exchange with Intrepid Energy, and advised ARCO British in the transfer of operatorship in a number of southern North Sea fields to ExxonMobil. **Clients** Talisman Energy (UK); BP Exploration Operating Company; Kerr-McGee North Sea; Dana Petroleum; First Oil.

SCOTLAND   ELECTRICITY

SHEPHERD+ WEDDERBURN (see firm details p.1130) Its reputation for electricity work north of the border is "*unparalleled.*" The team is picking up "*better work than ever*" through its close relationship with ScottishPower. **James Saunders** (see p.344) is dual qualified and heads the team. He was commended to researchers for his "*breadth of experience*" encompassing trading contracts at home and in Europe. Last year he led teams completing trading contracts for ScottishPower, advising on arrangements for trading between Scotland, Northern Ireland and the Republic of Ireland, and acting on several oil and gas transactions. **Clients** ScottishPower; Scottish Electricity Settlements; Manweb; Electricity Association; CRE Energy; Shell Renewables UK; Natural Power; Electricity Supply Nominees; Waverley Mining Finance; Fergusson Coals; Cairn Energy; Edinburgh Oil & Gas; Transco.

BIGGART BAILLIE (see firm details p.871) This respected team is best known for handling consumer-facing contracts for ScottishPower in Scotland and Northern Ireland. As the boundaries between gas and power are increasingly blurred, the firm has captured a more diverse portfolio of work. The team handles all ScottishPower's gas purchasing and is heavily involved in gas storage projects. The "*redoubtable*" **David Ross** remains the most famous face here; he led a team advising ScottishPower on the proposed 60 million therms underground gas storage project in Cheshire. The team also advised ScottishPower on the renegotiation of its gas supply contract for the Rye House power station, recently purchased from Powergen. **Clients** ScottishPower; Shell; BP.

SCOTLAND/THE LEADERS ■ ENERGY & NATURAL RESOURCES

ENERGY: ELECTRICITY
■ SCOTLAND

1
- Shepherd+ Wedderburn Edinburgh

2
- Biggart Baillie Glasgow
- Dundas & Wilson CS Edinburgh
- MacRoberts Glasgow

3
- Burness Edinburgh, Glasgow
- McGrigor Donald Glasgow

4
- Harper Macleod Glasgow

LEADING INDIVIDUALS

1
- CUMMING Donald Dundas & Wilson CS
- DICKSON Ian MacRoberts
- ROSS David Biggart Baillie
- SAUNDERS James Shepherd+ Wedderburn

This book is the product of 6,582 1/2 hour interviews. See p.7 for BMRB audit. Within each band, firms are listed alphabetically. See individuals' profiles p.341.

DUNDAS & WILSON CS (see firm details p.943) An acclaimed broad utilities-focused practice, it operates across the UK and is noted for its electricity work, both in projects and regulatory matters. The firm's extrication from Andersen Legal is anticipated to have little effect in this sector. The group has acted on several NETA generated matters, where it "*held its own*" against English firms. It has acted for Scottish and Southern Energy (SSE) on the separation of its business into dedicated subsidiaries under the Utilities Act 2000, and is set to continue its involvment with these subsidiaries. Researchers found a staunch following at the Bar, where commentators rate its contentious practice "*amongst the best.*" Partners advised SSE in its Court of Session litigation with British Energy and ScottishPower over the price of the output of Scotland's nuclear plants. Acting for each of the three Scottish Water authorities across the board, the team was notably connected with the Loch Katrine project. Commentators flagged up the team's "*considerable oil and gas capability*" on the trading, transport and finance sides. **Donald Cumming** heads the energy team and is one of the best known and admired names in Scotland. **Clients** Scottish and Southern Energy; BizzEnergy; Tullis Russell Papermakers; EPR Scotland; Transco; water authorities.

MACROBERTS (see firm details p.1049) Clients like this firm because it comprises "*good businessmen and great lawyers.*" The team is noted for its work in the nuclear sector and for its contribution on contentious matters. **Ian Dickson** (see p.236) leads a practice that acts for "*top clients*" on a range of matters. **Clients** British Energy; Scottish Nuclear; Nuclear Energy.

BURNESS Operating out of its offices in Edinburgh and Glasgow, this team has an acknowledged reputation in power projects and, increasingly, renewables. It remains "*highly respected*" for its work on power generators. John Miller heads the projects practice and has expertise in the water and waste water sectors. It has acted for Shanks Group in its bid to manage Argyll and Bute Council's PPP waste project.

MCGRIGOR DONALD (see firm details p.1065) This team's reputation is for quality corporate work and it wins plaudits for its work on the Scotland Northern Ireland Interconnect. The group operates under the firm's broader projects practice and has expertise in a range of issues including waste water.

HARPER MACLEOD (see firm details p.985) The group is respected by our interviewees for "*quality in its niche;*" it is most closely associated with minerals mining, waste management and coal. It undertakes both transactional and contentious work for its principal client, the Scottish Coal Company (SCC). The team is led by Rod McKenzie, a litigation specialist who handles SCC's contractual disputes, and the team has acted for SCC in the acquisition of the Miller Group's coal mining interests. **Clients** SCC; Aardvark TMC.

THE LEADERS IN ENERGY

BIRCHALL, David
Denton Wilde Sapte, London
(020) 7242 1212

BLAKE, Peter
Clifford Chance, London
(020) 7600 1000
peter.blake@cliffordchance.com
Specialisation: Banking and finance. Partner specialising in general company and commercial work, energy, oil, gas, natural resources and project finance.
Career: Partner since 1983.

BOND, Richard
Herbert Smith, London
(020) 7374 8000
richard.bond@herbertsmith.com
Specialisation: Senior partner since 2000. Wide ranging experience of corporate transactions, particularly in the fields of energy and privatisations.
Prof. Memberships: Council member of the Section on Energy and Natural Resources Law (SERL) of the International Bar Association.
Career: Qualified in 1969. Partner with *Herbert Smith* since 1977.

BRENNAN, Paul
Martineau Johnson, Birmingham
(0121) 678 1527
paul.brennan@martjohn.com
Specialisation: Advises energy companies and major users on emissions and energy trading, transportation CHP and renewable energy projects, also advises on competitive water supply. Career highlights include international litigation involving production assets in Kazakhstan, de-merger of British Gas plc and associated gas purchase and transportation arrangements, drafted Network Codes for Phoenix Natural Gas and East Midlands Pipelines Ltd, advised on the establishment of EnMO, an online energy market.
Prof. Memberships: Law Society, UK Energy Lawyers Association, Society for Computers & Law.
Career: Stonyhurst College, Durham University; Leeds University; College of Law; articled *TV Edwards & Co*. Various positions BG plc. Partner, *Martineau Johnson Solicitors* 1997.
Publications: Editor: 'Code Update'.
Personal: Born 1961, resides Warwick with wife and two children. Interests - cricket, football and the other arts.

BRETTON, Linda
Lawrence Graham, London
(020) 7379 0000

CALLADINE, Paul
Knight & Sons, Newcastle-under-Lyme
(01782) 619225
Specialisation: Specialises in mines and minerals, landfill, public law, property aspects of privatisation in respect of water utilities, vehicle and equipment leasing, vehicle maintenance workshops and joint ventures.
Prof. Memberships: Honorary Secretary of the West Midlands Branch of the Institute of Quarrying.
Career: 1985-88, Assistant Solicitor with *Cutts and Solicitors*; 1988-92, Deputy Group Solicitor with Steetly PLC; 1992-93, Company Solicitor with Burmah Petroleum Fuels Limited; 1993-94, Commercial Department of Boots Company PLC, also self-employed consultant and locum Solicitor; 1994-95, Company Solicitor (sole legal advisor) and Company Secretary with Alfred McAlpine Minerals Limited; 1995-97, Legal Advisor with Lex Transfleet Limited; 1997-current, Partner in Property Department.
Personal: Education: Trent Polytechnic, Nottingham (BA Hons) Legal studies; College of Law, Chester. Leisure interests: motor sports, motorcycling and gardening. Married with two children.

CARVER CBE, Jeremy
Clifford Chance, London
(020) 7600 1000
jeremy.carver@cliffordchance.com
Specialisation: Litigation and Dispute Resolution. Partner specialising in state and diplomatic immunity, status, privileges and immunities of international organisations, upstream oil and gas operations, international economic sanctions, maritime and territorial boundary issues, world trade law, jurisdiction, conflicts of laws, extraterritoriality.
Career: Qualified 1969; Partner since 1974; *Coward Chance* 1969-87; *Clifford Chance* 1987; Resident Manager Brussels 1973-74; Resident Partner Singapore 1982-83.
Personal: Trinity College, Cambridge (MA Engineering).

CLOUGH, Adrian
Herbert Smith, London
(020) 7374 8000
adrian.clough@herbertsmith.com
Specialisation: Partner in *Herbert Smith's* energy and infrastructure group. Has a general commercial background, specialising in public private partnerships and regulated utilities, including privatisations, restructurings and infrastructure projects. Has extensive experience of advising both private and public sector organisations, particularly in relation to contractual and regulatory issues. His practice covers the energy, transport and defence sectors.
Career: Educated at Christ Church, Oxford (MA). Qualified as a Solicitor 1998. Partner at *Herbert Smith* 1995. Was seconded as an Assistant Director to the Office of Passenger Rail Franchising between 1993 and 1995 and was closely involved in the development of the contractual and regulatory structure of the UK railway industry.

www.chambersandpartners.com

341

ENERGY & NATURAL RESOURCES ■ THE LEADERS

COFFELL, Howard
Field Fisher Waterhouse, London
(020) 7861 4000
fhc@ffwlaw.com
Specialisation: Partner Commercial Property Department. Head of Pipeline Services Unit. Practice covers acquisition, disposal and development of commercial property including industrial sites, oil and gas terminals and facilities and the construction of cross-country pipelines. Acts for a number of major UK oil and gas companies, pipeline operators and other industrial concerns.
Prof. Memberships: Law Society.
Career: Qualified 1974, having joined *Field Fisher Waterhouse* in 1972. Became a Partner in 1978.
Personal: Born 23 November 1948. Attended King Henry VIII School, Coventry and Magdalen College, Oxford.

CUMMING, Donald
Dundas & Wilson CS, Edinburgh
(0131) 228 8000

CUTHBERT, Michael
Clifford Chance, London
(020) 7600 1000
michael.cuthbert@cliffordchance.com
Specialisation: Banking and finance and capital markets. Partner specialising in securities, corporate, natural resources and privatisation work.
Career: Trainee *Slaughter and May* 1978-80; Assistant Solicitor 1980-82; Assistant Solicitor *Clifford-Turner* 1982-86; Partner since 1986.
Personal: 1977 University College, London (LLB) faculty medal and Andrews Prize winner.

DALLAS, James
Denton Wilde Sapte, London
(020) 7242 1212

DANN, Adam
Dewey Ballantine, London
(020) 7456 6000
adann@deweyballantine.com
Specialisation: Partner specialising in all aspects of energy and corporate law. A London based partner in the firm's international corporate, projects and energy groups, specialising in energy law and particularly oil and gas, M&A and asset transactions.
Career: Joined *Dewey Ballantine* in September 2000 after having spent three and a half years as legal manager of Hardy Oil and Gas Plc and British-Borneo Oil & Gas Plc. Counsel to a number of energy and oil and gas companies. Speaker at energy conferences.

DAVEY, Henry
Herbert Smith, London
(020) 7374 8000
henry.davey@herbertsmith.com
Specialisation: Partner with over ten years experience in the energy industry. Advises clients on a wide range of matters and jurisdictions, including projects in India, Kazakhstan, the Middle East, Northern Ireland, Pakistan, the Philippines and Portugal. Has been closely involved in the privatisation of the UK electricity industry since 1990, and in the subsequent restructurings that have occurred. Deals include mergers and acquisitions within the energy sector, energy projects, power generation and transmission, and oil and gas developments.
Prof. Memberships: Member of IBA. Member of the United Kingdom Energy Lawyers Group. Representative on the SERL Oil Committee.
Career: MA Cantab (Queens' College), Law. Qualified 1988. Partnership 1996.

DICKSON, Ian
MacRoberts, Glasgow
(0141) 332 9988
ian.dickson@macroberts.com
See under Corporate Finance, p.236

ELDER, Ian
Allen & Overy, London
(020) 7330 3000
ian.elder@allenovery.com
Specialisation: Head of *Allen & Overy's* Global Energy Group, has extensive experience of mergers, acquisitions and joint ventures, as well as a large number of energy transactions, both in the UK and internationally. Companies acted for include ICI, BG, RWE-DEA, Lattice, British Energy, Duke, Degussa, Courtaulds and SWEB, as well as a number of UK IPPs. Co-led the A&O team on the UK nuclear privatisation (British Energy). Advises clients on the implications of the de-regulation and restructuring of the European Energy Markets.
Prof. Memberships: Law Society (England and Scotland), IBA, City of London Solicitors Company.
Career: Articled *Dundas & Wilson*; qualified Scotland (1977), England (1984); Solicitor ICI Legal Department (1977-87); Associate, *Allen & Overy* (1987-89), Partner (1989).
Personal: St Andrew's University (1972 MA); Edinburgh University (1974 LLB). Born 1951.

GREENO, Ted
Herbert Smith, London
(020) 7374 8000
ted.greeno@herbertsmith.com
Specialisation: Partner with extensive experience of litigation and arbitration across a range of industry sectors including energy, media, construction and accounting. In particular, he advises a number of major oil companies on a wide range of matters including disputes relating to the price of oil and gas from the North Sea, unitisation disputes and disputes arising under exploration, production sharing and transportation agreements. He has conducted High Court litigation on various energy related matters. In particular, he has recently conducted a number of cases relating to gas sales, transportation, and drilling agreements.
Career: Qualified 1983; Partner at *Herbert Smith* since 1989.

Personal: Educated at King's College, London.

GRIFFIN, Paul
Herbert Smith, London
(020) 7374 8000
paul.griffin@herbertsmith.com
Specialisation: Partner with 20 years experience in the energy sector, with wide experience in the oil, gas and power sectors gained from high profile international projects. Transactions range from the provision of advice in the development of major gas and oil pipeline projects, to regulatory and competition work, power projects, privatisations, financing and acquisitions. He has also been much involved in contentious energy work (in litigation, arbitration and expert determinations) and the restructuring of long-term energy contracts for short-term markets. This has also resulted in considerable expertise in the emerging trading of gas (including LNG), power and coal. Writes and lectures widely.

HAMLETT, David
Wragge & Co, Birmingham
(0870) 903 1000

HIGGINSON, Antony
Baker Botts, London
(020) 7726 3416
antony.higginson@bakerbotts.com
Specialisation: Partner, specialises in energy and natural resources in the United Kingdom and internationally on energy projects and transactions including: petroleum concessions; production sharing contracts and risk service contracts; joint ventures; corporate and asset acquisitions and disposals; farm-ins, downstream refining and product sales; sale and purchase of natural gas and LNG; pipelines; generation and supply of electricity; drilling and service contracts.
Prof. Memberships: International Bar Association; Institute of Petroleum; Association of International Petroleum Negotiators.
Career: Articled *Herbert Smith*; legal advisor Vickers Plc, 1974-76; attorney Phillips Petroleum Company Europe - Africa and Phillips Petroleum Company, Oklahoma 1976-84; General Counsel Sun Oil International; Managing Director Sun Oil Britain Limited, Far East Regional Manager, Sun Oil, 1984-92; partner *Lovell White Durrant* 1996-99. Partner *Baker Botts* from 1 January 2000.
Personal: MA, Emmanuel College, Cambridge (1971); Graduate PMD Harvard Business School 1987.

HURST, Philip
Ashurst Morris Crisp, London
(020) 7638 1111
philip.hurst@ashursts.com
Specialisation: Partner in Energy, Transport and Infrastructure Department. Heads mining team. Leading practitioner in natural resources law, especially in Africa, Middle East and South Asia. Extensive experience in advising privatisations in natural resources sector. Currently advising on major greenfield mining projects in Peru, Honduras and Dominican Republic, and on other resources projects in Zambia, Tanzania and Kenya. Visiting lecturer in natural resources law, Imperial College, London.
Career: BA, LLB (ANU), MA, LLM (Virginia) FRGS. 1981-85 associate *White & Case*, New York; 1985-87, Counsel, World Bank, Washington DC; 1988-92, solicitor *Linklaters & Paines*, London.

JONES, Gareth
Nabarro Nathanson, London
(020) 7524 6209
g.jones@nabarro.com
Specialisation: Partner in *Nabarro Nathanson* energy group. Acts for developers/other contract parties of generation distribution and infrastructure projects. Advises on power and gas supply, upstream petroleum issues and electricity and gas licensing.
Prof. Memberships: Law Society; contributes to energy law and regulation in the EU.
Career: Qualified in 1980. Joined *Nabarro Nathanson* 1983 (Partner in 1986).

KELLY, Christopher
Linklaters, London
(020) 7456 3600
christopher.kelly@linklaters.com
Specialisation: Corporate Partner specialising in corporate finance and commercial matters including mergers and acquisitions, equity offers and the provision of general corporate advice. Also a specialist in mining-related corporate and projects work.
Career: 2000 to date: Partner, *Linklaters*; 1997-2000: Senior Assistant Solicitor, *Linklaters*; 1999: Solicitor of the Supreme Court of England and Wales; 1995-97: Assistant Solicitor, *Linklaters* London; 1992-95: Solicitor with *Allen, Allen & Hemsley*, including a 12 month secondment to MIM Holdings Limited; 1992: Solicitor to the Supreme Court of Queensland; 1990: Commenced Articles of Clerkship with *Feez Ruthning* (now *Allen, Allen and Hemsley*) in Australia. 1987-92: University of Queensland, LLB (Hons); 1987: University of Queensland, Bachelor of Commerce (Accounting and Business Finance).

KING, Ronnie
Ashurst Morris Crisp, London
(020) 7638 1111
ronnie.king@ashursts.com
See under Litigation, p.561

LANE, Mark
Masons, London
(020) 7490 6214
mark.lane@masons.com
Specialisation: Head of *Masons'* Water Sector Group. Specialises in contact drafting (much of it on a PPP/BOT basis) and dispute resolution both nationally and internationally. Advises extensively on water and waste water treatment projects (concession agreements construction issues and O&M issues). Contract drafting on water-related

THE LEADERS — ENERGY & NATURAL RESOURCES

projects includes projects in India, the Philippines, Australasia and Scotland. Led the legal team for the preferred bidder on the £63m Levenmouth PPP waste water project in Scotland. Currently leading the team advising the Sri Lankan government on the Negombo water privatisation project. Current projects include filtration plant in Israel, desalination plant in Abu Dhabi and a water and wastewater concession in Bulgaria. Editor-in-chief of 'Masons' Water Year book'. Has extensive African experience (much of it FIDIC related) including matters in Nigeria, Gambia, Ghana, Mozambique, Kenya, Mali, the Maldives and Ethiopia. In 1998, led *Masons*' team acting for the Government of Ukraine in negotiations to establish the Project Management Unit to manage the project to render the Chernobyl Nuclear Reactor No. 4 safe. (ongoing). Experienced conference speaker nationally and internationally
Prof. Memberships: Society of Construction Law; IBA (Committee T) Past Chairman of Sub-committee on International Procurement in Construction Projects; European Construction Institute (member of Executive Committee).
Career: Qualified in 1975. Partner at *Masons* since 1988.
Personal: Born 18 March 1950. Educated at Cranleigh School 1962-67 and Trinity College, Cambridge 1968-72. Lives in London.

LANE CBE, Robert
CMS Cameron McKenna, London
(020) 7367 3000
robert.lane@cmck.com
Specialisation: Partner specialising in utilities law and regulation, with over 14 years extensive experience of electricity projects, restructurings and privatisations in the UK and overseas. Work includes advice on Grid Codes, connection arrangements, trading rules, ancillary services arrangements, PPAs, licences, legislation and all related issues. Advisor to The National Grid Company plc. Recent projects include the £14 billion merger of National Grid and Lattice Group Transco. Provides restructuring and regulatory advice for the England and Wales electricity industry. Also advises on the development and reform of market structure. Advisor in Northern Ireland for Northern Ireland Electricity plc where he recently introduced the new market structure to implement the IME Directive. Has advised on restructuring of other energy markets including Eire, State of Victoria (Australia), Orissa (India), Ontario (Canada) and South Africa. Following the European IME Directive he has advised on its implementation in a number of countries. Appointed CBE in 2001 by the UK Government in recognition of services to commercial and legal interests overseas, reflecting his extensive work.
Prof. Memberships: International Bar Association (member of Section on Energy and Natural Resources Law and co-chairman of Utilities Law Committee). Member of UK government's Power Sector Working Group.

LOGAN, Niall
Nabarro Nathanson, Sheffield
(0114) 279 4000
n.logan@nabarro.co.uk
Specialisation: Mineral development and extraction, royalty agreements, post extraction landfill schemes, coalbed methane gas exploitation. From 1992 to 1995 worked on the restructuring and privatisation of the UK coal industry. Recent projects include advising mineral owners on large scale extension to workings at Boulby Potash Mine in North Yorkshire, advising Lafarge Aggregates on a number of projects in County Durham and advising on the disputed ownership of brickshale at an opencast coal site in Scotland.
Career: Qualified 1981. British Coal Legal Dept, 1982-90; Partner, *Nabarro Nathanson* 1990.

LYNCH, Malcolm
Wrigleys, Leeds
(0113) 244 6100
law@malcolmlynch.com
See under Charities, p.130

MCKNIGHT, Elizabeth
Herbert Smith, London
(020) 7374 8000
elizabeth.mcknight@herbertsmith.com
See under Competition/Anti-trust, p.172

MILLAR, Stephen
Paull & Williamsons, Aberdeen
(01224) 621621
samillar@paull-williamsons.co.uk
Specialisation: All areas of oil and gas law and in particular: offshore developments whether in the form of new projects or revised commercial and contractual arrangements for existing developments; acquisition and sale of interests in oil and gas acreage and related infrastructure, including platforms, pipelines and terminals.
Prof. Memberships: Law Society of Scotland.
Career: Joined *Paull & Williamsons* as trainee in 1994. Became an associate in 1999 and a partner in 2000.
Personal: Born 22 November 1972. Studied at University of Dundee from 1989-94 and graduated with LLB (Hons)/DipLP. Thereafter, part-time post graduate study (whilst working at *Paull & Williamsons*) at Centre for Petroleum Mineral Law & Policy, Dundee and graduated with LLM (Natural Resources & Mineral Law).

PICTON-TURBERVILL, Geoffrey
Ashurst Morris Crisp, London
(020) 7638 1111
geoffrey.picton-turbervill@ashursts.com
Specialisation: Partner in energy and projects groups. Commercial lawyer specialising in energy and natural resources law, in particular upstream and downstream oil and gas and power both in the UK and overseas. His work covers all aspects of oil and gas and electricity industries, and he has particular expertise in mergers and acquisitions and project work. Represents many UK and international energy clients on corporate, project and regulatory matters.
Prof. Memberships: Association of International Petroleum Negotiators; UK Energy Lawyers' Group; Institute of Petroleum; IBA Section on Energy and Resources Law (member of Gas Committee); City of London Law Society Energy Sub-Committee.
Publications: Various articles on oil and gas and electricity including 'Structuring Cross-Border Pipeline Projects'; India editor of 'Oil & Gas Law & Taxation Review', and the author of the chapter on 'Oil and Gas Acquisition Agreements' for Sweet & Maxwell.

PUGH, Chris
Freshfields Bruckhaus Deringer, London
(020) 7936 4000
christopher.pugh@freshfields.com
Specialisation: Partner specialising in commercial litigation. He heads *Freshfield Bruckhaus Deringer's* Energy Disputes Group and handles litigation, arbitration and mediations across the energy sector. He has acted in a number of the highest profile upstream disputes, including those with multijurisdictional elements and those arising out of investments in emerging markets.
Career: Qualified 1983; Partner 1991.
Personal: Educated University College, London.

REES, Jonathan
Freshfields Bruckhaus Deringer, London
(020) 7936 4000
jonathan.rees@freshfields.com
Specialisation: Head of the *Freshfields* Energy Group; specialises in M&A, commercial and regulatory work in the oil and gas, electricity and natural resource sectors. Clients include oil companies, government, utilities and investment banks.
Prof. Memberships: International Bar Association (Section on Energy and Natural Resources Law), Member Institute of Petroleum, Vice Chair of the American Bar Association, Section on International Energy and Resources.
Career: *Freshfields* 1982, qualified in 1984 and became a partner in 1992.
Personal: Educated at Wadham College, Oxford (MA).

REEVES, Tony
Kent Jones and Done, Stoke-on-Trent
(01782) 202020

RENGER, Mike
Nabarro Nathanson, Sheffield
(0114) 279 4130
m.renger@nabarro.com
Specialisation: Extensive energy, industrial and property client base. Projects include privatisation of coal industry, construction and modification of power stations, waste to energy plants, CHP Schemes. Clients include UK Nirex, all major UK coal operators, US and UK owned oil companies and regional electricity companies.
Prof. Memberships: Legal Associate of RTPI; Associate of Institution of Mining Engineers; Member of the Law Society's Planning Panel; contributor to 'Energy Law and Regulation in the European Union'.

ROSS, David
Biggart Baillie, Glasgow
(0141) 228 8000

ROWEY, Kent
Freshfields Bruckhaus Deringer, London
(020) 7936 4000
kent.rowey@freshfields.com
Specialisation: Head of *Freshfields'* international project finance group, with over 15 years experience representing lenders, sponsors and suppliers in independent power projects and other project financing throughout Europe, Asia and the Americas. Currently involved in projects in Israel, Croatia, Australia, Russia and the Indian Sub-continent.
Prof. Memberships: State Bar of California, American Bar Association, International Bar Association.
Career: BA Philosophy, University of California, Los Angeles, (Magna cum laude) JD New York University. Partner, *Perkins Coie*, London. Associate *Milbank, Tweed, Hadley & McCloy*, Los Angeles, London.
Personal: Lives in Oxfordshire with wife Rosalie and two children, Allison and Austin. Avid (but average) golfer.

RUDDIMAN, Robert
Ledingham Chalmers, Aberdeen
(01224) 408515
bob.ruddiman@ledinghamchalmers.com
Specialisation: Oil and gas exploration and production. Bidding agreements; licence applications; joint operating agreements; production sharing agreements; unitisation; pipeline and transportation agreements; trading in field and licence interests; onshore/offshore construction agreements; drilling contracts; integrated services agreements; logistics agreements; all aspects of contracting and operational philosophy.
Prof. Memberships: Law Society of Scotland, The Law Society.
Career: Qualified in Scots law 1989, English law 1994. Articled and assistant with *Shepherd & Wedderburn WS* 1987-91. Legal counsel Elf Exploration 1991-93. *Cameron Markby Hewitt* 1993-97. Partner *Ledingham Chalmers* 1997.

SALT, Stuart
Linklaters, London
(020) 7456 5912
stuart.salt@linklaters.com
Specialisation: Expertise in project financings, privatisations and structured acquisitions in a variety of industry sectors. Advises a number of leading participants in the power generation, development and transmission sectors.
Career: Partner *Linklaters*. 1992 to date: Solicitor, *Linklaters* 1986-92; admitted as a Solicitor 1985. Law Society Qualifying

www.ChambersandPartners.com

ENERGY & NATURAL RESOURCES ■ THE LEADERS

Examinations 1983; Southampton University LL.B (Hons) 1982.

SAUNDERS, James
Shepherd+ Wedderburn, Edinburgh
(0131) 473 5288
james.saunders@shepwedd.co.uk
Specialisation: Partner in Corporate Department. Main areas of practice are energy law and IP (including computer law). Advises on electricity agreements and on IP agreements including licensing and turnkey.
Career: Qualified in 1984. Trainee with *McClure Naismith*, Glasgow 1983-85. Worked for ICI plc 1986-87 and *Freshfields* 1987-93. Joined *Shepherd+ Wedderburn* in 1993.

SAUNDERS, Mark
Dewey Ballantine, London
(020) 7456 6121
msaunders@deweyballantine.com
Specialisation: Partner specialising in all aspects of energy law and corporate law. A London-based partner in the firm's International Corporate, Projects and Energy Groups specialising in all aspects of energy law, particularly oil and gas. Seconded to a major oil and gas company in the mid 1980s. Outside counsel to a number of the integrated majors as well as service companies within the sector. Also solicitor to oil industry environmental response collective. Frequent speaker at energy conferences worldwide, contributed to Sweet & Maxwell's 'Upstream Oil and Gas Agreements' and to 'Energy Law & Regulation in the European Union'. Listed in Chambers Survey of Leading UK Commercial Lawyers as one of the eight leading commercial lawyers in the United Kingdom 1997-98. Listed in 'The Best of the Best - Energy & Natural Resources' for each of 2000 and 2002 as one of the world's leading energy lawyers.

SCRIVEN, John
Allen & Overy, London
(020) 7330 3000
john.scriven@allenovery.com
Specialisation: Partner specialising in advising on major projects worldwide including water, power, road, telecommunications and other infrastructure projects. He advises sponsors, project companies, lenders and contractors on UK private finance institution (PFI/PPP) schemes for hospitals and healthcare, water treatment, light rail and prison construction and operations. Has a particular interest in construction law and related issues and heads the Construction Law Group, which is an integral part of the *Allen & Overy* Projects Group. In addition, he has advised in a number of property development transactions acting for employers, investors, lenders and tenants.
Publications: Editor and co-author of 'A Constructional Guide to Major Construction Projects' (1999) and regular contributor to Construction Land Review. Contributor to 'Future Direc-

tions in Contribution Law' (1992), 'Risk Management and Prosecution' (1995) and 'Handbook of Construction Law' (2000).
Personal: Trinity College Cambridge (MA 1979). Born 1953.

SMITHERS, Tim
Veale Wasbrough, Bristol
(0117) 925 2020
tsmithers@vwl.co.uk
See under Real Estate, p.736

STACEY, Paul
Slaughter and May, London
(020) 7600 1200
paul.stacey@slaughterandmay.com
Specialisation: Main areas of practice include electricity-related work, banking and project finance.
Prof. Memberships: The Law Society.
Career: Qualified with *Slaughter and May* 1983. Partner 1990.
Personal: Born 1959.

STANGER, Michael
Lovells, London
(020) 7296 2000
michael.stanger@lovells.com
Specialisation: Practice covers a wide range of energy and projects work; energy work related primarily to the gas industry; heavily involved in the structural changes in the UK, acting on behalf of gas shippers in relation to the drafting of the Network Code and the 'Claims Validation' agreements; and acting for the Bacton Agent's Group in relation to gas flows through the Interconnector to Belgium. Practice covers gas trading, gas supply, gas storage and independent gas pipeline systems, with frequent involvement in transactions in Continental Europe.
Prof. Memberships: Law Society, City of London Solicitors Company, Institute of Petroleum, UK Energy Lawyers Group.
Career: Field Engineer in the oil industry for SPE Schlumberger, mainly in Africa, 1975-78; articled *Lovells*; qualified 1981; partner 1986.

TEMPLE, Richard
CMS Cameron McKenna, London
(020) 7367 3000
richard.temple@cmck.com
Specialisation: Head of water in the Energy Projects and Construction Group at *CMS Cameron McKenna*. Specialises in infrastructure projects and advised the World Bank on the water and sanitation toolkit: a manual on how to implement water and sewerage projects worldwide. Has advised on water projects in Romania, Bulgaria, India, the Czech Republic, Panama, Oman, Bolivia, Poland, Peru, Ghana, Kazakhstan, Hungary, England and Scotland.
Prof. Memberships: Vice-president Europe, Africa and Middle East of the International Private Water Association; the Water Sector Group of the Department of Trade and Industry; Committee Member of the Overseas Forum of British Water; International Bar Association; Project Finance Law Sub-commit-

tee of the IBC; Law Society of England and Wales.
Career: Partner, *CMS Cameron McKenna* 1997. Solicitor 1987-95 *Lovell White Durrant*, 1996-97 *Ashurst Morris Crisp* .
Personal: Tennis and squash.

TOWNER, Chris
Herbert Smith, London
(020) 7374 8000

TRINICK, Marcus
Bond Pearce, Southampton
(023) 8072 0750
mtrinick@bondpearce.com
See under Environment, p.363

TUDWAY, Robert
Nabarro Nathanson, London
(020) 7524 6421
r.tudway@nabbarro.com
Specialisation: Head of Energy Group *Nabarro Nathanson*. Energy law. Advises developers and other parties on electricity distribution and generation contracts, electricity and environmentally compatible forms of energy production; notably, combined heat and power in industry, district heating schemes and renewables.
Career: International Bar Association. Statute Law Society, member of the Developer's Forum of the Combined Heat and Power Association and Policy Committee, Cogen Europe. Qualified in 1973. Joined *Nabarro Nathanson* as a partner 1995.
Publications: General editor, 'Energy Law and Regulation in the European Union', (Sweet & Maxwell).

TURTLE, Trevor
Herbert Smith, London
(020) 7374 8000
trevor.turtle@herbertsmith.com
Specialisation: Practice includes joint ventures and consortium arrangements, acquisitions and disposals, restructurings and refinancings, flotations, rights issues and placings, and regulatory and statutory interpretation work. Also has a substantial non-contentious insurance practice, with particular emphasis on insurance insolvency. Specialises in water and water related projects.
Prof. Memberships: International Bar Association, Utilities Section. UK Environmental Law Association.
Career: BA and LLB Cambridge; Qualified 1975, Partnership 1987.

UPTON, Neil
Wragge & Co, Birmingham
(0870) 903 1000

VERRILL, John
Lawrence Graham, London
(020) 7379 0000

WAKE, Brian
Wake Dyne Lawton, Chester
(01829) 773101
bdw@wdl.co.uk
See under Environment, p.363

WALKER, Mark
Allen & Overy, London
(020) 7330 3000
mark.walker@allenovery.com
Specialisation: Partner in energy and projects group specialising in all areas of energy law, in particular electricity and downstream gas projects. He has acted on a number of power projects (for example Immingham CHP, Rugeley B, Sutton Bridge, Teesside, Humber, South East London CHP, Arcos de la Frontera (Spain), SADAF Refinery CHP (Saudi), Afsin Elbistan B (Turkey)) and has significant experience of gas tolling and merchant trading arrangements. He also advises on gas and electricity trading arrangements generally. He continues to advise industry participants in relation to the liberalisation of the European energy markets and the new electricity trading agreements in the UK.
Prof. Memberships: United Kingdom Energy Lawyers' Group; Society of Construction Law.
Career: Articled *Allen & Overy*, 1989-91; Associate *Allen & Overy* 1991-2000; Partner *Allen & Overy* 2000. Secondments: Midland Bank (1991-92); Enron Europe Limited (1996).
Personal: Leeds University (1987 LLB (Hons)); Kings College London (1995 MSc).

WALLACE, Patrick
Freshfields Bruckhaus Deringer, London
(020) 7936 4000
patrick.wallace@freshfields.com
Specialisation: Advised on establishing the UK electricity market structure at privatisation. Acted on a wide range of electricity projects in the UK and internationally. Advises on energy and natural resources, project financing, regulatory issues, privatisation, commercial contracts and corporate transactions. Speaks English, German and French.
Career: Holds degrees from London, Paris and Harvard Universities. Qualified in 1986. Partner since 1992.
Personal: Born 1959. Educated King's College, London. University of Paris and Harvard Law School.

WARNE, Penelope
CMS Cameron McKenna, Aberdeen
(01224) 622002
penelope.warne@cmck.com
Specialisation: Practice covers commercial agreements and advice of all types associated with oil and gas exploration and production; dealings in oil and gas interests, farm-ins and farm-outs; unitisation and joint operating agreements; partnering, alliances and joint ventures; and service contracts including pipeline, construction and drilling contracts.
Prof. Memberships: Honorary fellow of Centre for Energy, Petroleum and Mineral Law and Policy, University of Dundee.
Career: Qualified in English law in 1981. Articled and Assistant Solicitor with *Slaughter and May* 1976-83. Thereafter in-house legal advisor to Marks &

THE LEADERS ■ ENERGY & NATURAL RESOURCES

Spencer plc before establishing own practice in Aberdeen. 1993 joined *CMS Cameron McKenna* to establish the Aberdeen office. Became a partner in 1994. Also qualified in Scots law.

WHITAKER, Neil
Pinsent Curtis Biddle, Leeds
(0113) 244 5000
neil.whitaker@pinsents.com
Specialisation: Partner in commercial property department. Head of mines, minerals and landfill unit, specialising in transactions involving minerals extraction and utilisation of airspace. Acts for nationally known clients in this field including Hanson Aggregates.
Career: University of Leeds; qualified 1987; partner *Pinsent Curtis Biddle* 1996.

WHITEHEAD, Andrew
Martineau Johnson, Birmingham
(0121) 678 1528
andrew.whitehead@martjohn.com
Specialisation: Head of Energy and Projects team acting for a broad client base of electricity, gas and water companies. Heavily involved in ongoing reviews of electricity and gas trading arrangements for several major utilities. Leads a team advising The National Grid Company plc on contractual, regulatory and trading issues, in particular the procurement of balancing services. Also leads a team advising on a variety of accommodation PFI projects in the education and transport sectors. Advised on creation of the world's first reactive power market.
Prof. Memberships: Law Society.
Career: South Hunsley School, Birmingham University (1985 LLB). College of Law, Chester (1986). Articled *Ryland Martineau* (now *Martineau Johnson*). Qualified 1988; partner 1994.
Personal: Born 1963, resides Warwick with wife and daughter. Music (plays piano and oboe). Member UK Energy Lawyers Association. Associate London College of Music, piano, curries.

WOOD, Charles
Denton Wilde Sapte, London
(020) 7242 1212

WOOLF, Fiona
CMS Cameron McKenna, London
(020) 7367 3000
fiona.woolf@cmck.com
Specialisation: Electricity restructurings and privatisations, regulation and the introduction of wholesale and retail competitive markets in the power sector, power station and transmission projects and financings. Acted for The National Grid Company plc on the restructuring of the Electricity Supply Industry in England and Wales and advised on the Northern Ireland Electricity restructuring. Advised Electricidade de Portugal on the Tapada do Outeiro and Pego power projects. Independent transmission projects in Pakistan and Malaysia. Privatisation of the transmission system of Argentina. Has worked on power sector restructurings, utility regulation and privatisations in Australia, Canada, India, the US, South Africa, the Republic of Ireland, Central America, the Far East and Russia. Was made a Commander of the British Empire (CBE) in recognition of her work around the world, for her contribution to the UK's Knowledge Economy and invisible earnings.

ENVIRONMENT

London: 346; The Regions: 350; Scotland: 356; Profiles: 357

Research approved by BMRB For this edition, **Chambers'** researchers conducted 6,582 interviews – 3,900 with law firms, 511 with barristers and 2,171 with clients. The validity of the research was scrutinised by BMRB International, who audited both the methodology and the results at our offices in London. They interviewed **Chambers'** researchers and cross-checked sample interviews. Details of the audit appear on page 7.

OVERVIEW Development in environmental law as a whole progresses at a pace, with the IPPC regulations expected to replace IPC frameworks, developed in the 1990s, by 2007. The EC landfill sites directive is due to be implemented in July 2002, and there will be a sustained increase in sites affected by regulation in a range of industry sectors. Contaminated land continues to dominate, not least because of government backing for brownfield development and the consequent regeneration of former industrial sites. Ravenscraig Steelworks in Lanarkshire, Scotland, is the largest such site in Britain, on which an £800 million development will finally go ahead after a four-year public inquiry. Though human rights actions have not been as successful as expected following Alconbury, there have been some successes, such as in Hatton (night flights from Heathrow) and Marcic (liability for waste). On a short-term basis, BSE and foot-and-mouth have had a sustained impact. Despite continued interest in the need for separate environmental courts, this remains a subject more for academic study than an imminent reality. While legislation has made it imperative for corporations to consider the environmental impact of their business, public pressure through direct action has also come to the fore. At a global level, carbon trading has also become a major focus within the discipline. Environmental insurance policies, previously only talked about at conferences, have also become a serious reality in the day-to-day running of environmental practices.

LONDON

ENVIRONMENT
LONDON

1. Freshfields Bruckhaus Deringer
2. Allen & Overy
3. Ashurst Morris Crisp
   Barlow Lyde & Gilbert
   CMS Cameron McKenna
   Linklaters
   Mayer, Brown, Rowe & Maw
   Simmons & Simmons
   Slaughter and May
4. Berwin Leighton Paisner
   Clifford Chance
   Denton Wilde Sapte
   Gouldens
   Hammond Suddards Edge
   Herbert Smith
   Leigh, Day & Co
   Nabarro Nathanson
   Norton Rose
   SJ Berwin
5. Lawrence Graham
   Lovells
   Nicholson Graham & Jones
6. Stephenson Harwood
   Theodore Goddard
   Trowers & Hamlins

This book is the product of 6,582 1/2 hour interviews. See p.7 for BMRB audit. Within each band, firms are listed alphabetically.

FRESHFIELDS BRUCKHAUS DERINGER (see firm details p.964) Commended for having "*developed a team like no one else*," the firm was thought to have a slight edge over its rivals, gained from a "*focused approach to both contentious and non-contentious work*". A "*big character and obviously an excellent lawyer*", **Paul Watchman** (see p.363) is the standout practitioner in the international environmental planning and regulatory group, his approach being "*straight down the line*." He led the environmental advice to Trillium subsidiary, Telereal, on the acquisition of £2.4 billion of BT property assets, negotiating liabilities associated with sale and leaseback securitisation, facilities management and redevelopment of strategic sites. Highlights for the firm include advising on structuring environmental risk between LUL and infrastructure companies and advising Powergen on the disposal of coal-fired power stations to ScottishPower.

The practice is also considered "*unique in developing a strong niche litigation practice.*" This is led by **Paul Bowden** (see p.357), characterised to *Chambers'* researchers as "*a hardball player but plain talking.*" The large corporate defendant group also includes "*high calibre toxic tort litigator*" **Jonathan Isted** (see p.360), who successfully defended a series of ground-breaking challenges to the operation of the British Nuclear Fuels Sellafield MOX plant, including those brought by the Irish Government under the UN's Law of the Sea Convention and the OSPAR Convention.

While **Malcolm Forster** (see p.359) is seen as having "*taken a sideways step*" into public international law, he is still recognised by interviewees for his "*wealth of environmental expertise*" and contributes to the team's work on this basis. "*Conscientious and massively experienced,*" **Daniel Lawrence** (see p.360) is included in the rankings following the weight of market opinion; he recently acted as the lead environment lawyer to ScottishPower on the sale of Southern Water. **Clients** Abbey National; Financial Security Assurance; Babcock & Brown; MOD; Compass; Conoco; ScottishPower; Powergen; BNFL; Rank; Cinven; Solvay.

ALLEN & OVERY (see firm details p.841) The firm is best known for its "*pure volume of trans-*

TOP IN-HOUSE LAWYERS

Bridget MARSHALL, Scottish Environmental Protection Agency

Stephen SYKES, Legal Director, Certa

Peter Kellett has left the Environment Agency's legal department to join a policy team. At SEPA **Bridget Marshall** *provides an "excellent service" and has attracted sufficient commendation to be included in the list for the first time.* **Stephen Sykes** *of Certa is said to be "making the area his own," and benefiting from "valuable, composite experience gained from employment in both private practice and the business world"* – he is portrayed as an "innovative solicitor" in the environmental insurance field.

In-house lawyer's profiles p.1201

actions and the broad range of its environmental work." A high degree of standalone work also contributes to a strong profile as the team continues to expand, most recently acquiring Justine Thornton from Simmons & Simmons. Growth areas include advice on environmental insurance and health and safety-related matters. **Owen Lomas** (see p.360) continues to be recognised as "*a genuine star*" attracting clients with his "*huge range of knowledge,*" particularly in waste disposal and management. He is also credited by peers with successfully managing the firm's integrated European environmental law services team and has worked with senior solicitor **Matthew Townsend** (see p.363) ("*always dynamic*") on two important work highlights. Together they advised Phillips Petroleum on the refloat and export to Norway of one of its North Sea oil platforms (Maureen), including its eventual recycling – one of the first major decommissionings since Brent Spa. They also represented a major European chemical company on obtaining environmental insurance during its proposed merger with another chemicals corporation.

346 | INDEX TO LEADING LAWYERS: PAGE 1693 ■ IN-HOUSE LAWYERS PROFILES: PAGE 1201

LONDON ■ ENVIRONMENT

LEADING INDIVIDUALS

[1]
- **BOWDEN Paul** Freshfields Bruckhaus Deringer
- **FAIRLEY Ross** Allen & Overy
- **LOMAS Owen** Allen & Overy
- **WATCHMAN Paul** Freshfields Bruckhaus Deringer

[2]
- **DAY Martyn** Leigh, Day & Co
- **FOGLEMAN Valerie** Barlow Lyde & Gilbert
- **FORSTER Malcolm** Freshfields Bruckhaus Deringer
- **HAVARD-WILLIAMS Vanessa** Linklaters
- **KEEBLE Ed** Slaughter and May
- **LOOSE Helen** Ashurst Morris Crisp
- **MAY Caroline** Hammond Suddards Edge
- **MYLREA Kathy** Simmons & Simmons
- **O'KEEFFE Jacqui** Denton Wilde Sapte
- **RICE Paul** Lawrence Graham
- **SHERIDAN Paul** CMS Cameron McKenna
- **WAITE Andrew** Berwin Leighton Paisner

[3]
- **DEANESLY Clare** Gouldens
- **GARBUTT John** Nicholson Graham & Jones
- **NASH Mike** Simmons & Simmons
- **WISEMAN Andrew** Trowers & Hamlins

[4]
- **BRUMWELL Mark** SJ Berwin
- **CUCKSON David** Stephenson Harwood
- **DOOLITTLE Ian** Trowers & Hamlins
- **GREENWOOD Brian** Norton Rose
- **HOBLEY Anthony** Baker & McKenzie
- **ISTED Jonathan** Freshfields Bruckhaus Deringer
- **LLOYD Deborah** Ashurst Morris Crisp
- **REDMAN Michael** Clifford Chance
- **SHEPPARD Claire** Theodore Goddard
- **VALLANCE Philip** Berrymans Lace Mawer

[5]
- **HUTCHINSON Michael** Mayer, Brown, Rowe & Maw
- **LAWRENCE Daniel** Freshfields Bruckhaus Deringer
- **MARSHALL Anna** Nabarro Nathanson
- **MOORE Louise** Lovells
- **SHARP Cate** Mayer, Brown, Rowe & Maw
- **TOWNSEND Matthew** Allen & Overy

UP AND COMING
- **DAVIES Paul** Macfarlanes
- **KEELE Helen** Travers Smith Braithwaite
- **SHERGOLD Stephen** Denton Wilde Sapte

ASSOCIATES TO WATCH
- **DE WIT Elisa** Berwin Leighton Paisner
- **ENRIGHT Joanna** Ashurst Morris Crisp
- **SHORT David** CMS Cameron McKenna

See individuals' profiles p.357

Consistently spoken of as a "*serious player*", **Ross Fairley** (see p.359) is "*a leading representative of the new generation of environment lawyers.*" He advised TXU in the disposal of a sizeable portion of its UK power generation portfolio, including coal-fired and gas-fired power stations. In addition to a strong pan-European presence, the firm's continued recruitment in the US strengthens transatlantic links. **Clients** Valpak; ICI; HSBC; United Waste; UK Steel; GE Capital; Pennon Group; Hyder; Degussa UK Holdings; Marconi; Vivendi; ABN AMRO; Barking Power; Saville Gordon; Lasmo; ASW.

ASHURST MORRIS CRISP (see firm details p.852) The group is judged by our interviewees to "*have done exceptionally well*" this year, not least due to the performance of the firm's corporate and property departments. It also works closely with the firm's PFI/projects department in acting for a range of construction, engineering, chemical and energy clients. "*Energetic*" Helen Loose (see p.361) is considered by peers as being "*ahead of her years, having built up immense knowledge acting for quality clients.*" An expert on environmental insurance, emissions trading and energy and waste matters, she heads up the environmental risk management group. In a major highlight, Loose acted for BT in the outsourcing of its UK property portfolio (£2.38 billion) to Telereal. Other transactional highlights for the firm included acting for National Express Group on the £241 million sale of its airport division and advising Cinven on its acquisition of Burmah Castrol's metallurgical and releasants chemicals divisions.

Standalone highlights include acting for Ballast Phoenix in the waste to energy sector on regulatory action taken by the Environment Agency (EA). The firm also possesses an established specialist group within litigation, dealing with claims of breach of environmental warranties, and advising clients on workplace exposure litigation (chemical, asbestos and radiation). It benefits from the recent arrival of "*personable and knowledgeable*" Deborah Lloyd (see p.360). **Clients** BAE Systems; Carillion Group; NRG Energy Group; JPMorgan; Northern Foods; United News and Media; The Laird Group; BT Property; Automotive Products Ltd; Enviros.

BARLOW LYDE & GILBERT (see firm details p.858) This environmental group continues to expand its range of specialist liability and insurance and reinsurance matters, acting on both contentious and non-contentious matters. These services span UK, European and US jurisdictions. Interviewees agreed that Valerie Fogleman (see p.359) has "*worked hard and is now reaping the rewards.*" Both US and UK qualified, she leads "*an excellent environmental insurance practice.*" The group was recently instructed for the first time by St Paul International Insurance Company on pollution issues.

Other matters include receiving instructions from new client ECS Claims Administrators to handle claims against XL Europe's environmental insurance policies. The team also advises leading brokers' firms on environmental issues in warranty and indemnity policies. The practice incorporates transactional support work to UK and international companies and lenders, and continues to handle Environment Agency prosecutions. **Clients** Reliance National Insurance Company; Trelleborg; Zurich London; Qual-Effic Services.

CMS CAMERON MCKENNA (see firm details p.914) Despite the loss of Anthony Hobley to Baker & McKenzie, there is consensus that this remains "*an excellent team of broad expertise,*" which will "*weather the changes.*" "*Quietly knowledgeable,*" Paul Sheridan (see p.362), who heads the group, typifies its range. Interviewees agree that the practice continues to provide a "*service that goes beyond corporate support,*" where it advises on transactions led by the firm's competition, property, banking and dispute resolution departments. Specialist areas include Climate Change Levy, waste and water regulation, risk management, landfill tax and packaging law. The team acted for the buyer on the £1.9 billion acquisition of the Le Méridien chain of hotels, and advised the preferred bidder for two of the three infracos in the London Underground PPP.

A considerable portion of the firm's work is standalone, featuring instructions on environmental, economic and fiscal instruments: highlights include advice to a new client, The Waste and Resources Action Programme, in its £20 million capital support for a new reprocessing facility in the newsprint sector. The contentious environment law practice is thriving, having successfully acted for the Atomic Weapons Establishment in the Court of Appeal on a judicial review concerning the continued production and maintenance of the UK's independent nuclear deterrent – this involved many aspects of domestic, EU and international law. **Clients** Delphi Automotive Systems; Waste Recycling Group; Aventis; Lattice; Atomic Weapons Establishment; Heathrow Airport; Eastman Chemicals; Pegasus Retirement Homes; National Australia Bank.

LINKLATERS (see firm details p.1043) A "*commercial edge,*" for which this environmental law practice is almost universally praised, continues to give it an advantage in the marketplace. Areas of growth are contentious cases and international project finance-related advice, which draws upon the foundations laid by acting for the firm's existing clients. Notable transactional highlights include advising Billiton on its merger with BHP and two Innogy transactions. Real estate and the management of contaminated land problems, parent company liability for the acts and omissions of subsidiaries and environmental aspects of insolvency matters feature strongly in its workload.

A "*good all-round environmental lawyer,*" Vanessa Havard-Williams (see p.359) leads the practice, which is acknowledged by peers to be actively developing the sector. She advised BP on the disposal by Burmah Castrol of certain chemicals businesses to Cinven and also on the acquisition by BP of a 50% interest in Veba Oil. The firm also advised Rio Tinto on establishing an independent scheme to examine claims against a former subsidiary and the smelting operations it performed. **Clients** AMEC; Anglo American; Cargill; AstraZeneca; Honeywell; J Sainsbury; Balfour Beatty; Deutsche Bank; Railtrack; BP Amoco; Barclays Capital; London Electricity.

ENVIRONMENT ■ LONDON

MAYER, BROWN, ROWE & MAW (see firm details p.1060) A number of peers indicated that, if met on the other side, they "*would be more concerned with these lawyers than almost any other currently.*" The market awaits with interest the results of the merger with US firm Mayer, Brown & Platt. A transactional focus leads to regular crossover work with the property, banking and projects teams. The group is also supported in litigious matters, and is often seen acting for insurers on contamination and health and safety claims. This experience is complemented by a growing regulatory practice with special expertise in waste and packaging regulations.

The team sustains its high profile in the chemicals sector, and has advised ICI on all environmental aspects of the sale of its large Hillhouse site in the North West. It also advised Powell Duffryn on the environmental due diligence and contractual documentation for the €150 million sale of the Geesink Norba group of companies to Oshkosh Truck Corporation. **Cate Sharp** (see p.362) ("*tough and well prepared*") remains widely regarded, while the promotion to partner in 2001 of "*fierce negotiator*" **Michael Hutchinson** (see p.360) was often referred to by interviewees as evidence of the firm's sustained commitment to an environmental practice. The team has advised the Waste Recycling Group on its acquisition of Integrated Waste Management for £30.9 million, involving over 60 sites nationwide. **Clients** ICI; Syngenta; Hunstman Tioxide; Unilever; Cable & Wireless; Waste Recycling Group; Marley; Aquila Energy; Chemical Industries Association; DHL International (UK); IP Powerhouse.

SIMMONS & SIMMONS (see firm details p.1136) Long established in the market, the firm is "*one of the few genuine stand alone environment outfits,*" and enjoys the steady hand of **Kathy Mylrea** (see p.361) at its helm. Contentious and non-contentious matters have been combined into one pure environmental group, located within the litigation department, and the team is most often seen catering for the chemicals, energy and waste sectors. Recent growth areas such as nature conservation and renewable energy have helped to preserve a well-balanced practice, which provides complex due diligence advice and contractual negotiations. **Mike Nash** (see p.361) ("*as good an environment lawyer as there is,*") advised English Nature on various issues including a public inquiry and a forthcoming amendment of the Habitats Regulations. He also advised Ofgem on the development of the new Renewables Obligation and on its functions under the Climate Change Levy.

Litigious highlights include acting for Anti-Waste against two local authorities for recovery of waste recycling credits, and advising a US multinational defending a claim based on its manufacture of a product which entered waters. **Clients** Akzo Nobel; English Nature; British Sugar; Cleanaway; MOD; Railtrack; Shell UK; Shell International; Vivendi UK; The Scotch Whisky Association; Invensys; British Alcan Aluminium; Interbrew; Bass Brewers.

SLAUGHTER AND MAY (see firm details p.1140) Although peers link the profile of the firm's environmental law unit in "*direct proportion to the firm's corporate department,*" clients point to the high-quality advice proffered across the board. A "*brilliant negotiator on transactions,*" **Ed Keeble** (see p.360) advised Unilever on its disposal (worth $1.6 billion) of DiverseyLever institutional and industrial cleaning business, involving a major environmental due diligence exercise concerning 100 sites. The firm recently concluded its advice to Huntsman on its €205 million purchase of the European surfactants business of Albright & Wilson from Rhodia, which included the shared use of a large industrial site post-closing. The team's contaminated land expertise has also been called upon in advice to Mitchell Cotts (now part of Dow Chemicals) during the negotiation with the EA for remediation of a contaminated site. Operating authorisations, packaging laws, Climate Change Levy and corporate environmental policy also feature in the workload. **Clients** Degussa Laporte; Marconi; Blue Circle; Tomkins; Shell; Croda International; Huntsman.

BERWIN LEIGHTON PAISNER (see firm details p.866) The combined planning and environment practice is considered by peers well placed for contaminated land and other planning or property-related issues. The practice also covers waste management, environmental insurance and habitats and conservation-related issues. **Andrew Waite** (see p.363) is respected for "*putting environment on the agenda at a European level*" and dubbed "*a true specialist.*" He led advice to Shell on the sale of a contaminated site by the River Thames, and advised Petroplus on regulatory issues concerning the shipment of oil waste for recovery in the UK. The merger with Paisner & Co has led to a successful consolidation of the practice, which has seen the group advise one of a clutch of new clients, British Benzol. **Clients** English Partnerships; ICI; Lex; Mercury Asset Management; Newcastle Estates; Petroplus; National Power; Blue Circle; Prudential; Tesco; Waste Facilities Audit Association.

CLIFFORD CHANCE (see firm details p.911) This "*leading international practice*" is well suited to providing due diligence on cross-border transactions through its European environment group. Telecoms, energy and utilities sectors continue to dominate as the team's principal areas of influence. The group has advised Dynegy on the environmental issues arising from its £421 million acquisition of BG Storage, including the negotiation of the environmental indemnity, and provided UK and EU advice to AEP Energy Services on its acquisition of two coal-fired power stations in the UK. **Michael Redman** (see p.361), who continues to command the market's respect as "*a leading figure at the coalface,*" featured on the AEP Energy deal and also recently advised Lafarge on UK emissions trading proposals. Regulatory advice adds depth to the practice, which recently advised General Electric on its UK responsibilities under the producer responsibility (packaging) regulations, and represented Acordis on contaminated land at sites in the UK, Netherlands, Germany and the US. A contentious strand to the practice is also in evidence, and the team has represented Acordis on indemnity claims. **Clients** Emerson Electric Company; AEP; The Coca-Cola Company; British Energy; Edf; Kohlberg Kravis Roberts & Son; CVC Capital Partners; Enodis.

DENTON WILDE SAPTE (see firm details p.935) The firm is unusual in having an environment, health and safety practice attached to its energy department. It was praised by clients for providing a "*seamless service,*" and is best known for offering regulatory expertise, where the advice increasingly focuses on renewable energy and integrated waste policies, alongside its strong transactional support. "*Great lateral thinker*" **Jacqui O'Keeffe** works on both non-contentious and contentious issues. Together with "*sensible and level-headed*" **Stephen Shergold**, she advised London Electricity on the environmental aspects in the £1.45 billion purchase of Eastern Electricity and 24 Severn from TKU Europe. The group also advised the Royal Bank of Scotland and Fuelforce on environmental issues arising from a £120 million MBI (involving the acquisition of over 190 petrol filling stations), and has acted for English Partnerships on old landfill and other brownfield sites, including the regeneration of former colliery sites under the land stabilisation programme. On the contentious side, O'Keeffe advised Mayer Parry in a judicial review (referred to the ECJ) concerning packaging waste and the definition of waste under European and domestic law. The group also handles the defence of criminal prosecutions and acted on a judicial review of the grant of an IPC authorisation. **Clients** Mayer Environmental; Wastepack; English Partnerships.

GOULDENS (see firm details p.976) A highly thought of, dedicated environmental practice with a developed standalone base, specialising in minerals, waste management, packaging waste, contaminated land, mines and minerals and water industry matters. **Clare Deanesly** (see p.358) ("*has her teeth in some fairly meaty environmental cases*") is principally credited with this achievement, and she was recently instructed by the Waste Recycling Group on a number of waste contracts. The practice has also had a long-term relationship with Biffa, advising on planning and waste management licensing in relation to Patteson Court, Surrey. This involved a landmark four-week public appeal hearing, resulting in a successful licensing modification appeal to the Environment Agency. Though our interviewees place the profile of the firm on its standalone work, the practice also provides support to an enviable base of corporate and property clients. **Clients** Hanson; Biffa Waste Services; Mid Kent Water; Mayr-Melnhof Karton; Thames Waste Management; Pillar Property.

HAMMOND SUDDARDS EDGE Commended by peers for its "*broad-based environmental strategy,*" the London office deals with high-profile corporate commercial environmental work with an emphasis on the utilities sector. The team is also well supplied with acquisition and disposal instructions, acting for institutions, property developers and manufacturing companies. Peers value its "*excellent all-round knowledge and a commercial approach,*" while there is a consensus that, under the stewardship of **Caroline May**, the group's profile has significantly increased. Heading up the London branch of the national safety, health and environment group, she has recently drafted a number of significant environmental insurance policies. Other areas of specialism include negotiating contracts for recycling credits, packaging waste regulations, groundwater pollution and contaminated land-related matters. The team has been appointed to one of the new private companies formed to run the London Underground post-PPP. International work includes advising the Japanese Government (via a Japanese consultancy) on a pollutant release and transfer register, and access to environmental information systems operated in Europe. The practice defends prosecutions and has civil and criminal litigation capabilities. **Clients** London Electricity; TXU Europe; John Mowlem and Company; Norwest Holst; ONDEO; PPG Industries; Sigma Coatings; Surrey Local Council's Recycling initiative; Waverley Borough Council; South East England Development Agency; Cookson Group.

HERBERT SMITH (see firm details p.992) Praised by clients for its PFI credentials, the firm has a contentious and non-contentious practice that remains best known for its transactional support. Deborah Lloyd has recently moved to Ashurst Morris Crisp. Prior to this, the team advised Anschutz in its successful bid for the Dome and the apportioning of environmental liabilities. It was also involved in advising Northern Electric on the environmental aspects of the disposal of its supply business and acquisition of Innogy's electric distribution business. Other areas of activity have been in the chemical manufacturing and processing industries, food, automotive and transport sectors and instructions relating to the negotiation of insurance.

Equipped with a renowned litigation capacity, the practice has also advised a UK plc on a multimillion dollar claim arising out of a catastrophic fire at a chemical plant in Georgia, USA, and is advising BAA on a potential action concerning the retention of statutory compensation in a contaminated property matter. **Clients** EMI; British Energy; Royal & SunAlliance; Apogent Technologies; Simon Group; GE Capital; Onyx Aurora; Johnson Matthey; South West Water.

LEIGH, DAY & CO (see firm details p.1036) "*The claimant firm,*" it is respected by all sources for its "*high degree of specialisation,*" and has been described by one peer as "*world-class in its sector.*" Recent highlights include the settlement agreed for victims of asbestos-related disease arising from Cape's mining operations in South Africa, establishing the liability of UK-based multinational companies for their overseas subsidiaries. "*The founding father of toxic tort theory,*" **Martyn Day** (see p.670) continues to be recognised for his experience in presenting class action cases; for many competitors he remains key to the firm's success. He is currently acting in a case for compensation from the British Geological Survey on behalf of hundreds of victims of arsenic poisoning in Bangladesh, following water exploration operations. Nuisance and PI claims related to landfill sites or contaminated land contribute to the workload and the practice has proven its expertise in carbon monoxide leakages and water pollution. **Clients** Individual and group claimants.

NABARRO NATHANSON (see firm details p.1080) Now recognised as "*serious players,*" the London team with **Anna Marshall** (see p.361) at its head was emphatically portrayed by peers as "*having arrived.*" Marshall is experienced in advising US-based clients on environmental risks issues – on a pan-European basis – with much of her success stemming from a buoyant property market. Highlights include acting for a JV between Westbrook Partners and a Jones Lang LaSalle private equity fund in the acquisition of a mixed use portfolio of 20 properties, involving the apportioning of liabilities and environmental due diligence. Marshall also acted for an overseas investor on the £300 million acquisition of a mixed use portfolio of 45 properties from a major insurance company, calling for expertise on closed landfill and former colliery sites. In co-operation with the Sheffield office, the practice has also developed expertise in environmental reporting in corporate governance and investment policies. Other recent work includes advising clients on land remediation tax relief and pension fund trustees on their potential exposure to environmental liability. **Clients** DigiPlex; Merrill Lynch Investment Managers; Land Securities; Access Storage Group; GE Capital; Inchcape Motors; Costco UK; London Development Agency.

NORTON ROSE (see firm details p.1084) As "*an excellent planning team with environmental overtures,*" the practice sustains a high environmental profile. Illustrating its dual capacity, interviewees pointed to the group's involvement in the Dibden Bay planning inquiry, where it advised a new client, Associated British Ports. **Brian Greenwood** (see p.359) is portrayed as "*always urbane and on top of the matter,*" and has recently been active in contamination, industrial land and ecology matters. The team has been instructed by Castle Cement in a judicial review relating to IPPC permits and the use of waste as a fuel in the cement manufacturing process. Other areas of practice include corporate support, especially involving transactions in the power sector, where the firm advised AES on the disposal of the Partington Power project to TXU. **Clients** Castle Cement; BMW; ScottishPower; AES; Royal Bank of Scotland; Associated British Ports; Siemens; Taylor Woodrow; London Underground.

SJ BERWIN (see firm details p.867) The firm is endorsed by peers for its work on transactional matters, particularly financing-related issues, with an environmental expertise covering compulsory purchases, waste management licensing, landfill tax, environmental audits and nature conservation controls. It also has a strong planning-related string to its bow, and has acted recently for Mercia Waste Management on a proposed integrated waste management facility, which includes a waste to energy plant in Kidderminster. Recognised by the market as "*a big name,*" **Mark Brumwell** (see p.358) has advised J Sainsbury on its strategy for the redevelopment of contaminated sites, and represented the Royal Bank of Scotland on complex environmental aspects of financing the purchase and redevelopment of 11 retail parks. He continues to advise the EA on flood defence schemes in South East England and Southern Water on infrastructure projects. Contentious work relating to water pollution, land contamination and judicial review matters are also handled. **Clients** Southern Water; Asda Properties; J Sainsbury; Environment Agency; British Land; London City Airport; Marylebone Warwick Balfour; The Crown Estate.

LAWRENCE GRAHAM (see firm details p.1031) Having "*excelled in the field as an individual,*" the market awaits with interest the impact made by **Paul Rice** in consolidating the firm's environmental practice profile. The team is based in commercial property and supported by partners in the planning and litigation practices, Rice handles both contentious and non-contentious matters with strengths, *inter alia*, in waste, renewables and climate change. Recent highlights have included acting for Scottish & Newcastle on disposals of 646 hotels, restaurants and public houses (total value of

ENVIRONMENT ■ LONDON/THE SOUTH

£340 million) to Noble House and Enterprise Inns. He also advised GATX Corporation under the contaminated land regime on the letting of its Avonmouth Terminal property from The Bristol Port Company to GATX Terminals. **Clients** Legal & General; GATX Terminals; GATX Corporation; J Sainsbury Developments; NFUMIS.

LOVELLS (see firm details p.1045) The team advises on the environmental aspects of corporate banking and property transactions (UK and cross-border), while also possessing a standalone and contentious capacity. There remains consensus stretching beyond London that **Louise Moore** (see p.361) is *"a high-quality operator;"* she consistently appears as a lead environmental solicitor to Tube Lines on the JNP (Jubilee, Northern and Piccadilly lines) PPP, and also advises a number of major pension funds on environmental liabilities and risk management. Moore has also recently acted on all aspects of the UK Emissions Trading Scheme for companies with Climate Change Levy Agreements. **Clients** Cory Environmental; IKEA; Prudential.

NICHOLSON GRAHAM & JONES (see firm details p.1083) Adjudged by clients *"excellent on planning-related environmental issues, especially regarding IPPC,"* the firm retains its profile as an outstanding specialist practice. **John Garbutt** (see p.359), classed as *"an immensely experienced waste regulatory practitioner,"* also has a high profile in minerals and leisure developments. The group advises on appeals, development plans, environment disputes, audits and policy and compulsory purchase. Garbutt led advice to SITA on a public inquiry into a multi-million pound project for a new mass burn waste to energy incinerator. Advice to the UK Renderers Association continues, on a judicial review challenge and in an appeal to the Court of Appeal against the former Secretary of State for the Environment, Transport & the Regions under the Environmental Protection Act 1990. The firm has also advised Warner Jenkinson on proceedings brought by the EA for breach of its process authorisation and LondonWaste on the proposed relocation of its facility. **Clients** London-Waste; Blue Circle Industries; UK Renderers Association; Strong & Fisher (Holdings).

STEPHENSON HARWOOD (see firm details p.1147) Areas of expertise include property-related matters, corporate support and waste management regulation. A former UKELA chairman, **David Cuckson** (see p.358) remains highly regarded and recently advised Macdonald Hotels on the environmental aspects of its £235 million acquisition of Heritage Hotels. The group also draws upon the strengths of practitioners from other departments to deal with planning, criminal and regulatory offences, marine pollution and insurance matters. Further highlights include instructions from Landwell to carry out environmental due diligence on the acquisition by a Danish company of a UK agri-chemicals business, and advising AEA Technology on waste management matters for a major waste disposal authority. **Clients** AEA Technology; Cenargo; Heart of Thames Gateway; Peel Holdings; Kuwait Investment Office; Sorin Biomedica; Caird Group; Elementis.

THEODORE GODDARD (see firm details p.1158) The practice covers transactional support, including PFI-related, property finance and corporate matters, as well as providing development-related and regulatory advice. A *"significant waste experience via the planning department"* is provided by **Claire Sheppard** (see p.362), commended for her property-related environmental and contaminated land advice. The team recently advised Entergy on the environmental aspects of the £571 million disposal of Saltend Power Station to Calpine, and acted for the Katsouris family on the £102 million disposal of UK Katsouris Fresh Foods to the Icelandic Bakkavor Group. The firm has also worked with the planning department in advising Hampshire Waste Services and SITA on three waste management projects. **Clients** Associated British Foods; Burdale Financial; Delta; Lakeside Energy from Waste; Minosus; Monteagle Barlow Trust; Royal Bank of Scotland.

TROWERS & HAMLINS (see firm details p.1168) The team is highly valued by clients for its advice on contaminated land, an area in which it principally advises local authorities, both in their capacity as regulator and landowner. Success in this sphere is in part attributed to the launch of a confidential e-mail discussion forum for local authorities. Lead partner **Ian Doolittle** (see p.359) remains well respected on the housing association side, while **Andrew Wiseman** (see p.359) was appreciated by clients for *"cutting through the complexities of contaminated land issues with ease."* Together they advised Wellingborough Borough Council in negotiations with the Environment Agency over a closed landfill site. The practice incorporates transactional work, advising the firm's housing association clients on the redevelopment of brownfield sites, and continues to build relations with US law firms; it has been instructed by one such firm on the purchase of a large chemical facility owned by a multinational. Another area of specialisation is waste cases, often undertaken on behalf of trade associations in the secondary metals sector. **Clients** Borough Council of Wellingborough; local authorities; housing associations.

OTHER NOTABLE PRACTITIONERS Anthony Hobley (see p.359), having moved from CMS Cameron McKenna to Baker & McKenzie, continues to attract a weight of market opinion, most typically pointing to his *"outstanding strategic judgement."* Expert in emissions and climate change, he continues to work on contaminated land issues and general environmental law. **Philip Vallance** (see p.363) has now settled as in-house counsel at Berrymans Lace Mawer, having moved from 4-5 Gray's Inn Square. He will continue to undertake wide-ranging environmental liability work, and retains a strong profile for advising insurers on pollution claims. Dubbed a *"significant new arrival"* at Macfarlanes, **Paul Davies** was commended by interviewees as possessing the expertise gained from his time as health, safety and environmental counsel for Eastern Hemisphere Operations at Schlumberger. **Helen Keele** (see p.360) of Travers Smith Braithwaite recently advised Pinewood and 3i on the acquisition of Shepperton Studios, and acted for Titanic Properties on the redevelopment of the former shipbuilding yards in Belfast.

THE SOUTH

BOND PEARCE (see firm details p.879) Nationally renowned, it is the pre-eminent renewables practice – its onshore and offshore wind projects advice stands out in the region. The Southampton office co-operates closely with Plymouth and the joint planning and environment practice offers support to corporate and property transactions as well as standalone compliance advice. A clear leader and according to one peer, *"the best environment lawyer in the South,"* **Marcus Trinick**'s (see p.363) practice dovetails with his planning prowess. He has been involved in ongoing advice to Associated British Ports on the environmental issues raised by the proposed Dibden Terminal project at Southampton port. Other areas of expertise include landfill sites, urban regeneration, waste to energy projects and advising developers on European habitat regulations. Though primarily a non-litigious practice, the group has recently defended emissions prosecutions. **Clients** Associated British Ports; Devonport Management; Sid Knowles Waste; ScottishPower.

BLAKE LAPTHORN (see firm details p.877) This well-respected practice in Southampton and Portsmouth is thought to produce *"thorough work,"* and its property-based environmental expertise has been bolstered by the merger with Sherwin Oliver and Andrew

THE SOUTH/SOUTH WEST ■ ENVIRONMENT

ENVIRONMENT
■ THE SOUTH

1 Bond Pearce *Southampton*
2 Blake Lapthorn *Portsmouth, Southampton*
Brachers *Maidstone*
DMH *Brighton*
Stevens & Bolton *Guildford*
3 Horsey Lightly Fynn *Newbury*

LEADING INDIVIDUALS

1 TRINICK Marcus *Bond Pearce*
2 ABRAHAM Henry *Brachers*
ALLEN Tony *DMH*
DAVEY Catherine *Stevens & Bolton*
PAWLIK Andrew *asb law*
RAYNER David *Blake Lapthorn*

This book is the product of 6,582 1/2 hour interviews. See p.7 for BMRB audit.
Within each band, firms are listed alphabetically. See individuals' profiles p.357

Peck's arrival. Further areas of expertise include advising regional and national companies under the packaging waste regulations and international corporations under the Radioactive Substances Act and The Transfrontier Shipment of Waste Regulations. **David Rayner** retains his market position; he has recently acted for a major motor business on environmental liabilities, and provided corporate and lending support to manufacturing businesses on warranties and indemnities issues. He is particularly well-versed in contaminated land issues. **Clients** Hillier Nurseries; Planned Maintenance Engineering; Webb Country Foods; Chelton.

BRACHERS (see firm details p.886) Much of the firm's recent profile lies with its strong agricultural offering, and this small practice has recently advised farmers on the impact of waste regulation upon large-scale agricultural land raising operations. Operating in conjunction with its town and country planning practice, clients comment that the firm provides a "*first-rate service.*" Typical highlights include acting for a landowner on flooding and related contamination matters and securing a waste management licence for a waste business. **Henry Abraham** (see p.357) remains respected for both non-contentious and contentious cases, with the latter including the defence of waste and noise-related prosecutions. Douglas Horner has retired. **Clients** Manufacturing and waste companies; landowners.

DMH (see firm details p.940) A recognised strength in planning has provided the foundations for the firm's developing expertise in environmental matters. Clients rate the team as "*on the ball and up to date with legislation.*" **Tony Allen** (see p.649) heads the planning and environmental group, which has seen an increase in demand for contaminated land advice. Due diligence on corporate and property transactions, and planning applications, have been a feature of the workload. Recent highlights include waste to energy plant proposals, advising the International Study Centre on water pollution and providing environmental support to Brighton and Hove Albion FC's planning application for a new stadium. Environmental litigation specialists bolster the team's strength, assisting on statutory nuisance appeals and defending environmental prosecutions, noise and odour complaints and judicial reviews. **Clients** Cory Environmental; Reprotech; Crawley Abattoir; Compco Holdings; Brighton Health Care NHS Trust.

STEVENS & BOLTON (see firm details p.1149) Endorsed regionally by peers as a "*mover and a shaker,*" **Catherine Davey** (see p.358) heads up the environmental department, combining this speciality with planning. The practice has seen relations with existing clients strengthened, providing environmental due diligence on acquisitions and disposals as well as standalone advice on commercial agreements for a waste to energy operator. The team advises private investment companies, local authorities and local residents' groups on environmental issues. **Clients** Hays; ENER.G; BOC.

HORSEY LIGHTLY FYNN The planning department headed by Lionel Fynn continues to attract praise for its environmental expertise, particularly in advising on urban regeneration schemes and preparing environmental statements pursuant to Environmental Impact Assessment Regulations. Core strength lies in its experience with planning applications concerning the EC Birds Directive, Coastal SSSI's and protected lowland. The team also handles all aspects of advocacy for environmental work, including statutory nuisance notice appeals and defence of criminal environmental prosecutions. **Clients** Bowlplex; Murco Petroleum.

OTHER NOTABLE PRACTITIONERS Andrew Pawlik (see p.361) of asb law was recognised this year as an emerging talent specialising in waste management licensing and prosecutions.

SOUTH WEST

ENVIRONMENT
■ SOUTH WEST

1 Bond Pearce *Plymouth*
Burges Salmon *Bristol*
Osborne Clarke *Bristol*
2 Clarke Willmott & Clarke *Bristol, Taunton*
3 Bevan Ashford *Bristol*
Veale Wasbrough *Bristol*

LEADING INDIVIDUALS

1 BAKER Neil *Clarke Willmott & Clarke*
GIBBS Kevin *Osborne Clarke*
HOLMES Sarah *Bond Pearce*
JOHN Alan *Osborne Clarke*
SALTER Ian *Burges Salmon*
2 HAYDEN Tim *Clarke Willmott & Clarke*
SCOTT Peter *Toller Beattie*

This book is the product of 6,582 1/2 hour interviews. See p.7 for BMRB audit.
Within each band, firms are listed alphabetically. See individuals' profiles p.357

BOND PEARCE (see firm details p.879) Well regarded regionally, **Sarah Holmes** (see p.360) remains the standout practitioner in the Plymouth-based planning and environment team. She has recently worked on the lawfulness of radioactive discharge consent and the Radioactive Substances Act 1993 and on human rights issues both for due diligence projects and judicial reviews. Working in close co-operation with the Southampton office, the group advised Associated British Ports on Dibden Terminal, and continues to act on a wide range of development projects subject to environmental impact assessment. Transactions in the waste and mineral sector include landfill issues and the impact of European legislation, while environmental liability advice to the firm's corporate clients is a key feature of the work. **Clients** Associated British Ports; Devonport Management; Renewable Energy Systems; Aggregate Industries; National Wind Power; Pennon Group; Taylor Woodrow.

BURGES SALMON (see firm details p.894) Peers commend the firm as quick to establish itself in the sector, especially for its niche nuclear expertise, and foresee "*excellent prospects.*" The recruitment of former DETR solicitor William Wilson, new client wins (including the Carbon Trust) and the firm's appointment to the Ofgem panel are indicative of its environmental stature amid the market. "*Emerging front runner*" **Ian Salter** (see p.362) is widely endorsed for building a "*strong and distinct environmental practice.*" Drawing clients nationally and internationally, the firm has advised Brightstar Environmental on the establishment of a substantial number of waste-to-energy plants across the UK and Ireland, a transaction that recently featured the £25 million Derby project. This follows advice to Nirex on nuclear waste disposal and advice to the MOD on Aldermaston and Burghfield nuclear establishments. The firm continues to service its existing clients within the transport industry. **Clients** MOD; Sevalco; United Kingdom Nirex; Institute of Waste Management; FirstGroup.

ENVIRONMENT ■ SOUTH WEST/WALES

OSBORNE CLARKE (see firm details p.1090) While the firm's environmental profile rests principally on providing transactional support on an array of corporate and property acquisitions, the practice is also increasingly focused on renewables. Other areas of expertise include waste management, indemnity negotiations and contaminated land. Sitting in the environmental and energy group, lead lawyer **Alan John** was described as an *"outstanding, highbred corporate finance lawyer with a strong interest in environment."* **Kevin Gibbs** is recognised for his contribution to the group's development, particularly his work on urban regeneration and CHP projects. Quarry acquisitions and disposals have featured heavily in the workload recently; a further highlight was advising Novera Energy Europe on its acquisition of a portfolio of UK renewable energy businesses. The team often works in co-operation with the planning, agriculture and litigation departments, and fields a qualified scientist. **Clients** Churngold Waste Management; Hanson; Recycling Services Group; SITA Holding UK; St Regis Paper Company.

CLARKE WILLMOTT & CLARKE (see firm details p.907) Peers acknowledged the consistent efforts of the lead solicitors to develop environmental expertise within a planning-based practice, resulting in new recruits and the firm's recent appointment to the NFU panel. Split between Bristol and Taunton offices, it has experience in defending waste and water pollution cases, waste management and both contentious and non-contentious environmental issues relating to minerals. City-trained **Neil Baker** (see p.357) is well received for his transactional support, most recently exercised in landfill acquisitions for a waste company. His standalone work is also held in high esteem, advising The Scotts Company on peat harvesting activities under the EU Habitats Directive and Regulations and acting for Countryside Residential on a South Wales brownfield development. Formerly a prosecutor for HMIP, **Tim Hayden** (see p.359) also remains a well-respected litigator. **Clients** The Scotts Company (UK); Pfizer; Classic Mouldings (UK); Countryside Residential (South West); Hydraulic Lias Limes.

BEVAN ASHFORD (see firm details p.869) The firm's environmental practice is bolstered this year by the recruitment of an associate from the Environment Agency, and retains its share of public authority clients. Brownfield development, clinical waste, municipal waste disposal and collection contracts and IPPC are all areas of focus for the team. Spanning planning, health and safety and PFI disciplines, the team is led by David Wood. Recent highlights include successfully acting for City Hospital NHS Trust (Birmingham) (leading the EA to drop its prosecution) and advising Gloucestershire County Council on its waste disposal contract. **Clients** Energy Power Resources; City Hospital NHS Trust (Birmingham); Gloucestershire Health Authority; University Hospital Birmingham NHS Trust.

VEALE WASBROUGH (see firm details p.1174) Now led by newly recruited associate Peter Harvey, the team has consolidated its client base of local authorities and national property developers, while also attracting an increasing number of mineral operators. Ongoing advice to Bath & North East Somerset Council on resisting judicial review challenges and work with Esso on nature conservation issues arising from pipeline projects continue to feature as highlights. Other strengths include waste management planning, landfill development and acquisition and contaminated land remediation schemes. Litigious work includes defence of water pollution and statutory nuisance prosecutions. **Clients** Esso Petroleum Company; TotalFinaElf; Hemmings Waste Management; Bristol City Council; Nicholson Properties.

OTHER NOTABLE PRACTITIONERS *"Devoted practitioner"* **Peter Scott** (see p.362) of Toller Beattie is a widely recognised specialist in water quality and sewage law. He advises local authorities on habitats (under European regulations), and retains a niche practice in fishery law acting for health authorities and fishery and shellfish interests throughout the UK and Ireland.

WALES

ENVIRONMENT ■ WALES

1. **Morgan Cole** Cardiff
2. **Edwards Geldard** Cardiff
   Eversheds Cardiff
3. **Hugh James** Bargoed, Cardiff

LEADING INDIVIDUALS
1. **BOSWALL Julian** Morgan Cole

This book is the product of 6,582 1/2 hour interviews. See p.7 for BMRB audit. Within each band, firms are listed alphabetically. See individuals' profiles p.357

MORGAN COLE (see firm details p.1075) Considered by some interviewees to be *"the only firm with a seriously dedicated practice in Wales,"* its environmental operation now centres on the Cardiff office and is headed by **Julian Boswall**, a recognised expert in the field. The team conducts its own advocacy in a broad range of environmental prosecutions, covering waste licensing, packaging waste and water pollution. It has defeated one prosecution on the grounds of a breach of Article 6 under the Human Rights Act, currently the subject of an appeal by the Environment Agency. A strong non-contentious practice boasts energy, mining and waste sector expertise, providing transactional support for acquisitions and disposals, including those conducted by the property department. It advised an industrial company on a claim under environmental indemnity for a heavily contaminated site. **Clients** Cardiff and Vale NHS Trust; HSBC Trust Company; NFU Services; PHS Group; Welsh Development Agency; Corus; LAS Waste; Liberty Properties; TotalFinaElf.

EDWARDS GELDARD (see firm details p.944) A steady year for Huw Williams' team, which defends packaging waste prosecutions and is active on the corporate support front. Drafting environmental warranties in property transactions and advising on contaminated land in the context of site disposals under both English and Welsh regulations provides the mainstay for the practice. The team advises public authorities on reclamation and redevelopment schemes, lending breadth to the practice. **Clients** Welsh Development Agency.

EVERSHEDS (see firm details p.949) This remains a well-regarded practice amongst market commentators, albeit ancillary to the firm's environmental strongholds in England. Jonathan Richards oversees the office's environmental and regulatory work, which covers transactional support, appeals against enforcement authorities and the defence of prosecutions. It is particularly valued for its contaminated land and landfill tax advice. **Clients** Allied Bakeries; Celtic Energy; British Aluminium Plate; Jewson; Solutia UK.

HUGH JAMES (see firm details p.1004) This expanding claimant practice is recommended for the first time in *Chambers* following endorsement for its litigious environmental expertise. Its group actions experience encompasses air, water, land and noise pollution, planning challenges, and toxic tort and flooding-related matters. A recent highlight was being appointed to represent over 100 claimants seeking damages, both in nuisance and in negligence, for personal injury, against the former operators of Nantygwyddon Landfill Site in the Rhondda. Its small environmental group is based in the firm's claimant division, and is headed by senior associate Neil Stockdale. **Clients** Individual and group applicants.

MIDLANDS

ENVIRONMENT
MIDLANDS

1. **Wragge & Co** Birmingham
2. **Eversheds** Birmingham, Nottingham
   Pinsent Curtis Biddle Birmingham
3. **Browne Jacobson** Birmingham, Nottingham
   Hammond Suddards Edge Birmingham
   Kent Jones and Done Stoke-on-Trent

LEADING INDIVIDUALS

1. **SHINER Philip** Public Interest Lawyers
   TURNER John Wragge & Co
2. **MACKINLAY Hannah** Putsman.wlc
3. **BARLOW Richard** Browne Jacobson

This book is the product of 6,582 1/2 hour interviews. See p.7 for BMRB audit. Within each band, firms are listed alphabetically. See individuals' profiles p.357

WRAGGE & CO (see firm details p.1197) There is virtually no disagreement among practitioners that the group has made its mark in the region and beyond, with clients praising its approach to understanding the environmental aspects of their business. A "*well-informed environmental advisor with long experience,*" **John Turner** is judged largely responsible for the team's success. He is a senior magistrates' advocate in environmental prosecutions, and recent highlights include the defence of a high-value foot-and-mouth case and a matter concerning the illegal shipment of waste. The team is busy providing due diligence for sale, acquisition and finance transactions to corporate clients, while other instructions include advice to developers on the regeneration of contaminated sites and the negotiation of environmental warranties and indemnities. Expertise in coal-fired power plant emissions adds to the team's capabilities in advising electricity industry clients. **Clients** HSBC; Cadbury; Burmah Castrol; Royal & SunAlliance; PwC; British Energy.

EVERSHEDS (see firm details p.949) Co-headed by David Young and David Gordon, the team has acknowledged strengths in providing environmental support to developers in mixed use regeneration projects, alongside its thriving contentious practice. It is a sizeable operation, spread across Birmingham and Nottingham offices, and has recently recruited Kevin Elliot from Wragge & Co. Acting for a broad range of manufacturing, mining, construction, engineering and retail clients, the firm's highlights include advising SimsMetal UK on its recent group reorganisation, involving the transfer of nearly 100 environmental authorisations. The firm is also experienced in environmental due diligence, IPPC, climate levy, waste management and environmental water and highway law. **Clients** Bass Leisure Retail; Bellway Homes; East Midlands Development Agency; McDonald's Restaurants; TRW.

PINSENT CURTIS BIDDLE (see firm details p.1102) Martin White heads up the planning and environment team, which now lacks Hannah Mackinlay following her departure to Putsmans.wlc. Corporate support, handling warranties and indemnities and advising on environmental aspects of property transactions remain the mainstay work for the group. Contentious defence work undertaken by the commercial litigation department has included watercourse pollution, statutory nuisance and waste disposal infringements. Non-contentious highlights include advising Abbot Group on the environmental aspects of its strategic disposal of non-core subsidiaries. **Clients** Onyx; Severn Waste Services; Daventry District Council; Johnson Controls; Glanbia.

BROWNE JACOBSON (see firm details p.891) Our researchers were informed that the group possesses "*real specialists,*" whose environmental work is shared by Nottingham and Birmingham offices. It gains recognition in the table, having been retained on panels for English Nature and the Countryside Council for Wales. Incorporating members of the firm's public authority and commercial litigation groups, barristers characterised team leader **Richard Barlow** (see p.357) as "*committed, personable and practical,*" with highly valued expertise in statutory nuisance prosecutions and nature conservation law. The firm has successfully acted for English Nature in a two-week public inquiry into extracting sand from the Ribble Estuary, and advised in a human rights-based injunction and judicial review concerning sites in Hampshire and Norfolk. **Clients** English Nature; Countryside Council for Wales; Express Dairies; Midland Glass Processing.

HAMMOND SUDDARDS EDGE A "*respectable*" if lower profile practice following the departure of Gwyn Williams, it operates from the firm's national safety, health and environment group. The team is led by Chris Green and remains active in the waste and mining industries. Waste management, contaminated land issues and regulatory work relating to water pollution feature among the team's areas of expertise. It recently advised Jabil Circuit on the environmental aspects of its acquisition from Marconi of its electronic circuit board business at five locations throughout Europe and the USA. **Clients** Waste and mining sectors.

KENT JONES AND DONE (see firm details p.1020) The planning and environment group is considered to have sustained its strong presence, especially in the waste and mineral spheres. Led by Grant Anderson, typical work has included advising clients on the establishment of a new waste collection business and on a project to minimise potential environmental liabilities in 100 disused mines. Other areas of expertise include contaminated land issues. **Clients** Laporte; Norcros Adhesives; Bliss Sand & Gravel Co.

OTHER NOTABLE PRACTITIONERS Peers "*admire the spirit*" of **Phil Shiner**'s practice and his "*sometimes ingenious challenges*" to existing environmental, planning and human rights procedures. Operating under the Public Interest Lawyers aegis, he has seen Court of Appeal action with his continued involvement in Marchiori, the Aldermaston nuclear submarine case, and acted for the applicants in separate challenges to permission granted by Daventry District Council and Derbyshire County Council to incinerate animal carcasses and extend waste disposal sites respectively. The cases appeared together in the Court of Appeal, with the former continuing to the House of Lords. Widely considered "*a key player*" among environmental practitioners, **Hannah Mackinlay** (see p.361) has recently moved from Pinsents to Putsman.wlc. Operating on the non-contentious side, she is especially well respected for her technical ability within a project finance or transactional context.

EAST ANGLIA

MILLS & REEVE (see firm details p.1071) This high-profile planning outfit also tops the region's environment table, with its considerable strength and depth of expertise, operating primarily in the development, waste management, property and corporate sectors. **David Brock** (see p.649) has a national reputation and is "*able to provide real insight into the big cases.*" He played a notable role in Aggregates Industries v English Nature, a leading case in the application of human rights law to wildlife protection. "*Enthusiastic*" **Rebecca Carriage** (see p.358) recently acted for Norfolk Environmental Waste Services, achieving a time extension in a planning appeal with complex environmental implications, concerning a major landfill site. The team proffers comprehensive litigious and regulatory advice on liabilities, and has acted on an increasing number of prosecutions with an emphasis on those under the Water Resources Act for pollution of controlled waters. **Clients**

ENVIRONMENT ■ EAST ANGLIA/NORTH WEST

ENVIRONMENT
■ EAST ANGLIA

1 Mills & Reeve Cambridge, Norwich
Richard Buxton Cambridge
2 Eversheds Norwich
Hewitson Becke + Shaw Cambridge

LEADING INDIVIDUALS
1 BUXTON Richard Richard Buxton
2 BRYCE Andrew Andrew Bryce & Co
3 BROCK David Mills & Reeve
CARRIAGE Rebecca Mills & Reeve
4 JEWKES Penny Eversheds

This book is the product of 6,582 1/2 hour interviews. See p.7 for BMRB audit.
Within each band, firms are listed alphabetically. See individuals' profiles p.357

Norfolk Environmental Waste Services; Ugbrooke Environmental; Jarrold Printing; UEA; NHS Trusts; landowners.

RICHARD BUXTON Adjudged the claimant litigation and judicial review specialists in environmental impact, the firm attracts warm and wide-ranging commendation for its "inventive approach, which often achieves ground-breaking results." Richard Buxton was commended by barristers for "always developing arguments of greater refinement and sophistication," while solicitor peers admire him as a practitioner "who really gets things done." This is reflected in a recent favourable judgment at the ECHR in Hatton, the Heathrow night flights case. The firm also has a proven expertise in nature conservation cases. **Clients** Residents' groups; individual objectors.

EVERSHEDS (see firm details p.949) Transactional support for property, commercial and corporate departments remains at the core practice, with Penny Jewkes (see p.360) as a full-time specialist. Highly rated by peers, she recently advised Petchey Holdings on due diligence for the acquisition of 400 petrol stations. A key practice area is advice to high-profile property developers on contaminated land liabilities, while environmental impact assessment, packaging issues and waste management licences also feature. **Clients** Electricity Supply Nominees; Lancaster; Borough Council of King's Lynn and West Norfolk.

HEWITSON BECKE + SHAW (see firm details p.993) Continue to enjoy a "fair showing," representing corporate defendants, farmers and individuals under the leadership of Peter Brady in Cambridge. Also co-operating closely with the Northampton office, the planning-based team focuses on waste management and disposal issues, while also advising on environmental warranties and indemnities in property and corporate transactions. **Clients** Shanks Waste Services; University of Cambridge; Norfolk Homes; Medical Research Council; RSPB.

OTHER NOTABLE PRACTITIONERS "Easily capable of competing with the best London practitioners," sole practitioner Andrew Bryce is highly respected for his "well-rounded" environmental practice, defending UK and international corporate clients on a range of issues. With construction contractors, waste management agencies and oil companies among his clientele and a large environmental consultancy to boot, it is in the field of waste management and licensing that he is best known.

NORTH WEST

ENVIRONMENT
■ NORTH WEST

1 Eversheds Manchester
Leigh, Day & Co Manchester
2 Addleshaw Booth & Co Manchester
Hammond Suddards Edge Manchester
Masons Manchester
Wake Dyne Lawton Chester

LEADING INDIVIDUALS
1 SHEPHERD Elizabeth Eversheds
SHEPHERD Michael Hammond Suddards Edge
2 WAKE Brian Wake Dyne Lawton

This book is the product of 6,552 1/2 hour interviews. See p.7 for BMRB audit.
Within each band, firms are listed alphabetically. See individuals' profiles p.357

EVERSHEDS (see firm details p.949) City practitioners agree that this team is the region's preferred transactional operation. It enjoys a heavy preponderance of both UK and US clients. Elizabeth Shepherd (see p.362) retains a strong presence as national head of non-contentious environmental law. Recent highlights for the firm include advising HSBC and Caradon Plumbing Holdings on the disposal of Caradon's Mira Showers and Bathrooms divisions (total £383 million) and acting for SPX on the acquisition from EIS Group of its Plenty division, which services the oil and gas, chemical and water industries. The firm has also advised ARDEX on its multi-jurisdictional acquisition of the ceramic tiles adhesives division of Norcros (Holdings). Asbestos issues, environmental impact assessment and EHS policy statements also contribute to the workload. **Clients** DuPont (UK); AstraZeneca; Waste Recycling Group; BFGoodrich; Solectron; Ineos Acrylics UK; Anglo American; Renold.

LEIGH, DAY & CO (see firm details p.1036) The group retains its top tier ranking for its environmental plaintiff work under the leadership of Gisele Bakkenist. A substantial force in the region, its core strength is to be found in toxic tort expertise. This contentious practice represents individuals in civil suits and multi-party claims for environmental damages, and the team's specialism in carbon monoxide poisoning cases remains at the fore. **Clients** Individual applicants.

ADDLESHAW BOOTH & CO (see firm details p.838) Interviewees judged this "an important regional practice," both for transactional and advisory work. Its profile has been affected by the departure of Michael Kenworthy, who formerly headed up the Manchester arm of the planning and environmental team. The bulk of the workload consists of environmental assessment in the preparation of planning applications. The team also advises international clients on environmental due diligence in corporate and property transactions, particularly in the utilities sector. **Clients** Barclays Private Equity; Borden Chemicals UK; English Partnerships; Northwest Development Agency; GeoDelft Environmental.

HAMMOND SUDDARDS EDGE The pre-eminent figure here is Michael Shepherd, litigator and national head of the safety, health and environment group. Practitioners have made inroads on the non-contentious front, providing advice on environmental permits and EC law. The team advised INEOS Fluor on environmental issues concerning the acquisition and disposal of assets, waste disposal facilities and contaminated land. As well as preserving its niche in advising chemical producers and distributors, the team is active in the environmental aspects of PFI projects. The group has represented Bryant Homes on brownfield acquisitions for multimillion pound residential developments, and acted for Guardian Industries on its PPC permit obligations prior to the development of its first UK manufacturing plant. **Clients** AES Drax Power; Guardian Industries; Great Lakes Chemical; London Electricity; NOVA International Services.

MASONS (see firm details p.1057) A traditional construction base guarantees a steady stream of environmental work. The planning, environment and public law team is perceived by interviewees to come into its own in the North West, though the Manchester office works in close collaboration with its London-based colleagues. A diet of housing development-related environmental advice for the likes of Peel Holdings and Crest Nicholson Residential (South) has recently been a central feature. This has involved advising on infrastrucure improvements and the protection of wildlife, environmental liabilities and insurance. Other highlights include advising North Shropshire District Council on the compulsory purchase of a listed building in a conservation area with a potential public inquiry looming. Karen Cooksley in London heads up the national team. **Clients** Trafford Borough Council; Roland Bardsley; Morris Homes; Peel Holdings.

WAKE DYNE LAWTON (see firm details p.1177) Minerals, waste, planning and road haulage sectors form the bedrock of this practice, which sustains its market position with **Brian Wake** (see p.363). The defence of environmental prosecutions on the contentious side has increased, while the bulk of its instructions remain on brownfield development sites, mining-related permit applications and transactional support, including environmental insurance. Other areas of expertise include advising on wind farm projects. **Clients** RTZ.

NORTH EAST

ENVIRONMENT
NORTH EAST

1. **Eversheds** Leeds
2. **Nabarro Nathanson** Sheffield
3. **Addleshaw Booth & Co** Leeds
   DLA Sheffield
4. **Dickinson Dees** Newcastle upon Tyne
   Hammond Suddards Edge Leeds
   Pinsent Curtis Biddle Leeds

LEADING INDIVIDUALS

★ **SMITH Paul** Eversheds
1. **CLARKE Ray** Nabarro Nathanson
   HITCHCOCK Teresa DLA
   RENGER Mike Nabarro Nathanson
2. **BELL Stuart** Eversheds
   BERESFORD Amanda Addleshaw Booth & Co
   DOWEN Denise Dickinson Dees
   PIKE John Addleshaw Booth & Co

This book is the product of 6,582 1/2 hour interviews. See p.7 for BMRB audit.
Within each band, firms are listed alphabetically. See individuals' profiles p.357

EVERSHEDS (see firm details p.949) "*A strong office with a substantial national client base.*" Market commentators endorse its litigious corporate defence practice, which covers a variety of toxic tort, insurance, water pollution and nuisance cases and judicial reviews. The team is best known for its crisis management expertise, often involving criminal proceedings, and it also conducts transactional support and compliance work for its chemicals, utilities and manufacturing clients. Applauded as an "*excellent environmental litigator,*" Paul Smith (see p.362) recently advised DuPont on the establishment of the UK Emissions Trading System and on lobbying DEFRA and negotiating baseline trading agreements. Smith and the academic **Stuart Bell** (see p.357) successfully advised British Waterways in a case that went to the House of Lords, following a Court of Appeal hearing against Severn Trent Water, regarding the right to discharge water from its sewers into canals. **Clients** British Waterways Board; McCain Foods; EWS; DuPont; Mothercare; Waste Recycling Group.

NABARRO NATHANSON (see firm details p.1080) Peers contend that this firm has come of age, "*successfully branching out with further minerals and mining work,*" resulting in an "*extensive environmental practice*" with many interviewees aware of its national impact. Highly rated for the "*instrumental role he takes in transactions,*" **Mike Renger** (see p.361) advised Fenner on environmental due diligence in its acquisition of Dunlop-Enerka, which involved the investigation of sites across the US and Europe. He is also contact partner for UK Nirex and offers policy advice on long-term solutions for radioactive waste. Other non-contentious work at the firm has encompassed advising corporate clients at board level on the drafting of environmental policy. **Ray Clarke** (see p.358) is equally well regarded, particularly for his "*no-nonsense approach and fabulous expertise.*" He retains his profile for regulatory advice and civil and criminal environmental litigation. This has included judicial reviews involving mixed human rights and environmental issues and waste licensing and planning. Extensive contaminated land advice to both the public sector and to clients owning multi-sites countrywide has also featured among the group's recent achievements. **Clients** Balfour Beatty; Biffa Waste Services; The Coal Authority; UK Nirex; Waste Recycling Group; Leicester City Council; Syngenta.

ADDLESHAW BOOTH & CO (see firm details p.838) The better known of the firm's two Northern offices, it is an "*advanced environmental operation,*" particularly on property and planning-related matters. **Amanda Beresford** (see p.357) was applauded by clients for her "*top-notch advice on complex contaminated land issues.*" She represented NPL Estates on a 1,400-acre urban regeneration scheme at a former ICI site, which included a proposed energy park. Beresford also advised Fenner on the environmental aspects of a disposal, involving an environmental covenant relating to several European countries. The team has also been newly appointed as panel lawyers to English Nature. Peers also singled out **John Pike** (see p.734), who benefits from a strong property background, and the firm takes advantage from the services of an environmental consultant in Victoria Joy. **Clients** Fenner; NPL Estates; Kvaerner Estates; Kvaerner Energy.

DLA This strong regulatory team features specialist **Teresa Hitchcock**. The firm concentrates on non-contentious matters but also possesses the capacity for litigious matters, and it covers mining and metals, chemical and waste management sectors. The team has advised corporations on environmental report issues, Climate Change Levy and IPPC.

DICKINSON DEES (see firm details p.938) Part of a wider regulatory practice, the environment group covers corporate due diligence, stand-alone and litigious environmental work. Peers agree that the team is seen on the "*majority of environmental prosecutions*" in the region, and it is commended for the breadth of its client base. Recent matters have involved defending allegations arising from imported pesticides, civil claims regarding environmental pollution and contaminated land issues. **Denise Dowen** (see p.359) heads the team and has a focus on the contentious side. **Clients** Chemical company; food manufacturer; local authority; waste management company.

HAMMOND SUDDARDS EDGE Interviewees perceived this team, headed by David Williams and David Goodman, to be at its strongest in environmental litigation. Drawing on its ample utilities sector client base, the team defended Scottish and Southern Electricity in a prosecution brought by the Environment Agency relating to groundwater pollution caused by a leak of coolant oil from underground electricity cables. It also sustains a significant profile advising on environmental liabilities in chemicals, food and drink and healthcare sectors, while possessing niche expertise in environmentally sensitive planning projects. **Clients** ICI; BASF; Royal Bank of Scotland; Rank Group; Kelda; KPMG; Horizon; ScottishPower; The National Grid Company; BNFL; John Mowlem & Company.

PINSENT CURTIS BIDDLE (see firm details p.1102) Much of the firm's environmental profile lies with supporting advice to its corporate team, but the team also brings to bear expertise

ENVIRONMENT ■ NORTH EAST/SCOTLAND

on property and planning matters. Peter Atkinson leads the team, which is distributed between Birmingham and Leeds offices. With a wide-ranging regulatory practice, it covers the defence of prosecutions by enforcement authorities, environmental assessments, accident management and negotiations on warranties in corporate deals. **Clients** Abbott Laboratories; Hanson; Tesco; Premdor; Schneider Electric; OSS Group; Viridor Waste Management; Powell Duffryn; IMI; SIG.

SCOTLAND

ENVIRONMENT ■ SCOTLAND

1. **Brodies** Edinburgh
2. **Maclay Murray & Spens** Glasgow
   McGrigor Donald Glasgow
3. **Bishops Solicitors** (Formerly Morison Bishop) Glasgow
   Dundas & Wilson CS Edinburgh
   MacRoberts Glasgow
4. **Burness** Edinburgh
   Tods Murray WS Edinburgh

LEADING INDIVIDUALS

1. **SMITH Charles** Brodies
2. **BROWN Vincent** Semple Fraser
   ROSS Kenneth Bishops solicitors
3. **GRANT James** MacRoberts
4. **AMNER Neil** Biggart Baillie
   SALES Martin Burness
   TAYLOR Douglas Maclay Murray & Spens
   UP AND COMING
   AITCHISON Karen Dundas & Wilson CS

This book is the product of 6,582 1/2 hour interviews. See p.7 for BMRB audit. Within each band, firms are listed alphabetically. See individuals' profiles p.357

BRODIES (see firm details p.889) Though not unanimous, the dominant opinion among interviewees was that it remains "*far and away number one.*" The firm's current position is due in no small part to possessing "*one of the best in the country,*" **Charles Smith** (see p.362). Lead partner in the environmental law group, he recently advised the Scottish Environment Protection Agency (SEPA) on the first transfrontier shipment of an oil rig from Scottish waters to Norway, effected under EC regulations for dismantling and decontamination. Smith also commented on the Scottish Executive consultation paper for the EU Water Framework Directive. Other highlights for the firm include advising British Waterways on mercury contamination in a canal and South Lanarkshire Council on the transfer of liability in relation to chromium contamination in the disposal of land. The practice covers corporate, commercial property and litigation matters. **Clients** Corus UK; Dalgleish Associates; Dumfries & Galloway Council; Crop Chemicals; BOCM PAULS; Ashdale Land & Property Company.

MACLAY MURRAY & SPENS (see firm details p.1048) "*One of the main players,*" it incorporates standalone and transactional environment advice. A fully-fledged planning and environmental team offers expertise in environmental insurance contracts, waste management licensing, clinical waste incineration, Climate Change Levy and IPC/IPPC regimes. Andrew Primrose has now retired, while **Douglas Taylor** (see p.363) has been widely recognised for his "*specialist role at the firm.*" The team recently advised Wilson Bowden on the Ravenscraig Steelworks mixed development, and acted for a private landfill licensee in a successful appeal against SEPA. It also advised a major river management trust on interpreting the EU Water Framework Directive during negotiations with manufacturers. **Clients** British Waterways Board; Allied Distillers; Bank of Scotland; DuPont Teijin Films; Compaq Computer Manufacturing.

MCGRIGOR DONALD (see firm details p.1065) Led by partner Jennifer Ballantyne, this planning and environment team specialises in waste management, minerals, renewable energy and contaminated land issues, and is supported by its London and Belfast offices. The practice has witnessed a growth in advice on off- and onshore wind energy schemes and continues to advise on PFI-related matters. An established waste management practice advises local authorities and the MOD on outsourcing projects. **Clients** MOD; BP; Lattice Property Holdings; Clyde Port; Forth Port Authority; Dexter Corp.

BISHOPS SOLICITORS (see firm details p.1076) The firm is led in this sphere by well-renowned contaminated land expert **Kenneth Ross** (see p.361), who also heads up the commercial property department. Although felt by our interviewees to be lower in profile over the last year, the firm continues to act on land contamination issues – recently with regard to sites owned by a major chemical company – general environmental liabilities, waste management licences and litigation. Other specialist areas include providing due diligence for property acquisitions and disposals and IPC/IPPC. **Clients** ICI; Greenpeace; Motorola; AstraZeneca.

DUNDAS & WILSON CS (see firm details p.943) The group is commended for cultivating new talent in the form of assistant solicitor **Karen Aitchison**, who received praise among peers as a "*talented full-time specialist,*" bringing experience gained on secondment to SEPA. Aitchison featured in advice to HypoVereinsbank on potential environmental exposure in its £102 million funding of the acquisition by MWB Leisure of various leisure developments, and instructions from WOSWA on environmental aspects of its effluent treating plants, including advice on EC directives. The team enjoys an extensive list of institutional clients, and the mainstay of the practice continues to be transactional support within chemicals, water, technology and engineering sectors. Expertise in environmental impact assessment exists within the planning and PFI spheres, and the team also fields an assistant with experience as environmental counsel to the government of Hong Kong. **Clients** Bank of Scotland; West of Scotland Water Authority; Tilbury Douglas; Abbey National Treasury Services; SEPA; Micron Technologies.

MACROBERTS (see firm details p.1049) PFI specialist **Jamie Grant** (see p.359) heads a combined planning and environmental unit that is renowned in Scotland and beyond. The practice has recently advised on landfill sites, waste treatment facilities, the financing of a waste management licence, wind farms and contamination insurance for site development. Highlights include advising GlaxoSmithKline on proposals to change its method of disposal of trade effluent under Urban Waste Water Treatment Regulations, acting for Catchment Moray in negotiations with SEPA and advising the Scottish Executive on proposals for a sludge drier under IPPC regulations. Other long-standing strengths include advising on Scottish waste water PFI projects and contaminated land matters for NHS Trusts. **Clients** Yorkshire Environmental Solutions; B&S Visual Technologies; Scottish Nuclear; AMEC Construction; Royal Infirmary of Edinburgh NHS Trust; Texaco.

BURNESS The firm is building on its environmental expertise, with the recruitment of a solicitor from New Zealand and new instructions from Yorkshire Water and Alfred Stewart Properties. Based in the property department, the team's focus is on minerals, waste, PFI and planning applications. **Martin Sales** remains respected for his mining and waste sector expertise; he recently advised Shanks Group in the Argyll and Bute and Dumfries and Galloway waste water projects. The team has also won standalone instructions from William Munro on its PPC permit application for a raised landfill site in the Highland region. Further highlights include advising a major bank in a regeneration project at a former minerals working site and defending an enforcement order in relation to waste water. The team has also advised exten-

NORTHERN IRELAND/THE LEADERS ■ ENVIRONMENT

sively on nuclear contamination of sites. **Clients** Brown Brothers (Rolls Royce); Royal Bank of Scotland; Lothian Hospital Trust; DERA; Caledonian Paper; Shanks Group; Lafarge Redland Aggregates.

TODS MURRAY WS (see firm details p.1164) Clients told *Chambers'* researchers they valued "*wide and varied environmental advice*" from this integrated planning and environment team, led by Ian McPake. It remains best known for construction, PFI, incinerator and sewage-related expertise, and has some litigation capacity. Recent matters include new instructions from The States of Guernsey on a waste to energy project, and acting for a national house builder on historic land contamination. Long-standing clients have been a source of instruction, including Aberdeen Environmental Services on UK and EC water quality requirements and Dundee Energy Recycling on the transportation of clinical waste. **Clients** Aberdeen Environmental Services; Dundee Energy Recycling; Forestry Commission; Nevis Range Development Company; RSPB; WWF; Woodland Trust.

OTHER NOTABLE PRACTITIONERS Praised by peers for his "*determined and personal approach,*" **Vincent Brown** (see p.358), already recognised as a pure environmental lawyer, is seen as benefiting from a strong corporate practice at Semple Fraser. As well as advising on contaminated land in brownfield developments, he is also known for the cross-border dimension to his practice and his involvement with a wide range of inward investors. He is retained by Oiltools (Europe) and The Greenbelt Group of Companies, and has advised the latter on the acquisition of the secure containment facility and treatment plant at the former Ravenscraig Steelworks site. **Neil Amner** at Biggart Baillie specialises in contaminated land, IPC/PPC and waste management licensing. Peers confirm that he has increased his profile, focusing on both standalone and transactional advice in the energy sector; he advised on the sale of BP's fuels marketing and distribution business in mainland Scotland.

NORTHERN IRELAND

ENVIRONMENT
■ NORTHERN IRELAND

1. **Cleaver Fulton Rankin** Belfast

LEADING INDIVIDUALS

1. **FARIS Neil** Cleaver Fulton Rankin

This book is the product of 6,552 1/2 hour interviews. See p.7 for BMRB audit.
Within each band, firms are listed alphabetically. See individuals' profiles p.357

CLEAVER FULTON RANKIN (see firm details p.910) The firm remains unique in Northern Ireland as the only one to boast a significant environmental profile. It has advised on contaminated land in the context of property transactions and brownfield redevelopment on industrial sites. The group has grown environmental insurance as a niche area of expertise. Led by **Neil Faris** (see p.359), it acted for a Northern Irish council on a waste disposal licence appeal with human rights implications. It has also defended companies against pollution claims and acted for both claimants and NGOs. Planning-related environmental issues also contribute to the practice. **Clients** Water Service; Belfast City Airport; Antrim Borough Council.

THE LEADERS IN ENVIRONMENT

ABRAHAM, Henry
Brachers, Maidstone
(01622) 690691
henryabraham@brachers.co.uk
See under Planning, p.649

AITCHISON, Karen
Dundas & Wilson CS, Edinburgh
(0131) 228 8000

ALLEN, Tony
DMH, Brighton
(01273) 744451
tony.allen@dmh.co.uk
See under Planning, p.649

AMNER, Neil
Biggart Baillie, Glasgow
(0141) 228 8000

BAKER, Neil
Clarke Willmott & Clarke, Bristol
(0117) 941 6658
nbaker@cw-c.co.uk
Specialisation: Partner specialising in environmental and planning law including planning and other development applications, agreements, appeals, public inquiries, High Court proceedings, pollution control under the Environmental Acts, defending environmental prosecutions and advice on minerals, waste and contaminated land. Recent experience has included advising a waste disposal company on the acquisition of landfill sites in Hampshire and Berkshire and acting for a major horticultural company in connection with environmental issues that surround its peat harvesting activities.
Prof. Memberships: Vice-Chairman UKELA South West.
Career: Articled with *Nicholson Graham & Jones*; qualified in 1994. Joined *Clarke Willmott & Clarke* in 1999. Partner 2001.
Personal: Attended Bristol University (BSc Hons Biochemistry). Leisure interests include golf, squash and the theatre.

BARLOW, Richard
Browne Jacobson, Nottingham
(0115) 976 6208
rbarlow@brownej.co.uk
Specialisation: Partner dealing with a broad range of environmental law. Advising at a strategic level upon the impact of legal developments in environmental policy. Head of Countryside Team, acting for both English Nature and the Countryside Council for Wales. Regular trial and public inquiry advocate. Key member of firm's Insurance and Public Risk Department concentrating upon devising environmental risk management solutions.
Prof. Memberships: UKELA, Legal Associate of the RTPI and Nottingham Green Partnership Steering Group.
Career: Articled with Hertfordshire County Council, joined *Browne Jacobson* in 1990, becoming a Partner in 1999.
Publications: Practitioner's contributions to Garner's Rights of Way.
Personal: Oulder Hill School, Rochdale (1978-83), University of Sheffield LLB Hons (1983-86). Diploma in Local Government Law and Practice. Continues to participate in many sports despite declining level of achievement.

BELL, Stuart
Eversheds, Leeds
(0113) 243 0391
stuartbell@eversheds.com
Specialisation: Consultant. Main area of practice is environmental law. Advises on the whole range of environmental issues with particular emphasis on commercial and regulatory matters. Institutional clients include the Environment Agency, the Australian Commonwealth Environmental Protection Agency, the World Health Organisation and the European Commission. Commercial clients include chemical companies, utilities and retailers. Editor of the Environmental Law Reports and Water Law. Editorial board member of the Journal of Planning and Environment Law. *Eversheds* Professor of Environment Law at Nottingham Law School.

BERESFORD, Amanda
Addleshaw Booth & Co, Leeds
(0113) 209 2325
amanda.beresford@addleshawbooth.com
Specialisation: All planning work including retail, leisure, industrial, residential and advocacy at Public Inquiries. Comprehensive environmental advice including pollution control, energy, waste, transport, contaminated land and due diligence. Clients advised include major development and manufacturing companies, utilities, banks and local authorities. Particular expertise in environmental and planning issues in urban regeneration projects. Recognised authoress and speaker at conferences.
Prof. Memberships: Qualified planner. Member UKELA.
Career: Qualified in 1985, joined *Addleshaw Booth & Co* in 1997. Partner and Head of Environmental and Planning Unit, *Addleshaw Booth & Co*.

BOSWALL, Julian
Morgan Cole, Cardiff
(029) 2038 5385

BOWDEN, Paul
Freshfields Bruckhaus Deringer, London
(020) 7936 4000
paul.bowden@freshfields.com
Specialisation: Partner in Litigation Department. Multi-party litigation and

357

ENVIRONMENT ■ THE LEADERS

judicial review cases in the environmental and product fields.
Prof. Memberships: Membership: Joint Bar/Law Society Working Party on Civil Justice (1992-93); Lord Woolf's advisory committee on multi-party actions (1995-96); Chairman of Nottingham Law School.
Career: Qualified with *Freshfields* in 1981. Partner in 1987, qualified in Hong Kong, 1986.
Personal: Born 1955. Educated: Bristol University 1973-78.

BROCK, David
Mills & Reeve, Cambridge
(01223) 222 438
david.brock@mills-reeve.com
See under Planning, p.649

BROWN, Vincent
Semple Fraser, Glasgow
(0141) 221 3771
vincent.brown@semplefraser.co.uk
Specialisation: Environmental law, with emphasis on (1) contractual work associated with contaminated land redevelopment – remediation contracts, building contracts, indemnity contracts, environmental liability insurance contracts, professional team appointments, (2) waste management and regulation, (3) regulatory issues, negotiation and appeals, (4) advising industrial corporates in sensitive areas (eg oil, chemicals, steel, waste industries) on all aspects of environmental compliance and liability, (5) environmental taxation, including landfill tax, corporation tax relief for contaminated land, the aggregates levy and the climate change levy, (6) EU environmental impact and policy and (7) nature conservation and other ecological liability.
Prof. Memberships: Law Society of Scotland, British Urban Regeneration Agency (BURA), Lanarkshire Environmental Business Club.
Career: Shepherd and Wedderburn, Edinburgh (2 years); *Dorman Jeffrey and Co*, Glasgow (10 years, 6 as Partner); *Dundas and Wilson/Anderson Legal* (4 years as partner), *Semple Fraser WS*, partner, June 2001.
Personal: University of Glasgow: MA, LLB. Married with two children (11 and 5).

BRUMWELL, Mark
SJ Berwin, London
(020) 7533 2784
mark.brumwell@sjberwin.com
Specialisation: All areas of environmental law with particular emphasis on environmental aspects of corporate and property transactions, due diligence, contaminated land, land use planning, water, waste and nature conservation. Recent work has included advice on contaminated land on development for a supermarket, leisure uses and housing, upgrading of wastewater treatment works, and compliance issues for a pharmaceutical plant and power station. Has also advised on other environmental and health and safety issues for the property, banking, private equity, engineering, utilities, construction, pharmaceutical, plastics and automotive sectors. Has particular expertise of infrastructure projects, especially flood alleviation schemes, sewage treatment plants and railways.
Prof. Memberships: Member of the Law Society's Planning Panel. Legal Associate of the Royal Town Planning Institute; Council Member of the United Kingdom Environmental Law Association, Co-ordinator of all UKELA's Working Groups and former Convenor of its Water Working Group. Associate of the Institute of Environmental Science.
Career: University of Bristol – LLB (Hons). Articled with *Simmons & Simmons*. With *Ashurst Morris Crisp* for seven years including a period of secondment to the London Docklands Development Corporation. Environment Group at *S J Berwin & Co* since March 1996. Partner since May 1998.
Personal: Married and lives in Hertfordshire. Leisure interests include motorsport, photography, mountain walking, golf and badminton.

BRYCE, Andrew John
Andrew Bryce & Co, Coggeshall
(01376) 563123

BUXTON, Richard
Richard Buxton, Cambridge
(01223) 328933

CARRIAGE, Rebecca
Mills & Reeve, Norwich
(01603) 693228
rebecca.carriage@mills-reeve.com
Specialisation: Environmental (including health and safety and food safety) and town and country planning (including compulsory purchase). Recent work includes major mineral and waste planning appeals and development plan work; defence of statutory nuisance, environmental and health and safety prosecutions; referrals to the Lands Tribunal involving questions of law and valuation; waste management licenses and IPPC law; advice on strategic coastal defence strategies.
Prof. Memberships: Member of Steering Group of East Anglian Business Environment Club. Associate member of Environmental Services Association. Panellist on BBC Radio Norfolk's monthly legal slot.
Career: Articled *Hill & Perks* (now *Eversheds*, Norwich). Moved to *Mills & Reeve* 1988. Associate 2000.

CLARKE, Ray
Nabarro Nathanson, Sheffield
(0114) 279 4028
r.clarke@nabarro.com
Specialisation: Civil litigation including defending high profile multi-party actions. Environmental and health and safety prosecutions including advocacy; waste and other enforcement appeals, industrial nuisances, water, contamination, air pollution, PPC, COMAH and WML issues. Lead advisor to waste and chemical international. Acquisitions and disposals. Privatisation – mines and chemicals. Urban regeneration with particular emphasis on brownfield sites. Human rights issues. Management of large development schemes including town centres, sub-regional shopping centre (Trafford centre). Judicial review and public inquiries. Crisis and awareness training for directors and managers.
Prof. Memberships: Former member of UKELA Council. Fellow of the Institute of Quarrying. Visiting tutor on environmental, regeneration and human rights issues at International Development Law Institute, Rome.

CUCKSON, David
Stephenson Harwood (incorporating Sinclair Roche & Temperley), London
(020) 7809 2505
david.cuckson@shlegal.com
Specialisation: Partner, property department and head of environmental law group. He covers most aspects of environmental law. Specific work includes issues relating to contaminated land, corporate mergers and acquisitions and waste management. He also handles property law work relating to education, local government and other public bodies, including PFI projects. Has written articles and lectured extensively on environmental law topics.
Prof. Memberships: Chairman of UK Environmental Law Association 1999-2001, also member of Contaminated Land and Waste Working Parties.
Career: Qualified October 1978. Held various posts in different local government authorities, most recently as Borough Secretary and Solicitor for Test Valley Borough Council 1988-89. Joined *Stephenson Harwood* in 1989 and became partner in 1992.

DAVEY, Catherine
Stevens & Bolton, Guildford
(01483) 734234
Specialisation: All aspects of environmental law including contaminated land, statutory nuisances, waste disposal, corporate support. Highways and commons law. Town and country planning.
Prof. Memberships: Law Society; Council Member United Kingdom Environmental Law Association; Trustee Environment Law Foundation; FRGS.
Career: Woking County Grammar School for Girls, University of Exeter (BA Hons). Joined *Stevens & Bolton* 1988 from local government, becoming a Partner in 1989.
Publications: Contributor to 'Sustainable Architecture, European Directives & Building Design' (Butterworths). Editor: 'E-law' – e-journal of United Kingdom Environmental Law Association.
Personal: Leisure interests are foreign travel, photography, sailing, film, theatre, the arts and virtual reality gardening. Trustee New Ashgate Gallery.

DAVIES, Paul
Macfarlanes, London
(020) 7831 9222

DAY, Martyn
Leigh, Day & Co, London
(020) 7650 1200
See under Product Liability, p.670

DE WIT, Elisa
Berwin Leighton Paisner, London
(020) 7760 1000

DEANESLY, Clare
Gouldens, London
(020) 7842 6144
chd@gouldens.com
Specialisation: Partner and Head of Environmental Law Group. Principal area of practice is environmental law, dealing with minerals, waste management, landfill and contaminated land cases. Also handles general commercial property work including landlord and tenant matters and retail and development work. Major transactions include: 1986 acted on sale of London Brick Landfill to Shanks & McEwan; 1993 acted for the Landfill Division of ARC (Greenways) in their acquisition of Econowaste from Tarmac plc; 1993 and 1996 acted for London Brick Property Limited on sale of substantial landfill void to Shanks & McEwan; 1996 acted for minerals division of ARC in Midlands joint venture with Tarmac plc; 1998 acted on landfill and minerals sites in connection with sale of Hanson Properties; 1999 acted on sale of Hughes Waste Management Limited; 2000 acted on sale of Hanson Waste Management to Waste Recycling Group plc. Other major clients include Hanson Brick Limited, SITA, Biffa Waste Management and Waste Recycling Group plc. Has also advised on landfill tax and environmental bodies. Contributor to ESA training seminars on Duty of Care and on Transfer Stations and MRF's; speaker on waste management issues at conferences and seminars.
Prof. Memberships: Law Society, UKELA, ESA. Member of UKELA Waste Working Party. Member of ICC Committee on Environment, ESA Public Affairs Committee and ESA General Planning Committee.
Career: Qualified in 1977 while at *Field Fisher Martineau*. Joined *Gouldens* in 1978 and became a Partner in 1980.
Publications: Author of Badlands 'Essential Environmental Law for Property Professionals' (1993) and author of various articles on waste management property issues for professional publications.
Personal: Born 30 May 1953. Attended Edgbaston C of E College for Girls, Birmingham 1957-71, then Southampton University 1971-74 (LLB Hons). Leisure pursuits include family, skiing, walking, tennis, travel, theatre and opera. Lives in London.

THE LEADERS ■ ENVIRONMENT

DOOLITTLE, Ian
Trowers & Hamlins, London
(020) 7423 8000
idoolittle@trowers.com
See under Social Housing, p.762

DOWEN, Denise
Dickinson Dees, Newcastle upon Tyne
(0191) 279 9215
law@dickinson-dees.com
Specialisation: Practice covers all aspects of environmental law in relation to company and property transactions including EIAs, waste management, water pollution, process authorisations and contaminated land. Acts for developers, lending institutions and waste management companies.
Prof. Memberships: Law Society. Member of CBI Environment Committee.
Career: Qualified in 1990. Trained with Avon County Council before moving to private practice. Joined *Dickinson Dees* in 1994.
Personal: Born July 1965. Read Law at the University of Leeds.

ENRIGHT, Joanna
Ashurst Morris Crisp, London
(020) 7638 1111

FAIRLEY, Ross
Allen & Overy, London
(020) 7330 3000
ross.fairley@allenovery.com
Specialisation: Involved in all aspects of UK and EU environmental and health and safety law particularly in areas such as policy, management and audit, contaminated land, power, renewables and infrastructure projects and lender liability. A regular speaker and author on environmental matters.
Prof. Memberships: Law Society, United Kingdom Environmental Law Association, Institute of Environmental Management and Assessment. Sits on the DTI's Innovation and Growth Team for the Environmental Goods and Services Sector.
Publications: Legal Editor of Gee's 'Environmental Risk Manager' and 'Premises, Health and Safety' and Tolley's 'Environmental Law and Procedures Management'.
Personal: Interests include all sports, particularly hockey, cricket and driving an old Austin Healey 'Frogeye' Sprite. Born 1968. Leicester University (LLB 1990).

FARIS, Neil
Cleaver Fulton Rankin, Belfast
(028) 9024 3141
n.faris@cfrlaw.co.uk
Specialisation: Environmental law.
Prof. Memberships: Council Member of the United Kingdom Environmental Law Association; founder Member and Chair 1998-99 Environmental & Planning Law Association of Northern Ireland.
Career: Qualified in 1977 and Managing Partner and Head of Consultancy Department (1998-2002).
Personal: Born 1950, educated in Belfast and at Trinity College Dublin and University of Cambridge.

FOGLEMAN, Valerie
Barlow Lyde & Gilbert, London
(020) 7247 2277
vfogleman@blg.co.uk
Specialisation: All aspects of environmental law including environmental liability, particularly contaminated land and water pollution, environmental insurance policies, environmental insurance coverage claims, due diligence and criminal and civil environmental litigation.
Prof. Memberships: Convenor, United Kingdom Environmental Law Association (UKELA) Insurance and Liability Working Party; Chair, Construction Industry Research and Information Association Contaminated Land and Urban Regeneration Working Party. Memberships include Lloyd's European Environment Working Group; UKELA Council; City of London Law Society Planning and Environmental Law Subcommittee.
Career: Solicitor and member of Texas State Bar; practised environmental and insurance law in Texas before joining *Barlow Lyde & Gilbert* in 1992; became partner in 1998. University of Illinois (1992 LLM); Texas Tech University (1989 MSc, 1989 JD, 1983 BLA).
Publications: Numerous books and articles on environmental liabilities and environmental insurance in UK and US publications including regular articles in Insurance Day; frequent speaker in UK and overseas.

FORSTER, Malcolm
Freshfields Bruckhaus Deringer, London
(020) 7936 4000
malcolm.forster@freshfields.com
Specialisation: Partner dealing with environmental aspects of corporate transactions and financings, handling environmental indemnity and warranty disputes, negotiating with regulatory agencies over environmental remediation requirements for contaminated land and groundwater, production and management of environmental impact assessments.
Prof. Memberships: International Bar Association, Selden Society. Professor of International Environmental Law, University of Kent.
Career: Qualified 1992. Partner 1995. Director of the Centre for Environmental Law at the University of Southampton 1973-84 and 1987-91. General Counsel for the Commission on Environmental Law at the International Union for Conservation of Nature and Natural Resources, Bonn, Germany, 1984-87.
Publications: Editor of 'Environmental Law & Management'.
Personal: Born 1948. Attended University of Southampton 1967-70.

GARBUTT, John
Nicholson Graham & Jones, London
(020) 7360 8208
john.garbutt@ngj.co.uk
Specialisation: Head of Planning and Environment Unit. Planning and environmental law, including appeals, development plans, environment disputes, audits and policy, compulsory purchase, rating, Lands Tribunal, major planning inquiries concerning minerals, waste management, leisure developments, and judicial reviews.
Prof. Memberships: UKELA, Environmental Services Association. The firm is a member of the Land Pollution Consortium.
Career: Qualified in 1963. Local government 1965-69. Blue Circle Industries (1978-85), Chief Executive, Blue Circle Industrial Minerals (1986-88) and Blue Circle Waste Management (1989). *Nicholson Graham & Jones,* Partner 1991.
Publications: 'Environmental Law – A Practical Handbook'; 'Waste Management Law: A Manager's Handbook'. Contributor, 'Commercial Environmental Law and Liability'.

GIBBS, Kevin
Osborne Clarke, Bristol
(0117) 917 3000

GRANT, James
MacRoberts, Glasgow
(0141) 332 9988
jamie.grant@macroberts.com
Specialisation: Main areas of practice are planning and environmental law, although also does some commercial property work (mainly development work involving planning or contamination issues).
Prof. Memberships: Law Society of Scotland.
Career: Edinburgh University 1979-84. *Mitchells Roberton* 1984-88 (Trainee/Assistant). *Maclay Murray & Spens* 1988-91 (Assistant/Associate). *MacRoberts* 1991-present (Assistant/Associate/Partner –1993).
Publications: Co-author of planning and environmental chapter in 'Building Law and Development – Scots Law and Procedure'.
Personal: Born 29 June 1961. Lives Glasgow. Leisure interests include sailing, music and gardening.

GREENWOOD, Brian
Norton Rose, London
(020) 7283 6000
greenwoodbj@nortonrose.com
Specialisation: Corporate acquisitions, disposals and funding; environmental due diligence, project finance, waste, water and IPPC including appeals and advocacy; international practice with considerable experience in Eastern Europe. Current clients include BMW (sale of Rover/Land Rover); Castle Cement Ltd., environmental challenge being referred to European Court; Associated British Ports, Dibdon Terminal, Southampton, public enquiry.
Prof. Memberships: Former chairman Law Society's Planning and Environmental Law committee, CBI Environmental Protection panel; UKELA.
Career: Qualified in local government, chief solicitor at Bedfordshire County Council. Joined *Norton Rose* in 1985, partner in 1988.
Publications: Author 'Butterworths Planning Law Service'. Co-author 'Environment Regulation and Economic Growth'. Editor 'Butterworths Planning Law Handbook'.

HAVARD-WILLIAMS, Vanessa
Linklaters, London
(020) 7456 4280
vanessa.havard-williams@linklaters.com
Specialisation: Member of the firm's environmental unit since 1990 and founder partner of the Environmental Law Group. Specialist in all aspects of environmental work (including corporate, advisory and litigious) and commercial, including EC litigation.
Career: 1999 to date: Partner, *Linklaters* London (Environmental Law Group); 1994-99: Assistant Solicitor, *Linklaters* London (Litigation Department); 1991-93: Assistant Solicitor, *Linklaters* Brussels; 1990-91: Assistant Solicitor, *Linklaters* London (Litigation Department); 1988-90: Trainee Solicitor, *Linklaters.* 1987-88: College of Law, Law Society Final Examinations; 1984-87: Oxford University, BA (Hons).

HAYDEN, Tim
Clarke Willmott & Clarke, Taunton
(01823) 445204
thayden@cw-c.co.uk
Specialisation: Partner and one of the leading specialist environmental lawyers in the South West. As a Solicitor Advocate, he practises in the Magistrates Courts and in the Crown Courts. Previously was a prosecutor for HM Inspectorate of Pollution. Has wide experience relating to waste management, contaminated land, air and water pollution and statutory nuisance including noise and odour abatement. Also has a substantial workload in relation to food safety, animal welfare, health and safety, and rights of way. Is an NFU Panel Solicitor.
Prof. Memberships: Member of the United Kingdom Environmental Law Association.
Career: Qualified in 1981. Joined *Clarke Willmott & Clarke* in 1979, becoming a Partner in 1985. Qualified as a Higher Courts Advocate in 1995.
Personal: Attended Bristol Grammar School 1968-74, University College Cardiff 1974-78 and College of Law Guildford 1978-79. Leisure interests include golf and cricket.

HITCHCOCK, Teresa
DLA, Sheffield
(08700) 111111

HOBLEY, Anthony
Baker & McKenzie, London
(020) 7919 1000
anthony.hobley@bakernet.com
Specialisation: Senior Associate in both the Environmental Law Group and the Global Climate Change and Clean Energy Group. Handles a wide range of environment law matters with particular emphasis on the environment aspects of

359

ENVIRONMENT ■ THE LEADERS

national and international corporate, banking and property transactions. Advises regularly in relation to contaminated land and its redevelopment; regulatory and enforcement issues and major infrastructure projects; waste; trading of economic environment instruments; lender liability issues; environmental liability in the context of insolvency; landfill tax, the terms and coverage of environment insurance products. Increasingly advising on climate change issues, permit trading, climate change levy energy efficiency agreements, emissions reduction projects, energy efficiency, renewable energy and related matters. He is regularly invited to speak at public conferences on a range of issues and has had a number of articles published on issues such as contaminated land and greenhouse gas emissions. He is the co-ordinator for his firm's central European Environment Law Group and travels regularly to central Europe in this capacity.
Prof. Memberships: Law Society, UK Environmental Law Association, graduate of the Royal Society of Chemistry.
Career: 1st Class Honours Degree in Chemistry with Physics. Qualified as a Solicitor in 1994. Joined *Baker & McKenzie* in August 2001.
Personal: Born 24 November 1966.

HOLMES, Sarah
Bond Pearce, Plymouth
(01752) 266633
sholmes@bondpearce.com
Specialisation: Associate specialising in environmental and planning law with MA (Oxon) and Master of Arts in Environmental Law (1997). National reputation for work in renewable energy having been at the forefront of the industry since 1991. Advises on all stages of the planning process, including environmental impact assessment, with clients in public and private sector. Extensive environmental practice includes contaminated land remediation, risk minimisation and allocation, environmental insurance, complex landfill tax issues, European Sites (nature conservation) and consents/permits. Active involvement in major waste, minerals, food and motor deals with due diligence on many further transactions.
Prof. Memberships: Council Member of UK Environmental Law Association; Secretary of UKELA South West and member of British Wind Energy Association.
Career: Qualified 1991 with *Bond Pearce*, becoming Associate 1997.

HUTCHINSON, Michael
Mayer, Brown, Rowe & Maw, London
(020) 7782 8164
michael.hutchinson@eu.mayerbrownrowe.com
Specialisation: Environmental aspects of corporate, property and finance transactions, as well as standalone UK and EU advisory work. Recent clients from a variety of sectors including waste, energy, chemicals, pharmaceuticals and banking.
Prof. Memberships: United Kingdom Environmental Law Association.
Career: Qualified and practised for three years at *Linklaters & Paines*. Assistant Solicitor, *Freshfields* (1996-2000). Joined *Rowe & Maw*, 2000. Partner in 2001.

ISTED, Jonathan
Freshfields Bruckhaus Deringer, London
(020) 7936 4000
jonathan.isted@freshfields.com
Specialisation: Defence of multi-party toxic tort claims, including Sellafield childhood leukaemia cases, electromagnetic field cases, judicial review and product liability actions, disaster litigation and contaminated land liability claims. Also general commercial litigation. Member of Lord Woolf's Advisory Group on Multi-Party actions.
Prof. Memberships: Law Society, UKELA.
Career: Qualified 1989. LLM (with Distinction) in Advanced Litigation from Nottingham Trent University in 1996. Partner in *Freshfields* 1998. CEDR Accredited Mediator in 2000.
Personal: Born 5 May 1964. Educated at Newport Free Grammar School and Durham University, College of Law (Chester) 1987. Leisure activities include golf, squash, running and travel. Reform Club.

JEWKES, Penny
Eversheds, Norwich
(01603) 272727
pennyjewkes@eversheds.com
Specialisation: Handles a broad range of environmental matters including property support and due diligence audits arising in the course of major property and commercial transactions, regulatory compliance (advisory and defence), civil liability, waste management and packaging issues. Also practices on the planning/environment interface. Increasingly involved with liability issues concerning petrol filling stations. Major clients include machinery manufacturers, food producers, government bodies, charities and premier car dealerships. Regular speaker at conferences and seminars.
Prof. Memberships: Barrister (non-practising). United Kingdom Environmental Law Association (UKELA), Chair, East Anglian Branch.
Career: Called to the English Bar in 1974 and the Hong Kong Bar in 1976. Crown Counsel in Hong Kong. Lecturer in law at Hong Kong University and from 1990 at the University of East Anglia specialising in planning and environmental law. Returned to practice in 1997.
Publications: Has published in the 'Journal of Occupational Safety and Health' on Corporate Killing. Article published in the 'Journal of Planning and Environment Law' on Light Pollution frequently referred to in planning and committee meetings.

JOHN, Alan
Osborne Clarke, Bristol
(0117) 917 3000

KEEBLE, Ed
Slaughter and May, London
(020) 7600 1200
edward.keeble@slaughterandmay.com
Specialisation: Wide range of environmental matters, including major transactions, due diligence, contaminated site issues and general environmental law advice.
Prof. Memberships: United Kingdom Environmental Law Association.
Career: Qualified in 1988 and became a partner at *Slaughter and May* in 1995.
Personal: Ipswich School; Cambridge University.

KEELE, Helen
Travers Smith Braithwaite, London
(020) 7295 3278
Helen.Keele@TraversSmith.com
Specialisation: All areas of environmental law with a particular focus on contaminated land and environmental regulatory compliance. Advising on environmental issues in corporate, commercial and property transactions, environmental insurance, environmental taxation, remediation projects and lender liability issues.
Prof. Memberships: UKELA and Environmental Law Foundation.
Career: Graduated with BSc in physical geography with environmental science from Queen Mary's College, London. Advisor for National Farmers Union. Qualified with *Denton Hall* and joined Environment Team at *Allen & Overy* in 1997. Joined *Travers Smith Braithwaite* in 2000.
Publications: Published articles in 'Estates Gazette', 'Property Law Journal', 'Environmental Law Review'.
Personal: Interests include travelling, cycling and spending time with family.

LAWRENCE, Daniel
Freshfields Bruckhaus Deringer, London
(020) 7936 4000
daniel.lawrence@freshfields.com
Specialisation: All aspects of environmental advice in mergers and acquisitions, disposals, flotations, privatisations, corporate financings and reorganisations. Has significant experience of water and sewerage, chemicals, power, electricity, telecommunications, biotechnology and nuclear sectors. Dispute resolution experience includes environment-related criminal defence work, civil and administrative litigation.
Prof. Memberships: Law Society; UK Environmental Law Association (UKELA) Council, 2001-date; Member UNED Forum 2001-date; Convenor UKELA Biotechnology Working Group 2002-date.
Career: Qualified 1989. *Lovells*, 1989-2000. *Freshfields Bruckhaus Deringer*, 2000-date.
Personal: Enjoys cycle touring, travel and photography.

LLOYD, Deborah
Ashurst Morris Crisp, London
(020) 7638 1111
Specialisation: Advising on the full range of environmental and health and safety matters with a certificate in occupational health and safety. She has advised and assisted buyers, sellers and financiers on managing environmental risk on a range of transactions across numerous industries and businesses and has been involved with major infrastructure and privatisation projects. She has provided standalone advice on environmental and health and safety issues to various businesses and managed incidents, regulatory investigations and the defence of prosecutions in environmental and health and safety matters.
Prof. Memberships: Law Society, United Kingdom of Environmental Law.
Career: Admitted as a barrister and solicitor of the Supreme Court of Victoria and High Court, Australia 1995 practising in environmental law. Commenced work in the UK in 1997 (admitted UK 1998) and has continued to specialise in environmental law.

LOMAS, Owen
Allen & Overy, London
(020) 7330 3000
owen.lomas@allenovery.com
Specialisation: Corporate Partner and Head of Environmental Law Services. Specialist in the strategic management of environmental and health and safety issues arising in day to day business and in the context of mergers, acquisition, divestitures and corporate finance, property transactions and energy/infrastructure projects. Particular areas of expertise include new forms of environmental regulation involving use of economic and fiscal instruments – notably in relation to climate change and emission trading; project responsibility and recycling in areas such as packaging and electrical goods; waste management and liability for land contamination – focusing, in particular, on managing legacy properties.
Prof. Memberships: Chair of the Environmental Industries Commission, Law and Policy Working Group; Editorial Board of Utilities Law Review and Water Law Journal; member, the Council of Management of the UK Environmental Law Association, 1988-97; past chairman of UK Environmental Law Association working party on air pollution; member of the working parties on integrated pollution control and environmental liability; Law Society; member of the Executive Committee of the Environmental Law Association (ELF).
Career: Qualified 1980. Lecturer in Law University of Birmingham (1979-88), University of Warwick (1988-91), Professor in Law University of Trier Germany (1991-91); Senior Associate *Allen & Overy* (1992-95), Partner (1995).
Publications: Co-author 'UK Packaging Waste Regulations' (Pira International

THE LEADERS — ENVIRONMENT

1999); joint editor looseleaf 'Commercial Environmental Law and Liability' (Sweet and Maxwell); 'Frontiers of Environmental Law' (Chancery 1991); editor of 'Environmental Law', the journal of UK Environmental Law Association (1988-97).
Personal: London University (LLB 1976), Solicitor (1980), University of Birmingham (LLM 1987).

LOOSE, Helen
Ashurst Morris Crisp, London
(020) 7638 1111
helen.loose@ashursts.com
Specialisation: Head of the Ashurst environmental risk management group which specialises in both transactional and advisory environmental and health and safety matters both on a standalone basis and in relation to corporate, major projects, banking and real estate transactions.
Prof. Memberships: Council member of United Kingdom Environmental Law Association; member of the Sustainability Unit of London First; member of the Energy Recovery Forum and Public Affairs Sub-Committee of the Environmental Services Association; member of the Renewable Power Association; and on the editorial board of Asbestos Risk Management (Croners.CCH); chair of the UKELA Climate Change Working Group.
Career: Trained at *Freshfields*, qualified in 1992; Partner in 2000.
Personal: Resides in London.

MACKINLAY, Hannah
Putsman.wlc, Birmingham
(0121) 237 3000
hannah.mackinlay@pwlc.co.uk
Specialisation: Advising in relation to the environmental issues involved in property transactions including brownfield regeneration, contaminated land issues and advising on waste issues such as licensing and landfill. Also advising in relation to corporate mergers and acquisitions, handling UK and multinational matters. Recent signification deals for GTRM, Lex Service Group, Corus, 3i and Onys.
Prof. Memberships: Graduate Member of Institute of Wastes Management. Member of the UK Environmental Law Association.
Career: LLB (Hons) Sheffield. Qualified 1981. MA (Environmental Law) Distinction, De Montfort University. Partner *Shoosmiths & Harrison*, Northampton 1986-95. Association, *Pinsent Curtis Biddle* 1995-2002. Partner, *Putsman.wlc* 2002-present.
Publications: Co-author of 'What Every Manager Needs to Know about Environmental Law'.
Personal: All aspects of new technology, snowboarding, piano.

MARSHALL, Anna
Nabarro Nathanson, London
(020) 7524 6000
a.marshall@nabarro.com
Specialisation: Non-contentious environmental work with particular emphasis on risk assessment and apportionment in context of corporate and property transactions; advice on contaminated land issues in context of developments, property portfolio management and landlord and tenant issues; advice on environmental policy and management systems. Clients include a wide range of UK property investment companies seeking advice on environmental risk on cross-border transactions.
Prof. Memberships: UKELA.
Career: 1983-87 *Freshfields* (qualified 1985); 1988-92 *Hay Management Consultants* (working as a management consultant specialising in strategy and organisation); 1992-94 *Norton Rose*; 1994-present, *Nabarro Nathason*.
Personal: Education: Girton College, Cambridge (MA(Hons)); University of Bath (MBA). Interests include tennis, skiing, football, ballet, opera and gardening.

MAY, Caroline
Hammond Suddards Edge, London
(020) 7655 1000

MOORE, Louise
Lovells, London
(020) 7296 2000
louise.moore@lovells.com
Specialisation: Environment, health and safety. Advising on the environmental aspects of corporate and finance transactions, defending EHS prosecutions and landfill tax litigation (including the successful Taylor Woodrow appeal in 1998).
Prof. Memberships: UKELA; IchemE Environmental Protection Subject group.
Career: Articled *Lovells*; qualified 1992; Partner 1999.
Publications: Contributor to numerous publications including 'Property Week', 'European Counsel', 'Oil and Gas Law' and 'Taxation Review', environment chapter in Butterworths' 'Commercial Property Disputes', and Tolley's 'Company Secretary's Review'.

MYLREA, Kathy
Simmons & Simmons, London
(020) 7628 2020
kathryn.mylrea@simmons-simmons.com
Specialisation: Head of Environmental Law Group. Advises on all aspects of UK and EU environmental law including transaction work involving allocation of environmental liabilities and co-ordination of due diligence, advice on authorisations and permits, criminal and civil litigation, in particular defence of criminal prosecutions. Particular expertise in contaminated land, water pollution, IPPC and waste management issues. Organises and conducts training seminars on the application of environmental law to individual businesses and business sectors. Major clients include Rohm & Haas, Owens Corning, Vivendi Water UK and Associated British Ports.
Prof. Memberships: Law Society, International Bar Association, UK Environmental Law Association.
Career: Qualified in Ontario, Canada in 1986 and in England and Wales in 1992. With *McKenna & Co* 1988-92. Joined *Simmons & Simmons* in May 1992.
Personal: Born 6 November 1958. Educated at Brown University, Providence, Rhode Island, USA (BA 1980) and the University of Toronto (LLB, 1984). Outside interests include skiing, scuba diving and ballet. Lives in London. Married with one son and one daughter.

NASH, Mike
Simmons & Simmons, London
(020) 7628 2020
mike.nash@simmons-simmons.com
Specialisation: Practises in all areas of UK, EU and international environmental law with particular emphasis on waste, renewable energy and emissions trading, contaminated land, chemicals, nature conservation and water law and their application to commercial transactions and contracts and in litigation. Significant recent matters include ongoing advice on settling third party claims and site remediation/disposal of a heavily contaminated site; advising a participant in the UK Emissions Trading Scheme on presenting and maximising its entitlements under the scheme; advising on the acquisition of a water and sewerage undertaker; advice on the new tax relief for land remediation and the new aggregates levy; advising OFGEM, the Northern Ireland Department of Enterprise and commercial clients on renewables legislation including the Renewables Obligation. Clients over the last year include OFGEM, Akzo Nobel, Associated British Ports, British Sugar, Invensys, CLA, NFU, Waste Recycling Group, George Wimpey, English Nature.
Prof. Memberships: Law Society of England and Wales.
Career: BA (First Class Honours) New College, Oxford University. Joined *Booth & Co*, 1991. Joined *Simmons & Simmons* 1994 and became a Partner in 2002.
Publications: Editor of the 'Encyclopaedia of Environmental Law' and co-author of 'The Environment Acts 1990-95 (annotated)'.

O'KEEFFE, Jacqui
Denton Wilde Sapte, London
(020) 7242 1212

PAWLIK, Andrew
asb law, Maidstone
(01622) 656500
andrew.pawlik@asb-law.com
Specialisation: Partner in the Property Services Group and a member of the Planning and Environment Team. Specialises in contentious matters with emphasis on those involving contaminated land, air and water pollution and damage caused by flooding. Has particular experience dealing with litigation arising from land fill. Also advises on waste management issues and works with other members of the Team in planning matters involving significant environmental issues.
Career: Qualified in 1978. Assistant and Partner with *Argles & Court* 1978-99. Partner with *asb law* 1999-date.
Personal: Born in 1954. Married with three children and lives in Kent. Leisure interests include all sports, gardening and travel.

PIKE, John
Addleshaw Booth & Co, Leeds
(0113) 209 2000
john.pike@addleshawbooth.com
See under Real Estate, p.734

RAYNER, David
Blake Lapthorn, Southampton
(023) 8063 1823

REDMAN, Michael
Clifford Chance, London
(020) 7600 1000
michael.redman@cliffordchance.com
Specialisation: Planning and Environment Unit. Solicitor Advocate in Planning and Environment Unit.
Career: Barrister 1975-86; solicitor – admitted 1986; Member Law Society's Planning Panel 1994; joined *Clifford Chance* 1985.
Personal: St John's College, Oxford 1971-74.

RENGER, Mike
Nabarro Nathanson, Sheffield
(0114) 279 4130
m.renger@nabarro.com
Specialisation: Extensive industrial, energy, waste and property client base. Projects include construction and modification of power stations, waste to energy plants, regional waste facilities, major commercial property and mineral developments. Privatisation of coal industry. Practice includes environmental regulation, due diligence and litigation (both civil and criminal). Chaired Environment Agency/CIRIA project 'Building a Cleaner Future'. Legal Member of Environment Steering Group of Institute of Chartered Accountants.
Prof. Memberships: Legal Associate of RTPI; Law Society's Planning Panel; UKELA.

RICE, Paul
Lawrence Graham, London
(020) 7379 0000

ROSS, Kenneth
Bishops Solicitors (formerly Morison Bishop), Glasgow
(0141) 248 4672
kenneth.ross@bishopslaw.biz
Specialisation: Partner in charge of commercial property division. Head of environmental law group. All aspects of environmental law, with particular emphasis on contaminated land and waste. Frequent lecturer to conferences.
Prof. Memberships: Convenor of Law Society of Scotland Environmental Law Committee; member of the National Council of UK Environmental Law Association (UKELA); Chair of the Scottish Committee of UKELA.

ENVIRONMENT ■ THE LEADERS

Career: Qualified in 1982, partner since 1984.
Publications: Author of chapter on Contaminated Land in Second Edition of 'Greens Guide to Environmental Law in Scotland'. Author of articles regarding a variety of environmental law topics, particularly contaminated land and its connection with commercial property transactions, waste management licences and other waste issues.
Personal: Born 30th September 1958. Graduate of Glasgow University (LLB 1st Class Hons 1980). Spare time interests include archaeology. Lives in Glasgow.

SALES, Martin
Burness, Edinburgh
(0131) 473 6000

SALTER, Ian
Burges Salmon, Bristol
(0117) 939 2225
ian.salter@burges-salmon.com
Specialisation: Environmental and energy. Particular expertise in the waste, PFI and projects, transport, chemical, nuclear and food/agricultural sectors. Advises on all aspects of waste law; radioactive waste and nuclear licensing; IPPC; IPC; LAAPC; water law and abstraction licensing; contaminated land and remediation notices; packaging waste; related criminal prosecutions; corporate due diligence.
Prof. Memberships: Legal Associateship Royal Town Planning Institute; Law Society's Planning panel; Chairman St UKELA (South West); International Nuclear Law Association.
Career: Joined *Burges Salmon* 1990, Partner 1999.
Publications: Joint author Tolley's 'Environmental Law and Procedures Management' and Butterworths 'Forms and Precedents' (agriculture and the environment).
Personal: Ian enjoys golf and spending time with his family.

SCOTT, Peter
Toller Beattie, Barnstaple
(01271) 375821
solicitors@tollerbeattie.co.uk
Specialisation: Water law, drainage, fisheries. Involved in various cases including Bowden v South West Water; R v Falmouth & Truro Port Health Authority ex parte SNU; Moase & Lomas v SSETR.
Prof. Memberships: Member of Water and Mature Conservation Working Groups of United Kingdom and Environmental Law Association.
Career: Admitted 1971, Assistant with *Stephens & Scowen St Austell* 1975-82 in between two periods in local government practice; Assistant/Associate with *Toller Beattie* since 1985.
Publications: Reports to European Commission on shellfish waters and freshwaters fishwaters directives as implemented in the UK. Articles in 'Water Law', 'Property Law Journal', 'Ukela Journal'.
Personal: Educated Truro School, Keble College, Oxford. Married with four children. Interests include walking, ecology, chess and music.

SHARP, Cate
Mayer, Brown, Rowe & Maw, London
(020) 7782 8891
csharp@eu.mayerbrownrowe.com
Specialisation: Extensive experience in a wide range of environment related work, particularly in the chemicals and manufacturing fields. Has a particular expertise in transactional support as well as standalone regulatory advice on a broad variety of environmental issues such as waste management, the climate change levy and contaminated land. Recently advised ICI plc on all the environmental aspects of the sale of its worldwide Chlor-Chemicals, Klea and Crosfield businesses to Ineos. This involved drafting and negotiating complex environmental documentation covering many jurisdictions and advising on permit transfer issues and property documentation. She also lectures regularly on a wide range of environmental topics and most recently on the contaminated land regime and the PPC Regulations.
Prof. Memberships: United Kingdom Environmental Law Association.
Career: Graduated from London University with an environmental BSc (Biology & Geography combined Hons). Articled to *Rowe & Maw* in 1991. Qualified and has been a member of the Environment Group since 1993. Partner in 2000.

SHEPHERD, Elizabeth
Eversheds, Manchester
(0161) 831 8000
elizabethshepherd@eversheds.com
Specialisation: Environmental and health and safety. Head of Manchester Environmental, Health and Safety Team advising on corporate and property transaction related environmental issues and general environmental compliance, carrying out legal environmental audits and formulating on behalf of clients corporate environmental policies and management systems.
Prof. Memberships: UKELA (United Kingdom Environmental Law Association). CBI North West Environment Business Forum, GMEA (Greater Manchester Environmental Association) and Law Society Environmental Law Sub-Committee.
Career: Cambridge University, Churchill College MA First Class Honours. Admitted as a solicitor in October 1984. Articled with *Eversheds Alexander Tatham* in Manchester and appointed partner of *Eversheds* in 1988.
Personal: Elizabeth lives near Knutsford, Cheshire. Her interests include classical music, skiing and gardening.

SHEPHERD, Michael
Hammond Suddards Edge, Manchester
(0161) 830 5000

SHEPPARD, Claire
Theodore Goddard, London
(020) 7606 8855
clairesheppard@theodoregoddard.co.uk
Specialisation: Partner in the Planning and Environment Unit specialising in transactions and commercial related advice. Provides environmental and health and safety advice on all types of corporate, banking, property and PFI transactions. Also provides regulatory advice and represents clients in environmental and health and safety prosecutions. Has particular experience in energy related matters and expertise in contaminated land issues. Contributor to Tolley's Environmental Law and Procedures Management.
Career: Articled *Linklaters & Alliance* (1989-1991), assistant in the environmental unit and litigation department of *Linklaters & Alliance* (1991-1998), joined *Theodore Goddard* 1999 and made a partner in November 1999.

SHERGOLD, Stephen
Denton Wilde Sapte, London
(020) 7246 7000

SHERIDAN, Paul
CMS Cameron McKenna, London
(020) 7367 2186
pfs@cmck.com
Specialisation: Partner and Head of the Environment Law Group. The environment law group is dedicated to providing a full environment law service. He advises numerous national and international clients on a wide range of domestic and international non-contentious and contentious matters. Non-contentious matters include transactional services in share and asset transactions, joint ventures, PFI/PPPs, major infrastructure projects, contaminated land transfers and developments, lenders transactions and business recoveries; advice on the insurance of environment risks; climate change renewables and energy efficiency; regulatory compliance advice; environment, economic and fiscal instruments; packaging and producer responsibilities; and the compilation of databases on both domestic and international environment laws. Is very active in contentious environment matters both civil and criminal. Has acted for parties in many high profile test cases. Is regularly involved in water, waste and licence/permit related prosecutions. Is particularly involved with environment issues relating to waste, water, contaminated land, IPPC energy, climate change, nuclear installations, hazardous substances, transport and construction. Is a regular speaker at UK and overseas conferences, has contributed to several environment law textbooks and is the author of several articles.

SHINER, Philip
Public Interest Lawyers, Birmingham
(0121) 702 2110

SHORT, David
CMS Cameron McKenna, London
(020) 7367 3000

SMITH, Charles
Brodies, Edinburgh
(0131) 228 3777
charles.smith@brodies.co.uk
Specialisation: Partner in Corporate Department. Advises on environmental law and liability generally and in respect of land, water and air pollution, sales and purchases of land, assets and shares, leases and security/banking transactions. Also handles major commercial contracts (including PFI and privatisations) and banking transactions. Advises companies on environmental compliance, housebuilders on environmental liability, contractors on waste management licensing and the landfill tax, and numerous clients on contaminated land. Continues to advise on Ravenscraig Steelworks Site.
Prof. Memberships: Law Society of Scotland; United Kingdom Environmental Law Association; Royal Society of Arts, Manufactures and Commerce; National Society for Clean Air & Environmental Protection; Scottish Environmental Industries.
Career: Qualified in 1987 having joined *Brodies* in 1985. Became a Partner in 1990.
Publications: Co-author of 'Pollution Control: The Law in Scotland', published in November 1997.
Personal: Born in 1960. Attended Perth Academy 1972-78, Exeter College, Oxford 1978-82, then University of Edinburgh 1982-85. Lives in Edinburgh.

SMITH, Paul
Eversheds, Leeds
(0113) 243 0391
paulsmith@eversheds.com
Specialisation: Partner in Commercial Litigation Department. Main area of practice is environment and health and safety law. Heads *Eversheds*' national corporate criminal defence group, having established the unit in 1988. Acts principally for major industrial companies in the UK, US and Europe in civil and criminal proceedings. Successfully took the River Derwent test case to the House of Lords. In the crisis management field he acted in the Hickson & Welch Castleford incident, the Hickson International Cork incident and the Associated Octel fire at Ellesmere Port. *Eversheds* client partner for Du Pont in the UK. Visiting Professor of Environmental Law at Nottingham Law School.
Prof. Memberships: UKELA, Law Society, ABA, IBA.
Career: Qualified in 1982, having joined *Freshfields* in 1980. Joined *Eversheds Hepworth & Chadwick* in 1984 and became a Partner in 1987.
Publications: Co-author of 'College of Law Environment Law' and 'Environmental Manual' published by CCH Publications. Regular contributor to BBC radio programmes.

THE LEADERS ■ ENVIRONMENT

Personal: Born 14 November 1956. Attended Warwick University 1975-79, winner Sweet and Maxwell prize. Governor of Richmond House School. Director Nottingham Law School Limited. Member Reform Club. Professional Puppeteer. Lives in Menston, West Yorks.

TAYLOR, Douglas
Maclay Murray & Spens, Glasgow
(0141) 248 5011

Specialisation: Practises exclusively in the field of environmental law with in-depth knowledge and experience of advising on all types of environmental issues including contaminated land, waste management licensing appeals, sewerage and drainage issues, the integrated pollution prevention and control regime, environmental due diligence, environmental warranties and indemnities, clinical and animal waste incineration and the climate change levy. Recently advised on the regeneration of industrial sites, the acquisition of fuel depots, the disposal of drilling cuttings and the regulation of asbestos in premises.

Prof. Memberships: CBI Scotland Environment Taskforce, Associate member of Institute of Environmental Management and Assessment (AIEMA), Director of Scottish Environmental Industries Association, UK Environmental Law Association Climate Change Levy Working Group, Law Society of Scotland Environmental Law Committee, Scotland Europa Environmental Group.

Career: University of Aberdeen, (LLB 1st Hons, 1994); University of Dalhousie, Canada, (LLM Environmental Law, 1998).

Publications: Published articles in Canada, the United States, Scotland and the UK. Contributed to the Scottish editing of Garners 'Environmental Law', Butterworths 'Environmental Regulation', Tolley's 'Environmental Law and Procedures Management'. Presented papers at various conferences and seminars.

Personal: Married.

TOWNSEND, Matthew
Allen & Overy, London
(020) 7330 3000
matthew.townsend@allenovery.com

Specialisation: Senior Associate in Environmental Law Group. Experience in advising on environmental issues, corporate and property acquisitions and disposals, new issues, projects and financings. This includes advising clients on dealing with potential environmental liabilities such as drafting and negotiating complex indemnities and obtaining environmental insurance. He also has particular experience in environmental and health and safety litigation (including prosecutions and judicial review) and recently advised Hunting- BRAE Ltd (previous operators of the Atomic Weapons Establishment) on an Environment Agency prosecution. He has advised on aspects of producer responsibility in relation to packaging waste and waste electrical and electronic equipment, together with environmental levies and renewable energy projects. He advises clients in areas such as waste (including the transfrontier shipment of waste), IPC and IPPC. He has recently represented a major trade association in its negotiations to obtain a reduction in the climate change levy on behalf of its members.

Prof. Memberships: United Kingdom Environmental Law Association (including Chairman of the Association's Contaminated Land Regime); Institute of Wastes Management.

Career: Admitted as solicitor 1996; solicitor *CMS Cameron McKenna* 1996-99; Associate *Allen Overy* since 2000.

Publications: Contributor to and receiver of 'Environmental Law and Procedures Management Handbook' and 'Health, Safety and Environment Cases' (Butterworths Tolley). Numerous articles – for several years he wrote the environmental law update of the 'Law Society Gazette'.

Personal: Born 18 February 1971. BA Hons University of Birmingham 1992; Diploma in Law, College of Law, York 1993; Diploma in Legal Practice College of Law 1994, York.

TRINICK, Marcus
Bond Pearce, Southampton
(023) 8072 0750
mtrinick@bondpearce.com

Specialisation: Partner and Head of the Specialist Planning and Environmental Group. Over twenty years experience of project development (often in large teams) in all parts of the UK. Advocate at over 320 public inquiries. Especial experience in energy generation, port development, retail work, nature conservation law, EU environmental law and Environmental Impact Assessment (EIA), as well as commercial, retail and housing development.

Prof. Memberships: Board Member of British Wind Energy Association and member of European, US Wind Energy Associations. Legal Associate member of the RTPI and member of UK Environmental Law Association.

Career: Qualified in 1983, joined *Bond Pearce* in 1990, becoming Partner in 1991.

TURNER, John
Wragge & Co, Birmingham
(0870) 903 1000

VALLANCE, Philip
Berrymans Lace Mawer, London
(020) 7638 2811
philip.vallance@blw-law.com

Specialisation: Principal area of practice is professional negligence and indemnity/liability insurance, especially in the construction and environmental context. Cases range from Anns v Merton (1978) to Cambridge Water v E Counties Leather (1994). Also advises extensively on environmental law (contaminated land, 'waste', pollution exclusion clauses, nuisance etc), where clients include major insurance companies, water companies, local authorities and waste disposal/landfill operators.

Prof. Memberships: TEC CON, Bar Association, London Common Law and Commercial Bar Association.

Career: Called to the Bar 1968 and joined *Berrymans Lace Mawer* as employed counsel (with full rights of audience) 2002. Took Silk in 1989.

Personal: Educated at Bryanston School and New College, Oxford (Scholar; BA Modern History). Born 20 December 1943. Lives in London.

WAITE, Andrew
Berwin Leighton Paisner, London
(020) 7760 1000
andrew.waite@blplaw.com

Specialisation: Partner, Planning and Environment Department. Specialist in environmental liability and pollution controls, dealing principally with contaminated land, waste management, noise, water resources issues, integrated pollution controls, air pollution and nature conservation. Advises on environmental liabilities in corporate and property transactions, lender liability issues, environmental litigation and legal issues involved in establishing and operating environmental management systems. Clients advised include English Partnerships, Blue Circle, Lattice Property Holdings (formerly BG plc), Tesco, Royal Bank of Scotland, Girobank, Prudential Property Management, Philips and Drew Fund management, Legal & General, Kronospan, WH Smith, Harnischfeger Industries, Transamerica, Schenectady inc and Petroplus. Advises Waste Facilities Audit Association on waste management issues and the Brownlands Group on law and policy developments relating to contaminated land.

Prof. Memberships: President of the European Environmental Law Association; co-founder and former Secretary of the UK Environmental Law Association; Vice-chairman (western Europe) of the IUCN Commission on Environmental Law; member of the International Court of Environment Arbitration and Conciliation; Chairman of CBI ad hoc working party on environmental liability; former chairman of the UKELA working party on contaminated land.

Career: Qualified 1975. Lecturer in law at Southampton University from 1980-88. Head of Environmental Law Group at *Masons* 1988-90 and co-ordinator of the Environment Group at *Linklaters & Paines* 1990-93. Joined *Berwin Leighton* in 1993, Partner 1996.

Publications: Co-author of Environmental Law in Property Transactions (2nd ed. Butterworths' 2001); Editor of Butterworths' Environmental Handbook (3rd edn 2001) and author of numerous articles on environmental law. Frequent speaker at national and international conferences on environmental law, with TV and radio experience.

Personal: Born 25 February 1950. Attended Lincoln College, Oxford, 1969-72, BA (Hons) 1972, MA 1977. Leisure interests include history, archaeology, wildlife, theatre, cinema and walking in the countryside. Lives in Chandlers Ford, Hampshire.

WAKE, Brian
Wake Dyne Lawton, Chester
(01829) 773101
bdw@wdl.co.uk

Specialisation: Mineral extraction, waste management, land reclamation and environmental law. Acts for major mineral companies and landowners, and advises regularly on contaminated land and pollution control matters.

Prof. Memberships: Fellow of the Institute of Quarrying. United Kingdom Environmental Law Association.

Career: Qualified 1978 with *Linklaters & Paines*. Tarmac Quarry Products 1981-86.

Personal: Born 1953 in Hong Kong. Speaks Cantonese. LLB Liverpool 1975.

WATCHMAN, Paul
Freshfields Bruckhaus Deringer, London
(020) 7936 4000
paul.watchman@freshfields.com

Specialisation: Property department: environment group. Principal area of work is environmental law, including contaminated land, water pollution, waste management, energy and minerals. Other main area of work is planning law, covering mineral developments (including coal mining and coastal superquarries), planning inquiries and retail office and business developments. Author or co-author of books and articles on environmental planning and public law. Lectures regularly on planning and environmental law.

Prof. Memberships: Law Society, Law Society of Scotland.

Career: Qualified as a Scottish Solicitor in 1977 and as an English Solicitor in 1994, partner *Freshfields*, 1995.

Personal: Born 1952. Lives in Surrey.

WISEMAN, Andrew
Trowers & Hamlins, London
(020) 7423 8000
awiseman@trowers.com

Specialisation: Practice covers the full range including waste, contaminated land, noise, pollution and planning. Former member of London Waste Regulation Authority. Visiting lecturer at Brunel University. Has addressed numerous conferences and been interviewed on TV and radio.

Prof. Memberships: Vice-Chairman UK Environmental Law Association; City of London Law Society (Planning and Environmental Law Sub-Committee); Member Institute of Wastes Management.

Career: Qualified in 1989. Former Partner at *Shindler & Co*, and *Wiseman Solicitors*.

Publications: Joint Editor 'Butterworths Environmental Law Bulletin'. Practice Editor of Garner's 'Encyclopedia of Environmental Law'.

Personal: Fellow of the Royal Society of Arts.

FAMILY/MATRIMONIAL

London: 364; The Regions: 366; Scotland: 373; Profiles: 374

Research approved by BMRB For this edition, **Chambers'** researchers conducted 6,582 interviews – 3,900 with law firms, 511 with barristers and 2,171 with clients. The validity of the research was scrutinised by BMRB International, who audited both the methodology and the results at our offices in London. They interviewed **Chambers'** researchers and cross-checked sample interviews. Details of the audit appear on page 7.

OVERVIEW While most departments featured exist within full-service firms, there is a continuing trend, in London at least, towards the creation of niche firms, specialising in family law and family law alone. Nationwide, the squeeze on public funding has convinced many of the larger firms to move away from legal aid work, which is now increasingly the province of the smaller high street practices and looks set to be yet more unavailable. In terms of pure law, a period of flux seems inevitable. Following the case of White v White which attempted to alter the approach to ancillary relief, it is anticipated that imminent rulings will further define the situation, while changes in cohabitant law seem equally nigh. Those handling high profile clients may be resting uneasy as Allen v Clibbery has highlighted the likelihood of increased publicity in family proceedings. Potentially most destructive of all, the spectre of Europe is casting its shadow. Brussels II has caused some difficulty already and Brussels III (planned regularisation of ancillary relief throughout the European Union) looks set to outstrip it in terms of disruption.

LONDON

FAMILY/MATRIMONIAL
■ LONDON

1
- Manches
- Withers LLP

2
- Alexiou Fisher Philipps
- Charles Russell
- Collyer-Bristow
- Hughes Fowler Carruthers
- Levison Meltzer Pigott
- Miles Preston & Co
- Payne Hicks Beach
- Sears Tooth

3
- Bindman & Partners
- Clintons
- Dawson Cornwell
- Goodman Ray
- Kingsley Napley
- Mishcon de Reya

4
- Farrer & Co
- Gordon Dadds
- International Family Law Chambers
- Reynolds Porter Chamberlain
- The Family Law Consortium

5
- Anthony Gold
- Barnett Sampson
- Cawdery Kaye Fireman & Taylor
- Dawsons
- Fisher Meredith
- Forsters
- Hodge Jones & Allen
- Osbornes
- Russell-Cooke
- Stephenson Harwood

This book is the product of 6,582 1/2 hour interviews. See p.7 for BMRB audit. Within each band, firms are listed alphabetically.

MANCHES (see firm details p.1052) Commentators believe that this flagship department of the firm "*has an edge over the majority of its rivals*." Tackling ancillary relief matters of the greatest complexity and value, its reputation is founded on the continued efforts of "*a phalanx of long-serving quality practitioners*." At the helm, **Jane Simpson** (see p.382) is recognised as "*a true cornerstone of the family law world*" who can rely on the huge talents of the "*tireless and committed*" **Richard Sax** (see p.382) and **Helen Ward** (see p.383): "*an intimidating presence*" who "*peremptorily demands the very best both from her staff and herself*." Excellent support is provided by the likes of ex Freshfield's man **William Massey** (see p.379) whose "*unassuming efficiency*" has been duly noted. Encouragingly for a firm sometimes accused of being too weighted towards the older practitioner, two new names also enter the table this year. **Louise Spitz** (see p.382) is an "*organised, careful and intelligent lawyer*" who sits on the Law Society Family Law Committee, while **Debbie Chism** (see p.376) impresses as "*a feisty one who isn't afraid to talk straight*." The team has appeared in recent significant cases such as Cornick-No.3 and L v L (Financial Provision: Contributions) and further handles private children, abduction and cohabitation work.

WITHERS LLP (see firm details p.1194) Already celebrated as having the largest private client base in Europe, the firm's merger with US trust and tax law firm Bergman, Horowitz & Reynolds has now given it an extra international dimension. Its specialism is high value ancillary relief, often stretching into the many tens of million pounds bracket, all handled in a "*get-ahead, modern style*." **Diana Parker** (see p.380) has assumed responsibility as the firm's managing partner but remains a "*fantastically assured practitioner*." This move has coincided with former partner James Harcus' decision to set up on his own. It has been widely agreed, however, that the slack has been more than adequately taken up by performers of the magnitude of **Gill Doran** (see p.376), who "*has seen it all*," the "*talented*" **Mark Harper** (see p.378) and **Marcus Dearle** (see p.376). The latter's ability was confirmed recently in his successful action on behalf of the mother in the highly publicised surrogate twins case in the High Court. Further support results from the superior quality of the department's breed of junior partners and assistants as epitomised by the highly popular **James Copson** (see p.376). Seen as "*a natural*" his "*youthfulness and brio*" have now been allied to a "*maturity that will see him going places in years to come*."

ALEXIOU FISHER PHILIPPS (see firm details p.840) Although only constituted in its present incarnation for just over a year now, this firm of devoted specialists has "*bedded in just as brilliantly as one would have expected*." It handles all aspects of family law, covering the full spectrum of divorce, separation, cohabitation and children's issues. It caters for an eclectic client base that accommodates professionals, the aristocracy and media figures. The driving force here is **Douglas Alexiou** (see p.374), a "*dignified figure of great integrity*" who is a "*magnet for the wealthier client*." In common with his other partners, **Susan Philipps** (see p.380) and the "*intellectually able*" **Jeremy Fisher** (see p.377), he also doubles up as a trained mediator.

CHARLES RUSSELL (see firm details p.904) "*A name in this field since time began*," claimed one observer. This firm has expanded rapidly in recent times and now encompasses 19 lawyers. The emphasis lies on acting for wealthy individuals (both old and new money) on financial and children work, with many cases having an international aspect. Part of a wider commercial firm, the team, led by pensions expert **David Davidson** (see p.376), can instantly draw on expertise in other departments and regularly pits itself against the best-known names in the field. Leading individuals include **William Longrigg** (see p.379), who is "*user-friendly but can call on a mean streak when the situation dictates*," and "*dyed in the wool family expert*" **Maryly La Follette** (see p.379). **Erica Shelton** (see p.382) also prompts admiration for her "*commercial*

LONDON ■ FAMILY/MATRIMONIAL

LEADING INDIVIDUALS

[1]
- **ALEXIOU Douglas** Alexiou Fisher Philipps
- **HUGHES Frances** Hughes Fowler Carruthers
- **PARKER Diana** Withers LLP
- **SAX Richard** Manches
- **SIMPSON Jane** Manches
- **WARD Helen** Manches
- **DORAN Gill** Withers LLP
- **LEVISON Jeremy** Levison Meltzer Pigott
- **PRESTON Miles** Miles Preston & Co
- **SHACKLETON Fiona** Payne Hicks Beach
- **TOOTH Ray** Sears Tooth

[2]
- **COLLIS Pamela** Cawdery Kaye Fireman & Taylor
- **DAVIDSON David** Charles Russell
- **DRAKE Michael** Collyer-Bristow
- **FOWLER Pauline** Hughes Fowler Carruthers
- **HARCUS James** Harcus Sinclair
- **HUTCHINSON Anne-Marie** Dawson Cornwell
- **PARRY Richard** Farrer & Co
- **RAE Maggie** Clintons
- **RUTTER Geoffrey** Collyer-Bristow
- **CORNWELL John** Dawson Cornwell
- **DAVIS Sandra** Mishcon de Reya
- **FISHER Jeremy** Alexiou Fisher Philipps
- **GIEVE Katherine** Bindman & Partners
- **HARPER Mark** Withers LLP
- **LONGRIGG William** Charles Russell
- **PIGOTT Simon** Levison Meltzer Pigott
- **RAY Peggy** Goodman Ray

[3]
- **CARRUTHERS Alex** Hughes Fowler Carruthers
- **DEARLE Marcus** Withers LLP
- **LA FOLLETTE Maryly** Charles Russell
- **MARCO Alan** Collyer-Bristow
- **MONRO Pat** Darlington & Parkinson
- **PHILIPPS Susan** Alexiou Fisher Philipps
- **TRUEX David** International Family Law Chambers
- **COPSON James** Withers LLP
- **KEIR Jane** Kingsley Napley
- **LEVERTON David** Payne Hicks Beach
- **MASSEY William** Manches
- **PEARSON Philippa** The Family Law Consortium
- **SHELTON Erica** Charles Russell

[4]
- **BAKER Miranda** Kingsley Napley
- **BRUCE Simon** Farrer & Co
- **READHEAD Siobhan** Miles Preston & Co
- **SPITZ Louise** Manches
- **WILLIAMS Elaine** Sears Tooth
- **BISHOP Gillian** The Family Law Consortium
- **PEMBRIDGE Eileen** Fisher Meredith
- **RODGERS Hilary** Forsters
- **STANCZYK Julia** Miles Preston & Co

UP AND COMING
- **BROWN Fiona** Payne Hicks Beach
- **NICE Anna** Miles Preston & Co
- **STEWART James** Reynolds Porter Chamberlain
- **CHISM Debbie** Manches
- **NICHOLSON John** Hughes Fowler Carruthers

See individuals' profiles p.374

---

awareness" on cases with a complex trust and tax element.

COLLYER-BRISTOW (see firm details p.917) Large enough to be "*more than capable of handling a big fight,*" this team has the advantage of being able to offer specialist in-house support on tax, trust, property and commercial issues. Its caseload comprises, in the main, high-value ancillary relief, private children and child abduction work, and prenuptial and cohabitation advice all delivered on behalf of a predominantly business and professional clientele. Prominent among its array of "*seasoned and unflappable partners*" are head of department Michael Drake (see p.377), Geoffrey Rutter (see p.381) and Alan Marco (see p.379), all of whom are "*far too wise and learned to be easily gulled.*" Indicative of the complexity of many of the cases undertaken, the team has of late been enmeshed in a private Children Act case that has been before the High Court on 11 occasions.

HUGHES FOWLER CARRUTHERS (see firm details p.1004) Active since July 2001, this firm, which incorporated the entirety of Bates, Wells & Braithwaites' respected family department, is "*a niche practice that is clearly working.*" It conducts complex, high value cases, many with an international flavour, and has negotiated a number of matters with assets in excess of £1 billion. Its life-force is provided by Frances Hughes (see p.378), a highly popular figure amongst her peers, who is "*tough, tremendously well informed and never unreasonable.*" All the partners within the team are highly rated including Pauline Fowler (see p.377) who is "*direct, fair and something of an expert on private children work,*" and new recruit John Nicholson (see p.380), "*an intelligent, rational opponent.*" The "*accommodating*" Alex Carruthers (see p.375), praised for his "*serenity in the face of seemingly intractable cases,*" has "*successfully shaken the monkey off the back of countless harrassed clients.*"

LEVISON MELTZER PIGOTT (see firm details p.1040) Anticipating the trend towards niche family practices, this firm was one of the first to set itself up on those lines and enjoys a reputation as being "*a tight, well-organised outfit.*" Jeremy Levison (see p.379) negotiates the usual diet of high net worth ancillary relief and concomitant children work with "*an effortless ease and charm born of many years' practice.*" He is ably complemented by the "*approachable and constructive*" Simon Pigott (see p.381). Rivals commented on the "*consistently pragmatic view*" taken by the team, which ensures "*a speedy and painless resolution of often seemingly intractable problems.*"

MILES PRESTON & CO (see firm details p.1070) Name partner Miles Preston (see p.381), "*an exceptionally popular and complaisant figure,*" presides over a compact specialist practice that "*offers a lavish service.*" Business people, professionals, landowners and media personalities alike benefit from the services of Siobhan Readhead (see p.381), the "*battling*" Julia Stanczyk (see p.382) and the "*inventive and linguistically talented*" Anna Nice (see p.380). Financial and children matters are handled both domestically and internationally.

PAYNE HICKS BEACH (see firm details p.1097) For the second year running this firm climbs the rankings largely due to the presence of Fiona Shackleton (see p.382). Notable for being lawyer to the Prince of Wales, "*her reputation as the best client winner in the business is unassailable.*" "*Solution-oriented,*" she is "*completely straight-talking*" and receives "*wonderful support*" from her "*clever, economic and quick*" assistant, Fiona Brown (see p.375). Having arrived only a year or so ago she has strengthened an already healthy team that includes David Leverton (see p.379), "*a rock-solid performer that the client can really lean on.*" The team acts in the main for professionals, businessmen, landowners and the aristocracy in big money cases.

SEARS TOOTH (see firm details p.1124) Ray Tooth's (see p.383) reputation in the family law world is taking on legendary proportions. "*Often combative but never unfair,*" he has a distinctive style deployed in the most tangled of big money cases where his undoubted flair for asset tracing comes to the fore. While his approach is not to everybody's taste our researchers did note a "*genuine affection and admiration*" for him amongst his peers. He further has the support of Elaine Williams (see p.383), included in the tables this year in recognition of her "*sensitivity to the client and strength of purpose.*" The team handles a high proportion of non-disclosure cases and disputes into quantum.

BINDMAN & PARTNERS (see firm details p.872) Despite the presence of an experienced matrimonial finance expert in the shape of Felicity Crowther, it is in the area of children law that this team really shines. "*Magnificent and virtually unrivalled,*" the team is particularly renowned for childcare and child abduction cases. Katherine Gieve (see p.377) "*amalgamates intellectual rigour with the greatest sensitivity*" and can be seen on cases of the greatest importance, of which her representa-

www.ChambersandPartners.com

FAMILY/MATRIMONIAL ■ LONDON/THE SOUTH

tion on behalf of 'Jodie' in the conjoined twins case is but one example. Other work handled includes custody disputes and adoption with the department enjoying the benefit of an immigration group for those cases with an international element.

CLINTONS (see firm details p.912) Able to advise across the board on family matters, sources judged this to be "*a trustworthy, middle-ranking team.*" Typical of many of the very best firms in this area it has expertise on international matters including forum shopping, international disputes and the investigation of offshore assets. Its prime mover, **Maggie Rae** (see p.381), is well known on the lecture circuit and is lauded for her "*often highly creative solutions to the difficult cases she has to handle.*"

DAWSON CORNWELL (see firm details p.931) This is a mixed practice combining high-end ancillary relief with a children's department that is "*the envy of many.*" **John Cornwell** (see p.376) handles the money side, and as befits one of the pioneers of mediation work in this country, is noted for his "*reasoned, problem-solving approach.*" **Anne-Marie Hutchinson** (see p.378) heads the children team, and is a nationally renowned expert on child abduction and forced marriages. Skilled in "*the minutiae of children's law,*" sources claim she "*knocks back the opposition at a canter.*" Recent cases for the firm include Re S, a case on asylum and abduction.

GOODMAN RAY (see firm details p.973) In a table, which by necessity features a high proportion of matrimonial finance experts, interviewees stressed the need for recognition of this firm's "*tireless endeavours in the children sphere.*" Children law experts, both solicitors and barristers, praised **Peggy Ray** (see p.381) as "*an energetic ambassador in the childcare field deserving of the highest accolades for her pioneering work.*"

KINGSLEY NAPLEY (see firm details p.1023)

This youngish team is broad in its scope, handling big money financial cases often involving foreign jurisdictions. It comes to the fore chiefly, however, on international child abduction where "*briskly efficient*" team leader **Jane Keir** (see p.379) lends her expertise. Other children issues undertaken include custody disputes and surrogacy questions, an area in which **Miranda Baker** (see p.374) is carving a reputation. The highlight of another successful year has undoubtedly been the department's representation of Mr Allan in Clibbery v Allan, a matter of signal importance which defined the public versus private debate in family law proceedings.

MISHCON DE REYA (see firm details p.1072) Traditionally celebrated for appearing in cases that attract media attention, the team has a diverse clientele embracing professionals, business people and figures from the entertainment industry. High-value ancillary relief is the order of the day, although child abduction and children matters generally are also handled. The mainstay of the practice is **Sandra Davis** (see p.376), "*a forthright character,*" who is particularly adept at negotiating complex settlements with offshore issues.

OTHER NOTABLE FIRMS Farrer & Co have yet to discover a high-profile star to rival the departed Fiona Shackleton but it retains "*the nucleus of a good team.*" Head of department **Richard Parry** (see p.380) and his colleague **Simon Bruce** (see p.375) are noted as being "*always open to constructive suggestions.*" Similarly hampered by the recent defection of key partners, the team at **Gordon Dadds** has "*made a concerted effort to boost its profile*" and is seen to offer "*a gilt-edged service.*" The Family Law Consortium "*has a following you can't ignore*" and handles top-end ancillary relief and child abduction. **Gillian Bishop** (see p.375) is "*crafty but not one for nasty surprises*" while **Philippa Pearson** (see p.380) is well versed in cohabitation issues having had two books published on the subject. As the name suggests International Family Law Chambers receives a number of referrals from overseas and has lawyers qualified in England and Wales, Australia, Germany, Sweden and the US. Pre-eminent among these is **David Truex**, chair of the SFLA International Committee and "*impressive on the children side of international law.*" "*Belying his years through his mature control,*" Reynolds Porter Chamberlain's young head of department, **James Stewart** (see p.383), enters the tables this year. His work for clients with substantial assets, many of whom have an Irish connection, was commended to our researchers. Riding high in the rankings, **Pamela Collis** (see p.376) of Cawdery Kaye Fireman & Taylor is "*wonderfully bright*" and leads a "*handy, little team.*" Seeking to do something similar, **James Harcus** (see p.378) has left Withers to set up Harcus Sinclair, a niche practice, which combines the specialisms of trusts and tax planning with family law. While observers felt it too early to include a firm so much in its infancy in the tables, no such reservations were attached to Harcus himself. "*A magnificent adversary,*" he was viewed as "*highly underrated*" by a number of sources. **Pat Monro** of Darlington & Parkinson enjoyed fulsome backing from her peers in the world of children law, who cited her as "*one of the trailblazing, unsung heroes of the profession.*" **Eileen Pembridge** (see p.380) of Fisher Meredith and **Hilary Rodgers** (see p.381) of Forsters were described as "*co-operative, solution-seekers.*" Illustrating that the family law world is not all about private client ancillary relief, a number of firms were commended for their legal aid practices. **Anthony Gold** and Hodge Jones & Allen are both popular referral firms, while Osbornes merits inclusion for offering "*a full service, individually tailored to the client.*" Dawsons, Barnett Sampson, Russell-Cooke and Stephenson Harwood were also commended to our researchers as being "*straight down the line, reliable family practitioners.*"

THE SOUTH

LESTER ALDRIDGE (see firm details p.1038) Abjuring the provincial character of many of its rivals, sources believe that this regional market leader "*would put many London firms in the shade.*" Its cases run into the multimillion pound bracket, many of them resulting from referrals from top City practices. Team leader **Stephen Foster**, (see p.377) has demonstrated his "*drive and enthusiasm*" by successfully creating a practice with an international flavour, as evidenced by a cluster of overseas referrals, most notably from the Tokyo offices of some of the big global players. Keen to challenge the esteemed firms in London, the team has signalled this intent through the recruitment of Clare Trotter, a former assistant from Manches' London office, who worked on the celebrated Picasso case.

BRACHERS (see firm details p.886) Predominantly catering for high net worth clients, many of whom are in the business and agricultural communities, this team is viewed as "*a real contender.*" Able to fall back on specialist corporate and tax departments, it handles the complex financial cases, while also advising on cohabitation and public law children work. At the helm is **Mary Raymont** (see p.381), a lawyer "*who never plays games.*" Recently she has successfully concluded a case for a celebrity client with a net worth of £4-6 million.

PARIS SMITH & RANDALL (see firm details p.1093) "*Rivalling the very best in the region,*" this firm handles multimillion pound settlements and complex child matters for high net worth individuals across the south of England. Whilst international matters form but a small proportion of the workload, the team has the clout to attract many of the richest members of the media and the professions and handles cases up to the £15 million mark. Felt to have "*more strength in depth than most,*" it is led by Neil

THE SOUTH/THAMES VALLEY — FAMILY/MATRIMONIAL

FAMILY/MATRIMONIAL
THE SOUTH

1 Lester Aldridge *Bournemouth*
2 Brachers *Maidstone*
   Paris Smith & Randall *Southampton*
   Thomson Snell & Passmore *Tunbridge Wells*
3 Blake Lapthorn *Portsmouth*
   Coffin Mew & Clover *Portsmouth*
   Cripps Harries Hall *Tunbridge Wells*
   Ellis Jones *Bournemouth*
   Horsey Lightly Fynn *Newbury*
   Max Barford & Co *Tunbridge Wells*

LEADING INDIVIDUALS
1 FOSTER Stephen *Lester Aldridge*
2 WRIGHT Barbara *Thomson Snell & Passmore*
3 DAVIES Neil *Paris Smith & Randall*
   RAYMONT Mary *Brachers*

This book is the product of 6,582 1/2 hour interviews. See p.7 for BMRB audit. Within each band, firms are listed alphabetically. See individuals' profiles p.374

Davies, one of the first to push mediation in the area. In the past year his team has worked on a £7.5 million farming case and on a matter where the client is the beneficiary of a multimillion pound US trust.

THOMSON SNELL & PASSMORE (see firm details p.1161) Acting for a multitude of agricultural and commercial clients, this firm's caseload is heavily slanted toward ancillary relief. Observers commend **Barbara Wright** (see p.384) for her "*good sense and mettle*" allied to a "*flair for forensic accounting,*" which "*has bedevilled many an evasive spouse.*" Best known on the financial side, she also handles private children work.

HORSEY LIGHTLY FYNN The firm has a strong presence in the area with ancillary offices in Oxford and London. Complex money matters and private children cases form the staple, many of the cases having an international element. The team is included in recognition of its "*commendable approach and established consistency over the years.*"

OTHER NOTABLE FIRMS Blake Lapthorn offers a full service with particular emphasis on proceedings relating to the welfare of children. An expertise in child abduction is becoming increasingly discernible. **Coffin Mew & Clover** has a strong connection with the armed forces and has developed an expertise in army pensions within the framework of a general practice handling cases over the million pound threshold. Negotiating matters of a similar complexity and value, **Cripps Harries Hall** services a clientele including celebrities, company owners and professionals. **Max Barford & Co** continues to be rated for its general practice. **Ellis Jones** joins the tables following recommendations from its peers. Housing "*battle-hardened lawyers with London training,*" it provides "*a sophisticated service*" in high-value ancillary relief cases.

THAMES VALLEY

FAMILY/MATRIMONIAL
THAMES VALLEY

1 Blandy & Blandy *Reading*
   Manches *Oxford*
2 Boodle Hatfield *Oxford*
   Darbys *Oxford*
   Henmans *Oxford*
   Iliffes Booth Bennett (IBB) *Uxbridge*
   Morgan Cole *Oxford*

LEADING INDIVIDUALS
1 DON Andrew *Blandy & Blandy*
   EDDY Catherine *Darbys*
   MITCHELL Jane *Manches*
   SIMPSON Barbara *Boodle Hatfield*
2 BLORE Siân *Blores Solicitors*
   HOWARD Jenni *Morgan Cole*
   MCQUAY Elizabeth *Sole Practitioner*

This book is the product of 6,582 1/2 hour interviews. See p.7 for BMRB audit. Within each band, firms are listed alphabetically. See individuals' profiles p.374

BLANDY & BLANDY (see firm details p.878) This popular firm receives a sizeable number of referrals, many of them from London firms. Its forte has always been big money cases for clients based both regionally and in the capital. Some public children matters are undertaken at present but this is likely to change as the firm examines the economic viability of its legal aid franchise. The team is headed by **Andrew Don** (see p.376) who has "*a strong commercial attitude and never personalises matters.*"

MANCHES (see firm details p.1052) "*London-quality work at a competitive regional price,*" proclaimed our interviewees. Many of the team here have been trained in the capital and have extensive experience of cases of the greatest value and complexity. **Jane Mitchell** (see p.380) ("*dedicated and procedurally excellent*") attracts clients from the medical, academic and professional worlds, while also benefiting from referrals provided by the firm's flagship City office. One recent matter involved representing the grandparents of three children whose mother had been murdered by their father, as to questions of finance and contact.

BOODLE HATFIELD (see firm details p.881) A firm "*definitely on the rise*" following recent recruitment and re-configuration. The practice is run in tandem out of the London and Oxford offices and services an international client base. Matters undertaken include matrimonial finance, cohabitation, forum shopping and children work marshalled on the Oxford side by the "*well-tried and tested*" **Barbara Simpson** (see p.382), who also sits as a Deputy District Judge. The team has recently been augmented by the arrival of an assistant from Manches' head office.

DARBYS (see firm details p.926) Following a firm-wide expansion into the commercial arena, this practice is now finding itself more preoccupied with private ancillary relief work. It maintains, however, a distinct interest in both private children and public childcare cases, where "*sense and sensitivity are its watchwords.*" **Catherine Eddy** (see p.377) is the dominant figure known among solicitors and barristers for her "*calmness and unwillingness to unnecessarily up the ante.*"

HENMANS (see firm details p.990) Representing something of a niche practice in a largely commercial firm, the family group handles exclusively private client work. Leaning heavily towards the financial side, some private children matters are undertaken. Maureen Clarke leads a team that has a "*spirited and determined approach.*"

ILIFFES BOOTH BENNETT (IBB) (see firm details p.1007) Operating from two offices, this team covers the full gamut of family work. In Chesham, private ancillary work is tackled with settlements worth £5 million plus being regularly handled, while children matters are the province of the Uxbridge branch. The group, led by Shon Roberts, also advises extensively on domestic violence issues.

MORGAN COLE (see firm details p.1075) Specialising in all areas, but with a bias towards complex financial matters, this team is thought to be "*getting a hold in the larger cases.*" In acknowledgement of this, the team has expanded to five fee-earners of which **Jenni Howard** is the best known personality who "*breathes purpose into her every case.*" The respected Helen Goss has now transferred her talents to employment law but observers nevertheless still contend that this is "*a fine private client practice.*"

OTHER NOTABLE PRACTITIONERS Siân Blore (see p.375), recommended by barristers for her "*meticulous preparation,*" has left Blandy & Blandy to set up on her own, advising now as Blores Solicitors. Similarly, **Elizabeth McQuay** (trading as Elizabeth McQuay-Sole Practitioner) is flourishing as a sole practitioner. Formerly with Gordon Dadds, she has "*a London touch*" and "*the depth of knowledge to tackle the most tangled of cases.*"

FAMILY/MATRIMONIAL ■ SOUTH WEST

SOUTH WEST

FAMILY/MATRIMONIAL
■ SOUTH WEST

1
- **Burges Salmon** Bristol
- **Foot Anstey Sargent** Plymouth
- **TLT Solicitors** Bristol
- **Tozers** Exeter, Plymouth, Torquay
- **Wolferstans** Plymouth

2
- **Clarke Willmott & Clarke** Bristol
- **Gill Akaster** Plymouth
- **Ian Downing Family Law Practice** Plymouth
- **Stephens & Scown** Exeter

3
- **Hooper & Wollen** Torquay
- **Stone King** Bath
- **Stones** Exeter
- **Woollcombe Beer Watts** Newton Abbot

4
- **E David Brain & Co** St Austell
- **Ford Simey** Exeter
- **Hartnells Family Law Practice** Exeter
- **Veale Wasbrough** Bristol
- **Withy King** Bath

LEADING INDIVIDUALS

1
- **ASHLEY Jacqueline** Gill Akaster
- **BONNER Margaret** Foot Anstey Sargent
- **HALLAM Catherine** Burges Salmon
- **SHAKESPEAR Felicity** Clarke Willmott & Clarke
- **THORNEYCROFT Phil** Wolferstans
- **WOODWARD David** TLT Solicitors

2
- **DOWNING Ian** Ian Downing Family Law Practice
- **KIDD Philip** Tozers
- **SCOFIELD Ian** Hooper & Wollen
- **WOODS Paul** Wolferstans

3
- **ALLEN Elizabeth** Stephens & Scown
- **DODD Andrew** Tozers
- **JURY Susan** Wolferstans
- **LAMBERT Tracy** Tozers
- **PAYNE Peter** Stephens & Scown
- **SHRIMPTON Julie** Tozers

ASSOCIATES TO WATCH
- **STEPHENS Lindy** Hooper & Wollen

This book is the product of 6,582 1/2 hour interviews. See p.7 for BMRB audit.
Within each band, firms are listed alphabetically. See individuals' profiles p.374

BURGES SALMON (see firm details p.894) Home to "*skilled practitioners,*" this firm advises on the legal implications of separation, marriage breakdown and more abstruse areas such as surrogacy. Attending to the needs of a client base comprised chiefly of members of the commercial, professional and landowning communities, the team is led by **Catherine Hallam** (see p.378). A Fellow of the International Academy of Matrimonial Lawyers (one of only two outside London), she is an SFLA-accredited specialist on substantial asset cases and pensions and described by peers as "*unfailingly courteous and a pleasure to be against.*" Her team also includes an expert on cohabitation issues.

FOOT ANSTEY SARGENT (see firm details p.958) Strengthened by the absorption of former rival Bond Pearce's family department, this practice boasts respected family and childcare teams. Children work makes up 70% of the caseload and is attended to by a team, that includes four members of the Law Society Children Panel and an expert in child abduction. The remaining portion is taken up with high-value matrimonial work handled out of both the Plymouth and Exeter offices. The department is headed by Vanessa Priddis and includes **Margaret Bonner** (see p.375) renowned as "*top-notch on adoption and care work.*"

TLT SOLICITORS (see firm details p.1163) This team enjoys "*strength in depth with lawyers who know how to do things properly.*" Financial cases and children are handled *pari passu* with much of the work containing an international element. "*Professional and well-mannered,*" **David Woodward** (see p.384) heads up the department and conducts much of his own advocacy in the high-value matrimonial cases he handles.

TOZERS (see firm details p.1165) This multi-office firm spans the region and makes "*a significant contribution in the children law sphere.*" A crop of highly rated individuals includes **Philip Kidd**, "*a favourite of guardians ad litem,*" and former local authority worker **Julie Shrimpton**, who "*has an abundance of experience and contacts.*" **Andrew Dodd** and **Tracy Lambert** complete an impressive line-up.

WOLFERSTANS (see firm details p.1195) Interviewees commented that this full-service practice was "*coming along nicely.*" An impressive cast of practitioners handles children and ancillary relief matters with distinguished team leader **Phil Thorneycroft** (see p.383) having a foot in both camps. "*Sharp, pragmatic and straight as a die,*" he impresses alongside "*sassy performer*" **Paul Woods** (see p.384) and the "*gifted*" **Susan Jury** (see p.378). The group also incorporates a trained mediator and a unit for dealing with emergency injunctions in instances of domestic violence.

CLARKE WILLMOTT & CLARKE (see firm details p.907) Insolubly linked to the agricultural community, the firm gained widespread praise in the wake of its appearance in the headline case of White v White. The increase in instructions resultant upon that was further fuelled by the effect of foot-and-mouth disease on the farming sector, leading to an extremely busy year for the practice. The dominant personality here is **Felicity Shakespear** (see p.382), "*a class act,*" who is a recognised expert on farming partnerships, pensions and care proceedings.

GILL AKASTER (see firm details p.971) Legally-aided and mid-range ancillary relief cases are handled, but the emphasis here remains firmly on public law and private children matters. **Jacqueline Ashley** is "*a top-league children's lawyer with a forceful personality,*" lauded by her contemporaries as "*a highly visible presence in the region.*"

IAN DOWNING FAMILY LAW PRACTICE A "*finely tuned specialist practice*" reliant upon the skills of **Ian Downing** (see p.376), who is an "*expert in pensions and always calm in the eye of the storm.*" Private client ancillary relief forms the basis of the practice with private children work handled where appropriate. The firm is a keen proponent of mediation and has increased its role in this area in the past year.

STEPHENS & SCOWN Operating from a number of satellite offices across the region, the practice tackles all aspects of family law and has particular expertise in handling business and family divorces. Private and public law children work constitutes a sizeable proportion of the caseload with adoption, international abduction and surrogacy issues all featuring. The "*excitable and energetic*" **Peter Payne**, directs operations, receiving the assistance of **Elizabeth Allen**, who was described to researchers as "*a big player in ancillary relief.*" The firm also offers a comprehensive mediation service.

HOOPER & WOLLEN (see firm details p.1001) The team possesses a legal aid franchise, but remains distinctly weighted towards high-value ancillary relief and public care work. On the financial side, **Ian Scofield** is "*always willing to talk*" and "*takes the heat out of contentious situations.*" Alan Brookes controls children's affairs acting, *inter alia*, for guardians *ad litem*. Mediation work is also undertaken.

OTHER NOTABLE PRACTITIONERS Stones is relocating to a site nearer the new court complex in Exeter and is expected to further develop its respected practice. **Stone King** and **Woollcombe Beer Watts** have both proved themselves to be "*solid and competent practices.*" Following a potentially disastrous fire in 1999, **E David Brain & Co** has built up a locally prestigious practice and joins **Ford Simey**, **Hartnells**, **Veale Wasbrough** and **Withy King** in being warmly recommended during the course of the research.

WALES

FAMILY/MATRIMONIAL
WALES

1
- **Hugh James** Cardiff
- **Larby Williams** Cardiff
- **Nicol Denvir & Purnell** Cardiff

2
- **Martyn Prowel Solicitors** Cardiff
- **Robertsons** Cardiff
- **Wendy Hopkins & Co** Cardiff

3
- **Harding Evans** Newport
- **Leo Abse & Cohen** Cardiff

LEADING INDIVIDUALS

1
- **NICOL Frazer** Nicol Denvir & Purnell
- **POWELL Mark** Hugh James
- **WILLIAMS Frances** Larby Williams
- **WILLIAMS Jane** Larby Williams

2
- **EDWARDS Robert** Martyn Prowel Solicitors
- **GREGORY-JONES Rosemary** Leo Abse & Cohen
- **WILLIAMS Ian** Robertsons

3
- **FORD Lindsay** Lindsay Ford Solicitors
- **HAMER Melanie** Wendy Hopkins & Co
- **HOPKINS Wendy** Wendy Hopkins & Co
- **NAYLOR Lynne** Avery Naylor
- **WILLIAMS Gail** Robertsons

This book is the product of 6,582 1/2 hour interviews. See p.7 for BMRB audit. Within each band, firms are listed alphabetically. See individuals' profiles p.374

HUGH JAMES (see firm details p.1004) The recent demerger from Ford Simey has had no discernible effect on this large operation. The firm retains a myriad of offices across the region, which soak up a high proportion of the legal aid work in Wales in addition to a smaller number of high-value ancillary relief matters. It really earns its spurs, however, in public law. Mark Powell (see p.381) leads the way and has sufficient knowledge of the area for commentators to believe him "*likely to be made a judge.*" Particularly strong on mental health issues, he also advises on childcare, capacity, domestic and international adoption and abduction.

LARBY WILLIAMS This highly versatile practice contains two members of the Children Panel and is possessed of a legal aid franchise and "*stacks of matrimonial*" work. Jane Williams has a fine reputation especially in the fields of adoption and mediation, while Frances Williams complements her by being "*a leading light in ancillary relief.*"

NICOL DENVIR & PURNELL "*Capable and with a wealth of experience,*" this is "*one of the premier firms for children work.*" Of the four solicitors here on the Children Panel, Frazer Nicol impresses most as "*a luminary, whose expertise in care proceedings is virtually unparalleled.*" He represents guardians ad litem, parents and local authorities among others, while his team also handles ancillary relief work and mediation.

MARTYN PROWEL SOLICITORS (see firm details p.1056) Chairman of the local Law Society, Bob Edwards raises the profile of this "*hard-working, smaller firm.*" Children matters are undertaken but ancillary relief dominates with the advice proffered being "*straight and to the point.*"

ROBERTSONS Adjudged by peers "*one of the top two names in Cardiff for children work,*" the firm has two highly prized practitioners. Ian Williams is "*a monument to calmness and sensitivity,*" while colleague Gail Williams is "*experienced in the care and mediation spheres.*"

WENDY HOPKINS & CO Founded upon the estimable talents of the "*redoubtable*" Wendy Hopkins, this practice is seen to be subtly changing. Following her decision to work only two days a week the practice is increasingly more reliant on the skills of Melanie Hamer. Adopting a less forthright approach, she is hailed by her peers as having "*a sensible approach which gets results.*"

OTHER NOTABLE FIRMS Observers agreed that Rosemary Gregory-Jones at Leo Abse & Cohen is "*thorough, fair and never runs up costs.*" Sole practitioner Lindsay Ford is "*a long-standing lawyer always on song*" who rivals Lynne Naylor of Avery Naylor as one of "*the torch-bearers for care work in Wales.*" Harding Evans was endorsed for its broad practice.

MIDLANDS

FAMILY/MATRIMONIAL
MIDLANDS

1
- **Blair Allison & Co** Birmingham
- **Challinors Lyon Clark** West Bromwich
- **Rupert Bear Murray Davies** Nottingham

2
- **Nelsons** Nottingham
- **Tyndallwoods** Birmingham

3
- **Hadens** Walsall
- **Lanyon Bowdler** Shrewsbury
- **Wace Morgan** Shrewsbury
- **Young & Lee** Birmingham

4
- **Benussi & Co** Birmingham
- **Blythe Liggins** Leamington Spa
- **freethcartwright** Nottingham

This book is the product of 6,582 1/2 hour interviews. See p.7 for BMRB audit. Within each band, firms are listed alphabetically.

BLAIR ALLISON & CO (see firm details p.876) Melding high-value ancillary relief with public/private children work, this firm "*can turn a deft hand to anything.*" A number of the lawyers are professionally accredited on the Childcare and Law Society Panels and offer a full mediation service. Heading "*a team with real depth,*" Mari Meisel (see p.379) wins plaudits from interviewees for her "*commitment to the cause*" and strong negotiating skills.

CHALLINORS LYON CLARK This eight-strong team handles ancillary relief and children work in equal measure. Both private client and legal aid work is undertaken, and the firm inspired universally positive sentiment. Its specialisms include adoption and abduction and it is well known for generating a great deal of work from local authorities.

RUPERT BEAR MURRAY DAVIES (see firm details p.1119) "*A first-class outfit,*" this team has enjoyed an enviable standing in the region for a number of years. Its driving force is Murray Davies (see p.376) who "*works like a Trojan*" and displays "*solid judgement*" in big money cases for clients from the business, professional and farming communities. Child care matters remain a specialism, but are likely to disappear as the firm has made clear its intention to dispense with its legal aid franchise in the future.

NELSONS (see firm details p.1082) "*Vast and impressive with tentacles across the region,*" this firm has the numbers to handle volume work. A respectable private client base ensures participation in some of the larger financial cases, while a significant proportion is made up of legal aid matters. A complementary care practice exists, comprising four lawyers on the Childcare Panel. The most prominent of these is John Appleby (see p.374), "*a major asset to the team, who has inspired confidence for many years.*"

TYNDALLWOODS (see firm details p.1172) Fundamentally reliant on legal aid work, the practice also encompasses some mid- to high-value financial cases. Its reputation rests primarily, however, on its childcare practice where Sally Jones is active. 24-hour emergency advice is available.

FAMILY/MATRIMONIAL ■ MIDLANDS/EAST ANGLIA

LEADING INDIVIDUALS

1. **CARTER Barbara** Barbara Carter
   DAVIES Murray Rupert Bear Murray Davies
2. **APPLEBY John** Nelsons
   FLINT Peter Lanyon Bowdler
   McDONALD Roberta Sole Practitioner
   MEISEL Mari Blair Allison & Co
   MESSENGER Mercy Sole Practitioner
   YOUNG Ian Young & Lee

See individuals' profiles p.374

HADENS "*A solid practice, good across the board,*" agree interviewees. The team works variously out of six offices with divorce, ancillary relief and care proceedings providing the bread and butter of the workload. Core clients are drawn from the business and professional communities, although legal aid work continues to make up the bulk of the instructions.

LANYON BOWDLER This compact practice was described by rivals as "*easy to deal with and clear in its advice*." Evenly split between legal aid and private client work, it has in **Peter Flint** "*a canny, thoughtful strategist.*"

WACE MORGAN Housing five fee-earners and a specialist mediator, the team has a sizeable legal aid practice. Advice is available on all aspects of divorce, separation and cohabitation and children work is handled by two lawyers co-opted onto the Children Panel. The firm also provides a 24-hour TraumaLine.

YOUNG & LEE Recent times have seen a concerted effort to bolster the financial side of this practice through the recruitment of a specialist practitioner to service a client base from the business and professional worlds. The spotlight though, remains on childcare where **Ian Young** has "*an excellent name*" and is known for "*always putting the needs of the client first.*"

FREETHCARTWRIGHT (see firm details p.963) Personal recommendation, a large private client base and an expanding commercial practice ensure plenty of referrals come into this busy department. Many of the financial settlements weigh in at over the £1 million mark, as befits a practice dealing with company directors, professionals and figures from the world of sport. Acting for local authorities, guardians and parents, the children's team has a broad caseload. The departure of respected Hugh Young late last year is seen as a blow but the general perception is still of "*a highly credible firm.*"

OTHER NOTABLE FIRMS Name partner Diane Benussi has built up **Benussi & Co** to be "*a popular choice for the monied client.*" Although she is less hands-on than in the past, her reputation and well-thought of team shoulder an impressive practice. Other recommended firms include **Blythe Liggins**, which offers "*a good traditional service.*" Sole practitioner **Roberta McDonald** further gained praise for her heavyweight caseload. **Barbara Carter** and **Mercy Messenger** (see p. 380) also received warm recommendation from our interviewees.

EAST ANGLIA

FAMILY/MATRIMONIAL ■ EAST ANGLIA

1. **Mills & Reeve** Norwich
2. **Buckle Mellows** Peterborough
   Greenwoods Peterborough
   Hunt & Coombs Peterborough
   Silver Fitzgerald Cambridge
4. **Cozens-Hardy & Jewson** Norwich
   Hatch Brenner Norwich
   Ward Gethin King's Lynn

LEADING INDIVIDUALS

1. **CARMICHAEL Graeme** Graeme Carmichael
   WILSON Bruce Mills & Reeve
2. **BAMBER Roger** Mills & Reeve
   HENSON John Hunt & Coombs
   O'REGAN Tim Rudlings & Wakelam
   PROCTOR Jane Greenwoods
   SILVER Raphael Silver Fitzgerald
3. **FIFE Peter** Ward Gethin
   ILIFF Catherine Fosters
   O'DONNELL Caroline Marchant-Daisley
   SISSON David Hansells
   WHITE Denis Hunt & Coombs
   WHITE Iain Cozens-Hardy & Jewson

This book is the product of 6,582 1/2 hour interviews. See p.7 for BMRB audit.
Within each band, firms are listed alphabetically. See individuals' profiles p.374

MILLS & REEVE (see firm details p.1071) Widely regarded as "*the major force*" in the region, this is a practice with "*gravitas.*" Its primary focus is on high value cases, many of which are handled on behalf of the agricultural community. The pivotal figure here is **Bruce Wilson**; "*out of the class of the majority of his local peers*" to the extent that one commented: "*he's so good that we'll all rest easier in our beds once he retires.*" Skilled at financial analysis, he is complemented by **Roger Bamber** (see p.374) who provides pensions expertise and "*great enthusiasm*" from the sister office in Cambridge. A respected mediation service is available.

BUCKLE MELLOWS Having jettisoned its legal aid franchise, the emphasis at this firm is solidly on higher quality ancillary relief cases and private children work. "*A healthy practice staffed by competent lawyers,*" it expends much of its efforts on behalf of agricultural clients.

GREENWOODS (see firm details p.978) Housed within a large commercial firm, this "*small-scale but dedicated*" family team has made the decision to concentrate solely on private client work. Its caseload is inevitably, therefore, limited but of a high quality. Featured individual **Jane Proctor** is "*a joy to work with*" and "*the epitome of the SFLA ethos.*"

HUNT & COOMBS Despite following the trend towards greater private client work, this firm has more of a commitment to legal aid work than most. It has a not inconsiderable childcare practice, but devotes most of its resources to ancillary relief, servicing spin-off clients from its commercial department as well as figures from the professional and business communities. **John Henson** "*knows where to draw the line and has a lovely style in court,*" while **Dennis White** "*tackles both financial and children matters with aplomb.*"

SILVER FITZGERALD (see firm details p.1135) Guardians, local authorities and parents all flock to this firm due to its acknowledged "*outstanding reputation in children law.*" **Raphael Silver** (see p.382) is particularly strong on the care and adoption side and is, according to interviewees, cited more often in the court reports than any other lawyer in the region. An ex-criminal lawyer, he has "*a skilful and abrasive adversarial style*" and is "*a delight to watch in court.*" His team also handles ancillary relief cases.

OTHER NOTABLE FIRMS Sole practitioner **Graeme Carmichael** is "*an undoubted leader*" in children work. "*A personable, technically gifted advocate,*" he acts extensively for guardians ad litem but can also turn his hand to ancillary relief matters. Similarly prominent in children's work is **Tim O'Regan** (see p.380) of Rudlings & Wakelam, "*a flamboyant performer*" who "*knows more than most put together.*" **Iain White** (see p.383) at **Cozens-Hardy & Jewson** has a more eclectic practice, handling both finance and public law work, and is felt by rivals to be "*competent and as helpful as can be.*" In King's Lynn, **Ward Gethin** is "*a sensible firm, head and shoulders above the opposition,*" whose family department is run by the "*sound and approachable*" **Peter Fife**. In Norwich, **Hatch Brenner** is "*a straightforward matrimonial practice.*" Other featured individuals include **Catherine Iliff** (see p.378) of Fosters, "*a keen proponent of media-*

EAST ANGLIA/NORTH WEST ■ FAMILY/MATRIMONIAL

tion," and **David Sisson**, formerly of the now defunct Eversheds family department, and presently with Hansells where he *"features in the higher end of cases."* Following a similar course, *"constructive, pleasant and sensible"* **Caroline O'Donnell** has left Miller Sands after the demise of its family team and has relocated to Marchant-Daisley.

NORTH WEST

FAMILY/MATRIMONIAL
■ NORTH WEST

1
- **Pannone & Partners** Manchester

2
- **Cobbetts** Manchester
- **Cuff Roberts** Liverpool
- **Farleys** Blackburn

3
- **Addleshaw Booth & Co** Manchester
- **Burnetts** Carlisle
- **Green & Co** Manchester
- **Jones Maidment Wilson** Manchester
- **Laytons** Manchester
- **Mace & Jones** Knutsford, Liverpool
- **Stephensons** Leigh

4
- **Morecroft Urquhart** Liverpool
- **Rowlands** Manchester

LEADING INDIVIDUALS

1
- **DEVLIN Michael** Stephensons
- **JONES Catherine** Pannone & Partners
- **WILKINS Beth** Pannone & Partners

2
- **ATKINSON Carole** Mace & Jones
- **COTTRELL Patricia** Cuff Roberts
- **GREEN Michael** Green & Co
- **HUGHES Kathryn** Farleys
- **MILBURN Paula** Jones Maidment Wilson

3
- **BARKER Christine** Laytons

UP AND COMING
- **NEWBURY Andrew** Pannone & Partners

This book is the product of 6,582 1/2 hour interviews. See p.7 for BMRB audit. Within each band, firms are listed alphabetically. See individuals' profiles p.374.

PANNONE & PARTNERS (see firm details p.1092) *"The largest and best"* family department in the region caters for a client base made up of professionals, businessmen and the occasional sports personality. Intricate high-value cases provide the stuffing to the practice, which is then seasoned with a limited amount of private children work. The team *"impresses from top to toe."* **Catherine Jones** (see p.378) is *"direct but always open to new ideas,"* while her fellow joint head of department, **Beth Wilkins** (see p.383) is known for her *"integrity and wonderful client skills."* Having grown up under the tutelage of these two, **Andrew Newbury** (see p.380) is in much the same mould, proving *"pragmatic and technically astute."* The team has a specialist unit to handle CSA matters and benefits from the services of an in-house financial services department, which advises on the implications of pension sharing.

COBBETTS (see firm details p.914) Drawing upon the resources of a large commercial firm, this tightly knit unit confines itself to big-ticket cases. Rivals from the larger departments across the region praised David Pickering's team for making *"infrequent but telling appearances in cases of the highest complexity."*

CUFF ROBERTS Head of department **Patricia Cottrell** has had *"a long and distinguished career"* and peers value that she is *"a lawyer's lawyer, straight-talking and thoroughly objective."* She applies herself to ancillary relief, private children work and abduction and leads a team commonly held to be *"the best in Liverpool."*

FARLEYS (see firm details p.951) Lacking the scope of the larger firms in the region, this team represents nevertheless *"a big fish in a small pond."* Home to three members on the Family Law panel, it concentrates on private client financial and children matters, with a smattering of publicly funded children work. At its heart lies **Kathryn Hughes** (see p.378), whose *"aggressive, robust style"* is tempered by *"a geniality that allows her to get on with fellow lawyers and judges alike."*

ADDLESHAW BOOTH & CO (see firm details p.838) Despite not enjoying quite the heightened reputation of its illustrious counterpart in Yorkshire, this department *"gets its fair share of high-value ancillary relief."* Led by Nigel Shepherd, it offers a full service with all the attendant back-up of a successful corporate firm in terms of specialist tax and trust advice. Co-ordinating with its Leeds office, it can draw on the highest expertise on pension issues and is *"renowned for untangling the nastiest financial imbroglios."*

BURNETTS Garnering clients both locally and from across the region, this firm is *"approachable and imbued with the SFLA spirit."* Financial and children work are undertaken in equal measure, although the real plaudits go to the *"splendid childcare team,"* which boasts three panel members and impressive contacts with guardians *ad litem.*

GREEN & CO A firm capable of handling the full range of family matters but judged by peers to be *"supremely adept at children work."* Such is its reputation that many of the larger firms are happy to refer work here, relying on the skills of **Michael Green**. *"Painstaking, sensitive and res-* *olute, he is always keen to put his shoulder to the wheel on behalf of his client."*

JONES MAIDMENT WILSON This firm has recently tried to put the practice on more of an ancillary relief footing but remains predominantly known on the children side. *"Clear leader along with Green & Co,"* it handles both public and private matters, representing a host of guardians and receiving numerous referrals from Cafcas and Relate. **Paula Milburn** heads affairs and cuts *"a versatile and sympathetic figure."*

LAYTONS (see firm details p.1032) A financially focused firm *"popular among the wealthy Cheshire society."* The client base is composed mainly of members of the professional and business classes, some of whom are referred up from the firm's London office. Team leader **Christine Barker** (see p.375), although now immersed to some extent in a management role, *"has been catching the bigger fish for many years"* and *"is never discomfited whatever the size of case."*

MACE & JONES (see firm details p.1047) A firm with multiple offices that *"dovetail nicely to give a rounded service."* The Knutsford office handles legally-aided matters, while the Liverpool branch rivals the larger concerns on big money matters. *"Eminently fair and consistent,"* the firm attracts clients from industry, politics and the entertainment world, and has in **Carole Atkinson** (see p.374), *"a bright and sensible lawyer."*

STEPHENSONS All aspects are handled by four partners spread across a variety of offices. Peers commented that the team *"gives its all, no matter how large or small the case."* Ancillary relief work exists in abundance but particular praise was reserved for **Mike Devlin**'s work with children. *"Technically excellent and forever in demand,"* he is renowned for his skill in complex contact and childcare matters.

OTHER NOTABLE FIRMS Morecroft Urquhart has *"large numbers of both lawyers and clients"* and was commended for its work in the adoption sphere, while **Rowlands** retained market support for its general commitment to the discipline, especially on behalf of clients in rundown areas.

www.ChambersandPartners.com

371

FAMILY/MATRIMONIAL ■ YORKSHIRE/NORTH EAST

YORKSHIRE

FAMILY/MATRIMONIAL
■ YORKSHIRE

1
- Addleshaw Booth & Co Leeds

2
- Gordons Cranswick Solicitors Bradford
- Grahame Stowe, Bateson Leeds
- Irwin Mitchell Leeds, Sheffield
- Jones Myers Gordon Leeds

3
- Andrew M Jackson Hull
- Zermansky & Partners Leeds

4
- Crombie Wilkinson York
- Kirbys Harrogate

LEADING INDIVIDUALS

1
- SALTER David Addleshaw Booth & Co

2
- JONES Peter Jones Myers Gordon
- LOXLEY Martin Irwin Mitchell
- STAKES John Gordons Cranswick Solicitors
- STOWE Marilyn Grahame Stowe, Bateson
- TAYLOR Norman Zermansky & Partners
- WAY Philip Addleshaw Booth & Co

3
- AYRTON Lyn Gordons Cranswick Solicitors
- BRAITHWAITE Anne Lupton Fawcett
- MANNING Richard Walker Morris
- MYERS John Jones Myers Gordon

This book is the product of 6,582 1/2 hour interviews. See p.7 for BMRB audit. Within each band, firms are listed alphabetically. See individuals' profiles p.374

ADDLESHAW BOOTH & CO (see firm details p.838) Competitors expressed no reservations about this firm's position at the head of our rankings. "*Leader by a country mile,*" it "*commands respect due to the quality of both caseload and individual lawyer.*" Separation, divorce, children, premarital agreements and pension sharing are all tackled on behalf of a client base that encompasses the rich and famous both in the region and beyond. Pensions expert **David Salter** (see p.381) is a national figure "*big on personality,*" who is "*set apart from the rest through sheer legal knowledge.*" One of only two fellows of the International Academy of International Lawyers outside London, he has in **Philip Way** (see p.383) an admirable foil and a "*dedicated, technically proficient lawyer utterly at home on the big money cases.*"

GORDONS CRANSWICK SOLICITORS Strong in both Bradford and Leeds, this "*talented, informed and committed team,*" has the clout to attract high-end cases from outside the region. Big-ticket financial cases are the order of the day, many of them involving assets in the £1-5 million bracket. Instrumental in conducting these is **John Stakes** (see p.382), a nationally known figure who is "*excellent, thorough and with a strong SFLA reputation.*" His counterpart in Bradford, **Lyn Ayrton** (see p.374), looks set to match his reputation in the future, being described to researchers as "*intelligent, non-contentious and with a greater judgement on whether to fight than many of her so-called superiors.*"

GRAHAME STOWE, BATESON "*A practice of some size and importance,*" note peers, which handles volume work out of its six offices. Commentators noted that the firm's well-oiled marketing machine has seen it obtain increasing numbers of instructions in high-value cases, some of which have an international element. **Marilyn Stowe** (see p.383) provides the impetus but is "*something of an acquired taste*" due to her "*ruthless pursuit of weakness*" - she is universally recognised as "*a major player one ignores at one's peril.*"

IRWIN MITCHELL (see firm details p.1009) A shift in strategy has seen this firm abandon care work and greatly reduce its public law operation. Playing to its strengths, it now concentrates on big-ticket cases. In its Leeds office Louise Walker tends to service the firm's corporate clients, while at the firm's flagship Sheffield office **Martin Loxley** (see p.379) handles the bulk of the practice. "*A consummate performer firmly committed to the SFLA,*" he enjoys widespread acclaim.

JONES MYERS GORDON This broad family law practice scores well on both the children and financial fronts. **Peter Jones** manages "*a friendly, well-drilled operation,*" blending public and private law work. "*Disarming in his approach,*" he has nurtured good connections in his many years of practice and "*attracts the very best financial cases.*" Children cases are the province of **John Myers**, a new entrant to our tables this year.

ANDREW M JACKSON (see firm details p.845) Offering expertise in every branch of family law, the team acts for business people, professionals and the agricultural community. Specialisms include children, domestic violence and ancillary relief matters across the financial spectrum. The department, led by Andrew Haines, also provides a full mediation service.

ZERMANSKY & PARTNERS (see firm details p.1200) This is a sizeable team whose legal aid franchise allows it to cover the whole range of family matters. Ancillary relief dominates, but it is the firm's specialist childcare unit that really catches the eye. Architect of the practice **Norman Taylor** (see p.383), proved a popular choice in our research due to his "*professionalism, integrity and good humour.*"

OTHER NOTABLE PRACTITIONERS Researchers detected the presence of talented individual practitioners tucked away in predominantly commercial firms. **Anne Braithwaite** of Lupton Fawcett is the treasurer of the local SFLA and "*a thoughtful lawyer devoted to the cause of mediation,*" while **Richard Manning** (see p.379) of Walker Morris, chiefly known for his white-collar crime practice, can provide "*well-orchestrated family advice.*" Other recommended practices include **Crombie Wilkinson**, known for its "*zest and determination,*" and **Kirbys**, which has "*carved out a niche in Harrogate.*"

NORTH EAST

FAMILY/MATRIMONIAL
■ NORTH EAST

1
- Dickinson Dees Newcastle upon Tyne

2
- Sinton & Co Newcastle upon Tyne

3
- Hay & Kilner Newcastle upon Tyne
- Mincoffs Newcastle upon Tyne
- Samuel Phillips & Co Newcastle upon Tyne
- Ward Hadaway Newcastle upon Tyne

4
- Askews Redcar

This book is the product of 6,582 1/2 hour interviews. See p.7 for BMRB audit. Within each band, firms are listed alphabetically.

DICKINSON DEES (see firm details p.938) In terms of size, national reach and quality of case, this practice "*comfortably outstrips others in the region.*" Benefiting from a considerable private client base, it regularly conducts cases over the £5 million mark for professionals, celebrities and media figures among others. Able to draw on tax, trusts and pension advice it has prompted some interviewees to proclaim that it offers a "*deluxe service.*" The firm has been further strengthened by a Tyne Tees office to complement its headquarters in Newcastle. Head of the group **Lyn Rutherford** (see p.381) is "*a force to be reckoned with and his own man,*" favouring "*a vigorous approach to litigation.*" As evidence of his skills, he has appeared in cases over the last year to the value of £50-80 million.

SINTON & CO (see firm details p.1139) A "*thoroughly dependable*" practice, which handles children work and ancillary relief cases for clients of all income levels. Commentators expressed a willingness to refer work to **Tim Gray** (see p.377), "*a sharp, personable character with commercial acumen.*"

NORTH EAST/SCOTLAND ■ FAMILY/MATRIMONIAL

LEADING INDIVIDUALS

1
- GRAY Tim *Sinton & Co*
- RUTHERFORD Lyn *Dickinson Dees*
- SMITH Michael *Mincoffs*

2
- CARLISLE Kenneth *Hay & Kilner*
- GLENDINNING David *Ward Hadaway*
- SPEKER Barry *Samuel Phillips & Co*

See individuals' profiles p.374

HAY & KILNER The team offers a full range of services for both privately and publicly funded clients. The recent acquisition of what was Evershed's private client team is viewed as a boon, which has resulted in a greater proportion of mid-to-high value ancillary relief and increased visibility across the market. Key individual **Kenneth Carlisle** is the local chairman of the SFLA and brings a "*pro-active, non-confrontational approach*" mirrored in the group's commitment to mediation.

MINCOFFS This moderately sized team embraces all facets of family law. Led by the "*highly experienced and amenable*" **Michael Smith**, the team provides "*a consistency of service which does it credit.*"

SAMUEL PHILLIPS & CO (see firm details p.1122) The presence of three members on the Children Panel attests to this firm's recognised specialism in private and public children law. Skilled in the areas of adoption and child abduction it has in **Barry Speker** (see p.155), the legal advisor to both Barnardo's and Durham Family Welfare. High-value, complex matrimonial cases also feature strongly here.

WARD HADAWAY (see firm details p.1180) The family team services this commercial firm's corporate clients, while attracting outside work through its own reputation. High-value ancillary relief, contact, residence and adoption issues all form the staple, with a smaller proportion of legally aided work handled by the firm's South Shields office. **David Glendinning** (see p.377) acts for a client base drawn predominantly from the professional, business and agricultural communities and was commended as a "*straight down the line, pragmatic lawyer.*"

OTHER NOTABLE FIRMS **Askews** is recommended as a wide-ranging practice offering a quality service.

SCOTLAND

FAMILY/MATRIMONIAL
■ SCOTLAND

1
- Anne Hall Dick & Co *Glasgow*
- Morton Fraser, Solicitors *Edinburgh*
- Turcan Connell *Edinburgh*

2
- Balfour & Manson *Edinburgh*
- Erskine MacAskill & Co *Edinburgh*
- Mowat Dean WS *Edinburgh*

3
- Brodies *Edinburgh*
- Drummond Miller WS *Edinburgh*
- Patience & Buchan *Aberdeen*
- Russel & Aitken *Edinburgh*
- Russells Gibson McCaffrey *Glasgow*

LEADING INDIVIDUALS

1
- DICK Anne *Anne Hall Dick & Co*
- LOUDON Alasdair *Turcan Connell*

2
- BALLANTINE Tom *Mowat Dean WS*
- BRUCE LOCKHART Karen *Brodies*
- CATTO Joan *Ledingham Chalmers*
- ERSKINE Sarah *Erskine MacAskill & Co*
- GIBB Andrew *Balfour & Manson*
- GRAHAM Caroline *Macleod & MacCallum*
- MAIR Leonard *Morton Fraser, Solicitors*
- PATIENCE Iain *Patience & Buchan*
- SCANLAN Margaret *Russells Gibson McCaffrey*
- SHEEHAN Wendy *Mowat Dean WS*
- SMITH Caroline *Russel & Aitken*
- TAIT Fiona *Drummond Miller WS*

3
- BARKER Sheila *Morton Fraser, Solicitors*
- FOTHERINGHAM John *Ross & Connel*
- SMITH Shona *Balfour & Manson*

This book is the product of 6,582 1/2 hour interviews. See p.7 for BMRB audit. Within each band, firms are listed alphabetically. See individuals' profiles p.374

ANNE HALL DICK & CO The firm advises on all issues contingent upon divorce, separation and cohabitation. It has a conciliatory spirit setting great store by mediation and displaying an accent upon the needs of children. **Anne Dick** is "*a sensible, efficient negotiator*" who has written extensively on family law.

MORTON FRASER, SOLICITORS (see firm details p.1077) An impressive team with wide experience of both the Court of Session and Sheriff Court. It participates in many of the big family cases and has been recently bolstered by the arrival of **Sheila Barker** (see p.375), a refugee from the dismantling of the respected family department at Loudons. She joins the "*renowned and highly experienced*" **Leonard Mair** (see p.379), one of the first in Scotland to be accredited as a solicitor mediator and a man "*always prepared to get down to brass tacks.*" All major sectors of children work are also undertaken, including residence, contact, adoption and care.

TURCAN CONNELL (see firm details p.1170) After a year or so, the firm's newly constructed family department is felt by observers to have bedded in well. Built around the considerable talents of **Alasdair Loudon** (see p.379), "*an incisive, considered practitioner of many years standing,*" it generates high-value financial work both from within and without the firm. Children work is also undertaken as individual cases dictate.

BALFOUR & MANSON (see firm details p.856) One of the larger practices, it is well-placed to negotiate volume ancillary relief as well as private and public children work. A strong private client base is serviced by **Andy Gibb** (see p.377), "*an excellent negotiator who always gives it his best shot,*" and the "*quietly efficient*" **Shona Smith** (see p.382), both of whom appear in major cases, many of which have an international dimension.

ERSKINE MACASKILL & CO (see firm details p.948) A practice with "*a strong vocational thread*" its members are recognised for their commitment to the needs of the young and victims of domestic violence. The majority of its work is legally-aided leading to regular appearances in the Sheriff's Court where team leader **Sarah Erskine** demonstrates her "*inexhaustible spirit.*"

MOWAT DEAN WS This practice is active in cases across the board and heavily reliant on the axis of its two major protagonists. **Tom Ballantine** (see p.374), co-author with Anne Dick of a respected text on family law, is noted for his "*frankness and accessibility,*" while handling convoluted financial cases. Colleague **Wendy Sheehan** (see p.382) "*places a heavy stress on mediation*" and has been to the fore recently through her involvement in a celebrated case on lesbian adoptions.

OTHER NOTABLE FIRMS The family practice at **Brodies** is very much centred around the celebrated talents of **Karen Bruce Lockhart**, (see p.375) "*a feisty opponent who gets to the heart of things.*" The team handles big money cases for a client base dominated by members of the landed classes and has specialisms in Hague Convention child abduction cases. **Drummond Miller** has offices dotted around Edinburgh, Glasgow and central Scotland and enjoys "*a strong reputation in litigation.*" Its impetus comes from **Fiona Tait** (see p.383) who is "*pugnacious and undaunted in court.*" **Iain Patience** (see p.380) continues to impress in his attempts to establish **Patience & Buchan** as a major player, and his firm is now judged to be

FAMILY/MATRIMONIAL ■ NORTHERN IRELAND/THE LEADERS

"*doing well and getting a lot of business.*" At **Russel & Aitken**, **Caroline Smith** "*deals with things efficiently and doesn't give up*," while **Maggie Scanlan** of **Russells Gibson McCaffrey** is praised as "*honest, direct and effective but above all good fun.*" Other recommended individuals include **John Fotheringham** (see p.377) at Ross & Connel, "*one of the main men for CSA work*," "*compassionate*" **Caroline Graham** (see p.377), of Macleod & MacCallum and "*best in Aberdeen*" **Joan Catto** (see p.375), who has left Burnett & Reid to kickstart the family department at Ledingham Chalmers.

NORTHERN IRELAND

FAMILY/MATRIMONIAL
■ NORTHERN IRELAND

1
- **Babington & Croasdaile** Londonderry
- **Flynn & McGettrick** Belfast
- **Thompsons** Newtownards

2
- **Carnson Morrow Graham** Bangor
- **Peden & Reid** Belfast
- **Wilson Nesbitt** Belfast

LEADING INDIVIDUALS
1 **CALDWELL Anne** Flynn & McGettrick
See individuals' profiles p.374

This book is the product of 6,582 1/2 hour interviews. See p.7 for BMRB audit. Within each band, firms are listed alphabetically.

All firms listed are recommended for offering a good general service. Of particular note is **Anne Caldwell** of Flynn & McGettrick, "*a master of all trades*" who has "*a keen eye for the needs of the client.*"

THE LEADERS IN FAMILY/MATRIMONIAL

ALEXIOU, Douglas
Alexiou Fisher Philipps, London
(020) 7409 1222
dalexiou@afp-law.co.uk
Specialisation: Covers all areas including divorce, judicial separation, financial disputes, co-habitation, children and international aspects (including recognition and enforcement). Lectures, gives TV, radio, magazine and newspaper interviews.
Prof. Memberships: Law Society; Solicitors Family Law Association (chairman of London Regional Group 1992-96); founding fellow and current president International Academy of Matrimonial Lawyers (president, European Chapter 1998-2000); member of the Family Mediators Association; member of the International Bar Association.
Career: Qualified in 1970. Joined *Gordon Dadds* in February 1971, and was made a partner later that year. Became senior partner in 1986. Founding partner *Alexiou Fisher Philipps* 2001. Director of Tottenham Hotspur Football Club from 1980-98. Chairman 1982-84. Director of Tottenham Hotspur plc 1983-91 and 1993-98. Member of 1996 British Olympic Appeal Council.
Personal: Born 24 May 1942. Attended St Paul's School 1955-59, Kings College, London (LLB Hons) 1965 and College of Law. Leisure interests include golf, tennis, association football and collecting old fountain pens. Lives in Kingston-upon-Thames.

ALLEN, Elizabeth
Stephens & Scown, Exeter
(01392) 210700

APPLEBY, John
Nelsons, Nottingham
(0115) 989 5327
john.appleby@nelsons-solicitors.co.uk
Specialisation: Family law with emphasis on high value financial and pension related matters.
Prof. Memberships: SFLA, Law Society (Children Panel).
Career: Admitted 1970. Formerly managing partner of Trumans in Nottingham (prior to its merger with Nelsons in 1999). Solicitor Higher Court Advocate. Recorder on Midland Circuit.
Publications: Contribution to Organisation and management of a solicitor's practice.
Personal: Leisure interests include theatre, cinema, travel and wine.

ASHLEY, Jacqueline
Gill Akaster, Plymouth
(01752) 512000

ATKINSON, Carole
Mace & Jones, Liverpool
(0151) 236 8989
Specialisation: Family – high value ancillary relief claims. Acted for national know figures. Many very high asset cases.
Prof. Memberships: Law Society, Solicitors Family Law Association.
Career: Nottingham University, Chester College of Law. Joined *Mace & Jones* upon qualifying in 1979. Partner since 1982. Appointed Deputy District Judge in 2000.
Publications: Magazine articles, newspaper editorial.
Personal: Married with children.

AYRTON, Lyn
Gordons Cranswick Solicitors, Bradford
(01274) 202202
lyn.ayrton@gordonscranswick.co.uk
Specialisation: Complex/high value financial settlements, in particular those involving owner managed businesses and pension issues.
Prof. Memberships: Solicitors Family Law Association; member of SFLA Procedure Committee and former Press Officer for North and West Yorkshire; Law Society's Family Law Panel.
Career: Qualified at *Booth and Co* (now *Addleshaw Booth and Co*), Leeds; joined *Gordons Wright and Wright* (now *Gordons Cranswick*) as a partner in 1997; head of department since April 2000.
Publications: Contributor to 'Humphreys Family Proceedings' and 'Debt and Insolvency on Family Breakdown'; joint author of 'Residence and Contact: A Practical Guide'.
Personal: Lives in Leeds. Interests include cinema, music, architecture and regular holidays!

BAKER, Miranda
Kingsley Napley, London
(020) 7814 1200
mbaker@kingsleynapley.co.uk
Specialisation: All aspects of family law, including complex children and ancillary relief applications. Advice in relation to the legal implications of surrogacy arrangements. Occasional writer and lecturer on family law. SFLA trained mediator. Law Society Family Law Panel member.
Prof. Memberships: SFLA (member of the editorial team for the Review, member of Children Committee since 1989 and chair of its Surrogacy sub-committee), National Council for Family Proceedings.
Career: Qualified 1981. With *Collyer-Bristow* 1983-86, *Rubinstein Callingham* 1986-94 (partner from 1989) and *Manches & Co* (following the merger with *Rubinstein Callingham*) 1994-95. Joined *Kingsley Napley* as a partner in 1995.
Personal: Born 16 May 1956. Attended Wimbledon High School, then New Hall, Cambridge (1974-77). Leisure interests include travel, opera, football, cycling and swimming. Lives in London.

BALLANTINE, Tom
Mowat Dean WS, Edinburgh
(0131) 555 0616
tom.ballantine@mowatdean.co.uk
Specialisation: Main area of practice is family law covering separation, divorce, children, financial issues and child protection. Accredited by Law Society of Scotland as a specialist in family law and a family mediator. On Law Society Mediation Accreditation Committee and Scottish Adoption Association.
Prof. Memberships: Law Society of Scotland, Family Law Association, CALM.
Career: Qualified 1986, set up *Mowat Dean* Family Law Department in 1994.
Personal: Born 3 May, 1959, obtained MA at Cambridge University 1978-81, LLB at Edinburgh University 1982-85. Leisure interests include walking, football and reading. Lives on outskirts of Edinburgh.

BAMBER, Roger
Mills & Reeve, Cambridge
(01223) 222203
roger.bamber@mills-reeve.com
Specialisation: Partner in Family Department. With newly appointed partner Nick Stone and senior appointment Roger Gurney, who was formerly a

374 INDEX TO LEADING LAWYERS: PAGE 1693 ■ IN-HOUSE LAWYERS PROFILES: PAGE 1201

THE LEADERS — FAMILY/MATRIMONIAL

partner in a Peterborough firm, leads the largest and most specialist team in the region. Lectures extensively within the legal profession, including to District Judges for the Judicial Studies Board. Work centres on complex financial cases and high net worth individuals, involving businesses, trusts and pensions. Member of the SFLA Pensions Committee. Practises as a mediator.
Career: Qualified in 1981. Joined *Mills & Reeve* as a partner in 1989.
Publications: Co-author of 'Pensions and Insurance on Matrimonial Breakdown'. Editor of 'The Family Through Divorce', which is a comprehensive guide to the personal, financial and legal aspects of family breakdown. He is author of divorce.co.uk – a leading website dealing with all aspects of family breakdown.
Personal: Born 5 February 1955. MA Cantab. Leisure interests include music, art and rowing.

BARKER, Christine
Laytons, Manchester
(0161) 834 2100
Specialisation: Divorce, ancillary relief (high value cases), contact and residence disputes; Fournier v Fournier.
Prof. Memberships: SFLA member.
Career: Family lawyer for past 24 years. Qualified October 1978. Law degree, Nottingham University. Moved to *Laytons* 1992, set up department.
Personal: Married to hotelier and restauranteur. Two children aged 13 and 15. Hobbies; travel, food and wine.

BARKER, Sheila
Morton Fraser, Solicitors, Edinburgh
(0131) 247 1000
Specialisation: Practises exclusively in the field of family law with experience in both Sheriff Court and Court of Session. Particular interest in cross-border and international cases including child abduction and jurisdiction issues.
Prof. Memberships: Law Society of Scotland, Family Law Association, Comprehensive Accredited Lawyer Mediators.
Career: Qualified 1993 after traineeship with *Balfour & Manson*; Solicitor with *Loudons WS* 1994-2001, becoming partner in 1999.
Publications: Articles in various Family Law publications.
Personal: Edinburgh University – MA (Hons), German 1971, Dip Ed 1973, LL.B (Dist) 1991. Chair of Dalkeith & District CAB. Board Member of Family Mediation Lothian. Married with two grown up children. Lives in Midlothian. Enjoys music, walking and sailing.

BISHOP, Gillian
The Family Law Consortium, London
(020) 7420 5000
gb@tflc.co.uk
Specialisation: Partner. Expertise in all types of ancillary relief including high net worth and international cases. Children issues including permanent removal from the jurisdiction applications. Mediation.
Prof. Memberships: Solicitors Family Law Association (Member Education Committee and National Committee), Family Mediators Association, Board Member of the Family Mediators Association. Co-author 'Divorce Reform: A Guide for Lawyers and Mediators'.
Career: Qualified 1982. Partner at *Brecher & Co* 1988-95; Co-Founder of *The Family Law Consortium* in 1995.
Personal: Born 25 September 1958. Educated at The Old Palace School 1972-76. Queen Mary College, London (LLB Hons. 1979). Leisure pursuits include walking, cooking, choral singing and supporting Liverpool Football Club. Lives in Sevenoaks.

BLORE, Siân
Blores Solicitors, Henley-on-Thames
(01491) 579265
seb@blores.co.uk
Specialisation: Advice on all areas of family law with particular emphasis on complex and substantial financial issues (including those with an international element) arising from matrimonial and relationship breakdown.
Prof. Memberships: Law Society Family Law Panel, SFLA.
Career: Qualified 1985. Specialised in family law at *Theodore Goddard*; joined *Farrer & Co* in 1989 and became partner in 1993; joined *Blandy & Blandy* as partner in 1996 having decided to leave London to work nearer home and family. Set up own firm, specialising entirely in family law, in December 2001.
Personal: Born 1961. Attended University College of Wales, Aberystwyth. Lives in Henley-on-Thames with husband and three young sons.

BONNER, Margaret
Foot Anstey Sargent, Plymouth
(01752) 675080
margaret.bonner@foot-ansteys.co.uk
Specialisation: Partner; acts in cases involving children, in both public and private law. Work includes adoption and child abduction.
Prof. Memberships: Member of SFLA, Law Society's Children Panel; Association of Lawyers for Children; Association of Women Solicitors, Plymouth Child Care Support Group; past National Secretary SFLA 1994-2000; Conference Chairman at the SFLA fifth National Conference in 1993.
Career: Qualified in 1985. Joined *Foot Anstey Sargent* in 1986, becoming a partner in 1987. Previously Nursing Auxiliary in geriatric hospital, personal assistant to Editor of cookery publications and personal assistant to clinical psychologist.
Personal: Born 31 August 1946. Attended University of Sussex 1965-68. Leisure interests include opera, gardening, walking and planning holidays.

BRAITHWAITE, Anne
Lupton Fawcett, Leeds
(0113) 280 2000

BROWN, Fiona
Payne Hicks Beach, London
(020) 7465 4300
fbrown@paynehicksbeach.co.uk
Specialisation: All aspects of high net worth ancillary relief cases; many cases contain an international element with potential and actual forum disputes; prenuptial contracts; cohabitation issues; children disputes; experience of many high profile cases, since 1994.
Prof. Memberships: SFLA.
Career: Articled at *Herbert Smith* 1992-94; assistant solicitor at *Farrer & Co* 1994-2000; associate – Payne Hicks Beach 2001.
Personal: Education: Magdalen College, Oxford 1986-89 (1st class Hons, Mod. Hist.). Leisure: running (triple blue – Oxon). Family: married with two daughters.

BRUCE, Simon
Farrer & Co, London
(020) 7242 2022
sjb@farrer.co.uk
Specialisation: Partner and Deputy Head of Family Team, specialising in family law cases involving 'big money', tax and international aspects.
Prof. Memberships: Law Society, Solicitors Family Law Association. Member of the SFLA Procedure Committee since 1994, and as such co-author of the SFLA Precedents for Consent Orders, and Precedents for Separation Agreements and Pre-Marital Agreements. Accredited by the SFLA as a specialist family lawyer with particular specialisms in Substantial Assets and in Emergency Procedures in financial relief. Appointed examiner for the SFLA Substantial Assets accreditation paper in 2002. Member of the President of the Divisions Ancillary Relief Advisory Group since 2001.
Career: Joined *Farrer & Co* in 1984. Qualified in 1986; became a partner in 1993.
Publications: Co-author of 'Matrimonial Consent Orders and Agreements' (published by FT Law and Tax), and 'Butterworths Family Law Guide'.
Personal: Born 4 February 1959, educated at Trinity College Oxford 1978-82 with a degree in Classics and French. Married with four children. Churchwarden of St Peter's Church, Hammersmith.

BRUCE LOCKHART, Karen
Brodies, Edinburgh
(0131) 228 3777
karen.brucelockhart@brodies.co.uk
Specialisation: Partner in litigation department and heads the family law team. A family law practitioner for 30 years. Deals herself mostly with high value or complicated divorces in the Court of Session. Her team acts both in the Court of Session and the Sheriff Court and handles Legal Aid. Proud of settling most cases and seldom getting involved in fought divorces. The team also specialises in international child abduction.
Prof. Memberships: International Academy of Matrimonial Lawyers; Scottish Family Law Association; Writer to the Signet; APIL; Law Society of Scotland Personal Injuries Panel; accredited for medical negligence.
Career: School in Canada and New Zealand. Edinburgh University 1966-70 (LLB and MSc in Forensic medicine 1998-2000). Partner *Courtney Crawford & Co* 1974-77. Partner *Brodies WS* since 1978.
Personal: Born in 1942. Leisure interests: walking, reading and skiing. Lives in Edinburgh and Cumbria.

CALDWELL, Anne I M
Flynn & McGettrick, Belfast
(028) 9024 4212

CARLISLE, Kenneth
Hay & Kilner, Newcastle on Tyne
(0191) 284 2818

CARMICHAEL, Graeme
Graeme Carmichael, Ipswich
(01473) 252159

CARRUTHERS, Alex
Hughes Fowler Carruthers, London
(020) 7421 8383
a.carruthers@hfclaw.com
Specialisation: Partner in niche family law practice. Work includes complex international financial cases; private children's law including child abduction.
Prof. Memberships: SFLA; previously founder member of YSFLA (London); IBA.
Career: Articled *Bates, Wells & Braithwaite*, qualified 1994; partner 1999; co-founder of *Hughes Fowler Carruthers* 2001.
Personal: Born 1967. Resides London and Cambridge. Interests include bridge.

CARTER, Barbara
Barbara Carter, Birmingham
(0121) 441 3238

CATTO, Joan
Ledingham Chalmers, Aberdeen
(01224) 408610
joan.catto@ledinghamchalmers.com
Specialisation: Sole area of practice family law. Deals with numerous divorce cases including ancillary issues such as financial arrangements and residence and contact orders. Also handles child law.
Prof. Memberships: Member of Family Law Association, Member of Family Mediation (Grampian); Member of Scottish Legal Group of BAAF.
Career: Qualified in 1968. Joined *Ledingham Chalmers* 1 May 2002.
Personal: Born 30 April 1946. Attended Aberdeen High School for Girls and Aberdeen University. Vice-Convenor of Business Committee, General Council, Aberdeen University; Committee Member, Aberdeen Civic Society; Assessor to Dean of Guild, Aberdeen. Leisure interests include needlework and walking. Lives in Aberdeen and Glenbuchat.

375

FAMILY/MATRIMONIAL ■ THE LEADERS

CHISM, Debbie
Manches, London
(020) 7404 4433
debbie.chism@manches.co.uk
Specialisation: Partner in family department. Advises on all areas of family law, specialising in cases with complex financial issues, particularly those with an international element as well as cohabitation issues and disputes relating to children.
Prof. Memberships: Solicitors Family Law Association, Law Society.
Career: Qualified in 1993 at *Frere Cholmeley Bischoff*. Joined *Manches* in 1995, became a partner in 2000.
Personal: Born 19 September 1968. Educated at Tiffin Girls' Grammar School and Mansfield College, Oxford (1987-90). Enjoys reading, travel and football. Married with one child.

COLLIS, Pamela
Cawdery Kaye Fireman & Taylor, London
(020) 7431 7262
pcollis@ckft.com
Specialisation: Head of Family Department. International and domestic family law work, particularly financial aspects of marriage and cohabitation breakdown, pre-nuptial contracts and Children Act work. Contributor to legal journals and speaker on matters relating to family law.
Prof. Memberships: Fellow of the International Academy of Matrimonial lawyers and member of the SFLA and of the Family Law panel of the Law Society.
Career: Qualified 1981. Partner and head of family law at *Kingsley Napley* 1984-99. Joined *Cawdery Kaye Fireman & Taylor* in 1999 as partner and head of family.
Personal: Born 9 March 1957. Attended Rosemead School for Girls, then Bristol University (LLB 1978). Leisure pursuits include sailing, cycling, books and family life. Lives in London.

COPSON, James
Withers LLP, London
(020) 7597 6044
james.copson@withersworldwide.com
Specialisation: Family law with emphasis on the resolution of substantial money and international cases. Represented the successful appellant in Wicks v Wicks [1998] 1 FLR 470 confirming the law on interim capital arrangements in divorce and the successful respondent in Re A (Specific Issue Order: Parental Dispute) [2001] 1 FLR 121, both in the Court of Appeal.
Prof. Memberships: Solicitors Family Law Association, SFLA Pensions Committee, American Bar Association (associate member).
Career: Qualified at *Withers* 1991. Partner at *Withers* since 1998.
Personal: Born 20 May 1966. Educated at Wellingborough School and the University of Birmingham. Interests Chelsea Football Club, sport and travel. Lives in Fulham and the South of France.

CORNWELL, John
Dawson Cornwell, London
(020) 7242 2556
cornwellj@dawsoncornwell.co.uk
Specialisation: Has practised family law as a specialist since 1970; particular specialism in ancillary relief and pensions on divorce. Has practised as a mediator in family law since 1985. Practises as a mediator under the auspices of the SFLA. Spent the summer term of 1999 at Wolfson College, Oxford as visiting fellow at the Institute for Socio-Legal Studies. Lectures on pension in divorce.
Prof. Memberships: Solicitors' Family Law Association, founder, chairman 1982-87; Family Mediators Association, co-founder 1988; has chaired the SFLA Children committee and the SFLA Mediation committee; member of the Law Society Family Law committee 1993-99; Deputy District Judge at the Principal Registry of the Family Division, 1986 to date.
Career: Qualified in 1969. Founding partner of *Dawson Cornwell* in 1972. Founder of the SFLA, chairman 1982-87 and returned to the committee in 1994. Co-founder of FMA, vice chairman 1992-93 and board member from inception until 1994. Deputy District Judge since 1987.
Personal: Born 21 September 1943. Educated at St. Paul's School 1957-62 and Bristol University 1962-65. Leisure interests include theatre, cricket and Georgian architecture. Lives in London.

COTTRELL, Patricia
Cuff Roberts, Liverpool
(0151) 237 7777

DAVIDSON, David
Charles Russell, London
(020) 7203 5114
davidd@cr-law.co.uk.
Specialisation: Partner in Family Law Department. Handles all areas of family law with emphasis on substantial financial applications, frequently with an international aspect. Author of 'A Guide to Pensions and Marriage Breakdown'. Contributor of chapters on pensions to 'Essential Family Practice' and 'Encyclopaedia of Financial Provision in Family Matters'. Joint author 'Precedents for Pre-Marital Agreements', 'Precedents for Consent Orders'. Featured regularly in national and legal press.
Prof. Memberships: International Academy of Matrimonial Lawyers. Solicitors Family Law Association.

DAVIES, Murray
Rupert Bear Murray Davies, Nottingham
(0115) 924 3333
Specialisation: Murray Davies has over 20 years experience of matrimonial and family law, with a particular specialisation in the financial aspects of divorce and separation.
Prof. Memberships: Member of SFLA.
Career: Admitted in 1978, Murray has gained experience within prominent firms in Nottingham before joining *Rupert Bear* in partnership, in the firm of *Rupert Bear Murray Davies*.
Personal: Born in 1951, Murray is married with four children. Interests include walking, bird watching and bricklaying.

DAVIES, Neil
Paris Smith & Randall, Southampton
(023) 8048 2482

DAVIS, Sandra
Mishcon de Reya, London
(020) 7440 7000
Specialisation: Head of Family Department with over 20 years experience in the field. Work includes international and domestic 'big money' cases with a specialisation in high profile and high net worth individuals attracting media attention, international child abduction, divorce and separation, cohabitation disputes and contact and residency disputes. Author of 'International Child Abduction' and numerous articles. Frequently lectures at various national and international events. Lord Chancellor's Department panel solicitor.
Prof. Memberships: Solicitors Family Law Association; Law Society; fellow of the International Academy of Matrimonial Lawyers.
Career: Qualified with *Mishcon de Reya* in 1981, becoming a partner in 1984.
Personal: Born 3 July 1956. Attended University of Sussex 1974-78 and Universite Aix-en-Provence, France, reading European Studies/Law. Languages: French and German. Leisure interests include travel, painting and photography. Lives in London. Married with two children.

DEARLE, Marcus
Withers LLP, London
(020) 7597 6000
marcus.dearle@withersworldwide.com
Specialisation: Exclusively family law and, in particular, substantial financial and complex children cases including those with an international element. Also deals with surrogacy and medico-legal issues. Has broadcast on TV and radio and regularly written articles for the national press. Represented the surrogate mother in the international surrogacy case of W and B v H (child abductions: surrogacy) [2002] 1 FLR 1008.
Prof. Memberships: Law Society. SFLA 1990 to date. SFLA International Committee 1992 to date.
Career: Articled *Eversheds Daynes Hill & Perks*. Qualified January 1990. Joined *Withers'* family law department in September 1990. Partner at *Withers* 1995.
Publications: Contributor to family section 'Practical Civil Court Precedents' (Sweet & Maxwell). Co-contributor to SFLA International Committee's 'Guide to Family Law in Europe' (1992) and 'International Aspects of Family Law, A Guide to Good Practice and Procedure' (2000).
Personal: Born 6 May 1964. Educated at Bryanston School and University of East Anglia. Interests include modern history, theatre, music and cinema. Married and lives in Horsell, Surrey.

DEVLIN, Michael
Stephensons, Salford
(0161) 832 8844

DICK, Anne
Anne Hall Dick & Co., Glasgow
(0141) 636 0003

DODD, Andrew
Tozers, Plymouth
(01752) 206460

DON, Andrew
Blandy & Blandy, Reading
(0118) 951 6800
Andrew_Don@blandy.co.uk
Specialisation: Head of one of the largest family departments in the Thames Valley region consisting of seven specialist lawyers. Involved with substantial financial/property matters and children issues arising from divorce and separation. An experienced mediator having trained with the FMA in 1990. In the past has trained other solicitors to be mediators. Member of the UK College of Mediators.
Prof. Memberships: Solicitors Family Law Association. Family Mediators Association.
Career: Parachute regiment 1976-79. Qualified with *Blandy & Blandy* in 1981 and became a partner in 1984. Deputy District Judge.
Personal: Born 1 December 1952. Educated at Malvern College and Liverpool University. Lives in Hampshire. Married with four sons. Enjoys outdoor and sporting activities which include playing rackets and rough gardening.

DORAN, Gill
Withers LLP, London
(020) 7597 6108
gill.doran@withersworldwide.com
Specialisation: Principal in and Head of the Family Law Department. Has specialised in family and matrimonial work for 20 years. Has written articles about family matters, addressed conferences and done committee work for the Solicitors Family Law Association (SFLA).
Prof. Memberships: International Academy of Matrimonial Lawyers (IAML), Family Mediators Association (FMA).
Career: Qualified in 1974. Joined *Gordon Dadds* (1979-96). Joined the Family Law Department at *Withers* in 1996.
Personal: Born 28 September 1949. Educated at The Abbey School 1960-68 and Manchester University 1968-71. Leisure interests include music, opera and horses. Lives in London.

DOWNING, Ian
Ian Downing Family Law Practice, Plymouth
(01752) 226224
ian@famply.co.uk
Specialisation: Family law generally, and particularly: high asset ancillary relief claims involving company/business matters and pensions; Inheritance Act

THE LEADERS — FAMILY/MATRIMONIAL

claims; cohabitee disputes.
Career: Qualified 1984. Family law partner, *Bond Pearce*, 1990. Left to set up specialist family practice 1997.
Publications: Contributing writer to 'Pensions and Insurance on Family Breakdown', 'Debt and Insolvency on Family Breakdown', and 'Humphreys Family Proceedings'.
Personal: Born 20 September 1959. Newcastle-upon-Tyne University LLB (Hons). Married. Interests include windsurfing, skiing, scuba diving, theatre, travel.

DRAKE, Michael
Collyer-Bristow, London
(020) 7242 7363
michael.drake@collyerbristow.com
Specialisation: Head of Matrimonial Department. Handles all areas of matrimonial and family law, particularly where there is a commercial, financial or international element. Also advises on business law, including contract and commercial advice.
Prof. Memberships: SFLA (National Committee 1987-94); Assessor to the Law Society Family Law Panel.
Career: Qualified in 1971. Joined *Collyer-Bristow* as a partner in 1984.
Publications: Author of various textbooks, SFLA publications, articles. Co-author of 'Divorce and the Family Business', first published in 1997 by Jordans; second edition published in 2001. Has lectured and broadcast on radio and television, and continues to feature in a series of family law videos for The Law Channel.
Personal: Born 14 August 1947. Educated at Haberdasher's Askes's Elstree (to 1965) and Selwyn College, Cambridge (to 1968). Recreations include travel, arts reading and tennis. Lives in London.

EDDY, Catherine
Darbys, Oxford
(01865) 811703
ceddy@darbys.co.uk
Specialisation: Senior member of one of the largest family teams in Oxford. Experienced in dealing with substantial finance/property disputes on marriage/relationship breakdown.
Prof. Memberships: Law Society's Family Law Panel, Solicitors Family Law Association.
Career: Qualified 1970, Partner, senior member of Family Team, family law specialist for over 20 years.

EDWARDS, Robert
Martyn Prowel Solicitors, Cardiff
(029) 2047 0909

ERSKINE, Sarah
Erskine MacAskill & Co, Edinburgh
(0131) 622 6062

FIFE, Peter R G
Ward Gethin, King's Lynn
(01553) 660033

FISHER, Jeremy
Alexiou Fisher Philipps, London
(020) 7409 1222
jfisher@afp-law.co.uk
Specialisation: Partner. Specialises in the problems arising out of the breakdown of family relationships. Particular expertise in complex financial and trust structures both domestic and international.
Prof. Memberships: International Academy of Matrimonial Lawyers; International Bar Association.

FLINT, Peter
Lanyon Bowdler, Shrewsbury
(01743) 280280

FORD, Lindsay
Lindsay Ford Solicitors, Caerphilly
(029) 2088 2441

FOSTER, Stephen
Lester Aldridge, Bournemouth
(01202) 786161
Specialisation: Head of family law unit, leading a team of seven specialist lawyers dealing with all areas of family law work, financial and children. Specialises in dealing with substantial financial and property matters within divorce and cohabitee proceedings, including related shareholding and other company disputes. Cases often involve an international element. Team includes two SFLA qualified mediators. Also specialises in solicitors' negligence covering all areas of family law.
Prof. Memberships: Solicitors Family Law Association (Good Practice committee member).
Career: Qualified 1986. *Bircham & Co Westminster* 1986-92 as lead family lawyer and member of the commercial litigation team. Joined *Lester Aldridge* in 1993 as a partner to head up large family law unit. Qualified SFLA mediator 1998.
Personal: Born 1959. Educated at Newport High School and University of Wales, University College Swansea (1980 BA History). Lives near Dorchester, Dorset. Interests include his two young daughters, English and American literature, swimming and tennis.

FOTHERINGHAM, John M
Ross & Connel, Inverkeithing
(01383) 414104
jfotheringham@ross.connel.co.uk
Specialisation: Accredited specialist in child law and family law. Also specialises in general family law. Author of articles in JLSS and SLT on child and family law. Lectures to CPD courses. Extensive experience of Child Support Act cases.
Career: Qualified 1977. Partner with *Ross & Connel* since 1983. Writer to the Signet since 1986.
Personal: Born 24 July 1953. Educated at Edinburgh University.

FOWLER, Pauline
Hughes Fowler Carruthers, London
(020) 7421 8383
p.fowler@hfclaw.com
Specialisation: Partner in niche family law practice. Work includes complex financial matters, often where consideration of commercial implications is necessary and regularly with off-shore assets and an international dimension; private children's law including international adoption; mediation, particularly in complex financial matters.
Prof. Memberships: SFLA; IBA; FMA (Vice Chair).
Career: Qualified 1983; *Bates, Wells & Braithwaite* 1985 (partner 1990); co-founded niche practice of *Hughes Fowler Carruthers* in 2001. Accredited FMA mediator. Lectures and writes on family law.
Personal: Born 1955; lives in London; leisure interests include chamber music.

GIBB, Andrew
Balfour & Manson, Edinburgh
(0131) 200 1250
andrew.gibb@balfour-manson.co.uk
Specialisation: Partner in litigation department. Accredited family law specialist. Has a substantial practice in family law in both the Court of Session and Sheriff Court, also involving drafting of separation agreements with particular regard to financial provision. Is involved in all aspects of education law including contract disputes, disciplinary matters, criminal prosecutions and accident cases. Provides employment law advice to both employers and employees. Solicitor to The Educational Institute of Scotland, the main teaching union in Scotland. Joint editor of 'The Family Law Bulletin' and regular contributor to 'Update' (Education Department of Law Society of Scotland) on family law matters.
Prof. Memberships: Law Society of Scotland; Family Law Association; member International Academy of Matrimonial Lawyers; chair, Family Law Accreditation Panel of Law Society of Scotland.
Career: Qualified in 1971. Became a partner in *Balfour & Manson* in 1975. Member of Council of Law Society of Scotland 1981-93 and president of Law Society of Scotland 1990-91.
Personal: Born 17 August 1947. Educated at Perth Academy 1959-65 and Edinburgh University 1965-69. Chairman, Management Committee Lothian Allelon (probation hostel). Leisure interests include golf and music. Lives in Edinburgh.

GIEVE, Katherine
Bindman & Partners, London
(020) 7833 4433
info@bindmans.com
Specialisation: Partner in and Head of Family Department. She has an established reputation as a leader in the field in work concerning children, 'possibly the market leader'. Her range of expertise covers public law and private law children cases; adoption; abduction; declarations of parentage; surrogacy; issues of medical treatment for children. She is instructed by Children's Guardians, Cafcass Legal and the Official Solicitor. She has represented children in landmark cases on child abduction and was appointed by the Court to represent 'Jodie' as her Guardian ad Litem in the case of the conjoined twins.
Prof. Memberships: Member: Law Society Children's Panel; Solicitors Family Law Association (currently Chair of the Children Committee); Association of Lawyers for Children.
Career: Joined *Bindman & Partners* 1988 and became Partner in 1991.
Publications: Co-author, 'Co-habitation Handbook'.
Personal: Born 1949, educated Merchant Taylor's School for Girls, Liverpool: St Anne's College, Oxford. Resides in London.

GLENDINNING, David
Ward Hadaway, Newcastle upon Tyne
(0191) 204 4000
Specialisation: Head of family law specialising in high value ancillary relief cases, many involving a foreign trust element.
Prof. Memberships: Law Society; Solicitors Family Law Association.
Career: LLB London. Qualified 1974. Appointed partner with *Ward Hadaway* 1986.
Personal: Married with three children. Golf and fell walking in Lake District.

GRAHAM, Caroline J M
Macleod & MacCallum, Inverness
(01463) 239393
mail@macandmac.co.uk
Specialisation: Partner in Court Department. Specialist in family law. Accredited Family Law Mediator. Extensive experience in family law: divorce, separation, child law. Curator ad Litem in court proceedings and Reporting Officer. Safeguarder to children in Children's Panel proceedings and Sheriff Court referrals and appeals. Accredited as a Family Law Mediator: has made presentations at family law seminars and been involved in training for Children's Panel members. A member of the Scottish Partnership on Domestic Abuse.
Prof. Memberships: Member of Family Law Association. Member and former convenor of CALM (Family Law Mediators in Scotland)
Career: Qualified in 1977. Worked in Inverness since 1976. Previous experience in criminal court work leading to full time speciality in family law.
Personal: Born 9 March 1954. School education – Glasgow. Edinburgh University. Married, three children.

GRAY, Tim
Sinton & Co, Newcastle upon Tyne
(0191) 212 7800
t.gray@sinton.co.uk
Specialisation: Substantial ancillary relief work especially involving participators in limited companies, professional partnerships etc. Has handled a large number of cases involving assets in excess of £1 million and settlements of similar size particularly in the last two years. Considerable work load in dealing

FAMILY/MATRIMONIAL ■ THE LEADERS

with cases under the Inheritance (Provision for Family & Dependants) Act 1975.
Prof. Memberships: Member of SFLA. Member of the Law Society Family Law panel.
Career: MA (Cantab). Qualified 1978. Articled clerk, assistant solicitor and then partner in the firm of *Sinton & Co* (1980). Specialist in family law work and especially ancillary relief throughout that time.
Personal: Devotee of Newcastle United Football Club and 'The Times' crossword puzzle.

GREEN, Michael
Green & Co, Manchester
(0161) 834 8980

GREGORY-JONES, Rosemary
Leo Abse & Cohen, Cardiff
(029) 2038 3252

HALLAM, Catherine
Burges Salmon, Bristol
(0117) 939 2245
catherine.hallam@burges-salmon.com
Specialisation: Advice about separation, divorce and related financial/children issues. Particular specialist knowledge of high asset value and complex financial settlements, restructuring of family businesses and pensions on marriage breakdown. Also settlements with an international element.
Prof. Memberships: Fellow, International Academy of Matrimonial Lawyers; SFLA; accredited specialist (pensions and substantial asset cases); member of Law Society Family Law Panel; Solicitors Family Law Association Pensions Committee.
Career: Qualified 1984. Worked in London until 1988. Partner at *Burges Salmon* since 1990. Regular contributor to legal journals and lecturer on family law issues. Co-author of 'Pensions and Insurance on Family Breakdown'. (Jordans 1999).
Personal: Jesus College, Oxford 1977-80. Married with two children.

HAMER, Melanie
Wendy Hopkins & Co, Cardiff
(029) 2034 2233

HARCUS, James
Harcus Sinclair, London
(020) 7583 7353
james.harcus@harcus-sinclair.co.uk
Specialisation: Partner in Family Law Department. Specialises in divorce, matrimonial finance and taxation, children, cohabitation and pre-marital contracts (including international cases). Acted in Robinson v Robinson 1982 (case involving setting aside for material non-disclosure) and Cornick v Cornick (Barder principles).
Prof. Memberships: Fellow of the International Academy of Matrimonial Lawyers (IAML). Treasurer of the Solicitors Family Law Association (1982-87).
Career: Qualified December 1974; Partner (*Gordon Dadds*) 1981-96; Partner (*Withers*) 1996-2001; Senior Partner (*Harcus Sinclair*) 2002 to date.

Publications: Author of articles in Family Law (Pre-Nuptials/Term Maintenance). Has lectured for the Solicitors Family Law Association and the Institute of Financial Planning.
Personal: Born 1949. Educated at Exeter University (1968-71). Leisure interests include riding, skiing, sailing and gardening. Lives in London.

HARPER, Mark
Withers LLP, London
(020) 7597 6043
mark.harper@withersworldwide.com
Specialisation: Principal in Family Law Department. Exclusively family law and in particular, substantial financial cases including those with an international element and involving trusts and cohabitation disputes.
Prof. Memberships: SFLA National Committee 1992-98, SFLA Family Law Bill team, SFLA Cohabitation Working Group Chairperson 1995-97, SFLA Press Officer 1997-98, Law Society Family Law Committee 1998 to date.
Career: Qualified in 1988. Became a partner in 1990 at *Anthony Gold* after articles with the firm. Head of Family Law Department 1991-99. Joined *Withers* February 1999.
Publications: Author of articles in Family Law and SFLA Newsletter. Author of 'Model Letters for Family Lawyers' (Jordans). Has broadcast on TV and radio and been quoted regularly in national press.
Personal: Born 2 February 1962. Educated at Malvern College and Pembroke College, Oxford. Enjoys travel, architecture and classic cars. Lives in Balham, South London.

HENSON, John S
Hunt & Coombs, Peterborough
(01733) 565312

HOPKINS, Wendy
Wendy Hopkins & Co, Cardiff
(029) 2034 2233

HOWARD, Jenni
Morgan Cole, Oxford
(01865) 262 600

HUGHES, Frances
Hughes Fowler Carruthers, London
(020) 7421 8383
f.hughes@hfclaw.com,
j.hall@hfclaw.com
Specialisation: Senior partner of family law niche practice. Practice covers the full range of family law, especially international cases and cases involving trust law or complex offshore corporate entities, as well as complex children's work. Clients include City professionals, entertainment clients and other lawyers.
Prof. Memberships: International Academy of Matrimonial Lawyers; vice-president of the European Chapter of IAML; SFLA; coordinator of SFLA Mediation Training (1996-99). Accredited SFLA and FMA Mediator.
Career: Qualified in 1981. Assistant at *Theodore Goddard*. Joined *Bates Wells & Braithwaite* to establish the family department in 1983 and became a partner in 1984. Set up *Hughes Fowler Carruthers* in 2001.
Publications: Former contributing editor 'Butterworths Family Law Service'. Writes, lectures and broadcasts on family law, nationally and internationally.
Personal: Born 15 June 1954. Oxford 1973-76. School governor. Enjoys opera and gardening. Lives in London and Wiltshire. FRSA.

HUGHES, Kathryn L
Farleys, Blackburn
(01254) 606060
klh@farleys.com
Specialisation: Partner in family law department. Main areas of practice are childcare and ancillary relief in divorce together with the law relating to cohabitants. Handles all aspects, privately paid and publicly funded, and public and private law cases. Children Panel member, Law Society Family Law Panel member, SFLA Accredited Specialist (advocacy-ancillary relief and children law – private). Ancillary relief – substantial assets cases and high volume of such work; Children – care work in particular, but also adoption. Past contributing author to Butterworth's 'Family Law Service'.
Prof. Memberships: Law Society Family Law Committee member representing the Law Society on other Committees, SFLA, Child Concern.
Career: Qualified in 1985; past member of the Bar (called 1977); joined *Farleys* in 1983, becoming a partner in 1985; Recorder, sitting on crime, civil and family.
Personal: Born 5 June 1954. Leisure interests include walking, swimming and reading. Lives in Hale, Cheshire.

HUTCHINSON OBE, Anne-Marie
Dawson Cornwell, London
(020) 7242 2556
mail@dawsoncornwell.co.uk
Specialisation: Practises exclusively in family law, with particular specialism in international family law, international custody disputes and child abduction. SFLA accredited specialist. Is currently engaged in extensive research into forced marriage and has represented many victims of forced marriage. Awarded the inaugural UNICEF Child Rights Lawyer Award, 1999. Received an OBE for services to international child abduction and adoption in the 2002 Queen's New Year's Honours List.
Prof. Memberships: Chair of Reunite International Child Abduction Centre; Solicitors' Family Law Association; International Society of Family Law; International Bar Association; Association of Lawyers for Children; National Council for Family Proceedings; The Society for Advanced Legal Studies; management committee member of the AIRE Centre (Advice on Individual Rights in Europe), member of New Scotland Yard's child protection steering group; member of Metropolitan Police forced marriage project board; member of steering group of the International Centre for Missing and Exploited Children; member of the Adoption Forum.
Publications: Consultant editor Hershman and McFarlane 'Children Law and Practice' and co-author 'International Parental Child Abduction'. International correspondent: 'International Family Law'. Editorial Contributor 'Family Law in Europe', to be published 2003.

ILIFF, Catherine
Fosters, Norwich
(01603) 620508
Specialisation: Bungay (01986) 895251. Partner in *Fosters*' substantial Family Law Department. Highly experienced in all aspects of family work for private clients. Accredited as a family mediator in 1991 and now has substantial mediation practice across East Anglia.

JONES, Catherine
Pannone & Partners, Manchester
(0161) 909 3000
catherine.jones@pannone.co.uk
Specialisation: Partner and Joint Head of Family Department. Work includes divorce, separation, financial provision and children including contested adoption and cohabitation, with special emphasis on the settlement of complex financial issues for corporate, other business, professional and high net worth clients.
Prof. Memberships: Law Society, Manchester Law Society, SFLA.
Career: Qualified 1977. Joined *Pannone & Partners* in 1982. North West SFLA Committee Member, solicitor representative to Greater Manchester Adoption Committee and founder member of Manchester Family Forum.
Personal: Leisure interests include walking, sailing, theatre and travel. Lives in Altrincham.

JONES, Peter
Jones Myers Gordon, Leeds
(0113) 246 0055

JURY, Susan
Wolferstans, Plymouth
(01752) 663 295
sjury@wolferstans.com
Specialisation: Family/matrimonial. Family law – all areas of divorce work; ancillary relief; children, private and public law; cohabitee and domestic violence.
Prof. Memberships: Member of SFLA and special accredited member – children's matters; member Law Society, Children Panel, trained SFLA family mediator. Committee member of Devon and Cornwall SFLA.
Career: Tavistock School; Huddersfield University; Chester College of Law; LLB. Articled *Wolferstans* 1987, qualified 1990, became a partner 1995.
Personal: Year of birth: 1964; town of residence: Christow. Main leisure activities: skiing, running, aerobics, reading and caring for three small children.

THE LEADERS — FAMILY/MATRIMONIAL

KEIR, Jane
Kingsley Napley, London
(07887) 571050
jkeir@kingsleynapley.co.uk
Specialisation: Partner since 1992 and Head of the Department of Family Law since 1999. Specialises in all aspects of family law work particularly dealing with the complexities which can arise in negotiating financial settlements and the arrangements that divorcing or separating couples may need to work out in relation to their children. The department is already highly regarded for its work in the field of child abduction and enjoys an enviable and growing reputation in the field of financial dispute resolution when working with both the married and unmarried family.
Prof. Memberships: Accredited Member of the Law Society's Family Law Panel and accredited by the Solicitors Family Law Association; former Chair of its International Committee and current member of its Media Committee. Fellow of the Society for Advanced Legal Studies and member of its previous working party looking at the issues arising from the cross-border movement of children. International Bar Association; the City Women's Network and Reubite.
Career: Qualified in December 1987 having been articled at *Henmans*. Joined *Kingsley Napley* in 1989 and became a partner in the Department of Family Law in November 1992.
Publications: Contributing author to 'Evidence in Family Proceedings' published by Jordans Publishing Limited and 'International Aspects of Family Law – A Guide to Good Practice and Procedure' published by the SFLA in 2000. Has also been published twice in 2002 in New Law Journal ('Discretion Absolute') and in the SFLA Review – ('Bare Talaq not enough'). In demand for comment from the media in relation to issues thrown up about paternity testing following the Liz Hurley/Steve Bing story.
Personal: Born 4 March 1962. Lives in London and enjoys horses and National Hunt racing, fine wines, running, travel and needlepoint.

KIDD, Philip
Tozers, Newton Abbot
(01626) 207020

LA FOLLETTE, Maryly
Charles Russell, London
(020) 7203 5059
marylylf@cr-law.co.uk
Specialisation: Partner in the Family Department. International divorce, ancillary relief and child related work (private law).
Prof. Memberships: Solicitors Family Law Association; Family Mediators Association.

LAMBERT, Tracy
Tozers, Torquay
(01803) 407020

LEVERTON, David
Payne Hicks Beach, London
(020) 7465 4300
Specialisation: Senior Partner in Family Law Department. Founder member of International Academy of Matrimonial Lawyers. Very experienced specialist in all aspects of matrimonial law with particular expertise in complex financial matters and in negotiating financial settlements.
Career: Qualified 1958 at *Ridsdale & Son* of Westminster: joined *Payne Hicks Beach* in 1959. Became Partner in 1963. Former Managing Partner of firm. Member of Solicitors Disciplinary Tribunal.
Personal: Born 8 September 1935. Educated at The Haberdashers' Askes' School, Hampstead. Enjoys fine art, music and rugby. Lives in London.

LEVISON, Jeremy I
Levison Meltzer Pigott, London
(020) 7556 2400
jlevison@lmplaw.co.uk
Specialisation: Along with leading practitioners Claire Meltzer and Simon Pigott opened the specialist divorce and family law firm, *Levison Meltzer Pigott*. Now joined by new partner Alison Hayes. Handles all aspects of matrimonial work, with particular interest in high worth clients, cohabitation, cases with a foreign element, children and, particularly more recently, pre-nuptial contracts.
Prof. Memberships: International Academy of Matrimonial Lawyers. Solicitors' Family Law Association. American Bar Association (Family Section).
Career: Qualified in 1974 and worked for *Theodore Goddard* until 1980. *Collyer-Bristow* 1980-98. *Levison Meltzer Pigott* from 1 June 1998.
Personal: Born 3 February 1952. Educated at Charterhouse School 1965-69 and the University of Kent 1970-73. Enjoys fine art, music, cricket, classic cars and France. Married and lives in London.

LONGRIGG, William
Charles Russell, London
(020) 7203 5096
williaml@cr-law.co.uk
Specialisation: Partner in Family Department. Main areas of practice are divorce, ancillary relief and child-related work (private law).
Prof. Memberships: International Academy of Matrimonial Lawyers; Past Chairman Solicitors Family Law Association London Region.
Publications: Joint Author of Butterworths' 'Family Breakdown and Trusts' (with Sarah Higgins).

LOUDON, Alasdair
Turcan Connell, Edinburgh
(0131) 228 8111
ajl@turcanconnell.com
Specialisation: Sole area of practice is family law, including divorce cases, particularly those involving claims for capital payments or property transfer orders. Also handles substantial number of cases involving the negotiation of separation agreements. Acts in principally Court of Session. Former tutor in criminal advocacy at Edinburgh University. Accredited by the Law Society of Scotland as a specialist in family law.
Prof. Memberships: WS Society, Edinburgh Bar Association (past president), Family Law Association. Member of Sheriff Court Rules Council for Scotland.
Career: Qualified in 1978. Apprentice at *Tods, Murray & Jamieson WS* 1978-80. Qualified assistant at *Warner & Co* 1980-82 and partner 1982-92. Founded *Loudons WS* in 1992. Joined *Turcan Connell* as a partner, 2001.
Personal: Born 7 April 1956. Attended Dundee University 1974-78. Leisure interests include golf (member of Bruntsfield Links and Luffness New) football (Hearts season ticket holder) and food and wine. Lives in Edinburgh.

LOXLEY, Martin
Irwin Mitchell, Sheffield
(0870) 1500 100
loxleym@irwinmitchell.co.uk
Specialisation: High value ancillary relief including pension cases, cohabitation disputes, private Children Act cases.
Prof. Memberships: Law Society; National Committee of SFLA; Chair of Procedure Committee SFLA; SFLA Accredited Specialist in High Value and Pension (ASE).
Career: Articled at *Irwin Mitchell* 1978-80; partner at *Irwin Mitchell* 1981 to date; head of family law at *Irwin Mitchell* since 1986.
Publications: Editor of SFLA Consent Order Precedents 1998, editor of SFLA Separation and Pre-Marital Agreements 2001.
Personal: Educated at High Storrs, Sheffield and Trent Polytechnic, Nottingham. Leisure interests include sport, music and family. Keen interest in the failing fortunes of Sheffield Wednesday FC. Married with two daughters.

MAIR, Leonard
Morton Fraser, Solicitors, Edinburgh
(0131) 247 1000
lm@morton-fraser.com
Specialisation: Partner in Civil Litigation Division. Head of Family Law Team. Main areas of practice are family law, negotiating financial divorce settlements, Child Law, ADR and mediation and defamation. Has covered a wide range of work over a 28 year period and has developed mediation skills since 1993. Mediator with Family Mediation Service; Accredited 'solicitor-mediator' with Law Society of Scotland.
Prof. Memberships: Law Society of Scotland, Writers to the Signet, UK College of Family Mediators.
Career: Qualified in 1975. Joined *Morton Fraser* in 1973, becoming a Partner in 1977.
Personal: Born 5 September 1949. Attended Stirling University 1967-71 and Edinburgh University 1971-73. Former Vice Chairman of Lothian Marriage Counselling Service. Former part-time Chairman CSAT. Former board member Family Mediation Lothian. Council Member Step Family Scotland. Leisure interests include fly fishing, sailing and the arts. Lives in East Lothian.

MANNING, Richard
Walker Morris, Leeds
(0113) 283 2500
Prof. Memberships: Deputy District Judge (Magistrates Court).

MARCO, Alan
Collyer-Bristow, London
(020) 7242 7363
alan.marco@collyerbristow.com
Specialisation: Partner, Matrimonial Department. Handles all areas of family and matrimonial law with emphasis on financial provision applications. Deputy District Judge at Principal Registry of the Family Division.
Prof. Memberships: Solicitors Family Law Association.
Career: Qualified in 1965. Partner at *Baileys Shaw & Gillett* 1972-96. Partner *Collyer-Bristow* 1996.
Personal: Born in Devon. Married with three children.

MASSEY, William
Manches, London
(020) 7404 4433
william.massey@manches.co.uk
Specialisation: Practises exclusively in family and matrimonial law.
Prof. Memberships: Solictor's Family Law Association, SFLA London Regional Committee (Treasurer), SFLA Accredited Specialist (Big Money and International Cases), London Guildhall University LPC Advisory Panel.
Career: Qualified in 1990 at *Freshfields*. *Penningtons* 1991-94. Joined *Manches* in 1994, became partner 1999.
Personal: Born 3 May 1964. Educated at Oundle School and Exeter University. Married with three young children. Enjoys family, friends, sports, outdoors and constructive solutions.

MCDONALD, Roberta
Roberta McDonald - Sole Practitioner, Birmingham
(0121) 449 6821

MCQUAY, Elizabeth
Elizabeth McQuay - Sole Practitioner, Kidlington
(01869) 351 229

MEISEL, Mari
Blair Allison & Co, Birmingham
(0121) 233 2904
Specialisation: Large wealth ancillary relief cases. All aspects of pension sharing, mediation.
Prof. Memberships: SFLA. UK College of Mediators. Accredited member of the Law Society of Family Law Panel.
Career: LLB Law, University of Leeds. Senior Partner of *Blair Allison & Co* since 1983.

FAMILY/MATRIMONIAL ■ THE LEADERS

MESSENGER, Mercy
Mercy Messenger – Sole Practitioner, Solihull
(01564) 779427
family@mercymessenger.co.uk
Specialisation: High value ancillary relief; strong focus on companies and pensions aspects; handles the cases personally. Xydhias v Xydhias Court of Appeal (winning side) and now in the textbooks.
Prof. Memberships: SFLA.
Career: Qualified 1966. Founded present firm 1983.
Personal: Family – two grown up sons; husband is company law specialist and consultant to the practice. Leisure interests – gardening and renovating old houses.

MILBURN, Paula
Jones Maidment Wilson, Manchester
(0161) 832 8087

MITCHELL, Jane
Manches, Oxford
(01865) 722 106
jane.mitchell@manches.co.uk
Specialisation: Advises on all areas of family law, particulary complex financial and children issues arising from matrimonial and relationship breakdown.
Prof. Memberships: Solicitors Family Law Association, Law Society.
Career: Qualified in 1988. Has practised at *Manches* since then, first in London and then, in 1995, moving to their Oxford office to set up its family law department. Partner since 1997.
Publications: Contributing editor to 'Current Law Weekly'.
Personal: Born 17 May 1963. BA Hons (English and Related Literature). Married with three children. Leisure interests include theatre and gardening.

MONRO, Pat
Darlington & Parkinson, London
(020) 8998 4343

MYERS, John
Jones Myers Gordon, Leeds
(0113) 246 0055

NAYLOR, Lynne
Avery Naylor, Swansea
(01792) 463 276

NEWBURY, Andrew
Pannone & Partners, Manchester
(0161) 909 3000
andrew.newbury@pannone.co.uk
Specialisation: Specialises in financial settlements on divorce, in particular high net worth cases and those involving the family business and pensions.
Prof. Memberships: Chair of Solicitors Family Law Association Training Committee; Chair of Manchester SFLA; Member of SFLA National Committee and media team.
Career: Qualified 1991. *Frere Cholmeley*, London to 1996. Joined *Pannone & Partners* 1996 and became a partner in 1998.
Personal: Born 1967. Wirral Grammar School and University of Nottingham. Interests include music, reading, wine, my wife and our three cats (but not necessarily in that order).

NICE, Anna
Miles Preston & Co, London
(020) 7583 0583
anna.nice@milespreston.co.uk
Specialisation: All aspects of family law, particularly cases involving substantial assets and/or disputes relating to children, including those with an international element.
Prof. Memberships: Solicitors' Family Law Association.
Career: *Manches* 1994-97; *Miles Preston & Co* 1997; partner 2000; SFLA Accredited Specialist (substantial assets, advocacy: ancillary relief and children (private)); accredited member of Law Society's Family Law Panel.
Personal: Born 1968. Educated University College, London.

NICHOLSON, John
Hughes Fowler Carruthers, London
(020) 7421 8383
j.nicholson@hfclaw.com
Specialisation: Partner in niche family law practice. Works principally in complex, high value ancillary relief cases.
Prof. Memberships: SFLA.
Career: Called to the Bar (Middle Temple) 1994; joined *Manches & Co*, 1995, solicitor 1998. joined *Hughes Fowler Carruthers* as partner, 2002.
Publications: 'Ancillary Relief: A Guide to the New Rules' [Butterworths, 2000] (with Nicholas Mostyn), frequent contributor to legal periodicals and lecturer for the SFLA.
Personal: Education: Wilson's School, Wallington (governor since 1995); Jesus College, Oxford. Born 1962, resides London. Interests include conversation, bridge and food.

NICOL, Frazer
Nicol Denvir & Purnell, Cardiff
(029) 2079 6311

O'DONNELL, Caroline
Marchant-Daisley, Cambridge
(01223) 443333

O'REGAN, Tim
Rudlings & Wakelam, Thetford
(01842) 754151
Specialisation: Specialises in child law, particularly child care and adoption. Original member of the Children Panel. Head of Child Law Department at *Rudlings & Wakelam*.
Prof. Memberships: Member Children Committee of the Solicitors Family Law Association, Member of the Association of Lawyers for Children etc.
Career: Admitted as solicitor in 1975, partner since 1978. Writes and lectures regularly on child law and adoption and is a Solicitors Family Law Association Specialist Accredited Solicitor for Child Law and Adoption

PARKER, Diana
Withers LLP, London
(020) 7597 6042
diana.parker@withersworldwide.com
Specialisation: Principal in Family Law Department. Exclusively family law. The Chairman of *Withers LLP* but still handling heavy caseload of complex cases.
Prof. Memberships: Solicitors Family Law Association (SFLA); Family Mediators Association (FMA); International Academy of Matrimonial Lawyers (IAML).
Publications: Co-author of 'Longman's Practical Matrimonial Precedents' and 'Know How for Family Lawyers'. Author of articles in professional journals and elsewhere. Occasional lecturer, speaker at conferences and contributor to the media.
Personal: MA; MPhil. Lives in London and Oxford.

PARRY, Richard
Farrer & Co, London
(020) 7242 2022
rwp@farrer.co.uk
Specialisation: Partner in family team. Main area of practice is family law.
Prof. Memberships: Solicitors Family Law Association.
Career: Qualified in 1976. Joined *Farrer & Co* in 1974, becoming a partner in 1983.
Personal: Born 6 December 1951. Educated at Eton College (1964-69) and Balliol College, Oxford (1970-73). Governor of Downe House. Leisure interests include golf, bridge and music. Lives in London.

PATIENCE, Iain
Patience & Buchan, Aberdeen
(01224) 588333
iain@patienceandbuchan.com
Specialisation: Partner. Law Society of Scotland accredited specialist in Family Law and Family Mediation.
Career: Admitted December 1979. Previously one of the senior partners at *Iain Smith & Company*. With a fellow Family Law specialist Lorna Buchan set up the dynamic and expanding firm *Patience & Buchan* in August 2000. This is the only Aberdeen legal firm specialising exclusively in Family Law. A member of the Law Society of Scotland and Family Law Association. Qualified mediator – member of CALM.

PAYNE, Peter
Stephens & Scown, Exeter
(01392) 210700

PEARSON, Philippa
The Family Law Consortium, London
(020) 7420 5000
pp@tflc.co.uk
Specialisation: Main aim is to deal with family issues in a conciliatory but firm manner so that, particularly where children are involved, the parties are able to communicate effectively after the legal process is over.
Prof. Memberships: Member of the SFLA National Committee and chair of its Legal Aid Committee for six years.
Career: Qualified 1988, previously head of family law at *Osbornes*.
Publications: Regularly writes (including Butterworths 'Family Law Service' and 'Cohabitation Law and Precedents', 'Cohabitation Rights'), lectures and appears in the media to talk about family law matters.

PEMBRIDGE, Eileen
Fisher Meredith, London
(020) 7622 4468
eileenp@fishermeredith.co.uk
Specialisation: Senior Partner and Head of Family Department. Deals with all aspects of family law, but especially complex ancillary relief on divorce and other financial matters. Has always taken on Legal Aid work. Has written various opinion pieces on family law and the legal profession, lectured and addressed sessions on family law at the Solicitors Annual Conference.
Prof. Memberships: Law Society; Council Member for London South since 1990; Family Law Committee 1990 to date (Chair 1990-94); Courts and Legal Services Committee from 1987; now Vice-Chair Access to Justice Committee. International Human Rights Working Party for five years from 1993 and Equal Opportunities Committee since 1994, (Chair from 1999). LAPG (Committee Member since 1982 and Chair 1987-88); SFLA; International Family Law Association; Chair of Law Society Reputation Working Party; Member, Law Reform Board 2001 to date; 1999-2001, Member Institute of Advanced Legal Studies.
Career: Worked as a freelance interpreter for the UN 1967-73 and casually thereafter until 1983. Qualified in 1975. Co-founder of *Fisher Meredith* in 1975, now 110 strong. Challenged Law Society convention by standing for election as President, July 1995. Co-author of the 'Law Society's Family Law Protocol' launched 2002 and member of its Working Party reviewing Ancillary Relief Law and Procedure (2002).
Publications: General Editor and now Consulting Editor, Sweet and Maxwell 'Legal Aid Practice Manual'.
Personal: Born 15 March 1944. Educated at Worcester Girls' Grammar School; Newnham College, Cambridge (Natural Sciences degree and postgraduate French and Russian), and Bath University (postgraduate language studies). FRSA. Interests include sailing, animal welfare, children's activities, hill-walking, vegetable-growing and reading novels in French, Russian and Spanish. Lives in Dulwich Village, London with her two young children and husband (a judge).

PHILIPPS, Susan
Alexiou Fisher Philipps, London
(020) 7409 1222
sphilipps@afp-law.co.uk
Specialisation: Partner. Covers all areas of family and matrimonial law. SFLA trained mediator.
Prof. Memberships: Solicitors Family Law Association. Serves on Education committee of the SFLA.
Career: Qualified in 1984. Joined *Ward Bowie* in 1982 and became a partner in

THE LEADERS — FAMILY/MATRIMONIAL

1986 on merger with *Penningtons*. Head of family law department since 1994 until joined *Gordon Dadds* in 1999. Founding partner *Alexiou Fisher Philipps* 2001.
Personal: Born 9 April 1957. Lives in London.

PIGOTT, Simon
Levison Meltzer Pigott, London
(020) 7556 2400
spigott@lmplaw.co.uk
Specialisation: Along with leading practitioners Jeremy Levison and Claire Meltzer opened *Levison Meltzer Pigott*. Now joined by new partner Alison Hayes. Handles all aspects of matrimonial work including cases involving complex financial issues and children. Practising family mediator. Lecturer and broadcaster.
Prof. Memberships: Solicitors Family Law Association. American Bar Association (Family Section). Family Mediators Association. United Kingdom College of Family Mediators. International Academy of Matrimonial Lawyers.
Career: Qualified 1982. *Wright Webb Syrett* 1978-83; *Theodore Goddard* 1983-85; *Collyer-Bristow* 1985-98 (partner from 1987); *Levison Meltzer Pigott* 1998.
Personal: Born October 1956. Mill Hill School 1970-74. University of Southampton 1974-77. Lives in Wolverton, Hants. Married with three daughters.

POWELL, Mark
Hugh James, Bargoed
(01443) 822022
mark.powell@hughjames.com
Specialisation: Partner and head of family group. Public childrens law, mental health.
Prof. Memberships: Association of Lawyers for Children (Past Chair).
Career: Rugby School. University College, London. Admitted as solicitor 1977. Barrister and Solicitor of the High Court of New Zealand (admitted 1990). Assistant Recorder 1995. Made Recorder in the year 2000.

PRESTON, Miles
Miles Preston & Co, London
(020) 7583 0583
miles.preston@milespreston.co.uk
Specialisation: Practises exclusively in matrimonial and family law.
Prof. Memberships: Solicitors Family Law Association, International Academy of Matrimonial Lawyers.
Career: Qualified in 1974. Partner with *Radcliffes & Co* (1979-94). Founding partner *Miles Preston & Co* (1994). Served on Sir Gervaise Sheldon's Family Law Liaison Committee 1982; founder member SFLA 1982; served on Main Committee of SFLA 1982-88; chaired working party on procedure 1982-88; founder member of IAML 1986; Governor IAML 1986-89; Parliamentarian to Main Committee 1989; president of English Chapter 1989; president of European Chapter 1989-92; president Elect of Main Academy 1992-94. President of Main Academy 1994-96; Counsel to Executive Committee (2000-). Member of the President's International Family Law Committee (chaired by Lord Justice Thorpe) since 1993.
Personal: Born 1950. Educated Shrewsbury School 1963-68. Leisure interests include food, travel and classic cars. Lives in Chelsea, London.

PROCTOR, Jane
Greenwoods, Peterborough
(01733) 887700

RAE, Maggie
Clintons, London
(020) 7395 8425
maggie@clintons.co.uk
Specialisation: Partner. Family Department. Work includes divorce, children, adoption, employment and education. Also all aspects of family and children work. Lectures at Warwick University. Undertakes frequent teaching, lecturing and writing assignments.
Prof. Memberships: Solicitors Family Law Association, Education Law Association, British Association for Adoption and Fostering, Inter Country Adoption Lawyers Association, International Academy of Matrimonial Lawyers, members of the Government's consultation panel on Pensions and Divorce, the President of the Family Division's International Committee, Special Adviser to the Social Security Select Committee in relation to Pensions and Divorce, Fellow of the RSA.
Career: Qualified in 1973. Barrister 1973-77. Partner at *Hodge Jones & Allen* 1978-92. Joined *Mishcon de Reya* in 1992, becoming a Partner in 1993. Joined *Clintons* in 1999.
Publications: Author of 'Women and the Law', 'Children and the Law', 'First Rights' and 'Child Care Law' – Co Author with Robin Ellison of 'Pensions & Matrimonial Breakdown'.
Personal: Born 20 September 1949. Attended Great Yarmouth High School 1961-68 and University of Warwick 1968-71. Leisure interests include walking, cooking and gardening. Lives in London.

RAY, Peggy
Goodman Ray, London
(020) 7254 8855
peggyray@goodmanray.com
Specialisation: Practice covers all areas of childcare work including both public and private law cases, adoption and associated areas such as judicial review and administrative law. Speaker and trainer in childcare. Former member of the Law Society Family Law Committee, current member of Solicitors Family Law Association children committee, member of the Expert Witness Group, former member of the Inner London Children Act Business committee. Member of the Law Society Children panel since 1985. Member of Funding Review committee, member of President's Interdisciplinary committee, member of Family Appeals Review Group.
Prof. Memberships: Solicitors Family Law Association, Association of Lawyers for Children, NaGALRO, BAAF.
Career: Qualified 1980. Established own practice with Judith Goodman in Hackney in 1985. Awarded Unicef Child Rights Lawyer of the Year 2001. Awarded Unicef Child Rights Lawyer of the Year 2001.

RAYMONT, Mary
Brachers, Maidstone
(01622) 776426
maryraymont@brachers.co.uk
Specialisation: Divorce and ancillary relief: high net worth; private children: contact and residence; public child: care acting mainly for child through Court approved guardian; adoption; cohabitees; mediation (trained by SFLA).
Prof. Memberships: Solicitors Family Law Association; Association of Lawyers for Children; Law Society; Kent Law Society; Kent Solicitors Family Law Association; Law Society Advanced Family Panel; SFLA Advanced Panel; Law Society Children Panel.
Career: LLB Degree University of London, 1989; Trainee Solicitor *Penningtons*, 1990-92; Assistant Solicitor, *Brachers* 1992-97; Partner at *Brachers*, 1997
Personal: Teaching Diploma in Litigation; Committee Member of Kent SFLA. Interests: running, yoga and travel.

READHEAD, Siobhan
Miles Preston & Co, London
(020) 7583 0583
siobhan.readhead@milespreston.co.uk
Specialisation: All areas of matrimonial and family law, including resolution of financial issues on divorce and separation; all issues relating to children; pre-marriage and cohabitation contracts.
Prof. Memberships: Solicitors Family Law Association; International Academy of Matrimonial Lawyers.
Career: *Radcliffes* 1982-94; partner 1989; founding partner *Miles Preston & Co* 1994; SFLA Accredited Specialist (Advocacy: Ancillary Relief and Substantial Assets; Trustee of Mediation in Divorce).
Personal: Born 1957. Educated Southampton University; married, two children; resides Richmond.

RODGERS, Hilary
Forsters, London
(020) 7863 8333
hrodgers@forsters.co.uk
Specialisation: Head of family law practice, specialising in complex financial divorce settlements and children matters. Also experienced in issues of jurisdiction, taxation, trusts and pensions in relation to matrimonial matters.
Prof. Memberships: Solicitors Family Law Association treasurer; SFLA; chair of the Cohabitation committee; International Bar Association; International Academy of Matrimonial Lawyers.
Career: Admitted 1987. Assistant at *Theodore Goddard*. Joined *Frere Cholmeley Bischoff* 1991. Partner 1994. Founder partner of *Forsters*, August 1998.
Personal: Born 1962. Married with two children. Lives in North London.

RUTHERFORD, Lyn
Dickinson Dees, Newcastle upon Tyne
(0191) 279 9229
lyn.rutherford@dickinson-dees.com
Specialisation: Partner and head of family law department. The practice covers a full range of family law matters. In particular specialisation in high net worth private clients and major ancillary matters.
Career: Qualified 1972. Thereafter one year at *Clayton Mott* in Nottingham. Joined *Dickinson Dees* in January 1974. Became a partner in 1976.
Personal: Born 20 January 1948. Educated at Hookergate Grammar School and Liverpool University – LLB Degree. Interests include sports, particularly horse racing, football and reading. Lives in Newcastle upon Tyne.

RUTTER, Geoffrey
Collyer-Bristow, London
(020) 7242 7363
geoffrey.rutter@collyerbristow.com
Specialisation: Many years experience in family law, principally involving substantial financial issues resulting from marriage breakdown, including forum issues. Considerable knowledge of and experience in the investigative elements of domestic and international work including offshore trusts and structures. Regularly advises on the commercial and tax considerations involved in financial negotiations and settlements.
Prof. Memberships: Solicitors Family Law Association (accredited specialist), International Academy of Matrimonial Lawyers. Committee member of the London Regional Committee of the Solicitors Family Law Association.

SALTER, David
Addleshaw Booth & Co, Leeds
(0113) 203 2454
david.salter@addleshawbooth.com
Specialisation: Partner and head of family law department. Handles all aspects of family law, but principally financial relief with an emphasis on pensions. Frequent lecturer on family law topics.
Prof. Memberships: SFLA (Chairman 1997-99). Chairman of SFLA Accreditation and Pensions Committees. International Academy of Matrimonial Lawyers (Fellow; Member, Management Committee, European Chapter).
Career: Qualified 1972. Joined the firm in 1975, becoming a Partner in 1978. Recorder (North Eastern Circuit); Former member of the Family Committee of the Judicial Studies Board.
Publications: Author or joint author of 'Humphreys Family Proceedings', 'Matrimonial Consent Orders and Agreements', 'Family Finance and Tax' and 'Family Courts: Emergency Remedies and Procedures'. Editor of 'Pensions and Insurance on Family Breakdown' and 'Longman Litigation Practice'. Contribu-

FAMILY/MATRIMONIAL ■ THE LEADERS

tor to 'Insolvency on Family Breakdown' and 'Butterworths Family Law Service'.
Personal: Educated Pembroke College, Cambridge.

SAX, Richard
Manches, London
(020) 7404 4433
richard.sax@manches.co.uk
Specialisation: Partner in family department. Advises on all areas of family law, particularly complex financial and children issues arising from matrimonial and relationship breakdown including international, trust and tax aspects.
Prof. Memberships: Solicitors Family Law Association, International Academy of Matrimonial Lawyers, Law Society.
Career: Qualified in 1967. 1968 Partner and subsequently Managing Partner at *Rubinstein Callingham* (which merged with *Manches* in 1994). Since 1990 has sat as a Deputy District Judge at the Principal Registry. Past Chairman of the Solicitors Family Law Association. President International Academy of Matrimonial Lawyers European Chapter. Member of the DSS Consultation Panel on Pension Sharing.
Publications: Co-Author 'Know how for Family Lawyers', published by Longmans. Joint General Editor Butterworth's 'Family Law Service'.

SCANLAN, Margaret
Russells Gibson McCaffrey, Glasgow
(0141) 332 4176

SCOFIELD, Ian
Hooper & Wollen, Torquay
(01803) 213251

SHACKLETON, Fiona
Payne Hicks Beach, London
(020) 7465 4300
Specialisation: Partner in family team. Principal area of practice is family law. Solicitor to HRH The Prince of Wales and TRH Princes William and Harry since 1996.
Prof. Memberships: SFLA, IAML.
Career: Qualified in 1980. Became a partner with *Brecher & Co* in 1982. Joined *Farrer & Co* in 1984; became a partner in 1987. Joined *PHB* in 2001 as a partner.
Publications: Co-author of 'The Divorce Handbook'.
Personal: Born 26 May 1956. Attended Benenden School and Exeter University. Governor of Benenden School since 1985. Leisure pursuits include calligraphy, cooking, opera and bridge. Lives in London.

SHAKESPEAR, Felicity
Clarke Willmott & Clarke, Taunton
(01823) 445450
fshakespear@cw-c.co.uk
Specialisation: Partner dealing with all areas of family law, with particular expertise in high asset ancillary relief claims involving companies, pensions and farmers, and also public law child care. Acted for Mr White in the House of Lords regarding the division of assets on dissolution of marriage which is the leading authority in this field. As a result of the case has received numerous new instructions and heads up a team of eight specialist family lawyers.
Prof. Memberships: Solicitors Family Law Association, member of the Children Panel, Family Law Panel assessor.
Career: Southampton University (LLB); articled with *Moore & Blatch*; admitted in December 1973; Partner with *Darlington & Parkinson* (Ealing, London) 1985-86; joined *Clarke Willmott & Clarke* October 1986.

SHEEHAN, Wendy
Mowat Dean WS, Edinburgh
(0131) 555 0616
wendy.sheehan@mowatdean.co.uk
Specialisation: Practises solely in family law both in the Sheriff Court and Court of Session dealing with inter alia financial provision on divorce, parental rights, residence and contact cases, spousal maintenance/CSA and separation agreements. Appointed as an independent court reporter in child residence and contact cases. Also accredited by the Law Society of Scotland as a family law specialist and mediator with a substantial mediation practice.
Prof. Memberships: Family Law Association, Notary Public, Convenor of C.A.L.M.
Career: Born 26 December 1968. Educated at St. George's School for Girls and University of Aberdeen. Admitted as a solicitor in 1991.
Personal: Lives in Edinburgh. Author for 'Butterworths Family Law Service', Chair of Couple Counselling Lothian. Leisure interests include music and water sports.

SHELTON, Erica
Charles Russell, London
(020) 7203 5000
ericas@cr-law.co.uk
Specialisation: Family law, ancillary relief, particularly experienced in dealing with big money cases with an international element where there are complex tax and trusts issues. Acted for wife in Conran v Conran. Also deals with private law Children's Act disputes often with an international angle.
Prof. Memberships: Law Society, SFLA, Association of Contentions Trust and probate practitioners.

SHRIMPTON, Julie
Tozers, Plymouth
(01752) 206460

SILVER, Raphael
Silver Fitzgerald, Cambridge
(01223) 562001
Specialisation: Senior litigation partner. Childcare, Care Standards Regulation.
Prof. Memberships: Law Society Children Panel. SFLA. Associate Member NAGALRO and BAAF.
Career: Admitted October 1984. Former Duty Solicitor. Children Panel member since 1991.
Publications: ADHD 'Family Law' 1998.
Personal: Born 1960, Liverpool. Graduated Durham University. Married. Lives in Saffron Walden. Interests include cricket, gardening and wine.

SIMPSON, Barbara
Boodle Hatfield, Oxford
(01865) 265128
bsimpson@boodlehatfield.com
Specialisation: Highly experienced in handling substantial financial cases, including those with an international element or complex commercial issues. Practice also includes dealing with all types of private children and ancillary relief issues. Experienced in emergency work including injunctions and strong contacts with London office.
Prof. Memberships: SFLA (was the first chair of the Solicitors Family Law Association in Oxford); Deputy District Judge in the Principal Registry of Family Division since 1995.
Career: Qualified 1974. Assistant at *Herbert & Gowers* from 1975-76. Head of the *Cole & Cole* (now *Morgan & Cole*) family law department from 1984. Joined *Boodle Hatfield* as a partner in 1999.
Personal: Born 1948. Educated at Durham University. Enjoys squash, cinema, chess and singing.

SIMPSON, Jane
Manches, London
(020) 7753 7519
jane.simpson@manches.co.uk
Specialisation: Partner and Head of Family Law Department. Deals in particular with divorce and complex financial issues, children, tax, and the commercial implications of divorce and separation; international aspects of divorce and separation and forum shopping. Has lectured extensively.
Prof. Memberships: Founder member of International Academy of Matrimonial Lawyers. Non-executive Director and Vice-Chairman of the Tavistock Portman NHS Trust.
Career: Qualified in 1967. Marriage Guidance Counsellor 1972-77. Founded *Manches* Family Law Department in 1977. Co-founder of Solicitors Family Law Association in 1982 and chairman 1993-95. Member of Ancillary Relief Advisory Group 1991-2000. Member of Lord Chancellor's Advisory Board on Family Law 1996-2001. 2002 – Member of President's Interdisciplinary Family Law Committee.
Personal: Born 15 July 1942. Educated at Channing School, Highgate and University College, London. Enjoys music, reading, travel. Has two adult daughters and one son.

SISSON, David
Hansells, Norwich
(01603) 615731

SMITH, Caroline
Russel & Aitken, Edinburgh
(01324) 822194

SMITH, Michael
Mincoffs, Newcastle upon Tyne
(0191) 281 6151

SMITH, Shona
Balfour & Manson, Edinburgh
(0131) 200 1238
shona.smith@balfour-manson.co.uk
Specialisation: Partner in the Family Law Team. Accredited by the Law Society of Scotland as a family law specialist.
Prof. Memberships: Law Society of Scotland (member of the Family Law Committee); Treasurer of the Family Law Association; Child Law Centre.
Career: Qualified in 1991. Joined *Balfour & Manson* in 1996. Board member Child Law Centre 1997-2000; Chair Family Law Association 1999-2001.
Personal: Born 17 November 1966. Edinburgh University 1984-89. Lives in Edinburgh.

SPEKER, Barry
Samuel Phillips & Co, Newcastle upon Tyne
(0191) 232 8451
barryspeker@samuelphillips.co.uk
See under Clinical Negligence, p.155

SPITZ, Louise
Manches, London
(020) 7404 4433
louise.spitz@manches.co.uk
Specialisation: Partner in Family Department. Advises on all aspects of family breakdown and its financial and general legal consequences; cohabitation and pre-marriage planning and disputes concerning children.
Prof. Memberships: Solicitors Family Law Association.
Career: Qualified 1989. Joined *Manches* 1994 in merger with *Rubinstein Callingham*. Partner 1997. Member of Law Society Family Law Committee since 2000.
Personal: Born 3 July 1951. Married with two adult children. Educated Universities of the Witwatersrand (Johannesburg), Sheffield and University College London. Enjoys home and garden, fine food and wine and reading cookbooks, biographies and novels.

STAKES, John Anthony
Gordons Cranswick Solicitors, Leeds
(0113) 245 2450
john.stakes@gordonscranswick.co.uk
Specialisation: Main area of practice financial settlements on divorce/separation.
Prof. Memberships: National SFLA Regional Press Officer and former Chairman of West and North Yorkshire SFLA. Accredited member of the SFLA; Member of Law Society's Family Law Panel.
Career: Qualified 1971. Partner 1975.
Personal: Married with two children and three stepchildren. Leisure interests include walking, amateur dramatics and cricket.

STANCZYK, Julia
Miles Preston & Co, London
(020) 7583 0583
julia.stanczyk@milespreston.co.uk
Specialisation: Financial cases, often involving complex and international issues; pre-marriage contracts; cohabitation cases and private Children Act cases.

THE LEADERS — FAMILY/MATRIMONIAL

Instructed in the leading case on reciprocal enforcement of maintenance orders: K v M, M and L (Financial Relief: Foreign Orders) 1998 2 FLR 59.
Prof. Memberships: SFLA.
Career: Articled *Radcliffes*; partner 1990; partner *Miles Preston & Co* 1994. One of the first SFLA accredited specialists (substantial assets/emergency relief) 1999.
Personal: Educated Haberdashers' Aske's Girls' School, Elstree and Southampton University.

STEPHENS, Lindy
Hooper & Wollen, Torquay
(01803) 213251

STEWART, James
Reynolds Porter Chamberlain, London
(020) 7307 9530
jhs@rpc.co.uk
Specialisation: Partner and Head of Family Department. Deals with all aspects of family law, especially complex financial cases which often have an international dimension. Has acted in a number of high profile cases, most recently in the landmark family/Human Rights Act case of Clibbery v Allan [2002] 1 FLR 565.
Prof. Memberships: Solicitors Family Law Association, SFLA Education Committee.
Career: Admitted 1990. Became a Partner at *Reynolds Porter Chamberlain* in 2000 after joining the firm from *Stephenson Harwood*. SFLA Accredited Specialist 2001.
Personal: Born 2 May 1964. Educated at Coleraine Academical Institution and at the University of Essex. Lives in London.

STOWE, Marilyn J
Grahame Stowe, Bateson, Leeds
(0113) 260 6191
famlaw@grahame-stowe-bateson.co.uk
Specialisation: Deals in particular with divorce and complex financial issues, children, tax, commercial implications of divorce and separation.
Prof. Memberships: The Law Society, The Law Society Family Law Panel.
Career: Career: Qualified in 1980. Former lecturer in English Law at University of Le Mans, France. Partner in *Grahame Stowe, Bateson* 1982. Chair Child Support Appeals Tribunal 1993. Chair Social Security Appeals Tribunal 1994. Chief Assessor and Chief Examiner of the Law Society's Family Law Panel 1998 to date. Appointed Chief Assessor and Chief Examiner of the Advanced Tier of the Law Society's Family Law Panel 2001.
Publications: Author; 'Divorce – A New Beginning' published 1993; 'No Looking Back' published 2002.
Personal: Married with one son. Lives in Leeds. Leisure interests include distance running.

TAIT, Fiona
Drummond Miller WS, Edinburgh
(0131) 226 5151
ftait@drummond-miller.co.uk
Specialisation: Partner. Head of *Drummond Miller's* family law team which deals with divorce, financial provision, child law, child abductions and children's hearings. Accredited specialist in family law. Tutor at the University of Edinburgh LLB course in Commercial Law (1990-97).
Prof. Memberships: Law Society of Scotland, Edinburgh Bar Association Council Member (1993-96).
Career: Qualified in 1991. Joined *Drummond Miller* in 1989, becoming a partner in 1996.
Publications:
Personal: Born 9 January 1966. Attended University of Edinburgh: LLB (Hons) 1988, DipLP 1989. Lives in Edinburgh.

TAYLOR, Norman
Zermansky & Partners, Leeds
(0113) 245 9766
nst@zermansky-solicitors.com
Specialisation: Ancillary relief in divorce and cohabitation disputes.
Prof. Memberships: Law Society Family Law Panel; West and North Yorkshire SFLA Committee.
Career: Qualified July 1975. With *Zermansky & Partners* since February 1974. Senior Partner and Head of Family Department.
Personal: Born 14 January 1951. Educated at University of Newcastle upon Tyne (LLB). Married with three children. 1st Dan Black Belt Japan Karate Association (retired). Lead guitarist in charity rock band.

THORNEYCROFT, Phil
Wolferstans, Plymouth
(01752) 663295
pthorneycroft@wolferstans.com
Specialisation: Partner 1990. Head of family office. Main areas of practice are childcare and ancillary relief. Acts on behalf of parents and children, and Children's Guardians, in care proceedings and related matters. Acts for private and legally aided clients in divorce and ancillary relief. Has made a number of appearances on local radio dealing with such issues as sexual abuse, cohabitation contracts and the effect of pensions on divorce.
Prof. Memberships: Chair of the Devon & Cornwall Solicitors Family Law Association committee; a member of the Children panel; founder member of the Plymouth Childcare Support group. Associate member of the National Association of Guardians ad Litem and reporting officers. SFLA trained family mediator. SFLA accredited specialist (advocacy, ancillary relief and children's law).
Career: Qualified in 1982. Joined *Wolferstans* in 1982, becoming a partner in 1990.
Personal: Born 2 December 1957. Attended Chesterfield Grammar School 1970-76, Hull University 1976-79 and Chester Law College 1979-80. Leisure interests include hockey, skiing, music and Sheffield Wednesday. Lives in Plymouth.

TOOTH, Ray
Sears Tooth, London
(020) 7499 5599
Specialisation: All aspects of matrimonial matters with particular emphasis on financial cases, often of an international nature particularly in relation to cases involving the Middle East. Has habitually been involved in difficult cases.
Prof. Memberships: The Law Society.
Career: Dragon School. Oxford. Kings School, Canterbury. University College Oxford.
Personal: Extensive horse racing interests, including breeding. Carlton Television produced a half-hour documentary about Mr Tooth, 'Tooth and Nail' in August 1997 demonstrating the practice of matrimonial law.

TRUEX, David
International Family Law Chambers, London
(020) 7583 5040

WARD, Helen
Manches, London
(020) 7404 4433
helen.ward@manches.co.uk
Specialisation: Partner in family law department. Handles all areas of family law, particularly complex financial aspects of matrimonial and relationship breakdown often involving an international element.
Prof. Memberships: Solicitors Family Law Association, International Academy of Matrimonial Lawyers, Law Society.
Career: Qualified in 1978. Partner at *Ward Bowie* from 1978, which subsequently became *Penningtons*. Joined *Manches* as a partner in July 1994. Deputy District Judge in the Principal Registry and Recorder.
Personal: Born 28 May 1951. Attended King Alfred School, London 1955-69 and Birmingham University 1970-73. Family come first but leisure interests include music, theatre, tennis and gardening.

WAY, Philip
Addleshaw Booth & Co, Leeds
(0113) 209 2000
philip.way@addleshawbooth.com
Specialisation: Partner in the firm's family law department. Deals with all aspects of marriage and relationship breakdown. Wide experience of the financial issues arising on divorce including those surrounding the family business and pensions. Typically represents successful business and professional people where the family assets exceed £1m. SFLA trained mediator.
Prof. Memberships: Chairman of the West & North Yorkshire SFLA and member of the SFLA Good Practice Committee. Accredited SFLA specialist family lawyer with particular expertise in dealing with substantial assets on divorce and emergency financial procedures on divorce. Associate of UK College of Family Mediators.
Career: Joined the firm in 1990 as a trainee, qualified into the firm's family law department in 1992 and became a partner in 2001.
Publications: Contributor to 'Humphreys Family Proceedings', 'Pensions on Family Breakdown' and 'Insolvency on Family Breakdown'. Regular author of articles for legal journals.
Personal: Educated at Durham University. Married with two children. Lives in Wakefield.

WHITE, Denis
Hunt & Coombs, Peterborough
(01733) 565312

WHITE, Iain
Cozens-Hardy & Jewson, Norwich
(01603) 625231
Specialisation: Family department. Specialises in child-related work, divorce and matrimonial finance.
Prof. Memberships: Original member of the Children panel. Member of the Family Law panel and Solicitors Family Law Association. Representative on the Norwich Family Court Business committee.
Career: Qualified 1977. Partner 1986.

WILKINS, Beth
Pannone & Partners, Manchester
(0161) 909 3000
beth.wilkins@pannone.co.uk
Specialisation: Partner and joint head of family department. Handles all aspects of marriage breakdown, matrimonial finance and private law relating to children. Advises on co-habitation and pre-nuptial agreements. A large percentage of work comprises acting for professionals and high net worth individuals, and in cases with a corporate/business element.
Prof. Memberships: Member of SFLA National Committee and Chair of Good Practice Committee; SFLA North West Branch press officer.
Career: Qualified in 1981. Formerly partner and head of family department at *Maurice Rubin Clare* (now *DAC*); partner *Pannone & Partners* 1995. Regular speaker, lecturer and broadcaster on family law topics.
Personal: Leisure interests include gluttony, theatre, cinema, the arts and travel. Lives in Greater Manchester.

WILLIAMS, Elaine
Sears Tooth, London
(020) 7495 2970
elainewilliams@searstooth.co.uk
Specialisation: Expertise in ancillary relief cases of high net worth, often incorporating and international aspect. Reported cases include El Fadl, Tavoulareas, Mubarak, Cornick No.1, Cornick No.2, Cornick No. 3, Fax, Q v V (Costs: Summary Assessment).
Prof. Memberships: Law Society; Solicitors Family Law Association.
Career: Articled *Hudgell Yeates & Co*; qualified 1988; *Malkin Janners* 1988-89; *Sears Tooth* 1989 to date; Partner 1995.
Personal: Born 1961, resides London. Attended Washington School; Manchester University LLB (Hons); leisure interests include design, travel.

FAMILY/MATRIMONIAL ■ THE LEADERS

WILLIAMS, Frances
Larby Williams, Cardiff
(029) 2047 2100

WILLIAMS, Gail
Robertsons, Cardiff
(029) 2023 7777

WILLIAMS, Ian
Robertsons, Cardiff
(029) 2023 7777

WILLIAMS, Jane R
Larby Williams, Cardiff
(029) 2047 2100

WILSON, Bruce
Mills & Reeve, Norwich
(01603) 660155

WOODS, Paul
Wolferstans, Plymouth
(01752) 663295
pwoods@wolferstans.com
Specialisation: Family/matrimonial specialising in divorce clients, including ancillary relief and advocacy. SFLA accreditation for 'Big money cases' and 'co-habitation'.

Career: Qualified in 1975. Senior partner *Wolferstans*. Part-time chairman Social Security Appeal tribunal 1988 to date; president Plymouth Law Society 1996-97; founder member and past committee member of Devon and Cornwall SFLA.
Personal: Wellfield Grammar School, Durham; Liverpool University; LL.B 1972. Year of birth: 1949. Town of residence: Plymouth. Main leisure activities golf, rugby and theatre. Clubs: President of Plymouth Albion Rugby FC; member St Mellion and Yelverton Golf Clubs.

WOODWARD, David
TLT Solicitors, Bristol
(0117) 917 7501
dwoodward@tltsolicitors.com
Specialisation: Partner in family law team. Main areas of practice are divorce, ancillary relief and children. Acted in Richardson 1994 1FLR 188, B v B 1995 IFLR 9 and Richardson (No 2) 1996 2 FLR 617. Contributor to Western Daily Press. Experience includes cable television work, LNTV and occasional lecturing.
Prof. Memberships: SFLA, Law Society, Chairman Bristol SFLA. Member of Family Law panel. Accredited member of SFLA. Director Bristol Family Mediators Association.
Career: Qualified in 1975. Joined *Trumps* in 1979, becoming a partner in 1981. *Trumps* merged with Bristol law firm *Lawrence Tucketts* to become *TLT Solicitors* on 1 May 2000. Heads up family law team of 13.
Personal: Born 10 January 1950. Holds an LLB from Bristol. Leisure interests include cycling, badminton and cricket. Lives in Bristol.

WRIGHT, Barbara
Thomson Snell & Passmore, Tunbridge Wells
(01892) 510000
bwright@ts-p.co.uk
Specialisation: Partner and Head of Family Department. Deals with all areas of family breakdown. Particular interest in financial aspects.
Prof. Memberships: Member of Solicitors Family Law Association. Founding chair of Kent Solicitors Family Law Association and member of National Committee of SFLA from March 1997-98. Vice-president Tonbridge, Tunbridge Wells & District Law Society January 2002.
Career: Qualified 1979. Joined *Thomson Snell & Passmore* in 1987. Equity partner from 1995. Honorary legal advisor to West Kent Relate. Accredited mediator trained by the Family Mediators Association.
Personal: Born 16 March 1955. Honours Law degree Sheffield University. 2nd Class (Hons) in Part II Law Society's examinations. Interests include English and French history, current affairs, cuisine. Lives in the Tunbridge Wells area.

YOUNG, Ian
Young & Lee, Birmingham
(0121) 633 3233

FINANCIAL SERVICES

London: 385; The Regions: 387; Scotland: 388; Profiles: 389

Research approved by BMRB For this edition, **Chambers'** researchers conducted 6,582 interviews – 3,900 with law firms, 511 with barristers and 2,171 with clients. The validity of the research was scrutinised by BMRB International, who audited both the methodology and the results at our offices in London. They interviewed **Chambers'** researchers and cross-checked sample interviews. Details of the audit appear on page 7.

OVERVIEW The new regulatory regime ("N2") under the Financial Services and Markets Act 2000 came into force at the end of November 2001. However it seems that the "*mini-boom*" in preparation for its impact has turned out to be "*a phoney war*," with the amount of new work generated not representing the peak anticipated by most practitioners. Although some work is being lost to in-house compliance departments, most firms report that there is "*lots of work on the boil.*" Practitioners sense that the FSA will be active on its enforcement policy, regulating by theme rather than by firm within the context of a politically driven agenda. Beyond market abuse, other areas identified as potential "*trophies*" include depolarisation and senior management responsibility across a wider sector range to include insurance, accountancy and e-commerce. Outside London, practitioners predict that many firms with strong sector focus in corporate, banking or funds will choose to expand their expertise in this "*growing and profitable*" sector. This is certainly the case in Scotland, where investment funds and corporate finance are the primary bases for most compliance work. This reinforces the view of one leading specialist, that the best financial services lawyers are those who are "*good all-rounders with knowledge in areas such as contract and tort, who have a strong feel for the markets and who are not purely focused on procedure – they need to be alert to new icebergs*" that the morass of law and regulation incurs.

LONDON

CLIFFORD CHANCE (see firm details p.911) This "*machine of international contacts*" impresses with its "*fabulous*" continental coverage. Interviewees observed that the broadly-based practice, which is "*heavily geared*" towards global securities houses and the investment banking community has "*years of experience.*" Competitors praise the team for its "*fantastic reputation*" among exchanges and clearing houses, while clients report that it is "*great for taking a different view*" on matters that include wholesale derivatives and energy. **Tim Herrington** (see p.390) continues to elicit resounding peer approval, as "*an extremely experienced all-rounder with an encyclopaedic grasp of the law,*" while clients concur that he is "*everything one would want a senior financial services lawyer to be.*" He advised JPMorgan Chase on the disposal of Fleming Private Banking, and advised the Financial Services Compensation Scheme on the establishment of a compensation scheme and merger of existing compensation schemes under the old legislation. Envied by peers for his "*huge input*" on market-driven industry matters, **Chris Bates** (see p.389) is "*a down-to-earth, details lawyer*" with "*incredible energy*" who "*thinks about the subject in terms of new developments.*" He advised Cedel International, the 50% owner of Clearstream International, on the €1.75 billion offer by Deutsche Börse, and advised The Futures and Options Association on its standard documentation protection. Also commended for his regulatory expertise, **Mark Harding** (see p.390) advised LIFFE on its £555 million acquisition by Euronext. **Clients** International Swaps and Derivatives Association; British Bankers' Association; LIFFE; London Clearing House; FSA; Bank of America; JPMorgan Chase; Citigroup; Deutsche Bank.

FRESHFIELDS BRUCKHAUS DERINGER (see firm details p.964) "*A high-quality practice that is saturated in the regulatory culture.*" Competitors admire the team for its "*broad-ranging perspective*" and "*targeted*" approach towards tax structuring and unregulated matters, while clients attest to its "*excellent strength and depth*" and "*Rolls-Royce service.*" **Guy Morton** (see p.390) continues to attract market-wide plaudits as being "*dynamic and fearfully bright;*" a lawyer who some reckon possesses "*the most detailed understanding of the area aside from the Financial Services Authority.*" One leading practitioner pronounced that he is "*expert at administering conciliation and reaching agreement in divergent situations,*" while clients observe that "*despite being in high demand, he always makes himself available for us.*" He advised Dresdner Bank on Allianz's €24 billion agreed takeover bid for it and represented the London Stock Exchange on regulatory aspects of its admission to the Official List. Her peers commend "*clever*" **Annabel Sykes** (see p.390) for her "*deep technical knowledge.*" An "*energetic*" participant in consultative committees, she has recognised expertise in the context of takeovers. She advised AMP on its acquisition of Towry Law and on its disposal to Churchill Insurance of the right to act as underwriter for the Pearl general insurance portfolio and the right to reinsure Pearl's existing general insurance business. Blue-chip finance houses deem **Mark Kalderon** (see p.390) to be "*wonderfully responsive*" on large-scale bank finance and regulatory issues. He advised CIBC on the merger of its Caribbean financial services and banking businesses with Barclays Bank to form First Caribbean International Bank. **Clients** ABN AMRO; Bank of England; Citigroup; Deutsche Bank; Dresdner Kleinwort Wasserstein; FSA; Goldman Sachs; Lazard; Legal & General; Morgan Stanley; NM Rothschilds; Société Générale; Takeover Panel; UBS Warburg.

LINKLATERS (see firm details p.1043) The financial markets group is widely admired by its competitors for having "*developed an extremely successful model*" with the Blue Flag product and associated client-driven services, which are geared towards the global corporate and investment banking community. In addition to praise for its "*excellent service and timely advice,*" clients enthuse about their "*marvellous therapy sessions*" with the team, which entail "*wonderfully practical*" support systems such as the FSMA bi-weekly Breakfast Briefings. The group launched the new online service, Blue Flag FSMA Litigation, in response to potential investigatory activity by the FSA. Market sources rank the team firmly on a par with its peers in regard to its cross-continental strength with existing relationship counsel and "*comprehensive*" reach across the globe. His peers regard "*individualistic and highly experienced*" **Paul Nelson** (see p.390) as a "*clear leader,*" while clients say that "*upcoming star*" **Michael Kent** (see p.390) is "*always good for a sensible view.*" He spearheads matters relating to exchanges, e-commerce and multi-jurisdictional work for key investment bank clients. The team has been heavily involved in major whole implementation projects under N2, including infrastructure and market abuse for blue-chip finance houses. It continues to act for BrokerTec, OTC Derivatives and SwapsWire, in relation to e-commerce ATS platforms. **Clients** Lehman Brothers; JPMorgan Chase; Salomon Smith Barney/Citigroup; Goldman Sachs; Toronto Dominion Bank; CSFB; Merrill Lynch; Dresdner Kleinwort Wasserstein; Bear Stearns; OTC Derivatives.

ALLEN & OVERY (see firm details p.841) "*A superb quality outfit,*" according to industry users and competitors alike. One blue-chip client opined that the team has "*worked extremely hard to attain expert levels in the financial services arena and it is now paying off.*" It boasts an "*impressive range of expertise*" across

385

FINANCIAL SERVICES ■ LONDON

FINANCIAL SERVICES
■ LONDON

1
- Clifford Chance
- Freshfields Bruckhaus Deringer
- Linklaters

2
- Allen & Overy
- Slaughter and May

3
- CMS Cameron McKenna
- SJ Berwin
- Travers Smith Braithwaite

4
- Lovells
- Norton Rose
- Simmons & Simmons

5
- Herbert Smith

6
- Dechert
- Macfarlanes
- Stephenson Harwood

LEADING INDIVIDUALS

1
- **ABRAMS Charles** SJ Berwin
- **HERRINGTON Tim** Clifford Chance
- **MORTON Guy** Freshfields Bruckhaus Deringer
- **NELSON Paul** Linklaters

2
- **BATES Chris** Clifford Chance
- **CHAMBERLAIN Margaret** Travers Smith Braithwaite
- **MORRIS Simon** CMS Cameron McKenna
- **SYKES Annabel** Freshfields Bruckhaus Deringer

3
- **FOX Ruth** Slaughter and May
- **LITTLE Tamasin** SJ Berwin
- **STONES Richard** Lovells

4
- **PHILLIPS Paul** Allen & Overy
- **SLATER Richard** Simmons & Simmons

5
- **HARDING Mark** Clifford Chance
- **KALDERON Mark** Freshfields Bruckhaus Deringer
- **KENT Michael** Linklaters
- **MANSFIELD Rachel** Travers Smith Braithwaite

UP AND COMING
- **GLEESON Simon** Allen & Overy
- **REYNOLDS Carmen** Norton Rose

ASSOCIATES TO WATCH
- **BEVAN Peter** Linklaters

This book is the product of 6,582 1/2 hour interviews. See p.7 for BMRB audit.
Within each band, firms are listed alphabetically. See individuals' profiles p.389

---

statutory and regulatory legislation that is perceived to rest largely within the context of its work for the firm's commercial banking client base. Capital adequacy and income generation are key features of the practice that flow from its financial markets focus on structured products, derivatives, eurobonds and corporate work. Head of the European financial services regulatory group, **Paul Phillips** (see p.390) ("*studious and thorough*") continues to advise a number of major custodians with an "*extremely sound knowledge of the market.*" "*Entertaining*" **Simon Gleeson** (see p.389) advises on capital markets and derivatives-related matters with emphasis on new investment structures. The group has been involved in the development of new investment structures for the UK retail market; clients include CSFB, including securitised (Andrea IV) and deposit (TOISA) products, Merrill Lynch, Deutsche Bank, Citibank and HSBC. It also advised on a number of significant new investment exchanges including TradeWeb, Imarex, Swiss Re and Nordpool, and it advised ISDA as to several aspects of the Basel II process. **Clients** CSFB; Alliance & Leicester; Deutsche Bank; Merrill Lynch; TradeWeb.

SLAUGHTER AND MAY (see firm details p.1140) Widely judged as "*strong performers,*" despite being relatively new in the field, the group continues to combine regulatory support for the firm's "*A1*" transactional work with freestanding regulatory advice for clients that "*genuinely range beyond corporates.*" Examples include assisting with the establishment of new regulated entities and involvement in the consultation process with the Treasury and the FSA for development of the new regulatory regime. Her peers are "*great admirers*" of **Ruth Fox** (see p.389), whom they describe as "*eminently sensible and talented.*" The team advised Cater Allen (Abbey National's subsidiary) on its acquisition of Fleming Premier Bank from JPMorgan Chase, and acted for AMP in the Royal Bank of Scotland's acquisition of shares in Virgin One from its joint venture partners AMP and the Virgin Group. The group has also been advising Consignia on the establishment of arrangements to permit benefit payments to be made through Post Offices to recipients who have no other bank account. **Clients** Abbey National; Standard Chartered; Euroclear Bank; Schroders; Consignia.

CMS CAMERON MCKENNA (see firm details p.914) A "*cohesive team of specialists*" with a "*prime*" reputation in retail and insurance products, it typically advises medium-sized corporates and smaller financial institutions on regulatory and standalone matters. Adjudged by clients as "*easy to get on with,*" the team's reputation is primarily associated with **Simon Morris** (see p.390), who peers rate as "*a class performer.*" Viewed by the Scottish market as "*the first port of call on regulatory matters,*" clients praise him as "*an intelligent, persistent operator*" who displays "*an analytical but practical understanding*" of contentious regulatory and disciplinary matters. His key work of late includes advising a major UK high-street bank on the establishment of its UK wealth management division and handling a blue-chip fund provider's market re-entry as an internet-based provider of life/fund products and IFA servicing. He also successfully represented six product providers in FSA/SRO enforcement cases, while the team has advised M&G/Prudential and GISC among other financial institutions, on N2 review and compliance preparations. **Clients** Co-operative Insurance Society; Legal & General; Lloyds TSB; M&G; Royal Bank of Scotland; Old Mutual.

SJ BERWIN (see firm details p.867) "*A star among the smaller players.*" The "*experienced*" team's reputation for handling "*a lot of high-level standalone work*" marries comfortably with the firm's overall reputation in private equity funds and VC limited partnerships. Clients attest to the team's "*prompt, focused, bespoke service*" and "*phenomenal grasp*" of UK and European regulatory systems. "*Paid-up member of the profession*" **Charles Abrams** still handles an "*astonishing amount of work,*" while retaining his respected profile among his peers as a "*genius with great enthusiasm for the subject.*" "*Focused, concise, precise*" **Tamasin Little** gains widespread admiration as a "*sensible, effective performer who handles matters beautifully.*" The team acted for Pershing Securities in the expansion of its clearing and settlement activities in Europe and its clearing relationships with UK and overseas brokers and fund managers. Further highlights include handling the regulatory aspects of the buyout of Mercury Private Equity (now HgCapital) from Merrill Lynch, and the structuring of its new fund. It also acted for the Apax group on its €4.4 billion Europe V fund and related restructuring and management arrangements for optimal pan-European regulatory and tax treatment. **Clients** Bridgepoint Capital; Close Fund Management; Dresdner Kleinwort Wasserstein; Electra Managers; HgCapital; Pershing Securities.

TRAVERS SMITH BRAITHWAITE (see firm details p.1166) A "*prominent, self-contained*" group, whose "*first-class name*" in the regulatory structuring of secondary trading vehicles is founded on its experience in advising the Stock Exchange and CRESTCo. Competitors admire its "*exceptional focus*" and aptitude for attracting "*original and interesting*" clients. Clients report that it "*excels*" in its advice on matters such as netting projects, international links, switch to central bank money (CBM) and payment for purchase of securities, and that the firm works in close conjunction with the Treasury to effect its advice. Popular with her peers, **Margaret Chamberlain** (see p.389) is said to embody an "*exceptionally fine combination of technical skills with commercial good sense.*" She led teams on two major projects relating to structural developments in the London securities markets, namely the electronic transfer of title (ETT) for UK securities and DvP settlement in central bank money for sterling and euro payments. **Rachel Mansfield** (see p.390) also gains strong client commendation. Among transactional highlights, the team acted for CRESTCo, advising on the legal and regulatory framework required for the establishment of the business model that formed the basis for its merger with Euroclear, and advised CRESTCo on the establishment of a delivery-versus-payment link with the Swiss settlement system, in order to launch the Virt-X Exchange. It also advised Western Union on two new online trad-

LONDON/SOUTH WEST ■ FINANCIAL SERVICES

ing e-payment products launched in the UK and Europe. **Clients** CRESTCo; Bloomberg LP; Bloomberg Tradebook Europe; Western Union Financial Services; Royal Bank of Scotland; KAS Bank.

LOVELLS (see firm details p.1045) The team is best known for its "*exceptional*" regulatory retail practice that extends across funds, e-commerce and the insurance sectors. Clients report that the "*incredibly user-friendly*" team "*delivers speedy, relevant advice*" on regulatory aspects of matters ranging from the transactional to new product development. Held in high regard by peers, investment and funds specialist **Richard Stones** (see p.390) is "*genial, thoughtful and thinks hard about points.*" Enjoying some "*enviable clients,*" he led the team advising Depository Trust & Clearing on the process of the FSA's recognition of the European Central Counterparty (EuroCCP) as a clearing house under legislation. Further team highlights include advice to Egg on the sale of its products under Microsoft's MSN portal, and advising AMP on the introduction of franchise arrangements for its tied sales force. **Clients** AMP/Henderson; Barclays; Britannic Money; INVESCO; Thomas Cook; Lloyds TSB; Bank of Scotland; Merrill Lynch Asset Management; Abbey National; Egg.

NORTON ROSE (see firm details p.1084) "*We expect to see more of them in the future*" claimed one competitor. The practice is perceived to be regaining its profile while maintaining its "*solid*" reputation in funds and investment trust-related work. Clients speak of "*competence in abundance*" and "*thorough, high-quality support*" within the team, with one noting a "*family feel*" to its service. Her peers single out **Carmen Reynolds** (see p.390) as "*a good person to bounce ideas off.*" Formerly seconded to the Treasury to draft the new Financial Services bill (while at Slaughter and May), she has advised Bank of Ireland F Sharp on the establishment of its website 'Fsharp', the world's first offshore internet bank and on the offshore bank's compliance with UK regulations. Demonstrating its focus on cross-border and European transactions, the team assisted ISMA in its launch of isma.info, an online integrated information service, involving the firm's offices in Belgium, Germany, France and Italy and counsel in six other jurisdictions. It also advised easyMoney in relation to the development of new financial products, including the launching of an online credit card service. **Clients** Bank of Ireland; Bank of Ireland F Sharp; FSA; Friends Ivory & Sime; HSBC; ISMA; LIFFE; Pictet; Seymour Pierce; TD Waterhouse; Visa International.

SIMMONS & SIMMONS (see firm details p.1136) "*An interesting practice - they do a superb job*" in the derivatives and hedge funds market, according to market sources. Regulatory and funds specialist, the "*understated*" **Richard Slater** (see p.390) retains high regard from peers and clients alike, as an "*extremely competent practitioner.*" On the advisory side, the team acted on the establishment of Weather Xchange, a joint venture between the UK Meteorological Office and two prominent City brokers, as the first brokerage house dealing exclusively in the European weather derivatives market. Among further highlights, it advised Ofgem in relation to setting up trading facilities for Renewable Obligations Certificates (ROCs), and advised Sempra in its acquisition of Enron Metals. **Clients** AIB Govett; AIG International; Barclays; Merrill Lynch Investment Management; Ofgem; Prudential-Bache; Sempra; Swiss Exchange.

HERBERT SMITH (see firm details p.992) "*A strong, industrious team.*" The newly formed financial institutions group (headed by David Willis) advises on a broad range of contentious and non-contentious regulatory and transactional matters. Its competitors voice their "*great respect*" for its views on regulatory issues, particularly in relation to funds, transfer disputes and market abuse. The team provided multi-jurisdictional regulatory advice to the Bank of Scotland on its merger with the Halifax Group. It has also been advising a range of clients including professional bodies and major accountancy firms, on the implications of the new FSMA provisions in the context of professional body status, client agreements, compliance procedures and potential liability. **Clients** Bank of Scotland; Goldman Sachs; Equitable Life; J Rothschild Assurance; Royal London Mutual Insurance; Lazard Brothers.

DECHERT (see firm details p.934) "*They've made a splash,*" according to interviewees who acknowledge the team's derivatives and hedge funds-related regulatory expertise. Clients praise its "*reliable*" technical ability on structuring-related matters. The team, headed by Peter Astleford, assisted the ongoing acquisitions of four major East European private equity funds, namely, the Baltic Republics Fund and three funds of Société Générale (Ladenburg Thalmann Ukraine, Romania and Central and Eastern European Opportunities). The team continues to act for applicants to regulatory organisations in the UK, US and other jurisdictions. **Clients** Advisory European Equity Market Neutral Fund (American Express); Falcon US Long/Short Equity Fund; Gartmore European Analysts Fund; Lindsell Train Japan Fund; Lindsell Train Global Media Fund; Groupama; American Express.

MACFARLANES (see firm details p.1047) "*A well-focused practice*" that market sources perceive to be expanding its reputation beyond its "*sterling*" regulatory investment funds and private equity practice. Clients commend the team, headed by Bridget Barker, as "*pleasant, solid and dependable.*" Highlights include advising Legal & General in settling its product distribution arrangements with Alliance & Leicester, acting for Deutsche Bank on several cross-border notional co-investment plans, and advising Hawkpoint on N2 compliance matters. **Clients** Fidelity; Deutsche Asset Management; Legal & General.

STEPHENSON HARWOOD (see firm details p.1147) A "*top-notch*" investment funds client base underpins the team's "*sound*" reputation in regulatory work. The funds and financial services group, headed by Andrew Sutch, handles financial services work as an integral part of its funds practice, ranging from authorisation to market abuse. The team advised HSBC on the outsourcing of their cheque and credit paper clearing service business to joint venture company, iPSL and advised on financial promotion and other regulatory issues in relation to the Merrill Lynch/HSBC joint venture. It also provided N2 and other regulatory compliance advice to Standard & Poor's and to the corporate finance arm of PricewaterhouseCoopers. **Clients** HSBC; KPMG; PricewaterhouseCoopers; Standard and Poor's; Merrill Lynch/HSBC; FSA; RZB; Ample Interactive Investor.

SOUTH WEST

FINANCIAL SERVICES
■ SOUTH WEST

1 Burges Salmon Bristol

This book is the product of 6,582 1/2 hour interviews. See p.7 for BMRB audit. Within each band, firms are listed alphabetically.

BURGES SALMON (see firm details p.894) "*They get some great work,*" acknowledge market sources. The team, headed by Chris Godfrey, enjoys a "*well-respected*" profile among leading London specialists, particularly in relation to its work on collateral investment schemes. Highlights include providing N2-related advice to the Nationwide Building Society, and advising on two major share placings for Exeter Asset Management, including £21 million in the Exeter Enhanced Income Fund. **Clients** Exeter Investment; St James's Place Capital; Bristol & West; Nationwide Building Society; Premier Fund Managers; Sarasin Investment Managers.

FINANCIAL SERVICES ■ MIDLANDS/THE NORTH/SCOTLAND

MIDLANDS

FINANCIAL SERVICES
■ MIDLANDS

1. Pinsent Curtis Biddle Birmingham
   Wragge & Co Birmingham

This book is the product of 6,582 1/2 hour interviews. See p.7 for BMRB audit. Within each band, firms are listed alphabetically.

PINSENT CURTIS BIDDLE (see firm details p.1102) Leading practitioners are "*happy to recommend*" the team for its expertise on contentious matters, which covers pensions disputes and insurance. The team, headed by Andrew Long, is moving towards a more even balance with its transactional work, as demonstrated by its regulatory advice to major pension trust funds in London and professional firms including actuaries. It has also provided the N2 risk assessment of Benfield's financial services subsidiary, Orbit. Key highlights on contentious matters include multimillion pound reinsurance cases arising from pension mis-selling, and warranty and indemnity claims on corporate transactions for losses from pension mis-selling. **Clients** Benfield Group; New York Life (UK); DBS; Britannic Assurance; Pointon York Vos (PYV).

WRAGGE & CO (see firm details p.1197) "*Strongly focused*" on non-contentious and the advisory regulatory aspects, interviewees remark that the team, led by Jonathan Denton, has "*made an impact on the market*" with its "*energetic*" approach. Its purported focus is on capital markets-related matters, and the team has acted for Derbyshire Building Society on a £1 billion MTN programme. It also advised several building societies on FSMA N2 compliance arrangements, and has established a mortgage brokerage operation for a US subsidiary. It has also advised on the purchase of a Consumer Credit Act loan portfolio by Amber Credit. **Clients** Alliance & Leicester; Bank of Scotland; Britannic Assurance; Derbyshire Building Society; HSBC.

THE NORTH

FINANCIAL SERVICES
■ THE NORTH

1. Addleshaw Booth & Co Leeds
   Dickinson Dees Newcastle upon Tyne

LEADING INDIVIDUALS

1. GERVASIO James Keeble Hawson
   LYNCH Malcolm Wrigleys

This book is the product of 6,582 1/2 hour interviews. See p.7 for BMRB audit. Within each band, firms are listed alphabetically. See individuals' profiles p.389

ADDLESHAW BOOTH & CO (see firm details p.838) Clients commend the team's "*thorough and competent*" approach on general regulatory advice and its assistance on acquisitions and transactional work. Servicing a broad range of corporates, building societies and insurers, the team's work covers mergers and acquisitions, debt portfolios and mortgage acquisitions. Jointly headed by David Heffron (financial services group) and Adam Bennett (financial regulation group), the team acted for the Hospital Saving Association in its proposed merger with Leeds Hospital Fund, and advised Portman Building Society on the £95 million purchase of Sun Bank. Further team highlights include the Derbyshire/Ilkeston and Yorkshire/Gainsborough building society mergers and 13 separate mortgage portfolio transfers with £425 million aggregate value. **Clients** Royal Bank of Scotland; National Australia Group; Britannia Building Society; Portman Building Society; Royal & SunAlliance; Scottish Equitable; HSA; TD Waterhouse Investor Service (Europe).

DICKINSON DEES (see firm details p.938) Well known in the regions for its work for high-profile regional funds such as Northern Rock, the team, headed by David Rewcastle, advises on a range of FSMA-related matters such as market abuse. It advised on regulatory and compliance matters relating to a number of regional VC fund formations, including One North East's Investment Funds 1, 2 and 3, which provide loan and equity funding totalling £10 million for investment in North East SMEs. It also advised on Capital North East, a £20 million regional joint VC fund launched by One North East and Northern Enterprise. **Clients** NE Regional Investment Fund; NE Seed Capital Fund; NE Regional VC Capital Fund; Northern Enterprise; Northern Venture Manager.

OTHER NOTABLE PRACTITIONERS James Gervasio (see p.389) of Keeble Hawson attracts commendation as an "*extremely competent VC trusts specialist*," while **Malcolm Lynch** (see p.390) of Wrigleys continues to demonstrate his expertise in the charities sector. He advised CityLife and Portsmouth Housing Association on zero bond issues (£50 million and £5 million, respectively) for regeneration purposes involving money laundering regulations and relevant exemptions under FSMA. He also assisted on the launch of Renewable Energy Investment Club and advised on approvals of financial promotions for social economy companies.

SCOTLAND

DUNDAS & WILSON CS (see firm details p.943) "*They will continue to prosper*," according to market sources, referring to the firm's severance from the Andersen Legal network. Competitors rate its "*sturdy regulatory practice*" that represents "*big-name*" funds and corporates. The team handles the full scope of general financial services work, including compliance, regulatory and financial promotion matters. His peers commend **Philip Mackay** as "*an able, personable technician*." He led the team advising on the acquisition by Royal Bank of Scotland of Virgin's stake in the Virgin One Account, on Britannic Investment Managers' launch of an investment trust, and on reductions of capital for Britannic UK Income Trust and Britannic Global Income Trust. The team also acted on Britannic Smaller Companies Trust's investment management arrangements and Abbey National Financial and Investment Services' establishment of an administration outsourcing business. **Clients** Scottish Widows Group; National Australia Group Europe; Royal Bank of Scotland; Bank of Scotland; Abbey National; Britannic Group.

DICKSON MINTO WS (see firm details p.938) Interviewees commended the team's "*solid*" regulatory and compliance advice in the context of buyouts, mergers and reconstructions of investment trusts. Its competitors rate the "*excellent group of individuals*," distinguishing "*charismatic rainmaker*" **Bruce Minto** (see p.390) as its best-known member. The team was involved in the launch of UK Balanced Property Trust and acted as its sponsor in its listing with the UKLA (£150 million raised). It also advised Platinum Fund Managers and Albany Fund Managers in establishing FSA regulation. **Clients** Standard Life; Scottish Widows; Aberforth Partners; Artemis; Edinburgh Fund Managers; Friends Ivory & Sime.

MACLAY MURRAY & SPENS (see firm details p.1048) The team is perceived to handle financial services work as an integral part of its work for corporates, financial institutions and investment funds. His peers commend head of practice **Michael Livingston** (see p.390) as a

SCOTLAND/THE LEADERS ■ FINANCIAL SERVICES

FINANCIAL SERVICES
■ SCOTLAND

1. **Dundas & Wilson CS** Edinburgh
2. **Dickson Minto WS** Edinburgh
3. **Maclay Murray & Spens** Glasgow
   McGrigor Donald Glasgow
   Shepherd+ Wedderburn Edinburgh
   Tods Murray WS Edinburgh

LEADING INDIVIDUALS

1. **ATHANAS Chris** Tods Murray WS
   MACKAY Philip Dundas & Wilson CS
   MINTO Bruce Dickson Minto WS
   THURSTON SMITH Martin Tods Murray WS
2. **DORAN Frank** McGrigor Donald
   LIVINGSTON Michael Maclay Murray & Spens

This book is the product of 6,582 1/2 hour interviews. See p.7 for BMRB audit. Within each band, firms are listed alphabetically. See individuals' profiles p.389

"*great all-rounder and deal-doer*" with strong connections with Edinburgh financial institutions. **Clients** Lloyds TSB; Scottish Widows.

MCGRIGOR DONALD (see firm details p.1065) The team has a "*respectable*" profile advising fund and corporate clients on investment, insurance, retail banking and credit-related matters from within a broadly-based practice. His peers are "*really impressed*" by **Frank Doran**, whom they merit as "*a successful player*" in the market. The team acted for Britannic Asset Management in the acquisition of Blairlogie Capital Management, an Edinburgh-based fund management company. **Clients** Abbey National Life; Clydesdale Bank; Scottish Life International; Scottish Friendly Society; Britannic Investment Managers; Intelli Corporate Finance; Direct Line Life.

SHEPHERD+ WEDDERBURN (see firm details p.1130) Interviewees opined that the Edinburgh-based team, headed by Marian Glen, "*looks set to raise its profile*," having undergone internal reorganisation. The team advises on financial services matters as part of its "*broader focus*" covering corporate finance and offshore and onshore investment funds. It retains its market reputation as a key adviser to Friends Ivory & Sime, which it advised on the reorganisation of eight exempt unit trust funds (including arrangements for unit holders to transfer their investments into other funds), and in its £128.9 million acquisition of the retail investment business and managed pension fund business of FPLO. **Clients** Friends Ivory & Sime; Edinburgh Fund Managers; Baillie Gifford; Colonial First State Investments; McInroy & Wood.

TODS MURRAY WS (see firm details p.1164) An "*upcoming team of diligent individuals*," according to its competitors, who perceive the main thrust of its financial services expertise to lie within the context of investment funds, advising on behalf of unit trust managers. Typical work includes regulatory, compliance and marketing issues, investigations, disputes, and drafting documentation relating to investment management, outsourcing, and custody and registration agreements. **Chris Athanas** (see p.389) maintains his market image as an "*inimitable*" unit trusts technician, while **Martin Thurston Smith** (see p.390) gains good press for being "*trusted with very important work*" because he "*thinks things through carefully and simply gets on with it.*" The team advised on the financial services aspects of the Bank of Scotland/Halifax merger. **Clients** HBOS; Edinburgh Unit Trust Managers/Edinburgh Investment Company ICVC and Edinburgh Portfolio; Baillie Gifford; AEGON Fund Management UK/Asset Management UK; Scottish Value Management; Britannic Fund Managers/Asset Management/Investment Managers.

THE LEADERS IN FINANCIAL SERVICES

ABRAMS, Charles
SJ Berwin, London
(020) 7533 2222

ATHANAS, Chris
Tods Murray WS, Edinburgh
(0131) 226 4771
chris.athanas@todsmurray.com
See under Investment Funds, p.501

BATES, Chris
Clifford Chance, London
(020) 7600 1000
chris.bates@cliffordchance.com
Specialisation: Banking and finance. Partner specialising in advice to financial institutions.
Career: Articled Clifford Chance; qualified 1982; Partner since 1987.
Personal: 1978 Christ Church, Oxford (MA Law), 1979 Columbia University, New York (LLM).

BEVAN, Peter
Linklaters, London
(020) 7456 2000

CHAMBERLAIN, Margaret
Travers Smith Braithwaite, London
(020) 7295 3000
margaret.chamberlain@traverssmith.com
Specialisation: Specialist in trading, clearance, settlement, investment management and custody issues. Part of team at *Travers Smith Braithwaite* which advised The Bank of England and CREST Co Limited on the legal arrangements for the introduction of CREST and continues to advise CREST Co, including on links to overseas settlement systems, central counter party development, dematerialisation of money-market instruments and central bank money. Advises on custody relationships; on the legal and regulatory requirements relevant to the establishment and management of funds; on a wide range of general regulatory and legal issues arising from the conduct of financial services business.
Prof. Memberships: Chairman regulatory committee of the British Venture Capital Association and member of BVCA Council. Chairman of City of London Law Society Regulatory Sub-Committee. Contributor to Tolley's 'Company Law' and Butterworth's 'Financial Regulation Service'. International Bar Association; chairman of sub-committee on regulation of markets and exchanges.
Career: Qualified September 1985. Partner *Travers Smith Braithwaite* 1991.
Personal: Educated at University College, Oxford. Married.

DORAN, Frank
McGrigor Donald, Glasgow
(0141) 248 6677

FOX, Ruth
Slaughter and May, London
(020) 7600 1200
ruth.fox@slaughterandmay.com
Specialisation: Practice covers a wide range of regulatory work for banks, investment firms and insurance companies, both in relation to the establishment and structure of regulated businesses and the regulatory issues arising in connection with mergers and acquisitions in the financial services sector. Has acted extensively for banks and also for building societies, including in relation to conversions, and for corporate trustees.
Prof. Memberships: The Law Society.
Career: Qualified in 1979 with *Slaughter and May*. Became a partner in 1986.
Personal: Born 3 October 1954. Educated at St Helena School, Chesterfield and University College, London. Married with three sons. Lives in London and Hertfordshire.

GERVASIO, James
Keeble Hawson, Leeds
(0113) 279 9590
jimgervasio@keeblehawson.co.uk
Specialisation: Jim specialises in regulatory compliance, with particular reference to venture capital fund management. He graduated first in economics and then in law before qualifying as a solicitor. He has a particular interest in all aspects of private equity work and venture capital deals, structuring investment funds and financial services regulation. He is company secretary to a number of companies including three venture capital trusts.
Prof. Memberships: Member of the Securities Institute.
Career: BSc Econ (Hons); LLB; FNA Compliance Officer.
Personal: Married with two adult daughters. Enjoys walking and the theatre.

GLEESON, Simon
Allen & Overy, London
(020) 7330 3000
simon.gleeson@allenovery.com
Specialisation: Partner specialising in financial services regulation and investigations. He is a former stockbroker who has particular expertise in the regulation of the securities and financial markets and also specialises in custodianship, investment vehicles and bank capital regulation.
Career: Admitted as solicitor in England and Wales (1995). Stockbroker Williams de Broë 1986-91; qualified as barrister 1991; barrister 1991-94; associate *Richards Butler* 1994-97; partner *Richards Butler* 1997-98; senior associate *Allen & Overy* since 1998. Joined *Allen & Overy* in 1998 as a member of the financial services regulatory team.
Publications: Editor of 'International Banking Law and Regulation' (Sweet & Maxwell), 'Tolleys Company Law' (Tolleys) and 'International Capital Markets Law and Regulation' (West Publishing) and is the author of 'Personal Property Law' (Sweet & Maxwell, 1997).
Personal: Born 1962. MA Hons (Medieval History) St Andrews; LLB London University.

www.ChambersandPartners.com

FINANCIAL SERVICES ■ THE LEADERS

HARDING, Mark
Clifford Chance, London
(020) 7600 1000
mark.harding@cliffordchance.com
See under Commodities, p.160

HERRINGTON, Tim
Clifford Chance, London
(020) 7600 1000
tim.herrington@cliffordchance.com
Specialisation: Corporate Department. Partner specialising in financial services including mutual funds, asset management and investment trust work, securities and derivatives, regulatory issues, mergers and acquisitions and other corporate work for the financial services industry.
Career: Articled *Clifford Chance*; qualified 1978; Partner since 1985.
Personal: Queen Mary's Grammar School, Basingstoke; Bristol University (LLB).

KALDERON, Mark
Freshfields Bruckhaus Deringer, London
(020) 7936 4000
mark.kalderon@freshfields.com
Specialisation: Partner Corporate Department. Main area of practice is capital markets, particularly involving securitisation and structured finance. Also handles banking and financial services regulation.
Career: Qualified in 1983, having joined *Freshfields* in 1981. Became a Partner in 1990. Worked in Tokyo office 1989-92.
Personal: Born 1 March 1957. Attended Balliol College, Oxford, 1976-79, University of Chicago Law School 1979-80. Lives in London.

KENT, Michael
Linklaters, London
(020) 7456 3772
michael.kent@linklaters.com
Specialisation: Specialist with over 10 years' experience in financial markets regulation, including acting for investment banks, investment managers, life companies, credit institutions, regulators and exchanges.
Career: *Linklaters*: articled clerk 1984-86; solicitor *Linklaters* 1986-93 and solicitor/consultant 1995-99; partner 1999 to date.
Personal: First Class LLB Liverpool University 1983.

LITTLE, Tamasin
SJ Berwin, London
(020) 7533 2222
tamasin.little@sjberwin.com
Specialisation: Specialises in financial markets and regulatory matters including structuring, funds, derivatives and other investment products and advising investment managers, banks, financial services groups, brokers, venture capitalists, insurance companies and other investment firms on regulatory and related matters.
Prof. Memberships: City of London Law Society Regulatory Sub-Committee, International Bar Association, Futures and Options Association Legal Scrutiny committee, Financial Services Authority Advisory panel on Authorisation Manual, EVCA Fiduciary Duties.
Career: 1st class BA Jurisprudence, Oxford; LLM London School of Economics. Legal associate seconded to the Bank of England's Legal Risk Review committee 1991/2. Partner *Stephenson Harwood* 1992-96. Partner *SJ Berwin* financial services group 1996-date.
Publications: Editor of 'Bond Markets: Law & Regulation' (Sweet & Maxwell 1999). Articles on marketing funds and an overview of the regulation of OTC derivatives in 'Swaps and Off-Exchange Derivatives Trading' (FT Law and Tax) and contributor to 'Issues in Derivative Instruments' (Kluwer), Butterworth's 'Financial Services Law Guide and 'The Practitioners Guide to the FSA Handbook'.

LIVINGSTON, Michael
Maclay Murray & Spens, Glasgow
(0141) 248 5011
mbl@maclaymurrayspens.co.uk
See under Corporate Finance, p.241

LYNCH, Malcolm
Wrigleys, Leeds
(0113) 244 6100
law@malcolmlynch.com
See under Charities, p.130

MACKAY, Philip
Dundas & Wilson CS, Edinburgh
(0131) 228 8000

MANSFIELD (née FORD), Rachel
Travers Smith Braithwaite, London
(020) 7295 3000
rachel.mansfield@TraverSmith.com
Specialisation: Specialises in advising financial institutions and pension fund trustees on regulatory, investment management, custody and securities trading issues.
Career: Trained at *Travers Smith Braithwaite*, qualifying there in 1992.
Personal: Born 1967. Educated at Sidney Sussex College, Cambridge.

MINTO, Bruce
Dickson Minto WS, Edinburgh
(0131) 225 4455
bruce.minto@dmws.com
See under Corporate Finance, p.243

MORRIS, Simon
CMS Cameron McKenna, London
(020) 7367 2702
sm@cmck.com
Specialisation: Partner in financial services group. Establishing financial institutions in the United Kingdom and advising on financial sector acquisitions and disposals; handling corporate reorganisations of onshore and offshore fund managers and insurers; advising on internet projects for banks, brokers and insurers; working on novel products and distribution structures such as a wholesale tracker fund for pension investment, a retail timeshare bond and converting an insurer's salesforce into a franchise; representing brokers, managers and insurers in over 40 FSA disciplinary cases and in a further 60 enforcement and investigation actions. An advisor to HM Opposition on FSM Bill.
Career: Qualified in 1982, having joined *Cameron Markby* (now *CMS Cameron McKenna*) in 1980. Became a partner in 1988.
Publications: Author of 'Financial Services: Regulating Investment Business' (3rd edn forthcoming).
Personal: Born 24 January 1958. Attended Cambridge University. Member of Council, London Topographical Society. Leisure interests include travel and cartography. Lives in Islington.

MORTON, Guy
Freshfields Bruckhaus Deringer, London
(020) 7936 4000
guy.morton@freshfields.com
Specialisation: Head of the financial services group. Practice covers a wide range of financial services, regulatory and banking work. Specialises in banking and securities regulation, payment systems and trading law, repos and securities lending. Is particularly experienced within the banking, securities dealing, investment trading and insurance sectors. Has given evidence to the Joint Committee on Financial Services and Markets on the Financial Services and Markets Bill.
Prof. Memberships: Member and former Chairman of the City of London Law Society Regulatory Sub-Committee.
Career: Became partner in *Freshfields* in 1986. Corpus Christi College, Oxford.

NELSON, Paul
Linklaters, London
(020) 7456 3766
paul.nelson@linklaters.com
Specialisation: Specialises in regulation of markets and financial institutions including investment banks, securities houses and their affiliates in the UK and internationally.
Career: 1996 to date: Head of Financial Markets Group; 1987 to date: Partner in *Linklaters*; 1981-87: Assistant solicitor, *Linklaters*; 1979-81: Articled clerk, *Linklaters*. 1978: Law Society Final Examination; 1978: Corpus Christi College, Cambridge, BA in Law (First Class), George Long Prize for Jurisprudence.

PHILLIPS, Paul
Allen & Overy, London
(020) 7330 3000
paul.phillips@allenovery.com
Specialisation: Partner dealing with financial services law, including investment management, custody services, marketing investments, securities and derivatives, regulation of banking and financial services, collective investment schemes and insurance. Clients include banks and financial institutions, fund management groups, brokers and securities dealers.
Career: Barrister (1983-87); Assistant *Allen & Overy* (1987-94); seconded to the SFA 1991-92; Partner (1994).
Publications: Co-author of 'Encyclopedia of Banking Law'.
Personal: Downing College, Cambridge (1982, MA Law 1st). Born 1961.

REYNOLDS, Carmen
Norton Rose, London
(020) 7444 3774
reynoldsc@nortonrose.com
Specialisation: Partner and Head of the Financial Services Group. Solicitor dealing with project related and day to day financial services advice for a broad range of financial institutions.
Prof. Memberships: Law Society of England and Wales. Law Society's Financial Services Working Party.
Career: Qualified 1993, *Slaughter and May*. Partner, *Norton Rose* 2001.
Personal: Exeter University.

SLATER, Richard
Simmons & Simmons, London
(020) 7628 2020

STONES, Richard
Lovells, London
(020) 7296 2000
richard.stones@lovells.com
Specialisation: Advises financial services businesses, mostly on regulatory matters, the establishment and marketing of unit trusts and other investment funds and other legal issues affecting the industry. Has a general corporate and commercial training, and deals with corporate transactions involving businesses in his sector. Also advises a number of major pension funds on investment management issues. Has contributed to the CCH 'Financial Services Reporter' and 'Securities Transactions in Europe'. He regularly speaks at seminars on regulatory and investment fund topics.
Prof. Memberships: He is a member of the Securities Institute, and of the City of London Law Society Regulatory Working Party.
Career: Joined *Lovells* 1977; qualified 1980; Partner 1987.

SYKES, Annabel
Freshfields Bruckhaus Deringer, London
(020) 7936 4000
annabel.sykes@freshfields.com
Specialisation: Partner dealing with regulatory and other issues for asset managers, custodians, broker-dealers and other institutions in the financial services and insurance sectors. Has advised Lloyd's on various regulatory matters including the admission of corporate capital and the market's reconstruction and renewal and the 1998 premiums trust deeds revision.
Prof. Memberships: Law Society; Member of the Financial Services Working Party of the Law Society Company Law Committee; Member of the Financial Services Authority's advisory group on its rules and guidance handbook.
Career: Trinity College, Cambridge; University of Auckland.
Personal: Born 1961.

THURSTON SMITH, Martin
Tods Murray WS, Edinburgh
(0131) 226 4771
martin.thurston.smith@todsmurray.com
See under Investment Funds, p.503

FRANCHISING

London: 391; Profiles: 392

Research approved by BMRB For this edition, **Chambers'** researchers conducted 6,582 interviews – 3,900 with law firms, 511 with barristers and 2,171 with clients. The validity of the research was scrutinised by BMRB International, who audited both the methodology and the results at our offices in London. They interviewed **Chambers'** researchers and cross-checked sample interviews. Details of the audit appear on page 7.

OVERVIEW The franchising industry continues to flourish. However, with a clutch of the leading lights now less visible at the frontline, the legal landscape of this practice area looks set to change.

NATIONWIDE

FRANCHISING
■ NATIONWIDE

[1]
- **Eversheds** London, Newcastle upon Tyne
- **Field Fisher Waterhouse** London

[2]
- **Wragge & Co** Birmingham

[3]
- **Pinsent Curtis Biddle** Birmingham

[4]
- **Brodies** Edinburgh
- **Mundays** Cobham
- **Owen White** Slough

[5]
- **Dundas & Wilson CS** Edinburgh
- **Hammond Suddards Edge** Manchester
- **Leathes Prior** Norwich

LEADING INDIVIDUALS

[1]
- **ABELL Mark** Field Fisher Waterhouse

[2]
- **BATES Anton** Owen White

[3]
- **PRATT John** Pinsent Curtis Biddle

[4]
- **HARRIS Gordon** Wragge & Co
- **VOGE Julian** Brodies
- **WORMALD Chris** Eversheds

[5]
- **BROWN Victoria** Wragge & Co
- **CHAMBERS John** Chambers & Co
- **COWIE Pauline** Hammond Suddards Edge

This book is the product of 6,582 1/2 hour interviews. See p.7 for BMRB audit. Within each band, firms are listed alphabetically. See individuals' profiles p.392

EVERSHEDS (see firm details p.949) This national outfit is proclaimed an "*undisputed leader*" once again, due to the team's size and "*fantastic relationships with US franchisors.*" According to interviewees, it is "*highly regarded for both international and domestic work,*" with cross-border matters comprising over half of its workload. On the European side, the team in London and Newcastle works in tandem with the firm's Paris and Amsterdam offices. It regularly handles advice to start-ups, domestic structuring, inbound and outbound work, as well as acting on internet and IT issues and competition law restrictions. Now a consultant, Martin Mendelsohn remains one of the area's best-known figures. **Chris Wormald** (see p.392) was recently appointed chief European counsel to Budget Rent a Car and is steadily building a top reputation. Recent highlights have included advising Mothercare on international projects including the termination of its agreement with a major Japanese franchisee, and advising Whirlpool on establishing a franchised service, sales and repair network. **Clients** Whirlpool; PayShop; Whitegates; McDonald's (Netherlands); Mothercare.

FIELD FISHER WATERHOUSE (see firm details p.954) Alongside Eversheds, this is the other market leader. "*Enviably well-resourced*" according to peers, the team possesses "*critical mass*" and a top-rate "*national reputation.*" Much of its profile is attributed to the presence of "*vocal and visible*" **Mark Abell** (see p.392). Described by one peer as "*the guru of franchising,*" he has a wide and enthusiastic following in the field. Clients appreciate the team's "*hands-on and responsive*" attitude, as well as its "*contacts across the jurisdictions.*" Recent instructions include representing Regus on rollouts in a large number of countries, advising Arcadia on rewriting its franchise agreements and assisting Laura Ashley with its online franchising operations. **Clients** Regus; Arcadia; Marks &Spencer; Body Shop; National Car Rental; Laura Ashley.

WRAGGE & CO (see firm details p.1197) Operating within the firm's IP department, the team boasts several leading players and is emerging as one of the area's most respected practices. According to clients, "*fees sit comfortably with the quality on offer*" and the group provides "*consistently sound advice and support.*" **Gordon Harris'** "*knowledge and experience*" has long been recognised, while **Victoria Brown** is known to handle a high volume of franchising work and is increasingly popular. The team recently franchised the Land Rover Experience, which included managing the national and international elements of the franchise and providing strategic advice on structure. It also advised BT on franchising the sales agency to SME customers. **Clients** Rosemay Conley Diet & Fitness Clubs.

PINSENT CURTIS BIDDLE (see firm details p.1102) "*First-rate for day-to-day work,*" the firm is fostering a growing reputation among an impressive range of major franchisors. "*Hugely experienced and charmingly eccentric*" **John Pratt** (see p.392) spearheads the team. Author of *Franchising Law and Practice*, he is particularly recommended for his advice on international agreements. He recently acted for Amtrak in revising its various franchise agreements, devising and implementing a strategy, including roadshows across the UK, for the roll-out of the new agreements. The team also assisted Prontaprint with complex litigation against a competitor who was seeking to poach franchisees. **Clients** Kall Kwik; Dollond & Aitchison; Amtrak; Prontaprint; Rainbow International.

BRODIES (see firm details p.889) "*Clear market leaders in Scotland,*" the group regularly advises both franchisors and franchisees on agreements and dispute resolution, and possesses niche expertise in the hotel and leisure industry. At the helm, **Julian Voge** (see p.392) specialises in franchising, corporate and contract law. Competitors say that he was "*an expert before franchising became fashionable.*" The firm was recently reappointed by the SRA to advise on all aspects of the ScotRail franchise. **Clients** Strategic Rail Authority.

MUNDAYS (see firm details p.1078) The departure this year of leading figure Manzoor Ishani has caused the team's profile to drop. It remains to be seen who will replace him as its spearhead, and commentators are following the group's fortunes with interest. It continues to act for franchise clients on contentious, corporate and property-related matters. **Clients** Pronuptia; Sevenoaks Sound & Vision.

OWEN WHITE The "*know-how is there*" according to rivals, largely due to the dominant reputation of **Anton Bates** (see p.392), legal advisor to the BFA. The practice is best known for advising franchisees, both associations and individuals. Litigation and employment in the franchising context are also areas of strength. **Clients** Franchisees.

DUNDAS & WILSON CS (see firm details p.943) Operating under the umbrella of the corporate department, the practice, led by Eric Galbraith, is attracting a growing number of franchisees. Franchisor work has included assisting long-standing client Scotwork International on operations in eastern Europe and South America. Clients are impressed by the firm's "*quality across the board.*" **Clients** Scotwork International; Airtec; Toni&Guy (Scotland).

FRANCHISING ■ LONDON/THE LEADERS

HAMMOND SUDDARDS EDGE Headed by the "*eminently capable*" **Pauline Cowie**, the team operates on a national basis, advising a wide range of franchisor clients on franchise sale and purchase agreements, e-commerce and contentious matters. Recent highlights include advising Aggregate Industries on establishing a franchise, Kodak on a photo processing franchise, and Virgin Cosmetics as franchisor in South Africa. **Clients** Bradford & Bingley; Virgin Cosmetics; Kodak.

LEATHES PRIOR The team, led by head of commercial, Jonathan Chadd, advises a mixture of franchisors and franchisees. Drawing on the team's IP, licensing and dispute resolution expertise, it provides a comprehensive service. Franchisor clients considering international expansion benefit from the firm's membership of the EU-LEX network of international lawyers and tax advisors. **Clients** Franchisees and franchisors.

OTHER NOTABLE PRACTITIONERS John Chambers of Chambers & Co has impressed all in the field with his "*absolute dedication*" and is known to be attracting a high volume of work.

THE LEADERS IN FRANCHISING

ABELL, Mark
Field Fisher Waterhouse, London
(020) 7861 4000
pma@ffwlaw.com
Specialisation: Partner heading the brands technology, media and telecommunications department. Main areas of practice are franchising and licensing of intellectual property. Work covers negotiating, drafting and advising generally on international and domestic matters, area and unit franchises, development agreements, concessions, subordinated equity arrangements, technology transfers, merchandising, endorsement and sponsorship. Expert to the United Nations WIPO advising on the appropriate legal regime for franchising and trademark licensing and evaluation of IP in developing countries. Originator of the FBI (franchise buyin) and FBO (franchise buyout). Acted in the Moosehead decision of the EC Commission, an important trademarks and anti-trust case. Clients include Bodyshop, National Car Rental and Regus plc. External examiner at University of London. Lectures regularly in the USA, Japan, PRC and Europe. Editorial board member of 'Trade Mark World' and 'Franchise Law and Business Review' and 'IP World'. Creator and editor of europeanfranchising.com
Prof. Memberships: IFA, IBA, INTA, UIA, LES, Society of Franchising, British Franchise Association (BFA).
Career: Qualified in 1984.
Publications: Author of 'The Franchise Option', 'The International Franchise Option', 'European Franchising-Law and Practice in the European Community Vol I & II', 'International Technology Transfer for Profit', 'Franchising in India', Volume on Franchising in Butterworth's Encyclopaedia of forms and precedents. Chapters in ten textbooks and over 300 articles on franchising, licensing and IP.
Personal: BFA Legal committee member. Leisure interests include Japanese, Chinese and Thai culture (Japanese speaker), scuba diving, opera, and his family.

BATES, Anton
Owen White, Slough
(01753) 876818
antonbates@owenwhite.com
Specialisation: Leads the commercial department. Main area of practice is franchising. Legal advisor to British Franchise association since advising founder members and drafting constitution in 1977. Chairman of BFA legal committee and BFA representative on European Franchise Federation legal committee. Has advised scores of franchisors and franchisees including companies engaged in international franchising. Acts for many household names in the franchising industry. Author of many articles in various specialist magazines and newspapers. Organiser and speaker at numerous seminars in the UK (for the BFA) and abroad.
Prof. Memberships: Law Society, Chartered Institute of Arbitrators, ADR Mediator.
Career: Qualified in 1967. After 5 years as a Partner in a large city firm, joined *Owen White* as a Partner in 1973.

BROWN, Victoria
Wragge & Co, Birmingham
(0870) 903 1000

CHAMBERS, John
Chambers & Co, Norwich
(01603) 616155

COWIE, Pauline
Hammond Suddards Edge, Manchester
(0161) 830 5000

HARRIS, Gordon
Wragge & Co, Birmingham
(0870) 903 1000

PRATT, John
Pinsent Curtis Biddle, Birmingham
(0121) 200 1050
john.pratt@pinsents.com
Specialisation: Partner, Birmingham office. Main area of practice is franchising. Drafts franchise agreements, advises on international franchising and prepares documentation. Expertise also in competition law including anti-trust compliance programmes, notifications and general advice. Acts for 100 UK franchisors including FTSE 100 companies.
Prof. Memberships: Law Society; Birmingham Law Society.
Career: Qualified in 1976. Worked at *Lovell White Durrant* from 1974-83, then *Needham & James* 1983-93. Joined *Pinsent Curtis Biddle* as a partner in 1993. Previously chairman of Young Solicitors of England and Wales.
Publications: Author of 'Franchising Law & Practice', and 'Franchising'. Contributor to 'New Frontiers in Competition Law' and 'Il Franchising Internazionale'. Lectures in the UK and overseas.
Personal: Born 1951. Attended Dulwich College 1960-69; Oxford University 1969-72; Universite D'Aix-Marseille 1972-73. Interests include theatre, wine, food and sport.

VOGE, Julian
Brodies, Edinburgh
(0131) 228 3777
julian.voge@brodies.co.uk
Specialisation: Main areas of practice are corporate and contract law, including franchising and licensing.
Prof. Memberships: Law Society of Scotland, Writer to the Signet. Also admitted as a solicitor in England and Wales.
Career: Qualified in 1982. Articled at *Tods Murray*. Then worked at *Brodies* and *Berwin Leighton* before re-joining *Brodies* as a partner in 1987.
Publications: Author of chapters on Scots law for 'Franchising Law and Practice' and 'International Franchising Law'.
Personal: Born in 1958. Attended Daniel Stewarts & Melville College 1964-76, then University of Edinburgh 1976-80. Lives in Edinburgh.

WORMALD, Chris
Eversheds, London
(020) 7919 4862
wormaldc@eversheds.com
Specialisation: Main areas of practice for over 19 years – franchising and other variants of business system expansion; substantial volume of international work in addition to domestic UK practice; related EC competition law; acts primarily for franchisors, master franchisees and franchisee associations. Joined McDonald's European headquarters in 1984 as their first European General Counsel and became a Vice-President of McDonald's Europe two years later. During 10 years with McDonald's played a key role in developing the local teams as the system grew to 2000 restaurants in Europe. Hired and managed outside lawyers; negotiated master, development and joint venture franchise arrangements throughout Europe, North Africa and the Middle East; and designed and implemented franchise arrangements for new jurisdictions. Trained European real estate and franchising teams and was responsible for the legal side of the property acquisition programme. General Counsel role also involved him in trouble-shooting, litigation, lobbying and multinational group restructuring in view of his international tax origins. In 1996 joined Martin Mendelsohn to strengthen *Eversheds*' experienced franchising group as it began its international joint venture with Horwath International to form a global franchise consultancy. Today he leads the firm's London team. Specialises in strategic advice to businesses ranging from start-ups to the largest multinationals, reviewing their expansion options and considering re-engineering and international expansion, and to government organisations. Works across commercial sectors – from hotels, restaurants and retail to IT, insurance and financial services, manufacturing, distribution and the public sector. He speaks French and German and has lived and worked in Brussels and Frankfurt.
Prof. Memberships: IBA, American Bar Association, International Franchise Association, British Franchise Association, Law Society.
Career: Qualified with *Simmons & Simmons* 1979 - international tax and commercial structuring for six years. McDonald's Europe - European General Counsel and vice-president; partner *Eversheds* London 1996.
Publications: Writes and speaks frequently worldwide on legal and business aspects of system expansion, most recently co-authoring for specialist UK publishers 'The Guide to Franchising in UK Pubs and Restaurants'.
Personal: Born 1954. Law degree from Sidney Sussex College, Cambridge University. Leisure interests include IT, sailing, fishing, travel and family.

392 INDEX TO LEADING LAWYERS: PAGE 1693 ■ IN-HOUSE LAWYERS PROFILES: PAGE 1201

FRAUD (CRIMINAL)

London: 393; The Regions: 394; Profiles: 396

Research approved by BMRB For this edition, **Chambers'** researchers conducted 6,582 interviews – 3,900 with law firms, 511 with barristers and 2,171 with clients. The validity of the research was scrutinised by BMRB International, who audited both the methodology and the results at our offices in London. They interviewed **Chambers'** researchers and cross-checked sample interviews. Details of the audit appear on page 7.

LONDON

FRAUD: CRIMINAL
LONDON

1
- Burton Copeland
- Kingsley Napley
- Peters & Peters

2
- Dechert
- Irwin Mitchell

3
- Russell Jones & Walker
- Simons Muirhead & Burton

4
- Claude Hornby & Cox
- Corker Binning Solicitors
- Garstangs
- Victor Lissack & Roscoe

LEADING INDIVIDUALS

★ **BURTON Ian** Burton Copeland
RAPHAEL Monty Peters & Peters

1
- **CORKER David** Corker Binning Solicitors
- **MURRAY Christopher** Kingsley Napley
- **OLIVER Keith** Peters & Peters
- **POLLARD Stephen** Kingsley Napley
- **TRAVERS Harry** Burton Copeland

2
- **BINNING Peter** Corker Binning Solicitors
- **BYRNE David** Dechert
- **CAPLAN Michael** Kingsley Napley
- **COWELL Adam** Irwin Mitchell
- **DELAHUNTY Louise** Peters & Peters
- **FLETCHER Rod** Russell Jones & Walker
- **KIRK David** Simons Muirhead & Burton
- **SPIRO Brian** Burton Copeland

3
- **CARNELL Bernard** Simons Muirhead & Burton
- **CORNTHWAITE Richard** Garstangs
- **FRANKLAND Matthew** Dechert
- **HARDING John** Kingsley Napley
- **ROBINSON Kevin** Irwin Mitchell
- **WOOLLEY Linda** Kingsley Napley

UP AND COMING
- **GENTLE Stephen** Kingsley Napley
- **GLASS Jane** Burton Copeland

This book is the product of 6,582 1/2 hour interviews. See p.7 for BMRB audit. Within each band, firms are listed alphabetically. See individuals' profiles p.396

BURTON COPELAND (see firm details p.895) This firm is home to a number of high-profile fraud specialists, who are frequently found on CPS, SFO, DTI and Inland Revenue prosecutions. It has achieved success in an approach, that sees these lawyers "*meticulous in their preparation and sensitive to the clients' needs.*" Senior partner **Ian Burton** (see p.396) has been credited with the development of this "*talented bunch,*" and he remains endorsed for his "*technical nous and tactical ability.*" **Harry Travers** (see p.399) is perceived to be "*one of the leading lights;*" his straight-talking approach has won him a following, a trait shared by **Jane Glass** (see p.397). "*Feisty, no-nonsense and intelligent,*" barristers commended her as a practitioner who "*has her feet on the ground and works bloody hard.*" Catherine Mather and Karen Peacock support the team in their roles as consultants. **Brian Spiro** (see p.399) has impressed competitors with his work on the Jubilee Line case.

KINGSLEY NAPLEY (see firm details p.1023) Portrayed by peers as "*one of the hot firms*" in the marketplace, it is currently representing a pharmaceutical company on allegations of a price-fixing cartel. The "*skilful*" **Stephen Pollard** (see p.398) is heavily involved in the Bloody Sunday Inquiry. **John Harding** (see p.397) is representing a defendant in phase two of a prosecution involving allegations of Green Form fraud. "*Technical prowess*" is a key attribute possessed by **Michael Caplan QC** (see p.396), who is leading the defence team for the Henry Sweetbaum SFO Wickes case. Respected as a "*polished performer,*" **Christopher Murray** (see p.398) is the man to go to "*if you need the weight of enormous experience.*" He has a forte in mutual assistance and is currently advising on a large US corruption investigation. "*Universally liked, self-deprecating and conscientious,*" **Stephen Gentle** (see p.397) led the successful defence of Erik Langaker as the remaining defendant in the Morgan Grenfell case. **Linda Woolley** (see p.399) is "*hard-working, good with clients and consistently gets results.*"

PETERS & PETERS (see firm details p.1100) "*Rainmaker*" **Monty Raphael** (see p.398) leads the team and remains key to much of its profile in the sector, although observers were keen to endorse its depth of talented practitioners. "*A superb performer,*" he "*knows the law inside out.*" He is ably accompanied by the "*extremely capable*" **Louise Delahunty** (see p.397), "*a tenacious litigator, who does everything for her clients.*" The firm has recently established a dedicated money laundering compliance unit in line with client demand. Highlight cases include the defence of Trefor Llewellyn, the ex-finance director of Wickes and the representation of Carl Cushnie of the Versailles Group. **Keith Oliver** (see p.398) retains strong market commendation although he has had a bias towards civil fraud of late. Peter Binning has now left the practice to join forces with former colleague David Corker.

DECHERT (see firm details p.934) One of the few firms to display expertise in both the criminal and civil arenas, it continues its commitment to legal aid matters. The team includes "*globetrotting litigator*" **David Byrne** (see p.396). Perceived by interviewees as the firm's figurehead, he is "*a dominant character in litigation,*" whose "*lateral thinking*" is the envy of many. "*Enthusiastic and thorough*" **Matthew Frankland** (see p.397) has an expertise in large restraint and confiscation matters. He conducted the successful appeal of Michael Villiers in a £68 million diversion fraud, and is leading the Wallace Duncan Smith appeal, the first SFO matter to be referred to the Court of Appeal by the Criminal Cases Review Commission.

IRWIN MITCHELL (see firm details p.1009) The business crime unit operates across this national firm and is judged by interviewees to have "*broken into the field, pursuing interesting cases with some vigour.*" Head of department and "*rising star*" **Adam Cowell** (see p.397) is "*hands-on and technically astute.*" The "*ubiquitous*" **Kevin Robinson** (see p.398) boasts "*an engaging personality*" and peers rate his litigation prowess. The unit is currently instructed on several major financial services investigations, DTI prosecutions and has been involved in actions brought by the DTI in the High Court seeking disqualification of directors. The group is representing defendants in the Jubilee Line Extension fraud, and the CWS and Baxendale-Walker cases.

RUSSELL JONES & WALKER (see firm details p.1120) "*Consummate performer*" **Rod Fletcher** (see p.397) was applauded by the marketplace as "*bright and hard-working.*" He leads an expanding team structured on a national basis. Substantial SFO, Customs & Excise, Inland Revenue and FSA investigations form the backbone of the practice. A recent highlight case involves an SFO prosecution of the first ever internet-based investment fraud.

SIMONS MUIRHEAD & BURTON (see firm details p.1137) A full-service criminal fraud firm, it offers advice on Customs & Excise prosecutions, VAT frauds, advance fee and investment fraud, Inland Revenue and accounting cases, and money laundering. The "*technical*

www.ChambersandPartners.com

393

FRAUD CRIMINAL ■ LONDON/THE SOUTH & SOUTH WEST/WALES

and academic" David Kirk (see p.398) heads the group, which also enjoys the services of "*highly experienced*" Bernard Carnell (see p.396). This past year has seen the conclusion of the Deutsche Morgan Grenfell case, resulting in the acquittal of the firm's client. Expertise in confiscation and mutual assistance is also an acknowledged part of this firm's portfolio.

CLAUDE HORNBY & COX (see firm details p.909) The firm handles fraud matters by dint of its healthy criminal practice. Cases arrive via referrals on a range of matters, including customs, VAT and DTI prosecutions.

CORKER BINNING SOLICITORS This firm is a new entry to the tables this year. "*Academic*"

David Corker (see p.396) has recently been joined by former Peters & Peters colleague Peter Binning (see p.396), said to be "*down-to-earth and experienced.*" The resultant practice is already gaining plaudits from the marketplace, which predicts "*a fine combination, who will do well.*" The team handles the broad spectrum of fraud matters from VAT and credit card cases through to customs and organised crime. Money laundering and investor fraud also features in its caseload. Although the bulk of the work is defence, prosecutions are also catered for by the team.

GARSTANGS Viewed as an "*active force in the area,*" the firm has enjoyed an increased workload in Customs & Excise matters, while confiscation and money laundering also form part of the repertoire. The group represents both individuals and large corporations facing prosecution brought by a wide range of bodies, including the SFO and Customs & Excise. "*Able and experienced*" Richard Cornthwaite (see p.396) leads the team.

VICTOR LISSACK & ROSCOE (see firm details p.1175) This is a respected crime practice, boasting a fraud capability as part of its greater criminal repertoire. Commentators considered the team "*highly reliable.*" All-rounder Robert Roscoe leads the team, which advises on VAT and Customs & Excise prosecutions. It has recently acted on allegations of fraud in the NHS.

THE SOUTH & SOUTH WEST

FRAUD: CRIMINAL
■ SOUTH & SOUTH WEST

1. Bobbetts Mackan Bristol
2. Blake Lapthorn Fareham
   DMH Brighton
   Hodkinsons Locks Heath

LEADING INDIVIDUALS

1. MITCHELL John Blake Lapthorn

This book is the product of 6,582 1/2 hour interviews. See p.7 for BMRB audit. Within each band, firms are listed alphabetically. See individuals' profiles p.396

BOBBETTS MACKAN (see firm details p.879) "*Still regarded as clearly at the top,*" the firm has one of the largest criminal practices in Bristol.

White-collar crime is a strong feature for the team, which advises on multimillion pound regulatory and large-scale investigatory cases.

BLAKE LAPTHORN (see firm details p.877) This commercial firm, which has a sound fraud offering, is led by John Mitchell, "*a sensible operator,*" who peers rate highly. Fraud is dealt with under the firm's regulatory umbrella, where the team defends clients accused of a range of offences and is involved in the recovery of assets. The client base is composed of individuals and corporates, while an impressive roster of professional bodies also provides a steady stream of work.

DMH (see firm details p.940) The criminal fraud practice is run from within the firm's commercial litigation group. Clients range from companies and partnerships to public bodies and charities. The past year has seen the team acting on a cheque fraud, involving a claim for several hundred thousand pounds, which resulted in a successful recovery.

HODKINSONS The firm handles purely criminal work, and boasts three ex-police officers and a full-time barrister on its roster of staff. Led by Nigel Hodkinson, the team handles substantial fraud matters including an immigration-related fraud, tax and VAT frauds.

WALES

FRAUD: CRIMINAL
■ WALES

1. Martyn Prowel Solicitors Cardiff
2. Huttons Cardiff
   Roy Morgan & Co Cardiff

LEADING INDIVIDUALS

1. PROWEL Martyn Martyn Prowel Solicitors
2. MORGAN Roy Roy Morgan & Co

This book is the product of 6,582 1/2 hour interviews. See p.7 for BMRB audit. Within each band, firms are listed alphabetically. See individuals' profiles p.396

MARTYN PROWEL SOLICITORS (see firm details p.1056) The firm benefits from its strong reputation in criminal representation, a profile that is also afforded to its white-collar crime, VAT and duty evasions work. "*Professional and pragmatic*" Martyn Prowel (see p.398) leads a team that is warmly endorsed by the market.

HUTTONS (see firm details p.1007) "*Solid and well-organised,*" the firm is another strong criminal practice undertaking white-collar crime as part of its repertoire. Individuals and companies are both catered for by this respected team. VAT fraud continues to be a specialism of the firm, while its expert handling of fraudulent matters arising out of the hi-tech arena continues to grow.

ROY MORGAN & CO "*Thorough and committed*" Roy Morgan heads the fraud team of this major practice, which also handles general criminal matters. The firm boasts a specialised investigation unit dealing with a number of hefty multi-jurisdictional financial fraud cases. Investigations into frauds by opticians on the NHS is just one stream of specialism. The team has spent much of its time on a Green Form fraud case which resulted in the acquittal of the firm's client. A further highlight has been defending a client accused of obtaining fraudulent restaurant licences.

MIDLANDS

FRAUD: CRIMINAL
MIDLANDS

1. **Cartwright King** Nottingham
   Nelsons Nottingham
2. **Glaisyers** Birmingham
3. **Hammond Suddards Edge** Birmingham
   Varley Hadley Siddall Nottingham

LEADING INDIVIDUALS

1. NELSON Richard *Nelsons*
   THURSTON Michael *Cartwright King*
   WILSON Mark *Cartwright King*
2. ROYLE Charles *Glaisyers*

This book is the product of 6,582 1/2 hour interviews. See p.7 for BMRB audit. Within each band, firms are listed alphabetically. See individuals' profiles p.396

CARTWRIGHT KING A strong team advises on the whole gamut of fraud cases from VAT and Customs & Excise matters to the counterfeiting of MP3 music CDs and videos. The "*dynamic*" **Mark Wilson** (see p.399) retains market commendation. He has represented a mobile telephone wholesaler accused of an alleged £16 million VAT fraud by the Customs & Excise National Investigation Service. "*Technically adept*" **Michael Thurston** (see p.399) profits from an engineering background, which he puts to good effect on new technology frauds. The team is currently defending an offshore bank and investment company accused in a $350 million money laundering case.

NELSONS (see firm details p.1082) Rivals commended a "*thorough team that knows its way around the complexities.*" Led by the "*experienced and capable*" **Richard Nelson** (see p.398), the team deals with a good mix of work ranging from Inland Revenue cases to VAT fraud. Regulatory and professional disciplinary work has also proved to be a source of instruction of late. The firm is currently defending an accountant allegedly involved in a large VAT fraud, and has acted for the defence on the 'dirty chicken case', involving the importation of food unfit for human consumption.

GLAISYERS Observers agreed that this strong criminal practice "*knows what they are talking about in white-collar crime.*" It is led in this respect by the high-profile "*leader in the field,*" **Charles Royle**. The team's portfolio covers a range of fraud matters as part of its wider criminal practice.

HAMMOND SUDDARDS EDGE The team deals with contentious regulatory matters, defending companies and individuals allegedly involved in misdemeanours. Contact partners Chris Green and Françoise Snape have both handled prosecutions on behalf of Birmingham City Council relating to frauds perpetrated by employees. The team has defended an individual alleged to be involved in insider dealing, resulting in his acquittal.

VARLEY HADLEY SIDDALL This is a general crime practice offering the capability to handle fraud as part of a wider remit. The team acts on Customs & Excise cases and is respected for its continuing work on prescription frauds.

THE NORTH

FRAUD: CRIMINAL
THE NORTH

1. **Cooper Kenyon Burrows** Manchester
2. **Betesh Fox & Co** Manchester
   DLA Manchester
   Irwin Mitchell Sheffield
   Pannone & Partners Manchester
3. **Garstangs** Bolton
4. **Burton Copeland** Manchester
   Russell Jones & Walker Manchester

LEADING INDIVIDUALS

1. BURROWS Lesley *Cooper Kenyon Burrows*
   KENYON Michael *Cooper Kenyon Burrows*
   SMYTH Richard *DLA*
2. COOPER Ian *Cooper Kenyon Burrows*
   FOX Stephen *Betesh Fox & Co*
   TAYLOR Paul *Pannone & Partners*
3. BARNFATHER Anthony *Pannone & Partners*
   KENYON Andrew *Burton Copeland*

This book is the product of 6,582 1/2 hour interviews. See p.7 for BMRB audit. Within each band, firms are listed alphabetically. See individuals' profiles p.396

COOPER KENYON BURROWS (see firm details p.919) A new offering of "*tried-and-tested thoroughbreds,*" this team is composed of Ian Cooper, Michael Kenyon and Lesley Burrows, and is "*expected to do phenomenally well.*" The team handles the whole gamut of fraud matters, including corporate and commercial fraud and Inland Revenue and Customs & Excise investigations. The outstanding reputations of the three lead partners ensures it the top spot in our tables. **Ian Cooper** (see p.396) is "*absolutely top flight,*" while **Lesley Burrows** (see p.396) is respected by peers as "*an aggressive practitioner committed to her clients.*" **Michael Kenyon**'s (see p.397) "*long experience*" makes him the prime choice of many for complex, large-scale frauds. The team is currently acting on a £110 million VAT fraud.

BETESH FOX & CO (see firm details p.868) The "*well-respected*" team handles diversion frauds, Customs & Excise and VAT evasion cases, often with an overseas element. Derivative fraud also features, while the team continues to act on a high-profile Green Form scheme fraud. Senior partner and head of crime **Stephen Fox** (see p.397) was perceived as the group's lead figure. The firm is likely to find itself tested following the departure of Andrew Kenyon to Burton Copeland.

DLA Peers recommended **Richard Smyth** as a leading light in the fraud market. This well-regarded team acts on SFO, investigatory and regulatory matters for its corporate client base.

IRWIN MITCHELL (see firm details p.1009) Peers applauded this young team as one that is growing in stature. The fraud department is led by Kevin Robinson, a leading individual in our London table, he splits his time between the London and Sheffield offices. Major SFO cases are the order of the day with the team currently acting on a matter concerning Anglo American.

PANNONE & PARTNERS (see firm details p.1092) "*Increasingly involved in large-scale cases,*" this "*expanding team*" deals with the spectrum of fraud cases. Solicitor accounting cases, SFO investigations, Customs & Excise and Inland Revenue matters are all catered for here. Money laundering scams have also occupied the firm of late. Team leader **Paul Taylor** (see p.399) is "*an extremely capable individual,*" while **Tony Barnfather** (see p.396) was commended as a "*down- to-earth*" practitioner, "*thorough*" in his handling of complex cases.

GARSTANGS Fraud matters handled by this firm range from SFO, Customs & Excise matters and confiscation, to money laundering. A strong presence in the North is bolstered by the firm's thriving London office.

BURTON COPELAND (see firm details p.896) The fraud department has undergone a relaunch since the departure of Ian Cooper, Michael Kenyon and Lesley Burrows to form their own practice. It has bolstered the current team with the recent recruitment of **Andrew Kenyon** (see p.397) from Betesh Fox. He is "*a delight to work with,*" according to peers, and "*technically extremely capable.*" His recruitment

FRAUD CRIMINAL ■ THE LEADERS

ensures that the team remains on the SFO panel. The firm continues to advise on a range of fraud-related work.

RUSSELL JONES & WALKER (see firm details p.1120) Nick Holroyd runs the team since the departure of David Hanman to form his own practice. The team undertakes Customs & Excise fraud as well Inland Revenue investigations as an offshoot of its strong white-collar crime practice.

THE LEADERS IN FRAUD (CRIMINAL)

BARNFATHER, Anthony
Pannone & Partners, Manchester
(0161) 909 3000
anthony.barnfather@pannone.co.uk
Specialisation: Main area of specialisation encompasses all aspects of business crime. Prime areas of expertise include representation of corporations and individuals subject to investigation by regulatory agencies. Present/recent case load includes Customs & Excise, FSA, Inland Revenue, Office of Fair Trading and SFO work. Also assists a number of corporations including multinationals regarding quasi-criminal investigations brought by such agencies as the Environment Agency and Health and Safety Executive. (Presently advising on a number of fatal accidents). Acts for professional clients in respect of allegations of serious/complex crime.
Prof. Memberships: The Law Society.
Career: Anthony Barnfather's initial involvement with criminal litigation was in his role as a police officer. He served with the West Yorkshire Police and thereafter continued this investigative role in the tax haven of Bermuda. He gained his law degree in Leeds, later becoming a partner in a Leeds practice. He joined *Pannone & Partners* in 1998 and is now a partner in their business crime unit.
Personal: Interests include Rugby League, motorcycling and hillwalking.

BINNING, Peter
Corker Binning Solicitors, London
(020) 7353 6007
pb@corkerbinning.co.uk
Specialisation: All aspects of business crime and other complex criminal cases, including extradition, mutual legal assistance, tax and customs fraud, money laundering and data protection. Regulatory inquiries involving the DTI and FSA as well as other regulatory bodies such as the Health and Safety Executive. Current cases include first ever extradition request from the UAE and major SFO and National Crime Squad prosecutions.
Prof. Memberships: Justice Executive Board, Treasurer, London Criminal Courts Solicitors Association and IBA.
Career: Called to the Bar: 1985. Crown Prosecution Service: 1989-94. Serious Fraud Office: 1994-96. *Peters & Peters*: 1996 - partner 1998-2001: Partner at *Corker Binning* from December 2001.
Publications: Articles in legal journals and responses to consultation papers. Numerous broadcasting appearances. Contributor to the 'Law of International Fraud' Sweet & Maxwell 2001.
Personal: Resides London. Sailing, ski mountaineering. Member of Royal Ocean Racing Club, Royal Geographical Society.

BURROWS, Lesley
Cooper Kenyon Burrows, Manchester
(0161) 834 7374
lesleyburrows@c-k-b.com
Specialisation: Commercial fraud defence work including liquidation, banking, stock market, loan and leasing and mortgage and property fraud. Considerable experience of SFO investigations and prosecutions having acted in several such cases including for the principal defendants in the Arrows and Butte Mining prosecutions. Experienced in Customs & Excise and Inland Revenue investigations and is currently acting in the series of cases relating to London City Bond. Serious Fraud Panel Supervisor.
Career: Qualified 1980; Partner at *Burton Copeland* from 1990; Founding Partner *Cooper Kenyon Burrows* 2002.
Personal: Attended Arnold School in Blackpool and the University of Sheffield. Lives in Cheadle, Cheshire.

BURTON, Ian
Burton Copeland (London), London
(020) 7430 2277
Specialisation: Commercial fraud, tax investigations, company investigations, problem solving.
Prof. Memberships: International Bar Association; London Criminal Courts Solicitors Association.
Career: Qualified 1971. Founded *Burton Copeland* 1982.
Personal: Lives London and Cheshire.

BYRNE, David
Dechert, London
(020) 7775 7415
david.byrne@eu.dechert.com
Specialisation: Partner and head of litigation and investigations, London. Responsible for all aspects of investigation work. He specialises in civil and criminal fraud for both claimants and defendants and has acted in numerous high profile cases brought by the SFO, city regulators, Inland Revenue and Customs & Excise. David is also co-ordinating the firm's growing practices in the financial services field and in corporate manslaughter.
Prof. Memberships: Law Society; Association of Business Recovery Professionals.
Career: Qualified in 1978. Articled at *Norton Rose*. Solicitor *Norton Rose* 1978-83. *Clifford Turner* (now *Clifford Chance*) 1983-85 Partner T*itmuss Sainer & Webb* (now *Dechert*) since 1987.
Personal: Born 1951. Attended Kings College London, Masters degree in tax, corporate and insurance law, Sweet & Maxwell prize for company law. Interests include golf and fell walking.

CAPLAN QC, Michael
Kingsley Napley, London
(020) 7814 1200
mcaplan@kingsleynapley.co.uk
Specialisation: Partner in Criminal Litigation Department. Work includes criminal law, advocacy, extradition, casino applications, gaming and licensing, and prosecuting for and advising professional and regulatory bodies. Sits as a Recorder. Rights of audience in the Crown Court. Chairman of the Solicitors Association of Higher Court Advocates.
Career: Qualified in 1977. Joined *Kingsley Napley* in 1978 and became a partner in 1982.
Personal: Born 3 May 1953. Attended Kings College, London: LLB (Hons), AKC. Leisure interests include family, sport and reading. Lives in London.

CARNELL, Bernard
Simons Muirhead & Burton, London
(020) 7734 4499
bernard.carnell@smab.co.uk
Specialisation: Work includes commercial fraud and insider dealing. Particular experience of legal aid regulations and international and financial investigations. Acted in R v Kellard and Others (Britannia Park Fraud trial, the longest in English history); BCCI Investigation; R v Fisher (the first insider dealing trial); R v Adelaja and Others (the first trial using computers).
Prof. Memberships: Law Society.
Career: Qualified in 1972. Joined *Offenbach & Co* in 1976, becoming a Partner in 1982. Joined *Simons Muirhead & Burton* as a consultant in 2001.
Personal: Born 1947. Attended LSE. Lives in London.

COOPER, Ian
Cooper Kenyon Burrows, Manchester
(0161) 834 7374
iancooper@c-k-b.com
Specialisation: Partner specialising in business and corporate fraud, particularly fraudulent trading, investment, offshore and tax fraud, mortgage and property fraud, professional misconduct matters, share and securities fraud and money laundering. Has acted in a number of high profile SFO prosecutions including Barlow Clowes and Arrows and in the successful defence of 'high yield bank instrument' trials. Serious Fraud Panel Supervisor.
Career: Qualified 1987; solicitor *Hugh Pond & Co* 1987-89; solicitor *Burton Copeland* 1989-91, Partner 1991. Founding Partner *Cooper Kenyon Burrows* 2002.
Personal: Born 1949. Attended King Edward VII School and Liverpool University (1973 BA Hons). Leisure interests include skiing, golf, wine, travel, family.

CORKER, David
Corker Binning Solicitors, London
(020) 7353 6007
dc@corkerbinning.co.uk
Specialisation: Specialist in white collar crime/general crime and regulatory. Author of 'Disclosure in Criminal Proceedings' (Sweet and Maxwell, 1998) and 'Abuse of Process and Fairness in Criminal Proceedings' (Butterworths, 2000). Conducts seminars with, inter alia, the Judicial Studies Board, SFO, CPS, DTI, Criminal Bar Association, LCCSA and Bramshill Police College. Major cases include DTI v Maxwell, Wickes and Barrymore.
Career: BA from Oriel College Oxford, MA from University of Sheffield. Police Officer 1984-87. Qualified 1990, *Peters and Peters* 1990-2000.
Personal: Born 1961.

CORNTHWAITE, Richard
Garstangs, London
(020) 7242 4324
r.cornthwaite@garstangs.co.uk
Specialisation: Specialises in the defence of fraud cases, including SFO, Inland Revenue, HM Customs and Excise and DTI prosecutions. Also handles ancillary commercial litigation, particularly in relation to fraud and asset recovery in the Chancery Division. Acted in the Guinness, Eagle Trust, Thermastor and Brent Walker cases. Also secured the acquittal of Kevin Taylor in the 'Stalker Affair'. Recently represented a principal defendant in Chancery proceedings brought by Jyske Bank (Gibraltar) Limited. Currently acting for defendant in Hungarian International Bank (SFO prosecution) and three major HM Customs and Excise investigations and two money laundering prosecutions.
Prof. Memberships: Law Society. Serious Fraud Panel.
Career: Qualified in 1977. Joined *Garstangs* as a partner in 1990.
Personal: Born 12 November, 1951. Keele University 1970-74. Lives in London and Manchester.

THE LEADERS — FRAUD CRIMINAL

COWELL, Adam
Irwin Mitchell, London
(0870) 1500 100
cowella@irwinmitchell.co.uk
Specialisation: Partner in Company Regulation Group, specialises in SFO, FSA and DTI investigations and advises on regulatory matters including S447 enquires, CDDA proceedings and Inland Revenue investigations. Currently instructed in Jubilee Line Extention Fraud and SFO prosecution of internet company, BCCI related litigation (Gokal-v-UK) and numerous DTI, FSA (insider dealings) and tax investigations and related civil cases. Also responsible for developing *Irwin Mitchell's* compliance and risk assessment initiatives.
Prof. Memberships: Hon. Secretary of International Criminal Law Association; Committee member LCCSA and Association of Regulatory and Disciplinary Lawyers; Law Society.
Career: Qualified 1989. Solicitor *Bindman & Partners*, then partner at *Moss & Co.* 1993-98. Partner *Irwin Mitchell* 1998.
Publications: Regular lecturer and writer on Company Investigations (including White Collar Crime Conferences 2000 & 2001), FSA powers (Eurolegal 2001), Business Crime and Internet (ICLA Conference 2000) and Business Crime and Human Rights, Tax Investigations and Asset Recovery (ICLA 2001) and Director Responsibilities (White Collar Crime Conference 2002).
Personal: Lives in London. Enjoys golf.

DELAHUNTY, Louise
Peters & Peters, London
(020) 7629 7991
ldelahunty@petersandpeters.co.uk
Specialisation: Partner specialising in all aspects of fraud and regulatory work and money laundering compliance. Has wide experience in acting for professionals, including solicitors and also deals with company fraud investigation work. Is well known for her international work in extradition and frequently advises on litigation in other jurisdictions. Lectures widely both here and abroad and regularly provides legal commentary on television and radio. Was admitted as a solicitor in the Republic of Ireland in 2000. Is a member of the firm's specialist Money Laundering Compliance Unit and regularly advises professional firms and financial institutions in this area. Was recently involved in the firm's launch, together with the Law Society, of a CD Rom-based money laundering training and compliance programme for law firms.
Prof. Memberships: Law Society; The City of Westminister Law Society; London Criminal Courts Solicitors Association (LCCSA); International Bar Association; Hong Kong Law Society. Chairman of the Law Society's Money Laundering and Serious Fraud Task Force, a member of the government-appointed Money Laundering Advisory Committee and member of the Law Society Criminal Law Committee.
Career: Having qualified with *Peters & Peters* in 1984, spent four years in Hong Kong practising in commercial and criminal litigation. Returned to *Peters & Peters* in 1990 and became a partner in 1991.
Publications: Numerous.

FLETCHER, Rod
Russell Jones & Walker, London
(020) 7837 2808
Specialisation: Partner and Head of Criminal and Business Investigations Department. Main area of practice is criminal defence. Has particular involvement with white collar/ business crime and major miscarriage of justice cases. Also regularly instructed in disciplinary cases. Represents individuals attending a number of government and other public inquiries: examples include the Scott Inquiry, the Stephen Lawrence Inquiry, the Marchioness Inquiry and the Bloody Sunday Inquiry. Acted in many miscarriage of justice cases, including the representation of the police officers prosecuted following the Birmingham Six, Guildford Four and Broadwater Farm investigations. Acted in the Maxwell, Barings and Bute Mining cases. Currently acting in international corruption investigations, a unique FSA investigation and SFO investigations and prosecutions in pensions, tax, investment and price-fixing.
Prof. Memberships: Law Society, LCCSA, IBA
Career: Qualified in 1981. Worked with *Kingsley Napley* , 1979-83. Left to join *Russell Jones & Walker* in 1983, becoming a Partner in 1985.
Personal: Born 21 April 1957. Attended Berkhamstead School, then Birmingham University 1975-78. Leisure interests include sailing, golf, cricket and music. Lives in London.

FOX, Stephen
Betesh Fox & Co, Manchester
(0870) 998 9000
stephen.fox@fraud.co.uk
Specialisation: Senior Partner. International and UK Fraud, Commercial Crime and Defendant injunctive work including defence of DTI, Excise and Revenue prosecutions, Solicitors Tribunal and professional proceedings. Defence of Extradition proceedings.
Prof. Memberships: The Law Society, The Manchester Law Society.
Career: Instructed by Defendants in Eagle Trust, BCCI, Arrows, IRL Group Australia (Malcolm Johnson), Kevin Taylor (the Stalker Affair), Jyske Bank, Alliance Resources, Hamilton Wines, Harrovian Property, G Grosberg, A Mandelberg and other Solicitor Defendants.
Personal: Born 8 October 1948. Educated Manchester GS College of Law. Interests: Rugby League and writing.

FRANKLAND, Matthew
Dechert, London
(020) 7583 5353
matthew.frankland@eu.dechert.com
Specialisation: Partner in the Investigations Department. Specialises in the defence of national and international fraud/white collar crime cases, including those brought by the SFO, DTI, CPS, Inland Revenue and Customs & Excise. He has particular experience of Crown Court confiscation, High Court restraint proceedings and large money laundering investigations. He also jointly heads a team that specialises in financial services regulatory investigations including those by the FSA and lectures on this topic. He advises on investigations by professional institutes including fraud enquiries at the General Medical Council and the General Dental Council. He has conducted litigation arising from criminal law in the House of Lords and European Court of Human Rights.
Prof. Memberships: Law Society; Criminal Law Solicitors' Association; The London Criminal Courts Solicitors' Association; Assocation of Business Recovery Professional; The Association of Regulatory and Disciplinary Lawyers; Serious Fraud Association.
Career: Qualified in September 1991. Joined *Titmuss Sainer Dechert* (now *Dechert*) in 1995.
Personal: Born 1964, attended University of Wales, resides London. Leisure interests include sport, travel and art.

GENTLE, Stephen
Kingsley Napley, London
(020) 7814 1200
sgentle@kingsleynapley.co.uk
Specialisation: Main area of practice is serious fraud and business crime, extradition and international legal assistance, city regulatory matters. Successfully defended Erik Langaker, the broker in the Morgan Grenfell case.
Prof. Memberships: International Criminal Law Association; London Criminal Courts Solicitors Association.
Career: Articled *Kingsley Napley* 1993-95. Qualified 1995. Became a Partner in 2001.
Publications: Numerous contributions to professional journals. Contributor to 'Mutual Legal Assistance in Criminal Matters' (Murray Harris).
Personal: Born 17 January 1964. Educated at Wymondham College, Norfolk and Wadham College, Oxford University.

GLASS, Jane
Burton Copeland (London), London
(020) 7430 2277
jglass@burtoncopeland.co.uk
Specialisation: Principal area of practice is commercial fraud defence work. Substantial experience of acting in major cases involving investigations and prosecutions brought by the SFO, Customs & Excise and DTI.
Prof. Memberships: Law Society.
Career: Qualified 1996. Partner at *Burton Copeland* from 1997.
Personal: Born 1964. Attended Bolton School (Girls Division) and University of Essex. Resides London.

HARDING, John
Kingsley Napley, London
(020) 7814 1200
jharding@kingsleynapley.co.uk
Specialisation: Partner in Criminal Litigation Department dealing with white collar and general crime. Recent cases include SFO and Inland Revenue Investigations, and International case work involving sanctions legislation and fraud and mutual legal assistance. Currently involved in the Jubilee Line Extension case and the criminal prosecutions of the staff and partners of Robinson's, solicitors.
Prof. Memberships: Law Society; LCCSA; CLSA; BAFS.
Career: Qualified in October 1988. Joined *Kingsley Napley* in 1990 and became a partner in 1994.
Personal: Born 9 April 1963. Educated at Derby School and Brunel University.

KENYON, Andrew
Burton Copeland (North), Manchester
(0161) 827 9500
Specialisation: Partner in Serious and Commercial Crime Department. Commercial Fraud and Business Crime including defence of cases instituted by SFO, DTI, Inland Revenue and Customs and Excise: and other areas of white collar crime.
Prof. Memberships: The Law Society and the Manchester Law Society.
Career: Qualified 1970. Practised in both Private Practice and Crown Prosecution Service. Joined *Betesh Fox & Co* as Partner in 1993. Instructed by Defendants in Arrows, Financial Services Group plc, Ahmed (British Telecom Fraud), Herr Peter Tuegel, Allgemeine Handels und Effectenbank AG, BancEurope, Robinsons (Legal Aid Fraud).
Personal: Born 13 March 1946. Educated Oundle School and Leeds University. Interests include sport, walking, theatre and cinema.

KENYON, Michael
Cooper Kenyon Burrows, Manchester
(0161) 834 7374
michaelkenyon@c-k-b.com
Specialisation: Commercial fraud investigation and defence including prospectus fraud, loan and leasing fraud, insider dealing, fraudulent trading, frauds on investors, property and mortgage fraud, corruption and tax investigations. Considerable recent experience of advising and defending in large scale customs duty and VAT cases. Defended numerous solicitors charged with fraud and money laundering offences. Serious Fraud Panel Supervisor.
Career: Qualified 1980; Partner at *Chafes* in Stockport 1985-86; Senior Crown Prosecutor in Manchester 1987-89;

FRAUD CRIMINAL ■ THE LEADERS

Partner at *Burton Copeland* 1990. Founding Partner *Cooper Kenyon Burrows* 2002.
Personal: Born 1956. Attended Manchester Grammar School and Kent University (1977 BA Hons). Leisure interests include salmon fishing, game shooting, opera and European military history. Lives in Cheshire and Scotland.

KIRK, David
Simons Muirhead & Burton, London
(020) 7734 4499
david.kirk@smab.co.uk
Specialisation: Head. Fraud Department. Commercial Fraud (including SFO, DTI, Inland Revenue and Customs & Excise investigations), Regulation, Investigations. Co-author of 'Serious Fraud - Investigation and Trial' (2nd Edition, Butterworths 1997).
Prof. Memberships: Law Society, LCCSA, IBA.

MITCHELL, John
Blake Lapthorn, Fareham
(01489) 579990

MORGAN, Roy
Roy Morgan & Co, Cardiff
(029) 2039 8511

MURRAY, Christopher
Kingsley Napley, London
(020) 7814 1200
cmurray@kingsleynapley.co.uk
Specialisation: Partner and Head of the Criminal Litigation Department. Specialises in both white collar and general crime with a strong emphasis on the international aspects and pre-inquiry stages of this area. Particular expertise in money laundering, corruption, fraud and mutual assistance cases. Involved in many highly publicised cases including Maxwell, Polly Peck, Guinness, Banco Ambrosiano. Curently acting for Henry Sweetbaum in the SFO prosecution against Wickes and recently advised the Nigerian Government in its mutual assistance proceedings to recover the ABACHA funds. Speaks regularly at national and international conferences and writes on money laundering, lawyer confidentiality and international co-operation in white collar crime. Regular contributor to TV and radio on criminal law matters. Vice Patron Missing Persons Helpline.
Prof. Memberships: Member of Criminal Justice Consultative Council; London Criminal Courts Solicitors Association (LCCSA) (President 1997/8); LCCSA Committee on Disclosure (Chairman); Law Society Criminal Law Committee; Law Society Criminal Law Sub-committee on Juries in Serious Fraud Trials; Law Society Evidence to House of Lords on EU Corpus Iuris Anti-fraud proposals; City of London Solicitor's Society (sub-committee on Judicial Appointments for City Solicitors) CLSA, IBA (Co-Chairman of Committee W - Business Crime), British Academy of Forensic Sciences; Justice (Sub Committee on Serious Fraud).
Career: Qualified 1972. Partner at *Kingsley Napley* since 1974. Recorder of the Crown Court.
Publications: Numerous, including jointly with Lorna Harris 'Mutual Assistance in Criminal Matters,' Sweet & Maxwell, 2000.
Personal: Educated at Kings College, Taunton 1961-65, and University College, London (LLB) 1966-69. Member of the Athenaeum and 2 Brydges Place. Leisure pursuits include music, theatre, modern art and design, 20th Century English literature. Born 6 November 1947.

NELSON, Richard
Nelsons, Nottingham
(07000) 150160
richard.nelson@nelsons-solicitors.co.uk
Specialisation: Leads substantial business defence department comprising in-house Solicitors and Barristers covering full range of business related investigation and defence, acting for companies and individuals. Practice involves cases over wide geographical area throughout England and Wales often with international element. Current casework of fraud involves many multimillion pound cases, including money laundering, confiscation, corruption, conspiracy, Revenue and Customs & Excise investigations (including Tax and Duty evasion prosecutions), Trading Standards and OFT, Companies Act, DTI and Insolvency offences, Regulatory and Environmental, Professional Disciplinary Conduct and Management issues, Corporate and other individual crime and SFO investigations. Significant HSE cases, particularly involving serious injury and death and attendant Prohibition Notices and Inquests. Casework often involves pursuit and consideration of large volumes of evidence in various forms (several million documents in individual cases) and liaison with technical and forensic experts. The firm also has a separate department dealing with civil law implications and further department dealing with general and other serious crime.
Prof. Memberships: Vice-Chairman and Secretary, Serious Fraud Association. Founder member Complex Case Practitioners' Group. Notts Criminal Justice Strategy Committee. Notts Law Society Criminal Business Committee (former Chairman). Former Council Member Notts Law Society. Solicitors' Assistance Scheme.
Career: Qualified 1975. *J A Bright Richards & Flewitt* 1972-77. *Freeth Cartwright & Sketchley* 1977-83 (partner from 1980). Formed *Nelson, Johnson & Hastings* (now *Nelsons*) with two partners and no staff in 1983. *Nelsons* is now one of the largest firms in the region, based in several cities.
Personal: Born 14 June 1950. Educated Nottingham High School and Bristol University. Interests include sport and comedy. Vice-Chairman Nottinghamshire Hospice. Governor Trent College. Director of private companies.

OLIVER, Keith
Peters & Peters, London
koliver
(020) 7629 7991
See under Litigation, p.565

POLLARD, Stephen
Kingsley Napley, London
(020) 7814 1200
spollard@kingsleynapley.co.uk
Specialisation: Partner in criminal and regulatory department. Practice covers all criminal work, but particularly white collar fraud and 'city crime'. Also handles regulatory work including disciplinary proceedings before the FSA. Recently represented the football manager David Jones, acquitted of child abuse allegations and a defendant in the Deutsche Morgan Grenfell SFO prosecution. Is currently part of the team representing 450 former soldiers in Lord Saville's Inquiry into 'Bloody Sunday'. Has various clients involved in current FSA proceedings. Appears regularly on TV and radio on criminal law matters.
Prof. Memberships: London Criminal Courts Solicitors' Association.
Career: Qualified 1985. Worked at *Payne Hicks Beach* 1982-87, including 1984-85 as a Member of Secretariat of the European Commission of Human Rights, Strasbourg. One year with the Crown Prosecution Service 1987-88. Joined *Kingsley Napley* in 1989, becoming a partner in 1990.
Personal: Born 5 September 1958. Attended Manchester Grammar School 1972-77, and Pembroke College, Oxford 1977-80. Leisure interests include reading, sport, theatre and family. Lives in Putney, London. Married with four children.

PROWEL, Martyn
Martyn Prowel Solicitors, Cardiff
(02920) 470909
mprowel@mped.globalnet.co.uk
Specialisation: Complex fraud trials, commercial and VAT/revenue fraud and other serious crime trial defences. Prosecutions undertaken for RSPCA. General crime, magistrates and crown court defence.
Prof. Memberships: Law Society. South Wales Duty Solicitors Regional committee member. Serious Fraud panel.
Career: LLB (Hons) Wales 1962-65. European Law Studies 1965-66 Nancy Univ. France. Qualified 1970. Former senior partner Hallinans solicitors and South Wales Duty Solicitors' Regional committee member.
Personal: Married with two children.

RAPHAEL, Monty
Peters & Peters, London
(020) 7629 7991
montyr@petersandpeters.co.uk
Specialisation: Senior Partner specialising in fraud and regulatory matters, money laundering and tax investigations. When not practising he publishes widely and travels the world lecturing and training governmental and commercial organisations on numerous aspects of fraud. He acts for corporate and individual clients, financial institutions and professional firms, dealing with a wide variety of fraud-related matters. Areas of his work include regulatory enquiries, compliance advice (particularly money laundering), tax and Customs & Excise enquiries, securities infractions and a range of related commercial litigation matters. He is a member of the firm's specialist Money Laundering Compliance Unit and was recently involved in the firm's launch, together with the Law Society, of a CD Rom based money laundering training and compliance programme for law firms.
Career: Qualified 1962; Senior Partner of *Peters & Peters*. In 1979 became the first advocacy training officer appointed by the London Criminal Courts Solicitors' Association (president 1982-84). Provided detailed written and oral evidence on the prosecution and trial of commercial fraud to the Roskill Committee and to the Royal Commission on Criminal Justice. Founder and past chairman of the Business Crime Committee of the Section on Business Law of the International Bar Association. Served as a member of the Home Office Working Party advising on the proposed alterations to 'right to silence' in 1988-89. Assisted the Council of Europe in its programme to help the emergent economies of Eastern Europe in their transition to a market economy. Honorary solicitor to the Howard League for Penal Reform. Member ICAEW Fraud Advisory Panel. Chair IBA Anti-Corruption Working Group.
Publications: Numerous.
Personal: Lives in London.

ROBINSON, Kevin
Irwin Mitchell, London
(0870) 1500 100
robinsonk@irwinmitchell.co.uk
Specialisation: Partner heading Business Crime Unit. Based in London. Acted in the major Iraqi arms export cases and also Astra/BMARC disqualification proceedings. Represents company directors, managers and professionals subject to investigation or charged with fraud, particularly SFO prosecutions, fraudulent trading, VAT Inland Revenue and like offences. Also represents corporations including multinationals and Plcs in criminal proceedings arising out of their commercial activities.
Prof. Memberships: Member International Bar Association. Legal Reds.

Committee member Solicitors Association of Higher Court Advocates, London Criminal Courts Solicitors Association. **Career:** Qualified in 1973. Joined *Irwin Mitchell* in 1974 became a partner in 1975. Former Treasurer of Criminal Law Solicitors Association. Higher Courts Rights of Audience 1995.

ROYLE, Charles
Glaisyers, Birmingham
(0121) 233 2971

SMYTH, Richard
DLA, Manchester
(08700) 111111

SPIRO, Brian
Burton Copeland (London), London
(020) 7430 2177
bspiro@burtoncopeland.co.uk
Specialisation: Partner. Criminal defence litigation, specialising in business crime, drugs law and serious offences against the person. Also fraud investigation and international consultancy work. Regular contributor to legal journals and broadcaster.
Prof. Memberships: Law Society, LCCSA, IBA, AIJA, Lawyers for Liberty.
Career: Qualified in 1984, Partner of *Simons Muirhead & Burton* (1986-2001). Partner of Burton Copeland (London) from April 2001.
Publications: Author of 'Police Station Advisers' Index' (Sweet & Maxwell).

TAYLOR, Paul
Pannone & Partners, Manchester
(0161) 909 4556
paul.taylor@pannone.co.uk
Specialisation: All aspects of business crime, fraud and related proceedings. Advising and representing individuals and corporations at all stages of investigation and litigation by the SFO, Customs & Excise, DTI, Fraud Investigation Group, Trading Standards, Health and Safety Executive, and other regulatory authorities. Significant experience in representing solicitors and accountants in a wide range of fraud cases, including those with an international dimension, money laundering and in serious/complex criminal cases generally. Successfully acted in a number of recent major cases for a solicitor charged with perverting the course of justice; a chartered accountant charged with a VAT cash accounting fraud; a solicitor in connection with a SFO investigation; a solicitor in connection with a Customs & Excise investigation and other substantial work.
Prof. Memberships: Law Society of England & Wales and Hong Kong; former member of the Criminal Law Sub-committee Hong Kong; Complex Case Practitioners Group; Serious Fraud Panel Supervisor.
Career: Admitted in England & Wales 1980; admitted in Hong Kong 1985: Head of business crime *Alsop Wilkinson* Hong Kong 1989-93; Head of business crime *Pannone & Partners* 1995 to date.
Personal: Born 1955. Graduated University College of Wales 1977. Keen sportsman and enjoys traveling.

THURSTON, Michael
Cartwright King, Nottingham
(0115) 958 7444
mthurston@cartwrightking.co.uk
Specialisation: All types of fraud, defending businesses, companies, directors and professionals. SFO, Fraud Squad, DTI, Customs & Excise, Inland Revenue cases and regulatory investigations and prosecutions by the HSE, Environment Agency, Trading Standards, etc. Consultancy advice to commerce to prevent and detect and deal with the aftermath of fraud. LSC Serious Fraud Panel Supervisor. *Cartwright King* is a specialist corporate crime (and general criminal defence) practice, and is a member of the LSC Serious Fraud Panel.
Career: Engineering graduate and worked in industry prior to qualification. Criminal Litigation partner in *freethcarthwright* 1974-99. De-merged to set up *Cartwright King* in January 2000. Remains consultant to *freethcartwright*.
Personal: Born 1948. Leisure: tennis, golf, skiing.

TRAVERS, Harry
Burton Copeland (London), London
(020) 7430 2177
htravers@burtoncopeland.co.uk
Specialisation: Partner specialising in white-collar crime, including tax fraud, corruption, insolvency/banking/insurance fraud/insider dealing and money laundering. Also specialises in regulatory and disciplinary work (e.g. Lloyds, FSA), Inland Revenue and Customs & Excise investigations, directors' disqualifications, and prosecutions for breach of environmental protection/health and safety legislation. Has substantial experience in securing negotiated financial settlements with the Inland Revenue and/or bringing Judicial Review proceedings in respect of their actions, particularly in relation to the conduct of raids under Section 20C TMA 1970. Acted for Darius Guppy, Dieter Abt, George Hendry (the European Leisure case), Hisham Alwan (R v Allcock & Others) and Victoria Aitken. Disciplinary work has included acting for Derek Walker (Lloyd's Disciplinary Proceedings relating to Gooda Walker). Fluent French speaker.
Prof. Memberships: LCCSA (sub-committees relating to fraud), BISLA.
Career: Qualified as a barrister in 1986, a solicitor in 1990. 1987-91: *Berwin Leighton* Tax & Trusts Dept specialising in tax investigations, trusts and tax avoidance litigation including Craven v White up to House of Lords. 1991 joined *Burton Copeland* Commercial Fraud Dept. Partner February 1995. Educated at Manchester Grammar School and St Edmund Hall, Oxford (BCL MA).
Personal: Leisure interests include Manchester United, golf, languages and music.

WILSON, Mark
Cartwright King, Nottingham
(0115) 958 7444
mwilson@cartwrightking.co.uk
Specialisation: Commercial and professional fraud and regulatory crime. LSC Serious Fraud Panel Supervisor. Recent experience of investigations and prosecutions by all fraud investigation agencies, DTI, Revenue, HMC&E, Trading Standards, HSE, Environment Agency, for corporations and individuals. Mainly defence representation but also prosecutions for regulatory bodies and advice to commerce the subject of fraud. *Cartwright King* is a niche commercial crime (and general criminal defence) practice, and is a member of the LSC Serious Fraud Panel.
Career: Partner in *freethcartwright* White Collar Crime department 1990-99. De-merged to set up *Cartwright King* on 1 January 2000. Remains a consultant to *freethcartwright*.
Personal: Born 1961. Leisure: Family, motor racing, mountain biking.

WOOLLEY, Linda
Kingsley Napley, London
(020) 7814 1224
lwoolley@kingsleynapley.co.uk
Specialisation: Practice includes all areas of criminal work, but particularly serious fraud and business crime, extradition, international crime and mutual legal assistance. Also handles public inquiries, tax investigations and professional disciplinary matters.
Prof. Memberships: Committee member, London Criminal Courts Solicitors Association; International Bar Association; Criminal Law Solicitors Association; City of London Solicitors Company; Amnesty International.
Career: Joined *Kingsley Napley* 1990; qualified 1992; partner 1998.
Publications: Articles on extradition and international law, 'Solicitors' Journal', IBA publications.
Personal: University of Warwick (1983); College of Law (1990). Leisure – arts, reading, travel.

HEALTH & SAFETY

London: 400; The Regions: 400; Profiles: 402

Research approved by BMRB For this edition, **Chambers'** researchers conducted 6,582 interviews – 3,900 with law firms, 511 with barristers and 2,171 with clients. The validity of the research was scrutinised by BMRB International, who audited both the methodology and the results at our offices in London. They interviewed **Chambers'** researchers and cross-checked sample interviews. Details of the audit appear on page 7.

OVERVIEW This is a burgeoning area due to a number of factors: firstly, a leaner and hungrier HSE is keeping the marketplace on its toes, with cases such as Friskies Petcare (UK) and, more latterly, Colthrop Board Mill indicating to the market that fines are on the increase. A new head of legal, a relaunch of its enforcement policy statement and the establishment of a construction division are just a few of the changes introduced to the HSE in the past year. Legislation on corporate manslaughter still looms large, while the continuing saga of the rail industry has led to the establishment of a rail safety inspectorate. Employers, particularly the larger organisations, are responding with training on up-to-the-minute policies.

LONDON

HEALTH & SAFETY
LONDON

1. CMS Cameron McKenna
2. Masons
   Simmons & Simmons
3. Davies Arnold Cooper
   Kennedys

LEADING INDIVIDUALS

1. SCOGGINS Mark *Fisher Scoggins LLP*
   TYLER Mark *CMS Cameron McKenna*
2. THOMAS Margaret *Davies Arnold Cooper*

This book is the product of 6,582 1/2 hour interviews. See p.7 for BMRB audit. Within each band, firms are listed alphabetically. See individuals' profiles p.402

CMS CAMERON McKENNA (see firm details p.914) The firm retains its poll position in this area, with **Mark Tyler** (see p.403) at the helm boosting the practice with his "*ability to reassure clients.*" He was praised by peers and clients as "*a pure health and safety practitioner; he is an absolute leader in the field.*" A repertoire of corporate governance, regulatory advice and defence work is bolstered by the firm's corporate client base. The Ladbroke Grove inquiry saw the team representing the train owners, and, in Part 2 of the inquiry, the rolling stock leasing companies. It is also involved in project work on the London Underground PPP for shortlisted bidders. **Clients** Rail companies; construction companies.

MASONS (see firm details p.1057) The team provides a national health and safety service alongside its Leeds office, building on its strengths and outstanding client base in the construction market. Dubbed by peers "*a major practice,*" it advises on major PFI/PPP projects to ensure proper risk allocation and management. Advice following fatal accidents, subsequent prosecutions by the HSE and the drafting of response crisis protocols also play their part. **Clients** Property developers; construction; engineering.

SIMMONS & SIMMONS (see firm details p.1136) A strong health and safety presence runs in tandem with the firm's respected environmental team. The team is led by head of environmental law, Kathy Mylrea, while team members range from construction and employment to environmental law practitioners, who are held in "*the highest esteem*" by peers. The past year has seen advice to a chemical company on the distribution of products containing a prohibited substance within the UK and its potential prohibition under EC health and safety legislation on the classification and labelling of dangerous substances. The firm also advised on a successful appeal to a French administrative court against a statutory enforcement notice leading to an independent Advocate General notice being quashed. **Clients** Rail; electronics; chemical and pharmaceutical companies.

DAVIES ARNOLD COOPER (see firm details p.930) A new entry to our table this year, the firm was acknowledged by interviewees as having a presence in the area. Ex-health and safety inspector **Margaret Thomas** (see p.403) is "*as straight as a die and a class act.*" She is part of a team that has been involved in defending clients from, inter alia, fatal accident and serious injury prosecutions, from the time of accident through to the end of prosecution. **Clients** Engineering; pharmaceutical; construction.

KENNEDYS (see firm details p.1019) Historically associated with the British Railways Board, the group enjoys a high profile through its rail work. Peers acknowledged that the "*right background*" provides an advantage. Work involves major accident response including inquiries, subsequent prosecutions and civil claims. Civil liability from the Selby rail crash is one of the issues currently being advised on, while roles in Ladbroke Grove and Hatfield continue. Numerous improvement notices were also handled over the past year. **Clients** NHS Trusts; construction; rail companies.

OTHER NOTABLE PRACTITIONERS "*Excellent chap*" **Mark Scoggins** has left Elborne Mitchell together with Alan Fisher to form Fisher Scoggins LLP. He was showered with commendation from peers and clients who had "*great admiration for his technical knowledge.*" The past year has seen work on rail inquiries (in particular, Hatfield), prohibition notice cases and pre-incident advisory work. Risk management for the water industry and emergency services has also featured, together with defence of fatalities and serious injuries within the construction and light industry sectors.

THE SOUTH & SOUTH WEST

BOND PEARCE (see firm details p.879) The firm has risen in the rankings this year in recognition of the nationwide commendation for **Jon Cooper** (see p.402), a "*pre-eminent person in the field.*" "*Fair, efficient and a worthy opponent,*" clients lauded "*his analytical skills – he is incredibly commercially aware and sensitive*" – while "*a strong, tight team*" was also recognised as part of the equation. The firm is acclaimed for balancing defence for a range of clients – from businesses and insurers to individual directors – with prosecuting for the HSE. This year the team concluded the prosecution arising from the Avonmouth Bridge gantry collapse. **Clients** HSE; Nuclear Safety Directorate; major retailers.

OSBORNE CLARKE (see firm details p.1090) The "*extremely knowledgeable*" **Richard Bretton** possesses expertise in property industry accidents, and clients praised his "*timely advice; he's practical and commercial.*" The team, including the "*sensible*" **Dale Collins**, was also the subject of client endorsement for giving "*strong, immediate feedback; they are good communicators.*"

THE SOUTH & SOUTH WEST/WALES/MIDLANDS ■ HEALTH & SAFETY

The group handles mostly defence work, with some prosecutions for the HSE. It also advises on employers' liability and public liability claims and occupational injuries. **Clients** Retail; transport; waste management; food; property developers.

BURGES SALMON (see firm details p.894) Although the team advises on a wide array of contentious and non-contentious matters, it remains most renowned in the market for its rail work. The group advised on all aspects of Southall, Ladbroke Grove and Hatfield with representation at four public inquiries before Lord Cullen. Partner expertise in employment, insurance and commercial litigation sectors bolsters this practice and has ensured that construction and logistic companies are attracted to the firm. **Clients** Rail companies (passenger and freight); construction; logistics.

BEVAN ASHFORD (see firm details p.869) The firm's workload encompasses a range of matters, including policy development and implementation, investigations and prosecutions, typically for NHS Trusts, educational establishments and private sector companies. Contentious work is a strong feature, involving liaising with regulators and preliminary investigations. Head of the team **David Wood** (see p.403) was described as "*sensible, professional and measured*" by peers. **Clients** NHS Trusts; manufacturers; builders; contractors; educational establishments.

LESTER ALDRIDGE (see firm details p.1038) A solid offering is headed by the popular **Richard Byrne** (see p.402) who was highly recommended by the marketplace. A heavily contentious workload sits alongside the preparation of policies, training, corporate killing advice, and monitoring and management on health and safety issues. The team provides out of hours emergency advice in accident situations. **Clients** HSE; construction; care homes.

WALES

EVERSHEDS (see firm details p.949) This office benefits from the national network, which provides health and safety advice. Head of the property litigation team Jonathan Richards deals with matters which include defence, prosecutions and pre-accident enquiries. **Clients** Contractors; manufacturers.

HUGH JAMES (see firm details p.1004) The firm continues to provide its health and safety advice under the guidance of Graham Rees of the Merthyr Tydfil office. The team has concluded the Cleveland Bridge prosecution, while insurers continue to give a steady stream of work.

OTHER NOTABLE PRACTITIONERS Acclaimed by clients to be "*constructive and fair*" **Robin Havard** of Morgan Cole acts on contentious and non-contentious matters. Recent cases include the defence of two directors accused of corporate manslaughter and representation on an investigation into a fatality at an organisation which has Crown Immunity.

MIDLANDS

HEALTH & SAFETY
■ MIDLANDS

1. **Eversheds** Birmingham
2. **Hammond Suddards Edge** Birmingham
3. **Shoosmiths** Northampton

LEADING INDIVIDUALS

1. **REID Ron** Shoosmiths

This book is the product of 6,582 1/2 hour interviews. See p.7 for BMRB audit.
Within each band, firms are listed alphabetically. See individuals' profiles p.402

EVERSHEDS (see firm details p.949) Active in this area, the Birmingham office has been bolstered by the addition of Kevin Elliot as an associate from Wragge & Co. Defending clients on a number of fatalities is a core part of the practice, and this year the firm acted on a lorry crash into a funeral cortège, which killed three people. **Clients** Major corporates in the power, technology and retail sectors.

HAMMOND SUDDARDS EDGE Interviewees felt that this team was "*interesting to lock horns with*" and experienced in risk management and compliance issues. Prosecutions and disputes also form a large part of the workload. The group, under the guidance of national head of safety, health and environment Michael Shepherd, has acted on numerous fatalities and advised on the drafting of health and safety policies, while a rapid response service is on hand for clients. **Clients** Chemical, construction, manufacturing, nuclear and food sectors.

SHOOSMITHS (see firm details p.1133) A new entrant to the tables this year, the team was perceived by our interviewees as having "*a big intention to give value added service.*" **Ron Reid** (see p.403), head of the team, was praised by clients for possessing "*an encyclopaedic knowledge; he is a good advocate and down to earth.*" Advice on prosecutions and civil claims has been a feature of this year's workload. **Clients** Major food companies; police; retailers.

www.ChambersandPartners.com 401

HEALTH & SAFETY ■ THE NORTH/THE LEADERS

THE NORTH

HEALTH & SAFETY
■ THE NORTH

1 **Eversheds** Leeds, Manchester

2 **Addleshaw Booth & Co** Leeds, Manchester
Hammond Suddards Edge Leeds, Manchester
Nabarro Nathanson Sheffield

3 **DLA** Manchester, Sheffield
Masons Leeds, Manchester

LEADING INDIVIDUALS

1 **BURNLEY Paul** Eversheds
ELLIKER Michael Addleshaw Booth & Co
PARRINGTON Simon Hill Dickinson
SHEPHERD Michael Hammond Suddards Edge
WATKINS Gareth Nabarro Nathanson

UP AND COMING
GRICE Helen Masons
MCLOUGHLIN Kevin DLA
MCPHERSON Lyn Nabarro Nathanson

This book is the product of 6,582 1/2 hour interviews. See p.7 for BMRB audit. Within each band, firms are listed alphabetically. See individuals' profiles p.402

EVERSHEDS (see firm details p.949) A strong regulatory team that includes "*specialist lawyers who are good at upsetting the apple cart,*" including the highly respected **Paul Burnley** (see p.402). Work includes the defence of a high-profile prosecution by the HSE and defence on fatalities. **Clients** Major corporates in the power, technology and retail sectors.

ADDLESHAW BOOTH & CO (see firm details p.838) **Michael Elliker** (see p.402) is respected for his trading standards and regulatory crime work; indeed, peers pointed to him as "*an expert in the field.*" Derailments, fatalities, breaches of airport regulations, collapsed buildings and factory accidents have all provided the team with a rich source of prosecution work for the HSE. The firm also handles defence work for local authorities. Highlights of the year include repeated prosecutions for breach of asbestos regulations. **Clients** Construction; transport; manufacturers; servicing industries.

HAMMOND SUDDARDS EDGE The Manchester office, complemented by a burgeoning Leeds office, was praised by peers as "*a player*" that handles a large volume of work. National head of safety, health and environment **Michael Shepherd** was recommended as "*number one in the North.*" The team has handled numerous fatalities, reviews and audits. **Clients** Chemical, construction, manufacturing, nuclear and food sectors.

NABARRO NATHANSON (see firm details p.1080) This group of lawyers stands out as "*knowledgeable and easy to deal with,*" claim peers. **Gareth Watkins** (see p.403) provides "*excellent advice,*" and clients noted that he "*handles things sensitively and at the right pitch.*" The advocacy skills of senior assistant **Lyn McPherson** (see p.403) were also singled out by clients, who claim "*she is on our level and wave-length.*" Matters range from risk and crisis management to audits on reviews and enforcement actions. The team secured hazardous substance consent for a new product, where there was substantial opposition. **Clients** Power; education; rail; construction and manufacturing.

DLA A team of "*specialist lawyers who are growing in the area*" features the "*sensible*" **Kevin McLoughlin**. Big on regulatory, the team represents insurers in respect of prosecutions and regulatory matters, as well as providing advice to hospitals, nursing and residential homes who may face investigation.

MASONS (see firm details p.1057) The Leeds office of this national practice is bolstered by a team steeped in practical experience and commended by clients for "*delivering what they say they will.*" **Helen Grice** (see p.403) was recommended by both peers and clients as "*well informed, efficient, with a 'can-do' attitude – she cannot be bettered for health and safety.*" The team provides a full service on the defence of prosecutions.

OTHER NOTABLE PRACTITIONERS "*First and foremost a gentleman,*" **Simon Parrington** (see p.403) of Hill Dickinson was singled out by peers as "*extremely competent, straight-up and hard-working.*" He handles mainly prosecutions for the HSE, hazardous installations, technology and engineering matters.

THE LEADERS IN HEALTH & SAFETY

BRETTON, Richard
Osborne Clarke, Bristol
(0117) 917 3000

BURNLEY, Paul
Eversheds, Leeds
(0113) 243 0391
paulburnley@eversheds.com
Specialisation: Principal area of practice is acting for corporate/commercial clients and other directors in complex civil and criminal, health and safety litigation. Known for his extensive experience of crisis management, having represented clients in major incidents, large scale disasters and product recall. He and his team undertake all their own advocacy where possible. Experienced in all aspects of health and safety issues including Coronor's Court. A "no-nonsense" advocate. Invited to many venues as a guest speaker on corporate and individual director liability.
Prof. Memberships: UKELA.
Career: Qualified April 1980. Nine years as a prosecuting solicitor, he joined *Eversheds* in 1989 becoming a partner in May 1996. A gamekeeper turned poacher!
Personal: Born 31 August 1955.

BYRNE, Richard
Lester Aldridge, Bournemouth
(01202) 786121
richard.byrne@lester-aldridge.co.uk
Specialisation: Advises on all aspects of health and safety legislation, company health and safety policies and their management. Provides representation in connection with Health and Safety at Work Act and associated regulatory prosecutions. Advises and represents the health and safety executive in prosecutions. Part time employment tribunal chairman. Lectures nationwide, and a visiting lecturer at Bournemouth University in health and safety law.
Career: Qualified in 1978. Joined *Lester Aldridge* 1983, becoming a partner in 1984.
Publications: Regular contributor to the 'Employment Lawyer' covering health and safety issues in the employment context.
Personal: Born 1955. Lives near Romsey, Hampshire. Fellow of the Royal Geographic Society.

COLLINS, Dale
Osborne Clarke, Bristol
(0117) 917 3000

COOPER, Jon
Bond Pearce, Plymouth
(01752) 677802
jcooper@bondpearce.com
Specialisation: Partner and Head of the Health and Safety Group. Specialises in all aspects of health and safety including prosecutions in all Courts. Also judicial review proceedings and advisory work relating to health and safety, health and safety policies, risk management, and health and safety due diligence issues in corporate transactions. The work arises from all sectors of industry and commerce ranging from the nuclear industry to agriculture.
Prof. Memberships: Member of the Law Society Personal Injury Panel; member of the Editorial Advisory Board for 'Tolley's Health and Safety at Work' publication.
Career: Qualified in 1984 with *Bond Pearce*, becoming a Partner in 1989.

ELLIKER, Michael
Addleshaw Booth & Co, Leeds
(0113) 209 2233
mike.elliker@addleshawbooth.com
Specialisation: Senior solicitor in Litigation and Dispute Resolution Group. Specialises in health and safety matters but also deals with trading standards and environmental cases. An experienced advocate who frequently conducts prosecutions on behalf of the Health and Safety Executive.
Prof. Memberships: Law Society and Leeds Law Society.
Career: Articled at *Booth and Co.* and qualified in 1974; with *R.C. Moorhouse and Co.* from 1977 to 1984; rejoined *Booth & Co.* in 1984. Deputy District Judge from 1988-98.

THE LEADERS ■ HEALTH & SAFETY

Publications: Contributor to 'Litigation Practice' (Sweet and Maxwell). Regularly contributes articles to legal journals on topical health and safety issues.
Personal: Born 11 December 1949. Educated at St. Michael's College Leeds and University of London (Queen Mary College). Lives in Leeds.

GRICE, Helen
Masons, Manchester
(0161) 234 8234
helen.grice@masons.com
Specialisation: Solicitor in *Masons'* expanding national Health and Safety Team. Provides advice on the full range of health and safety issues including: proactive safety management systems, risk allocation in projects, crisis management guidance following major incidents, advice during police and Health and Safety Executive investigations and defending prosecutions. Also provides a stand-alone safety consultancy and training service on health and safety legal issues.
Prof. Memberships: Law Society. Member of the Institution of Occupational Safety and Health and the Society for Radiological Protection.
Career: Worked as a health and safety professional for British Nuclear Fuels plc at Sellafield for 7 years before leaving to study law. Joined *Masons'* Leeds office in 1996 and became a specialist health and safety lawyer on qualification in 1998. Moved to *Masons'* Manchester office in July 2002.
Publications: Writes regularly for trade journals, and has recently written a chapter for Butterworths' forthcoming practitioner text: 'Corporate Manslaughter Service'.
Personal: Born 21 January 1966. Graduated from Bristol University in 1987 with a BSc in Physics and obtained a Diploma in Law in 1995 from the College of Law in York. Leisure pursuits include gardening, travelling and scuba diving. Married and lives in West Cumbria.

HAVARD, Robin
Morgan Cole, Cardiff
(029) 2038 5385

MCLOUGHLIN, Kevin
DLA, Sheffield
(08700) 111111

MCPHERSON, Lyn
Nabarro Nathanson, Sheffield
(0114) 279 4104
L.Mcpherson@nabarro.com
Specialisation: Health and safety criminal litigation, including advocacy; appeals against improvement/prohibition notices; fire certificate appeals;

statutory nuisance appeals; appearing at inquests; litigation in appeal courts. Due diligence on property/corporate transactions. General advisory work. Advises waste and manufacturing internationals.

PARRINGTON, Simon
Hill Dickinson, Chester
(01244) 896600
Specialisation: Personal injury specialist with an interest in health and safety. Much of his work is handling employers' liability and public liability for insurers but a significant portion of his work is in the handling of prosecutions brought by the Health and Safety Executive. He has been involved in a number of high profile prosecutions of major industrial companies including the Associated Octel case which settled law in relation to sections 2 and 3 of the Health & Safety at Work Act 1974 and other major cases concerning hazardous installations, construction, dangerous pathogens and GM crops.
Prof. Memberships: Law Society.
Career: Law Society's Civil Litigation committee member. Formerly member of Lord Woolf's working group on the fast track. Deputy District Judge. Admitted 1975. Partner *Hill Dickinson*.
Personal: Gardening, country sports, skiing, music, theatre.

REID, Ron
Shoosmiths, Northampton
(01604) 543000
Specialisation: Specialises in all health and safety issues, both contentious and non-contentious. Has led the launch of *Shoosmiths* Occupational Safety, a department dedicated to offering straightforward advice on all safety matters. Has set up a specialist training department to handle the requirements of national and international companies for in-house training from director to shop floor level. He is a regular speaker at conferences and seminars, often alongside senior Health & Safety Executive officials.
Prof. Memberships: Secretary to the Food Industrial Regional Safety Team, East Midlands and the Northamptonshire Occupational Safety and Health Association. Director of The Radon Council. Legal advisor to and Honorary Member of Executive Committee of Inter-Company Consumer Affairs Assocation, a trade association of Consumer Care Managers in the food and drinks manufacturing industry. Member of The Food Law Group.
Career: Qualified in 1983, having previously been a F.I.L.Ex. Joined *Shoosmiths & Harrison* in 1974. Became a Partner in 1985.

SCOGGINS, Mark
Fisher Scoggins LLP, London
(020) 7489 2035

SHEPHERD, Michael
Hammond Suddards Edge, Manchester
(0161) 830 5000

THOMAS, Margaret A M
Davies Arnold Cooper, London
(020) 7936 2222
Specialisation: Solicitor in Product Liability and Mass Tort. Principal area of practice is personal injury litigation with emphasis on asbestos related claims. Also represents defendants in health and safety prosecutions. Acted in numerous reported asbestos related cases. Clients include insurance companies.
Prof. Memberships: Member Law Society and Association of Women Solicitors.
Career: Qualified in 1977. Articled with *Cole and Cole*, Oxford 1971-75. Clerical Officer and subsequently HM Inspector of Health and Safety with the Health and Safety Executive 1976-81. Joined *Brian Thompson and Partners* as Assistant Solicitor 1981-83 and *Young Jones Hair and Co*. 1983-86. Joined *Davies Arnold Cooper* in 1986.
Personal: Born 26 July 1949. Educated at Oxford High School For Girls 1960-67 and University of Exeter 1968-71. LLB College of Law 1976 and Imperial College of Science and Technology 1979 (Advanced Certificate of Occupational Safety and Health). Leisure interests include playing classical music in various orchestras and chamber groups and singing in choirs large and small.

TYLER, Mark
CMS Cameron McKenna, London
(020) 7367 3000
mlt@cmck.com
Specialisation: Product liability and health and safety. Co-author of 'Product Safety' and 'Safer by Design'; consultant editor of 'Health and Safety Liability and Litigation'. Contributor to 'Buildings and Health: The Rosehaugh Guide to the Design Construction and Management of Buildings', 'A New Balance: A Guide for Property Owners and Developers', 'Environmental Issues in Construction' - CIRIA Special Report, CIOB Handbook Facilities Management and 'Medicines, Medical Devices and the Law', 'PLC Legal Risk Management Manual'.
Prof. Memberships: Law Society, Institution of Occupational Safety and Health (IOSH), CBI Health and Safety Panel, CBI Consumer Affairs Panel, International Association of Defense Counsel.
Career: Joined *McKenna & Co* in 1984; qualified in 1986; became Partner in 1992.

Personal: Born 10 October 1960. Educated at Borlase School, Marlow, Worcester College, Oxford and Kings College, London.

WATKINS, Gareth
Nabarro Nathanson, Sheffield
(0114) 279 4000
Specialisation: Head of Sheffield litigation department. Main area of practice is health and safety. Gives advice to clients on health and safety policies, organisation, inquests, public inquiries and Health and Safety at Work Act prosecutions. Lead partner for defendant in the Coal Industry Respiratory Disease Litigation, the largest multi-party trial to come before the English courts. Has published numerous papers and articles in professional journals, magazines and newspapers. Regular conference speaker. Edits the 'Encyclopedia of Health & Safety at Work' and published the 'Health and Safety Handbook' in 1997. Appointed Deputy District Judge 2000.

WOOD, David
Bevan Ashford, Bristol
(0117) 975 1635
david.wood@bevanashford.co.uk

HEALTHCARE

London: 404; The Regions: 405; Profiles: 407

Research approved by BMRB For this edition, Chambers' researchers conducted 6,582 interviews – 3,900 with law firms, 511 with barristers and 2,171 with clients. The validity of the research was scrutinised by BMRB International, who audited both the methodology and the results at our offices in London. They interviewed Chambers' researchers and cross-checked sample interviews. Details of the audit appear on page 7.

OVERVIEW Healthcare lawyers have been much in demand to ease the integration of health and social services through Section 31 (Partnership in Action) schemes and the implementation of Primary Care Trusts (PCTs). Another area of growth is private sector work, in part due to the gradual implementation of the Care Standards Act (which subjects private nursing and care home providers to new regulations). In addition, many firms without places on the NHSLA panel for clinical negligence claims have specialised increasingly in constitutional, commercial and PFI work, defining themselves as pure healthcare practices that are not tied to claims litigation. Meanwhile, some of those firms in the NHSLA circle have benefited, with the recruitment of the excluded firms' foremost practitioners. Further developments are awaited following the massive funding injection promised for the NHS.

This year, mental healthcare has merged considerably with health and social care thanks to the NHS shake-ups, in a bid to stop patients slipping through the system. The Human Rights Act has been the impetus for important reforms relating to issues such as consent to treatment, criteria for detention and patient confidentiality. The preparations for the new Mental Health Act have been the subject of lively debate. Although the individuals listed in this section of *Chambers* are without doubt at the top of the field, it should be noted that there is a large body of excellent work handled by lesser-known names like Tony Harbour and Camilla Parker, among dozens of others.

LONDON

HEALTHCARE ■ LONDON

1. Capsticks
2. Bevan Ashford
   Hempsons
3. Beachcroft Wansbroughs
4. Pinsent Curtis Biddle
   RadcliffesLeBrasseur

LEADING INDIVIDUALS

1. **LEIGH Bertie** Hempsons
2. **HOLMES John** Hempsons
   MASON David Capsticks
3. **FRANCIS Barry** Pinsent Curtis Biddle
4. **BARBER Janice** Hempsons
   BLACKWELL Hilary Capsticks
   BROADHURST Marisa Beachcroft Wansbroughs
   LESLIE Alex RadcliffesLeBrasseur
   SMITH Janice Capsticks
   SUMERLING Robert RadcliffesLeBrasseur
   WILDER Gay Browne Jacobson

This book is the product of 6,582 1/2 hour interviews. See p.7 for BMRB audit. Within each band, firms are listed alphabetically. See individuals' profiles p.407

CAPSTICKS (see firm details p.900) Exclusively dedicated to healthcare law, the firm has sustained its reputation as the number one NHS practice in the capital. Competitors praise its work in mental health, clinical negligence and its use of IT systems in particular, stressing its "*innovative, integrated approach*" across the board. The group is expanding into the private care homes market and advising on PFI projects, partnerships, PCT formation and LIFT schemes. On the litigation side this year, it represented the NHS in the Victoria Climbié Inquiry. **Janice Smith** (see p.409) is noted for her contributions to the clinical law team, while our interviewees deemed **Hilary Blackwell** (see p.407) to be "*good news – realistic and friendly.*" **David Mason**'s (see p.408) depth of experience remains respected. **Clients** Over 150 NHS bodies; some private sector work.

BEVAN ASHFORD (see firm details p.869) Our researchers were impressed with the clear communication between the firm's offices in London, Bristol and Birmingham. In London, the renowned Christian Dingwall is a "*figurehead*" for the firm but specialises purely in contentious work. Although the healthcare team lacks star individuals, it is recognised as attracting excellent coverage thanks to its "*fresh approach*" and "*tightly run ship.*" The firm covers the complete range of healthcare law from constitutional advice to LIFT and fertilisation issues, and has won provision of care contracts with local councils in view of the increasing partnership between health and social care.

HEMPSONS (see firm details p.989) The firm has a strong presence nationally, with the London branch winning the respect of many interviewees. Two thirds of its work is clinical negligence related to the Alder Hey organ retention scandal nationally, and its constitutional and commercial work on healthcare is also respected. The firm has recently recruited heavily while retaining its prestigious, well-known names, such as the clinical disciplinary expert, **Janice Barber** (see p.407). The "*formidable and inscrutable*" **Bertie Leigh** (see p.408) inspires both competitors and clients; he is "*a real lawyer's lawyer*" and a "*stalwart defender of the medical profession.*" Litigator and mental health expert **John Holmes** (see p.408) has impressed many interviewees with his "*always thoughtful and rounded approach*" to his cases. **Clients** Seven health authorities, 17 NHS Trusts and several major national NHS bodies; GPs.

BEACHCROFT WANSBROUGHS (see firm details p.22) Having lost its place on the NHSLA panel, the London branch of the firm has moved towards specialising in commercial work. Our interviewees judged the group as "*still a force*" with its considerable expertise. **Marisa Broadhurst** (see p.407) is working on major PPP/property work for NHS Estates. **Clients** Nationally, over 200 NHS bodies; some private work.

PINSENT CURTIS BIDDLE (see firm details p.1102) The advent of high-profile **Barry Francis** (see p.408) and his team has raised the profile of Pinsent Curtis Biddle in healthcare, and many recognised it as being the firm of choice when it comes to property, project and PFI work; "*you can't touch their PFI practice.*" The firm also specialises in employment and IT for healthcare bodies. **Clients** 15 NHS bodies; private clients.

RADCLIFFESLEBRASSEUR (see firm details p.1107) The merger in December 2001 has given RadcliffesLeBrasseur a London healthcare team of over 60 lawyers. Despite losing its place on the NHSLA panel, the firm covers the whole range of healthcare law and represents medical and dental defence organisations. Its involvement in care homes has grown and the mental health team is respected. Peers recommend **Robert Sumerling** (see p.409) and NHS employment expert **Alex Leslie** (see p.408). **Clients** NHS bodies; GPs; private providers.

OTHER NOTABLE PRACTITIONERS While Browne Jacobson is best known in the Midlands, it is expanding into London, where the "*excellent*" **Gay Wilder** (see p.409) runs the healthcare department. Peers warmly endorsed her sensitivity: she has "*a feel for what the clients want.*"

THE REGIONS ■ HEALTHCARE

THE SOUTH, THAMES VALLEY, SOUTH WEST & WALES

HEALTHCARE
■ SOUTH, THAMES VALLEY, SOUTH WEST & WALES

[1] **Bevan Ashford** Bristol
[2] **Beachcroft Wansbroughs** Bristol, Winchester
[3] **Brachers** Maidstone
Morgan Cole Cardiff

LEADING INDIVIDUALS
[1] **ANNANDALE Richard** Bevan Ashford
SHEATH John Brachers

This book is the product of 6,582 1/2 hour interviews. See p.7 for BMRB audit. Within each band, firms are listed alphabetically. See individuals' profiles p.407

BEVAN ASHFORD (see firm details p.869) Endorsed to our researchers as "*undoubted leaders in the South West,*" the Bristol office is "*strong across the board*" in healthcare. This year, the dedicated health and social care department, led by **Richard Annandale** (see p.407), has worked on Section 31 and LIFT schemes and advised on PCT formation. It has also won 22 PFI projects nationally. **Clients** Nationally, over 150 NHS bodies; 95% public sector.

BEACHCROFT WANSBROUGHS (see firm details p.860) Under the guidance of Nigel Montgomery, the firm has flourished in the region, with its presence on the NHSLA panel ensuring a high profile for its Bristol and Winchester offices. Alongside its clinical negligence work, the firm has been instructed by NHS Estates on property deals of over £400 million this year. It has also covered risk management and major PPP projects involving IP and IT procurement. **Clients** Over 150 NHS bodies.

BRACHERS (see firm details p.886) The firm's place on the NHSLA panel has been firmly secured, and three quarters of the work handled is clinical negligence. In general constitutional healthcare, the group works on PCTs, partnerships and PFI schemes, as well as mental health and employment issues. Head of department **John Sheath** (see p.409) was commended to our researchers as "*a good, strong litigator with the interests of the NHS at heart.*" **Clients** Over 20 NHS bodies; GPs.

MORGAN COLE (see firm details p.1075) The firm has restructured its healthcare group, which, led by Eve Piffaretti, advises on NHS law, mental health, fertility and genetics and community care law. The practice also covers employment law, IP, property and PFI/PPP work. Its litigation against the NHS for an IVF clinic regulator has been acclaimed. **Clients** 43 NHS bodies; private clients.

MIDLANDS & EAST ANGLIA

HEALTHCARE
■ MIDLANDS & EAST ANGLIA

[1] **Browne Jacobson** Birmingham, Nottingham
[2] **Bevan Ashford** Birmingham
Mills & Reeve Cambridge
Weightman Vizards Birmingham

LEADING INDIVIDUALS
[1] **BARBER Paul** Bevan Ashford
PICKUP Raith Mills & Reeve
YEAMAN Anthony Weightman Vizards

This book is the product of 6,582 1/2 hour interviews. See p.7 for BMRB audit. Within each band, firms are listed alphabetically. See individuals' profiles p.407

BROWNE JACOBSON (see firm details p.891) The firm has emerged this year as the leader in the Midlands, satisfying clients with its "*good professional advice.*" The firm handles the bulk of its healthcare work in Nottingham under the leadership of Paul Southby, but is expanding in Birmingham and London. An NHSLA panel member, it has built a substantial clinical negligence department. Recent highlights include acting for a NHS Trust in the first ever appeal against the Broadcasting Standards Commission and advising on on-site residential PFI schemes for trusts. IP work for trusts and NHS employment advice also feature in the workload. Clients pronounce the team "*extremely accessible and deadline-focused – other firms are nowhere near as efficient or responsive.*" **Clients** 70 NHS healthcare bodies.

BEVAN ASHFORD (see firm details p.869) Since the firm opened its Birmingham practice in May 2001, it has challenged the Midlands market with the same breadth of services as its more established offices in the South. The firm's PFI work is highly rated, and **Paul Barber** (see p.407) is noted by peers as experienced in litigation and mental health issues.

MILLS & REEVE (see firm details p.1071) The firm spans the whole range of healthcare issues including PFI/property work, e-government, PCT formation and clinical negligence litigation, but it is **Raith Pickup**'s (see p.409) Cambridge PFI practice which draws the most comment from our interviewees. This PFI work is "*on a completely different level from anyone else in East Anglia.*" Although the Birmingham office has lost its place on the NHSLA panel, this branch, under Sheila Waddington, has gained contracts with 40 local councils in an initiative to amalgamate public sector work in the light of PCTs and partnerships. **Clients** Over 140 public sector bodies including over 100 NHS bodies.

WEIGHTMAN VIZARDS (see firm details p.1183) The merged firm of Weightman Vizards now boasts a national healthcare practice uniting two NHSLA panel firms and spanning London, Birmingham, Leicester and Liverpool, with Richard Foster as the national head of department. It is home to **Tony Yeaman** (see p.409), acquired from Beachcroft Wansbroughs in London, a respected and knowledgeable lawyer whom peers agree has "*a wide perspective*" of the field. While providing the full range of healthcare law advice, 15% of the firm's work is clinical negligence, the latter part producing work on high-profile cases. **Clients** 38 NHS bodies.

www.ChambersandPartners.com

405

HEALTHCARE ■ THE NORTH

THE NORTH

HEALTHCARE
■ THE NORTH

1. **Beachcroft Wansbroughs** Leeds
   Eversheds Leeds, Newcastle upon Tyne
   Hempsons Harrogate, Manchester
   Hill Dickinson Liverpool, Manchester
2. **George Davies** Manchester

LEADING INDIVIDUALS

1. **BATCHELOR Claire** George Davies
   HALLATT Diane Beachcroft Wansbroughs
   HARRISON Frances Hempsons
   MOWAT Allan Hill Dickinson
   PARKER Adrian Hempsons

This book is the product of 6,582 1/2 hour interviews. See p.7 for BMRB audit. Within each band, firms are listed alphabetically. See individuals' profiles p.407

BEACHCROFT WANSBROUGHS (see firm details p.860) The firm was recommended by competitors for its high-quality advice on a range of general healthcare issues, despite losing its place on the NHSLA panel. Head of department **Diane Hallatt** (see p.408) "*knows her stuff*" and is particularly rated for her clinical negligence work.

EVERSHEDS (see firm details p.949) Peers contend that, with its commercial outlook, the firm "*has thrown itself into the healthcare market.*" It specialises in project/PFI work, the formation of PCTs, partnerships and litigation. The Newcastle branch, headed by David Weatherburn, is on the NHSLA panel, while the Leeds branch is dubbed "*switched on*" and attracts clients from the Midlands. **Clients** Over 40 NHS bodies.

HEMPSONS (see firm details p.986) The firm has created a NHS constitutional and commercial law team by merging its community care and healthcare departments, which has seen the team in the North expand by 12 new fee earners this year. **Adrian Parker** (see p.408), acquired from Bevan Ashford, is a "*procurement guru,*" praised by clients as responsive and accessible. The team, headed by Louise Holroyd in Harrogate and the "*extremely competent*" **Frances Harrison** (see p.408) in Manchester, specialises in PCT and SHA formation and partnerships. **Clients** 52 NHS bodies.

HILL DICKINSON (see firm details p.995) Adjudged a focused healthcare team, led by "*experienced NHS lawyer*" Allan Mowat (see p.408), it has seen a growth in its workload since retaining its position on the NHSLA panel. It provides the full spectrum of services to the NHS, with an emphasis this year on PCT work and litigation, in which field Mowat has been acting locally in the Alder Hey organ retention enquiry. **Clients** Over 50 NHS bodies.

GEORGE DAVIES (see firm details p.968) Although a smaller offering than others in our table, the firm continues to attract a high level of commendation. A member of the NHSLA panel, the firm is strong not only in litigation (where it is best known for working on the Shipman Inquiry) but also in constitutional work and clinical governance. Head of department **Claire Batchelor** (see p.407), who specialises in risk management, is respected by competitors as a "*knowledgeable*" lawyer, skilled at offering clients a tailored service.

MENTAL HEALTH: REPRESENTING PATIENTS

LEADING INDIVIDUALS

1. **SCOTT-MONCRIEFF Lucy** Scott-Moncrieff, Harbour & Sinclair
2. **EDWARDS Peter** Peter Edwards Law
   MACKINTOSH Nicola Mackintosh Duncan

See individuals' profiles p.407

Lucy Scott-Moncrieff Unanimously acknowledged as "*certainly the best legal aid practitioner working on the individual's behalf,*" peers claim Scott-Moncrieff inspires the utmost confidence. She is at the cutting edge of mental health reforms, initiating argument for the rights of restrained patients to refuse treatment and for compliant patients to be discharged if accompanied. "*A fierce and passionate advocate for her clients, the whole world knows Lucy.*"

Peter Edwards "*The Scott-Moncrieff of the North,*" he has a "*huge reputation*" as "*an honest man at the cutting edge.*" He represents individual patients "*conscientiously*" in light of the Mental Health Act and the Human Rights Act, and in 2001 was elected President of the Mental Health Lawyers Association.

Nicola Mackintosh Forging ahead in her niche of representing unrestrained patients, she handles "*a huge volume of case work*" with a consistently positive attitude. She acts on judicial reviews for patients suffering from healthcare rationing as well as running a well-known social care practice. Market sources endorse her as "*committed to her clients.*"

MENTAL HEALTH: REPRESENTING HOSPITALS

LEADING INDIVIDUALS

1. **ELDERGILL Anselm** Anselm Eldergill
2. **PARSONS Andrew** RadcliffesLeBrasseur
3. **IRONS Ashley** Reid Minty

See individuals' profiles p.407

Anselm Eldergill (see p.407) The sage of mental health law, he is renowned for being "*hugely clever*" and "*a highly respected academic and commentator*" with "*the best theoretical approach.*" A heavyweight practitioner who chairs and is involved in judicial enquiries nationwide, he advises foreign states and is currently redrafting Mental Health Act proposals for the Department of Health.

Andrew Parsons (see p.409) With an enormous reputation in the field, sources agree that he is "*always readily accessible and has a clear, broad knowledge of mental health law that is rare.*" "*A tough litigator,*" he represents a large number of NHS Trusts and private providers, and works for judicial reviews examining human rights issues among others.

Ashley Irons (see p.408) Noted by competitors as a "*model*" in mental health, he has been representing special hospitals and advising on issues such as patient confidentiality and compulsory treatment. He is also involved in issues surrounding learning disabilities and the integration of health and social care.

THE LEADERS IN HEALTHCARE

ANNANDALE, Richard
Bevan Ashford, Bristol
(0117) 975 1656
richard.annandale@bevanashford.co.uk
Specialisation: Partner in the Public Sector Division specialising in clinical governance, medical law and the law relating to reproductive and medical technologies. Experience includes working on three Group Actions involving the treatment of patients with cancer where independent reports, involving reports commissioned by the Chief Medical Officer, led to radical changes in national standards of clinical practice and governance. Also advised nationally on issues arising from the retention of organs at post mortem which have resulted in governmental reports and summit called by the Chief Medical Officer and will result in radical changes to the law. Recent work includes the Re V posthumous insemination case and advice to centres licensed under the Human Fertilization and Embryology Act 1990 on regulatory and criminal issues.
Career: Qualified 1977. Partner since 1993. Director of QRM Healthcare Limited (*Bevan Ashford's* healthcare risk management company) since 1993.
Personal: Educated at Manchester University (LLB) 1968-71.

BARBER, Janice
Hempsons, London
(020) 7839 0278
jcb@hempsons.co.uk
Specialisation: Managing Partner. Has wide experience of all areas of healthcare law, though she specialises in disciplinary and employment law. Has undertaken variously: medico-legal advice to and representation of defendant Health Authorities, NHS Trusts and individual practitioners covering all areas of hospital and general practice; professional disciplinary and other tribunals and statutory inquiries; defence of serious criminal charges and employment law, particularly in relation to hospital practice. Leading cases include R v Cox 1992: manslaughter, euthanasia, acting for the defendant; Howard v E Dorset Health Authority 1993: hospital, negligence, applicability of res ipsa loquitur principle in medical negligence cases, for the defendant; Thomson v Blake-James CA 1997: re. forseeability; WG Dick v Brookmount Estates Limited & Ford Sellar Morris Developments Limited CA 1992: successful recovery of fees, under Order 14, acting for Plaintiff, a quantity surveyor; The Orkney Child Abuse Inquiry, Stanley Royd Hospital Inquiry: Salmonella Inquiry, led to the lifting of Crown Immunity for hospital kitchens and the BSE Inquiry; United Leeds Hospital v Duncan Walker 1997: Disciplinary Inquiry under HSG(95)25 and subsequent appeal to the Secretary of State.
Career: Graduated with a 1st Class Hons BA at the University of Reading. Was articled at *Hempsons* and admitted in 1983. Has been a partner since 1984. Often conducts seminars and lectures in all the specialist areas of practice set out above.

BARBER, Paul
Bevan Ashford, Birmingham
(0121) 634 5006
paul.barber@bevanashford.co.uk
See under Clinical Negligence, p.149

BATCHELOR, Claire
George Davies, Manchester
(0161) 236 8992
Specialisation: Partner and head of healthcare/clinical negligence department. Specialises in defendant healthcare related law advising NHS Trusts, PCT's and Health Authorities. Principal area of work is in the field of clinical negligence handling a wide spectrum of claims including complex high value obstetric and neurosurgical claims. Work also involves all areas of NHS advisory work including administrative law, representation at inquests and advice on risk management strategies.
Prof. Memberships: Law Society and Manchester Medico-Legal Society.
Career: Joined *George Davies* in 1985. Qualified in 1987 and became a Partner in 1991. Deputy District Judge.
Personal: Educated at Manchester High School for Girls. Bristol University 1980-83 LLB. Trinity Hall Cambridge 1983-84 LLM. Leisure interests include the arts, walking and yoga. Lives in Altrincham, Cheshire.

BLACKWELL, Hilary
Capsticks, London
(020) 8780 2211
h.blackwell@capsticks.co.uk
Specialisation: Partner specialising in commercial, property and administrative law cases on behalf of the NHS, including acute hospital PFI and continuing care schemes. Currently Lead Partner on £30m Brighton Children's Hospital PFI reprovision project. Also acting on the first joint NHS/local authority PFI for Neighbourhood Resource Centres, Lead Partner on a second wave NHS Lift Pilot and acting on a wide range of section 31 agreements for partnership working between NHS and local authorities.
Prof. Memberships: Law Society.
Career: LLB (Hons) University of Bristol, College of Law, Guildford. Articled *Veale Benson* (now *Veale Wasborough*). 1992 joined *Capsticks* to head Property and Commercial Department, 1993 Partner. Member of firm's management committee.

BROADHURST, Marisa
Beachcroft Wansbroughs, London
(020) 7242 1011
mbroadhurst@bwlaw.co.uk
Specialisation: All aspects of estates and commercial property transactions, with particular emphasis on development. Currently lead partner acting for the Secretary of State for Health on the public private partnership involving the disposal of £400 million worth of NHS properties and the Trading Group.
Prof. Memberships: Law Society, Women in Property
Career: Admitted 1970, articles at *Max Bitel Greene & Co*, a Partner from 1970-71, the Greater London Council from 1971-76, the London Residuary Body from 1988-89 and *Beachcroft Wansbroughs* from 1989 to present, a Partner from 1991, elected Regional Senior Partner for London, Fetter Lane in 2001.
Personal: Born in Spain. Educated in Spain, France and at The Convent of Our Lady of Sion London. Interests include cinema and theatre, travelling and reading. Lives in Wimbledon, London.

EDWARDS, Peter
Peter Edwards Law, Hoylake
(0151) 632 6699

ELDERGILL, Anselm
Anselm Eldergill, London
(020) 7284 1006
medicolegal@hotmail.com
Specialisation: Specialist in mental health law. Practice includes NHS and social services inquiries, legislative drafting, conferences, lecturing, policy development, drafting, representation and training for NHS trusts and local authorities, agency and consultancy work. Chairman, Mental Health Act Commission Legal & Ethical Committee, 1997-98. Discussant, XXIIIrd International Congress on Law and Mental Health, Sorbonne (1998). Chairman, IBC Conference, Mental Health Law, Regents Park (1998). Keynote speaker, 1st National Conference on Risk Management in Mental Health, Royal College of Physicians (1998). Keynote speaker, Institute of Mental Health Law Conference on Mental Health Review Tribunals, Law Society's Hall (1998). Speaker, Institute of Mental Health Act Practitioners Conference on the Code of Practice, Royal College of Physicians (1999). Speaker, Infolog Conference, Mental Health 2000 and Beyond, Barbican Centre (2000). Speaker, Institute of Mental Health Act Practitioners' Mental Health Act Green Paper Conference, Royal College of Physicians (2000). Speaker, Ad Idem Conference, The Human Rights Act 1998 and Mental Health Law, Royal College of Physicians (2000). Speaker, Institute of Mental Health Conference, Lessons from recent homicide inquiries, King's Fund Centre (2000). Speaker, Institute of Mental Health Act Practitioners' Annual Conference, Legal remedies for patients, Royal College of Physicians (2000). Keynote address, IBC Conference, Mental Health Law: The Implications of the Review Explained, London (2000). Speaker, Capital Conference, Mental Health Services and the Law, London (2000). Keynote address, Mental Health Lawyers Association Annual Conference, Regent's Park (2000). Keynote speaker, Laing-Buisson Conference, The Review of Mental Health Legislation, London (2000). Consultant, Department of Health - Legislation Branch, Reform of the Mental Health Act 1983 (2001). Visiting Professor in Mental Health Law, University of Northumbria (2001). Keynote speaker, Reforming the Mental Health Act 1983, Institute of Mental Health Act Practitioners' Annual Conference, Royal College of Physicians (2001). Speaker, Institute of Mental Health Conference, Reforming the Mental Health Act 1983, King's Fund Centre (2001). Speaker, European Convention on Human Rights and Mental Health, Institute of Mental Health Act Practitioners, London (2001). External Confidential Review of the X Eating Disorders Unit (2001). Law Society video, Human Rights and Mental Health (2001). Legal chairman of eight independent NHS and social services inquiries into homicides committed by psychiatric patients (1999-2001). Advising foreign states on the reform of their mental health legislation (1999-2001). Textbook (Mental Health Review Tribunals - Law & Practice) reprinted (2001); Advisor, Mental Health Bill, Department of Health (2001-02); Legal chairman of two further independent NHS homicide inquiries (2002); UK's first Visiting Professorship in Mental Health Law (2002); Speaker, Law Society Royal College of Psychiatrists Conference on Mental Health Law Reform, London (2002); Speaker, Institute of Mental Health Act Practitioners' Annual Conference, London (2002).
Career: London School of Economics, Oxford University, The College of Law. Mental Health Act Commissioner, 1992-2000. Alexander Maxwell Law Trust Scholar. David Hallett Prize for Government. Visiting Professor in Mental Health Law, University of Northumbria.
Publications: Mental Health Review Tribunals - Law & Practice (Sweet & Maxwell, 1998, lxxvii, 1333pp., nominated for a Nobel Prize). 'The Falling Shadow and the Deteriorating Patient' Mental Health Act Commission Discussion Paper, 1998. 'Psychopathy, the law and individual rights' Princeton University Law Journal, Volume III, Issue 2, Spring 1999. 'The legal logistics of independent inquiries: Common steps and principles for navigating through tragedy' British Journal of Health Care Management, May 1998. 'A greater evil' The Guardian, 20 July 1999. 'Reforming Inquiries following Homicides' Journal of Mental Health Law, October 1999. 'The law and individual rights' in The treatment of the personality disordered offender (ed. R Blackburn, et al., Butterworth-

HEALTHCARE ■ THE LEADERS

Heinemann, 2000). 'The European Convention and Mental Health Review Tribunals' Journal of Mental Health Law, June 2001. 'White Paper: Reform of the Mental Health Act' (Editorial) Journal of Forensic Psychiatry, August 2001. The Mental Health Act Commission, Ninth Biennial Report, 'Journal of Mental Health Law', February 2002; The Mental Health Act Commission, 'Journal of Forensic Psychiatry', March 2002; The Legal Structure of Mental Health Services, 'Journal of Mental Health Law', September 2002.

FRANCIS, Barry
Pinsent Curtis Biddle, London
(020) 7418 7340
barry.francis@pinsents.com

Specialisation: Public/private interface transactions including PPP, PFI projects and other commercial transactions in the health and other public sectors; including public sector/private sector joint ventures, outsourcing contracts and procurement and administrative law advice. Current projects include major hospital building and services projects (PFI). Regular speaker at conferences and seminars. Contributor to a range of specialist publications including Butterworths' 'PFI Manual'. A member of the editorial board of 'The PFI Report'.
Prof. Memberships: Law Society.
Career: Admitted 1977, at *Beachcroft Hyman Isaacs* (now *Beachcroft Wansbroughs*). Associate 1979-80, Partner 1980-99, Managing Partner *Buchanan Ingersoll* 2000. Partner and Head of Major Projects (London) *Pinsent Curtis Biddle* 2001.
Personal: Born 1953. Educated at Enfield Grammar School and University of Bristol. Interests include travel, history and food.

HALLATT, Diane
Beachcroft Wansbroughs, Leeds
(0113) 251 4700
dhallatt@bwlaw.co.uk

Specialisation: Partner specialising in medical negligence inquests, major untoward incidents and all aspects of medical and health service law. Has 22 years experience in the public sector, 17 years for the NHS and has a wide range of experience in public administrative law/corporate and clinical governance issues. Has defended many judicial reviews, health and safety prosecutions and has advised in several major untoward incidents, including Hillsborough, Allitt, Kiberu and Jenkinson. Also advises in mental health, consent, children, care in the community, data prosecution and ethical issues.
Career: Qualified 1980. Trent Regional Health Authority 1986-89. Partner at *Oxley & Coward* 1989-95. Partner at *Wansbroughs Willey Hargrave* from February 1995. 1999 Partner in *Beachcroft Wansbroughs*.

HARRISON, Frances
Hempsons, Manchester
(0161) 228 0011
fah@hempsons.co.uk

Specialisation: Partner in Medical & Healthcare Department and Senior Partner in the firm's Manchester office. Principal area of practice is the law relating to hospitals and general practice. Work includes medico-legal advice to, and representation of, Health Authorities, NHS Trusts and individual practitioners in medical negligence actions. Advises on ethics in relation to healthcare and also concerning the conduct of, and representation at, enquiries. Other main areas of practice are defamation and the law relating to children. Major cases include Re: A (Minor) Conjoined Twins: (seperation) CA Sept 2000.
Prof. Memberships: Law Society.
Career: Qualified in 1978 and joined *Hempsons*. Became a Partner in 1982. Moved to Manchester in 1990 to lead the firm's Manchester office.

HOLMES, John
Hempsons, London
(020) 7839 0278
j.holmes@hempsons.co.uk
See under Clinical Negligence, p.152

IRONS, Ashley
Reid Minty, London
(020) 7318 4444

Specialisation: Specialises in mental health law advice to managers and doctors in public and private sector hospitals. His work covers detained, including forensic, patients, as well as those who are informal. In the last two years, he has been instructed by hospitals in over 28 Judicial Review challenges. No policy written by him has ever been successfully challenged. He represents hospital clients at public and other inquiries, MHRTs, and claims. In October 2001, he represented Broadmoor Hospital in the widely reported Wilkinson case under which the Court of Appeal held that patients' human rights were not adequately safeguarded under S.58 of the Mental Health Act. This is the leading authority on capacity and compulsory treatment of detained patients. He represented Ashworth Hospital in the House of Lords on 6 March 2002 concerning the 'Daily Mirror' challenge to a Court of Appeal decision whereby they must disclose the source from whom they obtained (and paid) for clinical notes of a patient (Judgment awaited). This case is already the leading authority on medical records confidentiality. He lectures widely at national conferences on mental health issues and writes two quarterly mental health law newsletters, including for Informa's Medical Law Monitor.

LEIGH, Bertie
Hempsons, London
(020) 7839 0278
mamsl@hempsons.co.uk

Specialisation: Senior Partner. Principal area of practice is medical law, with particular interest in cases involving obstetrics, anaesthesia, paediatrics, orthopaedics, neurosurgery and general practice. Other main area of expertise is National Health Service Acts and associated Regulations. Has dealt with a number of Court of Appeal cases including Gregory v Pembrokeshire (1989), Forest (1991), and Bull & Wakeham v Devon Health Authority (1989), DeFreitas v O'Brien (1994), R v Nottingham HA (1996), Re MB (1997) and Thomas v Brighton HA in the House of Lords (1998). Major clients include the Association of Anaesthetists and the Royal College of Paediatrics and Child Health of which he is an Hon. Fellow. Author of chapters in 'Ethics & Obstetrics & Gynaecology' (RCOG 1994) and 'Safe Practice in Obstetrics & Gynaecology' (1994), Dewhursts 'Obstetrics' 1999 and 'Neonatology' (Ed Roberton & Rennie) 1997. Lectures regularly to lawyers and doctors. Delivered the John Snow Lecture to the Association of Anaesthetists in 1999
Prof. Memberships: Medico-Legal Society.
Career: Qualified in 1976, having joined *Hempsons* in 1973. Became a Partner in 1977.
Personal: Born 30 August 1946. Educated at St. Christopher School, Letchworth 1960-65 and the University of East Anglia 1966-69. Lives in Clapham.

LESLIE, Alex
RadcliffesLeBrasseur, London
(020) 7227 6706
alex.leslie@rlb-law.com

Specialisation: Partner with 20 years' experience in health service law. Principal area of practice is employment and regulatory work in the NHS. Work for NHS and commercial clients in employment law. Important cases include acting for the NHS trust in Re: G, the Health Authority in Re: C and the Health Authority in X v A Health Authority. Has presented lectures and seminars for Health Services clients. He has appeared on the BBC Select TV/Legal Network on a number of topics and contributed a chapter to a textbook on NHS Law and Practice.
Prof. Memberships: Law Society.
Career: Admitted in February 1981. Partner in *Le Brasseur J Tickle* since 1985. Born 1956. Graduated LLB (Hons) from Birmingham University in 1977.
Personal: Sailing.

MACKINTOSH, Nicola
Mackintosh Duncan, London
(020) 7357 6464

MASON, David
Capsticks, London
(020) 8780 4701
dmason@capsticks.co.uk

Specialisation: Now concentrating on healthcare litigation and advisory work specialising in public law, mental health and inquiries after many years of mainly defending clinical negligence claims. Recent cases include acting as advocate for all four NHS bodies involved in the Victoria Climbie Inquiry; successfully defending two different judicial reviews arising as advocate in a successful benefits appeal tribunal following the withdrawal of benefits from 80 residents in a learning disability scheme: the successful appeal saved the NHS £1.7 million per annum. Was the only defence lawyer on Lord Woolf's Steering Group for Medical Negligence and was the defence Solicitor on the Clinical Disputes Forum from 1996-2001. Also lectures to senior health service managers and clinicians and appears on radio and television on a variety of medico-legal topics. He is Honorary Legal Advisor to the College of Health.
Career: Called to the Bar 1984. Employed barrister with *Thomas Watts & Co* 1986-88. Joined *Capsticks* in 1988 as employed Barrister. Requalified as Solicitor and became a Partner in 1990. Elected Fellow of the Society for Advanced Legal Studies 1998.
Publications: Co-author of 'Litigation - A risk management guide for midwives', published by the Royal College of Midwives. He was also co-author of the Clinical Disputes forum 'Pre-Action Protocol for the Resolution of Clinical Disputes' and the CDF 'Guidelines on experts' discussions in the context of clinical disputes'.
Personal: Born 1955. Attended Winchester College 1969-73, then Oriel College, Oxford 1974-77 (MA in experimental psychology). Dip L (City University) 1983. Lives in Wimbledon.

MOWAT, Allan
Hill Dickinson, Liverpool
(0151) 236 5400

Specialisation: Head of Health Department at *Hill Dickinson*, specialising in healthcare law, particularly medical negligence, nursing home registration and advisory work for NHS bodies. Clients include NHS Trusts and PCTs, Health Authorities, the NHSLA, the National Care Standards Commission and healthcare related insurance companies. Successfully defended the NHS in Benzodiazepine class action. Appeared on behalf of Alder Hey Childrens Hospital at the Redfern Inquiry and currently acting on behalf of the NHS in the organ retention group action Royal Liverpool Childrens Litigation.
Prof. Memberships: Law Society, Liverpool Law Society.
Career: Qualified in 1980; in-house legal advisor to Mersey Regional Health Authority 1982-90; Partner *Hill Dickinson Davis Campbell* 1990; Appointed Head of Health Department at *Hill Dickinson* 1994.

PARKER, Adrian
Hempsons, Harrogate
(01423) 842557
a.parker@hempsons.co.uk

Specialisation: Team leader of NHS Commercial and Constitutional Law

THE LEADERS ■ HEALTHCARE

Team. Specialist in non-contentious commercial advice to NHS bodies. Principal areas of practice include: EU procurement law, statutory powers and corporate governance, contracting and outsourcing, grant funding, equipment PFI schemes.
Career: Articled at *Wansbroughs Willey Hargrave* (now *Beachcroft Wansbroughs*). Admitted 1994. *Bevan Ashford* 1994-2001. Joined *Hempsons* in 2001.
Personal: Educated at Durham University (History and Philosophy).

PARSONS, Andrew
RadcliffesLeBrasseur, London
(020) 7227 7282
andrew.parsons@rlb-law.com
Specialisation: Partner in Litigation Department (Head of Health Marketing Group). Specialises in healthcare law, especially mental health law and human rights. Advises extensively on the administration and powers of the NHS. Extensive experience of psychiatric related issues and advocacy at inquests. Advises on relationships with local authorities and other healthcare contracts. Has wide experience in drug related fatal cases and drug testing protocols. Acts for Health Authorities and NHS Trusts, Teaching Hospitals, private clinics and health insurers. Also acts for institutional, property investment funds and NHS clients in connection with property and general commercial litigation matters.
Prof. Memberships: Law Society, City of Westminster and Holborn Law Society and Royal Society of Medicine.
Career: Qualified in 1987 having been at *Radcliffes* since 1985. Became a Partner in 1992.
Publications: Author of 'Tenant Default Under Commercial Leases' (1993, 3rd edition published 1999). 'Labour Ward Manual' (legal chapter), 'Mental Health Law Compendium' (2000), and 'Health Service Law' (mental health chapter, Butterworths 2001). Lectures widely to doctors, nurses and other NHS staff.
Personal: Born 5 February 1963. Educated at Norwich School 1971-80 and the University of Reading 1981-84. Leisure pursuits include music, sports and handicrafts. Member of Mensa and RAC. Lives in London.

PICKUP, Raith
Mills & Reeve, Cambridge
(01223) 222283
raith.pickup@mills-reeve.com
Specialisation: Head of PFI at *Mills & Reeve*. Considerable experience of advising on capital projects in the NHS. Completed PFI schemes for several NHS trusts and the NHS Executive with projects including acute facilities, mental health schemes, staff accommodation, nurse training facilities and car parks. Work includes joint ventures between NHS trusts and other public sector bodies or the private sector; EC procurement and tendering; Concode compliance, income generation schemes. Is a regular speaker at NHS seminars.

SCOTT-MONCRIEFF, Lucy
Scott-Moncrieff, Harbour & Sinclair, London
(020) 7485 5588

SHEATH, John
Brachers, Maidstone
(01622) 680401
johnsheath@brachers.co.uk
See under Clinical Negligence, p.155

SMITH, Janice
Capsticks, London
(020) 8780 2211
Specialisation: Partner in clinical law department specialising in clinical negligence claims with a particular interest in cases involving obstetrics, orthopaedics and A&E, also deals with a variety of NHS advisory matters. Co-ordinates *Capsticks*' clinical governance programme including running training for Trust Boards. Advises Trusts on their risk management arrangements, particularly helping to identify high risk specialities and develop incident reporting schemes. Regular lecturer on *Capsticks*' Diploma in Risk Management and also lectures on various aspects of medical law.
Prof. Memberships: Law Society and its committees concerning issues of clinical negligence.
Career: Qualified in 1985. Assistant Solicitor with *Herbert Smith* 1985-86. Assistant solicitor at *Beckman & Beckman* 1987-90. Joined *Capsticks* in 1990 and became a partner in 1991, member of firm's Management Committee.
Personal: Born 24 March 1960. Attended Tunbridge Wells Grammar School for Girls 1971-78, then Leeds University 1978-81 before taking a year out to work for the Boys Brigade. Vice President of London District Boys' Brigade and Director of Oasis Trust. Lives in Bicester.

SUMERLING, Robert
RadcliffesLeBrasseur, London
(020) 7227 6710
robert.sumerling@rlb-law.com
Specialisation: Major and varied experience in most fields of health related law, including administrative law. Current specialisms are mental health, fitness to practise defence at GMC and GDC, and general practice partnership. Frequent lecturer to management and clinical staff. Mental Health Review Tribunal part-time legal member.
Prof. Memberships: The Law Society. Institute of Mental Health Act Practitioners.
Career: Admitted in 1969. Partner in 1975.

WILDER, Gay
Browne Jacobson, London
(020) 7539 4950
gwilder@brownej.co.uk
Specialisation: Partner in Medical Negligence Department and Head of Health Law Group. 20 years' experience in health law and advises health providers on a wide range of medico-legal issues, NHS and public law. Special interest in clinical risk management. Regular contributor of articles to health publications and a frequent speaker at conferences and seminars on medico-legal issues.
Prof. Memberships: Law Society.
Career: Qualified in 1982. With *Hempsons* 1980-88 (Partner from 1985). Joined *Beachcroft Stanleys* in 1988 and became a Partner in 1989. Joined *Browne Jacobson* 1 July 1999.
Personal: Educated at Reading University 1976-79 (LLB).

YEAMAN, Anthony
Weightman Vizards, Birmingham
(0121) 200 8108
tony.yeaman@weightmanvizards.com
Specialisation: Partner in Health Law Group. Principal area of practice is high value and complex medical negligence, handling claims for Health Service bodies and advising on all aspects of health service law, particularly issues concerning patient care consent and complaints. Has dealt with multi-party litigation, structured settlements and internal NHS inquiries. Acts for health service bodies throughout England and including major teaching hospitals. Frequent speaker at conferences and seminars on medico-legal and related issues. *Weightman Vizards* is on the panel for the NHS Litigation Authority (NHSLA).
Prof. Memberships: Law Society and Birmingham Medico-Legal Society.
Career: Qualified in 1988. Assistant Regional Solicitor to former Wessex Regional Health Authority 1988-94. Joined *Beachcroft Stanleys* in 1994, before joining *Weightman Vizards* in 2001.
Personal: Born 11 November 1961. Educated at Middlesex University 1983-85, The College of Law, Guildford 1985-86 and Bournemouth University 1991-99 MBA.

HUMAN RIGHTS

London: 410; The Regions: 411; Profiles: 412

Research approved by BMRB For this edition, **Chambers'** researchers conducted 6,582 interviews – 3,900 with law firms, 511 with barristers and 2,171 with clients. The validity of the research was scrutinised by BMRB International, who audited both the methodology and the results at our offices in London. They interviewed **Chambers'** researchers and cross-checked sample interviews. Details of the audit appear on page 7.

OVERVIEW The past 12 months have been eventful ones for lawyers involved in civil liberties work. Post September 11th, many have been busy representing individuals and organisations that fell foul of subsequent anti-terrorist policy. The work of a number of human rights lawyers resulted in a ruling delivered by the special immigration appeals commission in July 2002, stating that the detention of 11 Muslim men under the Anti-Terrorism, Crime and Security Act 2001 was unlawful. After sustained effort, practitioners from the UK aided in the abolition of the mandatory death sentence in several Caribbean countries this year. The case of Diane Pretty has forced examination of the relationship between the HRA and the right to die with dignity. Prisoners rights, death in custody and actions against the police are main areas of focus for the majority of practitioners, whilst the related fields of employment, immigration, discrimination and mental health have significant civil liberties elements. This section is concerned predominantly with lawyers involved in traditional civil liberties work. Commercial clients should note, however, that lawyers such as Andrew Lidbetter of Herbert Smith and Michael Smyth of Clifford Chance also take an active interest in the implications of the HRA.

LONDON

HUMAN RIGHTS
LONDON

1. Bindman & Partners
2. Bhatt Murphy
3. Christian Fisher Khan
   Hickman & Rose
4. Birnberg Peirce & Partners
   Deighton Guedalla
5. Simons Muirhead & Burton
   Taylor Nichol
   Thanki Novy Taube
   Winstanley-Burgess
6. Irwin Mitchell
   Scott-Moncrieff, Harbour & Sinclair

LEADING INDIVIDUALS

1. **BHATT Raju** Bhatt Murphy
   BINDMAN Geoffrey Bindman & Partners
   GROSZ Stephen Bindman & Partners
   PEIRCE Gareth Birnberg Peirce & Partners
2. **CHRISTIAN Louise** Christian Fisher Khan
   KHAN Sadiq Christian Fisher Khan
   MACHOVER Daniel Hickman & Rose
   MURPHY Fiona Bhatt Murphy
   NICHOL James Taylor Nichol
3. **CHARALAMBOUS Louis** CCL
   CONRATHE Paul Coningsbys
   CREIGHTON Simon Bhatt Murphy
   DEIGHTON Jane Deighton Guedalla
   KHAN Imran Imran Khan & Partners
   SCHWARZ Michael Bindman & Partners
   WILLIS-STEWART Marcia Thanki Novy Taube
   WISTRICH Harriet Thanki Novy Taube

UP AND COMING
   KING Vicky Thanki Novy Taube
   MURPHY Tony Bindman & Partners

This book is the product of 6,582 1/2 hour interviews. See p.7 for BMRB audit.
Within each band, firms are listed alphabetically. See individuals' profiles p.412

BINDMAN & PARTNERS (see firm details p.872) Its ability to deal with the full spectrum of human rights law has earned this outfit the title "*Rolls-Royce of firms*" amongst the civil liberties community. Size, resources and breadth of practice set it apart, and it is visible in actions against the police, public order work (handling cases relating to large-scale demonstrations), prison law, judicial review and mental health. Senior partner **Geoffrey Bindman** (see p.412) retains a formidable reputation for human rights work, while judicial review specialist **Stephen Grosz** (see p.413) is described as a "*doyen of his field.*" **Michael Schwarz** (see p.414) is renowned for his public order and environmental work, and "*rigorous and committed*" **Tony Murphy** (see p.414) is rapidly making a name for himself in actions against the police. The firm represented Lord Melchett and Greenpeace on charges of destroying GM crops. It also secured a landmark judgement in R v Sec State Home Department ex parte Simms, allowing prisoners access to journalists in miscarriage of justice cases.

BHATT MURPHY This undisputedly high-quality operation is only a fraction short of the top spot according to competitors. It excels in prison law and police actions and is known for meticulous preparation and producing "*great stuff, always really professionally done.*" It also has a reputation for employing top quality staff throughout the firm. "*Incredibly rigorous*" **Raju Bhatt** is an expert in police actions and has recently acted against the Criminal Cases Review Commission in a case regarding Article 6 of the Human Rights Act (HRA). **Fiona Murphy** was felt by interviewees to be "*good at being honest with clients.*" She has dealt with a number of actions against the police and a recent case against the Police Complaints Authority concerning its investigative process. **Simon Creighton**'s forte is representing prisoners against the Home Secretary. He appeared in the Madezia case, a challenge to the legality of a policy refusing temporary releases from prison to lifers awaiting deportation.

CHRISTIAN FISHER KHAN (see firm details p.906) The firm handles inquests, actions against the police, mental health, medical negligence and immigration. It is driven by the "*fantastic match*" of **Louise Christian** (see p.413) and **Sadiq Khan** (see p.413). Christian's highest profile recent case involved appealing to the British government on behalf of the Guantanamo Bay detainees, and she continues to be involved in the Ladbroke Grove inquiry. Peers rate her "*global*" practice and ability to speak effectively on behalf of clients. An "*impressive operator*" and chair of Liberty, Khan's work has a sex and race discrimination bent. He recently acted on behalf of the former vice-president of the Law Society in the first sex discrimination case brought against them, and for a black teacher abused by pupils.

HICKMAN & ROSE (see firm details p.995) An "*increasing presence,*" according to peers, the firm's judicial review practice and prisoners' rights work are praised throughout the market. It also tackles mental health and police matters and is considered a "*mature*" operation. Notable recent cases include the P&Q case concerning the separation of mothers and their babies in prison and a significant judgement on whether the Home Office can be sued directly. **Daniel Machover** (see p.413) is credited with the "*exponential growth*" of the civil side of the practice, and is widely praised for his "*fantastic*" ongoing work with inmates of Wormwood Scrubs.

BIRNBERG PEIRCE & PARTNERS Criminal cases constitute the core of the firm's workload, with its immigration practice also reputedly

410

LONDON/MIDLANDS ■ HUMAN RIGHTS

strong. "*Tenacious and hard-working*" **Gareth Peirce** is the driving force of the operation. A big name for criminal cases, her activity on behalf of 'terrorist' organisations and individuals over the past year has earned universal acclaim from peers. She has recently been occupied representing the Muslim men who's detention under the 2001 Anti-Terrorism, Crime and Security Act was ruled unlawful in July 2002. "*Unsurpassed*" for this type of work, competitors believe that her profile in human rights is rising rapidly.

DEIGHTON GUEDALLA The firm is particularly involved in discrimination, police protection and immigration-related work. It recently undertook a duty of care claim against the Metropolitan Police on behalf of one of the friends of Stephen Lawrence traumatised and injured by the attack. **Jane Deighton** stands out from a strong and energetic department. Peers rate her a "*committed and conscientious*" practitioner.

SIMONS MUIRHEAD & BURTON (see firm details p.1137) This practice is best known in the human rights community for its focus on death row cases. Its persistent campaigning against the mandatory death penalty in the eastern Caribbean came to fruition last year when Law Lords ruled it unlawful. **Saul Lehrfreund** has been leading the team campaigning for its abolition for six years, while **Anthony Burton** continues to oversee all aspects of human rights work in the firm, including ongoing work for Friends of the Earth and Greenpeace.

TAYLOR NICHOL This enthusiastic team is accomplished in a range of human rights work but is particularly strong in miscarriages of justice cases, and handles a significant amount of youth crime work. Standing out from the team, **James Nichol** is felt to excel in the former and is described by peers as having "*brought another dimension to human rights.*"

THANKI NOVY TAUBE (see firm details p.1158) The firm is visible in a wide range of work including actions against the police, inquests, deaths in custody and prison law. **Harriet Wistrich**'s (see p.414) police action work is highly commended and she has recently represented inmates of Wormwood Scrubs allegedly assaulted by officers. **Vicky King** (see p.413) is "*good on prisoners' rights,*" while **Marcia Willis-Stewart** (see p.414), formerly of Birnberg Peirce, is characterised by competitors as "*calm and reassuring to clients*" and is commended for the time she devotes to cases. The firm has strength in mother and baby prison cases and appeals on behalf of battered women accused of killing their partners.

WINSTANLEY-BURGESS (see firm details p.1193) This team is particularly respected by peers for "*taking immigration challenges to the forefront of human rights law.*" The firm is known for its strong immigration and asylum-based practice, with human rights work flowing from that. A strong and enthusiastic team is headed by **David Burgess**.

IRWIN MITCHELL (see firm details p.1009 This firm is felt by interviewees to have been "*doing some good things*" recently. Working closely with its highly rated Sheffield office, it is involved in a range of civil liberties cases and continues to represent multi-applicant parties and individuals, including animal rights activists. It has recently been in Strasbourg challenging the Inland Revenue's search and seize powers and questioning current law allowing the post of bankrupt people to be automatically diverted to their creditors. **Sara Leslie** has left the firm and **Michael Napier** is now head of department.

SCOTT-MONCRIEFF, HARBOUR & SINCLAIR Described by peers as "*the leading mental health firm,*" its recent work concerning the human rights implications of the Mental Health Act (MHA) has made an impression on the market. It obtained the first ever declaration of incompatibility leading to the amendment of discharge criteria under the MHA. It has also recently initiated a number of judicial reviews using the HRA, including one that challenged the Home Office's policy of recalling patients at the end of their sentence. The team, including **Lucy Scott-Moncrieff**, is also involved in judicial reviews relating to prison law.

OTHER NOTABLE PRACTITIONERS **Louis Charalambous** (see p.412) of CCL's freedom of expression-related work has won acclaim from peers. He recently acted on behalf of a child whose image was used without authorisation on the cover of a local authority health brochure. "*Significant in the field,*" **Imran Khan** (see p.413) of Imran Khan & Partners was widely commended for his human rights work in cases such as Stephen Lawrence and Victoria Climbié. **Paul Conrathe** (see p.413) of Coningsbys appeared in the Leonard Cheshire care home judicial review case. He represented The Society for the Protection of Unborn Children in the Dianne Pretty case.

MIDLANDS

HUMAN RIGHTS
■ MIDLANDS

1. **Tyndallwoods** Birmingham
2. **McGrath & Co** Birmingham

LEADING INDIVIDUALS
1. **PHILLIPS Mark** Tyndallwoods

This book is the product of 6,582 1/2 hour interviews. See p.7 for BMRB audit.
Within each band, firms are listed alphabetically. See individuals' profiles p.412

TYNDALLWOODS (see firm details p.1172) The firm's human rights practice can loosely be split into immigration and public law-related work. In the former category, **Margaret Finch** heads a team that handles asylum-related judicial reviews. It has recently been involved in one such appeal against the Home Office's decision to refuse asylum applications lodged in Yemen. The public law operation deals with criminal and judicial review cases as well as local government-related human rights issues. It continues to run training projects for other solicitors. The firm (led by **Natalia Garcia**) represented two of the eleven Mulsim men who's detention under the 2001 Anti-Terrorism, Crime and Security Act was ruled unlawful in July 2002. **Mark Phillips** (see p.414) is highly regarded for his work in this field.

MCGRATH & CO This respected team undertakes a lot of civil actions against the police, including cases relating to assaults and deaths in custody. It is currently involved in claims on behalf of victims of police discrimination and breaches of privacy. Much of its activity relates to unlawful arrest and false imprisonment and it has also been visible representing inmates assaulted by prison guards. **Emma Guilfoyle-Carey** heads the group.

HUMAN RIGHTS ■ THE NORTH/THE LEADERS

THE NORTH

HUMAN RIGHTS ■ THE NORTH

1
- AS Law Liverpool
- Harrison Bundey & Co Leeds
- Howells Sheffield
- Irwin Mitchell Sheffield

2
- David Gray Solicitors Newcastle upon Tyne
- Robert Lizar Manchester

LEADING INDIVIDUALS

1 BUNDEY Ruth Harrison Bundey & Co
2 SIMPSON Danny Howells
3 ABRAHAMSON Elkan AS Law
LOCKLEY Andrew Irwin Mitchell

UP AND COMING
PRICE Richard Howells

This book is the product of 6,582 1/2 hour interviews. See p.7 for BMRB audit.
Within each band, firms are listed alphabetically. See individuals' profiles p.412

AS LAW The firm's large prison practice is held in high regard in the North, and market opinion confirms that the firm is highly visible in connection with civil liberties work connected with prisoners' rights. **Elkan Abrahamson** regularly advises at the ECHR and has earned the respect of peers across the region.

HARRISON BUNDEY & CO This nationally renowned operation boasts an extremely impressive reputation for human rights. Much of it is down to the high standing of **Ruth Bundey** (see p.412) who was praised by interviewees as an outstanding civil liberties lawyer. The team has experience of police inquest work and was recently involved in an inquiry into the death of a detainee at Hull police station. With its strong asylum department, the firm also has a particular focus on the plight of Asian women in violent marriages.

HOWELLS (see firm details p.1002) This widely respected, "*hard-working*" team covers a full range of civil liberties work, including actions against the police, prisoners' rights, deaths in custody and miscarriages of justice. It has recently been in the Court of Appeal on a judicial review of a decision by the Police Complaints Authority not to release details of an incident in which a young black man was run over by police officers. It is also involved in an ongoing miscarriage of justice case concerning a man serving a 20-year sentence. The "*energetic and committed*" **Danny Simpson** (see p.414) heads the department and works alongside "*dedicated*" **Richard Price** (see p.414).

IRWIN MITCHELL (see firm details p.1009) This strong team works well in combination with its impressive London office to form a nationally renowned operation. "*Smart lawyer*" and head of department **Andrew Lockley** (see p.413) has successfully acted in a recent case involving the sale of personal data to commercial interests. The firm also undertakes actions against the police and has dealt with several death in custody cases as well as representing an innocent man arrested in Rome. It has also been visible representing animal rights' campaigners, including ones demonstrating against the use of Shamrock monkeys for vivisection.

DAVID GRAY SOLICITORS Although best known for its expertise in immigration and asylum, the firm handles a wide range of civil liberties-related work. The team boasts particular strength in police and mental health cases, and has recently been involved in a number of cases regarding access of imprisoned mothers to their children. The group, headed by Mike Bishop, also has experience of handling right-to-life cases.

ROBERT LIZAR This prominent practice is known principally for its police and prisons work. It has recently acted in a death in custody case at Strangeways Prison and represents a man imprisoned for 25 years for a murder he claims not to have committed. With a sound knowledge of mental health law, the team has assisted a pregnant patient detained under the MHA who was seeking a termination but prevented by a doctor's decision concerning her mental capacity.

THE LEADERS IN HUMAN RIGHTS

ABRAHAMSON, Elkan
A S Law, Liverpool
(0151) 707 1212

BHATT, Raju
Bhatt Murphy, London
(020) 7253 7744

BINDMAN, Geoffrey
Bindman & Partners, London
(020) 7833 4433
info@bindmans.com
Specialisation: Senior partner. Specialises in civil liberties and human rights, media law, defamation, anti-discrimination and general litigation. Author of numerous articles in the professional and national press on these subjects, and has broadcast frequently. Has represented the ICJ, IBA, Amnesty International, and other bodies in human rights missions in many countries.
Prof. Memberships: Law Society; president, Discrimination Law Association; president, Client Interviewing Competition of England and Wales.
Career: Established *Bindman & Partners* in 1974. From 1966-76 was legal advisor to the Race Relations Board and thereafter until 1983 to the Commission for Racial Equality. Visiting professor, UCLA (1982); currently visiting professor of law at University College London; honorary fellow Society of Advanced Legal Studies; Hon LL.D (De Montfort University); Liberty and Law Society Gazette Award for Lifetime Human Rights Achievement 1999.
Personal: Born 3 January 1933. Attended Newcastle RGS and Oriel College, Oxford.

BUNDEY, Ruth
Harrison Bundey & Co., Leeds
(0113) 237 4047
ruth.bundey@harrisonbundey.co.uk
Specialisation: Partner specialising in crime, immigration and inquests. Acted in the Helen Smith inquest, the case of the Bradford 12 and of Anwar Ditta, and numerous Yorkshire drug operations, and cases involving women who kill violent men. Contributor to the Liberty Guide 'Know Your Rights' and member of the Liverpool Eight Inquiry which published 'Loosen the Shackles'. Involved more and more with inquests into deaths in custody and currently instructed by the sister of Christopher Alder who died on video in Hull Police Station on 1 April 1998.
Prof. Memberships: Law Society, Leeds Law Society, Liberty, Law Society Immigration Law Committee, Inquest Lawyers Group, Stonewall Immigration Group, National Civil Rights Movement.
Career: Qualified in 1980. Formed *Ruth Bundey & Co* in 1986. Merged in 1993 to form *Harrison Bundey & Co*.
Personal: Educated at the University of Kent (BA Hons in English & American Literature). Awarded Honorary Master of Arts Degree for services to law in November 1995: University of Kent. Member of West Yorkshire Justice for Women. Lives in Chapeltown, Leeds.

CHARALAMBOUS, Louis
CCL, London
(020) 7253 2277
louis@cclsolicitors.com
Specialisation: Criminal, media and public law. Special expertise in representing clients in high profile cases or causes. Recent cases include representing Brian Pretty (husband of Diane Pretty in 'right to die' case); Lotfi Raissi (Algerian pilot sought by US authorities) in defamation matters; Josephine Smith in CCRC referral back to Court of Appeal for murder of husband in 1993 and successful breach of confidence/privacy case against LBNewham, achieving record damages. Also member of Abdullah Ocalan legal team against Turkey in Strasbourg proceedings in leading death penalty case. Clients include National Union of Journalists, Channels 4 and 5, Guardian Newspapers, Med TV, Voluntary Euthanasia Society, Rex Features and National Union of Teachers.
Prof. Memberships: Criminal Appeal Lawyers Association, Police Action Lawyers Group and Serious Fraud Panel (supervisor).
Career: University of Bradford (BA Hons) and University of Leeds (MA). Qualified in 1987. Practised as a Partner with both *Ruth Bundey and Co* and *John Pickering and Partners* before returning to London in 1994 to head the Crime and Public Law Team with media specialists *Stephens Innocent*, becoming a partner in 1998. Founded *CCL* in January 2001 in partnership with Sarah Cul-

412

INDEX TO LEADING LAWYERS: PAGE 1693 ■ IN-HOUSE LAWYERS PROFILES: PAGE 1201

THE LEADERS — HUMAN RIGHTS

shaw. Former NUJ Legal Officer Sally Gilbert also joined as a Consultant.
Personal: Born 1957. Educated at St. Marylebone Grammar School (1968-75).

CHRISTIAN, Louise
Christian Fisher Khan, London
(020) 7691 4381
louisec@christianf.co.uk
Specialisation: Partner in civil litigation department. Main area of practice is administrative law/judicial review, public inquiries, inquests, medical negligence, personal injury and disaster law, actions against government departments, and Human Rights Act litigation. Solicitor for rail crash victims in public inquiry.
Prof. Memberships: Senior Fellow of the College of Personal Injury Law, Chair of INQUEST, board member of the Centre for Corporate Accountability, Law Society Personal Injury and Clinical Negligence Panel member.
Career: Qualified in 1978 while at *Lovell White & King*. Solicitor, Plumstead Community Law Centre 1979-81, then Advisor to the GLC Police Committee 1981-84. Co-founded *Christian Fisher* with Michael Fisher in November 1985.

CONRATHE, Paul
Coningsbys, Croydon
(020) 8680 5575
paulconrathe@coningsbys.co.uk
Specialisation: Challenges brought against central and local government in areas such as education, community care, health and disability issues. Particular expertise in ethical issues such as the right to life, abortion, reproductive technology and end of life decisions. Specialism includes media disputes (freedom of expression) and religious liberty.
Prof. Memberships: The Education Law Association. Is the convenor of the Special Educational Needs Tribunal Users Group for the Education Law Association. Honorary Legal Advisor to Parents for Early Intervention in Autistic Children (PEACH), Legal Advisor to Society for Protection of Unborn Children and honorary Legal Advisor to the Pro-Life Alliance. Honorary Legal Advisor to the Christian Institute.

CREIGHTON, Simon
Bhatt Murphy, London
(020) 7253 7744

DEIGHTON, Jane
Deighton Guedalla, London
(020) 7359 5700

GROSZ, Stephen
Bindman & Partners, London
(020) 7833 4433
s.grosz@bindmans.com
Specialisation: Partner in public law and litigation department. Specialises in public and administrative law and human rights handling applicant work on behalf of pressure groups and individuals in civil liberties and environmental cases including European Community law. Also handles respondent work on behalf of the Law Society and the Office for the Supervision of Solicitors. Major clients have included Friends of the Earth, the World Development Movement War on Want, Campaign Against Arms Trade, Tapol, Mencap and Amnesty International. Frequently writes articles on public law and human rights. Co-author, with Jack Beatson QC and Peter Duffy QC, of 'Human Rights: the 1998 Act & the European Convention'.
Prof. Memberships: Administrative Law Bar Association, United Kingdom Environmental Law Association, Solicitors European Group, Executive Committee of Public Law Project and Governor of British Institute of Human Rights, Member of the Council of JUSTICE. Member of the Advisory Board of Judicial Review quarterly; Member of the Advisory Board of Education, Public Law & the Individual; Member of the Council of Liberty.
Career: Qualified in 1978. Entire career spent at *Bindman & Partners*. Partner since 1981.
Personal: Born April 1953. Graduate in Law of Cambridge University and in European Law of Université Libre de Bruxelles.

KHAN, Imran
Imran Khan & Partners, London
(020) 7636 6314
info@imrankhanandpartners.co.uk
Specialisation: Main areas of practice are crime; actions against the police; race discrimination; immigration, inquests and inquiries. Major cases include the Stephen Lawrence Case; Victoria Climbie inquiry; Amin v Home Secretary (Zahid Mubarek case); represented main defendant in Stansted (Afghan) Hijack case; representing victims in Leeds footballers case/ Najeib v Bowyer; representing family of Jason McGowan (inquest into 'Telford Hangings').
Prof. Memberships: Editorial Board of 'Independent Lawyer'; Patron of North Lambeth Law Centre; Vice President of National Civil Rights Movement.
Career: Trainee solicitor with *Birnberg & Partners*. Set up *Imran Khan and Partners* in November 2000 with specific emphasis on developing human rights based 'Impact Cases'.
Publications: Currently working on book called 'Empowering Victims of Race Crime'.
Personal: Lectured extensively in the UK and abroad on issues of race, the criminal justice system, human rights and civil liberties. Honorary doctorates from Oxford Brookes University; University of East London and Staffordshire University. Lawyer of the Year 1999 (The Lawyer Newspaper).

KHAN, Sadiq
Christian Fisher Khan, London
(020) 7831 1750
sadiqk@christianf.co.uk
Specialisation: Partner. Main area of practice is actions against the police, employment and discrimination law, judicial reviews, inquests. Involved in all areas of human rights work. Has given oral evidence to the Home Affairs Select Committee. Won landmark cases including: in police damages (Hsu v Met Police), negligence (Reeves v Met Police), discriminations (Bahl v Law Society; Murray v CAB), police discipline (Logan v Met Police), Inquests (Bentley v HM Coroner District of Avon; inquest into death of Rocky Bennett). Human Rights Act (Farrakhan v S of S of Home Dept), Chairman of Liberty (NCCL). Vice-chair of LAG (Legal Action Group).
Prof. Memberships: Police Action Lawyers Group, Executive Committee of Legal Action Group and Liberty, Inquest Lawyers Group, APIL. Member of The Law Society's Equal Opportunities Committee. Panel member of EOC Solicitors and DRC Solicitors. Member of Discrimination Law Association.
Career: Trainee Solicitor with *Christian Fisher & Co* where he is now a Partner. He is a visiting lecturer in Employment Law at the University of North London.
Publications: Has authored various articles on legal reform and writes extensively on human rights issues.
Personal: Awarded Sweet & Maxwell Law Prize, Governors Award, Windsor Fellowship, Esso Law Bursary and Awarded Society of Black Lawyers bursary. Councillor in London Borough of Wandsworth since 1994. Representative on Racial Incidents Panel. Involved in human rights visits to Turkey and has lectured in Poland on the ECHR on behalf of Justice. Member of Institute of Advanced Legal Studies Advisory Committee examining civil legal aid and Advisory Committee of Liberty examining independent police complaints system. Member of advisory committee looking into inquests. Member of Steering Group Camden Community Legal Services Partnership and Member of Working Party looking into Pre Action Protocol for Police actions.

KING, Vicky
Thanki Novy Taube, London
(020) 7485 5558
info@tntlaw.co.uk
Specialisation: Acting for prisoners in challenging the conditions of their imprisonment. Practice includes a large volume of judicial review cases. Also considerable experience of representing defendants in criminal trials arising within the prison context - especially prison mutiny/riots and serious offences of violence on prison officers/prisoners.
Prof. Memberships: Prisoners' Advice Service, Liberty, Justice, Prison Reform Trust.
Career: Early career spent as a caseworker in various organisations in the voluntary sector. Set up and developed the Prisoners' Advice Service in 1991. Left to pursue career in private practice, arriving at *Thanki Novy Taube* when newly qualified. Partner from 2000.
Publications: 'Prisoners and the Law' (published Butterworth, 2nd edition 2000), contributor to the 'Prisons' Handbook' (published annually by Waterside Press).

LOCKLEY, Andrew
Irwin Mitchell, Sheffield
(0114) 274 4658
lockleya@irwinmitchell.co.uk
Specialisation: Admin and Public law, especially with Human Rights angle; acted in R v Chief Constable of Derbyshire ex parte Bramley; R v LAB ex parte Rafina (OAO Robertson; R v Wakefield Metropolitan District Council & SSHD; R (OAO Jarrett) v LSC & Lord Chancellor. The last three of these were in the past year.
Prof. Memberships: Law Society; Education Law Society
Career: Admitted 1979; Official of Law Society of England and Wales 1982-96, including Director of Legal Practice (1987-95); Director of Corporate and Regional Affairs 1995-96; *Irwin Mitchell* 1996-present (Partner and Head of Public Law); Part time Chair of Special Needs Tribunal (1996-present); Honorary Fellow University of Sheffield (1999-present).
Publications: The Pursuit of Quality – A Guide For Lawyers (Tolley – 1993 Edition); Articles in legal and national press.
Personal: Read Classics at Oriel College, Oxford. Resides Sheffield. Three children; Keen on growing fruit and vegetables, choral singing, reading and walking.

MACHOVER, Daniel
Hickman & Rose, London
(020) 7700 2211
dmachover@hickmanandrose.co.uk
Specialisation: Civil remedies to all problems experienced by people within the criminal justice system, including actions against the police, judicial review of chief officers of police, magistrates, prison governors and the Home Secretary, inquests and claims arising out of assaults by prison officers. Represents over fifty alleged victims of assaults at HMP Wormwood Scrubs.
Prof. Memberships: Founder of Lawyers for Palestinian Human Rights, member of Council of Liberty, Inquest Lawyers Group, Prisoners' Rights Legal Group and APIL.
Career: Qualified 1988, worked at North Kensington Law Centre, Liberty's legal department (locum) and *Christian Fisher* before joining *Hickman and Rose* in January 1997 as head of the civil litigation department. Partner since March 1998.
Personal: LLB, LLM in International Human Rights Law.

MURPHY, Fiona
Bhatt Murphy, London
(020) 7253 7744

HUMAN RIGHTS ■ THE LEADERS

MURPHY, Tony
Bindman & Partners, London
(020) 7833 4433
tmurphy@bindmans.com
Specialisation: Specialises predominantly in civil claims against the Commissioner of Police of the Metropolis and Chief Constables nationwide. Also strong track record in assisting clients negotiate the police complaints system, including a recent successful criminal prosecution of an officer. Particular expertise in challenging police racism and violence, and large scale public order arrests (including May Day). Currently has conduct of a number cases issues issued under the Race Relations (Amendment) Act 2000, including against the Chief Constable of Lancashire for systemic racism, and on behalf of the Commission for Racial Equality member injured by police during the Burnley disturbances. Also successful this year before the European Court of Human Rights in a police phone-tapping case, where the government was found in breach of Article 8. Reputation for securing high awards, including one of the highest in respect of exemplary damages on behalf of Winston Silcott, and more recently for loss of liberty on behalf of an asylum seeker under the Home Office Miscarriages of Justice Scheme. Works closely with the Mental Health Department at *Bindmans*, and just secured a record amount of compensation for a Section 3 Mental Health Act detainee, who successfully sued a NHS Trust for false imprisonment and assault. Also represents mandatory life sentence prisoners in parole reviews (including Winston Silcott) and regularly appears on behalf of other lifers before oral hearings of the Parole Board. Sits as practitioner member on Home Office Oral Hearings User Group.
Prof. Memberships: Law Society, Police Action Lawyers Group, Prisoners Legal Rights Group, Mind Legal Network, Inquest Lawyers Group, Irish Consultative Committee on Policing, GALOP.
Career: LLB Queens University Belfast. Joined *Bindman & Partners* on qualification in 1998.

NICHOL, James
Taylor Nichol, London
(020) 7272 8336

PEIRCE, Gareth
Birnberg Peirce & Partners, London
(020) 7284 4620

PHILLIPS, Mark
Tyndallwoods, Birmingham
(0121) 624 1111
Mark_Phillips@tyndallwoods.co.uk
See under Immigration, p.424

PRICE, Richard
Howells, Sheffield
(0114) 249 6666
rprice@howells-solicitors.com
Specialisation: Human rights, public law (civil and criminal), civil liberties, community care, prison law, disability right, social security benefits. Decision of Court of Appeal in Middleton dismissing Secretary of State's appeal and revisiting Jamieson decision concerning deaths whilst in care of state.
Prof. Memberships: Law Society, Howard League.
Career: Trainee solicitor with small high street practice, thereafter worked with youth homeless project as deputy project leader and welfare rights officer with Sunderland city council. Admitted and returned to practice as solicitor, employed by Wolverhampton CAB, then employed by *Glaisyers* (Birmingham). For last four years at *Howells* as head of community law.
Personal: Lives in Sheffield. Education: Ashfield Comprehensive School, Wolverhampton Polytechnic (LLB Hons), City of London Polytechnic (Law Society Finals). Admitted 1993.

SCHWARZ, Michael
Bindman & Partners, London
(020) 7833 4433
Specialisation: Specialist in criminal defence work, including fresh evidence appeals to the Court of Appeal and in inquests, extradition, police complaints, applications to the European Court of Human Rights. Acts for political activists and campaigners on environmental, animal rights, peace / disarmament, race, social justice issues. Particular experience of public order arrests and multi-defendant trials. Has represented anti-roads protesters at Twyford Down, the M11 and Newbury. Represents Greenpeace campaigners on genetic modification, Star Wars, climate change, incineration, rainforest destruction. Represented campaigners facing serious public order charges at anti-capitalism and anti-globalisation demonstrations. Represents family of Michael Menson, the black musician set alight by racists in North London, at inquest, Old Bailey prosecution, police complaint and case to the European Court of Human Rights. Represented Animal Defenders in successful prosecution of Chipperfields for circus animal cruelty.
Career: Qualified in 1992. Partner at *Bindmans* since 1995.
Personal: Degree in law (Oxford) and postgraduate degree in European Law (College of Europe, Brugge, Belgium).

SIMPSON, Danny
Howells, Sheffield
(0114) 2496612
dsimpson@howells-solicitors.com
Specialisation: Partner and Head of Criminal Law Department. All aspects of criminal law, including miscarriage of justice cases and a range of civil liberties issues.
Prof. Memberships: Law Society.
Career: BA (Hons) Degree, Exeter College, Oxford, in Politics, Philosophy and Economics; qualified as a solicitor in 1984 and employed at *Bindman & Partners* solicitors. Became a Partner in 1989 before moving to Sheffield in 1990 as a Partner. Head of Department at *Howells* solicitors.
Personal: Lives in Sheffield, married to GP practising locally, with three children.

WILLIS-STEWART, Marcia
Thanki Novy Taube, London
(020) 7485 5558
Specialisation: Civil liberties practice specifically in respect of complaints and/or actions against detaining authorities. Including deaths in custody. Leading practice in respect of 'babies in prison', most notably the case of Q & QB v SSHD, a landmark judgement, which crossed the parameters of administrative and family law, heralding a significant human rights victory for prisoners.
Prof. Memberships: Police Lawyers Action Group (PLAG), Association of Personal Injury Lawyers (APIL), Association of Child Abuse Lawyers (ACAL) and Rights of Women (ROW).
Career: Extensive public sector experience – government and voluntary sector. Change of career in the 90s to pursue career in law (private practice). Joined *TNT* in 1999. Partner 2002.

WISTRICH, Harriet
Thanki Novy Taube, London
(020) 7833 5800
harrietwistrich@tntlaw.co.uk
Specialisation: Acting for 'battered women who kill' – mainly at appellant and CCRC stages; third party interventions at house of Lords on provocation (R v Morgan James Smith) and on rape (R v A). Actions against the police and the prison service; inquests (especially death in custody); advising victims of sexual abuse and rape; women's rights as human rights.
Prof. Memberships: Founder Member of Justice For Women; founder and trustee of Emma Humphreys Memorial Prize; Police Action Lawyers Group; Inquest Lawyers Group; Association of Child Abuse Lawyers; Justice; Lawyers for Liberty.
Career: Prior to training as a lawyer, worked in the independent film industry; in community video training and production, film editing and as an independent film-maker.
Publications: Articles published in Legal Action, Liberty newsletter, Rights of Women Bulletin. Speaker at national and international conferences and seminars on range of issues from domestic violence to women in prison.

IMMIGRATION

London: 415; The Regions: 419; Profiles: 421

Research approved by BMRB For this edition, **Chambers'** researchers conducted 6,582 interviews – 3,900 with law firms, 511 with barristers and 2,171 with clients. The validity of the research was scrutinised by BMRB International, who audited both the methodology and the results at our offices in London. They interviewed **Chambers'** researchers and cross-checked sample interviews. Details of the audit appear on page 7.

OVERVIEW The sector experienced a noted decline in the number of immigration applications from corporate clients in the latter half of 2001. Weak global markets combined with the effects of the September 11th terrorist attacks have slowed the movement of staff. However, in 2002 the frequency of applications has begun to recover. The skills threshold for work permit applications has been lowered in response to a shortage evident in many sectors, especially healthcare, teaching and IT. This has been aided by new initiatives such as the Highly Skilled Migrant Programme (HSMP) in the UK and the new Spousal Work Authorization regulations in the US. After a slow start, HSMPs have taken off as prime choice for corporate clients, in preference to the Innovators' Programme for Entrepreneurs. The HSMP is designed to attract individuals without a prior job offer, who would not otherwise be capable of gaining permission to enter the UK. It is seen as a more flexible, easier way to attract and introduce entrepreneurial individuals to the UK, who can act as catalysts for improvement in the economy. Companies have also increased their usage of naturalisation applications, seen by many as the most efficient way to relocate staff in the current climate. In personal immigration, the Government's dispersal programme for asylum seekers, coupled with the decision to make enforcement rulings appealable, have ensured a stream of high-profile work. The problems experienced by many firms under the Legal Services Commission (LSC) funding regime have prompted several to abandon the franchise. The increasing use of the European Convention of Human Rights (ECHR) in immigration cases, particularly Articles 3 (prohibition of torture) and 8 (right to respect for private and family life), has helped bring the sector into line with international standards. However, the Government's Anti-Terrorism, Crime & Security Act is just one example of how quickly the goal-posts can move.

LONDON

BUSINESS

IMMIGRATION: BUSINESS
LONDON

[1] **CMS Cameron McKenna**
   Kingsley Napley
[2] **Bates, Wells & Braithwaite**
   Reed Smith Warner Cranston
[3] **Baker & McKenzie**
   Eversheds
   Magrath & Co
[4] **Gherson & Co**
   Mishcon de Reya
   Sturtivant & Co
[5] **Fox Williams**
   Gulbenkian Harris Andonian
   Harbottle & Lewis
   Lovells
   Norton Rose
   Penningtons
   Pullig & Co
[6] **DJ Webb & Co**
   Taylor Wessing

This book is the product of 6,582 1/2 hour interviews. See p.7 for BMRB audit. Within each band, firms are listed alphabetically.

CMS CAMERON MCKENNA (see firm details p.914) This, the largest corporate immigration team in the country offers enormous expertise, and does not secure its place in *Chambers*' top band on size alone. It continues to have an undeniable impact across the corporate immigration sector. An extensive European network and established links with the US and the Far East enable the firm to provide a comprehensive service to businesses requiring immigration assistance. The last year has seen the addition of a number of international household names to its already extensive client portfolio. The team has a high success rate on HSMP applications, advising on the first ever entry, and actively pursuing them since on a 'no-win, no-fee' basis. It has dealt with a considerable increase in naturalisation applications, and represents high net worth individuals in the fields of entertainment and sport. Satisfied clients speak of "*well-qualified people and a good value, full service.*" **Julia Onslow-Cole** (see p.424) leads a uniform, integrated team. She has been involved in national and international consultations, addressing immigration issues such as security. She is also a frequent policy advisor to the Home Office and DTI. Such is her profile that she has in the past eclipsed her talented colleagues. However, *Chambers* research showed that their market profiles are beginning to strengthen. The team has assisted a US charitable family trust on a number of visa applications, and advised several investment banks on relocations and processed large volumes of visa applications, for which it has developed its own bespoke package. **Clients** BNP Paribas; financial institutions; manufacturers; private clients.

KINGSLEY NAPLEY (see firm details p.1023) Interviewees felt that the firm was pushing hard against CMS Cameron McKenna with a "*solid team of interesting and exciting individuals providing an all-round service.*" The efficient department was particularly commended for its wide spectrum of expertise and commitment to high-quality work secured without losing its personal approach. Department head **Hilary Belchak** (see p.422) is "*a high-powered specialist*" with considerable experience. Admired for her European knowledge, **Elspeth Guild** (see p.423) can count the European Commission and governments among her clients as well as corporate and private individuals. "*Conscientious team player*" **Nicolas Rollason** (see p.425) also impressed with his strong European skills, particularly on European Economic Area Association Agreements (EAAs). Work permit applications have comprised the mainstay of the firm's recent activity, particularly in the energy and insurance markets. The firm continues to service the banking and finance, telecoms, entertainment and sports sectors on their immigration requirements. It has added a further string to its bow with its work on HSMP applications. The team has been instrumental in clarifying and broadening some of the boundaries of the new programme: it established that a foreign lawyer involved in a higher court case meets the HSMP 'significant achievement' criterion, as do software consultants involved in unusual or complex projects. As well as its leading corporate focus, the firm continues to handle personal applications on behalf of individuals. It successfully obtained Home Office guidance that Turkish nationals could establish businesses in the UK, on the basis of immigration rules utilised prior to the stricter, present-day regime. **Clients** Construction companies; financial institutions; IT and telecoms organisations; law firms; media and entertainment groups; professional service firms.

BATES, WELLS & BRAITHWAITE (see firm details p.859) This knowledgeable team was commended to *Chambers* for its commitment across a wide range of matters, including HSMP

www.ChambersandPartners.com 415

IMMIGRATION ■ LONDON

LEADING INDIVIDUALS

1
- **BELCHAK Hilary** Kingsley Napley
- **GUILD Elspeth** Kingsley Napley
- **ONSLOW-COLE Julia** CMS Cameron McKenna

2
- **ALFANDARY Peter** Reed Smith Warner Cranston
- **DEVINE Laura** Eversheds
- **HAQUE Tony** Baker & McKenzie
- **MAGRATH Chris** Magrath & Co
- **MEHMET Gülay** Penningtons
- **ROLLASON Nicolas** Kingsley Napley
- **STURTIVANT Karen** Sturtivant & Co
- **TROTT Philip** Bates, Wells & Braithwaite

3
- **BARTH Philip** Mishcon de Reya
- **DIXON Marian** Lovells
- **KEMP Lesley** Reed Smith Warner Cranston
- **MOSS Peter** Bates, Wells & Braithwaite
- **POPE Caron** Reed Smith Warner Cranston

4
- **ANDONIAN Bernard** Gulbenkian Harris Andonian
- **BALCOMB Anne** Harbottle & Lewis
- **GHERSON Roger** Gherson & Co
- **MANN Jane** Fox Williams
- **WEBB David** DJ Webb & Co

See individuals' profiles p.421

---

work for noted individuals. Successes in this area have included assistance to author Bud Smith on his relocation, and advice to former astronaut David Scott on his move to the UK to pursue a design role – becoming the first individual to switch from visitor status to HSMP status, despite the absolute prohibition contained in the terms of the scheme. **Philip Trott** (see p.425) "*knows immigration inside out and still cares about getting the results for clients.*" **Peter Moss** (see p.424) was also recommended for his provision of business immigration advice. The firm has focused on representations to visa officers on behalf of employers or individuals over adverse work permit decisions. The firm also undertakes a proportion of personal immigration work, including advice to professionals who wish to be economically active in the UK, such as civil engineers and doctors. **Clients** David Scott; Bud Smith.

REED SMITH WARNER CRANSTON (see firm details p.1109) Buoyed by the effect of its US merger last year, the firm has seen an influx of new clients, and is considered by some to be a one-stop shop for multinationals seeking immigration advice. The team was appreciated for its ability to integrate well with the HR departments of its clients. It has dealt with a range of work permits, sole representatives and business applications across all sectors, witnessing an increase in applications from manufacturing, pharmaceutical and hi-tech companies. It has also represented a number of individuals under the Innovator category. Observers described **Peter Alfandary** (see p.421) as a "*stylish opera-*

tor" and "*good problem solver.*" Team leader, he is well known for his work on behalf of national and multinational corporations looking to set up subsidiaries in the UK. Thorough and approachable in her methods, **Lesley Kemp**'s (see p.423) corporate advice centres on the convergence of UK and European immigration law and the effects on individuals coming to live and work in the UK, which includes issues of family dependency. She has advised individuals in the arts and entertainment world. Clients recommended the "*expert and highly professional*" **Caron Pope** (see p.424) for her "*quick and attentive approach.*" She has recently arrived from Norton Rose with an assistant, and although it is too early to judge her effect on the practice, it does demonstrate the team's commitment to this field. **Clients** Hitachi; LCC International; Marsh & McLennan; Saatchi & Saatchi.

BAKER & McKENZIE (see firm details p.855) The ability to call on and interact with its considerable international network is the firm's strongest asset. It has advised on mainstream work permit applications for both sole representatives, and for international corporates undergoing large-scale transfers. The group has ties with companies in Japan, from which senior paralegal Shizuko Fujimoto receives a steady stream of instructions, including the likes of Toyota Motor Manufacturing UK. The department's international coverage also ensures that it represents a significant number of US-based clients. **Tony Haque** (see p.423) is the most visible member of this well-resourced team. He is involved in several Home Office policy reviews and provides training to immigration practitioners and regulatory bodies. He was recommended to *Chambers* for his ability to empathise and his "*bright, clear thinking.*" The firm has been most active in the telecoms and financial services sectors, transferring over 40 software developers and management staff to the UK for Sharp Telecommunications following a major acquisition. **Clients** Manufacturers; new media organisations; pharmaceutical groups; publishing companies; Sharp Telecommunications; Toyoda Gosei; Toyota Motor Manufacturing UK; TS Tech.

EVERSHEDS (see firm details p.949) The firm has experienced a considerable increase in the overall amount of work it has conducted on Innovator category applications, HSMP instructions and general corporate immigration concerns. It advises four international business schools on immigration matters, and was involved in influencing the policy concerning the reconsideration of HSMP applications. The majority of interviewees identified the team's growing presence in the sector, based around the "*dynamic, experienced and talented*" **Laura Devine** (see p.422). An effective team builder, Devine led on the successful pitch to represent a large telecoms company, establishing its global

immigration service. She also oversaw several hundred instructions from a major consulting group. The practice is further augmented by the use of two US dual-qualified lawyers working full-time on work for US clients, a dedicated practice launched in November 2001. **Clients** Business schools; HSMP applications; telecoms companies.

MAGRATH & CO (see firm details p.1050) A pragmatic, down-to-earth and transaction-based approach to the sector may account for the lower market visibility of this large and highly skilled team. It has busied itself with a number of HSMP and Innovator applications, as well as related employment and remuneration advice and assistance on the relocation of dependents. The well-resourced unit advises international finance companies, music industry groups and an expanding client base of private individuals. Of a large team, "*highly effective*" group leader **Chris Magrath** stood out in our research for his longevity in the sector and for his network of contacts here and in the US. The department has continued to develop its active links with US firms to assist a packed roster of multinational clients.

GHERSON & CO (see firm details p.970) Although the volume of the firm's corporate-related work has fluctuated in the wake of the September 11th attacks, appeals work concerning national security for the Special Immigration Appeals Court (SIAC) has risen to fill the gap. The interest shown by its clients in HSMP applications has been matched by a similar growth in the Innovator category. Considered an "*under-rated*" department by some interviewees, it has been heavily instructed on investor applications by a combination of overseas companies and individuals seeking to build businesses in the UK, assisting also on the commercial and human rights elements that arise. According to a leading barrister, name partner **Roger Gherson** (see p.423) "*has a commitment to his clients and successes that are unmatched*" by many in the market; "*a substantial presence and clientele – he gets results.*" The majority of the firm's work is business-oriented, but a third of its caseload is associated with personal immigration matters from same sex applications to political asylum.

MISHCON DE REYA (see firm details p.1072) The small team practises immigration work with a decidedly corporate flavour. Instructions on work permit applications and related matters make up the lion's share of its workload. It has focused on the Chinese market and on assistance to IT and hi-tech companies in India. The firm has advised on some HSMP applications, but assistance to high net worth individuals remains an area of greater activity. While the firm does not carry out asylum work, the influence of civil liberties law has meant that it is more involved in cases involving nationality issues. **Philip Barth** (see p.421) has "*a proactive approach to litigation.*" He has successfully appealed against the exclusion by the Home Office of an accountant refused leave to remain in the country on the grounds that his presence was not conducive to the public good.

STURTIVANT & CO (see firm details p.1154) This immigration practice is anchored around the capable and professional **Karen Sturtivant** (see p.425). She applies her considerable experience in the sector to the full range of business immigration work, including applications for both corporate clients and sole representatives. While her own ability is without question, peers considered that the department's small size would be a barrier for assistance on volume transactions, or cases requiring considerable depth of resources.

FOX WILLIAMS (see firm details p.962) "*Prompt, professional and comprehensive,*" the practice has seen a marked increase in the number of applications received from the energy and insurance sectors. This has been in addition to a central core of advice to corporate clients in the financial services, technology and property sectors. The team has also witnessed an increase in HSMP instructions. Possessed of a "*calm, reassuring approach,*" **Jane Mann** (see p.424) heads a small group with particular expertise in employment-related matters. The team occupies a niche in the sector, assisting foreign law firms and professional partnerships on the establishment of new offices in London, including all the necessary associated immigration clearances. **Clients** DigiTerra; GNI; Quintiles; XL Winterthur International.

GULBENKIAN HARRIS ANDONIAN (see firm details p.980) An immigration and nationality specialist, the firm offers a bespoke, personal service. The committed partner-led department remains a favourite of peers, who claim that the firm "*speaks the same language .*" Bucking the general market trend, the firm has seen more work on behalf of clients under the Innovator programme than using the HSMP. Many of these have been in connection with e-commerce companies transferring staff from abroad to the UK. Other application work has been on behalf of wealthy business individuals from abroad looking to settle in the UK, and for sole representatives of particular organisations. **Bernard Andonian** (see p.421) is a "*forceful advocate*" of the immigration rights of companies and individuals. The firm undertakes non-legally aided asylum work, and has been involved in a number of judicial reviews. This has included successfully arguing that applicants could have a right of appeal in the UK to apply for asylum. The team was also successful in a case against the Secretary of State, concerning the right of an applicant's wife to remain in the UK under Article 8 of the European Convention of Human Rights (ECHR), as her children were in education here.

HARBOTTLE & LEWIS (see firm details p.983) Commended to *Chambers* by clients for its smooth, consultative style, the "*efficient, helpful and practical*" immigration team is led by **Anne Balcomb** (see p.421). "*Always directly available,*" report clients, she spends a third of her time on non-legally aided personal immigration matters. The team specialises in work permit applications for the entertainment and media sectors, representing actors, producers and musicians on several prominent productions in the last year. This has included bringing four US nationals to the UK to be employed in senior positions relating to a terrestrial television series. High-profile work is illustrated by the team's assistance to Dramatico to bring a Canadian national to the UK to be employed as a member of classical group The Planets. It also secured a work permit for Paris Hilton to star in the film 'Nine Lives' on behalf of A&A Films. Aside from its media base, the team has assisted Oxxon Pharmaccines to bring a biotechnology specialist into the country to be employed as a Director of Operations. **Clients** 19 Management; Attenda; Carlton Television; Dazed & Confused magazine; DISCO International; Dramatico; Fairbourne Films; Golden Pride Clothing; ICM; Los Angeles Times International; Oxxon Pharmaccines; Untitled Management.

LOVELLS (see firm details p.1045) The firm's respected reputation is due in large part to "*professional and on the ball*" **Marian Dixon** (see p.422). Experienced and resolute, she is particularly noted for the insight gained from her parallel role as a part-time Immigration Appeals Adjudicator. The firm has dealt with instructions from organisations in the oil and retail sectors, on both specific work permit applications and ongoing advice on their immigration procedures and strategies. Recent applications have included advice on the Innovator programme to an architectural design company concerning a Korean employee, and work alongside an international engineering and construction group to swiftly conclude the application of a senior management figure and Russian national. The firm is also involved in pro bono representations on behalf of NGOs concerning the drafting of immigration legislation and the promotion of possible amendments. **Clients** Bechtel; Enterasys (UK); Information Services International; McCann-Erickson EMEA.

NORTON ROSE (see firm details p.1084) The departure of Caron Pope to Reed Smith Warner Cranston has diminished its capacity and dedication in this sector. Based in the firm's employment and pensions department, under Timothy Russell, the unit advises on the full range of business immigration matters from high-volume transfers to more complex, individual applications. It has recently made successful applications under Home Office policy concessions, and advises on the application of European law to the UK. **Clients** Financial groups; high net worth individuals; insurance providers; overseas law firms based in London; pharmaceutical companies; software and related services; travel and shipping organisations; utilities.

PENNINGTONS (see firm details p.1098) Positively recommended by firms dealing on both sides of the immigration fence, roughly a quarter of its work is taken up with a personal immigration caseload. All-rounder **Gülay Mehmet** (see p.424) handles predominantly corporate matters, such as for accountancy firms and a Japanese company involved in the construction of the HSBC building at Canary Wharf. Judicial reviews and appeals also form part of her caseload. Peers agree that "*she has raised the firm's profile enormously.*" It has advised the former mayor of Istanbul's financial district, applying for permission for her to remain in the UK due to her marriage in the face of a subsequent extradition request from Turkey. **Clients** Work permits for commercial clients.

PULLIG & CO Gooch Heer leads a "*spirited*" team, built on business immigration and European Economic Area Association Agreements (EAAs). In common with several smaller departments in our tables, it also has a strong sideline in family immigration matters, judicial reviews and some asylum work. The team has regrouped since the loss of its key partner, and in the past year has seen an increase in the amount of work the practice has undertaken for American and Central European companies. New media and the internet has proved a valuable source of instruction, while assistance to medical organisations has also been prominent. **Clients** EAAs; LSC franchise asylum work; family immigration; media and internet companies; medical companies.

DJ WEBB & CO David Webb's team comprises several highly experienced individuals. These include a founder member of ILPA and a former immigration barrister, and the team possesses a broad range of long-term experience from nationality to asylum matters. The compact, proactive unit has registered success in both business and personal immigration matters, particularly the latter.

TAYLOR WESSING (see firm details p.1156) New to our tables this year, the well-sized group's unambiguous approach and international reach was reflected in the comments of interviewees. A leading advisor to US and Australasian clients, its particular focus is on advice to management consultancies and relocation companies concerning applications on behalf of

IMMIGRATION ■ LONDON

entrepreneurial and technical groups. This has led to an increase in the number of cross-practice referrals. Advice on work permits and assistance to sole representatives make up the majority of its efforts. Gavin Jones leads a group endorsed by clients for its depth and efficiency.

Clients Citrix; Concha y Toro; Digital Impact; McKinsey & Company; Montgomery Watson; Novartis.

LONDON   PERSONAL

IMMIGRATION: PERSONAL
■ LONDON

1
- Bindman & Partners
- Birnberg Peirce & Partners
- Wesley Gryk
- Winstanley-Burgess

2
- Coker Vis Partnership
- Deighton Guedalla

3
- Bartram & Co
- Gill & Co
- Glazer Delmar
- Luqmani Thompson
- Powell & Co
- Wilson & Co

LEADING INDIVIDUALS

1
- **BURGESS David** Winstanley-Burgess
- **COKER Jane** Coker Vis Partnership
- **GRYK Wesley** Wesley Gryk
- **GUEDALLA Vicky** Deighton Guedalla
- **RANDALL Christopher** Winstanley-Burgess
- **STANLEY Alison** Bindman & Partners

2
- **DAVIES Matthew** Wilson & Co
- **HANLEY Michael** Wilson & Co
- **LINDSLEY Fiona** Winstanley-Burgess
- **LUQMANI Jawaid** Luqmani Thompson
- **RIPLEY Fiona** Winstanley-Burgess
- **WOODHOUSE Sarah** Birnberg Peirce & Partners

3
- **BARTRAM Peter** Bartram & Co
- **BYE Eileen** Luqmani Thompson
- **HUNTER Alison** Wesley Gryk
- **HUSSAIN Belayeth** DJ Webb & Co
- **LESKIN Nigel** Birnberg Peirce & Partners
- **PEIRCE Jacqueline** Glazer Delmar
- **PENROSE Martin** Winstanley-Burgess
- **THOMPSON Sally** Luqmani Thompson

This book is the product of 6,582 1/2 hour interviews. See p.7 for BMRB audit.
Within each band, firms are listed alphabetically. See individuals' profiles p.421

BINDMAN & PARTNERS (see firm details p.872) The team is well respected and highly experienced in this field and the related issues of family, housing and childcare law. It excels in the provision of a comprehensive, all-round service. Market-leading assistance on the rights of children and their families, and the concomitant effects of immigration decisions is a specialism of the firm. Peers "*would recommend them without hesitation.*" In a sub-sector dominated by individuals rather than departments, the tenacious **Alison Stanley** (see p.425) is a leading light. "*Formidable, sharp and extra-determined,*" she was also described to *Chambers* as unfailingly helpful. She possesses a broad knowledge built on long experience; she "*plays it close to the net, acting proactively on behalf of her clients.*" Advice on trafficked-women cases and work permit applications for the voluntary sector is matched with legal aid, asylum appeals and judicial review work, including deportation cases. The team has also dealt with a smaller number of business-related matters.

BIRNBERG PEIRCE & PARTNERS Long established in the sector, the team employs a "*thorough, committed and imaginative*" approach. Recently focused on the twin issues of internment and compensation, it has been involved in matters of the highest profile. The group has pursued compensation claims concerning the wrongful imprisonment of asylum seekers under Article 31 of the UN Convention on Refugees (UNCOR). It can also count the judicial review of benefits and HIV cases as areas of concerted attention. Peers considered that the effects of Fiona Lindsley's departure to Winstanley-Burgess have been somewhat redressed by the increased profile of **Sarah Woodhouse**. "*A force to be reckoned with;*" counsel considered that "*she has the most penetrating analysis and is about as good as you can get in her generation.*" Woodhouse's "*complete dedication*" has assisted Erdem Bulbul in the Sepet and Bulbul case, concerning the asylum position on conscientious objectors, which has proceeded to the House of Lords. **Nigel Leskin** has assisted six of the eight individuals detained indefinitely under the Anti-Terrorism, Crime & Security Act, following its introduction in late 2001 after the September 11th terrorist attacks. This has made good use of Leskin's dual abilities in criminal and immigration work.

WESLEY GRYK (see firm details p.1184) A team of "*highly committed individuals*" eschews a large volume of cases in preference to significant actions dealing with civil liberties. This has included assisting women brought to the UK for marriage and subsequently abused in the first year, to stay, as well as political asylum cases involving unaccompanied minors. The firm is well known for its activities on applications concerned with sexuality, and the availability of combination therapy for applicants with HIV/AIDS. Perhaps most notably, the firm has represented the UNHCR as interveners in the Sepet and Bulbul case. **Wesley Gryk** (see p.423) leads an energetic team that goes "*well beyond the call of duty*" to assist its clients. A specialist in same sex cases, his tenacious and analytical style has proved popular, and he is said to have been instrumental in formulating Government policy in this area. A new entrant to the tables, **Alison Hunter** (see p.423) is one team member carving a profile for herself. She is respected for her representation of self-employed persons and Eastern Europeans under EAAs.

WINSTANLEY-BURGESS (see firm details p.1193) The firm is judged by peers to be "*absolutely top-notch and incredibly thorough.*" Preceded by its reputation for involvement in key asylum cases in recent years, the firm has maintained a high level of consistency across its varied areas of work. **David Burgess** was described to *Chambers* as "*probably the most inspirational lawyer in immigration*" for his innovative and tactical approach to cases. He heads a team "*several layers deep in highly committed individuals.*" Interviewees highlighted **Christopher Randall**'s practical approach and intellectual ability. The arrival of "*innovative creative thinker*" **Fiona Lindsley** from Birnberg Pierce & Partners has strengthened an already powerful squad. "*Hard-working,*" **Fiona Ripley** was considered an effective client handler. The profile of **Martin Penrose** has increased in recent months due to his representations on behalf of Zimbabwean asylum seekers.

COKER VIS PARTNERSHIP The practice was particularly commended by observers for its "*highly professional and fiercely dedicated*" ethos. **Jane Coker** (see p.422) personifies this approach. A highly influential lawyer "*prepared to tackle issues of principal at a high level,*" she was in the spotlight this year as a result of her action on behalf of a Nigerian woman against the Lord Chancellor. The case alleged discrimination concerning his appointment, without advertising the post, of a personal friend to be his special advisor. She is one of only a handful of lawyers in the sector to be charged with undertaking peer review, and is also a children's lawyer.

DEIGHTON GUEDALLA The practice has its foundations in the "*extremely thorough, determined and meticulous*" **Vicky Guedalla**. "*Her knowledge is quite extraordinary – she is a perfectionist in preparation and presentation and she doesn't let the Home Office or the Immigration Service get away with anything,*" claimed one peer. She continues to assist Yasin Sepet in the ongoing Sepet and Bulbul legal process, and

LONDON/THE SOUTH, THAMES VALLEY & SOUTH WEST ■ IMMIGRATION

represented Martha Osamor, the second appellant in the discrimination action brought against the Lord Chancellor over the appointment of his special advisor.

BARTRAM & CO This small unit works predominantly on individual immigration cases and mainstream immigration work on behalf of families and businesses. It has witnessed an increase in the volume of its appeals work concerning human rights and the enforcement of decisions. Impressing interviewees with its lively approach, the firm accepts both private and legally aided instructions. **Peter Bartram**'s (see p.422) "*forthright and upfront*" signature style has assisted many self-employed people, particularly on behalf of Lithuanian individuals. He has also been involved in two Colombian cases, concerning individuals seeking leave to remain in the UK and the precise nature and definition of the activity that caused them to leave, whether economic or political.

GILL & CO Avtar Gill's well-supported team deals primarily with asylum cases for Iraqi Kurds and Romanies. The firm acted in the Gardi test case, concerning an appeal under Article 1 of the ECHR relating to the repatriation of an Iraqi Kurd. It has also seen an increase in HIV-related matters and private immigration cases brought by individuals, often on behalf of American artists and musicians following the September 11th attacks.

GLAZER DELMAR This dedicated asylum firm has expanded in the past year, boosting its available resources and capacity. Latin American cases dominate the caseload, which also comprises HIV cases, domestic violence-related instructions and work on behalf of unmarried persons. Peers agree that the firm "*knows how to represent clients in the best way - committed and careful.*" **Jacqueline Peirce** is the most high profile of a number of individuals at the firm recommended to researchers by interviewees. An "*assertive personality,*" she represented Diriye in the Saad, Diriye and Osorio case, concerning whether an individual who has exceptional leave to remain (ELR) may appeal the refusal of refugee status. She further assisted the appellant in the McPherson case, based on Articles 3 and 8 of the ECHR. The practice has continued to broaden out with non-asylum work and immigration-related human rights cases a feature.

LUQMANI THOMPSON A human rights and asylum specialist, the department focuses on strategic casework tackling discrimination across immigration, education and public law. It has brought key cases against the Government concerning the withholding of education to the children of asylum seekers, and over the delay experienced by successful applicants in receiving rights-granting documentation. The creative **Jawaid Luqmani** (see p.424) is the firm's lead player; he is described as "*bright and quick on his feet.*" The firm assisted two of the claimants in the Saad, Diriye and Osorio case concerned with the status of those granted ELR. **Sally Thompson**'s (see p.425) work covers a wide base, with a proportion relating to vulnerable individuals from children to those with disabilities. She has made representation on behalf of a young African girl who was profoundly deaf. **Eileen Bye** (see p.422) was "*committed to her clients.*"

POWELL & CO (see firm details p.1105) Frank Kiangala heads a team that has observed an increase in applications relating to human rights, specifically Articles 2, 3, and 8 of the ECHR. The firm has been involved in formulating the boundaries of the Government's 'safe country' list for the repatriation of refugees, taking on cases concerning the status of Greece and Pakistan. In the latter case, ex parte Javed, the firm successfully acted against the Secretary of State in establishing both that the woman involved should not be returned to Pakistan for fear of persecution, and that the court was entitled to review the subordinate legislation under which the decision was made. The unit has also acted on behalf of several Palestinian individuals. It receives regular referrals on matters concerning HIV/AIDS and same sex relations, and has represented Kenyan families affected by the UK's voucher system.

WILSON & CO (see firm details p.1191) A large legal aid practice, its successful challenge to the Government over the high-profile Oakington Reception Centre resulted in a great deal of publicity. The court ruled that the Government's internment of four Iraqi Kurd terrorist suspects under the Anti-Terrorism, Crime & Security Act 2001 to enable their applications to be determined more quickly, was unlawful and breached Article 5 of the ECHR, the provision guarding against discrimination. **Matthew Davies** was particularly recommended for his expertise on HIV and same sex applications, while **Michael Hanley** was applauded by peers for his personal direction of the Oakington case.

OTHER NOTABLE PRACTITIONERS
Belayeth Hussain at DJ Webb & Co was rated highly by market observers.

THE SOUTH, THAMES VALLEY & SOUTH WEST

IMMIGRATION
■ THE SOUTH, THAMES VALLEY & SOUTH WEST

1. **Bobbetts Mackan** Bristol
   Darbys Oxford
   Eric Robinson & Co Southampton

LEADING INDIVIDUALS
1. **HARVEY** Jennifer Darbys
   TURPIN Philip Turpin & Miller

This book is the product of 6,582 1/2 hour interviews. See p.7 for BMRB audit.
Within each band, firms are listed alphabetically. See individuals' profiles p.421

BOBBETTS MACKAN (see firm details p.879) The firm operates out of Bristol, as well as from a drop-in law unit in Easton. Derek McConnell's team has a largely localised focus, assisting on immigration, asylum and related concerns. Interviewees spoke of a well-prepared firm with a proactive approach to its clients.

DARBYS (see firm details p.926) Asylum matters for a largely Kosovan and Afghani clientele make up the majority of this firm's growing caseload. Working closely with its criminal and family departments, the practice is undertaking more privately paying immigration work, in addition to its Legal Services Commission (LSC) instructions. **Jenny Harvey**'s (see p.423) team has also been making moves to boost its commercial immigration work, assisting Formula 1 racing teams, engineering companies and hospitality organisations with their immigration requirements.

ERIC ROBINSON & CO The firm has given up its legal aid franchise in favour of private client immigration, of which work permits are a notable focus. A small percentage of private asylum work exists. It has experienced an increase in the use of HSMP applications, and cases involving nationality issues and representations on behalf of children joining dependents or relatives. Astrid Grafton was involved in a successful human rights appeal under Article 8 of the ECHR concerning the right to respect for private and family life, on behalf of a married couple.

OTHER NOTABLE PRACTITIONERS
Philip Turpin, formerly of Dukes Arnold Du Feu, now of his own firm **Turpin & Miller**, was recommended to researchers for his experience and knowledge. Observers anticipate that his practice will flourish in a dedicated immigration environment.

IMMIGRATION ■ MIDLANDS/EAST ANGLIA/THE NORTH

MIDLANDS

IMMIGRATION
■ MIDLANDS

1. **Tyndallwoods** Birmingham
2. **Nelsons** Nottingham

LEADING INDIVIDUALS

1. **CONLAN Sue** Tyndallwoods
   FINCH Margaret Tyndallwoods
   PHILLIPS Mark Tyndallwoods
   SMITH David Nelsons

This book is the product of 6,582 1/2 hour interviews. See p.7 for BMRB audit.
Within each band, firms are listed alphabetically. See individuals' profiles p.421

TYNDALLWOODS (see firm details p.1172) Interviewees consider the firm to be "*head and shoulders above the others in the region.*" Predominantly an asylum practice, it deals with cases via the LSC, and carries out a small proportion of personal and business immigration work. **Sue Conlan** (see p.422) has been involved in a number of cases that have set precedents, while **Margaret Finch** (see p.422) is said to "*go the extra mile in research and effort.*" Of **Mark Phillips** (see p.424), competitors claimed: "*Tenacity must be his middle name.*" The team has dealt with two of the eight current matters brought under the Anti-Terrorism Crime & Security Act, including one relating to a recognised refugee, who the Secretary of State claims is excluded from the protection of the ECHR and the UN Refugee Convention. The firm, which carries out all of its own representations, has also successfully brought a judicial review of the refusal to consider applications from asylum seekers at the British Embassy in Yemen.

NELSONS (see firm details p.1082) The firm became one of the highest profile examples of a practice, contracted to the LSC, to totally withdraw from asylum work and legally aided instructions. It now covers all other areas within immigration on a privately paying basis. Consultant David Smith deals with both business and personal immigration matters, with a practice weighted towards the latter, and focused predominantly in the East Midlands.

EAST ANGLIA

IMMIGRATION
■ EAST ANGLIA

1. **Gross & Co** Bury St Edmunds
   Leathes Prior Norwich
   Wollastons Chelmsford

LEADING INDIVIDUALS

1. **CARY Tim** Leathes Prior
   KIRK Graeme Gross & Co

This book is the product of 6,582 1/2 hour interviews. See p.7 for BMRB audit.
Within each band, firms are listed alphabetically. See individuals' profiles p.421

GROSS & CO (see firm details p.979) **Graeme Kirk** (see p.424) (chairman of The Immigration & Nationality Committee of The International Bar Association) leads a responsive team at this broad-based practice. A corporate immigration firm, it represents British companies seeking work permits for foreign citizens, and those individuals applying to the UK under the HSMP on behalf of foreign companies. Related family and dependent matters are also featured. Its instructions emanate from a broad range of disciplines, although the majority of applications have been in the IT and accountancy sectors. Its abilities are well respected by peers and it receives referrals from both regional and London-based firms.

LEATHES PRIOR The firm's immigration practice trades as Immigration Assist, a dedicated unit set up in 2001. **Tim Cary** heads the unit, comprising trained and experienced fee-earning paralegals. In the last year, it has experienced an increase in its caseload across the board and has doubled its workforce. While asylum is still the mainstay of the practice, work permit applications for those with hi-tech skills, for restaurant and hotel staff from the Far East and Asia and for agricultural workers from Eastern Europe, occupy much of the team's time. It has also been involved in some High Court applications and judicial reviews.

WOLLASTONS (see firm details p.1196) The firm is almost a pure business immigration concern, occupying a specialist niche in its work for TV commercial companies and the film industry. It obtains permits for directors, actors and technicians from outside the European Economic Area. Although overseen by commercial partner Nicholas Burnett, the team includes full-time immigration manager Janice Leggett, who deals with the majority of applications. The "*efficient and helpful*" team also assists non-EAA nationals on shortages in the agricultural industry, and processes individual applications for private businessmen and their families.

THE NORTH

DAVID GRAY SOLICITORS Considered "*head and shoulders above the others in the region,*" the firm's team ethos make it a favourite amongst interviewees. Peers were quick to praise the firm's efforts on both asylum and non-asylum matters, including family immigration and nationality applications. In their experience, the unit "*tends to win, especially at the appeals stage.*" Practice head **David Gray** was considered "*the best immigration man for anything complex*" with an intelligent, committed approach allied to considerable experience.

AS LAW A committed focus has maintained the firm's reputation as specialists in asylum and immigration work. "*A first-class legal technician,*" **Peter Simm** heads the team. He is recommended by peers and counsel alike for his "*attention to detail and deep knowledge of asylum and related areas.*" He sets the standard for the team in his ability to combine tenacity with a willingness to listen to new ideas.

HARRISON BUNDEY & CO Acknowledged personal immigration specialists, the firm's main focus is asylum matters. In receipt of a LSC franchise for immigration, this work is carried out by a stand-alone, six-person team headed by caseworker Vladimir Mikeljevic. **Ruth Bundey** (see p.422) handles all non-asylum matters, including HIV/AIDS cases involving sudden diagnosis and subsequent appeals against Home Office decisions. Well known also for her civil liberties experience, leading peers consider her cross-fertilisation of practice areas to be a key factor in her success. The team has expertise in same sex immigration matters. It is also involved in domestic violence concession cases, concerning female immigrants who have entered the country as a spouse or partner and who have subsequently been the victim of domestic abuse within the probationary 12 month period specified under immigration rules.

HOWELLS (see firm details p.1002) One of the largest immigration teams in the North, the firm deals with the full range of immigration

THE NORTH/THE LEADERS ■ IMMIGRATION

IMMIGRATION
■ THE NORTH

1
- **David Gray Solicitors** Newcastle upon Tyne

2
- **AS Law** Liverpool
- **Harrison Bundey & Co** Leeds
- **Howells** Sheffield

3
- **Jackson & Canter** Liverpool
- **James & Co** Bradford

4
- **Davis Blank Furniss** Manchester
- **Samuel Phillips & Co** Newcastle upon Tyne
- **Thornhill Ince** Manchester

LEADING INDIVIDUALS

1
- **BUNDEY Ruth** Harrison Bundey & Co
- **GRAY David** David Gray Solicitors
- **SIMM Peter** AS Law

2
- **DONKERSLEY John** Howells
- **JAMES Charles** James & Co

3
- **HOLROYD Andrew** Jackson & Canter
- **SAFFER Laurence** Henry Hyams

This book is the product of 6,582 1/2 hour interviews. See p.7 for BMRB audit.
Within each band, firms are listed alphabetically. See individuals' profiles p.421

---

work, with a focus on the personal side including both asylum and non-asylum work. Its "*precise*" team works with a variety of nationalities as a result of the Government's dispersal policy, notably assisting Yemeni, Somali, Afghan and Pakistani clients at adjudications and at tribunal level. **John Donkersley** (see p.422) heads the group; he is "*committed to clients, optimistic in his approach and always cheerful.*" One of several firms in the region to hold an LSC franchise, it also acts on disability, same sex and HIV cases.

JACKSON & CANTER (see firm details p.1011) Asylum work makes up more than half of this firm's immigration caseload. In common with other firms in the North, the Government's dispersal policy has magnified its instructions, particularly among Iraqi Kurds sent to Liverpool and the surrounding area. These matters are dealt with by a large team that counts non-practising barristers among its numbers. Practice head **Andrew Holroyd** (see p.423) also represents professionals on their work permit applications and has assisted on a number of HSMP applications for doctors.

JAMES & CO (see firm details p.1012) Out-and-out immigration specialists, the firm splits its work between the business and personal elements of the sector. Of the former, it is regularly instructed on work permits for those coming to the UK for business purposes, particularly for individuals in the building trade. On the personal side, its asylum work has included a number of appeals against Home Office decisions made on allegedly incorrect information. **Charles James** has much experience and a "*solid grounding in immigration and asylum work.*" He leads a compact, proactive team.

DAVIS BLANK FURNISS The firm pursues a deliberately broad-based approach. As a result, it represents IT and technology companies, hotels and leisure groups and multinationals as well as private individuals with asylum needs. This confident unit comprises lawyers with additional expertise in employment and family law, with Guy Robson benefiting from his ongoing role sitting as a part-time immigration adjudicator.

SAMUEL PHILLIPS & CO (see firm details p.1122) Work permit applications and those concerning nationality are the mainstay of the firm. It specialises in applications on behalf of individuals from the Far East, as well as those from inward investment companies and electronic goods manufacturers. Closer to home, the team has been instrumental in assisting local hospitals and restaurants to fulfill their requirements for medical staff and specialist chefs. Head of department Barry Speker leads a small team that has ceased its LSC-funded asylum work, although it continues to work on a number of refugee and asylum cases brought privately.

THORNHILL INCE Robin Ince's firm continues to assist on most types of immigration work, including asylum, for a predominantly local clientele.

OTHER NOTABLE PRACTITIONERS Laurence Saffer of Leeds-based Henry Hyams enjoys a solid reputation locally for leading a "*knowledgeable*" LSC-funded team, and for his dogged approach – "*he will push through a case for the positive result.*"

THE LEADERS IN IMMIGRATION

ALFANDARY, Peter
Reed Smith Warner Cranston, London
(020) 7403 2900
palfandary@reedsmith.co.uk
Specialisation: Partner and head of UK and US corporate immigration department. Corporate immigration. 17 years of experience advising national and multinational corporations on work permits and related immigration issues with the Home Office and Work Permits (UK). Advice on nationality law, overseas investor rules and business related immigration for individuals. Author of chapter on immigration in 'CCH Employment Contracts Manual'.
Prof. Memberships: Law Society; Immigration Law Practitioners Association.
Career: Articled *Lovell White & King*; qualified 1979 followed by a year in industry and a year with a leading firm of French avocats. Joined *Warner Cranston* as a partner in 1982. Managing partner 1991-93.
Personal: Born 10 January 1953, resides in London. Educated at Lycée Francais de Londres, University of Kent and London School of Economics. Interests include Theatre, Music and Anglo-French relations. Deputy-President French Chamber of Commerce; decorated by the French Government as a *Chevalier dans L'Ordre Nationale du Mérite* in 1991.

ANDONIAN, Bernard
Gulbenkian Harris Andonian, London
(020) 7937 1542
Specialisation: Partner in immigration department. Principal areas of practice are UK and US business immigration for multinational companies and foreign business executives. Deals with work permit applications and business investor and inter-company applications; preparation, submission of business and investor plans; independent means. Contributor to numerous business immigration articles. Lectures on business immigration. Has recently reviewed 'Law and Practice' by Michael Supperstone QC and Declan O'Dempsey; appointed by the Lord Chancellor as part-time Immigration Adjudicator and Special Adjudicator.
Prof. Memberships: Member of Immigration Law Practitioners Association, and former Executive Committee Member, the International Bar Association, Law Society, Holborn Law Society.
Career: Qualified 1985 while at *Gulbenkian Harris Andonian*, and became a partner in 1986.
Personal: Born 11 September 1949. Attended City of London and Thames Valley Universities. Obtained Distinction in Intellectual Property for MA Degree. Leisure pursuits include reading, rambling, table tennis, snooker, swimming. Lives in Osterley, Middlesex.

BALCOMB, Anne
Harbottle & Lewis, London
(020) 7667 5000
anne.balcomb@harbottle.com
Specialisation: All aspects of immigration and nationality law; advising corporate and private clients, in particular on employment and business-related matters. Head of the Immigration Group.
Prof. Memberships: Law Society; Immigration Law Practitioners' Association.
Career: Worked as a teacher from 1964-78; qualified as a solicitor in 1982; practised in immigration and nationality law since 1986; worked for *Simmons and Simmons* from 1990-93 and for *Pullig & Co* from 1993-2000. Joined *Harbottle & Lewis* 2001.
Publications: Various articles in professional journals.
Personal: St Anne's College Oxford 1960-63; BA Hons Modern Languages 1963. College of Law 1978-79. Fluent in French. Lives in London and Devon.

BARTH, Philip
Mishcon de Reya, London
(020) 7440 7000
philip.barth@mishcon.co.uk
Specialisation: Specialises in all aspects of immigration and nationality law other than asylum. Having a background as an experienced company/commercial lawyer, his combination of expertise is of particular benefit for all businesses, corporates and persons who wish to move to the UK to pursue economic activities. He is regulary involved in cases at the cutting-edge of business immigration practice and has many years experience

421

IMMIGRATION ■ THE LEADERS

in providing practical immigration advice within the wider commercial context to meet the needs of business. Writes and speaks regularly on business immigration topics.
Prof. Memberships: Immigration Law Practitioners Association; co-chair of the Employment & Business Sub-committee; Law Society.
Career: Rugby School; Magdalene College, Cambridge University. 1980-82 articles with *Malkin Cullis & Sumption*; 1983-86 Assistant solicitor at *Clintons*; 1986-88 assistant solicitor at *Walters Fladgate*, 1988-98 partner in successor firm, *Fladgate Fielder*, 1998-present: partner *Mishcon de Reya*.

BARTRAM, Peter
Bartram & Co, Hounslow
(020) 8814 1414
Specialisation: Head of a West London practice (near Heathrow Airport) devoted to all aspects of UK immigration and asylum law with Community Legal Service contract in immigration law.
Prof. Memberships: Law Society Immigration Law Panel; Immigration Law Practioners Association.
Career: Qualified 1981. Immigration specialist since 1984. Has worked in law centres, advice centres and in private practice. Established own firm, *Bartram & Co*, in 1994.
Personal: Born 21 August 1957. Bristol University (LLB, 1978) and Brunel University (MA, 1988). Spanish and French speaker.

BELCHAK, Hilary
Kingsley Napley, London
(020) 7814 1200
hbelchak@kingsleynapley.co.uk
Specialisation: Partner and head of immigration department. Main areas of practice are UK immigration and nationality law. Has 18 years experience in this field. Presently covering corporate immigration such as work permits, immigration advice to entrepreneurs, the highly skilled and high net worth individuals wishing to invest and settle in the UK, and nationality issues. Numerous articles including in the 'International Quarterly', 'Offshore Investment', the new quarterly publication 'Immigration and Employment Law', as well as being deputy editor of that journal. Has spoken at ILPA and the immigration committees of AILA, IBA and IPBA annual conferences as well as conferences of the Centre for International Legal Studies CBI Employee Relocation Council, IBC UK, Employment Lawyers Association, the Japan Institute for Overseas Investment and In-house Seminars. Recently prepared contribution for the Croner's publication 'Managing Internationally Mobile Employees', as well as articles for its monthly bulletin. Also contributed to a publication by FL Memo (publication date Autumn 2002).
Prof. Memberships: ILPA, IPBA, AILA, ABA. Chair IPBA's Immigration Committee 1997-99. Secretary of ILPA 1995-97.

Career: Qualified in 1984. Senior lecturer at North London Polytechnic 1971-81; worked at *Winstanley Burgess* 1982-84 and *Clinton Davis & Co.* 1984-88. Joined *Simmons & Simmons* in 1988, becoming a partner in 1994. Joined *Kingsley Napley* February 1999.
Personal: Born 17 March 1949. Holds an LLB (1970) and LLM (1971). Leisure interests include opera and cinema. Lives in London and Suffolk.

BUNDEY, Ruth
Harrison Bundey & Co., Leeds
(0113) 237 4047
ruth.bundey@harrisonbundey.co.uk
See under Human Rights, p.412

BURGESS, David
Winstanley-Burgess, London
(020) 7278 7911

BYE, Eileen
Luqmani Thompson, London
(020) 8365 7800
Specialisation: Immigration and related areas of public law, including prisons, social welfare, discrimination, European community and work-related law; taking cases in civil and administrative law up to House of Lords and European Court of Human Rights.
Prof. Memberships: ILPA, Law Society, founder member and director of Bail for Immigration Detainees (BID), vice-chair of Detention Advice Service (DAS), director of Central London Law Centre.
Career: Qualified in 1994 with many years experience in human rights NGO and alternative dispute resolution.
Publications: Co-author 'JCWI Handbook'; contributor to other public law textbooks; occasional public law articles.
Personal: Committed to training others to improve delivery of public services, including local authority prison, probation staff as well as other practitioners.

CARY, Tim
Leathes Prior, Norwich
(01603) 610911

COKER, Jane
Coker Vis Partnership, London
(020) 8885 1415
Specialisation: Partner specialising in immigration. Work includes deportation, asylum, appeals representation and judicial review, and contempt of court. Author of numerous articles for Immigration Nationality Law Journal, LAG. Lectures on ILPA, LNTV and LAG courses. Addresses WNS, UKCOSA and medical conferences. Numerous TV and radio interviews. Joint author of 'Putting Children First: a Guide for Immigration Practitioners' (LAG) 2002, and 'Best Practice Guide to Making an Asylum Application' (ILPA) 2002.
Prof. Memberships: Immigration Law Practitioners Association, Law Society
Career: Qualified 1980. Set up *Jane Coker & Partners* in 1982. Now *Coker Vis Partnership*.
Personal: Born 11 July 1954. Holds a BSc in Biological Sciences.

CONLAN, Sue
Tyndallwoods, Birmingham
(0121) 624 1111
Specialisation: All aspects of immigration, including asylum, family reunion, illegal entry, deportation and detention. Experienced and special interest in advocacy before Adjudicators and Immigration Appeal Tribunal. Experienced in Judicial Review (including emergency cases) and in preparing appeals for Court of Appeal. Visiting lecturer in Immigration Law (with particular emphasis on asylum law and practice) for MA in Immigration Law, Policy and Practice at University of Central England (UCE) and the Legal Practice Course at UCE.
Prof. Memberships: Immigration Law Practitioners' Association. Immigration Panel of the Law Society.
Career: Graduated with a B.A. (Hons.) Law degree from Kingston Polytechnic (1980) and with an LLM (Welfare Law) from Leicester University (1990). Specialised in immigration law since July 1987. Joined *Tyndallwoods* in March 1996.
Personal: Born 14 November 1958, Birmingham.

DAVIES, Matthew
Wilson & Co, London
(020) 8808 7535

DEVINE, Laura
Eversheds, London
(020) 7919 4856
devinel@eversheds.com
Specialisation: Head of *Eversheds* Immigration and Nationality Team which she established in 1996. She is a prominent immigration lawyer, widely recognised as one of top ten executive specialists in the UK, advising on all areas of UK and US immigration law. Qualified as a solicitor at *Cameron Markby Hewitt* (now *CMS Cameron McKenna*) and established the immigration practice at *Coopers & Lybrand* (now *PWC*). She has an LLM from the London School of Economics and the School of Oriental and African Studies. She is due to be admitted to the Bar of the State of New York. She is a visiting lecturer at Hull University and gives presentations to the business community in the UK and abroad.
Publications: She is the author of numerous articles and publications, including: 'A Practical guide to the immigration aspects of employing overseas nationals in the UK' to be published in 2002, 'Immigration for Employment – Fast Tracking for Business' (2nd edition) published by Palladian in 2000 and 'Key Techniques in Employing Overseas Nationals under the Work Permit Scheme' published by Thorogood in 1999. Laura is featured in 'An International Who's Who of Corporate Immigration Lawyers' and in 'The Legal Experts Directory' as being an international immigration authority.

DIXON, Marian
Lovells, London
(020) 7296 2000
marian.dixon@lovells.com
Specialisation: Solicitor and Head of Immigration Unit. Over 19 years' experience in all areas of UK immigration and nationality law. Concentrates primarily on employment and business-related immigration issues such as business and commercial permits, training and work experience permits, business and self-employed applications, innovators, the Highly Skilled Migrant Programme, sole representatives, writers, composers and artists, entertainers and sportspeople, investors and business visitors. Also deals with citizenship applications, European Community law (including the European Community Association Agreements) and immigration appeals. Regular writer and speaker on immigration matters.
Prof. Memberships: Law Society, Immigration Law Practitioners' Association, The American Immigration Lawyers Association, International Bar Association.
Career: HM Immigration Officer, Heathrow Airport 1975-82, Immigration Advisor and Consultant with *Norton Rose* from 1984-87. Qualified in 1990. Worked for the Government Legal Service from 1990-92, then *McGrath & Co* from 1992-93 and 1994-97. Joined *Lovells* in January 1998 as Head of Immigration Unit. Appointed by the Lord Chancellor as a part-time immigration appeal adjudicator in 1997.
Personal: Educated at Newcastle upon Tyne University; College of Law, Chancery Lane. Lives in London and Warwickshire. Married. Leisure pursuits include tennis, music and reading.

DONKERSLEY, John
Howells, Sheffield
(0114) 249 6666
Specialisation: All aspects of immigration, in particular Kosovan, Yemeni and Somali asylum cases, HIV/AIDS, family reunion cases and judicial review. The team he heads has now grown to six solicitors, seven caseworkers and six support staff and he is an external supervisor for another firm's immigration work.
Prof. Memberships: Law Society, ILPA.
Career: Welfare Rights worker and freelance trainer 1985-88. Articled, and qualified 1991 at current firm where cut teeth representing detained Iraqis during Gulf War.
Personal: Born 1 December 1961. Attended London School of Economics (University of London), LLB (Hons) 1985. Leisure interests include building computers and Linux.

FINCH, Margaret
Tyndallwoods, Birmingham
(0121) 624 1111
Specialisation: Has practised immigration exclusively since qualification in 1993. Asylum and human rights work forms approximately 80% of current

THE LEADERS — IMMIGRATION

case-load, but other personal immigration work also handled. Conducts own advocacy when possible. Has strong track-record of investigating and substantiating asylum cases which have previously been rejected.
Prof. Memberships: ILPA, Law Society, member Law Society Immigration Law Panel.
Career: Graduated 1984. Taught English in Palestinian refugee camps in the Gaza Strip and worked in Switzerland before undertaking law conversion course. Trained at *John Howell & Co* before moving to *Tyndallwoods* in 1993.
Personal: Born 22 February 1962. BA English Literature 1984. Fluent French speaker.

GHERSON, Roger
Gherson & Co, London
(020) 7724 4488
roger@gherson.com
Specialisation: Widely experienced principal of a niche immigration firm, which practises exclusively in immigration and nationality. Work covers the full spectrum of business/employment-related immigration and personal immigration matters. Particularly expert in national security cases. Political asylum claims (private only) also covered, whether in the context of extradition/national security proceedings or otherwise. Extensively experienced in providing practical immigration advice and in dealing with the resolution of complex immigration issues. Expert in human rights law affecting all the firm's areas of practice. Business/employment expertise includes work permit applications and applications relating to visitors, sole representatives, business, investors, innovators, retired persons of independent means, ancestry, writers/composers/artists; as well as all free movement rights under European Community law, such as rights of establishment under the EC Association Agreements. Advises start-up companies; multinational companies relocating employees to the UK; overseas companies seeking to establish a business in the UK for the first time; individual overseas nationals wishing to establish a UK business; a wide range of enterprises including e-commerce/IT businesses; and individuals in a number of capacities. Work also includes appeals before immigration adjudicators, the Immigration Appeals Tribunal and the Special Immigration Appeals Commission; and judicial review matters in the High Court.
Career: Qualified in 1981.

GRAY, David
David Gray Solicitors, Newcastle upon Tyne
(0191) 232 9547

GRYK, Wesley
Wesley Gryk, London
(020) 7401 6887
wesley@gryklaw.com
Specialisation: All areas of UK immigration and nationality law.
Prof. Memberships: Law Society, Immigration Law Practitioners Association, Association of the Bar of the City of New York.
Career: Qualified in 1990, admitted to the Bar of New York in 1976. Federal Judicial Clerk to Judge Constance Baker Motley, Southern District of New York, 1975-76; associate, *Shearman & Sterling*, New York and Hong Kong, 1976-80; Deputy Representative and Legal Advisor, UN High Commissioner for Refugees, 1980-81; Deputy Head of Research Department, Amnesty International, 1981-86; *B.M. Birnberg & Co*, London, 1988-94; established own firm 1995.
Personal: Born 12 May 1949; attended East Catholic High School, 1963-67; Harvard College, 1967-71, BA; Warsaw University, 1971-72, Fulbright Scholar; Harvard Law School 1972-75, JD. Active in the work of Stonewall. Has travelled widely on human rights missions for Amnesty International, Human Rights Watch, and Article 19.

GUEDALLA, Vicky
Deighton Guedalla, London
(020) 7359 5700

GUILD, Elspeth
Kingsley Napley, London
(020) 7814 1200
eguild@kingsleynapley.co.uk
Specialisation: Partner, immigration department. Primarily specialises in European Community law relating to free movement of persons including the transfer of staff from companies in one Member State to another Member State, the right of self-employment and provision of services. Wide expertise in UK immigration and nationality issues. Author of numerous books including, 'Immigration Law in the European Community', 'Free Movement of Persons in the European Union,' and 'Developing Immigration and Asylum Policy of the European Union.' She is also Professor of European Immigration Law at the University of Nijmegen, and Visiting Fellow at the London School of Economics, where she also lectures.
Prof. Memberships: Chair of the Immigration Law Practitioners' Association European Group; Member of the Council of Justice; British representative of the European Sections of the International Commission of Jurists; Member of the Executive Committee, Centre of European Law, Kings College London.
Career: 1989-97 *Baileys Shaw & Gillett*: Head of immigration department. Joined *Kingsley Napley* as a partner in March 1997.

HANLEY, Michael
Wilson & Co, London
(020) 8808 7535

HAQUE, Tony
Baker & McKenzie, London
(020) 7919 1000
tony.haque@bakernet.com
Specialisation: Solicitor, business immigration group. Specialising in all areas of UK immigration and nationality work and related European Community law with emphasis on employment and business related applications. Acts principally for multinational companies and other corporate clients, entrepreneurs and high net worth individuals offering creative solutions to effect international transfers as expediently and cost-effectively as possible. Client base is particularly strong in the information technology sector. Also extensively involved with the firm's leading Japanese practice. Works closely with *Baker & McKenzie's* worldwide network of offices, particularly in the North America and Asia Pacific regions, to assist clients who require advice upon relocation issues outside of the UK. Member of the firm's International Executive Transfer Practice Group which provides advice on a broad range of related corporate, tax and labour law issues. Has published articles and spoken at seminars on a wide number of immigration issues in the UK and abroad.
Prof. Memberships: Law Society, Immigration Law Practitioners' Association, International Bar Association.
Career: 1994-97 *Baileys Shaw & Gillett*; qualified at *Kingsley Napley*; joined *Baker & McKenzie* as an associate in November 1997.

HARVEY, Jennifer
Darbys, Oxford
(01685) 811719
jharvey@darbys.co.uk
Specialisation: All aspects of immigration work including family reunion, work permit applications and other business/employment matters including increasing involvement in the field of Formula One motor racing. Extensive experience in the field of asylum law, with large caseload of Kosovan, Sudanese and Algerian asylum seekers.
Prof. Memberships: Law Society, Immigration Law Practitioners Association, Joint Council for Welfare of Immigrants.
Career: Degree in Modern History at Lady Margaret Hall, Oxford (2:1), worked in Sydney Legal Centre, Australia upon completion of law finals. Qualified October 1994, partner and head of immigration team.

HOLROYD, Andrew
Jackson & Canter, Liverpool
(0151) 282 1732
Specialisation: Partner in immigration department. Covers all aspects of immigration law including business immigration matters.
Prof. Memberships: Law Society Council Member and member of Law Society Immigration Sub-Committee. Past President of Liverpool Law Society. ILPA. Immigration Law Panel member.
Career: Qualified 1974 in Liverpool, joined *Jackson & Canter*. Became a partner in 1977.
Personal: Born 13 April 1948. Attended Nottingham University.

HUNTER, Alison
Wesley Gryk, London
(020) 7401 6887
alison@gryklaw.com
Specialisation: All areas of UK immigration and nationality law with particular emphasis on EU free movement law, asylum and human rights law.
Prof. Memberships: Law Society; Executive Committee Member of the Immigration Law Practitioners' Association; Management Committee Member of the Centre for Advice on Individual Rights in Europe.
Career: Qualified in 1997 after training at *Freshfields*. Since 1997, assistant at *Wesley Gryk Solicitors*. Visiting lecturer at Westminster University.
Publications: European Journal of Migration and Law, 'Between the domestic and the international: the role of the EU in providing protection for unaccompanied children in the UK'.
Personal: Educated in Switzerland, Germany and the UK. LLB with French law (London); LLM in Human Rights Law (London). Maintains close links with German lawyers and academics working in the field of immigration.

HUSSAIN, Belayeth
DJ Webb & Co, London
(020) 7247 9933

JAMES, Charles
James & Co, Bradford
(01274) 729900

KEMP, Lesley
Reed Smith Warner Cranston, London
(020) 7403 2900
lkemp@reedsmith.co.uk
Specialisation: Partner, business immigration department. Primarily specialises in business/employment related immigration. Advises both small and large scale global organisations in the relocation process for expatriates transferring to the UK; individual entrepreneurs and overseas firms seeking to establish a business in the UK; professionals in the entertainment, arts and media fields. Expertise in all aspects of UK immigration and nationality law including personal applications for investors; retired persons of independent means; spouse and family applications.
Prof. Memberships: Lectures and has published articles on immigration issues. Member of Immigration Law Practioners' Association (ILPA) (past treasurer and member of the Executive Committee of ILPA 1995-97).
Career: Qualified February 1989. Assistant solicitor 1989-93, *Kingsley Napley*; assistant solicitor and partner 1993-95, *Magrath & Co*; returned to *Kingsley Napley* as a partner, 1995-2000, to establish the firm's immigration department. Joined *Warner Cranston* as a partner in March 2000.

IMMIGRATION ■ THE LEADERS

Personal: Born 1960. Tiverton Grammar School; University of Kent at Canterbury (BA Hons); College of Law, Chancery Lane.

KIRK, Graeme
Gross & Co, Bury St Edmunds
(01284) 763333
gdk@gross.co.uk

Specialisation: Senior partner and head of immigration. Principal area of practice is immigration and nationality law. Also deals with company/commercial work for private companies and businesses, including foreign businesses seeking to establish a UK presence. Handles highly skilled migrant cases, work permits, self-employment, investor, business, sole representative, independent means innovator and all other immigration cases. Addressed IBA conferences regularly since 1991 and has spoken at seminars throughout the world inlcuding the AILA 2002 Global Immigration Summit in New York. Acts as consultant in immigration law to solicitors firms throughout the UK and overseas. Has lectured on business immigration for CLT. Client base includes international banks, major foreign and UK corporations, IT and high tech companies, entrepreneurs and high net worth individuals. Recognised as one of the leading UK corporate immigration specialists in 'International Who's Who of Business Lawyers'.
Prof. Memberships: Law Society, IBA, ILPA.
Career: Qualified in 1981. Assistant solicitor with *Radcliffes & Co*. 1981-84, then joined *Gross & Co*. in 1984 becoming a partner in 1986. Currently chairman of the Immigration & Nationality Committee of the International Bar Association, and member of the Law Society Immigration Law Panel.
Personal: Educated at Westminster School and University of East Anglia. A member of Bury St. Edmunds Rotary Club. Lives in Bury St. Edmunds.

LESKIN, Nigel
Birnberg Peirce & Partners, London
(020) 7284 4620

LINDSLEY, Fiona
Birnberg Peirce & Partners, London
(020) 7284 4620

LUQMANI, Jawaid
Luqmani Thompson, London
(020) 8365 7800
jawaid@luqmanithompson.com

Specialisation: Partner specialising in immigration. Work includes Administrative Court and Court of Appeal litigation in immigration law and related fields of education, crime and civil actions against the immigration service. Cases include inter-relationship between asylum and terrorism, asylum and crime and free movement entitlements for non EU nationals in particular rights of Eastern European nationals.
Prof. Memberships: Executive Committee Member for ILPA since 1992, current Treasurer of ILPA, appointed by the Law Society as Immigration Assessor since 1999, member of the Law Society.
Publications: Co-author of 'Recent Developments in Immigration' for Legal Action Group and author of immigration sections in 'Defending Suspects at Police Stations'. Lecturer for ILPA, LAG, UKCOSA and CAB. Numerous TV and radio interviews in respect of topical immigration issues.

MAGRATH, Chris
Magrath & Co, London
(020) 7495 3003

MANN, Jane
Fox Williams, London
(020) 7628 2000
jemann@foxwilliams.co.uk
See under Employment, p.327

MEHMET, Gülay
Penningtons, London
(020) 7457 3000
mehmetg@penningtons.co.uk

Specialisation: Solicitor, immigration department. Specialising in all areas of UK immigration and nationality and related Community law. Advises corporate/business and private clients including applications for work permits, business persons, entrepreneurs, investors, rights of establishment under the EC Association Agreement with Turkey and family reunion. Also has experience of immigration appeals, judicial review and extradition. Clients include international companies, including leading Indian companies and financial institutions; international accountants; first division and premiership football clubs; internationally renowned chef. Has been involved in training and spoken at seminars including International Bar Association Conference 2001.
Prof. Memberships: Law Society Immigration Committee, ILPA European Group, International Bar Association, Trustee to the Immigration and Nationality Research and Information Charity.
Career: Liverpool University, College of Law. 1991-94 Assistant Director, Joint Counsel for Welfare of Immigrants.
Personal: Bilingual Turkish. Trustee of Refugee Legal Centre.

MOSS, Peter
Bates, Wells & Braithwaite, London
(020) 7551 7777
p.moss@bateswells.co.uk

Specialisation: Immigration and Nationality Advisor. Advises on immigration and nationality matters and conducts advocacy in appeals. Main area of practice covers commercial immigration: work permits and applications for entry clearance as businessmen, overseas representatives, and under the Europe Agreements with Eastern European countries. Also specialises in applications outside the immigration rules for long term residents and applications for couples who cannot marry. Has provided expert opinions on immigration status for other solicitors acting in family law matters. Other main area of work for private clients includes persons of independent means, self-employed artists and family settlement cases. Author of articles for 'Immigration Law and Practice' and the 'Hong Kong Law Society Gazette'. Frequent lecturer on ILPA training course.
Prof. Memberships: Treasurer of Immigration Law Practitioners' Association, 1992-96. Many years service on the Executive of ILPA, and its European sub-committee.
Career: HM Immigration Officer, Dover 1973-75. Immigration Counsellor with the United Kingdom Immigrants Advisory Service 1975-76, then Senior Counsellor 1976-89. Immigration and Nationality Advisor with *Thomson Snell & Passmore* 1989-92, then joined *Bates Wells & Braithwaite*.
Personal: Born 11 July 1949.

ONSLOW-COLE, Julia
CMS Cameron McKenna, London
(020) 7367 3000
julia.onslow-cole@cmck.com

Specialisation: Partner and Head of the Global Immigration and Nationality Group at *CMS Cameron McKenna*, which is the largest Executive immigration practice in the UK. The team is ranked No.1 by all legal directories. *CMS Cameron McKenna* is a top ten law firm in Europe with offices worldwide, and the Global Immigration and Nationality Group offers commercial immigration advice to corporate and individual clients in the UK, US, Hong Kong, Eastern Europe, the Far East and Africa. Julia's team of 24 provide, accurate, cutting-edge advice to financial institutions, international conglomerates, IT companies and other major multinationals. Julia's dedicated team also advise individuals, particularly Highly Skilled Migrants, investors, innovators, business persons and entertainers and sportspeople. The Group has an impressive track record, taking an innovative approach to providing solutions to client problems. Julia's team submitted the first successful application under the Highly Skilled Migrant Programme in January 2002 and has had a 100% success rate to date.
Prof. Memberships: Immediate past Chair of International Bar Association, Immigration Committee and current council member, Co-convenor of Immigration Law Practitioners Association's Business and Employment Sub-Committee, Member and Assessor of the Law Society's Immigration Law Panel, Member of the UK Association for European Law, Fellow of the Society for Advanced Legal Studies, immigration consultant to office of the Immigration service commissioner, member of American Immigration Lawyers Association.
Career: Qualified 1984. British Coal 1982-86, then *Simmons & Simmons* as head of UK immigration and nationality department 1986-90. Joined *Cameron Markby Hewitt* in 1990 as head of immigration and nationality group, partner from 1991.
Publications: Contributing co-editor to several leading textbooks on immigration law including Butterworth's 'Handbook and Immigration Service' and Sweet and Maxwells loose leaf service.
Personal: Born 30 September 1959. Took an LLB (Hons) in 1981, Law Society exams in 1982.

PEIRCE, Jacqueline
Glazer Delmar, London
(020) 7639 8801

PENROSE, Martin
Winstanley-Burgess, London
(020) 7278 7911

PHILLIPS, Mark
Tyndallwoods, Birmingham
(0121) 624 1111
Mark_Phillips@tyndallwoods.co.uk

Specialisation: Partner and head of immigration department. Area of practice is immigration and public law, mainly refugee, marriage and family reunion cases. Undertakes advocacy and judicial review work. Author of 'Tenants Control' (Council Housing Co-operatives). Has lectured for LIBERTY on civil liberties issues (especially policing and Human Rights Act) and for ILPA and IISA on judicial review and immigration appeals advocacy. Member of Amnesty International and Joint Council for the Welfare of Immigrants. Member of the Law Society Immigration Law Committee, Chairperson Midland Immigration Practitioners (MIP). Member of Region 6 Legal Services Commission Review Committee.
Prof. Memberships: Law Society, Birmingham Law Society, Immigration Law Practitioners Association, Assessor and Member Law Society Immigration Law Panel.
Career: Paralegal advisor at Stepney Green Law Centre 1973-75. Action/research project on tenant's co-operatives 1975-77. Articled clerk at *T.V. Edwards* 1978-81. Assistant solicitor at *Geffens* 1981-83. Senior solicitor at Handsworth Law Centre, Birmingham, 1983-85. Joined *Tyndallwoods* in 1985, becoming a partner in 1988.
Personal: Born 10 May 1947. Educated at Lymm Grammar School, Cheshire, 1958-64; Dame Allen's School, Newcastle-on-Tyne, 1964-66, Hull University 1967-70; then London School of Economics 1970-71. Married with two children. Leisure interests include mountain biking. Lives in Walsall.

POPE, Caron
Reed Smith Warner Cranston, London
(020) 7403 2900

Specialisation: Caron has specialised in UK business immigration law since qualification in 1990 and has extensive experience in the full range of business immigration applications. She has been ranked among the leading UK immigration lawyers for several years. Particular areas of expertise include work permit applications, particularly obtaining per-

THE LEADERS — IMMIGRATION

mits for outside hires which have not been advertised or which do not fully meet the requirements of the work permit scheme she has 100% success rate for work permit applications. In addition, Caron has made numerous applications for sole representatives and other permit free employment categories, applications for businessmen, applications under Home Office concessions and settlement and naturalisation applications. She has also made a number of applications for investors and the innovator category which was introduced in September 2000. She also advises on the application of European Law.

Prof. Memberships: Immigration Law Practitioners Association. Associate member - Canada/UK Chamber of Commerce; Member Inter Pacific Bar Association (IPBA).

Career: Croydon High School for Girls 1977-84. University of East Anglia, Norwich 1984-87 (LLB Hons). Guilford College of Law. *Cameron Markby Hewitt* 1988-96. Articled Clerk (1988-90). Solicitor, Immigration & Nationality Law Group (1990-96). *Norton Rose* (1996 - 2002) Head of Business Immigration Team. July 2002; *Reed Smith Warner Cranson* - partner - business immigration. Caron has lectured and written on UK immigration issues in the UK and overseas and is recognised in all the leading legal directories.

RANDALL, Christopher
Winstanley-Burgess, London
(020) 7278 7911

RIPLEY, Fiona
Winstanley-Burgess, London
(020) 7278 7911

ROLLASON, Nicolas
Kingsley Napley, London
(020) 7814 1200
nrollason@kingsleynapley.co.uk

Specialisation: All areas of business and personal immigration and nationality law with particular emphasis on EU free movement law and the rights of establishment under the EC Asssociation Agreements with central and eastern Europe. Substantial experience of immigration appeals, judicial review and proceedings before the ECJ and Court of First Instance in Luxembourg. Reported cases before the ECJ include Case C-356/98 Kaba v SSHD and C-416/96 El Yassini v SSHD. Frequent lecturer on EU free movement and related human rights issues. Rapporteur to the European Commission on free movement 1996-2002.

Prof. Memberships: Member of the ILPA European Subcommittee since 1996, Law Society.

Career: Qualified in 1996. Assistant in immigration department *Baileys Shaw and Gillet* 1996-97. Joined *Kingsley Napley* in March 1997.

Personal: Born 1968. Attended Oxford University 1986-89. Lives in London.

SAFFER, Laurence
Henry Hyams, Leeds
(0113) 243 2288

SIMM, Peter
A S Law, Liverpool
(0151) 707 1212

SMITH, David
Nelsons, Nottingham
(0115) 989 5225
david.smith@nelsons-solicitors.co.uk

Specialisation: Partner, head of immigration unit. Developed immigration work from scratch at *Nelsons* since 1989. Works across full range of individual and corporate immigration cases.

Prof. Memberships: Law Society, Immigration Law Practitioners Association. Panel solicitor for Stonewall and Refugee Legal Centre. Member of and Assessor for Law Society Immigration Panel.

Career: After ten years in social work qualified as a solicitor in 1989. Partner at *Nelsons* 1995-2002. Now part-time consultant.

Personal: Born 5 March 1954. BA Philosophy 1976, Master in Social Work 1978.

STANLEY, Alison
Bindman & Partners, London
(020) 7833 4433

Specialisation: Practice covers all aspects of immigration, asylum and nationality law.

Prof. Memberships: Deputy Chair of the Law Society's Immigration Law Sub-Committee; Member of the Law Society's Access to Justice Committee; Member of Immigration Law Practitioner's Association; Member of the Justice Administrative Law Panel; Member of the Refugee Women's Legal Group.

Career: Trained at *Winstanley Burgess*, subsequently worked for 4.5 years as the solicitor to the Joint council for the Welfare of Immigrants. Joined *Bindman & Partners* in 1994, became partner and Head of Immigration Department in May 1995.

Publications: Co-author of 'Putting Children First', a guide for immigration practitioners published by the Legal Action Group 2002.

STURTIVANT, Karen
Sturtivant & Co, London
(020) 7486 9524
visas@sturtivant.co.uk

Specialisation: Principal. Runs a practice devoted entirely to UK Immigration and Nationality law. Emphasis on business clients, but covers the full range of private client immigration work, although legal aid not undertaken. Author of numerous articles and has spoken widely at seminars in the UK and abroad.

Prof. Memberships: Immigration Law Practitioners Association, American Immigration Lawyers Association, International Bar Association, Law Society Immigration Law Sub-Committee, Deputy Assessor Immigration Law Panel.

Career: Qualified in 1980. Founded *Sturtivant & Co.* in 1985.

THOMPSON, Sally
Luqmani Thompson, London
(020) 8365 7800
sally@luqmanithompson.com

Specialisation: Partner specialising in immigration work with emphasis on human rights issues. Work includes administrative court litigation. Main client base includes unaccompanied children and clients assessed as particularly vulnerable.

Prof. Memberships: ILPA, Law Society.

Career: Articled in London and Reading, qualified in 1991. Working exclusively in immigration since qualifying. Founding partner of *Luqmani Thompson & Partners* from December 1998.

TROTT, Philip
Bates, Wells & Braithwaite, London
(020) 7551 7777
p.trott@bateswells.co.uk

Specialisation: Partner in Immigration and Employment Department. Commercial immigration law, advising individuals and corporations on how they can be economically active in the UK and advising on Home Office and Department of Employment unpublished practices and concessions. Regular lecturer on professional courses on immigration and employment law issues. Contributed to the debate with the Home Office on the reform of economic immigration law including the introduction of the Highly Skilled Migrant Programme. Regular contributor for TV and radio broadcasts on immigration and extradition issues. Expert witness on Immigration law.

Prof. Memberships: Immigration Law Practitioners' Association (executive committee member), Joint Chair of its Business and Employment sub-committee, Employment Lawyers Association, American Immigration Lawyers' Association, Law Society. Member of the Advisory Panel to the Office of the Immigration Services Commissioner.

Career: Qualified in 1979. Assistant Solicitor *Lawford & Co* 1979-82. Partner *Lawford & Co* in 1982. Joined *Thomson Snell & Passmore* as Head of Immigration and Employment Law Department in 1989, and moved to *Bates, Wells & Braithwaite* in 1992, Head of Immigration Department.

Publications: Co-author of 'McDonald's Immigration Law and Practice' (5th Edition) and 'Immigration Law and Practice' (Jackson 3rd Edition).

Personal: University College, London 1973-76. Fluent in French.

TURPIN, Philip
Turpin & Miller, Oxford
(01865) 308 200

WEBB, David John
DJ Webb & Co, London
(020) 7247 9933

WOODHOUSE, Sarah
Birnberg Peirce & Partners, London
(020) 7284 4620

INFORMATION TECHNOLOGY

London: 426; The Regions: 429; Scotland: 433; Profiles: 434

Research approved by BMRB For this edition, **Chambers'** researchers conducted 6,582 interviews – 3,900 with law firms, 511 with barristers and 2,171 with clients. The validity of the research was scrutinised by BMRB International, who audited both the methodology and the results at our offices in London. They interviewed **Chambers'** researchers and cross-checked sample interviews. Details of the audit appear on page 7.

OVERVIEW Business process outsourcing has been the flavour of the year, with many companies requiring advice on their back-room operations. Government work has also been particularly buoyant, in a year in which traditional companies have cut back on IT outsourcing and infrastructure deals.

LONDON

INFORMATION TECHNOLOGY — LONDON

1
- Baker & McKenzie
- Bird & Bird
- Clifford Chance

2
- Allen & Overy
- Lovells
- Masons
- Taylor Wessing

3
- Denton Wilde Sapte
- Field Fisher Waterhouse
- Olswang
- Osborne Clarke
- Tarlo Lyons

4
- Freshfields Bruckhaus Deringer
- Herbert Smith
- Kemp Little LLP
- Linklaters
- Shaw Pittman
- Slaughter and May

5
- Ashurst Morris Crisp
- Berwin Leighton Paisner
- Bristows
- CMS Cameron McKenna
- DJ Freeman
- Mayer, Brown, Rowe & Maw
- Nabarro Nathanson
- Simmons & Simmons
- Theodore Goddard

This book is the product of 6,582 1/2 hour interviews. See p.7 for BMRB audit. Within each band, firms are listed alphabetically.

BAKER & McKENZIE (see firm details p.855) Celebrated by clients for its "*superb understanding of the IT industry*" and seamless international network, this broad-based team undertakes contentious and non-contentious work, from big-ticket outsourcing deals to international litigation. "*Powerhouse litigator and master technician*" **Harry Small** (see p.438) achieved recent notoriety representing Levis in its high-profile grey imports case against Tesco, prompting speculation amongst rivals that he was taking on more IP work, however, he remains committed to IT. He recently acted for ICL on a major dispute with the Co-operative Group, concerning the interpretation and enforceability of exclusions and limitation clauses in software procurement agreements. **Michael Hart** (see p.435) has been recommended for non-contentious work, and boasts an impressive range of clients including Apple and Hewlett-Packard. The team has maintained a good flow of work despite the downturn, continuing to act on cutting-edge deals. It advised Hutchison 3G on its agreement with BBC Technology for the construction and operation of a 3G production facility, one of the first of its kind. **Clients** Cisco Systems; Compaq; Symbian; ntl; Hutchison 3G.

BIRD & BIRD (see firm details p.874) European reach and big-ticket government work helps to give this firm its breadth and reputation as "*true specialists.*" "*Fantastic litigator,*" **Graham Smith** (see p.438) was recommended for a range of work, including advice on the e-commerce aspects of large IT deals. **Hamish Sandison** (see p.438) has been busy in his role as non-executive chairman, however he maintains a high standing in the market. He recently advised the Cabinet Office on a pioneering deal licensing Microsoft to exploit the technology underlying the Government Gateway project. Microsoft's success in selling packages involving this technology to other governments and businesses will result in royalties being paid back to the government. **Roger Bickerstaff** (see p.434) is especially rated by peers for his public sector practice, and acted for the FCO on establishing high-security worldwide IT solutions for its back office functions. On the supplier side, Dun & Bradstreet has instructed the firm on all its European IT work, which includes substantial data protection advice. **Hilary Pearson** (see p.437) also gained her share of market approval. **Clients** Steria; Microsoft; Citigroup; UBS Warburg; Belron.

CLIFFORD CHANCE (see firm details p.911) The market is divided as to whether the loss this year of Chris Millard to Linklaters will adversely affect the practice. Nevertheless, clients are quick to recommend the team, whose international presence and top-class client base are regarded as unparalleled, while peers point to "*a blue-chip environment, fully focused on big-ticket work.*" The financial services sector is an area of particular expertise for the team, which can combine its IT knowledge with the firm's wide experience of specialist markets. It has been advising NTT DoCoMo on the licensing of the i-mode technology to a series of mobile telecoms operators in Europe and Asia. The practice now centres around the highly respected figure of **David Griffiths** (see p.435), whose talent and serious commitment to the work gains him the respect of his peers. **Raj Parkash** (see p.437) enters the tables this year on the back of clients' admiration of his flair for outsourcing work. Highlights for the team have included advising LIFFE on electronic trading projects, and Diageo on various e-commerce projects. **Clients** NTT DoCoMo; Diageo; LIFFE.

ALLEN & OVERY (see firm details p.841) For most commentators, this firm is snapping at the heels of Clifford Chance, but for at least one competitor it is "*the pre-eminent magic circle firm.*" The team is noted for its financial services and convergence work, gaining instructions from major suppliers and users. Standout practitioner **Laurence Jacobs** (see p.436) is appreciated for his profound technical skill: as one peer commented "*someone of his calibre is always a pleasure to deal with.*" He recently acted for Accenture on the outsourcing of Sainsbury's IT function. Outsourcing work has been a particular feature of the last year for the team, and it has also handled several large outsourcing deals for EDS. **Colleen Keck** (see p.436) was praised for her expertise within systems development agreements. **Clients** EDS; Lloyds; Barclays; Sunguard; Unisys.

LOVELLS (see firm details p.1045) This well-resourced team is felt to possess strength in depth, making it a genuine standalone outfit doing more than just corporate support. It remains the first choice amongst certain clients for major outsourcing work. **Conor Ward** (see p.439) moves up the tables following a raft of warm recommendations. As one client explains: "*it just clicks with him, I come away from a session feeling I've got where I want to be.*" He has assisted a well-known supplier of postal services in one of the largest outsourcing deals in the UK, with a projected value of £3.8 billion. "*Cool customer*" **Quentin Archer** (see p.434) has acted for CGNU on an IT services arrangement with

LONDON ■ INFORMATION TECHNOLOGY

TOP IN-HOUSE LAWYERS

Richard ALLNUTT, Group Counsel, Fujitsu Services
Tanya HERMAN, Legal Director, Capita Group
Robert MARCUS, Counsel, Business Innovations/Service, IBM
Jane McELHATTON, Senior Corporate Counsel, Cable & Wireless
Jane REEVES, European Counsel, Thompson Financial
David WITT, Senior Counsel, Europe, Middle East and Africa, Litigation and Intellectual Property, IBM

Richard Allnutt has "done great things" for Fujitsu. The "absolutely excellent" **Jane Reeves** maintains high standards, amassing a string of recommendations. **Tanya Herman** and **Jane McElhatton** continue to attract praise, in particular for their "commercial awareness." The IBM team "greatly impresses," with **Robert Marcus** and **David Witt** once again being singled out for having "a high level of intellect and market knowledge."

In-house lawyers' profiles p.1201

Abbey National in which CGNU agreed to underwrite insurance business sold though Abbey National branches. **Heather Rowe** (see p.438) ("possesses the full range of expertise") is noted for her intelligent analysis of the sector. Litigation instructions have included acting for a major engineering company on a software dispute with British Airways. **Clients** Standard Chartered Bank; O2; Nortel Networks; Deutsche Telekom; Granada Media.

MASONS (see firm details p.1057) Competitors admire the firm's technology client base, while clients appreciate its Far East network and celebrated litigation expertise. Non-contentious work, in particular data protection advice, forms a growing share of its caseload. The team is advising Invensys on the outsourcing of its global IT systems to IBM, a ten-year, £4 billion deal involving the provision of IT Services in 18 countries and the transfer to IBM of 700 Invensys staff worldwide. **Rob McCallough** (see p.436) remains "the lynchpin of the Masons' team," according to competitors, while **Iain Monaghan** (see p.437) has been described as "one of the best non-contentious IT strategists and negotiators around." He advised Fujitsu on the £319 million Libra project to introduce national IT systems to support magistrates courts throughout England and Wales. On the contentious side, the team was instructed by United Assurance in its 31-day High Court hearing against Unisys, which settled out of court. With a burgeoning national reputation, especially for her data protection expertise, "hugely commercial" **Shelagh Gaskill** (see p.435) joins the team from the Leeds office. **Clients** Zurich Financial Services; Fujitsu; a leading UK manufacturing plc.

TAYLOR WESSING (see firm details p.1156) "A high-profile team which just keeps winning top-class work," one peer admits, pointing out its enviable relationship with US suppliers and US companies investing in the UK. Clients praised the team's excellent drafting skills and its thorough understanding of IT procurement and outsourcing issues, particularly within the financial services sector. "True IT specialists," the team advised MWB Business Exchange on a range of contractual IT work including the procurement of IT goods and services for its business centres and onward supply to customers. **Glyn Morgan** (see p.437), who rises in the tables this year following sustained recommendations, was described by one client as "outstanding; he can do a mix of everything." The team is active on M&A-related work, advising Huon Holdings on the £181 million reverse takeover of the Innovation Group. **Clients** eBay; Google.com; MWB Business Exchange Limited; Liberate; Requisite.

DENTON WILDE SAPTE (see firm details p.935) Not as well known as it deserves to be, according to some sources, the team was recommended for its focus in this area. Much of its most impressive work is for the public sector, including representing the MoD on the restructuring of its IT outsourcing and development contract with EDS, covering payroll and pensions for all three armed services. This put a high-profile public sector IT deal, which was perceived to have gone wrong, back on course. **Nick Higham** (see p.794) comes highly recommended by the market, and recently acted for Opodo.com on the establishment and rollout of its pan-European online travel agency. "Genuine specialist" **John Worthy** (see p.439) is co-ordinating a series of projects for Wirebird, a provider of IT outsourcing and consultancy services. The team has also advised Northgate Information Systems on a dispute in the Californian courts concerning the supply of software to a US company. **Clients** London Electricity; EDS; Sainsbury's; Bertelsmann; WIPRO.

FIELD FISHER WATERHOUSE (see firm details p.954) With a particularly high profile for e-commerce, the team is recognised for its considerable all-round IT expertise. It has won major government instructions, recently acting for the London Borough of Lewisham on a £60 million IT procurement. "Academic" **Michael Chissick** (see p.434) assisted Accenture with one of its largest ever contracts for the supply of business process re-engineering and outsourcing services to a FTSE 100 company, with a value in excess of £350 million. **Nigel Wildish** (see p.439) who was described by one client as "a sound choice if you want to win," also assisted Accenture on IT contracts with companies, including AXA and the Johannesburg Stock Exchange. On the contentious side, the team advised Gentia Software on various disputes, including proceedings against a distributor in the Netherlands over a breach of licence and distribution agreements. **Clients** Dell; Apple; London Underground; NBA Quantum; Logica.

OLSWANG (see firm details p.1087) The team has not been as visible in the market this year, with its highest profile coming in the area of media-based IT deals. One such example was advising Channel 4 on the procurement of technology licences and support services from BSkyB for the interactive Big Brother service. The acquisition of Garretts' Reading office was widely expected to increase the firm's standing as a technology practice. One large supplier client is software development company Tao Group, which the team advised on a $17 million refinancing from a consortium of trade and financial investors. It also advised Whitbread on various strategic outsourcing deals. The firm's standout practitioner remains **Kim Nicholson** (see p.437) who, despite being less visible in the market this year due to her maternity leave, nevertheless retains a high-market profile. **Clients** Amdocs; Gateway; Criterion Software; Grant Thornton; Kingfisher.

OSBORNE CLARKE (see firm details p.1090) The firm's profile was perceived by market sources to have dropped slightly with the downturn in the technology market. Nevertheless, **Rory Graham** continues to elicit substantial praise from competitors as a "well-balanced opponent" with a profound knowledge of the industry. The firm's office in California's Silicon Valley is felt to give it an edge within the US market, helping it to win instructions from US firms such as Bytemobile, a software producer for the telecoms sector, which it recently assisted in licensing matters with Vodafone. The team is also well known for representing large-scale users, banks in particular, and it acted for Citibank on its outsourcing deal with Consignia. **Simon Rendell** and **Paul Gardner** are recommended by clients for their broad based approach. **Clients** Hewlett-Packard; British Airways; Cable & Wireless; Prudential Corporation; Cambista.

TARLO LYONS (see firm details p.1155) This outfit wins substantial praise from clients and competitors alike, and is especially admired for the way it has "grown from a boutique into an established, thriving practice." Newly ranked **John Mawhood** (see p.436) is recognised by the market for his IT expertise. He recently advised a leading bank on a system migration project, relocating the bank's services to a new data centre. On the supplier side the team acts for a major network services provider, while on the user side it has assisted a blue-chip company on audio and video conferencing agreements. The team was widely admired by clients for its outsourcing expertise, and is active on both contentious and non-contentious work. **Clients** Banks; insurance companies; technology providers.

FRESHFIELDS BRUCKHAUS DERINGER (see firm details p.964) Renowned for the corporate side of IT deals, clients value the firm's interna-

INFORMATION TECHNOLOGY ■ LONDON

LEADING INDIVIDUALS

1
- **MILLARD Christopher** Linklaters
- **GRIFFITHS David** Clifford Chance
- **KEMP Richard** Kemp Little LLP
- **REES Chris** Herbert Smith
- **WARD Conor** Lovells
- **SMALL Harry** Baker & McKenzie
- **JACOBS Laurence** Allen & Overy
- **MAUGHAN Alistair** Shaw Pittman
- **SMITH Graham** Bird & Bird

3
- **ARCHER Quentin** Lovells
- **BICKERSTAFF Roger** Bird & Bird
- **GARDNER Nick** Herbert Smith
- **LISTER Richard** Freshfields Bruckhaus Deringer
- **ROWE Heather** Lovells
- **SWYCHER Nigel** Slaughter and May
- **WESTMACOTT Philip** Bristows
- **BARRETT David** Simmons & Simmons
- **CHISSICK Michael** Field Fisher Waterhouse
- **GRAHAM Rory** Osborne Clarke
- **MCCALLOUGH Robert** Masons
- **SANDISON Hamish** Bird & Bird
- **TURNER Mark** Herbert Smith

4
- **DAVIES Clive** DJ Freeman
- **HART Michael** Baker & McKenzie
- **MORGAN Glyn** Taylor Wessing
- **RENDELL Simon** Osborne Clarke
- **WEBSTER Michael** Nicholson Graham & Jones
- **GASKILL Shelagh** Masons
- **HIGHAM Nicholas** Denton Wilde Sapte
- **PEARSON Hilary** Bird & Bird
- **SINGLETON Susan** Singletons
- **WILDISH Nigel** Field Fisher Waterhouse

5
- **BURNETT Rachel** Bristows
- **DINSDALE Danelle** DLA
- **LUBBOCK Mark** Ashurst Morris Crisp
- **MAWHOOD John** Tarlo Lyons
- **MOYLE Andrew** Shaw Pittman
- **PARKASH Raj** Clifford Chance
- **ROBERTSON Ranald** Robertson & Co
- **CAROLINA Robert** Landwell
- **GARDNER Paul** Osborne Clarke
- **MARTINDALE Avril** Freshfields Bruckhaus Deringer
- **MONAGHAN Iain** Masons
- **NICHOLSON Kim** Olswang
- **PRINSLEY Mark** Mayer, Brown, Rowe & Maw
- **WORTHY John** Denton Wilde Sapte

UP AND COMING
- **CHAPMAN Richard** Berwin Leighton Paisner
- **CROZIER John** Linklaters
- **KECK Colleen** Allen & Overy

See individuals' profiles p.434

---

tional reach, while competitors recognise that this impressive team is "*up-to-speed on the technical issues.*" It led the work for Hewlett-Packard on its merger with Compaq, assisting with the harmonisation of websites, and working on the IT infrastructure. At the other end of the scale, it also acts for IT start-up companies, and recently advised Yodlee, a Palo Alto venture offering internet account aggregation services, on its successful entrance into the European market. Another highlight was the £2 billion British Telecom/Trillium outsourcing transaction. "*Pragmatic and commercial*" **Richard Lister** (see p.436) won plaudits from clients, while **Avril Martindale** (see p.492) is described by peers as "*a great rainmaker, excellent at client relations.*" **Clients** Deutsche Bank; Financial Times; Ford; Nokia; London Stock Exchange.

HERBERT SMITH (see firm details p.992) This firm is increasingly making its mark at the corporate end of the sector with a string of big-ticket deals. Favoured by substantial supplier clients as a "*litigator who understands the key issues*," **Nick Gardner** (see p.435) defended NATS in a £42 million breach of contract action brought by EDS following its decision to terminate EDS's software development contract. In the non-contentious sphere, it has advised University College London Hospitals on the procurement of the complete IT infrastructure for a new teaching hospital. "*Commercial expert*," **Chris Rees** (see p.438) has been active for IMS on complex database licensing work, while highly-rated **Mark Turner** (see p.439) has assisted Abbey National on a £300 million software development and outsourcing contract with Capita. **Clients** Cisco; AOL; EMC; Abbey National; Time.

KEMP LITTLE LLP (see firm details p.1019) Though a small team, it gains enormous approbation from clients for its grasp of "*complex, strategic work and understanding of our business.*" The core of the team's caseload has comprised commercial and contractual advice, such as the recent outsourcing work for air transport communications provider, SITA, on the UK law aspects of its strategic agreement with Equant. The "*outstanding*" **Richard Kemp** (see p.436) remains prominent here. He advised QBE on its outsourcing arrangements with Logica for the upgrading of its systems to include a superior internet function. Along with growth in corporate instructions for suppliers, the practice has witnessed an increase in work for the financial sector, winning new clients such as Standard Chartered, which it advised on the acquisition of IT services. **Clients** EDS; Expedia; SunGard; AFR Consortium; DZ Bank.

LINKLATERS (see firm details p.1043) The recruitment this year of Clifford Chance's "*star*," **Chris Millard** (see p.437), has convinced commentators that boon times are ahead for the firm, though they acknowledge that it is too early to be certain. Millard gains access to an enviable extant client roster, including the likes of Hewlett-Packard, which the firm advised on a three-year, $260 million outsourcing contract with Nokia, spanning Asia, Europe and North America. **John Crozier** (see p.434) enters the tables this year. One client praised him for "*giving us the commercial advantage.*" He led the work for Centrica on a ten-year collaborative agreement with Accenture. The team also advised BBC Technology on a deal with Hutchison 3G to supply content production facilities and services. **Clients** Microsoft; Hewlett-Packard; BP; JP Morgan; Tiscali.

SHAW PITTMAN (see firm details p.1128) Clients and competitors agree that this team has made an outstanding mark in the field of outsourcing, undertaking some of the largest deals and possessing remarkable technical expertise. One competitor enthused "*I have not seen a more impressive IT team,*" while a client described it as "*head and shoulders above the rest for outsourcing.*" However, competitors consider it much less visible across the rest of the IT spectrum. Newly ranked **Andrew Moyle** (see p.437) is "*a tough cookie who really delivers for his clients.*" He led the group acting for Equant in one of the largest IT transactions of the year, the ten-year $6 billion deal to provide SITA with network services. On the public sector side, **Alistair Maughan** (see p.436) continues to "*push the practice forward.*" The team is advising the Inland Revenue on the planning, completion and management of its ten-year ASPIRE project, worth £300-400 million per year due to be awarded in 2004. **Clients** Deutsche Bank; E-government solutions; PricewaterhouseCoopers; Cable & Wireless; Prudential.

SLAUGHTER AND MAY (see firm details p.1140) Perceived by the market to have "*got its act together and brought IT to the fore,*" it is acknowledged to be more than a support function, though it is also "*exposed to interesting deals due to its corporate client base.*" These include Steria's acquisition of most of Bull's IT services business in exchange for newly issued Steria shares. The client base is weighted slightly towards users, such as Schroders, who the team advised on the outsourcing of its IT infrastructure and support service to Computer Sciences Corporation. **Nigel Swycher** (see p.439) receives praise, not simply for being "*a classic IT/IP lawyer,*" but for "*fielding a good team.*" This team also assists in dispute management, such as a recent case for KwikFit against ICL relating to system development. **Clients** Consignia; Abbey National; Ericsson; HSS; Enigma.

ASHURST MORRIS CRISP (see firm details p.852) "*A class outfit,*" its strength is felt to lie in the corporate side of IT work. The team recently advised UBS Warburg as the financial advisor to Guardian iT on the acquisition of Safetynet Group for £170 million. Leader of the team is **Mark Lubbock** (see p.436) who, as well as acting on substantial IT deals, has considerable IP experience. The team advised Alba, and its subsidiary Bush Internet, on the procurement of internet portal services from ITV active. Litigation work has included representing an IT supplier on a CEDR mediation and copyright infringement claims. **Clients** IBM; Thus; Royal & SunAlliance; Amey; BT.

BERWIN LEIGHTON PAISNER (see firm details p.866) The practice boasts a formidable reputation for government-related IT work. A major client has been the NHS, and it acted for Greenwich Healthcare Trust on the country's first completed NHS IT PFI project, which was ground breaking in its implementation of a PACS system. Former software engineer **Richard Chapman** (see p.434) is the team's rising star; as one client states "*I've never met a better lawyer.*" On the data protection side, the team represented Tesco in connection with the adoption and implementation of a group-wide data protection compliance programme. It also boasts niche expertise in acting for IT suppliers specialising in the financial services sector, such as Aon. **Clients** Financial Times; Tesco; Sophos; IntelliFlo; London Borough of Richmond.

BRISTOWS (see firm details p.888) While many in the market perceive the firm's profile to be based principally on its IP strength, clients claim that the team possesses "*a real understanding of the IT industry.*" **Philip Westmacott** (see p.439) is lauded by clients and peers alike for his technical aptitude. He represented British Airways on data protection issues and the acquisition of IT systems and services. On the supplier side, the team has been acting for software developer Finsoft on software development and joint venture agreements in relation to online betting. "*Real specialist*" **Rachel Burnett** (see p.434) joins the team from Salans Hertzfeld & Heilbronn to head up the non-contentious side of the practice. **Clients** IBM; BBC; Philips; Thomson Multimedia; Symbian.

CMS CAMERON MCKENNA (see firm details p.914) This integrated contentious and non-contentious team is an "*important player*" according to the market. Headed by John Armstrong, it has been particularly active on outsourcing deals for major technology suppliers. It advised Nestlé on the licensing and development of MIS and production software systems and, on the user side, assisted DST Systems on the purchase of IT assets from a major supplier to the financial services industry. The team has also acted on a range of IT disputes, both for supplier and user clients. **Clients** Consignia; ABN AMRO; Bank of Scotland; Home Office and Treasury; NSB Retail Solutions.

DJ FREEMAN (see firm details p.939) Felt by competitors to have been less visible in the market this year, the team nonetheless acted on major mail automation contracts for Consignia. **Clive Davies**, who leads the team, has been instrumental in assisting Bull Information Systems on the negotiation of an £85 million pathfinder PFI IT project with Norwich City Council. On the litigious side, the team successfully represented Axon Solutions as a third party in a £5 million IT claim brought by WH Smith against Fujitsu Siemens Computers and Siemens plc. **Clients** Belron; BPI; Channel 4; Energis; Rebus Insurance Systems.

MAYER, BROWN, ROWE & MAW (see firm details p.1060) This team can be relied upon to do a good job, according to competitors. Head of department **Mark Prinsley** (see p.438), who boasts expertise in IP as well as IT, acted for Marconi on a joint venture with Oxford Glyco-Sciences to market IT solutions to the biotech sector. Generally visible, undertaking non-contentious work for international IT users, the group assisted M&G International Investments in outsourcing its sub-transfer agency services to First European Transfer Agent SA. This involved financial services, regulatory and data protection issues in Luxembourg and Germany. **Clients** Bank of America; Cable & Wireless; EMI; Unilever; Halogen.

NABARRO NATHANSON (see firm details p.1080) A team with a focus upon pure IT outsourcing and IT-related BPOs, it has a growing reputation in the public sector, and was recently appointed by the London Borough of Greenwich on the strategic outsourcing of its entire IT function. On the supplier side, the firm represented CSL on implementing and integrating Oracle database technology and new e-commerce platforms for the London Borough of Croydon. Another highlight of the year was acting for Jupiter Asset Management on an IT and BPO service with HSBC. **Clients** Hammerson; Guardian iT; Deloitte Consulting; British Land; Metropolitan Police Authority.

SIMMONS & SIMMONS (see firm details p.1136) The presence here of highly rated **David Barrett** (see p.434), a "*traditional IT lawyer,*" ensures the firm its place in the tables. With a strong profile for government-related work, the team has been advising the Cabinet Office on the procurement of IT services for the development and running of the Citizens' Portal (ukonline.gov.uk). Its strength is felt by peers to lie in corporate-related work, such as acting for Geneva Technology shareholders on the $692 million merger with Convergys. **Clients** Home Office; MOD; Interbrew; HFC; Telewest.

THEODORE GODDARD (see firm details p.1158) Led by Paddy Grafton Green, this team, which boasts a broad range of work, has been assisting SAIC with the licensing aspects of its acquisition from Oracle of Oracle Energy Downstream. It has also advised Ericsson in relation to outsourcing arrangements. Litigation is handled within the group, and it acted for the British Horseracing Board on its successful database rights case concerning William Hill's website. **Clients** Lufthansa Revenue Services; Signet Trading; Internet Security Systems; Raft International; Ericsson.

OTHER NOTABLE PRACTITIONERS Susan Singleton (see p.438) of Singletons is renowned for "*acting for the people who matter,*" and was said by one peer to be "*as good as Millard on data protection.*" **Michael Webster** (see p.439) of Nicholson Graham & Jones is singled out for his corporate slant on IT work, while **Ranald Robertson** (see p.438) of Robertson & Co also won market plaudits. **Danelle Dinsdale** of DLA moves up the tables, winning praise for her impressive client base and her ability to "*seal the deal.*" **Robert Carolina** has moved from Tarlo Lyons to join Landwell, pronounced "*a true specialist, as good a lawyer as he is a speaker.*"

THE SOUTH

INFORMATION TECHNOLOGY
■ THE SOUTH

1	**Bond Pearce** Southampton
	Clyde & Co Guildford
	DMH Brighton

BOND PEARCE (see firm details p.879) The firm has capitalised upon its retail client base, and focuses upon the non-contentious side of the market. **Julian Hamblin** (see p.435), praised by clients for his "*keen eye for detail,*" is leading the team in advising a major national retailer on its exploitation of a software product it developed. A key client is elata plc, a supplier of software which enables mobile network owners to identify the forms of technology mobile phone users are employing on 3G telephones. **Clients** COR Systems; B&Q; Courts; AssureSoft; Skandia Life.

CLYDE & CO (see firm details p.913) Drawing strength from its London office, the team, led by

INFORMATION TECHNOLOGY ■ THE SOUTH/THAMES VALLEY

LEADING INDIVIDUALS
1. **HAMBLIN Julian** Bond Pearce

See individuals' profiles p.434

Sally Shorthose, has been active on acquisitions and disposals for IT suppliers. Recent work includes advising Microgen on the project management of the build and delivery phase of a bespoke database project. On the user side, it advised the Pacific Cyberworks group on negotiating contracts for a new IT system with IBM. **Clients** Marconi Medical Systems; Hypercom Europe; Invensys; Nokia; Eurosoft Systems.

DMH (see firm details p.940) It has been a year of growth for the firm, particularly within the areas of financial services systems and data protection. The team has undertaken major projects for HFC Bank, advising on all IT contracts, including multimillion pound transactions. Led by Tim Ashdown, it is also involved in dispute resolution, recently advising Hosiden Besson on a software decompilation dispute involving a large telecoms company. **Clients** SEEBOARD; KBC Advanced Technologies; Security Partnerships; Copy-Data; Eyretel.

THAMES VALLEY

INFORMATION TECHNOLOGY
■ THAMES VALLEY

1. **Nabarro Nathanson** Reading
   Osborne Clarke Reading
   The Law Offices of Marcus J O'Leary Wokingham
2. **Manches** Oxford
   Olswang Reading
3. **Clark Holt** Swindon
   Willoughby & Partners Oxford
4. **Boyes Turner** Reading

LEADING INDIVIDUALS
1. **HARRINGTON Alison** Olswang
   O'LEARY Marcus The Law Offices of Marcus J O'Leary
2. **BAILES Tony** Nabarro Nathanson
   ELLACOTT Sara Nabarro Nathanson
   GORNALL-KING William Boyes Turner
   HOLT Jeremy Clark Holt
   TIGHE David Manches
3. **BOWYER Russell** Osborne Clarke
   GOODGER Ben Willoughby & Partners
   NEWTON Jeremy Nabarro Nathanson

This book is the product of 6,582 1/2 hour interviews. See p.7 for BMRB audit. Within each band, firms are listed alphabetically. See individuals' profiles p.434

NABARRO NATHANSON (see firm details p.1080) The arrival of **Jeremy Newton** (see p.437) from his in-house position at Sun Microsystems to head up non-contentious IT has been hailed by the market as a coup for the team. Major IT multinationals continue to provide the core of its instructions. These include advising Oracle on a sub-contract for the supply of database software and services, in connection with McKesson's $480 million contract for the provision of a new NHS electronic staff records system. Procurement instructions have increased from user clients, such as Hi-Q systems, for whom the firm has reviewed software licenses and hardware and support agreements. **Tony Bailes** (see p.279) is noted for his contentious expertise, while **Sara Ellacott** (see p.435) garners warm recommendations from a number of sources including the London bar. **Clients** Sun Microsystems; Siemens; Nextra; Deloitte & Touche; Jarvis.

OSBORNE CLARKE (see firm details p.1090) City quality advice at a reasonable cost is the verdict of the market, causing the team to move to the top of this year's tables. Head of department, **Russell Bowyer** is newly ranked, having been praised by clients for "*understanding our objectives and being adept at defining our risk.*" Crossover IT/e-commerce deals have included the negotiation for Clarus of online auction and e-procurement trading exchange solutions with Barclays B2B. The team also advised British Gas on the procurement of group-wide IT systems from Accenture and PwC. Key strengths of the practice lie in its understanding of the financial services sector and large outsourcing transactions. **Clients** Agilent Technology; npower Communications; Compuserve; Lloyds TSB Development Capital; Vodafone.

THE LAW OFFICES OF MARCUS J O'LEARY (see firm details p.1030) With many dedicated IT practitioners, the team is noted for its international client base. "*Superb contracts man,*" Marcus O'Leary (see p.437) is said by rivals to be "*always a name to be reckoned with.*" IT represents a core specialism of the firm, which represents an impressive roster of blue-chip corporations on both the user and supplier sides. **Clients** High technology companies, industry bodies.

MANCHES (see firm details p.1052) Recognised by the market as a strong team, **David Tighe** (see p.439) in particular, is singled out by competitors as "*an IT whiz.*" The team has particular expertise in procurement and software development in the financial service sector. One such deal included negotiating agreements for the development and implementation of a financial services system on behalf of a New York bank. A key client is the Natural Environment Research Council, whom the team advised over the failed implementation of an accounts system in the run-up to Y2K. **Clients** Deutsche Bank; Electrocomponents; Grant Thornton; Rebus; Intelligroup.

OLSWANG (see firm details p.1087) In the wake of the break-up of Anderson Legal, the move of the Garretts' team to Olswang is felt to bode well for the future, as is the presence of "*ambitious, talented player,*" **Alison Harrington** (see p.435). On the supplier side, the team is advising Network Appliance on negotiations for a multimillion pound software and hardware supply contract with a major telecoms company. It has also assisted Motorola on software and technology licensing agreements with its customers. **Clients** Vodafone; Direct Image; RP Scherer; Ebbon-Dacs; Timberland.

CLARK HOLT (see firm details p.907) Although perhaps not yet a majority view, at least one peer considers this niche player "*streets ahead of anyone else in the market.*" Not just a talented lawyer, **Jeremy Holt** (see p.436) is said by peers to be "*extremely knowledgeable about computers.*" He leads a team whose strength lies in its knowledge of the industry. Highlights have included preparing an outsourcing agreement for a Polish supplier in relation to the Estonian national telephone system, and acting on a number of strategic alliances between major international IT suppliers. **Clients** AIT Group; Equinet; Blick; CQ Systems; MessageLabs.

WILLOUGHBY & PARTNERS (see firm details p.1189) The firm is identified by market sources with IT/IP crossover work, particularly on software patents. **Ben Goodger** (see p.435) is singled out by peers for his IT expertise. He represented Net Solutions Europe in connection with its supply of software for a real time information database for media use during the World Cup. Data protection work has included advice to Tracker, the stolen vehicle recovery system. The team undertakes a range of contractual IT work, from facilities management agreements to hosting agreements. **Clients** Tracker; a leading supplier of digital images; users and suppliers of software and hardware.

BOYES TURNER (see firm details p.883) Visible in the local marketplace, the firm benefits from the presence of "*impressive operator,*" **William Gornall-King** (see p.435). The core of the team's instructions derives from suppliers, for example advising Pink Roccade on the supply of outsourcing solutions to one of the largest services companies in the UK, involving detailed negotiation of the service delivery risk and reward mechanism. Public sector work has included advising the Met Office on a software supply contract with Belgian air traffic control. **Clients** Geac Computer Systems; Impact Europe; Information Resources; i-documentsystems group; IKON Office Solutions.

430   INDEX TO LEADING LAWYERS: PAGE 1693 ■ IN-HOUSE LAWYERS PROFILES: PAGE 1201

SOUTH WEST

INFORMATION TECHNOLOGY
■ SOUTH WEST

1 Osborne Clarke Bristol
2 Beachcroft Wansbroughs Bristol
   Bevan Ashford Bristol
   Burges Salmon Bristol
3 Foot Anstey Sargent Plymouth
   Laytons Bristol

This book is the product of 6,582 1/2 hour interviews. See p.7 for BMRB audit. Within each band, firms are listed alphabetically.

OSBORNE CLARKE (see firm details p.1090) Maintaining poll position, due to its national reach and a reputation as *"proactive deal makers,"* Andrew Braithwaite's team has historically focused upon technology companies. These include Cramer Systems, for which it is handling telecoms operating system customer agreements across Europe. Increasingly attracting instructions from user clients, the team is representing Profund Systems on a substantial licensing agreement for AON. A recent coup has been its appointment by Microsoft to act on piracy litigation. **Clients** Allied Domecq; Brann; Future Publishing; Somerfield Stores; Elixent.

BEACHCROFT WANSBROUGHS (see firm details p.860) The firm drew recommendations from international clients and London practitioners, who see the team as *"well versed in IT projects,"* and possessing a particularly good grasp of IT/IP crossover work. Acting for a broad client base including both suppliers and users of varying sizes, instructions come from a number of sectors. **Clients** Software suppliers.

BEVAN ASHFORD (see firm details p.869) Spanning the public and private sectors and covering all major areas of IT law, the team, led by Gareth Jones, is a recognised player in the marketplace. It boasts specialist expertise in the procurement of strategic health systems, and acted for the South West EPR collaboration representing 27 NHS Trusts on the £400 million procurement of electronic patient record services. In the private sector, the team acted for a consortium of hi-tech companies in establishing a co-ordinated database and information service designed to reduce freight crime in the IT hardware sector. **Clients** Intel; Lucent Technologies; AssureSoft; Welsh Health Supplies; Inventures.

BURGES SALMON (see firm details p.894) A growing team, the core of whose work is transactional, it enjoys niche expertise in the provision of IT systems for hospitals. Most visible in public sector work, the team is receiving increasing numbers of private sector instructions, such as acting for Reuters on the development of worldwide framework agreements for the procurement of internet measurement software application tools. On the supplier side, it advised Science Systems on software distribution and licensing arrangements in connection with its international VAR network. **Clients** PassGo Technologies; Nationwide Building Society; United Biscuits; Bristol & West; Orange.

FOOT ANSTEY SARGENT (see firm details p.958) This team is especially recommended by clients for its expertise in litigation. Recent contentious work has included advice to a legal software provider concerning the function and quality of software. The team, led by Edmund Probert, continues to work on the Planning Portal and Casework projects for the Planning Inspectorate, involving contract negotiations with IBM and Unisys as well as other government bodies. It also assists a number of software designers. **Clients** ISPs; Eclipse; Planning Inspectorate.

LAYTONS (see firm details p.1032) Gaining plaudits from London practitioners as well as local peers, the team has received a boost in the form of its merger with Lochners Technology Solicitors. Led by Richard Brown, it typically acts for suppliers, with recent work including advising Dan Network Solutions on contractual arrangements for networking services. Instructions from purchaser clients have included assisting Somerfield with licence agreements. **Clients** INTY; Zuken; Business Link; Dan Network Solutions.

WALES

INFORMATION TECHNOLOGY
■ WALES

1 Edwards Geldard Cardiff
   Eversheds Cardiff
   Morgan Cole Cardiff

LEADING INDIVIDUALS
1 DELEMORE Ceri Edwards Geldard

This book is the product of 6,582 1/2 hour interviews. See p.7 for BMRB audit. Within each band, firms are listed alphabetically. See individuals' profiles p.434

EDWARDS GELDARD (see firm details p.944) Enjoying a lower market profile this year, according to competitors, the team, led by *"genuine specialist"* Ceri Delemore (see p.488), has nevertheless participated in a number of top-flight deals, including advising Peter Evans on the supply and maintenance of back office systems for major financial services clients. In an active year for procurement, the team has also assisted Baxi Heating with the procurement of a major IT system. **Clients** British Chambers of Commerce; Chubb; CITEL Technologies; Molecular Light Technology; Pendragon.

EVERSHEDS (see firm details p.949) This commercial team is respected by the market for its international capability. Led by Heather McNabb, it is advising the National Assembly for Wales on the procurement of a high-profile ICT system, a major project which will involve the rest of the Eversheds network. The team has also represented Halifax Card Services on the acquisition of an IT system for use in call centres. While work derives principally from the user market, suppliers such as Cotec Computing Services are key clients. **Clients** ABN AMRO; Cogent Defence Systems; Welsh Development Agency; First Plus Financial Group.

MORGAN COLE (see firm details p.1075) The firm, which has elicited plaudits nationwide, is joined this year by data protection specialist Tamzin Matthew from The Law Offices of Marcus J O'Leary. Acting for a mix of users and suppliers, the firm's regional network was held to be an advantage by clients. **Clients** RAC; British Energy; Philips; Categoric Software; Unipalm.

INFORMATION TECHNOLOGY ■ MIDLANDS & EAST ANGLIA/THE NORTH

MIDLANDS & EAST ANGLIA

INFORMATION TECHNOLOGY
■ MIDLANDS & EAST ANGLIA

1 Wragge & Co Birmingham
2 Eversheds Birmingham, Nottingham
3 Hewitson Becke + Shaw Cambridge, Northampton
  Pinsent Curtis Biddle Birmingham
  V-Lex Ltd Worksop

LEADING INDIVIDUALS

1 JONES Bill Wragge & Co
  YATES John V-Lex Ltd
2 ARNOLD Michael Eversheds
  SASSE Sarah Wragge & Co

This book is the product of 6,582 1/2 hour interviews. See p.7 for BMRB audit. Within each band, firms are listed alphabetically. See individuals' profiles p.434

WRAGGE & CO (see firm details p.1197) Pulling away from the rest of the pack, the firm is said by competitors to be "*making real inroads into the London scene,*" and is perceived to have the greatest strength in depth within the region. **Bill Jones** is admired for the way he has built up an excellent team. He acted recently for a major US investment bank on the European elements of a global desktop outsourcing project to IBM. Representing some of the largest suppliers of IT, the team has advised Cap Gemini Ernst & Young on over 120 instructions with a contract value of approximately £1 billion. Highly recommended for public sector expertise, the team has advised Sandwell Borough Council on the procurement of IT systems for a new revenues and benefits system to meet e-government requirements. **Sarah Sasse** elicits praise for her knowledge of the IT industry. **Clients** 186K; AT&T; London Borough of Croydon; BT; ITNET.

EVERSHEDS (see firm details p.949) This commercial team is felt by peers to possess "*quality all the way down*" from partners to assistants. Particularly praised for his dedication and technical skills was **Michael Arnold** (see p.434), who has been acting for Hays on the establishment of a supplemental website to the government's e-conveyancing project, linked to the National Land Information Service. The firm's strong national network helps it to service a superb client base spanning major users and suppliers. **Clients** Hays; Six Continents Retail.

HEWITSON BECKE + SHAW (see firm details p.993) This is a small team but nevertheless it attracts an international client roster, including Microsoft Research. The department, led by Bill Thatcher, boasts a broad range of specialisms including strength in relation to internet search software, bio-informatics and geographical information systems. Instructions are derived from suppliers and users for a range of issues, from licensing to procurement. **Clients** Users and suppliers.

PINSENT CURTIS BIDDLE (see firm details p.1102) The firm boasts expertise in public and private sector work, and a niche in data protection. Led by Cerys Wyn Davies, the team recently advised Premier International Foods on the renewed outsourcing of its group IT services. On the public sector side, it assisted the NHS Information Authority on the £320 million National HR and Payroll IT procurement, including negotiations with Oracle and IBM. The team continues to undertake high-profile dispute resolution. **Clients** Ramesys; Smith & Nephew; Bull Information Services; Worcestershire County Council.

V-LEX LTD (see firm details p.1176) The team led by **John Yates** (see p.439) ("*runs rings around the competition*") has gained recognition from the market as "*an excellent set of individuals, particularly for outsourcing work.*" It has been visible on numerous high-profile instructions, including the outsourcing of Swinton Insurance's DLP insurance business. The team also received praise for its international litigation expertise, acting recently on behalf of a large multinational IT supplier in a multimillion pound dispute relating to the establishment of a new net market. **Clients** Nottingham City Council; Rebus HR; CSC Computer Services; Metapath Software International; KW International.

THE NORTH

INFORMATION TECHNOLOGY
■ THE NORTH

1 Addleshaw Booth & Co Leeds, Manchester
  Masons Leeds, Manchester
2 Eversheds Leeds
  Pinsent Curtis Biddle Leeds
3 Halliwell Landau Manchester
4 Hammond Suddards Edge Leeds, Manchester
  Irwin Mitchell Leeds

LEADING INDIVIDUALS

1 SAMPSON Ian Addleshaw Booth & Co
2 MOAKES Jonathan Halliwell Landau
  PEETERS Michael Pinsent Curtis Biddle
3 DAVIS Dai Nabarro Nathanson
  UP AND COMING
  HARVEY Margaret Addleshaw Booth & Co

This book is the product of 6,582 1/2 hour interviews. See p.7 for BMRB audit. Within each band, firms are listed alphabetically. See individuals' profiles p.434

ADDLESHAW BOOTH & CO (see firm details p.838) "*A focused, quality team,*" it stands out in particular for big-ticket litigation. The highlight of the year, however, has been infrastructure work, with the team negotiating outsourcing and procurement contracts for Airtours. The Commonwealth Games in Manchester also provided a wealth of instructions for the firm, such as advising on contracts relating to the timing and scoring computer systems. It also negotiated with Microsoft involving software and consultancy services. Another field in which the team has witnessed increased work is data protection. **Ian Sampson** (see p.438) moves up the tables, having been recommended by clients for offering "*city quality legal advice without overcharging you.*" **Margaret Harvey** (see p.435) also gains her share of peer approval. **Clients** BAE Systems; CGNU; Granada Media; Manchester United; Trinity Computer Services.

MASONS (see firm details p.1057) The team has faced change this year with its star name Shelagh Gaskill relocating to London and Rosemary Jay becoming a consultant. Nevertheless it continues to be acclaimed by clients as "*brilliant at outsourcing.*" Currently advising Clariant International on the global outsourcing of its wide area network, other highlights include its appointment by the Department of Trade and Industry to advise on the £34 million reprocurement of its accounts function. Data Protection is an area of niche expertise, and the team was instructed by *Hello!* to advise on the data protection aspects of its case against the UK magazine over celebrity photographs. **Clients** DTI; Balfour Pension Trust; Kettering NHS Trust; Equifax; IBA Technology.

EVERSHEDS (see firm details p.949) With Rex Parry's move to London, Paula Barrett has stepped up to take charge of the team. "*Pre-eminent in Leeds,*" according to some competitors, it boasts a group of highly-rated individuals and a top-class client base. Noted for its capacity to undertake large outsourcing deals and a niche within public sector work, the team has advised Bedfordshire County Council on the IT aspects of its 12-year £267 million outsourcing to Hyder Business Services, a deal which is expected to bring revenue savings to the Council of around £16 million per year. Litigation work has increased, and the firm has advised on a range of multimillion pound IT project disputes. **Clients** Link Interchange Network; Bedfordshire County Council.

PINSENT CURTIS BIDDLE (see firm details p.1102) The team ascends the tables this year, recognised by the market for its national reach

THE NORTH/SCOTLAND ■ INFORMATION TECHNOLOGY

and "*huge skill in the public sector.*" "*Academically strong*" **Michael Peeters** (see p.437) is the group's standout name. Among a long list of impressive recent work, he advised the Department of Health on its £350 million outsourcing of payroll and HR services. The team also boasts substantial contentious expertise, and has acted on a range of IT disputes with claims of up to £20 million. **Clients** Accenture; BT; Pace Micro Technology; Norwich Union; Logica.

HALLIWELL LANDAU (see firm details p.982) Adept at attracting entrepreneurial clients, the team is visible acting for both users and suppliers. It is led by "*sensible opponent*" **Jonathan Moakes** (see p.492), who won particular praise from peers for his expertise in high-value procurements. A recent example of these has been the software and system procurement which the team undertook for Edison Mission Marketing Services in connection with the new electricity trading arrangements (NETA). It also acts for Time Computers on large-scale PFI tenders. **Clients** University of Manchester; NettGain Solutions; Knowledge Management Software; Manchester Chamber of Business Enterprises.

HAMMOND SUDDARDS EDGE Though the team boasts City quality lawyers, certain commentators feel that its profile in the region is not as high as it might be. The group in Manchester, led by Andrew West, has been handling a number of outsourcing instructions, for example advising Jabil Circuit on the outsourcing of Marconi's European and US telecoms equipment manufacturing operations. Meanwhile the Leeds practice, headed by Mike Henley, has been acting for various software companies, including LiveDevizes, on software licensing and customer documentation. **Clients** Halifax; B&Q; Co-operative Group; GB Group; Manchester Airport.

IRWIN MITCHELL (see firm details p.1009) An important presence in Sheffield, it undertakes high-value transactions for leading software houses, quoted companies and institutional clients. The team, led by Joanne Palframan, has advised the multimedia division of University of Leeds Innovations on joint development agreements and licensing activities. Gaining a reputation for data protection work, it is carrying out a data protection audit for Ufi, which runs the Learn Direct Initiative. **Clients** Build Assured; Fretwell-Downing Group; Eiger Systems; Bewise.

OTHER NOTABLE PRACTITIONERS Dai Davis (see p.434) of Nabarro Nathanson is well known in the market for his niche within safety-related systems.

SCOTLAND

INFORMATION TECHNOLOGY
■ SCOTLAND

1 Maclay Murray & Spens — Edinburgh, Glasgow
2 McGrigor Donald — Edinburgh, Glasgow
3 Dundas & Wilson CS — Edinburgh
   Shepherd+ Wedderburn — Edinburgh
4 MacRoberts — Glasgow
   Masons — Edinburgh

LEADING INDIVIDUALS

1 FLINT David — MacRoberts
2 CAMERON Gillian — Maclay Murray & Spens
   MACPHERSON Shonaig — McGrigor Donald
   NICOLSON Fiona — Maclay Murray & Spens
3 BOAG-THOMSON Joanna — Shepherd+ Wedderburn
   MCROBB Liz — Shepherd+ Wedderburn
   ORR Alistair — Maclay Murray & Spens

This book is the product of 6,582 1/2 hour interviews. See p.7 for BMRB audit. Within each band, firms are listed alphabetically. See individuals' profiles p.434

MACLAY MURRAY & SPENS (see firm details p.1048) "*Rightly placed at number one,*" concede competitors, a joint IT/IP group deals with a large volume of non-contentious work, while IT litigation is handled by a discrete group. Active over the past year on outsourcing work, the firm has represented the Bank of Scotland on procurement and outsourcing. Led by the widely respected **Fiona Nicholson** (see p.493), it acts for both user and supplier clients, from start-ups to universities. Success has been achieved within litigation, where the firm represented a major global software provider in a multimillion pound dispute with a blue-chip company. **Gillian Cameron** (see p.434) is described by clients as "*pragmatic; she can see the salient issues,*" while **Alistair Orr** also continues to gain market plaudits. **Clients** Picsel Technologies; Scottish Enterprise; FAST; Ascom IT; Mona Computing.

MCGRIGOR DONALD (see firm details p.1065) The firm's connection with KLegal has been viewed with interest, and commentators remain unsure about whether it will benefit the practice. What isn't in doubt is the high calibre of the lawyers produced by this IT/IP team. **Shonaig Macpherson** (see p.492) has been involved in a management role, however she continues to be act on IT-based PPP deals for Visitscotland and Glasgow Schools. In the financial sector, the team has given advice to Intelligent Finance on establishing the infrastructure contracts for internet banking. System disputes are another focus area, in particular in the field of software licensing. **Clients** Intelligent Finance; Visit Scotland; Mitel; Cerner.

DUNDAS & WILSON CS (see firm details p.943) Singled out by clients for its finance expertise, the team has been lauded for its work on "*legally complex and innovative transactions.*" It acts for a range of user and supplier clients on the spectrum of IT work, including advice on outsourcing, supply and procurement agreements. **Clients** Software suppliers and users.

SHEPHERD+ WEDDERBURN (see firm details p.1130) Standing out from the team, leading names **Joanna Boag-Thomson** (see p.434) and **Liz McRobb** have been acting for the Scottish Executive in providing advice to Scottish Criminal Record Office on an IT PPP project concerning criminal record disclosures. Alongside its notable public sector experience, it works extensively with private sector users and suppliers. It has been newly instructed by Cap Gemini Ernst & Young on its e-procurement agreement with the Scottish Executive. The opening of a London office focusing on TMT is expected to give the practice a broader reach. **Clients** Independent Newspaper; West LB; Scottish Parliamentary Corporate Body; Scottish Enterprise; Scottish Power.

MACROBERTS (see firm details p.1049) **David Flint** (see p.488), described by one commentator as "*remarkably knowledgeable in IT and internet matters,*" continues to attract warm market recommendations. The team, which boasts strength within the global aspects of internet technology, has advised Calligraphix on various internet projects. Outsourcing work has also been active, particularly in the context of PFI, and it has undertaken procurement instructions for public sector education clients. **Clients** University of Strathclyde; Initiative Software; Scottish Internet Exchange; Dunedin International; Giltech.

MASONS (see firm details p.1057) One London-based practitioner expressed admiration for the firm, which "*held its own and worked hard*" on a recent deal. The team, led by John Salmon, has been active on outsourcing and procurement work within the financial sector, acting for a Scotland-based UK financial services company on a £10 million IT procurement. Contentious work has included advising a supplier on the defence of a £3 million claim. **Clients** The Mindwarp Pavillion; Realise; The Games Kitchen.

INFORMATION TECHNOLOGY ■ THE LEADERS

THE LEADERS IN INFORMATION TECHNOLOGY

ARCHER, Quentin
Lovells, London
(020) 7296 2000
quentin.archer@lovells.com
Specialisation: Partner specialising in all aspects of IT law, both contentious and non-contentious, particularly computer contracts (including projects under the Private Finance Initiative), electronic commerce and the introduction of new technology. One of the first lawyers to move (in 1985) from the IT industry back into private practice. Most clients outside the IT sector are in the financial services, defence and media fields.
Prof. Memberships: Law Society; US Computer Law Association; Treasurer, British Czech and Slovak Law Association.
Career: Qualified 1981. In-house solicitor at Acorn Computer Group PLC, 1984-85. Rejoined *Lovells* in 1985, partner 1987.

ARNOLD, Michael R
Eversheds, Birmingham
(0121) 232 1141
michaelarnold@eversheds.com
Specialisation: System development, outsourcing, e-commerce. Head of *Eversheds* IT group.
Prof. Memberships: Society for Computers and Law.
Career: MA (Cantab). Qualified with *Eversheds* 1984. Partner 1990.
Personal: Cricket.

BAILES, Tony
Nabarro Nathanson, Reading
(0118) 950 4700
See under E-commerce, p.279

BARRETT, David
Simmons & Simmons, London
(020) 7628 2020
david.barrett@simmons-simmons.com
Specialisation: Partner and head of information technology practice. Responsible for practice in information technology, communications, computer technology transfer, information systems and business systems outsourcing, IT and telecommunications procurement and supply, and multimedia and international projects.

BICKERSTAFF, Roger
Bird & Bird, London
(020) 7415 6000
roger.bickerstaff@twobirds.com
Specialisation: Principal area of practice is information technology. He is Co-head of the Information Technology group. His particular work focus is large-scale IT-infrastructure projects, including outsourcing, partnering and PFI projects and e-commerce infrastructure development. Other specialities include IT contract management and IT dispute resolution, protection of rights, e-commerce, the impact of EC legislation and impact of new technology. Also advises on all aspects of EC/GATT procurement law. Clients include many government departments and major private sector IT purchasers.
Prof. Memberships: Society for Computers and Law.
Career: Qualified in 1990. At *Linklaters & Paines* 1990-92. Joined *Bird & Bird* in 1992 and became a Partner in 1995.
Personal: Born 1961. Attended King's College, Cambridge 1980-84. Lives in London.

BOAG-THOMSON, Joanna
Shepherd+ Wedderburn, Glasgow
(0141) 566 8570
joanna.bt@shepwedd.co.uk
Specialisation: Accredited by Law Society of Scotland as a specialist in intellectual property law. Principal areas of practice are IP/IT and e-commerce, with a focus on B2B e-commerce.
Prof. Memberships: Law Society of Scotland; Licensing Executives Society; TIPLO; Scottish Society for Computers and Law.
Career: Trained *Wright Johnston & Mackenzie*, Glasgow and Edinburgh 1988-90. Assistant *Wright Johnston & Mackenzie* 1990-91. Assistant *Bird Semple Fyfe Ireland* 1991-93. Assistant, associate then partner *MacRoberts* 1993-2000. Partner in Media and Technology Group at *Shepherd+ Wedderburn* 2000 to date.
Publications: Numerous magazine and newspaper articles. Co-edited Greens' 'Scottish E-commerce Handbook'; regular column in Greens' 'E-Law Review'.
Personal: Educated Craighome School, Glasgow, then LLB and Dip LP at Edinburgh University. Interests - theatre, travel, reading and writing.

BOWYER, Russell
Osborne Clarke, Reading
(0118) 925 2000

BURNETT, Rachel
Bristows, London
(020) 7400 8000
rachel.burnett@bristows.com
Specialisation: Partner specialising in information technology. Practice covers contract negotiation, drafting and related commercial advice for the full range of IT and e-commerce industry transactions. Acts for major vendors, system integrators, software publishers, data licensors, service providers, resellers, major corporate and financial services sectors. Co-author of 'Drafting and Negotiating Computer Contracts' (Butterworths, 1994), author of 'Outsourcing IT - The Legal Aspects' (Gower, 1998). Editor of the IT Law Guides Series for the Institute of Chartered Accountants. Writes and lectures widely on IT-related matters.
Prof. Memberships: Institute for Information Systems Management Chairman; Worshipful Company of Information Technologists (Court Livery Member); British Computer Society (Vice-President, Management); Society for Computers & Law; Law Society.
Career: Qualified 1980. Former IT professional.
Personal: Exeter University (BA Soc. Studies, Hons). Associate, Institute of Linguists (French). Chair, Association of Women Solicitors, 1990-91.

CAMERON, Gillian
Maclay Murray & Spens, Glasgow
(0141) 248 5011
gjc@maclaymurrayspens.co.uk
Specialisation: Partner in IP and Technology Department. Specialises in IP generally and non-contentious IT/internet work in particular for a wide range of clients, including advising Scotland's largest dot.com start-up and various ISPs. Accredited as an IP specialist by the Law Society of Scotland and an honorary lecturer at Strathclyde University's Hunter Centre for Entrepreneurship.
Career: LLB (Hons) Edinburgh University (1987); Dip LP (1988); joined *Maclay Murray & Spens* in 1996; previously headed Technology Law Unit at *Bird Semple* (now DLA).

CAROLINA, Robert
Landwell, London
(020) 7212 1616

CHAPMAN, Richard
Berwin Leighton Paisner, London
(020) 7427 1219
richard.chapman@blplaw.com
Specialisation: Commercial work in the IT, telecoms and e-commerce sectors. Focus on major IT and telecoms projects for both private and public sector. Outsourcing, managed services, systems development, software development and licensing, hardware procurement and maintenance, e-commerce.
Prof. Memberships: Law Society, Society for Computers and Law.
Career: Logica (1986-93) software engineer and project manager. *Clifford Chance* (1995-99), *Berwin Leighton Paisner* (2000-date).
Personal: Born 1966. Educated City of London School, University of Kent (BSc(Hons) Physics with Astrophysics), College of Law (London).

CHISSICK, Michael
Field Fisher Waterhouse, London
(020) 7861 4000
mpc@ffwlaw.com
Specialisation: Head of IT and e-commerce law group which comprises a team of seven partners and 18 specialist lawyers. Main areas of practice include outsourcing projects, IT programming, data protection, digital mixed media, electronic commerce and m-commerce contracts.
Prof. Memberships: Law Society; Solicitors European Group; FAST Legal Advisory Group; Computer Law Association.
Career: 1st Class Degree in Law (LLB); Law Society Finals 1st Class; Masters Degree in IT and Telecommunications.
Publications: Author of 'Internet Law' published in October 1997 by FT Publications and co-author of 'Electronic Commerce Law and Practice' published in 1999, 2000 and 2001 by Sweet & Maxwell.

CROZIER, John
Linklaters, London
(020) 7456 5778
John.Crozier@linklaters.com
Specialisation: Partner in the dedicated Information Technology and Communications Group. He is a commercial lawyer specialising in outsourcing, transactions where technology is a key feature (including system design and build agreements, distribution agreements, software development agreements and licensing joint ventures), data protection and commercial telecommunications. He is a member of a number of IT related professional associations including the Computer Law Group.
Career: 1989-91, *Hesketh Henry*; 1993-95, *Masons*, 1995-99, Assistant Solicitor, *Linklaters* London; 2000 to date, Partner, *Linklaters* London.
Personal: Kings College, London LLM; University of Auckland, LLB.

DAVIES, Clive
D J Freeman, London
(020) 7583 4055

DAVIS, Dai
Nabarro Nathanson, Sheffield
(07785) 771721
d.davis@nabarro.com
Specialisation: Consultant. Main areas of practice are computer, internet and technology law. Advises on sale of computer systems, licensing of computer systems, intellectual property, joint ventures, development agreements and facility management agreements. Expert in internet and e-commerce legal issues. Clients range from start-up dot.coms to large PLCs. Also advises on product safety for technological products and on compliance with technology related European Union legislation such as the CE Marking Directive. Member of the Executive of the IEE Management Network. Speaker at many national and international conferences; co-opted legal expert to BSI committee DS/1/1 and convenor of IEC Committee TC56 Legal Working Group.
Prof. Memberships: Solicitor; Member of Institution of Electrical Engineers; Chartered Engineer; Member of Royal Academy for the Arts, Manufacture and Commerce; Honorary Scientific Member of International Association of Cybernetics; Honorary Member of Centre for International Legal Studies; Member of Licensing Executives Society.
Career: Joined *Eversheds Hepworth & Chadwick* in 1987; became a partner in 1992; head of *Eversheds* national IT law practice 1995-98.
Personal: Born 2 March 1958. Took a Physics MA at Keble College, Oxford 1976-79; then MSc Computing Science at Newcastle University 1981-83. Leisure interests include tennis, reading and cooking. Lives in Boston Spa.

434   INDEX TO LEADING LAWYERS: PAGE 1693 ■ IN-HOUSE LAWYERS PROFILES: PAGE 1201

THE LEADERS ■ INFORMATION TECHNOLOGY

DELEMORE, Ceri
Edwards Geldard, Cardiff
(029) 2023 8239
ceri.delemore@geldards.co.uk
See under Intellectual Property, p.488

DINSDALE, Danelle
DLA, London
(08700) 111111

ELLACOTT, Sara
Nabarro Nathanson, Reading
(0118) 925 4616
s.ellacott@nabarro.com
Specialisation: Internet related and e-commerce issues, with particular expertise in e-mail issues, cybersquatting, domain names and Meta-tags; largescale IT disputes, mainly acting for large IT suppliers; advising internet start-ups on aspects of setting up and running their businesses.
Prof. Memberships: TIPLO. Thames Valley Commercial Lawyers Association.
Career: *Turner Kenneth Brown*, trainee solicitor (March 1989-91); solicitor (March 1991-May 1995). *Nabarro Nathanson*, solicitor (May 1995-May 1998); partner (May 1998).
Publications: Email scanning may breach privacy - 'Computing' (May 2000). IT companies need to prepare for new email privacy rights - 'Corporate Briefing' (April 2000). Private Lives - privacy, human rights and e-mail - 'IT Consultant' (March 2000). Use of emails within the working environment ('Charity Finance Yearbook 2000'). Domain names explained - 'The Business Magazine' (October 1999). The Year 2000: issues of conformity, discovery and legal privilege - 'IT, Communications and Law' (February 1999), 'Commercial Litigation' (January 1999).
Personal: Lincoln College Oxford - BA Hons in Jurisprudence. Post Graduate Diploma in UK and European Copyright and Related Rights - Kings College London. Married, two children.

FLINT, David
MacRoberts, Glasgow
(0141) 332 9988
df@macroberts.com
See under Intellectual Property, p.488

GARDNER, Nick
Herbert Smith, London
(020) 7374 8000
nick.gardner@herbertsmith.com
Specialisation: Partner specialising in matters involving technical issues in the computing and electronics field. Solicitor Advocate with rights of audience in all civil proceedings.
Prof. Memberships: Chartered Institute of Patent Agents; National Computing Centre Legal Group; Intellectual Property Lawyers Association.
Career: A number of years experience in the electronic and computing industries before becoming a solicitor. Qualified in 1988 and became a partner at *Herbert Smith* in 1994.
Personal: LLB (University of Nottingham).

GARDNER, Paul
Osborne Clarke, London
(020) 7809 1000

GASKILL, Shelagh
Masons, London
(020) 7490 4000
shelagh.gaskill@masons.com
Specialisation: Partner and Head of Data Protection Group. Industrial and commercial IT outsourcing deals, information law, data protection law, database design, international data flows, electronic and new media and major infrastructure projects.
Prof. Memberships: Associate Member of BCS.
Career: Lecturer - Faculty of Law, University of Leeds 1979-84. Qualified 1986. At *Dibb Lupton Broomhead* 1984-94 (Partner from 1993). Joined *Masons* as a Partner in 1994.
Personal: Interests: opera and bridge.

GOODGER, Ben
Willoughby & Partners, Oxford
(01865) 791990
bgoodger@iprights.com
Specialisation: Partner in Intellectual Property Department. Advises on all aspects of the commercial exploitation and management of IP. Specialist areas: internet, e-commerce and IT law; technology transfer, patenting and biotechnology; trademarks and brand management; IP audits and strategy consulting. Also handles other general IP and commercial law, including advertising and trading standards.
Prof. Memberships: Past President of Licensing Executives Society; past Secretary: Society for Computers & Law (Thames Valley Group); IPI; INTA, on Editorial Boards for 'Global eCommerce' and 'Euro Watch' journals.
Career: Exhibition to Keble College, Oxford; *Frere Cholmeley* 1986-90; *Denton Hall* 1990-93; *Dallas Brett* 1993-97. *Willoughby & Partners* 1997 to date.
Personal: Married with three children; plays the bassoon; architecture; drama; drawing.

GORNALL-KING, William
Boyes Turner, Reading
(0118) 959 7711
wgornall-king@boyesturner.com
Specialisation: Partner and head of technology and commerce group. Main areas of practice are technology and computer law including intellectual property. Advises on e-commerce, internet, multimedia and software development, integration, distribution as well as technology licensing and outsourcing contracts. Clients include major multinationals in software, including GEAC Computer Systems Ltd (Canada's leading software house) and Intermec Technologies (mobile rugged computing); data and storage products including Information Resources Inc (CPG data); the Met Office (weather data) and CommVault Inc (data storage and warehousing) as well as peripherals suppliers (Kyocera-Mita, Tally) and ISPs and ASPs. Advises clients on e-commerce strategies and data protection issues.
Prof. Memberships: Law Society, Society for Computers and Law, British Computer Society, ISPA, TVCLA, SEG and Data Protection Forum.
Career: *Clarks* 1980-88 (partner from 1985). Joined *Boyes Turner* as partner 1988. Elected Partnership Chairman 2001.
Publications: Contributes articles of topical interest in technology field for 'Business Magazine' and other publications.
Personal: Brighton College (1971-76); LLB (Hons) University of Exeter (1979). Married with two children. Vice President Redingensians RFC, coaches mini-rugby; cycling; opera and military history. Vice Chairman Reading Area Committee Thames Valley Chamber of Commerce.

GRAHAM, Rory
Osborne Clarke, London
(020) 7809 1000

GRIFFITHS, David
Clifford Chance, London
(020) 7006 8013
david.griffiths@cliffordchance.com
Specialisation: Corporate Department. Partner specialising in e-commerce, information technology and telecoms industry work including systems procurement, technology licensing, outsourcing, encryption regulation and regulation of e-business services.
Career: Articled *Clifford-Turner/Clifford Chance*, qualified 1983; Partner since 1990.
Personal: Cambridge (MA Law).

HAMBLIN, Julian
Bond Pearce, Southampton
(023) 8082 8888
jhamblin@bondpearce.com
Specialisation: Partner and Head of the Information Technology and Intellectual Property Groups. Specialises in information technology, intellectual property, internet and data protection issues. Acting for major retailers, government bodies, universities, and software companies. Focus is on development and licensing of computer software, outsourcing, online services and e-commerce.
Prof. Memberships: The Intellectual Property Lawyer's Organisation and the Society for Computers and Law.
Career: Qualified 1987 following articles with *Pickering Kenyon*. Joined *Boodle Hatfield* 1987 and *Bond Pearce* in 1995 following the firm's acquisition of *Boodle Hatfield's* Southampton office.

HARRINGTON, Alison
Olswang, Reading
(0118) 952 3354
afh@olswang.com
Specialisation: Practice covers all aspects of computer and technology law including media and communications. Areas of practice include electronic commerce, computer software development, systems integration, network maintenance, information provision, IT distribution, outsourcing, data protection, internet and new media related work. Work also includes the protection and exploitation of copyright, trademarks, designs, patents and confidential information.
Prof. Memberships: Law Society; Committee Member Thames Valley branch of the Society for Computers and Law; Federation Against Software Theft.
Career: Qualified in 1989 - *Denton Hall* (1987-94), *Garretts* (1994-May 2002) (Head of Technology Group - *Garretts*, Reading). *Olswang* (June 2002 - date).
Personal: Born 13 July 1963. Educated at Harrogate College/Harrogate Grammar School and St Edmund Hall, Oxford University. Lives in Henley-on-Thames. Leisure interests include sailing and family.

HART, Michael
Baker & McKenzie, London
(020) 7919 1000
michael.hart@bakernet.com
Specialisation: Principal area of practice is contentious and non-contentious IP and IT Law. Work includes copyright, trademarks and passing off, patents and trade secrets, computer copyright disputes, broadcasting and media law. Also deals with government regulations and trade libel. Has represented various trade bodies in lobbying activities relating to UK and EU legislative proposals, including the copyright in the Information Society Directive. Has acted in numerous IP court actions representing companies such as Fila, McLaren, Seiko, Versace, Apple Computer and Sony.
Prof. Memberships: Anti-counterfeiting Group, AIPPI, Intellectual Property Lawyers Association.
Career: Qualified in 1983, with *Linklaters & Paines* 1983-87. Joined *Baker & McKenzie* in 1987 and became a Partner in 1990.
Personal: Born 12 August 1959. Educated at City of London School 1970-77 and Exeter College, Oxford 1977-80. Leisure activities include theatre, cinema, horse racing and tennis. Lives in London.

HARVEY, Margaret
Addleshaw Booth & Co, Manchester
(0161) 934 6348
margaret.harvey@addleshawbooth.com
Specialisation: Technology law including major IT supply and implementation projects and e-commerce related advice. Particular speciality in outsourcing both technology related and business process outsourcing.
Prof. Memberships: Computer Law Group; Society for Computers and Law; Computer Law Association.
Career: Qualified with *Boodle Hatfield* in 1987, legal counsel IBM 1988-93, head of legal for Price Waterhouse Management Consultants 1993-98; partner *Shaw Pittman* 1998-2000; partner *Addleshaw Booth & Co* 2000-.
Publications: Various articles on technology and outsourcing related issues.

435

INFORMATION TECHNOLOGY ■ THE LEADERS

Contributing author 'IBC Distance Learning Course on IT and Telecommunications'; regular speaker on IT and outsourcing Sheffield University LLB 1984.
Personal: Walking, sailing, friends, family.

HIGHAM, Nicholas
Denton Wilde Sapte, London
(020) 7242 1212
nach@dentonwildesapte.com
See under Telecommunications, p.794

HOLT, Jeremy
Clark Holt, Swindon
(01793) 617444
Specialisation: Partner specialising in computer law. Advises on all aspects of non-contentious work including internet related contracts, software rights, system purchase agreements and maintenance contracts.
Prof. Memberships: Society for Computers and Law, British Computer Society.
Career: Qualified in 1980, co-founded *Clark Holt* Commercial Solicitors in 1995.
Personal: Born 1956. Leisure interests include military history, five-a-side football and reading computer magazines.

JACOBS, Laurence
Allen & Overy, London
(020) 7330 3000
laurence.jacobs@allenovery.com
Specialisation: Partner specialising in outsourcing, information technology, e-commerce and related intellectual property matters. Advises on system development and integration projects, outsourcing, public procurement, electronic commerce, technology joint ventures and on policy matters relative to the development of new digital media.
Prof. Memberships: Chairman of the International Communications Round Table Working Party on copyright and new media.
Career: Qualified *Clifford Chance* 1990. Partner *Allen & Overy* 1997.
Personal: Born 1960. Educated Queens College, Cambridge University (1982).

JONES, Bill
Wragge & Co, Birmingham
(0870) 903 1000

KECK, Colleen
Allen & Overy, London
(020) 7330 3000
colleen.keck@allenovery.com
Specialisation: Partner specialising in corporate and commercial law in intellectual property/information technology intensive industries, particularly in relation to the pharmaceutical, media, publishing, e-commerce, IT, internet and outsourcing sectors.
Prof. Memberships: Alberta Law Society; Canadian Bar Association; International Trademarks Association; Licensing Executives Society; associate member Pharmaceutical Trademarks Group.
Career: Articled *Bennet Jones* (Calgary); qualified Alberta, Canada 1983, England 1988; barrister and solicitor, Home Oil Company Limited 1983-88; assistant solicitor *Allen & Overy*, partner 1992. Speaks and publishes frequently in the area of IP/OT/e-commerce.
Personal: University Saskatchewan (1982 LLB; 1985 BA); University of London (1987 LLM).

KEMP, Richard
Kemp Little LLP, London
(020) 7710 1610
richardk@comlegal.com
Specialisation: Practice covers intellectual property, competition/EU regulatory and general business law for the full range of IT, e-commerce and telecoms sectors, acting for both suppliers and acquirers.
Prof. Memberships: Law Society; Chartered Institute of Patent Agents; Computer Law and Security Reports – editorial board member. Guide to the World's Leading IT Lawyers (1999); one of top 20 global IT lawyers ('Best of the Best') (2000 and 2002); board member, Computer Law Association (2001).
Career: *Clifford-Turner* (1978-84); *Hopkins & Wood* 1984-91 (partner 1985); *Hammond Suddards* 1991-95 (Head of IT Group; founder partner London office); *Garrett & Co* (partner 1995, IP/IT London office group head 1996; IP/IT European Service Line head, 1997). Set up *Kemp & Co* in November 1997 to specialise in business and technology work. Became *Kemp Little LLP*, the first UK law firm LLP in July 2001. Firm now has 20 lawyers and 30 staff.
Personal: Born 8 July 1956. Educated Oakham School, St. Catharine's College Cambridge, Université Libre de Bruxelles.

LISTER, Richard
Freshfields Bruckhaus Deringer, London
(020) 7936 4000
richard.lister@freshfields.com
Specialisation: IT/telecoms transactional work (procurement, outsourcing, joint ventures) for customers and suppliers. Advises on e-commerce projects and online services generally (contract, intellectual property, data protection, security.)
Prof. Memberships: Law Society. American Bar Association. Society for Computers and Law.
Career: Joined *Berwin Leighton* 1989 and became a partner in 1997. Partner at *Freshfields* 1999.
Personal: Born 1966. Educated Manchester Grammar School and University College, Cardiff. Married with two children.

LUBBOCK, Mark
Ashurst Morris Crisp, London
(020) 7638 1111
mark.lubbock@ashursts.com
Specialisation: IT/e-commerce/IP.
Prof. Memberships: Law Society; Society for Computers & Law; Associate Member of Trade Mark Agents; and Computer Law Group.
Career: Articles *McKenna & Co* (1982-84), *McKenna & Co* (1984-88); and *Ashurst Morris Crisp* (1988-date).
Publications: Intellectual Property Section of Sweet and Maxwell's 'Practical Commercial Precedents'; Intellectual Property Section of Sweet and Maxwell's 'Practical Commercial Checklists'; 'E-Commerce - Doing Business Electronically, A Practical Guide'. Published by The Stationery Office, 2000.
Personal: Education: Cranleigh and Peterhouse, Cambridge. Interests: rugby, cricket, tennis, modern art and lately, toddlers.

MACPHERSON, Shonaig
McGrigor Donald, Edinburgh
(0131) 777 7000
shonaig.macpherson@mcgrigors.com
See under Intellectual Property, p.492

MARTINDALE, Avril
Freshfields Bruckhaus Deringer, London
(020) 7936 4000
avril.martindale@freshfields.com
See under Intellectual Property, p.492

MAUGHAN, Alistair
Shaw Pittman, London
(020) 7847 9562
alistair.maughan@shawpittman.com
Specialisation: Partner in Global Technology Group. Acts for major technology users and vendors, government departments, banks and manufacturing entities. Focus on complex and strategic technology projects, particularly outsourcing and e-commerce. Involved in major IT PFI projects (Inland Revenue - NIRS2, ASPIRE; Home Office - Police mobile radio replacement project). Specialises in IT, e-commerce and technology acquisition supply contracts. Work is mainly non-contentious and divided equally between major government contracts and contracts for private sector clients. Author of several articles on computer law. Lectures on outsourcing, e-commerce and acquiring computer systems. Contributing author to Sweet and Maxwell's 'Outsourcing Practice Manual'.
Prof. Memberships: Law Society, New York State Bar, Society for Computers and Law, Computer Law Association.
Career: Qualified in 1987. With *Boodle Hatfield* 1985-89, then *Crowell & Moring* in Washington D.C, 1989-92. Qualified in New York in 1990. At *Theodore Goddard* 1992-93, before joining *Dibb Lupton Broomhead* in 1993. Became a partner in 1994. Joined *Shaw Pittman* in 1998.

MAWHOOD, John
Tarlo Lyons, London
(020) 7405 2000
john.mawhood@tarlolyons.com
Specialisation: For more than 10 years he has specialised in legal issues affecting the internet, computer and telecommunications sectors. His early work included securing changes to the European Software Directive and the UK's copyright legislation in 1988. He chaired the Society for Computers and Law submission that proposed legislation prior to the UK's Computer Misuse Act in 1990. During his career he has advised on a number of notable outsourcing and international commercial transactions as well as dispute resolution. Recent examples of transactions he has advised on range from the listing of a leading internet domain registration company on the London Stock Exchange to the resolution of a major e-commerce licensing dispute through to exploitation of software patents on internet technology.
Prof. Memberships: Founding member of euroTcounsel®; member of Society for Computers and Law; Computer Law Group; Computer Law Association; International Bar Association.
Career: University of Cambridge (BA, History and Law, 1980). Qualified 1986.
Publications: Co-inventor of Deal-Builder™ and devised Felix™, a conferencing system used by UK judiciary. Co-author and other works: joint author of chapter entitled Laws and the Internet in 'Internet Ethics' (published by Macmillan, Feb 2000); Legal Guidelines on Millennium Date Change Issues, 'Tarlo Lyons', 1997'; 'Croners Guide to IT Purchasing & Supply', contracts section, 1994; contributor, 'Service Level Agreements', A Hiles, 1992; 'Society for Computers and Laws', response to Law Commission working paper on computer misuse, 1989.
Personal: Cambridge Lightweight Rowing Blue, accredited Amateur Rowing Association Coach. Horse riding, water sports.

MCCALLOUGH, Robert
Masons, London
(020) 7490 6236
rob.mccallough@masons.com
Specialisation: Partner and Head of Information and Technology Group. Has international experience in handling large commercial and technology-related disputes involving arbitration, litigation and Alternative Dispute Resolution relating to hardware and software procurement, project management, product liability, licensing, outsourcing and PFI contracts. He specialises in legal risk management and dispute resolution for the computer, telecommunications and other technology-related industries. He also lectures widely upon commercial and legal issues relevant to the IT industries.
Prof. Memberships: Hong Kong Law Society; English Law Society; the N.C.C.; European workshop for resolution of telecommunications disputes and the Worshipful Company of Information Technologists.
Career: Qualified in 1975. At *Hill & Perks*, Norwich 1975-78. Member of Attorney General's Chambers in Hong Kong 1978-83. Joined *Masons* (Hong Kong) in 1983. Became a Partner in 1984.

THE LEADERS ■ INFORMATION TECHNOLOGY

MCROBB, Liz
Shepherd+ Wedderburn, Glasgow
(0141) 566 9900

MILLARD, Christopher
Linklaters, London
(020) 7456 2676
christopher.millard@linklaters.com
Specialisation: Head of ITC Practice.
Career: Manchester Grammar School; University of Sheffield (LLB Hons 1980); University of Toronto (MA 1982, LLM 1983). Partner *Clifford Chance* since 1992; partner *Linklaters* 2002.

MOAKES, Jonathan
Halliwell Landau, Manchester
(0161) 835 3003
jmoakes@halliwells.co.uk
See under Intellectual Property, p.492

MONAGHAN, Iain
Masons, London
(020) 7490 6239
iain.monaghan@masons.com
Specialisation: Partner Information and Technology Group. Iain has advised on some of the UK's largest and most innovative ICT and business process outsourcing transactions. Has led teams handling PFI-funded ICT and business process procurement and the first private sector property outsourcing. In e-commerce, deals with procurement of services for prospective businesses and advises clients, particularly in the financial sector, upon the customer/commercial interface.
Prof. Memberships: Law Society.
Career: MA (Cantab).
Publications: Publications include 'The Complete Contracts' section of 'The Commercial Contracts Practice Manual' (PLC)'.

MORGAN, Glyn
Taylor Wessing, London
(020) 7300 7000
g.morgan@taylorwessing.com
Specialisation: All aspects of intellectual property and information technology law, including litigation and transactional work. Substantial expertise in copyright infringement actions relating to computer software, disputes relating to the supply of computer systems and in major IT-related transactions including outsourcing and IT systems supply and procurement.
Prof. Memberships: The Society for Computers and The Law, Computer Law Association.
Career: Qualified 1988. At *Woodham Smith* 1986 to 1990. Joined *Taylor Joynson Garrett* 1990 (Partner from 1994).
Personal: Born 23 January 1963. Educated Royal Hospital School, Holbrook and University College, Cardiff, University of Wales (LLB). Interests include skiing, film, literature, food and wine.

MOYLE, Andrew
Shaw Pittman, London
(020) 7847 9561
andrew.moyle@shawpittman.com
Specialisation: Partner in *Shaw Pittman's* Global Technology Group. Advises private and public sector clients on information technology and intellectual property law. Specialises on structuring, negotiating, implementing and managing complex technology and telecom transactions, strategic alliances, business process transformation and other technology-based collaborations. Has provided advice to clients on some of the largest technology transactions undertaken in recent times including advising AstraZeneca on its multi-billion dollar global outsourcing to IBM and advising Equant on its multibillion dollar strategic network services agreement with SITA. He is a regular speaker at technology conferences on outsourcing, best practices in procurement, sourcing strategies, software development and systems integration and is a regular contributor to various IT journals and publications.
Prof. Memberships: Law Society, Law Society of Victoria, Law Society of New South Wales.
Career: Qualified in Melbourne, Australia in 1989. With *Corrs Chambers Westgarth* from 1988 before joining *Freehill Hollingdale & Page* in 1992. Partner at *Freehill Hollingdale and Page*, 1995. Joined *Shaw Pittman* 1996.

NEWTON, Jeremy
Nabarro Nathanson, Reading
(0118) 925 4673
j.newton@nabarro.com
Specialisation: Principal areas of expertise are IT, e-commerce and intellectual property. Jeremy's practice focuses on non-contentious work for suppliers and users on major IT projects, including outsourcing, systems integration and software development contracts. Lectures and publications in 2001-02 include 'Practical IT Contracts' (Centre for Commercial Law Studies, University of London) and a 'Limitations of Liability in Computer Contracts' (Law Society Commerce & Industry Group) and a series on European e-commerce developments contracts to the current edition of 'Computer Law' (Blackstone Press) and is on the editorial panel of 'Electronic Business Law Magazine' (Butterworths).
Prof. Memberships: Law Society, British Computer Society (and law specialist group), Computer Law Association.
Career: Highlights include *Slaughter and May* 1989-94 (trainee and assistant in the Intellectual Property Group), Assistant General Counsel at Sun Microsystems 2000-01, partner at *Nabarro Nathanson* 2001 to date.
Personal: Married with two children. Lives near Fleet, Hampshire. Leisure interests include drama, running and spending time with his children.

NICHOLSON, Kim
Olswang, London
(020) 7208 8731
kan@olswang.com
Specialisation: Partner and Head of IT and Telecommunications Unit. Practice covers on the corporate side: corporate finance, venture capital, syndicated equity funding, mergers and acquisitions, IPOs, takeovers, all within the online, communications and technology industries; on the commercial side: contracts for exploitation of products, licensing, content deals, distribution exploitation and carriage deals in, or related to, the online and communications industry, for clients ranging from multinational plcs through to internet start-ups, for example Thus plc, Sportal International Limited, Raw Communications Limited, UUNet Technologies Inc and Motorola Inc.
Career: Qualified 1985. Joined *Olswang* as a partner in 1993.
Personal: Born 30 November 1960. Educated at Birmingham University and College of Law, London. Interests include opera, music, hill walking, art and antiques.

NICOLSON, Fiona
Maclay Murray & Spens, Glasgow
(0141) 248 5011
fmmn@maclaymurrayspens.co.uk
See under Intellectual Property, p.493

O'LEARY, Marcus
The Law Offices of Marcus J. O'Leary, Wokingham
(0118) 989 7110
Specialisation: IT: main area of practice is IT, including the drafting and negotiation of computer and software distribution, development, tpm, outsourcing, evaluation, VAR and licensing arrangements. All areas covered especially internet and e-commerce issues, (including cybersquatting), multimedia, disaster recovery, database, software piracy, data protection matters and disputes generally. IP: other principal area of practice is intellectual property where experience encompasses copyright and designs generally, patents, biotechnology, trademarks, branding, passing off, confidential information, trade libel, music, media and entertainment (particularly the new methods of music delivery), franchising and character merchandising, as well as intellectual property health checks and IP litigation. Advertising and Sales Promotion: healthy advertising and marketing practice involving copy advice on marketing/advertising and promotional campaigns on TV, in print, on the internet and in direct marketing - including multimedia material. Dealing with agency/client relationships including drafting suitable contracts. Acts for some of the world's leading international technology companies.
Prof. Memberships: Law Society, Society for Computers and the Law, British Japanese Law Association and member of the legal advisory group to FAST.
Career: Over 20 years experience in the IT industry. Previously an accountant, then qualified as a Barrister, later requalifying as a Solicitor, Manager of Legal Affairs at Hewlett Packard and was negotiating IT contracts for them as long ago as 1978. In-house as an Intellectual Property Lawyer for the United Biscuits Group in the mid 1980s, moving to *Pitmans* in 1989 and forming their IP/IT Department. With two others founded the Reading office of *Garrett & Co* in 1994 and set up *Garrett's* IP/IT function including a worldwide network of IP/IT lawyers. Launched The Law Offices of Marcus J. O'Leary in 1995, which has gone from strength to strength since that date.
Personal: Born 31 October 1952. Educated at London University and the Inns of Court School of Law. Enjoys sailing, writing, and scrambling in the mountains. Lives in Eversley, Hampshire.

ORR, Alistair C
Maclay Murray & Spens, Edinburgh
(0131) 226 5196

PARKASH, Raj
Clifford Chance, London
(020) 7600 1000
Rajiv.Parkash@cliffordchance.com
Specialisation: Corporate Department. Partner specialising in general company and commercial with a focus on the information technology industry and e-commerce.
Career: Partner since 1988.

PEARSON, Hilary
Bird & Bird, London
(020) 7415 6000
hilary.pearson@twobirds.com
Specialisation: Partner in Intellectual Property Department. Main areas of practice are intellectual property and computer law. Barrister in patent chambers then worked in Silicon Valley 1980-83, Houston 1983-90. Has represented a wide range of hardware, software, semi-conductor manufacturing equipment and component suppliers. Work generally IT-related; patent litigation, contract litigation and non-contentious.
Prof. Memberships: American Bar Association, Computer Law Association, Licensing Executives Society, American IP Law Association.
Career: Qualified 1976. New Court, Temple 1977-80; *Rosenblum, Parrish & Bacigalupi*, San Francisco 1980-83; *Arnold White & Durkee*, Houston 1983-90. *Simmons & Simmons*, London 1990-95. Joined *Bird & Bird* in 1995. Member of the Californian Bar 1981 and Texas Bar 1985; US Patent Attorney.
Publications: Author of 'Computer Contracts' (1983) and 'Commercial Exploitation of Intellectual Property' (1990). Contributor to 'Internet Law and Regulation' (1996, 1997, 2002).
Personal: Born 1943. Holds BA/MA (Oxon) Hons Physics 1965-69, and LLB (London) 1975.

PEETERS, Michael
Pinsent Curtis Biddle, Leeds
(0113) 244 5000
michael.peeters@pinsents.com
Specialisation: Head of Technology and Media Group in Leeds. Principal area of practice is information technology law

www.ChambersandPartners.com 437

INFORMATION TECHNOLOGY ■ THE LEADERS

including major IT procurement and outsourcing contracts, data protection, telecommunications, e-commerce, software licensing and distribution, and dispute resolution. Other main area of work is intellectual property law, particularly international software copyright. Frequently addresses seminars and conferences. Registered Trade Mark Agent.
Career: *Clifford Chance* 1986 until 1992, then became Head of IT Unit at *Simpson Curtis* (now *Pinsent Curtis Biddle*) in Leeds.

PRINSLEY, Mark
Mayer, Brown, Rowe & Maw, London
(020) 7782 8900
mprinsley@eu.mayerbrownrowe.com
Specialisation: Head of IT Group, specialising in major IT projects. Works particularly on outsourcing transactions. Advises on all aspects of corporate transactions and covers work for e-commerce and internet businesses, in particular, internet infrastructure businesses such as vignette and a variety of 'incubating' new media businesses.
Career: Articled *McKenna & Co* 1979-81; Assistant Solicitor 1981; Assistant Solicitor *Rowe & Mawe* 1984-98; Partner 1987 to date.
Personal: Born 1956. Educated Brasenose College, Oxford (1978 Law).

REES, Chris
Herbert Smith, London
(020) 7374 8000
christopher.rees@herbertsmith.com
Specialisation: Partner with 20 years experience of the IT industry advising on all types of IT related issues. His practice covers system supply, outsourcing, mergers and acquisitions and joint ventures for IT based companies. Has a particular interest in the protection and use of content (database ownership and data privacy).
Prof. Memberships: National Computing Centre (Chairman of Legal Affairs Committee); International Bar Association (Chairman of Computers and Database Committee).
Career: Qualified *Freshfields* 1979; Data General, European Counsel 1985-90; *Bird & Bird*, 1990-2000 (Managing Partner 1993-96); *Herbert Smith* 2001 - Head of IT group.
Publications: Co-editor 'Database Law' (Jordans) 1998.
Personal: Christ's College Cambridge.

RENDELL, Simon
Osborne Clarke, London
(020) 7809 1000

ROBERTSON, Ranald
Robertson & Co, Technology Law Practice, London
(020) 7731 4626
Specialisation: Focus of practice is IT law, with over 20 years' experience in this field within the computer industry and private practice. Advises an international client base of users and vendors. Work includes major IT procurement projects (outsourcing, software development, systems integration, distribution agreements, software licensing, e-commerce/internet issues, international data protection and hi-tech start-ups.
Prof. Memberships: British Computer Society, Computer Law Association, Worshipful Company of Information Technologists, London Computer Law Group, Founder Chairman of 13 country pan-European IT Law Group/Europe network of which *Roberston & Co* is UK member.
Career: Legal Services Manager with CAP/SEMA (1980-87); Partner and head of IT groups at *Stephenson Harwood*, *Field Fisher Waterhouse* and *Taylor Johnson Garrett* (1987-97). Set up *Robertson & Co* in September 1997 to provide clients with senior expertise and experience on computing, software and internet matters at an affordable and reasonable cost. Qualified 1980.
Publications: Author of 'Legal Protection of Computer Software' and Computer Contracts section of Butterworths 'Forms and Precedents'. Co-author of 'European Computer Law' and Sweet & Maxwell 'Outsourcing Practice Manual'. Editorial Panel of 'IT Law Today'.
Personal: Born 1948. Graduated Auckland University, New Zealand 1972. Married with 2 children.

ROWE, Heather
Lovells, London
(020) 7296 2000
heather.rowe@lovells.com
Specialisation: Non-contentious information technology, telecommunications and multimedia work, including matters relating to electronic commerce, electronic banking, electronic data interchange and agreements and regulation; consultant editor, 'IT Law Today' and 'Computer Law and Security Report'; correspondent 'Computer and Telecommunications Law Review'; editorial panel 'World Telecoms Law Report', and 'World Internet Law Report'; World Data Protection Report; editorial Board 'Butterworths Journal of International Banking and Financial Law' and 'Butterworths E-Journal'.
Prof. Memberships: Past Co-chairman of Committee R (technology and e-commerce), IBA; Chairman ICC International Working Party on Data Protection and Privacy; Chairman ICC UK Computing, Telecommunications and Information Policies Committee; member International Telecommunication Users Group and Telecommunications Users Association.
Career: Articled *Wilde Sapte*, London: Qualified 1981 with *Wilde Sapte* ; Assistant Solicitor, *S J Berwin & Co*. Assistant Solicitor, *Lovells*; Partner 1988.

SAMPSON, Ian
Addleshaw Booth & Co, Leeds
(0113) 209 2000
ian.sampson@addleshawbooth.com
Specialisation: Head of firm's technology unit within the technology, media and intellectual property department. Advises on all non-contentious aspects of information technology contracts, including outsourcing, e-commerce and systems procurement.
Prof. Memberships: LES, IBA, Society for Computers and Law.
Career: Qualified in 1987. Joined the firm in 1988, partner in 1992.
Personal: Educated at University of Kent. Enjoys competitive distance running.

SANDISON, Hamish
Bird & Bird, London
(020) 7415 6000
hamish.sandison@twobirds.com
Specialisation: Partner in Company Department and Co-chair of Information Technology Group. Elected Non-Executive Chairman of *Bird & Bird* in 2000. Main area of practice is IT law. Acts for both public bodies and private sector companies on IT procurement, including major IT PFI projects. Heads teams representing Office of Government Commerce, Prescription Pricing Authority, Dresdner Kleinwort Wasserstein. Member of DWP legal advisors panel and intellectual property, e-commerce and multimedia work is also covered, especially advising on copyright law. Lectures frequently in both UK and US. Often interviewed on TV and Radio.
Prof. Memberships: Council of Intellectual Property Institute, FAST Legal Advisory Group, Intellectual Property Committee of the British Computer Society.
Career: Admitted to Washington DC Bar 1980. Qualified in UK 1989. Joined *Bird & Bird* 1992 as a Partner.
Publications: Co-author of 'Computer Software Protection Law', 1989. Contributing Editor 'International Copyright and Neighbouring Rights', 1990.
Personal: Born 1952. Attended University College School, London 1960-70, Jesus College, Cambridge 1971-74, then University of California, Berkeley 1974-75. Lives in Usk, Monmouthshire.

SASSE, Sarah
Wragge & Co, Birmingham
(0870) 903 1000

SINGLETON, Susan
Singletons, London
(020) 8866 1934
susan@singlelaw.com
Specialisation: Principal of firm since 1994. Main areas of practice are commercial law, competition law and IT/IP law. Handles compliance, competition law, litigation and complaints, and EU law generally. Advises on internet law, copyright, trademarks and patents, ownership of rights, licences, EU IT/IP directives, general commercial law, agency (particularly Commercial Agents (Council Directive) Regulations), distribution and contract law.
Prof. Memberships: Competition Law Association, Licensing Executives Society, Law Society, Society of Computers and Law and Computer Law Association.
Career: Admitted 1985 after training at *Nabarro Nathanson. Slaughter and May* EC/Competition Department 1985-88. *Bristows* 1988-94.
Publications: Author of 20 books including 'Business, Internet and the Law' (Tolley), Gower, 'E-Commerce - A Practical Guide to the Law' (2nd edn, 2002), 'Commercial Agency' (Butterworths 1998), 'Legal Guide to Online Business' (Lawpak 2nd edn 2002), Tolley's 'Data Protection Handbook' (2nd edn 2002), 'Blackstone's Guide to the Competition Act 1998'. Editor of 'Comparative Law of Monopolies' looseleaf. Writes and speaks widely on legal issues.
Personal: Born 14 December 1961. Attended Westfield School, Newcastle upon Tyne 1972-79, then Manchester University 1979-82 and Chester Law College 1982-83. Married with five children. Lives on Pinner Hill.

SMALL, Harry
Baker & McKenzie, London
(020) 7919 1000
harry.small@bakernet.com
Specialisation: Partner specialising in information technology law including both contentious (IT and telecoms disputes and software protection) and non-contentious (outsourcing, facilities management and multijurisdictional software licensing). Other main area of work is IP law, covering enforcement of IP rights, copyright and designs law and multimedia contracts. Acted in many significant computer systems and high technology disputes including, amongst others, Exel v Dun & Bradstreet Software and Vodafone v Orange. Regularly addresses conferences and is lecturer on designs for Bristol University Intellectual Property Diploma course.
Prof. Memberships: Society for Computers and Law (Chairman); Member of Editorial Board of 'IT Law Today'; Expert to the EC Economic and Social Committee on EC IT Harmonisation Measures.
Career: Qualified England and Wales 1981; qualified Hong Kong 1987; *Baker & McKenzie* Hong Kong 1986; *Baker & McKenzie* London 1987; Partner 1990-present.
Publications: Contributor to Sweet & Maxwell 'IT Encyclopaedia' and Sweet & Maxwell 'Outsourcing Practice Manual'. Author of numerous articles on IP and IT law for various legal periodicals.
Personal: St Alban's Boys Grammar School 1968-75; Oriel College, Oxford (1978 BA; 1981 MA) Born 1957; resides London.

SMITH, Graham
Bird & Bird, London
(020) 7415 6000
graham.smith@twobirds.com
Specialisation: Computer project disputes, commercial litigation in computer and telecommunications industries. Evidence, document imaging and computer records. Internet law including domain name disputes, website advice, internet/email use policies and regulatory issues. Intellectual property disputes.

THE LEADERS ■ INFORMATION TECHNOLOGY

Gave evidence to the House of Lords Science and Technology Select Committee on Digital Images as Evidence. Advised Guernsey on its electronic transaction legislation.
Prof. Memberships: American Intellectual Property Law Association; Computer Law Association; eCentre Legal Advisory Group; Fellow of the Society for Advanced Legal Studies.
Career: Qualified 1978. Joined *Bird & Bird* 1983. Partner 1985.
Publications: Contributes a section on Non-Contractual Liability to the looseleaf 'Encyclopaedia of Information Technology Law' (Sweet & Maxwell). Editor and a co-author of the book 'Internet Law and Regulation' (Sweet & Maxwell, 3rd edition January 2002). Speaks and writes regularly in the UK and abroad mainly on IT and internet legal issues.
Personal: Born 1953. Educated Bristol University (LLB, 1975). Lives London.

SWYCHER, Nigel
Slaughter and May, London
(020) 7600 1200
nigel.swycher@slaughterandmay.com
Specialisation: Intellectual property and information technology law; including the IP and IT aspects of acquisitions, disposals, flotations and privatisations; involved in technology, licensing and transfer, franchising and sponsorship and IT procurement and development. Co-head of the firm's Technology, Media and Telecoms Group.
Prof. Memberships: ITMA.
Career: Admitted 1987 with *Slaughter and May*. Partner 1994.
Personal: Born 6 June 1962. Educated at Denstone College, Staffordshire and Durham University. Magician.

TIGHE, David
Manches, Oxford
(01865) 722106
Specialisation: Main area of practice is IT, dealing with all types of commercial IT agreements and with corporate finance work in the IT sector. Commercial work includes software licensing, distribution and marketing agreements, software development contracts, facilities management outsourcing and computer bureau agreements, system supply agreements, and internet and e-commerce issues. Corporate finance work ranges from start-ups and venture capital deals to acquisitions/disposals and flotations. Also writes articles on IT issues.
Prof. Memberships: Society for Computers and Law.
Career: Attended Marist College, Hull and Trinity College, Cambridge. Qualified as a solicitor in 1982. At *Boodle Hatfield* from 1980-85. Head of legal services at Logica plc from 1986-88. *Manches* since 1989. Partner since 1990.

TURNER, Mark
Herbert Smith, London
(020) 7374 8000
mark.turner@herbertsmith.com
Specialisation: Partner specialising in transactional and advisory work in the IT and e-business industries. Has particular expertise in major systems procurement and software development projects, outsourcing and IT service provision. Also advises extensively on electronic commerce, internet and digital media issues. Partner at the forefront of developments in e-commerce, advising leading companies on trading, contracts and payment on the internet and regulation of business online.
Prof. Memberships: International Chamber of Commerce; International Bar Association; Society for Computers and Law; Computer Law Association.
Career: Qualified 1983. *Macfarlanes* 1981-85. *Denton Hall* 1985-95 (Partner 1988). *Garretts* 1995-97. *Herbert Smith* 1998.

WARD, Conor
Lovells, London
(020) 7296 2000
conor.ward@lovells.com
Specialisation: Partner in the firm's computer, communications and media unit. Work includes advising on the contentious and non-contentious aspects of systems acquisition and development; facilities management and outsourcing (including telecommunications services); electronic commerce, electronic data interchange encryption technologies, anti-piracy and computer crime. Practises exclusively in the information technology field, often where the technological issues are most complex. Recent work includes advising in relation to the setting up of public key infrastructures in the UK and abroad advising in relation to various outsourcing arrangements (including the largest IT outsourcing project in the UK in 2002) and advising an e-financial institution on the launch of a data aggregation service.
Prof. Memberships: The British Computer Society Legal Affairs Committee, The Computer Law Association, member of editorial board of the Computer and Telecommunications Law Review published by Sweet and Maxwell. Appointed a Director of the Federation Against Software Theft (FAST) and Chairman of the legal advisory group of FAST.

WEBSTER, Michael
Nicholson Graham & Jones, London
(020) 7360 8101
michael.webster@ngj.co.uk
Specialisation: Computer and telecoms, software and service supply contracts, ranging from software development and distribution contracts, VAR and franchising, turnkey supply and systems integration agreements, internet, EDI, ASP, e-commerce and website issues, multimedia rights, joint ventures, technology transfer, outsourcing and long term supply of services agreements.
Prof. Memberships: Society for Computers & the Law, British Computer Society, Computer Law Group, Software Business Network, Worshipful Company of Information Technologists.
Career: Articled *Herbert Smith*, qualified in 1967, partner *Rowe & Maw* 1973. Long term involvement with specialisations has led to many invitations to speak and write articles on a number of topics such as outsourcing, joint ventures and liability arising from IT systems contracts.
Personal: Born 1942. Educated at Berkhamsted School and Bristol University (LLB Hons). Interests include tennis, golf, long distance walking and tree felling. Member of The Honourable Artillery Company.

WESTMACOTT, Philip
Bristows, London
(020) 7400 8000
philip.westmacott@bristows.com
Specialisation: Partner in Intellectual Property Department and Head of IT Practice. The full range of intellectual property work, contentious and non-contentious, with an emphasis on disputes involving, and advice to, the IT and computer industries. Has given evidence as an expert on UK IP law in US proceedings. Cases include, for the plaintiff, Philips v VDC, IBM v Phoenix, Monsanto v Maxwell M Hart and Monsanto v Stauffer and, for the defendant, Smith Myers Communications Ltd v Motorola, Iomega v Nomai, and Intel v VIA Technologies. Lecturer and marker on the Bristol University Diploma in Intellectual Property Law and Practice.
Prof. Memberships: Law Society, Associate of Chartered Institute of Patent Agents, London Computer Law Group, AIPPI, Society for Computers and Law.
Career: Undergraduate trainee at Tube Investments Ltd 1971-74. Joined *Bristows* on qualification in 1978 and became a Partner in 1985.
Personal: Born 15 April 1954. Educated at Cambridge University 1972-75 (Engineering and Law). Enjoys sailing, walking, skiing and cycling. Lives in London and Yorkshire.

WILDISH, Nigel
Field Fisher Waterhouse, London
(020) 7861 4000
ndw@ffwlaw.com
Specialisation: IT Law: acting for suppliers and customers in relation to a wide range of IT contracts, including systems and software development and procurement, networking, marketing and distribution agreements, outsourcing contracts and service level agreements. Electronic Publishing, Electronic Commerce and Internet Law: drafting and negotiating all kinds of e-commerce contracts including web development and exploitation agreement, and linking affinity agreements; advising on all legal aspects of the internet, including contracts over the internet, cross-jurisdictional liability and name/brand protection. Mergers and Acquisitions in IT, Telecoms and E-commerce: due diligence, joint ventures, acquisitions and sales. Data protection: advice, drafting contracts and audits.
Prof. Memberships: IBA (Technology and Intellectual Property Committees); National Computing Centre (Member, Law Group); Computer Law Association.
Career: Clare College, Cambridge. Partner: *Turner Kenneth Brown* (1974-95); *Nabarro Nathanson* (1995-97); *Osborne Clarke* (1997-99); *Field Fisher Waterhouse* (1999-date).
Personal: Married with 2 children. Active in squash, golf, cricket. Active member of Church of England. Member: MCC.

WORTHY, John
Denton Wilde Sapte, London
(020) 7242 1212
jnw@dentonwildesapte.com
Specialisation: Partner in Technology, Media and Telecoms Group. Electronic banking, e-commerce, internet, IT system integration, software development, facilities management, encryption, export control; data transfer, data protection, multimedia; telecoms transactions and privatisations, joint ventures, regulatory issues, network services, satellite transponder leases, satellite construction and launch, satellite financing.
Prof. Memberships: Law Society. Telecommunications Managers Association. Editorial Board, Computer Law and Security Report.
Career: *McKenna & Co* 1983-92; *Allen & Overy* 1992-96; *Denton Wilde Sapte*, Partner, 1996. In-house counsel at British Aerospace (1992) and News Digital Systems (1994).

YATES, John
V-Lex Ltd, Worksop
(01909) 544017
john.yates@v-lex.com
Specialisation: Chief Executive Officer. Main area of practice is computer law, including computer contracts and disputes. Author of numerous articles on all aspects of computer law. Regular speaker on outsourcing and computer disputes.
Prof. Memberships: Joint Chairman of Society of Computers and Law. Vice-Chairman of CSSA Legal and Contracts Group.
Career: Qualified in 1984. IBM in-house lawyer 1984-87. Partner at *Theodore Goddard* in Computer Group, 1987-93. Joined *Oxley & Coward* as a Partner in 1993. Co-founder of *V-Lex Limited* in June 2000.
Personal: Born 8 May 1959. Attended Leeds University (LLB) and Oxford University (BCL). Leisure interests include mountaineering and rock climbing. Lives near Sheffield.

INSOLVENCY/CORPORATE RECOVERY

London: 440; The Regions: 445; Scotland: 453; Profiles: 455

Research approved by BMRB For this edition, **Chambers'** researchers conducted 6,582 interviews – 3,900 with law firms, 511 with barristers and 2,171 with clients. The validity of the research was scrutinised by BMRB International, who audited both the methodology and the results at our offices in London. They interviewed **Chambers'** researchers and cross-checked sample interviews. Details of the audit appear on page 7.

OVERVIEW Practitioners have been kept busy over the past year with increasing numbers of insolvencies and restructurings. The headlines have been filled with references to matters such as Railtrack's administration and the Equitable's compromise scheme, while the world economy continues to reel from shock waves sent out by high-profile company collapses such as Enron and WorldCom. Additionally many jurisdictions have undergone legislative development in relation to procedural streamlining – in the UK, the Insolvency Act 2000 has partially come into force. The multi-jurisdictional locations of funding entities further reinforce the global nature of work. In London, the market continues to converge: clients find it "*more difficult to distinguish between the top ranking firms – they are all just as good as each other.*" Factors that "*give the top-tier the edge*" are restructuring expertise ("*a good source of work and prestige*") and strong banking divisions ("*it helps to understand these issues*"). Some industry players warn that "*cosy*" relationships between IPs and their favoured representatives may have costs implications for the future, a view that contrasts with the regional outlook that no IPs dominate the market that is likely to continue shrinking following mergers such as Andersen/Ernst & Young.

LONDON

INSOLVENCY/CORPORATE RECOVERY
■ **LONDON**

1
- Allen & Overy
- Clifford Chance

2
- Denton Wilde Sapte
- Linklaters

3
- Cadwalader, Wickersham & Taft
- CMS Cameron McKenna
- Freshfields Bruckhaus Deringer
- Lovells

4
- Herbert Smith
- Norton Rose
- Simmons & Simmons
- Slaughter and May
- Travers Smith Braithwaite

5
- Ashurst Morris Crisp
- Bingham McCutchen LLP
- Hammond Suddards Edge
- Lawrence Graham
- Nabarro Nathanson
- Stephenson Harwood

6
- Berwin Leighton Paisner
- Eversheds
- Isadore Goldman
- Osborne Clarke
- Richards Butler
- Sprecher Grier Halberstam LLP
- Taylor Wessing
- Weil, Gotshal & Manges

This book is the product of 6,582 1/2 hour interviews. See p.7 for BMRB audit. Within each band, firms are listed alphabetically.

ALLEN & OVERY (see firm details p.841) "*The gap is closing*" on this "*top-tier*" team. Interviewees perceived that it is buoyed up by "*historical*" relationships with several key finance houses. It nevertheless continues to enjoy a "*rounded*" profile in "*the biggest ticket*" contentious and non-contentious matters, including formal insolvencies and restructurings, corporate rescue, workouts and other insolvency-related issues. Cross-border assistance from its international network also gives this team a clear market advantage. Clients detail their experiences as "*extremely professional.*" His peers extol head of the global business restructuring group **Gordon Stewart** (see p.463) as a "*class act*" who "*casts a big shadow*," having "*clocked up many miles*" on high-profile matters such as the Marconi restructuring. "*Cerebral superstar*" **Nick Segal** (see p.463) "*tips the scales*" for clients with a "*commercial acumen that sets him apart from the rest.*" In conjunction with teams in New York, Amsterdam and Brussels, he advised the Dutch and US finance companies of SAir Group in the collapse of Sabena and SwissAir, the latter involving a $2 billion debt. **Ian Field** (see p.458) shares his "*solutions-orientated*" approach. He advised Investcorp and the key group companies in the debt restructuring of the Polestar Group, thought to be the first successful European high yield debt restructuring. The team also advised on the Brunner Mond high yield debt restructuring (involving $175 million and £50 million of debt), completed the complex European Kvaerner group restructuring (involving over NOK20 billion of debt and bonding), and advised Barclays Capital as co-ordinator of a number of financial creditors of Railtrack, in relation to unique proposals concerning its administration. **Clients** Big five accountancy firms; city firms; major clearing, international, merchant and investment banks.

CLIFFORD CHANCE (see firm details p.911) Its competitors acknowledge that the team has had "*a blistering year,*" particularly within the languishing telecoms sector. Interviewees commend it as a "*high-profile, top-notch outfit*" that boasts a "*multiplicity of resources*" enabling it to offer "*truly full-service*" restructuring and insolvency capability. Key players perceive that the team's involvement in the highest profile insolvency and restructuring assignments is a testament to its global strength and depth, particularly in New York.

His clients rate group head **Mark Hyde** (see p.460) as "*first rank for large, complex jobs*" because he is "*interested in practical outcomes and doesn't get bogged down with theory.*" He advised the UK and Swiss syndicates on the complex arrangements in connection with the ntl debt restructuring, the largest ever corporate debt restructuring in the UK. **Nick Frome** (see p.458) "*thinks proactively*" and "*gives the right answer at the right time,*" according to clients. He advised Barclays Capital and HSBC as co-ordinators of the bank group on the Marconi restructuring. His peers opine that "*switched-on*" insurance expert **Adrian Cohen** (see p.457) has "*established himself well*" within the team. Clients single out "*intelligent*" **David Steinberg** (see p.463) for his "*commercial*" approach on insurance-related insolvency matters and also commend "*rising star*" **Philip Hertz** (see p.460) for his "*strong assistance*" on the most complex of matters. Among its further highlights, the team advised Kvaerner on its debt restructuring including NOK9 billion of funded debt and additional liabilities, and it acted for the senior lenders on the successful financial restructurings of Derby Cycle Corporation and the Polestar Group. It also advised Barclays Capital and Citibank as joint co-ordinators on the refinancing of the bank debt of Cooksons, a £450 million secured deal, and acted for the lenders to the European Polaroid group of companies in relation to the impact of the Polaroid Corporation Chapter 11 proceedings. **Clients** Bank of America; Barclays Bank; Citibank; JPMorgan Chase; KPMG; PricewaterhouseCoopers; Nomura.

DENTON WILDE SAPTE (see firm details p.935) Interviewees commend the team's strong performance on domestic matters. Clients perceive that it is "*continuing to build*" upon its

440 INDEX TO LEADING LAWYERS: PAGE 1693 ■ IN-HOUSE LAWYERS PROFILES: PAGE 1201

LONDON ■ INSOLVENCY

LEADING INDIVIDUALS

[1]
- **ANDREWS Mark** Denton Wilde Sapte
- **FROME Nicholas** Clifford Chance
- **SEGAL Nicholas** Allen & Overy
- **ELLIOTT Robert** Linklaters
- **HYDE Mark** Clifford Chance
- **STEWART Gordon** Allen & Overy

[2]
- **ANDERSON Hamish** Norton Rose
- **FOSTER Stephen** CMS Cameron McKenna
- **ROOME James** Bingham McCutchen LLP
- **WHITE John** CMS Cameron McKenna
- **BUGG Tony** Linklaters
- **GALE Stephen** Herbert Smith
- **SHANDRO Sandy** Freshfields Bruckhaus Deringer

[3]
- **BARNETT Nigel** Denton Wilde Sapte
- **GREGORY Deborah** Lovells
- **MORRIS Howard** Denton Wilde Sapte
- **STEINER Michael** Denton Wilde Sapte
- **WILKINSON Andrew** Cadwalader, Wickersham & Taft
- **COHEN Adrian** Clifford Chance
- **HOUGHTON John** Simmons & Simmons
- **RUSHWORTH Jonathan** Slaughter and May
- **VERRILL John** Lawrence Graham

[4]
- **BAIRD Ken** Freshfields Bruckhaus Deringer
- **GAINES Keith** Lovells
- **GODFREY Patricia** Nabarro Nathanson
- **HAMILTON Dan** White & Case
- **MANNING Peter** Simmons & Simmons
- **WALSH Jeremy** Travers Smith Braithwaite
- **FLETCHER Ian** Stephenson Harwood
- **GILL Mark** Denton Wilde Sapte
- **GRIERSON Christopher** Lovells
- **MALLON Christopher** Weil, Gotshal & Manges
- **SCHAFFER Danny** Isadore Goldman

[5]
- **BLOXHAM Peter** Freshfields Bruckhaus Deringer
- **CROUCHER Yvette** Cadwalader, Wickersham & Taft
- **GRIER Ian** Sprecher Grier Halberstam LLP
- **PIKE Nicholas** Lawrence Graham
- **WOOLF Geoffrey** SJ Berwin
- **BORDELL Keith** Travers Smith Braithwaite
- **FIELD Ian** Allen & Overy
- **LOWE Rita** CMS Cameron McKenna
- **SELIGMAN George** Slaughter and May

[6]
- **BAINES Richard** Osborne Clarke
- **GORDON-SAKER Paul** Stephenson Harwood
- **MCCARTHY Michael** Richards Butler
- **BERRY Christopher** Edwin Coe
- **HIGHAM John** Stephenson Harwood
- **RAJANI Shashi** Davies Arnold Cooper

UP AND COMING
- **ANTHONY Rachel** Denton Wilde Sapte
- **NORLEY Lyndon** Kirkland & Ellis
- **WITHYMAN Tom** Lawrence Graham

See individuals' profiles p.455

LEADING INDIVIDUALS INSURANCE INSOLVENCY

[1]
- **SPENCER Robin** Lovells
- **STEINBERG David** Clifford Chance

[2]
- **FRENCH Matthew** Lovells
- **WILKINSON Andrew** Cadwalader, Wickersham & Taft
- **MONTGOMERY Nigel** DLA
- **YORKE Jon** Richards Butler

[3]
- **TYRELL Vivien** DJ Freeman

UP AND COMING
- **ELLIOTT Laurence** Herbert Smith
- **HERTZ Philip** Clifford Chance

See individuals' profiles p.455

---

merged resource capability with "*the right attitude and good ethics.*" Handling the full range of insolvency and restructuring work from personal bankruptcy to workouts, it offers additional expertise in insurance and reinsurance-related matters. Clients recommend head of practice **Mark Andrews** as their "*first choice,*" for his "*undoubted technical abilities and sheer presence.*" He advised the administrators in the restructuring of Federal-Mogul's activities in the UK, part of one of the largest cross-border restructuring proceedings in history. They also consider "*technically astute*" **Michael Steiner** as "*still one of the top investigative lawyers who is good at digging for evidence on difficult matters.*" He advised the joint provisional liquidators of the Independent Insurance Group and its subsidiaries on the cause and potential third party claims to be made in relation to the company's collapse. Clients vouch that "*you couldn't ask for anyone better on a complex insolvency matter*" than **Nigel Barnett**, who acted for the administrators of The Money Channel, while they regard **Howard Morris** as "*flavour of the month*" for his "*good-humoured attention to detail.*" He advised on various aspects of RSL Communications Group's major international telecommunications insolvency on behalf of Weil, Gotshal & Manges. **Mark Gill** brings to bear his corporate and banking expertise in the field, whilst **Rachel Anthony** can "*draw together a tangled web of technical issues and prioritise practically*" on litigious insolvency matters. She acted for PwC, receivers of the Cammell Laird Group on all major issues arising out of the receiverships of several of its operating subsidiaries. The team advised United States Aviation Underwriters with regard to London market schemes of arrangement, and acted for Dolphin Telecommunications in the attempted reconstruction of their European operations, and subsequently on the formal insolvency proceedings in relation to the UK sub-group of companies. **Clients** Big five accountancy firms; leading clearing banks.

LINKLATERS (see firm details p.1043) Interviewees point to this firm's involvement in "*top-notch jobs,*" most notably, Enron. Clients list among its strengths the "*huge depth and high quality of its resources,*" with "*canny*" non-partner lateral hires and greater European focus. As regards inter-departmental support, a key market source vouched that it "*paraded experts on every aspect of tax, pensions, litigation, and insolvency*" on a highly complex matter." First division, polished" head of restructuring and insolvency **Robert Elliott** (see p.458) gains client plaudits as "*one of the most recognised lawyers in the restructuring market.*" A "*team builder who adds value to the overview of the term sheet,*" he advised RBS and National Australia Bank as joint co-ordinators of several banks and other financial creditors on the restructuring of John Laing, the disposal of its construction division and its completion of a £76.8 million rights issue. Clients recommend the "*high energy*" of **Tony Bugg** (see p.457) on litigious matters. He advised Sabena and Sabena Interservices Centre in the collapse of the SwissAir Group. Having advised Enron Europe on its options in the Dynergy rescue, the team represented PwC as administrators of Enron Europe and related European subsidiaries. It also advised the Strategic Rail Authority in the ongoing financing arrangements in relation to Railtrack and issues arising from its subsequent failure and administration. **Clients** Barclays Group; Citigroup; HSBC; Goldman Sachs; JPMorgan Chase; PwC; Schroder Salomon Smith Barney.

CADWALADER, WICKERSHAM & TAFT (see firm details p.898) Interviewees concurred that the team, which is typically seen handling the full range of restructuring and issuing work for US bondholders, has "*made a strong impact.*" Credited by some sources as having pioneered high yield note restructuring in Europe, the team is "*highly focused and aggressive*" in its expansion strategy. In this respect it is aided by its strong connections with US and European investment banks and hedge funds. Heading the London team, "*big-hitter*" **Andrew Wilkinson** (see p.464) "*combines good party rapport with sound commercial nous and strong technical knowledge*" on general and insurance-related matters. He acted for Brunner Mond Group on its innovative debt and capital restructuring involving full high yield bond equitisation in

INSOLVENCY ■ LONDON

addition to a full refinancing of the company's senior debt. Clients opine that **Yvette Croucher** (see p.457) has "*all the qualities to be one of the best – she gets on with people, runs with the deal and keeps the client informed.*" She advised a committee of noteholders regarding a potential restructuring of Brokat, a German technology company. Among other highlights, the team advised KPMG as joint administrators of Cammell Laird, and advised the ad hoc committees of The Polestar Corporation and RSL Communications. **Clients** Alliance Capital; Brunner Mond; Close Brothers; KPMG; Morgan Stanley; Oaktree Capital.

CMS CAMERON MCKENNA
(see firm details p.914) Clients "*have a high regard*" for the "*strong team*" on domestic, medium-sized matters. They commend its "*solid technical skill set,*" "*superb team-work*" and "*wide-ranging*" resources. On contentious matters, it is "*a winner with clout*" in court. Offering full service reconstruction and insolvency expertise, the team acts for banks, bondholders and other creditors, businesses and IPs. **John White** (see p.464) displays "*gravitas with his excellent strategic judgement*" on matters such as advising DTLR on Railtrack's administration, while "*thoughtful, co-operative*" **Stephen Foster** (see p.458) is a "*practical operator who gets results.*" He advised Equitable Life on one aspect of the proposed scheme of arrangement. "*Capable*" **Rita Lowe** (see p.461) advised the joint administrators of the Save Group of companies (Ernst & Young) in completing contracts for the sale of their properties, business and assets to a consortium that included one of the largest independent energy companies in the UK. The team also acted for Andersens as joint administrators of the companies in the Action Leisure Group, in disposing of the business and assets. It also advised KPMG as receivers of the Albert Fisher Group. **Clients** Andersen; Deloitte & Touche; Equitable Life; Ernst & Young; Grant Thornton; Kroll Buchler Phillips; Lloyds TSB; RBS.

FRESHFIELDS BRUCKHAUS DERINGER
(see firm details p.964) The team is "*making its presence known in the market as a serious heavyweight in major restructurings and insolvencies.*" Although notably smaller than some of its competitors, clients credit the team with "*all-round strength and high-quality expertise,*" while many opine that it is "*bulked by the international network*" and is "*great on knowledge-sharing.*" Describing its approach as "*on the ball and forward thinking,*" a key industry player claimed that it is "*particularly good on advising when to go for a strike-out or when to settle.*" **Sandy Shandro** (see p.463) is highly regarded by clients for his "*tremendous intellect married with keen commercial sense.*" A "*flexible, deal-doer,*" he is often seen on overseas matters such as advising Teleglobe's global group of companies on the development of a restructuring strategy. Clients also seek out "*greatly respected*" head of group **Peter Bloxham** (see p.456) "*for the big stuff,*" such as major corporate restructurings. He advised the liquidators in England of various companies in HIH, the second largest insurance group in Australia that has commenced insolvency proceedings with a minimum shortfall of A$2.7 billion. "*Sensible, self-effacing, commercial*" **Ken Baird** (see p.455) displays "*excellent business sense*" on innovative cross-border work such as advising KPMG as FLAG Telecom's provisional liquidators in Bermuda.

The team has advised several counterparties affected by the collapse of ITV Digital, and also advised Garuda in its successful multibillion dollar finance restructuring. **Clients** Abbey National; Andersen; Deloitte & Touche; Ernst & Young; KPMG; Nomura; PwC; RBS.

LOVELLS
(see firm details p.1045) As one client summed up: "*Nick Frome's departure to Clifford Chance was a loss, but to be fair, the team still has tremendous strength in depth.*" Other loyal industry users claim that it is "*our favourite for the big stuff*" on account of their "*special relationship*" with the team. It typically handles domestic rescue and restructuring work for a range of financial institutions, accountants and corporates, enjoying a strong reputation for its specialist expertise in the insurance sector. Group head on the insurance side **Robin Spencer** (see p.463) is "*cerebral, determined and extremely easy to work with,*" claim clients. He led the team that advised Equitable Life Assurance Society on the drafting of a Section 425 scheme of arrangements to restructure its £20 billion with-profits fund. He is ably assisted by **Matthew French**, who clients report "*gives his seniors a run for their money*" with his "*exceptional personal skills and enormous brain.*" They also commend "*massively experienced*" **Deborah Gregory** (see p.459) as one who "*gives 110% to put her clients first.*" She advised Grant Thornton and KPMG on the largest ever UK receivership in the motor retail sector. Blue-chip clients vouch that they "*haven't had a failure yet*" with "*the best litigator around,*" **Christopher Grierson** (see p.558). He and "*sound operator*" **Keith Gaines** (see p.557) continue to advise Deloitte & Touche as English, Luxembourg and Cayman liquidators of BCCI, which they successfully represented in the House of Lords against the Bank of England. Among further highlights, the team was instructed by creditors, including institutional shareholders, ALSTOM and Bechtel, in the Railtrack administration, and it continues to act for ING in the partial settlement of the Barings audit litigation. **Clients** Bank of Scotland; Barclays; CSFB; Dresdner; Ford Credit; Kroll Buchler Phillips; MCI Worldcom; RSM Nelson Wheeler.

HERBERT SMITH
(see firm details p.992) Interviewees perceive that this "*quality*" team is in the process of building a "*magnificent practice*" with the backing of a strong corporate department. It is a "*recognised player*" in international restructurings and reorganisations, insurance insolvency, litigation and arbitration. Involvement in the high-profile Independent Insurance case demonstrated that it is "*clearly able to handle bigger jobs,*" according to clients. "*Well-organised*" head of corporate recovery **Stephen Gale** (see p.458) advised PwC as the provisional liquidators of the insurance company, in the run-off of the insurance book, valued in excess of £1 billion. Clients declare that they would choose him for "*brutal negotiations.*" New partner **Laurence Elliott** (see p.458) is "*making a name for himself*" on insurance-related matters.

The team advised the Brunner Mond Bondholder Committee on the restructuring of Brunner Mond Group's £50 million and $125 million high yield bonds, which led to control of the company being passed to its bondholders. It also advised various energy, utility and trading companies and investment banks in the UK and US on the Enron collapse. **Clients** Begbies Traynor; Brunner Mond Bondholder Committee; PPB; big five accountancy firms.

NORTON ROSE
(see firm details p.1084) Clients commend it as a "*steady*" practice that handles a range of restructuring, turnaround work and formal insolvencies, primarily on behalf of the firm's existing banking client roster. It has increased its focus in the telecoms, technology and insurance sectors. "*Balanced lawyer*" **Hamish Anderson** (see p.455) "*doesn't get emotionally involved.*" His clients report that he is "*an excellent technical lawyer – give him a bundle of documents and he'll be happy.*" He acted for the principal supplier and secured creditor of Axxon, in a security and repossession enforcement action that led to insolvency proceedings in Germany, The Netherlands and Belgium. The team advised a syndicate of banks led by CIBC World Markets as secured creditors of the Dolphin Telecommunications Group in its administration. Among further highlights, it represented the Rail Regulator in Railtrack's administration, acted for the credit providers in Garuda's restructuring deal, and advised numerous counterparties including BP and Norsk Hydro in relation to Enron. **Clients** Big five accountancy firms; BP; CIBC; HSBC; JPMorgan Chase; RBS.

SIMMONS & SIMMONS
(see firm details p.1136) "*Gravitating to the top,*" clients "*have no doubt*" that the firm "*has the resources to cover the banner of work*" in insolvency and recovery, including large bond administrations. One put it down to its "*uncanny ability for finding bright young people – all the assistants are exceptional.*" Several expressed the view that while "*not the cheapest,*" it presents an "*effective, sensible approach*" in protecting the client's interests. "*Energetic*" head of the corporate recovery

LONDON ■ INSOLVENCY

group John Houghton (see p.460) is "*good at keeping everyone in the loop as a team*" and "*delivers a quality service,*" according to clients. One testified that he is "*great to have on your side – he does a good 'angry man' when needed, but is not gratuitously aggressive.*" They also have "*no difficulty*" in advising "*reasoned, knowledgeable and commercial*" Peter Manning (see p.461). The team advised pan-European telecoms group GTS in a scheme of arrangement involving converting $550 million of bond debt into equity. It also advised Ofgem, numerous counterparties and a purchaser of Enron's metal business, and has acted for the company, directors and Ernst & Young in relation to Railtrack's administration. **Clients** Deloitte & Touche; Grant Thornton; GTS; KPMG; RSM Robson Rhodes; Singer & Friedlander.

SLAUGHTER AND MAY (see firm details p.1140) "*Small but impressive*" sums up the market view of the team, which has enjoyed a high profile in "*significant restructurings*" that include Railtrack and Barings. In the former, the team, led by respected Jonathan Rushworth (see p.463), acted for four members of Ernst & Young who were appointed as special railway administrators. "*Thorough and pragmatic*" George Seligman (see p.463) also advised Ernst & Young as the liquidators of various companies in the Barings group, involving a scheme of arrangement to settle litigation against Coopers & Lybrand, and acted on a £70 million restructuring debt for Boosey & Hawkes. Among further highlights, the team advised the Polaroid Group on the UK aspects of its financial difficulties, and acted for Carlton and Granada in relation to ITV Digital's collapse. **Clients** Major accountants; IPs; banks; corporate clients.

TRAVERS SMITH BRAITHWAITE (see firm details p.1166) Clients endorse the "*superior quality*" of the team's output on traditional insolvency, restructuring and turnarounds, particularly in the banking and private equity sectors. It also advises on solvent liquidations as part of corporate restructurings. "*Good on the detail,*" Jeremy Walsh (see p.464) displays "*the right empathy to bring parties together and close the deal,*" according to clients that have worked with him on both sides. Head of department, he advised Bridgepoint Capital on the restructuring and acquisition of Betterware Holdings, and advised Kroll Buchler Phillips in the liquidation of vehicle removal and storage operator Bells of Richmond. "*Proactive*" Keith Bordell (see p.456) (formerly of Berwin Leighton Paisner) advised ntl on its recapitalisation, involving restructuring up to $20 billion of debt. The team has advised Miller Fisher on its debt and equity restructuring through new money facilities and a debt/equity swap. It also advised Ernst & Young as administrative receivers of toy retailer Beatties of London. **Clients** Bank BNI; Bank of Scotland; Barclays; Crestco; big five accountancy firms.

ASHURST MORRIS CRISP (see firm details p.852) Clients "*can't say enough to praise*" a team that offers "*quality that is second to none.*" One declared that "*life would be easy if every firm was like them.*" The "*highly cohesive*" team demonstrates "*extraordinary backup*" and "*clear, thorough advice that gets to the heart of the matter.*" It has enjoyed "*increasing prominence*" in bond restructuring work as debt advisers acting for "*high-quality*" corporates among its incumbent clients. Head of department Ben Tidswell leads a team that has an "*accommodating and responsive*" style. Among various highlights, the team acted for the administrators of Atlantic Telecom, represented Railtrack Group on the administration of its subsidiary, and advised on a £700 million restructuring of a company close to the Enron collapse. Its heightened profile in telecoms-related restructuring and insolvency work attaches to Atlantic Telecom, Centrica's purchase of OneTel, RSL Communications and WorldxChange. **Clients** PwC; Railtrack Group; Arthur Andersen Singapore; Ernst & Young; Kroll Buchler Phillips; Levy Gee.

BINGHAM MCCUTCHEN LLP (see firm details p.872) "*Well- recognised players*" in high yield bond restructuring on behalf of creditors, clients also commend the team for its expertise in transactions involving notes. It typically handles matters in the £50-300 million range in the mid-corporate market. His peers report that "*pragmatic specialist*" James Roome (see p.462) is "*creating a lot of heat and light*" in UK and US public listed bonds work. He advised the public bondholders of Marconi in its restructuring. He also represented the convertible bondholders of the largest Polish conglomerate, Elektrim, on the complex negotiations for recovery of their claims outside bankruptcy. The team negotiated the complex workout of blue-chip construction company John Laing, and advised bondholders of Versatel in its restructuring. **Clients** Leading insurance institutions; investment funds and banks; hedge funds.

HAMMOND SUDDARDS EDGE The team's inclusion on "*large, complex*" matters flows from its "*strong allegiances*" in the banking community. Clients regard it as "*the market leader*" in factoring work, which it handles with a "*cerebral*" approach that "*always adds a new dimension.*" Andrew Visintin "*runs a fantastic team in recovery and is the client's favourite.*" The team successfully acted for the joint liquidators of Leyland Daf upholding the first instance judgment before the Court of Appeal in their favour regarding priority of liquidation expenses over the claims of floating chargeholders. Among further highlights, it advised Arthur Andersen on the administration of the City Truck Group, which involved 2,500 vehicles throughout the UK, and advised the R3 general technical committee on the implications of the Brumark decision and in relation to the Enterprise Bill. **Clients** Leading accountants and financial institutions.

LAWRENCE GRAHAM (see firm details p.1031) Market sources note that the team is "*making a push,*" having "*established its presence*" in mid-market corporate recovery and asset sales work. "*Enormously bright and practical*" John Verrill heads "*an experienced department with deep resources.*" He advised on the reconstruction and sale of Euro Sales Finance. Key advisor on mid-tier personal and corporate insolvency, Nick Pike ("*clever*") handled investigative work for the Insolvency Practitioners' Association, the UK's largest regulator of IPs. Also recommended, Tom Withyman advised PwC on the continued recoveries for London Trust Bank in administration. The team advised on the administrative receivership of Demaglass Holdings for Arthur Andersen and Bank of America. **Clients** Insolvency Practitioners' Association; Arthur Andersen; PwC; Ernst & Young; KPMG.

NABARRO NATHANSON (see firm details p.1080) Market sources commended this team for its expertise in a breadth of mid-level corporate work that covers the TMT, hotel and leisure, and healthcare sectors, including wrongful trading matters. Clients report that its "*bright partners*" are "*responsive, will cover all the angles and take a view.*" Patricia Godfrey (see p.458) heads the team that "*draws together different skill sets proficiently*" and has "*great connections*" overseas. Among highlight matters, it successfully defended one of the directors of Continental Assurance Company of London (in liquidation) on a wrongful trading claim brought by the liquidators of the company, and advised the Heart Hospital on its widely publicised purchase by the NHS. **Clients** Grant Thornton; BDO Stoy Hayward; Kroll Buchler; Begbies Traynor; Moore Stephens; Deloitte & Touche; Ernst & Young; HSBC; Bank of Scotland; Barclays Bank; HSBC Ventures; GE Capital; NewMediaSPARK ; Executive Interim Management.

STEPHENSON HARWOOD (see firm details p.1147) Clients give a "*pretty high*" rating to the "*well-established*" team on insolvency and corporate recovery work. One of those who enjoy s a "*long-standing relationship*" with the team described it as a "*good mix of dedicated people.*" Leading the team as "*one of the market's better-known names,*" Paul Gordon-Saker (see p.459) is "*quite a street fighter ,*" according to clients. He acted for the administrators, including BDO Stoy Hayward , and for NatWest, in the administrations of leisure companies in the Fairmont Group. "*Useful expert on Scottish law*" Ian Fletcher (see p.458) and John Higham QC (see p.460) also gained strong market endorsement.

www.ChambersandPartners.com   443

INSOLVENCY ■ LONDON

The team acted for the liquidator of Allwines, and advised the administrators of Enron in relation to claims against various counterparties under diverse contractual arrangements. It also concluded the bankruptcy of Jonathan Aitken for Baker Tilly. **Clients** Deloitte & Touche; KPMG; PwC; Ernst & Young; Baker Tilly; Grant Thornton; BN Jackson Norton; Begbies Traynor; Benedict Mackenzie; Kroll Buchler Phillips; Levy Gee.

BERWIN LEIGHTON PAISNER (see firm details p.866) The "*robust*" practice is now headed by David Leibowitz following Keith Bordell's departure to Travers Smith Braithwaite. It covers a broad range of work from individual insolvencies to corporate rescues and reorganisations, business disposals and controlled wind-down programmes. Clients describe it as a "*time- and task-oriented*" team that delivers a "*prompt and speedy service*." It fields "*experienced, easy-going*" lawyers that can "*take in their stride any intricate problems.*" One client typically recommended that it is "*on top of the subject*" in respect of crisis management involving IPs or pensions elements. The team completed its work in winding down the affairs of the New Millennium Experience Company, which operated the Dome. It also acted for BDO Stoy Hayward as administrators of six companies within the insolvent Alpha Group. **Clients** BDO Stoy Hayward; Baker Tilly; Begbies Traynor; Connolly Leather; Chorion; Deloitte & Touche; First Leisure Corporation; Grant Thornton; KPMG; Kroll Buchler Phillips; Levy Gee; New Millennium Experience Company.

EVERSHEDS (see firm details p.949) Clients commend a "*capable, knowledgeable team*" although some clients observe that it can be "*slightly stretched*" at times. At the time of going to press, Jeff Drew has joined from the Birmingham office to head the team. Covering restructuring, workouts and insolvency matters, the practice aims to represent a spread of major banks and other financial institutions, major accountants, niche corporate recovery players and ABLs. The team acted for the partners in Begbies Traynor as the administrative receivers appointed by the Bank of Ireland, in relation to a number of companies within the USIT group, the largest student travel company in the UK (previously trading as Campus Travel). Among other highlights, it represented Margent Capital Management in its successful application for compulsory winding-up and the appointment of a provisional liquidator, the first such application by an insolvent corporate member, which set a case precedent. Working in tandem with foreign law firms and with the firm's Paris office, the team has also been advising directors of the UK entities in two very large multinational groups of companies whose US parent companies have gone into, or are shortly to enter, Chapter 11 proceedings. **Clients** Begbies Traynor; Margent Capital Management.

ISADORE GOLDMAN "*You just can't beat firms like this,*" opined one industry player. Interviewees applauded its "*small but very active*" niche practice in personal insolvency and corporate work. "*Reliable and confident*" specialist **Danny Schaffer** is popular with clients who consider him to be a "*leader in personal insolvency work, but equally good on corporate matters.*" The team acted for the liquidator of Floor 14 in a Court of Appeal case involving liquidation of expenses construed as assets of the company. It also successfully represented the respondent in GVDC v Koshy in a Court of Appeal case involving the interpretation of debenture documentation. **Clients** RBS/NatWest; KPMG; Harris Lipman.

OSBORNE CLARKE (see firm details p.1090) The team is active across the spectrum from corporate rescues to receiverships, liquidations and bankruptcies, representing major clearing banks, accountants and IPs. Flowing from the firm's sector strength, the team specialises in turnaround advice to TMT corporates in financial difficulties. "*Bright lawyer*" **Richard Baines** retains the highest profile in the team that represented Henderson & Co concerning Marin Sobey (in bankruptcy) in complex litigation involving £200 million of claims from creditors. It also advised the Weir Group on the acquisition of the business of Diametric from its administrative receivers, and represented Grant Thornton on the receivership of Craftworld Trading. **Clients** Barnes & Noble; Brown, Shipley & Co; Chesterton; Close Brothers; Communications Collateral; Ernst & Young; Grant Thornton; Levy Gee; PwC; RBS/NatWest.

RICHARDS BUTLER (see firm details p.1112) Interviewees noted that the team has "*pretty good depth,*" having "*made efforts to bulk up.*" Clients "*have no hesitation in picking up the phone*" to group head **Jon Yorke** (see p.464), a "*user-friendly, all-rounder*" who they credit with having handled some "*interesting work,*" particularly within the insurance sector. He acted on the administrative receivership and CVA of Web2U, and advised PwC on the provisional liquidations and schemes of arrangement for both the North Atlantic Insurance Company and the Black Sea & Baltic General Insurance Company. Clients also commend "*practical*" **Michael McCarthy** (see p.461) who "*doesn't mind getting his hands dirty in difficult situations.*" He advised on the administrative receivership of Jentique Furniture and the provisional liquidation of City Vintners. The team has also been advising Deloitte & Touche on various ancillary matters relating to Drake Insurance Company. **Clients** PwC; Deloitte & Touche; Royal Bank of Scotland.

SPRECHER GRIER HALBERSTAM LLP This specialist niche practice handles a broad range of personal and corporate insolvency matters. Still the team's best-known personality, **Ian Grier** (see p.459) garnered definitive client approbation: "*Sometimes you need to battle, protect your position; if you want a rottweiller, he's your man.*" **Clients** Big five accountancy firms; IPs; clearing banks; corporates.

TAYLOR WESSING (see firm details p.1156) Clients commend the growing team's "*fantastic*" work on mid-corporate matters, particularly within the IP and telecoms sectors. Michael Frawley heads a "*robust, lateral-thinking*" team that clients approve for being solutions-oriented and "*receptive to discussion.*" One declared that it "*always gives an excellent service.*" Among its highlights, the team acted for Deloitte & Touche as administrators of Dolphin Telecommunications. It also represented Smith & Williamson as receivers of the Britannic Group, and as liquidators of VK Vintners in relation to wrongful trading, preference and transactions at an undervalue action against the company's directors. **Clients** KPMG; PwC; Smith & Williamson; Baker Till; Begbies Traynor; Deloitte & Touche.

WEIL, GOTSHAL & MANGES (see firm details p.1183) According to market sources, "*there is great potential here – the team will generate significant work on both sides of the pond.*" Clients praised **Chris Mallon** (see p.461), its leader, who recently joined from Freshfields, as "*technically strong, hard-working and committed.*" The team represented Enron and Global Crossing on the UK and other non-US aspects of their restructurings. It also acted for Netia on its restructuring across Poland, Holland and the US. **Clients** Enron; KPMG; Abbey National Treasury Services.

OTHER NOTABLE PRACTITIONERS On the insurance side, clients recommend former accountant **Nigel Montgomery** of DLA as a "*safe pair of hands,*" an attribute shared by **Vivien Tyrell** of DJ Freeman. Known by his peers to "*take a commercial view,*" **Geoffrey Woolf** (see p.464) of SJ Berwin "*does good work*" for building industry sector clients. Clients recommend "*unflappable*" **Shashi Rajani** (see p.462) who has left Nicholson, Graham & Jones to join Davies Arnold Cooper. A "*technical lawyer with an academic approach,*" he deals "*thoroughly with complex problems.*" Interviewees also rated **Christopher Berry** (see p.456) of Edwin Coe for his personal insolvency expertise, particularly in relation to directors disqualifications. **Dan Hamilton** (see p.460) has recently moved from CMS Cameron McKenna to join White & Case. Clients appreciate his "*pragmatic, cost-effective advice;*" he advised the administrators of Scotia Holding and its subsidiaries, working on an innovative scheme for the distribution of funds to creditors. **Lyndon Norley** (see p.462) of Kirkland & Ellis was recommended by peers and clients as a "*skilled technical lawyer*" who appears on "*interesting*" matters.

THE SOUTH

INSOLVENCY/CORPORATE RECOVERY
■ THE SOUTH

1
- asb law Crawley
- Blake Lapthorn Fareham, Portsmouth

2
- Lester Aldridge Bournemouth, Southampton

3
- Bond Pearce Southampton
- Paris Smith & Randall Southampton

4
- Cripps Harries Hall Tunbridge Wells
- Paul Davidson Taylor Horsham

LEADING INDIVIDUALS

1
- BROCKMAN Christopher Blake Lapthorn
- DOBSON Julian Julian Dobson Solicitors
- KEITLEY Nicholas Blake Lapthorn
- NIEKIRK Malcolm Lester Aldridge
- OLIVER David Blake Lapthorn
- TAYLOR Andrew asb law

2
- JEFFRIES Graham Bond Pearce
- LE BAS Malcolm Paris Smith & Randall
- MUNRO Rick Lamport Bassitt

3
- BARKER Matthew Lester Aldridge
- COOK Nigel Paul Davidson Taylor
- CRAIG Nigel Blake Lapthorn

This book is the product of 6,582 1/2 hour interviews. See p.7 for BMRB audit. Within each band, firms are listed alphabetically. See individuals' profiles p.455

ASB LAW (see firm details p.851) Clients acknowledge that this is an "*extremely approachable and able team*" that handles a range of corporate and personal insolvency work. Niche strengths exist in DTI matters and voluntary arrangements. Clients also singled out "*excellent litigator*" **Andrew Taylor** for being able to "*handle anything we throw at him.*" Typical of the team, he "*takes a practical, commercial view – he gives you the options then points out the best one.*" The firm has also increased the level of workout advice it offers. The firm has acted for a creditor in the provisional liquidation of Daewoo, advising on cross-border issues and the use of the provisional liquidator model. It also advised on the VK Vinters High Court disqualification trial. **Clients** Major regional IPs.

BLAKE LAPTHORN (see firm details p.877) Market sources opine that the team, having merged with Sherwin Oliver, is "*now a leader in the region with good strength in depth,*" handling larger corporate-related matters. Highly rated by his peers and popular with clients, **Nicholas Keitley** handles defence contract and construction work "*extremely diligently.*" His highlights include advising administrative receivers Grant Thornton in relation to Basys Technology, and acting for PwC in relation to Rival Bowman Yachts. He also advised 4th Wave Technologies, and subsequently, its administrators PwC, on the administration of the company. Clients noted the team's "*technically sound expertise*" in liquidation and insolvency for small to mid-sized corporates. Clients gave equal commendation to former Sherwin Oliver partners **Christopher Brockman**, **David Oliver** and **Nigel Craig**. The three share commercially focused attributes: "*practical and sensible,*" they take "*a tough line in negotiations*" but never lose sight of the deal. They acted for the purchaser of the business of Camper & Nicholson Yachts, a subsidiary of Cammell Laird, dealing with the acquisition of the business from the administrators, and several post-completion disputes. They also acted on numerous applications for administration orders. **Clients** Grant Thornton; PwC; Fanshawe Lofts; Tenon Recovery; Buchanans.

LESTER ALDRIDGE (see firm details p.1038) Clients confirm that they can rely on the team to "*have the bodies*" and to "*perform well under pressure.*" The team provides a "*rapid response*" on contentious and non-contentious matters. Clients also commend team leader **Malcolm Niekirk** (see p.462) as "*a thorough technician*" on non-contentious matters, particularly restructuring debentures. **Matthew Barker** (see p.455) is "*commercially robust*" in his advice. Both licensed IPs, they have niche expertise in advising football clubs and supporters' groups in England, Wales and Northern Ireland. Team highlights include advising in the aerospace and aviation sectors in connection with a major flying school, a small private airline and a precision engineering business manufacturing aerospace components. **Clients** Major accountants and IPs.

BOND PEARCE (see firm details p.586) Interviewees commended the team's "*strong performance at the front end of insolvency,*" particularly in the agribusiness market. They opine that leading banking specialist **Graham Jeffries** (see p.106) is "*such a good lawyer*" that he is "*in extremely high demand.*" The team has handled restructuring and turnaround work across a range of sectors including Enron-related fallout. It also advises on recovery work including insolvency proceedings for finance houses and banks. The firm has assisted on several trading receiverships, including court-appointed receiverships for a Midlands manufacturer and within the leisure sector. **Clients** IPs; accountants; corporates.

PARIS SMITH & RANDALL (see firm details p.1093) The "*growing*" team, led by **Malcolm Le Bas**, typically handles corporate restructuring and contentious work on behalf of licensed IPs. Among its highlights, the team handled two large, complex reconstructions under Section 110 of the Insolvency Act 1986, completed two large purchases from receivers of business and assets, and dealt with urgent sales by administrative receivers and liquidators. Among its successful cases, the team represented directors in a disqualification case, and a foreign client in annulling a bankruptcy order. It also defended an alleged transaction at undervalue, and obtained reimbursement of funds for a liquidator in relation to a pre-liquidation preference payment. **Clients** KPMG; Radfords; Roger Evans.

CRIPPS HARRIES HALL (see firm details p.922) The team, led by Peter Ashford, typically handles personal insolvency matters, failed IVAs, complex bankruptcy matters and administrations for the 'big five' accountancy firms. Its highlights include acting for the receiver of a large motor trader, and acting for the liquidators of a company in a members' voluntary winding up, which involved the disposal of contemporary artwork as part of its assets. The team also acted for the trustees in bankruptcy in obtaining a number of possession orders of high-value houses leading to recovery of several million pounds. **Clients** Major accountants; IPs.

PAUL DAVIDSON TAYLOR Clients identify the team as "*solid niche factoring specialists*" on mid-tier work. They commend it as "*user-friendly, commercial and capable,*" but "*extremely aggressive when required,*" particularly on non-contentious and contentious asset-based lending work. "*Approachable*" **Nigel Cook** (see p.457) heads up the team that acted for receivers appointed over companies with businesses covering the manufacturing, retail and services sectors. It advised the administrator of Amraf, in a matter that involved consideration of a claim by Barclays to set off credit balances in the company's bank account. **Clients** Smith & Williamson; Baker Tilly; Benedict Mackenzie; Tenon.

OTHER NOTABLE PRACTITIONERS **Rick Munro** (see p.462) of Lamport Bassitt was endorsed by peers as a "*sound and sensible*" litigator. **Julian Dobson** (see p.457) of Julian Dobson Solicitors continues to impress both clients and peers. He is an "*approachable, commercial, high-calibre operator,*" who is particularly skilled in directors disqualification issues.

INSOLVENCY ■ THAMES VALLEY/SOUTH WEST

THAMES VALLEY

INSOLVENCY/CORPORATE RECOVERY
■ THAMES VALLEY

1 Boyes Turner Reading
2 Pitmans Reading
3 Clarks Reading
 Darbys Oxford
 Matthew Arnold & Baldwin Watford
 Morgan Cole Reading

LEADING INDIVIDUALS

1 BRANSON Christopher Boyes Turner
2 BROOKER Suzanne Pitmans
 TAYLOR Elizabeth Darbys
3 ARCHER David Pitmans
 BACON Alistair Matthew Arnold & Baldwin
 POTTER Bruce Morgan Cole
 SMITH Phillip Boyes Turner

See individuals' profiles p.455

BOYES TURNER (see firm details p.883) "*The leading firm in the Thames Valley,*" claimed our interviewees. It is able to "*boast a strong reputation*" for its advice to IPs and LPA receivers. The work here ranges from commercial insolvency on large corporate failures to large IVAs and personal insolvency matters. Possessing "*vast experience,*" head of department **Christopher Branson** (see p.456) is "*dynamic and straightforward.*" Clients particularly commended his "*ability to handle difficult litigation.*" **Phillip Smith** acts for liquidators and receivers in corporate insolvencies and advises trustees in bankruptcy. Highlights for the team include advice to the administrators on the sale of Ascot Drummond. It also acted for the court appointed administrators of three companies following a disputed minority shareholders action in the High Court. **Clients** Main accountancy firms.

PITMANS (see firm details p.1103) The market acclaims "*a team of substance,*" that acts on contentious and non-contentious recovery matters. IPs, directors, lenders, creditors and employees provide the bulk of the firm's instructions, while the group has seen an increase in its advice on administration orders. **Suzanne Brooker** (see p.456) is perceived as the key figure here. She was lauded by rivals as "*easy to deal with – she delivers sound advice.*" Consultant **David Archer** (see p.610) is head of the recovery and insolvency department, which has been further bolstered by the recruitment of barrister Robert Foote from Dechert. **Clients** Main IPs.

CLARKS (see firm details p.908) The team, led by David Clark, acts on receiverships, administration orders, liquidations and IVAs for a broad spectrum of clients. Market observers acknowledge that the team provides "*realistic advice*" that displays its "*thorough knowledge*" of the field. **Clients** IPs; accountants.

DARBYS (see firm details p.926) The "*highly experienced*" **Elizabeth Taylor** (see p.464) is "*a reliable choice*" and key to much of the firm's profile in this market. She and the team advise on bankruptcy and voluntary arrangements. Contentious matters are also handled here. **Clients** Main accountants; IPs.

MATTHEW ARNOLD & BALDWIN (see firm details p.1058) A specialist offering, the firm enters our tables this year. It operates for clients in London and the South East and is noted for its close relationship with Barclays Bank. Business reconstructions, administrations and receiverships all form part of the firm's portfolio. Peers endorsed **Alistair Bacon** (see p.455), co-head of the insolvency and corporate recovery department with Adrian Hyde. Bacon is thought to possess a "*heavyweight*" practice that attracts "*top-quality work.*" The team has recently been appointed to act for the administrators of the fish! restaurant chain, as a going concern. Further highlights include acting for RSM Robson Rhodes as liquidators of The Wap Store, including the disposal of assets. The team has also advised on the sale of the fashion boutique Voyage by the liquidator. **Clients** Main accountancy firms; IPs; Barclays Bank.

MORGAN COLE (see firm details p.1075) Observers perceived that the firm derives an advantage from its string of national offices, which offer a great depth of resources. It is envied for its "*loyal clients.*" Head of the firm's technology practice **Bruce Potter** retained the commendation of the marketplace. **Clients** Big five accountancy firms; major IPs.

SOUTH WEST

INSOLVENCY/CORPORATE RECOVERY
■ SOUTH WEST

1 Bond Pearce Bristol, Plymouth
 Osborne Clarke Bristol
2 Foot Anstey Sargent Plymouth
3 Burges Salmon Bristol
4 Clarke Willmott & Clarke Bristol
 CMS Cameron McKenna Bristol
 Laytons Bristol
 TLT Solicitors Bristol
5 Bevan Ashford Bristol
 Meade-King Bristol

This book is the product of 6,582 1/2 hour interviews. See p.7 for BMRB audit. Within each band, firms are listed alphabetically.

BOND PEARCE (see firm details p.879) Interviewees gave strong approbation for this "*incredibly experienced team of specialists.*" Boasting "*uniformly good quality,*" it "*makes a difference*" to clients, who appreciate its "*practical, business-oriented approach*" that "*produces the right option every time.*" Clients also endorse the team's "*cost-effective and rapid response,*" hailing its "*cool, calm and collected*" leader **Victor Tettmar** (see p.464) as "*the one who puts it ahead of the rest.*" Banks and IPs applaud his "*unflinching personal attention*" and ability to advise on complex matters "*with aplomb.*" The team maintains its emphasis on turnaround work for banks and boards of directors including businesses in the energy, retail and construction sectors. It has been advising on matters relating to fallout from Enron, and been involved in high-profile administrations including that of a football club. **Clients** Big five accountancy firms and regional IPs; Begbies Traynor; KPMG Southern Region; Lloyds TSB Bank; Agricultural Mortgage Corporation; Department of Trade & Industry.

OSBORNE CLARKE (see firm details p.1090) Market sources continue to regard the team as "*extremely impressive in strength and depth.*" Clients endorse its "*commercial lawyers who don't drop the ball – they cross every T and cover every angle.*" Some declare that new partner and team leader **Nigel Boobier** is their "*first port of call for corporate banking and debt restructuring.*" They also sanction section head **Patrick Cook** as "*strong on the banking side,*" and commend **Claire Bundy** as a "*sterling team member.*" The team acted for Ernst & Young as administrative receivers in the sale of the business and assets of Aston Electronics as a going concern, and advised Grant Thornton as administrative receivers on the sale of the business and assets of Hill Leigh as a going concern. **Clients** Big five and smaller accountancy firms and niche insolvency practices; RBS/NatWest; GE Capital; The Insolvency Service (Disqualification Unit); 3i; Bank of Scotland.

FOOT ANSTEY SARGENT (see firm details p.958) The team gains recognition for its "*first-rate*" expertise in individual insolvency, bankruptcy and LPA receiverships. It also repre-

SOUTH WEST ■ INSOLVENCY

LEADING INDIVIDUALS

[1] TETTMAR Victor Bond Pearce

[2] ASKEW Martin Clarke Willmott & Clarke
BOOBIER Nigel Osborne Clarke

[3] ALLINSON Stephen Clarke Willmott & Clarke
BON Gordon Bevan Ashford
COOK Patrick Osborne Clarke
STOBART Guy Burges Salmon
WILTSHIRE Peter CMS Cameron McKenna

[4] AGAR Nick CMS Cameron McKenna
BOUMPHREY Patrick Burges Salmon
HARRIS Anthony Laytons
HARRIS Clare Meade-King
MAY Philip TLT Solicitors
SMITH Gillian Foot Anstey Sargent

UP AND COMING
BUNDY Claire Osborne Clarke

See individuals' profiles p.455

sents claimants in disqualification cases. Her peers admire team leader **Gillian Smith** (see p.463) as a "*sound technician*" on DTI director's arrangements, while clients give special mention to consultant Stephen Lawson's assistance on individual voluntary arrangements. The "*efficient*" team has maintained its coverage of personal and corporate contentious and non-contentious insolvency matters; the team serves on Lloyds TSB's nationwide litigation panel. **Clients** National, regional and local practices and IPs; private clients.

BURGES SALMON (see firm details p.894) Drawing on resources from across the firm, the insolvency, rescue and recovery team is not perceived to have the level of sector focus of its competitors. Nevertheless, interviewees concur that it "*features strongly because of talented individuals*" and in particular, for its "*deep knowledge*" in agricultural insolvency matters. Clients report that it "*always produces good results*," commending lead partner **Guy Stobart** (see p.463) as "*excellent on standard security orders*," although some "*struggle to get hold of him*." They also single out **Patrick Boumphrey** (see p.456) for his banking and insolvency expertise. The team acted for ATOC and on behalf of a number of train operating companies individually (including Great Eastern Trains, Great Western Trains and North Western Trains) in relation to the recent Railtrack railway administration. It also advised Bayerische Landesbank and Bristol Water on the Enron administration, and advised Bristol International Airport on the Belgian airline Sabena's insolvency. **Clients** Big five accountancy firms; AMC; HBOS; Bayerische Landesbank; GMAC; Lloyds TSB; HSBC; UCB; Lombard Leasing; Lombard North Central; Nationwide Building Society.

CLARKE WILLMOTT & CLARKE (see firm details p.907) Licensed IP **Stephen Allinson** (see p.455) heads a team that has a broad practice in contentious and non-contentious insolvency matters. It has specialist expertise in representing IPs in respect of corporate and personal recoveries. Clients peg "*assertive*" **Martin Askew** (see p.455) (formerly of Beachcroft Wansbroughs) as "*the man to watch*" because he "*gets results*." One declared: "*If I want someone to start a fight, I go to him.*" The team successfully acted for KPMG Bristol as trustee in bankruptcy in recovering a 50% shareholding in a company that had been expatriated to offshore interests in the Pacific. It also advised Ernst & Young as trustee in bankruptcy on the negotiation of a settlement of ongoing employment litigation with the bankrupt's former employer, and subsequently, on the successful sale of the bankrupt's large shareholding in the same company. **Clients** PwC; RBS/NatWest; Baker Tilly; KPMG; Smith & Williamson.

CMS CAMERON MCKENNA (see firm details p.914) Market sources commended it as a "*high-quality team*" that is well known as dedicated lawyers for Lloyds TSB in Bristol. The Bristol based team can draw upon the expertise of partners based in London. A "*long-established favourite*" among clients, **Nick Agar** (see p.455) is a "*solid pair of hands*" on realising security and related issues, while **Peter Wiltshire** (see p.109) is a banking and finance specialist who offers "*strong advice on trickier matters.*" His emphasis lies with restructuring advice to banks and corporates. The team advises IPs, banks; directors and shareholders. **Clients** Local IPs; Lloyds TSB.

LAYTONS (see firm details p.1032) The team maintains its focus on liquidations, voluntary arrangements and turnarounds across a range of sectors that include road transport, shipping, aviation, rail and the motor industry. It also has acted on matters arising from the IT, engineering, construction, healthcare and agribusiness sectors, and handles company director disqualification cases for the DTI. Clients singled out licensed IP **Anthony Harris** (see p.460) as a sector specialist. Among its highlights, the team acted for Enterprise in relation to the purchase of shares in Dewsbury Civil Engineering in administration. **Clients** IPs in predominantly Bristol-based accountancy firms; clearing banks and building societies; creditors, troubled businesses and their directors.

TLT SOLICITORS (see firm details p.1163) Clients confirm that they are "*more than happy to use*" the team on corporate rescue, receivership and general insolvency matters. Administrative orders and receiverships, LPA receiverships, liquidations, voluntary arrangements, bankruptcies and disqualification proceedings all feature in the team's workload. Clients regard **Philip May** (see p.461) as "*extremely sound*" on insolvency litigation and reconstruction matters. Among its highlights, the team acted for the Official Receiver in Mulkerrins v PwC, a case that involved issues regarding the proper meeting of proceeds, resulting in payment of personal and property damages. **Clients** KPMG; Ernst & Young; PwC; Grant Thornton; Moore Stephens Booth White; Baker Tilly; The Insolvency Service (Official Receiver); Barclays; Lloyds TSB; Triodos Bank; DTI; Woolwich.

BEVAN ASHFORD (see firm details p.869) "*Technically strong*" **Gordon Bon** (see p.456) (formerly of Laytons) heads the newly launched team that clients regard as a "*well-respected*" player in the region. Credited for having "*recruited some strong individuals*," he "*knows when to fight.*" The team handles a range of non-contentious and contentious insolvency and turnaround matters, including financial restructuring, refinancing, downsizing and non-core asset disposals. It acted for Moore Stephens in relation to a Section 110 reconstruction of a group of business services companies, which involved an AIM flotation and a members' voluntary liquidation, holding £1 million on retention to meet potential tax liabilities. The firm also advised Baker Tilly on a CVA for a printing company with £6 million turnover and 79 staff. **Clients** Begbies Traynor; Bishop Fleming; BKG Haines Watts; BN Jackson Norton; Grant Thornton; Houghton Stone; Moore Stephens; PwC.

MEADE-KING "*Well-respected*" **Clare Harris** (see p.460) leads a "*solid*" team that advises on a range of corporate, personal and property-related insolvency matters. Directors disqualification and defence work also forms a healthy portion of the practice. The team is also supported by the firm's property, commercial and corporate lawyers. **Clients** IPs.

447

INSOLVENCY ■ WALES/MIDLANDS

WALES

INSOLVENCY/CORPORATE RECOVERY
■ WALES

1. **Eversheds** Cardiff
2. **Edwards Geldard** Cardiff
3. **Hugh James** Cardiff
   Morgan Cole Cardiff
4. **Hunt & Morgan** Cardiff

LEADING INDIVIDUALS

1. **VAUGHAN Philip** Eversheds
2. **BARANSKI Karl** Edwards Geldard
   HUNT Matthew Hunt & Morgan
3. **PAY Alex** Morgan Cole
   REES Bleddyn Morgan Cole

This book is the product of 6,582 1/2 hour interviews. See p.7 for BMRB audit. Within each band, firms are listed alphabetically. See individuals' profiles p.455

EVERSHEDS (see firm details p.949) Rivals acknowledge that the firm is both "*well-established*" in the region and able to handle the crème de la crème of insolvency matters. It is bolstered by the presence of the head of the corporate and commercial department, **Philip Vaughan** (see p.464). Clients endorsed his "*commercial acumen and long-standing experience*." The team has acted for KPMG on the receivership of HMG Group. It also advised the Japanese company, SNK, in the insolvencies of Castillion Engineering and AST and on the subsequent purchase of the businesses of those companies from the administrators. Deloitte & Touche instructed the firm on the administrative receivership of MC Sheet Metals. **Clients** Major accountants; IPs; clearing banks; finance houses; surveyors.

EDWARDS GELDARD (see firm details p.944) The team acts on receiverships, liquidations, administrations, corporate rescues and bankruptcies. "*Well-thought-of by IPs*," **Karl Baranski** (see p.455) is "*thorough, technical and professional*" while offering expertise on "*a broad range of matters.*" A highlight for the firm has been its advice to the defendant in the Smith (Administrator of Cosslett (Contractors) Ltd) v Bridgend County Borough Council, landmark case that reached the House of Lords. **Clients** Big five accountancy firms; IPs; accountants.

HUGH JAMES (see firm details p.1004) The insolvency and corporate recovery group, led by Ian Herbert, handles the whole range of insolvency work from administrative receiverships to personal bankruptcy. The team is noted for its strength on contentious and personal insolvency matters. Highlights include the successful conclusion of a misfeasance action on behalf of the joint liquidators of Pathways Residential & Training Centres against its former officers; a full recovery was made. The team has also acted on behalf of Hire One on an acquisition of a business from the administrative receivers of a company in the Brunswick Holdings group. **Clients** Grant Thornton; PwC; KPMG; Solomon Hare; McCambridge Duffy.

MORGAN COLE (see firm details p.1075) Operating on a cross-office basis, the team continues to maintain its respected position in the marketplace. A qualified banker, **Alex Pay** is considered "*the main figure*" here, representing clients based both inside and outside Wales. Corporate partner **Bleddyn Rees** has fingers in many pies, one of which is insolvency. Highlights for the team include acting on two successful corporate turnaround projects for Grant Thornton. The group is also advising a liquidator on the Brumark priority dispute case. KPMG instructs the firm on a range of bankruptcy/recovery matters. The team has also acted for Julian Hodge Bank on a LPA receivership for substantial investment property. **Clients** Grant Thornton; KPMG.

HUNT & MORGAN "*An adept practitioner,*" **Matthew Hunt** retains his heavy involvement in mid-tier cases. His "*energetic*" handling of matters has won him many fans. Liquidators and trustees in bankruptcy form the bulk of the client base.

MIDLANDS

INSOLVENCY/CORPORATE RECOVERY
■ MIDLANDS

1. **Eversheds** Birmingham
2. **Wragge & Co** Birmingham
3. **Martineau Johnson** Birmingham
4. **Gateley Wareing** Birmingham
   Irwin Mitchell Birmingham
5. **DLA** Birmingham
   Hammond Suddards Edge Birmingham
6. **Actons** Nottingham
   Harvey Ingram Owston Leicester
   Pinsent Curtis Biddle Birmingham
   Shoosmiths Northampton

This book is the product of 6,582 1/2 hour interviews. See p.7 for BMRB audit. Within each band, firms are listed alphabetically

EVERSHEDS (see firm details p.949) Clients report that the "*highly professional*" team displays "*a good combination of approaches – both street wise and gentlemanly,*" on a range of contentious and non-contentious insolvency and reconstruction matters. **Jeff Drew** (see p.457) divides his time equally between the London and Birmingham offices. He heads the national group and was described to researchers as "*a first-class operator, utterly practical and commercially focused.*" Clients continue to commend **Louise Pheasant** (see p.462) as an insolvency and corporate recovery specialist. Some interviewees perceived that she is the main contact in this office and "*a worthy successor to Drew.*" The team represented PwC as administrative receivers of Beck Foods, in a Court of Appeal case concerning administrative receivers' liability for rates, and in relation to worldwide freezing orders against delinquent directors of Tyre City in liquidation. Among other highlights, it advised KPMG as administrative receivers of Cherub, and advised Baker Tilly on a provisional liquidation of Coin TV, which involved cross-border jurisdictional issues and recognition of CVA procedure in a foreign jurisdiction. **Clients** Ernst & Young; Grant Thornton; Baker Tilly; KPMG; Kroll Buchler Phillips.

WRAGGE & CO (see firm details p.1197) Interviewees commended it as a "*highly sought after*" team, while clients "*greatly value*" its advice on a range of matters overlapping among insolvency, restructuring and banking. **Julian Pallett's** style may be "*understated*" but competitors agree that "*he's no pushover.*" He is thought to attract "*the real blue-chip clients*" and is the "*first choice*" of many for intricate matters. **Nicola Mumford** typifies the depth of the team, and she was commended for carving a name in the region. The firm handles directors disqualification cases for the DTI and is skilled in rescue and restructuring matters. **Clients** Accountants; banks.

MARTINEAU JOHNSON (see firm details p.1056) Market sources respect the "*thoroughly professional*" team for its "*successful track record*" in turnarounds and reconstructions, while clients report that it "*responds quickly*" to instructions. **Ian Baker** (see p.455) is well regarded for his "*astute understanding of the practicalities,*" while **Helen Readett** (see p.462) provides "*high-quality advice*" and is a "*great team player.*" The team acts for a range of accountants, banks and corporates on issues arising out of administrative receiverships and IVAs, and liability issues. **Clients** Lloyds TSB; Allied Irish; HBOS; PwC; Andersen; Deloitte & Touche; BDO Stoy Hayward; HLB Kidsons; Baker Tilly; Mazars Neville Russell; Grant Thornton.

GATELEY WAREING (see firm details p.967) Peers acknowledge that this smaller team "*punches above its weight*" and has "*long estab-*

MIDLANDS/EAST ANGLIA ■ INSOLVENCY

LEADING INDIVIDUALS

[1]
- **BAKER Ian** Martineau Johnson
- **DREW Jeff** Eversheds
- **PALLETT Julian** Wragge & Co
- **PHEASANT Louise** Eversheds

[2]
- **MCGEEVER Brendan** Gateley Wareing
- **READETT Helen** Martineau Johnson

[3]
- **BOWDEN Jeremy** DLA
- **DOLPHIN Huw** DLA

UP AND COMING
- **MUMFORD Nicola** Wragge & Co

. See individuals' profiles p.455

lished presence" in the Midlands. It is also increasingly working further afield. **Brendan McGeever** is "*lively and fun to work with*" and respected for his "*sound judgement and technical knowledge.*" The team acts for receivers, administrators and liquidators. It also has a healthy local corporate client base that has resulted in instructions from directors on liability issues. **Clients** Accountants; IPs.

IRWIN MITCHELL (see firm details p.1009) Boasting "*strong relationships*" with industry players, the team is popular with clients for "*just getting on with it.*" Led by Steven George, it "*makes everything simple*" by delivering "*straightforward, unfussy advice.*" The team advises IPs across the range of personal and corporate insolvency procedures, and also represents major clearing banks and asset based financiers. Among its highlights, the team advised KPMG on the receivership of Willoughby Holdings Group, and advised Smith & Williamson on the administration of Telford Pressings. It also acted for PwC on a receivership under Section 37 of the Supreme Court Act 1981. **Clients** PwC; KPMG; Kroll Buchler Phillips; Smith & Williamson; BDO Stoy Hayward; Deloitte & Touche; Moore Stephens Booth White.

DLA Jeremy Bowden and Huw Dolphin are the respected figures in this team that handles the range of insolvency matters for banks, accountants and IPs.

HAMMOND SUDDARDS EDGE The team, headed by Chris Harlowe, handles a range of insolvency and reconstruction matters with niche expertise in asset finance and invoice discounting sectors. The team is respected for its work in both administrations and turnaround, for banks, accountants, IPs and corporate clients.

ACTONS The niche insolvency and reconstruction practice handles corporate and personal insolvency matters, representing IPs, accountants, directors and banks based in the Midlands and London. The team is jointly headed by licensed IPs, Richard Leman and Nicky Calthrop-Owen. It has acted for administrators, liquidators and receivers of companies across a range of sectors including health and leisure, manufacturing, light industry, agriculture, retail and IT. It also acted on bankruptcies to recover and trace substantial assets for trustees in bankruptcies and liquidators.

HARVEY INGRAM OWSTON (see firm details p.988) This Leicester-based firm was commended as a "*sensible outfit*" for mid-tier matters. Its clients range from small owner-managed businesses to larger plcs. It advises on turnaround and administrations. Roy Botterill is a member of the non-contentious insolvency team, that advises accountants and IPs.

PINSENT CURTIS BIDDLE (see firm details p.1102) The team is now led by head of corporate recovery Jonathan Jeffries, based in Leeds, following David Cooke's appointment as a District Judge. It continues to advise primarily in relation to regionally based insolvencies for banks, IPs, corporates and insurance companies. Among its highlights, it acted for the receiver of Staffordshire Tableware, one of the region's largest manufacturers and distributors of chinaware with 671 employees. It also acted for Tenon Recovery as receivers of Dudley Die Forgings, and was appointed as independent trustee to the UEF pension scheme comprising over 1,500 members following the company's administration. **Clients** PwC; KPMG.

SHOOSMITHS (see firm details p.1133) Neil Bradshaw heads the department that continues to handle insolvency and restructuring work for major accountancy firms. It also maintains a niche practice in advising company directors concerning ongoing trading in the context of pension funds. The team has represented IT and media sector companies on restructuring and asset disposals, acting for both purchasers and vendors in this context. Among its highlights, the team advised BDO Stoy Hayward as the receivers of Burall Carwood on matters that included complex security issues. It also acted for PwC in the receivership of Wakefield Storage Handling. **Clients** IPs and major accountants.

EAST ANGLIA

INSOLVENCY/CORPORATE RECOVERY
■ EAST ANGLIA

[1]
- **Eversheds** Cambridge, Norwich
- **Mills & Reeve** Cambridge, Norwich
- **Taylor Vinters** Cambridge

[2]
- **Prettys** Ipswich

[3]
- **Leathes Prior** Norwich
- **Nicholsons** Lowestoft

LEADING INDIVIDUALS

[1]
- **MCGURK Anthony** Eversheds
- **SHORT John** Taylor Vinters
- **WAINE Ian** Prettys
- **WHEATLEY Jamie** Mills & Reeve

[2]
- **NICHOLSON Mark** Nicholsons

UP AND COMING
- **BRUMBY Frank** Leathes Prior

This book is the product of 6,582 1/2 hour interviews. See p.7 for BMRB audit.
Within each band, firms are listed alphabetically. See individuals' profiles p.455

EVERSHEDS (see firm details p.949) Clearly one of the main players in the region, the firm fields a "*commercially aware*" team that has the capacity to advise on a range of insolvency matters. The non-contentious side of the practice is well known under the stewardship of Cambridge-based head of corporate **Anthony McGurk** (see p.461). Clients commend him as "*a sharp operator – sensible and accurate in his advice.*" The contentious side of the practice is led by Paul Matthews. The team advises both companies and directors on liability issues, and is active in reconstructions and administrative receiverships. **Clients** Accountants; corporates.

MILLS & REEVE (see firm details p.1071) Adjudged "*a healthy operation*" by market sources, the team advises clients within the engineering, technology and food production sectors. It has of late experienced an increase in turnaround work and CVAs. **Jamie Wheatley** (see p.464) is a partner in the commercial disputes team. Clients reported that he is "*sensible and practical*" and while "*a robust negotiator,*" he remains approachable. He specialises in corporate and insolvency litigation, and has advised a major creditor in the Metro court-appointed receivership. Further highlights for the team include acting for BDO Stoy Hayward in the administration of Zephyr Cams and acting for PwC on the administrative receiverships of East Anglian-based food producers. **Clients** Banks; accountants and IPs.

TAYLOR VINTERS (see firm details p.1156) Clients believe that **John Short** (see p.246) is "*perhaps the best insolvency brain in the region.*" He leads a team that is lauded as "*commercial, practical and easy to deal with,*" while peers acknowledge its depth of resources and capacity to handle "*some of the best work.*" The group advises on insolvency issues from corporate turnarounds and IVAs to representing office holders and creditors during disputes. It also enjoys a close relationship with corporate recovery specialists at the major accountancy firms

INSOLVENCY ■ EAST ANGLIA/NORTH WEST

and practitioners within Lloyds TSB. **Clients** Ernst & Young; Grant Thornton; Lloyds TSB.

PRETTYS (see firm details p.1106) This Ipswich-based team operates from the corporate department. It is led by **Ian Waine** (see p.464) who combines insolvency-related matters with his respected corporate activities. This year has seen insolvency advice provided to a number of local industry initiatives, including administrative receiverships, liquidations, and a court appointed receivership. The group has also undertaken defence work on the Company Directors Disqualification Act. **Clients** Grant Thornton; Ensors; IPs.

LEATHES PRIOR The firm was endorsed by both clients and competitors for its offering of a "*traditional practice undertaking personal insolvency work.*" **Frank Brumby** is the key figure here; "*pleasant to deal with – you will get a good result with him,*" agree clients. The team handles corporate recovery and turnaround procedures. Voluntary and compulsory liquidation and receiverships are also dealt with. Directors disqualification proceedings, defended misfeasance and wrongful trading actions against directors have been a feature of this past year. **Clients** Accountants; IPs.

NICHOLSONS Clients reported that this is "*a boutique worth looking at.*" It specialises in litigious personal bankruptcy. The team also handles company liquidations and administration orders. **Mark Nicholson** (see p.462) is a "*highly respected*" local practitioner. He acted on the administration of Zephyr Cams. **Clients** BDO Stoy Hayward; Lovell Blake.

NORTH WEST

INSOLVENCY/CORPORATE RECOVERY
■ NORTH WEST

1 Addleshaw Booth & Co Manchester
2 DLA Liverpool, Manchester
   Hammond Suddards Edge Manchester
3 DWF Liverpool
   Eversheds Manchester
   Halliwell Landau Manchester
4 Cuff Roberts Liverpool
   Mace & Jones Manchester

LEADING INDIVIDUALS
★ BROOKS Egan Addleshaw Booth & Co
1 HAYMES Duncan LCL Law
2 JOYCE John Addleshaw Booth & Co
3 BUCHANAN Andrew Halliwell Landau
   GREGORY Andrew DWF
   PRESTON Dermot Hammond Suddards Edge
   SPENCER Shân DLA
   WALLER Simon Eversheds
4 BARNES Ged Addleshaw Booth & Co
   COATES Philip Pinsent Curtis Biddle
   GOODMAN Nick NJ Goodman & Co
   SOMEKH Peter DLA
   TWEMLOW Tony Cuff Roberts
   UP AND COMING
   GRAY David Eversheds
   KELLY Susan Hammond Suddards Edge

This book is the product of 6,582 1/2 hour interviews. See p.7 for BMRB audit.
Within each band, firms are listed alphabetically. See individuals' profiles p.455

ADDLESHAW BOOTH & CO (see firm details p.838) Interviewees hail the team as "*absolutely top rank,*" crediting "*outstanding*" head of department **Egan Brooks** (see p.456) as "*the key*" to its market status. Clients find the team "*friendly and extremely willing to help,*" sanctioning the "*enormous breadth of experience and knowledge*" that enables it to handle the scope of insolvency work. Acclaimed as "*a luminary in the Manchester market*" with "*a brain the size of a planet,*" Brooks remains "*in a class of his own.*" His seniority finds him less at the coal face, while key clients see **John Joyce** (see p.461) "*all the time.*" They praise his "*excellent service that combines solid business appraisal with a technical answer.*" Sharing these attributes, **Ged Barnes** (see p.456) is "*a strong prospect for the future.*" Clients vouch that they can "*rely totally*" on his "*common sense advice.*" Among highlights, the team advised Andersen as the receivers and debenture holder of Euro Sales Finance in connection with the receiverships of the four textile companies comprising the Wills Group. It advised DTE as receivers, and Yorkshire Bank on the receivership of The Hill Construction Group of four companies, and represented the directors and administrators of Caxios, a UK subsidiary of Enron. On the contentious side, the team has acted for the agricultural receivers, SHM Smith Hodgkinson and the mortgagee, the successful party, in the Court of Appeal case, National Westminster Bank v Jones, concerning transaction at undervalue. **Clients** Co-operative Bank; HSBC; Lloyds TSB; RBS/NatWest; Yorkshire; Euro Sales Finance; Five Arrows Commercial Finance.

DLA The majority of interviewees opined that the team has gained a good focal point and is more cohesive than previously. The additional clout of the Chaffe Street team should see the team flourish. Observers recommended former Addleshaw's practitioners **Shân Spencer** and **Peter Somekh**, who replaced Philip Coates following the latter's departure to Pinsent Curtis Biddle.

HAMMOND SUDDARDS EDGE Clients reported that the team's "*increased investment in the market*" with its "*enhanced ability to service work*" now makes it "*the first port of call*" for some on larger matters. The team will, however, be tested by the departure of leading figure Duncan Haymes to found his own practice, LCL Law. **Dermot Preston** and **Susan Kelly** "*do a great job*" and typify the firm's team ethos. The firm has acted for Andersen on the successful administration of Seyfert, a £25 million turnover, 250-employee paper and packaging company, resulting in its sale as a going concern. It also acted for BDO Stoy Hayward, appointed by GMAC Commercial Credit as administrative receivers of The Swordword Group, a multi-site textile group of six companies with a £30 million turnover. The team was involved in the RBS/Ernst & Young's regional administrative receivership of listed company Snackhouse. **Clients** Andersen; BDO Stoy Hayward; KPMG; Begbies Traynor.

DWF (see firm details p.943) Interviewees perceive that the team is "*working the firm's corporate client base well and will expand from there*" within the middle-tier market. Clients affirm that it "*makes a good impression*" with its "*plain-speaking*" style and ability to "*see through the clutter.*" These lawyers can "*deal with awkward cases extremely competently.*" **Andrew Gregory** (see p.459) was praised for his "*proficient*" team leadership and technical ability. He advised the directors and workforce of Dennis Ruabon, a 30-year-old tile manufacturer based in North Wales in buying back the business from the receivers, saving over 100 jobs. The team advised the receivers of Gray Dunn, a biscuit factory in Glasgow, in an asset finance transaction that led to the appointment of Deloitte & Touche as administrative receivers. It also represented the receivers of Tristan Sailing in the sale of company assets including a 70-foot pleasure vessel from a dry dock in Liverpool. This matter involved aspects of maritime law and European legislation. **Clients** Kroll Buchler Phillips; Ernst & Young; Davenham Trust.

EVERSHEDS (see firm details p.949) According to market sources, this team, which is "*smaller in relation to its competitors*" is "*effective and keen to grow.*" It provides the firm's Leeds office with spare capacity for its overflow work, and is growing its own profile in Manchester. **Simon Waller** (see p.464), national head of corporate recovery and insolvency, gains recognition for having "*been around a long time,*" while clients regard **David Gray** (see p.459) as "*a sensible operator.*" The team acted for Andersen as receivers of the production companies for the childrens television programmes, 'Melvyn P Otter MD' and 'The Lampies', and Trident Analytical and G Cus-

NORTH WEST/YORKSHIRE ■ INSOLVENCY

sons. It also acted for Begbies Traynor as receivers of F Bode & Son and advised Ernst & Young as receivers of Stately Developments. **Clients** KPMG Corporate Recovery; PwC; Deloitte & Touche; HSBC; HBOS.

HALLIWELL LANDAU (see firm details p.982) Market sources who "*rate the team highly*" opine that it is "*missing out on opportunities because it needs to let people know it's there,*" particularly in relation to the profile of its junior lawyers. Clients trust "*understated*" department head **Andrew Buchanan** (see p.457) to "*give a black and white response on grey, esoteric matters.*" The team is thought to be "*excellent on the technical aspects,*" and has advised on a range of transactional issues following the acquisition by KTH of the automotive division of Transtec, with Andersen acting as the administrative receivers. It also advised PwC as administrative receivers on the sale of Yamato International, a group of industrial sewing machine manufacturers. It also represented AIG's interest in the administration of the Save Group of petrol station companies. **Clients** Kingston Smith; PKF; Deloitte & Touche; Begbies Traynor; Andersen.

CUFF ROBERTS The firm has a loyal following in the Liverpool market, advising on corporate and personal insolvency matters. **Tony Twemlow** brings "*many years of experience*" to the field, and has attracted major financial institutions and accountancy firms to this practice.

MACE & JONES (see firm details p.1047) Graeme Jump leads a "*solid*" team that is best known for its expertise in agricultural receiverships, employment and disqualification proceedings. It acted for the supervisor in enforcing the provisions of its voluntary arrangement against the estate of the deceased debtor, and has advised the trustee in bankruptcy in recovering pension entitlements from a debtor. It also acted for a receiver appointed under a charge granted by a self build housing association arising out of the collapse of the association in the context of a half-completed development. **Clients** Accountants.

OTHER NOTABLE PRACTITIONERS Interviewees rate Altrincham-based sole practitioner **Nick Goodman** (see p.459) of NJ Goodman & Co as "*absolutely great*" and "*extremely efficient*" on smaller matters, while former DLA partner **Philip Coates** (see p.457) is raising the profile of the "*well-placed*" new practice at Pinsent Curtis Biddle. He is "*an imperative source for a worried board of directors*" on account of his "*extremely clear advice.*" "*Top-notch insolvency lawyer*" **Duncan Haymes** has left Hammond Suddards Edge to found LCL Law. He remains popular for his "*professional, managerial style,*" while key players enthuse that he "*brings in a lot of chutzpah with his weight of experience*" and "*holds great sway with clients.*"

YORKSHIRE

INSOLVENCY/CORPORATE RECOVERY
■ YORKSHIRE

1 DLA Leeds, Sheffield
Walker Morris Leeds

2 Addleshaw Booth & Co Leeds
Pinsent Curtis Biddle Leeds

3 Hammond Suddards Edge Leeds

4 Eversheds Leeds

5 Brooke North Leeds

6 Carrick Read Insolvency Leeds
Keeble Hawson Sheffield

LEADING INDIVIDUALS

1 CRANSTON Peter DLA
MUDD Philip Walker Morris

2 BALLMANN William Addleshaw Booth & Co
BRIGGS Graham Addleshaw Booth & Co
BROWN Robert Keeble Hawson
FRIEZE Steven Brooke North
FRITH Stuart Brooke North
HINCHLIFFE David Walker Morris
JACKSON Mark DLA
JEFFRIES Jonathan Pinsent Curtis Biddle

3 LAYCOCK Andrew Carrick Read Insolvency
OBANK Richard DLA
RIDLER Graham Eversheds

4 MARSHALL Richard Lupton Fawcett

UP AND COMING
ALDERTON John Charles Hammond Suddards Edge
FERGUSSON Richard Keeble Hawson

This book is the product of 6,582 1/2 hour interviews. See p.7 for BMRB audit. Within each band, firms are listed alphabetically. See individuals' profiles p.455

DLA The business support and restructuring group is thought by interviewees to benefit from a network of national offices. It handles asset disposals, property sales, investigation work and recovery matters for banks, accountants, professional managers and investors. Peers appreciated the intelligence and practicality of **Peter Cranston**. He is assisted by **Mark Jackson**, and **Richard Obank**.

WALKER MORRIS (see firm details p.1178) "*Some bloody strong lawyers*" are housed at a firm which has the capacity to advise on the whole range of insolvency matters. **Philip Mudd**'s (see p.461) return to full-time fee earning from his role as managing partner was welcomed by clients and rivals. They appreciated that he is "*ideal to have with you on negotiations,*" since he "*combines specific technical expertise in a broader, commercial context.*" **David Hinchliffe** is experienced in administrations, liquidations and voluntary arrangements. Highlights for the team include representing PwC as administrators of UK- and USA-listed Eurotelecom. This involved the disposal of several businesses in diverse locations and the subsequent obtaining of an administration order. The team also acted on the administration of Carnography, a multi-site retailer with 37 outlets, advising the administrators Kroll Buchler Phillips. The team also acted on the liquidation of Salco, a company with turnover in excess of £30 million and debts of more than £10 million. **Clients** Lloyds TSB; RBS; Barclays; big five accountancy firms.

ADDLESHAW BOOTH & CO (see firm details p.838) The insolvency and corporate recovery group handles large scale and complex administration and receiverships alongside its activities in personal insolvency work. Corporate voluntary arrangements and directors disqualifications are also a feature of the workload. "*Quietly efficient*" **Graham Briggs** (see p.456) is "*a good technician who will give a considered opinion.*" He specialises in corporate reconstruction and recovery as well as all aspects of insolvency and banking law. Clients find that **William Ballmann**'s "*energy is infectious.*" He possesses a "*strong personality*" and a "*commercial approach.*" The team acted for Arthur Andersen on matters arising from the administration of the East Lancs Group. The team also acted for on the administrative receivership of the Just Tyres group. This involved the successful disposal of both the wholesale and retail divisions of the group. In a further highlight, it advised the investors and subsequently the administrative receivers (PwC) of ESM. **Clients** 3i Group; HSBC; RBS; Lloyds TSB; leading accountants and IPs.

PINSENT CURTIS BIDDLE (see firm details p.1102) The team has had "*a cracking year*" according to peers, with involvement in "*interesting and intricate*" matters. The departure of Patrick Corr to Sidley Austin Brown & Wood was perceived by the marketplace to be a loss to the team. It has recruited Andy Smith from Hammond Suddards Edge, a move, that should reinforce the team's capacity. The standout figure here is "*hands-on*" **Jonathan Jeffries**. (see p.460) "*Experienced, respected and genuinely nice to deal with,*" he acted for PwC in relation to the administration of Famous Army Stores. Further highlights for the team include acting on the

INSOLVENCY ■ YORKSHIRE/NORTH EAST

financial restructuring of a foreign company. It is also acting for Ernst & Young on the receivership of Brooke Industrial Holdings and a number of its subsidiaries. **Clients** Banks; accountants.

HAMMOND SUDDARDS EDGE Clients commended a firm, that possesses "*gravitas*" and has the depth of individuals to "*provide a consistently thorough service.*" The client base ranges from large corporates through to local IPs and bankers. Although the business finance and recovery Group has been tested by the departure of Andy Smith, peers agree that it "*still has the breadth of resources required.*" "*Up-and-coming*" John Charles Alderton specialises in contentious and non-contentious insolvency, workouts and reconstructions. The team has acted for the joint administrative receivers of IMS in the sale of this, a £33.5 million turnover business. It also acted for the liquidators of Viasystems, particularly advising on a £7 million subrogation claim.

EVERSHEDS (see firm details p.949) The corporate recovery group acts for the big five accountancy firms and mid range accountants as well as banks and corporates on the whole gamut of insolvency matters. Graham Ridler (see p.462) was perceived to have successfully established the Leeds practice as a popular choice. He advises IPs on contentious and non-contentious insolvency work as well as offering expertise in receivership and administrations. The team acted for KPMG on the administration of Discovery Stores, and is acting for Bayford on the £47 million acquisition from the administrators of Save. The team have also acted on the receivership of the Appleby Group of companies for RSM Robson Rhodes. **Clients** KPMG Corporate Recovery; PwC; RBS; HBOS; HSBC.

BROOKE NORTH Commended by clients as "*small but highly active in personal insolvency,*" the firm is also endorsed for its corporate capability. The head of debt recovery litigation Steven Frieze (see p.458) is "*a leading light in personal insolvency,*" who was applauded for his "*huge academic mind.*" He concentrates on insolvency and debt recovery litigation in work that frequently has a cross-border element to it. "*Shrewd operator*" Stuart Frith (see p.458) "*knows how to negotiate his way through the issues.*" He focuses on corporate and individual insolvency. **Clients** Accountants; banks; corporates.

CARRICK READ INSOLVENCY This is a specialist insolvency practice with one of the largest dedicated teams in the North of England. It acts on behalf of, and as, insolvency practitioners. It also advises parties wronged by banks, financial institutions and insolvency practitioners. The split from Read Hind Stewart was perceived to have enabled the "*aggressive and tenacious litigator*" Andrew Laycock to concentrate fully on insolvency matters. The team acted in the administration of Shimla Pinks, a national group of restaurants, which culminated in a substantial trade sale. The firm also acted on the liquidation of K&C Timber. **Clients** Accountants/IPs; banks; corporates.

KEEBLE HAWSON "*Thorough, professional and accurate*" practitioner Robert Brown (see p.457) leads the team. He handles personal insolvency and administrations, asset disposals, receiverships and contentious investigations and was lauded by clients as "*a bright guy who communicates well and takes a commercial view.*" "*Rising star*" Richard Fergusson (see p.458) has strong handling client skills that he puts to good effect in his work in personal insolvency, mainly on the non-contentious side of matters. The year has seen an increase in instructions from administrative and fixed charge receivers in the mid-market sector. It has acted for an administrative receiver of an electrical contractor appointed by RBS in the disposal of its assets on a going-concern basis. **Clients** Accountants/IPs; banks; corporates.

OTHER NOTABLE PRACTITIONERS Richard Marshall of Lupton Fawcett maintains his reputation as "*a focused practitioner who knows his onions.*" He acts for insolvency practitioners and accountants on all aspects of corporate and individual insolvencies.

NORTH EAST

INSOLVENCY/CORPORATE RECOVERY
■ NORTH EAST

1 Dickinson Dees Newcastle upon Tyne
2 Eversheds Newcastle upon Tyne
3 Hay & Kilner Newcastle upon Tyne
Robert Muckle Newcastle upon Tyne
Ward Hadaway Newcastle upon Tyne
Watson Burton Newcastle upon Tyne

LEADING INDIVIDUALS

1 ANDERSON John Eversheds
SANDERSON Gordon Dickinson Dees
2 BLAIR Jonathan Dickinson Dees
PENNIE John Dickinson Dees
3 GILL Julian Watson Burton
HARROLD Neil Hay & Kilner
4 DUTTON Paul Eversheds
JAMES Jim Ward Hadaway
MCNICOL Stephen Robert Muckle

This book is the product of 6,582 1/2 hour interviews. See p.7 for BMRB audit. Within each band, firms are listed alphabetically. See individuals' profiles p.455

DICKINSON DEES (see firm details p.938) Clients applauded the team as "*all talented lawyers and well-managed.*" It has "*the depth of resources to handle the more complex cases.*" The department also boasts "*strong juniors coming through the ranks.*" Mainstream insolvency work and disqualification work is the order of the day here, while the team also provides training on insolvency matters. Clients commended head of banking Gordon Sanderson (see p.463) as one who "*adopts a sound, practical approach*" while providing "*good advice relevant to your problem.*" He advises on all aspects of personal and corporate recovery. Jonathan Blair (see p.456) gives "*proactive advice*" on corporate insolvencies, receiverships and administrations. As leader of the directors disqualification team, he handles the whole of the DTI contract to provide legal services in respect of the proceedings in the North East. He also acted for the liquidators of the companies in the EWE and Beaver Groups, where a multimillion pound fraud was revealed and significant monies recovered. John Pennie (see p.462) is "*a confident operator who plays with a straight bat.*" Interviewees thought him "*illustrative of the depth of the team.*" He advised Deloitte & Touche on the administrative receivership of Penguin Confectionery, resulting in the successful sale of the business as a going concern. **Clients** Deloitte & Touche; Ernst & Young; Grant Thornton; PwC; KPMG; Tenon; RMT.

EVERSHEDS (see firm details p.949) A strong regional presence is a benefit to this team, which can draw upon support from across the network. Its corporate turnaround practice continues to grow. John Anderson (see p.455) is "*supremely knowledgeable and possesses a love of the law.*" "*Thorough and meticulous,*" he advised Grant Thornton on the group receivership and administration of Avanti and Kingsway and the subsequent sales. Clients claimed to be "*absolutely delighted*" with the receivership work of "*go-getter*" Paul Dutton (see p.457) since his arrival from Robert Muckle. Peers commend him as a client-friendly operator. He advised PwC on the liquidation of Gill Aviation. The team is also co-advising Bank of Scotland (jointly with KPMG) for the group review and restructure of the EWS Group with subsequent sales. **Clients** KPMG Corporate Recovery; PwC; Grant Thornton; Deloitte & Touche.

HAY & KILNER The firm undertakes a broad mix of corporate and personal insolvency work, placing an emphasis on investigations. Neil Harrold, head of department and licensed insolvency practitioner, has the capacity to be "*tough*" in negotiations, while clients applauded his ability to conclude "*the more difficult contentious personal insolvency matters, where you*

NORTH EAST/SCOTLAND ■ INSOLVENCY

need to go away and look at the books." The team has advised a well-known sportswear manufacturer on retention of title issues arising from the insolvency of a major chain of sports retailers. This resulted in the successful recovery of its debt, and advising the respondent on an ongoing preference action where a substantial six-figure sum is being claimed by the liquidator. **Clients** IPs; major accountants.

ROBERT MUCKLE Peers endorsed this firm as "*one of the main players, which crops up again and again,*" highlighting its "*good client relations and resources*" as reasons for its continued prominence. "*Commercial*" **Stephen McNicol** (see p.107) leads the business restructuring unit, which focuses on restructuring, turnaround work and corporate insolvency. The team is advising the directors of a plc in relation to a proposed restructuring and rescue package. It has also successfully acted for existing shareholders in the rescue of the production company that makes the 'Melvyn P Otter MD' children's television programme. The team has represented an MBO team in its acquisition of Waste Tyre Solutions from the joint administrative receivers. **Clients** Big five accountancy firms; The Co-operative Bank; Lloyds TSB.

WARD HADAWAY (see firm details p.1180) The team advises on preventative methods to avoid insolvency, alongside its work on receiverships, directors disqualification and voluntary arrangements. Head of department **Jim James** (see p.460) possesses "*a distinctive style; he is tenacious and has innovative ideas,*" while he is "*able to command the respect of lenders.*" Recent highlights include advice on the purchase of several companies from the receivers. **Clients** Major accountancy firms.

WATSON BURTON The firm adopts a cross-departmental approach to the insolvency arena, drawing on support from both its litigation and banking specialists. The team has advised on a number of insolvencies, receiverships and bankruptcies this year. Advice to companies on the purchase of assets and businesses is also a feature of the workload. "*Sound operator*" **Julian Gill,** (see p.458) a former Robert Muckle litigator, is perceived to have injected new life into the department. He is "*good behind his desk and strong in court – he's not afraid of the advocacy.*" The team has acted for a receiver of the property of a large leisure venue worth in excess of £1 million, and has advised a liquidator of a dot.com business, previously worth more than £100 million. In a further highlight, the team represented the purchaser of contracts valued in excess of £10 million from a liquidator for the supply of fire engines to a European airforce. **Clients** Large accountants.

SCOTLAND

INSOLVENCY/CORPORATE RECOVERY
■ SCOTLAND

1. **Dundas & Wilson CS** Edinburgh, Glasgow
2. **Shepherd+ Wedderburn** Edinburgh
3. **Burness** Glasgow
   DLA Glasgow
   Iain Smith & Company Aberdeen
   Maclay Murray & Spens Glasgow
4. **Biggart Baillie** Glasgow
   MacRoberts Glasgow
   McGrigor Donald Glasgow
5. **Paull & Williamsons** Aberdeen
6. **Boyds** Glasgow

This book is the product of 6,582 1/2 hour interviews. See p.7 for BMRB audit. Within each band, firms are listed alphabetically.

DUNDAS & WILSON CS (see firm details p.943) "*Number one by a country mile;*" clients commended a "*dedicated team*" that provides "*quality beyond the key partners.*" Despite the firm's decision to leave the Andersen Legal network, it retains "*the greatest volume of work, and the juiciest clients*." Clients also endorsed head of corporate recovery **Ian Cuthbertson** as "*commercially focused and solutions-based,*" while peers agreed that he is "*good to have on board for the complex transactions.*" He acted for Bank of Scotland and Deloitte & Touche on the receivership of the MRW Technologies Group of six companies and in the restructuring and subsequent realisation of other subsidiaries. **Yvonne Brady** possesses "*a wealth of experience and does not get bogged down by the detail.*" Focusing on receiverships, she has recently acted for Bank of Scotland and Ernst & Young in the disposal of assets and businesses in England, Malaysia and the USA, which involved five separate deals and hive downs of the Wadkin Group of five companies. **David Gibson** tackles restructuring and administrations. He was commended by clients for his "*invaluable technical skills*" and acted for the Royal Bank of Scotland and PwC in the receivership of Donside Paper Group, including all trading issues and subsequent restructuring and sales. **Graeme Henry** retains commendation from the marketplace for his work in restructurings and for his "*quality documentation.*" A further highlight for the team was its advice to Clydesdale Bank and KPMG on the receivership and disposal of Glenfield & Kennedy to Danish purchasers. **Clients** Deloitte & Touche; KPMG; Kroll Buchler Phillips; National Australia Bank.

SHEPHERD+ WEDDERBURN (see firm details p.1130) The firm continues to handle VAT enforcement work for Customs & Excise in Scotland. Head of the corporate recovery group and licensed insolvency practitioner **Gillian Carty** (see p.457) is a "*rising star, growing in experience,*" who was praised for the quality of her technical work. She led the team acting for the joint provisional liquidators of Web Metering in concluding a deal for the sale of its business and assets. Chief executive of the firm, **Paul Hally** (see p.459), is perceived to be less at the coal face. He retains market approval as a valuable advisor and "*a shrewd operator – technically astute and highly commercial.*" He gives opinions on solvency issues in the financial services sector for the London market. The group was instructed by a City law firm to advise on the Scottish aspects of the appointment of administrators and a provisional liquidator to the Independent Insurance Group. This was the first Scottish insurance company insolvency appointment since the introduction of the Insolvency Act 1986. **Clients** Customs & Excise; HSBC; DTI; RBS; Bank of Scotland.

BURNESS This team was commended by clients as having "*the quality of a big firm, but not the fees.*" It has the capacity to provide "*seamless advice*" covering a spectrum of corporate insolvency and restructuring issues and remains "*a pleasure to work with.*" The team is envied for its high-profile cases for major corporates. Head of department **Andrew Sleigh** is "*commercial, focused on getting results and rigorous in his analysis.*" He continues to act for Gordon & Innes on a contentious litigation against the receivers. A further highlight for the team has been its advice to the first creditors administration petition in Scotland. The group also acted in the receivership of Residence International, owner of hotels and prestige time-share outlets in Edinburgh and Paris. **Clients** Main accountants; financial institutions.

DLA IPs, accountants and corporates form the client base for the team, which focuses on contentious matters in the insolvency arena. The firm was perceived to benefit from the combination of the Bird Semple depth of practice and a national client base. **Gordon Hollerin** was endorsed for his strong negotiation skills.

IAIN SMITH & COMPANY Clearly endorsed by interviewees as "*the best in Aberdeen,*" this firm covers the whole range of insolvency matters including turnaround work. Insolvency litigation is also a key strength of the practice,

www.ChambersandPartners.com   453

INSOLVENCY ■ SCOTLAND/NORTHERN IRELAND

LEADING INDIVIDUALS

1
- **BRADY Yvonne** Dundas & Wilson CS
- **CUTHBERTSON Ian** Dundas & Wilson CS
- **ROXBURGH Roy** Iain Smith & Company

2
- **FLINT David** MacRoberts
- **HALLY Paul** Shepherd+ Wedderburn
- **HOLLERIN Gordon** DLA
- **MACFARLANE John** McGrigor Donald
- **SHAW Murray** Biggart Baillie
- **SLEIGH Andrew** Burness

3
- **GIBSON David** Dundas & Wilson CS
- **GRANT Rachel** Semple Fraser
- **HENRY Graeme** Dundas & Wilson CS
- **HUGHES Michael** Maclay Murray & Spens
- **MCNIVEN Alan** Paull & Williamsons

UP AND COMING
- **CARTY Gillian** Shepherd+ Wedderburn
- **JONES Calum** Boyds

See individuals' profiles p.455

and the firm acts both for and against IPs. "*Technically first-class*," both peers and clients commended head of department Roy Roxburgh (see p.463). Clients IPs; accountants; corporates.

MACLAY MURRAY & SPENS (see firm details p.1048) "*Unassuming*" Michael Hughes (see p.460) has won a loyal fan base with his ability to "*steadily get on with things*." Based within the corporate department, he represents receivers, liquidators and administrators. The team has acted on the sale of assets for trustees, and has advised directors on company restructurings. Litigation is also catered for by this team, that can draw upon cross-departmental strength. Clients IPs; accountants; corporates.

BIGGART BAILLIE (see firm details p.871) A team that was applauded by clients for "*giving sensible advice*" includes Murray Shaw, "*a joy to negotiate with, hard but fair.*" The team has been bolstered by the merger with Steedman Ramage and an appointment to act on behalf of the Insolvency Service in respect of directors disqualification cases. The team has also been instructed by the Insolvency Practitioners Tribunal in relation to an appeal by an IP against the refusal of eth Secretary of State to grant an Insolvency Licence in terms of the Insolvency Act. The group also act on behalf of BP. Clients IPs; accountants; corporates.

MACROBERTS (see firm details p.1049) The team continues to undertake significant insolvency work by dint of its strong corporate practice. Receiverships, liquidations and pre-emptive advice are all on the agenda here. The "*ubiquitous*" David Flint (see p.488) possesses "*a devilish sense of humour, is technically adept and gets things done.*" Peers rate his contentious skills, particularly in hi-tech matters. Clients Grant Thornton; Deloitte & Touche.

MCGRIGOR DONALD (see firm details p.1065) The team operates on a cross-departmental basis. The lead figure here is John Macfarlane, a partner within the banking department. Clients commend him as "*an extremely able and commercially sensible lawyer.*" He acts for IPs in receiverships, liquidations, general corporate insolvencies and reconstructions. The cross-border aspects of insolvencies are a particular expertise of the firm. Clients Banks; accountants.

PAULL & WILLIAMSONS (see firm details p.1096) Reconstructions and insolvency matters are dealt with under the banner of the firm's corporate department. It has a sizeable presence in the Aberdeen market. "*First-class talent*" Alan McNiven (see p.461) displays "*immense experience,*" although insolvency is only one part of his mixed practice. Clients IPs; accountants; corporates.

BOYDS (see firm details p.882) Market sources pointed to a team, that is "*building up its reputation in the field.*" It is led by "*pragmatic and energetic*" Calum Jones (see p.460). He acted on the restructuring of a large family company, which included the division of the existing trading entities among the members of the family. Banks and accountants form part of the firm's client base, which also has a healthy profile for personal insolvency matters. Clients Accountants.

OTHER NOTABLE PRACTITIONERS Rachel Grant (see p.459) of Semple Fraser retained strong market commendation. A recent arrival from Steedman Ramage, she is said to be building a team in the insolvency arena.

NORTHERN IRELAND

INSOLVENCY/CORPORATE RECOVERY
■ NORTHERN IRELAND

1
- **Napier & Sons** Belfast

2
- **John McKee & Son** Belfast

3
- **Elliott Duffy Garrett** Belfast
- **McManus Kearney** Belfast

LEADING INDIVIDUALS

1
- **GORDON John** Napier & Sons

2
- **ROSS Alexander** John McKee & Son

3
- **KEARNEY Mary** McManus Kearney
- **WILSON Michael** Elliott Duffy Garrett

This book is the product of 6,582 1/2 hour interviews. See p.7 for BMRB audit.
Within each band, firms are listed alphabetically. See individuals' profiles p.455

NAPIER & SONS The team retains top spot this year following market commendation, that typically described it as "*the leading insolvency firm in Northern Ireland.*" Licensed insolvency practitioner John Gordon leads the team and has a focus on voluntary arrangements. While the firm has previously enjoyed a strong reputation for individual insolvency work, the nature of the current market has ensured that corporate insolvency has come to the fore this year. The team acted for a large pvc water pipe manufacturer on the successful implementation of a voluntary arrangement. A further highlight for the team is its representation of the franchisees of Dunkin' Donuts on its insolvency in Northern Ireland. Clients IPs; accountants and corporates.

JOHN MCKEE & SON (see firm details p.1015) This team was roundly praised by peers as one that can boast a "*substantial defence litigation practice.*" The firm advises both banks and corporates, and has a following amongst local IPs. Lex Ross (see p.462) is renowned for his work in the banking and finance sectors. He was endorsed by clients as "*efficient, steady and pragmatic,*" while peers thought him "*a pleasure to deal with, and a man you can trust.*" His work on receiverships was particularly commended. Clients IPs; accountants and corporates.

ELLIOTT DUFFY GARRETT (see firm details p.947) This firm was applauded by competitors for its "*high standards.*" It offers the depth of resource necessary to service its long established corporate and banking client base. "*Pleasant, practical and capable,*" Michael Wilson is the key figure for the team. Like the whole, he was commended as "*easy to deal with.*" The firm handles insolvency and business recovery work as part of the reconstruction, reorganisation and insolvency practice. Clients IPs; accountants and corporates.

MCMANUS KEARNEY Led by the "*knowledgeable and thorough*" Mary Kearney, (see p.461) the firm is renowned for its work for finance companies. Personal bankruptcy is also a strong feature of the firm's repertoire. The team has witnessed an increase in voluntary arrangements. Referrals from the mainland provide a steady stream of work. Clients IPs; accountants and corporates.

THE LEADERS IN INSOLVENCY

AGAR, Nick
CMS Cameron McKenna, Bristol
(0117) 9300 200
nick.agar@cmck.com
Specialisation: Nick advises banks and insolvency practitioners on all aspects of corporate and personal insolvency and on debt recovery. He is a partner in the firm's Bristol office, which he established in 1990.
Personal: Born 1955. Educated at King's College, London.

ALDERTON, John Charles
Hammond Suddards Edge, Leeds
(0113) 284 7000

ALLINSON LIP, Stephen
Clarke Willmott & Clarke, Taunton
(01823) 445207
sallinson@cw-c.co.uk
Specialisation: Partner holding both the Licensed Insolvency Practitioner qualification and also accredited as a LPA Registered Property Receiver and specialising in all areas of insolvency (corporate and personal). He also has extensive experience of commercial litigation with particular expertise in professional negligence and debt recovery issues for Insolvency Practitioners. He acts for banks, accountants and other insolvency professionals as well as undertaking general insolvency advocacy for creditors and debtors. Recent highlights include a major rescue scheme for a farmer's co-operative (Friendly Society) resulting in the continuation of the business and the maintenance of a particular well known food brand in the West Country. Substantial litigation for an Arts Centre against an architectural company which had gone into liquidation resulting in recoveries which enabled the Arts Centre to survive.
Prof. Memberships: Law Society, Fellow of the Association of Business Recovery Professionals (South West Branch Committee Member); The Institute of Credit Management (South West Branch Committee Member); The Non Administrative Receivers Association; The Insolvency Lawyers Association; Chairman of the ACCA Admissions and Licensing Committee.
Career: Guildford College of Law; Bristol University (LLB); trained with *Clarke Willmott & Clarke* 1982; admitted October 1984; Partner January 1989; Member of the firm's Management Board from May 1999.
Publications: Author of Debt Recovery (3rd edition published May 2001); Legal Update contributor to Credit Today and numerous other legal and professional journals on Insolvency and Debt Recovery issues. Regular lecturer on these subjects for national training providers.

ANDERSON, Hamish
Norton Rose, London
(020) 7238 6000
andersonh@nortonrose.com
Specialisation: Partner in the insolvency group. His work covers all aspects of insolvency under the Insolvency Act 1986 and he specialises in cross-border insolvency and restructurings. He has had extensive recent experience in the telecoms, aviation and motor sectors. Has acted as an expert witness on English insolvency law in US chap II proceedings.
Prof. Memberships: Past president Insolvency Lawyers' Association. Council member, R3. Member, Law Society and City of London Law Society Insolvency sub-committees. Publications officer, committee J (creditors' rights) International Bar Association. Member, editorial board 'Insolvency Law & Practice'.
Career: Admitted 1973. Licensed insolvency practitioner since 1987. Partner, *Bond Pearce* 1977-1996. Partner, *Norton Rose* since 1996. Author of several insolvency textbooks and numerous articles.

ANDERSON, John
Eversheds, Newcastle upon Tyne
(0191) 241 6285
johnanderson@eversheds.com
Specialisation: All aspects of insolvency, corporate and personal, acting for secured and unsecured creditors, office holders and debtors; banking; asset tracing and recovery. Particular interests include landlord and tenant, pensions in bankruptcy and directors disqualification. Ensuring the conversion of the technicalities into results.
Prof. Memberships: The Law Society. Incorporated Law Society of Newcastle upon Tyne.
Career: Education: Royal Grammar School, Newcastle upon Tyne 1976-83. Newcastle University 1983-86. Articles: *Wilkinson Maughan* 1987-89. Partner: 1997 (when *Wilkinson Maughan* joined *Eversheds*).
Personal: Interests include cricket, ancient history and legal history.

ANDREWS, Mark
Denton Wilde Sapte, London
(020) 7246 7000

ANTHONY, Rachel
Denton Wilde Sapte, London
(020) 7246 7000

ARCHER, David
Pitmans, Reading
(0118) 958 0224
darcher@pitmans.com
See under Pensions, p.610

ASKEW, Martin
Clarke Willmott & Clarke, Bristol
(0117) 943 5906
maskew@cw-c.co.uk
Specialisation: Partner specialising in all aspects of personal and corporate insolvency with considerable experience in dealing with investigations and pursuing antecedent transaction claims. Has successfully attacked a number of off-shore trusts in the Channel Islands, the Isle of Man and Vanuata in the South Pacific. Regularly advises on appointment and security issues and also on directors duties. Highlights from the year include acting for the liquidator of a group of companies in the recruitment business where the business had been sold, prior to liquidation, to a company in which the principal shareholder and managing director retained an interest. The transaction was clearly at an undervalue, having valued the goodwill of a £15,000,000 pa business at £3. The liquidator obtained an injunction preventing the new company from rebranding the transferred business, commenced substantive proceedings to set aside the transaction as one at an undervalue and obtained an order appointing himself as Court Appointed Receiver of the business to preserve the status quo while the case was litigated. The case was settled with an order restoring the transferred business to the companies in liquidation. (Walker v W A Personnel Limited [2002] BPIR 620). Also acted for a trustee in bankruptcy, in his capacity as a 50% shareholder in a company, in relation to an s459 Companies Act 1985 petition, to ensure that the interests of the trustee were fairly represented in the running of the company.
Career: University of Sheffield; articled with *Nabarro Nathanson*; joined *Dibb Lupton Broomhead* and admitted 1992; joined *Wansbroughs Willey Hargrave* (now *Beachcroft Wansbroughs*) 1996-2001 and appointed partner in 1998. Joined *CW&C* in 2001 as partner.

BACON, Alistair
Matthew Arnold & Baldwin, Watford
(01923) 690020
alistair.bacon@mablaw.co.uk
Specialisation: Insolvency. Acting for the liquidators of Organic Clothing, the administrative receivers of the Wap Store Ltd and the administrators of Fish!. A panel lawyer for Barclays Bank plc and one of the small number of firms which receive regular instructions in recovery matters.
Career: Trained at *Braby & Waller*; qualified 1992 *Sprecher Grier* 1993-94. Assistant at Lloyd's of London (Financial Recovery Department) 1994-96; Senior Associate *Sinclair Roche & Temperley* 1996-2001, *Matthew Arnold & Baldwin* Partner 2001 to date.
Publications: Specialist journals, notably insolvency intelligence and insolvency law and practice.
Personal: Born 1966. Resides London. Interests: golf, rugby and wine.

BAINES, Richard
Osborne Clarke, London
(020) 7809 1000

BAIRD, Ken
Freshfields Bruckhaus Deringer, London
(020) 7936 4000
ken.baird@freshfields.com
Specialisation: Finance Department. Partner specialising in restructuring and insolvency; has worked extensively on both domestic and cross-border reconstructions. Recent deals include ICO (US/Bermuda/Cayman, including provisional liquidation and chapter ii); Boo.com and RKB (Latvian Bank).
Prof. Memberships: Liveryman of City of London Solicitors Company; Law Society and the Law Society of Scotland.
Career: Qualified in Scotland 1987; admitted England 1990; regular contributor to periodicals and various speaking engagements.
Personal: Born 1964. University of Glasgow (LLB Hons Dip LP). Keen clay pigeon shot; golf.

BAKER, Ian
Martineau Johnson, Birmingham
(0121) 678 1575
ian.baker@martjohn.com
Specialisation: Advises on banking and debt finance of all kinds including acquisition and project finance, restructurings and security issues and all aspects of non-contentious insolvency.
Prof. Memberships: Associate member of the Securities Institute, member of R3.
Career: Qualified 1983; partner 1987.
Personal: Arts, cricket, rugby, soccer. Church - missionary and development work in Europe and Africa. Married, two children.

BARANSKI, Karl
Edwards Geldard, Cardiff
(029) 2023 8239
karl.baranski@geldards.co.uk
Specialisation: Non-contentious corporate insolvency work including administrative receivership, LPA receivership, administration and liquidation. Instructed by major accountancy practices. Also has wide experience in banking and finance in relation to secured lending, acquisition finance, project finance and Housing Association lending. Acted for the administrators in the administration of semi-conductor company Newport Wafer-Fab Ltd and for Barclays Bank plc in the funding of the Millennium Stadium in Cardiff.
Prof. Memberships: Law Society.
Career: A graduate of Aberystwyth University. Joined *Edwards Geldard* in 1980 as a trainee, qualified in 1982 and became a partner in 1987.
Personal: Born 24 April 1958. Leisure interests include hill walking, mountain biking and swimming. He is also an elder in a local baptist church. He is married with one three year old daughter.

BARKER, Matthew
Lester Aldridge, Southampton
(023) 8082 0407
matthew.barker@lester-aldridge.co.uk
Specialisation: Work includes all aspects of insolvency, business rescue and turn-around relating to companies and individuals. Acts for insolvency practitioners

INSOLVENCY ■ THE LEADERS

and directors and creditors of companies in financial difficulties. Also acts for invoice discounters and other financiers. Advises on corporate reorganisations and solvent liquidations.
Prof. Memberships: Law Society; Association of Business Recovery Professionals.
Career: Qualified in 1995 following articles with *Blake Lapthorn*. Solicitor in the Insolvency and Business Rescue Group at *Blake Lapthorn* until December 2000. Licensed insolvency practitioner in 2000. Joined Lester Aldridge in January 2001 as an associate in the corporate recovery team.
Personal: Born 1969. Married. Recreations include hockey, tennis, film, music and walking.

BARNES, Ged
Addleshaw Booth & Co, Manchester
(0161) 934 6656
ged.barnes@addleshawbooth.com
Specialisation: All aspects of corporate recovery and insolvency work, including turnaround and reconstruction, and associated banking and security arrangements.
Career: Articled *Slater Heelis*. Joined *Addleshaw Booth & Co* as an assistant solicitor in 1998. Senior solicitor from 2000.
Personal: Born 1971. Educated at Maricourt High School and Manchester University (1993 LLB Hons). LPC at Chester Law School (1994 Distinction). Resides Greenfield, Saddleworth. Leisure interests include golf and football (Everton FC).

BARNETT, Nigel
Denton Wilde Sapte, London
(020) 7246 7000

BERRY, Christopher
Edwin Coe, London
(020) 7691 4000
Specialisation: Personal insolvency and all other areas including disciplinary licensing and disqualification proceedings.
Prof. Memberships: Law Society. Association of Business Recovery Professionals, AEPPC, Insolvency Lawyers Association (Technical Committee).
Career: Partner *Edwin Coe*. Crown Court Recorder. Chartered arbitrator. Law Society Nominee, Insolvency Court Users-Committee. Several books, numerous articles.
Personal: Early morning squash. Chairman, Warman Sports Trust.

BLAIR, Jonathan
Dickinson Dees, Newcastle upon Tyne
(0191) 279 9219
jonathan.blair@dickinson-dees.com
Specialisation: Partner, corporate recovery, head of directors disqualification team. Work includes corporate recoveries, administrations and receiverships as well as individual insolvency work. Jonathan heads up the 10 man strong directors disqualification team working for the insolvency service across the North of England. The team was successful in tendering for the expanded North East region in autumn 2000.
Prof. Memberships: Law Society; Committee Member of SPI (North East Region)
Career: LLB; training with *Wragge & Co* 1987-89; 1989 to date *Dickinson Dees*. Partner at *Dickinson Dees* 1997.
Personal: Married, two children; keen mountaineer and rock climber.

BLOXHAM, Peter
Freshfields Bruckhaus Deringer, London
(020) 7936 4000
peter.bloxham@freshfields.com
Specialisation: Head of restructuring and insolvency practice. He has worked on many large insolvencies, including the initial stages of the BCCI collapse, Canary Wharf and aspects of Barings. Recent work includes advising: Lloyd's of London on the banking and insolvency aspects of its R&R proposals and the settlement structure and various aspects of their funding; banks, investment banks and debtors on consensual restructurings including bond issue reschedulings; KPMG as the English provisional liquidators of HIH.
Publications: Author with Ken Baird of the chapter on cross-border issues in Tolley's 'Insolvency Law'.
Personal: St John's College, Cambridge. Speaks fluent French.

BON, Gordon
Bevan Ashford, Bristol
(0117) 918 8914
gordon.bon@bevanashford.co.uk
Specialisation: Partner in the Commercial Department and Head of the firm's Professional Services Division, specialising in insolvency (contentious and non-contentious). Acting for major, medium-sized and small accountancy firms, with insolvency practitioners as well as for British and foreign banks and other commercial clients. Cases include refinancing and restructuring businesses in financial crisis.
Career: Torquay Boys' Grammar School; Queen Mary College, London. Called to the Bar 1983, qualified as a solicitor 1986. Joint insolvency exam 1995. Partner at *Laytons* since 1994. Joined *Bevan Ashford* as partner 2001.
Personal: Born 1959. Lives in Bristol.

BOOBIER, Nigel
Osborne Clarke, Bristol
(0117) 917 3000

BORDELL, Keith
Travers Smith Braithwaite, London
(020) 7295 3000
keith.bordell@traverssmith.com
Specialisation: Partner, joint head of business reconstruction and insolvency group. Advises on all aspects of business rescues and reconstructions, workout and insolvency law. Clients include distressed companies, company doctors, accountants and insolvency practitioners, investors, lenders and other creditors.
Prof. Memberships: Law Society; Association of Business Recovery Professionals; Insolvency Lawyers' Association; AEPPC/ EIPA.
Career: Trained at *Cameron Markby*. Qualified 1988. *Watson, Farley & Williams* 1989-95, *Allen & Overy* 1995-98. Partner *Berwin Leighton* 1998-2002. Partner *Travers Smith Braithwaite*.
Personal: Born 1963. Educated at Chigwell School and the London School of Economics. Married with two sons.

BOUMPHREY, Patrick
Burges Salmon, Bristol
(0117) 939 2261
patrick.boumphrey@burges-salmon.com
Specialisation: Leading the Burges Salmon team which advised the MoD on the recent PPP procurement of future offshore patrol vessels on an innovative capability based lease structure; advising a number of train operating companies (including Great Eastern Railway, Great Western Trains and North Western Trains) and ATOC on the recent Railtrack plc railway administration; advising Bristol Water plc in connection with the recent ENRON administration; advising a number of corporate clients in relation to the restructuring of their finances or the turnaround of their business including the recent rescue of the Solsoft IT business; advising the Administrative Receivers of Poplar Plastics Limited generally, including on the sale of the business to certain of the management team; advising both lenders and receivers in relation to residential nursing homes and care homes facing financial difficulties. Patrick has advised on more than 50 such cases in the last year; and advising the Administrative Receivers of Kishen & King Limited generally, including on the validity of their appointment and on the sale of the business to the management team.
Career: Qualified 1994; Partner *Burges Salmon* 2001.

BOWDEN, Jeremy
DLA, Birmingham
(08700) 111111

BRADY, Yvonne
Dundas & Wilson CS, Glasgow
(0141) 222 2200

BRANSON, Christopher
Boyes Turner, Reading
(0118) 952 7205
cbranson@boyesturner.com
Specialisation: Partner in insolvency. Principal area of practice is corporate and individual insolvency. Acts for receivers, liquidators and administrators in corporate insolvency situations and for trustees in bankruptcy as well as nominees and supervisors in CVAs and IVAs. Acts for office-holders in areas of fraud and asset tracing, often abroad. Advises banks and financial institutions on security and lending issues. Clients include all the major accountancy firms, plus many smaller regional firms. Has lectured at IBC Conferences, R3 conferences and Jordans Insolvency Practice Conferences. Charge-out rate of £210 per hour.
Prof. Memberships: Law Society; IPA; fellow R3; Insolvency Lawyers Association; member Insolvency Courts Users committee.
Career: Qualified in 1981. Partner at *Boyes Turner* from 1988. Insolvency practitioner 1989.

BRIGGS, Graham
Addleshaw Booth & Co, Leeds
(0113) 209 2000
graham.briggs@addleshawbooth.com
Specialisation: Insolvency, turnaround and banking law. Graham's broad based skills as an advisor to banks and insolvency practitioners were further enhanced by a one year secondment to a major UK bank as lead advisor to a commercial debt management project.
Prof. Memberships: Leeds Law Society. Insolvency Lawyers Association. Association of Business Recovery Professionals.
Career: Joined *Addleshaw Booth & Co* upon qualifying as a solicitor in 1984. Developed his expertise from a background in bank litigation and bank advisory work.
Personal: Married with 3 children, lives in Menston near Ilkley. He is the holder of a Motor Sports Association competition license and competes in the Thoroughbred Sportscar Championship in a race prepared MGB.

BROCKMAN, Christopher
Blake Lapthorn, Portsmouth
(023) 9222 1122

BROOKER, Suzanne
Pitmans, Reading
(0118) 958 0224
sbrooker@pitmans.com
Specialisation: Licensed Insolvency Practitioner with extensive experience in all areas of formal rescue and insolvency procedures for individuals, partnerships and companies. Continues to act on contentious insolvency matters including claims arising under the Insolvency Act 1986, the Companies Act 1985 and the Company Directors Disqualification Act 1986, and non-contentious insolvency business sales and restructuring.
Prof. Memberships: Law Society; Member of Association of Business Recovery Professionals (ABRP); Committee Member for Southern Region for ABRP; Member of Insolvency Practitioners Association.
Career: Joined Pitmans in 1992. Qualified Licensed Insolvency Practitioner 2000.
Personal: Married. Leisure pursuits: sport and reading.

BROOKS, Egan
Addleshaw Booth & Co, Manchester
(0161) 934 6000
egan.brooks@addleshawbooth.com
Specialisation: Partner in corporate recovery, insolvency, banking and security law practice.
Prof. Memberships: The Law Society

THE LEADERS ■ INSOLVENCY

(Chairman, Insolvency Law sub-committee 1999-). Licensed Insolvency Practitioner, Society of Practitioners of Insolvency and Notary Public.
Career: Qualified 1966. *Slater Heelis* 1964-98. Partner 1969. Joined firm 1998 as Partner.
Personal: Educated at Manchester Grammar School and Manchester University (LLB Hons). Lives in Hale. Leisure interests include motoring, architecture and walking.

BROWN, Robert
Keeble Hawson, Leeds
(0113) 244 3121
robertbrown@keeblehawson.co.uk
Specialisation: Robert is a partner and head of department at *Keeble Hawson*. He deals with all aspects of insolvency, Directors' Disqualification proceedings, insolvency litigation and recovery both personal and corporate. Robert has particular expertise in dealing with contentious claims arising out of insolvency situations both for the insolvency practitioners and the respondents.
Prof. Memberships: The Law Society; SPI; ILA; IPA; Licensed Insolvency Practitioner; member of Association of Business Recovery Professions; member of Insolvency Practitioners Association. Member of Leeds Law Society Civil Litigation committee.
Career: Articled *RC Moorhouse & Co*. Qualified 1979, partner 1981.
Personal: Born Harrogate 1955. Resides Wetherby. Educated Leeds University (LLB). A retired goalkeeper now concentrating on mountain biking and tennis.

BRUMBY, Frank
Leathes Prior, Norwich
(01603) 610911

BUCHANAN, Andrew
Halliwell Landau, Manchester
(0161) 831 2970
abuchanan@halliwells.co.uk
Specialisation: Head of Insolvency and Corporate Recovery. Specialises in corporate and personal insolvency and turnaround, receives instructions from clearing banks, secondary banks, invoice discounters, public and private companies and all major firms of insolvency practitioners. He has extensive industry within a wide range of sectors, including manufacturing, food, automotive, public sector, financial services and technology.
Prof. Memberships: Law Society.
Career: Partner with *Haliwell Landau* since joining in March 1999.
Publications: Accountancy books, including 'Corporate Recovery Health Check'.
Personal: Stockport Grammar School, Sheffield University, Trent Polytechnic, member of Heaton Moor and Elgin golf clubs, member of Heaton Mersey cricket club, Rugby, Walking. Father is a retired medical practitioner.

BUGG, Tony
Linklaters, London
(020) 7456 4470
tony.bugg@linklaters.com
Specialisation: Experienced in all aspects of insolvency related work, advising banks and financial institutions, insolvency practitioners and corporate clients in relation to recovery, reconstruction or distressed debt problems. Has acted on a wide range of administrations, receiverships, liquidations and schemes and voluntary arrangements and workouts in relation to major international and UK companies.
Prof. Memberships: Council Member and Past President, Insolvency Lawyers Association.
Career: Qualified 1981. Partner *Dibb Lupton Broomhead* and its predecessor 1982-97. Joined *Linklaters* 1998 as partner.

BUNDY, Claire
Osborne Clarke, Bristol
(0117) 917 3000

CARTY, Gillian
Shepherd+ Wedderburn, Edinburgh
(0131) 473 5138
gillian.carty@shepwedd.co.uk
Specialisation: Corporate recovery/insolvency (all aspects) and directors disqualification (for DTI).
Prof. Memberships: Licensed Insolvency Practitioner (through Law Society of Scotland). Accredited by Law Society as specialist in insolvency law.
Career: Qualified 1995. Assumed as partner in May 2001.
Personal: Educated at Hutchesons Grammar School, Glasgow, LLB (Hons) and Dip LP at Edinburgh University.

COATES, Philip
Pinsent Curtis Biddle, Manchester
(0161) 247 8282
Specialisation: Licensed Insolvency Practitioner specialising in business support and reconstruction. Involved in numerous leading cases including Charnley Davies, re International Bulk Commodities and re Cosslett Contractors.
Prof. Memberships: SPI and Insolvency Lawyers Association.
Career: BA Politics and Economics, Newcastle upon Tyne 1977. LLB Leeds 1979. Qualified 1982. Trained Mediator. Partner: *Simpson Curtis* 1988-94; Consultant: 1994-97. Solicitor: *Hammond Suddards*, 1997-99. May 1999 onwards: Partner *Dibb Lupton Alsop*. 2002 to date - partner *Pinsent Curtis Biddle*.

COHEN, Adrian
Clifford Chance, London
(020) 7600 1000
adrian.cohen@cliffordchance.com
Specialisation: Banking and Finance Department. Partner specialising in all aspects of domestic and international non-contentious insolvency and corporate reconstruction.
Career: Called to the Bar 1988; Barrister at law 1988-90; joined *Clifford Chance* Corporate Practice 1990 and Insolvency Group 1991.
Personal: London School of Economics; Queen Mary and Westfield College, London (LLB (Hons) 1985, LLM 1987).

COOK, Nigel
Paul Davidson Taylor, Horsham
(01403) 831213
ncook@pdt.co.uk
Specialisation: Corporate insolvency, particularly administrative and LPA receiverships and administrations. Within past year has acted for insolvency practitioners in respect of insolvencies in the manufacturing and retail sectors. Also specialises in advice to directors of companies in financial difficulties or who face disqualification proceeds.
Prof. Memberships: Associate member of the Insolvency Lawyers Association.
Career: Assistant Solicitor: commercial department *Clifford Turner* (1976-81). Head of legal department First National Commercial Bank (1982-89); Partner: *Paul Davidson Taylor* (1995-).
Personal: MBA; BA (Oxon) Jurisprudence. Keen golfer and cricketer. Trustee of penal affairs charity, The Inside Out Trust.

COOK, Patrick
Osborne Clarke, Bristol
(0117) 917 3000

CRAIG, Nigel
Blake Lapthorn, Portsmouth
(023) 9222 1122

CRANSTON, Peter
DLA, Leeds
(08700) 111111

CROUCHER, Yvette
Cadwalader, Wickersham & Taft, London
(020) 7170 8714
yvette.croucher@cwt-uk.com
Specialisation: Senior associate in the London Financial Restructuring Department. She has comprehensive experience of complex corporate insolvencies and restructurings, particularly in advising bondholder committees. She also advises on insurance company run-offs, restructurings and investigations. Ms Croucher has advised companies, banks, bondholders and creditors generally and also directors and office holders on their respective duties and liabilities. She is also a licensed insolvency practitioner.
Prof. Memberships: R3 Association of Business Recovery Professionals.
Career: Graduate of Exeter University. Trained and qualified at *Simmons & Simmons*. Spent six months on secondment to the Royal Bank of Scotland, Specialised Lending Services in 1997. Joined *Cadwalader* in February 1998.

CUTHBERTSON, Ian
Dundas & Wilson CS, Glasgow
(0141) 222 2200

DOBSON, Julian
Julian Dobson Solicitors, Brighton
(01273) 693567
jcd@juliandobson.com
Specialisation: Solicitor and licensed insolvency practitioner by examination, specialising exclusively in insolvency law; full range of insolvency work carried out for insolvency practitioners and other clients including administrations, bankruptcies, CVAs, IVAs, liquidations, PVAs and receiverships. Registered IPA Property Receiver. Regularly instructed by Top Five accountancy firms.
Prof. Memberships: Insolvency Lawyers Association. R3. Law Society.
Career: Articled *Hawley & Rodgers*; qualified 1986; assistant solicitor *Bunkers & Co* 1986-91; partner *Bunkers* 1991; passed JIEB examination to become Insolvency Practitioner 1993.
Personal: Born 1959; resides Lewes. Swimming, golf.

DOLPHIN, Huw
DLA, Birmingham
(08700) 111111

DREW, Jeff
Eversheds, Birmingham
(0121) 232 1000
jeffdrew@eversheds.com
Specialisation: Partner in insolvency and banking group. Chairman of *Eversheds* corporate recovery and insolvency group. Advises insolvency practitioners and banks in connection with all aspects of corporate recovery and insolvency law and banks in connection with the taking and realising of charges. Speaks widely at conferences and seminars.
Prof. Memberships: Association of Business Recovery Professionals.
Career: Qualified in 1980. Worked at *Wragge & Co* 1978-82, then *Edge & Ellison* 1982-92 (from 1984 as a partner). Joined *Eversheds* as a partner in 1992.
Personal: Born 12 October 1954. Attended Solihull School and St Edmund Hall, Oxford 1974-77. Leisure interests include tennis, squash and badminton. Lives in Birmingham.

DUTTON, Paul
Eversheds, Newcastle upon Tyne
(0191) 241 6229
paulnsdutton@eversheds.com
Specialisation: Partner and head of corporate recovery and insolvency. Clients include all the big five accountancy firms, as well as regional specialist insolvency practitioners such as Tait Walker, Tenon Jennings Johnson, JB Taylor & Co and BKR Haines Watts. The firm also acts for HSBC Bank, National Westminster Bank, Royal Bank of Scotland, Bank of Scotland, Lloyds TSB and Co-op Bank. Advises insolvency practitioners, banks and other secured lenders and businesses on all aspects of corporate recovery and insolvency regimes. Particular specialism in non-contentious business recovery bank work, including administrative receiverships and administrations, work outs, turn around and intensive care work, security reviews and advice on corporate restructures and bank refinancing. Involved in most high profile recoveries in the North East

www.ChambersandPartners.com

457

INSOLVENCY ■ THE LEADERS

during and since the recession including Stanley Miller plc, Slaley Hall and Swan Hunter. The most notable case dealt with is the landmark decision on fixed and floating charges in New Bullas Trading Company limited and he can also claim the dubious accolade of renaming the case following the sale of the company's name by the receiver.
Prof. Memberships: Law Society Committee, R3 Committee Tyne and Wear Region, Insolvency Lawyers' Association.
Career: Date of birth: 6 August 1965, Northumbria University LLB (Hons), Chester Law School. Joined *Robert Muckle Solicitors* 1989, qualified 1991, partner 1993, head of insolvency and banking since 1994. Joined *Eversheds* (Newcastle) in January 2001 as head of corporate recovery and insolvency.
Personal: Cricket, Northumberland CCC, golf and football.

ELLIOTT, Laurence
Herbert Smith, London
(020) 7374 8000
laurence.elliott@herbertsmith.com
Specialisation: Partner specialising in corporate recovery and insolvency, with particular emphasis on insurance insolvency and restructuring. Currently acting for the provisional liquidation of Independent Insurance Company and Ocean Marine Mutual. Also currently advising the US Futures Representative on issues arising out of the bankruptcy of Federal Mogul.
Career: *Lovell White Durrant* 1991-99. Qualified 1993. Joined *Herbert Smith* 1999. Partnership 2002.

ELLIOTT, Robert
Linklaters, London
(020) 7456 4478
robert.elliott@linklaters.com
Specialisation: Head of restructuring; specialist in corporate recovery and insolvency. Wide experience of syndicated and bilateral facilities (secured and unsecured), cross-border financing, leveraged and acquisition finance.
Career: Leeds Grammar School; London University; Queen Mary College (LLB) 1973. Qualified in 1976. Assistant Solicitor *Wilde Sapte* 1976-81. Partner, *Wilde Sapte* 1981-90. Joined *Linklaters* 1990 as a Partner. Co-head corporate recovery and insolvency *Linklaters*.

FERGUSSON, Richard
Keeble Hawson, Leeds
(0113) 244 3121
richardfergusson@keeblehawson.co.uk
Specialisation: Licensed insolvency practitioner dealing with all forms of corporate and personal insolvency and recovery on behalf of practitioners, banks and building societies and debtors. Deals with a full range of contentious and non-contentious insolvencies from bankruptcy to trading receiverships and administrations. Also has experience of court appointed, agricultural and LPA receiverships as well as director disqualification proceedings.

Prof. Memberships: Law Society and ABRP.
Career: Trained at *Dibb Lupton Broomhead* 1989 to 1991; joined *Booth & Co* (now *Addleshaw Booth & Co*) September 1992; partner *Keeble Hawson* June 2000.
Personal: Educated at Batley Grammar School and Leeds University. Interests include hill walking, reading, travelling, food and wine.

FIELD, Ian
Allen & Overy, London
(020) 7330 3000
ian.field@allenovery.com
Specialisation: Partner dealing with all types of corporate reconstruction and insolvency work, acting for banks and other financial institutions, insolvency practitioners and corporations. Latterly involved in major restructuring in Thailand.
Prof. Memberships: Law Society's Insolvency Law Sub-Committee.
Personal: Born 1966. Exeter College, Oxford University (1988, MA).

FLETCHER, Ian
Stephenson Harwood (incorporating Sinclair Roche & Temperley), London
(020) 7809 2025
ian.fletcher@shlegal.com
Specialisation: Partner, Corporate. Specialist in restructuring work and corporate recovery, and also in acquisition finance (MBO's MBI's) against a general corporate and financial background with a significant international element. An authorised insolvency practitioner and former member of the Government Party which considered insolvency regulation in the UK.
Prof. Memberships: Council of the Association of Business Recovery Professionals (R3); Former Council Insolvency Lawyers' Association (President 1995/96).
Publications: Joint author 'The Law Practice of Corporate Administrations' 1994, 1st edition, 2nd edition (2003). Joint Editor 'Cross Border Insolvencies' incorporating contributions from 35 jurisdictions published by Oceana Publications Inc 1999. Joint editor, 'The Law and Practice of Receivership in Scotland' 2nd Edition, 3rd Edition 2003.
Personal: Educated Glasgow University (LLB). Qualified Scotland 1971, England 1978.

FLINT, David
MacRoberts, Glasgow
(0141) 332 9988
df@macroberts.com
See under Intellectual Property, p.488

FOSTER, Stephen
CMS Cameron McKenna, London
(020) 7367 3000
stephen.foster@cmck.com
Specialisation: Partner in Banking and International Finance Department. Principal areas of practice are banking, reconstruction and insolvency. Work includes advising banks and corporates on domestic and international banking questions and pre-insolvency issues, including options to maximise recovery. Also advises insolvency practitioners in receiverships, administrations and liquidations. Other main areas of practice are domestic, European and cross-border reconstructions, distressed debt issues and advising on documentation and insolvency issues. Has lectured to the Institute of Bankers, R3 and for various commercial lecture providers on banking and insolvency topics and written various articles.
Prof. Memberships: Member of Law Society; Insolvency Lawyers Association; R3; IBA Committee J; Insol Europe.
Career: Qualified in 1989. Became a Partner at *Cameron Markby Hewitt* (now *CMS Cameron McKenna*) in 1991.
Personal: Born 4 January 1958. Educated at Pembroke College, Cambridge. Interests include walking, music and film. Lives in London.

FRENCH, Matthew
Lovells, London
(020) 7296 2000

FRIEZE, Steven
Brooke North, Leeds
(0113) 283 2100
Specialisation: All aspects of contentious insolvency with a bias towards personal insolvency but including cross border issues.
Prof. Memberships: R3, ILA, Commercial Law League of America, Licensed Insolvency Practitioner.
Career: Leeds Grammar School; Trinity College, Oxford (1965-1968). Admitted 1971. Partner 1976. Deputy District Judge 1982-1994. Author of Handbook of Personal Insolvency, Weavings Notes on Bankruptcy, Compulsory Winding Up Procedure, and Practice Note: Insolvency in their various editions from 1982 to date.
Personal: General editor of Insolvency Intelligence (1988 to date).

FRITH, Stuart
Brooke North, Leeds
(0113) 297 9000
sif@brookenorth.co.uk
Specialisation: Contentious insolvency of all types for banks, insolvency practitioners, debtors and creditors. Acted for the successful bank in Bank of Ireland v Hollicourt (Contracts) Ltd [2001] 1 All ER 289 (CA); acted for the liquidator in Khalastchi v Walker Morris [2001] 1 BCLC 1; acted in relation to Anglo Manx Trust Ltd v Aitken - applicability of Limitation Act in bankruptcy.
Prof. Memberships: Law Society; immediate Past-President of the Insolvency Lawyers' Association; R3; IPA.
Career: Qualified October 1983; Articled at *Jacksons Monk & Rowe*, Middlesbrough; joined *Brooke North* in 1984; Partner 1989; Licensed Insolvency Practitioner 1989.
Personal: Born 6 December 1957; educated Spalding Grammar School; Leeds University.

FROME, Nicholas P
Clifford Chance, London
(020) 7600 1000
nicholas.frome@cliffordchance.com
Specialisation: Banking and Finance Department. Partner specialising in all aspects of insolvency, business rescues and restructuring.
Career: *Lovells*, 1975-2001, Partner since 1983; Partner at *Clifford Chance* since 2001.
Personal: Marlborough College and University London College, London.

GAINES, Keith
Lovells, London
(020) 7296 2000
keith.gaines@lovells.com
See under Litigation, p.557

GALE, Stephen
Herbert Smith, London
(020) 7374 8000
stephen.gale@herbertsmith.com
Specialisation: Partner and head of corporate recovery. Has extensive experience of all aspects of insolvency and corporate recovery practice both in the UK and Asia. Solicitor and licenced insolvency practitioner. Lectures widely on insolvency-related issues.
Prof. Memberships: Law Society, Institute of Credit Management, IPA, AEPPC, Institute of Directors, IBA Committee J.
Career: Qualified in 1982. Associate with *Simpson Curtis* 1984, then partner with *Masons & Marriott* in Hong Kong, 1985. Joined *Hammond Suddards* in 1987 as a partner. Partner *Herbert Smith* January 1998.

GIBSON, David
Dundas & Wilson CS, Glasgow
(0141) 222 2200

GILL, Julian
Watson Burton, Newcastle upon Tyne
(0191) 244 4444
Specialisation: Advising banks and insolvency practitioners on recoveries and insolvency procedures as well as companies in relation to shareholder and commercial contract disputes.
Prof. Memberships: Insolvency Lawyers Association.
Career: Articled *Wilkinson Kimbers*; qualified 1989; assistant solicitor *Alsop Wilkinson* 1989-92; assistant solicitor *Robert Muckle* 1992-94; partner 1994; *Watson Burton*; partner 2001. Educated at Tudor Grange School, Solihull; Sheffield University (1985 LLB Hons).
Personal: Football, cricket, golf.

GILL, Mark
Denton Wilde Sapte, London
(020) 7246 7000

GODFREY, Patricia
Nabarro Nathanson, London
(020) 7524 6000
Specialisation: Head of insolvency and corporate recovery group; handles all aspects of insolvency, rescue, turnaround

and reorganisation.
Career: Council member German-British Chamber of Industry and Commerce, director and trustee, German British Forum. Regular conference speaker R3 and INSOL Europe.
Publications: Associate editor: Tolley's 'Insolvency Law & Practice'. Regular contributor: Legal Network TV. Joint author: Tolley's 'Company Secretarial Manual' - Insolvency Section. Member of both R3's London region and education courses and conferences committees. Head of firm's German group and joint author 'Englische Gesekshaften in der Insolvenz', a guide to UK insolvency proceedings written in collaboration with German-British Chamber of Industry and Commerce.

GOODMAN, Nick
NJ Goodman & Co, Altrincham
(0161) 928 0990
nick@njgoodman.co.uk
Specialisation: Specialist with wide experience acting for officeholders in all types of insolvency cases, both personal and corporate. Expertise acquired as a partner within the banking and insolvency groups of two Top 20 law firms. Undertakes director defence work including disqualification proceedings.
Prof. Memberships: ABRP; Law Society.
Career: Qualified 1982; *N J Goodman & Co* (2000); *Addleshaw Booth & Co* (1995-00); *Dibb Lupton Broomhead* (1989-95); Hong Kong (1982-88).
Personal: Attended Southampton University. Leisure pursuits include golf and family. Lives in Cheshire.

GORDON, John Gerard
Napier & Sons, Belfast
(028) 90244602

GORDON-SAKER, Paul
Stephenson Harwood (incorporating Sinclair Roche & Temperley), London
(020) 7809 2367
paul.gordon-saker@shlegal.com
Specialisation: Partner, litigation. Head of recovery and insolvency. Paul has specialised in insolvency work for 32 years and has substantial experience in all types of insolvency procedures in the UK together with more general experience of procedures in the United States, Europe and Hong Kong. He has special expertise in cross-border insolvency and is heavily involved in reconstruction and workouts for banking clients. He acts for all the major accountancy practices, banks and building societies. He is involved with many reported decisions of the High Court, Court of Appeal and House of Lords and has a prestigious reputation throughout the insolvency world. He is a frequent lecturer on insolvency topics.

GRANT, Rachel
Semple Fraser, Glasgow
(0131) 273 3771
rachel.grant@semplefraser.co.uk
Specialisation: Specialising in corporate recovery and insolvency for more than 12 years. Is accredited by The Law Society of Scotland as a specialist in insolvency law and is well known for her work in this area. Over the years she has acted for a wide range of clients including government departments, banks, insolvency practitioners and businesses of all sizes as well as individual clients. Was the first solicitor in Scotland to act for the DTI Insolvency Service in conducting director disqualification cases. Has specialist knowledge of all aspects of corporate recovery and insolvency including director's disqualification, liquidation, receivership, administration, CVAs and personal insolvency, and lectures on all of these topics. Also has a wide ranging general corporate litigation practice.
Prof. Memberships: Law Society Insolvency Representative on the Joint Insolvency Committee (JIC); member of the Law Society Insolvency Committee; member of R3 (the Association of Business Recovery Professionals) Technical Committee; Chair of Edinburgh Insolvency Discussion Group.
Career: 1985-87, Trained *D.R. Calder & Williams*, Dundee; 1987-88, *Alex Morrison & Co*; 1988-99, Head of the Corporate Recovery and Insolvency Team at *Shepherd & Wedderburn*; 1999-2001, Partner and Head of Corporate Recovery & Insolvency Unit at *Steedman Ramage*; 2001-present, Partner at *Semple Fraser*.
Personal: Education: University of Edinburgh 1981, LLB (Hons); Dundee University, 1983, Dip LP.

GRAY, David
Eversheds, Manchester
(0161) 831 8000
dgray@eversheds.com
Specialisation: Associate in the corporate recovery and insolvency department. Acts for all major banks and accountancy practices and advises corporate clients on restructurings and refinancings. Acted for Andersens as administrative receivers of the Trident Group of companies, and Lampies Limited. Advised RSM Robson Rhodes as administrators of Bury FC and Begbie Traynor as receivers of F Bodie & Sons Limited.
Prof. Memberships: R3 - licensed insolvency practitioner.
Career: Trained *Slater Heeks* 1993-95. *Addleshaw Booth & Co* 1995-98. *Chaffe Street* 1998-99. *Eversheds* since 1999.
Personal: Sheffield University (LLB Hons), Law Society finals (1st Class Honours). Interests include golf and walking. Resides Buxton. Married with one daughter.

GREGORY, Andrew
DWF, Manchester
(0161) 228 3702
andrew.gregory@dwf.co.uk
Specialisation: Heads up the Business Recovery Team at DWF, which has grown and developed significantly in the last 12 months. Andrew and his team's specialisms have broadened over the past year to include not just the traditional areas including receiverships, administrations and liquidations but is becoming increasingly involved in turnaround projects and workouts for banks and asset based lenders.
Prof. Memberships: Law Society; Association of Business Recovery Professionals.
Career: Partner *Davies Wallis Foyster* 1992 (head of insolvency and banking).
Publications: Editorial board 'The Insolvency Lawyer' (Sweet & Maxwell).
Personal: Paramount Secondary School; St Helens College of Technology; Liverpool John Moores University; walking; reading; theatre; resides Macclesfield.

GREGORY, Deborah
Lovells, London
(020) 7296 2000
deborah.gregory@lovells.com
Specialisation: Partner in *Lovells*' business restructuring and insolvency group. A licensed insolvency practitioner who has specialised in restructuring and insolvency work since 1984. Deals with all aspects of corporate insolvency including voluntary arrangements, schemes of arrangements, administrations, receiverships, liquidations and all forms of corporate restructurings. Led the legal team on the administration of the British & Commonwealth Group and acted for ING on the Barings acquisition, Proton on the acquisition of Lotus, the receivers of Yorkshire Food Group Plc and its 27 subsidiaries, a consortium of 28 leasing financiers and two banks who had a multi-million dollar exposure to Newport Wafer-Fab Limited, a major western bank on the restructuring of an exposure arising from repo agreements with a group trading in Russia and a multi-million pound restructuring of a debt arising from equity options, a restructuring and receivership of two groups of nursing homes and a major telecoms carrier on the restructuring of two multi-million pound debts owed to it.
Prof. Memberships: Fellow of and Council Member of the Association of Business Recovery Professionals ('R3'), Chairman of the Constitution Committee of R3, Member of INSOL Europe, INSOL, International Association of Insurance Receivers, International Women's Insolvency & Restructuring Confederation (IWIRC), British Insurance Law Association, the Law Society Insolvency Sub-Committee and a member of the Insolvency Court Users' Committee.
Career: Articled *Lovell White & King* 1982-84; qualified 1984; assistant solicitor 1984-89; non-contentious business restructuring and insolvency department since 1983; partner *Lovell White Durrant* 1989-99; consultant 2000; partner 2001.
Personal: Educated at Nuneaton High School for Girls; King Edward VI Sixth Form College; Manchester University (1980 LLB Hons); Guildford College of Law (Law Society Part II).

GRIER, Ian Stephen
Sprecher Grier Halberstam LLP, London
(020) 7544 5555
iang@sghlaw.com
Specialisation: Head of Litigation and Insolvency Department. Deals with all aspects of corporate and individual insolvency, principally working for administrative receivers, liquidators and trustees in bankruptcy as well as for banks and creditors. Substantial involvement in rescue schemes for limited companies, partnerships and individuals by way of corporate and individual voluntary arrangements. Also has considerable experience in relation to court appointed receiverships and LPA receiverships. Other main area of practice is corporate litigation including contractual disputes, construction work, intellectual property, banking litigation and debt recovery. Important cases have included Re Brightlife Limited (leading case on fixed and floating charges); Re Cranley Mansions Limited (leading case in relation to individual voluntary arrangement); Scottish Enterprise v Bank of East Asia Limited. Clients include merchant banks, a substantial number of firms of insolvency practitioners and major firms of accountants, international employment agencies and many companies in the IT and technology sectors. Lectures widely to the Association of Business Recovery Professionals (R3), firms of chartered accountants and other professional bodies in relation to the law and practice of insolvency.
Prof. Memberships: Law Society; fellow of the Association of Business Recovery Professionals.
Career: Qualified in 1972. Joined with David Sprecher to form *Sprecher Grier* in 1984.
Publications: Co-author of three published works on corporate and individual insolvency and of numerous articles.
Personal: Born 23 February 1945. Educated at London University (LLB 1967, LLM 1968). Former local councillor. Leisure interests include theatre, playing poker and bridge. Lives in London.

GRIERSON, Christopher
Lovells, London
(020) 7296 2000
christopher.grierson@lovells.com
See under Litigation, p.558

HALLY, Paul
Shepherd+ Wedderburn, Edinburgh
(0131) 473 5183
paul.hally@shepwedd.co.uk
Specialisation: Chief executive and partner in corporate department. Main areas of practice are corporate finance and corporate recovery. Author of Scots law opinions to the Stock Lending and Repo Committee Capital Adequacy Directive Working Group on various international stock lending master agreements and netting provisions used therein.
Prof. Memberships: Law Society of Scotland, Society of Writers to the Signet, Institute of Directors.
Career: Trained *Fyfe Ireland* (1982-84); assistant *Shepherd+ Wedderburn* (1984-87), partner (1987-). Lecturer to Joint

INSOLVENCY ■ THE LEADERS

Insolvency Training Courses (1990-). Member of Law society of Scotland Insolvency Committee (1998-). Qualified Insolvency Practitioner.
Personal: Born 23 June 1959. Holds an LLB (Hons) Dip LP Edinburgh (1977-84).

HAMILTON, Dan
White & Case, London
Specialisation: Partner in banking group. Principal area of practice is insolvency and reconstruction. Has wide experience of insolvency and rescue work including receiverships, administrations, liquidations, corporate and individual voluntary arrangements and schemes of arrangements. Also has wide experience of advising directors of troubled companies, banks and creditor groups on restructuring and rescues. The firm acts for the leading firms of accountants and insolvency practitioners and has numerous banks among its clients. During Summer 1998 he was a member of the team establishing the firm's corporate rescue and recovery practice in Hong Kong and South East Asia. Has recently been advising the UK government with Railtrack Plc and its administrators. Regular lecturer to clients and occasional conference speaker.
Prof. Memberships: Associate of Business Recovery Professionals; Insolvency Lawyers Association.
Career: Qualified in 1988. Joined *Cameron Markby* in 1986 and became a partner at *Cameron Markby Hewitt* (now *CMS Cameron McKenna*) in 1994.
Personal: Educated at Reigate Grammar School 1973-80 and Worcester College, Oxford 1981-84.

HARRIS, Anthony
Laytons, Bristol
(0117) 930 9500
Specialisation: Bristol senior partner and part of the Company, Commercial & Insolvency Group. Specialises in all aspects of insolvency law and is a licensed insolvency practitioner. Practice also covers company and commercial work including mergers and acquisitions, corporate finance and banking.
Prof. Memberships: Association of Business Recovery Professionals; Insolvency Lawyers Association.
Career: Qualified 1971. Partner at *Laytons* 1977. Editor of 'Laytons Insolvency'.
Personal: Educated at Kings School, Rochester and St. Johns College, Cambridge 1962-66. Born 14 May 1946. Lives near Bath.

HARRIS, Clare
Meade-King, Bristol
(0117) 914 2568
ch@meadeking.co.uk
Specialisation: All aspects of personal and corporate insolvency. Predominantly contentious. Acts for a broad range of medium-sized and smaller insolvency practitioners.
Prof. Memberships: Law Society, MABRP, ILA, Licensed Insolvency Practitioner.
Career: LLB London University. Qualified at *Meade-King* 1989. Insolvency practitioner since 1992. Partner from 1994.
Personal: Born 1962. Married with young family. Lives in Bristol.

HARROLD, Neil
Hay & Kilner, Newcastle upon Tyne
(0191) 232 8345

HAYMES, Duncan
LCL Law, Manchester
(07850) 785 727

HENRY, Graeme
Dundas & Wilson CS, Edinburgh
(0131) 228 8000

HERTZ, Philip
Clifford Chance, London
(020) 7600 1000
philip.hertz@cliffordchance.com
Specialisation: Banking and Finance Department. Partner specialising in insurance insolvency and 'special situations', including insurance reconstruction and schemes of arrangement.
Career: Trainee solicitor at *Clifford Chance*, qualified as a solicitor, 1993; Partner since 2002.
Personal: City of London School; University College, London (LLB (Hons), First Class); Downing College Cambridge (LLM, First Class).

HIGHAM, John QC
Stephenson Harwood (incorporating Sinclair Roche & Temperley), London
(020) 7809 2347
john.higham@shlegal.com
Specialisation: Commercial litigator - particularly experienced in the fields of corporate insolvency, company law, banking, financial services, insurance and professional negligence.
Career: Partner *Stephenson Harwood* 2000. Called to the Bar in 1976. From 1978 to 1999 he was a practising barrister and a member of a leading insolvency set of chambers. He was appointed a QC in 1992. In 1999 he requalified as a solicitor advocate. He is also a Recorder on the Midlands and Oxford Circuit.
Publications: 'The Law and Practice of Corporate Administrations' (Joint Editor/Published 1994). MA, LLM Churchill College, Cambridge (1971-75).

HINCHLIFFE, David
Walker Morris, Leeds
(0113) 283 2500

HOLLERIN, Gordon
DLA, Glasgow
(08700) 111111

HOUGHTON, John
Simmons & Simmons, London
(020) 7628 2020
john.houghton@simmons-simmons.com
Specialisation: Head of corporate recovery. Rescues and turnarounds: Railtrack Group plc; The Dome; Bookers plc's standstill; Heron. Work-outs: The Brent Walker Group plc. Receiverships: Connolly Leather Limited; 96 branch estate agency chain; hotels group; multinational polyester manufacturer; de Savary receiverships; Colorvision plc. Administrations and CVAs: Railtrack plc; NRC Refrigeration; Richmond Rugby Club; Oxford United FC's CVA; Portsmouth FC on its administration application; Team Lotus; Travers Morgan (construction and surveying consultancy).
Prof. Memberships: R3, Insolvency Lawyers' Association, European Insolvency Practitioners Association and City of London Law Society Insolvency Committee.
Career: LLB, LLM. Partner 1994.

HUGHES, Michael
Maclay Murray & Spens, Glasgow
(0141) 248 5011
mjh@maclaymurrayspens.co.uk
Specialisation: Head of Corporate Recovery Unit. Principally based in Glasgow office. Extensive experience of corporate recovery and insolvency work for over 10 years. Principally involved in receiverships and larger administrations and liquidations and restructuring work. Recent matters include the administration of Atlantic Telecom Group plc and Arthur D Little Limited. The receiverships of the Buko Group, APC, Oregon Developments, CRT Displays Group, Blue Sky Technology, Gilcomston Construction, Omnia Books, liquidation of Atlantic Telecom Group plc, acquisition of the assets of Applecraft Limited from receivership, acquisition of the assets of Aerpac (UK) (In Administration), advising the board of Semple Cochrane plc.
Career: Trained at *Allan McDougall and Co*; qualified 1988; University of Glasgow (LLB, Dip LP); assistant *McGrigor Donald* 1989-92; assistant/associate/partner *Dundas and Wilson* 1992-97; partner *Maclay Murray and Spens* 1997.
Personal: Born 1964. Running, walking, tennis, golf.

HUNT, Matthew
Hunt & Morgan, Cardiff
(029) 20341234

HYDE, Mark
Clifford Chance, London
(020) 7600 1000
mark.hyde@cliffordchance.com
Specialisation: Litigation and Resolution Department, Banking and Finance. Partner specialising in contentious and non-contentious insolvency work and restructuring work often with a cross-border element.
Career: Articled *Philip Conway Thomas*; joined *Clifford Turner* on qualification in 1984; admitted to practice in Hong Kong and Brunei; Partner since 1993.
Personal: Bootham School, York; 1980 Birmingham University (LLB Hons).

JACKSON, Mark
DLA, Leeds
(08700) 111111

JAMES, Jim
Ward Hadaway, Newcastle upon Tyne
(0191) 204 4000
Specialisation: (i) Extensive experience in advising lenders, companies, directors, individuals and creditors on the options available when a business is in crisis or has failed. Has advised banks, insolvency practitioners, directors and creditors on issues as diverse as receiverships of quoted companies, voluntary arrangements for "ex" multi-millionaires and negotiations with banks when businesses are in financial difficulty. Has also been involved in major litigation involving complex construction frauds.(ii) Experience in dealing with Directors' Disqualification and attending creditors' meetings on behalf of creditors. (iii) Is also the partner responsible for the management of the firm's debt collection unit.
Prof. Memberships: Member of Law Society, associate member of R3.
Career: University of Bristol BSc in Politics. Qualified 1990. Employed at *Walker Morris* 1988-98. Joined *Ward Hadaway* 1998 as a partner.

JEFFRIES, Graham
Bond Pearce, Southampton
(023) 8082 8868
gjeffries@bondpearce.com
See under Banking & Finance, p.106

JEFFRIES, Jonathan
Pinsent Curtis Biddle, Leeds
(0113) 244 5000
jonathan.jeffries@pinsents.com
Specialisation: Partner, licensed insolvency practitioner, heavily involved with financial institutions. Advises insolvency practitioners on all aspects of insolvency, and banks and other financial institutions on re-financing and security. Acted for the directors of DC Cook Group plc; the administrators of United Kitchens plc; receivers of O'Hare Limited, the administrator of Evans Group Limited and the administrators of Famous Army Stores. Also successfully managed turnaround for a number of major corporates. Advises a number of banks on financial recovery strategies. Presents workshops to banks and accountants on corporate recovery, debt recovery and banking law.
Prof. Memberships: Fellow of the Association of Business Recovery Professionals - R3; Fellow of the Insolvency Practitioners Association; Member of the Education Courses and Conference Committee of R3.
Career: Qualified 1983. *Pinsent Curtis Biddle* 1981 to date.

JONES, Calum
Boyds, Glasgow
(0141) 221 8251
calum.jones@boydslaw.com
Specialisation: Head of the Corporate and Insolvency Department and areas of work cover insolvency (both contentious and non-contentious), corporate finance, debt factoring and invoice dis-

THE LEADERS ■ INSOLVENCY

counting. Acted for: the Receivers of Scotcrest Ltd during the trading of the business and its ultimate sale; the Administrator of Motherwell Football Club; the management of one of Scotland's biggest mining companies in restructuring the business and turning it around; the Liquidator of Apollo Engineering Limited in developing a CVA proposal and having it approved by the creditors; the former Receiver of Glen Scotia Whisky Distillery Co. Limited and the firm of Pannell Kerr Forster in defending an action for negligence being pursued by the Liquidator; the Accountant in Bankruptcy in connection with two landmark cases involving the rights of trustees and of the beneficiaries of deceased debtors and the rights of trustees and of secured creditors; the largest independent debt factoring business in action against its fraud insurers which created precedent in this area. Calum Jones was also asked to assist the Scottish Law Commission in its comments on the Law Commission report on Electronic Commerce. The Law Commission was particularly concerned to ensure that the position of factors who are increasingly dealing with their clients electronically, was not ignored.
Prof. Memberships: Accredited by the Law Society of Scotland as a specialist in Insolvency Law. Member of Insolvency Lawyers Association. Subscriber member of Association of Business Recovery Professionals (R3). Committee member of Scottish Committee of R3. Secretary of Glasgow Insolvency Forum. Convener of Law Society of Scotland Insolvency Conference.
Career: Trained, *Kidstons & Co* ; Qualified 1989; partner in present firm, 1999. 1987-89, trainee solicitor, *Kidstons & Co* , 1989-90, assistant solicitor, *Kidstons & Co* ; (litigation); 1990-91, associate, *Kidstons & Co* ; (insolvency); 1991-99, partner, *Kidstons & Co* (Head of Corporate Law and Insolvency); 1999-date, partner, *Boyds* (Head of Corporate and Insolvency).
Personal: Main leisure activities: reading, walking, gardening and golf.

JOYCE, John
Addleshaw Booth & Co, Manchester
(0161) 934 6180
john.joyce@addleshawbooth.com
Specialisation: Head of corporate recovery practice. Deals with all non-contentious and contentious aspects of corporate insolvency work as well as corporate reconstructions and turnaround.
Career: Qualified 1988. Joined firm as Partner in 1998.
Personal: Educated at De La Salle College Salford and Manchester University (1985 LLB Hons). Law Society Finals (1986 Second Class Hons). Resides Chorley.

KEARNEY, Mary Frances
McManus Kearney, Belfast
(028) 9024 3658
kearney@mcmk.co.uk
Specialisation: Licensed Insolvency Practitioner. Specialised in all aspects of personal and corporate insolvency. Also handles general corporate work. Advisor to Insolvency Practitioners.
Prof. Memberships: Law Society of Northern Ireland and Committee Member of the Association of Business Recovery Professionals.
Career: Qualified in April 1986. Partner in the firm of *McManus Kearney* in 1990. Authorised by Law Society of Northern Ireland to carry on insolvency practice since 1996.

KEITLEY, Nicholas
Blake Lapthorn, Southampton
(023) 8063 1823

KELLY, Susan
Hammond Suddards Edge, Manchester
(0161) 830 5000

LAYCOCK, Andrew
Carrick Read Insolvency, Leeds
(0113) 246 7123

LE BAS, Malcolm
Paris Smith & Randall, Southampton
(023) 8048 2482

LOWE, Rita
CMS Cameron McKenna, London
(020) 7367 2798
rita.lowe@cmck.com
Specialisation: Member of the banking department of *CMS Cameron McKenna*, specialising in insolvency and corporate reconstruction.
Prof. Memberships: Association member of R3 (Association of Business Recovery Professionals); member of Education, Courses & Conferences committee of R3; member of Insol Europe.
Career: Queens University Belfast (LLB); University of London (LLM). Called to the Inn of Court of Northern Ireland and converted to solicitor in 1993.
Publications: Associate editor of 'Insolvency Law & Practice'. Contributor to other publications.
Personal: Married with four children.

MACFARLANE, John
McGrigor Donald, Edinburgh
(0131) 777 7000

MALLON, Christopher
Weil, Gotshal & Manges, London
(020) 7903 1180
christopher.mallon@weil.com
Specialisation: Partner and head of London office's restructuring practice. All areas of insolvency law and asset tracing. Particular expertise in cross-border insolvency and complex bank fraud.
Prof. Memberships: Insolvency Lawyers Association, City of London Solicitors Company.
Career: Qualified in Australia in 1982. Practised at *Jackson McDonald*, Perth, 1982-85, *Allen & Overy* 1985-86. Joined *Lovell White & King* 1987. Admitted in England 1987. *Biddle* July 1995-99. *Freshfields* 1999-2001.
Personal: Born 6 May 1956. Attended Aquinas College, Perth, Western Australia and the University of Western Australia. Lives in Stockwell.

MANNING, Peter
Simmons & Simmons, London
(020) 7628 2020
peter.manning@simmons-simmons.com
Specialisation: Partner, corporate recovery. Corporate insolvency, reconstructions, banking and security reviews. Regular lecturer on banking and insolvency issues. Recent instructions include GTS/Esprit Telecom, Railtrack, Enron (for the purchaser of its metals division) and ITV Digital.
Prof. Memberships: Law Society, Association of Business Recovery Professionals, Insolvency Lawyers Association.
Career: Qualified 1986. Partner *Alsop Wilkinson* 1990 to 1999. Joined *Simmons & Simmons* in 1999 as a partner.
Personal: Born 1959. Attended Hertford College, Oxford 1978-82.

MARSHALL, J Richard
Lupton Fawcett, Leeds
(0113) 280 2000

MAY, Philip
TLT Solicitors, Bristol
(0117) 917 7912
pmay@tltsolicitors.com
Specialisation: Acts for official receivers and insolvency practitioners nationally. Also acts in relation to corporate restructuring and recovery. For biographical details see Litigation (Commercial) section.

MCCARTHY, Michael
Richards Butler, London
(020) 7772 5738
mpm@richardsbutler.com
Specialisation: Specialises in both contentious and non-contentious insolvency matters, dealing with administrations, administrative receiverships, liquidations and in particular provisional liquidations on behalf of the Official Receiver. Acts for major clearing banks as well as insolvency practitioners from the major accountancy firms. Acted for Liquidators of GlobalCentre (UK) Limited (part of Global Crossing) and the Administrative Receivers of Jentique Furniture Limited, and for the Official Receiver in various high profile Provisional Liquidations.
Prof. Memberships: Insolvency Lawyers Association.
Career: Qualified 1989; Associate Partner, *Dibb Lupton Broomhead* -1991; partner, *Hill Taylor Dickinson* -1993; partner, *Richards Butler* 1999.
Personal: Finchley Catholic High School; Southampton University LLB (Hons) 2:1; Law Society Finals (Hons). Interests: films, gardening. Married with two children. Lives in London.

MCGEEVER, Brendan
Gateley Wareing, Birmingham
(0121) 234 0000

MCGURK, Anthony
Eversheds, Cambridge
(01223) 443 204
anthonymcgurk@eversheds.com
Specialisation: Handles all aspects of corporate insolvency and reconstruction work, including acting for insolvency practitioners in connection with administrative receiverships, LPA receiverships, administrations, IVAs and liquidations. In addition, specialises in company/corporate work, including mergers and acquisitions and fundraising, in particular with regard to start up and early stage companies.
Prof. Memberships: Eastern Region Committee member of ABRR; Institute of Directors.
Career: Qualified in September 1989. Became a partner at *Eversheds* in May 1995 and relocated to the Cambridge office in December 1998.
Personal: Educated at Downside School, Nr. Bath, Graduated in Law from Hull University. Obtained First Class Honours in Law Society finals.

MCNICOL, Stephen
Robert Muckle, Newcastle upon Tyne
(0191) 244 2904
smcnicol@robertmuckle.co.uk
See under Banking & Finance, p.107

MCNIVEN, Alan
Paull & Williamsons, Aberdeen
(01224) 621621
armcniven@paull-williamsons.co.uk
Specialisation: Partner in corporate department, specialising in company acquisitions/disposals/investment; MBOs, MBIs; reconstructions; general corporate and insolvency law. Licensed insolvency practitioner and accredited by Law Society as insolvency specialist.
Prof. Memberships: Law Society of Scotland; Society of Advocates in Aberdeen; Joint Insolvency Specialists Group.
Career: Apprentice *AC Bennett & Son*, Edinburgh 1972-74; joined *Paull & Williamsons* 1974 (partner since 1980).
Personal: Educated Alloa Academy (1962-68); Edinburgh University (1968-72). Married with three children. Leisure interests: golf, football, skiing.

MONTGOMERY, Nigel
DLA, London
(08700) 111 111

MORRIS, Howard
Denton Wilde Sapte, London
(020) 7246 7000

MUDD, Philip
Walker Morris, Leeds
(0113) 283 2500
Specialisation: Head of banking and insolvency department. Deals with insolvency and banking issues for lenders, insolvency practitioners and corporate clients with an emphasis on debt restructuring and corporate rescue in addition to mainstream insolvency, lending and realisation work. Recent work includes administrations of US and UK listed EuroTelecom Corporation Limited, and UK listed companies Totalise plc and IMS Group plc. Acted for the purchaser on rescue of Hull City AFC. Speaker at

461

INSOLVENCY ■ THE LEADERS

local and regional R3 conferences.
Prof. Memberships: Fellow of Association of Business Recovery Professionals; member, Insolvency Lawyers Association; Licensed Insolvency Practitioner.
Personal: Born 19 January 1959. Attended Bristol University 1977-80. Leisure interests include music, skiing and sailing. Lives in Huddersfield.

MUMFORD, Nicola
Wragge & Co, Birmingham
(0870) 903 1000

MUNRO, Rick
Lamport Bassitt, Southampton
(023) 8083 7777
rick.munro@lamportbassitt.co.uk
Specialisation: Rick Munro covers all aspects of corporate and personal insolvency, particularly in liquidations and bankruptcies; fraud/asset tracing work; acting primarily for insolvency practitioners. Recent work includes acting for liquidators in preference, transaction at under value and wrongful trading claims against former directors, acting for trustees in bankruptcy in realising assets such as the matrimonial home and personal pension policies.
Prof. Memberships: Hampshire Incorporated Law Society; Association of Business Recovery Professionals; Accredited mediator with CEDR and ADR Group.
Career: Qualified in 1992 following articles with *Lovells*; assistant solicitor with *Lovells*, London (1992-94) and in Hong Kong (1994-97); joined *Lamport Bassitt* in January 1998. Partner in January 2000.
Publications: Contributor to Tolley's 'Insolvency Law and Practice'.
Personal: Born 1967. Birmingham University (LLB Hons) 1985-88. Married with two children. Interests include cricket, golf, diving.

NICHOLSON, Mark
Nicholsons, Lowestoft
(01502) 532 324
mnicholson@nicholsons-uk.com
Specialisation: Bankruptcy and personal insolvency and liquidations. Acts for insolvency practitioners.
Career: Qualified May 1977. Licensed insolvency practitioner.
Personal: Born 14 June 1952.

NIEKIRK, Malcolm
Lester Aldridge, Southampton
(023) 8082 0405
malcolm.niekirk@lester-aldridge.co.uk
Specialisation: Head of the corporate recovery and insolvency team. Licensed insolvency practitioner. Deals almost exclusively with non-contentious corporate insolvency, including turnaround work and restructuring as well as the full range of formal insolvency procedures. Usually advises banks and other financial institutions, insolvency practitioners and sometimes businesses buying assets from receivers and companies in financial difficulties. He has received public attention for his work with insolvent football clubs. Occasional conference speaker. Supports plain English drafting. One of his documents was commended in the 1999 Clarity awards.
Career: Articled *Moore & Blatch*, Southampton; qualified 1987. Joined *Lester Aldridge* 1990. Partner 1994. Insolvency practitioners licence 1998.
Personal: Born 1963. Educated Royal Grammar School, High Wycombe; Southampton University (1984 LLB Hons). Lives in Lyndhurst.

NORLEY, Lyndon
Kirkland & Ellis, London
(020) 7816 8851
lyndon_norley@uk.kirkland.com
Specialisation: Partner, member of the firm's Restructuring, Workout & Bankruptcy Group; specialising in insurance insolvency and reorganisations, bond restructuring and general insolvency.
Prof. Memberships: Insolvency Lawyers Association; Association of Business Recovery Professionals; International Association of Insurance Receivers; European Insolvency Practitioners Association.
Career: Trained *Clifford Chance*, qualified 1992; solicitor *Cadwalader Wickersham & Taft* 1997-2000; partner 2000; Partner, *Kirkland & Ellis* 2002.
Personal: University of London; College of Law.

OBANK, Richard
DLA, Leeds
(08700) 111111

OLIVER, David
Blake Lapthorn, Portsmouth
(023) 9222 1122

PALLETT, Julian
Wragge & Co, Birmingham
(0870) 903 1000

PAY, Alex
Morgan Cole, Cardiff
(029) 2038 5385

PENNIE, John
Dickinson Dees, Newcastle upon Tyne
(0191) 279 9255
john.pennie@dickinson-dees.com
Specialisation: A specialist in both personal and corporate insolvency, heading a team of nine lawyers. JIEB Moderator in personal insolvency. Member of the Law Society Insolvency Authorisation Casework Committee. Licensed insolvency practitioner.
Prof. Memberships: Law Society, Fellow of the Association of Business Recovery Professionals.
Career: MA (Cantab). Partner with *Dickinson Dees* since 1985.

PHEASANT, Louise
Eversheds, Birmingham
(0121) 232 1154
louisepheasant@eversheds.com
Specialisation: Banking, corporate recovery and insolvency. Acts for lenders and insolvency practitioners on all aspects of insolvency law, reconstructions, security and asset realisations.
Prof. Memberships: R3, Association of Business Recovery Professionals.
Career: Birmingham University (1st Class Hons). Midland Bank plc 1979-83; BBC 1983-84; *Eversheds* 1988. Became partner in 1997.
Personal: Cinema, contemporary art, West Bromwich Albion.

PIKE, Nicholas
Lawrence Graham, London
(020) 7379 0000

POTTER, Bruce
Morgan Cole, Reading
(0118) 955 3000

PRESTON, Dermot
Hammond Suddards Edge, Manchester
(0161) 830 5000

RAJANI, Shashi
Davies Arnold Cooper, London
(020) 7648 9000
shashi.rajani@ngj.co.uk
Specialisation: All aspects of corporate rescue and insolvency matters, acting for accountants and banking and corporate clients. Also advises banking and individual clients on personal insolvency matters. Particularly skilled in director disqualification cases and international aspects of turnarounds and insolvencies. Acts as consultant to the other departments and groups of the firm on insolvency matters. Licensed Insolvency Practitioner since 1986.
Prof. Memberships: The Law Society, including Chief Insolvency Assessor; The City of London Solicitor's Company; The City of London Law Society and its Insolvency Law Sub-Committee; Association of Business Recovery Professionals (R3) and its Membership Committee; INSOL International; INSOL Europe; Appeal Committee of ACCA.
Career: Partner and head of corporate rescue and insolvency group from 1994 to date. In practice as an advocate in Dar es Salaam, Tanzania and Tabora (1956-64). Appointed in 1964 to the Tanzanian Civil Service as Assistant Administrator General. Promoted to Senior Assistant Administrator General in 1967. Coopers & Lybrand London as manager in insolvency department (1970-77). *Linklaters & Paines*, senior assistant solicitor (1977-88). *Cameron Markby Hewitt*, partner (1989-93); *Nicholson Graham & Jones*, partner (1994-2002); partner and Head of Business Recovery Group, *Davies Arnold Cooper* since May 2002.
Publications: Author of Tolley's 'Corporate Insolvency Law Handbook' (1990); Tolley's 'Corporate Insolvency' (1995); chapters in Tolley's 'Company Law on Insolvency'; chapter in 'Theory & Practice' (Sweet & Maxwell, 1993) on 'Equitable Assistance in the Search for Security' in insolvency law; and Tolley's 'Insolvency Fees and Costs' (1995-2000). Chief editor of Tolley's 'Insolvency Law & Practice' and joint consulting editor of Tolley's 'Insolvency Law' (1996). Writes for a number of international journals.

READETT, Helen
Martineau Johnson, Birmingham
(0121) 678 1576
helen.readett@martjohn.com
Specialisation: Advises insolvency practitioners on all types of insolvency work and banks and lending institutions on putting security in place and maximising realisations.
Prof. Memberships: Licensed insolvency practitioner and member R3. Law Society member.
Career: Qualified 1982. *Edge Ellison* partner until 1998. Now with *Martineau Johnson*.
Personal: Married with young son.

REES, Bleddyn
Morgan Cole, Cardiff
(029) 2038 5385

RIDLER, Graham
Eversheds, Leeds
(0113) 243 0391
ridlerg@eversheds.com
Specialisation: Partner and head of insolvency for Leeds. Advises insolvency practitioners on both contentious and non-contentious insolvency work. Advises banks on security and intensive care issues. Particular specialism in receivership, administration and corporate restructuring work.
Prof. Memberships: Law Society, SPI.
Career: Leicester University LLB (Hons), qualified 1987 - joined *Pinsent Curtis*, made partner 1993, joined *Eversheds* as partner in 1996.
Personal: Resides Leeds, leisure interests include golf, shooting and weight training.

ROOME, James
Bingham McCutchen LLP (formerly Bingham Dana LLP), London
(020) 7661 5317
james.roome@bingham.com
Specialisation: Partner in financial restructuring group. Corporate law, including insolvency and reconstructions. Specialist experience in corporate insolvency, including work-outs and reconstructions. Particular experience in multinational insolvency and bondholder representations. He is a licensed insolvency practitioner and has spoken at conferences on topics ranging from professional liability to financial institution insolvency.
Personal: Born 7 October 1958.

ROSS, Alexander
John McKee & Son, Belfast
(028) 9023 2303
lex_ross@jmckee.co.uk
Specialisation: Advises banks and financial institutions on lending and security matters and has particular expertise in acting for funders in private finance initiative work. Also advises insolvency practitioners, particularly administrative receivers, on all legal matters arising from corporate recovery and insolvency including sales of businesses and assets and claims by creditors.
Prof. Memberships: Law Society of

Northern Ireland.
Career: Qualified 1967; Partner in *John McKee & Son* from 1972.
Personal: Born 23 December 1942. Educated at Strathallan School, Perthshire and Queens University, Belfast.

ROXBURGH, Roy
Iain Smith & Company, Aberdeen
(01224) 654831
roy@iainsmith.com
Specialisation: Partner in Company and Commercial Department. Main areas of practice are mergers and takeovers, MBOs, MBIs and corporate insolvency, acting for both purchasers and vendors of businesses, investors both private and institutional, and receiverships. Involvement in insolvency is generally on a specialist basis. Author of a chapter on diligence for the ICAS 'Insolvency Case Book'. Convener 1993 to 1995 of the Law Society/ ICAS's Insolvency Specialist Group.
Prof. Memberships: Law Society of Scotland (Member of Insolvency Solicitors Committee since 1992, and Insolvency Specialist Accreditation Panel since 1994), R3 (Member of Scottish Technical Committee).
Career: Qualified in 1974. Joined *Iain Smith & Co* as a Partner in 1977. External Examiner JIEB from 1993 (administration and Receiverships) to 2000. Notary Public.
Personal: Born 29 September 1950. Educated at Dunfermline High School 1961-68 and Edinburgh University 1968-72. Recreations include skiing, golf, bridge, chess and football. Lives in Aberdeen.

RUSHWORTH, Jonathan
Slaughter and May, London
(020) 7600 1200
jonathan.rushworth@slaughterandmay.com
Specialisation: Partner with a wide-ranging company, corporate finance and capital markets practice both domestic and international, acting in particular for listed and other companies, for partnerships and also for corporate trustees in capital markets issues. He has a particular interest and specialisation in corporate recovery and insolvency work, advising companies and their directors, banks and other creditors and also insolvency practitioners on refinancing and insolvency issues. His practice involves domestic, overseas and cross-border insolvency matters. He has been involved in numerous large restructurings and insolvencies, in particular acting for the administrators of the Barings Group and Railtrack plc. He has lectured extensively on the subjects of corporate recovery and insolvency, written many papers on the subject and has written a book on receivership.
Prof. Memberships: Creditors' Rights Committee of the International Bar Association and the Law Society's Standing Committee on Company Law.

SANDERSON, Gordon
Dickinson Dees, Newcastle upon Tyne
(0191) 279 9348
law@dickinson-dees.com
Specialisation: Practice covers advising banks and other lending institutions on all aspects of personal and corporate recovery, term loan and other security documentation, enforceability of directors guarantees and other third party security and general banking issues.
Career: Qualified 1985. Joined *Dickinson Dees* in January 1990. Became partner in 1993 and head of firm's banking unit in 1995. Former lecturer in Banking Law at the University of Northumbria.

SCHAFFER, Danny
Isadore Goldman, London
(020) 7242 3000

SEGAL, Nicholas A
Allen & Overy, London
(020) 7330 3000
nick.segal@allenovery.com
Specialisation: Partner dealing with banking, commercial law, reconstruction and insolvency with an emphasis on international restructurings; worked on restructuring of BCCI, Heron Group and Queens Moat House; recently involved in major restructurings in Thailand and Russia, insolvency proceedings in England, USA and Cayman and cross-border litigation in England/USA.
Personal: St Peter's College, Oxford (1979 MA First Class). Born 1956.

SELIGMAN, George
Slaughter and May, London
(020) 7600 1200
george.seligman@slaughterandmay.com
Specialisation: Secured and unsecured loan financings, securitisations, structured financings, banking advisory matters, restructuring and insolvency.
Career: Partner in *Slaughter and May* since 1984.

SHANDRO, Sandy
Freshfields Bruckhaus Deringer, London
(020) 7936 4000
sandy.shandro@freshfields.com
Specialisation: Partner in Restructuring and Insolvency Group. Advises on all aspects of insolvency from risk-avoidance to formal insolvencies to restructuring. Also advises officeholders in formal insolvency proceedings. Much cross-border experience. Fluent French. Frequent speaker and author. Member of editorial board of Receivers, Administrators & Liquidators Quarterly.
Prof. Memberships: Vice Chairman, City of London Law Society Insolvency Law Sub-Committee, Insolvency Lawyer's Association, INSOL and INSOL Europe, R3, Canadian Bar Association.
Career: Qualified in 1978 (British Columbia) and 1992 (England & Wales). Solicitor Advocate. CEDR Accredited Mediator.
Personal: Born 1951. Educated in Canada (BA, Alberta, 1972; MA McGill, 1974) and at Oxford University (BA 1976, BCL 1978). Past President, Canada-UK Chamber of Commerce. Lives in London.

SHAW, Murray
Biggart Baillie, Glasgow
(0141) 228 8000

SHORT, John
Taylor Vinters, Cambridge
(01223) 225 158
john.short@taylorvinters.com
See under Corporate Finance, p.246

SLEIGH, Andrew
Burness, Glasgow
(0141) 248 4933

SMITH, Gillian
Foot Anstey Sargent, Exeter
(01392) 411221
gillian.smith@foot-ansteys.co.uk
Specialisation: Handles all aspects of personal and corporate insolvency, contentious and non-contentious, particularly personal contentious work. Acts for major national insolvency practitioners and for the Insolvency Service in conducting directors' disqualification proceedings under the CDDA 1986. Interested in agricultural insolvency. Law Society CPD course assessor.
Prof. Memberships: Law Society.
Career: BA Birmingham University. Qualified in 1981. LLM at University College London, before moving to Devon in 1982. Partner with *Foot Anstey Sargent* since 1989. Licensed insolvency practitioner since 1990.
Personal: Leisure interests include riding, sailing and skiing.

SMITH, Phillip
Boyes Turner, Reading
(0118) 959 7711

SOMEKH, Peter
DLA, Liverpool
(08700) 111111

SPENCER, Robin
Lovells, London
(020) 7296 2000
robin.spencer@lovells.com
Specialisation: Insolvency and business restructuring group specialising in general insolvency, insurance, company reconstruction, insurance-related insolvency matters and troubled financial services companies, as well as other more general types of insolvency and restructuring. Major assignments include Mentor Insurance Limited; Drexel Burnham Lambert Group; British & Commonwealth Merchant Bank plc; OIC Run-Off (formerly The Orion Insurance Company plc); The London and Overseas Insurance Company Ltd; Sovereign Marine & General Insurance Company Limited; New Cap Reinsurance Corporation (Bermuda) Limited and New Cap Re (Australia); Equitable Life Assurance Society; TransTec; Japan Leasing; RBG Resources plc (in liquidation).
Prof. Memberships: Member of International Association of Insurance Receivers, Association of Business Recovery Professionals.
Career: Qualified as Barrister 1981; solicitors' office HM Customs & Excise 1983-86; joined *Lovells* 1987 (including two year secondment to *Appleby, Spurling & Kempe*, attorneys, Bermuda); requalified as solicitor 1991; partner 1994.
Personal: Born 1958. Educated at Birkenhead School (1969-76); Pembroke College, Cambridge (1980 BA Hons (Cantab)); 1984 MA (Cantab)). Resides Chesham, Buckinghamshire.

SPENCER, Shân
DLA, Manchester
(08700) 111111

STEINBERG, David
Clifford Chance, London
(020) 7600 1000
david.steinberg@cliffordchance.com
Specialisation: Banking and Finance Department. Partner specialising in insurance reconstruction and insolvency, general restructuring and general insolvency.
Career: Articled *Clifford Chance*; qualified 1988; Partner since 1994.
Personal: King Edward VI Grammar School, Southampton; 1983 St John's College, Cambridge (BA Hons 2(1)).

STEINER, Michael
Denton Wilde Sapte, London
(020) 7242 1212

STEWART, Gordon
Allen & Overy, London
(020) 7330 3000
gordon.stewart@allenovery.com
Specialisation: Partner dealing with all types of corporate and personal insolvency, reconstruction, reorganisation and turnaround work, acting for banks and other financial institutions, insolvency practitioners, corporations and private individuals.
Prof. Memberships: Society of Practitioners of Insolvency (past President); Chairman of Law Society's insolvency law sub-committee.
Career: Articled *Cameron Markby*; qualified 1980; solicitor and partner *Cameron Markby* 1980-88; partner *Allen & Overy* 1989, Head of Business Reconstruction and Insolvency Group; past president of the Society of Practitioners of Insolvency (SPT) - now the Association of Business Recovery Professionals (R3).
Publications: Author of 'Administrative Receivers and Administrators', published CCH Editions Limited 1987; contributor to 'Leasing Law in the European Union', published by Euromoney Books 1994; contributor of legal update column to 'Recovery', the quarterly journal of SPI.
Personal: University College, Oxford (MA 1977). Born 1956.

STOBART, Guy
Burges Salmon, Bristol
(0117) 939 2241
guy.stobart@burges-salmon.com
Specialisation: Corporate rescue and recovery and general insolvency. Major clients include Lloyds TSB, Bank of Scotland and Standard Chartered Bank. His finance work also covers a diverse spectrum of banking transactions and general banking law.
Prof. Memberships: Law Society, mem-

INSOLVENCY ■ THE LEADERS

ber of the Association of Business Recovery Professionals and the Insolvency Lawyers Association and a licensed insolvency practitioner.
Career: Trained and worked at *Slaughter and May* for five years before joining *Burges Salmon* in 1983, becoming a partner in 1986. He was managing partner from 1995-99.

TAYLOR, Andrew
asb law, Brighton
(01273) 828000

TAYLOR, Elizabeth
Darbys, Oxford
(01865) 811 711
etaylor@darbys.co.uk
Specialisation: Deals with all aspects of individual and corporate insolvency, from administration to IVAs. Acts for a number of insolvency practitioners.
Prof. Memberships: Law Society; LawNet Insolvency Unit; Member of the Association of Business Recovery Professionals. Licenced insolvency practitioner.
Career: Qualified 1992. Oxford University. Partner *Parrott & Coales* 1997-1999. Joined *Darbys* as a Partner September 1999.

TETTMAR, Victor
Bond Pearce, Bristol
(0117) 929 9197
vtettmar@bondpearce.com
Specialisation: Partner and Head of the Banking and Insolvency Group. Licensed insolvency practitioner and Registered Property Receiver specialising in all aspects of insolvency, bank recovery and turnaround. Particular expertise in corporate insolvency, security issues, restructuring and the agribusiness sector.
Prof. Memberships: Full member of the Association of Business Recovery Professionals (R3) and Chairman of South West and South Wales region; Council member of the Insolvency Lawyers Association and member of the Non Administrative Receivers Association.
Career: Manchester University. Remained with *Bond Pearce* on qualifying in 1985, becoming Partner 1991.
Publications: Editor of Jordans' 'Agricultural Lending: Security and Enforcement' published 1999. Co-author of Distribution chapter in 'Tolley's Insolvency Law'.

TWEMLOW, Tony
Cuff Roberts, Liverpool
(0151) 237 7777

TYRELL, Vivien
D J Freeman, London
(020) 7583 4055

VAUGHAN, Philip
Eversheds, Cardiff
(029) 2047 1147
Specialisation: Practice covers a wide-range of non-contentious banking and finance work and includes transactional work (including acquisition finance), regulatory advice and drafting of standard documentation for banks, building societies, centralised mortgage lenders and finance companies. Has a particular expertise in consumer credit work. Also involved in a wide range of non-contentious insolvency work acting for receivers, administrators and liquidators and advising lenders on enforcement of security and restructuring/refinancings.
Career: Qualified 1984. Formerly with *Clifford Chance* and National Westminster Bank Legal Department. Joined current firm in 1987 and became partner in 1988.
Personal: Born 14 December 1958. Educated at Haverfordwest Grammar School, St Edmund Hall, Oxford (M.A.) and Emmanuel College, Cambridge (LLM).

VERRILL, John
Lawrence Graham, London
(020) 7379 0000

WAINE, Ian
Prettys, Ipswich
(01473) 232 121
iwaine@prettys.co.uk
Specialisation: Main areas of work include company law, mergers, acquisitions and reorganisations, corporate finance MBOs, insolvency and advice on directors' responsibilities. Works with both private and public companies.
Prof. Memberships: A Member of the IP City Initiative, and active with the rapidly growing Ipswich Cambridge Hi Tech sector.
Career: Qualified 1986. Partner at *Prettys* since 1989.

WALLER, Simon
Eversheds, Manchester
(0161) 831 8000
simonwaller@eversheds.com
Specialisation: Partner; National Head of corporate recovery and insolvency. Specialises in insolvency and corporate reconstruction. Acts for all of the main accountancy practices and for a number of banks and secondary lenders; previously acted (whilst at *Wilde Sapte*) for the receivers of Leyland Daf Limited and the administrators of Paramount Airways Limited amongst others. Currently advising the administrator of Bury FC, the receivers of Lampies Limited (childrens TV programme) and BDO Stoywood as administrators of Power X Limited.
Prof. Memberships: SPI.
Career: Articled *Booth & Co*; qualified 1989; *Wilde Sapte* to 1996; partner *Halliwell Landau* 1996-98; partner *Eversheds* 1998; sits on editorial board of 'Receivers, Administrators and Liquidators Quarterly'.
Personal: St Cuthbert's School; Durham University (BA Hons Law). Interests include sport, cinema and reading. Resides Didsbury, has one daughter.

WALSH, Jeremy
Travers Smith Braithwaite, London
(020) 7295 3500
Jeremy.Walsh@TraversSmith.com
Specialisation: Partner specialising in corporate rescue, reconstruction and insolvency, acting for banks, companies, insolvency practitioners, creditors and investors. Has wide experience including rescues, reconstructions, administrations, receiverships, liquidations, voluntary arrangements and schemes of arrangement. Licensed insolvency practitioner since 1994.
Prof. Memberships: Law Society; Association of Business Recovery Professionals; Insolvency Lawyers Association; INSOL Europe; International Bar Association.
Career: Qualified in 1985. Partner in *Travers Smith Braithwaite* since 1994.
Personal: Born 4 November 1960. University of Manchester. Interests include family, films, theatre, swimming and music.

WHEATLEY, Jamie
Mills & Reeve, Cambridge
(01223) 222206
jamie.wheatley@mills-reeve.com
Specialisation: Practises in commercial and insolvency litigation.

WHITE, John
CMS Cameron McKenna, London
(020) 7367 3000
john.white@cmck.com
Specialisation: Partner and head of banking and insolvency group. Insolvency work includes multi-bank support operations, administrations and administrative receiverships. Banking work includes clearing bank lending, property and project finance, trade finance and syndicated facilities. Acted for the administrators of Polly Peck, the examiner of the Maxwell Communication Corporation, the administrators of Air Europe and the Department of Transport on Railtrack. Addresses around 20 conferences per year.
Prof. Memberships: Law Society; Chartered Institute of Bankers; R3, Insolvency Lawyers Association; International Bar Association; City of London Solicitors Company; Insol International; Insol Europe; International Insolvency Institute.
Career: Qualified in 1963. Having joined the firm in 1957, became a partner in 1964. Fellow of the Chartered Institute of Bankers.
Personal: Born 6 July 1938. Leisure interests include hockey, cricket and port. Lives in London. Clubs: Athenaeum and West Herts.

WILKINSON, Andrew
Cadwalader, Wickersham & Taft, London
(020) 7170 8740
andrew.wilkinson@cwt-uk.com
Specialisation: Partner in the London Financial Restructuring Department, Managing Partner of the London offices and a member of the firm's management committee. Mr Wilkinson has wide experience in both insurance restructuring and general restructuring and insolvency. He has pioneered the use of schemes of arrangement for the work out of troubled insurance companies and is currently acting for investment banks, related hedge funds and insolvency practitioners on general restructuring and insolvency matters. He is a licensed insolvency practitioner. He also writes and lectures extensively on all aspects of restructuring and insolvency.
Prof. Memberships: CLLS insolvency law sub-committee.
Career: Graduate of Jesus College, Oxford. Joined *Cadwalader* in 1998 from a major City firm.

WILSON, Michael
Elliott Duffy Garrett, Belfast
(028) 9024 5034

WILTSHIRE, Peter
CMS Cameron McKenna, Bristol
(0117) 934 9300
prw@cmck.com
See under Banking & Finance, p.109

WITHYMAN, Tom
Lawrence Graham, London
(020) 7379 0000

WOOLF, Geoffrey
SJ Berwin, London
(020) 7809 2012
Specialisation: Partner in Banking Department. Principal area of practice is banking, corporate insolvency, reconstruction and debt restructuring. Advises a clearing bank on its standard forms and procedures. Has acted as an expert witness in a number of cases. Regularly speaks at conferences and publishes articles.
Career: Qualified in 1970 after articles at *Stephenson Harwood*. Former Head of the Property Department and former Finance Partner.
Personal: Born 1946. Educated at Harrow County Grammar School and King's College, London (LLB 1967).

YORKE, Jon
Richards Butler, London
(020) 7772 5925
jy@richardsbutler.com
Specialisation: Specialises in all aspects of corporate insolvency in particular receiverships, administrations, liquidations and voluntary arrangements. He has been involved in a number of larger insolvencies over the last decade with considerable involvement in cross border cases. In recent years he has specialised in the insolvency of insurance companies acting for PricewaterhouseCoopers in the North Atlantic and Black Sea and Baltic provisional liquidations.
Prof. Memberships: Society of Practitioners of Insolvency, Law Society European Insolvency Practitioners Association, Insolvency Lawyers Association.
Career: University of Essex LLB (Hons). Qualified as a solicitor 1986; licensed insolvency practitioner 1990; partner at *Richards Butler* 1992.
Personal: Cycling, skiing, sailing, paragliding and trying to get fit. Married with two children.

INSURANCE

London: 465; The Regions: 470; Scotland: 472; Profiles: 472

Research approved by BMRB For this edition, **Chambers'** researchers conducted 6,582 interviews – 3,900 with law firms, 511 with barristers and 2,171 with clients. The validity of the research was scrutinised by BMRB International, who audited both the methodology and the results at our offices in London. They interviewed **Chambers'** researchers and cross-checked sample interviews. Details of the audit appear on page 7.

OVERVIEW The insurance market has witnessed some adjustments this year. There have been job losses and many industry commentators consider this to be the start of a troubled period. It would be impossible to ignore the events of September 11th in helping to exacerbate this. However, the developments in the life assurance industry surrounding Equitable Life, and the insolvency of a number of insurers, including Independent Insurance, have also shaken up the market. Non-contentious lawyers have found it a lean year with relatively few major deals announced. For insurance insolvency specialists, however, and lawyers operating in the contentious side of the field, these are boom times. There has been a sharp increase in disputes and a hardening of attitudes amongst insurers and reinsurers. Looking forward, sources expect more insolvencies, and await the results of the FSA's review of the regulation of the industry with interest.

LONDON

GENERAL CLAIMS

INSURANCE: GENERAL CLAIMS
■ LONDON

1. Barlow Lyde & Gilbert
2. Clyde & Co
3. CMS Cameron McKenna
   Reynolds Porter Chamberlain
4. Herbert Smith
   Ince & Co
   Kennedys
5. Beachcroft Wansbroughs
   Clifford Chance
   Davies Arnold Cooper
   Freshfields Bruckhaus Deringer
   Holman Fenwick & Willan
   Lovells
   Mayer, Brown, Rowe & Maw
6. Berrymans Lace Mawer
   Charles Russell
   DJ Freeman
   Elborne Mitchell

LEADING INDIVIDUALS

1. **BAKES Martin** Herbert Smith
   GREENLEY Simon Reynolds Porter Chamberlain
   PAYTON Michael Clyde & Co
   SCHOFIELD Belinda CMS Cameron McKenna
2. **HIGGINS David** Herbert Smith
   SMITH Rod Clyde & Co
3. **CONNOLLY Sean** Mayer, Brown, Rowe & Maw
   FARTHING Peter Clyde & Co
   HARDY Tim Barlow Lyde & Gilbert
   KENDALL David DJ Freeman
   LEONARD Paul Freshfields Bruckhaus Deringer
   PARKER Raj Freshfields Bruckhaus Deringer
   PERRY Bill Charles Russell

This book is the product of 6,582 1/2 hour interviews. See p.7 for BMRB audit. Within each band, firms are listed alphabetically. See individuals' profiles p.472

BARLOW LYDE & GILBERT (see firm details p.858) This specialist insurance firm again gets the highest level of recommendation from peers and clients across all sectors. Aviation, marine and professional negligence are areas of expertise. This is, however, not a firm that produces a raft of star individuals, rather one that promotes a strong team ethos, which is the envy of many: "*an excellent practice, which can always offer superb levels of back-up.*" The team had a momentous twelve months in which it helped with the insurance-related repercussions of the World Trade Centre attacks. It has also advised on the cancellation of the Ryder Cup and assisted in contingency claims relating to the Wimbledon Championships 2002 and various music events. The team is heavily involved for insurers/reinsurers on the high-profile 'gap' film finance policies, in a case which involves trans Atlantic litigation and exposure in excess of $1 billion. Respected **Tim Hardy** (see p.474) is described by sources as "*effervescent, with enthusiasm for a wide spectrum of matters.*" **Clients** Ace Global Markets; Allianz Cornhill; Aon Holdings; Chartwell Group; Churchill Insurance; General Cologne Re; Hiscox Group; Lloyd's; Munich Re; St Paul's International Insurance; Zurich Municipal.

CLYDE & CO (see firm details p.913) The "*exceptional*" **Michael Payton** (see p.475) remains the "*much admired*" head of this successful insurance practice. It is renowned for its traditional skills in marine, aviation and professional negligence. The team has enjoyed a busy year with a number of high-profile cases and transactions and these days is regarded as "*only a cat's whisker*" behind Barlow Lyde & Gilbert in profile. The team has advised on the after-effects of the September 11th attacks, including acting for a Bermudan insurer on the Silverstein Insurance of the World Trade Centre. It has also acted on the conclusion in the House of Lords of the Piper Alpha litigation, where judgement was given in favour of Clyde & Co's clients and costs were recovered. The team contains a number of "*excellent people*" standing out in particular are the "*clever and brilliant*" **Peter Farthing** (see p.473) and **Rod Smith** (see p.476) ("*a safe pair of hands*"). **Clients** Ace; Hiscox; Equitas.

CMS CAMERON MCKENNA (see firm details p.914) Liam O'Connell leads this "*seasoned*" team, which has "*the great ability to step back and see the wider issues.*" It has provided liability matters and claims advice to large multinational companies following September 11th. The firm has also continued its efforts in an aviation-related patent infringement dispute, where the sums involved exceed $100 million. The ongoing 'gap' film finance dispute has also occupied this team. The "*busy and ebullient*" **Belinda Schofield** (see p.476) remains the name most often cited by peers; she is acting on behalf of the managing agents in a case to recover cash call sums due from underwriting names in P&B v Woolley. **Clients** Insurers.

REYNOLDS PORTER CHAMBERLAIN (see firm details p.1111) **Simon Greenley** (see p.474) continues to "*ride a wave of high-quality insurance work*" and retains his place as the leading light in this "*sizeable, talented*" firm. Handling a remarkable range of insurance clients, the firm received a number of instructions in the wake of the World Trade Centre attacks. It has also been involved in D&O transactions, primarily concerned with the high-profile failures in the insurance and pensions markets. Much of the workload features matters for Lloyd's insurers, and it has a niche strength in cases which concern claims against other solicitors' firms. **Clients** Black Sea & Baltic General Insurance Company; PwC; Stirling Cooke Brown.

HERBERT SMITH (see firm details p.992) Often found in the limelight over the past year, the firm retains its interest in high-value, complex cases which frequently have an international element. Solicitor advocate **David Higgins** (see p.474) ("*impressive to cross swords with*") leads this widely respected team. Its has represented Royal & SunAlliance on film finance-related matters. Sitting at the "*top of the tree,*" **Martin Bakes** (see p.472) was instructed by PwC, the provisional liquidators of Independent Insurance Company, advising them on various matters arising from the insolvency. The team also acted for Fortis Insurance regarding issues arising from the Selby rail crash. **Clients** Advizas; CGNU; Fortis Insurance; NTL; PwC; Royal & SunAlliance.

www.ChambersandPartners.com 465

INSURANCE ■ LONDON

> ### TOP IN-HOUSE LAWYERS
>
> **Bob BRITTON**, Solicitor, Hiscox Syndicate 33
>
> **Peter MAYNARD**, Group Legal Services Director, Prudential Plc
>
> **Jane OWEN**, Senior Lawyer, Aon Ltd
>
> **Dan PRIMER**, General Counsel, Catlin Underwriting
>
> **Humphrey TOMLINSON**, Legal Director, Royal & SunAlliance Insurance
>
> **Vyvienne WADE**, Group Legal Director, Jardine Lloyd Thompson
>
> **Rich WEBB**, General Counsel and Senior Vice President, Excel London Market Ltd
>
> The only new addition to this year's list is **Dan Primer**, with recommendations coming from leading industry practitioners. "Seasoned" **Bob Britton** and **Humphrey Tomlinson** continue to attract praise for their effective handling of matters. Private practitioners commend **Peter Maynard** as "highly efficient," while **Vyvienne Wade** and **Rich Webb** are endorsed for their "good commercial knowledge." "Bright" **Jane Owen** received numerous recommendations.
>
> In-house lawyers' profiles p.1201

INCE & CO (see firm details p.1008) This "*impressive*" firm is perhaps best known for its outstanding trade and maritime skills, but maintains a broad insurance base of experience. The team, which includes Alan Weir, has advised on the aftermath of the World Trade Center terrorist attacks and representing a major broker in a high-profile dispute arising out of the US version of '*Who Wants To Be A Millionaire*'. IMG instructed the firm in a dispute with contingency underwriters over the cancellation of the Sahara Cup. Interviewees endorsed the team's "*clear commitment to providing quality insurance advice.*" **Clients** Large insurance institutions.

KENNEDYS (see firm details p.1019) The national coverage of this firm ensures its prominence in the market place and commentators believe that it has the "*skills to match anybody's.*" Nick Williams, Geoff Lord and the group act across a range of sectors including construction, engineering, personal injury, banking and clinical negligence. Litigation remains a key strength of the team. It has recently acted on claims arising from the Selby rail crash and it has been instructed in relation to a £100 million claim to do with a large fire at CenterParcs. **Clients** Large insurers.

BEACHCROFT WANSBROUGHS (see firm details p.860) This "*responsive and sharp*" team was commended by a client for its "*consistent offering – satisfaction guaranteed.*" Trevor Chamberlin's team enjoys a broad client roster and has a track record in claims management, litigation and mediation. The group has recently been involved in the high-profile Callery v Gray case in the House of Lords; a matter pertaining to funding litigation. Sources also acknowledged its experience in professional negligence, fraud and education liability. **Clients** AXA; Cornhill; Ecclesiastical; Royal & SunAlliance; Zurich.

CLIFFORD CHANCE (see firm details p.911) The global back-up that accompanies this firm and its envied international client base ensure that the insurance practice is a "*definite competitor*" for so many included in this chapter. Terry O'Neill's team has acted on major insurance claims across Europe with particular strengths in professional liability and political risk insurance. The group has also been instructed on matters pertaining to the collapse of Enron and represented Johnson Higgins in the Aneco case, which went to the House of Lords. **Clients** Aon; CSFB; Deloitte & Touche; Sun Life of Canada.

DAVIES ARNOLD COOPER (see firm details p.930) This "*outstanding*" insurance practice retains its prominence in the sector, instructed by a loyal client base of large insurers. The team has advised insurers in the last year on losses and issues relating to the Hatfield and Selby train crashes, the combined figures of which runs into tens of millions. It has also represented the insurers in a £15 million dispute arising from the refurbishment of Royal Brompton Hospital, a matter which is set to go to the House of Lords. Michael Dobias is a key member of the team. **Clients** Large insurers.

FRESHFIELDS BRUCKHAUS DERINGER (see firm details p.964) Much admired expertise in litigation has ensured that the firm plays an important role in this aspect of the insurance market. High-profile cases of late include representing the Royal Bank of Canada against film financing insurers. It has also acted for Lloyd's in the Jaffray litigation, a case concerning allegations that Lloyd's fraudulently withheld information from the Names concerning asbestos-related liabilities that hit the market in the eighties. Head of department **Paul Leonard** (see p.562) is characterised by peers as one who "*creates an air of calm when dealing with even the most complex issues,*" while **Raj Parker** (see p.565) is a "*quick-witted thinker and a tough litigator.*" **Clients** Aon Risk Services; Lloyd's; Royal Bank of Scotland.

HOLMAN FENWICK & WILLAN (see firm details p.999) This "*distinctively classy*" practice is well regarded by clients and peers alike. The team has acted in a number of high-volume, complex international insurance and reinsurance cases. Involvement in the HIH film finance litigation, which went to the Court of Appeal, has afforded it a leading profile. The team has also acted on the Gold Medal/Hopewell arbitration in Bermuda, which involved a claim in excess of $200 million. The contact partner here is Paul Wordley. **Clients** Large international publicly-listed companies.

LOVELLS (see firm details p.1045) The team, which is headed by John Powell, has been involved in a number of "*interesting, satisfying*" deals over the last year. Although primarily acting for the corporate insured against the insurers, the practice has advised CNA Insurance Company in obtaining a judgement against a managing general agent for £10.8 million, with regards to a premium collected by the defendant on behalf of CNA. The team has also represented KPMG in the on-going film finance matters. **Clients** Ace; CGNU; CAN; Wellington.

MAYER, BROWN, ROWE & MAW (see firm details p.1060) Thanks in part to the firm's recent US merger, many interviewees spoke of a team "*growing in stature and standing across the marketplace.*" It advises corporate insurers and Lloyd's syndicates both in the London market and on an international level. The profile of Sean Connolly (see p.680) is one that has risen in the past year. He is described as "*outstanding – a lawyer who truly takes the bull by the horns.*" The team has advised on a multibillion dollar utilities project involving a number of complex technical issues across different jurisdictions. Directors' liability cases are also an area of skill. **Clients** Large international insurers.

BERRYMANS LACE MAWER (see firm details p.865) Although the practice is perhaps best known for its work in the personal injury field, it remains active nationwide on a broad spectrum of insurance matters. Charlotte Capstick and the team handle volume insurance for a respected client base. It has recently been involved in a number of industrial disease cases, including one claim which reached the House of Lords. The firm has also represented insurers' interests in a catastrophic injury claim – a case which was the second highest value injury claim ever to come before the Royal Courts of Justice. **Clients** Insurers.

CHARLES RUSSELL (see firm details p.904) This "*busy*" practice is seen as "*securing interesting work.*" The team is led by **Bill Perry** (see p.476), whose advice "*forms a strong foundation for any case.*" It has acted on a number of high-profile international cases such as its advice to Sovereign General Insurance on a £2 million claim, which involved two actions, one in Israel and one in England. The team has also represented underwriters in the high-profile Matalan v Raymond Cladding, a £1.5 million 'reasonable precaution' action. **Clients** AA Mutual Insurance Company; The City Fire Insurance Co; General Accident Fire & Life Assurance; Le Assicurazioni d'Italia; NPA Group.

DJ FREEMAN (see firm details p.939) The chief face of this insurance firm is the "*phenomenal*" David Kendall, who, although slightly better known for his reinsurance work, enjoys "*a healthy slice of the insurance pie.*" Handling work for large banks and companies, the firm has

LONDON ■ INSURANCE

secured its involvement in some high-profile cases over the past year. It has represented GNER against the Avon Insurance Company in the Court of Appeal, in a case surrounding policy wording and other matters. **Clients** ABB Insurance Company; Axa Corporate Solutions; Markel; St. Paul.

ELBORNE MITCHELL (see firm details p.946) The firm was recommended by clients as "*a good firm to go to for the smaller cases*," and endorsed for its "*watchmaker's precision in handling them*." The team, which is headed by Tim Brentnall, has been involved in a number of aviation matters. It has acted for Transamerica on Syndicate 959 and advised on matters relating to carving out personal injury insurance and insuring it separately. **Clients** ACE; GE Frankoma; LIMIT; Markel International; PwC.

LONDON — REINSURANCE

INSURANCE: REINSURANCE
■ LONDON

[1]
- Barlow Lyde & Gilbert
- CMS Cameron McKenna
- Holman Fenwick & Willan
- Ince & Co

[2]
- Clifford Chance
- Clyde & Co
- Lovells

[3]
- DJ Freeman
- Freshfields Bruckhaus Deringer

[4]
- Charles Russell
- Herbert Smith
- Lawrence Graham
- Reynolds Porter Chamberlain

[5]
- Berwin Leighton Paisner
- Denton Wilde Sapte
- Elborne Mitchell
- LeBoeuf, Lamb, Greene & MacRae
- Norton Rose
- Richards Butler

This book is the product of 6,582 1/2 hour interviews. See p.7 for BMRB audit. Within each band, firms are listed alphabetically.

BARLOW LYDE & GILBERT (see firm details p.858) This "*pre-eminent*" reinsurance firm combines "*client-oriented skills, with a deep pool of knowledge*." Led by the "*masterly*" **Colin Croly** (see p.473), assisting in negotiations following the events of September 11th between various concerned parties into the possibility of a reorganisation of insurance arrangements. He is described by peers as being in his "*performance and his arrangements the most skilful of all*." Also dealing with the World Trade Center arrangements was **Michael Mendelowitz** (see p.475), of whom it is is said: "*complex technological matters are his bread and butter*." He was involved on the Government backed UK aviation rescue plan – 'Troika'. The "*sublime*" **Clive O'Connell** (see p.475) is respected as "*a determined opponent*." He has been involved in a number of alternative risk transfer transactions, primarily in the area of credit derivatives risk. **Ed Stanley** (see p.476) is "*on his way to becoming a heavyweight player*," and has been active recently in advising US, Israeli and Venezuelan companies with reinsurance problems. **Clients** Large insurance, reinsurance and banking bodies.

CMS CAMERON MCKENNA (see firm details p.914) This practice can boast a team of top-class solicitors, with "*a gold mine of knowledge on reinsurance matters*." Particular shining lights include **John Hall** (see p.474), "*a superb guy and sensible to deal with*," while **Mark Elborne** (see p.473) is described by peers as "*a highly professional operator with a sharp intellect*." The latter has been advising a global power company, and its worldwide reinsurance subsidiaries, on World Trade Center liabilities and claims. The group has also been involved on a number of multimillion pound insurance industry disputes and has acted on the largest ever single event contractors' all-risk claim, in relation to an earthquake in Turkey. The firm enjoys a truly international client base and offers advice on health spiral issues and matters relating to large reinsurance disputes. **Clients** Domestic and international insurers.

HOLMAN FENWICK & WILLAN (see firm details p.999) This "*wonderfully efficient firm*" rises in the tables this year thanks to the strong recommendations of both clients and parties on the other side. **John Duff** (see p.473) leads the team and is portrayed as "*an expert technician, combining sharpness and common sense*." The team has been involved in a case relating to the loss of 15 aircrafts and numerous spare parts belonging to the Kuwait Aircraft Corporation during the Iraqi invasion of 1990. The case involves over 25 reinsurers and is being eagerly watched in the wake of the September 11th terrorist attacks. Two further names to standout in the marketplace are the "*truly on-the-ball*" **Andrew Bandurka** (see p.472) and the "*most impressive*" **Ian McKenna** (see p.475). An acknowledged skill in personal accident insurance spiral disputes is also on offer. **Clients** Large international plcs.

INCE & CO (see firm details p.1008) Although in some quarters better known for its shipping work, the practice's reinsurance expertise is clearly acknowledged as "*placing them in the top three or four in the capital*." The firm has been active in the reinsurance repercussions of the terrorist attacks of September 11th. It has also represented a large publicly listed insurance company in an American arbitration. **Peter Rogan** (see p.476) heads up the group, but managerial duties do not appear to have impacted on his profile; "*he remains extremely impressive on the groundwork*." **Allan Hepworth** (see p.474) is described as "*someone who always makes it interesting on the other side*." The firm has been advised on honourable engagement causes, in the high profile case of Home and Overseas v Mentor. **Clients** Large insurance bodies.

CLIFFORD CHANCE (see firm details p.911) This practice stands at the head of the worldwide Clifford Chance operation, ready to lend or receive support from offices in New York, Washington, Düsseldorf and Hong Kong. Instructions flow from various banks and financial institutions, and the firm has dealt with the after effects of the collapse of Independent Insurance, Enron and Equitable Life. The firm also continues its involvement with the Unicover arbitration. The "*impressive*" **Terry O'Neill** (see p.475) leads this team and holds a reputation as "*one of the best performers in the market - he really has the best interests of his clients at heart*." Some interviewees believe that **Nicholas Munday** (see p.475) is "*by far the busiest guy there*," while **Stephen Lewis** (see p.475) has "*an eye for detail*." **Clients** Aon; CSFB; Deliotte & Touche; ESG; Manulife Financial; St. Paul.

CLYDE & CO (see firm details p.913) This "*striking*" firm is recommended for the "*pure depth*" of its reinsurance work. The team is headed up by "*spitfire*" **Michael Payton** (see p.475) who "*is able to train his skills onto multiple targets*." The team has been involved in a major litigation involving Personal Accident workers' compensation retrocessions. Matters pertaining to the collapse of Fortress Re pool and the insolvency of Taisei have recently occupied the team. Expert **Nigel Brook** (see p.473) was endorsed by peers and clients, and like the team he holds a strong niche in aviation reinsurance work. **Clients** Ace; Commercial Union; Gard; Hiscox; Kiln.

LOVELLS (see firm details p.1045) An "*efficient, knowledgeable, professional*" unit agree clients. John Powell's team has been involved in a large transaction for the Yasuda Fire and Marine Insurance Company, handling a disposal of a subsidiary simultaneously with a reinsurance of Yasuda. It has also acted in a large recovery for Syndicate 957. **Clients** Large international insurers.

DJ FREEMAN (see firm details p.939) David Kendall is a lawyer who "*combines technical

467

INSURANCE ■ LONDON

LEADING INDIVIDUALS

1
- **CROLY Colin** Barlow Lyde & Gilbert
- **DUFF John** Holman Fenwick & Willan
- **KENDALL David** DJ Freeman
- **ROGAN Peter** Ince & Co

2
- **BANDURKA Andrew** Holman Fenwick & Willan
- **BRADLEY Nicholas** Lawrence Graham
- **BROOK Nigel** Clyde & Co
- **ELBORNE Mark** CMS Cameron McKenna
- **HALL John** CMS Cameron McKenna
- **MACKIE Francis** Norton Rose
- **MCKENNA Ian** Holman Fenwick & Willan
- **O'NEILL Terry** Clifford Chance

3
- **CARTER Stephen** Charles Russell
- **DOBIAS Michael** Davies Arnold Cooper
- **ENOCK Roger** Freshfields Bruckhaus Deringer
- **GOLDSPINK Robert** Morgan, Lewis & Bockius
- **HEPWORTH Allan** Ince & Co
- **LEWIS Stephen** Clifford Chance
- **MENDELOWITZ Michael** Barlow Lyde & Gilbert
- **MUNDAY Nicholas** Clifford Chance
- **O'CONNELL Clive** Barlow Lyde & Gilbert
- **PAYTON Michael** Clyde & Co
- **SCHWARTZ Peter** Baker & McKenzie
- **STANLEY Ed** Barlow Lyde & Gilbert

See individuals' profiles p.472

knowhow with tactical intuition," and as such is strongly recommended for both his insurance and reinsurance expertise. He supervised a team acting for AXA Corporate Solutions in the ongoing 'Gap' film finance disputes. This action has seen disputes on both sides of the Atlantic, with the team acting on over a dozen cases in London. It is also involved in a number of high profile arbitrations, and litigation arising from the music industry. **Clients** Axa Corporate Solutions; Chartwell; Chubb; KWELM; Markel; St. Paul; XL America.

FRESHFIELDS BRUCKHAUS DERINGER (see firm details p.964) Peers perceive that this firm has increased its level of activity in the reinsurance markets over the last few years. It has advised a large insurer in matters relating to the collapse of Independent Insurance in June 2001, and has acted on the reinsurance aspects of film finance claims and the aftermath of the World Trade Center attacks. The star litigator on the reinsurance side is felt to be **Roger Enock** (see p.473), who is recommended as "*a heavyweight in court*." **Clients** Aon; Lloyd's.

CHARLES RUSSELL (see firm details p.904) Market sources commended this firm as "*a definite presence in the reinsurance scene*." Although he has a focus on corporate insurance, **Stephen Carter** (see p.473), remains best known for his reinsurance expertise. The team has been involved in the international dispute concerning Nationwide's participation in the Rutty pool. Wide-ranging experience in litigation has seen it involved in matters concerning run-off reinsurance coverage and administration liabilities. **Clients** AA Mutual International Insurance; Axa; British Aviation Insurance; Nationwide Mutual Insurance; ReAC; Singapore Aviation & General; Zurich International Insurance.

HERBERT SMITH (see firm details p.992) Peers agree that this firm is home to litigation partners who are "*truly getting to grips with the subtleties of reinsurance law*." David Higgins' team has been instructed by PwC in reinsurance issues relating to the insolvency of Independent Insurance. It has also advised Willis in a reinsurance dispute between La Reunion Arienne and ACE, flowing from the Air France Concorde crash. **Clients** Pool Re; PwC; Royal & SunAlliance; Willis.

LAWRENCE GRAHAM (see firm details p.1031) "*One of the most client-oriented firms in the business*," say interviewees. It is home to **Nicholas Bradley**, who is described by clients as "*highly effective, a smart operator*." The team has been heavily involved advising Phoenix Life Insurance in relation to its various PA/LMX spiral reinsurance disputes. It is also involved in a test case arbitration, which will deal with the reinsurance treatment of asbestos, pollution and health hazard losses. **Clients** Global insurance companies.

REYNOLDS PORTER CHAMBERLAIN (see firm details p.1111) This firm has seen reinsurance work grow into a major part of its practice. It is praised by peers and clients for its "*technical astuteness and informed communication skills*." Paul Nicholas's team has been instructed on some of the major reinsurance cases of the last year, including advising on financial losses in South America through the London market. The team has also advised the London market on claims arising from public disturbances in Indonesia. **Clients** Large global insurers.

BERWIN LEIGHTON PAISNER (see firm details p.866) Clients endorsed the "*enthusiasm and effectiveness*" of these lawyers, who "*really know our business*." Jonathan Sacher's team has been involved in high- profile and high-value cases in the last year. These include acting for London market reinsurers on accident and death claims arising from the terrorist attacks of September 11th. It has also advised a major European reinsurer on the consequences of losses arising from the escape of GM products beyond its authorised use. **Clients** London and World insurers and reinsurers.

DENTON WILDE SAPTE (see firm details p.935) A new entry to the *Chambers*' tables this year, following recommendations from both peers and clients for this growing reinsurance team. "*Able to make common sense out of the most complex case*," it offers a "*a top-notch team*." The group, which includes Michelle George, has acted for AIG Europe (UK) in film finance insurance disputes, valued in excess of $200 million. It has also represented London reinsurers in connection with a $15 million loss suffered by an Argentinian bank. **Clients** AIG; Markel Group.

ELBORNE MITCHELL (see firm details p.946) A favourite among clients who perceive its advice to be "*as steady as a rock*." Spanish speaker Jolyon Patten is a member of a team dealing with large-scale arbitrations. It has also advised London reinsurers in a number of jurisdictional and substantive disputes relating to Latin American risks. **Clients** Lloyd's syndicates; Large insurers.

LEBOEUF, LAMB, GREENE & MACRAE (see firm details p.1033) A new entry to the tables this year, the firm is perceived as being "*at the spearhead of the emerging American firms*," which is no surprise considering its long-standing insurance expertise in the US. Peter Sharp and the team have a track record in cross-border reinsurance and high-value insolvency matters. It has been instructed in sensitive issues regarding the events of September 11th and the firm is a growing presence on high-value cases. **Clients** Ace Syndicates; Generali; Hiscox; Munich Re; Wellington.

NORTON ROSE (see firm details p.1084) A smaller team, but one which still "*carries a reputation for expertise*." Led by "*the impeccable*" **Francis Mackie** (see p.475). He has acted for E&O underwriters in connection with the recent US extended warranty problems. The team has also acted for a major US company on a complex finite reinsurance transaction. The firm acts on a range of international issues, including marine reinsurance cases. **Clients** AIG; Allianz Cornhill; AXA Reinsurance; Gerling Global; Sirius International Insurance; SCOR.

RICHARDS BUTLER (see firm details p.1112) The firm continues to impress with its "*well-rounded teams and sharp commercial skills*." Headed up by Mark Connoley, the firm is representing North Atlantic Insurance Company in disputes arising out of the operation of the Rutty Pool. It has also been active on Sphere Drake v Stirling Cooke Brown and others, a major piece of litigation relating to personal accident excess of loss contracts. **Clients** North Atlantic Insurance Company; PwC; Stirling Cooke Brown; Willis Corroon Group.

OTHER NOTABLE PRACTITIONERS At Baker & McKenzie, **Peter Schwartz** (see p.476) was described as "*a strong and lively presence*" by peers, while **Michael Dobias** (see p.473) of Davies Arnold Cooper was described as "*prompt and responsive*." New to this year's rankings is **Bob Goldspink** (see p.474) of Morgan, Lewis & Bockius, perceived to be "*a name very much in the ascendancy*."

LONDON

NON-CONTENTIOUS

INSURANCE: NON-CONTENTIOUS
■ LONDON

1
- Lovells

2
- Clifford Chance
- Freshfields Bruckhaus Deringer
- Herbert Smith

3
- Linklaters
- Norton Rose
- Slaughter and May

4
- Ashurst Morris Crisp
- Barlow Lyde & Gilbert
- Clyde & Co

5
- DJ Freeman
- Eversheds
- Lawrence Graham

6
- Allen & Overy
- Dechert

LEADING INDIVIDUALS

1
- YOUNG John *Lovells*

2
- BATESON James *Norton Rose*
- COATES Katherine *Clifford Chance*
- EVENETT Hilary *Clifford Chance*
- HILL Jeremy *Ashurst Morris Crisp*
- HOLDERNESS Andrew *Clyde & Co*
- JAMES Glen *Slaughter and May*
- MADDOCK Geoffrey *Herbert Smith*
- MIDDLEDITCH Matthew *Linklaters*
- RONALDSON Cheryl *Norton Rose*

3
- BARKER Alan *Linklaters*
- BROWNING Stephen *Barlow Lyde & Gilbert*
- DAVIDSON John *Lovells*
- POYNTON Ian *Freshfields Bruckhaus Deringer*

This book is the product of 6,582 1/2 hour interviews. See p.7 for BMRB audit. Within each band, firms are listed alphabetically. See individuals' profiles p.472

LOVELLS (see firm details p.1045) An "*epic*" presence in the non-contentious insurance market, clients claim that the team is "*detailed in its knowledge, utterly responsive and sympathetic to our needs.*" Its star performer is team leader **John Young** (see p.476). A "*true doyen,*" many believe that he is "*a vital prop in the insurance industry.*" He has advised Equitable Life on the sale of its business to Halifax Group for £1 billion. The team has also advised Natural Mutual on its demutualisation and sale to GE Capital. Peers commended **John Davidson** (see p.473) as one who provides "*a mountain of support for clients.*" **Clients** Equitable Life; Liverpool Victoria; National Mutual Life Assurance; Prudential.

CLIFFORD CHANCE (see firm details p.911) Recommended by clients for providing "*a truly excellent level of service,*" the firm has a strong focus on this sector and an admired international back-up for cross-border transactions. The team is headed by the "*indomitable*" **Katherine Coates** (see p.473) who has "*a reputation that wins clients and gravitas galore.*" She has recently advised Royal Liver on its acquisition of the industrial insurance business of FPLO and Irish Life & Permanent. **Hilary Evenett** (see p.473) is a name that continues to grow in prominence, due to her "*subtlety and intelligence.*" She has worked extensively with members of the Lloyd's market, and has acted for Hiscox in its recent rights issue. **Clients** AXA/Sun Life; Britannic; CGNU; GE Insurance Holdings; Hiscox Group; Lloyd's; Royal Liver Assurance; Sun Life Financial Services of Canada.

FRESHFIELDS BRUCKHAUS DERINGER (see firm details p.964) Observers agree that this "*cracking*" practice has "*settled and consolidated its place in the insurance market.*" It has advised on the establishment of The Troika Insurance Company, an instruction carried out for HM Treasury to ensure that commercial airliners could continue to fly in the UK in the wake of September 11th. The deal was handled by the "*expert*" **Ian Poynton** (see p.476) "*an excellent man to have stood at your side.*" He has also advised Prudential on its proposals to merge with American General and acted for Zurich Financial Services on its relations with Deutsche Bank. **Clients** AIG; AMP; Aon Capital Markets; Cologne Re; Equitas Reinsurance; Lloyd's; Prudential; Scottish Widows; Zurich Financial Services.

HERBERT SMITH (see firm details p.992) Commentators typically believed that "*there was always going to be a shift when Marion Pell retired - but this is a strong team building nicely.*" The team is headed by "*versatile performer*" **Geoffrey Maddock** (see p.475), whom clients endorse as "*impressive and competitive – he understands how to forge a good working relationship.*" He has represented Friends Provident on its £4 billion demutualisation and flotation, and advised PwC on the proposed liquidation of Independent Insurance, valued in excess of £1 billion. The team also represented GE Capital on its successful £570 million bid to acquire National Mutual. **Clients** Equitable; Friends Provident; GE Capital; PwC; Royal London; Standard Life.

LINKLATERS (see firm details p.1043) Although holding a slightly lower profile than some of its competitors, the firm is envied for its involvement in some big-ticket work in the past 12 months. Corporate partner **Matthew Middleditch** (see p.475) is described as "*someone who adapts himself to this work beautifully.*" He is recommended for offering "*one of the highest levels of knowledge and understanding in this sector.*" "*The ever reliable*" **Alan Barker** (see p.472) remains "*an incredibly useful operator to have on your side.*" The team has advised Halifax on its £1 billion purchase of the business assets of Equitable Life, and advised Merrill Lynch on the demutualisation and listing of Friends Provident – a transaction worth £3.7 billion. **Clients** Allianz; Halifax; Merrill Lynch.

NORTON ROSE (see firm details p.1084) This practice is recognised as "*gradually building up an excellent team,*" is "*knowledgeable on regulatory matters and responsive to clients.*" "*Slick operator*" **James Bateson** (see p.472) is portrayed by peers as "*an absolute master of cross border transactions.*" He led the team, that advised AIG on its £200 million investment in Lloyd's through the formation of Ascot Underwriting Company. He is aided by the "*experienced*" **Cheryl Ronaldson** (see p.476), who last year advised the Financial Services Authority on the collapse of Equitable Life. **Clients** AIG; AXA; Budget Insurance Company; Citigroup; HSBC Insurance Old Mutual; Royal & SunAlliance; SVB Holdings.

SLAUGHTER AND MAY (see firm details p.1140) **Glen James** (see p.475) stands out as the public face of this firm's activities in the insurance market. A respected corporate lawyer, he has acquired "*all the skills necessary for insurance matters.*" The team is clearly distinguished by clients as "*one of the sharpest transactional firms around, offering top-drawer advice.*" It was involved in a £1.2 billion hybrid capital issue. For Abbey National, it acted on its £1.8 billion acquisition of Scottish Provident. **Clients** Aegon UK; CGNU; Cox Insurance; GE Capital; Legal & General; Old Mutual; Scottish Mutual.

ASHURST MORRIS CRISP (see firm details p.852) The "*superb*" **Jeremy Hill** (see p.474) is thought by interviewees to be one who "*embodies the spirit of tenacity within the team.*" The firm has acted on a number of complex, high value schemes, including advising Goshawk Insurance Holdings on its placing and open offer to raise £100 million to finance a new reinsurance business in Bermuda. A highly regarded, user-friendly firm, clients agree that these lawyers "*pass the main test - when deals get heavy, you don't mind sitting with them till three o'clock in the morning.*" **Clients** Benfield Group; CBS Insurance; Goshawk Insurance Holdings; Ockham Holdings; Royal & SunAlliance.

BARLOW LYDE & GILBERT (see firm details p.858) Heartily recommended for its skills on the "*nuts and bolts aspects of deals,*" the firm has a reputation for "*competence, care and attention*" in the most demanding of transactions. **Stephen Browning** (see p.473) is praised by peers as "*an all-rounder with a sound background and great knowledge.*" He has acted for CAN Financial on its disposal of its Lloyd's interests to Chaucer and has advised the shareholders of Morgan, Read & Sharman - a Lloyd's aviation and non-marine insurance broker - on

INSURANCE ■ LONDON/THE REGIONS

the sale of the company. He is able to draw upon the support of respected consultant Verner Southey. **Clients** ACE Insurance; Chubb Insurance Company of Europe; Heath Lambert; Munich Re Underwriting; QBE International Insurance; SVB Holdings; Windsor.

CLYDE & CO (see firm details p.913) **Andrew Holderness** (see p.474) leads a group that is regarded by peers and clients as a "*friendly, efficient team.*" It has been occupied of late on the sale of the Bishopscourt Group Insurance broking business to Liverpool Victoria Friendly Society for £10 million. The team has also acted for Ensign Holdings on its £85 million syndicate acquisition from Limit. Peers acknowledge that the firm uses "*its key strengths wisely on these corporate deals.*" **Clients** ACE; Brit; Ensign; March; Radian Asset Assurance; Skandia Group; Swiss Re; Winterthur Life UK; XL Capital.

DJ FREEMAN (see firm details p.939) The team, led by Toby Greenbury and Ashwani Kochhar, is "*heavily recommended, particularly for structured transactions.*" It has secured instruction in a number of sizeable deals, including political risk transactions worth over $200 million and credit default swaps worth over half a billion dollars in total. **Clients** Large insurers; UK P&I clubs.

EVERSHEDS (see firm details p.949) This focused team is praised by clients and competitors alike, described as "*competent and pragmatic*" employing a "*smoothly impressive*" approach to transactions. Anton Eisdell and the group have acted for Sun Life Financial of Canada, on the outsourcing of the run-off of its closed book of individual pensions. The team has also acted for the Leeds Hospital Fund in its merger with The Hospital Savings Association. **Clients** Leeds Hospital Fund; Legal & General; Sun Life Financial of Canada.

LAWRENCE GRAHAM (see firm details p.1031) Although lacking the profile in the market of some of its rivals, Robert Smith's team is still regarded as a good producer of quality work. In the last year, it has advised a large financial body on various warranty and indemnity insurance matters. It also advises on alternative risk transfer transactions for various offshore insurers and insureds. **Clients** Axa; HSBC Insurance Brokers; Isle of Man Assurance; QBE International Group; West Risk Management; Zurich.

ALLEN & OVERY (see firm details p.841) Regarded as an "*enthusiastic*" practice, it received warm endorsement for its combined skills in insurance and derivatives. Headed up by Michael Brown, the team has acted for Sun Life of Canada Group on its disposal of its UK asset management and pooled pension business to Credit Suisse Asset Management. It also acted for Aon, Marsh and Willis on the setting up of Troika – a UK Government backed insurance scheme providing terrorist cover post September 11th. **Clients** Aon; Marsh; Sun Life of Canada Group; Willis.

DECHERT (see firm details p.934) New to the tables this year, this combined contentious/non-contentious practice is "*becoming one of the major competitors in technical Lloyd's work.*" Robin Williams heads the team, which has acted for Berkshire Hathaway on the reinsurance of CGNU's Global Roles and London market business, as well as advising Brit Insurance Holdings on a £150 million risks placing. **Clients** Berkshire Hathaway; Brit Insurance Holdings; Chaucer Holdings; City 3K; Heath Lambert.

THE REGIONS

INSURANCE ■ THE REGIONS

1 **Beachcroft Wansbroughs** Birmingham, Bristol, Leeds, Manchester
Berrymans Lace Mawer Birmingham, Liverpool, Manchester, Southampton
2 **Keoghs** Bolton
Weightman Vizards Liverpool
3 **Bond Pearce** Exeter
James Chapman & Co Manchester
4 **Browne Jacobson** Nottingham
Crutes Law Firm Newcastle upon Tyne
Hill Dickinson Liverpool
Jacksons Gateshead
Wragge & Co Birmingham
5 **Cartwrights Insurance Partners** Bristol
Davies Arnold Cooper Manchester
DWF Liverpool, Manchester
Eversheds Newcastle upon Tyne
Halliwell Landau Manchester, Sheffield
Mills & Reeve Cambridge, Norwich
Morgan Cole Cardiff
Ricksons Preston

This book is the product of 6,582 1/2 hour interviews. See p.7 for BMRB audit. Within each band, firms are listed alphabetically.

BEACHCROFT WANSBROUGHS (see firm details p.860) This "*superior*" insurance firm has strength in depth across the nation, and is regarded by peers as offering "*a top notch service from all its offices.*" Acting for major insurers, the firm runs a specified 'Mutual Law' approach, which allows it to focus on all aspects of insurance litigation. Tom Corrigan's team has in the last year represented Cornhill Insurance v DE Stamp Felt Roof and Contractors - a case that was heard in the Court of Appeal. **Clients** ACE Global Markets; CGNU; Markel; QBA; RSA; Zurich.

BERRYMANS LACE MAWER (see firm details p.865) This is a "*dedicated team*" handling claims and other insurance matters out of a network of offices, and possessed of "*a reputation you can but admire.*" The group, which includes Jason Nash, has acted on a multi million pound arbitration, has a strong track record in cases regarding occupational and industrial diseases. Observers praised the team for its "*tenacity and spirit,*" while clients recommend its skills in handling "*top-end bulk work*" with the utmost ease. **Clients** Aon; Allianz Cornhill; Endsleigh; Norwich Union; St Paul International Insurers; Zurich International.

KEOGHS (see firm details p.1021) Rival firms agree that this outfit "*gets a good press when talking to insurance companies*" and single out its "*dynamism when faced with high intensity work.*" The team is active for four of the five top UK insurers, as well as 20 other UK insurers. David Tyson's team also carries out work for loss adjusters, insurance brokers and claims handling agents. Its reach stretches far beyond its Bolton base. **Clients** Large insurance companies.

WEIGHTMAN VIZARDS (see firm details p.1183) This group is praised nationally as a "*sharp Northern firm, which always offers value for money.*" Based in Liverpool, the team is rightly hailed as one of the best in the country. In the past year, the group has been involved in 14,000 insurance claims on behalf of major insurers. The firm is recognised for its expertise in EL/PL, industrial disease and public sector related claims. Lynne McFaul is a key member of this team. **Clients** Large Insurers.

BOND PEARCE (see firm details p.879) Carrying a strong presence across the South of the country, Erik Salomonsen's team continues to be described as "*a prime choice for insurance work.*" The group has been active in the last year on a large cross-border dispute involving an underwriter's claim in the construction industry. It is also occupied by the run off work and disputes originating from the Solicitor's Indemnity Fund. **Clients** Hiscox Insurers; NFU Mutual Insurance Society; Norwich Union; Royal & SunAlliance; Solicitors Indemnity Fund; St Paul International Insurance Company; Zurich Professional.

JAMES CHAPMAN & CO (see firm details p.1012) Following recommendations for it describing "*an expanding firm in both size and profile,*" the practice moves up the rankings this year. The team, which includes Kevin Finnegan, has worked on a multitude of cases in the last year. Highlights included the successful defence of a £2 million claim for Zurich Commercial, just one of a number of high value cases. Peers typically thought of this as a "*strong firm, which can handle anything clients throw at them.*" **Clients** AGF; Horizon; NFU Mutual; Zurich Commercial

BROWNE JACOBSON (see firm details p.891) The strong Midlands practice is described by sources as "*very much a firm to admire.*" On the panel of a number of insurers, public bodies and corporate organisations, it has a strong focus on risk assessment and litigation. Nick Parsons' team has been involved in a number of high-value cases in the last twelve months. **Clients** Hiscox; NHSLA; NFU Mutual Insurance Company.

CRUTES LAW FIRM (see firm details p.924) Clients applauded the firm for its ability to "*communicate effectively, efficiently and promptly*" and for fielding "*lawyers who are genuinely there to help you.*" Paul Hughes's team holds the respect of commentators from the insurance community. The group advises both large insurance companies, and local authorities in the North. It can also boast a designated fast-track unit, which handles high volume work, and personal injury claims are a forte of the firm. **Clients** Norwich Union; St Paul.

HILL DICKINSON (see firm details p.995) Manchester based partner David Scott leads this insurance litigation practice, which was commended during research for its "*wide breadth of expertise.*" It handles insurance matters for clients in the public sector, retail, travel and the motor industry, while professional negligence is a key source of instruction. It has recently set up a specialist claim management division under the title One Liability Services. The team has been involved in the last year on a number of cases in the House Of Lords. **Clients** Insurer's Panels; Large Corporate/Commercial Entities.

JACKSONS (see firm details p.1011) This sizeable North East team is now prominent handling cases on a nationwide basis. It has particular strengths in EL/PL, disease work, asbestos claims and road traffic accidents for large insurers. Richard Clarke's team includes a fast track group, and was applauded by peers as "*one of the most efficient firms around.*" **Clients** AXA; other large insurers.

WRAGGE & CO (see firm details p.1197) The market regards this as "*a firm with depth and a strong regional presence.*" Mark Hick's team receives a healthy flow of instruction from Lloyd's syndicates and major insurers. It is also heavily involved in the emerging markets, including e-commerce, warranty and indemnity insurance. The firm has advised underwriters on a £60 million part disposal of a property company. **Clients** ACE Europe; Chubb Insurance; Hiscox; Independent; Norwich Union; Reliance National; Royal & SunAlliance; SVB Syndicate.

CARTWRIGHTS INSURANCE PARTNERS This specialist practice is described by its clients as having "*a twenty-twenty focus which few others firms can manage.*" Ian Poole's team handles a full range of general insurance work, including industrial disease, EL/PL, indemnity work, as well as high value catastrophic work. It has been retained on the panels of a number of large insurers **Clients** AXA; First Group; NU; Royal & SunAlliance.

DAVIES ARNOLD COOPER (see firm details p.930) This Manchester based team falls under the auspices of the wider London department. Led in the North by Stephen Gorman, the group has a strong combative presence with ninety percent of its insurance work being litigation. The remit here stretches across the disciplines of commercial litigation, construction, environmental and professional negligence. It is currently handling a case with 110 claimants. **Clients** Insurers.

DWF (see firm details p.943) Operates between Liverpool and Manchester, the firm enjoys a "*good reputation across a wide spectrum of insurance matters.*" The team, which includes David Lund, represents major insurers on injury claims, ranging from public liability to disease. It also handles commercial issues of construction and engineering insurance. The team fields in-house investigators and an in-house barrister, and its skill in ADR was singled out. **Clients** Large insurers.

EVERSHEDS (see firm details p.949) This national practice is regarded by peers as having first rate skills on the life insurance side, and praised for being able to handle "*top notch matters as well as small regional work.*" It has in the last year handled a complete redesign and redrafting of the rules and policy wordings of Sunderland Marine Mutual Insurance Company. The team is led from Newcastle by Lex Dowie, and handles large professional indemnities as well as some matters of reinsurance. **Clients** Citadel Group Representatives; Sunderland Marine Mutual Insurance Company.

HALLIWELL LANDAU (see firm details p.982) Peers applaud the firm as one "*successful in generating insurance work,*" while clients appreciated that it has "*a listening ear which doesn't dictate.*" Industrial accidents and health and safety issues are all to be found in the teams portfolio. Victor Rae-Reeves' team also handles cross border policy disputes. The firm has been involved over the last year in matters relating to the Hatfield derailment. **Clients** AIG Europe; Endsleigh Insurance; Norwich Union.

MILLS & REEVE (see firm details p.1071) This East Anglia based practice, has a subsidiary London office, and is praised as "*getting to the crux of the matter quickly.*" The team, which includes Geoff Barrett, carries out work on policy disputes and binding authority problems. Domestic and foreign brokers also feature on the client roster. **Clients** AIG; Goshawk; TL Clowes; Talbot; XL Insurance.

MORGAN COLE (see firm details p.1075) The firm enters the *Chambers* rankings this year thanks to high praise from a range of insurance companies, with its national team described by clients as "*supportive and responsive to our needs.*" The firm's offering in this section is split into two teams: general insurance and regulatory. It handles a wide range of work including personal injury, public liability, health and safety and licensing. Elizabeth Carr is a key member of the team. **Clients** Insurers.

RICKSONS Retained on the panels of a number of high profile national insurers, the practice is described as "*riding high on insurance work.*" The team, which includes Anthony Hughes, has a focused disease department, which brings in a good level of instruction. The team has displayed expertise on abuse cases and health and safety issues, and its involved in a number matters with Lloyd's syndicates. **Clients** Iron Trades; Garwin; Zurich Municipal.

INSURANCE ■ THE REGIONS/SCOTLAND/THE LEADERS

THE REGIONS

REINSURANCE

INSURANCE: REINSURANCE
■ THE REGIONS

1. Humphreys & Co Bristol

This book is the product of 6,582 1/2 hour interviews. See p.7 for BMRB audit. Within each band, firms are listed alphabetically.

HUMPHREYS & CO (see firm details p.1005) "*The only reinsurance firm outside London worthy of note*" acknowledged one commentator. Peter Montgomery leads a team that handles work for a broad base of international reinsurance clients. It has been active in the past year handling a case for an American company at a civil tribunal in Rome and has advised on the after-effects of the collapse of a French reinsurance pool. **Clients** International reinsurers.

SCOTLAND

INSURANCE

INSURANCE
■ SCOTLAND

1. Simpson & Marwick Edinburgh
2. HBM Sayers Glasgow
3. Biggart Baillie Glasgow
   Brechin Tindal Oatts Glasgow
   Dundas & Wilson CS Edinburgh

This book is the product of 6,582 1/2 hour interviews. See p.7 for BMRB audit. Within each band, firms are listed alphabetically.

SIMPSON & MARWICK (see firm details p.1138) As one commentator put it "*you'd have to be daft or naive not to believe they're the premier insurance firm.*" Paul Wade's team offers advice on policy drafting and interpretation, with experience of revising the policy conditions of major UK insurers. Have been handling various high profile matters over the last year, including work on a case which relates to security of a composite policy which reached the House of Lords. **Clients** Lloyd's Syndicates; insurers

HBM SAYERS Clients and peers praised this firm's "*substantial all round skills.*" The team handles the full range of insurance work, including road traffic accidents, EL/PL, fraud and catastrophic injury. The firm's great litigation skills have helped distinguish it from its competitors, and it is thought to have a healthy volume of instruction. George Moore is a contact member at the firm. **Clients** Axa; Allianz Cornhill; Direct Line; Norwich Union; Royal & SunAlliance.

BIGGART BAILLIE (see firm details p.871) Although perceived to lack the broad focus of some of its closest competitors, this practice retains "*a strong interest in and knowledge of niche areas*." The team, which includes Alison Grant, is one of the few firms in Scotland to act for solicitors in negligence cases. It also handles professional disputes involving other professions, and has the capacity to advise on risk management matters. The firm is recommended for its work in the health and safety sector. **Clients** Iron Trades; Scottish Power; Zurich Municipal.

BRECHIN TINDAL OATTS Observers pointed to "*some dedicated people and a long track record in insurance,*" and the practice remains a force in the region. Headed by Bill Speirs, the team advises on policy interpretation and avoidance, contractual claims, indemnities and major losses. It does have experience of a number of cross-border policy disputes, and has undertaken a major professional indemnity case that reached the House of Lords. **Clients** Major insurers.

DUNDAS & WILSON CS (see firm details p.943) The focus here is perceived to lay on the professional indemnity side of the insurance market. Clients agree that these lawyers are "*a constant source of support.*" Colin MacLeod and the team represent a broad range of industry sectors. A key matters has been the firm's defence of a high value stress claim on behalf of insurance clients. **Clients** NFU Mutual; Norwich Union; Royal & SunAlliance.

THE LEADERS IN INSURANCE

BAKES, Martin
Herbert Smith, London
(020) 7374 8000
martin.bakes@herbertsmith.com
Specialisation: Partner with extensive expertise in insurance and reinsurance law. His work includes advising on policy disputes of all kinds between insureds and insurers. Has acted in a wide variety of subrogated actions involving claims against professionals. Also has wide experience of conducting overseas litigation on behalf of UK insurers and their insureds and in relation to reinsurance disputes.
Prof. Memberships: Law Society; British Insurance Law Association.
Career: Qualified in 1980. Became a partner at *Herbert Smith* in 1987.
Personal: Educated at Downing College, Cambridge.

BANDURKA, Andrew
Holman Fenwick & Willan, London
(020) 7264 8404
andrew.bandurka@hfw.co.uk
Specialisation: Partner in insurance/reinsurance department. Well known for his work on marine, aviation and PA spirals. Principal area of practice is large insurance claims and reinsurance related. Work covers large insurance claims and reinsurance and professional negligence (insurance/reinsurance brokers and managing agents). Successfully took the Kuwait Aviation Test Case to the High Court on behalf of the retrocession market. Author of numerous articles in 'Lloyd's List', 'Mealey's' and other publications. Regular speaker at seminars world wide on arbitration and reinsurance. Sits as an arbitrator. This department of 26 lawyers specialises in all aspects of insurance and reinsurance contentious and non-contentious work.
Prof. Memberships: British Insurance Law Association.
Career: Degrees in Mathematics and Statistics. Masters degree in Operational Research. Called to the Bar in 1985. Qualified as a solicitor in 1989. Became a Partner at *Holman Fenwick & Willan* in 1993.
Personal: Born 31 December 1956. Married with three children.

BARKER, Alan
Linklaters, London
(020) 7456 3388
alan.barker@linklaters.com
Specialisation: Partner 1986. Corporate Department. Deals with a wide range of corporate work including acquisitions, disposals, joint ventures, reconstructions, regulatory problems, etc., particularly in relation to insurance companies. Advises a number of leading UK insurance companies, both life and non-life and both listed and mutual. In addition, advises many non-UK insurance companies on UK and European legal matters (eg companies from other European countries, North America and elsewhere).
Career: 1970 Cambridge, BA in Economics & Law; 1973-78, Assistant Solicitor, *Linklaters* Trusts Department; 1980-86, Assistant Solicitor, *Linklaters* Corporate Department; 1986 to date, Partner, *Linklaters*, responsible for the firm's insurance companies practice.

BATESON, James
Norton Rose, London
(020) 7444 3528
batesonjgd@nortonrose.com
Specialisation: Head of the firm's Corporate and Regulatory Insurance Practice. Advises on the establishment, regulation, sale and purchase of insurance companies and related business in the UK and Europe and in relation to Lloyd's matters. A member of the Insurance Law sub-committee, City of London Solicitors Company. Part of the team which advised AXA on its takeover of Guardian Royal Exchange plc for £3.4 billion. Led the team advising the Law Society in relation to the new Professional Indemnity Scheme.
Prof. Memberships: Law Society; City of London Solicitors Company.
Career: Aldenham School; Southampton University (LLB). Articled *Norton Rose*. Qualified 1986; partner since 1995.
Personal: Born 1961. Resides Harpenden.

THE LEADERS ▪ INSURANCE

BRADLEY, Nicholas
Lawrence Graham, London
(020) 7379 0000

BROOK, Nigel
Clyde & Co, London
(020) 7623 1244
Nigel.Brook@clyde.co.uk
Specialisation: Partner, head of reinsurance. Handles international reinsurance disputes, mainly for London market. On the direct side, his main specialisations are credit insurance, brokers' professional indemnity, art and regulatory. Drafts and advises on wordings.
Career: Qualified 1981, partner 1985.
Publications: Author of various articles and many of *Clydes*' 'Reinsurance Updates'.

BROWNING, Stephen
Barlow Lyde & Gilbert, London
(020) 7247 2277
sbrowning@blg.co.uk
Specialisation: Partner in corporate department; chairman of corporate and regulatory insurance group. Handles a wide variety of transactional, regulatory and general corporate work in the Lloyd's, London and international insurance markets including start-ups, acquisitions, disposals, reorganisations, demergers and joint ventures concerning insurance/reinsurance companies, underwriting agents (including Lloyd's managing agencies), insurance intermediaries and broker teams and insurance/reinsurance run-off and consulting businesses. Major involvement in the consolidation and restructuring of the Lloyd's market, including numerous syndicate mergers and more than 20 Lloyd's capacity offers.
Prof. Memberships: The Law Society; City of London Solicitors Company.
Career: Joined *Barlow Lyde & Gilbert* in January 2000. *Clyde & Co* 1986-99 (partner 1996).
Publications: Author of articles in various publications on insurance regulatory matters and the Lloyd's market. Contributing author to 'A Practitioner's Guide to the FSA Regulation of Lloyd's'.
Personal: Born 1963. Lives in Sussex. Married with three children. Leisure interests include motor racing and classic cars.

CARTER, Stephen
Charles Russell, London
(020) 7203 5000
Specialisation: Reinsurance, international insurance and coverage issues, both contentious and non-contentious; practice includes international arbitration and litigation, problems arising from reinsurance pools, underwriting agency relationships and run-off as well as advice on contract wordings and new products.
Prof. Memberships: International Insurance Society; Federation of Defense and Corporate Counsel; Association of Run-off Companies (Sub-committee Member); British Insurance Law Association;

ARIAS (UK); Associate of the Chartered Institute of Arbitrators.
Career: *Wansbroughs* (1978-81); *Reynolds Porter Chamberlain* (1981-85); *Charles Russell* (1985 to the present, including a full time secondment with Market Run-Off Services (1985-87). Currently Head of *Charles Russell*'s Insurance and Reinsurance Group.
Personal: Educated at University of Durham and The College of Law, Guildford. Married with two children. Pastimes include shooting, swimming, spectator sports and music.

COATES, Katherine
Clifford Chance, London
(020) 7600 1000
katherine.coates@cliffordchance.com
Specialisation: Corporate Department. Partner specialising in non-contentious insurance matters including UK and European regulation, start-ups, mergers and acquisitions, demutualisations, capital raising distribution arrangements, product development, Lloyd's, investment funds including in particular private equity funds and other financial services matters.
Career: Articled *Coward Chance/Clifford Chance*; qualified 1983; Partner since 1990.
Personal: King Edward VI High School for Girls, Edgbaston, Birmingham; Somerville College, Oxford (MA Jurisprudence); Law Society Finals.

CONNOLLY, Sean
Mayer, Brown, Rowe & Maw, London
(020) 7327 4144
sconnolly@eu.mayerbrownrowe.com
See under Professional Negligence, p.680

CROLY, Colin
Barlow Lyde & Gilbert, London
(020) 7247 2277
ccroly@blg.co.uk
Specialisation: Partner and Head of Reinsurance and International Risk team, and Chairman ART Practice group. Advises on all areas of reinsurance and international risks, including contract wording and dispute resolution. Joint Editor 'Reinsurance Practice and the Law', published by Informa. Speaks regularly on a number of aspects relating to reinsurance/insurance at various conferences, including such matters as drafting and construction of reinsurance contracts, alternative risks transactions and coverage issues in respect of asbestos, environmental and tobacco issues.
Prof. Memberships: Secretary General of AIDA (Association Internationale de Droits des Assurances), Board member, Federation of Defence and Corporate Counsel (FDCC), Chairman of the AIDA Reinsurance Working Party, and Chairman, Reinsurance Section, FDCC, Government Appointed member Insurance Brokers Registration Counsel (IBRC) 1997-98.
Career: Qualified in 1971 in the Republic of South Africa. Practising attorney in Transvaal 1974-75. Qualified in England and Wales 1980. Joined *Barlow Lyde & Gilbert* 1976, Partner 1980.
Personal: Born 9 October 1949. Read economics and law at Cape Town University, followed by a Masters Degree in International Law at London University. Recreations include gardening, reading, theatre, gym. Lives in Central London.

DAVIDSON, John
Lovells, London
(020) 7296 2000
john.davidson@lovells.com
Specialisation: Is a member of Lovells' Corporate Finance Group, specialising in public and private UK and cross-border mergers and acquisitions and joint ventures, international equity offerings and private equity investments, and is a member of the firm's market-leading corporate insurance practice.
Career: Articled *Lovells*, qualified 1985; Partner 1991; Resident Partner New York office 1991-95.

DOBIAS, Michael
Davies Arnold Cooper, London
(020) 7936 2222
mdobias@dac.co.uk
Specialisation: Partner and head of reinsurance and professional indemnity group. Main area of practice is insurance, particularly professional indemnity, financial institutions and directors and officers; also reinsurance matters, both domestic and international, covering arbitration and litigation. Includes facultative and treaty contracts. Represents insurers, reinsurers and brokers. Author of 'The Trials of Treaty Disputes' jointly with David McIntosh and 'The Scales of Justice: the Need for a Defence Bar Representation Body'. Visiting lecturer at London and Singapore Colleges of Insurance. Lectures extensively at conferences and seminars on insurance and reinsurance issues.
Prof. Memberships: Law Society, International Association of Defence Counsel, London Solicitors Litigation Association.
Career: Joined *Davies Arnold Cooper* in 1973. Qualified in 1975. Partner 1980. Head of Reinsurance Interest Group.
Personal: Born 28th September 1950. Attended Birmingham University 1969-72. Leisure pursuits include sport, cinema and wine tasting. Lives in Chigwell, Essex.

DUFF, John
Holman Fenwick & Willan, London
(020) 7264 8344
john.duff@hfw.co.uk
Specialisation: Partner in Insurance/Reinsurance Department. Main area of practice is non-marine and marine reinsurance. Author of various articles and a frequent speaker worldwide.
Career: Qualified in 1982. Joined *Holman Fenwick & Willan* in 1983, becoming a Partner in 1987.

ELBORNE, Mark
CMS Cameron McKenna, London
(020) 7367 3057
me@cmck.com
Specialisation: Principal areas of practice involve acting in claims and disputes for insurers and reinsurers of banks and financial institutions, directors and officers, accountants, financial advisors and stockbrokers, Lloyd's agents and Lloyd's brokers; advising insurers and reinsurers on policy wordings and construction in insurance and reinsurance contracts; acting in major reinsurance arbitration and litigation disputes and advising reinsurers generally with clients in the London market, Europe, Middle and Far East, USA and Bermuda. Lectured in Bermuda at International Reinsurance Congress and in Hong Kong and London at various conferences on financial institutions insurance, directors' and officers' liability cover and on reinsurance.
Prof. Memberships: Law Society, Chartered Institute of Insurers, Society of Insurance Receivers.
Career: Qualified 1983 and became a Partner of *CMS Cameron McKenna* in 1988.
Personal: Born 22 January 1958. School Trustee. Leisure pursuits include golf, swimming, tennis, shooting and opera. Lives near Uppingham, Rutland. Married with five children.

ENOCK, Roger
Freshfields Bruckhaus Deringer, London
(020) 7936 4000
roger.enock@freshfields.com
Specialisation: Litigation Department. Partner specialising in commercial litigation with an emphasis on insurance and reinsurance disputes, banking and arbitration.
Prof. Memberships: American Bar Association; British Insurance Lawyers Association.
Career: Qualified 1984.
Personal: Born 1957. Lancaster University; City of London Polytechnic. Tennis, music, walking.

EVENETT, Hilary
Clifford Chance, London
(020) 7600 1000
hilary.evenett@cliffordchance.com
Specialisation: Corporate Department. Partner specialising in non-contentious insurance matters, including UK and European regulation, new authorisations, mergers and acquisitions, portfolio transfers, demutualisations, Lloyd's corporate capital transactions, and other financial service matters.
Career: Called to Bar 1986; requalified as solicitor with *Clifford Chance* 1990; Partner since 1997.
Personal: King Edward VI High School for Girls, Birmingham; Merton College, Oxford (MA Jurisprudence).

FARTHING, Peter
Clyde & Co, London
(020) 7623 1244
Peter.Farthing@clyde.co.uk

www.ChambersandPartners.com

473

INSURANCE ■ THE LEADERS

Specialisation: Partner in insurance and reinsurance department. Has covered almost every aspect of insurance and reinsurance: marine – hull, cargo, war and liability, contract frustration; non-marine – property, jewellers' block, fine art, goods in transit, kidnap and ransom, E&O, D&O, pollution, personal accident, personal stop loss, employers' liability, product liability, performance guarantee, contractors' all risks; reinsurance – excess of loss, quota share, run-off covers, LMX, pools, commutations; brokers' liabilities; issues involving Lloyd's Names, Managing and Members' Agents; significant insurance cases include Napier v Kershaw (1993) (subrogation) and Commercial Union v NRG Victory (1998) ('follow the fortunes'). Member of Council of Law Society (non-constituency, insurance matters); worked on implementation of open market for solicitors' professional indemnity insurance.
Career: *Clyde & Co* 1973 to date. Became a partner in 1977.

GOLDSPINK, Robert
Morgan, Lewis & Bockius, London
(020) 7710 5517
rgoldspink@morganlewis.com
Specialisation: Partner and head of international litigation in London. Main areas of practice are international commercial litigation and arbitration. Has particular experience in heavy, multi-jurisdictional cases and in advising companies affected by fraud. Cases include Alexander Howden, PCW, Lloyds litigation, Lonrho v Fayed, 'Operation Cheetah' (Liverpool and Derek Hatton), Canada Trust Company and Others v W.O. Stolzenberg and Others, Grupo Torras litigation, Anaconda arbitration, and JP Morgan Chase v HIH and others (film finance litigation cases). Member of 1993 joint working party of the general counsel of the Bar and the Law Society which reviewed Britain's civil courts and made wide ranging recommendations for the reform of the English Civil Litigation process. Member of the 'Mariott' committee which produced draft legislation for the reform of British arbitration law, eventually taken up by the DTI. Member of Court of Appeal ADR steering committee. CEDR accredited mediator. Teaches law regularly at conferences and seminars. Co-editor of 'International Commercial Fraud', published by Sweet and Maxwell.
Prof. Memberships: City of London Law Society, London Litigation Solicitors' Association.
Career: Qualified in 1975. Joined *Denton Hall* in 1980, becoming a Partner in 1981. Joined *Morgan Lewis and Bockius* as a Partner in 1997.
Personal: Born 8 August 1949. Attended Eltham College 1959-67, then Cambridge University 1968-72 (receiving an MA and LLM).

GREENLEY, Simon
Reynolds Porter Chamberlain, London
(020) 7242 2877
skg@rpc.co.uk
Specialisation: Partner in insurance, reinsurance and professional indemnity department. Main areas of practice are insurance, reinsurance, coverage litigation and arbitration, financial institutions, first party property and professional liability litigation. Work includes litigation for London market underwriters, including banks, fund managers and other financial institutions, Directors and Officers, Bankers' bond, financial services industry, insurance brokers, and other professionals. Acts in a wide range of non-marine insurance and reinsurance disputes for Lloyd's syndicates and company underwriters, including commercial property risks, liability and contingency. Special studies of financial institutions and 1st party property risks; also handles international insurance and reinsurance and liability litigation (US, South America, European).
Prof. Memberships: Law Society. British Insurance Law Association.
Career: Qualified in 1980. Became a partner in 1984.
Personal: Born 29 January 1957. Leisure interests include golf, tennis, rackets, squash, 20th century art, antique furniture. Hurlingham Club and Walton Heath Golf Club. Married with two children and lives in Central London.

HALL, John
CMS Cameron McKenna, London
(020) 7367 3000
john.hall@cmck.com
Specialisation: Reinsurance, contingency insurance, general insurance advice and professional indemnity. Major cases in recent years include Pan Atlantic v Pine Top (for the brokers, BRS), DSG Retail v QBE International, Alfred McAlpine v BAI (Run-off) Limited and HIH Casualty & General v Chase Manhattan Bank. Currently acting for US reinsurers in relation to the personal accident LMX spirals and retrocessional issues arising from the Unicover debacle. Advising Lloyd's Underwriters with regard to the Riot Damages Act claim arising from the fire at the Yarl's Wood Immigration Centre.
Career: Ardingly College (1958-67); Sidney Sussex College, Cambridge University (1968-71); *Parlett Kent & Co* (1980-82); *Berrymans* (1982-86); *Hewitt Woollatt & Chown*; subsequently *Cameron Markby Hewitt*; subsequently *Cameron McKenna* (1986-date): Became a partner 1989.

HARDY, Tim
Barlow Lyde & Gilbert, London
(020) 7247 2277
thardy@blg.co.uk
Specialisation: For over 20 years has advised upon policy construction issues and handled coverage disputes, litigation and arbitration for the insurance and reinsurance markets worldwide. A founder member of the firm's Reinsurance and International Risk team and Head of its War Risks and Political Risks group, has extensive experience of long-tail liability, aggregation and agency/binder problems, international liability/property programmes, credit and political risk insurance and more innovative forms of risk transfer. Has advised extensively upon war and terrorism issues in wake of September 11 losses.
Prof. Memberships: BILA; CII; BExA; IBA.
Career: *Barlow Lyde & Gilbert* since qualifying, 1982; Partner since 1987; Past Chairman/present committee member, BILA ; member IUA Clauses sub-committee; CEDR accredited mediator,1998; trustee/director, Insurance Charities; trustee, BILA Charitable Trust.
Publications: Numerous articles, papers and presentations in UK and abroad; co-author of 'Reinsurance Practice and the Law (LLP, 1993, looseleaf); editorial board member, 'Commercial Conflict of Laws' (Informa).
Personal: Educated RGS High Wycombe and Balliol College, Oxford, graduating in Jurisprudence. Lives in London.

HEPWORTH, Allan
Ince & Co, London
(020) 7623 2011
allan.hepworth@ince.co.uk
Specialisation: Specialises in marine, non-marine and aviation reinsurance litigation. In recent years his practice has had particular emphasis on London market reinsurance problems arising out of the marine, aviation and personal accident LMX spirals, Unicover, and the reinsurance of US workers compensation business. He has also handled major reinsurance disputes such as the 'Pan Atlantic v Pine Top' litigation, one of the disputes arising out of the death of Robert Maxwell.
Career: Educated at Rugby School and obtained a Law with French degree from Birmingham University. He joined *Ince & Co* as an articled clerk in 1986, qualified in 1988 and became a partner in 1995. In the early 1990s, spent 15 months on secondment to the Legal Department of the reinsurance division of a major US insurance and reinsurance company.

HIGGINS, David
Herbert Smith, London
(020) 7374 8000
david.higgins@herbertsmith.com
Specialisation: Partner specialising in insurance and reinsurance law and private international law. Also has extensive experience of handling disputes in every area of law generally involving insurers, ranging from most aspects of contract and tort arising in complex commercial disputes to personal injury and fraud.
Prof. Memberships: Recorder of the Crown Court; Solicitor Advocate with higher court rights in all courts in all proceedings both civil and criminal; Chairman of the Insurance Law Sub-Committee of the City of London Law Society; Member of the Committee of the City of London Law Society.
Career: Qualified 1970; joined *Herbert Smith* 1971; Partnership 1977.

HILL, Jeremy
Ashurst Morris Crisp, London
(020) 7859 1748
jeremy.hill@ashursts.com
Specialisation: Partner in company/commercial department. Head of insurance. Lloyd's of London and London Market: handles all non-contentious matters, particularly policy wordings; acquisition, disposal, flotation of agencies, brokers and insurance and reinsurance companies; regulatory issues; captive insurance vehicles; insurance reconstructions and insolvencies; and creation and registration of Lloyd's Corporate Members. Has advised on numerous capacity offers in the Lloyd's market (both for cash and securities) as well as conversion schemes. Acted for Iron Trades on the disposal of Iron Trades Insurance Company to QBE; acted for CBS on the largest conversion scheme at Lloyd's, CBS 2000; acted for the St Paul Companies on the sale of Minet to Aon and for Goshawk Insurance Holdings plc on its takeover of Matheson Lloyds Investment Trust plc; acted for Ockham Holdings PLC on its takeover of New London Capital PLC; acted for Benfield Greig Group plc on its merger with E W Blanch, and for the IVA and LPC in the creation of the 'Ins-sure' joint venture. Author of 'Willis Guide to Directors' and Officers' Liability', and of articles in publications on Lloyd's and the London Insurance market.
Prof. Memberships: Chartered Insurance Institute, Law Society.
Career: Qualified in 1984. Joined *Ashurst Morris Crisp* in 1982, spending a year seconded to Lloyd's of London in 1985, and becoming a partner in 1992.

HOLDERNESS, Andrew
Clyde & Co, Guildford
(01483) 555555
Andrew.Holderness@clyde.co.uk
Specialisation: Principal area of practice is corporate finance covering flotations, mergers, acquisitions and disposals (both public and private), MBOs/MBIs, joint ventures, private equity transactions and general corporate advice for the Lloyd's and the companies market. Also specialises in the introduction and structuring of corporate capital to Lloyd's, formation of new Lloyd's Managing Agents and Syndicates. Acted for Wren plc on the £250 million merger with BRIT Insurance Holdings plc; Fairfax Financial Holdings on the US$600 million takeover of TGI Holdings, Inc; management of Euclidian plc on the £30 million MBO; Chartwell Re, Swiss Re and Thomas Miller on the new US$50 million joint venture marine hull syndicate; Wren plc on the £130 million group reorganisation; management of Ensign

on the £145m syndicate MBO and Cathedral Capital plc on the Offer for Subscription raising £15m.
Prof. Memberships: Law Society.
Career: Articled at *Titmuss Sainer Dechert* 1985-87, became a partner in 1992, joined *Clyde & Co* as a partner in 1997.
Personal: Born 15 February 1962. Educated Marlborough College 1975-80, Exeter University 1981-84. Leisure pursuits include golf, tennis and skiing.

JAMES, Glen
Slaughter and May, London
(020) 7600 1200
glen.james@slaughterandmay.com
Specialisation: Practice covers all work in the fields of company and corporate finance, including mergers and acquisitions, issues and flotations and corporate restructurings. Additional interest in non-contentious insurance and reinsurance work.
Prof. Memberships: The Law Society; Securities Institute.
Career: Qualified 1976. Articled at *Slaughter and May* 1974-76. Assistant solicitor 1976-83. Partner since 1983.
Personal: Born 22 August 1952. Educated at King's College School, Wimbledon and New College, Oxford

KENDALL, David
D J Freeman, London
(020) 7583 4055

LEONARD, Paul
Freshfields Bruckhaus Deringer, London
(020) 7936 4000
paul.leonard@freshfields.com
See under Litigation, p.562

LEWIS, Stephen
Clifford Chance, London
(020) 7600 1000
stephen.lewis@cliffordchance.com
Specialisation: Litigation and Dispute Resolution Department. Partner specialising in insurance and reinsurance, ADR arbitration litigation and advisory work, including reinsurance treaty and policy drafting and review.
Career: Qualified 1974; Partner since 1985 worked with the Law Commission, a branch of the British Government concerned with law reform 1975-80 concentrating particularly on reform of insurance law and the law concerning liability for defective products.
Personal: 1970 St Catherine's College, Oxford (1st Class Hons Philosophy, Politics and Economics); 1980 University of London (LLB).

MACKIE, Francis
Norton Rose, London
(020) 7283 6000
mackiefo@nortonrose.com
Specialisation: Partner practising in the international commercial insurance and reinsurance market, with clients being from the London market (Lloyd's and company market) and the international insurance market. The practice involves both contentious matters and policy advisory work. Current high profile cases include Marc Rich Oil/Sugar claims (in arbitration), the London market film financing insurance/reinsurance disputes, the travel insurance litigation. The practice currently has an emphasis on political risk/CF advise and disputes and also energy related risks.
Career: Admitted 1976. After qualification practised for two years in Newcastle and then moved to London, becoming a partner at *Clyde & Co* in 1984. In November 1993 he moved over to *Norton Rose* to become a partner in the insurance group.

MADDOCK, Geoffrey
Herbert Smith, London
(020) 7374 8000
geoffrey.maddock@herbertsmith.com
Specialisation: Partner working principally on corporate finance transactions in the insurance sector. Has experience of demutualisations of life assurance companies, acquisitions, disposals, joint ventures and related transactions in the sector. Also has particular experience of transfers of insurance business under the Insurance Companies Act.
Prof. Memberships: Law Society; City of London Solicitors Company.
Career: Qualified in 1990 and became a partner in 1997.
Personal: Educated at Gonville & Caius College, Cambridge.

MCKENNA, Ian
Holman Fenwick & Willan, London
(020) 7264 8222
ian.mckenna@hfw.co.uk
Specialisation: Partner specialising in all aspects of insurance and reinsurance dispute resolution on behalf of cedants, reinsurers and brokers in both the London and overseas insurance and reinsurance markets. Also specialises in brokers' E&O disputes, and disputes arising from the operation of underwriting agencies/reinsurance pools. Has a wide experience of conducting litigation, arbitration and mediation both in London and in various overseas jurisdictions.
Prof. Memberships: British Insurance Law Association; The Law Society.
Career: Belfast Royal Academy; University of Birmingham; University of Limoges (France); Munich Re (London) 1985 to 1987; trained and qualified *Holman Fenwick & Willan* (1988-91); *Barlow Lyde & Gilbert* (1992-94); rejoined *Holman Fenwick & Willan* in 1994. Became partner in 1997.
Personal: Born 1962. Married with two children, resides in Hertfordshire. Interests include reading and watching sport, particularly rugby (Saracens RFC) and football (Aston Villa FC).

MENDELOWITZ, Michael
Barlow Lyde & Gilbert, London
(020) 7247 2277
Specialisation: Partner in reinsurance division. All aspects of insurance and reinsurance, with emphasis on complex reinsurance claims, environmental and other long-tail problems, insurance insolvency and disputes concerning interpretation of contracts or materiality of underwriting information.
Prof. Memberships: Association Internationale de Droit des Assurances (Assistant Secretary-General), British Insurance Law Association, UK Environmental Law Association, Law Society and Chartered Insurance Institute.
Career: Practised as a barrister in South Africa before joining *Barlow Lyde & Gilbert* in 1987. Re-qualified as a solicitor in 1989 and became a partner in 1990. Frequent speaker at conferences in UK and overseas on topics ranging from arbitration and alternative dispute resolution in reinsurance to liability for pollution and toxic torts. Numerous articles published in legal and market journals. Co-author and co-ordinating editor of 'Reinsurance Practice and the Law' (Lloyd's of London Press, 1993).
Personal: Born 1952. Educated at University of the Witwatersrand (BA, LLB) and Oxford University (BCL) as a Rhodes Scholar. Lives in North-West London. Interests include family, music and skiing holidays.

MIDDLEDITCH, Matthew
Linklaters, London
(020) 7456 3144
matthew.middleditch@linklaters.com
Specialisation: Specialist in UK corporate finance and company law advising both corporate clients and investment banks. Main areas of practice include: public and private mergers and acquisitions, joint ventures and general corporate work.
Career: 1990 to date: Partner, *Linklaters*; 1988-90; Assistant Solicitor, *Linklaters*; 1986-88: Assistant Solicitor, *Mills & Reeve*, Norwich; 1982-86: Assistant Solicitor, *Linklaters*; 1980-82: Articled Clerk, *Linklaters*. 1979-80: College of Law, Law Society Final Examinations; 1976-79: Trinity College, Cambridge, MA Law.

MUNDAY, Nicholas
Clifford Chance, London
(020) 7600 1000
nicholas.munday@cliffordchance.com
Specialisation: Litigation and Dispute Resolution Department. Partner specialising in insurance and reinsurance, project finance insurance and political risk and Lloyd's matters including Lloyd's regulatory issues.
Career: Qualified 1985; articled *Barlow Lyde & Gilbert*; joined *Clifford Chance* 1990; Partner since 1995.
Personal: Forest School, Snaresbrook; BA Law P London – South Bank.

O'CONNELL, Clive
Barlow Lyde & Gilbert, London
(020) 7643 8477
coconnell@blg.co.uk
Specialisation: Reinsurance law, primarily of a contentious nature; handling reinsurance disputes in arbitration and court in London, the US, Continental Europe and elsewhere. Advising on various aspects of reinsurance law and regulation and allied areas including, particularly, the development of new risk transfer products.
Career: Qualified 1982; joined Reinsurance and International Risk team at *Barlow Lyde & Gilbert* 1984; partner 1989.
Publications: Contributing author to 'Reinsurance Practice and the Law'; chapters for two Chartered Institute of Insurers Coursebooks; Chapter for 'Alternative Risk Strategies' (ed Morton Lane 2002); regular column in 'The Review – Worldwide Reinsurance' and articles in numerous other publications.
Personal: Born 1957, resides Islington; Married with two daughters; flies power kites and supports Chelsea.

O'NEILL, Terry
Clifford Chance, London
(020) 7600 1000
terry.oneill@cliffordchance.com
Specialisation: Litigation and Dispute Resolution Department. Partner specialising in contentious and non-contentious insurance, reinsurance, Lloyd's and professional indemnity.
Career: Called to the Bar, Lincoln's Inn 1973; joined *Clifford-Turner* 1977; Partner since 1980.
Personal: Educated Ratcliffe College, Leicester; 1962-65 University College, London (LLB); 1973 University College, London (PhD).

PARKER, Raj
Freshfields Bruckhaus Deringer, London
(020) 7936 4000
raj.parker@freshfields.com
See under Litigation, p.565

PAYTON, Michael
Clyde & Co, London
(020) 7623 1244
Michael.Payton@clyde.co.uk
Specialisation: Partner in Insurance and Reinsurance Department. Adviser to insurers worldwide on most of the major international insurance problems of recent years, notably (and in no particular order) 'Piper Alpha'; the invasion of Kuwait; collapse of US Savings & Loans Banks; breast implants; US environmental and pollution claims; break up of the former Yugoslavia; Scandinavian credit reinsurance; loss of Sleipner GBS; the kidnap of 'Shergar', the ships 'Braer', 'Estonia', and 'Sea Empress'; Chernobyl related contamination of food crops; and the Lloyd's litigation including reconstruction and renewal, in particular the reinsurance aspects; implications of the break up of the former USSR for the oil and gas industries from an insurance perspective. US and Canadian extended warranty insurance problems; Hatfield rail crash; loss of Rig P.36; WTC.
Prof. Memberships: Chairman, Solicitors' Indemnity Mutual Insurance Association. Chairman, British Maritime Law Association. 1995-96 Member of the Working Party of the President of the Law Society on Professional Indemnity

INSURANCE ■ THE LEADERS

Insurance. 1997 Chairman – Energy Employers Mutual Insurance Association.

PERRY, Bill
Charles Russell, London
(020) 7203 5288
billp@cr-law.co.uk

Specialisation: Practice involves both contentious and non-contentious work in national and international insurance and reinsurance; in particular direct property insurance coverage disputes (especially high risk property and fine art); property reinsurance (facultative and treaty); alternative risk transfer programmes. Recent reported cases include the Callaghan litigation, Aetna Re v Central Re, etc. Also competition and trust litigation work. Lectures and writes internationally.
Prof. Memberships: Chartered Institute of Arbitrators; International Association of Defense Counsel; British Insurance Law Association; Institute of Management; International Bar Association; City of London Solicitors Company; Law Society.
Career: *Norton Rose* 1974-85 (qualified with Honours 1977); *Pickering Kenyon* 1985-95 (senior partner 1990-95); *Charles Russell* 1995-date.
Personal: Educated University College, Oxford. Fellow, Royal Society for Arts. Married to Jane; children: Alexandra, Caroline and Michael.

POYNTON, Ian
Freshfields Bruckhaus Deringer, London
(020) 7936 4000
ian.poynton@freshfields.com

Specialisation: Corporate Department. Partner specialising in M&A and corporate transactions, with particular emphasis on the insurance sector and other financial institutions.
Career: Partner *Freshfields* 1998.
Personal: Born 1965. Corpus Christi College, Oxford. Languages: French and German.

ROGAN, Peter
Ince & Co, London
(020) 7623 2011
peter.rogan@ince.co.uk

Specialisation: Became senior partner of the firm in May 2000. Specialises in advising in the insurance and reinsurance fields and is Chairman of the *Ince & Co* Insurance Business Group. Reinsurance practice is litigation oriented and diverse, acting for clients both in London and abroad on high profile non-marine, aviation and marine reinsurance disputes, including, such high profile matters as the PA LMX Spiral & Unicover. Past cases included setting a number of important precedents in areas of legal difficulty, such as Pine Top on non-disclosure, and PCW on moral hazard. In direct insurance work, his practice is almost as broad, encompassing a variety of classes, most significantly professional indemnity insurance matters for brokers, accountants and banks and others in a range of high value cases arising from major market losses and disputes since the late 1980s.
Prof. Memberships: Aside from the IBA, he is a Committee member of ARIAS (UK).
Career: Educated at Stellenbosch University and Kings College, London, he spent two years at London brokers *Willis Faber* before joining *Ince & Co* in 1977, becoming a partner in 1982.
Personal: Born 1950, resides London, leisure interests include family, theatre, tennis, golf and skiing.

RONALDSON, Cheryl
Norton Rose, London
(020) 7444 3323
ronaldsonca@nortonrose.com

Specialisation: Partner in the corporate insurance group at *Norton Rose*. Has a strong reputation for corporate and regulatory insurance, particularly within the Lloyd's market. Experience covers a broad range of private and public company transactions for insurance companies in all sectors of the insurance industry, Lloyds' managing agencies, brokers and corporate members. Also has expertise in advising participants in the market on a wide variety of insurance regulatory matters – both life and non-life, and on alternative risk products and structures.
Prof. Memberships: The Law Society.
Career: Partner *Norton Rose* Jan 1999. Solicitor *Clifford Chance* 1994-98. Solicitor *Barlow Lyde & Gilbert* 1990-94. Trainee *Barlow Lyde & Gilbert* 1988-90. King's College London – LLB (Hons). Leicester High School for Girls.

SCHOFIELD, Belinda
CMS Cameron McKenna, London
(020) 7367 3000
belinda.schofield@cmck.com

Specialisation: Principal areas of practice are handling professional indemnity claims against accountants, actuaries, financial institutions, insurance brokers and directors' and officers' liability. Acting for insurers and insureds. Growing and significant area of practice is in the field of regulation and risk management acting for professionals and insurers in risk control and avoidance projects, due diligence exercises and advising on the impact of regulatory controls, including representing individuals in regulatory proceedings and monitoring such proceedings for insurers. Work also includes general insurance and reinsurance advice and drafting and construction of policy wordings. Experienced in handling large commercial disputes. Speaks at numerous market seminars.

SCHWARTZ, Peter
Baker & McKenzie, London
(020) 7919 1000
peter.schwartz@bakernet.com

Specialisation: Peter is Chair of the European insurance group. He deals with all aspects of liability insurance and non-marine reinsurance, including commercial and financial risks; commercial agreements; discontinued operations; cross-border reinsurance issues; professional liabilities; agency-intermediary relationships; new solutions; dispute resolution.
Prof. Memberships: International Bar Association; British Insurance Law Association; ARIAS; Chartered Insurance Institute.
Career: Trained *Alexander Howden Group Ltd*; qualified 1978; partner *Wilde Sapte* 1991-96; partner *Sonnenschein, Nath & Rosenthal* 1996-99; partner *Baker & McKenzie* 1999 to date.
Publications: Peter contributes articles regularly to professional trade press and is a regular speaker at conferences and seminars both in the UK and worldwide.
Personal: Peter was born in 1953 and resides in Chalfont St Giles. He enjoys all sports, particularly tennis, athletics and football, music, ballet (watching!) and travel. Education: Wembley County Grammar/Alperton High; Leeds University (LLB Hons); College of Law, London.

SMITH, Rod
Clyde & Co, London
(020) 7623 1244
roderick.smith@clyde.co.uk

Specialisation: Partner in Insurance and Reinsurance Department. Acts for London market and overseas insurers in a wide range of insurance and reinsurance disputes, frequently of an international nature. Work areas include marine and non-marine insurance including cargo, goods in transit, jeweller's block, Fine Art, contingency, business interruption, credit, political and financial risks, and personal accident including Key Man insurance. Handles all aspects of reinsurance disputes and has extensive involvement in the drafting and review of insurance and reinsurance wordings including new product development.
Career: Admitted as an attorney in South Africa 1976. Joined *Clyde & Co*. 1977. Admitted as a solicitor in England and Wales 1980. Partner *Clyde & Co*. 1982.

STANLEY, Ed
Barlow Lyde & Gilbert, London
(020) 7643 7503
estanley@blg.co.uk

Specialisation: Partner in Reinsurance and International Risk Team. Reinsurance and all areas of commercial insurance litigation, notably professional indemnity disputes involving brokers and underwriting agencies.
Career: Articled *Elborne Mitchell*, Qualified 1984. Assistant Solicitor *Elborne Mitchell* 1984-98. Partner *Elborne Mitchell* 1989-97. Partner *Hammond Suddards* 1997 to 1999. Partner *Barlow Lyde & Gilbert* 1999 to date.
Personal: Born 1959. Educated at St Brendan's College, Bristol and Exeter College, Oxford. Leisure: football and playing keyboards. Resides: London.

YOUNG, John
Lovells, London
(020) 7296 2000
john.young@lovells.com

Specialisation: Advises on the formation, regulation, sale and purchase of insurance companies and businesses in the UK and internationally. Co-ordinates the activities of *Lovells* lawyers who advise the insurance industry on non-contentious matters. Has acted on numerous transactions within the industry, including several recent life assurance demutualisations. Regularly speaks on topics relating to the regulation of insurance and mergers and acquisitions in the industry.
Prof. Memberships: Law Society. Member ICC Committee on Insurance. Immediate past President of the Society of Scottish Lawyers in London.
Career: Articled *Lovells* 1979-81; qualified 1981; partner 1987.
Publications: Author of various articles on insurance; author of the insurance chapter in the 'CCH Common Market Reporter' (1996); consulting editor of 'A Practitioner's Guide to the FSA Regulation of Insurance' (City and Financial Publishing, 2002).

INTELLECTUAL PROPERTY

London: 477; The Regions: 481; Scotland: 486; Profiles: 486

Research approved by BMRB For this edition, **Chambers'** researchers conducted 6,582 interviews – 3,900 with law firms, 511 with barristers and 2,171 with clients. The validity of the research was scrutinised by BMRB International, who audited both the methodology and the results at our offices in London. They interviewed **Chambers'** researchers and cross-checked sample interviews. Details of the audit appear on page 7.

OVERVIEW The market has proved buoyant as companies increasingly view their IP rights as one of their greatest assets. Image rights are gaining sway, in particular for top sports personalities who wish to register their names as trademarks. The convergence of IT and IP continues, with cases such as WWF v WWF displaying the impact of domain names upon trademark agreements. The tables have been renamed, firstly to recognise the patent licensing work of many firms which feature in the general tables, and secondly to highlight the specific expertise of patent litigators.

LONDON

INTELLECTUAL PROPERTY
PATENT LITIGATION ■ LONDON

1
- Bird & Bird
- Bristows

2
- Linklaters
- Simmons & Simmons
- Taylor Wessing

3
- Herbert Smith
- Lovells
- Wragge & Co

4
- Baker & McKenzie
- Clifford Chance
- Eversheds
- Roiter Zucker

5
- Allen & Overy

This book is the product of 6,582 1/2 hour interviews. See p.7 for BMRB audit. Within each band, firms are listed alphabetically.

BIRD & BIRD (see firm details p.874) The firm maintains its position "*in a field of its own,*" claim peers who endorse its "*informed and proactive*" lawyers, while clients appreciate its ability to "*seamlessly*" manage an international case. A new office launched in The Hague has bolstered this pan-European team, leading to an increase in cross-border instructions. The team has represented Aventis in the case against Kirin-Amgen regarding the use of genetic engineering to produce erythropoietin. In this, one of the longest running UK patent trials, three of the four infringement claims against Aventis were found to be invalid. The case was led by "*the doyen of IP,*" **Trevor Cook** (see p.488), who is particularly regarded for his litigation expertise. "*Tough yet commercially astute*" **Morag Macdonald** (see p.491) led the landmark case in which the Estate of James Joyce obtained an injunction against Macmillan Publishers and editor Danis Rose to publish an edition of *Ulysses* that infringed the copyright of manuscripts and draft documents belonging to the Estate. **David Harriss** (see p.489) provides valuable support in the field of patent litigation, while Miles Gaythwaite is now a consultant with the group. **Clients** Aventis; Pfizer; Fuller, Smith & Turner; Emap; Compaq Computer.

LINKLATERS (see firm details p.1043) Competitors "*can't fault this superb IP practice: they don't just rely on a corporate client base, they are creative about collaring new work.*" The team rises to the lead in the general tables this year in recognition of its trademarks strength, as the market pointed our researchers to "*sterling clients and practitioners, equal to those firms within the top tier.*" The group's profile has benefited from the headline-catching Davidoff case, which the team took to the ECJ, thereby reversing the judgment reached in the UK courts. **Jeremy Brown**'s (see p.487) "*inimitable*" presence presided over the recently settled Novartis v American Home Products case, while **Anna Carboni**'s (see p.487) "*first-class*" trademark expertise has propelled her up the tables due to sheer weight of peer and client recommendation. Robert Swift is now a consultant with the group, and is a valuable resource as an IP strategist, while Nigel Jones is on secondment to Cologne, forming a vital link within multi-jurisdictional patent work. **Robin Whaite** (see p.495) has advised Hewlett-Packard on trademark enforcement proceedings in several European jurisdictions concerning UK ink-jet cartridges, while **Ian Karet** (see p.491) has acted for Ciba Specialty Chemicals Holding in a patent infringement case concerning pigments. **Clients** Johnson & Johnson; American Home Products; GlaxoSmithKline; Hewlett-Packard; Gucci.

TAYLOR WESSING (see firm details p.1156) The group maintains the top spot in our general tables, while an impressive array of commendation for the patent team suggests a narrowing gap between themselves and the top tier firms. A competitor views it as "*one of the leaders for pharmaceutical work,*" while clients appreciate the high quality expertise and hands-on approach of the patent partners. **Mark Hodgson** (see p.489) acted for Eli Lilly and ICOS in their successful hearing in the Court of Appeal to revoke the monopolisation by Pfizer of the Viagra compound. He is viewed by clients as "*always on top of the facts, a great strategist.*" **James Marshall** (see p.492) has been singled out for the clarity of his legal and business advice within the patent field. **Gary Moss** (see p.493) has been acting for Kirin-Amgen and Ortho Biotech in their high-profile litigation regarding the patent for erythropoietin, although there is a perception that his role as managing partner has limited his visibility at the coalface. **Richard Price** (see p.493) is regarded for his expertise within the contentious side of patent and trademark work. Aside from patent litigation, the team is endorsed as "*masters of the commercial game.*" In particular, newly ranked **Jason Rawkins** (see p.494) impressed the market with his "*robust*" and successful handling of the trademark infringement action brought by PepsiCo against French Connection. **Clients** Kirin-Amgen; SC Johnson; University of Cambridge; Citibank; Pharmacia & Upjohn.

TOP IN-HOUSE LAWYERS

Bob BOAD, Assistant Head of Group Trademarks, BP

Alan COX, Global Head of Trademarks, GlaxoSmithKline

Marc DALBY, Legal Director, Merck Sharpe and Dohme

Richard HEATH, Head of Corporate Trademarks and General Trademark Counsel, Unilever

Sheila HENDERSON, Trademarks Director, Reckitt & Benckiser

Evie KYRIAKIDES, Market Property Manager, Mars

Frederick MOSTERT, Chief Intellectual Property Counsel, Richemont International

Chris PETTY, AstraZeneca

David ROBERTS, Director & Senior Vice President, Corporate Intellectual Property, GlaxoSmithKline

Louis J VIRELLI Jr, Senior Vice President, General Patent Counsel, Unilever

New additions to this year's list include **Chris Petty**, *who is "bright – he knows his field backwards," and* **Louis J Virelli Jr** *who comes "extremely highly recommended", as does* **Marc Dalby**, *the latter praised for being a "clear instructor." The "exceptional" and "scarily knowledgeable"* **Bob Boad** *is again highly commended.* **Alan Cox**, **Sheila Henderson** *and* **David Roberts** *are acclaimed for their "vast experience" in the sector. The "efficient"* **Richard Heath** *and "excellent"* **Evie Kyriakides** *are thoroughly deserving of their place on the list, while the "knowledgeable and commercial"* **Frederick Mostert** *received numerous recommendations.*

In-house lawyers' profiles p.1201

477

INTELLECTUAL PROPERTY ■ LONDON

INTELLECTUAL PROPERTY
GENERAL ■ LONDON

1 **Bird & Bird**
  Linklaters
  Taylor Wessing

2 **Bristows**
  Simmons & Simmons

3 **Baker & McKenzie**
  Lovells
  Willoughby & Partners
  Wragge & Co

4 **Allen & Overy**
  Clifford Chance
  Denton Wilde Sapte
  Eversheds
  Herbert Smith
  Olswang
  Slaughter and May

5 **Ashurst Morris Crisp**
  Field Fisher Waterhouse
  Freshfields Bruckhaus Deringer
  Gouldens
  Roiter Zucker
  Shook, Hardy & Bacon
  SJ Berwin

6 **Briffa**
  Dechert
  Hammond Suddards Edge
  KLegal
  Mayer, Brown, Rowe & Maw

This book is the product of 6,582 1/2 hour interviews. See p.7 for BMRB audit.
Within each band, firms are listed alphabetically.

BRISTOWS (see firm details p.888) A "*focused*" team, according to peers, producing "*consistently excellent quality: they are able to do the job properly, with bona fide partner involvement.*" Patent work is perceived to be the group's forte, with trademark and 'soft' IP work slightly lower in profile this year. Commended as a "*litigation powerhouse*," it led the co-ordination of European, US, Canadian and Japanese patent infringement proceedings issued by Pharmacia against Merck in relation to its painkiller, Vioxx. "*Straight-dealing, clearly expert*" **Edward Nodder** (see p.493) led the team representing CIBA Vision in its patent infringement case. Competitors cite **Sally Field** (see p.488) as a "*first-class, tough opponent,*" who has been working alongside **Paul Walsh** (see p.494) on trademark disputes for Guinness UDV. Walsh was commended to our researchers for his excellent judgement, while peers singled out **David Brown** (see p.487) and **Ian Judge** (see p.490) for their prowess in patent litigation. A new bioinformatics group has been set up in response to the publication of the first draft of the human genome. **Clients** 3M; Novartis; Affymetrix; Guinness UDV; Sony Computer Entertainment.

SIMMONS & SIMMONS (see firm details p.1136) This "*crack team*" of patent lawyers was commended to our researchers for its consistently high quality advice. The group is best known for its expertise in multi-jurisdictional litigation, and has obtained the only interim injunction in a patent case to be awarded to GlaxoSmithKline in the past five years. An active participant in this case, **Kevin Mooney** (see p.493) has been cited by peers as "*the doyen of patent law.*" **Gerry Kamstra** (see p.490) maintains market approval for his co-ordination of European patent litigation proceedings concerning the protection of the AstraZeneca patent, Losec. "*One of the best patent litigators in London,*" **Rowan Freeland** (see p.489) has been judged a "*safe pair of hands*" in the most complex of cases; he acted on the SmithKline Beecham v Generics [UK] case, regarding two 'Belgian torpedoes' and two 'Italian torpedoes'. On the 'soft' side of IP, the team "*continues to secure top end work.*" The "*skilful*" **Helen Newman** (see p.493) has been responsible for the expansion of the trademark prosecution practice to offer a fully-fledged one-stop shop. The team continues to act for Interbrew, recently advising on the sale of certain brands, including Carling and Caffrey's, to American brewer Coors. **Clients** GlaxoSmithKline; Procter & Gamble; Interbrew; Bacardi-Martini Group; Burberry.

BAKER & McKENZIE (see firm details p.855) The firm houses a hugely respected patent and general practice, although our researchers found that its market profile is felt to be higher on the general side. Patent cases range from pharmaceutical issues to disputes regarding the Sony Walkman. The group, which included **Stephen Jones**, acted for Pfizer in the high-profile Pharmacia and Pfizer v Merck case. The department boasts high-profile branding work, and, according to clients, fields "*an excellent trademark team, who don't over-lawyer things.*" Perhaps better known for his IT prowess, Harry Small has led a team in one of the most important trademark cases of the past year, the Levi Strauss case against Tesco and Costco, which encompasses seven European jurisdictions. Peers endorsed his "*creative*" approach, and contend that he is a "*walking encyclopaedia.*" The "*solution-focused*" **Michael Hart** (see p.435) acted on a significant case in which Universities UK successfully reduced the cost of licences from the Copyright Licensing Agency, thereby reducing the costs for higher education over years to come. **Clients** Pfizer; Sony; Versace; Tommy Hilfiger; BP Chemicals.

LOVELLS (see firm details p.1045) The department, which is perceived to maintain "*great stature in patent litigation,*" is gaining in cross-border strength due to its successful merger with Boesebeck Droste, and more recently with French and Dutch firms. "*The maverick who is full of good ideas,*" **Robert Anderson** (see p.486) has represented Korean company Daesang in the Europe-wide patent dispute with Japanese company Ajinomoto, relating to artificial sweeteners. The "*supremely talented*" **Nick Macfarlane** (see p.492) acted for Merck in the Monsanto and Searle v Merck case, in which Merck was accused of patent infringement for NSAIDs; the Court of Appeal found the patent invalid in 2001. Non-contentious work has included acting for Mars on a worldwide licence for the rights in Harry Potter confectionery products. **Clients** 3i; Estée Lauder; Novo Nordisk; Reuters; Janssen Pharmaceutica.

WILLOUGHBY & PARTNERS (see firm details p.1189) A team that moves up the tables this year due to sheer weight of peer and client recommendation for its trademark work. The "*superb*" team is "*full of dynamic up-and-comers,*" thus not relying solely on the inimitable **Tony Willoughby** (see p.495), who retains "*the edge over everyone else for tough litigation matters.*" The London office concentrates mainly on contentious work; it has advised Cartier on design right protection for one of its new ranges of watches. The firm continues to act for GlaxoSmithKline on the parallel import of Zovirax and Seroxat. The practice also covers patent litigation, biotech- and media-related work. **Clients** GlaxoSmithKline; The Generics Group; Celltech Group; Celador Productions; Guinness UDV.

WRAGGE & CO (see firm details p.1197) "*If you want a firm with a different approach, you should use them,*" claim industry experts. The firm is seen to be "*really emerging to take on the market,*" both on the patent and non-patent side. The majority of contentious work is led by the London team. It recently acted on the Elida Fabergé v Colgate-Palmolive patent case concerning a toothbrush with a hinge in the brush head. The "*unstoppable*" **Gregor Grant** (see p.270202), unanimously perceived to be "*one of the greats*" of the patent world, recently won the Amersham v Millipore patent appeal regarding chromotography columns. **Adam Cooke** is well regarded for his biotech work, while David Gibbins is now a consultant with the group. On the non-patent side, anti-counterfeiting has been a particular area of growth within its branding work. **Clients** Unilever; British Airways; Elida Fabergé; Icon Health and Fitness.

ALLEN & OVERY (see firm details p.841) The team is best known for its non-contentious work; however, our researchers found it warmly endorsed by experts within the patent litigation field. Our interviewees agreed that this is "*a specialist patent practice, not simply corporate support,*" which acted for Ishida on a patent infringement matter relating to Ishida's VFFS machine for bagging snack food products. "*Contentious expert*" **Catriona Smith** (see p.494) is lauded for "*building up a great practice,*" while **Robert Barry** (see p.487) gains the

LONDON — INTELLECTUAL PROPERTY

LEADING INDIVIDUALS

[1]
- **COOK Trevor** Bird & Bird
- **GRANT Gregor** Wragge & Co
- **MACDONALD Morag** Bird & Bird
- **WILLOUGHBY Tony** Willoughby & Partners
- **FIELD Sally** Bristows
- **HODGSON Mark** Taylor Wessing
- **MOONEY Kevin** Simmons & Simmons

[2]
- **BROWN Jeremy** Linklaters
- **FREELAND Rowan** Simmons & Simmons
- **MACFARLANE Nicholas** Lovells
- **WALSH Paul** Bristows
- **DAVIES Isabel** Eversheds
- **JUDGE Ian** Bristows
- **NODDER Edward** Bristows

[3]
- **ANDERSON Robert** Lovells
- **MARTINDALE Avril** Freshfields Bruckhaus Deringer
- **PERKINS David** Clifford Chance
- **STARR Ian** Ashurst Morris Crisp
- **COHEN Laurence** McDermott, Will & Emery
- **NEWMAN Helen** Simmons & Simmons
- **SMITH Catriona** Allen & Overy

[4]
- **BROWN David** Bristows
- **HARRISS David** Bird & Bird
- **JONES Stephen** Baker & McKenzie
- **LLEWELYN David** White & Case
- **MOODIE Bill** Herbert Smith
- **SWYCHER Nigel** Slaughter and May
- **WHAITE Robin** Linklaters
- **CARBONI Anna** Linklaters
- **INGLIS Andrew** Olswang
- **KARET Ian** Linklaters
- **MARSLAND Vanessa** Clifford Chance
- **MOSS Gary** Taylor Wessing
- **THORNE Clive** Denton Wilde Sapte

[5]
- **BRIFFA Margaret** Briffa
- **HARRIS Paul** Eversheds
- **MACDONALD-BROWN Charters** Gouldens
- **RICH Andrew** Herbert Smith
- **TAYLOR Peter** Clifford Chance
- **COOKE Adam** Wragge & Co
- **HART Michael** Baker & McKenzie
- **PRICE Richard** Taylor Wessing
- **SHILLITO Mark** Herbert Smith

[6]
- **BARRY Robert** Allen & Overy
- **GARE Stephen** Mayer, Brown, Rowe & Maw
- **KAMSTRA Gerry** Simmons & Simmons
- **MARSHALL James** Taylor Wessing
- **RAWKINS Jason** Taylor Wessing
- **WOOD Ian** Mayer, Brown, Rowe & Maw
- **DANILUNAS Marija** Hammond Suddards Edge
- **IRVINE James** Shook, Hardy & Bacon
- **LEVINE Simon** Denton Wilde Sapte
- **MCKAY Anna** Roiter Zucker
- **TURNER Catrin** KLegal

UP AND COMING
- **MIDDLEMISS Susie** Slaughter and May
- **ROSE David** SJ Berwin

See individuals' profiles p.486

---

respect of his peers for his work in the EPO. The non-contentious practice recently acted on one of Europe's largest biotech product deals to license CDP 870, an injectable medicine for rheumatoid arthritis and Crohn's Disease, to Pharmacia. **Clients** William Hill; JP Morgan Securities; Bass; British Telecommunications.

CLIFFORD CHANCE (see firm details p.911) Clients were keen to recommend this patent and general team for its ability to carry out multi-jurisdictional litigation, while peers pointed to an emphasis outside the UK. One such example was the Sun v Ciba case, a patent revocation and amendment case concerning pigments for use in engineering substrates, with corresponding cases in Germany and Holland. **David Perkins** (see p.493) is respected for his wide-ranging expertise, particularly in patent and trademark work. **Vanessa Marsland** (see p.492) holds a slightly lower profile this year, but was nevertheless singled out for her pragmatism. **Peter Taylor** (see p.494) ("*an excellent all-rounder*") has acted for Malaysia Dairy Industries in a long-running dispute with Yakult concerning the right to register the container shape as a trademark. **Clients** Honda; Whitbread; Sun Chemical; Mars; Reuters.

DENTON WILDE SAPTE (see firm details p.935) "*A stellar team*" for general IP work, its "*quality inspires confidence*" in rivals, and remains best known for its contentious expertise. The non-contentious side of the practice is growing, with clients such as easyGroup and Sony instructing the team for brand management and strategy as well as enforcement proceedings. Newly ranked **Simon Levine** (see p.491) is lauded by clients for "*really understanding our business.*" He acted for the Estate of EH Shepard on one of the largest publishing deals of the year: the sale of Winnie the Pooh rights to Disney. The "*underrated*" **Clive Thorne** (see p.494) gains the respect of his peers for the depth of his knowledge. **Clients** Marks & Spencer; Pinnacle Insurance; Virgin Mobile; Hamleys; Magnex Scientific.

EVERSHEDS (see firm details p.949) Packed with "*knowledgeable people,*" the London office of this large national and international firm offers a broad range of advice. Alongside high-profile work in trademarks, copyright and design work, the team has been involved in cutting-edge non-contentious work advising Catalyst BioMedica on IP and regulatory matters affecting its research institutions, which include the Human Genome Project. High-profile **Isabel Davies** (see p.488) has been cited as "*one of the best patent litigators in London,*" while **Paul Harris** (see p.489) is highly rated by peers. The team has defended patent litigation commenced by Commtel against Amstrad concerning connectors for set-top satellite receivers. **Clients** Guinness; Intel; Black & Decker; Lonza Biologics; Gant.

HERBERT SMITH (see firm details p.992) This team enjoys a reputation for "*cutting-edge advocacy*" on the patent side and specialist litigation expertise on the general side of IP. Non-contentious work generally derives from corporate support. **Andrew Rich** (see p.494) has been labelled "*the biotech patent lawyer,*" attracting attention for his work on the high-profile erythropoietin patent litigation, while **Bill Moodie** (see p.492) successfully represented Yorkshire Dales on the patent action brought by Unilever, whose ice cream patent was subsequently declared invalid. **Mark Shillito** (see p.494) has been lauded for his hands-on approach. He has recently been heavily involved in issues as to whether human gene sequences arising out of the Human Genome Project should be patented. **Clients** Roche/Genetics Institute; Formula One Administration; Vodafone; Colgate-Palmolive.

OLSWANG (see firm details p.1087) A "*technically astute*" practice which gains plaudits for its continued success in the Dyson v Hoover case, winning the appeal in October 2001. In addition, it's almost unique patent filing practice, alongside its trademark filing practice, is felt to give the firm a certain advantage in the market. The "*sharp performer*" **Andrew Inglis** (see p.490) leads the team, which recently acted for Gendaq on its acquisition by Sangamo BioSciences, in a case that dealt with the complex issues of warranties and disclosure. **Clients** The Sunday Telegraph; BSkyB; Oxxon Pharmaccines; Procter & Gamble; Carphone Warehouse.

SLAUGHTER AND MAY (see firm details p.1140) A "*quality practice*" recognised for its blue-chip client base and singled out by barristers for its "*bright assistants.*" The team is headed by **Nigel Swycher** (see p.439), who, according to peers, is "*willing to get his hands dirty.*" The team represented Ladbrokes in the high-profile copyright and database right infringement actions brought by William Hill. Non-contentious work is regarded by many as the strength of the practice: it advised iFormation on a deal with BT relating to the licensing and enforcement of approximately 14,000 patents in the US and Japan. The biotech side of the practice benefits from the "*quietly forceful*"

INTELLECTUAL PROPERTY ■ LONDON

Susie Middlemiss (see p.492), who "*manages a case beautifully.*" **Clients** GlaxoSmithKline; Oxford GlycoSciences; Unilever; Adolph Coors Company; British Airways.

ASHURST MORRIS CRISP (see firm details p.852) A firm recognised for its stand-alone IP expertise outside corporate support and its "*inimitable business sense,*" according to clients. With slightly more focus on non-contentious work, the team has nonetheless acted on notable litigation cases, such as the successful defence of Rem Koolhaas on a Dutch copyright infringement claim by architect Gareth Pearce. "*Superb trademark litigator*" **Ian Starr** (see p.494) acted for Ritz Hotel Casino, issuing proceedings against various defendants concerning the potential infringement of the Ritz trademark in online gaming services. **Clients** Virgin; Imperial Tobacco; SkyePharma; Kraft Foods.

FIELD FISHER WATERHOUSE (see firm details p.954) Gaining a reputation for trademark and passing off cases, the firm boasts a vast and successful trademark prosecution practice, now managing 17,000 live trademarks. The firm also fields a fledgling patent prosecution practice. While its core client base is technology-focused, clients also derive from the publishing, luxury goods, food industry and financial services sectors. The litigation team, headed by Nick Rose, acted for Phonenames on the landmark 800 FLOWERS trademark case, which set out for the first time the Court of Appeal's opinion on what constitutes the use of a trademark in the UK on the internet. **Clients** Glynwed Pipe Systems; DaimlerChrysler; Dell Computer; Warner Brothers.

FRESHFIELDS BRUCKHAUS DERINGER (see firm details p.964) A firm admired by peers for its pan-European capacity, it fields a team that is credited for "*taking IP seriously.*" "*Doing the top-draw, non-contentious work,*" the firm was recently instructed by Hewlett-Packard, following the demerger with Agilent, to co-ordinate the transfer of approximately 20,000 patents around the demerged business. The "*eminently capable*" **Avril Martindale** (see p.492) has "*really built up the team,*" which is acting for Colgate-Palmolive on its patent dispute with Unilever and advising Yves Saint Laurent in a copyright infringing parody of its Opium perfume advertisement. **Clients** British Telecom; Nomura; Granada Compass; Bio-Medical Research.

GOULDENS (see firm details p.976) Best known for its trademark expertise and "*top-notch clients,*" the firm acted for GlaxoSmithKline in the high-profile case against Dowelhurst concerning the rights of parallel importers to overlabel or repackage the genuine product and import it into the UK. This "*bright, hard-working team really under-stands the business,*" agree clients. The team also handles design right, copyright and patent litigation, and has recently been boosted by the arrival of the former Head of Trade Marks at Glaxo Wellcome, Lesley Edwards, as a consultant. **Charters Macdonald-Brown** (see p.491) heads the department and brings his wealth of experience to the team. **Clients** GlaxoSmithKline; Eidos; Rank Hovis McDougall; WestLB Panmure.

ROITER ZUCKER (see firm details p.1115) A successful, "*impressive*" niche firm, which draws the majority of its work from the life sciences field. The newly ranked **Anna McKay** (see p.492) is recommended for her strength in biotech work, garnering plaudits from peers on a national basis. While the core of the team's work comprises high-profile contentious work, non-contentious work also features on the roster. **Clients** IVAX Pharmaceuticals UK; generic companies; parallel importers; biotech companies.

SHOOK, HARDY & BACON (see firm details p.1132) This year has seen the merger between US litigation giant Shook, Hardy & Bacon and the niche City practice, Arnander Irvine & Zietman. Clients have a particular regard for the firm's litigation expertise, perceiving an "*increased capability and focus*" among the ranks. Many US clients are drawn to the firm's capacity to handle large litigation cases. **James Irvine** (see p.490) leads the team, which continues to represent Hoover's interests against Dyson, seeking the revocation of one of Dyson's UK patents. The team is skilled in the range of IP issues, from biotech advisory work to software and technology licensing. **Clients** Hoover; AstraZeneca; South African Rugby Football Union; Reader's Digest.

SJ BERWIN (see firm details p.867) Considered an "*underrated, specialist*" practice, it moves up the tables this year. The team is valued by its clients, who believe it "*commercially aware and on top of the issues.*" Holding a high profile within trademark work, the team continues to advise the World Wrestling Federation in its dispute with the Worldwide Fund for Nature concerning a co-existence agreement entered into in the early 1990s. It has also taken action against 100 parallel importers of Smirnoff Ice on behalf of Guinness. Trademark prosecution and licensing work, alongside copyright and design right work, also forms a large part of the group's workload. The newly ranked **David Rose** (see p.494) is judged by our interviewees as tenacious and "*a good addition to the team.*"

BRIFFA (see firm details p.887) A respected niche practice which derives its core strength from its trademark and branding expertise. It is one of the few firms to boast a design registry practice, which sits alongside its trademark registry practice. High-profile trademark litigation includes the action brought against the 'Pop-stars' band, Liberty, by the owner of a chain of nightclubs with the same name. It now handles appeals from the Trade Marks Registry, and is currently acting on an appeal for Silverspring. The team, headed by the "*innovative*" **Margaret Briffa** (see p.487), also specialises in industrial design work and domain name disputes. **Clients** Cobra Beer; Uniqlo; Elocation; Tomy Toys.

DECHERT (see firm details p.934) Commended to our researchers as a team with depth across the board, it provides clients with "*clear, business-orientated advice.*" Particularly active on trademark and copyright work this year, the team, led by Paul Kavanagh, was involved in successfully opposing the application to register Diana Princess of Wales as a trademark, not only in the UK, but in various countries worldwide. Trademark registration work has been flourishing. The team is rated for its breadth of expertise, which includes brand protection, domain name protection and copyright. **Clients** Fiat; Asprey & Garrard; Campbell Foods; Thomas Cook.

HAMMOND SUDDARDS EDGE Best known for its trademarks branding work, the team has acted on the high-profile RFU and Nike case against Cotton Traders, which involved the use of the red rose symbol on rugby shirts. The team is headed by **Marija Danilunas**, who is highly recommended by clients. It advises on domain name disputes, and recently advised on copyright issues concerning the film, 'Gosford Park'. **Clients** Kodak; Aventis; Harrods.

KLEGAL (see firm details p.1025) The move from H$_2$O to KLegal has been lauded by clients as "*a positive step, which will give the team greater capacity.*" Gaining its name from the Tesco case against Levi Strauss, the team continues to act for Tesco on the international exhaustion campaign. The team, headed by the "*charismatic*" **Catrin Turner** (see p.494), has acted on a domain name dispute for Cussons. The non-contentious side of the practice continues to thrive, and has undertaken the launch of the 'go racing' website for the attheraces consortium. **Clients** Arena Leisure; Fuller, Smith & Turner; Standard Life Group; Tottenham Hotspur Football Club.

MAYER, BROWN, ROWE & MAW (see firm details p.1060) Clients point to "*a cohesive team, with a hands-on approach and partner attention.*" **Ian Wood** (see p.282794) was singled out for his "*bright ideas*" by interviewees, scoring a significant win in the BP Amoco action against Kelly Fuels, in which the judgment upheld BP's colour marks. The team also undertook the acquisition of Guinness World Records' IP rights for Gullane Entertainment in which trademark issues were prevalent. **Stephen Gare** remains respected by clients for his commercial awareness. **Clients** AstraZeneca; Cable & Wireless; Morgan Stanley.

THE SOUTH/THAMES VALLEY ■ INTELLECTUAL PROPERTY

OTHER NOTABLE PRACTITIONERS
Adjudged an "*outstanding practitioner*" by our interviewees, **David Llewelyn** (see p.491) of White & Case is still regarded as the standout name here. He recently advised John Lewis in a successful copyright infringement action against Peacock Stores concerning bed linen designs. **Laurence Cohen** (see p.488) of McDermott, Will & Emery has been described as "*a dynamic litigator, who will fight to the end.*" He advised BT and mmO2 on the defence of the O2 trademarks.

THE SOUTH

INTELLECTUAL PROPERTY
■ THE SOUTH

1. **Laytons** Guildford
2. **DMH** Brighton
3. **Blake Lapthorn** Fareham
   Lester Aldridge Bournemouth

LEADING INDIVIDUALS
1. **LOCHNER Ludi** Laytons
2. **ASHDOWN Tim** DMH

This book is the product of 6,582 1/2 hour interviews. See p.7 for BMRB audit. Within each band, firms are listed alphabetically. See individuals' profiles p.486

LAYTONS (see firm details p.1032) Following the merger of Lochners Technology Solicitors with Laytons, the firm is felt to have an IP practice that "*really stands out in The South.*" **Ludi Lochner** (see p.491) is the lynchpin of the team and a "*true patent specialist.*" He was also recommended by peers for his trademark expertise. Clients pointed out: "*he deals with the complex issues and gets the results we want.*" The team handled one of the highest profile trademark cases of the year, in its successful defence of McChina in its dispute with McDonald's over the use of the prefix 'Mc.' The non-contentious side of the practice has seen an upturn in areas such as licensing, joint ventures and R&D agreements. **Clients** British Airways; Nokia; Reckitt Benckiser; Sauflon Pharmaceuticals.

DMH (see firm details p.940) The firm is singled out by clients as "*quick to get to the heart of the matter.*" Predominantly a contentious practice, the team's expertise spans copyright, design right and trademark. Head of department **Tim Ashdown** (see p.486) has been described as "*on the ball,*" by clients, while peers endorse his efforts in higher profile patent work. The team is acting for the patent owner in a worldwide infringement of the patent for 'flame effect' flame machine technology. **Clients** University of Sussex; Arcadia Group; HFC Bank; Fender Europe.

BLAKE LAPTHORN (see firm details p.877) A newcomer to the tables, whose clients believe that the team is "*streets ahead of London firms.*" Head of department, Chris McClure, leads the team acting for defendants Agform on a patent infringement claim in which a spring board injunction was sought. The sizeable team undertakes contentious and non-contentious work, with a niche in technology licensing work and trade marks. **Clients** Dicon Group; Thomson Travel; Chelton; WPL.

LESTER ALDRIDGE (see firm details p.1038) The IP team is particularly involved in internet domain name work, while non-contentious licensing forms another of its strengths. The group advised on the European licensing rights for Ruff Ryders, the US-owned hip hop clothing brand allied to the record label. The team, headed by Richard Byrne, successfully completed a copyright and design infringement action on behalf of RTK Marine, concerning raiding craft constructed for the Royal Marines. Patent work and trademark prosecution also feature in the team's workload. **Clients** Future 3000; Halma Group; Paragon Publishing Magazine.

THAMES VALLEY

INTELLECTUAL PROPERTY
■ THAMES VALLEY

1. **Willoughby & Partners** Oxford
2. **Nabarro Nathanson** Reading
   Olswang Reading
   The Law Offices of Marcus J O'Leary Wokingham
3. **Manches** Oxford
4. **Osborne Clarke** Reading

LEADING INDIVIDUALS
1. **BOOY Anna** Willoughby & Partners
2. **HARRINGTON Alison** Olswang

This book is the product of 6,582 1/2 hour interviews. See p.7 for BMRB audit. Within each band, firms are listed alphabetically. See individuals' profiles p.486

WILLOUGHBY & PARTNERS (see firm details p.1189) The firm is adjudged a "*top ranking, tremendous practice, with long-standing IP expertise,*" by our interviewees. The team largely concentrates on non-contentious work, and has recently advised on the construction of a database for Entertainment UK, which involved complex cross-licensing issues. **Anna Booy** (see p.487) was described to researchers as "*committed and willing to get stuck in,*" while possessing sound technical skills. The group has advised Oxford University Press on licensing and brand management issues. Trademark registration is undertaken, managed by its allied company, Rouse & Co International. **Clients** Kodak; Celador; Sega; The Stationery Office.

NABARRO NATHANSON (see firm details p.1080) The firm boasts an impressive niche in e-commerce-related IP. This "*first rate team*" is headed by Sara Ellacott, and has advised Nikon Europe on the establishment of its European Fotoshare operation, comprising branding and web site advice. The group also acted for Pentium Coastal Defence in its defence to trademark infringement and passing off proceedings brought by Intel, regarding the use of the word 'pentium' in the company name. Particular focus is given to copyright, domain name and branding work. **Clients** Jarvis; Deloitte Consulting; Sun Microsystems.

OLSWANG (see firm details p.1087) Formerly part of Garretts, this practice is recommended for its sound knowledge of the technology and pharmaceutical industries. The team, headed by the "*illustrious*" **Alison Harrington** (see p.435), advised on the licensing of new technology for Cardinal House. It has seen an increase in patent work, which has included work on the software and computer programs for an interactive television company. **Clients** Motorola; Timberland; Hallmark Cards.

THE LAW OFFICES OF MARCUS J O'LEARY (see firm details p.1030) *Chambers*' researchers found that the firm has a higher profile for IT than IP work, perhaps due to its world-class technology client base. It was nevertheless praised by peers for its commercial, professional team. The firm has been advising on the copyright rules for psychometric tests. The range of work comprises copyright, patents, biotech and passing off. **Clients** Leading IT and software companies.

MANCHES (see firm details p.1052) The firm is perceived by peers to have the "*Oxford market wrapped up,*" with its particular expertise in university-related work. The firm has expertise in patents, copyright issues, trademarks and designs.

OSBORNE CLARKE (see firm details p.1090) While our researchers were impressed by the

INTELLECTUAL PROPERTY ■ THAMES VALLEY/SOUTH WEST/WALES

market endorsement for the non-contentious side of the practice, both competitors and clients felt that the firm "*still needs a while to make its mark.*" The team, headed by Russell Bowyer, has experienced a growth within the exploitation of specialised technology. It has negotiated patent and know-how licensing deals for Cambridge Display Technology. A highlight of the year has been the involvement in branding acquisition advice for Woods of Windsor. **Clients** Porsche; Cambridge Display Technology; 3i.

SOUTH WEST

INTELLECTUAL PROPERTY
■ SOUTH WEST

1. Osborne Clarke Bristol
2. Beachcroft Wansbroughs Bristol
   Bevan Ashford Bristol
   Burges Salmon Bristol
3. Humphreys & Co Bristol
4. Laytons Bristol

LEADING INDIVIDUALS

1. BRAITHWAITE Andrew Osborne Clarke
   JONES Gareth Bevan Ashford
2. HUMPHREYS Robert Humphreys & Co
   WOOD Alan Beachcroft Wansbroughs

This book is the product of 6,582 1/2 hour interviews. See p.7 for BMRB audit. Within each band, firms are listed alphabetically. See individuals' profiles p.486

OSBORNE CLARKE (see firm details p.1090) This is a team that "*never falters when it comes to technical expertise,*" claim national commentators, who also point to its highly respected non-contentious work. The firm has recently advised Bristol & West on the high-profile dispute with easyJet regarding the Easy Life account, which settled before trial. The team is led by the "*doughty competitor*" **Andrew Braithwaite**, who has been particularly involved in patent licensing for technology spin-out companies allied to the University of Bristol. Anti-counterfeiting work, copyright and branding are all features of the workload. **Clients** Bristol & West; Communication 2000 Group; The Morgan Motor Company; Rotork.

BEACHCROFT WANSBROUGHS (see firm details p.860) **Alan Wood** (see p.495) was endorsed by his peers as "*an experienced lawyer, offering excellent advice.*" He works with a team skilled in both IT and IP issues, which is often seen advising the firm's first-class healthcare clientele.

BEVAN ASHFORD (see firm details p.869) The firm is renowned for its public sector client base, and it also boasts top private sector clients such as Orange and Biotrace International. "*Top company lawyer*" **Gareth Jones** (see p.490) is particularly recognised for his technology transfer work. He recently acted for Biotrace International in the establishment of a joint venture company with the Defence Science and Technology Laboratory, for the development and manufacture of defence-critical reagents. Areas of expertise range from patent infringement to passing off. **Clients** Border Biofuels; Intel; Pittards.

BURGES SALMON (see firm details p.894) Our interviewees agreed that the firm is "*seriously investing in its IP practice, now establishing a concentrated, specialised outfit.*" Patent litigation has seen an upturn with the arrival of Andrew Allan-Jones from Linklaters, and the team advised the administrative receivers of Collag on patent infringement issues. On the non-contentious side, the trademark filing practice continues to grow, while new media work has involved advising the Royal Botanic Gardens in Kew on database licensing arrangements for its biotech and plant variety data. **Clients** United Biscuits; Reuters; Nationwide Building Society.

HUMPHREYS & CO (see firm details p.1005) The firm was endorsed to *Chambers'* researchers as a niche litigation outfit. "*Energetic litigator*" **Robert Humphreys** (see p.490) concentrates on the 'hard' side of IP, with particular expertise within computer software and database rights. He leads a team involved in patent litigation, inventions and know-how, and design and copyright. **Clients** Food and drinks manufacturers.

LAYTONS (see firm details p.1032) The team is considered to hold a profile lower than its competitors, although commentators pointed to its important trademark protection work for Somerfield Stores in its aim to register 'price check' as a trademark. Non-contentious work is the focus here, with the core of instruction deriving from copyright work for software products. The firm also undertakes patent licensing and infringement work.

WALES

INTELLECTUAL PROPERTY
■ WALES

1. Edwards Geldard Cardiff
2. Eversheds Cardiff
3. Morgan Cole Cardiff

LEADING INDIVIDUALS

1. DELEMORE Ceri Edwards Geldard
2. LINDSEY Michael Morgan Cole
   MCNABB Heather Eversheds

This book is the product of 6,582 1/2 hour interviews. See p.7 for BMRB audit. Within each band, firms are listed alphabetically. See individuals' profiles p.486

EDWARDS GELDARD (see firm details p.944) Clients point to a team with great scientific expertise, particularly adept at negotiating licenses for cutting-edge technology. The "*astute*" **Ceri Delemore** (see p.488) "*doesn't waste any time,*" and has advised Life Fitness on a sponsorship agreement with Arsenal Football Club involving trademark issues surrounding the club logo. Advising educational institutions is another strength of the team, and it has assisted further education colleges in Wales to draw up IPR policies. The practice also spans patent litigation and design right work. **Clients** Pulse Home Products; Royal Bank of Scotland; Molecular Light Technology; Welsh Development Agency.

EVERSHEDS (see firm details p.949) This practice stands out for its non-contentious work, and draws an advantage from its place in the national network of IP expertise. "*Commercial and reliable performer*" **Heather McNabb** (see p.492) has acted for Alliance Pharmaceuticals on the acquisition of IP and know-how portfolios for the manufacture of pharmaceutical products from Novartis and Eli Lilly. The full-service team has also advised on the IP aspects of setting up and operating business incubation centres throughout Wales. **Clients** Sun Life of Canada; Alliance Pharmaceuticals; UWIC.

MORGAN COLE (see firm details p.1075) The firm is heavily endorsed by our interviewees for contentious IP work, while the department draws a clear distinction between IP and IT work, possessing a discreet IP team. **Michael Lindsey** has acted for Novum (Overseas) in its design right infringement proceedings against Iceland Foods and Austria Haustechnik. The team also represents Gyrus on research and development issues, and patent agreements. **Clients** Cardiff International Airport; HSBC; Swansea Institute of Higher Education.

MIDLANDS

INTELLECTUAL PROPERTY
■ MIDLANDS

[1] **Wragge & Co** Birmingham

[2] **Martineau Johnson** Birmingham
Pinsent Curtis Biddle Birmingham

[3] **Browne Jacobson** Nottingham
Shoosmiths Northampton

[4] **Eversheds** Birmingham, Nottingham

LEADING INDIVIDUALS

[1] **HARRIS Gordon** Wragge & Co

[2] **ASSIM Gary** Shoosmiths
BARKER William Martineau Johnson
BARRON David Wragge & Co
ELLIS Peter Browne Jacobson
LUCKMAN Michael Wragge & Co
WYN DAVIES Cerys Pinsent Curtis Biddle

[3] **DRISCOLL Helen** Martineau Johnson

This book is the product of 6,582 1/2 hour interviews. See p.7 for BMRB audit.
Within each band, firms are listed alphabetically. See individuals' profiles p.486

WRAGGE & CO (see firm details p.1197) The team has garnered plaudits for its "*City approach*" and commerciality, which are perceived by researchers to be the results of the fluid movement of resources between London and Birmingham. This "*stellar IP team*" is skilled in non-contentious work and litigation, while branding has been the principal area of growth, and the team has been involved in a mass anti-counterfeiting campaign. The "*sophisticated, superb technician,*" **Michael Luckman**, has advised Centura Foods, the owner of the Robertson's food brand, on the replacement of the Robertson's Golly with characters from the World of Roald Dahl. Standout litigator **Gordon Harris** is the joint head of department; he has spent part of his time in London on high-profile patent cases such as SEB v De Longhi. Further areas of specialism include media- and internet-related disputes, enhanced by the appointment of Cerryg Jones to Nominet's expert panel on domain name disputes. **David Barron** has been less visible in the market this year; however, he recently enjoyed success in the representation of Icon Health and Fitness on a patent dispute. **Clients** British Telecommunications; McDonald's; Dyson Appliances; UBC Media; Nominet.

MARTINEAU JOHNSON (see firm details p.1056) The team is highly regarded by peers and clients, particularly for its part in the cutting-edge Scholes v Magnet window frames case, which definitively established what is meant by a 'commonplace' design. Focus is largely placed upon patent and design rights, with patent work forming a lion's share of the workload. A highlight of the year included a patent ownership dispute on the packaging system for pinch/pull bags. The team is headed by **Bill Barker** (see p.487), who has been seen less at the coalface this year. Non-contentious work generally derives from corporate support, such as the IP due diligence on the $764 million purchase by Convergys of Geneva Technology. The team is responsible for the establishment and protection of IP rights for various universities. **Helen Driscoll** (see p.488) gains market recognition for her patent and biotech work. **Clients** BODUM (UK); Magnet; BMW; Convergys; Manganese Bronze.

PINSENT CURTIS BIDDLE (see firm details p.1102) A chorus of recommendations from commentators elevates the firm within the tables this year. Its transactional work is highly rated by our interviewees, in particular for clients such as Indigo Photonics, which the team represented on the IP aspects of its acquisition of the fibre bragg business of Oxford Fiber Optic Tools. With national recommendations for her non-contentious work, **Cerys Wyn Davies** (see p.495) leads a team active on high-profile trademark work, such as MG Rover's national anti-infringement programme. On the contentious side, patent infringement work forms the core of the workload, with design right issues for clients such as Brintons Carpets also at the fore. **Clients** Maersk Medical; Siemens; Portmeirion Group; David S Smith Group.

BROWNE JACOBSON (see firm details p.891) Adjudged by interviewees as a "*professional*" team, it is felt to have made good progress in the past year, particularly on the contentious side. The team successfully negotiated a settlement on the infringement claims brought by Eidos regarding its Tomb Raider 4 game. On the non-contentious side, the rights for Charnos' Bioform patent were licensed to Speedo International. There is a strongly international flavour to the team; it has represented CANAL+ in trademark actions involving the US firm Gemstar Development. Trademark and copyright disputes are a mainstay of the firm's work, and **Peter Ellis** (see p.488) "*has a good handle on his cases*" as the standout practitioner in the field. **Clients** Joseph; Kelly Hoppen; Charnos.

SHOOSMITHS (see firm details p.1133) Commentators believe that the firm has "*gone in for the bulldog approach, which has worked in their favour.*" Contentious patent work is a particular strength of the team, which acted for the Waters Corporation in the high-profile case against Agilent Technologies regarding the infringement of water pumps. The trademark practice has broadened, and now represents Mattel on its trademarks, which include Barbie and Harry Potter. Within the education sector, the team has advised The Open University on the establishment of spin-out companies. The "*cool-headed*" **Gary Assim** (see p.486) has been described as "*a master draftsman with an excellent reputation.*" **Clients** BP Oil; Volkswagen Group (UK); Conran Design Group.

EVERSHEDS (see firm details p.949) Our researchers found that the firm is best known for its London capacity and national work, rather than for a local presence. The year's highlight has been acting for Diageo in the sale of Guinness World Records. The team is headed by Philip Atkinson, and has enjoyed Court of Appeal success with UCI Logistics. The team has also been involved in trademark litigation for Abercrombie & Fitch, and has acted for MG Rover on the purchase of Powertrain. **Clients** UCI Logistics; J&J Crombie; Diageo; MG Rover.

INTELLECTUAL PROPERTY ■ EAST ANGLIA/NORTH WEST

EAST ANGLIA

INTELLECTUAL PROPERTY — EAST ANGLIA

1 Eversheds *Ipswich, Norwich*
Mills & Reeve *Cambridge, Norwich*
2 Greenwoods *Peterborough*

LEADING INDIVIDUALS

1 FARRANT Patrick *Eversheds*
NAPPER Isabel *Mills & Reeve*
POORE Alasdair *Mills & Reeve*

This book is the product of 6,582 1/2 hour interviews. See p.7 for BMRB audit. Within each band, firms are listed alphabetically. See individuals' profiles p.486

EVERSHEDS (see firm details p.949) Clients point to the firm's edge over its competitors due to its industry expertise within the biotech field. Patrick Farrant (see p.488) is renowned for his ability to "*get to the heart of the matter;*" he led the team in its representation of Ionix Pharmaceuticals on IP agreements and due diligence supporting the £8 million investment by Apax and The Wellcome Trust. The team's patent expertise has been demonstrated by its work for QXYZ on a patent entitlement dispute with the University of Cambridge. The technology practice is growing apace, undertaking domain name and trademark disputes, and joint ventures. **Clients** DuPont; Amstrad; Convergys; Bespak.

MILLS & REEVE (see firm details p.1071) This "*impressive, thorough*" team gained plaudits from City firms. Patent litigation has been particularly active this year, with the highly respected Alasdair Poore (see p.493) working on the mediation of a major US patent infringement dispute in the electronics field. The "*businesslike*" head of department, Isabel Napper (see p.493), has been advising the NHS on the implementation of its IP management framework for all NHS Trusts in England and Wales. The team boasts a niche within copyright infringement claims relating to house designs. **Clients** University of Cambridge; Macrovision; Zeus Technology; AVEVA Group.

GREENWOODS (see firm details p.978) Our interviewees have recommended the firm for its greater visibility on larger cases, and it is reputed to be "*developing its niche in the East Anglian market.*" The team, headed by Philip Sloan, generally undertakes contentious work, in particular for various international technology companies on patent infringement issues. The workload spans trademarks, copyright and design right, and media-related work. **Clients** Hi-tech companies.

NORTH WEST

INTELLECTUAL PROPERTY — NORTH WEST

1 Addleshaw Booth & Co *Manchester*
Halliwell Landau *Manchester*
2 Eversheds *Manchester*
Hill Dickinson *Manchester*
3 DLA *Manchester*
4 Hammond Suddards Edge *Manchester*
Kuit Steinart Levy *Manchester*
Taylors *Blackburn*
5 Berg & Co *Manchester*
Cobbetts *Manchester*
Lawson Coppock & Hart *Manchester*

LEADING INDIVIDUALS

1 MOAKES Jonathan *Halliwell Landau*
WOODS Philip *Hill Dickinson*
2 BENTHAM Paul *Addleshaw Booth & Co*
GOLD Antony *Eversheds*
JONES Patricia *Hammond Suddards Edge*
ORCHISON Graeme *DLA*
STOKER Robert *Addleshaw Booth & Co*

This book is the product of 6,582 1/2 hour interviews. See p.7 for BMRB audit. Within each band, firms are listed alphabetically. See individuals' profiles p.486

ADDLESHAW BOOTH & CO (see firm details p.838) A "*robust*" offering, it is particularly rated for its non-contentious expertise, stalwartly maintaining its lead in the region. The standout name here is the "*commercially astute*" Paul Bentham (see p.487), who has been advising Manchester United Football Club on the launch of its new brand, MU Finance, and on licensing it to various financial services providers. Robert Stoker was endorsed as a "*thorough lawyer.*" On the contentious side, the team has defended William Lomas Carpets on High Court copyright infringement proceedings brought by Stoddard Templeton. Inroads have been made by the department in the international acquisition, protection and exploitation of IP rights. This is supported by a highly respected trademark prosecution practice. **Clients** British American Tobacco (Investments); Reckitt Benckiser; MBNA Europe Bank; PwC.

HALLIWELL LANDAU (see firm details p.982) A top-flight team, which "*gets to the heart of the matter,*" according to its clients. Jonathan Moakes (see p.492) has been referred to as "*as good as it gets in the IP world,*" successfully upholding a patent for The Ninja Corporation in relation to children's pop up tents against Worlds Apart, Woolworths and Argos. The team has been noted for its representation of spin-out companies in the education sector, advising Kaiku, a business spun out of UMIST, on its technology and research agreements. Non-contentious and contentious matters are handled by all members of the team. Richard Boardman is now a consultant and remains active on branding work. **Clients** Fibreguide; Swinton Group; Kaiku; The Ninja Corporation.

EVERSHEDS (see firm details p.949) Clients endorsed the practice as true specialists in the field. The team, headed by "*sensible opponent*" Antony Gold (see p.489), is acting for Ultraframe on high-profile, multimillion pound, multiparty design right proceedings relating to its roof system. Non-contentious work has included advising Coats on the disposal of international trademark portfolios, with associated licences such as Van Heusen. Well known for its university-related work, the firm acts for Manchester Innovation, a spin-out company from The University of Manchester. **Clients** Ultraframe; Kellogg; Manchester Innovation; Tepnel Life Sciences.

HILL DICKINSON (see firm details p.995) The move from Stockport to Manchester has been hailed by peers as "*a great move for the team, it will raise their profile.*" While the team is highly respected for its contentious work, there have been questions raised by market commentators as to the depth of the team behind Philip Woods (see p.495). The "*great pragmatist,*" Woods undertakes a variety of work, spanning architectural and engineering copyright disputes, outsourcing agreements and IT procurement contracts. Patent litigation involving thermoplastics technology and auto industry components forms a large part of the practice.

DLA The strength of the team is perceived to be in Leeds rather than Manchester. Graeme Orchison is featured in the tables this year for his litigation prowess.

HAMMOND SUDDARDS EDGE One client pointed researchers to the need to draw upon the London branch of the firm for the depth of IP expertise. Nevertheless, Patricia Jones has been hailed as "*extremely bright*" by our interviewees, and is particularly involved in anti-counterfeiting work for brand owners. With a slight bias towards litigation, strength lies in contentious trademark and patent work. On the non-contentious side, the team has a niche in research and development agreements, particularly those involving clinical trials. **Clients** Kickers International; Boots; Lambert Howarth; Kappa.

NORTH WEST/NORTH EAST ■ INTELLECTUAL PROPERTY

KUIT STEINART LEVY (see firm details p.1026) Peers commend the firm for its quality work for a loyal client base. The team, headed by Colin Hoffman, has acted on acquisitions of healthcare brands and technical matters relating to Medicines Act regulations and Medical Devices Regulations. The team is also active on the commercialisation and licensing of patents, and trademark licensing. **Clients** SSL International; Wisdom Toothbrushes; Accurist Watches; Karrimor International.

TAYLORS Peers endorsed the firm as a niche offering, "*aggressive, but they do get the results.*" The firm specialises in textiles copyright work.

BERG & CO (see firm details p.864) The IP team formerly of Philip Conn & Co has moved to this practice, thereby greatly strengthening its IP capability. Know-how work forms the lynchpin of the practice, and the team has advised UMIST on the funding and exploitation of IP work for its spin-out companies. The firm also undertakes big-ticket trademark work, both licensing and disputes.

COBBETTS (see firm details p.914) The firm joins the rankings this year following market endorsement for its "*precise*" approach to IP. The team, which is headed by Robert Roper, was involved in a highlight of the year: defending Matalan regarding the Burberry trademark. Another success included obtaining a doorstep injunction at four premises for IGT (UK). **Clients** Cussons; The Great Universal Stores; Datel Electronics.

LAWSON COPPOCK & HART The firm is best known for its work on distributorship agreements with a trademark angle. The team, led by Roger O'Brien, undertakes a variety of instructions, from patent licensing to design right work. A growth area has been copyright infringement work within the textiles sector. **Clients** Textile companies; manufacturers; mail order companies.

NORTH EAST

INTELLECTUAL PROPERTY
■ NORTH EAST

1
Addleshaw Booth & Co Leeds
Pinsent Curtis Biddle Leeds

2
DLA Leeds
Eversheds Leeds
Hammond Suddards Edge Leeds

3
Irwin Mitchell Leeds
Walker Morris Leeds

4
Dickinson Dees Newcastle upon Tyne
Lupton Fawcett Leeds

LEADING INDIVIDUALS

1
CHANDLER Stephen Pinsent Curtis Biddle
KEMPNER Richard Addleshaw Booth & Co

2
LOVE James Irwin Mitchell
TULLEY Christopher DLA

3
CLAY Andrew Hammond Suddards Edge
HEAD-RAPSON Niall Martineau Johnson
JACKSON Stuart Addleshaw Booth & Co
SYKES John Lupton Fawcett

This book is the product of 6,582 1/2 hour interviews. See p.7 for BMRB audit. Within each band, firms are listed alphabetically. See individuals' profiles p.486

ADDLESHAW BOOTH & CO (see firm details p.838) Highly regarded by clients, who compare the practice favourably to City firms: "*they know IP law inside out.*" **Richard Kempner** (see p.491) has been singled out for his "*authoritative style and fantastic client care;*" he led the case for IBM in IBM v Websphere, a trademark infringement action regarding computer software. The team has been advising the Commonwealth Games in anti-counterfeiting matters relating to the staging of the games in Manchester in July 2002. The team is split into contentious and non-contentious specialists, boasting a thriving trademark prosecution practice. **Stuart Jackson** (see p.490) has been singled out by clients for his technical expertise. **Clients** British Airways; BASF; AstraZeneca; Ferrari; Granada Media.

PINSENT CURTIS BIDDLE (see firm details p.1102) The team is renowned for winning new business and for fielding a "*crack team of up-and-comers.*" These lawyers support the "*class act,*" **Stephen Chandler** (see p.487), who has been singled out by London practitioners for his smooth management of a case. The team advised Pace Micro Technology on a high value patent litigation case against Thomson Licensing and Deutsche Thomson-Brandt relating to five digital television patents. BT is another high-profile client, and the firm has acted on a multimillion pound deal granting exclusive agency to iFormation to exploit BT's patent portfolio in the US, Canada and Japan. A further strength of the team is its trademark expertise and trademark prosecution practice. **Clients** Smith & Nephew; BOC; DEFRA; Energis Squared.

DLA The firm is prominent in the region and the emphasis here is on TMT-related work. **Christopher Tulley** was recommended to our researchers.

EVERSHEDS (see firm details p.949) The team pools its resources in both Leeds and Manchester under the leadership of Antony Gold, and is widely known for its non-contentious work. Advice was given to Stanelco on its deal with drug delivery company, RP Scherer, to jointly complete the development and commercialisation of Stanelco's patented capsule making technology. The team has advised on international licensing and brand strategy for The Woolmark Company, concerning its international portfolio of trade and certification marks. **Clients** Stanelco; AEA Technology; BNFL; Ineos.

HAMMOND SUDDARDS EDGE Although much of the firm's profile lies in London, industry experts point to the advantages of this capability, given its numerous contentious instructions. **Andrew Clay** has been cited by our interviewees as "*a credible force; aggressive while also being pragmatic.*" The team is currently acting for Automotive Products on a major patent entitlement dispute with Luk Leamington. A large part of the year's workload has comprised acting for UK manufacturing companies on know-how and patent licensing agreements with overseas companies. **Clients** Associated Octel; BSkyB; Britannia Building Society; Supaturf Products.

IRWIN MITCHELL (see firm details p.1009) The firm is adjudged "*an important presence in the contentious sphere.*" The team has successfully prosecuted one of the first cases issued under the new US cybersquatting laws for a leading professional ice skate manufacturer, HD Sports, following the virtual hijacking of two of their leading brand names. "*Litigation animal*" **James Love** (see p.491) was endorsed for his work on patent disputes; he has been acting on a multi-jurisdictional concrete industry patent dispute spanning the US, Germany and Italy. Non-contentious work continues to hold its own, particularly in the field of branding advice. **Clients** Minit UK; Anglo-Danish Fibre Industries; Hydro Products; Sheffield Wednesday Football Club.

WALKER MORRIS (see firm details p.1178) The firm's trademark filing practice was warmly recommended to our researchers. The team, headed by Patrick Cantrill, has successfully negotiated and settled a substantial damages claim in favour of City Technology, a spin-out of City University, London, arising out of a patent infringement action. A further achievement involved obtaining the removal of defamatory and infringing materials from a website on behalf of Northern Foods. Domain name work has generally been on the increase, and the firm has acted for a range of household name clients on over 50 domain name disputes. **Clients** Fox's Biscuits; ICI; Jarvis; Philip Treacy; Selfridges.

INTELLECTUAL PROPERTY ■ NORTH EAST/SCOTLAND/THE LEADERS

DICKINSON DEES (see firm details p.938) "*If you want IP work done in Newcastle, go to them,*" advised one peer. Headed by Mark Pearce, the team is advising Go-Ahead on several domain name disputes. Particular strength lies in the representation of educational institutions: the department is currently involved in ten technology transfer projects with universities. A range of advice is offered, from branding to patent infringements. **Clients** Formica; University of Durham; Northern Venture Managers.

LUPTON FAWCETT A small team celebrated for its "*rainmaker,*" **John Sykes**, who is respected by industry experts as a lawyer who "*does a good job, without bragging about it.*" On the transactional side, the team is involved in the exploitation, distribution and franchising of IP rights.

OTHER NOTABLE PRACTITIONERS Niall Head-Rapson (see p.489) has joined Ward Hadaway from Martineau Johnson. He remains respected for his patent and biotech work.

SCOTLAND

INTELLECTUAL PROPERTY
■ SCOTLAND

1
- Maclay Murray & Spens Glasgow
- McGrigor Donald Edinburgh

2
- Dundas & Wilson CS Glasgow
- MacRoberts Glasgow

3
- Shepherd+ Wedderburn Edinburgh

LEADING INDIVIDUALS

1
- MACPHERSON Shonaig McGrigor Donald
- NICOLSON Fiona Maclay Murray & Spens

2
- FLINT David MacRoberts
- GRASSIE Gill Maclay Murray & Spens

This book is the product of 6,582 1/2 hour interviews. See p.7 for BMRB audit. Within each band, firms are listed alphabetically. See individuals' profiles p.486

MACLAY MURRAY & SPENS (see firm details p.1048) The firm maintains a strong lead due to its acclaimed technology expertise. Head of department **Fiona Nicolson** (see p.493) led the team that has settled Scottish trademark cases for the owners of JOOP! and Davidoff perfume brands following the ECJ's decision regarding parallel imports. A major patent infringement dispute was undertaken for a multinational oil company in relation to North Sea oil technology. The team is also winning a profile in software-related disputes and cybersquatting cases. **Gill Grassie** (see p.489) has been recommended for her pragmatic and commercial approach by peers. **Clients** GlaxoSmithKline; ICI; easyGroup; Deutsche Bank.

MCGRIGOR DONALD (see firm details p.1065) Clients agree that with this "*blue-chip firm, if something comes from them, you know it's going to be good.*" Headed by **Shonaig Macpherson** (see p.492), ("*you know she'll do a good job*") the team is particularly well known for software acquisition work, and has acted for Digital Bridges regarding an investment by Apax Partners. Contentious work has been growing; the team has prevented a patent infringement claim coming to trial for a client involved in developing WAP applications. **Clients** Meconic; Intelligent Finance; Arrayjet; PPL Therapeutics.

DUNDAS & WILSON CS (see firm details p.943) "*We chose them for their excellent niche expertise within education-related IP,*" commented one client. Team leader Laurence Ward is advising Ardana Bioscience on the commercialisation of the research conducted by the Medical Research Council's Human Reproductive Sciences Unit. The firm also advises the University of Glasgow on the licensing of its patent rights concerning the spin-out company, Adaptive Screening, established in conjunction with Imperial College of Science Technology and Medicine, London, and Scientific Generics. The core of the department lies within technology transfer work, not only for educational clients, but also within the pharmaceutical and biotech sectors. **Clients** Quantanova; Crusade Laboratories; Intense Photonics; Heriot-Watt University.

MACROBERTS (see firm details p.1049) Peers commented that the firm is "*able to handle the broad range of work.*" The "*commercial*" David Flint (see p.488) "*has masses of experience,*" recently advising Giltech on the international licensing of medical products. On the educational side, the team has advised the University of Strathclyde on various technology spin-outs. Particular expertise is enjoyed within internet- and e-commerce-related IP. **Clients** Initiative Software; The Scottish Internet Exchange; Railtrack; British Energy.

SHEPHERD+ WEDDERBURN (see firm details p.1130) Our researchers found that the firm is better known within the market for IT rather than IP expertise. Joanna Boag-Thomson leads a team that has a niche in biotech fundraising. The firm advised on the IP aspects of a £30.5 million fundraising for Strakan Group, an early stage pharmaceutical company specialising in skin and bone disease therapies. Instructions from The Royal and Ancient Golf Club of St. Andrews have included work on the licensing arrangements for putting the Rules of Golf onto CD-ROM. **Clients** Scottish Rugby Union; Cairn Energy; The Royal College of Surgeons; Scottish & Newcastle; WestLB.

THE LEADERS IN INTELLECTUAL PROPERTY

ANDERSON, Robert
Lovells, London
(020) 7296 2000
robert.anderson@lovells.com
Specialisation: Intellectual property and technology. Patent litigation – he has particular experience of cases with a chemical, pharmaceutical and biotechnological content. Designs, copyright, trade secrets and trade marks. R&D agreements and acquisitions and joint ventures involving technology based businesses. Also other matters involving computers, pharmaceuticals, biotechnology or otherwise having a high technology content. Lectures on patent litigation for the Bristol University IP Diploma.
Prof. Memberships: European Patent Lawyers Association; AIPPI; Associate Member Chartered Institute of Patent Agents; Solicitors European Group; City of London Law Society Intellectual Property Sub-committee; IPLA.
Career: BSc Edinburgh (Natural Sciences), 1968. Admitted 1972; joined Lovells 1974; Partner 1978; IP practice area leader.

ASHDOWN, Tim
DMH, Crawley
(01293) 605079
tim.ashdown@dmh.co.uk
Specialisation: Intellectual property and IT; Head of Innovation and Media Group. Emphasis on dispute resolution in all areas of intellectual property and IT law. Experienced in trademark, copyright, design and patent infringement work. Also handles breach of confidence issues. Partner leading IT dispute resolution team handling disputes focusing on outsource and system supply, software development and copyright matters, domain name and internet-related disputes. Focus is on technology, internet and media industries. Additionally, he handles disputes in the pharmaceutical sector involving parallel imports and product recalls.
Prof. Memberships: Society for Computers and Law.
Career: Qualified with DMH in 1992; Partner in DMH, 1996 to date.
Personal: Born 1968.

ASSIM, Gary
Shoosmiths, Milton Keynes
(01908) 488 411
gary.assim@shoosmiths.co.uk
Specialisation: Partner specialising in intellectual property, practice covers trade mark and copyright infringement with particular expertise in parallel importing and anti-counterfeiting; acted on the case of Mackie Designs Inc v Behringer and Others 1999 RPC 717, the leading case on copyright/design rights in electronic circuit boards and S.51 CDPA 1988; acts for retailers and brand owners alike in a variety of business sectors including automotive and tech-

nology.
Prof. Memberships: Institute of Directors; International Trade Mark Association; British Association for Sport and Law; Board Member of Milton Keynes Economic Partnership.
Career: Trained *Travers Smith Braithwaite*, qualified 1990; joined *Shoosmiths* 1997; Partner *Shoosmiths* 1998
Publications: Joint author of Enforcement of US judgements in England: an Update, 'International Commercial Litigation' (1996); Letters Rogatory: an English Legal Perspective, 'New York Law Journal' (1996); joint author of four articles on 'Copyright Made Simple' in 'The Bookseller' (1997); one of the first lawyers to be quoted in the press ('The Times', 'Drapers Record') on the ECJ Opinion in Silhouette v Hartlauer regarding parallel importing and rights of trade mark owners (1998).
Personal: Durham University (1987 BA Hons Law); Chester College of Law 1988; Born 1961; resides Bedfordshire; married with two children; leisure interests include rugby, cricket and walking his dogs.

BARKER, William
Martineau Johnson, Birmingham
(0121) 678 1632
william.barker@martjohn.com
Specialisation: Senior partner, head of intellectual property department. Areas of practice include contentious and non-contentious intellectual property and computer law. Experienced in anti-counterfeiting and has particular experience of trademarks, copyright and patents. Has written various articles on the protection and enforcement of intellectual property rights and has addressed seminars in Birmingham, Singapore, Sydney, Seattle, Munich and Cincinnati. Experienced in the application and execution of Anton Piller Orders and is on the Birmingham Law Society list of supervising solicitors.
Prof. Memberships: Anti-counterfeiting Group; Licensing Executives Society; TIPLO (The Intellectual Property Lawyers Organisation).
Career: Articled: *Laces & Co*, Liverpool. Qualified 1986; assistant solicitor, *Pinsent & Co* 1986-90; associate, 1990-91; partner, *Martineau Johnson* 1992.
Personal: Born 4 January 1962. Educated at Merchant Taylors School, Crosby, Liverpool. BSc in Law and Mathematics. Leisure interests include tennis, member Edgbaston Priory LTC and golf. Member Moor Hall Golf Club.

BARRON, David
Wragge & Co, Birmingham
(0870) 903 1000

BARRY, Robert
Allen & Overy, London
(020) 7330 3000
robert.barry@allenovery.com
Specialisation: Partner in the Litigation Department specialising in intellectual property. He has considerable experience of the full range of intellectual property litigation, with a particular emphasis on patents and trademarks. After obtaining a degree in pharmacy from London University, he spent a post-graduate year at Guy's Hospital before qualifying as a pharmacist. He then read for the Bar and, after pupillage with Nicholas Pumfrey (now Mr Justice Pumfrey of the Patents Court), he joined the intellectual property department at *Bird & Bird*; where he became a partner in 1991. In 1997, he joined *Eversheds* as a partner and Head of Intellectual Property North. He joined *Allen & Overy* in May 2000 to lead the firm's patent practice. Robert has acted in many major patent disputes in the High Court and the European Patent Office, covering a range of technologies in several industry sectors, including the pharmaceutical, electronic, chemical and bioscience industries.
Prof. Memberships: Royal Pharmaceutical Society of Great Britain; International Bar Association; Associate member of the Chartered Institute of Patent Agents; The International Association for the Protection of Industrial Property.
Career: Called to the Bar 1983; pupillage at 11 South Square, Gray's Inn; associate *Bird & Bird* (1985), partner (1991); partner *Eversheds* (1997), head of intellectual property litigation North; partner *Allen & Overy* (2000).
Personal: Kings College Chelsea (Pharmacy 1979). City University (Dip Law 1981).

BENTHAM, Paul
Addleshaw Booth & Co, Manchester
(0161) 934 6337
paul.bentham@addleshawbooth.com
Specialisation: Partner in Technology, Media and Intellectual Property Department, Commercial Services Group, specialising in intellectual property and technology including patents, trademarks, passing off, copyright and designs, trade secrets and confidential information and related areas of competition law. Particular expertise in information technology contracts including e-commerce, the acquisition of computer systems, the licensing of computer software and databases, and outsourcing agreements. Also has considerable experience in technology licensing and advising on intellectual property matters in respect of corporate acquisitions and joint ventures.
Prof. Memberships: Licensing Executives Society, Solicitors European Group and The Society for Computers and Law.
Career: Qualified in 1989 and became a Partner in 1995.
Personal: Educated at the University of Leicester (1984-87), (LLB Hons, Law with French) Universite de Strasbourg (Diplome d'Etudes juridiques francaises). Leisure interests include foreign travel and supporting Manchester United.

BOOY, Anna
Willoughby & Partners, Oxford
(01865) 791 990
abooy@iprights.com
Specialisation: Consultant in Intellectual Property Department. All transactional intellectual property work especially in the industry areas of computer software, the internet, multimedia, publishing, music and entertainment, the fine arts, advertising and brand management. Was recently nominated by the 'Legal Business' magazine as one of the best lawyers in the provinces in its '40 under 40' feature.
Prof. Memberships: SCL, IPI, SEG.
Career: Qualified both UK and Australia.
Personal: Born 19 June 1962. Educated at the University of Queensland (BA, LLB Hons) and University College, London. (LLM in Intellectual Property).

BRAITHWAITE, Andrew
Osborne Clarke, Bristol
(0117) 917 3000

BRIFFA, Margaret
Briffa, London
(020) 7288 6003
Specialisation: Principal of highly regarded intellectual property practice *Briffa & Co*. All aspects of Intellectual Property and Information Technology law. Acts for a wide range of clients across all industries.
Career: Qualified in 1987. *Boodle Hatfield* 1987-91, *Clifford Chance* 1991-92, *Rouse & Co*. 1992-95, Established *Briffa & Co*. in 1995.
Personal: Born 18 September 1961. Educated Ursuline High School, East London and London School of Economics. Enjoys dancing, boats, travel and family pursuits.

BROWN, David
Bristows, London
(020) 7400 8000
david.brown@bristows.com
Specialisation: Senior Partner and Head of Intellectual Property Department. Practice covers the full range of intellectual property and includes disputes in relation to patents, copyright, design rights, trade secrets and anti-trust issues. Co-ordinates multi-forum disputes. Acts for international companies in the manufacturing, pharmaceutical, electronic and engineering industries. Had conduct of major cases such as Pilkington v PPG and Glaxo v Generics. Recent cases include Electrolux v Dyson, Texas Instruments v Hyundai, and Novartis v AHP.
Prof. Memberships: Member Royal Corps of Naval Constructors 1960-66.
Career: Joined *Bristows* 1966. Qualified as solicitor in 1973; Partner from 1974; Member of Editorial Board of 'Patent World'.
Personal: Born 8 May 1942. Educated at Royal High School Edinburgh, Royal Naval Engineering College Plymouth and Royal Naval College Greenwich (Honours Degree in Naval Architecture). Interests include the Turf.

BROWN, Jeremy
Linklaters, London
(020) 7456 5748
jeremy.brown@linklaters.com
Specialisation: Global and London Head of Intellectual Property, Technology and Communications (IPTC) Practice. Specialist in intellectual property and technology-related matters with experience in commercial and litigious matters involving intellectual property rights and technology-related issues. Particular knowledge of, and experience with, issues affecting the healthcare, chemical, computer, and luxury goods industries. Main areas of practice include patent, copyright, trade marks and trade secrets litigation; licensing of intellectual property rights and technology transfer generally including EC and UK anti-trust and competition law considerations; pharmaceutical law; computer law.
Prof. Memberships: Past President LES International, 1995-96; Past President 1991-92 and Member of Council (1988 to date) LES Britain and Ireland; Member of Council of AIPPI United Kingdom 1989 to date; Chartered Institute of Patent Agents (Associate Member); South African Institute of Intellectual Property (Fellow); American Intellectual Property Law Association.
Career: Partner, *Linklaters* 1982 to date. Associate, *Linklaters* 1978-82. *Spoor & Fisher*, Patent Attorneys, South Africa 1971-78.

CARBONI, Anna
Linklaters, London
(020) 7456 5810
anna.carboni@linklaters.com
Specialisation: Specialist in contentious and non-contentious intellectual property and information technology work with particular expertise in trade marks, passing off and anti-counterfeiting litigation and breach of confidence matters. Specialisms include contentious intellectual property work, trade mark portfolio management and brands and commercial IP/IT work.
Career: 1996 to date Partner *Linklaters*; 1995 to date Head/Co-Head of the Trade Mark and Design Filing and Prosecution Practice, *Linklaters*; 1989 secondment to Italian intellectual property firm, *Jacobacci & Perani*; 1988-96 assistant solicitor, *Linklaters*; 1986-88 articled clerk, *Linklaters*. 1984-86 College of Law, Lancaster Gate, Common Professional Examination and Law Society Finals; 1981-84, Girton College, Cambridge, Natural Sciences BA (converted to MA, Cantab).

CHANDLER, Stephen
Pinsent Curtis Biddle, Leeds
(0113) 244 5000
stephen.chandler@pinsents.com
Specialisation: Group Head of Technology and Media. Intellectual property, including protection, exploitation and

INTELLECTUAL PROPERTY ■ THE LEADERS

enforcement of patents, trademarks, copyrights, design rights and trade secrets, as well as consultancy in the management of IP. Acted in Thomson Multi-media v Pace Microtechnology (digital TV patent infringement); 3M v NAMSA (patent infringement); PLM v Redfearn; for Smith & Nephew plc in healthcare patent matters; for Sema Schlumberger; worked for the NHS in developing a framework for the management of its intellectual property; a number of NHS Hospital Trusts.
Career: Qualified in 1980. Partner in 1985.
Personal: Born 1955. Educated St John's College, Cambridge 1974-77.

CLAY, Andrew J
Hammond Suddards Edge, Leeds
0113 284 7000

COHEN, Larry J
McDermott, Will & Emery, London
(020) 7577 6909
lcohen@europe.mwe.com
Specialisation: Partner – Intellectual Property. Contentious and non-contentious intellectual property matters including patents, trademarks, copyright, domain name and metatags, design right and trade secrets. Also deals with regulatory law, particularly in the area of agrochemicals and medicines and genetically modified organisms. Acted in Chiron v Murex (client), Gillette v Unilever, Harrods Limited (client) v Harrods (Buenos Aires) Limited, Diskxpress v Phillips, Kodak v Polaroid, Hitachi v Storage Computer, Baby Dan v Brevi, R v MAFF ex p Watson, Agrevo v Genetix Snowball.
Prof. Memberships: CIPA, ITMA, INTA, IBA, Law Society.
Career: Qualified 1976. Assistant Solicitor with *Bristows Cooke & Carpmael* from 1976, and became a Partner in 1981. Joined *Hammond Suddards* in 1992. Joined *McDermott, Will & Emery* in 2000 and is currently Head of Contentious Intellectual Property.
Publications: Author of 'World Litigation Law and Practice: Unit B1 England and Wales' (1986) and CIPA/ ITMA Trademarks Handbook section on Civil Litigation (1992). Contributor of numerous articles to a variety of specialist publications on intellectual property topics and regular conference speaker.
Personal: Born 12 September 1951. Attended Emmanuel College, Cambridge 1970-73. Leisure pursuits include tennis, cycling and skiing. Lives in Radlett, Hertfordshire.

COOK, Trevor
Bird & Bird, London
(020) 7415 6000
Specialisation: Partner in intellectual property department. Main areas of practice are litigation, transactional and advisory work in relation to patents, copyright, other intellectual property rights and associated regulatory law issues, particularly in the information technology and pharmaceutical/biosciences sectors.
Prof. Memberships: Treasurer of the International Association for the Protection of Industrial Property (AIPPI) (UK Group), member of Licensing Executives Society, associate member of Chartered Institute of Patent Agents, Secretary of British Copyright Council Working Group on Copyright & Technology.
Career: Qualified in 1977. Joined *Bird & Bird* in 1974, became a partner in 1981.
Publications: Contributor to 'Information Technology and the Law', 'CIPA Guide to Patents Act' and 'European Patents Handbook', 'Database Law'; co-author of 'Pharmaceuticals Biotechnology and the Law' and 'Practical Intellectual Property Precedents'; author of 'The Protection of Regulatory Data', and 'A User's Guide to Patents'.
Personal: Born 1951. Attended Southampton University (BSc Chemistry, 1973).

COOKE, Adam
Wragge & Co, London
(0870) 903 1000

DANILUNAS, Marija
Hammond Suddards Edge, London
(020) 7655 1000

DAVIES, Isabel
Eversheds, London
(020) 7919 4555
daviesi@eversheds.com
Specialisation: Chairman of the *Eversheds* National IP Group. Her experience spans all aspects of intellectual property, including trademarks, patents, design, copyright, confidential information and trade libel. Early in her career she represented Reckitt & Colman Plc in the Jif Lemon case and has been involved in high profile IP cases ever since. Recently she has been to the Court of Appeal to successfully defend a patent infringement action and she has been involved in a confidentiality action against a client's ex-employee, which also includes a claim to entitlement of IP. Many aspects of her work have an international angle, with litigation in overseas jurisdictions and crossing national boundaries, and involve cross-border injunctions. She is actively involved in various IP organisations, including the International Trademark Association of which she is a board member, the Institute of Trademark agents, the Chartered Institute of Patent Agents and the Law Society IP Sub-Committee. She has lectured and written extensively and is the legal editor to the 'Journal of Brand Management', on the editorial board of 'Trademark World', a country contributor for 'EIPR' and editor of Sweet & Maxwell's 'European Trademark Litigation Handbook'.
Prof. Memberships: ITMA, CIPA, INTA, ACG. Member of Intellectual Property Sub-committee of the Law Society.
Career: Qualified in 1976. Partner at *Wragge & Co*, 1979-85. Joined *Woodham Smith (Taylor Joynson Garratt)* as partner in 1986, then *Jaques & Lewis* (now *Eversheds*) in 1994.
Personal: Born 30th May 1952. Attended St Albans Girls' Grammar School, Leicester University and Guildford College of Law. Leisure interests include travel, theatre, squash, skiing, food and wine. Lives in Chelsea.

DELEMORE, Ceri
Edwards Geldard, Cardiff
(029) 2023 8239
ceri.delemore@geldards.co.uk
Specialisation: Partner, head of intellectual property/information technology. All aspects of intellectual property and information technology law including transactional work, research and collaboration agreements, licensing, assignments, trade mark and design applications, IT procurement, FM and outsourcing contracts, bespoke software developments and IP and IT related litigation. Also handles media work.
Prof. Memberships: The Intellectual Property Lawyers Organisation. The Law Society's Solicitors' European Group. Society for Computers & The Law. Licensing Executives Society.
Career: Articled *Slaughter and May*, qualified 1986; *Slaughter and May* 1984-88; joined *Edwards Geldard* 1988: partner 1991.
Publications: Author of 'Copyright Explained' published by RIBA.
Personal: BA (Hons) English and French Law Class 1, University of Kent at Canterbury; Diplome de droit francais de l'université de Paris-Sud.

DRISCOLL, Helen
Martineau Johnson, Birmingham
(0121) 678 1635
helen.driscoll@martjohn.com
Specialisation: Intellectual property specialist, principally dealing with contentious work. Particular expertise: trademark and passing off actions, design right and copyright actions, injunctions and contempt.
Prof. Memberships: AIPPI. Law Society's European Group.
Career: Articled *Eversheds*, qualified 1993, associate 1996, *Freeth Cartwright, Hunt Dickins* 1997, partner 1998; partner *Martineau Johnson* 2001. Education: University College, Cardiff; Leicester University.
Personal: Interests include choral singing, fast cars and languages.

ELLIS, Peter
Browne Jacobson, Nottingham
(0115) 976 6269
pellis@brownej.co.uk
Specialisation: Practises in all aspects of intellectual property litigation and dispute resolution including patents, copyright and design rights (registered and unregistered), trademarks and passing-off. Also general litigation, including confidential information. Acts for businesses involved with IT; telecoms; engineering and fashion. Recent cases include trademark disputes for fashion house, assisting clients in US patent litigation, representing a US retail business in connection with UK and European trademarks; representing UK manufacturer in patent disputes in Ireland and in dispute with French competitor.
Prof. Memberships: LES, AIPPI.
Career: Qualified 1976. At *Wells & Hind* 1976-80. *Browne Jacobson* 1981 to present (Partner from 1984).
Personal: Born 3 June 1952. Interests include family, golf, cricket and sports generally. Lives in Nottingham.

FARRANT, Patrick
Eversheds, Cambridge
(01223) 443 666
patrickfarrant@eversheds.com
Specialisation: A commercial lawyer specialising in the exploitation of intellectual property, in particular biotechnology related, and the interaction between IP and competition law. Head of national Biosciences Group.
Prof. Memberships: Solicitors European Group, AIPPI, Licensing Executive Society, BIA.
Career: Trained with *Frere Cholmeley*; qualified in 1989; joined *Eversheds* in 1990; partner in 1995.
Personal: Three children; Swiss and British national; fluent French speaker.

FIELD, Sally
Bristows, London
(020) 7400 8000
sally.field@bristows.com
Specialisation: Partner in Intellectual Property Department. Intellectual property litigation. Work covers advising on full range of intellectual property including patents, trademarks, copyright, designs and confidential information. Cases include Allen & Hanbury's (Glaxo) v Generics, IBM v Phoenix and Kimberly-Clark v Procter & Gamble.
Prof. Memberships: Law Society, Associate Member Chartered Institute of Patent Agents, Associate Member Institute of Trade Mark Agents.
Career: Articled with *Clifford Turner* 1979-81, then moved to *Bristows* in 1983. Became a Partner in 1987.
Publications: Writes articles for specialist periodicals. Regular speaker at intellectual property conferences and seminars.
Personal: Born 16 May 1957. Attended Durham University 1975-78. Leisure pursuits include golf, tennis and skiing. Lives in London.

FLINT, David
MacRoberts, Glasgow
(0141) 332 9988
df@macroberts.com
Specialisation: Partner in IP and Technology Law Group. Corporate and commercial matters including commercial contracts, patents, trademarks, copyright and other intellectual property licensing, computer and technology contracts, agency and distribution agreements, restrictive practices and competition law in terms of both EU and UK law. Author of 'Liquidation in Scotland'; EU Compe-

THE LEADERS ■ INTELLECTUAL PROPERTY

tition Law section of 'Stair Memorial Encyclopaedia of the Laws of Scotland'; executive editor 'Greens Scottish E-commerce Handbook'. Extensive lecturing experience on a variety of legal and IT subjects.
Prof. Memberships: Licensing Executives Society; Insolvency Practitioners Association; Association of Business Recovery Professionals; Institute of Credit Management; The Computer Law Association Inc; Union Internationale des Avocats; UK Association for European Law; American Bar Association (associate); member of Joint Working Party of Scottish, English and Northern Irish Law Societies and Bars on Competition Law (since 1981); member of CBI Competition Panel; member of Law Society of Scotland Intellectual Property Law and International Relations Committees; licensed insolvency practitioner.
Career: Qualified 1979. Assistant in *MacRoberts* company and commercial department 1979-84; Partner May 1984. Admitted Notary Public 1980. Chairman of Scottish Lawyers European Group 1985-95.
Personal: Educated at High School of Glasgow 1964-73, University of Glasgow (LLB 1976 and LLM 1982), and Europa Institut, Universiteit van Amsterdam (Diploma in European Integration 1978). Director of Giltech Ltd, The Shareholding & Investment Trust Ltd, Renfrewshire Chamber of Commerce and Advoc Ltd.

FREELAND, Rowan
Simmons & Simmons, London
(020) 7628 2020
rowan.freeland@simmons-simmons.ccm
Specialisation: Intellectual property litigation particularly patents and designs. Major cases include SmithKline Beecham v Generic UK, Rambus v Hyundai Electronics, Texas Instruments v Hyundai Electronics, Allied Colloids v American Cynamid, General Instrument v Intel, Southco v Dzus and Hallen v Brabantia. Also IT law.
Prof. Memberships: AIPPI, AIPLA, TIPLO.
Career: Born 1956. Education Wellington, St Catherines College Oxford (BA 1978). Joined *Simmons & Simmons* 1980, qualified 1982, partner 1988.
Personal: Married with three daughters. Interests: Reading, gardening, opera.

GARE, Stephen
Mayer, Brown, Rowe & Maw, London
(020) 7782 8814
sgare@eu.mayerbrownrowe.com
Specialisation: Founder and Head of *Mayer, Brown, Rowe & Maw's* Intellectual Property and IT Group in London. Has over 25 years of experience in handling all aspects of intellectual property, including trademark and passing-off advice and litigation over a very wide range of goods and services, patent litigation and acting in many copyright and design matters. Has advised in numerous corporate and commercial transactions and is actively involved in *Mayer, Brown, Rowe & Maw's* media practice.
Prof. Memberships: Member of the Law Society, the City of London Solicitors Company Intellectual Property Sub-committee, AIPPI and the Institute of Patentees and Inventors. Is also an Associate of the Chartered Institute of Patent Agents. Served for several years on various INTA Committees.
Career: Joined *Rowe & Maw* in 1974 after reading Law at Cambridge. Partner in 1981. In 1986 obtained a Masters Degree in Business Law, specialising in intellectual property and anti-trust.
Publications: Co-editor of 'Blackstone's Statutes on Intellectual Property' and is an editor of 'Media World'.

GOLD, Antony
Eversheds, Manchester
(0161) 831 8000
antonygold@eversheds.com
Specialisation: Head of intellectual property team, *Eversheds* Leeds/Manchester and head of commercial department at *Eversheds* Manchester. Former Chairman of *Eversheds* national litigation group. Area of practice is intellectual property, particularly internet-related disputes and advice as well as passing off, trade mark, patent and copyright litigation. Other previous experience includes acting in Brady v Brady (House of Lords, 1988), Barlow Clowes, BCCI, Lancashire and Yorkshire Assurance Society. Most recent reported case is Arrow Nominees v GR+MM Blackledge Plc (Court of Appeal July 2000). Has extensive media experience.
Prof. Memberships: Law Society, International Bar Association, International Arbitration Club. Member INTA Committee on the Internet. Expert appointed by Nominet, the UK naming authority, under its dispute resolution service.
Career: Qualified in 1983, joined *Eversheds Alexander Tatham* in 1984 and became a partner in 1988. Chairman of *Eversheds'* National Litigation Group 1993-98.
Personal: Born 26th August 1958. Attended Birkenhead School 1969-76, then Manchester University 1976-79 and Chester College of Law 1979-80. Leisure interests include climbing and mountaineering. Lives in Adlington, Cheshire. Married, three children.

GRANT, Gregor
Wragge & Co, London
(0870) 903 1000

GRASSIE, Gill
Maclay Murray & Spens, Edinburgh
(0131) 226 5196
gg@maclaymurrayspens.co.uk
Specialisation: Contentious IP and technology partner specialising in trademarks, domain name disputes, patents, copyright and confidential information/trade secret and increasing number of software and internet related disputes. Recent cases included House of Lords copyright appeal case - Redrow Homes v Bett; numerous Scottish parallel imports trademarks cases including landmark Davidoff/Joop v M&S Toiletries; first Scottish domain name case for Scottish Widows; multi-jurisdictional patent/trade secret case acting for BCI Asia in mediating dispute with Scottish website design company. Clients include Microsoft, Glaxo Smith Kline, ICI, BMW, Kymata Ltd, Iwerks, WL Gore & Associates, Peregrine Systems Limited, Business Software alliance, and Yale.
Prof. Memberships: Law Society IP committee member; Law Society specialist accreditation in IP law; associate member of CIPA; member and regular attendee of TIPLO and INTA.
Career: Edinburgh University (LLB Hons 1984). Writer to the Signet. Worked for *Bristows* IP litigation department, London (1991-92) and *Drostes*, Munich (1992-93).
Publications: Scottish correspondent for CIPA guide. Member of editorial committee for Sweet & Maxwell 'European Trade Mark Reports' and 'European Copyright and Design Reports'; author of Scottish chapters of Sweet & Maxwell 'European Trade Mark Litigation Handbook' and of Monitor Press 'IT 2000 Handbook'.
Personal: Born 1963. Interests: running; skiing; scuba diving; travelling.

HARRINGTON, Alison
Olswang, Reading
(0118) 952 3354
afh@olswang.com
See under Information Technology, p.435

HARRIS, Gordon
Wragge & Co, Birmingham
0870 903 1000

HARRIS, Paul
Eversheds, London
(020) 7919 4500
harrisp@eversheds.com
Specialisation: Partner *Eversheds* London Intellectual Property Group. Patents, trademarks, copyright, designs. Notable cases include Coloplast (1993); Wagamama v City Centre Restaurants (1995); Electrolux v Black & Decker (1996). Author of various IP articles; regular lecturer including Bristol University: IP Diploma course.
Prof. Memberships: ITMA; CIPA; INTA; AIPPI; UNION; Royal Society of Chemistry; Chairman of the Whittington Committee of the City of London Law Society.
Career: Qualified in 1987. *Bristows Cooke & Carpmael*; *McKenna & Co* (1988-92); *Taylor Joynson Garrett* (1992-94); *Eversheds*, formerly *Jaques & Lewis* (1994-), became Partner in 1995.
Personal: Born 17th May 1961; Keele University; Leisure interests include fitness; running; theatre; Italian wine. Lives in Westminster.

HARRISS, David
Bird & Bird, London
(020) 7415 6000
david.harriss@twobirds.com
Specialisation: Partner in the intellectual property department. Main area of practice is intellectual property litigation. Includes UK and international patent infringement litigation, trademark infringement, passing off, copyright infringement, design infringement and breach of confidence. Acted in Akzo/Du Pont, PLG/Ardon, BP/Hoechst Celanese, BP/Union Carbide and Exxon/Lubrizol.
Prof. Memberships: Chairman of Law Society IP Working Party; Chartered Institute of Patent Agents (Fellow).
Career: Qualified as Patent Agent 1969. Worked for *AA Thornton & Co* 1965-70, then *Langner Parry* from 1970-73 (Chartered Patent Agents). Joined *Bird & Bird* in 1973. Qualified as a solicitor 1977. Partner 1977. Senior partner 1993.
Publications: Member of Editorial Board of 'Patent World'; co-editor of 'International Intellectual Property Litigation'.
Personal: Born 1943. Educated Christ's College, Cambridge. Lives in Chobham, Surrey.

HART, Michael
Baker & McKenzie, London
(020) 7919 1000
michael.hart@bakernet.com
See under Information Technology, p.435

HEAD-RAPSON, Niall
Ward Hadaway, Newcastle upon Tyne
(0191) 204 4230
Specialisation: Partner, intellectual property.
Prof. Memberships: AIPPI, INTA, LES, AURIL.
Career: CPE/LSF Nottingham Law School; Kings College, London – Biotechnology BSc (Hons) 2:1; Diploma in intellectual property – Queen Mary's College, London; Articled and qualified *Gouldens*. *Freshfields*; *McKennas*, *Eversheds*.

HODGSON, Mark
Taylor Wessing, London
(020) 7300 7000
m.hodgson@taylorwessing.com
Specialisation: Partner in intellectual property department. Head of pharmaceutical and medical group. Specialises in patent litigation in the UK courts and in the European Patent Office. Also handles pharmaceutical, medical device and biotechnology matters, including regulatory issues, product liability, advertising, parallel importation and clinical trial contracts. Acted in respect of Smith Kline and French Laboratories Ltd (Cimetidine) Patents, Bonzel v Intervention, R v Licensing Authority ex p Smith Kline and French Laboratories Ltd Merck/SB v Primecrown, Smithkline Beecham v Norton/LEK, Eli Lilly & Co v Novo Nordisk, Biogen v Medeva and, most recently, on behalf of Lilly Icos in their successful action to revoke Pfizer's

INTELLECTUAL PROPERTY ■ THE LEADERS

UK patent for the use of sildenafil (Viagra) to treat impotence. Has written articles for legal and pharmaceutical journals and lectures extensively on matters such as EC medical device regulations, parallel importation and harmonisation of European patent litigation.
Prof. Memberships: Member Law Society; AIPPI; IBA; member of City of London Solicitors' Company (IP sub-committee) and Chairman of Intellectual Property Lawyers Association.
Career: Qualified in 1983 whilst at *Woodham Smith* 1981-85. Joined *Simmons & Simmons* in 1985 where he became a partner in 1989. Joined *Taylor Joynson Garrett* in 1998.
Personal: Educated at Barnard Castle School 1969-77 and at Emmanuel College Cambridge 1977-80. Chester Law School 1981. Leisure interests include Newcastle United FC and chauffeuring his children to parties. Lives near Kimbolton, Hunts.

HUMPHREYS, Robert
Humphreys & Co, Bristol
(0117) 929 2662
Specialisation: Senior Partner in commercial department. Intellectual property, commercial and reinsurance.
Prof. Memberships: Law Society.
Career: Qualified 1981. With *Simmons & Simmons* 1979-85. Partner *Cartwrights* 1985-86. Co-founded *Humphreys & Co* 1986.
Personal: Born 1953. Educated Dr Morgan's School, Bridgwater and New College, Oxford. Leisure interests include cricket. Lives near Bristol.

INGLIS, Andrew
Olswang, London
(020) 7208 8975
api@olswang.com
Specialisation: Partner specialising in intellectual property, particularly patents and trademarks. He also deals with copyright issues for media clients of the firms. Heads *Olswang*'s Intellectual Property Group which comprises over 20 lawyers. The practice spans substantial patent and trademark practices (including patent and trade mark filing practices), as well as meeting the needs of the more traditional clients of the firm in the areas of media, IT and e-commerce. A substantial portion of his trademark practice concerns online issues. He splits his time between litigation and deals with branding strategy, advertising and promotional issues. He acted for Dyson in their recent patent win against Hoover in the High Court and Court of Appeal and is currently acting for it in its damage claim. Other important reported cases he has handled include British Coal Corporation v Glaverbel SA, R Bance & R Bance & Co Ltd's Licence of Right (copyright) Application, Mecklermedia v DC Congress, and Anheuser-Busch Ince v Budejovicky Budvar Navdoni Podnik.
Career: Originally qualified in Australia in 1981 where he practised before moving to England. After qualifying in England in 1990 he was a partner at *Nabarro Nathanson* from 1991-97, and has been a partner at *Olswang* since 1997. Active in contributing articles to publications such as the 'European Intellectual Property Review' and public speaking on intellectual property issues at various seminars.

IRVINE, James
Shook, Hardy & Bacon, London
(020) 7842 5400
jirvine@shb.com
Specialisation: Partner. Specialises in IP litigation, particularly major patent and trademark litigation and anti-counterfeiting work for international companies. Clients in industries ranging from computer software to fashion accessories. Co-author of chapter on Hong Kong in book about IP rights in Hong Kong and other countries. Lectures on IP issues. Regular contributor of articles to IP magazines.
Prof. Memberships: Institute of Trade Mark Agents (Associate Member), Chartered Institute of Patent Agents, Marques, Law Society of Scotland, AIPPI, INTA.
Career: Admitted in Scotland in 1983, Hong Kong in 1984 and England and Wales 1995. With *Johnson Stokes & Master* in Hong Kong 1984-88. Joined *Denton Hall* in 1988 and became a partner in 1990. In their Hong Kong office 1988-92. Joined *Llewelyn Zietman* in November 1997. Joined *Shook, Hardy & Bacon* in July 2002.
Personal: Born 24th August 1959. Educated at Aberdeen University 1977-82 (LL.B Hons, DLP). Interests outside the law include golf and bridge.

JACKSON, Stuart
Addleshaw Booth & Co, Leeds
(0113) 209 2391
stuart.jackson@addleshawbooth.com
Specialisation: Both litigation and licensing in all areas of intellectual property, with a concentration on patents and other areas involving high technical or scientific content. As a Chartered Chemist who has worked as a scientist in the healthcare industry for many years, he specialises particularly in matters involving chemical and pharmaceutical patents. Recent matters include BASF v Smithkline Beecham, action for revocation of patent for major antidepressant drug, paraxetine (seroxat) and Nutrinova (Hoechst) v Scanchem, concerning alleged infringement of process patent by importing from China acesulphame-K synthetic sweetener. Acted for Sir Roger Penrose in copyright action against Kimberly Clark regarding use of embossing pattern on toilet paper. Also acted for Clayton Plant Protection as intervener in judicial review by Monsanto against decision by MAFF to approve generic glyphosate, including successful reference to ECJ regarding interpretation of European Directive on pesticides.
Prof. Memberships: Law Society,Royal Society of Chemistry (C Chem, MRSC).
Career: Flavour chemist with *Brewing Research Foundation* (1975-77). Project Manager in R & D for *Johnson & Johnson Patient Care Limited* (1997-99). Joined *Addleshaw Booth & Co* in 1994 and qualified as a solicitor in 1996.
Publications: Named inventor on a number of patents. Has published many papers and articles on intellectual property topics, wound healing and chemistry of beer. The author of the chapter 'Parallel Imports into and within the European Union' in 'Intellectual Property in the Global Market Place' (1999).
Personal: BSc Hons (First Class) in chemistry, Imperial College (1969-72); MSc, Oxford University (1972-75). Leisure interests include cycling (racing and touring), running, fell-walking.

JONES, Gareth
Bevan Ashford, Bristol
(0117) 975 1687
gareth.jones@bevanashford.co.uk
Specialisation: Head of the Intellectual Property and Information Technology Group. Advises on technology transfer transactions for both licensors and licensees in various sectors but particularly in the metallurgical, medical and biochemical fields. Has acted for a variety of clients, licensing technology to many organisations throughout the world. Also acts for public sector bodies in high value procurements of IT systems frequently involving the use of the Private Finance Initiative and PPP. Has recently advised on a number of transactions for delivery of Electronic Patient Record solutions.
Prof. Memberships: Licensing Executives Society; Society for Computers and Law; The Intellectual Property Organisation.
Career: University College Wales, Aberystwyth – LLB (Hons). Qualified 1980. 1985-91, partner *Eversheds* Cardiff (formerly *Phillips & Buck*). 1991-date, partner – *Bevan Ashford*.
Personal: Golf, rugby, skiing.

JONES, Patricia
Hammond Suddards Edge, Manchester
(0161) 830 5000

JONES, Stephen
Baker & McKenzie, London
(020) 7919 1000
stephen.jones@bakernet.com
Specialisation: Partner specialising in intellectual property, in particular patents, trademarks and designs; involved in both contentious and non-contentious areas of practice with an emphasis on litigation and dispute resolution; qualified patent agent and registered trademark agent as well as Solicitor. Partner in charge of the London office Trade Marks Unit and member of the Pharmaceuticals/Healthcare and E-commerce practice groups.
Prof. Memberships: Chartered Institute of Patent Agents (fellow); Institute of Professional Representatives before the European Patent Office (EPI); Institute of Trade Mark Agents (ITMA); European Communities Trademark Association (ECTA); Licensing Executives Society (LES); AIPPI (UK); International Trademark Association (INTA); Pharmaceutical Trade Marks Group; Competition Law Association; Royal Society of Chemistry (Associate); Law Society.
Career: Began career at *Frank B Dehn & Co* 1978-83; qualified 1981 as patent agent; IP department *Linklaters & Paines* 1983-85, Head of Trademarks Unit 1987-93; Patent Department ICI Pharmaceuticals 1985-87; Partner, Head of Intellectual Property *Boodle Hatfield* 1993-95; *Allen & Overy* 1995-99; Partner *Baker & McKenzie* 1999.
Publications: Editor 'CIPA Guide to Patents Acts'.
Personal: Imperial College, London (1977 BSc Chemistry); University of London (external) (1990 LLB). Born 22 January 1956; married with three children.

JUDGE, Ian
Bristows, London
(020) 7400 8000
ian.judge@bristows.com
Specialisation: Intellectual property. Ian is a consultant to the firm having been a partner in the intellectual property department of the firm for 33 years. He is one of over 70 lawyers handling intellectual property matters in the firm together with 20 other intellectual property partners: David Brown, John Allcock, Philip Westmacott, Edward Nodder, Sally Field, Paul Walsh, Kevin Appleton, Alan Johnson, Pat Treacy, Tim Powell, Dr Penny Gilbert, Matthew Warren, David Wilkinson, Simon Ayrton, Christine Hore, Laura Anderson, Justin Watts, Andrew Lykiardopoulos, Ralph Cox and Alastair McCulloch. Work covers litigation and licensing of the full range of intellectual property, including patents, trademarks, copyright, designs and confidential information. Has had conduct of major patent cases such as Bristol-Myers ats Beecham and Du Pont v Akzo (both H.L.), Monsanto v Stauffer, Chiron v Organon Teknika and Chiron v Evans Medical. Speaker at seminars on specialist intellectual property topics.
Prof. Memberships: Law Society, Chartered Institute of Patent Agents (Associate Member), Chairman – Intellectual Property Lawyers Association (1997-2001), AIPPI, AIPLA.
Career: Joined *Bristows* 1964, qualified as a solicitor in 1967, became a Partner in 1969. Head of Intellectual Property Department 1992 to 2002.
Personal: Born 4 December 1941. Attended Cambridge University (BA Natural Sciences and Law 1963, MA 1967).

KAMSTRA, Gerry
Simmons & Simmons, London
(020) 7628 2020
gerry.kamstra@simmons-simmons.com
Specialisation: Partner in Intellectual Property Department. Principal area of practice is intellectual property law, including financings, commercial trans-

actions and litigation within the pharmaceutical and biotechnology industries. Clients include AstraZeneca, Aventis, 3M, Bayer, Bristol-Myers Squibb, GlaxoSmithKline, Guidant Corporation, Alizyme plc and Inhale Therapeutic Systems. Has written numerous articles and lectures widely.
Prof. Memberships: Member Intellectual Property Advisory Committee of BioIndustry Association and Intellectual Property Committee of the Association of the British Pharmaceutical Industry and Associate Member of Chartered Institute of Patent Agents.
Career: Qualified in 1986. Joined *Simmons & Simmons* 1986 where he became a partner in 1992.
Personal: Born 13 May 1954. Educated at Hymers College, Hull, Keble College, Oxford (Psychology & Physiology), Leicester University (Ph.D in Neuroendocrinology) and Trent Polytechnic.

KARET, Ian
Linklaters, London
(020) 7456 5800
ian.karet@linklaters.com
Specialisation: Specialist in intellectual property and information technology. Main areas of practice include IP aspects of patent litigation, SPCs, jurisdiction issues, anti-counterfeiting, licensing disputes, joint ventures and IPOs. Main areas of practice also include the IT aspects of outsourcing, litigation and arbitration of failed computer systems, software infringement and ownership, data protection and privacy advice and disputes.
Prof. Memberships: Deputy Reporter General of AIPPI. Fellow of the Chartered Institute of Arbitrators. Member of the Royal Society of Chemistry. Associate Member of the Chartered Institute of Patent Agents.
Career: 1997 to date: Partner, Intellectual Property and Technology Department, *Linklaters*; 1990-97: Assistant Solicitor, *Linklaters*; 1987-89 Articled Clerk, *Linklaters*. Oxford University, MA (Chemistry). Leo Baeck College, MA (Jewish Studies).

KEMPNER, Richard
Addleshaw Booth & Co, Leeds
(0113) 209 2000
richard.kempner@addleshawbooth.com
Specialisation: Partner and Head of Intellectual Property. Handles both disputes and transactions involving patents, copyright, trademarks, designs and confidential information. Voted the UK's Top Trade Marks Rising Star for 2000 by the 'Insider Guide to Brands and Trade Marks' and as being "very knowledgeable" and "bright, friendly and proactive". Clients include Asda, MyTravel, BASF and Ferrari. Recent High Court reported cases include Stoddards v Ryalux (copyright), United Biscuits v Asda (TMs), BASF v Smithkline Beecham (patents) and Nutrinova v Stanchem (patents) and in the ECJ in R v Maff ex p Monsanto. Speaks and writes extensively on protection, licensing and enforcement.
Prof. Memberships: LES, INTA, CIPA, IPLA, ITMA.
Career: BA Hons Law (1st Class), *Linklaters* (1985-90). Partner of *Addleshaw Booth & Co* since 1992.

LEVINE, Simon
Denton Wilde Sapte, London
(020) 7320 6533
srl@dentonwildesapte.com
Specialisation: Specialises in intellectual property, information technology and media law, advising on all aspects of copyright and related rights, advertising, design right, trademark rights, passing off, breach of confidence and patents. He has acted for well-known individuals, trusts and charities, and companies in many industries, in particular media, new media, sport and manufacturing. He has been involved in all aspects of litigation and arbitration and has experience in the High Court, the Copyright Tribunal, the Court of Appeal, the House of Lords and the Privy Council, as well as Trademark Registry. A number of these matters have been reported and have been the subject of media interest.
Prof. Memberships: Member of the Intellectual Property Lawyers Organisation (TIPLO); member of the International Trademark Association (INTA); member of the IP Committee of the City of London Law Society (CLLS); member of the IP Committee of the International Chamber of Commerce (ICC); close associations with the IP and IT Bar.
Career: September 1988-July 1998: solicitor and Partner, *Frere Cholmeley Bischoff*, London. August 1998 joined *Denton Wilde Sapte*, Partner; May 2001 Head of Intellectual Property Group.

LINDSEY, Michael
Morgan Cole, Cardiff
(029) 2038 5385

LLEWELYN, David
White & Case, London
(020) 7397 3607
Dllewelyn@whitecase.com
Specialisation: Partner in *White & Case's* London office specialising in intellectual property law. Main area of practice is intellectual property. Deals with all aspects, both contentious and non-contentious. Also covers information technology, e-commerce and pharmaceutical law. Has been involved in a number of major IP related transactions and cases, many cross-border. Clients come principally from the cosmetics, food and drink, pharmaceuticals and retail sectors. Also computer companies (especially software) and multimedia. Senior Visiting Fellow in Intellectual Property, Centre for Commercial Law Studies, Queen Mary College, London.
Prof. Memberships: Law Society, Pharmaceutical Trade Marks Group, International Trade Mark Association.
Career: Research Fellow at Max Planck Institute for Patent, Copyright and Competition Law, Munich 1980-81. Qualified in 1985. With *Linklaters & Paines* 1982-87, then Partner at *McKenna & Co* 1987-94. Founded *Llewelyn Zietman* in July 1994. Joined *White & Case's* London office in September 1999.
Publications: Joint author of leading textbook Kerly's 'Law of Trade Marks and Trade Names' (13th ed, 2001). Author of numerous articles published in legal journals. Has also delivered many conference papers in the UK and abroad.
Personal: Born 15th July 1956. Educated at Wallingford Grammar School 1967-74, Southampton University 1974-77 (LLB) and Worcester College, Oxford 1978-79 (BCL, 1st Class Hons). German speaker. Lives in London SW7.

LOCHNER, Ludi
Laytons, Guildford
(01483) 407022
ludi.lochner@laytons.com
Specialisation: Intellectual Property Law.
Prof. Memberships: Chartered Institute of Patent Agents; Institute of Trade Mark Agents; AIPPI; Competition Association; Licensing Executives Society; FICPI; Surrey Law Society; Member of the CBI's Technology & Innovation Committee.
Career: Qualified 1981; Head of IP at *Stephenson Harwood* 1982-94; established *Lochners Technology Solicitors* to specialise in legal work requiring an understanding of technology and ancillary areas of law such as trademarks and copyright. In November 2001, *Lochners Technology Solicitors* merged with *Laytons Solicitors* and became a Partner of *Laytons*. Handled successfully two of the most important patent infringement actions to come before the English Courts. Represented Remington successfully up to the European Court of Justice in the trademark infringement proceedings brought by Philips.
Publications: Author of the UK Chapter of 'International Patent Litigation' published by the Bureau of International Affairs, Inc, Washington, USA. Numerous articles.
Personal: Born in 1938. A keen offshore yachtsman, skippered City of Springs in the first Cape Town to Rio de Janeiro Yacht Race. BSc (Chemistry and Physics); LLB; Registered Attorney and Patent Agent (South Africa).

LOVE, James
Irwin Mitchell, Leeds
(0113) 234 3333
lovej@irwinmitchell.co.uk
Specialisation: Intellectual property. Extensive experience in relation to patent, trade marks, copyright, designs, confidentiality, counterfeiting and search and seize orders. Recent work includes: handling an oil industry patent dispute which was one of only half a dozen cases since 1977 to reach the House of Lords in connection with the Patents Act 1977; handling defence of dispute featured on national television concerning the extent of Dyno-Rods alleged monopoly in Day-Glo painted vans; major international litigation in US and throughout Europe. Chairman of seminar at this year's International Trade Mark Association meeting in Washington DC.
Prof. Memberships: Chartered Institute of Patent Agents. Institute of Trade Mark Agents.
Career: 1989-94: *Bristows*, London. 1994-96: *Eversheds*, Leeds. 1996 to date *Irwin Mitchell*, Leeds (partner from 1997). Named as one of Yorkshire's top three lawyers under 40 in 1999 and as one of the region's leading young professionals. The only young lawyer to win two awards in the inaugural Yorkshire Lawyer Awards 2000, and recently cited as one of the leading young lawyers outside London in 'Legal Business'.
Publications: Articles in a wide variety of general and specialist press.
Personal: 1984-87: Queens College, Cambridge (Sciences). 1987-89: The College of Law, Chancery Lane. 1992-93: Diploma in Intellectual Property, Bristol University.

LUCKMAN, Michael
Wragge & Co, Birmingham
0870 903 1000

MACDONALD, Morag
Bird & Bird, London
(020) 7415 6000
morag.macdonald@twobirds.com
Specialisation: Partner and head of international IP group. Work includes litigation, transactional and advisory work in relation to all intellectual property rights. In particular, handles pharmaceutical, biotechnology, electronics and software patents and trademarks. Acted in Mentor/Hollister, Compaq/Dell, Richardson Vicks/Reckitt & Colman, Chocosuisse/Cadbury, Research Corporations SPC, Swiss Miss, Baxter/Pharmacia Upjohn and Genetics Institute, Stolt Comex Seaway/Coflexip, Novo Nordisk/DSM, Estate of James Joyce/Macmillan, Stannah/Freelift.
Prof. Memberships: CIPA, ITMA, INTA, ECTA, British Computer Society.
Career: Called to the Bar 1984. Joined *Bird & Bird* 1985. Partner 1989.
Publications: Contributor on IP issues to 'Internet Law and Regulation' (Sweet & Maxwell, 3rd edition, December 1997), UK section of 'The New Role of Intellectual Property in Commercial Transactions' (Wiley 1994). Co-author of 'Designs & Copyright Protection of Products: World Law & Practice' (Sweet & Maxwell), Enforcement chapter 'CTM Handbook'.
Personal: MA in Mathematics, Physics and Law from Cambridge.

MACDONALD-BROWN, Charters
Gouldens, London
(020) 7583 7777
cmb@gouldens.com
Specialisation: Advised in numerous patent, trademark, copyright design and IP cases. In the last year, acted for two major pharmaceutical companies in a

INTELLECTUAL PROPERTY ■ THE LEADERS

High Court trademarks/parallel imports case, in which the ECJ has just delivered judgment and the case will now return to the High Court in London (Glaxo-SmithKline and Boehringer Ingelheim); acted for the successful claimant in an important design right case (Fulton v Grant Barnett) and two recent patent cases will be reported: One on costs (McGhan Medical Ltd v Nagor Ltd) and the other (Punduit v Band-It) where he was successful in the Court of Appeal. All cases cited are reported.
Prof. Memberships: Law Society, IBA, CIPA, ITMA, IPLA, TIPLO, AIPPI, ABA, AIPLA, INTA, ECTA, Pharmaceutical Trade Mark Group and LES.
Career: Trained with *Gouldens*, Partner 1977, founder of IP Group and its head. Executive Council of AIPPI (UK) and INTA Committee member. Honorary Advisor to the Legal and Parliamentary Committee of the Royal Society of Chemistry. Lectures on IP Diploma Course at Bristol University.
Publications: Numerous papers and articles for INTA, CIPA, PTMG, EIPR, Bristol University and others.

MACFARLANE, Nicholas
Lovells, London
(020) 7296 2000
nicholas.macfarlane@lovells.com
Specialisation: Patents; trade marks; passing-off; copyright; misuse of confidential information; trade libel and other allied areas of competition law; largely involved in litigation. Involved in many leading intellectual property cases concerning inter alia; patentability of software; the movement of patented pharmaceuticals within the EU; extent of relief in Anton Piller Orders; comparative advertising and counterfeiting.
Prof. Memberships: Founder Member of and former Secretary of Intellectual Property Lawyers Association; Council Member British Group of AIPPI; associate member Chartered Institute of Patent Agents and Institute of Trade Mark Agents.
Career: Lancaster University 1974 BA (Hons). Articled *Richards Butler*, qualified 1977. *Faithfull Owen & Fraser* partner 1980. 1985 amalgamated with *Durrant Piesse*, now *Lovells*.

MACPHERSON, Shonaig
McGrigor Donald, Edinburgh
(0131) 777 7000
shonaig.macpherson@mcgrigors.com
Specialisation: Senior Partner (Scotland) and Head of Technology Unit. Handles all aspects of intellectual property and information technology work. Advises on protection strategies, funding for technology projects, licensing, research contracts, litigation and dispute resolution with particular expertise in biosciences. Speaker at Glasgow IT summits in 1993 and 1994, and at the International Science Festival in Edinburgh in 1992, 1993 and 1994, Chicago 1996.
Prof. Memberships: Law Society (England and Wales), Law Society (Scotland), Licensing Executives Society, Royal Society, Scottish Biomedical Association, Scottish Biomedical Research Trust. Visiting Professor at Heriot-Watt University, Society for Computers and the Law.
Career: Qualified in 1984 in England and Wales with *Norton Rose*. Assistant Company Secretary (Legal) Storehouse plc, then Legal Director of Harrods 1987-89. Partner at *Calow Easton* in London 1989-91. Qualified in Scotland 1991. Joined *McGrigor Donald* in 1991 and became a Partner in 1992. 2002, Senior Partner, Scotland.
Personal: Born 29 September 1958. Director of Edinburgh Chamber of Commerce and Enterprise. Recreations include theatre, opera and reading. Lives in Edinburgh.

MARSHALL, James
Taylor Wessing, London
(020) 7300 7000
j.marshall@taylorwessing.com
Specialisation: All areas of intellectual property, both contentious and non-contentious. In particular, patent, trademark, copyright and breach of confidence litigation; licences and other agreements concerning exploitation of intellectual property including in competition law context.
Prof. Memberships: Solicitors Association of Higher Courts Advocates; Associate of Chartered Institute of Patent Agents; AIPPI; AMIEE.
Career: BSc (Mathematics and Physics), University of Bristol. Called to the Bar in 1986 with pupillage in Chambers of (then) Stephen Gratwick QC. 1987 joined *Lovell White Durrant*, subsequently requalifying as a solicitor. 1995 obtained solicitor advocate (Higher Courts Civil) qualification. 1997 joined partnership of *Taylor Joynson Garrett*.

MARSLAND, Vanessa
Clifford Chance, London
(020) 7600 1000
vanessa.marsland@cliffordchance.com
Specialisation: Litigation and dispute resolution. Partner specialising in intellectual property including copyright, patents, trademarks and designs particular emphasis on digital products and online exploitation.
Career: Admitted 1981; Intellectual Property Partner since 1987.
Personal: St Leonard's Mayfield, King's College, Cambridge.

MARTINDALE, Avril
Freshfields Bruckhaus Deringer, London
(020) 7936 4000
avril.martindale@freshfields.com
Specialisation: Partner specialising in intellectual property. Main area of practice covers non-contentious intellectual property and information technology. Deals with commercial, advisory and transactional aspects of intellectual property and information technology.
Prof. Memberships: Law Society of England & Wales, Law Society of Scotland, Licensing Executives Society, Competition Law Society, INTA.
Career: Qualified in Scotland in 1985. With Scottish firm *Dickson Minto WS* 1985-88, then *McKenna & Co.* 1988-92. Qualified in England & Wales in 1992. Joined *Bristows Cooke & Carpmael* and became a partner in 1993. Joined *Freshfields* August 1997.
Personal: Born 1961. Educated at Glasgow University.

MCKAY, Anna
Roiter Zucker, London
(020) 7644 8913
amckay@roiterzucker.co.uk
Specialisation: Intellectual property/competition law. Head of *Roiter Zucker's* IP Department: well known for work concerning pharmaceuticals, in relation to patents, trademarks and competition law. Acted for Dowelhurst and Medihealth (Swingward) against Glaxo, Boehringer Ingelheim, SKB and Eli Lilly (Glaxo v Dowelhurst) and for the BAEPD in relation to its application for judicial review of the 1999 PPRS. Acts for pharmaceutical companies in the US and throughout Europe, including IVAX, Niche Generics, the British Association for European Pharmaceutical Distributors, and Pharming Group.
Prof. Memberships: IPLA, ITMA.
Career: Trained at *Breechers*: qualified 1983. *Christopher B Mitchell* 1984, Partner 1986: Partner *Roiter Zucker* 1991. Regularly contributes articles to 'Patent World', 'Trademark World', 'Commercial Lawyer', 'ERA News', 'Pharmaceutical Technology' and other intellectual property law publications
Personal: Loughborough High School, University of Sussex (1979 - BA Law). Theatre, architecture, 20th century furniture, children.

MCNABB, Heather
Eversheds, Cardiff
(029) 2047 1147
heathermcnabb@eversheds.com
Specialisation: Partner and Head of Intellectual Property and Information Technology Unit. Specialises in all aspects of intellectual property and IT work. Practice covers the full range of contentious and non-contentious IP. Advises on the protection, maintenance and exploitation of intellectual property rights. Particular interest in technology-based businesses and the internet. Extensive experience of exploiting and protecting IP and drafting and negotiating all types of IT contracts, including agreements for licensing and maintenance, turnkey, facilities management, and outsourcing arrangements, (including PFI work). Also particular interest in e-commerce dealing with clients on the supplier and customer side.
Prof. Memberships: Member of the Licensing Executives Society; Member of the Society for Computers and Law; Member of the Intellectual Property Lawyers Association and the New Media Development Group.
Career: University of Wales, Cardiff (LLB Hons 1986). Qualified in 1989. Joined *Eversheds* in 1994, becoming a Partner in 1995.
Personal: Married and resides in South Wales.

MIDDLEMISS, Susie
Slaughter and May, London
(020) 7600 1200
susie.middlemiss@slaughterandmay.com
Specialisation: Partner in the Intellectual Property Group, dealing particularly with contentious matters in relation to the full range of intellectual property rights, focusing on patent and trademark issues.
Career: Qualified New South Wales 1986; England and Wales 1991; *Clifford Chance* 1987-95; *Slaughter and May* 1995; partner 2000.
Personal: Education; University of Sydney (BSc; LLB). Resides London.

MOAKES, Jonathan
Halliwell Landau, Manchester
(0161) 835 3003
jmoakes@halliwells.co.uk
Specialisation: Partner and Head of Intellectual Property. Work includes patents, copyright, designs, trade secrets, technology transfer and exploitation agreements, trademarks and disputes. Particular experience in acting for high tech business and in technical litigation. His other main area of practice is Computer Law, including software licensing, supply contracts and disputes. Author of 'International Information Technology Law- England and Wales' and the 'Encyclopaedia of Information Technology Law'. Has addressed numerous conferences on Intellectual Property and Computer Law issues.
Prof. Memberships: Committee Member of North West Branch of the Licensing Executives Society, Society for Computers and Law, Solicitors European Group.
Career: Qualified 1984. Worked at *Baker & McKenzie* 1982-88, then *Halliwell Landau*, becoming a partner in 1989.
Personal: Born 1960. Attended Queens' College, Cambridge 1978-81. Leisure interests include sailing, skiing, fell walking, tennis and playing the violin. Lives in Wilmslow.

MOODIE, Bill
Herbert Smith, London
(020) 7374 8000
bill.moodie@herbertsmith.com
Specialisation: Head of the intellectual property and technology department. Partner with extensive experience of intellectual property covering both contentious and non-contentious work. Has handled several major patent cases (validity, infringement and enforceability) primarily in the electronics and communications fields as well as numerous cases involving copyright (software), technical confidential information and trademarks.
Prof. Memberships: CIPA; AIPLA; IPLA.
Career: South African patent agent and

THE LEADERS ■ INTELLECTUAL PROPERTY

attorney, 1975; solicitor in England and Wales, 1979; partner at *Herbert Smith*, 1984.
Personal: University of Cape Town (B.Sc Elec. Eng.) First Class Honours, 1969; University of South Africa (LLB), 1975.

MOONEY, Kevin
Simmons & Simmons, London
(020) 7628 2020
kevin.mooney@simmons-simmons.com
Specialisation: Senior Partner in Intellectual Property Department. Principal area of practice is patent litigation. Clients include GlaxoSmithKline, Aventis Crop Science, Bristol Myers Squibb, Pharmacia & Upjohn, 3M, Union Carbide, Procter & Gamble, Gallaher and Norsk Hydro. Member of Nuffield Bioethics Council Working Party on Human Tissue (April 1995). Experienced speaker at conferences.
Prof. Memberships: ABA, AIPLA, AIPPI, City of London Solicitors Company (Member of Intellectual Property Sub-committee).
Career: Qualified in 1971. Partner at *Simmons & Simmons* since 1973.
Personal: Born 14 November 1945. Educated at Bristol University (LLB 1968). Leisure activities include gardening and supporting QPR. Lives in Ealing, West London.

MOSS, Gary
Taylor Wessing, London
(020) 7300 7000
g.moss@taylorwessing.com
Specialisation: UK Managing Partner and member of *Taylor Wessing's* Intellectual Property Department. Practice covers all areas of intellectual property, but with particular emphasis on patents, biotechnology, information technology and technology transfers. Examples of important cases handled are Pall Corporation v Commercial Hydraulics, SKM v Wagner Spraytech, Single Buoy Moorings v Brown Brothers and Vickers plc, Brugger v Medic-Aid Limited, Amgen v Roche Diagnostics & Genetics Institute (major litigation relating to biotechnology patents) Amgen v Aventis (ditto) and Taylor v Ishida Co Limited. Clients include Amgen Inc, Visa, Pall Corporation, Haberman Associates, Avery Denison, Geron Corporation Biocompatibles plc, Generics Group AG and SkyPharma plc. Member of the editorial boards of 'The Biotechnology Law Report' and the 'Journal of Brand Management'. Has spoken at seminars on life sciences and information technology, both protection and issues arising on acquisitions of technology based companies.
Prof. Memberships: Law Society (member of Intellectual Property Sub-committee).
Career: Qualified in 1977. With *Clifford Turner* 1977-79, then *Woodham Smith* 1979-90 (partner from 1981). Joined *Taylor Joynson Garrett* as a partner in 1990.
Personal: Born 7 April 1953. Educated at the University of Leicester 1971-74 (1st Class Hons) and the College of Law (1st Class Hons). Recreations include theatre, opera and golf. Lives in London.

NAPPER, Isabel
Mills & Reeve, Cambridge
(01223) 222379
isabel.napper@mills-reeve.com
Specialisation: Strong City background dealing in all aspects of intellectual property law. Her move to Cambridge, where she has acquired a substantial reputation, enables her to use that experience to the advantage of clients. Enjoys handling a wide variety of IP issues relating to patents, designs, trademarks and confidential information, including advising companies of all sizes on how to deal with their intellectual property in order to protect and exploit it efficiently. Frequently lectures and gives seminars to clients and professional bodies. Extensive practical experience of litigation and licensing. Has a particular interest in technology transfer and biotechnology.
Prof. Memberships: Chartered Institute of Patent Agents, Society for the Application of Research, Licensing Executives' Society.
Career: MA (London). Qualified 1984. Specialist IP lawyer with *Lovell White Durrant*. 1991 IP partner *Hopkins & Wood*. 1994 to 1998, IP team at *Taylor Vinters*. 1998 partner in IP team *Mills & Reeve*.
Personal: Born 1958. Keen on good food, wine and enjoying life.

NEWMAN, Helen
Simmons & Simmons, London
(020) 7628 2020
helen.newman@simmons-simmons.com
Specialisation: Partner and Managing Partner of the firm's Intellectual Property Group. Principal area of practice is advising on the acquisition, disposal, re-structuring and exploitation of intellectual property rights portfolios (including merchandising deals). Involved in trademark filing and prosecution for clients for an extensive range of global brand owners. Conducts enforcement litigation for merchandising campaigns handles other intellectual property litigation in the United Kingdom and co-ordinates corresponding overseas litigation.
Prof. Memberships: International Trademark Association, Institute of Trademark Agents, MARQUES, Anti-counterfeiting Group, European Communities Trade Mark Association.
Career: Articled with *Simmons & Simmons*. Qualified 1980 and became a partner in 1985.

NICOLSON, Fiona
Maclay Murray & Spens, Glasgow
(0141) 248 5011
fmmn@maclaymurrayspens.co.uk
Specialisation: Partner and head of IP and technology department. Specialises in intellectual property and information technology work for clients both national and international, including start-ups, listed companies, venture capitalists and educational institutions.
Prof. Memberships: Past President - Licensing Executives Society, 'Britain and Ireland' council member. Chairman of the Law Society of Scotland panel for accreditation of intellectual property. Member, Scottish Committee Bioindustry Association; member Steering Group, Hillington Innovation Centre, Glasgow; non executive director of YABA Limited and St Andrews Clinic for Children.
Career: Joined *Maclay Murray & Spens* in 1993. Previously partner and head of IP at *Bird Semple*, *Fyfe Ireland*.
Personal: Glasgow University MA (1974) LLB (1983). Born 1954.

NODDER, Edward
Bristows, London
(020) 7400 8000
edward.nodder@bristows.com
Specialisation: Partner in intellectual property department. Advises on the full range of contentious and non-contentious intellectual property, including patents, trademarks, copyright, designs and confidential information, computers and IT, pharmaceuticals and biotechnology. This includes advice on European competition and harmonisation laws as they impact on intellectual property, including the European Patent Office and the Community Trade Mark Office. Amongst numerous reported cases, acted for the claimant in 3M v Rennicks (patent infringement and licensing), Gillette v Edenwest (trademark infringement and passing off), 3M v Plastus (cross-border injunction) and 3M v NCI (stay pending EPO opposition) and for the defendant in Kastner v Rizla (patent claim contruction). Has been involved in opposition proceedings at European Patent Office for 3M, British Gas and other clients. Currently responsible for Patents Court, High Court and Appeal Court patent and brands litigation on behalf of 3M, Novartis, Sara Lee (Douwe Egberts), CibaVision and closely involved with Novartis v AHP in Court of Appeal and House of Lords.
Prof. Memberships: Law Society, Associate Member of Chartered Institute of Patent Agents, AIPPI.
Career: Joined *Bristows* in 1978. Became a Partner in 1986.
Publications: Author of articles for specialist periodicals such as 'Patent World' and 'Managing Intellectual Property'. Regular speaker at intellectual property conferences and seminars.
Personal: Born 1956. Educated at Cambridge University 1974-77 (MA in Natural Sciences and Law). Enjoys opera, chamber music, tennis, skiing, gardening and the Languedoc.

ORCHISON, Graeme
DLA, Manchester
(08700) 111111

PERKINS, David
Clifford Chance, London
(020) 7600 1000
david.perkins@cliffordchance.com
Specialisation: Litigation and dispute resolution. Partner specialising in patents, trademarks, designs and pharmaceuticals.
Career: Partner since 1975.
Personal: Newcastle Preparatory School; Uppingham School; Newcastle University.

POORE, Alasdair
Mills & Reeve, Cambridge
(01223) 222248
alasdair.poore@mills-reeve.com
Specialisation: Wide range of intellectual property work including commercial (licensing and other agreements, computer contracts, competition law and mergers and acquisitions) and litigation and dispute resolution. Experience and particular interest in high-tech areas including electronics, computers and software, and also chemicals and biotechnology. Recent work has included a substantial patent action involving electronic copy protection technology, strategic advice on listing of new engine technology company, licensing negotiations on world beating refining process, licensing and advice on a significant web browsing technology, negotiation of Pathfinder PFI project in the IT sector.
Prof. Memberships: Chartered Patent agent, Registered Trade Mark agent, former council member of CIPA and chairman General Laws' committee, Patent Litigators' Association, Licensing Executives' Society, INTA.
Career: MA (Cantab) Law and Natural Sciences; Shell International Petroleum Co; *Lovell White Durrant*; *Clyde & Co*; *Mills & Reeve*, partner 1996.
Personal: Squash, real tennis, mountaineering, music.

PRICE, Richard
Taylor Wessing, London
(020) 7300 7000
r.price@taylorwessing.com
Specialisation: Intellectual property partner, specialising in patents, trade marks, copyright, confidential information, trade libel litigation, IP intensive acquisitions, disposals and licensing. Important cases include successful defence of SC Johnson & Son, Inc. (2000) in patent infringement proceedings brought by Sara Lee and on appeal (October 2001); in 1998-2000 acting successfully (first instance, Court of Appeal and House of Lords) for Healing Herbs Ltd in revocation action against BACH trade mark registrations for flower remedies (leading case on generic marks); acting successfully for Hoechst Celanese Corporation in patent infringement proceedings against BP Chemicals, first instance and appeal; proceeding to first account of profits in a patent case for 100 years, successful settlement shortly before Judgment (1998); in 1997, successful for Canon in last civil appeal from Hong Kong to the Privy Council

INTELLECTUAL PROPERTY ■ THE LEADERS

(patent and copyright issues); in 1991 successful appeal to House of Lords concerning Asahi Chemical's Patent Application (genetic engineering – priority of competing patent claims and the need for enabling disclosure); in 1988 acted for Reckitt and Colman winning the leading case on trade dress/passing off (JIF Lemon, House of Lords).
Prof. Memberships: Chairman, 1994-97 The Intellectual Property Lawyer's Association (formerly Patent Solicitors Association), City of London Solicitors' Company, Law Society's Intellectual Property Working Party, Solicitors European Group, AIPPI (UK). Lecturer Bristol University post-graduate IP Diploma.
Career: Qualified in 1970. With *Joynson-Hicks & Co* 1968-75 (partner 1973-75), then partner at *Courts & Co* 1975-77 and at *Woodham Smith* 1977-90. Joined *Taylor Joynson Garrett* as a partner in 1990.
Personal: Born 7th January 1946. Educated at Kingston Grammar School 1957-64 and Bristol University (LLB) 1964-67. Leisure interests include natural history, tennis and sailing. Trustee, British Ornithologist's Union. Lives in West Berkshire. Married with three sons.

RAWKINS, Jason
Taylor Wessing, London
(020) 7300 7000
j.rawkins@taylorwessing.com
Specialisation: Partner in Intellectual Property Department. Litigation and general advice in all areas of intellectual property, particularly trade marks (and brand protection), copyright/designs and domain names. Cases handled include Visa International v Sheimer, PepsiCo v French Connection and Canon v Green Cartridge. Writes articles for specialist periodicals and is a regular speaker at conferences and seminars. Appointed Nominet expert for domain name disputes.
Prof. Memberships: Law Society; member of INTA sub-committee.
Career: *Taylor Joynson Garrett* since 1990, qualifying in 1992. Became a Partner in 1998.
Personal: Educated at Uppingham School and Merton College, Oxford (1984-88). Interests include tennis, scuba diving, Norwich City F.C. and North Norfolk pubs. Lives in Herne Hill.

RICH, Andrew
Herbert Smith, London
(020) 7374 8000
andrew.rich@herbertsmith.com
Specialisation: Partner experienced in all areas of intellectual property law. Has acted on a wide range of contentious intellectual property matters including the worldwide patent litigation relating to the recombinantly produced protein enythropoietin, Roche's PCR technology, slow release pharmaceuticals and parallel imports. Also advises clients on the negotiation and drafting of intellectual property licences and IP rights clearance.
Prof. Memberships: Member of the Intellectual Property Advisory Committee of the BioIndustry Association. Member of Council of the AIPPI UK Group, member of IPLA and associate member of CIPA and ITMA.
Career: BSC (Marine Biology), from Liverpool University – 1984. College of Law, Guildford – 1987; qualified – 1989, Partnership – 1996.

ROSE, David
SJ Berwin, London
(020) 7533 2782
david.rose@sjberwin.com
Specialisation: Intellectual property - litigation and advisory; branding and design portfolio management. Major cases 2001-02: Cairnstores v AB Hassle; SmithKlineBeecham v Generics UK.
Prof. Memberships: TMA; SCL; INTA.
Career: Qualified 1994; Partner 2001.
Publications: Contributor to 'EIPR', 'MIP', 'Trademark World' and Sweet & Maxwell's 'Readings on Intellectual Property'.
Personal: LLB (Hons) University of Manchester; LLM (Intellectual Property) QMW, University of London.

SHILLITO, Mark
Herbert Smith, London
(020) 7374 8000
mark.shillito@herbertsmith.com
Specialisation: Partner with a broad practice covering the full spread of IP work, both contentious and non-contentious. Has extensive trial experience and has acted in a number of leading cases in the field of patents, copyrights, design right, plant variety rights and trademarks. Has also specific expertise in the law relating to genetically modified organisms.
Prof. Memberships: AIPLA; CIPA; ITMA; INTA; IPLA; TIPLO.
Career: Articled at *Herbert Smith*; qualified 1989; partner 1996. University College London (LLB Hons). Queen Mary & Westfield College, London (Dip.IP).

SMITH, Catriona
Allen & Overy, London
(020) 7330 3000
catriona.smith@allenovery.com
Specialisation: Partner specialising in intellectual property and information technology disputes from patents to software contracts. Has wide experience of pharmaceutical and healthcare disputes, protecting well-known trademarks and acting in international patent litigation. Is familiar with all aspects of litigation, from immediate injunctions to arbitration and full trials, and is also experienced in settlement negotiations. Is a member of various IP organisations and a regular speaker on IP-related topics.
Prof. Memberships: Secretary to the British Group of the Union of European Practitioners in Industrial Property; Member Intellectual Property Lawyers Association; AIPPI; Committee Member, International Trademark Association; American Intellectual Property Association; The Intellectual Property Lawyers Organisation.

Career: Assistant *Clifford Chance* (1982-89); Assistant *Allen & Overy* (1989-92), Partner 1992.
Personal: University of St Andrew's (1977, MA Hispanic Languages and Literature).

STARR, Ian
Ashurst Morris Crisp, London
(020) 7638 1111
ian.starr@ashursts.com
Specialisation: Partner in Intellectual Property and Technology Group. Principal area of practice is litigation and arbitration in relation to disputes relating to intellectual property rights and technology. Particular interest in cross-border disputes on patents and trademarks and disputes relating to the interaction between competition law and the enforcement of IP rights.
Career: Qualified in 1979. *Clifford Chance* 1980-93 (partner 1984-93). *Ashurst Morris Crisp* 1993-date (head of IP group).
Personal: Family and golf.

SWYCHER, Nigel
Slaughter and May, London
(020) 7600 1200
nigel.swycher@slaughterandmay.com
See under Information Technology, p.439

SYKES, John
Lupton Fawcett, Leeds
(0113) 280 2000

TAYLOR, Peter D
Clifford Chance, London
(020) 7600 1000
peter.taylor2@cliffordchance.com
Specialisation: Litigation and dispute resolution. Partner specialising in intellectual property, patents, trademark, copyright, registered design and design right law, contentious and non-contentious, related aspects of competition law, passing off, trade libel and misuse of confidential information.
Career: Articled *Needham & Grant*; qualified 1984; Partner *Clifford Chance* since 1990.
Personal: LLB Hons Law, Birmingham.

THORNE, Clive
Denton Wilde Sapte, London
(020) 7320 6953
cdt@dentonwildesapte.com
Specialisation: Partner in intellectual property group. Specialises in contentious IP work, including copyright law, patents, trade marks, passing off, marketing law, computer law and trade secrets. Also commercial litigation, arbitration and employment law.
Prof. Memberships: Founding member of The Intellectual Property Lawyers Organisation. Fellow of the Chartered Institute of Arbitrators. Member of Patent Solicitors Association; International Trade Mark Association; Institute of Trade Mark Agents; Anti-counterfeiting Group; Computer Law Group; Chartered Institute of Patent Agents; panel of arbitrators WIPO and Patents County Court.

Career: Qualified in 1977. Articled *Clifford Turner*. Admitted in Hong Kong in 1984 and Victoria, Australia in 1985. Joined *Denton Wilde Sapte* as a partner in 1987.
Publications: Co-author of 'Intellectual Property – the New Law,' joint author of 'Sony Guide to Home Taping' and 'Users Guide to Copyright.'

TULLEY, Christopher
DLA, Leeds
(08700) 111111

TURNER, Catrin
KLegal, London
(020) 7694 8909
catrin.turner@klegal.co.uk
Specialisation: Intellectual property, information technology, privacy and data protection. IP aspects and launch of Learndirect and Arena contribution to go Racing consortium. Advisor to Tesco on IP matters including European case against Levi. Management of reputation risk arising from e-commerce and insurance of those risks.
Prof. Memberships: INTA, ITMA (Associate), Pharmaceutical Trade Marks Group. Fellow of the Royal Society of Arts, Sciences and Maunufacturing.
Career: Qualified 1989 with niche IP/IT firm. *Davies Arnold Cooper* 1991-99. *H2O* since 1999.
Personal: Interests: Africa, carpentry.

WALSH, Paul
Bristows, London
(020) 7400 8000
paul.walsh@bristows.com
Specialisation: Partner in Intellectual Property Department. Practice spans both contentious and non-contentious intellectual property matters including computer contracts and related disputes. Legal advisor to the British Brands Group, an alliance of leading manufacturers in the FMCG industry concerned with lookalike products. Also interested in emergency interlocutory applications, search and seizure and asset freezing orders, and has been appointed by the High Court to supervise in the conduct of such orders. Cases include Pilkington v PPG (confidential information arbitration), PPG v Pilkington (anti-trust arbitration), Assidoman Multipack v Mead Corporation and Altertext Inc. v Advanced Data Communications Ltd.
Prof. Memberships: Licensing Executives Society, Associate Member of the Institute of Trade Mark Agents, European Community Trade Mark Association, Law Society.
Career: Qualified and joined *Bristows* in 1983. Became a Partner in 1988.
Publications: Lecturer on technology transfer litigation, trademark law, biotechnology law and Anton Piller Orders. Author of various articles for 'Trade Mark World' and 'Corporate Briefing'.
Personal: Born 21st December 1956. Educated at Salvatorian College 1968-75 and Oxford University 1976-79. Leisure

interests include tennis, squash, literature and wine. Lives in London.

WHAITE, Robin
Linklaters, London
(020) 7456 5828
robin.whaite@linklaters.com

Specialisation: Specialist in intellectual property and technology-related matters. Particular knowledge of issues in the healthcare, chemical and computer industries. Areas of practice include patent, copyright, trade marks, trade secrets litigation, cross-border litigation; technology joint ventures, IP aspects of M&A and corporate finance; technology transfer generally, including European and UK anti-trust and competition law considerations and pharmaceutical law.
Prof. Memberships: Committee Member of the IP Lawyers Association. Represents the British Chamber of Commerce on the UK Government's Standing Advisory Committee on IP. Editorial Board of 'Managing Intellectual Property'.
Career: Since 1989: Partner, Intellectual Property Department, *Linklaters*; 1986-89: Assistant Solicitor, *Linklaters*; 1978-86: Articled Clerk/Assistant Solicitor, *Herbert Smith & Co*. 1977-80: Cambridge University, BA, MA; 1978: Law Society Final Exams.

WILLOUGHBY, Tony
Willoughby & Partners, London
(020) 7345 8888
twilloughby@iprights.com

Specialisation: Senior Partner. All areas of intellectual property, but particularly litigation relating to trademarks, passing off, copyright, designs and confidential information. Has particular experience of parallel imports/grey market and anti-counterfeit litigation, and the Anton Piller Order and Mareva Injunction. He is an arbitrator for the WIPO ICANN and Nominet UK domain name dispute resolution procedures.
Prof. Memberships: ITMA, INTA, LSLA, TIPLO, Law Society.
Career: 1970 The Distillers Co. Ltd. 1973 *Herbert Smith*. 1994 *Willoughby & Partners*.
Publications: Various papers relating to subjects such as parallel imports; search orders; freezing orders; domain names.
Personal: Born 29 September 1944. Educated at Westminster School. Interests include music, sport and wine. Member of the Governing Body of Westminster School (1990-2000).

WOOD, Alan
Beachcroft Wansbroughs, Bristol
(0117) 918 2000
awood@bwlaw.co.uk

Specialisation: Partner in projects department. Main areas of practice are computer and IT, competition and public procurement, and intellectual property. Acts for both public bodies and private sector companies. IT projects range from complex, high-value IT system procurements, with advice on tendering procedures, review and incorporation of technical specifications, contract drafting and award and ongoing contract support, to advice on standard supply, licence and maintenance terms. Also includes advice on public procurement rules, the Private Finance Initiative, outsourcing and facilities management. Intellectual property advice includes both contentious and non-contentious aspects of IP protection, licensing agreements both national and international, technology led joint ventures and technology transfer generally.
Career: Qualified at *Linklaters & Paines* in 1975. With *Linklaters & Paines* 1975-87. *Osborne Clarke* 1987-97. Joined *Wansbroughs Willey Hargrave* May 1997. Partner in *Beachcroft Wansbroughs* 1999.

WOOD, Ian
Mayer, Brown, Rowe & Maw, London
(020) 7782 8632
awhite@eu.mayerbrownrowe.com

Specialisation: Partner Intellectual Property Department. All aspects of intellectual property law, including patents, trademarks and copyright and allied rights, although primarily involved in the area of dispute resolution. Acts for a broad range of clients from large multinational corporations to smaller more locally based businesses, covering a broad spectrum of industries and services extending from those involved in newly emergent technologies to those in more established areas of business. Responsible for the conduct of several notable actions in the High Court, including the following leading reported patent infringement actions: Molnlycke v Procter & Gamble; Nidek v VISX; Unilever v Akzo and Chefaro; Honeywell v ACL. Other leading cases include Burton v Burton Snowboards and BP Amoco v Kelly. Also advising the European Commission in connection with WTO disputes regarding international obligations on patents. Author of several articles and regularly invited to speak at conferences and seminars (including those attended by fellow professionals).
Prof. Memberships: CIPA; ITMA; INTA; AIPPI; IPLA.
Personal: Born 1950. Attended Durham University (BSc Physics and MSc Nuclear Physics). Qualified as a solicitor in 1977.

WOODS, Philip
Hill Dickinson, Manchester
(0161) 429 6767

Specialisation: Partner in Technology and Intellectual Property Group of *Hill Dickinson* specialising in all aspects of intellectual property and computer law, both contentious and non-contentious.
Prof. Memberships: Chartered Institute of Patent Agents (Associate); Institute of Trade Mark Agents (Associate); UNION; FICPI; AIPPI; Society for Computers and Law; Chairman of Committee of LES (North West Group); TIPLO (founder member).
Career: Qualified 1974. Admitted Hong Kong 1975. *Deacons* (Hong Kong) 1975-81. Partner, *Wilkinson & Grist* (Hong Kong) 1981-89. Partner, *Eversheds Alexander Tatham* (Head of IP Department) 1989-94. Chairman of *Eversheds* National IP Group until 1994. Partner, *Philip Woods & Co* 1994-97. Presently Partner *Hill Dickinson*.
Personal: Leisure pursuits include classic cars, wines, walking, reading and gardening. Lives in Prestbury, Cheshire. Born 23 December 1950.

WYN DAVIES, Cerys
Pinsent Curtis Biddle, Birmingham
(0121) 625 3056
cerys.wyn-davies@pinsents.com

Specialisation: Technology partner. Advises on intellectual property, information technology, e-commerce/e-business and data protection, emphasis on non-contentious matters including technology and biotechnology licensing; multimedia licensing; research and development and collaboration agreements; confidentiality arrangements; trademarks and designs advice and licensing and IP/IT due diligence and audits.
Prof. Memberships: Licensing Executives Society. TIPLO. FAST. Intellectual Property Lawyers Association. ICC.
Career: Qualified 1985. *Coward Chance* 1983-87 and *Clifford Chance* 1987-95. Joined *Pinsent Curtis Biddle* in 1995 as partner.
Personal: Born 1961. Graduated from Exeter University 1982 (LLB) 1st Class and Sweet and Maxwell prize winner. Diploma in Intellectual Property Law, University of London 1991 – Distinction in all four heads. Interests include theatre, walking and skiing.

INVESTMENT FUNDS

London: 496; The Regions: 499; Scotland: 500; Profiles: 501

Research approved by BMRB For this edition, Chambers' researchers conducted 6,582 interviews – 3,900 with law firms, 511 with barristers and 2,171 with clients. The validity of the research was scrutinised by BMRB International, who audited both the methodology and the results at our offices in London. They interviewed **Chambers'** researchers and cross-checked sample interviews. Details of the audit appear on page 7.

OVERVIEW The year has seen a fragile investment trust sector. Against the background of FSMA investigations, "*the story of the split capital shakedown is hanging over the market,*" according to commentators. Across the industry, practices have been noting the shortfall in new fund activity and adjusting accordingly. Beyond restructuring of existing funds, the hedge funds and alternate investment industry has matured. Investment banks and US fund managers are beginning to feature these as part of the stable of asset offerings and are establishing new product lines throughout Europe. Real estate, a hitherto under-invested asset class, continues to outperform the market with assistance from the euro.

LONDON

This book is the product of 6,582 1/2 hour interviews. See p.7 for BMRB audit. Within each band, firms are listed alphabetically.

CLIFFORD CHANCE (see firm details p.911) Interviewees agree that this "*long established*" practice has "*always had a strong franchise across the entire sector.*" Competitors rate its performance in private equity downstream work, unit trusts, and funds including property, retail, offshore funds and split capital investment trusts. Clients believe that the team figures "*among the leaders in the global game,*" noting its "*dominant presence*" in the sector across the UK, Europe and increasingly the US. They also endorse the "*enormously talented, experienced individuals*" that comprise the "*user-friendly, well-integrated team.*" As one client said: "*It provides solutions and cracks the whip to get the work done to a high standard.*" **Tim Herrington** (see p.390) is "*always regarded as a big name*" and remains hugely respected in regulatory and fund matters, such as advising UBS Asset Management in the establishment of the pan-European Fresco Exchange Traded Fund. **Andrew Hougie**'s (see p.502) "*outstanding*" market reputation lies in his technical expertise on closed-end funds and listed vehicles, particularly in the context of takeovers. He advised Aberdeen Preferred Income Trust on the placing and open offer of preference shares and the issue of new ZDP shares. **James Barlow** (see p.501) is still "*well respected*" for his retail expertise. The team advised recently on the establishment of a further ten private equity funds comprising part of the DTI's Regional Venture Capital Funds, the Government's programme for providing risk capital finance to start-ups and small companies within the 'equity gap'. **Clients** Aberdeen Asset Managers; Man Investment Products; Citibank; Gartmore; Industri Kapital; JPMorgan Chase Fleming; Duke Street Capital; Merrill Lynch; Morgan Stanley.

LINKLATERS (see firm details p.1043) "*Nothing ever goes wrong with deals the firm is on – it makes everything easy,*" report satisfied clients, while rivals pay tribute to the team's "*fabulously blue-blooded*" client base of major institutional investment funds and trusts. Leading global finance houses testify that it "*provides an extensive and extremely high-quality package*" with a "*pragmatic, solution-oriented approach,*" while some clients suggest that it is "*best-placed*" for pan-European fund launches. "*First-class leader*" **Tim Shipton** (see p.503) impressed industry players with "*high-powered*" pitches, particularly in relation to offshore and public markets matters. He advised a fund of hedge funds and the split capital dual-listed investment company, MAGIC, on a major investment in Morley Alternative Investment Strategy Fund (MAISF), a Guernsey protected cell company subsidiary. Clients endorse the "*father of funds in the City,*" **Paul Harris** (see p.502), who can "*make esoteric areas accessible.*" He recently advised on the reconstruction of GAM Diversity, a $1.8 billion open-ended investment company incorporated in the British Virgin Islands. Peers hold "*impressive corporate generalist*" **Matthew Middleditch** (see p.502) in high regard for his expertise in complex onshore matters. He advised on the capital structure reorganisation of the Monthly High Income Trust and MHIT Securities, and completed Section 110 Insolvency Act schemes for three different UK-listed investment trusts (M&G Income, M&G Recovery and Fleming Income and Capital). Clients commend "*user-friendly*" **Jonathan Perkins** (see p.502) as "*the main port of call*" for fund products and linked businesses because "*he provides an excellent service for cutting-edge products.*" With expertise in private equity, real estate investment trusts and capital markets, he advised on the launch of the AXA Secondary Fund II, which closed at $480 million. Expert in the establishment, marketing and listing of investment funds for US and international clients, "*commercial, pragmatic*" **John Kilner** (see p.502) is esteemed as "*a consummate professional with huge stores of knowledge.*" He acted for Govett High Income Investment Trust on its innovative restructuring to restore its capital base. The team also advised Real Estate Investment Managers (REIM) in France on the structuring and launch of the AFrench Development Venture. **Clients** Morgan Stanley; Terra Firma Capital Partners; JPMorgan Fleming Asset Management; Morley Fund Management; BC Capital Partners; Govett Investment Management; PRICOA Capital Group ; ING Real Estate; AXA Investment Managers Private Equity Europe; Credit Suisse First Boston International; Lend Lease Investments; Triton Advisers (UK); Janus International.

HERBERT SMITH (see firm details p.992) Clients say that this team is "*at the forefront of developments*" in investment trusts and public quoted funds matters, including reconstructions, new issues and corporate finance loan stocks. Though not quite as visible for its authorised and retail unit trusts practice, it commands a growing profile in that part of the sector as well. Competitors praise its strength in depth of "*solid, highly experienced*" individuals, while clients admire its ability to "*simplify complicated matters*" and "*think creatively to ensure that objectives are met.*" One declared that the team "*has expertise at its fingertips and is highly responsive with timely opinions.*" Retaining his outstanding name for investment trusts work,

LONDON ■ INVESTMENT FUNDS

> ### TOP IN-HOUSE LAWYERS
>
> **Karen BIRCH**, The Bank of New York
>
> **Pamela EDWARDS**, Executive Director of Legal Services Europe, Fidelity Investments International
>
> **Kenneth GREIG**, Head of Legal Services, Scottish Widows Investment Partnership
>
> **Lucy LYNCH**, Head of Law and Compliance for Europe, Morgan Stanley
>
> **Alexander MARSHALL**, Executive Director and Senior Counsel, Goldman Sachs Asset Management
>
> **Simon MARTIN**, Legal Manager, Gartmore Investment Management
>
> **Jonathon THOMAS**, Executive Director and Counsel, Goldman Sachs Asset Management International
>
> **Jane THORNTON**, Head of Legal, Gartmore Investment Management
>
> **Josephine TUBBS**, Head of Legal and Secretarial, Framlington Group
>
> **Karen Birch** joins the list following recommendation of her "*extremely practical approach – she is very determined.*" **Kenneth Greig** received recommendations from the top law firms in the industry. **Pamela Edwards** and **Jonathon Thomas** are acclaimed for their "*great intelligence.*" Private practitioners find both **Simon Martin** and **Lucy Lynch** a "*pleasure to work with,*" while the "*pragmatic*" **Alexander Marshall** remains a well-known figure in the sector. **Jane Thornton** is an "*excellent communicator,*" while **Josephine Tubbs** is "*concise and to the point.*"
>
> In-house lawyers' profiles p.1201

"*exceptional*" **Nigel Farr** (see p.502) advised the British Portfolio Trust on its flotation, the first launch of a non-split capital investment trust since 1999. Regarded by his peers as "*an authority*" on retail unit trusts, "*thoughtful, affable*" **Dominic Clarke** (see p.501) advised Royal & SunAlliance on the establishment of its Equity Income Fund, and the OEIC conversion of its North American Unit Trust. "*Bright, diligent*" **Michael Shaw** (see p.503) advised Real Estate Opportunities on its establishment and initial fund-raising of about £800 million. The team also advised on the innovative launch, and flotation on the LSE, of Close Assets Funds, a new Guernsey-incorporated umbrella investment company. **Clients** Royal London; Collins Stewart; Close Fund Management; Royal & Sun Alliance; Henderson Investors; UBS Warburg; Gartmore; Dresdner RCM Global Investors; BFS Investments.

NORTON ROSE (see firm details p.1084); The team enjoys "*a powerful market position,*" according to rivals, having broadened its base to include offshore work, split capital launches, hedge funds, reconstructions and rollovers. Its competitors consider it to be "*technically well versed with bags of experience,*" while clients commend its "*pragmatic, common-sense advice and ability to think around the problem.*" They admire "*fantastically commercial, distinctive*" leader, **Tim Marsden** (see p.502), whose broad practice encompasses the range of investment trusts work. He acted on the launch of Henderson European Micro Trust and on the hostile approach by Henderson Euro Trust to Charter European Trust. Clients also recommend **Simon Cox** (see p.501) as a "*likeable, focused practitioner,*" and "*diligent, solid*" **Andrew Mitchell** (see p.502), who is said to possess particular expertise on complex onshore matters. He acted on the successful restructuring of Investors Capital Trust, a long-established investment trust managed by Friends Ivory & Sime. Exhibiting its international muscle, the team advised Goldman Sachs International/Deutsche Investment Trust, in Germany, on the creation of a wrapper product for a fund of hedge funds. **Clients** Merrill Lynch Investment Managers; Henderson Global Investors; F&C Management; Jupiter Asset Management; Britannic Investment Management; Friends Ivory & Sime; Massachusetts Financial Services; SUEZ Group.

EVERSHEDS (see firm details p.949) The firm's position in this sector is founded on its "*mastery*" of domestic authorised unit trusts and OEICs. Market sources resoundingly endorsed its strength in 'plain vanilla' retail investment matters, while competitors commented that it has done well in growing its offshore practice with some "*high-quality*" work. Regarded as "*the force behind the team,*" **Pamela Thompson** (see p.503) is "*professional, effective and knows the subject inside out.*" Under her aegis the team has gained a reputation for "*looking after its clients extremely well.*" She advised M&G Securities on the OEIC conversion of its entire unit trusts range, comprising funds under management exceeding £10 billion. She also acted for JPMorgan on the establishment of its second OEIC and the OEIC conversion of a range of its retail and Fleming institutional unit trusts. Further team highlights included advice on the transfer of Barclays unit trusts and associated ISA and PEP arrangements to Legal & General, and four new OEIC launches for Friends Ivory & Sime. **Clients** JPMorgan; AXA Fund Managers; Finsbury Worldwide Pharmaceutical Trust; M&G Securities ; New Star Asset Management.

DECHERT (see firm details p.934) A "*highly successful name*" in hedge funds and alternative investments, and "*increasingly visible*" in pitches, its competitors note that "*it has excelled in picking up a lot of business.*" Interestingly, given its UK hedge funds niche, market sources dub it "*the Eversheds of the US,*" in reference to its leading reputation for "*top-quality*" transatlantic open-ended and unit trusts work. Clients rate "*big personality*" **Peter Astleford** (see p.501) for his hedge funds expertise and "*great work in building the practice,*" noting "*able assistance*" from **Stuart Martin** (see p.502). Highlights for the team included advice on hedge fund launches for Gartmore, including Prometheus European, Gartmore European Analysts and Alphagen funds Avior, Cepheus, Pictor and Hokuto. **Clients** Société Générale; Deutsche Asset Management; Gartmore; Zurich Scudder Investments; American Express; T Rowe Price; Malta Financial Services Centre.

MACFARLANES (see firm details p.1047) Interviewees regard this "*compact, high-quality practice*" as a "*highly skilled player*" in private equity funds, domestic retail investments, VC and limited partnership work. Clients appreciate the team's "*hands-on*" approach, rating **Tim Cornick** as "*an established name and one of the most knowledgeable practitioners*" on quality domestic retail funds. He advised on INVESCO Perpetual's rationalisation of its unit trust s range. A "*growing force*" in the sector, **Stephen Robinson** assisted Coutts & Co with the formation of its fund of private equity funds. The team acted for HSBC Private Equity in raising its new pan-European private equity fund, with a £1 billion anticipated closing value. **Clients** Alchemy Partners; HSBC Private Equity; Legal & General Ventures; Morgan Grenfell Private Equity; Fidelity; Gerrard; Lazard.

SIMMONS & SIMMONS (see firm details p.1136) Widely recognised as "*a key instigator*" in hedge funds and alternative investment work, the team has a "*full, rounded*" practice in the offshore and domestic markets, with a strong focus on start-ups, options and retail investment funds. Clients wax lyrical about the team's "*enormous expertise*" and "*proactive approach in progressing transactions,*" praising it for its overall strength and for "*going the extra length.*" Peers single out "*great all-rounder*" **Richard Slater** (see p.503) as "*the established figure whom boards of trusts like and respect.*" He advised Swiss incorporated fund of funds Altin and Deutsche Bank on the $190 million introduction of the fund to the London Stock Exchange. Leading hedge funds expert **Iain Cullen** (see p.501), "*an extremely strong performer*" with "*a tremendous client following,*" advised Merrill Lynch Investment Managers on the launch of a series of hedge funds, and advised Beaumont Capital on its establishment and £33.5 million sale to Schroders. Team highlights include advising Schroders on the launch of new fund of funds products, advising CSFB on the launch of a multi-manager alternative investment strategy fund established in the Cayman Islands and other hedge fund projects, and advising the shareholders of Momentum Holdings on its sale to Pioneer Global Asset Management, a subsidiary of UniCredito Italiano, for $110 million. **Clients** CSFB; INVESCO Perpetual; Henderson Global Investors; Merrill Lynch Investment Management; Jupiter Asset Management; New Star Asset Management; Schroders.

SJ BERWIN (see firm details p.867) A "*star performer,*" the firm's success is founded upon its

INVESTMENT FUNDS ■ LONDON

LEADING INDIVIDUALS

1
- **FARR Nigel** Herbert Smith
- **HERRINGTON Tim** Clifford Chance
- **SHIPTON Tim** Linklaters

2
- **CORNICK Timothy** Macfarlanes
- **CULLEN Iain** Simmons & Simmons
- **HARRIS Paul** Linklaters
- **MARSDEN Tim** Norton Rose
- **MIDDLEDITCH Matthew** Linklaters
- **SLATER Richard** Simmons & Simmons
- **THOMPSON Pamela** Eversheds

3
- **ASTLEFORD Peter** Dechert
- **BLAKE Jonathan** SJ Berwin
- **BROUGH Gordon** City Law Partnership
- **CRIPPS James** Slaughter and May
- **HOUGIE Andrew** Clifford Chance
- **STONES Richard** Lovells
- **SUTCH Andrew** Stephenson Harwood

4
- **BAILLIE Kirstene** Field Fisher Waterhouse
- **IVE David** Mayer, Brown, Rowe & Maw
- **PERKINS Jonathan** Linklaters
- **WALSOM Roger** Ashurst Morris Crisp
- **WATTERSON Mark** Freshfields Bruckhaus Deringer

5
- **BARLOW James** Clifford Chance
- **CLARKE Dominic** Herbert Smith
- **COX Simon** Norton Rose
- **MCWHIRTER Anthony** Freshfields Bruckhaus
- **MITCHELL Andrew** Norton Rose
- **SAUNDERS William** Stephenson Harwood

6
- **KILNER John** Linklaters
- **ROBINSON Stephen** Macfarlanes
- **SHAW Michael** Herbert Smith
- **WILKINSON Charles** Lawrence Graham
- **YOUNGHUSBAND Victoria** Lawrence Graham

UP AND COMING
- **BUDD Elizabeth** Speechly Bircham
- **CLARK John** Jones, Day, Reavis & Pogue
- **MARTIN Stuart** Dechert
- **THOMPSON Blair** SJ Berwin

ASSOCIATES TO WATCH
- **COCHRANE Scott** Herbert Smith

See individuals' profiles p.501

---

large volume of private equity-related work. The practice extends to alternative asset classes including offshore, hedge and property funds. It operates within the context of structuring, regulatory and UK and European fund formation in Spain, France and Germany. "*Outstanding*" **Jonathan Blake** (see p.662) garners unequivocal market endorsement as "*the man who got the funds and private equity practice going.*" He advised Barclays Private Equity on the first closing of its European Fund. Deemed "*an acknowledged specialist,*" **Blair Thompson** (see p.503) worked on Bridgepoint Capital's Second European Private Equity Fund, which closed with commitments exceeding €2 billion. The team also advised on over 100 private equity fund-raisings including Barclays Private Equity European Fund and PAI Europe III (Paribas). **Clients** Apax Partners; Bridgepoint Capital; PRICOA Capital Group; Schroders; Matrix Securities; AXA Equity; Regent Capital; Close Fund Management; Quilter & Co.; Barclays Private Equity; Advent; Nomura.

ASHURST MORRIS CRISP
(see firm details p.852) Market sources continue to endorse this "*strong, determined team*" for its private equity funds and investment trusts expertise, though competitors believe its profile has decreased over the past year. Interviewees commended its solid transactional expertise in relation to listed investment fund vehicles, and increasing focus on hedge funds. Clients rate **Roger Walsom** (see p.503) as an "*extremely capable, hands-on*" practitioner who "*beavers away to produce results,*" particularly on endowment and split capital trusts. He acted for INVESCO Asset Management following its removal as investment manager by the board of investment trust GT Japan. He and his team also advised Merrill Lynch International as sponsor and financial advisor on the admission of Aberdeen Growth VCT I and II to the official list of the UKLA, and to trading on the LSE. **Clients** Dresdner RCM Global Investors (UK); Legal & General Investment Management; INVESCO Asset Management; Carlyle Partners; MVM; Coller Capital.

FIELD FISHER WATERHOUSE
(see firm details p.954) "*A technically driven*" practice, it is primarily noted for its retail funds expertise, of which competitors claim: "*It has built something really substantial.*" The team offers specialist knowledge on pensions and insurance products. Peers praise **Kirstene Baillie** (see p.501) for "*speaking knowledgeably*" on the industry, describing her as a "*pleasant and effective performer.*" The team advised Bradford & Bingley on the transfer of its £750 million PEP and ISA business into AXA multi-manager funds. Further team highlights include assisting with JPMorgan Fleming Asset Management's rationalisation of its worldwide funds, and with the establishment of the Catalyst EIS funds and the Lacomp British Enterprise EIS Funds. **Clients** Fidelity; Bradford & Bingley; LeggMason Investors; B & CE Unit Trust Management; SG Asset Management; JPMorgan Fleming; Legal & General; Chase Flemin g; Virgin Direct.

FRESHFIELDS BRUCKHAUS DERINGER
(see firm details p.964) The team was adjudged by interviewees to be "*superb investors' counsel,*" particularly on the private equity funds side. Consisting of "*brainy people,*" it is noted for working closely with the firm's first-class tax practice. Peers rate "*top-quality technician*" **Mark Watterson** (see p.503) for specialist unregulated matters such as limited partnerships investing in real estate, while "*clever tax expert*" **Anthony McWhirter** (see p.502) has a good name for general funds matters. The team advised Scottish Widows on the establishment with Henderson Investors of a limited partnership to invest in Covent Garden. **Clients** AMP Asset Management; Apollo Funds and Portfolio Holdings; AXA REIM; Babcock & Brown; Barclays Capital; Blackstone Group; Citigroup; Compass Partners; Deutsche Bank; Goldman Sachs/Whitehall Funds; JP Morgan; Land Securities Trillium; Lone Star (US) Fund II; Manhattan Investment Fund; Morgan Stanley Dean Witter; Orion Capital Management; Rothschild; Scottish Widows; State Street Global Advisors; Thornhill Investment Management; UBS.

LOVELLS
(see firm details p.1045) "*Extremely knowledgeable*" on asset management, according to market commentators, its competitors know the team best for its work as investors' counsel on property and offshore investment funds matters. Clients praise "*donnish*" **Richard Stones** (see p.390) as "*diligent, on the ball and great for sensible answers to difficult questions.*" He advised Merrill Lynch Investment Managers on the migration of the Merrill Lynch Property Fund to Jersey. The team advised on the proposed launch of Doughty Hanson & Co Fund IV. It also co-ordinated multi-jurisdictional reviews for Henderson Private Capital and Prudential Corporate Asia in respect of the permissibility of marketing certain fund products worldwide. **Clients** AMVESCAP/INVESCO; Global Asset Management; Henderson Investors; Merrill Lynch Investment Managers; Prudential; Threadneedle.

SLAUGHTER AND MAY
(see firm details p.1140) Interviewees admire this team's "*high-quality, complex*" structuring work for its base of "*mature, established*" investment trusts clients. From a group of "*technically excellent*" practitioners, clients singled out "*bright*" **James Cripps** (see p.501) for his expertise in limited partnerships matters; one observed that "*he can interpret the law in creative ways to deliver the best commercial outcome.*" He advised Consulta on the launch and listing of Consulta Hedge Funds, a closed-end Guernsey fund of hedge funds with a Dublin listing and redemption facility. He also advised Polar Capital Partners on its establishment as a fund manager, involving the launch of three hedge funds and rollover vehicles. The team advised Schroders on the launch and listing of Schroder Private Equity Fund, a closed-end umbrella with a redemption facility. **Clients** Primera; 3i; Abbey National; ING Barings; Baring Asset Management; Schroder s; Sierra Trading.

STEPHENSON HARWOOD
(see firm details p.1147) "*Commercially and technically proficient – a great outfit,*" according to market leaders, and the team is commended for its share of top-quality clients like HSBC and ABN Hoare Govett. Senior partner **Andrew Sutch** (see p.503) maintains "*considerable gravitas*" as a "*thoughtful, measured operator*" on closed-end matters,

LONDON/THE REGIONS ■ INVESTMENT FUNDS

while **William Saunders** (see p.503) is *"commercial, pragmatic and good to work with,"* according to clients. The team advised BFS on the launch of its property fund, raising £200 million, and acted for Jupiter on the launch of a series of hedge funds. It also advised on split capital fund transactions for Framlington Split Income Trust, Exeter Enhanced Income Fund, BC Income & Growth Fund, and BC Property Income & Growth Fund. **Clients** BC Asset Management; BFS Investments; Framlington; Hoare Govett; Collins Stewart; HSBC Investment Funds (UK); Julius Baer; Jupiter.

ALLEN & OVERY (see firm details p.841) The team gains strong market endorsement for its *"considerable depth and specific knowledge"* of specialised structured products such as securitised derivatives. With its focus on offshore transactions, including funds work in Luxembourg, Amsterdam and Hong Kong, competitors comment that its profile in domestic work is correspondingly lower. Led by Simon Gleeson, the team has advised a range of institutional investors, including 30 venture capital/private equity funds, real estate funds, offshore hedge funds and other regulated and unregulated vehicles, on various investments. It has also been involved in developing new investment structures for the UK retail market, including CSFB's Andrea IV programme and Merrill Lynch's MLDR offerings. **Clients** Bank of Scotland; Bear Stearns Asset Management; CSFB; Deutsche Bank; Merrill Lynch International; Schroder Exempt Property Unit Trust.

LAWRENCE GRAHAM (see firm details p.1031) This is *"a user-friendly, efficient"* outfit for investment trusts work, according to interviewees. It gains especially strong recognition for its activity on behalf of small to mid-cap entities, such as split capital investment trusts work for key client, Brewin Dolphin Securities.

Clients say that *"bright, commercial"* head of department **Charles Wilkinson** is *"good at holding our hands,"* while *"experienced technician"* **Victoria Younghusband** also gained wide market approval. The team advised on the launch of the Premier Recovery Trust. Other highlights include the launch of Falcon Investment Trust and the establishment of the Thomas More Square Partnership. **Clients** Pavilion Asset Management; Unicorn Asset Management; Gartmore Investment Management; Old Mutual Securities; Premier Asset Management; St David's Investment Trust.

MAYER, BROWN, ROWE & MAW (see firm details p.1060) This well-respected practice has a particular name in retail funds work for smaller fund managers, such as key client M&G. Interviewees commended *"intellectual"* **David Ive** (see p.502) as being *"particularly on the ball with the tax aspects of retail funds."* Said by competitors to have *"a mind like a steel trap,"* he has *"a thorough grasp of issues and comes up with novel solutions to problems."* **Clients** M&G Charifund.

SPEECHLY BIRCHAM (see firm details p.1141) *"Driving forward,"* this practice has a sound profile in retail OEICs, authorised funds, unit trusts and insurance funds. **Elizabeth Budd** (see p.501) gained peer-wide endorsement as its *"prime specialist"* on the retail side. The team acted for Scottish Life on the acquisition of the International Press Centre via a limited partnership, and advised the Bank of New York Trust & Depositary Company on several OEIC launches and reorganisations, including the umbrella OEIC for National Australia, and Smartinvest for First Direct. **Clients** Bank of New York Trust & Depositary Company; Ecclesiastical Insurance Group; Royal Bank of Scotland; Royal London Mutual Insurance Society (Scottish Life).

TRAVERS SMITH BRAITHWAITE (see firm details p.1166) The investment funds group, led by head of tax Alasdair Douglas, integrates financial services, tax and corporate finance expertise. Its clients include private equity funds, venture capital trusts, investment trusts and fund management groups. Clients praise its *"helpful, efficient approach"* and *"good quality service provision."* The group advised on the launch of two funds for European Acquisition Capital, raising €400 million, and advised Beeson Gregory on the initial and subsequent funding of its seed technology exploitation vehicle IP2IPO. **Clients** Barings Private Equity; European Acquisition Capital; Fleming Technology Trust; Gartmore Investment Management; Geocapital Partners; Singer & Friedlander Investment Management.

OTHER NOTABLE PRACTITIONERS *"Lively, likeable, rounded practitioner"* **Gordon Brough** (see p.501) of City Law Partnership retains market approval for his *"superb"* work on investment trusts and split capital matters. It is said to be his great relationship with Aberdeen Asset Managers that *"lies beneath the firm's remarkable reputation."* He has been busy recently advising this key client, and several others, on the problems surrounding the split capital investment trust sector, and also acted on the launch of two new funds for property and hedge fund clients Westbury Asset Management. *"Impressive, knowledgeable"* **John Clark** (see p.501), of Jones, Day, Reavis & Pogue, heads a team that interviewees perceive to be *"muscling in on the scene,"* advising on fund launches and merger matters. As part of his integrated corporate finance practice, he acted on the court-approved merger of HL Income & Growth Trust and Aberdeen High Income Trust, and assisted Collins Stewart in connection with offers by Technology & Income Trust for European Income & Technology Trust in a takeover code-governed transaction.

THE REGIONS

INVESTMENT FUNDS
■ THE REGIONS

1. **Burges Salmon** Bristol

LEADING INDIVIDUALS

1. **GODFREY Christopher** Burges Salmon

This book is the product of 6,582 1/2 hour interviews. See p.7 for BMRB audit.
Within each band, firms are listed alphabetically. See individuals' profiles p.501

BURGES SALMON (see firm details p.894) A *"credible, respected"* regional practice, it displays *"City expertise"* in retail and authorised funds work as part of its general commercial, funds and regulatory offering. Leading specialists commend the team as *"an attractive choice"* for fund managers seeking independent advice, aside from that sought on behalf of investors. Clients list *"immediate partner access,"* *"fabulous response times"* and the *"consummate ability to field questions on diverse matters"* as top-scoring attributes of the team. *"Extremely knowledgeable"* **Christopher Godfrey** (see p.238) led the team advising Exeter Investment Group on its acquisition of Duncan Lawrie Unit Management and of two funds from Sanwa Asset Management. It also assisted with Premier Fund Managers' amalgamation of OEIC subfunds. **Clients** Asset Management Investment Company (AMIC); Premier Portfolio Managers; Exeter Investment Group; Hargreaves Lansdown; Sarasin Investment Management.

INVESTMENT FUNDS ■ SCOTLAND

SCOTLAND

| **INVESTMENT FUNDS** |
| **■ SCOTLAND** |
| **[1]** **Dickson Minto WS** Edinburgh |
| **Dundas & Wilson CS** Edinburgh |
| **Tods Murray WS** Edinburgh |
| **[2]** **Maclay Murray & Spens** Glasgow |
| **McGrigor Donald** Glasgow |
| **[3]** **Shepherd+ Wedderburn** Edinburgh |

| **LEADING INDIVIDUALS** |
| **[1]** **ATHANAS Chris** Tods Murray WS |
| **[2]** **MACKAY Philip** Dundas & Wilson CS |
| **MINTO Bruce** Dickson Minto WS |
| **[3]** **DORAN Frank** McGrigor Donald |
| **DUNSIRE David** Tods Murray WS |
| **POLSON Michael** Dundas & Wilson CS |
| **THURSTON SMITH Martin** Tods Murray WS |
| **TODD Andrew** Dickson Minto WS |

This book is the product of 6,582 1/2 hour interviews. See p.7 for BMRB audit. Within each band, firms are listed alphabetically. See individuals' profiles p.501

DICKSON MINTO WS (see firm details p.938) Adjudged "*a towering strength*" on private equity downstream work, and boasting the largest investment trust s client base in Scotland, many interviewees believe that it takes "*pole position*" in closed-end funds. Standing out from the "*well-focused, commercial, high-quality*" team, **Andrew Todd** (see p.503) is perceived to have "*come on strongly for the practice,*" while **Bruce Minto**'s (see p.243) "*strong name generates a lot of business – a lot of clients swear by him.*" The team advised on the launch of Aberforth Geared Capital & Income Trust, raising £70 million, and on bond issues by the Scottish American Investment Trust and British Assets Trust, following on from the £150 million bond issue by the Scottish Investment Trust. It also acted on a number of reconstructions and reorganisations, including those of Edinburgh New Tiger Trust, Piccadilly Growth Trust, American Opportunities Trust and Enterprise Capital Trust. **Clients** Aberforth Partners; Standard Life Private Equity; Edinburgh Fund Managers; Baillie Gifford Pacific Horizon Investment Trust.

DUNDAS & WILSON CS (see firm details p.943) The firm is envied by its competitors for its "*incredible franchise and astonishing client loyalty.*" Interviewees perceive a balanced practice with a "*healthy, all-round client base,*" and a number of enthusiastic, talented lawyers who are rated highly by clients and competitors alike. These include "*excellent*" **Philip Mackay**, who maintains a relatively low profile but is respected for his experience of open-end funds work, and **Michael Polson** who has a solid reputation for investment trusts work. The team acted for Scottish Widows in relation to the rationalisation of its portfolios of unit trusts and OEICs, and advised on the launch of the Britannic UK Income Trust, raising £270 million. It also advised on the reconstruction of the Martin Currie Capital Return Trust (about £140 million). **Clients** Scottish Widows Services; Britannic Asset Management; Martin Currie Investment Management.

TODS MURRAY WS (see firm details p.1164) "*Sector leaders*" in unit trusts, open-end retail and collective investment schemes work, this "*prominent*" team continues to feature widely, according to its competitors. Peers consider "*technically superb and dogged*" **Chris Athanas** (see p.501) "*the mainstay*" of the practice, describing him as "*distinctively thorough – he likes to have his Is dotted and his Ts crossed.*" "*Knowledgeable, technically capable*" practitioners, **David Dunsire** (see p.502) and **Martin Thurston Smith** (see p.503), assist him. The team acted for AEGON Fund Management and AEGON ICVC in the successful same day integration of 11 former Guardian Royal Exchange authorised unit trusts into AEGON ICVC by separate amalgamations (aggregate value exceeding £1 billion). It also advised on the integration of 11 fund of funds authorised unit trusts into a new umbrella fund of funds OEIC, with an aggregate value of around £200 million, under the new financial services regime post-N2. **Clients** Edinburgh Fund Managers; Baillie Gifford; AEGON; Scottish Value Management; Britannic Fund Managers.

MACLAY MURRAY & SPENS (see firm details p.1048) This "*excellent*" practice, jointly headed by Michael Livingston and Ian Lumsden, is a winner with clients for its mixture of investment and unit trusts expertise. It boasts a particular name for limited partnerships and private equity funds-related work. An impressive deal list includes advice to long-standing client Brewin Dolphin Securities on a number of trust reorganisations and fund-raisings, including those of the Aberdeen Preferred Income Trust (about £65 million), St David's Investment Trust (£29 million), Media and Income Trust (£46 million) and Gartmore Monthly Income Trust (£79 million). **Clients** Brewin Dolphin Securities; INVESCO Continental Smaller Companies Trust; Glasgow Income Trust; Shires Income; Shires Smaller Companies; Edinburgh Investment Trust.

MCGRIGOR DONALD (see firm details p.1065) Competitors rate this team for its solid, reliable handling of investment trusts work. Competitors and clients alike were full of praise for "*good operator*" **Frank Doran** and his group of technically assured, competent practitioners. It represents a broad range of clients but is weighted towards fund managers and fund management companies. OEIC and unit trust s work comprises a smaller but still important facet of the total practice. **Clients** Aberdeen Murray Johnstone; Scottish Friendly Assurance Society ; Clyde s dale Bank; Gartmore.

SHEPHERD+ WEDDERBURN (see firm details p.1130) Retaining "*a good base of clients*" in investment trusts and collective investments, the funds and financial services team, led by Malcolm Gillies, provides a range of advice to fund managers and funds, including investment trusts, unit trusts, OEICs and limited partnerships. The team advised Friends Ivory & Sime in connection with both the reorganisation of eight exempt unit trust funds, and its £128.9 million acquisition of the retail investment and managed pension fund businesses of the Friends Provident Life Office (FPLO). **Clients** Franklin Templeton; Martin Currie; Friends Ivory & Sime; Edinburgh Fund Managers; Baillie Gifford & Co.

THE LEADERS IN INVESTMENT FUNDS

ASTLEFORD, Peter
Dechert, London
(020) 7583 5353
peter.astleford@eu.dechert.com
Specialisation: Partner and Head of the Financial Services and Investment Management Group, London. Specialises in all aspects of onshore and offshore mutual funds and attendant legal and regulatory issues applicable to the funds and their promoters/investment managers/other service providers. His unit also provides a one-stop-shop dealing with UK and US regulatory issues including dual purpose compliance manuals. Frequent contributor to the financial press and speaker at related conferences.
Career: Qualified in 1986. Specialised in financial services/investment funds with a leading City of London law firm and subsequently became Group Legal Advisor and then Head of Corporate Services at the London listed holding company to a major international financial services group. In 1997, appointed a partner of *Dechert*.
Personal: Born 1962.

ATHANAS, Chris
Tods Murray WS, Edinburgh
(0131) 226 4771
chris.athanas@todsmurray.com
Specialisation: Specialises in corporate financial services and investment funds; all aspects of collective investment schemes including open-ended investment companies (OIECs), unit trusts, investment trust companies, investment products (including PEPs and ISAs), related regulatory and compliance law.
Prof. Memberships: Law Society of Scotland; Society of Writers to the Signet; Notary Public.
Career: Qualified 1966 *Paull & Williamsons*, *Dundas & Wilson* 1968, corporate department partner 1969-96 and member of strategy board 1991-95; partner *Tods Murray* since 1996.
Personal: Born 1941. Attended Fettes College, Edinburgh; Aberdeen University (1962 MA) 1964 (LLB); WS Leisure: the arts, collecting, walking, golf, angling; Blairgowrie golf club; Luffness new golf club; the Royal Burgess Golfing Society.

BAILLIE, Kirstene
Field Fisher Waterhouse, London
(020) 7861 4000
kmb@ffwlaw.com
Specialisation: Financial services – Head of Investment Funds and Products Group. Advises fund managers, insurance companies, and banks on a wide range of retail and institutional investment funds, insurance and pension products – and related financial services regulatory issues.
Prof. Memberships: City of London Solicitors Company; Association of Pension Lawyers; Life Assurance Legal Society.
Career: Qualified *Bischoff & Co* 1987; partner *Frere Cholmeley Bischoff* 1995-98; partner *Field Fisher Waterhouse* 98 to present.
Publications: Writes the financial services chapter of Sweet & Maxwell's textbook on e-commerce (now in the third edition); wrote the chapter on collective investment scheme and other special cases for the City & Financial Publishings Practitioner's Guide to the FSA Regulation of Designated Investment Business (published 2002); contributes one of the lead articles to the FT Unit Trust and Oeic Directory and Review regarding UK investment funds (in 2000, 2001, and 2002).

BARLOW, James
Clifford Chance, London
(020) 7600 1000
james.barlow@cliffordchance.com
Specialisation: Corporate Department. Partner specialising in financial services and investment funds.
Prof. Memberships: Chartered Institute of Taxation (Associate).
Career: Partner since 1980.
Personal: Mill Hill School; Nottingham University (LLB).

BLAKE, Jonathan
SJ Berwin, London
(020) 7533 2222
jonathan.blake@sjberwin.com
See under Private Equity, p.662

BROUGH, Gordon
City Law Partnership, London
(020) 7253 5505
gordon@citylaw.com
Specialisation: Corporate with emphasis on fund management and fund transactions including flotations, acquisitions and mergers. Specialist interest in partnership law.
Prof. Memberships: Association of Partnership Practitioners.
Career: Founded *Brough Skerrett* (now *City Law Partnership*) in 1994. Formerly a partner with *Bird Semple Fyfe Ireland WS* and prior to that, *Thorntons WS*.
Publications: 'Private Limited Companies: Formation and Management'. 'The Law of Partnership in Scotland'.
Personal: An enthusiastic socialiser and writer (resting). Married with two children.

BUDD, Elizabeth
Speechly Bircham, London
(020) 7427 6520
elizabeth.budd@speechlys.com
Specialisation: Acts for fund managers and depositaries on structuring of authorised and unauthorised funds, their promotion, restructuring and winding up as well as providing ongoing regulatory advice. Also advises insurance companies and other financial services providers generally on regulation including assisting clients to obtain authorisation, producing a broad range of agreements and documentation for operating on authorised business.
Prof. Memberships: Law Society.
Career: Qualified 1991. Joined *Speechly Bircham* 1997 and became Partner 1999.
Publications: Articles for 'PLC Magazine' and 'Investors Chronicle'.
Personal: Graduated from University of Bristol 1988.

CLARK, John
Jones, Day, Reavis & Pogue, London
(020) 7634 9328
jclark@jonesday.com
Specialisation: Main practice areas are investment funds, capital markets, public M&A and general corporate finance. Particular expertise in closed end onshore and offshore funds, property investment and hedge funds and other investment vehicles. Acting for funds, investment managers, financial advisors, brokers and banks on launches, reorganisations, restructurings and mergers/takeovers. Also extensive experience in advising investment banks and brokers on non-fund related equity and debt issues and contested and recommended takeovers.
Career: Articled at *Theodore Goddard* 1984. Partner 1992. Head of Corporate Finance 1994-2000. Joined *Jones, Day, Reavis & Pogue* in 2000.
Personal: St Edmund Hall, Oxford. Interests include golf, rugby, wine and travel.

CLARKE, Dominic
Herbert Smith, London
(020) 7374 8000
dominic.clarke@herbertsmith.com
Specialisation: Specialises in investment funds within the UK and overseas and in the regulation of the financial services industry. His work in connection with investment funds includes the formation and restructuring of unit trusts, open-ended investment companies, investment trusts, limited partnerships, common investment funds for charities, offshore funds and other investment vehicles. His regulatory practice covers the formation of new businesses, product documentation, drafting of relevant agreements and regulatory procedures and advising clients in respect of their relationship with regulators.
Career: Admitted 1975. Partnership 1987.
Personal: LLB (Leeds University).

COCHRANE, Scott
Herbert Smith, London
(020) 7374 8000

CORNICK, Timothy
Macfarlanes, London
(020) 7831 9222

COX, Simon F T
Norton Rose, London
(020) 7283 6000
Specialisation: Partner in corporate finance department. Has a wide-ranging securities and corporate practice with an emphasis on collective investment and international and domestic corporate finance. Contributor to 'A Practitioner's Guide to the Stock Exchange Yellow Book' and author of various articles. Has spoken at a number of UK and overseas conferences on funds, stock exchange and Financial Services Act issues and on investment in the former Soviet Union.
Prof. Memberships: Securities Institute, IBA, Law Society, City of London Solicitors Company.
Career: Qualified in 1980, having joined *Norton Rose* in 1978. Became a partner in 1988.
Personal: Born 17th January 1956. Attended Eton College 1967-73 and Trinity College, Oxford 1974-77. Trustee of two Charitable Trusts. Lives in London.

CRIPPS, James
Slaughter and May, London
(020) 7600 1200
james.cripps@slaughterandmay.com
Specialisation: Partner in commercial department. General and international corporate and corporate finance practice with emphasis on listed and unlisted collective investment schemes (including private equity and emerging markets) and advice (including regulatory advice) to providers of financial services and financial products. Co-ordinator of Asset Management Practice.
Prof. Memberships: Juvenile Diabetes Research Foundation (director); The Law Society; Securities Institute; Worshipful Company of Fullers (Court Member) and the City of London Solicitors' Company.
Career: Joined *Slaughter and May* 1978; qualified 1980; partner 1989.
Personal: Born 15 March 1956. Educated Eton and St. Catharine's College, Cambridge. Married, three sons, two daughters. Lives in London and Buckinghamshire. Leisure interests include farming, forestry, opera and golf.

CULLEN, Iain
Simmons & Simmons, London
(020) 7628 2020
iain.cullen@simmons-simmons.com
Specialisation: Partner in financial markets department. Handles all types of work relating to commodities, futures and options, unit trusts, offshore funds and investment management. Author of numerous articles in the professional press. Regular speaker at conferences and seminars.
Prof. Memberships: Law Society, International Bar Association, American Bar Association, Alternative Investment Management Association, Board of Editors of Futures and Derivatives Law Report, Advisory Board of World Securities Law Report.
Career: Qualified in 1980, having joined *Simmons & Simmons* in 1977. Became a Partner in 1986.
Personal: Born 13th May 1953. Took a BA in Law in 1975. Lives in London.

INVESTMENT FUNDS ■ THE LEADERS

DORAN, Frank
McGrigor Donald, Glasgow
(0141) 248 6677

DUNSIRE, David
Tods Murray WS, Edinburgh
(0131) 226 4771
david.dunsire@todsmurray.com
Specialisation: Partner in corporate department. Specialises in financial services particularly unit trusts, acting principally for trustee. Also handles corporate finance and general corporate work, with an emphasis on acquisitions and disposals, MBOs and start-ups.
Prof. Memberships: Law Society of Scotland.
Career: Qualified 1982, having joined Tods Murray WS in 1980. Partner Tods Murray WS 1986. Departmental managing partner 1998.
Personal: Born 1958. Attended Buckhaven High School, Fife 1970-76, then Edinburgh University 1976-80 (LLB). Leisure: family, gardening and music.

FARR, Nigel
Herbert Smith, London
(020) 7374 8000
nigel.farr@herbertsmith.com
Specialisation: Partner specialising in corporate finance work, his principal field of activity being the investment funds sector where he has been involved in numerous flotations, secondary money raisings, reorganisations, unitisations and reconstructions. Increasingly, his practice includes work with UK and offshore open-ended companies. Also has extensive general corporate finance and mergers and acquisitions experience.
Career: Joined Herbert Smith in 1985; Admitted 1987; Partner in 1994.
Personal: Gonville & Caius College, Cambridge (MA Cantab).

GODFREY, Christopher
Burges Salmon, Bristol
(0117) 939 2219
chris.godfrey@burges-salmon.com
See under Corporate Finance, p.238

HARRIS, Paul
Linklaters, London
(020) 7456 3104
paul.harris@linklaters.com
Specialisation: Specialises in investment funds matters. Has over 25 years experience in structuring, creating and organising funds for investment in property of all types (securities, derivatives, financial instruments, real estate, etc) onshore and offshore, domestic and international, public and private, retail and institutional.
Career: Partner, Linklaters 1976 to date; 1969-1976: Assistant solicitor, Linklaters. University of Birmingham, LLB (First Class Hons), LLM.

HERRINGTON, Tim
Clifford Chance, London
(020) 7600 1000
tim.herrington@cliffordchance.com
See under Financial Services, p.390

HOUGIE, Andrew
Clifford Chance, London
(020) 7600 1000
andrew.hougie@cliffordchance.com
Specialisation: Corporate Department. Partner specialising in investment companies, closed end funds and other collective investment funds as well as transactional and advisory work in the funds, financial institutions and asset management sectors generally and general corporate finance.
Career: Articled Slaughter and May 1994; qualified 1986; joined Clifford Chance 1996; Partner since 1999.
Personal: Stockport Grammar School; 1983 Gonville & Caius College, Cambridge (MA).

IVE, David
Mayer, Brown, Rowe & Maw, London
(020) 7782 8609
dive@eu.mayerbrownrowe.com
Specialisation: Partner in Corporate Taxation Department. Experienced in all aspects of taxation, especially in relation to financial services, collective investment schemes, unit trusts, offshore funds, life assurance taxation and also taxation matters relating to trusts generally, and tax litigation. Author of articles in various tax journals, including 'British Tax Review' and 'Tax Journal'. Lecturer on tax topics, especially collective investment schemes and unit trusts. Former member of the Taxation Committee of the Associators of Unit Trusts and Investment Funds. Member Law Society Revenue Law Stamp Duty Committee.
Prof. Memberships: Law Society.
Career: Qualified in 1972. Worked with Allen & Overy 1976-84. Spent six months at the Tax Bar (1984-85), then joined Rowe & Maw in June 1985. Became a Partner in 1986.
Personal: Born 2nd January 1950. Attended Highgate School 1963-68, then Birmingham University 1968-71. Chairman of the Association of Liberal Democrat Lawyers. Joint author of a number of Liberal Democrat publications on constitutional reform. Parliamentary candidate for 1979, 1983 and 1987 General Elections. Leisure pursuits include opera and swimming. Lives in London.

KILNER, John
Linklaters, London
(020) 7456 2000
john.kilner@linklaters.com
Specialisation: Specialist in investment funds matters. Has 25 years' experience in structuring, creating, marketing and reconstructing onshore and offshore investment funds of all types (securities, private equity, derivatives, financial instruments, real estate etc) and handling their related M&A transactions.
Career: Partner, Linklaters (London and Paris) 1985 to date; Assistant Solicitor Linklaters 1976-85; Gonville & Caius College, Cambridge, MA (Law) 1973.

MACKAY, Philip
Dundas & Wilson CS, Edinburgh
(0131) 228 8000

MARSDEN, Tim
Norton Rose, London
(020) 7283 6000
Specialisation: Partner in Corporate Finance Department. Corporate finance with particular emphasis on financial services operations and collective investment schemes, both onshore and offshore. Advises on acquisitions and disposals in the financial services sector and advises both public and private sector entities on financial services regulation generally. Commonly advises on corporate and collective investment transactions involving emerging markets. Lectures on financial services, investment trusts and unit trusts.
Career: Qualified 1984; Barrister 1984-85. Joined Norton Rose 1986. Partner in 1993.
Personal: Born 9th September 1961. Honorary solicitor to DEBRA. Leisure interests include sport and social activities.

MARTIN, Stuart
Dechert, London
(020) 7775 7542
advice@eu.dechert.com
Specialisation: Partner, financial services group, London. Specialises in advising on the establishment and structuring of asset management and financial service businesses, financial products and related corporate finance work, retail and institutional funds established in the UK and abroad including emerging fund markets, hedge funds, multi-manger funds, property funds and venture capital funds. Also advising on fund mergers and re-organisation involving UCITS and non-UCTIS funds and UK investment trusts and on collateralised debt obligation issues.
Prof. Memberships: Member of the International Bar Association.
Career: Qualified 1985. Specialised in corporate finance, investment fund and financial services work with a leading City of London law firm between 1987 and 1993, later becoming Head of Legal at a major asset management group. Stuart joined the financial services group of Titmuss Sainer Dechert (now the merged firm of Dechert) as a partner in 1997.
Publications: Publications include the new Financial Services Edition of 'The Encyclopaedia of Forms and Precedents'.
Personal: Born 1960. Graduate of Manchester University.

MCWHIRTER, Anthony
Freshfields Bruckhaus Deringer, London
(020) 7936 4000
anthony.mcwhirter@freshfields.com
Specialisation: Partner in tax department. Main practice area is investment funds. Advises on all aspects of the structuring, operation and winding up of investment funds and other collective investment arrangements including tax planning and regulation. Author of various articles; has spoken widely at conferences.
Prof. Memberships: Law Society of City of London, AUTIF.
Career: Qualified in 1979, having joined Freshfields in 1977. Became a Partner in 1985.
Personal: Born 1954. Attended Downing College, Cambridge.

MIDDLEDITCH, Matthew
Linklaters, London
(020) 7456 3144
matthew.middleditch@linklaters.com
Specialisation: Specialist in UK corporate finance and company law advising both corporate clients and investment banks. Main areas of practice include: public and private mergers and acquisitions, joint ventures and general corporate work.
Career: 1990 to date: Partner, Linklaters; 1988-90: Assistant Solicitor, Linklaters; 1986-88: Assistant Solicitor, Mills & Reeve, Norwich; 1982-86: Assistant Solicitor, Linklaters; 1980-82: Articled Clerk, Linklaters. 1979-80: College of Law, Law Society Final Examinations; 1976-79: Trinity College, Cambridge, MA Law.

MINTO, Bruce
Dickson Minto WS, Edinburgh
(0131) 225 4455
bruce.minto@dmws.com
See under Corporate Finance, p.243

MITCHELL, Andrew
Norton Rose, London
(020) 7444 3502
mitchellas@nortonrose.com
Specialisation: Partner in the corporate finance department where he specialises in investment fund and financial services related work. He has acted for UK and overseas financial services and fund management groups, dealing with merger and acquisition transactions and all aspects of the launch, operation and restructuring of UK domestic and overseas investment funds. His clients include asset management houses, investment banks and property development companies.
Career: Joined Norton Rose 1988; qualified 1990; partner 1997.
Personal: Born 1964. University of York.

PERKINS, Jonathan
Linklaters, London
(020) 7456 3049
jonathan.perkins@linklaters.com
Specialisation: Investment Management Group, Corporate Department. Principal areas of practice include all aspects of investment fund work for managers, promoters and investors, including the structuring, establishment and reorganisation of different forms of collective investment vehicles (open and closed companies, unit trusts and limited partnerships), in both domestic and offshore domiciles and for institutional and retail investors. Recent work includes private

THE LEADERS ■ INVESTMENT FUNDS

equity and real estate funds and repackaging structures for investment products. Also advises on general corporate law matters.
Career: 2000: Partner, *Linklaters*; 1992-2000: Solicitor, *Linklaters*; 1990-92: Trainee solicitor, *Linklaters*.

POLSON, Michael
Dundas & Wilson CS, Edinburgh
(0131) 228 8000

ROBINSON, Stephen
Macfarlanes, London
(020) 7831 9222

SAUNDERS, William
Stephenson Harwood (incorporating Sinclair Roche & Temperley), London
(020) 7809 2138
william.saunders@shlegal.com
Specialisation: Partner, Corporate: Head of Funds and Financial Services Group. Particular areas of expertise: the structuring and restructuring of investment trusts and offshore funds and hedge funds; a thorough knowledge of the regulatory regime governing financial services. Transactions: a number of flotations; takeovers and reorganisations; mainstream corporate activities including mergers and acquisitions, international joint ventures and schemes of arrangement. Recent highlights: Launch of Deanhill Property Limited Partnership and Polunin Capital – management company and hedge fund.
Career: Qualified September 1994. Became a partner in November 1999.
Personal: Educated at the University of Kent and the University of Grenoble (English and French Law 2:1 and first in French Law). Captain Old Citizens Cricket Club.

SHAW, Michael
Herbert Smith, London
(020) 7374 8000
michael.shaw@herbertsmith.com
Specialisation: Partner specialising in corporate law, with particular emphasis on takeovers, domestic and international equity issues, mergers and acquisitions, corporate restructurings, investment funds and joint ventures.
Career: *Clifford Chance* 1988 to 1992. Admitted 1990. Joined *Herbert Smith* 1992. Became a Partner 1997. Seconded as Joint Secretary to the panel on Takeovers and Mergers 1996-98.
Personal: St John's College, Cambridge.

SHIPTON, Tim
Linklaters, London
(020) 7456 3100
tim.shipton@linklaters.com
Specialisation: Corporate department. Specialist in offshore fund work advising domestic and foreign clients on the corporate, regulatory and tax aspects of structuring, creating, organising and marketing funds for investment in property of all types (securities, derivatives, financial instruments, debt, real estate, onshore and offshore, domestic and international, public and private, retail and institutional).
Career: Head of Investment Management Group. 1988 to date: Partner, *Linklaters*, Corporate Department; 1980-88: Assistant Solicitor, *Linklaters* London and New York. 1979: Trinity Hall, Cambridge, MA Law; 1977: Trinity Hall, Cambridge, BA Law. Hitchin Grammar School.

SLATER, Richard
Simmons & Simmons, London
(020) 7628 2020
richard.slater@simmons-simmons.com
Specialisation: Partner in financial markets department. Corporate and regulatory work with a particular emphasis on the financial services industry. Work covers regulatory advice on the formation and promotion of investment vehicles of all types, the acquisition and disposal of financial services businesses and the reconstruction and merger of investment trust companies, unit trusts and other investment entities. Transactional advice includes public and private company takeovers and acquisitions, joint ventures, initial share offerings and flotations.
Career: Qualified in 1977, after joining *Simmons & Simmons* as an articled clerk in 1975. Partner in 1981.
Personal: Born 9 November 1950. Attended City University 1979-82, then Cambridge University 1982-84. Lives in London.

STONES, Richard
Lovells, London
(020) 7296 2000
richard.stones@lovells.com
See under Financial Services, p.390

SUTCH, Andrew
Stephenson Harwood (incorporating Sinclair Roche & Temperley), London
(020) 7809 2100
andrew.sutch@shlegal.com
Specialisation: Senior Partner, Partner in Corporate, Member of Funds and Financial Services Group. Specialises in investment funds, both UK and offshore, and has considerable depth of experience in his specialist field of financial services regulation. Transactional work has involved a number of investment fund flotations, takeovers and restructurings. Has been involved in a number of split capital investment and trust reconstructions, including the first Channel Islands funds to issue zero dividend preference shares. Also has considerable experience of emerging market funds and advises on open-ended funds in the UK, including unit trusts and OEICs. Lectures on open-ended investment companies (OEICs) and other aspects of financial services law.
Prof. Memberships: Law Society, IBA.
Career: Qualified October 1979. Grindlays Bank (1974-76) trained for five months in Beirut; Assistant Operations Manager in Calcutta; *Stephenson Harwood* 1979 as Assistant Solicitor; seconded *Stephenson Harwood & Lo*, Hong Kong 1982-86. Partner in 1984 and Head of Corporate Department in 1997. Senior Partner in 2002.
Personal: Born 10 July 1952. Educated at Haileybury College; Oriel College, Oxford (1970-74) 1974 Literae Humaniores (MA Oxon). Interests include running, theatre, former member of the TA (Intelligence Corps). Languages: French and some Russian. Resides London.

THOMPSON, Blair
SJ Berwin, London
(020) 7533 2776
blair.thompson@sjberwin.com
Specialisation: Member of *SJ Berwin's* Corporate Finance Group specialising in structuring, establishment and operation of private equity, property and other investment funds and advising on venture and development capital investments.
Prof. Memberships: Law Society of England and Wales; New Zealand Law Society.
Career: Qualified in New Zealand in 1995; *Buddle Findlay* 1995-97; *SJ Berwin* 1997-present.
Personal: Educated at University of Canterbury (LLB (Hon) B.Comm).

THOMPSON, Pamela
Eversheds, London
(020) 7919 4500
thompspm@eversheds.com
Specialisation: Partner and head of financial services group. Main areas of practice are collective investment schemes, pooled investments and financial services regulatory work. Handles onshore and offshore funds and products including authorised and unauthorised unit trusts, open ended investment companies and limited partnerships both retail and institutional. Advises on the structuring of such products. Also handles insurance company products – life and pensions pooled funds. Also handles general financial services work, including regulatory advice, taxation and promotion of financial products.
Prof. Memberships: Association of Women Solicitors.
Career: Qualified in 1982, having joined *Bischoff & Co* in 1980. Became a partner in 1986.
Personal: Born in 1956. Attended St Hilda's College, Oxford 1975-78.

THURSTON SMITH, Martin
Tods Murray WS, Edinburgh
(0131) 226 4771
martin.thurston.smith@todsmurray.com
Specialisation: Partner in Corporate Department. Specialises in pension schemes, non-contentious employment law and employee share schemes. Also handles other corporate and commercial work including collective investment schemes.
Prof. Memberships: Law Society of Scotland; Association of Pension Lawyers.
Career: Joined *Tods Murray* 1974. Qualified 1977. Partner 1978.
Personal: Born 1951. Attended The Edinburgh Academy 1957-69 and Christ's College Cambridge 1970-74. Leisure: family, hillwalking, wine, classical music and jazz. Fluent in German and French.

TODD, Andrew
Dickson Minto WS, Edinburgh
(0131) 225 4455
andrew.todd@dmws.com
Specialisation: Main areas of practice are investment funds, financial services, private equity funds and venture capital work.
Prof. Memberships: Law Society of Scotland, Writer to the Signet.
Career: Joined *Dickson Minto* in 1987; Partner 1995.
Personal: Born 1964. Edinburgh University 1982-87.

WALSOM, Roger
Ashurst Morris Crisp, London
(020) 7859 1780
roger.walsom@ashursts.com
Specialisation: A partner in the company department involved in a wide range of corporate work including corporate finance and investment funds. Advises on all aspects of investment fund work, including in particular investment trusts and venture capital funds, and has been involved in the launch and restructuring of numerous investment vehicles. Also has substantial experience of a wide range of other corporate transactions, particularly in relation to the raising of capital, mergers and acquisitions and capital restructuring.
Prof. Memberships: Law Society.
Career: Qualified in 1980. Joined *Ashursts* in 1983. Became a partner in 1988.

WATTERSON, Mark
Freshfields Bruckhaus Deringer, London
(020) 7936 4000
mark.watterson@freshfields.com
Specialisation: Specialises in transactional and advisory work in the investment funds sector, including the structuring, marketing and taxation of investment funds, including property funds and joint ventures, and structuring fund-based financial products and tax-driven financing transactions.
Prof. Memberships: Law Society, City of London Solicitors Company.
Career: Attended Wymondham College 1974-81; Churchill College, Cambridge 1982-85. Joined *Freshfields* 1986, qualified 1988 and became a partner 1997.
Personal: Born 1963. Leisure interests include golf and motor racing (Le Mans 24 hours).

WILKINSON, Charles
Lawrence Graham, London
(020) 7379 0000

YOUNGHUSBAND, Victoria
Lawrence Graham, London
(020) 7379 0000

LICENSING

London: 504; The Regions: 505; Scotland: 510; Profiles: 511

Research approved by BMRB For this edition, **Chambers'** researchers conducted 6,582 interviews – 3,900 with law firms, 511 with barristers and 2,171 with clients. The validity of the research was scrutinised by BMRB International, who audited both the methodology and the results at our offices in London. They interviewed **Chambers'** researchers and cross-checked sample interviews. Details of the audit appear on page 7.

LONDON

LICENSING — LONDON

1
- Berwin Leighton Paisner
- Jeffrey Green Russell
- Joelson Wilson & Co

2
- Field Fisher Waterhouse
- KSB Law
- Pinsent Curtis Biddle
- Richards Butler

3
- Davenport Lyons
- Pullig & Co

LEADING INDIVIDUALS

1
- **BAYLIS Craig** Berwin Leighton Paisner
- **CLIFTON David** Joelson Wilson & Co
- **GLAZEBROOK Peter** Field Fisher Waterhouse
- **SOUTHORN Elizabeth** Richards Butler

2
- **DAVIES Suzanne** Joelson Wilson & Co
- **EDNEY Robert** KSB Law
- **HALLIWELL Tilly** Jeffrey Green Russell
- **HARRIS Julian** Pinsent Curtis Biddle

3
- **HEPHER Christopher** Pullig & Co
- **SKEENS Julian** Jeffrey Green Russell

This book is the product of 6,582 1/2 hour interviews. See p.7 for BMRB audit. Within each band, firms are listed alphabetically. See individuals' profiles p.511

BERWIN LEIGHTON PAISNER (see firm details p.866) "*A growing team, with a superb client base,*" according to practitioners. **Craig Baylis** (see p.511) has achieved success in the challenge to Westminster City Council's Entertainment Licence Policy on behalf of Chorion (now Urbium). Liquor and entertainment work forms the core of the group's workload, with gaming and betting taking a less prominent, but nonetheless important, role. Instructions in this field have included acting for Gaming Insight on commercial agreements with Harrods Casino and idTV. **Clients** JD Wetherspoon; Tote; Aspinalls Online; Frogmore Developments; Whitbread Hotel Company.

JEFFREY GREEN RUSSELL (see firm details p.1013) This is one of the leading London firms according to several interviewees. Liquor licensing forms the mainstay of the team's work, with its "*key player,*" **Tilly Halliwell** (see p.513), acting for the Soho House club in obtaining a 2am licence for the Electric Cinema in Portobello. Another highlight for the unit has been the representation of Pacha, the Ibiza-based nightclub brand, on the opening of the first Pacha club in the UK, in Victoria. **Julian Skeens** (see p.516) has been pronounced "*great on entertainment work,*" by the market. **Clients** fish!; Glendola Leisure; Hard Rock Café; City Bars & Restaurants; Grange Hotel Group.

JOELSON WILSON & CO (see firm details p.1014) The team is well received by the market, "*shining out from the rest in the field of gaming.*" **David Clifton** (see p.512) was singled out for his advocacy skills; he is, according to one barrister, "*exceptionally well prepared for court, the best licensing lawyer I have come across.*" Alongside him, **Suzanne Davies** (see p.512) "*is a real team player.*" The department spans liquor, betting, late-night entertainment licensing, lotteries and internet gaming. Solicitors appear as advocates before local authorities throughout England and Wales. **Clients** Prominent operators in the pub, nightclub, casino, betting and internet gaming fields.

FIELD FISHER WATERHOUSE (see firm details p.954) This firm has its reputation rooted firmly in its "*premier client base.*" **Peter Glazebrook** (see p.513) is this team's leading light. The practice is centred around liquor and entertainment work, with a niche in planning matters. Westminster City Council remains an important client, which the group represents in various licensing arrangements. **Clients** Jamies; Unwins; London Clubs; Selfridges; Burberry.

KSB LAW (see firm details p.1026) The team is well reputed for its representation of traditional brewers. Recommendations centre around **Robert Edney** (see p.513), the unit's "*reliable, experienced advocate.*" The team works closely with the commercial property department on acquisitions of new and existing licensed premises. Liquor licensing and public entertainment form a key focus for the team. **Clients** Fullers; Tootsies Restaurants; Oddbins; Pitcher & Piano.

PINSENT CURTIS BIDDLE (see firm details p.1102) "*Heavily involved in gaming work,*" the team enjoys a substantial client base in this area. **Julian Harris** (see p.513) "*has built up quite a practice in the gaming sphere,*" eliciting respect from his peers for his deep experience. A highlight for the group has included obtaining two of the first five online gaming licences in the Isle of Man: one was for SunOnline, a division of Sun International Hotels, the second for Action Online. The team also advises various overseas operators of casinos interested in operating in the UK. **Clients** Sun International; A&S Leisure Group; Stanley Casinos.

RICHARDS BUTLER (see firm details p.1112) A complement of liquor and gaming expertise stands the team in good stead within the market. The "*enormously experienced*" **Elizabeth Southorn** (see p.516) "*electrifies a room with her fearsome intellect.*" She has been involved in licensing a new £54 million hotel in Victoria for Park Plaza International. The unit has obtained a betting office licence for a new flagship Coral shop at Canary Wharf. **Clients** Marylebone Warwick Balfour; Sir Terence Conran; Rank Group; Thistle Hotels; Manhattan Loft Corporation.

DAVENPORT LYONS (see firm details p.927) David Lavender has adopted a consultancy role with the team. His successor, Alun Thomas, arrives from Eversheds with "*a hard act to follow,*" but the depth of experience enjoyed by the group is anticipated to stand it in good stead. The team is characterised by a prominent West End clientele, and has successfully challenged Westminster City Council on Bar Soho's application for a variation of licence. It also acted for the Sports Café and Planet Hollywood, successfully obtaining early liquor licences for the World Cup football matches. **Clients** The Stork Room; Sugar Reef; Che; Café Grand Prix; Divina Commedia.

PULLIG & CO This small yet "*competent*" outfit is focused on liquor and entertainment licensing. **Christopher Hepher** is widely respected by peers. The team has applied for various waivers of prohibitions imposed by councils on lap dancing. It continues to act for the owners and catering operators in four London exhibition centres.

THE SOUTH

LICENSING — THE SOUTH

1. **Blake Lapthorn** Portsmouth
   Horsey Lightly Fynn Newbury
2. **asb law** Maidstone
   DMH Brighton
   Lester Aldridge Bournemouth
   Trethowans Southampton
3. **Girlings** Herne Bay
   Lamport Bassitt Southampton

LEADING INDIVIDUALS

1. **CRIER Phil** Blake Lapthorn
   FYNN Lionel Horsey Lightly Fynn
   MESSENT Michael Trethowans
2. **DAY Philip** Horsey Lightly Fynn
   HARTWELL Roger DMH

This book is the product of 6,582 1/2 hour interviews. See p.7 for BMRB audit. Within each band, firms are listed alphabetically. See individuals' profiles p.511

BLAKE LAPTHORN (see firm details p.877) "Leading the pack in the South," the firm is perceived by interviewees to have "come on hugely since Phil Crier joined them." Crier, who acted on five new licences for Waitrose in the Canary Wharf development, has been praised for his "thorough, client-oriented" approach. This "efficient" team has witnessed a rise in the numbers of applications for special hours certificates Sunday variations, processing near to 100 applications over the past year. **Clients** Six Continents Retail; Costa Coffee; Balfour; Clear Channel Entertainment.

HORSEY LIGHTLY FYNN A key presence in the South, the firm garnered recommendations from the Bar, clients and fellow practitioners. Julia Palmer has left the firm to go in-house; however **Lionel Fynn** (see p.513) remains a prominent figure in the market. He is joined by the newly ranked **Philip Day**, whose work for Corals Betting was judged to be "*the equal of any*." The team undertakes advocacy work for Corals from Cornwall through to Kent. The liquor and public entertainment side of the practice is just as buoyant, and the team has recently processed over 20 new licence applications for SFI Group. **Clients** Grosvenor Casinos; SFI Group; Corals; Wadworth's Brewery; Bowlplex.

ASB LAW (see firm details p.851) Peers endorsed this outfit for its expertise in liquor licensing, which remains its key focus. The team has organised licensing for concerts at historic buildings in the South East, including Leeds Castle. It also acts for a national chain of off-licences covering the Kent, London and M25 area, and has assisted on applications for first special hours certificates in the high-street area of Welwyn Garden City. A forte of the department lies in its advocacy skills. Department head Stephen Thomas recently obtained the Certificate of Advocacy to appear in the Crown Court. **Clients** Leeds Castle; Mexxa Mexxa Chain; ASDA; Gallery Group.

DMH (see firm details p.940) The team possesses a "*good knowledge of the local licensing laws,*" according to clients. **Roger Hartwell** (see p.513) gains respect for his commercial outlook, leading a unit with a broad base of clients. A successful appeal was lodged against the decision of a magistrate on behalf of the Tin Drum in Brighton. The group also worked on the new application for Hotel du Vin in Brighton. **Clients** Drum at the Dials; Sarumdale; Hotel du Vin.

LESTER ALDRIDGE (see firm details p.1038) This established firm is generally seen on licensing and entertainment projects. Active in advocacy work, the team, led by Colin Patrick, is often embroiled in contentious matters for large, local nightclubs. It works alongside the insolvency practice, advising receivers and liquidators on the licensing aspects of insolvent venues. Betting and casino licence applications also form part of the workload. **Clients** Nightclubs; country house hotels; restaurants.

TRETHOWANS (see firm details p.1167) **Michael Messent** (see p.515) is the epicentre of the practice, and observers contend that "*his betting expertise is second to none.*" The firm's instructions encompass contested betting matters for Ladbrokes, including operations at football grounds. Instructions are largely won from large-scale clients, such as Pizza Hut, for which the team undertakes all the liquor licensing throughout England and Wales. **Clients** Ladbrokes; Pizza Hut; Santa Fe; Tower Casino Group.

GIRLINGS The firm is recognised by the market for its presence in Herne Bay. Instructions are undertaken on the range of licensing work, including gaming. The team acts for brewers, pubs, hotels and off-licences, amongst all other types of licensed premises.

LAMPORT BASSITT (see firm details p.1027) The team, led by Adrian Lightfoot, has been busy acting for independent late-night clubs, and has a full service, which includes liquor and public entertainment licensing. Specialisms exist in special hours certificates and straightforward and contested transfers. Contested hearings form a large section of the group's workload, for which the firm conducts all its own advocacy. **Clients** Southampton University; De Vere Grand Harbour; Meridian Taverns; Montague Ventures.

THAMES VALLEY

LICENSING — THAMES VALLEY

1. **Morgan Cole** Oxford
2. **Allan Janes** High Wycombe
   Blandy & Blandy Reading
   Field Seymour Parkes Reading
   McLellans Hertford
   Turbervilles with Nelson Cuff Uxbridge

LEADING INDIVIDUALS

1. **HAY David** Allan Janes
   ROCHE Paddy Morgan Cole
   SMITH David Turbervilles with Nelson Cuff
2. **DOWLING Susan** Blandy & Blandy

This book is the product of 6,582 1/2 hour interviews. See p.7 for BMRB audit. Within each band, firms are listed alphabetically. See individuals' profiles p.511

MORGAN COLE (see firm details p.1075) Maintaining the "*clear blue water*" between itself and its rivals, the team boasts the presence of the experienced **Paddy Roche**. His practice includes new licence applications covering the south of England, special hours certificates and public entertainment licences. The firm has been appointed to the panel of Bass Take Home to act on off-licence applications for petrol forecourts. **Clients** Youngs Brewery; Blanc Restaurants; Punch Taverns; Milton Inns; Sound Exchange Banbury.

ALLAN JANES The "*knowledgeable advocate*" **David Hay** leads the team on liquor and betting licensing work. Liquor licensing is carried out for smaller pub groups and private licensees, and betting is undertaken for the diminutive betting concerns. **Clients** The Richardson Family; Dan Bruce Bookmakers; WR Bird.

BLANDY & BLANDY (see firm details p.878) The team was warmly recommended by the market for its work with major sports grounds. It successfully secured a new on-licence to cover all of the bars in Twickenham Stadium, previously run on a piecemeal basis. The "*expert*" **Susan Dowling** (see p.513) has a broad knowledge of licensing matters.

FIELD SEYMOUR PARKES Tim Child takes up the reins as head of department, following a number of departures. The team continues to work for Swindon Town FC on the licensing of

LICENSING ■ SOUTH WEST

the terraces. The practice has witnessed an increase in public entertainment licence applications for hackney carriages and private hire vehicles. Gaming and betting work also form a part of the unit's workload. **Clients** Greene King; Swindon Town FC.

MCLELLANS (see firm details p.1066) Much of the profile of this firm is tied up with its strong ties to key client JD Wetherspoon, which it has advised on the development of the Lloyds No. 1 chain, involving applications for public entertainment licences and special hours certificates throughout England and Wales. Led by Clare Eames, the team has witnessed an increase in contested hearings. It scored a success for new client, Barracuda Group, gaining a new licence in Redditch, which was granted despite police objection. **Clients** JD Wetherspoon; Barracuda Group; McMullen & Sons; Faces nightclubs; Caffe Nero.

TURBERVILLES WITH NELSON CUFF (see firm details p.1169) This highly regarded local firm undertakes a range of licensing work. **David Smith** (see p.516) is admired for his presence in the courtroom, and his down-to-earth approach. The team has undertaken new licence applications for the Iceland Group and for Holmes Place. Night café licence applications have also been undertaken for Diageo Group. **Clients** Sheraton Hotels; Bookes; Budgens Stores; World Duty Free.

SOUTH WEST

LICENSING ■ SOUTH WEST

1. **Bond Pearce** Bristol
2. **Osborne Clarke** Bristol
3. **Clarke Willmott & Clarke** Bristol
   Foot Anstey Sargent Plymouth
   Gregg Latchams Quinn Bristol
4. **Bevan Ashford** Bristol
   Crosse & Crosse Exeter
   Rickerbys Cheltenham
   Stephens & Scown Exeter
   Stones Exeter

LEADING INDIVIDUALS

★ **PHILLIPS Jeremy** Osborne Clarke
1. **DAVIES Tim** Bond Pearce
   PARROTT Michael Bond Pearce
2. **CROSS James** Kitson Hutchings
   EARDLEY Kathryn Bond Pearce
   GREGG Andrew Gregg Latchams Quinn
   HAYDEN Tim Clarke Willmott & Clarke
   PHIPPS Matthew Osborne Clarke
   UP AND COMING
   MACGREGOR Ewen Bond Pearce

This book is the product of 6,582 1/2 hour interviews. See p.7 for BMRB audit. Within each band, firms are listed alphabetically. See individuals' profiles p.511

BOND PEARCE (see firm details p.879) "*Bond Pearce continues to go from strength to strength since acquiring Cartwrights*," choroused the market. Clients point to the team for its expertise in complex licensing issues. The "*quietly confident*" **Tim Davies** (see p.512) is "*always well prepared*," while **Michael Parrott** (see p.515) is singled out for his deep knowledge. **Kathryn Eardley** has been less visible with her management commitments; however, she is noted for her courtroom prowess. Associate **Ewen MacGregor** (see p.514) "*has grown into his role - he gives a calm and polite presentation to magistrates*." This "*crack team*" has been instrumental in enabling 'Puppetry of the Penis' to play in the West End, arguing that it was a play within the scope of the Theatres Act, thereby not in breach of Westminster City Council's no nudity conditions. **Clients** Aberdeen Steak Houses; First Quench; Forte UK; Mecca Bingo; Scottish & Newcastle.

OSBORNE CLARKE (see firm details p.1090) The leading light of the practice remains **Jeremy Phillips**, who the market agrees is "*one of the best in the country*." **Matthew Phipps** "*has done some sturdy work*." A strength of the practice lies in the area of law reform, particularly in its representation of the British Beer and Pub Association and Scottish & Newcastle in the licensing issues that preceded the World Cup 2002. The team challenged the 1978 ruling regarding liquor licences, eventually taking the case to the House of Lords, and creating a precedent for the World Cup 2002 licences. **Clients** City Centre Restaurants; Earl's Court/Olympia; SFI Group; Oddbins; Shell UK.

CLARKE WILLMOTT & CLARKE (see firm details p.907) "*An excellent firm*," according to commentators, buoyed by the presence of the knowledgeable and diligent **Tim Hayden** (see p.359). Nightclubs, pubs, retailers and hotels are all found on the firm's client roster, and a wide range of licensing issues are handled.

FOOT ANSTEY SARGENT (see firm details p.958) Pronounced "*a good local firm*" by interviewees, the team acts for major operators in Devon and Cornwall regarding all aspects of liquor licensing. Senior consultant Tony Daniel leads the team, and he has conducted numerous high-profile cases relating to bottle bans. Particular expertise is enjoyed within public entertainment, hackney carriage, and amusement machine licensing. **Clients** Public houses; clubs; hotels; leisure facilities.

GREGG LATCHAMS QUINN The practice gains respect from the market, particularly as home to **Andrew Gregg** (see p.513). Well known for its entrepreneurial client base, the team predominantly advises on public entertainment and liquor licensing, including the crossover with food safety law. **Clients** A large brewery chain; restaurants; off-licences; pubs; clubs.

BEVAN ASHFORD (see firm details p.869) The team's workload spans a range of licensing issues, from liquor to gaming licences. Led by David Wood, the department's sphere of activity includes advice on new on and off-licences, structural alterations and gaming machine permits. Its advocacy comprises contested licensing applications and various appeals. **Clients** Breweries; retail supermarkets; private businesses.

CROSSE & CROSSE This is a successful licensing outfit, well known by London practitioners. The loss of James Cross has been counterbalanced by the growth of the team, which now possesses the capacity to undertake the majority of different licensing instructions. The unit is led by Tim Selley, and continues to act on substantial entertainment licences, particularly for nightclubs. **Clients** Sainsbury's; Tesco; nightclubs.

RICKERBYS (see firm details p.1113) An established player in the market, the firm impresses interviewees with the number of specialists it can field. The team, which includes Maggie Smith, has obtained a provisional liquor licence for a new stand at a racecourse. On the betting side, permits have been obtained for a number of Irish bookmakers. **Clients** Racecourses; festivals; educational institutions; bookmakers.

STEPHENS & SCOWN The firm has a significant presence in the Cornwall region. The team, led by Martin Clayden, has handled acquisitions involving licensing applications. The client base largely comprises institutional clients, and small companies and individuals involved in the holiday industry.

STONES (see firm details p.1152) Paul Keeling leads the team, which has been particularly active in obtaining new on and off-licences. Typical instructions include occasional licences, special orders of exemption and new club registrations. **Clients** Private landlords; clubs; a bowling club.

OTHER NOTABLE PRACTITIONERS The "*pugilistic*" **James Cross** (see p.512), formerly of Crosse & Crosse, has moved to Kitson Hutchings.

WALES

LICENSING — WALES

1. **Morgan Cole** Cardiff
2. **Cartwrights Adams & Black** Cardiff

LEADING INDIVIDUALS

1. **FREEMAN Bill** Freemans Solicitors
   RAWLE Claire Morgan Cole
2. **CHILDS Christopher** Cartwrights Adams & Black
   MORSE John John Morse Solicitors

This book is the product of 6,582 1/2 hour interviews. See p.7 for BMRB audit. Within each band, firms are listed alphabetically. See individuals' profiles p.511

MORGAN COLE (see firm details p.1075) Although the firm overall has refocused its efforts on a smaller number of sectors, it maintains a significant licensing presence in the region, advising numerous local establishments on mainstream licensing applications. It further assists on national ongoing contracts for brewers, and on petrol forecourt licences. **Claire Rawle** was commended to *Chambers* for her fine presentation skills, and was considered a valuable asset in this area.

CARTWRIGHTS ADAMS & BLACK This firm is a regional player with a handful of major national clients. The group acts on a broad range of licensing duties and specialises in liquor and entertainment matters. **Christopher Childs** heads up an experienced team.

OTHER NOTABLE PRACTITIONERS Long experienced in the field, **Bill Freeman** of Freemans Solicitors is well regarded for his concentration on licensing matters for local operators. Similarly well established is **John Morse** (see p.515) of John Morse Solicitors, who has dealt with the majority of applications for businesses on Cardiff's St Mary Street, with advice on betting increasing to match that of liquor licences.

MIDLANDS

LICENSING — MIDLANDS

1. **Poppleston Allen** Nottingham
2. **Anthony Collins Solicitors** Birmingham
3. **Hammond Suddards Edge** Birmingham
   Kenneth Curtis & Co Birmingham
4. **Challinors Lyon Clark** West Bromwich
   Nelsons Nottingham
   Young & Pearce Nottingham
5. **Berryman Shacklock** Nottingham
   Eversheds Birmingham
   freethcartwright Nottingham

LEADING INDIVIDUALS

1. **ALLEN Jeremy** Poppleston Allen
   COLLINS Anthony Anthony Collins Solicitors
   CURTIS Anthony Kenneth Curtis & Co
2. **LUCAS David** Nelsons
   POPPLESTON Susanna Poppleston Allen
   POTTS Andrew Hammond Suddards Edge
   SHAW Deborah Anthony Collins Solicitors
3. **PEARCE John** Young & Pearce
   WHUR Paddy Poppleston Allen
   WILSON Robin Berryman Shacklock
4. **LEE Trevor** Challinors Lyon Clark
   RADCLIFFE Malcolm freethcartwright
   SHARKEY Lisa Poppleston Allen
   YOUNG David Eversheds

This book is the product of 6,582 1/2 hour interviews. See p.7 for BMRB audit. Within each band, firms are listed alphabetically. See individuals' profiles p.511

POPPLESTON ALLEN (see firm details p.1104) This boutique firm has unrivalled expertise. Proactive and devoted to the sector, it is undoubtedly the largest team in the country, commanding comprehensive national coverage for franchises such as PizzaExpress. It has maintained its tradition as an on-licence specialist to the late-night sector, providing "*sterling service*" to clients. Keeping pace with increasing liquor and public entertainment applications from both plcs and independents, the firm applied for over 300 Sunday licences nationwide following the deregulation of Sunday opening hours. Betting and gaming licences have featured in its workload, and it provides frequent advice to Leicestershire Constabulary concerning objections. It holds the coveted post of licensing consultee to the Government and is also legal advisor to BEDA, of which the charismatic **Jeremy Allen** (see p.511) is the legal director. The archetypal licensing lawyer, Allen's "*thorough, persuasive and charming*" approach has won him many fans across the country. Peers considered **Susanna Poppleston** (see p.515) a "*formidable opponent.*" Formerly of Addleshaw Booth & Co, **Paddy Whur** (see p.516) has quite a reputation in the betting and gaming fields, obtaining instructions from Ladbrokes for the north of England and promoting internet betting. His "*practical, down-to-earth manner*" has stood him in good stead. **Lisa Sharkey** (see p.515) is perhaps best known for her work for NUSFL, securing over 30 licensing applications from student unions. Ultimate Leisure instructed the firm in obtaining the first purpose-built nightclub in Newcastle upon Tyne. The well-resourced team acts for several developers; it has worked with Clearwater Estates & Properties on its 23 site licences at the Greenwich Reach retail and leisure development. **Clients** Clearwater Estates & Properties; Henry J Beans; Leicestershire Constabulary; Luminar Leisure; Megabowl; NUSFL; Pizza Express; Taylor Woodrow; Ultimate Leisure; Yo! Sushi Soho.

ANTHONY COLLINS SOLICITORS (see firm details p.845) The firm's commercial attitude pleased many interviewees: "*Really pleasant to work with, they took us through the process,*" reported clients. The team combines ongoing licensing work for national and regional operations with the more substantial cases. The department has this year secured work on behalf of the Spirit Group (formerly Punch Retail) in the Birmingham area and the licensing work of the La Tasca and Bank restaurant chains. **Anthony Collins** (see p.512) has championed the group with his "*organised, helpful and efficient*" stance, agree clients. **Deborah Shaw** (see p.516) offers a combination of technical ability and combative litigation skills. They have worked on licensing matters at several high-profile venues: at Millennium Point they worked on both Thinktank (Birmingham's Museum of Science and Discovery) and the new IMAX Theatre. Alongside its relicensing duties on behalf of the Birmingham Hippodrome, the firm was also retained for the licensing of several units by The Mailbox, a multi-use building that will also be home to the BBC in Birmingham. **Clients** Bank; Birmingham Hippodrome; Brindleyplace; Churchill Vintners; City Centre Restaurants; The Mailbox; National Amusements UK; Thinktank, Millennium Point.

HAMMOND SUDDARDS EDGE The practice is structured around the esteemed **Andrew Potts**. Based in the firm's dispute resolution group, he is said to deal with high-quality work on a wide range of licensing matters from liquor through to gaming, for both regional and national clients.

KENNETH CURTIS & CO Considered "*proficient*" at mainstream off-licence work, the firm holds its own in the region despite its relatively smaller team. **Anthony Curtis** remains a regular and "*combative*" sight at the local courts on most aspects of licensing.

CHALLINORS LYON CLARK **Trevor Lee** (see p.514) leads a small team that represents a wide range of clients including pub chains and major

507

LICENSING ■ EAST ANGLIA

breweries, nightclubs and off-licences. The department comes highly recommended and can call on additional commercial expertise within the firm for matters involving acquisitions, disposals and funding for licensed premises.

NELSONS (see firm details p.1082) Although **David Lucas**' (see p.514) team is not large, it has captured a healthy proportion of the regional market. Lucas was considered by peers to be "*a pure licensing lawyer – thorough and level-headed, with some excellent clients.*" The team has advised Scottish & Newcastle on licences for its new head office, and also secured a proportion of Interbrew UK's licensing work. Most notably, the firm has achieved success for brewer Hardys & Hansons on its licence extensions for the duration of the World Cup. In the gaming sphere, the team aided the Horse Race Betting Levy Board on its revocation of a bookmaker's permit. It also acted on the licensing aspects of Wilson Connolly's development work. **Clients** Derbyshire Police; Everards; Hardys & Hansons; Horse Race Betting Levy Board; Interbrew UK; Scottish & Newcastle; SFI Group; Wilson Connolly.

YOUNG & PEARCE Gathered around Nottingham and its environs, **John Pearce**'s (see p.515) team has continued its traditional focus on the betting and gaming sectors. It acts for major gaming operators, breweries and public houses and nightclubs. The firm also deals with a variety of licensing-related matters, including health and safety, and food safety.

BERRYMAN SHACKLOCK The firm attracts clients in the licensed trade and leisure industries. Interviewees agreed that **Robin Wilson** has an "*efficient and dependable*" presence in the sector. The team successfully contested an application for a late licence for Garben Enterprises, and the objector to this matter subsequently instructed the firm on a series of other applications. Ongoing work has included a series of late licence applications for snooker club chain Spot On Leisure, while Sunday dancing and licensing regulations round out the practice. **Clients** Garben Enterprises; Spot On Leisure; Home Farm; Inn Time Leisure; Nottinghamshire County Cricket Club.

EVERSHEDS (see firm details p.949) In common with other branches of the firm, the Birmingham office has realigned its well-sized team to concentrate specifically on higher value deals. This aim was underlined by its work with Six Continents Hotels and Town & Country Inns on the licensing aspects of several units in the Summer Row/Lionel Street redevelopment in Birmingham. **David Young** (see p.516) heads the department, which carries out its licensing instructions in conjunction with the national network. It continues to assist both Eldridge Pope and Stanley Racing on developments and betting licenses respectively across a number of sites. **Clients** Eldridge Pope; Six Continents Hotels; Six Continents Retail; Stanley Casinos; Stanley Racing; Town & Country Inns.

FREETHCARTWRIGHT (see firm details p.963) Head of department **Malcolm Radcliffe** (see p.515) acts for Aldi Supermarkets on a nationwide basis and also assists Leicestershire Police on its revocations work. This small group has obtained licences covering the Donington Park Race Circuit and for a major new South London nightclub. **Clients** Leicestershire Police; Aldi Supermarkets.

EAST ANGLIA

LICENSING
■ EAST ANGLIA

1 Howes Percival Norwich
2 Belmores Norwich
    Eversheds Norwich
3 Kenneth Bush King's Lynn
    Mills & Reeve Norwich

LEADING INDIVIDUALS
1 KEFFORD Alan Howes Percival
    PARTRIDGE Malcolm Eversheds
2 NICHOLLS Simon Belmores
    WELLS Harriet Mills & Reeve

This book is the product of 6,582 1/2 hour interviews. See p.7 for BMRB audit. Within each band, firms are listed alphabetically. See individuals' profiles p.511

HOWES PERCIVAL (see firm details p.1003) The proactive market leader in East Anglia has continued to work with the Norfolk & Norwich LVA on training matters. These have been expanded on with the inclusion of the National Licensees Drugs Certificate, which focuses on drug abuse in licensed premises of any type. On the transactional level, **Alan Kefford**'s (see p.514) sizeable, regional team acts for several pub companies, including Gold Cater in the Home Counties. Its capable members also assist the Number 10 group of tenpin bowling centres on its licensing applications, including for three of its new greenfield sites. **Clients** Gold Cater; Number 10.

BELMORES Much of the practice's profile is built around the talents of **Simon Nicholls**, who many commend as a "*good listener, who knows what he's doing.*" The firm is particularly well known for its licensing work on behalf of pubs.

EVERSHEDS (see firm details p.949) Well reputed in the region, **Malcolm Partridge** (see p.515) heads an experienced team that is considerably weighted towards on-licence instructions. This group is able to pull on a national network focused on this sector. Highlights have included applications on behalf of a UK holiday firm for its hotels throughout the country, and obtaining licences for two private hospitals. The firm also conducts a number of matters as an agency firm for those further north, who make good use of its local knowledge and expertise. **Clients** Eldridge Pope; Six Continents Hotels; Six Continents Retail; Stanley Casinos; Stanley Racing; Town & Country Inns.

KENNETH BUSH Notwithstanding its small size, the firm is rated by leading figures in the sector. Managing partner Nigel Dodds is the key contact here. The group as a whole is said to play to its strengths in local knowledge and litigation on behalf of hotels, off-licences and leisure companies.

MILLS & REEVE (see firm details p.1071) Liquor licensing comprises the majority of hard-working **Harriet Wells**' (see p.516) time. Litigation takes up the remainder, and she has successfully applied for a public entertainment licence for a new nightclub in Norwich on behalf of Peri's Leisure. The firm has a bias towards work for larger companies and it has seen its market share grow, primarily due to new client Park Resorts and its 13 holiday parks nationwide. It also continues to advise The Forum Trust on all licensing issues relating to the Millennium Building in Norwich. **Clients** The Forum Trust; The National Trust; Norwich City FC; Park Resorts; Peri's Leisure.

NORTH WEST

COBBETTS (see firm details p.914) The consistent professionalism of the firm impressed interviewees, and its size ensures a high profile in the region. Traditionally linked with the brewing sector, it has extended its reach with public entertainment applications and work on special hours certificates. Health and safety, food hygiene and trading standards regulations are all elements of its experience. The firm's move into Leeds via the acquisition of Read Hind Stewart is expected to increase its workload. The "*tactical and astute*" **Hamish Lawson** (see p.514) was recommended for his technical ability, possessing "*a greater in-depth knowledge of the subject than many in the field.*" He oversaw the firm's application work for a number of major operators, including De Vere Hotels & Leisure, convenience stores and petrol forecourts. His colleague, **Simon Jones**, (see p.514) was recommended for his "*straightforward*" approach. Orbit Development instructed the firm on multiple applications for a variety of end-users at a development in Salford Quays.

Clients De Vere Hotels & Leisure; Honeycombe Leisure; Lime Entertainments; Orbit Development; Scottish & Newcastle; Village Leisure; Warner Brothers; Whitbread.

WEIGHTMAN VIZARDS (see firm details p.1183) The firm is respected for its work in the off-licence sector in Liverpool, servicing a cross-section of clients. It operates out of its commercial division and a quarter of its workload comprises contested matters. The Manchester office has assisted Coliseum on applications for the new Sports Café and long-term clients such as Grosvenor Casinos. The Liverpool branch has aided clients as diverse as bookmaker Done Brothers and Liverpool FC. Betting specialist **Mark Owen** (see p.515) was singled out as "*authoritative and disciplined,*" while **Anthony Horne** (see p.514) was noted for his strong entertainment and gaming experience. In addition to its own work, the department takes on agency work on behalf of other firms of solicitors. **Clients** Coliseum; Cream; Done Brothers; Gatecrasher; Grosvenor Casinos; Menzies Hotels; Rank Leisure Division; SFI Group; UMIST.

ELLIOTTS (see firm details p.947) **Barry Holland** (see p.514) sits at the heart of this team, which has concentrated on petrol forecourts work for Esso, Shell and TotalFina, via retail consultants Lockett & Co. Competitors consider Holland's "*great presence and flamboyancy*" to have a stabilising effect on transactions. Accomplished at handling clients and "*technically on the ball,*" he is said to have "*the ability to inject a bit of humour into proceedings.*" The unit was re-appointed to the legal panel to advise Whitbread's subsidiary Tragus on licensing matters, and it continues to advise on the roll-out of the new Woolworth's concept nationally. Holland continues to act on several food-related prosecutions. **Clients** Brannigans; Coral Racing; Esso; Lockett & Co; Majestic Wine Warehouses; Safeway Stores; Shell; TotalFinaElf; Tragus (formerly Pelican Group); Vernons Pools; Woolworth's.

A HALSALL & CO Dominant in the Wirral, **Christopher Johnson** (see p.514) leads the licensing efforts at the firm, which assists national co-operatives as well as a broad range of licence applicants. "*Consistently busy*" with for the most part, specifically regional issues, he is said by peers to use his local knowledge to particularly good effect.

PANNONE & PARTNERS (see firm details p.1092) This knowledgeable team has seen petrol forecourt work take up a large slice of its licensing work, assisting Fuel Force on the potential licensing of 20 sites. The group's two partners possess technical training qualifications for liquor licensing. **Nick Dickinson** (see p.512) stood out in our research. He worked with Daniel Thwaites over the refusal of a special licence application by Bolton licensing justices. **Clients** Daniel Thwaites; Fox Group; Jennings Brothers; Late Leisure; Texaco.

DWF (see firm details p.943) The firm is known for having an even spread of work across the sector. Partner Carl Bruder leads a small unit that also acts on licensing matters in Scotland. It works exclusively with TM Retail on all of its applications and also handles a proportion of Safeway's off-licence requirements relating to new stores.

HALLIWELL LANDAU (see firm details p.982) This small but dedicated practice led by Chris Eddlestone has aided Entrepreneurial Leisure on the structure of the company, and all its licensing matters. The team has advised Rocco Forte on licensing matters for the new Lowry Hotel, and offered mainstream advice to Macdonald Hotels concerning all its licensing matters throughout the UK. The firm has also worked with Randombet.com on the legal aspects of the development of its internet gaming service. **Clients** Entrepreneurial Leisure; Macdonald Hotels; Randombet.com; Rocco Forte.

YORKSHIRE

GOSSCHALKS Market feedback singled out the firm as one pulling clear of its local competition. "*An outfit with excellent national reach,*" it received strong recommendations nationwide for its experience in betting, gaming and liquor licensing. The combined expertise of **Andrew Woods** ("*he holds the team together well*") and **Clare Johnson** heads this well-resourced group. On-licence work takes up almost all of its time, with specialist knowledge being in late licences, the keystone of the practice. The firm continues to work with a number of national franchises on their applications as well as local clients. It was involved in the licensing aspects of Nomura's acquisition of the Voyager Pub Estate from Bass as well as the sale of Inn Partnership by Nomura to Pubmaster. **Clients** Georgica; Spirit (formerly Punch Taverns); Wizard Inns.

DLA The team, under regulation partner **Martin Cowell**, works with a broad portfolio of local and some national clients on all aspects of licensing and associated regulatory matters.

JOHN GAUNT & PARTNERS (see firm details p.1015) The firm concentrates on liquor licensing and related commercial litigation matters.

509

LICENSING ■ NORTH EAST/SCOTLAND

LEADING INDIVIDUALS
1. WOODS Andrew Gosschalks
2. COWELL Martin DLA
   GAUNT John John Gaunt & Partners
   JOHNSON Clare Gosschalks

See individuals' profiles p.511

John Gaunt (see p.513) leads a highly experienced and dedicated team from the front, further developing its existing nationwide client base. The unit has sufficient resources to handle volume transactions, and the group has been retained by several major franchises, including the Laurel Pub Company, which took on 800 managed houses and 1,500 tenanted properties when it acquired the pubs and bars division of Whitbread. The firm is active in the licensing and development of greenfield sites, it licensed half of Debenhams Department Stores this year. **Clients** Albion Pub Contracts; Brannigans Estate; Inn-spired Group; Laurel Pub Company; Old English Inns; Pub Estate Company; Queens Moat Hotels; J Sainsbury's; Whitbread; The Wolverhampton & Dudley Breweries.

NORTH EAST

LICENSING
■ NORTH EAST
1. McKenzie Bell Sunderland
2. Dickinson Dees Newcastle upon Tyne
   Freemans Newcastle upon Tyne
   Mincoffs Newcastle upon Tyne

LEADING INDIVIDUALS
1. TEMPERLEY William McKenzie Bell
2. ARNOT Richard Dickinson Dees
   FREEMAN Keith Freemans
3. SMITH Sarah Mincoffs

This book is the product of 6,582 1/2 hour interviews. See p.7 for BMRB audit. Within each band, firms are listed alphabetically. See individuals' profiles p.511

MCKENZIE BELL (see firm details p.1066) This firm retains its prominence in the North East with **William Temperley** (see p.516) considered by some to be "*the best lawyer in the area.*" Experience is on his side, and his technical ability is described as "*impressive.*" The team has a strong local client base including nightclubs, individuals and the Northumbria Police. Late licensing matters in North Tyneside have also kept the team occupied. **Clients** Northumbria Police; major breweries; nightclubs; sports clubs.

DICKINSON DEES (see firm details p.938) "*Charismatic*" **Richard Arnot** (see p.511) is head of this "*expert*" team. The group focuses exclusively on liquor licensing and counts Scottish & Newcastle Retail, Enterprise Inns, Northumbria Police and Thistle Hotels amongst its clients. Instructions from the national supermarket chain Iceland are a significant acquisition and the group is developing its presence in the North West, Leeds and the Tees Valley. **Clients** Scottish & Newcastle Retail; Northumbria Police; Thistle Hotels; Trafalgar Leisure; Enterprise Inns.

FREEMANS The well-known **Keith Freeman** is praised by contemporaries as "*experienced and able.*" His team undertakes licensing work on behalf of retail pub chains on both a local and national basis. **Clients** Voyager Pub; breweries.

MINCOFFS In the wake of Austen Science's retirement, **Sarah Smith** (née Robinson) (see p.516) leads the majority of the group's caseload. Peers endorse her capabilities and told researchers that her presence shows the firm still has "*a decent capacity*" for licensing work. It recently obtained the first high-street cash bingo licence in Hull on behalf of major client RAL. Acting for individual proprietors, it has secured a number of permits for pubs in the North, allowing the operation of mini bingo. The recruitment of former chief inspector of the Gaming Board Bill Galston as a consultant strengthens the firm. **Clients** RAL; Absolute Leisure; Ultimate Leisure; Wessex Taverns; individual proprietors.

SCOTLAND

LICENSING
■ SCOTLAND
1. Brunton Miller Glasgow
   Dundas & Wilson CS Edinburgh
   R & JM Hill Brown & Co Glasgow
2. Harper Macleod Glasgow
   McGrigor Donald Glasgow
3. Blackadders Dundee
   Hasties Edinburgh
   Lindsays WS Edinburgh

This book is the product of 6,582 1/2 hour interviews. See p.7 for BMRB audit. Within each band, firms are listed alphabetically.

BRUNTON MILLER (see firm details p.891) One of the "*main players*" in Scotland, the firm is judged to have "*gone from strength to strength.*" The group's "*big-name clients*" ensure that it remains a clear leader for licensing work. **Archibald Maciver** (see p.514) was commended by clients and peers alike as "*the best licensing lawyer in the country,*" while **Douglas Dalgleish** (see p.514) has "*the most amazing charisma.*" **Robin Morton** (see p.515) is deemed a "*pragmatic*" and highly knowledgeable lawyer. The firm offers a full range of services, handling liquor, betting and entertainment licensing. **Clients** Bass; SFI Group; Safeway; Debenhams; Whitbread; De Vere Hotels.

DUNDAS & WILSON CS (see firm details p.943) The firm is home to **John Loudon**, who is said to be "*a formidable force;*" sources agree that he is a "*leading light in Edinburgh.*" Competitors credit him with developing one of the "*most influential firms in the region.*" Recent highlights included obtaining a new public house licence for Jenners Store at Lomond Shores, Balloch. Advice on ongoing acquisitions of various new betting offices for Stanley Racing and amusement arcades for RAL has also kept the team busy. The existence of a dedicated hospitality and leisure team continues to give the firm an advantage in the marketplace. **Clients** Scottish Rugby Union; Odeon Cinemas; Alldays; Stanley Racing; RAL; Carlton Group.

R & JM HILL BROWN & CO (see firm details p.995) **Jack Cummins** (see p.512) is widely respected throughout the market as "*a leading expert on all types of licensing.*" He has won a following with his "*authoritative*" approach. The team is bolstered by the presence of "*pragmatic and realistic*" **Peter Lawson** (see p.514). It has received instructions from the Noble House Pub Company this year, and was assisting Chorion in its introduction of the Tiger Tiger brand to Glasgow. The firm retains a sizeable off-sales workload for Tesco and Somerfield. **Clients** Carnegies; Luminar; First Leisure; Scottish & Newcastle.

HARPER MACLEOD (see firm details p.985) "*Getting better all the time,*" the firm continues to build on its profile in this sector. **Joanna Brynes** (see p.512) is the standout practitioner at this firm. Her "*talented*" team has a strong betting and gaming profile, alongside its full-service offering to major breweries. **Clients** Breweries; restaurants; pubs.

NORTHERN IRELAND ■ LICENSING

LEADING INDIVIDUALS

[1] **BATTERS John** John Batters & Co
CUMMINS Jack R & JM Hill Brown & Co
LOUDON John Dundas & Wilson CS
MACIVER Archibald Brunton Miller
[2] **DALGLEISH Douglas** Brunton Miller
LAWSON Peter R & JM Hill Brown & Co
[3] **FERRIE Audrey** McGrigor Donald
JOHNSTON Tom Young & Partners
[4] **BRYNES Joanna** Harper Macleod
MORTON Robin Brunton Miller

See individuals' profiles p.511

MCGRIGOR DONALD (see firm details p.1065) Audrey Ferrie (see p.513) typifies the team's approach, which is commended as "*straightforward and effective.*" Her group advises on betting, casino and liquor licensing for a client base that includes a number of hotels and the Glasgow Royal Concert Hall. Rivals have noted the group's increased profile over the past 12 months, and its gaming work was particularly endorsed during research. **Clients** Glasgow Royal Concert Hall; SFI Group; Ladbrokes; hotels.

BLACKADDERS (see firm details p.876) The team was described by interviewees as "*thorough and always good value.*" Led by Ken Glass, it generally undertakes licensing work relating to entertainment, public houses and hotels. It also acts as an agent on behalf of Edinburgh and Glasgow firms. Work highlights included representing VIS iTV in registering pool betting on computerised horse racing, which is to be accessed via the internet and interactive television. The team has also represented an applicant in a successful taxi licence appeal. **Clients** Pubs; hotels.

HASTIES Alistair Macdonald is the key partner in this "*confident local practice.*" It acts predominantly for small local companies and single outlet operators. The team is currently advising pub clients on the introduction of entertainment and promotions as they face competition from English chains newly arrived in Edinburgh. **Clients** Pubs; hotels; nightclubs.

LINDSAYS WS (see firm details p.1042) The group, led by David Reith, tackles a range of betting and gaming licensing with particular focus on liquor. It handles a large amount of licensing for temporary, large, outdoor events, and has recently been involved with off-sale licensing matters. **Clients** Victoria Wines; Granada Group; BHS in Scotland; Sodexho; Bell Haven.

OTHER NOTABLE PRACTITIONERS Sole practitioner **John Batters** brings his "*long experience*" in licensing matters to the market, and was described by peers as "*hugely influential.*" **Tom Johnston** of Young & Partners "*remains central to the game*" and is a "*powerful advocate,*" whose remit focuses on the Fife region.

NORTHERN IRELAND

LICENSING
■ NORTHERN IRELAND

[1] **E & L Kennedy** Belfast
Shean Dickson Merrick Belfast
[2] **O'Reilly Stewart** Belfast

LEADING INDIVIDUALS

[1] **MCGRATH Roisin** E & L Kennedy
MCKAY Maura Shean Dickson Merrick

This book is the product of 6,582 1/2 hour interviews. See p.7 for BMRB audit.
Within each band, firms are listed alphabetically. See individuals' profiles p.511

E & L KENNEDY "*Sound and sensible*" Roisin McGrath is the standout partner at this firm. Clients appreciate that she "*puts herself out for us and knows everyone in the business.*" The team has been advising Tesco on the conversion of its free-standing licence units into in-store units. It also represented Wine Flair on new licences for off-licence units within its convenience stores. The support of a consultant skilled in licensing matters is a boost to the group. **Clients** Wine Flair; Tesco.

SHEAN DICKSON MERRICK (see firm details p.1129) Maura McKay (see p.515) was praised by clients for her "*highly competent and businesslike*" approach to licensing work. The Millennium Project generates ongoing work for the team, and it has also been involved in the opening of restaurants, bowling alleys and pubs. **Clients** Hard Rock Café; Sheridan Group.

O'REILLY STEWART (see firm details p.1089) Garrett O'Reilly heads this "*quality*" outfit, which tackles work on behalf of hotels, pubs, individual landlords, restaurateurs and bookmakers. It has a healthy track record in the arrangement of liquor, betting and gaming licences. It has recently represented the Hastings Group regarding five hotels in Northern Ireland. **Clients** Hastings Group; Queens University; Andras House; hotels.

THE LEADERS IN LICENSING

ALLEN, Jeremy
Poppleston Allen, Nottingham
(0115) 953 8500
jeremy@popall.co.uk
Specialisation: Licensing and leisure work, including liquor, public entertainment, betting and gaming and regulatory crime. Recognised for expertise in hotly contested applications and large retail leisure developments. Legal Director of late-night leisure industry association BEDA. Member of Home Secretary's Advisory Committee on drugs, consulted by the government in respect of licensing reform. Legal correspondent of Night, Theme and Sleeper Magazines. Clients include many leading industry operators: Butlins/Bourne Leisure, Carluccios, Henry J Beans, Ladbrokes, Luminar Leisure, PizzaExpress, Scottish & Newcastle, Signature Restaurants, Spirit Group, Urbium (formerly Chorion plc), Wilson Bowden, Yo!Sushi, various developers and more student unions than any other solicitor.
Prof. Memberships: Law Society; member of Home Office Review of Procedure Committee; current Chairman of Advocacy Training Sub-Committee.
Career: Qualified 1970. Articled at *Johnstone Sharp & Walker* 1962-68; Raleigh Industries 1968-72; joined *Hunt Dickins* 1972, Partner 1973, Managing Partner 1987. Co-founded *Poppleston Allen*, 1994, 'Law Firm of the Year' Award 1999.
Personal: Born 1944; married (three children); resides in Nottingham.

ARNOT, Richard
Dickinson Dees, Newcastle upon Tyne
(0191) 279 9000
richard.arnot@dickinson-dees.com
Specialisation: Specialises in liquor licensing law and has presided over a rapidly expanding licensing practice which is well on its way to becoming a national presence.
Prof. Memberships: British Institute of InnKeepers. Association of Licensing Practitioners.
Career: Articled at *Mincoffs* and qualified in 1992. Spent a number of years specialising in criminal advocacy before being recruited by the Chief Constable of Northumbria Police to represent the force in licensing matters. In 1998 he was asked to join *Dickinson Dees* to establish and develop a licensing department.
Personal: Enjoys most sports.

BATTERS, John A
John Batters & Co, Glasgow
(0141) 427 6884

BAYLIS, Craig
Berwin Leighton Paisner, London
(020) 7760 1000
craig.baylis@blplaw.com
Specialisation: Partner in regulatory department and head of the business regulation unit. Main area of practice is licensing and leisure. Handles all aspects for the leisure, retailing and brewing industries including advocacy at all levels throughout the UK. Other area of expertise is business protection and environmental law. Advises and represents on all regulatory matters, health and safety, food safety, trading standards and environmental health. Author of 'Food Safety: Law and Practice' and 'Environmental Regulation – Its Impact on Foreign Investment'.
Prof. Memberships: Food Law Group.
Career: Qualified 1981. Solicitor for the

www.ChambersandPartners.com 511

LICENSING ■ THE LEADERS

Metropolitan Police 1981-84; Partner at *Field Fisher Waterhouse* 1984-92. Joined *Paisner & Co* (now *Berwin Leighton Paisner*) in 1992 and became a Partner in 1993.
Personal: Born 9th February 1957. Attended Exeter University 1975-78. Lives in London.

BRYNES, Joanna
Harper Macleod, Glasgow
(0141) 221 8888
joanna.brynes@harpermacleod.co.uk
Specialisation: Licensing and leisure. Represents The Scottish Licensed Trade Association, OKO Restaurants in the first sushi conveyor belt restaurant in Scotland, Cairngorm Chairlift Company in the highest restaurant in Scotland, Lidl, and RW Cairns Ltd.
Prof. Memberships: Law Society of Scotland.
Career: Qualified 1996; trained at *Harper Macleod*; associate August 2000.
Personal: Educated at Balfron High School, Stirlingshire; University of Glasgow 1991-96; lives in Glasgow; enjoys visiting some of the licensed premises she represents; cinema and reading.

CHILDS, Christopher
Cartwrights Adams & Black, Cardiff
(029) 2046 5959

CLIFTON, David
Joelson Wilson & Co, London
(020) 7580 5721
drgc@joelson-wilson.co.uk
Specialisation: Partner in charge of licensing/leisure department. Many years' experience in liquor and late-night entertainment licensing. Acknowledged as one of the UK's leading specialists in betting, gaming and lottery law with considerable experience in the developing area of internet/interactive gambling. Acts for a range of leading public companies, appearing as advocate in magistrates courts and crown courts and before local authorities throughout England and Wales. Advises two of the leading trade organisations in the leisure field which has resulted in involvement in the drafting of national licensing legislation and membership of working parties on licensing law reform. 'Legal Expert' for 'The Publican' Newspaper and featured on Sky Television's 'Inn Business' programme. Clients include leaders in the casino, bingo, betting, internet gaming, pub, hotel, restaurant and nightclub fields.
Prof. Memberships: Law Society; International Association of Gaming Attorneys; Association of Licensed Multiple Retailers; Interactive Gambling, Gaming and Betting Association.
Career: Attended Wellingborough School (1963-74) and University of Reading (1974-78). Articled at *Joelson Wilson & Co* in 1979; appointed partner in 1983, head of litigation department 1988 and head of licensing/leisure department in 1993.
Publications: Contributing editor, Smith & Monkcom, 'Law of Betting Gaming & Lotteries' (2nd edition) and 'Halsbury's Laws of England: Betting, Gaming and Lotteries'. Regularly speaks at seminars and conferences.
Personal: Born 14 March 1955. Lives in West Sussex. Leisure interests include family, theatre and cricket.

COLLINS, Anthony
Anthony Collins Solicitors, Birmingham
(0121) 212 7420
Specialisation: Heads up the licensing and leisure law department of the firm. Specialises in licensing applications of all types, particularly for national brewers and entrepreneurs. The majority of the applications are concentrated within the West Midlands conurbation but clients are also advised throughout England and Wales. The firm also arranges secured lending for breweries.
Prof. Memberships: Co. Chairman Association of Licensing Practitioners 2000. President Birmingham Law Society.
Career: Articled *Wragge & Co* and qualified 1970, joined *Tilley Carson & Finlay* in Toronto 1970 and admitted as a Barrister and Solicitor to the Law Society of Upper Canada 1972. Founded *Anthony Collins Solicitors* in 1973.
Personal: Married. Three children. Bradfield College. Family history and fly fishing.

COWELL, Martin
DLA, Sheffield
(08700) 111111

CRIER, Phil
Blake Lapthorn, Portsmouth
(023) 9222 1122

CROSS, James
Kitson Hutchings, Newton Abbot
(01626) 203366
james.cross@khlaw.co.uk
Specialisation: Liquor and entertainment licensing (regulatory offences and commercial litigation). Has acted for brewers, national chains, hotels, holiday complexes and entertainment venues. Particular emphasis on advocacy, having 10 years experience before licensing committees and local authorities in the South West.
Career: Qualified 1992. Partner Head of Licensing *Crosse and Crosse*, moving to the recently merged *Kitson Hutchings* in September 2002.
Personal: Born South Wales 22 August 1963, married with three children. Interests include swimming, surfing, walking and when possible reading the newspapers.

CUMMINS, Jack
R. & J. M. Hill Brown & Co, Glasgow
(0141) 333 0636
jcc@hillbrown.co.uk
Specialisation: Partner in Licensing Department. Handles licensing, gaming, leisure and retail matters, representing a wide range of restaurant, retail and entertainment interests in the licensed trade. Author of 'Licensing Law in Scotland' (Butterworths, 2nd edition, 2001); Consultant Editor to the licensing volume in Butterworths Scottish Legislation series; contributor to 'Scots Law Times', 'Journal of the Law Society of Scotland' and 'Scottish Licensed Trade News'; reporter for 'Scottish Civil Law Reports' and Editor of 'Scottish Licensing Law and Practice'. Contributed chapter on Scottish Licensing Law to 'Licensing Law Guide' (Butterworths, 1998). Accredited as a specialist in liquor licensing law by The Law Society of Scotland. Keynote speaker or Chairman, National Conferences for Licensing Boards 1994-99 and 2001. Contributor to various radio and television programmes. Law Society of Scotland 'Update' speaker. Convenor of Certificate in Liquor Licensing Course, Central Law Training; Convenor and keynote speaker Annual Licensing Conference, Central Law Training 1996-2002. Keynote speaker 'ACPO' Conference, York, November 1998 and IBC Licensing Conference, London, 2002. Member of Licensing Law Committee of the Law Society of Scotland.
Prof. Memberships: Law Society of Scotland.
Career: Joined *R & JM Hill & Brown & Co.* in 1976. Qualified in 1978 and became a Partner in 1980.
Personal: Born in 1952. Educated at the University of Glasgow (MA, 1974, LL.B. 1976) and University of Montpellier (1972-73). Leisure pursuits include motoring. Lives in Glasgow.

CURTIS, Anthony G
Kenneth Curtis & Co, Birmingham
(0121) 356 1161

DALGLEISH, Douglas S
Brunton Miller, Glasgow
(0141) 337 1199
douglasdalgleish@bruntonmiller.com
Specialisation: Senior partner. Has been involved in licensing work for over 30 years. Widely experienced, acting for several major breweries and supermarket chains. Also handles general commercial work. Regular contributor to various licensed trade publications. Has addressed numerous conferences and seminar groups. Scottish Legal Advisor to Scottish Golf Union.
Prof. Memberships: Law Society of Scotland.
Career: Qualified in 1956. Became senior partner of *Brunton Miller* in 1974. Member of Law Society Working Party on licensing law.
Personal: Born 26 December 1927. Attended Glasgow University 1949-55. Chairman of Dumbarton FC; Past President of Scottish Golf Union; Chairman of Caledonian Golf Travel Limited. Leisure interests include golf and football. Lives in Helensburgh.

DAVIES, Suzanne
Joelson Wilson & Co, London
(020) 7580 5721
scd@joelson-wilson.co.uk
Specialisation: Partner in licensing/leisure department. Liquor, betting, gaming and late night entertainment licensing, together with associated compliance and regulatory matters, including health and safety, food safety, trading standards and criminal prosecutions. Appears as advocate in courts throughout England and Wales. Acts for, amongst others, Regent Inns plc, IG Index plc, Grosvenor Casinos Limited, Association of Licensed Multiple Retailers and Hard Rock Cafe. One of the firm's legal experts who writes for 'The Publican'.
Prof. Memberships: Hotel Property Network, International Association of Gaming Attorneys.
Career: Manchester University, American Studies BA (Hons) 1982-86, Pennsylvania State University, USA 1986-87, College of Law, Chester – CPE and LSF 1987-89.
Personal: Interests include theatre, cinema and travelling.

DAVIES, Tim
Bond Pearce, Bristol
(0117) 929 9197
tdavies@bondpearce.com
Specialisation: Partner and Head of Licensing at *Bond Pearce* (formerly *Cartwrights*). 18 years continuous specialisation in liquor, gaming and entertainment licensing. Advises on strategy and specific cases and appears as advocate nationally. Examples of clients include Gala Casinos, Tesco Stores and Hilton Hotels. Co-ordination with commercial partners on licensed property acquisitions and disposals. Consultant to British Retail Consortium.
Career: Qualified 1978 with *Cartwrights*, becoming Partner in 1984. Joined *Bond Pearce* in 2001 on merger.

DAY, Philip J
Horsey Lightly Fynn, Newbury
(01635) 580858

DICKINSON, Nick
Pannone & Partners, Manchester
(0161) 909 4503
nick.dickinson@pannone.co.uk
Specialisation: Represents major clients throughout the United Kingdom, one of very few English solicitors regularly appearing before Licensing Boards in Scotland. Special interest in petrol station forecourt licensing. Has lectured extensively on licensing-related matters. Has written staff training manuals and written and produced training videos for clients.
Prof. Memberships: Law Society and Association of Licensing Practitioners. Holds MBII Training Professional qualification.
Career: Qualified in 1975. Partner since joining *Pannone & Partners* in 2000, previously head of licensing at *Davis Wallis Foyster*.
Personal: Born 3rd June 1943. Educated at Uppingham School 1956-61. Leisure interests include shooting and sailing.

THE LEADERS — LICENSING

DOWLING, Susan
Blandy & Blandy, Reading
(0118) 951 6829
Sue_dowling@blandy.co.uk
Specialisation: Partner in charge of Liquor Licensing and Gaming Department. The department has considerable experience in sports related liquor licensing, often dealing with licensing issues for football, rugby and cricket grounds. This year the department acted for The Rugby Football Union/Twickenham Experience Ltd and successfully applied for a new On Licence (and numerous specific licensing orders/certificates), to cover the whole of Twickenham Rugby Stadium. Also acts for Wembley (London) Ltd on licensing matters relating to Wembley Exhibition Halls, Arena, Conference Centre and Bingo Hall. Continues to act for Debenhams PLC, recently being instructed to make numerous licensing applications for its Stores in London, the South and the Midlands. The department provides a complete service from advising on proposed licensing operations at new venues, advising on improvements to existing licensing operations, making appropriate applications and conducting the advocacy at hearings.
Prof. Memberships: The Law Society. Thames Valley Commercial Lawyers Association.
Career: Articled at *Blandy & Blandy*. Associate (1991), partner 1992 to date.
Personal: LLB (Hons) Business Law (Coventry), College of Law (Guildford). Leisure interests include family, travel, dance, renovation of antique furniture.

EARDLEY, Kathryn
Bond Pearce, Bristol
(0117) 929 9197

EDNEY, Robert
KSB Law, London
(020) 7447 1200
redney@ksblaw.co.uk
Specialisation: Partner and Head of Licensing Department. Acts for major retail clients and others in the leisure industry at all levels in relation to liquor and entertainment licensing and related work.
Career: Qualified in 1970, having joined *Kingsford Stacey* in 1968. Became a Partner in 1972.
Personal: Born 8 September 1946. Educated at Cambridge University (MA 1968). Chairman of local tennis club. Enjoys tennis, food and wine. Lives in Aston, near Stevenage with his wife and family.

FERRIE, Audrey
McGrigor Donald, Glasgow
(0141) 567 9289
audrey.ferrie@mcgrigors.com
Specialisation: Liquor, betting, gaming and civic government licensing, acting for a wide range of clients in the hotel, restaurant, pub, casino and bookmaking sectors. A regular speaker at industry conferences throughout the UK. Accredited as a specialist in liquor licensing by the Law Society of Scotland.
Prof. Memberships: Law Society of Scotland.
Career: Educated Notre Dame High School, Glasgow and Glasgow University, trained with *Hughes Dowdall Solicitors*, Glasgow and joined *McGrigor Donald* in 1985 on merger with *Moncrieff Warren Paterson*.
Personal: Married to a Glasgow lawyer, two children. Leisure interests include travel and attempting to keep up with children on the ski slopes.

FREEMAN, Bill
Freemans Solicitors, Lower Chepstow
(01291) 623225

FREEMAN, Keith Michael
Freemans, Newcastle upon Tyne
(0191) 222 1030

FYNN, Lionel
Horsey Lightly Fynn, Newbury
(01202) 551991
Specialisation: Partner and Head of Environmental, Licensing and Planning Departments. Regular advocate in a wide range of planning, environmental and licensing matters. Has personally conducted numerous cases involving liquor licensing, betting and gaming and noise related proceedings at Magistrates Court and Crown Court level, as well as many Town Planning Inquiries. Recently involved in substantial cases concerning village greens, waste disposal proposals and affordable housing matters. Specialises in High Court Challenges/Judicial Review.
Prof. Memberships: Member of BISL, Associate Member of The Institute of Acoustics.
Career: Lectures at national seminars on licensing and planning matters. Produced 'cassette law' audio series with Oyez IBC and Law Society. Has produced two licensing videos and a third on children's certificates to wide acclaim. Latest production a town planning video entitled 'Planning by Design'.

GAUNT, John R T
John Gaunt & Partners, Sheffield
(0114) 266 8664
Specialisation: Main area of practice is licensing and leisure with over 20 years experience in this field. Has developed a wide client base including many plcs and operates nationally. Exclusively retained by many clients. Has handled a number of high profile licence applications (including the licensing of multi-faceted leisure centres) attracting significant media attention and coverage, particularly in recent years.
Career: Qualified in 1976. Became a partner in *Wake Smith* in 1977 and latterly a member of the firm's Management Committee. Co founded *John Gaunt & Partners* in 1995, a specialist commercial litigation and property practice particularly for the liquor and leisure industries. The practice now handles in excess of 5,000 licence applications per annum and has over 19 people dedicated to the field of licensing.

GLAZEBROOK, Peter
Field Fisher Waterhouse, London
(020) 7861 4000
Specialisation: Partner and Head of the Licensing Department. Primary area of practice is liquor and entertainment licensing law. Work includes applications to the licensing justices for liquor licences for public houses, hotels, clubs, wine bars and off-licences including supermarkets and applications to local authorities for public entertainment licences for nightclubs and bars and conducting appeals through to the Crown Courts where appropriate. Frequently involved in issues of environmental and health and safety law related to licensed premises. In recent times, has been engaged in applications for betting office permits for online businesses.
Prof. Memberships: A representative and member of the North & South Westminster Court User Forum.
Career: Qualified in 1970. Joined *Field Fisher Waterhouse* in 1974 and became a partner in 1977.

GREGG, Andrew
Gregg Latchams Quinn, Bristol
(0117) 906 9400
andrew.gregg@glqlaw.co.uk
Specialisation: All aspects of law concerning food, licensing, employment and health and safety. Acts for wide variety of food and drink manufacturers, processors and retailers. See R v Gateway Foodmarkets Ltd C.A. TLR 2.1.97. Notary Public.
Prof. Memberships: Secretary Food Law Group, Past President Bristol Law Society, Council Member Notaries Society.
Career: The Dragon School Oxford, The Kings School Canterbury. Solicitor D.o.A. 1970, Notary Public D.o.A. 1984. For 20 years partner with a leading Bristol firm before setting up own niche practice in 1992.
Personal: Born 12 September 1943. Interests include rugby, sailing, motor racing and restoration of vintage cars. Owns and campaigns a 1933 Lagonda. Chairman of Young Bristol.

HALLIWELL, Tilly
Jeffrey Green Russell, London
(020) 7339 7000
tih@jgrlaw.co.uk
Specialisation: Liquor and entertainment licensing. Work includes liquor and public entertainment licensing (and allied matters) for bars, restaurants, clubs etc. She has a reputation for problem solving and detail and, due to her originally corporate background, for a 'commercially astute' approach. Clients include Hard Rock Cafe, Glendola Leisure and Shoeless Joe's. Recent projects include establishment of Pacha Nightclub in London, reinstatement of Seen public entertainment licence, and Electric Cinema/Club and Brasserie.
Prof. Memberships: Law Society.
Career: LLB (Hons), Manchester. Qualified in 1970. Joined *Jeffrey Green Russell* as a Partner in 1994.

HARRIS, Julian
Pinsent Curtis Biddle, London
(020) 7667 0110
julian.harris@pinsents.com
Specialisation: Partner in Litigation Department, specialising in gambling and licensing law with particular emphasis on internet gambling, advising internet businesses and obtaining the necessary regulatory permits. The firm has advised sports betting operators moving their internet operations offshore, the Fantasy League and several gambling and other sporting websites. The firm acts for several major casino, leisure and food/catering groups, and recently obtained two of the first internet gaming licences in the Isle of Man. Spent six years with the solicitors for the Gaming Board. In the past year has represented the British Casino Association. In addition, the firm represents two major casino operators in the UK, with casinos both in London and in other major cities. The firm also advises overseas operators interested in establishing a UK presence. Well known regular contributor to gambling and internet-related seminars and international conferences.
Prof. Memberships: International Association of Gaming Attorneys, International Internet Gaming Association, European Forum for the Study of Gambling and the International Masters of Gaming Law.
Career: Qualified 1980; partner *Gregory, Rowcliffe & Co* 1983-86, *Nicholson Graham Jones* 1986-88 and *Shoosmiths* 1988-93 where he was Head of Litigation. Joined *Biddle* 1993 where he is Head of the Gaming & Leisure Group.
Personal: Born 15 May 1955. Magdalene College, Cambridge.

HARTWELL, Roger
DMH, Worthing
(01903) 235026
roger.hartwell@dmh.co.uk
Specialisation: All forms of liquor and entertainment licensing, as well as associated property work for both large and small operations. Undertakes own advocacy including appeals.
Career: Qualified 1966. Prosecuting solicitor, Brighton Borough Council 1966-69. Joined *Donne Mileham & Haddock* (now *DMH*) in 1970 and became a partner in 1973. Managing Partner 1994-97.
Personal: Born 1943. Education: Magdalen College School Brackley and Bristol University 1960-63. Interests: endurance sports, astronomy, theatre and gardening. Lives in Worthing.

HAY, David Leslie
Allan Janes, High Wycombe
(01494) 521301

LICENSING ■ THE LEADERS

HAYDEN, Tim
Clarke Willmott & Clarke, Taunton
(01823) 445204
thayden@cw-c.co.uk
See under Environment, p.359

HEPHER, Christopher
Pullig & Co, London
(020) 7353 0505

HOLLAND, Barry
Elliotts, Manchester
(0161) 834 9933
barry.holland@elliott-law.co.uk
Specialisation: Notary Public 1980. Head of Licensing and Food Safety Department. Acts for major off licence chains in England and Wales and for a national bookmaker and a pools company. Also handles entertainment and liquor licensing for major brewing clients and night club operators. Other areas of practice are food safety and health and safety at work acting on a nationwide basis for national supermarket chains. Chairman of the Food Law Group. Cases have included a leading authority in the field of petrol stations, convenience stores and the preparation of rules for an 'on line' National Lottery game. Has lectured for the Law Society and given both in-house and client seminars on liquor, betting, licensing, food safety and health and safety.

HORNE, Anthony
Weightman Vizards, Manchester
(0161) 833 2601
anthony.horne@weightmanvizards.com
Specialisation: Sole area of practice is licensing and leisure. Work includes liquor, gaming and public entertainment. Successfully represented Coliseum Plc in the high profile application relating to the new sports cafe in Manchester. Acted in the first new casino licence to be granted in Manchester for more than 30 years. Major clients include Gatecrasher, Rank Leisure Division Ltd, Menzies Hotels plc, Grosvenor Casinos Ltd, UMIST and Manchester University, SFI Group plc.
Prof. Memberships: Law Society. Fellow to the Society of Entertainment Licensing Practitioners. Manchester Doorsafe committee.
Career: MA (Cantab) 1983. Admitted 1985. Progressed to *Weightman Vizards* as a licensing partner March 1999.

JOHNSON, Christopher R
A Halsall & Co, Birkenhead
(0151) 647 6323
Specialisation: Head of licensing department. All aspects of liquor licensing including off licence work. Acting for National Companies England and Wales.
Career: Qualified 1971. Partner 1973.

JOHNSON, M Clare
Gosschalks, Hull
(01482) 324252

JOHNSTON, Tom
Young & Partners, Glenrothes
(01592) 630890

JONES, Simon
Cobbetts, Manchester
(0161) 833 5621
simon.jones@cobbetts.co.uk
Specialisation: Partner specialising in licensing and leisure work including all aspects of liquor licensing, public entertainment and Gaming Act matters; representing a wide range of brewing, restaurant and retail interests in the licence trade. Increasingly provides assistance and representation in Health and Safety Prosecutions and related regulatory matters – food safety, consumer protection, trading standards and environmental protection. Has extensive experience in appearing before courts and committees throughout England and Wales and in dealing with enforcing authorities.
Prof. Memberships: Law Society, Manchester Law Society, Food Law Group.
Career: Articled with *Leak Almond & Parkinson* which subsequently became *Cobbett Leak Almond* and qualified in 1978. Became a partner in 1982.
Personal: Born 28 March 1953. Educated at Birkenhead School 1965-71 and Oxford University 1972-75.

KEFFORD, Alan
Howes Percival, Norwich
(01603) 762103
Specialisation: Managing partner for East Anglian office and head of firm's liquor and leisure division. Main area of practice covers all aspects of liquor and entertainment licensing. Also includes gaming matters. Alan is a staunch believer in the principle of providing a one-stop service to the leisure sector. He has made applications throughout East Anglia and the South East on a regular basis. He acts for two major breweries on licensing matters in East Anglia and counts amongst his clients a number of major hotels in Norfolk. Instrumental in *Howes Percival* being licensed by the Awarding Body of the British Institute of Innkeeping to run courses and examinations for the National Licensee Certificate in four centres: Lowestoft, Great Yarmouth, Thetford and Ipswich. Alan is a director of Anglian Archives plc and his family have close links with the hotel industry. He has spoken at various seminars for representatives of the leisure industry.
Personal: Born 1 May 1944. Attended University College, London 1963-66. Leisure pursuits include walking, cricket and golf. Lives in Norwich.

LAWSON, Hamish K
Cobbetts, Manchester
(0161) 833 5260
hamish.lawson@cobbetts.co.uk
Specialisation: Partner in Commercial Property Department. Main area of practice is licensing. Acts for most of the breweries and major licensed retail operators represented in the north west, especially with regard to new site applications. Also handles food law, acting for two major national food manufacturers. Acted in Drury & Samuel Smith Old Brewery (Tadcaster) v Scunthorpe Licensing Justices on surrender of licences. Firm advises North West Brewers and Licensed Retailers Association. Has addressed numerous conferences and seminars including 'The 24 Hour City' in Manchester in 1993.
Prof. Memberships: Law Society of England and Wales, Manchester Law Society.
Career: Qualified in 1978. Joined *Cobbett Leak Almond* in 1976, becoming a partner in 1981.
Personal: Born 23 June 1951. Attended Oxford University 1969-72. Leisure interests include theatre (acting and directing) and sport. Lives in Bramhall, Cheshire.

LAWSON, Peter J
R. & J. M. Hill Brown & Co, Glasgow
(0141) 332 3265
plawson@hillbrown.co.uk
Specialisation: Partner in Licensing Department. Principal area of practice is licensing. Deals with new licence applications, provides an advice service to multiple operators and individuals, court representation (including trading standards, consumer protection, etc) and renewal/review service for existing clients. Also handles commercial and conveyancing, in particular with regard to licensed premises, providing a full commercial service and advice. Clients include pub companies, supermarket chains and national entertainment companies. Has written various articles for trade magazines and lectured on Central Law Training licensing courses.
Prof. Memberships: Law Society of Scotland.
Career: Qualified in 1981. Partner at *McSherry Halliday, Irvine* 1984-90. Joined *Hill Brown* as a Partner in 1990.
Personal: Born 25 March 1958. Educated at Glasgow University. Holds various directorships. Committee member, BAFTA Scotland. Chairman of Tron Theatre, Glasgow. Leisure interests include theatre. Lives in Glasgow.

LEE, Trevor
Challinors Lyon Clark, Edgbaston
(0121) 455 6333
tal@challinors.co.uk
Specialisation: Licensing (gaming, betting and liquors). Leisure. Heads an enlarged licensing team with wide client base throughout West Midlands in all forms of licensed premises. Undertakes work for Bass Taverns Enterprise Inns and instructed by Richardson Brothers for licensing work at prestigious development of Merry Hill Waterfront.
Prof. Memberships: Past President of Birmingham Law Society.
Career: Admitted 1969. Worked in licensing since then with present firm where he is Senior Partner.
Personal: Married, sons 21 and 22. Golf, cricket, skiing, good wines.

LOUDON, John
Dundas & Wilson CS, Edinburgh
(0131) 228 8000

LUCAS, David
Nelsons, Nottingham
(0115) 989 5353
david.lucas@nelsons-solicitors.co.uk
Specialisation: Works exclusively in the areas of liquor and entertainment licensing and gaming. Head of department that represents a wide spectrum of clients from plcs to individual operators and police authorities advising on a diverse range of applications around the country.
Prof. Memberships: Association of Licensing Practitioners, Association of Entertainment Licensing Practitioners, Member of British Institute of Innkeeping.
Career: Articled at Nottingham City Council joining private practice in 1981. Moved from mixed civil practice to concentrate solely on licensing in 1996.
Publications: Contributor to LNTV video on licensing law, provides material and training to clients and organisations involved in licensing work.
Personal: Vice President of Nottingham Rugby Football Club, Member of Nottinghamshire County Cricket Club.

MACGREGOR, Ewen
Bond Pearce, Bristol
(0117) 929 9197
emacgregor@bondpearce.com
Specialisation: Liquor licensing and gaming.
Prof. Memberships: Law Society.
Career: Qualified in 1992 following articled with *Cartwrights*. Joined Licensing Team in 1996 being made an Associate in 2000.
Personal: Educated Gordonstoun 1978-83. Keele University 1984-88, Chester Law School 1988-89.

MACIVER, Archibald D
Brunton Miller, Glasgow
(0141) 337 1199
archiemaciver@bruntonmiller.com
Specialisation: Partner. Main area of practice is licensing. Extensive experience in all aspects of liquor licensing work. Also involved heavily in licensing under Civic Government (Scotland) Act such as public entertainment licences, street traders and late hours catering licences. Regular columnist in various trade papers. Has addressed many seminar groups on licensing matters. Scottish Legal Advisor to BEDA.
Prof. Memberships: Law Society of Scotland, Scottish Law Agents Society, Glasgow Bar Association.
Career: Qualified in 1982. Worked at *Levy & McRae* 1981-88, from 1984 as a partner. Joined *Brunton Miller* in 1988 as a partner. Accredited by the Law Society of Scotland as a Specialist in Liquor Licensing Law in 1993.
Personal: Born 13 December 1959. Attended Hutchesons' Grammar School 1972-77 and University of Strathclyde 1977-81. Leisure interests include sport (especially football), cinema and reading. Lives in Glasgow.

THE LEADERS — LICENSING

MCGRATH, Roisin
E & L Kennedy, Belfast
(028) 9023 2352

MCKAY, Maura
Shean Dickson Merrick, Belfast
(028) 9032 6878
mauram@shean-dickson-merrick.com
Specialisation: All aspects of liquor licensing with particular strengths in public house, off licence, restaurant, hotel, airport, registered club and entertainment licensing. Has advised the Law Society of Northern Ireland on draft licensing legislation. Represents a wide range of brewing and retail interests and acts for Northern Ireland Federation of Registered Clubs. Contributor to Law Society magazine and licensed trade publications. Lectures to trade bodies on licensing issues.
Career: Qualified 1986, Partner 1990 - with *Shean Dickson Merrick*; specialist licensing practitioners since qualification.
Personal: Born 1962. Married with two children.

MESSENT, Michael
Trethowans, Southampton
(023) 8032 1000
michael.messent@trethowans.com
Specialisation: Head of licensing department with extensive experience as advisor and advocate in betting, gaming and liquor licensing law. Retained by Ladbrokes, Tower Casinos, Pizza Hut and other leisure companies. Regularly instructed as Ladbrokes advocate in contested betting licensing cases.
Career: Qualified 1971. Joined *Woodford & Ackroyd* 1973. Partner since 1976.
Personal: Educated KCS Wimbledon and Southampton University. Interests include golf, walking, travel, food and drink.

MORSE, John
John Morse Solicitors, Swansea
(01792) 648111
mail@johnmorse.co.uk
Specialisation: Licensing, Leisure and Commercial work.
Prof. Memberships: The Law Society, past President of the Swansea Law Society.
Career: Admitted 1967. Formed own practice in 1970. Experienced in all forms of licensing including liquor, betting and gaming. Acted for major brewers in the acquisition of new liquor licenses in Wales, West Country London and Northern England. Represented three of the major bookmaking firms in betting and gaming applications and objections and represented casino operators in Wales, the Midlands and other areas.
Personal: Educated at Swansea Grammar School and The College of Law. Married with three grown up children. Horse racing, rugby and golf.

MORTON, Robin J M
Brunton Miller, Glasgow
(0141) 337 1199
robinmorton@bruntonmiller.com
Specialisation: Mobile telephone no: 07970 272953. Consultant in licensing department. Handles liquor licensing, leisure and entertainment law. Acts for major organisations as well as individuals in obtaining and operating liquor licences, appearing at many boards throughout Scotland. Also acts for banks, purchasers and sellers in the property and commercial aspects relating to licensed premises. Has been involved in a number of reported cases, including one which resulted in a change of law (Mount Charlotte Investments v City of Glasgow District Licensing Board). Accredited by the Law Society of Scotland as a specialist in liquor licensing. Regular contributor to 'Scottish Licensed Trade News' Legal Clinic. Frequently lectures on liquor licensing law.
Prof. Memberships: Law Society of Scotland.
Career: Qualified in 1975. With *Brunton Miller* 1975-78. Assistant Director of Legal Aid for the Hong Kong Government 1978-81. Partner with *Brunton Miller* 1981-88. Joined *McClure Naismith Anderson & Gardiner* as a partner in 1988, established *Robin Morton Solicitors* in 1995. Consultant with *Brunton Miller* 1996-date.
Personal: Born 1 October 1951. Educated at Glasgow Academy 1961-69, then Glasgow University 1969-72. Leisure pursuits include music and football. Lives in Glasgow.

NICHOLLS, Simon
Belmores, Norwich
(01603) 617947

OWEN, Mark
Weightman Vizards, Liverpool
(0151) 227 2601
mark.owen@weightmanvizards.com
Specialisation: Head of the firm's licensing department – handles all areas of liquor licensing as well as public entertainment and betting and gaming. Represents most of the major breweries and major licensed retail operators – particular expertise in new site applications. Acts exclusively for the sixth largest bookmaker in the country. Regularly appears before committees across the country. Acted for the successful party in the landmark Hestview decision. Clients include Done Bookmakers, University of Liverpool, Liverpool Football Club and Cream.
Prof. Memberships: Law Society. Founder member of the Association of Licensing Practitioners. Secretary to the Liverpool Licencees Association.
Career: Qualified 1987 – partner 1992.

PARROTT, Michael
Bond Pearce, Bristol
(0117) 929 9197
mparrott@bondpearce.com
Specialisation: Formerly with *Cartwrights*, Michael is a partner specialising in all aspects of licensing law including liquor, gaming, entertainment and cinema licences on behalf of major plcs. Practice has involved applications for judicial review of interpretation and implementation of licensing justices' policy. Has carried out due diligence excercises in relation to the acquisition and disposal of licensed premises and estates. Also acts for national food retailers on food law matters.
Career: Articled in Magistrates Court Service, qualified 1979 and joined *Cartwrights* in 1985, becoming Partner in 1987. Joined *Bond Pearce* in 2001 on merger.

PARTRIDGE, Malcolm
Eversheds, Norwich
(01603) 272660
malcolmpartridge@eversheds.com
Specialisation: Specialisations include all aspects of liquor and entertainment licensing for both independent operators and national concerns.
Prof. Memberships: Norfolk and Norwich Law Society (Former President), Employment Lawyers Association.
Career: Qualified 1970. Partner in Norwich since 1976. Considerable advocacy experience. Specialist in licensing law for 20 years.
Personal: Born 16 January 1945. University of Sheffield 1964-67.

PEARCE, John
Young & Pearce, Nottingham
(0115) 959 8888
Specialisation: Partner in Licensing and Leisure and Commercial Department. Experienced in licensing and leisure work involving public houses, clubs of all types, casinos, bingo halls, betting offices, leisure centres, off-licences and restaurants. Acts for major breweries and other PLCs in the East Midlands and elsewhere in the UK, as well as for many individuals and groups. Deals with acquisitions and sales of businesses as well as licensing. Has been involved in the licensing work for new public houses for major breweries, bingo halls, casinos and betting offices for other companies and individuals as well as other leisure complexes for golf, tennis and indoor cricket including the UK holiday villages for Center Parcs. Reviewed 'Betting, Gaming and Lotteries' by K Barker and DJ Hamilton. Has delivered various lectures and is available to address conferences and seminars.
Prof. Memberships: Law Society, Nottinghamshire Law Society.
Career: Has been senior partner of *Young & Pearce* since qualifying in 1965. Member of the Young Solicitors Group London Committee 1970-77. Past President of the Nottinghamshire Law Society (1994-95).
Personal: Born 8 April 1940. Educated at Nottingham High School 1953-57. Chairman of Rufford Parish Council. Trustee of the Nottingham Union Rowing Club. Owner of 27 foot steam launch and 3 vintage tractors. Enjoys rowing, DIY, boating, painting and playing the drums. Lives in Rufford, near Newark.

PHILLIPS, Jeremy
Osborne Clarke, Bristol
(0117) 917 3000

PHIPPS, Matthew
Osborne Clarke, Bristol
(0117) 917 3000

POPPLESTON, Susanna
Poppleston Allen, Nottingham
(0115) 953 8500
susanna@popall.co.uk
Specialisation: Licensing and leisure work, including liquor, public entertainment, betting and gaming and regulatory crime. Particularly recognised for expertise in late-night licensing, pay parties and table dancing applications; specialist knowledge of Westminster. Legal correspondent for 'Leisure and Hospitality Business'. Consulted by the government in respect of licensing reform. Clients include many leading industry operators: Butlins/Bourne Leisure, Carluccios, Henry J Beans, Ladbrokes, Luminar Leisure, PizzaExpress, Scottish & Newcastle, Signature Restaurants, Spirit Group, Urbium (formerly Chorion plc), Wilson Bowden, Yo!Sushi, various developers and more student unions than any other solicitor.
Prof. Memberships: Past President Nottinghamshire Law Society; Law Society.
Career: Qualified 1972. Articled at *Shacklocks*, set up criminal department 1972, Partner 1974. Co-founded *Temple Wallis* 1979, merged to create *Hunt Dickins* 1987. Co-founded *Poppleston Allen*, 'Law Firm of the Year' Award 1999.
Personal: Born 1948; married (two sons); resides in Nottingham.

POTTS, Andrew
Hammond Suddards Edge, Birmingham
(0121) 222 3000

RADCLIFFE, Malcolm
Freethcartwright, Leicester
(0116) 201 4000
malcolm.radcliffe@freethcartwright.co.uk
Specialisation: Partner in licensing and commercial department. Principal area of practice is licensing. Also handles commercial conveyancing. Major clients include Aldi Stores and Leicestershire police.
Prof. Memberships: Law Society, Solicitors Benevolent Association.
Career: Qualified in 1972. With *Ironsides* from qualification and became a partner in 1974. Partner in *Freeth Cartwright Hunt Dickins* (now Freethcartwright) 1998.
Personal: Born 22 November 1948. Educated at Oakham School 1959-66. Parish Councillor and Chairman of local primary school governors.

RAWLE, Claire
Morgan Cole, Cardiff
(029) 2038 5385

ROCHE, Paddy
Morgan Cole, Oxford
(01865) 262600

SHARKEY, Lisa
Poppleston Allen, Nottingham

LICENSING ■ THE LEADERS

(0115) 953 8500
l.sharkey@popall.co.uk

Specialisation: Licensing and leisure work, including liquor, public entertainment, betting and gaming and regulatory crime. Firmly established national licensing advocate with recognised expertise in late-night licensing, table dancing applications and student unions. Legal correspondent for 'Trading News', the NUSSL magazine. Consulted by the government in respect of licensing reform. Clients include many leading industry operators: Butlins/Bourne Leisure, Carluccios, Henry J Beans, Ladbrokes, Luminar Leisure, PizzaExpress, Scottish & Newcastle, Signature Restaurants, Spirit Group, Urbium (formerly Chorion plc), Wilson Bowden, Yo!Sushi, various developers and more student unions than any other solicitor.
Prof. Memberships: Law Society; Committee Member of Society of Entertainment Licensing Practitioners.
Career: LLB: (Hons) Leeds 1989. Lectured Law at University of Derby. Articled *Hunt Dickins* 1992. Left in 1994 with Jeremy Allen and Susanna Poppleston when they founded *Poppleston Allen*; Partner in January 2001.
Personal: Born 1968; resides in Nottingham.

SHAW, Deborah
Anthony Collins Solicitors, Birmingham
(0121) 212 7435
deborah.shaw@anthonycollinssolicitors.com

Specialisation: Deborah Shaw is a partner in the firm's licensing and leisure department specialising in licensing applications of all types, particularly for national chains and entrepreneurs. Applications are made throughout England and Wales but with a special concentration in the West Midlands. Deborah has wide experience of handling betting and gaming licensing. The firm's licensing expertise incorporates a licensing property department with a substantial secured lending emphasis.
Career: Qualified in 1984. Deborah has 15 years experience with two leading licensing practices.
Personal: Educated at Birmingham University; interests include mountaineering, fell walking, films and theatre, reading, travel when time and family permit.

SKEENS, Julian
Jeffrey Green Russell, London
(020) 7339 7018
jms@jgrlaw.co.uk

Specialisation: Partner in charge of Licensing and Gaming Law Department. Specialist in liquor licensing, betting gaming, public entertainment and lotteries; undertakes cases throughout the UK including Scotland and Northern Ireland. Described as being at the cutting edge of licensing; known for his creative approach and for successfully challenging traditional views. Represented the industry in the leading case of Shipley. Dealt with the leading case of R v Preston Crown Court ex parte Gosling (changing the constitution of the Crown Court on appeals). Other cases successfully handled include the UK's first multi-activity centre, the UK's first 24 hour public entertainment licence and the UK's largest licensed premises.
Prof. Memberships: Law Society, Business in Sport and Leisure (Director), Solicitor for the Study of Gambling, International Association of Gaming Attorneys, European Society for the study of Gambling. Society of Entertainment and Licensed Practitioners, Society for Advanced Legal Studies and sits on the National Licensing Forum. Solicitor to the Westminster Licensees Association.
Career: Qualified 1980. Joined *Jeffrey Green Russell* in 1987 as a partner to establish the now thriving Licensing and Gaming Department.
Personal: Born 26 December 1951. LLB (Hons) (1974).

SMITH, David
Turbervilles with Nelson Cuff, Uxbridge
(01895) 201700
david.smith@turbervilles.co.uk

Specialisation: Partner and Head of Licensing Department. Specialises in all aspects of liquor and entertainment licensing. Clients include major retailers and wholesalers, nightclubs, health clubs, football clubs, golf clubs, hotel groups and airport retailers. Substantial local following. His firm has been accredited by the British Institute of Innkeeping as a training and examination centre for National Licensees Certificates. Defends in criminal proceedings, prosecutes for RSPCA.
Prof. Memberships: Law Society, Association of Licensing Practitioners.
Career: Qualified in Magistrates Courts Service. Admitted in 1981, Private Practice from 1984, Partner at *Turbervilles* from 1986.
Personal: Born 1 Feb 1953. Married with two children. Lives in Ickenham. Leisure – football, music, fine wines.

SMITH, Sarah
Mincoffs, Newcastle upon Tyne
(0191) 281 6151
sjrobinson@mincoffs.co.uk

Specialisation: Leisure Department Head. Main area of practice is licensing, covering liquor, gaming, amusements and planning. Handles applications and objections on behalf of national and local companies, individuals and residents associations.
Prof. Memberships: Member of British Amusement Catering Trades Association (BACTA) – Fellow of the Society of Entertainment Licensing Practitioners.
Career: Qualified in 1994. Articled with *Mincoffs* and became a partner in 2000.
Personal: Born 1969. Interest in sport, leisure, food and drink (for research purposes).

SOUTHORN, Elizabeth
Richards Butler, London
(020) 7816 3729
es@richardsbutler.com

Specialisation: Partner, head of licensing unit specialising in the licensing of liquor, betting, gaming, internet gambling, and UK bookmaking permits; late night entertainment and large new multi-leisure sites; acts for major players in the leisure industry including the Rank Organisation, the Royal Opera House, The BBC; Thistle Hotels, Mezzanine group plc, national bookmakers Coral, Sir Terence Conran, Park Plaza Europe and many of the most active development companies such as Marylebone Warwick Balfour and Centros Miller.
Prof. Memberships: Business in Sport and Leisure; Association of London Brewery Solicitors; the Law Society; Fellow of the Society of Entertainment Licensing Practitioners.
Career: Articled *Oswald Hickson Collier & Co.*; qualified in 1974; *Clyde & Co* 1980-82; *Crossman Block & Keith* 1982-88; partner and head of licensing at *Penningtons (London)* 1988-93. Joined *Richards Butler* in 1993. Currently partner and Head of Licensing Unit.
Personal: St Anne's College, Oxford 1968-71; (MA Jurisprudence 1975). Leisure interests include family, sailing, opera and reading.

TEMPERLEY, William
McKenzie Bell, Sunderland
(0191) 567 4857
mckbell@dial.pipex.com

Specialisation: Partner in licensing and leisure department. Principal area of work covers liquor and public entertainment licensing including sports grounds, betting and theatre licences and all types of applications and offences under the Licensing Act 1964. Handles applications to Justices and local authorities and Appeals to Crown Court throughout five North Eastern counties. Handles objections and applications for late licences, revocations and opposed renewals on behalf of police and licensees.
Prof. Memberships: Association of Licensing Practitioners. Fellow of the Society of Entertainment Licensing Practitioners.
Career: Articled with *McKenzie Bell* and became a partner in 1966.
Personal: Born 1940. Attended Bristol University 1958-61. Leisure pursuits include theatres and railways. Lives in Sunderland.

WELLS, Harriet
Mills & Reeve, Norwich
(01603) 693239
harriet.wells@mills-reeve.com

Specialisation: Head of Licensing Department, specialising in liquor, entertainment and gaming. Harriet has extensive experience across the range of liquor licensing applications, betting and gaming, theatre and public entertainment licensing. Her licensing portfolio has a wide client base including the leisure and entertainment industries, educational establishments, theatres, department stores and private enterprises across the country.
Prof. Memberships: The Law Society, The Association of Licensing Practitioners and the Licensed Victuallers' Association.
Career: Geography (BSc Hons) Liverpool University; qualified as a solicitor 1980.

WHUR, Paddy
Poppleston Allen, Nottingham
(0115) 953 8500
p.whur@popall.co.uk

Specialisation: Licensing and leisure work, including liquor, public entertainment, betting and gaming and regulatory crime. Firmly established national licensing advocate with recognised expertise in betting and gaming, internet betting, high profile licensing and major leisure/retail developments. Consulted by the government in respect of licensing reform. Clients include many leading industry operators: Butlins/Bourne Leisure, Carluccios, Cowies Bookmakers, First UK Racing, Henry J Beans, James Racing, Ladbrokes, Luminar Leisure, Needwood Racing, PizzaExpress, Scottish & Newcastle, Signature Restaurants, Spirit Group, technologies4tv (formerly randombet.com), Urbium (formerly Chorion plc), Wilson Bowden, Yo!Sushi, various developers and more student unions than any other solicitor.
Prof. Memberships: Law Society; British Institute of Innkeeping.
Career: Qualified 1991. Articled at *Gosschalks*, under Les Green. Moved to *Walker Morris*, Leeds, before joining *Addleshaw Booth & Co*, 1999. Joined *Poppleston Allen* as a partner in April 2002.
Personal: Born 1967; single; resides in Leeds and moving to Nottingham shortly.

WILSON, Robin
Berryman Shacklock, Nottingham
(0115) 945 3700

WOODS, Andrew
Gosschalks, Hull
(01482) 324252

YOUNG, David A
Eversheds, Birmingham
(0121) 232 1000
davidyoung@eversheds.com

Specialisation: Partner in Litigation Department. Acts principally for retail and leisure clients. Work covers all aspects of food, environment, health and safety, product liability and trading law. Acts for a number of recognised operators.
Prof. Memberships: Law Society, Food Law Group.
Career: Qualified in 1984. Became a Partner at *Eversheds* in 1993.
Personal: Born 11 October 1959. Educated at Solihull School 1971-78, University College, London 1978-81 and The College of Law, Chancery Lane 1981-82. Leisure time devoted to his children and partner, sport and travel. Lives Solihull.

LITIGATION GENERAL COMMERCIAL

General Commercial: 517; Banking & Finance: 537; Civil Fraud: 540; Pensions: 542; Real Estate: 544; Profiles: 552

Research approved by BMRB For this edition, **Chambers'** researchers conducted 6,582 interviews – 3,900 with law firms, 511 with barristers and 2,171 with clients. The validity of the research was scrutinised by BMRB International, who audited both the methodology and the results at our offices in London. They interviewed **Chambers'** researchers and cross-checked sample interviews. Details of the audit appear on page 7.

OVERVIEW Whilst commercial litigation is the province of many, there are wide variations across firms as to the organisational approach taken. Some opt for centralised departments, whereas others prefer to deal on an ad hoc basis, plucking individual practitioners from specialised groups to handle matters as they arise. In this section of *Chambers* we feature recognised generalist litigators, undertaking cases across a number of disciplines, as well as specialists in the field of banking and finance, civil fraud, pensions and property litigation. Overall, researchers have detected a continuation of the post-Woolf trend to obviate the need for trials. Whilst the number of disputes is as high as ever, there are real changes in the way they are being handled with ADR, and more especially mediation, increasing the potential for sensible discussion of issues at an early stage. Generally welcomed by all, this has ushered in a new era of co-operation without entirely flushing out the traditional red meat litigators of yesteryear.

LONDON

40+ LITIGATORS

LITIGATION: GENERAL COMMERCIAL (40+ LITIGATORS)
LONDON

1. Herbert Smith
2. Clifford Chance
   Freshfields Bruckhaus Deringer
   Lovells
3. Allen & Overy
4. Linklaters
5. Ashurst Morris Crisp
   Norton Rose
   Simmons & Simmons
   Slaughter and May
6. Barlow Lyde & Gilbert
   CMS Cameron McKenna
   Denton Wilde Sapte
   Richards Butler

This book is the product of 6,582 1/2 hour interviews. See p.7 for BMRB audit. Within each band, firms are listed alphabetically.

HERBERT SMITH (see firm details p.992) Still ahead of the field, albeit by an ever-thinning margin, this firm maintains "*a fantastic branding everybody would kill for*." The practice is felt to stand out by virtue of being driven independently of its corporate base and containing "*litigators who really hold their nerve.*" All forms of litigation are handled by a team of "*tough individuals who always seem to get to the gun first.*" Prominent among these are **David Gold** (see p.558), a "*practitioner with the wow factor who enjoys signal success,*" and department head **Harry Anderson** (see p.552), who is known for his "*rigour and affability.*" Commentators were particularly fulsome regarding **Christa Band** (see p.553), a "*clever and intelligent litigator,*" who is felt to best reflect the more conciliatory side of the practice. Similarly approachable is **Campbell McLachlan** (see p.563), who particularly impresses on public international law and was cited as "*doing with his brain what others do with their brawn.*" **Ted Greeno** (see p.342) ("*one of the best*") continues to be a leader in the energy sector and represented Amoco on the Gorilla V oil platform case, while the "*unnervingly calm*" **Charles Plant** (see p.566) also brings experience to bear in this sector, having recently acted in the BHP Liverpool Bay case for a consortium in relation to claims arising out of a gas reinjection pipeline failure. At the more junior end, **Paula Hodges** (see p.560) is praised by peers for bringing "*exuberance*" to the myriad headline cases that fall to the practice. Examples of the high quality of the firm's work include acting for Fruit Shippers Ltd in the dispute between members of the Noboa family for control of the Fruit Shippers group, and advising British American Tobacco in the context of a lengthy DTI investigation into its activities. **Clients** Arthur Andersen; British American Tobacco; Equitable Life; PwC; BP Amoco; Royal & SunAlliance.

CLIFFORD CHANCE (see firm details p.911) Historically known as a finance firm, the litigation team in this global giant has only truly come to the fore in recent years. Litigation now forms up to 25% of the turnover of a firm whose size and reach allows it to handle complex, multi-jurisdictional work through one centrally co-ordinated team. Its sheer scale means that, as one leading QC put it, "*the team possesses the resources to make a real difference,*" a view endorsed by one client who felt it to be "*excellent for full-blown, heavyweight, no-holds-barred litigation.*" Although some still feel it has not quite the litigation focus to produce a raft of star names, there is no doubting that the team as a whole appears in many of the causes célèbres of the day. **Jeremy Sandelson** (see p.567), for example, has appeared in the Thyssen litigation and is known for "*his charisma, confidence and ability to constantly keep the lines of communication open.*" **Simon Davis** (see p.556) received praise for his "*organisation, tactical awareness and commercial good sense,*" which were displayed on behalf of Philip Morris in a successful action against Rothmans. Active in many keynote cases, the team as a whole has further appeared in the Barings litigation and has acted for Kuwait's oil sector in its major claims to the UNCC for compensation for lost oil and gas production and depletion of resources. **Clients** ABN AMRO; Commerzbank; FSA; Kuwait Petroleum Corporation; Philip Morris; Sumitomo Bank; Whitbread.

FRESHFIELDS BRUCKHAUS DERINGER (see firm details p.964) Not one of the highest profile players a decade or so ago, this team has now "*overwhelmed the market by quality work.*" Differing in approach from great rival Herbert Smith, it is a smaller practice with a "*thoughtful and challenging aspect,*" which concentrates on multimillion pound headline litigation. Clients point to the offering of an "*utterly professional and smooth service;*" it is distinguished from its nearest rivals by having an altogether more youthful team composed of a significant number of lawyers in their thirties and forties. Leading individuals include **Raj Parker** (see p.565), an "*unruffable and well-regarded operator,*" and **Paul Lomas** (see p.562), who is a "*sharp cookie with a real brain.*" Youthful vigour notwithstanding, the team further encompasses respected senior figures such as **Paul Leonard** (see p.562) who is noted for his considered approach. The team also has the satisfaction of drawing upon its first-rate litigators with a more specialist focus, such as Paul Bowden (environment) and Chris Pugh (energy). Representation of Lloyd's in the Jaffray litigation and The Estate of Francis Bacon in its claims against the Marlborough Art Gallery are testament to the practice's ability to attract the choicest work. The firm also acted for the defendant in Amoco v British American Offshore, a dispute concerning the Arbroath oilfield. **Clients** Abbey National; BNFL; FSA; Government of Brunei; ICI; Lloyd's; PowerGen; Rank; Sotheby's.

LOVELLS (see firm details p.1045) Of all the mainstream firms investigated in our research, this was the one many commentators were happiest to deal with. "*More constructive than most,*" it is "*dedicated to seeing the major points*

517

LITIGATION GENERAL COMMERCIAL ■ LONDON

LEADING INDIVIDUALS

★ **GOLD David** Herbert Smith	**STYLE Christopher** Linklaters
1 **ANDERSON Harry** Herbert Smith	**DAVIES Valerie** Norton Rose
GREENO Ted Herbert Smith	**MACKIE David** Allen & Overy
MCLACHLAN Campbell Herbert Smith	**PARKER Raj** Freshfields Bruckhaus Deringer
SANDELSON Jeremy Clifford Chance	
2 **FAGAN Neil** Lovells	
FORDHAM John Stephenson Harwood	
HOUSE Tim Allen & Overy	**LEONARD Paul** Freshfields Bruckhaus Deringer
PEARSON Nick Baker & McKenzie	**PLANT Charles** Herbert Smith
REYNOLDS John McDermott, Will & Emery	**SPARROW Edward** Ashurst Morris Crisp
TAYLOR Tim SJ Berwin	
3 **CANNON Lista** Richards Butler	**GOLDSPINK Robert** Morgan, Lewis & Bockius
GOOD Diana Linklaters	**GRIERSON Christopher** Lovells
HENDERSON Guy Allen & Overy	**KELLY Jonathan** Simmons & Simmons
KING Ronnie Ashurst Morris Crisp	**MICKLETHWAITE Neil** DLA
NICHOLSON Brinsley Linklaters	**SLEIGH Russell** Lovells
TURNBULL John Linklaters	**WATSON Peter** Allen & Overy
YORK Stephen Vinson & Elkins LLP	
4 **BAND Christa** Herbert Smith	**HUMPHRIES Mark** Linklaters
HUNTLEY Graham Lovells	**LOMAS Paul** Freshfields Bruckhaus Deringer
POLLACK Craig SJ Berwin	**SHERRINGTON Patrick** Lovells
TROTTER John Lovells	
5 **ARCHER Nick** Slaughter and May	**BACON Gavin** Simmons & Simmons
DAVIS Simon Clifford Chance	**DE WALDEN Ludovic** Lane & Partners
FINKLER Deborah Slaughter and May	**HEARN Andrew** Dechert
MAGNIN John Nicholson Graham & Jones	**RANDS Harvey** Memery Crystal
SLOWE Richard SJ Berwin	**TOUT Liz** Denton Wilde Sapte
VAUGHAN Philip Simmons & Simmons	
6 **COLE Margaret** White & Case	**FRASER David** Baker & McKenzie
FRIEDMAN Paul Baker & McKenzie	**GILL Judith** Allen & Overy
GRANDISON Richard Slaughter and May	**GRAY Nick** Slaughter and May
HEWETSON Charles Richards Butler	**HODGES Paula** Herbert Smith
MALONEY Tim Eversheds	**SKREIN Michael** Richards Butler
WOOD Jonathan Clyde & Co	

See individuals' profiles p.552

without being unduly aggressive." Described as "*the thinking man's litigators,*" the team is extremely broad in its overall outlook and covers all the main areas, while largely reflecting the firm's bias towards insolvency work. Seen as progressive even before the advent of the Civil Justice Reforms, it places a premium on mediation and ADR, a field in which **Patrick Sherrington** (see p.673) is particularly well known. Touted as equally approachable is **Neil Fagan** (see p.557), "*an old school practitioner always on the lookout for a solution,*" who recently appeared in the Equitable Life litigation. His colleague, the "*meticulous*" **Russell Sleigh** (see p.567), is heavily involved in the Barings litigation and "*never misses a trick,*" while **Christopher Grierson** (see p.558) has impressed many through marshalling a huge team in the BCCI saga. Perennially in the biggest litigation, the firm has also acted for Standard Chartered Bank in an action in deceit against Pakistan National Shipping Company, and has been making the headlines in acting for the institutional shareholders in Railtrack Group, where **Graham Huntley** (see p.560) has proved "*incredibly bright and totally unflappable.*" The team also includes **John Trotter** (see p.683), who is recommended in particular for his environmental work. **Clients** Equitable Life; Granada; Trinity Mirror; BP Amoco; Liquidators of BCCI; Nortel Networks; Xerox.

ALLEN & OVERY (see firm details p.841) This firm, according to one member of the Bar, is "*supremely adept at those massive pieces of litigation that have a life of their own.*" The practice "*feeds off the firm's traditional strength in finance*" and is split into a number of discrete practice groups focusing on specialist areas of work, benefiting in particular with the growth of the corporate department. Incorporating "*a host of first-class people,*" the team is headed up by former barrister **David Mackie QC** who is committed to putting all of his litigators through Higher Rights training. Its leading lights include **Guy Henderson** (see p.559), "*a powerful force with a practical approach,*" and **Tim House** (see p.560), who "*cuts to the chase, unerringly getting to the bottom of the issue.*" **Judith Gill** (see p.558) was, similarly, highly commended, while **Peter Watson** (see p.570), "*an effective litigator who sees the broad horizon,*" was praised for his involvement on a number of litigation-related committees. Client backing was particularly pronounced for this practice with many commenting on the "*useful training courses and general events aimed at the layman's increased understanding.*" A busy year has seen the team appearing for Marlborough International Galleries in the Francis Bacon litigation, and acting for the UK dealers of Mercedes-Benz following the termination notices of their dealership agreements. A further highlight was the representation of First Rand Bank of South Africa in proceedings brought by AIG International in a dispute relating to a joint venture to engage in the gold derivatives business in South Africa. **Clients** British American Tobacco; BT; Citibank; CSFB; Ericsson Mobile Communications; HSBC Bank; Punch Taverns; The Telstar Entertainment Group; William Hill.

LINKLATERS (see firm details p.1043) Unusual for a magic circle firm in having a dual focus on M&A and finance work, this particular quality has afforded the practice involvement in a number of high-end deals. Arbitration remains a key strength here. In terms of size, the team is in a lower league in comparison to some of its arch-rivals but nevertheless "*does very nicely on the back of its corporate reputation.*" Peers agree that it "*undoubtedly contains a number of quality practitioners.*" Chief amongst these is **Christopher Style** (see p.568), "*a gifted black letter lawyer*" with an "*understated but ruthless, tactical approach,*" who has led the team on behalf of Abbey Life's multimillion pound professional negligence claim against Rowe & Maw. **Mark Humphries** (see p.560) has spearheaded the team's commitment to in-house advocacy, and **Diana Good** (see p.558) was involved in acting for Centrica in litigation against HFC Bank. **Brinsley Nicholson** (see p.564) continues to be one of the elder statesmen of the practice, and was praised for his intuitive approach, while **John Turnbull** (see p.569) is recommended for his corporate finance, M&A and professional negligence work. The recent high spot for the team as a whole came in the successful action on behalf of International Power on an appeal before the House of Lords in a landmark pensions litigation case. **Clients** Agency for Restructuring of Credit Organisations; Centrica; International Power; JPMorgan Chase; PwC.

ASHURST MORRIS CRISP (see firm details p.852) Following a year in which this firm has further strengthened its litigation presence on the Continent through strategic alliances, the

LONDON ■ LITIGATION GENERAL COMMERCIAL

London end of the operation remains buoyant. Rivals concluded that this is "*a tactically sound firm with a hands-on approach. Sensible in its dealings, there is no argument for the sake of it.*" Its key players are team leader **Ed Sparrow** (see p.568), who is "*a shrewd and tough negotiator*," and **Ronnie King** (see p.561), a "*quick-witted jack-in-the-box whose instinct is to engender debate.*" Amongst the firm's recent highlights are continued involvement in the Sumitomo and Barings affairs, and representation of TvDanmark on the judicial review of a decision from the ITC relating to listed events on television. The team also represented Railtrack Group on contentious matters concerning its administration. **Clients** Allied Domecq; Canary Wharf; Deutsche Bank; Imperial Tobacco; Motorola; Railtrack Group; Sumitomo.

NORTON ROSE (see firm details p.1084) Viewed by many as "*a genuine litigation practice,*" it is divided into three teams (shipping and insurance/construction/general commercial litigation), each under the stewardship of Peter Rees. Commentators remarked on the very "*detailed approach*" undertaken and a general air of co-operation that results in an "*absence of skirmishing over minor points.*" Unlike other practices it relies less on internal referral and more on the standalone reputation of celebrated lawyers such as **Valerie Davies** (see p.556), who is known for her "*commercial acumen*" and "*good, down-to-earth advice.*" Examples of recent cases include acting in the Equitable Life case and successful representation of the policyholder in the Needler v Taber pensions misselling case. The team has further appeared in the Thyssen case and has advised Braehead in its successful defence of a summary judgment obtained by Bovis. **Clients** ABN AMRO; BNP Paribas; FSA; PwC.

SIMMONS & SIMMONS (see firm details p.1136) This "*group of sensible, straightforward litigators*" concentrates on a smorgasbord of finance, telecom, energy and general commercial matters. Presented overall as "*measured, capable and commercial,*" the team is headed by **Philip Vaughan** (see p.569), "*a strong claimants man and a constructive force for good,*" who acted on the Unilever pensions fund case. **Jonathan Kelly** (see p.561) "*displays a great depth of understanding*" on the banking and financial services side, while **Gavin Bacon**'s (see p.552) "*measured approach*" wins many fans. Well capable of appearing in the largest cases, the team acted for HFC against British Gas and Centrica in a case concerning the Goldfish credit card, and represented clients sued by the US Armco Group in relation to a management buyout. It also acted for Railtrack Group in the Government's application to put Railtrack into administration. **Clients** Amerada Hess; Barclays; Close International Private Banking, Guernsey; HFC Bank; ITC; Railtrack; Shell UK.

SLAUGHTER AND MAY (see firm details p.1140) The firm handles all forms of commercial dispute resolution for a blue-chip client base derived predominantly from the corporate and financial sectors. A different animal to its magic circle rivals, it represents more of "*a lean machine*" in terms of size and handles matters of a highly complex and international nature. Largely seeking to address the needs of its existing clients, while picking up a smaller proportion of work through its litigation reputation *per se*, it relies on an "*elite band of dedicated litigators.*" Its "*sober and assured*" head, **Richard Grandison** (see p.558), is joined by the likes of **Nick Gray** (see p.558), described by clients as a "*tower of strength,*" and **Deborah Finkler** (see p.557), "*a savvy operator who is like a dog with a bone.*" **Nick Archer** (see p.552) was commended by peers for complex litigation, often in the financial sphere. Recent cases have included acting for the liquidators in the Barings saga and representing Unilever Superannuation Trustees in the claim arising out of Mercury Asset Management's mishandling of Unilever's pension fund. The group continues to act for the administrators of Railtrack in all aspects of the Railway Administration proceedings ongoing since October 2001. **Clients** Abbey National; Deutsche Bank; Ernst & Young; Inchcape; Unilever; Willis.

BARLOW LYDE & GILBERT (see firm details p.858) A process of diversification has seen this firm move towards areas such as IT, banking, aviation and shipping. Inevitably, however, its litigation capability continues to be founded on a bedrock of insurance, reinsurance and professional negligence. Cited by users as being "*efficient and good value for money,*" this reputation has seen the firm in recent years attracting new clients of the calibre of National Express and Dixons solely on the basis of its name for litigation. The move to pure mainstream litigation, however, remains as yet unfulfilled in terms of its market profile, although retention on the panels of the likes of Del Monte, Hutchison 3G and Bank of America bodes well for the future. Led by David Arthur, the team has continued its lead role on behalf of Cooper & Lybrand in respect of the Barings litigation, and has acted for Metro Trading in the Glencore v Metro Trading litigation in the Commercial Court. It has also advised Premier Product Tankers in a dispute with US bond holders over a fleet of six 'H' class product tankers. **Clients** Dixons; Ernst & Young; National Express; PwC.

CMS CAMERON MCKENNA (see firm details p.914) Praised by clients as "*industrious and clear-thinking,*" this team of "*tough-minded individuals*" scored well in our research in its focus areas of construction, insolvency and insurance. Although the team does not have the vast portfolio of corporate clients enjoyed by its rivals, its ambitions outside its traditional core areas are evident, with banking, for example, providing a fertile source of work. Recent cases include acting for German investment bank DEG in long-running litigation concerning its investment in a large-scale farming project in Zambia. The team also acted in High Court proceedings on claims against London & Regional companies arising out of an agreement for lease for the redevelopment of the Crystal Palace site. **Clients** DSND Subsea; First Union National Bank; Post Office.

DENTON WILDE SAPTE (see firm details p.935) Versatility is the key here. Capabilities exist in the areas of energy, banking, media, sports, insolvency and insurance: this practice can truly live up to its reputation as "*one of the better generalists.*" Rivals commented on the partners' complaisant natures, agreeing that **Liz Tout**, in particular, is "*pragmatic and takes things in well,*" qualities recently displayed on behalf of the defendant in the case of ScottishPower v ELEXON. Well capable of attracting big-ticket litigation, the firm has acted for major insurance market participant AIG Europe in the high-profile film finance insurance disputes and represented Crédit Lyonnais in the $200 million dispute between Glencore International and Metro Trading International. **Clients** AIG; Copyright Licensing Agency; Crédit Lyonnais; Kroll Buchler Philips; Royal Bank of Scotland.

RICHARDS BUTLER (see firm details p.1112) This practice has a much greater scope than its traditional shipping and insurance tag would suggest. The department provides up to 50% of the firm's work and is notionally split into three teams: finance and banking, media and technology, and professional negligence and employment. In reality, however, the team acts as one and was commended by clients as being "*highly responsive in time-critical situations.*" Possessing a slightly different ethos to some, clients point to "*a feel of true partner involvement in every case,*" which many found reassuring. The team is led by **Charles Hewetson** (see p.559) and features **Lista Cannon** (see p.554), who is "*superb at thinking right the way round a problem,*" and **Michael Skrein** (see p.567) whose "*true forte lies in media cases.*" Its recent highlights include acting for DaimlerChrysler UK in defending litigation arising out of its decision to restructure its car distribution system. It continues to act on a regular basis for Bar Mutual Indemnity Fund and advises FACT (Federation Against Copyright Theft). **Clients** Bar Mutual Indemnity Fund; BBC; Channel 4; DaimlerChrysler UK; Gerrard; PwC.

www.ChambersandPartners.com

LITIGATION GENERAL COMMERCIAL ■ LONDON

LONDON
FEWER THAN 40 LITIGATORS

LITIGATION: GENERAL COMMERCIAL (FEWER THAN 40 LITIGATORS)
■ LONDON

1
- Baker & McKenzie
- SJ Berwin

2
- Dechert
- Eversheds
- Gouldens
- Stephenson Harwood

3
- Clyde & Co
- D J Freeman
- Nabarro Nathanson
- Nicholson Graham & Jones

4
- Berwin Leighton Paisner
- Macfarlanes
- Mayer, Brown, Rowe & Maw
- Reynolds Porter Chamberlain
- Taylor Wessing
- Travers Smith Braithwaite

5
- Hammond Suddards Edge
- Ince & Co
- Lawrence Graham
- Theodore Goddard

6
- Charles Russell
- Lane & Partners
- Lewis Silkin
- Masons
- Memery Crystal
- Mishcon de Reya
- Pinsent Curtis Biddle
- Shook, Hardy & Bacon
- Watson, Farley & Williams
- White & Case

This book is the product of 6,582 1/2 hour interviews. See p.7 for BMRB audit.
Within each band, firms are listed alphabetically.

BAKER & McKENZIE (see firm details p.855) Unsurprisingly, considering its worldwide reach, this firm has a reputation for involvement in multi-jurisdictional disputes. The litigation department proper concentrates on general breach of contract and commercial problems, dispensing advice in an "*effective and concise*" manner. Head of the group **Nick Pearson** (see p.565) is an "*excellent team co-ordinator*" who continues to display his "*organisational genius*" in the byzantine Grupo Torras fraud litigation. Supporting him are **David Fraser** (see p.557) and **Paul Friedman** (see p.557), who is "*commercially minded and results-oriented.*" In the past year, the team has undertaken two commercial disputes for a major sports retailer and represented Cooper Industries in an action against Emess arising out of the acquisition of the latter's JSB electrical goods distribution business. **Clients** Sony; JPMorgan; Intel; Grupo Torras; Cooper Industries; Ingram Micro.

SJ BERWIN (see firm details p.867) Unanimously regarded as correctly placed at the top of our tables, this "*tight, professional outfit*" continues to attract high-quality work. Its caseload, a third of which emanates from outside the firm, comprises of fraud, shipping, shareholder and regulatory disputes, and general interlocutory applications. Once again, commentators described a distinct slant towards international disputes, the result of contacts cultivated with lawyers in foreign jurisdictions. At the helm is **Tim Taylor** (see p.568), a "*mercurial and marvellous figure*" who combines well with the "*doughty and tenacious*" **Richard Slowe** (see p.567) and **Craig Pollack** (see p.566), a "*blunt speaker whose drive is tempered with an openness to negotiation.*" Matters successfully handled by the team include representing The Walton Group in its dispute with Liverpool City Council over the interpretation of an agreement to enter into a lease in the Chavasse Park retail development. The firm also acted for Dalmore Holdings in a complex dispute over the ownership and produce of 14 fishing super-trawlers. **Clients** ANZ Investment Bank; Carlton Television; Diageo, Express Newspapers; Marks & Spencer; SES ASTRA.

DECHERT (see firm details p.934) With a foot in camps as diverse as property, insurance, IP, insolvency and defamation, this is a firm that was readily identifiable by its peers. "*Tough and gritty competition,*" the team garnered many plaudits as lead lawyers in the Abacha case, where it "*handled the most complex litigation imaginable quite beautifully.*" It possesses strong US links and has in **Andrew Hearn** (see p.559) "*a personable and tireless performer*" who has been championing mediation and ADR. Recent highlights for the firm include acting for ELONEX in a multi-jurisdictional dispute against the likes of Dell, Sony and Philips. **Clients** Abacha family; Dixons; ELONEX; Oasis Group; Telegraph Newspapers; William Hill.

EVERSHEDS (see firm details p.949) Well-known nationally, but less so in London itself, this firm was described by clients as "*aggressive in style but easy on the pocket.*" It has the capability to draw on large numbers of lawyers, including the "*bright*" **Tim Maloney** (see p.562), making it well able to handle the larger matters in its core areas of media, insurance and the financial sectors. Respected for the international flavour of the practice, it acted for Jardine and Heath, two global insurance brokers, in a series of claims relating to film financing, and has also had a role in the Abacha case. The firm also acted as sole advisors to the Government in defence of claims arising out of the foot-and-mouth epidemic. **Clients** DEFRA; Heath Lambert Group; Twenty First Artists; Jardine Lloyd Thompson Group; Clariden Bank.

GOULDENS (see firm details p.976) "*A high-quality, economic alternative to the larger firms.*" Operating around a general commercial core, much of the work is on behalf of financial institutions incorporating a specialism in actions on behalf of banks and hedge funds in proceedings against sovereign states. Hailed by clients as "*tough and technically adept,*" the Bar confirms that "*this is a firm one cannot take lightly.*" Key cases include a success in the Court of Appeal on behalf of Credit Suisse First Boston in setting aside court orders under the Hague Evidence Convention. The team, which includes Craig Shuttleworth, also concluded a successful mediation in settlement of claims brought by the executors of Matthew Harding's estate against PricewaterhouseCoopers and Benfield Greig. **Clients** Credit Suisse First Boston; Sir Robert McAlpine; Norwich Union; PEMEX.

STEPHENSON HARWOOD (see firm details p.1147) This firm is "*always on the lookout for a tactical advantage and never guilty of letting cases go to sleep,*" acknowledged a barrister. The firm draws most of its caseload from the financial services industry but further busies itself in sectors as diffuse as IP, employment, fraud and shipping. **John Fordham** (see p.557) heads up affairs and was lauded as a "*courteous, ideas man and a redoubtable fighter.*" Building on the firm's reputation for asset tracing, his team acted for City of Westminster in pursuit of £26 million ordered by the District Auditor. Other cases include continued involvement in the Abacha affair and an action on behalf of Prost Grand Prix against Jaguar Racing and Pedro de la Rosa. **Clients** Noga; Christie's; Getronics; Royal Bank of Scotland.

CLYDE & CO (see firm details p.913) Years of involvement in the shipping and international insurance markets have culminated in this practice being "*very much at home in multi-jurisdictional disputes.*" It also handles financial services-related litigation and maintains strong contacts with the DTI. **Jonathan Wood** (see p.571) has built his name on insurance work but has now successfully metamorphosed, as the Bar commented, into "*a strong generalist who provides well-ordered briefs.*" His recent cases include acting for the Turkish Government on an insurance claim relating to the construction of the Anatolian Highway, a matter where the client recovered $110 million. The team has also appeared in a £2 million retention of title case arising out of the Kingswood insolvency. **Clients** CGU; EULER Trade Indemnity; Export Credits Guarantee Department; NCM Credit Insurance.

D J FREEMAN (see firm details p.939) Having enjoyed prominence in the Hamilton v Al Fayed litigation, this firm continues to secure a role in

LONDON ■ LITIGATION GENERAL COMMERCIAL

a healthy number of headline cases. Described as "*dedicated, hard-working and thoughtful,*" the team, led by Kevin Perry, has had roles in both the Abacha and the recent film financing cases, where it acted for AXA, the insurer with the largest involvement. Relatively eclectic in approach, the practice has nurtured relationships with the likes of Invensys, Corus and Shell for whom it handles contractual disputes involving substantial sums of money. **Clients** Corus; Harrods; Invensys; Shell International.

NABARRO NATHANSON (see firm details p.1080) "*Focused and diligent,*" this compact team handles general company and commercial litigation with a slant towards shareholder disputes and cross-border litigation. Its international ambitions are reaping success, with its continuing role as advisor to the US Securites and Exchange Commission on a variety of matters. Examples of its prowess in shareholder disputes include actions on behalf of Nottingham Forest and NewMedia SPARK in its Section 459 Petition against a variety of defendants in the technology and telecommunications sector. **Clients** Eaton Corporation; Granada; International Management Group; US Securities and Exchange Commission; Trans World International.

NICHOLSON GRAHAM & JONES (see firm details p.1083) Travel, sport, banking, financial services and insolvency-related matters form the staple diet of this "*dependable practice.*" Clients adverted to the team's "*instinctive understanding of business*" and felt it to be "*a highly cost-effective alternative to the bigger players.*" Recommended here is **John Magnin** (see p.562), said to have "*a practical approach and a gift for understanding the cardinal issues in a case.*" Recent key cases for the firm include acting for ABTA in successfully appealing a decision of the Director General of Fair Trading forcing ABTA members with involvement with travel insurance to become members of GISC. The team has also acted for Dame Shirley Porter in the Westminster Council 'Homes for Votes' case, and advised Ryder Cup Ltd on the consequences of the postponement of the 2001 Ryder Cup. **Clients** Windsor Life; Sanyo Industries; British Film Institute; Six Continents; Britvic; Ryder Cup Ltd.

BERWIN LEIGHTON PAISNER (see firm details p.866) Last year's merger now having bedded in, the fruits of this marriage have become apparent. Existing litigation capability has been enhanced by the injection of insurance expertise and the experience of ex-Paisner partners in dealing with entrepreneurs of the likes of Forte. Commercial instructions have increased in volume and the IP, IT and media markets are being pushed to the fore. Clients welcome the "*unambiguous advice*" on offer and "*the knack of keeping feet firmly on the ground.*" Significant cases include acting for WestLB in the defence of proceedings issued concerning a letter of credit claim in connection with the collapse of Enron. It has further been involved in a professional negligence claim in relation to advice given to NMEC over the roofing contract for the Millennium Dome. **Clients** Chorion; Courts; Del Monte Foods International; Forte; Lillywhites; Southern Water; Tesco Stores.

MACFARLANES (see firm details p.1047) One rival commented that this firm "*offers as high quality a service as the magic circle but at a fraction of the price.*" Drawing on a strong corporate base, the litigation department largely services existing clients, while further specialising in property, IP and employment matters. Its reputation is such, however, that it can attract standalone work, obtaining, for example, a role in the AIG affair advising on fraud proceedings arising out of investments in privatisations in Azerbaijan. Other matters include acting in the British Airways Pension Trustees case and the Eastgate/Hambro Legal Protection litigation. The group, led by Willie Manners, has also appeared in the injunction proceedings and trial on behalf of ICAP against one of its senior brokers who was seeking to join Cantor Fitzgerald International. **Clients** AIG; Eastgate Group; Pret A Manger; Anheuser-Busch; JD Wetherspoon; Carlton; Cordiant; Kingfisher; KirchGruppe; Walkers Snack Foods.

MAYER, BROWN, ROWE & MAW (see firm details p.1060) This year's merger adds further scope to a practice already engaged in big-ticket litigation. Now with a pronounced US capability, its main areas comprise pensions, financial services, banking and insolvency. Examples of recent international work include acting for Bank of America in the BCCI litigation, and successfully concluding 12 years of work in the Magill v Porter Westminster Council 'Homes for Votes' case. The team, jointly headed by David Allen and Sean Connolly, has also acted for Bull Information Systems in a £42 million claim by Consignia for alleged breach of contract. **Clients** Argos; Associated British Foods; AstraZeneca; Bank of America; EMI; NBC; Trinity Mirror Group; Unilever.

REYNOLDS PORTER CHAMBERLAIN (see firm details p.1111) Insurance-based work and all its myriad facets lie at the foundations of this "*constructive, commercial and proactive practice.*" Once closely linked to SIF work, it is now involved in more dispute work including shareholder, contract, fraud and product liability cases. In the last year it has acted for the shareholders of Dalkia in a £5 million environmental dispute with a local authority over a waste to heat conversion plant. The firm, which houses Duncan Harman-Wilson, also represented Saint-Gobain Glass UK in a major claim arising out of the construction of one of their factories. **Clients** Associated Newspapers; AstraZeneca; AXA Sun Life; Christie's; Vivendi.

TAYLOR WESSING (see firm details p.1156) Clients rate this as "*a straight, hard-nosed litigation team who are good if you need a fire putting out.*" Sophisticated litigation is handled in arbitration, fraud corruption, insolvency and to an increasing extent in the TMT sector, where the downturn has led to a growth in insolvency and dispute resolution work. Recent highlights include acting for Casio Computer Company in a $30 million fraud case involving 18 defendants, and successfully representing VK Vinters in a claim against its director for wrongful trading. The team, led by Neil White, has also been instructed by the NFU on behalf of members in group litigation relating to non-payment of subsidies by DEFRA. **Clients** Casio Computer Company; GE Capital Commercial Finance; Lloyds TSB; Psion; National Farmers' Union; Toyota (GB).

TRAVERS SMITH BRAITHWAITE (see firm details p.1166) Rivals perceive this team as "*guaranteeing a hard fight.*" It has an eye firmly fixed on the international market, receiving a number of referrals and possessing an on the ground presence in both Paris and Berlin. The bulwark of the practice remains financial services work, although increased activity has been espied in the IP and TMT sectors of late. The department, headed by John Kingston, undertook complex multinational litigation for a Russian corporate client concerning disputed ownership of oilfields in Siberia to a value of $500 million. It also acted for First ANZ Modaraba in pursuing $6 million of finance lease charges against a publicly quoted firm in Bangladesh, and has recently concluded proceedings on behalf of a 'big five' accountancy firm involving a claim of alleged negligence in connection with an investment made by venture capitalists in a public company. **Clients** Interros Holding Company; MGN Pension Trustees; Lloyds Disciplinary Committee.

HAMMOND SUDDARDS EDGE Constituting the second biggest department in the firm, the litigation team, headed by Simon Price, handles disputes in the fields of energy, telecoms, fraud, media and advertising. In addition, its incorporation of Townleys has led to a yet stronger footing in sports work where it has represented The Football League in relation to the question of financial irregularities at Chesterfield FC. Other highlights include advising a client on allegations of corruption regarding a $20 million procurement contract in Africa. It also acted for an energy generator operator over a dispute relating to one of its power stations. **Clients** Amateur Boxing Association; Banking Ombudsman; British Energy; The Football League; One 2 One; Viatel.

INCE & CO (see firm details p.1008) Shipping and insurance provide the bread-and-butter caseload of this practice, although other fields such as construction, fraud, partnership and telecoms feature. Its marine expertise inevitably

LITIGATION GENERAL COMMERCIAL ■ LONDON

exposes the practice to work of an international nature and makes it one of the main users to be found in the Commercial Court. Led by Peter Rogan, the firm has acted on a number of breach of warranty claims arising out of the sale and purchase of businesses ranging in value from £700,000 to $202 million. It also acted on behalf of the liquidators of HIH in a dispute between a creditor and the estate, as to whether the proceeds of an LOC draw down are available to the creditor. **Clients** BNP Paribas; ABN AMRO; Fyffes International; Royal & SunAlliance; Hong Kong Shanghai Bank.

LAWRENCE GRAHAM (see firm details p.1031) An old-established firm with a relatively blue-chip client base, it handles financial, property and contractual warranty claims. "*Efficient and easy to deal with,*" the firm has, to boot, a not insignificant body of US clients. For example, it has acted in the Roto Packing Materials case for an Oman-based trading family defrauded by way of secret commissions by former directors. The group has also appeared for DiaSys, a US- and UK-based manufacturer and worldwide supplier of biomedical products, in relation to breaches by the UK directors and employees of contractual and fiduciary duties. Pam Bryan is the leader of the group. **Clients** Scottish & Newcastle; AXA PPP Healthcare; Eastgate.

THEODORE GODDARD (see firm details p.1158) Strong in a broad spectrum of industries, ranging from institutional banking through to fraud, media, product liability and pharmaceuticals. Led by Monica Burch, the team was praised for its "*versatility and commercialism.*" It has been active on behalf of The Law Debenture Trust Corporation, the largest single creditor of Railtrack and Barings. It also acted for Dimpco in an action brought against Hoover for breach of contract, and represented a Swiss bank in relation to a $10 million trade finance facility rendered to a bunkering business, which became insolvent in the oil crash of 1998. **Clients** Anglo Irish Bank; Crédit Agricole Indosuez; Diageo; GlaxoSmithKline; The Times; Ryanair.

CHARLES RUSSELL (see firm details p.904) Complementing specialist insurance, clinical negligence and IP teams, the core commercial litigation department here is staffed by a "*collection of fine generalists*" and includes John Sykes. It has a particular name in the TMT arena, where clients value its "*industry knowledge, enthusiasm and fast turnaround of papers.*" It has, for some time, represented Gary Kemp (Spandau Ballet) in the protection of his copyrights and has advised Hello! magazine on claims by Michael Douglas and Catherine Zeta-Jones that paparazzi photographs of their wedding breached their privacy. The team has also advised ntl in relation to the judicial review decision by a Crown Court Judge to apply PACE 1984 rather than RIPA 2000, an issue of major interest to major ISPs. **Clients** ntl; Hello!; Gary Kemp; Scoot.com; Cable & Wireless; Sotheby's.

LANE & PARTNERS (see firm details p.1028) This firm's litigation practice is synonymous with its lead lawyer **Ludovic de Walden** (see p.556), who is known for his "*charisma and approachability.*" It has achieved its strong reputation by trading off a "*great client base for a small firm*" and offering a high level of partner input. Rare in having a specialism in art world litigation, he is also something of a generalist who acts for a number of Lloyd's Underwriters. **Clients** Corporates and corporate subsidiaries; private individuals.

LEWIS SILKIN (see firm details p.1041) This compact department, led by Tom Coates, concerns itself with contract, breach of warranty, partnership, utilities and shareholder disputes. It has a strong link with Mohamed Al Fayed, having represented him personally on a claim for damages against the Commissioner of Police for wrongful arrest in relation to a safe deposit at Harrods, hired by Tiny Rowland. It also undertakes litigation on behalf of Harrods itself, having defended it against a £27 million claim by Suisse American for an alleged wrongful termination of a licence agreement. Other matters include defending GE Capital IT Solutions against a British Airways claim for unpaid fees following a contract to install systems for the airline's worldwide cargo operation. **Clients** Al Fayed; Bass Group; Bonhams; House of Fraser; London Electricity Group; Telegraph Group; Trafficmaster.

MASONS (see firm details p.1057) Portrayed as "*the contractor's standard choice for litigation,*" the firm inevitably devotes a large contingent of its resources to servicing clients in this field. It has, however, succeeded in widening its reach and can boast expertise in IT, contract and sale of goods, and energy disputes, where it has represented major international utilities in determining adjustments to the pricing formula in long-term energy supply agreements. The team, which includes Ray Werbicki, acted for a Nigerian insurers' consortium against Aon in claiming $13 million arising from the placement of risk on the London market, of the assets of the Nigerian National Petroleum Company. It also represented Courage in a test case before the European Court of Justice in a matter concerning the tie-in provisions in leases of public houses. **Clients** Babcock International Group; Courage; TXU Europe Group; ICL; Pathfinder Properties.

MEMERY CRYSTAL (see firm details p.1067) "*A small colony of dedicated litigators,*" managing a "*focused, niche corporate practice.*" Insurance, regulatory, shareholder and media litigation are all undertaken, although peers point especially to the firm's expertise in specialist fraud work. **Harvey Rands** (see p.566) particularly shines in this field, adopting a "*pugnacious*" style. **Clients** Lloyd's Underwriters; Morant; Seymour Pearce & Ellis; Wembley Corporation.

MISHCON DE REYA (see firm details p.1072) Characterised by its impressive private client base, this firm handles fraud, employment, media and entertainment, and defamation-based work in the main. An "*energetic bunch,*" the Bar rates the team, headed by Larry Nathan, as "*the bee's knees for fraud claimant work*" where it has been retained by Microsoft to assist on its European strategy for anti-counterfeiting. Cases include Breasy Medical Equipment & Ors v Hayek, concerning breach of confidentiality obligations and allegations of passing off. It has also acted for Lord Hanson and the McAlpine family in resisting claims for contributions towards Mohamed Al Fayed's costs in defending Neil Hamilton's unsuccessful libel action. **Clients** Auto Credit Trust; Blacks Leisure Group; Euromoney Institutional Investor; Lord Archer; Lord Hanson; Microsoft; Sir Robert McAlpine.

PINSENT CURTIS BIDDLE (see firm details p.1102) Continuing to reap the benefits of its recent merger, this practice has extended its scope to include contract, shareholder, fraud, professional negligence, product liability and breach of warranty disputes. The London office operates in the context of a national network, and, enjoying the relative rarity of in-house forensic accountancy capability, has had a role over the years in cases of the scale of Maxwell, BCCI and Equitable Life. More recently, the team, which is fronted by Bill Dixon, has acted for the defendant in Dubai Aluminium v Salaam, a $10 million appeal case, and has appeared in the multimillion pound litigation arising out of the collapse of Metro Trading. **Clients** Alexander Forbes; Bar Mutual; 3663; Cedar; Dawson.

SHOOK, HARDY & BACON (see firm details p.1132) The result of a merger between Arnander Irvine & Zietman and US firm Shook, Hardy & Bacon, this is something of a peculiarity in our tables, being a specialist commercial litigation and IP firm that eschews other types of work. The firm targets the referral market, picking up work from firms outside the jurisdiction and those in this country who find themselves conflicted. Commentators highlighted the practice's aptitude in complex fraud litigation and those matters of an international character. It has acted for DaimlerChrysler Canada and its pensions fund in a substantial multi-jurisdictional fraud claim, and represented Purolite International in a major dispute with the EBRD. It also represented RIT Capital in connection with a conspiracy involving a claim against the client and others to the value of $240 million. **Clients** AIG Europe; Bio-Tek Instruments; Cedar Group; DaimlerChrysler; Pillsbury Europe; Swiftcall; 3D Aluminium.

LONDON/THE SOUTH ■ LITIGATION GENERAL COMMERCIAL

WATSON, FARLEY & WILLIAMS (see firm details p.1181) Readily associated by its peers with shipping litigation, this perception doesn't tell the whole story. Finance litigation, international arbitration, construction and offshore oil and gas also form a healthy slice of a practice that often pits itself against the biggest names in the field. It has defended International Industrial Bank on an international arbitration claim valued at CHF200 million brought by Deutsche Bank, and represented Vivendi in a shareholder dispute with Deutsche Telekom over a controlling block of shares in PTC, Central Europe's largest mobile phone operator. The group also acted for Petroleum Geo-Services in ongoing litigation arising out of the Banff Field FPSO project in the North Sea. **Clients** Advance Agro; Bankgesellschaft Berlin; Petroleum Geo-Services.

WHITE & CASE (see firm details p.1185) "*In the vanguard of the US firms*," this department is "*beginning to cement its reputation after a comparatively short time in the market.*" Drawing its lifeblood from its bedrock of impressive clients, it displays a pronounced slant towards banking and finance issues and is led by the "*conciliatory and sensible*" **Margaret Cole** (see p.555). Cases include acting for International Finance Corporation against Utexafrica in a claim based on an alleged moratorium arising from the political and economic situation in the Congo. It has also acted for LuK, a large car parts manufacturer, in a Commercial Court action concerning the transfer to a joint venture company of a patent portfolio. **Clients** IBM; Lloyds TSB; EBRD; IFC; Skanska.

OTHER NOTABLE PRACTITIONERS John Reynolds (see p.566) of McDermott, Will & Emery is characterised as "*an attentive lawyer who provides an iron fist in a velvet glove,*" while Neil Micklethwaite (see p.563) of DLA received warm recommendation for his involvement in complex cases. Robert Goldspink (see p.474) of Morgan Lewis & Bockius impresses as "*astute and pleasant to deal with*" and is warmly endorsed alongside Stephen York (see p.76) of Vinson & Elkins LLP whose "*foresight and ability to come up with solutions*" was widely commented upon.

THE SOUTH

LITIGATION: GENERAL COMMERCIAL
■ THE SOUTH

[1] **Blake Lapthorn** Fareham, Southampton
[2] **Bond Pearce** Southampton
    Cripps Harries Hall Tunbridge Wells
    DMH Brighton
    Thomas Eggar Chichester, Reigate, Worthing
[3] **asb law** Crawley, Maidstone
    Brachers Maidstone
    Clyde & Co Guildford
    Lester Aldridge Bournemouth
    Paris Smith & Randall Southampton
    Stevens & Bolton Guildford
[4] **Barlows** Guildford
    Charles Russell Guildford
    Shoosmiths Fareham

LEADING INDIVIDUALS

[1] **ASPINALL Tim** DMH
   MURFITT Stephen Blake Lapthorn
   THOMSON Clive Paris Smith & Randall

This book is the product of 6,582 1/2 hour interviews. See p.7 for BMRB audit. Within each band, firms are listed alphabetically. See individuals' profiles p.552

BLAKE LAPTHORN (see firm details p.877) Competitors agree that this firm remains the main player in the region due to its depth of "*talented litigators*" and imposing client portfolio. Describing the team as "*honourable,*" one interviewee stated that it "*is pleasant to deal with and doesn't cut corners.*" Extremely knowledgeable, its practitioners can also draw on the firm's expertise in various fields, including construction, insolvency, pensions and export credit, while its merger with Sherwin Oliver is providing the team with growing amounts of IP and IT-related work. The downturn in the telecoms market has led to an increased amount of telecoms litigation, and the group continues to prosecute cases before the Disciplinary Committee of the General Optical Council. Although David Higham is no longer visible in the market, **Stephen Murfitt** is filling his shoes: peers commend him as "*able, methodical and consistent; he doesn't compromise standards.*" **Clients** Alcatel; General Optical Council; Kerry Group; GB Holiday Parks.

BOND PEARCE (see firm details p.879) "*Principal players*" in the South West, according to some sources, the firm's bases in Bristol, Plymouth and Exeter give it an enviable spread. The team, led by Tony Askham, handles a wide range of litigation, including minority shareholder disputes, pensions and IP litigation. The Plymouth and Exeter offices boast expertise in dealer recovery claims, having gained much experience working for Peugeot Wholesale, while the Bristol office concentrates on pensions, insolvency and EC-related litigation and has seen considerable expansion over the past year. The firm is representing one of the largest road transport companies in the UK in connection with matters arising from a pension scheme merger, and recently assisted Swansea City AFC in its successful defence of a hostile administration petition. **Clients** Gul International; Peugeot Wholesale; Post Office; Epwin; The National Trust; Pennon Group.

CRIPPS HARRIES HALL (see firm details p.922) A big hit with competitors and clients alike, this firm is a "*big commercial presence*" in the region. It continues to undertake large numbers of warranty claims arising from the sale of businesses, while the acquisition of Peter Garry strengthens the firm's capacity in the area of partnership disputes. The department handles work on behalf of a wide variety of clients, much of it standalone work won by virtue of the team's outstanding reputation. Sizeable recent cases include a $10 million breach of contract dispute with a Czech investment fund. It also represented a high-street bank in pursuing former partners of a dissolved law firm to recover loans worth £10 million. **Clients** High-street bank; football club manager; US manufacturing company.

DMH (see firm details p.940) A high-profile operation covering a broad base of commercial disputes, the team is headed by "*pleasant and experienced*" **Tim Aspinall** (see p.552). Its caseload typically involves contractual and shareholder conflicts for its top-flight client base of large and medium-sized corporates and public bodies, as well as contentious work in its niche area of factoring and invoice discounting. It is currently acting for a manufacturer of Formula 1 components in a product liability issue. Another recent highlight is its work for a major bank in a commercial action against a technology company. **Clients** Arcadia Group; Thomson Intermedia; Capital Radio; GMAC Commercial Credit; KPMG; Croydon London Borough Council; University of Sussex.

THOMAS EGGAR (see firm details p.1160) This "*big player*" is respected in the market for combining a traditional, established image with up-to-the-minute expertise. Its commercial litigation practice is divided between different offices, with Worthing focusing on insolvency and cross-border asset tracking, while Reigate undertakes major one-off litigation and Chichester provides a more general commercial service including fringe litigious activities such as licensing. As a whole, the firm has strength in professional negligence, shareholder and partnership disputes and international fraud. Tom McKeown heads the department from the London office. **Clients** Building societies.

ASB LAW (see firm details p.851) The commercial litigation team of what competitors

523

www.ChambersandPartners.com

LITIGATION GENERAL COMMERCIAL ■ THE SOUTH/THAMES VALLEY

consider a "*major force in the region*" has undergone restructuring of late, divesting itself of its property litigation unit and hiring two new partners. Areas of expertise include commercial fraud, shareholder disputes and IP-related litigation. Over the past year the team has been involved in some large and complex work, such as assisting a multinational aircraft supplier in a dispute with a Columbian airline, representing a tour operator in a food poisoning group action, and acting for a receiver in obtaining a freezing injunction and disclosure orders against a former matron of a nursing home. The department is headed by Andrew Pawlik. **Clients** An aircraft supplier; a tour operator.

BRACHERS (see firm details p.886) This "*methodical and sensible*" outfit is headed by John Sheath. Its litigation strength is bolstered by a superb debt recovery practice, which has assisted the team in winning important clients like Eurotunnel, while an increase in corporate and commercial instructions throughout the firm has generated new commercial litigation challenges. The team focuses on insurance-related work and has represented insurer clients in resisting fraudulent fire and flood claims. Other important recent cases include claims against retailers, local authorities and two airlines. It has also acted in a successful challenge to the UK Government against security directions imposed contrary to the Treaty of Canterbury and Sangatte protocol. **Clients** Eurotunnel; FirstAssist.

CLYDE & CO (see firm details p.913) The Guildford branch of this City firm is known in the market as a quality operation. It boasts the capacity to represent big-ticket clients on high-value claims, often with an international element. With an efficient operation at the volume debt recovery end, a large proportion of its commercial litigation is insurance-driven, though its broad expertise encompasses insurance fraud, jurisdiction disputes, IP and energy litigation. Art is an interesting niche area for the firm; it has been involved in litigation surrounding artefacts from the Middle East. The team, led by Jonathan Wood, also recently acted in a $500 million case concerning the destruction of an oil rig. **Clients** Oracle; Dell; Carphone Warehouse; Glencore; Tate & Lyle; East Point Holdings.

LESTER ALDRIDGE (see firm details p.1038) The firm has built up a good name for itself and is said by competitors to "*attract quality work by virtue of its reputation.*" Areas of specialism include construction technology, product liability and insurance, and it has recently acted in a spate of freezing orders involving alleged theft of clients' money by senior company employees. The increasingly international flavour of its work has seen the team tackle cases in the US, Canada, Nigeria, Pakistan and South Korea, as well as European countries. It advises a number of football clubs on the rescue and restructuring of their businesses after its success with Bournemouth FC. Richard Byrne and Michael Giddins lead the team. **Clients** McCarthy & Stone.

PARIS SMITH & RANDALL (see firm details p.1093) This practice has impressed competitors with its "*professional and diligent*" approach. It was praised to researchers for producing work of a consistently high quality, and boasts particular strength in insolvency-related claims. **Clive Thomson** is considered a good litigator and a "*safe pair of hands.*" Major recent instructions have included acting for the local port authority on licensing and liability matters, and representing three company directors in relation to proceedings brought by the DTI under the Company Director's Disqualification Act. **Clients** ABP; Southampton Institute; Radfords, Licensed Insolvency Practitioners; Mondial Assistance (UK).

STEVENS & BOLTON (see firm details p.1149) A solid and consistent outfit, with "*realistic and commercial*" lawyers; peers say simply "*good name, good firm.*" It has recently consolidated its commercial litigation operation, and is now based entirely in Guildford, where it acts in a range of work, including contractual and M&A-related disputes. Richard King heads a department that has recently assisted an international pharmaceutical company in recovering £6 million, along with IP rights worth £20 million, from ex-employees. It has also represented a consortium, including Europe's largest construction company, in an action against Portsmouth City Council concerning an abortive millennium tower project. **Clients** WS Atkins Group; Unilever; Gerling Namur Insurances of Credit.

BARLOWS A "*pleasant and helpful*" outfit, according to competitors, which includes Hamish Cameron-Blackie. Its profile is highest in connection with construction, design rights and general IP-related litigation. Clients range from public authorities and local retailers to construction companies, for which it has recently handled work relating to the supply of defective concrete. Expertise in mediation bolsters its contentious offering. **Clients** Retailers; public authorities; construction companies.

CHARLES RUSSELL (see firm details p.904) The Guildford team enters our tables this year after enthusiastic recommendations for its "*able, professional approach.*" Competitors rated it as a growing force in the region, while clients raved about its "*fantastic work; it has the ability to handle complex financial cases.*" The team, which is led by Duncan Elson, conducts a wide range of commercial disputes and debt recovey actions for clients from sectors including technology, transport and financial services. **Clients** Local and national corporates.

SHOOSMITHS (see firm details p.1133) Recommended for the efficiency with which it handles a high volume of work, the Fareham office of this national operation excels in IP litigation and boasts a broad practice including lots of contractual disputes. Professional indemnity also generates a substantial caseload, and the team is handling an increasing number of adjudications under the Housing Grants Act. Richard Cook heads the department. **Clients** Shaftfield Group; Toys 'R' Us; Letsure; Spicer Haart; Wates Residential.

THAMES VALLEY

LITIGATION: GENERAL COMMERCIAL
■ **THAMES VALLEY**

1. **Clarks** Reading
   Morgan Cole Oxford, Reading
   Nabarro Nathanson Reading
2. **Boyes Turner** Reading
   Pitmans Reading
   Shoosmiths Reading

This book is the product of 6,582 1/2 hour interviews. See p.7 for BMRB audit. Within each band, firms are listed alphabetically.

CLARKS (see firm details p.908) The firm enjoys a steady stream of IT and IP-related work and is visible in increasing amounts of injunction litigation involving search and seizure and freezing orders. Popular amongst peers, "*able*" Antony Morris (see p.564) leads a team that is said to "*really know its market.*" It represented a listed media company in breach of confidentiality claims against former employees and is currently acting for an international company on a £10 million claim. The recent addition of multinational management company SITA to an already impressive client base has been a considerable bonus for the group. **Clients** Allegis; BMW; The BOC Group; The University of Reading; Thames Water; SITA; Global Crossing.

MORGAN COLE (see firm details p.1075) Despite recent partner losses, the general consensus amongst rivals is that the firm is "*competent and going places.*" Anthony Hughes and Philip Jones head teams in Oxford and

THAMES VALLEY/SOUTH WEST ■ LITIGATION GENERAL COMMERCIAL

LEADING INDIVIDUALS

[1] **CLARK Tim** Olswang
MORRIS Antony Clarks
ROBINSON Michael Boyes Turner
ROWE Claire Shoosmiths

See individuals' profiles p.552

Reading respectively. IT-related litigation is a particular niche for the team, and it is acquiring new clients in the finance and transport sectors, including developing links with RAC. Recent high-profile work includes representing a man accused of cheating in the TV show 'Who Wants to be a Millionaire?' **Clients** Banks; educational institutions; national and international plcs.

NABARRO NATHANSON (see firm details p.1080) "*Tough and knowledgeable*" say solicitors of this successful operation. Peter Sheppard heads a team that services a blue-chip, multinational client base, including telecoms companies, banks, finance outfits and medium-sized corporates. It also has a niche in charity dispute work, and recently acted for Arthritis Care in a dispute with a photocopier supplier. Drawing on the firm's exceptional property expertise, the team has also advised a number of leading institutional and corporate landlord and tenant clients on a variety of contentious property-related matters. **Clients** Save the Children; RSPCA; National Trust; Atmel; Boxclever; Direct Wines; Singer & Friedlander; Sun Microsystems.

BOYES TURNER (see firm details p.883) "*Respected litigator*" **Michael Robinson** (see p.566) leads a team that boasts strength in property, IT and IP, professional negligence, directors' disqualification and mortgage-related litigation. Increasingly busy in construction and shareholder disputes, it has recently represented a motor dealership in connection with claims arising from international car sales fraud. Current work includes assisting a provider of IT security systems and services in a claim for damages against ex-employees. **Clients** Barratt North London; Grenco UK; Kelly Services; IG Index; Baumatic.

PITMANS (see firm details p.1103) The firm enters *Chambers'* tables this year on the strength of its high-class team and reputation for expertise in a range of areas, including financial and international litigation. It services commercial clients with particular reference to post-acquisition work, and has conducted a substantial number of insolvency cases as well as minority shareholder disputes. Construction and professional negligence are other focuses for the team, which is headed by Sue O'Brien. A recent highlight involved a breach of contract claim against a foreign airline. **Clients** AFN; Barratt Homes; De Beers; Dura Automotives; Hewlett-Packard; Fujitsu Siemens Computers.

SHOOSMITHS (see firm details p.1133) Praised by competitors for its "*reasonable, commercial*" attitude, the Reading branch of the nationwide firm is headed by highly regarded **Claire Rowe** (see p.567). Clients include banks, accountants, corporates and professional bodies. A multimillion pound claim arising from a corporate acquisition, a £1/2 million warranty claim and a number of high-value contract disputes are typical examples of the firm's recent caseload. **Clients** ACE Insurance; Fired Earth; McLarens Toplis.

OTHER NOTABLE PRACTITIONERS "*Impressive*" **Tim Clark** (see p.554) is head of litigation and dispute resolution at Olswang's Reading office, following its absorption of Garrett's office.

SOUTH WEST

LITIGATION: GENERAL COMMERCIAL
■ SOUTH WEST

[1] **Burges Salmon** Bristol
Osborne Clarke Bristol

[2] **Beachcroft Wansbroughs** Bristol
Bevan Ashford Bristol, Exeter
Bond Pearce Bristol, Exeter, Plymouth
Veale Wasbrough Bristol

[3] **Clarke Willmott & Clarke** Bristol, Taunton
Foot Anstey Sargent Exeter, Plymouth
TLT Solicitors Bristol

[4] **Laytons** Bristol
Michelmores Exeter

LEADING INDIVIDUALS

[1] **HAGGETT Paul** Burges Salmon
MAY Philip TLT Solicitors
MORRIS Peter Burges Salmon
PIZZEY Simon Veale Wasbrough
PUDDICOMBE Nigel Veale Wasbrough

[2] **CLOUGH Peter** Osborne Clarke
METCALFE Stephen Beachcroft Wansbroughs
ROBINSON Clare Osborne Clarke

This book is the product of 6,582 1/2 hour interviews. See p.7 for BMRB audit.
Within each band, firms are listed alphabetically. See individuals' profiles p.552

BURGES SALMON (see firm details p.894) Considered by some sources the "*strongest and most pre-eminent*" litigation team in the region, it is clearly at the top of its game and is commended by peers for its multifaceted expertise and clout. It boasts an impressive client base, and its "*skilled practitioners*" were praised for their professional approach and ability to collaborate effectively. With strength in banking, pensions, professional negligence and competition, as well as general contractual claims, its acknowledged rail expertise has seen it win instructions relating to the Selby rail crash. Head of group **Paul Haggett** (see p.559) is best known for his expertise in financial litigation, while **Peter Morris** (see p.564) has a high profile in disputes relating to property and professional negligence. Experienced in multi-jurisdictional work, the team has recently advised a major European bank on potential liabilities arising from the collapse of Enron. It also represented a multinational in a dispute over the tender process for the supply of its power requirements in the UK. **Clients** Bayerische Landesbank; Bristol & West; English Welsh & Scottish Railways; HSBC; Kimberly-Clark; Nationwide Building Society; Paragon Finance.

OSBORNE CLARKE (see firm details p.1090) An "*outstanding*" practice with a national reputation, rivals feel it to be particularly strong in corporate finance-related claims for its exceptional blue-chip client base. Praised to researchers for its "*high-quality service,*" a busy year has witnessed the recruitment of two new partners and an increase in cross-European work and international arbitration. Boosted by a number of recent client gains in the media, telecoms and IT sectors, industry-focused teams service the litigation needs of the firm's clients across these specialist areas and others such as construction and banking. Leading the group, **Clare Robinson** won considerable praise from the market, while **Peter Clough**, though less visible this year, also retains a respected profile. Over the past year the firm has handled a number of contentious matters for Nortel and acted in several policyholder claims for Equitable Life. **Clients** Transco; Yahoo!; BSkyB; Tesco; Innogy; 3i; Vodafone; Marks & Spencer; Nortel.

BEACHCROFT WANSBROUGHS (see firm details p.860) Particularly known and rated in the market for its insurance expertise, the firm gets a steady stream of cases from this sector, but also boasts a number of standalone clients. Growth areas have included warranty claims and international commercial disputes. Recent highlights have included successfully defending a £15 million case on behalf of Equifax, and advising Marks & Spencer on a continuing dispute with one of its suppliers. High-profile name **Stephen Metcalfe** (see p.563) is described by peers as "*a terrific litigator.*" **Clients** Marks & Spencer; Equifax; KPMG; Ryder; Allied Pickfords.

BEVAN ASHFORD (see firm details p.869) An established presence in this region, the firm retains a formidable reputation for public sector and health-related work, and is felt by both

LITIGATION GENERAL COMMERCIAL ■ SOUTH WEST/WALES

clients and competitors to be "*strong across the board.*" Its top-class client base includes foreign states, government departments, banks, NHS Trusts and software companies, and much of its work is now national or international in flavour. Recent examples of the team's high-profile caseload include acting in a lengthy dispute surrounding a US TV game show and representing a railway brake company in a multiparty Anglo-French contractual claim. Patricia Mitchell heads the department. **Clients** Zurich Financial Services; Orange; Westlea Housing Association; Liverpool Victoria Friendly Society.

BOND PEARCE (see firm details p.879) "*Principal players*" in the South West, according to some sources, the firm's bases in Bristol, Plymouth and Exeter give it an enviable spread. The team, led by Tony Askham, handles a wide range of litigation, including minority shareholder disputes, pensions and IP litigation. The Plymouth and Exeter offices boast expertise in dealer recovery claims, having gained much experience working for Peugeot Wholesale, while the Bristol office concentrates on pensions, insolvency and EC-related litigation and has seen considerable expansion over the past year. The firm is representing one of the largest road transport companies in the UK in connection with matters arising from a pension scheme merger, and recently assisted Swansea City AFC in its successful defence of a hostile administration petition. **Clients** Gul International; Peugeot Wholesale; Post Office; Epwin; The National Trust; Pennon Group.

VEALE WASBROUGH (see firm details p.1174) Competitors describe this firm as "*good to deal with*" and "*thoroughly on the ball.*" It has an impressive client base, including local authorities and corporates, which it represents in a wide range of commercial claims. It also acts in partnership disputes for solicitors and doctors and is targeting the IT market. The team recently advised an international shipping company in a dispute concerning containers in the UK and US, and acted for Gloucester City Council in prosecuting two traders for breach of food safety regulations. Simon Pizzey (see p.565) is a "*highly visible*" figurehead for the team, while Nigel Puddicombe (see p.566) was described by peers as a "*solid performer.*" **Clients** Gunns International Transport & Shipping; Edward Ware Homes; Bar Mutual Indemnity Fund.

CLARKE WILLMOTT & CLARKE (see firm details p.907) The recruitment of partner Huw Davey and several new assistants to the Taunton office augments the profile of this "*powerful outfit.*" Considered a "*shrewd and sharp*" team by competitors, it is particularly well known for insolvency-related litigation. It has recently created a specialist construction disputes unit and also enjoys expertise in property, agriculture, IT and IP. A growing international profile has recently seen it appear in a $100 million cross-border arbitration, and represent a retail client against a consortium of Italian manufacturers in a case concerning European regulations on the slicing of Parma ham. The firm was also lead solicitors in the judicial review into the foot-and-mouth inquiry. **Clients** ASDA; NFU; David Wilson Homes; Prowting Group; Gloucestershire County Council; Hygrade Foods; University of Bristol.

FOOT ANSTEY SARGENT (see firm details p.958) Some competitors consider this "*good medium-sized firm*" the "*main force*" in its area, while clients appreciate its "*highly efficient*" approach. The Exeter office has been boosted recently by new recruits and the firm is working towards greater integration between its Plymouth and Exeter operations. Angus McNicol heads a department that is known for its probate litigation and includes two team members who belong to the Association of Contentious Trust and Probate Specialists. Other areas of expertise include commercial agency disputes, accountants' negligence and partnership disputes, and it has been seeing a lot of insolvency-related work over the last year. It has recently acted for two clients in earn out disputes with their former companies, each worth several hundred thousand pounds. **Clients** Newspaper groups; communications companies.

TLT SOLICITORS (see firm details p.1163) "*Dynamo*" Philip May (see p.563) is a leading light in this reputable outfit. Divided into teams specialising in financial, property and general commercial litigation, the department boasts an impressive client base made up largely of medium-sized corporate clients. These include Cameron Balloons, the largest balloon manufacturer in the UK, which the team represented in a large IP-related case. Other recent work includes assisting Parragon Book Service on various contractual matters, while its strong reputation for partnership law sees it handling a large number of disputes for solicitors and accountants. Clients; Aardman Animations; Imperial Tobacco; Avon Rubber; Proton Cars (UK); Alfred McAlpine.

LAYTONS (see firm details p.1032) Said by interviewees to "*shine in construction litigation,*" the firm also undertakes a range of general commercial cases including insolvency-related claims. Bill Brydon heads a department that has recently advised in, *inter alia*, several large breach of warranty claims arising out of share purchase agreements. Another interesting recent case concerned an alleged breach of contract following a failure to supply tickets for a major international sports tournament. **Clients** Hamptons International; Gullivers Sports Travel; Somerfield Stores; Zuken.

MICHELMORES (see firm details p.1068) Described by one competitor as "*the main commercial force in Exeter,*" the firm's highly reputed litigation department handles a range of work, including construction, family and property disputes, as well as general commercial cases. Tim Richards heads a team that was established upon his arrival two years ago from Pinsent Curtis Biddle. The firm displayed its international credentials recently by representing Dutch clients in a shopfitting dispute, while other highlights of the year have included a contractual dispute in the energy industry. **Clients** Retailers and other corporates.

WALES

EDWARDS GELDARD (see firm details p.944) A powerful force in Wales, this "*credible*" team has "*established and well-regarded lawyers.*" Led by "*sensible, straightforward and effective*" Paul Hopkins (see p.560), the group wins market respect in a range of areas, including professional negligence, product liability, defamation and shareholder and IT disputes. Servicing clients across the UK, it recently defended the Arts Council of Wales in defamation proceedings brought by the director of the Chapter Arts Centre in Cardiff. Another highlight of the year was representing major water client Hyder and three of its subsidiaries in a £3.7 million claim brought against it by a specialist computer software company. **Clients** Hyder and subsidiaries; Baxi Group; Citigroup; Pendragon; Chevron UK; Welsh Development Agency (WDA); Arts Council of Wales; Chubb.

EVERSHEDS (see firm details p.949) This highly regarded outfit is said by rivals to be a team of "*smart operators.*" Its large banking and recovery team is considered an asset and its approach to training is widely admired. Peter Jones (see p.561) remains the department's standout name, with much of his work now felt by peers to be conducted on a national level. Less visible, Mark Rhys-Jones (see p.566) also maintains a solid profile. Experienced in a broad range of work, the team has particular expertise in technology cases and product liability. Getting onto the Virgin panel was a highlight of the year, and the team is assisting Energy Power Resources in an ongoing £12 million dispute with another energy company. It successfully represented the Ice Hockey Super-

WALES/MIDLANDS ■ LITIGATION GENERAL COMMERCIAL

LITIGATION: GENERAL COMMERCIAL
■ WALES

1
- Edwards Geldard Cardiff
- Eversheds Cardiff
- Hugh James Cardiff
- Morgan Cole Cardiff, Swansea

2
- Palser Grossman Cardiff Bay

LEADING INDIVIDUALS

1
- HOPKINS Paul Edwards Geldard
- JONES Peter Eversheds

2
- JEFFERIES Michael Hugh James
- JONES Michael Hugh James
- NOTT Christopher Palser Grossman
- RHYS-JONES Mark Eversheds
- WILLIAMS Gareth Hugh James
- WILSON Allan Morgan Cole

This book is the product of 6,582 1/2 hour interviews. See p.7 for BMRB audit. Within each band, firms are listed alphabetically. See individuals' profiles p.552

HUGH JAMES (see firm details p.1004) "*Strong in Wales*," the recent demerger has done nothing to damage the profile of this firm in litigation. Peers praise a large and efficient department, which includes **Michael Jefferies** (see p.561), who has experience in a range of cases but is especially renowned for his construction forte. **Michael Jones** (see p.561) was less visible this year, while **Gareth Williams** (see p.570) is best known for his high-profile work on behalf of the Welsh Rugby Union (WRU). Representing local authorities and large- and medium-sized corporates, IP-related litigation has been a growth area. The team demonstrated its growing global reach recently in handling a substantial claim against defendants in Belgium and the USA. Contentious probate disputes, partnership disputes and defamation are other areas of focus. **Clients** WRU; Welsh Water; AIT.

MORGAN COLE (see firm details p.1075) The litigation group in Wales is split between the firm's Cardiff and Swansea offices. The team at the former has expertise in agriculture, banking and defamation cases, whilst the latter focuses on energy-related litigation and debt recovery. Over the last year the firm has seen a steady league against the Sheffield Steelers over the question of the ownership of their franchise. **Clients** National Assembly for Wales; WDA; Tarmac Southern Ltd; Energy Power Resources.

increase in contentious finance and insolvency cases for big-name clients like Grant Thornton and KPMG. It remains heavily involved in litigation stemming from the foot-and-mouth crisis and does a lot of work for energy companies such as TotalFinaElf and BP, much of it on a national level. A recent highlight was representing a freezer manufacturer in relation to an alleged design right infringement worth £1 million. "*Fine lawyer*" **Allan Wilson** has a niche skill in injunctions. **Clients** Bank of Scotland; Grant Thornton; HSBC; Mitel; NFU; KPMG.

PALSER GROSSMAN **Christopher Nott** is a big presence in the local market with a distinctive style. He heads a department with a reputation for solid and commercial advice on contractual and corporate shareholder disputes. Large-scale civil fraud and partnership disputes have also occupied the team recently. Highlights of the last year include winning a case concerning part of a deceased businessman's estate and representing one of the owners of a leading Welsh sports organisation in an ownership dispute. **Clients** Julian Hodge Bank; The American Furniture Group; TRW; International Greetings; Cardiff Athletic Club.

MIDLANDS

LITIGATION: GENERAL COMMERCIAL
■ MIDLANDS

1
- Wragge & Co Birmingham

2
- Pinsent Curtis Biddle Birmingham

3
- Eversheds Birmingham, Nottingham
- Hammond Suddards Edge Birmingham
- Martineau Johnson Birmingham

4
- Browne Jacobson Nottingham
- DLA Birmingham
- Gateley Wareing Birmingham
- Lee Crowder Birmingham

5
- Bell Lax Litigation Birmingham
- Challinors Lyon Clark West Bromwich
- Freethcartwright Nottingham
- Kent Jones and Done Stoke-on-Trent
- Moran & Co Tamworth
- Shakespeares Birmingham
- Shoosmiths Northampton
- The Wilkes Partnership Birmingham

This book is the product of 6,582 1/2 hour interviews. See p.7 for BMRB audit. Within each band, firms are listed alphabetically.

WRAGGE & CO (see firm details p.1197) "*Top of the tree in terms of breadth and depth*," with a dedicated commercial litigation team of nine partners, "*quality at every level*" and seamless efficiency make this the "*most together firm*" according to the market. Clients and peers particularly praised the group's "*willingness to think laterally*." Its size enables it to undertake the largest and most complex cases, and it handles a large volume of disputes involving breach of warranty on purchase and sale agreements, and negligence claims, for its high-profile, blue-chip client base. Highlights of the past year include acting for a former director in litigation relating to Ciro Citterio Menswear, and representing a FTSE 250 company in an £18 million fraudulent misrepresentation and breach of warranty claim. Head of department **Paul Howard** is known amongst peers for doing "*the big stuff*." He has support from **Andrew Manning Cox**, who is highly experienced in the High Court and Commercial Court, and **Nicola Mumford**, who competitors praise for her "*extremely professional*" approach. **Clients** Arvin Meritor; Bank of Scotland; BI Group; Cadbury Schweppes; Halifax; HSBC Bank; Lloyds TSB.

PINSENT CURTIS BIDDLE (see firm details p.1102) With its superb corporate client base and cohorts of talented, "*practical*" lawyers, this operation is felt by peers to "*present a strong face to the opposition.*" Clients praise its "*ability to deal with messy situations*" and do a "*professional, quality job*" in tough circumstances. Led by "*strong individual*" **Greg Lowson** (see p.562), the department's highest profile name is "*first-rate*" **Carl Garvie** (see p.558), who some commentators consider "*head and shoulders above the rest*" of the players in the market. "*Sensible operator*" **Jonathan Fortnam** (see p.557) also won sustained plaudits from his peers. The team undertakes high-value contractual and warranty disputes and major construction claims. It is representing AXA in defending a £10 million contractual dispute and successfully acted for Siemens in a £3.5 million action centring on the construction of a waste treatment plant. **Clients** AXA; Rolls-Royce; Saint-Gobain; Marconi; New York Life.

EVERSHEDS (see firm details p.949) The Midlands branches of this national corporate powerhouse are renowned for the quality work they win for their household name blue-chip clients. While much of the team's caseload is spin-off work for existing clients, a sizeable proportion is standalone, often one-off, disputes, gained by virtue of its high market standing. Competitors and clients have a healthy respect for the team's doggedness and efficiency, but comment that it is not as visible as the two leading groups, and the lack of a high-profile player may contribute to this. Recent work includes representing a former board director in a DTI investigation, and the team acted for MG Rover in its widely reported £500 million post-completion dispute with BMW. The acquisition of work from DEFRA has been another highlight for the firm both nationally and regionally. Sue Green is the head of department. **Clients** Hays; MG Rover Holdings; Smiths Group; Britax.

HAMMOND SUDDARDS EDGE An aggressive team of tough, commercially aware lawyers, it has made a name for itself with its involvement

www.ChambersandPartners.com — 527

LITIGATION GENERAL COMMERCIAL ■ MIDLANDS

LEADING INDIVIDUALS

1 GARVIE Carl *Pinsent Curtis Biddle*
HOWARD Paul *Wragge & Co*
2 ROSE Digby *Hammond Suddards Edge*
3 DAVIES Peter *Gateley Wareing*
MANNING COX Andrew *Wragge & Co*
MUMFORD Nicola *Wragge & Co*
SINGLETON Bernard *Lee Crowder*
SPOONER Andrew *Martineau Johnson*
4 GOODRHAM Stephen *Gateley Wareing*
LAX Peter *Bell Lax Litigation*
LOWSON Greg *Pinsent Curtis Biddle*
WILLETTS Jayne *Hammond Suddards Edge*

UP AND COMING
FORTNAM Jonathan *Pinsent Curtis Biddle*

ASSOCIATES TO WATCH
LOWETH Craig *Wragge & Co*

See individuals' profiles p.552

---

in "*some really huge stuff.*" In the minds of many competitors is the Dunkin' Donuts litigation, a huge action with proceedings in Birmingham and the US. This success boosted the standing of "*shrewd litigator*" **Digby Rose**, whose stock is currently riding high as head of department and the team's best known name. Less visible but still highly rated is **Jayne Willetts**. The firm covers all areas of litigation but boasts particular expertise in engineering and IT claims, breach of warranty claims, partnership disputes and defamation. It is placing emphasis on developing its own advocacy and mediation techniques. Major recent successes include advising a US outsourcing company on claims and settling a £1 million computer dispute on the first day of trial in the Technology and Construction Court. **Clients** Scottish & Newcastle; Adare Group; Allied Domecq; Calor Gas.

MARTINEAU JOHNSON (see firm details p.1056) A solid, established name, admired for its "*great clients*," the firm is best known for its strengths in education and IT. It services a high-class client base consisting of educational organisations, local authorities and plcs on issues including corporate fraud, professional negligence, hi-tech claims and regulatory matters. A recent success was acting in a compensation claim under the Commercial Agents Regulations and achieving a settlement immediately before a Court of Appeal hearing. The team has also advised a local authority on claims, potentially worth £5 million, arising from the development of a landfill site, and assisted a number of educational institutions involved in possible prosecutions for the escape of asbestos. **Andrew Spooner** (see p.568) leads the team and is described by clients as "*practical and user-friendly.*" **Clients** ALSTOM UK; The Patrick Whitehead Partnership; local authorities; universities.

BROWNE JACOBSON (see firm details p.891) Peter Ellis heads this respected Nottingham-based team. It represents an impressive mix of local corporates and big-name multinationals like Siemens on a range of contentious matters. Experienced in alternative dispute resolution the firm has expertise in breach of contract, product litigation and regulatory prosecutions. It recently represented Triumph Motorcycles in a large product litigation case against a supplier. **Clients** Express Dairies; GeoPost UK; Siemens.

DLA This prominent local player has a reputation amongst peers for breeding tough and "*aggressive*" litigators. With the resources of the national firm to draw upon, including particular expertise in contentious work connected to the financial, regulatory and hi-tech fields, it numbers retailers, financial services companies and consumer goods manufacturers amongst its enviable list of clients. James Sharkey heads the department in Birmingham. **Clients** Local and national corporates.

GATELEY WAREING (see firm details p.967) This "*good quality outfit*" has impressed its rivals over recent months with its determination and commitment to the sector. Felt to be "*firing up,*" some leading players consider this "*one of the best of the medium-sized firms.*" Led by "*switched-on*" **Stephen Goodrham**, the team is bolstered by the presence of "*clever litigator*" **Peter Davies**. An "*astute*" group, it recently extracted a corporate client from a dispute with a major logistics company concerning invoices for haulage services. Other areas of strength include IP-related disputes and claims involving breach of contract and breach of confidence. **Clients** Plcs; manufacturers.

LEE CROWDER (see firm details p.1035) "*A growing force*" according to some competitors, commentators have been impressed by the firm's methodical expansion and "*increasing involvement in significant cases.*" Its broad range of litigation experience includes exposure to a number of directors' disqualifications, warranty claims and a recent dispute over terms and conditions involving the National Employment Agency. Another recent highlight was representing a motor parts distributor against a multinational supplier. The team, which also boasts strength in employment and professional negligence, includes highly rated and prominent **Bernard Singleton** (see p.567). **Clients** William M. Mercer; NSG Ltd; Teneco Walker.

BELL LAX LITIGATION Maintaining its market reputation as a small but effective outfit, the firm handles a broad range of work but is best known for engineering, construction and employment-related claims. The team is headed up by **Peter Lax** (see p.562), who was praised by researchers as skilful and "*committed.*" It continues to act internationally, recently representing a large Netherlands-based company in its UK activities. **Clients** Owner-managed businesses.

CHALLINORS LYON CLARK This team has impressed market sources with its drive and profile, and enters *Chambers*' tables following sustained market plaudits. A group of "*skilled litigators,*" including Peter Lowe, earns high marks from competitors for its ability to "*punch above its weight*" on a range of disputes, including high-profile, multimillion pound telecoms and pollution litigation. **Clients** Telecoms companies.

FREETHCARTWRIGHT (see firm details p.963) Philippa Dempster heads the commercial litigation department of this large East Midlands outfit. It has experience in a wide variety of contentious work, including fraud, judicial reviews and breach of contract claims for a client base spanning local authorities and big-name corporates. Capable of handling complex, high-value work, it recently acted in a £10 million commercial dispute and a £1.5 million claim for Centrica arising from the closure of one its showrooms. **Clients** Nottinghamshire County Council; HMV (Media); Waterstone's; Bombardier Transportation; David Wilson Homes; Centrica; Experian.

KENT JONES AND DONE (see firm details p.1020) Graham Neyt leads this Stoke-based team that continues to handle commercial disputes for its steady clients. Typical work includes winding up petitions and claims related to warranties for sale and purchase. The team has particular expertise in mining subsidence as well as contentious property, professional negligence and insolvency work. Recent highlights include representing two large utility companies on coal mining issues and successfully acting for a foreign client in a contract dispute involving carriage of goods. **Clients** JCB Group.

MORAN & CO (see firm details p.1074) Barristers in particular praise this niche firm as "*first class; it's very small but handles top-quality work.*" Banking, solicitors' negligence and employment are key areas. Over the last year the team has successfully defended Vauxhall Motors in claims totalling £1.9 million and acted in a commercial banking dispute for over £3 million. Patrick Moran heads the group. **Clients** Allied Irish Banks; Coors Brewers; Vauxhall Motors; Leeds Leasing; Haydock Finance.

SHAKESPEARES (see firm details p.1127) This solid, impressive firm is acknowledged by peers to have a good name in the West Midlands. Sources comment on the well-organised and "*efficient*" way in which it handles a complex caseload. The group has particular expertise in banking litigation and restraint of trade, and experience of undertaking cross-

MIDLANDS/EAST ANGLIA ■ LITIGATION GENERAL COMMERCIAL

jurisdictional disputes. Mark Beesley heads the team and has particular expertise in trust disputes and injunctions. **Clients** Banks.

SHOOSMITHS (see firm details p.1133) "*Strong in its region,*" the firm excels in banking, construction and insurance work. The international reach of the practice is exemplified by its involvement in UK litigation on behalf of Portuguese clients and in litigation in New Jersey for a Nottingham-based company. Members of the team, ably led by John Hill, have particular expertise in pensions and trusts, IP and trademarks and consumer credit. **Clients** Barclays Bank; Royal Bank of Scotland; Paragon Group; Barclaycard; Winterthur Life; Kier International.

THE WILKES PARTNERSHIP (see firm details p.1188) The firm continues to command a strong market position and wins praise from peers as a "*quality operation.*" Peter Ewin heads up a commercial litigation team that is involved in a broad range of disputes for a diverse client base, which includes national names as well as local businesses and established private clients. **Clients** Banks.

EAST ANGLIA

LITIGATION: GENERAL COMMERCIAL
■ EAST ANGLIA

1 Eversheds Cambridge, Norwich
  Mills & Reeve Cambridge, Norwich
2 Hewitson Becke + Shaw Cambridge
  Taylor Vinters Cambridge
3 Greenwoods Peterborough
  Prettys Ipswich
4 Birketts Ipswich
  Steele & Co Norwich

LEADING INDIVIDUALS
1 CALLAGHAN Edward Mills & Reeve
  HIGGS Rachel Mills & Reeve
  MATTHEWS Paul Eversheds
  ROESSLER Max Eversheds
2 BLAKE Peter Prettys
  PERROTT Edward Taylor Vinters

This book is the product of 6,582 1/2 hour interviews. See p.7 for BMRB audit.
Within each band, firms are listed alphabetically. See individuals' profiles p.552

EVERSHEDS (see firm details p.949) The "*sensible teams*" at the firm's East Anglian offices won sustained praise from clients and competitors alike for their ability to handle seamlessly whatever is thrown at them. With the firm's powerful corporate client base and national reach, rivals point to its superb network of offices and note that "*strong panel appointments get it lots of good work.*" Considered by some competitors "*the main player*" in the region, its reputation for efficiency has also gained it some impressive standalone cases. The Cambridge office is well known for its strength in IP and biotech-related claims, while Norwich has a bent towards defamation and insolvency. Exhibiting its burgeoning international reach, the firm has been acting for Seaweld Engineering as defendant in proceedings brought in Texas in relation to a restraint injunction. It also recently represented an oil company as claimant in a contractual dispute with a North Sea oil contractor. "*Effective*" Paul Matthews (see p.563) and "*experienced*" Max Roessler (see p.566) are its standout practitioners. **Clients** Ipswich Borough Council; Epron International; Seaweld Engineering.

MILLS & REEVE (see firm details p.1071) A "*substantial presence*" in the local marketplace, with a national reach and a top-class client base, competitors praised the quality and business sense of this "*top team*" of solicitors. It undertakes a wide range of litigation for business and public sector bodies and has noticed particular growth in contentious IP instructions. Around 40% of the team's workload has an international element and it has recently appeared in litigation in California, Trinidad and Tobago, Australia, Canada and Germany. It represented an Austrian bank in a 40-party litigation relating to a dispute over oil cargo in the Middle East. Instructions from the many hi-tech companies based in Cambridge include patent litigation in the US and global trademark enforcement. The firm has also acted in high-profile discrimination claims against public sector clients and undertakes warranty claims related to M&A and shareholder disputes. "*Pragmatic*" Edward Callaghan (see p.554) was highly rated by peers for his knowledge and commerciality, while Rachel Higgs (see p.559) was widely praised to researchers as "*sensible and pleasant to deal with.*" **Clients** AVEVA Group; Zeus Technology; Neopost; Potton.

HEWITSON BECKE + SHAW (see firm details p.993) This sensible team of lawyers was described by peers as "*solid opposition.*" The department, led by Dominic Hopkins, offers services in a range of contentious areas, including competition, pensions, partnership, IT and insolvency-related disputes, and corporate recovery. A recent highlight from its varied caseload was representing shareholders of Barings in proceedings concerning the settlement of claims against auditors. It also represented the UK arm of a US telecoms company in mediation proceedings relating to contractual and systems integration agreements. **Clients** US-owned private companies; pharmaceutical companies; local authorities; manufacturers; private healthcare providers.

TAYLOR VINTERS (see firm details p.1156) Described by interviewees as "*a competent and well-established firm,*" the group is noted for some interesting niche work. Currently forging ahead in engineering and telecoms-related claims, it also undertakes large amounts of regulatory and professional negligence matters. Over the last year the team has acted for Philips Electronics UK in a £4 million case against a nuisance litigator, and appeared in a breach of warranty claim against the vendor of a business. Head of department Edward Perrott (see p.565) remains a respected figure in the market. **Clients** Philips Electronics UK; pharmaceutical companies; telecoms companies.

GREENWOODS (see firm details p.978) This impressively commercial oufit undertakes a broad mix of general contentious work for a sizeable client base, which includes large names from the publishing, manufacturing, financial services and IT sectors. James Maxey heads a department that is currently developing its contentious asset recovery work and growing its caseload in the fields of internet and e-business disputes. It has recently acted in database-related claims and asset recovery cases for accountancy firms. **Clients** Accountancy firms; publishers; manufacturing companies.

PRETTYS (see firm details p.1106) A respected name in the region, Peter Blake (see p.553) leads an efficient team that has recently been occupied with a number of directors' disqualifications and IT, IP and insolvency-related disputes. It is best known in the market for the steady stream of agricultural claims that flows from its place on the NFU panel. It also undertakes, as part of an international network, cases with multi-jurisdictional elements, and recently undertook a high-value arbitration case. **Clients** NFU; IT companies.

BIRKETTS (see firm details p.875) Though not felt by interviewees to be a highly visible presence in the market, local solicitors praise the team's solid efficiency. The department handles litigation for established commercial clients, but has also built a standalone practice, and has a

LITIGATION GENERAL COMMERCIAL ■ EAST ANGLIA/NORTH WEST

particularly good reputation in the construction sector. Other areas of strength include IT and IP-related claims, property, licensing and inheritance disputes. Bob Wright heads the team and has experience in professional negligence, banking and insolvency. **Clients** National pub chain; construction companies; banks; building contractors.

STEELE & CO (see firm details p.1145) Competitors heaped praise on what they consider a "*progressive*" practice with "*truly specialist*" commercial litigators. Chris Gilbert heads a team that, over the past 12 months, has been involved in IP-related disputes and actions for local authorities. Recent highlights include successfully representing two local councillors against a trade union and local newspaper, and acting in a multimillion pound automotive engineering dispute in the Technology and Construction Court. **Clients** Canon; Zenith Windows; Danisco Pack Bux.

NORTH WEST

LITIGATION: GENERAL COMMERCIAL
■ NORTH WEST

1 DLA Liverpool, Manchester
2 Addleshaw Booth & Co Manchester
   Eversheds Manchester
3 Brabners Chaffe Street Liverpool, Preston
   Cobbetts Manchester
   Halliwell Landau Manchester
   Hammond Suddards Edge Manchester
4 Berg & Co Manchester
   DWF Liverpool, Manchester
   Hill Dickinson Liverpool
   Wacks Caller Manchester
5 Cuff Roberts Liverpool
   Rowe Cohen Manchester
6 Kershaw Abbott Manchester
   Kuit Steinart Levy Manchester
   Mace & Jones Liverpool, Manchester
   Pannone & Partners Manchester

LEADING INDIVIDUALS

1 CLAVELL-BATE Michael Eversheds
   HARRIS Andrew DLA
   SORRELL Kit Wacks Caller
2 GATENBY John Addleshaw Booth & Co
   GOSLING John Addleshaw Booth & Co
   MANLEY Mark Brabners Chaffe Street
   MATTISON Mark Eversheds
   ROPER Robert Cobbetts
   WINTERBURN Anthony DLA
3 AMSDEN Mark Addleshaw Booth & Co
   AUSTIN Ian Halliwell Landau
   CHERRY Peter Addleshaw Booth & Co
   KERSHAW Anne Kershaw Abbott
   KHAN Charles Berg & Co
   WHITTELL Mark Cobbetts
4 BLAKEMORE Craig Mace & Jones
   GRAY David DLA
   JOHNSON Paul Pannone & Partners
   RAWLINSON David Cuff Roberts
   RYAN Geraldine Hill Dickinson
   SMALL Graham Rowe Cohen

This book is the product of 6,582 1/2 hour interviews. See p.7 for BMRB audit. Within each band, firms are listed alphabetically. See individuals' profiles p.452

DLA The team is viewed by the market to have pulled away from the rest of the pack, winning fans with its aggressive style, rendering many interviewees to proclaim it the leading player in Manchester. **Andrew Harris** "*takes no prisoners*" while maintaining his eye for detail. **Anthony Winterburn** pleases interviewees by "*always producing ingenious ideas.*" **David Gray** is noted for his commercial outlook.

ADDLESHAW BOOTH & CO (see firm details p.838) "*A polished team,*" renowned for "*complex, meaty cases and enjoying a blue-chip client roster.*" The "*thorough*" **John Gatenby** (see p.558) is lauded for his ability to "*delve to the heart of the matter.*" He has acted for the Royal Exchange Theatre Company in a dispute with Birse Construction over payment for Birse's work on the refurbishment of the theatre in the aftermath of the IRA bomb in Manchester. Interviewees view **John Gosling** (see p.558) as formed from "*a quieter mould, but technically astute;*" he advised a major utility company on a dispute following the termination of a £4 million contract for the provision of an IT package. **Mark Amsden** (see p.552) has secured a following for his "*hard-hitting approach – he cuts to the chase.*" He has impressed in his advice to an international banking corporation on a multi-million pound IT development project. The team has also placed an emphasis upon mediation as successfully rounding out its dispute resolution offering. **Clients** BAE Systems; IBM; Airtours; British Airways; United Utilities.

EVERSHEDS (see firm details p.949) The practice continues to elicit praise for the strength of its cohesive national network and quality client base. **Michael Clavell-Bate** (see p.555) is deemed "*an excellent advisor and litigator*" by peers; however, researchers were warned: "*there is steel behind the silk.*" He acted for Delta Sound PA on a high-value case in the High Court against Federal Signal. **Mark Mattison** (see p.563) is revered as "*technically expert, one of the old school litigators;*" he is lower in profile in the general commercial circles as his work is taking on a greater construction focus. Antony Gold's workload is now heavily concerned with IP-related matters. A truly general commercial litigation team, undertaking commercial, contractual and tortious matters, with a niche in product liability and professional negligence. **Clients** Delta Sound PA; The Drinks Company; British Aerospace; United Utilities.

BRABNERS CHAFFE STREET (see firm details p.885) The team has moved up the tables this year; the merger with Chaffe Street has produced a perception of not simply a larger team, but one with increased impact. Interviewees proclaim that it is "*really emerging into the market.*" **Mark Manley** (see p.272) has been described to researchers as "*switched-on – a bit of a Rottweiler, but with a practical approach to problem-solving.*" He represents large corporate clients particularly on breach of warranty transactions. Defamation provides a steady flow of instruction, representing broadcasters and publishers in a variety of matters, including a claim of libel by a businessman against a magazine commenting on his involvement in criminal offences. The team also undertakes shareholder disputes, IP cases, property litigation and professional negligence. **Clients** Emap; Union Railways; Laings.

COBBETTS (see firm details p.914) Adjudged a "*gentlemanly outfit, with a well-established client base,*" it has a particular flair for property litigation. There is an increased emphasis upon mediation, and matters relating to directors' disqualification have come to the fore of late. The team generally undertakes franchisee and shareholder disputes, banking recovery, chancery and guarantee work. Leading light **Robert Roper** (see p.566) has been noted for his specialism within IP, while **Mark Whittell** (see p.570) is viewed by interviewees as "*super-enthusiastic and technically proficient.*" The broad client base ranges from government departments to owner-managed businesses. **Clients** P&O Properties; Britannia Building Society; Cussons; Matalan; Northern Rock.

HALLIWELL LANDAU (see firm details p.982) "*A diligent team,*" it is often to be seen on high-profile litigation cases, such as a conspiracy to defraud case in the Court of Appeal brought by shopfitting contractors against Time Group regarding the opening of retail stores. The department is characterised by its "*good people at junior level as well as stars at the top – aggressive in pursuing claims but good at settling them too.*" The team generally undertakes claimant professional negligence, construction and brewery-related litigation. Interbrew has instructed the team on litigation and recovery matters. Newcomer to the tables, **Ian Austin** (see p.552)

NORTH WEST/YORKSHIRE ■ LITIGATION GENERAL COMMERCIAL

has been described as "*tigerish in his approach.*" He recently acted for the Swinton Group on a commercial contract dispute in which it was established that the franchisers could terminate franchise agreements. **Clients** Abbey National; Alfred McAlpine Homes; Bethell Construction; NUKEM Nuclear; Pilkington.

HAMMOND SUDDARDS EDGE The team is commended as "*robust litigators,*" with particular prowess displayed in insolvency and the use of ADR. Philippa Hayes has moved to the role of professional support lawyer, while Lucci Dammone now heads the team. An upturn has been seen in health and safety cases, while the core of the practice lies in defendant professional indemnity, construction, insurance and personal injury work. With the majority of litigation partners as mediators, the emphasis here is upon dispute resolution. **Clients** BASF; Cleanaway; Royal Bank of Scotland; Bradford City AFC; Rank Group.

BERG & CO (see firm details p.864) Interviewees endorsed this "*small, ambitious and well-geared up outfit,*" which has **Charles Khan** (see p.561) ("*aggressive*") at its helm. The team is involved in contractual disputes, shareholders' actions, professional negligence and matters arising from the IP and insolvency sectors. The firm is well-versed in mediation and arbitration as well as litigation.

DWF (see firm details p.943) "*Bouncing back after a difficult phase, they have consolidated and are bigger and better than ever.*" The team is geared towards dispute resolution, with an emphasis on early case assessment. Insolvency, construction and property are areas of expertise and the team is involved in all forms of mediation, arbitration and litigation including injunctions.

HILL DICKINSON (see firm details p.995) The team is renowned for insurance litigation and defendant personal injury work; however, its litigious range extends to construction, banking, insolvency and property. **Geraldine Ryan** (see p.567) has been described as "*terrier-like – she gets the best results for her clients.*" The department promotes a pragmatic, partner-intensive approach, and is supported by a litigation team in London. **Clients** Peel Holdings; Merchant Navy Officers Pensions.

WACKS CALLER (see firm details p.1177) The firm enjoys a rising profile largely due to the leadership of **Kit Sorrell** (see p.568), who attracts "*incredible work for the size of the firm.*" He has been described by peers as "*a bulldog in litigation; his style is perfectly suited to Northern businesses.*" The team has seen a rise in property litigation cases, acting for Liverpool and Lancashire Properties on its case against B&Q, which defined commercial landlords' rights over common parts. Asset finance litigation, defamation and IP cases have particularly been sources of instruction in the past year. **Clients** Anglo International Holdings; Scottish & Newcastle; Total Fitness. Liverpool and Lancashire Properties.

CUFF ROBERTS Although "*not a noisemaking firm,*" it is one that can boast quality work, particularly within partnership cases. **David Rawlinson** (see p.566), whose main strength lies within construction, has been nevertheless described as "*a real generalist, who does well for his clients.*" Mediation is another string to the firm's bow, with four accredited mediators within the team and pre-litigation advice forming an essential element of the practice. Areas of focus include shareholder disputes, health and safety, property and defamation. **Clients** Littlewoods Leisure; Johnson Cleaners.

ROWE COHEN (see firm details p.1118) "*A streetwise firm, developing well,*" it has impressed market commentators as one "*clued up on the issues.*" **Graham Small** (see p.568) leads the team, which possesses "*a nice balance of being aggressive without being pushy.*" The team is perceived to be taking on some high-quality work that has a greater international dimension, building up a practice within cross-border contractual disputes. **Clients** National associations; commercial clients.

KERSHAW ABBOTT (see firm details p.1022) The firm's status is firmly based around the presence of **Anne Kershaw** (see p.561), whose "*love or loathe her*" reputation should not mask her ability as a "*formidable opponent, who fights hard for her clients.*" She leads a small but experienced team that has a track record in the construction, insurance, employment and insolvency sectors, and a recognised expertise in the field of partnership.

KUIT STEINART LEVY (see firm details p.1026) "*The young bloods*" coming into the market, whose expertise within company disputes has been singled out by interviewees. Jeff Lewis leads the department, which advised Cambos on its action against a landlord for breach of covenant and successfully defended a claim for forfeiture on a property. The team has recently acted on an arbitration in a copyright dispute concerning engineering equipment. **Clients** Associated Tyre Specialists; H Mears Ltd; Cambos.

MACE & JONES (see firm details p.1047) "*Property experts,*" the team lays claim to some high-quality instructions. "*True generalist*" **Craig Blakemore** (see p.553) heads up the Liverpool branch of the team, which has been involved in the conduct of a contractual appeals procedure worth £50 million. The Manchester team has been active on Barrett McKenzie v Escada UK, the first reported case on compensation under the Commercial Agents Regulations. The firm is also well-versed in professional negligence cases against solicitors. **Clients** Grant Thornton; Maclean & Nuttall; Co-operative Group; Peel Holdings.

PANNONE & PARTNERS (see firm details p.1092) **Paul Johnson** (see p.561) enters the tables following recommendatons that portrayed him as "*a team player, tenacious, always well prepared.*" A recent coup for the team within the IP field has been its success acting in the Cotton Traders case against Nike and the RFU, concerning rights to national emblems on sports shirts. The practice embraces insolvency and property litigation. **Clients** The Compass Group; Texaco; Royal Bank of Scotland; Manchester Airport.

YORKSHIRE

ADDLESHAW BOOTH & CO (see firm details p.838) "*A proactive team that stacks up well when compared to City firms,*" claim clients, who agree that its profile has been bolstered by large, complex cases. **Simon Kamstra** (see p.561) is appreciated by clients as "*commercially sharp,*" while peers like to have him on the other side; "*he can think round a problem.*" Peers respect **Peter Cherry** for his "*great intellect*" and long experience. The team recently represented 18 Mercedes-Benz dealerships in a dispute with DaimlerChrysler, following its termination of all its dealership agreements on one year's notice. Particularly strong in the tax field, the team acted for Halifax in a £7 million VAT case. It also frequently participates in corporate warranty claims, financial services, pensions and insolvency. There is an increasingly international element to the team, acting on various ICC arbitrations. **Susan Garrett** (see p.557) continues to garner her share of market approval. **Clients** 3i Group; British Airways; Comet; United Utilities.

DLA Renowned for its skill in heavyweight litigation, this team is also felt by peers to possess a sensible approach to mediation. **Paul Stone** has been singled out during the research.

EVERSHEDS (see firm details p.949) "*A sterling team,*" well known for its public sector work, which includes the high-profile Bloody Sunday inquiry. This should not, however, obscure the "*commercially driven*" outlook of the team, which also enjoys a substantial corporate client

www.ChambersandPartners.com

531

LITIGATION GENERAL COMMERCIAL ■ YORKSHIRE

LITIGATION: GENERAL COMMERCIAL
■ YORKSHIRE

1
- **Addleshaw Booth & Co** Leeds
- **DLA** Leeds, Sheffield
- **Eversheds** Leeds
- **Hammond Suddards Edge** Leeds

2
- **Irwin Mitchell** Sheffield
- **Pinsent Curtis Biddle** Leeds
- **Walker Morris** Leeds

3
- **Gordons Cranswick Solicitors** Bradford, Leeds
- **Keeble Hawson** Leeds
- **Lupton Fawcett** Leeds
- **Rollits** Hull

4
- **Andrew M. Jackson** Hull

5
- **Brooke North** Leeds
- **Cobbetts** Leeds
- **Gosschalks** Hull

LEADING INDIVIDUALS

1
- **KAMSTRA Simon** Addleshaw Booth & Co
- **SINCLAIR Jonathan** Eversheds

2
- **CROSSLEY Peter** Hammond Suddards Edge
- **HEAPS John** Eversheds
- **KISSACK Nigel** Pinsent Curtis Biddle
- **STONE Paul** DLA

3
- **CHAPMAN Stuart** Pinsent Curtis Biddle
- **CHERRY Peter** Addleshaw Booth & Co
- **DAVIES Gwendoline** Walker Morris
- **GILBERT Ralph** Rollits

4
- **ROTHWELL Charles** Keeble Hawson
- **SMITH Hugh** Andrew M. Jackson

UP AND COMING
- **GARRETT Susan** Addleshaw Booth & Co

This book is the product of 6,582 1/2 hour interviews. See p.7 for BMRB audit.
Within each band, firms are listed alphabetically. See individuals' profiles p.552

---

base. Recommended by clients for "*always seeing the opportunities,*" **Jonathan Sinclair** (see p.567) continues to act for ASDA in the high-profile case concerning Parma ham, which has gone to the ECJ. This branch leads the litigation and dispute management work undertaken for DEFRA, arising out of the foot-and-mouth crisis. "*Strategic thinker*" **John Heaps** (see p.559) heads up the national team. Dispute management forms a major part of the team's caseload, offering a meticulous approach to early case assessment and fielding several trained mediators within the team. Telecoms, IT and competition matters are areas of great strength for the team. **Clients** mmO2; Terra Industries; DEFRA; ASDA.

HAMMOND SUDDARDS EDGE "*The top players in Leeds,*" the firm is home to a collection of "*impressive, dynamic partners.*" **Peter Crossley** is "*very much in the limelight, a real competitor,*" according to rivals. The group is active on multi-jurisdictional fraud, recently undertaking a case worth £13 million involving parties in the US and UK. With a flair for IT-related disputes,

the team has acted on a claim against Cable & Wireless regarding IT services. Further highlights include multimillion pound manufacturing contract disputes, often with a product liability angle. The mediation-oriented team also boasts several US-qualified lawyers and expertise within pensions, shareholder disputes and warranty claims. **Clients** Austin Reed; Bradford & Bingley; Harrods; The National Grid Company.

IRWIN MITCHELL (see firm details p.1009) This is a firm best known for bulk class actions; however, this should not detract from its sizeable commercial client base and attendant cases. Retail petrol and oil is a particular area of specialism; the team has worked for Esso in a group litigation order regarding claims brought on behalf of former retailers. Peter Bellamy heads the group, which is actively involved in ADR. It recently represented a local university in a dispute following the termination of a distance learning agency agreement, where claims in excess of £500,000 were settled for a significantly smaller sum via mediation. The team also undertakes professional negligence and partnership, shareholder and supply of goods disputes. **Clients** AXA Sun Life Services; British Steel; Alfred McAlpine; Henry Boot; Minit UK.

PINSENT CURTIS BIDDLE (see firm details p.1102) Chasing the leaders for the top spot, these "*successful, old-style litigators know how to put together a good case.*" National head of litigation **Nigel Kissack** (see p.562) is still very much on the scene, "*a master tactician, who gets to the nub of the matter.*" He led the team on a multi-party product liability litigation involving the PVC industry, on behalf of a subsidiary of IMI. **Stuart Chapman** (see p.554) is appreciated for his "*calm, analytical approach,*" and heads the Leeds team. The emphasis here is upon early case assessment. IT disputes, fraud, pensions and competition work are thriving areas, and the team boasts a niche in forensic accounting. **Clients** Pace Micro Technology; Tesco; Groupe Schneider; E&E Ltd; Northgate Information Solutions.

WALKER MORRIS (see firm details p.1178) "*A commercially sensible team*" seen mostly on regional cases, and its banking work is especially well regarded. Peers contend that **Gwendoline Davies** (see p.556) is "*passionate about her cases; she is good to have on your side.*" She led the team acting for the Bank of Scotland on a complex guarantee action against Henry Butcher, a firm of surveyors and valuers. The team has acted in a significant number of successful injunction cases, for clients such as Intelligent Finance, Foot Locker and CALA Homes. The diverse client base ranges from corporates to wealthy individuals and trusts. **Clients** BUPA; Brown & Jackson; Debenhams; Northern Foods Group; Persimmon Homes.

GORDONS CRANSWICK SOLICITORS "*Stronger on the back of its merger,*" this firm, which has a reputation for adeptly handling "*decent cases,*" has broadened its sphere of expertise. Asset finance litigation specialist Jennifer Johnson heads the department, which also covers interference with goods, penalty clauses, relief from forfeiture and allegations of misrepresentation. **Clients** A major supermarket group; an internet banking company; finance companies; owner-managed businesses; construction companies.

KEEBLE HAWSON Clients select the firm for its "*unparalleled understanding of our business.*" The "*confident, committed*" **Charles Rothwell** (see p.567) leads a team endorsed for its technical strength. It has attracted 40 new corporate clients over the past year. Partnership, IP, property and contract disputes are all facets of the team's experience. **Clients** Volvo Financial Services; Tarmac Central; Yorkshire Bank; MICE Group; Trianco Redfyre.

LUPTON FAWCETT "*Leaders of the medium-sized firm pack,*" it can boast an "*expanding team.*" Accredited mediator Paul Houghton undertakes a broad range of mediations, including professional negligence, contract disputes and personal injury disputes, with values ranging from £20,000 to £9 million. Early case analysis is an essential component of the team's ethos. Its base of experience extends to property litigation, competition issues, IP and IT disputes. **Clients** BAT.

ROLLITS (see firm details p.1115) A number of our interviewees endorsed this as "*the best firm in Hull, with an impressive, established client base.*" "*Lateral thinker*" **Ralph Gilbert** (see p.558) is respected for his sound judgement, particularly within property litigation matters. An emphasis upon dispute resolution, and an increasingly European flavour, can be found here, and the team's dual-qualified German lawyer has advised two German organisations in commercial disputes where the jurisdiction of the English court was at issue. Construction has proved to be a source of instruction this year, alongside IP, product liability and landlord and tenant work. **Clients** American Standard Plumbing (UK); Fenner; Wabco Automotive UK; Bonus Electrical.

ANDREW M. JACKSON (see firm details p.845) A growing team, characterised for many by its experience within admiralty litigation. However, the team has been involved in notable disputes outside this remit, such as the resolution by negotiation of ASD v Michael Barugh Steel Stockholding, which concerned proceedings against a financial institution on behalf of a limited company for a breach of contract and negligence. "*Battler*" **Hugh Smith** (see p.568) possesses a niche within food law litigation, in

YORKSHIRE/NORTH EAST ■ LITIGATION GENERAL COMMERCIAL

which his depth of experience is celebrated by market commentators. International disputes have become an increasingly prominent feature of the firm's workload, particularly within the area of sale of goods. **Clients** MFI Properties; Dixons; Seven Seas; Central Land Developments.

BROOKE NORTH "*A developing practice,*" which reaches well beyond its strong reputation in insolvency. The team has recently been occupied with a £4 million pension fraud case, which involved a five-week trial. Head of department Richard Stockdale leads the team, whose scope extends to professional negligence, IP and construction. Property work has afforded greater contentious work this year; the team was involved in one such trial concerning a sum of £20 million. Arbitration is another facet of the team, particularly within the construction sector. **Clients** The Evans Group; LinPAC Plastics; US clients.

COBBETTS (see firm details p914) The merger between Leeds-based Read Hind Stewart and Manchester's Cobbetts has proved to be a fruitful alliance, producing a "*technical, on-the-ball team,*" which is commended for getting the results.

GOSSCHALKS Clients singled out the firm's clear, professional advice to our researchers. The team, led by Nick Dean, has recently enjoyed success in a patent trial, in which infringement proceedings were turned into a revocation action. The core of the team's work is made up of contractual disputes, within the fields of commercial fraud, property and insurance. **Clients** Dixon Motors; Thompson Plastics; East Yorkshire Aluminium & Glass; William Hill; Punch Retail.

NORTH EAST

LITIGATION: GENERAL COMMERCIAL
■ NORTH EAST

[1] **Dickinson Dees** Newcastle upon Tyne
Ward Hadaway Newcastle upon Tyne
[2] **Eversheds** Newcastle upon Tyne
[3] **Robert Muckle** Newcastle upon Tyne
Watson Burton Newcastle upon Tyne
[4] **Hay & Kilner** Newcastle upon Tyne

LEADING INDIVIDUALS
[1] **COLLINSON Ian** Ward Hadaway
ELLIOTT Robert Ward Hadaway
HARVEY Guy Dickinson Dees
[2] **SOLOMAN Martin** Hay & Kilner

This book is the product of 6,582 1/2 hour interviews. See p.7 for BMRB audit. Within each band, firms are listed alphabetically. See individuals' profiles p.552

DICKINSON DEES (see firm details p.938) It retains the regional crown acknowledge interviewees, due to its "*commercial nous and blue-chip client base.*" Much work is derived from the existing corporate client base; however, its increasing amount of standalone work is typical of this firm's national reach. Professional negligence has provided a steady flow of instructions of late. The "*figurehead*" of this department, **Guy Harvey** (see p.559), has been advising on serious fraud cases. This "*expanding team, with City standard expertise,*" has advised on a potential £4 million claim against DEFRA for payment of clean-up costs following the foot-and-mouth epidemic. Shareholder disputes, property litigation and warranty claims are all areas of specialism. **Clients** Plcs; US-based companies.

WARD HADAWAY (see firm details p.1180) Market commentators spoke of a firm that is aiming for a greater volume share of the litigation market. Competitors agree that high-profile individuals and a broad base of work render this a formidable team. "*Civilised opponent*" Robert Elliott (see p.557) has an emphasis upon mediation; with an "*academic approach, he gets his head around the details.*" The "*energetic*" Ian Collinson (see p.555) "*gives logistical direction to a case.*" He specialises in professional negligence, achieving recent success in the Court of Appeal.

EVERSHEDS (see firm details p.949) This team was recommended for its "*thorough and committed approach,*" and is respected for its Europe-wide client base. With the Eversheds commitment to dispute resolution, this team is advising DEFRA on the regional claims following the foot-and-mouth epidemic. The team, led by Susan Howe, is particularly adept at competition litigation, representing a Northern business client, which was the subject of a dawn raid by European commissioners. The team was subsequently called upon to supervise an investigation by officials. **Clients:** Rolls-Royce; Fermex International; Invensys.

ROBERT MUCKLE The firm has moved up the tables due to overwhelming client endorsement. Clients depict a hard-hitting team, which "*did not need to be aggressive in our case, so thorough were they in preparation.*" The arrival of Paul Jonson from Pinsent Curtis Biddle to head up the department has been welcomed, and the team has recently undertaken some substantial cases. One such example has been the professional negligence claim of Labelling Dynamics against Watson Burton solicitors, recovering a six-figure sum for the former. The team also scores well with its involvement in cross-border matters and shareholder and warranty disputes. **Clients** Fone Logistics; International Maritime Group; Rowan Specialist Interiors; Sevcon.

WATSON BURTON A team best known for its construction work, but which has various spheres of expertise. Rob Langley heads the department, which has recently enjoyed success in the High Court, where the team defended Premier Direct Group on a claim from Reader's Digest. Devoted to education clients, the team undertakes litigation for the University of Durham colleges and the University of Sunderland. Confidentiality; sale of goods; banking; partnership and shareholder disputes are all strengths of the department. **Clients** Co-operative Wholesale Society; Northern Land; Premier Direct Group; Ultimate Leisure; Metnor Group.

HAY & KILNER Clients point to a "*small, efficient outfit*" renowned for its niche within railway work. On the construction side, the team has acted on a claim for £1.1 million on an engineering and construction project, where it was involved in several mediation meetings. Head of department **Martin Soloman** has the confidence of peers who refer work to him. The team is also active in professional negligence, partnership, IP and minority shareholder disputes. **Clients** Insurance bodies; partnerships; owner-managed companies.

www.ChambersandPartners.com 533

LITIGATION GENERAL COMMERCIAL ■ SCOTLAND

SCOTLAND

LITIGATION: GENERAL COMMERCIAL
■ SCOTLAND

1
- **Brodies** Edinburgh
- **Dundas & Wilson CS** Edinburgh, Glasgow
- **Maclay Murray & Spens** Edinburgh, Glasgow
- **McGrigor Donald** Edinburgh, Glasgow

2
- **Shepherd+ Wedderburn** Edinburgh

3
- **Simpson & Marwick** Edinburgh

4
- **Anderson Strathern WS** Edinburgh
- **Bishops Solicitors** (formerly Morison Bishop) Glasgow
- **Burness** Edinburgh, Glasgow
- **MacRoberts** Edinburgh, Glasgow

5
- **Anderson Fyfe** Glasgow
- **Balfour & Manson** Edinburgh
- **Biggart Baillie** Edinburgh, Glasgow
- **Henderson Boyd Jackson WS** Edinburgh
- **Levy & McRae** Glasgow
- **Morton Fraser, Solicitors** Edinburgh

LEADING INDIVIDUALS

1
- **ANDERSON Peter** Simpson & Marwick
- **CONNAL Craig** McGrigor Donald
- **MACLEOD Colin** Dundas & Wilson CS
- **WILLIAMSON David** Brodies

2
- **CULLEN Joyce** Brodies
- **EASTON Ewan** Maclay Murray & Spens
- **SWANSON Alayne** Maclay Murray & Spens

3
- **DONALD Hugh** Shepherd+ Wedderburn
- **HAYWOOD Brent** Biggart Baillie
- **TYLER Alfred** Balfour & Manson
- **WATSON Peter** Levy & McRae

This book is the product of 6,582 1/2 hour interviews. See p.7 for BMRB audit. Within each band, firms are listed alphabetically. See individuals' profiles p.552

BRODIES (see firm details p.889) Traditionally a leading firm in Scottish litigation, there are strong teams on offer here in the related areas of property, employment and professional indemnity. Respected William Holligan has retired from the firm to become a full-time Sheriff, but the firm remains home to some outstanding litigators. **David Williamson** (see p.570) is one of three solicitor advocates at the firm and for a long time has been "*the leading litigator in Scotland*" with "*extensive experience and a degree of judgement greater than many.*" He also has an additional role as a part-time Sheriff. A leading player in the Scottish employment market, **Joyce Cullen** (see p.555) is the new head of commercial litigation, and has advised a major financial institution in an action against a joint venture partner. Peers consider her "*excellent – she rolls her sleeves up and gets stuck in.*" This large team is prominent on the regulatory side, and has instigated judicial review proceedings to challenge the decision of Edinburgh Council to grant planning permission for the construction of a waste water treatment plant. "*Easy to deal with and responsive,*" the team has further assisted on a claim for damages arising from a major bank's failure to adhere to the terms of its mandate, and was instructed on a contract claim for £1.5 million over the installation of an IT system. The younger generation at the firm, while numerous, has had a less prominent market profile than its established players; the market awaits the effect of new, internal appointments in throwing the spotlight on the depth of this "*quality team.*" **Clients** AGF Insurance; Allied Carpets; CIS Insurance; De La Rue; FMC Technologies; Forth Ports Authority; GKN Group Services; John Menzies; Norfrost; Royal & SunAlliance; Samuel Smith (Old Brewery) Tadcaster; Scottish Higher and Further Education Funding Councils; The Scottish Prison Service; South Lanarkshire Council; TM Retail.

DUNDAS & WILSON CS (see firm details p.943) The team is respected by clients for its "*efficiency, high level of expertise and accessibility,*" while peers point in particular to its insurance-related work. A long-standing reputation and a large team ensure that "*it is still considered big players,*" despite its departure from the Andersen Legal network. High-profile **Colin Macleod** is spoken of as a "*talented and pragmatic commercial litigator,*" skilled in professional indemnity and banking work. The team has acted for a UK plc in defence of a £3 million warranty claim and advised a major UK bank on a number of Court of Session's actions. The firm has represented a European distributor seeking enforcement and recognition of €18 million Scottish judgment, and was instructed by several major trust funds seeking approval of their cancellation of share premium accounts and share capital reduction. **Clients** Clydesdale Bank; Digital Animation; The Institute of Chartered Accountants of Scotland; KPMG; West of Scotland Water.

MACLAY MURRAY & SPENS (see firm details p.1048) Rivals laud the firm for its "*commercial awareness – it seeks to achieve what is reasonable.*" Its IP/IT and property litigation teams are especially well respected; internal restructuring has placed these groups inside their respective departments, refocusing the firm's commercial litigation practice on judicial reviews and tax-related matters. The firm is assisting Harrods in a judicial review case against the Inland Revenue and has conducted a further appeal on behalf of Scottish Provident Institution. **Ewan Easton**'s (see p.556) star is in the ascendant, with peers believing him "*a real lateral thinker and hyperintelligent,*" while clients appreciate that "*he doesn't take stupid points and you can always understand him even if you disagree.*" The team, considerable in its size and reach, has represented 110sport in an action against the World Snooker Association concerning a dispute over the staging of an alternative snooker tour. Head of department **Alayne Swanson** (see p.568) ("*a feisty opponent*") acted as a solicitor advocate for the pursuers in the case of Caledonia Subsea v Micoperi SRL, where it was held that Scots law applied to a contract in which a Scottish company was contracted to provide diving services for an Italian company on a construction project in Egypt. The firm has also acted for Ayrshire and Arran Health Board in two statutory appeals concerning devolution and human rights issues. **Clients** Allied Distillers; Amerada Hess; 110 Sport; Harrods; Lithgows; Margaret Blackwood Housing Association; Precision Technology Group; Scottish Provident Institution.

McGRIGOR DONALD (see firm details p.1065) The firm remains a leader in construction litigation and has seen an increase in its work on regulatory issues. The recent link-up with the KLegal network is anticipated to broaden the firm's client base, although the network formerly lacked an existing Scottish base. **Craig Connal QC** (see p.555), Scotland's first appointed solicitor advocate silk, received impressive market feedback. "*Straight down the middle – industrious, bright and not overly aggressive,*" he is also known for his planning expertise. The return of Jim Cormack to the firm after five years at the Bar should also strengthen the unit's capability. The firm has continued to represent BP concerning health and safety regulatory issues at its Grangemouth complex, and William Grant has retained the department's services on a passing off action, a matter that has now gone to the House of Lords. The firm has conducted a judicial review on behalf of the Law Society of Scotland concerning a disciplinary tribunal and has acted for the US insurers in the fatal accident inquiry into a light aircraft crash in Paisley. **Clients** BP; Imperial Tobacco; Law Society of Scotland; William Grant & Sons.

SHEPHERD+ WEDDERBURN (see firm details p.1130) This traditional litigation firm has increased both its work before the commercial courts and the volume of mediation in which it is involved. It has assisted clients on the restructuring matters and the regulation of interim payments between parties pending the outcome of an action. Much of the firm's reputation in this field rested on the shoulders of the hugely experienced Ian MacLeod, who retired from the firm in May 2002. One of the most "*formidable and outstanding figures in Scottish litigation for 25 years,*" the market now awaits the impact of his departure. The firm is, however, not lacking in well-known individuals; medical negligence and aviation specialist **Hugh Donald** (see p.151) comes highly recommended, with "*lots of experience in a varied practice – smart and switched-on.*" He worked on the King v Bristow Helicopters case (appealed to the House of Lords), relating to a critical interpreta-

SCOTLAND · LITIGATION GENERAL COMMERCIAL

tion of the Warsaw Convention. **Clients** Bredero Pipe Coaters; Bryant Homes; General Accident; HSBC; Orange; Pillar Property; Royal London & Mutual Assurance; Scottish Power; Scottish Provident; Shell UK; Thus.

SIMPSON & MARWICK (see firm details p.1138) Professional negligence work makes up much of the firm's specialist defendant litigation practice, with more general instructions, aviation and personal injury assistance contributing the rest. Peers speak of a firm with both "*volume and quality*" in its caseload. As well as professionals and insurers, the client base includes small- to medium-sized industrial companies and electronics boutiques (both software and hardware disputes). Clients told us that the partner-led firm has an open approach: it "*states its ground and is good for advising on positions.*" It has assisted the manufacturer of a cash transactions software package in an action concerning alleged fault and loss. The team has assisted a building contractor in a dispute over the alleged design failure of a bridge and its components. "*A good advocate and a class player,*" solicitor advocate **Peter Anderson** (see p.552) "*has his finger on the pulse*" and was particularly recommended for his insurance expertise. **Clients** Small- to medium-sized commercial industrial companies; electronics companies; professionals; insurers.

ANDERSON STRATHERN WS (see firm details p.844) This mid-sized team divides its labours between a strong banking litigation focus and more general assistance, working in conjunction with its commercial and corporate banking teams. The firm acted on the multimillion Labinski v BP Oil Development case and a connected case involving GS Brown, arising from the exercise of a servitude right by BP preventing land development. The team fields solicitor advocates and has a track record in insolvency, employment and IP rights disputes. The past year has also seen a particular increase in constructive trusts work, where the firm has been working with a Scottish bank on a series of 'class' claims against surveyors and solicitors. **Clients** Buccleuch Estates; Clydesdale Bank; The Coal Authority; Crown Estates Commission; Dumfries & Galloway Council; Napier University; PwC; Royal Bank of Scotland; Scottish Rugby Union; Zurich Commercial.

BISHOPS SOLICITORS (see firm details p.1076) Headed by David Whyte, the litigation unit is respected among peers for providing a good service in defendant personal injury and insurance reparation work. The team is also active in construction, employment and insolvency issues. The market awaits the impact of the firm's demerger this year.

BURNESS Property, media and technology-based disputes comprise the main focus areas for the group. The departure of respected Brent Haywood to Biggart Baillie was considered by several interviewees to have affected the firm's profile over the past year. Clients did commend the team of dispute resolution head Philip Rodney as "*absolutely committed to the case,*" employing a "*light touch.*" A major retail developer has instructed the firm on a claim for multiple design and installation defects at a retail park. Rodney has led an integrated, cross-departmental unit, which has successfully brought a privacy claim concerning unauthorised photographs against OK! Magazine on behalf of JK Rowling. It has also advised on an interdict and damages action against Channel 4 regarding a documentary on an expedition to Everest, which resulted in the death of a climber. The team has conducted a breach of contract claim against Ericsson, and been instructed by a UK insurance company over a £700,000 claim on a performance bond. **Clients** BBC; Class 98; HarperCollins; The Harris Tweed Association; Health Care International; Highland Spring; JK Rowling; The Leith Agency; News Group Newspapers; Scottish Equitable; The Scottish Football Association; SMG; Standard Life; Which? Magazine.

MACROBERTS (see firm details p.1049) A respected employment litigation team and a market-leading construction practice has led to the creation of separate units at the firm for these areas. Spin-off work from the property, corporate and IP/IT department continues to keep the team busy. Partner David Arnott acted for British Energy in a dispute concerning the supply of electricity to the Hunterston and Torness nuclear generating stations. This expanding team advised the Royal Bank of Scotland in a VAT appeal in connection with the disposing of bank notes from ATM machines. Demonstrating the breadth of its expertise, the team represented Carillion and Karl Construction on two separate actions, which were the first cases in Scotland to hold that inhibition and arrestment procedures were contrary to Article 1 of the first protocol to The European Convention on Human Rights (ECHR). **Clients** AMEC; British Energy; Carillion; Crouch Mining; Johnston Press; Railtrack; Royal Bank of Scotland; Safeway; Scottish Equitable; Scottish Qualifications Authority.

ANDERSON FYFE (see firm details p.843) A small but robust unit, it has a particular track record in banking and commercial contract work, allied to the firm's insolvency department. Solicitor advocate and partner Roddy McIlvride is a member of this respected team. It has been active in matters relating to directors' warranties in share purchase transactions and professional claims over allegedly negligent advice.

BALFOUR & MANSON (see firm details p.856) Fred Tyler (see p.637) is the most prominent member of this large department, which is headed by Maggie Neilson; he is also recommended for his professional indemnity and clinical negligence work. Covering the broad base of commercial litigation, the team has acted in King v Bristow Helicopters, deciding whether the term 'bodily injury' incorporates psychiatric illness. It assisted on the Tehrani v UKCC matter, a judicial review and eventual confirmation of the impartiality and independence of the professional body for nurse, midwives and health visitors under Article 6 of the ECHR. The group has also advised on a judicial review of the method of entitlement to residential care.

BIGGART BAILLIE (see firm details p.871) A good general litigation firm with noted specialist areas in insurance reparation and insolvency. The firm has recently been appointed to deal with half of all directors' disqualifications proceedings of The Insolvency Service of the DTI. Head of the department and construction specialist Murray Shaw leads a large and growing team that derives referrals from both its own departments and from other firms. The arrival of **Brent Haywood** from Burness is a sign of this expansion and is anticipated to strengthen the team.

HENDERSON BOYD JACKSON WS The overall contentious work of the firm is split between general commercial litigation and insolvency instructions, which are dealt with by a linked but separate asset retrieval unit called Recovery Solutions. For the second consecutive year, the firm was said to be moving forward and developing its expertise, with peers identifying it as "*a well-organised player that hasn't got carried away with itself.*" Litigation head Maggie Moodie heads up a group that has assisted on a £3.3 million IT action over an alleged breach of contract against a major bank. It has worked on an ongoing instruction concerning patents, now in the House of Lords, as well as insolvency-based litigation on behalf of liquidators, receivers and trustees.

LEVY & MCRAE (see firm details p.1041) "*A strong, ballsy, if small, firm,*" its lawyers are "*always on the mark.*" Senior partner, head of litigation and part-time Sheriff **Peter Watson** (see p.275) has a particular expertise in media law. Historically noted for its work on high-profile matters such as Piper Alpha and Lockerbie, his team has assisted a major commercial client in Holland on a dispute concerning software problems. The group also assists on copyright and publishing issues and on contractual disputes in engineering.

MORTON FRASER, SOLICITORS (see firm details p.1077) A small team under divisional manager Peter Braid assisted Scottish & Newcastle in an international dispute concerning the supply and installation of a motion simulation

LITIGATION GENERAL COMMERCIAL ■ SCOTLAND/NORTHERN IRELAND

ride at an amusement park. The Civil Aviation Authority instructed the team in a month-long fatal accident inquiry into the crash of a Cessna aircraft, and it has been involved in a dispute where a company secretary tried to assume control of his employees bank account by issuing controlling shares to a company owned by him. The team has also represented an international organisation concerning the use of allegedly fraudulent documents during the course of a litigation. It has also been instructed by Clydesdale Bank in a defence of a £2 million damages claim concerning an alleged failure to exercise reasonable care in the sale of a farm over which they had security. **Clients** Bank Austria; Halifax; National Australia Group; Nationwide Building Society; Scottish & Newcastle; The Scottish Agricultural College; Skipton Building Society; UKAEA.

NORTHERN IRELAND

LITIGATION: GENERAL COMMERCIAL
■ NORTHERN IRELAND

1
- **Carson McDowell** Belfast
- **Elliott Duffy Garrett** Belfast

2
- **C & H Jefferson** Belfast
- **Cleaver Fulton Rankin** Belfast
- **L'Estrange & Brett** Belfast
- **McKinty and Wright** Belfast
- **Mills Selig** Belfast

3
- **Johns Elliot** Belfast
- **Johnsons** Belfast
- **Tughans** Belfast

LEADING INDIVIDUALS

1
- **BECKETT Sam** L'Estrange & Brett
- **LYNCH Michael** Elliott Duffy Garrett
- **TURTLE Brian** Carson McDowell
- **WILSON Michael** Elliott Duffy Garrett

2
- **CRAWFORD Sandra** McKinty and Wright
- **FOX Brendan** Cleaver Fulton Rankin
- **O'DRISCOLL Pat** Cleaver Fulton Rankin
- **SPRING Paul** Mills Selig

3
- **CURRY Adam** Mills Selig

This book is the product of 6,582 1/2 hour interviews. See p.7 for BMRB audit. Within each band, firms are listed alphabetically. See individuals' profiles p.552

CARSON MCDOWELL (see firm details p.901) The firm's first-rate company department feeds into this broad litigation practice, which has a particular emphasis on IP disputes. **Brian Turtle** (see p.569) heads the firm's litigation and employment teams and is a leading figure in professional negligence. Recommended by interviewees for complex disputes, he assisted Multimedia Infotech in its defence of an action by Philips alleging a compact disc patent infringement. The firm also advised an internet bookseller in its defence over the sale of copies of a book banned in Northern Ireland, clarifying the enforceability of Northern Irish judgments in courts abroad. Partnership disputes, IT and licensing law matters also feature strongly in the caseload. **Clients** Multimedia Infotech; internet booksellers.

ELLIOTT DUFFY GARRETT (see firm details p.947) Peers endorsed this general commercial litigation practice for the depth of its experience. Additionally noted for his planning expertise, head of litigation **Michael Lynch** (see p.562) "*does a prodigious amount of work*" and is liked by clients for his "*down-to-earth approach – he looks at the overall picture.*" Corporate head **Michael Wilson** is held in high regard for his litigation work. A leader in the product liability field, his work in the insolvency sector was also highlighted by interviewees.

C & H JEFFERSON (see firm details p.1013) The firm's litigation practice interlinks with its professional negligence work and insurance client base, resulting in "*attention to detail and the ability to negotiate complex matters,*" according to clients. This "*upfront, on the ball*" team fields Gareth Jones. A young group focusing on defendant litigation, it assists professionals and insurers in various areas, including construction-related work. The firm also advises on issues of public liability and frequently acts as Northern Irish agents for City-based and other mainland firms.

CLEAVER FULTON RANKIN (see firm details p.910) This broad-based, partner-led practice has an emphasis on insurance, construction, fraud and debt. Head of the department **Brendan Fox** (see p.195) has specialist IP and construction knowledge. His "*commercial*" style is mirrored in his fellow partner **Pat O'Driscoll** (see p.565). Highlight work for the team has included acting for the Oil Promotion Federation in opposition to a grant given to an Irish company by the Northern Ireland Assembly for a pipeline between Dublin and Derry. The small but growing team worked with the National Federation of Retail Newsagents in an action against local newspapers for a breach of the then Restricted Trade Practices Act. The past year has also seen a rise in IP cases, such as the firm's successful assistance to Wedgwood on a trademark infringement and passing off action. **Clients** Ballygowan Water; Oil Promotion Federation; Wedgwood; National Federation of Retail Newsagents.

L'ESTRANGE & BRETT (see firm details p.1039) The firm has one of the strongest commercial client bases in the province, stemming from its thriving commercial property team. A correspondingly robust litigation practice under the "*cool, reflective and level-headed*" **Sam Beckett** (see p.192) is the result. Also a construction specialist, his "*straightforward*" approach has aided a local developer on a major arbitration brought by a contractor and subcontractor arising out of the construction of a residential care home. The firm undertook a successful judicial review brought by a private landowner refused planning permission for a proposed housing development. It has also assisted professional practices on a number of partnership disputes, advised on professional negligence claims and acted on several separate allegations of unfair treatment by minority shareholders. **Clients** BP; developers; landowners; professionals.

MCKINTY AND WRIGHT (see firm details p.1066) One of the most established and largest litigation teams in Northern Ireland, it is recommended by peers for insurance and shipping work. The team has also seen an increase in media and employment-related instructions as part of a refocusing of the department. Partner **Sandra Crawford** (see p.555) has defended a major bank in its defence of a negligence claim, and has defended another claim by the owners of a newly constructed hotel. A strong professional negligence practice assists solicitors, medical practitioners and structural engineers in the defence of claims.

MILLS SELIG (see firm details p.1072) A company commercial firm that has successfully restructured to broaden out its client base, although peers recognise that defamation and related areas remain its best known specialities. **Paul Spring** (see p.274) in particular has led the way in the libel arena. New to our tables this year, partner **Adam Curry**'s (see p.556) no-nonsense approach prompted peers to consider him their first port of call.

JOHNS ELLIOT (see firm details p.1016) The firm makes good use of its company commercial and property arms, from which it derives many of its litigation instructions. Partner Ronnie Robinson typifies the firm's respected expertise on defamation matters. The small team is one of only two firms to be assisting the Northern Ireland Housing Executive with its arbitration work. It has advised Dunloe Ewart on a number of planning judicial reviews, including objections against the development proposals for Victoria Square. Other high-profile work has included a judicial review on behalf of the Police Ombudsman on a report concerning the Omagh bomb explosion, and advice to Westfield Shoppingtowns concerning the Castle Court shopping centre in Belfast. Clients; Dunloe Ewart; Police Ombudsman; Veterinary Defence Society; Westfield Shoppingtowns.

JOHNSONS (see firm details p.1016) The firm remains best known for its defamation work on behalf of plaintiffs, issuing 50 writs against several internet sites over the sale and distribution of the book, *The Committee*. Paul Tweed is an example of one of the specialists in this area.

The firm is also rightly respected for its insurance defendant work, enjoying a comprehensive insurance client base.

TUGHANS (see firm details p.1169) Respected by peers and clients alike for its insurance defence work, its corporate and property departments additionally provide a steady stream of spin-off litigation. Under senior partner and head of litigation Michael Gibson, the firm also has a good base in both employers' and public liability work. It has been involved on the 'D5 Inquiry' at the House of Lords, acting for a property developer on the judicial review of the granting of planning permission for the development of a large site. It has also assisted a Northern Irish supplier in an action against the British Government concerning EU procurement provisions, and has assisted a US computer company on IP issues and on an alleged breach of contract. The firm continues to enjoy the benefits of working in conjunction with a linked firm in Dublin, receiving referrals from a number of mainland firms. **Clients** Property developers; housing providers.

LITIGATION BANKING & FINANCE

OVERVIEW "*Watch out – it's becoming hairier*," warned one practitioner, in reference to how regulatory and contentious banking matters are becoming increasingly interwoven in the wake of the Enron catastrophe. Top practitioners are seeing an upturn in potential global investment litigation, ADR and class actions, while across the board, practices are gearing up to the client's increasing need for risk management advice in addition to litigation expertise. Many predict that the increasing trend in innovative fund raisings and fund restructurings will result in related litigation. Despite noting that investment banks tend to "*shop around more,*" one leading practitioner observed that "*it is strong institutional relationships between product areas at every level of seniority that still provides the leverage*", although this clearly gives rise to conflicts which open out the market somewhat. However, at this level, it is those with specialist expertise in "*understanding the product,*" and only the "*very best litigation practices,*" which emerge as the main contenders.

LONDON

LITIGATION: BANKING & FINANCE
■ **LONDON**

1. **Allen & Overy**
   Clifford Chance
   Freshfields Bruckhaus Deringer
2. **Linklaters**
3. **Herbert Smith**
   Lovells
4. **Norton Rose**
   Slaughter and May
5. **Ashurst Morris Crisp**
   Simmons & Simmons
6. **CMS Cameron McKenna**
   Denton Wilde Sapte
   Richards Butler
   Stephenson Harwood

This book is the product of 6,582 1/2 hour interviews. See p.7 for BMRB audit. Within each band, firms are listed alphabetically.

ALLEN & OVERY (see firm details p.841) The firm is admired by competitors for its consummate ability to leverage "*fantastic*" work from its top-level banking client base. "*Hugely experienced and well integrated,*" the team has consolidated "*a hell of a lot of expertise,*" including bond issues and Euromarkets matters. Peers report that "*well- rounded*" head of the banking and finance litigation group, **Tim House** (see p.560) is "*faultless at hitting the right note in whatever aspect he's handling.*" He has been advising a leading investment bank on a $300 million arbitration arising from an emerging markets acquisition in the financial services sector (includes cross-border regulatory issues). Head of litigation **Peter Watson** (see p.570) is described by clients as "*a pleasure to work with;*" he has advised a US investment bank on a bonds default worth $50 million, and represented a bank in dispute with a clearing system regarding a fine imposed for its failure to deliver 200 million of bonds. "*Highly focused and efficient,*" **John O'Conor** (see p.565) is commended by peers as a "*tough, clever litigator*" with expertise in derivatives matters, while blue-chip clients rave about his "*superb technical ability and highly responsive style.*" He has been acting for First Rand Bank in a $200 million claim concerning a gold derivatives joint venture in South Africa. The team has also been acting for a group of former non-executive directors of Equitable Life in defence of the £3.3 billion claim brought against them by the Society and acting for an investment bank in connection with the South African Government investigation into the dramatic decline of the rand. **Clients** ABN AMRO; CSFB; JPMorgan Chase; Nomura International; Standard Chartered Bank; Royal Bank of Scotland; UBS.

CLIFFORD CHANCE (see firm details p.911) "*Juggernaut litigators.*" The team is highly favoured by in-house counsel for its "*consensual, user-friendly*" work ethic, fielding partners who are "*incredibly responsive and thorough.*" Among those said to underpin team quality, **Roger Baggallay** (see p.553) gains peer endorsement as an "*impressive, knowledgeable and highly experienced*" litigator. He has been acting for Dresdner Kleinwort Benson in a restitution case against Glasgow resulting from void interest rate swaps, now proceeding in Scotland following hearing in the European Court of Justice. Returning to the fold following completion of the Bermudan Thyssen case, **Jeremy Sandelson** (see p.567) garners solid endorsement as a "*sharp, clever operator*" whom banks regard as "*a leading player,*" while "*class performer*" **Simon Davis** (see p.556) is said by clients to be "*frightfully talented.*" He acted for Commerzbank and its subsidiary (Jupiter International Group) in a high-profile dispute with the latter's former chief executive.

Market commentators point beyond the team's "*broad-ranging expertise*" to its leading cross-border capability, which establishes its presence as the top choice for complex, high-profile matters. Examples include settling a dispute concerning a defaulted debt on behalf of the buyer against the Central Bank of Yemen, involving litigation in London with parallel attachments obtained in Frankfurt. **Clients** ABN AMRO; Bank of New York; Citigroup; Commerzbank; Creditanstalt Group; Crédit Lyonnais Rouse; CSFB; Deutsche Bank; HSBC; JPMorgan Chase; Lehman Brothers; Merrill Lynch; Morgan Stanley; UBS.

LITIGATION BANKING & FINANCE ■ LONDON

LEADING INDIVIDUALS

1
- **ARCHER Nick** Slaughter and May
- **HOUSE Tim** Allen & Overy
- **STYLE Christopher** Linklaters
- **TAYLOR Ian** Freshfields Bruckhaus Deringer

2
- **BAGGALLAY Roger** Clifford Chance
- **BAND Christa** Herbert Smith
- **FAGAN Neil** Lovells
- **KELLY Jonathan** Simmons & Simmons
- **SANDELSON Jeremy** Clifford Chance
- **WATSON Peter** Allen & Overy

3
- **BAGGE James** Norton Rose
- **CAVE Tim** Freshfields Bruckhaus Deringer
- **DAVIES Valerie** Norton Rose
- **FINKLER Deborah** Slaughter and May
- **FORDHAM John** Stephenson Harwood
- **GILL Mark** Denton Wilde Sapte
- **GOOD Diana** Linklaters
- **GRANDISON Richard** Slaughter and May
- **WARNE David** Richards Butler

4
- **CANNON Lista** Richards Butler
- **DAVIS Simon** Clifford Chance
- **FOORD Roland** Stephenson Harwood
- **GODDARD John** Freshfields Bruckhaus Deringer
- **GWYNNE Richard** Stephenson Harwood
- **HART Andrew** Freshfields Bruckhaus Deringer
- **O'CONOR John** Allen & Overy
- **SPARROW Edward** Ashurst Morris Crisp
- **TURNBULL John** Linklaters

UP AND COMING
- **DUNCAN Michelle** Cadwalader, Wickersham & Taft
- **HOLLAND Jon** Lovells
- **PARISH Philip** Linklaters

See individuals' profiles p.552

FRESHFIELDS BRUCKHAUS DERINGER (see firm details p.964) "*Sheer astounding dedication – the Freshfields ethos*" sums up the market approval of this "*highly professional, slick operation.*" Distinguished by its "*Rolls-royce*" approach to "*big ticket*" litigation, the team also gains top marks for its "*pristine*" quality and team structuring, and its "*measured, methodical*" approach to devising strategies. Securitisation and regulatory work are key strands that flow from its premier corporate investment banking practice. "*Practical*" **Ian Taylor** (see p.568) services a "*formidable*" client base and "*knows the law inside out.*" A "*key attraction*" for US clients, his peers admire **Tim Cave**'s (see p.554) ability to communicate complex legal principles with "*total clarity.*" He successfully represented Morgan Grenfell in its defence of an appeal brought by SACE (Italian export credit agency) that related to the recovery of £100 million of export credit transactions in Hungary and Equatorial New Guinea. Clients endorse "*imaginative*" **Andrew Hart** (see p.559) as "*incredibly responsive*" – "*a lawyer who adds value at every stage and commercially assists in decision-making.*" He and Taylor have been advising financial institutions on inquiries conducted by major regulatory bodies in the UK and abroad. "*Hard-hitting*" **John Goddard** (see p.558) propounds his impressive reputation as a key advisor to the Bank of England, most recently preparing for a House of Lords trial arising from claims brought by depositors in BCCI for major damages arising from the Bank's alleged failure to supervise BCCI. **Clients** Bank of England; Clearstream; CSFB; Deutsche Bank; Lehman Brothers; Morgan Stanley; Rothschild; RBS; Société Générale.

LINKLATERS (see firm details p.1043) "*First class operators.*" Somewhat less visible than its peers, the team receives strong market commendation as a "*serious player*" in regulatory matters, which it handles for the firm's blue-chip investment banking clients and as part of its FSMA Blue Flag service line. Clients sanction the team's "*good value and efficient service on chunky matters,*" praising its "*scrupulously-researched, timely advice.*" Head of litigation and arbitration, **Christopher Style** (see p.568) maintains a "*huge reputation*" in the international arena. Described as "*efficient and imaginative,*" he is noted as a "*clear expositor*" on derivatives-related transactions. "*Extremely hands-on*" litigator **Diana Good** (see p.558) is described as a "*gutsy fighter for her clients*" while both "*experienced*" **John Turnbull** (see p.569) and "*derivatives and regulatory wizard*" **Philip Parish** (see p.565) receive strong recommendations. **Clients** Citigroup; CSFB; JPMorgan Chase; Merrill Lynch; Morgan Stanley; RBS Warburg.

HERBERT SMITH (see firm details p.992) Against the backdrop of an "*awesome litigation profile,*" the team receives unequivocal endorsement for its ability to "*litigate among the best*" in banking matters. Its burgeoning market profile relates to its prolific work on behalf of the firm's corporate client base and a prime ability to attract work in conflict situations. Clients' appreciate its "*innovative, imaginative, proactive*" approach. Approving the team's "*sound business judgement,*" one client explained that it "*takes matters beyond miserable litigation by coming at problems from every angle to find solutions or resolution.*" "*Classic litigator*" **Christa Band** (see p.553) is still the highlight of the "*well-trained*" team, which she has led on advice to leading investment banks in complex matters. This includes a multi-party claim relating to the flotation of a company and a multi-jurisdictional asset securitisation that failed to meet investor expectations. Further team highlights include advising investment banks on foreign debt obligations, financial advisory and prospectus liability. **Clients** Goldman Sachs; CSFB; Merrill Lynch, JPMorgan; Standard Chartered Bank; Deutsche Bank; Bear Stearns; Coutts; Close Brothers Corporate Finance; Schroder Salomon Smith Barney; Rabobank.

LOVELLS (see firm details p.1045) "*A terrific practice – top of the tree for retail work.*" Prevailing market opinion denotes a large pool of "*aggressive but gentlemanly*" litigators with "*all-round, sharpened knowledge*" of banks' operations and dispute objectives "*beyond being merely litigation providers.*" Leading counsel endorse the team's pedigree of experience that stands it in good stead to handle "*high profile, tricky knockabout dispute work with consummate skill.*" Among the team's best-known personalities, **Neil Fagan** (see p.557) exemplifies the "*mature, experienced*" practitioner with his "*sensible, balanced*" judgement. Joint-head of the practice group, **Jon Holland** (see p.560) is hailed by the bar as "*outstanding – a clever spark with a strong following.*" He successfully represented the EBRD and OPIC in the High Court and related arbitration proceedings to enforce US dollar loans to a Romanian borrower. The team continues to advise ING Barings and the liquidators of BCCI in ongoing high-profile proceedings. It also represents Barclays on a range of domestic and international issues, including those arising from the collapse of a pyramid selling scheme, a substantial constructive trust claim and various international cross-border disputes. **Clients** EBRD; BCCI; ING; Barclays; Standard Chartered Bank; Commerzbank; Lloyds TSB; Fidelity Investment Services; Invesco; Federal Bank of the Middle East.

NORTON ROSE (see firm details p.1084) An "*impressive, dependable*" team, commended by its opponents for taking a "*balanced, experienced*" view in disputes. In addition to strengths in insolvency and fraud, it is noted for its "*proficient*" handling of trading disputes for investment banks. **James Bagge** (see p.553) retains an "*excellent*" market reputation for his expertise in regulatory investigations work, which includes continuing involvement in the Thyssen case involving international trust litigation, and advising Ronnie Baird, the FSA's director in connection with his review of the regulation of Equitable Life. "*Highly motivated*" **Valerie Davies** (see p.556) creates positive impressions with her peers as one who "*thinks from the client's perspective.*" She acted on behalf of Visa International Service Association regarding Morgan Stanley Dean Witter's complaint to the European Commission about its exclusion from Visa's credit card issuing network. The team has also been conducting litigation on behalf of Komercni Banka (one of the largest banks in the Czech Republic) in matters arising out of a $250 million letter of credit fraud perpetrated on it, involving civil and criminal proceedings in the Czech Republic, Ireland and England. **Clients** ABN Amro; BHF Bank; Crédit Agricole Indosuez; Crédit Lyonnais; HSBC; Komercni Banka; RBS.

LONDON ■ LITIGATION BANKING & FINANCE

SLAUGHTER AND MAY (see firm details p.1140) As one leading practitioner commented, "*its exceptional to see them, but when you do – they're superb.*" The team's profile correlates to major litigation that it handles primarily for its celebrated corporate client base. **Nick Archer** (see p.552) boasts a leading profile in Middle Eastern and Indian banking operations. His peers describe him as a "*skilful tactician and unique lateral thinker,*" while clients are impressed by how he supervises with "*close personal involvement and enormous attention to detail.*" He successfully represented Crédit Industriel et Commercial against China Merchants Bank in a key case regarding letters of credit, and also acted for the Central Bank of Yemen in a multi-million dollar promissory note dispute with a debt trader arising out of a World Bank-sponsored debt restructuring programme. Clients think **Deborah Finkler** (see p.557) is "*terrific*" on the regulatory side, while counsel endorse her "*independent approach to the right way forward.*" She has acted for Deutsche Bank on several matters, including multi-million dollar proceedings regarding promissory notes issued by Garuda, and complex proceedings regarding a purchase of shares in the major German telecommunications company EMTV. **Richard Grandison** (see p.558) gains strong peer recommendation for his "*absolutely charming client manner*" and "*astute*" handling of matters. He continues to act for the liquidators of Barings in their £1 billion claim for negligence against Coopers & Lybrand and Deloitte & Touche, in respect of the collapse of the Barings Group. **Clients** Deutsche Bank; JPMorgan Chase; Abbey National; Schroders; ABN AMRO; Standard Chartered Bank; Dresdner Kleinwort Benson; Société Générale; Crédit Lyonnais; Banque Worms; Sakura Bank; KBC Bank; Crédit Industriel et Commercial; Riyad Bank.

ASHURST MORRIS CRISP (see firm details p.852) This "*cohesive*" team is said to be "*moving forward*" in terms of market reputation and is backed by a strong finance practice. It does "*a great job*" in mid-tier disputes, while also handling agency work for US firms without litigation capacity in the UK. Recently instructed by Nomura International, senior litigator **Ed Sparrow** (see p.568) gains peer credit for his "*impressive*" performance in complex litigation. The team continues to work on behalf of claimants in the Barings and Sumitomo matters, and has acted for two major international finance houses in issues arising from the Russian market collapse. Further highlights include acting for WestLB in a dispute regarding enforcement of on-demand guarantees with various Israeli counterparties, and acting for a major Dutch insurer on its claim against the asset management subsidiary of a French investment bank in relation to its failure to put in place a currency hedge. **Clients** Morgan Grenfell Private Equity; Close Brothers; Indosuez International Finance; Barings Futures (Singapore); NM Rothschild; WestLB; Nomura International; Sumitomo.

SIMMONS & SIMMONS (see firm details p.1136) "*They did a bloody good job,*" asserted one client. Having enjoyed heightened profile acting for Merrill Lynch Investment Managers against a claim by Unilever's pension fund (which ended in a mid-trial settlement), the team of "*accomplished litigators*" continues to garner peer respect as "*worthy opponents.*" Clients attest to a "*well-run*" practice, providing "*sensible, sound*" advice that "*progresses the case.*" **Jonathan Kelly** (see p.561) is said to display "*sound judgement.*" In addition to heading the team in the Merrill/Unilever case, he acted for Prudential Bache defending ten Commercial Court actions brought by various Latin American investors seeking recovery of losses following alleged miss-selling of leveraged structured Eurobonds. The team also acted for UBS in its dispute with Bank of China concerning a world-wide freezing order in respect of assets held by third party banks outside the jurisdiction, in conflict with the third party's local civil obligations. **Clients** Merrill Lynch; Prudential Bache; CSFB; Refco Overseas; UBS Warburg; Lloyds TSB.

CMS CAMERON MCKENNA (see firm details p.914) The team attracts widespread compliments for its "*effective, low key*" negotiating style on "*substantial*" litigation matters. It retains strong market recognition for retail banking and capital markets work, particularly derivatives disputes. The team, led by Duncan Aldred, advised a large overseas investment bank on its position on trades in light of the financial difficulties of SwissAir. It also advised a major bank on issues relating to its lending to a high profile company in financial difficulties. **Clients** Lloyds TSB; RBS; DEG; AIB; Crédit Lyonnais; KBC.

DENTON WILDE SAPTE (see firm details p.935) Its peers endorse the team's "*commercial*" approach to disputes, while its reputation on insolvency-related matters remains undiminished. Clients attest to its "*splendid analysis and thorough advice*" – one observed, "*it doesn't work in a vacuum.*" **Mark Gill** has been described by his peers as a "*ferocious litigator who looks at every single angle and doesn't give up,*" He leads the team that has been acting for Crédit Lyonnais in a $200 million dispute between Glencore International and Metro Trading International (and others). The team provides ongoing advice to the FSA in its enforcement work, most recently in the provisional liquidation and eventual compulsory liquidation of a PIA firm. **Clients** RBS; Bank of Scotland; Bank Leumi (UK); Bank One; Allied Irish Bank; Crédit Lyonnais; GE Capital; Cyprus Commercial Bank; Bank of Egypt.

RICHARDS BUTLER (see firm details p.1112) Industry experts deem it "*a force to be reckoned with,*" commending its "*staunch approach*" to banking litigation. Clients applaud the team's "*perceptive*" strategy, "*well-balanced*" negotiation skills, and adept handling of the law - "*they squeeze every ounce out of the documentation.*" Describing him as an "*extremely shrewd operator,*" peers tip **David Warne** (see p.570) as "*a dangerous opponent.*" Clients rave about "*superbly dedicated*" **Lista Cannon** (see p.554), ascribing her with "*immense credit*" for empowering the practice. She is leading the team advising the Co-operative Group on the performance of its £2 billion WS Pension Fund, which has been managed by Merrill Lynch Investment Managers (MLIM). The team also acted for an Iranian company in relation to recovery of payments made in error by a French bank under terms of a letter of credit issued in London relating to the supply of lead ingots in Sweden. **Clients** Bank of Scotland; Lloyds TSB; Maple Investments; Morgan Stanley; National Bank of Kuwait; The Co-OperativeGroup; Société Générale.

STEPHENSON HARWOOD (see firm details p.1147) "*The first port of call if there is a conflict,*" according to some clients. The team of "*adept litigators*" has established roots as an advisor to a raft of London-based banks. Clients "*naturally warm to*" **John Fordham** (see p.557), while peers respect this "*old hand*" with his "*vast knowledge*" and "*unflappable manner.*" He represented RBS in a multi-million pound claim under the Bankers' Blanket Bond insurance policy to recover losses sustained as a result of having lent to Versailles Trade Finance against fictitious book debts. He is ably supported by **Richard Gwynne** (see p.558), whom leading counsel endorse as "*a pragmatist who tells it straight,*" albeit with "*a marvellous client touch,*" and **Roland Foord** (see p.557) who handles difficult situations "*impeccably,*" according to clients. The team represented Standard Bank London (for a syndicate of banks) against Canara Bank in claims concerning bank guarantees, and is acting for HSBC in a matter before the House of Lords relating to the effect of a garnishee order abroad. **Clients** RBS; HSBC; Standard Bank; Den norske Bank; KBC Bank; Dresdner Bank; British Arab Commercial Bank; RZB-Austria.

OTHER NOTABLE PRACTITIONERS Operating within the Financial Restructuring Group of Cadwalader, Wickersham & Taft, "*tough, effective*" litigator **Michelle Duncan** (see p.556) is distinguished for representing the 1986 Noteholders Steering Committee, comprised of the senior creditors of Barings, in highly complex insolvency proceedings of the company.

www.ChambersandPartners.com 539

LITIGATION CIVIL FRAUD

LITIGATION: CIVIL FRAUD
LONDON

1. Allen & Overy
   Clifford Chance
   Freshfields Bruckhaus Deringer
   Herbert Smith
   Linklaters
   Lovells
   Norton Rose
2. Ashurst Morris Crisp
   Baker & McKenzie
   Slaughter and May
3. CMS Cameron McKenna
   Denton Wilde Sapte
   Richards Butler
   Simmons & Simmons
   Stephenson Harwood
4. Dechert
   Kingsley Napley
   Mishcon de Reya
   Peters & Peters
   SJ Berwin
   Theodore Goddard
5. DLA
   Eversheds
   Macfarlanes
   Withers LLP

This book is the product of 6,582 1/2 hour interviews. See p.7 for BMRB audit. Within each band, firms are listed alphabetically.

ALLEN & OVERY (see firm details p.841) Adjudged true specialists in the civil fraud arena, competitors conceded that this "*professional outfit*" was "*rightly at the forefront of the market.*" Clients praised a team, which takes a "*quick and efficient*" approach. The client base comprises investment banks, and wealthy individuals, and the team draws on the specialist knowledge of offshore jurisdictions belonging to its private client lawyers. **Robert Hunter** (see p.560) is "*a robust team leader, who deserves every accolade*" according to peers, while clients commended him as one who "*keeps your commercial interests at the forefront of proceedings.*" He is joined in the tables this year by **Mona Vaswani** (see p.569), who is "*growing in reputation and stature.*" She led the team in the successful defence of Marlborough Liechtenstein in a case brought by the estate of Francis Bacon. The regulatory investigations group acts for banks and financial institutions, and handles the whole gamut of regulatory work. Led by the "*cool, calm and collected*" **Sidney Myers** (see p.564), the group enjoys a reputation as "*utterly knowledgeable – the ones to turn to.*" It has been bolstered by the recruitment of John Mansell from the Financial Services Authority. Recent work has involved dealing with several major investigations by the SFA into suspected breaches of its rules and advising clients on the provisions of the Financial Services and Markets Act.

CLIFFORD CHANCE (see firm details p.911) The firm's client base includes investment banks, parties to securities transactions and listed companies. Its track record in regulatory matters was particularly commended to researchers. The German and US offices are of increasing importance for this practice, and it clearly attracts clients for its multi-jurisdictional expertise. An increasing emphasis of its workload has been asset tracing, where the team works closely with the Regulator. The "*figurehead*" of the practice remains **George Staple QC** (see p.568), a former head of the SFO. "*Hugely bright*" **Jeremy Sandelson** (see p.567) is a "*colourful and ebullient character*" who has spent a portion of his time overseas this year working on the Thyssen case. **John Potts** (see p.566) retained market commendation. The team acts for regulators and official bodies on their disciplinary procedures, and handles a steady flow of instruction arising out of UK Listing Authority investigations. A recent highlight has seen the firm handle the first test case relating to profits warnings, in which the jurisdiction of the Quotations Appeals Committee was tested. Following N2, the firm has also been instructed on a major market abuse investigation.

FRESHFIELDS BRUCKHAUS DERINGER (see firm details p.964) Clients commended the group as one which provides "*a Rolls-Royce service.*" Acting under the umbrella dispute resolution department, the team is well-placed to handle the multi-jurisdictional aspects of fraud proceedings, advising on potential criminal proceedings and remedies where necessary. Contact partner **Ian Taylor** (see p.568) was acknowledged as "*a fine project manager – he sees the bigger picture.*" Highlights include acting for Lloyd's in the Jaffray litigation and acting for HRH Prince Mohamad Bin Fahad Bin Abdulaziz Al Saud relating to an alleged embezzlement of $200 million from his personal bank account. The team continue to act on regulatory matters for financial institutions, including advice on investigations by the FSA, SFO, DTI, LME, the Stock Exchange and overseas regulatory authorities.

HERBERT SMITH (see firm details p.992) "*Commercial specialists created by a large litigation practice*" was how one interviewee described this offering, and many thought its litigation expertise formed a solid foundation for the fraud practice. The typical instructions here are asset tracing and advising banks, professional firms and companies on money laundering issues. Highlights include continuing to represent Riggs Bank in its action against a customer in relation to a fraud perpetrated through an invoicing discounting facility. The team is bolstered by the presence of "*gutsy litigator*" **Christa Band** (see p.553), who impresses peers as "*client focused at all times.*" Highly respected litigator, **Sonya Leydecker** (see p.562) is a new entry to our tables this year, "*calm and thoughtful, she thinks out a strategy and then achieves the desired result.*" The team act for professional advisors and banks on investigations by the DTI, the SFO, IR and Customs & Excise, inter alia.

LINKLATERS (see firm details p.1043) **Alan Walls** (see p.569), head of the fraud and regulatory litigation practice was applauded by market commentators as "*bright, thorough and tenacious.*" The firm's roster of overseas offices is put to good effect on cross-border matters. The team acted for the Agency for Restructuring of Russian Credit Organisation (ARCO) in the recovery of assets of SBS Agro Bank, which involved arbitration and litigation in a number of jurisdictions across the world. The core of the practice sees it acting for investment banks in instances of market manipulation, market abuse, insider dealing and money laundering. Interviewees also singled out **Philip Parish** (see p.565) as one who consistently "*shows good judgement.*" The team continue to advise the extensive client base on disciplinary procedures.

LOVELLS (see firm details p.1045) A buoyant international practice complements the team's growing fraud capability. Peers acclaimed a firm "*growing in stature,*" while clients commended its "*high-quality advice.*" **Jeremy Cole** (see p.555) was lauded as "*friendly, responsive, and conscientious*" and one skilled in handling multi-jurisdictional issues. He is currently acting for Grant Thornton on the RBG Resources case. **Keith Gaines** (see p.557) has a reputation as a "*punchy litigator,*" who enjoys "*an excellent track record.*" Highlights include acting for BCCI liquidators in their case against the Bank of England. The team has been further bolstered by the recruitment of Annie Hockaday from 3 Verulam Buildings. The group also acts on disciplinary matters as and when required by its corporate client base.

NORTON ROSE (see firm details p.1084) The team profits from a respected corporate client base, and advises on the whole gamut of fraud matters. It is also blessed with "*some heavyweight*" individuals. "*Formidable litigator*" **Deirdre Walker** (see p.569) is "*a good motivator*" who possesses "*a huge fund of experience and solid judgement.*" She acted for the State Bank of Saurashtra (a wholly-owned subsidiary of the State Bank of India) in actions brought against it by a Chinese shipping company pursuant to various letters of indemnity. The "*thorough and statesmanlike*" **James Bagge** (see p.553) is "*a leading light*" in regulatory matters. The firm has advised Komercni Banka (one of the largest banks in the Czech Republic) on matters arising out of a $250 million letter of

LONDON ■ LITIGATION CIVIL FRAUD

LEADING INDIVIDUALS

1
- BAGGE James *Norton Rose*
- HUNTER Robert *Allen & Overy*

2
- FORDHAM John *Stephenson Harwood*
- GAINES Keith *Lovells*
- GERRARD Neil *DLA*
- MYERS Sidney *Allen & Overy*
- POLLARD Stephen *Kingsley Napley*
- STAPLE George *Clifford Chance*
- TAYLOR Ian *Freshfields Bruckhaus Deringer*
- WALLS Alan *Linklaters*

3
- BAND Christa *Herbert Smith*
- BARRETT Elizabeth *Slaughter and May*
- FINKLER Deborah *Slaughter and May*
- OLIVER Keith *Peters & Peters*
- POTTS John *Clifford Chance*
- RAPHAEL Monty *Peters & Peters*
- SANDELSON Jeremy *Clifford Chance*
- WALKER Deirdre *Norton Rose*
- WOODCOCK Tony *Stephenson Harwood*

4
- BYRNE David *Dechert*
- COLE Jeremy *Lovells*
- KELLY Jonathan *Simmons & Simmons*
- LEYDECKER Sonya *Herbert Smith*
- PEARSON Nick *Baker & McKenzie*

UP AND COMING
- PARISH Philip *Linklaters*
- VASWANI Mona *Allen & Overy*

See individuals' profiles p.552

---

credit fraud. It has also co-ordinated the Bank's attempts to trace assets in several European jurisdictions.

ASHURST MORRIS CRISP (see firm details p.852) The firm's fraud practice is run from the litigation department where it can call upon "*talented litigators, who take a sensible approach.*" Fee earners based in the Paris, Frankfurt, Munich and Milan offices complement the London offering. Much of the work involves confidential investigations for corporate clients, relating to internal fraud and irregularities. The group continues to act for the liquidators of Barings Futures (Singapore) in claims against it by the former auditors of the company for nearly £1 billion. The team also represented Sirte Oil company in proceedings against a former employee and others, including the administrators of Channel Island trust companies, for fraud, which involved claims for knowing assistance and receipt. The case proceeded to trial and judgement was given in Sirte's favour. The team advise corporate clients under investigation by regulatory bodies.

BAKER & MCKENZIE (see firm details p.855) Defendants and claimant work is undertaken here, derived from a client base, which features banks and major corporates. The London office acts as the hub for an extensive network of overseas offices. Sources pointed to **Nick Pearson** (see p.565) as "*a great strategist and tactician,*" appreciating that he is "*a pleasure to deal with.*" He is currently managing the enforcement proceedings in the Grupo Torras litigation. The team has acted for a bank in a significant asset tracing and recovery exercise co-ordinating proceedings in Switzerland, Germany, the USA, British Virgin Islands and the Bahamas, to obtain asset freezing injunctions and disclosure orders on an emergency basis. The team also provide advice to clients on money laundering issues.

SLAUGHTER AND MAY (see firm details p.1140) Housed within the litigation and arbitration department, the civil fraud team acts for clients in both the commercial and financial sectors. The group has been involved in a number of high-profile asset tracing inquiries of late. It acted for the Liquidators of Barings following the collapse of the Barings Group, and advised Deutsche Bank following the Peter Young affair. The commendation elicited by this practice centres around its two leading lights: **Deborah Finkler** (see p.557) has won her following for her commitment and an impressive pedigree of top-flight cases, while **Elizabeth Barrett** (see p.553) was described as "*a doughty fighter and fine client handler.*"

CMS CAMERON MCKENNA (see firm details p.914) The department, which is headed by Duncan Aldred and Tony Marks, acts for corporates and banks on a broad spectrum of civil fraud matters. Highlights include advising the former chairman of Christie's in the price-fixing case in the US Courts. The group has also obtained emergency injunctive relief and pursued fraud claims on behalf of a major clearing bank, and has acted for a bank on a fraud-related constructive trusts dispute. The team also give advice on preventative and contingency planning for banks and advises on disciplinary matters as and when they arise.

DENTON WILDE SAPTE (see firm details p.935) The team acts for institutions and individuals faced with investigations and disciplinary proceedings. It has recently advised Deloitte & Touche as Trustees of Bre-X, in a case alleging that drilling samples were fraudulently salted. The Trustees successfully defended an appeal by the estate of the former chief executive and principal shareholder to the Privy Council to set aside the worldwide Mareva Injunction. The team also advises clients on disciplinary investigations.

RICHARDS BUTLER (see firm details p.1112) Lista Cannon heads a group, which represents a client base independent to that of the rest of the firm. Clients commended the team as "*prompt and accurate,*" appreciating its "*clear thinking and communication.*" Institutions and individuals are catered for and the team also wins a healthy proportion of its instructions via referrals from other solicitors. The team employs a good friends policy across many jurisdictions, ensuring that cross-border matters are dealt with immediately. The team has acted for a number of Brazilian investors in claims against an English investment bank and its Brazilian affiliate. It acted for a French company in relation to a prime bank instrument fraud, and has co-ordinated the multi-jurisdictional aspects of the proceedings. Rare among its peers, the firm places strong emphasis on its regulatory and investment practice. Expertise is offered on money laundering problems, while preventative advice is also placed high on the agenda.

SIMMONS & SIMMONS (see firm details p.1136) The civil fraud offering is based in the finance litigation department as part of the umbrella financial markets department. Its client base comprises investment banks and other financial institutions. The emphasis for the firm lies on regulatory matters. Non-contentious regulatory issues, Stock Exchange regulations and advice on contentious matters have all been a feature this year. **Jonathan Kelly** (see p.561) is the key figure here. The team advised Barclays Bank on its strategic alliance with Legal & General relating to the promotion by Barclays of the former's pension, savings and protection products.

STEPHENSON HARWOOD (see firm details p.1147) This growing department acts for a substantial client roster, derived from the UK and overseas. Its recent merger with Sinclair Roche and Temperley is hoped to bolster the breadth of instruction as well as extending the international client base. Peers agree that head of litigation **John Fordham** (see p.557), "*can handle everything, and is a fantastic, amiable lawyer.*" The team's highlights include acting for a US bank and a major Italian corporation in the enforcement of a $5 million judgement obtained in a fraud claim, which involved enforcement proceedings in England and Switzerland. Peers also reported that they would refer work to **Tony Woodcock** (see p.571), for his track record in appearing for and against the regulatory authorities.

DECHERT (see firm details p.934) This firm is a rare creature amongst City players, with feet firmly placed in both the civil and criminal camps. Head of Litigation **David Byrne** (see p.554) garnered the lion's share of comment as a "*great rainmaker*" and one who is "*dogged in litigation.*" Acting for claimants and defendants, the team draws its instructions from individuals and corporate clients. The firm continues to represent the interests of the Abacha family. Fraud involving investment funds and insider dealing is a key facet of the workload, and the team is also advising on an SFA investigation

www.ChambersandPartners.com 541

LITIGATION PENSIONS ■ LONDON

and on related insolvency and DTI matters. It has also advised three foreign exchange bureaux that have been targeted in the recent crackdown by Customs & Excise.

KINGSLEY NAPLEY (see firm details p.1023) A favourite among City players for referrals, the team uses its highly rated criminal practice as a platform to build an increasingly prominent civil practice. The team boasts the presence of **Stephen Pollard** (see p.398) (*"outstanding legal knowledge"*), although he is currently involved in the Bloody Sunday Inquiry. Inland Revenue, Customs & Excise and DTI investigations all form part of the caseload, and the team is currently advising on a large FSA investigation into a multinational bank. It has also been advising on international insider dealing investigations conducted by the DTI.

MISHCON DE REYA (see firm details p.1072) Gary Miller is head of the firm's special investigations and fraud litigation group. A *"technically savvy"* team stands out from its peers with its creation of a dedicated brand protection group, which acts in the anti-counterfeiting arena and tracks the recovery of traced assets. It remains most closely associated with its key client Microsoft and is retained by the company to advise on its European Strategy for anti-counterfeiting. It conducts multisite and multiparty search and seize operations as a result. The team also acts for various banking, financial services and technology clients. Clients reported that the firm is *"exceptionally quick, and superbly responsive to our needs."* The integrated team also works with and advises private enquiry agents. It continues to advise on DTI, FSA and IMRO investigations.

PETERS & PETERS (see firm details p.1100) *"Always stimulating and challenging opponents"* claimed competitors, this firm of "*smooth operators*" secures a healthy share of referrals from other law firms. A growing reputation in the civil arena enables the team to command instructions in its own right. **Monty Raphael** (see p.398) possesses "*a wealth of knowledge and is a great tactical player,*" while head of the firm's specialist civil fraud unit, **Keith Oliver** (see p.565) retains commendation for his "*exceptional ability.*" The team is acting for the claimants on the case of Luiz Vicente Barros Mattos Junior and others v Amaka Martina Anajemba Chief Innocent Anajemba and others, in trying to trace and recover the proceeds of a $240 million fraud.

SJ BERWIN (see firm details p.867) The team acts for claimants and defendants, and has a discernible institution bias. It has acted for Viktor Kozeny in AIG Group v Kozeny, in his defence of a $20 million fraud claim brought by AIG and others relating to a voucher privatisation scheme in Azerbaijan. The team also acted for the minority shareholder claimants in Konamaneni and others v Rolls-Royce Industrial Power (India) Limited and others. The shareholders brought a derivative action in England on behalf of SPGL in order to pursue a multimillion pound claim for bribery against Rolls Royce. The team acts for clients under investigation by the regulatory authorities.

THEODORE GODDARD (see firm details p.1158) The specialist fraud and asset recovery unit acts for companies, governments, banks and individuals who are the victims of fraud in asset tracing. It also represents corporate clients under investigation by the regulatory bodies, and was endorsed by interviewees for its skills in asset tracing and investigatory proceedings.

DLA Ex-police officer, **Neil Gerrard** attracted commendation from peers for his expertise in asset tracing. The firm acts for a broad range of clients on regulatory matters.

EVERSHEDS (see firm details p.949) Much of the firm's civil fraud instructions are derived from its respected litigation practice and an extensive network of nationwide offices with growing overseas connections. Clients are assisted on the whole range of fraud matters including defence work. The firm also has the capability to represent clients under investigation by the regulatory authorities.

MACFARLANES (see firm details p.1047) Possessed of an outstanding corporate client base, the firm is also the recipient of civil fraud related referrals from peers on a regular basis. This practice operates as part of the litigation and dispute resolution group. The team acted for AIG and others in fraud proceedings against Viktor Kozeny and others.

WITHERS LLP (see firm details p.1194) The firm makes an entry into our tables this year following market commendation. It appears frequently on trust-related matters, utilising its private client and equities expertise. The team is acting for the beneficiaries of Sheik Fahad Mohammed Al Sabah's Jersey family trusts in the long running Grupo Torras case. It is also acting for the three defendants on the CIBC Mellon Trust Company and Others v Stolzenberg and Others involving a £200 million fraud on the Daimler Chrysler pension fund. The team are seeking to set aside judgement entered against two of the defendants and discharge of freezing orders worth in excess of $30 million.

LITIGATION PENSIONS

EVERSHEDS (see firm details p.949) "*Sensible combatant*" and operational head **Giles Orton** (see p.565) stays steady in the top spot, according to interviewees, thanks to his "*extensive*" knowledge base and a personality that "*you warm to instantly.*" His move last year from Derby to London, as part of the firm's national integration strategy, is believed to have bolstered the London office's clout, though he still spends time in the regional offices. Joining him in the rankings this year is **Harold Lewis** (see p.562), who is recognised by market sources as a "*talented specialist.*" The team is known in the market for handling an enormous volume of pension work smoothly and efficiently. It took on 1,700 claims for various clients this year, following on from the Preston case in the House of Lords. A highlight was handling a dispute before the Pensions Ombudsman regarding £0.5 million in loans made by the former trustees of an insolvent company. **Clients** Pension scheme trustees.

LINKLATERS (see firm details p.1043) **Mark Blyth** (see p.553) is the star of this show, described by peers as "*sharp, professional and positive.*" Thanks to his efforts at the helm, the team rises in our rankings this year, gaining considerable respect from peers, clients and industry bodies. The group acts for employers, trustees, insurance/life companies, representative members, scheme advisors and pension professionals. Clients with multi-jurisdictional requirements benefit from a tightly integrated network of offices across Europe. Last year, the team acted successfully for Save & Prosper Group v Scoot in a crucial appeal against a decision by the Pensions Ombudsman. This concerned the ambit of a trustee's duty to provide certain information to the beneficiaries. **Clients** Pension professionals; trustees; insurance companies.

LOVELLS (see firm details p.1045) This historically strong unit includes two standout practitioners, **Angela Dimsdale Gill** (see p.556) and **Craig Monty** (see p.564). "*Strong-minded*" Gill, who heads the pension fund litigation group, is well known for the breadth of her legal learning, while her "*sturdy right-hand man*" Monty, draws glowing recommendations for

LONDON ■ LITIGATION PENSIONS

LITIGATION: PENSIONS
■ LONDON

1
- Eversheds
- Linklaters
- Lovells

2
- Mayer, Brown, Rowe & Maw
- Pinsent Curtis Biddle
- Sacker & Partners

3
- CMS Cameron McKenna
- Freshfields Bruckhaus Deringer
- Nabarro Nathanson
- Slaughter and May

LEADING INDIVIDUALS

1
- **BLYTH Mark** Linklaters
- **DIMSDALE GILL Angela** Lovells
- **ORTON Giles** Eversheds

2
- **CARRUTHERS Andrew** Mayer, Brown, Rowe & Maw
- **COOMBS Monica** Sacker & Partners
- **MONTY Craig** Lovells

3
- **ATKINSON Mark** CMS Cameron McKenna
- **LEWIS Harold** Eversheds
- **NURSE-MARSH Isabel** Pinsent Curtis Biddle
- **WARNE Jonathan** Nabarro Nathanson

This book is the product of 6,582 1/2 hour interviews. See p.7 for BMRB audit.
Within each band, firms are listed alphabetically. See individuals' profiles p.552

---

his intellect and professionalism. The group continued to act this year for the trustees of the BT Pension Scheme in court proceedings concerning the entitlements of thousands of members taking voluntary redundancy. It also dealt with a dispute for Industry-Wide Coal Staff Superannuation Scheme Trustees Ltd, a scheme set up to provide for coal workers following the privatisation of the industry. The dispute was over the interpretation of the scheme's provisions for members leaving early due to ill health. **Clients** Pension fund trustees.

MAYER, BROWN, ROWE & MAW (see firm details p.1060) The pension litigation team is thought to have benefited from the professional indemnity experience of the firm's insurance team with which it was amalgamated this year. The group receives instructions from companies across the pension sector on behalf of their institutional clients, as well as directly from major underwriters and an increasing number of actuaries. It recently acted for the employers in a sizeable surplus dispute relating to Lonrho's John Holt Scheme. Peers and clients were enthusiastic in their applause for lead partner **Andrew Carruthers** (see p.554), who was described as a "*pragmatic chap with a wealth of understanding.*" **Clients** Lonrho.

PINSENT CURTIS BIDDLE (see firm details p.1102) The small but "*unflappable*" pension litigation team, operates out of the main pension department and fields "*sharpshooting*" **Isabel Nurse-Marsh** (see p.564). This year the group brought a number of cases before the Pensions Ombudsman. A notable highlight was acting for the trustees of the former National Power scheme in a landmark House of Lords case concerning the allocation of a £400 million surplus. **Clients** Trustees of the Innogy (formerly National Power) Group of the Electricity Supply Pension Scheme.

SACKER & PARTNERS (see firm details p.1121) "*Accomplished,*" **Monica Coombs** (see p.555) heads this popular and "*hard-working*" unit, drawing particular commendations for her experience in professional negligence and trust law as pertaining to pensions litigation. This year the team represented Hogg Robinson Trustees, independent trustees to the Earby Light Engineers Ltd Group Pension Scheme, in its claim against the scheme's former investment advisors. This concerned the charge that the advisors were negligent in their investment strategy, and a settlement was eventually reached by mediation. The group also acted successfully for Syntegra Ltd in a claim for compensation against its pension scheme insurers, Scottish Equitable. **Clients** Hogg Robinson Trustees; Syntegra Ltd.

CMS CAMERON MCKENNA (see firm details p.914) This "*sure-footed*" firm, highly visible in cases brought before the Pensions Ombudsman, prides itself on its technical aptitude. It includes **Mark Atkinson** (see p.610), who clients consider "*keen as mustard and extremely clever.*" The team acted this year for an independent trustee drawn into litigation and threatened with cost orders and cross-examination under oath. This involved negotiating with both administrative receivers and fellow trustees. Another highlight was a successful application to the High Court concerning the administration of trusts for the Coloroll Carpets Works Scheme. **Clients** Black & Decker; British Land; Consignia; Motorola; Siemens.

FRESHFIELDS BRUCKHAUS DERINGER (see firm details p.964) Although this firm is better known for its non-contentious pension work, the pension litigation team has been quietly increasing its workload. Three substantial cases are in the development stages at the time of going to press. The department has particular experience in the use of mediation in reaching settlements for its clients. It assists an impressive client base of pension trustees, employers, pension professionals and scheme advisors on a range of contentious matters, being assisted in cross-border matters by its network of international offices. **Clients** Pension trustees; investment companies; blue-chips.

NABARRO NATHANSON (see firm details p.1080) **Jonathan Warne** (see p.570), who sits on the Pension Litigation Court Users' Committee, always works hard to achieve the right results for his clients, according to peers. With an "*easy style,*" he leads a team that was involved recently in a Court of Appeal case for two representative beneficiaries of the Airway Pension Scheme. Other key matters include acting on behalf of British Coal in connection with a dispute regarding tax liability. The group has also continued to handle various matters relating to the Maxwell case. **Clients** British Coal.

SLAUGHTER AND MAY (see firm details p.1140) Small but top-quality, this "*sensible and knowledgeable*" team, headed by Richard Clark, won warm praise from clients for its ability to "*deploy arguments with panache and conjure up unexpected solutions.*" With particular experience of pension mis-selling cases, it appeared in one of the most high-profile cases of the year, representing the Unilever trustees in its claim against Merrill Lynch Investment Management, formerly Mercury Asset Management. Though relating more to investment management than pensions per se, it was nonetheless one of the biggest cases concerning pension funds for some time. The group also handled a Stockholm Chamber of Commerce arbitration relating to the mis-selling of pensions. **Clients** Unilever; William M Mercer; Marsh & McLennan; Prudential Assurance Company.

LITIGATION REAL ESTATE

LONDON

LITIGATION: REAL ESTATE — LONDON

1. **Linklaters**
   Nabarro Nathanson
2. **Berwin Leighton Paisner**
   Lovells
3. **Ashurst Morris Crisp**
   Clifford Chance
   DJ Freeman
   Dechert
   Denton Wilde Sapte
   Herbert Smith
   Lawrence Graham
4. **CMS Cameron McKenna**
   Masons
   Mayer, Brown, Rowe & Maw
   Simmons & Simmons
   SJ Berwin
5. **Boodle Hatfield**
   Macfarlanes
   Olswang
   Speechly Bircham
6. **Beachcroft Wansbroughs**
   Charles Russell
   Dewar Hogan
   RadcliffesLeBrasseur

This book is the product of 6,582 1/2 hour interviews. See p.7 for BMRB audit. Within each band, firms are listed alphabetically.

LINKLATERS (see firm details p.1043) Winning the utmost respect from its opponents, this practice is a byword for "*great quality control*" and lawyers that are "*generally both excellent and right*." "*Strong, firm and very, very effective*," **Katie Bradford** (see p.554), is the area's undisputed star. Said to rule her "*awesome team*" firmly and intelligently, commentators report that she is "*developing her assistants well*" and that the team demonstrates real depth and cohesion. The recent creation of a joint property and finance litigation team indicates both the firm's core finance strength and its commitment to property litigation. Much of the team's work lies in assisting the firm's stunning corporate and property client base, and its workload consists largely of landlord & tenant, professional negligence and finance-related work. There has also been considerable activity in relation to insolvencies over the last year. The team acted for PricewaterhouseCoopers, against accusations by Silven of undervaluing properties. It also acted for Moss Bros against Cadogan over a matter of contract provisions. **Clients** BP Pension Fund; Lloyds TSB Pension Fund; Canary Wharf Company; PricewaterhouseCoopers.

NABARRO NATHANSON (see firm details p.1080) With a "*long and honourable history*" and a "*fabulous client base*," this "*true and original property firm*" still commands deep respect in an increasingly competitive marketplace. Though other firms continue to make inroads into the top tier, competitors acknowledge it unlikely that anybody could actually squeeze out the cup-holders. Though some sources raise questions about the consistency of the assistants, most commentators believe that the team is strong and growing; ("*rugged and professional.*") and that it boasts one of the most extraordinary property litigation practices around. Best known for landlord & tenant work, with an emphasis on rent reviews and redevelopment, the team sustains a high profile with numerous reported cases for industry names. The telecoms sector has proved especially productive for the team. "*Efficient and friendly*" **Jennifer Rickard** (see p.566) is credited with a "*good combination of the best and most necessary skills.*" She "*always makes excellent points.*" "*Decisive and forceful*" **Iain Travers** (see p.569) is revered by peers as the "*surefooted grandfather of the industry*" who "*knows a trick or two.*" The team acted for Allied Dunbar v Homebase on the use of collateral agreements to avoid alienation restrictions, and for Ravenseft v Hall in a matter concerning the validity of statutory notices under the Housing Act. **Clients** Land Securities; Allied Dunbar; Capital & Counties; Annington Properties; London Institute.

BERWIN LEIGHTON PAISNER (see firm details p.866) Possessing a great client base since the merger, and a team with "*both the numbers and the get-up-and-go*," this "*heavy-duty*" outfit is tipped for an eventual top-tier position. The practice is continuing to settle after the merger and commentators refer approvingly to a growing efficiency and sense of purpose. Known for both top-end and mainstream work, the team is noted for its landlord & tenant expertise. Chief name here is the "*always accurate and innovative*" **Roger Cohen** (see p.555), who is commended as a "*good lateral thinker.*" Key client British Land uses "*smooth operator*" **David Cox** (see p.555), who peers describe as "*superb, sensible and effective.*" "*Excellent analyst*" **Ros Morshead** (see p.564) "*continues to fight the good fight for Liverpool City Council*," according to competitors, and led a team acting for the Council against Walton Group, which dealt with the interpretation of an option agreement granted by the Council to Walton. The team also acted for Legal & General in obtaining vacant possession of a development site in the City. **Clients** Allied London Properties; British Land; Brown & Jackson; Capital & Regional.

LOVELLS (see firm details p.1045) This "*efficient and aggressive*" firm is praised by market sources for "*going its own way*" and, with its team experiencing growth in pre-action advice, it is developing into arguably the leader in the field for litigation avoidance. Commentators note that the team boasts "*some great clients.*" It retains the respect of peers for its "*client-driven style and service*," and is said to be "*getting better and stronger.*" "*Absolutely superb*" **Nicholas Cheffings** (see p.554) ("*a shining example*") was felt to have been slightly less active in pure property litigation last year as he "*develops a niche*" in outsourcings, which fits well with the property practice's increasing pre-action expertise. **Anne Waltham** (see p.570) is respected by clients and competitors alike for her "*no-nonsense dialogue*," and is regarded as a "*good administrator who runs a good case.*" The team acted for Six Continents in Trusthouse Hotels v Burford, and for Millennium Park (Grimsby) in an action brought by North East Lincolnshire Council alleging breach of obligations under a development agreement. **Clients** Six Continents; Millennium Park (Grimsby); Forte.

ASHURST MORRIS CRISP (see firm details p.852) Regarded throughout the marketplace as a "*fine group*," the team is noted for "*combining expertise from different sectors superbly well*" and "*deploying the firm's resources to the best effect.*" "*Great team leader*" **Michael Madden** (see p.562) is perceived by peers as "*tough*" but also "*fun and enjoyable.*" All agree, however, that he is very much in control, and "*one of the few solicitors willing and able to resolve litigation problems himself.*" The team acted for Ipswich Town Football Club in successfully resisting proceedings brought by local residents opposed to the development of the club's grounds. It also acted for Friends Provident seeking judicial review of the Secretary of State's decision not to call in a planning application for a proposed scheme. **Clients** BT; Lattice Property; Thames Water; Hemingway; IBM (UK); Berkley Homes; Reuters.

CLIFFORD CHANCE (see firm details p.911) This small team is visible on "*top-end, high-value stuff*" and always works to "*the highest standards.*" It attracts a diverse range of clients, including developers, hoteliers, retailers and manufacturers. Servicing a decent property practice with a hotels specialism, the team is associated with complex, finance-related work, and has been busy with contract disputes, rent reviews, and development-linked matters. Its lawyers have a reputation in the market as "*careful, quality litigators*," and chief amongst them is the "*consistent and polished*" **John Pickston** (see p.565). He is regarded by competitors as "*a hard-working intellectual.*" The team acted for

LONDON — LITIGATION REAL ESTATE

LEADING INDIVIDUALS

★ **BRADFORD Katie** Linklaters

[1]
CHEFFINGS Nicholas Lovells
KING Vivien DJ Freeman
MADDEN Michael Ashurst Morris Crisp
RICKARD Jennifer Nabarro Nathanson

[2]
COHEN Roger Berwin Leighton Paisner
FRANCIS Penelope Lawrence Graham
FREYNE Michele Mayer, Brown, Rowe & Maw
HUTCHINSON Lucy Herbert Smith
PEET Carole Denton Wilde Sapte
PICKSTON John Clifford Chance
TRAVERS Iain Nabarro Nathanson
WALTHAM Anne Lovells
WEBBER Lesley Beachcroft Wansbroughs

[3]
BRIERLEY Ian DLA
CONWAY Keith Dechert
COX David Berwin Leighton Paisner
CROSS Siobhan Masons
FOX-EDWARDS Jane Lawrence Graham
HEWSON Carol Simmons & Simmons
HIGHMORE Robert Charles Russell
MOLYNEUX Anne Masons
THOMAS Martin Herbert Smith
WALKER Andrew CMS Cameron McKenna

[4]
BARCLAY Marcus Olswang
HINDLE Andrew Boodle Hatfield
HOGAN Ronald Dewar Hogan
HUNTER Jason Russell-Cooke
ISRAEL Jennifer Jennifer Israel & Co
MASTERS David Dawsons
METLISS Michael SJ Berwin
MORSHEAD Ros Berwin Leighton Paisner
TUGWELL Andrew Osborne Clarke

See individuals' profiles p.552

Tishman Speyer, negotiating and settling rights of light claims at the Marsh Centre, Tower of London. It also defended the Burford Group in a claim in the High Court for damages arising out of the refurbishment of the Trocadero/London Pavilion. **Clients** Burford Group; Tishman Speyer; Grantchester Group; Railtrack; Canary Wharf Group.

DJ FREEMAN (see firm details p.939) Undoubtedly a high profile name in the area, this "*strong team*" has a "*gritty style*" and garners the admiration and respect of peers and clients. The team, which sits with lawyers from other specialisms, is composed of litigators who are said by peers to be "*all property specialists.*" They undertake 1954 Act work and rent renewals, as well as higher profile jobs, such as big rent reviews. "*Unforgettable*" Vivien King, though "*larger than life*," is "*definitely one of the world's good guys.*" "*Passionate about her subject*," she is considered "*outstandingly good,*" by

clients and competitors alike. Her team acted for Petra Investments in settling a complicated funding agreement regarding a shopping centre with MAB. **Clients** Benchmark; AXA Sun Life; Land Securities; Carillion; Karen Millen.

DECHERT (see firm details p.934) Based around a "*traditional tenants' practice for retail clients,*" this "*committed team*" is confident across the board in property litigation matters. Commentators remark that these days "*it is not just for retailers.*" They note that the team's reputation is strengthening in areas it was not traditionally associated with, and that it is winnig new clients like The Crown, and Land Securities. Keith Conway (see p.555) is "*respected for heavyweight stuff*" and has been called "*an effective rottweiler.*" The practice gained experience of handling major contentious matters for the Secretary of State for Environment, Transport & the Regions, defending the department against a dilapidations claim brought by P&O, and an action for specific performance brought by the Asha Foundation. **Clients** Secretary of State for Environment, Transport & the Regions; British Land.

DENTON WILDE SAPTE (see firm details p.935) Much of this practice's work is run out of Milton Keynes, and some commentators expressed wariness of this "*split-campus*" approach. Researchers discovered, however, a broad endorsement for this "*efficient*" practice, known for producing good quality work, especially in the areas of portfolio management and landlord & tenant disputes. The team also boasts an admired record of rent reviews for Sainsbury's. Bestriding both offices as the team's most recognised personality is "*down to earth*" Carole Peet, who is "*tough, committed and a tried campaigner.*" She led the team advising Sainsbury's on the rent review of a store at Coldhams Lane in Cambridge. **Clients** Barclays Bank; Sainsbury's; English Partnerships.

HERBERT SMITH (see firm details p.992) The firm is well known for big-ticket disputes for "*genuine property clients*" run out of "*an outstanding litigation practice.*" The practice here also covers pre-emptive advice, contract renegotiations, Lands Tribunal and rent review work. Clients tend to be big property companies and funds, but the team counts occupiers on its list as well. Active in the appeal courts, it is said to have "*an awful lot of experience of running major litigation.*" Lucy Hutchinson (see p.561) is said to exemplify "*the tough HS approach, coupled with academic excellence.*" Although she has fingers in other pies, including construction, over half her practice is in property litigation. The "*hard-working*" and "*increasingly prominent*" Martin Thomas (see p.568) is said to be "*developing a nice punch.*" He led a team defending Severn Trent Water against a trespass claim, and advised Guinness/Diageo in a dispute over the value of development land

at Paddington Basin. **Clients** Severn Trent Water; Guinness/Diageo; London & Continental Stations & Property; Hermes.

LAWRENCE GRAHAM (see firm details p.1031) Commentators were united in their praise for this "*serious, efficient and hungry team,*" which has a reputation for big rent review cases, and other high-end work. The group has plenty of freestanding clients for whom it carries out "*classic property litigation*" work, including advice on redevelopment. Despite her new duties as managing partner, the "*bright, skilled, and effervescent*" Penny Francis is "*keeping her hand in.*" Researchers were told of her "*cracking personality*" and "*great finesse and skill.*" She acted for London & Regional in its abortive acquisition of the Strand Palace Hotel. Offering her able support is the "*ever more pivotal*" Jane Fox-Edwards, widely regarded as "*Penny's gifted number two.*" Competitors describe her as "*a first class operator who gives you a run for your money.*" She acted recently for London & Regional in litigation relating to the proposed development site at Crystal Palace. **Clients** Universities Superannuation Scheme; Scottish & Newcastle; Legal & General.

CMS CAMERON MCKENNA (see firm details p.914) Nestled within the property department, this practice advises investor, developer, retail and public sector clients, often pre-emptively. It has an acknowledged and respected niche in opposed lease renewals and right to light claims, and handles a large volume of contentious work for landlords relating to portfolio management. Though the team lost the Crown Estate tender, it has in fact gained clients and increased its workload over the year, and remains highly regarded for its "*punchy*" style and "*good quality casework by good calibre people.*" It continues to act for the Crown Estate on special projects. Andrew Walker (see p.569) is "*assured and accomplished,*" and respondents agree that he "*speaks with authority.*" The team advised the London Borough of Bromley in High Court proceedings against London & Regional companies arising out of an agreement for lease for the Crystal Palace development. **Clients** Britannic Asset Management; The Crown Estate Commissioners; Dunnes Stores.

MASONS (see firm details p.1057) A highly rated team for construction-related matters, competitors believe it "*deserves wider recognition outside construction*" too. The calibre of the lawyers is deemed excellent, and commentators applaud their "*meticulous attention to detail*" and observe that "*they keep their clients very happy.*" The team has expertise in development work, and also in licensed premises matters. It handles volumes of landlord & tenant work and has a growing outsourcings and health & safety-related practice. Competitors rate "*tough and together*" Siobhan Cross (see p.555) highly, and

545

LITIGATION REAL ESTATE ■ LONDON

Anne Molyneux (see p.564) garners respect for her loyal client base and "*excellent sense of humour.*" The team acted for the landlord in Plummer v TIBSCO, a case concerning options in leases. It also acted for P&O Trans European on a significant rent review. **Clients** Inntrepreneur; Portman Estate; Unique Pub Company; Nomura International.

MAYER, BROWN, ROWE & MAW (see firm details p.1060) Considered "*a smallish but high-class practice,*" this team has niche expertise in disputed notices, leases, and environmental injunctions. It services both landlords and tenants from across the commercial world. "*Level-headed*" Michele Freyne (see p.557) is a 1954 Act and service charges specialist. Admired for her "*feisty*" style, she is "*always taken seriously*" by rivals who admire her " *eye for the big picture.*" She led the team representing the successful party in Ashworth Frazer v Gloucester City Council, and represented a subsidiary of Unilever in a compensation case in the Lands Tribunal. **Clients** Funds; retail houses.

SIMMONS & SIMMONS (see firm details p.1136) A "*commercial and pragmatic*" group, which co-operates closely with the firm's property department, it handles such matters as arise for the firm's commercial clients. Mainly visible assisting landlords, the team noticed a rise last year in rent review activity. Heading the team is "*seriously good litigator*" Carol Hewson (see p.559), who has "*a good eye for the merit*" in a case. She acted for Deka Immobilien Investment, as landlord of the Lloyd's Building, and for Eagle Star as the landlord of the Heal's building, on rent reviews that went to arbitration. **Clients** Deka Immobilien Investment; Eagle Star; Henderson Global Investors; Kvaerner International.

SJ BERWIN (see firm details p.867) A team "*full of exciting mavericks,*" "*well-deployed*" in the service of a wide spread of clients. Much of the caseload is advisory work under the 1954 Act and involves pre-emptive work for clients such as Brixton Estates and The Crown. Most work arises from existing commercial clients, though free-standing work for clients like CLS Holdings also figures. The name here is "*extraordinary character*" Michael Metliss (see p.563), who led the team acting for The Crown Estate on a site clearance in Regent Street. He also acted for British Land in successfully appealing a declaration concerning the status of a tenancy. **Clients** British Land; Delancey; AXA Sun Life; Merivale Moore; Chelsfield.

BOODLE HATFIELD (see firm details p.881) The firm has a unified litigation practice in which property litigation features prominently. It covers the range of traditional work in this field, including lease renewals, contested applications for new tenancies, dilapidations, rent reviews and service charge disputes. Though mostly active on landlord work, the team has an acknowledged niche in enfranchisement claims for tenants. A solid private client base keeps the practice ticking along nicely, and the team is well known for its work for key client Grosvenor. Best-known practitioner here is the experienced and respected Andrew Hindle (see p.560). He recently represented a market trader in Chelsea threatened with the withdrawal of a licence of 20 year's standing. **Clients** Grosvenor Estates; The Bedford Estates; St Giles Hotel; urban estates; Oxford colleges.

MACFARLANES (see firm details p.1047) The team acts for landlords and tenants across the range of contentious property matters, and boasts a growing practice in insolvency-related matters. It represents a number of offshore trusts, developers and existing commercial and institutional clients. Willie Manners heads this "*class outfit with a good client base,*" which has acted for Royal London in a number of contested lease renewals. **Clients** Royal London; Checkpoint Meto; Magnohard; offshore trusts.

OLSWANG (see firm details p.1087) This team is making a name for itself on the strength of some fine property clients, mostly landlords and investors, but also some tenants. It has dealt with a number of substantial dilapidations claims over the year, as well as a range of possession actions, rent reviews, service charge issues, and other landlord & tenant disputes. Lead figure here is Marcus Barclay (see p.553), who is "*popular with professionals.*" The team acted for Helical Bar in a substantial claim for dilapidations involving warehouse space. **Clients** Minerva; Helical Bar; Prestbury Group; Phillips & Drew; Green Property (UK); Capital & Regional.

SPEECHLY BIRCHAM (see firm details p.1141) This small, creditable team of dedicated property litigators acts for a range of clients, including entites like de Walden Estates and P&O. Much of its work is standalone contentious advice for clients who appreciate the firm's "*straightforward and solid*" service. Commentators declare that "*it has the potential to grow rapidly.*" Graham Ling leads the team, which acted for Hollybrook on a site clearance in London's East End. **Clients** RBS/NatWest; Royal London; Sun Life of Canada.

BEACHCROFT WANSBROUGHS (see firm details p.860) A relatively small but "*pretty high-quality*" team that undertakes a variety of work, especially on adjoining owner issues, dilapidations, development, and rent reviews. It also conducts major overage disputes and legal assessor work, and has a recognised niche in the public sector. More than half of the department's work is freestanding. Peers expressed tremendous regard for the "*truly great*" rent review specialist Lesley Webber (see p.570) whose "*forthright manner delights her clients.*" The team represented Lloyd's of London in the rent review of its headquarters building in the City, and recently won instructions from the BBC. **Clients** Balfour Beatty; Jaeger; Guy's & St Thomas' NHS Trust; Mid Kent Water.

CHARLES RUSSELL (see firm details p.904) Working closely with teams in Guildford and Cheltenham, this practice services a "*credible client base*" that includes some impressive institutions. It handles landlord & tenant matters for residential and institutional clients, and has valuable experience in adverse possession claims. The firm has been boosted by the recruitment of "*bright, competent and popular*" ex-Radcliffes partner Rob Highmore (see p.559), who is widely regarded as "*the crux of the practice.*" The team handled a large dilapidations claim against a local authority, and a land clearance for a noted developer. It has also noted an increase in mediations as a way of resolving dilapidations. **Clients** Sun Life Financial of Canada; Vodafone; Lincoln Assurance; Osborne Group; MAB; Milton Group; Lemon Land.

DEWAR HOGAN (see firm details p.936) This "*unique*" group of pure property litigators has a "*sound niche residential practice.*" Its caseload includes contract-based work, renewal work, and also negligence claims and residential disputes. Clients include property companies, funds, public authorities, banks, private investors and individuals. They are mostly tenants, especially retailers. Active in the appeal courts, the team tends not to handle planning or construction matters. Founder Ronald Hogan (see p.560) is a "*recognised specialist*" with "*great experience in the industry.*" The team recently represented a developer with the benefit of rights of pre-emption over land for a proposed retail park, and defended another developer of a retail park from a £1.3 million claim by a tenant for a contribution towards fitting out. **Clients** Tesco; Vodafone; Deutsche Asset Management; English Partnerships.

RADCLIFFESLEBRASSEUR (see firm details p.1107) The clients of this "*traditional*" practice have remained loyal since the departure of Rob Highmore. An active team handling complex cases for substantial clients, it enjoys a steady volume of landlord & tenant litigation for both landlords and tenants, and has a reputation for residential work. The team acted on several environmental contamination claims arising from petro-carbon contamination of an industrial estate, and on a precedent-setting LVT case regarding the recoverability of service charges. **Clients** The Church Commissioners; Portman Estate; The Crown Estate; Hermes Property Unit Trust.

OTHER NOTABLE PRACTITIONERS "*Bright*" Ian Brierley of DLA is regarded by peers as "*switched-on.*" Russell-Cooke's Jason Hunter (see p.560) "*looks to be a real one to watch,*" striking commentators as "*impressive, sensible and knowledgeable.*" His practice includes commercial and residential work fed from larger firms, as well as mediations. New to our tables is **Jennifer Israel** of **Jennifer Israel & Co**, who comes highly recommended for leasehold enfranchisement. **Dawsons'** **David Masters** (see p.563) wins praise, as does **Osborne Clarke's** **Andrew Tugwell**, whose "*profile is on the up and up.*"

THE SOUTH & THAMES VALLEY

LITIGATION: REAL ESTATE
■ THE SOUTH

1. **DMH** Brighton
2. **Brachers** Maidstone
   Cripps Harries Hall Tunbridge Wells
   Thomson Snell & Passmore Tonbridge
3. **asb law** Crawley
   Coffin Mew & Clover Portsmouth

LEADING INDIVIDUALS
1. **ALLEN Martin** DMH
   WAKEFORD Carol Cripps Harries Hall

This book is the product of 6,582 1/2 hour interviews. See p.7 for BMRB audit. Within each band, firms are listed alphabetically. See individuals' profiles p.552

DMH (see firm details p.940) A "*regional heavyweight*" with "*great strength in all divisions,*" this large team handles volumes of litigation for charities and public sector clients as well as household name banks and corporates. Tina George heads a public sector-focused team that works for local government, housing associations and commercial investment clients, while highly respected **Martin Allen** (see p.552) heads a team focused on specialist and complex work, largely for house builders. He acted for the CSMA when a development company retained to construct leisure villages went into receivership. **Clients** Local authorities; housing associations; Dorrington Investments; TM Retail; Lloyds TSB; University of Sussex; Civil Service Motoring Association.

BRACHERS (see firm details p.886) Peers applaud the team for being "*careful in its development, which has paid off.*" Working closely with a highly regarded planning practice on a broad range of traditional property litigation issues, John Sheath heads a team admired by clients and competitors alike for "*quality service.*" The team recently acted for principal client Eurotunnel on litigation concerning the Sangatte refugee hostel near the French terminal of the Channel Tunnel. **Clients** Eurotunnel.

CRIPPS HARRIES HALL (see firm details p.922) The team undertakes a fair volume of government-related work, often opposite London firms, and commentators acknowledge that "*it's really got the ability.*" Typical work includes site clearances for clients with major redevelopment schemes, and portfolio estate management for a number of Government departments, pension funds and property investment and holding companies. "*Active and accomplished*" **Carol Wakeford** leads a team that has acted in compulsory purchase compensation referrals to the Lands Tribunal, for the Channel Tunnel Rail Link developer. **Clients** Crown Prosecution Service; HM Customs & Excise; Union Railways (South).

THOMSON SNELL & PASSMORE (see firm details p.1161) Regarded as "*well established*" in the region, the team handles a healthy volume of work in landlord & tenant matters, lease disputes and lease enfranchisements. Peter Radula-Scott heads a team catering to a range of solid property players, including private clients, and renowned in the market for "*great quality.*" Lawyers in the department have acted on a challenge, based in the Human Rights Act, regarding rent officers' assessment of fair rents. **Clients** Marley Properties; Antler Homes; Royal British Legion Industries; Colas.

ASB LAW (see firm details p.851) Continuing to make inroads into the market, the team, based in the planning and environmental and commercial litigation groups, handles property litigation issues for a range of national clients. Interviewees applaud its "*great service,*" efficiency and responsiveness. The team, led by Rex Cowell, handles matters across the range of property litigation in the service of an active client base. **Clients** Marley Pension Fund; private investors.

COFFIN MEW & CLOVER Robert Wassall's litigation team handles the range of commercial matters, including dilapidations, forfeiture, rent and service charge arrears, right to buy and boundary disputes. A thriving residential practice supports the firm's social housing group. The team acted for Bellway Homes when a planning authority's decision to grant permission for a development was challenged. **Clients** Bellway Homes; Purvers International; housing associations.

SOUTH WEST

BURGES SALMON (see firm details p.894) Admired by peers for its "*sheer breadth and size,*" this firm is said to be focusing more and more on the commercial side of property litigation. The practice was recently boosted by winning the Crown Estate as a client. Specialising in commercial property disputes, including landlord & tenant issues, core work continues to be complex disputes and flagship agricultural cases. Commentators report that the team is "*very thorough,*" and "*sets a case up well.*" **Richard Bedford** (see p.553) is considered "*hard-working and thoughtful,*" and renowned for his "*great attention to detail.*" "*Young and thrusting*" **Neil Ham** (see p.559) deals with a broad range of contentious property matters, including rent review, service charge dilapidations, contested lease renewals, restrictive covenants, forfeiture, and contaminated land disputes. The team was recently involved in Barrett v Morgan (House of Lords) and Pye v Graham (Court of Appeal). **Clients** Orange First Group; Lattice; New Zealand Milk; Southern Electric.

OSBORNE CLARKE (see firm details p.1090) A "*strong and competent*" team, it services a commercial client base with a retail and leisure focus, and often acts for investment and development clients. Considered a leader in this field, and active across a range of sectors, it is "*recruiting hard*" and growing rapidly. Researchers were told that the "*intelligent and conscientious*" **Leona Briggs** is "*up there with the best,*" and respondents were also full of praise for **Jane Rogers**. The team was recently involved in a dispute over the wording of a pipeline easement, and has been advising a retailer on a damages claim against a landlord for a breach of covenant. **Clients** Benchmark Group; Bovis Homes; British Airways Pensions.

MASONS (see firm details p.1057) This "*respected and admired*" team acts on a range of commercial landlord & tenant disputes, with a focus on dilapidations and portfolio and industrial estate management. The year has seen an increase in advice to landlords with insolvent tenants, and in service charge disputes. An "*established and trusted*" outfit, loyal clients praise its "*great care and thoroughness.*" "*Efficient*" **Bonnie Martin** (see p.563) is respected as a "*good technician*" by peers, who consider "*her excellent reputation is well-deserved.*" She defended Bourne Leisure in injunction proceedings alleging breach of a restrictive covenant relating to the location of amusement machines. New partner **Nicola Seager** (see

LITIGATION REAL ESTATE ■ SOUTH WEST/WALES

LITIGATION: REAL ESTATE
■ SOUTH WEST

1
- Burges Salmon Bristol
- Osborne Clarke Bristol

2
- Masons Bristol

3
- Beachcroft Wansbroughs Bristol
- Bond Pearce Bristol
- Veale Wasbrough Bristol

4
- Bevan Ashford Bristol
- Lyons Davidson Bristol
- TLT Solicitors Bristol

LEADING INDIVIDUALS

1
- BRIGGS Leona Osborne Clarke

2
- BEDFORD Richard Burges Salmon
- HAM Neil Burges Salmon
- MARTIN Bonnie Masons

3
- BASTOW Martin Lyons Davidson
- PUDDICOMBE Nigel Veale Wasbrough
- SEAGER Nicola Masons

UP AND COMING
- BARLEY Mark Bond Pearce
- ROGERS Jane Osborne Clarke

This book is the product of 6,582 1/2 hour interviews. See p.7 for BMRB audit. Within each band, firms are listed alphabetically. See individuals' profiles p.552

p.567) is warmly recommended by commentators for her "*energy and discipline*," and "*dedication to the field*." She led an action for Wereldhave on a contested business lease renewal on premises in Truro. **Clients** Wereldhave Property Corporation; Park Resorts; Somerfield Property Company; WPD Property Investments.

BEACHCROFT WANSBROUGHS (see firm details p.860) A "*reliable*" practice that is "*gain-ing in stature and respect*" thanks to its "*astute management.*" Philip Hands leads a team that acts for a wide range of institutional and development clients, including Bristol & West. During the past year it has also been appointed to act for a number of property funds. Respondents note its reputation for "*good work in the health sector*" in particular. **Clients** Bristol & West; Hill House Hammond; C & J Clark International.

BOND PEARCE (see firm details p.879) An "*always impressive*" team that is "*expanding and doing seriously good stuff.*" Considered by market commentators to be "*rising*," it now provides "*strong service*" out of offices across the South West. It has particular expertise in retail, public sector, banking, insolvency and licensing-related work. Landlord & tenant disputes figure prominently in its caseload. Respondents were warm in their praise for "*surefooted*" Mark Barley (see p.553), who is "*definitely one to keep an eye on.*" The team was involved for The Crown Estate in Ipswich Borough Council v Duke and Moore. **Clients** West Country HA; B&Q; Safeway; Comet; The National Trust.

VEALE WASBROUGH (see firm details p.1174) The team is said by peers to be "*bulking up*" and improving in its market position. This owes much to the efforts of Nigel Puddicombe (see p.566), who is "*proving himself a great lawyer and strategist.*" The versatile property litigation team has been amalgamated with the firm's planning and environmental lawyers to form the new Land Use Team, providing an integrated service to clients. It acted for Reading Borough Council in settling a dispute with a local business occupying a landmark site. It also represented the buyers of a farm affected by the foot and mouth clean-up, an action involving an extensive environmental counterclaim. **Clients** Defence Estates; PACE; DETR; HPH; OGC; Crest Nicholson Properties.

BEVAN ASHFORD (see firm details p.869) This "*thorough and reliable*" team boasts an acknowledged specialism in health authority work. Clients are drawn largely from the firm's impressive public sector client base, and the team "*pulls off some gems*" for them. Led by Kane Kirkbride, it successfully represented the landowner in a Court of Appeal matter relating to lock-out agreements. **Clients** Allied Domecq; Orange; Linden Homes; Places for People; Westlea Housing Association.

LYONS DAVIDSON (see firm details p.1045) The practise is respected for its work for commercial lenders, LPA receivers and pension fund holders, and has experienced an increase in commercial landlord & tenant disputes and dilapidations claims. Well-known figure Martin Bastow (see p.553) has a broad practice and wins plaudits for his "*down-to-earth practicality.*" **Clients** Corporate clients; individuals; landlords; tenants; lenders.

TLT SOLICITORS (see firm details p.1163) A small group of dedicated property litigators, it is known to service a diverse roster of clients from the worlds of commerce, leisure, housing and finance. Commentators feel that the team has "*really found its level.*" Julia Lucas heads a team that commands a growing profile within and beyond the region. She also heads the team's leisure team. **Clients** Punch Pub Company; Brandon Hire; First Choice Holidays; Hanson; Lloyds TSB; The Spirit Group.

WALES

LITIGATION: REAL ESTATE
■ WALES

1
- Hugh James Cardiff
- Morgan Cole Cardiff

2
- Edwards Geldard Cardiff

LEADING INDIVIDUALS

1
- JONES Siân Morgan Cole
- MORGAN Neil Hugh James

UP AND COMING
- MEGGITT Edward Edwards Geldard

This book is the product of 6,582 1/2 hour interviews. See p.7 for BMRB audit. Within each band, firms are listed alphabetically. See individuals' profiles p.552

HUGH JAMES (see firm details p.1004) The highly regarded landlord & tenant experts at this newly demerged firm act on a broad range of matters for a mostly landlord client base. "*One of the most focused*" teams in the region, it is "*highly visible in the market.*" Commentators are full of admiration for its work for housing associations, and the team recently acted on a boundary dispute between two of them. "*Well-known*" Neil Morgan (see p.564) has a "*broad range of experience*" and wins the respect of peers. The team successfully defended a Government agency in a £2 million dilapidations claim. **Clients** Registered Social Landlords; Government agencies; Cardiff City Council.

MORGAN COLE (see firm details p.1075) Conducting a broad range of predominantly commercial litigation for "*high-profile clients,*" the team is experienced in 1954 Act dilapidations issues, and boasts a significant residential practice with housing associations on the books. The practice, known for "*quality work,*" is described by peers as "*a solid M4 corridor firm, all the way to Reading.*" Team leader Siân Jones is "*thorough, tough and fair,*" and highly experienced acting for corporate clients throughout Wales and England. This year has seen the team active on a number of interesting cases, including assisting a landlord in a dilapidations matter against a public body. **Clients** HSBC Bank; National Farmers' Union.

EDWARDS GELDARD (see firm details p.944) A "*sound commercial practice,*" it was praised to researchers for its reliability and efficiency, and for co-operating well with the other offices in its network. The team provides services to a broad range of clients in both the public and private sectors. Ed Meggitt (see p.563) has "*shown his calibre and earned his place*" in our tables, according to competitors. His team has been engaged in the disposal of 16 industrial estates for Rhondda Cynon Taff Borough Council, and has advised Dwr Cymru Cyfyngedig/Glas Cymru in defending against damages claims. **Clients** Chubb; Pendragon; Powergen; Spectrum Technologies; Bass Developments; Chevron UK.

548 | INDEX TO LEADING LAWYERS: PAGE 1693 ■ IN-HOUSE LAWYERS PROFILES: PAGE 1201

MIDLANDS

LITIGATION: REAL ESTATE
MIDLANDS

1. **Wragge & Co** Birmingham
2. **Eversheds** Birmingham
   Hammond Suddards Edge Birmingham
3. **Martineau Johnson** Birmingham
   Pinsent Curtis Biddle Birmingham
4. **Anthony Collins Solicitors** Birmingham
   Browne Jacobson Nottingham

LEADING INDIVIDUALS
1. **LLOYD HOLT Suzanne** Wragge & Co
2. **KENT Paul** Pinsent Curtis Biddle
   O'BRIEN Gary Eversheds
   SCOTT Gordon Hammond Suddards Edge

UP AND COMING
EDWARDS Martin Martineau Johnson

This book is the product of 6,582 1/2 hour interviews. See p.7 for BMRB audit. Within each band, firms are listed alphabetically. See individuals' profiles p.552

WRAGGE & CO (see firm details p.1197) Commentators are full of admiration for this "*fine group*" of "*client-focused*" lawyers. Competitors admire the firm's "*successful strategy to conquer the West Midlands*," which has seen it enjoy steady growth in its client base and attract increased local authority work this year. Celebrated for her "*great experience and talent*," team head **Suzanne Lloyd Holt** specialises in rent review, 1954 Act issues, dilapidations, service charges and property management. Also a trained arbitrator, competitors admire her "*unquestionable distinction*." She led the team advising London & Associated Properties on a tenant's claim for the specific performance of landlord's repairing covenants in connection with a shopping mall. The team also acted for V&P Midlands in High Court litigation with respect to a development site. **Clients** British Waterways Board; Calthorpe Estates; Castlemore Securities; HSBC Bank.

EVERSHEDS (see firm details p.949) Market sources comment on this team for its "*intellectual edge*" and "*sound reputation.*" The practice continues to grow, with billings and fee-earner numbers up on last year, and commentators have been impressed with its consolidation in the East Midlands. Clients contend that it "*doesn't miss a shot.*" It has acknowledged strength in resolving commercial disputes between landlords and tenants, and disputes inhibiting property development. It also has a name in residential work, including private challenges to developments. National team head **Gary O'Brien** (see p.564) is "*sound, and straightforward.*" His team acted for Priory Hospitals in a Lands Tribunal hearing, and for The Birmingham Alliance on a succession of opposed lease renewals on Phase II of the Martineau Galleries development. **Clients** Royal Bank of Scotland; Bournville Village Trust; The Birmingham Alliance.

HAMMOND SUDDARDS EDGE Acting chiefly for landlords and developer clients, this is a "*sensible and professional*" team. The heart of the practice is **Gordon Scott**, who is admired by peers for his "*great ability and attitude*" The group covers the range of traditional and more complex property disputes, including landlord & tenant work for its impressive client base. Its national network provides it with enormous resources for larger cases. Some market sources, however, consider that its profile has not been as high in the past year. **Clients** Corporates; property companies; developers.

MARTINEAU JOHNSON (see firm details p.1056) A "*competent and practical*" team with a "*strong penetration of the education sector,*" it has gained a national reputation for education-related property disputes. The client base includes corporates and Government agencies, and the practice is well known for university and charity clients. "*Cautious and sound*" **Martin Edwards** (see p.556) leads the team. His is a versatile practice, specialising in commercial landlord & tenant matters, including 1954 Act lease renewals, boundary disputes, dilapidations and disrepair claims. He led the team acting for a large private company securing compensation from its landlord arising out of the termination of a lease. The group also defended a public authority client in a multiparty trespass action. **Clients** Environment Agency; ALSTOM UK.

PINSENT CURTIS BIDDLE (see firm details p.1102) Known for "*top-quality*" work, this practice is said to be relatively small but high calibre. **Paul Kent** (see p.561) leads a team that handles complex, high-end work. Commentators consider him a "*good operator who gets results.*" His team acted recently for I M Properties on the issue and completion of proceedings regarding a dispute break clause. It also handled Shrewsbury Borough Council's recovery of a prime development site from a defaulting tenant. **Clients** Lex Service Group/RAC/BSM; I M Properties; ANC; Shrewsbury & Atcham Borough Council; English Partnerships.

ANTHONY COLLINS SOLICITORS (see firm details p.845) This "*thriving*" public sector property litigation practice is focused on local government and the social housing sector. Clients include several large national housing associations. Andrew Lancaster heads the commercial and property litigation team, which acts mainly for claimants. The lawyers are regarded by peers as "*worthy opponents, and honourable.*" The team handled claims on behalf of Wolverhampton & Dudley Breweries against surveyors for negligent property surveys. **Clients** Housing associations.

BROWNE JACOBSON (see firm details p.891) David Potts' team continues to provide advice to commercial clients in a range of property litigation matters. The team has experience of working with, and for, liquidators, administrators and receivers. It acted recently for the landlord of a national retail company that went into receivership with rent arrears. It also represented a landowner in Chancery Division proceedings over a claim for breach of contract in the sale of development land. **Clients** Landowners; tenants.

EAST ANGLIA

LITIGATION: REAL ESTATE
EAST ANGLIA

1. **Eversheds** Norwich
   Mills & Reeve Norwich
2. **Hewitson Becke + Shaw** Cambridge
3. **Greenwoods** Peterborough

LEADING INDIVIDUALS
1. **FALKNER James** Mills & Reeve

This book is the product of 6,582 1/2 hour interviews. See p.7 for BMRB audit. Within each band, firms are listed alphabetically. See individuals' profiles p.552

EVERSHEDS (see firm details p.949) Following the departure of John Scannell, some market sources consider that the team has maintained a low profile over the last year. This group can draw on national resources to assist its brisk practice in commercial landlord & tenant work, development, and freehold and title disputes. The team acted for Ipswich Borough Council in a Court of Appeal case concerning charges for mooring on a tidal river. **Clients** Crawford & Company Adjustors (UK); Rentokil; The Gap; TXU Europe; St Matthew Housing; Ipswich Borough Council.

MILLS & REEVE (see firm details p.1071) A "*great quality*" and "*good sized,*" with a varied practice, it has grown over the last year to meet demand from its institutional, education and developer clients. It also has a coveted reputation for work for landed estates. The team is led by **James Falkner** (see p.557), who specialises in landlord & tenant matters covering all management and contentious aspects of commercial, agricultural and residential premises. **Clients** Educational institutions; corporates; landowners.

LITIGATION REAL ESTATE ■ NORTH WEST/NORTH EAST

HEWITSON BECKE + SHAW (see firm details p.993) The "*credible*" team at the Cambridge office is led by Janet Rees. Its work covers landlord & tenant renewals and disputes, professional negligence and contentious probate. It also acts in all types of possession proceedings, dilapidations, service charge disputes, title and boundary disputes as well as advice to mortgagees and mortgagors. **Clients** Educational institutions; corporates.

GREENWOODS (see firm details p.978) This large and respected team enjoys recognised strength in residential possessions. Dealing with a high volume of possession actions and related issues, it has an established reputation for its housing law expertise. Particular expertise is offered in nuisance and injunction work in relation to anti-social behaviour cases. The team is headed by housing expert Michael Taylor. **Clients** Legal expense insurers; housing societies and associations; Government agencies; property managing agents; property companies.

NORTH WEST

LITIGATION: REAL ESTATE
■ NORTH WEST

1
- **Cobbetts** Manchester

2
- **DLA** Liverpool
- **Eversheds** Manchester
- **Hammond Suddards Edge** Manchester

3
- **Addleshaw Booth & Co** Manchester
- **Pannone & Partners** Manchester

LEADING INDIVIDUALS

1
- **JENNINGS Steven** DLA
- **RANSON Lee** Eversheds
- **STONE Peter** Cobbetts

2
- **HOATH Helen** Hill Dickinson
- **LEVINSON Jan** Hammond Suddards Edge
- **O'FARRELL Vincent** Pannone & Partners
- **WALKER Alan** Cobbetts

This book is the product of 6,582 1/2 hour interviews. See p.7 for BMRB audit. Within each band, firms are listed alphabetically. See individuals' profiles p.552

COBBETTS (see firm details p.914) A "*closely-knit*" and client-focused team comprising "*exceptionally sound practitioners,*" it is widely regarded as "*the most impressive group in the North West.*" The firm handles 1954 Act renewals and dilapidations, as well as more unusual and complex matters. The focus of the practice has moved towards property management, and the "*sound, non-aggressive, and professional*" team focuses on pre-emptive advice to avoid disputes. It services "*a storming client base*" with a strong brewery and leisure element, and is led by "*elder statesman*" Peter Stone (see p.568), admired for his "*great ability.*" He makes a "*super double act*" with Alan Walker (see p.569), who has a reputation for "*skill and professionalism.*" The team acted for Yaslou Properties in a High Court dispute over whether an option agreement constitutes a disposal of property. **Clients** Bruntwood Estates; Burger King; Peel Holdings.

DLA A strong commercial property department with good clients, it has some high-profile work assisting shopping centres. **Steven Jennings** is seen as something of an "*elder statesman.*" He heads a practice with expertise across the spectrum of property litigation and the capacity to undertake large and complex cases. **Clients** Developers; tenants; landlords.

EVERSHEDS (see firm details p.949) A "*constructive and focused*" team run out of Manchester, but handling work across the trans-Pennine region in conjunction with its Leeds outfit. Clients include prestige names, and there have been some impressive new additions this year. The "*reasonable and reliable*" team has a niche in development disputes. It is led by "*outstandingly good*" **Lee Ranson** (see p.566), who now splits his time between his Manchester base and Leeds, where he is charged with building up a practice. "*Personable and sensible*" with "*a fine business razzamatazz,*" clients confirm that he is "*quick to cut to the important points.*" The team has acted for English Partnerships on a number of high value claims concerning government funding, involving claw back, fraud and overage provisions. **Clients** Asda Group; Hammerson UK; United Norwest Co-operatives; Westport Developments; Littlewoods.

HAMMOND SUDDARDS EDGE Regarded as "*dependable and positive,*" this team has been active within the region and is highly visible. Some commentators find its "*forceful*" style not to their taste but most appreciate "*a team that you can have a sensible relationship with.*" Team leader **Jan Levinson** in particular is described as a "*pleasant man you can do business with,*" and is well known for dispute resolution expertise. **Clients** Corporates; developers; investors.

ADDLESHAW BOOTH & CO (see firm details p.838) A small team, with "*solid*" lawyers who "*know what they're doing,*" commentators continue to monitor its progress. Many now believe that it "*remains a force,*" and that "*Charles Jagger will buck it up.*" The group is experienced across the range of landlord & tenant work, and has special expertise in residential tenancies. It successfully defended a £1 million professional negligence action (Leicestershire County Council v Gordon Hewitt Associates) in the Technology and Construction Court. **Clients** AMEC; Manchester University; GEHE; Barlows.

PANNONE & PARTNERS (see firm details p.1092) A "*partner-led*" practice known for its "*tactical approach,*" it covers the range of landlord & tenant work, and is experiencing growth in Lands Tribunal cases. Clients are drawn from diverse backgrounds, and the team has been particularly busy acting for key client GMPTE. The best known name here is **Vincent O'Farrell** (see p.565), who impresses with his "*ability to do everything.*" The team acted for Malory Enterprises v Cheshire Homes, winning in the Court of Appeal. **Clients** Texaco; Jennings Brothers; Timpson; Milliken Industrials; GMPTE; Family HA.

OTHER NOTABLE PRACTITIONERS Observers are watching closely to see how "*competent and assertive*" **Helen Hoath** (see p.560) will do following Gorna and Co's merger with Hill Dickinson. Admired by peers for her "*good technique,*" she is particularly rated for adverse possessions and boundary disputes.

NORTH EAST

DLA Highly respected throughout the region, commentators report a "*professional and highly competent*" group, which "*combines property knowledge and litigation skills well.*" Clients regard them as "*on the ball and responsive.*" Acting for a broad client base, the team is visible on a range of traditional property litigation matters, and undertakes high-value, top-end matters. **Clients** Developers; tenants.

PINSENT CURTIS BIDDLE (see firm details p.1102) This strong team comprises "*top grade lawyers*" who are dedicated to work drawn from the property market. Its active client base includes both private companies and public sector bodies, and the team handles extensive property portfolios, and advises on all aspects of property litigation for owners of industrial and

NORTH EAST/SCOTLAND — LITIGATION REAL ESTATE

LITIGATION: REAL ESTATE
NORTH EAST

1
- **DLA** Leeds
- **Pinsent Curtis Biddle** Leeds

2
- **Addleshaw Booth & Co** Leeds
- **Dickinson Dees** Newcastle-Upon-Tyne
- **Eversheds** Leeds
- **Hammond Suddards Edge** Leeds
- **Nabarro Nathanson** Sheffield
- **Walker Morris** Leeds

LEADING INDIVIDUALS

1
- **BECK Andrew** Walker Morris
- **BELCHER Penny** Hammond Suddards Edge
- **HERBERT Alan** Pinsent Curtis Biddle
- **O'LOUGHLIN Philip** Addleshaw Booth & Co

UP AND COMING
- **OLDFIELD Alison** Eversheds

ONES TO WATCH
- **BILLING Petra** DLA

This book is the product of 6,582 1/2 hour interviews. See p.7 for BMRB audit.
Within each band, firms are listed alphabetically. See individuals' profiles p.552

---

office space. National head of the property litigation team **Alan Herbert** (see p.559) is widely admired by competitors, who consider him a "*dependable, affable and sensible bloke.*" **Clients** Landlords; investors; developers.

ADDLESHAW BOOTH & CO (see firm details p.838) A "*traditionally strong*" team servicing the property group's client base, it is recognised for its expertise in management-related work, as well as dilapidations, breaches of covenant and professional negligence matters. Commentators report a slightly reduced profile this year. Highly respected **Philip O'Loughlin** (see p.565) heads the team, which represented the successful claimant landlord in Gibson Investments v Chesterton, a large dilapidations claim. **Clients** AMEC; Manchester University; GEHE; Barlows.

DICKINSON DEES (see firm details p.938) A dedicated property litigation group with a "*fine reputation,*" it has struck observers with its "*constant flow of work.*" "*Dominating Newcastle,*" the team has experience in all aspects of mainstream property litigation, including lease renewals, dilapidations, breaches of covenant, rent review, trespass and possession actions. Jen Smurthwaite's team has been "*seen around on some top cases,*" including a Court of Appeal hearing regarding the interpretation of a contract for sale, and a £500,000 claim for misrepresentation against a development company. **Clients** HJ Banks & Co; Cheviot Investment; Durham University; Helical Properties Investment.

EVERSHEDS (see firm details p.949) Manchester-based Lee Ranson has been tasked with developing the Leeds property practice. He may well be the leader the market has been waiting for, and commands firm respect for his skills. Supporting him in Leeds is "*bright and sensible*" **Alison Oldfield** (see p.565), who rivals say is "*good to have on the other side.*" She led the team advising Hammerson UK Properties and Standard Life Assurance on a redevelopment scheme for the Brent Cross Shopping Centre. **Clients** Asda Group; Hammerson.

HAMMOND SUDDARDS EDGE This team enjoys considerable experience in the property arena, and is regarded by market commentators as having "*the makings of a fine group.*" It undertakes 1954 Act work, dilapidations, easements, and agricultural matters, and was recently heavily engaged in handling substantial Land Compensation Act claims. The market recognises the "*aggressively excellent*" **Penny Belcher**. **Clients** Tenants; landlords.

NABARRO NATHANSON (see firm details p.1080) Stephen Scott heads the team in Sheffield, which has a reputation for acting for retailers, and assisting blue-chip clients with major management and portfolio work. The group acted for boxclever on the rationalisation of its nationwide portfolio of retail outlets, and for the defendant in Hallam Land v UK Coal Mining. **Clients** Capital Shopping Centres; The Coal Authority; GE Capital; Grosvenor Estate; boxclever.

WALKER MORRIS (see firm details p.1178) A dedicated property litigation team, it is felt by some sources to have "*unsurpassed strength in Leeds.*" It offers a full range of services to clients, both locally and nationally, and, amongst others, has acted over the last year for Halifax, Debenhams, Arcadia and Top Shop Estates, mostly in commercial landlord & tenant work. **Andrew Beck** (see p.553) is "*acute and effective,*" according to rivals. **Clients** Retail clients; banks and building societies; house builders; Halifax; Arcadia Group; Tops Estates.

SCOTLAND

LITIGATION: REAL ESTATE
SCOTLAND

1
- **Dundas & Wilson CS** Edinburgh
- **Maclay Murray & Spens** Glasgow

2
- **Semple Fraser** Glasgow
- **Shepherd+ Wedderburn** Edinburgh

3
- **Brodies** Edinburgh
- **Burness** Edinburgh
- **McGrigor Donald** Glasgow

4
- **Biggart Baillie** Edinburgh, Glasgow
- **McClure Naismith** Edinburgh

LEADING INDIVIDUALS

1
- **CUMMING Kenny** Shepherd+ Wedderburn
- **EASTON Ewan** Maclay Murray & Spens

2
- **WEBSTER Sheila** Dundas & Wilson CS

This book is the product of 6,582 1/2 hour interviews. See p.7 for BMRB audit.
Within each band, firms are listed alphabetically. See individuals' profiles p.552

DUNDAS & WILSON CS (see firm details p.943) This is a "*first-class*" practice with a solid property client base and "*skilled and honourable practitioners.*" Having left the Andersen Legal network, commentators believe that it looks "*set to strengthen across the board.*" "*Sensible and commercial*" **Sheila Webster** has her "*head screwed on,*" according to competitors. She led the team acting successfully for Legal & General in a Court of Session case concerning alleged unreasonable withholding of consent in relation to changes to a retail park. **Clients** Standard Life; Legal & General; Land Securities; Somerfield; Alldays; Scottish Widows.

MACLAY MURRAY & SPENS (see firm details p.1048) A "*reasonable and experienced*" team that competitors say is "*great to deal with.*" The lawyers handle the gamut of commercial work, with a focus on lease-related matters for landlords, especially retailers. This year has seen an upsurge in investment and industrial work, and a rise in insolvencies and work from surveyors. Lead figure is the "*extremely sharp and able*" **Ewan Easton** (see p.556). He acted recently for Montague Evans on a partnership matter. **Clients** Sears; Stannifer; Capital & Regional; Montague Evans; Jones Lang LaSalle; Hazelmere Estates.

SEMPLE FRASER (see firm details p.1125) A dedicated team with "*great support*" and excellent clients, it is known in the market for its "*exceptionally high quality*" and "*good volume of work.*" Peers applaud the team for its "*innovative approach,*" and for "*pushing the boundaries.*" Headed by Alison Gow, it acted for Bass Developments challenging the decision by Glasgow Council to promote a compulsory purchase order and convey property in Buchanan Street, central Glasgow, to a rival developer. **Clients** Tesco; The British Land Corporation; Clydeport Operations; Scudder Threadneedle Property Fund Managers.

SHEPHERD+ WEDDERBURN (see firm details p.1130) A team that market sources believe is "*on the up and up*" since pulling off the "*coup*" of recruiting **Kenny Cumming** ("*knowledgeable and commercial*"). This "*takes it into the serious league*" according to competi-

LITIGATION ■ THE LEADERS

tors. The firm undertakes a range of property litigation for its growing client base. **Clients** Developers; tenants.

BRODIES (see firm details p.889) Renowned for its "*strong, top quality property work,*" this group is deemed by peers to be "*capable of handling all the issues and fighting its clients' corner well.*" Property litigation work has grown over the year, particularly for retailers, and commentators expressed "*high hopes for the future.*" The team gains strength from the firm's top-quality planning department. **Clients** Retailers and other tenants; developers.

BURNESS This "*solid*" team is considered "*a worthy opponent*" by peers. Associated with "*lower profile cases,*" it is adept at everything from rent recoveries and common repairs to the law of irritancy. It also handles the termination of leases and arbitration of rent reviews and land values. Philip Rodney leads the team, which recently advised a major retail developer in a £700,000 claim for multiple design and installation defects at a retail park. **Clients** British Land Universal; Highland Spring; Newcastle Building Society; Zurich GSG.

MCGRIGOR DONALD (see firm details p.1065) Admired for its planning practice, this "*assertive*" litigation team handles property matters as they arise for a range of public and private clients. **Clients** Banks and building societies; property developers and managers.

BIGGART BAILLIE (see firm details p.871) The acquisition of many of the Steedman Ramage team has boosted this practice considerably. Commentators are waiting to see how things fall out, but commend a "*quiet, solid, quality*" practice with "*real strength in the retail sector.*" The firm boasts a blue-chip client base in the financial, industrial and utilities sectors, which helps to generate balanced work across the whole range of property activity. **Clients** Retailers; banks; utilities companies; developers.

MCCLURE NAISMITH (see firm details p.1062) "*Emerging as a force,*" peers acknowledge this practice as "*tenacious without being unduly aggressive.*" The last year has seen a large increase in the volume of its property work, with a consequent rise in contentious matters. Commentators are increasingly impressed by the team, which includes Ewen Brown. It handles a diverse range of cases including enforcement of obligations in leases, termination of leases, rent reviews, and dilapidations. It acted for the landlords in both of the CIN Properties v Dollar Land (Cumbernauld) cases. **Clients** La Salle Investment Management; Keith Macdonald.

THE LEADERS IN LITIGATION

ALLEN, Martin
DMH, Brighton
(01273) 744324
martin.allen@dmh.co.uk
Specialisation: Partner with wide experience of all contentious property related matters, professional negligence, title and covenant cases, arbitrations (rent review, options etc), construction and insolvency, with particular expertise in commercial leases. Acts for a range of investors, developers, businesses with multiple property holdings as well as public authorities, charities and institutions; has handled numerous cases relating to commercial leases, (eg privity, rent reviews, user and keep-open covenants and repairs).
Career: Qualified 1972. Partner *Donne Mileham & Haddock* (now *DMH*) 1976. Head of litigation group, 1982-94; head of commercial property 1996-2000.
Personal: Interests include sailing, jazz, naval history and sport.

AMSDEN, Mark
Addleshaw Booth & Co, Manchester
(0161) 934 6195
mark.amsden@addleshawbooth.com
Specialisation: IT. Litigation, Commercial Disputes. Engineering, e-commerce. (1) Acting for a major US finance company in relation to their customer account software (2) Lead Partner in a tens of million pound breach of contract software supply case (ongoing) (3) Various internet related disputes (4) Numerous telecoms disputes (5) Extensive experience of warranty and company acquisition related disputes
Career: Solicitor and Barrister Victoria, Australia – admitted 1987, Solicitor admitted England 1992. *Slater Heelis* 1990-98, partner 1996. *Addleshaw Booth & Co* 1998-date. Partner 1998.
Personal: Educated Melbourne Grammar, Monash University, Melbourne. Married, one son. Cricket, rugby, travel.

ANDERSON, Harry
Herbert Smith, London
(020) 7374 8000
harry.anderson@herbertsmith.com
Specialisation: Head of litigation and arbitration division. Specialises in commercial litigation and has substantial experience in a wide variety of cases, particularly those arising out of corporate transactions, as well as fraud-related and professional negligence cases.
Career: Joined *Herbert Smith* as an articled clerk in 1968. Qualified 1970. Partner since 1976. Founded *Herbert Smith's* Hong Kong office in 1982; Returned to London 1987.
Personal: Educated at Jesus College, Cambridge.

ANDERSON, Peter
Simpson & Marwick, Edinburgh
(0131) 557 1545
peter.anderson@simpmar.com
Specialisation: Work includes professional negligence, personal injury, commercial litigation and aviation litigation. Acted in the Lockerbie inquiry (for Pan-Am) and all related claims, advocacy for C.A.A. in litigation and inquiries including Cormorant Alpha, Brent Spar, for Boeing Helicopters in passenger cases, commercial aviation contract cases.
Prof. Memberships: Law Society of Scotland, International Association Defence Counsel, I.B.A., senior lecturer Edinburgh University.
Career: Qualified 1977, Partner since 1980. Solicitor Advocate 1993. Legal Adviser - Royal Incorporation of Architects in Scotland; Legal Adviser - Royal Fine Art Commission for Scotland.

ARCHER, Nick
Slaughter and May, London
(020) 7600 1200
nick.archer@slaughterandmay.com
Specialisation: Area of practice is commercial litigation and arbitration. Handles a wide variety of domestic and international disputes in the commercial context. Has particular experience in banking disputes.
Prof. Memberships: The Law Society; International Bar Association; Indian Council of Arbitration.
Career: Qualified in 1981 with *Slaughter and May* and became a Partner in 1988.
Personal: Attended Durham University. Lives in London.

ASPINALL, Tim
DMH, Brighton
(01273) 744319
tim.aspinall@dmh.co.uk
Specialisation: Managing partner. Focuses on resolving heavyweight commercial litigation cases. Deals with high value commercial disputes on behalf of national and international clients. These cases often pose significant threats to the clients' business or reputation. Particularly recognised for his skill at managing difficult and complex cases to a successful conclusion and working closely with his clients. Has been involved in resolving numerous major disputes of this kind over the years in the High Court and ICC arbitrations. Regularly speaks at conferences and lectures to other lawyers throughout the country on litigation topics including the strategy and tactics of winning cases and risk management.
Prof. Memberships: Institute of Directors. Managing Partners Forum. Arts and Business.
Career: York University 1975-78 BA (Hons); qualified in 1982 and joined *DMH* 1983, partner in 1987; appointed information technology partner 1989; appointed head of litigation in 1994; appointed managing partner 1997.
Publications: Contributor to the new 'Civil Litigation Handbook', published by the Law Society.
Personal: Born 1956. Interests are visual arts, golf, gardening.

ATKINSON, Mark
CMS Cameron McKenna, London
(020) 7367 3000
mark.atkinson@cmck.com
See under Pensions, p.610

AUSTIN, Ian
Halliwell Landau, Manchester
(0161) 835 3003
idaustin@halliwells.co.uk
Specialisation: Partner and Head of Litigation and Corporate Recovery. Work includes complex and high value commercial disputes. Particular experience with interpretations of commercial contracts, disputes with regard to quality of goods supplied under commercial contracts, disputes in setting up contracts, disputes concerning company legislation especially Section 459 petitions, construction disputes and property litigation.
Career: Articled at *Phillips & Buck*, qualified in 1986, joined *Halliwell Landau* in 1987, made partner in 1992.
Personal: Born 1961, resides Foulridge, Lancs. Enjoys rugby and running.

BACON, Gavin
Simmons & Simmons, London
(020) 7825 4334
gavin.bacon@simmons-simmons.com
Specialisation: Commercial litigation and dispute resolution; regulatory issues. Acted for the majority shareholders of BCCI, Novartis and Railtrack amongst

others.
Prof. Memberships: Law Society of England and Wales; IBA; ABA.
Career: Qualified in 1982; partner 1988. Worked in the following *Simmons & Simmons* local offices: Adu Dhabi (1993-95); Hong Kong (1995-97); Shanghai (1997-99). Relocated to *Simmons & Simmons*' London office in April 1999.
Personal: Bristol University. Married with two children.

BAGGALLAY, Roger
Clifford Chance, London
(020) 7600 1000
roger.baggallay@cliffordchance.com
Specialisation: Litigation and dispute resolution. Partner specialising in commercial and financial litigation.
Career: Joined *Clifford Chance* 1976; Partner since 1987; Head of Litigation in Hong Kong 1982-85.

BAGGE, James
Norton Rose, London
(020) 7283 6000
baggejs@nortonrose.com
Specialisation: Partner in commercial litigation department. Practice focuses on fraud and the regulation of investment and banking business, in particular advising on all forms of investigations, statutory or private, and associated legal proceedings involving the SFO, DTI, SRO and Revenue authorities. Advised the Board of Banking Supervision on the Barings inquiry. Has acted for LIFFE in relation to market investigations and enforcement actions. Conducted the Banking Act inquiry into Hambros involvement with the aborted bid for the Co-operative Wholesale Society. Represented the trustee of the Thyssen Bornemisza Trust in action commenced by Baron Thyssen in Bermuda. Acts for three global investment banks in relation to ongoing regulatory investigations. Assisted with the Baird enquiry into the FSA's supervision of the Equitable Life.
Prof. Memberships: International Bar Association.
Career: Qualified 1979. Spent eight years at the Criminal Bar and two years on secondment to the Serious Fraud Office. Joined *Norton Rose* in 1990 and became a partner in 1993.

BAND, Christa
Herbert Smith, London
(020) 7374 8000
christa.band@herbertsmith.com
Specialisation: Partner whose practice covers a wide variety of general commercial litigation with a particular emphasis on banking and financial services litigation including advice and litigation in relation to the contractual and other duties of banks, bond issues, derivatives, enforcement of security, constructive trust and asset recovery claims.
Prof. Memberships: Solicitors' Association of Higher Court Advocates; City of London Solicitors Company Litigation Committee.
Career: Trinity Hall, Cambridge (BA 1985, MA 1988); Inns of Court Law School (Bar Finals 1986); St. Edmund Hall, Oxford (BCL 1987). Qualified 1993; Barrister, London, 1987-90; worked with major solicitors' firm, Sydney, Australia, 1990-92; Solicitor Advocate, all Courts (1994). Partner *Herbert Smith* since 1996.

BARCLAY, Marcus
Olswang, London
(020) 7208 8888
Specialisation: Principal area of practice is property litigation. Handles all aspects of commercial property litigation, including contentious lease renewals, forfeiture actions, rent review arbitrations, service charge disputes and privity actions. Also deals with insolvency including security enforcement for banks, and acting for liquidators and administrative receivers on all matters arising out of liquidations or receiverships. Important cases include Ropemaker Properties v Noonhaven Ltd, Ivory Gate Ltd v Spetale.
Prof. Memberships: Law Society; Property Litigation Association; Accredited CEDR Mediator.
Career: Qualified in September 1988. At *Rubinstein Callingham Polden & Gale* 1986-90. Joined *Simon Olswang* in August 1990. Became a Partner at *Olswang* in May 1994.
Personal: Born 12th December 1961. Educated at Holland Park School 1971-76, Abingdon School 1976-78 and Warwick University 1981-84. Leisure pursuits include music, sports, cooking, theatre and cinema. Lives in London.

BARLEY, Mark
Bond Pearce, Plymouth
(01752) 266 633
mbarley@bondpearce.com
Specialisation: Associate specialising in business and residential tenancy disputes, lease renewals, dilapidations, restrictive covenants, adverse possession and property-related professional negligence claims.
Prof. Memberships: Member of the Property Litigation Association, the Forum of Insurance Lawyers and a committee member of the Plymouth Law Society.
Career: Oxford University Exhibitioner (French and Latin) 1982-85; Guildford Law College (CPE and LSF 1985-87). Qualified 1989 with *Bond Pearce*, appointed Associate 1999.

BARRETT, Elizabeth
Slaughter and May, London
(020) 7600 1200
elizabeth.barrett@slaughterandmay.com
Specialisation: Partner in litigation department. Principal area of practice is commercial litigation including civil and commercial fraud and corporate crime, and extensive experience of a broad range of statutory, regulatory and disciplinary investigations and enquiries.
Prof. Memberships: The Law Society.
Career: Qualified 1981. Partner *Peter Carter-Ruck and Partners* 1982-1986. Joined *Slaughter and May* 1986; partner 1989.
Personal: Born 23 November 1956. Attended University College, London (LLB Hons 1978).

BASTOW, Martin
Lyons Davidson, Bristol
(0117) 904 5898
mbastow@lyonsdavidson.co.uk
Specialisation: Partner and Head of Commercial Litigation Department. Experienced in all aspects of property litigation with particular emphasis on landlord and tenant disputes and complex security enforcement. Work includes dilapidations, forfeiture, 1954 Act renewals, arbitration, possession proceedings, property-related prosecutions and acting for LPA receivers.
Prof. Memberships: Associate of the Chartered Institute of Arbitrators; PACT panel member; member of Property Litigation Association, and LSC Funding Review Committee.
Career: Joined *Lyons Davidson* on qualification in 1988. Partner since 1994.

BECK, Andrew
Walker Morris, Leeds
(0113) 283 2500
Specialisation: Partner and head of property litigation group. Specialist areas include service charge disputes, lease renewals, removing squatters and landlord and tenant disputes. Andrew has been involved in a number of reported cases including Postel Properties Limited v Boots the Chemist Limited involving a substantial service charge dispute in respect of a shopping centre.
Prof. Memberships: Andrew is a CEDR accredited mediator and a member of the Association of Northern Mediators, Member of the Property Litigation Association.
Career: Qualified in 1988, joined *Walker Morris* 1989.
Personal: Born 1958, resides Leeds, hobbies include family and sport.

BECKETT, Sam
L'Estrange & Brett, Belfast
(028) 9023 0426
sam.beckett@lestrangeandbrett.com
See under Construction, p.192

BEDFORD, Richard
Burges Salmon, Bristol
(0117) 902 2749
richard.bedford@burges-salmon.com
Specialisation: As a specialist property litigator, he deals with professional indemnity claims, agricultural insolvency related matters and real property disputes. Particular specialism is banking disputes relating to agriculture. He has lectured on numerous subjects including agricultural law, secured lending and specialist areas of landlord and tenant law.
Prof. Memberships: Law Society.
Career: Joined *Burges Salmon* in 1983 as a trainee and became a partner in 1992. Joint author of RICS publication, 'Farm Receiverships'.

BELCHER, Penny
Hammond Suddards Edge, Leeds
0113 284 7000

BILLING, Petra
DLA, Sheffield
(08700) 111111

BLAKE, Peter
Prettys, Ipswich
(01473) 232121
plb@prettys.co.uk
Specialisation: Commercial litigation, including construction, sale of goods and cross-border disputes. Clients include: construction, engineering and transport companies and professional practices.
Prof. Memberships: Law Society; Faculty of Building.
Career: Qualified in 1987. Commercial litigation partner *Prettys* from 1991.
Personal: Born 1963. Education: King Edward VI School Norwich 1973-81, Exeter University 1981-84, Guildford College of Law. Ipswich-East Suffolk Hockey Club (past Chairman).

BLAKEMORE, Craig
Mace & Jones, Liverpool
(0151) 236 8989
craig.blakemore@maceandjones.co.uk
Specialisation: Commercial contract disputes, professional negligence actions (particularly solicitors), insolvency, computer/IT law and intellectual property.
Prof. Memberships: Society for Computers and Law. Association of Business Recovery Professionals.
Career: Articled *Mace & Jones* –1980-82. Solicitor *Mace & Jones* – 1982-86. Partner *Mace & Jones* –1986 onwards. Head of litigation for the firm.
Personal: Interests include rugby, squash, motorcycling.

BLYTH, Mark
Linklaters, London
(020) 7456 4246
mark.blyth@linklaters.com
Specialisation: Full-time specialist in all types of pensions litigation. Typical matters include proceedings by members to challenge a surplus repayment made by trustees to the employer; proceedings brought by way of interpleader by trustees facing competing claims by members and employer to pension benefits; proceedings involving representative members to sanction a compromise reached between trustees and the employer in relation to a scheme surplus; proceedings involving representative members to sanction the compromise of litigation against trustees for breach of trust; proceedings involving representative members to determine the construction of scheme rules on benefit entitlement, claims by the trustees to reduce the payment of benefits to the 'correct' level and recover overpayments to members; proceedings brought by members against trustees for failure to pay ill health early retirement pensions; Pen-

LITIGATION ■ THE LEADERS

sion Ombudsman complaints; the appeal of determinations of the Pensions Ombudsman to the High Court; claims of professional negligence against scheme actuaries/professional advisers and scheme administrators; regulatory issues with OPRA; defending claims by trustees against employers for contributions to fund scheme deficits (including 'good faith' issues); pensions mis-selling issues; defending claims against Life Offices in relation to pensions issues.
Prof. Memberships: Association of Pensions Lawyers. Advisory Panel Member – Occupational Pensions. Association of Contentious Trust & Probate Specialists.
Career: Articled to *Allen & Overy* 1988-90. 1990-2001, Consultant, *Linklaters*. Associate Partner, 2001 to date.

BRADFORD, Katie
Linklaters, London
(020) 7456 4234
katie.bradford@linklaters.com
Specialisation: Property litigation, including tenant default, rent review, dilapidations actions, and insolvency advice. Clients include pension funds and banks (landlords) retailers and financial institutions (tenants) lenders, insolvency practitioners, developers and property companies. Has conducted in excess of 65 trials plus appeals to Court of Appeal and House of Lords. Listed in the 'Guide to the World's Leading Real Estate Lawyers' and the 'Guide to the World's Leading Arbitration Lawyers'. Specialist in rent review arbitration and determination by experts; acting for landlords and tenants in cases determined by written submissions and by oral evidence; advising arbitrators and independent experts on points of law. Expert in property disputes; right of light, right of way, party wall disputes, title and adverse possession claims; restrictive covenants and easements, vendor and purchaser actions; specific performance, mortgage actions. Also public law and judicial review in property context. Expert in professional negligence cases involving property professionals, valuations disputes, conveyancing problems, advising lenders, property owners and insurers.
Prof. Memberships: CEDR accredited mediator; arbitrator and independent expert: Law Society Panel: RICS Panel: PACT trained; founding member of Property Litigation Association (Chair 1997-98); Facilitator of Women in Property Litigation Group.
Career: 2001 to date, Head of Property and Finance Litigation; 1997 to date, Partner *Linklaters*; 1992 to date, Head of the Property Litigation Unit; 1992-97, Assistant Solicitor and Head of the Property Litigation Unit, *Linklaters*, 1984-91, *Lovell White Durrant* (formerly *Lovell White & King*); 1982-84, *Osmond Gaunt & Rose* (trainee solicitor 1981-82).
Personal: London University, LLM (Merit); College of law, Lancaster Gate; University College, London LLB (Hons).

BRIERLEY, Ian
DLA, London
(08700) 111 111

BRIGGS, Leona
Osborne Clarke, Bristol
(0117) 917 3000

BYRNE, David
Dechert, London
(020) 7775 7415
david.byrne@eu.dechert.com
Specialisation: Partner and head of litigation and investigations, London. Responsible for all aspects of investigation work. He specialises in civil and criminal fraud for both claimants and defendants and has acted in numerous high profile cases brought by the SFO, city regulators, Inland Revenue and Customs & Excise. David is also co-ordinating the firm's growing practices in the financial services field and in corporate manslaughter.
Prof. Memberships: Law Society; Association of Business Recovery Professionals.
Career: Qualified in 1978. Articled at *Norton Rose*. Solicitor *Norton Rose* 1978-83. *Clifford Turner* (now *Clifford Chance*) 1983-85 Partner *Titmuss Sainer & Webb* (now *Dechert*) since 1987.
Personal: Born 1951. Attended Kings College London, Masters degree in tax, corporate and insurance law, Sweet & Maxwell prize for company law. Interests include golf and fell walking.

CALLAGHAN, Edward
Mills & Reeve, Cambridge
(01223) 222 242
ed.callaghan@mills-reeve.com
Specialisation: Main areas of practice include building and engineering litigation, arbitration and adjudication. Also covered is professional indemnity work relating to architects, surveyors, engineers and solicitors. Has addressed seminars to audiences in the construction industry.
Prof. Memberships: Law Society, Legal panel. Technology & Construction Solicitors' Association.
Career: Qualified with *Mills & Reeve* in 1974. Became Partner in Commercial Litigation Department in 1979.
Personal: Born 25th February 1950 in Middlesex. Attended Franciscan College, Buckingham 1961-68, then Exeter University 1968-71. Leisure pursuits include squash, reading and viticulture. Lives Norfolk Broads.

CANNON, Lista
Richards Butler, London
(020) 7772 5702
lmc@richardsbutler.com
Specialisation: Lawyer qualified in New York (1975) and England and Wales (1974); practice covering the full range of commercial litigation work with particular emphasis on transnational (cross-border) commercial disputes and litigation, sovereign immunity issues, risk assessment and dispute resolution and government advisory work. Has a strong banking, finance and regulatory practice. Work includes ICC arbitration and energy-related contract disputes.
Prof. Memberships: In September 1998, seconded for six months to the Financial Services Authority as a Senior Legal Advisor and Acting Head of Enforcement. Law Society, admitted to New York State Bar in 1976, Federal Bar Council, ICC UK Environmental Committee.
Career: Litigation lawyer at *Sullivan & Cromwell*, New York, 1975-80. Established Commercial Litigation Department, (*Boodle Hatfield*), London 1980-92; Member of the Partnership Board of *Richards Butler* since May 1998.
Publications: Recently contributed a chapter on 'Regulatory Issues' to Sweet & Maxwell's new major publication entitled 'International Commercial Fraud' – a worldwide collaboration between over 20 leading fraud specialists.
Personal: Educated at New York University 1969; University of London LLB (hons) 1971. Trustee British American Educational Foundation since 1980, member of India House, New York and Reform Club.

CARRUTHERS, Andrew
Mayer, Brown, Rowe & Maw, London
(020) 7782 8809
acarruthers@eu.mayerbrownrowe.com
Specialisation: Pensions litigation and domestic and international arbitration and mediation.
Prof. Memberships: Law Society; Association of Pensions Lawyers; CEDR; LCIA; Chartered Institute of Arbitrators; Secretary of Pensions Litigation Committee of the Association of Pensions Lawyers.
Career: Solicitor *Lovell White & King* 1975-1977; Solicitor *Bond Pearce* 1977-1980; Solicitor *Linklaters & Paines* 1980-1983; Solicitor *Rowe & Maw* 1983-present; Partner 1985; Head of Litigation and Dispute Resolution Department 1995.
Publications: 'Pensions Litigation' – Tolley's; 'Pensions Law' (2000).
Personal: Educated at Harrow County Boy's School; Pembroke College, Oxford (1972 Jurisprudence; 1975 MA). Enjoys music, travel, family, history and gardening.

CAVE, Tim
Freshfields Bruckhaus Deringer, London
(020) 7936 4000
timothy.cave@freshfields.com
Specialisation: Partner in the dispute resolution department dealing with commercial litigation and specialising in banking and property litigation.
Career: Articled *Freshfields*. Qualified 1986. Partner 1994.
Personal: Born 1960. Educated at Bristol University.

CHAPMAN, Stuart
Pinsent Curtis Biddle, Leeds
(0113) 244 5000
stuart.chapman@pinsents.com
Specialisation: Partner and head of litigation, Leeds. Independently acknowledged expert in resolution of both commercial and IT disputes.
Prof. Memberships: Chairman, Society for Computers & Law (Northern Group)
Career: *Linklaters* (1989-1994). *Eversheds*, Leeds (1994-1998). *Pinsent Curtis Biddle*, Leeds (1998-Date).
Personal: Born 1965 and educated in Grimsby. Leisure interests include family, football, sailing, cricket, most other sports.

CHEFFINGS, Nicholas
Lovells, London
(020) 7296 2000
nicholas.cheffings@lovells.com
Specialisation: Partner and head of group of 13 PACT arbitrators. ADR-Net (1991) and CEDR (2000) accredited mediator and has sat as a mediator and mentor on a number of occasions; also a fellow of the Chartered Institute of Arbitrators (1993) and acts as a legal assessor to surveyor arbitrators and experts. Specialises in all aspects of contentious property work from advisory to House of Lords, such as landlord and tenant (including major rent reviews), planning/judicial review, rights of light, lands tribunal work, professional negligence, agency and vendor/purchaser and joint venture disputes; acted on several reported cases; member of the RICS President's Independent Expert Quality Initiative.
Prof. Memberships: ARBRIX; Chartered Institute of Arbitrators; Property Dispute Resolution Forum; Property Litigation Association; Law Society
Career: Qualified 1983; partner *Nabarro Nathanson* 1990; partner *Lovells* 1999.
Publications: General editor of 'Commercial Property Disputes: Law and Practice' (1999); author of numerous articles and regular speaker at conferences; Blundell Memorial lecturer.
Personal: Born 1960. Educated at Caistor Grammar School; University of Leicester (LLB 2(1) Hons). Interests include holidays, dining, theatre etc, watching virtually any sport and occasionally complete inactivity. Resides Chelsfield.

CLARK, Tim
Olswang, Reading
(0118) 952 3380
TGC@Olswang.com
Specialisation: Complex commercial litigation, arbitration and dispute resolution. Recent cases include information technology disputes, minority shareholders actions, finance and leasing, professional negligence and energy sector disputes. Recently acted for Thames Water Utilities Ltd in complex litigation concerning the sale and supply of renewable energy. Clients include multinational corporations, major listed plcs and technology companies based in the Thames Valley.
Prof. Memberships: Thames Valley Commercial Lawyers Association.
Career: *Eversheds* London (formerly *Jaques & Lewis*) 1985-96; *Garretts* (1996-2002); *Olswang* (June 2002 to date).

Personal: Leisure interests include family, golf, all sports. Married with two children.

CLAVELL-BATE, Michael
Eversheds, Manchester
(0161) 831 8000
michaelclavellbate@eversheds.com
Specialisation: Head of the Commercial Litigation Team in Manchester. All areas of management of commercial disputes including mainstream commercial litigation and ADR. Also specialises in all areas of defamation. Received national press coverage following the Football Association's withdrawal of its charges against Brian Clough. Also hit the headlines last year acting for Ros Marks, former nanny to Cherie and Tony Blair. Contributed to a chapter on 'Defamation on the Internet' for a legal text published April 2000. Reported cases include Secretary of State v Secure & Provide plc. Current major cases include two very high profile defamation cases, a multi-party product liability case (approx. £50m) and a professional negligence case with a damages claim in excess of £20m.
Prof. Memberships: Chairman of the Civil Litigation Committee of the Manchester Law Society. Council Member of the Manchester Law Society. President of Manchester Law Society.
Career: Qualified with *Eversheds* in 1990 and became a Partner in 1997.
Personal: Born 25 March 1966. Attended Newcastle University and Chester College of Law. Resides in Trawden, North East Lancashire. Leisure interests include all sport.

CLOUGH, Peter
Osborne Clarke, Bristol
(0117) 917 3000

COHEN, Roger
Berwin Leighton Paisner, London
(020) 7760 1000
roger.cohen@blplaw.com
Specialisation: Litigation and dispute resolution partner. Main areas of practice are real estate disputes and ADR. Represents Prudential, Legal & General, Central Government, UBS and Tesco.
Prof. Memberships: CEDR registered mediator; Fellow Chartered Institute of Arbitrators. Professional member: Law Society Civil/Commercial Mediation Panel.
Career: Articled with *Donnelly & Elliott* in Gosport, then joined *Matthew Arnold & Baldwin* in Watford. Joined *Berwin Leighton* in 1984 and became a partner in 1989. Head of real estate disputes group and co-chair of *Berwin Leighton Paisner* Israel desk.

COLE, Jeremy
Lovells, London
(020) 7296 2000
jeremy.cole@lovells.com
Specialisation: Contentious insolvency and international fraud litigation. Head partner on the collapse of RBG Resources plc.
Prof. Memberships: R3; AIJA; Society of English American Lawyers; AEPPC.
Career: Qualified in 1985. Has worked in *Lovells*' offices in Hong Kong and New York and spent extensive periods of time in Abu Dhabi and Cayman Islands. Previous matters are: Derby v Weldon, acting for Prince Jefri in Jefri v KPMG and for the liquidation of BCCI.
Publications: Co-editor of Sweet and Maxwell publication 'International Commercial Fraud'.

COLE, Margaret R
White & Case, London
(020) 7397 3609
mrcole@whitecase.com
Specialisation: One of the country's leading advisors in commercial litigation.
Prof. Memberships: Law Society of England & Wales, registered CEDR mediator.
Career: Joined *White & Case*, London as partner, 1995.
Personal: MA Cambridge University 1982. Interests include opera and competitive horse riding.

COLLINSON, Ian
Ward Hadaway, Newcastle upon Tyne
(0191) 204 4000
Specialisation: Head of commercial litigation with particular expertise in professional negligence, insurance and defamation.
Career: Birkenhead School and Kings College, London. Qualified in 1982. Articled and subsequently partner with *Dawson & Co*, London. Head of litigation 1989. Moved to Newcastle and *Ward Hadaway* 1991. Partner 1992. Head of litigation 1993.
Personal: Golf, sailing and fishing.

CONNAL QC, Craig
McGrigor Donald, Glasgow
(0141) 248 6677
craig.connal@mcgrigors.com
Specialisation: Partner in Commercial Litigation Unit. Appointed Scotland's first Solicitor Advocate, Queens Counsel in February 2002. Many years experience of advising on and appearing at tribunals, courts and inquiries in contentious and high profile matters. Recent cases ranged from construction to employment negligence, to property and insolvency and trusts, in addition to appearances in planning inquiries and litigation.
Prof. Memberships: Law Society of Scotland, SSC (Solicitor in the Supreme Courts), Council member, Royal Faculty of Procurators in Glasgow 1995-98. Member of the Scottish Law Commission Working Party on Partnership Law. External Examiner, University of Aberdeen.
Career: Joined *McGrigor Donald* in 1977 on qualification, becoming a Partner in 1980.
Publications: A regular lecturer and author of many articles, from the 'Financial Times' to, for example, 'Estates Gazette' and 'JPEL'. Contributor, 'Stair Memorial Encyclopaedia of Scots Law'.
Personal: Born 7 July 1954. Educated at Glasgow University (LLB, 1st Class Honours 1975). Rugby referee.

CONWAY, Keith
Dechert, London
(020) 7583 5353
keith.conway@eu.dechert.com
Specialisation: Partner, specialising in property litigation and commercial litigation. Keith deals with all property and landlord and tenant matters. In recent years, Keith has had extensive experience of dealing with major rent review arbitrations and encourages the use of self-help remedies. He also deals with corporate, joint venture and partnership disputes, and commercial, banking and insolvency litigation and arbitration. Keith is featured in the 'Legal Business' Legal Experts list of highly recommended lawyers. Some of Keith's significant cases include Argyll Stores v CIS (House of Lords) – Keep Open, Banner Homes Group Plc v Luff Developments Ltd – Joint Venture Dispute (Court of Appeal), Belvedere Court v Frogmore Estates Plc and Harley House (Marylebone) Ltd v Michaels – both Court of Appeal 1987 Act, London & Leeds v Paribas (Court of Appeal) – Rent Review. Currently dealing with; BHP Petroleum v Chesterfield Properties – original Landlord release of personal/developers covenants under the 1995 Act and liability for defects and the Broadgate Rent Reviews.
Prof. Memberships: Property Litigation Association, Member of Chartered Institute of Arbitrators, Member of Joint Working Party – Limitation of Actions. ADR Accredited Mediator.
Career: Qualified 1984. Partner in 1990.
Publications: Contributor to the 'Landlord & Tenant Factbook' published by Franey & Co in 1992, Joint Editor of 'Property Law Journal', regularly writes on property and commercial law and litigation practice. Spoken at numerous conferences.

COOMBS, Monica
Sacker & Partners, London
(020) 7329 6699
monica.coombs@sacker-partners.co.uk
Specialisation: Specialising in pensions litigation and mediation particularly professional negligence, trust law and asset tracing and recovery.
Prof. Memberships: Association of Pension Lawyers. Association of Pensions Lawyers Pensions Litigation Committee. Law Society.
Career: Admitted in Western Australia 1990. Qualified in England 1996. Partner at *Sacker & Partners* since 1999.
Personal: Educated at the University of Western Australia. Leisure activities include travel, diving and walking.

COX, David
Berwin Leighton Paisner, London
(020) 7427 1328
david.cox@blplaw.com
Specialisation: Specialises in a whole range of property-related disputes, including rent collection and service charge disputes, forfeitures, rent reviews, lease renewals, dilapidations claims, title and right to light disputes and professional negligence claims. Clients include institutional investors, retail groups, developers and owner-occupiers. Has led seminars recently on the proposed Landlord & Tenant Act reforms and insolvent tenants and has had articles published in 'Estates Gazette' and 'Property Law Journal'.
Prof. Memberships: Law Society, Property Litigation Association.
Career: Qualified 1979. Partner *Lovells* 1985-97. Partner Berwin Leighton *Paisner* 1998.

CRAWFORD, Sandra
McKinty and Wright, Belfast
(028) 9024 6751
post@mckinty-wright.co.uk
Specialisation: Practises in all types of commercial litigation including professional negligence, claims arising out of the carriage of goods and marine matters. Also extensive employment law practice, both advisory and litigation, acting for employers.
Prof. Memberships: Law Society of Northern Ireland, Northern Ireland Employment Lawyers Group.
Career: Graduated Queen's University of Belfast in Law (LLB) 1985. Qualified 1987. Partner in *McKinty & Wright* since 1995.
Personal: Born 1962. Married, two children.

CROSS, Siobhan
Masons, London
(020) 7490 6277
siobhan.cross@masons.com
Specialisation: Partner in property litigation group. Practice covers all areas of property litigation and dispute resolution including landlord and tenant matters such as rent reviews, dilapidations, possession proceedings, and lease renewals and other property related disputes including disputes over development of land, relevant professional negligence claims and rights of way, light and air. Experienced in alternative methods of dispute resolution including mediation, arbitration and expert determination.
Prof. Memberships: Property Litigation Association.
Career: Qualified in 1987. Joined *Masons* in 1988 and became a partner in 1993.
Personal: Born 21 July 1962 and lives in North London.

CROSSLEY, Peter
Hammond Suddards Edge, Leeds
0113 284 7000

CULLEN, Joyce
Brodies, Edinburgh
(0131) 228 3777
joyce.cullen@brodies.co.uk
Specialisation: Head of Litigation Department and member of the Employment Law Group providing a full

LITITGATION ■ THE LEADERS

range of advice to companies, institutions, partnerships and individuals, including a major Scottish Bank, national retailers, colleges, professional firms and clients in the industrial and manufacturing sectors. Extensive experience as an advocate in Employment Tribunals, EAT and the Court of Session.
Prof. Memberships: Member of the Management Committee of the Employment Lawyers Association, Industrial Law Group, Institute of Directors. Member of the General Teaching Council, Scotland.
Career: Qualified in 1981. With *Brodies*, initially as an Assistant Solicitor, then as a Partner since 1986. Accredited specialist in employment law and Solicitor Advocate with extended rights of audience in the Civil Courts.
Personal: Born in 1958. Educated Leith Academy, Edinburgh and Dundee University. Married with three children. Interests include travel and playing the cello.

CUMMING, Kenny
Biggart Baillie, Glasgow
(0141) 228 8000

CURRY, Adam
Mills Selig, Belfast
(028) 9024 3878
adam.curry@nilaw.com
Specialisation: Commercial litigation, employment law, IPR and injunctions. Frequently advises on employment related issues in major corporate transactions including the recent client purchase of Bow Street Mall, Lisburn for £30.5m. Mainly acts for employers. Also acts in a substantial number of injunctions arising out of employment and IPR disputes. Extensive experience in injunction work including regular instructions to oversee the execution of Anton Pillar Orders as supervising solicitor.
Prof. Memberships: Law Society of Northern Ireland.
Career: Qualified 1990. Joined *Mills Selig* 1998. Became Partner 2002.
Personal: Sailing.

DAVIES, Gwendoline
Walker Morris, Leeds
(0113) 283 2500
gxd@walkermorris.co.uk
Specialisation: Partner and Head of Commercial Dispute Resolution Group engaged in a wide range of High Court and commercial dispute resolution for corporate clients, institutional clients and insolvency practitioners. Emphasis on contractual disputes, sale and purchase disputes, breach of warranty disputes, defective products, banking and insolvency. Member of firm's Lender Services Group. Involved in a number of recent Court of Appeal cases including successfully acting in a leading case on agency defending a bank's right to charged assets (Triffit Nurseries v Salads Etcetera Limited) and also successfully acting in a landmark House of Lords case involving relief from forfeiture of finance leases and the effect of an order for sale made by the Court pursuant to RSC Order 29 Rule 4 (now CPR 25.1 (c) (v)) [2002] 2 WLR 919.
Prof. Memberships: Society of Practitioners of Insolvency (subscriber status); Law Society; Leeds Law Society; CEDR accredited mediator.
Career: Whitland Grammar School; Leicester University (LLB); College of Law, Chester. Articled *Herbert Smith* 1996-98; qualified 1998 with *Herbert Smith* until December 1992, *Mallesons Stephen Jacques* (Australia – six months); joined *Walker Morris* in 1992 and partner May 1994.
Personal: Born 1964; resides Luddendenfoot. Leisure interests include reading, walking, sport, travel and family.

DAVIES, Peter
Gateley Wareing, Birmingham
(0121) 234 0000

DAVIES, Valerie E M
Norton Rose, London
(020) 7444 2673
daviesvem@nortonrose.com
Specialisation: Partner in Commercial Litigation Department. Handles a wide variety of domestic and international disputes of a commercial nature with particular emphasis on banking, corporate and financial litigation, insolvency and commercial fraud. Experienced in tracing and recovering assets. Heads *Norton Rose's* insolvency litigation team and has extensive experience of cross border international insolvency. A CEDR accredited mediator and mediates actions being appealed from a first instance decision to the Court of Appeal. Also handles some high profile defamation cases.
Prof. Memberships: Law Society; City of London Solicitors Company; International Bar Association.
Career: Qualified as a solicitor in 1979 and became a partner in *Norton Rose* in 1986. Was appointed as an Assistant Recorder in 1997 and a Recorder in 2000.

DAVIS, Simon
Clifford Chance, London
(020) 7600 1000
simon.davis@cliffordchance.com
Specialisation: Litigation and dispute resolution. Partner specialising in corporate litigation and product liability, advising on effective dispute avoidance and resolution.
Career: Articled *Clifford-Turner*; qualified 1984; Partner since 1994; Recruitment Partner since 1995.
Personal: Wellington College, Magdalen College, Oxford (MA).

DE WALDEN, Ludovic
Lane & Partners, London
(020) 7242 2626
dewaldenl@lane.co.uk
Specialisation: Complex multinational litigation and arbitration, art law problems.
Prof. Memberships: Chartered Institute of Arbitrators; IBA; Institute of Art and Law.
Career: Litigation and arbitration partner since 1985.
Personal: Interests: the arts, opera, theatre, skiing, shooting, golf, reading. Married with three children. Lives Chelsea and Oxfordshire.

DIMSDALE GILL, Angela
Lovells, London
(020) 7296 2000
amdg@lovells.com
Specialisation: Commercial chancery, pension fund disputes, professional negligence and fraud. Significant cases include Re Courage, National Power plc v Feldon, British Coal Corporation v British Coal Superannuation Scheme Trustees Ltd and the largest fraud claim arising out of collapse of BCCI. Extensive experience of high value pension and trust disputes and professional negligence work. Advises OPRA and Solicitors Indemnity Fund.
Prof. Memberships: City of London Law Society Litigation Sub-Committee, Association of Pension Lawyers and Pension Litigation committee of that association, Pensions Litigation Court Users' Committee, City of London Law Society Pro Bono Sub-Committee (Chair), Trustee Solicitor's Pro Bono Group.
Career: Qualified 1982, partner *Lovells* 1988.

DONALD, Hugh
Shepherd+ Wedderburn, Edinburgh
(0131) 473 5159
hugh.donald@shepwedd.co.uk
See under Clinical Negligence, p.151

DUNCAN, Michelle
Cadwalader, Wickersham & Taft, London
(020) 7170 8734
michelle.duncan@cwt-uk.com
Specialisation: Partner in the Financial Restructuring Department in London specialising in banking and corporate litigation. Recent experience includes acting for the bondholders of Barings Plc in proceedings to replace the Liquidators of the company and in the negligence actions against Coopers & Lybrand and Deloitte & Touche; acting for Alvaro Noboa, a leading businessman in Ecuador in proceedings concerning ownership and control of Fruit Shippers Ltd; acting for Messrs GP and SP Hinduja in connection with the Parliamentary Inquiry into Keith Vaz; and acting for certain reinsurers in connection with the administration of the Federal Mogul group of companies. In addition to her banking and finance litigation experience, Ms Duncan has advised bondholders in a number of restructurings such as Versatel, Kvaerner, Asia Global Crossing and NTL. Ms Duncan also helps *Cadwalader's* corporate attorneys assess legal risk intransactions involving banks and the capital markets.
Career: LLB University of Otago, New Zealand; admitted to practice in New Zealand in 1985 and England and Wales in 1991.

EASTON, Ewan
Maclay Murray & Spens, Edinburgh
(0131) 226 5196
ere@maclaymurrayspens.co.uk
Specialisation: Partner in Commercial Litigation and Advocacy. Specialises in property litigation, planning issues and employment law. Initiated the series of 'stay open' clause litigations in Scotland which have resulted in orders requiring banks, a supermarket and numerous other traders to keep trading operations alive. Has acted for Haslemere in shopping centre repossession, and for WISCO in environmental judicial review against the Scottish Executive. Instrumental in the first business petition to the new Scottish Parliament suggesting new Scottish legislation on landlord and tenant Law.
Career: University of Glasgow (LLB) 1980). Member of the Arbitration committee of the Law Society of Scotland. Worked for *Herbert Smith*, London (1984-85).
Personal: Born 1958.

EDWARDS, Martin
Martineau Johnson, Birmingham
(0121) 200 3300
Specialisation: Head of *Martineau Johnson's* property litigation team specialising in high quality property litigation and advises on all manner of disputes concerning property but principally commercial landlord and tenant matters including all aspects of lease renewals under the 1954 Act, boundary disputes, claims concerning rights of way and restrictive covenants, breaches of lease; forfeiture; all aspects of rent recovery; contested rent reviews, termination of leases; pursuing and defending interlocutory injunctions; nuisance actions; professional negligence claims against surveyors and Solicitors relating to property matters, and has particularly specialised knowledge of dilapidations and disrepair claims. Recent cases include: final settlement before trial of a £15m multi-party trespass action in so far as it concerned our public authority client as one of the defendants; acting for a large private company securing payment from its landlord of a significant sum of compensation arising out of termination of its Midlands office headquarters lease and other associated issues; acting for a private individual in defence of interference with his valuable fishing rights by a neighbouring landowner at one of the premier private fishing sites in the UK.
Prof. Memberships: Member of Property Litigation Association.
Career: Articled *Johnson & Co*; qualified 1988; Partner, *Martineau Johnson* 2000.
Publications: Contributor to 'Higher Education Law' Editors, Palfreyman and Warner.
Personal: University of Birmingham (1986 LLB Hons). Born 1963; resides Solihull. Leisure: family and gardening.

THE LEADERS — LITIGATION

ELLIOTT, Robert
Ward Hadaway, Newcastle upon Tyne
(0191) 204 4319
bob.elliott@wardhadaway.com
Specialisation: Partner dealing with wide range of commercial litigation, primarily heavy/light engineering, IT/hi-tech, and other manufacturing businesses. Particular interest in intellectual property, IT sector disputes, company/business sales disputes, faulty machinery/manufacturing processes, EU/international, defamation. CEDR accredited mediator. Independent expert for Nominet UK.
Career: Attended RGS Newcastle, then Manchester University. Qualified 1983. Practised in London 1981-93; *Herbert Smith*, *Clifford Chance*, *Richards Butler* (partner). Returned to Newcastle 1994 joining *Ward Hadaway* as Partner in 1996.
Personal: Lives in Wall (nr Hexham); married, two daughters; interests: hill walking, gardening and cooking.

FAGAN, Neil
Lovells, London
(020) 7296 2000
neil.fagan@lovells.com
Specialisation: Senior partner of 'city litigation group' specialising in financial, corporate finance and commercial litigation, regulatory issues and commercial dispute resolution. He also heads the firm's public policy practice.
Prof. Memberships: Member of the City of London Solicitors' Company and former Chairman, Employment Law Sub-Committee City of London Solicitors' Company; member International Bar Association Commercial Litigation and Labour Law Committee.
Career: Articled *Lovells*; qualified 1971; partner 1975.

FALKNER, James
Mills & Reeve, Norwich
(01603) 693230
james.falkner@mills-reeve.com
Specialisation: Agricultural, commercial and residential property and landlord and tenant disputes.
Prof. Memberships: Law Society; Property Litigation Association; Agricultural Law Association.
Career: Joined *Mills & Reeve*, 1980. Partner 1988.

FINKLER, Deborah
Slaughter and May, London
(020) 7600 1200
deborah.finkler@slaughterandmay.com
Specialisation: Broad range of commercial litigation including advising Unilever Superannuation Fund in its negligence claim against Mercury Asset Management, as well as a wide range of financial regulatory matters for a number of global financial institutions.
Career: Partner 1991.

FOORD, Roland
Stephenson Harwood (incorporating Sinclair Roche & Temperley), London
(020) 7809 2315
roland.foord@shlegal.com
Specialisation: Partner specialising in general commercial litigation, often with a significant international element and with particular focus on professional negligence work, particularly for chartered accountants and auctioneers and valuers. Regularly advises a Big Four firm and a leading auction house. Also experienced in representing clients in regulatory and disciplinary enquiries and proceedings. Cases include Prince Jefri v KPMG, Sasea Finance Limited v KPMG, RZB v Five Star General Trading and Gulf Bank v Mitsubishi Heavy Industries.
Career: Articled *Stephenson Harwood*; qualified 1985; Partner since 1989.
Personal: Born in 1958. Educated at Eton College and King's College, London (1982 LLB).

FORDHAM, John
Stephenson Harwood (incorporating Sinclair Roche & Temperley), London
(020) 7809 2300
john.fordham@shlegal.com
Specialisation: Partner, Head of Litigation, *Stephenson Harwood*. Extensive dispute resolution experience: High Court; international arbitrations; international investigations; asset-tracing; multi-jurisdictional disputes; commercial, banking, insolvency, fraud litigation. Regulatory enquiries. Alternative dispute resolution: advocate and mediator. Led team representing liquidators of the Maxwell pension trustee company – approximately £400 million recovered for pensioners. Lectures on litigation and fraud matters.
Prof. Memberships: CEDR – Accredited Mediator.
Career: *Stephenson Harwood* 1972; qualified 1974; partner 1979; Head of Litigation 1995.
Personal: Born 1948. Educated at Dulwich College; Gonville & Caius College, Cambridge, 1st in Law. Married with two children. Interests include theatre, cinema, art, tennis and cricket. Foreign languages French. Resides Cheam, Surrey.

FORTNAM, Jonathan
Pinsent Curtis Biddle, Birmingham
(0121) 626 5712
jonathan.fortnam@pinsents.com
Specialisation: Experienced in a wide variety of high value and complex commercial disputes that have in recent years focused on financial services and IT-related matters. Important cases: Radiant Shipping Co Limited v Sea Containers Limited [1995] CLC 976 (the enforceability of a lock out and underwriting agreement in the context of negotiations for the purchase of a company); Young v Purdy [1995] TLR 572, CA (whether wrongful termination of a solicitor's retainer was the cause or occasion of loss); Crawley Borough Council v Bradford and Bingley Building Society (1998), CA (unreported) (rectification of a sub-ordinated loan agreement); Kidd v AXA Equity & Law Life Assurance Society Plc [2000] IRLR 299 (the limits of the liability of a provider to the subject of a reference) and Heaton and others v AXA Equity & Law Life Assurance Society Plc [2002] 2 WLR 1081, HL (effect of a settlement agreement on claims against successive contract breakers).
Career: 1987, LLB (Hons) University of Liverpool; 1988, Law Society Final Examination, College of Law, 1990; Solicitor *Pinsent & Co*; 1998, Partner *Pinsent Curtis Biddle*; 2001, ADR Net Mediator. Member of the Society for Computers and Law.
Publications: Numerous articles on the effect of the Woolf reforms, expert evidence, mediation and IT-related issues, both in the UK and abroad.
Personal: Local church, cooking, sports and jazz music.

FOX, Brendan
Cleaver Fulton Rankin, Belfast
(028) 9027 1325
b.fox@cfrlaw.co.uk
See under Construction, p.195

FOX-EDWARDS, Jane
Lawrence Graham, London
(020) 7379 0000

FRANCIS, Penelope
Lawrence Graham, London
(020) 7379 0000

FRASER, David
Baker & McKenzie, London
(020) 7919 1000
david.fraser@bakernet.com

FREYNE, Michele
Mayer, Brown, Rowe & Maw, London
(020) 7782 8796
mfreyne@ev.mayerbrownrowe.com
Specialisation: Main area of practice is property litigation. Started first specialist team in 1980 which has grown into team which she heads of six including two partners. Also specialises in matrimonial law (about 15% of total workload).
Prof. Memberships: Property Litigation Association, Solicitors Family Law Association.
Career: Qualified in 1978. Joined *Rowe & Maw* in 1979, became Partner in 1984. Group Managing Partner, commercial litigation 1993-94.

FRIEDMAN, Paul
Baker & McKenzie, London
(020) 7919 1000
paul.friedman@bakernet.com
Specialisation: Specialises in litigation, arbitration and dispute resolution. Qualified in England and Wales as a Solicitor and Advocate having obtained his higher rights qualifications. Has substantial experience of commercial disputes including banking litigation, commercial fraud, trust litigation, breach of warranty and general contractual and tortuous claims. Clients include major multinationals, financial institutions and clients in the sports and media industries. Has been involved in litigation in courts in the UK and elsewhere and has worked on international arbitrations and on mediations. Listed as being a leader in his field as a commercial litigation expert.
Prof. Memberships: Association of Contentious Trust and Probate Specialists; Confederation of British Industry, Judicial Issues Group; Solicitors Association of Higher Court Advocates; Law Society of England and Wales.
Career: Graduated in law from the London School of Economics in 1988. Qualified as a Solicitor with *Clifford Chance* before joining *Baker & McKenzie* in London. Spent a year in the firm's Sydney office (1995-96) before becoming a Partner in 1999.
Publications: Frequent writer on legal issues and regularly speaks at conferences and seminars. Is also often asked to provide in-house training to clients. Articles have recently appeared in publications such as 'The Banker', 'Global Counsel', 'The British Bankers' Association Newsletter' and 'PLC'.
Personal: Born in South Africa. He is married to Debbie with a little son called Yonatan.

GAINES, Keith
Lovells, London
(020) 7296 2000
keith.gaines@lovells.com
Specialisation: Principal areas of work: contentious insolvency, commercial fraud, asset tracing. Wide experience with emphasis on cross-border situations encompassing many jurisdictions from USA through Caribbean to Europe and Far East. Advised on several key legal developments in last 15 years; acted on several high profile cases, including liquidation of BCCI. Advises UK accountants, overseas lawyers, UK and overseas financial institutions. Experienced in dealings with Serious Fraud Office and other regulatory bodies. Worked for the administrators of British and Commonwealth, ING in the Barings collapse, the receivers of Rosehaugh, Liquidation of RBG, and other large corporate collapses.
Prof. Memberships: The Law Society, International Bar Association, Society of Practitioners of Insolvency, AEPPC. Committee O. Author of several articles and talks on insolvency.
Career: Qualified 1981; seconded to New York 1984-86; partner 1986, London; admitted Hong Kong solicitor 1986.

GARRETT, Susan
Addleshaw Booth & Co, Leeds
(0113) 209 2450
susan.garrett@addleshawbooth.com
Specialisation: Commercial litigation, human rights and professional negligence with particular expertise in tax, insurance and construction disputes.
Personal: Interests include skiing.

www.ChambersandPartners.com   557

LITIGATION ■ THE LEADERS

GARVIE, Carl
Pinsent Curtis Biddle, Birmingham
(0121) 625 3088
carl.garvie@pinsents.com
Specialisation: Partner specialises in corporate and commercial litigation including warranty claims, shareholder disputes, fiduciary duty claims and commercial contractual disputes. Considerable experience in injunctive relief applications, including acting as the court-appointed supervisor of search orders.
Prof. Memberships: Law Society.
Career: MA Trinity Hall, Cambridge. Articled at *Pinsent & Co* (now *Pinsent Curtis Biddle*). Qualified in 1986. Partner in 1991.
Personal: Soccer, music, gymnasium.

GATENBY, John
Addleshaw Booth & Co, Manchester
(0161) 934 6548
john.gatenby@addleshawbooth.com
Specialisation: Partner. Advises English and overseas private and public companies on international litigation, arbitration and alternative dispute resolution, including the enforcement of foreign judgements, and arbitral awards, commercial contract disputes and partnership law. Lectures regularly on civil procedure matters including international litigation, arbitration, ADR and documentary evidence.
Prof. Memberships: Law Society, Chartered Institute of Arbitrators (Fellow), Institute of Credit Management, IBA, SEG, LSLA, Commonwealth Lawyers Association, Non-exec Director of CEDR. CEDR and ADR Group registered mediator. Chartered Institute of Arbitrators mediator panel.
Career: Qualified in 1975. Joined the firm in 1984; Partner since 1985.
Personal: Educated at Trinity Hall, Cambridge 1968-72.

GERRARD, Neil
DLA, London
(08700) 111 111

GILBERT, Ralph
Rollits, Hull
(01482) 323 239
ralph.gilbert@rollits.com
Specialisation: Full range of commercial disputes including contentious insolvency and commercial property work.
Career: Qualified at *Rollit Farrell & Bladon* (1990), Partner (1999).
Personal: Educated at University of Hull (1987). Married with three children. Interests include church and charity work.

GILL, Judith A E
Allen & Overy, London
(020) 7330 3000
judith.gill@allenovery.com
Specialisation: Judith Gill has been a Partner in the Litigation Department since 1992. She has extensive experience in all forms of arbitration proceedings: both local and international. She also has wide-ranging litigation experience with an emphasis on commercial disputes, insurance-related work and pensions litigation. She is a co-author of a new edition of 'Russell on Arbitration' and has produced a number of articles in her capacity as News Section Correspondent for the 'International Arbitration Law Review'. Judith is also a member of the Board of Directors of the London Court of International Arbitration, a committee member of the International Arbitration Club, a fellow of the Institute of Advanced Legal Studies and a fellow of the Chartered Institute of Arbitrators.
Prof. Memberships: Chartered Institute of Arbitrators; International Arbitration Club; member of the Board of Directors of the London Court of International Arbitration; fellow, the Society of Advanced Legal Studies; member of the ICC UK Arbitration Group.
Career: Articled *Allen & Overy*. Qualified (1985). Partner (1992). Director of the London Court of International Arbitration. Solicitor Advocate (1998).
Publications: Co-Author of the 21st Edition of 'Russell on Arbitration'.
Personal: Worcester College, Oxford University (1982, MA Jurisprudence). Diploma in International Commercial Arbitration, University of London (1990, Distinction).

GILL, Mark
Denton Wilde Sapte, London
(020) 7246 7000

GODDARD, John
Freshfields Bruckhaus Deringer, London
(020) 7936 4000
john.goddard@freshfields.com
Specialisation: Partner in dispute resolution department, specialising in banking litigation (principally for the Bank of England) and commercial litigation, usually involving company law and shareholder disputes.
Career: Qualified 1980.
Personal: Born 1955. Educated at Magdalene College, Cambridge.

GOLD, David
Herbert Smith, London
(020) 7374 8000
david.gold@herbertsmith.com
See under Partnership, p.600

GOLDSPINK, Robert
Morgan, Lewis & Bockius, London
(020) 7710 5517
rgoldspink@morganlewis.com
See under Insurance, p.474

GOOD, Diana
Linklaters, London
(020) 7456 4328
diana.good@linklaters.com
Specialisation: Commercial litigator advising clients, settling and fighting a wide range of commercial disputes, including financial services and insurance sector disputes (including professional negligence and regulatory investigation in relation to fraud, insider dealing, market abuse etc). EU litigation: experience of resolving disputes in relation to EU and UK competition law including investigations, acting on behalf of both claimants and defendants in Article 81 and 82 disputes, judicial review, human rights and challenge to regulators. Joint head of the EU Litigation Unit. International litigation: co-ordinating and strategic lead in multi-jurisdictional disputes and tax litigation. Joint head of *Linklaters* Contentious Tax Unit.
Prof. Memberships: Solicitor Advocate with Rights of Audience in the Higher Courts. Part-time judicial appointment as a Recorder. CEDR accredited mediator. Member of the Executive Committee and Council of the British Institute of International and Comparative law.
Career: 1988 to date: Partner, *Linklaters* London; 1989-92 Partner, *Linklaters* Brussels; 1982-88: Assistant Solicitor, *Linklaters*. 1982: Aix-en-Provence International Law D.E.S.U; 1978: Oxford University BA Jurisprudence.

GOODRHAM, Stephen
Gateley Wareing, Birmingham
(0121) 234 0000

GOSLING, John
Addleshaw Booth & Co, Manchester
(0161) 934 6565
john.gosling@addleshawbooth.com
Specialisation: Commercial litigation and mediation for major corporate and insurance clients, including professional negligence work. Accredited mediator.
Prof. Memberships: Law Society, Manchester Law Society.
Career: Qualified in 1984; Partner since 1990. Appointed Head of Group in May 1998.
Personal: Educated at Durham University 1978-81. Leisure pursuits include sport and family.

GRANDISON, Richard
Slaughter and May, London
(020) 7600 1200
richard.grandison@slaughterandmay.com
Specialisation: Head of commercial litigation and arbitration department. Extensive experience in commercial litigation, arbitration and commercial judicial review for a wide range of corporate clients in commercial disputes in England and overseas.
Prof. Memberships: The Law Society and City of London Solicitors' Society.
Career: Qualified in 1978 with *Slaughter and May*. Partner since 1987. Educated at Fettes College, Edinburgh and Pembroke College, Cambridge.

GRAY, David
DLA, Manchester
(08700) 111111

GRAY, Nick
Slaughter and May, London
(020) 7600 1200
nick.gray@slaughterandmay.com
Specialisation: Partner specialising in a wide range of commercial disputes in the English Courts, in arbitration proceedings in England and abroad and in judicial review proceedings. Regularly involved in overseeing litigation and co-ordinating local advice in other jurisdictions.
Career: Qualified 1988. Joined *Slaughter and May* in 1988. Partner since 1996.
Personal: Born 1964; resides London. Educated at Daniel Stewert's and Melville College, Edinburgh and at Sidney Sussex College, Cambridge. Leisure interests include music, sport, theatre and Italy.

GREENO, Ted
Herbert Smith, London
(020) 7374 8000
ted.greeno@herbertsmith.com
See under Energy, p.342

GRIERSON, Christopher
Lovells, London
(020) 7296 2000
christopher.grierson@lovells.com
Specialisation: International and domestic litigation with particular emphasis on insolvency, fraud and asset recovery matters, and insurance and reinsurance. Has acted in a number of prominent cases, including Laker Airways, Mentor Insurance, BCCI, Barings and EMLICO. Has acted for Prince Jefri of Brunei in the KPMG 'Chinese Walls' litigation and in defence of the proceedings brought by the Government of Brunei. Is now also acting for the liquidators of BCCI in their claim against the Bank of England. Licensed insolvency practitioner.
Prof. Memberships: International Bar Association, American Bar Association, American Bankruptcy Institute, European Association of Insolvency Practitioners, London Solicitors Litigation Association, The Law Society (England), City of London Solicitors' Company.
Career: 1976-80 Assistant Solicitor in *Durrant Piesse*; 1980 Partner *Lovells*; 1991-94 partner in New York office and 1992-94 managing partner of that office.

GWYNNE, Richard
Stephenson Harwood (incorporating Sinclair Roche & Temperley), London
(020) 7809 2321
richard.gwynne@shlegal.com
Specialisation: Partner, litigation department. Wide experience of all types of commercial litigation, international arbitration and ADR. Specialises in particular in banking litigation, shareholder disputes and jurisdiction issues. Major cases include: multi-party litigation against investment banks and professional advisers arising out of the acquisition of a substantial computer leasing company involving claims of over £500m; successfully defending a shareholders dispute in connection with a satellite broadcasting company; several reported cases involving letters of credit and performance guarantees.
Career: Qualified 1979. Became a partner in November 1986.
Publications: Author of the chapter on enforcement of foreign judgments in England and Wales in 'International Execution against Judgment Debtors' (Oceana 1999).
Personal: Educated at Trinity College, Cambridge.

THE LEADERS ■ LITIGATION

HAGGETT, Paul
Burges Salmon, Bristol
(0117) 939 2262
paul.haggett@burges-salmon.com
Specialisation: Head of Litigation Department. Responsibility for firm's contentious banking and insolvency litigation practice. Lead Partner of Nationwide Managed Litigation project and team leader for Burges Salmon's involvement in Paragon Managed Litigation Project.
Career: Trained at *Freshfields*. Qualified in 1985. Manager (*Freshfields* Litigation Department) 1985-89. Assistant/associate *Burges Salmon* – 1989-92. Partner *Burges Salmon* – 1992-date. Head of Commercial Litigation Department – 1997-date.
Personal: Born 1960, resides Bristol. Interests – golf, vegetable gardening, reading, family.

HAM, Neil
Burges Salmon, Bristol
(0117) 902 2747
neil.ham@burges-salmon.com
Specialisation: Commercial property disputes including rent and service charge disputes; contested rent reviews and arbitrations; disrepair claims; contested lease renewals; professional negligence claims; risk assessment for major landowners and developers; non-litigious dispute resolution.
Prof. Memberships: Law Society and Property Litigation Association.
Career: Qualified in 1987 and continued with *Simmons & Simmons*, joined *Burges Salmon* in 1991 and became a partner in 1996.

HARRIS, Andrew
DLA, Manchester
(08700) 111111

HART, Andrew R
Freshfields Bruckhaus Deringer, London
(020) 7936 4000
andrew.hart@freshfields.com
Specialisation: Partner specialising in litigation (particularly in the financial sector and fraud) and contentious regulatory matters. Head of the Contentious Banking and Financial Services Group. Publications editor of 'Freshfields on Financial Services: Investigations and Enforcement'.
Career: Articled *Freshfields*. Qualified 1988.
Personal: Born 1962. Educated at Keble College, Oxford.

HARVEY, Guy
Dickinson Dees, Newcastle upon Tyne
(0191) 279 9237
law@dickinson-dees.com
Specialisation: Head of Commercial Disputes Group. Practice covers a full range of litigation problems including fraud, disaster recovery and disputes management. Recent matters include Ladbroke Grove Rail Inquiry, substantial local government arbitration, three large professional negligence claims and major trust litigation.
Prof. Memberships: Member of ILA, trained mediator.
Career: Qualified 1976; *Simpson Curtis* (now *Pinsent Curtis Biddle*) 1974-77; Partner 1978-96; *Dickinson Dees* Partner 1997-.
Personal: Born 1951, educated at Stowe School and Trinity College, Cambridge. Interests include the arts, shooting, France. Married with two children. Lives near Darlington.

HAYWOOD, Brent
Biggart Baillie, Edinburgh
(0131) 226 5541

HEAPS, John
Eversheds, Leeds
(0113) 243 0391
johnheaps@eversheds.com
Specialisation: Partner. National head of litigation and dispute management. Main area of practice is the management and negotiation of business disputes. Particular expertise in the fields of cross border disputes, information technology, business risks and product liability.
Prof. Memberships: Senior Vice-Chairman to Committee 12 (Civil Litigation SLP) International Bar Association. Fellow of The Chartered Institute of Arbitrators.
Career: Qualified 1978 *Hepworth & Chadwick*, Leeds. *Freshfields* 1978-84. Joined *Eversheds*, Leeds 1984, partner 1985.
Personal: Born 8th July 1953. Ratcliffe College then Liverpool University 1972-75. Lives near Harrogate, North Yorkshire.

HEARN, Andrew
Dechert, London
(020) 7775 7466
andrew.hearn@eu.dechert.com
Specialisation: Litigation Partner and Solicitor-Advocate (Higher Courts Civil). Specialises in the resolution of commercial disputes and also in the areas of intellectual property and libel (in which areas his broad client base is well represented in the publishing and retail sectors). His work is both national and international in nature and extends to international arbitrations and mediations. Examples of its range recently have been a substantial commercial court trial and its connected litigation in several other jurisdictions involving claims of over $1 billion by the State of Nigeria; working with *Dechert's* New York office on successful enforcement proceedings to recover a multimillion dollar judgment from the State of Peru; acting in High Court proceedings and ICC arbitration and related foreign proceedings all concerning entitlement of various parties to the assets of a substantial Liechtenstein entity; obtaining emergency injunctive relief on behalf of a retail client claiming malicious falsehood in respect of a competitor's promotional materials; acting in the defence of an action for patent infringement and passing off on behalf of a national retail chain.
Prof. Memberships: Solicitor-Advocate (Higher Courts Civil); Fellow of the Chartered Institute of Arbitrators; CEDR Accredited Mediator and on W.I.P.O. List of Mediators; former member of the City of London Law Society's Litigation Sub-Committee.
Career: Graduated in law in 1979 from St John's College, Oxford. Was articled to *Titmuss Sainer & Webb* (now *Dechert*), qualified in 1982 and became a Partner in 1986.
Personal: Born 1957. Married with three sons. Skiing, tennis, the arts, member of Old Gowers Club and Campden Hill Tennis Club.

HENDERSON, Guy
Allen & Overy, London
(020) 7330 3000
guy.henderson@allenovery.com
Specialisation: Guy Henderson became a partner in 1990 and currently heads the London office's Commercial Litigation Group. He has a wide experience of both domestic and international commercial disputes. He led the firm's litigation and dispute resolution practice in Hong Kong from 1993-97, where he served as a member of the Compliance Committee of the Law Society of Hong Kong and the Securities and Futures Appeals Panel of Hong Kong. He is an associate of the Chartered Institute of Arbitrators and a CEDR accredited mediator.
Prof. Memberships: Member, Law Society of England and Wales; member, Law Society of Hong Kong; Securities and Futures Appeals Panel of Hong Kong 1994-97; associate, Chartered Institute of Arbitrators; appointed lay member Insider Dealing Tribunal Hong Kong 1995; appointed to committee of Hong Kong International Arbitration Centre, reporting to the Attorney General on reforming Hong Kong's arbitration law 1996; member, Compliance Committee of the Law Society of Hong Kong 1996-97; CEDR accredited mediator 1998.
Career: Qualified in 1982, partner *Allen & Overy* 1990. Head of Litigation and Dispute Resolution, *Allen & Overy*, Hong Kong 1993-97. Head of Corporate and Commercial Litigation Group, *Allen & Overy*, London since 1998.
Personal: Downing College, Cambridge University (1980, MA).

HERBERT, Alan
Pinsent Curtis Biddle, Leeds
(0113) 244 5000
alan.herbert@pinsents.com
Specialisation: All aspects of property dispute resolution and litigation including landlord and tenant, development disputes, dilapidations, portfolio management, rent reviews, rating, possession, vendor/purchaser disputes, enforcement and protection of security, enforcement of restrictive covenants. Arbitration, litigation, mediation and lands tribunal work.
Prof. Memberships: Property Litigation Association.
Career: Articled with *Ashurst Morris Crisp*. Qualified 1989. Joined *Pinsent Curtis Biddle* 1993. Partner and Head of Property Litigation Team 1996.
Personal: Walking, fly fishing.

HEWETSON, Charles
Richards Butler, London
(020) 7772 5722
cmh@richardsbutler.com
Specialisation: Commercial disputes – particularly banking, financial services and professional negligence related work.
Prof. Memberships: Law Society.
Career: *Boodle Hatfield* 1987-92; *Richards Butler* 1992 to date. Partner 1996 to date; Head of Commercial Disputes Nov 2000 to date.
Publications: Banking.
Personal: Winchester College, Durham (BA) Hons. Interests include golf and bridge. Married with two sons.

HEWSON, Carol
Simmons & Simmons, London
(020) 7628 2020
carol.hewson@simmons-simmons.com
Specialisation: Partner in litigation department. Main area of practice is commercial litigation, with particular experience in all aspects of commercial property and landlord and tenant litigation. Has extensive experience in rent review disputes, including arbitration, service charge disputes, forfeiture claims and litigation under the Landlord and Tenant Act 1954. Experienced in all aspects of property insolvency. Addressed seminars for Central Law Training on commercial property and also for Euroforum on commercial lease insolvency.
Prof. Memberships: Law Society; City of London Solicitors Company; member of Property Litigation Association; member of Women in Property Litigation.
Career: Kings College, London 1974-77; qualified in April 1980; partner in 1986.
Personal: Member of the Board of Management of Affinity Homes Group.

HIGGS, Rachel
Mills & Reeve, Norwich
01603 693 233
rachel.higgs@mills-reeve.com
Specialisation: Commercial litigator, specialising in contract disputes, warranty claims, boardroom disputes, professional negligence and infringements of intellectual property rights. Particular expertise in disputes relating to restrictive covenants and confidential information. Experienced mediator and exponent of alternative dispute resolution. Willing to take cases on a conditional fee basis.
Prof. Memberships: ADR Group (Eastern Region); Mediators in East Anglia; Norwich Businesswomen's Network.
Career: LLB Nottingham University; qualified 1984; partner 1990; LLM in Advanced Litigation, Nottingham Law School 1997; head of commercial dispute resolution team, Norwich.
Personal: Born 1960; resides Norwich. Leisure interests include family, cooking, reading, theatre and film.

HIGHMORE, Robert
Charles Russell, London
(020) 7203 5201
roberth@cr-law.co.uk
Specialisation: Litigation partner and Head of Property Litigation and Dispute

LITIGATION ■ THE LEADERS

Resolution Team. Principal area of practice covers full range of property and landlord and tenant litigation and dispute resolution including commercial and residential property and professional negligence actions. Acts for both landlords and tenants including major institutions, pension funds, banks and life assurance companies.
Prof. Memberships: Chairman 1998-99 and founder committee member of Property Litigation Association; active member of British Property Federation; Law Society; City of Westminster Law Society.
Career: Qualified 1982. Partner *Radcliffes & Co* 1987. Partner *Charles Russell* 2001.
Personal: Born 9 February 1957. Educated at Cambridge and County High School (1968-71), Beverley Grammar School, East Yorkshire (1971-75), Trinity Hall, Cambridge (1976-79). Leisure pursuits include squash and Ceroc. Lives in Bromley, Kent.

HINDLE, Andrew
Boodle Hatfield, London
(020) 7318 8131
ahindle@boodlehatfield.com
Specialisation: Main areas of practice include property and commercial litigation for both domestic and foreign clients, covering issues relating to business tenancies; residential tendencies, including the Rent Acts and the Housing Act; rent and debt recovery; breaches of covenant; forfeiture and possession; corporate, contractual and employment disputes. In addition, a broad range of general litigation, including insolvency matters and construction disputes, and significant experience in acting for clients in the agrochemical industry.
Prof. Memberships: Lord Chancellor's department: civil procedures for Housing and Land Actions Working Group; Property Litigation Association.
Career: Qualified 1979. Appointed an associate of *Boodle Hatfield* in 1996.
Publications: Articles in 'New Law Journal', 'Estates Gazette' and 'Landlord and Tenant Review'. Editorial board of 'Landlord and Tenant Review' (Sweet & Maxwell).
Personal: Born 11 July 1955. Educated at Marlborough and Trinity College, Oxford. Lives in London. Married with two children. Leisure interests include travel, food and wine, theatre and music.

HOATH, Helen
Hill Dickinson, Manchester
(0161) 817 7200
helenhoath@hilldicks.com
Specialisation: Property litigation; break clauses; dilapidations; rent reviews; contested business tenancy renewals; specific performance; restrictive covenants; easement disputes; 'rights to light' Allied London Industrial Properties Ltd v Castleguard Properties Inc 1997 EGCS 18; Jolley v Carmel Limited 2000 2EGLR 153; 2000 3 EGLR 68.
Prof. Memberships: Law Society; Association Women Solicitors; Property Litigation Association; Women in Property; MCIA.

Career: Qualified 1985. *Kramer & Co* 1983-87; *McKenna & Co* 1987-94; joined *Gorna & Co* 1995, partner 1995; *Gorna & Co* merged with *Hill Dickinson* 2002.

HODGES, Paula
Herbert Smith, London
(020) 7374 8000
paula.hodges@herbertsmith.com
Specialisation: Partner with wide range of experience in commercial litigation and international arbitration but advises for the most part on multimillion pound disputes in the energy and IT/ telecoms industries. Has been closely involved in several high profile cases before the High Court in London, and has also appeared before the Court of Appeal and House of Lords.
Prof. Memberships: Member of the United Kingdom Energy Lawyers Group; and Institute of Petroleum.
Career: Qualified 1989; Partner 1996.
Publications: Contributor to PLC 'Legal Risk Management Manual' (2000).
Personal: Read law at Cambridge University. Undertakes significant legal pro bono work in the UK and overseas.

HOGAN, Ronald
Dewar Hogan, London
(020) 7822 7400
ronhogan@dewarhogan.co.uk
Specialisation: All types of contentious property matters and related litigation in connection with commercial and residential property. Instructed in relation to property management disputes (including dilapidations, arrears, forfeiture, and rent reviews); professional negligence cases involving solicitors and valuers; enforcement of securities and other insolvency related work; leasehold enfranchisement and estate management schemes. Instructed in a number of reported cases, author of articles in the property press and speaker at conferences on property issues. Former Chairman of the Property Litigation Association.
Career: Formed the niche property litigation practice of *Dewar Hogan* in 1991. Formerly at *Nabarro Nathanson*.

HOLLAND, Jon
Lovells, London
(020) 7296 2000
jon.holland@lovells.com
Specialisation: Commercial litigation, with particular experience in the fields of banking and finance, including financial services. Speaks and writes regularly on issues in these areas. Active member of The Banking and Technique and Practice Committee of ICC UK.
Prof. Memberships: Admitted in England and Wales, Hong Kong and Australia (ACT). Law Society of England and Wales. City of London Solicitors' Company.
Career: Articled *Lovells* 1986-88. *Lovells* Hong Kong 1988-91. Partner 1998. Higher Courts (civil proceedings) Qualification 2001.
Personal: Born 1964. Bristol Cathedral School followed by Exeter University (1985 LLB). Leisure interests include sport, classical music, opera, arts and crafts, furniture and architecture.

HOPKINS, Paul
Edwards Geldard, Cardiff
(029) 2023 8239
paul.hopkins@geldards.co.uk
Specialisation: Head of commercial dispute resolution at *Edwards Geldard* and also the firm's international services partner. He specialises in large scale High Court commercial litigation and commercial dispute resolution including negotiation, arbitration and ADR. CEDR accredited mediator.
Prof. Memberships: Member of the Law Society; Associate Member of the American Bar Association; Member of the International Bar Association; Fellow and Member of Congress of the Center for International Studies, Saltzburg; Chairman of the South Wales Exporters Association; Committee Member of Wales Commercial Law Association.
Career: Educated at University College, Oxford. Trained at *Slaughter & May*. Joined *Edwards Geldard* in 1988 from *Slaughter & May's* litigation department. Made a partner in 1992.
Personal: Interests include: history, rugby and music.

HOUSE, Tim
Allen & Overy, London
(020) 7330 3000
tim.house@allenovery.com
Specialisation: Partner in the Litigation Department and Head of Banking and Finance Group in London. He specialises in commercial dispute resolution in the banking and finance sector and has wide experience of acting for financial institutions and quoted companies in complex litigation and regulatory disputes. He currently acts for leading US/European banks and other financial institutions in all areas of contentious business, risk management and reputational risk including regulatory. He also has particular experience in derivatives disputes.
Career: Admitted as a solicitor in England (1986) and in Hong Kong (1988). Assistant solicitor, *Allen & Overy*, London (1986-88); assistant solicitor, Hong Kong (1988-90); assistant solicitor, London (1990-92). Partner since 1992.
Personal: Education: University of London (1982, LLB).

HOWARD, Paul
Wragge & Co, Birmingham
0870 903 1000

HUMPHRIES, Mark
Linklaters, London
(020) 7456 4250
mark.humphries@linklaters.com
Specialisation: Commercial litigation and arbitration: experience of handling a wide range of commercial disputes but with an emphasis on industrial, employment, insurance and professional negligence cases. Advocacy: extensive experience of conducting cases in the High Court, County Courts, Court of Appeal and other courts including trial advocacy; substantial experience of advocacy before tribunals including ICC, LCIA and market arbitrations. As experienced solicitor-advocate who was one of the first solicitors to be granted a Higher Courts Qualification following the changes in rights of audience brought about by the Courts and Legal Services Act 1990. Extensive experience of civil (and some criminal) advocacy. The first solicitor to appear in the English Commercial Court in a contested action in open court and one of the first solicitor-advocates to appear in the Court of Appeal.
Career: Since 1993 Partner, *Linklaters*; 1994 to date: Solicitor-Advocate (Higher Courts, Civil); 1986-93: Assistant Solicitor, *Linklaters*; 1988: Secondment to *Morgan, Lewis & Bockius*, Washington DC; 1984-86: Articled Clerk, *Winters*, Huntingdon. 1987: MA Cantab; 1983: BA (Hons) Cantab; 1983-84: The College of Law, Guildford; 1980-83: St Catharine's College, Cambridge.

HUNTER, Jason
Russell-Cooke, London
(020) 7405 6566
hunterj@russell-cooke.co.uk
Specialisation: All aspects of both commercial and residential property disputes.
Prof. Memberships: Property Litigation Association and its Law Reform committee. Mediator (ADR Net).
Career: Qualified at *Russell-Cooke* in 1992. Partner in 1997.

HUNTER, Robert
Allen & Overy, London
(020) 7330 3000
robert.hunter@allenovery.com
Specialisation: Partner and head of the Trust, Asset Tracing and Fraud Group. Widely known as one of the leading fraud specialists in the country, has extensive experience in trust litigation, asset tracing and civil fraud cases ranging from claims involving bribery and secret commissions to commodities fraud and advance fee frauds. He has acted in proceedings in all major offshore centres. He is Secretary of the Association of Contentious Trust and Probate Specialists and writes and lectures internationally on fraud and trust litigation. He is a CEDR accredited mediator.
Career: Admitted as a solicitor 1984; assistant solicitor, *Allen & Overy* 1984-90; partner in the litigation department since 1991.
Personal: Educated at York University (BA Psychology); UCL (LLM); City of London Polytechnic (MA Business Law).

HUNTLEY, Graham
Lovells, London
(020) 7296 2000
graham.huntley@lovells.com
Specialisation: Main areas of practice include corporate and finance litigation, M&A disputes, contentious regulatory and financial services matters, regulatory and corporate investigations and professional negligence. Manager of *Lovells'* Corporate and Financial Litigation Group.
Prof. Memberships: Secretary of London Solicitors Litigation Association. Director of RCJ Advice Bureau.
Career: Solicitor since 1986.
Personal: Durham University (BA Hons).

THE LEADERS — LITIGATION

HUTCHINSON, Lucy
Herbert Smith, London
(020) 7374 8000
lucy.hutchinson@herbertsmith.com
Specialisation: Head of property litigation. Practice involves major property and landlord and tenant disputes relating in the main to commercial, retail and industrial property, in particular covering rent review work including court proceedings arising from that and advising arbitrators. Also does regulatory work including FSA and DTI investigations, disciplinary procedures as well as general commercial litigation.
Prof. Memberships: Property Litigation Club; Property Litigation Association.
Career: Qualified in 1982. Became a partner at *Herbert Smith* in 1989.
Personal: Educated at Southampton University.

ISRAEL, Jennifer
Jennifer Israel & Co, London
(020) 8445 3189

JEFFERIES, Michael
Hugh James, Cardiff
(029) 2022 4871
michael.jefferies@hughjames.com
Specialisation: Partner in construction and civil engineering department. Has specialised in construction law for over 20 years, engaged in major litigation and arbitration for all sectors of the industry, as well as advising on non-contentious matters. Particular emphasis on professional indemnity matters, acting on behalf of a variety of professionals including architects, engineers, surveyors and their insurers (including contractor's design liability insurers). Important cases handled include Mid Glamorgan C.C. v Devonald Williams; H.H.C v W.H.T.S.O and Mid Glamorgan C.C. v Land Authority for Wales. Member of Salford University Working Party on Intelligent Authoring of Building Contracts. Lead partner for the Welsh Rugby Union redevelopment of the National Stadium.
Prof. Memberships: Institute of Arbitrators.
Career: Joined *Hugh James* in 1970. Qualified and became a partner in 1972.
Personal: Born 21st November 1947. Educated at University College, London. Lives in Cardiff.

JENNINGS, Steven
DLA, Manchester
(08700) 111111

JOHNSON, Paul
Pannone & Partners, Manchester
(0161) 909 3000
Specialisation: Commercial litigation, civil regulatory work, contentious corporate recovery, professional negligence, shareholder disputes and tax disputes.
Prof. Memberships: The Law Society, CEDR accredited mediator.
Career: Qualified in 1990. Joined *Pannone & Partners* in 1992; became a partner in 1995.
Personal: Born 28 December 1963. Educated St Josephs R.C. comprehensive school, Port Talbot, Brunel University and Chester College of Law. Enjoys rugby league and union, and sport in general. Lives in Dobcross, Saddleworth, Lancashire.

JONES, Michael
Hugh James, Cardiff
(029) 2022 4871
michael.jones@hughjames.com
Specialisation: Partner in commercial litigation department. Handles a wide variety of commercial litigation work including intellectual property. Acts for numerous clients including advertising agencies, building companies and manufacturers. Also handles construction arbitration and litigation matters acting for housing associations and architects amongst others. Cases handled include R v South Glamorgan County Council ex parte Evans concerning parents' choice in education. High Court Advocate. Lecturer on civil advocacy courses at Cardiff Law Society.
Prof. Memberships: Chartered Institute of Arbitrators, past President of Cardiff Law Society, Law Society Welsh Spokesman for over 30 years.
Career: Joined *Hugh James* in 1963. Qualified in 1966 and become a partner the same year. Senior partner in 1970.
Personal: Born 14 January 1943. Educated at Neath Boys' Grammar School 1953-60 and Jesus College, Oxford 1960-63. School Governor. Past chairman and current secretary of Parents for Welsh Education. Leisure pursuits include gardening and music. Lives in Peterston-S-Ely, Cardiff.

JONES, Peter Watkin
Eversheds, Cardiff
(029) 2047 1147
peterjones@eversheds.com
Specialisation: Commercial dispute management, particularly for the public sector. Has considerable experience in major construction disputes and professional negligence in relation to earthworks design and claims for loss and expense. Also advises on matters of defamation. Is joint lead partner for the provision of legal services to the National Assembly for Wales. Peter is the national Head of the Inquiries and Investigations Unit which is now in its fourth year of working for Lord Saville's Bloody Sunday Inquiry. The Unit also worked this year for the Inquiry into the deaths and issues raised by the activities of Harold Shipman. Has practised as a mediator and is an accredited mediator with CEDR and the ADR Group.
Prof. Memberships: Fellow Chartered Institute of Arbitrators; member of the Law Society.
Career: Articled with *Phillips & Buck*, now *Eversheds*. Partner 1986.
Personal: Educated University of Wales; University of Aix-en-Provence; has a university doctorate in Comparative Law. Fluent French and Welsh speaker. Is a semi-professional musician.

JONES, Siân
Morgan Cole, Cardiff
(029) 2038 5385

KAMSTRA, Simon
Addleshaw Booth & Co, Leeds
(0113) 209 2000
simon.kamstra@addleshawbooth.com
Specialisation: Partner in Commercial Litigation. Specialising in company and shareholder disputes; sports law; mergers and acquisition related claims; trusts and trustee law; misfeasance and directors duties issues; professional negligence; engineering; arbitration and mediation.
Prof. Memberships: IBA. Leeds Law Society.
Career: Educated at University of Manchester (LLB). Partner 1996.
Personal: Interests include music, cricket and photography.

KELLY, Jonathan
Simmons & Simmons, London
(020) 7628 2020
jonathan.kelly@simmons-simmons.com
Specialisation: Partner in Financial Markets Department and Head of the Finance Litigation Group. Main areas of practice are banking and financial services litigation, specialising in asset management, securities, commodities and derivatives disputes, and regulatory issues arising in these areas. Experienced in corporate disputes and large scale commercial fraud actions. Clients include UK, US and European commercial and investment banks, investment institutions, brokers and commodity houses.
Prof. Memberships: Law Society, Society of English and American Lawyers.
Career: Qualified in 1989 after articled at *Simmons & Simmons*. Became a partner in 1995.
Personal: Born 11 August 1964. Educated at Stonyhurst College 1972-82, Balliol College, Oxford 1983-86.

KENT, Paul
Pinsent Curtis Biddle, Birmingham
(0121) 200 1050
paul.kent@pinsents.com
Specialisation: Partner in property litigation. All aspects of property dispute resolution for major corporate and Government Departments including the tactical value of disputes in corporate transactions in development work and site acquisition. Rent review, Lands Tribunal work, dilapidations claims, rates disputes and all contentious landlord and tenant matters. Recovery of environmentally sensitive areas from activists and trespassers. Reported cases: Banks v Kokkinos
Prof. Memberships: Property Litigation Association.
Career: 15 years in wholesale food distribution prior to qualification as solicitor. Several years of commercial litigation and for nine years specialising in property litigation. Joined *Pinsent Curtis Biddle* 1993. Partner 1998.
Personal: Sailing, large-scale landscape gardening, English furniture and ceramics.

KERSHAW, Anne
Kershaw Abbott, Manchester
(0161) 839 0998
mail@kershaw-abbott.co.uk
Specialisation: Practises in the field of commercial dispute resolution with particular emphasis on professional partnership disputes, professional liability and commercial and construction disputes.
Prof. Memberships: Member of Association of Partnership Practitioners; Deputy Vice-Chairman Pro Manchester; Past President Manchester Law Society; Member of Society of Construction Lawyers; CEDR Accredited Mediator.
Career: Admitted 1975. Practised in North West all working life. Co-founder of *Kershaw Abbott* as niche practice in 1991. Appointed Tax Commissioner in 1995.
Personal: Lives in Ribble Valley with judicial husband and son. Music lover and devoted gardener.

KHAN, Charles
Berg & Co, Manchester
(0161) 833 9211
charlesk@berg.co.uk
Specialisation: Charles Khan is a partner in the commercial litigation department. He specialises in commercial litigation, including contract disputes (special expertise in disputes in the textile and clothing sector), concerning quality, title, non-payment; professional negligence; landlord and tenant; advising office holders, companies and individuals on insolvency related matters.
Prof. Memberships: Law Society; Manchester Law Society.
Career: Qualified in 1980. Joined *Berg & Co* in 1982 and became partner in 1984. Appointed Deputy District Judge in the Northern Circuit in 1994.
Personal: Born 21 June 1956. Educated Stand Grammar School and Hull University. Enjoys cycling, football, cricket, cinema. Lives in Prestwich, Greater Manchester.

KING, Ronnie
Ashurst Morris Crisp, London
(020) 7638 1111
ronnie.king@ashursts.com
Specialisation: Commercial litigation and arbitration, both domestic and international with particular experience in oil and gas, power, engineering and projects. Also acts on general contract claims including warranty claims and disputed completion accounts.
Career: Articled *Ashurst Morris Crisp* 1984-86. Assistant solicitor 1986-94. Partner 1994.
Personal: Educated at the Belfast Royal Academy and St Catharine's College, Cambridge (Simmons scholar); MA, LLM.

KING, Vivien
D J Freeman, London
(020) 7583 4055

LITIGATION ■ THE LEADERS

KISSACK, Nigel
Pinsent Curtis Biddle, Leeds
(0113) 294 5226
nigel.kissack@pinsents.com
Specialisation: National Head of Dispute Resolution and Litigation and Managing Partner in Leeds. Commercial litigation: recent cases include product liability/contract claim against a supplier for £6m; defending a major electric company in product liability and contract claim against it for £6m; trade libel/malicious falsehood/ASA claim for a corporate client in relation to a competitor's sales campaign; advising majority shareholder in £50m business on acquisition of the minority stake.
Career: Partner *Alsop Wilkinson* 1980-96. Partner *Dibb Lupton Alsop* 1996-97. Partner and National Head of Dispute Resolution and Litigation *Pinsent Curtis Biddle* 1997-date.
Personal: King William's College, Isle of Man. Sheffield University LLB (Hons). Married with two children. Reading, travel, arts and motorcycling.

LAX, Peter
Bell Lax Litigation, Birmingham
(0121) 355 0011
PeterLax@belllax.com
Specialisation: Partner in specialist commercial and accident litigation firm. Main area of practice is commercial litigation. Handles construction and engineering litigation, professional negligence and employment matters. Pioneer of no-win no-fee agreements for commercial litigation and professional negligence claims. Reported cases include North West Holdings (advertising public interest petitions) and Fishel and University of Nottingham (employee's entitlement to undertake paid outside work). Has addressed Society of Practitioners in insolvency, Midlands Association of Insolvency Lawyers, Midlands Guild of Newspaper Editors.
Career: Qualified in 1982. Worked with *Duggan Lea & Co* 1980-85, then *Pinsent & Co* 1985-93, from 1988 as a Partner. Joint founder with Heather Bell of specialist litigation practice *Bell Lax Litigation*.
Personal: Born 27 March 1958. Attended Barnard Castle School 1969-75, then Durham University 1976-79. Leisure interests include drinking real ale (occasionally) and sipping wine (repeatedly!). Lives in Lichfield.

LEONARD, Paul
Freshfields Bruckhaus Deringer, London
(020) 7936 4000
paul.leonard@freshfields.com
Specialisation: Partner in litigation department. Main areas of practice are international litigation, arbitration and mediation. Cases include Ocean Island case (Tito v Waddell), Westinghouse Uranium Contract litigation and the Alexander Howden insurance fraud cases. Acting in numerous ICC arbitrations. Also involved in insurance insolvency litigation, acting in the KWELM and Electric Mutual (EMLICO) cases. A CEDR accredited mediator.
Prof. Memberships: Law Society.
Career: Articled at *Freshfields*. Qualified in 1966. Partner in 1972. Head of litigation department 1988-91.
Personal: Born 14th January 1942. Educated at Finchley Grammar School and Sheffield University (LL.B). Leisure interests include cricket, contemporary art and an old Aston Martin.

LEVINSON, Jan
Hammond Suddards Edge, Manchester
(0161) 830 5000

LEWIS, Harold
Eversheds, London
(020) 7919 4707
haroldlewis@eversheds.com
Specialisation: As a pensions lawyer he specialises in dealing with disputes as well as giving advice to trustees and acting for companies on the pensions aspects of mergers and acquisitions. He has dealt with many complaints to the Pensions Ombudsman and under the internal dispute resolution procedures established in accordance with the Pensions Act 1995. Recent high profile cases include two House of Lords appeals: National Grid, about employer's use of pension fund surplus, and Preston v Wolverhampton NHS, the part-timer/sex discrimination test case referred to the European Court of Justice on time limits. Further test issues in the part-time cases (which number about 60,000 in total) remain to be decided.
Prof. Memberships: Association of Pension Lawyers (member of International Committee), CEDR mediator).
Career: Having received a BA in Politics from Sydney University in 1972 he moved to England where he obtained a BA in Law with 1st Class Honours from Sussex University. Admitted as a Solicitor in 1980 and became Partner with *Eversheds* in 1985.
Personal: Born 1952. Married with three daughters. Interests include golf and music.

LEYDECKER, Sonya
Herbert Smith, London
(020) 7374 8000
sonya.leydecker@herbertsmith.com
Specialisation: Partner in one of the general commercial litigation groups which has a strong bias towards banking and professional negligence work, particularly in relation to accountants. Acts for banks in commercial disputes and has been involved in numerous asset recovery claims. Also has wide experience of freezing injunctions and search and seize orders.
Prof. Memberships: Committee of the London Solicitors Litigation Association.
Career: Qualified *Herbert Smith* 1984; Partnership 1991.

LLOYD HOLT, Suzanne
Wragge & Co, Birmingham
0870 903 1000

LOMAS, Paul
Freshfields Bruckhaus Deringer, London
(020) 7936 4000
paul.lomas@freshfields.com
Specialisation: Particular interests: EC and anti-trust; ECHR; financial services and banking; regulatory or economics dominated cases; art law; crises.
Prof. Memberships: Law Society, Solicitors' European Group, INSEAD Alumni Association.
Career: Sciences and Law, Emmanuel College, Cambridge; *Freshfields* Litigation Department; MBA INSEAD; *Freshfields* Brussels office in 1989; partner 1990; Litigation Department, London from 1993.
Personal: Interests: anything that you can do on a mountain, on a beach or in France, music, food and wine, family (one wife and two daughters); not necessarily mutually exclusive or in that order.

LOWETH, Craig
Wragge & Co, Birmingham
0870 903 1000

LOWSON, Greg
Pinsent Curtis Biddle, Birmingham
(0121) 200 1050
greg.lowson@pinsents.com
Specialisation: Joint Managing Partner in Birmingham and Birmingham Head of Dispute Resolution and Litigation. Specialises in commercial litigation; arbitration and construction including four recent and significant power generation arbitrations, one of which was successfully determined in the Court of Appeal and which set the first law on the M/F1 form of engineering contract. Currently engaged on a $188 million breach of contract claim. Also regularly obtains Mareva injunction relief without using counsel for a number of financial institutions on a national basis. Trained mediator.
Prof. Memberships: Law Society; Insolvency Lawyers Association.
Career: Qualified 1984. Joined *Pinsent & Co* as partner in 1981 from *Ashurst Morris Crisp*.
Personal: Tennis; golf.

LYNCH, Michael
Elliott Duffy Garrett, Belfast
(028) 9024 5034
michael.lynch@edglegal.com
Specialisation: Head of Litigation Department. Main areas of practice are commercial litigation, judicial reviews, professional negligence and general property disputes. Solicitor to the Assembly Ombudsman for Northern Ireland and the Social Fund Commissioner.
Prof. Memberships: Law Society for Northern Ireland, Belfast Solicitors Association.
Career: Qualified in 1972. Became a partner upon the foundation of *Elliott Duffy Garrett* in 1973.
Personal: St Malachy's College Belfast and Queen's University Belfast.

MACKIE QC, David L
Allen & Overy, London
(020) 7330 3000

MACLEOD, Colin
Dundas & Wilson CS, Edinburgh
(0131) 228 8000

MADDEN, Michael
Ashurst Morris Crisp, London
(020) 7859 1539
michael.madden@ashursts.com
Specialisation: Partner in charge of the property litigation group at *Ashurst Morris Crisp*. He specialises in development agreement disputes, property financing actions, landlord and tenant disputes and other general property disputes. Acts for both landlords and tenants in contested rent review arbitrations and expert determinations. Also advises on both liquor and gaming licensing matters.
Prof. Memberships: Accredited mediator with CEDR; FCIArb; Past Chairman of Property Litigation Association; Law Reform Committee.
Career: Qualified as a solicitor in 1987. Joined *Ashursts* in 1993. Partner in litigation since 1995.
Publications: Contributor to 'Commercial Property Disputes: All England Legal Opinion'.

MAGNIN, John
Nicholson Graham & Jones, London
(020) 7360 8168
john.magnin@ngj.co.uk
Specialisation: Involved in all aspects of commercial litigation, UK and international, including shareholder disputes; contractual, warranty and agency claims; fraud; defamation; confidential information; boardroom disputes and departures; restrictive covenants; proceedings under the Companies, Insolvency, Financial Services and Company Directors Disqualification Acts; financial services, regulatory and disciplinary proceedings. Recent work includes metals and currency trading litigation; limited partnership disputes; contingency insurance claims; acting for financial services, media and sports companies.
Career: Joined *Nicholson Graham & Jones* in 1985, qualified in 1987, became Partner in 1992. Head of Litigation, 2001. Solicitor Advocate.
Personal: Attended UCL 1981-84. Interests include family, golf, cricket, football, running and the trumpet.

MALONEY, Tim
Eversheds, London
(020) 7919 4721
timmaloney@eversheds.com
Specialisation: International litigation, arbitration and alternative dispute resolution. Highlights include: acting for Sir Elton John and his companies in their professional negligence action against PricewaterhouseCoopers; acting for Jardine Lloyd Thompson in film finance litigation against Law Debenture Trust Corporation and Lexington Insurance Company.
Prof. Memberships: The Law Society. Associate member: The Law Society of Singapore.
Career: 1973-75 *Lawford & Co*; 1975-96 *Jaques & Lewis*; 1996-date *Eversheds*.
Personal: Exeter University. Soccer (Chelsea FC); cricket (associate member of MCC); golf. Married; two children.

MANLEY, Mark
Brabners Chaffe Street, Liverpool
(0151) 600 3000
mark.manley@brabnerscs.com
See under Defamation, p.272

MANNING COX, Andrew
Wragge & Co, Birmingham
0870 903 1000

THE LEADERS ■ LITIGATION

MARTIN, Bonnie
Masons, Bristol
(0117) 924 5678
bonnie.martin@masons.com
Specialisation: Specialises in property litigation. Acts for a number of companies relating to a range of property disputes arising from their retail and leisure outlets. Advises on numerous landlord and tenant problems arising out of all aspects of commercial leases including dilapidations, forfeiture and the Landlord & Tenant Act 1954. Acts for a number of landlords of industrial estates advising on all aspects of management. Has acted for parties to a number of significant Lands tribunal appeals, a high profile arbitration concerning the financial effects of boundary changes and arbitrations relating to land values. Has a particular interest in rent review and arbitration law as it relates to property. Is an appointed arbitrator under the Professional Arbitration on Court Terms (PACT) scheme, a member of ARBRIX, an appointed member of the RICS Presidents Initiative relating to the training of independent experts and a qualified mediator.
Prof. Memberships: ARBRIX; BURA; UKELA (UK Environmental Law Association); BPAA (Bristol Property Agents Association); BPF; British Council of Offices; TCPA; Law Society; Property Litigation Association.
Career: Admitted 1985 – partner *Masons* London before moving to set up property litigation department in Bristol in 1990.
Personal: Lives in Somerset with partner and two small boys.

MASTERS, David
Dawsons, London
(020) 7421 4869
d.masters@dawson-legal.com
Specialisation: All aspects of property litigation including landlord and tenant advice, commercial property disputes, enforcement of restrictive covenants, rent reviews, forfeiture claims, dilapidations and disrepairs claims, applications under the Landlord & Tenant Act 1954, the Housing Act 1988, Leasehold Reform Act 1967 and Leasehold Reform, Housing and Urban Development Act 1993. Acts for large and small property companies, housing associations, landed estates and private individuals.
Prof. Memberships: Property Litigation Association, The Institute of Continuing Professional Development, Law Society.
Career: Qualified 1981. *Speechly Bircham* 1988-98 (Partner from 1990) *Dawsons* since 1999 (Partner).
Personal: Born 7 November 1956. Educated at Felsted School and Reading University. Married. Lives in Coggeshall, Essex. Interests include skiing, hiking, tennis, member of the Royal Horticultural Society, Director of Ski Club of Great Britain.

MATTHEWS, Paul
Eversheds, Norwich
(01603) 272 727
paulmatthews@eversheds.com
Specialisation: Partner in commercial litigation department. Principal area of practice is contract-based commercial dispute management including sale of goods and services in various commercial and industrial sectors (chemicals, manufacturing, agriculture, motor retail and public sector). Also handles insolvency matters. Acts for insolvency practitioners in pursuing and defending a wide variety of claims arising during mainly corporate insolvencies. Has been involved in a wide variety of high value corporate disputes, including shareholders disputes and warranty claims. Has also acted in disputes arising in the course of and following completion of PFI projects in the public sector. Insolvency work has included ROT cases, challenging IVA's, director disqualification, wrongful trading and preferences. Has handled disputes in Italy, France, Belgium, the Netherlands and Scandinavian countries and has dealt with numerous disputes involving issues of European law. Experienced in various forms of alternative dispute resolution.
Career: Qualified in 1982. Became a partner at *Eversheds Daynes Hill & Perks* in 1985. Has obtained CEDR Mediator accreditation. Member of CEDR Solve.
Personal: Born 25 September 1953. Educated at Culford School 1966-71, Hatfield Polytechnic 1971-75 (BA Hons in Business Studies) and the College of Law. Leisure activities include golf, shooting, wine and food. Lives in Weybread, Suffolk.

MATTISON, Mark
Eversheds, Manchester
(0161) 831 8000
markmattison@eversheds.com
Specialisation: Partner in commercial litigation department. Main area of practice is construction and engineering litigation.
Prof. Memberships: Law Society. Past President of Manchester Law Society. Member, Chartered Institute of Arbitrators, Chairman of North West Branch, Member Society of Construction Law. CEDR - SOLVE. Registered and practising mediator.
Career: Articled at *Alexander Tatham* (now *Eversheds*) 1972-74 and became a Partner in 1978.
Personal: Born 26 April 1951. Attended Liverpool College and studied Law in Liverpool. Leisure pursuits include cycling, swimming and overseas travel. Lives in Hale, Cheshire.

MAY, Philip
TLT Solicitors, Bristol
(0117) 917 7912
pmay@tltsolicitors.com
Specialisation: Principal area of practice is business breakdown and insolvency. Extensive experience of general commercial disputes, including search and seize orders, freezing orders, cross-border litigation, arbitration and mediation. Acts as arbitrator in commercial disputes. Charge-out rate is £220 per hour. See also Insolvency/Corporate Recovery and Partnership.
Prof. Memberships: Law Society; Bristol Law Society; Insolvency lawyers Association; Association of Business Recovery Professionals; Chartered Institute of Arbitrators; Bristol Chancery Court Users committee.
Career: Educated Southend-on-Sea, Essex and Lincoln College, Oxford. Articled *Osborne Clarke*, Bristol 1982-84. Assistant solicitor to partner *Osborne Clarke*, Bristol 1984-95. Joined *Trumps* as partner 1995. *Trumps* merged with Bristol law firm *Lawrence Tucketts* to become *TLT Solicitors* on 1 May 2000.
Personal: Born 16 March 1959. Married with two children. Lives near Bristol. Leisure pursuits include golf, snooker and skiing.

MCLACHLAN, Campbell
Herbert Smith, London
(020) 7374 8000
campbell.mclachlan@herbertsmith.com
Specialisation: Well known specialist in the field of international commercial litigation and arbitration. Is particularly respected for his work on matters involving private and public international law, representing multinational corporations and sovereign states.
Prof. Memberships: Vice-Chairman of the IBA Committee on International Litigation.
Career: Qualified New Zealand 1984 and England and Wales 1991. Partner at *Herbert Smith* since 1992. Solicitor-Advocate (Higher Courts, Civil) 2001.
Publications: His book, 'Transnational Tort Litigation', is published by OUP.
Personal: Educated at Victoria University of Wellington, New Zealand, the University of London (PhD) and Hague Academy of International Law (Diploma cum laude).

MEGGITT, Edward
Edwards Geldard, Cardiff
(029) 2023 8239
ed.meggitt@geldards.co.uk
Specialisation: All aspects of property dispute resolution and litigation. This includes advising on numerous landlord and tenant issues arising from commercial leases such as forfeiture; break notices; distraint; breaches of covenant (particularly dilapidations); security of tenure and advice and Court proceeding relating to the Landlord and Tenant Act 1954. Other areas include conveyancing problems such as misrepresentation; specific performance; professional negligence and rectification. Also, involved in issues arising from developments including nuisance/negligence; easement disputes and trespass/adverse possession claims.
Prof. Memberships: Law Society; Property Litigation Association; Member of Regional Committee of the Property Litigation Association (South West and Wales).
Career: Articled *Edwards Geldard*, qualified in 1993 and became a partner in 2002.
Personal: Interests include cricket (captain Cardiff Cricket Club 1999 & 2000); golf (Llanishen Golf Club); rugby and travel. Educated at St Illtyd's College, Cardiff and the University of the West of England. Married to Karen with a young daughter, Ella.

METCALFE, Stephen
Beachcroft Wansbroughs, Bristol
(0117) 918 2000
smetcalfe@bwlaw.co.uk
Specialisation: Commercial litigation, particularly involving IT and financial institutions.
Prof. Memberships: Law Society.
Career: *Durrant Piesse* 1981-85. *Beachcroft Wansbroughs* 1985-date. Partner 1988.
Personal: BA (Hons) New College, Oxford. Married with four children. Interests: Music, theatre, literature, walking.

METLISS, Michael
SJ Berwin, London
(020) 7533 2222
michael.metliss@sjberwin.com
Specialisation: Michael regularly advises property companies, institutional owners and retailers on a wide range of property issues; from redevelopment to rent review, from disclaimer to distraint, from rights of way to dilapidations, from professional negligence to nuisance, from service charges to forfeiture, from tenant insolvency to trespass and from rectification to misrepresentation. He has written articles for the Property Press, has lectured to the Property Managers' Association, at the Royal Institute of Chartered Surveyors, for IBC UK Conferences and extensively at SJ Berwin's inhouse property seminars. He also acts as an advocate in mediation.
Prof. Memberships: Professional memberships: Property Litigation Association
Career: Articled *Bartletts De Reya*, qualified 1984. Partner *SJ Berwin* 1991.
Publications: Articles in 'Estate Gazette', 'Property Week': has lectured to IBC UK Conferences, Property Managers Association, RICS.
Personal: Football, golf, music, Middle East, film.

MICKLETHWAITE, Neil
DLA, London
(08700) 111111
neil.micklethwaite@dla.com
Specialisation: Auditors negligence, civil fraud, Companies Acts, corporate defence, crisis management, defamation, disciplinary tribunals, DTI investigations, financial services and market abuse, insider dealing, shareholder disputes.
Prof. Memberships: ABA, IBA.
Career: To date *DLA*, Head of Business Solutions Division and Board Member 1994-2000 *DLA*, Head of Commercial Litigation 1993-94 *DLA*, Head of Banking Litigation 1992-93 *DLA*, Partner and Head of Commercial Investigations Unit 1986-92 *Gouldens* 1984-86 Chambers of Colin Ross Munro, 2 Hare Court.
Publications: Various articles and lectures on financial services matters
Personal: University: Warwick University, LLB (Hons) Law 1983. Called to the Bar July 1984.

LITIGATION ■ THE LEADERS

MOLYNEUX, Anne
Masons, London
(020) 7490 4000
anne.molyneux@masons.com
Specialisation: Partner and head of property litigation group. Handles all areas of High Court litigation. Cases have included Passmore v Morland (House of Lords interpretation of EC Treaty). Courage v Crehan (reference to Luxembourg – right to damages/illegality), Langton v Inntrepreneur (House of Lords – set-off), Little v Courage (covering status of option). Has addressed conferences on the licensed trade, dilapidations, insolvency, litigation and rent review.
Prof. Memberships: Law Society.
Career: Qualified in 1983. Associate at *Lawrence Messer & Co*, before joining *Masons* in 1987. Became a partner in 1989. Appointed Recorder in 2000.
Personal: Born 12 January 1959. Member of Ealing and Fulham Book Club. Lives in Ealing. Has two children.

MONTY, Craig
Lovells, London
(020) 7296 2000
craig.monty@lovells.com
Specialisation: Partner in the commercial litigation sector with particular emphasis on professional indemnity work, trust and pensions disputes (important cases include: British Coal Corporation v British Coal Staff Superannuation Scheme Trustees Limited (1995) 1 All ER 912; National Power plc v Hugh Feldon & Others (1999:CA) and product liability work.
Prof. Memberships: Member London Solicitors Litigation Association; associate member of Association of Pension Lawyers.
Career: Articled *Lovells*; qualified 1988; partner 1998.
Personal: Education: Our Lady and St. Bede's Roman Catholic Comprehensive School, St. Mary's Sixth Form College, University of Newcastle upon Tyne (LLB 1st Class Hons); College of Law, Chester (Law Society Finals). Personal: Born 1964; resides Harpenden. Leisure: All sports, particularly football (Middlesbrough FC) and horse racing.

MORGAN, Neil Christopher
Hugh James, Cardiff
(029) 2039 10221
neil.morgan@hughjames.com
Specialisation: Partner. Head of the firm's Property Litigation Department. He is based in Cardiff. Extensive experience in all aspects of property litigation, commercial and residential. Highly regarded in the area of landlord and tenant. Clients include government agencies, local authorities, insurance companies, housing associations, surveyors, property developers, property management companies, estate agents and letting agents, commercial landlords and tenants, residential landlords and residents associations. Cases include: successfully defended a £1m dilapidations claim against a government agency; instructed by local authorities and their insurers in defending disrepair claims; several substantial boundary dispute cases, successfully represented RSL's in possession actions and injunctions for anti-social behaviour, advised Welsh Federation of Housing Association and its members on the issue of rent increase notices under s13 Housing Act 1988, advised RSL's and residential homes on the Care Standards Act 2002, drafting of tenancy agreements on behalf of RSL's.
Prof. Memberships: Member of the Property Litigation Association. Committee Member for South Wales and South West.
Career: Graduate of Aberystwyth University and Chester College of Law. Qualified in 1991. Joined the firm in 1991. Partner in 1997. Welsh speaker. Lives in Cardiff and is married with one child.

MORRIS, Antony
Clarks, Reading
(0118) 960 4646
antonymorris@clarks-solicitors.co.uk
Specialisation: Partner and Head of the Commercial Litigation Team at *Clarks*; specialises in the resolution of corporate and commercial disputes. His extensive experience includes advice on major contract disputes; warranty claims and shareholder disputes; IT and telecoms contracts; property, landlord and tenant and property-related negligence claims, as well as specific expertise in commercial injunction work, including search and freezing orders. Antony also has considerable experience in alternative dispute resolution techniques and has successfully concluded many mediations on behalf of clients.
Prof. Memberships: Past Chairman of Berkshire and Oxfordshire Young Solicitors Group.
Career: Qualified 1988. Partner 1993.

MORRIS, Peter
Burges Salmon, Bristol
(0117) 902 7721
peter.morris@burges-salmon.com
Specialisation: Partner in Burges Salmon's Commercial Litigation Department. Particularly undertakes commercial contract disputes; commercial property disputes; professional negligence (mainly for claimants, especially against solicitors and surveyors); and risk management. Clients include Bristol and West, Co-op group and Rhodia.
Prof. Memberships: Law Society, Property Litigation Association.
Career: Trained with *Kenwright & Cox* (Chancery Lane, London) and qualified in 1982. Became a Partner at *Kenwrights & Cox* (Chancery Lane, London) in 1985: Partner at *Holt Phillips* (Bristol) in 1986; Partner at *Eversheds* (Bristol) in 1994 and a Partner at *Burges Salmon* (Bristol) in 2001.
Personal: Peter likes hill walking, fine food, wine and beer.

MORSHEAD, Ros
Berwin Leighton Paisner, London
(020) 7760 1000
ros.morshead@blplaw.com
Specialisation: Partner in litigation and dispute resolution. Main area of practice is property litigation including landlord and tenant, planning-related litigation, disputes as to all aspects of real property and professional negligence. Represents retailers, institutions, developers and local government.
Prof. Memberships: The Law Society; Property Litigation Association; member of the Education and Training Sub-committee.
Career: Articled with *Clifford Chance*, September 1990-September 1992. Joined *Berwin Leighton* in 1997 and became partner *Berwin Leighton Paisner* in 2001.
Publications: Regular contributor of articles to property press and presenter at conferences and client seminars.
Personal: Lives in North London. Interests include cinema, theatre, music and socialising.

MUMFORD, Nicola
Wragge & Co, Birmingham
0870 903 1000

MURFITT, Stephen
Blake Lapthorn, Fareham
(01489) 579990

MYERS, Sidney A
Allen & Overy, London
(020) 7330 3000
sidney.myers@allenovery.com
Specialisation: Partner and head of Regulatory Investigations Group; advises both institutional and individual clients, principally in the banking and financial services sectors, on a variety of regulatory investigations and disciplinary and enforcement proceedings. In addition, he has extensive experience of litigating and negotiating a broad range of commercial disputes, including judicial review proceedings involving decisions both of financial regulatory bodies and UK tax authorities.
Career: Admitted as a solicitor in England (1984) and Hong Kong (1995). Assistant solicitor, *Allen & Overy* 1984-90; partner, *Allen & Overy*, London since 1991; partner, *Allen & Overy* Hong Kong (1994-96). CEDR accredited mediator.
Personal: Education: Worcester College, Oxford (1980 BA Hons PPE).

NICHOLSON, Brinsley
Linklaters, London
(020) 7456 4364
brinsley.nicholson@linklaters.com
Specialisation: Commercial litigation: practised in proceedings before the High Court of Justice and in the Commercial Court; experience in obtaining urgent injunctions (particularly to freeze assets), dealing with jurisdictional issues, questions of conflict of laws and handling substantial disputes. Experience in domestic and international arbitration, insolvency disputes arising out of the crashes of 1974, 1981, 1987 (Hong Kong) and 1990; acting for liquidators, administrative receivers and administrators; all forms of disputes in the securities field including Stock Exchange work, defaults and recoveries; representing clients and witnesses before regulators; inspectors appointed under the Companies Act and the Financial Services Act and insider dealing investigations; banking, documentary credits, international finance, including bond issues, syndicated loans and swaps, domestic banking problems including conflict problems, negligence, recoveries and realisations, borrower reschedulings and defaults, state immunity and the effect of blocking or expropriatory legislation; white collar crime.
Career: 1992-99: Head of Litigation Department, *Linklaters*; 1986-89: Partner, *Linklaters* Hong Kong; 1977 to date: Partner, *Linklaters*, 1972-77; Solicitor, *Linklaters*; 1965-71: Articled Clerk, *Peacock & Goddard*. Educated at Winchester College.

NOTT, Christopher
Palser Grossman, Cardiff Bay
(029) 2045 2770

NURSE-MARSH, Isabel
Pinsent Curtis Biddle, London
(020) 7606 9301
isabel.nurse-marsh@pinsents.com
Specialisation: Head of pensions litigation group and full-time specialist in pensions litigation. Experience includes winding up disputes, claims over surplus, breach of trust, asset tracing and rectification actions, construction of scheme documentation issues, applications to the High Court and Pensions Ombudsman claims. Particular interest in professional negligence claims – bringing and defending claims against pensions professionals. Registered mediator and active promoter of use of mediation in pension disputes. High profile cases include acting for the National Power trustees in the House of Lords surplus case.
Prof. Memberships: Association of Pension Lawyers; member of Association of Pension Lawyers' Pension Litigation Sub-Committee; member of Centre for Effective Dispute Resolution's Faculty: Member of Association of Contentious Trust and Probate Specialists.
Career: 1989-92 *Slaughter and May*; 1992-2001 *Biddle*; 2001 *Pinsent Curtis Biddle*.
Publications: Writes and lectures frequently on pensions litigation and mediation.
Personal: Lincoln College, Oxford. Dual nationality – English and French.

O'BRIEN, Gary
Eversheds, Birmingham
(0121) 232 1362
garyobrien@eversheds.com
Specialisation: Head of property litigation team in Birmingham and National Chairman of property litigation product group in *Eversheds* which handles all types of landlord and tenant disputes. Gary has particular specialisation in freehold property developments involving difficult restrictive covenants or major boundary and easement disputes as well as enforcement of sale and purchase contracts and clearance of sites for redevelopment schemes.
Career: Qualified in 1985. Joined *Simpson Curtis* in 1987. Partner at *Simpson Curtis* 1990 and at *Eversheds* from 1996.
Personal: Born 1959. Attended KEGS Aston and St. John's College, Oxford. Interests include opera and Aston Villa Football Club.

THE LEADERS — LITIGATION

O'CONOR, John
Allen & Overy, London
(020) 7330 3000
john.o'conor@allenovery.com
Specialisation: Partner specialising in banking, financial disputes and financial regulatory proceedings, as well as advising on banks generally on litigation risk issues. In particular, he has acted in many reported cases in London dealing with the derivatives markets which have, on a number of occasions, involved jurisdictional disputes with important anti-suit and inconvenient forum contests. In addition, he has substantial experience of arbitration proceedings held both in London and overseas in the financial, insurance and other sectors before the ICC, LCIA and other arbitral bodies in Sweden, Japan, Switzerland and the United States. He has considerable knowledge of banking and international capital markets and specialist knowledge of derivatives and other financial instruments.
Career: Qualified in 1990; Assistant Solicitor *Allen & Overy* 1990-97; Partner since 1997.
Personal: Radley College; Gonville and Caius College, Cambridge University (1986 BA, 1989 MA); Law Society Finals (1988).

O'DRISCOLL, Pat
Cleaver Fulton Rankin, Belfast
(028) 9027 1311
p.o'driscoll@cfrlaw.co.uk
Specialisation: Commercial litigation, serious fraud, multi-document litigation, intellectual property, product liability, judicial review and admiralty.
Prof. Memberships: The Law Society of Northern Ireland.
Career: Educated at Glenstall Abbey School, Republic of Ireland and Queen's University of Belfast (BSc Econ). Qualified 1972. Became a Partner in *Cleaver Fulton Rankin* 1975.

O'FARRELL, Vincent
Pannone & Partners, Manchester
(0161) 909 3000
vincent.o'farrell@pannone.co.uk
Specialisation: Partner and Head of Department in Commercial Litigation. He specialises in land disputes, contentious probate and trust issues, civil fraud, judicial review, defamation, contract and pre-emptive remedies. He is also a notary public.
Prof. Memberships: Member of ACTAPS (Association of Contentious Trust and Probate Specialists).
Career: Vincent was admitted in 1971, when he joined *Howards*, a predecessor to *Pannone & Partners*.
Personal: Leisure interests include theatre, sport and music. Lives in Bury.

OLDFIELD, Alison
Eversheds, Leeds
(0113) 200 4660
alisonoldfield@eversheds.com
Specialisation: Specialises in all areas of property litigation, acting for institutional landlords and retail occupiers on property disputes arising from their leasehold interests as well as advising developers on land assembly issues. Particular niche areas include applications to the Lands Tribunal and Judicial review proceedings. Clients include Asda, Hammerson UK Properties plc, Next plc and British Waterways.
Prof. Memberships: Property Litigation Association (Past Chairman Northern Regional Group); Women in Property.
Career: Articled with *Macfarlanes*; joined *Eversheds*, London on qualification in 1994; transferred to *Eversheds*, Leeds February 1995.
Personal: Educated Harrogate Grammar School; Durham University.

OLIVER, Keith
Peters & Peters, London
(020) 7629 7991
Specialisation: Partner specialising in commercial, regulatory and insolvency litigation who heads the firm's specialist civil fraud team. Has extensive experience in asset tracing, including the use of emergency relief procedures, and is often involved in multijurisdictional actions. Lectures widely on issues such as insider trading, money laundering, abuse of process and jurisdictional issues. Represents both individuals and major corporate clients in Companies Act and Financial Services and Markets Act investigations and prosecutions.
Prof. Memberships: Association Internationale de Jeunes Avocats (AIJA), President AIJA Business Crime Sub-Commission, International Bar Association, Law Society, British Italian Law Association.
Career: Qualified in 1980, having joined *Peters & Peters* in 1978. Became a Partner in 1983.
Personal: Lives in London.

O'LOUGHLIN, Philip
Addleshaw Booth & Co, Leeds
(0113) 209 2000
philip.oloughlin@addleshawbooth.com
Specialisation: Head of Property Litigation Department, Commercial Property Group. Practice covers all landlord and tenant and property litigation, in particular rent reviews, dilapidations, property related professional negligence. Work also includes Landlord and Tenant 1954 applications, forfeiture, tenant default.
Career: Qualified 1986; joined the firm 1991, becoming a Partner in May 1995.
Personal: Attended Cambridge University 1979-82. Leisure interests include fellwalking, landscape photography, archaeology.

ORTON, Giles
Eversheds, London
(020) 7919 4739
gilesorton@eversheds.com
Specialisation: Head of pensions. Main area of practice is pensions litigation, conducting disputes over pension schemes, particularly regarding surplus and winding up. Leading cases include Falconer v Aslef and NUR, Imperial Tobacco, Mirror Group, Lloyd's Bank Pension Scheme. Author of numerous articles on pensions law and Pensions Ombudsman procedure.
Prof. Memberships: Member of Main Committee of Association of Pension Lawyers. Chairman of Pensions Litigation Committee of Association of Pension Lawyers.
Career: Qualified in 1983. Joined *Eversheds* 1987, associate 1988, partner 1989. Head of litigation, East Midlands 1994-2001.
Personal: Born 18 August 1959. Attended King Edward VII School, Sheffield 1970-77; The Queen's College, Oxford (Hastings Exhibition) 1977-80 and Chester College of Law 1980-81. Derby City Councillor 1988-92.

PARISH, Philip
Linklaters, London
(020) 7456 4282
philip.parish@linklaters.com
Specialisation: Expertise in all aspects of financial markets litigation, including: contentious regulatory matters, including enforcement and disciplinary matters; representing financial institutions and witnesses in investigations conducted by regulatory authorities, inspectors or by other disciplinary bodies; litigation and regulatory issues arising in respect of investments and securities and dealing activities of financial institutions; disputes, investigations and regulatory matters in relation to derivatives and other complex investment banking activity; cross-border financial litigation including conflicts of laws issues, anti-suit injunctions, overseas enforcement litigation, co-ordination of foreign legal teams; expertise in the procedural and tactical issues in respect of preparations for trial and conduct at trail. Rights of audience in all civil courts.
Career: 2001 Associate Partner, *Linklaters*, 1999-2000 Consultant, *Linklaters* London (Financial Markets Litigation); 1996 Admitted as a Solicitor-Advocate; 1991-99 Assistant Solicitor, *Linklaters* London (Litigation); 1991 requalified as a Solicitor of the Supreme Court; 1989-90 Assistant Solicitor, *Linklaters* London (Corporate); 1988-89 pupillage at Erskine Chambers and 13 Old Square.

PARKER, Raj
Freshfields Bruckhaus Deringer, London
(020) 7936 4000
raj.parker@freshfields.com
Specialisation: Partner in litigation department, Solicitor Advocate. Main area of practice is insurance and reinsurance work. Regular speaker at insurance industry seminars. Substantial general commercial dispute resolution practice. Also deals with sports law, acting for the Football Association in advisory and contentious work.
Prof. Memberships: Society of Solicitor Advocates. Nominated Court of Arbitration for Sport ('CAS') Arbitrator. Member of British Insurance Law Association, British Association for Sport and the Law. CEDR accredited mediator.
Career: Joined *Freshfields* in 1986 and became a partner in 1993. Appointed recorder in 2002.
Personal: Born 1960. Educated Southampton University. Recreations include sport, music, theatre and ornithology.

PEARSON, Nick
Baker & McKenzie, London
(020) 7919 1000
nick.pearson@bakernet.com
Specialisation: Head of the Commercial Dispute Resolution Group with emphasis on multijurisdictional disputes; commercial fraud and insolvency; Head of Business Recovery Practice Group and licensed insolvency practitioner; managing the multijurisdictional Kuwait Investment Office driven Grupo Torras litigation in London, Jersey, the Bahamas, Switzerland and elsewhere ($800 million international fraud), 1993 and continuing.
Prof. Memberships: Society of Practitioners of Insolvency; Insolvency Lawyers Association; Insol Europe.
Career: Qualified 1976; *Herbert Smith* 1974-79; *Baker & McKenzie* Hong Kong 1979-88; Partner 1982; Partner *Baker & McKenzie* London 1988-present.
Publications: 'International Tracing of Assets' – Sweet & Maxwell.
Personal: Education: King Edward School, Birmingham; Lincoln College, Oxford (1970 BA Jurisprudence). Born 1951; resides London; married with two children.

PEET, Carole
Denton Wilde Sapte, Milton Keynes
(01908) 690260

PERROTT, Edward
Taylor Vinters, Cambridge
(01223) 225 140
edward.perrott@taylorvinters.com
Specialisation: Partner and Head of Commercial Litigation Team. Specialises in leading edge technology, biotech and high quality manufacturing clients. Litigation and regulatory issues, including Competition Act/Office of Fair Trading matters, contractual disputes, IP claims and professional negligence.
Prof. Memberships: Law Society.
Career: Jesus College, Cambridge 1965-68. Retail business owner in Beirut 1968-73. Trained and practised in London with *Crossman Block and Keith* 1974-1980. Joined *Taylor Vinters* in 1981. Registered mediator.
Personal: Interests include skiing, sailing and cricket.

PICKSTON, John
Clifford Chance, London
(020) 7600 1000
john.pickston@cliffordchance.com
Specialisation: Litigation and Dispute Resolution Department. Partner dealing with all types of litigation and advice relating to contentious property matters including contractual disputes, development issues, rent review, professional negligence.
Career: Qualified 1986; Partner since 1996.

PIZZEY, Simon
Veale Wasbrough, Bristol
(0117) 925 2020
spizzey@vwl.co.uk
Specialisation: Managing Partner. Commercial litigation in the fields of banking, commercial fraud, business breakdown (corporate and partnership) and professional negligence. Clients include

LITIGATION ■ THE LEADERS

building societies, banks, local authorities, central government agencies, professional partnerships and corporates.
Prof. Memberships: Bristol Law Society Panel of supervising solicitors for the enforcement of search and seize orders.
Career: Qualified 1982. Joined *Veale Wasbrough* in 1987. Partner in 1989. Head of *Veale Wasbrough*'s Litigation Department. Managing Partner since 1998.
Personal: Born 1957. Birmingham University.

PLANT, Charles
Herbert Smith, London
(020) 7374 8000
charles.plant@herbertsmith.com
Specialisation: Partner dealing with all aspects of commercial disputes and specialising in international arbitrations in the construction, oil and gas and media industries.
Prof. Memberships: Law Society, International Bar Association (Secretary of the International Litigation Committee).
Career: Qualified in 1969 while at *Herbert Smith*. Became a partner in 1976. Head of litigation department 1988-95. Member Legal Services Consultative Panel (appointed December 1999.) Governor of College of Law. CEDR Addredited mediator.
Publications: Editor: Blackstone's 'Civil Practice 2001'; 'Civil Procedural Rules' (Blackstone 2000).
Personal: Born 1944. Attended Cambridge University 1963-66.

POLLACK, Craig
SJ Berwin, London
(020) 7533 2222
craig.pollack@sjberwin.com
Specialisation: Complex commercial litigation often with multijurisdictional aspects; cross-border fraud and asset tracing and shareholder disputes. Also acts as a mediation advocate. Clients include major public companies, banks and venture capital houses as well as governments.
Prof. Memberships: Law Society. Israel Bar Association.
Career: Joined *SJ Berwin* in 1991. Partner commercial litigation 1997.
Personal: BA (Cape Town); LLB (Jerusalem); LLM (London). Qualified as an advocate in Israel 1989.

POLLARD, Stephen
Kingsley Napley, London
(020) 7814 1200
spollard@kingsleynapley.co.uk
See under Fraud, p.398

POTTS, John
Clifford Chance, London
(020) 7600 1000
john.potts@cliffordchance.com
Specialisation: Litigation and Dispute Resolution Department. Managing Partner of litigation specialising in commercial litigation, regulatory disputes and tribunals, statutory enquiries, white-collar crime, fraud and asset recovery, financial services, investigations and tribunals
Career: Articled *Clifford-Turner*; qualified 1982; Partner since 1987.
Personal: Worksop and Exeter Schools; 1968 Manchester University (BSc Hons 2.1).

PUDDICOMBE, Nigel
Veale Wasbrough, Bristol
(0117) 925 2020
npuddicombe@vwl.co.uk
Specialisation: All aspects of property litigation principally acting for lenders and landlords. Clients include breweries and pub companies, life companies, distribution companies, property companies, and local authorities.
Prof. Memberships: President, Bristol Law Society 2000. Chairman, Bristol Law Society. Civil Courts committee 1993-98.
Career: Qualified 1979. Partner with *Cartwrights* from 1987. Joined *Veale Wasbrough* as Partner 2001.
Personal: Born 1954. Southampton University.

RANDS, Harvey
Memery Crystal, London
(020) 7242 5905
dhrands@memerycrystal.com
Specialisation: Head of litigation; leads groups specialising in commercial, commodities, insurance and shipping litigation; company and regulatory enquiries and white-collar crime; intellectual property; directors' and officers' liability.
Prof. Memberships: Chartered Institute of Arbitrators
Career: Articled *Charles Mazillius & Co*; qualified 1976; Solicitor *Rubinstein Callingham* 1977; Solicitor *Stilgoes* 1977; Partner *Stilgoes* 1978; Partner *Memery Crystal* since 1980.
Personal: Pilgrim School, Bedford; The City University (1972 BSc Philosophy and Physics); College of Law (1976 Solicitors finals). Born 1951; resides in London. Leisure interests include family and country pursuits.

RANSON, Lee
Eversheds, Manchester
(0161) 831 8000
leeranson@eversheds.com
Specialisation: Property litigation – acting for commercial and institutional landlord clients in Retail, Local Authority and Banking sectors. Specific niche areas include resolution of property disputes in the education and leisure industries. Has a particular interest in property related professional indemnity claims.
Prof. Memberships: Law Society. CEDR qualified mediator. Member of Property Litigation Association.
Career: Qualified 1990. *Jaques & Lewis* (merged *Eversheds* 1994). Transferred to *Eversheds* Manchester, Jan 1997. Partner May 1999.
Personal: Born 16.12.64. Educated Wilmslow Grammar School & Hull University. Married, two children. Interests include golf, football, cricket. Lives in Bramhall.

RAPHAEL, Monty
Peters & Peters, London
(020) 7629 7991
montyr@petersandpeters.co.uk
See under Fraud, p.398

RAWLINSON, David
Cuff Roberts, Liverpool
(0151) 237 7777
david.rawlinson@cuffroberts.co.uk
Specialisation: Commercial contract, construction (and related professional negligence), arbitration, adjudication, alternative dispute resolution, defamation, and non-contentious construction contracts, appointments, warranties.
Prof. Memberships: Law Society; Liverpool Law Society; Member of Chartered Institute of Arbitrators; member of Society of Construction Law; Chairman Society for Computers and Law Liverpool Group.
Career: Qualified 1976. Assistant Solicitor, then Partner (1978) *Banks Kendal Taylor & Gorst*, merged with *Cuff Roberts* 1987. Chairman of firm's Executive Board 1999 to date. Past member of Young Solicitors' Group National committee. Past Chairman YSG Liverpool Group.
Personal: Nottingham University (1970-73). Married, two children. Lives West Kirby, Wirral. Interests include golf, cycling, walking, local and family history. Supporter Tranmere Rovers FC.

REYNOLDS, John
McDermott, Will & Emery, London
(020) 7577 6994
jreynolds@europe.mwe.com
Specialisation: International commercial litigation and arbitration.
Prof. Memberships: Law Society. International Bar Association.
Career: 1985-87: *Lickfolds Wiley & Powles*, London (Articles); 1987-99: *Herbert Smith*, London (New York 1989-90; Partner 1994); 1999 to date: *McDermott, Will & Emery*, London (Partner)
Personal: Born 1963. Educated at Clifton College, Reading University and UCL. Married with two children. Lives in Highgate. Leisure: rugby, Formula One motor racing, cooking, music (loud/quiet/dance). Member of the Groucho Club.

RHYS-JONES, Mark
Eversheds, Cardiff
(029) 2047 1147
markrhysjones@eversheds.com
Specialisation: Partner in the Dispute Resolution and Commercial Litigation Department at *Eversheds* Cardiff office. Specialises in conducting litigation in all areas of IT, intellectual property, product liability and general contractual disputes of a substantial value; accredited mediator with the Centre for Dispute Resolution (CEDR) and the ADR Group; Chair of the *Eversheds* Technology Litigation Group.
Prof. Memberships: Wales Commercial Law Association; Society for Computers and Law; British Computer Society; Advisory Board of Centre for Professional Legal Studies, Cardiff Law School.
Career: Educated at Merton College, Oxford (1987 BA Hons Jurisprudence). Articled with *Eversheds*, qualified 1990; became a Partner in 1995.
Personal: Born 1966 and resides in Cardiff.

RICKARD, Jennifer
Nabarro Nathanson, London
(020) 7524 6000
j.rickard@nabarro.com
Specialisation: Partner property litigation department. All aspects of property litigation. Acted in Mannai Investment Company Ltd v Eagle Star Assurance Ltd, Checkpoint v Strathclyde Pension Fund, Lewisham Investment Partnership v Morgan, Straudley Investment v Mount Eden Land, Grundy v Summit Group Holdings and Pontsarn v Kansallis Osake Panke. Speaker at Blundell Memorial Lectures, Henry Stewart conferences, RICS, ISVA, IBC conferences, Euroforum, and Contract Property Training, Central Law Training. Speaker on Owlion cassettes on Dilapidations 1996, Lease Renewals 1998, Rent Reviews 1998 and Property law updates 1997-2002.
Career: Qualified 1983. Partner 1989.
Publications: Joint author of 'The Rooftop Rents' report on mobile phone base stations, which won the UK Design and Marketing award 2000 in the research category.

ROBINSON, Clare
Osborne Clarke, Bristol
(0117) 917 3000

ROBINSON, Michael
Boyes Turner, Reading
(0118) 959 7711
mrobinson@boyesturner.com
Specialisation: Partner in dispute resolution group, specialising in commercial litigation. Particular expertise in professional negligence claims for claimants (including the recovery of £2m in a claim against a firm of solicitors) and intellectual property disputes.
Prof. Memberships: Property Litigation Association; Environmental Law Foundation; Institute of Credit Management; OSS Negligence Referral Panel.
Career: With *Boyes Turner* since 1978. Qualified 1980; Partner 1985.
Personal: Stowe School, Magdalene College, Cambridge. Married with three children. Interests include golf, carp angling, gardening and Reading FC.

ROESSLER, Max
Eversheds, Norwich
(01603) 272727
maxroessler@eversheds.com
Specialisation: Professional Negligence, Product Liability.
Prof. Memberships: Law Society.
Career: Admitted 1981. Partner 1986.

ROGERS, Jane
Osborne Clarke, Bristol
(0117) 917 3000

ROPER, Robert
Cobbetts, Manchester
(0161) 833 5214
robert.roper@cobbetts.co.uk
Specialisation: Principal area of practice is intellectual property. Work includes litigation on all types of trademark, pass-

THE LEADERS — LITIGATION

ing off, copyright and design right matters as well as mechanical and electrical patent proceedings. Also handles commercial litigation and dispute resolutions including large commercial contract disputes with overseas elements and/or competition law issues. Has considerable experience in injunction work including Anton Piller Orders both in intellectual property matters and commercial litigation. Important cases handled include McMillan Graham & Others v R R UK Ltd (contempt of court for breach of interlocutory undertakings in passing off/copyright case); DTI v D C Wilson and others (acted for the major intermediaries sued by the DTI in the Barlow Clowes collapse); Watson & Watson v Duton Forshaw and Others (commercial court London – restrictive trade practice and conspiracy to injure by unlawful means); MIG v CSH (2001, commercial court London – commercial agent regulations).
Prof. Memberships: Law Society, Manchester Law Society, Licensing Executive Society.
Career: Qualified in 1979 while at *Cobbett Leak Almond*. Became a partner in 1983.
Personal: Born 11 August 1953. Educated at Altrincham Grammar School 1964-71 and the University of Wales Institute of Science and Technology 1973-76 (LLB Hons). Married with two children. Narrowboating, golf, training.

ROSE, Digby H
Hammond Suddards Edge, Birmingham
(0121) 222 3000

ROTHWELL, Charles
Keeble Hawson, Leeds
(0113) 244 3121
charlesrothwell@keeblehawson.co.uk
Specialisation: Partner specialising in commercial litigation matters, particularly of a heavyweight nature. Main areas of practice are building and engineering disputes, partnership disputes and professional negligence. The practice covers commercial disputes, construction and property litigation, and expertise in mediation and arbitration.
Career: Articled at, and assistant with *Biddle and Co*. Qualified in 1993. Assistant at *Dibb Lupton Broomhead* 1995 to 1997. Partner at *Keeble Hawson* 1998.
Personal: Born 1968. Resides at Holmfirth. Educated at Queen Elizabeth Grammar School, Wakefield and the University of Liverpool. Interests; horse riding, gardening and walking.

ROWE, Claire
Shoosmiths, Reading
(0118) 965 8959
claire.rowe@shoosmiths.co.uk
Specialisation: Head of dispute resolution unit. Insurance lawyer advising major insurers, loss adjusters, loss assessors and self-insured companies. Experience in prosecuting and defending claims for business interruption and consequential loss. Also handles a range of commercial litigation relating to general commercial contract disputes, IT contracts, various internet related disputes, product liability cases and warranty and company acquisition related disputes. Recently has advised on dispute resolution tactics and risk management procedures to a number of companies in the technology, media and telecommunications sector, including the tactics to be adopted to achieve the successful resolution of a £5 million claim against a software developer in relation to the development of an interactive web site.
Prof. Memberships: Member of the Law Society
Career: Joined *Shoosmiths* in 1984 as a trainee. Qualified in 1986. Associate in 1987. Salaried Partner in 1990 and Equity Partner in 1999.

RYAN, Geraldine
Hill Dickinson, Manchester
(0151) 236 5400
gryan@hilldicks.com
Specialisation: Commercial litigation and insolvency. Main areas of practice on the commercial litigation side are contractual disputes, shareholder disputes, fiduciary duty claims. Clients include the full range of corporate entities plcs, SME's and OMB's.
Prof. Memberships: Manchester and Liverpool Law Societies Factors and Discounters Association.
Career: 1990-97 *Davies Wallis Foyster*, Manchester; 1997-date *Hill Dickinson*.
Personal: Born 31 December 1965. Education: St Anselm's, Oldham, University of Sheffield. Interests include gym, literature, good company, food and wine. Lives in Liverpool.

SANDELSON, Jeremy
Clifford Chance, London
(020) 7600 1000
jeremy.sandelson@cliffordchance.com
Specialisation: Litigation and dispute resolution. Partner specialising in commercial litigation, including securities disputes, mergers and acquisitions litigation and regulatory investigations.
Career: Qualified 1981; Partner since 1988.
Personal: Charterhouse School, Cambridge University.

SCOTT, Gordon
Hammond Suddards Edge, Birmingham
(0121) 222 3000

SEAGER, Nicola
Masons, Bristol
0117 970 5206
nicola.seager@masons.com
Specialisation: Partner in the property litigation group. Acts for pension funds, property developers, property managers and construction companies, a leading supplier of gas and electricity services, retailers, and local authorities on all aspects of commercial landlord and tenant and general property disputes. Particular specialisms include contested lease renewal proceedings under the Landlord and Tenant Act 1954, dilapidation and service charge disputes; portfolio management; disputes arising on land development including rights of light and way party walls; advising landlords and insolvency practitioners on their rights and remedies on tenant insolvency; possession proceedings; promoting and contesting compulsory purchase orders and compensation claims arising on compulsory acquisition.
Prof. Memberships: Property Litigation Association (current Chair of the South West and South Wales group).
Career: Qualified 1991. Joined *Masons* in 1996 and became partner in 2001.
Personal: Lives in Somerset.

SHERRINGTON, Patrick
Lovells, London
(020) 7296 2000
patrick.sherrington@lovells.com
See under Product Liability, p.673

SINCLAIR, Jonathan
Eversheds, Leeds
(0113) 200 4686
jonathansinclair@eversheds.co.uk
Specialisation: Head of Litigation and Dispute Management Department for Leeds and Manchester and of the core Commercial Dispute Management Group in those offices. Specialises in the management and resolution of major business disputes for corporate clients. He has extensive experience in a range of substantial corporate and commercial dispute including warranty claims, auditors' negligence claims, product liability and IT disputes. He has developed a particular expertise in contentious competition work including anti-trust litigation and OFT and EU Commission Dawn Raids. He acted for Asda on its challenges to resale price maintenance on OTC pharmaceuticals and on the widely published Parma Ham case in the European Court of Justice (February 2002).
Prof. Memberships: Law Society.
Career: Qualified in 1987. *Clifford Chance*, London 1985-89. Joined *Eversheds*, Leeds 1989. Partner 1992.
Personal: Born 1961. Oxford University (1st) 1979-82. Lives in Ilkley. Leisure: mainly keeping up with son and two daughters at football, tennis etc.

SINGLETON, Bernard
Lee Crowder, Birmingham
(0121) 236 4477
Specialisation: Civil litigation.
Career: Partner 1976.
Personal: Tennis.

SKREIN, Michael
Richards Butler, London
(020) 772 5720
spms@richardsbutler.com
Specialisation: Partner specialising in litigation; Head of Media and Technology Team in the Commercial Disputes Group. His Team's work won 'The Lawyer 2001 Litigation Team of the Year Award'. Specialises in administrative law (notably in the aviation field) and competition law, insurance, intellectual property, media and sports law. Clients include Direct Line, EUROCONTROL, MTV and Nike, among others, some of which he has represented for 25 years. He is familiar with international law, judicial review and multijurisdictional disputes.
Prof. Memberships: Fellow of the Society for Advanced Legal Studies; Law Society; The City of London Solicitors' Company; The Baltic Exchange; British Literary and Artistic Copyright Association; Royal Television Society.
Career: Articled *Richards, Butler & Co* 1971; qualified 1973; partner since 1976; head of litigation department 1990-96; lectured on advertising law, copyright infringement, intellectual property and defamation implications of the internet, libel and trade marks; chair of the market leading 'Protecting the Media' series of conferences; chair of the committee drafting the Civil Procedures Rules Pre-action Protocol on Intellectual property; partner in charge of *Richards Butler's* pro bono programme.
Personal: Born 1947. Educated at Oxford University (MA, Modern History) and the University of Southern California (AM *magna cum laude* International Relations). Honor Society of *Phi Kappa Phi*.

SLEIGH, Russell
Lovells, London
(020) 7296 2000
russell.sleigh@lovells.com
Specialisation: International commercial litigation, in particular corporate, banking and regulatory disputes and multijurisdictional fraud issues. Acted on numerous official investigations on behalf of the authorities and of other parties involved. Also experienced in media law issues.
Career: Qualified 1973. Partner 1980. New York office 1977-80. Paris office 1990-93. Managing Partner, Litigation and Dispute Resolution Practice, 1997-2001. Currently Managing Partner, US Practice.

SLOWE, Richard
SJ Berwin, London
(020) 7533 2345
richard.slowe@sjberwin.com
Specialisation: Partner in Litigation Department and Head of Advocacy Group. Main area of practice is commercial litigation. 15 years commercial and common law experience at the Bar as Head of Chambers at 4 King's Bench Walk, Temple. Acted for the working miners throughout the 1984 strike. Successfully defended Michael Fagan after he had visited the Queen's bedroom and acted for numerous pop groups and 'Private Eye'. His speciality was, and remains, the Freezing Order. At *SJ Berwin*, has handled various actions arising out of the Lloyd's debâcle, including the leading case of Clementson, alleging infringement by Lloyd's of European Community Competition Law, for which he was shortlisted as Advocate of the Year by 'Legal Business'. Represented British Land in litigation relating to the acquisition of Broadgate, Astra in its claim arising out of the Iraqi supergun affair and APAX in the Oasis litigation. Recent matters include defending Viktor Kozeny in a $200 million claim concerning Azerbajani privatisation vouchers and Northern & Shell in a tax claim arising out of its acquisition of Express Newspapers.
Prof. Memberships: Secretary of West London Law Society 1972-75. Vice-chairman of Solicitors Association of Higher Court Advocates 1995-97.
Career: Qualified in 1970. Called to the bar in 1975. Joined *SJ Berwin & Co* in 1990 as a Partner. First solicitor advocate

LITIGATION ■ THE LEADERS

to exercise rights of audience in the High Court.
Personal: Leisure interests include tennis, cricket, skiing and family. Lives in London.

SMALL, Graham
Rowe Cohen, Manchester
(0161) 830 4600
Specialisation: Extensive experience in commercial litigation and dispute resolution handling very significant and high profile claims with an increasingly international emphasis. Often seen as a 'must have' lawyer by clients and is highly regarded for both his blend of technical acumen and his commercial approach to problem solving. Acts for both domestic and international clients and is presently involved in cases in Taiwan, Vietnam, Dubai, North America, Zimbabwe and across Europe. Acted for the defendant in a claim for wrongful arrest brought by Mohammed Al Fayed and others which has twice been to the Court of Appeal on interim matters.
Prof. Memberships: Law Society; British Association for Sport and Law.
Career: Joined the firm in 1998. Since his arrival at *Rowe Cohen* he has played a major part in raising the firm's profile. Head of Commercial Litigation Department.

SMITH, Hugh
Andrew M. Jackson, Hull
(01482) 325242
hes@amj.co.uk
Specialisation: Substantial area of practice involves retail law covering trading standards, health and safety, consumer protection and consumer safety. Particular expertise in the vitamin and fish industry. Commercial litigation work includes contractual disputes both international and domestic, company and partnership disputes, commercial property disputes, professional negligence, defamation and passing off. Represents finance houses in respect of consumer complaints/recoveries.
Prof. Memberships: Member of the Law Society and the Food Law Group. Also an ADR Mediator.
Career: Admitted 1983. Joined present firm in 1989, becoming a Partner in 1991 in charge of the commercial litigation division.
Personal: Born 16 January 1959. Attended Nottingham University (LLB Hons).

SOLOMAN, Martin
Hay & Kilner, Newcastle upon Tyne
(0191) 232 8345

SORRELL, Kit
Wacks Caller, Manchester
(0161) 957 8888
Ksorrell@wackscaller.com
Specialisation: Partner and Head of the Commercial Litigation and Insolvency Team. Specialises in high value commercial litigation, professional negligence, property litigation and shareholder disputes.
Prof. Memberships: Manchester Law Society, Liverpool Law Society.
Career: BSC (Econ) London, MA (Sheffield). Assistant Solicitor, *Bremner Sons & Corlett*, Liverpool 1979-82. Assistant Solicitor, *Bermans*, Liverpool 1982-83. Partner and Head of the Commercial Litigation Department, *Davies Wallis Foyster*, Liverpool, 1983-2000. Since 2000 with *Wacks Caller*.
Personal: Educated at Liverpool Collegiate; North Staffs Polytechnic 1969-72; Sheffield University 1973-74; Liverpool Polytechnic 1974-75. Born 25 October 1949. Lives in Caldy.

SPARROW, Edward
Ashurst Morris Crisp, London
(020) 7859 1573
edward.sparrow@ashursts.com
Specialisation: General commercial litigation and dispute resolution (corporate acquisition and disposal and financial disputes; City regulation; mergers and acquisitions; Stock Exchange transactions and management and trading of securities/other financial instruments); professional negligence, insolvency and insurance; corporate fraud claims.
Prof. Memberships: Law Society.
Career: Ampleforth College; Lincoln College, Oxford. Articled *Ashurst Morris Crisp*; qualified 1977; partner 1981; head of litigation department 1993.
Personal: Born 1953; resides London.

SPOONER, Andrew
Martineau Johnson, Birmingham
(0121) 200 3300
andrew.spooner@martjohn.com
Specialisation: Partner and head of litigation department. Main area of practice is commercial litigation including major claims for breach of contract and tort. In particular, handles claims arising from product liability and defective goods and machinery. Has acted in a variety of large claims involving landfill sites and the engineering industry, including robots, cranes, mining equipment, furnaces, diesel trains, power stations, industrial conveyors, plastic extrusions, boilers, radiators computers and hi-tech devices. Addressed seminars on Trading Conditions, the Woolf Reforms and resolving disputes by mediation.
Prof. Memberships: Chartered Institute of Arbitrators, Centre for Dispute Resolution, Association of Midlands Mediators.
Career: Qualified in 1978. Head of litigation in 1989. Fellow of the Chartered Institute of Arbitrators. Accredited Mediator (CEDR). Solicitor member of the Solicitors Disciplinary tribunal.
Personal: Holds an LLB. Leisure interests include golf, cricket, walking the dogs and the Arts.

SPRING, Paul
Mills Selig, Belfast
(028) 9024 3878
paul.spring@nilaw.com
See under Defamation, p.274

STAPLE, George
Clifford Chance, London
(020) 7600 1000
george.staple@cliffordchance.com
Specialisation: Partner in London office specialising in all forms of commercial litigation and arbitration in the UK and abroad but especially fraud and regulatory investigations.
Career: Qualified as a solicitor in 1963; Queens Counsel, Honoris Causa, 1997. Joined *Clifford Turner* in 1964; made partner in 1967; Member Commercial Court Committee 1977-92; appointed by the Secretary of State for Trade and Industry as a Companies Act Inspector 1986 and 1988; partner *Clifford Chance* 1987; a Chairman of the Authorisation and Disciplinary Tribunal of The Securities Association and Securities and Futures Authority 1987-91; Treasurer of the Law Society 1989-92; Director of the Serious Fraud Office 1992-97; partner *Clifford Chance* 1997; Chairman Fraud Advisory Panel. Member, Senior Salaries Review Body 2000. Hon Bencher, Inner Temple 2000.

STONE, Paul
DLA, Leeds
(08700) 111111

STONE, Peter
Cobbetts, Manchester
(0161) 833 5246
peter.stone@cobbetts.co.uk
Specialisation: Over 25 years experience in litigation for national and regional blue chip clients. Particular expertise in commercial property litigation (forfeiture, dilapidations, covenants, contested lease renewals, brewery/licensed retailer work) and in defamation (plaintiff and defendant) for individual and media clients.
Prof. Memberships: Law Society. Notaries Society.
Career: Articled at *Cobbetts*, 1974. Qualified 1976, partner 1979.
Personal: Born 1951. Educated at Rossall School and Liverpool University (LLB Hons 1st class). Leisure interests include fell walking, climbing and mountain biking.

STYLE, Christopher
Linklaters, London
(020) 7456 4286
christopher.style@linklaters.com
Specialisation: Specialises in commercial litigation and arbitration. Has practised in proceedings before the High Court of Justice and Commercial Court, and has advised on questions of international public law before international tribunals. Has conducted numerous arbitrations, both ad hoc and institutional (ICC, LMAA, LCIA etc). Also advised on multijurisdictional disputes, financial services disputes, professional negligence, corporate litigation, oil and gas disputes and shipping disputes.
Career: Partner and Head of Litigation and Arbitration, 1985 to date. 1979-85: Assistant Solicitor, *Linklaters* London; 1983: six months with the Litigation Department of *Sullivan & Cromwell* New York; 1977-79: Articled Clerk, *Linklaters*. 1978: MA Law; 1976-77: City of London Polytechnic, Law Society Part II; 1973-76: Trinity Hall, Cambridge, BA Law (Cantab).

SWANSON, Alayne
Maclay Murray & Spens, Glasgow
(0141) 248 5011
aes@maclaymurrayspens.co.uk
Specialisation: Head of Commercial Litigation and Advocacy; solicitor advocate with 18 years of commercial litigation experience who appears regularly in the Court of Sessions; specialist areas include contractual disputes, judicial review, commercial actions. Major repented cases include minority shareholder petitions, commercial agents, misrepresentation and leading case on application law.
Career: Attended University of Edinburgh (LLB Hons, Dip LP). Articled at *Shepherd & Wedderburn* 1982-84; assistant solicitor Glasgow 1984-85; foreign associate at *Hughes Hubbard & Reed*, New York 1986-87; assistant solicitor *Bird Semple Fyfe* Ireland 1987-90; partner 1990-93; partner *Dundas & Wilson* 1994-97; solicitor advocate 1996.
Personal: Born 1959. Resides Glasgow. Leisure interests include music, playing cello and piano, walking.

TAYLOR, Ian
Freshfields Bruckhaus Deringer, London
(020) 7936 4000
ian.taylor@freshfields.com
Specialisation: Partner in Litigation Department. Main area of practice is commercial litigation, particularly in relation to banking and financial services, fraud and asset recovery. Also represents financial institutions in regulatory, DTI and SFO inquiries.
Prof. Memberships: Law Society; Member of Commercial Court Committee.
Career: Qualified in 1976, having joined *Freshfields* in 1974. Became a Partner in 1982.
Personal: Born 1951. Attended Gonville & Caius College, Cambridge 1969-73. Lives in London.

TAYLOR, Tim
SJ Berwin, London
(020) 7533 2222
tim.taylor@sjberwin.com
Specialisation: Commercial litigation and arbitration. Co-author of Sweet and Maxwell's 'European Litigation Handbook'. Major cases in the last 12 months include acting in Federal Republic of Nigeria v General Abacha (deceased), Brunei Investment v Agency Prince Jefri Bolkiah, Bergen Industries v Dalmore Products, World Wildlife Fund v World Wrestling Federation.
Prof. Memberships: International Bar Association; American Bar Association.
Career: MA Oxon.

THOMAS, Martin
Herbert Smith, London
(020) 7374 8000
Specialisation: Partner and solicitor advocate with extensive experience of all aspects of property litigation including: all aspects of landlord and tenant (1954 Act claims, dilapidation, forfeiture, possession actions, rent reviews etc); Land Tribunal compensation claims; contractual, nuisance and negligence actions; and insolvency and corporate recovery matters relating to real property.
Prof. Memberships: Property Litigation Association; Solicitors Pro Bono Group; Solicitors' Association of Higher Court Advocates.
Career: Joined *Herbert Smith* 1987, qualified 1989, partner 1997.

Publications: Contributes to 'Estates Gazette' and 'Property Law Journal'. Also speaks at public lectures and seminars on property litigation topics.
Personal: Worcester College Oxford.

THOMSON, Clive
Paris Smith & Randall, Southampton
(023) 8048 2482

TOUT, Liz
Denton Wilde Sapte, London
(020) 7242 1212

TRAVERS, Iain
Nabarro Nathanson, London
020 7524 6283
i.travers@nabarro.com
Specialisation: Head of Property Litigation. Property litigation and arbitration generally.
Prof. Memberships: Chairman of Property Litigation Association. Member of London Court of International Arbitration. Member of ARBRIX. Accredited mediator. Appointed by President of Law Society and RICS as Arbitrator on property disputes.
Career: Qualified 1977. Partner 1980. Fellow of Chartered Institute of Arbitrators.
Publications: Joint author of 'Distress for Rent' (Jordans).

TROTTER, John
Lovells, London
(020) 7296 2000
john.trotter@lovells.com
See under Professional Negligence, p.683

TUGWELL, Andrew
Osborne Clarke, London
(020) 7809 1000

TURNBULL, John
Linklaters, London
(020) 7456 4310
john.turnbull@linklaters.com
Specialisation: Specialising in corporate finance litigation, all contentious aspects of mergers and acquisitions work and professional negligence.
Career: Since 1989: Partner, *Linklaters*, Litigation Department; 1988-89: Assistant Solicitor, *Linklaters* London; 1985-87: Assistant Solicitor: *Linklaters* Hong Kong; 1983-85: Assistant Solicitor, *Linklaters* London; 1980-82: Articled Clerk, *Philip Ross & Co.* 1979: Leicester University, LLB.

TURTLE, Brian
Carson McDowell, Belfast
(028) 9024 4951
Specialisation: Commercial litigation (30 years of practice in all major areas) to include contractual and tortious disputes. Intellectual property. Professional negligence. Employment law/industrial relations to include unfair dismissal, race, religious and sex discrimination claims.
Prof. Memberships: Law Society of Northern Ireland.
Career: 1968: LLB – QUB; joined *Carson & McDowell* 1968. Admitted as solicitor 1971. Partner in *Carson & McDowell*.

TYLER, Alfred
Balfour & Manson, Edinburgh
(0131) 200 1210
fred.tyler@balfour-manson.co.uk
See under Personal Injury, p.637

VASWANI, Mona
Allen & Overy, London
(020) 7330 3000
mona.vaswani@allenovery.com
Specialisation: Partner dealing with a variety of banking and finance disputes, with a special emphasis on fraud and asset tracing as well as trust litigation. In the latter context, she has substantial experience in advising banks and trustees, in particular offshore trustees in the co-ordination of trust litigation in several jurisdictions. Has acted in a variety of claims in the High Court involving allegations of fraud, constructive trust and breach of fiduciary duty; also has experience of conducting internal inquiries and investigations for a number of corporate and banking clients.
Career: Qualified 1993; Partner *Allen & Overy* 2001.
Personal: University of East Anglia (LLB).

VAUGHAN, Philip
Simmons & Simmons, London
(020) 7628 2020
Specialisation: Partner and Head of Commercial Litigation Department. Experienced in all forms of dispute resolution: High Court litigation, arbitration, expert determination and mediation. Frequently instructed by clients in the pharmaceuticals, energy and telecommunication sectors. Also acts for regulators or regulated industries, advising on commercial judicial review proceedings. Solicitor-Advocate (Civil).
Prof. Memberships: Law Society, City of London Law Society Litigation Sub-Committee, International Bar Association and Fellow of the Chartered Institute of Arbitrators.
Career: Qualification in 1979. Admitted as a solicitor in Hong Kong in 1986, having joined *Simmons & Simmons* in 1981. Partner since 1985.
Personal: Born 1 May 1955. Attended Jesus College, Cambridge 1973-76. Leisure interests include choral music, skiing, windsurfing and numerous children. Lives in London.

WAKEFORD, Carol
Cripps Harries Hall, Tunbridge Wells
(01892) 506116
caw@crippslaw.com
Specialisation: Specialises in all forms of property-related disputes including property-related insolvency, judicial review, planning litigation and Lands Tribunal work. Her experience extends to all aspects of landlord and tenant work including rent reviews, dilapidations, tenant default, landlord's withholding of consent and opposed lease renewals with particular emphasis on redevelopment and site regeneration. Reported cases: Bass Holdings v Morton Music; Midland Bank v Chart Enterprises; Lloyds Bank SF Nominees v Hassan; Ballard (Kent) v Oliver Ashworth (Holdings).
Prof. Memberships: Women in Property; Property Litigation Association; R3.
Career: Articled with *Nabarro Nathanson* 1983-85; assistant solicitor with *Nabarro Nathanson* 1985-90; became a partner in the property litigation department of that firm 1990. Joined *Cripps Harries Hall* as a partner in 1996.
Personal: University College London (LLB). Speaks fluent French. Married to chartered surveyor, two children. Enjoys horseriding, sailing, reading, entertaining and France.

WALKER, Alan
Cobbetts, Manchester
(0161) 833 7413
alan.walker@cobbetts.co.uk
Specialisation: All aspects of property litigation work, with particular emphasis on landlord and tenant matters, including dilapidations, rent reviews, opposed lease renewal proceedings, breaches of covenant and associated aspects of property management work.
Prof. Memberships: Law Society. Property Litigation Society.
Career: Magdalene College, Cambridge (MA, LLM). Articled 1989-91. Admitted 1991; Partner 2000.
Personal: Leisure interests include swimming, walking and theatre.

WALKER, Andrew
CMS Cameron McKenna, London
(020) 7367 2710
andrew.walker@cmck.com
Specialisation: Partner and head of Property Litigation and Dispute Resolution group. Main area of practice covers all types of property disputes including landlord and tenant (breaches of covenants, rent reviews, statutory renewals of commercial leases, breaches of statutory obligations, insolvency and applications to the Leasehold Valuation tribunal for Estate Management Schemes); claims arising out of contracts for the sale and purchase of land/buildings; breach of statutory obligations; disputes on boundaries, trespass, rights of way, professional negligence by surveyors or solicitors in relation to property matters.
Prof. Memberships: Law Society, Property Litigation Association, The City of London Property Association.
Career: Qualified 1986 and became a partner and head of Property Litigation group in 1993.
Personal: Born 8 December 1959. Leisure pursuits include horse-riding, gardening, cars and family life. Lives in London and Ross-on-Wye.

WALKER, Deirdre
Norton Rose, London
(020) 7444 2633
walkerdm@nortonrose.com
Specialisation: Partner in commercial litigation department specialising in corporate and fraud related litigation. She has extensive experience of urgent applications for Freezing Orders and ancillary relief and in the recovery of assets. Previous instructions include advising beneficiaries in connection with a dispute involving the tracing and recovery of assets wrongfully disposed of in an effort to avoid tax liabilities in several jurisdictions, obtaining a freezing injunction in this jurisdiction, ancillary relief in the British Virgin Islands and Jersey and eventually recovering in excess of £120m misappropriated assets; advising Towry Law plc in connection with its warranty claims against Hogg Robinson plc arising out of the disposal of Advizas Limited and the subsequent 'hole' discovered in connection with the pensions misselling provision; successfully defending TBI plc against a claim by London & Regional Investments Limited alleging breach of fiduciary duty, breach of contract and misrepresentation for approximately £20 million and obtaining summary judgment on a counterclaim of £20 million (the Court of Appeal recently upheld the decision at first instance); advising a major international bank in relation to a multimillion pound letter of credit fraud which involved obtaining a Freezing Order and later summary judgment against the fraudster; advising the Pell Frischmann Group in connection with its dispute with Trevor Osborne regarding the diversion of assets from a joint venture; advising a plc in respect of its recovery of confidential information unlawfully disseminated through third parties by a previous director of the company and obtaining an injunction to prevent further disclosure; advising in connection with the Wickes fraud and advising and reporting to the Bank of England following a failed bid for the CWS.
Career: Called to the Bar in 1985. She joined *Norton Rose* in 1989 and became a partner in 1997. Appointed Head of the Corporate and Banking Litigation team in 2000 and has recently been elected London Managing Partner (a role which will allow her to continue to practice).

WALLS, Alan
Linklaters, London
(020) 7456 4258
alan.walls@linklaters.com
Specialisation: Specialist in contentious commercial practice, principally fraud investigation and asset recovery, insolvency and banking – encompassing regulatory investigations and other types of commercial dispute. Extensive experience of acting in a wide variety of commercial disputes for major clients including banking and finance: representing parties to a diverse range of banking and finance transactions in connection with issues and disputes arising, including litigation in the higher courts, domestic and international arbitration, interlocutory applications and use of alternative methods of dispute resolution; insolvency and asset recovery: acting for secured and unsecured creditors, for officeholders and for insolvent or potentially insolvent companies in relation to the wide range of issues arising in insolvency and pre-insolvency situations, including emergency steps to preserve or recover assets, often in an international context, and litigation aimed at setting aside preferential transactions or transaction at an undervalue and recovery from directors or shadow directors involved in wrongful or fraudulent trading; investigations: leading a series of major and sometimes high profile investigations into financial misconduct, most significantly investiga-

LITIGATION ■ THE LEADERS

tions into the affairs of financial institutions and public companies in England and overseas liaising with regulatory and prosecuting authorities and representing the client and witnesses in deadline with those authorities; general commercial litigation and arbitration: over a very wide spectrum, including contractual disputes and regulatory issues, commonly (but not exclusively) in the financial services sector and often involving fraud and/or insolvency; labour disputes; individual employment issues including issues arising from the poaching or defection of teams of employees or from executive dismissals; litigation involving pension funds and investment funds; shareholder disputes; professional negligence claims and defamation in the corporate.commercial context.
Career: 1987 to date: Partner, *Linklaters*; 1981-87: Assistant solicitor, *Linklaters*; 1979-81: Articled clerk, *Linklaters*. 1978: Trinity Hall, Cambridge University, Law MA (Cantab).

WALTHAM, Anne
Lovells, London
(020) 7296 2000
anne.waltham@lovells.com
Specialisation: A partner in the property litigation group. Specialises in property litigation, dealing with a wide variety of landlord and tenant and real property disputes, including advising the firm's property department on potentially litigious matters. Particular expertise in rent review disputes acting for leading institutional landlords. Familiar with running substantial landlord and tenant cases and has also dealt with a number of property related professional negligence cases, arbitrations and development related disputes. Regularly presents seminars on aspects of property litigation, to clients and externally, most recently on expert witnesses post Woolf and rent review update.
Prof. Memberships: Law Society; Property Litigation Association.
Career: Qualified in 1982 and joined *Lovells* in 1989; Partner 1998.
Publications: Contributes to a number of publications including the 'Estates Gazette', 'Property Week', 'Property Law Journal' and 'Commercial Lawyer'.

WARNE, David
Richards Butler, London
(020) 7772 5709
dgw@richardsbutler.com
Specialisation: Commercial litigation. Partner specialising in the banking, insolvency and regulatory fields, nationally and internationally; specialises particularly in cases involving international conflict of law issues, has acted successfully for Barclays Bank in connection with US and UK jurisdictional issues arising in the MCC Administration; has also acted for creditors and bond holders in the Brent Walker reconstruction, for creditors in the Heron reconstruction and has had substantial involvement with the regulatory issues arising out of the collapse of Barings and the losses suffered by Morgan Grenfell by reason of the Peter Young affair; has successfully represented the Personal Investment Authority in connection with judicial review of decisions relating to certain high-profile compensation of investor issues; on the international front, has recently been involved in a very substantial trust dispute in the courts of the Bahamas and Australia, a jurisdiction dispute involving the US and UK courts in respect of the affairs of a US company in chapter 11, and a case for Lloyd's Bank involving evidence of Turkish banking law which raises significant issues for clearing banks in relation to the collection of foreign cheques and the application of Section 4 of the Cheques Act 1957 (see 'The Times' 8th February 1999); succeeded in the Court of Appeal and successfully resisted a petition for leave to appeal to the House of Lords in relation to a trust dispute raising significant issues on the law of constructive trust (Walker v Stones) concerning French and Hong Kong companies and property in France; is acting in relation to a challenge to the English courts jurisdiction under the Brussels Convention raising issues as to domicile; a substantial mis-selling case involving long dated step-down bonds sold to Brazilian investors; a Prime Bank Instrument fraud claim involving England and continental jurisdictions; has recently been successful in trial in the commercial court concerning a claim for the return of substantial funds wrongly paid to a French Bank under a Letter of Credit and a claim against a well-known inspection agency for negligent certification.
Prof. Memberships: The Law Society.
Career: Qualified 1972; joined *Richards Butler* 1972.
Publications: Joint editor 'Banking Litigation' (Sweet & Maxwell). Is contributing a chapter on 'Parallel Proceedings' to 'Transatlantic Litigation', shortly to be published by Oceana.
Personal: Born 1947. Leisure: walking, wine, cricket, food and literature.

WARNE, Jonathan
Nabarro Nathanson, London
(020) 7524 6000
j.warne@nabarro.com
Specialisation: Extensive experience of a range of company/commercial disputes, including asset tracing and fraud, frequently involving multijurisdictional issues and pensions litigation. Recent high profile cases: successfully acting in leading pensions cases, ranging from Maxwell to National Bus and the Court of Appeal British Airways case; acting in a range of shareholder disputes, including NewMedia Spark plc in its Section 459 petition; successfully representing a non-executive director of Continental Assurance in the five and a half month trial, unusually resulting in an award of indemnity costs in favour of client; representing Slough Heat & Power Limited in its challenge to the New Electricity Trading Arrangements.
Prof. Memberships: Law Society and APL.
Career: Head of the firm's Commercial Litigation and Dispute Resolution Department and Pensions Litigation Team.

WATSON, Peter
Allen & Overy, London
(020) 7330 3000
peter.watson@allenovery.com
Specialisation: Managing Partner of the Litigation Department of *Allen & Overy*. Has substantial experience in a wide range of contentious commercial and financial matters, judicial review and aviation disputes. From 1997-2001 was a member of the Lord Chancellor's Civil Procedure Rules Committee responsible for producing new court rules as part of the implementation of Lord Woolf's reforms.
Prof. Memberships: Member of the Civil Procedure Rules Committee (1996-2000); CEDR Board Member.
Career: Assistant Solicitor *Allen & Overy* 1981-86, seconded to *Allen & Overy* Dubai office 1984-86; Partner *Allen & Overy* 1987.
Personal: Oxford University (BA, 1978). Born 1956.

WATSON, Peter
Levy & McRae, Glasgow
(0141) 307 2311
peterwatson@lemac.co.uk
See under Defamation, p.275

WEBBER OBE, Lesley
Beachcroft Wansbroughs, London
(020) 7894 6699
lwebber@bwlaw.co.uk
Specialisation: Partner, head of property litigation and planning. Principal area of practice is property litigation including rent reviews, lease renewals, dilapidations and service charge disputes. Also acts as arbitrator and as legal assessor to arbitrators. Other main area of work is town and country planning covering planning applications, agreements and appeals, local planning advice and representation, compulsory purchase orders and environmental assessments. Acted in PHIT v Holding & Management, Zubaida v Hargreaves, Sterling Estates v Pickard, Morgan Sindall v Sawston Farms, Fluor Daniels v Shortlands Investments. Member of Law Society/RICS Working Party on Landlord and Tenant Act 1954 and co-draftsman of PACT scheme for lease renewals. Member of Property Advisory Group to the Office of the Deputy Prime Minister. Awarded the OBE for services to the property industry.
Prof. Memberships: Fellow of the Chartered Institute of Arbitrators, honorary member of Arbrix, Blundell Memorial Lecturer 1999.
Career: Qualified 1980 while with *Freshfields*. Joined *Masons* in 1984 and became a partner in 1985. Partner London office of *Dibb Lupton Broomhead* from 1993. Joined *Beachcroft Stanleys* in 1997.
Personal: Born 10 April 1956. Attended Birmingham University 1974-77. Winner of SLSS Prize for Planning Law.

WEBSTER, Sheila
Dundas & Wilson CS, Edinburgh
(0131) 228 8000

WHITTELL, Mark
Cobbetts, Manchester
(0161) 833 5252
mark.whittell@cobbetts.co.uk
Specialisation: Commercial litigation including banking professional negligence, franchise disputes, insolvency.
Prof. Memberships: CEDR, accredited mediator.
Career: Articled 1980-82. Assistant solicitor, *Glass Bagshawe Miller*, 1982-84; assistant solicitor, *GW Towells*, 1984-86; *Cobbetts* 1986-present – made partner, 1989.
Personal: 44 years old. Three children. Educated Marple Hall Grammar School and Sheffield University. Lacrosse player at international and veteran international level. Enthusiastic sportsman. Interested in wine, travel.

WILLETTS, Jayne
Hammond Suddards Edge, Birmingham
(0121) 222 3000

WILLIAMS, Gareth
Hugh James, Cardiff
(029) 2022 4871
gareth.williams@hughjames.com
Specialisation: Partner and Head of Business Litigation Division. Has acted for insurers for more than 20 years and undertaken usual range of personal injury work with heavy emphasis on maximum severity claims. One of the two lead partners advising the Welsh Rugby Union on regulatory and constitutional issues.
Prof. Memberships: Law Society; FOIL.
Career: Joined *Hugh James* in 1975 and qualified in 1976. Became a Partner in 1978. First solicitor in Wales to be appointed a Licensed Insolvency Practitioner. Deputy District Judge from 1991 to date.
Personal: Born 5 September 1951. Educated at Glan Clwyd High School 1962-69 and University College of Wales, Aberystwyth 1969-72 (Morgan Owen Law Prizeman). Leisure pursuits include sport, reading and music. Lives in Cowbridge.

WILLIAMSON, David
Brodies, Edinburgh
(0131) 228 3777
david.williamson@brodies.co.uk
Specialisation: Solicitor Advocate handling general commercial litigation and specialising in intellectual property, employment law, partnership disputes and professional negligence. Experienced speaker at conferences and seminars. Lectured for over five years at University of Edinburgh in civil procedure.
Career: Qualified in 1971. With *Simpson & Marwick* 1969-75, latterly as Partner. Joined *Brodies* as a Partner in 1976. Part-time Employment Tribunals Chairman and part-time Sheriff. Criminal Injuries Compensation Panel member. Fellow of the Chartered Institute of Arbitrators.
Personal: Born in 1949. Educated at Royal High School, Edinburgh and University of Edinburgh. Leisure interests include cricket and hill walking. Lives in Edinburgh.

WILSON, Allan
Morgan Cole, Cardiff
(029) 2038 5385

WILSON, Michael
Elliott Duffy Garrett, Belfast
(028) 9024 5034

WINTERBURN, Anthony
DLA, Manchester
(08700) 111111

WOOD, Jonathan
Clyde & Co, London
(020) 7623 1244
Jonathan.Wood@clyde.co.uk
Specialisation: Co-ordinating partner of Commercial Dispute Resolution and Recovery Department. Main area of practice is insurance and banking work, within the Department. Involves advising on export credit guarantee insurance, financial institution insurance, fraud, reinsurance and insolvency matters. International trade work also covered, including conflict of laws, trading contracts, trading disputes and political risk insurance. Increasingly involved in international commercial arbitrations and mediations. Frequent speaker on insurance and reinsurance, insolvency, fraud and export credit and political risk insurance.
Prof. Memberships: Law Society, IBA. Vice Chairman of Committees on International Trade, Member of Insurance, Insolvency and International Litigation Committees, Member of London Court of International Arbitration, ABA and DRI.
Career: Qualified 1977. Joined *Clyde & Co* 1984. Partner in 1987. Legal Advisor to Export Credits Guarantee Department, Cardiff 1987.
Personal: Born 11 June 1953. Attended Stockport Grammar, Sheffield University 1971-74. Leisure pursuits include tennis, skiing and scuba diving. Lives in Farnham.

WOODCOCK, Tony
Stephenson Harwood (incorporating Sinclair Roche & Temperley), London
(020) 7809 2349
tony.woodcock@shlegal.com
Specialisation: Partner – litigation; Head of investigation and regulation group. Main area of practice is financial services and professional regulation; fraud; insider dealing; directors liability; white collar crime including health and safely and environmental regulation. Also deals with financial and professional investigations, conducting investigations for regulatory bodies in financial services, accounting and insolvency and advising institutions on money laundering avoidance procedures.
Career: Office of the DPP 1979-85 and the Office of Treasury Solicitor 1985-87. *Slaughter and May* 1987-90. *Stephenson Harwood* 1990; partner, 1994. Solicitor-Advocate (All Courts) 1996.
Publications: Co-author of 'Serious Fraud: Investigation and Trial' (Butterworths). Contributor to Butterworth's 'Financial Law Services'.
Personal: LLB (Hons), LLM; Joseph Hume Law Scholar (UCL); Montague Prizeman & Harmsworth Scholar (Middle Temple); Languages: French. Resides London.

YORK, Stephen
Vinson & Elkins LLP, London
(020) 7065 6033
syork@velaw.com
See under Arbitration, p.76

LOCAL GOVERNMENT

London: 572; The Regions: 573; Scotland: 576; Profiles: 577

Research approved by BMRB For this edition, **Chambers'** researchers conducted 6,582 interviews – 3,900 with law firms, 511 with barristers and 2,171 with clients. The validity of the research was scrutinised by BMRB International, who audited both the methodology and the results at our offices in London. They interviewed **Chambers'** researchers and cross-checked sample interviews. Details of the audit appear on page 7.

LONDON

LOCAL GOVERNMENT — LONDON

1
- Nabarro Nathanson

2
- Mayer, Brown, Rowe & Maw
- Sharpe Pritchard

3
- Ashurst Morris Crisp
- Berwin Leighton Paisner
- Lawrence Graham
- Léonie Cowen & Associates
- Trowers & Hamlins

4
- Denton Wilde Sapte
- Herbert Smith

5
- Clifford Chance
- DJ Freeman
- Dechert
- Jenkins & Hand
- Winckworth Sherwood

LEADING INDIVIDUALS

1
- CHILD Tony Mayer, Brown, Rowe & Maw
- COWEN Léonie Léonie Cowen & Associates
- ILEY Malcolm Nabarro Nathanson

2
- CURNOW Tony Ashurst Morris Crisp
- FORGE Anna Mayer, Brown, Rowe & Maw
- GRIFFITHS Trevor Sharpe Pritchard
- RANDALL Simon Lawrence Graham

3
- DOOLITTLE Ian Trowers & Hamlins
- HAND Catherine Jenkins & Hand
- RANDALL Helen Nabarro Nathanson
- SERRELLI Roseanne Sharpe Pritchard

UP AND COMING
- SHARLAND John Sharpe Pritchard

This book is the product of 6,582 1/2 hour interviews. See p.7 for BMRB audit. Within each band, firms are listed alphabetically. See individuals' profiles p.577

NABARRO NATHANSON (see firm details p.1080) "*Clearly strong across the board,*" observers agree that the firm secures its position at the forefront of the market with "*the biggest team and the best clients.*" "*An impressive public sector record*" has been won by a "*talented and committed team.*" Peers were full of praise for the long-established and "*thoroughly knowledgeable*" **Malcolm Iley** (see p.578). The team also includes "*focused and informed*" **Helen Randall** (see p.578). Local authorities, regional development agencies, government departments, all feature on the client roster here. The team also advises statutory and regulatory agencies including the Audit Commission and the Commission for Racial Equality. It has expertise in strategic partnerships, e-government, PPP/PFI work and joint ventures. In particular e-government instructions have increased, and the firm has closed a PPP between E-Government Solutions and the Association of Colleges concerning an online procurement hub for FE colleges. It has been appointed to act on strategic partnerings by Peterborough and West Berkshire councils. A further highlight this year has been the completion of a major outsourcing of integrated waste collection and disposal facilities for the London Borough of Haringey. **Clients** LB of Haringey; local authorities.

MAYER, BROWN, ROWE & MAW (see firm details p.1060) Of the wide range of cases the firm has undertaken recently, it is most closely associated with and commended for its Audit Commission work and involvement in the Dame Shirley Porter 'homes for votes' case. **Tony Child** (see p.577) is an "*extraordinarily able*" practitioner and respected for his strong relationship with the Audit Commission, while **Anna Forge** (see p.577) "*knows her job backwards.*" Areas of focus for the group include property, local government reorganisation and PFI. Advice to councils on ethical matters is also a string to its bow. Expertise in education has come into play in its involvement in a challenge to the closure of a 6th form college and expulsion cases. The team has advised on the matter of a girl seeking home tuition after being deemed too unwell to go to school. Transport for London and the Mayor of London continue to instruct the team and the firm is regularly involved in health and planning matters. **Clients** Local authorities.

SHARPE PRITCHARD (see firm details p.1127) Adjudged an "*organised*" outfit, some interviewees agreed that it was home to some of "*the best local government solicitors in London.*" Its foundations in this sector lie with litigation on behalf of local authorities. The team has also advised on non-contentious procurement issues and PPP/PFI. **Trevor Griffiths** (see p.577) is a "*highly visible*" presence in the market; he specialises in judicial review, planning appeals and injunctions, and environmental issues. **Roseanne Serrelli** (see p.578) is "*impressive*" across the spectrum of public sector contracting, including waste management and social services PFI, while **John Sharland** (see p.578), has been commended for his clear advice on matters such as contracting and procurement. **Clients** Local authorities.

ASHURST MORRIS CRISP (see firm details p.852) Town regeneration work ensures that the firm remains at the forefront of the market, and **Tony Curnow** (see p.650) is widely recognised for his skill in compulsory purchase. The team acts for a large number of London authorities and has represented Hackney in planning matters and development agreements. Commended for its work in the rail sector, the firm has also developed a niche in infrastructure agreements and town centre schemes. Urban regeneration of brownfield sites is a forte and its remit spreads nationwide, with matters handled in Manchester and Leeds. **Clients** LB of Hackney; LB of Ealing; LB of Brent.

BERWIN LEIGHTON PAISNER (see firm details p.866) Considered by observers to be "*one of the main players*" in the sector, the firm is thought to derive an advantage from its recognised property expertise and its relationship with local authorities. It currently acts for around 70 authorities nationwide. Within its local government practice, the team handles educational, IT and housing matters, and advises lenders on public sector transactions. It draws from a cross-departmental team and has strong links fortified by partner Candice Blackwood. Recently the team has been involved in IT work for the London Boroughs of Hackney and Southwark. **Clients** City of Westminster; Department for Social Development for Northern Ireland; Liverpool CC; LB of Enfield; Maidstone BC; Northampton BC; Solihull MBC; LB of Merton.

LAWRENCE GRAHAM (see firm details p.1031) **Simon Randall** is head of department at this "*effective*" outfit. The two main prongs of its practice are housing and the transferral of leisure and heritage assets on behalf of local authorities. It has handled over £2 billion worth of voluntary transfers during the past 12 months. The team has also transferred leisure centres to charitable entities on behalf of local authorities in Southwark and Canterbury. Its commercial property capability is expanding and it advises several authorities on town centre regeneration. Compulsory purchase, contamination, governance and conflicts of interest are other areas of focus. **Clients** Walsall MBC; Wealden DC; Chiltern DC; Coventry CC; Denbighshire CC; Pendle BC; Thurrock Council.

LÉONIE COWEN & ASSOCIATES (see firm details p.1038) This boutique practice is rated by larger firms for the high quality of work and innovation on offer. Clients avow to being able to "*rely on*" and "*respect the judgement*" of Léonie Cowen (see p.577). The team tends to focus on the transferral of leisure assets such as arts venues and libraries on behalf of local authority clients. It recently completed the transfer of leisure services to a charitable organisation on behalf of Hertsmere Borough Council, which owns some of the most modern facilities in the UK. It has been instructed in the disposal of the Discovery Visitors' Centre on behalf of Dover District Council, and has recently completed a grant for a new theatre on behalf of the Arts Council of Wales. The team is currently finalising an appraisal of the entire leisure service of Bracknell Forest BC. Social services, public procurement and contracting advice are other areas of focus. **Clients** Hertsmere BC; Bracknell Forest BC; Wrexham County BC; Dover DC; LB of Newham; Southwark Council; LB of Tower Hamlets.

TROWERS & HAMLINS (see firm details p.1168) This regeneration and social housing-oriented team is "*clearly knowledgeable*" and is headed up by "*talented*" **Ian Doolittle** (see p.762). Alongside this niche expertise sits a wide-ranging experience in local government law, and the team is commended for its "*detailed*" approach to cases. Stock transfers for Birmingham and Glasgow City Councils have been a key achievement in the last 12 months, and it is involved in ongoing related advisory work in Bradford, Sheffield and Walsall. Capable of handling high- value transactions with ease, the team has recently advised on a stock transfer for Sunderland City Council worth £520 million. **Clients** Glasgow CC; Sunderland CC; Oxfordshire CC; Birmingham CC.

DENTON WILDE SAPTE (see firm details p.935) An established presence, clients appreciate the "*real range*" of work the team is able to undertake. The three main strands of its practice are planning, PFI and property, including town centre regeneration, and procurement is a particular forte. The team has been appointed by the London Borough of Camden to act in the redevelopment of the Kings Cross area including the station and tube. It is representing three local authorities in promoting the Elstow Garden Village in Bedfordshire. David Danskin is the head of department here, and the team remains on the English Partnerships legal panel. In transactional matters, it has advised the British Waterways Board on the acquisition of the residual estate of the Port of London properties. **Clients** LB of Camden; Manchester CC; Essex CC; LB of Barking & Dagenham; Stevenage BC.

HERBERT SMITH (see firm details p.992) This respected practice is best known for the litigation it undertakes on behalf of local authorities. Andrew Lidbetter and Chris Tavener are key partners in the team. Cases undertaken of late include advising Swindon Borough Council on proposals for a mixed-use development near Swindon including 4,500 houses, four schools and a stadium. It has represented one of the London boroughs on the redevelopment of an old people's home, and acted for Sheffield City Council on the development of a new retail quarter. **Clients** Swindon BC; Oxfordshire CC; LB of Hackney; Sheffield CC; Audit Commission

CLIFFORD CHANCE (see firm details p.911) The thrust of the firm's local government practice involves representing local authorities with significant landholdings. It is no surprise that real estate finance for local authority clients is what distinguishes this firm from rivals in the field. It also advises public and private bodies, including banks, on their local authority lending. The team has been advising the Corporation of London on a proposed joint venture regarding a development at Spitalfields, set to create a 700,000 square foot office. Work continues for the Historic Royal Palaces in relation to the Tower Environs Scheme for the Tower of London. The highly respected PFI practice often straddles the local authority sphere. **Clients** Corporation of London; East Hertfordshire DC; Hastings BC; LB of Hounslow LBC; Manchester CC; Spelthorne BC; West Dorset DC.

DJ FREEMAN (see firm details p.939) Ted Totman heads the department that is involved in the drafting, negotiation and exchange of joint venture development agreements on behalf of local authorities. Recent cases include a conditional agreement for the development of a leisure centre at Swiss Cottage on behalf of the London Borough of Camden. The firm also advised Fareham Borough Council on the development of Fareham town centre. **Clients** LB of Camden; Fareham BC.

DECHERT (see firm details p.934) The group handles local authority work from within its respected property department. A recent coup has been the successful tender for a portfolio of work relating to the development and improvement of Regent Street for the Crown Estate. The team is also immersed in leisure schemes for a number of local authorities and has acted for Winchester City Council in a regeneration scheme. Michael Hallowell leads the team. **Clients** Brent LBC; Corporation of London; Dacorum BC; LB of Hillingdon; Mole Valley DC; Swansea C&CC.

JENKINS & HAND (see firm details p.1014) **Catherine Hand** heads a team, which is devoted to pure local government work. It typically handles stock transfer and outsourcing and derives an advantage in the market from its social housing and residential expertise. Work for the District Audit Service is regularly undertaken and it has recently been advising authorities on the Local Government Act 2000. Highlight cases include stock transfers for Crewe and Nantwich Borough Council. It also handled the outsourcing of Westminster City Council's domiciliary care service, which involved the transfer of several hundred staff. **Clients** Crewe & Nantwich BC; Nantwich BC; Westminster CC.

WINCKWORTH SHERWOOD (see firm details p.1192) Andrew Murray is head of this "*sound*" operation. It covers a broad spectrum of work for local authorities including education, housing, police and infrastructure projects. In recent years, it has augmented the scope of its practice to cover PPP and urban regeneration, while litigation also retains its prominence. The firm acts for over 100 local authorities and receives instructions from healthcare providers and the National Audit Office.

SOUTH WEST

LOCAL GOVERNMENT
■ SOUTH WEST

1. **Bevan Ashford** Bristol, Exeter
2. **Bond Pearce** Bristol, Exeter

This book is the product of 6,582 1/2 hour interviews. See p.7 for BMRB audit. Within each band, firms are listed alphabetically.

BEVAN ASHFORD (see firm details p.869) Market sources agree that the team has had a "*prosperous*" 12 months, and is deservedly rated top. Peers see the recruitment of Bethan Evans from Syniad, the improvement and development agency for local government in Wales, as an "*important acquisition,*" as she brings with her particular knowledge of the Local Government Act 2000. The firm's workload includes PFI, PPP, schools projects, urban regeneration, leisure and waste disposal. It regularly offers advice on 'best value' and procurement issues, and has been reappointed as legal advisor to both the South West Regional Development Agency and the South East England Development Agency. It has advised Swindon Borough Council on proposals for a new arts centre, intended to be the catalyst for the regeneration of its surrounding area. **Clients** South Somerset DC; Swindon BC; Somerset CC; Rhondda Cynon Taff CBC; Bristol CC.

BOND PEARCE (see firm details p.879) This highly esteemed operation is headed by Emrys Parry. He and the team have particular expertise

LOCAL GOVERNMENT ■ WALES/MIDLANDS

in compulsory purchase issues, and have received instructions on two major schemes in Reading relating to the improvement of a road junction and town centre regeneration. Other work highlights include acting for South Oxfordshire District Council in a town centre regeneration operation, and advising Dorset County Council on a compulsory purchase matter. **Clients** South Oxfordshire DC; Dorset CC; Caradon DC; Penwith DC; Plymouth CC; Reading BC.

WALES

LOCAL GOVERNMENT
■ WALES
1. **Eversheds** Cardiff
2. **Edwards Geldard** Cardiff
3. **Morgan Cole** Cardiff, Swansea

LEADING INDIVIDUALS
1. **EVANS Eric** Eversheds
2. **COLE Alun** Morgan Cole
   WILLIAMS Huw Edwards Geldard

This book is the product of 6,582 1/2 hour interviews. See p.7 for BMRB audit. Within each band, firms are listed alphabetically. See individuals' profiles p.577

EVERSHEDS (see firm details p.949) "*Definitely number one,*" market commentators "*can't fail to acknowledge*" the firm's presence in Wales. Long-established Eric Evans (see p.577) heads a group that has recently been advising the National Assembly for Wales on various public law matters, including procurement. It has advised five Welsh local authorities on the outsourcing of a large consultancy practice, which they operate. It also offers advice to the WDA on vires and public law matters, and assisted Cardiff County Council on defamation issues. **Clients** National Assembly for Wales; WDA; Cardiff CC.

EDWARDS GELDARD (see firm details p.944) Huw Williams (see p.49) is the "*experienced and effective*" head of this "*sensible*" operation. Current endeavours include a town centre regeneration project, an out-of-town retail project and the disposal of an entire industrial estate portfolio to a private investor. The team is undertaking an increasing amount of property-related work on compulsory purchase orders (CPOs). It advises the WDA on joint projects with various Welsh local authorities, and further afield has been instructed by Derbyshire County Council on a public/private regeneration scheme near Chesterfield. A place on the panel advising the East Midlands Development Agency has also been secured. **Clients** Derbyshire CC; WDA; Newport CC.

MORGAN COLE (see firm details p.1075) The firm has an "*acknowledged expertise*" in local government law and acts for clients across the UK. It is currently advising an authority in the Midlands on its IT system. The team offers expertise in outsourcing and property matters and PPP, and has advised authorities in the Channel Islands on drugs issues. Team leader Alun Cole is described by peers as "*approachable and reliable.*" **Clients** Cardiff CC; WDA.

MIDLANDS

LOCAL GOVERNMENT
■ MIDLANDS
1. **Wragge & Co** Birmingham
2. **Pinsent Curtis Biddle** Birmingham
3. **DLA** Birmingham
   Eversheds Birmingham, Nottingham
4. **Anthony Collins Solicitors** Birmingham
   Mills & Reeve Birmingham

LEADING INDIVIDUALS
1. **KEITH-LUCAS Peter** Wragge & Co
2. **MATTHEW Stephen** Eversheds
   STEPHENS Hugo Pinsent Curtis Biddle
3. **COOK Mark** Anthony Collins Solicitors
   KNOX Martin Anthony Collins Solicitors

This book is the product of 6,582 1/2 hour interviews. See p.7 for BMRB audit. Within each band, firms are listed alphabetically. See individuals' profiles p.577

WRAGGE & CO (see firm details p.1197) At "*the forefront of the market*" the team is esteemed by peers, barristers and clients alike. Clients praise its "*rapid response time,*" while peers point to its ability to "*produce something, not just talk.*" Its work on the Local Government Act 2000 is widely acclaimed, as is its town centre development and property-related work. This small core team is bolstered by specialists based in other departments. The group has a national remit, and has recently been involved in a number of partnership arrangements and urban regeneration schemes. Highlight cases include advising Buckinghamshire County Council on the transfer of care homes to Heritage Care, and advising the GLA on the promotion of the multi-ethnic Respect festival. It has also advised South Bedfordshire District Council on the development of a joint venture theatre and arts project in Dunstable. Rated by clients for his "*depth of understanding and experience,*" Peter Keith-Lucas is renowned for his drafting skills and detailed advice on constitutional matters. He has advised 15 authorities on the drafting of their executive constitutions under the LGA 2000, and assisted four authorities on probity and complaints issues. **Clients** Basingstoke & Deane BC; Birmingham CC; Blackpool BC; Brighton & Hove CC; Canterbury CC; Coventry CC; Derby CC; English Heritage; Leicestershire CC; LB of Tower Hamlets.

PINSENT CURTIS BIDDLE (see firm details p.1102) A strong presence in the Midlands is enjoyed by this firm, particularly basking in the light of its expert PFI and stock transfer work. Among this "*well co-ordinated*" team is Hugo Stephens (see p.765), who specialises in advice on large-scale voluntary transfers. The team has advised on a LSVT for Birmingham City Council involving 92,000 units. The firm's local government practice breaks down into the areas of projects/PFI, commercial property, planning, housing and education. It has acted for Pathfinder street-lighting projects in areas as diverse as Islington, Walsall and Sunderland. It is leading a team in London, on behalf of the London Borough of Newham regarding the provision of £30 million worth of new schools. It has also advised Worcestershire County Council on IT procurement issues. **Clients** LB of Newham; Nuneaton & Bedworth BC; Brighton & Hove CC; Stoke-on-Trent CC; Worcestershire CC; LB of Islington; Rushcliffe BC; Solihull MBC.

DLA This established team has strength in high-value work such as PFI projects and transportation and infrastructure issues for local authorities.

EVERSHEDS (see firm details p.949) An outstanding reputation in the public sector and long relationships with local authorities are enjoyed by this firm. In the local government sphere much of the work revolves around PFI/PPP matters, at which Stephen Matthew (see p.697)'s "*commitment*" shines. Outsourcing work as well as PFIs for schools, fire and police stations have occupied the team, which also advised on the Nottingham tram project. Middlesbrough Council represents an important client acquisition, instructing the team in a high-profile PPP involving the outsourced provision of public access services, IT, telecoms, property management and financial services. The group has also been acting on an ICT and network communications-based learning partnership for Sandwell Metropolitan Borough

Council. It advised Milton Keynes and Northamptonshire councils on their first major joint authority strategic partnership with the private sector. **Clients** Middlesbrough Council; Braintree DC; Northamptonshire CC; Cornwall CC.

ANTHONY COLLINS SOLICITORS (see firm details p.845) Housing and regeneration matters are high on the agenda at this practice, which is headed by **Martin Knox** (see p.764). Notable achievements of recent times include being appointed as legal advisors to 15 areas involved in the 'New Deal for Communities', each running a £50 million programme. It has represented North East Derbyshire District Council on a housing PFI project, and acted for Breckland Council in a proposed public/private partnership for IT and e-commerce matters. **Mark Cook** (see p.577) is considered "*co-operative and proactive.*" **Clients** Prime Focus; Knowsley Housing Trust; Accord Housing Association; NE Derbyshire DC; Knowsley MBC.

MILLS & REEVE (see firm details p.1071) The firm's success in obtaining two significant contracts from Birmingham City Council, in the fields of adult social services litigation, and property and public law, is testimony to the wisdom of its relocation to this region. It has particular expertise in employment law and educational matters, and has secured a two-year extension to its contract for the provision of advice on property, commercial and education law, with the London Borough of Barking & Dagenham. This has included giving advice on a partnering arrangement regarding the sharing of IP rights in a school maths programme. It has also advised Maldon District Council in Essex on the £1 million extension of a leisure centre, and assisted in the drafting of a new operating contract for a partnered firm to run it. Nicholas Hancox heads the team. **Clients** Birmingham CC; Leicester CC; LB of Barking & Dagenham; Blaby DC; Kent CC; Mid Beds DC; Hertfordshire CC.

EAST ANGLIA

LOCAL GOVERNMENT
■ EAST ANGLIA

1 Steele & Co Norwich

This book is the product of 6,582 1/2 hour interviews. See p.7 for BMRB audit. Within each band, firms are listed alphabetically.

STEELE & CO (see firm details p.1145) The only significant presence in the region, this "*capable*" firm has recently increased its client base and is now advising around one third of London's borough councils. Its workload entails contract work for the City of Swansea and general advice to Southampton City Council. Department head Richard Hewitt operates from both London and Norwich. The firm's local authority capability includes specialist housing and public sector groups, although it remains predominantly based in the public law department. Areas of expertise are procurement, regeneration, environmental health, planning and property matters. **Clients** Bath & North East Somerset Council; Boston BC; Suffolk CC; Swansea CC; LB of Bromley; LB of Croydon; LB of Ealing; LB of Hounslow; Westminster CC.

THE NORTH

LOCAL GOVERNMENT
■ THE NORTH

1 Eversheds Leeds
2 Pinsent Curtis Biddle Leeds
3 Walker Morris Leeds
4 Cobbetts Manchester
  Masons Leeds
  Pannone & Partners Manchester

LEADING INDIVIDUALS
1 CIRELL Stephen Eversheds
2 DOBSON Nicholas Pinsent Curtis Biddle
  KILDUFF David Walker Morris

This book is the product of 6,582 1/2 hour interviews. See p.7 for BMRB audit. Within each band, firms are listed alphabetically. See individuals' profiles p.577

EVERSHEDS (see firm details p.949) The northern offices of this nationally regarded operation are thought to stay ahead of the pack by dint of their "*talented and well-resourced teams.*" Leading light **Stephen Cirell** (see p.577) is department head, described by peers as "*one of the most recognised figures in the local authority world.*" Of late, the firm has been advising Dacorum Borough Council on strategic outsourcing, and acting for the Greater Manchester Police on PFI matters. It has also represented Lancashire County Council on a large-scale waste management matter worth over £100 million. Advice on partnering arrangements, with particular focus on the use of technology, has been given to several councils around the UK, and the firm has expertise in constitutional advice. It undertook a legal services 'best value' review for the London Borough of Haringey, and assisted on e-government work for South Norfolk District Council. The team has also prepared new political constitutions for Lichfield District Council, Walsall Metropolitan Borough Council and Southend-on-Sea Unitary Council. **Clients** South Norfolk DC; Lichfield DC; Walsall MBC; Southend-on-Sea UC.

PINSENT CURTIS BIDDLE (see firm details p.1102) This highly regarded practice fields the "*technically excellent*" **Nicholas Dobson** (see p.577). It excels in e-government, PPPs, audit, 'best value' and employment law issues. The recent acquisition of e-government work from five local authorities in the Midlands (the Welland Partnership) has been a significant coup for the team. It has also offered 'best value' advice to Birmingham City Council. Other highlights include representing Coventry City Council in a large joint venture and advising the chief finance officer in the London Borough of Redbridge on the drafting of a certificate in a major PFI. **Clients** Birmingham CC; Cardiff CC; Colchester BC.

WALKER MORRIS (see firm details p.1178) **David Kilduff** (see p.578) was endorsed by competitors as "*a trusted hand*" on the most complex of matters. His team advises local authorities and private entities on issues such as partnering, development and asset management. This practice can be divided broadly into two areas: advice on governance issues such as auditing and compliance, and commercial advice relating to partnerships and PFIs. A recent development has been the cementing of a partnering relationship with Wakefield City Council, including procurement issues. The team has also advised Leicester City Council on a complex land transaction connected to the National Space Centre. Transport has proved a fruitful area with the group appointed by the South Yorkshire Passenger Transport Executive to be its overall partner, and advice has been given to a Scottish authority on transport outsourcing. **Clients** Associated British Ports; Bradford MDC; City of Wakefield MDC; Environment Agency; Liverpool CC; Scarborough BC; Stirling Council.

COBBETTS (see firm details p.914) This is a "*solid*" firm that peers perceived to be "*increasingly prominent*" in the North West. Its local government team is headed by Tony Fitzmaurice. The group sits on the panel for commercial, partnership and PFI work of Lancashire County Council, and also advises on pensions and property matters. **Clients** Local authorities.

LOCAL GOVERNMENT ■ SCOTLAND

MASONS (see firm details p.1057) The firm applies its expertise in the construction, utilities and outsourcing sectors to its local authority client base. It is led by construction partner, Mark Richards, and considered "*proficient*" by contemporaries. The partnership set up with North Yorkshire County Council continues to be fruitful. Appointment to the panel of Yorkshire Forward has generated instructions, such as acting for Bradford Metropolitan City Council on the redevelopment of the Manningham Mills area post-riot. The firm is advising a number of regional small education action zones. **Clients** Leeds CC; North Yorkshire CC; local authorities.

PANNONE & PARTNERS (see firm details p.1092) Adjudged an "*organised and professional*" operation, the team has been occupied of late with Metrolink Phase 3 (the Manchester tram system), one of the largest ever transport infrastructure projects outside London. It completed the purchase of the airports division of National Express, with a deal value of £241 million, on behalf of local-authority owned Manchester Airport. The group has also advised the North West Regional Assembly on issues relating to its legal status and the possibility of incorporation. Steven Grant is the head of department. **Clients** Greater Manchester Passenger Transport Executive; Oldham MBC; Association of Greater Manchester Authorities.

SCOTLAND

LOCAL GOVERNMENT
■ SCOTLAND

1
- Dundas & Wilson CS Edinburgh
- Shepherd+ Wedderburn Edinburgh

2
- McGrigor Donald Glasgow
- Simpson & Marwick Edinburgh

3
- Brodies Edinburgh
- Burness Edinburgh
- Tods Murray WS Edinburgh

LEADING INDIVIDUALS
1 SHAW Kate Simpson & Marwick

This book is the product of 6,582 1/2 hour interviews. See p.7 for BMRB audit. Within each band, firms are listed alphabetically. See individuals' profiles p.577

DUNDAS & WILSON CS (see firm details p.943) Recognised as a "*strong firm*" that covers a range of local government work, it has had particular success in securing "*inroads into PFI projects.*" The arrival of John Watchman, former in-house legal advisor to the Scottish Executive, is a significant acquisition for the group. Recent highlights are the completion of the City of Edinburgh Schools PPP on behalf of the City Council, and the three-year extension of a partnering agreement with Stirling City Council. The group, which is led by PFI partner Michael McAuley, has been appointed to advise on the preparation of Edinburgh City Council's proposal for central traffic management. **Clients** City of Edinburgh Council; Stirling City Council; Glasgow CC; South Lanarkshire Council; The Moray Council.

SHEPHERD+ WEDDERBURN (see firm details p.1130) A "*robust*" team, it was commended by peers for its dedicated local government practice. After the retirement of Ian MacLeod, Kenny Cumming has stepped in as head of the local government team. It draws on the expertise of various specialist partners in areas such as environment, employment, PPP/PFI and property litigation. Over the past year, the team has defended several councils in the Court of Session. It has advised on some substantial planning work for Midlothian Council and acted in an inquiry for Aberdeenshire Council. Amongst a significant number of education PFI projects undertaken, the firm acted in the provision of one newly built and five refurbished secondary and primary schools in West Lothian. **Clients** East Dunbartonshire Council; North Lanarkshire Council; Highland Council; Aberdeenshire Council; West Lothian Council; Midlothian Council; City of Edinburgh Council.

MCGRIGOR DONALD (see firm details p.1065) The team advises private sector clients, as well as local authorities, on statutory interpretation and legislative matters. It is headed by director of public law and procurement specialist, Alan Boyd. Typical work includes LSVTs and related tax advice. It is also involved in a number of substantial PFIs, including waste management matters. It continues to work on joint ventures and partnerships, and has expertise in marine work. The firm recently advised a government department in Northern Ireland on issues relating to ports and harbours. **Clients** Local authorities in Scotland, England and Northern Ireland.

SIMPSON & MARWICK (see firm details p.1138) Kate Shaw (see p.49) has an "*impressive client base*" and is commended by peers for her constructive approach. Her team regularly represents local government in judicial reviews in the Court of Session and House of Lords. Its track record includes defending actions involving school closures, special payments and housing problems. **Clients** Local authorities.

BRODIES (see firm details p.889) Neil Collar is the head of this "*impressive*" operation. It undertakes a range of work on behalf of local authorities, and has recently witnessed an increase in the number of cases that have a human rights element. Local authority clients are advised on policy, regulatory issues and procurement issues. Expertise is also on hand in commercial property, construction, environment and PFI. **Clients** Local authorities.

BURNESS Headed by Stephen Phillips, this "*focused*" team has a strong relationship with the City of Edinburgh Council and Midlothian Council. It has been developing corporate structures and land option arrangements, which will drive the largest single property development project in the UK (the South East Wedge project, estimated final value £500 million). It has also been advising the Scottish Borders Council on its proposed joint venture with a private sector partner on economic development projects. **Clients** Scottish Borders Council; Department of Social Security; East Lothian Council; Fife Council; North Ayrshire Council; South Edinburgh Partnership.

TODS MURRAY WS (see firm details p.1164) The team has expanded to include ex-McClure Naismith partner, Alistair Burrow, as a partner. Of late it has advised East Dunbartonshire Council on a possible large-scale voluntary transfer of its housing stock, and represented South Lanarkshire Council on its Centre West Development. The firm continues to represent long-standing client, Angus Council. **Clients** Angus Council; Derbyshire CC; Dundee CC; Scottish Archive Network; South Lanarkshire Council.

THE LEADERS IN LOCAL GOVERNMENT

CHILD, Tony
Mayer, Brown, Rowe & Maw, London
(020) 7782 8686
tchild@ev.mayerbrownrowe.com
Specialisation: Practice covers the full range of public and administrative law. Specialist in local government and NHS law. Acts for public bodies and those who deal with them. Advisor to local government and NHS external auditors. Renowned expertise and experience in acting for both applicants and respondents in judicial review and public law proceedings. This includes the first successful challenge in any commonwealth jurisdiction to the adequacy of a government consultation exercise; bringing down the Rate Support Grant (RSG) and ratecapping regime in 1985; overcoming retrospective legislation on RSG; having interest rate swaps declared by the House of Lords to be ultra vires local authorities; 'Bookbinder v Tebbit (No. 2)' (1992); 'Allsop v North Tyneside MBC' (1992); 'Burgoine and Cooke v Waltham Forest LBC' (1996) Lasaethes v the Incorporated Froebell Institute (2000), the first successful challenge to the expulsion of a pupil from a private school. Porter v Magill (2002), acting for the successful auditor in the 'homes for votes' case involving Dame Shirley Porter.
Career: Articled Redbridge London Borough Council; qualified 1971. Assistant Solicitor 1971-74. Senior Solicitor 1974-76. Chief Solicitor Greenwich LBC 1976-79. Assistant Chief Executive and Solicitor 1979-83; Deputy Chief Executive 1983-87; Solicitor to Audit Commission 1987-95; Partner *Rowe & Maw* 1995. Education: Ilford County High School; University College, London (LLB First Class Hons).
Personal: Born 1947. Resides Chelmsford. Interests include football (player/manager Braintree and Bocking United FC), cricket (wicket-keeper, batsman, Redbridge Parks CC), sports generally, crosswords.

CIRELL, Stephen
Eversheds, Leeds
(0113) 243 0391
stephencirell@eversheds.com
Specialisation: Partner in National Local Government Group. Principal area of practice covers public sector advice and administrative laws, Best Value, major commercial transactions such as under the Private Finance Initiative, partnership outsourcing and public sector contracting generally. Lectures frequently on local government law and related matters for commercial course organisers, professional organisations, local authorities and in-house.
Prof. Memberships: Law Society.
Career: Qualified 1984 while with Stockport MBC. Assistant Solicitor, then Principal Solicitor with Dudley MBC 1984-88, then Head of Common Law/Assistant Director at Leeds City Council 1988-93. Joined *Eversheds Hepworth & Chadwick* as a Partner in the Local Government Group in October 1993.
Publications: Co-author of 'CCT- Law & Practice' (FT 1990), 'Municipal Trading' (FT 1992), 'Competitive Tendering for Professional Services' (FT 1994), 'Private Finance Initiative for Local Authorities' (FT 1997) 'Best Value: Law and Practice' (Sweet & Maxwell 1999), and 'E Government, Best Value and the Law' (SOCITM 2001). Specialist editor to 'Encyclopaedia of Local Government Law'. Specialist correspondent to the 'Local Government Chronicle' and author of numerous articles for professional publications.
Personal: Born 3 July 1960. Attended University College of Wales Aberystwyth 1978-81. Leisure pursuits include motorcycling and golf. Lives in Leeds.

COLE, Alun
Morgan Cole, Cardiff
(029) 2038 5385

COOK, Mark
Anthony Collins Solicitors, Birmingham
(0121) 212 7472
mark.cook@anthonycollinssolicitors.com
Specialisation: Partner heading the Best Value Projects Group at *Anthony Collins Solicitors*. Public sector commercial lawyer, with particular experience of 'public/private partnerships' in the local government, regeneration, NHS and education sectors. Advising principally upon service delivery, strategic procurements, facilities management and the Private Finance Initiative, with considerable involvement in EC public procurement, UK competitive tendering legislation and vires issues, along with Best Value.
Prof. Memberships: Law Society.
Career: Joined *Anthony Collins* in 1997. Prior to that worked with *Pinsent Curtis* where he was extensively involved in local government work. Contributor to Butterworths 'Best Value Manual' and 'Joseph Rowntree Foundation Report' "Community Benefits in Contracts", Member of legal and technical team of ODPM Strategic Partnering Taskforce for local authorities.
Personal: Leisure interests: World music, real ale, football and walking. Married with two children. Chair of Aston Law Centre. Trustee of Lawyers' Christian Fellowship.

COWEN, Léonie
Léonie Cowen & Associates, London
(020) 7604 5870
leonie.cowen@lcowen.co.uk
Specialisation: Local Authority professional work and consultancy, especially public private partnerships, companies, joint ventures, PFI, project finance, Best Value and quality, high level sensitive investigations and inquiries, social services, education, employment and public procurement. Has advised over 100 local authorities. Recent projects include advising WS Atkins in the externalisation of Southwark's education services, acting for Southwark in the transfer of their residential homes to Anchor Trust, advising Barking & Dagenham on a homes re-provisioning programme and developing standard form social services procurement contracts, Mile End Park (an acclaimed multi-million pound Millenium project), transfers of leisure services for Hertsmere, Dover, Ellesmere Port, Hounslow (a first for libraries) and others, a PPP for a new theatre in North Wales and externalising Enfield's theatre, acting for school governors in PFI projects, advising on museums in Basingstoke, Grimsby and elsewhere, community-led social and economic regeneration companies. Regular speaker at conferences and seminars.
Prof. Memberships: Law Society, Association of District Solicitors, Charity Law Association, Education Law Association.
Career: 15 years in local government, latterly as Chief Solicitor to Barnet and Director of Law & Administration/ Deputy Chief Executive at Camden. Founded her own practice in 1989.
Personal: Born 1950. Leisure interests include music and her family.

CURNOW, Tony
Ashurst Morris Crisp, London
(020) 7638 1111
See under Planning, p.650

DOBSON, Nicholas
Pinsent Curtis Biddle, Leeds
(0113) 244 5000
nicholas.dobson@pinsents.com
Specialisation: National Head of Local Government Law and Partner. Advises on local authority law, audit issues, constitutional and administrative law, Best Value, TUPE and local government modernisation generally. Advises local authorities and others (public and private).
Prof. Memberships: Association of Council Secretaries and Solicitors.
Career: Qualified in 1984 (also qualified in teaching and social work). Has worked as a lawyer with six local authorities. In 1999 left Doncaster MBC (Chief Solicitor). 1999 *Pinsent Curtis*, Partner.
Publications: Writes and lectures extensively on local government law (eg 'Journal of Local Government Law'). Books: 'Best Value: Law and Management' (Jordan Publishing Limited June 2000); TUPE, 'Contracting-Out' and 'Best Value' (Sweet and Maxwell, December 1998).

DOOLITTLE, Ian
Trowers & Hamlins, London
(020) 7423 8000
idoolittle@trowers.com
See under Social Housing, p.762

EVANS, Eric
Eversheds, Cardiff
(029) 2047 1147
Specialisation: Partner in Commercial Property Department and Head of the Projects, Planning and PFI Units. Specialises in all aspects of property law including complex planning obligations, major town centre regeneration/shopping schemes, site assembly, agreements for the construction of major highways associated with developments, public/private sector joint ventures, planning gain, valuations, urban development/regeneration grants and land reclamation. 30 years public sector experience, dealing with all areas of local government. Extensive experience of PFI and led one of the first PFI/PPP deals in Wales, at University Hospital of Wales NHS Trust. Has since advised on numerous deals including Newport Southern Distributor Road, Chepstow Community Hospital, Wiltshire's grouped schools scheme, 'Waste to Energy' scheme at Neath and schemes at Oxford and West Sussex.
Prof. Memberships: Member of Law Society's Planning Panel.
Career: Qualified in 1980. Town Clerk, Borough of Blaenau Gwent (1981-89). Deputy Chief Executive and Legal Advisor, Land Authority for Wales (1989-92). Partner *Eversheds* 1992.
Personal: Director of Silent Valley Waste Services. Lives in Abertillery.

FORGE, Anna
Mayer, Brown, Rowe & Maw, London
(020) 7782 2011
aforge@eu.mayerbrownrowe.com
Specialisation: Partner in the firm's Public Law Group; concentrates on work for local authorities; provides advice on statutory powers and administrative law requirements, local authority finance and interest in companies, compulsory purchase and land disposal, EC and domestic grants, housing matters, local government reorganisation disputes, public procurement, pensions issues relating to local government, statutory transfer schemes and the public and finance law implications of a variety of commercial contracts involving public bodies including PFI contracts, 'partnership' arrangements, best value contracts; redevelopment and regeneration schemes.
Prof. Memberships: Administrative Bar Association.
Career: Qualified 1982. LB Southwark; 1979-89; *Berwin Leighton* 1989-99, Partner 1996; Partner *Rowe & Maw* 1999.
Personal: Born 1951. Leisure interests include ballet, theatre, travel, reading. Two children. Lives in Hove.

GRIFFITHS, Trevor
Sharpe Pritchard, London
(020) 7405 4600

LOCAL GOVERNMENT ■ THE LEADERS

Specialisation: Partner specialising in judicial review, statutory and planning appeals, in the Administrative Court, conducts appeals to Court of Appeal and House of Lords. In addition deals with assessment of costs and environmental and planning injunction work.
Career: Joined *Sharpe Pritchard* in 1982, qualified in 1984 and became a partner in 1987.
Personal: Born 6 December 1957. Educated at Bishop Wordsworth School 1969-76 and UWIST 1976-79. Recreations include golf and cricket. Lives in London.

HAND, Catherine
Jenkins & Hand, London
(020) 7222 5002

ILEY, Malcolm
Nabarro Nathanson, London
(020) 7524 6909
m.iley@nabarro.com
Specialisation: Main practice area in public law relating to local government, central government departments and increasingly the private sector on public sector issues generally. Experience in public sector outsourcings, asset transfer, regeneration, compulsory purchase, planning, education, competition and PFI, including the consideration of wider European involvement. Currently advising on one of the first 'best value' partnership joint venture pathfinder projects in LEA outsourcings, and PFI Housing, Waste and Accommodation projects. Clients have included London boroughs, district and county councils, government departments, local authority related companies, higher and further education, LAWDAC and urban development corporations. Media advisor and broadcaster on public sector legal and commercial issues. Contributor to the public sector press.
Career: Qualified in 1976. Began career in the private sector, transferred to local government and later became a senior lawyer with Leeds City Council. Appointed City Solicitor and Deputy Chief Executive for Plymouth City Council. Held other senior posts in Lancashire, Sussex and Norfolk. Joined *Nabarro Nathanson* in 1997 as a partner and Head of the Public Sector Group.
Personal: Born 12 April 1950. College Governor. F.E. Governor, company director, advisor to DTLR and government on public/private partnerships.

KEITH-LUCAS, Peter
Wragge & Co, Birmingham
(0870) 903 1000

KILDUFF, David
Walker Morris, Leeds
(0113) 283 2500
Specialisation: All aspects of public administrative law including powers, joint ventures, audit law, procurement and commercial contracts under best value and PPP. Leads an innovative Human Rights Advisory Service for public bodies and advises the Institute of Waste Management on best value. Substantial major projects experience across the public sector in local government, education, Government Department and health. Current appointments include a number of high and innovative regeneration highways, accommodation and IT projects.
Prof. Memberships: Law Society: Former member of the specialist Law Society Planning Panel.
Career: Training: Calderdale MBC; Qualified in 1982. Appointments include Assistant Chief Solicitor Stockton on Tees, Deputy Secretary Ashford Borough Council then Borough Secretary and Solicitor 1988-95. Former secretary and honorary legal advisor to the Kent Association of District Councils. Joined *Walker Morris* as Head of Public Sector & PFI in May 1999 from *Eversheds*.
Personal: Born 26 July 1958. Attended the University of Kent. Married with three children. Lives in Shipley.

KNOX, Martin
Anthony Collins Solicitors, Birmingham
(0121) 212 7450
martin.knox@anthonycollinssolicitors.com
See under Social Housing, p.764

MATTHEW, Stephen
Eversheds, Nottingham
(0115) 950 7000
See under Projects/PFI, p.697

RANDALL, Helen
Nabarro Nathanson, London
(020) 7524 6665
h.randall@nabarro.com
Specialisation: Main practice area is public private partnerships including PFI and local government outsourcings acting for both public and private sector clients. Experience in closing PFI pathfinders and firsts and has led teams of innovative best value partnerships in education, libraries, waste, ICT and housing, as well as regeneration and planning. Particular experience in European public procurement especially use of the negotiated procedure. Clients have included London Boroughs, government department, unitary, county and district councils and private sector service providers and funders.
Career: Qualified in 1991. Began career at a City firm, transferred to local government and joined *Nabarro Nathanson* in 1996 and was admitted as a partner in 2001.
Publications: Only lawyer member of Sir Ian Byatt's Procurement Review Taskforce; co-author of Butterworth's 'Guide to the Local Government Act 1999'; contributor to IPPR's 'Report on Public Private Partnerships'; Sweet and Maxwell's 'Outsourcing Practice Manual'; the 'New Local Government Network's' reports – 'Achieving Best Value' and 'Strategic Partnerships'. Helen writes a column on procurement for 'Municipal Journal' and is a regular speaker at national conferences.
Personal: 14 May 1962. Non-executive director of New Local Government Network.

RANDALL, Simon
Lawrence Graham, London
(020) 7379 0000

SERRELLI, Roseanne
Sharpe Pritchard, London
(020) 7405 4600
rserrelli@sharpepritchard.co.uk
Specialisation: All areas of public sector contracting but especially public/private partnerships and PFI. Particular specialities – waste management, social services PFI, leisure provision, information technology procurement, schools PFI and housing regeneration.
Prof. Memberships: Law Society.
Career: Articles *Sharpe Pritchard* 1992-94. Partner *Sharpe Pritchard* 1997.
Publications: Lectures: PFI standardisation documents, waste management, IT contracts and case law.
Personal: Ursuline School; New Hall, Cambridge.

SHARLAND, John
Sharpe Pritchard, London
(020) 7405 4600
jsharland@sharpepritchard.co.uk
Specialisation: Partner specialising in local government law including advice on local authority powers, local government finance, public sector contracting, housing regeneration, town and country planning.
Prof. Memberships: Law Society.
Publications: TUPE and the 'Acquired Rights Directive' (co-editor) 1996. 'A Practical Approach to Local Government Law', Blackstones 1997. Articles in various publications. Lectures and presentations to seminars and conferences.
Personal: Educated Dulwich College, LSE, City of London Polytechnic. Leisure interests include history of art and architecture, swimming, walking and theatre.

SHAW, Kate
Simpson & Marwick, Edinburgh
(0131) 557 1545
kate.shaw@simpmar.com
See under Administrative & Public Law, p.49

STEPHENS, Hugo
Pinsent Curtis Biddle, Birmingham
(0121) 212 1828
hugo.stephens@pinsents.com
See under Social Housing, p.765

WILLIAMS, Huw
Edwards Geldard, Cardiff
(029) 2023 8239
huw.williams@geldards.co.uk
See under Administrative & Public Law, p.49

MEDIA & ENTERTAINMENT

London: 579; The Regions: 586; Scotland: 586; Profiles: 587

Research approved by BMRB For this edition, **Chambers'** researchers conducted 6,582 interviews – 3,900 with law firms, 511 with barristers and 2,171 with clients. The validity of the research was scrutinised by BMRB International, who audited both the methodology and the results at our offices in London. They interviewed **Chambers'** researchers and cross-checked sample interviews. Details of the audit appear on page 7.

OVERVIEW This year has seen the musician triumph over the record company, with Bruce Springsteen winning his copyright case against Masquerade Music, which was attempting to release some of his early recordings against his wishes. It has also seen the proposed IPO of theatre *share* plc, an innovative new way of financing theatrical productions. In the publishing world, the copyright infringement and passing off claims of the Estate of James Joyce against Macmillan over the newly edited *Ulysses* have captured the headlines, while September 11th has resulted in film finance litigation between insurers/reinsurers and film financiers that is likely to run for some time.

LONDON

FILM FINANCE / FILM & TV PRODUCTION / BROADCASTING

MEDIA & ENTERTAINMENT: FILM FINANCE — LONDON

1. Richards Butler
   SJ Berwin
2. Davenport Lyons
   Denton Wilde Sapte
   Olswang
3. The Simkins Partnership
   Theodore Goddard

MEDIA & ENTERTAINMENT: FILM & TV PRODUCTION — LONDON

1. Olswang
2. Harbottle & Lewis
   Lee & Thompson
   Theodore Goddard
3. Davenport Lyons
   Richards Butler
   The Simkins Partnership
4. Denton Wilde Sapte
   Harrison Curtis
   Simons Muirhead & Burton
   SJ Berwin

This book is the product of 6,582 1/2 hour interviews. See p.7 for BMRB audit. Within each band, firms are listed alphabetically.

RICHARDS BUTLER (see firm details p.1112) "*Superb all-round entertainment lawyers,*" this team is the first port of call for many banks due to its expertise in "*real film finance work and excellent international contacts.*" Particularly adept at gap financing, it has a superb reputation for acting for lessors in sale and leaseback deals. The "*professor-like, lawyer's lawyer*" **Richard Philipps** (see p.591) is in many people's eyes the "*clear leader in this field,*" and has recently been visible advising N1 European Film Produktions on a complex re-financing arrangement for 'Sin Eater' starring Heath Ledger. **Michael Maxtone-Smith** (see p.589) is renowned amongst peers for being "*great in times of crisis.*" He recently assisted Cobalt Media Group in concluding two slate deals with German tax funds. Felt to be increasing its production capability, the firm boasts the expertise of **Barry Smith** (see p.591), who was praised as "*media-savvy with the knowledge to back it up,*" and recently assisted with the production work on 'Gosford Park'. A well-known player on the regulatory side of broadcasting, **Stephen Edwards** (see p.588) acted for BBC Worldwide on the supply of BBC 1 and BBC2 to BSkyB. **Clients** NatWest; DZ Bank; Channel 4; MTV; BBC.

SJ BERWIN (see firm details p.867) A "*stellar team, very good with banks,*" it is perceived by industry sources as a leading firm for sale and leaseback, and co-production work. **Nigel Palmer** (see p.590) was described as a "*finance guru: formidable, yet painstaking.*" He represented Société Générale on the pre-sale commitment for Woody Allen's 2002 project. Experienced in representing financing distributors, **Tim Johnson** (see p.589) ("*ahead of the game*") acted for Alliance Atlantis on the financing of 'Double Down'. **Peter McInerney** (see p.589) is highly regarded by producers for his format protection work, most recently for the 'Popstars' programme. Within the broadcasting field, interviewees highlighted the team's competition expertise. It recently advised mm02 on the content licensing of its Genie WAP internet services. **Clients** MGM/UA; Dexia Banque; Channel 4; The Jim Henson Company; Société Européenne des Satellites.

DAVENPORT LYONS (see firm details p.927) The firm is favoured by banks for finance work, and possesses particular expertise in gap financing. **Leon Morgan** (see p.590) was described by one industry expert as "*one of the best media lawyers in London; he will tell you how it is.*" He has been busy advising the Royal Bank of Scotland on the risk-managed gap financing of '24 Hour Party People'. **Sam Tatton-Brown** (see p.592) "*will be a major player,*" according to market sources, and was recently visible representing Barclays on the financing of 'A Christmas Carol', featuring Simon Callow. Gaining a name for international co-productions, the team structured a UK/Italian co-production of 'Hotel', directed by Mike Figgis and starring John Malkovich. **Richard Moxon** (see p.590) "*knows his way round the deals,*" and has represented UK production company Studio Eight on co-productions with its Canadian partners. With strength in the traditional areas of broadcasting, the team acts for Radio Investments Group, most recently on the sale of its interest in Brighton & Hove's 'Surf' Radio to Forever Broadcasting. **Clients** Barclays Bank; Coutts & Co; Entertainment Rights; GMG Radio Holdings; SKA Films.

DENTON WILDE SAPTE (see firm details p.935) Rapidly becoming "*the first port of call for sale and leaseback work,*" for certain US clients, its "*thrusting style*" has attracted many warm recommendations. **Ken Dearsley** (see p.588) has been lauded by clients as "*streets ahead of other individuals,*" and is gaining a high profile for his work for US studios, while **Chris Hanson** (see p.589) gains market recognition for, *inter alia*, advising Coutts & Co on the financing of 'Swept Away', starring Madonna. Production work has included advice to Jamie Oliver on the creation of his new production company. The jewel in the crown of the media practice, however, is its broadcasting expertise, which competitors admire for its "*all-round strength, particularly on the competition aspects.*" **Michael Ridley** (see p.591) was recommended to researchers for his expertise in television work, and advised Discovery Communications on its wholly owned channels and joint ventures with BSkyB and the BBC. **Nick West** (see p.592) enters the tables following a raft of recommendations from lawyers and industry experts. He "*knows the business, particularly rights agreements,*" according to competitors, and has advised the FA Premier League on the exploitation of various rights, including international audio-visual and mobile rights. **Clients** Universal Studios; Paramount Pictures; ITV Network; Pearson Television; Royal Bank of Canada.

OLSWANG (see firm details p.1087) A "*focused, creative team*" to whom production clients turn "*for advice on crucial aspects of the business,*" its roll-call of top-class instructions includes acting for SKA Films on the production of 'Swept Away', directed by Guy Ritchie and starring

www.ChambersandPartners.com

MEDIA & ENTERTAINMENT ■ LONDON

LEADING INDIVIDUALS: FILM FINANCE/FILM & TV PRODUCTION

1
- **PALMER Nigel** SJ Berwin
- **PHILIPPS Richard** Richards Butler

2
- **ANTONIADES Reno** Lee & Thompson
- **BERGER Jonathan** Theodore Goddard
- **DEARSLEY Ken** Denton Wilde Sapte
- **DEVEREUX Mark** Olswang
- **JOHNSON Tim** SJ Berwin
- **MORGAN Leon** Davenport Lyons
- **SAVILL Lisbeth** Olswang

3
- **GOSTYN Antony** The Simkins Partnership
- **HURT Jacqueline** Olswang
- **JONES Medwyn** Harbottle & Lewis
- **MAXTONE-SMITH Michael** Richards Butler
- **MOORE Charles** Olswang
- **STORER Robert** Harbottle & Lewis

4
- **BENNETT Nigel** The Simkins Partnership
- **CURTIS Tim** Harrison Curtis
- **GAWADE Jeremy** Lee & Thompson
- **GOLDBERG Simon** Simons Muirhead & Burton
- **HANSON Christopher** Denton Wilde Sapte
- **LOM Nicholas** Simons Muirhead & Burton
- **MCINERNEY Peter** SJ Berwin
- **MOXON Richard** Davenport Lyons
- **PAYNE Abigail** Harbottle & Lewis
- **SMITH Barry** Richards Butler

UP AND COMING
- **BLAIR Jonathan** Theodore Goddard
- **TATTON-BROWN Sam** Davenport Lyons

See individuals' profiles p.587

Madonna. Expert in the complete range of production work, it has also been advising HBO on its deal with British Equity to engage Equity members on HBO films, including 'Conspiracy'. **Mark Devereux** (see p.588) was described by competitors as "*seasoned and civilised; he has done it all.*" **Charles Moore** (see p.590) is renowned for his enviable Hollywood film work, while **Lisbeth Savill** (see p.591), "*a tough negotiator*," acted for Fox Searchlight on the co-production financing of Jim Sheridan's 'East of Harlem'. **Jackie Hurt** (see p.589) has been singled out by market sources, not only for her cerebral qualities, but for being "*keen to do well for her clients.*" On the broadcasting side, the team retains poll position, and is lauded by clients for its ability to "*immediately see the key issues.*" **David Zeffman** (see p.592) is considered a "*sharp, intelligent player.*" He gained praise from peers for his work on the acquisition of the media rights to British horse racing for Channel 4 and the at the races consortium. **Selina Potter** (see p.591) also continues to garner recommendations for her broadcasting expertise. **Clients** Miramax; Buena Vista International; Icon Productions; Canal +; MTV Europe; Sony Pictures.

THE SIMKINS PARTNERSHIP (see firm details p.1136) A firm boasting clients from across the media spectrum, from talent to large film studios, it is well regarded for high-profile financing and production work, including projects like the feature film 'Iris'. "*Technically astute*" **Antony Gostyn** (see p.588) led the team acting for the production company, Fox Iris, responsible for producing and financing the film, and dealing with the human rights issues surrounding the depiction of living people. The firm also represented The Film Consortium on the Anglo-Canadian production '51st State'. **Nigel Bennett** (see p.587) is well regarded by peers for his expertise in film work, in particular for his representation of talent. Broadcasting work has included advising the ITV network on broadcasting Champions League football matches. **Clients** US studios; Coutts & Co; Ingenious Media; The Film Consortium; Channel 4 Television.

THEODORE GODDARD (see firm details p.1158) The team is felt by peers to undertake "*legitimate production work,*" and is viewed by some clients as "*the best for film production work.*" **Jonathan Berger** (see p.587) was recommended to researchers for his ability to conceptualise deals for an independent client base, including Renaissance Films, whom he recently assisted with 'Safety of Objects'. **Jonathan Blair** (see p.587) moves into the up-and-coming category, receiving praise for his work for Pacificus Films and Big Fish Films on 'Before You Go'. Also seen on film finance work, the team has advised on over 40 sale and lease-back transactions for producers and financiers. **Clients** DNA Films; Royal Bank of Scotland; Universal Studios; Cloud 9 Screen Entertainment; Andell Entertainment.

HARBOTTLE & LEWIS (see firm details p.983) An important player in the production arena, it is renowned for a high-quality independent client base. Although less visible this year, **Bob Storer** (see p.592) is respected in the field for his diverse workload, ranging from production and finance advice for Fragile Film's 'The Importance of Being Earnest', to advising 19 Management on film and television projects for S Club 7. **Medwyn Jones** (see p.589) is highly rated for his knowledge, experience and client relation abilities, while **Abigail Payne** (see p.591) is commended for her hard-working approach. The team acted for Ecosse Films on the financing and production of 'Charlotte Gray'. On the broadcasting side, the firm is recommended for its work on internet rights, and recently advised on a joint venture between Chrysalis Holdings, Capital Radio, UBC Media Group, GMG Radio Holdings and Trafficlink (UK) on the start-up of a new company, Digital News Network. **Clients** Merchant Ivory Productions; Tiger Aspect Films; Talkback Productions; CNBC; International Sportsworld Communicators.

LEE & THOMPSON A high-profile production practice, it is singled out for its sizeable spread of clients and co-production expertise. On the film side, the department has worked on major feature films such as 'Bend It Like Beckham', and has seen an increase in work for talent-led production companies such as Michael Winterbottom's Revolution Films. Independent television drama production is another string to the firm's bow. It has advised Red Productions on projects including 'Clocking Off', and is newly instructed by Elisabeth Murdoch's Shine. Animation work also continues to thrive, with

High-profile Media Cases

Parties	Lawyers	Significance
The Football League v Carlton/Granada	The Football League – Lawrence Graham Carlton/Granada – Slaughter and May	A crucial case of the last year, relating to whether the two broadcasters owed monies left outstanding by the collapse of their company ITV Digital. The Football League claimed they were owed £131 million, but their claim was described by the judge as failing at the "*first and fundamental*" hurdle.
Eddie Irvine v Talksport	Talksport – Rosenblatt (superseded Olswang) Eddie Irving – Fladgate Fielder	The case concerned the use of implied celebrity endorsements in advertisements. Talksport sent out a publicity brochure including a picture of Eddie Irvine, doctored to look like an advert for the station. Mr. Irvine won, after the judge ruled it satisfied the requirements of a 'passing off' claim.
Aprilla v Spice Girls Limited (appeal)	The Spice Girls – Lee & Thompson	Appeal launched following earlier ruling that the Spice Girls had misled their sponsor. Ruling upheld.
Ludlow Music v Robbie Williams, BMG, EMI	Robbie Williams/BMG/EMI – Harbottle & Lewis Ludlow Music – Sheridans	Ludlow Music sued Robbie Williams over claims that one of his songs infringed the copyright of a Woody Guthrie song on their catalogue. Their claim was successful.
Bruce Springsteen v Masquerade Music	Bruce Springsteen – Hamlins	The House of Lords refused to let the record company appeal over earlier ruling concerning ownership of recordings.

LONDON — MEDIA & ENTERTAINMENT

MEDIA & ENTERTAINMENT: BROADCASTING
LONDON

1
- Denton Wilde Sapte
- Olswang

2
- Ashurst Morris Crisp
- Clifford Chance

3
- Goodman Derrick
- Wiggin & Co

4
- Allen & Overy
- DJ Freeman
- Davenport Lyons
- Field Fisher Waterhouse
- Harbottle & Lewis
- Herbert Smith
- Richards Butler
- SJ Berwin
- The Simkins Partnership

5
- Lovells
- Travers Smith Braithwaite

LEADING INDIVIDUALS: BROADCASTING

1
- GHEE Tony Ashurst Morris Crisp
- JAMES Sean Wiggin & Co
- ZEFFMAN David Olswang

2
- EDWARDS Stephen Richards Butler
- RIDLEY Michael Denton Wilde Sapte
- SANDELSON Daniel Clifford Chance

3
- BALLARD Tony Field Fisher Waterhouse
- SWAFFER Patrick Goodman Derrick
- WEST Nick Denton Wilde Sapte

UP AND COMING
- POTTER Selina Olswang

This book is the product of 6,582 1/2 hour interviews. See p.7 for BMRB audit. Within each band, firms are listed alphabetically. See individuals' profiles p.587

productions such as 'Bounty Hamster', a 26-part series for ITV. A key player in the production world, **Reno Antoniades** is praised for his "*no-nonsense approach,*" while **Jeremy Gawade** also gains his share of peer approval. **Clients** Box TV; Kudos Productions; Footprint Films; Lolafilms; Peafur Productions.

HARRISON CURTIS (see firm details p.987) Though a small outfit, the quality and volume of its work belies its size. **Tim Curtis** was described by peers as "*bright without being flashy – a fine lawyer.*" He has led the team on such projects as the contractual arrangements for the child actors involved in 'Harry Potter & the Philosopher's Stone'. The group has also advised the National Film Trustee Corporation on its role in the financing of many of the year's celebrated films, including 'Iris' and 'Gosford Park'. The practice boasts a wide variety of independent television production clients, including Blakeway Productions, a major documentary maker, which produced 'The Queen's Life' for the Golden Jubilee. **Clients** The Film Council; Zone Vision Enterprises; RDF Television; 4Learning.

SIMONS MUIRHEAD & BURTON (see firm details p.1137) This firm has made a big impact upon the market since acquiring the "*experienced*" Nicholas Lom (see p.589). Commentators describe him as "*good in times of crisis.*" The team, which is admired by peers for its "*long-term approach,*" is led by the "*indispensible*" Simon Goldberg (see p.588), to whom clients turn on difficult deals; "*he is user-friendly for the other side while getting the best deal for me.*" The department has acted for Natural Nylon Entertainment on its production of the film 'Cromwell & Fairfax', and for Union Pictures on its new BBC television series 'Rockface'. **Clients** Natural Nylon; Autonomous; Richard Jobson; Union Pictures; Brook Lapping.

ASHURST MORRIS CRISP (see firm details p.852) Known in the market as "*a focused team, with fantastic regulatory expertise,*" it fields "*solution-oriented, commercial expert*" Tony Ghee (see p.588). With a spread of large corporate and independent clients, the team has been involved in various media rights deals, including representing Kirch Media on the sale of media rights for the 2002 and 2006 World Cups, and advising on its complaint to the OFT concerning the joint bidding position of ITV and the BBC. On the corporate side, it has recently acted for United Business Media on the shareholder negotiations with RTL concerning Channel 5. **Clients** TV Danmark1; UPC Media; Kingston Communications; Fox New s Networks.

CLIFFORD CHANCE (see firm details p.911) Particularly noted for banking and regulatory expertise, this pan-European team "*always gets the deal done.*" The "*specialist*" Daniel Sandelson (see p.591) "*runs an impressive ship.*"

GOODMAN DERRICK (see firm details p.973) Renowned for its ability to compete with the top firms, this team possesses a core of traditional media clients, many of whom it has helped with the transition into the digital age. It has advised ITV, Channel 4, Channel 5 and S4C on various digital broadcasting arrangements. The team, which includes "*formidable player*" Patrick Swaffer (see p.592), boasts expertise in a range of work from commercial and regulatory issues to clearance and litigation work for programme makers and broadcasters. It continues to advise the BBFC on film and video classification issues. **Clients** ITV; Channel 4; Channel 5; BBFC.

WIGGIN & CO (see firm details p.1186) The firm is well known in the market for its media and IT practice, in comparison to its rivals. It boasts a "*focused, City-calibre approach*" according to peers who commend its style and expertise, in particular for cable and satellite projects. Clients single out **Sean James** (see p.589), who they describe as "*commercial and experienced ; he doesn't over-lawyer things.*" He acted for UKTV on the liquidation of ITV Digital. **Clients** Flextech; SBS; Super 12 Racing; Granada; EMAP.

ALLEN & OVERY (see firm details p.841) With a growing presence for corporate work, the firm's pan-European capability is said by clients to give it a real advantage. The London media team is headed by Sasha Haines and John Wotton, whose particular strength is felt to lie in regulatory work. A highlight of the past year has been representing News Group on its disposal of Fox Family Worldwide to Walt Disney for £3.7 billion. It has also advised BT and United Business Media on the sale of their jointly owned portal and internet service provider,

TOP IN-HOUSE LAWYERS

TELEVISION

Martin BAKER, Commercial Director, Content, Carlton Television

Deanna BATES, Head of Legal, BSkyB

Colin CAMPBELL, Director of Legal and Business Affairs, Channel 5 Broadcasting

Antonia DOWNEY, Head of Legal UK, Jim Henson Company

Svenja GEISSMAR, Senior Vice President, Corporate Business Affairs & General Counsel, MTV

Simon JOHNSON, Director of Rights and Business Affairs, ITV

Sarah TINGAY, Director of Legal and Business Affairs, FremantleMedia

Kathryn WILLIAMS, Senior Business Affairs, Channel 4

Simon Johnson possesses "*good commercial knowledge and a strong understanding of legal aims.*" **Sarah Tingay**, **Martin Baker** and **Colin Campbell** are recognised, in particular for their "*extensive experience*" in the sector. **Deanna Bates** and **Svenja Geissmar** are commended for their excellent technical acumen, and **Antonia Downey** and **Kathryn Williams** are included in the list for their "*vast commercial knowledge.*"

FILM

Andrew HILDEBRAND, Director of Business Affairs, FilmFour

Cameron McCRACKEN, Deputy Managing Director, Pathé UK

Angela MORRISON, Chief Operating Officer, Working Title Films

Mark PYBUS, Head of Business Affairs, Company Pictures

Sheeraz SHAH, Head of Legal and Business Affairs, Working Title Films

James SHIRRAS, Head of Business and Legal Affairs, Film Finances

The Working Title Films team receives strong recommendations, with **Angela Morrison** *and* **Sheeraz Shah** *receiving particular praise for their "efficiency."* **Mark Pybus** *and* **Cameron McCracken** *are commended for being "easy to work with" and "innovative," while* **James Shirras** *and* **Andrew Hildebrand** *command respect for their "commercial awareness."*

In-house lawyers' profiles p.1201

MEDIA & ENTERTAINMENT ■ LONDON

LineOne , to Tiscali. **Clients** Bell Media (Canada) ; MTV; Radio Authority; Twentieth Century Fox.

DJ FREEMAN (see firm details p.939) Best known for its expertise on the traditional side of broadcasting, the team, led by Tony Leifer, acted recently on the demerger and flotation of Pilat Media Global, a provider of software to the broadcasting industry. Further highlights of the year have included acting for Xtreme Information Services on the sale of Xtreme Information Group for £37 millon. **Clients** Airstream Film; Working Title Televison; Itinerant Films; Four Ventures; Strange Dog.

FIELD FISHER WATERHOUSE (see firm details p.954) "Pushing the boundaries of media work," this practice is involved in cutting-edge new media transactions, such as Ordnance Survey's new digital database, MasterMap, and location-based services with mobile phone operators. The team has also been acting for Quadriga on the launch of Genesis, an on-demand digital entertainment and communications system for hotel guests and hoteliers. The "*intellectual*" Tony Ballard (see p.587) had a lower market profile this year. **Clients** BBC; Channel 4; Television Monitoring Services; SSVC.

HERBERT SMITH (see firm details p.992) Prized by its clients, the firm's corporate expertise is felt to ensure it an enviable position on the transactional side of the sector, especially when taken together with its competition and litigation prowess. Stephen Wilkinson heads the group which, together with Cravath, Swaine & Moore, advised Time in its £1.15 billion acquisition of UK consumer magazine publisher IPC Media. On the contentious side, the department advised SMG on the termination of its arrangements with Chris Evans. Clients : AOL Time Warner; B S kyB; Trinity Mirror; Granada.

LOVELLS (see firm details p.1045) Recognised for its "*fine corporate client base,* " the team, which includes Lindy Golding, is best known in the market for its work for Granada, which it recently advised in negotiating the agreement for the broadcast of a new motor racing championship. A place on the BBC panel has led to advice on digital cable carriage, involving conditional access systems and electronic programme guides. The client base is not limited to corporate clients, however, and the team is representing the Radiocommunications Agency in ongoing advice concerning the disposal of the 40 GHz band spectrum. **Clients** Granada; BBC; Saga Group; Skandia Media Invest.

TRAVERS SMITH BRAITHWAITE (see firm details p.1166) Perceived by competitors to have had "*a fantastic run with NTL,* " corporate work remains the mainstay of the practice. The team has advised NTL on various transactions, including its internet joint ventures with Glasgow Rangers, Leicester City and Middlesbrough. Now attempting to broaden its client base in the wake of NTL's decision to file for US bankruptcy, the team has been assisting Channel 5 on its shareholding and management structure. **Clients** NTL; Premium TV; Pace Micro T echnology.

LONDON   PUBLISHING

MEDIA & ENTERTAINMENT: PUBLISHING
■ LONDON

1. **Denton Wilde Sapte**
2. **Taylor Wessing**
   The Simkins Partnership
3. **Finers Stephens Innocent**
   Harbottle & Lewis
   Lovells

LEADING INDIVIDUALS

1. **WILLIAMS Alan** Denton Wilde Sapte
2. **MITCHELL Paul** Taylor Wessing
   NYMAN Bernard B M Nyman & Co
3. **KAYE Laurence** Laurence Kaye
   RUBINSTEIN John Manches
   SOLOMON Nicola Finers Stephens Innocent

This book is the product of 6,582 1/2 hour interviews. See p.7 for BMRB audit. Within each band, firms are listed alphabetically. See individuals' profiles p.587

DENTON WILDE SAPTE (see firm details p.935) "*The top for publishing and internet work,*" according to many rivals, the firm is felt to be keeping up with the times, while retaining "*superb copyright expertise.*" It recently acted for Macmillan on High Court litigation concerning claims of copyright infringement and passing off surrounding the newly edited *Ulysses*. "*The best publishing lawyer around,*" according to clients, **Alan Williams** (see p.592) acted for The Society of Authors on the successful recovery of the domain names of leading authors, including Louis de Bernières and Margaret Drabble, in a dispute heard by a panel of the World Intellectual Property Organi zation. **Clients** Macmillan; Random House; Copyright Licensing Agency; FT Magazines; Yale University Publications.

TAYLOR WESSING (see firm details p.1156) Highly regarded for the contractual side of publishing work, the team is felt to benefit from a strong technology presence which its recent merger can only improve. "*Knowledgeable*" **Paul Mitchell** (see p.590) leads the team, which recently advised the Design & Artists ' Copyright Society on its arrangements with the Copyright Licensing Agency and the Newspaper Licensing Agency. On the contentious side, the team has acted for Associated Newspapers on various libel actions. **Clients** Macmillan; Oxford University Press; HarperCollins; Condé Nast; Dahl & Dahl.

THE SIMKINS PARTNERSHIP (see firm details p.1136) This team was described by one client as "*red-hot; it really knows the publishing world.*" Headed by the experienced Julian Turton, it has provided pre-publication advice to IFG in connection with publications including *Viz* , *Fortean Times* and *Bizarre*. The team also advised the group of photographers engaged by Getty Images on their standard form agreements. **Clients** Everyman; The Association of Photographers; Alex Garland; Gillon Aitken Associates; Aurum Press.

FINERS STEPHENS INNOCENT (see firm details p.955) An "*efficient outfit,*" it has a reputation for celebrity clients and defamation work. **Nicola Solomon** (see p.592) is praised by clients as "*pragmatic and to the point.*" She recently advised Turnaround Books regarding the publication of Ian Brady's book on serial murderers. A growth area for the team has been electronic publishing within the academic field, including advising the LSE on electronic and database rights, alongside copyright and defamation in journals and e-mail. **Clients** Anthea Turner; The Society of Authors; Time Magazine; Arcadia Books.

HARBOTTLE & LEWIS (see firm details p.983) A respected firm, its market profile has been boosted by highly visible work such as representing Helen Fielding on the syndication of *Bridget Jones's Diary* , including acting on the rights for the Comic Relief book and recovering the domain name from cybersquatters. On the transactional side, the team, led by Rachel Atkins, recently advised Chrysalis Books on its £2 million takeover of C&B Publishing. **Clients** Penguin Books; Comic Relief; Sue Townsend; The Los Angeles Times.

LONDON — MEDIA & ENTERTAINMENT

LOVELLS (see firm details p.1045) An important presence in the market, it recently advised MGN on a Court of Appeal case relating to a competition run in certain Trinity Mirror newspapers. The team, which includes Michael Golding on print, Lindy Golding on electronic and Jennifer McDermott on newspaper publishing, also advised Trinity Mirror on the acquisition of additional newspaper titles and on its online interests. Another significant client, for whom the team provides defamation and IP advice, alongside general corporate and commercial advice, is the Guardian Media Group. **Clients** Guardian Media Group; Trinity Mirror; Playboy Enterprises.

OTHER NOTABLE PRACTITIONERS Sole practitioner **Bernard Nyman** is regarded by the market as "*a true specialist; vastly experienced,*" while, at Manches, **John Rubinstein** (see p.590) has attracted attention for his work for Condé Nast, and was recommended as "*a great publishing lawyer.*" **Laurence Kaye** (see p.280), now an Oxfordshire-based sole practitioner following the demise of Garretts, is a recognised expert within electronic publishing.

LONDON — MUSIC

MEDIA & ENTERTAINMENT: MUSIC — LONDON

1. Russells
2. Clintons
3. Lee & Thompson
4. Sheridans
   The Simkins Partnership
   Theodore Goddard
5. Bray & Krais
   Harbottle & Lewis
   Mishcon de Reya
6. Davenport Lyons
   Denton Wilde Sapte
   Eversheds
   Hamlins
   Harrison Curtis
   Marriott Harrison
   Searles
   Spraggon Stennett Brabyn

This book is the product of 6,582 1/2 hour interviews. See p.7 for BMRB audit. Within each band, firms are listed alphabetically.

RUSSELLS (see firm details p.1120) Although Clintons is snapping at the firm's heels, the consensus of market opinion is that Russells retains the music crown. Lauded for its "*outstanding pure music expertise,*" it is "*always seen on the high-profile cases,*" and competitors acknowledge that the team "*plays hardball!*" Its unparalleled market position is largely due to the formidable duo of "*doyen of music litigation,*" **Brian Howard**, described as "*aggressive, yet shrewd,*" and **Tony Russell**, singled out by some peers as "*the leading practitioner, a fantastic negotiator and rainmaker.*" "*Star*" **Chris Organ** rises up the tables this year. Competitors and clients appreciate the way "*he gets difficult deals done,*" while "*tough lieutenant*" **Steven Tregear** is admired for his experience in litigation. **Mark Sinnott** also gains his share of market recommendations. **Clients** Major and independent labels; major artists.

CLINTONS (see firm details p.912) Perceived by the market to be closing the gap with Russells, particularly within litigation, the group wins praise from many industry experts, who recognise "*a top-quality, focused team, with a commercial approach.*" For some, "*the best music litigation lawyer in the UK,*" **Andrew Sharland** (see p.591) is recognised for the breadth of his clientele, from major labels to independent talent. A newcomer to the tables, "*tough competitor*" **Jacqueline Brown** (see p.587) acted for Gut Records on a dispute with Don Reedman over the profits from the Tom Jones album 'Reload', managing to settle the dispute on the first day of trial. On the commercial side, the team has been advising on the joint venture between Poptones and Telstar, and on the sale of Cheeky Records to BMG. **Andrew Myers** (see p.590) makes his debut in the tables, following praise from clients for "*always pushing the deal and using plain English.*" **David Landsman** (see p.589) is well known for representing U2. **Clients** Sony; Universal; Ministry of Sound; Stereophonics; Go!Beat.

LEE & THOMPSON A niche entertainment firm, with a team of "*real experts who understand the industry,*" it remains best known for its impressive artist client base, but is starting to break into the corporate market. The team is gaining a profile for litigation prowess, with the "*experienced*" **Gordon Williams** acting for Food Records in its successful and much reported battle with EMI over entitlement to Blur royalties. The "*uncompromising and highly experienced*" **Robert Lee** boasts an enviable client base of artists and managers, and has acted for Queen on download deals with EMI and Hollywood Records. **Robert Horsfall** is also highly regarded by clients, and represents various Scandinavian artists, such as Lene Marlin, while **Andrew Thompson** is best known for his work with the Spice Girls, and remains active on management agreements for Victoria Beckham, Emma Bunton and Melanie Chisholm. **Mike Brookes** and **Sophia Robb** have both been active on copyright disputes, a particular strength of the team. **Clients** Victoria Beckham; Tom Jones; Paul Oakenfold; EMI.

SHERIDANS (see firm details p.1131) This firm enjoys a mix of highprofile contentious and non-contentious work for its broad base of industry clients. The respected and "*reliable*" **Howard Jones** represents an impressive array of artists including ABBA, for whom he has renegotiated recording and publishing contracts. On the commercial side, the team has been involved in setting up and running a number of joint ventures including Riverhouse Records and Ministry of Sound. **Clients** MPL; Diesel Music; Rolling Stones; Kylie Minogue; industry executives.

THE SIMKINS PARTNERSHIP (see firm details p.1136) With strength across the board, the team is applauded by peers for doing "*proper music litigation.*" The rise of **Dominic Free** (see p.588) in the tables is due to his litigation prowess and links with major clients such as EMI. He is praised by industry experts for "*asking the right questions.*" **Julian Turton** (see p.592) represented Bond on major sponsorship and long-term publishing deals. The team has recently grown its profile amongst European artists, and is representing such successes as Italy's Zucchero. **Clients** Universal-Island Records; RAK Publishing; Geri Halliwell; Leftfield; industry executives.

THEODORE GODDARD (see firm details p.1158) Best known for its corporate work, market sources also acknowledge the strength of its artist practice. In this field, the team has recently advised Björk on renegotiating her recording contract with One Little Indian Records. Finance expertise forms another string to the firm's bow, boasting as it does the talents of **Paddy Grafton Green** (see p.589) who is "*second to none in terms of tax.*" The group has been particularly active this year in new media work, and advised EMI records on its online joint venture with Queen Productions. **James Harman** (see p.589) was singled out by interviewees as "*incredibly hard-working and excellent for contracts.*" **Clients** Universal Music; Telstar Records; David Bowie; Sade; Tina Turner.

BRAY & KRAIS Recommended by commentators for its "*high-quality legal advice,*" the team's highest profile figure is **Richard Bray** who rivals acknowledge "*knows how to get a deal done.*" **Clients** Artists.

HARBOTTLE & LEWIS (see firm details p.983) "*A fine set of lawyers,*" the team is well regarded

MEDIA & ENTERTAINMENT ■ LONDON

LEADING INDIVIDUALS

1
- **GRAFTON GREEN Paddy** Theodore Goddard
- **HOWARD Brian** Russells
- **RUSSELL Tony** Russells
- **SHARLAND Andrew** Clintons

2
- **BRAY Richard** Bray & Krais
- **FREE Dominic** The Simkins Partnership
- **GILMORE Laurence** Hamlins
- **GLICK David** Mishcon de Reya
- **HARMAN James** Theodore Goddard
- **LEE Robert** Lee & Thompson
- **ORGAN Chris** Russells
- **TURTON Julian** The Simkins Partnership

3
- **ALLAN Robert** Denton Wilde Sapte
- **HORSFALL Robert** Lee & Thompson
- **JONES Howard** Sheridans
- **THOMPSON Andrew** Lee & Thompson
- **TREGEAR Steven** Russells

4
- **ABRAMSON Lawrence** Harbottle & Lewis
- **BROOKES Mike** Lee & Thompson
- **LANDSMAN David** Clintons
- **SEARLE Helen** Searles
- **SINNOTT Mark** Russells
- **WARE James** Davenport Lyons
- **WILLIAMS Gordon** Lee & Thompson

UP AND COMING
- **BROWN Jacqueline** Clintons
- **MYERS Andrew** Clintons
- **ROBB Sophia** Lee & Thompson

This book is the product of 6,582 1/2 hour interviews. See p.7 for BMRB audit. Within each band, firms are listed alphabetically. See individuals' profiles p.587

in this sphere for its litigation expertise. **Lawrence Abramson** (see p.587) was described to researchers as "*forceful, yet tenacious.*" He successfully concluded an action between EMI, BMG, Robbie Williams and Ludlow Music in February 2002, over the use of lyrics from a 1961 Woody Guthrie song. The team's workload is not confined to litigation, however, and it acted for Chrysalis on the £60 million securitisation of its global music publishing catalogue. **Clients** Robbie Williams; 19 Management; Estate of Eva Cassidy; Gareth Gates; Mushroom Records.

MISHCON DE REYA (see firm details p.1072) With Michael Eaton moving into a consultancy role, the firm was felt by interviewees to have had a slightly lower profile this year. Its best-known figure is now "*heavyweight negotiator*" **David Glick** (see p.588), who is admired throughout the market for his tenacity and "*American style: he will battle hard for his client.*" An impressive roster of artists includes Enya, Craig David and Charlotte Church. On the corporate side, the team recently concluded the sale of Trojan Records to Sanctuary. **Clients** Relentless Records; Eric Clapton; Christina Aguilera; A1; major record labels.

DAVENPORT LYONS (see firm details p.927) The team is especially recognised in the market for its transactional expertise. "*Straightforward*" head of department **James Ware** (see p.592) leads the music practice, and has acted on publishing deals with various acts including Turin Brakes. The team has a strong US client base, and acts for recording artists such as Beenie Man. It represented the record company VP Music Group on establishing its UK operation and drafting distribution agreements. **Clients** Bob Dylan; Mediaeval Baebes; Adelphoi Records; Music Choice.

DENTON WILDE SAPTE (see firm details p.935) This firm's expertise is felt to lie within large corporate music deals. **Robert Allan** (see p.587) heads a team that advised 3i on its acquisition of a 20% stake in Ministry of Sound for £25 million. Aside from corporate work, it acts for artists such as the 'Pop Idol' finalists. It assisted the Edward Kassner Music Company on an exclusive songwriting agreement with Philip Oakey of The Human League. **Clients** EMI; Virgin Music; Windswept Music; Concept Music; Jamie Needle.

EVERSHEDS (see firm details p.949) The strength of the music practice is felt to lie in its loyal, high-profile clients such as Elton John. The team, headed by Patrick Isherwood, has advised Elton John and the Estate of George Harrison on various commercial transactions. On the contentious side, it has represented AEI Music in a copyright tribunal with PPL. **Clients** Elton John; Michael Ball; Estate of George Harrison; AEI Music.

HAMLINS (see firm details p.983) The firm received recommendations this year for its expertise in litigation and its industry knowledge. Led by "*major litigation player*" **Laurence Gilmore** (see p.588), it successfully represented Bruce Springsteen in a Court of Appeal copyright case against Masquerade Music, preventing it from proceeding to the House of Lords. He is also representing Ozzy Osbourne in his defence against band members who are suing him for royalties. On the industry side, the team represents the BPI on piracy work. **Clients** Sony UK; Bruce Springsteen; BPI; Liberty X; BMG.

HARRISON CURTIS (see firm details p.987) A small team, it nonetheless acts on big deals. Lawrence Harrison heads a group that represented Sony in negotiations regarding a joint venture and label arrangements with Fat Boy Slim's Southern Fried Records. It is advising the members of S Club Juniors in their arrangements with 19 Recordings and Polydor. **Clients** Sony Independent Network Europe; BMG; Madison Avenue; S Club Juniors.

TOP IN-HOUSE LAWYERS

MUSIC

Julian FRENCH, Director of Business Affairs, EMI

Alisdair GEORGE, Vice President of Legal and Business Affairs, Sony

James RADICE, Senior Director Legal & Business Affairs, Polydor

Claire SUGRUE, Director of Legal and Business Affairs, Universal Island

John WATSON, Commercial and Business Affairs Director UK, Warner Music

Julian French is described as "*highly talented*" and joins the list this year. **John Watson** and **Claire Sugrue** were both praised for "*good commercial awareness.*" Many would find it hard to deny that the "*outstanding*" **Alisdair George** is "*the pick of the bunch.*" **James Radice** continues to receive recommendations following a move to Polydor.

MUSIC PUBLISHING

Jane DYBALL, Director of Legal and Business Affairs, Warner Chappell

Grenville EVANS - 19

Nick FOLLAND, Company Secretary and Group General Director, Emap

Sarah LEVIN, Head of Legal and Business Affairs, Universal Music Publishing

Chris MILESON, Director of Legal and Business Affairs, EMI Publishing

Rakesh SANGHVI, General Manager, Sony Publishing

New to this year's list is **Nick Folland**, who is "*experienced and talented.*" **Jane Dyball** and **Chris Mileson** are included for their "*excellent commercial knowledge,*" while **Sarah Levin** and **Rakesh Sanghvi** have been praised for being "*easy to work with.*" **Grenville Evans** retains his place following his move to 19.

In-house lawyers' profiles p.1201

MARRIOTT HARRISON (see firm details p.1054) Newly ranked this year, the firm is recommended by clients for its commercial and pragmatic outlook. The team, led by Tony Morris, has been involved in major litigation, advising Sanctuary Music Group on its protection of the Immediate catalogue, which culminated in a two-week trial. On the commercial side, it advised independent record producer Eagle Rock Entertainment on the £34 million disposal of a controlling interest to HG Capital. **Clients** Eagle Rock Entertainment; ZYX Music; Delta Music; Andrew Powell; Black Dog.

SEARLES (see firm details p.1124) This artist-led practice is rated by the market for its work in the independent sector. **Helen Searle** (see p.591) "*has built up a great practice,*" according to competitors, acting not only for musicians, but also for managers, labels and music publishers. The team has been busy in the past year renegotiating artists' contracts. **Clients** Artists; managers.

LONDON — MEDIA & ENTERTAINMENT

SPRAGGON STENNETT BRABYN A "*young, lively*" practice, it is renowned for picking up new artists. Focusing on the independent side of the sector, the firm has set up recording and publishing deals for artists such as Sugababes and The Prodigy. It also works for independent recording artists, producers and songwriters. **Clients** Independent talent.

LONDON — THEATRE

MEDIA & ENTERTAINMENT: THEATRE
LONDON

1. Clintons
   Tarlo Lyons
2. The Simkins Partnership
3. Bates, Wells & Braithwaite
   Campbell Hooper
   Harrison Curtis
4. Harbottle & Lewis
5. Theodore Goddard

LEADING INDIVIDUALS

1. COHEN John — Clintons
   SHAW Barry — Sole Practitioner
2. EGAN Sean — Bates, Wells & Braithwaite
   FRANKS David — The Simkins Partnership
   HARRISON Lawrence — Harrison Curtis
   MEADON Simon — Tarlo Lyons

This book is the product of 6,582 1/2 hour interviews. See p.7 for BMRB audit. Within each band, firms are listed alphabetically. See individuals' profiles p.587

TOP IN-HOUSE LAWYERS

THEATRE

Jonathon HULL, Legal & Business Affairs Manager, Really Useful Group

Despite few in-house lawyers in this specific sector, "top expert" Jonathon Hull *received numerous highly positive recommendations for his work.*

In-house lawyers' profiles p.1201

CLINTONS (see firm details p.912) This team is envied by rivals for "*acting for the major producers*," such as Clear Channel Entertainment, the producers of 'Chicago' and 'Singin' In the Rain'. The "*leading light*" of musical theatre, **John Cohen** (see p.587) is renowned for acting for talent, producers, lyricists and playwrights. He is currently representing the producers of the American production of 'The Graduate' on Broadway. **Clients** Tim Rice; Andrew Lloyd Webber; Don Black; Stanhope Productions.

TARLO LYONS (see firm details p.1155) A top-ranking firm, it is highly rated by peers and clients, who "*go to them with the complex issues.*" The "*doyen of theatre law,*" Michael Rose has moved into a consulting role; his shoes, however, have been amply filled by **Simon Meadon** (see p.590), who clients say "*really understands production work and has masses of experience.*"

THE SIMKINS PARTNERSHIP (see firm details p.1136) A firm felt by competitors to be "*at the cutting edge of things*," it has been advising the Royal National Theatre on its contract with Sir Cameron Mackintosh for its production of 'My Fair Lady', including the transfer to the West End, Broadway and overseas tours. **David Franks** (see p.588) "*knows the business inside out,*" and has recently acted for the Really Useful Group on commissioning music, lyrics and a book for the new musical 'Bombay Dreams'. **Clients** Really Useful Group; Chorion IP; Nigel Havers; Theatrenow.

BATES, WELLS & BRAITHWAITE (see firm details p.859) The firm boasts the talents of the "*supremely knowledgeable*" **Sean Egan** (see p.588), who provides "*good tactical advice*" according to clients. The practice acts for a client base spanning commercial producers and small arts organisations, and has been advising on all production aspects of the Boy George musical 'Taboo'. It has also recently represented Watermans Arts Centre on restructuring and a joint venture for the venue. **Clients** ENO; RSC; Katharine Dore Management; Random Dance Company.

CAMPBELL HOOPER (see firm details p.899) The team is felt by the market to be less visible following the loss of Carolyn Jennings. However, it is still perceived as a "*heavy hitter when it comes to disputes.*" Consultant David Wills heads the department that, alongside litigation, has worked on the production of 'Oklahoma!' in New York and the new Queen musical, 'We Will Rock You', in London. **Clients** Trevor Nunn; Theatre of Comedy; Peter O'Toole; Chichester Festival Theatre.

HARRISON CURTIS (see firm details p.987) Traditionally visible acting for a variety of big-name producer clients, the firm has recently won appointments to act for the Theatre of Comedy and the Shaftesbury Theatre, its first major theatre-owning client. The "*highly specialised*" **Lawrence Harrison** acted for Background Production on the revival of 'Top Girls' at the Aldwych. The firm has also been representing Mark Goucher on the West End production and national tour of 'Rent'. **Clients** Theatre of Comedy; Drill Hall Theatre; Guy Chapman Productions; The Sarah Mitchell Partnership.

HARBOTTLE & LEWIS (see firm details p.983) The team was particularly recommended to researchers for its financial services expertise, something amply demonstrated recently by its success in advising on the funding and launch of theatre*share* plc, an innovative way of financing and co-producing plays. The team, headed by Colin Howes, has also recently advised Tiger Aspect productions on the development of the musical 'Our House', based on the songs of Madness. **Clients** Queen Theatrical Productions; Really Useful Theatres; Hampstead Theatre; Society of London Theatres.

THEODORE GODDARD (see firm details p.1158) The team is best known in the market for representing the Ambassador Theatre Group on various creative collaborations. Recent examples include a joint venture with the Natural Nylon Theatre Company, which will bring actors such as Jude Law, Sadie Frost and Ewan McGregor to the stage. The team has also advised ATG on the acquisition of the Fortune Theatre in the West End. **Clients** Ambassador Theatre Group; producers; theatres.

OTHER NOTABLE PRACTITIONERS "*The star of the theatre,*" sole practitioner **Barry Shaw** (see p.591) is a colourful and high-profile figure in the market. Peers respect his expertise and commitment.

MEDIA & ENTERTAINMENT ■ THE REGIONS

THE REGIONS

MEDIA & ENTERTAINMENT
■ THE REGIONS

1
- **Manches** Oxford
- **McCormicks** Leeds
- **Wiggin & Co** Cheltenham

2
- **Eversheds** Leeds
- **Morgan Cole** Cardiff, Swansea

LEADING INDIVIDUALS

1 ANDERSON Frances Lee Crowder

2 LEWIS Emyr Morgan Cole

MCCORMICK Peter McCormicks

This book is the product of 6,582 1/2 hour interviews. See p.7 for BMRB audit. Within each band, firms are listed alphabetically. See individuals' profiles p.587

MANCHES (see firm details p.1052) The Oxford branch of this outfit collects recommendations from across the country, particularly for its niche within publishing work. Cathleen Blackburn heads the department, which has been active on work for the Tolkien Estate. Protection and exploitation work is undertaken for photographers and designers. **Clients** Tolkien Estate; photographers; designers.

MCCORMICKS (see firm details p.1063) An important presence in the market, it boasts particular expertise in sports-related media work. The team is headed by the commercially minded **Peter McCormick** (see p.589), who handled the £50 million national radio broadcasting agreements with Radio Five Live and TalkSPORT. The team represents celebrity clients such as Jenny Pitman and Nell McAndrew on media and publishing negotiations, and acts for talent in the film, television and music industries. **Clients** BBC; Music Factory Entertainment Group; Love Promotions; talent agencies.

WIGGIN & CO (see firm details p.1186) The epicentre of the firm lies within its Cheltenham offices, which have been immersed in large corporate deals. The team acted on the disposal of TV Travel Shop to USA Networks for a consideration of £100 million. It was also active on the establishment of a joint venture between Telewest and BBC concerning new television channels. **Clients** Discovery Communications Europe; Universal; Global Crossing; Sima TV; SBS.

EVERSHEDS (see firm details p.949) Well known for its negotiation of television deals, the team, led by Joanna Berry, benefits from the London connection. It has recently advised Granada TV in connection with formats and format option agreements, and is involved in online music deals.

MORGAN COLE (see firm details p.1075) This team is experiencing a growth in animation work, with the arrival of the former head of legal at Disney in Asia. The highly respected **Emyr Lewis** has worked for the Avanti Group, owners of the Pop Factory, on copyright and project work, and the team also represents the production company of Dave Edwards, the creator of 'Superted'. **Clients** Agenda Group; Parkville; Avanti Group.

OTHER NOTABLE PRACTITIONERS Frances Anderson (see p.587) of Birmingham-based Lee Crowder is highly rated by the market for "*going out on her own.*"

SCOTLAND

MEDIA & ENTERTAINMENT
■ SCOTLAND

1
- **Dundas & Wilson CS** Edinburgh, Glasgow
- **Tods Murray WS** Edinburgh

2 **Levy & McRae** Glasgow

3
- **Anderson Strathern WS** Edinburgh
- **Bannatyne, Kirkwood, France & Co** Glasgow
- **McGrigor Donald** Glasgow
- **Wright, Johnston & Mackenzie** Glasgow

LEADING INDIVIDUALS

1 FINDLAY Richard Tods Murray WS

2 SIBBALD Graham Dundas & Wilson CS

WATSON Peter Levy & McRae

This book is the product of 6,582 1/2 hour interviews. See p.7 for BMRB audit. Within each band, firms are listed alphabetically. See individuals' profiles p.587

DUNDAS & WILSON CS (see firm details p.943) "*First class, with a blue-chip client base,*" according to its competitors, the firm has a cross-media focus. The team is headed by **Graham Sibbald**, who has "*a fine knowledge of ownership rules*" according to clients. He advised Scottish Radio Holdings on its acquisition of Southampton radio station 'Wave 105 FM' for £18 million and Irish national radio station 'Today FM' for £36.4 million. Not restricted to corporate deals, the firm is particularly active in the publishing and licensing aspects of new media, including advising DigMedia on an interactive music site and on agreements for the digital distribution of music with artists including Neil Finn of Crowded House, and Daft Punk. **Clients:** Scottish Radio Holdings; Torridon; SCORE Digital; Mecca.

TODS MURRAY WS (see firm details p.1164) Leaders in its field, according to various interviewees, it was particularly singled out for theatre expertise. The team acts for theatre companies and venues, including the producers of the musical 'Opera Galactica', which is now on a national tour. **Richard Findlay** (see p.588) received a raft of recommendations from peers for the depth of his expertise. He has led teams on important film financing and production work, including advising the UK producers on the Canadian co-production of the feature film 'Passing Strangers'. The team also undertakes a range of music, publishing and animation instructions. **Clients** RPM Arts; Reign of Sound; RoughCut Comics; Blackwatch Productions.

LEVY & MCRAE (see firm details p.1041) Well respected by peers, this firm is best known for its contentious expertise. The team is led by the "*talented*" **Peter Watson** (see p.275), who competitors say, "*can turn his hand as deftly to litigation as to copy review.*" The team has particular expertise in newspaper issues, and has been handling instructions regarding the Press Complaints Commission. **Clients** Scottish Media Group; Trinity Mirror.

ANDERSON STRATHERN WS (see firm details p.844) A team recognised by the market within the sphere of location licensing, acting for the National Trust for Scotland on a location filming licence for the television remake of the film '*Les Liaisons Dangereuses*'. Simon Brown leads the team on instructions from a new publishing client on the establishment, protection and exploitation of multimedia rights in a series of children's stories, including character and brand merchandising. **Clients** The Union Advertising Agency; The National Trust for Scotland; publishing clients.

BANNATYNE, KIRKWOOD, FRANCE & CO (see firm details p.856) Acting for a wide range of clients, the team has an emphasis on litigation. Led by Martin Smith, it regularly undertakes newspaper cases, including litigation and contractual work. Aside from print media, it also acts for Scotland Equity. **Clients** Associated Newspapers; Scotsman Publications; The Guardian; Scotland Equity.

MCGRIGOR DONALD (see firm details p.1065) A largely non-contentious outfit, its media work is thought to have an IP bias. The team, headed by Niall Scott, has been active on acquisition and contract work for newspapers, including the Scottish *Daily Record* and *Sunday Mail*. It acts for children's animation company Storyland on IP rights and fund-raising. **Clients** Phonographic Performance; Sunday Mail; Northcliffe Newspapers; Digital Bridges.

WRIGHT, JOHNSTON & MACKENZIE The team retains a presence in the market due to its niche within finance for creative industries. The department, led by Yvonne Dunn, has advised the Glasgow Film Fund, producers of such films as 'Shallow Grave', on the creation of a private sector film fund. It also represented Zentropa Film, producers of 'Breaking the Waves', on its decision to enter into co-production with Scottish film producers. **Clients** Glasgow Film Fund; Short Film Fund; Signa Films.

THE LEADERS IN MEDIA & ENTERTAINMENT

ABRAMSON, Lawrence
Harbottle & Lewis, London
(020) 7667 5000
lawrence.abramson@harbottle.com
Specialisation: Specialist litigator in all areas of the entertainment and media industries, including music, television, film, computer games, publishing and sport.
Prof. Memberships: International Association of Entertainment Lawyers.
Career: Trained at *Sheridans*. Solicitor with *Denton Hall* 1988-97. Joined *Harbottle & Lewis* in 1996.
Personal: Educated at the British School of The Netherlands, University of Manchester, Chester College of Law (LLB 2:1). Married with two children. Interests include sport, music, theatre, travel and entertaining.

ALLAN, Robert
Denton Wilde Sapte, London
(020) 7320 6516
rwa@dentonwildesapte.com
Specialisation: Partner in TMT Group and Head of the Music Group. Works with music industry clients on music publishing; recording; 'due diligence' reviews of music companies and their assets; music business mergers and acquisitions; video licensing; negotiations with rights bodies and other contractual matters. Advises users of music and IPOs, eg TV programme makers and broadcasters, film production companies and advertisers regarding clearances. Also works on the 'talent' side of the music business. Published widely in leading professional journals and the trade press. Lectured at MIDEM and New Music Seminar in New York and Beverly Hills Bar Association.
Career: Qualified in 1967. Partner: *Roney & Co* 1970-73, *Simons Muirhead & Allan* 1973-86. *Denton Hall* partner 1986-current.

ANDERSON, Frances
Lee Crowder, Birmingham
(0121) 236 4477
frances.anderson@leecrowder.com
Specialisation: Non-contentious work in music, television, film, the arts, new technology and computer law.
Prof. Memberships: Law Society; Women in Film and Television; PACT; Society for Computers & Law.
Career: Qualified in 1989 at *Wragge & Co*; set up own practice in 1995 and joined *Lee Crowder* in 2000.
Personal: Former chairman and currently a director of Birmingham International Film & Television Festival. Company Secretary and a director of the Grand Theatre, Wolverhampton.

ANTONIADES, Reno
Lee & Thompson, London
(020) 7935 4665

BALLARD, Tony
Field Fisher Waterhouse, London
(020) 7861 4000
jab@ffwlaw.com
Specialisation: Main area of practice is communications with a recent focus on network platforms at the leading edge of recent developments in this field, advising both established operators and new entrants on the new technologies. Acting for television network and service providers in both public and private sectors, including established broadcasters and new entrants. Also acting for telecoms companies entering the content market. Specialisms extend to all forms of broadcasting as well as major feature film production and distribution, competition, copyright and administrative law. Arbitrator on International Arbitration panel of American Film Marketing Association and trained mediator for alternative dispute resolution. Frequent speaker at conferences.
Prof. Memberships: International Bar Association, Communication Lawyers Association, Royal Television Society, Copinger Society and chairman of UK branch of European Centre for Space Law.
Career: Qualified in 1974, having joined *Allison & Humphreys* in 1971. Became a partner in 1975. Merged with *Field Fisher Waterhouse* in 1998.
Personal: Born 21 August 1945. MA (Cantab) 1964-68. Fellow of Royal Anthropological Institute. Leisure interests include astrophysics, sailing and painting. Lives in London and Suffolk. Athenaeum.

BENNETT, Nigel
The Simkins Partnership, London
(020) 7907 3011
nigel.bennett@simkins.com
Specialisation: Partner in Film & TV and Sport Groups. Main practice areas cover media finance, production and distribution (particularly in fields of film, television and radio). Advising media groups, producers, distributors, broadcasters and financiers on copyright, financing agreements, production contracts and distribution arrangements world-wide. Other areas include sport (particularly exploitation of sports rights) and publishing.
Prof. Memberships: Law Society, International Bar Association, American Bar Association, Royal Television Society, BAFTA.
Career: Qualified with *Rubinstein Nash*. Joined *The Simkins Partnership* 1973; Partner 1975.
Personal: Educated Dulwich College and Clare College, Cambridge. Interests include golf, cricket, sailing, films, jazz guitar.

BERGER, Jonathan
Theodore Goddard, London
(020) 76068855
jonathanberger@theodoregoddard.co.uk
Specialisation: Main area of practice covers legal and business affairs advice on the production, finance and distribution of feature films and television programming. Acts for leading independent producers and distributors. Regular speaker on the film and television industry.
Prof. Memberships: British Academy of Film & Television Arts; Producers Association for Cinema & Television.
Career: Qualified in 1986 with *Bartletts de Reya* and became a Partner in *Mishcon de Reya* in 1990 and joined *Theodore Goddard* as a Partner in the Media & Entertainment Group in 1995.
Personal: Born 1962. Educated Charterhouse and the University of Kent at Canterbury. Leisure interests include supporting Chelsea FC, cooking and golf.

BLAIR, Jonathan
Theodore Goddard, London
(020) 7880 5696
jonathanblair@theodoregoddard.co.uk
Specialisation: Film production, film financing, new media exploitation (broadband and convergence technology). Major cases (matters for 2001 - 2002): advising producers on the production Before You Go (starring Julie Walters, John Hannah, Victoria Hamilton, Tom Wilkinson, Patricia Hodge and Joanne Whalley) to be released by Entertainment in the Summer; advising producers of the film Heart of Me (starring Helena Bonham Carter and Olivia Williams); advising film council in its investment on Dr Sleep and Importance of Being Ernest.
Prof. Memberships: Member of the Experts Panel for the Media Training Programme - Brussels.
Career: Qualified 1994 at *Mishcon de Reya* (1992-96); *Theodore Goddard* 1996-to date; Partner from November 2001.
Publications: Article in Entertainment Law Review entitled 'Mobile Business: Legal Implications of Business on the Move' (dated March 2002).
Personal: Education: Watford Boys Grammar School; Magdalene College Cambridge (History MA). Leisure Interests: sport (watching and playing football), theatre and travel.

BRAY, Richard
Bray & Krais, London
(020) 7493 8840

BROOKES, Mike
Lee & Thompson, London
(020) 7935 4665

BROWN, Jacqueline
Clintons, London
(020) 7395 8477
jb@clintons.co.uk
Specialisation: Advises on contentious matters including intellectual property rights and contract law with reference to the music industry, sport and entertainment generally. Clients include celebrated sports people and entertainers, managers, sports agents and marketing consultants and multinational entertainment groups (especially recording and publishing companies). Has been involved in the following landmark cases: for U2/Polygram against the Performing Rights Society (including before the Monopolies and Mergers Commission), for the Stone Roses against Zomba and for Sony against George Michael. Recent cases include representing Big Life Management in proceedings against Richard Ashcroft and Mel Stein against Paul Gascoigne. Particular knowledge and experience of restraint of trade issues in entertainment and sports.
Prof. Memberships: Member of British Association for Sport and Law.
Career: Educated in Scotland and at Birmingham University (LLB). Articled at *Clintons* in 1990. Partner from 1996.
Personal: Born 12th January 1966. Owns and competes two showjumpers, member of the British ShowJumping Association.

COHEN, John
Clintons, London
(020) 7395 8404
jc@clintons.co.uk
Specialisation: Partner in Entertainment Department. Principal area of practice is theatre, representing most of the leading British creators of music theatre - Andrew Lloyd Webber, Tim Rice, Don Black and the Late Lionel Bart as well as directors, designers and a number of producers. He also continues to represent a number of recording artists and television personalities. In addition han-

MEDIA & ENTERTAINMENT ■ THE LEADERS

dles corporate matters in the entertainment business. Among this year's projects have been 'Bombay Dreams' and various productions of 'The Graduate'.
Career: Qualified 1960. Joined Clintons in 1968 and has remained there throughout career, becoming a Partner in 1972.
Personal: Born 14th February 1946. Attended University College London 1964-67. Trustee of Mercury Workshop and the Arts Foundation. Lives in London.

CURTIS, Tim
Harrison Curtis, London
(020) 7611 1720

DEARSLEY, Ken
Denton Wilde Sapte, London
(020) 7320 6547
krd@dentonwildesapte.com
Specialisation: Partner in technology, media and telecoms group. Specialises in all aspects of film financing with special expertise and reputation in UK sale/leaseback transactions, tax based financing arrangements and working with the major studios, other leading US and European film companies, banks and other lending institutions. Wide experience in film and television production and distribution, video distribution, 'due diligence' reviews in the media industry and copyright matters generally. Has lectured on a wide number of industry subjects in London, America, India and Far East.
Prof. Memberships: International Bar Association.
Career: Has been with *Denton Wilde Sapte* since articles. Qualified in 1974. Became a partner in 1979.

DEVEREUX, Mark
Olswang, London
(020) 7208 8888
mjd@olswang.com
Specialisation: Senior partner. Main area of practice is film and television finance, production and distribution. Responsible for all areas of work covered by entertainment, media and communications. Regular contributor to media trade press.
Prof. Memberships: Law Society, State Bar of California.
Career: Qualified in 1981, joining *Simon Olswang & Co* in the same year and becoming a partner in 1982.
Personal: Born 2 August 1956. Attended Lycée Français de Londres 1961-74, then University College London 1975-78. Leisure interests include tennis, skiing, diving and photography. Lives in London.

EDWARDS, Stephen
Richards Butler, London
(020) 7772 5849
se@richardsbutler.com
Specialisation: Broadcasting law including ITC licence applications; satellite and cable transmission and programme contracts; production financing, distribution and co-production agreements and European regulation. Other copyright and media/entertainment work including sports agreements; copyright collecting society transactions; print and multimedia publishing agreements; talent contracts; website agreements; copyright tribunal hearings and music industry agreements. Regular speaker at media industry conferences.
Career: Qualified in 1976. Joined the BBC in 1978, and was head of copyright 1981-90. Joined *Richards Butler* as a partner in 1990.
Personal: Attended University of the Witwatersrand, Johannesburg 1968-70 and Trinity Hall, Cambridge 1971-73. Leisure pursuits include sailing, cricket and music.

EGAN, Sean
Bates, Wells & Braithwaite, London
(020) 7551 7777
s.egan@bateswells.co.uk
Specialisation: Partner and head of the Arts and Media department. Acts for leading theatre, film, and television producers, talent and other media organisations. Specialist areas include copyright law, film and television production, charity law and the financing of theatre and film production. Regular lecturer and author.
Prof. Memberships: Law Society, RSA.
Career: Qualified in 1988. At *Clifford Chance* 1986-88, *Harbottle & Lewis* 1988-98, joined *Bates, Wells & Braithwaite* in 1999.
Personal: Born 1961. MA Queens' College, Cambridge. Charity trustee. Leisure interests include film, theatre, Fives, and golf.

FINDLAY, Richard
Tods Murray WS, Edinburgh
(0131) 226 4771
richard.findlay@todsmurray.com
Specialisation: Entertainment and media law partner. Practices exclusively in entertainment and media law acting for a wide range of clients throughout the film, television and music industry sectors and also for companies in the fields of theatre, festival and event management and the arts generally.
Prof. Memberships: International Association of Entertainment Lawyers.
Career: Partner *Ranken & Reid* (1979-90); Partner *Tods Murray* (1990).

FRANKS, David
The Simkins Partnership, London
(020) 7907 3030
david.franks@simkins.com
Specialisation: Partner in Music Group and head of Theatre Group. In the music sector David has increasingly found himself in recent years acting for record companies in relation to label deals, and for music publishers in relation to catalogue acquisitions and disposals. In relation to theatre David's main expertise lies in the structuring of contractual and financial arrangements for the staging of major musicals. Clients include producers and investors as well as individual members of the 'creative team'.
Prof. Memberships: The Law Society, IAEL.
Career: Qualified 1973, *The Simkins Partnership* 1974 to date.

FREE, Dominic
The Simkins Partnership, London
(020) 7907 3050
dominic.free@simkins.com
Specialisation: Partner in Litigation Group. Main area of practice is disputes in the music industry. Has a particular interest in music technology and new media. Acts for several major record companies, music publishers, collecting societies and recording and performing artists. Also acts for those in the film and television, print publishing and advertising industries and on intellectual property disputes particularly copyright and trade mark matters.
Career: Qualified in 1985. Partner *Richard Butler* 1989-92. Partner *The Simkins Partnership* 1993.
Personal: Born 16 November 1956. Educated in New Zealand (LLB, Auckland 1979) and the USA (LLM, Cornell University 1982).

GAWADE, Jeremy
Lee & Thompson, London
(020) 7935 4665

GHEE, Tony
Ashurst Morris Crisp, London
(020) 7859 1310
tony.ghee@ashursts.com
Specialisation: Media and entertainment and telecommunications. Regulatory, corporate and commercial advice for cable and telecommunications operators, terrestrial and satellite broadcasters and film and television production companies. Particular expertise: all aspects of satellite and broadcasting law including digital media. Speaks and writes regularly on the convergence of broadcasting, telecoms and information technology industries and broadcasting regulation.
Prof. Memberships: IBA, ICC and BSAC.
Career: Worked: *Blake Dawson Waldron* and *TEN* television network in Australia. *Denton Wilde Sapte* and partner at *Ashursts* in UK.
Personal: Married.

GILMORE, Laurence
Hamlins, London
(020) 7355 6000
lgilmore@hamlins.co.uk
Specialisation: A Managing Partner and Head of the Entertainment and Intellectual Property Department. Specialises in all aspects of related litigation including copyright, trademark, contract disputes, monopolies and mergers and EC competition law. Practice also covers defamation and passing off actions. Acts for prominent organisations, corporations and individuals from the world of entertainment.
Prof. Memberships: International Association of Entertainment Lawyers.
Career: Articled at *Davenport Lyons* 1984-86. Assistant Solicitor *Taylor Joynson Garrett* 1986-87. Partner, *Hamlins* (previously known as *Hamlin Slowe*) since 1988.
Personal: Educated at Preston Manor Grammar School and Trinity Hall, Cambridge. Writes occasional newspaper articles. Leisure pursuits include theatre, music and sport. Born 17 April 1959. Lives in London.

GLICK, David
Mishcon de Reya, London
(020) 7440 7000
Specialisation: All areas of entertainment and media law with particular emphasis on music, television, film and sport. Music client base ranges from new and emerging artists/bands to 'superstar artists'. Corporate clients include major record and publishing companies as well as a number of independent record labels and publishing companies in relation to their various spheres of activities. A specialist in co-ordinating substantial joint venture and other 'label' structures, he bridges the gap between the media business and the City.
Career: Qualified in 1989 and co-founded *Eatons* in 1990. *Eatons* merged with *Mishcon de Reya* in 2000.

GOLDBERG, Simon
Simons Muirhead & Burton, London
(020) 7556 3120
simon.goldberg@smab.co.uk
Specialisation: Film and television: production lawyer for 'To Kill a King', Natural Nylon's latest feature on the lives of Cromwell and Fairfax; '16 Years', Richard Jobson's first feature film as director for Scottish Screen and Metro Tartan; 'Diana - Story of a Princess' landmark ITV series for Brook Lapping; 'Rockface' Union Pictures drama for BBC; also advises Channel 4 and wide range of media clients; legal advisor to the Royal Court Theatre and on IP matters to Friends of the Earth.
Prof. Memberships: PACT, Law Society, Royal Society of Television.
Career: Qualified at *Simons Muirhead and Burton* 1989; Partner 1992; Head of Non-contentious Media and Entertainment Department having developed the fields of film, television and theatre. Also part-time lecturer in Media Studies at University of Warwick.
Publications: Legal advisor to 'WRAP', new film production monthly magazine.
Personal: MA in Classics, St John's College Cambridge; Solicitors' Finals, College of Law, London. Member of MCC; fellow of the Zoological Society of London; secretary of local squash team; member of Soho House and on management committee at Century.

GOSTYN, Antony
The Simkins Partnership, London
(020) 7907 3015
antony.gostyn@simkins.com
Specialisation: Film and television production, finance and distribution agreements, acting for broadcasters, producers, lending institutions and individuals. Author of 'Pact Model Contracts' (1991,

THE LEADERS ■ MEDIA & ENTERTAINMENT

1998 and 1999 Editions).
Prof. Memberships: International Association of Entertainment Lawyers.
Career: Qualified 1975. With Thorn EMI 1976-82. Partner at *DJ Freeman* 1986-95. Joined *The Simkins Partnership* as a partner in 1995. Sits on PACT Finance Committee and has attended Council Meetings of Design and Artists' Copyright Society since its inception.

GRAFTON GREEN, Paddy
Theodore Goddard, London
(020) 7880 5685
paddygraftongreen@theodoregoddard.co.uk
Specialisation: Work includes advice on (i) copyright issues in relation to recordings, musical compositions and theatrical productions and (ii) production, distribution, management concert appearance, sponsorship and merchandising agreements. Advice on taxation both within the UK and overseas of income derived by businesses and artists. Cases have included acting as Chairman of BPI Tribunal into chart hyping, and for BMG in the MMC Enquiry into Recorded Music, for PolyGram and Universal Music in relation to a variety of corporate and commercial transactions including PolyGram Filmed Entertainment's acquisition of ITC in 1995 and sale in 1999 and PolyGram's acquisition (1991) and disposal (1999) of its interest in The Really Useful Group, in the sale in 1999 of London Records to the Warner Group, for major companies and artists in structuring international transactions including concert tours (Tina Turner, Michael Jackson, Janet Jackson, Lionel Richie and The Rolling Stones), for David Bowie in relation to the "Bowie Bonds" and Iron Maiden in relation to the securitisation of income. Lecturer and seminar chairman for IBC Legal Studies and others.
Prof. Memberships: Law Society.
Publications: Occasional articles in legal journals.
Personal: Born 30 March 1943. Attended Ampleforth College 1957-62; holds an MA (Oxon), 1963-65. Leisure interests include music and cricket. Lives in London.

HANSON, Christopher
Denton Wilde Sapte, London
(020) 7320 6576
czh@dentonwildesapte.com
Specialisation: Specialist in all areas of media financing, film and television production and distribution, copyright and sports sponsorship. Work undertaken includes 'off-balance sheet' finance, single project loans, revolving credit facilities, equity investment, sale and leaseback and other tax based financing, structuring international co-productions and the commissioning, production, licensing, sponsorship, merchandising and exploitation of film and television product. Clients include leading US and European banks in this sector, US 'Hollywood' studios, independent producers, distributors and broadcasters.
Career: Qualified 1992. Partner *Denton Wilde Sapte* 1999.

HARMAN, James
Theodore Goddard, London
(020) 7606 8855
Specialisation: Specialises in entertainment industry work, including music business, multi-media publishing and conventional book and magazine publishing. Other specialisations include non-contentious intellectual property law, including advice on copyright, passing-off and a variety of copyright based commercial contracts.

HARRISON, Lawrence
Harrison Curtis, London
(020) 7611 1720

HORSFALL, Robert
Lee & Thompson, London
(020) 7935 4665

HOWARD, BK
Russells, London
(020) 7439 8692

HURT, Jacqueline
Olswang, London
(020) 7208 8888
jmh@olswang.com
Specialisation: Partner in the media and communications group, advising on all aspects of media and communications law specialising in the financing, production and distribution of films and television programmes. Has particular experience and expertise in the financing of independent feature films and, in that connection, the structuring of a combination of any one or more of government subsidies, co-productions, grants, distribution pre-sales and bank financing. Also advises producers and acquirers of films on tax driven sale and leaseback transactions.
Prof. Memberships: Law Society, Women in Film & Television.
Career: Trained at *SJ Berwin & Co* qualified 1991, partner at *SJ Berwin & Co* 1998. Joined *Olswang* as a partner in 2000.

JAMES, Sean
Wiggin & Co, London
(020) 7290 2424
sean.james@wiggin.co.uk
Specialisation: Partner specialising in cable, satellite, analogue and digital terrestrial, on-line, internet and other television operations and programming including sports media rights, regulatory compliance, programming acquisitions, licences, co-productions and commissions, telecommunications and satellite agreements including uplink, transponder capacity, encryption and compression, facilities agreements, conditional access and subscriber management contracts and licence agreements, cable affiliation agreements and direct-to-home distribution agreements.
Prof. Memberships: Royal Television Society.
Career: Articled *Wiggin & Co*; qualified 1990; 18 months secondment to United Artists 1991-92; Assistant Solicitor with *Wiggin & Co* until May 1996; Partner 1996.
Personal: Born 1965. Interests include squash, cars, windsurfing and rowing.

JOHNSON, Tim
SJ Berwin, London
(020) 7533 2202
tim.johnson@sjberwin.com
Specialisation: Film production, financing (including co-production structuring and use of local incentives) and distribution, satellite communications, digital media, broadcasting and telecommunications (including communications infrastructure procurement and communications services outsourcing).
Career: MA, Sidney Sussex College, Cambridge. *Denton Hall* 1987-93, *Yusef & Leader* 1993-94, *SJ Berwin* 1994-date. Partner 1995.
Personal: Married with one son. Interests include rugby, travel, food and wine, history and the West Country.

JONES, Howard
Sheridans, London
(020) 7404 0444

JONES, Medwyn
Harbottle & Lewis, London
(020) 7667 5000
medwyn.jones@harbottle.com
Specialisation: Partner and Head of the Broadcasting Group. Main area of practice is film and television production, financing, and distribution and broadcasting. Work includes television and film commissioning, licensing and financing agreements, programme content, sponsorship, broadcasting legislation, carriage and transmission agreements and joint ventures.
Prof. Memberships: Law Society, Royal Television Society, BAFTA.
Career: Qualified in 1980. Worked at *Theodore Goddard* 1978-81, then *Walker Martineau* 1981-92 (from 1983 as a Partner). Joined *Cameron Markby Hewitt* as a Partner in 1992 and *Harbottle & Lewis* as a Partner in 1994. Regular lecturer at conferences and seminars.
Personal: Born 1955. Attended Scorton Grammar School, Chester Grammar School, Sheffield University and College of Law. Leisure interests include skiing, regular exercise and good wine. Lives in Richmond.

KAYE, Laurence
Laurence Kaye, Radlett
See under E-commerce, p.280

LANDSMAN, David
Clintons, London
(020) 7395 8422
dml@clintons.co.uk
Specialisation: Partner in Entertainment Department. Deals with music, TV, video, film, merchandising, media and leisure work.
Prof. Memberships: Law Society.
Career: Qualified 1970. Founding partner of *DM Landsman & Co*, which merged with *Clintons* in 1990.
Personal: Born 14 March 1946. Educated at Haberdashers' Aske's School. Leisure pursuits include music, reading, sport and family. Lives near London.

LEE, Robert
Lee & Thompson, London
(020) 7935 4665

LEWIS, Emyr
Morgan Cole, Swansea
(01792) 634634

LOM, Nicholas
Simons Muirhead & Burton, London
(020) 7734 4499
nicholas.lom@smab.co.uk
Specialisation: Entertainment and commercial lawyer; main areas of practice - non-contentious internet, film, television, video, music, publishing, multimedia and copyright matters.
Career: Prior to entering law, worked as a script editor at the BBC and in independent production. Qualified in 1982. Articled at *Wright Webb Syrett* before. Formed *Schilling & Lom* in 1984. Moved to *Simons Muirhead & Burton* in 2001.
Personal: Born 29 April 1949. Attended Westminster School and Pembroke College, Cambridge (MA Cantab). Member of the Groucho Club. Leisure interests include his children, chess and book collecting.

MAXTONE-SMITH, Michael
Richards Butler, London
(020) 7772 5481
mjs@richardsbutler.com
Specialisation: Advises banks, financiers, distributors and sales agents in connection with all aspects of financing film and television both in Europe and the USA including the granting of security over intellectual property rights. Clients include Cobalt Media Group LLC, DZ Bank A.G., Deutsche Zentral - Genossenschaftsbank, Royal Bank of Scotland and Societe Generalé.
Career: Articles at *McKenna & Co* (1986-88); assistant at *Richards Butler* (1988-98); partner at *Richards Butler* (1998-).
Personal: Educated at Nottingham High School and St Catharine's College Cambridge. Married with three sons. Leisure interests: playing the piano, cricket and literature.

MCCORMICK OBE, Peter
McCormicks, Leeds
(0113) 246 0622
p.mccormick@mccormicks-solicitors.com
Specialisation: Substantial area of practice is media and entertainment (allied to extensive portfolio of sports law) with considerable experience in both contentious and non-contentious aspects. Advises a number of sporting bodies, clubs and individuals on contractual matters as well as media and entertainment law issues. Clients include The FA Premier League, Leeds United FC, a number of sporting personalities such as Leslie Ash, Lee Chapman, Billy Pearce,

MEDIA & ENTERTAINMENT ■ THE LEADERS

Freddie Trueman, Richard Whiteley and a number of television presenters, actors, actresses and journalists. Advises on all aspects of broadcasting. Has advised on three radio franchise bids. Deals with a number of defamation actions and advice on behalf of leading public figures, including politicians and personalities. Handles complaints on broadcasting and press issues. Lectures on media and entertainment. Advises a number of clients in the music industry including performers and managers. Considerable experience of broadcast sponsorship and similar issues. Negotiates contracts for personal benefits, corporate sponsorship and ancillary matters. Has 20 years experience of tax investigation and enquiry work, both Revenue and VAT and serious fraud cases. Resident legal expert on Radio Leeds, Yorkshire Television and the Yorkshire Post.
Publications: Author of 'Sport, Business and the Law' published by Jordans.
Personal: Chairman of the Yorkshire Young Achiever Awards. Member of the Advisory Board, Sports Law Centre, Anglia University; vice-president of The Outward Bound Trust; solicitor to The Duke of Edinburgh's Award; member of the Legal Working Party of the FA Premier League; patron, Harrogate Junior Chamber of Commerce; trustee, Friends of War Memorials. Inaugural Yorkshire Lawyer of the Year 2000.

MCINERNEY, Peter
SJ Berwin, London
(020) 7533 2521
peter.mcinerney@sjberwin.com
Specialisation: Partner in the Media and Communications Groups. Specialist in media industries including television and film production, distribution and finance, merchandising, sponsorship, advertising and publishing. Also specialist in sports broadcasting rights exploitation.
Career: Royal National Theatre (1981-83). Thames Television (1983-89). SJ Berwin (1989 to date).

MEADON, Simon
Tarlo Lyons, London
(020) 7405 2000
simon.meadon@tarlolyons.com
Specialisation: Having practised as an entertainment lawyer for over 10 years both in private practice and in industry, he then worked as a theatre producer with Bill Kenwright Ltd for five years presenting over 50 theatrical productions in the West End of London and on Broadway. Principal area of practice is theatre and related work particularly for the Donmar Warehouse, New Adventures Ltd, SFX Backrow Ltd and Cameron Mackintosh Limited. He also acts for theatrical agents and personal management companies. In addition, his long experience of film production and financing enables him to advise on these and related matters.
Prof. Memberships: Law Society.
Career: Qualified in 1983.

Personal: Born 25 August 1958, in Staffordshire, England. Educated at North Staffordshire Polytechnic where he graduated in 1979 with a BA (Hons) in Law. Leisure pursuits include theatre, film, tennis and bridge.

MITCHELL, Paul
Taylor Wessing, London
(020) 7300 7000
p.mitchell@taylorwessing.com
Specialisation: Partner in intellectual property department. Principal area of practice is entertainment and media law including copyright and related work in various areas of the entertainment and media industry including music, books, films, television and multimedia. Other main area involves company law aspects of the acquisition and disposal of companies and joint ventures in the entertainment and media industry. Contributes articles to various professional publications and is co-author of Joynson-Hicks on UK Copyright Law. Addresses various conferences on topics related to entertainment and media law.
Prof. Memberships: Law Society.
Career: Qualified in 1976 while with *Joynson-Hicks* and became a partner in 1978.
Personal: Born 2 November 1951. Attended Canford School 1965-69, then Bristol University 1970-73. Roald Dahl Foundation (Advisory Board member). Leisure pursuits include family life, sailing and walking. Lives in London.

MOORE, Charles
Olswang, London
(020) 7208 8699
chm@olswang.com
Specialisation: Partner in media and communications group. Specialist in the development, production, financing, distribution and acquisition of feature films and television programmes. Work includes helping clients structure the financing of productions, including co-production deals, subsidies and UK sale and leaseback deals. Clients include independent producers and major financiers and distributors and, in particular, US studios given unique US experience (see below). Runs the Film Business School in Spain and contributes to the National Film and Television School Finance Module for its Producers Course. Only European member of the Advisory committee for the annual UCLA Business Affairs Symposium for the motion picture industry.
Prof. Memberships: Law Degree from University of Manchester 1984. Qualified as an English solicitor in 1988. Qualified as California lawyer in 1991.
Career: Joined *Olswang* from qualification in 1988. Rejoined *Olswang* in 1998 after four years in Los Angeles working as attorney in motion picture group at Paramount Pictures Corporation (1994-95) and as vice-president, legal affairs at Twentieth Century Fox Film Corporation (1995-97).

MORGAN, Leon
Davenport Lyons, London
(020) 7468 2600
lmorgan@davenportlyons.com
Specialisation: A specialist in the production, financing and distribution of films, television and other audio visual material and IP rights generally. Advises funds specialising in film and television sale and leaseback transactions and other similar financing or investment schemes. Major clients include Barclays Bank plc, The Royal Bank of Scotland, Equity Bank, Bank Leumi, Ed Victor Limited, The Mersey Television Company and many individuals including Phil Redmond, Matthew Vaughn, Guy Ritchie, Douglas Adams, Richard Harris and Sylvie Guillem. Is regularly quoted in industry periodicals.
Prof. Memberships: Law Society
Career: Qualified and joined *Davenport Lyons* in 1964. Became a partner in 1969.
Personal: Born 3 July 1939. Educated at Westcliff High School, 1951-58. Leisure interests include film, books, art, theatre, music and opera. Lives in London

MOXON, Richard
Davenport Lyons, London
(020) 7468 2600
rmoxon@davenportlyons.com
Specialisation: Main area of practice is film and television production and finance including animation and children's programming together with involvement in merchandising and character licensing. Has also been particularly active in the area of tax-based financings, film library acquisitions and so-called 'sale and leaseback' transactions.
Prof. Memberships: PACT Council, BAFTA and a co-opted member of the British Screen Advisory Board.
Career: Imperial Tobacco legal department, 1975-77; *Denton Hall & Burgin* 1977-84 (partner 1982); Lorimar Productions 1984-86 (head of legal and business affairs); *Marriott Harrison* 1986 - January 1999, (partner); *Davenport Lyons* January 1996 to date.
Personal: Queen Elizabeth Grammar School, Wakefield. University of Birmingham LLB (Hons) 1969-72, College of Law, Guildford 1972. Interests include singing, cinema, golf. Lives Sunbury-on-Thames.

MYERS, Andrew
Clintons, London
(020) 7395 8468
amm@clintons.co.uk
Specialisation: Partner in Entertainment Department. Principal areas of practice are music and theatre representing high profile artists, song writers, producers, managers and industry executives, major and independent record labels and theatre producers. Particular expertise in the creation of joint ventures with majors and independents, in the sale and purchase of record companies and the sourcing of recording deals for new bands.
Prof. Memberships: The Law Society.

Career: Joined *Clintons* on qualification in 1995 from *Clifford Chance* and became a partner in 1998.
Personal: Born 18 November 1969. Studied law at Leeds University, attaining a 1st class honours degree.

NYMAN, Bernard
B M Nyman & Co, London
(020) 8365 3060
bernie.nyman@iname.com
Specialisation: Principal area of practice is non-contentious work in publishing (books, magazines, journals, etc), dealing with contracts for all aspects of publishing including electronic publishing, acting for publishers, authors, literary agents, printers, distributors and learned societies. Libel reading (ie pre-publication advice) and dealing with libel complaints post-publication. General intellectual property work including advice on copyright, trademarks and passing off, and agreements in the entertainment industry generally.
Prof. Memberships: Law Society, European Communities Trade Mark Association, The Media Society, Trustee of The Enid Blyton Trust for Children (appointed 2000).
Career: Qualified in 1979. Partner at *Rubinstein Callingham* from 1983. Partner at *Manches & Co* 1994-98. Proprietor *BM Nyman & Co* 1999.
Publications: Author of the copyright section of 'The Encyclopaedia of Forms & Precedents' (5th edn re-issue, 1999, Vol 21(2)), precedents for Adams: 'Character Merchandising' (2nd edn, 1996, Butterworths). Regular contributor to 'Entertainment Law Review'. Specialist contributor to the 14th edn of 'Copinger & Skone James on Copyright' (Sweet & Maxwell, 1999 and 1st supplement 2002).
Personal: Born 1954. Educated at Royal Liberty School 1965-72 and Sheffield University 1972-75 (BA in Law). Leisure interests include jazz, film and cricket. Lives in North London.

ORGAN, CD
Russells, London
(020) 7439 8692

PALMER, Nigel
SJ Berwin, London
(020) 7533 2265
nigel.palmer@sjberwin.com
Specialisation: Head of Media and Communications Group. Main area of practice is media and entertainment work, including film financing, tax shelter financing, merchandising, film and television production, publishing and video distribution. Involved in financing of many notable feature films, and tax based film financing. Lawyer to 'Thomas the Tank Engine' company from back bedroom to public company. Author of Longman's 'Practical Commercial Precedents on Merchandising'. Member of editorial board of 'Yearbook of Copyright and Media Law'.

THE LEADERS — MEDIA & ENTERTAINMENT

Prof. Memberships: International Bar Association, Fellow of Royal Society of Arts.
Career: Joined *Denton Hall & Burgin* in 1976, qualifying in 1979. Partner *Denton Hall Burgin & Warrens* 1983-88. Left to join *SJ Berwin & Co* as a partner in 1988.
Personal: Born 12 May 1950. Attended St Edward's School, Oxford 1963-67, then Christ Church, Oxford 1968-71. Leisure pursuits include swimming, reading and music. Lives in Greenwich.

PAYNE, Abigail
Harbottle & Lewis, London
(020) 7667 5000
abigail.payne@harbottle.com
Specialisation: Main areas of practice are film and television production, financing, distribution and copyright issues. Particular expertise in structuring international co-productions to obtain subsidies and tax incentives. Clients include major US production companies and sales agents, leading UK producers, sale and leaseback partnerships, insurance underwriters and talent agencies.
Career: Qualified in 1995, worked at *Theodore Goddard* 1993-95, then BBC (Independent Drama) 1995-97. Joined *Harbottle & Lewis* in 1997. Became Senior Associate in 2000 and Partner in 2002.
Personal: Born 1968. Attended Lockleaze School 1981-86, then Bath University. Leisure interests include tennis, skiing, gym and cinema.

PHILIPPS, Richard
Richards Butler, London
(020) 7772 5840
rpsp@richardsbutler.com
Specialisation: Partner in media group. Specialises mainly in film finance work, acting for leading banks and other financial institutions active in the market, distribution companies and major overseas organisations. He also acts for leading UK based producers.
Prof. Memberships: BAFTA.
Career: Qualified 1978. Partner at *Richards Butler* since 1985.
Personal: Born 1952. Educated at Queens College, Cambridge.

POTTER, Selina
Olswang, London
(020) 7208 8734
skp@olswang.com
Specialisation: Broadcasting and publishing industries. Advises on all commercial aspects of broadcasting, including channel launches, licensing sports, movies and other content, distribution deals and ad sales agreements. Particular expertise in technical aspects of broadcasting, such as satellite and uplink contracts, conditional access, electronic programme guide and interactive television deals. Advises on all commercial elements of book and magazine publishing.
Career: Qualified in 1989 with *Frere Cholmeley*; joined *Olswang* in 1994; became a partner 1995.
Personal: Educated, New College, Oxford.

RIDLEY, Michael
Denton Wilde Sapte, London
(020) 7320 6526
mfr@dentonwildesapte.com
Specialisation: Partner in technology, media and telecoms group. Practice encompasses all aspects of television industry, especially the establishment and carriage of new television channels, and also includes commissioning, distribution, co-production agreements for films and television, sponsorship agreements, broadcasting regulation, copyright law. Frequently lectures on broadcasting, television production and copyright.
Prof. Memberships: Law Society, Royal Television Society.
Career: Qualified in 1980. Rights manager, National Theatre 1980-81. Senior solicitor, London Weekend Television 1981-89. Joined *Denton Hall* in 1989 and became a partner in 1990.
Personal: Chairman of St Paul's Arts Trust and Pop Up Theatre Company.

ROBB, Sophia
Lee & Thompson, London
(020) 7935 4665

RUBINSTEIN, John
Manches, London
(020) 7404 4433
john.rubinstein@manches.co.uk
Specialisation: All aspects of media law and electronic publishing; defamation, malicious falsehood, copyright, obscenity, trade mark infringement, passing off, rights of privacy and personality. Also practices in publishing, multimedia and computer law. Has appeared on BBC and Sky TV. Recent cases include Stern v Piper (CA) 1998, Bremner v Westview Press Inc, Cardata Ltd v RAC Motoring Services Ltd and representation of Southwest Water in the leading computer law case against ICL. Also led a 22 person team Anton Piller search for Business Software Alliance against The Mirror Group.
Prof. Memberships: International Bar Assocations (Co-Chairman of Art and Cultural Property Law Committee 1997-2000), Media Society, TIPLO, Association of the Bar of the City of New York.
Career: Admitted in 1977; admitted to New York Bar and Federal Courts ED and SD New York 1979; with *Manches* since 1994 on merger with *Rubinstein Callingham Polden & Gale*.

RUSSELL, AD
Russells, London
(020) 7439 8692

SANDELSON, Daniel
Clifford Chance, London
(020) 7006 8237
daniel.sandelson@cliffordchance.com
Specialisation: Corporate. Partner specialising in commercial law relating to the media industries.
Career: Articled *Allen & Overy*; qualified 1988; Partner *Clifford Chance* since 1996.
Personal: St Catherines; Oxford University (BA Philosophy, Politics & Economics).

SAVILL, Lisbeth
Olswang, London
(020) 7208 8888
ljs@olswang.com
Specialisation: Partner and Head of Media and Communications Group. Specialist in the production, financing, distribution and acquisition of feature films and television programmes. Work includes structuring finance therefor, including loans, subsidies, and tax-based leasing deals. Clients include independent producers, television broadcasters, major US studios and film financiers (including banks). Runs the Film Business School in Spain and contributes to the National Film and Television School ('NFTS') Finance Module for its Producers Course.
Prof. Memberships: Women in Film and Television; sits on NFTS Producer Course Advisory Panel and British Film Committee Advisory Panel.
Career: Arts/Law degree from University of New South Wales, 1980; litigation solicitor *Clayton Utz*, Sydney 1981; international finance work for *Linklaters* in New York and London 1985-89; joined *Olswang* in 1989 (Partner 1991).

SEARLE, Helen
Searles, London
(020) 7371 0555
helen@searles-solicitors.co.uk
Specialisation: Intellectual property. The firm represents a large number of successful international artists, as well as independent publishers, record companies and distributors. The firm is particularly strong in e-commerce activities.
Career: Became a partner at the now defunct *Siefert Sedley Williams* in her mid-twenties. Joint founding partner of *Searles Solicitors*, a niche practice. Helen has been actively engaged in private practice for the past fourteen years.
Publications: Regularly lectures to both industry and university audiences on the field of agreements relating to the entertainment industry and contributes articles to the music, legal and academic press.

SHARLAND, Andrew
Clintons, London
(020) 7396 8480
ajs@clintons.co.uk
Specialisation: A leading partner in the litigation department of *Clintons*. Over the last 12 years, his practice has developed from one near-exclusively music-based to one which now encompasses clients within several fields of the entertainment world, including film and video production companies, sporting personalities and representatives, actors and actresses, comedians and television presenters. His interest in popular music and in its creation and production has ensured that his practice retains a strong music bias, increasingly in the field of dance music. Together with David Davis, he represented Sony in the litigation brought by George Michael and has separately brought or defended actions for EMI Music Publishing Limited, Robert Smith (The Cure), Nigel Martin-Smith (the former manager of Take That), Virgin Records and A&M Records. He successfully represented Island Records following the seizure by the Police on the grounds of obscenity of the Album 'Niggaz 4 Life' by the band NWA.
Career: Called to the bar 1986. Partner *DM Landsman & Co* 1988, *Clintons* 1990 (upon its merger with *DM Landsman & Co*).

SHAW, Barry
Barry Shaw, London
(020) 8297 8899
barhanelth@compuserve.com
Specialisation: Drafting of documents in connection with theatrical presentations not only in and for the United Kingdom but also overseas. Invariably, but not always, acts for the Producer. Normally involved in the negotiation and preparation of all material documents for clients. Thereafter acts on the further licensing of rights in the ventures. Recent projects have included dealing with the production documents for 'Mamma Mia'; 'Chitty Chitty Bang Bang'; 'Humble Boy'. Additionally specialises in music copyright matters, publishing and defamation.
Prof. Memberships: Has been associated with a number of subsidised theatres; has sat on numerous boards and is a Director and Secretary of Greenwich Theatre and a Director of Almeida Productions Limited. Is also actively involved with Blackheath FC (Rugby Union) where he is the Honorary Secretary.
Career: Articled to Oscar Beuselinck and followed him when he rejoined *Wright & Webb* in 1963. Stayed in *Wright & Webb* (which in due course merged with *Syrett & Sons*) until *Wright Webb Syrett* decided to join another firm in 1995 at which point he set up practice on his own.

SIBBALD, Graham I
Dundas & Wilson CS, Glasgow
(0141) 222 2200

SINNOTT, Mark
Russells, London
(020) 7439 8692

SMITH, Barry
Richards Butler, London
(020) 7772 5845
bhs@richardsbutler.com
Specialisation: Partner advising on all aspects of copyright law, film and television finance distribution and production, particular expertise in all aspects of sale and leaseback transactions including representing lenders to lessor partnerships. Advises on the Internet, multimedia and other forms of publishing, and on music agreements, also advises clients on character merchandising and licensing, trademarks, passing off and other forms of protection.
Career: Qualified 1974; partner *Richards Butler* 1980.

MEDIA & ENTERTAINMENT ■ THE LEADERS

SOLOMON, Nicola
Finers Stephens Innocent, London
(020) 7344 7652
nsolomon@fsilaw.co.uk
Specialisation: Nicola Solomon is head of publishing and intellectual property at *Finers Stephens Innocent*. She has considerable expertise in all areas of law relating to publishing and book selling. She and her team are unique in that as well as advising a broad range of publishers, both British and international, they also provide specialist advice to rights holders such as authors, illustrators, journalists, photographers and their representatives including agents, literary estates and professional organisations. Nicola advises on both contentious and non-contentious issues, including drafting and negotiating contracts, advice on copyright, moral rights, contractual disputes, passing off and trademark infringement, brand management, defamation and literary estates. Clients include the Wall Street Journal, The Society of Authors, The Association of Illustrators and The British Association of Picture Libraries and Agencies, as well as many individual publishers, creators and agents.
Career: Nicola qualified in 1984 and has been a partner since 1988. She also sits as a Deputy District Judge.
Publications: Writes extensively in this area, including a regular column in 'Author' magazine.

STORER, Robert
Harbottle & Lewis, London
(020) 7667 5000
robert.storer@harbottle.com
Specialisation: Partner and Head of the Film & TV Production & Finance Group. Main areas of practice are film and television production and finance and copyright issues. Has over 25 years' experience representing leading producers, including Merchant Ivory Productions, Fragile Films and Kismet Films, as well as Film Finances Limited, the completion guarantors and various film financiers. Involved in the production and financing of numerous films and television series and programmes, including Mr Bean, Spice World - The Movie, Ideal Husband, Honest, Golden Bowl, Lucky Break and The Importance of Being Earnest and the S Club TV Series. Addressed a number of conferences on media issues.
Prof. Memberships: Law Society, International Bar Association, Director of Association of Independent Producers (early 1980s), Director of Film Finances Ltd (1983-88).
Career: Joined *Harbottle & Lewis* in 1969, qualifying in 1971. Became Partner in 1974, and Senior Partner in 1999.
Personal: Born 1947. Attended Buxton College 1960-65, then London School of Economics 1965-68. Leisure pursuits include family, golf, tennis and cinema. Lives in Barnes, London.

SWAFFER, Patrick
Goodman Derrick, London
(020) 7404 0606
law@gdlaw.co.uk
Specialisation: Partner in the Media Department. Main areas of practice are broadcasting and publishing. Includes pre and post-publication advice on defamation, contempt, confidence and copyright, rights exploitation, contractual issues and regulatory advice for the broadcasting industry.
Career: Joined *Goodman Derrick* in 1974. Qualified 1976. Became Partner in 1979 in the Media Department.
Personal: Born 12 February 1951. Lives in London.

TATTON-BROWN, Sam
Davenport Lyons, London
(020) 7468 2600
stattonbrown@davenportlyons.com
Specialisation: Practice includes production, financing and distribution of films and television. Particular expertise and experience in film finance work, acting for The Royal Bank of Scotland, Barclays Bank, sale and leaseback partnership and other film financiers.
Prof. Memberships: Qualified at Frere, Cholmeley, Bischoff in 1998. *Clifford Chance* 1998 - 99. Joined *Davenport Lyons* in 1999.
Personal: Educated at Durham University. Pleasure interests include cinema, playing judo badly, boogie boarding and walking in beautiful scenery.

THOMPSON, Andrew
Lee & Thompson, London
(020) 7935 4665

TREGEAR, Steven
Russells, London
(020) 7439 8692

TURTON, Julian
The Simkins Partnership, London
(020) 7907 3040
julian.turton@simkins.com
Specialisation: Media and entertainment with emphasis on music industry but also publishing, art and new media. Represents artists, composers, publishers and record companies, book publishers, authors, performers. Editor of books on Neighbouring Rights, Competition Law and Effects of Digitisation on the Music Industry. Author of numerous specialist articles. Lectured on a wide variety of music industry themes. Member of Management Board. Expert in many recent music industry disputes.
Prof. Memberships: President of the International Association of Entertainment Lawyers 1998-2001 and now committee member; BAFTA.
Career: 1980 Qualified and joined *The Simkins Partnership*. (Partner since 1985).
Personal: Born 23 July 1952. Attended Bristol University (1974). Interests include family, golf, reading and Arsenal F.C.

WARE, James
Davenport Lyons, London
(020) 7468 2600
jware@davenportlyons.com
Specialisation: Copyright and copyright tribunal and has an extensive knowledge of transactional broadcast clearing practice, music industry, broadcasting, entertainment, merchandising, rights administration, theatre, computer media. Clients include substantial independent music publishers and specialist entertainment businesses on the one hand and well-known composers and artists on the other.
Prof. Memberships: International Association of Entertainment Lawyers, International Managers Federation. Deputy chairman of the Guildford School of Acting.
Career: St Johns College, Oxford. Virgin Group, director; CBS Songs, European regional vice-president; *Davenport Lyons*, partner since 1986.
Personal: Music, theatre and hill walking. Members: Athenaeum, MCC.

WATSON, Peter
Levy & McRae, Glasgow
(0141) 307 2311
peterwatson@lemac.co.uk
See under Defamation, p.275

WEST, Nick
Denton Wilde Sapte, London
(020) 7242 1212
Specialisation: Partner in the Technology Media and Telecoms group, specialising in television work, particularly in relation to analogue and digital pay television. He also has experience in sports law, sponsorship and TV broadcast of sporting events, as well as satellite work including contracts for the launch and construction of satellites and transponder leases.
Career: Partner, *Denton Wilde Sapte* 1993; Re-joined *Denton Wilde Sapte* 1991; Solicitor, *Wigan & Co* 1989; Solicitor, *Denton Wilde Sapte* 1983.

WILLIAMS, Alan
Denton Wilde Sapte, London
(020) 7320 6249
apw@dentonwildesapte.com
Specialisation: Head of digital media practice. Work includes digital media and e-commerce, electronic publishing, copyright, libel, commercial contract, traditional publishing and theatre. Lectures for Hawksmere, PIRA and others.
Career: Qualified in 1969, having joined *Denton Hall & Burgin* in 1967. Became a partner in 1972.
Publications: Co-author with Michael Flint and Clive Thorne of 'Intellectual Property: the New Law'; contributes to 'Publishing Agreements' edited by Charles Clark and 'International Media Liability' published by John Wiley. Author with Duncan Calow of 'Digital Media: Contracts, Rights and Licensing' (2nd edn 1998 Sweet & Maxwell). Edited Halsbury's Laws of England section on 'Press, Printing and Publishing'.

WILLIAMS, Gordon
Lee & Thompson, London
(020) 7935 4665

ZEFFMAN, David
Olswang, London
(020) 7208 8888
dcz@olswang.com
Specialisation: Partner media and communications group. Principal area of practice involves commercial and corporate aspects of television, sport, music and e-commerce businesses.
Prof. Memberships: IBA, IAEL.
Career: Qualified 1983 while with *Frere Cholmeley* and became a partner in 1989. Appointed head of company and commercial department, *Frere Cholmeley Bischoff* in 1993. Joined *Simon Olswang & Co* as partner in 1994.
Personal: Born 28 February 1958. Attended Haberdashers' Aske's School 1969-76, then Brasenose College, Oxford 1977-80. Lives in London.

PARLIAMENTARY & PUBLIC AFFAIRS

London: 593; Profiles: 594

Research approved by BMRB For this edition, **Chambers'** researchers conducted 6,582 interviews – 3,900 with law firms, 511 with barristers and 2,171 with clients. The validity of the research was scrutinised by BMRB International, who audited both the methodology and the results at our offices in London. They interviewed **Chambers'** researchers and cross-checked sample interviews. Details of the audit appear on page 7.

OVERVIEW Transport and Works Act (TWA) and Harbour Orders continue to comprise the lion's share of work in this sector, with the number of private bills presented to Parliament remaining static and low. In public affairs, the year has seen a reduced level of work from commercial clients and public affairs groups. Taking its place has been a flow of public policy work, centred on human rights, devolution and the monitoring of the legislative process. The devolved parliaments have seen a rise in private legislation with a consequent increase in demand for specialist legal services. Some interviewees noted that a number of City firms were making their first concerted inroads into this market, a trend that will be followed with interest.

LONDON

PARLIAMENTARY AGENCY
LONDON
1
- Bircham Dyson Bell
- Rees & Freres
- Winckworth Sherwood

2
- Sharpe Pritchard

LEADING INDIVIDUALS
1
- DURKIN Joseph Rees & Freres
- THOMPSON Paul Bircham Dyson Bell

2
- GORLOV Alison Winckworth Sherwood
- IRVING Paul Winckworth Sherwood
- OWEN Robert Bircham Dyson Bell

3
- BROWN Nicholas Bircham Dyson Bell
- LEWIS Alastair Sharpe Pritchard
- MCCULLOCH Ian Bircham Dyson Bell
- PETO Monica Rees & Freres

This book is the product of 6,582 1/2 hour interviews. See p.7 for BMRB audit. Within each band, firms are listed alphabetically. See individuals' profiles p.594

BIRCHAM DYSON BELL (see firm details p.873) This highly respected team stands out from the other firms in our table as, according to the market, the only one that can offer a genuine and leading service for both agency and public affairs work. The large and relatively young group covers the range of agency work from general planning and public law advice to the promotion of private and local legislation, particularly on local transport schemes. Clients confirm that it is *"switched on, grasps what you need quickly, has good resources and the right attitude."* Bucking the market trend, it has acted on an increased number of private bills this year. *"Outrageously well-researched and thorough,"* **Paul Thompson** (see p.595) recently acted on the South Hampshire Rapid Transit TWA Order for Hampshire County Council (CC) and Portsmouth City Council. **Robbie Owen** (see p.595) has worked for Merseytravel promoting the Mersey Tunnels Bill concerning the levying of tolls for their use. Clients say that he *"puts a lot of effort into really understanding our needs and really goes the extra mile."* The *"impressive expertise"* of **Nicholas Brown** (see p.594) has recently been put to use on the HSBC Investment Banking Bill, to allow for the bank's restructuring, while senior partner **Ian McCulloch** (see p.595) (*"well informed and on the ball"*) has been instructed by the Countryside Agency over the designation of the New Forest National Park and by landowners on the Land Reform (Scotland) Bill, currently before the Scottish Parliament. Work on heavy rail enhancements has also been a feature of the last year, with the whole team representing landowners affected by the construction of the Channel Tunnel Rail Link. **Clients** Countryside Agency; Docklands Light Railway; City of Edinburgh Council; English Welsh & Scottish Railway; Environment Agency; Gallagher Estates; Gloucester Harbour Trustees; The Highland Council; HSBC; Merseytravel; Peterhead Harbour Trustees; Trinity House Lighthouse Service.

REES & FRERES (see firm details p.1110) Harbour work in Scotland and a noted nationwide ability in the railway sector were considered by many interviewees to be the firm's greatest assets. A growing team, which includes three 'Roll A' parliamentary agents and a parliamentary draftsman, is said by clients to have a refreshingly clear approach. It works closely with the firm's property department on related planning and environmental issues. Lead partner **Joseph Durkin** (see p.594) is, in the eyes of some, *"becoming the doyen of parliamentary agents; the most senior and authoritative."* He is said to form an impressive double act with **Monica Peto** (see p.595) (*"she sticks to her guns."*) The firm has acted on two of the biggest schemes ever undertaken under TWA Orders. It has continued working with Railtrack on the public inquiries concerning the Thameslink 2000 and the West Coast Main Line upgrades, and has also been involved on the scheme to enlarge the operating area of the Port of Felixstowe by means of reclamation and the construction of the new quay. **Clients** Harwich International Port; Railtrack.

WINCKWORTH SHERWOOD (see firm details p.1192) The department continues to grow, with the arrival of new members to the team. It

PARLIAMENTARY AGENCY

is working on a large number of LRT schemes and has won new instructions relating to heavy rail (the first new railways for decades and the first railway Bills in the Scottish Parliament,) harbour development and energy projects. These last include several wind farm schemes, one of which has become the Scottish Parliament's first Private Bill. Devolution has resulted in public Bill drafting work for both the Scottish Parliament and the Northern Ireland Assembly. Our researchers were told that the department *"represents its clients well and is reasonable in a negotiating forum."* Parliamentary agent **Alison Gorlov** (see p.595) has continued to work with the Corporation of London on the reform of their electoral franchise and East Riding of Yorkshire Council on the Yorkshire Marina regeneration project at Bridlington. On behalf of Cheshire County Council she has promoted the first TWA Order to be made authorising a guided busway. **Paul Irving** (see p.595) (*"extremely strong intellectually"*) continues to act for Associated British Ports over the deepwater container terminal scheme at Dibden Bay. **Clients** Associated British Ports; Corporation of London; Cheshire CC; East Riding of Yorkshire Council; National Audit Office; West Yorkshire PTE; West Midlands PTE; Northern Ireland Assembly; Scottish Parliament.

SHARPE PRITCHARD (see firm details p.1127) The small team assists London boroughs and local authorities nationwide on TWA Orders. Several harbour authorities have instructed the firm on constitutional issues and harbour projects. It also supplies general advice on government legislation and works closely with the firm's planning department. *"A delight to deal with,"* **Alastair Lewis** (see p.595) has recently promoted five private bills relating to the environment and public health in London and advised on highways and parking issues. The unit has also assisted a port authority on the reconstitution of its board and on new powers of investment. **Clients** Local authorities; development agencies.

www.ChambersandPartners.com

PARLIAMENTARY & PUBLIC AFFAIRS ■ LONDON

LONDON

PUBLIC AFFAIRS

PARLIAMENTARY: PUBLIC AFFAIRS
■ LONDON

1. Bircham Dyson Bell
   Clifford Chance
   DLA
   Lovells
   SJ Berwin

LEADING INDIVIDUALS

1. **THOMAS Richard** Clifford Chance
2. **BRACKEN Jonathan** Bircham Dyson Bell
   CLEMENT-JONES Tim DLA
3. **HOLMES Simon** SJ Berwin

This book is the product of 6,582 1/2 hour interviews. See p.7 for BMRB audit. Within each band, firms are listed alphabetically. See individuals' profiles p.594

BIRCHAM DYSON BELL (see firm details p.873) The department has particular expertise in drafting public legislation and advising on parliamentary and legislative procedure. Although the team arguably enjoys a higher market profile for its parliamentary agency work, the practice undertakes a roughly equal amount of public affairs work, with many of its agency experts also contributing to this sector. The unit has recently widened its reach, drafting bills for the Northern Ireland Assembly. **Jonathan Bracken** (see p.594) has lobbied on behalf of the theatre industry regarding the implementation of the Fixed Term Work Directive and has drafted amendments to the Health and Social Care Bill on behalf of community pharmacies. "*A Westminster specialist, he knows the place inside and out*" according to competitors, and has advised the Health Professions Council and its predecessors on the implementation of the Health Professions Order 2001. **Clients** Countryside Agency; Environment Agency; Health Professions Council; Merseytravel; Royal Yachting Association; Trinity House Lighthouse Service.

CLIFFORD CHANCE (see firm details p.911) Although small in size, the team has the advantage of an established client base and extensive global contacts. It undertakes public policy work and monitors developments on behalf of commercial clients, civil servants and regulators. Recognising the increasing importance of EU decisions for the domestic business community, the team has refocused its practice and boasts a permanent representative stationed in Brussels. With experience at the OFT, **Richard Thomas** (see p.595) "*knows a lot of people – and he has the energy to keep that up.*" Competitors commended his "*masterly grasp of strategy and tactics.*" He successfully implemented a campaign for IMS HEALTH to remove a clause from the government's Health and Social Care Bill that threatened its activities. The firm's "*commercial, pragmatic approach*" has also assisted Driver Technologies Association in its efforts to persuade the government to drop its proposals preventing the use of enforcement detection devices. **Clients** Battelle Foundation; Driver Technologies Association; GALA Holding; GECAS; GKN; Hunters & Frankau; IMS/Source Informatics; Innisfree; Japanese Embassy; LIFFE; London Transport Users Council; National Consumer Council; Radio Authority; Safeway Stores; Standard Life Healthcare.

DLA The strategic communications and public affairs practice is led by solicitor and Liberal peer **Tim Clement-Jones**, said by interviewees to "*hustle about the marketplace with style.*" The team is made up of a mixture of legal and communications professionals, based in London, Scotland and Brussels, and is said by some sources to "*focus extensively on the political side of the business.*" Clement-Jones' team monitors policy initiatives and lobbies for policy and legislative changes on behalf of domestic groups and foreign companies in the UK. It also provides wider media relations, crisis management functions and other related services. **Clients** Corporates; professional bodies.

LOVELLS (see firm details p.1045) Corporate and regulatory partner Neil Fagan oversees a large, partner-led public policy steering group, assisted by new head of public policy Francesca Arcidiaco. "*Well informed about how government works,*" the unit conducts a range of public policy services, providing legislative monitoring and strategic advice, issue management and political training programmes. It works in close collaboration with its Brussels office and other elements of its international network. The biotech and pharmaceutical industries continue to be a leading area of activity, while work on matters relating to tobacco and food has increased. The team was praised to researchers for getting to know its markets well and is aiming to widen its sphere of influence into e-commerce and telecommunications. It recently advised on the opportunities of extending patent protection for a medicinal product and recommended a lobbying strategy to influence the amendment process of the Bermuda constitution. **Clients** Corporates; professional bodies.

SJ BERWIN (see firm details p.867) The firm has proactively expanded its work in the EU and competition sectors and can call on a large number of partners if required. **Simon Holmes** (see p.595), who is also active in competition law, was described by clients as "*a super networker*" and was praised for his ability "*to approach problems with a legal and a business attitude.*" The firm has worked with a UK bookmaker to overturn the prohibition of online betting in countries outside the UK, and assists Coca-Cola Enterprises in its communications programme. It opposed the merger between Mars and Royal Canin on behalf of a client and has lobbied successfully on behalf of a number of UK electricity generators against a licence modification. Abroad, it led the campaign against the German 'Green Dot' recycling system, involving complaints before the European Commission and lobbying at both the regional and national levels. **Clients** Coca-Cola Enterprises; Kobayashi; Laura Ashley; Mediaset; Qantas; Samuel Strapping; Sumitomo; Warner Brothers.

THE LEADERS IN PARLIAMENTARY & PUBLIC AFFAIRS

BRACKEN, Jonathan
Bircham Dyson Bell, London
(020) 7227 7000
jonathanbracken@bdb-law.co.uk
Specialisation: Principal areas of practice are public affairs, lobbying, legislative drafting, parliamentary procedure and advice on public policy and public law issues. During the past year he has worked on the Police Reform Bill, Firearms (Amendment) Bill, Animal Sanctuaries (Licensing) Bill, Office of Communications Bill, the Animal Health Bill and the Health Professional Order.
Prof. Memberships: Law Society; Society for Advanced Legal Studies (Associate Fellow); Institute of Public Relations (Government Affairs Group); Administrative Law Bar Association.
Career: Partner *Bircham Dyson Bell* (then *Bircham & Co*) 2000; Scholar in Residence, US Law Library of Congress.

BROWN, Nicholas
Bircham Dyson Bell, London
(020) 7227 7000
nicholasbrown@bdb-law.co.uk
Specialisation: Specialises in infrastructure legislation. Advisor to charities and trustees. Is presently engaged in promoting various Harbour Orders and promoting HSBC Investment Banking Bill.
Career: Articled *Bircham Dyson Bell* (then *Bircham & Co*) 1979. Qualified as a Solicitor in 1983. Partner and Roll A Agent 1985. Chairman of Executive Committee 1997-to present.
Personal: Attended Westminster School and Jesus College, Oxford. Plays cricket and golf and is a qualified soccer referee. Two children.

CLEMENT-JONES, Tim
DLA, London
(08700) 111111

DURKIN, Joseph
Rees & Freres, London
(020) 7222 5381
Specialisation: Senior partner and specialist in administrative and public law, railways and tramways, highways and harbours, planning, environmental law and compulsory acquisition. 30 years experience of promoting and opposing legislation on behalf of the Central Government, local authorities, major public

THE LEADERS — PARLIAMENTARY & PUBLIC AFFAIRS

and private sector transport operators, port authorities, universities and colleges and major national and multinational corporations. Publications include 'Blackstones Guide To The Transport & Works Act 1992' (co-author). Regularly addresses conferences on the parliamentary and legislative process, Royal Charter, harbour law, infrastructure, and Transport & Works projects.
Prof. Memberships: Society of Parliamentary Agents (President). Law Society.
Career: 1961-70 solicitor in general practice in the City. 1970-73 Government parliamentary draftsman with the Office of the Parliamentary Counsel. Partner, *Rees & Freres* since 1973, senior partner since 1981.
Personal: Educated at Sheffield University (LL.B). Born 2nd January 1938.

GORLOV, Alison
Winckworth Sherwood, London
(020) 7222 0441
amhgorlov@winckworths.co.uk
Specialisation: Senior parliamentary partner and parliamentary agent. Specialist in legislation and legislative drafting, parliamentary and legislative procedures, administrative and public law, public sector bodies, commercial undertakings. Particular expertise in transport and other infrastructure (railways, harbours, tramways, utilities). Long experience of acting for central and local government, major transport undertakers, port authorities, utility undertakers, banks, building societies, charities and educational bodies.
Prof. Memberships: Law Society. Society of Parliamentary Agents (past president).
Career: Joined *Sherwood & Co.* (now *Winckworth Sherwood*) in 1971. Qualified as a solicitor in 1975, became a partner and Roll A Agent in 1978.

HOLMES, Simon
SJ Berwin, London
(020) 7533 2222
simon.holmes@sjberwin.com
Specialisation: European, competition and trade law. Major cases include some of the largest anti-dumping, competition and single market law cases involving lobbying in Brussels, London and other member state capitals.
Prof. Memberships: Recent Chairman, Solicitors' European Group.
Career: 1st Class Honours, Law and Economics from Cambridge. Grande Distinction, Licence Speciale en Droit Européen, Brussels University.
Personal: Married, two daughters. Walking, cycling, film.

IRVING, Paul
Winckworth Sherwood, London
(020) 7593 5000
pirving@winckworths.co.uk
Specialisation: Partner in Parliamentary Department. Specialises in drafting, promoting and opposing legislation in Parliament and delegated legislation (including Orders under the Transport and Works Act and the Harbours Act) and in advising on railways, harbours and other infrastructure projects.
Prof. Memberships: Society of Parliamentary Agents. Law Society.
Career: Called to the Bar 1986. Requalified as solicitor 1991. Partner at *Sherwood & Co* (now *Winckworth Sherwood*) since 1992.
Personal: Educated at Trinity College, Oxford (MA and D.Phil). Born 7 November 1956.

LEWIS, Alastair
Sharpe Pritchard, London
(020) 7405 4600
alewis@sharpepritchard.co.uk
Specialisation: Specialisation: promotion of and opposition to private and hybrid bills, transport and works orders and harbour revision orders. Work on government bills including drafting amendments and monitoring. Promoting five private bills in current session, including major local authority general powers and transport bills, and bills for a development agency and a major harbour authority. Editor of Parliamentary section of Butterworths 'Forms and Precedents'.
Prof. Memberships: Society of Parliamentary Agents.
Career: Qualified at *Sharpe Pritchard* 1992, Partner 1996.
Personal: Football, walking, cycling.

MCCULLOCH, Ian
Bircham Dyson Bell, London
(020) 7227 7000
ianmcculloch@bdb-law.co.uk
Specialisation: Parliamentary strategy and procedure, tactics and lobbying with much work in Scotland as well as Westminster. Promoting and opposing primary and subordinate legislation for statutory companies, local authorities, trade associations, transport undertakers, banks, property companies, harbours, charities and sporting and amenity bodies.
Prof. Memberships: Society of Parliamentary Agents (Hon Sec 1989-95; President 1995-98). City of Westminster Law Society (President 1994-95). Law Society. Statute Law Society.
Career: Admitted as a Solicitor 1976. Partner since 1977. Enrolled as a Roll A Parliamentary Agent 1979. Senior Partner (1997-).
Personal: Born 13 May 1950. Educated Edinburgh Academy and University of Dundee (LLB Hons jurisprudence and philosophy).

OWEN, Robert
Bircham Dyson Bell, London
(020) 7227 7000
robertowen@bdb-law.co.uk
Specialisation: Main areas of practice continue to be parliamentary and public affairs, town and country planning, transport and environmental law. Over the past year highlights have been: promoting for Docklands Light Railway Limited an order under the Transport and Works Act (TWA) to authorise an extension of the DLR to Silvertown and London City Airport and, prospectively, a TWA order to authorise a further DLR extension to Woolwich Arsenal; being appointed by Merseyside Passenger Transport Executive and Nottinghamshire County and Nottingham City Councils to promote TWA Orders for, respectively, a Mersey tram system and extensions to the Nottingham Express Transit System; Promoting for the Merseyside Passenger Transport Authority a private bill to change the tolling regime for the Mersey Tunnels; acting for objectors in relation to various orders proposed to be made under the TWA for transport infrastructure; continuing to act for EWS and other landowners affected by the proposed Channel Tunnel Rail Link; advising in relation to various other light rail schemes and railway re-openings; advising the Environment Agency Wales in relation to various matters including byelaws for the river Wye and a review of its role as Conservancy Authority for the River Dee; advising various ports, harbours and conservancies on local legislation and the Government's new ports policy.
Prof. Memberships: Law Society; United Kingdom Environmental Law Association; Society of Parliamentary Agents.
Career: University of London: 1983-86; College of Law: 1986-87; Qualified as a Solicitor 1989; Partner with *Bircham Dyson Bell* since 1991.
Personal: Married with three children.

PETO, Monica
Rees & Freres, London
(020) 7222 5381
monica.peto@1thesanctuary.com
Specialisation: Partner at *Rees & Freres*, Parliamentary Agent and specialist in public law, transport and infrastructure, and legislative drafting. Experienced in drafting, promoting and opposing legislation, including that for the construction and operation of transport infrastructure projects on behalf of major public sector transport operators, port authorities, local authorities. Publications include 'Blackstone's Guide to the Transport & Works Act' 1992, and 'Blackstone's Guide to the Environment Act' 1995 (co-author).
Prof. Memberships: Society of Parliamentary Agents, Law Society.
Publications: Publications include Blackstones 'Guide to the Transport & Works Act' 1992'; Blackwell's 'Guide to the Environment Act 1995' (co-author).
Personal: Born 16 August 1947.

THOMAS, Richard
Clifford Chance, London
(020) 7600 1000
richard.thomas@cliffordchance.com
Specialisation: Public policy. Director of public policy specialising in political, legislative and regulatory activity arising from Whitehall, Westminster and Brussels.
Career: Qualified as a solicitor in England and Wales 1973; 18 year career in UK public sector, rising to Director at Office of Fair Trading 1986-92; joined *Clifford Chance* in 1992; member of several governmental and commercial boards, advisory committees etc.

THOMPSON, Paul
Bircham Dyson Bell, London
(020) 7227 7000
paulthompson@bdb-law.co.uk
Specialisation: Advice on parliamentary and legislative procedures and tactics, legislative drafting, lobbying and public affairs and the promotion of and opposition to local legislation. Has acted for a wide range of public and private sector bodies including national, local, port and transport authorities, banks and other financial institutions, major plcs, utilities, trade and amenity associations and religious and other charitable bodies. Currently, particularly involved in advising various interests on, and assisting them in relation to, new government legislation and devolved matters, whilst also heavily engaged in the promotion of light rail schemes by Transport and Works Order and port-related work.
Prof. Memberships: Law Society, Society of Parliamentary Agents.
Career: Called to the Bar 1977. Partner in *Dyson Bell & Co* 1982. Partner and Solicitor at *Bircham & Co* and *Dyson Bell Martin* since 1990.
Personal: Born 26th March 1954.

PARTNERSHIP

London: 596; The Regions: 597; Scotland: 598; Profiles: 600

Research approved by BMRB For this edition, **Chambers'** researchers conducted 6,582 interviews – 3,900 with law firms, 511 with barristers and 2,171 with clients. The validity of the research was scrutinised by BMRB International, who audited both the methodology and the results at our offices in London. They interviewed **Chambers'** researchers and cross-checked sample interviews. Details of the audit appear on page 7.

OVERVIEW Contentious work in this area has risen as the fluctuating economic climate has prompted a discernible increase in the number of partners being axed or moving on. The most noticeable market trend, however, concerns the effect of the introduction of Limited Liability Partnerships (LLPs) in 2001. The initial excitement induced by these vehicles, which allow the traditional internal partnership to trade with limited liability, seemed to have died down until, that was, the Enron scandal and its exposure of accountancy giant Arthur Andersen to crippling losses. Unsurprisingly, firms are now seeing heightened interest in the concept as accountancy firms, in particular, scramble to limit their vulnerability. A keen, although more limited, interest is being taken by law firms and greater activity in this area is widely predicted.

LONDON

PARTNERSHIP ■ LONDON

1. Allen & Overy
   Fox Williams
   Mayer, Brown, Rowe & Maw
2. Herbert Smith
   Kingsley Napley
3. Finers Stephens Innocent
   Reynolds Porter Chamberlain
4. Bristows
   Field Fisher Waterhouse
5. Wright Son & Pepper

LEADING INDIVIDUALS

1. **FOX** Ronnie *Fox Williams*
   LINSELL Richard *Mayer, Brown, Rowe & Maw*
   TURNOR Richard *Allen & Overy*
2. **GOLD** David *Herbert Smith*
   SACKER Tony *Kingsley Napley*
   WILLIAMS Christine *Fox Williams*
3. **MAYER** Stephen *Reynolds Porter Chamberlain*
   SIMMONS Michael *Finers Stephens Innocent*
4. **MCARTHUR** Colin *Field Fisher Waterhouse*
   MURRAY Clare *Fox Williams*
   WRIGHT Nicholas *Wright Son & Pepper*

PARTNERSHIP: LARGE INTERNATIONAL MERGERS ■ LONDON

1. Allen & Overy
   Herbert Smith
   Linklaters
   Slaughter and May

LEADING INDIVIDUALS

1. **GODDEN** Richard *Linklaters*
   TRIGGS Jeff *Slaughter and May*
   UP AND COMING
   COHEN Raymond *Linklaters*

This book is the product of 6,582 1/2 hour interviews. See p.7 for BMRB audit.
Within each band, firms are listed alphabetically. See individuals' profiles p.600

ALLEN & OVERY (see firm details p.841) This "*first-rate practice*" stands at the forefront of this area of the law largely due to the presence of **Richard Turnor** (see p.602). Possessed of a "*superior intellect*" and a distinguished private client base, a mark of his standing is his position as chairman of the Association of Partnership Practitioners. More involved in the non-contentious side of affairs, he acts mainly, although not exclusively, for professional partnerships offering advice on all partnership-related matters, including mergers, conflict procedures and limited liability issues. In the past year the firm has advised a firm of pension consultants on incorporation as an LLP, and a Jersey firm on its partnership and international structure. **Clients** Accountants; law firms; international investment banks.

FOX WILLIAMS (see firm details p.962) "*Innovative experts on disgruntled partner work,*" this firm fields an array of quality practitioners. **Ronnie Fox** (see p.323) is hailed as "*a tenacious, pioneering spirit*" who has immersed himself for many years in the world of partnership law, negotiating arrangements for partners to leave one firm and join another. His colleague **Tina Williams** (see p.602) has a fine reputation on the transactional side, handling mergers and the formation and structure of partnership agreements. Testament to the firm's "*creative approach*" is its 'Law Firms New to London' initiative, which seeks to advise those law firms planning to set up and develop offices in London, a programme in which **Clare Murray** (see p.601) is heavily involved. On the contentious front the firm has recently dealt with a complex dispute, arguing that the behaviour of leaving partners amounted to grounds for expulsion, whilst on the non-contentious side it has advised a number of accountancy and law firms on the implications of a move to LLP status. **Clients** Solicitors; accountants.

MAYER, BROWN, ROWE & MAW (see firm details p.1060) Active on mergers, demergers, general partnership disputes and LLP issues, **Richard Linsell** (see p.601) co-ordinates affairs in "*a highly polished*" fashion. Often at the cutting edge, he advised Ernst & Young on its conversion to the first GB LLP, and has acted for long-standing client Baker Tilly on its agreed merger with HLB Kidsons to form a £150 million accounting services firm. **Clients** Solicitors; accountants; commercial organisations.

HERBERT SMITH (see firm details p.992) Leading light **David Gold** (see p.600) advises on major disputes and all aspects of partnership structure and constitution (often on an international scale), claiming clients ranging from medium-tier firms to the largest accountancy partnerships. "*Delightfully blunt,*" he is "*superb at the larger case*" and noted by rivals for his "*ability to keep partners' feet firmly on the ground in tense negotiations.*" Obtaining a large amount of spin-off work from the firm's renowned corporate base, the practice acted for PwC in a wide-ranging review of its global governance arrangements and advised Arthur Andersen on claims made against it in connection with the collapse of the Bond Group in Australia. **Clients** Accountants; law firms; legal networks.

KINGSLEY NAPLEY (see firm details p.1023) Consultants to a number of other legal firms, this practice is heavily biased towards non-contentious work and involves itself in innumerable partnership exit and agreement exercises. **Tony Sacker** (see p.601) is "*a savvy figure, good at knocking people's heads together*" who has been consulted on law reform in this area. He has drafted a number of partnership agreements for accountancy firms and acted for Jordans in consulting the company formations agents. **Clients** Solicitors; accountants.

FINERS STEPHENS INNOCENT (see firm details p.955) Although partnership is not a core area of the firm's business, the practice receives solid repeat work from businesses in difficulties and is relatively active in the disciplinary field. Proficient on both the contentious and non-contentious side, **Michael Simmons**

LONDON/THE REGIONS ■ PARTNERSHIP

(see p.601) is seen by market sources as "*something of a guru in partnership management*," adept at handling the needs of both individuals and teams. Advice is offered on partnership agreements and exits, LLPs and the drafting of deeds. **Clients** Accountants; solicitors; actuaries; architects.

REYNOLDS PORTER CHAMBERLAIN (see firm details p.1111) Equally happy with contentious and non-contentious matters, this firm advises on partnership agreements, restructuring, mergers and disposals. **Stephen Mayer** (see p.601) leans more towards dispute-based work and was praised to researchers for his "*rational approach.*" As one barrister commented, he is "*a practical sort of chap, never one to rush carelessly into an already inflamed situation.*" **Clients** Solicitors; accountants; estate agents; surveyors; farming and veterinary partnerships.

BRISTOWS (see firm details p.888) This smaller practice offers advice to professionals on both contentious and non-contentious issues. Its services include negotiating and drafting partnership agreements, advising individuals on the terms upon which they intend to join existing partnerships and providing assistance on mergers, de-mergers and dissolutions. Led by John Lace, the team also lays a stress on alternative dispute resolution in handling partner disagreements. **Clients** Solicitors; accountants; surveyors; veterinary surgeons; architects.

FIELD FISHER WATERHOUSE (see firm details p.954) Liaising closely with its commercial litigation department and with access to specialist tax advice, this practice advises professionals on the full spectrum of partnership issues. The cynosure of the practice remains **Colin McArthur** (see p.601) who is "*switched on to Law Society regulations*" and "*brings calm assurance to the most heated of disputes.*" **Clients** Accountants; solicitors; architects and other professionals.

WRIGHT SON & PEPPER (see firm details p.1198) **Nicholas Wright** (see p.602) and his team, although capable of handling general dispute and negligence issues, remain primarily celebrated by peers in the disciplinary arena. His experience in dealing with Law Society disciplinary procedures is "*second to none*" and he continues to be "*a great man to have on your side if you are hauled up before the Official Solicitor.*" **Clients** Solicitors; accountants; surveyors.

LINKLATERS (see firm details p.1043) Ideally placed by virtue of its global coverage, the firm has enjoyed an excellent year in this field. Richard Godden (see p.600), "*a great lawyer who really takes command,*" has steered his team through many major deals over the past year. Examples include advising Ernst & Young on the reconstitution of its global network and assisting KPMG on its conversion to LLP status. The firm has done a considerable amount of work with PwC, advising it on the IPO of its management consultancy business and the conversion of its UK business into an LLP. In these matters, in particular, commentators have been quick to praise the efforts of the warmly recommended **Raymond Cohen** (see p.600). **Clients** Major accountancy firms.

SLAUGHTER AND MAY (see firm details p.1140) Historically this firm has not enjoyed a high profile in this sector, but peers believe that it is now "*increasingly getting a slice of the pie.*" **Jeff Triggs** (see p.602) heads up affairs and is "*an able and commercial lawyer who works hard with the opposition to get a deal done.*" His recent highlights include advising Bacon & Woodrow on demerger of a partnership and assisting Cazenove on incorporation in preparation for IPO. The firm also acted for KPMG in the UK regarding the takeover of Arthur Andersen following the Enron scandal. **Clients** Accountants; actuaries; large professional and commercial partnerships.

THE SOUTH & THAMES VALLEY

PARTNERSHIP
■ THE SOUTH & THAMES VALLEY

1. **Lester Aldridge** Bournemouth
   Linnells Oxford
   Mundays Cobham

LEADING INDIVIDUALS

1. **CORKE Andrew** Lester Aldridge
   MISCAMPBELL Andrew Linnells

This book is the product of 6,582 1/2 hour interviews. See p.7 for BMRB audit.
Within each band, firms are listed alphabetically. See individuals' profiles p.600

LESTER ALDRIDGE (see firm details p.1038) Handling both contentious and non-contentious work, this team, led by the knowledgeable **Andrew Corke** (see p.600), offers specialist advice on medical partnerships. Its expertise stretches, however, to other professions, with the firm regularly advising on and preparing partnership agreements for accountants, lawyers and veterinary professionals. **Clients** Medical practitioners; accountants; solicitors; other professionals.

LINNELLS (see firm details p.1044) **Andrew Miscampbell**, respected for his "*even-handed approach,*" handles the majority of the non-contentious work in this practice. Some contentious work is also undertaken but the main thrust lies in advising on LLP and medical partnership issues and catering to the needs of other professionals. **Clients** Medical partnerships; solicitors.

MUNDAYS (see firm details p.1078) Respected commercial operator David Irving commits approximately a third of his time to partnership matters, advising on LLPs and medical partnerships in a non-contentious context. The firm also undertakes contentious work for a range of professionals. **Clients** Professional partnerships.

SOUTH WEST

PARTNERSHIP
■ SOUTH WEST

1. **Burges Salmon** Bristol
   TLT Solicitors Bristol
2. **Bond Pearce** Bristol
   Osborne Clarke Bristol
   Veale Wasbrough Bristol

This book is the product of 6,582 1/2 hour interviews. See p.7 for BMRB audit.
Within each band, firms are listed alphabetically.

BURGES SALMON (see firm details p.894) Visible on the professional and trading partnerships front, the firm advises on compulsory retirement, expulsion and general partnership issues. **Adrian Llewellyn Evans** (see p.601) primarily conducts contentious work in a "*forthright but fair*" style as part of a team that also includes well respected **David Marsh** (see p.601). Recent highlights include having acted in the first contentious LLP. **Clients** Farming partnerships; accountants; surveyors; solicitors.

TLT SOLICITORS (see firm details p.1163) A firm able to call on both "*contentious and non-contentious experts who dovetail beautifully.*" **Nick Moss** (see p.601) (non-contentious) is an expert in the GP sector while **Philip May** (see p.563) handles the dispute side and is noted by peers for his excellence in "*drawing up agreements and playing fair with all the partners.*" Advice is proffered on structure, partner relations, incoming and outgoing partner issues and exit strategies and is increasingly involved

www.ChambersandPartners.com

PARTNERSHIP ■ THE REGIONS

LEADING INDIVIDUALS
1 LLEWELYN EVANS Adrian Burges Salmon
MAY Philip TLT Solicitors
2 BELLEW Derek Veale Wasbrough
MARSH David Burges Salmon
MOSS Nicholas TLT Solicitors
MOULE Jos Osborne Clarke
STARKS Brian Bond Pearce

See individuals' profiles p.600

in LLP issues. The team acted on the transfer of the NMGW accountancy practice into Numerica Group on its AIM float, incorporating a partnership with Levy Gee and Jayson Newman. **Clients** Doctors; solicitors; accountants; dentists; vets; surveyors; architects.

BOND PEARCE (see firm details p.879) Dispute resolution expert **Brian Starks** (see p.601) is that *rara avis*: a full-time partnership practitioner. Heading a team, which also handles non-contentious work, he "*always does the best for his client and never takes an entrenched position.*" Recent matters have included the settlement of a number of professional disputes, some involving High Court proceedings, and the acquisitions of several vets' practices for consolidated veterinary services. **Clients** Solicitors; accountants; doctors; business and family partnerships.

OSBORNE CLARKE (see firm details p.1090) Heading a team of six, **Jos Moule** was recommended to our researchers as having "*a watertight grasp of partnership law*." Possessed of a broad reach, the team advises *inter alia* on disputes, LLPs, exit strategies and questions of whether commercial joint ventures can be construed as partnerships. The firm continues to act for Solomon Hare, one of the largest firms of accountants in the country with a single office location, and has recently advised two professional partnerships in relation to their incorporation as LLPs. It also advised in relation to the successful dissolution of a partnership where one of the partners had defrauded the partnership of a sum in excess of £300,000. **Clients** Accountants; solicitors; actuaries; commercial partnerships.

VEALE WASBROUGH (see firm details p.1174) Firmly focused on the medical sector, this team handles all areas of legal work required by GPs' practices. **Derek Bellew** (see p.600) received fulsome praise, particularly from clients, who prize him as a "*responsive, strategic thinker who is something of a guru in this area.*" Over the past year his team has been involved in the structuring of a number of major health centre developments and has given advice to around 200 medical practices within and beyond the region. The practice further encompasses work on behalf of other professionals, advising on partnership agreements and general disputes. **Clients** Medical partnerships; solicitors; accountants; veterinaries; pharmacists.

MIDLANDS

PARTNERSHIP ■ MIDLANDS
1 Hammond Suddards Edge Birmingham

This book is the product of 6,582 1/2 hour interviews. See p.7 for BMRB audit.
Within each band, firms are listed alphabetically.

HAMMOND SUDDARDS EDGE On the contentious side Digby Rose dovetails nicely with Baljit Chohan who handles non-contentious matters. The pair advise on LLPs, restrictive covenants and general partnership issues and have of late dealt with disputes emanating from an increasing number of commercial as well as professional partnerships. **Clients** Lawyers; accountants; surveyors.

THE NORTH

PARTNERSHIP ■ THE NORTH
1 Cuff Roberts Liverpool
Kershaw Abbott Manchester
Mace & Jones Manchester
2 Cobbetts Manchester

LEADING INDIVIDUALS
1 KERSHAW Anne Kershaw Abbott
TWEMLOW Tony Cuff Roberts
2 JUMP Graeme Mace & Jones

This book is the product of 6,582 1/2 hour interviews. See p.7 for BMRB audit.
Within each band, firms are listed alphabetically. See individuals' profiles p.600

CUFF ROBERTS Our researchers detected a universal enthusiasm for **Tony Twemlow**, whose work on the formation, dissolution and disputes inherent within partnerships was much praised. Possessing a "*very sensible head on his shoulders*," he brings "*a calm and realistic approach which negates the emotional side of the most testy disputes.*" **Clients** Surveyors; accountants; solicitors; doctors.

KERSHAW ABBOTT (see firm details p.1022) "*Determined, steely and vigorous*," **Anne Kershaw** (see p.600) is known for her strength of purpose in contentious matters. Whilst the practice edges towards medical partnership work, it is still in the area of expulsions and exits that this firm's true forte is seen to lie. **Clients** Solicitors; accountants; doctors.

MACE & JONES (see firm details p.1047) Ex-president of the Manchester Law Society, **Graeme Jump** (see p.600) is a well-known figure who has utilised his insolvency and litigation background to good effect. Active on both the contentious and non-contentious sides, he acts for a range of professionals but has a particular reputation within the medical sector. **Clients** GPs; dentists; solicitors; accountants.

COBBETTS (see firm details p.914) This large regional firm has had an involvement in partnership law for many years. All matters are undertaken but there is a pronounced slant towards non-contentious work which includes the preparation of new partnership deeds, demergers, retirements and start-ups. Recent highlights include the setting up of LLPs for commercial clients involved in new ventures, and advice on the acquisition of a regional office of a national firm. **Clients** Medical partnerships; accountants; solicitors.

SCOTLAND

DUNDAS & WILSON CS (see firm details p.943) "*Innovative and pioneering,*" this team, led by Christian Hook, largely confines itself to the weightier, commercial end of the market, drawing up complex partnership structures for its corporate clients. Typical of its cutting-edge work has been its advice on the use of limited partnerships as vehicles in property investment and in corporate deals. A highlight of the past year has been its deployment of Scottish limited partnerships in the Lloyd's insurance market. **Clients** Commercial partnerships; professional partnerships.

MACLAY MURRAY & SPENS (see firm details p.1048) On the traditional partnership front the

THE REGIONS — PARTNERSHIP

PARTNERSHIP — SCOTLAND

1
- Dundas & Wilson CS — Edinburgh, Glasgow
- Maclay Murray & Spens — Glasgow
- McGrigor Donald — Edinburgh, Glasgow

2
- Burness — Edinburgh
- Fyfe Ireland WS — Edinburgh

3
- Tods Murray WS — Edinburgh

LEADING INDIVIDUALS

1
- STUBBS Ian — Maclay Murray & Spens

This book is the product of 6,582 1/2 hour interviews. See p.7 for BMRB audit. Within each band, firms are listed alphabetically.. See individuals' profiles p.600

firm continues to advise its client base of solicitors, accountants and other professionals. Increasingly, however, it acts for entertainment and media clients and is visible in the corporate sector handling cross-border partnership law issues and dealing with the structure of US/UK partnerships. **Ian Stubbs** (see p.829) again received high praise for his acumen in the sphere of partnership formation and, as part of the team, advised a group of partners leaving chartered surveyors firm Rydens, a matter that attracted pronounced media attention. **Clients** Doctors; surveyors; lawyers; media and entertainment figures.

MCGRIGOR DONALD (see firm details p.1065) Renowned among its peers for involvement in disputes concerning the fund management community in Edinburgh, this firm is strong in the field of corporate partnerships. "*Never bogged down in the legal detail*" its reach in this area extends from workaday partnership disputes for professional clients to the use of LLPs as vehicles for financing and venture capital projects. **Clients** Chartered surveyors; law firms; accountants.

BURNESS "*Seasoned campaigners*" in this sphere, according to interviewees, the team led by Alan Soppitt has a "*limited but telling role*" in dispute and Scottish limited partnership work. Rival firms were especially impressed by its endeavours in disputes where property is involved. **Clients** Limited and professional partnerships.

FYFE IRELAND WS (see firm details p.966) Based within the corporate department, Andrew Cubie's team acts for professional, medical, farming and leisure partnerships. It also has a marked interest in LLPs. It has advised on the potential of harnessing LLPs as joint venture vehicles for property-based funds, and has assisted two solicitors' firms on the potential implications of conversion to LLP status. **Clients** Doctors; hoteliers; farmers.

TODS MURRAY WS (see firm details p.1164) Partnership law represents a growth area for this team led by Granger Brash. In the past year advice has been given to nine professional firms on partnership demergers or reorganisations, and the team has acted for the proprietors of an Edinburgh hotel in the creation of one of the first LLPs in Scotland. Its new-found prominence in the field is confirmed by its success in being retained by an international bank in connection with a substantial tax planning structure for the bank's wealthy private clients. This alone has involved the creation of 200 limited partnerships. **Clients** Professional firms including lawyers and accountants.

NORTHERN IRELAND

PARTNERSHIP — NORTHERN IRELAND

1
- L'Estrange & Brett — Belfast

2
- Elliott Duffy Garrett — Belfast

LEADING INDIVIDUALS

1
- IRVINE John — L'Estrange & Brett

This book is the product of 6,582 1/2 hour interviews. See p.7 for BMRB audit. Within each band, firms are listed alphabetically.. See individuals' profiles p.600

L'ESTRANGE & BRETT (see firm details p.1039) The highly regarded **John Irvine** (see p.239) leads a team that focuses on providing advice to the big five accountancy firms and assisting individuals in professional firms in relation to the terms of their agreements. The past year has seen the team advising one of the partners involved in the dissolution of a leading firm of criminal law practitioners. **Clients** Solicitors; accountants; estate agents.

ELLIOTT DUFFY GARRETT (see firm details p.947) Largely eschewing non-contentious work, Michael Lynch's team concentrates on meeting the needs of commercial and smaller professional partnerships. Commentators welcome the firm as being "*approachable and easy to deal with*." **Clients** Accountants; solicitors.

NATIONAL — MEDICAL

PARTNERSHIP: MEDICAL — NATIONAL

1
- Hempsons — London

2
- BrookStreet Des Roches — Witney
- Payne Marsh Stillwell — Southampton
- Veale Wasbrough — Bristol

3
- Clarkson Wright & Jakes — Orpington
- Mace & Jones — Liverpool
- TLT Solicitors — Bristol

LEADING INDIVIDUALS

1
- ABBESS Lynne — Hempsons
- BELLEW Derek — Veale Wasbrough
- GREGAN Paddy — BrookStreet Des Roches

2
- JUMP Graeme — Mace & Jones
- STILLWELL Kevin — Payne Marsh Stillwell

This book is the product of 6,582 1/2 hour interviews. See p.7 for BMRB audit. Within each band, firms are listed alphabetically.. See individuals' profiles p.600

HEMPSONS (see firm details p.989) Although undertaking cases for other professional bodies, this firm receives its laurels for being "*the biggest and best*" in medical partnerships. Handling hundreds of cases at any one time, the team is led by **Lynne Abbess** (see p.600) who works closely with bodies such as the General Practitioners Committee at the BMA, and "*has forgotten more than most people know about NHS-related law.*" Recent matters undertaken include acting on Cost Planning Agreements for practices in relation to their ownership of partnership property. The team also advised on goodwill issues and goodwill payments in respect of NHS practices. **Clients** Doctors; solicitors; accountants; architects.

BROOKSTREET DES ROCHES (see firm details p.890) Despite being by no means confined to medical issues, it is in this area that **Paddy Gregan**'s (see p.600) reputation burns the brightest. "*Wholly reliable and a delight to deal with,*" he handles non-contentious work in the main, advising on partnership mergers and exits. Indicative of his standing in partnership law generally, he has recently contributed to a new publication for the Institute of Chartered Accountants in England and Wales to assist in partnership planning and succession issues. **Clients** GPs; lawyers; farmers; chartered surveyors.

PAYNE MARSH STILLWELL (see firm details p.1097) **Kevin Stillwell** (see p.602) retains his reputation as "*one of the true specialists in medical partnership law.*" "*Solution-oriented,*" he avoids litigation where possible, utilising his background in property law to resolve the difficulties of his clients. **Clients** GPs.

VEALE WASBROUGH (see firm details p.1174) See the South West editorial. (see p.598)

PARTNERSHIP ■ THE LEADERS

CLARKSON WRIGHT & JAKES (see firm details p.909) Michael North co-ordinates a team of four, experienced in property and commercial matters. Its core work concerns formations and expulsions in the medical sector, but the group has been looking to broaden its scope of late. Recently it resolved two massive partnership disputes, one concerning architects, the other veterinary surgeons. **Clients** Medical practitioners and other professional partnerships.

MACE & JONES (see firm details p.1047) See the North editorial. (see p.598)

TLT SOLICITORS (see firm details p.1174) See the South West editorial. (see p.597)

THE LEADERS IN PARTNERSHIP

ABBESS, Lynne
Hempsons, London
(020) 7839 0278
lma@hempsons.co.uk
Specialisation: Partner and head of the Professional Practice Department. Principal area of practice is partnership law, encompassing advice on partnership formation, disputes, termination and associated property matters (in particular NHS GP's cost rent schemes and other surgery developments). Acts for doctors, dentists, solicitors, accountants and other professional partnerships. Advises the BMA/GPC on policy issues relating to partnerships and surgery developments affecting all NHS GPs in England and Wales. Author of chapters on partnership in 'The Law and General Practice' and 'When Partners Fall Out' and numerous articles in a variety of professional publications. Co-author of 'Primary Healthcare Premises: An Expert Guide' and 'A Practitioner's Guide to Partnership and LLP Law and Regulation'. Frequent lecturer on partnership issues. Legal correspondent for 'Medeconomics' and regular contributor to the journal 'GP'.
Prof. Memberships: Law Society. Founder member and currently Hon Sec of Association of Partnership Practitioners.
Career: Qualified 1982 with *Hempsons*. Partner since 1985.

BELLEW, Derek
Veale Wasbrough, Bristol
(0117) 925 2020
dbellew@vwl.co.uk
Specialisation: Partner in Company Commercial Department. Chairman. Work covers company sales and purchases, MBOs, corporate finance and professional partnerships. Specialist practice in medical partnerships.
Career: Qualified 1967. Managing Partner of *Veale Wasbrough* 1993-98. Chairman since 1998.
Personal: Born 1942. St John's College, Oxford 1961-64. Chairman St George's Music Trust.

COHEN, Raymond
Linklaters, London
(020) 7456 3556
raymond.cohen@linklaters.com
Specialisation: Specialist in UK corporate finance and company law with wide ranging international experience, having spent nearly 10 years in Hong Kong. Main areas of practice include public and private mergers and acquisitions, issues, joint ventures and general corporate advice. Member of *Linklaters* Asian Business Group with particular focus on Hong Kong, China and Taiwan. Experienced in private mergers and acquisitions and joint ventures; public mergers and acquisitions; reorganisations including restructuring; flotations and listings.
Career: 1996 Partner *Linklaters* London; 1992-96 Partner Corporate Finance Department *Linklaters* Hong Kong; 1987-92 Assistant Solicitor Corporate Finance Department *Linklaters* Hong Kong; 1985-87 Assistant Solicitor Corporate Department *Linklaters* London; 1983-85 articled clerk *Linklaters* London. 1982 Brasenose College, Oxford University, BA Jurisprudence.

CORKE, Andrew
Lester Aldridge, Bournemouth
(01202) 786132
andrew.corke@lester-aldridge.co.uk
Specialisation: Commercial litigator specialising in partnership (particularly professional partnership) disputes. Particular specialisation in medical partnership litigation and in the statutory and financial implications of dissolution in GP practices.
Career: Articled *Thomas Eggar Church Adams* (London). Qualified 1980. Solicitor and partner *Coffin Mew & Co* (Southampton) 1980-87. Partner *Lester Aldridge* 1988.

FOX, Ronnie
Fox Williams, London
(020) 7614 2517
rdfox@foxwilliams.com
See under Employment, p.323

GODDEN, Richard
Linklaters, London
(020) 7456 3610
richard.godden@linklaters.com
Specialisation: Specialist in general corporate advisory work and corporate transactions. Advises a wide range of corporate clients, professional services organisations and investment banks on public mergers and takeovers, joint ventures, private merger and acquisition transactions, reorganisations, flotations, other corporate equity fundraising and equity sales and general corporate advice.
Career: 1990 to date: Partner, Corporate Department, *Linklaters*, 1988-90: Secretary to Takeover Panel; 1987-88: Assistant Solicitor, Corporate Department, *Linklaters* London; 1985-87: Assistant Solicitor, *Linklaters* Hong Kong; 1982-85: Assistant Solicitor, Commercial Department, *Linklaters* London; 1980-82: Trainee Solicitor, *Linklaters* London. 1979-80: College of Law; 1976-79: Trinity Hall, Cambridge University, MA First Class.

GOLD, David
Herbert Smith, London
(020) 7374 8000
david.gold@herbertsmith.com
Specialisation: Large-scale commercial litigation, much of it with an international dimension. Has considerable experience of conducting litigation in various jurisdictions. In addition to general contract disputes, deals with joint venture, partnership and shareholder disputes, banking (notably derivatives related) litigation, commercial fraud, professional indemnity claims, computer-related litigation and defamation. Has wide experience of all types of injunctive remedy. Leads the *Herbert Smith* Israel Business Group.
Prof. Memberships: Law Society.
Career: Qualified in 1975. Joined *Herbert Smith* in 1973, becoming a Partner in 1983.
Personal: Attended LSE 1969-72.

GREGAN, Paddy
BrookStreet Des Roches, Witney
(01993) 771 616
paddy@bsdr.com
Specialisation: All aspects of business law including company acquisitions and disposals, corporate finance, partnership and joint ventures and company restructuring. Also advises on insolvency law. Particularly regarded for his work on behalf of professional partnerships and individual partners. Acts for a wide range of corporate clients, institutions and professionals.
Prof. Memberships: Law Society, Thames Valley Commercial Lawyers Association, Association of Partnership Practitioners, Employment Lawyers Association.
Career: Qualified in 1987. Joined *BrookStreet Des Roches* in 1997 as a partner.
Publications: Contributions to Butterworths 'Encyclopaedia of Forms and Precedents' partnership volume and CCH/ICAEW joint publication 'Succession Planning and Retirement'.
Personal: Leisure interests include all kinds of sport, mountains and spending time with family.

IRVINE, John
L'Estrange & Brett, Belfast
(028) 9023 0426
john.irvine@lestrangeandbrett.com
See under Corporate Finance, p.239

JUMP, Graeme
Mace & Jones, Manchester
(0161) 236 2244
graeme.jump@maceandjones.co.uk
Specialisation: Senior partner. Head of Insolvency and Recovery Department. Licensed insolvency practitioner (1989). Insolvency assessor to the Law Society's post-qualification Case Work Committee (1992). President of the Insolvency Lawyers Association (1997-98). Fellow of the Association of Business Recovery Professional. Member of the Insolvency Practitioners Association. Member of the American Bankruptcy Institute. Member of AEPPC.
Prof. Memberships: Member of the Association of Partnership Practitioners; president, Manchester Law Society, 1991-92; honorary treasurer, Manchester Law Society 1995-98; founder member and honorary secretary of the Northern Arbitration Association (1990); Associate of the Chartered Institute of Arbitrators (1997). Member of the Chartered Institute of Arbitrators (1999). Chairman of Legalink, the international grouping of independent law firms.
Career: Admitted 1969. Joined *Mace & Jones* in 1971. Partner, 1973. Senior partner 1997.

KERSHAW, Anne
Kershaw Abbott, Manchester
(0161) 839 0998
mail@kershaw-abbott.co.uk
Specialisation: Practises in the field of commercial dispute resolution with particular emphasis on professional partnership disputes, professional liability and commercial and construction disputes.
Prof. Memberships: Member of Association of Partnership Practitioners; Deputy Vice-Chairman Pro Manchester; Past President Manchester Law Society; Member of Society of Construction Lawyers; CEDR Accredited Mediator.
Career: Admitted 1975. Practised in North West all working life. Co-founder of *Kershaw Abbott* as niche practice in 1991. Appointed Tax Commissioner in

THE LEADERS — PARTNERSHIP

1995.
Personal: Lives in Ribble Valley with judicial husband and son. Music lover and devoted gardener.

LINSELL, Richard
Mayer, Brown, Rowe & Maw, London
(020) 7782 8806
rlinsell@eu.mayerbrownrowe.com
Specialisation: Partnership and commercial law. Acts for leading partnerships in all areas of professional practice. Work undertaken ranges from mergers, demergers and strategic alliances, through partnership defections and a wide range of partnerships disputes, to partner assessment and remuneration schemes and regulatory and disciplinary issues. Gave evidence to the House of Commons Trade and Industry Select Committee on the subject of LLPs and remains closely involved with the movement, including lecturing and writing on these and other professional topics. Also regularly advising on the adoption of improved partnership agreements with particular emphasis on partner retention, profit sharing and succession issues. He is also a CEDR Accredited Mediator.
Prof. Memberships: IBA, APP.
Career: Jesus College, Cambridge 1966-69; Articled *Rowe & Maw*; Partner 1976.

LLEWELYN EVANS, Adrian
Burges Salmon, Bristol
(0117) 939 2272
adrian.llewelyn-evans@burges-salmon.com
Specialisation: Broadly-based heavyweight litigation and arbitration with a bias towards technical subject matter, often with an international element. Recent work includes substantial product liability cases for insurers; Competition Act investigations; corporate finance claims; professional indemnity claims; engineering equipment failure in the defence, marine and aircraft industries; partnership disputes of all descriptions; a flourishing practice as a mediator.
Prof. Memberships: Registered mediator CEDR and ADR Group; FCI Arb; Law Society; Bristol Mercantile Court Users Committee; Tecsa.
Career: Trained at *Linklaters*, qualifying in 1979 and joining *Burges Salmon* in 1982, becoming a partner in 1984.
Personal: University College of Durham 1973-76. Leisure interests include gardening, walking, fishing and music.

MARSH, David
Burges Salmon, Bristol
(0117) 939 2288
david.marsh@burges-salmon.com
Specialisation: Main areas of practice are company/commercial and corporate finance work, and partnerships. Various directorships.
Prof. Memberships: Law Society.
Career: Joined *Burges Salmon* in 1971, became a Partner in 1972, Managing Partner in 1990 and Senior Partner from 1995-2001.
Personal: University College, Oxford 1962-65. Leisure interests include skiing, music and golf.

MAY, Philip
TLT Solicitors, Bristol
(0117) 917 7912
pmay@tltsolicitors.com
See under Litigation, p.563

MAYER, Stephen
Reynolds Porter Chamberlain, London
(020) 7242 2877
sdm@rpc.co.uk
Specialisation: Head of dispute resolution. A substantial and increasing area of his practice consists of advice on partnership disputes. His work includes the negotiation of settlements with or for retiring partners, acting in arbitrations, and advising on restrictive covenants in partnership agreements. Clients include professional and commercial partnerships. Also acts in employment disputes.
Prof. Memberships: Law Society; International Bar Association; Media Society; Association of Partnership Practitioners.
Career: Educated at St Paul's School and Oriel College, Oxford. Qualified in 1974. Partner at *Reynolds Porter Chamberlain* since 1977.
Personal: Married with three children. Leisure interests include erratic golf and slightly less erratic tennis.

McARTHUR, Colin
Field Fisher Waterhouse, London
(020) 7861 4175
cma@ffwlaw.com
Specialisation: Partner in company and commercial department. Handles all aspects of corporate and partnership law, including establishment, mergers and acquisitions, sales, retirements, dissolutions and joint ventures. Also deals with commercial contracts.
Prof. Memberships: Law Society, IBA, Institute of Directors.
Career: Qualified in 1969, having joined *Waterhouse & Co* (now *Field Fisher Waterhouse*) in 1967. Became a partner in 1974.
Publications: Co-author of 'A Director's Guide – Duties, Liabilities and Company Law' (1990), and contributor to 'A Directors Guide to Accounting and Auditing' (1991) and to 'A Practitioners Guide to Partnership and LLP Law and Regulation' (2001).
Personal: Born 5 November 1944. Educated at Fettes College 1958-63 and Cambridge University 1963-66. Leisure interests include golf and aphorisms. Lives in London.

MISCAMPBELL, Andrew
Linnells, Oxford
(01865) 248607

MOSS, Nicholas
TLT Solicitors, Bristol
(0117) 917 7777
Specialisation: Involved in all areas of corporate and commercial law but main area of practice is partnership and quasi-partnership law. Has wide experience providing strategic and business advice to a large number of professional partnerships, including doctors, dentists, vets, solicitors, accountants, surveyors and architects.
Prof. Memberships: Association of Partnership Practitioners; Insolvency Lawyers Association.
Career: Qualified 1982; joined *Trumps* (now merged with *Lawrence Tucketts* to form *TLT*) 1985; partner since 1988.
Personal: Born 1955, lives in Bristol. Recreations include motorbike, trekking and golf.

MOULE, Jos
Osborne Clarke, Bristol
(0117) 917 3000

MURRAY, Clare
Fox Williams, London
(020) 7614 2554
cmmurray@foxwilliams.com
Specialisation: Employment and partnership law. Claire has a particular interest in international employment law, contracts and disputes. Over the last year she has advised a large number of US and UK law firms on partnership arrangements in the UK, particularly team moves and partner retirement.
Prof. Memberships: Founder member and past Honorary Secretary of the Association of Partnership Practitioners, International Committee of the Employment Lawyers Association, Labour and Employment Law Section of the American Bar Association.
Career: Articles at *Jacques & Lewis* (subsequently *Eversheds*), qualified 1993, joined *Fox Williams* 1996, appointed partner at *Fox Williams* May 1999.
Publications: Editor of Fox Williams' weekly online employment law information service, www.hrlaw.co.uk. Provides regular comments on employment and partnership law issues in Legal and National newspapers and television.
Personal: Member of the panel of the Peter Wolff Theatre Trust, a charitable trust set up to promote new British playwrights; regular theatre goer; running and playing tennis.

SACKER, Tony
Kingsley Napley, London
(020) 7814 1200
tsacker@kingsleynapley.co.uk
Specialisation: Head of partnership unit. Main area of practice is partnership law. Over 20 years experience advising and negotiating in this area. Also deals with charities.
Prof. Memberships: Association of Partnership Practitioners, City of London Law Society, Westminster Law Society, Association of Charity Lawyers.
Career: Qualified in 1963. Partner from 1967 at *Egerton Sandler*, which merged with *Kingsley Napley* 1989. Partner at *Kingsley Napley* since 1989. President Westminster Law Society 1987-88. Chairman City of London Law Society 1998-2001. Committee Member Association of Partnership Practitioners 1997 to date. Official Solicitor Consultant to the Law Commission.
Publications: Author, 'Practical Partnership Agreements' (Jordans). Consultant Editor 'Practitioners Guide to Partnership and LLP Law Regulation' (City and Financial Publishing).
Personal: Born 2nd March 1940. Educated at Owens School to 1958. Recreations include doing communal work and improving computer skills. Lives in London.

SIMMONS, Michael
Finers Stephens Innocent, London
(020) 7323 4000
msimmons@fsilaw.co.uk
Specialisation: Partner in Company and Commercial Department. Handles general company and commercial work, with particular reference to partnership matters. Deals with partnership formation, growth, management and remuneration issues, consultancy advice, disposal of unproductive partners, partnership disputes and dissolution. Acts for partnerships and for individual partners. Also deals with cross-border transactions and other international matters, with particular reference to inward investment into the UK. Has a wide overseas clientele. Regular speaker at management and marketing conferences for professionals both at home and abroad. Has appeared many times on television and radio as a legal spokesman on various topics. Standard charge out rate £300 per hour.
Prof. Memberships: International Bar Association (Immediate past Chairman of Committee dealing with Professional Practice and Technology), Law Society, American Bar Association, Fellow and Trustee of the College of Law Practice Management, Association of Partnership Practitioners and Chairman Designate of Society of English and American Lawyers.
Career: Qualified in 1958. First Class Honours in Law Society Final and Clements Inn Prize. National Service Commission in Secretarial Branch Royal Air Force 1959-61. With *Malkin Cullis & Sumption* 1961-90, as a Partner and as Senior Partner from 1964. Joined *Finers Stephens Innocent* as a Partner in 1990.
Publications: Author of 'Anatomy of Professional Practice', published by Gazette Publications, and 'Successful Mergers: Planning Strategy and Execution' published by Waterlows. Also many articles published in UK and overseas law journals.
Personal: Born 19 May 1933. Educated at St. Paul's School 1947-52 and Emmanuel College, Cambridge 1952-56 (MA and LLM). Leisure interests include music, (especially jazz, football, cricket, tennis, eating, cooking and travelling. Lives in Highgate and Italy.

STARKS, Brian
Bond Pearce, Plymouth
(01752) 677605
bstarks@bondpearce.com
Specialisation: Partner in the Commer-

PARTNERSHIP ■ THE LEADERS

cial Litigation Group. Specialises in partnership disputes and in particular professional partnerships eg solicitors, accountants, doctors, surveyors and valuers, and family farming partnerships.
Prof. Memberships: Member of the Association of Partnership Practitioners.
Career: Qualified 1972 with *Bond Pearce*, becoming Partner in 1977.

STILLWELL, Kevin
Payne Marsh Stillwell, Southampton
(023) 8022 3957
kevinstillwell@pms.solicitors.co.uk
Specialisation: Advising GPs (practices and individuals) constitutes the vast majority of his work: partnership formations and restructuring – admissions and retirements – surgery relocation, leasing and building schemes, interpartner disputes. His approach is practical, drawing on extensive experience of general medical practice. Regularly delivers lectures to GPs.
Prof. Memberships: Law Society; Hampshire Law Society; Association of Partnership Practitioners.
Career: LLB Southampton, London articles, qualified 1979, two years with *Ashford Sparkes* in Exeter then relocated to Hampshire in 1981.
Personal: Born 1954. Married with three sons. Carriage driving is his main hobby.

STUBBS, Ian
Maclay Murray & Spens, Glasgow
(0141) 248 5011
ims@maclaymurrayspens.co.uk
See under Trusts & Personal Tax, p.829

TRIGGS, Jeff
Slaughter and May, London
(020) 7600 1200
jeff.triggs@slaughterandmay.com
Specialisation: General corporate/commercial practice. Recent matters include the merger of *Price Waterhouse* and *Coopers & Lybrand*; the takeover of the Savoy Group by Blackstone; the renegotiation of the contracts for the automation of post office counters among ICL, the DSS and Consignia plc; the joint venture between Consignia plc, TNT Post Group NV and Singapore Post Pte Limited relating to international cross-border mail business; and the demerger of Bacon & Woodrow, the merger of part of its business with *Deloitte & Touche* and the proposed merger of the remainder of its business with Hewitts.
Prof. Memberships: The Law Society.
Career: Gorleston Grammar School; University College, London (LLB, Hons).
Personal: Leisure interests include playing trombone in a jazz band, sport and keeping fit.

TURNOR, Richard
Allen & Overy, London
(020) 7330 3000
richard.turnor@allenovery.com
Specialisation: Partner, specialising in partnership law and estate planning for private clients, private banks and trustees, and heritage and cultural property. Published legal update on partnership law for 'Commercial Lawyer' (1996). Articles on liability of partners (1995-97), 'Sale Trustees of Private Companies' (October 1988), 'Export Licensing Rules in the UK and the Waverley Criteria' (1992), 'Effective decision making in larger professional partnerships' (1999), 'Trust Law Committees Consultation on Capital and Income Trusts' (1999).
Prof. Memberships: Serves on working party of Trust Law Committee (1996 to date) and Committee of Association of Partnership Practitioners (1998 to date); chaired Association of Partnership Practitioners working party on Limited Liability Partnerships (1998 to date); serves on the Law Society's Regulation Review Working Party (1999 to date).
Career: Articled *Allen & Overy*; qualified 1980; partner 1985. Formed and leads *Allen & Overy's* professional partnerships practice group (1995 to date).
Publications: Author of legal chapters in Tolleys 'Professional Partnerships Handbook' (1996, 1988).
Personal: Oxford University (BA 1977). Born 1956.

TWEMLOW, Tony
Cuff Roberts, Liverpool
(0151) 237 7777

WILLIAMS, Christine
Fox Williams, London
(020) 7628 2000
cjwilliams@foxwilliams.com
Specialisation: Specialises in international M&A and capital raising. Has won recognition in Euromoney survey as one of the world's leading mergers and acquisitions lawyers. Within the context of her corporate work, also acts for many professional partnerships, advising on partnership agreements, mergers, incorporations and conversion to LLP status.
Prof. Memberships: Law Society, City of London Law Society, International Bar Association, Association of Partnership Practitioners.
Career: Qualified in 1977. Partner at *Oppenheimers* 1981-88. Formed and joined *Fox Williams* as a partner in 1989.
Personal: Born 15 February 1953. Educated at St Anne's College, Oxford 1971-74. Leisure interests include theatre and cinema. Lives in Buckinghamshire.

WRIGHT, Nicholas
Wright Son & Pepper, London
(020) 7242 5473
Specialisation: Head of Partnership and Professional Department. Main area of practice is partnership law. Advises on partnership creation, disputes and dissolutions, including interventions and practice management of other firms. Member of the Solicitors Assistance Scheme and solicitor member of Defendants' Friends (ICA). Has considerable commercial experience and acts for both UK and overseas corporations.
Prof. Memberships: Law Society. Holborn Law Society, Association of Partnership Practitioners.
Career: Qualified in 1970, having joined *Wright Son & Pepper* in 1960. Became a Partner in 1979.
Personal: Born 2 February 1943. Educated at Charterhouse 1956-60.

PENSIONS

London: 603; The Regions: 606; Scotland: 610; Profiles: 610

Research approved by BMRB For this edition, **Chambers'** researchers conducted 6,582 interviews – 3,900 with law firms, 511 with barristers and 2,171 with clients. The validity of the research was scrutinised by BMRB International, who audited both the methodology and the results at our offices in London. They interviewed **Chambers'** researchers and cross-checked sample interviews. Details of the audit appear on page 7.

OVERVIEW With the jolts being delivered to the stock market, it is hardly surprising that the pensions market has focused this year on contentious work. Lawyers report that litigation has been a growth area, though, perhaps surprisingly, some claim that the Pensions Ombudsman has been relatively quiet. The pensions aspects of restructurings and the winding-up of insolvent companies have also occupied practitioners' time. It has been a good year for the traditional top four who retain their position in *Chambers*' tables, though they are being pressed by the second tier. In Scotland, the big news was the move of a team from Morison Bishop to Biggart Baillie, an event coming shortly before Morison Bishop's decision to demerge.

LONDON

PENSIONS — LONDON

[1]
- Freshfields Bruckhaus Deringer
- Linklaters
- Mayer, Brown, Rowe & Maw
- Sacker & Partners

[2]
- Baker & McKenzie
- Lovells
- Slaughter and May

[3]
- Allen & Overy
- Clifford Chance
- CMS Cameron McKenna
- Travers Smith Braithwaite

[4]
- Nabarro Nathanson
- Pinsent Curtis Biddle

[5]
- Eversheds
- Hammond Suddards Edge
- Herbert Smith

[6]
- Macfarlanes
- Norton Rose
- Simmons & Simmons

This book is the product of 6,582 1/2 hour interviews. See p.7 for BMRB audit. Within each band, firms are listed alphabetically.

FRESHFIELDS BRUCKHAUS DERINGER (see firm details p.964) The firm's superb corporate client base and its "*exceptionally good lawyers*" are said to offer the key to its pensions success. Highly commended for its international network, the team is experienced in handling cross-border, multi-jurisdictional work. Less well known for its standalone pensions profile, competitors nonetheless acknowledge that this is an "*absolutely top-rate*" practice. Typical work includes the establishment and reorganisation of funded and non-funded schemes, and the merging and winding-up of schemes. Elected chairman of the APL in 2001, "*immensely intellectual, technical genius*" **David Pollard** (see p.614), has been involved in the pensions aspects of the demerger of BT and mmO2. Perhaps less visible last year than in the past, according to competitors, "*safe pair of hands*" **Kenneth Dierden** (see p.611) acted for Agilent Technologies on the international retirement benefits aspects of the sale of its medical systems businesses to Philips. This involved formulating a retirement benefits strategy both globally and with specific regard to 31 local jurisdictions. "*Young, enthusiastic*" **Daniel Schaffer** (see p.615) is considered "*hard-working and effective*" by clients. He recently handled the industry-wide defined contribution arrangements for Railway pension scheme trustees. **Clients** Agip; AMP; Balfour Beatty; CIBC; Citibank; Compass; Goldman Sachs; Hays; Hewlett-Packard; ICI; Marconi; Powergen; Rolls-Royce; Somerfield.

LINKLATERS (see firm details p.1043) "*Always competitors for the best work from FTSE companies*" and blue-chips worldwide, according to peers, the team is known to represent leading corporates and trustees of large schemes. Commended by clients for its "*high-powered, go-ahead, modern*" pensions practice, the "*young, vibrant*" team handles standalone issues as well as providing advice on the pensions aspects of corporate led transactions. "*Absolute star*" **Ruth Goldman** (see p.612) advised Lex Service and its trustees on the merger of the RAC pension scheme into that of Lex. She also assisted with the merger of the Royal Bank of Scotland and NatWest schemes. In another highlight for the firm, "*brilliant*" **Tim Cox** (see p.611) advised the trustees of the CGU staff pension scheme on the merger of the Norwich Union Group pensions and life insurance non-contributory plan and the London & Edinburgh Insurance Group retirement and death plan into the CGU scheme. Acclaimed for "*thinking outside of the box,*" interviewees say he handled this transaction, involving assets in excess of £4.5 billion with "*incisive technical knowledge.*" "*Focused*" **Claire Petheram** (see p.614) advised the trustees of the Rothmans International UK pension fund on its merger with the BAT pension scheme. Exhibiting its international reach, the team also handled the pensions aspects of the disposal of a business located in 47 jurisdictions. **Clients** Allied Domecq; BAE Systems; Halifax; Hilton Group; Orange; Plumbing Industries Pension Scheme; PwC; Rank Group; Royal Bank of Scotland; Tesco; TDG; Total Oil Pensions Scheme; WestLB; WH Smith.

MAYER, BROWN, ROWE & MAW (see firm details p.1060) "*The firm was in this business before many of the others and it shows,*" according to commentators. Add to this traditional expertise the weight lent by its recent merger and you have a winning recipe. A good choice for corporate-led deals, the "*well-organised*" team also handles a volume of standalone work for its loyal client base of employers and large occupational pension scheme trustees. With a broad and varied practice, **Stuart James** (see p.613) retains his reputation as a "*standout, practical pensions expert.*" **Anna Rogers** always does a "*fantastic job*" according to clients, for whom she "*sits at the top of the pack.*" Competitors also praise **Andrew White** (see p.616) whose "*in-depth knowledge*" of the industry means he "*always understands the important issues.*" The team advised the trustees of the BAT pension scheme on its merger with the Rothmans scheme. It also handled the wind-up of HSBC's pension unit trusts and the transfer of the assets to HSBC Life's unitised funds. After acting for the Kingfisher trustees on a demerger of schemes following the flotation of Woolworth Group, the firm advised on the establishment of two new pension schemes. **Clients** Abbey National; British American Tobacco; Corus; Kingfisher Group; London Regional Transport; Nestlé; Prudential; The Pensions Trust.

SACKER & PARTNERS (see firm details p.1121) "*A solid, unique and traditionally purely pensions-centred*" practice, competitors are especially impressed with its trustee scheme advice work. A true leader in the field, with a remarkable team, competitors note that it is "*going from strength to strength.*" **Mark Greenlees** (see p.612) is "*the one to go to if you're looking for the solution*" according to one client. He was recently involved in planning and establishing harmonised pensions arrangements following the merger of Glaxo Wellcome and

603

www.ChambersandPartners.com

PENSIONS ■ LONDON

LEADING INDIVIDUALS

1
- **BENNETT Philip** Slaughter and May
- **GOLDMAN Ruth** Linklaters
- **POLLARD David** Freshfields Bruckhaus Deringer
- **STANNARD Paul** Travers Smith Braithwaite
- **COX Tim** Linklaters
- **GREENLEES Mark** Sacker & Partners
- **SLOAN Derek** Allen & Overy
- **WEST Robert** Baker & McKenzie

2
- **ARTHUR Hugh** Macfarlanes
- **FORD Peter** Norton Rose
- **MARSHALL Jane** Hammond Suddards Edge
- **MULLEN Chris** Pinsent Curtis Biddle
- **QUARRELL John** Nabarro Nathanson
- **SAMSWORTH Jane** Lovells
- **SERES Jonathan** Sacker & Partners
- **DIERDEN Kenneth** Freshfields Bruckhaus Deringer
- **JAMES Stuart** Mayer, Brown, Rowe & Maw
- **MOORE Nigel** CMS Cameron McKenna
- **PITTAWAY Ian** Sacker & Partners
- **ROGERS Anna** Mayer, Brown, Rowe & Maw
- **SCHAFFER Daniel** Freshfields Bruckhaus Deringer
- **WHITE Andrew** Mayer, Brown, Rowe & Maw

3
- **ANDREWS Sue** Pinsent Curtis Biddle
- **BENNEY Belinda** Field Fisher Waterhouse
- **DOCKING Peter** Sacker & Partners
- **GAULT Ian** Herbert Smith
- **KOWALIK Mark** CMS Cameron McKenna
- **SAUNDERS Carolyn** Taylor Wessing
- **SMITH Stephanie** Travers Smith Braithwaite
- **TIER Sarah** Sacker & Partners
- **ATKINSON Mark** CMS Cameron McKenna
- **COX Helen** Clifford Chance
- **FENTON Jonathan** DLA
- **ITO Stephen** Lovells
- **LEWIS Roger** Eversheds
- **SHERWIN Nick** Clifford Chance
- **STRACHAN Russell** Lovells

4
- **BERKELEY Christopher** Pinsent Curtis Biddle
- **CLOSE Chris** Sacker & Partners
- **GRANT Mark** CMS Cameron McKenna
- **JACOBS Howard** Slaughter and May
- **PEARSON John** Lovells
- **POWELL Andrew** Hammond Suddards Edge
- **BROWNING Lesley** Norton Rose
- **FENN Jonathan** Slaughter and May
- **GREENSTREET Ian** Hammond Suddards Edge
- **MEEKS Alastair** Pinsent Curtis Biddle
- **PETHERAM Claire** Linklaters
- **WYMAN Michael** Simmons & Simmons

UP AND COMING
- **HOLLAND Jeanette** Baker & McKenzie
- **STIMPSON Maria** Ashurst Morris Crisp

See individuals' profiles p.610

SmithKline Beecham. **Ian Pittaway** (see p.614) "*slices through the details to get to the main issues*" according to rivals. He was visible throughout the year advising the trustees of the Blagden pension scheme in their high-profile dispute with the liquidator of Blagden. "*Well-established in the industry*," but less visible than in the past, according to interviewees, **Jonathan Seres** (see p.615) is "*very constructive and not a point-scorer.*" "*Great guy*" **Peter Docking** (see p.612) also "*doesn't play games*," while **Sarah Tier** (see p.616) was also recommended by market sources. **Chris Close** (see p.611), "*eager to cut to the chase*," completes a team of ranked practitioners, which "*exudes confidence*." The team acted for BT in establishing its new money purchase scheme, and has since advised the trustees in other matters. **Clients** AXA Sun Life; BBC; Citibank; Dixons Group; Jarvis Hotels; Nationwide Building Society; Powergen Energy; Reuters Group; Yorkshire Bank.

BAKER & MCKENZIE (see firm details p.855) Having "*strengthened its numbers and depth*" in pensions, the firm is said by competitors to be "*strong on products and the investment side.*" Market sources are impressed by the way in which the team has successfully built a stand-alone pensions practice, servicing a lot of UK pension schemes, alongside its international work, and it duly rises in this year's ranking. Headed by **Robert West** (see p.616), an "*all-rounder who communicates well with clients*," the team is "*friendly to work with and doesn't try to score unnecessary points.*" West advised Sony on pensions matters relating to its joint venture with Ericsson to merge their mobile phone businesses worldwide. "*Extremely bright*" **Jeanette Holland** (see p.613) is a young partner who clients say "*efficiently holds her ground.*" She acted for BP Chemicals on pensions issues relating to its agreement with Solvay concerning participation of their polypropylene and engineering polymer businesses in European and US joint ventures. Other highlights include advice to the trustees of the Swallow Hotels pension scheme on its merger with the Whitbread pension fund. **Clients** Avis UK Pension Plan; Avon Cosmetics; Co-Operative Insurance Society Pension Scheme; Emerson Electric; Hanson Industrials Pension Scheme; Merchant Navy Officers Pension Fund.

LOVELLS (see firm details p.1045) "*A large practice with quality lawyers*" is the market perception of this impressive and friendly team. It enjoys a broad base of "*top pensions clients*" who commend the team for its "*strong transactional advice*" and long-standing expertise. "*Doing a cracking job*" **Jane Samsworth**'s (see p.615) name is associated with the firm's major recent highlight – its involvement in Equitable Life. **Stephen Ito** (see p.613) is said by clients to be capable of "*breaking the mould.*" He handled the restructuring of the Civil Aviation Authority pension scheme as part of the National Air Traffic Services PPP. **Russell Strachan** (see p.616) is an "*old hand in pensions matters,*" but competitors say that he is less visible now on the front line, **John Pearson** (see p.614) remains "*highly regarded*". Its representation of Equitable Life naturally kept the team busy this year, and it played an important role in the scheme arrangement approved by the High Court in February. Other highlights for the firm include advising the Bank of Scotland on a project launching a stakeholder pension and a range of special pension products including a self-invested personal pension plan. **Clients** BAA; Land Rover Group; NATS; Pension Provision Group; Army Benevolent Fund.

SLAUGHTER AND MAY (see firm details p.1140) The firm boasts a "*fantastic*" practice advising "*excellent pensions clients*" many of them from its blue-chip client base, of which peers confess to being "*hugely envious.*" Though best known for its advice on major transactions, a healthy proportion of the department's work is self-generated. Praised by clients for his "*encyclopaedic knowledge of pensions,*" **Philip Bennett** (see p.611) is "*phenomenally hard-working.*" He advised the Royal London Mutual Insurance Company on a transaction involving the harmonisation of future service benefits across five group pension schemes as well as the transfer of assets from the Refuge Assurance Superannuation Fund. "*Dynamic employment expert*" **Howard Jacobs** (see p.613) also cuts a dash in the pensions world, while "*efficient*" **Jonathan Fenn** (see p.294) was praised by clients for "*quietly getting on with things.*" He advised Boots on changes to the investment policy of its pension scheme. The firm also represented Unilever in multinational pensions issues surrounding its sale of the DiverseyLever industrial cleaning business to Johnson Wax Professional. **Clients** Adolph Coors Company; Boots Company; Chubb; Ericsson; GM Investment Trustees; Unilever; Vauxhall Motors.

ALLEN & OVERY (see firm details p.841) Considered by sources to be most visible on the pensions aspects of large transactional work, this compact, "*high-quality*" team acts for a range of pensions clients across sectors including manufacturing, financial services, banking, the privatised utilities and voluntary organisations. The workload includes matters concerning age and sexual discrimination, the rights of part-timers and casual workers, conversion to money purchase, and advice on corporate governance and executive remuneration. Easily the firm's standout practitioner, **Derek Sloan** (see p.615) is "*first class at getting straight to the heart of matters.*" Continuing to advise Mobil on pensions matters, the team recently acted for Centrica on the reorganisa-

LONDON ■ PENSIONS

> **TOP IN-HOUSE LAWYERS**
>
> **Mark McKEOWN**, Litigation Counsel, William Mercer
> **Val VARDY**, Principal, Towers Perrin
>
> The "*knowledgeable*" **Val Vardy** *retains her place in the list, and likewise the "excellent"* **Mark McKeown**. *Both lawyers were commended by sources as good to deal with.*
>
> In-house lawyers' profiles p.1201

tion of its management grade pension arrangements and on introducing new benefit structures for managers. **Clients** ASW; Bass; CGU; Consignia; Ericsson; Global Crossing; The Lucas Pension Scheme.

CLIFFORD CHANCE (see firm details p.911) With its "*heavy-hitting corporate clients*," the pensions practice is predominantly visible in a transactional context; however, it also offers standalone advice to trustees, employers and product providers. Commended by peers for the strength of its international network, it has a big profile for assisting its top-drawer financial institution client base in cross-border pensions matters. Head of group, **Helen Cox** (see p.611), and **Nick Sherwin** (see p.615), who handle matters "*with justified confidence*," make up the core of the team. Highlights of the past year have included advice to Prudential in relation to its flexible annuity product, and to Yell on splitting its pension arrangements from BT. The team also acted for Dynegy on the pensions aspects of its acquisition of the gas storage business from BT. **Clients** AGA Foodservice Group; Alcatel Telecom; BAE Systems; British Energy; Jaguar Cars; JPMorgan Chase; Prudential; Nationwide; Nomura.

CMS CAMERON MCKENNA (see firm details p.914) According to the market this "*young, enthusiastic bunch of 30-somethings*" is "*doing well and winning pitches.*" The team has had a busy year advising on final salary schemes and on the pensions aspects of mergers. "*Energetic client man*" **Mark Atkinson** (see p.610) advised on the merger of seven pension schemes to form the Iceland Group pension scheme, and has since acted for the trustees of the merged scheme. "*Pragmatic*" **Mark Grant** (see p.612) advised the trustees of Independent Insurance pension scheme in relation to the impact of Independent Insurance's administration and the winding-up of the scheme. **Mark Kowalik** (see p.613), who was praised by interviewees for "*always doing the best for his clients*," handled various merger-related pensions issues for First Group. Heading the team is "*experienced and commercially sensitive*" **Nigel Moore** (see p.614), who assisted with the report for the court in relation to aspects of the Equitable Life compromise scheme. **Clients** Bestfoods Pension Scheme; First Group Trustees; Independent Insurance; Iceland Group Trustees.

TRAVERS SMITH BRAITHWAITE (see firm details p.1166) Though smaller than many of its rivals, this firm wins commendations from peers for doing "*quality work*" for an "*excellent client base*" weighted towards the insurance industry. "*Effective*" head of department **Paul Stannard** (see p.615) can be relied upon to "*see the wood for the trees*," while **Stephanie Smith**'s (see p.615) "*detailed work is liked by clients.*" Together they have handled the 'career average' scheme for Cadbury Schweppes. Following market trends, the team has become more involved of late in advising on the investment side of running pension schemes. Alongside its employment department, the group advised on a number of claims from part-timers against several different clients for backdated pension scheme memberships. **Clients** Associated British Foods; AXA; Clarks Shoes; Hanson; Trinity Mirror.

NABARRO NATHANSON (see firm details p.1080) The firm is said to be "*bouncing back, rather than falling over*" following last year's departure of two partners to Norton Rose. Rivals believe that the team has retained loyal clients and is recovering nicely. Heading the team, **John Quarrell** (see p.614) has an "*historical reputation which is not to be underestimated.*" They represented the trustees of Invensys pension scheme in managing their £4 billion investment transition project. This high-profile transition involved negotiating investment management and custodian agreements with companies such as Merrill Lynch, HSBC, Morgan Stanley, Goldman Sachs and Schroders. The team also acted for the trustees of the AMP UK Staff pension scheme in its merger with Towry Law. **Clients** AMP UK Staff Pension Scheme; IBM UK Pension Plan; Invensys Pension Scheme; Pirelli Common Investment Fund.

PINSENT CURTIS BIDDLE (see firm details p.1102) Market sources consider last year's merger, adding Pinsent Curtis' national weight to Biddle's expertise, to have been a huge success, creating a "*chunky team, which does some chunky work without making too much noise about it.*" **Chris Mullen** (see p.614) is said to have been "*pushing things hard since Hugh Arthur left*," while "*punchy*" **Sue Andrews** (see p.610) "*gets to the point in a practical and sensible way.*" Together they acted on a three-way pension scheme merger for the UK subsidiary of a leading US manufacturer, involving assets in excess of £100 million. "*Meticulous*" **Christopher Berkeley** (see p.611) represented the trustees of the former National Power scheme in a House of Lords case concerning allocation of a £400 million surplus. Also highly recommended, **Alastair Meeks** (see p.614) "*quietly gets the job done with an academic touch.*" The team acted recently in the merger of the Rhône-Poulenc pension fund with the Aventis CropScience UK pension fund. **Clients** Aventis CropScience UK Pension Fund; Babcock International Group; Eaton UK; Shell International; Trustees of Innogy Group of the Electricity Supply Pension Scheme; Vivendi Water UK.

EVERSHEDS (see firm details p.949) The "*strength of its regional backing*" helps to guarantee this firm its place in our tables, where it "*gives the City firms a run for their money.*" A top-class, high-volume pensions litigation practice is also a boon. Competitors wait to see how the departure of Robin Ellison to private consultancy will affect the practice. It leaves **Roger Lewis** (see p.614), well known for his advice in electricity industry schemes, now "*holding the fort.*" He acted recently for National Grid in its successful House of Lords appeal regarding the use of a surplus. The team also assisted J Sainsbury in drafting and negotiating investment management agreements with 20 fund managers for over £2 billion assets, and advised the One 2 One pension scheme on a wide range of issues. **Clients** The National Grid Company; One 2 One Pension Scheme; J Sainsbury Pension Scheme.

HAMMOND SUDDARDS EDGE This sizeable team has undergone recent restructuring, which, say competitors, should give it "*fire in its belly.*" They predict that it could easily make much more of an impact in the London market than it has currently achieved. Covering trustee advice work, as well as the corporate angle, the firm advises on a number of asset management agreements and investment matters. "*Not to be underrated*" according to competitors, practice head **Jane Marshall** "*does her homework.*" You also have to get up early to catch out "*bright*" **Ian Greenstreet** who clients acknowledge can "*easily think through difficult problems.*" "*Entertaining*" **Andrew Powell** is also praised for offering "*solid advice.*" **Clients** ICI; Allied Dunbar Assurance; Northern Electric.

HERBERT SMITH (see firm details p.992) Busy assisting the firm's highly rated corporate practice with the pensions elements of major transactions, the firm is not felt by market sources to have a high profile for standalone advice, though it does offer an all-round pensions package. Its standout partner is **Ian Gault** (see p.612), who clients say "*will often come up with an entirely new angle.*" He and his team have recently acted for Northern Electric, advising on the pensions aspects of the sale of its supply and metering business to Yorkshire Electricity. Another highlight for the team was its advice to Time on the pension aspects of its £1.15 billion acquisition of IPC Media. **Clients** Capita; Onyx Environmental; QinetiQ; Royal London Mutual Insurance Society.

MACFARLANES (see firm details p.1047) Known in the market as "*primarily a transaction-based practice*," it is building on last year's recruitment of **Hugh Arthur** to establish a pensions profile. Peers consider him "*phenomenally*

PENSIONS ■ THE SOUTH & SOUTH WEST/THAMES VALLEY

good at cutting through the pensions mess," though they believe his profile has dipped slightly with his move. The team provided advice to one of the groups of beneficiaries in the well-publicised National Bus litigation. It has also been instructed by Thorn over an application to OPRA for a modification order. This sought to permit a repayment of surplus in exchange for benefit improvements under the Thorn pension scheme. It also assisted new client Aventis CropScience in the merger of the Rhône-Poulenc pension fund with the Aventis CropScience UK pension fund. **Clients** Addis; British Airways Trustees; Cordiant Communications Group; Royal Doulton; Saatchi & Saatchi; United Carriers Group.

NORTON ROSE (see firm details p.1084) Following last year's recruitment of two partners from Nabarro Nathanson, peers acknowledge that the firm's "*profile has risen in the market*," making it "*a force to be reckoned with*." "*First-class*" head of department **Peter Ford** (see p.612) acted for McDermott International on the wind-up of its UK pension plan and return of surplus, including a high-profile dispute in Scotland. **Lesley Browning** (see p.611), "*efficient and to the point*," advised Towry Law on the merger of its pension arrangements with AMP. The firm has also assisted BMW on general UK pensions matters, and took part in the House of Lords hearing in the Equitable Life test case. **Clients** AIG; Hanover International; Goldman Sachs International; Thomson Multimedia; Xansa.

SIMMONS & SIMMONS (see firm details p.1136) Though better known for its leading employment practice, the team has nonetheless handled quality pensions work. **Michael Wyman** (see p.616) ("*sticks to his guns*") heads a team that has recently represented the trustees of Zurich Financial Services UK pension scheme on its merger with the Allied Dunbar and Zurich Insurance schemes. It also advised the Ministry of Defence on the pensions aspects of its DERA public private partnership and assisted Merrill Lynch Investment Managers in the landmark litigation brought by Unilever's pension fund. **Clients** Barclays Life; BASF; Cadbury Schweppes; GlaxoSmithKline; Railtrack; William Hill; Xerox; Next; Zurich Financial Services.

OTHER NOTABLE PRACTITIONERS "*Helpful and determined*" **Belinda Benney** (see p.611) of Field Fisher Waterhouse is said to take an "*analytical approach*" to pensions problems. "*Hard-working and constructive*" **Carolyn Saunders** (see p.615) at Taylor Wessing made a lasting impression on the market with the "*fantastic job*" she made of the National Bus case. At DLA, **Jonathan Fenton** is respected as an "*experienced practitioner*." Competitors say that **Maria Stimpson** (see p.615) at Ashurst Morris Crisp has "*taken the practice in both hands and is making a name for herself*."

THE SOUTH & SOUTH WEST

BURGES SALMON (see firm details p.894) "*Pre-eminent in the South West*" according to some commentators, the team works on a large number of scheme mergers, mostly as standalone work. It is also handling a fair amount of transactional work for clients seeking to escape City prices. "*Extremely bright and accomplished*" Tim Illston (see p.613) heads the pensions and incentives group. He acts for Western Power Distribution on all pensions matters, including those relating to the Electricity Supply pension scheme with assets in excess of £1 billion. The team was appointed this year as the advisor to the trustees of TI Automotive, and to QinetiQ, for which it has handled final salary scheme issues. **Clients** AT&T ISTEL; FirstGroup; Group 4; Prospect (IPMS).

OSBORNE CLARKE (see firm details p.1090) Together with Burges Salmon, this is "*the other serious player*" in the region. "*A heads-up pensions team*," it has acted for the Imperial Tobacco pension fund, a 48,000-member scheme, on various matters including investment issues such as currency hedging and stock lending, and arranging a new final salary scheme for new starters. "*Sensible and steady*" Mark Womersley heads the team, which has also assisted Scottish Widows, Abbey National and Lincoln National on an array of pensions matters. **Clients** Abbey National; Blick UK; Environment Agency's Active Pension Fund; Imperial Tobacco Pension Fund; Kier Group Pension Scheme; Scottish Widows.

BLAKE LAPTHORN (see firm details p.877) Like its regional rivals, only on a "*slightly smaller scale*," the team is visible in the pensions aspects of transactional work for its growing roster of corporate clients. Recent client wins include work for the trustees of the Western Provident Association pension scheme, Beales and the trustees of the Isle of Wight Private Hospital pension scheme. "*Up-and-coming*" **Maria Riccio** has handled a great deal of Ombudsman and High Court pension work, recently obtaining a Court Order for the trustees of the Bournemouth Orchestras retirement benefits scheme and undertaking two cases with OPRA. **Clients** Beales; George Gale & Co Pension Scheme; LM Asic Pension Plan; Marlborough Underwriting Retirement Benefits Plan.

THAMES VALLEY

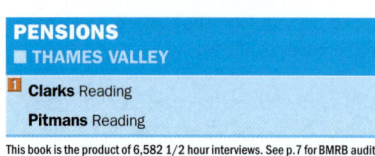

CLARKS (see firm details p.908) A "*long established*" practice, it concentrates on a mix of standalone work and corporate support. Key player **David Clark** covers pensions as part of a varied practice including other corporate matters. Clients praise his "*technical expertise*." The team is visible advising small- to medium-sized schemes and local businesses. **Clients** Local businesses; pension trustees.

PITMANS (see firm details p.1103) Undertaking the full range of pensions work this "*strong*" department has been particularly busy advising on scheme mergers, wind-ups and documenta-

606

WALES/MIDLANDS ■ PENSIONS

LEADING INDIVIDUALS

1 ARCHER David *Pitmans*
   CLARK David *Clarks*

tion. "*Experienced*" group head, **David Archer** (see p.610), is a high-profile player in the regional market. His expanding team has recently recruited another pensions partner from Burges Salmon. The firm received several new appointments by independent trustees during the year, and has recently been busy assisting the Ferguson Group Scheme in various matters. **Clients** Ferguson Group.

WALES

PENSIONS
■ WALES

1 Eversheds *Cardiff*

LEADING INDIVIDUALS

1 DAVIES Ian *Eversheds*

EVERSHEDS (see firm details p.949) Clear leaders in Wales, the main element of the firm's work is advice on scheme mergers. With his "*reputation reaching to London,*" head of department **Ian Davies** (see p.611) works "*effectively, even though he is often extremely busy.*" The past year has seen work for Alcoa on the merger of its pension schemes following the acquisition of part of the business of British Aluminium. The team also assisted Luxfer Group in implementing a pension scheme restructuring following the sale of a large part of its business. **Clients** Alcoa; Heinz; Luxfer Group; Spontex; Technicolor.

MIDLANDS

PENSIONS
■ MIDLANDS

1 Wragge & Co *Birmingham*
2 Hammond Suddards Edge *Birmingham*
3 Eversheds *Birmingham*
   Pinsent Curtis Biddle *Birmingham*
4 Martineau Johnson *Birmingham*

LEADING INDIVIDUALS

1 COCKERILL Vivien *Wragge & Co*
   FORREST Ian *Hammond Suddards Edge*
   RYLAND Glyn *Wragge & Co*
2 BLACK Richard *Wragge & Co*
   FALLON Liz *Eversheds*
   HINGLEY Gerald *Wragge & Co*
   RAMSHAW Simon *Pinsent Curtis Biddle*
   SHELLEY Daniel *Pinsent Curtis Biddle*
3 DAVIS Richard *Browne Jacobson*
   EVERSON Ingrid *Eversheds*
   GRAVILL Robert *Hammond Suddards Edge*
   LAIGHT Simon *Martineau Johnson*
   MILES Helen *DLA*
   MILTON Kevin *Wragge & Co*

WRAGGE & CO (see firm details p.1197) The number one in the area, it stands alone at the top of our list. Its strong pensions team offers all-round pensions advice, much of it of the standalone variety, to its blue-chip client base. Admitted to have the "*quality edge on the other firms*" in the region, its "*technical excellence*" is appreciated by clients. Head of department **Glyn Ryland** has an "*unmatched grasp*" of the sector and a knack of "*getting to the heart of the matter.*" He acted this year on a transfer from a private sector scheme back into the Principal Civil Service pension scheme. Also admired is "*likeable and intelligent*" **Vivien Cockerill**, who advised a leading multinational recently on benefit structures. "*Determined*" **Gerald Hingley** is praised by clients for always exceeding their expectations, while **Richard Black** is said to "*manage clients with ease.*" He demonstrated his expertise recently in a scheme merger, involving a household name petrochemical company, with a total merged value of £1.3 billion. The team also includes "*commercial and pragmatic*" **Kevin Milton** who was described as "*technically tops*" by one interviewee. The group also has a dedicated pensions litigation team resolving issues before the High Court and Ombudsman. **Clients** Adepta; BA; Britannic Assurance; Europcar; Peugeot; Windsor Group.

HAMMOND SUDDARDS EDGE This "*massive outfit,*" described as "*a strong regional player,*" is thought by peers to retain an independent identity rather than just being a satellite of London. Pensions advisory work makes up a large part of the team's workload, and it assists in matters such as wind-ups, mergers, documentation and trusteeship work. Clients apparently love "*extremely commercial*" **Ian Forrest** and his "*loyal team.*" His colleague, "*bright and practical*" **Robert Gravill**, handles a large volume of documentation and is expert on advice to trustees. As a team, they have acted on full-service briefs for Allied Carpets as well as for other new clients such as Land Rover, East Midlands Airport and Hagemeyer. **Clients** Allied Dunbar; British Midlands Airways; ICI; United Utilities.

EVERSHEDS (see firm details p.949) Best known for its work on the pensions elements of transactional advice, the firm co-operates closely with its London office, and is said by peers to contribute a lot to the national network. Head of department **Liz Fallon** (see p.612) gives "*good commercial advice*" according to clients. She has recently assisted IBM with various pension scheme matters including transactional support and advice on adding new employees to its scheme. "*Sensible*" **Ingrid Everson** (see p.612) has acted on the pensions elements of a range of PFI projects such as public service takeovers. The team established a new pension scheme last year for the Laurel Pub Company, including final salary and money purchase elements. **Clients** Alexander Forbes Trustee Services; Alliance & Leicester; Centrefile; Ernst & Young; Staples; Trustees Scapa Tapes UK Limited Pension Plan; Wyko Group.

PINSENT CURTIS BIDDLE (see firm details p.1102) Market sources consider that the book is still open on this office since the merger. "*It may be catching up*" say some, and there is little dispute that eventually Biddle's pensions expertise will help it to "*rise to the top.*" The team, which concentrates on merger advice, is headed by "*extremely energetic and bright*" **Simon Ramshaw** (see p.614), who competitors consider a "*skilled client-winner*" as well as a good lawyer. Recently appointed by the independent trustee to the UEF pension scheme, following the company's administration, he showed considerable skill in handling this 1,500 plus member scheme. Clients also appreciate the "*traditional technical strength*" of **Daniel Shelley** (see p.615). He handled the reorganisation of pension schemes for Hillsdown Holdings and the introduction of new benefit structures for the Cadbury's pension scheme. **Clients** Arriva; Cadbury Schweppes; Devonport Royal Dockyard; GKN Group; Kalamazoo.

MARTINEAU JOHNSON (see firm details p.1056) Competitors admire the way this small team has "*made a name for itself.*" They attribute this success to "*personable*" **Simon Laight** (see p.614), who is said to be "*full of energy and enthu-*

PENSIONS — EAST ANGLIA/NORTH WEST

siasm." The team has continued to work for Pointon York, having assisted in establishing the group's SIPP, a new concept in pension provision. It also defended an educational body against 180 claims brought by part-time employees seeking retrospective membership of its occupational pension scheme. Another highlight has seen the group offer advice in relation to a major multiparty scheme merger involving assets in excess of £1 billion. **Clients** Britannic Assurance; Bullough; Pointon York; University of Aston; University of Coventry.

OTHER NOTABLE PRACTITIONERS Richard Davis (see p.611) of Browne Jacobson is a well-respected pensions lawyer, while peers praise **Helen Miles** of DLA for "*delivering clear advice with technical strength.*"

EAST ANGLIA

PENSIONS — EAST ANGLIA

1 Eversheds Norwich

LEADING INDIVIDUALS

1 SCOTT Harry Mills & Reeve

This book is the product of 6,582 1/2 hour interviews. See p.7 for BMRB audit. Within each band, firms are listed alphabetically. See individuals' profiles p.610

EVERSHEDS (see firm details p.949) Covering a mixture of pensions and share schemes advice, the national firm enjoys a pre-eminence in the region. Ben Goodfellow is a member of the respected team, which acted for Lancaster on a scheme merger and rule changes, and also handled the changes to Eastern Counties Newspapers Group's scheme as a result of a Section 425 reorganisation. Other typical work includes updating and consolidating scheme documentation. **Clients** Appleyard Group; Eastern Counties Newspapers Group; Lancaster plc.

OTHER NOTABLE PRACTITIONERS "*Established*" Harry Scott (see p.615) handles the pensions work at Mills & Reeve and is respected for his thoroughness.

NORTH WEST

PENSIONS — NORTH WEST

1 Addleshaw Booth & Co Manchester
   DLA Liverpool, Manchester
2 Eversheds Manchester
   Hammond Suddards Edge Manchester
3 Masons Manchester

LEADING INDIVIDUALS

1 WRIGHT David DLA
2 ASHLEY TAYLOR Andrew Hammond Suddards Edge
   GRAHAM Ronald Eversheds
   GRIFFITHS David Addleshaw Booth & Co
   KENNEDY Patrick Masons
3 HARRIS Jeremy DLA
   SCHOLEFIELD Stephen Pinsent Curtis Biddle
   SOUTHERN Steve Hammond Suddards Edge

This book is the product of 6,582 1/2 hour interviews. See p.7 for BMRB audit. Within each band, firms are listed alphabetically. See individuals' profiles p.610

ADDLESHAW BOOTH & CO (see firm details p.838) "*Ahead by a nose*" according to some sources, this solid pensions outfit is commended by competitors as "*good to work with.*" Head of department **David Griffiths** (see p.613) is praised for "*covering all the angles in detail.*" As a team they have handled a number of pension scheme mergers over the past year, and have also been busy advising companies and trustees on scheme deficits, closure of final salary schemes and application of debt legislation. The team has also recently assisted in an actuarial consultancy with an OPRA investigation. **Clients** Cussons (International); Kellogg's; Trinity Mirror; Ciba Specialty Chemicals.

DLA The firm's strength is thought by market sources to remain in Liverpool where it has a "*large presence*" offering its clients support on a range of pensions matters including advice in connection with mergers. "*Courteous and competent*" David Wright is the renowned name here. He enjoys support from a team including "*combative but constructive*" Jeremy Harris. **Clients** Trustees; local companies.

EVERSHEDS (see firm details p.949) With Jacqui Timmins' relocation to the Leeds office, interviewees consider that the profile of the team in Manchester has dipped, though Ronald Graham (see p.612), a pensions expert praised by competitors as "*easy to get on with,*" is visible in the local market. He and his team, in conjunction with the Leeds office, advised Hopkinson Trustees on the wind-up and return of surplus of its scheme. Other highlights include the establishment of a new final salary scheme for Arkady Craigmillar. **Clients** Arkady Craigmillar; Akzo Nobel Trustees; Ideal Standard; Hopkinson Trustees.

HAMMOND SUDDARDS EDGE Though considered lower-profile than some of its regional competitors, this team is felt by rivals to be "*strong and stable.*" Handling scheme mergers and general trustee advice as well as product development work, it has the backing of its national support network. "*Polite and charming*" Andrew Ashley Taylor is a respected name for pensions law. Competitors also admire Steve Southern for "*getting a good job done for his clients.*" **Clients** British Midlands Airways; Imperial Home Decor Group.

MASONS (see firm details p.1057) "*A strong, dependable team*" according to clients, it covers a range of standalone work for a wide variety of pension schemes, as well as undertaking transactional support related to PFI/PPP projects, IT outsourcing and commercial transactions. Head of department Patrick Kennedy (see p.613) is "*constructive and keen to ensure a sensible result*" according to clients. The team recently advised the Metropolitan Police Authority on matters relating to pension scheme drafting and clauses of the project agreement governing the transfer of staff. It also acted on the merger of two pension schemes sponsored by London Scottish Bank. **Clients** Metropolitan Police Service; London Scottish Bank; Simon Carves.

OTHER NOTABLE PRACTITIONERS The "*highly commercial*" Stephen Scholefield (see p.615) has moved from Addleshaw Booth & Co to join the budding Manchester office of Pinsent Curtis Biddle.

NORTH EAST

PENSIONS
NORTH EAST

1
- Addleshaw Booth & Co — Leeds
- Hammond Suddards Edge — Leeds

2
- DLA — Leeds, Sheffield

3
- Eversheds — Leeds

4
- Dickinson Dees — Newcastle upon Tyne
- Pinsent Curtis Biddle — Leeds
- Wrigleys — Leeds

5
- Nabarro Nathanson — Sheffield
- Walker Morris — Leeds

LEADING INDIVIDUALS

1
- AINSCOE Raymond — Wrigleys
- MCKENNA Catherine — Hammond Suddards Edge
- RAWNSLEY Rachel — Addleshaw Booth & Co

2
- HOLMES Leigh — Wrigleys
- JENKINS Martin — Dickinson Dees
- MASSARANO SALT Vikki — DLA
- PAYNE Kate — DLA
- TIMMINS Jacqueline — Eversheds
- TURNBULL Andrew — Walker Morris

3
- ALLISON Margaret — Nabarro Nathanson
- RIDLER Mark — Hammond Suddards Edge
- SAEEDI Terry — Hammond Suddards Edge
- TAYLOR Anne — Irwin Mitchell
- THOMAS-GREEN Susan — Pinsent Curtis Biddle

This book is the product of 6,582 1/2 hour interviews. See p.7 for BMRB audit.
Within each band, firms are listed alphabetically. See individuals' profiles p.610

ADDLESHAW BOOTH & CO (see firm details p.838) The team boasts a good client base, including manufacturers, banks and financial institutions, and covers standalone and corporate support work. Though it is close at the top, many consider that this team has a slight edge over its regional rivals. **Rachel Rawnsley** (see p.615) is said by competitors to have "*done a good job at taking over where Neville Peel left off.*" With her "*helpful, sound advice*" making her popular with clients, she has worked on numerous pension scheme mergers. Other work over the past year has included the wind-up of schemes, including one scheme which transferred into more than ten other schemes. The team continues to advise clients on scheme funding difficulties, including applications to OPRA for time extension for contribution rates. **Clients** ASDA; Bradford & Bingley; Skipton Building Society; Logica; Regional Independent Media Group; Water/Mirror Image Pension Scheme.

HAMMOND SUDDARDS EDGE This broad practice, with a healthy dose of standalone work, is respected by peers and clients alike for its skilful and efficient style. **Catherine McKenna** is said by clients to "*always do a perfect job.*" High on her list of resources are "*negotiating flair and technical skill.*" **Mark Ridler** has "*made his way well*" in the field, while **Terry Saeedi** was also said to be "*moving up.*" The team acted for the Kalon pension scheme in relation to its merger with 13 other schemes of the TotalFinaElf Group. It also advised North Yorkshire County Council on the pensions implications of outsourcing its roads and maintenance services, and assisted new client Alumasc Group on investment agreements relating to its pension arrangements. **Clients** BBA Group; Fenner; Kalon Pension Scheme; Kelda Group; VAW; Northern Electric Group; Redcats.

DLA Though not a huge practice, it is seen by rivals to enjoy some good work, particularly in relation to mergers and acquisitions, and to be a genuine competitor in the region. **Kate Payne** is described by market sources as "*a safe pair of hands*" who is "*good with clients.*" Her colleague, "*commercial and proactive*" **Vikki Massarano Salt**, is also respected in the field. **Clients** Trustees; local businesses.

EVERSHEDS (see firm details p.949) Arriving from the Manchester office, "*ambitious*" **Jacqui Timmins** (see p.616) "*has her focus firmly on the client,*" and is expected to boost the visibility of the firm. Over the last year she has worked for Ideal Standard, in conjunction with the firm's Manchester office, handling the pension scheme merger with the Create scheme. **Clients** Britannia Building Society; Akzo Nobel Trustees; Hophold Pensions Trustees.

DICKINSON DEES (see firm details p.938) The firm has "*the Newcastle market in its hands*" according to competitors. The team's standout practitioner is group head **Martin Jenkins** (see p.613) who was said by interviewees to be "*superb with clients.*" The group offers advice on scheme mergers and general pensions matters for domestic employees and trustees. Recent client wins include an appointment by Taylor Woodrow, which has increased the team's spread. The firm is also on the panel of advisers for OPRA, and offers contentious as well as non-contentious advice. **Clients** ARRIVA; Go-Ahead Group; Procter & Gamble; Northern Electric; Northern Rock; Railways Pension Scheme; UCB.

PINSENT CURTIS BIDDLE (see firm details p.1102) "*Raising its profile*" in the market, the firm is thought by competitors to be upping its game and playing in a higher league. The "*smallish but high-quality*" firm has been particularly active assisting in the pensions elements of transactional work. "*Sensible and tough*" **Susan Thomas-Green** (see p.616) leads a team that has recently been appointed to assist the Hydra International pension scheme. A highlight of the year was advising on the merger of three pension schemes with combined assets of £250 million. **Clients** AMP; Hydra International Pension Scheme; Koppers UK; Jacuzzi; Thistle.

WRIGLEYS (see firm details p.1199) This team certainly has the resources, and competitors expect that its profile will also take off soon. **Raymond Ainscoe** (see p.610) has a varied practice and is admired by rivals for his grasp of detail and for "*not giving anything away.*" Tim Knight supports the team with his tax and trust background. "*Thorough*" **Leigh Holmes** (see p.613) also wins market plaudits. Work includes ongoing pensions advice and transactional support, and it is growing its standalone practice and attracting pension scheme trustees. **Clients** Pension scheme trustees; charities; private clients.

NABARRO NATHANSON (see firm details p.1080) Recently arriving from Addleshaw Booth & Co, head of department Neville Peel, though a consultant, is said by peers to bring about the needed boost to the firm's pension practice. He and his team advised the London Borough of Haringey and Accord on the transfer of some of the authority's employees to the contractor. This is just one of a number of PFI/outsourcing projects on which the firm has advised. The team's focus in this area has also led UNITE Group to seek its advice on a pathfinder project concerning the University of Sheffield's halls of residence. **Margaret Allison** (see p.610) advised Sheffield City Council on the transfer of employees. **Clients** Dew Pitchmastic; Middlesbrough Council; Shaws Petroleum; Audit Commission, Bristol; Tractel UK.

WALKER MORRIS (see firm details p.1178) This respected team is said to offer sound advice and to pick up a lot of conflict work. It is especially experienced in advising trustees and providing independent trustee services. "*Pragmatic*" **Andrew Turnbull** (see p.616) "*gets things done,*" according to clients. He recently provided pensions advice on a number of commercial transactions, assisting the sellers in a transaction with a value of approximately £70 million. The team has also been appointed as statutory independent trustees on various schemes, including acting as a trustee in a wind-up involving a pension scheme of £25 million. **Clients** Bradford & Northern Housing Association; Cattles; John Foster & Son; Kelda Group; Servelec; Killgerm Group; Trustees of Atlas Ward Pension Scheme.

OTHER NOTABLE PRACTITIONERS Head of department at Irwin Mitchell, **Anne Taylor** (see p.616) is said to "*never miss a technical point.*"

PENSIONS ■ SCOTLAND

SCOTLAND

PENSIONS
■ SCOTLAND

1 **Shepherd+ Wedderburn** Edinburgh
2 **Burness** Glasgow
   McGrigor Donald Glasgow
3 **MacRoberts** Glasgow

LEADING INDIVIDUALS

1 **FLEMING Andrew** Burness
   GORDON Ian McGrigor Donald
   HOLEHOUSE Andrew Shepherd+ Wedderburn
   TALMAN Iain Biggart Baillie
2 **CROMBIE June** Biggart Baillie
   KNOX Louisa Shepherd+ Wedderburn
   TROTTER Peter MacRoberts
3 **THURSTON SMITH Martin** Tods Murray WS

UP AND COMING
   HILL Alistair Dundas & Wilson CS

This book is the product of 6,582 1/2 hour interviews. See p.7 for BMRB audit.
Within each band, firms are listed alphabetically.. See individuals' profiles p.610

SHEPHERD+ WEDDERBURN (see firm details p.1130) This is widely acknowledged to be "*the number one firm in Scotland*" thanks to its size, its "*good team and its established client base.*" "*Friendly but shrewd*" Andrew Holehouse (see p.613) is especially liked by clients, while Louisa Knox (see p.613) is said to be "*hyper-efficient and particularly valuable in difficult situations.*" Together they have acted for Scottish Transport Group pension schemes on a wind-up, which continued throughout the year. The team also advised ScottishPower on the outsourcing to Aon of the administration of all group pension schemes. Typical work includes assistance with wind-ups, reorganisations and documentation. **Clients** Brintel; Church of Scotland Pension Scheme; Coats Viyella; Edinburgh Fund Managers Pension Scheme; Scottish Amicable; ScottishPower; Scottish Life Pension Scheme; Scottish Transport Group.

BURNESS "*Heavyweight*" Andrew Fleming is at the forefront of this improving practice. Considered a "*dashed good lawyer who knows his stuff and is very thorough,*" he has recently advised members of the Post Office pension scheme on procedures for dealing with the pensions rights of divorcing members. He has also acted for the trustees of company pension schemes that had funds invested in Equitable Life. One scheme merger that he was involved with in the past year saw him assisting the Royal Bank of Scotland staff pension scheme in its £2 billion union with the National Westminster Bank pension fund. **Clients** Bison Group Limited Pension Scheme; Clyde Marine; Dawson International; Lees of Scotland; Riley Dunn & Wilson; Standard Life.

MCGRIGOR DONALD (see firm details p.1065) The firm is acknowledged for the acuity of its advice on the pensions elements of transactional work; it also undertakes standalone work, including wind-ups. Clients say of Ian Gordon (see p.612) that he "*researches the details of cases thoroughly and offers sound, practical opinions.*" Over the past year the firm has handled work for newly acquired clients like Polaroid and BSW Timber. Public to private transfer work is also on the increase to fill the gaps left by a subdued M&A market. **Clients** Andrews Holding; BSW Timber; Polaroid.

MACROBERTS (see firm details p.1049) Covering a great deal of professional independent trustee work, the firm is said to handle an interesting caseload. Peter Trotter (see p.296) is universally praised by market sources: "*everybody speaks highly of him – including his assistants.*" Admired for his technical skill and knowledge, he recently advised the trustees of the Richards Group pension scheme in connection with the decision of Aberdeen-based Richards to terminate contributions for future service accrual. The team also assisted RJ McLeod and the trustees of its occupational pension scheme in changing from a defined benefit to a defined contribution scheme. **Clients** Airdrie Savings Bank; Campbell Distillers; Johnston Press; Mitre Pensions; Peter Walker Group.

OTHER NOTABLE PRACTITIONERS The whole pensions team from now-demerged Morison Bishop has moved to build a pensions practice at Biggart Baillie. "*Practical and experienced*" June Crombie and "*academic*" Iain Talman lead the way. At Tods Murray WS, Martin Thurston-Smith (see p.503) retains his reputation as a thorough and knowledgeable specialist. Alistair Hill of Dundas & Wilson CS is still said to be "*finding his focus.*"

THE LEADERS IN PENSIONS

AINSCOE, Raymond
Wrigleys, Leeds
(0113) 244 6100
raymond.ainscoe@wrigleys.co.uk
Specialisation: Partner in commercial department. Area of practice is pensions. Contributed to 'Pensions World' and 'Pensions Management'. Lectured to Leeds Metropolitan University. Addressed APL, NAPF and PMI conferences.
Career: Qualified 1980 with *Stephenson Harwood*. 1983 joined *Nicholson Graham & Jones*. Joined *Hepworth & Chadwick* 1985. Partner 1987. Joined *Wrigleys* as a Partner in 2000.
Personal: Born 28 April 1954. Attended Bolton School 1965-72, St. Catherine's College, Oxford (BA) 1972-75, BCL 1977. Trustee of Yorkshire Spinal Deformity Trust, Leeds. Leisure pursuits include Italian racing motorcycles. Author of four books.

ALLISON, Margaret
Nabarro Nathanson, Sheffield
(0114) 279 4004
m.allison@nabarro.com
Specialisation: Work covers almost every aspect of pension law, including advising trustees and companies on the re-organisation of schemes and the updating of scheme documentation. In the last year, has advised increasingly on the pension aspects of local government PFI projects of disposals by several plcs. Enjoys speaking engagements and trustee training.
Prof. Memberships: Full APL member.
Career: Qualified 1987. Specialised in pensions since 1988. Joined *Nabarro Nathanson* 1994 to establish their Sheffield pension team.
Personal: Born 1962. Has lived and worked in Sheffield since 1985. Interests include horses and cats.

ANDREWS, Sue
Pinsent Curtis Biddle, London
(020) 7606 9301
susan.andrews@pinsents.com
Specialisation: Partner in Pensions Group of *Pinsent Curtis Biddle*. Advises on all areas of pensions law including trustees' duties and liabilities, winding-up, investment management and custody, mergers and acquisitions and stakeholder.
Prof. Memberships: Member and secretary of the Association of Pensions Lawyers; Fellow of the Pensions Management Institute and director of the governing council.
Career: Qualified as barrister in 1984. Requalified as solicitor in 1991. Worked in-house 1986-89, entering private practice in 1989. Joined *Pinsent Curtis Biddle* in February 2001.
Personal: Born 1 July 1961 and holds an LLB from Thames Valley University. Leisure interests include squash and golf. Lives in Hertford with her daughter.

ARCHER, David
Pitmans, Reading
(0118) 958 0224
darcher@pitmans.com
Specialisation: Commercial and personal insolvency; commercial litigation and corporate pensions. Acts as an independent trustee to corporate pension schemes of insolvent companies.
Prof. Memberships: Insolvency Lawyers Association; INSOL Europe; Associate Member of R3.
Personal: Christianity, skiing and sailing.

ARTHUR, Hugh
Macfarlanes, London
(020) 7831 9222

ASHLEY TAYLOR, Andrew M
Hammond Suddards Edge, Manchester
(0161) 830 5000

ATKINSON, Mark
CMS Cameron McKenna, London
(020) 7367 3000
mark.atkinson@cmck.com
Specialisation: Advises trustees and companies on all aspects of pensions law including scheme mergers and demergers, Pensions Act compliance, documentation, litigation, issues arising from corporate transactions, Pensions Ombudsman complaints and other member disputes. Established the stakeholder team across pension and financial

THE LEADERS ■ PENSIONS

services groups. Speaks for APL and commercial conference organisations. Secretary to Coloroll Pension Trustees Limited.
Prof. Memberships: Association of Pension Lawyers member of the Legislative and Parliamentary Sub-committees, Associate of the Pensions Management Institute.
Career: Qualified 1994 *Cameron McKenna*.
Personal: Born 1968. Attended Pembroke College, Cambridge.

BENNETT, Philip
Slaughter and May, London
(020) 7600 1200
philip.bennett@slaughterandmay.com
Specialisation: Partner in pensions/employment department. Main area of practice is pensions work. Author of 'Pension Fund Surpluses' (Longman, 2nd ed 1994).
Prof. Memberships: Association of Pensions Lawyers, Past Chairman Legislative & Parliamentary Sub-Committee of the Association of Pensions Lawyers, Former Member, Main Committee of the Association of Pensions Lawyers.
Career: Qualified 1979. Partner 1986 with *Slaughter and May* in London.
Personal: Born 2 March 1954.

BENNEY, Belinda
Field Fisher Waterhouse, London
(020) 7861 4190
bxb@ffwlaw.com
Specialisation: Partner in Pensions Department. Full-time pensions specialist since 1986 when switched from private client work. Since then has covered full range of pensions work: documentation and rule drafting, sex discrimination, mergers and acquisitions, severance terms, application of surplus, scheme deficits and winding-up, trustee duties and liabilities, and all aspects of pension investment. Frequent speaker at pensions seminars and trustee training courses. Author of 'A Guide to the Pensions Act 1995' (Butterworths), and the pensions chapter in the 'Administration of Estates' practitioners' manual published by Tolley's. Appointed to the Board of the Occupational Pensions Regulatory Authority (OPRA) in April 2000.
Prof. Memberships: National Association of Pension Funds, Association of Pension Lawyers, Law Society, Institute of Chartered Accountants Pensions Sub-Committee.
Career: Qualified in 1981. Joined *Field Fisher Waterhouse* in 1996 as head of the pensions practice.
Personal: Holds an LL.B from the University of Bristol.

BERKELEY, Christopher
Pinsent Curtis Biddle, London
(020) 7667 0147
christopher.berkeley@pinsents.com
Specialisation: Partner in pensions group. Acted in 2001 for the trustees of the Innogy Group of the ESPS in the National Grid/International Power allocation of surplus case that was decided in the House of Lords. Advises on the legal aspects of pension scheme investment. He has recently been appointed as legal advisor to the trustees of a number of pension schemes in the engineering and transport sectors.
Prof. Memberships: APL, Member of APL Investment Sub-Committee, Member of the Committee of the City & Eastern Group of the National Association of Pension Funds; Co-opted member of the NAPF Investment Committee 2000-01; City of London Solicitors Company. Has spoken at both NAPF and APL conferences.
Career: Educated at Sherborne School (1967-71) and Brasenose College, Oxford (1972-76) where he gained a Second Class Honours degree in Classics; MA (1980); articled at *Lemon & Co*, Swindon (1977-79); qualified as a solicitor with *Lemon & Co* in May 1980; commercial property solicitor with *Wansbroughs* in Bristol (1981-85); Assistant Parliamentary Counsel (1985-90); assistant solicitor in the Pensions and Employment department of *Lovell White Durrant* (1990-96); Partner in the Pensions Group of *Biddle* (now *Pinsent Curtis Biddle*) (1996-present).
Personal: Married with three children; armchair cricket and rugby union enthusiast. Membership of MCC and London Wasps RFC.

BLACK, Richard
Wragge & Co, Birmingham
(0870) 903 1000

BROWNING, Lesley
Norton Rose, London
(020) 7444 2448
browningla@nortonrose.com
Specialisation: Experience of all types of pensions related work including general advisory work for employers and trustees, corporate transactions (including PFI), pension scheme mergers, winding-up of pension schemes, investment and custodian agreements and insurance related issues. Also has extensive pensions litigation experience, having been involved in the British Airways, National Bus and Hillsdown Holdings cases as well numerous complaints to the Pensions Ombudsman.
Prof. Memberships: Association of Pension Lawyers (and currently serving on the Education and Seminars sub-committee and the Main Committee), NAPF City and Eastern Group, IPEBLA.
Career: Joined *Norton Rose* in June 2001 having previously been a partner at *Nabarro Nathanson* where she also trained. Studied at Keble College, Oxford and the College of Law and qualified in 1991.
Publications: Contributor to Butterworths 'Pensions Law Handbook' and 'Whitehouse on Revenue'.
Personal: Married. Enjoys reading, cinema, theatre and eating out.

CLARK, David
Clarks, Reading
(0118) 958 5321

CLOSE, Chris
Sacker & Partners, London
(020) 7329 6699
chris.close@sacker-partners.co.uk
Specialisation: Partner in specialist law firm. All aspects of law relating to pension schemes. Represented the employer in South West trains case. Acted on a number of high profile scheme mergers and demergers. Experienced in transactions including TUPE. Lectures at conferences, seminars and workshops.
Prof. Memberships: Association of Pensions Lawyers.
Career: Qualified in April 1987; became a partner at *Sackers* in June 1987.
Personal: Born 14 December 1954, University of York 1973-76. London University (external) 1981-85. Interests: family, cricket, Charlton Athletic, real ale, walking and backgammon. Lives in Sevenoaks.

COCKERILL, Vivien
Wragge & Co, Birmingham
(0870) 903 1000

COX, Helen
Clifford Chance, London
(020) 7600 1000
helen.cox@cliffordchance.com
Specialisation: Tax, pensions and employment. Partner and Head of the Pensions Group in London specialising in all aspects of pensions law and practice including pension scheme documentation, the establishment, merger and winding-up of pension schemes, the pensions aspects of corporate mergers and acquisitions, sales, flotations and privatisations and international pension arrangements
Career: Articled *Coward Chance*; qualified 1977; Partner since 1989.
Personal: Barry County Grammar School for Girls; 1974 University College, London (LLB 1st Class Hons).

COX, Tim
Linklaters, London
(020) 7456 3692
tim.cox@linklaters.com
Specialisation: Specialist advice on all aspects of pensions law including the establishment and winding-up of schemes; advice on employment and regulatory issues; advice on the application of tax and social security legislation affecting different kinds of pension arrangement; advice on the pension aspects of corporate takeover and merger work.
Career: 1980-83 Downing College, Cambridge BA (Law, First Class Hons). 1983-84 College of Law. 1984-85 Magdalen College, Oxford, BCL. Trainee *Linklaters* 1985-87, Assistant Solicitor *Linklaters* 1987-96. 1989-90 seconded to the Office of Solicitor, Department of Social Security. Partner, *Linklaters* 1996 to date.

CROMBIE, June
Biggart Baillie, Glasgow
(0141) 228 8000

DAVIES, Ian
Eversheds, Cardiff
(029) 2047 1147
iandavies@eversheds.com
Specialisation: Partner in the Pensions Unit within the Human Resources Group. Handles all aspects of establishing and running pension schemes; documentation; scheme mergers; winding-up; advice to trustees, acting as independent trustee; and pensions aspects of M&A. Has particular experience of handling multi-scheme mergers and providing SSAS documentation and advice to pensioner trustees. Also handles taxation work, including share option schemes, ESOPs, business and capital taxation. Has published several articles on pensions and tax issues.
Prof. Memberships: APL.
Career: Qualified in 1984. Joined *Phillips & Buck* (now *Eversheds*) in 1982, becoming a Partner in 1988.

DAVIS, Richard
Browne Jacobson, Nottingham
(0115) 976 6549
rdavis@brownej.co.uk
Specialisation: Partner in Pensions Department. Specialises in occupational pension schemes. Covers documentation, transactional work, scheme mergers, reconstructions and wind-ups, insolvency advice and independent trusteeship. Has handled several major scheme mergers.
Prof. Memberships: NAPF; APL; Law Society.
Career: Qualified in 1977. At *Overbury Steward & Eaton* 1978-88. Joined *Eversheds* (*Wells & Hind*) in 1988 and was a Partner 1989-97. Joined *Edge Ellison* in 1997.
Personal: Born 29 April 1952. Attended Leeds University 1970-73.

DIERDEN, Kenneth
Freshfields Bruckhaus Deringer, London
(020) 7936 4000
ken.dierden@freshfields.com
Specialisation: Partner in employment, pensions and benefits department. Work covers all aspects of the establishment and operation of pension schemes (both private and public sector). Experienced in pensions litigation and has wide involvement of the pensions aspects of privatisations. Acts for employers and trustees.
Prof. Memberships: Former Chairman of the Association of Pension Lawyers (APL). Associate of the Institute of Taxation. Member of the legislative and parliamentary sub-committee of the Association of Pension Lawyers.
Career: Qualified in 1977. Lecturer at College of Law 1977/80. Joined *Freshfields* 1980. Partner 1987.
Personal: Born 1952.

PENSIONS ■ THE LEADERS

DOCKING, Peter
Sacker & Partners, London
(020) 7329 6699
peter.docking@sacker-partners.co.uk
Specialisation: Partner in specialist pensions law firm. Principal area of practice is pensions law. Covers all aspects including litigation, sales and purchases, trust law issues and life office matters. Frequent lecturer and contributor to pensions and academic journals. Former Chairman of APL's Education Committee. Current member of the APL's International Committee. Steering group member of IPEBLA (International Pension and Employee Benefit Lawyers Association).
Prof. Memberships: Association of Pensions Lawyers, Law Society.
Career: Qualified in 1987. Partner at *Nicholson Graham & Jones* 1991-96. Joined *Sacker & Partners* as a partner in 1996.
Personal: Born 1 June 1961. Educated at Sutton Manor High School for Boys and the University of Exeter. Leisure activities include mountaineering, climbing, walking, skiing and travel.

EVERSON, Ingrid
Eversheds, Birmingham
(0121) 232 1493
ingrideverson@eversheds.com
Specialisation: Partner specialising in all aspects of pensions work, advising companies and trustees and including support in various corporate, commercial, employment and property. Through *Eversheds* Pension Trustees Limited responsible for several trusteeships.
Prof. Memberships: Association of Pensions Lawyers, Midlands Life & Pensions Society and student member of the Pensions Management Institute.
Career: Articled at *Wragge & Co*, qualified 1982. Joined *Eversheds* in 1992 and became a Partner in 2001.
Personal: Educated at Bristol University. Sits as part-time Support Child Support Appeal Tribunal Chairman. Hobbies – attempting to learn golf and to keep fit.

FALLON, Liz
Eversheds, Birmingham
(0121) 232 1000
Specialisation: Partner. Handles all aspects of pensions law including transactional work, scheme reorganisation, advice to insolvency practitioners, establishment of schemes and scheme documentation. Is also a director of *Eversheds* Pension Trustees Limited, which has a substantial portfolio of institute trusteeships. Has spoken at the Institute of Actuaries Annual Conference and for the Pensions Management and is a regular lecturer for a number of professional training organisations including Industrial Relations Services. Also regularly involved in Trustee training courses.
Prof. Memberships: Law Society, Association of Pension Lawyers, National Association of Pension Funds.
Career: Qualified 1983. Joined *Eversheds* 1981. Became a Partner 1997. Heads up Human Resources Group in Birmingham.
Personal: Born 17 February 1959. Attended University of Kent, BA Law and German. Interests include keeping up with two young sons, skiing and horse riding.

FENN, Jonathan
Slaughter and May, London
(020) 7600 1200
jonathan.fenn@slaughterandmay.com
See under Employee Share Schemes, p.294

FENTON, Jonathan
DLA, London
(08700) 111111

FLEMING, Andrew
Burness, Edinburgh
(0131) 473 6000

FORD, Peter
Norton Rose, London
(020) 7444 2711
fordp@nortonrose.com
Specialisation: Partner with experience in all aspects of pensions including corporate transactions, scheme mergers and reorganisations, scheme winding-up, investment and custody and pensions litigation.
Prof. Memberships: Previously a member of the Main Committee of the Association of Pensions Lawyers (APL). He also previously chaired the APL Education Sub-Committee and was a member of the JWG Actuarial Committee. Also a member of a number of pensions organisations including the National Association of Pensions Funds and the IEBA. Currently a 'secondee' to the Department of Work and Pensions 'Pickering' Review on simplification of pensions legislation.
Career: Qualified April 1988. Partner *Nabarro Nathanson* in 1993. Partner *Norton Rose* 2001.
Personal: Born 8 December 1962. Attended John Fisher School, Purley 1974-81 and the University of Hull 1981-84.

FORREST, Ian
Hammond Suddards Edge, Birmingham
(0121) 222 3000

GAULT, Ian
Herbert Smith, London
(020) 7374 8000
ian.gault@herbertsmith.com
Specialisation: Partner with extensive experience of advising on all aspects of pensions law and practice. Currently on the Legislative and Parliamentary sub-committee of the Association of Pensions Lawyers, the executive committee of the Pensions Research Accountant's Group and the Council of the Society of Pensions Consultants. Is also involved in advising the Faculty and Institute of Actuaries on issues connected with their role as regulatory body for the actuarial profession. Is also currently a member of the Consultation Panel assisting the Department for Work and Pensions on the replacement to the Minimum Funding Requirement.
Prof. Memberships: Association of Pensions Lawyers.
Career: Qualified 1977. Partnership 1988.
Personal: Educated at Clare College, Cambridge.

GOLDMAN, Ruth
Linklaters, London
(020) 7456 3689
ruth.goldman@linklaters.com
Specialisation: Specialises in pensions law. Considerable experience in all main areas of pension law practice including trust law aspects, documentation, mergers and acquisitions, flotations and industry-wide schemes, as well as international pensions.
Prof. Memberships: Chair of International Committee of Association of Pension Lawyers 1993-99. Chair of *Linklaters & Alliance* European Pensions Group. Elected Member of NAPF Council.
Career: 1992 to date: Partner, *Linklaters*; 1985-92: Assistant Solicitor, *Linklaters*; 1983-85: Articled Clerk, *Linklaters*. 1981-83: College of Law, Chancery Lane; 1981: Warwick University, MA Industrial Relations; 1980: Lady Margaret Hall, MA Politics, Philosophy and Economics.

GORDON, Ian
McGrigor Donald, Glasgow
(0141) 567 9269
ian.gordon@mcgrigors.com
Specialisation: Principal area of practice is employee benefits, pension schemes, share incentive schemes, option schemes, and employee share ownership arrangements for listed and unlisted companies. Also advises employees and trustees on pensions law. Work includes establishment of and ongoing advice in relation to approved and unapproved pension arrangements. Frequent lecturer on pensions and taxation issues. Has given TV and radio interviews on pension issues.
Prof. Memberships: Association of Pension Lawyers, Association of Share Scheme Lawyers.
Career: Joined *McGrigor Donald* as a trainee in 1979. Qualified in July 1979. One year secondment to *Thomson McLintock CA* in 1983. Became a Partner at *McGrigor Donald* in the same year. Director of Scotia Pacific Trustees Limited.
Personal: Educated at Edinburgh University 1975-79. Born 15 August 1957. Lives in Glasgow.

GRAHAM, Ronald
Eversheds, Manchester
(0161) 831 8000
ronaldgraham@eversheds.com
Specialisation: All aspects of pension law, including trust documentation and advice (approved and unapproved schemes), sales and acquisitions, scheme mergers, dispute resolution, investment matters, statutory schemes and independent trusteeship. Director, *Eversheds* Pension Trustees Limited.
Prof. Memberships: Full Member APL, Member and Former Secretary NAPF Manchester Group, NWAPL, Law Society.
Career: Qualified 1985 at *Alexander Tatham* (now *Eversheds* Manchester) and became a Partner in 1990.
Personal: Attended Kendal Grammar School, Merton College, Oxford (MA in Jurisprudence) and Corpus Christi College, Cambridge (Diploma in Criminology). Interests include theatre, birds and travel. Lives in Chapel-en-le-Frith, Derbyshire.

GRANT, Mark
CMS Cameron McKenna, London
(020) 7367 2325
msg@cmck.com
Specialisation: Advises on all aspects of pensions law. Established firm's Pensions Ombudsman Unit. Acted for trustee of Coloroll schemes in landmark ECJ case on sex equality issues.
Prof. Memberships: APL, IPEBLA.
Career: Trained *McKenna & Co*, qualified 1992; secondment to pensions practice of New York firm *Winthrop, Stimson, Putnam & Roberts*, 1995; Law Society Working Committee on Pensions Bill, 1995; Partner *CMS Cameron McKenna* 1999; winner of APL's Wallace medal for excellence in pensions writing, 2001.
Publications: Co-editor 'International Pension Lawyer' 1995-97; assistant editor 'OPLR' 1997-; author of 'The Pensions Ombudsman; Powers, Procedures and Decisions' (Sweet & Maxwell) 1998.
Personal: Married with two children. Interests: Newcastle United and cycling.

GRAVILL, Robert
Hammond Suddards Edge, Birmingham
(0121) 222 3000

GREENLEES, Mark
Sacker & Partners, London
(020) 7329 6699
mark.greenlees@sacker-partners.co.uk
Specialisation: Senior Partner in specialist pensions law firm. All aspects of law relating to occupational pension schemes. Represented the male beneficiaries in the 'Coloroll' reference to the European Court. Acted for vendor in what was then the second largest MBO in UK business history. Regular contributor to pensions periodicals; regular speaker at major conferences and seminars. Past Chairman of the Association of Pension Lawyers.
Prof. Memberships: Association of Pension Lawyers.
Career: Qualified in 1979. Joined *Sacker & Partners* in 1977, becoming a partner in 1982. Chairman of APL 1997-99. Member of the Main Committee of APL 1991-96. Chairman of Legislative and Parliamentary Committee of APL 1992-94. Chairman of Legislation Committee of SPC 1991-92. Member of SPC Council.
Personal: Born 18 April 1954. Attended Berkhamsted 1964-71 and Oxford

University 1972-76. Leisure interests include family, old cars and Watford FC. Lives near Berkhamsted.

GREENSTREET, Ian Alexander
Hammond Suddards Edge, London
(020) 7655 1000

GRIFFITHS, David
Addleshaw Booth & Co, Manchester
(0161) 934 6233
david.griffiths@addleshawbooth.com
Specialisation: Partner in Pensions Department, Commercial Group. Pensions law, covering advice to individuals, employers and/or trustees in relation to the maintenance and conduct of occupational pension schemes, scheme mergers and reconstructions, contentious pensions issues and the pensions aspects of mergers and acquisitions. Provides full legal document service.
Prof. Memberships: Association of Pension Lawyers. Currently serving on their Legislative and Parliamentary Sub-Committee.
Career: Qualified as a solicitor in 1990 with the firm. Associate 1993. Partner 1996.
Personal: Educated at the University of Edinburgh, (MA English Language and Literature). Interests include music, literature, hill walking and badminton. Lives in Bolton.

HARRIS, Jeremy
DLA, Manchester
(08700) 111111

HILL, Alistair
Dundas & Wilson CS, Edinburgh
(0131) 228 8000

HINGLEY, Gerald
Wragge & Co, Birmingham
(0870) 903 1000

HOLEHOUSE, Andrew
Shepherd+ Wedderburn, Edinburgh
(0131) 473 5192
andrew.holehouse@shepwedd.co.uk
Specialisation: Partner and Head of Pensions Group. Deals with all legal aspects of pensions law, including establishment, winding-up and ongoing advice for major occupational pension schemes, advice to life offices, pensions aspects of company sales, acquisitions, mergers and flotations, pensions litigation and EC aspects. Also handles employee share schemes. Has written journal articles and regularly speaks at seminars on pensions law.
Prof. Memberships: Committee member and past Chairman Scottish Group Association of Pensions Lawyers, Law Society Pensions Law Accreditation Panel, Law Society Working Party on Pensions Law, Committee member National Association of Pension Funds Scottish Group.
Career: Qualified in England and Wales 1981. With *Rooks Rider*, London 1981-87 (partner from 1984). Joined *Shepherd+ Wedderburn* in 1988. Qualified in Scotland 1989. Became an associate at *Shepherd+ Wedderburn* in 1990 and a partner in 1992.
Personal: Born 8 December 1955. Leisure activities include malt whisky, fine wines, opera, classical music, rugby. Lives in Edinburgh.

HOLLAND, Jeanette
Baker & McKenzie, London
(020) 7919 1000
jeanette.holland@bakernet.com
Specialisation: Partner with a wide range of experience in all aspects of pensions work advising both company and trustees in connection with the trust law aspects of pension schemes, regulatory matters, surplus, sales and purchases, including multijurisdictional transactions and the preparation of documents. She also advises in connection with independent trusteeships and litigation matters relating to pension funds. She has spoken at many conferences, trustee training seminars and workshops on multiple aspects of pensions law.
Prof. Memberships: A member of the Association of Pension Lawyers, the International Committee of the APL, the International Pensions and Employee Benefits Lawyers Association (IP&EBLA) and the Society of Pensions Consultants (SPC).
Career: Articled *Baker & McKenzie*; qualified 1991; Partner 1997 to date.
Publications: Regular contributor to the *Baker & McKenzie* 'Pensions Newsletter' and has also contributed to the 'Pension Lawyer' and 'European Legal Developments Bulletin'.

HOLMES, Leigh
Wrigleys, Leeds
(0113) 244 6100
leighholmes@eversheds.com
Specialisation: Senior solicitor in commercial department. Advises on all aspects of pensions law. Has recently advised on scheme amendments, wind-ups, restructuring of pension arrangements for corporate clients and on pension aspects of sales and acquisitions. A contributor to Butterworths/Tolleys 'Pensions Law' textbook.
Prof. Memberships: Full member of the Association of Pension Lawyers.
Career: Degree in law obtained from St Hilda's College, Oxford University in 1991. Qualified in 1994 with *Eversheds*, Leeds. Worked in the pensions unit at *Eversheds* until joining *Wrigleys* in 2001.
Personal: Born 1970. Leisure interests include photography.

ILLSTON, Tim
Burges Salmon, Bristol
(0117) 939 2284
tim.illston@burges-salmon.com
Specialisation: Head of Pensions and Employee Benefits Unit. Has expertise in independent trusteeships, trust law, unapproved retirement benefits schemes, public sector schemes, pension fund trustee training, investment management agreements and establishment, merger and winding-up of pension schemes. Drafts insurance company and pension scheme documentation. Also has expertise in all types of share incentive schemes.
Prof. Memberships: Law Society, Association of Pension Lawyers, NAPF, Society of Pension Consultants, PMI and IPEBLA.
Career: Moved from *Freshfields* to *Burges Salmon* in 1988, becoming a Partner in 1990.
Personal: University of Manchester 1977-80. Leisure interests include hockey, guitar and cycling.

ITO, Stephen
Lovells, London
(020) 7296 2000
stephen.ito@lovells.com
Specialisation: Principal area of practice is pensions law with a particular emphasis on corporate mergers and acquisitions related work including multijurisdiction transactions. Otherwise involved in all aspects of UK pensions law acting mainly for UK, US and EU corporate clients.
Prof. Memberships: Law Society, Association of Pension Lawyers.
Career: Former Barrister (qualified 1984): qualified as a solicitor 1992 *Lovells*, partner 1995.

JACOBS, Howard
Slaughter and May, London
(020) 7600 1200
howard.jacobs@slaughterandmay.com
Specialisation: Pension scheme restructurings, general pension advice.
Prof. Memberships: City of London Solicitors' Company Employment Law Sub-committee.
Career: *Slaughter and May* since 1975.
Personal: Winchester College. Pembroke College, Cambridge. Married, three children. Interests: family and gardening.

JAMES, Stuart
Mayer, Brown, Rowe & Maw, London
(020) 7782 8613
sjames@eu.mayerbrownrowe.com
Specialisation: Senior Partner Pensions Department and member of the International Policy and Planning Committee which governs the firm. Pensions law and related trust, tax and commercial law matters. Other main area of work is unit trusts and retail financial services. Member of the Pension Law Review Committee 1992-93.
Prof. Memberships: Law Society, Association of Pensions Lawyers (Past Chairman), Reliance Insurance Group (Chairman), M&G Securities Limited, Fellow, Pensions Management Institute.
Career: Articled with *Rowe & Maw*. Qualified in 1967, then joined *Warren Murton & Co*. 1967-77. Returned to *Rowe & Maw* as a Partner in 1977. Senior Partner 1996.
Personal: Born 3 March 1944. Attended Reed's School 1958-62. Lives in Surrey. Enjoys skiing, flying, diving and reading.

JENKINS, Martin
Dickinson Dees, Newcastle upon Tyne
(0191) 279 9528
martin.jenkins@dickinson-dees.com
Specialisation: Pensions law in all its aspects.
Prof. Memberships: Association of Pensions Lawyers; Secretary National Association Pension Funds (Northern Counties Group).
Career: Joined *Dickinson Dees* from *Eversheds* in 1992. Now leads a team of twelve pension specialists.
Personal: Cycling and socialising (sometimes simultaneously!).

KENNEDY, Patrick
Masons, Manchester
(0161) 234 8234
patrick.kennedy@masons.com
Specialisation: Partner in *Masons'* National Pensions Group, the only national pensions group based in the North West. He is accustomed to giving legal advice on all aspects of pensions and is a Director of *Masons* Trustees Limited, the market leader separate independent trustee company in the North West. He is a full member of the Association of Pension Lawyers and has spoken on a wide variety of pensions legal topics including pensions and insolvency, Data Protection and the pensions aspects of corporate transactions and been involved in liaison between the Association of Corporate Trustees, the Association of Pension Lawyers and the Society for Practitioners of Insolvency.
Career: Graduated in Law from London University in 1988. Qualified as a Solicitor in 1990. Joined *Masons* in 1999.

KNOX, Louisa
Shepherd+ Wedderburn, Edinburgh
(0131) 473 5216
louisa.knox@shepwedd.co.uk
Specialisation: Partner in Pensions Group 1998. Deals with all aspects of pensions law, writes journal articles and regularly speaks at seminars.
Prof. Memberships: Committee Member of the Association of Pension Lawyers (Scottish Group), Member of the Association of Pension Lawyers.
Career: Glasgow University (LLB Hons); qualified 1993; specialised in pensions law since then.
Personal: Hill walking; mountain biking; swimming; socialising – food and drink.

KOWALIK, Mark
CMS Cameron McKenna, London
(020) 7367 3000
mak@cmck.com
Specialisation: All aspects of law relating to occupational pension schemes, including documentation, mergers and acquisitions, privatisations, Ombudsman complaints and scheme wind-ups. Handles day to day work for several major pension funds.
Prof. Memberships: Association of Pension Lawyers (Treasurer of APL 1996 to 2000, Member of Education & Seminars Committee since 1993 becoming the Committee's Chairman in January 2002).
Career: Qualified in 1988. Whole career

PENSIONS ■ THE LEADERS

has been at *McKenna & Co* and then *CMS Cameron McKenna*.
Personal: Born 17 September 1962. Educated at King Henry VIII School, Coventry (1973 to 1981) and St John's College, Oxford (1982 to 1985). Interests include fine art, international athletics and football (Member of Coventry City London Supporters Club).

LAIGHT, Simon
Martineau Johnson, Birmingham
(0121) 678 1334
simon.laight@martjohn.com
Specialisation: Handles all aspects of law relating to pension schemes. Acts mainly for trustees of large occupational schemes and employers. Specialises in development work for pension product providers and insurance companies. Experienced in public sector pension issues, in particular pension aspects of PFIs/PPPs.
Prof. Memberships: APL, NAPF (Midlands Region), Committe member of Midlands Life & Pensions Society.
Career: Worked exclusively in pensions since qualifying in 1992 at *Ellison Westhorp*. Norwich Union 1994. Associate at *Martineau Johnson* in 1998 and partner in 2000.
Personal: Educated at London University (BA). Interests include family and cycling.

LEWIS, Roger
Eversheds, London
(020) 7919 4815
lewisr@eversheds.com
Specialisation: Head of London Pensions Group. Advises employers and trustees in relation to all aspects of corporate pension arrangements.
Prof. Memberships: Law Society, APL, NAPF.
Career: Qualified 1978. Employed IBM 1966-68, GEC 1968-72 and Commission of the European Communities 1973-75. Joined *Lewis, Lewis & Co.* (now *Eversheds*) in 1976, becoming a partner in 1979.
Personal: Born 14 April 1945. Attended UCS 1958-63, then Balliol College, Oxford 1963-66 (BA [Hons], MA [Oxon] Physics). Governor of Hebrew University of Jerusalem, trustee of Sobell Foundation. Married with two children. Leisure interests include golf, tennis and theatre.

MARSHALL, Jane
Hammond Suddards Edge, London
(020) 7655 1000

MASSARANO SALT, Vikki
DLA, Leeds
(08700) 111111

MCKENNA, Catherine M P
Hammond Suddards Edge, Leeds
(0113) 284 7000

MEEKS, Alastair
Pinsent Curtis Biddle, London
(020) 7606 9301
alastair.meeks@pinsents.com
Specialisation: Advising trustees and employers on all aspects of the law relating to occupational pension schemes. Clients include Charter plc and ITN.
Prof. Memberships: APL, Associate of the Pensions Management Institute.
Career: Joined *Biddle* (now *Pinsent Curtis Biddle*) on qualification 1992. Partner in 1997.
Publications: Author of 'Tolley's Pension Cases'; assistant editor of 'Occupational Pensions Law Reports'; on editorial committee of 'Occupational Pensions' magazine; regular writer of pensions press articles.
Personal: Born 1967. BA (Hons) Law Durham 1985-88. Lives in London.

MILES, Helen
DLA, Birmingham
(08700) 111111

MILTON, Kevin
Wragge & Co, Birmingham
(0870) 903 1000

MOORE, Nigel
CMS Cameron McKenna, London
(020) 7367 3000
nigel.moore@cmck.com
Specialisation: Partner and Head of Pensions Team. Work includes advising on administration of pension schemes; drafting trust deeds; mergers and acquisitions; litigation in courts and tribunals; investigations by Pensions Ombudsman. Acted in Coloroll's application to European Court. Speaking experience includes NAPF courses, APL and ACA annual conferences.
Prof. Memberships: Law Society, City of London Solicitors Company, Association of Pension Lawyers (Chairman of International Committee). OPAS advisor.
Career: Qualified 1986. Articles *Radcliffes & Co* 1984-86. Joined *McKenna & Co* (now *CMS Cameron McKenna*) in 1986. Partner 1994.
Personal: Born 13 June 1962. Attended St Albans School 1973-80, Warwick University 1980-83, College of Law 1983-84 and City of London Polytechnic (MA in Business Law) 1984-86. Leisure interests include golf and football. Lives in Welwyn Garden City.

MULLEN, Chris
Pinsent Curtis Biddle, London
(020) 7606 9301
chris.mullen@pinsents.com
Specialisation: Partner in and Head of *Pinsent Curtis Biddle*'s 25-lawyer strong Pensions Group. Advises companies and scheme trustees on all aspects of pensions law, relating principally to occupational pension schemes. Heavily involved in complex mergers and pension scheme reorganisations and conversions; negotiations concerning settlement of employer liabilities to schemes in deficit; advising trustees and employers on member disputes and Ombudsman complaints; documentation advice, drafting and large-value transaction advice. Specialist knowlege of data protection issues for pension schemes.

Clients include Heinz, Lloyd's, Costain Group plc, Vivendi Group, Aventis Cropscience and the NSPCC as well as other UK and US Law firms seeking specialist pensions support.
Prof. Memberships: APL, Member of APL Main Committee, City of London Solicitors Company. Editor of 'Pension Lawyer' magazine. Conference Speaker for IBC, NAPF, APL among others.
Career: Qualified in 1986 after articles at *Biddle* . Became a partner in 1990. Head of pensions group since 1998. Non-executive member of *Pinsent Curtis Biddle* board.
Personal: Born 1960. Educated at Jesus College, Cambridge 1979-82 (MA in Law). Married, with three children, a beagle and a swimming pool.

PAYNE, Kate
DLA, Sheffield
(08700) 111111

PEARSON, John
Lovells, London
(020) 7296 2000
john.pearson@lovells.com
Specialisation: Partner in pensions and employment group. Advises employers, trustees and others on all aspects of pensions law and documentation relating to occupational and personal pension schemes and pension products; reorganisations; offshore schemes; pensions aspects of company sales, purchases and insolvencies; and pensions litigation. Acted for Mirror Group Newspapers post-Maxwell in sorting out its pensions problems. Has given many pensions related talks, including one in French.
Prof. Memberships: Law Society, City of London Solicitors Company, Association of Pension Lawyers, International Pension and Employee Benefit Lawyers Association.
Career: Qualified in 1971. Joined *Lovells* and became a partner in 1986.
Personal: Attended King's College, London (LLB 1968).

PETHERAM, Claire
Linklaters, London
(020) 7456 3676
claire.petheram@linklaters.com
Specialisation: Specialist in pensions law with 10 years experience. Typical matters include drafting pension scheme documentation; dealing with pensions aspects of sales and disposals; considering trust law issues; advising in relation to pension scheme mergers; considering equalisation issues; investment management matters; dispute resolution.
Career: 1997 to date: Partner, *Linklaters*, Employment and Employee Benefits; 1989-97: Assistant Solicitor, *Linklaters*; 1987-89: Trainee Solicitor, *Nabarro Nathanson*. College of Law, Lancaster Gate; University of Leeds, LLB (Hons).

PITTAWAY, Ian
Sacker & Partners, London
(020) 7615 9506
ian.pittaway@sacker-partners.co.uk
Specialisation: Partner in specialist pensions law firm. Covers all aspects of pension law including acting as trustee, arbitrator and expert witness. Author of numerous articles and lectures. Former Chairman and Secretary of APL.
Prof. Memberships: Law Society, Association of Pension Lawyers, Justice.
Personal: Born 28 July 1956. Attended the University of Hull 1974-77. Leisure interests include gardening, wine and reading.

POLLARD, David
Freshfields Bruckhaus Deringer, London
London (020) 7936 4000
email@freshfields.com
Specialisation: Partner in Employment, Pensions and Benefits Department, and group of over 30 lawyers covering the whole range of pensions, employment and benefits work. Acted for trustees in Drexel pension case. Author of book 'Corporate Insolvency: Employment and Pension Rights' and contributor of chapters to Tolley's 'Employment Law' and Tolley's 'Insolvency Law'. Co-Editor 'Trust Law International' magazine. Editor of 'Guide to the Pensions Act 1995' book. Editorial Board, Occupational Pensions Law Reports. Main Committee of the APL. Awarded APL 'Wallace Prize' in 1998.

POWELL, Andrew M
Hammond Suddards Edge, London
(020) 7655 1000

QUARRELL, John
Nabarro Nathanson, London
(020) 7524 6000
Specialisation: Partner and Head of Pensions Department. Work covers all aspects relating to occupational and personal pension schemes, including investment legalities, overseas provision, equality issues, litigation matters and dispute resolution. Acts for and advises most leading firms of accountants, many pension providers and a number of firms of pensions consultants and actuaries. Has acted in a large number of leading cases. Author of numerous articles and papers. Lectures at home and abroad.

RAMSHAW, Simon
Pinsent Curtis Biddle, Birmingham
(0121) 200 1050
simon.ramshaw@pinsents.com
Specialisation: Partner and Regional Head of Pensions Group. Main area of practice is pensions, covering documentation, transactional work, scheme mergers, reconstructions and wind-ups, insolvency advice and independent trusteeship. Has handled several major scheme mergers and acted as independent trustee to schemes run by a part of a nationalised industry, a national clothing company, three quoted public companies and a professional practice which is a world leader in its field. Author of various articles for technical publications and regular lecturer for Professional Associations and pension consultancies. Organiser of and speaker at various trustee training courses.

THE LEADERS ■ PENSIONS

Prof. Memberships: NAPF, APL, IPEBLA, Law Society.
Career: Qualified 1981, working at *Robert Muckle* from 1979-83. Then joined *Edge Ellison*, becoming Partner in 1986. Joined *Pinsent Curtis Biddle* in 2000.
Personal: Born 28 January 1958. Attended Newcastle upon Tyne University, 1975-78.

RAWNSLEY, Rachel
Addleshaw Booth & Co, Leeds
(0113) 209 2290
rachel.rawnsley@addleshawbooth.com
Specialisation: Partner in Employee Benefits Department, Commercial Group. Advises corporate clients and trustees on all aspects of ongoing pension schemes, setting up new schemes, winding-up and merging established schemes. Advises insolvency practitioners, including on independent statutory trusteeships.
Prof. Memberships: Association of Pensions Lawyers, National Association of Pension Funds.
Career: Joined the firm in January 1993. Partner in 1997.
Personal: Educated at Cambridge University 1983-86 (MA in Law). Lives in Ilkley.

RICCIO, Maria
Blake Lapthorn, Fareham
(01489) 579990

RIDLER, Mark
Hammond Suddards Edge, Leeds
(0113) 284 7000

ROGERS, Anna
Mayer, Brown, Rowe & Maw, London
(020) 7248 4282

RYLAND, Glyn
Wragge & Co, Birmingham
(0870) 903 1000

SAEEDI, Terry
Hammond Suddards Edge, Leeds
(0113) 284 7000

SAMSWORTH, Jane
Lovells, London
(020) 7296 2000
jane.samsworth@lovells.com
Specialisation: Partner advising on all aspects of pension law and documentation, including establishment, management and termination of occupational pension schemes, (both approved and unapproved and personal pensions); reorganisation and scheme mergers; pension aspects of company sales and acquisitions; pension litigation; pensions in insolvency; advising clients in their relations with the regulatory authorities including the preparation of submissions to the Pensions Ombudsman. Co-author of 'Guide to the Pensions Act 1995'; regular contributor to seminars and conferences on pension issues.
Prof. Memberships: Fellow Pensions Management Institute; Member of Investment Sub-Committee of Association of Pension Lawyers, Member of the Council of OPAS Ltd; Council Member SPC; Law Society; City of London Solicitors; Director *Lovells* Pension Trustees Ltd.
Career: Qualified 1978. 1978-83 Greater London Council. 1983-87 British Telecommunications plc; 1987 joined *Lovells*; Partner 1991.

SAUNDERS, Carolyn
Taylor Wessing, London
(020) 7300 7000
c.saunders@taylorwessing.com
Specialisation: Partner in Employment Department and Head of the Pensions Group. Has specialised in pensions law since qualifying at *Baker & McKenzie* in 1987 and advises employers, trustees and individuals on all aspects - contentious and non-contentious. Regular conference speaker.
Prof. Memberships: Association of Pension Lawyers (current member of the Association's Education and Seminars sub-committee); NAPF Local Group Committee member.
Career: Qualified at *Baker & McKenzie* in 1987, subsequently working at *Travers Smith Braithwaite* before joining *Taylor Joynson Garrett* in February 1995. Became a partner in 1997.
Personal: Educated at North London Collegiate School and Cambridge University (MA Law). Leisure interests include singing, mountain walking, tennis and theatre.

SCHAFFER, Daniel
Freshfields Bruckhaus Deringer, London
(020) 7936 4000
daniel.schaffer@freshfields.com
Specialisation: Partner in employment, pensions and benefits group. Pensions. Advises on all aspects of pensions.
Prof. Memberships: Association of Pension Lawyers (Member of International Committee). Sir John Vinelott Trust Law Committee. Sat on Financial Law Panel working party on 'commercial dealings with trustees'. Regular speaker.
Career: Joined *Freshfields* in 1988. Part-time tutor in trusts at LSE (1987-88), Merton College, Oxford (1987-90) and Balliol College, Oxford (1988-92).
Personal: Born 1963. Educated at Haberdashers' Aske's School, Elstree 1971-82, Bristol University 1983-86 (LLB, Simmons Scholar) and Merton College, Oxford 1986-87.(BCL 1st Class). Leisure pursuits include travelling in France. Fluent in French; working knowledge of Spanish.

SCHOLEFIELD, Stephen
Pinsent Curtis Biddle, Manchester
(0161) 250 0147
stephen.scholefield@pinsents.com
Specialisation: Advises on all aspects of pensions law, including the pensions aspects of corporate disposals and acquisitions, pension scheme mergers, trustee issues, contentious matters and documentation.
Prof. Memberships: Association of Pension Lawyers; Society of Pension Consultants.
Career: Qualified as a solicitor in 1996; *Addleshaw Booth & Co* 1997-2002; *Pinsent Curtis Biddle* 2002.
Personal: Educated at Cambridge University.

SCOTT, Harry
Mills & Reeve, Norwich
(01603) 693 249
harry.scott@mills-reeve.com
Specialisation: Pensions ie law and practice relating to occupational pension schemes including documentation, advice, Pensions Ombudsman Cases and acting as a pension scheme trustee through *Mills & Reeve*'s corporate trustee, Francis House Trustees Limited. Full member of the Association of Pension Lawyers.

SERES, Jonathan
Sacker & Partners, London
(020) 7329 6699
jonathan.seres@sacker-partners.co.uk
Specialisation: Partner in specialist pensions law firm of over 40 pensions lawyers. Experienced in all aspects of pension schemes, covering establishment, alteration, merger, booklets, related employment law, Financial Services and Markets Act work, common investment funds and investment management and custody agreements. Advises employers, trustees, trade unions and charities. Acted in application to the ECJ in the Coloroll matter (*Sacker & Partners* were acting for the four classes of male beneficiaries). Acted for GEC Plan in 1999 on £2.5bn separation of MES. Author of 'Pensions: A Practical Guide' (4th edition 1997, FT Law & Tax, 450 pages). Appeared as pensions tax expert on Channel 4's City Programme. Has led on scheme mergers within HSBC Group. Immediate past Senior Partner. Continues client work.
Prof. Memberships: Association of Pension Lawyers, National Association of Pension Funds, Society of Pension Consultants, Law Society.
Personal: Born 13 June 1945. Oxford University PPE (Hons) 1966. Leisure interests include sailing, history and charities. Lives in London.

SHELLEY, Daniel
Pinsent Curtis Biddle, Birmingham
(0121) 200 1050
daniel.shelley@pinsents.com
Specialisation: All aspects of pension law.
Prof. Memberships: Association of Pension Lawyers.
Career: Articles - *Slaughter and May*; *Pinsent Curtis Biddle* - partner 1995.
Personal: Born 1958.

SHERWIN, Nick
Clifford Chance, London
(020) 7600 1000
nick.sherwin@cliffordchance.com
Specialisation: Tax, pensions and employment. Partner specialising in pensions, advising employers, trustees and product providers.
Career: Articled *Clifford-Turner*; Assistant Solicitor *Clifford-Turner/Clifford Chance* 1986-93; Partner since 1993.
Personal: Manchester Grammar School; 1982 St John's College, Cambridge (MA Hons); 1983 University of Pennsylvania (LLM); ATII; Gilbert Burr Medal Winner.

SLOAN, Derek
Allen & Overy, London
(020) 7330 3000
derek.sloan@allenovery.com
Specialisation: Partner and Head of Employment, Pensions and Incentives Department. Practice covers all areas of pensions work including establishing, reorganising, merging and terminating schemes, conversion of schemes from defined benefit to defined contribution, investment management and custody arrangements, the pensions implications of business sales, reorganisations and insolvencies, funding issues and equal treatment. Regular speaker at conferences.
Prof. Memberships: Law Society, Association of Pension Lawyers, Chairman of APL Legislative and Parliamentary sub-committee 1998-2001, Pensions Research Accountants Group.
Career: Qualified 1973. Partner 1977.
Personal: Oxford University (1970, BA Jurisprudence). Born 1948.

SMITH, Stephanie
Travers Smith Braithwaite, London
(020) 7295 3000
Stephanie.Smith@TraversSmith.com
Specialisation: Partner in Pensions Department. Handles all aspects of pensions law. Regular public speaker.
Prof. Memberships: Association of Pensions Lawyers.
Career: Qualified in 1986. Joined *Travers Smith Braithwaite* in 1993, becoming a Partner in 1994.
Personal: Born 22 March 1962. Holds an LLB from Queen Mary College, London (1983). Lives in London.

SOUTHERN, Steve
Hammond Suddards Edge, Manchester
(0161) 830 5000

STANNARD, Paul
Travers Smith Braithwaite, London
(020) 7295 3000
Paul.Stannard@TraversSmith.com
Specialisation: Partner in Pensions Department. All aspects of pensions law.
Prof. Memberships: Fellow of the Pensions Management Institute.
Career: Qualified 1982. Joined *Travers Smith Braithwaite* as a Partner in 1989.
Personal: Born 1957.

STIMPSON, Maria
Ashurst Morris Crisp, London
(020) 7859 1114
maria.stimpson@ashursts.com
Specialisation: All aspects of pensions law and practice, including establishing, merging and winding-up schemes, unapproved pension provision, legisla-

PENSIONS ■ THE LEADERS

tive and regulatory compliance, discrimination issues and the pensions aspects of corporate transactions.
Prof. Memberships: Association of Pensions Lawyers (currently serving on investment sub-committee), National Association of Pension Funds.
Career: Qualified 1989 *Shoosmiths*, 1995-98 *Freshfields*, 1999 to date partner and head of pensions *Ashurst Morris Crisp*.
Publications: Include chapter on equalisation, Tolley's 'The Guide to the Pensions Act 1995'.
Personal: LLB Business Law, married living in Surrey, interests include health, theatre, walking and travel.

STRACHAN, Russell
Lovells, London
(020) 7296 2000
russell.strachan@lovells.com
Specialisation: Pension law in all its applications, particularly: negotiating scheme reorganisations and mergers, benefit design, sales and acquisitions, conflicts of interest and trustee problems, winding-up, equal pay and contentious issues, investment and regulatory matters, scheme documentation and member communications. Clients include multinational and UK employers, trustees, insurance companies, investment companies and professional advisors.
Prof. Memberships: Law Society, Association of Pension Lawyers, National Association of Pension Funds; Pension Research Accountants Group.
Career: Articled *Lovells* qualified 1970; Partner 1975.

TALMAN, Iain
Biggart Baillie, Glasgow
(0141) 228 8000

TAYLOR, Anne
Irwin Mitchell, Leeds
(0113) 234 3333
taylora@irwinmitchell.co.uk
Specialisation: Partner and National Head of Pensions Department. Director of Queen street Trustees Limited. Specialises in the winding-up and merger of pension schemes, advice on the pensions aspects of transfers of business and the impact of the Transfer of Undertakings legislation, dealing with litigious pensions issues including claims against companies, advising on potential breaches of the Pensions Act 1995, actions involving the Pensions Ombudsman.
Prof. Memberships: NAPF, PMI, APL.
Career: Qualified 5 September 1990.
Personal: Educated at Bradford Girls' Grammar School. Recreations include sailing, skiing, cars.

THOMAS-GREEN, Susan
Pinsent Curtis Biddle, Leeds
(0113) 244 5000
susan.thomas-green@pinsents.com
Specialisation: Partner in Pensions Group and Head of Leeds Team. Acts for trustees and employers in relation to scheme mergers. Director of *Pinsents* Trustees Ltd. Public sector pension arrangements, pensions disputes and changes to benefits and contributions, conversions to money purchase, and winding-up schemes.
Prof. Memberships: Association of Pensions Lawyers; Pensions Management Institute and on its Trustee Committee; Society of Pensions Consultants.
Career: Partner *Pinsent Curtis Biddle* and Leeds Head of Pensions 1994 to date: *Dundas & Wilson* 1991-94 (established Pensions Unit), *Freshfields* 1987-91. *Nicholson Graham & Jones* 1985-86.
Personal: University of Leicester. Golf, astronomy, swimming and good holidays. Married.

THURSTON SMITH, Martin
Tods Murray WS, Edinburgh
(0131) 226 4771
martin.thurston.smith@todsmurray.com
See under Investment Funds, p.503

TIER, Sarah
Sacker & Partners, London
(020) 7329 6699
sarah.tier@sacker-partners.co.uk
Specialisation: Partner in specialist pensions law firm. Deals with all aspects of pensions law including public sector and post-privatisation schemes, scheme mergers, advising trustees and pensions on divorce. Lectures at professional conferences, seminars and workshops. Writes for the professional and specialist press.
Prof. Memberships: Law Society, Association of Pension Lawyers, National Association of Pension Funds.
Career: Qualified in 1986. At *Clyde & Co* 1986-87. Joined *Nicholson Graham & Jones* in 1987 and became a Partner in 1991. Joined *Sacker & Partners* as a Partner in 1996.
Personal: Born 21 November 1960. Educated at the University of Southampton 1980-83. Interests include reading and hill-walking. Lives in Highgate, London.

TIMMINS, Jacqueline
Eversheds, Leeds
(0113) 243 0391
jacquelinetimmins@eversheds.com
Specialisation: Partner in Human Resources Group. Pensions law including scheme mergers, amalgamations, establishment of schemes, documentation, trusteeship matters, sales and acquisitions and dispute resolution.

Presented at APL and external seminars.
Prof. Memberships: Full member APL, secretary to North West APL, secretary and committee member of Manchester NAPF Group and a member of SPC.
Career: Qualified in 1991. Joined *Eversheds* in 1995.
Personal: Born 1965. Married, two sons. Leisure interests include wine (vineyard partner 'La Chevalerie' in the Loire Valley), hill walking and windsurfing.

TROTTER, Peter
MacRoberts, Glasgow
(0141) 332 9988
peter.trotter@macroberts.com
See under Employee Share Schemes, p.296

TURNBULL, Andrew
Walker Morris, Leeds
(0113) 283 2500
Specialisation: Practice covers the full range of pension work and includes creation and administration of schemes, scheme mergers, transactions and wind-ups whether acting as an individual independent trustee or through Walker Morris Trustees Limited.
Prof. Memberships: North Eastern Group of the Association of Pension Lawyers.
Career: Qualified 1983. Joined *Walker Morris* after qualification becoming a partner in 1985.
Personal: Born 19 April 1957. Educated at Shrewsbury and Birmingham University. Interests include golf, tennis and keep fit.

WEST, Robert
Baker & McKenzie, London
(020) 7919 1000
robert.west@bakernet.com
Specialisation: Partner in Pensions Department. Principal area of practice involves advising on all legal aspects of pensions including trust aspects, litigation, surpluses, sales and purchases, drafting and advice to independent trustees. Other areas of work are employee benefits and share schemes. Acted in AMP litigation South West Trains v Wightman, National Bus, The Times Pension Fund litigation, the Drexel Pension Scheme litigation and in the sex discrimination case in the European Court, Neath v Hugh Steeper. Contributor on pensions to Butterworths' 'Legal Service' and author of articles for 'Pensions World' and 'Pensions Management'. Addressed many conferences in UK, USA and Canada.
Prof. Memberships: Law Society, Former Chairman of Association of Pension Lawyers, former Secretary of International Employee Benefits Association, Member of the Legal Advice Committee of the Occupational Pensions Advisory Service.
Career: Joined *Baker & McKenzie* in 1982 and became a Partner in 1985.
Personal: Attended Maidenhead Grammar School and Clare College, Cambridge. Leisure pursuits include sport and archaeology. Lives in Wargrave, Berkshire.

WHITE, Andrew
Mayer, Brown, Rowe & Maw, London
(020) 7782 8632
awhite@eu.mayerbrownrowe.com
Specialisation: Partner in Pensions Department. All aspects of law relating to company and personal pension schemes. Also handles life insurance, advising insurance companies on life policies and other products. Author of 'Pensions Issues in Mergers and Acquisitions' (FT Law and Tax, 2nd edition 1996); writes a regular monthly article in 'PLC Magazine'. Frequent speaker at conferences.
Prof. Memberships: Law Society, formerly a member of the Main Committee of the Association of Pension Lawyers. Former Chairman of Association's Legal and Parliamentary sub-committee. Current Chairman of Association's Divorce sub-committee.
Career: Qualified 1974. Joined *Rowe & Maw* 1977, becoming a partner in 1979.
Personal: Born 1 January 1950. Attended Manchester Grammar School 1961-68, then University College, Oxford, 1968-72. Leisure pursuits include reading. Lives in London.

WOMERSLEY, Mark
Osborne Clarke, Bristol
(0117) 917 3000

WRIGHT, David
DLA, Liverpool
(08700) 111111

WYMAN, Michael
Simmons & Simmons, London
(020) 7628 2020
michael.wyman@simmons-simmons.com
Specialisation: Partner in pensions group, which covers the whole range of pension work.
Prof. Memberships: Member of European Sub-committee, Society of Pension Consultants. Previously a member of the Legislative Sub-Committee of the Association of Pension Lawyers.
Career: Slaughter & May, 1976-85. With *Simmons & Simmons* since 1985.
Publications: Contributor to 'The Acquisition of Private Companies and Business Assets' 1989, 1992 and 1997; 'Pensions: The New Regime', 1998; Sweet & Maxwell's 'The Law of Pension Schemes', 1998-, and Joint Ventures and Shareholders' Agreements', 2000.

PERSONAL INJURY

London: 617; The Regions: 619; Scotland: 628; Profiles: 630

Research approved by BMRB For this edition, **Chambers'** researchers conducted 6,582 interviews – 3,900 with law firms, 511 with barristers and 2,171 with clients. The validity of the research was scrutinised by BMRB International, who audited both the methodology and the results at our offices in London. They interviewed **Chambers'** researchers and cross-checked sample interviews. Details of the audit appear on page 7.

OVERVIEW A tough year for personal injury solicitors has seen the abolition of legal aid in personal injury cases, while an increasing incidence of CFAs has resulted in a situation summarised by one interviewee as "*it's become harder than ever to get paid.*" In response, law firms and barristers' chambers have implemented training schemes to get staff up to speed on new and efficient ways of working. Claimant solicitors suffered a blow when the Fairchild ruling stated that where there is asbestos exposure from more than one source and it is not possible to prove which source caused mesothelioma, then the claim must fail. Firms have experienced an increase in stress claims – now the main reason for employees taking time off work – and post-traumatic stress disorder (PTSD) continues as Falklands and Gulf War veterans fight to obtain compensation.

LONDON

MAINLY CLAIMANT

PERSONAL INJURY: MAINLY CLAIMANT – LONDON

[1]
- Irwin Mitchell
- Leigh, Day & Co
- Russell Jones & Walker

[2]
- Evill and Coleman
- Pattinson & Brewer
- Stewarts
- Thompsons

[3]
- Anthony Gold
- Field Fisher Waterhouse
- Hodge Jones & Allen
- Rowley Ashworth

[4]
- Bolt Burdon
- Levenes
- OH Parsons & Partners

LEADING INDIVIDUALS

[1]
- ETTINGER Colin *Irwin Mitchell*
- LEE Terry *Evill and Coleman*
- NELSON-JONES Rodney *Field Fisher Waterhouse*

[2]
- ALLEN Patrick *Hodge Jones & Allen*
- CAHILL John *Stewarts*
- DAY Martyn *Leigh, Day & Co*
- KITSON Paul *Russell Jones & Walker*
- MARSHALL David *Anthony Gold*
- MCCARTHY Frances *Pattinson & Brewer*
- WALKER Ian *Russell Jones & Walker*

[3]
- MEERAN Richard *Leigh, Day & Co*
- PARKER Alison *Bolt Burdon*

This book is the product of 6,582 1/2 hour interviews. See p.7 for BMRB audit. Within each band, firms are listed alphabetically. See individuals' profiles p.630

IRWIN MITCHELL (see firm details p.1009) Frequently described to *Chambers'* researchers as "*impressive,*" the firm's stature in London now rivals that of its Sheffield office. It covers the full range of personal injury work, and is admired by peers for its "*tenacious*" approach to cases. A policy of treating cases as individuals and of doing the best for its clients by not taking needless points was noted and praised by interviewees, with the highest praise given by one fellow solicitor was that he would refer a family member to this group.

The firm has handled a number of maximum severity cases, and, in one instance, increased damages awarded to the victim of a traumatic brain injury to 80% more than previous lawyers had achieved. It is currently exploring potential effects of the Human Rights Act, including one case regarding the responsibility to grit roads. "*Top of the tree*" **Colin Ettinger** (see p.632) is omnipresent in this field; a member of the APIL executive committee and the Personal Injury Panel, he specialises in brain and spinal injury claims. On top of his practical expertise, he is considered "*a strong writer, an intellectual and a great commentator.*" **Clients** UNIFI; AMICUS; trade unions.

LEIGH, DAY & CO (see firm details p.1036) "*An outstanding practice, seated at the cutting edge,*" which has a strong, big group action bent (often with a foreign jurisdiction element). The Cape asbestos case, in which it represented 5,000 South African miners, settled for £21 million in 2001, and the firm continues to pioneer work on behalf of foreign victims of British organisations. It is currently acting on behalf of 200 Kenyan children injured by live bombs left by the British Army, and is advising several hundred Bangladeshis who suffered water poisoning.

Peers praise the quality of service provided by the group, which also maintains a reputable name for private client work. Maximum severity cases are a feature of the workload. As a figurehead for the practice, **Martyn Day** (see p.670) is perceived as "*tremendous,*" while **Richard Meeran** (see p.672) drew accolades during our research for his work on the Cape asbestos case. **Clients** Private clients.

RUSSELL JONES & WALKER (see firm details p.1120) Considered by many to be "*pre-eminent*" in union work, the firm has a comprehensive personal injury practice and is expanding its client base. The Cyclists' Touring Club is a valuable new addition, and private instructions are on the increase. Specialist teams deal with fast-track, multi-track, occupational disease, employers' liability and maximum severity claims. Within the latter, a designated group handles child abuse cases. RTA is an area of particular expertise, and the firm recently settled one of the largest ever fatal claims in the UK, £2 million, in favour of the widow of a RTA victim. It has also acted for the Porton Down veterans, a group of 450 servicemen used in the testing of nerve gas in the 1950s.

Ian Walker (see p.637) leads the firm's maximum severity department and is a senior fellow of the College of Personal Injury Law. "*Accomplished*" **Paul Kitson** (see p.634) is another key player, with a recognised strength in police work. **Clients** Cyclists' Touring Club; Usdaw; Police Federation; Royal College of Nursing; ISTC; PCS; TSSA; Prospect.

EVILL AND COLEMAN (see firm details p.950) The firm's niche maximum severity unit is admired by peers for its "*extremely talented people,*" and has recently handled a number of cerebral palsy claims around the £2 million mark. It appeared in the case of a dental anaesthetist accused of serious professional misconduct, and has acted against the National Blood Authority on several Hepatitis C cases. Managing an increase in asbestosis claims, accidents abroad and sporting injuries are other areas of expertise. **Terry Lee** (see p.634) is universally acknowledged as an expert; he has "*desperately important*" experience, and is described by our interviewees as "*efficient – he covers all bases and isn't afraid of difficult cases.*" His colleague, Liz Martinez, was recommended to *Chambers'* researchers for her maximum severity expertise. **Clients** Private clients.

PATTINSON & BREWER (see firm details p.1095) Respected for its large union practice, the firm is also increasing its private client base. It handles a large amount of occupational disease, employers' liability and accidents at work cases, and is organised into partner-led teams dealing with specific areas of personal injury.

617

www.ChambersandPartners.com

PERSONAL INJURY ■ LONDON

Head of department **Frances McCarthy** (see p.634) has been appointed as a member of the Civil Justice Council, and is widely respected amongst peers as someone who "*knows what she's talking about.*" Having served two years as president of APIL, she has recently been involved in a rehabilitation working party under the Insurance Underwriters Association, and has been developing the rehabilitation practice in her firm. **Clients** Private clients.

STEWARTS (see firm details p.1150) Niche maximum severity practice with particular focus on brain and spinal claims, the firm employs two independent, living advisors, both paraplegics, to assist catastrophically injured clients. It also fields a specialist abuse department, and has expertise in foreign jurisdiction claims and aviation disasters. Substantial recent claims include the recovery of £4.75 million for a teenage victim of criminal assault; the largest payout awarded to a British crime victim. The team also recovered £2.25 million on behalf of a hairdresser paralysed in a traffic accident.

The foreign jurisdiction team has acted on several cases involving UK citizens injured or killed abroad, including a major claim against a theme park and medical centre in Florida and claims from passengers injured in the Nevada coach crash. In cases such as these, the firm works in conjunction with an established network of lawyers in the States. Our researchers were told that **John Cahill** (see p.631) is committed and hands-on; "*a doer.*" He is a trustee of Headway. **Clients** Private clients.

THOMPSONS The name of this "*top TU firm*" carries weight in the market in light of the large volume of union claims it handles. It acts for a range of unions, and has seen an increasing number of occupational stress and asbestos-related claims. Damages were recovered for a fireman injured by tripping on tools in a fire station and for a BECTU member injured working in the Royal National Theatre. Total damages recovered by the London office in the past year are £12.5 million. Anthony Lawton is a key member of the team. **Clients** UNISON; GMB; AEEU; TGWU; PCS; FBU; ASLEF; GPMU.

ANTHONY GOLD (see firm details p.846) Acting almost entirely for individual claimants, the firm does not undertake bulk work for unions or insurers. It has long-standing experience of using conditional fees, the current trend in the personal injury world. Areas of expertise include brain and spinal injuries, stress at work, psychiatric and fatal claims. The team recently obtained £190,000 damages for the victim of PTSD following a relatively minor RTA and substantial damages for a man who suffered an injured back as a result of a defective canteen chair. The "*excellent*" **David Marshall** (see p.634) continues to impress peers with his effective working style and strong communication skills. **Clients** Private clients.

FIELD FISHER WATERHOUSE (see firm details p.954) The debacle surrounding the Fairchild ruling has disrupted proceedings for this largely asbestos-driven practice, as several multi-defendant cases have had to be put on hold. Nevertheless, the team has recovered £5 million in 85 successful asbestos claims in the last year. The team's approach is widely praised by peers: "*they research things properly and can deal with a novel point.*"

Asbestos specialist **Rodney Nelson-Jones** (see p.635) remains a pre-eminent practitioner, said to "*know his subject better than any other lawyer,*" and is "*prepared to pull his finger out.*" He acted for the claimant in the fatal mesothelioma case of O'Loughlin v Cape, in which the Court of Appeal upheld an award of £285,000 to the widow of an Irish property developer, and is on the team of solicitors appealing against the Fairchild decision. The firm has expertise in claims arising from air and rail disasters, as well as industrial and catastrophic cases. Nelson-Jones has recovered damages in claims stemming from crashes in Thailand, Nepal, Zambia and Guernsey, while partner Paul McNeil is on the steering committees for the Southall and Paddington rail crashes. **Clients** Private clients.

HODGE JONES & ALLEN (see firm details p.997) "*Good quality, solid practice,*" the firm's profile is considerably bolstered by the presence of soon to be APIL president **Patrick Allen** (see p.630). A multiparty specialist, he is currently leading a team handling Gulf War illness claims for UK veterans, and is described by peers as "*a good performer who knows what he's talking about.*" The firm is involved in approximately 650 claims at any one time on behalf of servicemen pursuing claims for PTSD relating to the Gulf War, Falklands and Northern Ireland. It also has expertise in criminal injury, accidents at work and RTAs. **Clients** Private clients.

ROWLEY ASHWORTH Endorsed by our interviewees as a "*strong team*" of union solicitors that "*prepares work well,*" it has the capacity and case management systems to handle a large volume of instructions from its traditional union client base. The group also attracts private clients, and draws strength from its six offices across England and Wales.

BOLT BURDON Still acting exclusively for accident victims, the firm excels in accidents at work and occupational disease. It recently picked up the claim of a nurse from the larger firms and represented a woman attacked by a DSS claimant. Fatal accidents, head injuries and accidents abroad are other areas of specialism. **Alison Parker** (see p.635) is rated by our interviewees as an "*extremely sensible*" lawyer.

LEVENES (see firm details p.1040) The firm was recommended to our researchers as an "*underrated*" operator in its work for both legal expense insurers and private claims. Working on a no win no fee basis, it handles RTA, accidents at work and slip and trip claims. **Clients** Legal expense insurers; private clients.

OH PARSONS & PARTNERS Largely an industrial trade union firm, much of its major work comes from the mining, construction and transport industries. It also handles claims on behalf of a limited number of private clients. Futher areas of expertise include local authorities and carpet weavers' claims. Paul Stanley is an active practitioner at the firm. **Clients** TGWU; UCATT; ISTC; GMB.

LONDON — MAINLY DEFENDANT

BARLOW LYDE & GILBERT (see firm details p.858) The firm is known amongst our interviewees for its "*contentious*" approach, and is thought of as the popular choice with insurers, a fact reflected by the expansion of its already comprehensive base of insurance clients. The firm mainly acts on EL/PL; it is on the NHSLA panel, and appeared for the Association of British Insurers in the seminal conditional fee cases Callery v Gray and Sarwar v Allan. Its specialist industrial disease unit has been bolstered by three new recruits, and is dealing with an increasing number of stress claims. Continuing his special interest in rehabilitation, **Graham Dickinson** (see p.632) is involved in the new Rehabilitation Case Managers Society; he is described by peers as "*the business.*" **Clients** Insurers.

BEACHCROFT WANSBROUGHS (see firm details p.860) Appreciated for its "*realistic*" attitude, this is a "*big player*" undertaking personal injury work for its large corporate insurance base. The firm is shedding its lower value claims to concentrate on top-end matters, and has dealt with an increasing number of occupational disease claims, including stress. The Eastcheap office has particular expertise in

LONDON/THE SOUTH ■ PERSONAL INJURY

PERSONAL INJURY: MAINLY DEFENDANT
■ LONDON

1
- Barlow Lyde & Gilbert
- Beachcroft Wansbroughs
- Berrymans Lace Mawer
- Kennedys

2
- Vizards Wyeth

3
- Badhams
- Davies Arnold Cooper
- Hextalls

LEADING INDIVIDUALS

1
- **DICKINSON Graham** Barlow Lyde & Gilbert

2
- **RENOUF Terence** Berrymans Lace Mawer
- **STAPLES Martin** Vizards Wyeth

3
- **NEILL Bryan** Prince Evans
- **OLIVER Timothy** Badhams
- **PARKER Andrew** Beachcroft Wansbroughs
- **SLESS Tania** Beachcroft Wansbroughs
- **WILSON Timothy** Kennedys

This book is the product of 6,582 1/2 hour interviews. See p.7 for BMRB audit. Within each band, firms are listed alphabetically. See individuals' profiles p.630

pharmaceutical and contraception-related cases. Other areas of focus include asbestos, RSI and RTA. Anthony Cherry has moved to the firm's Bristol office, leaving the highly rated **Tania Sless** (see p.636) and the "*capable*" head of FOIL, **Andrew Parker** (see p.635), as lead practitioners.

BERRYMANS LACE MAWER (see firm details p.865) The firm was described to *Chambers*' researchers as "*a pleasant, professional outfit*" that "*moves with the times.*" It is organised into units managing specialist areas such as catastrophic injury, industrial disease, police education, motor and local authority claims. The head of the catastrophic unit, Jenny Moates, has been appointed to the NFU's super panel of four solicitors dealing with high-value brain and spinal claims.

The team has been appointed to a variety of new panels such as ACE, British Railways Board, Hearing Aid Council and Thames Valley Police. **Terence Renouf** (see p.636) is respected as a practitioner who "*cares about cases.*" **Clients** ACE; Chubb Security; Generali; HSBC; Marks & Spencer; Royal & SunAlliance (RSA); St. Paul; Norwich Union (NU).

KENNEDYS (see firm details p.1019) Our interviewees believed that the firm's profile has increased recently, and recommended its lawyers for their "*commercial*" aptitude and "*hard but not stupid*" attitude. A tendency to make a well-judged offer early on in proceedings was admired by peers. It has a strong base of insurance panel clients, and won a recent tender for AXA work.

A broad range of personal injury cases is handled, including industrial disease, RTA and maximum severity, while it is moving towards higher value claims. In the industrial disease sector, the team deals with asbestos, industrial deafness and VWF. Previously ranked Mariel Irvine has left to set up her own practice in personal injury and railway-related work, and **Tim Wilson** (see p.637) has taken up the reins, including work in stress claims. He is considered "*excellent*" by fellow solicitors. **Clients** AXA; Zurich; Virgin Trains; Railtrack.

VIZARDS WYETH A merger with Dartford firm AE Wyeth & Co sees the majority of the firm's personal injury workload shift to a new Dartford office, although it will continue to operate with a reduced London presence. Its client base boasts a healthy number of insurance panels, including all of Zurich's. Noted for a particular expertise in handling claims for local authorities, the firm frequently undertakes dyslexia and failure to educate cases. Prominent ex-FOIL president **Martin Staples** (see p.636) ensures the firm's profile remains high, and is rated for his "*effective*" communication skills. He acted on one of the UK's first 'hot drinks' claims against McDonald's. Other focus areas include stress, disease and rehabilitation, as well as fast-track and multi-track work. **Clients** Iron Trades; Zurich; RSA; NU; QBE; NIG; Skandia; Prudential; Green Flag; The Underwriter.

BADHAMS (see firm details p.853) The arrival of **Tim Oliver** (see p.635) from Berrymans with a large team is a significant boost to this specialist insurance firm. Now heading the department, Oliver is endorsed by peers as "*straightforward – he knows his job backwards.*" Since his arrival the firm has undergone a major reorganisation with smaller, fast-track claims sent to the Croydon office and higher value claims handled by the London team. Specialist units have been formed to focus on travel, industrial disease and environmental claims, and partner-led teams exist to deal with specific major clients. **Clients** Direct Line; RSA; AXA; NU.

DAVIES ARNOLD COOPER (see firm details p.930) Market opinion differs on the firm's profile; while its impact has undoubtedly diminished over the past few years, our interviewees still perceived it as "*a force to be reckoned with on larger actions.*" The firm houses a specialist unit, which provides strength in sports injuries' claims, and John Smith continues to handle work for the football Premiership. Travel is another niche area, and the team is handling a mass food poisoning case in Spain. Other typical claims in this area relate to holiday and swimming pool accidents. The firm retains a sound base of insurance clients. **Clients** Aurora; Zurich Commercial; RSA; Tryg-Baltica; Rover Group.

HEXTALLS (see firm details p.994) Involved in a broad range of personal injury work, particularly employers' and public liability, the firm also handles a substantial number of motor claims. It recently represented Racing Lines and Medd Racing in a claim brought by a motorcyclist seriously injured when a wheel on his bike disintegrated, and substantially reduced the damages awarded. A specialist sport unit recently handled the case of Pitcher v Huddersfield Town FC, in which a footballer sued because of injuries sustained in a tackle; the claim was thrown out. Travel is also an area of expertise. Partner Joe McManus focuses on industrial disease claims, and is experienced in accidents overseas, and head and spinal injuries. **Clients** AIG; Place Hastings; ACE Europe; Chaucer Group; Generali; Crawfords.

OTHER NOTABLE PRACTITIONERS Bryan Neill (see p.634) of Prince Evans was also recommended for his defendant work.

THE SOUTH — MAINLY CLAIMANT

LAMPORT BASSITT (see firm details p.1027) This is predominantly a trade union firm with a strong asbestos-related disease practice and a lesser percentage of RTA. Its workload typically consists of employers' liability and disease claims, and it has niche expertise in noise induced hearing loss. Considered by peers to employ a "*pragmatic*" approach, the firm's technical knowledge also attracts accolades. A new Reading office handles an increased amount of trade union work, largely generated by main client TGWU. **Nick Rogers** (see p.636) is a leading practitioner who has moved from defendant to claimant work, and is deemed "*a good person to deal with – always to the point.*" **Clients** TGWU; hospitals.

GEORGE IDE, PHILLIPS (see firm details p.969) In its successful combination of legal expense and volume motor work with higher value serious claims, the firm is moving away from the bulk end of the market and handling an increasing amount of maximum severity cases. It has particular strength in brain injury work. **Tony Goff** (see p.633) is a widely known player in this region, considered by peers to be "*top-notch.*" **Clients** Auto Indemnity; Aftercare.

MOORE & BLATCH (see firm details p.1074) The firm is endorsed by interviewees as the "*best of the bunch*" in its understanding of the mechanics of the claimant market. David Thompson heads the unit rated for its "*strong*

PERSONAL INJURY ■ THE SOUTH

PERSONAL INJURY: MAINLY CLAIMANT ■ THE SOUTH

1
- Lamport Bassitt *Southampton*

2
- George Ide, Phillips *Chichester*
- Moore & Blatch *Southampton*
- Shoosmiths *Basingstoke*
- Thomson Snell & Passmore *Tunbridge Wells*

3
- Amery-Parkes *Basingstoke*
- Blake Lapthorn *Portsmouth*
- Pattinson & Brewer *Chatham*
- Warner Goodman & Streat *Fareham*

LEADING INDIVIDUALS

1
- GOFF Tony *George Ide, Phillips*
- ROGERS Nick *Lamport Bassitt*

This book is the product of 6,582 1/2 hour interviews. See p.7 for BMRB audit. Within each band, firms are listed alphabetically.. See individuals' profiles p.630

tradition" and fielding specialists in RTA, accidents at work and industrial disease. Clients include legal expense insurers and referral organisations. Alongside its work in general RTA and EL/PL claims, the firm handles brain and spinal injuries, including a recent recovery of £1.2 million on behalf of a brain damage victim. **Clients** Legal expense insurers; private clients.

SHOOSMITHS (see firm details p.1133) A *"large and successful"* team, it mainly handles bulk fast-track work from its legal expense and motor insurer clientele; it has attained a position on The Automobile Association's (The AA) newly formed ATE solicitors' panel. The firm also handles higher value claims, including accidents at work and industrial disease. It has dealt with RTA-related head injuries, including a settlement for £750,000 and a fibromyalgia claim. Head of department John Spencer is a national committee member of MASS. **Clients** Direct Line Group; The AA; Churchill Insurance Company; Capita; Green Flag; Saga.

THOMSON SNELL & PASSMORE (see firm details p.1161) The practice was recommended to our researchers for its work covering RTA, accidents at work and slip and trip claims. It also undertakes brain injury cases, and head of department Julie Reynolds is a member of Headway locally and nationally. The team recently settled a brain injury case for £450,000. **Clients** Private clients.

OTHER NOTABLE FIRMS Amery-Parkes is respected by peers for *"always providing good quality"* advice, with particular expertise in RTA claims. It also handles accidents at work, public liability and multiparty claims. Tom Risley is a member of the team. Blake Lapthorn is a *"well-managed"* firm dealing with claims ranging from RTA and fast-track to maximum severity head and back injury. The group draws on resources from both the Portsmouth and Southampton offices. It recently settled a back injury claim for £750,000. Areas of particular strength include abuse claims against LEAs and schools, and criminal injury compensation. Alison McClure is a respected member of the team. Niamh O'Brady is a partner in the Chatham office of **Pattinson & Brewer**, a largely trade union-driven firm. The team has expertise in complex cases and disease claims. **Warner Goodman & Streat** was commended to our researchers for its work in asbestos-related cases, accidents at work, RTA and slip and trip claims. The firm advises individuals, trade unions and insurance companies.

THE SOUTH

PERSONAL INJURY: MAINLY DEFENDANT ■ THE SOUTH

1
- Beachcroft Wansbroughs *Winchester*
- Berrymans Lace Mawer *Southampton*
- Bond Pearce *Southampton*
- Clarke Willmott & Clarke *Southampton*

2
- Davies Lavery *Maidstone*
- Palser Grossman *Southampton*
- Vizards Wyeth *Dartford*

LEADING INDIVIDUALS

1
- BRUFFELL Martin *Berrymans Lace Mawer*
- EVANS Rod *Clarke Willmott & Clarke*

This book is the product of 6,582 1/2 hour interviews. See p.7 for BMRB audit. Within each band, firms are listed alphabetically.. See individuals' profiles p.630

BEACHCROFT WANSBROUGHS (see firm details p.860) This highly thought of, insurance-based, personal injury team *"always provides good quality,"* predominantly tackling multi-track claims for its insurer clients. It is equipped to handle all from the lowest to the highest value cases, including catastrophic and tetraplegic. It is conveniently located to handle employers' liability claims on behalf of the MOD resulting from accidents on nearby naval bases, and undertakes accident work for local authorities and health trusts. Asbestos and stress claims are regular sources of work, and the team is developing niche expertise in latex allergies, asthma and dermatitis amongst nursing staff. Duncan Rutter is an active member of the team. **Clients** MOD; Cornhill; RSA.

BERRYMANS LACE MAWER (see firm details p.865) Lateral solicitor hires from Leo Abse & Cohen and Ensor Byfield have boosted the size of this highly rated office. It has secured new work from insurers, including Pearl, Aon and Marsh. Occupational and industrial disease claims constitute the majority of its instructions, and it has expertise in horse-riding related claims, recently winning the case of a woman injured by a fall. £1 million damages were also secured in a work-related stress claim, while other areas of focus include educational, abuse and leisure industry claims. A familiar sight in the market, **Martin Bruffell** (see p.631) heads the team. **Clients** Insurers; private individuals.

BOND PEARCE (see firm details p.879) This *"highly respected"* outfit has witnessed the move of Bettina Rigg to employment and health and safety law; she is replaced as head of department by Lea Brocklebank. The team acts for 22 insurer, self-insured, mutual fund and P&I club clients, and has handled a growth in serious claims arising out of collisions with farm machinery and motorcycles. The unit's Southampton base places it well to handle shipping claims, and it also receives instructions from the Channel Islands. It is one of four firms on the Post Office's national panel. **Clients** Post Office; NFU Mutual; insurers.

MAINLY DEFENDANT

CLARKE WILLMOTT & CLARKE (see firm details p.907) The firm is combining its work for a number of significant insurance panels with a move towards smaller, more specialist entities. Areas of focus include industrial disease, asbestos, severe injuries and sports injuries. **Rod Evans** (see p.632) concentrates on brain injury, and settled a recent case for over £1 million. He is described by contemporaries as *"a sensible, commercial litigator."* **Clients** Insurers; private clients.

OTHER NOTABLE FIRMS Davies Lavery works for a stable of insurance clients, and has expertise in RTA, EL/PL and product liability. It also handles fatal accidents and works for local authorities. Stephen Read is a member of the team. The largest of the **Palser Grossman** satellite offices is perceived as *"successful"* by competitors. Its team has expanded recently, and handles a mixture of RTA and employers' liability claims ranging from low-value to catastrophic. Disease claims, most often industrial asthma and asbestosis-related, are handled by two specialists. The main office of the merger between AE Wyeth & Co with Vizards Staples & Bannisters – **Vizards Wyeth** – is located in a newly established Dartford office. It maintains a strong insurance client base. Clients include insurers and local authorities.

THAMES VALLEY/SOUTH WEST ■ PERSONAL INJURY

THAMES VALLEY

MAINLY CLAIMANT

**PERSONAL INJURY:
MAINLY CLAIMANT
■ THAMES VALLEY**

1
- Boyes Turner Reading
- Osborne Morris & Morgan Leighton Buzzard

2
- Fennemores Milton Keynes
- Harris Cartwright Slough
- Henmans Oxford

LEADING INDIVIDUALS

1 OSBORNE Tom Osborne Morris & Morgan

2 DESMOND Adrian Boyes Turner

This book is the product of 6,582 1/2 hour interviews. See p.7 for BMRB audit. Within each band, firms are listed alphabetically. See individuals' profiles p.630

BOYES TURNER (see firm details p.883) Solicitors described the firm as "*committed to clients,*" and praised its "*complete service.*" Focusing mainly on catastrophic claims, the team has particular strength in RTA claims, including motorcycle accidents, bolstered recently by the appointment of an in-house accident investigator. The group includes a brain injury support group, and is headed by "*extremely good competitor*" **Adrian Desmond** (see p.150). It recently recovered £2.2 million for the victim of a tardily diagnosed brain tumour.

OSBORNE MORRIS & MORGAN Reputed brain injury specialist **Tom Osborne** heads this "*respected outfit.*" Alongside its multi-track instructions, the group undertakes serious injury claims for clients throughout the UK. It recently recovered £1.9 million on behalf of a baby injured because of an undisclosed pregnancy.

OTHER NOTABLE FIRMS "*Good for fast-track litigation,*" **Fennemores** handles RTA claims for legal expense insurers, as well as EL/PL. Kent Pattinson leads the team at **Harris Cartwright** that has particular strength in high-value catastrophic claims. Although dealing with some low-value claims, **Henmans**' claimant practice continues to undertake a substantial number of high-value catastrophic cases, typically handling 14 £1 million claims at any one time. Mary Duncan is one of the team's key players, advising a client base that includes legal expense insurers.

THAMES VALLEY

MAINLY DEFENDANT

**PERSONAL INJURY:
MAINLY DEFENDANT
■ THAMES VALLEY**

1 Morgan Cole Reading

2 Henmans Oxford

This book is the product of 6,582 1/2 hour interviews. See p.7 for BMRB audit. Within each band, firms are listed alphabetically.

MORGAN COLE (see firm details p.1075) The firm is the main defendant player in this region, widely endorsed by our interviewees as "*certainly the best.*" It has succeeded in remaining on a healthy number of insurance panels, and undertakes motor, EL/PL and fast-track claims, alongside substantial high-value claims. Elizabeth Carr heads the department. **Clients** NU; NFU; MMA; AXA Corporate Solutions; Highway; Tesco; Allianz Cornhill.

HENMANS (see firm details p.990) Set up to handle medium to large claims, the firm has secured a place on an admirable number of insurance panels, and is skilled in handling employers' liability claims. It frequently tackles substantial fatal cases, and has recently advised on a number of mesothelioma and RTA claims and a large multi-jurisdictional fatal claim. Finbar Cahill is a key member of this respected team. **Clients** St. Paul; Zurich; Hiscox; Stagecoach; Oxfordshire County Council.

SOUTH WEST

MAINLY CLAIMANT

**PERSONAL INJURY:
MAINLY CLAIMANT
■ SOUTH WEST**

1
- Bond Pearce Bristol, Plymouth
- Veale Wasbrough Bristol

2
- Lyons Davidson Bristol
- Russell Jones & Walker Bristol
- Thompsons Bristol

3 Rowley Ashworth Exeter

LEADING INDIVIDUALS

1
- HERBERT Andrew Thompsons
- ROBERTS Gavin Thompsons
- ROWE Bernard Lyons Davidson
- SOLLY Gillian Russell Jones & Walker
- THOMPSON Mark Bond Pearce
- WEBSTER John Veale Wasbrough

This book is the product of 6,582 1/2 hour interviews. See p.7 for BMRB audit. Within each band, firms are listed alphabetically. See individuals' profiles p.630

BOND PEARCE (see firm details p.879) Felt by some to be "*head and shoulders above the rest,*" this is a quality operation handling the full range of personal injury claims. The "*sensible and pragmatic*" team acts for private clients and individuals referred by fleet management and credit hire companies. It also acts for a trade union. The unit divides up into specialist teams for RTA, industrial disease and employers' liability. It handles an increasing number of high-value claims. Head of department **Mark Thompson** (see p.637) enjoys a good reputation with peers and clients.

VEALE WASBROUGH (see firm details p.1174) A 50% increase in cases has prompted this successful firm to hire three new solicitors. A respected union firm, its bedrock is union-funded employers' liability work. Multiparty cases remain an area of focus, and another busy area is RSI for lorry drivers. The team handles complex cases, including several £750,000 claims for claimants such as injured scaffolders and a significant claim on behalf of a woman who fell over on a broken shoe. Regional co-ordinator of APIL **John Webster** (see p.637) is said to have the right mix of "*knowing what he's doing and being realistic.*" **Clients** Private clients; trade unions.

OTHER NOTABLE FIRMS John Parkhouse operates from the Exeter office of **Rowley Ashworth**, which is best known for its work with trade unions. The "*highly knowledgeable*" **Bernard Rowe** (see p.636) heads the claimant department at **Lyons Davidson**, respected by peers for its legal expenses work. Areas of specialism include motor claims, handling 15 000 per annum ranging from small to catastrophic. Dedicated units deal with motorcycle, MIB, CFA, occupational health and head injury claims. Clients include RSA, DAS Legal Expenses Insurance Company and Direct Line. **Russell Jones & Walker**'s Bristol presence is described by peers as a healthy practice serving a strong base of trade union clients, which also handles

www.ChambersandPartners.com
621

PERSONAL INJURY ■ SOUTH WEST/WALES

work for private clients. The team includes well-regarded **Gillian Solly** (see p.636). The Bristol and Plymouth presence of **Thompsons** acts for union clients, and includes highly rated practitioners **Andrew Herbert** and **Gavin Roberts**, who are both felt to "*know exactly what they're about.*"

SOUTH WEST

MAINLY DEFENDANT

PERSONAL INJURY: MAINLY DEFENDANT ■ SOUTH WEST

1. **Beachcroft Wansbroughs** Bristol
2. **Bond Pearce** Bristol, Plymouth
   Cartwrights Insurance Partners Bristol
3. **Bevan Ashford** Bristol
   Palser Grossman Bristol
   Veitch Penny Exeter

LEADING INDIVIDUALS
1. **BEALE Robert** Beachcroft Wansbroughs
   BRADLEY Deborah Cartwrights Insurance Partners
   CHERRY Anthony Beachcroft Wansbroughs

This book is the product of 6,582 1/2 hour interviews. See p.7 for BMRB audit. Within each band, firms are listed alphabetically. See individuals' profiles p.630

BEACHCROFT WANSBROUGHS (see firm details p.860) "*Still got their noses out in front*" was the view of one interviewee, and the firm is generally regarded as the strongest in the region, possessing "*the most prominent name.*" The team has placed an emphasis on the development of its fast-track practice moving towards more multi-track work, the latter of which is handled by the designated mutual law group. Top-value cases that the firm has taken on include a £3 million product liability claim and a policeman injured on a training course. Catastrophic claims are also handled. The arrival of leading figure **Anthony Cherry** (see p.631) from London adds ballast to the team, and he is joined by James Morris, a partner from Palser Grossman. **Robert Beale** (see p.630) maintains a strong local profile. **Clients** Insurers.

BOND PEARCE (see firm details p.879) This respected defendant practice enjoys a substantial client base of insurers, self-insureds, mutual funds and P&I clubs. It has seen an increase in high-value serious injury claims arising out of collisions between heavy farm machinery and motorcycles, cases often handled on behalf of NFU Mutual. It is well located to handle shipping-related cases. The Post Office remains a key client, and the firm is one of four appointed to its national panel. **Clients** Marketform; NFU Mutual; Post Office; Groupama; St. Paul; Hiscox.

CARTWRIGHTS INSURANCE PARTNERS Deborah Bradley (see p.631) is a leading practitioner in the team, which has expertise in EL/PL, motor and product liability claims. It handles occupational disease and asbestosis claims, and acts for loss adjusters, insurers and the insured.

OTHER NOTABLE FIRMS The team at **Bevan Ashford** has placed a clear emphasis on its personal injury portfolio, and Paul Taverner now runs a dedicated team that has seen a recent increase in RTA claims, and at the time of research was handling four £2 million maximum severity head and back injuries. Stress is an area of particular expertise for the team, advising both its corporate clients and one insurer client, while Taverner gives regular talks to ALARM (The Association of Local Authority Risk Managers). Clients include Orange and NU. Much of **Palser Grossman**'s caseload in Bristol serves Zurich, while Angus McFarlane leads the team that also acts for AXA, NU and Green Flag. It predominantly handles multi-track claims up to £1 million in value. The personal injury unit at **Veitch Penny** is felt by peers to "*always know what they're doing.*" It acts for insurer clients, and is one of two firms in the South West to be on the RAC's panel. It has particular expertise in handling motorcycle-related claims. Clients include RAC.

WALES

MAINLY CLAIMANT

PERSONAL INJURY: MAINLY CLAIMANT ■ WALES

1. **Hugh James** Cardiff, Merthyr Tydfil
   Leo Abse & Cohen Cardiff
2. **Thompsons** Cardiff
3. **Loosemores** Cardiff
   Russell Jones & Walker Cardiff

LEADING INDIVIDUALS
1. **HARDING Andrew** Hugh James
   HARVEY Mark Hugh James
   HOPKINS Ian Leo Abse & Cohen
   WILLIAMS Robin Leo Abse & Cohen

This book is the product of 6,582 1/2 hour interviews. See p.7 for BMRB audit. Within each band, firms are listed alphabetically. See individuals' profiles p.630

HUGH JAMES (see firm details p.1004) The team specialises in high-value claims, and has recovered more than £9 million last year for victims of catastrophic injuries. It is also involved in a multiparty action relating to the Gerona air crash. Industrial disease is an area of strength for the firm; it recovered over £1 billion in damages last year for VWF victims, and handles a large number of respiratory claims. It has been appointed to the Lord Chancellor's Receivers' panel for Wales and the South West. **Mark Harvey** (see p.671) and **Andrew Harding** (see p.633) continue to be respected practitioners. **Clients** Royal College of Nursing; NACODS; pressure groups.

LEO ABSE & COHEN "*An effective and impressive*" outfit, the firm is rated by peers for its knowledge of a wide range of personal injury claims. **Robin Williams** and **Ian Hopkins** are both deemed "*reliable, safe pairs of hands*" by peers. **Clients** Trade unions.

OTHER NOTABLE FIRMS **Thompsons** continues its "*established*" presence in the region, respected primarily for its union practice. **Loosemores** tackles high-volume work on behalf of legal expense and motor insurers. A "*new outfit on the block,*" **Russell Jones & Walker** opened in Wales four years ago and has a dedicated personal injury team. It handles predominantly multi-track claims for trade unions, but has the capability to tackle fast-track and an increasing number of catastrophic cases. Michael Imperato leads the team, and has acted for the ISTC in the aftermath of an explosion at Port Talbot Blast Furnace in 2001. It recovered £100,000 on behalf of a police officer rendered deaf during the course of his employment.

WALES/MIDLANDS ■ PERSONAL INJURY

WALES

MAINLY DEFENDANT

PERSONAL INJURY: MAINLY DEFENDANT ■ WALES

[1] **Hugh James** Cardiff
Morgan Cole Cardiff
[2] **Palser Grossman** Cardiff Bay
[3] **Dolmans** Cardiff

LEADING INDIVIDUALS

[1] **CRADICK Simon** Morgan Cole
WILLIAMS Gareth Hugh James
[2] **MACWILKINSON Jeffrey** Dolmans
PRICE Hugh Morgan Cole

This book is the product of 6,582 1/2 hour interviews. See p.7 for BMRB audit. Within each band, firms are listed alphabetically. See individuals' profiles p.630

HUGH JAMES (see firm details p.1004) Mairwen Whittaker heads the defendant side of this "*major, quality firm.*" The team's approach is praised as "*proactive; not overly aggressive*". The group divides into three strands, handling fast-track, multi-track and maximum severity claims, and the latter practice area has recruited three new fee-earners from Keoghs' closed Southampton office. Clients include a large number of insurers and local authorities. Gareth Williams (see p.570) is a respected figurehead for the firm. **Clients** Prudential; NU; AIG; Zurich Municipal; Tokio Marine; The Underwriter; Chartwell; local authorities.

MORGAN COLE (see firm details p.1075) A "*strong operation*" in Wales, the firm handles a range of PI matters, including occupational disease and limb-related disorders, stress and asbestos. It undertakes maximum severity claims, and recently settled a severe injury case for £3.2 million on behalf of an insurer client. The presence of "*technically skilled*" Simon Cradick and Hugh Price ("*personable and brilliant with clients*") is a considerable boost to the team. **Clients** Insurers.

OTHER NOTABLE FIRMS Peers are impressed by the Cardiff office of Palser Grossman and its "*good client base.*" Dolmans is judged to be a "*good, solid, niche practice*" renowned for its local authority client base. Jeff MacWilkinson (see p.634) was recommended to researchers for his expertise in stress and bullying cases.

MIDLANDS

MAINLY CLAIMANT

PERSONAL INJURY: MAINLY CLAIMANT ■ MIDLANDS

[1] **Freethcartwright** Nottingham
Irwin Mitchell Birmingham
Rowley Ashworth Birmingham, Wolverhampton
Thompsons Birmingham
[2] **Barratt, Goff & Tomlinson** Nottingham
Russell Jones & Walker Birmingham

LEADING INDIVIDUALS

[1] **HENDERSON Stuart** Irwin Mitchell
[2] **BALEN Paul** Freethcartwright
GOULDING Jane Freethcartwright
PRAIN David Rowley Ashworth
ZINDANI Jeffry Russell Jones & Walker

This book is the product of 6,582 1/2 hour interviews. See p.7 for BMRB audit. Within each band, firms are listed alphabetically. See individuals' profiles p.630

FREETHCARTWRIGHT (see firm details p.963) This Nottingham-based firm was praised by peers as "*innovative and dynamic,*" while clients commended its "*quality of advice, prompt response and commitment.*" The personal injury team handles a wide range of claims, including RTA, accidents at work, industrial disease and criminal injury. It is focused on acting for individuals and has niche expertise in head and spinal claims. It is on the panel of the Royal College of Nursing and receives regular referrals from Headway. Jane Goulding (see p.633) was described to our researchers as a "*clever litigator,*" while Paul Balen (see p.149) drew accolades as "*someone who wants to move the boundaries.*" **Clients** Private clients.

IRWIN MITCHELL (see firm details p.1009) "*Outstanding for the big stuff,*" the Birmingham office of the personal injury giant handles everything from fast-track claims to high-value neurotrauma and complex liability cases. The presence of a separate LEI department provides an extra breadth of expertise. The unit also fields an international travel group that deals with injuries incurred by UK citizens abroad, and has specialist teams devoted to traumatic brain injury, asbestos claims and work-related accidents. As an example of a recent success, £1.5 million was recovered on behalf of the brain-injured victim of a road rage incident. "*Extremely effective, totally dedicated*" Stuart Henderson (see p.633) is thought by some interviewees to be "*the best of them all.*" He has particular expertise in spinal injuries, and has recently settled claims of this nature for £2.2 million and £3 million. **Clients** Private individuals.

ROWLEY ASHWORTH The firm has earned the respect of its peers across the Midlands, largely due to its ability to "*get the job done efficiently.*" Trade union and industrial disease claims form the core of the practice, and it is equipped to tackle personal injury matters ranging from RTA to major asbestos claims. Managing partner David Prain is adjudged a "*thorough and capable*" practitioner. **Clients** Private clients.

THOMPSONS The national firm's Birmingham office is extremely well-regarded by peers who consider its lawyers to be "*the people to beat.*" It continues to act for several trade unions. Sarah Goodman is the lead practitioner here. **Clients** Trade unions.

BARRATT, GOFF & TOMLINSON The lateral hire of former Kingsley Napley partner Alison Brooks strengthens a niche personal injury and clinical negligence practice, which has obtained £13 million on behalf of victims of spinal cord injuries in 2001. Maximum severity claims make up the bulk of its workload, but lower value accidents abroad and RTA cases are also undertaken. The team acted for a man who suffered delayed PTSD after involvement in the Kegworth air crash rescue, and represents several victims of the Soho pub bombing. Jill Barratt heads the personal injury unit, which includes six partners.

RUSSELL JONES & WALKER (see firm details p.1120) The group is best known for its work in disaster cases and its ability to handle large claims, and continues to make good progress in this region. It retains a strong union client base, and handles a large number of claims on behalf of the Royal College of Nursing. Specialist teams exist to deal with occupational disease, fast-track RTA and corporate manslaughter. A recent successful claim was brought by the team on behalf of an injured police officer against his chief constable. The group also takes advantage of Jeffry Zindani's (see p.637) high profile.

www.ChambersandPartners.com

PERSONAL INJURY ■ MIDLANDS/EAST ANGLIA

MIDLANDS

PERSONAL INJURY: MAINLY DEFENDANT
■ MIDLANDS

1
- **Beachcroft Wansbroughs** Birmingham
- **Browne Jacobson** Nottingham
- **Buller Jeffries** Birmingham
- **Weightman Vizards** Birmingham

2
- **Everatt & Company** Evesham

3
- **DLA** Birmingham
- **Palser Grossman** Birmingham

LEADING INDIVIDUALS

1
- **ADAMSON Derek** Buller Jeffries

2
- **ARKELL Catherine** Everatt & Company
- **DACE Nigel** Weightman Vizards
- **PERRY Timothy** Weightman Vizards
- **ROACH Andrew** Beachcroft Wansbroughs

3
- **CUTTS Dan** Weightman Vizards
- **MAY Sara** Beachcroft Wansbroughs

This book is the product of 6,582 1/2 hour interviews. See p.7 for BMRB audit.
Within each band, firms are listed alphabetically. See individuals' profiles p.630

BEACHCROFT WANSBROUGHS (see firm details p.860) Judged to "*run a tight ship and know what they're doing,*" the Birmingham team has seen significant growth, and has moved to larger premises as a result. The personal injury unit is split into partner-led teams handling catastrophic injury, RTA, EL/PL and sports injuries, and it is retained by a number of major insurance panels. Multinational product liability claims specialist **Andrew Roach** (see p.636) is considered by our interviewees to be "*extremely capable,*" and **Sara May** (see p.634) is "*on the ball.*" Recent cases handled by the team include a £3.6 million brain damage claim and a £2.5 million tetraplegic claim caused by an escaped animal. **Clients** AXA; NU; Zurich; Aon.

BROWNE JACOBSON (see firm details p.891) Our researchers found that the team is seen more and more by peers in the market, particularly with its growing presence in Birmingham and Nottingham. It also enjoys a strong insurance client base. The firm handles EL/PL for local authorities nationwide and major employers, and has teams dedicated to social service, failure to educate and serious injury-related claims. Major recent cases include acting in the South Wales Childrens Home litigation and a multiparty action by employees of a London borough alleging injury caused by sick building syndrome. Nick Parsons heads the team. **Clients** St. Paul; NFU.

BULLER JEFFRIES (see firm details p.892) The firm is respected for its traditional approach and sturdy team of "*capable people,*" with peers often pointing to its partner heavy recruitment policy. The firm covers the full gamut of fast-track work, and has particular strength in industrial disease (fielding a specialist asbestos team) and oil-based cancer claims. Regular clients include car manufacturers, local authorities and construction companies. Experienced practitioner **Derek Adamson** (see p.630) drew accolades from several interviewees, described as "*a first-rate litigator with excellent judgement.*" **Clients** Insurers.

WEIGHTMAN VIZARDS (see firm details p.1183) The Midlands offices of this strong Northern firm are described by peers as "*a big force in the region.*" Each office is organised into teams dedicated to employers' liability and disease, while members of the team have niche expertise in police, asbestos and stress claims. The firm is dealing with an increasing number of industrial disease cases. The "*excellent judgement*" of **Dan Cutts** (see p.632) was recommended to Chambers' researchers. **Nigel Dace** (see p.632) was endorsed by peers as an "*exceptional lawyer,*" while **Tim Perry** (see p.635) is "*an experienced operator.*"

EVERATT & COMPANY (see firm details p.948) Deemed a team of "*sensible lawyers, firm but fair,*" it is almost entirely dedicated to personal injury work and particularly employers' liability. The firm has been heavily involved in asbestos and work-related stress claims, and partners have expertise in large-volume industrial deafness, work-related upper limb disorder and hand-arm vibration syndrome cases. Minor to maximum severity RTAs are handled, and the team represents insurance companies in HSE and CPS inquiries into work-related stress. The presence of "*first-class solicitor*" **Catherine Arkell** (see p.630) strengthens the team. She is rated for her knowledge of law and procedure, and one barrister describes her as "*the best insidious disease solicitor around.*" **Clients** Insurers.

OTHER NOTABLE FIRMS DLA is recognised as a regional player, and the team is on the St. Paul panel. Interviewees remarked upon the strength of **Palser Grossman**'s Birmingham operation. It acts for Zurich, and Albert Powell has particular expertise in employers' liability claims.

EAST ANGLIA

PERSONAL INJURY: MAINLY CLAIMANT
■ EAST ANGLIA

1
- **Cunningham John** Thetford

2
- **Morgan Jones & Pett** Great Yarmouth
- **Taylor Vinters** Cambridge

3
- **Edwards Duthie** Ilford
- **Leathes Prior** Norwich

LEADING INDIVIDUALS

1
- **JOHN Simon** Cunningham John
- **JONES David** Morgan Jones & Pett

This book is the product of 6,582 1/2 hour interviews. See p.7 for BMRB audit.
Within each band, firms are listed alphabetically. See individuals' profiles p.630

CUNNINGHAM JOHN (see firm details p.925) An "*excellent*" firm whose national reputation ensures instructions from all over the UK. It divides work between multi-track tetraplegia, head and spinal claims in the Thetford office, while Bury St Edmunds handles fast-track and industrial injuries. International instructions have been a growth area, and the team settled the claim of a woman who suffered tetraplegic injury after diving into a pool in Saudi Arabia, for £1.6 million. Child pedestrian RTA claims also feature in the caseload. The team, headed by **Simon John** (see p.153), recovered £20 million damages this year.

MORGAN JONES & PETT "*Direct*" **David Jones** (see p.153) heads this Great Yarmouth-based operation, undertaking RTA, occupational disease and accidents at work claims. It has niche expertise in offshore, diving and sports-related cases, and recently achieved £1.3 million damages for a RTA victim.

TAYLOR VINTERS (see firm details p.1156) This respected operation deals mostly with high-value catastrophic personal injury, proffering expertise in severe brain and spinal claims. It receives referrals from the Law Society's Personal Injury Panel, National Accident Helpline, Headway and the Spinal Injuries Association panel. Paul Tapner heads the team.

OTHER NOTABLE FIRMS Edwards Duthie handles a large volume of accident claims, and received instructions from trade unions and legal expense insurers. Peers respect **Leathes Prior** for its work on both fast-track and multi-track claims.

EAST ANGLIA/NORTH WEST ■ PERSONAL INJURY

EAST ANGLIA

MAINLY DEFENDANT

PERSONAL INJURY: MAINLY DEFENDANT
■ EAST ANGLIA

1
- Eversheds Ipswich

2
- Mills & Reeve Norwich
- Prettys Ipswich

3
- Edwards Duthie Ilford
- Kennedys Brentwood

LEADING INDIVIDUALS

1
- CROOK Christopher Edwards Duthie
- PADFIELD Brendan Eversheds

This book is the product of 6,582 1/2 hour interviews. See p.7 for BMRB audit. Within each band, firms are listed alphabetically. See individuals' profiles p.630

EVERSHEDS (see firm details p.949) **Brendan Padfield** (see p.635) heads the firm's East Anglian operation. The team has a broad practice, including multiparty actions, employers' and public liability and stress claims, and acts for several insurers and local authorities. It was recently successful in several high-profile stress cases on behalf of Zurich. **Clients** Zurich Municipal; Transco; The AA; NFU Mutual.

OTHER NOTABLE FIRMS **Mills & Reeve** acts on spinal and head injury claims for various insurers, and Stephen King is an active member of the team. **Prettys** has a highly regarded defendant practice involved in claims against local authorities and the police, as well as industrial disease, motor and EL/PL claims. The firm's profile is such that it attracts commendation from peers on a national level. John Bucklow specialises in employers' liability and industrial disease. **Christopher Crook** (see p.632) is a key member of the well-regarded defendant team at **Edwards Duthie**. The Brentwood team of **Kennedys** was established to service defendant personal injury claims, and typically deals with EL/PL, motor and disease claims. It also handles high-value claims, including brain injury and asbestosis. The group is involved in an ongoing fibromylagia case with a value of £4.5 million. John Yates is an active partner.

NORTH WEST

MAINLY CLAIMANT

PERSONAL INJURY: MAINLY CLAIMANT
■ NORTH WEST

1
- Pannone & Partners Manchester

2
- John Pickering & Partners Oldham
- Leigh, Day & Co Manchester
- Russell Jones & Walker Manchester
- Thompsons Liverpool

3
- Donns Solicitors Manchester
- Hugh Potter & Company Manchester

4
- Alexander Harris Altrincham
- Linder Myers Manchester

LEADING INDIVIDUALS

1
- JACKSON Carol Pannone & Partners
- LEECH Catherine Pannone & Partners
- PATTERSON Frank Leigh, Day & Co
- PICKERING John John Pickering & Partners

2
- CHANDLER Pauline Pannone & Partners
- MCCOOL Geraldine Leigh, Day & Co
- POTTER Hugh Hugh Potter & Company

3
- CONNOR Michael Russell Jones & Walker

This book is the product of 6,582 1/2 hour interviews. See p.7 for BMRB audit. Within each band, firms are listed alphabetically. See individuals' profiles p.630

PANNONE & PARTNERS (see firm details p.1092) Competitors continue to judge the firm as clear leaders in the region, proffering "*realistic, quality opposition.*" A designated catastrophic injuries unit has been formed, comprising 14 specialist partners, which provides a full service to the victims of catastrophic injuries and their families. The firm also handles RTA and industrial disease claims, as well as bulk referrals from clients such as The AA and RAC. A trio of talented partners are one of the unit's key assets. **Carol Jackson** (see p.633) and **Cathy Leech** (see p.634) are "*strong and proactive,*" whilst **Pauline Chandler** (see p.631) is described by peers as "*first-rate for disease and asbestos.*" **Clients** Capita; Mondial; RAC; AA Legal Services.

JOHN PICKERING & PARTNERS The firm maintains a reputation for excellence in industrial disease; it is described by peers as "*professional and intellectually able.*" While asbestosis is its main area of strength, the group also handles asthma and other occupational disease claims, amid a broadening of its practice. Working on behalf of unions such as the NUT and TGWU, it tackles accidents at work and stress. **John Pickering** (see p.635) is regarded as an expert in his field. **Clients** NUT; TGWU; private clients.

LEIGH, DAY & CO (see firm details p.1036) The respected regional office of this leading London outfit has several areas of expertise, including carbon monoxide poisoning and aviation-related catastrophic injuries. It has recently seen an increase in the number of PTSD cases handled for primary and secondary victims, and works closely with RoadPeace, an organisation dealing with all aspects of RTA claims. **Geraldine McCool** (see p.634) specialises in aviation-related personal injury; she is on the panel of The Royal British Legion solicitors, and was involved in advising family members of victims of the World Trade Centre bombing. **Frank Patterson** (see p.635) is described by peers as "*an extremely good lawyer.*"

RUSSELL JONES & WALKER (see firm details p.1120) The firm has expertise in brain, spinal and fatal injuries, and operates fast-track and multi-track subgroups. Renowned for its work for the police, it also represents the Royal College of Nursing and the PFA. It recently settled a claim on behalf of a tetraplegic claimant for £2.7 million. **Michael Connor** (see p.631) is a prominent member of the team. **Clients** Police Federation; Professional Footballers' Association; Prospect; Royal College of Nursing.

THOMPSONS Strongly recommended during our research, the North-Western operation of this national union giant is said to "*consistently get its clients good results.*" The experienced team includes Stephen Allen.

OTHER NOTABLE FIRMS **Donns Solicitors** is an exclusively personal injury operation with a particular expertise in claims arising out of military service, and also handles maximum severity injuries and RTAs. A recent claim on behalf of a military victim settled for £3.5 million. Managing partner Hilary Meredith is an active practitioner, and the team's clients include The Royal British Legion, Colonnade Insurance Brokers and Argent Insurance. A member of APIL, the team at **Linder Myers** handles accidents at work and on the road, and has expertise in group actions claims relating to faulty products. Peter Hale is a member of the team. The niche firm's recent name change to **Hugh Potter & Company, Serious Injury Solicitors** reflects its main area of focus. **Hugh Potter** (see p.635) is responsible for much of the outfit's strong reputation, and is said to bring a depth of expertise to each case. The firm handles predominantly spinal, brain and cerebral palsy claims, and also undertakes RTA, industrial disease and criminal injury cases. It often acts for victims injured on holiday abroad. **Alexander Harris** is perceived by peers to be a "*quality regional operation.*" It has a dedicated multiparty action unit currently handling group actions into MMR claims and arsenic poisoning claims in Bangladesh. David Harris heads the team.

www.ChambersandPartners.com   625

PERSONAL INJURY ■ NORTH WEST/YORKSHIRE

NORTH WEST

MAINLY DEFENDANT

PERSONAL INJURY: MAINLY DEFENDANT — NORTH WEST

1
- James Chapman & Co Manchester

2
- Berrymans Lace Mawer Liverpool, Manchester
- Halliwell Landau Manchester
- Keoghs Bolton
- Weightman Vizards Liverpool, Manchester

3
- Beachcroft Wansbroughs Manchester
- Hill Dickinson Liverpool, Manchester

LEADING INDIVIDUALS

1
- BROOKS Roger James Chapman & Co
- FINNIGAN Kevin James Chapman & Co
- HOLT David Weightman Vizards

2
- WHITEHEAD Peter James Chapman & Co

This book is the product of 6,582 1/2 hour interviews. See p.7 for BMRB audit. Within each band, firms are listed alphabetically. See individuals' profiles p.630

JAMES CHAPMAN & CO (see firm details p.1012) "*Unquestionably the best*" claim our interviewees; the firm is a clear leader in personal injury in the North West. Solicitors, barristers and clients agreed on the quality of its work and "*gold standard*" clients. It is known for its pragmatic approach, "*taking reasonable points*" in an "*absolutely efficient*" manner. The lateral hire of Keoghs' Roger Brooks (see p.631) adds weight to the unit. Catastrophic claims are an area of particular expertise, and the firm is broadening its disease and volume work. It has an extensive insurance panel client base, and recently successfully defended a £2 million diving claim on behalf of Zurich. Head of department **Kevin Finnigan** (see p.632) is an "*accomplished, heavyweight litigator*," and his colleague **Peter Whitehead** (see p.637) is respected amongst his peers.

BERRYMANS LACE MAWER (see firm details p.865) A client base of insurance panels, local authorities and accountancy firms feeds the firm with a range of claims, including occupational disease and catastrophic cases. The group has been appointed nationally to Marsh's curriculum scheme, and handles a significant number of education-related claims, bolstered by its dedicated abuse unit. The team is headed by Andrew Relton, and is focusing increasingly on high-value cases. **Clients** AXA; Aon; Marsh; local authorities.

HALLIWELL LANDAU (see firm details p.982) The "*high-quality outfit*" is respected by peers and clients. Described as "*so switched on*," it undertakes insurance litigation for a strong base of insurers and corporate clients such as Balfour Beatty. It acted successfully in Fairchild v Glenhaven Funeral Services involving a mesothelioma claim, and represented Norwich Union in a large multiparty action of initially 3,000 claimants. Chris Phillips heads the department and has particular expertise in industrial disease. **Clients** NU; Balfour Beatty; Resolute Management Inc; AIG Europe (UK); XL Winterthur.

KEOGHS (see firm details p.1021) Our interviewees felt that the firm has maintained a "*strong market presence*," despite the loss of Roger Brooks; indeed, some placed it as "*one of the best for quality of service and quality of clients*." David Tyson heads the unit that primarily handles bulk claims on behalf of leading insurers. Other clients include loss adjusters, insurance brokers and claims handling agencies. **Clients** Insurers.

WEIGHTMAN VIZARDS (see firm details p.1183) The Liverpool and Manchester offices of this national firm have expertise in industrial disease, EL/PL and large loss. **David Holt** (see p.633) is head of the latter department, and was described to researchers as an "*experienced, tough opponent*." **Clients** Insurers.

OTHER NOTABLE FIRMS The **Beachcroft Wansbroughs** team carries out personal injury claims on behalf of its strong insurance client base. Iain Moore is head of the Manchester office. On the panels of several insurers, **Hill Dickinson** covers a wide range of personal injury claims, including EL/PL, occupational disease, RTA, stress and education-related claims (failure to educate and abuse). David Scott is head of the insurance department.

YORKSHIRE

MAINLY CLAIMANT

PERSONAL INJURY: MAINLY CLAIMANT — YORKSHIRE

1
- Irwin Mitchell Sheffield

2
- Pattinson & Brewer York
- Rowley Ashworth Leeds
- Russell Jones & Walker Leeds, Sheffield

3
- Bridge McFarland Solicitors Grimsby
- Morrish & Co Leeds

LEADING INDIVIDUALS

1
- ALLEN Simon Russell Jones & Walker
- CARSON Peter Rowley Ashworth
- PICKERING John Irwin Mitchell
- TUCKER Andrew Irwin Mitchell

2
- BRIDGE John Bridge McFarland Solicitors
- SMITH Blaise Ford & Warren

This book is the product of 6,582 1/2 hour interviews. See p.7 for BMRB audit. Within each band, firms are listed alphabetically. See individuals' profiles p.630

IRWIN MITCHELL (see firm details p.1009) "*Pre-eminent*," this is still the top firm in Yorkshire with "*a good spread of able litigators*." The office has the expertise to cover the gamut of personal injury claims, including asbestosis, VWF, RTA, stress and neurotrauma. Damages were recently recovered on behalf of a man who suffered head injuries as a result of falling off his bike on a poorly maintained road. Larger claims include a serious head injury settled for £1.1 million and £3.6 million awarded to a severely injured motorcyclist; the latter was CFA-funded. **Andrew Tucker** (see p.673) was commended by peers as "*one of the best personal injury solicitors in the country*," while head of department **John Pickering** (see p.154) was also warmly endorsed. **Clients** Private clients.

PATTINSON & BREWER (see firm details p.1095) This respected, mainly trade union, firm handles a large number of industrial disease and asbestosis claims from RMT, a legacy of the carriageworks formerly based in York. Other areas of focus include PTSD and RSI-related claims. Jane Radcliffe heads the team that recovered £6 million of damages during the last year, including £45,000 for a saturation diver traumatised after the death of a colleague during a North Sea dive. **Clients** Police Federation; TGWU; GMB; PCS.

ROWLEY ASHWORTH This strong team deals entirely with claimant personal injury, undertaking trade union-referred accidents and industrial disease claims, including asthma, dermatitis and asbestosis. It handles a steady stream of referrals from Headway and the Spinal Injuries Association, and has a busy RTA practice. A recent traffic accident claim was settled for £1.5 million. **Peter Carson** is considered by peers to be a prominent figure in the region. **Clients** Trade unions.

RUSSELL JONES & WALKER (see firm details p.1120) The Yorkshire offices handle predominantly trade union work, although private client referrals are on the increase, and the Sheffield team has recently set up a department called Child and Adult Survivors of Abuse to assist abuse victims. It has particular expertise in occupational disease, particularly asbestosis and VWF. A lot of police work is undertaken by the Leeds office, including a large number of noise induced hearing loss claims. In Sheffield £1.1 million damages were recovered on behalf of a paraplegic patient and £900,000 for an injured steelworker, the highest ever award recorded for the steelworkers' union (ISTC). Simon Allen

YORKSHIRE/NORTH EAST ■ PERSONAL INJURY

(see p.630) comes recommended. **Clients** ISTC; Police Federation; PCS.

OTHER NOTABLE FIRMS Morrish & Co undertakes mainly employers' and public liability and RTA claims, and can also handle maximum severity cases. It fields specialist industrial disease lawyers with particular expertise in noise induced hearing loss, asbestosis, asthma, dermatitis and VWF. Team member Martin Bare is a Fellow of the College of Personal Injury Law. Clients include trade unions and private clients. **Bridge McFarland Solicitors** is recommended for its niche expertise in accidents at sea, and this "*good outfit*" regularly acts for injured divers. The firm's reputation owes much to "*able*" **John Bridge** (see p.631), who is often consulted as a national specialist in this field. Clients include trade unions. "*Highly knowledgeable and tough*" **Blaise Smith** (see p.636) of Ford & Warren is a highly esteemed practitioner.

YORKSHIRE

MAINLY DEFENDANT

PERSONAL INJURY: MAINLY DEFENDANT
■ YORKSHIRE

1. **Beachcroft Wansbroughs** Leeds
   DLA Bradford, Leeds, Sheffield
2. **Irwin Mitchell** Leeds
   Nabarro Nathanson Sheffield
3. **Keeble Hawson** Leeds, Sheffield
   Langleys York
   Praxis Partners Leeds

LEADING INDIVIDUALS
1. **ANSON Peter** DLA
2. **GOODWILL Peter** Nabarro Nathanson
   GREGORY Tony Keeble Hawson
   THOMPSON David Langleys

This book is the product of 6,582 1/2 hour interviews. See p.7 for BMRB audit.
Within each band, firms are listed alphabetically. See individuals' profiles p.630

BEACHCROFT WANSBROUGHS (see firm details p.860) The team advises on fast-track and multi-track claims, with a particular focus on the latter, and is organised into motor, EL/PL, disease and catastrophic units. John Newman heads the department, which has successfully defended a number of RTA claims valued at over £1 million. **Clients** AXA Corporate Solutions; Cornhill Insurance; ICI; Liverpool Victoria; MMA Insurance; NU; RSA; Unilever; Zurich.

DLA The Yorkshire offices of this national firm were praised by our interviewees, who also pointed to the litigation skills of **Peter Anson**. **Clients** Insurers.

IRWIN MITCHELL (see firm details p.1009) The firm's defendant practice is somewhat overshadowed in the eyes of interviewees by its outstanding claimant strength. Nevertheless, the team provides a "*consistently quality*," fielding lawyers who are "*on the ball*."

NABARRO NATHANSON (see firm details p.1080) The group was endorsed by peers as "*sensible, with an intelligent approach*." It handles all defendant work for the DTI, including miners' claims for VWF, and advises on EL/PL and RTA claims. **Peter Goodwill** (see p.633) is considered a "*high-quality*" practitioner. **Clients** DTI; Co-operative Insurance Society; Crowe Insurance Group.

OTHER NOTABLE FIRMS Keeble Hawson fields a "*sensible bunch*" handling a broad range of personal injury claims, while **Tony Gregory** (see p.633) is admired for having "*pulled in some amazing work*." **Langleys** acts throughout the north of England, and was recommended to Chambers' researchers by peers and clients alike. Insurance clients find them "*geared towards our needs*," while one solicitor commented, "*my life's more difficult when they're on the other side*." The team acts for motor insurers, liability adjusters and local authorities on claims for EL/PL, disease, accidents at work and RTA. It deals with a limited number of catastrophic claims. "*Experienced litigator*" **David Thompson** is head of department. Clients include Avon Insurance, NFU Mutual, NIG, Drysdale and East Riding of Yorkshire Council. A "*good profile with insurers*" ensures that **Praxis Partners** has a busy workload. Jane Olive is a member of the team.

NORTH EAST

MAINLY CLAIMANT

PERSONAL INJURY: MAINLY CLAIMANT
■ NORTH EAST

1. **Thompsons** Newcastle upon Tyne
2. **Browell Smith & Co** Newcastle upon Tyne
   Marrons Newcastle upon Tyne
   Russell Jones & Walker Newcastle upon Tyne
3. **Hay & Kilner** Newcastle upon Tyne
4. **Beecham Peacock** Newcastle upon Tyne
   Gorman Hamilton Solicitors Newcastle upon Tyne

LEADING INDIVIDUALS
1. **ALLAN David** Marrons
   BROWELL Philip Browell Smith & Co
   PORTEUS Stephen Marrons
2. **BRADSHAW David** Hay & Kilner

This book is the product of 6,582 1/2 hour interviews. See p.7 for BMRB audit.
Within each band, firms are listed alphabetically. See individuals' profiles p.630

Thompsons is widely regarded as "*the best*" in the region, excelling in industrial disease-related trade union claims, which include VWF and asbestosis. Phil Smith is a member of the team. Peers respected **Browell Smith & Co** for its expertise in disease claims, and agree that "*steady performer*" **Philip Browell** is an asset to the team. The "*good team*" at **Russell Jones & Walker** is used by the Royal College of Nursing, and is known for its police work. Philip Andrews heads the group, which offers an occupational disease unit and has expertise in catastrophic injury. It is involved in representing a brain-injured schoolgirl in a high-value RTA claim. The bedrock of **Beecham Peacock**'s caseload is accident at work claims on behalf of trade union clients TGWU and Usdaw. David Lamb is a member of the team that has particular strength in disease claims. **Gorman Hamilton Solicitors** was recommended to our researchers for its motor expertise. **Marrons** is known for its involvement in high-value claims. The team fields "*able*" **David Allan** and "*experienced*" **Stephen Porteus**. The "*decent outfit*" at **Hay & Kilner** is headed by Spinal Injuries Association and Headway panel member **David Bradshaw**. The team specialises in severe head and spinal injuries, recently achieving damages of £2.2 million for a brain-injured RTA victim. It has expertise in sports claims related to karate, motorcross, swimming and horse-riding.

www.ChambersandPartners.com

PERSONAL INJURY ■ NORTH EAST/SCOTLAND

NORTH EAST

MAINLY DEFENDANT

PERSONAL INJURY: MAINLY DEFENDANT ■ NORTH EAST

[1]
- Eversheds Newcastle upon Tyne
- Hay & Kilner Newcastle upon Tyne
- Sinton & Co Newcastle upon Tyne

[2]
- Crutes Law Firm Newcastle upon Tyne
- Jacksons Stockton on Tees

LEADING INDIVIDUALS

[1]
- DIAS James Sinton & Co
- PESCOD Peter Hay & Kilner

[2]
- CLARKE Richard Jacksons
- DREWE David Crutes Law Firm
- SCOTT Toby Eversheds
- WILLIAMS Alun Hay & Kilner

This book is the product of 6,582 1/2 hour interviews. See p.7 for BMRB audit. Within each band, firms are listed alphabetically. See individuals' profiles p.630

EVERSHEDS (see firm details p.949) The firm acts for a range of insurance and corporate clients, and has been instructed by Norwich Union to defend claims by British Coal on behalf of 140,000 underground workers suffering lung disease, with total damages likely to exceed £2 billion. **Toby Scott** (see p.636) is leading these proceedings, and is considered a disease expert by his peers; an "*experienced and knowledgeable lawyer.*" **Clients** NU; NHSLA; ASDA; Transco.

HAY & KILNER The firm maintains a strong defendant practice alongside its claimant work. It has expertise in industrial disease and workplace stress, and typically defends stress, harassment, bullying and RSI claims. The team has recently acted in the PTSD claim of a witness to a fire, and has been involved in several head injury and paraplegic claims of over £1 million. "*Engaging and effective performer*" **Peter Pescod** and "*particularly well-regarded*" **Alun Williams** are key members of the team. **Clients** Insurers.

SINTON & CO (see firm details p.1139) A number of insurers count amongst this firm's client base, and while the firm is developing its claimant practice, it continues to maintain a strong defendant presence. Industrial disease claims, including VWF and carpal tunnel syndrome, are typical examples of work handled, and the team is also involved in stress, RTA and fatal cases. Researchers were told that **James Dias** (see p.632) is "*an effective insurance litigator.*" **Clients** NU; Provident; NIG; Tokio Marine; Zurich.

CRUTES LAW FIRM (see firm details p.924) Acting for all the local authorities in the North East, the firm is particularly involved in education claims involving abuse, stress, failure to educate and bullying. It also covers fast-track and multiparty cases, and acts for a wide range of insurers. **David Drewe** (see p.632) was recommended during our research. **Clients** NU; Zurich Municipal; St. Paul; local authorities.

JACKSONS (see firm details p.1011) The firm has maintained its position on several insurer panels, and deals predominantly with RTA and EL/PL claims. Disease is another area of strength, and it handles a small number of catastrophic cases. **Richard Clarke** is the standout practitioner here. **Clients** Insurance panels.

SCOTLAND

MAINLY PURSUER

PERSONAL INJURY: MAINLY PURSUER ■ SCOTLAND

[1]
- Thompsons Edinburgh, Glasgow

[2]
- Anderson Strathern WS Edinburgh
- Balfour & Manson Edinburgh
- Burnside Kemp Fraser Aberdeen
- Digby Brown Glasgow
- Lawford Kidd Edinburgh

[3]
- Drummond Miller WS Edinburgh
- Levy & McRae Glasgow

LEADING INDIVIDUALS

[1]
- KEMP Sandy Burnside Kemp Fraser
- SHORT David Lawford Kidd
- SMITH Sid Thompsons
- TYLER Alfred Balfour & Manson

[2]
- CARR Robert Anderson Strathern WS
- GARRETT Graeme Digby Brown
- LUMSDEN Lawrence Thompsons
- MAGUIRE Frank Thompsons
- STEVENSON David Biggart Baillie
- SWANNEY Robert Digby Brown

This book is the product of 6,582 1/2 hour interviews. See p.7 for BMRB audit. Within each band, firms are listed alphabetically. See individuals' profiles p.630

Peers agree that "*no one can compete*" with the amount of union work handled by **Thompsons**, and describe it as the "*best in terms of volume and ability.*" A strong team of leading solicitors includes "*able and experienced*" **Sid Smith**, "*well-respected*" **Frank Maguire** and "*capable*" **Lawrence Lumsden**. **Anderson Strathern WS**'s claimant practice is deemed "*a strong force*" by peers. It continues to handle a large amount of work for the Royal College of Nursing, including claims relating to back injuries, stress and assault. It has niche experience in child sex abuse claims and regularly undertakes catastrophic cases. The presence of highly rated **Robert Carr** (see p.631) is important to the firm's profile. "*Definitely a player,*" **Balfour & Manson** deals with a mixture of bulk referrals from unions and maximum severity claims, and had established a serious injury department to deal with the latter. A recent case involved the possibility of recovering damages for pure psychiatric injury under the Warsaw Convention. **Fred Tyler** (see p.637) is felt by some peers to be "*the mainstay of the firm,*" and is described as "*a highly skilled, first-class lawyer.*" **Burnside Kemp Fraser** is deemed a "*top-class*" outfit with particular expertise in handling claims for injuries sustained in the fishing and offshore oil industries. **Sandy Kemp** (see p.326) is described by peers as a "*first-class litigator.*" **Digby Brown** has a bent towards high-volume fast-track work, handling disease, RTA and accidents at work claims, as well as some maximum severity cases. It is felt to be a "*prominent*" player and acts for both union and individual clients, and **Graeme Garrett** has carved a profile as "*a well-known local rainmaker.*" His colleague **Robert Swanney** was also recommended and appears in our tables for the first time this year. At **Lawford Kidd**, claims for a healthy union client base are undertaken, including accidents at work, occupational disease, RTA, and sporting and head injuries. **David Short** (see p.636) is renowned for his work in this field, described to researchers as "*a well-respected grafter.*" **David Stevenson** of Biggart Baillie also received warm market recommendation. Our interviewees were impressed by the "*high-quality work*" handled by **Drummond Miller WS**, and its ability to advise on a variety of claims. Typically it deals with accidents at work, sporting injuries, occupational disease, RTA, offshore oil and diving and PTSD claims. It is a member of APIL, and managing partner Grant McCulloch is a key team member. **Levy & McRae** is rated for its "*good, strong client base.*" It deals with accidents at work, RTA and aircraft/shipping-related claims.

SCOTLAND

PERSONAL INJURY: MAINLY DEFENDER — SCOTLAND

1
- HBM Sayers *Glasgow*
- Simpson & Marwick WS *Edinburgh*

2
- Anderson Partnership *Glasgow*
- Biggart Baillie *Glasgow*
- Brechin Tindal Oatts *Glasgow*

3
- Anderson Strathern WS *Edinburgh*
- Bishop Solicitors (formerly Morison Bishop) *Glasgow*
- Paull & Williamsons *Aberdeen*

LEADING INDIVIDUALS

1
- ANDERSON Peter *Simpson & Marwick WS*
- KEYDEN Gordon *Simpson & Marwick WS*
- MOORE George *HBM Sayers*

2
- CRAWFORD Allan *HBM Sayers*
- FIFE Robert *Anderson Strathern WS*
- WOOD Michael *Simpson & Marwick WS*

This book is the product of 6,582 1/2 hour interviews. See p.7 for BMRB audit.
Within each band, firms are listed alphabetically. See individuals' profiles p.630

MAINLY DEFENDER

HBM SAYERS "*Growing and getting a bigger market share*" claim our interviewees; the acquisition of Balfour & Manson's insurance team is a considerable boost to the team. It acts for a range of insurer clients, as well as railway organisations, and has particular expertise in VWF claims. Other areas of focus include EL/PL, RTA and maximum severity claims, including tetraplegia. **George Moore**'s (see p.634) solicitor advocacy is rated by contemporaries who say he's "*straightforward, decisive*." His colleague, **Allan Crawford** (see p.632), is also endorsed by peers as one who "*knows when to fight or settles as necessary.*" **Clients** Direct Line; Allianz Cornhill; ACE; AXA.

SIMPSON & MARWICK WS (see firm details p.1138) Peers praise the firm for fielding "*practitioners who are a pleasure to work against.*" The firm handles occupational disease, including noise induced deafness and VWF, as well as catastrophic claims. The team includes "*adaptable*" **Peter Anderson** (see p.552), "*experienced*" **Gordon Keyden** (see p.633) and "*decisive*" **Michael Wood** (see p.637). **Clients** Insurers.

OTHER NOTABLE FIRMS **Anderson Partnership** is judged by peers to be a "*sound*" practice handling high-volume work for its insurance clientele. Known for its disease expertise, **Biggart Baillie** has strength in EL/PL, RTA and fatal accident inquiries. **Brechin Tindal Oatts** is perceived by some interviewees to be "*cropping up more and more.*" The firm handles personal injury claims on behalf of its insurance clientele. **Anderson Strathern WS** acts for several insurance companies in employers' liability cases, including CRU cases. **Robert Fife** (see p.632) is currently representing insurers in multiple claims arising from a fatal accident on a construction site in Edinburgh with a total value of over £1 million. Its clients include Zurich Commercial, Royal College of Nursing, Garwyn Liability Adjusters and AXA Insurance. A well-regarded defendant practice, **Bishops solicitors** handles claims for large general insurers, motor insurers, local authorites, trade unions and individuals. **Paull & Williamsons** has expertise in oil industry-related injury and accident claims.

NORTHERN IRELAND

PERSONAL INJURY: MAINLY CLAIMANT — NORTHERN IRELAND

1
- Agnew, Andress, Higgins *Belfast*

2
- Diamond Heron *Belfast*
- Eamonn McEvoy & Co *Lurgan*
- Edwards & Co *Belfast*
- Francis Hanna & Co *Belfast*

LEADING INDIVIDUALS

1
- AGNEW Seamus *Agnew, Andress, Higgins*
- ANDRESS Stephen *Agnew, Andress, Higgins*
- DIAMOND Maurice *Diamond Heron*
- MCEVOY Eamonn *Eamonn McEvoy & Co*

This book is the product of 6,582 1/2 hour interviews. See p.7 for BMRB audit.
Within each band, firms are listed alphabetically. See individuals' profiles p.630

MAINLY CLAIMANT

Peers recommended the union-based practice of **Agnew, Andress, Higgins**, which includes the highly rated **Seamus Agnew** and "*forceful*" **Stephen Andress**. **Diamond Heron** services mainly union clients, with a workload that is predominantly RTA. It handles criminal injury claims for prison worker clients, and has expertise in fishery and harbour-related cases. **Maurice Diamond** is a highly recommended member of the team. The team at **Edwards & Co**, which includes Dorcas Crawford, is best known amongst our interviewees for its police work. A comprehensive range of personal injury work is undertaken at **Francis Hanna & Co**, including industrial disease, accidents at work, RTA and criminal injuries. Gerry Daly heads the personal injury team. **Eamonn McEvoy** and his team were also recommended.

PERSONAL INJURY ■ THE LEADERS

NORTHERN IRELAND — MAINLY DEFENDANT

PERSONAL INJURY: MAINLY DEFENDANT — NORTHERN IRELAND

[1]
- **C&H Jefferson** Belfast
- **Johnsons** Belfast
- **Tughans** Belfast

[2]
- **Harrisons Solicitors** Belfast
- **McKinty and Wright** Belfast
- **Murphy & O'Rawe** Belfast

LEADING INDIVIDUALS

[1]
- **BOWDEN Ronnie** Harrisons Solicitors
- **CROSS John** McKinty and Wright
- **GIBSON Michael** Tughans
- **TWEED Paul** Johnsons

[2]
- **JEFFERSON Ian** C&H Jefferson
- **LOUGHLIN Grahame** Tughans

This book is the product of 6,582 1/2 hour interviews. See p.7 for BMRB audit.
Within each band, firms are listed alphabetically. See individuals' profiles p.630

C & H Jefferson is deemed by some peers to be "*the main firm,*" with its strong insurance client base, and **Ian Jefferson** (see p.633) is the standout practicitioner here. Esteemed as a "*growing*" firm, the team at **Johnsons** includes the highly regarded **Paul Tweed** (see p.637), described as "*proactive in winning good work.*" **Tughans'** recent growth has impressed peers, handling EL/PL as well as RTA claims. **Michael Gibson** (see p.633) and **Grahame Loughlin** (see p.634) are both esteemed practitioners here. The "*ubiquitous*" **Ronnie Bowden** (see p.631) leads a solid operation at **Harrisons Solicitors**. At **McKinty and Wright**, a wide range of defendant claims are undertaken, including RTA and accidents at work. **John Cross** (see p.632) is a well-regarded personal injury lawyer. **Murphy & O'Rawe** was strongly recommended to researchers for its work with insurer clients such as St. Paul.

THE LEADERS IN PERSONAL INJURY

ADAMSON, Derek
Buller Jeffries, Birmingham
(0121) 200 0437
derek.adamson@bullerjeffries.co.uk
Specialisation: Personal injury claims particularly fatal accidents, catastrophic injuries, industrial disease and medical negligence. High profile cases have included motorway disasters, asbestos litigation and products claims. Other principal areas include professional indemnity, fires, construction claims, policy interpretation and, particularly, local authority liabilities.
Prof. Memberships: Law Society; Birmingham Law Society; FOIL.
Career: Articles *Buller Jeffries* 1979-81. Partner 1985. Deputy District Judge 1993-97.
Personal: Born 1956. Birmingham University 1975-78. Leisure interests: mainly sport, manager of youth soccer team.

AGNEW, Seamus
Agnew, Andress, Higgins, Belfast
(028) 9032 0035

ALLAN, David
Marrons, Newcastle upon Tyne
(0191) 281 1304

ALLEN, Patrick
Hodge Jones & Allen, London
(020) 7482 1974
pallen@hodgejonesallen.co.uk
Specialisation: Principal area of practice – multi-party claims, clinical negligence, personal injury and miscarriage of justice claims. Member of Steering Committee of Plaintiff lawyers in the Kings Cross Fire and Marchioness litigation. Managed the MMR litigation 1998-99 and the Sheep Dip litigation 1998-2000. Since April 1998 co-ordinating and managing the Gulf War Illness and Kerrin Point group claims. Lecturer on legal aid, personal injury practice and costs.
Prof. Memberships: President of APIL May 2002; Senior Fellow, College of Personal Injury Law Oct 2001; Member of the Law Society Council since Sept 2001; Law Society Personal Injury Panel; AVMA Referral Panel; Society of Labour Lawyers; Legal Services Commission Funding Review Committee Chairman. Deputy District Judge.
Career: Articled *Offenbach & Co* 1974-76. Qualified 1977 and simultaneously set up *Hodge Jones & Allen* with Henry Hodge. Senior Partner of *Hodge Jones & Allen* and Head of Personal Injury Team.
Personal: Born 27 May 1950. St Catherine's College, Oxford 1969-72. Married to GP, two daughters. Lives Camden Town, London. Interests - windsurfing, sailing, hill walking, opera, theatre.

ALLEN, Simon
Russell Jones & Walker, Sheffield
(0114) 276 6868
s.j.allen@rjw.co.uk
Specialisation: Claimant personal injury. Involved specifically in industrial accidents, RSI cases, Asbestos cases, multi-handed fume and VWF cases and post-traumatic stress cases. Ran the Hillsborough Police PTSD Litigation which was successful before the Court of Appeal in October 1996 and set new law in the House of Lords in 1998. Has been involved in two of the top ten RSI settlements ever, winning over £0.5 million in damages in the year 2000.
Prof. Memberships: APIL. American Trial Lawyers Association. Member of Personal Injury Panel. Appointed Assessor for Personal Injury Panel in 2000. Member of Law Society Committee which produced the Pre-Action Protocol and is preparing the Disease protocol for the Lord Chancellors' Dept. Local contact point for Headway. Society of Labour Lawyers. Regular lecturer.
Career: Articled *Favell & Smith*, Sheffield. Qualified 1985. *Brian Thompson & Partners*, Sheffield 1985-89 (Partner 1987). *Russell Jones & Walker* 1989 to date (partner 1990). Local managing partner: Leeds 1996-97. Local managing partner: Sheffield (which he opened in 1997). Heads RSI, PTSD, VWF and Asbestos Units within the firm. Set up the firm's National Occupational Disease Group, which is the first of its kind in the UK, to research and develop knowledge of such illnesses.
Publications: 'Sol. Journal' 1993, 1994, 1997 and 2000; 'New Law Journal' 1997 and 2000; 'PMILL' 1996, 1997, 1998 and 1999; 'APIL Magazine' 1995, 1996, 1997, 1998 and 1999; 'Personal Injury Law Journal' 2002; 'Legal Times' 1996. Regular lecturer on PI and in particular on PTSD, RSI, stress, employers liability, Asbestos and procedure. 'PI Update' provider: Law Society Gazette 1996 to date with four published articles in 2002. Published Sweet & Maxwell paper on PTSD.
Personal: Family, photography. Trades Union Movement, Manchester United supporter.

ANDERSON, Peter
Simpson & Marwick, Edinburgh
(0131) 557 1545
peter.anderson@simpmar.com
See under Litigation, p.552

ANDRESS, Stephen
Agnew, Andress, Higgins, Belfast
(028) 9032 0035

ANSON, Peter
DLA, Sheffield
(08700) 111111

ARKELL, Catherine
Everatt & Company, Evesham
(01386) 769161
arkell@everatt.co.uk
Specialisation: Senior Partner. Acts for defendant insurers in a variety of personal injury claims. Work includes serious accident claims involving paraplegia, head injury, etc, and many disease cases including large volume deafness, asbestos-related, RSI, and hand/arm vibration claims. Has also dealt with large (over £1 million) fire-related claims for insurers. Defending HSE prosecutions is a particular interest.
Prof. Memberships: Law Society.
Career: Qualified in 1979. Became a Partner in *Everatt & Co* in 1980.
Personal: Born 1954. Educated at Westwood's Grammar School and Bristol University 1973-76.

BALEN, Paul
freethcartwright, Nottingham
(0115) 936 9369
paul.balen@freethcartwright.co.uk
See under Clinical Negligence, p.149

BEALE, Robert
Beachcroft Wansbroughs, Bristol
(0117) 918 2000
rbeale@bwlaw.co.uk
Specialisation: Partner. He has handled property, fraud and fire damage claims, advising on policy wording and coverage disputes on such claims. Now handles public and employer's liability and

motor claims, particularly in back injury and malingering cases and industrious diseases as well as product liability cases.
Prof. Memberships: Member of FOIL.
Career: Articled *Robins Hay*; qualified 1971; assistant solicitor *Burges Salmon* 1971. *Wansbroughs Willey Hargrave*, 1974.

BOWDEN, Ronnie
Harrisons Solicitors, Belfast
(028) 9032 3843
Ronnie.Bowden@harrisonll.com
Specialisation: Senior Partner Road Traffic, Employers Liability. Matters handled recently have included: serious injury (brain damage and quadriplegia); industrial disease claims; repetitive strain injury; stress in the workplace.
Prof. Memberships: Law Society of Northern Ireland.
Career: Educated at Methodist College, Belfast and Queen's University, Belfast.
Personal: Married: two adult children. Weekend golfer. Soccer fan.

BRADLEY, Deborah
Cartwrights Insurance Partners, Bristol
(0117) 943 9960
dbradley@cipartners.co.uk
Specialisation: Defendant insurance litigation including policy disputes, employer's liability, public liability, agricultural and road traffic claims. Special interest in claims involving injuries of the utmost severity, particularly head and spinal injuries.
Prof. Memberships: Bristol Law Society, Medicolegal Society and FOIL.
Career: 1985-87: *Davis Campbell & Co*, Liverpool (articled clerk). 1987-91: *Cartwrights* (Solicitor). 1991-2001: *Cartwrights* (Partner). 2001-: *Cartwrights Insurance Partners* (Partner).

BRADSHAW, David
Hay & Kilner, Newcastle upon Tyne
(0191) 232 8345

BRIDGE, John
Bridge McFarland Solicitors, Grimsby
(01472) 311711
jrb@bmcf.demon.co.uk
Specialisation: Main area of practice is accidents to seafarers, divers, offshore workers and dockers. Handles many cases in which conflicts of law and foreign elements are relevant.
Prof. Memberships: Law Society. Association of Personal Injury Lawyers.
Career: Qualified in 1975. Trainee Solicitor with *Blatchfords*, London: Assistant Solicitor with *Keeble Hawson Steele Carr & Co* Sheffield; Partner in present firm and its predecessors since 1976.
Personal: Married and lives in Louth, Lincolnshire. Interests include football, cycling, reading and cinema.

BROOKS, Roger
James Chapman & Co, Manchester
(0161) 828 8000
insurancelit@james-chapman.co.uk
Specialisation: Acts for insurers defending personal injury claims arising from EL, PL and road traffic accident liability. His particular speciality is high value claims arising from serious head and spinal injuries. He is one of a select group of solicitors from across the country to be appointed by a number of leading UK insurance companies to handle claims in excess of £1m.
Prof. Memberships: Law Society. FOIL.
Career: Partner. Articled 1980-82 at *Berrymans*, London. Qualified 1982. Partner at *Keoghs* from 1983. Joined *James Chapman & Co* in 2002 as Partner.
Personal: Born in 1958. Educated at The King's School, Ely. LLB Hons at University in Southampton. Resides Bolton. Married with three children. Enjoys tennis, walking, skiing.

BROWELL, Philip
Browell Smith & Co, Newcastle upon Tyne
(0191) 221 1611

BRUFFELL, Martin
Berrymans Lace Mawer, Southampton
(023) 8023 6464
martin.bruffell@blm-law.com
Specialisation: Senior Partner, Southampton, handles personal injury and commercial litigation claims with specialisation in occupational disease and employers' liability.
Prof. Memberships: Former President of FOIL, CEDR accredited mediator, Law Society, BILA, PEOPIL, Institute of Directors etc.
Career: Joined *Berrymans* 1979, partner 1984. Working parties for the Law Society, the LCD, DETR, DSS and ABI etc, covering the Ogden tables, Woolf, damages, CFAs, the tracing of EL insurers, rehabilitation, expert witnesses inter alia.
Publications: Contributor to 'Binghams and Berrymans Motor Cases', 'The Lawyer', 'Post Magazine', 'Law Society Gazette' and the publications of ILEX, the Association of District Judges, Butterworths and Tolleys. Radio appearance on BBC Radio 4 and 5Live. On the editorial team of JSB Guidelines on General Damages.
Personal: Born 1955, educated at RGS High Wycombe and Leeds University.

CAHILL, John
Stewarts, London
(020) 7242 6462
jcahill@stewarts-solicitors.co.uk
Specialisation: Managing Partner and head of personal injury and clinical negligence group. Specialises in foreign personal injury claims and ADR.
Prof. Memberships: Centre for Dispute Resolution; Law Society; Association of Personal Injury Lawyers; Richard Grand Society.
Career: Articled *Kingsford Stacey*. Qualified 1985; partner 1990; CEDR accredited mediator; member of Personal Injury Panel; founder of The Richard Grand Society; trustee of Headway, the Brain Injuries Association.
Publications: Spinal Injuries Case Studies; personal injury chapter in the 'New Penguin Guide to the Law'.
Personal: Born 1960. Educated at Oratory School and Bristol Polytechnic (1981 LLB Hons). Resides London and Wiltshire. Married with two daughters. Enjoys wine, golf, swimming, and time off in France.

CARR, Robert
Anderson Strathern WS, Edinburgh
(0131) 220 2345
robert.carr@andersonstrathern.co.uk
Specialisation: Partner in litigation department. Accredited by the Law Society of Scotland as a medical negligence specialist and admitted as a solicitor/advocate with extended rights of audience in the highest Scottish civil courts. Almost 20 years of practice in civil litigation covering all areas of court and tribunal work. One of a team involved in advising insurers, particularly in personal injuries and related actions, and in advising the Royal College of Nursing as their appointed Scottish agents. The RCN instructions cover the full spectrum of criminal and civil court work and employment law matters, including frequent advice on medical negligence issues and regular appearance at fatal accident enquiries. Also speaks and lectures to insurers, nurses and doctors on many aspects of civil law and court procedure and practice. Head of the firm's Parliamentary Unit; assisted the RCN in its evidence before the Scottish Parliament on the Adults with an Incapacity Bill. Represented the Denholm family at the much publicised recent fatal accident enquiry in relation to the death of Darren Denholm who died whilst undergoing dental surgery under general anaesthetic; the case resulted in a finding that dental surgery under general anaesthetic should no longer be conducted outside a hospital setting. *Anderson Strathern* also dealt with the case of Richard Adamson, one of the first medical negligence actions in Scotland to proceed before a jury for almost 50 years, which resulted in an award for pain and suffering of £100,000 for a young man whose only testicle was negligently removed by doctors at a hospital in West Lothian. Has also been pioneering in Scotland damages for children who have suffered disability as a consequence of their mothers undergoing anticonvulsant therapy whilst pregnant. Also acts for the Parole Board for Scotland and the Mental Welfare Commission for Scotland.

CARSON, Peter
Rowley Ashworth, Leeds
(0113) 244 2018

CHANDLER, Pauline
Pannone & Partners, Manchester
(0161) 909 3000
pauline.chandler@pannone.co.uk
Specialisation: Plaintiff personal injury work comprising industrial accidents and disease including asbestos claims: Owen v IMI (bystander asbestos case); Jeromson v Shell Tankers in the Court of Appeal (asbestos mesothelioma in marine engineers); asthma (including a series of groundbreaking AGM asthma cases settled in 2001); lead welders bronchitis (Knox and Others v Cammel Lairds); lung disease; deafness; vibration; repetitive strain; passive smoking cases; solvent damage (Jenkins v MOD, brain damage from trike); professional negligence; fatal disease and accident cases (William v Great Ormond Street Hospital).
Prof. Memberships: Law Society Personal Injury Panel Assessor.
Career: Degree at Manchester University. Admitted 1974. Specialised in personal injury and disease work for 25 years at *Thomsons*. Joined *Pannone & Partners* as a partner in 1999.

CHERRY, Anthony
Beachcroft Wansbroughs, Bristol
(020) 7894 6022
acherry@bwlaw.co.uk
Specialisation: Partner with extensive experience in corporate risk management and liability claims of all types. Special expertise in chemical, physical and biological agents in the workplace, through products and in the environment. Lectures regularly on risk management and liability.
Prof. Memberships: Past president of the Forum of Insurance Lawyers from 1995 to 1997. He is a member of the Law Society Civil Litigation committee and was a member of the Vice Chancellor's working party on Practice Direction.
Career: Admitted May 1979, articles at *Bates & Partners*, Medico Legal section at ICI Legal Department from 1980 to 1983 (developing an expertise in long-term exposure to chemical and physical agents in the work place through products and the environment), *Stanley Simpson North* (then *Beachcroft Stanleys*) from 1983 to date, a partner since 1985.

CLARKE, Richard
Jacksons, Stockton on Tees
(01642) 643643

CONNOR, Michael
Russell Jones & Walker, Manchester
(0161) 934 4897
m.j.connor@rjw.co.uk
Specialisation: Claimant personal injury principally on behalf of Trade Unions and Staff Organisations.
Prof. Memberships: APIL, PI Panel, Manchester Law Society Council Member since 1996.
Career: Articled at *Whittles*, Manchester and Leeds 1989-91. *Thompsons*, Liverpool 1991-93, *Thompsons*, Stoke-on-Trent 1993-96, appointed Partner 1995, *Thompsons* Manchester 1996-99, *Russell Jones and Walker* Dec 1999-date, appointed Partner Jan 2001. Appointed Acting Managing Partner Manchester office in May 2002.
Publications: Regular contributor to Trade Union and Staff Organisation Journals.
Personal: Married with two boys aged

PERSONAL INJURY ■ THE LEADERS

eight and six. Spare time spent playing tennis and supporting Blackburn Rovers FC.

CRADICK, Simon
Morgan Cole, Cardiff
(029) 2038 5385

CRAWFORD, Allan
HBM Sayers, Glasgow
(0141) 353 2121
allan.crawford@hbmsayers.com
Specialisation: Litigation for insurance companies, with particular reference to personal injury, employers liability and public liability claims. Specialist experience in contact disputes, industrial disease claims and veterinary defence cases.
Prof. Memberships: Member of the Law Society of Scotland, Solicitor to the Supreme Court, Solicitor-Advocate and Member of FOIL.
Career: Qualified MA LLB. Admitted as solicitor in 1971. Formerly Partner of *Cochran Sayers and Cook*, Glasgow and Edinburgh; now *HBM Sayers*. Qualified as a Solicitor-Advocate with civil rights of audience in 1994. Former Temporary Sheriff. Tutor in Civil Advocacy at University of Strathclyde.

CROOK, Christopher
Edwards Duthie, Ilford
(020) 8514 9000
Specialisation: A specialist in personal injury litigation since qualification. After many years acting for claimants, in the last 15 years has specialised on acting on behalf of insurers in claims of maximum severity. Acted for the successful claimant in Doyle v Wallace and for the defendant in the House of Lords case of Hunt v Severs and has been involved in several other reported cases. Was a member of the Disability Assessment Unit Working Party and has frequently spoken at seminars. Is currently a member of BICMA (the Bodily Injury Claims Management Association).
Career: Attended Royal Grammar School, Guildford. Articled with *Dale & Newbery* qualifying in 1972. Joined *E. Edwards Son & Noice* (now *Edwards Duthie*) in 1976, becoming a Partner 1977.
Personal: Hockey, wine and travel. Lives in Cobham, Surrey.

CROSS, John
McKinty and Wright, Belfast
(028) 9024 6751
post@mckinty-wright.co.uk
Specialisation: Motor claims for insurers and defending professional indemnity claims.
Prof. Memberships: Law Society of Northern Ireland and member of Contentious Business Committee of the Society.
Career: Qualified 1970. Partner in *McKinty & Wright* since 1975. Graduate of Trinity College Dublin (BA, LLB).
Personal: Leisure interests include trap shooting and computers.

CUTTS, Dan
Weightman Vizards, Leicester
(0116) 253 9747
dan.cutts@weightmanvizards.com
Specialisation: Maximum severity cases especially head injury. Stress cases. Local Authority work. Product liability work and large employment liability cases. Major case: Kaur v CTP Coil Ltd CA (2001) C.P. Rep 34.
Prof. Memberships: Chartered Insurance Institute and FOIL.
Career: Articled at Eking Manning, Nottingham. Qualified in 1984 and was appointed to partner level in 1986, becoming the head of insurance in 1996. Joined *Weightman Vizards* in 1999 and is the Regional Managing Partner of the Leicester office.

DACE, Nigel
Weightman Vizards, Birmingham
(0121) 233 2601
nigel.dace@weightmanvizards.com
Specialisation: Partner specialising in personal injury work, particularly clinical negligence and motor claims. Acts at both High Court and County Court level. Very considerable experience of cases involving paraplegic and tetraplegic damage, brain damage and cerebral palsy. Has lectured on behalf of Birmingham Law Society and Worcester Law Society on 'The Practice and Procedure in Personal Injury Claims'.
Prof. Memberships: Birmingham Medico-Legal Society.
Career: Qualified 1973. Trained in London. Partner with *George Green & Co* 1982-96. Partner with *Weightman Vizards* since May 1996.
Personal: Educated at Shrewsbury School 1963-67 and Liverpool University 1967-70. Leisure pursuits include playing golf and tennis, watching most sports, particularly football, and also theatre. Born 6 September 1949. Lives in Hagley, Worcestershire.

DAY, Martyn
Leigh, Day & Co, London
(020) 7650 1200
See under Product Liability, p.670

DESMOND, Adrian
Boyes Turner, Reading
(0118) 952 7219
adesmond@boyesturnerlegal.co.uk
See under Clinical Negligence, p.150

DIAMOND, W Maurice
Diamond Heron, Belfast
(028) 9024 3726

DIAS, James
Sinton & Co, Newcastle upon Tyne
(0191) 212 7800
j.dias@sinton.co.uk
Specialisation: Partner in personal injury department. Sole area of practice is personal injury and medical negligence. The personal injury is mainly on behalf of defendant insurers and the medical negligence on behalf of claimants.
Prof. Memberships: Law Society.

Career: Qualified in 1972 after articles with *John H Sinton & Co*. Became a Partner in 1974.
Personal: Born 1948. Educated at Austin Friars School, Carlisle and Leeds University. Deputy District Judge. Deputy District Chairman Appeals Service. Past President North of England Medico-Legal Society. Leisure interests where family commitments permit include sport and reading. Lives in Newcastle-upon-Tyne.

DICKINSON, Graham
Barlow Lyde & Gilbert, London
(020) 7247 2277
gdickinson@blg.co.uk
Specialisation: All aspects of insurance liability work but primarily employers liability, industrial disease, motor and public liability claims. Extensive experience in major injury and loss claims and defence of group action.
Prof. Memberships: Member of the Chartered Insurance Institute.
Career: Qualified 1978. Partner *Robin Thompson & Partners* 1980. Founding partner *Dickinson Simpson* (Birmingham) 1983. Senior partner *Rowley Dickinson* (Birmingham) 1989. Appointed head of general insurance division, *Barlow Lyde & Gilbert* 1994.

DREWE, David
Crutes Law Firm, Newcastle upon Tyne
(0191) 212 5600
Specialisation: Partner in Litigation Department. Main area of practice is personal injury, acting largely on behalf of insurers, and professional negligence, acting exclusively for defendants including solicitors, surveyors, brokers and accountants. Also acts for hospitals and other health bodies on ethical and other issues. Making growing use of mediation in both personal injury and professional indemnity matters.
Prof. Memberships: FOIL, Law Society, Vice President Newcastle Upon Tyne Law Society.
Career: Joined *Crutes* on qualifying in 1981. Became a Partner in 1986.
Personal: Born 15 July 1957. Educated at Merchant Taylor's School, Crosby 1968-75, and Newcastle University 1975-78. Leisure interests include walking, theatre, cinema and reading. Lives in Newcastle upon Tyne.

ETTINGER, Colin
Irwin Mitchell, London
(020) 7404 3600
Specialisation: Partner specialising in personal injury and trade union law; conducts catastrophic injury cases of a high value and has particular specialities in workplace accident cases and occupational health matters.
Prof. Memberships: Executive council member Association of Personal Injury Lawyers; convenor Health & Safety Group of the Society of Labour Lawyers; patron for the charity Roadpeace; member of the OSS Professional Negligence Panel. Consultant Editor of J.P.I.L.

Career: Articled *Robin Thompson & Partners*; qualified 1978; partner 1980-95; partner *Irwin Mitchell* 1995. Fellow of College of Personal Injury Law.
Personal: Born 1952, London. Interests: current affairs, circuit training, football, cinema, jazz.

EVANS, Rod
Clarke Willmott & Clarke, Southampton
(023) 8048 3260
rodevans@cw-c.co.uk
Specialisation: Partner acting for leading household names in the insurance industry. Deals with injuries of maximum severity and stress related claims and has a special interest in rehabilitation. Also advises in construction disputes and policy interpretation. Regular contributor of articles to legal journals and conducts in-house training for insurance clients.
Prof. Memberships: FOIL, committee member Rehabilitation Special Interest Group, Law Society.
Career: Qualified 1981, *Deacons Solicitors* Hong Kong 1982-85. *Ensor Byfield* 1985-2002. Senior Partner 1997. *Ensor Byfield* merged with *Clarke Willmott & Clarke* May 2002, joined as Partner and sits on management board.
Personal: Running, classic cars.

FIFE, Robert
Anderson Strathern WS, Edinburgh
(0131) 220 2345
robert.fife@andersonstrathern.co.uk
Specialisation: All areas of personal injury litigation acting on behalf of trade union clients and insurers. Particular interest in health and safety law. Regularly lectures to insurers and nursing profession. Also handles general commercial litigation, defamation, professional negligence and advising local authorities.
Career: Qualified 1978. Partner in Litigation Department 1982. Solicitor Advocate 1995. Part-time Chairman of Appeals Committee of the Institute of Chartered Accountants of Scotland. Part-time Sheriff 2000.
Personal: Born 2 September 1955. School Governor. Lives in Edinburgh.

FINNIGAN, Kevin
James Chapman & Co, Manchester
(0161) 828 8000
insurancelit@james-chapman.co.uk
Specialisation: Head of personal injury department. He has extensive experience in dealing with severe brain and spine injury claims involving maximum awards. He has pioneered successfully the development of a consensual approach with claimants' solicitors and insurers resulting in early economic settlement of the largest personal injury claims. He is one of a select group of solicitors from across the country to be appointed by a number of leading UK insurance companies to handle claims in excess of £1m.
Prof. Memberships: Northern Circuit Working Party on joint meetings in personal injury cases. Manchester Law Soci-

ety and FOIL.
Career: Educated at St Bedes College, Hull University LLB (Hons) - 1975. Articled at *James Chapman & Co.* Admitted 1978.
Personal: Born 18 December 1953. Married with three children. Enjoys hill walking particularly in Ireland, reading and consuming Guinness.

GARRETT, Graeme
Digby Brown, Glasgow
(0141) 566 9494

GIBSON, Michael
Tughans, Belfast
(028) 9055 3300
michael.gibson@tughan.co.uk
Specialisation: Graduated from Cambridge University and was admitted as a solicitor in 1970. Joined *Tughan & Co* as a partner in 1974 and is Head of the Litigation Department. Has extensive experience of commercial litigation involving the construction and manufacturing industries and also has considerable expertise in all aspects of employers liability and public liability. His authority has been recognised for many years by the independent 'Chambers Guide to the Legal Profession' where he was named as one of the leaders in the field of defence litigation in Northern Ireland. Has dealt with industrial chest disease claims, class actions on behalf of pharmaceutical companies, catastrophic injury cases (including both brain damage and spinal injury) and medical negligence.

GOFF, Tony
George Ide, Phillips, Chichester
(01243) 786668
tony.goff@chi.georgeide.co.uk
Specialisation: Claimant personal injury specialist. Partner and Head of personal injury department. Principal area of practice is catastrophic injuries, particularly brain injuries. Member of Headway Specialist panel and national committee member of Motor Accident Solicitors' Society. Has represented a number of amputees and was instructed in the high profile case of Westmoquette v Dean which was extensively reported. Has a special interest in, and has written a number of articles on, rehabilitation.
Prof. Memberships: Fellow of C.P.I.L., Personal Injury Panel and A.P.I.L.
Career: Qualified 1980. Joined *George Ide, Phillips* 1983. Partner 1985.

GOODWILL, Peter
Nabarro Nathanson, Sheffield
(0114) 279 4000
Specialisation: Personal injury - defendant only. Major cases: Stark v Post Office; King v RCO Services and Yorkshire Traction; Green v Yorkshire Traction.
Prof. Memberships: FOIL.
Career: *CW Nelson & Co*, *Gordons Cranswick*, *Nabarro Nathanson*.
Personal: Cockburn High School. University of Newcastle upon Tyne.

GOULDING, Jane
freethcartwright, Nottingham
(0115) 936 9369
Specialisation: Personal injury work for claimants. Specialising in head injury cases, spinal cord injury and all serious injury matters. Settled two cases with damages over £1 million in the last 12 months.
Prof. Memberships: Law Society Personal Injury Panel Member; APIL; Nottingham Medico-Legal Society; Head Injury Special Interest Group; Spinal Cord Injury Special Interest Group.
Career: Trainee Solicitor 1983-85; joined *Hunt Dickins* 1986; became Partner 1988; Head of Personal Injury 1994.
Personal: Education - BA law, Nottingham Trent University, 2:1.

GREGORY, Tony
Keeble Hawson, Sheffield
(0114) 272 2061
Specialisation: Managing Partner. Personal injury litigation in all types of accident/disease claims. Has handled many maximum severity claims and disease claims. Former North Eastern representative of FOIL. Former part-time Chairman of Social Security Appeals Tribunal.
Prof. Memberships: Law Society. Personal Injury Panel Member for Law Society.
Career: LLB (Hons) Leeds University. Sidney Herbert Clay Prize. Harrison Simpson prize for jurisprudence. Qualified 1967. Articled *Bury & Walker*, Barnsley. Joined *Keeble Hawson* in 1967.
Personal: Married. Four children.

HARDING, Andrew
Hugh James, Cardiff
(029) 2022 4871
andrew.harding@hughjames.com
Specialisation: Partner and head of the claimant personal injury litigation group in the firm's head office. Specialises in catastrophic injury claims with particular interest and speciality in claims involving head injury. Established the firm's Head Injury Unit in 1998. Also undertakes claims arising out of spinal cord injury.
Prof. Memberships: Member of the Law Society's Personal Injury Panel and the Association of Personal Injury Lawyers. Trustee and Chairman of Headway Cardiff and Childrens' Brain Injury Trust (CBIT) Cymru. Recorder sitting on Wales and Chester circuit. Member Headway and SIA Panel.
Career: Born 10 June 1961. Graduate of University College Cardiff. Joined the firm in 1982 and qualified in 1984. Partner since 1986.

HARVEY, Mark
Hugh James, Cardiff
(029) 2022 4871
mark.harvey@hughjames.com
See under Product Liability, p.671

HENDERSON, Stuart
Irwin Mitchell, Birmingham
(0121) 212 1828
Specialisation: Partner in personal injury department. Particular emphasis on catastrophic spinal cord and brain injury, fatal accident claims, clinical negligence and travel litigation. Heads firm's plaintiff personal injury department in Birmingham. Acted in a number of cases involving some of the highest award of damages in personal injury in the UK including the Leung case, (a record £3.4 million in 1994) and the Luhar case (a record £5.1 million in 2000). Acting in numerous major group actions for illness suffered by holiday makers against tour operators. Has extensive media experience and lectures in-house and externally.
Prof. Memberships: APIL, Law Society.
Career: Qualified in 1992. Joined *Robin Thompson & Partners* in 1979, becoming a partner in 1992. Partner at *Irwin Mitchell* from January 1995.
Personal: Born 20 February 1958. Attended UCE Birmingham.

HERBERT, Andrew
Thompsons, Bristol
(0117) 304 2400

HOLT, David
Weightman Vizards, Liverpool
(0151) 242 7921
david.holt@weightmanvizards.com
Specialisation: Partner in Litigation (Insurance) Department. Main area of practice is defendant insurance litigation. Acts for a large number of major insurers, advising at length on MIB and uninsured motorist cases and matters of policy interpretation. Has particular specialism in MIB law - acts for MIB and for MIB handling agents whilst also advising insurers on their liability under the Road Traffic Act 1988 and under Article 75 of the MIB Internal Regulations. Acted for MIB on the Judicial Review action commenced against the Secretary of State by MASS challenging the legitimacy of the 1999 Uninsured Drivers Agreement, which action has recently been discontinued. Has given numerous lectures to insurers, particularly on uninsured motoring and has addressed major claims conferences.
Prof. Memberships: Law Society, Liverpool Law Society.
Career: Qualified in 1986. Joined *Weightman Vizards* in 1984, becoming a Partner in 1990.
Personal: Born 29 March 1962. Attended Birmingham University (2:1 LLB); passed Law Society Finals with Honours 1984; won Liverpool Law Society prize for highest marks in Law Society Finals for Merseyside area. Leisure interests include tennis, cricket and snooker. Lives on the Wirral.

HOPKINS, Ian
Leo Abse & Cohen, Cardiff
(029) 2038 3252

JACKSON, Carol
Pannone & Partners, Manchester
(0161) 909 3000
carol.jackson@pannone.co.uk
Specialisation: Serious injuries, head, spine and fatal accidents. Successfully completed jurisdiction arguments in relation to a fatal accident in Lanzarote, in which the claimant's mother was killed and the claimant rendered catastrophically head injured and a semi-vegetative condition. Tragically much reduced life expectancy, settled £420,000. Also recently completed case for a young man's traumatic amputation of leg at the hip, £1 million. Settlement of paraplegic and head injury £3.45 million, primarily road traffic act claim with clinical negligence intervening. Settlement of serious head injury case after trial on liability, young man age 26, £2.2 million. Trial listed for July, a case involving a Hong Kong national with evidence from Hong Kong; serious head injury, value circa £4 million. Trial listed December for a young woman catastrophically head injured after a near drowning incident in the bath whilst in care of local authority, value circa £5.5 million.
Prof. Memberships: Law Society Personal Injury Panel, APIL, Fellow of CPIL, Headway, SIA and Richard Grand Society.
Career: Admitted as a solicitor in 1981, became partner with *Pannone & Partners* in 1994. Head of personal injury department.

JEFFERSON, Ian
C & H Jefferson, Belfast
(028) 9032 9545
ianjefferson@chjefferson.co.uk
Specialisation: Senior Partner specialising in personal injury work, primarily but not exclusively for defendants. Clients include major insurance companies and Lloyds syndicates. Considerable experience of cases involving catastrophic injuries including brain damage, spinal injuries and fatal accidents.
Prof. Memberships: Council of the Law Society of Northern Ireland; area representative of FOIL; Headway; Spinal Injuries Association; NI Medico-Legal Society; PEOPIL.
Career: Qualified Northern Ireland 1971. England 1990.
Personal: Fishing, sailing, hockey and theatre.

JOHN, Simon
Cunningham John, Thetford
(01842) 752401
See under Clinical Negligence, p.153

JONES, David
Morgan Jones & Pett, Great Yarmouth
(01493) 334700
david.jones@m-j-p.co.uk
See under Clinical Negligence, p.153

KEMP, Sandy
Burnside Kemp Fraser, Aberdeen
(01224) 327500
See under Employment, p.326

KEYDEN, Gordon
Simpson & Marwick, Edinburgh
(0131) 557 1545
gordon.keydon@simpmar.com

PERSONAL INJURY ■ THE LEADERS

Specialisation: Specialises in insurance-based litigation but is principally involved in personal injury claims. Handles claims ranging from catastrophic injury to industrial ailments as well as accidents at work and road traffic cases. Currently the Motor Insurer's Bureau appointed Solicitor in Scotland and has been involved in revising the wording of the new MIB Agreement from a Scottish Viewpoint.
Prof. Memberships: International Bar Association, Forum of Insurance Lawyers, British Insurance Law Association.
Career: Qualified 1978; Partner since 1980.

KITSON, Paul
Russell Jones & Walker, London
(020) 7339 6673
Specialisation: Claimant personal injury specialist. Has successfully pursued numerous claims for injuries on the sports field for footballers and rugby players. Acted for the appellants in Wells v Wells (the 'multipliers case').
Prof. Memberships: Past committee member of British Association of Sport & the Law; Member of the Association of Personal Injury Lawyers; Past co-ordinator of Greater London Regional Group of APIL; Member of Law Society Personal Injury Panel.
Career: Partner with *Russell Jones & Walker* since 1992.

LEE, Terry
Evill and Coleman, London
(020) 8789 9221
Terry.Lee@evillandcoleman.co.uk
Specialisation: Partner of personal injury/clinical negligence department. Main areas of practice are catastrophic injuries, clinical negligence, particularly brain damage at birth, head injuries, multiple injuries, fatal accident claims and Court of Protection work. Has been involved in a number of significant actions including Brown v Merton & Sutton Health Authority, Head v East Anglia Health Authority, Hall v Pirie and Lambert v Devon County Council. A further important case, Joyce v Wandsworth Health Authority, provided clarification of the judicial approach to causation in a clinical negligence case. Recently was involved in the well known sporting injury case which was the first of its kind brought against a rugby referee and which was successful. This was the case of Smoldon v Whitworth & Nolan. Further, the case of Dudley v East Dorset Health Authority is an important case relating to the removal of a litigation friend in an application that was contested. Has also been instrumental in dealing with a number of cases which involve the formation of a structured settlement. Is an assessor to the Personal Injury panel as well as a member of the Personal Injury panel of Solicitors. Is also a member of the Medical Negligence Specialist panel of Solicitors. Author of articles for legal magazines and a book on dealing with cases involving catastrophic injuries. Lectures extensively at conferences and seminars. Is also a referral solicitor to various organisations including AVMA, Spinal Injuries Association, Headway etc.
Prof. Memberships: Member of the Association of Personal Injury Lawyers, British Academy of Forensic Science and the Environmental Law Foundation.
Career: Qualified and joined *Evill and Coleman* in 1972. Became a Partner in 1976.
Personal: Educated at Wimbledon College. Recreations include golf and tennis. Lives in Esher, Surrey.

LEECH, Catherine
Pannone & Partners, Manchester
(0161) 909 3000
catherine.leech@pannone.co.uk
Specialisation: All types of personal injury work especially catastrophic injury claims (particularly spinal), aviation law and disaster litigation, product liability litigation and multi-party actions.
Prof. Memberships: Personal Injury Panel since 1995; APIL Co-ordinator Product Liability and Consumer Affairs SIG; Spinal Injury Association Panel; Association of Trial Lawyers of America. Fellow of the College of Personal Injury Law.
Career: Attended University of Wales, Cardiff and College of Law, Chester. Trained at *Ryland Martineau* then *Pannone and Partners*. Admitted September 1987. Became partner with firm May 1991. Lectures in PI law for Law Society/AWS Returners course and other continuing education suppliers.
Personal: Married with three children. Enjoys running, rowing and spending time with family. Member of SIA Ball committee.

LOUGHLIN, Grahame
Tughans, Belfast
(028) 9055 3300
grahame.loughlin@tughans.com
Specialisation: Wealth of experience of litigation in Northern Ireland's High Court, principally on behalf of insurers in the field of personal injury. Also considerable experience in the commercial field, representing plaintiffs and defendants in the Commercial Court.
Prof. Memberships: Law Society of Northern Ireland. Northern Ireland Employment Lawyers Group.
Career: Graduated in 1973 - Queens University, Belfast. Partner from 1981 to date.

LUMSDEN, Lawrence
Thompsons, Edinburgh
(0131) 225 4297

MACWILKINSON, Jeffrey
Dolmans, Cardiff
(020) 2034 5531
Jeffreym@dolmans.co.uk
Specialisation: Senior Partner and Head of Defendant Litigation Department. Specialises in personal injury. Acts for major insurance clients and a substantial number of local authorities. Handles specialist civil actions for police authorities. Leads a team handling multi-party actions and other high value cases. Nominated by insurers to handle specialist work including occupational stress cases and actions arising out of special educational needs.
Prof. Memberships: Law Society, Chartered Institute of Arbitrators, FOIL.
Career: Qualified in 1966. Partner with *Dolmans* since 1972. President of the Cardiff and District Law Society 2001-02. Part-time Chairman of Social Security Appeals Tribunal (1990-96). Deputy District Judge 1995-2000.

MAGUIRE, Frank
Thompsons, Glasgow
(0141) 221 8840

MARSHALL, David
Anthony Gold, London
(020) 7940 4000
mail@anthonygold.co.uk
Specialisation: Principal area of practice - personal injury and medical negligence work. Member of the Law Society's Personal Injury and Medical Negligence Panels. Acted in APIL campaigns on Legal Aid, Lord Woolf's Report and Conditional Fees.
Prof. Memberships: Law Society, APIL (Executive Committee Member since 1996, Treasurer since 1998, Vice-President 2002). Fellow of the Society for Advanced Legal Studies. CPIL Fellow.
Career: Joined *Anthony Gold* as a Trainee Solicitor in 1985, qualifying in 1987 and becoming a Partner in 1989. Managing Partner 1997.
Personal: Born 5 June 1962. Education - Queen's College, Oxford, 1980-83. Lives in Herne Hill, South London. Honorary Treasurer, Blackfriars Advice Centre. Leisure interests include foreign travel, history and contemporary fiction.

MAY, Sara
Beachcroft Wansbroughs, Birmingham
(0121) 698 5200
Specialisation: Regional Senior Partner in Birmingham. Has vast experience in all aspects of personal injury including employers, public and motor liability.

MCCARTHY, Frances
Pattinson & Brewer, London
(020) 7400 5100
fmccarthy@pattinsonbrewer.co.uk
Specialisation: Head of Personal Injury Department. Main area of practice is work accident and occupational disease claims. Also handles medical negligence and other areas of personal injury. Has handled successful appeals to the European Court of Justice on the question of equal treatment in matters of Social Security. Lectures and broadcasts regularly on personal injury matters.
Prof. Memberships: Law Society, Association of Personal Injury Lawyers, Association of Trial Lawyers of America, Environmental Law Foundation.
Career: Qualified in 1981. Joined *Pattinson & Brewer* in 1979, becoming a Partner in 1985. Immediate past President of APIL, Chair of the International Practice Section of the American Lawyers Association, Member of Civil Justice Council, Member of working party for pre-action protocols. Editorial Board of 'Journal for Personal Injury Law'.

MCCOOL, Geraldine
Leigh, Day & Co, Manchester
(0161) 832 7722
gmccool@leighday.co.uk
Specialisation: Main area of practice is aviation for claimants, product liability and MOD claims. Cases have included Lockerbie, British Midland at Kegworth, Piper Alpha and Chinook Mull of Kintyre crash 1994.
Prof. Memberships: APIL, ATLA. Past National Chairman of Young Solicitors Group. Member of Law Society's Personal Injury panel. On panel of mediators in Personal Injury for Court of Appeal cases. Vice-President Manchester Law Society.
Publications: Co-author of Longmans 'Know How PI', 'Multi Party Actions' by LAG and 'Civil Litigation Handbook' published by the Law Society.
Personal: Born 20 April 1961.

MCEVOY, Eamonn
Eamonn McEvoy & Co, Lurgan
(028) 3832 7734

MEERAN, Richard
Leigh, Day & Co, London
(020) 7650 1200
See under Product Liability, p.672

MOORE, George
HBM Sayers, Glasgow
(0141) 353 2121
george.moore@hbmsayers.com
Specialisation: Litigation for insurance companies with particular reference to personal injury, employers and public liability claims. Also specialist in advising on insurance company fraud, professional negligence and industrial disease claims. Dealt with the legal aspects of the 1997 E-Coli outbreak in Scotland including representing the insurers involved.
Prof. Memberships: Member of the Law Society of Scotland, Solicitor to the Supreme Court, Solicitor/Advocate and Member of FOIL.
Career: Admitted as a Solicitor in 1971, founding partner of *Hamilton Burns & Moore* in 1972, now *HBM Sayers*. Qualified as a Solicitor/Advocate with Rights of Audience in the Court of Session in 1994. Former Member of Sheriff Court Rules Council. Member of Coulsfield Committee on Court of Session Procedure.

NEILL, Bryan
Prince Evans, London
(020) 8567 2001
neillbryan@prince-evans.co.uk
Specialisation: Partner in charge of Personal and Medical Injury Department. Handles catastrophic injury claims: brain injuries, tetraplegia and paraplegia. Has recovered record UK awards of

THE LEADERS — PERSONAL INJURY

damages for clients. Numerous £1m+ cases. Commonly recovers between £6m and £10m damages for clients each year. Specialises in structured compensation and post-award fund protection and planning.
Prof. Memberships: Law Society; Association of Personal Injury Lawyers; ATLA; APLA; LSLA; Headway; Spinal Injuries Association; International Medical Society of Paraplegia; Richard Grand Society.
Career: Articled *Thompsons*; qualified 1979; Partner 1982-85; Partner *Prince Evans* 1985-date. Co-author Butterworths 'Structured Settlements - A Practical Guide'.
Personal: Born 1954. LLB (Hons) London University. Resides London.

NELSON-JONES, Rodney
Field Fisher Waterhouse, London
(020) 7861 4022
rnj@ffwlaw.com
Specialisation: Partner in charge of personal injury litigation department. Personal injury work includes asbestos, aviation and road accidents. Also handles medical negligence work. Cases have included the M1 Air Crash (Steering Committee Member), Bryce v Swan Hunter Group (mesothelioma), Prendergast v Sam & Dee (medical negligence), O'Loughlin v Cape plc (mesothelioma) and the House of Lords appeals of Mrs Fox and Mr Matthews (mesothelioma).
Prof. Memberships: Law Society. Richard Grand Society.
Career: Qualified in 1975. Worked at *Prothero & Prothero* 1973-77 and *L Bingham & Co* 1977-83. Joined *Field Fisher Waterhouse* in 1983.
Publications: Co-author of 'Product Liability - The New Law Under the Consumer Protection Act 1987' (2nd edn 1988), 'Medical Negligence Case Law' (2nd edn 1995) 'Personal Injury Limitation Law' (1994), 'Computing Personal Injury Damages' (4th edn 2001), 'Multipliers' (1998) and 'Butterworths Personal Injury Damages Statistics' (4th edn 2001). Contributor to 'Structured Settlements - A Practical Guide', 'Butterworths Personal Injury Litigation Service' and 'The Medical Accidents Handbook'.
Personal: Born on 11 February 1947. Educated at Repton School and Hertford College, Oxford (MA Oxon). Lives in London.

OLIVER, Timothy
Badhams, London
(020) 7242 4154
tim.oliver@badhams.net
Specialisation: Personal injury, employers liability, public liability.
Prof. Memberships: Travel and Tourism, Lawyers Association.
Career: Managing Partner of both *Badhams* and *plexus*, the firm's specialist professional indemnity division. Has spent many years acting for the insurance industry specialising in personal injury and in particular with travel litigation. Was a Partner at *Berrymans Lace Mawer* for some 10 years where he headed the London Personal Injury Department and was heavily involved in the national development team of the personal injury practice.
Publications: Binghams & Berrymans Motor Claims Cases 10th and 11th editions and supplements. Co-author Oliver and Dingemans on Employers Liability Cases (to be published 2002 by Butterworth).
Personal: Reading School, Exeter University. Borough Councillor (Elmbridge) 1999-date. Liveryman, married with three children.

OSBORNE, Tom
Osborne Morris & Morgan, Leighton Buzzard
(01525) 378177

PADFIELD, Brendan
Eversheds, Ipswich
(01473) 284428
brendanpadfield@eversheds.com
Specialisation: Head of claims management for *Eversheds* nationally and regional head of insurance/personal injury for the East of England. Works on behalf of insurance companies, large self-insureds and P&I clubs, dealing with road traffic employers and public liability claims.
Prof. Memberships: Law Society, Norfolk and Norwich Medico Legal Society, Suffolk Medico Legal Society, Association of Serious Injury Solicitors.
Career: Qualified 1984; became a partner in 1990.
Personal: Born October 1959. Attended University College Durham. Lives in Suffolk. Interests include regional history, wine and cooking.

PARKER, Alison
Bolt Burdon, London
(020) 7288 4700
Specialisation: Personal Injury.
Prof. Memberships: Law Society Personal Injury Panel, Association of Personal Injury Lawyers, College of Personal Injury Law. Secretary of APIL Transport Special Interest Group.
Career: 10 years specialising in personal injury law. Special interest in cases involving law of business opportunity.

PARKER, Andrew
Beachcroft Wansbroughs, London
(020) 7894 6232
aparker@bwlaw.co.uk
Specialisation: Partner in insurance litigation (predominantly personal injury), currently heads a team specialising in test litigation especially relating to funding. Also specialises in motor insurance, having spent a year on the claims floor of a major direct insurer advising on systems to control litigation and claims costs. Has acted in the past year for defendant insurers in the Court of Appeal/House of Lords in Callery v Gray and Warriner v Warriner (Discount Rates for Personal Injury multipliers) and for the Liability Insurers Group in Sarwar v Alam. He acted for the Association of British Insurers in the House of Lords in Fairchild v Glenhaven and others (the asbestos cases). Currently engaged in the Claims Direct Test Cases at first instance having also appeared in these cases in the Court of Appeal.
Prof. Memberships: Immediate past president of FOIL (the Forum of Insurance Lawyers) and Executive committee member since 1995. Member of the IUA Rehabilitation Working Party and contributed to the IUA/ABI 2nd Bodily Injury Awards Study in 1999. Committee member of the London Solicitors Litigation Association. Member of the Costs Practitioners' Group.
Career: Qualified 1983, has been a partner in *Wansbroughs Willey Hargrave* and *Beachcroft Wansbroughs* since 1997 having previously been a defendant insurance partner with *Keeble Hawson* in Sheffield and *Irwin Mitchell* in Birmingham.
Personal: Studied Modern Languages and Law at Corpus Christi College, Cambridge.

PATTERSON, Frank
Leigh, Day & Co, Manchester
(0161) 832 7722
fpatterson@leighday.co.uk
Specialisation: Maximum severity cases, including spinal injury and acquired brain injury litigation, acting exclusively on behalf of claimants. He is a member of the Spinal Injuries Association Specialist Panel and the Headway Specialist Panel. Deals with complex and high value industrial accident and industrial disease litigation on behalf of Trade Union clients. Experience of co-ordinating large multi-party PI actions, including international industrial disease litigation. A regular lecturer on specialist legal topics to the legal profession.
Prof. Memberships: Member of the Law Society's Personal Injury Specialist Panel.
Career: Qualified in 1986, having served articles with *Pannone & Partners*. Became a Partner in 1990, and Head of Personal Injury Litigation in 1993. Partner at *Leigh Day & Co* from December 1995.
Publications: Co-author 'PI Know How' - published by Longmans. Co-author 'Personal Injury Precedents & Pleadings' - published by Sweet & Maxwell, former General Editor 'Personal Injury Precedents & Pleadings.'
Personal: Born 6 December 1959, graduated from University of Manchester.

PERRY, Timothy
Weightman Vizards, Birmingham
(0121) 233 2601
tim.perry@weightmanvizards.com
Specialisation: Mainly defendant insurance and associated personal injury work. Predominantly deals with employers' liability and public liability claims, to include catastrophic injuries and asbestos, deafness and other industrial diseases.
Prof. Memberships: Law Society and Birmingham Law Society.
Career: Educated at Abraham Darby Comprehensive in Telford and then Hull University. After qualifying in 1974, was Assistant Solicitor at *Browne Jacobson*. Joined *William Hatton* in 1979. Became a Partner in 1981 before the firm became part of *Weightman Vizards*.
Personal: Married and lives in Birmingham. Interests include motor sport and football.

PESCOD, Peter
Hay & Kilner, Newcastle upon Tyne
(0191) 232 8345

PICKERING, John
Irwin Mitchell, Sheffield
(0114) 276 7777
pickeringj@irwinmitchell.co.uk
See under Clinical Negligence, p.154

PICKERING, John
John Pickering & Partners, Oldham
(0161) 834 1251
law@jpicks.u-net.law
Specialisation: Specialist in handling asbestos claims for Plaintiffs. Claims handled throughout the country. Much experience in other industrial disease claims, i.e. asthma, white finger, dermatitis, bladder cancer. Also experience in solicitor's and medical negligence claims. Instructed by trade unions for members. Devised Conditional Fee Agreement for trade unions. Pioneered byssinosis, i.e. cotton dust, claims in England. Acted for Plaintiff in Leeds neighbourhood asbestos trial of 'Margereson v J.W. Roberts Limited'. Handled many claims for citizens of Australia and for claimants in Malta, Ireland, Canada, South Africa, USA, New Zealand with claims to pursue in UK. One of his cases resulted in a change in the law so that companies no longer in existence can be put back on the register and sued.
Prof. Memberships: APIL. Personal Injury Panel. Legal Aid Franchise.
Career: Qualified 1965. Partner *W.H. Thompson* and *Brian Thompson & Partners* from 1968 until 1979. Founded own firm in Manchester 1979. Now four branches, Oldham, Manchester, Liverpool and Halifax.
Personal: Born 1939.

PORTEUS, Stephen
Marrons, Newcastle upon Tyne
(0191) 281 1304

POTTER, Hugh
Hugh Potter & Company, Serious Injury Solicitors, Manchester
(0161) 237 5888
hughpotterandcompany@hotmail.com
Specialisation: Mainly brain and spinal cord injury including medical negligence and professional negligence cases. Has growing caseload of English plaintiffs injured abroad. Recent settlements include the case of Roebuck for £4.8 million - see website for details.
Prof. Memberships: Fellow of the College of Personal Injury Law, Member of the Law Society Personal Injury and Medical Negligence Panels, Member of AVMA Panel, Richard Grand Society

PERSONAL INJURY ■ THE LEADERS

and ten year membership of APIL.
Career: Qualified in 1988, became a Partner in *Pannone Napier* and *Pannone & Partners* in 1990. Formed *Hugh Potter & Company Serious Injury Solicitors* on 1 May 1998. The firm has 10 fee-earners specialising in serious injury cases and has franchises for personal injury, clinical negligence and welfare benefits.
Personal: Born 8 June 1962. Fundraiser for Headway and Spinal Injuries Association.

PRAIN, David
Rowley Ashworth, Wolverhampton
(01902) 771551

PRICE, Hugh
Morgan Cole, Cardiff
(029) 2038 5385

RENOUF, Terence
Berrymans Lace Mawer, London
(020) 7638 2811
terry.renouf@blm-law.com
Specialisation: Personal injury acting for defendants in all aspects of liability insurance relating to insurers. Particular specialisation in disease related litigation.
Prof. Memberships: Liveryman of City of London Solicitors' Company.
Career: Admitted 1987, joined *Berrymans Lace Mawer* 1987, associate 1989, partner 1991. Member of Pre-Action Protocol Working Group assisting Lord Woolf on both interim and final 'Access to Justice' reports. Member of Law Society pre-action Protocols Working Group and Drafting Group of both Injury and Occupational Diseases Protocols.
Personal: Born 1960. Educated at Hautlieu School, Jersey, Durham University, Manchester Polytechnic.

ROACH, Andrew
Beachcroft Wansbroughs, Birmingham
(0121) 698 5200
ARoach@bwlaw.co.uk
Specialisation: Partner handling all types of personal injury work including serious motor cases and public and employers' liability claims. Specialises in particular in gradual and modern diseases and sports law. Ran the successful defence of the co-defendant in the groundbreaking case of Smoulden v Whitworth & Nolan, the first case where liability attached to a referee for his handling of a rugby game. Also acts on large loss claims, especially arson and product liability (recently acted for Laboratoires Garnier), and advises on policy disputes of all types. Has spoken at AIRMIC and numerous other conferences on trends in industrial diseases and sports law.
Prof. Memberships: BILA, FOIL.
Career: Qualified 1980; solicitor *Lawrence Graham* 1980-82. Solicitor *Herbert Smith* 1982-86. *Wansbroughs Willey Hargrave* (now *Beachcroft Wansbroughs*) 1986.

ROBERTS, Gavin
Thompsons, Plymouth
(01752) 253085

ROGERS, Nick
Lamport Bassitt, Southampton
(02380) 837778
Nick.Rogers@lamportbassitt.co.uk
Specialisation: Partner specialising in catastrophic injuries (head and spinal), fatal accidents and industrial disease claims, for claimants and defendants. Acted for the Defendant in Wake v Wylie (2001). All aspects of employers', motor and public liability claims undertaken.
Prof. Memberships: Law Society, APIL.
Career: Qualified 1990. *Bird & Bird* 1988-94. *Lamport Bassitt* since 1994. Partner from 1997.
Personal: Canford School, Dorset 1977-82 and Exeter University 1983-87. Married with two daughters. Away from the office time is spent with family, golf and sailing.

ROWE, Bernard
Lyons Davidson, Bristol
(0117) 904 5701
browe@lyonsdavidson.co.uk
Specialisation: Partner and Head of Personal Injury and Insurance. Principal area of practice is personal injury litigation arising from road traffic accidents. Heads a department of 270 personnel, handling personal injury and road traffic litigation for claimants and defendants. Has been involved in numerous substantial personal injury cases, including structured settlements. Experienced lecturer at legal conferences and seminars. Organised 3-day international Conferences on Whiplash Injuries (1997 and 2000), Psychological Injuries (1998) and Fibromyalgia 2001 Conference. Current project in Loss of Limbs conference 2002. Served on Working Party to establish the Disability Assessment Unit and now Treasurer of BICMA (Bodily Injury Claims Management Association).
Prof. Memberships: Motor Accident Solicitors Society (Chairman 1992-94), European Whiplash Association. Treasurer of BICMA.
Career: Qualified in 1976. Partner at *Ivesons* in Hull from 1977. Joined *Lyons Davidson* in 1986 and became a Partner in 1987. Managing Partner 1992-94.
Personal: Born 21 December 1951. Educated at Watford Grammar School 1963-70 and Hull University 1970-73 (BA, Politics and Law). Leisure pursuits: fly fishing. Lives in Bristol.

SCOTT, Toby
Eversheds, Newcastle upon Tyne
(0191) 261 1661
tobyscott@eversheds.com
Specialisation: Defendant personal injury. Particular interest and major area of practise is in insidious disease and technical claims. Much of the year has been devoted to advising on insidious disease exposure and other long term liabilities.
Prof. Memberships: Board Director of Northern Dispute Resolutions.
Career: Trained *Cohen Jackson/ Ingledows*. Qualified 1986. Assistant and subsequently Partner in *Linsley & Mortimer*, the niche insurance practice until merger with *Eversheds* in 2000.
Publications: Contributor to Insurance Day.
Personal: Born 1962. Resides Newcastle upon Tyne. Leisure interests include sailing, travel, wine.

SHORT, David
Lawford Kidd, Edinburgh
(0131) 225 5214
law@lawfordkidd.co.uk
Specialisation: Exclusively acts for victims. Extensive practice acting on behalf of Trade Unions including AEEU, UNISON, BALPA and FirstAssist for ULR claims. Main area of practice, work related accidents and disease cases. Particular specialisation in aviation related accidents mainly representing pilots. Past steering Committee Member of Piper Alpha and Brent Spar disasters.
Prof. Memberships: Law Society of Scotland, Society of Writers to Her Majesty's Signet. Past Executive Councillor - APIL. ATLA Member.
Career: Dundee and Strathclyde Universities, trained at *Lawford & Co*, London for period in 1980s. Qualified 1984.
Personal: Married - one son. Interests: golf and travel.

SLESS, Tania
Beachcroft Wansbroughs, London
(020) 7242 1011
tsless@bwlaw.co.uk
Specialisation: Head of, and Partner in, insurance litigation department specialising in employers', public, product liability claims and also serious motor injury claims. Particular expertise in work-related upper limb disorders, and stress claims. Clients include major retailers and motor manufacturers. Retains an interest in Irish claims, and has written and broadcast on comparative levels of compensation between this jurisdiction and Ireland.
Prof. Memberships: Member of Employers' Liability and Disease special interest group of FOIL.
Career: Articled *Miley & Miley*, Dublin. Qualified 1985 in Ireland, 1991 in England and Wales. *Miley & Miley* 1985-88; *Prudential Assurance Company Limited* 1988-90; *Davies Arnold Cooper* 1990-99 (partner 1993); *Beachcroft Wansbroughs* 1999-date.
Personal: Born 1961. Trinity College, Dublin 1978-82. Married with two sons. Resides Highgate. Interests - reading, cinema, theatre, art.

SMITH, Blaise
Ford & Warren, Leeds
(0113) 243 6601
Specialisation: Over 20 years experience of all aspects of personal injury and insurance law; acts for insurers in claims of maximum severity and for claimants in clinical negligence claims; has particular interest in head and spinal injury claims and fatal accidents; also has extensive experience in policy disputes, MIB and product liability claims and horse-related accidents; member of Law Society's Personal Injury and Clinical Negligence Panels; has recovered record damages against a health authority (exceeding £4m). Reported cases including Crabtree v Wilson (CA, assessment of damages for dependency) and Jones v Chief Constable of South Yorkshire (HL, remoteness of damage - nervous shock).
Career: Leeds University LLB 1976-79; joined *Ford & Warren* in 1980, admitted 1982, and Partner since 1985.
Personal: Leisure interests include horses and running (Tadcaster Harriers).

SMITH, Sid
Thompsons, Edinburgh
(0131) 225 4297

SOLLY, Gillian
Russell Jones & Walker, Bristol
(0117) 927 3098
g.c.solly@rjw.co.uk
Specialisation: Managing Partner since 1994. Clinical negligence and serious personal injury including Heil v Rankin Court of Appeal (the general damages case). Has specialised in clinical negligence and personal injury work for claimants since 1983. The clinical negligence caseload is varied and substantial, during the last year including several awards over £100,000.
Prof. Memberships: Founder member of APIL and first treasurer. Member Bristol Law Society, Bristol Medico-Legal Society APIL. Trustee Headway Bristol.
Personal: Educated at Beverley High School for Girls followed by Warwick University for law degree. Qualified April 1981. Joined current firm in 1983. Married with two children.

STAPLES, Martin
Vizards Wyeth, London
(020) 7400 9999
mrs@vizardswyeth.com
Specialisation: Introduced insurance litigation to *Vizards* in 1974 and became Senior Partner in its bicentenary year, 1997; spearheaded the development of all aspects of non-marine insurance litigation with the firm, culminating in the merger with *Bannisters* in 1999 and *A.E. Wyeth* in 2001 to create the presently named firm. Today, his concentration is upon policy construction and the resolution of major liability disputes; also has wide experience of medical negligence claims, having run for seven years the original Thalidomide litigation and acted in Shewan v Westminster Hospital; also dealt with the first industrial deafness case Berry v Stone Manganese and other evolving disease claims involving asbestos, mica dust, talcosis, hardwood dust, rubber compounds and recently the test cases involving organophosphates - the Farmers' 'Sheep Dip' claims; has also dealt with claims in respect of major disasters, employers' liability, professional indemnity and coverage; directly responsible for liability claims with BAA, McDonalds and Airtours nationwide and acts for Iron

THE LEADERS ■ PERSONAL INJURY

Trades, Royal & Sunalliance, Prudential QBE and The Underwriter.
Prof. Memberships: Past President Forum of Insurance Lawyers (FOIL); Member Fire Loss Association; Founder Member of BICMA - Bodily Injuries Claims Management Association - FOIL Representative on the Law Society Council.
Career: Articled *Wilkinson Kimbers & Staddon* 1962; Joined *Geoffrey Coombs & Co*. Partner 1971 then amalgamation with *Vizards* as Partner 1974; Senior Partner *Vizards* 1997; Vice President of Forum of Insurance Lawyers FOIL in 1997; President in 1999, when he developed the response of Insurance Lawyers to Conditional Fees and the Law Commission's Report on Non Pecuniary Loss culminating in Heil v Rankin. Senior Partner of *Vizards Wyeth* in 2001.
Personal: Born 1944. Educated Hounslow College. Resides Islington and Upper Dicker. Leisure: travel, sport, wine.

STEVENSON, David
Biggart Baillie, Glasgow
(0141) 228 8000

SWANNEY, Robert
Digby Brown, Glasgow
(0141) 566 9494

THOMPSON, David
Langleys, York
(01904) 610 886

THOMPSON, Mark
Bond Pearce, Plymouth
(01752) 677852
mthompson@bondpearce.com
Specialisation: Personal injury and clinical negligence.
Prof. Memberships: Solicitor, Law Society Personal Injury Panel, APIL and ATLA.
Career: Qualified October 1993, founded *Bond Pearce* 1988 and Partner 1991.
Personal: Liverpool University 1977-80.

TUCKER, Andrew
Irwin Mitchell, Sheffield
0870 1500 100
See under Product Liability, p.673

TWEED, Paul
Johnsons, Belfast
(02890) 240183
pt@johnsonslaw.co.uk
Specialisation: Defamation - the most well-known case being for B J Eastwood against the boxer Barry McGuigan, resulting in an award of £450,000. Currently acting for Van Morrison and Patrick Kielty in a number of high profile libel actions. Acted for Robert McCartney QC, the former MP for North Down, who was awarded £80,000 in a high profile case against 'The Irish Times' on the eve of the 1997 General Election, and for the actors Liam Neeson and Natasha Richardson against a number of Irish newspapers in relation to false reports regarding the state of their marriage. Has represented the Irish band The Corrs and is currently involved in multiple defamation actions against UK and US-based internet book distributors, requiring the issue of what is believed to be the largest number of writs in respect of the publication of one book. Acts for a number of other media, political, public, business and legal personalities and also on the defence side for newspapers (including 'The Sunday Times') and other publications, in both Belfast and Dublin. Other areas of media practice include copyright and related entertainment work. Personal injury - has had more than 20 years of experience in acting for a number of major insurance companies in both Northern Ireland and the Republic of Ireland.
Prof. Memberships: Incorporated Law Society of Northern Ireland (1978); Law Society of England and Wales (1993); Law Society of Ireland (1999).

TYLER, Alfred
Balfour & Manson, Edinburgh
(0131) 200 1210
fred.tyler@balfour-manson.co.uk
Specialisation: Partner in Litigation Department. Main area of practice is personal injury (with special interest in head and spinal injuries) and medical negligence (with a special interest in birth cases). Also handles general commercial (including defamation and professional negligence) and aviation matters including the House of Lords cases of Herd v Clyde Helicopters Ltd and King v Bristow Helicopters Ltd. Has extensive experience in major multi-party actions.
Prof. Memberships: SSC; NP; Association of Personal Injury Lawyers (EC Member); Spinal Injuries Association; Headway; Governor of Personal Injury Panel of the Law Society of Scotland.
Career: Qualified in 1975, having joined *Balfour & Manson* in 1973. Became a Partner in 1978.
Personal: Born 27 January 1951. Educated at Daniel Stewart's College, Edinburgh 1956-69 and Edinburgh University 1969-73. Enjoys golf. Lives in Edinburgh.

WALKER, Ian
Russell Jones & Walker, London
(020) 7339 6346
Specialisation: Chairman and joint senior partner of personal injury department. Has specialised in plaintiff personal injury since 1975. Acted in the then largest CICB award in 1988. Also the then largest ever court fatal award (£920,000) in 1991. Lead solicitor in the Kings Cross fire cases. Regular lecturer for IBC, Jordans, Euroforum, Hawksmere and others. Immediate past president of Association of Personal Injury Lawyers. Former co-chair, International Section of Association of Trial Lawyers of America. 1993-95, co-ordinator for Information Technology Group APIL. Member of Board of Governors, Association of Trial Lawyers of America. Member of ABI and IUA Rehabilitation working parties. Senior Fellow, College of Personal Injury Law. Member of Executive Board, College of Personal Injury Law. Member of Editorial Board, Journal of Personal Injury Litigation. CEDR - accredited mediator. Vice-president, Bodily Injury Claims Management Association.
Prof. Memberships: Association of Personal Injury Lawyers (hon life member); Association of Trial Lawyers of America; Law Society; Holborn Law Society; Medico-Legal Society; Association of Plaintiff Lawyers of Australia; Society for Computers and the Law; London Solicitors Litigation Association; South African Association of Personal Injury Lawyers.
Career: Qualified in 1974. Joined *Russell Jones & Walker* in 1968, becoming a partner in 1977.
Publications: Co-author of 'Tribunal Practice and procedure 1985', 'Know-How for Personal Injury Lawyers 1993 and 1997', and editor in chief of the 'Journal of Personal Injury Litigation 1994/5'.
Personal: Born 15 April 1950. Attended Whitgift School 1961-68. Governor of an independent school. Leisure interests include music, golf, gardening, cooking and walking. Lives in Caterham, Surrey.

WEBSTER, John
Veale Wasbrough, Bristol
(0117) 925 2020
jwebster@vwl.co.uk
Specialisation: Personal injury, acting for claimants in accident and disease cases. Special interest in head and spinal injury cases and fatal accident cases. Many asbestos injury and post-traumatic stress disorder cases. Much experience of employers' liability, road accidents (including multi-party cases, Paddington rail crash, South African bus crash, M4 Hungerford multi-vehicle and Avonmouth explosion) and product liability. Some interest in sports and holiday injury cases.
Prof. Memberships: Fellow of the College of Personal Injury Law; chairman of the Civil Courts committee, Bristol. Member of Bristol Law Society Council; Association of Personal Injury Lawyers; Bristol Medico Legal Society; panel member of Law Society Personal Injury Panel; Spinal Injuries Association; Headway; MIND; Roadpeace.
Career: Qualified 1985. Joined *Veale Wasbrough* 1988. Partner in 1994 and head of the firm's personal injury team since 1996.
Personal: Born 1961. Manchester University.

WHITEHEAD, Peter
James Chapman & Co, Manchester
(0161) 828 8000
insurancelit@james-chapman.co.uk
Specialisation: Acts for insurers defending catastrophic personal injury claims arising out of employers' liability, public liability and road traffic accidents. He is one of a select group of solicitors from across the country to be appointed by some of the UK's leading insurance companies to handle claims in excess of £1m.
Prof. Memberships: Law Society, FOIL, Manchester Law Society.
Career: Educated at Leeds Business School (1980 CPE, 1981 LSF), Leeds University (BA Hons English). Articled at *James Chapman & Co* 1981, Partner since 1985.
Personal: Born 1958, married with three children. Enjoys theatre, classical music, skiing, squash, cricket, football, rugby and long distance running.

WILLIAMS, Alun C
Hay & Kilner, Newcastle upon Tyne
(0191) 232 8345

WILLIAMS, Gareth
Hugh James, Cardiff
(029) 2022 4871
gareth.williams@hughjames.com
See under Litigation, p.570

WILLIAMS, Robin
Leo Abse & Cohen, Cardiff
(029) 2038 3252

WILSON, Timothy
Kennedys, London
(020) 7614 3683
t.wilson@kennedys.com
Specialisation: Head of *Kennedys'* General Liability Unit specialising in employers' liability, industrial disease, product and public liability claims. Has particular experience in the handling of catastrophic claims many involving rehabilitation. Practice includes coverage issues and also non-personal injury losses arising under public and product liability insurance policies. Over the last year, much time has been directed to personal injury claims following recent railway disasters and work related stress claims.
Prof. Memberships: FOIL; Member of the FOIL EL/PL special interest group.
Career: Qualified in 1979; appointed Partner with *Kennedys* in 1986.
Personal: Graduate of Birmingham University; after a training contract in Bristol has worked in London since qualification as a defendant/insurer solicitor. Interests include industrial archaeology and spending time in France.

WOOD, Michael
Simpson & Marwick, Edinburgh
(0131) 557 1545
michael.wood@simpmar.com
Specialisation: Represents a number of major insurers in complex personal injury claims, and acts for other professional bodies and local authorities in fatal accident and other inquiries. Has a particular interest in claims in the self-employed and on behalf of children.
Prof. Memberships: Law Society of Scotland.
Career: Qualified 1979, having obtained a first class honours degree from the University of Edinburgh. Partner in the Litigation Department since 1981.

ZINDANI, Jeffry
Russell Jones & Walker, Birmingham
(0121) 643 6800
Specialisation: Main area of practice is for claimant personal injury victims.

Acted for emergency service workers and steel workers in back injury claims. Developed one of the first corporate killing units in the UK and has advised both trades unions and family members in fatal accident cases. Also advises on professional negligence issues and has acted as an expert for the OSS.

Prof. Memberships: Member of the Law Society Personal Injury Panel and APIL.
Career: Qualified in 1989 and joined *RJW* the same year. Was a Partner from 1994 and managed their Birmingham office until May 2002 before setting up Forum Law, an online claimant personal injury practice.

Publications: Author of 'Manual Handling Law and Litigation', 1998 and 'Health and Safety Law: A Modern Guide', 2002, Emis Publishing. Several articles relating to personal injury and health and safety law and frequently lectures to practitioners.

Personal: Born on 4 July 1963. Attended Moseley Comprehensive School and has an MA in Industrial Relations from Keele. Can be contacted by email at forumlaw.co.uk

PLANNING

London: 639; The Regions: 642; Scotland: 647; Profiles: 649

Research approved by BMRB For this edition, **Chambers'** researchers conducted 6,582 interviews – 3,900 with law firms, 511 with barristers and 2,171 with clients. The validity of the research was scrutinised by BMRB International, who audited both the methodology and the results at our offices in London. They interviewed **Chambers'** researchers and cross-checked sample interviews. Details of the audit appear on page 7.

OVERVIEW The government's recently published Green Paper has been heralded as a reinvention of the planning system. After the problems highlighted by the four-year, £83 million inquiry into T5 at Heathrow, its objective is to speed things up and improve transparency. While it is anticipated that there will be fewer medium-sized inquiries as a result, most commentators believe that there is no substitute for large-scale inquiries for controversial major projects. A 'hot topic' throughout much of 2001, the effect of the Human Rights Act on the planning system has proven a damp squib following the House of Lords' judgement in the Alconbury case. Wranglings continue over third party right of appeal continue, with the industry blaming planning delays for substantial losses. The government's recent proposal that some large-scale developments be decided by MPs rather than inquiries, however, has provoked a backlash from environmentalists.

LONDON

PLANNING — LONDON

[1] Berwin Leighton Paisner
[2] Denton Wilde Sapte
SJ Berwin
[3] CMS Cameron McKenna
Herbert Smith
Linklaters
Nabarro Nathanson
[4] Clifford Chance
Lovells
Norton Rose
[5] Ashurst Morris Crisp
Osborne Clarke
Theodore Goddard
[6] DJ Freeman
Dechert
Fladgate Fielder
Forsters
Gouldens
Lawrence Graham
Macfarlanes
Olswang
Slaughter and May
Stephenson Harwood
Travers Smith Braithwaite

This book is the product of 6,582 1/2 hour interviews. See p.7 for BMRB audit. Within each band, firms are listed alphabetically.

BERWIN LEIGHTON PAISNER (see firm details p.866) According to clients and competitors, the team remains "*clearly ahead of the pack*" due to its critical mass, breadth and depth, national coverage, and fantastic client base. The firm's investment in the area continues to bear fruit with a group that is not only "*technically excellent*" but crucially comprises "*friendly people who are sensible to deal with.*" At the helm, **Ian Trehearne** (see p.655) possesses "*huge reserves of experience.*" Felt by clients to be "*one of the area's young guns,*" **Tim Hellier** (see p.652) continues to impress all who encounter him, whilst **Tim Pugh** (see p.653) is known for his "*meticulous mind.*" **Tim Smith** (see p.654) also won applause from clients. The group, which boasts a detailed understanding and experience of the public sector, continues to secure planning permission for development companies. Other clients include financial institutions, utilities and transport operators. The team was recently successful in securing an unchallengeable planning permission for the New Medway Cement Works for Blue Circle/Lafarge. Inquiry work has included acting for Peel Airports in the Doncaster Finingley Airport, representing Liverpool City Council in the inquiry into Paradise Walk, and assisted the Wiggins Group in the inquiry into the East London Racecourse. **Clients** Tesco; Blue Circle/Lafarge; Land Securities; Southern Water; University of Brighton; Sunley Homes; Westfield Shoppingtowns.

DENTON WILDE SAPTE (see firm details p.935) The "*large, strategically-minded*" team is felt to be of a higher calibre than many of its rivals. Underpinned by strength in related areas such as public law, PFI and property finance, it was strongly endorsed by interviewees for "*looking at planning situations in the context of a commercial deal.*" Clients benefit from the knowledge fostered through team members' secondments to public bodies like the GLA. The firm's extended national reach following the recent launch of its formal planning alliance with Leeds-based niche firm Wilbraham & Co, also gives it an edge. **Margaret Casely-Hayford** (see p.649) was praised by clients for providing an "*excellent service,*" whilst "*aggressive fighter*" **Stephen Ashworth** (see p.649) is admired for his "*style, knowledge and ease with clients.*" "*Pragmatic, intelligent, approachable*" **Sandra Banks** (see p.649) completes the triumvirate of ranked practitioners. The team advised Alexandra Research on the £150 million development of a 400 plus unit urban village on a site in Chigwell within the Metropolitan Green Belt. It also advised Grosvenor Ltd on all planning aspects of the redevelopment of Liverpool's main retail area, a 42 acre site, and Grantchester on the application for a retail park development. **Clients** Sainsbury's; Marks & Spencer; London Borough of Barking & Dagenham; English Partnerships; Carter Commercial; City Centre Restaurants; Department of the Environment, Transport & the Regions.

SJ BERWIN (see firm details p.867) This "*small, high-quality*" team continues to make its mark in the area. Among its "*first-class players,*" interviewees singled out **Patricia Thomas** (see p.654) for her "*assertive manner and extreme skill.*" She recently advised Walton Group on a major retail development in Liverpool City Centre, and Mercia Waste in connection with an integrated waste management facility. She is supported by "*clever and easy-going*" **Simon Ricketts** (see p.654). "*Co-operative with excellent people skills,*" and extremely popular with clients, he is said to provide a "*strong focus for his team.*" He was recently instructed by the London Eye Company on its proposal to retain the BA London Eye on a permanent basis. He also represented Prudential in connection with a compulsory purchase inquiry in Bradford, and has led judicial review proceedings brought against the London Borough of Hackney and London Underground by Planit Events relating to the East London Line Extension. **Clients** Walton Group; London City Airport; Prudential; Marks & Spencer; London Eye Company; British Land.

CMS CAMERON MCKENNA (see firm details p.914) The group regularly advises on a mix of large infrastructure projects, CPO, housing and retail developments, and is particularly rated by the market for its "*advocacy expertise.*" "*Skilled, knowledgeable*" **Tony Kitson** (see p.652) leads a team whose "*great people and excellent client base*" are acknowledged by clients and competitors alike. He advised Berkeley Homes on planning issues relating to the development of Chelsea Bridge Wharf, and on planning agreements for the Wellcome Trust's new headquarters. The team continued to act for the applicants, BAA, on the granting of planning

www.ChambersandPartners.com

PLANNING ■ LONDON

LEADING INDIVIDUALS

1
- **ASHWORTH Stephen** Denton Wilde Sapte
- **CUNLIFFE Michael** Forsters
- **GALLIMORE Michael** Lovells
- **GREENWOOD Brian** Norton Rose
- **HELLIER Tim** Berwin Leighton Paisner
- **JACKSON Ray** Linklaters
- **KITSON Tony** CMS Cameron McKenna
- **MAX Richard** Olswang
- **RICKETTS Simon** SJ Berwin
- **THOMAS Patricia** SJ Berwin

2
- **CASELY-HAYFORD Margaret** Denton Wilde Sapte
- **CURNOW Tony** Ashurst Morris Crisp
- **DYER Carl** Osborne Clarke
- **HALL Brian** Clifford Chance
- **HILLEBRON Richard** Slaughter and May
- **PUGH Tim** Berwin Leighton Paisner
- **QUAYLE Sophie** Herbert Smith
- **ROBINSON Patrick** Herbert Smith
- **TREHEARNE Ian** Berwin Leighton Paisner

3
- **BANKS Sandra** Denton Wilde Sapte
- **EVANS Douglas** Theodore Goddard
- **EVANS Martin** Nabarro Nathanson
- **HAWKINS David** Nabarro Nathanson
- **HUGHES Norna** Nabarro Nathanson
- **JEEPS Barry** Stephenson Harwood
- **LEA Alison** Travers Smith Braithwaite

4
- **BLANEY Trevor** Lawrence Graham
- **FONGENIE Wesley** Osborne Clarke
- **FRASER Moira** Fladgate Fielder
- **HOWARD Karen** DJ Freeman
- **JACKSON Andrew** Macfarlanes
- **QUALTROUGH John** Simmons & Simmons
- **SMITH Tim** Berwin Leighton Paisner
- **TRUE Justin** Dechert
- **WATKINS David** Linklaters
- **WELLS Martin** Stephenson Harwood

UP AND COMING
- **O'TOOLE Eliza** Macfarlanes

See individuals' profiles p.649

permission for Terminal 5 at Heathrow Airport. **Clients** BAA; Berkeley Group; Crest Nicholson Properties; Crown Estate Commissioners; Pricoa; Taylor Woodrow; Westminster City Council; Sainsbury's.

HERBERT SMITH (see firm details p.992) Commercial property, environment and PFI know-how provide a solid foundation for this "*large and dynamic*" team. With a reputation for handling major, one-off projects, it is described by peers as "*highly commercial with impressive clients*." Its "*bunch of young, keen assistants*" is led by "*brainy and ambitious duo*" Sophie Quayle (see p.654) and Patrick Robinson (see p.654). Advice is given in relation to the spectrum of major city office developments, large residential schemes and retail projects, with the team developing a niche profile for energy-related matters and river-related devel-opment. It has also advised on several judicial review cases on behalf of applicants and respondents. Recent instructions include advising Allied London Properties on a range of redevelopment proposals in Bracknell, St Albans, Leatherhead and Manchester. The group also advised Chelsfield on development proposals and regional planning guidance for the 1.5-million sq ft Merry Hill shopping centre and surrounding area. **Clients** Allied London Properties; CABE; Chelsfield; Circadian; Lattice Property Holdings; Selfridges; Sheffield City Council; Swindon Borough Council.

LINKLATERS (see firm details p.1043) A triumphant year for the "*dedicated, thorough*" team has seen its profile soar following its recent success on the controversial Heron project inquiry. Said by clients to be "*worth every penny*," the team is characterised by competitors as "*young and go-getting with plenty of commercial nous.*" With a client roster that features a string of headline names, Ray Jackson (see p.652) is said to be "*client-friendly with no airs or graces*" and to possess a "*good grasp of London issues.*" He spearheaded the team advising Heron Corporation on all aspects of the proposed tower, and the BBC on the planning application and environmental statement for its 1 million sq ft scheme at White City and on the redevelopment of Broadcasting House. Other highlights for the team include resisting a judicial review against Fulham Football Club's proposal for a new 30,000 seater stadium. David Watkins (see p.655) has been involved in some big deals this year, and retains a market profile. **Clients** Heron Corporation; BBC; Fulham Stadium; Lend Lease; SRA; Development Securities.

NABARRO NATHANSON (see firm details p.1080) The team handles the whole spectrum of work, including CPOs, local authority and regeneration schemes, and is praised by clients for its "*focus and enthusiasm.*" A slight dip in profile is attributed by peers to the recent loss of Gary Graves. Nevertheless, the "*reliable*" department continues to house a handful of stars, who advise many of the top UK property companies as well as local authorities. "*Superb in terms of client care*," veteran David Hawkins (see p.652) is widely respected as "*the CPO guru.*" Clients appreciate Martin Evans' "*strong, definitive*" advice, whilst department head Norna Hughes (see p.652) has built up a loyal following and is particularly noted for her projects expertise. The team recently advised Hammerson on Brent Cross, as part of a strategic partnership with the public sector and major stakeholders to regenerate Cricklewood by means of a 10-million sq ft mixed-use scheme. It also advised Spitalfields Development Group on the redevelopment of the remaining part of the Spitalfields Development site. **Clients** Costco; Spitalfields Development Group; Hammerson UK Properties; EniChem; Land Securities; Brunel University; London Borough of Hillingdon; Slough Estates.

CLIFFORD CHANCE (see firm details p.911) The group advises its base of large blue-chip clients on matters including conservation listings and infrastructure agreements. Deemed by interviewees to offer "*a blue-ribbon service*," recent work has involved advising on a range of major office schemes in the West End, City and Dockland areas. "*Unassuming*" Brian Hall (see p.651) remains at the helm and is held in high esteem by all in the field. The group continues to advise the Burford Group on a challenge to the validity of a 1959 planning permission for industrial development, covering some 170 hectares of land. It assists Safeway on all planning matters affecting its UK property portfolio, and has recently acted for Railtrack on the controversial Bishopsgate Goodsyard scheme. **Clients** Burford Holdings; Safeway; Railtrack; Gallagher Estates.

LOVELLS (see firm details p.1045) Regarded by peers as a "*rock-solid outfit*," it benefits from the expertise of an "*impressive young group of broad-based, competent planners*" presided over by "*excellent strategist*" Michael Gallimore (see p.651). Clearly one of the field's most eminent practitioners, he is widely admired for his "*strong, authoritative advice.*" He and his team recently assisted Argent St George on the planning aspects of the redevelopment of King's Cross Central. This will involve a site of over 50 acres next to King's Cross and St Pancras stations, which is due to become a major European transport interchange. **Clients** Ballymore Properties; Fairview New Homes; Cory Environmental; John Lewis; Argent Group; Land Securities; City and County of Swansea.

NORTON ROSE (see firm details p.1084) The department attracts high-quality work through an excellent reputation, which competitors attribute to its "*commercial outlook.*" Brian Greenwood (see p.651), an established name in the field, continues to receive warm recommendations for both planning and environmental matters. Particularly noted for its expertise regarding wind farm projects, recent highlights for the team include assisting Hammerson, the Corporation of the City of London and Spitalfields Development Group in securing planning permission for an office scheme of 1 million sq ft. It is also acting for Associated British Ports on the proposed development of a new 400-acre container terminal at Dibden in the Port of Southampton. **Clients** Hammerson; Associated British Ports; Castle Cement; English Heritage; Corporation of the City of London; Exxon Mobil; Spitalfields Development Group.

ASHURST MORRIS CRISP (see firm details p.852) Competitors feel that the department is going through a period of uncertainty with the

LONDON ■ PLANNING

defection this year of Karen Howard to DJ Freeman. "*Popular*" **Tony Curnow** (see p.650) is currently rebuilding the team, which is bolstered by the firm's excellent commercial property, PFI and corporate practices. It recently acted for the London Borough of Ealing on the proposed development of a 54-acre former industrial site in West London into Grand Union Village. This environmentally friendly scheme will include 705 residential 'eco-standard' homes, 177 of them available as affordable housing and a further 70 reserved for key workers. Other highlights include advising Tesco on planning and highways negotiations with Stockport Metropolitan Borough Council. **Clients** Tesco; Ipswich Town Football Club; London Borough of Ealing; Chelsfield; Port of London Authority; Polestar Properties.

OSBORNE CLARKE (see firm details p.1090) The team covers the gamut of planning issues, including retail, housing, leisure and transport sector advice, infrastructure development and urban regeneration, for its varied client base. Having absorbed the niche planning and property outfit McGuiness Finch in 2001, the firm continues to go from strength to strength. **Carl Dyer** is cementing his reputation as "*an impressive, focused lawyer, who is incredibly thorough and has a fantastic memory.*" He leads the department together with "*able and pleasant*" **Wesley Fongenie**. Recent highlights include assisting Raven Group with a 1.5-million sq ft leisure development at Unstone near Chesterfield, and securing planning permission for Asda for a major foodstore development at Thurmaston near Leicester. **Clients** Asda Stores; Bristol International Airport; Barratt Homes; DERA; Danish Bacon; Countryside Strategic Projects; Countryside Properties; HP Bulmer; Raven Group.

THEODORE GODDARD (see firm details p.1158) This has been a profitable year for the team, which is increasingly sought after by clients for its cutting-edge property and waste expertise. Solicitor advocate **Douglas Evans** (see p.650) is known and liked by peers and clients. He led the team advising Minosus on the public inquiry for its proposal to store hazardous waste in the UK's only rock salt mine. Other work includes advising Hampshire Waste Services on securing planning permission for a 165,000-tonne incinerator at Marchwood, near Southampton, and successfully defending the judicial review brought by third parties, challenging the grant under the Human Rights Act 1998. **Clients** Minosus; Hampshire Waste Services; Bryant Homes; Waste Recycling Group; Thames Water Utilities; Lakeside Energy; Persimmon Homes.

DJ FREEMAN (see firm details p.939) The arrival of **Karen Howard** from Ashursts has breathed new life into this department, following its loss of Richard Max to Olswang. Heaped with praise by rivals, she is said to have an "*excellent manner with clients,*" and to "*work tirelessly.*" Clients appreciate the dedicated team's "*superb service.*" Advice is given on large masterplan schemes, High Court challenges, appeal work, compulsory purchase and planning agreements. Recent work includes advising Fulham Stadium on the redevelopment of the existing stadium, involving replacement of existing structures and construction of a new 30,000 seat arena. The team has also acted for KICC on its proposal for a 30,000 sq ft regeneration project in Hackney. **Clients** English Partnerships; Fulham Stadium; Carillion; Elmbridge Borough Council; NHS Executive; Warner Estates Holdings; Land Securities; Cherokee; AXA Sun Life.

DECHERT (see firm details p.934) This multi-disciplinary practice is headed by former planning officer **Justin True** (see p.655). Though rivals claim that he has maintained a low profile this year, the firm's loyal clients praise his "*excellent grasp of the ins and outs of the planning process.*" The team advises a growing core of property, retail and investment clients on a broad range of planning and related issues. Recent examples include assisting Waitrose on securing planning permission for a replacement town centre store in Romsey, and successfully appealing against a refusal by Westminster Council for the use of premises near Regent Street as a wine bar/restaurant on behalf of Crown Estates. **Clients** Bhs; Chinacorp; Furnitureland; Qoin; Quadrant Estates; Rhodia; Waitrose.

FLADGATE FIELDER (see firm details p.957) **Moira Fraser** (see p.651) leads a small team, which is recognised by peers for its planning and advocacy expertise. It regularly advises on compulsory purchase and section 106 agreements, and is undertaking an increasing volume of advocacy work in the context of informal inquiries. The team recently acted for Capital & Regional on the relocation of Swansea Football Club to a new stadium, including the development of a new retail park. **Clients** Capital & Regional; Lower Mill Estate; Redrow Homes.

FORSTERS (see firm details p.960) A new addition to *Chambers*' rankings this year, commentators applaud the man many consider the country's "*foremost section 106 practitioner,*" **Michael Cunliffe** (see p.650), on his success since arriving at the firm. Supported by a good team, all agree that he is "*reeling in quality work.*" The group has acted recently for Gloucester City Council on the proposals by Granchester Properties to develop the former Gloucester Cattle Market site and adjacent land. **Clients** Gloucester City Council; Crown Dilmun; Chester City Council.

GOULDENS (see firm details p.976) Though planning colossus David Cooper has retired from the firm to set up on his own, the practice remains safe in the hands of Angela Turner and her team. Handling advice and advocacy in relation to a number of leading developments, recent highlights include submitting Arsenal Football Club's planning application for its proposed 3 million sq ft redevelopment of three sites in the Borough of Islington. It is also advising Pillar Property on a planning application to Barnet Borough Council involving a mixed-retail, office and residential development supported by a substantial new transport infrastructure. **Clients** Pillar Property; Arlington Securities; Kimberley Developments; Benchmark Group; Burford Holdings; Land Securities; Arsenal Football Club; Hawksmoor Estates.

LAWRENCE GRAHAM (see firm details p.1031) An "*energetic*" department, it is respected by rivals for its advice to local authorities and developers on a range of retail, leisure and waste schemes. Spearheaded by "*helpful*" **Trevor Blaney**, who undertakes a substantial amount of public inquiry advocacy, the team continues to attract lots of impressive work. It advised the major objectors, BT and Midlands Electricity, in defeating Gloucester City Council's major Blackfriars CPO, both in the High Court and at an eight-month CPO inquiry. It also assisted East Sussex County Council in successfully opposing Southern Water's proposed waste treatment works at Brighton. **Clients** BT; Midlands Electricity; East Sussex County Council; Waverley Borough Council; London Development Agency.

MACFARLANES (see firm details p.1047) The integrated planning and public law team is felt by peers to benefit from the firm's powerful property and corporate departments. It is credited with "*great clients and several excellent practitioners,*" and has been visible on large NHS schemes. "*Charming*" **Andrew Jackson** remains at the helm, while **Eliza O'Toole**'s reputation for major infrastructure work is flourishing. Described as "*incredibly hardworking with real flair,*" clients agree that she "*gets into the meat of things.*" The team advised P&O and Shell UK on the proposed development of the London Gateway on the North bank of the Thames at Thurrock, potentially the largest new commercial port of its type in Europe. **Clients** P&O; Shell UK; Oscar Faber; Weston Homes; Scottish Life.

OLSWANG (see firm details p.1087) "*Voluble, enthusiastic*" **Richard Max** (see p.653) heads the department. Chairman of the London Law Society Planning sub-committee, he is well known in the community as an "*irrepressible advocate.*" Alongside inquiry advocacy, the team is attracting an increasing volume of CPO work and continues to advise on major development projects, such as the proposed redevelopment of part of the Millennium Quarter for Capital & Provident/World Trade Centre London. It has also recently advised Pelham Homes on planning agreements for several newbuild housing

PLANNING ■ THE SOUTH/THAMES VALLEY

developments. **Clients** Great Portlands Estates; Pelham Homes; Capital & Provident.

SLAUGHTER AND MAY (see firm details p.1140) The property, construction and planning group continues to be visible, advising property and developer clients on securing planning permission and section 106 agreements. A senior assistant within the litigation department, **Richard Hillebron** (see p.652) was singled out by clients as "*terrific and jolly nice too.*" The group is assisting FMR Corp on the planning aspects of the redevelopment of 1 million sq ft of commercial space in the Docklands, and its relationship to other nearby schemes. **Clients** FMR Corp; City Inns; Derwent Valley.

STEPHENSON HARWOOD (see firm details p.1147) The team is maintaining its popularity and winning increasing instructions on larger long-term projects. Head of planning **Barry Jeeps** (see p.652) elicits an enthusiastic response. He is warmly praised by clients for "*getting deeply involved in cases*" and "*always coming up with brilliant ideas.*" Though lower profile, **Martin Wells** (see p.655) has been involved in some impressive deals. Recent highlights for the team include acting for Peel Holdings in the public inquiry into its proposed conversion of the former RAF Finningley airfield near Doncaster into a civil airport, and advising Canterbury College on a planning application for the proposed relocation of its main campus to a site on the edge of Canterbury. **Clients** Peel Holdings; Canterbury College; London Development Agency; Christie's; St. Martin's Property Group; KPMG.

TRAVERS SMITH BRAITHWAITE (see firm details p.1166) The firm continues to advise chiefly on town centre regeneration schemes, although it has also appeared on cases involving human rights and judicial review. The practice is built around "*extremely intelligent and switched on*" **Alison Lea** (see p.653). Recent instructions include assisting Lend Lease on major retail proposals in Norwich and the redevelopment of Solihull Town Centre, and advising Lafarge Redland Aggregates on the planning implications of the burning of solvent-derived fuel in lime kilns, which involved successfully defending judicial review proceedings at first instance and in the Court of Appeal. **Clients** Lend Lease Norwich; Multi Development Corporation; Lafarge Redland Aggregates.

OTHER NOTABLE PRACTITIONERS John Qualtrough (see p.654) of Simmons & Simmons has had a lower profile of late, but remains respected by market commentators.

THE SOUTH

PLANNING
■ THE SOUTH

1. **Bond Pearce** Southampton
2. **DMH** Brighton
3. **Brachers** Maidstone
   Horsey Lightly Fynn Newbury
4. **Lester Aldridge** Southampton

LEADING INDIVIDUALS

1. **TRINICK Marcus** Bond Pearce
2. **ABRAHAM Henry** Brachers
   ALLEN Tony DMH
3. **HIGNETT Andrew** Lester Aldridge

This book is the product of 6,582 1/2 hour interviews. See p.7 for BMRB audit.
Within each band, firms are listed alphabetically. See individuals' profiles p.649

BOND PEARCE (see firm details p.879) This team is recognised nationally for its "*intricate understanding*" of general planning and CPO issues. A hallmark of the practice is its focus on development projects subject to environmental impact assessment, including landfill sites, port development and, in particular, renewable energy schemes including on and offshore wind farms. The team, led by "*fantastically commercial*" **Marcus Trinick** (see p.363), continues to be visible on the headline Dibden Bay inquiry. In this case the team is acting for Associated British Ports for its 250-hectares Dibden Terminal proposal, which has proceeded to an ongoing public local inquiry that began in November 2001. **Clients** Associated British Ports; Devonport Management; Scottish Power; Renewable Energy Systems; Next Generation.

DMH (see firm details p.940) The "*enthusiastic and responsive*" planning group offers a complete multidisciplinary service to a varied regional clientele. Spearheading the team, "*thorough, careful*" **Tony Allen** (see p.649) advised Brighton & Hove Albion on its development project for a £50 million new football stadium. Other recent work includes advising on the Brighton library complex, a PPP between Brighton & Hove City Council and the Mill Group, which will involve the £45 million development of a prime city centre site to include hotels, shops, restaurants and housing as well as the library. **Clients** CSMA Leisure Properties; Brighton & Hove Albion.

BRACHERS (see firm details p.886) The firm maintains a solid reputation for handling development-related work for a variety of clients, both large and small. "*Sharp, articulate*" **Henry Abraham** (see p.649) is a respected figure in both the environmental and town planning fields. Recent highlights for the practice include advising on the redevelopment of a redundant hospital site for housing, which involved a planning appeal and affordable housing issues. It also represented clients over CPOs before the Lands Tribunal, and secured an acquittal representing clients in a tree preservation order prosecution in the Magistrates Court. **Clients** Manufacturers; developers; private landowners.

HORSEY LIGHTLY FYNN Fielding a mixed team of consultants, chartered town planners and lawyers, the department offers clients a 'one-stop shop.' With Lionel Fynn at the helm, it handles the range of general planning matters including urban regeneration, planning appeals, inquiries and High Court challenges, and is known in particular for its experience in one-day inquiries. **Clients** Flower Brothers; Murco Petroleum; Kings Oak; Bowlplex.

LESTER ALDRIDGE (see firm details p.1038) The group offers a comprehensive service with particular strength in compulsory purchase, public inquiries and compensation issues before the Lands Tribunal. It has a recognised national as well as regional presence, achieving visibility in a range of housing, industrial, commercial and retail schemes. **Andrew Hignett** heads the "*enthusiastic and efficient*" team. Recent highlights include advising on a detailed application for a high-profile factory outlet scheme and a 105-unit waterfront development, including handling a contested highway order and negotiating a section 106 agreement. **Clients** Goulden Properties; Ibstock; Portland Port.

THAMES VALLEY

CLARKS (see firm details p.908) The group's "*solid reputation*" for general planning work remains uncontested, though it is too early to gauge the effect of former practice head Simon Dimmick's departure to Blandy & Blandy. It is known to handle a steady stream of general advisory matters for those seeking planning permission, as well as enforcement appeal work. **Clients** Blue Circle/Lafarge.

THAMES VALLEY/SOUTH WEST ■ PLANNING

PLANNING
■ THAMES VALLEY

1 Clarks *Reading*
Jameson & Hill *Hertford*
Pitmans *Reading*

LEADING INDIVIDUALS

1 DIMMICK Simon *Blandy & Blandy*
DRUKARZ Daniel *Pitmans*
JAMESON Robert *Jameson & Hill*
VALENTINE Richard *Pitmans*

This book is the product of 6,582 1/2 hour interviews. See p.7 for BMRB audit.
Within each band, firms are listed alphabetically. See individuals' profiles p.649

JAMESON & HILL The staple diet of this practice, led by **Robert Jameson**, consists of planning inquiries and enforcement appeals, with the team undertaking its own advocacy. Its workload is divided between local authority and private client matters, with recent instructions relating to retail impact, housing appeals, and greenbelt issues. **Clients** Somerfield; London & Cambridge Properties.

PITMANS (see firm details p.1103) Litigator **Richard Valentine** (see p.655) and development specialist **Daniel Drukarz** (see p.650) form an "*ambitious*" partnership, which is distinguished from many regional rivals by its large, London-based workload. With considerable experience in major new town development and town centre refurbishment projects, as well as brownfield regeneration schemes, recent highlights include advising Tottenham Hotspur FC on its successful planning application to redevelop the East Stand at White Hart Lane, increasing capacity from 36,000 to 44,000. It also advised a landowner on the strategic planning aspects of a 250,000 sq ft mixed-use redevelopment scheme in Lewisham, incorporating a 27-storey landmark tower adjacent to a DLR station. **Clients** Alfred McAlpine Homes; Boots; London & Cambridge Properties; Safeway; Somerfield; Tottenham Hotspur; Brookmill Estates.

OTHER NOTABLE PRACTITIONERS Respected **Simon Dimmick** (see p.650) has moved from Clarks to Blandy & Blandy. It is anticipated that he will develop the planning practice at this firm.

SOUTH WEST

PLANNING
■ SOUTH WEST

1 Clarke Willmott & Clarke *Bristol*
2 Bevan Ashford *Bristol, Exeter*
Burges Salmon *Bristol*
Osborne Clarke *Bristol*
3 Davies and Partners *Gloucester*
Stephens & Scown *Exeter*
TLT Solicitors *Bristol*

LEADING INDIVIDUALS

1 ENGERT Nick *Clarke Willmott & Clarke*
PASTERFIELD Stephen *Clarke Willmott & Clarke*
ROBINSON Patrick *Burges Salmon*
2 BOSWORTH John *Bevan Ashford*
EVANS Katherine *TLT Solicitors*
GIBBS Kevin *Osborne Clarke*
WOOD David *Bevan Ashford*

This book is the product of 6,582 1/2 hour interviews. See p.7 for BMRB audit.
Within each band, firms are listed alphabetically. See individuals' profiles p.649

CLARKE WILLMOTT & CLARKE (see firm details p.907) The undisputed planning stars of the South West, peers and clients applaud the team on its winning combination of "*size, breadth and depth.*" It handles a high volume of local and national work and is recommended in particular for its house building expertise. "*Leading light*" **Nick Engert** (see p.650) is said by clients to be "*great for inquiry advocacy.*" In addition to planning applications, he regularly advises on environmental matters, development control, listed buildings and conservation. "*A reliable, sensible lawyer,*" **Stephen Pasterfield** (see p.653) is an experienced advocate in the planning and environmental fields. The team recently advised Countryside Residential (South West) in negotiating a complex planning obligation to allow the redevelopment of a brownfield site in Cardiff, with the construction of 40 apartments and eight town houses. **Clients** Countryside Residential (South West); Laing Homes; Torridge District Council; Prowting Homes (South East); NHS Estates; Edward Ware New Homes; Winchester Property Developments; Persimmon Homes South East; Westbury Homes.

BEVAN ASHFORD (see firm details p.869) A "*small but active*" outfit, it is seen to be motoring ahead with regional development and NHS-related work. The firm's property and PFI profile lends further weight to the practice, which has considerable expertise in urban regeneration and the redevelopment of brownfield sites. "*Personable*" **John Bosworth** (see p.649) spearheads the team, supported by **David Wood** (see p.656). It recently advised on the redevelopment of a number of former NHS sites, including Roundway Hospital, Devizes, which involved the conversion of listed curtilage buildings into over 200 houses. Recent inquiry work has included acting for South Somerset Council in connection with a discontinuance notice seeking the cessation of an agricultural contractors yard and repair business in Somerton. **Clients** SWRDA; SEEDA; NHS Executive South and West; Quada Developments; Capitec; Living Homes.

BURGES SALMON (see firm details p.894) "*Robust, good on his feet and incredibly thorough,*" **Patrick Robinson** (see p.654) enjoys considerable popularity amongst clients and heads a team best known for high-profile telecoms work and advocacy. While its "*adversarial*" approach may not be to everybody's taste, nobody doubts its regional and national planning muscle. Additional areas of expertise include minerals and compulsory purchase work. Recent highlights include advising 186K and Hutchison 3G on the construction of new national telecoms networks, and assisting COLAS with its application for a major landfill site and a review of mineral permission. **Clients** United Kingdom Nirex; Foster Yeoman; Orange; Basingstoke & Deane Borough Council; British Waterways; COLAS; Southern Electric.

OSBORNE CLARKE (see firm details p.1090) Planning and environment specialist **Kevin Gibbs** is deemed to be "*making his mark*" in the regional marketplace. With expertise in waste management, urban regeneration, energy and transport, he is dual-qualified as a solicitor and chartered town planner. Visible assisting its blue-chip corporate and developer client base in a range of planning matters, the team has recently advised Bristol International Airport on noise issues and general development proposals. **Clients** Somerfield Stores; HP Bulmer; Bristol International Airport.

DAVIES AND PARTNERS (see firm details p.929) The group, which includes Michael Morgan, retains its niche status for house building work. Recent advice has chiefly been in relation to application matters and planning agreements, and the outfit is finding that a higher proportion of its work is non-contentious than in the past. Town and village green issues in particular are rising to the fore. **Clients** Westbury; Persimmon; Crest.

STEPHENS & SCOWN Ian Lamond heads up a practice with expertise in rural planning issues. It handles planning matters for the regional mining and waste disposal, leisure and farming industries. The team recently represented a landowner when a local authority sought a judicial review of a permission it had granted for a factory outlet shopping centre. It also represented the Kaolin & Ball Clay Association at the Devon Minerals Local Plan inquiry. **Clients** Camping and holiday industries; farmers; regional housebuilders.

TLT SOLICITORS (see firm details p.1163) Housing and minerals lie at the heart of the

PLANNING ■ WALES/MIDLANDS

practice, which is led by "*confidence-inspiring*" **Katherine Evans** (see p.651). Work is mainly non-contentious and has recently included large volumes of residential development in Bristol. The team also regularly undertakes local plan inquiry work. Recent instructions include advising on a major house building proposal in Gloucester for Westbury Homes, Bovis Homes and Barratt Homes. Inquiry work has included a CPO claim relating to the Channel Tunnel Rail Link. **Clients** Edward Ware Homes; Hanson; Westbury Homes; Bovis Homes; Barratt Homes; private landowners; Crosby Group; Chase Homes.

WALES

PLANNING
■ WALES

1 Edwards Geldard Cardiff
   Eversheds Cardiff
   Morgan Cole Cardiff

LEADING INDIVIDUALS

1 BOSWALL Julian Morgan Cole
   EVANS Eric Eversheds
   MANSON Stephen Eversheds
   WILLIAMS Huw Edwards Geldard

This book is the product of 6,582 1/2 hour interviews. See p.7 for BMRB audit.
Within each band, firms are listed alphabetically. See individuals' profiles p.649

EDWARDS GELDARD (see firm details p.944) Firmly established as one of Wales' most active planning practices, the team handles a diet of development projects and enforcement matters on behalf of private individuals, local authorities and institutions. Head of department **Huw Williams** (see p.49), an expert in property and public law as well as planning, is warmly praised by clients for his "*supportive*" manner. The team recently advised Wrexham County Borough Council on the compulsory purchase of land for the Wrexham Industrial Estate improved access scheme. **Clients** Welsh Development Agency; Wales Millennium Centre; Wrexham County Borough Council; Rhondda Cynon Taff County Borough; Arts Council of Wales.

EVERSHEDS (see firm details p.949) Consistently recommended by competitors and clients for minerals and compulsory purchase matters, the team benefits from two leading players. **Eric Evans**' (see p.577) land authority background is felt to have provided him with a "*strong pedigree.*" Also involved in banking, PFI and property, he recently advised Bridgend County Borough Council on compensation claims in connection with the Bridgend Northern Distributor Road. **Stephen Manson** (see p.653) has also built up a substantial following and recently advised Hanson Aggregates South Wales on various minerals planning matters. **Clients** Bridgend County Borough Council; United News & Media; Hanson Aggregates; Tarmac; Blaenau Gwent County Borough Council.

MORGAN COLE (see firm details p.1075) This growing team, led by "*eminent*" **Julian Boswall**, advises a range of housing developers, development agencies, petrochemicals and property clients on the spectrum of planning issues. Renewable energy is an area of expertise, and the team works in tandem with the firm's property and PFI practices. Recent highlights include advising BP Oil on numerous planning issues arising out of its service station estate and other major sites. It also advised the Welsh Development Agency on planning issues relating to the development of a new business park next to the Cardiff International rail freight terminal. **Clients** Welsh Development Agency; Associated British Ports; Grosvenor Waterside; Persimmon Homes (Wales); TotalFinaElf; British Energy.

MIDLANDS

PLANNING
■ MIDLANDS

1 Marrons Leicester
2 Eversheds Birmingham
   Pinsent Curtis Biddle Birmingham
3 Wragge & Co Birmingham
4 Hewitson Becke + Shaw Northampton
   Shoosmiths Northampton
5 Browne Jacobson Nottingham
   Hammond Suddards Edge Birmingham
   Kent Jones and Done Stoke-on-Trent

LEADING INDIVIDUALS

1 BULL Rod Eversheds
   MARRON Peter Marrons
   THOMSON Morag Marrons
   WHITE Martin Pinsent Curtis Biddle
2 DAMMS Martin Pinsent Curtis Biddle
   HEMMING Dan Wragge & Co
   TAYLOR Peter Hewitson Becke + Shaw
3 EDMOND John Marrons
   GILBEY Iain Shoosmiths

This book is the product of 6,582 1/2 hour interviews. See p.7 for BMRB audit.
Within each band, firms are listed alphabetically. See individuals' profiles p.649

MARRONS (see firm details p.1055) Immensely respected by peers and clients, the team is felt to be "*well-resourced with great people.*" Rivals admitted "*it's nice to deal with a firm which knows what it's doing,*" while clients often prefer it for "*the more complex, high-profile*" cases. Experienced in the range of planning issues, including advocacy, the eponymous **Peter Marron** (see p.653) continues to preside over the team. He is supported by **John Edmond** (see p.650), who specialises in contentious town planning, compulsory purchase and public law, and "*extremely efficient*" **Morag Thomson** (see p.654), who draws on a wealth of contentious planning experience including judicial review and High Court challenges. The team advised on the proposed redevelopment of Alconbury Airfield in Cambridgeshire comprising up to 7 million sq ft of B8 development. This involved participating in the planning inquiry and conducting litigation under the Human Rights Act in the High Court and House of Lords. **Clients** Hallam Land Management; Prologis Developments; Wilson Bowden; Alconbury Developments; Persimmon Homes; Barratt East Midlands; Bryant Homes; local authorities.

EVERSHEDS (see firm details p.949) "*Enthusiastic advocate*" **Rod Bull** (see p.649) heads a practice that is known best for its litigation strength. Boasting a strong client base and able to draw upon the expertise of its national network, it advises house builders, local authorities and development agencies on general planning matters including compulsory purchase and listed buildings consent. Recent work includes advising Bryant Homes on major schemes in Swindon, including assisting with the necessary planning arrangements surrounding the construction of 4,500 houses and a football stadium. **Clients** Bryant Group; Northwest Development Agency; Wilcon Homes; Huntingdonshire District Council.

PINSENT CURTIS BIDDLE (see firm details p.1102) Peers and clients are quick to recommend the strong team, particularly for public sector work. It continues to build an excellent reputation, regularly acting for local authorities on large town centre schemes, often involving compulsory purchases. Clients singled out compulsory purchase expert **Martin White** (see p.655) for his "*strategic thinking and pragmatism.*" He acted for Bradford Metropolitan District Council on its regenerative compulsory order relating to the Broadway site. **Martin Damms** (see p.650) is also recommended for his work on regenerative projects for both the

MIDLANDS/EAST ANGLIA ■ PLANNING

public and private sectors. He recently handled issues including a section 106 agreement and an inquiry relating to an eight-hectare development in Denton, Manchester, for Reeb Properties. **Clients** IM Properties; Bradford Metropolitan District Council; Castlemore Securities; East Midlands International Airport; English Partnerships.

WRAGGE & CO (see firm details p.1197) A "*reliable team*," it is known for its activity for developers on town centre schemes. **Dan Hemming** is the name here, recommended to researchers for his "*quiet good sense and impressive knowledge.*" The group's client roster features a raft of well-known property companies, developers and house builders. Recent highlights include successfully appealing against an out of town retail development in Tunbridge Wells for Castlemore Securities, and acting for Taywood Homes on negotiating agreements for Grand Union Village, a mixed-use scheme including 600 dwellings and commercial developments. **Clients** Barteak Developments; Birmingham International Airport; Castlemore Securities; Lafarge Redland Aggregates; ProLogis Developments; Redrow Homes; Wimpey Homes.

HEWITSON BECKE + SHAW (see firm details p.993) Widely respected, "*clued-up*" **Peter Taylor** (see p.654) heads the firm's expanding Northampton team. Working in tandem with the commercial property group, it provides a comprehensive service on a national basis to public authorities, developers, landowners, investors and private individuals. This year has seen the team advise on the planning aspects of a number of major commercial schemes, including office developments for Scottish & Newcastle, and the development of two office blocks for Hampton Brook. **Clients** London Brick Properties; Fairclough Homes; Bellway Homes; Taywood Homes; Old Road Securities.

SHOOSMITHS (see firm details p.1133) Residential development remains the cornerstone of this practice, which acts for regional and national house builders, however the dedicated group is also building a reputation within the retail and leisure industries. The "*personable*" team led by **Iain Gilbey** (see p.651) recently advised Esso Petroleum and ExxonMobil on their objections to Associated British Ports' proposals for a new container terminal at Dibden Bay, Southampton. Local authorities also regularly feature as clients, and the team assisted Nottingham City Council on the £400 million redevelopment of the Broadmarsh Centre and the Nottingham Waterside project. **Clients** Esso Petroleum; ExxonMobil; Nottingham City Council; Thames Water Property Services; Crosby Homes Yorkshire; SEEDA.

BROWNE JACOBSON (see firm details p.891) Interviewees praised this Nottingham-based firm for its experience and enthusiasm. With **Brian Smith** at the helm, it undertakes a range of informal hearing work, inquiry advocacy and general planning advice in connection with urban regeneration and other development projects. The group recently handled advocacy for the Countryside Council for Wales at four wind farm inquiries, and advised the Countryside Agency in the development of its rural affordable housing initiative. **Clients** Shaw Group UK; local authorities

HAMMOND SUDDARDS EDGE A highly respected practice, it mainly covers non-contentious planning matters. The team, with **David Goodman**, recently acted for Wilson Bowden Developments in connection with a regional storage centre. It also advised on the development of retail and new council office space in Harlow town centre, and assisted Wilson Bowden City Homes with environmental and highway matters and section 106 agreements in relation to the Ocean Village in Southampton. **Clients** Aldi; Aston Villa FC; Wilson Bowden Developments.

KENT JONES AND DONE (see firm details p.1021) **Grant Anderson's** team of planning and environment specialists maintains its steady profile in the field. Areas of expertise include minerals, leisure, residential developments and town centre regeneration, with the team advising developers, landowners and minerals/waste operators. The team recently advised on planning matters for a town centre regeneration scheme comprising retail warehousing and a new link road. It also advised a developer on the development of a number of new health and fitness centres for a major leisure operator. **Clients** Laporte; Trent City Securities; Bliss Sand & Gravel; JCB Group.

EAST ANGLIA

PLANNING
■ EAST ANGLIA

1. **Mills & Reeve** Cambridge
2. **Hewitson Becke + Shaw** Cambridge
   Taylor Vinters Cambridge

LEADING INDIVIDUALS

1. **BRADY Peter** Hewitson Becke + Shaw
   BROCK David Mills & Reeve
2. **FIRTH Beverley** Mills & Reeve
   KRATZ Philip Taylor Vinters

This book is the product of 6,582 1/2 hour interviews. See p.7 for BMRB audit. Within each band, firms are listed alphabetically. See individuals' profiles p.649

MILLS & REEVE (see firm details p.1071) Considered pre-eminent due to the quality and breadth of its practice, the integrated planning and environment group is felt to have had a busy and successful year. In addition to attracting a handful of new clients, including several local authorities, it has been visible on a range of planning issues, both locally and further afield, in the urban renaissance, housing, industrial and retail spheres. An expert on planning matters relating to PFI, minerals and waste, "*big gun*" **David Brock** (see p.649) recently represented Aggregate Industries in a human rights-related case against English Nature and the Secretary of State. It concerned English Nature's designation of a completed landfill site with development potential as being of special scientific interest and a special protection area for birds. Clients admire him for his "*technical skills and depth of experience,*" and are impressed by his "*up-to-date knowledge.*" Solicitor advocate **Beverley Firth** (see p.651) handles High Court challenges, appeals and local plan representations, in addition to non-contentious work. She recently acted for Ashwells Group on a proposal for a major extension of the City of Cambridge into the greenbelt land. **Clients** Chelsea FC; Fairview New Homes; Addenbrookes NHS Trust; Aggregate Industries; City & St James Property; Mid Beds District Council; Thames Waste Management.

HEWITSON BECKE + SHAW (see firm details p.993) Widely known for estates work and its "*active developer and educational client base,*" the team advises across the spectrum of town and country planning issues on a local and nationwide basis. It regularly assists public authorities, landowners, investors and private individuals, and has particular expertise in waste management and disposal issues. The team, with "*reliable, consistent and commercial*" **Peter Brady** (see p.649), recently advised a landowner/funder consortium on promoting a 1,400 acre new settlement to the east of Plymouth. This comprises 3,500 dwellings, employment land, retail, schools, community facilities and public transport systems through the South Hams Local Plan. **Clients** Shanks Waste Services; Cambridge University; Old Road Securities; Durmast (Jersey); Barratt Eastern Counties; Norfolk Homes.

TAYLOR VINTERS (see firm details p.1156) "*Pleasant and popular*" **Philip Kratz** (see p.652) heads up a team, which is increasingly visible in the planning community advising an impressive raft of developers, house-builders, landowners and institutions. The team recently achieved outline planning permission for a large residential and commercial development in central Cambridge on behalf of Countryside Residential and Kajima Cambridge, and assisted Highland Homes in the redevelopment of Bury Hill House in Newmarket and sites in Cambridge. **Clients** Countryside Residential; Juddmonte Farms; Highland Homes.

PLANNING ■ NORTH WEST/YORKSHIRE

NORTH WEST

PLANNING
■ NORTH WEST

1 Addleshaw Booth & Co Manchester
Eversheds Manchester
Halliwell Landau Manchester
2 DLA Manchester
Wake Dyne Lawton Chester

LEADING INDIVIDUALS

1 LANCASTER Roger Halliwell Landau
WINTER Paul Eversheds
2 MORITZ John Wake Dyne Lawton
PIATT Andrew DLA
3 HOLMES John Halliwell Landau

This book is the product of 6,582 1/2 hour interviews. See p.7 for BMRB audit.
Within each band, firms are listed alphabetically. See individuals' profiles p.649

ADDLESHAW BOOTH & CO (see firm details p.838) Characterised by clients as "*proactive and creative thinkers*," the team is felt to be powering ahead with increased visibility on brownfield and regeneration work. The firm's Manchester and Leeds planning departments co-operate closely, both spearheaded by Amanda Beresford since Michael Kenworthy's retirement. The team recently advised Railtrack on the development of 116 hectares, including former colliery land, for a rail freight distribution facility. It also advised SCPD on the redevelopment of a site in Bristol for B1 use, and assisted AWG Developments on the redevelopment of a site in Chesterfield. **Clients** English Nature; SCPD; Railtrack; AWG Developments.

EVERSHEDS (see firm details p.949) Heralded by rivals as "*truly excellent,*" Paul Winter (see p.655) divides his time between Manchester and Leeds. He heads an expanding team that continues to attract a high volume of CPO, regeneration and PFI work, and is increasingly picking up instructions from the public sector. Winter recently acted for AstraZeneca on a public inquiry involving works at Severnside in Avon. Other recent highlights for the team include acting for the Northwest Development Agency on CPOs required for the North Manchester Business Park and the Ancoats Urban Village scheme, which involved complex planning and listed building issues. It also dealt with the planning aspects of the development of a major float glass manufacturing plant at Goole. **Clients** Asda; Tarmac Central; Halton Borough Council; Guardian Glass; London Borough of Hackney; Northwest Development Agency; AstraZeneca.

HALLIWELL LANDAU (see firm details p.982) Roger Lancaster (see p.652) continues to be applauded by all in the market for his tremendous advocacy skills. Head of the planning and environmental law team, much of his caseload relates to appeals on behalf of house builders, developers and retailers. He is supported by John Holmes (see p.652), who is also building up a solid reputation in the field. The team recently advised Fairclough Homes on an appeal against a decision by Congleton Borough Council to refuse consent for a residential development. It also advised The Baltic Consortium on an appeal against Maldon District Council's decision to refuse permission to build B1 accommodation and ancillary works on land at Sadd's Wharf. **Clients** Fairclough Homes; PH Property Holdings; Green Properties; Gafoor Poultry Products; The Baltic Consortium; Peel Holdings.

DLA The planning team operates as part of the real estate department and is led by **Andrew Piatt**. Winning respect from market sources for its technical skill and punchy style, it advises local authorities and developers on town centre developments, CPOs, minerals and transport. **Clients** Developers; local authorities.

WAKE DYNE LAWTON (see firm details p.1177) Spearheaded by "*frank and business-like*" **John Moritz** (see p.653), the team covers environmental, CPO and regeneration work for a mixture of private and small to medium-sized corporate clients. It has recently handled a variety of planning appeals for private clients, representing objectors over a proposal to bury toxic waste in a salt mine, and the uncontrolled development of a dairy operation. **Clients** Developers; residential groups.

YORKSHIRE

PLANNING
■ YORKSHIRE

1 Wilbraham & Co Leeds
2 Walker Morris Leeds
3 Eversheds Leeds
Hammond Suddards Edge Leeds
4 Addleshaw Booth & Co Leeds
Nabarro Nathanson Sheffield

LEADING INDIVIDUALS

1 WILBRAHAM Peter Wilbraham & Co
2 WADE-SMITH Richard Wilbraham & Co
WILLIAMSON Andrew Walker Morris
3 GOODMAN David Hammond Suddards Edge
4 BERESFORD Amanda Addleshaw Booth & Co
GRIFFITHS Marian Eversheds

This book is the product of 6,582 1/2 hour interviews. See p.7 for BMRB audit.
Within each band, firms are listed alphabetically. See individuals' profiles p.649

WILBRAHAM & CO (see firm details p.1187) The provision of "*specialist advice at a decent price*" ensures the firm's continued popularity amongst its varied clientele. A mix of solicitors, consultants and town planners, clients praise the large team for its "*excellent grasp of the commercial realities*" and the "*wonderful quality*" of its inquiry work. It has recently launched Coaxis, a formal planning alliance with Denton Wilde Sapte. Peter Wilbraham (see p.655) boasts a longstanding and unshakeable national reputation. He is recommended for his strategic experience, and has recently advised on planning matters relating to projects as varied as water treatment works, retail, residential and commercial developments, as well as listed buildings and compulsory acquisition compensation. "*Experienced*" renewable energy expert **Richard Wade-Smith's** (see p.655) expertise relates to the redevelopment of brownfield and contaminated sites for employment, retail or residential schemes. Highlights for the team include successfully advising CTP St James on obtaining planning permission for the first two stages of the Holbeck Urban Village regeneration project in Leeds, and assisting Capitec on the redevelopment of a redundant hospital cluster for residential and related purposes. **Clients** CTP St James; Capitec; Clugston Developments; Countryside Properties; Cussons; Doncaster Council; Eden District Council; First Group; Severn Trent Property; Landmark Development Projects; UK Coal Mining; University of Leeds.

WALKER MORRIS (see firm details p.1178) Generally agreed to be "*gaining ground,*" the team is rated for its "*good all-round performance*" particularly on the contentious side. It is felt by rivals to have extended its reach nationally and strengthened its presence on more complex work. Solicitor advocate **Andrew Williamson** spearheads the group. Recent highlights for him and his team include representing Barratt and Persimmon Homes on an inquiry relating to the impact of a proposed development on the site of the Battle of Newburn Ford, and acting for Hallam Land Management on proposals for motorway service areas in the forthcoming M25/M40/M4 circus inquiry. **Clients** Anglian Water Group; Crosby Homes; County Metropolitan Homes; Land Securities; Starbucks Coffee Co; Barratt Homes; British Waterways Board; 3C Waste; Asda Property Holdings; Bryant Homes.

NORTH EAST/SCOTLAND — PLANNING

EVERSHEDS (see firm details p.949) The team, with widely respected **Marian Griffiths** (see p.651), continues to garner support from clients and competitors alike for its planning and environment work. Co-operating closely with its superb Manchester outfit, it represents a mix of private and public sector clients on the spectrum of planning advice. It recently acted for Halton Borough Council on the CPO for the regeneration of Widnes town centre, including redevelopment of land for an Asda store. This involved acting as advocate at the public inquiry into objections to the CPO and related road closures. **Clients** Halton Borough Council; Asda Stores; Tarmac Central.

HAMMOND SUDDARDS EDGE Contentious work comprises the bulk of this "*approachable*" team's caseload, with other areas of special focus including energy distribution and renewable energy. Clients are particularly impressed by its CPO expertise. "*Top class*" **David Goodman** elicits its warm peer approval as "*a man you can do business with.*" He leads a team that recently advised Seascape on two offshore wind farms in Liverpool Bay, and represented Celtic Offshore Wind on a proposed scheme in North Wales. It has also acted for electricity companies regarding overhead lines, and for National Grid regarding a converter station in the North East. **Clients** Powergen Renewables; TXU; Celtic Offshore Wind.

ADDLESHAW BOOTH & CO (see firm details p.838) Despite having a lower profile, the firm continues to be active in the area. Highly respected by peers for her skill and dedication, **Amanda Beresford** (see p.357) leads a team that advises both public and private sector operations on town centre and other developments, CPO in the context of PFI projects, and urban regeneration. Members of the team have recently been appointed as panel lawyers to English Nature to advise on planning and environmental matters. **Clients** Railtrack; SCPD; AWG Developments.

NABARRO NATHANSON (see firm details p.1080) Energy, environment, mines and waste management are areas of expertise for the team led by Mike Renger. It recently advised Land Securities on planning matters relating to the York Shopping Centre, a mixed-use scheme providing 250,000 sq ft of retail accommodation, with offices, residential, restaurant and leisure uses. **Clients** Land Securities; developers.

NORTH EAST

PLANNING
■ NORTH EAST

1 Dickinson Dees — Newcastle upon Tyne

LEADING INDIVIDUALS
1 FINCH Paul — Dickinson Dees

This book is the product of 6,582 1/2 hour interviews. See p.7 for BMRB audit. Within each band, firms are listed alphabetically. See individuals' profiles p.649

DICKINSON DEES (see firm details p.938) The firm offers clients a multidisciplinary team, comprising lawyers and chartered town planners, with a substantial reputation for advocacy work, minerals, waste disposal and land reclamation issues. Although best known amongst interviewees for its regional work, the team handles planning matters across the UK, including London and the southern counties. Though Paul Taylor has now retired, solicitor advocate **Paul Finch** and his team continue to attract a high volume of inquiry work, including local plans, called-in applications, appeals against refusals of planning permission and CPOs. Recent instructions include preparing several planning applications and environmental statements relating to minerals and waste disposal schemes throughout the North East, and advice in relation to proposals for the New Tyne Crossing. **Clients** Govia; Grainger Trust; South Tyneside Metropolitan Borough Council; A&P Appledore; North Eastern Co-op; Arriva; Tyne & Wear PTA; Millhouse Developments; Thornfield Developments; Westmorland Motorway Services.

SCOTLAND

BRODIES (see firm details p.889) "*Incontrovertibly market leaders,*" the team is widely acclaimed for providing a "*genuinely specialist*" planning service. It has forged a strong profile for inquiry and appeal work, and is felt to possess considerable expertise in residential development issues. Viewed as the team's fulcrum, **Neil Collar**'s (see p.649) "*excellent organisational skills*" and "*deep knowledge*" are greatly appreciated by clients. He continues to nurture the team's developer and local authority client base, bolstered by the firm's retail, investment and property practice. The team recently advised Comhairle Nan Eilean Siar on an appeal by Lafarge Aggregates to the Scottish Ministers in relation to a superquarry proposal, which had been refused planning permission. It also advised Wimpey Homes on sites in Edinburgh and Midlothian, and successfully defended South Lanarkshire Council's appeal to the Court of Session against the Scottish Ministers' decision to grant a certificate of appropriate alternative development to a landowner for retail development at Rutherglen. **Clients** Comhairle Nan Eilean Siar; Wimpey Homes; Clackmannanshire Council; Renewable Energy Systems; Edinburgh's Telford College; Menzies Hotels.

DUNDAS & WILSON CS (see firm details p.943) Despite undergoing a phase of readjustment with its decision to quit the Andersen network and Frances McChlery's departure, researchers were told by competitors that the team retains its status in the community as "*one of the most rounded and credible planning departments in Scotland.*" At the helm, clients rely on **Ann Faulds** for "*consistently sound advice*" and are impressed by the level of team support. The group has recently advised retail, house builder, developer and local authority clients on a range of general planning matters. **Clients** Retailers; house builders; developers; local authorities.

PAULL & WILLIAMSONS (see firm details p.1096) Researchers found that this Aberdeen-based firm is making considerable headway locally and regionally, impressing peers and clients alike with its inquiry work and visibility on major projects. It is recognised in particular for its "*specialised niche in house building.*" Described by rivals as "*able, courteous and well-prepared*" **Bruce Smith** (see p.654) is known to handle high volumes of planning work. "*Dedicated and innovative*" **Elaine Farquharson-Black** (see p.651) is also carving out a solid reputation within the market. The team handles inquiries throughout Scotland, and recently acted for Homes for Scotland in its recent Court of Session challenge regarding the North East of Scotland Structure Plan. **Clients** Bett Homes; CALA Management; Stewart Milne Group; Malcolm Allan; A&J Stephen; Homes for Scotland.

SHEPHERD+ WEDDERBURN (see firm details p.1130) The team "*provides a bespoke service*" to a range of public and private sector clients. "*Pleasant and astute*" **Colin Innes** (see p.652) is felt by market sources to be driving the practice forward. Younger than many of his rivals, he is a respected advocate and possesses recognised expertise in environmental and energy matters. The team acted for Midlothian Council on the inquiry into the proposed Com-

PLANNING ■ SCOTLAND

PLANNING
■ SCOTLAND

1
- **Brodies** Edinburgh
- **Dundas & Wilson CS** Edinburgh

2
- **Paull & Williamsons** Aberdeen
- **Shepherd+ Wedderburn** Edinburgh

3
- **Archibald Campbell & Harley WS** Edinburgh
- **McGrigor Donald** Glasgow

4
- **Burness** Edinburgh
- **Maclay Murray & Spens** Glasgow
- **Semple Fraser** Glasgow

5
- **Anderson Strathern WS** Edinburgh
- **Ledingham Chalmers** Aberdeen
- **MacRoberts** Glasgow

LEADING INDIVIDUALS

1
- **COLLAR Neil** Brodies
- **FAULDS Ann** Dundas & Wilson CS

2
- **COCKBURN David** Archibald Campbell & Harley WS
- **CONNAL Craig** McGrigor Donald
- **INNES Colin** Shepherd+ Wedderburn
- **SMITH Bruce** Paull & Williamsons

3
- **MCCHLERY Frances** Simpson & Marwick
- **SALES Martin** Burness

4
- **FARQUHARSON-BLACK Elaine** Paull & Williamsons
- **GILLES June** Semple Fraser
- **GRANT James** MacRoberts
- **HARRIS Jacqueline** McGrigor Donald
- **MCKIE Alastair** Anderson Strathern WS

ONES TO WATCH
- **MACLEOD Ewan** Shepherd+ Wedderburn

This book is the product of 6,582 1/2 hour interviews. See p.7 for BMRB audit. Within each band, firms are listed alphabetically. See individuals' profiles p.649

---

munity Hospital, which had been called in by the Scottish Ministers, and on seven housing appeals, including a major appeal by Cala Management in Penicuik. It also represented Angus & City of Dundee councils on a public local inquiry relating to CPO and road orders for the A92 dual carriageway. **Clients** Midlothian Council; Angus & City of Dundee Councils; Waterfront Edinburgh; Blue Circle Industries; Orange Personal Communications Services; Scottish Power.

ARCHIBALD CAMPBELL & HARLEY WS
(see firm details p.847) Inquiry work forms the backbone of this established department. Peers describe the team as "*low-key, but active,*" although it is felt to lack the profile of some of its rivals. "*Senior and well known*" **David Cockburn** remains the lynchpin of the practice. The team has recently handled quarry-related inquiries and housing appeals. **Clients** Scottish National Heritage; Waste Recycling Group; The Miller Group.

MCGRIGOR DONALD
(see firm details p.1065) This broadly-based practice benefits from the firm's strength in areas such as PFI and commercial property. **Craig Connal QC** (see p.555) is distinguished as the only solicitor advocate to have taken silk, while **Jacqueline Harris** (see p.651) maintains her reputation in the market. The team covers town planning, compulsory purchase and public policy work, and was recently visible acting for I&H Brown on the long running inquiry into a local development project. **Clients** Farmfoods; North Lanarkshire Council; I&H Brown; Lattice Property Holdings; Quarry Products Association.

BURNESS
The group covers contentious and non-contentious work across a spectrum of sectors including retail, landfill and housing. Clients praise "*proactive*" **Martin Sales** for his skill in "*defining the issues at stake.*" The team recently advised on the redevelopment of the Royal Infirmary site, which involved heritage, transport and housing issues. It also assisted the BBC on the planning aspects of the construction of Finneston Bridge across the Clyde and associated infrastructure work at Pacific Quay. **Clients** AXA Reim; BBC; British Nuclear Fuels; Castle Leisure Group; Wimpey Homes; Lothian Universities Hospitals.

MACLAY MURRAY & SPENS
(see firm details p.1048) A "*successful, sound operation,*" led by Chris Smylie, it is felt to be "*making inroads*" into the market. The team's clients are drawn from both the public and private sectors, and are now offered a multidisciplinary service following the department's 2001 launch of its joint venture with consultants Farningham McCreadie. The team recently advised Bank of Scotland on the Legacy bid for the Millennium Dome. It also successfully represented Wiseman Dairies in relation to judicial review proceedings to quash a grant of residential planning consent. **Clients** Bank of Scotland; Wiseman Dairies; Southside Capital; Morrison Homes.

SEMPLE FRASER
(see firm details p.1125) The team, which includes highly respected **June Gilles** (see p.651), advises a mix of retailers, housebuilders, environmental pressure groups and developers on planning and environmental matters. It continues to assist Tesco on its strategic expansion throughout Scotland, recently representing them in challenging, by judicial review, the Scottish Ministers' decision not to hold the examination in public prior to the approval of the Glasgow and Clyde Valley Joint Structure Plan. **Clients** Tesco; Standard Commercial Property Securities; Royal & Sun Alliance; British Land.

ANDERSON STRATHERN WS
(see firm details p.844) New to *Chambers* rankings this year following substantial market endorsement, the firm is said by clients and competitors to be "*developing a solid practice.*" **Alastair McKie** (see p.653), the firm's standout practitioner, is becoming increasingly prominent advising on telecoms projects and rural estate development. **Clients** Crown Estates.

LEDINGHAM CHALMERS
(see firm details p.1034) The team, with John Curran, continues to advise house builders, landowners and other property clients on commercial and residential development locally and across Scotland's central belt. It recently acted for AGW Partnerships in an appeal against Aberdeen City Council's decision to refuse the client's application for planning permission for a mixed hotel, leisure and retail development at Justice Mill Lane. **Clients** AGW Partnerships; University of Aberdeen; Aggregate Industries.

MACROBERTS
(see firm details p.1049) **Jamie Grant** (see p.359) is the leading figure in this team, which has a recognised niche in renewable energy and waste-related matters. It recently advised GlaxoSmithKline on a proposed change of disposal method for trade effluent. It has also advised on potential liabilities for closed landfill sites, and on wind farms. **Clients** GlaxoSmithKline; Catchment Moray.

OTHER NOTABLE PRACTITIONERS
The move of the much admired **Frances McChlery** from Dundas & Wilson to Simpson & Marwick is taken by the market as a good sign of the firm's intention to build a capacity in this area.

THE LEADERS IN PLANNING

ABRAHAM, Henry
Brachers, Maidstone
(01622) 690691
henryabraham@brachers.co.uk
Specialisation: Partner in Planning and Environmental Law Department. Experienced in all aspects of planning applications and appeals, enforcement proceedings, development plans, integrated pollution control, all environmental matters under the EPA 1990, private bills procedure, compulsory purchase and highway orders. Occasional contributor to the 'Journal of Planning & Environment Law'.
Prof. Memberships: UK Environmental Law Association, Legal Associate Royal Town Planning Institute, Member of the Law Society's Specialist Planning Panel.
Career: Qualified in 1983. Joined *Brachers* in 1990 and became a Partner in 1994.
Personal: Born 8 June 1957. St. Dunstan's College. University of London. Leisure pursuits include rowing. Lives in London.

ALLEN, Tony
DMH, Brighton
(01273) 744451
tony.allen@dmh.co.uk
Specialisation: Partner who specialises in town planning, environmental law, waste management and contaminated land. Acted in: housing, leisure and retail developments; health authority and university cases, in cases regarding waste deposit licensing, waste transfer stations, planning and licensing, statutory nuisance prosecutions, listed buildings, a waste power plant and mineral extraction.
Prof. Memberships: UK Environmental Law Association.
Career: Qualified 1971; partner 1976; with *DMH* throughout – latterly specialising in town planning and environmental. Heads a multidisciplinary planning group of lawyers and chartered town planners.
Publications: Various articles on planning, listed buildings and environmental subjects. 'A Practical Guide to the Law on Contaminated Land and its Implications for Property Transactions' – (Part IIA Environmental Protection Act 1990). Writes for 'Heritage' and 'Period Ideas' periodicals.

ASHWORTH, Stephen
Denton Wilde Sapte, London
(020) 7242 1212
Specialisation: Partner, Planning and Public Law Group. Experience in planning law, including major development inquiries; judicial review; highway law; compulsory purchase orders; Private Finance Initiative Public Private Partnerships projects; waste proposals. Advises on developing policy issues on retailing; planning benefits; infrastructure funding; and town centre management.
Prof. Memberships: Urban Land Institute. Council Member of City Property Association.
Career: Articled *Denton Hall* 1986; qualified 1988; partner 1995; secondment to Sainsbury plc 1992-94; Harkness Fellowship at Lincoln Institute of Land Policy, Cambridge Massachussetts 1995-96 (researching American approaches to regeneration, provision of infrastructure and public participation in the planning process).
Personal: Born 1963; leisure activities include cycling, 19th century British history, dry-stone walling, cookery.

BANKS, Sandra
Denton Wilde Sapte, London
(020) 7242 1212
sab@dentonwildesapte.com
Specialisation: Main areas of practice are development projects (for both the private and public sectors), including transport and regeneration with associated appeals and judicial review. Current projects include the redevelopment of Battersea Power Station and its environs as a visitor attraction with new rail link, housing, hotels, theatres and offices; major improvements at Ascot Racecourse, 3,000 houses at Northampton SW Sector and the redevelopment of central Milton Keynes for English Partnerships; continuing advice on the development of up to 10,000 houses at Barking Reach and other regeneration projects for the London Borough of Barking and Dagenham; and advice to Bedford Borough, Mid Bedfordshire District and Bedfordhire County Councils on the development of 4,500 houses at Elstow new settlement, near Bedford.

BERESFORD, Amanda
Addleshaw Booth & Co, Leeds
(0113) 209 2325
amanda.beresford@addleshawbooth.com
See under Environment, p.357

BLANEY, Trevor
Lawrence Graham, London
(020) 7379 0000

BOSWALL, Julian
Morgan Cole, Cardiff
(029) 2038 5385

BOSWORTH, John
Bevan Ashford, Bristol
(0117) 975 1731
john.bosworth@bevanashford.co.uk
Specialisation: Head of the Regulatory Department at *Bevan Ashford* specialises in planning, urban regeneration and local government law. Special expertise in judicial review and compulsory purchase. Projects have included regional shopping centres, Canary Wharf, a new village in South Hampshire, renewable energy schemes, town centre regeneration schemes, Temple Quay, Bristol, many PFI schemes and the redevelopment of major brownfield sites. Clients include developers, local authorities and regional development agencies.
Prof. Memberships: Legal Associate of RTPI. Member of Law Society's Planning Panel.
Career: Qualified 1988. Articled Portsmouth City Council. Joined *Bevan Ashford* 1995, after six years working for *Ashurst Morris Crisp*.

BRADY, Peter
Hewitson Becke + Shaw, Cambridge
(01223) 532721
peterbrady@hewitsons.com
Specialisation: Planning, environment and waste disposal.
Prof. Memberships: Law Society's specialist planning panel.
Career: Leicester University 1973-6 LL.B (Hons). 1977-79: Cheshire County Council. 1979-81: Hertfordshire County Council. 1981-84: Northumberland County Council. 1984-88: *Jameson & Hill*, Hertford. 1988-90: *Berwin Leighton*. 1990: *Hewitson Becke + Shaw*.
Personal: Golf.

BROCK, David
Mills & Reeve, Cambridge
(01223) 222438
david.brock@mills-reeve.com

BULL, Rod
Eversheds, Birmingham
(0121) 232 1477
rodbull@eversheds.com
Specialisation: Head of national *Eversheds* Planning Group. Planning and compulsory purchase/environmental. Experienced advocate. Considerable experience of advising developers on large mixed-use schemes (especially residential). Also specialist in minerals/waste law.
Prof. Memberships: Law Society's Planning Panel, Legal Associate RTPI, UK Environmental Law Association, Associate of Institute of Quarrying.
Career: Educated Rugby, Hull University. Partner of *Eversheds* leading Planning and Environmental Team.
Personal: Married, resides Elford, near Lichfield, Staffs. Interests: walking, computers and reading.

CASELY-HAYFORD, Margaret
Denton Wilde Sapte, London
(020) 7242 1212
Specialisation: Partner and non-practising barrister, planning and public law group. Practice covers the full range of major project property planning and PFI advice (such as housing, multi-purpose stadium and concert venue developments, police station developments, shopping centres, superstores, hospital development and contaminated land redevelopment proposals, as well as major energy installations). Negotiates planning consents and related agreements, carries out planning audits for funders and developers and co-ordinates and advises on compulsory purchase and land assembly matters and public inquiries covering all regulatory matters related to site development, as well as High Court appeals and judicial review proceedings.
Prof. Memberships: Bar (England and Wales), Grays Inn, UKELA, Association of Women Barristers, firm's representative on Business in Sport and Leisure, Leisure Property Forum.
Career: Called to the Bar by Gray's Inn 1984. Pupilage 4-5 Gray's Inn Square 1985-87. In house counsel ADC. Joined *Denton Hall* in 1987, partner 1998.
Publications: Author of 'Practical Planning: Permission and the Application' published by FT Law and Tax, December 1995; Contributor, 'Sustaining Architecture'.
Personal: Educated at Streatham Hill High (Girl's Public Day School Trust) and Somerville College, Oxford.

COCKBURN, David
Archibald Campbell & Harley WS, Edinburgh
(0131) 220 3000

COLLAR, Neil
Brodies, Edinburgh
(0131) 228 3777
neil.collar@brodies.co.uk
Specialisation: Partner and Head of Planning Law Department, Legal Associate of the Royal Town Planning Institute, LLM for research into use of planning issues 1990. Handles town and country planning matters – planning applications, appeals and inquiries (including inquiry advocacy), court actions, planning issues in relation to land acquisition and disposal, Local Authority compulsory purchase, roads etc. Wide experience of private and public sector clients. Member of Editorial Board of Scottish Planning and Environmental Law and the Law Society's Planning Law Committee. Senior tutor for planning law at University of Edinburgh and speaker on aspects of planning law at several conferences. Legal Examiner for RTPI.
Prof. Memberships: Law Society of Scotland, Legal Associate of the RTPI.
Career: Qualified in 1992, having joined *Brodies WS* in 1990.
Publications: Author of 'Planning' and 'Planning and Human Rights', published by W. Green & Son and Sweet & Maxwell (Concise Scots Law Series), Executive Editor of 'Greens Scottish Planning Factbook', co-author of 'Pollution Control in Scotland' published by T&T Clark and a number of articles in journals.
Personal: Born 31 March 1967. Educated at the University of Glasgow 1984-88 and 1989-90 (LLB and Diploma) and Liverpool University 1988-89 (LLM). Enjoys playing the saxophone, lacrosse, hockey and touch rugby. Lives in Edinburgh.

CONNAL QC, Craig
McGrigor Donald, Glasgow
(0141) 248 6677
craig.connal@mcgrigors.com
See under Litigation, p.555

PLANNING ■ THE LEADERS

CUNLIFFE, Michael
Forsters, London
(020) 7863 8477
mdcunliffe@forsters.co.uk
Specialisation: Planning law acting for both developers and local authorities.
Prof. Memberships: Legal Associate of the Royal Town Planning Institute, Member of the Law Society's Planning Panel and Member of the City of London Law Society's Planning and Environmental Law Sub-Committee. Associate Fellow of the Society for Advanced Legal Studies and a Member of the Society's Planning and Environmental Law Reform Working Group.
Career: Qualified 1974. Joined *Ashurst Morris Crisp* 1983. Partner *Ashurst Morris Crisp*, 1987-2001. Partner *Forsters*, 2001.

CURNOW, Tony
Ashurst Morris Crisp, London
(020) 7638 1111
Specialisation: Partner and head of planning and public sector group. Advises local authorities and the private sector on planning, regeneration and public infrastructure projects. Major schemes include Channel Tunnel Rail Link, Crossrail and Docklands Light Railway, Chalkhill Estate for London Borough of Brent, Parkway/M602 in Trafford Park, Hackney Estates Regeneration Strategy, redevelopment of the Guinness Brewery at Park Royal, Southgate Shopping Centre in Bath and extension of Broadmead for Bristol City Council.
Prof. Membership: Law Society Planning Panel and Legal Associate RTPI.
Career: Qualified 1979. 11 years in local government. Joined *Ashurst Morris Crisp* 1988, Partner in 1996.

DAMMS, Martin
Pinsent Curtis Biddle, Birmingham
(0121) 200 1050
martin.damms@pinsents.com
Specialisation: Planning and environmental law. Increasingly involved in urban regeneration schemes requiring compulsory purchase proceedings and highways stopping up and diversion orders. Covers full range of contentious and non-contentious matters including advising and representing public bodies. Planning applications, appeals, development plan representations, judicial review, negotiating/drafting planning agreements, enforcement action, housing, commercial, retail and leisure development, highways issues, compulsory purchase proceedings, hazardous substances consents. Advocate.
Prof. Memberships: Law Society. Birmingham Law Society. Member of the Law Society's Planning Panel. Legal Associate R.T.P.I.
Career: Qualified 1976. In Local Government to 1989. Joined *Edge Ellison* in 1989. Partner from 1993. *Pinsent Curtis Biddle* 2000 to date.
Personal: Interests: football, reading, music.

DIMMICK, Simon
Blandy & Blandy, Reading
(0118) 951 6800
Specialisation: Town and Country Planning, highways law, environmental work relating to property development. Advice on local authority matters generally. Advocacy. Acts for land owners, developers and local authorities.
Career: Qualified in 1977. 1983-88 Assistant County Solicitor, Berkshire County Council. Joined *Blandy & Blandy* as the Planning Partner in 2002, having previously been a partner with *Clarks*, from 1989-2002.
Personal: Born 19 January 1952. Educated Kings School, Worcester, and University College, London – LLB 1974. Leisure time interests revolve around family.

DRUKARZ, Daniel
Pitmans, Reading
(0118) 958 0227
ddrukarz@pitmans.com
Specialisation: Planning department partner specialising in all aspects of planning law and practice, including judicial review and major inquiry work. Wide experience in office and business park schemes, urban regeneration initiatives and other large scale retail, residential and mixed use developments, often involving 'tall' buildings. Many projects endorsed by the GLA and CABE. Expertise in negotiating and drafting planning and infrastructure agreements. Acts for a variety of multinationals (including advice on EC wide environmental strategy), investment and development companies and amenity groups.
Prof. Memberships: Law Society; Member Institute of Petroleum.
Career: Articles *Titmuss Sainer & Webb*, qualified 1989, assistant solicitor with *Nabarro Nathanson* and *SJ Berwin* before joining *Fladgate Fielder* in 1994 to set up Planning Unit. Partner since 1997. Joined *Pitmans* as partner in December 2000.
Personal: Born 1960. Married with two children. Interests include family, Himalayan, African and South American trekking and five-a-side. Lives in London.

DYER, Carl
Osborne Clarke, London
(020) 7809 1000

EDMOND, John
Marrons, Leicester
(0116) 289 2200
johnedmond@marrons.net
Specialisation: Partner in planning, development and public law department. Has 16 years experience of specialist contentious town planning and associated work, including judicial review and High Court challenges to planning decisions under the 1990 Act, public law matters and compulsory purchase. Has conducted a wide range of cases and appeals including new village schemes, major urban regeneration schemes, contaminated land proposals, landfill proposals, motorway service areas, retail and leisure applications, applications involving Conservation Areas, Listed Buildings and Registered Parks; and in negotiating Section 106 agreements and related agreements relating to major infrastructure proposals. Major clients include Persimmon Homes, Barratt Homes, David Wilson Homes, Allison Homes, Bryant Homes, McCain Foods (UK) Ltd, Forte UK Ltd, Jelson Homes, Stapleford Park plc, Safeways, Wilson Bowden Properties, CWS. Conducted Local Plan Inquiries on behalf of Local Planning Authorities including Daventry District Council, South Derbyshire District Council and North West Leicestershire District Council.
Prof. Memberships: Law Society, Legal Associate of the Royal Town Planning Institute, Member of the Law Society's Planning Panel.
Career: Qualified in 1983, joined *Marron Dodds* in 1987 becoming a partner in 1988. Prior to joining *Marron Dodds* specialised in Magistrates Court/Crown Court prosecution and defence work. Educated at Hull Grammar School.
Personal: Born 8 February 1959. Attended Wolverhampton University (BA (Hons) Law 1980). Leisure interests include golf (member of Luffenham Health Golf Club), personal fitness and the arts. Lives on the Leicestershire/ Rutland border. Married with four children.

ENGERT, Nick
Clarke Willmott & Clarke, Taunton
(01823) 445202
nengert@cw-c.co.uk
Specialisation: Partner with a well-established reputation as a planning advocate undertaking regular appearances at Public Inquiries in most parts of England and Wales. He also advises large development companies, public and private institutions and land owners on contentious and politically sensitive issues relating to development proposals, including planning applications and appeals. He also negotiates and settles planning and road agreements. His work includes advice on enforcement notices, listed buildings and nature conservation. His practice encompasses wide variety of projects, including the promotion of land for future development and large and complex residential, commercial and industrial schemes. He also advises on compulsory purchase orders and disputed compensation claims. Recent appearances as advocate include Local Plan Inquiries in Dorset, Gloucestershire, Somerset, Sussex and Wiltshire, and Section 78 Inquiries in Cornwall, Devon, Dorset, South Gloucestershire and Somerset. Recognised, nationally, as one of the highest rated solicitor advocates (as chosen by leading solicitors and planners – 'Planning Magazine' 1999, 2000 and 2001).
Prof. Memberships: UKELA; Advisor to Somerset Strategic Partnership.
Career: Guildford Law School; Southampton University (LLB); articled with *Breeze & Wyles*; admitted in July 1973; joined *Clarke Willmott & Clarke* 1975; partner 1979.

EVANS, Douglas
Theodore Goddard, London
(020) 7880 5789
douglasevans@theodoregoddard.co.uk
Specialisation: Management of multi-disciplinary and inter-firm teams to successfully obtain planning and regulatory consents for some of the UK's most contentious development proposals. Advocacy, strategic advice and negotiation of planning permissions and agreements for all forms of development. Advice on environmental assessment and contaminated land is an important part of the practice. Preparation and submission of cases to emerging RPGs, structure and local plans is central to the strategic advice provided to clients. Major clients include multinational waste companies, utility, mining, power generation, commercial and residential developers. Current cases include acting for Onyx Environmental Group, successfully obtaining three EfW planning permissions in Hampshire; acting for SITA on the 25 year Surrey Waste Contract and securing planning permission for an EfW plant; acting for Minosus in promoting the UK's first underground special waste facility within a rock salt mine; developing Grundon's 480,000 tpa incinerator at Colnbrook; acting for a number of clients promoting major landfill extensions; Bryant Homes, promoting a 2,000 house development in Devon; a 2,250 allocation in Nottinghamshire; a 600 unit allocation in Oxfordshire and negotiating the form and content of a planning application and subsequent Section 106 Agreement for 1,200 dwellings in Hampshire; Fairview, securing planning permission for 500 dwellings at Ashford; Persimmon Homes, negotiating planning permissions in London, South East England and East Anglia; Countryside Homes, appearing at a Secretary of State Planning Inquiry in respect of an 850 dwelling proposal and also securing planning permission for 700 dwellings.
Prof. Memberships: Member of the Law Society Specialist Planning Panel, Legal Associate of the Royal Town Planning Institute, Member of the City of London Law Society Planning and Environment Law Sub-Committee, Member of the Environmental Services Association, Affiliate Member of the Chartered Institution of Wastes Management, Member Editorial Board Chartered Institution of Wastes Management Scientific and Technical Review, Member UKELA, Member Renewable Power Association.

EVANS, Eric
Eversheds, Cardiff
(029) 2047 1147
See under Local Government, p.577

THE LEADERS ■ PLANNING

EVANS, Katherine
TLT Solicitors, Bristol
(0117) 917 7777
kevans@TLTsolicitors.com
Specialisation: Specialises in all aspects of development including planning, highways, compulsory purchase/compensation, land acquisition. Also environmental law particularly contaminated land and environmental liability in corporate transactions. Experienced in High Court challenges and judicial reviews. Acts for developers, financial institutions, minerals and waste operators, local authorities, private landowners and individuals.
Prof. Memberships: Law Society, Royal Town Planning Institute.
Career: Qualified planner 1987, solicitor 1997. 1986-96 employed by national housebuilders to acquire and project manage major development sites. *Lawrence Tucketts* (now *TLT Solicitors*, the merged firm of *Trumps* and *Lawrence Tucketts*) since 1998.
Personal: Born 1962. Lives in Bristol. Interests include family and travel.

EVANS, Martin
Nabarro Nathanson, London
(020) 7524 6000

FARQUHARSON-BLACK, Elaine
Paull & Williamsons, Aberdeen
(01224) 621621
efarquharsonblack@paull-williamsons.co.uk
Specialisation: Partner in Planning and Environmental Law Department. Main area of practice is planning. Advises on planning applications, appeals, enforcement notice appeals, local and structure plans, compulsory purchase, judicial reviews on planning decisions and the conduct of public inquiries. Also handles environmental law issues in respect of heritable properties and company operations. Advises on waste disposal licences, river purification issues and other issues arising out of the Environmental Protection Act.
Prof. Memberships: Law Society of Scotland, Society of Advocates in Aberdeen. Law Society accredited specialist in Planning Law.
Career: Qualified in 1991. Joined *Paull & Willliamsons* in 1993, becoming a Partner in 2000.
Publications: Co-author of 'Scottish Planning Law and Procedure'.
Personal: Born 21 March 1968. Attended Aberdeen University 1985-89 (LLB). Leisure interests include golf. Lives in Aberdeen.

FAULDS, Ann
Dundas & Wilson CS, Edinburgh
(0131) 228 8000

FINCH, Paul
Dickinson Dees, Newcastle upon Tyne
(0191) 279 9000

FIRTH, Beverley
Mills & Reeve, Cambridge
(01223) 222 235
beverley.firth@mills-reeve.com
Specialisation: Partner in the Property Services Department, specialising in all aspects of planning law. Work includes advice on aspects of land development, negotiations with local authorities including planning agreements. Also includes advocacy in planning appeals and in local plan inquiries. Contentious work includes judicial review. Particular environmental expertise in land contamination and waste disposal including clinical waste. Also experienced in health and safety. Recent projects include local airfields, new settlement and University campus.

FONGENIE, Wesley
Osborne Clarke, London
(020) 7809 1000

FRASER, Moira
Fladgate Fielder, London
(020) 7323 4747
mfraser@fladgate.com
Specialisation: Partner and Head of Planning. Many years specialist experience in planning, CPO and compensation, highway and other infrastructure issues. Emphasis on inquiry work and appeals. Expertise in negotiating and drafting planning and infrastructure agreements. Advises on development plan policies. Acts for public authorities, private sector and amenity groups. Special expertise in large retail and listed buildings. Undertakes advocacy.
Prof. Memberships: The Law Society; Fellow of the Royal Society of Arts; Town and Country Planning Association.
Career: MA (Hons) Cantab. Articled 1977-79 *Norton Rose*, qualified 1979. Assistant solicitor at *Norton Rose* and then *Simmons & Simmons* 1979-88. *D J Freeman* 1988-99, *McGuinness Finch* 1999-2001. *Fladgate Fielder* 2001- .
Personal: Born 1955. Leisure pursuits include golf, art appreciation and family.

GALLIMORE, Michael
Lovells, London
(020) 7296 2253
michael.gallimore@lovells.com
Specialisation: Partner in Commercial Property Department and Head of Planning Group. Principal area of practice is property development with particular expertise in the planning and environmental aspects of major development and infrastructure projects. Wide experience in office and business park developments, retail schemes, new housing settlements, leisure projects and waste management schemes. Also experienced in development site acquisitions. Expertise includes negotiations and appeals for planning and associated consents and drafting and negotiation of s.106 agreements and related development/infrastructure agreements. Has acted on numerous judicial review applications and High Court challenges. Experience also on various PFI and PPP projects. Acts as an advocate at planning and local plan inquiries.

Prof. Memberships: Law Society Specialist Planning Panel, Law Society Planning and Environmental Law Committee, City of London Law Society Planning and Environmental Law Sub-Committee.
Career: Qualified 1983, Partner 1988.

GIBBS, Kevin
Osborne Clarke, Bristol
(0117) 917 3000

GILBEY, Iain
Shoosmiths, Northampton
(01604) 543000
iain.gilbey@shoosmiths.co.uk
Specialisation: Partner and Head of Planning Group. Town and country planning and environmental law. All aspects of property development. Specialises in providing strategic advice on residential, retail and other large scale commercial developments. Experienced in conducting major public inquiries and associated High Court litigation. Acts for privatised utilities, major national housebuilders, landowners, retailers and occupiers.
Prof. Memberships: Law Society and UKELA.
Career: Educated at Royal Grammar School, High Wycombe. Southampton University (LLB). College of Law, Guildford. Trained at *Berwin Leighton*. Qualified 1994. *Ashurst Morris Crisp* 1997-2000. Joined *Shoosmiths* January 2000. Partner May 2000.

GILLES, June
Semple Fraser, Glasgow
(0141) 221 3771
june.gilles@semplefraser.co.uk
Specialisation: Commercial property specialising in town and country planning. June has extensive experience of providing legal advice and support in planning inquiries and legal challenges, enforcement and negotiation of planning agreements in the retail, leisure, industrial, minerals and renewable energy sectors. She works with a number of significant clients including Tesco Stores in their Scottish expansion and on windfarm projects for Powergen Renewables.
Career: Trained *Maclay Murray & Spens*; qualified 1983. Spent six years working in property and planning with Motherwell District Council and then Dumbarton District Council. Returned to private practice with *Bird Semple Fyfe Ireland*. Joined *Semple Fraser WS* 1990, made Partner in 1997.
Personal: Born 1960. Educated at Hutchesons' Grammar School and Glasgow University. Interests include cinema, music, theatre, photography, reading and skiing.

GOODMAN, David
Hammond Suddards Edge, Leeds
0113 284 7000

GRANT, James
MacRoberts, Glasgow
(0141) 332 9988
jamie.grant@macroberts.com
See under Environment, p.359

GREENWOOD, Brian
Norton Rose, London
(020) 7283 6000
greenwoodbj@nortonrose.com
Specialisation: Corporate acquisitions, disposals and funding; environmental due diligence, project finance, waste, water and IPPC including appeals and advocacy; international practice with considerable experience in Eastern Europe. Current clients include BMW (sale of Rover/Land Rover); Castle Cement Ltd., environmental challenge being referred to European Court; Associated British Ports, Dibdon Terminal, Southampton, public enquiry.
Prof. Memberships: Chairman, Law Society's Planning and Environmental Law Committee, former Chairman City of London Law Society Planning and Environment Committee; UKELA; Law Society's Specialist Planning Panel.
Publications: Author of 'Butterworths Planning Law Service', co-author of 'Environmental Regulation and Economic Growth', editor of 'Planning Law Handbook' and 'Butterworths Planning Law Guidance'.

GRIFFITHS, Marian
Eversheds, Leeds
(0113) 243 0391
mariangriffiths@eversheds.com
Specialisation: Town and country planning, compulsory purchase. Main areas of practice are retail, minerals and waste disposal and housing, town centre regeneration.
Prof. Memberships: Law Society's Planning Panel. Legal Associate Royal Town Planning Institute.
Career: Law degree from Leeds and qualified as a solicitor in 1981. Articled in local government and worked in the public sector until 1991. Joined *Eversheds* in 1996.
Personal: Born Chester, educated in Wolverhampton. Married with twin daughters. Lives in Leeds.

HALL, Brian
Clifford Chance, London
(020) 7600 1000
brian.hall@cliffordchance.com
Specialisation: Partner and Head of firm's Planning and Environment Unit specialising in environment, local government and town planning
Career: Articled North Tyneside MBC; qualified 1980; Partner since 1988.
Personal: Rutherford Grammar School; King's College, London (LLB, DMA, FCIS).

HARRIS, Jacqueline
McGrigor Donald, Edinburgh
(0131) 777 7000
www.mcgrigors.com
Specialisation: Partner in Commercial Litigation Unit. Developed expertise in planning through dealing with litigation involving technical and scientific evidence and with plannning applications, appeals, public inquiries and judicial review. Has considerable experience of dealing with technical and scientific

PLANNING ■ THE LEADERS

issues arising in planning (and litigation) matters. Planning practice now includes advising on all aspects of planning, particularly in relation to major development and infrastructure projects, retail and mineral planning. Conducts advocacy at public inquiries. Planning clients include: The Post Office; Lattice Property Holdings Ltd, Forth Ports plc, I & H Brown Ltd, Glasgow Harbour Ltd. Other key areas of practice are commercial litigation and product liability.
Career: Qualified 1990; Partner *McGrigor Donald* 1999.

HAWKINS, David
Nabarro Nathanson, London
(020) 7524 6261
d.hawkins@nabarro.com
Specialisation: Partner in Planning Department from 1978 and Consultant from May 2002. Covers all aspects of planning and development, particularly large scale commercial developments, public inquiries and judicial review; also administrative law, Parliamentary work and compulsory purchase and compensation. Addresses seminars regularly.
Prof. Memberships: Law Society; Legal Associate, R.T.P.I.; Law Society Planning Panel.
Career: Member of Planning and Environmental Law Committee of the Law Society, FRSA.
Publications: Author of 'Compulsory Purchase' volume of the Encyclopaedia of Forms and Precedents and 'Boynton's Guide to Compulsory Purchase and Compensation'.
Personal: King's College, London: LLB (Hons).

HELLIER, Tim
Berwin Leighton Paisner, London
(020) 7760 1000
tim.hellier@blplaw.com
Specialisation: Wide experience in retail, housing, leisure, office developments and major urban regeneration schemes, compulsory purchase, contaminated land, risk management and infrastructure schemes and urban regeneration schemes. Acts as strategic planning advisor to Tesco, Westfield, ING (Real Estate). Currently acting on major urban regeneration schemes in Bracknell, Hull, Chester, Liverpool, Belfast Guildford, Swindon and Derby. Other major clients: Legal and General, Liverpool Council, Belfast Regeneration Office and BAA McArthur/Glen.
Prof. Memberships: Law Society, Associate Fellow of the Society of Advanced Legal Studies, UKELA.
Career: Strode College, Egham. Sheffield University LLB (Hons). Law Society Finals, City of London Polytechnic. Qualified 1986; partner *Berwin Leighton* (now *Berwin Leighton Paisner*) 1997.
Personal: Married with two children. Interests include rugby, running, general fitness, music and his children.

HEMMING, Dan
Wragge & Co, Birmingham
(0870) 903 1000

HIGNETT, Andrew
Lester Aldridge, Southampton
(023) 8082 0400

HILLEBRON, Richard
Slaughter and May, London
(020) 7600 1200
richard.hillebron@slaughterandmay.com
Specialisation: Specialises in all aspects of town and country planning from submission of an application through to decision and appeal, including compulsory purchase, negotiating highways and other agreements with local authorities and certificates of lawful use or development.
Prof. Memberships: Legal Associate of The Royal Town Planning Institute; Member of The Law Society's Planning Panel and Member City of London Law Society Planning and Environmental Law Sub-Committee.
Career: Qualified 1980.

HOLMES, John
Halliwell Landau, Manchester
(0161) 831 2678
jholmes@halliwells.co.uk
Specialisation: Specialises in both environmental and planning matters. Acts for a wide range of corporate clients in the UK. Has also contributed to a number of legal journals and is an examiner for the Institute of Fisheries Management.
Prof. Memberships: Law Society.
Career: Qualified in 1999. Senior legal advisor to the Environment agency in its North West Regional Office. Joined *Halliwell Landau* in 1999.
Personal: Born in 1959. BA (Hons) Government and Politics 1988. LLB (London) (Hons) 1993. Recreations include football, cricket, hockey and horse racing.

HOWARD, Karen
D J Freeman, London
(020) 7583 4055

HUGHES, Norna
Nabarro Nathanson, London
(020) 7524 6000
n.hughes@nabarro.com
Specialisation: Heads planning department. Handles all aspects of planning related work, particularly contentious planning and Judicial Review.
Career: Qualified in 1989. Joined *Nabarro Nathanson* in 1987, becoming a partner in 1989. Previously a Barrister specialising in planning, having been called to the Bar in 1983.
Personal: Leisure interests include family, friends, socialising and tennis. Lives in London.

INNES, Colin
Shepherd+ Wedderburn, Edinburgh
(0131) 473 5104
colin.innes@shepwedd.co.uk
Specialisation: Partner in Litigation Department. Head of the Planning and Environmental Group specialising exclusively in planning and environmental issues. Has substantial experience of advising on planning or related issues to clients both in the private and public sectors, including on the contentious side representation at public local inquiries, planning appeals and judicial review of planning decisions in the Court of Session. In relation to non-contentious work has extensive experience in providing advice on all types of planning projects and PFI schemes.
Prof. Memberships: Law Society (England and Wales), Law Society (Scotland) and UKELA, WS Society. Legal associate, Royal Town Planning Institute.
Career: LL.B (Hons) University of Aberdeen. LL.M (Environmental Law) University of Aberdeen.

JACKSON, Andrew
Macfarlanes, London
(020) 7831 9222

JACKSON, Ray
Linklaters, London
(020) 7456 4884
ray.jackson@linklaters.com
Specialisation: Head of the Planning and Environmental Group. Specialises in all aspects of town planning development work including compulsory purchase, highways, local government law and regulatory matters such as environmental impact assessments. Typical projects have included a wide selection of major property transactions including planning and TWA public inquiries for motorways and large infrastructure schemes and also compensation claims in the Lands Tribunal.
Prof. Memberships: Member of the Planning & Environment Committee of the British Property Federation; the London Office Review Panel of the GLA and founding Member of the City of London Law Society Planning and Environmental Law Sub-Committee.
Career: Joined *Linklaters* in December 1985, made Partner in May 1988.

JAMESON, Robert
Jameson & Hill, Hertford
(01992) 554881

JEEPS, Barry
Stephenson Harwood (incorporating Sinclair Roche & Temperley), London
(020) 7809 2513
barry.jeeps@shlegal.com
Specialisation: Partner Property, Head of Town and Country Planning Group. Extensive experience in all aspects of town and country planning, compulsory purchase and Transport and Works Act applications with particular emphasis on large-scale public inquiries and litigation. Planning advice in relation to London Bridge City (one of the largest urban regeneration projects in the country) and the Trafford Centre, Manchester (a major shopping centre) planning permission for which was defended successfully in the House of Lords.
Career: Joined *Stephenson Harwood* in 1980 and qualified in 1982. Partner and Head of Town and Country Planning Group in 1989.
Personal: Born 1958. Educated at St Catherine's College, Oxford.

KITSON, Tony
CMS Cameron McKenna, London
(020) 7367 3556
tony.kitson@cmck.com
Specialisation: Partner and Head of Planning Group. Advises on the planning aspects of all types of property development. Has handled numerous appeals involving retail, office, industrial and residential developments. Experienced in negotiating and drafting Section 106 Agreements and other development agreements. Advises on all aspects of local authority law and administration, and PFI schemes. Advises on compulsory purchase and compensation, and Transport and Works Act schemes, the clean-up of contaminated industrial sites and disposal for redevelopment.
Prof. Memberships: Law Society, Law Society's Panel of Planning Solicitors. City of London Law Society.
Career: Qualified in 1975. Local authority solicitor before joining *McKenna & Co* in 1988; became a Partner in 1990.
Personal: Born 14 February 1952. Lives in London.

KRATZ, Philip
Taylor Vinters, Cambridge
(01223) 225184
philip.kratz@taylorvinters.com
Specialisation: All aspects of town and country planning and environmental law. Experienced advocate. Work includes agreements, applications, appeals (including local inquiries), local plan and structure plan representations. Recent experience has included acting in connection with large scale residential proposals in Cambridge and the surrounding area; commercial proposals throughout the country; and complex s.106 planning obligations.
Prof. Memberships: Law Society; member of the Law Society's Specialist Planning Panel; Legal Associate member of the Royal Town Planning Institute.
Career: Qualified in 1982. District Solicitor and Head of Legal Services with East Cambridgeshire District Council from 1983-1992; Assistant Chief Executive until joining *Taylor Vinters* in May 1995. Head of Planning Development and Construction Team.
Personal: Leisure interests include cricket, Jaguar cars and military engineering.

LANCASTER, Roger
Halliwell Landau, Manchester
(0161) 831 2743
rlancaster@halliwells.co.uk
Specialisation: Partner and Head of Planning and Environmental Law Department. Specialises in town and country planning, environmental law, compulsory purchase matters, local government issues and general advocacy at inquiries. Has substantial house building

THE LEADERS ■ PLANNING

retail and developer clients and also acts for public sector authorities.
Prof. Memberships: Law Society.
Career: Qualified in 1975. Solicitor with Humberside County Council and Birmingham City Council. Joined *Halliwell Landau* as a Partner in 1982. Senior Partner 1995-2000.
Personal: Born in 1951. Educated at Biddulph Grammar School and Leicester University (LLB 1971). Recreations include cricket, squash and gardening.

LEA, Alison
Travers Smith Braithwaite, London
(020) 7295 3000
Alison.Lea@TraversSmith.com
Specialisation: Partner and head of planning and environment group. Specialises in all aspects of planning and environmental law including highway matters and compulsory purchase. Has recently acted on a number of successful judicial review applications and High Court challenges for Lafarge Redland Aggregates, Clearwater Estates and Lend Lease Norwich Ltd. Particular experience in negotiating consents for large retail, leisure and residential mixed use schemes including the drafting and negotiation of planning and infrastructure agreements.
Prof. Memberships: City of London Law Society Planning and Environment Law Sub-Committee. Legal associate of Royal Town Planning Institute.
Career: Trained *Norton Rose*; qualified 1989. *Norton Rose* 1987-97. *Travers Smith Braithwaite* 1997 to date; made partner in 1998.
Publications: Author of monthly Planning Focus in 'Property Law Journal', member of contributory board of 'Property Law Journal'. Articles in 'Journal of Planning and Environmental Law', 'Environmental Law Monthly' and 'Environmental Law Review'.
Personal: Educated at Rainford High School and Girton College, Cambridge. Interests include horse riding and playing classical piano and flute.

MACLEOD, Ewan
Shepherd+ Wedderburn, Edinburgh
(0131) 228 9900

MANSON, Stephen
Eversheds, Cardiff
(029) 2047 1147
stephenmanson@eversheds.com
Specialisation: Partner specialising in town and country planning, Private Finance Initiative/Public Private Partnership work together with general public sector development work. Former member of Government's Private Finance Panel Executive. Advises a number of local minerals developers on such matters as the current minerals review procedures. Advised United News and Media on planning appeal for alternative use of studio site in Cardiff. Acts for both public and private sectors on PFI schemes in a variety of areas such as education (advised Wiltshire County Council on its three schools deal – £30m), health (advised health trust on local hospital scheme in Cardiff – £15m) and transport (advised Newport County Borough Council on its Southern Distributor Road – £40m).
Career: Bristol University (LLB Hons). Bristol Polytechnic (LSF First Class Hons).
Personal: Recreations include windsurfing and badminton.

MARRON, Peter
Marrons, Leicester
(0116) 289 2200
petermarron@marrons.net
Specialisation: Senior partner in planning, development and public law department. Has 25 years' experience of contentious town planning, together with associated work advising the development industry. Also handles public law matters, compulsory purchase and judicial review. Has acted in cases ranging from new village schemes, landfill proposals and many other applications of strategic importance. Has given talks over the years to a number of bodies. Major clients include national housebuilders, major land promoters, commercial developers, local authorities and higher education institutions.
Prof. Memberships: Law Society, Chartered Institute of Arbitrators.
Career: Qualified in 1970. Founded *Marron Dodds* as a senior partner in 1978. DOT/ RYA Ocean Yacht Master with commercial endorsement. ACIArb 1990. Fellow of the Royal Society of Arts 1995. Legal Associate of the Royal Town Planning Institute. Member of International Bar Assocation. Member of Law Society's Planning Panel. Fellow of the Institute of Advanced Legal Studies.
Personal: Born 3 June 1944. Attended Liverpool University (LLB Hons 1966). Leisure interests include the arts and offshore sailing. Lives in Uppingham, Rutland.

MAX, Richard
Olswang, London
(020) 7208 8616
rdm@olswang.com
Specialisation: Partner in Property Group. Head of planning. Deals with all areas of planning law and practice as well as compulsory purchase and highways matters. Noted solicitor-advocate at planning inquiries. Represents both private and public sectors including developers, retailers, housebuilders and local authoritites.
Prof. Memberships: Law Society's Planning Panel; Chairman of the City of London Law Society Planning and Environmental Law Sub-Committee; Legal Associate and Council Member of the Royal Town Planning Institute.
Career: Qualified in 1988. Assistant solicitor at *Macfarlanes* 1988-93. Planning solicitor, Oxford City Council 1993. At *Radcliffes & Co* 1993-95. Joined *D J Freeman* in April 1995 – made partner in May 1997 and head of planning in 1999. *Olswang* – partner and head of planning 2001.
Personal: Born 1 September 1963. Educated at St Paul's School 1976-82, Oxford Polytechnic 1982-85 and The College of Law, Chester 1985-86. Interests include exhibiting and driving a convertible VW Beetle as well as skiing and cycling. Lives in London.

MCCHLERY, Frances
Simpson & Marwick, Glasgow
(0141) 248 2666

MCKIE, Alastair
Anderson Strathern WS, Edinburgh
(0131) 220 2345
Specialisation: Joint Head of Planning and Environmental Group with over 10 years experience in this area. Specialises in all areas contentious and non-contentious planning law including planning appeals, local plan inquiries, enforcement appeals, judicial review; planning agreements, compulsory purchase and due diligence. Particular area of expertise is inquiry advocacy. Practice covers a diverse portfolio of housing, commercial, transport and energy-related projects.
Prof. Memberships: Law Society of Scotland; Royal Town Planning Institute; Society of Writers to HM Signet.
Career: Qualified 1987. Partner at *Anderson Strathern WS* since 2001. Accredited as a specialist in planning law by the Law Society of Scotland; Elected Legal Associate of the Royal Town Planning Institute.
Personal: Educated at Lornshill Academy 1975-80, Dundee University 1980-84. Leisure pursuits include squash, hill walking and fishing. Born 15 June 1962. Lives in Edinburgh.

MORITZ, John
Wake Dyne Lawton, Chester
(01829) 773100
jmm@wdl.co.uk
Specialisation: Initially in local government. Has advised on a number of major development projects in the North West and nationally involving urban regeneration and contaminated land. Advises housebuilders, commercial developers waste management companies and local authorities on planning and infrastructure law, compulsory purchase and environment law.
Prof. Memberships: Member of the Law Society's Planning Panel and a Member of the United Kingdom Environmental Law Association.
Career: Qualified in 1973. Partner at *Lambert Storey* in 1990. Joined *Masons* in 1990 as a partner.
Personal: Born in Manchester, 20 September 1948. LLB Manchester University. Leisure interests include travel, theatre and viewing and appreciating art and architecture.

O'TOOLE, Eliza
Macfarlanes, London
(020) 7831 9222

PASTERFIELD, Stephen
Clarke Willmott & Clarke, Bristol
(0117) 941 6656
spasterfield@cw-c.co.uk
Specialisation: Partner specialising in planning, handling all issues relating to development including mineral extraction, waste disposal, urban regeneration, retailing, office and residential uses; also compensation and environmental law including waste management licensing, contaminated land, nuisance and water pollution. Acts for government departments, developers, financial institutions, minerals and waste operators, and local authorities as well as private individuals. Recent cases include appearing as advocate for Torridge District Council throughout its four month long local plan inquiry; appearing for a national housebuilder in a rare Purchase Notice Inquiry; appearing for a statutory undertaker at a CPO inquiry and in successful related negotiations on diversion of a large commercial canal and new swing bridge carrying city bypass in the South West; and acting for one of the firm's major clearing banks in planning appeals relating to listed branches in various parts of the country.
Prof. Memberships: Law Society's Planning Panel; Legal Associate of the Royal Town Planning Institute; UKELA.
Career: Birkenhead School; articled Watford Borough Council (1969-74); admitted 1974; principal assistant solicitor at Solihull Metropolitan Borough Council (1976-79); deputy city solicitor Winchester (1979-88); associate then partner *Lawrence Tucketts* (1992-99); joined *Clarke Willmott & Clarke* as partner 1999.

PIATT, Andrew
DLA, Manchester
(08700) 111111

PUGH, Tim
Berwin Leighton Paisner, London
(020) 7760 1000
timothy.pugh@berwinleightonpaisner.com
Specialisation: Partner; Co-Head Planning and Environment Department. Planning and Environmental Law. Particular areas of planning-related expertise: rail and infrastructure projects, urban regeneration, retail, industrial, warehousing, waste disposal, land reclamation and housing projects; compulsory purchase; highway orders; planning and infrastructure agreements; Transport and Works Act Orders. Particular areas of environment-related expertise: contaminated land; waste disposal; environmental impact statements; water law; environmental terms and conditions of contract.
Prof. Memberships: City of London Solicitors Company, IBA, Society for Advanced Legal Studies (SAALS). Member: Planning and Environment Committee of the British Property Federation; Planning and Environment Law Sub Committee of the City of London

PLANNING ■ THE LEADERS

Law Society; IBA's Committee on International Environmental Law; and SAALS Planning and Environmental Law Reform Group.
Career: Qualified 1984. Articled at *Donne Mileham & Haddock* 1982-84. Joined *Berwin Leighton* (now *Berwin Leighton Paisner*) 1984; Partner 1990.
Personal: Born 1959. Education Duffryn High School, Newport, Gwent; University College, London; and College of Law, Lancaster Gate. Leisure skiing, cycling and lying under old cars. Resides in Hove.

QUALTROUGH, John
Simmons & Simmons, London
(020) 7628 2020
john.qualtrough@simmons-simmons.com
Specialisation: Partner in Property Department. Advises on all areas of planning law and practice including appeals; objections and representations to local plans; and the drafting and negotiation of planning, highway and other infrastructure agreements; highways; compulsory purchase; and compensation issues. In addition he deals with commercial property matters where planning is a significant element, including option agreements, conditional contracts and sales coupled with overage/clawback provisions.
Prof. Memberships: Law Society; City of London Law Society (Committee member of Planning and Environmental Law Sub-Committee).
Career: Qualified 1978. Partner at *Simmons & Simmons* since 1988.
Personal: Born 30 April 1953. Holds a BA (1974).

QUAYLE, Sophie
Herbert Smith, London
(020) 7374 8000
sophie.quayle@herbertsmith.com
Specialisation: Partner specialising in planning matters. Advises on a range of matters including planning applications and associated documents, call-in inquiries, planning appeals, section 106 agreements and section 278/38 agreements and conditions, implementation of planning permissions, development plans, PFI projects and general planning/property development matters. Also advises on judicial review and statutory appeals in relation to planning matters.
Prof. Memberships: City of London Law Society Planning and Environmental sub-committee.
Career: *Herbert Smith* (1989 to date). Qualified 1991. Partner 1998.
Personal: LLB (Southampton University).

RICKETTS, Simon
SJ Berwin, London
(020) 7533 2768
simon.ricketts@sjberwin.com
Specialisation: Planning and local government law, advising institutions and developers on major retail/business/residential/leisure schemes, including negotiating related agreements, coordinating appeals and legal challenges. Extensive experience in compulsory purchase and related procedures.
Prof. Memberships: Member of Law Society, Member of PLC Property Editorial Board.
Career: Called to the Bar 1985. Member of planning group at *Lovell White Durrant* (now *Lovells*) 1988 before moving to *SJ Berwin* in 1997. Partner 1999. Requalified as a solicitor 1991.

ROBINSON, Patrick
Burges Salmon, Bristol
(0117) 902 2740
patrick.robinson@burges-salmon.com
Specialisation: Partner and head of planning unit with all planning issues, including negotiation on planning and other infrastructure agreements and appearing as an advocate at planning inquiries; recent projects have included advising the UK Nirex on Radioactive waste management issues, advising 186K on new fibre optic telecoms network.
Prof. Memberships: Legal Associate of the Royal Town Planning Institute and a member of the Law Society specialist Planning Panel.
Career: Before joining *Burges Salmon* in 1990, he worked as a planning solicitor with Southampton City Council. Became a partner and head of planning unit in 1995.
Personal: University of Leicester 1982-85. Enjoys his motorbike and yachting.

ROBINSON, Patrick
Herbert Smith, London
(020) 7374 8000
patrick.robinson@herbertsmith.com

SALES, Martin
Burness, Edinburgh
(0131) 473 6000

SMITH, Bruce
Paull & Williamsons, Aberdeen
(01224) 621621
gbsmith@paull-williamsons.co.uk
Specialisation: Partner in Planning and Environmental Law Department. Main area of practice is planning. Advises on planning applications, appeals, enforcement notice appeals, local and structure plans and the conduct of public inquiries. Also handles environmental law. Advises on waste disposal licences, river purification issues and other issues arising out of the Environmental Protection Act. Has acted in many of the major planning inquiries in Scotland over the last decade. Visiting Professor of Law at Robert Gordon University, Aberdeen.
Prof. Memberships: Law Society of Scotland, Society of Advocates in Aberdeen. Law Society accredited specialist in Planning Law.
Career: Qualified in 1967. Joined *Paull & Williamsons* in 1970, becoming a Partner in 1973.
Personal: Born 15 June 1947. Attended Aberdeen University 1964-67 (LLB). Chairman of Abernethy Trust which runs four residential outdoor pursuit centres in Scotland. Leisure interests include golf, skiing and sailing. Lives in Aberdeen.

SMITH, Tim
Berwin Leighton Paisner, London
(020) 7760 1000
timothy.smith@blplaw.com
Specialisation: Partner handling all aspects of Planning and Environmental work including inquires and court work, strategic advice, infrastructure agreements, compulsory purchase and highways. Acted for Chelsfield in relation to White City, and in relation to West Quay, Southampton. Other major clients include Tesco, British Land, Ministry of Defence, and Southampton City Council
Prof. Memberships: Member of Planning Inspectorate's advisory 'user group' panel.
Career: Educated at Thomas Beckett Upper School Northampton, and Nottingham University. Articled and qualified with *Hewitson Becke & Shaw*. Joined *Berwin Leighton* 1996.
Publications: Planning chapter of 'Commercial Transaction Checklists', and environmental chapter of 'CBI European Business Handbook 1999' (with Andrew Waite).
Personal: Leisure interests include rugby (lifelong supporter of Northampton RFC) and fell walking.

TAYLOR, Peter
Hewitson Becke + Shaw, Northampton
(01604) 233233
petertaylor@hewitsons.com
Specialisation: All planning work including advocacy at planning appeals and local plan inquiries; Section 106 Agreements; judicial reviews; enforcements and general planning law. Acts for companies, private individuals and local authorities.
Prof. Memberships: The Law Society; Legal Associate R.T.P.I.; Member of The Law Society's Specialist Planning Panel.
Career: Qualified in 1985; *Shacklocks Solicitors* Mansfield 1985-86; *Hewitson Becke + Shaw* Solicitors Northampton 1986 to date (Partner since 1989).
Personal: Born 2 October 1960; Educated at Brunts Grammar School, Mansfield; Birmingham University and Chester Law College. Interests include: athletics and marathon running.

THOMAS, Patricia
SJ Berwin, London
(020) 7533 2222
pat.thomas@sjberwin.com
Specialisation: Principal areas of practice are planning and local government law including highways, land drainage and water matters, conservation issues (natural and built heritage) and environment law including environmental impact assessment, compliance and due diligence audits, advice on IPC authorisations, water abstraction licences, pollution and waste cases. Extensive experience of airport and aviation-related developments. Editor of and main contributor to 'The Planning Factbook'. Editor of 'Environmental Liability' and 'Water Pollution: Law and Liability'. Contributed planning law chapter to 'The Surveyor's Factbook'. Lectures frequently on planning and environmental topics.
Prof. Memberships: Law Society (member of Committee on Planning and Environmental Law), City of London Solicitors' Company (member of Planning and Environment Committee), International Bar Association. Member of Law Society's Specialist Planning Panel. CBI Property Management Forum. Trustee, TC.PA. Trustee, Theatres Trust.
Career: Qualified 1974. Planning Solicitor and Advocate, Greater London Council and London Borough of Southwark 1975-79. Joined *Denton Hall Burgin & Warrens* in 1979 and became a Partner in 1981, then moved to *S J Berwin & Co.* in 1988 as a Partner and Head of Planning and Environment Group.

THOMSON, Morag
Marrons, Leicester
(0116) 289 2200
moragthomson@marrons.net
Specialisation: Partner in planning, development and public law department. Has extensive experience of specialist contentious town planning and associated work, including Judicial Review and High Court Challenges to planning decisions under the 1990 Act, public law matters and compulsory purchase. Previously worked in local government for eight years. Currently advises many national and local house builders, property developers and local authorities concerning a wide range of developments. Acknowledged planning advocate. Continues to advise local authorities in relation to local plans, planning appeals, enforcement matters and other planning related issues. Regularly involved in the formation of infrastructure and planning agreements in relation to large-scale developments. Currently acting for Alconbury Developments Ltd in relation to their proposals for 7 million sq ft of rail-served warehousing at Alconbury Airport and in relation to the leading human rights case, known as 'the Alconbury Cases', the subject of a recent landmark judgment by the House of Lords.
Prof. Memberships: The Law Society, Legal Associate of the Royal Town Planning Institute and Member of the Law Society's Planning Panel.
Career: Educated at Banbury School, Nottingham University and Guildford College of Law. Qualified in 1982, following articles with New Forest District Council. 1982-1988 Planning Solicitor with Charnwood Borough Council. 1988 moved into private practice.
Personal: Lives in Mountsorrel, Leicestershire with her husband. Leisure interests include violin playing, the arts generally, golf and football.

THE LEADERS ■ PLANNING

TREHEARNE, Ian
Berwin Leighton Paisner, London
(020) 7760 1000
ian.trehearne@blplaw.com
Specialisation: Planner and Barrister. Joint Head of Planning and Environment Department. Principal area of work is planning law covering advice and advocacy on development, including major retail and office schemes, transport related developement, airports, media and entertainment, factory outlet centres, housing, hotels, utility and waste disposal developments and local plan inquiries. Specialist active on conservation, historic building and design issues. Also environment law advising on contamination liability and threats and European Community matters. Advised on Ludgate development, Regents Place, Euston Centre and tower and other major office sites in London, Ebbsfleet Station and 8.5m sq. ft. development surrounding it, five-star hotel in Bloomsbury, 1.6m sq. ft. shopping in Croydon, the Channel Tunnel Rail Link and environmental cases such as Dartford including Thames Gateway and Medway Cement Works and Welbeck, as well as Finningley and Airports, station related development for Railtrack. PFI issues: redevelopment of DSS estate in Newcastle and Sunderland; rationalisation and rebuilding of University College Hospital, United Medical and Dental Schools and King's College, London. Numerous conferences and seminars. Lectured at City University 1982-84.
Prof. Memberships: Royal Town Planning Institute.
Career: London Borough of Newham, 1972-4, then joined the London Borough of Islington 1974-76. City of Westminster 1977-9. Joined the London Borough of Camden in 1979 and moved to *Berwin Leighton* in 1985. Admitted to Partnership in 1988. Called to the Bar 1980.
Personal: Born 17th May 1950. Attended Durham University 1968-71. Leisure pursuits include sailing, building, books and music. Lives in London.

TRINICK, Marcus
Bond Pearce, Southampton
(023) 8072 0750
mtrinick@bondpearce.com
See under Environment, p.363

TRUE, Justin
Dechert, London
(020) 7583 5353
justin.true@dechertEU.com
Specialisation: Head of the Planning Unit. Principal areas of practice include planning application, EIAs, planning appeals, highways, environment, local government, CPO and compensation work and judicial review for retailers, housebuilders, developers, corporate and public sector clients. Experienced advocate and professional witness. Negotiates complex planning and infrastructure agreements.
Prof. Memberships: Royal Town Planning Institute.
Career: Has a background in Local Government in London and the Home Counties between 1974 and 1985. Joined *Titmuss Sainer Dechert (now Dechert)* in 1985. Member and former Director of the Association of Town Centre Management (1994-2000). Member of the Planning Task Group of the British Retail Consortium (1996-2000).
Personal: Born 1955. BA Hons Planning Studies and Diploma in Town Planning, Oxford Brooks University. Leisure pursuits include golf, skiing and cycling. Lives in Surrey.

VALENTINE, Richard
Pitmans, Reading
(0118) 958 0224
rvalentine@pitmans.com
Specialisation: The co-ordination and implementation of strategies and tactics employed in relation to major planning proposals, particularly in connection with inquiries and judicial reviews. In the last five years, he has increasingly specialised in the judicial review process as a means of challenging planning decision and in the statutory appeal procedures. Notable involvements have involved Copas v Royal Borough of Windsor & Maidenhead; Jones v The Secretary of State for Wales; Somerfield Stores Limited v Hambleton District Council; Baber v SoSETR; McLean Homes Limited v SoSETR and Chelmsford Borough Council; Rockhold v SoSETR; Somerfield Stores Limited v Flintshire County Council.
Prof. Memberships: Law Society.
Career: Partner *Stephenson Harwood* 1973-77. Partner *Pitmans* 1977-.
Personal: Travel, fishing and shooting, classic cars and any lawful intellectual challenge.

WADE-SMITH, Richard
Wilbraham & Co, Leeds
(0113) 243 2200
Specialisation: Partner with wide experience in planning work but with special knowledge on environmental assessment for infrastructure and energy projects. Practice covers industrial, retail and leisure development; renewable energy development; on shore gas exploitation; electricity transmission; and water and sewage treatment. Recent projects include major employment schemes in the West Midlands, surface mining in the North East, a mix of renewable energy schemes throughout the UK; and substantial wind energy projects.
Prof. Memberships: Member of the Law Society's Specialist Planning Panel, loyal associate of Royal Town Planning Institute, consultant editor to the Environmental Law Reports, and lectures regularly on environmental and planning law issues.

WATKINS, David
Linklaters, London
(020) 7456 4852
david.watkins@linklaters.com
Specialisation: Planning and environmental law specialist. Experienced in all aspects of town planning and development activity, including obtaining all requisite planning and other consents, compulsory purchase orders, road closure orders, planning, highways and drainage agreements. Environmental law expertise includes advising on the contaminated land regime, the development of brownfield sites and the environmental implications of corporate disposals.
Career: 1997 to date: Partner, *Linklaters*, Environment and Planning Group; 1987-97: Assistant solicitor, *Linklaters*; 1985-87: Assistant solicitor *Shepherd & Wedderburn WS*; 1983-85: Trainee solicitor, *Shepherd & Wedderburn WS*. 1978-83: Edinburgh University, LLB (Hons).

WELLS, Martin
Stephenson Harwood (incorporating Sinclair Roche & Temperley), London
(020) 7809 2529
martin.wells@shlegal.com
Specialisation: Senior Associate Property: planning group. Advises on planning and related matters. Recent cases have included advising on major developments for the University of Greenwich, Accor Group, The Royal Bank of Scotland Group, Royal Albert Hall, Canterbury College, South East Essex College, East Berkshire College, London Development Agency, London Transport Property and KPMG. Regular speaker at internal training seminars.
Prof. Memberships: Legal Associate, RTPI; City of London Law Society's Planning and Environmental Law Sub-Committee.
Career: Legal posts in local government 1965-87; assistant, *Denton Hall Burgin & Warrens* 1987-88. Joined *Stephenson Harwood* in 1988 and became senior associate in 1989.
Publications: Contributions to 'Property Week', 'Planning', 'Planning in London'.

WHITE, Martin
Pinsent Curtis Biddle, Birmingham
(0121) 200 1050
martin.white@pinsents.com
Specialisation: Handles planning and related areas, including highways and environmental issues, with emphasis on town centre regeneration, planning appeal work, development plans, compulsory purchase, issues of planning gain, Section 106 agreements, rail-related scheme and waste matters. Has acted in appeals relating to major inward investment, airports and business parks, for local Planning Authorities and private sector clients. Also handles local government and public law generally. Author of articles, speaker at conferences and seminars on planning gain and general planning issues.
Prof. Memberships: Law Society (Member of Planning Panel), Legal Associate of Royal Town Planning Institute.
Career: Qualified in 1979. Articled at Solihull Council 1977-79. Joined *Pinsent & Co* in 1981. Partner in 1987.
Personal: Born 1953. Attended Cambridge University 1972-76; Newcastle Polytechnic 1976-77. Interests include drama and music.

WILBRAHAM, Peter
Wilbraham & Co, Leeds
(0113) 243 2200
peter.wilbraham@wilbraham.co.uk
Specialisation: Acts for public and private sector clients, who are involved in a wide range of development issues, including housing, employment, retail and infrastructure projects. Also undertaking sensitive listed buildings and conservation area projects on behalf of the National Trust and various public bodies. Leading teams involved in the planning process, formulating strategy and, normally negotiating a successful conclusion to meet client's requirements.
Prof. Memberships: Honorary Solicitor and Secretary to the Royal Town Planning Institute; a member of the Council of the RTPI; and a member of the Law Society's Specialist Planning Panel. Lectures regularly on planning law issues at professional conferences as well as at Leeds Metropolitan University; and gave the main paper at the planning law conference at the University of Ulster.
Career: Specialist in planning law for over 30 years. In 1994 founded *Wilbraham & Co* – a niche planning and environmental law practice which is consistently ranked as one of the leading firms in its specialism.

WILLIAMS, Huw
Edwards Geldard, Cardiff
(029) 2023 8239
huw.williams@geldards.co.uk
See under Administrative & Public Law, p.49

WILLIAMSON, Andrew
Walker Morris, Leeds
(0113) 283 2500

WINTER, Paul
Eversheds, Manchester
(0161) 831 8000
paulwinter@eversheds.com
Specialisation: Partner in Property Department. Main areas of practice are planning and environmental law. Experience includes major town centre schemes, large urban regeneration projects and residential development. Enjoys both the advocacy and the negotiation aspects. Particularly handles environmental aspects of property transactions (especially contaminated land), waste management and development. Contributed 'Contaminated Land' and 'Planning and the Environment' chapters in College of Law Environmental Law Book. Delivered a paper on Environmental Impact Assessment at the Law Society, Bar Council and RICS Oxford Joint Planning Law Conference in September 2000, having been heavily involved in this aspect of planning work.
Prof. Memberships: Law Society, Town & Country Planning Association (Policy Council). Member of Specialist Planning

Panel of the Law Society. Legal Associate of the Royal Town Planning Institute. Notary Public. Accredited Mediator (working on Planning Inspectorate's pilot study on mediation). Also, member of the Oxford Joint Planning Law Conference Committee.
Career: Qualified 1976. Joined *Eversheds Hepworth & Chadwick* as a Partner in 1989.
Personal: Born 24 April 1949. Attended Leeds University 1968-72. Leisure interests include music and opera, walking, travelling and reading. Lives near Leeds.

WOOD, David
Bevan Ashford, Bristol
(0117) 975 1635
david.wood@bevanashford.co.uk
Specialisation: Partner, Public Sector Division. Main area of practice is health and safety and environmental, planning and food law. Handled local authority planning work in Essex 1972-76; specialising in advocacy at Public Inquiries and the presentation and defence of regulatory offences while a partner in Bristol. Has acted on health and safety matters for both public and private sector clients and regularly prosecutes for HSE.
Prof. Memberships: Law Society, UK Environmental Law Association.
Career: Qualified in 1969. Worked at *Hatten, Jewers & Mepham* in Basildon, Essex 1969-76. Partner at *Harris & Harris*, Bristol 1976-88, then partner *at Bevan Ashford* since 1988.
Publications: Author of an article in 'Urban Regeneration'. Wrote planning law section for NHS Estates 'Estate Code' guidance to land transactions by Health Authorities and Trusts and guidance on the law of Commons and Town and Village Greens for NHS Estates.
Personal: Born 7 January 1946. Attended Taunton School, Somerset 1957-62. Interests: walking, gardening, cricket and history.

PRIVATE EQUITY

London – Buyouts & Investment: 657; Debt: 659; Fund Formation: 661; The Regions: 661; Profiles: 662

Research approved by BMRB For this edition, **Chambers'** researchers conducted 6,582 interviews – 3,900 with law firms, 511 with barristers and 2,171 with clients. The validity of the research was scrutinised by BMRB International, who audited both the methodology and the results at our offices in London. They interviewed **Chambers'** researchers and cross-checked sample interviews. Details of the audit appear on page 7.

OVERVIEW It has been a difficult year for many, given the paucity of premium transactions, fallout suffered by the TMT sector and general economic uncertainty. Certain dynamics are working against the market, such as a tendency on the part of investors to hold out for cheaper deals and the difficulty in accessing bank finance, however, there is still a lot of money around, bringing with it a degree of optimism. The movement away from technology has rekindled interest in property based deals, such as pubs and nursing homes.

LONDON

BUYOUTS & INVESTMENT

PRIVATE EQUITY
BUYOUTS & INVESTMENT ■ LONDON

1
- Ashurst Morris Crisp
- Clifford Chance

2
- Allen & Overy
- Macfarlanes

3
- Dickson Minto WS
- Lovells
- Travers Smith Braithwaite

4
- Freshfields Bruckhaus Deringer

5
- CMS Cameron McKenna
- Olswang
- SJ Berwin

6
- Nabarro Nathanson

LEADING INDIVIDUALS

1
- BAIRD James *Clifford Chance*
- DICKSON Alastair *Dickson Minto WS*
- GEFFEN Charles *Ashurst Morris Crisp*
- LAYTON Matthew *Clifford Chance*

2
- COMPAGNONI Marco *Lovells*
- HALE Chris *Travers Smith Braithwaite*
- HANTON Bruce *Ashurst Morris Crisp*
- MARTIN Charles *Macfarlanes*
- PAUL Alan *Allen & Overy*

3
- BARTER Charles *Travers Smith Braithwaite*
- BEDDOW Simon *Ashurst Morris Crisp*
- BOWN Christopher *Freshfields Bruckhaus Deringer*
- DAVIS Steven *SJ Berwin*
- MEEK Charles *Macfarlanes*
- MURRAY-JONES Allan *Skadden, Arps*
- WHITE Graham *Linklaters*

4
- BAIRD Derek *Lovells*
- CARPANINI Fabrizio *Olswang*
- SHEACH Andrew *CMS Cameron McKenna*
- TUFFNELL Kevin *Macfarlanes*

5
- GREAVES Adam *Gouldens*
- HOWARD Susan *Allen & Overy*
- MACKIE Chris *Olswang*
- PEARSON David *Clifford Chance*

UP AND COMING
- MCNAIR Martin *Dickson Minto WS*

This book is the product of 6,582 1/2 hour interviews. See p.7 for BMRB audit.
Within each band, firms are listed alphabetically. See individuals' profiles p.662

ASHURST MORRIS CRISP (see firm details p.852) Unanimously acclaimed during our research for its *"excellent track record and vast experience,"* the team remains in the vanguard, despite a quieter year. Underpinned by *"high quality cross-departmental support,"* especially for environmental matters, it is further bolstered by what the market sees as the firm's *"steadily improving"* international reach. A clear favourite amongst clients, *"talented generalist"* **Charlie Geffen** (see p.663) is said to *"reel in the business"*. He recently co-advised Cinven and other institutional vendors on the £1.15 billion sale of IPC Group to Time Inc. Geffen is complemented by *"diligent"* **Bruce Hanton** (see p.663) and cross-border M&A specialist **Simon Beddow** (see p.662). Beddow recently advised OAG Worldwide and funds managed by Electra Partners Europe on the cross-border MBI of the Official Airlines Guide, owned by Reed Elsevier. Recent highlights for the team include acting for Cinven on its proposed acquisition of Vivendi Universal Publishing in France (€2 billion), acting for Apax Partners on its €418.5 million acquisition of Azimut, the fund management division of Bipop-Carire, and advising Go Fly's management team on the MBO of Go Fly from British Airways for £110 million. **Clients** Cinven; Apax Partners; ABN AMRO Private Equity; Bridgepoint Capital; Legal & General Ventures; PPM Ventures; OAG Worldwide.

CLIFFORD CHANCE (see firm details p.911) *"A great practice – the strongest overall"* is a common reaction from competitors and clients. Frequently visible on the highest profile deals, peers appreciate the team's user-friendly approach (*"the deal moves along at the right speed,"*) whilst clients are attracted by additional strength on the debt side and the firm's *"unrivalled cross-border critical mass."* **Matthew Layton** (see p.664) and **James Baird** (see p.662) form a double spearhead. Of Layton one peer commented: *"There is no posturing with him – he grasps the essentials and applies common sense even when things are fraught."* He advised Royal Bank Private Equity and Patron Capital on the £200 million institutional buyout of iGroup, led by GE Capital and iGroup management. Baird co-led the team advising CVC Capital Partners on the Austrian public to private of Lenzing from Bank Austria, together with the associated merger with certain businesses of Acordis (total €700 million), and acted on the £186 million institutional buyout of Aventis Animal Nutrition. Corporate partner **David Pearson** (see p.244) is increasingly visible on private equity transactions and recently led the team advising Apax Partners on the €528 million leveraged buyout of the Ericsson Enterprise Solution Channel business. Further highlights for the team include advising HSBC Private Equity on its further equity investment into TMD Holding for the acquisition of the Ruetgers brakes business (€60 million). **Clients** Royal Bank Private Equity; CVC Capital Partners; Candover Investments; Nomura International; Apax Partners; HSBC Private Equity; UBS Warburg; EQT Northern Europe; West Private Equity; Duke Street Capital; PPM Ventures.

ALLEN & OVERY (see firm details p.841) The team has forged a strong reputation through its involvement in large buyouts. Its track record does involve a smaller deal volume than some rivals, but the firm can draw upon the widely acknowledged *"quality and experience"* of its team, which also handles VC investment work and occasionally advises management teams. Clients prize the firm's ability *"to deal with every aspect, including banking and securitisation."* Corporate heavyweight **Alan Paul** (see p.244) (*"an extremely impressive character"*) sits at the helm, supported by **Susan Howard** (see p.663). Paul recently advised DB Capital Partners on its £670 million joint purchase of Center Parcs and Pierre & Vacances. A recent highlight for Howard was advising the shareholders (including private equity houses) of Principal Hotels on the sale of Principal Hotels for £255 million to Nomura International's Principal Finance Group. Other high-profile deals for the team include advising WestLB ASPF, the principal financial backer of Pubmaster, on Pubmaster's £485 million hostile bid for The Wolverhampton & Dudley Breweries. It also advised the management team on the buyout of Homebase from Sainsbury's for £750 million. **Clients** DB Capital Partners; WestLB ASPF; Compass Partners; Bridgepoint Capital; CapVest; Carlyle; Charterhouse Development Capital; Cinven; Commonwealth Devel-

657

PRIVATE EQUITY ■ LONDON

opment Corporation; Compass Partners; Duke Street Capital; Investcorp; JPMorgan Partners; Nomura Principal Finance; Soros Private Equity.

MACFARLANES (see firm details p.1047) Bucking market trends, the team has had a successful year with heightened visibility on major deals. While mid-market transactions form the bulk of its caseload, high-profile deals with a more international flavour are featuring increasingly. Highlights this year include representing Soros in its €3 billion recommended cash offer for eircom, and 3i on its acquisition of Go Fly for £110 million. Described by competitors as "*one of the most charismatic operators around,*" **Charles Martin** was praised for his "*unwaveringly focused and pragmatic*" approach. Head of department **Charles Meek** and **Kevin Tufnell** have both maintained strong relationships with a range of prestigious private equity houses. Other recent transactions handled by the team include advising Royal Bank Private Equity on its £441 million recommended offer for Britax International and advising Alchemy on its £161 million recommended offer for Anglian. **Clients** 3i; Advent; Alchemy; Candover; Cinven; KBDC; Gresham Trust; Royal Bank Private Equity; Sand Aire Private Equity; Soros Private Equity.

DICKSON MINTO WS (see firm details p.938) Endorsed by industry commentators as a "*quality, niche operation,*" the firm's profile is felt to have diminished following recent high-profile departures. Led by the "*excellent*" **Alastair Dickson** (see p.663), the team focuses on a broad range of domestic deals for an "*extremely loyal*" nucleus of clients. **Martin McNair** (see p.664) continues to attract praise as one of the sector's "*young hopefuls.*" Not a firm to have gone down the international expansion route, it remains active in the field and continues to win new clients. Recent highlights include advising Charterhouse Development Capital on its buyout from HSBC and advising Close Brothers Private Equity on its investment in the £45 million MBO of Park Resorts, an operator of holiday camps/caravan centres. **Clients** McLaren Global Systems; Penta Capital Partners; Charles Letts; JO Hambro Capital Management; Close Brothers Private Equity; Charterhouse Development Capital; Henderson Private Equity.

LOVELLS (see firm details p.1045) Chambers researchers were informed by our interviewees that the firm is still amidst a "*phase of readjustment*" following the move of Allan Murray-Jones to Skadden, Arps, Slate, Meagher & Flom and the recruitment of **Derek Baird** (see p.662) from Dickson Minto. The group continues to secure instructions from Doughty Hanson (a key Murray-Jones relationship) and has been buoyed by the goodwill afforded to the technical expertise of Baird. Currently channelling resources into strengthening its European network, the firm takes advantage from its impressive debt expertise and its fund formation work. Clients are attracted to its "*substantial experience and cross-border strength*" and by an "*easy to work with, creative*" team, with **Marco Compagnoni** (see p.662) singled out for his "*admirable energy and positive attitude.*" The team recently handled both the equity and debt aspects of the acquisition by Kappa Packaging of the corrugated and containerboard business of AssiDomän. **Clients** Candover; HgCapital; TI Automotive Systems; Cinven; CVC.

TRAVERS SMITH BRAITHWAITE (see firm details p.1166) A good year for the team, which is seen to be "*moving up the scales.*" Described by peers as "*a mid-market practice with frequent forays into bigger deals,*" the team has flown in the face of the general downturn with an increased visibility on public to private transactions as well as impressive work on the investment side. The market strongly endorsed team head **Chris Hale** (see p.663) as a "*well-respected operator,*" while "*charming*" **Charles Barter** (see p.662) continues to attract market commendation. The team recently advised Pinewood Studios on its acquisition of a majority stake in Shepperton Studios (£100 million) and advised 3i as the main investor in Pinewood-Shepperton, approximately a 60% stake. Other highlights include assisting the firm's new Berlin office on the €418.5 million buyout of the Italian fund management group Azimut from Bipop-Carire. **Clients** 3i; Bridgepoint; ABN AMRO; Apax; JPMorgan Partners.

FRESHFIELDS BRUCKHAUS DERINGER (see firm details p.964) Visible exclusively on "*massive transactions,*" the London office may not be as entrenched in the private equity sector as many of its rivals, though it is clearly building up expertise with a strong team led by "*effective and aggressive*" **Chris Bown** (see p.662). Its first rate client base, enviable cross-border strength and developing debt capability have helped to ensure a secure foothold and major deals. Recent highlights for the team include advising Morgan Grenfell Private Equity on the acquisition of Whitbread's 3,000-strong pub estate for £1.62 billion, and on the disposal of 439 of these pubs to Enterprise Inns for £262.5 million. The group also advised the Valentia consortium on the acquisition of eircom. **Clients** Compass Partners; INEOS; Nomura Principal Finance; DB Capital; Cinven; Warburg Pincus; UBS Warburg.

CMS CAMERON MCKENNA (see firm details p.914) Our researchers were informed that, while the group occupies the mid-market, it is best known for its breadth of practice, assisting clients in the TMT, property and hotels field. A skilled player in the MBO market, the group also advises on buy-ins, take privates and institutional purchases. Clients agreed that the firm's "*service is outstanding*" and **Andrew Sheach** (see p.664) was praised for his "*extremely commercial approach.*" The group has advised ABN AMRO Capital on the £170 million MBO of Smith & Nephew, the UK medical services group, and represented the management team and bidder on the £100 million take private of Moorfield Group. **Clients** Lloyds TSB Development Capital.

OLSWANG (see firm details p.1087) A burgeoning team with **Chris Mackie** (see p.664) and **Fabrizio Carpanini** (see p.662) carrying much of the profile. It has carved out a niche for VC work in the TMT sector and increasingly undertakes work on the buyout side. The team has advised HgCapital on the £34 million management buyout of Eagle Rock Entertainment and advised the shareholders of Merlin Communications, the global facilities management company backed by 3i, on its acquisition by Vosper Thornycroft for £95 million. On the investment side, it has advised Radiant Networks, a broadband telecommunications network developer, on a further round of funding of up to £10 million from Advent, Sandler and NatWest Pension Fund. **Clients** HgCapital; Royal Bank Ventures; Frontiers Capital; Barclays Private Equity; Graphite Capital; ISIS Capital; Gresham Trust; Lloyds TSB Development Capital; Sovereign Capital.

SJ BERWIN (see firm details p.867) The team's profile in the buyout market has been hit by Graham White's departure to Linklaters. Although it continues to receive market recommendation for its "*obviously strong*" VC work, researchers found that its transactional work tends to be overshadowed by the firm's highly successful funds practice. This active team led by "*deal-doer*" **Steven Davis** (see p.663) has recently handled a range of impressive transactions for institutional clients, including the £200 million buyout of ERM backed by 3i. It also advised Nomura International on its agreement to grant independence to Guy Hands' principal finance group. **Clients** 3i; Cazenove Private Equity; Nomura International; Carlyle; Advent Venture Partners.

NABARRO NATHANSON (see firm details p.1080) It has been a good year for the firm's corporate practice as a whole, with the private equity team advising on a steady stream of VC transactions. Its relationships with houses such as NewMedia SPARK have meant that the group is most visible for its work in the TMT sector. The team, which is lead by Rhidian Jones, has recently acted for a range of management teams and institutions. Highlights include advising Alchemy Partners on its investment in Grand Hotels Holding Company, acting for MICE on its recommended takeover for Expocentric with a transaction value of £30.5 million and acting for Cazenove Private Equity

LONDON — PRIVATE EQUITY

in the third round financing of crocus.co.uk. **Clients** Cazenove Private Equity; HSBC Ventures; Benchmark; NewMedia SPARK; MTI Partners.

OTHER NOTABLE PRACTITIONERS Graham White (see p.664) recently moved to Linklaters, where he is accruing the respect of his peers for his development of what seems set to be a sizeable team. He acted for Candover/First Leisure on the sale of Brannigans Bars and on the investment by HgCapital in Axiom Systems Holdings, an inventory software company. **Allan Murray-Jones** (see p.664) of Skadden, Arps, Slate, Meagher & Flom remains a highly respected name in the market with a "*great client base,*" whilst peers agree that **Adam Greaves** (see p.663) at Gouldens "*really knows his stuff and gets fantastic instructions.*" A leading M&A figure, his focus now lies primarily in this fields, and his team recently acted for Banc-Boston Capital on European investments in MobilRom SA, Jamoa and Kongsberg Automotive.

LONDON — DEBT

PRIVATE EQUITY
DEBT ■ LONDON

1
- Allen & Overy
- Clifford Chance

2
- Ashurst Morris Crisp

3
- Lovells

4
- Shearman & Sterling

5
- Denton Wilde Sapte
- Dickson Minto WS

6
- Freshfields Bruckhaus Deringer
- Latham & Watkins
- Norton Rose
- White & Case

LEADING INDIVIDUALS

1
- GILLESPIE Stephen *Allen & Overy*
- JOHNSON James *Clifford Chance*
- WARD Anthony *Shearman & Sterling*

2
- BARRON Michael *Dickson Minto WS*
- COTTIS Matthew *Lovells*
- GORRIE Euan *Allen & Overy*
- POLGLASE Timothy *Allen & Overy*
- STEWART Mark *Clifford Chance*
- VICKERS Mark *Ashurst Morris Crisp*

3
- CAMPBELL Mark *Clifford Chance*
- KEAL Anthony *Allen & Overy*
- SWEETING Malcom *Clifford Chance*
- WARD Nigel *Ashurst Morris Crisp*

4
- BAMBER Andrew *Allen & Overy*
- GOALEN Iain *Shearman & Sterling*
- INGLIS Alan *Clifford Chance*

UP AND COMING
- EVANS Jacqueline *Allen & Overy*
- FREEMAN Adam *Lovells*

This book is the product of 6,582 1/2 hour interviews. See p.7 for BMRB audit. Within each band, firms are listed alphabetically. See individuals' profiles p.662

ALLEN & OVERY (see firm details p.841) Despite difficult market conditions, researchers found the firm to be forging ahead in the sector, with a prominence on cross-border transactions. Its raft of "*gifted technicians*" has recently been involved in the highest profile European buyouts, and in early 2002 its banking team secured a major coup with the arrival of four heavyweights from Norton Rose. Interviewees agree that "*great resources for complex international transactions*" ensure its precedence. Whilst **Stephen Gillespie** (see p.105), who advised Goldman Sachs International and Uni-Credit Banca Mobiliare as arrangers for the senior financing of the €375 million MBO of Azimut, retains his position as one of the area's most prominent figures, **Euan Gorrie** (see p.663) is attracting increasing recognition amongst clients and peers as "*a reasonable face; he knows what he's doing and gets it done.*" He advised WestLB on the £188 million senior debt financing to support the £208 million MBO of Jim Beam Brands (Greater Europe) by Kyndal International. "*Exceptionally knowledgeable*" **Tony Keal** (see p.106) is renowned for enthusiastically pursuing his client's position, while **Jacqueline Evans** (see p.663) received praise as a "*strong performer.*" Keal advised Rabobank as arranger of the £79 million senior and mezzanine facilities for the financing of the £128.5 million leveraged acquisition by WT Tiger 3 of WT Foods, and Evans recently advised Lehman Brothers on a loan to support the £1.6 billion acquisition of Whitbread's 3,000 pubs and bars by Morgan Grenfell Private Equity.

Ex-Norton Rose **Tim Polglase** (see p.664) brings with him "*a loyal following;*" a "*thorough, lateral thinker,*" he is said by some to be "*one of the best buyout lawyers around.*" **Andrew Bamber** (see p.662), also formerly of Norton Rose, was consistently endorsed to researchers.

Recent transactions handled by the team include advising CIBC World Markets and Merrill Lynch on the public to private institutional buyout of Le Meridien Hotels by Nomura (£1.9 billion) and advising BNP Paribas, Citibank/SSSB, Sumitomo and Caja Madrid on the acquisition of Sema by Schlumberger ($3 billion). **Clients** ABN AMRO; Bank of America; Barclays Capital; BNP Paribas; Citibank; Deutsche Bank; HSBC; Goldman Sachs; JPMorgan; Merrill Lynch; Royal Bank of Scotland.

CLIFFORD CHANCE (see firm details p.911) Undisputed market leaders in terms of volume and coverage: rivals respect the team's "*firepower*" and enviable client relationships, whilst clients prize the firm's "*geographical spread.*" Paris and Frankfurt are seen as strongholds within its European empire. Among the firm's many "*likeable characters,*" **James Johnson** (see p.664) was described to researchers as "*particularly easy to get along with*" and "*a force*" on domestic deals. He recently advised SSSB, Royal Bank of Scotland, BNP Paribas and Crédit Agricole Indosuez on CVC Capital Partner's acquisition of Lafarge's speciality division (value £620 million) and CSFB on Texas Pacific's acquisition of Findexa (value £453 million). Though less visible recently, **Mark Stewart** (see p.664) remains a "*leading name*" acting for the borrower. He recently advised Royal Bank Private Equity on its recommended cash offer for the NYSE-listed DONCASTERS (which included existing high yield debt), and the latter's combination with Ross Catherall. He also represented CVC Capital Partners on the buyout of Aventis Animal Nutrition. **Mark Campbell** (see p.104) is widely regarded as "*truly excellent;*" his clients include Barclays Capital, Bank of America and UBS Warburg. He recently advised Barclays Capital on the financing of Kappa Packaging to enable the purchase of AssiDomän (€1.9 million). **Malcolm Sweeting** (see p.109) and **Alan Inglis** (see p.663) have close ties to major clients, including SSSB, JPMorgan and Goldman Sachs. **Clients** Schroder Salomon Smith Barney; Goldman Sachs; JPMorgan; CSFB; Barclays Capital; Commerzbank; Royal Bank of Scotland; BNP Paribas; Bank of America; UBS Warburg; HypoVereinsbank.

ASHURST MORRIS CRISP (see firm details p.852) The swelling team maintains a powerful profile for leveraged and acquisition finance and secures the client's vote for its "*highly professional*" approach to the completion of a deal. The group is often characterised by competitors as "*impressive on UK deals,*" while the firm's international finance practice is also rapidly evolving, with European high yield a notable field of expertise. Head of banking **Nigel Ward** (see p.664) receives accolades for his "*technical mastery,*" whilst "*talented player*" **Mark Vickers** (see p.664) specialises in the debt funding of public to private takeovers. The team has recently advised Schroder Salomon Smith Barney as financial advisor to Schlumberger on its recommended cash offer for Sema, acted for Barclays Capital, Merrill Lynch International and UBS Warburg on their provision of €1.11 billion of financing to INEOS, and advised on the public to private of Cannons (value £360 million). **Clients** Royal Bank of Scotland; Barclays

www.ChambersandPartners.com 659

PRIVATE EQUITY ■ LONDON

Bank; Intermediate Capital Group; BNP Paribas; Dresdner Kleinwort Wasserstein; SEB Acquisition Finance.

LOVELLS (see firm details p.1045) Adjudged an "*extremely professional*" outfit, the group regularly advises on a wide range of re-financings, acquisitions, MBOs and LBOs. The firm has also spent much of last year strengthening its European capacity, with dedicated partners on the ground. Spearheading the team, "*amiable*" **Matthew Cottis** (see p.663) recently acted for Royal Bank of Scotland on the £100 million Milbury Community MBO, whilst **Adam Freeman** (see p.663), now a partner, led the team advising CIBC World Markets on an acquisition facility (value £220 million). The team acted for Doughty Hanson & Co. on the £270 million refinancing of Rank Hovis McDougall and advised Bank of Scotland on the £53 million public to private of Nightfreight. **Clients** Doughty Hanson & Co; CIBC World Markets; Bank of Scotland; Royal Bank of Scotland; Dresdner Kleinwort Wasserstein; Barclays Bank; Barclays Leveraged Finance; SEB Merchant Banking; Crédit Agricole Indosuez.

SHEARMAN & STERLING (see firm details p.1129) It has been an enormously successful year for the group, which combines expertise in US and UK law. The firm's reputation for debt issues has soared, with high-profile clients praising its team of "*excellent negotiators*" for their work across the spectrum of senior debt, mezzanine and high yield. Whilst peers note that it is "*a relatively small unit,*" this is offset by what clients have described as the team's "*fantastic multi-jurisdictional capability*" and "*impressive service.*"

"*Thoughtful yet purposeful*" **Anthony Ward** is pointed to as one of the area's leading lights. He is supported by "*rising star*" **Iain Goalen**. The group has recently acted for Merrill Lynch and CIBC as underwriters of the £1.45 billion senior and high yield bridge financing of the acquisition of the Yellow Pages business of BT by Hicks Muse. It represented Merrill Lynch on the senior and junior debt financing of the acquisition by DB Capital Partners of the Center Parcs business from Scottish & Newcastle and also acted for CVC/Lecta on the €900 million refinancing of loan facilities for the Lecta Group. **Clients** Merrill Lynch; Morgan Stanley; Deutsche Bank; UBS Warburg.

DENTON WILDE SAPTE (see firm details p.935) The team was commended to our researchers as a familiar sight advising lenders and borrowers on mid-market transactions. The cross-departmental leveraged finance team draws on property, tax and employment expertise. Sarah Coucher recently led the team advising Coutts & Co and Royal Bank of Scotland on the £40 million MBO of Eagle Rock Entertainment and Royal Bank of Scotland's investment (both debt and equity) into FuelForce. **Clients** Royal Bank of Scotland; Bank of Scotland.

DICKSON MINTO WS (see firm details p.938) This team of "*specialists*" maintains a relatively low-key profile in the market while continuing to supply a "*high quality*" service to its clients. Much of its reputation lies in the domestic equity market and its work for the borrowers; the group recently advised Charles Letts in the financing of its acquisition of Filofax, which involved operations across Europe, Australia and the US. Researchers found that peers hold a "*great admiration*" for **Michael Barron** (see p.662), who is widely considered "*a pleasure to work with.*" Highlights from the last year include advising Royal Bank of Scotland on its £180 million combined debt and equity funding to acquire Wightlink. **Clients** Royal Bank of Scotland.

FRESHFIELDS BRUCKHAUS DERINGER (see firm details p.964) The group, which includes Sean Pierce, operates alongside the equity team on a range of large, cross-border transactions. Mirroring the equity team's rise in profile, *Chambers* was consistently informed by the market that the debt group is "*increasingly picking up work from high-profile clients.*" The group recently advised Valentia consortium (which consisted of Providence Equity Partners, Soros Private Equity Partners, Goldman Sachs and the eircom ESOT) on the acquisition of eircom. **Clients** Goldman Sachs; JPMorgan; Lehman Brothers.

LATHAM & WATKINS (see firm details p.1030) The "*first port of call*" for a range of US clients, who rate the team of "*experienced attorneys*" for its high yield expertise. As yet, the firm is felt to lack critical mass on the UK law side, despite the arrival of UK mezzanine and senior finance expert James Chesterman to head the banking team. The team represented CSFB in connection with e-Island's offer for eircom. **Clients** CSFB; Lehman Brothers; ING Barings; Bank of America.

NORTON ROSE (see firm details p.1084) The leveraged finance group faces rocky times following the departures in early 2002 of four of its leading names, including Tim Polglase and Andrew Bamber to Allen & Overy. Tom Speechley provides the remaining group with high yield expertise; he led the team that advised NIB Capital Bank, WestLB and Intermediate Capital Group on the £240 million secondary buyout of Leisure Link. The firm also draws heavily on its debt capacity in Paris. The market awaits the result of the firm's current round of active recruitment and period of reorganisation. **Clients** NIB Capital Bank; JPMorgan; Bank of America.

WHITE & CASE (see firm details p.1185) Active in Paris and London, the acquisition finance team has increased its market visibility through advice on a number of high-profile European transactions. The team is widely felt by peers to be "*on the up,*" although critics told researchers that it has yet to achieve the strength in depth of some of its more established rivals. Clients are clearly impressed by the technical expertise of its junior partners, while more established figures such as Maurice Allen have the requisite experience and connections to make further inroads into the market. The team recently acted for Deutsche Bank and CSFB as lead arrangers on the €633 million senior and €180 million mezzanine bridge financing of the €925 million acquisition of Klöckner Pentaplast from Klöckner Werke by Cinven. It also advised ING, Natexis Banques Populaires and ICG on the financing of the €73.8 million acquisition of the speciality chemicals business of The Goodyear Tire & Rubber Company by Littlejohn & Co. **Clients** Deutsche Bank; CIBC World Markets; ING Bank (France); Morgan Stanley Dean Witter; PRICOA Capital.

LONDON

FUND FORMATION

PRIVATE EQUITY
FUND FORMATION ■ LONDON

[1] SJ Berwin
[2] Clifford Chance
[3] Ashurst Morris Crisp
   Macfarlanes

LEADING INDIVIDUALS

[1] BLAKE Jonathan SJ Berwin
[2] BARKER Bridget Macfarlanes
   GLOVER Jason Clifford Chance
[3] GOLD Josyane SJ Berwin
   MIFSUD Mark SJ Berwin
   SHELDON Jeremy Ashurst Morris Crisp

This book is the product of 6,582 1/2 hour interviews. See p.7 for BMRB audit.
Within each band, firms are listed alphabetically. See individuals' profiles p.662

SJ BERWIN (see firm details p.867) Researchers found interviewees unanimous: "*the team is the market leader – it has a clear dominion.*" Increasing investment from Europe has seen the firm advising on a broad spectrum of funds across the continent, including buyout, development capital, funds of funds, and secondaries, evergreen and business recovery. The team is active at the cutting edge of new structures, and through successful lobbying it has recently secured exemption from the 20-partner limit for certain types of investment fund. Jonathan Blake (see p.662) recently co-led the team advising on the Apax Europe V fund (at the time the largest European private equity fund), raising €4.4 billion. It involved pan-European structuring and had approximately 170 investors. Josyane Gold (see p.663) specialises in advising VC fund managers establishing UK and European investment funds and recently led the team on the Advent Private Equity Fund III; a large fund closing at £300 million, its investment focus is emerging growth technology businesses. Mark Mifsud (see p.664) led the team for the Abingworth Bioventures III, for which $225 million was raised for investment in life sciences in the US and Europe. **Clients** Bridgepoint Capital; Advent; Apax.

CLIFFORD CHANCE (see firm details p.911) The firm has established a prominent profile for all stages of private equity investment, including fund formation. Described by clients as "*excellent for documentation,*" this team of specialists has captured a significant market share advising a range of heavyweight UK, US and European clients. Interviewees singled out Jason Glover (see p.663) as particularly "*high profile,*" with expertise covering fund formation, MBOs, MBIs and venture capital. He recently advised UBS Warburg on the establishment of a leveraged co-investment scheme investing in underlying private equity assets. The scheme raised over $4425 million from UBS Warburg executives and UBS itself. **Clients** UBS Warburg; HSBC Private Equity; UK Government.

ASHURST MORRIS CRISP (see firm details p.852) The firm's increasing European presence has bolstered its capacity in this marketplace, while its traditional links to large private equity houses such as Cinven ensure its reputation continues. The team advises on conventional and specialist fund formations, and the creation of investment vehicles. It has displayed skill in its work for pension funds investing in PE, and investors for private funds. The respected head of private funds, Jeremy Sheldon (see p.664), recently acted for Cinven on the formation of the Third Cinven Fund, which has raised €3.5 billion for European buyouts. **Clients** Carlyle; Cinven; JZ Equity Partners; West Private Equity.

MACFARLANES (see firm details p.1047) The firm combines expertise in private equity, retail funds and financial services. Peers point to the "*rock solid*" team, which maintains its strong position in the area, advising on co-investment schemes and feeder funds. Led by Bridget Barker ("*she stands for funds at Macfarlanes*"), the team recently advised Legal & General Ventures on a new, annual, English limited partnership for pan-European investment (which raised over £135 million) and HSBC Private Equity on a new technology fund. **Clients** Sand Aire Private Equity; Scottish Equity Partners; ECI Ventures.

THE REGIONS

PRIVATE EQUITY
■ THE REGIONS

[1] Addleshaw Booth & Co Leeds, Manchester
   DLA Manchester
   Eversheds Birmingham
   Hammond Suddards Edge Leeds
   Osborne Clarke Bristol
   Pinsent Curtis Biddle Birmingham, Leeds
   Wragge & Co Birmingham

This book is the product of 6,582 1/2 hour interviews. See p.7 for BMRB audit.
Within each band, firms are listed alphabetically.

ADDLESHAW BOOTH & CO (see firm details p.838) The firm can draw on strength across the firm's offices, which also includes a fledgling team in London. The private equity group possesses an enviable client roster featuring a raft of heavyweight private equity houses, while 3i continues to deliver the volume of mid-market instructions. The Manchester and London offices recently advised Barclays Private Equity on an international buyout involving the acquisition of Creative Outsourcing Solutions International. **Clients** Barclays Private Equity; 3i; Advent Venture Partners; Bridgepoint Capital; Candover Investments; HSBC Private Equity.

DLA Peers told researchers that the team is active on both equity and debt transaction. Its profile remains strong despite the departure of Andrew Roberts, head of the group, with much of its strength concentrated in the North.

EVERSHEDS (see firm details p.949) The firm is a new addition to the *Chambers* ranking this year following consistent, strong market endorsement for the "*capable and efficient*" team. Corporate finance expert Mike Seabrook, based in Birmingham, recently advised Lloyds TSB Development Capital on the MBO of Visionex 2000 (£20 million) and acted for the management team on the IBO of the Whitbread pubs and bars business (£1.7 billion). The firm acts for the private equity arms of each of the main clearing banks on a regular basis. **Clients** Lloyds TSB Development Capital.

HAMMOND SUDDARDS EDGE Considered by our interviewees to be a force in the market, the firm takes advantage from a relatively strong London base and enviable client roster. Management buyouts, buy-ins and investment work are the order of the day. The Leeds office has acted for Bon Marche on its £40 million partial sale and refinancing.

OSBORNE CLARKE (see firm details p.1090) Adjudged a "*rounded*" practice by peers, the group operates across its offices in the Thames Valley and South West, with expertise in investments, buyouts, acquisition finance and fund formation. The firm has built up close ties within the TMT sector, although its recent downturn appears not to have affected the team's profile. Researchers were informed of the group's "*sterling work,*" whilst clients praised the team's "*obvious strength*" in the field. Recent transactions on the equity side include advising Parc Technologies on £15 million investment by CSFB, Cisco, Advent International and Soros. **Clients** 3i; Barclays Private Equity; BHP Billiton Investment Group; Bridgepoint; ECI Ventures; European Internet Capital; GATX; Kleinwort Capital; Royal Bank Ventures; Bank of Scotland; Royal Bank of Scotland.

661

PRIVATE EQUITY ■ THE REGIONS/THE LEADERS

PINSENT CURTIS BIDDLE (see firm details p.1102) The thriving team has developed a niche for TMT work and acts for institutional private equity providers, management teams and companies seeking funds. It enters the *Chambers* tables this year following increased visibility on a range of high-profile deals. Paul Harkin operates from the Birmingham office. The team recently acted for the management of Britax International on the £441 million public to private buyout by Seton House Acquisition and advised the Phoenix Partnership on the joint venture with HBOS to acquire Rover Financial Services for £340 million from BMW. **Clients** Barclays Private Equity; Royal Bank Private Equity; Aberdeen Murray Johnstone Private Equity.

WRAGGE & CO (see firm details p.1197) The firm is a clear favourite amongst clients, and researchers found that the "*strong, proactive and helpful*" team has built up an "*excellent reputation*" for buyout and investment work. The team, which includes Maurice Dwyer, recently acted for Royal Bank Private Equity on the £110 million buyout of Vickers from Rolls-Royce and advised Bridgepoint Capital on the £30 million buyout of Initial Personnel Services from Rentokil. The group also advised Barclays Private Equity on the £50 million investment in Teaching Personnel. **Clients** Bridgepoint Capital; 3i; Aberdeen Murray Johnstone Private Equity.

THE LEADERS IN PRIVATE EQUITY

BAIRD, Derek
Lovells, London
(020) 7296 2000
derek.baird@lovellss.com
Specialisation: Mergers and acquisitions (public and private), particularly institutional and leveraged buyouts; advising major financial institutions.
Prof. Memberships: Law Society and Law Society Scotland.
Career: Qualified in Scotland and England; Partner *Dickson Minto WS* 1999-2002; Partner *Lovells* 2002.

BAIRD, James
Clifford Chance, London
(020) 7006 1226
james.baird@cliffordchance.com
Specialisation: Corporate. Partner specialising in general company and corporate finance matters including company acquisitions, venture capital, takeovers and listings
Career: Articled *Pinsent & Co* (Birmingham); qualified 1978; Partner since 1985
Personal: 1975 University College, Oxford (BA Jurisprudence).

BAMBER, Andrew
Allen & Overy, London
(020) 7330 3000
andrew.bamber@allenovery.com
Specialisation: Andrew Bamber joined as a partner at *Allen & Overy* in 2002, from *Norton Rose*. He specialises in structured finance and corporate transactions, in both cases typically in the context of corporate acquisitions. His practice covers acting for corporates, banks and other finance providers and financial advisers. Investment grade-type acquisition financings: acting for the corporate including the Texas Utilities £3.6bn bid for The Energy Group, the Ciba £1.3bn bid for Allied Colloids, the Mannesmann £22bn bid for Orange, the AXA £3.4bn bid for Guardian Royal Exchange, the TXU Europe £3.045bn bid for Hydroelectrica Cantabrica, the Trinity £1.05bn merger with Mirror Group, and the Airline Group's £1.4bn acquisition from HM Government of National Air Traffic Services; acting for the banks including the Chase and Deutsche Bank financing for the US$2bn bid by Cemex for Southdown, JP Morgan on certain other bid financings, Deutsche Bank in respect of a series of acquisition financings for Enterprise Inns; and HSBC on Taylor Woodrow's £525m bid for Bryant Group. Private equity sponsored acquisition financings include over 30 MBO/MBI transactions acting for RBS, ICG, Fortis Bank, Bank of Scotland, HSBC and Chase Capital Partners. Notable recent deals in this sector include private MBOs/MBIs of Flagship Foods £172.6m; Mill House Inns £97.5m; Allflex US$156m and public-to-privates of Concentric £122m; Ward Homes £54.5m and Fairview Homes £287m. Also acted for Deutsche Bank as financial adviser on the take private of Powell Duffryn plc £507m. Other structured deals include acting for TXU Europe on a series of confidential transactions including its acquisition of Norweb Energi and for Kelda on the proposed mutualisation of its regulated water business. Other recent work includes the sale and restructuring of interests in Spitalfields and advising easyRentacar on its fleet financing and other fund raisings. He also acted for Fuji Bank on the US$2.5bn facility for British Airways and for the banks on numerous other aircraft financings for BA and DHL.

BARKER, Bridget
Macfarlanes, London
(020) 7831 9222

BARRON, Michael
Dickson Minto WS, London
(020) 7628 4455
michael.barron@dmws.com
Specialisation: Private equity transactions, especially structured debt finance, whole business securitisations, high yield securities and other financings for private equity clients. Acts for major financial institutions and banks active in the private equity market.
Career: Qualified as a solicitor in Scotland 1977 and in England 1986. Educated University of Edinburgh. Solicitor with 3i plc 1984 to 1987 then with *Dickson Minto WS*, as a partner since 1989.

BARTER, Charles
Travers Smith Braithwaite, London
(020) 7295 3000
Charles.Barter@TraversSmith.com
Specialisation: Partner in Corporate Finance Department. Corporate finance, in particular private equity, buyouts, buyins, disposals and reconstructions.
Prof. Memberships: Law Society, City of London Solicitors Company.
Career: Articled Clerk 1985; Partner 1995.
Personal: Motorcycling, Norfolk, Exeter Silver, Church.

BEDDOW, Simon
Ashurst Morris Crisp, London
(020) 7638 1111
simon.beddow@ashursts.com
Specialisation: UK and cross-border Corporate, Corporate Finance and venture capital.
Prof. Memberships: City of London Solicitors' Company. Society for Advanced Legal Studies.
Career: 1987-89 *Pinsent & Co* (Birmingham) (Articled Clerk), 1989-96 *Travers Smith Braithwaite* (Assistant), 1996- *Ashurst Morris Crisp* (Partner since 1998), Partner responsible for training (1999-), *Ashursts* Management Board (2000-).
Personal: Married with two daughters and one son.

BLAKE, Jonathan
SJ Berwin, London
(020) 7533 2222
jonathan.blake@sjberwin.com
Specialisation: Head of the corporate finance department and the private equity group advising generally on mergers and management buy-outs, venture and development capital investments and related taxation issues. He has a particular specialisation in advising private equity and venture capital fund managers in many countries in Europe and elsewhere on the structure of venture capital funds, management companies and carried interest incentive arrangements. Clients for whom he has established funds or carried interest incentive arrangements include ABN Amro, Apax, Bridgepoint Capital, Phoenix Equity Partners, Dresdner Kleinwort Capital, Electra Partners, HgCapital, PRICOA, Permira Advisers Limited and UBS.
Prof. Memberships: Associate of the Chartered Institute of Taxation (ATII); British Venture Capital Association; International Bar Association; Chairman - Tax and Legal Committee of the European Venture Capital Association.
Personal: Educated at Haberdashers' Aske's School, Elstree and Queens' College, Cambridge (MA LL.M). Qualified 1979. Born 7 July 1954.

BOWN, Christopher
Freshfields Bruckhaus Deringer, London
(020) 7936 4000
christopher.bown@freshfields.com
Specialisation: Partner in corporate department specialising in private equity and cross-border M&A transactions. Recent transactions include major multi-jurisdictional private equity purchase of chemical business, and other major acquisitions.
Prof. Memberships: Law Society.
Career: Qualified 1981, partner *Baker & McKenzie* 1987-98; partner *Freshfields* since 1998.
Personal: Born 1956, educated Queen's College, Cambridge.

CAMPBELL, Mark
Clifford Chance, London
(020) 7600 1000
mark.campbell@cliffordchance.com
See under Banking & Finance, p.104

CARPANINI, Fabrizio
Olswang, London
(020) 7208 8888
fcp@olswang.com
Specialisation: Specialising in private equity/venture capital transactions, acting for institutions and management teams on buyouts, buyins, institutional buyouts and development capital deals. Institutional clients include Graphite Capital, Gresham Trust, Lloyds TSB Development Capital, Sagitta Private Equity and Sovereign Capital Ltd.
Prof. Memberships: British Venture Capital Association. British Italian Law Association. Law Society.
Career: Joined *Olswang* as a Partner in the Corporate Group in February 2000, having previously been a Partner at *Berwin Leighton*.
Publications: A regular speaker at conferences on private equity and management buyouts.
Personal: Belmont Abbey School, Hereford & Bristol Poly. Leisure: Family, skiing, cycling and golf.

COMPAGNONI, Marco
Lovells, London
(020) 7296 2000
marco.compagnoni@lovells.com

Specialisation: Specialises in a range of mergers and acquisitions work and corporate law. A particular specialisation is private equity transactions (MBOs and MBIs) acting primarily for institutional investors. Equity institutions for whom he has acted regularly include HgCapital, Doughty Hanson and Advent International. He also has extensive experience of joint ventures, purchase and sales of companies and businesses (both domestic and cross border). Significant recent transactions include acting for ING in its purchase of Barings, advising Doughty Hanson on its purchases of the BTR Aerospace Business and the demerger of Ti Automotive from Smiths Group.
Prof. Memberships: Member of the British Venture Capital Association, the British Italian Law Association and the City of London Solicitors Company.
Career: Articled at *Lovells*; qualified in 1987 and became a partner in 1993.

COTTIS, Matthew
Lovells, London
(020) 7296 2000
matthew.cottis@lovells.com
Specialisation: Expertise in management buyouts/buyins, bids and takeovers and other types of acquisition finance, rescheduling, general banking work and syndicated loans.
Career: Articled *Lovells* 1985-87, Partner 1993.
Personal: King Alfred's Grammar School, Wantage; Keble College, Oxford (1984 BA Law); golf and other sports.

DAVIS, Steven
SJ Berwin, London
(020) 7533 2660
steven.davis@sjberwin.com
Specialisation: A diversified corporate practice covering mergers and acquisitions (private and public), leveraged buyouts, venture and development capital investments, flotations, corporate finance and corporate reconstructions, albeit with a particular focus on private equity transactions acting primarily for financial institutions. Equity institutions for whom he acts regularly include Apax Partners and UBS Capital. Significant recent transactions include the public to private of The Limelight Group, advising the management of ERM on their management buyout and Pierre et Vacances on the acquisition of Center Parcs European business.
Prof. Memberships: Member of the New York Bar.
Career: Qualified in 1987 with *SJ Berwin*. Seconded to *Debevoise & Plimpton*, New York office 1992-93 and became a partner in 1994.
Personal: Born 1965. Educated Clifton College, Bristol and Manchester University. Married with one child. Leisure pursuits include golf, squash and cooking. Lives in London.

DICKSON, Alastair
Dickson Minto WS, London
(020) 7628 4455
alastair.dickson@dmws.com

Specialisation: Mergers and acquisitions; leveraged buyouts; acting for major financial institutions and banks.
Prof. Memberships: Member of Law Society of Scotland; Writer to Her Majesty's Signet.
Career: Educated Edinburgh University 1971. *Dundas & Wilson* 1971-73. *Maclay Murray & Spens* 1973-76. *Dundas & Wilson* 1976-85 (partner from 1978). Founding partner of *Dickson Minto WS* 1985.
Personal: Golf, squash, hill walking.

EVANS, Jacqueline
Allen & Overy, London
(020) 7330 3000
jacqueline.evans@allenovery.com
Specialisation: Advising banks and private equity houses on debt financing of leveraged acquisitions including public bids.
Career: Joined *Allen & Overy* 1990. Qualified 1992. Partner 1999.
Personal: Education: Christleton High School; University of Manchester (1989 LLB); Chester College of Law (1990).

FREEMAN, Adam
Lovells, London
(020) 7296 2000
adam.freeman@lovells.com
Specialisation: Cross-border and domestic leveraged buyouts, buyins, take privates and other types of acquisition finance and general syndicated loans.
Career: Articled *Lovells*, qualified 1996.
Personal: Married (Louisa) with a daughter (Lily). Interests include rugby, cricket and golf. Education: Birmingham University and Chester College of Law.

GEFFEN, Charles
Ashurst Morris Crisp, London
(020) 7638 1111
charlie.geffen@ashursts.com
Specialisation: General corporate and corporate finance.
Career: Head of M&A and buyouts.
Personal: Married, four children.

GILLESPIE, Stephen
Allen & Overy, London
(020) 7330 3000
stephen.gillespie@allenovery.com
See under Banking & Finance, p.105

GLOVER, Jason
Clifford Chance, London
(020) 7006 1634
jason.glover@cliffordchance.com
Specialisation: Corporate. Partner specialising in private equity matters including funds establishment, management buyins and buyouts and venture capital.
Career: Articled at *Clifford Chance*; qualified 1991; Operations Director Hambro European Ventures (now Duke Street Capital) 1996-97; Operations Director Asian Infrastructure Fund 1997-98; Partner since 1998.
Personal: Nottingham High School; 1988 University of Bristol (LLB).

GOALEN, Iain
Shearman & Sterling, London
(020) 7655 5000

GOLD, Josyane
SJ Berwin, London
(020) 7533 2314
josyane.gold@sjberwin.com
Specialisation: Partner in the private equity group. She specialises in advising private equity and venture capital fund managers on the establishment of investment funds in the UK and many other countries across Europe. She also advises on the creation of investment management companies and carried interest and other incentive arrangements. She has extensive experience in private equity financing and other corporate finance and commercial work.
Prof. Memberships: Member of the EVCA Tax & Legal Committee.
Career: *Bartletts de Reya* 1979-87, qualified 1981, partner 1983; joined *SJ Berwin* as partner in 1988.
Personal: Born 1956; resides London. Educated at Bristol (LLB). Speaks French.

GORRIE, Euan
Allen & Overy, London
(020) 7330 3000
euan.gorrie@allenovery.com
Specialisation: He specialises in acting for banks, mezzanine lenders or borrowers in connection with acquisition finance, public bids and other leveraged or structured finance transactions, restructurings, syndicated loans and lending to investment funds.
Career: Trinity College, Glenalmond; New College, Oxford (BA, 1984); Birkbeck College, Oxford (MA); articled *Allen & Overy*, qualified 1989; assistant 1989-96 (on the secondment at the Mitsubishi Bank 1992); Partner 1996.
Personal: Born 1962. Married; two children.

GREAVES, Adam
Gouldens, London
(020) 7842 6188
acg@gouldens.com
Specialisation: Partner in company/commercial department and head of the private equity team. Very diversified practice covers private equity, mergers and acquisitions (private and public), flotations, corporate finance, corporate reconstructions and commercial agreements and joint ventures.
Career: Qualified in 1982. Joined *Nabarro Nathanson* in 1980, joining and becoming a Partner of *Gouldens* in 1986.
Personal: Born 9 July 1958. Attended Bradfield College 1972-76, Selwyn College, Cambridge 1976-79 and Guildford College of Law 1979-80. Leisure interests include fly fishing (member of the Red Sea Casters), bridge, hockey, walking and cooking. Lives in London.

HALE, Chris
Travers Smith Braithwaite, London
(020) 7295 3263
Chris.Hale@TraversSmith.com
Specialisation: Main area of practice: Head of *Travers Smith* Private Equity Group. Advises leading buyout houses in the UK. Also advises on new issues and a number of listed companies, financial advisors and larger private companies on equity raising and mergers and acquisitions. Known particularly for working on more complex, larger buyouts and cross-border transactions.
Prof. Memberships: Hon. Treasurer and Executive Committee member of Society of Advanced Legal Studies.
Career: Qualified as a solicitor in 1981 with *Kingsley Napley*, joined *Travers Smith Braithwaite* in 1983 and became Partner in 1987.
Personal: Educated at King's College School, Wimbledon, Emmanuel College, Cambridge (MA) and Wolfson College, Cambridge (LLM). Leisure interests include football, reading, gardening, walking and legal history.

HANTON, Bruce
Ashurst Morris Crisp, London
(020) 7638 1111
bruce.hanton@ashursts.com
Specialisation: Principal area of work is corporate finance particularly private equity transactions. Recent transactions include the acquisition of the Foseco and Releasants businesses of Burmah Castrol (Cinven), the IPO of Carphone Warehouse Group plc, the acquisition of the retail business of Allied Domecq plc by Punch Taverns Limited (Texas Pacific Group and Colony Capital) and the acquisition of William Hill (Cinven and CVC).
Prof. Memberships: Law Society.
Career: Qualified in 1988 with *Ashurst Morris Crisp*. Became Partner in 1996.
Personal: Born 7 February 1962. Educated Alleyn's School and Bristol University (LLB and LLM). Married with five children.

HOWARD, Susan
Allen & Overy, London
(020) 7330 3000
susan.howard@allenovery.com
Specialisation: Partner in Corporate Department. Area of practice is general corporate finance, public company work (including flotations and takeovers) and mergers and acquisitions, with a particular emphasis on private equity work, including management buyouts/buyins.
Prof. Memberships: The Law Society.
Career: Articled with *Allen & Overy*, qualified (1987), partner (1994).
Personal: Born 1962. Cheltenham Grammar School; Exeter College, Oxford University (1984, BA Hons Law).

INGLIS, Alan
Clifford Chance, London
(020) 7600 1000
alan.inglis@cliffordchance.com
Specialisation: Banking and finance. Partner specialising in banking, corporate finance, insolvency and corporate reconstruction.
Career: Articled *Clifford Turner/Clifford Chance*, qualified 1985; Partner since 1992.
Personal: Exeter School; Birmingham University (LLB).

PRIVATE EQUITY ■ THE LEADERS

JOHNSON, James
Clifford Chance, London
(020) 7600 1000
james.johnson@cliffordchance.com

KEAL, Anthony
Allen & Overy, London
(020) 7330 3000
anthony.keal@allenovery.com
See under Banking & Finance, p.106

LAYTON, Matthew
Clifford Chance, London
(020) 7006 1229
matthew.layton@cliffordchance.com
Specialisation: Corporate. Partner specialising in domestic and international management, leveraged buyouts and venture capital transactions as well as general corporate and corporate finance work.
Career: Qualified 1986; Partner since 1991.
Personal: 1982 Leeds LLB (Hons).

MACKIE, Chris
Olswang, London
(020) 7208 8888
cam@olswang.com
Specialisation: Private equity and venture capital advising institutions as well as general corporate work.
Prof. Memberships: Law Society.
Career: 1987-94 *Turner Kenneth Brown*. 1994-2000 *Berwin Leighton*, partner 1996. February 2000 – joined *Olswang* as a partner.
Personal: Married with three children. Lives in London.

MARTIN, Charles
Macfarlanes, London
(020) 7831 9222

MCNAIR, Martin
Dickson Minto WS, London
(020) 7628 4455
martin.mcnair@dmws.com
Specialisation: Private equity transactions acting for major financial institutions.
Prof. Memberships: Member of Law Society of Scotland. Writer to Her Majesty's Signet.
Career: Qualified as a solicitor in 1991. Educated University of Edinburgh. *Dickson Minto WS* since 1988 (partner since 1997).

MEEK, Charles
Macfarlanes, London
(020) 7831 9222

MIFSUD, Mark
SJ Berwin, London
(020) 7533 2222
mark.mifsud@sjberwin.com
Specialisation: Partner in the private equity team of the corporate finance department. Advises private equity managers in relation to the structuring and establishment of private equity investment funds, incentive schemes, carried interest arrangements and co-investment plans. Has extensive experience in a wide range of jurisdictions. Also advises on related matters and general corporate finance. Clients for whom he has established funds, carried interest arrangements or advised on other related matters include Aberdeen Murray Johnstone Private Equity, ABN Amro, Accel Partners, Benchmark Capital, Dresdner Kleinwort Capital, Electra Partners Europe Limited, Lloyds TSB Development Capital, nCoTec, Palamon Capital Partners, PRICOA Capital Group Limited and TLcom Capital Partners.
Prof. Memberships: International Bar Association; Holborn Law Society (Committee Member); Law Society.
Career: Qualified 1993; partner *SJ Berwin* 1999.
Personal: Born 1968. Educated at Magdalen College School and St Catherine's College, Oxford. Speaks Maltese and Italian.

MURRAY-JONES, Allan
Skadden, Arps, Slate, Meagher & Flom LLP, London
(020) 7519 7000
amurrayj@skadden.com
Specialisation: Partner specialising in M&A, particularly private equity. Experience includes cross-border M&A, all aspects of English law corporate finance and private equity fund raising.
Prof. Memberships: The Law Society.
Career: Qualified in Australia in 1976 and in England in 1981. Became a partner at *Durrant Piesse* in 1986, and joined *Skadden Arps* as a partner in 2001.
Personal: Educated at All Saints' College, Bathurst, and the Australian National University.

PAUL, Alan
Allen & Overy, London
(020) 7330 3000
alan.paul@allenovery.com
See under Corporate Finance, p.244

PEARSON, David
Clifford Chance, London
(020) 7006 1429
david.pearson@cliffordchance.com
See under Corporate Finance, p.244

POLGLASE, Timothy
Allen & Overy, London
(020) 7330 3000
timothy.polglase@allenovery.com
Specialisation: Principal area of practice is structured finance, including the financing of leveraged buyouts and public bids, telecoms finance and project finance.
Career: Articled *Norton Rose*, qualified 1986; seconded to *Milbank, Tweed, Hadley & McCloy* (New York) 1988-89; seconded to banking supervision division, Bank of England 1990-91; partner *Norton Rose* 1994-2002, partner *Allen & Overy* 2002 to date.
Personal: Born 1962. Educated at St John's College, Oxford.

SHEACH, Andrew
CMS Cameron McKenna, London
(020) 7367 2969
ajs@cmck.com
Specialisation: Specialises in all types of private equity transactions (management buyout/buyin, public to privates (PTPs) and development capital and exit work), mergers and acquisitions and Stock Exchange and Blue Book work. In the last year he has acted on a number of management buyouts/buyins for both equity investors and management teams.
Career: BA (Law) Pembroke College, Cambridge 1981-84; joined *Cameron Markby* 1985; Partner 1993.

SHELDON, Jeremy
Ashurst Morris Crisp, London
(020) 7638 1111
jeremy.n.sheldon@ashursts.com
Specialisation: Partner in Company Department and Head of the firm's Private Investment Funds Practice. Apart from quoted and unquoted investment funds his practice includes international buyouts. He recently acted for Given Limited on the formation of the €4.34 billion Third Given Fund, mergers and acquisitions, flotations and other Stock Exchange transactions.
Prof. Memberships: Member of the International Rd Associations specialised Investment Funds Committee.
Career: Qualified in 1980. Became a partner in 1987.
Personal: Born in 1952.

STEWART, Mark
Clifford Chance, London
(020) 7600 1000
mark.stewart@cliffordchance.com
Specialisation: Banking and finance. Partner specialising in general corporate banking with an emphasis on acquisition financings.
Career: Articled *Richards Butler*; qualified 1983; Trainee and Assistant Solicitor 1983-86; *Clifford Chance* 1986-90; Partner since 1990.
Personal: University College School, London; Bristol University.

SWEETING, Malcom
Clifford Chance, London
(020) 7600 1000
malcom.sweeting@cliffordchance.com
See under Banking & Finance, p.109

TUFFNELL, Kevin
Macfarlanes, London
(020) 7831 9222

VICKERS, Mark
Ashurst Morris Crisp, London
(020) 7638 1111
mark.vickers@ashursts.com
Specialisation: Corporate banking and international finance: specialising in UK and cross-border acquisition finance and leveraged acquisitions, particularly management buyouts/buyins and institutional purchases; structured finance; global syndicated lending. He is one of the market's leading experts on the debt funding of public to private takeovers.
Career: Joined *Ashurst Morris Crisp* in 1999 having been head of European acquisition finance at a top-10 UK law firm (1980-99).
Publications: Author: 'Senior Debt Market for Management Buyouts' and 'Public to Private Takeovers: The New Paradigms'.
Personal: Helicopter pilot. Owner of Saracen armoured personnel carrier.

WARD, Anthony
Shearman & Sterling, London
(020) 7655 5000

WARD, Nigel
Ashurst Morris Crisp, London
(020) 7859 1236
nigel.ward@ashursts.com
Specialisation: International and structured finance with particular emphasis on acquisition and bid finance and debt restructurings. Advises primarily leading US and European investment banks and venture capital houses. Recent transactions include the financing of the Alfa Laval buyout, WPP's bid for Tempus and the Finelist and Dunlop Slazenger debt restructurings.
Prof. Memberships: Member of Banking Law sub-committee of the City of London Law Society.
Career: Educated St Catherine's College, Oxford. Qualified in 1985. Partner in 1992.
Publications: Author of 'How stands the high yield investor in the European LBO market?' and 'Winning Mandates in the European LBO Market'.
Personal: Born 1961. Married with three children. Plays golf and tennis.

WHITE, Graham
Linklaters, London
(020) 7456 2598
graham.white@linklaters.com
Specialisation: Partner in the Corporate Department specialising in private equity transactions.
Prof. Memberships: Law Society of Scotland.
Career: Since 2001, Partner *Linklaters*. 1999-2001, Partner *SJ Berwin*; 1993-98 Partner *Dickson Minton WS*. 1988-93, Assistant Solicitor *Dickson Minto WS*; 1979-84 Strathclyde University, Glasgow, LL.B (Hons).

PRODUCT LIABILITY

London: 665; The Regions: 667; Scotland: 668; Food Law: 668; Profiles: 670

Research approved by BMRB For this edition, **Chambers'** researchers conducted 6,582 interviews – 3,900 with law firms, 511 with barristers and 2,171 with clients. The validity of the research was scrutinised by BMRB International, who audited both the methodology and the results at our offices in London. They interviewed **Chambers'** researchers and cross-checked sample interviews. Details of the audit appear on page 7.

OVERVIEW Opinion is divided upon the extent to which recent judgments will significantly change the status quo between defendant and claimant. What is certain is that issues such as the use of the state-of-the-art 'development risk defense' arising from the Hepatitis C judgment are to be further explored in future group actions. The recent landmark judgment in the Cape group litigation has prompted predictions that further claims against companies with headquarters in the UK will ensue. However, the issue of funding continues to be debated. A rise in the number of claims between companies has also sparked new debate over the stigma of an underlying ' compensation culture' attached to product liability cases. With the January 2002 European General Product Safety Directive due to be implemented at the beginning of 2004, it has been predicted that European legislation will increasingly drive new obligations on distributors and producers. Lastly, while every case is different, there was some agreement among solicitors that a renewed determination exists on the part of all parties to circumvent 'trench warfare' scenarios, and recourse instead to mediation and other alternative schemes to bring cases to a close.

LONDON — MAINLY DEFENDANT

PRODUCT LIABILITY: MAINLY DEFENDANT — LONDON

1. CMS Cameron McKenna
   Davies Arnold Cooper
2. Arnold & Porter
   Lovells
3. Ashurst Morris Crisp
   Beachcroft Wansbroughs
   Kennedys
4. Freshfields Bruckhaus Deringer
   Simmons & Simmons
5. Clifford Chance
   Herbert Smith
   Theodore Goddard

LEADING INDIVIDUALS

1. DODDS-SMITH Ian Arnold & Porter
   HODGES Christopher CMS Cameron McKenna
2. MELTZER John Lovells
   PEARL Simon Davies Arnold Cooper
   WARE Anne Davies Arnold Cooper
3. BOWDEN Paul Freshfields Bruckhaus Deringer
   KELLEHER John Theodore Goddard
   TYLER Mark CMS Cameron McKenna
4. ELVY Mark Ashurst Morris Crisp
   MCDOUGALL Arundel Ashurst Morris Crisp
   SAYERS Shane Kennedys
   SHERRINGTON Patrick Lovells
5. ALEXANDER Miles Simmons & Simmons
   EDGAR Andrew Clifford Chance
   EVANS John Ashurst Morris Crisp
   WILKES Chris Beachcroft Wansbroughs

UP AND COMING
   FREEMAN Rod Lovells

This book is the product of 6,582 1/2 hour interviews. See p.7 for BMRB audit. Within each band, firms are listed alphabetically. See individuals' profiles p.670

CMS CAMERON MCKENNA (see firm details p.914) While some interviewees still see it as possessing "*an unbeatable amalgam of skills,*" many felt that its exclusive top-tier status could no longer be justified following the departure of Ian Dodds-Smith and his pharmaceutical team, bringing to an end a long period of unrivalled dominance in the market. Nevertheless, the "*depth of expertise*" possessed by the remaining five-partner team, which is also part of a pan-European network, is still widely acknowledged. It is well supported by an international client base stretching as far a field as the US and Japan that includes insurance companies and electronics and motor manufacturers. Advice on complex chemical and medical matters, often in the context of multiparty actions, also distinguishes the practice. "*Extremely knowledgeable to a European level,*" **Christopher Hodges** (see p.671) helps to preserve the reputation for excellence with which the practice is synonymous. Able to provide "*first-rate regulatory advice,*" he is also intimately involved with law reform issues. **Mark Tyler** (see p.403) "*never fails to impress,*" according to peers, who are adamant that he is "*going places.*" He retains the MMR litigation on behalf of Aventis Pasteur MSD. **Clients** Dow Corning; Aventis Pasteur MSD.

DAVIES ARNOLD COOPER (see firm details p.930) The group is going "*from strength to strength*" and sits easily as one of the "*most experienced*" in the market. The "*tactical nous*" it displays in running complex product liability cases has greatly impressed interviewees. **Simon Pearl** (see p.672) is "*held in super high regard*" and has led advice to SmithKline Beecham in the MMR litigation, as well as successfully defending Bayer in the organophosphates litigation. "*Absolutely rock-solid and a bit of a fighter,*" **Anne Ware** (see p.673) advised the defendant in Afrika & ors v Cape. There is a clear transnational dimension to the practice; it also covers complex and unusual personal injury claims, and substantial repercussive medical negligence and related litigation. **Clients** NHSLA; GlaxoSmithKline; Roche Products.

ARNOLD & PORTER (see firm details p.848) Included in the tables for the first time, the firm received an enormous boost with the recruitment of "*legendary*" **Ian Dodds-Smith** (see p.670) and his pharmaceutical team from CMS Cameron McKenna. A stream of superlatives punctuated interviewees' descriptions of Dodds-Smith, who joins the firm as head of its European product liability practice group and co-head of its international regulatory group in partnership with the Washington office. Product liability is a major feature of a wider healthcare practice, whereby the team acts for pharmaceutical, biotechnology and healthcare companies, covering EC and national regulatory law relating to products and devices in both human and veterinary fields. Other areas of expertise include cosmetic, pesticide and biocide regulatory law. The team often appears in group actions and high-profile cases include acting for pharmaceutical companies in both the oral contraceptives and baby drinks litigation. **Clients** Pharmaceutical manufacturers; biotechnology companies ; healthcare companies.

LOVELLS (see firm details p.1045) With "*strength and depth second to none,*" the team continues to build up its Europe-wide experience, making it an influential force in the market. Recent litigation has included defending pharmaceutical companies in the MMR group action, a judicial review in relation to tobacco as well as other smoking and health claims, and involvement in the benzene and blood contamination claims. It has also undertaken advisory work in the pharmaceutical, cosmetic, telecoms, transport and food sectors. Observers noted that **John Meltzer** (see p.672) ("*outstanding in a number of areas*") is experienced in cross-border product liability claims, and was a lead solicitor in the MMR litigation.

PRODUCT LIABILITY ■ LONDON

"*An extremely shrewd and experienced litigator,*" **Patrick Sherrington** (see p.673) remains highly regarded for his tobacco work, as well as having taken the lead in recent benzene claims. **Rod Freeman** (see p.670) was deemed to be an "*increasingly well-established*" member of the team. He will support Meltzer, following the firm's appointment by the European Commission, in carrying out a study of the application of product liability laws across the European Union. **Clients** Merck; BAT; car manufacturers; mobile phone suppliers.

ASHURST MORRIS CRISP (see firm details p.852) A "*sophisticated outfit,*" it benefits from a robust litigation department, and enjoys a reputation in the field established primarily through its involvement in high-profile, Europe-wide tobacco litigation. Involvement in health and safety matters, product recalls and wide-ranging regulatory matters also contribute to the workload. It has built up a healthy pharmaceutical client base through co-operation with the firm's healthcare group, and is further strengthened by ties with an expanding European network. "*Heavily involved,*" **Mark Elvy** (see p.670) is best-known as a tobacco specialist, while **Arundel McDougall** (see p.672) upholds his reputation for pharmaceutical actions. Head of product liability **John Evans** (see p.670) has had sustained involvement in weighty product recall matters. **Clients** Imperial Tobacco; Aventis Pharma.

BEACHCROFT WANSBROUGHS (see firm details p.860) Held out by interviewees at the Bar as an "*exemplary practice*" on cases involving an international dimension, it is promoted in the tables principally on the basis of a hugely favourable reaction to the lead role it has taken in oral contraceptives litigation. Accordingly, lead solicitor for the case **Chris Wilkes** (see p.673) enters the tables, commended as a "*hard-working, big hitter.*" The team has continued to attract new clients, most recently in the chemical sector. **Clients** Major insurers; chemical manufacturers; pharmaceutical companies.

KENNEDYS (see firm details p.1019) Clients commended the firm for its "*talented staff giving high-quality advice,*" on which this niche products practice is founded. It retains a client base evenly balanced between insurers on the one hand, and pharmaceutical, medical devices and industrial manufacturers on the other. Accomplished in handling cases with a cross-border dimension, the team places considerable emphasis on the importance of risk management, offering advice on clinical trial procedures, product labelling and product recall. Recent highlights include successfully acting for the chemical manufacturer in the organophosphate class action. A "*canny operator,*" **Shane Sayers** (see p.672) continues to be admired by interviewees as reflecting "*the strength and depth of the practice.*" **Clients** Johnson & Johnson; Novartis; Celltech Group; motor vehicle manufacturers.

FRESHFIELDS BRUCKHAUS DERINGER (see firm details p.964) An "*outstandingly wide-ranging practice,*" it is best known for its advice on tobacco litigation, alongside its involvement in risk and crisis management in many regulatory and environmental law settings. Recent highlights include acting for a major international pharmaceutical company in the co-ordinated worldwide defence of cases concerning injuries (and in some cases death) allegedly caused by one of its market-leading drugs. The team also advised a leading alcoholic beverages manufacturer on the potential recall of millions of bottles of its product in 15 countries worldwide. Head of practice **Paul Bowden** (see p.357) remains at the forefront of his environmental specialism. Interviewees singled out his "*faultless handling of technical evidence and co-ordination of complex cases.*" The defence of smoking and health litigation in several jurisdictions throughout Europe, Asia and the Middle East continues to occupy the team. **Clients** JT International; arms manufacturers; multi-national domestic appliance manufacturers.

SIMMONS & SIMMONS (see firm details p.1136) This "*key player*" has established its reputation following heavy involvement in tobacco litigation, and has now branched out into providing advice to pharmaceutical and petrochemical companies. It is often seen acting on novel products and those cases with an international dimension. The team is also experienced in advising on risk assessment and risk management, as well as product recall. Partner **Miles Alexander** (see p.670) enters the table this year having garnered much praise for his "*proven case management ability.*" **Clients** Tobacco manufacturers; petrochemical manufacturers; pharmaceutical companies.

CLIFFORD CHANCE (see firm details p.911) The firm is envied by peers for its "*diverse client base,*" which is international in scope and continues to expand, notably in Japan and Europe. While in this respect it was conceded by interviewees that the firm's profile is unbeatable, it remains little seen in the London and domestic markets. This should not detract from its major matters, such as the team's recent advice to a number of manufacturers and retailers on liabilities in up to 35 countries worldwide in the event that their products would be used in terrorist attacks. Asbestos-related matters, product recalls and associated health and safety matters, also at an international level, contribute to the workload. Co-ordinating the firm's European product liability efforts is **Andrew Edgar** (see p.670), deemed an "*experienced and conscientious litigator*" by his peers. **Clients** Pharmaceutical companies; car manufacturers; mobile phone manufacturers.

HERBERT SMITH (see firm details p.992) The profile of this product liability practice is derived largely from its reputation as a "*formidable litigation giant,*" and it is the insurance litigation group that handles most work. Whether acting directly for industrial clients or for insurers, it has had a busy year. Multiparty actions have included representing the defence in the benzene litigation. Weapons, telecoms and the automotive manufacturing sector have also proved a source of instruction as have claims arising from the use of asbestos. The firm has also provided advice on the safety of mobile telephones, involving issues of causation, which are at the forefront of scientific and medical knowledge. Tony Dempster is a key partner in the team. **Clients** Major insurers; major corporate organisations.

THEODORE GODDARD (see firm details p.1158) Well received by a broad cross-section of interviewees, this remains a practice of considerable standing, albeit one that has not been in the limelight recently. The quality of its team was acknowledged, particularly head of litigation and lead products partner **John Kelleher** (see p.671) who has "*long been held in high regard*" by solicitors and clients alike. The defence of Myodil claims on behalf of Glaxo-SmithKline continues, and while the practice's core expertise remains in the pharmaceutical and healthcare sectors, it has also acted for toy manufacturers. **Clients** GlaxoSmithKline; MDU.

LONDON   MAINLY CLAIMANT

LEIGH, DAY & CO (see firm details p.1036) Endorsed for its "*inventive and proactive*" approach to the sphere, defendant solicitors recognise the firm's unique capacity to "*challenge the rules in a way that achieves results.*" Considered by some the pre-eminent claimant solicitor, **Martyn Day** (see p.670) is particularly respected for his grasp of the scientific side of cases. He heads the team acting for claimants in the oral contraceptives litigation. Defendant solicitors indicate that **Richard Meeran**'s (see p.672) presence "*demands a cautious approach.*" Meeran has an international reputation in the field following the successful Cape asbestos litigation.

THE REGIONS — PRODUCT LIABILITY

PRODUCT LIABILITY: MAINLY CLAIMANT — LONDON

1. Leigh, Day & Co
2. Alexander Harris

This book is the product of 6,582 1/2 hour interviews. See p.7 for BMRB audit. Within each band, firms are listed alphabetically.

LEADING INDIVIDUALS

1. DAY Martyn Leigh, Day & Co
2. MEERAN Richard Leigh, Day & Co

See individuals' profiles p.670

ALEXANDER HARRIS (see firm details p.839) A "*key claimant firm*" under the leadership of Richard Barr, it has a strong tradition of multi-party action work. Recent highlights include involvement in Gulf War claims, the sheep dip litigation and contributing to the co-ordination of the firm's generic MMR cases.

THE REGIONS

PRODUCT LIABILITY: MAINLY DEFENDANT — THE REGIONS

1. Eversheds Leeds, Nottingham
2. Wragge & Co Birmingham

LEADING INDIVIDUALS

1. LLEWELLYN Paul Eversheds

This book is the product of 6,582 1/2 hour interviews. See p.7 for BMRB audit. Within each band, firms are listed alphabetically. See individuals' profiles p.670

EVERSHEDS (see firm details p.949) This sizeable national team, which boasts "*brilliant litigators*," is judged by clients and practitioners alike as one that has "*a lot to offer.*" Defending wide-ranging claims, the firm has experience of criminal prosecutions and crisis management. It also provides "*helpful and proactive*" non-contentious advice. Industry sectors in which it is active include food and drink, electrical, children's toys, construction, agriculture, automotive and IT. A "*tough negotiator,*" commentators were particularly impressed by Nottingham-based **Paul Llewellyn**'s (see p.671) multiparty medical devices work. Highlights include the management, under a negotiated ADR protocol, of over 3,000 UK and European claims relating to Trilucent breast implants for Inamed, and claims arising from the 3M Capital Hip for 3M Health Care. The group has witnessed an increase in disputes between companies, while other highlights include acting for Terra Industries in the benzene litigation. **Clients** Pharmaceutical and medical device manufacturers; electrical and automotive manufacturers; construction companies.

MAINLY DEFENDANT

WRAGGE & CO (see firm details p.1197) While not considered to possess premier league specialist expertise, it is deemed to be one of the few regional players to have "*tangible depth*" in the field. Acting for corporate clients and insurers, its recent cases often involve multimillion pound claims, and have covered a crop spraying product, medical devices used to power wheelchairs and electrical equipment in the medical sector. The firm also advised on allegedly defective self-loading stretchers used by NHS Ambulance Trusts. Eddie Breen features as a partner in the team. **Clients** Insurers; NHS Trusts; medical device manufacturers.

THE REGIONS

PRODUCT LIABILITY: MAINLY CLAIMANT — THE REGIONS

1. Irwin Mitchell Sheffield
2. freethcartwright Nottingham
3. Alexander Harris Altrincham
4. Blackett Hart & Pratt Newcastle upon Tyne
   Leigh, Day & Co Manchester

LEADING INDIVIDUALS

1. BALEN Paul freethcartwright
   TUCKER Andrew Irwin Mitchell
2. BODY David Irwin Mitchell
   HARRIS David Alexander Harris
   PICKERING John Irwin Mitchell
3. HARVEY Mark Hugh James
   MCCOOL Geraldine Leigh, Day & Co

This book is the product of 6,582 1/2 hour interviews. See p.7 for BMRB audit. Within each band, firms are listed alphabetically. See individuals' profiles p.670

IRWIN MITCHELL (see firm details p.1009) The Sheffield-based office of this national practice is regarded in every quarter as having an "*outstanding group litigation profile,* and boasts a stable of "*top-class fee-earners.*" The "*top-notch*" **Andrew Tucker** (see p.673) is counted among the best practitioners in the country by interviewees. He recently advised claimants in breast implant litigation and covers a broad range of product safety work. Preserving an "*excellent reputation,*" **David Body** (see p.149) recently saw BSE litigation to a close, negotiating terms with the Department of Health for a £55 million CJD Compensation Trust, to provide for up to 250 victims. Body is also responsible for the firm's investigative work into Foetal Anti-Convulsant Syndrome (FACS). **John Pickering**'s (see p.154) chief area of specialisation is in tobacco litigation.

FREETHCARTWRIGHT (see firm details p.963) A designated department within personal litigation, interviewees agree it is "*well known and highly respected.*" The team boasts international experience, especially in the US, and has been involved in cases relating to breast implants, replacement hip joints, and the MMR vaccine. **Paul Balen** (see p.149) is considered "*something of a guru*" among peers, "*bright and energetic.*"

ALEXANDER HARRIS (see firm details p.839) This "*excellent specialist team*" has a strong expertise in pharmaceuticals and medical devices, and is able to boast experience of litigation in the US. "*Well-resourced, self-assured and instilling confidence,*" **David Harris** (see p.671) heads the group actions into MMR claims, and is overseeing investigations into potential claims in relation to the anti-smoking drug Zyban.

BLACKETT HART & PRATT The Hepatitis C litigation for which the firm is best known has continued to provide the practice with work. Lead solicitor for the case Tony Mallen still attracts rave reviews from barristers and solicitors alike, and remains active as a consultant for the firm, having retired from the partnership. Partners Paul Saxon and Blaine Ward are now the principal practitioners active for both insurers and claimants in product liability cases.

LEIGH, DAY & CO (see firm details p.1036) Military and commercial aviation product liability continues to be the focus of this niche practice. **Geraldine McCool** (see p.634) has a "*long-standing reputation*" and remains respected by market commentators.

OTHER NOTABLE PRACTITIONERS Considered a "*rising star*" in the field of pharmaceutical group actions, **Mark Harvey** (see p.671) of Hugh James re-enters the tables having received accolades from defendant and claimant solicitors alike.

PRODUCT LIABILITY ■ SCOTLAND/NORTHERN IRELAND/FOOD LAW

SCOTLAND

PRODUCT LIABILITY
■ SCOTLAND

1. **Burness** Edinburgh
   McGrigor Donald Glasgow
   Simpson & Marwick Edinburgh

This book is the product of 6,582 1/2 hour interviews. See p.7 for BMRB audit. Within each band, firms are listed alphabetically.

BURNESS While the departure of Marsali Murray is a blow for the firm, interviewees agreed that it "*continues to possess the overall strength*" to keep its profile intact. Head of dispute resolution Philip Rodney now oversees the team's work, which services a client base drawn from pharmaceutical, agrochemical and consumer product manufacturers.

MCGRIGOR DONALD (see firm details p.1065) The team has demonstrated "*serious ability*" in defending tobacco manufacturers, and sustained its activity in the petrochemical, pharmaceutical, food and drink and electronics industries. The team is led by Jacqueline Harris. **Clients** Tobacco manufacturers.

SIMPSON & MARWICK (see firm details p.1138) This "*formidable team of litigators*" is headed by Peter Anderson. Recent highlights include the successful defence of a US motorcycle manufacturer for an alleged design failure, and an alleged manufacturing failure. The team is also involved in the ongoing defence of a pharmaceutical company against alleged tranquilliser addiction. **Clients** Pharmaceutical manufacturers; motor vehicle manufacturers.

NORTHERN IRELAND

PRODUCT LIABILITY
■ NORTHERN IRELAND

1. **Elliott Duffy Garrett** Belfast
   McKinty and Wright Belfast
   Mills Selig Belfast
   O'Reilly Stewart Belfast

LEADING INDIVIDUALS

1. **SPRING Paul** Mills Selig
   STEWART Brian O'Reilly Stewart
   WILSON Michael Elliott Duffy Garrett

This book is the product of 6,582 1/2 hour interviews. See p.7 for BMRB audit. Within each band, firms are listed alphabetically. See individuals' profiles p.670

ELLIOTT DUFFY GARRETT (see firm details p.947) Possessing "*extremely experienced litigators*," this firm retains a healthy share of the market. A "*true specialist*," **Michael Wilson** remains a first port of call for advice on the finer points of product liability cases, having been instrumental as a key protagonist in the recent tobacco litigation. **Clients** Tobacco manufacturers; pharmaceuticalcompanies.

MCKINTY AND WRIGHT (see firm details p.1066) The team benefits from a broad-based client roster of insurers and manufacturers. Peers view it as "*easily capable of handling big league cases.*" These include defending a multinational manufacturer of injection needles, and advising a French manufacturer of hi-tech industrial healthcare equipment against claims for an allegedly faulty filling line. The team has also worked with the manufacturer of an agrochemical product supplied to apple growers. It has defended GlaxoSmithKline in relation to claims made against the drug Myodil, and has also defended food poisoning claims that include psychiatric implications. The team is led by Paul McDonnell. **Clients** GlaxoSmithKline; insurers; car manufacturers; supermarkets.

MILLS SELIG (see firm details p.1072) Lead partner **Paul Spring** (see p.274) established his reputation during tobacco litigation that led to him being retained by a multinational tobacco manufacturer. He is supported by an assistant solicitor, and continues to be active in defending electronic goods and motor vehicle manufacturers. The firm is well regarded for its "*proven specialist expertise.*"

O'REILLY STEWART (see firm details p.1089) **Brian Stewart** (see p.673) stands out from this respected team of "*expert litigators.*" It continues to be active in the pharmaceutical sector, most recently defending claims relating to an anti-epileptic drug. His established reputation following tobacco litigation means Stewart also retains a watching brief in this area. **Clients** Pharmaceuticalcompanies; insurers.

LONDON

FOOD LAW

BERWIN LEIGHTON PAISNER (see firm details p.866) This highly developed food law practice that provides due diligence advice and defends clients against enforcement agency actions remains unrivalled at the top of the table. Head of the regulatory practice group, **Craig Baylis** (see p.511) divides his time among food law clients in the catering, retail and restaurant sectors and licensing arena. Possessed of a "*vast knowledge and experience,*" he can provide both contentious and non-contentious advice. Interviewees agreed that **Hilary Ross** (see p.672) demonstrates a "*major commitment to the area,*" with unrivalled GMO expertise. She offers a "*great combination of scientific understanding and legal knowledge.*" She recently advised Tesco in its purchase of shares in NutriCentre, reviewing products and compliance procedures. Under the auspices of Ross, the firm has developed the food manufacturing and processing side, winning new instructions from clients such as Heinz. Kathryn Gilbertson has moved to Dechert, but the group continues to attract new recruits, most recently Jagdeep Tiwana from Pinsent Curtis Biddle. Other areas of the practice include advising US and Canadian firms on launching products in the UK and Europe. **Clients** Whitbread; Heinz.

COVINGTON & BURLING (see firm details p.921) "*Bright, intellectual and innovative,*" the London branch of this international US firm is judged by peers to have made its mark. It advises companies such as McNeil Consumer Nutritionals, and continues to attract clients from both sides of the Atlantic requiring advice on the placement of new products in UK and European markets. The team, overseen by Patricia Ponsonby, typically covers novel foods, herbal products and cholesterol-lowering ingredients. Its pharmaceutical expertise affords it an advantage with regard to borderline food and medicine products. Other niche strengths include related customs and advertising issues.

PINSENT CURTIS BIDDLE (see firm details p.1102) Adjudged to have "*built up an excellent client base,*" this national practice is overseen by

668 INDEX TO LEADING LAWYERS: PAGE 1693 ■ IN-HOUSE LAWYERS PROFILES: PAGE 1201

FOOD LAW ■ PRODUCT LIABILITY

PRODUCT LIABILITY: FOOD
■ LONDON

1 Berwin Leighton Paisner

2 Covington & Burling
  Pinsent Curtis Biddle
  Taylor Wessing

3 Bird & Bird
  Simmons & Simmons

LEADING INDIVIDUALS

1 ROSS Hilary *Berwin Leighton Paisner*

2 BAYLIS Craig *Berwin Leighton Paisner*

3 CODY Nick *Taylor Wessing*
  GILBERTSON Kathryn *Dechert*

This book is the product of 6,582 1/2 hour interviews. See p.7 for BMRB audit. Within each band, firms are listed alphabetically. See individuals' profiles p.670

Andrew Stacey, who is based in Birmingham. However it retains its position in the London table, being "*well-equipped to compete with City firms*" in the opinion of many interviewees. A sophisticated regulatory outfit deals with the defence of manufacturers and retailers against enforcement agencies, as well as food safety and labelling. Proactive risk management advice is also a key feature of the practice. **Clients** Tesco; Glanbia.

TAYLOR WESSING (see firm details p.1156) "*Heavily involved,*" the team retains its healthy market profile, resting in the "*safe pair of hands*" belonging to **Nick Cody** (see p.670) , its best-known practitioner. The defence of food safety prosecutions form the bulk of the work, while the practice also covers related IP and advertising issues.

BIRD & BIRD (see firm details p.874) Approaching the specialism from an IP perspective, the team has a deep vein of expertise running through patents, trademarks, and copyrights and design. It provides advice to an array of leading corporations on such matters, and also regulatory issues. Partner Jane Mutimear heads up the team. **Clients** Nestlé.

SIMMONS & SIMMONS (see firm details p.1136) Mark Dewar heads the firm's consumer law group, which provides a broad spectrum of regulatory advice to food and drink sector clients, including those from the US. An international practice in scope, with "*a well-established reputation,*" it covers novel and GM foods as well as food safety and labelling issues.

OTHER NOTABLE PRACTITIONERS Kathryn Gilbertson (see p.671) now heads up the Corporate Safety Group at Dechert. Observers regard her as a "*highly accomplished regulatory lawyer,*" and she retains a strong food law bent to her practice. She advises FTSE 100 companies and enforcement agencies on a broad range of regulatory and compliance issues.

THE REGIONS

FOOD LAW

PRODUCT LIABILITY: FOOD
■ THE REGIONS

1 Eversheds *Birmingham, Norwich*

2 DLA *Birmingham*
  Elliotts *Manchester*
  Shoosmiths *Northampton*

3 Andrew M. Jackson *Hull*
  Gregg Latchams Quinn *Bristol*
  Margetts & Ritchie *Birmingham*

4 Bevan Ashford *Bristol*
  Bond Pearce *Bristol*
  Hammond Suddards Edge *Birmingham*

LEADING INDIVIDUALS

1 HOLLAND Barry *Elliotts*
  YOUNG David *Eversheds*

2 REID Ron *Shoosmiths*

3 EDMONDS Steven *DLA*
  GREGG Andrew *Gregg Latchams Quinn*
  HETHERINGTON David *Margetts & Ritchie*
  SMITH Hugh *Andrew M. Jackson*
  TOZER Roy *DLA*
  WARNOCK Owen *Eversheds*

This book is the product of 6,582 1/2 hour interviews. See p.7 for BMRB audit. Within each band, firms are listed alphabetically. See individuals' profiles p.670

EVERSHEDS (see firm details p.949) There was a consensus amongst interviewees that this "*excellent practice*" has become the "*preferred regional player.*" David Young (see p.516) heads up the regulatory team in Birmingham, and is credited with having "*built up a huge practice.*" Food law prosecutions and inquiries continue to form the bulk of his work, which sits as part of an eclectic regulatory practice including environmental and licensing elements. Norwich-based **Owen Warnock** (see p.332) divides his time between food law and employment. The firm recently won the food company Glisten as a client. **Clients** Dairy Crest; MuscleTech.

DLA A broad consumer law practice, it covers food law, health and safety, consumer credit and trading standards. Contentious work in these areas is complemented by associated advertising and IP advice. **Steven Edmonds** and **Roy Tozer** are warmly recommended by market commentators for their work on behalf of pub and hotel chains and catering companies.

ELLIOTTS (see firm details p.947) "*At the sharper end of the sector,*" **Barry Holland** (see p.514) is often to be seen defending food retailers in Magistrates' Courts nationwide. Admired as the lynchpin of the firm's licensing and food safety practice, he is also rated for his specialist knowledge in applications for off-licences in petrol station and convenience stores. The small team continues to punch above its weight, recently attracting new instructions from another major supermarket chain. **Clients** Pelican Group; supermarket chains.

SHOOSMITHS (see firm details p.1133) "*Going from strength to strength,*" the firm is widely cited as a leading food law practice. It specialises in training personnel at food companies throughout the UK and Ireland, with a view to raising awareness of issues such as consumer care, due diligence and crisis management. The defence of labelling and safety prosecutions also contributes to its workload. "*Expert*" **Ron Reid** (see p.672) is respected by clients for "*rolling his sleeves up and getting the job done.*" **Clients** British Sugar.

ANDREW M. JACKSON (see firm details p.845) Trading standards and food labelling cases, particularly in the fisheries sector, have formed part of the recent workload of this highly respected operation. It has also branched out into advising on novel dietary products. "*Co-operative and knowledgeable*" head of litigation **Hugh Smith** (see p.673) has a niche expertise in food law. Other areas of expertise include advising on associated advertising matters. **Clients** Vitamin companies; pharmaceutical companies.

GREGG LATCHAMS QUINN Leading partner Andrew Gregg (see p.513) has sustained his composite licensing and food safety practice, for which he continues to be warmly recommended by peers. Supported by a team of associates, the practice also covers food labelling and associated matters. **Clients** Restaurants; pubs.

MARGETTS & RITCHIE A "*definite leader,*" David Hetherington (see p.671) remains at the head of this respected and busy group. "*Demanding opponents in court,*" the firm is highly rated for its contentious advice, which includes both criminal and civil elements. The storage and transportation of food, hygiene, labelling and imports have all featured in the firm's recent workload. The practice also covers misleading pricing and product liability. **Clients** NFMFT; supermarkets ; retailers; pubs.

BEVAN ASHFORD (see firm details p.869) Preserving a "*serious presence*" in the market, the

PRODUCT LIABILITY ■ THE LEADERS

team advises on the production, manufacture and retailing of food, including hygiene and labelling and marketing issues. Partner David Wood is responsible for this sector, which is handled by the firm's health and safety practice. **Clients** Allied Domecq; Meridian Leisure.

BOND PEARCE (see firm details p.879) A "*top regional firm*," it defends prosecutions on a range of matters including weights and measures and trade descriptions. Food safety and hygiene matters also form part of the workload of Michael Parrott's group. **Clients** Restaurants; supermarkets.

HAMMOND SUDDARDS EDGE The firm is involved in both prosecutions and due diligence for acquisitions and disposals. Observers agree that this team of two associates has built up an enviable following of national clients. The unit is led by Françoise Snape. **Clients** Hazelwoods.

THE LEADERS IN PRODUCT LIABILITY

ALEXANDER, Miles
Simmons & Simmons, London
(020) 7628 2020
miles.alexander@simmons-simmons.com
Specialisation: Specialises in product liability, product safety regulation and recall. Has advised a range of international manufacturers and distributors: pharmaceutical, telephony, medical devices, building materials, tobacco, household goods, industrial machinery. Advises on non-contentious product development, presentation and distribution. Advises on contentious matters: recall, crisis management, defence of claims, particularly multi-party and multi-jurisdictional. Recently or presently advising a UK pharmaceutical manufacturer, a far east distributor of Chinese manufactured medicines, a US domestic appliance manufacturer and a Japanese machinery manufacturer.
Prof. Memberships: Law Society, City of London Solicitors Company, London Solicitors Litigation Association, IBA.
Career: Qualified on 1989; Partner *Simmons & Simmons* in 1992.

BALEN, Paul
freethcartwright, Nottingham
(0115) 936 9369
paul.balen@freethcartwright.co.uk
See under Clinical Negligence, p.149

BAYLIS, Craig
Berwin Leighton Paisner, London
(020) 7760 1000
craig.baylis@blplaw.com
See under Licensing, p.511

BODY, David
Irwin Mitchell, Sheffield
(0870) 1500 100
Bodyd@irwinmitchell.co.uk
See under Clinical Negligence, p.149

BOWDEN, Paul
Freshfields Bruckhaus Deringer, London
(020) 7936 4000
paul.bowden@freshfields.com
See under Environment, p.357

CODY, Nick
Taylor Wessing, London
(020) 7300 7000
n.cody@taylorwessing.com
Specialisation: Advises on a wide range of consumer law issues, including consumer protection, consumer safety and trading standards. Also advises on advertising, sales promotions and related issues. Particular experience in advising clients operating in the food, cosmetics and toy industries.
Prof. Memberships: Member of Food Law Group.
Career: Joined firm in 1967 and has been advising clients on consumer law issues since 1972.
Personal: Leisure – watching cricket and football, walking, local community and family life.

DAY, Martyn
Leigh, Day & Co, London
(020) 7650 1200
Specialisation: Partner in environment and product liability department. Main area of practice is environmental and product liability law. Heads team of 14 lawyers specialising in representing groups of injured people in complex actions. Co-Author of 'Toxic Torts', 'Personal Injury Handbook', 'Multi-Party Actions' and 'Environmental Action: A Citizens Guide'. Regularly addresses lectures, seminars and media on environmental issues.
Prof. Memberships: APIL, Executive Committee Member of Society of Labour Lawyers, Director of Greenpeace.
Career: Qualified in 1981 with *Colombotti & Partners*. Moved to *Clifford Chance* and then *Bindman & Partners* in 1981. Left to set up *Leigh Day & Co* in 1987.
Personal: Born in 1957.

DODDS-SMITH, Ian
Arnold & Porter, London
(020) 7786 6100
ian_dodds-smith@aporter.com
Specialisation: Partner and head of European Product Liability Group with broad expertise in all aspects of the law relating to pharmaceuticals, medical and biotech products, and other healthcare products including those in the cosmetic and food sectors; specialist in licensing and related regulatory affairs (with public law cases conducted in National and European Court); and in the field of product liability with involvement in a large number of matters, many with a multinational element and including multi-claimant litigation including pregnancy tests, oral contraceptives, blood products, intra-uterine devices, human insulin, heart valves, benzodiazepines, breast implants, pesticides and various other food and chemical product claims.
Prof. Memberships: Fellow of the Royal Society of Medicine; Member various Royal College, WHO and MRC Working Parties on research and medico-legal issues.
Career: Articled McKenna & Co; qualified 1976; Assistant McKenna & Co 1976-83; secondment to Schering Health Care Ltd 1978-83; Partner McKenna & Co/*Cameron McKenna* 1984-2002; Partner *Arnold & Porter* 2002.
Publications: 'Product Liability for Medical Products' (in 'Medical Negligence' by Powers & Harris, Butterworths); 'Legal Liabilities in Clinical Trials' in 'Early Phase Human Drug Evaluation in Man' by O'Grady and Linet (RC); 'Data Protection and Abridged Applications for Marketing Authorisations' in 'Pharmaceutical Medicine' by Goldberg and Linbay (Cambridge University Press). Various other book chapters and articles on regulatory and medico-legal matters.
Personal: Born 1951. Educated at Solihull School, Warwickshire; Downing College, Cambridge (1972 BA Law, 1973 MA).

EDGAR, Andrew
Clifford Chance, London
(020) 7600 1000
Andrew.Edgar@cliffordchance.com
Specialisation: Litigation and Dispute Resolution Department. Partner specialising in product liability, food, corporate and commercial litigation.
Career: Called to Bar, Middle Temple 1975; qualified 1981; Partner since 1984.
Personal: Fetes College, Edinburgh; London University.

EDMONDS, Steven
DLA, Birmingham
(08700) 111111

ELVY, Mark
Ashurst Morris Crisp, London
(020) 7859 1567
mark.elvy@ashursts.com
Specialisation: Main area of practice is commercial litigation specialising in product liability and risk management in the health, safety and environmental fields. Particular expertise in the defense of multi-party product related claims and the defence of multi-jurisdictional claims with a focus on Europe. Advised on a number of product recalls.
Prof. Memberships: Law Society; International Association of Defense Council; Defense Research Institute; International Bar Association.
Career: Admitted as a solicitor of the Supreme Court of New South Wales in 1984. Admitted as a solicitor in England in 1991. Joined *Ashurst Morris Crisp* in 1987; partner 1994.
Publications: Contributing author to publication on Group Actions in England and Wales published by Oxford University press in March 2001. Co-author of chapter in the 'Risk Management Guide: 2001', published by the London Stock Exchange.
Personal: Born 20 April 1961; attended University of New South Wales (B Comm 1982, LLB 1984). Married with two children, Resides London.

EVANS, John
Ashurst Morris Crisp, London
(020) 7859 1545
john.evans@ashurst.com
Specialisation: Business litigation (eg Indosuez International Finance v National Reserve Bank (reported)) and product liability, environmental and health and safety issues (as arising in eg the Federal Mogul Chapter 11 proceedings and T&N Administration).
Prof. Memberships: International Association of Defense Council (Executive Committee 1998-2001); Law Society; ABA.
Career: Joined 1979; qualified 1981; Partner 1988.
Publications: Contributing Author 'Multi-Party Actions', OUP, March 2001 and the London Stock Exchange's 'Risk Management Guide: 2001', dealing with (1) product liability and (2) environmental and health and safety.
Personal: Cambridge University MA LLM. Coach – London Welsh U-17s.

FREEMAN, Rod
Lovells, London
(020) 7296 5256
rod.freeman@lovells.com
Specialisation: Main areas of practice are the defence of product liability litigation, and product safety law including recalls and risk management. Particular experience in 'mass tort' claims involving public health issues. Cases have involved products as silicone breast implants,

THE LEADERS — PRODUCT LIABILITY

asbestos, cosmetics, building products, electrical products, pharmaceuticals, toys, medical devices and tobacco. Also has extensive experience in railway safety issues. Is currently co-ordinating a major study on behalf of the European Commission to investigate the practical operation of product liability systems throughout the European Community, and to advise on possible reforms. He speaks at international product liability conferences, and his articles are regularly published in leading product liability journals.
Prof. Memberships: Defense Research Institute (Member of European Advisory Committee); National Product Liability Association of Australia; Law Society of England and Wales.
Career: Admitted in New South Wales in 1990. Specialised in product liability in Sydney before joining *Lovells* in 2000.
Publications: Editor of *Lovells* quarterly journal 'European Product Liability Review'; Editor of 'Product Safety in the European Union – A Practical Guide to the General Product Safety Directive', *Lovells*, May 2002.
Personal: Born in Sydney, 16 February, 1966. Studied at University of Sydney (BEc; LLB (Hons), LLM). Resides London with wife and two daughters.

GILBERTSON, Kathryn
Dechert, London
(020) 7775 7693
kathryn.gilbertson@eu.dechert.com
Specialisation: Partner heading up the Corporate Safety Group, advising leading companies on all aspects of regulatory law including food safety, hygiene and labelling matters. Kathryn has a reputation for an innovative approach to regulatory compliance issues and for her astute commercial awareness. Dual qualified as both an environmental health officer (1984), with extensive enforcement experience and as a solicitor, Kathryn has a unique insight into enforcement strategies and policies. In addition to her extensive defence work for leading companies, she has been called to advise Government agencies on the practical aspects of regulatory enforcement matters. Kathryn has extensive experience in advising directors on their personal and corporate liabilities. She writes and speaks frequently on food and safety matters.
Prof. Memberships: Food Law Group, European Food Law Association, Society of Food Hygiene Technology and Road Risk Forum.
Career: Graduate of the University of the West of England (1984) and admitted as a solicitor in 1994.
Personal: Married with a son. Lives in Hertfordshire. School Governor.

GREGG, Andrew
Gregg Latchams Quinn, Bristol
(0117) 906 9400
andrew.gregg@glqlaw.com
See under Licensing, p.513

HARRIS, David
Alexander Harris, Altrincham
(0161) 925 5555
Specialisation: Senior Partner specialising in group actions, including pharmaceutical product liability; currently heading and co-ordinating group actions into MMR vaccine damage claims, organ retention, claims arising out of Britain's nuclear testing in the 1950s and 1960s, claims for arsenic poisoning in Bangladesh and over-treatment claims against Manchester orthodontist Melvyn Megitt; investigating potential claims against the manufacturers of Zyban. Previous group litigations include Myodil, Hillsborough disaster, Opren, human insulin, LSD, under-dosing of radiation cases at North Staff Deneral Hospital, Trilucent breast implants and Listeriosis. Considerable experience in litigation in the USA, including Shiley heart valves, Teletronic pacemakers and silicon breast implant claims. Alexander Harris is one of only 18 firms on the multi-party action panel.
Prof. Memberships: Law Society, APIL, ATLA.
Career: Qualified in 1979 and then became co-founder of *Alexander Harris* in May 1989. First practice in this country specialising exclusively in clinical negligence and pharmaceutical product liability. The practice also has a specialist personal injury department. Deputy District Judge on the Northern Circuit since 1988. Assessor to Law Society Personal Injury Panel. CEDR Accredited mediator.
Personal: Born 23rd May 1949. Attended Hull University (LL.B 1972).

HARVEY, Mark
Hugh James, Cardiff
(029) 2022 4871
mark.harvey@hughjames.com
Specialisation: Personal injury, clinical negligence, product liability; representing victims of transport accidents including P&O Lifeboat; Maidenhead Rail Fire; co-ordinating the Gerona Air crash litigation and member of the steering committees of Southall and Ladbroke Grove rail crashes. Also household product failures including sanitary and cosmetic items.
Prof. Memberships: Secretary of APIL; PEOPIL; ATLA; National Back Pain Association and British Association of Sports and the Law; Editorial Board Wales Law Today; Holiday Travelwatch.
Career: 1987 Legal Executive, *Owen White*; qualified 1990 *Lawford & Co*; Partner *Smith Llewelyn Partnership* 1995-May 2001; Partner, *Hugh James Ford Simey*.
Personal: Born September 1962; wine bluffer; footballer; golfer and skier; resides Vale of Glamorgan.

HETHERINGTON, David
Margetts & Ritchie, Birmingham
(0121) 214 5001
david.hetherington@margetts-ritchie.com
Specialisation: Defends businesses and directors prosecuted by local authorities and government departments in relation to food safety, trading standards, environmental health, product safety, price indications, officers' requests for records, health and safety and recovers defence costs. Businesses represented include: national chains of food and non-food supermarkets and furniture retailers; frozen food storage and distribution company; toys importer and retail supermarket chain; breweries pubs and restaurant chains; liquor licensees; nut importers and wholesalers; organic food importers and wholesalers; doors and fire doors manufacturers, kitchens, glass and conservatory producers and installers; electrical distributors and retailers; producers of poultry, meat, scotch eggs, ice cream, yoghurt, pizza and wine; fish processors, importers and shellfish distributors; tinned and general food importers; restaurants, cafés, butchers, bakeries, grocers and delicatessen; holiday camp; golf professional; university. Recent cases include: breach of emergency prohibition notice; excess water in cured ham; EC Marketing Standards; butcher's licensing; misleading price indications; short measure beer; under-age sales; meat pies content and labelling – withdrawn; food past use-by-dates – withdrawn; officer's requests for price records withdrawn; under-cooked chicken – withdrawn; restaurant food hygiene – withdrawn; reduced strength whisky – withdrawn; under-age sale – withdrawn with costs; health and safety of food storage racking and pallet mover training; butchers' food hygiene; misleading seafood labelling – withdrawn; health claim on food – withdrawn; false descriptions in car and electrical servicing; Pesticides Safety Directorate – required to amend 'naming and shaming' report; Food Standards Agency poultry product recall; unsafe fire door – withdrawn; misleading telephone prices – withdrawn
Prof. Memberships: Law Society. Food Law Group.
Career: With *Margetts & Ritchie* 1975-2002: articles (1975-77), assistant solicitor (1978-84), and partner (1984-2002). Instructed as a Prosecution Solicitor agent: West Midlands Trading Standards, Environmental and Fire Service Departments (1981-86), West Midlands Probation Service (1986-91), Crown Prosecution Service (1987-91), Birmingham Trading Standards (1988-89) and M.A.F.F. (1990). Instructed as a Defence Solicitor: general criminal law offences (1978-99), Duty Solicitor (1979-96), West Midlands Fire Service drivers (1981-87), Trading Standards, Environmental Health, MAFF & DEFRA Wine & Marketing Standards cases (1987-2002). Food Law Consultant to The National Federation of Meat and Food Traders (2001-02)
Personal: English Ski Council Club Instructor.

HODGES, Christopher
CMS Cameron McKenna, London
(020) 7367 3000
christopher.hodges@cmck.com
Specialisation: Main areas of practice are product liability, product regulatory and safety law and product recall across a wide range of sectors, including medical devices, pharmaceuticals, automotives and electronics. Author 'Multi-Party Actions'. Editor of 'Product Liability: European Laws and Practice', and 'Product Safety', Chapters in 'Product Liability: Law and Insurance', 'The Textbook of Pharmaceutical Medicine' and various other books. Author of 1995 European Commission Study on the Product Liability Directive. Honorary Research Associate, New College, Oxford.
Prof. Memberships: Law Society, CBI Consumer Affairs Committee and Working Parties on Product Liability and General Product Safety, ABHI Council, International Association of Defense Counsel, Chair of International Bar Association Committee on Product Liability and Consumer Affairs, Chair of Legal Committees of EUCOMED, EDMA, ABHI and BIVDA.
Career: Worked at *Slaughter and May* and *Clifford Chance* before becoming Partner at *McKenna & Co* in 1990.
Personal: Born 19 March 1954. Educated at King Edward's School, Birmingham. Academical Clerk at New College, Oxford. Founder member and Trustee of 'The Sixteen'.

HOLLAND, Barry
Elliotts, Manchester
(0161) 834 9933
barry.holland@elliott-law.co.uk
See under Licensing, p.514

KELLEHER, John
Theodore Goddard, London
(020) 7880 5814
johnkelleher@theodoregoddard.co.uk
Specialisation: Product liability litigation, particularly for clients in the pharmaceutical industry. Represented Glaxo in the Myodil litigation and The Wellcome Foundation Limited in the MMR Vaccine Litigation. Has acted for pharmaceutical manufacturers in defending claims arising out of a range of therapeutic products including corticosteroids. Has recently advised major electronics company and electrical cable manufacturing companies on product recalls and related issues. Currently advising manufacturing clients on potential exposure for asbestos claims, pharmaceutical clients on vaccine claims and on issues arising in the food and drinks sector.
Prof. Memberships: Law Society, City of London Solicitors Company, IBA.
Career: Uppingham, Sheffield University, trained with *Theodore Goddard*, qualified in 1978, partner 1984, head of litigation 1990.
Personal: Married, three children.

LLEWELLYN, Paul
Eversheds, Nottingham

671

PRODUCT LIABILITY ■ THE LEADERS

(0115) 859 8705
paulllewellyn@eversheds.com
Specialisation: Exclusively involved in product liability litigation and ancillary regulatory advice principally for medical device and pharmaceutical companies. Major cases involve the continuing 3M Capital Hip and Trilucent breast implant claims. Extensive experience of negotiating and running bespoke innovative ADR agreements as an alternative to formal litigation. Also involved in formal group action work on behalf of defendants. Currently engaged in the coordination of pan-European medical device claims. Experience of US product liability claims.
Prof. Memberships: Law Society. Defense Research Institute. Founding member of DRI's International Special Litigation Group. Member of DRI's Medical Device and Pharmaceutical Committee.
Career: Admitted 1980. Partner in *Robin Thompson & Partners* 1982-87; partner *Shoosmiths & Harrison* 1990-95; became a partner in *Eversheds* in 1995.
Publications: Commissioned to write UK product liability section of a US product liability encyclopaedia. Member of the editorial board of Health Law.
Personal: Born November 1953. Educated at Dyffryn Comprehensive School and London School of Economics (LLB, 1976). Married with one son.

MCCOOL, Geraldine
Leigh, Day & Co, Manchester
(0161) 832 7722
gmccool@leighday.co.uk
See under Personal Injury, p.634

MCDOUGALL, Arundel
Ashurst Morris Crisp, London
(020) 7859 1095
annabel.mcdougall@ashursts.com
Specialisation: Commercial litigation, with special emphasis on product liability and consumer safety issues, in the healthcare industry.
Prof. Memberships: City of London Law Society, International Association of Defence Counsel; Defence Research Institute.
Career: Qualified in November 1978. Became a partner in 1986 at *Rowe & Maw* and joined *Ashursts* as a partner in 2000.
Publications: Monograph; 'Pharmaceutical Subsidisation and the National Institute of Clinical Excellence', (October 2000); 'Corporate Killing – Legal Liabilities of Companies and Directors when Crisis Occurs' (November 2000); contributing author to publication on Multi-party Actions in England and Wales published by Oxford University Press (March 2001); 'The Blood Transfusion Case and Its Implications for the Pharmaceutical Industry', Pharmaceutical Physician, March 2002, Vol 12 No 4; 'Appeals against NICE Appraisals: The Appeals Process in Pracice and Proposed Reforms', joint author with Richard Best, Ashurst Morris Crisp Newsletter, March 2002; 'Appeals Against the UK's NICE Appraisals', joint author with Richard Best, 'The Regulatory Affairs Journal', Vol 13, No 4, April 2002.
Personal: MA (Hons) Christ Church Oxford, 1972. Married with two children, lives in London. Interests: Rugby, rowing, running, music and field sports.

MEERAN, Richard
Leigh, Day & Co, London
(020) 7650 1200
Specialisation: Practice covers environmental, product liability and personal injury claims including actions for damage caused by chemicals, noise, lead paint and asbestos; property devaluation arising from contaminated land, overseas claimants against UK companies (several reported cases including Afrika and 7,500 others v Cape Plc, Connelly v RTZ, and Ngcobo v Thor Chemical), many of these actions being multiparty in nature. Numerous publications in scientific and legal journals and newspapers.
Prof. Memberships: APIL; London Legal Aid Area committee chair. Solicitors' Human Rights Group. International Law Association. Amnesty International UK Business Group.
Career: Admitted April 1988. Partner at *Leigh Day* since 1991.
Publications: Contributing editor 'Journal of Personal Injury Law'. More than 50 published articles.
Personal: Born 23 June 1961. BSc (London University 1983), LLM Advanced Litigation (Nottingham Law School) 1996.

MELTZER, John
Lovells, London
(020) 7296 2000
john.meltzer@lovells.com
Specialisation: Head of the firm's London product liability group whose clients include manufacturers and retailers of motor vehicles (and components), aircraft engines, tobacco, pharmaceutical products, asbestos, electronic goods, food, guns, toys and beverages. Main areas of practice are product liability litigation and product safety regulation. Particular experience in defending multi-party claims. Currently representing pharmaceutical companies in the MMR vaccine group action. Also has experience defending cross-border product liability claims. Has assisted UK companies in the co-ordination of the defence of claims in jurisdictions outside the UK including the US, Canada and Australia. As well as defending claims, advises on non-contentious issues such as product safety, risk management, labelling, product recalls, crisis management and media handling. This work is often for clients who have to deal with high profile 'public health' issues, such as EMF (mobile phones), dioxin contamination, ETS ('passive smoking') and BSE. Has also acted in several judicial reviews of the actions of governmental authorities at national and EU levels. Acted for the principal UK tobacco companies in the judicial review proceedings that resulted in the annulment of the EU Directive banning tobacco advertising and sponsorship. Leading the team appointed to advise the European Commission on possible reforms of product liability laws in the EU.
Prof. Memberships: London Litigation Solicitors Association; International Association of Defense Counsel.
Career: Qualified New South Wales, Australia 1982. Qualified England and Wales 1991. Solicitor at *Freehill Hollongdale & Page* 1984-86. Joined *Lovells* in 1987 and became a partner in 1997.

PEARL, Simon
Davies Arnold Cooper, London
(020) 7936 2222
spearl@dac.co.uk
Specialisation: Partner in Product Liability and Group Action Unit. Main areas of practice are product liability and negligence. Defends pharmaceutical companies and other manufacturers and their insurers. Also handles pharmaceutical regulatory work. Co-ordinating solicitor for the NHS in HIV Haemophilia litigation and defended the National Blood Authority in the Hepatitis C litigation. Defended in the whooping cough vaccine test case, Loveday v Renton. Represents GSK in the MMR vaccine litigation. Author of a chapter relating to Product Liability Insurance in Lloyd's of London's 'Product Liability and Insurance' publication, edited by Mark Mildred and 'European Product Liability' published by Monitor Press. Writes and speaks widely at conferences. Sits as a part-time Chair of the Special Educational Needs Tribunal.
Prof. Memberships: Law Society. Law Society's Working Party on Group Actions, Medico-legal Society. American Bar Associations Defence Research Institute.
Career: Qualified in 1977. Joined *Davies Arnold Cooper* in 1975, becoming a Partner in 1980.
Personal: Born 30 April 1953. Attended Horace Mann School, New York and Birmingham University (LLB (Hons) 1974). Leisure interests include road running, theatre, music and family. Lives in Harpenden, Herts.

PICKERING, John
Irwin Mitchell, Sheffield
(0114) 276 7777
pickeringj@irwinmitchell.co.uk
See under Clinical Negligence, p.154

REID, Ron
Shoosmiths, Northampton
(01604) 543000
Specialisation: Specialises in all health and safety issues, both contentious and non-contentious. Has led the launch of *Shoosmiths* Occupational Safety, a department dedicated to offering straightforward advice on all safety matters. Has set up a specialist training department to handle the requirements of national and international companies for in-house training from director to shop floor level. He is a regular speaker at conferences and seminars, often alongside senior Health & Safety Executive officials.
Prof. Memberships: Secretary to the Food Industrial Regional Safety Team, East Midlands and the Northamptonshire Occupational Safety and Health Association. Director of The Radon Council. Legal advisor to and Honorary Member of Executive Committee of Inter-Company Consumer Affairs Association, a trade association of Consumer Care Managers in the food and drinks manufacturing industry. Member of The Food Law Group.
Career: Qualified in 1983, having previously been a F.I.L.Ex. Joined *Shoosmiths & Harrison* in 1974. Became a Partner in 1985.

ROSS, Hilary
Berwin Leighton Paisner, London
(020) 7760 1000
hilary.ross@blplaw.com
Specialisation: Partner in Regulatory Department. Advises on EU and UK regulatory compliance issues for foods. Specifically advises US, Canadian and Australia manufacturers about how to successfully launch their products in the EU. This includes providing advice on composition, labelling, packaging, claims and advertising. Also advises clients about defending prosecutions for non-compliance issues and represents clients in Court. Has extensive experience in obtaining pre-market approval for novel foods and advises US, Asian and Dutch companies on this matter. Hilary advises many US companies about compliance issues particular to nutraceuticals and food supplements. In the last year has also advised several e-commerce businesses on compliance issues. A specialist in the regulation of GM foods advising manufacturers, retailers and caterers on this topic. International Conferences in Korea on this topic. Regularly participates in the PAGB's one day training course on food supplements.
Prof. Memberships: Food Law Group, European Food Law Association. Food & Drink Federation. Institute of Food Science and Technology. Society of Hygene Technology.
Career: Qualified in Scotland in 1993; Obtained English Practicing Certificate in April 1994; Solicitor in pharmaceutical department of *McKenna & Co* 1993-95; Joined *Paisner & Co* in 1998. Partner, *Berwin Leighton Paisner* 2001.
Publications: Has recently authored a report for Monitor Law Press called 'Novel Foods: A guide to the Law & Technology of GMOs in Europe'. Wrote concluding chapter for 'International Food Law'.

SAYERS, Shane
Kennedys, London
(020) 7650 5605
s.sayers@kennedys-law.com

THE LEADERS — PRODUCT LIABILITY

Specialisation: Leading product liability claims including acting for manufacturers and insurers on cases including organophosphate/sheep dip, toxic shock related to tampon use and on behalf of NHSLA in 3m Hip litigation.
Prof. Memberships: Member of CEDR qualified mediator.
Career: Qualified in 1981. Moved to *Barlow Lyde & Gilbert* and to *Kennedys* in 1983.
Publications: Regular contributor to leading specialist journals on legal issues including procedure and in 'The Times' in defective products.
Personal: Married with two young boys. Travels extensively with his family. Enjoys food, wine and American crosswords.

SHERRINGTON, Patrick
Lovells, London
(020) 7296 2000
patrick.sherrington@lovells.com
Specialisation: Commercial litigation. Extensive experience of international commercial litigation, arbitration and ADR, especially in the fields of banking and finance, energy, product liability and professional negligence. Heads the Litigation Practice at *Lovells* and also the firm's ADR practice and regularly sits as a mediator. Author of: 'Civil Litigation' published in Hong Kong by Longmans, 2nd edition 1996; writes and regularly speaks on his specialist areas of practice.
Prof. Memberships: Admitted in the UK, Hong Kong and Australia (NSW). Law Society of England & Wales, Solicitors' European Group, City of London Solicitors' Company, Fellow of the Chartered Institute of Arbitrators, Law Society of Hong Kong, Inter-Pacific Bar Association, LawAsia, International Bar Association.
Career: Articled *Lovells* 1978-80; resident in New York 1982-84; Partner 1985; resident in Hong Kong 1987-96; CEDR accredited mediator; Higher Courts (Civil proceedings) qualification; Law Society of Hong Kong Council Member 1990-96; Vice President 1993-96; Council Member Inter-Pacific Bar Association 1990-96; Governor Advocacy Institute of Hong Kong 1994-96.

SMITH, Hugh
Andrew M. Jackson, Hull
(01482) 325242
hes@amj.co.uk
Specialisation: Substantial area of practice involves retail law covering trading standards, health and safety, consumer protection and consumer safety. Particular expertise in the vitamin and fish industry. Commercial litigation work includes contractual disputes both international and domestic, company and partnership disputes, commercial property disputes, professional negligence, defamation and passing off. Represents finance houses in respect of consumer complaints/recoveries.
Prof. Memberships: Member of the Law Society and the Food Law Group. Also an ADR Mediator.
Career: Admitted 1983. Joined present firm in 1989, becoming a Partner in 1991 in charge of the commercial litigation division.
Personal: Born 16 October 1959. Attended Nottingham University (LLB Hons).

SPRING, Paul
Mills Selig, Belfast
(028) 9024 3878
paul.spring@nilaw.com
See under Defamation, p.274

STEWART, Brian J C
O'Reilly Stewart, Belfast
(028) 9032 1000
brian_stewart@oreilly-stewart.co.uk
Specialisation: Specialises in product liability defence and insurance defence generally, including pharmaceuticals.
Prof. Memberships: Member of the Council of the Law Society of Northern Ireland. Former Chairman of the Belfast Solicitors' Association. Member of the International Association of Defence Counsel.
Career: Qualified 1978. Admitted to the Republic of Ireland Roll of Solicitors 1991.

TOZER, Roy
DLA, Birmingham
(08700) 111111

TUCKER, Andrew
Irwin Mitchell, Sheffield
(0870) 1500 100
Specialisation: Litigation in respect of products giving rise to injury, particularly pharmaceutical products, medical devices, experience of multi-party litigation both product related and arising from transport disasters and occupational disease. Acted for Plaintiffs in many high profile cases including: Opren, Dalkon Shield, Benzodiazepines, Manchester Aircrash, 'Herald of Free Enterprise', Kegworth Aircrash, 'Marchioness'/'Bowbelle' collision, North Cornwall Water Pollution, Armley Asbestos, Human Growth Hormone/Creutzfeldt-Jacob Disease, tobacco, silicone implants, Mineworkers V.W.F. and Mineworkers Respiratory Disease.
Prof. Memberships: Law Society, Association of Personal Injury Lawyers, South Yorkshire Medico Legal Society, American Trial Lawyers Association, Australian Plaintiff Lawyers Association.
Career: Articled *Wallace Mitchell*, Nottingham. Qualified 1985. Partner, *Irwin Mitchell*, 1988.
Personal: Born October 1960, University of Liverpool, LL.B. Lives North Derbyshire.

TYLER, Mark
CMS Cameron McKenna, London
(020) 7367 3000
mlt@cmck.com
See under Health & Safety, p.403

WARE, Anne
Davies Arnold Cooper, London
(020) 7293 4062
aware@dac.co.uk
Specialisation: Specialist in product liability litigation with particular expertise in mass tort claims. Major pharmaceutical related litigation experience includes Pertussis, Opren, Benzodiazepines, Lariam; current caseload includes medical device claims; environmental and multi-jurisdictional litigation. Other areas include medical negligence; complex or unusual medically related and personal injury actions; work related stress, sexual harassment and abuse claims; veterinary, cosmetic and food product-related claims.

WARNOCK, Owen
Eversheds, Norwich
(01603) 272727
owenwarnock@eversheds.com
See under Employment, p.332

WILKES, Chris
Beachcroft Wansbroughs, London
(020) 7894 6844
cwilkes@bwlaw.co.uk
Specialisation: Partner, specialises in policy and reinsurance disputes – particularly product liability and disaster litigation. Acted in the Oral Contraceptive Action trial for manufacturer and is now engaged in Persona Group Action. Also acts in Aerospace, construction and engineering related product claims.
Career: Qualified 1980. Articled *Stanleys & Simpson North*. 1983 to date, partner *Beachcroft Wansbroughs*.

WILSON, Michael
Elliott Duffy Garrett, Belfast
(028) 9024 5034

YOUNG, David A
Eversheds, Birmingham
(0121) 232 1000
davidyoung@eversheds.com
See under Licensing, p.516

PROFESSIONAL NEGLIGENCE

London: 674; The Regions: 676; Profiles: 680

Research approved by BMRB For this edition, **Chambers'** researchers conducted 6,582 interviews – 3,900 with law firms, 511 with barristers and 2,171 with clients. The validity of the research was scrutinised by BMRB International, who audited both the methodology and the results at our offices in London. They interviewed **Chambers'** researchers and cross-checked sample interviews. Details of the audit appear on page 7.

OVERVIEW The insurance market has hardened this year. Two years after the Solicitors Indemnity Fund (SIF) went into run off, the legal professional indemnity market has been especially affected as a string of insurers have withdrawn from the market, including Independent Insurance, which went into insolvency. The solicitors professional indemnity market is now dominated by St Paul, Zurich and QBE. Important cases from the year include the highly publicised *Etridge* case, concerning the solicitors' duty to advise spouses/partners about security given over businesses, and *Cave v Robinson*, concerning the extension of limitation periods in bringing a claim.

LONDON

PROFESSIONAL NEGLIGENCE
LEGAL ■ LONDON

1
- Barlow Lyde & Gilbert
- Reynolds Porter Chamberlain

2
- Lovells

3
- Beachcroft Wansbroughs
- CMS Cameron McKenna
- Kennedys

4
- Ince & Co
- Mills & Reeve
- Pinsent Curtis Biddle

PROFESSIONAL NEGLIGENCE
FINANCIAL ■ LONDON

1
- Barlow Lyde & Gilbert

2
- CMS Cameron McKenna
- Herbert Smith
- Reynolds Porter Chamberlain

3
- Lovells

4
- Berrymans Lace Mawer
- Mayer Brown Rowe & Maw

This book is the product of 6,582 1/2 hour interviews. See p.7 for BMRB audit. Within each band, firms are listed alphabetically.

PROFESSIONAL NEGLIGENCE
INSURANCE ■ LONDON

1
- Barlow Lyde & Gilbert
- Reynolds Porter Chamberlain

2
- CMS Cameron McKenna

3
- Herbert Smith

4
- Clyde & Co
- Mayer Brown Rowe & Maw
- Squire & Co

5
- Beachcroft Wansbroughs
- Davies Arnold Cooper
- Ince & Co

PROFESSIONAL NEGLIGENCE
CONSTRUCTION ■ LONDON

1
- Beale and Company
- Fishburn Morgan Cole
- Mayer Brown Rowe & Maw

2
- CMS Cameron McKenna
- Kennedys
- Reynolds Porter Chamberlain

3
- Berrymans Lace Mawer
- Davies Arnold Cooper

4
- Barlow Lyde & Gilbert

5
- Hextalls

This book is the product of 6,582 1/2 hour interviews. See p.7 for BMRB audit. Within each band, firms are listed alphabetically.

BARLOW LYDE & GILBERT (see firm details p.858) The retirement of Ian Jenkins is thought by peers to have had little impact on a team of remarkable breadth and depth, which carries out big-ticket work with "*serious commercial clout.*" **David Arthur** (see p.680) has the experience to "*shine in significant cases.*" He successfully represented PricewaterhouseCoopers in proceedings brought by Sir Elton John and others and is acting for them in the appeal. Despite **Richard Dedman**'s (see p.681) promotion to senior partner in May 2001 he remains highly involved in solicitors' liability and in claims concerning IT and management consultants. **Stuart Hall** (see p.681) was described by peers as a "*leading light,*" who deals practically with large cases. He was recently involved in the MCC litigation. **Richard Harrison** (see p.681) enters the tables following sustained recommendations. Another new entry is **Clare Canning** (see p.680), who peers say has "*risen to great things.*" **Michael Wilson** (see p.683) retains his reputation on the financial side of the sector.

LEADERS ACROSS THE BOARD

Sarah Clover (see p.680) was widely commended for her work on a range of Professional Indemnity (PI) claims against solicitors. The team has also been acting for Coopers & Lybrand in the Barings litigation and for Smith & Williamson in the Eastgate group matter. **Clients** Ernst & Young; SIF; PricewaterhouseCoopers; Zurich Professional; SVB Syndicates; Admiral Underwriting; Brewin Dolphin Securities; Jones Lang LaSalle.

REYNOLDS PORTER CHAMBERLAIN (see firm details p.1111) The market considers this a practice of "*outstanding quality*" with "*leading people*" doing a wide variety of work. Barristers have a particularly high opinion of **Simon Greenley** (see p.474). His team has recently received instructions from GE Frankona relating to two South American bankers' bond cases. "*Mover and shaker*" **Barney Micklem** (see p.682) gets results in surveyors' and solicitors' cases through his "*constructive*" approach while peers view **Paul Nicholas** (see p.682) as one of, if not "*the leading professional negligence solicitor in the country*" with "*great technical expertise and a commercial manner.*"

Stuart White (see p.683) stands out for his experience and personable attitude and is a regular speaker on insurance-related matters. Newly ranked **Timothy Brown** (see p.680) is said by clients to be "*flexible, knowledgeable and good to deal with.*" This year the firm acted for Lloyd's brokers' E&O insurers on a claim made by General Dynamics concerning workers' compensation contracts. It has also recently been instructed by a top ten accountancy firm on a claim worth £15 million. **Clients** ACE; Grant Thornton; Mercers; Heath Lambert; Markel; SVB; Wren Managers; Wurttembergische; XL Brockbank.

LEADING FIRMS IN ALPHABETICAL ORDER

BEACHCROFT WANSBROUGHS (see firm details p.860) The London office of this nationally recognised firm does a large volume of work across all types of professional negligence but is especially regarded for legal and insurance cases. Alison MacLennan's retirement was not felt to seriously affect a competent and pragmatic team, which peers say can be relied upon to "*shake the guts out of a case.*" Typical clients include valuers, architects, accountants, solicitors and brokers. **Clients** Insurance panels.

674   INDEX TO LEADING LAWYERS: PAGE 1693 ■ IN-HOUSE LAWYERS PROFILES: PAGE 1201

LONDON ■ PROFESSIONAL NEGLIGENCE

LEADING INDIVIDUALS

1
- **ARTHUR David** Barlow Lyde & Gilbert
- **GREENLEY Simon** Reynolds Porter Chamberlain
- **MICKLEM Barney** Reynolds Porter Chamberlain
- **NICHOLAS Paul** Reynolds Porter Chamberlain
- **TESTER Stephen** CMS Cameron McKenna

2
- **CONNOLLY Sean** Mayer, Brown, Rowe & Maw
- **DEDMAN Richard** Barlow Lyde & Gilbert
- **ELBORNE Mark** CMS Cameron McKenna
- **HALL Stuart** Barlow Lyde & Gilbert
- **SCHOFIELD Belinda** CMS Cameron McKenna
- **WARD John** Beale and Company

3
- **BARRETT Geoff** Mills & Reeve
- **SMITH Antony** Beale and Company
- **TROTTER John** Lovells
- **WHITE Stuart** Reynolds Porter Chamberlain

4
- **BROWN Timothy** Reynolds Porter Chamberlain
- **CANNING Clare** Barlow Lyde & Gilbert
- **CLOVER Sarah** Barlow Lyde & Gilbert
- **GIBSON Simon** Kennedys
- **HARRISON Richard** Barlow Lyde & Gilbert
- **REGAN Michael** Mayer, Brown, Rowe & Maw
- **SEYMOUR Michael** Lovells
- **THOMAS Nick** Kennedys
- **WILSON Michael** Barlow Lyde & Gilbert

See individuals' profiles p.680

BEALE AND COMPANY (see firm details p.862) This is praised as a "*good, little niche practice,*" which comes consistently top for construction-related claims. John Ward (see p.683) and Antony Smith (see p.682) were praised for putting a "*commercial, practical approach*" alongside "*sound legal judgement.*" As well as work gained from being on the Norwich Union panel, the firm carries out construction claims for Thames Water and sits on its civil litigation panel. This year it has picked up increased levels of overseas work from Hong Kong, the Philippines and Malaysia. **Clients** Engineers; insurance panels.

BERRYMANS LACE MAWER (see firm details p.865) Although interviewees considered the team's profile to have diminished over the past 12 months, clients still commended it as "*proactive and adaptable*" and "*good value for money.*" Charlotte Capstick heads a department which continues to act for Oxford University. It has recently successfully defended a firm of accountants in the Isle of Man against a claim of negligence alleged by an offshore leisure company. **Clients** Surveyors; accountants; educational institutions.

CLYDE & CO (see firm details p.913) This quality outfit acts for insurers in London and overseas, including Dubai and Hong Kong. Angela Horne does much of the work and was involved in the case of Medcalf v Mardell and others, concerning a wasted costs order against a leading and a junior counsel. The team also continues to deal with the $10 billion BCCI litigation on the instructions of Ernst & Young's insurers. **Clients** Insurers.

CMS CAMERON MCKENNA (see firm details p.914) Complex, high value work for accountants, financial institutions and engineers is where this firm excels. Stephen Tester (see p.683) was praised to researchers as a "*thorough, personable and commercial*" lawyer who "*won't get lost in fine detail.*" He is involved in claims against architects, engineers and contractors. An "*excellent reputation has developed around*" Mark Elborne (see p.473), who acted for PricewaterhouseCoopers on the landmark House of Lords case, Aneco Reinsurance v Johnson & Higgins, while "*tenacious and meticulous*" Belinda Schofield (see p.476) is seen by peers and clients as the "*driving force behind the practice.*" **Clients** Lloyd's Underwriters; insurers.

DAVIES ARNOLD COOPER (see firm details p.930) The general opinion is that this is an "*effective and well-managed*" firm, with a respected professional negligence team and that its profile is improving. It acts for a range of professionals including accountants, barristers, fund managers and insurance brokers, with Daniel Gowan involved in architects' and engineers' professional indemnity claims. **Clients** Insurers.

FISHBURN MORGAN COLE (see firm details p.956) This practice is a class act for construction. John Cayton, the firm's divisional director, has handled claims against engineers, architects, project managers and surveyors. The team acted for the architect, Sheard Walshaw, in a successful appeal against a decision taken by the Technology and Construction Court. It also recently advised a design and building contractor and its insurers in a claim of around £4 million concerning the allegedly negligent design of a cheese factory's mechanical and electrical works. **Clients** Insurers.

HERBERT SMITH (see firm details p.992) Interviewees had nothing but praise for the firm's insurance and financial professional negligence practices. Barristers were impressed by its "*organisation and intelligence.*" Partner Sonya Leydecker has represented Coopers & Lybrand Singapore in connection with the litigation brought against them as auditors of Barings Futures Singapore. Other members of the team have represented Arthur Andersen in defending claims concerning its audit of the 1988 accounts of Bond, and acted for Somatra in the Commercial Court. **Clients** Arthur Andersen; PwC; Royal & SunAlliance; Willis; Marsh; Aon; SITA; Abbey National; BDO Stoy Hayward.

HEXTALLS (see firm details p.994) The firm was felt by the market to lack the visibility it had before the departure of Stuart White, but it continues to have a good construction team. It acted in proceedings concerning multiple glazing failures in a hotel development at Charles de Gaulle airport, and successfully settled an underwriting and coverage dispute between architects and their PI insurers over work at Canary Wharf. Jill Heaton is active in this sector. **Clients** Engineers; surveyors.

INCE & CO (see firm details p.1008) The "*clever people*" in this team are especially rated by peers for legal professional negligence. Giles Adams joined the firm as a partner in August 2001 and specialises, amongst other things, in professional indemnity. The team, praised as "*open-minded and thorough,*" has acted on several multi-million pound claims for insurance companies. **Clients** Insurance panels.

KENNEDYS (see firm details p.1019) This is considered a "*solid team which holds its own*" in the field. New in the rankings this year, Simon Gibson (see p.681) was picked out by barristers as an "*increasingly impressive*" practitioner. Despite his experience and seniority, Nick Thomas (see p.683) still devotes the majority of his time to cases. In the past year, the team has advised Lloyd's insurers on a $50 million accountants' claim, and acted on a case concerning the design of two North Sea oil platforms. It also represented a firm of solicitors on a claim concerning a defect to the claimant's house. **Clients** Norwich Union; Talbot Underwriting; Hiscox; AXA Corporate Solutions UK; Admiral Underwriting; Lloyd's; Charringtons.

LOVELLS (see firm details p.1045) A good quality practice, this is mainly involved in big-ticket City cases. Head of department John Trotter (see p.683) is considered to be consistently excellent and "*easy to deal with,*" while Michael Seymour (see p.682) also comes highly recommended. A particular leader for solicitors' negligence claims, although considered to lack the volume of the top two, it has an enviable reputation for complex, high value work and a superb record at trials. In one of these it successfully represented SIF and a major law firm accused of giving negligent advice on the title of goods located outside the country. The firm also receives instructions from all the major insurers. **Clients** SIF; insurers; solicitors.

MAYER BROWN ROWE & MAW (see firm details p.1060) Interviewees agreed that the firm retains its top class reputation, particularly in insurance- and construction-related professional negligence, but that it is too early to say what effect the US merger may have. Sean Connolly (see p.680) was praised to researchers as "*an effective client-getter*" while Michael Regan continued to receive weighty recommendations. This year the team has been appointed to the panel of the APIA Scheme on behalf of insurers,

PROFESSIONAL NEGLIGENCE ■ THE SOUTH/THAMES VALLEY/SOUTH WEST

dealing with claims against architects and engineers. **Clients** Contractors; subcontractors; insurers.

MILLS & REEVE (see firm details p.1071) A new entrant into the tables this year for its expertise in handling claims against solicitors, much of its success has been built on the growing reputation of "*quick and efficient*" **Geoff Barrett** (see p.680), who peers commend as a "*good analyst.*" Although less visible in other areas, the office has also been involved in claims involving a broad range of professionals including accountants, architects and surveyors, IFAs and computer software writers. The firm has been involved in a claim against a solicitor accused of acting negligently in relation to a trust for which he was also a trustee. **Clients** St. Paul; Hiscox; ACE Global Markets.

PINSENT CURTIS BIDDLE (see firm details p.1102) Despite the loss of several partners, the firm is still regarded as a leading professional negligence outfit. Fiona Heyes heads the department, which represented the Law Society in the important RBS v Etridge case in the House of Lords. It also defended SBJ in Commercial Court proceedings concerning notification of brokers' PI policies in a pensions misselling exposure. **Clients** Insurance panels.

SQUIRE & CO (see firm details p.1142) This "*forceful and tenacious*" niche practice continues to have a strong profile in insurance professional negligence. The firm acts on complex insurer broker cases for architects, surveyors, IFAs and barristers. **Clients** Insurers.

THE SOUTH

PROFESSIONAL NEGLIGENCE
■ THE SOUTH

[1] **Bond Pearce** Southampton
Cripps Harries Hall Tunbridge Wells
[2] **Blake Lapthorn** Fareham

LEADING INDIVIDUALS

[1] **TRAYHURN Neil** Bond Pearce
[2] **BROADIE Charles** Cripps Harries Hall
PORTLOCK Richard Blake Lapthorn

This book is the product of 6,582 1/2 hour interviews. See p.7 for BMRB audit.
Within each band, firms are listed alphabetically. See individuals' profiles p.680

BOND PEARCE (see firm details p.879) The Southampton office is still felt to lack some profile, but has grown over the past year and head of department, **Neil Trayhurn** (see p.683), is highly respected by his contemporaries. His team has recently handled a multi-party construction-related claim for Chartwell Underwriting in relation to a Jersey-based firm of engineers. It also acts on instructions from SIF and the new market insurers. **Clients** Insurance panels.

CRIPPS HARRIES HALL (see firm details p.922) This is a well regarded firm, which competitors believe to be "*doing well in the new market.*" **Charles Broadie** (see p.680) is a leading individual, perceived to have good client skills. The department's main area of practice continues to be solicitors' professional negligence, and it receives regular instructions from SIF, QBE and St. Paul. **Clients** Insurance panels.

BLAKE LAPTHORN (see firm details p.877) The firm's profile has dropped over the last 12 months with the demise of SIF, but it continues to do quality work and **Richard Portlock** remains a key player. He is a member of the Professional Indemnity Panel of PASS (Pension Advisors Support System), and this year was involved in the Court of Appeal decision in the Westbury v Sampson case. **Clients** SIF.

THAMES VALLEY

PROFESSIONAL NEGLIGENCE
■ THAMES VALLEY

[1] **Henmans** Oxford

LEADING INDIVIDUALS

[1] **DINGWALL Francis** Henmans
NURSE-MARSH Tony Henmans

This book is the product of 6,582 1/2 hour interviews. See p.7 for BMRB audit.
Within each band, firms are listed alphabetically. See individuals' profiles p.680

HENMANS (see firm details p.990) This firm received high praise from all quarters for its "*magic circle quality of service.*" Lead figure **Francis Dingwall** (see p.681) is held in high regard by clients and peers. He is joined in the rankings this year by **Tony Nurse-Marsh** (see p.682), who was commended as a "*pragmatic and sensible case-handler.*" He recently handled a £10 million claim against an architect for the architect's insurers, concerning the design of a supermarket which burnt down. The team acts for the insurers of 60% of the solicitors' profession and appears in claims involving surveyors, engineers, architects, insurance brokers, accountants and IT providers. It represented the solicitor defendants in the House of Lords in the Royal Bank of Scotland v Etridge (No 2) and other matters case. **Clients** Insurers.

SOUTH WEST

PROFESSIONAL NEGLIGENCE
■ SOUTH WEST

[1] **Beachcroft Wansbroughs** Bristol
Bond Pearce Bristol
[2] **CMS Cameron McKenna** Bristol
[3] **Burges Salmon** Bristol
Osborne Clarke Bristol

This book is the product of 6,582 1/2 hour interviews. See p.7 for BMRB audit.
Within each band, firms are listed alphabetically.

BEACHCROFT WANSBROUGHS (see firm details p.860) The firm's Bristol office has a particularly strong team, two members of which feature in the rankings for the first time this year. **Paul Redfern** (see p.682) is said to be "*highly competent*" and "*pro-active,*" while **Marcus Campbell** (see p.680) was praised by one barrister for his "*unflappable*" approach. The firm has picked up much work in the new market with Norwich Union, Alexander Forbes, Bar Mutual and New Line. **Clients** Insurers.

BOND PEARCE (see firm details p.879) "*A very high quality practice,*" according to market sources, which does a large volume of work across the South West. Three outstanding members of the team are **Richard Challands** (see p.680), who "*clearly knows his stuff,*" **Ian Peacock** (see p.682), who comes highly recommended to researchers by a number of competitors, and head of department, **Erik Salomonsen** (see p.682), who is still considered a strong player. The team has acted on a number of Court of Appeal cases during the last year, including Hall v Simmonds, which resulted in the repeal of advocate's immunity, and Lloyds Bank v Crosse & Crosse, concerning transaction/no transaction losses in lenders' cases. **Clients** Insurance panels.

CMS CAMERON MCKENNA (see firm details p.914) The professional negligence team in the Bristol office of this international firm continues to thrive. Peers see **Simon Hegarty** (see p.681) as

676 INDEX TO LEADING LAWYERS: PAGE 1693 ■ IN-HOUSE LAWYERS PROFILES: PAGE 1201

WALES/MIDLANDS — PROFESSIONAL NEGLIGENCE

LEADING INDIVIDUALS

[1]
- **CHALLANDS Richard** Bond Pearce
- **CORNISH Sarah** SJ Cornish
- **HEGARTY Simon** CMS Cameron McKenna
- **PEACOCK Ian** Bond Pearce
- **SALOMONSEN Erik** Bond Pearce

[2]
- **BARNES Jeremy** CMS Cameron McKenna
- **CAMPBELL Marcus** Beachcroft Wansbroughs
- **REDFERN Paul** Beachcroft Wansbroughs

See individuals' profiles p.680

a "*very sensible bet,*" while **Jeremy Barnes** (see p.680) was singled out for his commercial acumen. The firm handles a range of claims against solicitors, surveyors, accountants, engineers, academics and sports bodies. For instance, it successfully defended a claim against the former accountants of Lennox Lewis in a multi-million dollar dispute in New York. **Clients** Markel; Norwich Union; AIG; Chartwell; Chubb.

BURGES SALMON (see firm details p.894) Although not considered to be a high-profile team, clients appreciated its "*conciliatory approach*" and were especially complimentary about its claimant work. The firm has recently acted on a claim arising from a royalties review for an estate owner against a mining consultancy, and represented a dairy farmer in a claim against his former advisers valued at over £1 million. **Clients** Private clients.

OSBORNE CLARKE (see firm details p.1090) The firm makes its debut in this year's professional negligence ranking after sustained recommendation. Clients were full of praise for its "*learned, yet practical approach.*" It acts as Abbey National's sole panel firm for claims brought against solicitors; for Bristol & West in claims against solicitors and valuers; and for Hawk Residential in defending valuer negligence actions. **Clients** Abbey National; Bristol & West; Hawk Residential; Nationwide; Scottish Widows; Stroud & Swindon; private clients.

OTHER NOTABLE PRACTITIONERS Sarah Cornish (see p.681) remains an outstanding specialist in the field and was described by contemporaries as a "*formidable character,*" with a loyal client base.

WALES

PROFESSIONAL NEGLIGENCE
■ WALES

[1]
- **Morgan Cole** Cardiff

LEADING INDIVIDUALS

[1]
- **HUGHES-WILLIAMS Clare** Morgan Cole

This book is the product of 6,582 1/2 hour interviews. See p.7 for BMRB audit.
Within each band, firms are listed alphabetically. See individuals' profiles p.680

MORGAN COLE (see firm details p.1075) This "*pro-active*" firm remains "*good value for money*" and continues to lead the professional negligence field in Wales. It acts for solicitors, barristers, accountants and surveyors. The team is led by **Clare Hughes-Williams** who impressed the market with her focus on "*creative solutions.*" **Clients** SIF; Hiscox; Norwich Union.

MIDLANDS

PROFESSIONAL NEGLIGENCE
■ MIDLANDS

[1]
- **Browne Jacobson** Nottingham

[2]
- **Beachcroft Wansbroughs** Birmingham
- **Wragge & Co** Birmingham

[3]
- **Pinsent Curtis Biddle** Birmingham

LEADING INDIVIDUALS

[1]
- **PATON Andrew** Pinsent Curtis Biddle
- **RIDGWELL Robert** Browne Jacobson

[2]
- **HICK Mark** Wragge & Co
- **LONG Andrew** Pinsent Curtis Biddle

[3]
- **BAMBURY Derek** Browne Jacobson
- **STEEL Philip** Beachcroft Wansbroughs

This book is the product of 6,582 1/2 hour interviews. See p.7 for BMRB audit.
Within each band, firms are listed alphabetically. See individuals' profiles p.680

BROWNE JACOBSON (see firm details p.891) Clients and competitors were full of praise for the quality of this team. **Robert Ridgwell** (see p.682), in particular, was praised for taking a "*refreshingly common-sense approach*" to proceedings and recently handled a major pension fund mismanagement claim, while "*pro-active*" **Derek Bambury** (see p.680) acted on a major loss adjuster's claim valued at over £20 million. Together they won a claims handling contract for a leading professional indemnity insurer. **Clients** Hiscox; Norwich Union; St. Paul.

BEACHCROFT WANSBROUGHS (see firm details p.860) The firm is well known for professional negligence and retains a broad client base. **Philip Steel** (see p.682) was praised by peers for his "*commitmen*t" and "*down-to-earth leadership.*" Case highlights of the past year included a £7.5 million claim against solicitors concerning the registration of an agreement under the Restrictive Trade Practices Act; a £4 million claim against solicitors in connection with the drafting of a joint venture development agreement; and a £500,000 claim against IT consultants arising from the provision of websites and domain names. **Clients** Insurance panels.

WRAGGE & CO (see firm details p.1197) Not felt to have the volume of Beachcroft Wansbroughs, the Birmingham giant owes its position to its strong grip on top-end, quality claims. **Mark Hick** is the public face of the operation, and is especially recommended for his client skills. He recently advised on a £100 million warranty & indemnity policy. Other recent work includes a £6 million investment managers' professional indemnity claim for allegedly erroneous advice, and advising PI insurers on 200,000 allegedly mis-sold endowment policies. **Clients** Insurance panels.

PINSENT CURTIS BIDDLE (see firm details p.1102) Despite the well publicised loss of partners, clients remain loyal to the firm and its practitioners. **Andrew Paton** (see p.70) is hailed for his mediation skills and outgoing personality, while **Andrew Long** (see p.682) is also highly rated. The team recently acted for SIF in a multi-million pound recovery claim against accountants arising from a solicitor's dishonesty, and also froze an injunction for Lloyd's underwriters arising from misappropriation by a firm of financial advisors. **Clients** SIF; Pointon York Vos; Equitas; New York Life; Lloyd's syndicates; St. Paul.

PROFESSIONAL NEGLIGENCE ■ EAST ANGLIA/NORTH WEST/YORKSHIRE

EAST ANGLIA

PROFESSIONAL NEGLIGENCE
■ EAST ANGLIA

1 Mills & Reeve Cambridge

LEADING INDIVIDUALS

1 HODGSON Guy Mills & Reeve

This book is the product of 6,582 1/2 hour interviews. See p.7 for BMRB audit.
Within each band, firms are listed alphabetically. See individuals' profiles p.680

MILLS & REEVE (see firm details p.1071) The firm garnered much praise as the leading professional negligence practice in the region. This year it closed its Cambridge office to concentrate its energies in Norwich. **Guy Hodgson** (see p.681) was recommended as one of the top practitioners in the field. Active in legal sector claims, the team was recently involved in the Smith v Henniker-Major & Co case, arising from the representation of a company in a property transaction. It also acted in the First City Insurance Group v Orchard and Steven Gee QC case, where a loss of opportunity action was brought against the solicitors. **Clients** Insurance panels.

NORTH WEST

PROFESSIONAL NEGLIGENCE
■ NORTH WEST

1 James Chapman & Co Manchester
2 Weightman Vizards Liverpool
3 Addleshaw Booth & Co Manchester
 Hill Dickinson Liverpool

LEADING INDIVIDUALS

1 MAHER Frank Weightman Vizards
 TAYLOR Elisabeth James Chapman & Co
2 GAUL Patrick Weightman Vizards
 GRANT Mike Addleshaw Booth & Co

This book is the product of 6,582 1/2 hour interviews. See p.7 for BMRB audit.
Within each band, firms are listed alphabetically. See individuals' profiles p.680

JAMES CHAPMAN & CO (see firm details p.1012) This firm has impressed clients, barristers and peers nationwide with its "*professional, knowledgeable, civilised*" approach. **Elisabeth Taylor** (see p.683) was singled out as a star: one London solicitor described her as the "*flagship of the firm.*" Recent highlights include the successful defence of a large claim against pensioner trustees in issues involving a breach of trust. **Clients** Insurance panels.

WEIGHTMAN VIZARDS (see firm details p.1183) The team's high profile owes much to its two key practitioners. **Patrick Gaul** (see p.681) is an "*entertaining, well regarded*" solicitor, who has done some high-profile cases for SIF, while **Frank Maher** (see p.682) is seen as a "*slightly more serious*" figure, who is "*keen, on the ball and possesses an encyclopaedic knowledge*" of the field. The bulk of the team's work is still for solicitors, though it has recently acted for barristers, surveyors, accountants and brokers. **Clients** Insurance panels.

ADDLESHAW BOOTH & CO (see firm details p.838) The firm has been working hard at building up a professional negligence team in Manchester and it is starting to "*make a real mark*" in the field. Clients are impressed with **Mike Grant**'s (see p.681) "*friendly and commercial*" attitude. He has recently dealt with a claim arising from the construction of the world's largest sewage treatment works. **Clients** Insurance panels; Law Society.

HILL DICKINSON (see firm details p.995) This outfit has a reputation amongst its peers as a "*good player,*" with a "*straightforward approach*" to business. Ruth Lawrence is an active member of the team. It works for solicitors, construction professionals and the Veterinary Defence Society, which insures 90% of veterinaries. **Clients** Insurance panels.

YORKSHIRE

PROFESSIONAL NEGLIGENCE
■ YORKSHIRE

1 Beachcroft Wansbroughs Leeds
2 Addleshaw Booth & Co Leeds
 Hammond Suddards Edge Leeds
3 Irwin Mitchell Sheffield

LEADING INDIVIDUALS

1 GREENWOOD Duncan Beachcroft Wansbroughs
2 COULSON Edward Hammond Suddards Edge

This book is the product of 6,582 1/2 hour interviews. See p.7 for BMRB audit.
Within each band, firms are listed alphabetically. See individuals' profiles p.680

BEACHCROFT WANSBROUGHS (see firm details p.860) Considered by peers to be a "*respectable, pro-active*" firm, with "*very able team leader*" Duncan Greenwood (see p.681) at the helm. This year its profile in finance- and construction-related work has increased. Major cases include two legal negligence claims for a large UK firm, and a surveyor misappropriation case. **Clients** Engineers; solicitors; surveyors.

ADDLESHAW BOOTH & CO (see firm details p.838) The Leeds team, headed by John Gosling, comes highly recommended by competitors and clients. The firm has acted on several multi-million pound claims and recently completed a claim worth £1.1 million against a construction project manager. **Clients** Insurance panels.

HAMMOND SUDDARDS EDGE The firm has a very strong team in Leeds acting, *inter alia*, for solicitors, architects and consulting engineers. Peers told *Chambers* researchers that they had "*never heard a bad word against*" Edward Coulson. **Clients** Insurance panels.

IRWIN MITCHELL (see firm details p.1009) The firm holds a unique position as the largest firm in Yorkshire with a dedicated claimant professional negligence practice. The growing department deals with a high volume of cases, principally against solicitors, although its varied diet includes claims against financial advisors, surveyors, architects and accountants. These include cases like Farley v Skinner, a groundbreaking House of Lords decision concerning the instruction of professionals and the recovery of non-pecuniary damages for distress and inconvenience. Peter Wylde heads the department, which is split between the firm's Sheffield and London offices. **Clients** Avesta Sheffield Ltd; Environment Agency; Lloyds Bank; National Mutual; The Sheffield College.

NORTH EAST

PROFESSIONAL NEGLIGENCE — NORTH EAST

1
- Crutes Middlesbrough

2
- Hay & Kilner Newcastle upon Tyne

This book is the product of 6,582 1/2 hour interviews. See p.7 for BMRB audit. Within each band, firms are listed alphabetically.

CRUTES (see firm details p.924) Since the demise of SIF, the firm was thought to have been less visible. However, competitors agreed that its quality remains top-notch. Helen Ager is a leading member of a team which conducts a broad range of claims. **Clients** St. Paul; SIF.

HAY & KILNER The firm has flourished in the open market, picking up work in all areas of professional negligence. The team, headed by Ros Sparrow, also acts for clients outside the region, including London-based insurers. **Clients** Architects; accountants; surveyors.

SCOTLAND

PROFESSIONAL NEGLIGENCE — SCOTLAND

1
- Dundas & Wilson CS Edinburgh
- Simpson & Marwick WS Edinburgh

2
- Balfour & Manson Edinburgh
- Brechin Tindal Oatts Glasgow
- Brodies WS Edinburgh
- Bishops Solicitors Glasgow

3
- Shepherd+ Wedderburn WS Edinburgh

LEADING INDIVIDUALS

1
- ANDERSON Peter Simpson & Marwick
- MACLEOD Colin Dundas & Wilson CS
- WELSH John Bishops Solicitors

2
- ALLAN Derek Brechin Tindal Oatts
- DONALD Hugh Shepherd+ Wedderburn
- GRANT Alison Biggart Baillie
- KENNEDY Spencer Balfour & Manson
- WILLIAMSON David Brodies

This book is the product of 6,582 1/2 hour interviews. See p.7 for BMRB audit. Within each band, firms are listed alphabetically. See individuals' profiles p.680

DUNDAS & WILSON CS (see firm details p.943) The firm has a broad spread of work and this year our research showed that it leads the field alongside Simpson & Marwick. The team, said by clients to be "*pro-active*" and "*good value for money,*" is led by the well-reputed **Colin Macleod**, who keeps a "*thorough grip*" on his cases. This year he has worked on the Blyth & Blyth v Carillion Construction case, acting for the claimant engineers. This was the first case to explore the obligations of engineers under novation agreements. **Clients** Law Society panel; engineers.

SIMPSON & MARWICK WS (see firm details p.1137) Although not felt to enjoy the pre-eminence it once did, this firm is still thought to command the largest volume of professional negligence work in Scotland, and it comes highly recommended. **Peter Anderson** (see p.552) is the star turn here. A clear leader, he is especially known for his work as legal advisor to Scottish architects. **Clients** Engineers; architects; brokers; accountants; computer consultants; Law Society panel.

BALFOUR & MANSON (see firm details p.856) Variety is the firm's watchword, and it does work for clients ranging from marine surveyors to accountants. Acting for the Law Society and a number of claimants, **Spencer Kennedy** (see p.681) was described by one peer as a multi-talented practitioner, equally at home in the role of "*gamekeeper or poacher.*" **Clients** Law Society; accountants; surveyors.

BRECHIN TINDAL OATTS Derek Allan (see p.680) is very much at the heart of this firm's reputation in professional negligence. Much of his work involves acting as a nominated panel solicitor, investigating and defending claims against solicitors for alleged breach of contract or negligence. He has also defended accountants and surveyors in claims brought against them. He increasingly represents individuals and corporate clients. **Clients** Insurers; large financial institutions.

BRODIES WS (see firm details p.889) The professional negligence team here "*gets the job done efficiently*" and **David Williamson**'s (see p.683) experience earns him respect from his contemporaries. He is on the Royal & SunAlliance panel defending solicitors, and the firm also deals with a large number of defender solicitor professional negligence cases under the Law Society of Scotland master policy. Other clients are drawn from the accountancy and construction sectors. **Clients** Architects; engineers; surveyors.

BISHOPS SOLICITORS (see firm details p.1076) This outfit is best known for its work for the construction industry. In a solid and dependable team, **John Welsh** (see p.683) stands out and is praised by rivals for his hard work and industry knowledge. **Clients** Law Society; insurance panels; engineers.

SHEPHERD+ WEDDERBURN WS (see firm details p.1130) **Hugh Donald** (see p.151) is one of the panel solicitors appointed under the Law Society of Scotland master policy scheme by Royal & SunAlliance and is involved in a number of major claims directed against accountants. With his rising profile, the market agreed that the firm should also be ranked this year. It acts as Scottish agent for London-based underwriters. **Clients** Solicitors; accountants.

OTHER NOTABLE PRACTITIONERS Alison Grant of Biggart Baillie wins inclusion in the tables this year having impressed clients with her "*growing portfolio of works*" and commitment to the sector.

NORTHERN IRELAND

PROFESSIONAL NEGLIGENCE — NORTHERN IRELAND

1
- Agnew, Andress, Higgins Belfast
- Carson McDowell Belfast
- McKinty and Wright Belfast

2
- McCloskeys Belfast

LEADING INDIVIDUALS

1
- TURTLE Brian Carson McDowell

This book is the product of 6,582 1/2 hour interviews. See p.7 for BMRB audit. Within each band, firms are listed alphabetically. See individuals' profiles p.680

AGNEW, ANDRESS, HIGGINS The firm specialises in solicitors' professional negligence where it has a high standing in the market. Seamus Agnew is on the Northern Ireland solicitor's panel. **Clients** Solicitors.

CARSON MCDOWELL (see firm details p.901) The firm has a strong practice acting for solicitors and boasts the highly experienced and respected **Brian Turtle** (see p.569), who competitors agree is the biggest name in this sector. He holds a place on the Northern Ireland solicitors' indemnity panel. **Clients** Solicitors.

MCKINTY AND WRIGHT (see firm details p.1066) As well as acting for solicitors and being on the solicitors' indemnity panel, the firm's broad client base includes engineers, valuers, accountants and brokers. **Clients** Solicitors; surveyors; valuers.

MCCLOSKEYS (see firm details p.1061) A new entrant to the rankings, this firm was picked out by contemporaries for its solicitors' professional negligence work. An up and coming department, it is also on the Northern Ireland solicitors' indemnity panel. **Clients** Solicitors.

THE LEADERS IN PROFESSIONAL NEGLIGENCE

ALLAN, Derek
Brechin Tindal Oatts, Glasgow
(0141) 221 8012
dja@bto.co.uk

Specialisation: Principal area of practice is professional negligence, acting on behalf of insurance companies and corporate lenders in professional indemnity claims brought against solicitors, accountants and surveyors. Mainly defender orientated, but some pursuer/claimant work.
Prof. Memberships: The Law Society of Scotland. The Scottish Law Agents Society.
Career: Joined *Brechin Robb* as apprentice in 1978. Partner since 1984.
Personal: Golf, tennis, walking.

ANDERSON, Peter
Simpson & Marwick, Edinburgh
(0131) 557 1545
peter.anderson@simpmar.com
See under Litigation, p.552

ARTHUR, David
Barlow Lyde & Gilbert, London
(020) 7247 2277
darthur@blg.co.uk

Specialisation: Professional negligence disciplinary and regulatory experience involving accountants, insurance brokers, solicitors and financial institutions. Also insurance and reinsurance matters including drafting and construction of policy wordings.
Prof. Memberships: Law Society, International Bar Association, B.I.L.A.
Career: Qualified in 1978. Joined *Barlow Lyde & Gilbert* in 1981. Became a partner in 1984. Head of professional liability and commercial litigation department.

BAMBURY, Derek
Browne Jacobson, Nottingham
(0115) 976 6204
dbambury@brownej.co.uk

Specialisation: Professional indemnity and commercial disputes, particularly strong in accountants, solicitors, brokers and financial risks. Highlights of the last 12 months include: major JDS enquiry into the role of the auditors of a collapsed quoted company; £25m claim against insurance professionals; £20m+ claims against auditors; £4m claim against solicitors; £1.5m+ claim against employment professionals; increased activity in the area of risk analysis and management for accountants and solicitors.
Prof. Memberships: Member of ICAEW Members Friends Support Panel; Member of Chartered Institute of Insurance.
Career: LLB (King's College London), Admitted 1981 *Browne Jacobson*, Partner 1987 *Browne Jacobson*.
Personal: Sport (football, cricket, golf, racing). Married (Jennie) two children.

BARNES, Jeremy
CMS Cameron McKenna, Bristol
(0117) 930 0200
jeremy.barnes@cmck.com

Specialisation: Partner dealing with insurance matters with emphasis on defendant professional indemnity work, D&O and financial institutions policies. Extensive experience with financial services claims (including pensions misselling), accountants, brokers, architects and engineers.
Career: Qualified 1989. Partner 1995.
Personal: Born 1964. Married with three children.

BARRETT, Geoff
Mills & Reeve, London
(020) 7648 9230
geoff.barrett@mills-reeve.com

Specialisation: Partner in Insurance and Reinsurance Group. Principal areas of practice involve acting in claims and disputes for insurers and reinsurers. Has acted in numerous disputes involving professionals such as accountants, financial advisors, insurance brokers, members' agents, surveyors, solicitors and loss adjusters as well as problems concerning financial institutions and Directors' and Officers' liability cover, both for the Lloyds and company market. Also advises on general insurance and reinsurance matters including drafting and construction of policy wordings and problems arising from the granting of binding authorities.
Prof. Memberships: Law Society.
Career: Read Law at University College London following which he obtained articles with *Hewitt Woollacott & Chown*, as it then was, in 1979. Was admitted as a Solicitor in April 1981 and has been a Partner since 1986. Joined *Mills & Reeve* as a Partner on 1 February 2000.

BROADIE, Charles
Cripps Harries Hall, Tunbridge Wells
(01892) 506270
crb@crippslaw.com

Specialisation: Heads the team that carries out work for the Solicitors Indemnity Fund. Extensive experience in professional indemnity work.
Prof. Memberships: Member of Law Society and local Law Society. Part-time chairman, Pensions Appeal Tribunal.
Career: Education: Bradfield College; Sidney Sussex College, Cambridge University (1966 BA - now MA, 1968 LLB - now LLM); Université de Nancy, France. Articled *Field Roscoe*, London; qualified 1969; *Hedleys*, London 1970-72; secretariat of the European Commission of Human Rights, Strasbourg 1972-74; assistant solicitor *Cripps Harries Hall*, Tunbridge Wells, 1974-76; partner from 1976.
Personal: Reading, foreign languages, walking, local church.

BROWN, Timothy
Reynolds Porter Chamberlain, London
(020) 7242 2877
tcb@rpc.co.uk

Specialisation: Partner specialising in non-marine insurance, reinsurance, property and professional litigation. Areas of expertise include reinsurance, professional liability insurance involving financial institutions and the financial services industry, accountants, insurance brokers, IT consultants and other professionals; property insurance, directors and officers insurance, contingency insurance and regulatory issues concerning insurance brokers and insurers. Acts for Lloyd's Syndicates, London Market Insurers and foreign insurers in domestic and international insurance and reinsurance litigation and arbitrations. Currently acting in substantial multijurisdictional and multi-party reinsurance disputes for US, UK and European insurers and reinsurers. Areas currently being developed include credit risk and political risk insurance.
Prof. Memberships: BILA; IBA; London Solicitors Litigation Association.
Career: Trained at *Reynolds Porter Chamberlain*; qualified in 1979; Partner 1984; located at the City office since 1996; one of 14 partners and their teams resident at *Reynolds Porter Chamberlain's* expanding City office.
Publications: Is listed in a number of publications including the Legal Business 'Legal Experts' as a professional negligence expert.
Personal: Born 1954. Education: Maidstone Grammar; Newcastle Polytechnic (1976 BA Law). Leisure: motor racing, football, antiques and golf.

CAMPBELL, Marcus
Beachcroft Wansbroughs, Bristol
(0117) 918 2000

Specialisation: Partner specialising in defending a wide variety of professionals on instructions from London market insurers. Has a leading reputation in advising on directors and officers liability insurance and insurance coverage generally.
Prof. Memberships: 1996 - Partner, *Beachcroft Wansbroughs*.

CANNING, Clare
Barlow Lyde & Gilbert, London
(020) 7247 2277

Specialisation: Commercial litigation with an emphasis on professional indemnity - specialising in accountants. Also insurance and reinsurance litigation. Acted for Ernst & Young in Butte Mining and NRG litigation and for Price Waterhouse in Bank Austria/Sovereign litigation. Involved in Lloyd's litigation for Ernst & Young. Acting for PricewaterhouseCoopers in relation to successful defence of claim brought by Sir Elton John. Currently acting for Ernst & Young in relation to litigation arising out of events at Equitable Life Assurance Society.
Prof. Memberships: Member of the Law Society.
Career: Joined *Barlow Lyde & Gilbert* 1986 on qualification. Became a partner in 1992. One of the authors of 'Reinsurance Practice & The Law, LLP'. Identified by 'Euromoney' as a leading Insurance and Reinsurance lawyer.
Personal: Born 1962. Educated at St Anne's College and Girton College, Cambridge (Classics and Law). Leisure interests include theatre and music. Qualified as Transactional Analysis Psychotherapist.

CHALLANDS, Richard
Bond Pearce, Plymouth
(01752) 677801
rchallands@bondpearce.com

Specialisation: Partner in Dispute Resolution. Specialises in professional indemnity and partnership litigation. Handles work on behalf of accountants, brokers, solicitors, barristers and surveyors. Also deals with policy and coverage disputes and has wide experience of claims involving fraud.
Prof. Memberships: Member of the International Bar Association Insurance Group, the British Insurance Law Association and the Association of Partnership Practitioners.
Career: Qualified 1975. Joined *Bond Pearce* in 1973, becoming Partner 1978.

CLOVER, Sarah
Barlow Lyde & Gilbert, London
(020) 7247 2277

Specialisation: Leads the Solicitor's Professional Liability group at *BLG*. She has wide professional indemnity experience. Has advised on a range of professional indemnity claims against solicitors including claims involving corporate finance, tax, commercial property, company acquisitions and commercial contracts. One of the lead Partners co-ordinating the profession's response to claims against numerous firms by Nationwide Building Society.
Career: Qualified in 1983, joined *Barlow Lyde & Gilbert* in 1987. Became a Partner at *Barlow Lyde & Gilbert* in 1992.
Publications: Has spoken at numerous seminars on professional indemnity and written for a number of publications.
Personal: Educated at University College of London.

CONNOLLY, Sean
Mayer, Brown, Rowe & Maw, London
(020) 7327 4144
sconnolly@eu.mayerbrownrowe.com

Specialisation: Specialises in all areas of contentious non-marine insurance and reinsurance work including professional indemnity and product liability insurance matters. Has represented a wide range of merchant banks, accountants, insurance brokers, engineers and surveyors on professional indemnity matters. Has conducted a number of substantial mediations this year. Managing Partner of the firm's insurance and reinsurance group at Lloyd's since 1992. Group Managing Partner of Litigation and Dispute Resolution Department 1999. One of the early proponents of the use of ADR. Participant in market ADR initiative (MAC). Member of the international policy and planning committee which governs the firm.
Prof. Memberships: Law Society; Inter-

THE LEADERS ■ PROFESSIONAL NEGLIGENCE

national Bar Association; British Insurance Law Association.
Career: University of London 1982 (LLB). Articled *Rowe & Maw* 1982-84. Assistant Solicitor Commercial Litigation Department 1984-86. Solicitor Alexander & Alexander Europe Plc 1986-88. Lloyd's Office *Rowe & Maw* 1989-date.
Personal: Cricket, golf and skiing.

CORNISH, Sarah
SJ Cornish, Tiverton
(01884) 243377
sarah.cornish@sjcornish.co.uk
Specialisation: Founding partner of niche litigation firm. Specialises in professional indemnity and insurance litigation defending claims against a wide range of professionals including accountants, architects, brokers, engineers and surveyors. Also acts for insurers in insurance litigation and policy coverage disputes.
Career: Qualified in 1982 with City insurance firm. Moved to West Country. Partner with *Bond Pearce*. Set up own practice in 1991. Opened London office January 2001

COULSON, Edward W H
Hammond Suddards Edge, Leeds
(0113) 284 7000

DEDMAN, Richard
Barlow Lyde & Gilbert, London
(020) 7247 2277
rdedman@blg.co.uk
Specialisation: Professional liability; commercial litigation and arbitration; insurance.
Prof. Memberships: CEDR accredited mediator; Society of Computers & Law; Member of Society of Construction Law.
Career: Trained at *Lovell White & King*, from 1979 at *Barlow Lyde & Gilbert* where formerly joint head of professional liability and commercial litigation department until becoming senior partner in May 2001.
Personal: Born 1954; educated at Felsted School and Cambridge University (Clare College - modern languages and law); interests include tennis, golf, football, music and languages.

DINGWALL, Francis
Henmans, Oxford
(01865) 722181
francis.dingwall@henmans.co.uk
Specialisation: Partner and Head of *Henmans* Professional Negligence/Commercial Litigation Department comprising a team of 16 solicitors. Principally acts on behalf of insurers in professional indemnity claims, on behalf of solicitors, accountants, insurance brokers, surveyors and IT consultants among other purchasers of indemnity insurance products. Also handles broader commercial dispute resolution.
Career: Trained at *Barlow Lyde & Gilbert*. Admitted 1984. Assistant Solicitor at *Barlow Lyde & Gilbert* 1984-89. Assistant Parliamentary Counsel 1989-91. Joined *Henmans* 1991.

Personal: Born 1958. Educated at Stonyhurst College and Corpus Christi College, Oxford. Lives in Oxfordshire countryside. Interests include English Language and Literature and coping with young family.

DONALD, Hugh
Shepherd+ Wedderburn, Edinburgh
(0131) 473 5159
hugh.donald@shepwedd.co.uk
See under Clinical Negligence, p.151

ELBORNE, Mark
CMS Cameron McKenna, London
(020) 7367 3057
me@cmck.com
See under Insurance, p.473

GAUL, Patrick
Weightman Vizards, Liverpool
(0151) 227 2601
patrick.gaul@weightmanvizards.com
Specialisation: Professional indemnity mainly solicitors and barristers. Regularly lectures and writes on professional indemnity and has a particular interest in wasted costs. Important cases include Hall v Simons; Whitley v Cook Leathes & Bickerton and others; Ridehaleh v Horsefield; Globe Equities v Globe Legal Services; J v Oyston.
Prof. Memberships: Law Society.
Career: Oxford University BA Jurisprudence.

GIBSON, Simon
Kennedys, London
(020) 7638 3688
s.gibson@kennedys-law.com
Specialisation: Partner in Insurance Department specialising in professional indemnity, construction industry and coverage disputes. Acts in the defence of architects, engineers, project managers, solicitors, surveyors, financial advisors and accountants. Also expertise in CAR and property disputes.
Prof. Memberships: Law Society, TECSA.
Career: Joined *Kennedys* 1982. Qualified 1984. Partner 1989.
Personal: Born 1959. Educated Queen Elizabeths Barnet and Warwick University. Leisure interests include running and football.

GRANT, Alison
Biggart Baillie, Glasgow
(0141) 228 8000

GRANT, Mike
Addleshaw Booth & Co, Manchester
(0161) 934 6571
Specialisation: Defendant professional indemnity claims, involving all major professions - accountants, solicitors, engineers. Particular experience dealing with large claims made against construction industry professionals - presently dealing with £10m claims defending construction project manager. Many other multimillion pound claims ongoing.
Career: Articled *Percy Hughes & Roberts*, qualified 1988; partner 1990; joined *Weightmans* as Partner in January 1996;

joined *Addleshaw Booth & Co* as Partner in September 2000.
Publications: Contributor to insurance/commercial litigation journals.
Personal: Cardinal Godfrey School, Liverpool; Liverpool University; Chester College of Law. Married, two daughters. Hobbies: tennis, squash.

GREENLEY, Simon
Reynolds Porter Chamberlain, London
(020) 7242 2877
skg@rpc.co.uk
See under Insurance, p.474

GREENWOOD, Duncan
Beachcroft Wansbroughs, Leeds
(0113) 251 4700
dgreenwood@bwlaw.co.uk
Specialisation: Has specialised in the PI market for 10 years, particularly in the fields of surveying, engineering, architects, accountants and solicitors negligence. Also advises on policy wording/coverage issues and last year advised a pre-eminent insurer on their claims handling processes on entry into the new solicitors open market. Major cases have included Barclays Bank v Peter Wardle Associates (1997) cited by C.A. in Platform Home Loans v Oyston Shipways; Archer v Hickmotts (1998) C.A. NPC 132; Halifax Mortgage Services v Simpson & Others (1998) 64 Con. L.R. 17 and Cottingham v Attey Bower & Jones (1999) 3 W.L.R.873.
Career: Qualified in September 1990 with *Wansbroughs Willey Hargrave*, Associate 1994, Partner 1997 and joined the partnership of *BW* on merger in May 1999.
Publications: Articles written have appeared in the 'Estates Gazette', 'Insurance Post' and the 'Chartered Institute of Insurers Magazine'.

HALL, Stuart
Barlow Lyde & Gilbert, London
(020) 7247 2277
shall@blg.co.uk
Specialisation: Professional indemnity, especially accountants, directors' and officers' liability and commercial litigation.
Prof. Memberships: English and Hong Kong Law Societies.
Career: Cambridge University; admitted 1975; partner *Dawson & Co* 1976-85; partner *Barlow Lyde & Gilbert* 1985 to date.

HARRISON, Richard
Barlow Lyde & Gilbert, London
(020) 7247 2277
rharrison@blg.co.uk
Specialisation: Principal area of practice is acting in the defence of a wide range of professional indemnity claims involving solicitors and barristers, including many large commercial claims and claims relating to breach of trust and dishonesty. Also handles related insurance issues. Considerable experience of mediation and other forms of ADR. Recent cases include Dubai Aluminium v

Salaam, Balfour Trustees v Petersen and Hurlingham Estates v Wilde.
Prof. Memberships: Law Society.
Career: Joined *Barlow Lyde & Gilbert* 1986, qualified 1988, Partner 1996.
Personal: Born 1964. Educated at the Hulme Grammar School, Oldham, Sheffield University and College of Law, Guildford. Married with three children. Resides Amersham, Buckinghamshire. Interests include skiing, architecture, social history, family and friends.

HEGARTY, Simon
CMS Cameron McKenna, Bristol
(0117) 930 0200
Specialisation: Specialises in insurance litigation (particularly professional indemnity and directors' and officers' liability) and banking litigation.
Career: Trained and qualified with *Cameron Kemm Norden* (1979-81), served with the Royal Navy (1981-86), rejoined *Cameron Markby* (1987) becoming a partner in *Cameron Markby Hewitt* in 1992. Managing Partner of *CMS Cameron McKenna*'s Bristol office from 1994.
Personal: Children, amateur dramatics, folk dancing, beer and butterflies are continuing to replace rapidly deteriorating performances on the sports field.

HICK, Mark
Wragge & Co, Birmingham
(0870) 903 1000

HODGSON, Guy
Mills & Reeve, Norwich
(01603) 693221
guy.hodgson@mills-reeve.com
Specialisation: Partner in insurance group. Specialises in professional indemnity risks and coverage disputes for insurers, mutual funds and professional firms and D&O. Acts for all traditional and emerging professions dealing with claims brought against them and any related insurance issues. Advises on and drafts policy wordings. Joined *Mills & Reeve* in 1984 to develop their professional indemnity practice after gaining a number of years' experience working in the London market, and currently spends approximately half his time in *Mills & Reeve*'s London office. Regular speaker on professional indemnity matters.
Prof. Memberships: British Insurance Law Association. Law Society.

HUGHES-WILLIAMS, Clare
Morgan Cole, Cardiff
(029) 2038 5385

KENNEDY, A J Spencer
Balfour & Manson, Edinburgh
(0131) 200 1200
spencer.kennedy@balfour-manson.co.uk
Specialisation: Commercial and professional negligence litigation. Solicitor Advocate enjoying extended rights of audience in Supreme Civil Courts. Panel Solicitor under Law Society of Scotland Master Policy since 1990. Contributor to 'Ensuring Excellence' Risk Management

www.ChambersandPartners.com
681

PROFESSIONAL NEGLIGENCE ■ THE LEADERS

Handbook 1998 and associated seminars.
Prof. Memberships: Law Society of Scotland, SSC Society (Past President), Federation of Insurance Lawyers. Notary Public.
Career: Educated Royal High School and University of Edinburgh. Partner in *Nightingale & Bell* from 1973 and, after merger, partner in *Balfour & Manson* since 1991.
Personal: Born 3 May 1945. Lives in Edinburgh. Enjoys hill walking and horticulture.

LONG, Andrew
Pinsent Curtis Biddle, Birmingham
(0121) 200 1050
andrew.long@pinsents.com
Specialisation: Partner in Insurance Litigation and Head of Financial Services Litigation. Professional indemnity defendant work, specialising in acting for solicitors and for the financial services industry. Author, speaker and leading expert on financial services claims and regulation. Acts for mutuals, Lloyd's Underwriters, insurers and the financial services industry. Also sits as a Deputy District Judge of the High Court and County Court.
Career: Qualified in 1980. Joined *Pinsent Curtis Biddle* in 1986 becoming a Partner in 1989.
Personal: Born 1955. Educated at Exeter School and Pembroke College, Oxford. Interests include still trying to play sport and following Exeter City FC.

MACLEOD, Colin
Dundas & Wilson CS, Edinburgh
(0131) 228 8000

MAHER, Frank
Weightman Vizards, Liverpool
(0151) 242 7916
frank.maher@weightmanvizards.com
Specialisation: Head of professional indemnity team. Responsibility primarily for solicitors, but also accountants, bankers, engineers, surveyors, valuers. Numerous major fraud investigations, financial services claims, construction litigation and policy wording disputes. Acting for solicitors in 'Alford v West Bromwich Building Society' and others. Home income scheme group action. Advises insurers on professional indemnity policy wording and websites. Advises professionals on risk management.
Prof. Memberships: Law Society - past involvement nationally and locally. Former Chairman of National Committee of Young Solicitors Group, Member of civil litigation, council membership and professional and public relations committees of the Law Society and general committee of Liverpool Law Society. Joint working partner of the Bar Council and Law Society on the Civil courts - sub-committee Chairman.
Career: Liverpool University LLB. Educational Foundation Prize.

MICKLEM, Barney
Reynolds Porter Chamberlain, London
(020) 7242 2877
ctm@rpc.co.uk
Specialisation: Partner in professional indemnity litigation department. Professional indemnity litigation specialist. Work relates principally to solicitors, barristers and surveyors. Has addressed various professional indemnity seminars.
Prof. Memberships: Law Society.
Career: Qualified in 1974. Became a partner in 1977.

NICHOLAS, Paul
Reynolds Porter Chamberlain, London
(020) 7242 2877
Specialisation: Insurance and professional indemnity.
Career: Qualified in 1970, having joined *Reynolds Porter* in 1968. Became a Partner in 1972.
Personal: Born 24 April 1946. Educated at Mill Hill School 1959-63 and Emmanuel College, Cambridge (BA 1967, LLB 1968). Governor of Lockers Park School and Trustee of S.W. Hertfordshire Hospice Charitable Trust.

NURSE-MARSH, Tony
Henmans, Oxford
(01865) 722181
tony.nurse-marsh@henmans.co.uk
Specialisation: Partner in Professional Indemnity Department. Specialises in professional negligence disputes for all professions, and coverage and insurance disputes, acting for insurers and professionals. Acted in the Etridge appeals in the House of Lords (2001); the Nationwide managed litigation against Solicitors; G E Capital v Arthur Andersen & Others; Bank Austria v Price Waterhouse.
Prof. Memberships: British Insurance Law Association; FOIL; Law Society; Association of Higher Court Advocates.
Career: Joined *Henmans* from *Freshfields* in 1997; Higher Court Advocate.
Publications: Regularly writes and speaks on professional indemnity and insurance issues.
Personal: Oxford MA (First Class); LLM in Advanced Litigation (Distinction). Interests include sport, history and cinema.

PATON, Andrew
Pinsent Curtis Biddle, Birmingham
(0121) 200 1050
andrew.paton@pinsents.com
See under ADR, p.70

PEACOCK, Ian
Bond Pearce, Bristol
(0117) 929 9197
ipeacock@bondpearce.com
Specialisation: Partner in the Insurance Group and Head of *Bond Pearce's* professional indemnity practice in the Bristol office. Defends claims on behalf of solicitors, accountants, brokers and financial advisors. Also specialises in the Financial Services sector with particular emphasis on income protection claims.
Career: Qualified in 1984 in London. Joined *Bond Pearce* in 1990, becoming Partner 1992.

PORTLOCK, Richard
Blake Lapthorn, Fareham
(01489) 579990

REDFERN, Paul
Beachcroft Wansbroughs, Bristol
(0117) 918 2000
Specialisation: Partner in Professional Indemnity and Insurance Department. Principal area of practice is professional indemnity, acting for a wide range of professions particularly accountants but including surveyors, brokers, financial intermediaries and developing schemes with insurers and brokers for the 'new' professions. Also acts for insurers in litigation and policy coverage disputes and was involved in advising insurers and brokers on policy wording and strategy in entering the commercial market for solicitors. National client partner for Norwich Union Professional Risks and dealing brokers. Writes and lectures widely on issues affecting the professions and the insurance industry.
Career: Qualified in 1978, having joined *Beachcroft Wansbroughs* in 1976. Partner in 1981.

REGAN, Michael
Mayer, Brown, Rowe & Maw, London
(020) 7248 4282

RIDGWELL, Robert
Browne Jacobson, Nottingham
(0115) 976 6236
rridgwell@brownej.co.uk
Specialisation: Professional indemnity. Partner advising insurers on policy issues and policy drafting. Risk management and claims avoidance. Advising on commercial claims and professional indemnity litigation, including defending professional indemnity claims against surveyors, solicitors, accountants, intermediaries (financial/insurance/pension consultants). Financial product liability.
Prof. Memberships: Fellow of the Chartered Institute of Arbitrators; founder member of the Institute for Continuing Professional Development.
Career: Qualified 1979; partner *Browne Jacobson* 1984, Chartered Arbitrator (2001)
Personal: Born 1954; resides Southwell. Education: Lincoln School; Queens College; Cambridge (1976 Law).

SALOMONSEN, Erik
Bond Pearce, Exeter
(01392) 211185
esalomonsen@bondpearce.com
Specialisation: Partner and Head of the Insurance Group. Defends claims against a wide range of professionals, including medical professionals. Work also includes employers' and public liability claims including work in the farming industry. Panel Solicitor for Composites, Lloyd's underwriters and mutual funds. An accredited mediator.
Prof. Memberships: Member of the International Bar Association. Holder of High Courts Advocacy qualification for all courts.
Career: Qualified in 1975. Joined *Bond Pearce* in 1975, becoming a Partner 1979.

SCHOFIELD, Belinda
CMS Cameron McKenna, London
(020) 7367 3000
Belinda.Schofield@cmck.com
See under Insurance, p.476

SEYMOUR, Michael
Lovells, London
(020) 7296 2000
michael.seymour@lovells.com
Specialisation: Main areas of practice: professional negligence, commercial litigation and arbitration often involving an international dimension, particularly in the area of trade and business. Has acted for foreign governments in cases involving state immunity and for banks, insurers and other companies in contract fraud and property related cases.
Prof. Memberships: Law Society, Chartered Institute of Arbitrators, member (President: 1994-96) of London Solicitors Litigation Association, member of the joint working party of the Bar and the Law Society on the Civil Courts.
Career: Articled at *Lovells*; qualified 1974; Partner 1982.

SMITH, Antony
Beale and Company, London
(020) 7240 3474
Specialisation: Partner in professional negligence. Specialises in international and national construction dispute resolution and litigation. Acted in largest ever claim brought in the Technology and Construction Courts. Regularly defends prosecutions under health and safety law. Writes for 'Health and Safety at Work' Journal. Acts on all types of professional negligence claims including accountants, architects, engineers, IFAs and insurance brokers. Member of Law Society panel of solicitors acting on professional negligence actions. Since the end of SIF, acts for the commercial market in defending solicitors.
Prof. Memberships: Institution of Occupational Safety and Health; Centre for Dispute Resolution; Law Society; British Insurance Law Association.
Career: Partner with *Beale and Company* since 1985.
Personal: Liverpool University LLB. (Upper Second Class Hons.). Interests include family, rugby, football and triathlon.

STEEL, Philip
Beachcroft Wansbroughs, Birmingham
(0121) 698 5212
psteel@bwlaw.co.uk
Specialisation: Professional and financial risks for solicitors, accountants, bankers, surveyors and architects.
Prof. Memberships: Law Society, Birmingham Law Society, Council Member in Birmingham Law Society, Chairman Civil Litigation Committee Birmingham LS.

THE LEADERS ■ PROFESSIONAL NEGLIGENCE

Career: Qualified 1987. Partner 1996. Relocated from Leeds to Birmingham 1996.
Publications: Speaker at risk management seminars for lawyers and solicitors.
Personal: Newcastle Upon Tyne Polytechnic 1980-83. Leisure: sailing, cycling, family.

TAYLOR, Elisabeth
James Chapman & Co, Manchester
(0161) 828 8000
profindemnity@james-chapman.co.uk
Specialisation: Has specialised in professional negligence work for the past 10 years and now Head of Professional Negligence Department. Handles professional negligence claims on behalf of solicitors, barristers, surveyors, valuers, architects, accountants, insurance brokers and other professionals. Also heads the general insurance team dealing with policy disputes, product liability, property damage, environmental, construction risks and subrogation recoveries.
Prof. Memberships: The Law Society and The Manchester Law Society.
Career: Educated University of Bristol (LLB). Admitted April 1974. Joined *James Chapman & Co* 1976. Partner 1979. Managing Partner since 1998. Head of Professional Indemnity and General Insurance Department.
Personal: Married, three children. Interests include family, music and theatre.

TESTER, Stephen
CMS Cameron McKenna, London
(020) 7367 2894
skt@cmck.com
Specialisation: Practises in construction and surveyors' PI, Contractors All Risk Insurance, D&O and Transaction Support Insurance. Clients include insurance and reinsurance companies, Lloyds syndicates, insurance brokers and construction companies.
Prof. Memberships: Society of Construction Law.
Career: KCS Wimbledon and St. John's College Cambridge. Qualified 1981. Partner since 1988.
Personal: Interests include family and friends, golf and squash.

THOMAS, Nick
Kennedys, London
(020) 7614 3674
n.thomas@kennedys-law.com
Specialisation: Senior Partner. Also Partner in associated Northern Ireland and Hong Kong practices. Principal area of expertise is professional indemnity, particularly in the construction field and CAR/ALOP and property claims, particularly overseas (Middle East and India, Far East and the Americas). Also covers insurance work generally, including disputes as to whether insurers should respond and which insurers should respond. Acted in BBL v John D. Wood and others, and National Trust v Hayden Young; Heathrow Express Terminal collapse and Terminal 1 fire. Author of 'Professional Indemnity Claims (An Architect's Guide)', published by Architect's Press in 1981. Regularly addresses conferences and seminars, particularly for insurers.
Prof. Memberships: Member of the Law Society, Fellow of the Chartered Institute of Arbitrators. Also qualified as a solicitor in Hong Kong, Northern Ireland and the Republic of Ireland.
Career: Joined *Kennedys* in 1977 and qualified in 1980. Became a Partner in 1981. Became Senior Partner in 1997.
Personal: Born 16 October 1954. Attended Bristol University 1973-76. School Governor. Leisure pursuits include all sports, travel and the arts. Lives near Berkhamsted, Herts.

TRAYHURN, Neil
Bond Pearce, Southampton
(023) 8063 2211
ntrayhurn@bondpearce.com
Specialisation: Head of the firm's Professional Indemnity Group. Extensive experience of handling claims on behalf of a wide range of professionals including solicitors, surveyors and accountants. Also has experience of construction disputes and policy coverage issues. Based in the firm's Southampton and London offices.
Prof. Memberships: Member of the Forum of Insurance Lawyers.
Career: Qualified in 1989 following articles with *Wansbrough Willey Hargreave*. Joined *Bond Pearce* in 1992 becoming Partner 1995.

TROTTER, John
Lovells, London
(020) 7296 2000
john.trotter@lovells.com
Specialisation: Main area of practice is litigation and other dispute resolution involving insurance and reinsurance, including professional indemnity and product liability. Has been involved in numerous actions and arbitrations in these areas, including the defence of major claims against lawyers. Has written and spoken widely about dispute resolution, professional indemnity and issues affecting the insurance industry.
Prof. Memberships: Chairman of the Insurance Committee of the International Bar Association. Member of the London Solicitors Litigation Association and the City of London Law Society. Member British Insurance Law Association, co-author of 'Liability of Lawyers and Indemnity Insurance' (Kluwer/IBA).
Career: Qualified in 1977 with *Lovells*; based in New York office 1980-82; Partner in 1983. Managing Partner, litigation 1994-98.

TURTLE, Brian
Carson McDowell, Belfast
(028) 9024 4951
See under Litigation, p.569

WARD, John
Beale and Company, London
(020) 7240 3474
Specialisation: Partner in construction department. Has specialised in construction industry law since 1979, on both UK and overseas projects. Work includes advice on contractual structures, contracts, prevention of disputes, resolution of disputes, mediations, adjudications, litigation and arbitration, including ICC arbitrations, and professional indemnity work, especially for engineers and surveyors. A significant proportion of the work relates to projects outside the UK. Also handles health and safety in the construction industry. Work includes advice on duties and obligations under health and safety legislation on systems for compliance (eg CDM regulations) as well as defence of prosecutions brought by the Health and Safety Executive against professionals. Advises insurers and brokers on professional indemnity issues, including policy wordings, and specialist applications of professional indemnity policies. Experienced conference speaker and author of articles on a variety of topics.
Prof. Memberships: Law Society, International Bar Association, International Chamber of Commerce.
Career: Qualified in 1975. Partner with *Beale and Company* since 1977. Now managing partner.
Personal: Born 22 November 1950. Educated at University College, London 1969-72 (LLB Hons). Leisure interests include fly fishing, Formula 1 motor racing and football. Lives in Cobham.

WELSH, John
Bishops Solicitors (formerly Morison Bishop), Glasgow
(0141) 248 4672
john.welsh@bishopslaw.biz
Specialisation: Partner in the Litigation Division. Main area of practice is construction law, including professional negligence claims against engineers, architects and surveyors; also drafting and advising on construction law contracts, appointments and warranties. John Welsh speaks frequently at conferences and seminars on construction law and related topics including mediation. He also advises arbiters and clerks in arbitrations. More recently his practice has developed into advising generally on professional negligence and claims against solicitors and accountants.
Prof. Memberships: Law Society of Scotland, Royal Faculty of Procurators in Glasgow.
Career: Qualified in 1968. Assistant Solicitor and Partner at *Robertson Chalmers & Auld* 1969-86. Partner with *Bishop and Robertson Chalmers* (now known as *Morison Bishop*) from 1986. Accredited by the Law Society of Scotland as a Specialist in Construction Law in 1993 and as a Solicitor-Mediator in 1994.
Personal: Born 12 September 1945. Educated at Glasgow University 1963-66. Enjoys golf and fishing. Lives in Bearsden.

WHITE, Stuart
Reynolds Porter Chamberlain, London
(020) 7242 2877
sgw@rpc.co.uk
Specialisation: Partner in Insurance and Reinsurance Department. A significant area of practice is professional indemnity, principally construction related, for architects and engineers. Also handles general insurance work, covering insurance disputes, policy wordings and general liability and property litigation. Extensive experience of mediation. Acted in 'Investors in Industry v South Bedfordshire DC', 'Crown v Mowlem' (re final certificates), 'Citibank v Excess' (re costs liability of insurers), and was also involved in the personal accident claim following the death of Robert Maxwell. Major clients include insurance companies, mutual insurance associations and Lloyd's syndicates. Has given seminars on a range of topics including architects' liability, product liability, liability for pollution, drafting of policy wordings, 'Chapman v Christopher', the impact of the Woolf reforms on insurers, fraudulent insurance claims and 'True Professionalism'. Has addressed the Fire Loss Association, the Chartered Institute of Loss Adjusters and the British Insurance Brokers Association. Regularly contributes to various insurance publications.
Prof. Memberships: Society of Construction Law, British Insurance Law Association, CEDR, Fire Loss Association, Chartered Insurance Institute, FOIL.
Career: Qualified in 1984. Joined *Hextall Erskine* in 1980, becoming a Partner in 1987. Partner *Reynolds Porter Chamberlain* from 2001.
Personal: Born 1957. Attended The Queen's College Oxford, MA (Hons) 1975-78.

WILLIAMSON, David
Brodies, Edinburgh
(0131) 228 3777
david.williamson@brodies.co.uk
Specialisation: Solicitor Advocate handling general commercial litigation and specialising in intellectual property, employment law, partnership disputes and professional negligence. Experienced speaker at conferences and seminars. Lectured for over five years at University of Edinburgh in civil procedure.
Career: Qualified in 1971. With *Simpson & Marwick* 1969-75, latterly as Partner. Joined *Brodies* as a Partner in 1976. Part-time Employment Tribunals Chairman and part-time Sheriff. Criminal Injuries Compensation Panel member. Fellow of the Chartered Institute of Arbitrators.
Personal: Born in 1949. Educated at Royal High School, Edinburgh and University of Edinburgh. Leisure interests include cricket and hill walking. Lives in Edinburgh.

WILSON, Michael
Barlow Lyde & Gilbert, London
(020) 7247 2277
mgwilson@blg.co.uk
Specialisation: Professional indemnity litigation, in particular, claims against

domestic and international banks. Direct involvement in many of the leading cases against merchant banks arising as a result of takeover activities.
Prof. Memberships: Member of the Law Society; City of London Solicitors Company; Asia Pacific Lawyers Association; International Bar Association; Southwestern Legal Foundation; Inter-Pacific Bar Association; Freeman of the City of London; Fellow of the Royal Society of Art.
Career: Articled with *Slaughter and May*; qualified in 1975; assistant solicitor 1977-79; partner *Berwin Leighton* 1979-99; *Barlow Lyde & Gilbert* 1999 to date.
Personal: Golf, tennis, squash, swimming, travel, reading, music.

PROJECTS/PFI

London: 685; The Regions: 691; Scotland: 693; Profiles: 694

Research approved by BMRB For this edition, **Chambers'** researchers conducted 6,582 interviews – 3,900 with law firms, 511 with barristers and 2,171 with clients. The validity of the research was scrutinised by BMRB International, who audited both the methodology and the results at our offices in London. They interviewed **Chambers'** researchers and cross-checked sample interviews. Details of the audit appear on page 7.

LONDON

PROJECT FINANCE

PROJECTS — LONDON

1. Allen & Overy
2. Clifford Chance
   Linklaters
3. Norton Rose
   Shearman & Sterling
4. Denton Wilde Sapte
   Freshfields Bruckhaus Deringer
5. Lovells
   Milbank, Tweed, Hadley & McCloy
   Slaughter and May
   White & Case
6. Ashurst Morris Crisp
   Baker & McKenzie
   CMS Cameron McKenna
   Herbert Smith
   Masons
   Simmons & Simmons

This book is the product of 6,582 1/2 hour interviews. See p.7 for BMRB audit.
Within each band, firms are listed alphabetically.

ALLEN & OVERY (see firm details p.841) Clients claim this to be "*the default choice for banks,*" and also report that the group has "*high levels of expertise across the board.*" Central and Latin America have proved to be rich sources of instruction, while a highly developed network of international offices is on hand to smoothly manage the multi-jurisdictional aspects of financings and project development. Head of project finance **Graham Vinter** (see p.700) is perceived to be less at the coalface; however, he retains a reputation as "*a formidable operator,*" adept at troubleshooting. He is "*pragmatic, sound and sensible*" and sets high standards in market innovation. The "*commercial*" **Stephen Gillespie** (see p.105) brings "*a knowledge of structures which work*" to the table, while peers agree that **Tony Humphrey**'s (see p.106) long experience places him "*at the forefront of the market.*" Expert in a wide range of asset finance matters, **Brian Harrison** (see p.696) is a "*personable and results-oriented*" lawyer. Bimal Desai has relocated to the firm's Dubai office. Highlights for the group include acting for the arrangers on the $570 million Ras Laffan power and desalination project. The group also advised the Abu Dhabi Islamic Bank in relation to the project financing of the Islamic tranche for A1 Shuweihat power and desalination plant.

Clients The National Grid Company; Japan Bank for International Cooperation; The Industrial Bank of Japan.

CLIFFORD CHANCE (see firm details p.911) This team of "*commercial and robust negotiators*" advises a client roster evenly split between banks and borrowers. The group plays host to a number of high-profile individuals, including power specialist **Peter Blake** (see p.341). Clients commended his "*dedication - he works phenomenally hard,*" while competitors enthused about his commercial acumen. **Margaret Gossling** (see p.696) is respected for her comprehensive management of complex projects, while **Chris Wyman** (see p.700) ("*a walking brain*") proved popular for the innovation he brings to financings. Banking and finance partner **Dan Reynell** (see p.699) is "*a pleasure to work with,*" an attribute shared by **Ranbir Hunjan** (see p.697). The latter makes an entry to the tables this year following client recommendation, which singled him out as "*accurate and responsive to our needs – a future star.*" Highlights for the group include advice to the IFC and commercial banks on the $4 billion operation and development of the Chad/Cameroon pipeline. The group has also advised International Power on the Al Kamil IPP in Oman, which entailed the construction and operation of a 275 MW gas-fired power plant. It acted for the arranger of bank debt in the financing for the N1-N4 Platinum Toll Highway project. **Clients** Chase Manhattan; Petrobras.

LINKLATERS (see firm details p1043) A team that competitors acknowledge as "*superb on the sponsor side,*" which has continued to develop its strong relationships with the banks and other financial institutions. It acts on a range of projects in the infrastructure, energy and natural resources sectors. Interviewees report that **Stuart Salt** (see p.699) is "*a joy to see on the other side.*" Clients appreciate his "*can-do attitude,*" and he is a lawyer with "*an appealing combination of high standards and approachability.*" **Alan Black** (see p.694) is the head of global projects, energy and natural resources. He has advised the sponsors in connection with the development and limited recourse financing of a 34,000-barrels-per-day, gas-to-liquids project at Ras Laffan. **Clive Ransome** (see p.699) is a projects and banking specialist, who led on the Huntstown Power Project. The group has advised the lead arranger on the €219.6 million financing of the Viridian Group-owned 343 MW combined cycle, gas turbine, electricity-generating facility. **David Weber** (see p.700) acts for both sponsors and developers. He led the team acting for the sponsors on the Chad/Cameroon Oil Transportation System Project. **Clients** ABN AMRO; AMEC; Deutsche Bank; Shell.

NORTON ROSE (see firm details p.1084) The team ethos at this firm has generated lawyers who are "*professional, down-to-earth and focused on the deal.*" The team benefits from its "*renowned energy department*", while infrastructure projects are also handled for a balanced sponsors and lenders client base. Global head of the projects group **Jeffery Barratt** (see p.694) has "*a lot of common sense*" and knows when to adopt a "*conciliatory approach.*" He led the team on the Taweelah A1 Power Generation and Sea Water Desalination Project in Abu Dhabi, representing the lead arrangers on the $1 billion debt financing. **Peter Hall** (see p.696) was singled out for his construction skills and gleaned praise from clients as prime choice in "*negotiating with difficult contractors.*" The team also represented the mandated lead arrangers in the fast-track negotiation of the $400 million loan facility to fund the QAFCO 4 expansion. **David Crane** (see p.695) received strong commendation from clients for his no-nonsense approach. **Clients** Abbey National; ANZ Investment Bank; SACE; BNP Paribas; Edison Gas; LASMO Pakistan; Singapore Power.

SHEARMAN & STERLING (see firm details p.1129) Clients appreciate that this team "*understands project finance and the risk matrix.*" Peers acknowledged that the London group has continued to develop "*a dynamic, enthusiastic practice*" where a volume-based business is deliberately eschewed in favour of high-end transactions. A high proportion of partners make an appearance in our table including the popular **Ken MacRitchie** (see p.697), who was praised by clients as "*one of the best project finance lawyers around.*" Co-head of global projects **Nick Buckworth** is "*a commercial lawyer who won't let pedantry stall a deal.*" The two co-led the team advising the lead arrangers on the $1.6 billion international financing of the Shuweihat independent water and power project in Abu Dhabi. "*Commercially minded and sensible*" **Stephen Peppiatt** enters the tables following considerable market

www.Chambersandpartners.com 685

PROJECTS/PFI ■ LONDON

LEADING INDIVIDUALS

1
- **BARRATT Jeffery** Norton Rose
- **BLACK Alan** Linklaters
- **MACRITCHIE Kenneth** Shearman & Sterling
- **SALT Stuart** Linklaters
- **VINTER Graham** Allen & Overy

2
- **BLAKE Peter** Clifford Chance
- **FOX Jason** Herbert Smith
- **GILLESPIE Stephen** Allen & Overy
- **HUMPHREY Tony** Allen & Overy

3
- **BUCKWORTH Nicholas** Shearman & Sterling
- **CRANE David** Norton Rose
- **FINLAY Peter** White & Case
- **FLETCHER Phillip** Milbank, Tweed, Hadley & McCloy
- **HARRISON Brian** Allen & Overy
- **RANSOME Clive** Linklaters
- **ROWEY Kent** Freshfields Bruckhaus Deringer

4
- **GAINES Peter** Vinson & Elkins LLP
- **GOSSLING Margaret** Clifford Chance
- **MCCORMICK Roger** Freshfields Bruckhaus Deringer
- **MCQUATER Gavin** Lovells
- **STOPFORD Philip** White & Case
- **WYMAN Chris** Clifford Chance

5
- **BELLHOUSE John** White & Case
- **DARLEY Mark** Skadden, Arps, Slate, Meagher & Flom LLP
- **HALL Peter** Norton Rose
- **JOHNSTON Bruce** LeBoeuf, Lamb, Greene & MacRae
- **PEPPIATT Stephen** Shearman & Sterling
- **PHILLIPS Robert** CMS Cameron McKenna
- **PREECE Andrew** Herbert Smith
- **REYNELL Daniel** Clifford Chance
- **TEMPLETON-KNIGHT Jane** Hunton & Williams
- **WEBER David** Linklaters

UP AND COMING
- **HUNJAN Ranbir** Clifford Chance

See individuals' profiles p.694

approval. The growth in his practice belies comment, which ascribes the prominence of this team to MacRitchie and Buckworth alone. He co-led the team advising AES on all aspects of the development and financing of the $570 million Ras Laffan independent water and power project. **Clients** ABN AMRO; BG.

DENTON WILDE SAPTE (see firm details p.935) "*Responsive and amenable,*" clients reported that this group possesses the ability to "*field an extensive team as and when required,*" and that it is "*good at presenting difficult positions.*" The firm is commended for its work in the energy sector, while telecoms, water, rail and banking projects are all strings to its bow. Instructions from Asia, Africa and the Middle East are testament to the reach of this firm. It has represented the Omani Government on the Salalah Power Privatisation Project, the first vertically integrated concession to close in the Middle East. The group also advised AES Haripur on all aspects of the $180 million project financing of its 360 MW combined cycle, gas-fired IPP in Bangladesh. **Clients** ADGAS; Bank of China; Chevron; Mobil; Shell; Icelandic Investment Bank; Deutsche Bank; Citibank.

FRESHFIELDS BRUCKHAUS DERINGER (see firm details p.964) The team is perceived by interviewees to provide a 'one-stop shop' where projects and PFI financings interrelate. Kent Rowey (see p.343) ("*highly effective*") co-led representation of the Ex-Im Bank in the Hamaca extra heavy crude oil project, one of the first financings in which Ex-Im has provided a guarantee covering the construction phase as well as the operations phase of the project. "*Expert*" Roger McCormick (see p.698) was recommended for his complex project management skills. Further highlights for the team include its advice to Hutchison 3G UK on the project financing for its UK 3G network roll-out, which featured complex inter-creditor agreements between banks and vendor financiers. **Clients** EIB; Ex-Im Bank; Financial Security Assurance; Powergen.

LOVELLS (see firm details p.1045) Head of the project finance unit **Gavin McQuater** (see p.698) was praised by competitors for his "*ability to see the bigger picture.*" Clients appreciated him as an "*exceptional problem solver,*" and valued the depth of the team beneath him. Highlights for the group include advising the Leonardo Consortium and Aeroporti di Roma on the initial €2 billion financing for the partial privatisation of Rome Airport, and the subsequent restructuring and refinancing of the project. The team also represented the EIB on the first monoline wrapped EIB and bond refinancing of a Portuguese road project. The firm has extended its reach in Europe. It has acted for a German consortium on the €320 million central waste water treatment plant in Zagreb, which involved related construction and commercial issues. **Clients** NATS; Sport England; Bechtel; Innisfree; Amey; Barclays Capital; Bank of Scotland.

MILBANK, TWEED, HADLEY & MCCLOY (see firm details p.1070) First-rate resources and the support of the firm's global presence has ensured a busy year for this London group, particularly in Italy. Phillip Fletcher (see p.696) is the standout practitioner here; peers agree that he is "*lively and a sensible deal-doer.*" The firm has represented International Power and joint venture partner Ansaldo on the portfolio financing of approximately ten power projects aggregating 8,000 MW, a key highlight of the year. The group is also acting for Viridian and other joint venture parties in the development and financing of the 300 MW Huntstown Power Project. In Oman, the group acted for the lenders in the Salalah Project, while in Ankara, the group is advising Tractebel in its $500 million acquisition and development of the 770 MW 'build-own-operate' Baymina IPP. **Clients** Goldman Sachs; TotalFinaElf; Tractebel.

SLAUGHTER AND MAY (see firm details p.1140) Clients commended a firm of "*consistently good practitioners,*" who are "*constructive in negotiations.*" A highlight has been acting for the Infraspeed consortium in connection with its successful bid to win the concession to construct, finance and maintain the superstructure for the Dutch high-speed rail link. The team continues to represent Qatar Liquefied Gas Company in connection with the long-running development of an LNG plant in Qatar. The group is also advising the joint lead arrangers on the €256 million bond refinancing of the SCUT Algarve toll road project. Christopher Saunders is advising the lead arrangers on the $1.375 billion term loan and letter of credit facilities to refinance the original project debt of

Top Five Project Finance Deals in the UK (June 2001 to June 2002)

	Project	Sector	Borrower	Sponsor	Legal Advisors	Value (US$m)	Close Date
1	Spalding Gas-fired Power Plant	Power	InterGen Spalding Power	InterGen Energy	Lender – **Shearman & Sterling** Consortium – **Clifford Chance**	742.383	21/05/02
2	Immingham CHP Plant	Power	Immingham CHP	Conoco Global Power	Lender – **Allen & Overy** Consortium – **Freshfields Bruckhaus Deringer**	400.524	17/01/02
3	Rugeley Power Plant Acquisition	Power	Rugeley Power	International Power	Lender – **Linklaters** Consortium – **Clifford Chance**	249.929	08/03/02
4	Project Husky	Gas Pipeline	Inexus Group	Star Capital Partners	Lender – **Denton Wilde Sapte** Consortium – **Slaughter and May**	216.320	08/08/01
5	Alba Field Financing	Oilfield Development	Energy Africa	Energy Africa	Lender – **Clifford Chance** Consortium – **Herbert Smith**	50.000	19/12/01

Source: Dealogic ProjectWare

LONDON — PROJECTS/PFI

the Oman LNG project. Martin Roberts has now retired from the practice. **Clients** AES; Deutsche Bank; EIB.

WHITE & CASE (see firm details p.1185) "*Excellent around the world*," the team derives a great advantage from the success of its global projects practice. Head of project finance **Philip Stopford** (see p.699) was heavily endorsed by clients: "*For my money, he's one of the best in the business*" was a typical view. He led the team representing the Nigerian and commercial lenders on the financing of the fourth and fifth trains in the Nigeria LNG project. Focusing on emerging markets, **Peter Finlay** (see p.696) acted for the arrangers in the $660 million project financing of an ammonia/fertiliser project in the Sultanate of Oman, in which half the financing is covered by export credit agencies. "*Patient and sensible*" **John Bellhouse** (see p.694) was singled out for his finance and construction expertise. **Clients** International sponsors.

ASHURST MORRIS CRISP (see firm details p.852) The team is already acknowledged to have expertise in the transport sector, and has this year seen energy instructions come to the fore. The team has advised Kuwait Petroleum Corporation on its importation of pipeline gas from the EGU project in Qatar. The Middle East has yielded much of the work, and instructions here are undertaken by joint teams from the Singapore and London offices. The team, led by Mark Elsey, has advised the Lusoscut consortium as concessionaire on the financing of the €1.2 billion Beiras Litoral e Alta shadow toll road project in Portugal. It also acted for The South African National Roads Agency on the award of a concession for the N4 Platinum Toll Road project. **Clients** Kuwait Petroleum Corporation; ABN AMRO; Centrica; Mitsubishi.

BAKER & MCKENZIE (see firm details p.855) This strongly international practice is co-ordinated on a worldwide basis with the support of practitioners on the ground in local jurisdictions. The London group has witnessed the departure of Peter Gaines to Vinson & Elkins, but remains respected by clients as "*a personable team, highly competent and deserving of every accolade*." The firm acts for sponsors, lenders and public bodies, and it has been acknowledged for its skill in multilateral financings. A highlight has been acting for the EIB on the financing of the Chad/Cameroon pipeline project. Neil Donoghue is a key partner here, and the team continues to act for Petrobras on its $3.2 billion Barracuda and Caratinga projects. Telecoms financing is another arena which has remained active despite poor market conditions, with instructions from Siemens and Metromedia bolstering the team's broad repertoire of work. **Clients** The Industrial Bank of Japan; BNP Paribas; Petrobras; The Arab Banking Corporation; Canadian Highways; Nortel.

CMS CAMERON MCKENNA (see firm details p.914) The team has used its renowned expertise in PFI as a platform for promoting its increasingly high-profile involvement in international projects. The Eastern European network of offices has come to the fore, as the team has advised PSEG Global on the structuring and negotiation of all project documentation for the first coal-fired independent power plant in Poland. The team is active for both the public and private sectors, and has transferred its experience of transport models to Western Europe. Renowned infrastructure lawyer **Robert Phillips** (see p.698) acted for the Dutch Government on the HSL-Zuid Dutch high-speed rail link, a project which has recently closed. Jonathan Beckitt leads the team that represents the DTLR on the Channel Tunnel Rail Link's further restructuring. **Clients** Dresdner Kleinwort Wasserstein; WestLB; The Dai-Ichi Kangyo Bank.

HERBERT SMITH (see firm details p.992) Financial institutions, bidding consortia and a host of government bodies are all providers of major instructions for this group. Clients commended the team as "*good at the innovative aspects of financing and structuring*." **Jason Fox** (see p.696) attracted accolades from clients as "*an experienced problem solver*," who understands "*the dynamics of project financings*." He advised Centrica on the 860 MW gas-fired Spalding Power Project. **Andrew Preece** (see p.699) is respected by peers. He advised Zuid Rail in connection with its tender for the Dutch high-speed rail link. **Clients** Société Générale; JPMorgan Chase; EIB; London and Continental Railways; International Water.

MASONS (see firm details p.1057) Observers perceived the team to be "*extremely busy with great contacts*," acknowledging that it has built out from its PPP success with the Bloemfontein prison project. It has an international reach and acts for both lenders and project developers. This is a cohesive national group, led in the London office by Chris Brown. The team is advising a leading global hydrocarbon company on two major LNG terminal and port projects in Asia and South America. It has also advised Gauteng on the Johannesburg Light Rail project. Instructions have been secured from the top three developers for road projects in Ireland. **Clients** EIB; Government of Cyprus; Government of South Africa.

SIMMONS & SIMMONS (see firm details p.1136) Market commentators respected this firm for its expanding resources overseas. Its team members have experience in the financing, construction and facilities management issues facing major projects. Highlights include the representation of the EIB on the drawdown of its €570 million loan to Wind Telecomunicazioni. It also advised Black & Veatch as sponsor of the Arzew Power Desalination Project in Algeria valued at $330 million. **Clients** MOD; Railtrack; Greek Government; EIB.

OTHER NOTABLE PRACTITIONERS Formerly of Baker & McKenzie, **Peter Gaines** (see p.696) has joined the ranks of Vinson & Elkins. **Mark Darley** (see p.695) has joined Skadden, Arps, Slate, Meagher & Flom from Lovells as the new head of the European banking practice. His focus has subsequently incurred a greater level of pure finance transactions. The projects market commends his "*commercially astute character*." "*Impressive client handler*" **Bruce Johnston** has bolstered the team at LeBoeuf, Lamb, Greene & MacRae, while at Hunton & Williams, "*charming*" **Jane Templeton-Knight** (see p.699) was commended by peers as "*an extremely capable lawyer with a loyal client following.*"

LONDON — PFI

ALLEN & OVERY (see firm details p.841) This "*cool, calm, collected and professional*" team enjoys a reputation among clients and peers as "*a top-quality outfit.*" Singled out for praise was finance partner **Anne Baldock** (see p.694), who clients rate for her "*ability to make a difference*" at the deal table. She co-led the team acting for Financial Security Assurance (UK) and Royal Bank of Scotland (RBS) on the PFI pathfinder project for the University of Hertfordshire. This was financed by way of a limited price inflation (LPI) wrapped bond raising approximately £60 million. "*Deadpan*" PPP specialist **David Lee** (see p.697) was praised for his negotiation ability: "*he is thorough and good at getting back to the real world,*" said competitors. He led the team acting for Ambac on the recently closed Home Office Central London accommodation project. This raised approximately £311 million by way of index-linked and fixed rate wrapped bonds. The team, acting in conjunction with the Amsterdam office, also advised the lead arrangers on the €1.2 billion financing for the DBFO Dutch high-speed rail link (HSL). David Sedgley has now relocated to the firm's Bangkok office. **Clients** Amey Ventures; Barts and the London NHS Trust; all major international banks and insurers.

CLIFFORD CHANCE (see firm details p.911) Considered by peers to be "*a pleasure to work*

PROJECTS/PFI ■ LONDON

PFI
■ LONDON

1. Allen & Overy
   Clifford Chance
   Linklaters
2. Ashurst Morris Crisp
   Freshfields Bruckhaus Deringer
3. CMS Cameron McKenna
   Herbert Smith
   Lovells
4. Denton Wilde Sapte
   Masons
   Norton Rose
5. Berwin Leighton Paisner
   Simmons & Simmons
6. DLA
   Mayer, Brown, Rowe & Maw
   Slaughter and May
   Theodore Goddard
   Trowers & Hamlins

This book is the product of 6,582 1/2 hour interviews. See p.7 for BMRB audit. Within each band, firms are listed alphabetically.

with," while clients praised an ability to "*pull the threads together,*" the team is comprised of "*excellent senior people.*" Welcome at any deal table, "*first-class*" financing specialist **David Bickerton** (see p.694) is "*extremely intelligent, witty and incisive,*" while construction expert **Tim Steadman** (see p.699) was described to researchers as "*a character you can do business with.*" Clients appreciate him as "*pragmatic and good at seeing things from our point of view,*" and admire his work on contracts and concession agreements. Statesmanlike **Andrew Rolfe** (see p.699) is "*a good man for detailed work.*" **Gavin Teague** (see p.283744) was lauded by peers as "*an outstanding lawyer with the ability to see the legal and commercial aspects of a deal.*" The DTLR, MOD and Department of Health form an important triumvirate of deal originators for the firm's sponsor and funder client base. Significant closed projects include the £200 million Cornwall Schools PFI where the team advised the NewSchools consortium (WS Atkins, Innisfree and Mowlem), and Serco's £160 million traffic control centre project, a ten-year PPP with the Highways Agency. **Clients** MBIA; Barclays Capital; Innisfree; Skanska; Qinetiq; Thales.

LINKLATERS (see firm details p.1043) This team is praised by clients for its "*excellent service and accessibility in key areas,*" while contractors applauded "*commercial people who will tell you things straight.*" Acting for a mix of sponsors and lenders, competitors noted the exceptional thoroughness with which the group approaches the negotiating table. Researchers were overwhelmed by feedback for "*God's gift to project finance*" **Bruce White** (see p.700), who is "*creative in finding ways of getting people where they want to be*" and gifted at "*brinkmanship negoti-*ation." He led the team on the £95 million MOD Heavy Equipment Transporter Project. New partner **Stuart Rowson** (see p.699) enters Chambers' tables this year. Clients praised him as "*a good negotiator, strong analytically and great to work with.*" He assisted on the recently closed £180 million Dudley Hospitals PPP, involving multi-sourced financing including an EIB loan and a project bond issue. **Clients** Ambac; Barclays; FSA; Bovis Lend Lease; Carillion; London Electricity; Abbey National; Halifax; RBS.

ASHURST MORRIS CRISP (see firm details p.852) This "*on-the-ball, no-nonsense*" team was consistently praised by clients for its "*approachability.*" Already renowned for its impressive transport sector work, peers acknowledged that the group had had a good year and made progress in the quality of its deals, particularly acting for funders. Head of department **Mark Elsey** (see p.696) is "*a delight to work with: non-patronising, calming and commercially sharp,*" according to one client. "*Thorough and hardworking*" infrastructure projects lawyer **Logan Mair** (see p.697) is a newcomer to the tables this year. Clients appreciate his ability to "*switch from a legal to a commercial mindset.*" He is currently acting for NIB Capital and ABN AMRO on the East London Integrated Waste Project. **Philip Vernon** (see p.699) carries out a mix of large funder and sponsor work, which has seen him advising the funders to the Metronet consortium as preferred bidder on the BCV and SSL London Underground PPP projects. The team acted for BT on the outsourcing of its entire UK portfolio to Telereal Holdings for £2.38 billion. **Clients** Barclays Private Equity; FSA; Interserve; RBS; Group 4; Balfour Beatty; Atkins; CIBC.

FRESHFIELDS BRUCKHAUS DERINGER (see firm details p.964) This is a team with "*strong commercial sense,*" which has enjoyed a year of major projects. "*First-class*" **Nick Bliss** (see p.695) was easily the team's best-known player, winning sustained market applause. He advised the lenders on the £867 million financing of the Northern Road concession in Portugal, and assisted the Road Management Group in its monoline wrapped eurobond financing of the A419/A417 Swindon/Gloucester toll road concessions. Energy and infrastructure expert **Perry Noble** (see p.698) is a "*deal-doer*" who was commended for his government work. He is part of the team offering continuing advice to London Underground on its £20 billion PPP. The team is still representing Paradigm Secure Communications as preferred bidder to deliver the MOD's Skynet 5 project, a contract worth approximately £2 billion. **Clients** Barclays Capital; Innisfree; LUL; RBS; WS Atkins

CMS CAMERON MCKENNA (see firm details p.914) This team of "*respected senior people*" boasts a number of strong individuals, including "*affable and avuncular*" **Andrew Ivison** (see p.697). Praised for his ability to "*deal with complex issues in a sensible way,*" clients appreciated his "*balanced, knowledgeable*" approach. He led the team representing the lenders on financing the acquisition of a 46% interest in NATS. "*Smooth operator*" **Frank Dufficy** (see p.695) brings to bear strong process management capabilities while remaining "*logical and sensible to deal with,*" and **Jonathan Beckitt** (see p.694) is said to combine "*high-quality documentation with an effective, non-confrontational negotiating style.*" In the transport sector, the firm's rail practice is steaming ahead, and it continues to represent the Erin Route Consortium in bidding for three major road projects in Ireland. Health and defence are also burgeoning areas, with the team advising the sponsors on the Walsgrave PFI and acting for Aquatrine, which is a Thames Water-led consortium. **Clients** Dresdner Kleinwort Wasserstein; Barclays Capital; Balfour Beatty Capital Projects; Innisfree.

HERBERT SMITH (see firm details p.992) "*This is something the firm excels in*" according to one client. The team was felt by interviewees to have "*spread its wings*" by increasingly supplementing its traditional public sector client base with an impressive list of financial institutions and bidding consortia. Head of infrastructure **Nick Tott**'s (see p.699) high market standing is founded upon his technical skill and his ability to "*manage a client.*" He acted recently for the Halliburton-led consortium, Fasttrax, on the provision of heavy equipment transporters. Project specialist **Jason Fox** (see p.696) also received warm commendations from clients and competitors alike, while clients rated **David Wyles** (see p.700) "*extremely highly*" for his banking and finance expertise. He acted for the EIB in relation to the co-financing of the Dudley Hospitals PFI project. The group is providing ongoing advice on all aspects of the Channel Tunnel Rail Link for London and Continental Railways, and is acting for the British Waterways Board on a project involving using the canal network as a water transportation system. **Clients** MOD; British Waterways Board; Virgin Trains; Partnerships UK; Halifax Bank.

LOVELLS (see firm details p.1095) "*Competent, pleasant and less arrogant than most City firms*" was the clients' view of this dynamic team. Handling a mix of sponsor and lender work, the London group includes the "*quietly commercial and knowledgeable*" **Mike Matheou** (see p.697). "*Good at grasping strategy,*" he continues to advise the Tubes Lines Group on its successful bid for the Jubilee, Northern and Piccadilly lines PPP project. The team also recently assisted the English Sports Council on the proposed project financing of the new £700 million National Stadium. Meanwhile, the firm's growing international reach is confirmed with a string of major projects. These include representing the Leonardo Consortium on the initial financing of over €2 billion for the partial privatisation of Rome Airport, and its subsequent restructuring and refinancing. The group has advised on three Portuguese toll road projects, including the €600 million Litoral Centro Toll Road and the €300 million Algarve shadow toll road project. **Clients** NATS; Sport England; Bechtel; Innisfree; Amey; Barclays Capital; BRISA; Bayerische Landesbank; EIB; RWE.

DENTON WILDE SAPTE (see firm details p.935) This "*reliable, thorough and friendly,*" team acts for government, sponsors and lenders in the transport, infrastructure, IT and health arenas. A strong and growing international portfolio includes projects in Ireland, Portugal, Romania and the Gulf. "*Knowledgeable*" **Stan Gniadkowski** is the standout practitioner here, noted by peers for being pleasant and hardworking, while **Ellen Gates** also retains a strong reputation in the marketplace. The team continues to act on the MOD's nationwide water and waste water project, and is advising Equion on a £120 million PFI project with the Metropolitan Police Authority for the provision of four new police stations. Its strong presence in the Middle East is demonstrated by its representation of the joint venture company established by Black and Veatch International and Thames Water, on the first PPP project for the delivery of municipal services in the Gulf region. **Clients** MOD; Highways Agency; Newcourt Capital; Abbey National; Equion; Lord Chancellor's Department; Balfour Beatty.

MASONS (see firm details p.1057) Praised by clients for being "*highly responsive,*" the team profits from the support of a string of offices nationwide. Increasingly active both domestically and internationally, the group represents leading consortia in the education, health and roads sectors. Finance partner **Martin McCann** (see p.697) was singled out for particular praise by clients. Endowed with an ability to "*build confidence and get on with the other side,*" his "*sound commercial judgement*" won him many admirers. He is leading the team acting for AMEC, Bombardier and FirstGroup on Manchester Metrolink Phase 3, a £600 million PPP project. Head of the projects and finance group, **Chris Brown** (see p.695) was also praised for his "*user-friendly manner.*" He is leading the team advising PwC and the Ministry of Communications and Works on the £200 million-plus PPP concession to develop Larnaka and Pafos Airports. **Clients** EIB; Dexia Public Finance Bank; Bank Gesellschaft Berlin; ING Barings; RBS; Innisfree; Carillion.

NORTON ROSE (see firm details p.1084) The team, described as "*co-operative, practical and businesslike,*" enjoys a steady stream of smaller projects. Renowned for its knowledge of defence projects, the team also possesses a leasing expertise derived from a Rolls-Royce asset finance team combined with a strong banking client base. Although there were questions about the consistency below partner level, the firm boasts a number of strong individuals. "*Straightforward*" **Jon Ellis** (see p.695) is described by competitors as "*a superb lawyer who fights well.*" He advised the Bank of Scotland on financing the £300 million project to supply the Astute Class Training Service to the Royal Navy. **David Coulter** (see p.695) is "*a great man who will stand up and be counted,*" according to clients. He recently advised RBS and Lombard Financing on a £100 million project to provide a fleet of ferries. **Clients** Abbey

Top Ten PFI Deals in the UK (June 2001 to June 2002)

	Project	Sector	Borrower	Sponsor	Legal Advisors	Value (US$m)	Close Date
1	NATS Public Private Partnership	Airport Security	NATS En Route	British Midland Airways, Airtours, Britannia Airways, easyJet, British Airways, Virgin Atlantic Airways, JMC Monarch	Concession awarder – **Lovells, Slaughter and May** Lender – **CMS Cameron McKenna** Consortium – **Norton Rose**	2,080.344	26/07/01
2	Refinancing of the A1/M1 Road Link	Road	Yorkshire Link Holdings	Jarvis, Barclays Infrastructure	Lender – **Clifford Chance** Consortium – **Freshfields Bruackhaus Deringer**	586.000	04/09/01
3	Home Office & Prison Service Accommodation Project	Property	Annes Gate Property	Bouygues UK, Ecovert South, HSBC	Concession awarder – **Berwin Leighton Paisner** Lender – **Allen & Overy** Consortium – **Norton Rose**	455.053	26/03/02
4	UPP Refinancing	Property	Jarvis UPP Holdings	Jarvis, Barclays Infrastructure	Lender – **Linklaters** Consortium – **Eversheds**	330.460	02/05/02
5	DSS Newcastle Longbenton Estate Refinancing	Property	Newcastle Estate Partnership	AMEC, Building & Property Group	Lender – **Allen & Overy** Consortium – **Berwin Leighton Paisner**	247.700	26/06/01
6	M40 Motorway Refinancing	Road	UK Highways M40	John Laing, Transroute International, CDC IXIS, Hyder Investments, Carillion	Concession awarder – **Denton Wilde Sapte** Lender – **Allen & Overy** Consortium – **CMS Cameron McKenna**	188.600	15/10/01
7	Refinancing of the Joint Service Command and Staff College	Defence	Defence Management	Serco Group, Equion	Concession awarder – **Masons** Lender – **Allen & Overy** Consortium – **Clifford Chance**	168.960	20/06/02
8	Metropolitan Police SE London Stations Project	Defence	Services Support	Equion	Concession awarder – **Masons** Lender – **CMS Cameron McKenna** Consortium – **Denton Wilde Sapte**	152.600	19/10/01
9	Edinburgh Grouped Schools	Schools	Edinburgh Schools Partnership	Bank of Scotland, Miller Group, Quayle Munro, Amey Ventures	Concession awarder – **Dundas & Wilson** Lender – **McGrigor Donald** Consortium – **MacRoberts**	148.394	01/11/01
10	Heavy Equipment Transporter	Defence	Fasttrax	Halliburton, Brown & Root, Barclays Infrastructure, Noble PFI Fund	Concession awarder – **Shepherd & Wedderburn** Lender – **Linklaters** Consortium – **Herbert Smith**	140.000	14/12/01

Source: Dealogic ProjectWare

PROJECTS/PFI ■ LONDON

LEADING INDIVIDUALS

★ **BALDOCK Anne** Allen & Overy
WHITE Bruce Linklaters

[1] **BICKERTON David** Clifford Chance
BLISS Nick Freshfields Bruckhaus Deringer
ELSEY Mark Ashurst Morris Crisp
MATHEOU Michael Lovells
STEADMAN Tim Clifford Chance

[2] **DUFFICY Frank** CMS Cameron McKenna
GNIADKOWSKI Stan Denton Wilde Sapte
IVISON Andrew CMS Cameron McKenna
NOBLE Perry Freshfields Bruckhaus Deringer

[3] **ELLIS Jon** Norton Rose
MCCORMACK Carol Berwin Leighton Paisner
TOTT Nick Herbert Smith

[4] **BALLINGALL James** Theodore Goddard
BROWN Chris Masons
COULTER David Norton Rose
FOX Jason Herbert Smith
FRANCIS Barry Pinsent Curtis Biddle
MCCANN Martin Masons

[5] **ARMITAGE Richard** Simmons & Simmons
AUSTWICK Malcolm Beachcroft Wansbroughs
BECKITT Jonathan CMS Cameron McKenna
GATES Ellen Denton Wilde Sapte
GOLDIE Ian Slaughter and May
ROLFE Andrew Clifford Chance
TEAGUE Gavin Clifford Chance

UP AND COMING

ANDERSON Joanne Mayer, Brown, Rowe & Maw
LEE David Allen & Overy
LUCAS Richard Berwin Leighton Paisner
MAIR Logan Ashurst Morris Crisp
ROWSON Stuart Linklaters
VERNON Philip Ashurst Morris Crisp
WYLES David Herbert Smith

See individuals' profiles p.694

National; HBOS; RBS; Bouygues Construction; Norwest Holst; United Utilities; NATS; NHS-Lift Ballast; Bechtel.

BERWIN LEIGHTON PAISNER (see firm details p.866) Roundly endorsed by market sources for its "*efficiency,*" clients were full of praise for this "*talented bunch.*" The team acts for a balanced base of sponsors, awarding authorities and banks. Its best-known personality is "*good fun but tough*" Carol McCormack (see p.698), who was praised by clients and peers for her "*incredible ability to pull all the threads together; she can buzz from document to document and gives 110%.*" She acted for the Bouygues Consortium negotiating the first transaction to reach financial close using the NHS standard form contract. Newcomer to the rankings this year, Richard Lucas (see p.697) was also commended by clients as "*a nuts and bolts man who eats and sleeps a project.*" Acting primarily for contractors, he led the team on the Strategic Sealift Project, a shipping PFI valued at £950 million. A recent highlight for the team has been reaching financial close on the MOD Whitefleet Project for Lex. **Clients** Lex; Jarvis; Bouygues/Charterhouse; The Home Office/Partnerships UK; Connex.

SIMMONS & SIMMONS (see firm details p.1136) This is another firm renowned for its work for the MOD, and it also retains a strong reputation in the transport sector despite the problems of major client Railtrack. IT projects form a third string to the bow following recent recruitments, and the team has acted on government IT contracts for the Department of Health, Home Office and Cabinet Office. "*Good at client care,*" Richard Armitage (see p.694) retains a strong reputation amongst peers for his MOD work. A major highlight has been advising the MOD on the PPP of the Defence Evaluation and Research Agency. It is also co-advising the Greek Government and the Bank of America on the €4.9 billion PPP construction of six new motorways, and providing ongoing advice to the MOD on the £2.5 billion-plus Future Strategic Tanker Aircraft project. **Clients** MOD; Barclays Bank.

DLA The firm possesses a strong team with expertise in advising banks, consortia and public sector bodies on a range of issues related to PFI. Highlights include acting for AXA Investment Managers on the Wirral Schools project and representing West LB on the £70 million Highways Agency Traffic Control Centre. **Clients** Banks; consortia.

MAYER, BROWN, ROWE & MAW (see firm details p.1060) The firm is particularly noted for its work within the roads sector. Although Neil Morrison now works on a consultancy basis, "*effective deal-doer*" Joanne Anderson (see p.694) enters *Chambers*' rankings this year on the strength of warm client recommendations. Many in the market expect the recent merger with Mayer, Brown & Platt to bolster the finance and securitisation work of the practice. Highlights include advising Road Management Limited on the £200 million A1(M) Darrington to Dishforth DBFO Road Project. **Clients** Alfred McAlpine; AMEC; Brown & Root; Carillion.

SLAUGHTER AND MAY (see firm details p.1140) Noted as "*robust negotiators,*" the team is particularly respected for its involvment at the top end of the PFI market. Clients value the "*responsive attitude*" of these lawyers and their "*consistently high-quality advice,*" but some banks reported that this firm is "*a different beast - not a traditional PFI player.*" The team is acting for the EIB on the financing of the Thessaloniki Metro Project in Greece. Ian Goldie (see p.696) ("*a bold personality*") led the team that acted for the LINC Consortium in its bid to win the concessions to maintain and upgrade the BCV and SSL sections of the London Underground network. A further highlight was acting for the syndicate of banks financing the PFI project to refurbish and maintain the MOD's main building and other office facilities in Whitehall. **Clients** Chase Manhattan; Modus; LINC Consortium.

THEODORE GODDARD (see firm details p.1158) Praised to researchers for "*bringing a lot to the party,*" the team is "*competitive in terms of price*" and acts for a broad range of clients, in particular in the education, health and defence sectors. "*Hard-nosed negotiator*" James Ballingall (see p.694) does "*high-quality work while remaining customer-focused,*" according to interviewees. The team acted for Jarvis as successful bidder on the recently closed Jews Free School PFI project in Camden, as well as advising them as successful bidder on the Kirklees School Bundle, involving the construction and/or refurbishment of 20 schools. It also advised the Kier/Innisfree consortium on the West Berkshire NHS Trust PFI involving the first mental health PFI project to be signed. **Clients** National Audit Office; Jarvis Projects; Vosper Thornycroft; HBOS; Ballast; Bilfinger + Berger/MW Zander.

TROWERS & HAMLINS (see firm details p.1168) Its dominant position in the social housing market sees this firm involved in a number of projects. Clients praised the team's ability to "*pull out all the stops*" while adopting a "*calm, non-confrontational approach.*" The team, which recently recruited John Holden Ross from Carillion Private Finance, acted for Dexia Public Finance Bank, the senior lender, on the Tendring Schools project. It is also acting for a consortium, including Kier Project Investment and Ashley Homes, as preferred bidder on a local authority project for neighbourhood resource centres. **Clients** Ryhurst; Dexia Public Finance Bank; Carillion.

OTHER NOTABLE PRACTITIONERS
Malcolm Austwick (see p.694) continues to make progress as head of projects at Beachcroft Wansbroughs. Noted for his specialism in public sector healthcare, his work base is expanding to include accommodation and social service projects. Barry Francis (see p.408) is now fully ensconced as head of projects at Pinsent Curtis Biddle. He led the growing young team advising University Hospitals Coventry and Warwickshire NHS Trust and Coventry Healthcare NHS Trust on their £300 million project.

THE SOUTH & WALES

PROJECTS/PFI
THE SOUTH & WALES

1 Bevan Ashford Bristol
2 Burges Salmon Bristol
　Eversheds Cardiff
3 Masons Bristol
　Morgan Cole Cardiff

LEADING INDIVIDUALS

1 HUGHES Stephen Bevan Ashford
2 EVANS Eric Eversheds
　WHITFIELD Stuart Bevan Ashford
3 VICKERS Cathryn Masons

This book is the product of 6,582 1/2 hour interviews. See p.7 for BMRB audit. Within each band, firms are listed alphabetically. See individuals' profiles p.694

BEVAN ASHFORD (see firm details p.869) Retaining pole position, clients acclaimed this group as "*proactive, with a commercial approach to negotiations.*" Peers agreed that these lawyers are "*easy to deal with.*" The group possesses a national reputation, and its increased level of instruction from bidder clients has bolstered its growing private sector reputation. Renowned for his work in the health sector, **Stephen Hughes** (see p.697) was credited with the successful development of the department: "*he has taken up the baton and run with it.*" He advised on the standard form documentation to implement the NHS Local Improvement Finance Trust (LIFT), through a joint venture between Partnerships UK and the Department of Health. **Stuart Whitfield** (see p.700) retained market commendation for his work in the defence sector. He advised the supporting bidding consortium on the £13 billion Future Strategic Tanker Aircraft. **Clients** Bank of Ireland; RBS; Wessex Water; Bovis Lend Lease; Rolls-Royce; AMEC; Vosper Thornycroft; Total FinaElf.

BURGES SALMON (see firm details p.894) Clients spoke of a "*customer-focused and responsive*" group. The team enjoys a weighty profile in the public sector, across the fields of transport and rail. A "*good pedigree with the MOD*" has seen the team advising on the multibillion pound Skynet 5 project, a PFI for the provision of secure military satellite communications. Mark Paterson is a key member of the team that has been appointed to act for London Fire Emergency Planning Authority on a PPP project to cover the development of 130 fire stations. Private sector work has also increased. The group is advising First on its bids for the LUAS-Dublin Light Rail PPP and the Manchester Metrolink Phase 3 project. **Clients** British Railways Board; London Fire & Emergency Planning Authority; MOD; University of Bristol; West Somerset District Council.

EVERSHEDS (see firm details p.949) Private and pubic sector bodies provide the lion's-share of instructions for the team, which is led by **Eric Evans** (see p.577). Specialising in planning and compliance work, he acted on the DBFO waste handling scheme for West Sussex County Council valued at £100 million. The team also acted for Newport Borough Council on the southern distributor road, a £65 million PFI scheme. Acting for Swansea University in relation to the energy infrastructure PFI adds the new dimension of energy to the group repertoire. A first has been secured this year with the PFI of a radiology department where equipment was supplied as well as the structure. **Clients** Wiltshire CC; Newport BC; West Sussex BC; Neath CBC; Impreglio.

MASONS (see firm details p.1057) The firm acts for bodies in the health, education and governmental sectors. "*Practical*" **Cathryn Vickers** heads the team. She specialises in facilities management contracts and led the team advising AMEY BPO Services in closing the Edinburgh Schools project. A further highlight has been the firm's advice to on the procurement and outsourcing of haemodialysis services at the St George's Hospital, Tooting and Roehampton Hospital sites. The group is also advising on the facilities management aspects of a bid in respect of the Manchester Children's Hospital Project, which has a capital value of £260 million. **Clients** Amey Business Services; Ballast.

MORGAN COLE (see firm details p.1075) Retaining the commendation of the marketplace, the team, led by Alun Cole, is "*always a pleasure to deal with*" according to peers. notable for niche schemes involving police stations. The team acted on the relocation of the Wales Maritime and Industrial Museum to the Swansea City Waterfront Development. **Clients** Associated Holdings; Wales Tourist Board; Luton & Dunstable NHS Trust.

MIDLANDS & EAST ANGLIA

PROJECTS/PFI
MIDLANDS & EAST ANGLIA

1 Eversheds Nottingham
　Pinsent Curtis Biddle Birmingham
　Wragge & Co Birmingham
2 DLA Birmingham
　Mills & Reeve Cambridge

LEADING INDIVIDUALS

1 MATTHEW Stephen Eversheds
　RANDLE Anthony DLA
2 PICKUP Raith Mills & Reeve
3 KENNY Stephen Wragge & Co
　WOODROW Cameron Pinsent Curtis Biddle

This book is the product of 6,582 1/2 hour interviews. See p.7 for BMRB audit. Within each band, firms are listed alphabetically. See individuals' profiles p.694

EVERSHEDS (see firm details p.949) This team is deemed by clients to have "*proved its worth*" by providing an "*excellent technical advice and good availability.*" Head of the National Projects group, **Stephen Matthew** (see p.697) is "*calm, considered and experienced,*" while clients reported that his knowledge of public sector matters ensures "*he can understand our perspective.*" Private sector work is also on the increase within this firm. Highlights for the group include acting for the Sussex Police Authority on the first PFI of custody units. It has also acted for Cornwall County Council on the refurbishment and construction of 30 fire stations. **Clients** Sussex Police Authority; MOD; South Durham Health Care NHS Trust; Department for Environment, Food & Rural Affairs.

PINSENT CURTIS BIDDLE (see firm details p.1102) The team operates on a cross-office basis, which has afforded it a strong national presence. The client roster has recently been bolstered by the addition of Carillion, Group 4 and Alfred McAlpine. Esteemed finance partner, Patrick Twist heads the team, which acted on the transfer of 86,000 houses for Birmingham City Council, and advised Carillion/Group 4 Consortium on two secure training centres in Warwickshire and Kent for the Youth Justice Board. **Cameron Woodrow** (see p.700) is acclaimed for his work in the utility sector. The group is also acting on the Islington, Manchester and Newcastle Street Lighting Projects. **Clients** Sunderland Housing Group; London Borough of Islington.

WRAGGE & CO (see firm details p.1197) Clients applauded "*a degree of legal expertise matched by a practical understanding of a commercial environment*" that is on offer at this firm. Rivals acknowledged "*a team of sensible practitioners we would refer work to.*" Led by **Stephen Kenny**, the team has built on the firm's superb reputation in construction, to focus on key areas. Defence, transport, infrastructure and local authorities are important sectors, while a profile in the waste sector is also coming to the fore. The team is acting for the MOD on a partnering PPP under the Government's Wider Markets Initiative. A further highlight is advis-

PROJECTS/PFI ■ THE NORTH

ing Bombardier Transportation on the phase 3 bid of the Manchester Metrolink PFI, with a project value in excess of £500 million, and on the London Underground PPP. **Clients** MOD; Bombardier; Derbyshire County Council; East London Waste Authority; AMEC; TRW; MJ Gleeson.

DLA Respected for its work in the transport sector, the ubiquitous **Tony Randle** (see p.699)

leads this team. A major highlight has been the team's advice for Vickers Specialist Engines on its award of a £200 million contract under a MOD PFI.

MILLS & REEVE (see firm details p.1071) The lead figure at the heart of this team remains **Raith Pickup** (see p.409) who is said to be "*a bright and personable guy.*" He led the team acting for the

University of Hertfordshire on the £60 million University of Hertfordshire Project. The deal was a Higher Education Funding Council's pathfinder project and involved a deal for 1,600 student residences and a sports facility. The team also represented the Ashwell Group, a private sector consortium, on a £35 million MOD housing project. **Clients** NHS Trusts; universities.

THE NORTH

PROJECTS/PFI
■ THE NORTH

1
- Addleshaw Booth & Co Leeds, Manchester
- Pinsent Curtis Biddle Leeds

2
- Dickinson Dees Newcastle upon Tyne

3
- DLA Leeds, Manchester
- Eversheds Leeds, Manchester
- Masons Leeds, Manchester

4
- Nabarro Nathanson Sheffield

LEADING INDIVIDUALS

1
- O'CONNOR Mike Addleshaw Booth & Co

2
- COCKRAM Richard Addleshaw Booth & Co
- FELLOWS Alison Dickinson Dees
- LOVITT Arthur Pinsent Curtis Biddle

3
- BAKER Huw Masons
- CARE Tim Dickinson Dees
- CIRELL Stephen Eversheds
- COOKE Ken Masons
- ROUT Peter DLA
- SUTTIE Frank Beachcroft Wansbroughs

This book is the product of 6,582 1/2 hour interviews. See p.7 for BMRB audit. Within each band, firms are listed alphabetically. See individuals' profiles p.694

ADDLESHAW BOOTH & CO (see firm details p.838) A strong team with a national focus, it acts for a broad public sector client base, and private sector providers and funders. The team has recently streamlined its practice with the resultant departure of Frank Suttie to Beachcroft Wansbroughs. Peers acclaimed the head of PFI/projects unit **Mike O'Connor** (see p.698) as one of the leading figures in the sector; "*his drafting is superb and his knowledge is second to none.*" He has led the team advising St Helens and Knowsley NHS Trust and Salford Royal Hospitals NHS Trust on two wave 4 NHS PFI projects with a combined capital value of £400 million. Construction partner **Richard Cockram** (see p.193) led the team acting for the Met Office (MOD) for the relocation of the Met Office Bracknell to Exeter under a PPP agreement. It has also acted for the Bray consortium on Project Aquitrine. **Clients** Jarvis; MOD; NHS Trusts; Met Office; Tameside MBC; Conwy Council; Eric Wright Group.

PINSENT CURTIS BIDDLE (see firm details p.1102) Clients lauded a team that "*provides excellent service,*" while rivals spoke of "*practical people, who are good to deal with on difficult projects.*" The team has extended its representation of funders and bidders, while continuing to advise on several of the fourth and fifth wave NHS schemes. Clients could "*not speak more highly of*" **Arthur Lovitt** (see p.697). He advised RBS on The University of Sheffield's outsourcing of all its student accommodation. The team is also advising University Hospital Birmingham and South Birmingham Mental Health on a £310 million new hospitals project, and is acting for the Department of Health on a £300 million payroll outsourcing. **Clients** RBS; Nationwide Building Society; Barclays; Bovis.

DICKINSON DEES (see firm details p.938) Hailed by clients for its "*excellent service with a reasonable fee structure,*" the team was applauded by peers for its approach that includes "*no point scoring.*" Multi-site educational projects, the health sector and local authority work were all seen as areas of major expertise for the team. Head of the firm's commercial group, **Alison Fellows** (see p.696) "*knows her stuff on specialist issues,*" having been seconded to the NHS Executive Private Finance Unit in Leeds. Facilities management specialist **Tim Care** (see p.695) received strong client and peer recommendation in the research. He is leading the team on the development of a new £35 million cancer centre at Belfast City Hospital. The group acted on 11 health PFU schemes including major hospital redevelopments in Newcastle, Leeds, Blackburn, Belfast and Wakefield. It also acted on three education projects in South Yorkshire and Tyne and Wear, including the £45 million Newcastle City Council grouped schools scheme for Focus Education. **Clients** Newcastle Hospitals NHS Trust; HM Prisons; Newcastle CC.

DLA This is a team that is deemed to have "*cornered the market*" in transport matters. **Peter Rout** in the Manchester office is "*a workaholic.*"

EVERSHEDS (see firm details p.949) This group is nationally renowned for its public sector expertise, and has continued to expand its level of instruction from funders. A major boost to the team has been its appointment to the MOD panel. Highlights include advising Leeds City Council on the grouped schools project. **Stephen Cirell** (see p.577) brings "*enormous gravitas*" to the team afforded by his local government expertise. Health and major waste procurements are an increasing area of instruction. The team has also received instructions on waste issues from Medway Council, Anglesey Council and Lancashire County Council. The past year has seen the completion of the PPP between Newcastle International Airport and Copenhagen Airport, relating to the disposal of a 49% interest in Newcastle International Airport and a partnership agreement for the provision of business and technical support services. **Clients** Leeds City Council; East Sussex CC.

MASONS (see firm details p.1057) Peers were impressed by the firm's "*breadth and depth,*" and the Leeds office was said to enjoy a loyal following in the market. The team has recently acted on projects in the fields of criminal justice and education. "*Personable*" **Huw Baker** (see p.191) was endorsed by interviewees for his construction expertise. **Ken Cooke** (see p.695) has advised the operating subcontractor on the Leeds 7 Schools Project. Highlights for the firm include acting for the preferred bidder (Mowlem Courts) on the £22 million provision of new service Crown Court accommodation in Ipswich and Cambridge. The team also advised the DTI on the reprocurement of its accounts function, as well as advising the successful contractor in two NHS PFI IT transactions. **Clients** Aqumen Services; John Mowlem & Company; ING Barings; Carillion Construction; Innisfree; DTI; IBA.

NABARRO NATHANSON (see firm details p.1080) The group is deemed to possess "*all the requisite skills in one responsive team.*" Clients also spoke of lawyers who give "*straight-dealing, balanced advice, recognising the parameters you are meant to work within.*" Undertaking an even spread of public and private sector work, the team's repertoire has now extended to outsourcing. This "*impressive bunch*" is led by Tim Shaw. It has advised Bank of Scotland on the provision of senior debt financing for the Great Western

SCOTLAND ■ PROJECTS/PFI

Hospital staff accommodation PFI, and advised Unite Group on the PPP for the outsourcing of The University of Sheffield's student residential accommodation. The team has also advised Mill Group/Norwich Union PPP Fund on the Newham Schools PFI scheme. **Clients** Sheffield City Council; East Riding of Yorkshire Council.

OTHER NOTABLE PRACTITIONERS Frank Suttie, formerly of Addleshaw Booth & Co, has joined the Leeds office of Beachcroft Wansbroughs. He was acclaimed by peers for his "*wealth of experience; he is a true projects expert.*"

SCOTLAND

PROJECTS/PFI — SCOTLAND

1. **Dundas & Wilson CS** Edinburgh, Glasgow
2. **MacRoberts** Edinburgh, Glasgow
   McGrigor Donald Edinburgh, Glasgow
3. **Shepherd+ Wedderburn** Edinburgh
4. **Maclay Murray & Spens** Glasgow
   Masons Glasgow
   McClure Naismith Edinburgh
   Tods Murray WS Edinburgh
5. **Burness** Edinburgh

LEADING INDIVIDUALS

1. **MURPHY Michael** MacRoberts
2. **MCAULEY Michael** Dundas & Wilson CS
   NASH David Shepherd+ Wedderburn
3. **BROWN Steven** McClure Naismith
   CAMPBELL Alan Dundas & Wilson CS
   GRAHAM Drysdale McGrigor Donald
   HENDERSON David MacRoberts
   MACAULAY Iain McGrigor Donald
   MCEWAN Alastair Maclay Murray & Spens
   MCPAKE Ian Tods Murray WS
   READ Anthony Burness
   SIMMONS William Tods Murray WS

UP AND COMING
   WATSON Michael McGrigor Donald

This book is the product of 6,582 1/2 hour interviews. See p.7 for BMRB audit. Within each band, firms are listed alphabetically. See individuals' profiles p.694

DUNDAS & WILSON CS (see firm details p.943) The firm derives a great advantage from its renowned expertise in the banking sector. Peers commended a "*first-class, professional team,*" which is "*easy to negotiate with.*" It has the capacity to handle a volume of instructions and caters for a mix of private and bidding sector work. The team enjoys good relationships with Gleeson and Ballast. Administering "*straightforward and sound advice,*" Michael McAuley led the team for Edinburgh City Council on its pooled schools project valued at £120 million. Head of department Alan Campbell is "*non-confrontational and efficient – he resolves issues calmly.*" He led the team for Newcourt Capital as senior and mezzanine lender and equity provider for the £50 million financing for the Fife Schools project. A key highlight for the firm has been its advice to the Treasury Solicitor's department on Dungavel House, Scotland's first detention centre for asylum-seekers. **Clients** Scottish Water; Bank of Scotland; Newcourt Capital; MJ Gleeson; Renfrewshire Council.

MACROBERTS (see firm details p.1049) Interviewees agreed that this team "*punches above its weight.*" Its projects reputation has been built upon the foundations of a respected construction base. The team acts for an even spread of public, private and banking sector clients, and is commended as "*excellent at the big infrastructure projects.*" Head of projects Michael Murphy (see p.698) is "*highly commercial and knows where clients' interests lie.*" He concentrates on banking issues and the drafting of project agreements. Projects, engineering and construction specialist David Henderson (see p.696) is valued by clients as "*a stickler for detail.*" The team completed Edinburgh Schools and the Glasgow Schools PPP Project for the Amey/Miller Consortium, which involved the building and refurbishment of 30 secondary schools in Glasgow and 16 in Edinburgh. The team also acted for RBS on a £90 million defence housing project in Bristol and on the £70 million Moray Coast Wastewater Project, and for Abbey National on the financing of the Dalkeith Schools project. It also advised HBOS on the financing of a schools PPP project in Bolton. **Clients** Amey; HBOS; AWG; Abbey National.

MCGRIGOR DONALD (see firm details p.1065) Acknowledged by the market for possessing "*a deep pool of experience,*" the team is recognised for its expertise in advising banks as both lenders and equity providers. It adopts a "*sensible approach*" when dealing with contractors. Public sector advice is dealt with out of the Glasgow office, while Edinburgh undertakes advice to private sector consortia and their funders. The "*dynamic team*" includes Drysdale Graham (see p.696). "*Astute and direct,*" he led the team that advised the Tricomm Housing consortium on the Defence Housing Executive Bristol, Bath, and Portsmouth accommodation project. He also advised the NewSchools consortium on the Swanscombe Schools PFI project. Michael Watson (see p.700) was commended by sources as "*pragmatic – he understands the way banks work.*" He led the team advising Bank of Scotland and the EIB on the Edinburgh Schools PPP project. Banking partner Iain Macaulay (see p.697) represented Halifax on the Scottish aspects of the funding of the Glasgow Schools PPP. **Clients** MBIA Assurance; Royal Bank of Scotland.

SHEPHERD+ WEDDERBURN (see firm details p.1130) This team "*possesses great presence and really understands PFI.*" Peers also appreciated its user-friendly manner. Its reappointment to the MOD's panel is reaping dividends, while strong connections with the Scottish Executive also provide a rich seam of work. The "*fantastic*" David Nash (see p.698) "*has a great mind and understands the bigger picture.*" He led the team for ScottishPower on outsourcing matters. In a major highlight, the firm was acting on the Heavy Equipment Transporter pathfinder project for the MOD. The group also represented the Pinnacle Schools consortium, comprising Sir Robert McAlpine, Sodexho and Newcourt Capital, on the Fife Schools Project for the provision of three new build schools under the PPP banner. **Clients** MOD; Angus Council; East Renfrewshire Council.

MACLAY MURRAY & SPENS (see firm details p.1048) "*A good banking and bidding capability*" has held the firm in good stead, securing it some innovative PFI deals this year. A healthy proportion of its work is based south of the border. Head of department Alastair McEwan (see p.698) was endorsed by interviewees as "*pragmatic and commercially aware.*" He advised the Noble PFI Fund in its acquisition of Edison Capital's UK PFI investment portfolio of 14 projects, and advised on the subsequent restructuring of Noble Group's PFI investments. The capital value of the transaction was £460 million. The team also acted as Scottish legal advisors to the North Of Scotland Water Authority on the £60 million Moray Coast Wastewater Project. **Clients** Lloyds TSB Bank; Nationwide Building Society; Robertson Group (Scotland); Noble Group; Bank of Ireland.

MASONS (see firm details p.1057) This is praised as "*a quality outfit*" enjoying a "*big reputation.*" The firm is said to have made major inroads into the education, transport and health arenas. The work here ranges across Scotland to Ireland and England. Alastair Morrison is the point of contact based in the firm's Glasgow office. Highlights for the group include advising MJ Gleeson in relation to all work arising from the West of Scotland Water Authority £100 million design/construct water project at Loch Katrine. It also advised a bidder on the design, construction, operation and maintenance of the M77. The team has acted for a bidder on a shortlist for the extension of the existing Docklands Light Railway. **Clients** MJ Gleeson Group; AMEC Project Investments; Royal Bank of Scotland.

MCCLURE NAISMITH (see firm details p.1062) The firm is rated for its expertise in the

PROJECTS/PFI ■ THE LEADERS

health sector, and it enjoys a close relationship with key NHS Trusts. The team caters for both private and public sector instructions. Head of projects **Steven Brown** (see p.695) leads a multi-disciplinary team. He was commended by peers for his abilities as "*a tenacious negotiator.*" The team supported bidder clients in a range of projects in health, law and order and schools, and advised public sector clients in continuing procurements in health and law and order. A further highlight was achieving financial close on the Redcar & Cleveland Office Accommodation PFI. **Clients** HBG Construction; Robertson Group; Melville Dundas.

TODS MURRAY WS (see firm details p.1164) Clients valued this group highly: it provides an "*equally good if not better than City service.*" The firm conducts work on a national basis for private sector bidders and funders. Balfour Beatty is also an important client for the team. **Ian McPake** (see p.698) was commended for being "*a driven practitioner and a good project manager.*"

BURNESS Clients praised the firm as one that is "*proactive and makes things happen.*" A good mix of experience in public sector matters, construction and finance is enjoyed by the team, exemplified by the broad practice of **Anthony Read**. The group advised the BBC on its £70 million PPP to build a new Scottish HQ. Nederlands Engelse Water Services was represented by the group on the first privately financed waste water project in the Netherlands. **Clients** Ballast; Bank of Scotland; Jarvis; Shanks Group; BBC; Yorkshire Water Services.

THE LEADERS IN PROJECTS/PFI

ANDERSON, Joanne
Mayer, Brown, Rowe & Maw, London
(020) 7782 8697
janderson@eu.mayermayerbrownrowe.com
Specialisation: Expertise in acting on all aspects of PPP/PFI projects, advising with public and private sectors from the early stages through to and beyond financial close.
Career: Qualified in 1991; partner *Rowe & Maw* 2000.
Publications: Bristol University (BSc Hons). Reading and keeping fit.

ARMITAGE, Richard
Simmons & Simmons, London
(020) 7628 2020
richard.armitage@simmons-simmons.com
Specialisation: Partner specialising in PFI/PPP projects, privatisations and other transactions between the public and private sectors. Has particular experience of the defence sector, including the contractorisations of the Royal Dockyards and the Atomic Weapons Establishment, the privatisation of Devonport Royal Dockyard, the DERA PPP and PFI projects, such as the pathfinder Medium Support Helicopter Training Facility Project, and the Future Strategic Tanker Aircraft Project, the largest defence PFI project. He also advises on a wide range of commercial transactions such as partnering, facilities management and outsourcing contracts.
Career: Articled *Simmons & Simmons*, qualified 1982, partner since 1987
Publications: Author of the defence section of the 'Butterworth's PFI Manual'.

AUSTWICK, Malcolm
Beachcroft Wansbroughs, London
(020) 7894 6504
maustwick@bwlaw.co.uk
Specialisation: Projects work for both public and private sector. Concentrates mainly on health sector. Acted for Taylor Woodrow/Innisfree Consortium on the third PFI hospital scheme to achieve financial close with the South Buckinghamshire NHS Trust. Since then has led *BW* teams on a number of PFI deals including: acting for Dudley Group of Hospital NHS Trust on the largest PFI hospital scheme to date to adapt the standard form contract and now seen as a benchmark for subsequent health schemes; acting for the Kier/Tilbury Douglas/Charterhouse Consortium on the largest hopsital PFI scheme in Wales at Neath/Port Talbot. Was also instrumental in bringing Hereford Hospitals NHS Trust PFI scheme to financial close and a member of the *BW* team which closed the pathfinder school and office scheme for Pembroke County Council. Currently leading teams acting for both private and public sector clients in the health and MoD sectors as well as leading the *Beachcroft Wansbroughs* Projects Department.
Prof. Memberships: Law Society; PPP Forum, IPFA.
Career: Qualified: 1983, *Beachcroft Hyman Isaacs*. 1988, Partner *Beachcroft Stanleys* (now *Beachcroft Wansbroughs*).
Personal: LLB, Exeter University. Reliving childhood dreams on the touchline and other family pursuits. Married with three children.

BAKER, Huw
Masons, Manchester
(0161) 234 8357
huw.baker@masons.com
See under Construction, p.191

BALDOCK, Anne
Allen & Overy, London
(020) 7330 3000
anne.baldock@allenovery.com
Specialisation: Partner in the finance area of *Allen & Overy*, specialising in project, acquisition and structured finance; acting in equal part for banks, borrowers and multilateral agencies; her work includes major PPP projects in the UK and abroad, cross-border leveraged buyouts and major tax and structured financings.
Career: Articled at *Allen & Overy*; qualified 1984; partner 1990. Secondment with major US bank 1986-88.
Personal: London School Economics (1980 LLB).

BALLINGALL, James
Theodore Goddard, London
(020) 7606 8855
jamesballingall@theodoregoddard.co.uk
Specialisation: Head of PFI and Asset Finance Teams. Has led the teams on numerous hospital, schools, further education, colleges, prison, police and railway projects. Has also advised the National Audit Office on their review of nine PFI projects to date. Acts for both banks and consortia. Background in asset finance and banking. Other project finance work includes Euro Tunnel, BSB, Lakeside Thurrock Shopping Centre, and a major cementation project. Specialises in structured finance and lease work, particularly in the transportation field, having set up *Theodore Goddard's* Railways Group.
Prof. Memberships: Law Society, FRGS.
Career: Born 1958. Educated: Eastbourne College, Cambridge (Emanuel). Qualified 1984.
Personal: Interests include hiking, cycling, squash, piano, writing (wrote 'A Taste of China', published John Murrays 1984), carpentry.

BARRATT, Jeffery
Norton Rose, London
(020) 7283 6000
barrattjvc@nortonrose.com
Specialisation: Partner, head of global projects group. All areas of banking, financing and capital markets debt instruments, in particular project related financings. Involved in many complex infrastructure and other project financings in the UK and worldwide, acting for banks, sponsors, project companies, export credit agencies and multilateral agencies. On the editorial board of Butterworths 'Financial Law and Practice'.
Career: Qualified 1973, joined *Norton Rose* 1976, partner 1979. Established and ran Bahrain office 1979-82. Training partner 1987-91. Headed South East Asian project finance group, based in Hong Kong 1993-95. Chairman Partnership committee 1997 to date.

BECKITT, Jonathan
CMS Cameron McKenna, London
(020) 7367 2113
jonathan.beckitt@cmck.com
Specialisation: Jonathan is a partner in the energy, projects and construction group specialising in accomodation based PPP/PFI projects. Jonathan's recent transactions include advising Surrey Elderly Services, advising Surrey County Council on the externalisation of six residential care homes for the elderly; Tendring Schools PPP project, advising the sponsors and senior lenders in relation to this project for the refurbishment of 12 primary schools in Essex; advising the senior lenders in relation to 4 PFI projects: Cornwall Fire Station, Portsmouth Social Services, Bromley Hospitals Equipment and Brighton and Hove Schools; Channel Tunnel Rail Link, leader of the team advising the Department for Transport.
Career: Admitted 1984. Joined the firm in 1982 and in addition to London, has practised in the Far East and Japan, where he was the resident partner in the firm's Tokyo office from October 1991 to June 1994. Since 1994 he has been a partner in the London office.
Personal: LLB at Bristol (graduated 1981); solicitor of the Supreme Court of England and Wales (1984); licensed foreign lawyer in Japan (1991).

BELLHOUSE, John
White & Case, London
(020) 7397 3605
jbellhouse@whitecase.com
Specialisation: Partner specialising in all aspects of major infrastructure projects including project appraisal; project document drafting and negotiation; post contract advice and dispute resolution. In addition to appearing as counsel in arbitrations, he also sits as an arbitrator and on Dispute Review Boards.
Prof. Memberships: Law Society of England & Wales
Career: Partner *McKenna & Co* (London and Hong Kong) 1976-94; partner *White & Case* 1994 to date. Admitted as a solicitor in England and Wales and Hong Kong.
Personal: Born 1946. Resides London.

BICKERTON, David
Clifford Chance, London
(020) 7600 1000
david.bickerton@cliffordchance.com

BLACK, Alan
Linklaters, London
(020) 7456 5948
alan.black@linklaters.com
Specialisation: Main area of practice is

THE LEADERS — PROJECTS/PFI

international projects. Extensive experience of acting for governments, sponsors and lenders on major projects for transport, airports and aviation, oil, gas, and derivative products, and projects involving concessions granted by governments to private developers in both civil law and common law countries.
Career: 1973 Kings College, London LLB. 1974, College of Law, Guildford, Law Society Final Examinations. 1976, articled *Linklaters*, 1976-79, Assistant Solicitor, *Linklaters* London; 1979-81, Assistant Solicitor, *Linklaters* Paris; 1981-83, Assistant Solicitor, *Linklaters* London; 1983 to date, Partner *Linklaters*, 1984-91, Partner, *Linklaters* Hong Kong; 1991 to date, Partner London; 1993 to date, Head of Projects.

BLAKE, Peter
Clifford Chance, London
(020) 7600 1000
peter.blake@cliffordchance.com
See under Energy, p.341

BLISS, Nick
Freshfields Bruckhaus Deringer, London
(020) 7936 4000
nicholas.bliss@freshfields.com
Specialisation: Project finance and PFI/PPP. Acted for Road Management Group in the (March 1996) A1(M) and A419/A417 DBFO Road Projects: the first UK monoline insured eurobond infrastructure financing and, subsequently, the M6 DBFO Road monoline insured eurobond infrastructure financing, acting for FSA the monoline insurer. In June 1999 completed the first eurobond financing of a multi-project Programme (Investors Finance). Acted for Paradigm in the secure milsatcom Skynet 5 programme, and for TTSC in the future strategic Tanker Aircraft programme - the two largest MoD equipment procurements under PFI/PPP.
Prof. Memberships: Law Society.
Career: Corpus Christi College, Cambridge.

BROWN, Chris
Masons, London
(020) 7490 4000
chris.brown@masons.com
Specialisation: Head of projects and finance group. Specialises in major infrastructure projects, including advising and negotiating on funding and concession contracts as well as leading the project management of legal input. He also advises on a wide range of domestic and cross-border debt transactions, asset finance, leasing, capital markets and infrastructure finance.
Prof. Memberships: Qualified solicitor in England, Wales and Scotland.
Career: Having qualified in Scotland in 1986 he moved to London. In 1996 he moved to *Masons* as a partner in the projects and finance group. Became head of the group in 1999.
Personal: Born 30 April 1958. Graduated from University of Edinburgh with MA Hons in Economics in 1981 and LLB in 1983. Part time tutor in economics at the Universities of Edinburgh and Cape Town.

BROWN, Steven
McClure Naismith, Edinburgh
(0131) 220 1002
sbrown@mcclurenaismith.com
Specialisation: Project finance and PFI. Advises public sector, private sector consortia and banks. Practice covers many PFI sectors and holds overseas appointments on BOO/BOT schemes in power generation, water and sewerage. Represented NHS Trusts or consortia in a range of early major PFI projects in health and education, throughout the UK. Currently advising on a range of projects in health, education, law and order, local authority and transport.
Prof. Memberships: Society of Writers to HM Signet, Law Society of Scotland.
Career: Qualified in 1980. Partner in *McClure Naismith* since 1986, now head of projects group.
Personal: Born 20 November 1956. Educated at Irvine Royal Academy 1969-74, University of Edinburgh 1974-78. Lives near Edinburgh. Leisure pursuits include family, computers, music, golf. Past chairman of a charity for adults with learning difficulties.

BUCKWORTH, Nicholas
Shearman & Sterling, London
(020) 7655 5000

CAMPBELL, Alan
Dundas & Wilson CS, Edinburgh
(0131) 228 8000

CARE, Tim
Dickinson Dees, Newcastle upon Tyne
(0191) 279 9259
tim.care@dickinson-dees.com
Specialisation: PFI/Projects. In past year advised several NHS Trusts on PFI schemes and advised Newcastle City Council on their successful grouped schools project.
Career: Trained in London and worked for three years in the specialist finance group at *Freshfields*. Joined *Dickinson Dees* in 1988 and became a partners in 1990. Became head of the Projects Group in 2000.
Personal: Music, especially amateur musicals (performing). Married to Alison, a fellow PFI lawyer, with two children.

CIRELL, Stephen
Eversheds, Leeds
(0113) 243 0391
stephencirell@eversheds.com
See under Local Government, p.577

COCKRAM, Richard
Addleshaw Booth & Co, Leeds
(0113) 209 2000
richard.cockram@addleshawbooth.com
See under Construction, p.193

COOKE, Ken
Masons, Leeds
(0113) 233 8905
ken.cooke@masons.com
Specialisation: Specialises in major projects including PFI. Recent work includes projects in the fields of criminal justice and education. Also specialises in information and technology, including outsourcing projects for financial institutions and has recently advised the DTI on business services procurement.
Prof. Memberships: Law Society.
Career: Fellowship, University of York 1977-87. Qualified 1989 after training at *DLA*. Solicitor, *DLA* to 1994, partner in *Masons* 1998.
Publications: Co-editor of the 'Facilities Management Legal Update', a specialist legal journal for facilities managers.
Personal: MA, DPhil University of York.

COULTER, David
Norton Rose, London
(020) 7283 6000
coulterdx@nortonrose.com
Specialisation: Project finance, PFI, asset finance, public sector finance and banking – PFI projects in last year have included MoD Strategic Airlift PFI Project involving G R.R. Ferries; MoD Warship Support Agencies Maritime Services, PFI project involving 9 vessels; Islington, Newham, Camden and Reading HRA Housing PFI Projects; Eden Project; National Physical Laboratory; London underground sub-surface and JNP Deeplines Projects; National Air Traffic Services; Northlink (Orkney and Shetlands) Ferries Project.
Prof. Memberships: Law Society, Law Society of Scotland, City of London Solicitors Company.
Career: Mainholm Academy, Ayr to 1979; Edinburgh University LLB (1984), DIPLP (1985). Admitted Scotland (1986); Notary Public (Scotland) (1986); admitted England and Wales (1989).
Personal: Sailing, hill walking and travel. Married (Catriona Rose) – one daughter, Fiona, one son, Alasdair.

CRANE, David
Norton Rose, London
(020) 7283 6000
cranedr@nortonrose.com
Specialisation: Partner in the projects group, specialising in project finance and asset finance. He also handles general commercial work. He has advised on numerous major plant leasing transactions, on sales of leasing companies as well as other company acquisitions and joint ventures. He also has considerable experience of public sector financing, particularly relating to local authorities.
Prof. Memberships: Law Society.
Career: Articled at *Norton Rose*. Qualified 1975. Partner since 1985.

DARLEY, Mark
Skadden, Arps, Slate, Meagher & Flom LLP, London
(020) 7519 7160
mdarely@skadden.com
Specialisation: All forms of structured, limited recourse and acquisition finance, including projects, receivables, acquisitions and bid financing both in the UK and overseas. Recent transactions include advising on the financing for the Rome airport privatisation, bid financing for listed companies in Europe, private equity transactions in Europe and other leveraged acquisition financing.
Prof. Memberships: The Law Society.
Career: Bradford Grammar School and Manchester University (1983 LLB Hons). Qualified 1986. Partner at *Lovells* 1996 in the Banking and Project Finance Group. In April 2002, joined *Skadden, Arps, Slate, Meagher & Flom LLP* as a partner in the Banking Group.
Personal: Born 29 January 1961; resides London. Leisure interests include shooting and fishing.

DUFFICY, Frank
CMS Cameron McKenna, London
(020) 7367 2904
frank.dufficy@cmck.com
Specialisation: Frank Dufficy is a partner in the project finance group, with extensive experience of advising consortia on all legal aspects of PFI projects, including finance, design, construction, operation and maintenance, within the UK and overseas. In addition he is frequently appointed to manage and lead teams of lawyers highly experienced in the various aspects of PFI work. He has advised on a variety of projects in the defence, health, education, other accommodation and transport sectors in the UK. Frank has also advised on the development, financing, construction and operation of tolled motorways and power projects overseas. He is currently advising project company/sponsors on the Health and Safety Laboratory PFI, the Exeter Courts PFI, Walsgrave and Havering Hospitals PFIs and the A1 Darrington-Dishforth section. He has also advised in respect of infrastructure project financing in other countries, advised the Hungarian Government on the M1/M15; the M5 and M7 roads projects and advised the private sector on the Croatian toll motorway, Ron Brown Highway.
Prof. Memberships: The Law Society, City of London Solicitors Company.
Career: 1981-83; articled clerk - *Linklaters & Paines*. 1983-89; solicitor - *Linklaters & Paines*. 1990 to date; partner, *CMS Cameron McKenna*.
Personal: Education: St Michael's Prep School. St Michael's College. North Carolina State University; BA Political Science. City University; Diploma in Laws. College of Law; Law Society Finals. Leisure Interests: Diving (Olympic Competitor - Munich 1972, British Team 1969-75 inclusive), sailing, skiing, fell walking, shooting, tennis, fishing, golf. Family Details: Married to Alison with three children, Georgia, Jack and Thomas.

ELLIS, Jon
Norton Rose, London
(020) 7283 6000
ellisjh@nortonrose.com
Specialisation: Projects work, acting for

PROJECTS/PFI ■ THE LEADERS

banks, project companies, export credit agencies and multilateral agencies on various types of projects in the UK and internationally.

ELSEY, Mark
Ashurst Morris Crisp, London
(020) 7638 1111
mark.elsey@ashursts.com
Specialisation: Acting for governments, sponsors, contractors and lenders in relation to UK and international infrastructure and energy projects, including PFI/PPP projects. Head of the firm's projects group.

EVANS, Eric
Eversheds, Cardiff
(029) 2047 1147
See under Local Government, p.577

FELLOWS, Alison
Dickinson Dees, Newcastle upon Tyne
(0191) 279 9289
law@dickinson-dees.com
Specialisation: PFI projects. Lead partner acting for Carlisle Hospital NHS Trust on PFI project for the redevelopment of the Cumberland Infirmary, followed by six months secondment to Private Finance Unit of NHS Executive to assist with ongoing projects. Now acting on several further major NHS projects including the Newcastle Hospitals NHS Trust Strategic Review PFI, the Leeds Teaching Hospitals PFI project for St James' Hospital in Leeds, and the Mid Yorkshire Hospitals PFI projects for hospitals in Wakefield and Pontefract.
Career: Cambridge University 1980-83. *Field Fisher Waterhouse* 1985-88. *Dickinson Dees* 1988 to date. Married to Tim Care, also a partner at *Dickinson Dees*, two children.

FINLAY, Peter
White & Case, London
(020) 7397 3603
pfinlay@whitecase.com
Specialisation: Has a unique range of international project finance and M&A law expertise, focusing particularly on the energy sector.
Prof. Memberships: Law Society of England & Wales, Irish solicitor, New York Bar. French Avocat.
Career: Partner, *White & Case* London. Member of the firm's world-wide management board.

FLETCHER, Phillip
Milbank, Tweed, Hadley & McCloy, London
(020) 7448 3000
pfletcher@milbank.com
Specialisation: Leader of the firm's project finance group in London. Specialising in the development and financing of major infrastructure projects, including power plants, industrial facilities, pipelines, roads and satellites; including: Arianespace satellite financing, France; the Yanpet petrochemicals project, Saudi Arabia; the BGT LNG vessel project, Nigeria; the Birecik and Marmara Ereglisi power projects, Turkey; the Taweelah A1 power project, Abu Dhabi;

the Tapada power project, Portugal; the Jawa power project, Indonesia; the Yemen LNG project; the Medway, Shoreham and Drax power projects, UK; the Hvalfjordour Tunnel, Iceland; the Centro Energia, Ferrara, Serene, Lomellina and Rosen power projects, Italy.
Career: Has been with *Milbank, Tweed* since 1983 and was resident in the firm's Hong Kong office in 1987 and 1988.
Personal: Born 1957. Educated at Georgetown University School of Foreign Service (BS, 1979), Fletcher School of Law & Diplomacy (MA, 1983) and the University of California, Berkeley (JD, 1983).

FOX, Jason
Herbert Smith, London
(020) 7374 8000
jason.fox@herbertsmith.com
Specialisation: Partner, projects group. Advising the public sector, corporates and banks on all aspects of the structuring, development and financing of projects in a variety of sectors including oil and gas, power, water, property and public infrastructure. Main areas of practice are advising on PFI projects and oil, gas and power projects.
Career: Qualified in 1987 with *Herbert Smith* and became a partner in 1994. Seconded to the Private Finance Panel Executive February to September 1994.
Publications: Author (jointly with Nicholas Tott) of 'The Private Finance Initiative Handbook' (Jordans, December 1998).

FRANCIS, Barry
Pinsent Curtis Biddle, London
(020) 7418 7340
barry.francis@pinsents.com
See under Healthcare, p.408

GAINES, Peter
Vinson & Elkins LLP, London
(020) 7065 6039
pgaines@velaw.com
Specialisation: Peter Gaines, a partner, has extensive experience in project, acquisition, and structured finance, representing a wide array of international banks and financial institutions, as well as project sponsors. He has been included in the Euromoney Guides to the 'World's Leading Banking Lawyers', in the 'World's Leading Project Finance Lawyers', in 'Chambers Global – The World's Leading Lawyers' (described therein as "somebody you'd want on your side of the table"), and in Law Business Research's 2002 directory entitled 'An International Who's Who of Business Lawyers'. Peter was a member of the Privatisation International 2000 Legal Team of the Year.
Prof. Memberships: American Bar Association; International Bar Association.
Career: Qualified 1975 (Illinois); 1988 (New York); associate *Mayer, Brown & Platt*, Chicago 1975-81; partner *Mayer, Brown & Platt*, Chicago 1981-90; partner *Mayer, Brown & Platt*, London 1990-95; partner *Baker & McKenzie* 1995-2001;

partner *Vinson & Elkins* LLP 2001-present.
Publications: Peter contributes a variety of project finance articles to various publications.
Personal: Education: Peter has a BA from the University of Wisconsin (1972) and a JD from the University of Wisconsin Law School (1975). He was admitted to the Illinois Bar in 1975 and to the New York Bar in 1978. Born 1951 and resides in London.

GATES, Ellen
Denton Wilde Sapte, London
(020) 7242 1212

GILLESPIE, Stephen
Allen & Overy, London
(020) 7330 3000
stephen.gillespie@allenovery.com
See under Banking & Finance, p.105

GNIADKOWSKI, Stan
Denton Wilde Sapte, London
(020) 7246 7000

GOLDIE, Ian
Slaughter and May, London
(020) 7090 3113
ian.goldie@slaughterandmay.com
Specialisation: Energy and natural resources; infrastructure and PFI/PPP projects. Recent projects include: 2000 – London Underground PPP Project, HSL Zuid IP Project (The Netherlands), National Air Traffic Services PPP.
Prof. Memberships: Section on Energy and Natural Resources, International Bar Association; Institute of Petroleum.
Personal: Jesus College, Cambridge; BA, MA.

GOSSLING, Margaret
Clifford Chance, London
(020) 7600 1000
margaret.gossling@cliffordchance.com
Specialisation: Banking and Finance Department. Specialises in international project finance (especially power, oil, gas and natural resources), restructurings and bank mergers.
Career: Articled *Coward Chance*; qualified 1986; Partner since 1993.
Personal: 1980-83 St Anne's College, Oxford (MA Hons).

GRAHAM, Drysdale
McGrigor Donald, Edinburgh
(0131) 777 7070
drysdale.graham@mcgrigors.com
Specialisation: Partner in Projects Unit. Specialises in capital projects/PFI work, although has broad experience of corporate finance and general corporate work. Recent projects experience includes advising the NewSchools consortium on the Swanscombe and Merton Schools Projects, the Tricomm consortium on the Defence Housing Executive Bristol, Bath and Portsmouth Service Family Accommodation Project and the Scottish Ministers on the Digital Scotland Broadband Project. Currently working on various projects in the roads, schools, accommodation and street lighting sectors.

Prof. Memberships: Law Society of Scotland; Law Society of England and Wales; the Society of Writers to Her Majesty's Signet; Notary Public.
Career: Trained *Biggart Baillie*; qualified Scotland 1982; qualified England and Wales 1990; corporate department *Dundas & Wilson* 1982-84; company department *McGrigor Donald* 1984-87; manager corporate department *Freshfields*, London 1987-91; rejoined *McGrigor Donald*, London office for 18 months; returned to Scotland to become a partner in Edinburgh office 1992.
Personal: Born 1958; resides Edinburgh. Leisure interests include theatre, music, golf, gardening.

HALL, Peter
Norton Rose, London
(020) 7283 6000
hallpm@nortonrose.com
Specialisation: A partner in the construction and engineering group with considerable experience of infrastructure projects around the world, including PFI/PPP transactions. Currently acting for both commercial lenders and sponsors on a number of independent power projects and rail projects in the UK and overseas. Contentious work encompasses High Court and international arbitration claims.
Prof. Memberships: Member of the Technology and Construction Court Solicitors Association, an accredited adjudicator and an associate of the Chartered Institute of Arbitrators.

HARRISON, Brian
Allen & Overy, London
(020) 7330 3000
brian.harrison@allenovery.com
Specialisation: Senior partner in *Allen & Overy's* highly regarded international projects practice. Specialises in banking, project finance and telecommunications.
Career: Qualified New Zealand 1976, England 1985; assistant solicitor, *Johnson Stokes & Master*, Hong Kong 1980-83; assistant solicitor *Allen & Overy*, London and Dubai 1983-85; Partner New York and London 1987.
Personal: Born 1953. Auckland University (1975, LLB).

HENDERSON, David
MacRoberts, Glasgow
(0141) 332 9988
david.henderson@macroberts.com
Specialisation: Partner specialising in PPP/PFI projects and non-contentious construction.
Career: Qualified in 1979, having joined *MacRoberts* in 1977. Became partner in 1983.
Publications: Co-author of 'MacRoberts on Scottish Building Contracts' and contributor to Butterworths 'PFI Manual'; co-editor of 'Scottish Construction Law Review'.
Personal: Born 18 July 1955. Educated at Kilmarnock Academy and Edinburgh University.

THE LEADERS — PROJECTS/PFI

HUGHES, Stephen
Bevan Ashford, Bristol
(0117) 975 1612
steve.hughes@bevanashford.co.uk
Specialisation: Partner in the Commercial Department and Head of the firm's Built Environment Division specialises in PFI and projects in the health sector, working for the public and private sectors. Is recognised by 'Legal Business Magazine' as one of the leading regional PFI advisors in the UK and in January 2002 was named by a leading legal publication as one of its Top 100 lawyers in the country. Examples of recent work include advising Partnerships for Health (a joint venture of Partnerships UK and the Department of Health) on NHS LIFT, an initiative to invest over £1 billion into new primary healthcare facilities. Acting as lead partner on three of the 4th Wave acute PFIs Lewisham, Maidstone and Tunbridge Wells and Avon Mental Health Projects.
Prof. Memberships: Faculty of Building, Society of Construction Law.
Career: *Bevan Ashford* (partner 1993).

HUMPHREY, Tony
Allen & Overy, London
(020) 7330 3000
tony.humphrey@allenovery.com
See under Banking & Finance, p.106

HUNJAN, Ranbir
Clifford Chance, London
(020) 7600 1000
Specialisation: Partner specialising in banking, asset finance, project finance and leasing.
Career: Articled *Clifford Chance* 1990-92; qualified 1992; *Clifford Chance* Tokyo 1995-97; Partner since 2001.
Personal: University of Reading (LLB Hons) 1986-89; College of Law, Guildford 1989-90.

IVISON, Andrew
CMS Cameron McKenna, London
(020) 7367 3410
andrew.ivison@cmck.com
Specialisation: Project finance and banking partner, advising on major infrastructure, utilities, acquisition and development projects in the United Kingdom and overseas. Recent examples of major projects include the NATS Air Traffic Services PPP, the London Underground PPP and the financing of Section 2 of the Channel Tunnel Rail Link.
Career: Partner at *CMS Cameron McKenna* since 1987. Admitted as a solicitor in 1980.

JOHNSTON, Bruce
LeBoeuf, Lamb, Greene & MacRae, London
(020) 7459 5000

KENNY, Stephen
Wragge & Co, Birmingham
(0870) 903 1000

LEE, David P
Allen & Overy, London
(020) 7330 3000
david.lee@allenovery.com

Specialisation: Specialised in public-private partnerships since the PFI started and has acted for banks, project companies and the public sector. In particular has acted for banks on Bridgend Prison, the project company on Lowdham Group Prison, the financiers on the Channel Tunnel Rail Link and Docklands Light Railway as well as many other projects. International projects include the Istrian Toll Road in Croatia. In 1997, recruited to the Treasury Taskforce HM Treasury and worked on project across all PFI sectors and was the principal author of 'Treasury Taskforce - Standardisation of PFI Contracts' (1999).
Career: Associate *Allen & Overy* (1992-98), Partner (1998).
Personal: Pembroke College, Oxford (1988, MA) (1990, BCL). Born 1966.

LOVITT, Arthur
Pinsent Curtis Biddle, Leeds
(0113) 244 5000
arthur.lovitt@pinsents.com
Specialisation: Partner in property department and major projects team. Involved in significant property developments including a major business park in Rochdale for Wilson Bowden which closed in June 2002. PFI and Public Sector Partnership work includes: representing, as lead partner, North Durham Acute Hospitals NHS Trust on their PFI scheme; Royal Bank of Scotland plc on £47m major pathfinder community health PFI scheme in Leeds. In 2001 he led the teams advising Royal Bank of Scotland plc on two school schemes at Caerphilly and Fleetwood which closed in April and May respectively. He also led the team advising the MoD on new housing scheme at Wattisham which closed in May. He is currently working on various health, housing and student accommodation PFI schemes.
Prof. Memberships: Round Table (former chairman of Leeds Round Table), Institute of Directors.
Career: Bradford Grammar School and Nottingham University (LLB 2:1). Qualified with *Daynes Hill & Perks* (now *Eversheds*) in Norwich. Three years in commercial property department of *Linklaters & Paines*. Joined *Pinsent Curtis Biddle* in 1990. Partner in 1994.

LUCAS, Richard
Berwin Leighton Paisner, London
(020) 7760 4886
richard.lucas@blplaw.com
Specialisation: Private Finance Initiative and rail industry work normally acting for contractors and operators. Has been heavily involved in PFI since 1996 and since then he has led deals which have reached financial close in the defence (Strategic Sealift Project), education (Haringey Schools, Richmond Schools) and healthcare (King's Hospital, Denmark Hill) sectors. Has worked in the rail industry since privatisation and currently advises a range of operators, rolling stock leasing companies and track maintenance and renewal companies.

Recent deals include: advising AWSR Shipping Limited on the £950m Strategic Sealift Service PFI Project with the Ministry of Defence (closed June 2002); advising Jarvis plc on the Richmond upon Thames Primary School PFI Project (closed June 2002); advising a Connex/Bombardier joint venture company on a range of regulated depot access and maintenance agreements relating to the new Connex fleet (closed May 2002).
Career: *Lee, Bolton & Lee* 1988-90, articled clerk; *Dibb Lupton Alsop* 1990-98, associate; *Berwin Leighton* (now *Berwin Leighton Paisner*) 1998-date, partner.
Publications: Recent articles include 'Getting Rolling Stock onto the Network' in Railway Strategies (December 2001).
Personal: Education: Pocklington School, Pocklington, York. Married with two children, resides in London.

MACAULAY, Iain
McGrigor Donald, Glasgow
(0141) 248 6677
iain.macaulay@mcgrigors.com
Specialisation: Partner active in all areas of corporate and retail banking. All aspects of debt funding including PFI funding retail finance and consumer credit, especially involved in the impact of e-commerce in the banking environment.
Prof. Memberships: Law Society of Scotland.
Career: Qualified in 1984. Worked in-house with BP Petroleum Development Limited before joining *McGrigor Donald* in 1987. Following a period with *Cameron Markby Hewitt*, in London, returned to *McGrigor Donald* as Banking Partner in Scotland in 1992.

MACRITCHIE, Kenneth
Shearman & Sterling, London
(020) 7448 3000
kmacritchie@shearman.com
Specialisation: Managing partner of the London office. Advising clients on major infrastructure projects including transport infrastructure, power, telecom, mining and oil and gas. Clients include international banks and project developers.
Prof. Memberships: Law Society, Law Society of Scotland.
Career: Qualified in 1976. Partner, *Clifford Chance* 1991-94. *Milbank, Tweed, Hadley & McCloy* 1994-96. *Shearman & Sterling* partner, since 1996.

MAIR, Logan
Ashurst Morris Crisp, London
(020) 7638 1111
Specialisation: Partner in *Ashursts*' Energy, Transport and Infrastructure Department, specialising in advising both sponsors and funders on PFI/PPP projects across a variety of sectors, including road, education, health, defence, social housing and accommodation. His work also covers energy and natural resources law and in particular projects in the waste and waste to energy sectors.
Prof. Memberships: Law Society.

Career: Articles at *Ashursts* 1992-94; assistant at *Ashursts* 1994-2001; Partner 2001.
Personal: Educated at Merchiston Castle School, Edinburgh and Gonville & Caius College, Cambridge. Rugby (London Scottish XV) tennis and golf. Married with two daughters.

MATHEOU, Michael
Lovells, London
(020) 7296 2000
mike.matheou@lovells.com
Specialisation: Working in the firm's Project Finance Unit advising the private sector, financiers and the public sector on PPP/Private Finance Initiative projects (all sectors) and international limited recourse financial projects. Heavily involved in PFI/PPP work across a range of sectors including transport (London Underground PPP/DBFO Roads and light rail), Healthcare and Government Accommodation (DSS PRIME; STEPS project). Also worked on a range of infrastructure projects internationally including BOT Waste Water Project in Oman, Bauxite mine and harbour development in Guyana and Oil refinery and petro-chemicals project in India.
Prof. Memberships: Law Society.
Career: *Lovells*, London and Hong Kong since 1980, Partner 1989. LLB (Hons) Nottingham University.

MATTHEW, Stephen
Eversheds, Nottingham
(0115) 950 7000
Specialisation: Joined *Eversheds* in 1995, becoming a partner in 1997, having previously worked for fifteen years in the public sector. Acts for public sector project sponsors and for bidding contractors, primarily in the field of social infrastructure. Is head of *Eversheds* projects group.
Career: Educated at Farnham Grammar School, University of Sheffield and the College of Law, London. Began his career with South Yorkshire County Council, moved to Derbyshire County Council and joined Shropshire County Council in 1998.
Personal: Married with three children and lives on the outskirts of Nottingham.

MCAULEY, Michael
Dundas & Wilson CS, Glasgow
(0141) 222 2200

MCCANN, Martin
Masons, London
(020) 7490 4000
martin.mccann@masons.com
Specialisation: Martin McCann is a partner in *Masons* projects and finance group. He advises on all manner of domestic/ international PFI/ project finance/ asset finance transactions including: Rail: He advised the successful bidder on the first PFI light rail project to close, Nottingham Light Rail, and is now advising on Manchester, Leeds and South Hants Light rail schemes, plus several heavy rail franchises. Accommodation projects: He continues to advise

PROJECTS/PFI ■ THE LEADERS

leading developers and funders on a wide range of accommodation projects including schools, hospitals and courts. IT Projects: He is currently advising the British Government on one of the first multijurisdictional IT PFI projects. He separately advised Rolls Royce and British Aerospace on the funding of their multi billion pound, multijurisdictional outsourcing/corporate PPP project. Martin previously headed up *Masons* China practice and was recognised as a 'leader in the field' of project finance/restructuring work. He advised governments, developers and banks on all manner of project finance transactions in China, including toll roads, power plants and water projects.
Prof. Memberships: Qualified solicitor in England and Wales. Qualified solicitor in Hong Kong.
Career: Qualified in 1995 and has since been at *Masons*. Head of *Masons* China practice 1996-2001. From 1999-2001 he has been in *Masons'* projects and finance group.
Publications: Advisor to the Chinese government on project finance/asset finance. Legal advisor to British/Dutch/German governments in relation to project finance and investment in China. Currently advising British government on multijurisdictional PPP project.
Personal: Golf.

MCCORMACK, Carol
Berwin Leighton Paisner, London
(020) 7760 1000
carol.mccormack@blplaw.com
Specialisation: Partner in projects and public sector department. Principal area of work is advising government departments, health bodies, educational establishments, local authorities, private sector consortia and service providers on major commercial transactions such as those undertaken through the Private Finance Initiative, Public Private Partnerships. Has represented HM Treasury and the Home Office on major accommodation PFI projects and represented the Bouygues Ecovert/Charterhouse consortium on the first NHS PFI to use the standard form contract.
Career: Articled with *Berwin Leighton* 1983-85 and became a partner in 1989.
Personal: Born in Middlesbrough 22 February 1961, attended Selwyn College, Cambridge.

MCCORMICK, Roger
Freshfields Bruckhaus Deringer
London
(020) 7936 4000
roger.mccormick@freshfields.com
Specialisation: Project Finance (all sectors, all countries) and other financial/commercial transactions.
Prof. Memberships: International Bar Association.
Career: Partner of *Freshfields* since 1981. Head of Project Finance 1991-97.
Personal: Born 1951, Educated M.G.S. and Oxford.

MCEWAN, Alastair
Maclay Murray & Spens, Edinburgh
(0131) 479 2865
ajm@maclaymurrayspens.co.uk
Specialisation: Partner specialising in capital projects and PFI transactions. Completed deals last year included Chester-le-Street Community Hospital Project, Ingleby Barwick Community Campus PFI Project, Kingston University Accommodation PFI Project, Findlay House NHS Care Home Project, acquisition of Edison Capital's UK PFI Investment Portfolio by Noble Group and restructuring of Noble Group's Investments and West Lothian Schools Project. Previous deals include St George's Hospital PFI Project, Aberdeenshire Schools Project, Dumfries & Galloway Acute and Maternity Hospital Project, Kilmarnock Prison, Ninewells Hospital Car Park Project and Cairngorm Funicular Railway Project. Currently advising in connection with Stobhill ACAD Hospital Project, Midlothian Community Hospital Project, Highland Primary Care NHS Trust and Invergordon/ Alness Medical Grove PFI Project and Forfar Community Resource Centre Project.
Career: George Watson's College; Edinburgh University (LLB 1979); Scottish School of Business Studies (MBA 1980); Queen's University, Canada (LLM 1982). Articled *Brodies*, 1986-88; assistant solicitor, *Maclay Murray & Spens*, 1988-90, associate 1990-91; partner 1991.
Personal: Born 1958; resides Edinburgh. Enjoys cross country skiing, hill walking.

MCPAKE, Ian
Tods Murray WS, Edinburgh
(0131) 226 4771
ian.mcpake@todsmurray.com
Specialisation: Partner in Capital Projects Department. Work includes PFI, property and environmental law.
Prof. Memberships: Member of United Kingdom Environmental Law Association; convenor of UKELA Scottish Law Working Party.
Career: Qualified in Scotland in 1971. Articled *J & W Buchan*, Peebles, 1969-72. *Ranken & Reid SSC* 1972-90, partner 1973. Joined *Tods Murray WS* as a partner in 1990. Qualified in England in 2001.
Personal: Born 1948. Attended George Watson's College, Edinburgh and St Andrew's University (LLB 1969). Married with three daughters. Leisure: theatre, walking, skiing, reading. Lives in Edinburgh.

MCQUATER, Gavin
Lovells, London
(020) 7296 2188
gavin.mcquater@lovells.com
Specialisation: Project finance. Handles UK (including public/private partnership) projects and international limited recourse transactions, across a range of industries including transport, water and general infrastructure, dealing with sponsors, financial institutions and contracting authorities. Advises on transaction structuring, such as bankable risk allocation and the tender process. Experience of a wide spread of joint ventures, business set ups, corporate reorganisations and M&A transactions. International work includes Europe, Asia and Middle Eastern transactions.
Prof. Memberships: Law Society.
Career: Qualified with *Lovell White & King* in 1979; partner since 1985; 1990-1994 in Hong Kong office; now head of firm's project finance unit.

MURPHY, Michael
MacRoberts, Glasgow
(0141) 332 9988
michael.murphy@macroberts.com
Specialisation: Head of *MacRoberts'* Projects Group, specialising in project finance and PPPs. Acted for Amey/Halifax/Miller consortium on Glasgow Schools PFI (£400 million). Acted for Amey on Edinburgh Schools PFI (£100 million) and acting in relation to several other schools projects. Acting on numerous health and accommodation projects.
Career: *MacRoberts*. Qualified 1985; Assistant Solicitor 1986-89; Associate 1989-90; Partner 1990.
Personal: St Mirin's Academy; Glasgow University 1980, LLB (Hons) 1st Class.

NASH, David
Shepherd+ Wedderburn, Edinburgh
(0131) 473 5266
david.nash@shepwedd.co.uk
Specialisation: PFI/PPP outsourcing and procurement. Current projects include A92 DBFO, Glasgow Southern Orbital DBFO, MOD construction vehicles, PFI. Past projects include Aberdeenshire schools, MOD Field Electrical Power Supplies Midlothian schools; Northlink Orkney & Shetland Ferries; Greater Glasgow Sewage Treatment PFI, East Renfrewshire Schools PFI, Scottish Children's Reporters Administration IT PFI, M8 DBFO; M6 DBFO; New Scottish Office; Victoria Quay; Skye Bridge.
Prof. Memberships: Law Society of Scotland.
Career: George Watson University College, Edinburgh. Edinburgh University - Hons MA, LLB (1969-76). Scottish Office Legal Department 1983-98.
Personal: Music, travel, skiing.

NOBLE, Perry
Freshfields Bruckhaus Deringer
London
(020) 7936 4000
perry.noble@freshfields.com
Specialisation: Projects. PFI, transportation and telecommunications projects. Acted for London Underground on its major PFI projects. Advised Hutchinson Whampoa on all aspects of its European 3G strategy including licence acquisition, network financing and network sharing. Acted for Abbey National on the debt financing of Bristol airport. Acts for Babcock & Brown and Abbey National on secondary market acquisitions in PFI/PPP. Acted for One2One (now T-Mobile), First Mark, Virgin Mobile and Bouygues Telecom on telecom project financings.
Prof. Memberships: Law Society.
Career: Letchworth Grammar School, North East London Polytechnic, Bristol University (LLM Commercial Law).
Personal: Married, three sons. Interests: All sport, particularly cricket, dog walking and cinema.

O'CONNOR, Mike
Addleshaw Booth & Co, Manchester
(0161) 934 6000
michael.oconnor@addleshawbooth.com
Specialisation: National Head of PFI/Projects unit. Specialises in PFI, public private partnerships and project finance also in mainstream corporate banking; public/ private finance, structured finance; finance transactions involving public bodies of all types. Contributing editor to Butterworths 2 volume PFI Handbook. Contributes to CIPFA Handbook on PFI.
Prof. Memberships: Law Society. British South Africa Lawyers Association. Institute of Fiscal Studies.
Career: Qualified 1989. Partner 1996.
Personal: Leisure interests include horse-racing, electric guitar, travel, piano. Governor of Appleton Thorn County Primary School, non-executive director of Willow Park Housing Trust.

PEPPIATT, Stephen
Shearman & Sterling, London
(020) 7655 5000

PHILLIPS, Robert
CMS Cameron McKenna, London
(020) 7367 2500
robert.phillips@cmck.com
Specialisation: Partner in projects group. Principal area of practice is advising on transactions involving private/public sector participation with particular emphasis on major infrastructure and capital projects. Work covers specialist contract drafting, development with other consultants of a risk profile, and negotiating terms of project documents required for limited recourse financed infrastructure schemes. Major projects include independent power projects (both generation and transmission); road, rail (including high speed rail links), ports and airports transport schemes and information technology. Retained by the World Bank to assist in development courses for the introduction of competition for public/private sector partnerships. Areas of activity include Hong Kong, India, Sub-Saharan Africa, continental Europe and the UK.
Prof. Memberships: Major Projects Association.
Career: Partner at *McKenna & Co* (now *CMS Cameron McKenna*) since 1979, including period as senior resident partner in Hong Kong 1983-88. Admitted as a Solicitor, England and Wales 1971, Hong Kong, 1983 and as a Barrister and Solicitor, State of Victoria, Australia, 1986.

THE LEADERS ■ PROJECTS/PFI

Personal: Born 15th May 1947. Lives in Walton-on-Thames, Surrey.

PICKUP, Raith
Mills & Reeve, Cambridge
(01223) 222283
raith.pickup@mills-reeve.com
See under Healthcare, p.409

PREECE, Andrew
Herbert Smith, London
(020) 7374 8000
andrew.preece@herbertsmith.com
Specialisation: Partner with considerable experience in projects work and in financing, particularly project finance, lease finance and general commercial work. Has led the *Herbert Smith* projects group since its formation in 1994 and has been involved in many PFI and PPP projects since the private finance initiative was first instigated. Has also been involved in numerous North Sea oil and gas transactions and other international oil and gas financings.
Prof. Memberships: Law Society, International Bar Association, Major Projects Association, UK Energy Lawyers Group, Finance & Leasing Association.
Career: Qualified in 1970. Became a partner at *Herbert Smith* in 1977.
Personal: Educated at Selwyn College, Cambridge.

RANDLE, Anthony
DLA, Birmingham
(08700) 111111

RANSOME, Clive
Linklaters, London
(020) 7456 5904
clive.ransome@linklaters.com
Specialisation: Specialist in projects, project finance and banking law. Since joining *Linklaters* in 1985 has worked on a number of major projects, project financings and structured financings, involving LNG, refineries and other petrochemical and oil and gas projects in the UK, Africa and worldwide.
Career: 1992 to date: Partner in the Project Finance Group, London; 1985-92: Assistant solicitor, *Linklaters*, 1985; Admitted as a solicitor, 1982: University College, Cardiff, LLB (Hons); 1978: University of Southampton, BA (Hons).

READ, Anthony
Burness, Edinburgh
(0131) 473 6000

REYNELL, Daniel Humphrey
Clifford Chance, London
(020) 7600 1000
daniel.reynell@cliffordchance.com
Specialisation: Banking and Finance Department. Partner specialising in banking, project, asset-based and structured finance and debt restructuring.
Career: Articled *Coward Chance*; qualified 1979; Partner since 1987.
Personal: St John's College, Oxford.

ROLFE, Andrew
Clifford Chance, London
(020) 7956 0071
andrew.rolfe@cliffordchance.com

Specialisation: Real Estate Department. Partner specialising in major infrastructure project and real estate development work, with particular involvement in PFI/PPP projects.
Career: Qualified 1982; Assistant Solicitor *Hunt Dickins and Willatt*, Nottingham 1981-84; Assistant solicitor *Clifford-Turner* 1984-88; Partner since 1988.
Personal: Nottingham University (LLB Hons 1977).

ROUT, Peter
DLA, Manchester
(08700) 111111

ROWEY, Kent
Freshfields Bruckhaus Deringer London
(020) 7936 4000
kent.rowey@freshfields.com
See under Energy, p.343

ROWSON, Stuart
Linklaters, London
(020) 7456 5918
stuart.rowson@linklaters.com
Specialisation: Partner in the Projects Group. Highly experienced in projects pursuant to the UK's private finance initiative, and in energy projects.
Career: 1985-88 Lincoln College, Oxford (Juisprudence, 2:1); 1989-90 Law Society Finals; 1990-92 Trainee Solicitor; 1992-2001, Associate, Project Finance Department; 2001 to date, Partner, Project Finance Department London.

SALT, Stuart
Linklaters, London
(020) 7456 5912
stuart.salt@linklaters.com
Specialisation: Expertise in project financings, privatisations and structured acquisitions in a variety of industry sectors. Advises a number of leading participants in the power generation, development and transmission sectors.
Career: Partner *Linklaters*. 1992 to date: Solicitor, *Linklaters* 1986-92; admitted as a Solicitor 1985. Law Society Qualifying Examinations 1983; Southampton University LL.B (Hons) 1982.

SIMMONS, William
Tods Murray WS, Edinburgh
(0131) 226 4771
william.simmons@todsmurray.com
Specialisation: Work includes infrastructure projects and PFI, corporate finance, mergers and acquisitions, banking and general commercial work including joint ventures.
Prof. Memberships: Law Society of Scotland.
Career: Qualified 1981 *Bishop & Co*. Joined *Dorman Jeffrey & Co* 1983 (partner 1984). Joined *Tods Murray* as a partner in 1986.
Personal: Born 1958. Attended Hutchesons Boys Grammar School 1967-75 and Glasgow University 1975-79 (LLB Hons). Leisure: hill walking and skiing.

STEADMAN, Tim
Clifford Chance, London
(020) 7600 1000
tim.steadman@cliffordchance.com

Specialisation: Partner and Head of Construction Group. Member of PFI/PPP Group, specialising in concession and construction aspects of projects arising from the PPP programe in the UK and PFI/PPP schemes elsewhere.
Prof. Memberships: European Construction Institute; IBA committee "T"; CBI Modernising Government Committee; UK PPP Forum; UN/ECE PPP Forum.
Career: Hertford College; Oxford University. Trainee and assistant *Lovell White & King* 1976-82; associate *Baker & McKenzie* 1982-85; partner *Baker & McKenzie* 1985-97; partner *Clifford Chance* since March 1997.
Publications: 'History and Framework of PFI/PPP in the UK', July 2000; 'Public Private Partnerships - A Private Sector Perspective', June 2000; 'Rubbish!' (the future of integrated waste management PPP schemes), Oct 2000; 'BOT/PPP Projects - The Contractor's Perspective', July 2000.
Personal: Born 1955; resides London.

STOPFORD, Philip
White & Case, London
(020) 7397 3604
pstopford@whitecase.com
Specialisation: Partner specialising in corporate finance with emphasis on project financings particularly in oil and gas, power and infrastructure. Also handles construction and joint ventures. Head of *White & Case's* Europe, Middle East and Africa Energy, Infrastructure and Project Finance Group.
Prof. Memberships: Law Society of England and Wales, American Bar Association, New York State Bar Association.
Career: *White & Case* New York 1980-81 and 1986-88; *White & Case* Hong Kong 1981-83; *White & Case* Indonesia 1983-86 and 1988-91; *White & Case* Frankfurt 1991-93; *White & Case* London 1993 to present. Admitted as a solicitor in England and Wales; admitted to New York State Bar and to District of Columbia Bar.
Personal: Brunel University (1977 LLB Hons); University of Virginia Law School (LLM 1978).

SUTTIE, Frank
Beachcroft Wansbroughs, Leeds
(0113) 251 4700

TEAGUE, Gavin
Clifford Chance, London
(020) 7600 1000
gavin.teague@cliffordchance.com
Specialisation: Banking and Finance Department. Partner specialising in asset and project finance.
Career: Partner in *Clifford Chance* since 1997.

TEMPLETON-KNIGHT, Jane
Hunton & Williams, London
(020) 7246 5700
JTempleton-Knight@hunton.com
Specialisation: Partner in project finance group specialising in the development and financing of major power

and infrastructure projects often involving export credit agencies and multilaterals. Represented parties in relation to projects in Europe, Middle East, Asia and Africa including Shoreham Power, UK; North Chennai Power, India; Powergen Renewables, UK; Croydon Tramlink; Lisheen Zinc Mine, Ireland; Sea Launch satellite system; New Tagus Bridge, Portugal; Pego and Tapada Power Stations, Portugal; Rosen Power Station, Italy; the Serene group of power stations, Italy; Second Severn Bridge; Newport gold heap leaching project in Uzbekistan; South East London waste-to-energy plant; The Kasese Cobalt Mine, Uganda.
Career: Durham University, BA Honours (upper second), 1985. University of Newcastle-upon-Tyne, Solicitors Final Examination, 1986. *Allen & Overy*, London – qualified 1989. Associate 1989 to December 1995. *Milbank, Tweed, Hadley & McCloy*, London – January 1995 senior associate, elected partner October 1996.

TOTT, Nick
Herbert Smith, London
(020) 7374 8000
nicholas.tott@herbertsmith.com
Specialisation: Head of Infrastructure. Practice comprises all forms of financing and banking work with particular emphasis on asset and project finance, PFI and PPP projects. Was seconded to the Private Finance Panel Executive for 15 months with responsibility for PFI Projects in Scotland, Northern Ireland and the Ministry of Defence.
Prof. Memberships: Law Society; City of London Solicitors' Company.
Career: LLB (Edin), Qualified Scotland (1986), England and Wales (1991). Partner 1992.
Publications: Author of the chapter 'Public Finance in the UK' in Leasing Finance (Euromoney 1997, 3rd Edition). Co-author of 'The PFI Handbook' (Jordans).
Personal: Born 8 May 1960. Educated at Edinburgh University. Leisure pursuits include golf and skiing.

VERNON, Philip
Ashurst Morris Crisp, London
(020) 7859 1705
philip.vernon@ashursts.com
Specialisation: Partner in projects group. Principal areas of practice are infrastructure projects, privatisations and project finance, with particular experience in projects under the UK government's private finance initiative (including light rail, road, prison, hospital and other accommodation projects) and also power and energy projects in the Middle East and Indian subcontinent.
Career: Articled at *Ashurst Morris Crisp*; qualified 1989. Partner at *Ashurst Morris Crisp* since 1998.
Personal: BA (Hons) in Classics, Worcester College, Oxford University 1985: Fulbright Fellowship in US Securities Law 1994.

PROJECTS/PFI ■ THE LEADERS

VICKERS, Cathryn
Masons, Bristol
(0117) 924 5678

VINTER, Graham
Allen & Overy, London
(020) 7330 3000
graham.vinter@allenovery.com
Specialisation: Partner specialising in all aspects of project finance.
Career: Articled *Allen & Overy*; qualified 1982; partner 1988.
Publications: 'Project Finance – A Legal Guide' published Sweet & Maxwell (2nd ed, 1998); various articles.
Personal: Oxford University (BA, 1979); Ludwig-Maximilians University, Munich (1977-78). Born 1956.

WATSON, Michael
McGrigor Donald, Edinburgh
(0131) 777 7071
michael.watson@mcgrigors.com
Specialisation: Has particular expertise in project finance (both bank and the capital markets) and a regular conference speaker and contributor to the trade journals in the projects and PFI/PPP arena. Also has experience in all areas of finance and debt-related work including acquisition and property finance. Clients he has acted for recently include Bank of Scotland, European Investment Bank (Edinburgh Schools PPP), The Royal Bank of Scotland (Highland Schools and Swanscombe PPP), MBIA Assurance and The Royal Bank of Canada (Levenmouth PFI Project Bond).
Prof. Memberships: Law Society of Scotland and Law Society of England and Wales.
Career: Trainee 1993-95, Solicitor 1995-99, Associate to 2000, Partner 2000-date.
Publications: Articles in Infrastructure Journal, PFI Intelligence Bulletin, PFI Journal.
Personal: MA (Hons), Economics and Accounting - University of Edinburgh and University of Pennsylvania LLB, University of Edinburgh. Golf, cycling, skiing, French. Married to Sandra, two children Eilidh and Iona.

WHITE, Bruce
Linklaters, London
(020) 7456 5986
bruce.white@linklaters.com
Specialisation: Specialist in project finance concentrating particularly on its infrastructure projects under the UK government's private finance initiative as well as advising on major international infrastructure projects.
Career: 1995 to date: Partner in the Project Finance Department of *Linklaters*; 1986-95: Assistant Solicitor, *Linklaters*, 1984-86: Trainee solicitor, *Dorman Jeffrey & Co*, Glasgow. 1981-84: University of Dundee, LLB Law.

WEBER, David
Linklaters, London
(020) 7456 5879
david.weber@linklaters.com
Specialisation: Project and Project Finance Department. Specialising in the development and financing of major international projects, including infrastructure, power generation and oil and gas projects, acting for project sponsors, borrowers and lenders.
Career: 1984 to date: Partner, *Linklaters*, Projects Department; 1981-84: Assistant Solicitor, *Linklaters* London; 1980-81: Seconded to *Fulbride & Jaworski*, Texas; 1978-80: Assistant Solicitor, *Linklaters*, corporate tax; 1976-78: Articled clerk, *Linklaters*. 1979: MA; 1976: College of Law, Lancaster Gate; 1975: BA Law, Clare College, Cambridge. Haberdashers Aske's School, Hertfordshire.

WHITFIELD, Stuart
Bevan Ashford, Bristol
(0117) 975 1722
stuart.whitfield@bevanashford.co.uk
Specialisation: Partner in the Commercial Department and Head of the firm's Technology and Manufacturing Division. Advises public and private sector clients at the public/private sector interface. Has acted in these areas for Ministry of Defence, DTI, the Royal Mint, Magnox Electric plc, Fire Service College, Rolls-Royce plc, AMEC, Vosper Thornycroft, Bovis and a number of other well-known private sector organisations. Examples include acting for Miller/Parkwood on the Mulberry School education PFI; Future Strategic Tanker Aircraft: advised Rolls-Royce plc on their participation in this £9 billion PFI scheme, advising Partnerships for Health (a joint venture of Partnerships UK and the Department of Health) on NHS LIFT, an initiative to invest £1 billion into new primary healthcare facilities.
Career: Exeter University. Articled at *Bond Pearce*; qualified 1990; partner at *Veale Wasbrough* 1997. Joined *Bevan Ashford* 1998.
Personal: Lives in Bristol; Leisure interests include family, music and cars.

WOODROW, Cameron
Pinsent Curtis Biddle, Birmingham
(0121) 200 1050
cameron.woodrow@pinsents.com
Specialisation: Major projects; public-private partnerships (including PFI); privatisations; corporate restructuring; joint ventures; acquisitions and disposals; project management. Major transactions have included the pre-franchising reorganisation of the Central Trains Operating Unit of British Rail; the £150 million restructuring and refinancing of Birmingham International Airport; a US$150 million joint venture for LucasVarity; the £100 million concession based financing of London Luton Airport; the acquisition by GEC Alsthom/Tarmac of the Central Infrastructure Maintenance Unit of British Rail. Significant experience in advising both public bodies (including local authorities) and major private sector clients in the transport, automotive and engineering sectors. Expertise in commercial, company, contract and public law.
Prof. Memberships: Law Society.
Career: BA (Jurisprudence), Brasenose College, Oxford. *Freshfields* 1983-93 (qualified 1986). Partner *Pinsent Curtis Biddle* 1993 to date. Birmingham head and national practice co-ordinator for major projects 1997-2001. Awarded PFI Team of the Year by Legal Business for Birmingham Airport restructuring.
Personal: Common Purpose graduate.

WYLES, David
Herbert Smith, London
(020) 7374 8000
david.wyles@herbertsmith.com
Specialisation: Partner with extensive experience of banking and finance matters with a particular focus on PFI projects covering a wide range of sectors including health and education.
Prof. Memberships: City of London Law Society.
Career: Admitted 1989. Partnership 1996.
Publications: Contributor to 'The PFI Handbook' (Jordans March 1999).
Personal: Kings College, London and Sorbonne Panthéon, Paris.

WYMAN, Chris
Clifford Chance, London
(020) 7600 1000
chris.wyman@cliffordchance.com
Specialisation: Banking and Finance Department. Specialises in banking and project and acquisition finance, with a particular emphasis on energy, natural resources and infrastructure.
Career: Articled *Coward Chance/Clifford Chance*, qualified 1981; Partner since 1986.
Personal: Epsom College; Cambridge University.

REAL ESTATE

London: 701; The Regions: 707; Scotland: 722; Profiles: 725

Research approved by BMRB For this edition, **Chambers'** researchers conducted 6,582 interviews – 3,900 with law firms, 511 with barristers and 2,171 with clients. The validity of the research was scrutinised by BMRB International, who audited both the methodology and the results at our offices in London. They interviewed **Chambers'** researchers and cross-checked sample interviews. Details of the audit appear on page 7.

OVERVIEW Despite the doom-mongers' predictions, the property market has borne up well this year. Investment purchases and development schemes are still coming in, and the base lending rate has helped maintain market bouyancy, although in the aftermath of September 11th it has been subject to some unique tensions. Private investment work has stood up well because of the disappointing performance of equities, and there has been an increase in direct investment from the United States and Germany. The creation of massive international funds is also booming. The only cloud on the horizon at present is the suggestion that some institutional investors are feeling increasingly exposed to the levels of real estate in their portfolios, though there is no sign yet that they are preparing to offload assets. While the trend to 'Europeanisation' continues, it still has a way to go, so international depth, whilst crucial to the practices of two or three firms in our top table, remains a relatively minor consideration for most firms. Property continues to become more commercial and tax-driven, with innovative property finance becoming increasingly central to the sector, especially in high-end, complex 'corporatised' deals. A distinct group of large, well-resourced City firms is taking on these mega-deals. To reflect this we have divided our three tables more loosely this year according to deal size/type rather than team size. The first table is now made up of those firms which, with varying degrees of success, are players at the cutting edge. The next two tables comprise the more traditional practices, although that is not to say that some of these firms are not engaging in fine finance-driven work, albeit on a more modest scale.

Real Estate Survey Results

Position	Firm	Points
1	Linklaters	54
2	Nabarro Nathanson	41
3	Herbert Smith	38
4	Clifford Chance	37
5	Freshfields Bruckhaus Deringer	36
6	Wragge & Co	27
7	Ashurst Morris Crisp	27
8	DJ Freeman	24
9	SJ Berwin	17
10	Eversheds	15
11	Norton Rose	14
12	CMS Cameron McKenna	12
13	Mayer, Brown, Rowe & Maw	11
14	Berwin Leighton Paisner	7

Overview
This client-only survey is based on the recommendations of over 100 of the leading property companies in the market. The clients had a clear favourite this year: Linklaters, with its advantages of the extensive resources and the focused expertise proving most popular. Clients also reported increased tendency to use small, niche firms. Although these did not receive sufficient votes to enter the above table, the personal service and the speed of response were greatly appreciated. Almost a fifth of clients interviewed listed such firms as their first choice for everyday work.

LONDON — LARGER DEALS

REAL ESTATE: LARGER DEALS
LONDON

1
- Linklaters

2
- Clifford Chance

3
- Berwin Leighton Paisner
- Herbert Smith
- Lovells

4
- Ashurst Morris Crisp
- Freshfields Bruckhaus Deringer
- Nabarro Nathanson
- SJ Berwin

5
- Allen & Overy
- CMS Cameron McKenna

This book is the product of 6,582 1/2 hour interviews. See p.7 for BMRB audit. Within each band, firms are listed alphabetically.

LINKLATERS (see firm details p.1043) Long regarded by the market as "*a cut above everyone else for sheer quality*," this team has "*strong solicitors throughout, with an awesome and loyal client base*." "*Genuinely interested in property clients*," the team is known for "*stellar financial*" and development work, and has also cut a swathe in outsourcings. Recommended for "*spread and breadth*," its clients "*will always pay for the real quality*" on offer here, especially to take full advantage of one of the best international networks available. The team boasts a "*smart, thoroughbred*" standalone property practice, in addition to undertaking corporate support on top transactions. The "*high-class*" Martin Elliott (see p.729) has great development expertise, especially concerning retail and leisure schemes. Robert Finch (see p.729) commands an incredible reputation as the man who "*elevated property amongst City firms*." Though not as visible as in the past, he remains active, and represented Bank of America on Canary Wharf. "*Bright and perceptive*" Simon Clark (see p.727) is, in the opinion of some competitors, "*the only person who really understands property and tax*," and interviewees were also strong in their endorsement of "*all-round brick*" Patrick Plant (see p.735). Jeffrey Bailey (see p.725) received warm recommendations from clients, while the "*very commercial*" James Knox (see p.732) has "*built a well-rounded practice*" in which outsourcings figure prominently, and is "*definitely moving up the ranks*." The team acted for BP Amoco on the acquisition of its new global headquarters at 1 St James's Square, which was structured as a corporate transaction, and for its pension fund in the sale of its Berkeley Square Estate to overseas investors. It also acted for MEPC on the £190 million disposal of a mixed investment portfolio to Antler Investments. **Clients** Development Securities; BP Amoco; Royal & SunAlliance; MEPC; Swiss Re; Merrill Lynch; Lend Lease; iii-Fonds; TIAA-CREF; Richardsons; Heron; CIT Group.

CLIFFORD CHANCE (see firm details p.911) This "*huge*" group is best known at the high end of the real estate marketplace. Evolving ever more sophisticated financial and corporate structures, no group can claim greater experience or depth on funds, financing, and development work than this "*unbeatably international*" team. It remains particularly active in

TOP IN-HOUSE LAWYERS

Michael ASHLEY-BROWN, Group Legal Counsel, Canary Wharf Group

Mark KINGSTON, European General Counsel and Managing Director, Tishman Speyer

Terry NEVILLE John Lewis

Jayne WALTERS, Pinder, Fry and Benjamin, Director

The "*practical and commercial*" **Jayne Walters** again retains her place on the list. Deserving of particularly high praise, are **Mark Kingston** and the "*technically and commercially strong*" **Michael Ashley-Brown**. Both are commended for their "*user-friendly*" approach. **Terry Neville** is the only new addition to this year's list, having been highly recommended for his "*wide knowledge*" of the law.

In-house lawyers' profiles p.1201

701

REAL ESTATE ■ LONDON

LEADING INDIVIDUALS

1
- BRETHERTON Philip Berwin Leighton Paisner
- ELLIOTT Martin Linklaters
- FINCH Robert Linklaters
- HAMILTON Sophie Forsters
- KIDBY Robert Lovells
- MACGREGOR Robert Clifford Chance
- MORPETH Iain Clifford Chance
- RYLAND David SJ Berwin

2
- BARNES James Herbert Smith
- BRIAM Tony Clifford Chance
- CLARK Simon Linklaters
- FIELD Christopher Macfarlanes
- GNIADKOWSKI Stan Denton Wilde Sapte
- HARRISON Christopher Herbert Smith
- LE PARD Geoffrey Freshfields Bruckhaus Deringer
- NISSE Ian Ashurst Morris Crisp
- PLANT Patrick Linklaters
- SOLOMON Jonathan Clifford Chance
- STANCOMBE Michael Lovells
- TAYLOR David Herbert Smith
- WHITE Graham Slaughter and May
- WRIGHT David Nabarro Nathanson

3
- BAILEY Jeffrey Linklaters
- BENZECRY Edward CMS Cameron McKenna
- BROWN Nicholas CMS Cameron McKenna
- DE PURY Chris Herbert Smith
- HOWARD Amanda Nabarro Nathanson
- KUSTOW David Olswang
- LUST Graham Nabarro Nathanson
- MORRIS Christopher Freshfields Bruckhaus Deringer
- QUICKE Martin Denton Wilde Sapte
- RUDOLF Peter Berwin Leighton Paisner
- SAMSON John Nabarro Nathanson
- SANDERS Andrew Lovells
- VIVIAN Jon SJ Berwin
- WATSON Gary Ashurst Morris Crisp
- WILLSON Stephen SJ Berwin

4
- BATTISCOMBE David Finers Stephens Innocent
- BUTLER Alan Simmons & Simmons
- CLARK Paul D J Freeman
- CLEAL Adam Allen & Overy
- KNOX James Linklaters
- PICKUP Bryan SJ Berwin
- RICE Dermot Slaughter and May
- ROBERTS David Gouldens
- ROBINSON Patrick Herbert Smith
- WESTHEAD Tim Olswang

5
- HOLY Julian Julian Holy
- LAKE Tim Stepien Lake Gilbert & Paling
- OLMER Philip Olswang
- PATTERSON Anthony Forsters
- TAVENER Chris Herbert Smith

UP AND COMING
- COX Ian Herbert Smith
- NEWSTEAD Jackie Lovells

See individuals' profiles p.725

---

the non-institutional investment market, a field in which it is constantly attracting new clients. Competitors concede, "*hats off to what they're doing at Canary Wharf – they're the only ones who could pull it off,*" with the ability to field an enormous "*well-oiled and efficient*" team. The practice is not felt by interviewees to have quite the 'pure' property presence or client base of Linklaters, however, with the sophisticated financial/transactional work being run out of the real estate department proper, it has massive stand alone capability. The "*outstanding*" **Robert MacGregor** (see p.733) maintains his reputation amongst peers as a "*great team leader,*" and is complemented by "*precise*" **Iain Morpeth** (see p.734). Recommendations were also warm for **Tony Briam** (see p.727) and the "*charming and focused*" **Jonathan Solomon** (see p.736). The team acted for Standard Life on the establishment and structuring of a €300 million pan-European fund, and for Nomura Investments on the leveraged buyout of Le Meridien Hotels, including a £1.25 billion sale and leaseback with Royal Bank of Scotland. **Clients** AIG Global Real Estate Investment; Benchmark Group; Canary Wharf Group; Curzon Capital Partners; Gallagher Estates; Grantchester Group; Helical Bar; Heron UK; Kingfisher; MEPC.

BERWIN LEIGHTON PAISNER (see firm details p.866) Market sources agree that this is "*a unique, high-quality practice with its own definite style and combination of strengths.*" A high-class retail and investment practice dovetails neatly with a "*fantastic planning group,*" and the merger with Paisner & Co has brought a rise in top-end leisure work. Winning "*glittering instructions*" from "*half of the blue-chip property institutions in London,*" as well as star client Tesco, the team is also acknowledged to be "*making strides in property finance.*" Still heavily involved in the Dome project, it acts for both the public and private sectors in major regeneration projects and PFI schemes. It is led by the "*astute, commercial and colourful*" **Philip Bretherton** (see p.726), who "*doesn't waste anybody's time,*" and is admired by competitors for his local authority expertise. His practice covers general commercial real estate law, with particular emphasis on development work and tax-led real estate transactions. **Peter Rudolf** (see p.735) also comes highly recommended for his development expertise. The team advised recently on a joint venture between English Partnerships, AMEC and Legal & General to develop a £250 million investment fund, and also acted for Southwark Land Regeneration in the redevelopment of the Elephant & Castle in London. **Clients** Bank of Scotland; British Land; Compass Group; Costain Construction; Legal & General; Liverpool City Council; Marylebone Warwick Balfour; Prudential Portfolio Managers; Bass; Frontier Estates.

HERBERT SMITH (see firm details p.992) Possessing an excellent client base and a team that is "*terrific, right down to the assistants,*" this group is best known for regeneration and corporate property work. Commentators point out that the practice is "*genuinely property led,*" rather than spun out of a corporate group. Its main strengths include core planning expertise and free-standing, tax-driven advice. Joint ventures for US funds have been a notable success story, along with complex debt and equity deals, and outsourcings. **James Barnes** (see p.726) is admired by clients for his "*sophisticated work,*" and "*down-to-earth style.*" Researchers were told that **Christopher Harrison** (see p.730) has been less visible since the project agreement on Kings Cross Central, partly because he has been active on some highly confidential matters. **David Taylor** (see p.737) is praised by competitors for his ability as "*a serious client-getter,*" while "*technically skilled*" **Chris de Pury** (see p.728) is "*as good as any in this game*" according to peers. The "*absolutely superb*" **Patrick Robinson**'s (see p.654) practice has an emphasis on development, and he also brings planning expertise to any deal. The market continues to endorse **Chris Tavener** (see p.737), who acts for a range of property companies and investors, and **Ian Cox** (see p.728) also wins plaudits. The team acted for Anschutz on its proposals for the Dome, and for BT on the sale of its headquarters building at St Martin's le Grand. **Clients** AXA Sun life Services; BAA; British Land; Crown Estate Commissioners; Deutsche Bank; Hermes; London and Regional Properties; MOD; Royal & SunAlliance; Stanhope.

LOVELLS (see firm details p.1045) This "*smart, commercial property finance group*" has a "*good international spread,*" especially in Europe, which clients find increasingly valuable. Boasting a reputation for "*commitment*" to the property sector, the team is also admired by competitors for its "*cutting-edge*" outsourcing expertise. A high-profile deal list has included work on a healthy number of regeneration schemes. This has included assisting Argent St George in its recent acquisition and regeneration of the King's Cross development lands. The team is praised for its practical outlook, and is regarded by interviewees as "*well organised and on the ball.*" "*Charismatic*" **Robert Kidby** (see p.732) has a "*rapport with clients,*" who also value the "*speed of delivery and quality of advice*" of **Michael Stancombe** (see p.737), known for having an "*appropriate commercial understanding of the business.*" **Andrew Sanders** (see p.736) is praised as a "*real commercial talent,*" and commentators were also free with their approbation of **Jackie Newstead** (see p.734). The team acted for Barclays Bank in its move to new offices in Canary Wharf, and also assisted ALSTOM in its pan-European corporate property outsourcing transaction. **Clients** Prudential;

LONDON ■ REAL ESTATE

Consignia; John Lewis Partnership; Abbey National; Land Securities; IKEA; Dawnay Day; Doughty Hanson.

ASHURST MORRIS CRISP
(see firm details p.852) "*Unbeatable on the technical legal side,*" the practice is said to have a "*delicate touch that is good for nervous clients.*" Considered a traditional outfit delivering "*quality work, especially where finance is involved,*" clients also describe it as "*nicely tax led.*" An enviable client base includes institutions, developers, retailers and corporates. The leasings practice is doing well, and it is gaining an impressive reputation for establishing funds for European co-venturers. Maintaining the firm's strong relationship with Chelsfield, **Ian Nisse** (see p.734) is now firmly "*back in the fray,*" and proving again his credentials as a "*fine operator.*" **Gary Watson** (see p.738) is "*greatly admired*" by his peers, and is considered by many commentators to be the key to the firm's long-term success. As well as handling the high-profile £2.38 billion outsourcing by BT of its property portfolio to Telereal Holdings, the team advised Canary Wharf Group on the letting of headquarters space to Barclays Bank. **Clients** Chelsfield; Grantchester Holdings; Tesco Stores; Bovis Lend Lease; Canary Wharf Group; Countryside Properties; Harvey Nichols & Co; Lattice Property Holdings; Royal Ordnance; Transco.

FRESHFIELDS BRUCKHAUS DERINGER
(see firm details p.964) "*Undoubtedly central to the sector,*" this "*tightly managed and focused*" team has a predictably good reputation for "*high-class outsourcings and corporate support.*" An increasing volume of work comprises freestanding 'corporatised' deals, while it also boasts a growing outsourcings practice acting for the bidder. Commentators point to the "*fine quality of work*" for clients like Scottish Widows, and the "*sleek professionalism*" of its occupier work at Canary Wharf. Receiving warm endorsement from the marketplace, **Geoffrey Le Pard** (see p.732) and **Christopher Morris** (see p.734) are the "*most notable figures in a notable team.*" Highlights of the year include acting internationally for Granada Compass on the property aspects of its £3.5 billion disposal of the Granada/Forte hospitality business. It subsequently advised Compass Group on its £3.26 billion disposal of the Signature, Posthouse, Heritage and Meridien brands acquired through the demerger. The team also acted for Lehman Brothers on the pre-letting of 1 million sq ft of office space at Canary Wharf, and for Telereal in the BT outsourcing. **Clients** Scottish Widows; LS Trillium; London Transport; Lehman Brothers; Compass Group; Kingfisher; Pearson; P&O; London Underground.

NABARRO NATHANSON
(see firm details p.1080) Researchers were told that this team retains "*a powerful property client base which it services well in all traditional property matters.*" Clients value the "*litigation backup and reasonable pricing,*" and give it credit for improving capacity and sophistication in the tax and corporate aspects of the business. Best known for "*day-to-day asset management,*" the team is also acknowledged by peers to be "*top of the tree for limited partnerships.*" Despite concerns about depth of quality, there is a growing perception that "*the practice has turned a corner and raised its game.*" All agree that it fields some "*absolutely first-class partners,*" including the widely admired **David Wright** (see p.738). "*Savvy and on the ball*" **Amanda Howard** (see p.731) is experienced in structuring real estate investment funds, and heads up the team's drive to consolidate the finance side. **Graham Lust** (see p.733) is well known for his work on property financing documentation, while **John Samson** is respected as "*a good lawyer's lawyer.*" The team advised Quintain in the purchase and redevelopment of the Millennium Dome, and acted for Land Securities on the sale of about £250 million worth of shopping centres to a client of REIT Asset Management. **Clients** British Land; Land Securities; Great Portland Estates; Heron; Quintain; BBC Pension Trust; Morley Fund Managers; GE Capital Real Estate; Costco Wholesale.

SJ BERWIN
(see firm details p.867) Renowned for the "*finest quality work and top-calibre people,*" the team "*really plays with the big boys*" in all things finance-related. With a "*pretty amazing client base,*" it has established an enviable reputation for private equity and tax-efficient investment work, and cuts a dash in structured deals with property as the underlying asset. As well as acting for property dealers, the team represents retailers, developers and institutions. Possessing an "*unquestionably, absurdly great mind,*" **David Ryland** (see p.810) is "*hardworking and demanding,*" and focuses on funds work. He acted for Schroders in establishing the WELPUT fund to invest in West-End properties. Having brought his "*hugely strong abilities*" and some top-flight clients with him, **Jon Vivian** (see p.737) wins praise for his commercial outlook, while one client said of **Stephen Willson** (see p.738) that "*he's quite simply the best lawyer we've ever come across.*" He assisted British Land on pre-letting accommodation to Accenture at Plantation Place. "*Fair and straightforward*" head of department **Bryan Pickup** (see p.810) acts on pre-lettings and redevelopments for the likes of The Crown Estate and AXA. The team represented Peabody Global Real Estate on the £300 million purchase of the Cutlers Gardens Estate. **Clients** Schroders; British Land; Marylebone Warwick Balfour; The Crown; AXA; Hilton; Sainsbury's; Brixton Estates; Aberdeen Property Investors; Chelsfield; Matrix; Citigroup; Frontier; London & Regional; Invesco; Rotch; Brixton.

ALLEN & OVERY
(see firm details p.841) Traditionally the property practice has been seen by peers as an adjunct of the banking department, but recent developments have seen the team "*beefing up considerably.*" As finance becomes ever more central to the sector, "*everything is moving in the right direction for it.*" Undeniably close to the banks, the team handles property finance, structures and funds, and complex one-offs. As its practice broadens, the team is "*getting its act together in straight property*" and gaining property clients, who appreciate its expertise in intricate limited partnerships work and its international reach, recently boosted in Germany. Respected department head **Adam Cleal** (see p.727) represents landowners, investors, developers and lenders. The team recently acted for William Pears on the BT Outsourcing, and also handled the debt side for Citibank. It advised Ericsson on the restructuring of its UK property interests, including the sale of its London headquarters at 1 St James's Square. **Clients** CPUT; Marks & Spencer; TXU; William Pears; Citibank; Ericsson; HypoVereinsbank; Chelverton; Lend Lease.

CMS CAMERON MCKENNA
(see firm details p.914) This remains a "*good, driven bunch*" with an excellent client base and prodigious throughput. Working principally for landlords, it boasts a good proportion of development and financing work, and some for occupiers. Competitors testify to the "*superb performance*" of a team that retains the capacity for complex and international work. "*Extremely thorough*" department head **Edward Benzecry** (see p.726) is said to have "*a dry sense of humour and a superb brain.*" Clients praise him for being "*good fun, and cutting to the chase quickly.*" **Nicholas Brown** (see p.727) is admired by peers, and is "*known to thump the table if necessary.*" The team acted for Nomura on its acquisition of the Le Méridien chain of 150 hotels located in more than 55 countries. It also advised Lloyds TSB on its acquisition of a new registered office from Asticus UK, and the simultaneous disposal of its existing registered office to Asticus. **Clients** Anglo Irish Bank; Berkeley Group; Brixton; Britannic Asset Management; Consignia; Grantchester Holdings; Haslemere Estates; Sainsbury's; John Laing Property; Lloyds TSB Bank; Nomura; St George; PRICOA.

REAL ESTATE ■ LONDON

LONDON

MEDIUM DEALS

REAL ESTATE: MEDIUM DEALS
■ LONDON

1
- Dechert
- Denton Wilde Sapte
- Lawrence Graham
- Macfarlanes

2
- DJ Freeman
- Gouldens
- Norton Rose

3
- Forsters
- Mayer, Brown, Rowe & Maw
- Slaughter and May

4
- Eversheds
- Olswang
- Simmons & Simmons

5
- Field Fisher Waterhouse
- Richards Butler

This book is the product of 6,582 1/2 hour interviews. See p.7 for BMRB audit. Within each band, firms are listed alphabetically.

DECHERT (see firm details p.934) A broad and well-regarded practice with an established reputation in retail and development, and a growing profile in property finance. A prestigious client roster has been boosted this year by the acquisition of Land Securities and The Crown Estate tender, and an influx of foreign investment clients. The team is acknowledged by peers to be "*winning instructions now that it couldn't have won just a few years ago.*" With an increasingly free-standing workload, it has branched out well beyond its traditional base of retail occupiers into commercial leasing, securitisations, and investment work. The team acted for Blackfriars Investments on the formation of a limited partnership with Royal London for a development at 1 London Wall, and for Helical Retail on a variety of development projects, including the redevelopment of a site in Accrington town centre. **Clients** Blackfriars; Chelsfield; City of London Corporation; The Crown Estate; Dixons; Freeport Leisure; Frogmore; Land Securities; Royal & SunAlliance; Schroders.

DENTON WILDE SAPTE (see firm details p.935) "*You can't go wrong with DWS*" was the comment of one client, and it was echoed widely in our research. A strong retail occupier practice is just part of the workload of an "*always good and steady*" team that is "*snapping at the heels*" of larger competitors. Also handling development work and PFI, it is experienced in outsourcings and sale and leasebacks, and is increasingly "*getting into the swing*" of 'corporatised' deals. The Milton Keynes office works closely with London to service clients like Barclays. "*Driven and commercial*" **Stan Gniadkowski** impressed our respondents with his "*intelligence and hard work*," and boasts a prestigious and loyal client base. He is active on the development side, and acted for Manchester Police on the development of 16 new police stations under a PFI scheme. "*Practical and careful*" **Martin Quicke** was said by competitors to have "*an eye for detail and a commercial approach*" that "*drives the deal through.*" The team assisted Marks & Spencer on the £348 million sale and leaseback of 78 stores across the UK to Topland Group Holdings. **Clients** Morgan Stanley; Sainsbury's; Barclays Bank Group Property Services; Marks & Spencer; CGIS Group; Taylor Woodrow; Terrace Hill; Thornfield Properties; John Laing Properties; MOD.

LAWRENCE GRAHAM (see firm details p.1031) Property is the core of this firm, and the team has a reputation as "*a solid, traditional player.*" The practice includes a large amount of work managing retail portfolios for major institutions like Legal & General and AXA, and a hefty retail development component. Clients applaud the team for its "*ability and service,*" and commentators note that "*it's holding its own,*" in the developing market and "*growing nicely.*" Stephen Stephens heads a department that acted for Scottish & Newcastle in the sale of over 1,100 pubs to Enterprise Inns and Noble House. Other recent highlights include acting for AXA REIM in a joint venture with GIC Real Estate to acquire a stake in the Thomas More Square Partnership. **Clients** AXA Sun Life; Cellnet; J Sainsbury Developments; Universities Superannuation Scheme; Allied Dunbar; Legal & General; Helical Bar.

MACFARLANES (see firm details p.1047) Regarded as a "*relatively small, quality outfit,*" competitors note that it is responsible for a broad range of "*absolute cream, headlining work*" for its "*select and contented client base.*" With the firm's fine reputation for private equity work, it is hardly surprising that related property investments feature prominently in its deal list. Clients and peers are "*always happy to deal with*" the team and especially with "*extremely commercial*" **Christopher Field**, whose "*can-do attitude*" and intelligence enable him to "*always engineer a novel and effective solution.*" The team he heads is said by market sources to be "*laid-back but really excellent.*" It acted for Kingfisher on the £614 million sale and leaseback of the Woolworths stores in its portfolio, and for P&O on the proposed new container port at London Gateway. **Clients** CIT Group; P&O Developments; ING; Kingfisher; Derwent Valley Holdings; Royal London Assurance; Dunedin Property; Legal & General Industrial Property Fund; Canada Life; Allders.

DJ FREEMAN (see firm details p.939) Having lost a number of partners in recent years, this team continues to divide opinion, though a strong caucus points out that it "*retains good lawyers and still commands respect.*" The practice enjoys a steady workload in investment, joint ventures and development, for a client base consisting mostly of landlords. Clients confirm that they are happy with the levels of service and would recommend the team in particular for traditional property matters. The job of rebuilding the practice has fallen to "*pleasant*" **Paul Clark**, who focuses on development, shopping centres and leases. The team acted recently for CGNU on the purchase of two buildings, in Euston Square and Euston Road. It also advised Buckingham Estates on its £40 million purchase of a portfolio of freehold properties. **Clients** Argent Group; AXA Sun Life; Benchmark Group; Capital & Regional; Carillion; CGNU; Land Securities; Lattice Properties; European Land.

GOULDENS (see firm details p.976) Clients and peers were queueing up to heap praise on this "*pragmatic, profitable and dynamic*" team. "*Everything it does is done well*" was a typical observation and, with its ability to innovate and "*cut through the mire,*" it can often be relied upon to "*pull off something spectacular.*" Traditionally focused on bread-and-butter development work, it is increasingly turning to investment work as clients' models evolve. **David Roberts** (see p.735) displays "*great commerciality and weighs things up quickly,*" according to commentators. He specialises in development and joint ventures, and is a market leader in establishing unit trusts and other development funding techniques. The team recently acted on the expansion of Hercules into a £1.5 billion fund, and on setting up a limited partnership for Ashtenne with Morley/CGNU. Another highlight was advising Pillar Property and the Hercules Unit Trust on the £185 million sale of a portfolio of 11 retail parks to Morley Fund Management. **Clients** Pillar Property; Ashtenne Holdings; Arlington; Miller Developments; HUT; CLOUT; Arsenal FC; Delancey; Burford.

NORTON ROSE (see firm details p.1084) "*A smaller team than you might expect, with greater weight and power than you'd think,*" was one comment, which goes some way to summing up this "*highly leveraged*" outfit. Research shows that the practice is deliberately "*going corporate*," with an emphasis on high-value and complex transactions rather than property management work. The property finance practice is also strong and draws on the firm's banking and structuring capacity, and the firm as a whole is gaining a more international flavour. Robin Mitchell heads a department that acted for CGI on its purchase of 10-15 Lombard Street from a subsidiary of MEPC for a £75 million development of offices and retail units. It also acted for the Benchmark Group in its creation of a Jersey property unit trust with Schroders called The West End of London Property Unit Trust (WELPUT). **Clients** Bench-

704   INDEX TO LEADING LAWYERS: PAGE 1693 ■ IN-HOUSE LAWYERS PROFILES: PAGE 1201

mark group; CGI; HSBC; Persimmon Homes; Helical Bar; QBE International Insurance; Annes Gate Property; Bank of Scotland; Old Mutual.

FORSTERS (see firm details p.960) "*A splash of colour*" that is "*going from strength to strength,*" this group is admired for "*creating a great niche from a standing start.*" Taking work from top-flight competitors, the "*gutsy*" team services an impressive client roster composed of institutional investors, as well as occupiers, developers and even public sector bodies. The team is particularly known for disposals and split title work, and is gaining real expertise in tax-driven deals. The best-known name here is "*strong and fair*" **Sophie Hamilton** (see p.730), whose "*commercial outlook and superb abilities*" make her "*a delightful person that gets deals done.*" **Anthony Patterson** (see p.734) is also well regarded. The team acted for Crown Dilmun in its purchase of the Harrods Depository, and for a private investor in the £97 million acquisition of Royal Mint Court. **Clients** McDonald's; Clerical Medical; Crown Dilmun; Shops etc.; Benchmark; Chester and Swansea City Councils; AOL Time Warner; Schlumberger; Redevco.

MAYER, BROWN, ROWE & MAW (see firm details p.1060) This team is still known best for its strong institutional and pension funds practice and niche specialism in local authority advice. Typical work includes corporate end-user and M&A support, and it boasts a large free standing practice. Clients especially appreciate it where banking documentation and the settlement of joint ventures are involved. The firm has taken part in one of the most talked about mergers of the year, and most of its competitors believe that "*the Americans, with their global resources, will really help,*" and that "*the Rowe & Maw team now has increased leverage.*" Led by Jeremy Clay, the team acted for Unilever on the acquisition and proposed development of a distribution centre in Doncaster, and for The Football Association on the acquisition and development of a National Football Centre at Byrkley Park. **Clients** Unilever; Nationwide; St Modwen; Henderson Global Investors; British Gas Pension Funds; ICI; AT&T; Royal Bank of Scotland.

SLAUGHTER AND MAY (see firm details p.1140) "*Small but perfectly formed,*" this team boasts "*great individuals and superb quality work.*" Approaching the market from a corporate angle, courtesy of its outstanding corporate client base, the practice also undertakes free-standing work for the likes of Manchester City Council, Whitbread, and Land Securities, leading some commentators to dub this "*the best-kept secret in the market.*" The team has seen a marked rise in investment and outsourcings work, and acts for property funds and tenants. **Graham White** (see p.738) has been described as "*one of the greats,*" while "*top-notch*" **Dermot Rice** (see p.735) also enjoys considerable support. The team acted for HRO (UK) on the letting of 265 The Strand to Covington and Burling, and the subsequent sale to German pension fund, CGI. It also advised Grosvenor and Dresdner Kleinwort Benson on the establishment of the Grosvenor/Kleinwort Benson Residential Limited Partnership. **Clients** HRO; Manchester City Council; Derwent Valley; Whitbread; Grosvenor; Abbey National; London Underground; Noble House; Land Securities; George Wimpey.

EVERSHEDS (see firm details p.949) A "*big and busy*" practice with a reputation for PFI work and an impressive client base including local authorities and other public sector bodies. The workload includes large projects and acquisitions, redevelopment and, on the investment side, property work under management for pension fund clients. The team acted for Berkeley Square Holdings on the acquisition, and subsequent management, of the Berkeley Square Estate, and for the London Borough of Islington on the redevelopment of Arsenal Football Ground. **Clients** London Borough of Islington; Berkeley Square Holdings; Catalyst Capital; Shaftesbury; ScottishPower Pension Scheme; Marconi; BAE Systems; Royal Bank of Scotland; NatWest; Jarvis group of companies; Poole Borough Council.

OLSWANG (see firm details p.1087) Institutions, medium-sized property companies and City funds make up the backbone of an investment practice, with development capacity, which peers admit has "*come up the fast lane.*" A tax focus gels with a growing emphasis on venture capital. The team is described as "*a good, aggressive unit, which project manages work well,*" while clients rave about its "*great tax-efficient advice.*" Group head **Tim Westhead** (see p.738) is "*commercial, sensible and hard-working,*" while **David Kustow** (see p.732) has been described as "*the lynchpin*" of the practice. **Philip Olmer** (see p.734) is "*supremely client-focused and responsive.*" The team acted for Capital & Regional on the formation with Morley Fund Management of The Mall Limited Partnership, creating a fund with an initial value of £670 million. **Clients** Capital & Regional; UBS Asset Management; Liverpool Victoria; Formhill Properties; Barclay Group; Allied London; Delancey Estates; Green Property (UK); Helical Bar; Minerva; Thornfield Properties; Woolworths.

SIMMONS & SIMMONS (see firm details p.1136) With a "*high-class property client base,*" this is a core practice area for the firm, which boasts a broad range of traditional work as well as more complex investment and finance deals. Though it represents property companies and occupiers, the team is particularly associated with investors, especially German and Italian funds. **Alan Butler** has a respected name. Peers describe him as "*always reliable,*" while for at least one client he is "*the main reason we use the firm.*" The team acted for MEPC on its £87 million forward sale to Matrix Securities of Northgate House in Moorgate. **Clients** Abu Dhabi Investment Authority; Deka Immobilien Investment; Henderson Global Investors; BP; Halfords; Interbrew.

FIELD FISHER WATERHOUSE (see firm details p.954) This is a traditional style property practice, which boasts specialist groups in institutional and property finance, hotels and leisure, retail, development, and industrial property and infrastructure. Clients are drawn from amongst multinationals, pension funds, retail chains, energy and telecommunications companies, leisure operators and developers. The team, headed by John Pedder, is especially known in the market for its strong practice in the leisure and brewing sectors, including transactions involving portfolios of licensed premises. **Clients** Pension funds; occupiers.

RICHARDS BUTLER (see firm details p.1112) Jon Pike heads an expanding property group that has been boosted by the "*tasty additions to its client roster*" which last year's merger with Higby Hargreaves is said to have brought. Practice specialisms include investment, development, leisure and hotels, and the team has been commended for its "*great work for Rank.*" The team acted for Land Securities Trillium on the service partner agreements underlying a partnership with the BBC set up to manage London and Scottish estates. It also assisted The io Group on the purchase of £50 million in investments for the Industrial Trust. **Clients** The io Group; Land Securities Trillium; Credit Suisse Asset Management; Commercial Estates Management; GLE; GNER; Kenmore; The Rank Group; Parkview International.

REAL ESTATE ■ LONDON

LONDON

SMALLER DEALS

REAL ESTATE: SMALLER DEALS
■ LONDON

1
- Boodle Hatfield
- Maxwell Batley

2
- Manches
- Nicholson Graham & Jones
- Speechly Bircham
- Travers Smith Braithwaite

3
- Finers Stephens Innocent
- Fladgate Fielder
- Julian Holy
- Trowers & Hamlins

4
- Hamlins
- Mishcon de Reya
- Osborne Clarke
- Park Nelson
- Stepien Lake Gilbert & Paling
- Taylor Wessing

This book is the product of 6,582 1/2 hour interviews. See p.7 for BMRB audit. Within each band, firms are listed alphabetically.

BOODLE HATFIELD (see firm details p.881) This "*thunderous property practice*" is "*user-friendly, commercial and experienced, with a huge prestige client.*" Richard Maughan leads the team, and Tim Manning is the relationship partner for that key client, Grosvenor Estates. The client base is growing, however, and now includes a range of commercial entities. The team is kept busy with ongoing work for Grosvenor on its well-reported developments in Basingstoke and Liverpool. It advised them on the formation of a limited partnership with Hammerson UK Properties for a £40 million office and retail redevelopment in Victoria. It also acted for PMB Holdings on the £28.5 million disposal of a 40,000 sq ft office block in the City to an overseas investor. **Clients** Grosvenor Estates; PMB Holdings; Bedford Estates; Treasury Holdings; Clubcorp International; Primary Health Care Centres; Highland Developments; British Biotech.

MAXWELL BATLEY (see firm details p.1059) This highly respected team is experienced in joint ventures, development and investment. Its impressive client base includes funds and institutional investors. The workload is mainly for landlords, though the team is also undertaking an increasing volume of occupier work. As relationships with the smaller portfolios deepen, the group is steadily developing the skills and capacity to handle outsourcings. Head of department Nigel Wilson handles a range of matters, such as institutional development financing and acquisitions and disposals, including portfolio transactions. **Clients** Hermes; National Mutual; Ropemaker Properties; General Electric Pension Trust; Land Securities; British Land; Ballast Wiltshier.

MANCHES (see firm details p.1052) Primarily associated with retail, this "*fine team*" has a niche in development and conducts a healthy volume of investment work for the likes of Green, Marylebone Warwick Balfour and Quintain. It has managed to grow its client base considerably over the last year, adding some impressive funds and developers. Louis Manches heads a department that has been appointed by Argos to work on its active acquisition programme. The team acted recently for JE Robert Company on a joint venture with Grosvenor Estates for a central London development. **Clients** Burford Group; Green Property; Quintain Estates; Marylebone Warwick Balfour; Munroe K; BHS Pension Fund; JE Robert Companies; WH Smith; PerkinElmer.

NICHOLSON GRAHAM & JONES (see firm details p.1083) This team of "*technically astute lawyers*" gains solid endorsement from the marketplace. The year has seen it increase its activity in investment and development work, for which it boasts a growing reputation. The team also has a number of complex deals with sophisticated tax and structuring aspects under its belt. Headed by Piers Coleman, the group acts for investors, occupiers and landlords. It represented Henderson Global Investors on a development at London Wall, in conjunction with Greycoat and Hammersons. It also acted for Heron International on the sale of 1 Drummond Gate. **Clients** Henderson Global Investors; Jermyn Investment Properties; Windsor Life Assurance; Loftus Family Property; London Underground; Arena Leisure; Arrowcroft Group; Heron International; HVB Real Estate Capital.

SPEECHLY BIRCHAM (see firm details p.1141) Popular with City lawyers, this is a "*tight, high-quality practice.*" Principal areas of work are investments for institutions, including large portfolio deals, and development. Clients enthuse that the firm has also "*got the tax edge,*" which wins it some complex and interesting deals. Headed by Charles Palmer, the team represents an impressive client list including institutions, pension funds, banks, developers, owner-occupiers, property companies, retailers and local authorities. It acted recently for The Royal London Mutual Insurance Society in the £300 million disposal of the Iceni Portfolio. **Clients** The Royal London Mutual Insurance Society; Royal Bank of Scotland; SLC Langbourn; P&O Properties; Visa International Service Association; Credit Suisse Investment Management; Chelsfield; Resolution; Howard de Walden Estates; Lincoln Financial Group.

TRAVERS SMITH BRAITHWAITE (see firm details p.1166) Offering a broad, free-standing practice, as well as undertaking high-quality corporate support, the team focuses on investment and development and is building a growing expertise in complex schemes in Europe. The group has made a name for itself for "*great property finance*" and is "*pretty hot on the pure stuff, too,*" according to competitors. Robert Harman leads a team that acted for Lothbury Property Trust in its purchase of the Dolphin Retail Park in Salisbury. It also assisted Lend Lease on the £220 million Touchwood Shopping Centre development in Solihull. **Clients** Anglo Irish Assurance Company; Bankgesellschaft Berlin; Clearwater Estates; Crestco; Lattice Group Pension Scheme; Lend Lease Europe; London Underground; De Vere Group.

FINERS STEPHENS INNOCENT (see firm details p.955) This "*lively and busy*" practice is engaged in increasingly complex, multi-disciplinary deals in the development and investment arenas. Growing its client base and team, competitors note the large volume of deals it handles, while clients appreciate its "*pragmatic approach.*" Best known for tax and construction, retail has been a growth area since the acquisition of niche firm Nathan Silman, and the team has been appointed to the panel of Virgin. David Battiscombe (see p.726) is said to have "*built the practice well,*" and it is "*thriving under his leadership.*" It acted for the Tannen Group on a £33 million acquisition of properties in Victoria and Holborn from Heron. **Clients** Portland House Holdings; Marylebone Warwick Balfour Group; Pizza Hut; Scope; Mean Fiddler Group; Grosvenor Waterside Group; St George South London; Tannen Group.

FLADGATE FIELDER (see firm details p.957) A "*great West End practice,*" interviewees praise this growing team as "*more together and effective than ever.*" Increasingly combining traditional property and corporate skills, its strength in investment and secured lending is complemented by expertise in development and leisure. Commentators note with approval that Allen Cohen's group has "*got better and tidier.*" It acted recently for Capital & Regional on the creation of a £350 million investment fund with Morley Fund Management. It also advised Orb Developments on the acquisition of a Thistle hotel in Dorset for redevelopment. **Clients** Allied Irish Banks; AXA Equity & Law Life Assurance Society; Bank of Scotland; Capital & Regional; Europe-Israel (MMS); Nando's Chickenland; Orb Estates; Woolwich; Sun Microsystems.

JULIAN HOLY (see firm details p.1018) A "*well-known and unique*" outfit, the heart of the practice is "*colourful*" Julian Holy, who is said to "*really know what he's doing.*" Respected for working hard and "*getting the deals done,*" the practice is said to have good international contacts, particularly in the Middle East and Asia. A loyal client base includes developers and occupiers. **Clients** Occupiers; landlords.

TROWERS & HAMLINS (see firm details p.1168) This "*upright*" team boasts a good range of public and private sector clients and is known for its "*sound workmanship*" and strength in property finance. Working closely with its well-regarded social housing and construction practices, the team is headed by Elizabeth McKibbin. Clients appreciate its ability to assist with the property aspects of corporate work, and pension fund transactions, and admire the way it has "*managed to become a City firm without losing its clarity and transparency*." The team acted for GP Nominees Limited, a fund managed by Aberdeen Asset Management, on development sites at Lyon Way, Camberley, and at Arenson Way, Dunstable. **Clients** Castlemore Securities; Aberdeen Property Asset Managers; Smiths Group; Network Estates; Crabtree & Evelyn (Overseas).

HAMLINS (see firm details p.983) The team's "*extensive experience*" in commercial property means that clients often instruct it to assist with "*complicated jigsaw stuff, which needs finesse and understanding.*" It acts for occupiers, property investors, developers, lenders and tenants, and has a recognised niche in property-related debt recovery. The team represented City Office Developments in forward funding and project management agreements with CGI for Capital House 10-15 Lombard Street, Paternoster House and 1 Paternoster Square. It also acted for NCP in a joint venture with Licet Holdings for the redevelopment of a prime site in the centre of Bournemouth to provide a mixed-use scheme and a subterranean car park. **Clients** City Office Developments; NCP.

MISHCON DE REYA (see firm details p.1072) This "*capable and vibrant*" practice has extensive experience in the sale and purchase of investment portfolios, joint venture structurings, secured lending and site assembly. Clients come from a range of sectors, including developers, pension funds, banks, house builders, private investors and occupiers. It has a growing reputation in the retail and leisure sectors and in urban regeneration. Nick Doffman heads a team that acted on the £70 million sale of King's Reach Tower to Capital & Counties. It also assisted specialist developer Urban Catalyst on the acquisition funding and development of its £32 million Bermondsey Square mixed-use urban regeneration scheme. **Clients** Asda Property Holdings; Associates Capital; Dunbar Bank; Edward Ware New Homes; Frogmore Estates; Helical Bar; Heron International; Holmes Place; HSBC Bank; Urban Catalyst; Warner Estate.

OSBORNE CLARKE (see firm details p.1090) Last year's merger with McGuinness Finch added some serious property clients, especially on the development and planning sides. The team has since also won some powerful investment clients. A "*well-rounded*" practice, according to peers, it advises on investment, development, finance and corporate occupation. Simon Speirs heads a growing team with an expanding profile, particularly in the retail and residential sectors. It acted for Benchmark Group on the £100 million acquisition, development, letting and disposal of Stirling Square, St James, to WELPUT, and for Marks & Spencer on its £50 million disposal of 11 stores and investment properties. **Clients** Barratt Homes; British Airways Pension Fund; Railtrack; Chiltern Investment Properties; Wimpey Property Holdings; Tesco; Henderson Investors.

PARK NELSON (see firm details p.1093) Regarded by market sources as "*a niche retail player, and great at it,*" this team is dedicated to commercial property. It acts for many major retailers and specialises in franchising, licensing, retail development, planning applications, sales and acquisitions. **Clients** Retail occupiers.

STEPIEN LAKE GILBERT & PALING (see firm details p.1148) "*Charismatic*" Tim Lake (see p.732) and his team won consistent plaudits this year from clients and competitors alike. Commentators acknowledge that he is "*impressive,*" and his team is growing its development skills to supplement an established investment practice. The team acted for St George on the £49 million acquisition of Gargoyle Wharf, and for another client on its acquisition of a central London investment for nearly £200 million. **Clients** Property companies, developers and investors.

TAYLOR WESSING (see firm details p.1156) Clients are full of praise for this "*smart group.*" Its capable partners are said to be "*good at working with other firms*" and to "*proceed with brisk professionalism.*" This year's acquisition of Garretts' commercial property department promises to boost the team's profile further. The team focuses on investment work and on the corporate end-user and development markets. It advised BEP Acquisitions on the property aspects of its bid for Bourne Properties and a proposed £140 million refinancing, and acted for Prestbury Investment Holdings on the purchase of a £60 million freehold office building at Holborn Gate. **Clients** Avebury Group; MWB; Canada Life; Prestbury Investment Holdings; Resolution Property; Diageo; Anglo-Irish; BHF Bank; Kew Green Hotels; Legal & General Ventures.

THE SOUTH

BLAKE LAPTHORN (see firm details p.877) Already the premier property department in the South, its October 2001 merger with Sherwin Oliver has bolstered it with four new property partners, prompting interviewees to agree that it has "*consolidated its lead further.*" The team, headed by highly respected Carey Blake, continues to attract commendation from peers and clients across the country. It recently closed the sale of 550 pubs for Whitbread, and was appointed by Berkeley Homes (Hampshire) and Berkeley Commercial Development to advise on the redevelopment of the 44-acre Royal Clarence Yard in Gosport. The team has also been appointed to the SEEDA legal panel for the first time, where it has advised on the purchase of regeneration land in Hampshire. It also provides banking support work and secured lending advice. **Clients** Bellway Homes; Premier Marinas; JS Bloor.

BOND PEARCE (see firm details p.879) "*Gradually spreading its influence along the coast from Plymouth to Southampton,*" peers praised the team's steady growth and breadth of practice. While Nigel Pugh has become a consultant, Tim Baily (see p.725) attracted substantial applause from clients for his "*technical ability.*" Strong retail and development teams are founded on a healthy balance of regional and national clients. The Dibden Terminal project, involving site acquisitions and the negotiation of collateral agreements with landowners, has been a highlight of the year for this busy outfit. Its growing public sector practice includes an expanding client base of educational institutions, and has seen it advise The Crown Estate (Marine Division) on the negotiation and settlement of the first phase of offshore wind farm leases with energy providers. It also advises mainstream commercial lenders. **Clients** Associated British Ports; B&Q; Coral Estates.

PARIS SMITH & RANDALL (see firm details p.1093) "*Quietly efficient,*" this team continues to be well received throughout the region. Prominent in the public sector, it has acted for local authorities on a regeneration scheme and a sports-related property development, and assisted a sixth form college on phased land disposal for development. In the commercial sector it acted recently for a local technology park on a proposed development and for Alldays Stores on the buy-back of its regional development companies. The "*thorough and polite*" Mark Howarth heads up the operation, which also undertakes substantial acquisitions and disposals for investor clients. **Clients** Southampton Leisure Holdings; Alldays Stores; Portsmouth FC; Banks of Ireland and Scotland.

STEVENS & BOLTON (see firm details p.1149) Boasting an "*excellent all-round profile,*" it is typically to be seen acting for commercial and

REAL ESTATE ■ THE SOUTH

REAL ESTATE
■ THE SOUTH

1
- **Blake Lapthorn** Fareham, Portsmouth, Southampton

2
- **Bond Pearce** Southampton
- **Paris Smith & Randall** Southampton
- **Stevens & Bolton** Guildford

3
- **Clyde & Co** Guildford
- **Cripps Harries Hall** Tunbridge Wells
- **Thomas Eggar** Chichester, Horsham, Reigate, Worthing

4
- **Brachers** Maidstone
- **DMH** Brighton, Crawley
- **Laytons** Guildford
- **Lester Aldridge** Bournemouth
- **Steele Raymond** Bournemouth
- **Thomson Snell & Passmore** Tunbridge Wells

5
- **Coffin Mew & Clover** Portsmouth, Southampton
- **GCL Solicitors** Guildford
- **Moore & Blatch** Southampton
- **Penningtons** Basingstoke, Godalming, Newbury
- **Rawlison Butler** Crawley
- **Shoosmiths** Fareham

LEADING INDIVIDUALS

1
- **BAILY Tim** Bond Pearce
- **BLAKE Carey** Blake Lapthorn

2
- **BENNETT Graham** Shoosmiths
- **HOWARTH Mark** Paris Smith & Randall
- **MITCHELL James** Stevens & Bolton

3
- **BAILEY Michael** asb law
- **BERRY Paul** Clyde & Co
- **BURTON Carl** DMH
- **ELLIS Michael** Cripps Harries Hall
- **GREEN Gilbert** Thomson Snell & Passmore
- **NEIL Don** Coffin Mew & Clover

UP AND COMING
- **DODGSON Robert** Davies Lavery

This book is the product of 6,582 1/2 hour interviews. See p.7 for BMRB audit.
Within each band, firms are listed alphabetically. See individuals' profiles p.725

---

residential developers, private investment companies and educational establishments. Noted by peers for its "*City feel,*" City recruitments are much in evidence here, including most recently Howard Lupton, former head of property at Middleton Potts. Ex-Slaughter and May and highly rated, James Mitchell (see p.733) advised BOC on the lease and subsequent sale of its Guildford head office to Topland Ridgeway for an eight-figure sum. He also acted on the property aspects of the sale of Asquith Schools to West Private Equity for £66 million, involving the transfer of over 60 properties UK-wide. The department is well supplied with logistics sector clients. **Clients** BOC; Hays; Adecco.

CLYDE & CO (see firm details p.913) An "*active team building up a decent practice*" was the verdict of peers on this energetic department, while clients attested to its "*excellent expertise shown in the midst of complex transactions.*" It has retained major national clients such as The Carphone Warehouse and Frogmore Estates while securing instructions from a clutch of new hi-tech, finance and retail businesses. Specialising in property investment and development, interviewees continue to admire the personal and technical abilities of Paul Berry. He has been involved in securing multimillion pound Docklands pre-lets, an acquisition of central London office space and the development of a distribution centre. The team also manages the property portfolios of clients such as Unigate Dairies. **Clients** Frogmore Estates; The Carphone Warehouse; Kipling UK.

CRIPPS HARRIES HALL (see firm details p.922) Retaining its market position following a busy year, the firm is often seen acting on behalf of local authorities and central government. Recent highlights include ongoing advice to Gravesham Borough Council on a mixed commercial and residential scheme and a canal basin development. "*Level-headed*" Mike Ellis (see p.729) enters the tables for the first time, having built a strong reputation across the region for advising residential developers. The team represented Croudace on the acquisition of Portland Homes and assisted Sittingbourne Retail Park on the leasing of units. Co-operating closely with the firm's construction and planning, and environment departments, other areas of strength include property portfolio management, advising major landowners and providing corporate support. **Clients** Crown Prosecution Service; Rouse Kent; Berkeley Homes (Eastern).

THOMAS EGGAR (see firm details p.1160) Rising in the tables this year, the firm is considered by peers to "*have a wider range of clients than most practices in the South.*" With Chris Bell at the helm, it covers property investment, pension funds and high-value acquisitions and disposals and also has niche property expertise in the rail sector. Its broad practice is distributed among several offices in the region, with the Horsham operation rising to prominence in the wake of its important further education sector property work. The firm acted for the West Bromwich Mortgage Company on the property aspects of the acquisition of the residential mortgage portfolio of New World, the UK mortgage lending division of the Commonwealth Bank of Australia. **Clients** Railtrack; Gleeson Homes; Rydon Group; Woolwich.

BRACHERS (see firm details p.886) Noted throughout the region for its "*strong commercial presence,*" the property team has solid support from the firm's planning and environment department, enabling it to provide a comprehensive property service. The group wins promotion in this year's tables, having gained a large volume of market applause. Typical recent work has included a £30 million building agreement, linked to Government funding. This involved a multimillion pound development option agreement with associated tax planning, trust and agricultural holdings work. The team also won a contract to undertake all property work for a public utility. Led by Geoffrey Burr, it has recognised strength in acting for NHS Trusts on hospital disposals, acquisitions and PFI projects. **Clients** NHS Trusts; manufacturers; developers and development consortia; utilities.

DMH (see firm details p.940) Now operating from Brighton, Crawley and London, it is rated by peers for having "*excellent lawyers who make transactions go in the right direction,*" and continues to attract premium project-related property work in the region. "*One of the best residential development lawyers in the South,*" Carl Burton (see p.727) remains highly visible, recently acting for Crest Nicholson Group companies on site acquisitions and strategic options. Ongoing advice to Brighton and Hove Albion FC on the negotiation, land assembly and project development for its £50 million new first division football stadium remains a touchstone for the quality of work in which the team is involved. With strengths in leisure, licensing and public sector property development, other highlights include extensive nationwide lease renewal work for the TM Retail group. **Clients** Crest Nicholson Group; Catholic Diocese of Arundel and Brighton; University of Sussex.

LAYTONS (see firm details p.1032) Widely recognised in the market as one of the leading advisors to the land development and house building sector, the practice is led by Ian Cook. His dedicated team deals with the sale of over 2,000 new homes annually for developer clients. The team is offering ongoing advice to the consortia on a new settlement in Cambourne, Cambridgeshire, including a business park and leisure facilities, and on the development of the Greenwich Gateway project. Highlight acquisitions include advising Prowting on the £11.2 million purchase of land for the 500-unit Sovereign Harbour Development in Eastbourne. **Clients** Barratt Homes; Cambourne Development Project; Wimpey Homes.

LESTER ALDRIDGE (see firm details p.1038) Having "*made a huge effort in Southampton,*" where it recently opened an office, Bob Robertson's team is acknowledged by competitors to have gone from strength to strength. Focusing on development, company relocations, and site acquisitions, it advised Bournemouth Borough Council on a multimillion pound redevelopment around Boscombe Pier involving a joint venture with a house builder. The practice has been appointed sole solicitor for Portland Port's industry development portfolio. It also has a specialist practice in doctors' surgeries and nursing home-related property work. **Clients** Lloyds TSB; SWERDA.

THAMES VALLEY ■ REAL ESTATE

STEELE RAYMOND (see firm details p.1146) Headed by John Raymond, the department has seen sustained activity this year in the retail and development sectors. Clients appreciate its "*hands-on approach*" and consistent partner involvement. The team has completed the acquisition of substantial leasehold retail warehouses for Land of Leather, and represented the Troika Group on the purchase of office buildings in Hampshire and Dorset. Other highlights include advising the RNLI on a number of property matters, including the establishment of four lifeboat stations on the Thames. **Clients** WH White; Bournemouth International Airport.

THOMSON SNELL & PASSMORE (see firm details p.1161) Although less visible this year, according to competitors, the firm preserves its traditional niche with substantial work advising on site acquisitions and disposals. Typical work has included acting for the site owner on the redevelopment of a former industrial complex in the Medway area, and advising the LEA and school governors on a disposal of land for residential development to fund a new school. The team also acts on property transactions for pension funds, institutions and private individuals. Dealing with all types of commercial property transaction, "*effective operator*" **Gilbert Green** (see p.730) remains a prominent figure in the marketplace. **Clients** Colas; Marley Pension Fund; developers.

COFFIN MEW & CLOVER Valued by clients for its residential property expertise, it also handles substantial commercial property matters for its client-base of house builders, NHS Trusts, land dealers and commercial developers. Having seen growth in property-related banking work, highly regarded senior figure **Don Neil** (see p.734) and his team acted for new client NatWest on major securities work involving a land value of over £1 million. Property investment also features heavily in the firm's workload. Highlights include advice to Breamore Developments on the £1.1 million purchase and subsequent £2.5 million sale of an investment property in Hampshire. **Clients** Gieves & Hawkes; Bellway Homes; University of Portsmouth.

GCL SOLICITORS (see firm details p.968) This "*efficient team*" was endorsed by competitors and clients alike for its efficiency and expertise and is distinguished by its residential development profile. In addition to local developers it acts for two national house builders. With Tony Inkin active in this area, recent highlights include major residential developments in central London, one involving over 2,000 units. **Clients** House builders.

MOORE & BLATCH (see firm details p.1074) With a dedicated residential development practice that also covers associated planning matters, the firm was described by one interviewee as "*outstanding in this sphere.*" Retaining its market position under the leadership of Steve Ingram, recent highlights have included acting for Barratt Homes and Banner Homes on the purchase of multimillion pound sites across the South. **Clients** House builders; developers; local authorities.

PENNINGTONS (see firm details p.1089) With offices across the South, the firm covers a broad range of commercial property work, including landlord and tenant and commercial leases, for its client base of national house builders, developers, institutional landlords, commercial lenders and corporations. The Newbury team, headed by Tom Rossiter, advised the Greenham Common Trust on a site sale for a major regional retail depot at Greenham Business Park. In collaboration with Latham & Watkins, the firm also acted for a group of investors on the property and construction aspects of the securitisation of Southampton, Ipswich Town and Leeds Utd football stadiums. The team benefits from good working relations with the London operations of US and Australian law firms. **Clients** Audley Developments; Cherwell Land; Sun Life of Canada.

RAWLISON BUTLER Headed by Andrew King and Clive Prior, the firm maintains a sound property profile. Experienced in both commercial and residential property development, and landlord and tenant work, the team also provides support on the property aspects of corporate transactions. Continuing to attract new clients in the retail, leisure and childcare sectors, it recently advised Amadeus Services on the completion of the lease for its new headquarters building at the World Business Centre at Heathrow Airport. **Clients** Amadeus Services; Crown Sports; JT Davies & Sons.

SHOOSMITHS (see firm details p.1133) Clients confirmed that the team "*consistently puts in the effort to understand our business.*" Working closely with the Reading office, it has been appointed to the panel of new client SEEDA, heralding instructions on major regeneration projects. Focusing on portfolio management and commercial development, this growing practice also covers property finance work for a range of banks, and some residential development. "*Excellent*" property head **Graham Bennett** (see p.726) recently advised Esso on its objections to ABP's proposals for a new container terminal at Dibden Bay. **Clients** HJ Heinz; Esso Petroleum; ExxonMobil Chemical.

OTHER NOTABLE PRACTITIONERS Michael Bailey (see p.725) of asb law remains a respected figure in the market, recently acting for the landowners in negotiations with a consortium of developers over the sale of a high value site for residential development. **Robert Dodgson** (see p.728) of Davies Lavery enters *Chambers'* tables this year. He impressed clients by combining a "*human approach*" with "*thorough attention to detail and pure doggedness.*" Best known for residential development work, he has also begun to attract secured lending property-related instructions.

THAMES VALLEY

PITMANS (see firm details p.1103) "*Efficient and prompt,*" with a top-rank client base of major developers, investors, banks and occupiers, this team is now widely recognised by peers as the leading regional commercial property outfit. "*Affable and knowledgeable*" **James Burgess** (see p.727) recently acted for Madford Developments on its £70 million acquisition of an MEPC portfolio, involving the purchase of three properties via SPVs. He also advised software company Veritas on the leasing of buildings at Green Park, Reading, for its European headquarters. Best known for his residential development work, rivals commented of **Andrew Davies** (see p.728) that "*you always know you will get a fair and commercial deal done*" with him on the other side. **Clients** MEPC; Allied Bank of Pakistan; Barratt Homes; Porsche.

BROOKSTREET DES ROCHES (see firm details p.890) Rated by peers as "*an excellent firm with all-round property expertise and decent commercial lawyers,*" it has received new instructions this year from Cable & Wireless and McDonald's, managing a fair portion of both companies' property portfolios. The firm boasts a client base of industrial, telecoms and energy entities and commercial landlords. Highly regarded **Charlie Seaward** (see p.736) recently acted for The National Grid Company on the £20 million disposal of the former NGC Control and Computer Centre on London's South Bank. **Martin Billings** (see p.726) remains well reputed, acting for MEPC on all acquisition and lease work in connection with Milton Park. Other highlights include acting for Booker in connection with the disposal of a development site in Reading for £15 million. **Clients** Mitre Estates; Blockbuster; National Grid; MEPC.

REAL ESTATE ■ THAMES VALLEY

REAL ESTATE
■ THAMES VALLEY

1 **Pitmans** Reading

2 **BrookStreet Des Roches** Witney
Denton Wilde Sapte Milton Keynes

3 **Clarks** Reading
Harold Benjamin Littlejohn Harrow
Iliffes Booth Bennett (IBB) Uxbridge
Morgan Cole Oxford, Reading

4 **Linnells** Oxford
Matthew Arnold & Baldwin Watford

5 **Boyes Turner** Reading
BPC Business Lawyers Gerrards Cross
Fennemores Milton Keynes
Manches Oxford
Nabarro Nathanson Reading
Pictons Luton, St Albans
Stanley Tee Bishop's Stortford

LEADING INDIVIDUALS

1 **DAVIES Andrew** Pitmans

2 **BURGESS James** Pitmans

3 **BILLINGS Martin** BrookStreet Des Roches
PAUL Sarah Harold Benjamin Littlejohn
SEAWARD Charlie BrookStreet Des Roches
SILVA David Iliffes Booth Bennett (IBB)

This book is the product of 6,582 1/2 hour interviews. See p.7 for BMRB audit.
Within each band, firms are listed alphabetically. See individuals' profiles p.725

DENTON WILDE SAPTE (see firm details p.935) This team won widespread praise from clients and competitors for its experienced, commercial approach and "*helpful and thorough advice.*" It has been reappointed to the panel of high-profile client English Partnerships, which it advises on various projects, in particular the further development of Milton Keynes. Led by David Danskin and Chris Denny, it has also advised Nokia on a major development and continues to act for KFC on recent acquisitions. High-profile portfolio management work includes advising on the management of property portfolios for Whitbread and Thornfield. **Clients** English Partnerships; Barclays; London Borough of Barking & Dagenham.

CLARKS (see firm details p.908) "*Now a leading light in property terms,*" regional players acknowledge that the team is beginning to emerge as a major force in the area. It has recruited five new lawyers in the past year, including two who are City-trained and two from the in-house department of Blue Circle Industries. Derek Ching heads a department with expertise in the office, industrial and public sectors. It recently acted for a major landowner on disposals in excess of £30 million and the transfer of secured loans of over £7 million. Supported by the firm's construction, litigation, planning and environmental teams, a large portion of its property caseload consists of instructions from NHS Trusts. Other typical work includes acting on a major pre-let of an industrial warehouse and the disposal of pension fund investment property. **Clients** Bunzl Group; BMW; CMB.

HAROLD BENJAMIN LITTLEJOHN (see firm details p.985) With an enviable mixture of national and local clients, the firm attracts high praise from a range of interviewees. Applauded for "*always performing to high standards,*" it has separate teams dealing with commercial development and the acquisition and management of sites. A "*feisty and pragmatic lead partner,*" Sarah Paul (see p.734) continues to advise Ladbrokes on lease renewals and property development throughout England and Wales. She oversees leasing advice in relation to new office developments and restaurants, as well as in the residential sector. The firm has seen an increase in advice to joint venture partners on inner-city mixed developments. It has also advised Southern Syringe on the sale of its Southgate headquarters to Fairview New Homes. **Clients** Bellway Homes & Estates; Michael Grant Homes; Michael Shanly Group; Southern Syringe.

ILIFFES BOOTH BENNETT (IBB) (see firm details p.1007) "*A little gem of a firm that frequently outperforms its better known City rivals,*" it is carried up the tables this year by a considerable volume of praise from the market. With a growing investment property practice, the team has won instructions from new client Evolve Fund Services to advise on establishing investment funds with a projected first-year value of £50 million. It also acted for Cathedral Court, a joint venture company formed by RBS and Frontier Estates, on the £25 million acquisition of the Prudential Buildings in Birmingham. David Silva (see p.736) enters *Chambers*' tables following praise from developer clients for "*heading an excellent team,*" as well as for his legal skills, especially in property finance, a growing area for the firm. The team boasts expertise in commercial and residential development and landlord and tenant advice. **Clients** Bellway Homes; CGNU; Frontier Estates.

MORGAN COLE (see firm details p.1075) Showing considerable "*staying power*" despite its recent changes of personnel, peers confirm that this is still a force to be reckoned with. Retaining an enviable traditional client base, the team works closely with its energy department and is advising BP on the disposal of a former oil terminal, most recently completing the commercial development aspects of the project. Other highlights include acting for International Power on the purchase and refinancing of Rugeley B power station, worth £200 million, and assisting Hays on the £20 million purchase of a site in the City of London. Both deals were conducted out of the Oxford office, where Ruth Morgan plays a key role. **Clients** Hays; International Power; UK Atomic Energy Authority.

LINNELLS (see firm details p.1044) The firm has merged its commercial and residential practices to create a unified commercial property department. Though competitors consider that its profile has fallen this year, it has been involved in some enviable deals, including the sale by Blackwell Science of an office to Oxford University. Other highlights include winning a tender to become sole property lawyers to Christchurch College, Oxford, and the team, headed by Stanley Beckett, also assisted a US multinational on a sale and lease back transaction worth over £40 million. **Clients** Berkeley Homes; Coventry Building Society; Bon Marché; Speedy Hire.

MATTHEW ARNOLD & BALDWIN (see firm details p.1058) Clients confirm that this practice "*produces work to the highest standard.*" With its thriving insolvency practice, banks such as Barclays account for a large portion of the firm's property clients, as do restaurants, public houses and retailers. In addition to receivership and liquidator sales, sale and leaseback schemes throughout London and the Northern counties continue to feature in the team's workload. Richard Hanney heads up the department, which also has experience in all aspects of commercial and residential property development. **Clients** Cerplex; Eurocar; Watford FC.

BOYES TURNER (see firm details p.883) The team, headed by Mark Appleton, is considered by peers to be "*well versed in property matters*." It has successfully cemented relations with key clients, acting for Barratt Homes on the £9.25 million acquisition of a factory site in Bedfordshire and representing a local developer on the £3.25 million purchase of a site in Reading. Secured lending advice for major banks is an area of growth for the team. **Clients** Barratt North London; Barclays; Persimmon.

BPC BUSINESS LAWYERS (see firm details p.884) "*Fielding an impressive team,*" according to competitors, the firm recently advised a US company on its acquisition of a substantial mobile storage company in the UK, involving around 30 sites worth up to £45 million. Another recent highlight was its work assisting the vendor on the sale of a leisure management business for £10 million, featuring health clubs in central London. Justin Samuel is one of a seven-partner team. **Clients** Sixt Kenning Group; United Biscuits (Holdings); Montpellier Group.

FENNEMORES Retaining its market position, competitors consider this a "*robust property outfit.*" Headed by Simon Ingram, the team deals with acquisitions and disposals of land and property in the retail, office and industrial sectors, as well as landlord and tenant work, for its impressive client list of investors, developers and occupiers. **Clients** Nicholls Brasseries; Pharmacia; Scania (Great Britain).

MANCHES (see firm details p.1052) The firm's property profile was felt by peers to benefit from a strong corporate practice and a renowned social housing unit. The group can also draw on the firm's environmental and property tax expertise, while recent recruitment to the office's PFI/PPP group should further bolster its visibility in the property arena. A growing department, led by Richard Shaw, much of its caseload is development work for major corporate and property clients, while it also provides support to the firm's IT department. **Clients** Siemens Real Estate; British Energy; Black & Decker.

NABARRO NATHANSON (see firm details p.1080) A "*first-class outfit*" according to clients, it enjoys a traditional profile in the retail sector and recently assisted GAP on its retail expansion programme. Headed by Andrew Banton, the team also played a role in advising GE Capital as a joint venture partner in the £47.25 million acquisition of the Headrow Shopping Centre in Leeds. Acting on a range of acquisitions and disposals, often in conjunction with the outstanding London outfit, the office has recently expanded its roster of Thames Valley IT clients, having won the property work of Oracle. **Clients** GE Capital; Oracle; GAP.

PICTONS Led by Chris Brown, the team remains a force in its locality. It continues to focus on leisure and electronics companies, as well as advising leading banks on property-related security work. One recent highlight was acting for a major joint venture company on the redevelopment of a site in Hemel Hempstead. **Clients** Citylights Group; SPG; Hemel Hempstead Group of Companies.

STANLEY TEE (see firm details p.1145) Clients expressed enthusiasm for this "*driven and exceptionally good*" commercial property department, which enters the tables this year as a result. It covers PFI-related instructions from health and education sector clients, mid-market corporate acquisitions and disposals, and advice to farmers converting land to a commercial or residential use. Jeremy Gillham heads the team. **Clients** Health authorities; independent and foundation schools; corporations; private landowners; banks; breweries.

SOUTH WEST

REAL ESTATE
SOUTH WEST

[1] **Burges Salmon** Bristol
Osborne Clarke Bristol
[2] **Beachcroft Wansbroughs** Bristol
Bevan Ashford Bristol, Exeter, Plymouth, Taunton
Bond Pearce Bristol, Exeter, Plymouth
Michelmores Exeter
[3] **Clarke Willmott & Clarke** Bristol, Taunton
TLT Solicitors Bristol
[4] **BPE** Cheltenham
Davies and Partners Gloucester
Rickerbys Cheltenham
Stephens & Scown Exeter, Liskeard, St Austell, Truro
Veale Wasbrough Bristol
[5] **Charles Russell** Cheltenham
Clark Holt Swindon
Davitt Jones Bould Taunton
Foot Anstey Sargent Plymouth
Lyons Davidson Bristol
Thring Townsend Bath, Swindon

This book is the product of 6,582 1/2 hour interviews. See p.7 for BMRB audit. Within each band, firms are listed alphabetically.

BURGES SALMON (see firm details p.894) Universal commendation from peers for its "*breadth of practice and quality of people*" qualifies the firm for the top tier once again. Having established a "*successful national practice,*" it has a strong presence in the office, leisure, retail, transport, telecoms, energy and industrial sectors. Brownfield regeneration and PPP relocation and development projects have also featured in the team's workload. Its "*out-and-out professionalism*" is epitomised by practitioners like funding and portfolio management specialist **John Dunn** (see p.729), who advised Lattice Property Holdings on the £10 million sale of a 20-acre development site in Manchester, involving remediation and infrastructure negotiations. "*Punchy performer*" **Stephen McNulty** (see p.764) is known for his property development work and this year resumes his position as head of the team. Now head of property development, former Rowe & Maw partner and "*heavy-hitter*" **David Gidney** (see p.729) is building on his "*excellent reputation for regional work*" by assisting with the firm's expansion into the London property market. **Robert Smyth** (see p.736) manages property portfolios for the likes of Scottish and Southern Energy and NAAFI, while also sustaining a niche telecoms sector practice. He recently advised 186K on establishing and running a national property acquisition programme for England and Scotland. This year the practice gained a place on The Crown Estate's panel for the first time, dealing exclusively with all commercial urban estates outside London. Other recent highlights include the closing of acquisitions on behalf of Honda, Innogy and EMI for their respective HQs. Robin Battersby remains an active consultant for the firm. **Clients** Orange; Canadian & Portland Estates; CSFB; Nationwide Building Society.

OSBORNE CLARKE (see firm details p.1090) The South West property department was described by interviewees as "*impressively managed,*" with specialist teams working in the development, retail, leisure, residential and investment sectors. Clients praised a "*slick operation*" able to complete deals swiftly and with "*a high level of technical aptitude.*" Its "*ambitious expansion*" has helped create a network that has strong ties with London and offices across Europe. **Simon Speirs** oversees the work of the entire department, and has achieved an "*outstanding reputation.*" He recently acted for Imperial Tobacco Pension Trustees on the £25 million sale of a portfolio of five industrial estates. Other highlights include acting for Pubmaster on the property elements of the proposed £523 million acquisition of Inn Partnership with a portfolio of over 1,200 pubs. The team also represented Benchmark Group on the acquisition, development, letting and disposal of a central London site valued at £100 million. Its quality and profile have assured the group a stream of new clients, notably winning it appointment to the Marks & Spencer property panel and instructions from the likes of Rotch Property. Its ability to provide advice on related areas, such as environment, planning and tax, strengthens it further. **Clients** British Airways Pension Fund; Pubmaster Group; Railtrack.

BEACHCROFT WANSBROUGHS (see firm details p.860) Widely praised to researchers for its "*transactional prowess,*" the firm is noted for its strong public sector profile. The department boasts a specialist NHS property team that covers large-scale investment and development work as well as disposals. Other areas of expertise include property development, often incorporating joint ventures. The team is increasingly active in property portfolio management, with an emphasis on shopping centres, as well as secured lending. Relinquishing his post as head of property to become regional senior partner, "*extremely well-respected*" **Michael Bothamley** (see p.726) nevertheless retains his market profile as a leading development lawyer. Interviewees sensed a degree of regrouping following the retirement of Martin Davis Jones, though the group continues to grow through a series of intelligent recruitments, prompting one interviewee to comment that it "*has upped its game.*" PFI-related advice

REAL ESTATE ■ SOUTH WEST

LEADING INDIVIDUALS

1
- **BOTHAMLEY Michael** Beachcroft Wansbroughs
- **GUNN David** Bond Pearce

2
- **DUNN John** Burges Salmon
- **GIDNEY David** Burges Salmon
- **MCNULTY Stephen** Burges Salmon
- **PRITCHARD Nicholas** TLT Solicitors
- **SCOTT Peter** Bevan Ashford
- **SMITHERS Tim** Veale Wasbrough

3
- **BROTHWOOD Graham** Clark Holt
- **DUNN Ian** Bond Pearce
- **FABIAN Mark** Rickerbys
- **GLYNN Andrew** TLT Solicitors
- **HANDLEY Richard** BPE
- **HOGGETT Jonathan** Stephens & Scown
- **JACOMB Brian** Thring Townsend
- **JORDAN Geoffrey** Charles Russell
- **LOWLESS Peter** Michelmores
- **SMYTH Robert** Burges Salmon
- **SPEIRS Simon** Osborne Clarke

See individuals' profiles p.725

is a specialist area. **Clients**: NHS Trusts; Building societies; national retailers.

BEVAN ASHFORD (see firm details p.869) Highly praised for its public sector work, particularly on behalf of the NHS and regional development agencies, this firm's commercial property department was said by clients and competitors to succeed through its "*practical and technically accomplished lawyers.*" Operating from a network of offices that gives it superb regional coverage, the group has been active in PFI-structured deals and development schemes, and offers specialist expertise in property tax. "*Commercial and pragmatic*" Peter Scott (see p.736) has been heavily involved in mixed-use residential and commercial schemes as part of redevelopment projects in Plymouth. His specialisms include estate rationalisation and joint ventures. The department also has a following of clients in the leisure and retail sectors. **Clients** SWERDA; Devon County Council; Hanson Quarry Products Europe.

BOND PEARCE (see firm details p.879) Competitors continue to regard Plymouth as the hub of the firm's regional practice, and recent highlights include acting for P&O Properties on the site acquisition and anchor letting of that city's Drakes Circus project. The team received warm commendation from peers for its "*commercial approach*," something that also makes it the preferred choice for many clients. Standout partner David Gunn (see p.730) has recently advised Rokeagle Group on major investments and Midas Group on development acquisitions. Ian Dunn (see p.729) also retains a strong market profile and has advised on several large pub portfolio transactions. The team's strengths lie in the public, transport and waste sectors, mostly on the development side, while recent recruits from Eversheds and Cartwrights have strengthened its compulsory purchase and licensing expertise. **Clients** Defence Estates; English Heritage; National Assembly of Wales; Transport for London.

MICHELMORES (see firm details p.1068) Peers acknowledge the "*continued growth*" of this important regional player, and point to the expansion of its public sector client base. The team now acts for 11 government agencies, as well as representing owners of business parks, developers and institutional clients. With strength in the property aspects of PFI, the department recently acted for the Court Service on the Exeter Combined Court PFI. Peter Lowless continues to be singled out by clients for commendation. He recently assisted the Borough of Torbay in a regeneration project at Torquay Waterfront. This comprised three interdependent developments and involved public, private and charitable bodies. He also led the property advice for two higher education authorities on a joint venture to create a new campus in Cornwall. **Clients** Regional developers; local and national house builders; local government and public bodies.

CLARKE WILLMOTT & CLARKE (see firm details p.907) Most peers expressed approval of recent developments at the firm, whereby it has closed its Bridgewater volume conveyancing unit and established "*an effective focus*" on the Bristol and Taunton offices. Core areas include house building, the retail sector and property finance and it is enjoying an increase in public sector activity. The team acted for Allied Irish Bank on its loan to fund the establishment of a £25 million medical teaching facility at Plymouth University. It has also received new instructions from Burger King on the development of sites nationally and has been appointed by Oddbins as sole advisor on the management of its property portfolio. Roger Seaton heads the department. **Clients** Unique/Voyager; Burger King; Nationwide Business Finance.

TLT SOLICITORS (see firm details p.1163) "*A well-managed team of quality lawyers*" that has "*worked hard to gain access to a competitive market,*" it continues to earn the respect of peers. Supported by planning and environment teams, it has acted on a range of property financing and portfolio management matters. Interviewees agreed that Andrew Glynn (see p.730) and Nicholas Pritchard (see p.735) remain at the forefront of the firm's operation. Recent highlights for the group include a £16 million transaction involving the refinancing of a harbourside portfolio for the JT Group. It also advised a consortium of Stroud District Council, Stroud College and Gloucester County Council on the redevelopment of Dursley town centre. With national clients such as Hanson taking the firm's practice beyond its regional base, it continues to be bolstered with new recruits and new clients, including Swan Hill Homes. **Clients** The Rank Group; Barclays; Sun Life Pensions Management.

BPE (see firm details p.884) Moving up the tables, the core strength of this "*agile team of lawyers,*" according to clients, lies in property development. They claim that the firm owes much of its success to head of department Richard Handley (see p.730), who is "*a natural first choice*" of several interviewees. The team receives instructions in relation to retail parks and industrial estates and provides advice on managing investment portfolios. It recently represented Granchester, alongside Clifford Chance, principally on tenancy and CPO issues arising from a development in Gloucester. Lead solicitors to Rodamco Inversiones on its €150 million acquisition of a substantial part of a regional shopping and leisure scheme in Valencia, the team also acted for Wolseley on the purchase of its new head office. **Clients** Granchester; Rodamco Inversiones; Wolseley.

DAVIES AND PARTNERS (see firm details p.929) This firm is best known amongst peers for its "*superb residential property profile.*" With Peter Mitchell heading up the group, it also has a following of retail and commercial sector clients. Boasting six partners involved in site acquisitions and disposals, the team has experience of a range of commercial property work including advice on consortium agreements, land options and project finance. The Gloucester-based practice also covers related financing, tax and planning issues. **Clients** House builders; retailers; investment companies.

RICKERBYS (see firm details p.1113) "*Excellent lawyers servicing a sound and long-established client base*" was the verdict returned by the market on this impressive regional outfit. Covering a wide range of disciplines, including national licensed property work, the team advises private clients on sales and developments and was one of nine acting for Whitbread on the £1.6 billion buyout of its 3,000-pub portfolio by Morgan Grenfell. It continues to act for Whitbread's pub and bar estate. Well regarded by peers, Mark Fabian (see p.729) acted for a local property developer on the sale of a brownfield development site involving complex environmental and planning negotiations. The team also assisted the consortium that acquired Kemble Airfield from the MOD. **Clients** Whitbread; Group 4; British Waterways Board.

STEPHENS & SCOWN Best known for its involvement in major regional projects, the team continues to win wide-ranging work throughout the West Country and beyond, including instructions relating to residential and commercial developments. Niche expertise in minerals and mining-related transactions remains a core strength. Highlights of the year include securing the property work for a major telecoms company, involving advice on the London relocation of its head office. It also recently acted for a developer in a £30 million Thames Valley office redevelopment. "*Careful and thorough*" **Jonathan Hoggett** remains well regarded by peers. **Clients** Aggregate Industries; IMERYS Minerals; National Marine Museum of Cornwall; SWERDA.

VEALE WASBROUGH (see firm details p.1174) Possessing "*lawyers with a refreshingly commercial approach,*" according to interviewees, a busy year has seen the firm acting for Bristol & England Properties in a series of high-value transactions involving pre-letting, forward funding and forward sale. Continuing with the Bath Spa, Gloucester docks and Bristol Harbour regeneration projects, the team has also advised the MOD on substantial disposals. Other highlights include advising a major international partnership, with an estate of around 150 properties, on the property aspects of converting to a limited liability partnership. An established property development specialist, **Tim Smithers** (see p.736) sustains a "*strong market following.*" **Clients** Lloyds TSB; Defence Estates; Local authorities.

CHARLES RUSSELL (see firm details p.904) Providing "*advice of the highest order,*" the firm acts for lenders, corporate clients and investors on both a regional and national level. Its "*gentlemanly and clever*" head of department **Geoffrey Jordan** (see p.732) received commendation from peers and clients alike. He is leading ongoing advice on the development of the South West Bicester mixed-use development scheme. Other highlights for the group include the acquisition of properties to a value of £30 million within a new limited partnership fund managed by LaSalle Investment Management. The firm boasts a specialist planning and development unit and has a niche clientele of Irish-based companies operating throughout the UK. **Clients** Eagle Star; Fairbridge Estates; Montpellier Group.

CLARK HOLT (see firm details p.907) This "*hungry, young outfit,*" is said by peers to have "*picked up clients quickly,*" bringing it to prominence in the region and leading to its first appearance in the tables. Its success is felt by interviewees to be partly attributable to the strong profile of department head **Graham Brothwood** (see p.727), who recently led advice to Tyco Electronics on the freehold disposal, to Brookhouse Development, of a commercial development site in Swindon. Other highlights include advising Parkstead House on an £8 million disposal of a Grade 1 Listed former educational college in South London to an educational charity. Active for regional house builders on a number of site acquisitions, client wins this year include property instructions from GWR Group. **Clients** Fortis Bank; Bloor Holdings; First Property Online.

DAVITT JONES BOULD (see firm details p.931) Retaining "*substantial Government property work,*" the practice has also made inroads into the private sector. A three-year-old dedicated property firm with 14 former government lawyers, it covers large-scale disposals, leasehold work and contentious claims. Highlights include acting for the MOD on all property aspects of the privatisation of DERA and the creation of Qinetiq. It also acted for a public sector client on the granting of leases to a communications company for over 100 G3 masts, and for the Royal Parks on the impact of Heathrow Terminal 5 on Crown land. Madeleine Davitt oversees the team. **Clients** MOD; HM Prison Service; Royal Parks.

FOOT ANSTEY SARGENT (see firm details p.958) A "*well-respected practice,*" the team works closely with the firm's planning department, acting for owner-managed businesses from farmers to commercial property developers. The team, led by Simon Gregory in Exeter and Cindy Rai in Plymouth, acts on large amounts of tenancy work and has particular leisure sector experience as well as advising national house builders and local authorities. A recent highlight was assisting M Baker Property Holdings on assessing sites across the UK for the location of refrigeration disposal facilities in readiness for the 2002 disposal restrictions. Secured lending advice is a burgeoning area for the firm. **Clients** University of Plymouth; London and West Country Estates; Nationwide Business Finance.

LYONS DAVIDSON (see firm details p.1045) Specialising in the education and health sectors, recent highlights for the practice include acting for a major bank on multimillion pound security transactions, and for the Bristol Cancer Help Centre on the acquisition of new premises at Ham Green House. The team, headed by John Hicks, has experience in land development, investment and management. It acts on both commercial and residential estate conveyancing, and leasehold work in the retail, industrial, office and residential sectors. Winning instructions from London firms, it has also become the main solicitor for a major London developer. **Clients** Appleby Westward Group; University of the West of England; AXA Sun Life; a major national healthcare provider.

THRING TOWNSEND (see firm details p.1162) Interviewees confirmed that the firm "*continues to build on a successful merger.*" Split between the Swindon and Bath offices, the team in Swindon deals mainly with tenant work, but also advises pension funds and regional landlords. The Bath office advises on all property matters for a major charitable trust and recently assisted a major minerals company on the completion of leases for railway depots nationally. Well-regarded **Brian Jacomb** (see p.731) acted for Watson Petroleum on the property aspects of the purchase of Lincolnshire-based Brobot Petroleum. Other areas of specialisation include acquisitions and disposals of licensed premises and hotels, property options and development, infrastructure agreements and telecoms-related work. **Clients** Vodafone; MAN Truck; charities.

WALES

EVERSHEDS (see firm details p.949) The consensus amongst peers and clients is that the firm's property department has the coverage and quality to retain its exclusive top-tier status, with prominent showings in both the public and private sectors confirming an unrivalled breadth of practice. "*A fair-minded heavyweight, well liked by clients,*" **Eric Evans** (see p.729) is rated for large-scale PFI work, and enjoys a fantastic reputation built upon acting for the likes of Macob Projects. **Nefydd Jones** (see p.732) "*had a good year,*" according to rivals, assisting the Dartmoor Limited Partnership on the sale of Capitol Tower. **Alan Meredith**'s (see p.733) time is divided between his responsibilities as senior partner and his property practice, but he remains a renowned figure in the market. He acted for Elinia on the land acquisition and development agreement, as well as the letting and funding, for a BT data centre in Cardiff Bay valued at around £50 million. **David Watkins** (see p.738) has acted on significant acquisition, development and funding arrangements in the public sector. **Clients** Investec Bank; National Assembly for Wales; MOD.

BERRY SMITH This widely respected "*niche property practice*" sustains a raft of high-value commercial property work in Cardiff, under the aegis of **Roger Berry** (see p.726). "*Always a pleasure to work with,*" according to peers, he specialises in development and investment-related work, recently acting for the developer in the £10 million reorganisation of the Environment Agency's property portfolio. He also acted on the lettings of ten office buildings at a major business park, two of them to the National Assembly for Wales. **Chris Jones** (see p.726) retains a high market profile and recently completed a series of site acquisitions for residential developers. **Clients** Gilesport; Driving Standards Agency; British Medical Association; Lidl.

REAL ESTATE ■ MIDLANDS/WALES

REAL ESTATE
■ WALES

1 Eversheds *Cardiff*
2 Berry Smith *Cardiff*
Edwards Geldard *Cardiff*
3 Morgan Cole *Cardiff, Swansea*
4 Hugh James *Cardiff*
Palser Grossman *Cardiff Bay*
Robertsons *Cardiff*

LEADING INDIVIDUALS

1 BERRY Roger *Berry Smith*
DAVIES Rowland *Edwards Geldard*
2 GEEN Jonathan *Palser Grossman*
JAMES Robert *Morgan Cole*
JONES Michael *Edwards Geldard*
WILLIAMS Martell *Robertsons*
3 EVANS Eric *Eversheds*
GATES Kathryn *Edwards Geldard*
JONES Chris *Berry Smith*
JONES Nefydd *Eversheds*
MEREDITH Alan *Eversheds*
ROBERTS David *Hugh James*
WATKINS David *Eversheds*

This book is the product of 6,582 1/2 hour interviews. See p.7 for BMRB audit. Within each band, firms are listed alphabetically. See individuals' profiles p.725

EDWARDS GELDARD (see firm details p.944) Its "*ubiquitous presence*" wins the firm promotion in this year's tables. Rated by one rival as "*the best property lawyer in Cardiff,*" **Rowland Davies** (see p.728) recently advised Rhondda Cynon Taff County Borough Council on the disposal of its industrial estate portfolio. He also worked together with highly regarded **Kathryn Gates** (see p.729) assisting Chevron in disposing of its interest in 43-45 Portman Square, London, to Healey & Baker. Though some peers believe that **Mike Jones** (see p.731) "*hides his considerable talents under a bushel,*" he is respected as an "*excellent team leader*" and rises in the tables. He has received instructions on three town centre development schemes in Newport, Torfaen and St Austell, two from local authorities and the third from a developer. He also assisted with the property documentation issued in connection with the £90 million Wales Millennium Centre project. **Clients** Chevron; Chubb Common Investment Fund; Newport Holdings.

MORGAN COLE (see firm details p.1075) The firm continues to feature as a "*big name*" in Wales. Despite the loss of Rosemary Morgan and three other partners, it retains a substantial Cardiff team and is expanding in Swansea. An increase in secured lending for major banks has contributed to the team's growing workload, while other typical work includes large acquisitions and disposals. Currently developing the health and energy strands of its practice, it has acted on a London hospital redevelopment and property matters relating to renewable energy projects. An enviable client base also includes international corporations, regional property companies and a large public sector following. Admired for his skill with clients, standout practitioner **Robert James** retains a high profile. **Clients** Associated British Ports; Grosvenor Waterside; HSBC Trust Company; NHS Trusts; BP.

HUGH JAMES (see firm details p.1004) Having had a busy year, interviewees agree that the firm "*has taken on a competitive edge.*" Acting on a range of development matters, it is particularly well known for its residential work, but is also active in the commercial, industrial and retail sectors. "*Meticulous and dependable*" **David Roberts** (see p.735) is seen by peers as the lynchpin of the practice. Acquisitions on behalf of house builders, housing associations and pension funds have dominated the year's workload. The practice continues to attract new registered social landlord and small business clients and remains on the property panel for Welsh Rugby Union. **Clients** Welsh Water; Barratt Homes; Hafod Housing Association.

PALSER GROSSMAN Adjudged to have undergone "*big changes,*" peers believe the departure of Alison Ivin has reduced the team's visibility, though partner-level recruitments from Eversheds and Loosemores are expected to go some way towards countering this. Having been "*adept in establishing a high profile for the department,*" lead partner **Jonathan Geen** recently acted for the developer/landlord on one of the largest recent developments and lettings in the area, that of St William House to Lloyds TSB. He also acted on all the lettings at Caspian Point – the largest speculative office development ever in Wales. David Seligman has moved into a consultancy role. **Clients** Crosby Group; property investment companies.

ROBERTSONS Centred around "*popular local operator*" **Martell Williams**, the team is said by competitors to be "*feted by a good set of loyal clients,*" who chose the firm for "*providing an excellent service and trustworthy judgements.*" Typical work includes secured lending advice for institutional clients and site acquisitions for house builders and developers across Wales and the West Country, including Cardiff Bay. **Clients** Developers; house builders.

MIDLANDS

EVERSHEDS (see firm details p.949) With an "*excellent reputation for development projects in Birmingham,*" peers have been impressed by the volume of work this team handles and its increasingly national scope. "*Thoroughly engaging*" **Tim Webb** (see p.738) is described as a "*high-flying deal facilitator.*" He has been assisting Advantage West Midlands on the strategic regeneration of Birmingham Eastside and Masshouse and represented Lend Lease in its work on the Bluewater retail and leisure centre. According to peers **Parmjit Singh** (see p.736) "*has always been highly regarded*" for his technical skill and commerciality. He has recently been visible representing Advantage West Midlands on the redevelopment of Pebble Mill and seeing the Birmingham Mailbox project through to completion. With ongoing involvement in major house building schemes, the practice is also cultivating niche strength in advising developers on innovative utilities-related property packages. Meg Heppel has become managing partner of the Birmingham office. **Clients** Bryant Homes; Paramount; Advantage West Midlands; Mailbox.

WRAGGE & CO (see firm details p.1197) "*Dynamic, focused and tenacious,*" the property management team has proved it can win work from City firms, acting for British Airways in renegotiating its innovative property agreements for the Eurohub at Birmingham International Airport. Property finance has featured prominently in recent work, with the team assisting Hypothekenbank on the multi-million pound refinancing of various London properties.

"*Personable and astute*" **Mark Dakeyne** was widely praised by clients and competitors. He recently acted for a new Luxembourg company set up by the Richardson family for its investment in a range of designer outlet centres. **David Askin** remains a well-reputed figure in the market. His wide-ranging and long-term advice to Powergen on Hams Hall power station recently included the lease of the rail freight terminal to ABP. "*A particularly entrepreneurial development lawyer,*" according to one client, **John Burns** recently acted for Hilton Group on the expansion of Living Well health clubs, while **Peter Thorne** continues to attract commendation for his work across the commercial and residential spheres. "*Extremely efficient and competent*" **Mark Chester** was one of a team of solicitors advising The IO Group in the acquisition of several development sites at Arlington Development's business parks, including the recently completed £17.6 million Pegasus Centre. Robert Caddick is now committed to establishing a London base for the practice.

MIDLANDS ■ REAL ESTATE

REAL ESTATE
■ MIDLANDS

1
- **Eversheds** Birmingham, Nottingham
- **Wragge & Co** Birmingham

2
- **Hammond Suddards Edge** Birmingham
- **Pinsent Curtis Biddle** Birmingham

3
- **DLA** Birmingham
- **Lee Crowder** Birmingham

4
- **Browne Jacobson** Nottingham
- **Freethcartwright** Leicester, Nottingham
- **Shoosmiths** Northampton, Nottingham

5
- **Edwards Geldard** Derby, Nottingham
- **Harvey Ingram Owston** Leicester
- **Knight & Sons** Newcastle-under-Lyme
- **Martineau Johnson** Birmingham
- **Wright Hassall** Leamington Spa

LEADING INDIVIDUALS

1
- **DAKEYNE Mark** Wragge & Co

2
- **KORDAN Joel** Lee Crowder
- **WATSON Adrian** DLA
- **WEBB Tim** Eversheds

3
- **ASKIN David** Wragge & Co
- **BURNS John** Wragge & Co
- **NEWCOMBE Mark** Hammond Suddards Edge
- **O'MEARA Anne** Hammond Suddards Edge
- **SINGH Parmjit** Eversheds
- **THORNE Peter** Wragge & Co

4
- **ROWE Tim** Wright Hassall
- **YATES Andrew** Pinsent Curtis Biddle

UP AND COMING
- **CHESTER Mark** Wragge & Co

This book is the product of 6,582 1/2 hour interviews. See p.7 for BMRB audit.
Within each band, firms are listed alphabetically. See individuals' profiles p.725

Clients Mapeley; ProLogis; Castlemore Securities; MEPC; McDonald's.

HAMMOND SUDDARDS EDGE Many in the market agree that this firm "*comfortably leads*" the chasing group. Clients attest to its quality and praise the team as "*commercially and technically adept.*" Offering advice on all aspects of ownership, occupation and investment issues, it has a strong profile in property development and urban regeneration projects. The "*focal point for the department and the reason for its success,*" **Anne O'Meara** has now taken over as head of the Birmingham property unit. As lead partner and project co-ordinator for two Millennium Commission-funded projects, she advised Millennium Point on the largest millennium project outside London. Though now senior partner of the Birmingham office, **Mark Newcombe** "*maintains a strong presence.*" He acted for Alconbury Developments on the redevelopment of the former MOD airfield at Alconbury in Huntingdon. The two lead partners also recently secured instructions from Nottingham Waterside on the redevelopment of the South East of Nottingham. **Clients** BAA; Advantage West Midlands; Signet Group.

PINSENT CURTIS BIDDLE (see firm details p.1102) This "*property practice respected for its corporate slant*" retains a prominent market position. While Barry Brice now works as a consultant for the team, **Andrew Yates** (see p.739) has established an enviable reputation for his work in property development in both the private and public sectors. The firm is acting for English Partnerships on the Omega business park development, among the largest redevelopment projects in the UK, with potential to accommodate seven million sq ft and an estimated end value of £1 billion. The project involves Miller Development and Royal Bank of Scotland, as well as RDAs and local authorities. Other highlights include acting for Modus Properties on a joint venture for a major shopping centre development in Wigan with an estimated value of £85 million. The team has seen an increase in property investment work and advice on sale and leaseback schemes, which has included acting for IM Properties. **Clients** Lex Service; English Partnerships; TRW.

DLA With a strong base of retail clients, the team brings what one client describes as a "*refreshing approach, whereby a range of specialists are all equally approachable*" to corporate acquisitions, property finance and development. Recent highlights include acting for HSBC on the property aspects of the £220 million MBO of Dignity Caring Funeral Services, involving around one thousand properties. Heading the team, **Adrian Watson** remains a respected figure in the marketplace. **Clients** Selfridges; Aggregate Industries; T&S Stores.

LEE CROWDER (see firm details p.1035) "*Snapping at the heels*" of the national networks, peers recognised a serious competitor in this "*ambitious team.*" **Joel Kordan** (see p.732), who heads it up, continues to elicit the praise of peers and clients alike. Typical work includes acquisitions and disposals, property development, including joint ventures, and leases for the retail, industrial, commercial and leisure sectors. The team's expansion in telecoms recently included winning Orange's Midlands Estate Region. Also strong in residential schemes, highlights of the past year include advice on the regeneration of the Digbeth area of Birmingham. The group boasts niche expertise advising logistics sector clients such as Exel and acting for registered social landlords and charities. **Clients** Alfred McAlpine Special Projects; Miller Homes; Parkridge Residential.

BROWNE JACOBSON (see firm details p.891) Clients heap praise on this "*dedicated team,*" which they say "*is always willing to adapt.*" An increased workload in the retail and freight and logistics sectors, combined with a burgeoning property finance practice, has meant a busy year for the team headed by David Hibbert. One recent highlight was acting for Securitas UK on the property aspects of creating Securitas Cash Management, a new venture combining the sterling cash management operations of Securitas UK, HSBC and Barclays. The practice dovetails with the firm's local authority practice, recently advising Derby County Council as landowner in its negotiations over a large city centre retail and leisure scheme. The team has been appointed to the new Birmingham City Council panel for property and reappointed to the EMDA panel. **Clients** Parceline; Wilkinson Hardware Stores.

FREETHCARTWRIGHT (see firm details p.963) Considered by peers to "*consistently perform well in the East Midlands,*" the firm retains an impressive base of retail clients, including Paul Smith, for whom it has recently acquired leasehold properties in London and a unit in Portsmouth Retail Park. Led by George Taylor, it has been involved in large redevelopment projects, advising the Metropolitan group of companies on a £30 million redevelopment in Leeds City Centre. Property finance is a growing area for the team and it receives instructions from the likes of NatWest. Residential and commercial developers, educational institutions, hotels and licensed businesses all feature among the firm's clientele. **Clients** Barratt Homes; Brydon Developments; Multiyork Furniture.

SHOOSMITHS (see firm details p.1133) Rated by clients for its "*proactive*" approach to deals, this well-respected team was newly appointed to the Smiths property panel this year. Acting out of offices in Northampton and Nottingham, the property department, headed by John Temple, works closely with the firm's construction and planning teams to service the needs of its developer clients. Typical recent work has included high-value mixed-use city centre and urban residential acquisitions for national house builders. A highlight has been an acquisition for a joint venture company involving a US partner, including advice on tax structuring, financing and the setting up of a new corporate group to acquire and manage the properties. The firm also has expertise in property-related commercial lending. **Clients** NatWest; Barratt Homes; Volkswagen.

EDWARDS GELDARD (see firm details p.944) Clients of the firm claim that the level of service on offer compares favourably with that of firms at the top of the table. Its highlight of the year was being appointed by Derbyshire County Council to advise on all aspects of the Markham Employment Project Growth Zone. A £180 million redevelopment scheme to create a new business park on land surrounding the former Markham Colliery, it is led by head of commercial property David Williams. The team also

REAL ESTATE ■ EAST ANGLIA

advised Peveril Securities on a multimillion pound mixed-use development adjacent to the M65 in Darwen, including the provision of a service area. The Eking Manning merger has been well received by the market and is said to have strengthened the team's involvement in Nottingham city centre developments. **Clients** Miller Homes; Balfour Beatty; Royal Bank of Scotland.

HARVEY INGRAM OWSTON (see firm details p.988) Commended by clients for its "*all-round service*," the team led by Phillip Lane retains its market position, with a presence in the retail, warehouse and distribution and NHS sectors. Also active in land options and development, loan securitisation and pension funds, it acted on the acquisition of the freehold and leasehold properties of Jones Bootmaker in connection with a management buy-in. Other recent work includes the transfer of part of the assets and liabilities of the Leicestershire and Rutland Health Care NHS Trust to three new primary care trusts, involving approximately 20 properties.

Clients Everards Brewery; Persimmon Homes; Alliance & Leicester.

KNIGHT & SONS Well received by the market, especially for its property development work, the team has advised the Department for Work and Pensions on development agreements and leases for two large call centres. Other highlights have included advising the Caudwell Group on the acquisition of around 175 leasehold retail properties, and involvement in disposals, development and infrastructure agreements for a Sainsbury's supermarkets distribution centre in Stoke-on-Trent. The team is led by Karl Bamford. **Clients** Gladmans; AWG; Trillium; Phones 4U.

MARTINEAU JOHNSON (see firm details p.1056) With its niche education-related property workload continuing to expand, the practice also sustains a presence in the retail and leisure sectors, and an enviable list of local authority clients. It also acts for biotech and telecoms companies, recently advising a national pharmaceutical business on the property aspects of its reorganisation. The team, led by Simon Arrowsmith, also advised two telecoms operators on leasing arrangements for 3G mobile masts. With strong property investment and management elements, it co-operates closely with the firm's banking and corporate divisions. **Clients** CLA Homes (Midlands); IM Properties; Wolverhampton City Council; Lloyds TSB.

WRIGHT HASSALL (see firm details p.1197) "*Quick, efficient and on the ball*," according to clients, the team is led by highly rated **Tim Rowe** (see p.735). Recent highlights include acting for the British Waterways Board on several mixed commercial and residential projects in the south of England, worth £110 million in total. Other work includes the acquisition and development of a new headquarters building for Whitefriars Housing Group and the acquisition of the undeveloped part of the Middlemarch Business Park for the AC Lloyd Group. **Clients** British Waterways Board; Laing Homes; National Grid.

EAST ANGLIA

REAL ESTATE
■ EAST ANGLIA

1
- **Eversheds** Cambridge, Norwich
- **Hewitson Becke + Shaw** Cambridge
- **Mills & Reeve** Cambridge, Norwich

2
- **Taylor Vinters** Cambridge

3
- **Birketts** Ipswich

4
- **Ashton Graham** Bury St Edmunds, Ipswich
- **Greene & Greene** Bury St Edmunds
- **Greenwoods** Peterborough
- **Prettys** Ipswich
- **Wollastons** Chelmsford

5
- **Ellisons** Colchester
- **Few & Kester** Cambridge

This book is the product of 6,582 1/2 hour interviews. See p.7 for BMRB audit. Within each band, firms are listed alphabetically.

EVERSHEDS (see firm details p.949) With its property practice now concentrated in the Norwich and expanding Cambridge offices, this "*extremely efficient outfit*" is highly rated by clients for its "*sophisticated practitioners.*" Focusing on occupiers, recent activity has centred on nursing homes, residential developments, regeneration projects and educational property. The team also provides transactional support, with particular experience in the energy sector. Recognised for having the strength to complete major PFI property support, one client claims it has "*the greatest depth of experience of all the firms in the region.*" Highlights have included acting for St Albans-based Oaklands College on the £20 million sale of part of its campus to Fairview Homes. Specialising in site acquisition and development, and also responsible for the regional residential development team, **Bryan Gillery** (see p.730) continues to attract warm commendation from peers, guaranteeing his position at the top of the table. He is based in the Norwich office along with **Robert Gibbs** (see p.729), who majors in development work but received praise as a wide-ranging commercial property specialist. **Keith Hamilton** (see p.730) also retains his market position. Cornelius Medvei has moved to the London office to head up the national commercial property team. **Clients**; GAP; Bernard Matthews; TXU Europe Group.

HEWITSON BECKE + SHAW (see firm details p.993) Possessing "*a whole raft of excellent practitioners,*" this team was praised for the high level of partner involvement it sustains throughout transactions, which "*gives it the edge over the other top Cambridge firms,*" according to one interviewee. Growth in development projects, acting for both developers and end-users, has been achieved through close co-operation with the construction and planning departments. Standout practitioners are "*sensible and astute*" **Elizabeth Jones** (see p.731) and **Alan Brett** (see p.727), who remain highly regarded by market sources. Both acted for new client South Cambridgeshire District Council on the transactional arrangements for the relocation of its head office. Other highlights include acting for Millennium Pharmaceuticals on the development of a new European HQ, and for Accelrys on a pre-let in the Cambridge Science Park. Work for Turnstone Estates on the development of the city's first major leisure site continues. **Clients** University of Cambridge; Millennium Pharmaceuticals; Fairclough Homes.

MILLS & REEVE (see firm details p.1071) An "*immensely successful practice,*" hi-tech companies and developers continue to be its focus, while research indicates an increasingly national presence, especially amongst higher education and institutional clients. **Tony Cowper** (see p.728) is highly rated for "*his excellent judgement in weighing up the commercial and academic aspects*" of transactions. Clients also appreciate his forte in joint ventures and complex structures. His long-standing involvement with the Cambridge Science Park has most recently involved advising Trinity College on letting and development, as part of a joint venture with Trinity Hall. Also highly rated, **Herbert Robinson** (see p.735) has acted for Cranfield University on joint venture agreements for the expansion of Cranfield Technology Park and for the University of Essex on the establishment of a research park at Colchester. The expanding Cambridge office has experienced growth in its commercial lending practice, recently advising the Bank of Scotland on its funding and security arrangements for the management buyout of the May Gurney Group. **Robert Hutton** (see p.731) continues to garner plaudits as the lead partner in the Norwich office and is visible dealing with a range of lease matters and acquisitions. **Clients** University of Cambridge; East of England Development Agency; health clients.

TAYLOR VINTERS (see firm details p.1156) A "*cut above the chasing group in the Cambridge*

EAST ANGLIA ■ REAL ESTATE

LEADING INDIVIDUALS

[1]
- BRISTOL Jeremy Birketts
- COWPER Tony Mills & Reeve
- GILLERY Bryan Eversheds

[2]
- BRETT Alan Hewitson Becke + Shaw
- GIBBS Robert Eversheds
- HAMILTON Keith Eversheds
- JONES Elizabeth Hewitson Becke + Shaw
- ROBINSON Herbert Mills & Reeve

[3]
- BEACH Steven Taylor Vinters
- HENSON Michaela Taylor Vinters
- HUTTON Robert Mills & Reeve
- PASKELL Fraser Greene & Greene
- WARREN Jennifer Taylor Vinters

UP AND COMING
- SCHWER Chris Birketts

See individuals' profiles p.725

market," the weight of market commendation this year sees the firm edge ahead as the closest challenger to the leading triumvirate. Having experienced considerable property investment activity, highly regarded **Steven Beach** (see p.726) also advised the University of Cambridge on the construction of Microsoft's multimillion pound research laboratory, finalising complex buyback and leasing arrangements. The team, working closely with the firm's planning department, advised Countryside Residential North Thames and Kajima Cambridge on a PFI structure for purchasing a mixed-use site in Cambridge city centre. Widely respected **Michaela Henson** (see p.731) also acted for Countryside Residential North Thames on the acquisition of a large site for residential development. **Jennifer Warren** (see p.738), whose "*positive approach*" was highly valued by interviewees, enters the tables for the first time. A specialist in development agreements and major leasing work, she is the firm's lead partner on its Granta Park activity. **Clients** Granta Park; The Technology Partnership; BioWisdom.

BIRKETTS (see firm details p.875) Peers admit that, with its long history in the region, this team has secured an "*enviable position in the market.*" Now building on its dominance within Suffolk, it has recruited City lawyers and is attracting London work, recently winning London & County Estates as a new client. Led by standout practitioner **Jeremy Bristol**, the team has been involved in advising on the sale of a large warehousing estate and on a joint venture for the purchase of development land. It also has niche expertise in the health sector, advising primary care trusts countrywide. **Chris Schwer** (see p.736) was praised by clients for his "*ability to speedily resolve matters.*" **Clients** Port of Felixstowe; Associated British Ports; Greene King.

ASHTON GRAHAM Though better known in the market for its expertise in agricultural land transactions, an experienced commercial property team, including Andrew Roe, operates from the Bury St Edmunds and Ipswich offices. Involved in joint ventures and site assemblies, corporate support, acquisitions and disposals, it also receives regular landlord and tenant instructions. Boasting a growing practice for offshore developers, it has an established profile within the hotel and restaurant sector in the South East. **Clients** Residential and commercial developers.

GREENE & GREENE This "*outstanding local firm*" has a growing profile in the commercial development, leisure, entertainment and transport sectors. **Fraser Paskell** was highly rated by clients for "*providing full support on a range of property matters,*" recently advising biopharmaceutical corporations on three multimillion pound leases in the Cambridge Science Park. An expanding area for the firm has been advice to private clients on using private pensions to acquire property investments. **Clients** Vitech Group; Capio Healthcare; Schering Plough; Western Medical.

GREENWOODS (see firm details p.978) The leading property practice in Peterborough and "*able to compete with those in the higher tiers,*" it enjoys a growing profile across the region. Founding partner of the commercial property department, Stephen Illingworth heads up a team that has acted recently in high-value land sales for a regional corporation and a site acquisition for a regional developer. Undertaking acquisitions and disposals for the Highways Agency, including compulsory purchases, it is retained by Emap for leasehold work while continuing to receive instructions from the likes of Thomas Cook and Geest. **Clients** Emap; Highways Agency; Thomas Cook.

PRETTYS (see firm details p.1106) This well-respected practice, led by David Clark, possesses a notable capacity in secured lending and development. Recent highlights include acting for an offshore investor on wet dock-related disposals, most recently one worth £9 million, and for a regional hotel and leisure group on a site acquisition and related land options. It also has a niche practice in advising health trusts on establishing retail malls. **Clients** Citibank; Nationwide; Ipswich Town FC.

WOLLASTONS (see firm details p.1196) A highly regarded property team led by Nicholas Cook, it recently advised a major insurance and reinsurance group on the long lease for its new HQ. Other recent highlights include advising a softwood timber company on the redevelopment of an industrial timber factory, and assisting a management buyout team in the purchase of long leasehold property. The team works closely with the firm's corporate department on the property aspects of acquisitions and restructuring. **Clients** Elektron; Global Marine Systems; Trace Elliot.

ELLISONS Retaining its market position, the team's property work is overseen by Peter Powell. Recent highlights for the group include advising the developer on the investment sale of an industrial estate and assisting a housing association on a £5 million refinancing. **Clients** Property investment companies; commercial developers; retail tenants.

FEW & KESTER Though it provoked some mixed reactions, clients value the services of one of the few remaining independent Cambridge-based firms. Working on land options and contractual property matters, the practice is led by Charles Webb. Kept busy by its institutional client base, it also has social housing expertise. **Clients** Ashwell Property Group; charities; banks; building societies.

REAL ESTATE ■ NORTH WEST

NORTH WEST

REAL ESTATE
■ NORTH WEST

1
- **Addleshaw Booth & Co** Manchester
- **Bullivant Jones** Liverpool
- **Cobbetts** Manchester
- **DLA** Liverpool, Manchester
- **Eversheds** Manchester

2
- **Halliwell Landau** Manchester
- **Hammond Suddards Edge** Manchester

3
- **DWF** Liverpool, Manchester
- **Field Cunningham & Co** Manchester
- **Pannone & Partners** Manchester

4
- **Beachcroft Wansbroughs** Manchester
- **Mace & Jones** Manchester

5
- **Aaron & Partners** Chester
- **Brabners Chaffe Street** Liverpool
- **Cuff Roberts** Liverpool
- **Hill Dickinson** Chester, Liverpool, Manchester
- **Jones Maidment Wilson** Altrincham, Manchester
- **Walker Smith & Way** Chester

LEADING INDIVIDUALS

1
- **BECKETT Roy** DLA
- **GOODMAN Stephen** Hammond Suddards Edge
- **JONES Pamela** Bullivant Jones
- **SORRELL Stephen** Eversheds

2
- **BENSON Stephen** Cobbetts
- **BUCKLEY Liam** Hammond Suddards Edge

3
- **ASHWORTH Peter** Field Cunningham & Co
- **CRAVEN Diana** Addleshaw Booth & Co
- **LEONARD Tessa** Eversheds
- **MARKS Geoffrey** Halliwell Landau
- **PATTISON Mark** Beachcroft Wansbroughs
- **WEIGHTMAN Anita** DLA

4
- **CONROY Paul** Addleshaw Booth & Co
- **FITZMAURICE Anthony** Cobbetts
- **ROONEY Phillip** DLA
- **WALLIS Guy** DWF
- **WHITE Stephen** Cobbetts

5
- **BLACK Ian** Cuff Roberts
- **CHALCRAFT Stephen** Masons
- **EDGE Mike** Halliwell Landau
- **GREEN Andy** DWF
- **JACKSON Karl** Mace & Jones
- **JONES Michael** Pannone & Partners
- **WALDIE Roderick** Halliwell Landau

UP AND COMING
- **WORRALL Simon** Cobbetts

This book is the product of 6,582 1/2 hour interviews. See p.7 for BMRB audit. Within each band, firms are listed alphabetically. See individuals' profiles p.725

ADDLESHAW BOOTH & CO (see firm details p.838) "*Looming large*" on the horizon, this sizeable team is commended by competitors for its "*wealth of expertise and consistently high-quality service.*" The team is able to count clients of the calibre of Whitbread amongst its roster, and has been involved in a number of transactions as part of the company's £1.63 billion sale of its pub portfolio. The team also acted for Whitehall Green Partnership on the disposal of seven properties, at a price close to £45 million. As well as corporate transactional strength, the team also has an expertise in portfolio management, local development and regeneration issues. In a "*talent-packed team*," a number of heavy hitters stand out including the "*immensely practical*" Diana Craven (see p.728) Who received warm peer commendation. Paul Conroy (see p.728) ("*always performs to a high standard*") recently advised Highstone Estates on its £26.5 million purchase of prime Manchester office space. **Clients** Aberdeen Asset Managers; AMEC; Barlows; Green Property; Haslemere Estates; Kingfisher Group; NPL Estates; Railtrack; The Met Office; Yorkshire Bank.

BULLIVANT JONES (see firm details p.893) Despite being smaller than its closest competitors in the market, clients attest that "*its expertise and concentration on property issues marks it out as the first firm you go to.*" The "*superb*" Pamela Jones (see p.732) is described by observers as "*a fearsome opponent - one who is well worth having on your side.*" Although its retail side is the star around which its reputation circles, the firm also handles property investment, and landlord tenant matters. The team has been active in the past year on the development of a new North West regional distribution centre for Somerfield Stores, and has advised on the purchase, development and sale of a warehouse and distribution centre at Parc Menai, Bangor. The team has also advised the charitable trust of Alder Hey Hospital, regarding the property aspects of a new £6.7 million paediatric oncology unit. **Clients** Somerfield Stores; Watkin Jones & Son.

COBBETTS (see firm details p.914) This highly regarded firm is home to partners who are valued as "*worth their weight in gold.*" Observers dub Stephen Benson (see p.726) as "*one of the brightest and the best.*" He has recently led a team, that has secured a number of high-profile matters; as well as its involvement in the Whitbread disposals, it has acted for Matalan in the purchase of 20 new stores. The group has also advised Bellway Homes on the acquisition and development of a 215,000 sq ft site. Stephen White was recommended to researchers as an "*excellent technical*" lawyer who provides a "*stand out client-focused service,*" while both Anthony Fitzmaurice (see p.729) and Simon Worrall (see p.738) continue to enjoy a loyal fan base. With sharp skills in licensing, as well as landlord tenant work, the team attracts clients of a high calibre. Its recent merger with Read Hind Stewart is hoped to create a trans-Pennine brand name, which can compete on a national playing field. **Clients** Bellway Homes; Bruntwood Estates; Honeycombe Leisure; Matalan; Twin Valley Homes; Whitbread.

DLA Roy Beckett, Anita Weightman and Phillip Rooney are the high-profile members of this practice, which is respected for its expertise in development, regeneration and portfolio management.

EVERSHEDS (see firm details p.949) At the helm of this group stands Stephen Sorrell (see p.736), who some sources regard as "*one of the best property lawyers nationwide.*" Many credit his talents as being behind the firm's success in its appointment as sole supplier of property legal services nationally to Littlewoods. He has also been in action on the King's Waterfront development in Liverpool – a project that includes a £300 million arena and mixed-use scheme. He is backed up by a fine complement, which includes the "*important lieutenant*" Tessa Leonard (see p.732). A strong focus on commercial and residential developments exists alongside property finance. Both clients and peers applauded the firm's quality of documentation and responsive service. **Clients** ASK Property Developments; Chester City Council; Crosby Homes; English Partnerships; Littlewoods; Liverpool Vision; Redrow; Swinton Insurance Group; Urban Splash.

HALLIWELL LANDAU (see firm details p.982) "*Well on the road to recovery*" following losses at partner level, this firm has impressed peers with its pragmatic commercial approach to transactions. With strengths in business, commercial and residential developments the firm is seen as "*sticking to the tried and true.*" Many singled out top-flight Geoffrey Marks (see p.733) as providing the impetus behind the team, which benefits from his depth of experience in real estate matters. Mike Edge (see p.729) and Roderick Waldie (see p.737) are typical of the firm's pool of talent. Over the last year the team has advised on the acquisition, development and disposal of 200,000 sq ft of office space in Manchester. It represented Bruntwood (Official Property Partners to the 2002 Commonwealth Games) on two acquisitions in Salford Quays. **Clients** Aldi Stores; Bruntwood Estates; Dunlop Heywood Lorenz; Foden Investments.

HAMMOND SUDDARDS EDGE It has been a busy year for the Manchester office of this national firm; some interviewees pointed to it as a rising force across the North West. Active in high-value projects, particularly on the leisure and residential side, the firm has also aimed its sights at business and industrial work. Typical of its high-profile matters of late, is the team's involvement in The Spinningfields project, the largest city centre office and retail scheme in the

YORKSHIRE ■ REAL ESTATE

region, which has involved the letting of over 450,000 sq ft to The Royal Bank of Scotland. The "*larger than life*" **Stephen Goodman** is active on high-profile developments, including the Ford factory site at Dagenham. He is already said to have created an "*excellent dynamic*" partnership with the "*highly perceptive*" **Liam Buckley**. **Clients** British Aerospace; British Energy; English Partnerships; Intercity; Liberty Property; Transco.

DWF (see firm details p.943) This "*extremely reliable and practical firm*" is praised by both peers and clients, with particularly effusive nods given to their work on site sales and acquisitions. The "*straight-talking, stand-up guy,*" **Guy Wallis** (see p.737), recently led a team on the acquisition of a £50 million portfolio, which included a large retail park. The firm is also advising a Glasgow-based company in the freehold purchase and leaseback of Somerfield's distribution centre, in a deal worth in excess of £27 million. The highly regarded **Andy Green** (see p.730) is described as "*holding a good range of clients.*" **Clients** AEGON UK; Berkeley College Homes; Inventive Leisure; St Modwen Group.

FIELD CUNNINGHAM & CO (see firm details p.954) This "*small but highly experienced*" firm is well regarded by peers, especially for its work in the residential sector. Much of its reputation hangs on the "*gravitas*" of **Peter Ashworth**. The group has been involved in developments for the leisure market, as well as carrying out multi-million pound transactions in the residential sphere. **Clients** Large developers.

PANNONE & PARTNERS (see firm details p.1092) Praised highly by clients who regard this firm as "*the epitome of responsiveness,*" the practice continues to make a strong impression on the marketplace. It is skilled in residential and industrial work, alongside its experience in the public sector. The team, which includes **Michael Jones** (see p.732) ("*sensible, with a wealth of experience*"), has been involved in a number of important transactions in the last year. Highlights include representing Manchester Airport on its acquisition of both East Midlands and Bournemouth Airports, and advising on the acquisition and development of a Staffordshire business park, a project, that covers 24,000 sq metres. **Clients** Argyll Securities;

Crosby Homes; Great Lakes; Newell Group; Reality Estates; Seddon Group; Texaco; Urban Splash.

BEACHCROFT WANSBROUGHS (see firm details p.860) Observers described **Mark Pattison** (see p.734) as "*bright and sharp, a creative genius who thinks outside the box.*" He and the team handle work for residential, public sector and leisure developers. In the last year the team has sold the Furness House building in Manchester (a deal which ran into the millions), and acted on the outsourcing of MEPC Factory Outlets management to Realm. The firm is praised for its commercial astuteness and awareness of client needs. **Clients** Defence Estates; MEPC; Realm; Westfield.

MACE & JONES (see firm details p.1047) This "*top-flight, busy firm*" has been particularly active in urban regeneration over the past year, complementing its acknowledged skill with public client and leisure developers. It has advised Artisan Holdings on Albion Works, a development that includes 230 apartments and a 3000 sq metre office centre, and involves a £30 million investment. The firm is also working with various property companies on the redevelopment of Ormskirk and Sandbach town centres. **Karl Jackson** (see p.731) is "*the main name*" of this well regarded team. **Clients** Artisan Holdings; The Accident Group; Cavern City Tours; The Co-operative Bank; North West Development Agencies.

AARON & PARTNERS (see firm details p.837) A well-known presence in the Chester market and beyond, this firm has been active on the disposal of an employment/manufacturing unit in North Wales, a deal worth over £1 million. The team, which includes Christopher Tomkinson, has also acted on the lease of a mineral extraction site and purchase of offices in a business park. It handles a full range of property work, and is praised by peers for its "*depth and tenacity.*" **Clients** Large developers.

BRABNERS CHAFFE STREET (see firm details p.885) Consolidating its reputation as a "*true up-and-comer,*" the practice has continued to grow, bolstered by the firm's recent merger with Chaffe Street, a union that has brought together a well regarded leisure and retail team with a much admired residential unit. Sandy Chapple Gill's team has been involved in a number of significant transactions, including representing Home

Bargains in the acquisition and development of the largest distribution warehouse in the region. It has also acted for Chester City Council on the new lease of the Racecourse. **Clients** Cains Brewery; JD Wetherspoon; Mersey Docks & Harbour Company; Southern Medical.

CUFF ROBERTS The firm has carried out complex national work in the last year. Interviewees commended its "*technical prowess,*" and the team has been scored well with its involvement in a large office development in Liverpool. It has also carried out work on a flagship $45 million hotel development in Birmingham, and advised on a £25 million development in Derbyshire. It retains its highly recommended skills in retail work. **Ian Black** (see p.726) is viewed by peers as "*strong and efficient,*" while clients described him as "*the bee's knees.*" **Clients** Everton FC; Johnsons The Cleaners; Help the Aged; Littlewoods; Neptune Developments.

HILL DICKINSON (see firm details p.995) The firm has a sizeable presence and is seen to be "*punching its weight*" in the region. It has attracted attention over the past year with its merger with the respected property practice Gorna & Co, in a move thought to give the team a surer footing in Manchester. David Swaffield's team has been involved in a number of high-profile developments for David McLean Developments and NCP. **Clients** Box Clever; David McLean Developments; Elite Homes; NCP; Royal Liver Assurance.

JONES MAIDMENT WILSON This small team lacks some of the presence of its nearest competitors, but is still regarded as "*highly competent.*" Led by James Banfi, the firm is particularly active on development and regeneration work. **Clients** Investment clients.

WALKER SMITH & WAY This "*impressive*" Chester based firm is well regarded across the marketplace. The team, led by Gray Prestt, had been involved in a number of notable commercial transactions and developments, and has advised on the purchase of office space. **Clients** Developers and investors.

OTHER NOTABLE PRACTITIONERS Clients singled out **Stephen Chalcraft** (see p.727) of **Masons** for his "*sharp mind*" and "*efficient*" handling of transactions.

YORKSHIRE

ADDLESHAW BOOTH & CO (see firm details p.838) Still very much regarded as "*the firm to aim for,*" the practice has enjoyed another top-flight year in commercial property work. The "*superbly constructive*" **Paula Dillon** (see p.728) has led a team that completed one of the UK's largest retail property transactions, advising The Paul Sykes Group on its £46.25 million acquisition of The Victoria Quarter, Leeds. The firm has also advised on the property aspects of the £875 million securitisation of Meadowhall by British Land Company – a deal led by the "*strong and focused*" **Michael Reevey** (see p.735). Competitors feel that it is "*quite right to be blowing their trumpet for commercial work,*" but that these lawyers also handle top-drawer residential and leisure work. The firm carries a "*great deal of history and clout*" and the

REAL ESTATE ■ YORKSHIRE

REAL ESTATE
■ YORKSHIRE

1
- **Addleshaw Booth & Co** Leeds
- **Walker Morris** Leeds

2
- **DLA** Leeds, Sheffield
- **Pinsent Curtis Biddle** Leeds

3
- **Andrew M. Jackson** Hull
- **Cobbetts** Leeds
- **Eversheds** Leeds
- **Hammond Suddards Edge** Leeds

4
- **Gordons Cranswick Solicitors** Bradford, Leeds
- **Nabarro Nathanson** Sheffield

5
- **Denison Till** York
- **Gosschalks** Hull
- **Irwin Mitchell** Sheffield
- **Rollits** Hull

6
- **Keeble Hawson** Sheffield
- **The Frith Partnership** Leeds
- **Wake Smith** Sheffield

LEADING INDIVIDUALS

1
- **INNES Richard** Walker Morris
- **MCCLEA Nigel** Pinsent Curtis Biddle
- **MCLEAN Neil** DLA
- **PIKE John** Addleshaw Booth & Co

2
- **DILLON Paula** Addleshaw Booth & Co
- **FLOUNDERS Andrew** Cobbetts
- **STONE David** Andrew M Jackson

3
- **AYRE Paul** Gordons Cranswick Solicitors
- **CROCKER Nic** Hammond Suddards Edge
- **GRABINER Martin** Nabarro Nathanson
- **QUINLAN Andrew** Pinsent Curtis Biddle
- **REEVEY Michael** Addleshaw Booth & Co
- **WILFORD Nick** Pinsent Curtis Biddle

This book is the product of 6,582 1/2 hour interviews. See p.7 for BMRB audit. Within each band, firms are listed alphabetically. See individuals' profiles p.725

"*redoubtable*" **John Pike** (see p.734) – "*a man with a fine head on his shoulders*" remains at the forefront. **Clients** Aberdeen Asset Managers; AMEC; Barlows; Kingfisher Group; Miller Group; North West Development Agency; NPL Estates; Railtrack; Standard Life Investments; Transco; Yorkshire Bank.

WALKER MORRIS (see firm details p.1178) The practice, which has a high national regard, is endorsed by observers for its "*broad range of property lawyers who are certainly no slouches*." Most prominent amongst them is **Richard Innes** (see p.731), described by peers and clients as "*a top-flight negotiator*." The firm handles various developments in the residential and leisure sectors, with a particular focus on financing. It has acted for Bank of Scotland in the refinancing of the Hampton Trust property portfolio, a deal worth £52 million, while also representing it in the £19 million funding of the new Rockingham Motor Circuit. The team has also been instructed by Rockcliffe Development in connection with the £13 million redevelopment of Erith Town Centre. **Clients** Bank of Scotland; Bryant Homes; Bovis Homes; Caterpillar; Clydesdale Bank; Debenhams Retail; Halifax; Jarvis; Redcastle; Tay Homes; White Rose Homes.

DLA This well-regarded practice has a good reputation for its development and regeneration work. **Neil McLean** remains a standout name.

PINSENT CURTIS BIDDLE (see firm details p.1102) The team is praised by market commentators for its "*energy and enthusiasm*" and "*for being quick and responsive to a client's needs*." The "*legendary*" **Nigel McClea** (see p.733) retains his loyal following in the market, while the highly rated **Andrew Quinlan** (see p.735) is thought "*a crucial support*" on any type of transaction. **Nick Wilford** enters the tables following commendation for his "*pragmatic and commercial approach*." The team is perceived to train its sights on the areas of retail and leisure, as well as having strong acquisition and development experience forged on a nationwide scale. The team has advised on the acquisition of 400 units for Rubicon Retail, as well as the $45 million purchase of a central London property for Close Brothers Investment. **Clients** Close Brothers Investment; Concert; DEFRA; Potter Group; Rubicon Retail; Teesland Group; University of London.

ANDREW M JACKSON (see firm details p.845) This Hull-based practice is thought to dominate its local region, with particular plaudits given to its out-of-town retail expertise. The "*highly impressive*" **David Stone** (see p.737) is recommended by peers and clients across the region. The team is well known for its skills in retail and leisure, amid a full property offering. It has been active in the last year for MFI in the acquisition of a 480,000 sq ft distribution centre/warehouse in Brackmills, Northampton. It has also been instructed to act in the 'New Deal for Communities' scheme, an extensive urban regeneration scheme funded by the Government. **Clients** Associated British Ports; Cannons Health & Fitness; Carpetright; MFI Properties.

COBBETTS (see firm details p.914) The amalgamation of well-respected property firm Read Hind Stewart and this top Manchester firm is described by some peers as "*having the potential to score a masterly coup*." It joins together Cobbetts' well-regarded landlord and tenant work with the retail and industrial skills of this Yorkshire firm, affording "*an expert range*" of skills. The "*technically excellent*" **Andrew Flounders** (see p.729) remains at the forefront of this firm, and with the merger it is felt that "*the extra depth of support will be noticeable*." The team has been active in the last year on the letting of a 100,000 sq ft store in Bradford. It also acted on the sale of Exchange Buildings which has a proposal for development as a hotel and leisure scheme on the Newcastle Quayside. **Clients** Caddick Group; Landmark Development Projects.

EVERSHEDS (see firm details p.949) Although the practice is seen to have diminished in profile in the last year due to the departure of John Foster, the team continues to "*benefit from its national presence*." Observers respected the team's strong project management skills, handling large-scale industrial and investment work. **Eve Gregory** and the group have helped open new stores, and carry out development and management work for Asda Stores, which included a store under construction as part of Manchester's Commonwealth Games Stadium. The firm has also been involved in Project Quail, the purchase of five shopping centres for £113 million, a transaction which used both Leeds and London-based lawyers. **Clients** British Waterways Board; Hammerson; HJ Banks; Orange; Simon Estates.

HAMMOND SUDDARDS EDGE This "*ebullient, enthusiastic*" team has impressed market sources with its loyal client following in Yorkshire. Recommended for its involvement in high-level developments and disposals, the firm has a healthy track record in leisure and the public sector. Peers appreciate that **Nic Crocker** is a lawyer, who "*moves a deal ahead*." He has been involved in the acquisition and development of two hotels in the North, at a cost of £35 million. The firm also acted on the disposal of Cedar Court Hotel, Bradford for Sindar for £15 million. **Clients** Bellway Homes; Morrison Supermarkets; ScottishPower; Yorkshire Forward.

GORDONS CRANSWICK SOLICITORS This Bradford-based firm houses lawyers valued by clients as "*extremely proficient, with the brilliant skill of speaking plain English*." **Paul Ayre** (see p.725) in particular is lauded as "*having a client's best interests at heart*." The retail sector is still thought to be the firm's prime strength, and it remains well regarded for its knowledge of investments and development projects. The team has acted in the disposal of 21 acres of the former ICI site in Harrogate, and has advised JF Finnegan in a £11 million financing of a mixed leisure and retail site in Redditch. **Clients** Hornbeam Developments; Ponden Mill; Wm Supermarkets; Yorkshire Building Society.

NABARRO NATHANSON (see firm details p.1080) Enjoying "*a high plateau of influence and expertise*," the firm is rated as a major player in the region. Although based in Sheffield, the practice's scope of experience ensures that it is a nationwide player. The firm acted for Portsmouth City Centre on a £200 million redevelopment, and advised Dover District Council on the regeneration of the Dover Town Investment Zone. The team is particularly well regarded for its work in leisure and retail developments. Singled out by interviewees, **Martin Grabiner** (see p.730) is valued as "*a steady pair of hands*." **Clients** The Arkle Fund; British Waterways; Capital Shopping

Centres; The Coal Authority; GE Capital Corporation Real Estate; Hayes Chemicals.

DENISON TILL Peers commended this practice's involvement in some particularly interesting work over the last year. David Grice's team has been occupied on the purchase of two substantial hotels in the York area, while also acting on the development of a city centre site for retail and leisure uses. The firm has strong connections with the Higher Education sector, and advises on accommodation strategy. **Clients** Castle Howard Estate; Helmsley Group; Hovingham Estate; The University of York; York Diocesan Board of Finance.

GOSSCHALKS Although the firm has a strong reputation for its licensing work, the property practice is described by clients as "*not putting all their eggs in one basket, diversifying and giving great value for money.*" The team, which is led by Dick Llewellyn, has been involved in a number of large developments and disposals in the past 12 months. **Clients** Leisure sector; betting industry; local developers; motor industry.

IRWIN MITCHELL (see firm details p.1009) This successful Sheffield-based practice continues to be well regarded both for its work on a regional level and nationwide. It possesses a dedicated retail unit, which represents a large swathe of high street stores. Clients are attracted by the firm's strongly commercial reputation. Kevin Docherty and the team have also been involved in the purchase and development of a number of retail parks, and worked on various deals within the leisure industry. **Clients** Large developers.

ROLLITS (see firm details p.1115) Martyn Justice's team has carved itself a respected name in the region, described by one competitor as "*one of the most expert in transactions.*" It has carried out property work in the fields of shipping and power, and has recently been involved in a large retail transaction. This "*bright*" team has been recommended by clients as "*easily capable of providing a wide range of services.*" **Clients** Housebuilders; educational establishments; power companies.

KEEBLE HAWSON Clients appreciate that this practice has committed itself to building "*personable relationships*" and garnering an understanding of their businesses. Gareth Owen's team has acted for a leading academic institution on a multimillion pound restructuring/PFI deal, which involved the sale and leaseback of a major part of its property assets. It has also acted on a planning dispute involving an important residential development site. **Clients** Retail companies; large housing suppliers; educational bodies.

THE FRITH PARTNERSHIP Barney Frith leads this practice, which is envied by competitors for its healthy ties to developer clients. The firm has particular expertise in retail work, and has handled a number of substantial acquisitions and developments in the last year. **Clients** Developers.

WAKE SMITH This "*medium-sized, punchy firm*" has a fine profile amongst clients and competitors. Neil Salter's team has acted on the purchase of a city centre residential site for development, in a deal valued in the region of £4 million. The team has also advised in the ongoing acquisition of the site and development issues arising from a new medical centre. **Clients** Retail and other commercial entities.

NORTH EAST

REAL ESTATE
NORTH EAST

1. **Dickinson Dees** Newcastle upon Tyne
2. **Eversheds** Newcastle upon Tyne
3. **Robert Muckle** Newcastle upon Tyne
   Ward Hadaway Newcastle upon Tyne
   Watson Burton Newcastle upon Tyne

LEADING INDIVIDUALS

1. **BRAITHWAITE Neil** Dickinson Dees
2. **COMBE Jonathan** Robert Muckle
   MORGAN Claire Eversheds
   WARD Ian Dickinson Dees

This book is the product of 6,582 1/2 hour interviews. See p.7 for BMRB audit. Within each band, firms are listed alphabetically. See individuals' profiles p.725

DICKINSON DEES (see firm details p.938) It has been another buoyant year for the North East's top real estate practice. Competitors endorsed it clearly as "*the biggest and best – it is packed with talented, personable people.*" Constructing some of the largest deals in the North East, the firm provides support to the public service sector, as well as an admired client base of retail, industrial and residential developers. The firm is involved in the ongoing retail development at the Gateshead Quay, and has advised on the development of a new hotel by the central station. Although now holding the position of managing partner, **Neil Braithwaite** (see p.726), is still regarded as "*a quality performer,*" while **Ian Ward** (see p.737) was portrayed by commentators as one who "*truly shines a light*" on a transaction. **Clients** Bellway; GEHE UK; Morrison Group; Northern Electric; Procter & Gamble.

EVERSHEDS (see firm details p.949) Interviewees portrayed this practice as "*the next choice in the region*" but nonetheless viewing the Eversheds brand name as an assurance of high quality. The firm handles a wide range of work from landed estates to large property portfolios and investment deals. The team has acted for a third of the equity investors in a limited partnership purchase of the Cameron Toll shopping centre in Edinburgh, a deal valued in excess of £63 million. It has also been involved in a number of residential, commercial and office developments. **Claire Morgan** (see p.733) remains the key name in the department, admired for her ability to "*keep a number of balls in the air at the same time.*" **Clients** Bryants; HJ Banks; Kilmartin Property Group; One NorthEast; UK Land.

ROBERT MUCKLE The "*bright, enthusiastic*" **Jonathan Combe** (see p.728) continues to lead a well-regarded team, which is described by clients as "*first and foremost accessible, and responsive to our needs.*" The team has been heavily involved in the £25 million redevelopment of a cattle market site in Newcastle, using the land for a new 270-bedroom hotel. Office and residential projects also feature heavily in the workload. The team has advised on an office development at the Metro, Gateshead, and remains well regarded for its acquisition and development skills in the industrial sector. **Clients** Bank of Scotland; City and Northern Projects; Easter Developments; Miller Homes; McAleer & Rushe.

WARD HADAWAY (see firm details p.1180) Peers judged the team to be "*an increasingly active presence in the market,*" respected, in particular, for its development work. Richard Freeman-Wallace's team has acted recently on the acquisition, development, letting and sale of Sunderland Retail Park, a project worth £20 million. It has also advised on the sale of a £29 million portfolio of property. **Clients** Granchester Group.

WATSON BURTON This "*excellent, efficient*" team "*knows how to structure a good deal.*" Kenneth Millband's team has expertise in development issues. It has been instructed recently in various projects, including acquisitions and sales in the commercial and residential areas. **Clients** Large developers.

REAL ESTATE ■ SCOTLAND

SCOTLAND

REAL ESTATE
■ SCOTLAND

1
- **Dundas & Wilson CS** Edinburgh
- **McGrigor Donald** Edinburgh, Glasgow

2
- **Burness** Edinburgh
- **Maclay Murray & Spens** Edinburgh, Glasgow
- **Semple Fraser** Glasgow
- **Shepherd+ Wedderburn** Edinburgh, Glasgow

3
- **Brodies** Edinburgh
- **Fyfe Ireland WS** Edinburgh
- **MacRoberts** Edinburgh, Glasgow
- **Tods Murray WS** Edinburgh

4
- **Archibald Campbell & Harley WS** Edinburgh
- **Biggart Baillie** Edinburgh, Glasgow
- **DLA** Edinburgh, Glasgow
- **Ledingham Chalmers** Aberdeen
- **Paull & Williamsons** Aberdeen

5
- **Harper Macleod** Glasgow
- **Thorntons WS** Dundee

6
- **Anderson Strathern WS** Edinburgh
- **Davidson Chalmers WS** Edinburgh
- **Masons** Edinburgh
- **McClure Naismith** Edinburgh

This book is the product of 6,582 1/2 hour interviews. See p.7 for BMRB audit. Within each band, firms are listed alphabetically.

DUNDAS & WILSON CS (see firm details p.943) Although the firm has this year severed its ties with the Andersen Legal network, market commentators perceived the property team to be largely unaffected in its capacity to attract or advise on substantial property matters. The firm continues to be respected for its mastery of the "*epic*" property transaction. A "*talented team of some depth*" has been involved in a number of high-profile matters, including the acquisition and development of the Royal Bank of Scotland's world HQ at Gogarburn, Edinburgh. It also advised the bank on the lease of its combined HQ in Paris, a complex deal that involved transportation/road advice. Among a raft of well-known names, **Iain Doran** was singled out as "*an excellent leader who can guide through a deal.*" **David Steel** is best known for his technical drafting and depth of knowledge, particularly in the retail sector, while **Ian Paterson** is praised highly for his residential skills. **Clients** Abbey National; ASDA; CGNU; Land Securities; Lattice; Miller Group; National Car Parks; Odeon; One 2 One; Premier Properties; Royal & SunAlliance; Transco.

McGRIGOR DONALD (see firm details p.1065) "*A blue-chip firm for blue-chip transactions*" is the verdict of many commentators, who have had dealings with this practice. Involved in the full spread of property work, the team is also respected for its work in private equity and tax driven schemes. The "*quite excellent*" **David Bankier** (see p.725) is a "*straight-talker; he has no side to him,*" while the "*marvellous*" **Tom Anderson** (see p.725) "*produces documentation which is the envy of the whole profession.*" Key highlights include advising BT on the outsourcing and management of its 1700 Scottish properties. Work also continues on the Glasgow Harbour Development Project, one of the largest waterfront redevelopment schemes in the UK. The "*standout*" **Ewan Alexander** (see p.725) advised Hilton Group on aspects of a £300 million sale and leaseback, while **Alison Newton** (see p.734) was warmly commended for her efficiency and attention to detail. She brings a "*personal touch, which makes her great to front a deal.*" **Clients** Bellhouse Joseph; Forth Ports; Halladale Group; Hilton Group; Montagu Evans; Rank Leisure Division; Scottish Power; Tarmac Northern.

BURNESS Department head **Ian Wattie** boasts "*a good understanding of the ins and outs of every deal.*" He recently advised RBS Property Ventures in its acquisition of a company with substantial pub holdings, a deal valued at £270 million. This "*expert*" team also includes the well-regarded **Caroline Drummond** who acted for the Lothian University Hospitals NHS Trust on the £350 million disposal of the Royal Infirmary, Edinburgh. Sources also endorsed **Kenneth Ross**, **Lionel Most** ("*a leading name*") and the "*sharp and skilled*" **David Reid**. Alongside Drummond, **Richard Rennie** is part of the firm's younger generation carving a name in this field. The team is thought to possess "*wide-ranging skills*" across the retail, leisure and industrial sectors. **Clients** Allied Leisure; BSkyB; Compass Group; Granada; Ladbrokes; Miller Developments; Norwich Union; Peel Construction; Pizza Express; Sun Life; Welcome Break.

MACLAY MURRAY & SPENS (see firm details p.1048) "*One of the big three property firms in Scotland*" claim some sources. The practice continues to "*add new resources*" to an already broad-based team, led by the "*technically strong*" **Robin Garrett** (see p.729). The group is praised highly for its retail and leisure skills, and it has been involved in numerous high-value developments and acquisitions. It represented REIT Asset Management in its £46 million acquisition of the Oak Mall Shopping Centre in Greenock. It advised Citibank in the Scottish aspects of the securitisation of BT's property portfolio, and also acted for Eurohypo, which funded the transaction – the deal had a total value of £2.4 billion. The "*keen and switched-on*" **Jennifer Johnson** (see p.731) is recognised as being "*highly visible on the scene,*" while **Iain Macniven** (see p.733) brings his "*superb negotiating*" skills to the table. Clients believe that **Ian Quigly** is "*the perfect package of knowledge and experience,*" and that he brings a "*refreshing*" approach to a transaction. **Clients** Abbey Life; BBC; CGNU; Friends Provident; Kilmartin; Macdonald Estates; PizzaExpress; Prudential; Signet Group; The Wellcome Trust.

SEMPLE FRASER (see firm details p.1125) This "*small team of value-adding lawyers*" enjoys "*a wonderful client base.*" **Paul Haniford** (see p.730) has impressed with his ability to "*wade through the minutiae of deals,*" while the pragmatism of **Simon Etchells** (see p.729) has won him many fans, who claim that "*it's always good to see him on the other side.*" Development and disposals remain key facets of this team's experience. It has acted on the sale of Blythswood House, Glasgow (£10 million), and advised on the Pacific Quay Business Park development, Glasgow. The team has also represented Tesco Stores on its shop development programme within Scotland. **Clients** Allied Dunbar Assurance; Delancey Group; Friends Provident; Halifax; Royal & SunAlliance Property Investments; Tesco Stores; Whitbread.

SHEPHERD+ WEDDERBURN (see firm details p.1130) Clients report that they are "*highly impressed*" by "*the skill and enthusiasm*" of this firm. The team has a presence in major office, leisure and retail developments, acquisitions and disposals. The "*superb*" **Nick Ryden** (see p.736) is known as "*a bit of a character;*" he acted in the sale of the prestigious Edinburgh One office building for a sum in excess of £23 million. Highly visible across a range of transactions, **David Smith** (see p.736) was consistently applauded for his commercialism, while **James Dobie** (see p.728) is "*a man most definitely on the rise*" and one possessed of a "*fair-minded, practical nature.*" The team has acted for Helical Bar in its disposal of a Scottish industrial portfolio worth £15 million. **Clients** Anglo Irish Bank; Bank of Scotland; British Airways; Charterhouse; De Vere Group; Mars Pension Trustees; Rank Hovis; ScottishPower; Shell UK; Waterfront Edinburgh.

BRODIES (see firm details p.889) This "*quietly efficient*" firm has handled the Scottish aspects of the acquisition by Telereal of BT's property portfolio in Scotland, in a high-value, complex transaction, that relied on the team's skills in tax, banking and finance. It has also advised on aspects of Edinburgh's Telford College's proposed move to a new purpose-built campus in Edinburgh's Waterfront development area. The firm is able to boast a large and global client base, and was particularly endorsed for its experience of large retail projects. **Dale Strachan** (see p.737) remains a respected member of the team. **Clients** British Waterways; Corus; Gazeley Properties; Grantchester; Macdonald Estates; National Amusements.

FYFE IRELAND WS (see firm details p.966) A well-regarded firm, it has a "*strong core of excellent property people*" residing within its practice. The team is headed by **James Roscoe** (see p.735),

SCOTLAND ■ REAL ESTATE

LEADING INDIVIDUALS

[1]
- ANDERSON Tom McGrigor Donald
- GARRETT Robin Maclay Murray & Spens
- HANIFORD Paul Semple Fraser
- RYDEN Nick Shepherd+ Wedderburn
- SMITH David Shepherd+ Wedderburn
- STEEL David Dundas & Wilson CS

[2]
- BANKIER David McGrigor Donald
- DORAN Iain Dundas & Wilson CS
- JOHNSON Jennifer Maclay Murray & Spens
- MOST Lionel Burness
- WATTIE Ian Burness

[3]
- DALGARNO Leslie Paull & Williamsons
- DOBIE James Shepherd+ Wedderburn
- NEWTON Alison McGrigor Donald
- QUIGLEY Ian Maclay Murray & Spens
- REID David Burness
- REID Sandy Biggart Baillie
- STRACHAN Dale Brodies

[4]
- BRYMER Stewart Thorntons WS
- ETCHELLS Simon Semple Fraser
- KERR Steven Fyfe Ireland WS
- MACNIVEN Iain Maclay Murray & Spens
- MCHARDY Iain Biggart Baillie
- MOFFAT Douglas Tods Murray WS
- PATERSON Ian Dundas & Wilson CS
- ROSCOE James Fyfe Ireland WS
- ROSS Kenneth Burness
- WILSON Alistair Fyfe Ireland WS

UP AND COMING
- ALEXANDER Ewan McGrigor Donald
- DRUMMOND Caroline Burness
- RENNIE Richard Burness

See individuals' profiles p.725

regarded by commentators as "*an expert man on property issues.*" He has recently been involved in the purchase of a large retail park in Falkirk. The team also advised on the disposal of the GPO building in Edinburgh. **Steven Kerr** (see p.732) and **Alistair Wilson** (see p.738) are typical of the firm's highly commercial, constructive style. Retail and residential matters feature in this broad property practice, and it gathers plaudits for its skills in cross-border transactions. **Clients** Allied London Properties; B&Q; Deutsche Property Asset Management; Green Property; Keir Homes; Matalan; Morrison Homes; Nationwide Building Society; Pizza Hut; Teachers Insurance & Amenity Association; Woolworths.

MACROBERTS (see firm details p.1049) This "*steady*" firm is rated by peers not just for its track record in the property arena, but also for its extra expertise in projects. The team has acted for high-level investors in major Scottish development work. Headed up by Laurence Fraser in Glasgow and Allan MacKenzie in Edinburgh, the team has been occupied with development work on the railways. In the last 12 months, it has acted for Kincaid on the sale of Greenock shipyard, as well as the purchase of premises at Inchinnan Business Park. Representing a large number of commercial companies with interests in Scotland, the firm is also instructed by the London Stock Exchange in relation to its commercial property requirements in Scotland. **Clients** AMEC; Anglo Irish Bank; Bank of Scotland; Henry Boot; MB Property; Miller Group; News International; Rank Hovis; Royal Bank of Scotland; Safeway Stores.

TODS MURRAY WS (see firm details p.1164) Peers envied the firm its "*good volume of work in the last year.*" A healthy track record exists in investment work and complex projects, while the team is also involved in development and financing issues arising from the commercial, residential and industrial sectors. It has acted for Scottish Power UK on the property aspects of the dismantling of its retail division, which included the disposal of 61 properties. The "*strongest performer by far with his attention to detail*" is **Douglas Moffat** (see p.733). In a key highlight he advised on the purchase of George House, Glasgow for £14.55 million. **Clients** Anglo Irish Bank; Balfour Beatty; Bank of Scotland; Barratt Homes; Canada Life; Greenwich Group; Lloyds TSB; ScottishPower.

ARCHIBALD CAMPBELL & HARLEY WS (see firm details p.847) David Cockburn's team remains heavily endorsed for its work in the retail sector, which this year has included funding a number of acquisitions of retail parks. It has acted for the Cuckfield Group and Spectrum on multimillion pound office developments within Edinburgh. The Ashtenne Group has instructed the firm on a number of high-profile industrial deals. **Clients** Anter Group; Boots; Britannia Building Society; Direct Line Insurance; Dixons; MDI; Northern Rock; Safeway.

BIGGART BAILLIE (see firm details p.871) The firm's merger with high-profile property firm Steedman Ramage has brought together an "*exquisite*" retail team, within a firm that can also handle the heavy aspects of industrial work. The new team is headed by Peter Cruickshank, and has over the past year acted as the sole legal providers to Wilcon Homes in the development of 1,200 acres in Dunfermline. The "*decent and enthusiastic*" **Iain McHardy** continues to enjoy a wide commercial client base, while peers endorsed **Sandy Reid** as a senior figure. **Clients** EDI Group; Hasbro Group; IBM; McDonald's; National Provident Insurance; Next; ScottishPower; Shell.

DLA This is a well regarded outfit, that has interests in residential and retail work, acquisitions and developments.

LEDINGHAM CHALMERS (see firm details p.1034) John Curran leads this smaller "*user-friendly*" team. Clients and peers recommend its residential, commercial and business-related property activities. The team has acted on the development of the Spectrum Building in Glasgow, and advised on the proposed 216-acre mixed-development site at Bellsdyke. **Clients** Accenture; AGW Partnerships; Cala; Elf Exploration; John Wood Group; Macdonald Hotels; Nationwide Building Society; University of Aberdeen.

PAULL & WILLIAMSONS (see firm details p.1096) This well-regarded firm holds a range of influence that stretches far beyond its Aberdeen base. Development issues and acquisitions in the office and leisure sectors have proved a strong source of instruction, and the team has a particular foothold in the power industry. It has recently acted for BP in the acquisition of a site for new operational offices in Aberdeen. Its work on major residential sites includes advice on the former Glenury Distillery in Stonehaven. A leading figure in the market, **Leslie Dalgarno** (see p.728) is described as "*pragmatic and sensible.*" **Clients** BAA; Cromwell Properties; Bett Brothers; Essen Properties; European Development Company; Halliburton Dresser Group.

HARPER MACLEOD (see firm details p.985) Mark Dewar's "*highly competent*" team has carved a comfortable niche for itself in the Scottish market. It has been occupied with a number of high-profile commercial and office deals, including the purchase of a number of industrial units in Cumbernauld for WG Mitchell. The team has also acted for Allied Irish Bank in a £3 million funding over four investment properties in Edinburgh. **Clients** AIB Group (UK); Barclays Bank; BP International; Celtic; ICI; Luminar; Northern Bank; Pfizer; Talisker Properties; Travis Perkins.

THORNTONS WS (see firm details p.1162) Observers recommend **Stewart Brymer** (see p.228) for his "*erudite and knowledgeable views,*" and he continues to carry a good profile across the industry. The practice has witnessed steady growth in the last year, with increasing work for property developers and HE institutions. The team has carried out a number of deals in the commercial, office and retail sectors. **Clients** B&Q; Bett Brothers; Edge Property Investments; Imperial Tobacco Pension Trusts.

ANDERSON STRATHERN WS (see firm details p.844) Alan Menzies' team has been singled out by sources, impressed by its "*effort and enthusiasm.*" The team has a range of skills that it employs on issues as diverse as redevelopment work for former industrial areas, and works for The Crown Estate. Highlights of the past year include representing a private investor in a £20 million Edinburgh office investment, and acting for Thistle Hotels on the sale of eight of its hotels in Scotland. **Clients** Allied Irish Bank; Boxclever Group; Castle Rock Housing Association; Halifax; Merlin Entertainments Group; National Westminster Bank; Richmond Homes; Scottish Airports; William Baird.

REAL ESTATE ■ NORTHERN IRELAND

DAVIDSON CHALMERS WS (see firm details p.929) This team of "*competent, charming*" lawyers is headed by Andrew Chalmers. The spectrum of real estate work is undertaken here, often for large investors and developers. The firm was involved in the purchase of an industrial portfolio in central Scotland, and advised on the purchase of a landmark building in St Andrews. It is currently advising a consortium in connection with a large PPP project. **Clients** Property companies; developers; banks; house builders.

MASONS (see firm details p.1057) This highly rated construction firm fields a property team that is well regarded by clients as "*quick and efficient*" offering a "*value for money service.*" The property team offers advice and expertise to the firm's established construction clients, but sits as an independent group. It is led by Hugh Bruce-Watt and has acted for Pathfinder Properties in its £100 million mixed-use development in Glasgow. **Clients** Canonbury Estates; International Computers; Morgan Stanley Dean Witter; Sandown Capital.

MCCLURE NAISMITH (see firm details p.1062) Wilson Aitken's team has been engaged in advice to investors in the Scottish property market. There has been a focus in the leisure market, where the firm has advised on development projects. It has also acted for a major bank on the leasing out of a large property in its possession. **Clients** Bass; Brown & Jackson Group; Burford; Care First Group; Coal Pension Properties; Equitable Life Assurance; NHP Properties.

NORTHERN IRELAND

REAL ESTATE
■ NORTHERN IRELAND

[1] **Carson McDowell** Belfast
L'Estrange & Brett Belfast
[2] **Elliott Duffy Garrett** Belfast
[3] **C & H Jefferson** Belfast
Johns Elliot Belfast
Mills Selig Belfast
Tughans Belfast
[4] **Arthur Cox** Belfast
Cleaver Fulton Rankin Belfast
McKinty and Wright Belfast

LEADING INDIVIDUALS

[1] **MAHOOD Laurence** Elliott Duffy Garrett
REILLY Alan Carson McDowell
[2] **AGNEW Phyllis** Tughans
HENDERSON Brian L'Estrange & Brett
HEWITT Alan L'Estrange & Brett
LEITCH David Johns Elliot
TINMAN Mark C & H Jefferson
[3] **CARSON Rosemary** Carson McDowell
FARIS Neil Cleaver Fulton Rankin
HAM Brian Mills Selig
HILL Jeremy Carson McDowell
HOUSTON James Cleaver Fulton Rankin
HUDDLESTON Ian L'Estrange & Brett
WHITE Rowan Arthur Cox Northern Ireland

This book is the product of 6,582 1/2 hour interviews. See p.7 for BMRB audit.
Within each band, firms are listed alphabetically. See individuals' profiles p.725

CARSON MCDOWELL (see firm details p.901) Commonly regarded as "*the best firm in the region,*" the practice has had an impressive run of substantial transactions and development matters in the past year. Alan Reilly (see p.735) is described by interviewees as "*a massively influential figure in property.*" He has been involved on the large development at Belfast Harbour. Rosemary Carson (see p.727) has impressed as one who "*takes great care and attention,*" and has acted for LA Sports on its entry into the city. The team had also been involved in the development of six shopping centres over the last year. Jeremy Hill (see p.731) was singled out for his work in the retail sector. Clearly growing in the field of retail and commercial developments, the team remains well-regarded for its skills in industrial acquisitions. **Clients** Arcadia; Argos; Belfast Harbour Commissioner; Electronics Boutique; Forestside; HMV; MFI; Tesco; TK Maxx; Woolworths.

L'ESTRANGE & BRETT (see firm details p.1039) "*Busy and focused,*" this team of "*common-sense individuals*" is regarded as one of the leading practices in Belfast. Headed by the "*exceptional*" Alan Hewitt (see p.825), it has been involved in the Northern Irish aspects of the outsourcing of BT's UK property portfolio, a deal that in total is worth £2.3 billion. The team has also recently advised Cusp in the acquisition, construction and leasing of the new mixed-use Lisburn Square development. Brian Henderson (see p.106) typifies the firm's "*proactive, constructive*" approach, while Ian Huddleston (see p.731) is rated as "*a good man to have on your side in any transaction.*" While the overall group's residential, commercial and leisure work provokes nods of approval, its PFI skills are also the envy of of many. **Clients** Cusp; Laganside; Morrison Homes; Northwin Consortium; Queen's University; Sainsbury's.

ELLIOTT DUFFY GARRETT (see firm details p.947) Laurence Mahood (see p.733) remains one of the highest praised real estate lawyers in the province, described by peers as "*a heavyweight lawyer, a real class act.*" He has led a respected team through a number of high value commercial and retail deals in the last 12 months. These include representing British Land in its sale of the Connswater Shopping Centre and Retail Park for £45 million. The group has also acted for Land Securities in the sale of two shopping centres (part of a portfolio of six) to Rate. **Clients** British Land; C&A; Land Securities; Lattice; Legal & General; Mapeley; Schroders.

C & H JEFFERSON (see firm details p.1013) The name of Mark Tinman (see p.737) has emerged during our research as a strong force in Northern Ireland real estate. Peers described him as "*truly impressive*" in both negotiations and the drafting of documents. He and the team have been involved in a number of retail transactions over the past year, including the purchase of a large shopping centre in Belfast. Enjoying a significant commercial client base, this group has been commended as "*very much on the up.*" **Clients** Lidl; Monsoon; New Look; Oasis; Peacocks; Sports Contact.

JOHNS ELLIOT (see firm details p.1016) High quality transactions feature in the workload here. The firm has acted for Scottish Widows in the sale of some Belfast city centre property, and has acted for Dunloe Ewart in a multi-million pound development. Peers believe that the team has been immersed in significant residential property developments over the last year. David Leitch (see p.732) was endorsed for his constructive approach to transactions. **Clients** Belfast International Airport; Dunloe Ewart; MEPC; NCP; Northern Bank Pension Trust.

MILLS SELIG (see firm details p.1072) This team is described by clients as "*keeping good links with some major developers.*" It has been active in the purchase of a local supermarket for £35 million, and has advised the Spanish retailer Zara on its entry into Northern Ireland. The firm is also involved in a number of high profile lettings, including Millennium House, one of the largest office blocks in the province. "*Experienced*" Brian Ham (see p.730) has "*a good steady hand*" on real estate issues. **Clients** Local and national plcs.

TUGHANS (see firm details p.1169) This practice has impressed interviewees on the investment side. Phyllis Agnew (see p.725) stands out here, endorsed as a lawyer who is "*extremely keen on straight-talking.*" The team has acted for Reed Asset Management in relation to the purchase of two shopping centres, which were part of a portfolio, with a total value of £250 million. High profile clients have instructed the team on leisure developments. **Clients** Anglia & General Developments; Marks & Spencer; Michael Roden; Prudential; SV Morrison; Tesco.

ARTHUR COX (see firm details p.850) This "*highly competent*" firm has been involved with Musgrave Supervalu-Centra on a new distribution centre at Belfast Docks, in what has been a £20 million investment. It has also acted for the Bank of Ireland on its new flagship branch in Belfast. Peers singled out **Rowan White** (see p.738) for his "*brilliant mind on finance issues.*" **Clients** Bank of Ireland; Fitness First; Musgrave Supervalu-Centra.

CLEAVER FULTON RANKIN (see firm details p.910) Adjudged a "*solidly impressive*" firm, it has been active in the Northern Irish aspects of Project Warren, the outsourcing of BT's property portfolio. The group has also been occupied with the development of the Northern Ireland Science Park, which is based in the Titanic Quarter of the docks. **James Houston** (see p.731) is highly praised by peers for his depth of knowledge, while **Neil Faris** (see p.729) continues to be regarded as a top name. **Clients** BT Property; Cellnet; Consignia; Crown Castle Telecommunications; Lisburn Borough Council.

MCKINTY AND WRIGHT (see firm details p.281) The active consultant, Ivan Fraser, runs this small, well-respected team. It remains best known for its expertise in shopping centre developments, and boasts a large retail client base. The team has advised on an ongoing joint venture project with a large investor in the province. It has also advised another large retail company on a dispute concerning premises. **Clients** Large commercial entities.

THE LEADERS IN REAL ESTATE

AGNEW, Phyllis
Tughans, Belfast
(028) 9055 3300
phyllis.agnew@tughans.com
Specialisation: Partner and head of the commercial property department. Main area of practice is commercial property development including property finance, bank and institutional funding, institutional investment, joint venture arrangements and PFI projects.
Prof. Memberships: Law Society of Northern Ireland, IBA and European Lawyers Group.
Career: Qualified 1981. Assistant solicitor at *Tughans* 1981-88. Partner since 1988. Chairman of Special Educational Needs Tribunal.

ALEXANDER, Ewan
McGrigor Donald, Edinburgh
(0131) 777 7027
ewan.alexander@mcgrigors.com
Specialisation: Leisure, developments and landlord and tenant. Aspects of Hilton/Royal Bank £312m sale and leaseback. Ottakars plc acquisition of James Thin bookshop chain.
Prof. Memberships: Law Society of Scotland.
Career: Trained *McGrigor Donald*, Edinburgh and London 1989-91. Qualified *McGrigor Donald*, Edinburgh and Glasgow 1991 to date. Assumed January 1999.
Personal: Married with one daughter aged three. Participates in rugby and golf.

ANDERSON, Tom
McGrigor Donald, Glasgow
(0141) 248 6677
tom.anderson@mcgrigors.com
Specialisation: Partner dealing with property joint ventures, property finance development work generally and forward arrangements; recent transactions include acting for Taylor Clark Properties Limited in the joint venture with Wilson Bowden Developments Limited for the Equinox Building in Glasgow (and for the joint venture in the subsequent prelet to E-sure and forward sale); acting for Glasgow Harbour Limited (a joint venture between Clydeport and Bank of Scotland) in the Glasgow Harbour Development Project (one of the largest UK Waterfront regeneration projects with a projected value on completion in excess of £450 million); acting for Scottish Enterprise in the arrangements for the redevelopment of Ravenscraig and acting for Morrison Developments in a joint venture with Bank of Scotland relative to the development of a factory outlet centre in Rathdowney, South of Dublin.
Prof. Memberships: Law Society of Scotland.
Career: 1971-75 Edinburgh University (LLB Hons); 1980-89 *Biggart Baillie & Gifford*, Partner (Commercial Property/Corporate); 1989 to date *McGrigor Donald*, Partner (Commercial Property).
Personal: Two daughters. Leisure interests include golf, duplicate bridge and skiing.

ASHWORTH, Peter
Field Cunningham & Co, Manchester
(0161) 834 4734

ASKIN, David
Wragge & Co, Birmingham
(0870) 903 1000

AYRE, Paul
Gordons Cranswick Solicitors, Leeds
(0113) 213 1925
paul.ayre@gordonscranswick.co.uk
Specialisation: Specialist in all types of commercial property work. Clients include retailers, developers, investors and lenders. Recent projects include numerous superstore acquisitions for Wm. Morrison Supermarkets plc including schemes in Enfield, Grays and Cambourne. Procurement of a contract for the firm to represent Coors Brewers Limited in all lending work throughout England and Wales; acting on the development of Hornbeam Business Park which incorporates 300,000sq ft of offices, a hotel and a fitness centre. Acquisition of a series of business parks extending to over 500,000sq ft for Wharfedale Finance Company.
Career: Qualified in 1989: *Simpson Curtis* until 1993: *Gordons Wright & Wright*, now *Gordons Cranswick* 1993 to present; became partner 1994.
Personal: Born 4 November 1964: married with two children: lives Guiseley. Hobbies include football, skiing, golf and cinema. Newcastle United FC season ticket holder.

BAILEY, Jeffrey
Linklaters, London
(020) 7456 4756
jeffrey.bailey@linklaters.com
Specialisation: Real Estate Department. Property law specialist. All-round experience of all types of real estate transactions. Involved in a large number of portfolio and syndicated property transactions. Also handled the real estate implications of several privatisations. Specific involvement with overseas clients, particularly Dutch and German on inward investment into UK real estate.
Career: Attained LLB (Hons) from University of Wales 1971. Qualified in 1974. 1974-75, Assistant Solicitor, *Linklaters* Property Department. 1976-78, Assistant Solicitor, *Linklaters* Tax Department. 1978-80, Assistant Solicitor, *Linklaters* Property Department. Partner 1980 to date. Joint head of *Linklaters* European Property Practice.

BAILEY, Michael
asb law, Crawley
(01293) 603674
michael.bailey@asb-law.com
Specialisation: Head of Property Services Group. Specialises in commercial property. Work includes handling the development of new sites, construction work, joint ventures, landlord and tenant, sales and purchases of businesses and land transactions for charities. Provides solicitor expert reports on conveyancing practice.
Prof. Memberships: Law Society, Associate of School of Urban and Regional Studies, University of Sussex.
Career: Qualified in 1965. Assistant and Partner at *Gates & Co* in Brighton 1966-71. Partner in *Whitley Hughes & Luscombe/Donne Mileham & Haddock*, Crawley and Brighton from 1973-98.
Personal: Educated at Varndean Grammar School; Brighton and College of Law. Positions held include President Sussex Law Society 1995, Member of Legal Aid Area Committee from 1975, Chairman 1990-91. Member Know How Housing team to Eastern Europe. CAB Tutor 1974-84, University of Sussex and Brighton College of Technology part-time lecturer 1967-80.

BAILY, Tim
Bond Pearce, Southampton
(023) 8063 2211
tbaily@bondpearce.com
Specialisation: Associate in the Commercial Property Group. Wide experience of all aspects of commercial property work especially development and commercial landlord and tenant. Involved in a number of the firm's niche areas of work such as wind farms and waste and minerals. Current emphasis is on port and marine related work including offshore windfarms and calls and pipelines.
Career: Qualified 1987, becoming Associate 1997.

BANKIER, David
McGrigor Donald, Glasgow
(0141) 567 9242
david.bankier@mcgrigors.com
Specialisation: Senior Property Partner and Chairman of Belfast Office. Main area of practice is property development and investment within tax efficient structures, joint ventures and public/private sector initiatives in commercial property. Acted for BAA-McArthur/Glen in the development of their first designer outlet centre in Scotland, and for Resolution Property plc in their first major retail development in Scotland, a 50% interest in the £80m The Forge shopping centre, Glasgow. Advised Downing Corporate Finance as sponsor of major collective investment throughout Scotland, England and Northern Ireland. Advised Akeler Developments and Royal Bank on 'golden contracts' prior to the expiry of the Renfrewshire Enterprise Zone. Presently advising North Lanarkshire Council on Cumbernauld Town Centre redevelopment and Forth Ports PLC in relation to their property portfolio in Edinburgh.
Career: Qualified in 1972, having joined *McGrigor Donald* in 1970. Became a Partner in 1978.
Personal: Born 24 March 1949. Educated at Edinburgh University (LLB 1970). Leisure interests include travel, art history, Scottish contemporary paintings, sailing and skiing. Lives in Glasgow.

REAL ESTATE ■ THE LEADERS

BARNES, James
Herbert Smith, London
(020) 7374 8000
james.barnes@herbertsmith.com
Specialisation: Partner with a wide range of experience in commercial property and property related matters, particularly in relation to development projects, property joint ventures and property funding and security work. Most recent work includes advising on a wide range of UK infrastructure projects, including those promoted under the government's Private Finance Initiative.
Career: Queen's University, Belfast (LLB). Qualified 1980. Partner *Herbert Smith* 1989.

BATTISCOMBE, David
Finers Stephens Innocent, London
(020) 7344 5531
dbattiscombe@fsilaw.co.uk
Specialisation: Partner and Head of Property at FSI, specialising in all key areas of commercial conveyancing with a particular focus on developers. Client portfolio includes high profile developers Marylebone Warwick Balfour Group Plc. Current caseload includes major Docklands regeneration schemes as well as significant hotel and leisure projects. Has a wide experience of new-build and refurbishment, both speculative and pre-let relating to offices, leisure, industrial parks, residential and retail. Investment experience includes acquisitions for private and institutional clients and joint venture work. He acts for prominent leisure operators, managing their successful national acquisition programmes. Broad construction experience including collateral warranties, professional appointments and bonds. David features as a Highly Recommended Individual in Commercial Property in the 'Global Counsel 3000' directory which is published by the Practical Law Company in conjunction with PriceWaterHouseCoopers.
Career: Qualified 1983. Appointed Head of Property at mid-town *Baileys Shaw & Gillett* 1995 after having established Abu Dhabi office 1994. Left merged firm of *Baileys Shaw & Gillett* and *Speechley Bircham* to join *Finers Stephens Innocent* 1998. Appointed Head of Property at *Finers Stephens Innocent* 2000.
Personal: Lives in London. Has travelled extensively and his interests outside the law include music, particularly playing bass in his band '$100 Bills'.

BEACH, Steven
Taylor Vinters, Cambridge
(01223) 225174
steven.beach@taylorvinters.com
Specialisation: All types of commercial property transactions specialising in institutional investment, development, joint ventures, property insolvency and securities work; dilapidations.
Prof. Memberships: Law Society Member.
Career: Graduated in law at Oxford University and joined *Taylor Vinters* in 1983.

Qualified in 1985. Became a partner in 1989 and head of the commercial property department in 1994.
Personal: Enjoys amateur dramatics and sport.

BECKETT, Roy
DLA, Manchester
(08700) 111111

BENNETT, Graham
Shoosmiths, Fareham
(01489) 881010
graham.bennett@shoosmiths.co.uk
Specialisation: Partner in the Commercial Property Group. Specialises in development acquisition, leasing, financing and disposal work, advising a wide range of companies, developers, banks and charities in commercial property matters including those involved with brownfield sites. In 2000, advises Heinz UK on the property and financing issues relating to the development of a 350,000sq ft National Distribution Centre at Wigan (the largest high bay, automated warehouse in Europe) including the first use in the UK of a synthetic lease. Is presently advising Bournemouth International Airport Ltd with regard to its property interests and Esso Petroleum Company Ltd in connection with its concerns regarding ABP's proposals for a new container terminal at Dibden Bay, Southampton. Also advised Esso regarding the installation at Fawley Refinery of a four mile high pressure gas pipeline for a new CHP Plant. Other high value or novel property transactions that he has dealt with include the privatisation of Chatham Docks and Southend Airport; funding including the £38 million development loan made in respect of 1 Cockspur Street, Trafalgar Square; Roehampton Institute, London, in the legal aspects of restructuring and financing of five new halls of residence; development including the site acquisition and funding of the head office of the East Hampshire Housing Association.
Prof. Memberships: Law Society; Society of Practitioners of Insolvency; Charity Law Association.
Career: Articled *Ashurst Morris Crisp*, assistant *Clifford-Turner*, Partner *Wilde Sapte*, 1994 Partner *Shoosmiths*.
Publications: Joint author 'Housing Act 1988 – A Practical Guide'.
Personal: Golf, cricket, riding and sailing.

BENSON, Stephen
Cobbetts, Manchester
(0161) 833 5232
stephen.benson@cobbetts.co.uk
Specialisation: Head of Commercial Property Division. Commercial property in the retail and leisure sector. Acts for household name retailers and licensed premises operators in the pub, restaurant and hotel sector.
Prof. Memberships: Law Society. Associate member of American Bar Association.
Career: Educated at Manchester Univer-

sity and Chester College of Law. Qualified 1980.
Personal: Born 1955. Married with three children. Lives in Knutsford. Leisure interests, exercise, motor cars.

BENZECRY, Edward
CMS Cameron McKenna, London
(020) 7367 2741
edward.benzecry@cmck.com
Specialisation: Commercial property specialist and heads the Real Estate Group of *CMS Cameron McKenna*. Leads the client teams for the Wellcome Trust and the Prudential. Recent experience includes the acquisition of the new Lloyds TSB headquarters building and leading the team on Hutchison 3G's site acquisitions for its third generation network.
Prof. Memberships: Law Society.
Career: Articled with *Hamilin Slowe* 1985-87. Qualified January 1988, joining *Cameron Markby* (now *CMS Cameron McKenna*) simultaneously. Became a Partner in 1994.
Personal: Education: St John's School Leatherhead; Birmingham University; Guildford College of Law. Leisure: golf, tennis, family. Married with two children.

BERRY, Paul
Clyde & Co, Guildford
(01483) 555 555

BERRY, Roger John
Berry Smith, Cardiff
(029) 2034 5511
Specialisation: Full range of commercial property work including investment and development with particular emphasis on landlord and tenant. Also joint ventures and banking.
Career: Qualified 1978. Articled *Broomheads & Neals* (Sheffield). At *Simpson Curtis* (Leeds) 1978-81 and *Phillips & Buck* now *Eversheds*, Cardiff 1981-86. Established *Berry Smith* 1986.
Personal: Born 19 March 1952, Colne, Lancashire. Educated at Sedbergh School and Emmanuel College, Cambridge (MA). Interests: football and cycling.

BILLINGS, Martin J
BrookStreet Des Roches, Witney
(01993) 771616
martin@bsdr.com
Specialisation: Commercial property with wide ranging experience of property financing, development and portfolio management. Recent transactions include pre-let and speculative development projects and strategic acquisitions for MEPC in the UK and forward funding and development projects in the UK and Europe for Tech Data Corporation.
Prof. Memberships: The Law Society.
Career: Qualified 1988. *Cole & Cole/Morgan Cole* 1988-2000. Partner 1994. Joined *BrookStreet Des Roches* in 2000 as a Partner.

BLACK, Ian
Cuff Roberts, Liverpool
(0151) 237 7777

ian.black@cuffroberts.co.uk
Specialisation: An experienced commercial property lawyer who is highly regarded for being commercially aware. Has had considerable experience in a wide range of property work, especially in the retail sector. Advises a number of high profile clients in the retail sector and also acts for a number of quality developers, significant landlords and major lending institutions. This experience has given him a valuable understanding of the 'other side's' view, thereby expediting the negotiation of deals that are acceptable to each party and are fundable. Clients include, amongst others, Johnsons the Cleaners, Help the Aged, the Royal Bank of Scotland Plc, the Highneal Group of Companies, the Legendary Property Company Ltd, Denbighshire County Council, Neptune Developments Ltd and the Beetham Organization Ltd.
Prof. Memberships: Law Society; Liverpool Law Society.
Career: Trained at *Cuff Roberts*, qualifying in 1988. Became a Partner with the firm in 1993. Has been a member of the firm's executive board since its inception in 1998.
Personal: Born 1964. Interests include Alpine walking, antiques, architecture, art, classic cars, good food and fine wines.

BLAKE, Carey
Blake Lapthorn, Fareham
(01489) 579990

BOTHAMLEY, Michael
Beachcroft Wansbroughs, Bristol
(0117) 918 2000
mbothamley@bwlaw.co.uk
Specialisation: Acts for a range of national and regional developers, retailers and institutions. Has particular expertise in development work where current projects include a number of office, retail and leisure schemes. Also acts for several major residential portfolio investment companies.
Career: Durham University. 1980 joined *Wansbroughs Willey Hargrave*. Partner with *Wansbroughs Willey Hargrave* 1986. 1999, partner in *Beachcroft Wansbroughs*.

BRAITHWAITE, Neil
Dickinson Dees, Newcastle upon Tyne
(0191) 279 9233
law@dickinson-dees.com
Specialisation: Managing Partner. Handles urban regeneration, development agreements and property joint ventures, minerals and waste disposal work, building preservation trusts and historic house rescues.
Career: Trinity College, Cambridge MA. Law Society Finals. *Joynson Hicks* 1976-78. *Clifford Chance* 1978-80. *Dickinson Dees* 1980 to date. (Partner 1981 onwards - Head of Property from 1990-98). Managing Partner from 1998.

BRETHERTON, Philip
Berwin Leighton Paisner, London

726 INDEX TO LEADING LAWYERS: PAGE 1693 ■ IN-HOUSE LAWYERS PROFILES: PAGE 1201

THE LEADERS ■ REAL ESTATE

(020) 7760 1000
philip.bretherton@blplaw.com
Specialisation: Head of the Real Estate Group. Specialises in commercial property with particular emphasis on development and tax-led work and, more recently, in projects promoted under the Private Finance Initiative. In the past 18 months has acted for government offices for London on the contract for the new London Parliament building and for English Partnerships in relation to the Greenwich Peninsula. Continues to represent Norwest Holst and MEPC, the promoters of the Bute Avenue scheme in Cardiff, a scheme being promoted under the PFI. Is also advising Blenheim Norwest Limited on the redevelopment of Hounslow Town Centre.
Prof. Memberships: Member of the Law Society.
Career: Articled *Slaughter and May*; qualified 1974; Assistant Solicitor 1974-78; Assistant Solicitor *Simmons & Simmons* 1978-79; Property Partner *Simmons & Simmons* 1979-94; Partner *Berwin Leighton* 1994.
Personal: Born 1950, educated at Oxford University (MA). Leisure interests include opera, collecting 78s, tennis and reading. Lives in Maidenhead.

BRETT, Alan
Hewitson Becke + Shaw, Cambridge
(01223) 461155
alanbrett@hewitsons.com
Specialisation: Managing Partner of firm and Partner in Property Department dealing with all aspects of commercial property work, including property funding, development work, joint venture agreements, freehold, leasehold, landlord and tenant matters.
Prof. Memberships: Institute of Directors; Fellow of Centre for Law Firm Management (MBA in legal practice), Nottingham Law School; Chairman, Cambridge Interact; various management, property and local clubs; Law Society (national and local).
Career: Trained with *Eversheds*; qualified 1972; LLM (distinction); Diploma in international law; solicitor *Wild, Hewitson & Shaw* 1973-76, partner 1977-89; partner (following merger) *Hewitson Becke + Shaw* since 1989; membership of various committees with firm including the firm's Heads of Department Committee, Finance Committee, Marketing and Practice Development Committees, Management Committees and Merger Committee; Head of firmwide Commercial Property Department 1991-94, and Managing Partner since 1994; supervisor in company law at Cambridge University: 1974-76 Sidney Sussex College, 1975-76 Magdalene College. Lectured in conveyancing law for external London LLB students.
Personal: Resides Cambridge. Governor of The Perse School for Girls, Cambridge.

BRIAM, Tony
Clifford Chance, London
(020) 7600 1000
tony.briam@cliffordchance.com
Specialisation: Real estate. Partner advising on all equity aspects of commercial property, with particular emphasis on advising developers and landowners on major city centre office schemes.
Career: Articled *Boodle, Hatfield & Co*; qualified 1974; Partner *Clifford-Turner/Clifford Chance* since 1981
Personal: Stratton School, Biggleswade; Clare College, Cambridge (MA).

BRISTOL, Jeremy
Birketts, Ipswich
(01473) 232300

BROTHWOOD, Graham
Clark Holt, Swindon
(01793) 617444
grahamb@clarkholt.com
Specialisation: Partner specialising in building and development projects. Advisor to Bloor Homes, ARVAL PHH, TYCO Electronics, St James's Place and GWR Group plc.
Career: Qualified in 1988 (previously with *Taylor Joynson Garrett* in the City). One of three partners who co-founded *Clark Holt Commercial Solicitors* in 1995.
Personal: Born 1961. Educated at Marlborough College and Southampton University. Qualified with *Joynson-Hicks*. Resides near Malmesbury.

BROWN, Nicholas
CMS Cameron McKenna, London
(020) 7367 3000
nick.brown@cmck.com
Specialisation: Partner in Real Estate Group. Handles property development and investment work for national and international property companies, institutions and retailers. Work includes acquisition and disposal of investment properties, acquisition funding and disposal of office and retail properties and development sites, and leases of all types of commercial property. Examples of matters handled are the development of Bristol Harbourside; development of supermarkets; the structuring of joint investments in property; securitisation of property interests and the property aspects of the Channel Tunnel Rail Link.
Prof. Memberships: City of London Law Society, Land Law Committee/Investment Property Forum.
Career: Qualified in 1974. Became a Partner of *McKenna & Co* (now *CMS Cameron McKenna*) in 1980.
Personal: Born 21 November 1949. Educated at Bristol University 1968-71.

BRYMER, Stewart
Thorntons WS, Dundee
(01382) 229111
See under Education, p.228

BUCKLEY, Liam
Hammond Suddards Edge, Manchester
(0161) 830 5000

BURGESS, James
Pitmans, Reading
(0118) 958 0224
jburgess@pitmans.com
Specialisation: Considerable experience in commercial property matters, including acquisitions, sales, joint venture agreements, funding, investment and developments. He also has significant knowledge pertaining to residential development, land assembly and acquisition.
Prof. Memberships: Law Society.
Career: He qualified in 1982 and joined *Pitmans* in 1989.
Personal: Born 1957. Educated Radley College. Leisure interests include tennis, skiing and fishing.

BURNS, John
Wragge & Co, Birmingham
(0870) 903 1000

BURTON, Carl
DMH, Crawley
(01293) 605084
carl.burton@dmh.co.uk
Specialisation: Partner who deals with all aspects of residential development work including site acquisitions and disposals, strategic options, collaboration agreements and joint ventures. Acts for household name residential developer clients, local planning authorities and major public and private companies. Also deals with planning matters relating primarily, but not exclusively, to residential development sites.
Prof. Memberships: Member of Law Society's Planning panel; legal associate member of Royal Town Planning Institute.
Career: BA (Hons) in Law; diploma in Local Government Law. Qualified 1979; assistant solicitor Horsham District Council (HDC) 1979-81; principal solicitor HDC 1981-83; chief legal officer Dartford Borough Council 1983-85; senior solicitor *Rawlison & Butler* 1985-86, made partner in 1986; joined *DMH* in July 2000.
Personal: Born 1955. Golf, travel and football.

BUTLER, Alan
Simmons & Simmons, London
(020) 7628 2020

CARSON, Rosemary
Carson McDowell, Belfast
(028) 9024 4951
rosemary.carson@carson-mcdowell.com
Specialisation: Acquisition and disposal of commercial property including site assembly and onward development. Landlord and tenant work, in particular all matters relating to the Business Tenancies (Northern Ireland) Order 1996. Clients include national retailers such as Arcadia plc, Boxclever and Birthdays, leisure operators and public authorities. In the past year major transactions have included acting for Chartwell Land in respect of all Northern Irish aspects of Project Horizon which was the single largest high street property deal of 2001, LA Fitness plc in its acquisition of its first three health clubs in Northern Ireland and Petchy Holdings plc in its acquisition and onward disposal of a chain of petrol filling stations.
Prof. Memberships: Law Society of Northern Ireland – member of the Non-contentious Business Committee.
Career: LLB (First Class Honours): Queen's University, Belfast, 1993. 1993-97: *Johns Elliot*, Belfast (qualified 1995). 1997-date: *Carson McDowell*, Partner 2001.
Publications: Willing Landlords, Unresponsive Business Tenants 'Northern Ireland Legal Quarterly' Spring 2002. Currently co-writing text on the Business Tenancies (Northern Ireland) Order 1996 with Professor Norma Dawson of Queen's University, Belfast.
Personal: Interests include travel and theatre.

CHALCRAFT, Stephen
Masons, Manchester
(0161) 234 8234
stephen.chalcraft@masons.com
Specialisation: Partner and Manager of the Property Group in Manchester, providing legal and strategic advice on all aspects of property development, property joint ventures and PFI project work. Has considerable experience of co-ordinating large-scale development projects and is also a member of the firm's PFI team.
Prof. Memberships: Law Society.
Career: Qualified in 1990; joined *Masons* in 1999 as a Partner.
Personal: Born 24 February 1964 and educated at Jesus College, Oxford. Leisure interests include squash, tennis and hiking. Lives in South Manchester.

CHESTER, Mark
Wragge & Co, Birmingham
(0870) 903 1000

CLARK, Paul
D J Freeman, London
(020) 7583 4055

CLARK, Simon
Linklaters, London
(020) 7456 4902
simon.clark@linklaters.com
Specialisation: Specialist in the UK taxation of real estate transactions and investment structuring advising UK and non-UK institutions, property companies, developers and occupiers. Has long been involved in the UK property market's efforts to create listed tax-transparent real estate vehicles in the UK.
Prof. Memberships: Member of Economic and Legislative Affairs Committee of Association of Foreign Investors in US Real Estate.
Career: Articled at *Linklaters* and qualified in 1981, Assistant Solicitor *Linklaters* 1981-88, Partner *Linklaters* Property Department 1988-99. Head of Real Estate Department 1999 to date.

CLEAL, Adam
Allen & Overy, London
(020) 7330 3000
adam.cleal@allenovery.com

REAL ESTATE ■ THE LEADERS

Specialisation: Acts for landowners, developers and lenders. Specialises in property acquisitions and disposals, hotels, landlord and tenant transactions, property developments, project financing, cross-border property transactions, large scale voluntary transfers of housing stock by local authorities to housing associations, property joint ventures, management buyouts, business acquisitions, the sale and purchase of mortgage portfolios, financing transactions, land law arbitrations and securitisation issues.
Prof. Memberships: The Law Society, City of London Solicitors Company.
Career: LLB Leeds University. Qualified in 1982. Partner *Allen & Overy* since 1991. Head of real estate group since June 2000.
Personal: Cycling, scuba diving, opera, theatre, contemporary art.

COMBE, Jonathan
Robert Muckle, Newcastle upon Tyne
(0191) 244 2925
jwcombe@robertmuckle.co.uk
Specialisation: Large scale development projects (both brownfield and greenfield) principally acting on behalf of developers but also commercial lenders and investors. Joint ventures, grant and funding agreements and property investment.
Prof. Memberships: Newcastle upon Tyne Law Society.
Career: Qualified 1989, 1989-95 *Edge & Ellison*. Joined *Robert Muckle* 1995. Partner and Head of Property Group.

CONROY, Paul
Addleshaw Booth & Co, Manchester
(0161) 934 6525
paul.conroy@addleshawbooth.com
Specialisation: All aspects of commercial property with particular emphasis on property development and investment transactions acting for developers and occupiers. Extensive expertise in enterprise zone development projects.
Prof. Memberships: Law Society.
Career: *Field Cunningham & Co* 1992-95; *Hammond Suddards* 1995-96; *Halliwell Landau* 1996-2000 (Partner from 1999); *Addleshaw Booth & Co* 2001 to date.
Personal: Married, lives in Altrincham. Educated at St Thomas More RC High School and the University of Manchester. Leisure interests include travel, marathon running and cycling.

COWPER, Tony
Mills & Reeve, Cambridge
(01223) 222231
tony.cowper@mills-reeve.com
Specialisation: Partner with responsibility for commercial property and development and redevelopment issues.
Prof. Memberships: Law Society member, associate member of UKSPA, member of IPF.
Career: Client Partner to some of the largest property owning educational institutions in the country. Responsible for setting up Cambridge Science Park and all subsequent legal work associated with it. Now acting in connection with other Science/Business Parks (including site set-up, subsequent lettings and sales), complex joint ventures and major acquisitions and disposals.
Personal: Golf.

COX, Ian
Herbert Smith, London
(020) 7374 8000
ian.cox@herbertsmith.com
Specialisation: Partner dealing with all aspects of property law including landlord and tenant, investment sales/purchases and corporate support work. His practice has a particular emphasis on property finance, structured finance (including establishment of alternative vehicles for property investment) and property development. Having spent a period of secondment with the firm's international finance and banking group he now heads the firm's Real Estate Corporate Recovery Group.
Career: *Herbert Smith* trainee 1987-89. Qualified 1989. Partner 1996.
Personal: Educated at St. Brendan's College, Bristol and Exeter University.

CRAVEN, Diana
Addleshaw Booth & Co, Manchester
(0161) 934 6000
diana.craven@addleshawbooth.com
Specialisation: Partner in the Commercial Property Group. Wide ranging commercial property interests but specifically including development schemes, land reclamation, property partnerships and joint ventures and funding agreements. Clients include government agencies, plc developers, banks and companies with substantial property portfolios.
Prof. Memberships: Law Society, Association of Women Solicitors, Network.
Career: Joined firm in 1977 and became a Partner in 1981.
Personal: Interests include professional and managerial level womens groups, gardening and antiques.

CROCKER, Nic
Hammond Suddards Edge, Leeds
(0113) 284 7000

DAKEYNE, Mark
Wragge & Co, Birmingham
(0870) 903 1000

DALGARNO, Leslie
Paull & Williamsons, Aberdeen
(01224) 621621
lsdalgarno@paull-williamsons.co.uk
Specialisation: Head of commercial property department, advising private and public property companies and financial institutions on all aspects of property acquisition, development funding and disposal throughout the whole of Scotland. Acted for Stewart Milne Group Limited in a number of major acquisitions throughout Scotland and for Esson Properties in a recent substantial office development in Edinburgh.
Prof. Memberships: Law Society of Scotland and member of Investment Property Forum.
Career: Graduated from Aberdeen University in 1971, LLB with Distinction. Joined Messrs. *Paull & Williamsons* as trainee in 1971, becoming a partner in the commercial property department in 1977. Head of department since 1986. Notary Public.
Personal: Born 19 March 1950. Educated at Robert Gordon's College and Aberdeen University. Leisure pursuits include golf and football. Lives in Aberdeen.

DAVIES, Andrew
Pitmans, Reading
(0118) 958 0224
adavies@pitmans.com
Specialisation: Specialises in all aspects of commercial property, but in particular residential development, site acquisition by conditional contracts options, joint ventures with other residential developers. Clients include a number of publicly quoted residential developers.
Prof. Memberships: Law Society.
Career: Articles *Lovell White Durrant* and joined *Pitmans* in 1995.
Personal: Born in 1962. Educated Birkenhead School and Robinson College, Cambridge. Interests: cricket, rugby and golf. Married with three children.

DAVIES, Rowland
Edwards Geldard, Cardiff
(029) 2023 8239
rowland.davies@geldards.co.uk
Specialisation: Head of commercial property department at *Edwards Geldard*. Work includes development work, urban regeneration, investment, acquisitions and disposals. Acted for the Cardiff Bay Barrage Scheme and undertook the land assembly and project development for the Millennium Stadium, Cardiff. Is a consultant to Cardiff University Legal Practice Course.
Prof. Memberships: Law Society and Cardiff and District Law Society.
Career: Qualified in 1978. Joined *Edwards Geldard*, becoming a partner 1981.
Personal: Born 27 August 1953. Attended Cardiff High School 1964-71 and Downing College, Cambridge 1972-75. Leisure interests include art, music, literature, cinema, theatre and gardening. Is a founder member of the Academy for Design in Wales and a trustee of Ty Hafen Children's Hospice. Lives in Cardiff.

DE PURY, Chris
Herbert Smith, London
(020) 7374 8000
christopher.de-pury@herbertsmith.com
Specialisation: Partner with varied experience in all principal areas of commercial property law acting for institutions, property companies, developers and occupational tenants. Specialises in large scale infrastructure development projects, joint ventures and in particular, acting for government and quasi government departments and recently the private sector, on private finance initiative and corporate outsourcing schemes.
Prof. Memberships: Law Society.
Career: Qualified 1992. Partnership 1998.
Publications: Author of 'Property Aspects' for Jordans PFI handbook. Has written papers and lectured on different aspects of commercial property including joint ventures and corporate outsourcing
Personal: MA Oxon.

DILLON, Paula
Addleshaw Booth & Co, Leeds
(0113) 209 2000
paula.dillon@addleshawbooth.com
Specialisation: Specialises in commercial property. Particularly well regarded for development and development finance, acting for developers, funds, investors and occupiers. Recognised as a lawyer who will make deals happen. Skilled negotiator with ability to reconcile potentially conflicting interests.
Prof. Memberships: Law Society
Career: University of Manchester. Qualified 1986. Joined firm as Partner in 1999.
Personal: Walking, cycling, skiing.

DOBIE, James
Shepherd+ Wedderburn, Edinburgh
(0131) 473 5156
james.dobie@shepwedd.co.uk
Specialisation: Property Development and institutional investment. Acted for Freeport plc in development of first factory outlet centre in Scotland, and for Pillar Property plc in retail park developments. Acted for developers of Scotland's premier business park at Edinburgh Park on all lettings and onward sales and for the University of Edinburgh and Miller Developments in major land sales and large scale developments. Also involved in specialist telecommunication property acquisitions for Orange plc. Instructed on new development projects for Scottish & Newcastle plc and in new business park at Alba Campus.
Prof. Memberships: Law Society of Scotland. Writer to the Signet. British Council of offices.
Career: Educated at Edinburgh University. Joined *Shepherd+ Wedderburn* 1988 as trainee, became partner in 1995.
Personal: Born 14 August 1964. Leisure interests: football, literature, wine and East African culture.

DODGSON, Robert
Davies Lavery, Maidstone
(01622) 625657
robert.dodgson@davies-lavery.co.uk
Specialisation: Commercial property; development including local authority work and acting for ROS/NATWEST, Allied Irish Bank.
Career: *Godloves* (Leeds) 1990-94, *Days* (Maidstone) 1994-97, *Davies Lavery* (1997-date).
Personal: Leeds Grammar School; Newcastle University. Married, one child (daughter). Family, all sports.

728   INDEX TO LEADING LAWYERS: PAGE 1693 ■ IN-HOUSE LAWYERS PROFILES: PAGE 1201

THE LEADERS — REAL ESTATE

DORAN, Iain
Dundas & Wilson CS, Glasgow
(0141) 222 2200

DRUMMOND, Caroline
Burness, Edinburgh
(0131) 473 6000

DUNN, Ian
Bond Pearce, Bristol
(0117) 929 9197
idunn@bondpearce.com
Specialisation: Ian is a Partner in the Commercial Property Group of *Bond Pearce*, handling all aspects of acquisition and disposal of commercial property, particularly block property transactions in the leisure, licensing and transport sector. Specialisation includes conditional acquisition and disposal of development land; estate management work and business lettings; block property auctions; secured lending for institutions, breweries and other commercial lenders.
Career: Qualified in 1981, joined *Cartwrights* in 1988 becoming a Partner in 1990. Joined *Bond Pearce* in 2001 on merger.

DUNN, John
Burges Salmon, Bristol
(0117) 939 2256
john.dunn@burges-salmon.com
Specialisation: Widely experienced in complex commercial property transactions including portfolio management, development and funding.
Prof. Memberships: Law Society.
Career: Partner with *Cameron Markby* 1987-88. Partner with *Burges Salmon* since 1989.

EDGE, Mike
Halliwell Landau, Manchester
(0161) 835 3003
medge@halliwells.co.uk
Specialisation: Partner and Head of the Commercial Property Department. He advises on all aspects of commercial property, including site assembly and development acquisitions and disposals. He is an expert in environmental law.
Prof. Memberships: United Kingdom Environmental Lawyers' Association.
Career: Qualified 1982, Solicitor 1986-89, partner 1989-98 *Slater Heeks*. Made partner at *Halliwell Landau* in 1998.
Personal: Born 1958. Enjoys squash, tennis, skiing, football and theatre.

ELLIOTT, Martin
Linklaters, London
(020) 7456 4722
martin.elliott@linklaters.com
Specialisation: Partner and specialist with over 20 years' experience in all aspects of commercial property work with particular emphasis on development related work, shopping centre and retail development for developer and investment clients, property joint ventures; also considerable experience in relation to property aspects of company flotations, acquisitions, disposals and joint ventures.
Career: 1985 to date Partner *Linklaters*;
1979-85 Assistant Solicitor *Linklaters*; 1977-79 Articled Clerk *Linklaters*; 1976 Oxford University BA Law.

ELLIS, Michael
Cripps Harries Hall, Tunbridge Wells
(01892) 506104
mfe@crippslaw.com
Specialisation: Partner in the Commercial Property Department. Main area of work is commercial property, normally associated with residential development. Case work includes substantial commercial and institutional matters, as well as property investment work for clients domiciled in Asia.
Career: Articled *Cripps Harries Hall*; Head of Development Group.
Personal: Born 1949. Education: Sandown Court Secondary Modern, Tunbridge Wells. Resides Tunbridge Wells, Kent.

ETCHELLS, Simon
Semple Fraser, Glasgow
(0141) 221 3771
simon.etchells@semplefraser.co.uk
Specialisation: Commercial property partner and finance partner with a special interest in development work and commercial advice to industry. Active in Scotland for Dunloe Ewart plc, The Miller Group Limited, The Laird Group plc, SMG plc.
Prof. Memberships: The Society of Writers to her Majesty's Signet.
Career: Articled *W & J Burness WS*, qualified 1985; trainee 1985-87; *Bird Semple Fyfe Ireland WS*, 1987-90; *Semple Fraser WS* since 1990, partner since 1992.
Personal: Hermitage Academy; Edinburgh University (1984 LLB Hons; Diploma Legal Practice). Skiing, sailing, books and good wine.

EVANS, Eric
Eversheds, Cardiff
(029) 2047 1147
See under Local Government, p.577

FABIAN, Mark
Rickerbys, Cheltenham
(01242) 246420
mark.fabian@rickerbys.com
Specialisation: All aspects of commercial property, with particular emphasis on leasehold office acquisitions and renewals, including property development work. Recent transactions include acting on the multimillion pound freehold purchase of a 67 acre business park which was subject to some third party leases, 19 of which were leased back to the vendor.
Prof. Memberships: Institute of Directors.
Career: 19 years' experience as a commercial property expert. Articled clerk at *Watterson Todman*. Qualified October 1981. Appointed *Rickerby Watterson* Managing Partner April 1998.
Personal: Law degree from St Edmund Hall, Oxford.

FARIS, Neil
Cleaver Fulton Rankin, Belfast
(028) 9024 3141
n.faris@cfrlaw.co.uk
Specialisation: A major area of practice is advisory and transactional work for local authorities and a wide range of public bodies.
Prof. Memberships: Council Member of UKELA, Council Member for Irish Centre for European Law and Member Competition Working Party.
Career: Qualified in 1977 and Managing Partner and Head of Consultancy Department.
Personal: Born 1950, educated in Belfast and at Trinity College, Dublin and University of Cambridge.

FIELD, Christopher
Macfarlanes, London
(020) 7831 9222

FINCH, Robert
Linklaters, London
(020) 7456 4768
robert.finch@linklaters.com
Specialisation: Experienced in all aspects of commercial property transactions, including acquisition, development, funding, leasing and disposal of City, Regional and International properties. Also involved in development and/or investment property transactions in the USA, Middle East and Europe.
Prof. Memberships: 2000-01: Master of City of London Solicitors Company; Blundell Memorial Lecturer; 1999-2000: Sheriff of the City of London.
Career: Assistant solicitor *Linklaters* 1969-73. Partner of Real Estate Department 1974 - present, Head of Real Estate, *Linklaters* 1997-99.

FITZMAURICE, Anthony
Cobbetts, Manchester
(0161) 833 5227
tony.fitzmaurice@cobbetts.co.uk
Specialisation: Specialist in property (commercial, landlord and tenant, development/investment construction (non-contentious).
Career: Articled *Sydney Mitchell & Co* Birmingham; *Bromley Hyde & Robinson*, Ashton-Under-Lyne; qualified 1984.
Personal: Born 1958. Educated at De La Salle College; Birmingham University (LLB Hons); Trent Polytechnic. Resides Prestwich. Leisure – children, golf, skiing, tennis.

FLOUNDERS, Andrew
Cobbetts, Leeds
(0113) 246 8123
andrew.flounders@cobbetts.co.uk
Specialisation: Team leader within Property Division. Extensive experience in major out of town industrial retail and leisure schemes including financing and joint venture arrangements. Acts primarily for developers. Emphasis on constructive commercial approach.
Prof. Memberships: Law Society.
Career: Educated – Benton Park Grammar School and Manchester University. Qualified – *Read Hind Stewart* 1983 and partner since 1984.
Personal: Born 1958. Resides Bramhope.
Keen sports spectator and plays 5-a-side football. Leisure interests include family, cinema, theatre and Round Table.

GARRETT, Robin
Maclay Murray & Spens, Glasgow
(0131) 226 5196
rjg@maclaymurrayspens.co.uk
Specialisation: Head of Property Department. Main area of practice is development work for developers and occupiers, including site assembly, planning, letting and disposals. Also handles general acquisitions, including freehold purchases and assignations of leases. Has lectured and led groups at various seminars.
Prof. Memberships: Writer to the Signet.
Career: Qualified in 1983. Previously partner with *Steedman Ramage*. Joined *Maclay Murray & Spens* 1997.
Personal: Born 2 April 1959.

GATES, Kathryn
Edwards Geldard, Cardiff
(029) 2023 8239
kathryn.gates@geldards.co.uk
Specialisation: Partner in commercial property department. Experienced in all aspects of commercial and residential development, leasing, investment and funding.
Prof. Memberships: Law Society and Cardiff and District Law Society.
Career: Qualified in 1987. Joined *Edwards Geldard* in 1995 and became a partner in 1999.
Personal: Director Cywaith Cymru Artwork Wales. Interests include travel, rugby and art.

GEEN, Jonathan
Palser Grossman, Cardiff Bay
(029) 2045 2770

GIBBS, Robert
Eversheds, Norwich
(01603) 272 727
robertgibbs@eversheds.com
Specialisation: Property development (residential and commercial), investment and portfolio management. Acts for Stock Exchange quoted and non-quoted businesses. Considerable care home sector experience.
Prof. Memberships: Law Society.
Career: Trained in London before moving to East Anglia.
Personal: Upper Second LLB Honours Degree (Leeds). Plays tennis, golf and squash. Married with two children.

GIDNEY, David
Burges Salmon, Bristol
(0117) 902 2750
david.gidney@burges-salmon.com
Specialisation: Head of Property Department Unit acting for developers, public sector bodies and landowners. Also specialises in property investment. Recent or current transactions include acting for Orange on new headquarter offices at Paddington Basin; acting for Terrace hill on an office development in Bristol; acting for Rugby Estates plc on retail warehouse scheme in

REAL ESTATE ■ THE LEADERS

Salisbury; acting for Swansea City Council on proposed new national waterfront museum in joint venture with the National Museum and Galleries for Wales.
Prof. Memberships: Member of British Property Federation and Investment Property Forum. On Committee of South West and Wales Chapter of British Council for Offices.
Career: Trained, *Rowe & Maw*; qualified, 1977; made Partner at *Burges Salmon*, 1998.
Personal: 1st Class Honours in Literae Humaniores, Oxford. Born 1952. Resides South Somerset. Married with four children. Enjoys tennis, theatre.

GILLERY, Bryan
Eversheds, Norwich
(01603) 272727
bryangillery@eversheds.com
Specialisation: Residential development acquisitions, volume residential development sales and housing association work.
Prof. Memberships: Law Society, Cambridge Forum for the Construction Industry.
Career: Admitted April 1976. Joined *Eversheds* from local government in 1976. Became a partner in 1979.

GLYNN, Andrew
TLT Solicitors, Bristol
(0117) 917 7926
aglynn@tltsolicitors.com
Specialisation: Practising mainly in investment/asset management and secured lending/recoveries. Major transactions of the recent past include disposal of industrial property portfolio for administrative receivers and acquisition of strategic mineral reserves for Hanson and other aggregate companies.
Prof. Memberships: Mining and Minerals Law Group; Non-Administrative Receivers Association.
Career: Qualified with the firm in 1985, then worked in London for more than seven years, principally with City practice *Rowe & Maw*. Returned to the firm in 1992, partner 1994, head of property group 1999.

GNIADKOWSKI, Stan
Denton Wilde Sapte, London
(020) 7246 7000

GOODMAN, Stephen
Hammond Suddards Edge, Manchester
(0161) 830 5000

GRABINER, Martin
Nabarro Nathanson, Sheffield
(0114) 279 4261
m.grabiner@nabarro.com
Specialisation: Property regeneration with particular emphasis on urban and waterside regeneration. Joint venture arrangements involving both the private and public sector including financing arrangements. Real estate, and rolling stock financing in connection with the rail industry and railway station and depot access issues.
Prof. Memberships: Director of The Wakefield Metropolitan Theatre Trust.
Career: 1984-86, first in-house solicitor for the Wickes group of companies, London. 1986-88, Partner – *Boodle Hatfield*, London. 1989-98, Partner – *Dibb Lupton Broomhead* and *Dibb Lupton Alsop*, Leeds. 1998-date Partner *Nabarro Nathanson*, Sheffield.
Personal: Education: St Paul's School, London; Trinity College, Cambridge (MA); resides York. Leisure: Member of the Leeds Library, trekking.

GREEN, Andy
DWF, Manchester
(0161) 228 3702
andy.green@dwf.co.uk
Specialisation: Since joining *Davies Wallis & Co* in 1981, has practised in commercial property, specialising in the areas of development and investment. Acts for a number of well known developers and property companies based in the North West.
Prof. Memberships: The Law Society, Liverpool Law Society.
Career: Articles with *Maurice Hurst & Co*, Manchester 1976-78; lecturer at Chester College of Law 1978-81; *DWF* in Liverpool 1981-present; Partner in 1984. From May 2002 moved to *DWF*'s Manchester Office as Head of Department.
Personal: Leisure: piano, playing golf, tennis, skiing, rugby (but nowadays as a spectator only). A member of Heswall Golf Club and life member of Chester RUFC. Married with two teenage daughters. Education: Tudor Grange Grammar School, Solihull 1965-72, Grey College, Durham University 1972-75. Chester College of Law 1976 (Second Class Honours).

GREEN, Gilbert
Thomson Snell & Passmore, Tunbridge Wells
(01892) 701237
fggreen@ts-p.co.uk
Specialisation: The sale and purchase of land for development, particularly negotiation of options, conditional contracts and site assemblies. Works both for leading developers and landowners. Undertakes non-contentious planning work. Major cases last year include the disposal in lots of a business park, a disposal for a charity, the let of a school site for redevelopment and the acquisition of various residential development sites.
Prof. Memberships: Law Society and Agricultural Law Association.
Career: Joined *Thomson Snell & Passmore* as articled clerk in 1976, qualified 1978 and Partner 1980 in commercial property department. Heads Development Land Team and Deputy Head of Commercial Division.
Personal: Born 30 October 1953. Educated Harrow and Jesus College Cambridge. Married with four children. Interests include field sports, cricket, gardening, cookery and wine. Lives in East Sussex.

GUNN, David
Bond Pearce, Exeter
(01392) 211185
dgunn@bondpearce.com
Specialisation: Commercial property Partner dealing with development, investment and funding including joint ventures and major project management. Clients include leading banks, developers and investment companies. Runs a team providing specialist portfolio management services. Specialises in no-nonsense, pragmatic, results-driven, good-humoured approach. As a French speaker has worked on property and other commercial transactions involving French companies and organisations.
Prof. Memberships: Member of the Law Society, Association Des Juristes Franco-Britanniques.
Career: Qualified 1982. Joined *Bond Pearce* in 1980, becoming Partner in 1987.

HAM, Brian
Mills Selig, Belfast
(028) 9024 3878
brian.ham@nilaw.com
Specialisation: Property based litigation. Acts for a number of major local property developers. Other major areas of practice are commercial property work (primarily site acquisition and development) and construction law.
Prof. Memberships: Law Society of Northern Ireland, The Environmental & Planning Law Association for Northern Ireland.
Career: Qualified 1969. Joined *Mills Selig* 1971. Became partner 1984. Senior partner in 2000.
Personal: Sailing, gardening and architecture.

HAMILTON, Keith
Eversheds, Norwich
(01603) 272727
keithhamilton@eversheds.com
Specialisation: Landlord and tenant, investment acquisitions and disposals and development work.
Prof. Memberships: Law Society.
Career: Admitted June 1978. Read Jurisprudence at Merton College, Oxford. Spent several years with *Slaughter and May* in London before joining *Eversheds* in 1982. Became a partner in 1985.

HAMILTON, Sophie
Forsters, London
(0207) 863 8450
schamilton@forsters.co.uk
Specialisation: Broad-based commercial and institutional property practice including investment acquisition and funding (clients include Clerical Medical and Goldsmith's Company); acting for occupiers on major relocations; leisure (including Multiplex cinemas for Warner Village); shopping centres (Shops etc.); private trusts and residential developers.
Career: Educated St Mary's School, Calne; Marlborough College; Clare College, Cambridge. Qualified 1979; partner 1985; head of property department 1991-94 (all at *Frere Cholmeley Bischoff*); founding partner of *Forsters* 1998; senior partner 2001.
Personal: Married. Lives in London. Enjoys theatre, cinema, reading and cooking.

HANDLEY, Richard
BPE, Cheltenham
(01242) 248241
rdh@bpe.co.uk
Specialisation: Partner. Cases – acting for Bewise Limited in trading location. Acquisition of new head office for Wolseley plc. Assisting Grantchester plc in connection with the development of the cattle market in Gloucester.
Career: Trained *Campbell Hooper*, London, qualified 1979. Partner *BPE* 1980.
Personal: Born 1955; resides Cheltenham. Leisure – football and rugby. Education – King Edward's School, Birmingham; St Catherine's College, Cambridge (1976 2:1).

HANIFORD, Paul
Semple Fraser, Glasgow
(0141) 221 3771
paul.haniford@semplefraser.co.uk
Specialisation: Specialist in all aspects of commercial property transactions, including property investment and development, landlord and tenant work and customarily offers advice to a non-Scottish client base.
Prof. Memberships: Society of Writers to HM Signet, Law Society of Scotland.
Career: Articled *Fyfe Ireland and Co WS* 1978-80; legal assistant *Moncrieff Warren Paterson* 1980-81; legal assistant *Bird Semple* 1981-83; partner 1983-90; founding partner *Semple Fraser WS* 1990.
Personal: Born 1955. Educated at Glasgow Academy and Glasgow University (MA-LLB). Interests include skiing, squash, tennis and travel. Lives in Glasgow.

HARRISON, Christopher
Herbert Smith, London
(020) 7374 8000
christopher.harrison@herbertsmith.com
Specialisation: Institutional property development and investment. Has advised on a wide range of commercial development projects and various regional and Town Centre Schemes. Led the Law Society's representation on the Department of the Environment's Working Party, preparing the Code of Practice on commercial leases. Has spoken at numerous venues, including RICS national and regional conferences, on topics including value added tax, developments in landlord and tenant law and land registry practice.
Career: Harrow School, articled *Halliley & Morrison*. Joined *Herbert Smith* 1969.

HENDERSON, Brian
L'Estrange & Brett, Belfast
(028) 9023 0426
See under Banking & Finance, p.106

THE LEADERS ■ REAL ESTATE

HENSON, Michaela
Taylor Vinters, Cambridge
(01223) 423444
michaela.henson@taylorvinters.com
Specialisation: Commercial acquisitions, sales and lettings. Property development and investments. Corporate support work. Clients include property developers, educational establishments, high-technology businesses and a major airline. Current projects include development of a new Cambridge Technology Park.
Prof. Memberships: Law Society.
Career: Qualified in 1995 with London firm *Baileys Shaw & Gillett*. Joined *Taylor Vinters* in 1997. Specialist diploma in planning and environmental law in 1998. Became a partner in 2001.
Personal: Born 1970. Educated at Hinchingbrooke School, Huntingdon and New Hall College, Cambridge. Interests include sports and horses.

HEWITT, V Alan
L'Estrange & Brett, Belfast
(028) 9023 0426
alan.hewitt@lestrangeandbrett.com
See under Trusts & Personal Tax, p.825

HILL, Jeremy
Carson McDowell, Belfast
(028) 9024 4951
jeremy.hill@carson-mcdowell.com
Specialisation: Landlord and tenant - particularly retail. Acts for JD Sports plc; Tesco plc; Arcadia plc. Advises on management of portfolio properties for commercial clients, including the Northern Ireland Transport Holding Company. Highlights in the last year include advising HCL Technologies on acquisition of a major telephone call centre.
Prof. Memberships: Law Society of Northern Ireland.
Career: Whole career spent with *Carson McDowell* (qualified in 1986; made Partner in 1995).
Personal: Golf, football. Educated at Campbell College, Belfast; Queen's University, Belfast (LLB). Married with four children.

HOGGETT, Jonathan
Stephens & Scown, Exeter
(01392) 210700

HOLY, Julian
Julian Holy, London
(020) 7370 5443

HOUSTON, James
Cleaver Fulton Rankin, Belfast
(028) 9024 3141
Specialisation: Commercial property law.
Prof. Memberships: Law Society of Northern Ireland and Law Society of England and Wales.
Career: After qualifying in England joined *Cleaver Fulton Rankin* in 1990, becoming a Partner and Head of the Commercial Property Department in 1998.
Personal: Educated at Belfast Inst and University of Exeter. Leisure interests –

golf and rugby. Married with three children.

HOWARD, Amanda
Nabarro Nathanson, London
(020) 7524 6342
a.howard@nabarro.com
Specialisation: Head of the Property Finance Group at *Nabarro Nathanson*. Has extensive experience of structuring real estate investment funds, particularly on and offshore pooled investment vehicles and joint ventures for property investment, development and trading. Acts for property companies such as Hammerson and Land Securities, institutional investors such as Henderson Global Investors and Merrill Lynch, and overseas investors such as Caisse (the Quebec pension fund).
Career: Qualified as a solicitor at *Nabarro Nathanson* and was admitted as a Partner in 1995.

HOWARTH, Mark
Paris Smith & Randall, Southampton
(023) 8048 2482

HUDDLESTON, Ian
L'Estrange & Brett, Belfast
(028) 9023 0426
ian.huddleston@lestrangeandbrett.com
Specialisation: Partner, commercial property department. Practising in all aspects of commercial property but with particular emphasis on property development work and PFI. Retained by a number of major national lenders and the Council of Mortgage Lenders to advise in connection with NI aspects of regularisation and the preparation of standard documentation. Also advises on tax planning and trust issues and acts for a number of charities.
Prof. Memberships: Law Society of Northern Ireland; Society of Trust and Estates Practitioners.
Career: Admitted as a solicitor in Northern Ireland in 1991. Joined *L'Estrange & Brett* in 1991 and became a partner in 1993.
Personal: Born 1965. Educated at Queen's University of Belfast (LLB); University of Bristol (LLM). Former part-time lecturer at Queen's University of Belfast; Course Adviser and Tutor (company law and conveyancing) at the Institute of Professional Legal Studies, Belfast.

HUTTON, Robert
Mills & Reeve, Norwich
(01603) 693218
robert.hutton@mills-reeve.com
Specialisation: Commercial property.
Prof. Memberships: Law Society
Career: Articled *Clifford Chance*. Qualified 1977. Joined *Mills & Reeve* 1981. Partner *Mills & Reeve* 1985.
Personal: Educated St Dunstan's College, London; Magdalen College, Oxford. Married with two children.

INNES, Richard
Walker Morris, Leeds
(0113) 283 2500
rhi@walkermorris.co.uk

Specialisation: Retail property with emphasis on acting for anchor tenants and supermarkets.
Career: Qualified 1984. Partner *Walker Morris* since 1987.
Personal: Music and awaiting the day that both children will sleep through the night.

JACKSON, Karl
Mace & Jones, Manchester
(0161) 236 2244
karl.jackson@maceandjones.co.uk
Specialisation: Broad range of commercial property work with emphasis on commercial property development and in particular urban regeneration projects in the North West. Established Land Resources Alliance to advise on redevelopment of contaminated land.
Prof. Memberships: Law Society.
Career: Qualified in 1989 with *Vaudrey Osborne & Mellor*. Joined *Mace & Jones* in 1997. Partner since 1998.
Publications: Various published articles, lectured widely.
Personal: Born 1964. Married with a daughter and a son. Lives in Hale, Cheshire. Leisure pursuits: cinema and visual arts, running, sport and theatre. Trustee of Cornerhouse Arts Centre.

JACOMB, Brian
Thring Townsend, Swindon
(01793) 412613
bjacomb@ttuk.com
Specialisation: Commercial property work including site acquisitions, options and secured lending. Experience in insolvency work.
Prof. Memberships: Solicitors Benevolent Association.
Career: LLB London School of Economics 1970. Law Society finals 1971. Articled at *Coward Chance* and qualified in 1973. Worked in Dubai and the Sharjah offices of *Coward Chance* 1977-82, joining *Townsends* in 1983. Director of Commercial Department at *Thring Townsend* from 2000.
Personal: Honorary Solicitor to St Francis School, Pewsey and chairman of Marlborough Bridge Club.

JAMES, Robert
Morgan Cole, Cardiff
(029) 2038 5385

JOHNSON, Jennifer
Maclay Murray & Spens, Edinburgh
(0131) 226 5196
jdj@maclaymurrayspens.co.uk
Specialisation: Extensive experience in all aspects of commercial property work. Practice spans a wide range of transactions for occupiers, property companies, developers, institutions and banks including purchase and sale, development, funding and leasing. Has particular experience in cross-border property portfolios and the acquisition, letting and sale of shopping centres.
Prof. Memberships: Writer to the Signet and Notary Public.
Career: Edinburgh University. Qualified 1979. Partner in *Maclay Murray & Spens*

in 1988.

JONES, Chris
Berry Smith, Cardiff
(029) 2034 5511
Specialisation: Full range of commercial property work; investment, commercial and residential development; landlord and tenant and secured lending.
Prof. Memberships: Law Society.
Career: Qualified in 1992. Articled in *Eversheds*, Cardiff. Joined *Berry Smith* in 1994 and became a Partner in 1996. Welsh speaker, born 30 December 1966. Educated at University College Wales, Aberystwyth and Guildford College of Law.
Personal: Rugby and travel.

JONES, Elizabeth
Hewitson Becke + Shaw, Cambridge
(01223) 461155
elizabethjones@hewitsons.com
Specialisation: Specialises in commercial property law with particular emphasis upon property development including, in particular, pre-let agreements relating to specialised end users. Also specialises in retail property. Recent significant work: acting on a major pre-let at Cambridge Science Park; acting for the Medical Research Council on several new projects nationwide; also completed the 190th acquisition for the retailer, Home Entertainment Corporation plc (trading as 'Choices'); acted for South Cambridgeshire District Council on relocation to Cambourne Business Park and allied disposal of premises.
Prof. Memberships: Law Society; Cambridge Law Society; Cambridge Business and Professional Club; University Business Club.
Career: After articles with a firm in the City, joined the commercial property department of *Macfarlanes* for a few years; subsequently joined *Hewitson Becke + Shaw* in 1984, becoming a Partner in 1988 and is currently Head of Commercial Property in the firm's Cambridge office.
Personal: Leisure interests: reading, travelling.

JONES, Michael
Edwards Geldard, Cardiff
(029) 2023 8239
mike.jones@geldards.co.uk
Specialisation: Property development and funding, public/private sector joint ventures and inward investment. Includes £1.8 billion investment by LG at Newport and first Welsh PFI. Currently dealing with Wales Millennium Centre project, the development of Cardiff Gate Business Park, a £24 million spec. funding scheme in Thurrock, and three town centre development schemes.
Prof. Memberships: Law Society.
Career: Qualified in 1976 followed by 12 years in local government. Partner at *Edwards Geldard* since 1990.
Personal: Born 1950. Educated Maidenhead Grammar School then Durham University 1969-72. Interests include

REAL ESTATE ■ THE LEADERS

tennis and music.

JONES, Michael
Pannone & Partners, Manchester
(0161) 909 3000
michael.jones@pannone.co.uk
Specialisation: Commercial property, including development, urban regeneration, landlord and tenant. Development and related agreements re acquisition, development, management and letting of 228 bed student accommodation at Fredericks Road, Salford.
Prof. Memberships: Law Society.
Career: Articled to Manchester office of *Eversheds* predecessor *David Blank Alexander* 1968-70. Joined *Pannone & Partners* in 1973 and became partner in 1975. Part-time law lecturer.
Personal: Educated at The Manchester Grammar School and LSE. Married with four children. Leisure interests include golf; Manchester United supporter, Francophile, devotee of Devon.

JONES, Nefydd
Eversheds, Cardiff
(029) 2047 1147
nefyddjones@eversheds.com
Specialisation: Partner in *Eversheds*' Cardiff office leading an experienced team of seven commercial property lawyers. Deals in all aspects of commercial property, investment, development and financing including asset management, particularly for large commercial and institutional clients. Has recent significant experience in public sector development work through a number of high profile joint venture and grant aid transactions and also being appointed by the National Waterfront Museum Swansea Project. Recent private sector experience includes the sale of a major office and leisure scheme following comprehensive redevelopment, letting quoted as being the largest investment sale in Wales last year.
Prof. Memberships: The Law Society.
Career: Qualified in 1985. *Berwin Leighton* 1988-95. Partner *Eversheds* 1999.
Personal: Born 1961. Married with two daughters. Reluctant gardener; keen reader; motor racing fan; social golfer.

JONES, Pamela
Bullivant Jones, Liverpool
(0151) 227 5671
pj@bullivantjones.co.uk
Specialisation: Senior Partner in Commercial Property Department. Deals in all aspects of commercial property especially in development schemes and agreements, retail property for occupiers and as investment and landlord and tenant.
Prof. Memberships: Law Society. Liverpool Law Society.
Career: Qualified in 1977. Joined *Bullivant Jones* in 1973, becoming a Partner in 1978 and Senior Partner in 1994.
Personal: Born 7 January 1951. Attended Holyhead Comprehensive 1962-68. Leisure interests include reading, gardening and walking her dogs. Lives near Tarporley, Cheshire.

JORDAN, Geoffrey
Charles Russell, Cheltenham
(01242) 246 322
geoffrey@cr-law.co.uk
Specialisation: Planning and development work.
Prof. Memberships: Law Society, Legal Associate Royal Town Planning Institute.
Career: 1976-82: EMI legal department. 1982-84: Allied Suppliers Ltd. 1984-2002: Partner *Charles Russell*.
Personal: BA (Hons) LLB.

KERR, Steven
Fyfe Ireland WS, Edinburgh
(0131) 343 2500
skerr@fyfeireland.com
Specialisation: Broad experience of most aspects of commercial property work, particularly in the fields of commercial leasing, site acquisition and development and property related VAT issues. Acted for national retailers (B&Q, Woolworths and Matalan) in letting deals alone exceeding 600,000sq ft in the last year.
Prof. Memberships: Writer to the Signet. Notary Public.
Personal: Born 23 April 1954. Educated Daniel Stewarts College and Edinburgh University. Interests include cricket (playing), golf (striving to beat his son); rugby (spectating) and travel. Married with two active teenagers.

KIDBY, Robert
Lovells, London
(020) 7296 2000
robert.kidby@lovells.com
Specialisation: Property related financing, corporate property outsourcing, REPs, PFI, secured lending, institutional sales/ purchases/ management, property joint ventures and development projects including shopping centres, offices, airports and hotels. Has lectured extensively on property development and property investment to audiences in England, Europe and Japan.
Prof. Memberships: Policy Committee British Property Federation, Investment Property Forum, NACORE.
Career: Qualified as a solicitor in 1977 and has specialised in commercial property work ever since. Partner 1985 at *Lovells*. Head of Property since 1995.

KNOX, James
Linklaters, London
(020) 7456 4760
james.knox@linklaters.com
Specialisation: Experienced in all aspects of commercial property transactions, including sales and purchases of high value investment properties, property development (and funding), property financing, PFI, private real estate partnerships and joint ventures (including joint equity sharing leases, co-ownership trusts and partnership agreements).
Career: 1999 to date; Partner, *Linklaters*; 1987-99: Assistant Solicitor, *Linklaters*. Bristol University, LL.B (Hons).

KORDAN, Joel
Lee Crowder, Birmingham
(0121) 236 4477
joel.kordan@leecrowder.co.uk
Specialisation: All areas of commercial property development including lettings, sales, funding and joint venture agreements, with particular emphasis on large-scale industrial distribution/warehouse/factory schemes. Also, large residential property development practice. Clients include developers, contractors and end users, including many multinational companies.
Career: Articled *Wragge & Co*. Qualified 1990. Joined *Lee Crowder* as a Partner in 1997.
Personal: Born 1961, USA. Attended King Edward VI Five Ways Grammar School, Birmingham and LSE (BSc (Econ).

KUSTOW, David
Olswang, London
(020) 7208 8888
dhk@olswang.com
Specialisation: All aspects of commercial property law – investment, development retail centre and funding transactions. Acts for a variety of quoted and unquoted property companies, including large private investment vehicles and property based funds. Also serves the property requirements of various companies in the advertising and media sectors, particularly those involved in film, satellite and cable. Notable transactions recently undertaken include a single investment property disposal for a consideration of £105 million, the property aspects of a re-organisation of assets with values exceeding £200 million, the property aspects of a flotation and the acquisition of a number of investment/development properties for a single client, over a 12 month period, for an aggregate consideration exceeding £150 million.
Prof. Memberships: A Governor of the British Film Institute and chair of their Property Committee; a member of the International Real Estate Federation (FIABCI).
Career: Admitted 1973; 1970-91 – *Brecher & Co* (partner since 1975); 1991-present – *Olswang* (partner property group).
Personal: Married with two children. Principal leisure interests include reading (particularly modern history), travel, film and food.

LAKE, Tim
Stepien Lake Gilbert & Paling, London
(020) 7812 0900
tim@slgp.co.uk
Specialisation: Partner. Large-scale development work (commercial and residential) including joint venture and consortia arrangements with all attendant property finance issues. Acts for listed and unlisted developers and equity investors.
Career: Qualified December 1980. Set up own practice in 1985 and subsequently merged his practice with *Birkbeck Montagu's*. A founding Partner of *Stepien Lake Gilbert & Paling* in 1991.
Personal: Born December 1955. Educated Radley and Exeter University. Interests include shooting, tennis, golf and skiing. Lives in Oxfordshire.

LE PARD, Geoffrey
Freshfields Bruckhaus Deringer, London
(020) 7936 4000
geoffrey.lepard@freshfields.com
Specialisation: Handles all aspects of commercial property including landlord and tenant, investment, development, planning and finance.
Career: Qualified in 1981. Joined *Freshfields* in 1981, becoming a partner in 1987. Head of property department from 1993-2000.
Personal: Born 30 November 1956. Attended Purley Grammar School 1968-70, Brockenhurst Grammar School 1970-75, Bristol University 1975-78 and Guildford College of Law 1978-79. Lives In Dulwich.

LEITCH, David A
Johns Elliot, Belfast
(028) 9032 6881
david.leitch@johnselliott.com
Specialisation: Commercial property development, covering site assembly, construction and development, commercial lettings and disposal.
Prof. Memberships: Graduated QUB 1969. Qualified 1972. Partner 1974.
Career: Law Society of Northern Ireland.
Personal: An enthusiastic if not expert golfer.

LEONARD, Tessa
Eversheds, Manchester
(0161) 831 8000
tessaleonard@eversheds.com
Specialisation: Commercial development in particular town centre regeneration and business retail and leisure parks handling development funding and disposal. Also specialises in collaboration agreements and joint ventures between the public and private sector. Recent public sector projects include: acting for the North West Development Agency in relation to a proposed strategic business park in Rochdale; Chester City Council in relation to a mixed use regeneration and Kirklees Henry Book Partnership in relation to a new shopping centre and revitalisation of listed buildings. Recent/current private sector projects include: acting for AMEC Developments in relation to a new supermarket and leisure scheme in East Manchester and Redrow Commercial Developments in relation to a mixed office/retail development.
Career: Manchester High School for Girls; Birmingham University; articled *Halliwell Landau*, achieving Partnership; joined *Eversheds* 1990, Partner 1993.
Personal: Resides Wilmslow, married with one son. Leisure: theatre, books, skiing, gym.

THE LEADERS — REAL ESTATE

LOWLESS, Peter
Michelmores, Exeter
(01392) 436244

LUST, Graham
Nabarro Nathanson, London
(020) 7524 6200
g.lust@nabarro.com
Specialisation: Property finance specialist. Extensive experience in commercial property investment and development transactions for major property institutions, public property companies and public sector organisations. Has developed innovative forms of property financing documentation for inward investors including tax based property financings for multinational clients. Currently instructed on substantial office developments in Central London, portfolio acquisitions and financings and property joint ventures.
Prof. Memberships: Law Society.
Career: Qualified in New Zealand in 1974, and in England in 1979. Became a commercial property partner in 1980. Member of Property Finance Group.
Personal: Born 1950.

MACGREGOR, Robert
Clifford Chance, London
(020) 7600 1000
robert.macgregor@cliffordchance.com
Specialisation: Real estate. Partner specialising in domestic and international real estate development and finance; joint ventures; investment and pre-letting transactions.
Career: Articled *Titmuss Sainer & Webb*, qualified 1985; Partner *Clifford Chance* since 1992.
Personal: Berkhamstead School; Nottingham University (LLB Hons).

MACNIVEN, Iain
Maclay Murray & Spens, Glasgow
(0141) 248 5011
igm@maclaymurrayspens.co.uk
Specialisation: Commercial property partner with extensive experience of all aspects of commercial property work, including investment deals, development work and leasing. Clients include Scottish Amicable Life Assurance Society, ASDA plc and British Waterways Board. Particular areas of interest include joint venture development work, and specialist rent review advice as well as the education sector. Member of the Investment Property Forum and the British Council of Shopping Centres.
Career: Glasgow University (MA 1975, LLB 1977). Been with *Maclay Murray & Spens* throughout his professional career. Past examiner for the Law Society of Scotland.
Personal: Born 1953. Resides Glasgow and West Highlands. Leisure interests include travel, food and drink and crosswords.

MAHOOD, W Laurence
Elliott Duffy Garrett, Belfast
(028) 9024 5034
laurence.mahood@edglegal.com
Specialisation: Head of Commercial Property Department. Commercial property development, letting and investment, acquisitions and disposals. Current projects include major retail, office and leisure developments and has recently acted in a number of high value investment acquisitions and disposals for clients including Land Securities and British Land.
Prof. Memberships: Law Society of N Ireland. Representative on joint Law Society/RICS Forum.
Career: LLB Queens University, Belfast 1976. Admitted solicitor 1978. Law Society Silver Medal awarded. Partner since 1982.
Personal: Contributing author to Butterworth's 'Property in Europe – Law and Practice'.

MARKS, Geoffrey
Halliwell Landau, Manchester
(0161) 835 3003
gmarks@halliwells.co.uk
Specialisation: Deals with full range of property work including development and investment work and all property aspects of property secured lending.
Prof. Memberships: Member of the Royal Chartered Institute of Arbitrators.
Career: Articled *AH Howarth & Co*; qualified 1963; partner *AH Howarth & Co* (now *Howarth Goodman & Co*) 1965-74; partner *Maurice Rubin & Co* 1974-84; partner *Halliwell Landau* 1984.
Personal: Born 1941; resides Prestwich. Educated at Arnold School, Blackpool. Recreations include theatre and opera.

MCCLEA, Nigel
Pinsent Curtis Biddle, Leeds
(0113) 294 5282
nigel.mclea@pinsents.com
Specialisation: National Head of Property. Specialises in large scale commercial property projects, in public and private sectors (with particular focus on leisure, education and health). Major projects: Royal Armouries Museum, Leeds; Relocation of Sunderland Football Club; Redevelopment of Odsal Stadium, Bradford; Disposal of Epsom cluster of redundant hospital sites for Secretary of State; New residential settlement at Lichfield.
Prof. Memberships: Fellow of the Royal Society of Arts, Manufactures and Commerce. Friend of Historic Houses Association.
Career: Qualified 1975. Partner in *Simpson Curtis* (now *Pinsent Curtis Biddle*) 1978.
Personal: Born 1951. Educated at Ashville College, Harrogate and Queen's College, Cambridge.

MCHARDY, Iain
Biggart Baillie, Edinburgh
(0131) 226 5541

MCLEAN, Neil
DLA, Leeds
(08700) 111111

MCNULTY, Stephen
Burges Salmon, Bristol
(0117) 939 2250
stephen.mcnulty@burges-salmon.com
See under Social Housing, p.764

MEREDITH, Alan
Eversheds, Cardiff
(029) 2047 1147
alanmeredith@eversheds.com
Specialisation: Senior Partner. Head of Commercial Property Department. Work includes property joint ventures between private and public sector and commercial property development work. Also handles urban regeneration, acting for both public and private sector bodies. Has given seminars on contaminated land for the Chartered Surveyors Study Group.
Prof. Memberships: Law Society, Country Landowners Association.
Career: Qualified in 1976. Joined *Phillips & Buck* (now *Eversheds*) as a Partner in 1982. Currently Head of Commercial Property Department.
Publications: Has co-authored with his environmental partner, Martin Warren, a book entitled 'Contaminated Land – Managing Liabilities'.
Personal: Born 8 January 1952. Attended University of Wales, Aberystwyth. Member of Management Committee of Swansea Cricket and Football Club. Trustee of Dragons Rugby Trust. Leisure interests include golf, rugby and reading. Lives in Cowbridge near Cardiff.

MITCHELL, James
Stevens & Bolton, Guildford
(01483) 734232
james.mitchell@stevens-bolton.co.uk
Specialisation: Commercial property; specialises in the development and funding of major property projects on behalf of banks, institutions and developers.
Prof. Memberships: Law Society; Fellow of the Royal Statistical Society and Associate of the Royal College of Science.
Career: Trained *Slaughter and May*, qualified 1980. Assistant Solicitor *Slaughter and May* 1980-85. Partner *Barlow Lyde and Gilbert* 1985-95. Joined *Stevens and Bolton* as a Partner in 1995.
Personal: Leisure interests include chess, mathematical games and puzzles, satellite and computer technology, football and horse racing. Family; five children aged from 18 months to 16 years.

MOFFAT, Douglas
Tods Murray WS, Edinburgh
(0131) 226 4771
douglas.moffat@todsmurray.com
Specialisation: Commercial property. Purchase of multi-let George House, Glasgow for Catalyst Capital (£14.55 million); acting for Baillie Gifford & Co in their taking lease of 105,000sq ft of offices at Calton Square, Glasgow; acting for Nomura in acquisition of 110 Scottish pubs from Bass; purchase of Unit A3, Edinburgh Park (let to Morgan Chase Bank) for Commerz Grundbesitz-Spezialfonds GmbH (£11.55m).
Prof. Memberships: Law Society, WS Society, British Council of Shopping Centres (Scottish Secretary), British Council of Offices, Investment Property Forum.
Career: Edinburgh University – LLB, apprenticeship and then assistant – *Shepherd & Wedderburn WS* 1968-73, *Tods Murray WS* 1993-date (Partner 1974, Head of Property 1980-98, 2002-).
Personal: Golf, hill walking, squash. One daughter and one son.

MORGAN, Claire
Eversheds, Newcastle upon Tyne
(0191) 241 6151
clairemorgan@eversheds.com
Specialisation: Partner in commercial property department. All aspects of urban regeneration and development including site assembly, infrastructure agreements, joint ventures, public/private sector partnerships/PFI, particularly in the health sector, public sector grant funding agreements, portfolio acquisitions and disposals. Recent instructions include property joint ventures for town centre redevelopment business parks, acquisition of development sites, disposal of surplus sites for residential redevelopment conditional on planning, abnormal costs, listed building consent and overage, coalfield regeneration and formation of Sunderland URC.
Prof. Memberships: Law Society; Newcastle upon Tyne Law Society.
Career: University of Nottingham; qualified 1975. Partner 1979 onwards.
Personal: Married, three children, lives in Newcastle. Interests include walking, reading, built environment.

REAL ESTATE ■ THE LEADERS

MORPETH, Iain
Clifford Chance, London
(020) 7600 1000
iain.morpeth@cliffordchance.com
Specialisation: Real estate. Partner specialising in domestic and international real estate transactions including real estate funds, joint ventures and private equity; structured finance; project development; single asset and portfolio acquisitions; leasing.
Career: Qualified 1978; Partner since 1988.
Personal: Fettes College, Edinburgh; Bristol University.

MORRIS, Christopher
Freshfields Bruckhaus Deringer, London
(020) 7936 4000
chris.morris@freshfields.com
Specialisation: Commercial property, development, property finance and insolvency law.
Career: Qualified in 1984 and became a partner in 1991. Head of real estate department since May 2000.
Personal: Born 1960. Eastbourne Grammar School 1973-78. Lincoln College Oxford 1978-1981. Lives in Bromley. Interests include family, sport, music and Italy.

MOST, Lionel
Burness, Glasgow
(0141) 248 4933

NEIL, Don
Coffin Mew & Clover, Southampton
(023) 8033 4661
donneil@coffinmew.co.uk
Specialisation: Has headed the firm's commercial property practice in Southampton for many years and has an invaluable knowledge of the local market. Has very wide experience in acting for developers, investors and lessees in all aspects of commercial property work, with a particular expertise in the field of residential development sites.
Prof. Memberships: Member of the Notaries Society.
Career: (LLB) Bristol University, admitted 1966. Joined *Coffin Mew & Clover* in 1971 and became a partner in 1974.
Personal: Married with three children. Interests include fishing, skiing and sport.

NEWCOMBE, Mark
Hammond Suddards Edge, Birmingham
(0121) 222 3000

NEWSTEAD, Jackie
Lovells, London
(020) 7296 2000
jackie.newstead@lovells.com
Specialisation: All aspects of commercial property, particularly development, investment and financing. Last year acted for Prudential on its pre-let of 600,000sq ft at GreenPark Reading to Cisco Systems (plus options for further 600,000sq ft). Also acted for Land Securities Trillium on its bid for the London Underground LUPP.
Prof. Memberships: Law Society. British Property Federation. British Council of Shopping Centres.
Career: Trained *Durrant Piesse*; qualified 1986; partner *Lovells* 1997.
Personal: Educated Harrogate Ladies College and St Hugh's College, Oxford. (CBA in jurisprudence 1983); College of Law Lancaster Gate 1984. Leisure interests include opera, archaeology, old buildings, contemporary literature. Married, no children.

NEWTON, Alison
McGrigor Donald, Glasgow
(0141) 248 6677
alison.newton@mcgrigors.com
Specialisation: Partner, real estate, Glasgow office. Recent transactions have included: lease and disposal of major new call centre at Dundee Technology Park from One2One to Inland Revenue with rent in excess of £1m pa. Purchase of SPV for Liverpool and Victoria in relation to development in excess of £145m. Structure and development advice to Deka and phases 2 and 3 of St Enoch Centre Glasgow.
Prof. Memberships: Law Society of Scotland. Member of Committee of Scottish Branch of British Council of Shopping Centres, also director of The Lighthouse Trust, Glasgow, Scottish Youth Theatre and legal advisor to Glasgow City Centre Partnership.
Career: 1980-84 Dundee University (LLB, DIP.LP); 1984-86 Trainee, 1986-90 Assistant; 1990-94 Associate; 1994-99 Partner; January 1999 to July 2000 Managing Partner, Glasgow office; June 2000 to June 2001 Partner in Edinburgh office, charged with development of *McGrigor Donald's* new premises; July 2001 to date Partner based in Glasgow office.
Personal: Riding, skiing, cooking.

NISSE, Ian
Ashurst Morris Crisp, London
(020) 7638 1111
ian.nisse@ashursts.com
Specialisation: Commercial property matters with an emphasis on development projects, investment transactions and joint ventures. Clients for whom he is the lead partner include British Telecom, Chelsfield, Church Commissioners for England, Hemingway Pearson and Stanhope.
Career: Became a Partner at *Ashursts* in 1987.

OLMER, Philip
Olswang, London
(020) 7208 8888
pho@olswang.com
Specialisation: Philip is a partner specialising in all areas of office, industrial, retail and leisure property investment and development transactions with particular emphasis on joint ventures, limited partnerships and offshore structures for overseas investors. By way of example over the last year has acted for overseas investors in structuring over £250m of prime office investments using tax efficient structures. Other significant transactions have included: acting for a major institutional fund on the joint venture structuring and development of serviced office schemes in London, Middlesex and the West Country; acting for a major housebuilder on the redevelopment of a former utility company headquarters building in North London and a brownfield site in London Docklands as two major residential schemes comprising over 500 units; the acquisition of the former Gucci building in London's Old Bond Street and its redevelopment and letting to DKNY; acting for a major health club operator on the development and pre-leasing of numerous 40,000sq ft health clubs all over the country; the purchase and leaseback of a new Holiday Inn hotel in the Midlands.
Prof. Memberships: British Israel Chamber of Commerce.
Career: Trained *Campbell Hooper*, qualified 1985; assistant solicitor property, *Forsyte Kerman* 1985-87; assistant solicitor, property department, *Berwin Leighton* 1987-91; equity partner 1991-99; partner *Olswang* 1999.
Personal: Education: Christ's College Grammar School, London; City of London Polytechnic (1982 BA Hons Business Law); College of Law, Guildford (1983 Finals). Born 1960; resides London.

O'MEARA, Anne
Hammond Suddards Edge, Birmingham
(0121) 222 3000

PASKELL, F C
Greene & Greene, Bury St Edmunds
(01284) 762211

PATERSON, Ian J C
Dundas & Wilson CS, Edinburgh
(0131) 228 8000

PATTERSON, Anthony
Forsters, London
(020) 7863 8333
ajpatterson@forsters.co.uk
Specialisation: Broadly-based commercial practice with particular emphasis on investment and development work. Clients include: Benchmark Group Plc, City Leisure Plc, Denvale Trade Parks Limited, Harbour Property Group Limited, Hutley Land Limited, KUC Properties Limited, Maple Oak Plc, Malbrough Developments Limited, Rockmartin Plc, Rockwest Properties Limited, Sabre Developments Limited, Salmon Developments Plc, Salmon Harvester Developments Limited, Saxan Securities Limited, Translloyd Developments Limited.
Prof. Memberships: Investment Property Forum; 100 Property Club; Lansdowne Club, Law Society.
Career: Articled *Frere Cholmeley Bischoff* 1973; qualified 1975; partner 1980; head of property department 1994-98 (all at *Frere Cholmeley Bischoff*); various management committees; founding partner of *Forsters* 1998.
Personal: Divorced with three children. Educated St Joseph's College, Blackpool; University College London. Lives in Shepherds Market.

PATTISON, Mark
Beachcroft Wansbroughs, Manchester
(0161) 934 3000
mpattison@bwlaw.co.uk
Specialisation: Property development, strategic and tactical advice, landlord and tenant new letting and management, investment acquisitions and disposals cases. Deals include the redevelopment, extension and letting of a shopping centre; the planning and development of a new urban village at Warrington; the redevelopment of a factory outlet centre and outsource management contract for a portfolio of factory outlet centres.
Career: Articled *Vaudreys*; qualified 1982. Remained at *Vaudreys* until it merged with *Beachcroft Wansbroughs*. Directorships: Disley Properties Limited; Winters Nominees.
Personal: Born 1958, educated at Stockport Grammar School, Manchester University and College of Law Chester. Married with two daughters. Leisure interests include clay pigeon shooting, swimming, running, walking and fishing.

PAUL, Sarah
Harold Benjamin Littlejohn, Harrow
(020) 8422 5678
sarah.paul@hben.co.uk
Specialisation: Commercial landlord and tenant property development acting for landlords, developers and tenants; business leases and renewals especially in the office and retail sectors; acquisition, disposal and management of commercial investment property.
Prof. Memberships: Law Society.
Career: Articled *Lovell White & King* (now *Lovells*); partner *Harold Benjamin Littlejohn* since 1992; head of commercial landlord and tenant department.
Personal: Born 1954; North London Collegiate School; St Hilda's College, Oxford; lives in North London.

PICKUP, Bryan
SJ Berwin, London
(020) 7533 2468
bryan.pickup@sjberwin.com
See under Travel, p.810

PIKE, John
Addleshaw Booth & Co, Leeds
(0113) 209 2000
john.pike@addleshawbooth.com
Specialisation: Main area of practice is commercial property work, in particular development, banking, investment and private sectors. A particular specialism is land pollution and he frequently advises on land contamination and remediation, waste and lender risk.
Career: Qualified 1972. Partner 1976.
Personal: Jesus College Cambridge (MA: Hons). De Montfort University (MA: Environmental Law). Chairman of Governors Moorlands School, Leeds and Governor of St Peters School, York. Director of Urban Mines Limited and heavily involved in the Brownfields pro-

THE LEADERS ■ REAL ESTATE

ject as a member of the Advisory Group. Interests include sports and family.

PLANT, Patrick
Linklaters, London
(020) 7456 4718
patrick.plant@linklaters.com
Specialisation: Specialist in UK commercial property advising investors, developers, lenders and tenants on all aspects of commercial property in the UK. Also a specialist in hotel and leisure with particular expertise in negotiating management and franchise agreements for hotel and leisure projects.
Career: 1994 to date: Partner in the Commercial Property Department of *Linklaters*. 1990-94: Assistant Solicitor, *Linklaters*. 1989-90: Assistant Solicitor, *Mallesons Stephen Jacques*, Sydney. 1986-89: Assistant Solicitor, *Linklaters*.

PRITCHARD, Nicholas
TLT Solicitors, Bristol
(0117) 917 7947
npritchard@tltsolicitors.com
Specialisation: Has specialised in commercial property since 1972. Undertakes a wide range of commercial conveyancing transactions with particular emphasis on leisure and office development both town centre and out of town as well as in town residential developments. Widespread experience of site assembly, acquisition development funding and disposals. Now concentrates on 'problem' properties which are suited to his entrepreneurial approach.
Career: Qualified 1970, moved to Bristol and *Trumps* (now *TLT Solicitors*, the merged firm of *Trumps* and *Lawrence Tucketts*) in 1972, became partner in 1974.
Personal: Tennis, golf, sailing and generally enjoying life.

QUICKE, Martin
Denton Wilde Sapte, London
(020) 7242 1212

QUIGLEY, Ian
Maclay Murray & Spens, Edinburgh
(0131) 226 5196
isq@maclaymurrayspens.co.uk
Specialisation: Partner dealing in all aspects of commercial property work, including development and leasing pre-funding, development finance and regeneration projects.
Prof. Memberships: Writer to the Signet and Notary Public.
Career: Glasgow University, LLB (Hons) 1969.
Personal: Born 1946.

QUINLAN, Andrew
Pinsent Curtis Biddle, Leeds
(0113) 294 5280
andrew.quinlan@pinsents.com
Specialisation: Property investment and property development (options and joint ventures).
Prof. Memberships: Investment Property Forum.
Career: *Titmuss Sainer & Webb* 1984-88; *Pinsent Curtis Biddle* 1988 to date.

REEVEY, Michael
Addleshaw Booth & Co, Leeds
(0113) 209 2409
michael.reevey@addleshawbooth.com
Specialisation: Partner in Commercial Property Group. Substantial development projects; the financing of property assets and representing both landlords and tenants of retail property.
Career: Oxford University 1976-79; joined the firm in 1980; admitted as a solicitor 1982 and made a partner in 1988.

REID, David
Burness, Edinburgh
(0131) 473 6000

REID, Sandy
Biggart Baillie, Glasgow
(0141) 228 8000

REILLY, Alan
Carson McDowell, Belfast
(028) 9024 4951
alan.reilly@carson-mcdowell.com
Specialisation: Acquisition and disposal of commercial property and all types of interests therein. Development of commercial property. Traditional specialisation in retail property originally for tenants latterly more particularly for landlords including from site acquisition through development to initial letting and ultimately disposal. More recently diversification into commercial property services in higher education, leisure, culture and arts sectors. This year the sale of Bow Street mall Shopping Centre, Lisburn for Tesco, Northern Ireland Science Park 24 acres of development land at Queens Road, Belfast, three large warehouses at Edgewater Road the largest comprising 185,000sq ft of warehouses plus offices, department store for Debenhams plc as Phase II of Foyleside Shopping Centre, Londonderry.
Career: MA (Cantab). Whole career with *Carson & McDowell* (qualified 1976), partner 1978.
Personal: Married with two daughters.

RENNIE, Richard
Burness, Edinburgh
(0131) 473 6000

RICE, Dermot
Slaughter and May, London
(020) 7600 1200
dermot.rice@slaughterandmay.com
Specialisation: Specialises in all types of commercial property work including development, investment, securitisation and structured finance. Recent significant transactions include: acting for GMETRO, the landlord of Enron Europe Limited, in relation to 40 Grosvenor Place, acting for HRO International in connnection with the redevelopment of Victoria Plaza, and acting for Land Securities plc in relation to various projects connected with interests in the Thames Corridor.
Personal: Hull University (LLB Hons). Married with two children. Interests include family, wine, food and travel.

Career: Articled *Gamlens*; qualified 1984; partner *Slaughter and May* 1991.
Personal: Married, three children. Resides: London.

ROBERTS, David
Gouldens, London
(020) 7842 6263
dar@gouldens.com
Specialisation: Specialist in commercial property development and joint ventures. A market leader in the establishment of unit trusts, joint ventures, partnerships and limited partnerships, and associated property development funding techniques, including speculative funding agreements. Wide-ranging experience in the acquisition and development of business parks and retail parks, including dealing with all planning issues, infrastructure agreements, pre-lets, lettings, sales and funding.

ROBERTS, David
Hugh James, Cardiff
(029) 2022 4871
david.roberts@hughjames.com
Specialisation: Partner and Head of Commercial Property Department. Work includes site assembly and acquisition, including option work, agreement and grant of lease and forward sale agreements in relation to office, retail and industrial developments. Undertakes large scale land acquisition for large volume house builders, consortia and joint venture agreements. Specialises in Housing Association stock transfers and other social housing initiatives.
Prof. Memberships: Law Society.
Career: Qualified 1974. Joined *Hugh James* in 1972, becoming a Partner in 1975. Head of Commercial Property Department.
Personal: Born 1949. Attended Grove Park Grammar School, Wrexham and Selwyn College, Cambridge 1968-72 (MA, LLB). Cambridge Blue at athletics. Member of British Athletics Team 1974-78. Competed at European and Commonwealth Championships. Member of Hawks Club and Achilles Club. Legal advisor and board member of Welsh Sports Hall of Fame. Leisure interests include sport, particularly golf, athletics and rugby. Lives in Cardiff.

ROBINSON, Herbert
Mills & Reeve, Cambridge
(01223) 222233
herbert.robinson@mills-reeve.com
Specialisation: Partner specialising in property development advice and transactional work; option agreements; joint venture arrangements; 25 years' experience in the field of commercial property including: major project work for HEIs; setting up Granta Park, Abington, Cambridge; advice to EEDA on major development projects.
Career: Trained *Kenneth Brown Baker Baker*; qualified 1969; assistant solicitor *Taylors*, Newmarket 1970-72; partner 1972-87; partner *Taylor Vinters*, Cambridge 1988-99; chairman 1990-99; partner *Mills & Reeve* since 1999, leading property development team.
Personal: Resides Newmarket. Sailing, walking, military history.

ROBINSON, Patrick
Herbert Smith, London
(020) 7374 8000
patrick.robinson@herbertsmith.com
See under Planning, p.654

ROONEY, Phillip
DLA, Liverpool
(08700) 111111

ROSCOE, James
Fyfe Ireland WS, Edinburgh
(0131) 315 8155
jroscoe@fyfeireland.com
Specialisation: Qualified in both Scotland and England, with extensive experience of cross-border transactions. Main specialisms are property investment and property finance. Largely for English-based, American and German investors and lenders including Teachers Insurance, Helaba, Nationwide, Fortis Bank and Resolution Properties.
Prof. Memberships: WS, NP, admitted as a Solicitor in England and Wales.
Career: Qualified 1988. Partner with *Bird Semple Fyfe Ireland* and thereafter *Fyfe Ireland* since 1992. Head of Commercial Property Department.
Personal: Born 22 December 1960. Educated Dundee High School and Oxford and Edinburgh Universities. Interests include cycling and gardening.

ROSS, Kenneth
Burness, Edinburgh
(0131) 473 6000

ROWE, Tim
Wright Hassall, Leamington Spa
(01926) 886688
timr@wrighthassall.co.uk
Specialisation: All aspects of commercial property law with a particular emphasis on commercial developments. Acts for a number of household-name clients.
Prof. Memberships: Law Society.
Career: Articled *Boodle Hatfield*; qualified 1987. *Dibb Lupton Broomhead* 1989. Partner *Shoosmiths & Harrison* 1995. Partner *Wright Hassall* 1997.
Personal: Born 1964. Corpus Christi College, Cambridge (1984 BA Hons). Lives North Oxfordshire.

RUDOLF, Peter
Berwin Leighton Paisner, London
(020) 7760 1000
peter.rudolf@blplaw.com
Specialisation: Property development and investment. Recent transactions include the acquisition and development of The Mall, Cribbs Causeway (Prudential Assurance); redevelopment, letting and forward sale of 59 Gresham Street, London EC4 (Legal & General); acquisition and development of Serpentine Green regional shopping centre, Peterborough (Tesco); acquisition, development and forward sale of Midsummer Place shopping centre, Milton Keynes

REAL ESTATE ■ THE LEADERS

(London and Amsterdam Properties); acquisition, development and forward sale of New Bond Street shopping centre, Weymouth (Shearer Property Group); acquisition and development of London headquarters for Ove/Arup Partnership; conditional acquisition for large mixed-use development at St Stephens, Ferensway, Hull (London and Amsterdam Developments).
Prof. Memberships: Law Society.
Career: Bedford School; St Johns, Cambridge – MA 1st Class Honours.
Personal: Participation in sports.

RYDEN, Nick
Shepherd+ Wedderburn, Edinburgh
(0131) 473 5286
nick.ryden@shepwedd.co.uk
Specialisation: Commercial property, property developments and finance, and banking.
Prof. Memberships: Member, Governor and past Chairman of Anglo-American Real Property Institute; occasional lecturer Law Society of Scotland post-qualifying legal education and RICS; member of Investment Property Forum; member of Investment Property Forum Securitisation Working Party; member of BPF Scottish working party.
Career: Articled *Shepherd & Wedderburn*; qualified 1976; assistant solicitor 1976-78; partner 1978.
Personal: Born 1953; resides Edinburgh. Leisure interests: Travel, hill walking and photography. Education: Fettes College; Aberdeen University (LLB; WS).

RYLAND, David
SJ Berwin, London
(020) 7533 2222
david.ryland@sjberwin.com
See under Travel, p.810

SAMSON, John
Nabarro Nathanson, London
(020) 7524 6000

SANDERS, Andrew
Lovells, London
(020) 7296 2000
andrew.sanders@lovells.com
Specialisation: Commercial property partner with wide experience of the commercial property market, specialising in all aspects of development investment, joint venture and property finance work.
Prof. Memberships: Law Society.
Career: Articled Welsh Water Authority; qualified 1978; solicitor Islwyn Borough Council, solicitor The Post Office Company; solicitor United Friendly Insurance, partner *D J Freeman* 1990; joined *Lovells* as a partner 1999.
Personal: Born 1954. Interests include karate, cinema, watching most sport.

SCHWER, Chris
Birketts, Ipswich
(01473) 406 274
chris-schwer@birketts.co.uk
Specialisation: Commercial property specialist representing local and national investors, developers, lenders, retailers and healthcare trusts.
Career: Trained with *Birketts* 1986-88; *D J Freeman* 1989-97 (partner 1996); *Bell Gully Biddle Weir* (Auckland, NZ) 1998-2000; Partner with *Birketts* 2000.
Personal: Education: Deben High School, Felixstowe; Leicester Polytechnic; College of Law, Guildford. Admitted: England (1988) and New Zealand (1999). Personal: married with three children. Passionate family man and golfer.

SCOTT, Peter
Bevan Ashford, Bristol
(0117) 975 1611
peter.scott@bevanashford.co.uk
Specialisation: Head of Real Estate Department which is now integrated into the firm's substantial built environment division. Concentrating on commercial leisure development and regeneration schemes both for Regional Development Agencies (RDAs) (*BA* is now on the panel of three RDAs) and private sector developers. Has been particularly involved in the regeneration of the greater Temple Meads area in Bristol on behalf of SWRDA.
Prof. Memberships: Law Society.
Career: *Norton Rose* 1969-72; *Boodle Hatfield* 1972-75. Joined *Bevan Ashford* 1975; partner 1977.

SEAWARD, Charlie
BrookStreet Des Roches, Witney
(01993) 771616
charlie@bsdr.com
Specialisation: Investment work large scale portfolio management, secured lending, joint ventures, consortium agreements, particular experience in the energy sector.
Prof. Memberships: The Law Society.
Career: Qualified 1978. Subsequently with *Lovell White and King* (now *Lovells*). Joined *BrookStreet Des Roches* as a partner in 1997.
Personal: City of London Polytechnic.

SILVA, David
Iliffes Booth Bennett (IBB), Uxbridge
(01895) 207801
david.silva@ibblaw.co.uk
Specialisation: Head of Commercial Property Development Team, which is rated as a leading development practice in the south east. The team has completed development transactions with a value in excess of £250 million. Acts for a number of significant developers, including Frontier Estates Limited, Turnstone Estates Limited and Earth Property Ventures Limited. Recent highlights include acting on behalf of Turnstone Estates in connection with the acquisition of a portfolio of development/investment properties for a value in excess of £20 million. He is now developing expertise in relation to property finance related investment structures and has been retained by a fund management client in connection with the launch of a £50 million limited partnership.
Prof. Memberships: Law Society.
Career: Articled at *Frere Cholmeley Bischoff* and joined the commercial property department upon qualification in September 1990. Joined *Iliffes Booth Bennett* in September 1996 and made a partner in May 1998.
Personal: Born December 1962. Leisure interests include football, tennis and swimming. Lives in Gerrards Cross and is married with two children.

SINGH, Parmjit
Eversheds, Birmingham
(0121) 232 1410
parmjitsingh@eversheds.com
Specialisation: Development: clients include Birmingham Alliance, Birmingham Mailbox, Crosby Special Projects, RBS Property Development, Stoford Developments and Urban Box. Major projects in the last 12 months include advising RBS Development on its joint venture with Grosvenor Ltd for the redevelopment of Natwest's former headquarters, 41 Lothbury, London and ongoing work for the jv company. Urban regeneration: acts for Advantage West Midlands on various strategic schemes including its acquisition of the BBC's interest at Pebble Mill Birmingham for the development of a high technology park. Investment: clients include The Birmingham Alliance (Hammerson, Henderson and Land Securities) on the redevelopment of the new BullRing, Birmingham.
Prof. Memberships: Investment Property Forum.
Career: Trained *Eversheds*, qualified 1989, Partner 1997.
Personal: Born 1965. Warwick University, LLB (Hons). College of Law, Chester. Enjoys watching and playing football. Married, two children.

SMITH, David
Shepherd+ Wedderburn, Edinburgh
(0131) 473 5292
david.smith@shepwedd.co.uk
Specialisation: Partner in Commercial Property Department and Chairman of firm. Main areas of practice are development projects, leases and opinion work. Regular speaker at conferences and seminars.
Prof. Memberships: Law Society of Scotland, Society of Writers to the Signet.
Career: Joined *Shepherd+ Wedderburn* in 1969. Partner in 1974.
Personal: Born 17 November 1947. Edinburgh University 1966-69. Leisure pursuits include veterans' hockey, golf, skiing, hill walking, gardening and enjoying good food and wine in good company. Lives in Edinburgh.

SMITHERS, Tim
Veale Wasbrough, Bristol
(0117) 925 2020
tsmithers@vwl.co.uk
Specialisation: Partner in Property Services Department. Main areas of practice are development, energy and environmental law with specialisms in wastes management, contaminated land and Pipelines Act work. An editor of Butterworths' 'Property Law Service'. Author of 'Veale Wasbrough on Property Development' due to be published in July 2002 by Butterworths. Regular contributor to professional publications and speaker at seminars.
Prof. Memberships: Pipeline Industries Guild, Institute of Wastes Management, Environmental Services Association.
Career: Qualified 1982. Joined *Veale Wasbrough* in 1986, becoming a Partner in 1988.
Personal: Born 1958. University of Wales.

SMYTH, Robert
Burges Salmon, Bristol
(0117) 939 2224
bob.smyth@burges-salmon.com
Specialisation: Environmental law and property. Provides legal and strategic management advice to large corporate occupiers of property and to government bodies (Scottish & Southern Energy plc, NAAFI, MoD). World Bank accredited consultant (Eastern Europe) specialising in land reform and property markets.
Prof. Memberships: Fellow of the Society for Advanced Legal Studies; Law Society.
Career: Trained at *D J Freeman & Co*; short-term placement Bristol City Council; joined *Burges Salmon* 1983, Partner 1987. Established Planning Unit (1989) and Environmental Law Unit. *Burges Salmon* marketing partner 1988-99, business development partner 1999 to 2001, Deputy Managing Partner 2001.
Personal: Born Scotland. Degree in Economics, UCW 1975. Married; keen cyclist ('End to End' 1998); Director of Bristol Circus School (Circomedia) and Cycle West; business representative in Bristol's LA21 strategic process.

SOLOMON, Jonathan
Clifford Chance, London
(020) 7006 4024
jonathan.solomon@cliffordchance.com
Specialisation: Real estate. Partner specialising in major development, funding and investment transactions acting for developers, tenants, investors and lenders with extensive experience of the central London market and of real estate related joint ventures, partnerships and cross-border transactions.
Career: Partner at *Norton Rose* 1995-2000; Partner at *Clifford Chance* since 2000.
Personal: King Alfred School, Warwick University.

SORRELL, Stephen
Eversheds, Manchester
(0161) 831 8000
stephensorrell@eversheds.com
Specialisation: Partner and Head of *Eversheds* National Developer Group which provides integrated legal services to developers in the private and public sectors across England and in Europe. Acts as a leading legal advisor in strategic

property development and urban regeneration schemes for a number of significant private companies including AMEC Developments Limited, Urban Splash Limited, Redrow Commercial Developments Limited and Ask Property Developments Limited. Also advises public sector organisations such as Liverpool Vision, several of the Regional Development Agencies including North West Development Agency and Yorkshire Forward and is involved in relation to a number of town/city centre regeneration companies now established and for local authorities including Manchester, Preston and Liverpool. Has a national profile in the funding and property aspects of urban regeneration projects and public/private partnerships.
Prof. Memberships: Law Society. Director of Business in the Arts: North West and a trustee of the newly regenerated Manchester Art Gallery.
Career: Training, *Abson Hall* (Manchester and Stockport) Solicitor and Partner, *Eversheds* as Partner from 1989 to present.
Personal: Born 5 October 1959. Educated Marple Hall Grammar School, Manchester University (LLB Hons) and Chester College of Law. Leisure interests include cinema, music and Manchester City FC. Lives in Bramhall, South Manchester and is married with two children.

SPEIRS, Simon
Osborne Clarke, Bristol
(0117) 917 3000

STANCOMBE, Michael
Lovells, London
(020) 7296 2000
michael.stancombe@lovells.com
Specialisation: Investment, financing and development (acting for both institutions and developers). Investment structures and indirect investment vehicles. Management of major portfolios. Also acts for a major retail group on new developments. Client partner for many of the firm's leading property clients. Recur deals include Barclays relocation to Canary Wharf; the Shambles development, Manchester (anchored by Harvey Nichols); the sale of portfolio of six shopping centres for Coal Pension Properties.
Prof. Memberships: Member of the British Council for Offices, the Investment Property Forum and Urban Land Institute. Fellow of the Society for Advanced Legal Studies. Representative Member of the British Property Federation, City Property Owners Association, Global Real Estate Investors and Westminster Property Owners Association.
Career: Articled at *Durrant Piesse* (now *Lovells*); qualified 1979; Partner 1982.

STEEL, David A
Dundas & Wilson CS, Glasgow
(0141) 222 2200

STONE, David J
Andrew M. Jackson, Hull
(01482) 325242

djs@amj.co.uk
Specialisation: Wide range of experience in commercial property development schemes (retail, leisure, and industrial) for developers, funders, owners and tenants. Recent experience includes acquisition, letting and funding of several retail/leisure schemes, joint venture agreements (including joint venture for redevelopment of a regional town centre). Acts for major leisure operator on schemes nationwide.
Prof. Memberships: Law Society.
Career: King Henry VIII School, Coventry and Cambridge University.
Personal: Married, two children. Golf.

STRACHAN, Dale
Brodies, Edinburgh
(0131) 228 3777
dale.strachan@brodies.co.uk
Specialisation: Commercial property partner dealing with development, investment, property outsourcing and property PFI/PPP. Recent/current transactions include acting on behalf of Corus in joint venture arrangements for the redevelopment of approx 1,100 acres at the former Ravenscraig Steelworks, Motherwell to form Scotland's next 'new town' involving a long term, large scale mixed use scheme of development. Also acted on behalf of Land Securities Trillium/William Pears Consortium in the Scottish aspects of the UK-wide property outsourcing project with British Telecommunications plc devising innovative Scottish property and stamp duty saving structures.
Prof. Memberships: Society of Writers to Her Majesty's Signet; International Bar Association; Society of Construction Law.
Career: George Heriot's School Edinburgh. University of Aberdeen (1977 LLB). Articled, *Archibald, Campbell & Harley WS* Edinburgh; qualified 1979; assistant Solicitor *Brodies* 1979-83; partner since 1983.
Personal: Fishing, skiing, motorcycling, private flying.

TAVENER, Chris
Herbert Smith, London
(020) 7374 8000
chris.taverner@herbertsmith.com
Specialisation: Partner in real estate department. Acts for a wide range of property companies and investors. Advises on all matters concerning development and acquisition. Negotiates a wide variety of income sharing leases, acting for both landlords and tenants. Also advises on all aspects of commercial landlord and tenant law and has considerable experience of contentious property work, including rent review arbitrations and litigation.
Career: Became a partner of the firm in 1982.
Personal: Educated at RGS, Guildford and Christ Church, Oxford. Qualified 1973.

TAYLOR, David
Herbert Smith, London
(020) 7374 8000
david.taylor@herbertsmith.com
Specialisation: Main areas of practice are commercial property development and investment. Broad commercial practice including acquisition development and joint ventures with specialist involvement for local authority and public sector clients.
Career: *Lovell White & King* 1974-79; joined *Berwin Leighton* in 1980 and became a Senior Associate in 1987. Became Head of Property Department 1996. Joined *Herbert Smith* in 2000. Member of the editorial board of the 'Property Law Journal'. Trustee of museum in Docklands.

THORNE, Peter
Wragge & Co, Birmingham
(0870) 903 1000

TINMAN, Mark
C & H Jefferson, Belfast
(02890) 329545
Specialisation: Acquisition development and disposal of commercial property. Acting for a number of retail multiples, developers and banks.
Prof. Memberships: Law Society of Northern Ireland.
Career: Whole career with *C & H Jefferson*. Qualified 1987. Partner since 1993.
Personal: Born 1962. Education: Queens University Belfast (LLB) 1985. Institute of Professional Legal Studies, Belfast 1986.

VIVIAN, Jon
SJ Berwin, London
(020) 7533 2809
jon.vivian@sjberwin.com.
Specialisation: Commercial property. Recent matters include: acting on behalf of Brixton plc on the purchase of Polar Park, Heathrow; disposal of two large industrial estates and a variation of Greenford Premier Partnership Agreement; acting on behalf of Gazeley in connection with their development at Marsh Leys, Bedford.
Prof. Memberships: City of London Law Society.
Career: Rugby School, St John's College, Cambridge (LLB, MA). *CMS Cameron McKenna* 1989 to August 2001. *SJ Berwin* since August 2001.
Publications: Monthly column in 'Property Week'.
Personal: Sport and theatre.

WALDIE, Roderick
Halliwell Landau, Manchester
(0161) 835 2738
rwaldie@halliwells.co.uk
Specialisation: Partner in the Property Department. Work includes acquisitions, disposals and secured lending transactions. Has particular expertise in advising development and investment clients in relation to retail and leisure driven development and investment schemes.
Prof. Memberships: The Law Society.
Career: Articled at *Weightmans*, Liver-

pool, qualified as a solicitor in 1994, became a partner at *Weightmans* in 1999. Joined *Halliwell* as an equity partner in 2001.
Personal: Born 1968, educated at Giggleswick School and Manchester University. Lives in Altrincham with his wife and two daughters. Enjoys playing golf and squash.

WALLIS, Guy
DWF, Liverpool
(0151) 236 6226
guy.wallis@dwf.co.uk
Specialisation: More than 25 years experience in area of commercial property development with particular emphasis on out of town retail, shopping centres and waterfront retail/leisure schemes. Lead solicitor in a £60m town-centre shopping centre in the Midlands. Involved from the outset with the prestigious Albert Dock scheme in Liverpool, the waterfront scheme at Ocean Village, Southampton and Twelve Quays, Birkenhead. Handled the joint venture arrangements in respect of the London & Amsterdam joint venture with ING Real Estate at Milton Keynes and the arrangements between Legal & General and London & Amsterdam Developments Limited in relation to the redevelopment of the town centre of Bracknell. Dealt with the Development Agreement in respect of the Art Deco former airport terminal building and listed hangars at Liverpool Airport. Currently involved in major redevelopment of the Metropolitan Cathedral Precinct, Liverpool.
Prof. Memberships: The Law Society; Liverpool Law Society; Manchester Law Society; Society for Computers and Law.
Career: King William's College, Isle of Man; College of Law; founder partner of *Davies Wallis & Co* in 1977.
Personal: Golf (and not much time for that). Family: Two teenagers. Understanding wife.

WARD, Ian
Dickinson Dees, Newcastle upon Tyne
(0191) 279 9244
law@dickinson-dees.com
Specialisation: Urban regeneration, including public/private sector joint ventures, mixed use commercial/residential developments, business parks and town centre developments. Acts for developers, national housebuilders and public authorities such as urban development corporations and local authorities. Also actively engaged in PFI, especially in the NHS. Recent work includes Gateshead Council's Baltic Quays development beside the Millenium Bridge and Arts Centre. A major mixed use Jury's hotel, commercial and residential scheme beside Newcastle Central Station and town centre regeneration schemes on Tyneside, Teesside and in Ipswich, as well as new business parks in Darlington and Durham.
Prof. Memberships: Law Society.
Career: Articled at *Eversheds* (Newcas-

REAL ESTATE ■ THE LEADERS

tle). Qualified 1983, Partner 1989-97. Became a Partner at *Dickinson Dees* 1997 – Head of Property.
Personal: Durham University BA Hons Law 1980. Swimming and family holidays.

WARREN, Jennifer
Taylor Vinters, Cambridge
(01223) 423444
jennifer.warren@taylorvinters.com
Specialisation: Partner dealing with commercial property and specialising in property development and all property aspects of charity law. Lead partner for two science and biotech parks. Also acting for a wide range of charities and educational institutions, advising on the purchase, development, management and disposal of property holdings and investments, and the making and documentation of charitable grants. Recent transactions include: acting for Granta Park on the development and letting of laboratory premises; as part of a PFI acting for a residential property developer on the largest residential development within Cambridge; acting on two joint ventures for Cambridge University and for a major religious charity with substantial property holdings on compliance issues.
Career: Qualified 1981. With *Bischoff & Co* 1979-91. Associate partner from 1986. Joined *Bates Wells & Braithwaite* 1991 as head of property department. Partner 1992. Joined *Taylor Vinters* as Partner 1996.
Personal: Exeter University 1967-70. Arts administrator and Member of Tate Gallery Educational Committee 1971-77. Governor of Anglia Polytechnic University. Visual arts, reading, riding.

WATKINS, David
Eversheds, Cardiff
(029) 2047 7634
davidwatkins@eversheds.com
Specialisation: All areas of commercial property including acquisitions and disposals, joint ventures, secured lending, landlord and tenant, developments and forward funding arrangements.
Prof. Memberships: Law Society.
Career: *Lovells* 1991-98. Joined *Eversheds* in 1998 and made partner in 2000.
Personal: Educated at Gowerton School, Lancaster University, University of Illinois and Chester College of Law. Interests include rugby, golf and reading.

WATSON, Adrian
DLA, Birmingham
(08700) 111111

WATSON, Gary
Ashurst Morris Crisp, London
(020) 7638 1111
gary.watson@ashursts.com
Specialisation: All aspects of property law with particular emphasis on institutional investment and funding, property development, leasing and relocation work. Has acted in numerous large relocations including for a number of UK and overseas law firms as well as many tenants at Canary Wharf. Also has particular expertise in advising overseas investors.
Prof. Memberships: Investment Property Forum, Council Member of the International Council of the Urban Land Institute of America, British Property Federation.
Career: Qualified as a solicitor in 1979 and specialised in property law ever since. Assistant solicitor at *Clifford Turner* 1979-82; assistant solicitor *Lovell White Durrant* 1982-95; partner and head of London office *Hammond Suddards* 1995-2001; partner *Ashurst Morris Crisp* 2001-date.
Personal: Born August 1955. Educated at Oxford University (BA 1976). Leisure pursuits include travel, eating out, cinema and reading.

WATTIE, Ian
Burness, Edinburgh
(0131) 473 6000

WEBB, Tim
Eversheds, Birmingham
(0121) 232 1354
timwebb@eversheds.com
Specialisation: Development: developers include Chase Midland plc, John Mowlem & Co plc, Highbridge Properties plc, Taylor Woodrow and St Modwen Properties plc. Deals include leading on 1,100 acre development of Newcastle Great Park for Bryant/Beazer Homes and Enterprise Zone purchase and forward sales for Highbridge Properties. Major corporates: clients include Headlam Group plc, Hampson Industries plc, Hagemeyer, Volvo, Misys Plc, Mentmore Abbey plc. Urban Regeneration: Advantage West Midlands.
Prof. Memberships: Investment Property Forum. British Council for Officers (Birmingham Board Member). Institute of Directors. Director of Birmingham Contemporary Music Group (one of the leading orchestras of its type in the world).
Career: Qualified *Eversheds* Sept 1989. Partner May 1997. Head of property (Birmingham) November 2000.
Personal: Married to Sarah, two children, Lucy and Charles. Jazz, cooking, live music, film and shooting.

WEIGHTMAN, Anita
DLA, Manchester
(08700) 111111

WESTHEAD, Tim
Olswang, London
(020) 7208 8720
tew@olswang.com
Specialisation: Head of Property Group; specialises in commercial property investment and development with a specialisation in shopping centres and structured tax efficient schemes; recent transactions include acting on behalf of Capital & Regional plc in connection with its sale into a £670m partnership with Morley Fund Management of its eight UK shopping centres when at the same time Morley put in three shopping centres to create the initial fund; acted on behalf of Green Property Plc in relation to the recent sale of the company for an estimated £600m; also acted on behalf of The Whitehall Green Partnership in the acquisition of a £430m portfolio from P&O and its subsequent disposal over the following year; other transactions involve the acquisition, development and letting of Cathedral Hill, Guildford for Green Property Development Ltd which was let to Avaya Ltd at a rent of £3.3m; previously acted on £100m sale portfolios for MEPC and the acquisition of offices at Victoria Station for £100m for Delancey Estates.
Career: Articled *Stafford Clarke & Co* 1980-82; qualified 1982; assistant solicitor 1982-85; assistant solicitor *Stones Porter* 1985-96; Partner 1986-96). Partner *Olswang* 1996 to date.
Personal: Born 1958; resides Godalming. Education: Loughborough Grammar School, University of Newcastle upon Tyne (1979 LLB). Leisure interests: Triathlon, mountain biking, family.

WHITE, Graham
Slaughter and May, London
(020) 7600 1200
graham.white@slaughterandmay.com
Specialisation: Experienced in all aspects of commercial property work, including landlord and tenant matters, corporate property outsourcing, structured and tax-based finance, commercial property investment, secured lending and development work. Extensive landlord and tenant practice, frequently acting for tenants. Regular contributor to 'Property Week'. Member of the committee which produced the Standard Commercial Property Conditions.
Prof. Memberships: City of London Law Society Land Law Sub-committee; The Law Society.
Career: Qualified in 1980 after articles at *Slaughter and May*. Became a Partner in 1987.
Personal: Born 1955. Educated at Haberdashers' Aske's, Elstree and St. Catherine's College, Oxford.

WHITE, Rowan
Arthur Cox – Northern Ireland, Belfast
(028) 9023 0007
rwhite@arthurcox.ie
Specialisation: Broad based commercial property practice including acquisitions and disposals, development, investment and funding. Recent transactions include acting for Musgrave Group on development of a major distribution centre for N.I., acting for Bank of Ireland in acquisition of new flagship branch in Belfast city centre, development and funding arrangements for four star hotel in Londonderry. Currently acting on major mixed-use development project within Laganside redevelopment area.
Prof. Memberships: Law Society of N.I., Belfast Solicitors' Association (past Chairman), Law Society of N.I. Education Committee.
Career: Admitted as Solicitor in N.I. 1977 and in Republic of Ireland 1997. Partner in *Norman Wilson & Co.* 1985 and (on merger) in *Arthur Cox N.I.* 1996.
Personal: Educated at Campbell College, Belfast and Cambridge University (MA 1977).

WHITE, Stephen
Cobbetts, Manchester
(0161) 833 3333

WILFORD, Nick
Pinsent Curtis Biddle, Leeds
(0113) 244 5000

WILLIAMS, M H
Robertsons, Cardiff
(029) 20237777

WILLSON, Stephen
SJ Berwin, London
(020) 7533 2255
stephen.willson@sjberwin.com
Specialisation: Head of Property Division of *SJ Berwin*. Specialist in all aspects of commercial property.
Prof. Memberships: Law Society.
Career: Qualified 1971, articled and subsequently Partner at *Burton & Ramsden*, Partner *SJ Berwin* 1982.
Personal: Battisborough School Plymouth, Devon College of Law. Married with three children. Interests: squash and tennis.

WILSON, Alistair
Fyfe Ireland WS, Edinburgh
(0131) 343 2500
awilson@fyfeireland.com
Specialisation: Senior Partner in firm. Acts extensively for investors, retailers, finance providers and developers, with considerable experience of providing strategic commercial advice in substantial property transactions and in negotiating the necessary documentation. Has particular experience of cross-border property transactions involving conflict of laws.
Prof. Memberships: WS, NP.
Career: Qualified 1968. Partner with *Fyfe Ireland WS* since 1971.
Personal: Born 19 July, 1945. Educated Peebles High School and Edinburgh University. Interests include fishing, hill-walking and motorcycling.

WORRALL, Simon
Cobbetts, Manchester
(0161) 833 5272
simon.worrall@cobbetts.co.uk
Specialisation: Landlord and tenant, development and investment property, and licensed premises acquisitions.
Prof. Memberships: Law Society
Career: Articled to *Cobbett Leak Almond* 1987. Qualified 1989; partner *Cobbetts* 1999.
Personal: Married with two children. Hulme Grammar School Oldham; Sheffield University (LLB (Hons)); Chester College of Law. Interests include golf, theatre, cinema.

WRIGHT, David
Nabarro Nathanson, London
(020) 7524 6000

d.wright@nabarro.com
Specialisation: Real estate partner dealing exclusively with commercial property with emphasis on development projects and institutional investment; extensive experience of leading teams in acquisition, disposal and leasing of major property portfolios.
Career: Qualified 1971.
Personal: Born 1946. Bishop Vesey's Grammar School, Sutton Coldfield then Bristol University 1965-68. Member of Management Board of Investment Property Forum. Director of Direct Wines Limited. Leisure: golf, gardening.

YATES, Andrew
Pinsent Curtis Biddle, Birmingham
(0121) 625 3071
andrew.yates@pinsents.com
Specialisation: Property development, joint ventures and leading other major property projects, particularly town centre schemes.
Career: 1986-90, *Slaughter and May;* 1990-94, *Ashurst Morris Crisp;* 1994-2000, *Pinsent Curtis Biddle.*
Publications: Joint editor of the chapters of Sweet and Maxwells 'Local Government Precedents and Procedures' dealing with local authority partnership arrangements and joint ventures (D29-D41).
Personal: Interests include martial arts and playing lead guitar in the *Pinsent Curtis Biddle* band.

SHIPPING

London: 740; The Regions: 744; Scotland: 746; Profiles: 746

Research approved by BMRB For this edition, Chambers' researchers conducted 6,582 interviews – 3,900 with law firms, 511 with barristers and 2,171 with clients. The validity of the research was scrutinised by BMRB International, who audited both the methodology and the results at our offices in London. They interviewed Chambers' researchers and cross-checked sample interviews. Details of the audit appear on page 7.

OVERVIEW The market has hardened over the last year. It has been a difficult twelve months for shipping companies with many reporting a drop in turnover, which has encouraged them to handle more work in-house. In addition, firms report a drop in the number of casualties. However, there have been some huge cases, such as the Metro Litigation and the sinking of the Petrobas P36 oil platform, and those firms with the personnel and technology to handle major work like this are noting a resurgence of interest amongst larger clients like P&I clubs. This need to invest in resources may have been a factor in the merger this year of Stephenson Harwood with Sinclair Roche & Temperley. In the regions, Eversheds' retrenchment of its shipping practice to its Newcastle base was welcomed by the market.

LONDON

SHIPPING
■ LONDON

[1]
- Holman Fenwick & Willan
- Ince & Co

[2]
- Clyde & Co

[3]
- Hill Taylor Dickinson
- Richards Butler

[4]
- Bentleys, Stokes & Lowless
- Clifford Chance
- Holmes Hardingham
- More Fisher Brown
- Norton Rose
- Shaw and Croft
- Stephenson Harwood
- Waltons & Morse

[5]
- Barlow Lyde & Gilbert
- Jackson Parton
- Lawrence Graham
- Thomas Cooper & Stibbard

[6]
- Fishers
- Hill Dickinson
- Middleton Potts
- Watson, Farley & Williams

This book is the product of 6,582 1/2 hour interviews. See p.7 for BMRB audit. Within each band, firms are listed alphabetically.

HOLMAN FENWICK & WILLAN (see firm details p.999) Commended by commentators for dry and, in particular, wet work, this "*leading light*" of a firm has expertise in casualty, salvage and charter party work. It remains home to "*any number of stars of their field*," who manage to "*combine a range of skills and styles*" to suit all tastes and needs. The "*gentlemanly*" **Richard Crump** (see p.747) is described by peers as "*a superbly clever man, with a phenomenal knowledge of the law*." He shares the limelight with **James Gosling** (see p.748) whose "*expert skill on admiralty*" has won him a huge client following. He approaches the most complex cases with ease and "*has brain power on tap*." Both men have acted successfully for owners on the loss of a vessel, caused by containerised dangerous cargo. **Hugh Livingstone** (see p.750) is "*a great fighter who will hammer through the work*;" he has been occupied of late with advice to shipowners and others affected by the collapse of the Enron group. Senior partner **Robert Wilson** (see p.752) ("*bright and enthusiastic*") is known for his particular expertise in P&I and defence work. **Marcus Bowman** (see p.746) is regarded as "*a determined fighter – it's impressive how personally he takes the cases.*" He has acted for marine insurance underwriters in total loss claims against ship owners. **Hugh Brown** (see p.747) offers "*excellent technical knowledge*" and is endorsed as "*somebody who can get things done.*" He is the liaison officer for the Indian subcontinent, and has advised Indian shipowners. Chris Swart provides the team with commodities and trade finance advice. A highlight of the last year for the firm was its representation of the owners of fishing vessels in obtaining a judgment against former charterers for a sum in excess of $100 million. **Clients** P&I clubs; charterers; owners; shipyards; underwriters.

INCE & CO (see firm details p.1008) Clients and peers used superlatives when talking of this firm: "*supreme in admiralty*" it is thought to enjoy "*a dry practice which is nearly the equal of its legendary wet.*" Its partners dominate the field with their "*long-standing connections*" and "*astute knowledge of the key issues, that affect the industry.*" The firm possesses a strong base in the insurance market and its lawyers are "*litigators par excellence.*" On the dry side, **Bob Deering** (see p.747) remains "*clever, a speedy opponent*," who is "*to the point in all he does.*" Peers single out **Paul Herring** (see p.749), especially "*recommended for his top-class service to clients*," while **Patrick Shaw** (see p.750) was described by one client as "*one of the most plain-speaking, constructive lawyers I've ever come across.*" The team has advised on a number of major arbitrations, and regularly handles international disputes with values in the region of £200 million. Wet work remains "*the jewel in its crown*," with "*talented lawyers carrying out top-notch work.*" This team is headed by **James Wilson** (see p.751) ("*astute*") and **Chris Beesley** (see p.746) who is "*a quality choice for admiralty matters.*" Highlight cases include acting for owners and insurers in a multimillion dollar claim concerning the loss of an oil rig off Israel, and advising on the after effects caused by the grounding of a bulk carrier in which the value of property at risk was £26 million. **Colin de la Rue** (see p.747) is valued for his oil pollution expertise and has been described by clients as "*prime choice for any complex problem.*" **Clients** Cargo owners; charterers; insurers; P&I clubs; shipowners.

CLYDE & CO (see firm details p.913) As one commentator reported, this firm is a "*regular feature in the shipping market – we run into them constantly.*" Portrayed as an "*expert firm offering polished advice,*" it has "*a fantastic base of expertise and experience.*" Many interviewees endorsed its position as the one of the three highest profile firms despite its recent concentration on corporate matters and it retains "*a strong lead over all other competitors.*" It remains best known for its cargo work and displays experience in casualty, salvage, insurance and commodities work. **Derek Hodgson** (see p.749) "*brings a light touch to his cases*" and is best known for his owners/charterers work. The team has won high-profile instructions from P&I clubs and charterers. **Nick Greensmith** (see p.748) and **Simon Fletcher** (see p.748) both specialise in marine casualty work. Greensmith is praised as "*a smart man for collision matters,*" while such is the confidence in Fletcher that he is portrayed as having the "*steadiest hands in the business.*" They are joined in the rankings this year by **Stephen Pink** (see p.750), a "*top-class lawyer who plays it straight.*" **Tony Thomas** (see p.804) takes the lead in the cargo work and has seen a healthy level of instruction from UK and foreign-based insurers, particularly those in the Far East. The firm remains involved in the Metro litigation, a case in both the UK and Singapore courts concerning a multimillion dollar loss of oil from storage in Fujairah. The firm has also acted for hull insurers in the loss of the semi-submersible P-36 off Brazil, leading to claims in excess of $500 million. **Clients** ACE; AIG;

740   INDEX TO LEADING LAWYERS: PAGE 1693 ■ IN-HOUSE LAWYERS PROFILES: PAGE 1201

LONDON ■ SHIPPING

LEADING INDIVIDUALS

1
- **CRUMP Richard** Holman Fenwick & Willan
- **GOSLING James** Holman Fenwick & Willan
- **VLASTO Tony** Clifford Chance
- **WINTER Glenn** Holmes Hardingham

2
- **BARDOT Andrew** Bentleys, Stokes & Lowless
- **DEERING Bob** Ince & Co
- **EVANS John** Hill Taylor Dickinson
- **GINSBERG Roy** Waltons & Morse
- **HERRING Paul** Ince & Co
- **LAX Michael** Lawrence Graham
- **LIVINGSTONE Hugh** Holman Fenwick & Willan
- **TAYLOR Timothy** Hill Taylor Dickinson
- **WILSON James** Ince & Co

3
- **EAST Lindsay** Richards Butler
- **FISHER Nicholas** Fishers
- **JOHNSON Andrew** Hill Taylor Dickinson
- **TAYLOR Andrew** Richards Butler
- **THORP Clive** Barlow Lyde & Gilbert
- **WILSON Robert** Holman Fenwick & Willan

4
- **BROWNE Ben** Shaw and Croft
- **DE LA RUE Colin** Ince & Co
- **GHIRARDANI Paolo** Stephenson Harwood
- **GREENSMITH Nicholas** Clyde & Co
- **HODGSON Derek** Clyde & Co
- **PARTON Nicholas** Jackson Parton
- **ROOTH Tony** Watson, Farley & Williams
- **SHAW Patrick** Ince & Co
- **WALLIS Robert** Hill Taylor Dickinson

5
- **ATKINSON Joe** Stephenson Harwood
- **BEESLEY Chris** Ince & Co
- **BOWMAN Marcus** Holman Fenwick & Willan
- **BROWN Hugh** Holman Fenwick & Willan
- **DUNN Chris** Waltons & Morse
- **GRAY Edward** More Fisher Brown
- **GRIFFITHS Paul** Bentleys, Stokes & Lowless
- **HARRIS Graham** Thomas Cooper & Stibbard
- **JOHNSTON David** Holmes Hardingham
- **MOYLAN Adrian** More Fisher Brown
- **PINK Stephen** Clyde & Co
- **THOMAS Tony** Clyde & Co
- **WAGLAND Nigel** Barlow Lyde & Gilbert
- **WILLIAMS Paul** Norton Rose

6
- **ALLEN Tony** Hill Dickinson
- **ASPINALL Mark** Shaw and Croft
- **BROWN Anthony** AD Brown, Solicitors
- **FITZPATRICK Stuart** More Fisher Brown
- **FLETCHER Simon** Clyde & Co
- **HARVEY Richard** Richards Butler
- **HAWKES Ian** More Fisher Brown
- **MCFADYEN Laurence** Sach Solicitors
- **WATLING John** Jackson Parton

UP AND COMING
- **CONCAGH Anthony** Stephenson Harwood
- **JOHNSON Angus** Stephenson Harwood

See individuals' profiles p.746

AXA; BP; Charles Taylor; CGNU; Chubb; Glencore; Golden Union; Les Abeilles International; Marine & Fire; MOAC; North of England P&I Club; NYK; Pan Ocean; Precious Shipping; Premuda; Royal & SunAlliance; Shell; Société Générale; Thomas Miller; Tokio Marine & Fire; Tsavliris; West of England P&I Club.

HILL TAYLOR DICKINSON (see firm details p.996) This highly esteemed firm has built up a shipping department from its solid base of maritime insurance and reinsurance work. Boasting an international client base, that includes owners, charterers, P&I clubs, oil companies, banks and trading houses, interviewees agree that the firm is "*committed to shipping.*" John Evans (see p.747) is described as "*impressively smart, a thorough details man.*" He specialises in marine insurance, charter party disputes and sale/purchase disputes. In line with the firm as a whole, he is involved in both litigation and arbitration. Peers endorsed Timothy Taylor (see p.751) as "*a mediator of class and substance;*" he has a strong focus on professional indemnity and casualty risks. Andrew Johnson (see p.749) is an experienced seaman, who "*is always offering a straight focus, never over-complicating matters.*" He is commended for his management of large-scale contract disputes. Robert Wallis (see p.751) is "*a man you can trust to deal with any situation;*" he is skilled on salvage and collision matters, as well as charter party and contractual disputes. The firm was involved in the aftermath of the Petrobras P-36 oil platform sinking, one of the biggest losses in recent years. **Clients** ACE; Associated British Ports; AXA; Brockbank; Capital Professions Finance; Costa Cruises; Cunard; Festival Cruises; Fineline Group; Fleet Business Credit (UK); Hiscox; MSC; P&O Nedlloyd; P&I clubs; Primorsk Shipping; Société Générale; Stena Line; Titan Salvage; Toisa; Tokyo Leasing; Vendor Finance.

RICHARDS BUTLER (see firm details p.1112) Clients agree that this firm "*combines an encyclopaedic shipping knowledge with intellectual rigour.*" The team has key strengths in both wet and dry disciplines, and handles a broad spectrum of charter party disputes, cargo claims and marine insurance claims. Casualty and underwriting work for charterers, salvers and P&I clubs also forms part of the portfolio. Lindsay East (see p.747) is described as "*one of the best dry shipping lawyers in the land.*" He has acted for Frontline, the largest crude tanker company in the world, in relation to the acquisition by its subsidiary, Golden Ocean, of five VLCCs. The deal involved acquisition finance of $320 million. Andrew Taylor (see p.751) combines his role as chairman with "*top quality instructions.*" Possessor of "*an impressive depth of knowledge,*" he is active on both the wet and dry sides of the shipping work, and has expertise in charter and sale/purchase disputes, and high value salvage cases. Richard Harvey (see p.749) is making a strong impression on the wet market, and was described by a client as one who "*can make any crisis seem like a spring stroll.*" In the past year, he has been involved in a number of cases, including the 'Gudermes' collision with 'Saint Jacques II' in the Channel near Dover, involving a laden oil tanker. **Clients** CM Lemos; Elka Shipping; Far Eastern Shipping Company; Glencore Rotterdam; Louis Dreyfus Group; MSC Mediterranean Shipping; Niarchos; North of England P&I Club; Pan Ocean; P&O Bulk Carriers; Shinwa KK; Standard Steamship Owners P&I Association; Steamship Mutual; UK Mutual P&I Club.

BENTLEYS, STOKES & LOWLESS (see firm details p.863) "*A smaller firm, but one providing a definite mark of quality*" was the opinion shared by both clients and competitors. It is greatly respected for its skills in maritime insurance and salvage work. Although the firm's absence from the Greek market has been commented on, observers commended the "*expanding amounts of work*" taken from both Denmark and Italy. Andrew Bardot (see p.746) is described as "*the main name here - he gives his all on every matter.*" He is particularly well regarded for his work with owners and charter parties. Paul Griffiths (see p.748) has "*a sure touch on shipping that places him above most.*" In the last year, the team has acted for the owners of 'The Willy', carrying out a swift and efficient salvage operation. **Clients** Cargo companies; owners; P&I clubs; underwriters.

CLIFFORD CHANCE (see firm details p.911) The "*terrific*" Tony Vlasto (see p.751) possesses the "*skills and authority that bring the whole firm into another arena.*" Observers commended his approach, which has "*created a small firm culture in a big City firm - this is a magnificent, cohesive team that stands apart from other shipping practices.*" He handles admiralty matters and all aspects of casualty work, including charter party claims and offshore oil disputes. Marine insurance/reinsurance litigation and arbitrations also form part of the portfolio here. The team has acted in the worldwide litigation that has surrounded the 'Navigator' dispute, and it has had success in the drawnout 'Sea-Empress' case. **Clients:** Banks and financial institutions; clubs & insurers; owners and operators.

HOLMES HARDINGHAM (see firm details p.1000) Market sources believe that the firm is "*going through a wonderful spell.*" The team has been praised by clients for its "*common sense and thoughtful approach;*" it has the advantage of "*strength in depth*". It fields "*a dry department that is the envy of many*" and produces "*wet work you can always trust.*" On the dry side, the "*ubiquitous*" Glenn Winter (see p.752) is "*a major competitor in the market.*" He has a "*broad base of knowledge and experience both here and on the continent.*" In the past year, the team has been active on the Starsin case, a matter awaiting a House of Lords ruling, relating to

SHIPPING ■ LONDON

respective liabilities of shipowners and charterers under bills of lading. Wet work has seen the firm involved in the high-profile cases of 'Willy' and the 'Jody F Millenium'. The team has recently made a name for itself in the more specialised yachting sphere. Here **David Johnston** (see p.749) is described as "*a breath of fresh air on deals.*" **Clients** BP Amoco; CGU; Howard Smith; Royal & SunAlliance; Pacnav (Mexico); Skuld; Spliethoff; Stolt-Nielsen; TotalFinaElf.

MORE FISHER BROWN This "*sharp, diligent firm*" has been endorsed by interviewees as home to "*some top- quality individuals.*" Clients value it as "*a firm that knows exactly when to fight.*" It is recommended for its work with P&I clubs, and its chief strength remains dry work. Here the firm handles matters for a wide range of clients from Scandinavia, Korea, the USA and beyond. **Edward Gray** (see p.748) has recently settled a large ongoing litigation relating to cargo, and advised on lading-related contract work. He is described by peers as an "*excellent player who understands the market.*" **Adrian Moylan** (see p.750) ("*a great thinker and doer*") has strong connections with the international markets. **Ian Hawkes** (see p.749) is active on charter party work and cargo claims; he was applauded by clients for his "*efficient and commercial handling of the most complex cases.*" New to this year's rankings is **Stuart Fitzpatrick** (see p.748) whose "*skills are coming to the fore.*" **Clients** Charterers; offshore contractors; P&I clubs; shipowners.

NORTON ROSE (see firm details p.1084) Expert in litigation and asset financing, sources felt that the firm has "*set the standards on maritime law.*" It boasts a full-service shipping unit, with expertise in finance, corporate, employment and tax-related shipping matters. It is the contentious group for which the firm remains best known. "*Efficient, tenacious and quite brilliant in its arguments,*" the firm has been involved in a major litigation for an Asian corporate, which has seen two appeals to the commercial court and two hearings on liability. The star of the department remains **Paul Williams** (see p.751). He has won a following for his "*shoot-from-the-hip*" style, and his "*determination to get the right result for his clients.*" He has been involved in casualty work relating to a number of cruise ships including the 'Jupiter', 'Pegasus' and 'Romantica'. **Clients** Acomarit; Andhika; A Bilbrough & Co; ExxonMobil; Festival Cruises; Gard Club; Hyundai Heavy Industries; Louise Cruise Lines; Lukoil; Malta Shipbuilding; Mitsubishi; P&O Princess Cruises; Silversea Cruises; Skuld Copenhagen; Stena; Texaco; TotalFinaElf; UK Club (Thomas Miller); Wallem.

SHAW AND CROFT (see firm details p.1128) The firm has a strong focus on admiralty law, and displays expertise in collisions, salvage and pollution matters, alongside its advice on total loss. It fields a well-regarded litigation team, which leads disputes concerning charter parties, cargo and shipbuilding. This "*small firm, which never stops working*" is home to **Mark Aspinall** (see p.746). Respected for his skills on petroleum issues, he has advised on joint ventures, collisions and oil tanker disputes. **Ben Browne** (see p.747) is thought to enjoy "*a good following in the cargo market.*" He has been active in the cargo litigation relating to 'Christopher'. **Clients** Brokers; charterers; Insurers; oil companies; operators; owners; P&I clubs; salvagers; salvers; shipyards; yachtowners

STEPHENSON HARWOOD (see firm details p.1147) The market awaits the impact of the firm's merger with Sinclair, Roche & Temperley. However, with strong skills in both wet and dry matters and a skilled litigation team, one commentator remarked that "*the balance seems to be right.*" **Paolo Ghirardani** (see p.748) remains highly rated; he is portrayed as "*the engine of the team.*" He has been recently occupied on behalf of a major shipowner on a multimillion dollar damages claim for the loss of cargo. From the SRT team comes **Joe Atkinson** (see p.746), respected for his collision work, which sees him "*battle with the best of them.*" In **Anthony Concagh** (see p.747) and **Angus Johnson** (see p.749), the firm has two younger lawyers capable of "*balancing the technical side with commerciality in the most adept way.*" Both have been involved in major cases of late, including acting for a major oil trader in a pollution incident involving the 'Alambra', a case that has led to a claim worth several million dollars. **Clients** Cargo companies; large insurers; P&I clubs; ship builders; shipowners.

WALTONS & MORSE (see firm details p.1180) This firm enjoys a "*top-flight team of senior partners*" and is blessed with a "*wonderful group of people just below them.*" **Roy Ginsberg** is "*a true expert on cargo matters,*" while **Chris Dunn** continues to be a respected name. The practice is best known for its wet skills, with instruction emanating from major cargo insurers both in the UK and overseas. Significant cases over the last year include representing cargo interests in the 'Caster' and the 'CMA CGM Normandie' cases. The firm also garners a substantial level of work from the Japanese market. **Clients** Cargo underwriters; hull underwriters; foreign insurers; shipowners.

BARLOW LYDE & GILBERT (see firm details p.858) This "*sharp, impressive*" firm fields litigators who are "*capable of leading the opposition a merry dance.*" The team has expertise on both the wet and dry sides of the business, and acts for cargo insurers, owners, underwriters and P&I clubs. The "*legendary*" **Clive Thorp** (see p.751) remains a key figure; he is a "*valuable source of sage advice.*" Department head **Nigel Wagland** (see p.751) is "*hands-on and client-focused.*" Many credit him with building up a "*tremendous brand name*" in recent years. He has acted for charterers in the high profile 'Petro Ranger' case and advised cargo insurers in the 'Happy Ranger' case. The team has also acted for a major corporation on a multimillion pound, multi-jurisdictional dispute. **Clients** Brokers; international trade groups; marine insurance; owners and operators; P&I clubs.

JACKSON PARTON (see firm details p.1011) Adjudged a "*niche, efficient firm,*" peers agree that it "*knows the beauty of details.*" Ex-partner Philip Bush has established a conditional fee scheme under the name of 'UK Enforcer', which continues to fall under the auspices of Jackson Parton, and represents UK and international clients. The team is headed by "*the expert*" **Nicholas Parton** (see p.750), who has been active in a number of different arenas in the past year. The firm has an acknowledged expertise in dry work, and a growing prominence in wet matters. It has handled a number of charter party disputes, as well as providing large American and Japanese companies with high profile advice and litigation. **John Watling** (see p.751) joins the tables this year following the endorsement of clients, for whom there is "*no-one better to guide you through the process.*" **Clients** FD&D clubs; insurers; P&I clubs; shipowners.

LAWRENCE GRAHAM (see firm details p.1031) **Michael Lax** remains the outstanding star of this strong contentious shipping practice. Clients agree that the team has an "*excellent grasp of all the practicalities of a case.*" "*Sharp, efficient and tough - it offers sound and reasoned advice.*" In the last year the team has been involved in the 'Atlantic Splendour' case, a rare appeal concerning an arbitration award. Issues arising from both the 'Jody F Millennium' and the 'Navigator Gas' cases have also occupied the firm. It has also seen a growth in its commercial work, having put together a number of large ship building deals. The work here has an international flavour, and the team remains associated with instructions emanating from Eastern Europe and Russia. **Clients** Charterers Mutual P&I Club; CMB Group; Dynergy; Geogas Trading; Latvian Shipping; Meyer Werft; MT Maritime; Novorossiysk Shipping; Ocean Rig; Steamship Mutual Underwriting Association; Tankers International; West of England P&I Club.

THOMAS COOPER & STIBBARD (see firm details p.1159) The much-admired David Hebden has now taken a consultancy role at the firm. This has cast the spotlight on the "*superb*" **Graham Harris** (see p.748) and observers believe he will "*stamp his style on the team.*" Most of the firm's work takes place on a commercial front, winning instructions from large international shipowners and operators, and handling cases of the highest value. The team also has a track record advising on multi-juris-

LONDON ■ SHIPPING

diction cases, particularly concerning stranded vessels, and insurance claims on cruise liners and crisis management matters. It has recently been involved in the 'Green Lily' case, a total loss incident off the Shetland Isles. **Clients** English clubs; Scandinavian clubs; shipowners and operators.

FISHERS (see firm details p.957) "*Experienced and eminently trustworthy*" Nicholas Fisher (see p.748) is described by clients and competitors as "*offering a superb service with the support of a small team*." The bulk of the group's instructions remain on the dry side, with a volume of commercial work handled for shipbuilders, owners and large corporations. The team is also involved in some high-level contamination and insurance matters. Notable cases of the past year include matters arising from the loss of cargo in 'Kodima', and various substantial arbitrations. **Clients** BP Chemicals Trading; BP Shipping; Hapag-Lloyd; Lauritzen-Cool; The Miller Insurance Group; Rickmers-Linie.

HILL DICKINSON (see firm details p.995) Although strongly associated with the firm's well regarded shipping practice in the North, the London based team is best known for its niche expertise in yachting matters. "*Absolutely first-class on yachting and recreational craft work*," the firm is a slightly different beast when compared with its London competitors. The "*astute and experienced*" Tony Allen (see p.746) leads the team, which represents both individuals and companies, on issues arising from construction, commercial and transactional matters. Insurance and recovery work is also a feature of the practice. The team has strong cargo and debt recovery skills, and shadows the Manchester office in these matters. **Clients** Lloyds underwriters; insurance companies; P&I clubs; brokers; yachtowners; yacht builders.

MIDDLETON POTTS (see firm details p.1069) The retirement of Andrew Donoghue has deprived the firm of its key figure in the market. However, sources agree that this respected team has maintained its range of expertise. The team is now led by David Lucas, and is acknowledged to enjoy "*fine skills and a good clientele.*" It has had success in the last year, advising liner operators in regard to several disputes, one of which was against a freight forwarder in relation to unpaid container demurrage. Arbitration and litigation experience remains a key attribute of this firm, and it is instructed by owners, operators and charterers on a variety of disputes arising from charter parties, bills of lading and marine insurance. **Clients** Steamship Mutual Club; charterers; hull and marine underwriters; owners.

WATSON, FARLEY & WILLIAMS (see firm details p.1181) This firm is an industry favourite for its substantial ship financing expertise, a forte that overshadows its general shipping experience. The "*redoubtable*" Tony Rooth (see p.750) is well known in all quarters for his dry shipping knowledge. He and the team are particularly endorsed for charter party and bill of lading disputes. He has represented many of the P&I and defence clubs. Shipping teams in New York, Paris, Singapore and Piraeus support the London office and the team enjoys a breadth of international clients, and involvement on substantial multi-jurisdictional matters. **Clients** Charterers; insurers; operators; owners; P&I clubs.

OTHER NOTABLE PRACTITIONERS Anthony Brown (see p.746), formerly of More Fisher Brown, remains "*a definite presence in the market*" at AD Brown Solicitors. He handles claims and transactional matters and was described to researchers as "*clever and forward thinking*." Laurence McFadyen, formerly of Southampton's Lester Aldridge, is now at Sach Solicitors. Peers believe he has "*undoubted abilities across the board.*"

LONDON   SHIPPING FINANCE

SHIPPING: FINANCE
■ LONDON

1 Norton Rose
2 Stephenson Harwood
   Watson, Farley & Williams
3 Allen & Overy
   Clifford Chance

LEADING INDIVIDUALS
1 GIBB Jeremy Norton Rose
   HARTLEY Simon Norton Rose
   SHELTON John Norton Rose
2 DUNNE Frank Watson, Farley & Williams
   RUSSELL Mark Stephenson Harwood
   SMITH David Allen & Overy
   TURNER Paul Clifford Chance
   WATSON Martin Watson, Farley & Williams

This book is the product of 6,582 1/2 hour interviews. See p.7 for BMRB audit. Within each band, firms are listed alphabetically. See individuals' profiles p.746

NORTON ROSE (see firm details p.1084) Still regarded by market commentators as "*the busiest and the best*," the firm is blessed with "*a range of skills and expertise that place it at the forefront of ship financing.*" The group's expertise in asset finance is employed to good effect for a wide range of shipping clients, particularly on complex cross-border transactions. A deep bench of talent exists. Jeremy Gibb (see p.748) is described as "*a true all-rounder, who can handle anything you can possibly throw at him.*" Simon Hartley (see p.748) is "*technically astute and easy to deal with*," while clients find John Shelton (see p.751) "*helpful and constructive.*" Recently, the team has acted for a syndicate of banks in a $485 million transaction relating to deep water drilling. It has also acted on the merger of Ceres Hellenic and Coeclerici to form one of the world's largest bulk fleets, in a deal worth $350 million. **Clients** ANZ Bank; Banca Commerciale Italiana; Bank of Nova Scotia; Bank of Scotland; Crédit Lyonnais; Deutsche Schiffsbank; HSBC; Lloyds TSB; Premuda Group; Shipping Corporation of India; Société Générale; Sovereign Finance.

STEPHENSON HARWOOD (see firm details p.1147) The merger with Sinclair Roche & Temperley has taken the finance offering of this firm "*on to the next level.*" It undertakes a range of work for banks and owners, often multi-jurisdictional in nature. The "*expert*" Mark Russell (see p.750) heads the team; he was commended by one commentator as "*first-class - he holds a premier reputation in the UK and overseas.*" The team has acted for a major shipping group in the negotiation of the construction documentation of an LNG carrier, which entailed offering advice on complex tax matters in two jurisdictions. It has also advised an international shipowning group on one of the first finance leases into a tonnage tax company. **Clients** ABN AMRO; ANZ Bank; Benor Tankers; Lloyds TSB; PGS Production; Solstad Shipping.

WATSON, FARLEY & WILLIAMS (see firm details p.1181) "*A firm excellent at what it does,*" agree competitors. It boasts an impressive client base, that consists of both shipbuilders and banks. Frank Dunne (see p.747) was singled out to our researchers for his "*dedicated concentration and easy-going style,*" while Martin Watson (see p.751) was commended for his "*great breadth of knowledge and scope.*" The headline deals of late include advising Citibank on its provision of $175 million and $350 million facilities for CP Ships. The team has also acted for Fortis/Nedship in a $176 million financing of container vessels for Seaspan, and has been involved in a number of LNG finances. **Clients** Bank of New York; Bank of Nova Scotia; Crédit Lyonnais; Citibank; Fortis Bank; JPMorgan Chase Bank; Lloyds Bank; Overseas Maritime; P&O Nedlloyd; Pegasus Ocean Services; Tankers International; Tufton Oceanic.

ALLEN & OVERY (see firm details p.841) "*An excellent team, capable of genius,*" but felt to lose part of the marketplace by having no dedicated shipping finance team. It draws on the expert staff of its asset finance group, and is respected for its ability "*to handle any work - particularly adept on complex matters.*" David Smith (see p.84) is respected for his knowledge of shipping

SHIPPING ■ THE SOUTH & SOUTH WEST/EAST ANGLIA

industry issues. The team has acted for Barclays Structured Asset Finance on a number of UK tax-structured lease financings of several ships, with a total value of $400 million. It has also advised JPMorgan on two major syndicated financings, involving LNG carriers, with a total value of $350 million. **Clients** Barclays Structured Asset Finance; Celtic Pacific; Halifax; JPMorgan Chase; West LB.

CLIFFORD CHANCE (see firm details p.911) The "*outstanding*" **Paul Turner** (see p.751) remains key to much of the firm's success in this field. Some interviewees credited him with "*refocusing the team and picking up some classy clients.*" Its clientele includes large financial institutions and international banks, and it is no surprise to find that high-level financing work is the main priority of this team. It has been engaged on the restructuring of a $500 million revolving loan to a US tanker operator, and has advised on the $190 million financing of four VLCCs. Joint ventures and operating arrangements regarding LNGs both occupy the team. **Clients** Barclays; Citibank; Commerzbank; Deutsche VerkehrsBank; Islamic Development Bank; Kvaerner; Merrill Lynch; Nomura; Union Bank of Switzerland.

THE SOUTH & SOUTH WEST

SHIPPING
■ THE SOUTH & SOUTH WEST

1
- Davies, Johnson & Co Plymouth
- Foot Anstey Sargent Exeter, Plymouth

2
- Bond Pearce Plymouth, Southampton
- Lester Aldridge Southampton

LEADING INDIVIDUALS

1
- HATTERSLEY Charles Foot Anstey Sargent
- JOHNSON Jonathan Davies, Johnson & Co

2
- HORTON Nicholas Bond Pearce
- KELLY Russell Lester Aldridge
- RUSTEMEYER Alistair Rustemeyer & Co

This book is the product of 6,582 1/2 hour interviews. See p.7 for BMRB audit. Within each band, firms are listed alphabetically. See individuals' profiles p.746

DAVIES, JOHNSON & CO (see firm details p.930) This "*impressive firm*" has established itself as "*the citadel of shipping in the South West*" claimed one competitor. **Jonathan Johnson** (see p.749) remains "*a near legendary figure,*" praised nationally for his skills on P&I matters and FD&D. The "*calm and reasoned team*" handles a wide range of wet and dry work, including casualty and salvage matters, and bills of lading, charter party disputes, and pollution and finance issues. A highlight of the past year was its representation of the defendant in supply of Veba Oil Trading v Petrotrade, an important case in the oil industry, the dispute related to oil density. The firm attracts clients from both home and overseas, and has strong connections with both Northern Europe and Greece. **Clients** Commodities traders; owners; P&I Clubs.

FOOT ANSTEY SARGENT (see firm details p.958) "*A sharp firm with expertise in both wet and dry work*" acknowledged observers. This South West-based firm continues to win plaudits from clients and peers on a national level. **Charles Hattersley** (see p.749) has "*an excellent understanding of the industry and the issues that affect it.*" High-value sale/purchase and mortgage related transactions have occupied the firm. On the wet side, it has been involved in a heavyweight litigation case, and significant limitation liability work. **Clients** Atlantic Marine & Sales Charter; AXA; Devonport Management; Everend Insurance Brokers; Haliburton Group; JW Stevenson & Co; Lloyds TSB; Norwich Union; Royal & SunAlliance; Van Meyden Insurance Company; owners; P&I clubs.

BOND PEARCE (see firm details p.879) This broad practice is judged by clients to "*offer expert service at a reasonable price.*" Straddling the South and South West, it advises on charter party work, cargo claims, marine insurance, port and harbour matters, ship construction and marine finance. The team has also been active in casualty defence and other matters for P&I clubs. **Nicholas Horton** (see p.749) remains the main name here: a "*strong alternative to the London lawyers.*" The group also has interests in the more specialised area of super yachts. **Clients** Banks; insurers; operators; owners; shipyards.

LESTER ALDRIDGE (see firm details p.1038) Although the departure of Laurence McFadyen to Sachs Solicitors has diminished the profile of the firm, the team itself is viewed as possessing the "*skills and industry savvy to survive.*" It combines skills in both shipping and insurance, with a particular reputation for the wet side. The firm has recently represented the owners in relation to a collision between a chemical tanker and a container vessel. It has also acted on purchases in the yachting sector. **Russell Kelly** (see p.750) was recommended to researchers for his knowledge of the P&I club market. **Clients** Amicus Legal; Bank Of Scotland; Gard UK P&I Club; Geest Line; Lombard Marine Finance; Standard P&I Club; St. Margaret's Insurance; Sunseeker; UK P&O clubs.

OTHER NOTABLE PRACTITIONERS Formerly of DMH, **Alistair Rustemeyer** has established Rustemeyer & Co. He was described as "*a superb lawyer with a big name in the field*" and has recently been involved in the 'Baltic Surveyor' case.

EAST ANGLIA

SHIPPING
■ EAST ANGLIA

1
- Dale & Co Felixstowe
- John Weston & Co Felixstowe

2
- Prettys Ipswich

3
- Birketts Ipswich

This book is the product of 6,582 1/2 hour interviews. See p.7 for BMRB audit. Within each band, firms are listed alphabetically.

DALE & CO **Michael Dale** remains the main factor in the success of this Felixstowe practice. He was endorsed by clients for his "*clear, concise advice*" and has won a following for his "*hands on, practically minded approach – giving us all we could ask for.*" Insurance-flavoured shipping work is a forte of this firm, and a number of its instructions are derived from the Japanese and German markets. Commentators discerned "*a strong feel*" for cargo related work, and the team also handles commercial and financing matters. Arbitrations have also featured in the work load over the past year. **Clients** European logistics and distribution companies; ferry operators; international P&I clubs.

JOHN WESTON & CO **John Weston**'s reputation is the main attraction at this highly recommended firm. Clients value his "*good bedside manner – he's a sharp operator, straightforward and trustworthy.*" The firm has advised on a dispute relating to the international carriage of goods by sea, and has acted on an insurance policy dispute. A key attribute here is case management before trial, and the team has recognised skills in mediation. Much of its work is carried out on an international stage. **Clients** P&I clubs; insurers; recovery agents; owners.

PRETTYS (see firm details p.1106) Clients reported that this team is "*utterly professional and value for money;*" it fields lawyers who have "*great industry awareness.*" Primarily active in dry shipping matters, the firm is active in cargo and freight work. Highlights of the last year

THE NORTH ■ SHIPPING

LEADING INDIVIDUALS

1
- DALE Michael Dale & Co
- WESTON John John Weston & Co

2
- DICKIE Paul Prettys

ONES TO WATCH
- DORAI-RAJ Dinesh Prettys

See individuals' profiles p.746

include the recovery of debts for a shipping line following the insolvency of a multinational company. Clients appreciate **Paul Dickie** (see p.747) as one who has "*never let us down on a big case.*" Clients P&I clubs; shipping lines.

BIRKETTS (see firm details p.875) John Winn's team continues to impress with its "*highly competent attitude*" to both dry and wet shipping work. It handles claims and transactions for a global clientele. The team has advised the Felixstowe Dock & Railway Company on the consequences of a latex spill in the harbour. It has also been involved in a number of large-scale mediations and arbitrations in London. Clients Fred Olsen; P&O Ferrymasters; Port of Felixstowe; Port of Ipswich.

THE NORTH

SHIPPING
■ THE NORTH

1
- Andrew M Jackson Hull
- Eversheds Newcastle upon Tyne
- Mills & Co Newcastle upon Tyne
- Rayfield Mills Newcastle upon Tyne

2
- DLA Liverpool, Manchester
- Hill Dickinson Liverpool, Manchester

LEADING INDIVIDUALS

1
- HILTON Chris Eversheds
- MACKIN Stephen Eversheds
- MILLS Guy Mills & Co
- MILLS Stephen Rayfield Mills

2
- JACKSON Peter Hill Dickinson
- TAYLOR Silas Andrew M Jackson

3
- BOADEN Jon Mills & Co
- HILL Martin DLA
- KEMP Jonathan Eversheds
- RAYFIELD Richard Rayfield Mills
- SMITH Michael Mills & Co

This book is the product of 6,582 1/2 hour interviews. See p.7 for BMRB audit.
Within each band, firms are listed alphabetically. See individuals' profiles p.746

ANDREW M JACKSON (see firm details p.845) Competitors commented on the "*professional approach*" of the firm, while clients valued it as "*efficient and reliable in every aspect.*" The team is able to boast a national reputation for its wet work, and its expertise in casualty and total loss is well respected. Although it fields "*an excellent team,*" only one name in particular stands out. Team head **Silas Taylor** (see p.751) was described to researchers as a "*hands on lawyer, able to dove-tail with the needs of his clients.*" He has been successful in the Perks case, which reached the Court of Appeal, in a ruling that allowed jack-up rig workers to claim tax recoveries of approximately £100 million. The team has also acted for ABP in its dispute with Humber Pilots over strike action. The firm has a wide national and international client base, and a depth of experience in the fishing industry. Clients P&I clubs; P&O North Sea Ferries; Sunderland Marine Mutual Insurance; marine insurers; fish producer organisations; Humber area shipping and freight forwarding companies.

EVERSHEDS (see firm details p.949) The firm has relocated its respected Ipswich team, centralising its shipping efforts in the North East. The group is experienced in both wet and dry work, and handles P&I defence, bulk cargo, charter party claims, salvage, marine insurance and various super yacht matters. Team leader **Chris Hilton** (see p.749) is thought to be "*a magnet for top-quality work.*" He is assisted by ex-mariner **Stephen Mackin** (see p.750) who peers regard as "*an impressive bonus for any team.*" Associate **Jonathan Kemp** (see p.750) "*mastered his skills in East Anglia*" and is a respected member of the team. It has been active in the three SCOPIC/salvage cases, relating to one of the most significant developments in insurance/salvage work in the last few years. The firm has also advised the group, that located and raised the wreck of the 'Bluebird.' The past year has seen it engaged in the integration of Eversheds' shipping teams in the UK, Netherlands, Denmark and Singapore. Clients Graig Ship Management; NEPIA; Page & Moy; P&I Clubs; ferry operators; shipowners; port authorities.

MILLS & CO This long established firm continues to draw support from a nationwide clientele, and was described by one London practice as "*a beacon in the North.*" P&I work is the firm's forte and it represents many of the major clubs. It also has a good track record in insurance matters, shipbuilding and ship repairs. **Guy Mills** remains one of the "*pre-eminent names in the region.*" He combines "*knowledge and flair, and is incredibly popular with the clubs.*" He is joined in the tables by "*the stand out*" **Jon Boaden** and the "*incredibly clever*" **Michael Smith**, both of whom are felt to "*offer expert support,*" particularly in their dry shipping work. Clients British shipbuilders; P&I clubs; ship repair yards; industrial groups.

RAYFIELD MILLS This "*impressive unit*" earns plaudits for having "*a small yet highly competent team that is able to achieve so much.*" **Stephen Mills** remains "*undoubtedly a star name - he inspires confidence.*" The firm has been active in the Metro litigation, a multiparty dispute, where Mills and his team acted for ExxonMobil. The case was settled after mediation. The firm also has strong ties to local P&I clubs, and has built up a healthy shipping finance practice. **Richard Rayfield** maintains the support of a national client base. Clients ExxonMobil; North of England P&I Club; UK P&I Club; shipowners

DLA **Martin Hill** is well regarded in this practice, which handles both wet and dry work, and marine insurance.

HILL DICKINSON (see firm details p.995) Clients believe that **Peter Jackson** (see p.802) "*adds value*" in the cases he handles. The practice is split between Liverpool and Manchester, with the former handling deals with P&I clubs, ship operators and environmental matters, and the latter taking care of cargo and debt recovery issues. Many of the firm's instructions concern cargo and insurance, but over the past year it has been involved in a large environmental case. Clients Gard; Mersey Docks & Harbour; Skuld; Thomas Miller Group; Warta.

SHIPPING ■ SCOTLAND

SCOTLAND

SHIPPING
■ SCOTLAND

1. **Henderson Boyd Jackson WS** Edinburgh
2. **Mackinnons** Aberdeen
3. **Maclay Murray & Spens** Glasgow

LEADING INDIVIDUALS

1. **LOWE James** Henderson Boyd Jackson WS
   MACLEAN Duncan Henderson Boyd Jackson WS
   MACRAE Keith Mackinnons

This book is the product of 6,582 1/2 hour interviews. See p.7 for BMRB audit. Within each band, firms are listed alphabetically. See individuals' profiles p.746

HENDERSON BOYD JACKSON WS The firm holds the strongest presence in a relatively small Scottish shipping market. Clients described "*a team of up-front, forthright individuals who understand the varied aspects of shipping and do their best to see you through*." The firm carries out work for owners, operators, bankers and yards, with insurance being a particular forte. James Lowe (see p.750) is "*approachable and understands the client's needs*." He has been involved for Chevron in the conclusion of BP's appeal to the House of Lords, concerning their on-going dispute. It also acted for BUE Kazakhstan on the construction and purchase of specialised oil exploration vessels. Duncan MacLean (see p.750) has "*an expert knowledge of the fishing industry*." In the past year, he has been involved in matters relating to the collision of an oil production jacket with Erskine Bridge. **Clients** Britannia Steam Ship Insurance Association; BUE Kazakhstan; Clydeport; Coastal Marine Boatbuilders; GARD P&I Club; North of England P&I Association; Scottish Boatowners Mutual Insurance; Sunderland Marine Mutual Insurance.

MACKINNONS (see firm details p.1048) Rivals believe that the firm makes its Aberdeen location "*work for it,*" developing a "*expert knowledge*" of the fishing and oil markets. The team is also instructed by P&I clubs for their casualty work and hull investigation skills. Litigator Keith MacRae (see p.750) is judged "*spot-on in shipping insurance work - he brings dexterity and speed of thought to marine work.*" The team is skilled in the criminal aspects of marine law, including collision regulations, fisheries regulations and the Health and Safety Act. **Clients** Harbours; insurers; owners; operators; P&I clubs.

MACLAY MURRAY & SPENS (see firm details p.1048) Although the firm does not have a full-time shipping team, it continues to be endorsed as "*an efficient team, which services its clients effectively.*" Bruce Patrick leads a team that has particular strengths in shipping finance. It has advised on a number of complex arrangements, including the high-value financing of a vessel designed for the North Sea. The contentious team also garners plaudits. It has been involved in a successful appeal in the House of Lords on behalf of BP. **Clients** BP; Clyde Marina; J&A Gardner & Co; Lithgows; North of England P&I club; NUMAST; Schlumberger; Ship Mortgage Finance Company; Skuld; Steamship Mutual; West of England P&I club.

THE LEADERS IN SHIPPING

ALLEN, Tony
Hill Dickinson, London
(020) 7695 1000
aallen@hilldicks.com
Specialisation: Heads the firm's specialist yacht team which deals primarily with yacht insurance and yacht transactional/finance matters for underwriters, brokers, yards, owners and others in the recreational marine market in the UK and overseas.
Prof. Memberships: British Marine Federation, Yachtbrokers Designers Surveyors Association (subscriber), Professional Yachtmen's Association, Superyacht Society, Little Ship Club, Lloyd's Yacht Club.
Career: Qualified in 1985, *Linklaters and Paines* 1982-85, legal advisor to Royal Yachting Association 1985-88; Whitbread Round the World Race and subsequent adventure sailing business 1989-90; *Ingedew Brown Bennison & Garrett* 1991-94; *Berrymans Lace Mawer* 1996-99; Partner, *Hill Dickinson* 1999.

ASPINALL, Mark
Shaw and Croft, London
(020) 7645 9000
mark.aspinall@shawandcroft.com
Specialisation: Main areas of practice are split between all aspects of shipping litigation/arbitration but predominantly in Tanker operations (oil, LPG and chemical) covering unseaworthiness actions, cargo claims, charterparty disputes; and oil trading disputes for the Independents, covering crude and products sale contracts (physical and paper), processing and netback agreements and related problems concerning letters of credit and trade finance. Also experienced in shipping fraud, asset tracing and joint venture agreements (oil biased).
Prof. Memberships: Baltic Exchange, Institute of Petroleum.
Career: Articled *Shaw & Croft*. Qualified 1994. Partner 1998.
Personal: Born 1962. Lives in London. Leisure interests: football, golf, tennis, travel and occasional surfing.

ATKINSON, Joe
Stephenson Harwood (incorporating Sinclair Roche & Temperley), London
(020) 7329 4422
joe.atkinson@shlegal.com
Specialisation: Litigation, arbitration and public enquiry work arising from collisions, groundings, wreck removal, total partial loss, fire explosion, oil pollution. Emergency response.
Prof. Memberships: Association of Average Adjusters.
Career: Joined *Sinclair Roche & Temperley* in 1998 and from outset was involved in high profile casualties, eg Khark V, Kowloon Bridge, Herald of Free Enterprise. Became partner in 1995 and Head of Admiralty in 1996. Has been involved in many other major casualties including 'Nassia', 'Mighty Servant II', 'DG Harmony', 'ABT Summer', 'Patraikos II'. Became a Partner at *Stephenson Harwood* in 2002 when *Sinclair Roche & Temperley* and *Stephenson Harwood* combined to form an enlarged firm.
Publications: Many articles for the trade press on "wet" topics. Also a regular speaker at seminars in UK and overseas.
Personal: Born 30 November 1962.

BARDOT, Andrew
Bentleys, Stokes & Lowless, London
(020) 7782 0990
abardot@bentleys.co.uk
Specialisation: Qualified 1980. Partner 1982. Principal areas of practice: all aspects of dry shipping and insurance related litigation and arbitration and non-contentious matters, including sale and purchase and MOA matters. French speaker.
Prof. Memberships: London Maritime Arbitration Association supporting member. Baltic Exchange member.

BEESLEY, Chris
Ince & Co, London
(020) 7623 2011
Career: Chris Beesley joined *Ince & Co* in 1972 and soon thereafter moved into the firm's wet marine practice. In 1979 he assisted in opening the firm's Hong Kong office, travelling extensively throughout Asia on casualty related business. On his return to the London office in 1984 he concentrated on developing the firm's business closer to 'home' - particularly in Scandinavia and Greece. In recent years he has focused on cruise ship related business and has personally supervised the firm's involvement in most of the recent cruise ship casualties. This year, Chris has been involved in the innovative launch of Incite - a new claims service. He is a regular on the seminar circuit - both at home and abroad - on safety issues relating to casualty matters.
Publications: Articles on safety at sea and emergency response have been published in various periodicals including the 'Nautical Institutes' magazine and 'P&I Monthly'. He authored the chapter on salvage in the 'Nautical Institutes' publication for Masters - 'Command'.

BOADEN, Jon H
Mills & Co, Newcastle upon Tyne
(0191) 233 2222

BOWMAN, Marcus
Holman Fenwick & Willan, London
(020) 7264 8551
marcus.bowman@hfw.co.uk
Specialisation: Partner in shipping litigation department. Specialising in maritime litigation with emphasis on charterparty, bill of lading and marine insurance disputes; P&I claims handler for seven years.
Career: Oceanus P & I club, 1980-83; Britannia P&I club, 1983-87; articled *Holman Fenwick and Willan*; qualified 1990; partner 1993; solicitor of the Supreme Court of England and Wales. University of Cape Town (BA); University of London (LLM).
Personal: Born 1954. Resides London.

BROWN, Anthony
AD Brown, Solicitors, London
(07774) 415287
adb@adbrown.co.uk
Specialisation: Commercial shipping litigation, in particular dry cases, both P&I and defence, arising under charterparties, bills of lading, MOAs and insurance

746 INDEX TO LEADING LAWYERS: PAGE 1693 ■ IN-HOUSE LAWYERS PROFILES: PAGE 1201

contracts; sale and purchase transactions; drafting of joint venture, profit/loss sharing, shareholders' and other commercial agreements, mostly in shipping-related matters. Fluent German speaker, hence large client base in Hamburg. Also has a number of further contacts in the Dutch, Croatian, Korean and Taiwanese markets. Frequent speaker on shipping topics both in the UK and overseas.
Prof. Memberships: Law Society, LMAA.
Career: Exeter School and Trinity Hall, Cambridge (graduated 1978). Subsequently with *Richards Butler*, *Elborne Mitchell* and *More Fisher Brown*. Commenced own practice in November 2000.
Personal: Extensive sailing experience, including a number of professional yacht deliveries in the Biscay and Atlantic areas.

BROWN, Hugh
Holman Fenwick & Willan, London
(020) 7264 8445
hugh.brown.co.uk
Specialisation: Admiralty. Partner specialising in collisions, salvage, total loss and other casualty and hull/P&I insurance-related work; notable cases include the 'Abidin Daver' (HL) 1984 1LLR 339; Leigh and Silivan Ltd v Aliakmon Shipping Co Ltd (the 'Aliakmon') HL 1986 2LLR 1; the 'Devotion' and 'Golden Polydinamos' CA 1995 1LLR 589; 'Herceg Novi' and 'Ming Galaxy' CA 1998 2LLR 454.
Career: Qualified 1971; partner *Holman Fenwick & Willan* 1983.
Personal: Born 1947; resides Dorking.

BROWNE, Ben
Shaw and Croft, London
(020) 7645 9000
Ben.Browne@shawandcroft.com
Specialisation: Partner specialising in all aspects of shipping, in particular salvage, collision, oil pollution, general average, transhipments and disputes arising from contracts of carriage of goods by sea. Advises marine cargo, hull and P&I insurers, shipowners, charterers and oil companies on shipping problems. Advisor to the International Underwriting Association of London and Lloyd's Underwriters' Association on salvage matters. Member of Lloyd's Open Form (Salvage) Working Party, Salvage Liaison Group, three man SCOPIC Drafting Committee and British Maritime Law Association General Average Sub-committee and the CMI Working Party on General Average. Co-ordinated the Ocean Marine Mutual Members Action Group following the Provisional Liquidation of that P&I Club. Has contributed many articles, chapters and papers on salvage, collision, general average and oil pollution. Has a special interest in the Middle East where he helped establish *Clyde and Co*'s Dubai office.
Prof. Memberships: Member of Comite Maritime International and British Maritime Law Association, Subscriber to Average Adjusters' Association.
Career: Qualified in 1978 while at *Lovell White & King*, *Morrell Peel & Gamlen*, Oxford 1979-81. Joined *Clyde & Co* in 1981 becoming a Partner in 1985. Joined *Shaw and Croft* in 2001.
Personal: Born 18 May 1953. Educated Eton College and Trinity College, Cambridge.

CONCAGH, Anthony
Stephenson Harwood (incorporating Sinclair Roche & Temperley), London
(020) 7809 2626
tony.concagh@shlegal.com
Specialisation: Partner, shipping litigation. Specialises in commercial litigation with the emphasis being on shipping, insurance and international trade. He has a wide range of experience in relation to charterparties, cargo claims and construction disputes. He has particular interest and knowledge of advising on insurance issues arising in the marine energy and offshore industry. His clients include Lloyd's underwriters, insurance companies in England and abroad, insurance brokers, ship and oil platform owners and oil traders.
Career: Qualified 1992. Joined *Stephenson Harwood* 1999. Became partner 2002.
Publications: Various articles for Lloyd's List.
Personal: Born 1965. Education - Bancrofts School, Woodford Green, Essex and University of Southampton, LLB. Interests: naval and military history, in between raising two very energetic boys.

CRUMP, Richard
Holman Fenwick & Willan, London
(020) 7264 8245
richard.crump@hfw.co.uk
Specialisation: Partner in commercial litigation department. Practice encompasses all areas of shipping litigation, including charterparty disputes, cargo claims, ship sale disputes, joint venture and pool agreement disputes, marine insurance claims including total loss and related commercial litigation. Has spoken at seminars in Athens and Bombay. Accredited CEDR Mediator.
Prof. Memberships: Law Society member.
Career: Qualified in 1981 having joined *Holman Fenwick and Willan* in 1979. Became a partner in 1987.
Personal: Born 6 September 1957. Educated at St Paul's School, London 1970-74, Oriel College, Oxford 1975-78 and College of Law, Guildford 1979. Lives in London.

DALE, Michael
Dale & Co, Felixstowe
(07074) 794708

DE LA RUE, Colin
Ince & Co, London
(020) 7623 2011
colin.delarue@ince.co.uk
Specialisation: Has acted in most major oil pollution incidents worldwide in the last 15 years. On a day to day basis advises shipowners, oil companies, P&I clubs, marine underwriters and others on the ramifications of pollution from ships in various branches of maritime commerce. Has given papers on the subject at seminars and conferences in many countries around the world.
Prof. Memberships: British Maritime Law Association Pollution Sub-committee; elected titulary member of the Comité Maritime International in 1994.
Career: Bar Finals 1977; admitted as solicitor 1980; partner *Ince & Co* 1986; head of firm's pollution group.
Publications: General Editor of 'Liability for Damage to the Marine Environment' (LLP 1993) and co-author of 'Shipping and the Environment' (LLP, 1998), the main textbook on the subject.
Personal: Born 1953. Education: Elizabeth College, Guernsey and Pembroke College, Cambridge. Married with three children.

DEERING, Bob
Ince & Co, London
(020) 7623 2011
bob.deering@ince.co.uk
Specialisation: Joined *Ince & Co* in 1976; partner in 1985. Over the years has become involved in all aspects of the firm's shipping practice and heads its Dry Shipping Group which is regularly adjudged to be No 1 and which comprises some 85 partners and other lawyers. He represents a number of substantial ship owners, charterers and P&I clubs both in their own capacity and on behalf of their shipowner members. He also acts for underwriters in the investigation of hull claims and as a result, has experience of casualties from all sides of the fence.
Prof. Memberships: Law Society.
Career: Pembroke College, Cambridge. Joined *Ince & Co* 1976. Qualified 1978. Partner 1985.
Publications: Bob is a regular on both the UK and the international seminar circuit, speaking on matters as diverse as e-commerce and ship arrest.
Personal: Married, three children. Sport - both watching and playing.

DICKIE, Paul
Prettys, Ipswich
(01473) 232121
pdickie@prettys.co.uk
Specialisation: Shipping litigation, acting for owners, charterers and their insurers. Also advises in relation to commercial shipping including sale and purchase, shipbuilding and finance.
Prof. Memberships: London Maritime Arbitrators' Association (supporting member).
Career: Qualified in 1988. Worked for *Clifford Chance* 1988-97 in London and Hong Kong. Joined *Prettys* 1997; partner 2000.
Personal: Born 22 April 1964 in Turriff, Aberdeenshire. Robert Gordon's College, Aberdeen 1975-81 and Worcester College, Oxford 1982-85. Leisure interests include most sports, gardening and cooking.

DORAI-RAJ, Dinesh
Prettys, Ipswich
(01473) 232121

DUNN, Chris
Waltons & Morse, London
(020) 7623 4255

DUNNE, Frank
Watson, Farley & Williams, London
(020) 7814 8000
fdunne@wfw.com
Specialisation: Partner in International Finance Group. Practice encompasses a broad range of ship finance work for major international shipping finance lenders and commercial shipping transactions for major international shipowners, including joint ventures, charter structures, new building contracts, and ship acquisitions. He has also been engaged in structured finance transactions involving insurance products and has been involved in a number of high profile workout and dispute resolution situations.
Career: Articled *Norton Rose*, qualified 1980; established the firm's highly successful office in Piraeus 1984 spending five years there; partner in *Watson, Farley & Williams* since 1984.
Personal: Educated Downing College, Cambridge University (LLM).

EAST, Lindsay
Richards Butler, London
(020) 7772 5875
lte@richardsbutler.com
Specialisation: Partner. Former head of shipping and insurance group. Main area of practice is shipping and insurance. Acts for owners and charterers direct or through their insurers (P&I and defence clubs) in all contractual disputes, charterparty, bill of lading, MOA, and building contracts. Particular expertise in drafting and advising on club rules, charterparties, especially with reference to LNG, and shipbuilding disputes acting both for the Builder and the Buyer. Also handles general marine and non-marine insurance, acting for cargo insurers, reinsurers and war-risk underwriters. Cases have included 'Antaios', 'Antares', 'Antonis P Lemos', 'Standard Steamship v Gann, Aditya Vaibhav', 'Aegean Maritime v Flender Werft' and 'Sagheera'. Speaker at, and chairman of, various seminars.
Prof. Memberships: Baltic Exchange; Supporting Member LMAA.
Career: Qualified in 1973, having joined *Richards Butler* in 1971. Became a partner in 1977.
Personal: Born 24 March 1949. Attended Skinners School to 1966, then Worcester College, Oxford 1967-70 (MA Jurisprudence). Leisure interests include cricket, golf, opera and travel. Lives in Rickmansworth, Herts.

EVANS, John
Hill Taylor Dickinson, London
(020) 7283 9033
john.evans@htd-london.com
Specialisation: Shipping and insurance litigation. A partner for 21 years, who has practised shipping and marine insur-

SHIPPING ■ THE LEADERS

ance litigation/arbitration throughout his career. Wide experience of resolution of charterparty disputes and pursuit of claims arising from major maritime casualties including actual and constructive total losses of vessels. Group leader of one of the firm's maritime and insurance litigation groups, leading a team of professional staff, including two partners who were formerly Master Mariners. Reported cases of interest handled by the group include Ventouris v Mountain (Italia Express); Choko Star; Royal Volker Stevin v Mountain; ('Dutch Dredgers'); Star Sea; Apostolis; Tjaskemolen and 'Vergina'. He is the partner in London responsible for the firm's Piraeus office.
Prof. Memberships: A supporting Member of LMAA, and inter alia a Member of the British Italian Lawyers' Association, of the BMLA and the IBA. He is a liveryman of the Worshipful Company of Shipwrights.
Career: Llandovery College; University College of Wales, Aberystwyth (1972 LLB).
Personal: Resides Stebbing.

FISHER, Nicholas
Fishers, London
(020) 7709 7203
info@fishcity.co.uk
Specialisation: Partner specialising in commercial shipping litigation, insurance and reinsurance litigation. Handles commercial shipping litigation, including significant client base in container, reefer and tanker operations. Also insurance and reinsurance litigation involving brokers' PI claims.
Prof. Memberships: London Maritime Arbitrators Association (Supporting Member), Baltic Exchange, The City of London Solicitors' Company.
Career: Qualified in 1979. Partner at *Richards Butler* 1984-88. Founding partner of *More Fisher Brown* 1988-93. Founded *Fishers* in May 1993.
Personal: Educated at Glyn Grammar School, Epsom, then Clare College, Cambridge (MA).

FITZPATRICK, Stuart
More Fisher Brown, London
(020) 7650 1848
sfitzpatrick@m-f-b.co.uk
Specialisation: Dry shipping - bills of lading/charterparty/sale and purchase disputes - safe port claims, ship construction/modification and guarantee claims, ship/shore fire and explosion claims - commodities/trading disputes.
Career: Qualified 1978. *Sinclair Roche & Temperley* 1978-96 (Partner 1988). 1996 joined *More Fisher Brown* as a Partner.

FLETCHER, Simon
Clyde & Co, Guildford
(01483) 555555
Specialisation: Senior partner in marine casualty department. On the wet side: salvage, collision, transhipment, general average for cargo, ship, salvor and banking clients including cargo, hull, P&I and MII insurance matters - recent cases: Collision between Ever Decent and Norwegian Dream and the sinking of the Mighty Servant 2. On the energy litigation side: acting for insurers, oil companies and contractors, mainly in respect of insurance, construction and operating problems including Piper Alpha and Sleipner A. Seconded to an oil company for 18 months regarding an FPSO construction dispute and now involved in the loss of the P 36.
Prof. Memberships: The Law Society; chairman of the BMLA sub-committee for Offshore Structures.
Career: LLB (Hons) Manchester 1968. Qualified and joined *Clyde & Co* in 1971. Became a partner 1975.

GHIRARDANI, Paolo
Stephenson Harwood (incorporating Sinclair Roche & Temperley), London
(020) 7809 2612
paolo.ghirardani@shlegal.com
Specialisation: Partner, Head of Shipping Litigation. Paolo handles all areas of shipping litigation but has a specialist practice of shipping and insurance fraud - with a particular emphasis on Africa. He regularly represents the interests of leading shipowners, P&I Clubs and underwriters, investigating fraudulent claims. He has gained a reputation as a tough, determined and well respected lawyer with good investigative skills. His most recent and interesting case is the Dubai Valour (Gulf Azov Shipping v Idisi) Lloyd's Rep [2001] 727 which involved the successful recovery of a payment made to release a crew detained in Nigeria for two years.
Career: Qualified 1985. Joined *Stephenson Harwood* in 1989 and became partner in 1992.
Personal: Born 1959. University College Cardiff BA (Hons) Law and Spanish 1978-82. Married. Interests: wine making and photography. Languages: fluent Spanish, a little French and Italian.

GIBB, Jeremy
Norton Rose, London
(020) 7283 6000
gibbjsp@nortonrose.com
Specialisation: Partner in Banking Department. Principal area of practice is asset finance, especially for ships and aircraft. In particular has considerable expertise in domestic and cross-border leasing structures. In the shipping field has over 15 years experience in the City of London, acting for financiers and owners of all types of vessels, including cruise ships and offshore vessels, and has been involved in numerous FPSO financings. Also deals with acquisition finance, especially acquisition and disposal of leasing companies.
Prof. Memberships: Law Society, Connecticut Maritime Association.

GINSBERG, Roy
Waltons & Morse, London
(020) 7623 4255

GOSLING, James
Holman Fenwick & Willan, London
(020) 7264 8362
james.gosling@hfw.co.uk
Specialisation: Partner in admiralty department. Principal areas of practice are salvage, collision, total loss, pollution and wreck removal, acting mainly for salvors, shipowners, hull underwriters and P and I Clubs. Also handles marine insurance, general shipping and commercial law MOA disputes, charterparty disputes and cargo claims. Important cases have included Scandanavian Star, Europa collision with Inchon Glory, Happy Fellow collision with Darfur, Estrella Pampeana collision with Sea Parana, Smit Tak B.V. v Selco Salvage and Mineral Dampier Collision with Hanjin Madras. Clients include several leading salvage companies, ship owners, hull underwriters, ship managers, insurance brokers and one southern hemisphere tycoon. Is on the editorial board of the *International Maritime Law*. Has lectured on admiralty law in Mexico and Venezuela in Spanish, and in London and Piraeus.
Prof. Memberships: Member of the Instituto Ibero-Americano De Derecho Maritimo.
Career: Qualified in 1980. Became a partner in 1988.
Personal: Born 28 June 1955. Educated at Ampleforth College, York and at St Catharine's College, Cambridge. Leisure interests include rugby, skiing, tennis, sailing, rowing, motor cycling, antiques and crosswords. Speaks French and Spanish. Lives near Saffron Walden.

GRAY, Edward
More Fisher Brown, London
(020) 7247 0438
egray@m-f-b.co.uk
Specialisation: Principal area of practice is dispute resolution advice to ship owners and operators, and their insurers. Specialises in contractual and tortious disputes arising in connection with the carriage of goods by sea, and second-hand sale and purchase contracts and newbuilding contracts. Particular experience with tankers, container vessels and offshore vessels/offshore construction projects. Extensively involved in managing and co-ordinating worldwide multi-jurisdictional disputes. Also advises in contentious and non-contentious matters in the shipping area in connection with EU competition and regulatory matters, sales and acquisitions of businesses, and debt refinancing.
Career: *Richards Butler*, London 1979-83; *Richards Butler*, Hong Kong 1983-91; *More Fisher Brown* since 1992.
Personal: St Edmund Hall, Oxford - BA Jurisprudence, 1st Class Hons.

GREENSMITH, Nicholas
Clyde & Co, Guildford
(01483) 555555
nick.greensmith@clyde.co.uk
Specialisation: Partner in Marine Casualty Department. Main areas of practice are collision, salvage, total loss and wreck removal, general average, towage and ship repair disputes. Important cases include M Vatan (salvage); Reijin (cap-size/wreck removal); Ya Mawlaya/New World (collision); BOS 400 (towage dispute); Sea Empress (grounding/pollution/criminal prosecution).
Prof. Memberships: The Law Society; City of London Admiralty Solicitors Group; Admiralty Court committee; International Harbour Masters Association.
Career: Qualified in 1980. Became a partner in 1984.
Personal: Born 3 March 1955. Educated at William Hulme's GS Manchester and at St Catharine's College, Cambridge. Married with three children. Interests include rugby, football, skiing, golf and sailing.

GRIFFITHS, Paul
Bentleys, Stokes & Lowless, London
(020) 7782 0990
PGriffiths@bentleys.co.uk
Specialisation: The full range of marine, insurance and transport related disputes principally on the 'dry' side. Advice given to a broad spectrum of clients in connection with actual or potential problems and their resolution by negotiation, Court process or arbitration.
Career: Qualified 1979. Partner at *Bentleys, Stokes & Lowless* since 1985.
Personal: Married. Two children.

HARRIS, Graham
Thomas Cooper & Stibbard, London
(020) 7390 2315
graham.harris@tcssol.com
Specialisation: Wide experience of dispute resolution, commercial negotiation and e-commerce in the shipping and transportation industries including shipbuilding, sale and purchase, charterparties, bills of lading, through transport documentation and insurance.
Career: Qualified at *Norton Rose* in October 1981. Joined *Richards Butler* in 1983 as an assistant, becoming a partner in 1988. Graham joined *Thomas Cooper & Stibbard* in July 2001 as a partner. Lectures: E-commerce; Incorporation of charterparty terms into bills of lading; package limitations; letters of credit; electronic bills of lading; Brussels and Lugano Conventions and conflicts of laws; safe ports, agency, through transport issues, Hague-Visby & Hamburg Rules.
Personal: Born 28 September 1956. Educated at King's School, Canterbury and Oriel College, Oxford (MA Jurisprudence, First Class Hons). Lives in London.

HARTLEY, Simon
Norton Rose, London
(020) 7283 6000
hartleysr@nortonrose.com
Specialisation: Specialising in shipping finance representing shipping companies, lessors, banks, export credit agencies and other financial institutions in

connection with all types of ship lending and leasing, capital raising, and related financial arrangements. The shipping finance group is one of the leading shipping finance practices in London, working closely with other *Norton Rose* lawyers experienced in advising shipping industry clients on competition and regulatory matters, taxation, litigation, insurance, mergers and acquisitions and corporate finance for the shipping industry.
Prof. Memberships: Member of the Law Society and Baltic Exchange.
Career: Trained *Norton Rose*; qualified 1988; partner 1997.
Publications: Has been a regular contributor to the 'Economy Shipping Finance Annual' over the last few years.
Personal: Married with one child. Leisure interests are sport and hill walking.

HARVEY, Richard
Richards Butler, London
(020) 7247 6555
rhjph@richardsbutler.com
Specialisation: Heads the firm's casualty response team of mainly legally qualified ex-seafarers, which handles all types of casualty including fires and explosions, groundings, salvage, collisions, wreck removal, reef damage and pollution, and their associated insurance and general average issues. Acts for Clubs, Hull underwriters, shipowners and major salvors. Has handled for owners such cases as the Europa/Inchon Glory, MSC Samia/Carina, Lula 1/Graceous, Polydefkis P/Anna Spiritou collisions and the Sea-Land Mariner fire and explosion. Acted for salvors in the European Gateway and for owners in the salvage of the MSC Rosa M as well as in the Maersk Tokyo, Erika, World Discoverer and Ievoli Sun.
Prof. Memberships: Law Society; British Maritime Law Association; BMLA Arrest Convention sub-committee, City of London Admiralty Solicitors Group.
Career: Served as an officer in the British Merchant Navy before qualifying as a solicitor in 1980. Became a partner in *Richards Butler* in 1983.
Personal: Educated at Christ Church, Oxford (MA); Southampton College of Technology. Interests include sailing, gardening, music, photography and engineering.

HATTERSLEY, Charles
Foot Anstey Sargent, Plymouth
(01752) 675000
charles.hattersley@foot-ansteys.co.uk
Specialisation: Main area of practice is admiralty law including total losses, collision, salvage marine insurance and pollution together with fatal accidents and personal injury claims arising out of such casualties; ship repair and shipbuilding disputes; non-contentious work relating to ship finance, mortgage, security documentation and shipbuilding contracts; expertise in pilot age and Harbour Authority matters. Recent cases: 'Rema'; 'Fleur De Lys'; 'Margaretha Maria' (Court of Appeal); 'Baltic Surveyor' (Court of Appeal); 'Pietertje'.
Prof. Memberships: Nautical Institute; Institute of Directors; CBI; BMIA; BMLA.
Career: 1970-83: Deck officer in submarine service; 1985-89, *Holman Fenwick & Willan*; 1989-91, *Norton Rose*; 1993-2001, *Foot Anstey Sargent*, partner.
Publications: Articles for 'Seaways' (Nautical Institute), 'Lloyd's List', and numerous trade magazines.
Personal: Born 22 March 1949. Attended Marlborough College, 1963-68; Durham University, 1969-71; Law College, 1982-84. Interests include mountaineering, skiing and tennis. Married with three children. Lives in Yelverton, Devon.

HAWKES, Ian
More Fisher Brown, London
(020) 7247 0438
ihawkes@m-f-b.co.uk
Specialisation: Principal areas of practice are charterparty, bill of lading and ship sale and purchase disputes. Also regularly involved in disputes arising from contracts for the international sale of goods.
Career: *Baker & McKenzie*, London 1989-93; *More Fisher Brown* since 1994.

HERRING, Paul
Ince & Co, London
(020) 7623 2011
paul.herring@ince.co.uk
Specialisation: Specialises in carriage of goods by sea, charterparty, bills of lading, sale and purchase and new building disputes. Regular lecturer on charterparty, carriage of goods by sea, sale and purchase issues.
Career: First Class Honours Degree in Law from Leicester University. Articled at *Ince & Co* in 1979 and became a partner in 1987.
Personal: Golf.

HILL, Martin
DLA, Liverpool
(08700) 111111

HILTON, Chris
Eversheds, Newcastle upon Tyne
(0191) 241 6250
chrishilton@eversheds.com
Specialisation: Head of Shipping Department. Shipping and maritime law. Has over 25 years experience in London and Newcastle, including 15 years managing a mutual FD & D association. Experienced in all aspects of maritime law ('wet' and 'dry') and is an arbitrator. Also handles insurance policy work. On various drafting committees of BIMCO.
Prof. Memberships: Chartered Institute of Arbitrators (Fellow); member of the BMLA Committee on Carriage of Goods by Sea.
Career: Qualified 1975. Accredited mediator. Partner *Eversheds* 1976.
Publications: Contributor to 'Practical Guide to Multimodal Transport'.
Personal: Cambridge University 1968-71; Adelaide University in 1972. Enjoys opera, history, travel, sport; REA, Northumberland Golf Club Ltd.

HODGSON, Derek
Clyde & Co, London
(020) 7623 1244
derek.hodgson@clyde.co.uk
Specialisation: Partner in Marine Department. Shipping/marine/insurance. Experienced in representing shipowners/P&I clubs/hull underwriters, charterers and trading companies in High Court actions and arbitrations. Particular speciality in Thailand, Greece, South America and Africa.
Career: Peterhouse School, Marandera; Tonbridge School; UCL (LLB); joined *Clyde & Co* 1977 on qualification; Partner since 1981.

HORTON, Nicholas
Bond Pearce, Plymouth
(01752) 677603
nhorton@bondpearce.com
Specialisation: Partner specialising in shipping and marine work. Full legal service to shipping, insurance and marine industries with particular specialism in yachts, both in the UK and internationally; litigation and commercial contract work; marine insurance; sale and purchase; build and refit contracts; international litigation.
Prof. Memberships: Member of the British Marine Industries Federation, Royal Ocean Racing Club, Royal Western Yacht Club.
Career: Qualified 1986. *Ingledew Brown Bennison & Garrett* 1984-88. Partner *Davies Grant & Horton* 1990-97; co-founder of *Grant & Horton, Marine Solicitors*, 1997-2001; partner *Bond Pearce* 2001.

JACKSON, Peter
Hill Dickinson, Manchester
(0161) 278 8800
Jacko@HillDicks.com
See under Transport, p.802

JOHNSON, Andrew
Hill Taylor Dickinson, London
(020) 7283 9033
andrew.johnson@htd-london.com
Specialisation: Partner in Shipping and Maritime Law Department. Main area of practice is shipping litigation, covering charterparties, bills of lading, collision and salvage. Co-author of 'A Guide to the Hamburg Rules'; contributor to 'Marine Claims'.
Prof. Memberships: Law Society.
Career: Qualified in 1984, having joined *Hill Dickinson* in 1980. Became a Partner in 1987.
Personal: Born 5 February 1955. Lives in London.

JOHNSON, Angus
Stephenson Harwood (incorporating Sinclair Roche & Temperley), London
(020) 7809 2618
angus.johnson@shlegal.com
Specialisation: Partner, shipping litigation. Principal areas of specialisation include oil trading disputes, ship finance disputes and enforcement of security, offshore construction and insurance disputes such as the loss of the 'Mighty Servant 2', and shipping litigation generally in relation to charterparties, bills of lading, and bunker disputes. Important recent cases include Mamidoil Jetoil Greek Petroleum Company v OKTA Crude Oil Refinery (Court of Appeal) (No. 2) [2001] LLR 591; Shell UK Ltd v CLM Engineering & Others [2000] LLR 612; Mamidoil Jetoil Greek Petroleum Company v Okta Crude Oil Refinery [2000] LLR 554; The 'Fjellvang' Seabridge Shipping AB v AC Orssleff EFT A/S [1999] LLR 685; The 'Giuseppe di Vittorio' (No. 2) [1998] LLR 661.
Prof. Memberships: Chartered Institute of Arbitrators; International Bunker Industry Association.
Career: Articled *Stephenson Harwood*; qualified 1989; partner 1998.
Personal: Born 1964. Educated at Gonville and Caius College, Cambridge (1986 BA Hons).

JOHNSON, Jonathan
Davies, Johnson & Co, Plymouth
(01752) 226020
jj@djco.co.uk
Specialisation: Partner specialising in shipping and maritime law. Shipping and maritime law since 1976, also handles commercial litigation work.
Prof. Memberships: LMAA (Supporting), BMIA.
Career: Qualified in 1976. Worked at *Richards Butler* London and Hong Kong 1976-92, became partner in 1980. Joined *Davies Grant & Horton* in 1992 as partner. Founded *Davies, Johnson & Co* May 1997.
Personal: Born 31 March 1951. Attended Nottingham University, taking LLB in 1972. Lives in Plymouth.

JOHNSTON, David
Holmes Hardingham, London
(020) 7280 3200
david.johnston@hhlaw.co.uk
Specialisation: Shipping litigation. All aspects of law pertaining to yachts, including salvage, collision, racing disputes, construction, operation and management, purchase and sale. Particularly marine insurance disputes, policy advice and drafting. Recent cases include 'The Milasan' [2000] 2 LL L Rep 458.
Prof. Memberships: BMIF. Subscriber to YBDSA.
Career: Articled *Paola Wright & Wilkinson*, Durban 1971-72; admitted South Africa 1973. Joined *Ingledew Brown Bennison & Garrett*, London 1974, subsequently admitted in England and appointed partner. Founding partner *Holmes Hardingham* 1989. Managing partner 1989 to date.
Personal: B Com LLB (Natal). Extensive yachting experience under sail and power. Member RYA, CA and local sailing club. Other interests include woodland management and gardening.

SHIPPING ■ THE LEADERS

KELLY, Russell
Lester Aldridge, Southampton
(023) 8082 0416
russell.kelly@lester-aldridge.co.uk
Specialisation: Partner in the shipping and marine department (LA Marine). Specialises in shipping and maritime law; particularly charterparties and contracts for the carriage of goods, defending MCA prosecutions, passenger and crew injury claims, bunker suppliers' claims and claims by repairers and suppliers of goods and services to vessels. Clients include a number of the leading P&I Associations, cruise and ferry operators and overseas law firms. Regularly engaged in Commercial and Admiralty Court litigation and arbitration.
Prof. Memberships: London Maritime Arbitrators Association, BMLA.
Career: Qualified 1986 with *Thomas Cooper & Stibbard*, London, becoming a partner in 1990. Joined *Bond Pearce* 1997. Joined *Lester Aldridge* in 2000.
Personal: Born 1960. Married with two children. Lives near Winchester.

KEMP, Jonathan
Eversheds, Newcastle upon Tyne
(0191) 241 6346
jonathankemp@eversheds.com
Specialisation: Shipping and maritime law. Most work relates to charterparties and commercial shipping dispute resolution. Also deals with port and harbour law, marine insurance and superyacht claims. Acted as arbitrator in two collision claims.
Prof. Memberships: Nautical Institute. Law Society.
Career: Royal Navy (navigating officer) 1976-86. Qualified 1990. Joined *Sinclair Roche & Temperley* in 1988 for articles and practised in Singapore and London. Joined *Eversheds* in 1998.
Personal: Born 1958. Educated at Norwich School and King's College, London. Sports: sailing and skiing.

LAX, Michael
Lawrence Graham, London
(020) 7379 0000

LIVINGSTONE, Hugh
Holman Fenwick & Willan, London
(020) 7264 8547
hugh.livingstone@hfw.co.uk
Specialisation: Partner in commercial litigation department. Specialising in all types of marine litigation on behalf of shipowners, charterers and insurers (P and I and market), as well as sellers and buyers of ships.
Career: Educated University of Cape Town (BA LLB) and University College London (LLM). Admitted 1976 (South Africa), 1985 (England and Wales) and 1986 (Hong Kong). Partner in *Holman Fenwick & Willan* 1986. Resident partner in Hong Kong office 1986-88 and subsequently at London office.

LOWE, James
Henderson Boyd Jackson WS, Edinburgh
(0131) 226 6881
Specialisation: Principal maritime partner. Handles sale and purchase agreements, ship building and financing, ship registration as well as admiralty work; collisions, salvage, marine pollution, ship building and repair contract disputes.
Prof. Memberships: Law Society of Scotland, Honourable Company of Master Mariners, Writer to the Signet, British Maritime Law Association, Nautical Institute.
Career: Ship's Officer 1966-80. Gained Master Mariners Certificate in 1976. Qualified solicitor 1985; assumed partner 1986.
Publications: Author of Maritime Securities in the 'Stair Memorial Encyclopedia' and various articles for legal, marine and fishing industry press.
Personal: Lives East Lothian. Enjoys sailing.

MACKIN, Stephen
Eversheds, Newcastle upon Tyne
(0191) 241 6251
stephenmackin@eversheds.com
Specialisation: Charterparty and bill of lading disputes, particularly 'oil tanker' related disputes. Oil shortage, cargo contamination, off-hire, unsafe port/berth disputes and market loss claims. Liepaya [1999] 1 Lloyd's Rep. 649.
Prof. Memberships: Member of the Nautical Institute.
Career: Qualified 1994. Previously Navigating Officer - Shell Tankers (UK) Ltd (experience of: VLCCs, product tankers, LNG and OBOs).
Personal: Married with two children. Interests include golf and squash. Born 1964.

MACLEAN, Duncan
Henderson Boyd Jackson WS, Edinburgh
(0131) 226 6881
Specialisation: All aspects of contentious shipping and transport work including arrests, cargo claims (sea and land), collisions, marine pollution, personal injury claims in the merchant, offshore and fishing fleets, salvage, ship building and repair disputes, and general commercial disputes. Acts for P&I clubs, insurers, banks, owners, builders and repairers in court and in investigations.
Prof. Memberships: Law Society of Scotland; Writer to the Signet; British Maritime Law Association.
Career: Qualified 1988. Joined *Henderson Boyd Jackson* in 1994. Became partner in 1996.
Publications: Presented papers to marine underwriters, the Nautical Institute and fellow solicitors.
Personal: Married with two daughters. Interests include sports and the outdoors.

MACRAE, Keith
Mackinnons, Aberdeen
(01224) 632464
keith@mackinnons.com
Specialisation: Partner in maritime and litigation department. Acts for marine insurers, covering hull and machinery and P&I. Has particular experience in fishing vessel insurance and claims. Practice split between hull/admiralty work (collisions, salvage, total loss and casualty investigation) and P&I claims (in particular personal accident/employers liability claims from accidents on oil rigs and ships). Also handles oil pollution cases. Work includes on-site investigation on and offshore. Has a substantial case load in the Sheriff Court and Court of Session, acting for Defenders in personal injury claims and for Pursuers in ship repair and ship builders negligence claims and contractual disputes. Gave a paper to Law Society of Scotland's Second Maritime Law Seminar. Presents seminars on Marine Insurance to clients.
Career: Qualified in 1982. Joined *Mackinnons* in 1980, becoming a partner in 1983.
Personal: Born 23 May 1953. Attended Aberdeen University 1971-76 (MA(Hons)) and 1977-80 (LLB). Honorary Norwegian Consul in Aberdeen; Honorary Danish Vice-Consul in Aberdeen. Leisure interests include football, rock and jazz music and travelling. Lives in Catterline.

MCFADYEN, Laurence
Sach Solicitors, London
(020) 7680 1133

MILLS, Guy B
Mills & Co, Newcastle upon Tyne
(0191) 233 2222

MILLS, Stephen
Rayfield Mills, Newcastle upon Tyne
(0191) 261 2333

MOYLAN, Adrian
More Fisher Brown, London
(020) 7247 0438
amoylan@m-f-b.co.uk
Specialisation: Charterparty and bill of lading disputes. Commodity, especially sugar, arbitrations. Marine and non-marine insurance litigation. Reported cases include 'Lutetian', 'Mexico I' and 'Holstencruiser'.
Career: Partner *Richards Butler* 1987; founding partner *More Fisher Brown* 1988-date.
Personal: Cambridge cricket blue 1977, skiing novice, learning Norwegian slowly.

PARTON, Nicholas
Jackson Parton, London
(020) 7702 0085
n.parton@jacksonparton.com
Specialisation: One of the founding partners. Cargo claims, charterparty disputes, collision and salvage, general average, casualty investigations and international trade. Particularly experienced in Francophone Jurisdictions.

PINK, Stephen
Clyde & Co, Guildford
(01483) 555555
stephen.pink@clyde.co.uk
Specialisation: Marine casualty, salvage, collision, general average, 'Ever Decent/Norwegian Dream', 'MSCROSAM', 'MSC Carla', 'CMA Jakarta'.
Career: Joined *Clyde & Co* as school leaver 1969.
Personal: Forest Hill School. Music, golf, photography. Married with three children.

RAYFIELD, Richard
Rayfield Mills, Newcastle upon Tyne
(0191) 261 2333

ROOTH, Tony
Watson, Farley & Williams, London
(020) 7814 8000
trooth@wfw.com
Specialisation: Partner in International Litigation Group. Shipping litigation including charterparty, bill of lading disputes, cargo claiming, maritime casualties and marine insurance (co-editor 'Gard P&I Handbook'). Acts principally for shipowners, charterers, P&I and defence insurers. Focuses on Scandinavia, Continental Europe and Mediterranean countries, especially Greece and Turkey.
Career: Partner *Clyde & Co* 1979-98 (opened their Hong Kong office 1981). Partner *Watson, Farley & Williams* 1998.
Personal: BA Queen's College, Cambridge. Interests: horses, tennis, skiing, theatre.

RUSSELL, Mark
Stephenson Harwood (incorporating Sinclair Roche & Temperley), London
(020) 7809 2600
mark.russell@shlegal.com
Specialisation: Partner, head of banking and asset finance. All aspects of non-contentious shipping law, acting for lenders and shipowners. He specialises in project finance and in the energy, oil and gas and natural resources fields. Lectures on syndicated loans, loan transfers, loan participations and workouts.
Career: Qualified October 1983. *Simmons & Simmons* as assistant solicitor 1983-84. *Sinclair Roche & Temperley* in 1984 and became partner in 1989. Joined *Stephenson Harwood* in 1995 as partner. Head of Ship Finance Group in 1996 and Banking and Asset Finance Group in 2002.
Personal: Born 7 October 1958. Educated at Bradfield College; Bristol University, LLB 2:1 1980. Married with two children. Interests include pig breeding. Resides Harpenden.

RUSTEMEYER, Alistair
Rustemeyer & Co, Hove
(01273) 241807

SHAW, Patrick
Ince & Co, London
(020) 7623 2011
patrick.shaw@ince.co.uk
Specialisation: Has a broad based shipping practice covering both wet (collisions/salvage) and dry (charterparty/sale and purchase/bills of lading). Represents both owners and P&I insurers. Experience of investigating a number of high profile marine casualties.

THE LEADERS — SHIPPING

Career: Joined *Ince & Co* in 1983. 1989-92 in *Ince & Co* Hong Kong and 1992-97 in *Ince & Co* Singapore. Partner since 1991.

SHELTON, John H
Norton Rose, London
(020) 7283 6000
sheltonjh@nortonrose.com
Specialisation: Shipping finance, acting for owners, lenders, lessors, builders, and others.
Prof. Memberships: The Law Society, The Baltic Exchange.
Career: Articled at *Pinsent & Co*, Birmingham, joined *Norton Rose* on qualifying in 1981. Became partner 1987.
Personal: Married, four children. Principal interests: fatherhood and gardening.

SMITH, David
Allen & Overy, London
(020) 7330 3000
david.smith@allenovery.com
See Under Asset Finance, p84

SMITH, Michael J
Mills & Co, Newcastle upon Tyne
(0191) 233 2222

TAYLOR, Andrew
Richards Butler, London
(020) 7772 5881
adt@richardsbutler.com
Specialisation: Partner in shipping unit. Specialises in marine casualty response, charter disputes, cargo liabilities, pollution, marine insurance, P&I clubs, club rules and sale and purchase. Speaker at conferences. Co-author of 'Voyage Charters' - Lloyds of London Press.
Career: Qualified in 1980. Partner at *Richards Butler* since 1983.
Personal: Born 1952. Educated at Magdalen College School and Lincoln College, Oxford (MA).

TAYLOR, Silas
Andrew M. Jackson, Hull
(01482) 325242
swt@amj.co.uk
Specialisation: Main area of practice is marine casualty work. Acts on behalf of all main P&I clubs in collisions, salvage and major personal injury cases. Particular expertise in legal matters relating to the fishing industry. Also deals with disputes in respect of towage, pilotage and hull and machinery claims. Acts as a mediator in shipping and other cases.
Career: Qualified and joined *Andrew M Jackson* in 1975. Became partner in 1980.
Publications: Has contributed articles to 'Lloyd's Maritime and Commercial Law Quarterly', 'Seaways' and 'International Shipping and Transport Lawyer'.
Personal: Born 3 February 1953. Educated at Bedford Modern School 1964-71 and Hull University 1971-74. Leisure pursuits include salmon fishing, football and horticulture.

TAYLOR, Timothy
Hill Taylor Dickinson, London
(020) 7283 9033
tim.taylor@htd-london.com
Specialisation: Partner in Shipping and Insurance Department. Principal area of practice is major international insurance dispute resolution, including marine and war risks, energy, construction all risks, fraud investigation, professional indemnity, reinsurance, political risks and general coverage disputes. Major cases include the 'Stena Nautica', 'Popi M', 'Zinovia', 'Michael', 'Piper Alpha', 'Bowbelle/Marchioness', 'Wondrou, S&W Berisford v New Hampshire', 'Exxon Valdez', 'Goodwyn A', 'Ya Mawalaya' and 'P-36'.
Prof. Memberships: Chairman British Maritime Law Association Standing Committee on Marine Insurance.
Career: Qualified 1978 while with *Hill Dickinson & Co*, Partner 1982. CEDR Registered Mediator (since 1997). Occasionally sits as an arbitrator and writes and speaks regularly on a range of insurance and shipping issues.
Publications: Contributor to 'Communicating out of a Crisis' by Michael Bland (Macmillan Press, 1998).

THOMAS, Tony
Clyde & Co, Guildford
(01483) 31161
Tony.Thomas@clyde.co.uk
See under Transport, p.804

THORP, Clive
Barlow Lyde & Gilbert, London
(020) 7247 2277
cthorp@blg.co.uk
Specialisation: Consultant in the shipping department. Main areas of practice are charterparties, commodities, oil, freezing injunctions, search orders, payment of judgment debts, sovereign immunity and demurrage arbitrations. Also handles enforcement of judgments. Acted in 'Sonangol v Lundquist', privilege against self-incrimination; and 'Griparion' on indemnity costs. Lectures on Mareva injunctions, demurrage, time charters and shipbroker commissions.
Prof. Memberships: Member of Law Society Committee on Arbitration Act 1996.
Career: Qualified 1976. Worked at *Holman Fenwick and Willan* 1976-79, joining *Clyde & Co.* in 1979. Became partner in 1982. Joined *Barlow Lyde & Gilbert* as a consultant in 2001.
Personal: Born 28 August 1950. Attended Malvern College 1963-68, Hull University 1969-72 and College of Law. Common Councillor. City of London Committee Member London Court of International Arbitration. Vice President, Association for Research into Stammering in Childhood. Married, two children.

TURNER, Paul
Clifford Chance, London
(020) 7600 1000
Specialisation: Litigation and Dispute Resolution Department. Partner specialising in transactional shipping work of all kinds including shipbuilding and ship conversion projects, ship sale and purchase, joint ventures, corporate acquisitions and sales, financing, mortgage registration and enforcement.
Career: Articled *Clifford Chance*, qualified 1987; Partner since 1995.
Personal: Millford School; 1976-80 Peterhouse, Cambridge (MA); 1981 Called to the Bar, Middle Temple, London.

VLASTO, Tony
Clifford Chance, London
(020) 7600 1000
tony.vlasto@cliffordchance.com
Specialisation: Litigation and Dispute Resolution Department. Partner specialising in all aspects of casualty work and general maritime work including charterparty and bill of lading disputes, offshore oil disputes, marine insurance litigation/arbitration and sale and purchase disputes.
Career: Joined *Coward Chance* 1973; qualified 1975; Partner since 1981.
Personal: LLB 1972.

WAGLAND, Nigel
Barlow Lyde & Gilbert, London
(020) 7247 2277
nwagland@blg.co.uk
Specialisation: Head of Shipping, Transport and International Trade department. Acts for clients in all areas of shipping and marine insurance, for one of the world's largest parcel carriers and also in disputes relating to the rail industry. Clients also include large international trading companies, procurement agencies and the UK and overseas governments. High profile cases last year included 'PETRO RANGER' (High Court - piracy) and 'HAPPY RANGER' (Court of Appeal - bills of lading).
Prof. Memberships: LMAA and BMLA.
Career: Qualified 1980; *Field Fisher & Martineau* 1978-81; *William A Crump* 1981-91; *Barlow Lyde & Gilbert* 1991 to date.
Personal: School: Merchant Taylors School, Northwood. University: Birmingham. Married with two sons (ages 13 and 11).

WALLIS, Robert
Hill Taylor Dickinson, London
(020) 7283 9033
Specialisation: Admiralty law, particularly Collision, Salvage, Wreck Removal, Total Loss, Pollution Claims, Limitation of Liability and Marine Insurance Litigation.
Prof. Memberships: Law Society and Solicitors' European Group, British Maritime Law Association, CMI Sub-committee on LoF 95, International Bar Association, Asia-Pacific Lawyers' Association.
Career: Leicester University LLB 1972, qualified 1975, Partner with *Elborne Mitchell* 1976-88, joined *Hill Taylor Dickinson* as Partner 1988. Elected Chairman of Partnership 1999. CEDR accredited mediator.
Personal: Born 1950, married with two children. Interests include golf, tennis and rugby.

WATLING, John
Jackson Parton, London
(020) 7702 0085
j.watling@jacksonparton.com
Specialisation: Shipping and insurance litigation on behalf of cargo interests, charterers, shipowners, insurers. Last year represented the successful parties in the 'Mercandian Continent' a decision of the Court of Appeal concerning the Duty of Good Faith.
Prof. Memberships: The Law Society, supporting member of London Maritime Arbitrators Association.
Career: Assistant solicitor *Bentleys, Stokes & Lowless* 1985-91; Assistant solicitor *Waltons & Morse* 1991-93. Partner *Jackson Parton* 1993 to date.
Personal: Latymer Upper School, University of East Anglia, College of Law Lancaster Gate 1980-82. Sailing, swimming, music. Married with three children.

WATSON, Martin
Watson, Farley & Williams, London
(020) 7814 8000
mwatson@wfw.com
Specialisation: Partner in International Finance Group. Main area of practice is ship finance, covering international finance, commercial leasing, banking, asset finance and corporate restructuring.
Career: Founding Partner of *Watson, Farley & Williams* 1982.
Personal: Educated at St Catharine's College, Cambridge (BA).

WESTON, John
John Weston & Co, Felixstowe
(01394) 282527

WILLIAMS, Paul
Norton Rose, London
(020) 7283 6000
williamspl@nortonrose.com
Specialisation: Paul Williams is a partner in the shipping litigation group. Whilst involved in all aspects of shipping disputes, he specialises in major casualties on behalf of shipowners, P&I Clubs and underwriters, as well as personal injuries. Paul has become a particular expert in multi-party disaster litigation and has wide experience in court and arbitration proceedings, both in England and internationally.
Prof. Memberships: Paul is a member of the British Maritime Law Association and the Baltic Exchange. He is also a supporting member of the London Maritime Arbitration Association.
Career: Trained *Norton Rose*, qualified 1982 and made partner 1990.
Personal: Pembroke College, Cambridge (MA).

WILSON, James
Ince & Co, London
(020) 7623 2011
james.wilson@ince.co.uk
Specialisation: James initially worked mainly on the charterparty and cargo claims side of the firm's business. In later years however, he has concentrated more

www.ChambersandPartners.com 751

SHIPPING — THE LEADERS

on the 'wet' side of the practice and has been increasingly involved in marine casualties. James now leads *Ince & Co's* renowned casualty team which has acted for the owners of and insurers of nearly all the world's major casualties in recent years. His client base is drawn from across the maritime industry and includes owners, clubs and marine underwriters. James is qualified both in England and Hong Kong and has an active practice as a commercial mediator.
Prof. Memberships: CEDR registered mediator. Member of Baltic Exchange.
Career: James graduated from Cambridge with an Honours Degree in Law. He joined *Ince* in 1983. He became a partner in 1991.
Publications: Co-author of the admiralty section of 'Halisbury's Laws of England'.

WILSON, Robert
Holman Fenwick & Willan, London
(020) 7264 8340
robert.wilson@hfw.co.uk
Specialisation: Partner in commercial litigation department and senior partner of the firm. Principal area of practice is shipping and commercial law. Work covers commercial legal advice, handling and resolving disputes, negotiations, conducting litigation and arbitration including newbuildings; conversion and repair (ship/offshore); MOA; pools; charters; bills of lading; P and I and defence club work; marine insurance (including total losses); international trade, especially tankers and the oil trade. Also deals with insurance, commercial and banking law where related to shipping and trading interests. House of Lords and Court of Appeal cases include Delfini (title to sue), Kyzikos (laytime), Evpo Agnic (arrest), Arta (shipbrokers negligence), Apj Priti (safe berth) and Padre Island (P&I club/third party claims), Factortame (European law) and Haji-Ioannou v Frangos (European Convention and ship arrests).
Prof. Memberships: Law Society, London Maritime Arbitrators Association (supporting member).
Career: Qualified in 1977, having joined *Holman Fenwick & Willan* in 1975. Became a partner in 1982. Appointed senior partner in November 2000.
Personal: Born 8 February 1952. Educated at Watford Grammar School 1962-69 and Corpus Christi College, Cambridge 1970-74 (MA Maths, History; Law). Interests include family, golf and travel. Lives in Hadley Wood, Herts.

WINTER, Glenn
Holmes Hardingham, London
(020) 7280 3200
Glenn.Winter@HHLaw.co.uk
Specialisation: Main areas of specialisation are charterparty disputes and bulk liquid cargo claims. Major cases handled include 'The Mito' (1987), 'The Stena Pacifica' (1990), 'The Holstencruiser' (1992) and 'The Stolt Sydness' (1996), 'The Sun Sapphire' (1999) and 'The Erika' (2000).
Career: Qualified in 1982. Senior partner of *Holmes Hardingham*.
Personal: Attended Keble College, Oxford and the University of Illinois. Born 7 May 1956. Married with two children.

SOCIAL HOUSING

London: 753; The Regions: 756; Scotland: 760; Profiles: 761

Research approved by BMRB For this edition, **Chambers'** researchers conducted 6,582 interviews – 3,900 with law firms, 511 with barristers and 2,171 with clients. The validity of the research was scrutinised by BMRB International, who audited both the methodology and the results at our offices in London. They interviewed **Chambers'** researchers and cross-checked sample interviews. Details of the audit appear on page 7.

OVERVIEW The emphasis in the social housing sector has swung away from traditional, pure housing work towards larger, more complex transactions. Stock transfers, regeneration schemes and varied projects involving PFI, such as key worker accommodation, are all on the increase. The impact of the Care Standards Act 2000 has begun to be felt this year, with the sector receiving a greater focus as homes are brought up to the standards laid down in the Act. This has necessitated a rationalisation within the industry, with registered social landlords (RSLs) and housing associations (HAs) increasingly merging, acquiring or swapping stock in order to stay competitive. As a result, the way in which they do business is altering. Advice on corporate governance and housing management is now a major source of instructions for many firms. As HAs have expanded their capacity and services to meet market demands, employment issues have become more prominent, particularly those that relate to senior positions. Similarly, RSLs are looking again at their tenancy agreements to determine the precise parameters of their obligations and rights.

LONDON

SOCIAL HOUSING — LONDON

1
- Trowers & Hamlins

2
- Devonshires

3
- Jenkins & Hand
- Lewis Silkin
- Prince Evans
- Winckworth Sherwood

4
- Lawrence Graham

5
- Evans Butler Wade
- Maclay Murray & Spens

6
- Coudert Brothers
- GL Hockfield & Co
- Hodge Jones & Allen

LEADING INDIVIDUALS

1
- ADLINGTON Jonathan — Trowers & Hamlins
- BASTOW Gillian — Lewis Silkin
- GRAHAM Ian — Trowers & Hamlins
- JENKINS Keith — Jenkins & Hand
- MURRAY Andrew — Winckworth Sherwood
- ROBERT Louis — Prince Evans

2
- DOOLITTLE Ian — Trowers & Hamlins
- HAND Catherine — Jenkins & Hand
- MORLEY Trevor — Prince Evans

3
- BILLINGHAM Nick — Devonshires
- BROWN Duncan — Devonshires
- EVANS Chris — Evans Butler Wade
- FITTON Roger — Winckworth Sherwood
- GOODE Naomi — Jenkins & Hand
- HALL Gareth — Devonshires
- HAWKINS James — Trowers & Hamlins
- MURRAY Lynne — Lewis Silkin
- RANDALL Simon — Lawrence Graham
- SMITH Chris — Maclay Murray & Spens

This book is the product of 6,582 1/2 hour interviews. See p.7 for BMRB audit. Within each band, firms are listed alphabetically. See individuals' profiles p.761

TROWERS & HAMLINS (see firm details p.1168) Still commanding the sector imperiously, the team "*never lacks depth of resources.*" A leader on issues of banking, governance and stock transfers for RSLs, the experience and knowledge at the firm is unparalleled. It remains the first choice for clients involved in prominent or complex transactions. The sharp London office remains more than "*able to scoop the top-end work.*" It has recently focused on larger projects, frequently funded on a private finance basis, while still handling a high volume of transactions. Its capacious housing team now acts for over 250 RSLs in some capacity, with lawyers linking freely with the firm's partnership, construction and engineering units. For example, the team advised Broomleigh HA in the provision of student accommodation at The Bittoms, Kingston. This included the development of the residence, and subsequent leasing and facilities management services over a 30-year term.

Property head **Jonathan Adlington** (see p.761) has been instrumental in shaping the practice, according to competitors, via a combination of good client management skills and an easy-going approach. "*Practical, knowledgeable*" **Ian Graham** (see p.763) led a team assisting Hereward HA and the MHA Care Group on the transfer and subsequent leaseback of three homes from Cambridgeshire County Council. Commended to researchers for the quality of his market relations, he also acted on behalf of the Western Challenge and Medina Housing Groups on the creation of a new merged association. Public sector and environment head **Ian Doolittle** (see p.762) brings his own considerable local government experience to bear on housing issues, while **James Hawkins** (see p.763) was particularly recommended for his negotiation and transfer abilities. **Clients** Carillion; Horizon Housing Group; Moat Housing Group; Network HA; Presentation HA.

DEVONSHIRES (see firm details p.936) Known for its traditional approach, the group is described by peers as "*a forceful firm that stands up strongly and positively for its clients' interests.*" Working in conjunction with its property, public sector and PFI teams, the department has "*made great strides in acquisitions for HAs,*" swelling its already large caseload. A reputation for being good value, allied to increased referrals from public sector bodies and from within the care home sector, has helped to broaden the firm's appeal.

Large-scale, non-grant funded property work for developers and advice on particularly complex transfers are its most important spheres of activity, though it also has a high profile for funding transactions. The dedicated, good-sized team has applied its "*wide spectrum of expertise*" assisting several charities with enquiries concerning subsidiaries and *vires* issues. This has included advice to Flagship Group and Spelthorne Housing on their conversion to charitable status. It has also acted on the innovative creation of the first faith-based regeneration company, Faith in the Future, in North London. The firm's high profile in contentious matters continues, with several cases being conducted this year in the higher courts by **Nick Billingham**'s (see p.762) "*common sense, confident and practical*" housing management team. These ranged from considerations of a tenant's notice to quit to the subletting of RSL properties.

Duncan Brown (see p.762) of the firm's PFI and public sector team advises a growing number of local authorities and NHS trusts, while **Gareth Hall** (see p.763) has also contributed to its overall success, receiving warm recommendations from clients. The firm has aided Circle 33 Housing Trust on the £57 million acquisition of a Warner Estate company, and on a similar deal concerning the purchase of part of the former Leytonstone Hospital site from Tesco Stores for a mixed residential and commercial development. **Clients** Circle 33 Housing Trust; Flagship Group; Notting Hill Home Ownership; Spelthorne Housing; Ujima Housing Association.

SOCIAL HOUSING ■ LONDON

JENKINS & HAND (see firm details p.1014) Bursting with experience, the reputation of the firm's two eponymous partners is without question. They are said by peers to have "*a feel for the sector and what clients want.*" Able to handle "*intellectually challenging roles,*" the small size of the firm means that it is not generally seen in volume transactions or litigious work outside of employment. However, recent growth may indicate an organic approach to expansion.

Its "*considerable knowledge*" of group structures and corporate governance matters are the keystones of the practice. "*Innovative and adroit,*" with a practical approach, **Keith Jenkins** assisted Nucleus HA on its group reorganisation. Also admired by the market, **Catherine Hand** represented Hastings' 1066 HA in becoming part of the Amicus group, involving advice on rule changes and their implications. She is also well known for her work on domiciliary care contracts and charity-related matters, including work for Housing 21 on the Ash Grange scheme for elderly people in Liverpool, developing two tower blocks and associated land. Recently joining from Winckworth Sherwood, **Naomi Goode** (see p.763) has already made an impact among interviewees, who consider her "*a rising star.*" The firm took on the transfer of 300 TUPE staff contracts for a city council and is still involved on some stock transfers, such as one for Mid Bedfordshire District Council. It has also represented a number of tenants' groups, in connection with innovative schemes, including work for the tenants of Help the Aged. **Clients** 1066 HA; Housing 21; Mid Bedfordshire District Council; Solon Community Network; Tenant Participation Advisory Service; William Sutton Trust.

LEWIS SILKIN (see firm details p.1041) Interviewees believe that this property-oriented firm has been more visible during the past year. In addition to a general focus on regeneration projects, head of department **Gillian Bastow** (see p.761) has been busy on schemes to set up or reorganise the corporate structures and procedures of certain RSLs. Recommended by clients for her "*sound, practical advice,*" she acted for two RSLs purchasing former school playing fields for a housing development, which included affordable housing and a new sports facility. New to our tables this year, and a "*dominant presence*" in the market, **Lynne Murray** (see p.764) assisted Ealing Family HA in the transfer to it of 11 residential care homes from the London Borough of Barnet for a 15-year period. This included all drafting and advice on associated pension schemes, guarantees and bonds.

As well as the transfer market, the team has worked on a variety of acquisitions and regeneration schemes involving RSLs, local authorities and private developers. Contentious work has included a successful action on behalf of Waltham Forest CBHA concerning whether an assured tenancy that had lapsed due to non-occupation and subletting could be revived by a tenant. **Clients** Bede HA; Broomleigh HA; Cambridge Housing Society; Harding HA; Horizon Housing Group; Housing 21; Hyde Housing Group; Kelsey HA; Keniston HA; Passmore HA; Pavilion HA; Peabody Trust; St Pancras & Humanist HA; Waltham Forest CBHA.

PRINCE EVANS (see firm details p.1106) The team is buoyed by the presence of "*class operator*" **Louis Robert** (see p.764), who boasts "*a huge amount of experience in difficult areas, and is involved in every part of the transaction.*" He won enthusiastic praise from all corners of the market; however some interviewees questioned whether the team wasn't overdependent upon him for its market profile. He recently assisted funding vehicle Ealing Family HA on the establishment of a £125 million syndicated loan facility to assist a regeneration project in North London. Also respected by market sources, **Trevor Morley** (see p.764) distinguished himself by being recommended for both his development and his funding work. The firm has acted for Brent Council in establishing its Arms Length Management Organisation (ALMO) and the transfer of the management of its housing stock to it. It has also busied itself with a number of constitutional revisions and site redevelopments for housing groups. **Clients** Acton HA; Brent MBC; Ealing Family HA; London & Quadrant Housing Trust; Quintain Estates & Development; Teachers Support Network.

WINCKWORTH SHERWOOD (see firm details p.1192) Finding no evidence that departures from the team over the past few years have seriously affected its market profile, *Chambers* research instead indicates that the "*bright and switched-on*" figure of "*lynchpin*" **Andrew Murray** (see p.764) has not only steadied the ship but has set it moving forward once more. Clients speak of a team that has an "*understanding of the housing market, and is able to negotiate and define key issues.*" Described as proactive and responsive, **Roger Fitton** (see p.763) was also recommended.

Regeneration and special projects work has been a key factor in the firm's growth. It has advised Notting Hill Housing Trust and the Genesis Housing Group on the Grahame Park regeneration project with the London Borough of Barnet. Its expertise has been put to use in the development, leasing and financing of the second phase of further staff accommodation for the Special Trustees of Great Ormond Street Hospital, a project which mirrored the team's work on behalf of Thames Valley HA on the outsourcing of its own special needs accommodation to three RSLs. Hanover HA also instructed the firm on the transfer from the London Borough of Hackney of their sheltered housing stock. **Clients** Genesis Housing Group; Hanover HA; Hundred Housing Association; Notting Hill Housing Trust; Opendoor Housing Group; Parchment Housing Group; Pavilion HA; Southern Housing Group; Thames Valley HA.

LAWRENCE GRAHAM (see firm details p.1031) The firm's work in this sector is still overshadowed by its dominating presence in the LSVT market, where it has transferred nearly 200,000 homes over the past year. Perhaps less known in the wider market are the firm's financial and corporate efforts on behalf of clients following transfers, representing RSLs nationwide on facilities enabling them to purchase homes and fund further development. With additional experience from his chairmanship of Broomleigh HA, **Simon Randall** leads a small enthusiastic team with instant recourse to strong, related resources. He assisted West Wiltshire Housing society as it took charge of the District Council's remaining stock, including negotiating a £100 million refinancing deal and converting the Society to a company limited by guarantee. Clients say the team gives "*easily understandable, timely advice*" and is "*totally up to speed, professional and efficient.*"

The firm assisted two housing bodies on the creation of a group structure and assisted the London Borough of Brent on its involvement with Stonebridge Housing Action Trust to regenerate the Stonebridge estate. It is regularly instructed by RSLs over discrimination claims at industrial tribunals. **Clients** 1066 HA; Aldwyck HA; Atlantic HG; CDS Housing; Dane Housing (Congleton); East Dorset HA; Evesham & Pershore HA; Harding HA; Horizon HG; Hyelm; Rother Homes; South Oxfordshire HA; Spa HA; Twynham HA; West Wiltshire HS; Worthing Homes.

EVANS BUTLER WADE Although not as visible as some of its larger competitors, the housing group at the firm emerged from *Chambers*' research with its reputation enhanced. Clients' favourite **Chris Evans** was the beneficiary of some effusive praise from peers, who particularly highlighted his extensive workload. **Clients** Housing associations; RSLs.

MACLAY MURRAY & SPENS (see firm details p.1048) A smaller team working almost exclusively on non-contentious housing work, the group co-operates with other departments to provide a comprehensive service. London leader **Chris Smith** (see p.765) is considered by peers to be "*a specialist with lots of experience.*" His vigorous team has notably assisted three RSLs on the development of a completely new settlement in Cambridge. Acquisitions on behalf of RSLs constitute a large proportion of its work, exemplified by the purchase of a 250-home site with associated amenities on the South coast. The firm is also involved in funding work for lenders. **Clients** Beacon HA; Bradford & Bingley; Guinness Trust; Hanover HA; Kelsey HA; Pavilion HA; Royal Bank of Scotland.

COUDERT BROTHERS (see firm details p.920) Despite being better known for other areas of work, the firm can deal efficiently with clients in the social housing sector and bring in heavy-

LONDON ■ SOCIAL HOUSING

weight support as and when required. London property head Anne O'Neill's team has a particular focus in this field on acquisitions and development work for HAs and investors. Sample work has included advice on a mixed public/private residential development in North London and associated regeneration schemes. **Clients** Notting Hill Housing Trust Group; Soho HA.

GL HOCKFIELD & CO (see firm details p.997) James Garvey heads a compact, down-to-earth unit tilted towards contentious work. A "*well-managed*" and professional team represents HAs against anti-social tenants, on matters ranging from injunctions to possessions, while also advising a fair number of tenants. The firm does also act on some housing management issues and development projects as well as providing assistance on property and commercial leasework transactions for HAs. **Clients** Genesis Housing Group; North West London HA; Octavia Housing & Care; Peabody Trust; Southern Housing Group; Walterton & Elgin Community Homes.

HODGE JONES & ALLEN (see firm details p.997) Acting more on behalf of tenants and leaseholders than HAs, the firm's housing unit is an important, if smaller, part of its work. The friendly, legal aid-funded firm has experienced year-on-year growth and is praised for its accessibility, efficacy and cost-effectiveness. **Clients** Housing associations; RSLs.

ADVISING LENDERS – NATIONWIDE

SOCIAL HOUSING: ADVISING LENDERS
■ LONDON

1. Clifford Chance
2. Addleshaw Booth & Co
3. Denton Wilde Sapte
   Trowers & Hamlins
4. Allen & Overy
   Devonshires

LEADING INDIVIDUALS

1. **PANTELIA Despina** Clifford Chance
2. **CARTER Adrian** Trowers & Hamlins
   COWAN Andrew Devonshires
   PAPWORTH Richard Addleshaw Booth & Co
3. **HAYES Sarah** Trowers & Hamlins
   ROBERTS Ian Denton Wilde Sapte
   ONES TO WATCH
   ELPHICKE Natalie Denton Wilde Sapte

This book is the product of 6,582 1/2 hour interviews. See p.7 for BMRB audit. Within each band, firms are listed alphabetically. See individuals' profiles p.761

CLIFFORD CHANCE (see firm details p.911) The firm's reputation as a global financial powerhouse holds true. While some query its understanding of the intricacies of the social housing market, its related expertise in banking, project and property finance matters ensure it retains top billing. More importantly, clients referred to the "*seamless interface*" between dedicated teams, while peers would "*consider them first for large-scale, complex or innovative transactions.*" Comprehensively respected for her abilities and well-liked among both peers and clients, **Despina Pantelia** (see p.764) ("*well-networked*") continues to lead a small, personable core team with unrivalled support. Her pragmatic and commercial approach is considered valuable as is her "*great ability to simplify the most complex transactions.*" The firm has again maintained its choice role advising on the Government's transfer programme and its complex funding arrangements, including transfers to HAs within a group structure. **Clients** Abbey National; Bank of Scotland; Barclays Bank; BNP Paribas; Nationwide Building Society, Royal Bank of Scotland.

ADDLESHAW BOOTH & CO (see firm details p.838) Competitors acknowledge that the firm "*gives Clifford Chance a good run for its money.*" A lenders' firm only, its forthright approach has been applied on stock transfer funding work for the majority of building societies in the sector and across mainstream HA lending. **Richard Papworth** (see p.108) alone has been responsible for billions of pounds worth of financings in the sector and he is said to "*devote a considerable amount of time to personally making sure his clients get the service they want.*" He is backed by an experienced team that advised on Nationwide Building Society's purchase of Paribas' substantial social housing loan book. The team has also advised Bradford & Bingley on the £111 million financing for the transfer of Calderdale BC's housing stock to Pennine Housing 2000, and has assisted on Redcar's LSVT, one of the largest undertaken this year. Significantly, the firm is also offering wider, strategic advice to the Council of Mortgage lenders on proposed consultations and revisions to the Enterprise Bill, which is currently going through Parliament. **Clients** Bradford & Bingley; Britannia Building Society; Dexia Crédit Local; Leeds & Holbeck Building Society; NatWest Bank; Nationwide Building Society; RBS Housing Finance.

DENTON WILDE SAPTE (see firm details p.935) The firm was commended by interviewees for its capacity to field a robust, cross-departmental team. This is underlined by its appointment by the Royal Bank of Scotland to act as arranger on the £151 million group funding for the Swan Housing Group, a structure, that involved a charitable subsidiary comprising both general needs and key worker facilities. **Ian Roberts** (see p.765) leads a well-resourced unit. It has acted on behalf of a syndicate of lenders over the £283 million Bedfordshire Pilgrims HA LSVT refinancing. The same clients also instructed the firm as joint underwriters for a £350 million two-stage group funding for the Anglia Housing Group, which included the direct funding of a LSVT into a group structure. **Clients** Halifax; HBOS Group; Nationwide Building Society; Royal Bank of Scotland.

TROWERS & HAMLINS (see firm details p.1168) Belying its reputation as a borrowers counsel, work for lenders takes up the majority of this firm's time. Competitors respect its "*strength in depth and a 360-degree understanding of all the stakes.*" Clients reported that the team "*rarely drops the ball and the work is of a consistently high quality.*" **Adrian Carter** (see p.762) ("*a businessman, good at getting deals done,*") leads a credible, dedicated unit, which "*knows the specific issues.*" He has aided Dexia Crédit Local on its hedging transactions with Raglan HA and its £10 million loan facility for Hanover HA, which utilised income-based property covenants rather than the standard asset cover security test. The pragmatic **Sarah Hayes** (see p.763) assisted Abbey National Treasury Services on a £50 million bilateral loan to Home HA. "*A leading academic light,*" she has worked with Prime Focus Housing Group on its £210 million borrowing. **Clients** Abbey National Treasury Services; Bedfordshire Pilgrims HA; Dexia Crédit Local; Lloyds TSB Bank; BNP Paribas; Places for People; Prime Focus Finance; Town & Country HG.

ALLEN & OVERY (see firm details p.841) Clients told *Chambers* that the firm was certainly "*able to make the leap to specific social housing matters - but we didn't hire them for their expertise in that.*" Like other firms in this field, lead partners such as Andrew Joyce are derived from its banking and corporate arms. A market leader in bond issues, such transactions have been limited over the last year, which has resulted in a recent lowering of its visibility. The firm has advised on group structures and the increasing division of RSLs and their subsidiaries into charitable and non-charitable groups. **Clients** Abbey National; Halifax; Nationwide; Royal Bank of Canada Europe; Royal Bank of Scotland.

DEVONSHIRES (see firm details p.936) The firm's funding side now accounts for almost a third of the social housing work undertaken. A meticulous core team is commended by peers as "*battling on behalf of the borrower.*" Lead partner **Andrew Cowan** (see p.762) is renowned for his robust style: "*he is fantastic at getting out there*

SOCIAL HOUSING ■ THE SOUTH/THAMES VALLEY

and winning clients." He has led the team on a large number of transactions on both sides of the funding fence. These have included volume work for RSLs on vanilla borrowings and larger funding facilities, such as the £170 million loan for New Downland HA. On the lenders side, it has advised Lloyds TSB on five facilities. **Clients** Bradford & Bingley; Bondway; CDS Housing; Circle 33; Faith in the Future; Flagship Group; HBOS; Hyde Housing Association; Liver Housing (now Arena); Lloyds TSB; National Housing Federation; New Downland HA; Royal Bank of Scotland; Spelthorne Housing; Thames Reach.

THE SOUTH

SOCIAL HOUSING — THE SOUTH

1. **Coffin Mew & Clover** Portsmouth
2. **Cripps Harries Hall** Tunbridge Wells
   Marsons Solicitors Bromley
   Sharratts Westerham
3. **DMH** Brighton
   Penningtons Basingstoke, Newbury

LEADING INDIVIDUALS

1. **BENNETT Jennifer** Coffin Mew & Clover

This book is the product of 6,582 1/2 hour interviews. See p.7 for BMRB audit.
Within each band, firms are listed alphabetically. See individuals' profiles p.761

COFFIN MEW & CLOVER This dedicated, knowledgeable and expanding social housing unit is headed by **Jennifer Bennett** (see p.761). She was recommended to *Chambers*' researchers as a top choice, comparable to leading London practitioners "*for her knowledge of the market and practical, commercial take on various issues.*" She led a team, capable of handling large deals, on the securitisation of rent schemes for HAs, including one involving the completion of 200 certificates of title in 12 weeks. Commended for its "*expertise, high speed and quality,*" her team has been involved in several joint venture schemes for redevelopment and regeneration. The landlord-focused group majors on housing management matters, including advice on service charges for LSVTs and the validity of rent review notices for RSLs. It also offers assistance on corporate governance issues, and is making a movement into funding work, recently negotiating a £22 million facility for a large PFI key worker accommodation scheme. **Clients** Drum HA; Eastleigh HA; Hampshire Voluntary HA; Hermitage HA; Hyde HA; New Downland HA; Parchment HG; Portsmouth HA; Signpost HA; Testway Housing; Town & Country HG; Western Challenge HA; Winchester HA.

CRIPPS HARRIES HALL (see firm details p.922) Under the leadership of Michael Stevens, the firm has maintained steady progress. According to peers, it possesses "*a good development side*" and a range of experience in the funding and transactional side of the sector. In common with many firms in the region, it can draw on a wide range of clients. **Clients** Housing Associations; RSLs.

MARSONS SOLICITORS Strong in the contentious side of the sector, the firm boasts an outstanding reputation for its work on nuisance and adverse possession orders on behalf of RSLs. Gerard O'Toole heads up a team with broad experience of dealing with excessively noisy or abusive tenants. Updating housing officers on changes in the law is another area of staple activity for the group. **Clients** Housing associations; RSLs.

SHARRATTS Relocating from London this year to new premises in Westerham, the firm's straightforward attitude has been applied to all non-contentious, property-related aspects of social housing. A good portfolio of clients comprises RSLs and some national house builders. Richard Locke's compact team has particular experience of the purchase and disposal of shared ownership sites and affordable housing developments, including a 166-unit scheme in central London. **Clients** Crest Partnership Homes; Fairview New Homes; Moat Housing Group; Threshold Housing.

DMH (see firm details p.940) Co-operating closely with the firm's property litigation team, typical work tends to be split between planning and development, and property enforcement. Tina George heads up a confident team that, increasingly, is involved in judicial reviews and other cases in the higher courts. As an illustration, the firm acted successfully in London Borough of Wandsworth v Mowan, in the Court of Appeal. This concerned the council's liability for breach of covenant following noise nuisance suffered by a tenant, which was caused by a second tenant with mental health problems. Recent client wins include Reigate & Banstead HA. **Clients** Brighton HT; Reigate & Banstead HA; Sanctuary HA; Wandsworth BC; Warden HA.

PENNINGTONS (see firm details p.1098) Based within the firm's litigation group, Jonathan Rouse leads a balanced team with a particular speciality in property-related matters, from right to buy work through to shared ownership. The team has the advantage of operating from a network of regional offices, and its size compares favourably with many of its nearest geographical competitors. It represents two of the larger regional HAs on all matters barring rent collection and repossessions. **Clients** Sentinel HA; Sovereign HA.

THAMES VALLEY

SOCIAL HOUSING — THAMES VALLEY

1. **Owen White** Slough
2. **Manches** Oxford
3. **Sherrards** St Albans

LEADING INDIVIDUALS

1. **BRAUN Simon** Sherrards

This book is the product of 6,582 1/2 hour interviews. See p.7 for BMRB audit.
Within each band, firms are listed alphabetically. See individuals' profiles p.761

OWEN WHITE This partner-led team was applauded by clients for providing "*a comprehensive range of advice.*" The group is large enough to take on substantial transactions and is known for its work in development. The firm also provides in-house training to HAs on tenancy law, human rights and management issues. The unit has worked on several NHS stock transfers for existing clients, and on matters concerning low-cost home ownership and key worker accommodation. Partner Phil Lawrence and his colleagues have also assisted on several contentious matters, including the eviction of five tenants on drugs and firearms charges. **Clients** Housing associations; RSLs.

MANCHES (see firm details p.1052) The firm has consolidated its efforts over the past year, following the retirement of Richard Frost. Paul Butterworth's team is increasingly active in regeneration schemes and project development work. It has completed an NHS trust PFI deal to provide key worker accommodation, which is an area of focus for the team. It has also acted on Phase II of a regeneration scheme for Christian Action (Enfield) HA. The team is experienced in funding, predominantly on behalf of RSLs, and has acted in a refinancing exercise for Swan Housing Group that included intragroup transfers. The increase in contentious matters has led to the recruitment of a dedicated housing litigator to the team. **Clients** Christian Action (Enfield) HA; Granta Housing Trust;

SOUTH WEST/WALES ■ SOCIAL HOUSING

Guinness Trust; Hampshire Voluntary Housing Society; Jephson HA; Lee HA; Sanctuary HA; Sarsen HA; Swan HG; Vale HA; Wiltshire Rural HA.

SHERRARDS (see firm details p.1132) The team is endorsed by interviewees as social housing litigation specialists, particularly for complex outright possession and nuisance cases. Heading the litigation team, "*dogged and determined*" solicitor advocate **Simon Braun** (see p.762) won plaudits from clients for his work with anti-social tenants. The self-contained team is also involved in non-contentious advice on property acquisitions and disposals, right to buy and employment issues. **Clients** Aldwyck HA; Bedfordshire Pilgrims HA; East Hertfordshire DC; Granta HA; Network HA; Riversmead HA; St Albans DC.

SOUTH WEST

SOCIAL HOUSING
■ SOUTH WEST

1. **Trowers & Hamlins** Exeter
2. **Bevan Ashford** Bristol
   Burges Salmon Bristol
3. **Stones** Exeter

LEADING INDIVIDUALS

1. **KEULS Peter** Trowers & Hamlins
   MCNULTY Stephen Burges Salmon
2. **ACTON Joseph** Trowers & Hamlins
   DYER Nick Stones
   MORTIMER Ken Bevan Ashford

This book is the product of 6,582 1/2 hour interviews. See p.7 for BMRB audit.
Within each band, firms are listed alphabetically. See individuals' profiles p.761

TROWERS & HAMLINS (see firm details p.1168) The market leader's South West office benefits from the firm's national profile and resources, while retaining its own "*slightly more diverse practice,*" say clients. Although it is involved in litigious work, it is primarily a non-contentious practice, focusing particularly on development and regeneration work. Considered "*pre-eminent*" in the region by peers, it has extended its reach to assist on the first LSVT in South Wales.

A precise, able team includes **Peter Keuls** (see p.764) who advises RSLs on their group structures. Construction-related issues take up much of department head **Joseph Acton**'s (see p.761) social housing efforts. He has assisted RSLs and private sector developers on construction, partnering and building contracts, and worked with Midas Homes on acquiring sites for development. He has also acted as partnering advisor for Signpost HA on several construction projects. **Clients** Guinness Trust; Kennett Housing Society; Knapp New Homes; Midas Homes; Signpost HA; Sovereign HA.

BEVAN ASHFORD (see firm details p.869) A solid team, it enjoys a good record in assisting RSLs on day to day non-contentious and litigious matters, as well as on some more substantial projects. The team's standout practitioner, **Ken Mortimer** (see p.764), advised a consortium of RSLs on a £10 million scheme to acquire and redevelop run-down premises as affordable housing for local tenants. Noted for its developmental and transactional expertise, the group also worked with an HA on its acquisition of former office buildings in Bristol for use as private rental city centre accommodation. **Clients** Sarsen HA; Solon South West HA; Westlea HA.

BURGES SALMON (see firm details p.894) Well-regarded in the region, this confident team has concentrated on development and management advice for HAs as the LSVT market has contracted. Heading a growing unit, **Stephen McNulty** (see p.764) is considered "*thorough, quick and practical.*" His group advised South West Co-operative HA on its rules, structures and charitable status, and assisted Jephson HA on the acquisition of five units for development. Although still involved in contentious work for HAs, its market visibility in this part of the sector has been lower than in previous years. **Clients** Anchor Trust; Bristol Community Housing Federation; Brunelcare; English Churches HA; Hyde HA; Jephson HA; Knightstone HA; Oakfern HA; Priority Youth HA; Sanctuary HA; Solon South West HA; South West Co-operative HA.

STONES (see firm details p.1152) This regional player enjoys particular expertise in site acquisition and development for RSLs, including Section 106 planning agreements, and in management agreements with Health Trusts concerning supported housing. Although a small team, it is said by peers to have a proactive approach. Head of department **Nick Dyer** (see p.762) has advised Western Challenge HA on the acquisition of 38 residential care homes from a health authority, including the transfer of homes to RSLs. Related instructions have included relocating residents from an existing home during its acquisition, demolition and rebuilding to comply with new care standards, all carried out for East Dorset HA. **Clients** East Dorset HA; Magna HA; Medina HA; Sarsen HA; Tor Homes; Western Challenge HA.

WALES

SOCIAL HOUSING
■ WALES

1. **Eversheds** Cardiff
   Hugh James Cardiff
2. **Edwards Geldard** Cardiff
   Morgan Cole Cardiff

This book is the product of 6,582 1/2 hour interviews. See p.7 for BMRB audit.
Within each band, firms are listed alphabetically.

EVERSHEDS (see firm details p.949) Anne Hayward heads the national social housing group, which is experienced in housing regeneration work. Assistance to local authorities on housing schemes has been augmented by funding expertise. It advised Wales & West HA on its drawdown of a final tranche of £10 million from a £50 million facility. The firm has further assisted HAs on post-LSVT advice. **Clients** Home Housing; Mid-Wales HA; Orbit; Places for People; Wales & West HA.

HUGH JAMES (see firm details p.1004) Long established in the sector, the firm enjoys a strong HA client base. David Roberts and his team are highly visible within the social housing sphere. The team has advised the Welsh Federation of HAs on the issues surrounding rent increase notices under Section 13 of the Housing Act 1988. It also provides general assistance to HAs on loan facilities. On the contentious side, the team has been involved on behalf of landlords in several successful possession cases following anti-social behaviour, and has acted in a dispute with a local authority over residential care homes. **Clients** Bro Myrddin HA; Charter HA; Hafod HA; Wales & West HA.

EDWARDS GELDARD (see firm details p.944) Michael Jones' department was particularly commended for its advice on financial matters, with a third of its work in the past year conducted on behalf of clearing banks arranging substantial loans to HAs. Debt recovery work is handled via its independent offshoot, GoDebt. The small team has advised Group Agored HA and others on group structures, and it has also worked on management agreements and partnerships between HAs and charities. **Clients** Group Agored HA; Newydd HA; United Welsh HA.

www.ChambersandPartners.com

SOCIAL HOUSING ■ WALES/MIDLANDS

MORGAN COLE (see firm details p.1075) The departure of the Swansea office's property team has seen the firm's property-related capacity in Wales reduced. Demolish-and-rebuild regeneration schemes on behalf of two local authorities and a number of refinancing schemes have occupied the firm of late. A commercial property and housing specialist, Philip Stewart's realigned team has assisted on an intricate partnership between a local authority social services department, an RSL and an NHS trust for the provision of accommodation for mentally ill patients.

MIDLANDS

SOCIAL HOUSING — MIDLANDS

1. **Anthony Collins Solicitors** Birmingham
2. **Browne Jacobson** Nottingham
   Lee Crowder Birmingham
   Wright Hassall Leamington Spa
3. **freethcartwright** Nottingham
   Needham & James Stratford-upon-Avon
   Pinsent Curtis Biddle Birmingham
4. **Harvey Ingram Owston** Leicester

LEADING INDIVIDUALS

1. **KNOX Martin** Anthony Collins Solicitors
   STEPHENS Hugo Pinsent Curtis Biddle
2. **HEATH Philip** Wright Hassall
   HUDDLESTON David Browne Jacobson
3. **BALLARD Andy** Lee Crowder
   DUDLEY Andrew Needham & James
   MATTHEWS Carol Wright Hassall

This book is the product of 6,582 1/2 hour interviews. See p.7 for BMRB audit.
Within each band, firms are listed alphabetically See individuals' profiles p.761

ANTHONY COLLINS SOLICITORS (see firm details p.845) A long-time leader in innovative partnering arrangements, the firm's "*open book approach*" to client management garnered plaudits from many quarters. The social housing group is part of the firm's transformation team, which includes local government and charities. The team has acted on its first LSVT during the last year, transferring 17,000 homes on behalf of Knowsley MBC. Regeneration specialist **Martin Knox** (see p.764) heads a unit that continues to receive appointments to a large number of New Deals for Communities. Its broad-ranging expertise was demonstrated by its appointment by Derby City Council to set up housing companies to attract DTLR funding, and on its advice on the funding and succession strategy for new build housing and management for 1,400 dwellings. **Clients** Accord HA; Derby City Council; Knowsley MBC; Optima Community Association; Prime Focus.

BROWNE JACOBSON (see firm details p.891) The firm enjoys a reputation amongst peers as "*accessible and experienced.*" The development of new properties and the sale and shared ownership of flats at new sites have occupied the firm of late. "*Seasoned*" **David Huddleston's** (see p.763) balanced team assisted Metropolitan Housing Trust on several office and flat developments in Derby. It has also been busy with Leicester HA's PFI of the local Kingsmill hospital, refurbishing doctors' and nurses' accommodation and building a new conference centre. The firm has advised on refinancing for borrowers and lenders, and acted on a number of anti-social behaviour and housing disrepair orders. **Clients** Co-operative Bank; East Midlands HA; Leicester HA; Metropolitan Housing Trust; Riverside HA; Royal Bank of Scotland; Wyre Forest HA.

LEE CROWDER (see firm details p.1035) Much of the firm's work is taken up by Schedule 1 work for HAs, advising them on existing rules such as rent increases and on their ongoing operation. This has include a major internal fraud investigation for an HA. One of the largest social housing teams in the Midlands, peers consider it to be skilled in volume stock transfers and in post-transfer group structures. It supplements these key areas with assistance on anti-social behaviour orders and some funding work for HAs. **Andy Ballard's** (see p.761) name continues to be well recognised in the region. **Clients** Accord HA; Midland Area HA; Prime Focus HA; Tamworth MBC; Walsall MBC; Waterloo HA; Whitefriars HA.

WRIGHT HASSALL (see firm details p.1197) **Philip Heath** (see p.763) and the team have impressed the market by landing the coveted post of legal advisor to Glasgow City Council on the transfer of Glasgow Council's housing stock, the largest to take place so far. The deal has returned the firm to the national arena, and its professional and committed approach has countered any queries as to its depth of resources. As well as stock transfers, the partner-led group is able to give constitutional advice to HAs and assistance on their conversion to charitable status. A relatively youthful yet well-rounded department can also assist on loan financing and securitisation for HAs and lenders. **Carol Matthews'** (see p.764) profile has been raised of late, and she was commended for her ability to empathise with clients in the sector. **Clients** Glasgow City Council; HAs.

FREETHCARTWRIGHT (see firm details p.963) The firm fields a small social housing team, specialising in development work for RSLs. It has expanded its services to include the securitisation of portfolios, loan agreements and facilities for HAs, RSLs and national house builders. The group, under property partner Gary Reynolds, focuses its advice on landlords and can draw on a solid client base providing a stream of instructions regarding employment issues and tenancy disputes. This base has been expanded with the prize catch of Riverside HA to assist on its development work. The team has represented the association on the £15 million Clifton Retirement Village scheme, a joint partnership with the City of Nottingham and a registered charity. It has further worked with Nottingham Community HA and Derwent HA on development schemes totalling £100 million. **Clients** Advance HA; Derwent HA; Guinness Trust; Longhurst HA; Nottingham Community HA; Riverside HA.

NEEDHAM & JAMES The partner-heavy, open and approachable team has been particularly busy on housing management and constitutional issues. A regular player in the market, at least half of its work is of a transactional nature. "*Technically sound*" **Andrew Dudley** (see p.762) was praised by peers for his client-handling skills. His department has acted on stock transfers for Erewash HA and St Edmundsbury Borough Council (both for 6,000 homes). The arrival of Mike Stevens, a former group secretary of Orbit HA, should help to bolster the practice in this area. **Clients** Erewash HA; St Edmundsbury BC.

PINSENT CURTIS BIDDLE (see firm details p.1102) The firm pursues a more specialist housing agenda than many of its competitors, with stock transfers now comprising the majority of its high-value, low-volume work. The firm's profile is still riding high on the success of its Sunderland LSVT last year and this is due in no small part to the efforts of LSVT specialist **Hugo Stephens** (see p.765). The group has also targeted corporate and project-related transactions and larger scale property development. Considerable associate support aided the group on its advice to the Spa and Partnership Housing Groups, as they merged to form a single, larger RSL. The firm was further recommended by clients for its advice relating to employment and bond issues, exemplified by its assistance to Toynbee Housing Group on its £17.5 million loan facility from Barclays Bank. **Clients** Festival Housing Group; Newcastle-under-Lyme Housing; Pennine Housing 2000; Sunderland Housing Group; Toynbee Housing Group; Wyre Forest Community Housing.

HARVEY INGRAM OWSTON (see firm details p.988) East Midlands clients and transactions

NORTH WEST/NORTH EAST ■ SOCIAL HOUSING

form the bulk of this firm's focus, and this small and personable team receives a steady stream of property-related work. This has included acquisitions assistance on the leasing of units and advice on staircasing sales. Gordon Arthur's unit is also actively instructed on shared ownership deals. **Clients** Alliance & Leicester; BSS; Cadeby Homes; Cawrey; David Wilson Homes; de Montfort Housing Society; Foundation HA; Home Office; Leicester HA; Newbuild Homes; Riverside HA; Wolds HA.

NORTH WEST

SOCIAL HOUSING
■ NORTH WEST

1
- **Cobbetts** Manchester

2
- **Brabners Chaffe Street** Liverpool
- **Trowers & Hamlins** Manchester

3
- **Eversheds** Manchester
- **Howarth Goodman** Manchester

4
- **Bremner Sons & Corlett** Liverpool
- **Croftons** Manchester

LEADING INDIVIDUALS

1
- GASKELL Mike Cobbetts

2
- TURNER Graham Trowers & Hamlins

3
- BODE Adrian Trowers & Hamlins
- FLETCHER Alistair Bremner Sons & Corlett
- RHATIGAN Michael Eversheds
- WINROW Janet Trowers & Hamlins

This book is the product of 6,582 1/2 hour interviews. See p.7 for BMRB audit. Within each band, firms are listed alphabetically. See individuals' profiles p.761

COBBETTS (see firm details p.914) Peers commend this firm as "*substantial players*" in the region and beyond. It has developed new business models for RSLs, such as the Community Housing Mutual, established for transfers on behalf of the National Assembly for Wales. On a national basis, it advises on the application of RSLs' VAT regimes. The merger with Read Hind Stewart is anticipated to further increase in its market share in the North. Department head **Mike Gaskell** (see p.763) "*thoroughly understands what clients want,*" according to leading players in the field. The team has acted on a key worker housing scheme for Selhal Housing Group and a £130 million refinancing transaction for Progress Housing Group. It also advised on a stock transfer for Places for People in Sheffield. **Clients** Places for People Group; Progress Housing Group; Selhal Housing Group; Twin Valley Homes.

BRABNERS CHAFFE STREET (see firm details p.885) The property and litigation resources of the firm have increased with the arrival of staff from Berrymans Lace Mawer and Brabner Holden Banks Wilson, although the esteemed Lawrence Holden has recently retired from the practice. Ex-Garretts man Simon Jones is set to assume the mantle as group head. The combined unit has seen a rise in its work on employment issues. The firm has dealt with the redevelopment of King's Dock in Liverpool for Riverside HA, and handled a similar scheme for Liverpool Housing Trust (LHT) on the city's waterfront. It can also call on resources to deal with work on group structures and loan financing via its corporate arm. The firm has aided Maritime HA on its reorganisation and merger with Templar HA, and advised LHT on restructuring, with assets topping £200 million. **Clients** Cosmopolitan HA; Liverpool Housing Trust; Maritime HA; Riverside HA.

TROWERS & HAMLINS (see firm details p.1168) Department head **Graham Turner** (see p.765) is one of the longest serving partners in the North West in the sector. He worked on the St George's Parade Education Village Wolverhampton project, including the provision of flats with a lecture hall and other facilities for the adjoining Wolverhampton College. The firm's nationwide stock transfer expertise is repeated here, and peers endorsed the team's level of efficiency. "*Excellent to deal with,*" **Adrian Bode** (see p.762) oversaw the transfer of two estates in Knutsford from Manchester City Council. New to our tables this year, **Janet Winrow** (see p.765) transferred 170 staff resident units at Kettering General Hospital on behalf of Servite Homes, a transaction that involved elements of PFI and the New Build programme. **Clients** Bromford Carinthia HA; Equity Housing Group; Heanton HA; Manchester Methodist HA; Mosscare Housing; Servite Homes; Willow Park Housing.

EVERSHEDS (see firm details p.949) The firm is considered by competitors to be a strong property and business unit, offering advice on specialist social housing elements. The small sector-focused unit is led by property partner **Michael Rhatigan** (see p.764). "*An excellent manager,*" he advised Harvest Housing Group on its joint venture with Redrow Homes, and acted for Willow Park Housing Trust on its CPO of properties relating to the GMPTE airport tram extension. The firm was commended by clients for its commercial aproach; it "*understands the law but does not give overly academic responses.*" **Clients** Harvest Housing Group; Willow Park Housing Trust.

HOWARTH GOODMAN This traditional Manchester firm has a predominant focus on the property development and management aspects of social housing. Former Cobbetts lawyer Steven Baddiel leads a team that acts on stock transfers and funding issues.

BREMNER SONS & CORLETT A small firm, predominantly focused on local matters, it was commended by leading figures as "*knowledgeable and approachable.*" In a "*prompt, proactive and efficient*" team that has grown in size this year, partner **Alistair Fletcher** was singled out by a diverse cross-section of the market for his depth of experience. A landlord-only firm, it is involved in regeneration projects and partnering arrangements with providers in specific areas, such as the care homes sector. It carries out stock transfers and stock swaps for a client base of HAs. Although the group's work is predominantly non-contentious, it also has a niche specialism in nuisance claims.

CROFTONS The firm retains the loyalty of many Manchester-based clients, and social housing comprises a third of its workload. Its partner-led approach has been brought to bear on a broad sweep of social housing matters, particularly contractual and leasing disputes and on behalf of ethnic minority HAs. It has also provided financial advice for borrowers and some banks, including several multimillion pound facility agreements provided to RSLs.

NORTH EAST

DICKINSON DEES (see firm details p.938) The firm retains its dominant position in the North East, with considerable resources available and a strong client base, the majority of which is outside the region. **Mitch Brown** (see p.762) combines a "*flexible and pragmatic attitude*" with an acknowledged understanding of the sector. His large department has advised on the Walker Riverside regeneration project, a partnership between Newcastle City Council and the firm's clients (North British Housing and Places for People) to build 3,500 homes. In funding matters, it has advised on the disengagement of Banks of the Wear from Housing 21, and on its venture with the Tees Valley Group and subsequent £24 million refinancing. It also works with ten regional and national RSLs on sizeable litigation concerning the

SOCIAL HOUSING ■ NORTH EAST/SCOTLAND

SOCIAL HOUSING
■ NORTH EAST

1. **Dickinson Dees** Newcastle upon Tyne
2. **Eversheds** Newcastle upon Tyne
   Rollits Hull
   Walker Charlesworth & Foster Leeds
3. **Gordons Cranswick Solicitors** Bradford
   Savage Crangle Skipton

LEADING INDIVIDUALS

1. **BROWN Mitch** Dickinson Dees
2. **BIRTWISTLE Colin** Walker Charlesworth & Foster
   HURST Andrew Savage Crangle

This book is the product of 6,582 1/2 hour interviews. See p.7 for BMRB audit. Within each band, firms are listed alphabetically. See individuals' profiles p.761

wrongful serving of rent notices. The team has also been involved in a number of LSVTs. **Clients** ACIS; Anchor Trust; Blueroom Properties; Darlington HA; Durham County Council; Endeavour HA; Newcastle Building Society; Nomad Housing Group; Northumberland County Council; Stenham HA; Tees Valley Housing Group.

EVERSHEDS (see firm details p.949) Adrian Stanley leads a small team that focuses on property-based development work, and acquisition and borrowing matters. The firm provides assistance on PPPs and on the non-contentious construction elements of transactions for RSLs. Other elements of the practice assist on corporate, management and service level agreements,

and the team can draw upon the support of its respected national network.

ROLLITS (see firm details p.1115) Clive Gardner's partner-led team concentrates on servicing a client base of medium-sized HAs requiring specialist advice. The property development of sites, including acquisitions and disposals, on behalf of RSLs constitutes much of this work. It has advised on right to buy schemes and shared ownership issues. The firm is advising on the 540-unit New Osladwick Village development on behalf of the Joseph Rowntree Housing Trust, a partnership venture with Yorkshire City Council. It has also assisted the Peabody Trust by drafting funding-related initiatives for key worker house purchases in London. Construction litigation and some funding work is undertaken for Yorkshire Community Housing. **Clients** Hull Churches HA; Joseph Rowntree Housing Trust; Peabody Trust; Yorkshire Community Housing.

WALKER CHARLESWORTH & FOSTER (see firm details p.1177) The firm assists on the mortgaging and securitisation of property portfolios, mainly on behalf of landlords. Lead partner **Colin Birtwistle** (see p.762) was recommended to *Chambers* for his abilities on development and governance transactions; he acted on an SRB agreement with Leeds City Council to deal with subsidence and refurbishment issues at several sites in the city for Leeds Partnership Homes. The small group has worked with several clients on the acquisition of PPG3 developments and their subsequent

shared ownership disposals. It has also been involved in the transfer of 150 properties from Sheffield City Council to South Yorkshire HA and worked with RSLs on a number of VAT reclamation schemes. **Clients** Harewood Housing Society; Leeds Federated HA; Manningham HA; South Yorkshire HA; Yorkshire Community Housing; Unity HA.

GORDONS CRANSWICK SOLICITORS Rooted in its property department, partner Deborah Powell and the team scored a notable success this year in successfully securing a place on the panel for Anchor Trust's legal work in the North. The committed unit has acted on a number of site acquisitions for redevelopment into flats for the elderly on a shared ownership or rental basis.

SAVAGE CRANGLE (see firm details p.1123) Property development work and advice on care homes and PFI-funded children's homes remains a core strength. **Andrew Hurst**'s small team has worked on "*some hefty matters,*" including advice to an HA on a scheme to provide devolved care to individual properties in the community for people with learning disabilities and their carers. It has also assisted a private sector provider, working with a local authority, which is seeking to provide three children's homes using PFI funding. Group structures and advice on charities issues complete the picture. **Clients** RSLs, HAs, private sector companies.

SCOTLAND

SOCIAL HOUSING
■ SCOTLAND

1. **Harper Macleod** Glasgow
   TC Young Edinburgh, Glasgow
2. **Ledingham Chalmers** Aberdeen, Aberdeen
   Brechin Tindal Oatts Glasgow
   Henderson Boyd Jackson WS Edinburgh
3. **Burness** Edinburgh
   Dundas & Wilson CS Edinburgh
   Macleod & MacCallum Inverness

LEADING INDIVIDUALS

1. **FREEDMAN Len** Harper Macleod
2. **COWAN Andrew** TC Young
   DEWAR Kate Henderson Boyd Jackson WS
   EWING Mark TC Young
   HOGG Derek Ledingham Chalmers
   MACGREGOR Stephen TC Young
3. **ROBERTSON Andrew** TC Young
   THOMPSON Alison TC Young

This book is the product of 6,582 1/2 hour interviews. See p.7 for BMRB audit. Within each band, firms are listed alphabetically. See individuals' profiles p.761

HARPER MACLEOD (see firm details p.985) One of only a few dedicated social housing teams in Scotland, the large team is skilled in stock transfers and major projects. It is currently acting for the selling authorities on four LSVTs, including the Glasgow stock transfer of 80,000 homes. The team is assisted by the firm's associated employment and conveyancing units, and judged to offer a "*proactive and innovative approach*" to complex transfers. "*Accessible, active and responsive,*" lead partner **Len Freedman** (see p.763) also impressed clients as one who "*brings a dynamism to the whole process.*" This "*bright and able*" group continues to advise HAs on right to buy, debt recovery and employment issues. It has also consolidated its position within funding, working with the Nationwide Building Society, and it has been appointed to the social housing funding panel of the Bank of Scotland. **Clients** Bank of Scotland; Dumfries & Galloway Council; Glasgow HA; Nationwide Building Society; Scottish Borders Council.

TC YOUNG (see firm details p.1199) Although a smaller firm overall, it possesses a large social housing unit heavily weighted towards property

work, stock transfers and funding. Peers reported that its "*knowledgeable performers specialise in this area and you can't fault them.*" It also enjoys a 'best friends' relationship with market leaders Trowers & Hamlins. The expanding team has acted on the acquisition of the majority of Glasgow University's residential student letting accommodation on behalf of Glasgow Student Villages, an SPV of Sanctuary HA. It counsels on constitutional matters and group structures for over 100 HAs on an ongoing basis, while the development and regeneration unit has worked extensively on construction, PPP and partnering schemes. **Andrew Cowan** (see p.762) leads the firm's housing management and litigation sector, while head of department **Mark Ewing** (see p.763) is best known for his work in the care sector for landlords. Sharing their expertise, **Stephen MacGregor** (see p.764) is thought to have brought a greater corporate focus to the team. It advised Sanctuary HA on the transfer of houses from Dundee City Council, the largest NHP-funded stock transfer to date in Scotland. Cowan and MacGregor represented the Scottish Federation of HAs on aspects of the Housing

(Scotland) Act 2001 during its passage through the Scottish Parliament. **Andrew Robertson** (see p.765) and **Alison Thompson** (see p.765) were warmly recommended to *Chambers*. Thompson assisted on the first convergence of a Scottish HA with the group structure of an English-based HA. **Clients** Dexia Municipal Bank; Dunfermline Building Society; Employers In Voluntary Housing; HBOS; Nationwide Building Society; Royal Bank of Scotland ; Sanctuary HA.

LEDINGHAM CHALMERS (see firm details p.1034) This commercial mid-sized team is best known for its work on stock transfers and associated funding, such as that for the Scottish Borders HA on its transfer of 7,000 homes. Department head **Derek Hogg** (see p.763) ("*personable and straightforward*") leads a department that was retained as main external solicitors by Glasgow City Council on the Glasgow stock transfer and regeneration project. The group is building up the volume of its mainstream HA work and, since Hogg arrived from Skene Edwards, has been attracting clients such as Melville HA. The team has also witnessed an increase in instructions across employment, corporate governance and constitutional matters as well as on group structures. **Clients** Eildon HA; Glasgow City Council; Loretto HA; Melville HA; Orkney HA; Scottish Borders HA.

BRECHIN TINDAL OATTS Observers commended the team's "*good project and stock transfer skills.*" Transfers and their related funding remain the keystones here, acting for both borrowers and lenders. The firm has advised Scottish Homes on proposed LSVTs and it assists RSLs on the full ambit of work from care homes to constitutional issues, in particular those concerning Tenants' Choice transfers. Although tested by the departure of Stephen MacGregor to TC Young, the team remains a solid presence under the guidance of Karen Brodie, and she has been joined by Patrice Fabien from Scottish Homes. **Clients** Scottish Homes; lenders; RSLs.

HENDERSON BOYD JACKSON WS The firm has formed a bespoke housing group, comprising construction, corporate and constitutional and employment units. It has acted for Shetland Homes on the Shetland Islands Council's local authority stock transfer. It also focuses on the development and regeneration spheres, conducting grant-assisted work for several groups. It advised on the formation of local housing company Capital City Homes on behalf of the City of Edinburgh. Although some interviewees considered **Kate Dewar** (see p.762) to have an "*aggressive*" manner, clients rated both her and her team as an approachable unit, which "*gives straight answers to straight questions*" and is willing to "*approach problems from a different angle.*" Supported by two litigators, the firm is also able to deal effectively with a proportion of contentious work. The team has assisted East Lothian's Homes for Life Housing Partnership on a number of acquisitions of both properties and development sites. **Clients** Cairn HA; Capital City Holdings; City of Edinburgh Council; Homes for Life Housing Partnership; Miller Homes; Paragon HA; Renaissance Social Housing; Shetland Homes; Waverley Housing Management; West Lothian Housing Management.

BURNESS Operating through its corporate department, the firm is better known for its strength in third-market work for voluntary groups and charities. Through partners such as Paul Pia, it has acted for a leading HA in securing a long-term loan of £50 million, and advised the Scottish Federation of HAs on corporate governance and independence agreements and compliance-related issues. Link HA also instructed the firm on its corporate restructuring. **Clients** Abbeyfield Society; Abertay HA; Cruden Investments; Institute of Housing in Scotland; Link HA in Scotland; Partick HA; Scottish Borders HA; Scottish Federation of HAs; Viewpoint HA.

DUNDAS & WILSON CS (see firm details p.943) The firm has this year seen the departure of Andrew Meakin and Chris Dun to Maclay Murray & Spens, and housing finance specialist Jane Howat takes up the reins. Despite the loss, the firm's unquestionable ability in its specialist area of advice to funders remains respected. The team has assisted funders on a number of large-scale local authority stock transfers and syndicated refinancings.

MACLEOD & MACCALLUM The firm has a track record in stock transfers for funders. It has a particular focus on social housing advice to groups in the Highlands. Property partner Graham Watson is the firm's leading housing specialist.

THE LEADERS IN SOCIAL HOUSING

ACTON, Joseph
Trowers & Hamlins, Exeter
(01392) 217466
jacton@trowers.com
Specialisation: Advises upon all areas of Housing Association law and practice including acquisition and development, building contracts, partnering and construction issues, PFI matters, homelessness initiatives, funding and major consortium agreements and joint ventures. Speaks regularly at client seminars on matters of current interest.
Prof. Memberships: Member of the Law Society.
Career: Torquay Grammar School (1977-84); Magdalen College Oxford (1984-87); *Trowers & Hamlins* (1989-date). Partner from 1995.

ADLINGTON, Jonathan
Trowers & Hamlins, London
(020) 7423 8000
jadlington@trowers.com
Specialisation: Senior partner. Head of property department. Vast experience of housing law and the Housing Association movement having built a specialist practice over more than 25 years. Deals with all aspects of commercial and residential property, from purchases, sales and mortgages to development agreements, structures and funding. Instrumental in the development of private finance for social housing. Acts for Housing Associations, Local Authorities and lenders. Regular speaker at housing events and for funding bodies.

BALLARD, Andy
Lee Crowder, Birmingham
(0121) 236 4477
Specialisation: Heads the housing group at *Lee Crowder* which is one of the largest within the region advising in excess of 50 Registered Social Landlords. Lectures and trains nationally and locally on a full range of housing management and human resource issues.
Prof. Memberships: Law Society; Employment Lawyers Association.
Career: Qualified in 1981 before joining the Birmingham practice of *Rigbeys* in 1983. Became a partner in *Rigbeys* in 1985 which in due course merged with *Irwin Mitchell* in 1996. Became a partner in *Lee Crowder* when transferring his team in 1999.

BASTOW, Gillian
Lewis Silkin, London
(020) 7074 8029
gillian.bastow@lewissilkin.com
Specialisation: Partner and Head of Social Housing Group. All aspects of housing association activity including land acquisition and development, regeneration schemes, PPP/PFI projects and other arrangements involving RSLs, local authorities/health authorities, private and public finance, constitutional/corporate matters, group structures, care in the community schemes, landlord and tenant issues, and specialist work with housing co-operatives.
Prof. Memberships: Law Society, NHF Lawyers Sub-Group, Housing Association Committee Member.
Career: Qualified 1981 with *Lewis Silkin*. Partner 1984.
Personal: Born October 1953. Attended Somerville College Oxford (MA) and Leicester University (LLM). Lives in London.

BENNETT, Jennifer
Coffin Mew & Clover, Fareham
(01329) 825617
jenniferbennett@coffinmew.co.uk
Specialisation: Partner. Head of social housing department. Over 20 years experience in housing law, with particular interest in new housing initiatives and low cost home ownership schemes, but with a very broad expertise in this sector. Heads one of the largest teams of dedicated housing professionals outside London who provide comprehensive services to local and regional RSLs as well as funders.
Prof. Memberships: Affiliate Member of Chartered Institute of Housing.
Personal: Born 1955. Educated University College, London. Admitted 1979.

SOCIAL HOUSING ■ THE LEADERS

BILLINGHAM, Nick
Devonshires, London
(020) 7880 4272
nick.billingham@devonshires.co.uk
Specialisation: Property Litigation.
Career: *Prince Evans Solicitors* 1990-95 (trainee and assistant); *Devonshires Solicitors* 1995-present (partner 1998).
Publications: Jordans Housing Act 1996.
Personal: Resides Colchester.

BIRTWISTLE, Colin
Walker Charlesworth & Foster, Leeds
(0113) 297 2913
Specialisation: Housing Association Law and Practice particularly in the field of constitutional matters for Housing Associations e.g. dealing with several rule changes and mergers. Also heavily involved from 1989 with Leeds Partnership Homes which dealt with the transfer of £33m of City Council land largely for Housing Association development but also for outright sale. Now involved with the Single Regeneration Budget Agreement for Leeds and related sales. Also involved with Health Service Reprovision Agreements for two charities and, on a major hospital closure, a supported living project.
Prof. Memberships: The Law Society, and Solicitor Benevolent Fund Member.
Personal: Family: married with three children aged 23, 21 and 17. Outside interests - sport, fell walking and charity work.

BODE, Adrian
Trowers & Hamlins, Manchester
(0161) 211 0000
abode@trowers.com
Specialisation: A partner since 1983 and has acquired wide ranging experience. Particular specialisations are large-scale acquisitions and disposals, joint venture work and private finance.
Career: University of Nottingham. Qualified 1978. *Trowers & Hamlins* (1978 to date). Partner 1983.

BRAUN, Simon
Sherrards, St Albans
(01727) 832830
skb@sherrards.com
Specialisation: Partner in charge of Litigation and Housing Department. Acts for Local Authorities and Housing Associations with a particular specialism in anti-social tenant litigation. Team regularly acts for and advises clients experiencing anti-social tenant issues involving drugs, criminal damage, violence, noise, environmental issues, prostitution, racial and sexual discrimination and squatters. Is a Solicitor Advocate enabling him to meet all advocacy needs of clients up to and including the House of Lords. Also advises Local Authorities on Reviews and Appeals arising out of homelessness legislation. Also gives Seminars to Local Authorities and Housing Associations on housing litigation. Currently acts for 35-40 local authorities and housing associations and has one of the few teams in the country dedicated to the law relating to anti-social tenants.
Prof. Memberships: Law Society, Solicitors Association of Higher Court Advocates, Accredited CEDR Mediator.
Career: Qualified in 1990 with *Bennett Taylor Tyrell* in the West End. Became a Partner with *Sherrards* in 1998 where he currently heads the Litigation and Housing Departments. Qualified as a Solicitor/Advocate (Civil) in 1998 and as an Accredited Mediator in 1999.
Personal: Born 1966. School Governor. Married with two children. Lives in North West London. Leisure interests include reading, theatre and cinema.

BROWN, Duncan
Devonshires, London
(020) 7628 7576
duncan.brown@devonshires.co.uk
Specialisation: Partner, head of projects and public partnership group at *Devonshires*, acts for RSLs, NHS Trusts and Local Authorities in relation to Public Private Partnership and PFI Projects and has acted recently on a number of NHS Trust Accommodation Projects with RSLs, Housing PFIs, Leisure PFIs and Education PFIs. Also provides advice to RSLs on special needs projects and VAT and property.
Prof. Memberships: Society of Construction Law.
Career: Admitted as a solicitor 1974, Maurice Nordon Prize for contract law, joined *Devonshires* 1990. Partner 1991.
Personal: BSC (Econ) Hons 2:1. Resides Surrey, leisure interests gardening, swimming, fine art, antiques.

BROWN, Mitch
Dickinson Dees, Newcastle upon Tyne
(0191) 279 9291
law@dickinson-dees.com
Specialisation: Partner in the commercial property department and head of the public sector development group. Handles all aspects of RSL work in the fields of development, governance and finance. Has in the past year dealt with social housing lending facilities on behalf of RSLs and lenders, social housing PFI and PPP transactions, and the establishment of RSL Group structures.
Prof. Memberships: Law Society.
Career: Born 1962. Educated Royal Grammar School, Newcastle upon Tyne. University of Newcastle upon Tyne 1984 (LLB). Qualified 1987, became a partner in 1995.
Personal: Leisure interests include sport, music, art and reading. Married with three daughters.

CARTER, Adrian
Trowers & Hamlins, London
(020) 7423 8000
acarter@trowers.com
Specialisation: Partner, Housing Finance Group. Specialist in housing finance, acting for borrowers and lenders. Experience includes innovative work on group borrowing arrangements, hedging arrangements, stock and bond issues, as well as bilateral and syndicated lending and borrowing. Regular speaker.
Career: University of Exeter. *Trowers & Hamlins* 1987-date. Qualified 1989, partner 1994.
Personal: Married, four children.

COWAN, Andrew
Devonshires, London
(020) 7628 7576
andrew.cowan@devonshires.co.uk
Specialisation: Partner and head of finance. The RSL finance unit has negotiated over £2.5 billion of housing association funding and group structures since 1988 from the capital markets, banks, building societies and new initiatives; Andrew acts for 10 banks, building societies and over 165 RSL based all over England and Wales and a group association borrowing vehicle. Andrew and his team act for over 50 RSLs on their group structures, including in relation to mergers and private company acquisitions, PFI, and new initiatives. In the last year he has advised on three new pathfinder regeneration projects. Lectures widely on finance, group structures and RSL corporate governance.
Career: Articled *Hobson Audley*; qualified 1989; *Trowers & Hamlins* 1990-91; *Devonshires* 1991; partner 1993; regular speaker; credit committee member of an international charity.
Personal: Educated University of East Anglia. Born 1964: resides Sevenoaks. Leisure: backpacking, football, swimming, Latin America.

COWAN, Andrew
TC Young, Glasgow
(0141) 221 5562
asc@tcyoung.co.uk
Specialisation: Housing association tenancies and housing management issues. Representation in all areas of litigation and employment related disputes. Has an extensive knowledge of the regulatory regime for secured and assured tenancies and regularly contributes to training conferences and seminars. Has a developing caseload dealing with construction-related disputes. Currently extensively involved in a number of transfer of engagements between housing associations. Housing management expertise complements fellow *TC Young* partners' corporate funding, stock transfer and special projects specialisations.
Prof. Memberships: Law Society of Scotland and Chartered Institute of Arbitrators.
Career: Qualified 1987; *TC Young*, Partner 1995.

DEWAR, Kate
Henderson Boyd Jackson WS, Edinburgh
(0131) 226 6881
Specialisation: Worked extensively on a variety of innovative transactions promoting community ownership and regeneration for and involving housing associations, housing management companies, local housing companies and local authorities considering stock transfer. Involved in all aspects of large-scale voluntary transfers, in the legal formation of housing associations, housing companies and housing partnerships and following on from acting as one of the lead solicitors in one of the first New Housing Partnership deals in Scotland a few years ago. Has since acted in numerous similar deals since.
Prof. Memberships: Law Society of Scotland. Writer to the Signet. Notary Public.
Career: Qualified 1982; partner specialising in housing and public sector work.
Personal: Edinburgh University graduate; lives Edinburgh; interests include swimming and travelling.

DOOLITTLE, Ian
Trowers & Hamlins, London
(020) 7423 8000
idoolittle@trowers.com
Specialisation: Team leader on many housing stock transfers, first LSVT and more recently urban estate-based transfers. Now a specialist advisor on complex metropolitan transfers. At the forefront of establishing arms length housing organisations. Is an authority on public/private sector partnerships. Also specialist in environmental law.

DUDLEY, Andrew
Needham & James, Stratford-upon-Avon
(01789) 416317
andrewdudley@needhamandjames.com
Specialisation: Acted for Housing Associations since 1982. Specialises in LSVT, site acquisition and disposal, nomination rights, planning and planning agreements, infrastructure agreements and environmental issues. Lead solicitor in the following housing transfers: Orbit Bexley, Telford & Wrekin, Calderdale, Staffordshire Moorlands, Erewash and St Edmundsbury. Has also acted for a number of diverse bodies acquiring care homes for the elderly and homes for persons with learning disabilities.
Prof. Memberships: Law Society.
Career: Kings Norton Grammar School Birmingham. LLB (Hons) Wales (Cardiff). Qualified 1981.
Personal: Married. one child. Enjoys cricket, soccer, motor racing, theatre and travel. Past president Old Nortonians Association.

DYER, Nick
Stones, Exeter
(01392) 666819
nickdyer@stones-solicitors.co.uk
Specialisation: Specialised in social housing work for nearly 20 years. Experience of site acquisition and development funding, management and transfer agreements with health trusts and local authorities, shared ownership and LSE schemes, and a wide variety of other issues involving registered social landlords.
Career: Law graduate (Trinity Hall, Cambridge). Formerly partner (latterly

managing partner) in *Cann & Hallett* and now partner in *Stones* in charge of social housing work.

ELPHICKE, Natalie
Denton Wilde Sapte, London
(020) 7246 7000

EVANS, Chris
Evans Butler Wade, London
(020) 8858 8926

EWING, Mark
TC Young, Glasgow
(0141) 221 5562
mee@tcyoung.co.uk
Specialisation: Represents a large number of social housing providers with extensive experience in all aspects of stock transfers from local authorities, Scottish Homes, NHS and the Ministry of Defence. Has acted in numerous transfers of engagements between housing associations. Regularly provides advice on corporate structures and governance issues and has developed group structures for Scottish and UK organisations. Also experienced in preparing multi-agency and private sector development agreements. Currently instructed in relation to a number of New Housing Partnership stock transfers from local authorities throughout Scotland. Corporate and special projects expertise complements fellow *TC Young* partners' funding, stock transfer and housing management specialisations.
Prof. Memberships: Law Society of Scotland.
Career: Qualified in 1983; *TC Young*, Partner (1987).

FITTON, Roger
Winckworth Sherwood, London
(020) 7593 5000
drfitton@winckworths.co.uk
Specialisation: Housing law with emphasis on mixed public and private schemes, brownfield urban regeneration projects, externalisations in social services, staff, student and NHS projects and a wide range of charitable and constitutional work.
Prof. Memberships: Law Society.
Career: Oulder Hill Community School, Rochdale 1974-79; Exeter College, Oxford, Law 1980-83; Trained, *Boodle Hatfield* 1984-86; Assistant Solicitor, *Denton Hall* 1986-89; Assistant, then partner, *Winckworth Sherwood* 1989-2002.

FLETCHER, Alistair G
Bremner Sons & Corlett, Liverpool
(0151) 227 1301

FREEDMAN, Len
Harper Macleod, Glasgow
(0141) 221 8888
leonard.freedman@harpermacleod.co.uk
Specialisation: Leonard Freedman LLB NP Diploma in Business Administration qualified in 1979 and co-ordinates the firm's Public Sector and Housing Practice Group. He is also a qualified English solicitor. Len has led the firm's Public Sector and Housing Team in some 30 deals with a value in excess of £100 million since 1995 and is currently acting in potential LSVTs in Scottish Borders, Dumfries and Galloway and Shetland as well as in various local authority option studies. He is Scottish legal correspondent of the magazine 'Social Housing' and 'Housing Law Monitor' and is a regular and well known speaker on a range of social housing and public sector issues. Len comes from a corporate law background and has had particular involvement in both loan and equity funding and joint ventures. Len was for some years tutor in Company Law and Formation at University of Glasgow and also secretary to the UK based Mining and Mineral Law Group.

GASKELL, Mike
Cobbetts, Manchester
(0161) 833 7499
michael.gaskell@cobbetts.co.uk
Specialisation: Advising registered social landlords and local authorities on housing related matters; group structures and constitutional issues; joint ventures; tenant involvement; stock transfer; acquisition and development; landlord and tenant. Currently advising on a number of group structures, stock transfers and tenant involvement initiatives.
Prof. Memberships: Law Society.
Career: LLB Liverpool. Advising housing associations for 20 years.
Personal: Married with three children. Voluntary board member of Manchester Care and Repair.

GOODE, Naomi
Jenkins & Hand, London
(020) 7222 5002
naomi.goode@jenkinsandhand.co.uk
Specialisation: Has wide ranging social housing practice including: stock transfers (including from NHS Trusts); site acquisitions and development; constitutional matters; tenancy and leasehold management; private finance; and supported housing agreements. Frequently advises on legal aspects of RSLs' housing management policies. Regularly acts for tenant groups and independent tenants' advisors on stock transfers.
Career: Qualified 1990; 1991 Courtauld Institute of Art; 1991-94 *Norton Rose*; 1994-2000 *Winckworth Sherwood*; 2000-01 MSc housing London School of Economics; 2001 partner *Jenkins & Hand*; Board Member Threshold Housing & Support; Chair Threshold Key Homes; Member Editorial Board ROOF; Member National Housing Federation's Regulation Panel.
Publications: National Housing Federation's model 'Right to Acquire Lease'.

GRAHAM, Ian
Trowers & Hamlins, London
(020) 7423 8000
igraham@trowers.com
Specialisation: Partner, housing. Work for associations includes advising on PFI and PPP projects; group structures; governance and vires issues; joint ventures and partnership projects in health, care and urban regeneration. A prolific author and public speaker.

HALL, Gareth
Devonshires, London
(020) 7880 4351
gareth.hall@devonshires.co.uk
Specialisation: A broad finance and company/commercial practice, advising housing associations and general corporate clients. Advice includes banking for public private partnerships and social landlords and capital market finance; corporate/constitutional including group structures; mergers, acquisitions and joint ventures; IT supply and support contracts ranging from standard packages to bespoke projects; e-commerce.
Career: Trainee at *Lovell White & King* 1982-84; assistant (corporate) solicitor, *Simmons & Simmons* 1984-94; joined *Devonshires* 1994, partner since 1995.
Personal: Born 1959. Educated Manchester Grammar School and Merton College, Oxford. Lives in Beckenham. Leisure interests include playing and listening to music of all eras, cycling and the National Trust.

HAND, Catherine
Jenkins & Hand, London
(020) 7222 5002

HAWKINS, James
Trowers & Hamlins, London
(020) 7423 8330
jhawkins@trowers.com
Specialisation: Partner public sector department. Specialist in public/private sector partnerships. Is an authority on housing stock transfers and, in particular, urban transfers, local housing companies and regeneration schemes. Also specialises in group structure and residential care home transfers.
Career: University of Birmingham; Qualified 1989. *Trowers & Hamlins* 1991 to date. Partner 1996.

HAYES, Sarah
Trowers & Hamlins, London
(020) 7423 8000
shayes@trowers.com
Specialisation: Partner, Head of Housing Finance/Corporate Finance. General expertise in property finance, secured and unsecured. Particular specialism in housing finance, acting for borrowers and lenders. Experience covers hedging arrangements; bond issues (domestic and Eurobond, rated and insured, own name and group issues); syndicated lending; bonds and securities and a large number of group borrowing arrangements in which she has a particular specialism. Sarah also has an extensive practice relating to RSL corporate governance covering all aspects of Board responsibilities, constitutional issues, group structures, charity law and vires and regulatory controls. Experienced speaker at housing, charitable and funding events.

HEATH, Philip
Wright Hassall, Leamington Spa
(01926) 886688
philiph@wrighthassall.co.uk
Specialisation: Large scale voluntary transfer of housing stock. He has worked on some 30 completed projects the most recent being the transfer by Knowsley MBC to Knowsley Housing Trust. He has also recently completed the transfer by Erewash Borough Council to Erewash Housing Limited. He is currently working on proposed transfers by Glasgow City Council, Wolvern Housing (Crewe Borough Council), Teignbridge Districk Council and Carlisle City Council.
Prof. Memberships: Law Society.
Career: Called to the Bar by Grays Inn 1988. Assistant then Senior Assistant Solicitor (Barrister) with Oxfordshire County Council. Deputy District Secretary and then Head of Legal Services for South Northamptonshire Council. Joined *Lawrence Graham* 1994 as senior assistant in Local & Public Authority Unit. Admitted as solicitor January 2000. Joined *Wright Hassall* as partner October 2000.
Personal: LLB (Hons) UWE 1978; MA De Montfort 1994 (Environmental Law). Leisure interests include walking, choral music and literature.

HOGG, Derek
Ledingham Chalmers, Edinburgh
(0131) 200 1071
derek.hogg@ledinghamchalmers.com
Specialisation: All aspects of social housing work, specialising in stock transfers, corporate structures, funding and advisory work. Heads the firm's social housing team, responsible for all contractual and financial aspects of transactions. Acted for Fife Special Housing Association in largest Scottish LSVT to date. Major clients include Bridgewater, Cunninghame, Fife Special, Melville and Scottish Borders HAs. Currently acting for Glasgow City Council in the UK's biggest stock transfer proposal.
Prof. Memberships: Committee member of Kirk Care and Old Town Housing Associations.
Career: Trained with local authority. Joined *Skene Edwards* in 1988 and became partner in 1994. Joined *Ledingham Chalmers* as partner in 2000.

HUDDLESTON, David
Browne Jacobson, Nottingham
(0115) 976 6000
dhuddleston@brownej.co.uk
Specialisation: Partner in property department. Advising both local and national Housing Associations on acquisitions of sites for residential developments including a consortium of a number of Associations. Advising Housing Associations on private financing and security agreements. Continues to receive instructions in connection with large value security work for Housing Associations and from banks lending to the sector. Clients include Metropolitan Housing Trust, East Midlands Housing

SOCIAL HOUSING ■ THE LEADERS

Association, Leicester Housing Association, Riverside Housing Association, and SOHA Housing. Other work includes advising on acquisition of development sites for residential, office and industrial developments. Advising on development agreements associated with acquisition of sites and subsequent sales and leases. Acting for developers on the development of sites including financing and subsequent sales by either grant of leases (including industrial, retail and offices) or to investors of whole developments.

HURST, Andrew
Savage Crangle, Skipton
(01756) 794611

JENKINS, Keith
Jenkins & Hand, London
(020) 7222 5002

KEULS, Peter
Trowers & Hamlins, Exeter
(01392) 217466
pkeuls@trowers.com
Specialisation: Housing associations, local housing companies, group structures, large-scale voluntary transfers of housing stock: East Dorset; West Dorset; Penwith; North Dorset; Basingstoke and Deane; Kennet; Kerrier; West Somerset; West Devon; South Hams; Bath and North East Somerset; Restormel; North Devon; Weymouth Portland; Torbay; Mendip. PFI and PPP projects with educational bodies and local authorities.
Career: Worth School, Sussex; College of Law, Guildford. Qualified 1977. *Trowers & Hamlins* (1972-date), partner 1982.

KNOX, Martin
Anthony Collins Solicitors, Birmingham
(0121) 212 7450
martin.knox@anthonycollinssolicitors.com
Specialisation: Provides specialist legal services on housing and local government law to a significant number of Local Authorites and Registered Social Landlords and numerous community associations, charities and businesses. Pioneered significant iniatives for community regeneration and increased investment in the provision and management of social housing. Particular experience of major urban regeneration and transfer work including SRB, particularly local housing companies and recently NDCs.
Career: Qualified 1980. Worked as legal advisor to Sheffield and Birmingham City Councils' Housing Committees. Since joining *Anthony Collins Solicitors* in 1989, has been closely involved in creating innovative solutions to housing and regeneration in urban local authorities. Has developed the community association model in a number of locations throughout the country both for provision of new stock and improvement of existing council housing.

MACGREGOR, Stephen
TC Young, Glasgow
(0141) 221 5562
sxm@tcyoung.co.uk
Specialisation: Has acted on behalf of housing associations and housing co-operatives throughout his career and specialises in large-scale voluntary transfers and funding. Extensive experience in funding issues, and has had regular instruction by Scottish clearing banks and other UK and European lenders. Advises on constitutional and corporate structures. He was appointed by Scottish Homes to head a statutory inquiry into the affairs of Bridgeton and Dalmarnock Housing Association in 1999. Corporate, funding and stock transfer expertise complements *TC Young*'s recognised special projects and housing management skills.
Prof. Memberships: Law Society of Scotland.
Career: Qualified in 1983. Partner *BTO* 1986-2001. Partner *TC Young* 2001.

MATTHEWS, Carol
Wright Hassall, Leamington Spa
(01926) 886688
carolm@wrighthassall.co.uk
Specialisation: Solicitor in constitutional issues and structures for registered social landlords and housing groups. Solicitor in LSVTs in acting for both housing associations and councils and with property work. Advises on purchase of development sites and housing management issues. Gives seminars and lectures on all aspects of housing law.
Prof. Memberships: Law Society.
Career: Qualified in 1980. With *Winckworth & Pemberton* in Westminster before joining *Wright Hassall* in June 1995. Head of the housing and local government department.
Personal: Warwick University, History 2:1 BA Hons. Married with two daughters. Lives in Stratford-upon-Avon. Leisure interests include literature and theatre.

MCNULTY, Stephen
Burges Salmon, Bristol
(0117) 939 2250
stephen.mcnulty@burges-salmon.com
Specialisation: Commercial property development and large portfolio management for end-user clients. He has a wide experience of commercial property issues arising when working with large corporate clients, especially in the telecommunications and transport sectors. He is also head of the highly regarded social housing unit which advises on all aspects of Registered Social Landlords' legal requirements from regulation and group structures to development management and funding issues. Recent projects include sale and acquisition of a number of bus depot facilities for First Group and negotiation of pre-let agreements for office accommodation on behalf of Orange.
Prof. Memberships: Law Society, British Italian Law Association.
Career: Joined *Burges Salmon* in 1984, becoming a partner in 1988.

MORLEY, Trevor
Prince Evans, London
(020) 8567 3477
Specialisation: Managing partner and head of housing finance and low cost home ownership departments; considerable experience in advising both lenders and borrowers of housing and public sector finance; acting on behalf of numerous borrowers in a range of transactions from bilateral and syndicated loans to group borrowing arrangements and capital market issues; expertise in advising on all aspects of banking law; including treasury management and related issues; head of largest low cost home ownership unit in the UK responsible for land acquisition and low cost home ownership development schemes including mixed use/tenure regeneration projects primarily on behalf of registered social landlords; acts for the majority of London based low cost home ownership registered social landlord providers; recent projects include: conduct of the sale of shared ownership portfolios; acting for the consortium of developer and housing association in the Trowbridge Regeneration project in the London Borough of Hackney.
Career: Articled Cambridgeshire; qualified 1979; partner *Prince Evans* 1982.
Personal: Born 1953. Resides Cobham, Surrey.

MORTIMER, Ken
Bevan Ashford, Bristol
(0117) 975 1638
ken.mortimer@bevanashford.co.uk
Specialisation: Partner specialising in commercial property with particular emphasis on public sector clients including RSLs; development acquisition and disposals; planning and statutory agreements; nomination agreements; management agreements and other agreements with local and similar authorities.
Career: Qualified with *Bevan Hancock & Co* in 1975 and returned to *Bevan Ashford* in 1984 having worked in the mean time with *Laurence & Co*. Partner at *Bevan Ashford* 2001.
Personal: Married with three children and formerly in the Territorial Army for 28 years.

MURRAY, Andrew
Winckworth Sherwood, London
(020) 7593 5000
ajmurray@winckworths.co.uk
Specialisation: Partner in housing and local government. Main area of practice is public sector and housing law, with particular expertise in finance and projects. Addresses various seminars organised by professional bodies and clients.
Prof. Memberships: Law Society.
Career: Qualified in 1987. Joined *Winckworth Sherwood* in 1988, becoming a Partner in 1989.
Personal: Attended Manchester University 1978-81 (English Language and Literature). Lives in Richmond, Surrey.

MURRAY, Lynne
Lewis Silkin, London
(020) 7074 8002
lynne.murray@lewissilkin.com
Specialisation: Partner in housing and project finance; specialising in RSL work, in particular dealing with private finance, PFI/PPP, community care, governance and regeneration issues.
Prof. Memberships: Law Society, NHF Lawyers Sub-group; Housing Association Board member.
Career: Trained *Prince Evans*, qualified 1996; formerly Senior Manager with the Housing Corporation, Notting Hill Housing Trust and Network Housing Association; joined *Lewis Silkin* 1998. Made Partner 2000.
Publications: Contributes articles to housing press including in 'Social Housing', 'Housing' and 'Housing Today' as well as other trade journals.
Personal: University of Edinburgh (MA Hons) UCL (MPhil Town Planning). Enjoys sailing, walking, tennis.

PANTELIA, Despina
Clifford Chance, London
(020) 7600 1000
despina.pantelia@cliffordchance.com
Specialisation: Banking and Finance Department. Partner specialising in bank lending, housing association finance, university finance and public/private sector financing.
Career: *Clifford Chance* 1987-95; *Allen & Overy* 1996-97; *Clifford Chance* since 1997.
Personal: University of London (LLM European and Maritime Law).

PAPWORTH, Richard
Addleshaw Booth & Co, Leeds
(0113) 209 2310
richard.papworth@addleshawbooth.com
See under Banking & Finance, p.108

RANDALL, Simon
Lawrence Graham, London
(020) 7379 0000

RHATIGAN, Michael
Eversheds, Manchester
(0161) 831 8000
michaelrhatigan@eversheds.com
Specialisation: Partner in commercial property department. All property aspects for Housing Association law including acquisition development and letting of properties and funding.
Career: Partner *Maurice Rubin Clare* 1979-90; partner *Davies Arnold Cooper* 1990-95; partner *Eversheds* 1995.
Personal: Born 1952. Leisure interests include Bolton Wanderers and opera.

ROBERT, Louis
Prince Evans, London
(020) 8567 3477
lrobert@prince-evans.co.uk
Specialisation: Senior partner of *Prince Evans*. Specialises in innovative regeneration and development projects on behalf of public authorities and registered social landlords; recent and current projects

THE LEADERS — SOCIAL HOUSING

involve stock transfers, including TUPE and pension arrangements, HAT succession projects, Social Services Authorities and Health Authority reprovision schemes and PFI with VAT and capital finance efficiency, key worker and flexible tenure projects and joint venture company/off-balance sheet SPC transactions, innovative large funding arrangements with group borrowing vehicles and security trustee arrangements and acting on ALMOs; over twenty years experience in the care and housing sector; author of report to Audit commission/CMHD on legal and financial framework of NHS and board member and currently chairs Risk Assessment Panel at the Genesis Housing Group.
Career: Articled *Butcher & Barlow*; qualified 1968, partner *Prince Evans* 1972.
Personal: Manchester University (1965 LLB). Resides Kew, Surrey. Born 1943.

ROBERTS, Ian
Denton Wilde Sapte, London
(020) 7246 7056
imr@dentonwildesapte.com
Specialisation: Leads the *Denton Wilde Sapte* social housing finance team with substantial experience acting on a full range of matters in the social housing finance sector (primarily for funders), including LSVTs, group structures, trickle transfers, development, care homes and keyworker facilities. The team is a cross-departmental group of 15 experienced social housing finance and property lawyers, working closely together and supported by leading projects/PFI, construction and environmental specialists. The firm's property department also has expertise in the public sector acting for government departments as well as being on the legal advisor panel for DETR (including advising on the development of PFI/PPP practice), the MoD, the Home Office, certain local authorities and other similar public sector bodies. The firm is on the legal panel for a number of RSLs and has been retained to advise on a wide range of matters including construction disputes, planning issues and tenant consultation. The firm also has significant experience in acting for local authorities in relation to the disposal and development of social housing land and the administration and payment of social housing grants.
Career: Joined *Denton Wilde Sapte* in 1983, becoming a partner in 1990.
Personal: Read law at Pembroke College, Cambridge before joining *Denton Wilde Sapte*. He is married with three children. Interests include rugby, motor racing, reading and, more recently, skiing and his Yamaha Fazer.

ROBERTSON, Andrew
TC Young, Glasgow
(0141) 221 5562
aor@tcyoung.co.uk
Specialisation: Works for community based charitable and generalist housing associations as well as fully mutual and non-fully mutual Co-ops. Acts on behalf of housing associations across the whole field of their activity. Was instrumental in the forming of the first Employers' Federation for Housing Association Committees (now EVH) and provided full administrative and advisory support during its early years. Accredited specialist in charity law.
Prof. Memberships: Law Society of Scotland.
Career: Qualified 1967. Partner, *TC Young* 1968.
Personal: Chairman of the Lintel Trust (formerly the Scottish Housing Associations Charitable Trust) from 1992 to date. Trustee of HACT from 1991-97.

SMITH, Chris
Maclay Murray & Spens, London
(0171) 606 6130
cps@maclaymurrayspens.co.uk
Specialisation: Partner in social housing department. Principal area of practice covers all aspects of social housing work with particular expertise in employment law, constitutional work, urban regeneration and Care in the Community. Other main area of practice is development work including consortium arrangements. Currently engaged in a major south coast reprovision project involving 250 properties and associated amenities, and the social housing aspects of a new settlement in Cambridge.
Career: Qualified in 1978. Became a partner with *Asshetons* in 1980 and in the merged firm of *Manches & Co*, then joined *Stones Porter* as a partner in 1993, and *Maclays* (associated with *Maclay Murray & Spens*) in 1998.
Personal: Born 22 October 1953. Attended University College, Cardiff 1972-75. Leisure pursuits include golf and squash. Lives in Godalming.

STEPHENS, Hugo
Pinsent Curtis Biddle, Birmingham
(0121) 212 1828
hugo.stephens@pinsents.com
Specialisation: An acknowledged leader in this field with expertise in all forms of corporate, constitutional and finance work for registered social landlords. Has advised on all forms of housing stock transfer including Sunderland Housing Group on the largest transfer to date - 37,000 houses to seven companies; group structures, amalgamations and mergers; PFI/PPP projects, care home transfers and charities; particular expertise in housing finance acting for borrowers and lenders in over £5 million of loans; wrote the National Housing Federation's guide to understanding loan documentation and the loan and security documentation sections for their new revised Private Finance Manual.
Prof. Memberships: Law Society.
Career: Qualified in 1989 with *Trowers & Hamlins*, 1989-94, assistant solicitor *Trowers & Hamlins*; 1994-97, senior assistant solicitor *Prince Evans*; 1997, partner *Irwin Mitchell*; 2001, partner *Pinsent Curtis Biddle*.
Personal: Born March 1956. Member of the Magic Circle.

THOMPSON, Alison
TC Young, Edinburgh
(0131) 220 7660
amt@tcyoung.co.uk
Specialisation: Handles all aspects of social housing law including stock transfers, public/private housing partnerships, commercial contracts, funding, policy, corporate structures, tenancies, tenures, shared ownership developments, site acquisition and development.
Prof. Memberships: Law Society (Scotland), Notary Public.
Career: Qualified 1988; Partner *TC Young*, 2001.

TURNER, Graham
Trowers & Hamlins, Manchester
(0161) 211 0000
gturner@trowers.com
Specialisation: Partner, Head of Manchester Office. Has specialised in Housing Association law for 25 years, heading a team of six Manchester lawyers (four partners) who provide a comprehensive housing law service on a regional and national basis. Experience ranges from stock transfer major development and partnership projects, urban renewal and regeneration to private finance and group structures. Constitutional vires and PFI issues. All legal issues relating to the housing movement are covered by the Manchester office, including litigation, construction and environmental matters.

WINROW, Janet
Trowers & Hamlins, Manchester
(0161) 211 0024
jwinrow@trowers.com
Specialisation: Partner with wide experience of housing work. Leads a team of five lawyers dealing with RSL work, in particular stock transfers of council housing. Experienced in care schemes, housing management issues and funding for RSL developments.

SPORT

London: 766; The Regions: 769; Scotland: 770; Profiles: 771

Research approved by BMRB For this edition, **Chambers'** researchers conducted 6,582 interviews – 3,900 with law firms, 511 with barristers and 2,171 with clients. The validity of the research was scrutinised by BMRB International, who audited both the methodology and the results at our offices in London. They interviewed **Chambers'** researchers and cross-checked sample interviews. Details of the audit appear on page 7.

OVERVIEW The last year has witnessed a tumultuous time for sport; the collapse of ITV Digital and the break-up of the Kirch empire have followed in the wake of falling advertising revenues arising from the September 11th terrorist attacks. The large commercial/media firms have scored well with a number of big cases being played out, while both regional and regulatory firms have been involved in a range of contentious issues.

LONDON

REGULATORY

SPORT: REGULATORY
LONDON

1. Denton Wilde Sapte
2. Farrer & Co
   Hammond Suddards Edge
   Max Bitel, Greene
3. Charles Russell
   Simmons & Simmons
4. Freshfields Bruckhaus Deringer
   The Simkins Partnership

This book is the product of 6,582 1/2 hour interviews. See p.7 for BMRB audit. Within each band, firms are listed alphabetically

DENTON WILDE SAPTE (see firm details p.935) The "*pre-eminent*" firm, it boasts a range of regulatory expertise and is home to the "*superb*" Mark Gay (see p.772). Highlights of the last year include defending proceedings brought by leading players alleging anti-competitive behaviour in the World Professional Billiards and Snooker Association's (WPBSA) rules – the first such case brought under the Competition Act. The firm also conducted an investigation for The Racecourse Association into allegations that negotiations for the disposal of media rights were tainted. **Clients** WPBSA; The Racecourse Association; IAAF; Rugby Football Union (RFU).

FARRER & CO (see firm details p.952) The team retains its outstanding reputation in governance work, where it is particularly renowned for its focus on athletics issues. It has advised UK Athletics on doping policies, and has drafted and implemented an appeals procedure that relates to able-bodied and disabled athletes. The firm has also advised a number of sporting bodies on the implementation of UK Sport's anti-doping policy. Although much of the firm's profile remains with its regulatory work, it is moving steadily towards the commercial arena. Lead partner **Karena Vleck** (see p.774) was dubbed "*a true expert*" by our interviewees. **Clients** Amateur Athletic Association of England; British Athletic Foundation; The Commonwealth Games Council for England; The Football Association (The FA); Sport England; UK Athletics.

HAMMOND SUDDARDS EDGE The merger of boutique firm Townleys with the nationally respected sports practice of Hammond Suddards Edge has created a unit with "*a huge core and great personalities.*" Stephen Townley's move into a consultancy role has allowed the "*always able and enthusiastic*" Jonathan Taylor to take on the lead governance role. Aided by Birmingham-based Richard Alderson, he advises on governance issues for a range of bodies. The firm has acted for The Football League in its dispute with Wimbledon FC – concerning its move to Milton Keynes – and has been particularly active in the fallout of the ITV Digital collapse. **Clients** The Football League; International Tennis Federation.

MAX BITEL, GREENE (see firm details p.1058) The recruitment of **Mel Goldberg** (see p.772) ("*sharp mind*") is seen as "*pushing up an already talent-packed firm.*" He continues to advise on management and image issues for footballers, boxers, tennis players and assorted athletes. The main thrust of the firm remains **Nick Bitel** (see p.771), who has "*a feel and empathy for sports work which few others can match.*" As well as his nationally recognised work for the London Marathon, he is active with commercial and contractual matters for individuals and institutions throughout the market. The firm has been particularly involved with the consequences of the postponement of the Ryder Cup. **Clients** The London Marathon; Ryder Cup; sporting individuals.

CHARLES RUSSELL (see firm details p.904) The well-respected **Patrick Russell** (see p.773) stands out particularly for his work with The Jockey Club. Over the last year he has helped align The Jockey Club's regulations with the Human Rights Act, rewriting its rules and establishing an appeal board. The firm also advised in the high-profile case of the English RFU v Martin Johnson. **Clients** The Jockey Club; The Hurlingham Polo Association; Kookaburra Sport; Lennox Lewis.

SIMMONS & SIMMONS (see firm details p.1136) A niche in cricket and continued representation of the ICC affords this firm a strong profile. Over the last year, the team has been active in major cricketing events, including the Under 19 World Cup 2002 and the next Cricket World Cup in South Africa in 2003. The team, which includes Mark Dewar, is involved in qualification disputes that have surrounded past tournaments. It also advises on the commercial, IP and property aspects of sporting matters. **Clients** MCC; ICC; TWR/Arrows Grand Prix International.

FRESHFIELDS BRUCKHAUS DERINGER (see firm details p.964) Deemed an "*expert*" by his peers, **Raj Parker** (see p.773) received plaudits for his litigation work. He has advised The Football Association in a number of high-profile cases including the charges brought against Chesterfield FC concerning the under-report-

---

TOP IN-HOUSE LAWYERS

Heather BARTON, Head of Legal and Special Project, Scottish Football Association
Darren BERMAN, Company Solicitor, Football Association
Nic COWARD, Company Solicitor, Football Association
Sara FRIEND, Legal Director, British Olympic Association
Andy GRAY, Head of Legal Affairs, British Swimming Association
Jonathan HALLI, Secretary and Legal Officer, Rugby Football Union
Bruce MELLSTROM, Lawyer, Lawn Tennis Association
Holly ROPER-CURZON, Club Solicitor, MCC
Mark ROPER-DRIMIE, Solicitor, England & Wales Cricket Board
Sacha WOODWARD HILL, Lawyer, Formula One
Richard VEROW, Octagon

The "*excellent*" **Heather Barton** continues to be praised within the Scottish sports scene. At the English Football Association, both the "*expert*" **Darren Berman** and **Nic Coward** ("*thinks well on his feet*") are respected. **Sara Friend** of the BOA is "*top class,*" **Andy Gray** is a "*star on doping issues*" and **Jonathan Hall** is "*good to deal with.*" **Bruce Mellstrom** is praised for his "*detailed knowledge and enthusiasm.*" **Holly Roper-Curzon** is "*incredibly skilled*" and **Sacha Woodward Hill** is described as a "*pleasant perfectionist,*" while **Mark Roper-Drimie** is "*absolutely brilliant.*" Meanwhile on the sports rights side, **Richard Verow** is recommended as "*a top lawyer at every level.*"

In-house lawyers' profiles p.1201

766　　INDEX TO LEADING LAWYERS: PAGE 1693 ■ IN-HOUSE LAWYERS PROFILES: PAGE 1201

LONDON ■ SPORT

LEADING INDIVIDUALS

1. **GAY Mark** Denton Wilde Sapte
2. **BITEL Nicholas** Max Bitel, Greene
   TAYLOR Jonathan Hammond Suddards Edge
   VLECK Karena Farrer & Co
3. **GOLDBERG Mel** Max Bitel, Greene
   PARKER Raj Freshfields Bruckhaus Deringer
   RUSSELL Patrick Charles Russell

See individuals' profiles p.771

LONDON — COMMERCIAL/MEDIA

SPORT: COMMERCIAL/MEDIA — LONDON

1. Denton Wilde Sapte
2. Bird & Bird
   Hammond Suddards Edge
3. Nicholson Graham & Jones
   Olswang
   SJ Berwin
4. Freshfields Bruckhaus Deringer
   Harbottle & Lewis
   The Simkins Partnership
   Theodore Goddard
5. Ashurst Morris Crisp
   Clintons
   Collyer-Bristow
   Field Fisher Waterhouse
   Herbert Smith
6. Couchman Harrington Associates
   Memery Crystal

LEADING INDIVIDUALS

1. **BARR-SMITH Adrian** Denton Wilde Sapte
2. **WALKEY Justin** Bird & Bird
3. **BELL Alasdair** Olswang
   PHELOPS Warren Nicholson Graham & Jones
4. **FITZPATRICK Nick** Denton Wilde Sapte
   HORNSBY Stephen The Simkins Partnership
   KORMAN Andy Hammond Suddards Edge
   METLISS Jonathan SJ Berwin
   MILLICHIP Peter Hammond Suddards Edge
   REEVE Felicity Bird & Bird
   REID Fraser Theodore Goddard
   ZEFFMAN David Olswang
5. **BARRATT Richard** Norton Rose
   BLAIN John Freshfields Bruckhaus Deringer
   BURDON-COOPER Alan Collyer-Bristow
   COUCHMAN Nicholas Couchman Harrington Associates
   HARRINGTON Dan Couchman Harrington Associates
   HIGTON Jonathan Hammond Suddards Edge
   MITCHELL Bob Harbottle & Lewis
   STINSON Philip Clintons
   WATTS Alan Herbert Smith

This book is the product of 6,582 1/2 hour interviews. See p.7 for BMRB audit.
Within each band, firms are listed alphabetically. See individuals' profiles p.771

---

ing of gate receipts and other financial irregularities. He is currently involved in the high-profile replica kits case. Both Parker and Paris-based partner Jan Paulsson are appointed to the Court of Arbitration for Sport in Lausanne. **Clients** The FA; FIFA; South African Football Association.

THE SIMKINS PARTNERSHIP (see firm details p.1136) The quality of this firm's regulatory work is apparent to our sources and its profile in the market has grown. Litigation partner Roger Billins is a member of the team that boasts a strong rugby client base. The firm acted for Premier Rugby on a number of transfer and code of conduct disputes and advised on the Martin Johnson disciplinary proceedings. **Clients** Premier Rugby; Premier Rugby Partnership Wales; Saracens Rugby Club; Surrey County Cricket Club; West Ham United FC.

DENTON WILDE SAPTE (see firm details p.935) Our researchers have found that the firm has become a dominant force in London sports law, able to field a "*constructive and highly commercial*" team. Crucial to the commercial/media side of work is "*the genius figure*" of **Adrian Barr-Smith** (see p.771), who is able to "*see every shade of the sporting spectrum.*" Over the last year, he has advised on the abolition of the Horserace Betting Levy Board and been active in the OFT investigation into The British Horseracing Board (BHB) licensing policy. His team has also raised its profile in acting for The FA Premier League on the sale of the domestic and international rights for the Premiership until the end of the 2004 season. A key figure here is the "*dynamo,*" **Nick Fitzpatrick** (see p.771), "*a tough, problem-crunching lawyer.*" **Clients** England and Wales Cricket Board; The FA Premier League; The Racecourse Association; RFU.

BIRD & BIRD (see firm details p.874) The team was praised for "*exuding confidence on commercial and sponsorship issues*" and for the speed and veracity of its work. Our market sources pointed particularly to the teaming of **Justin Walkey** and **Felicity Reeve** (see p.773) as key to much of the firm's success – they are described as "*superb standard-bearers for quality sports work.*" The representation of media bodies and rights' holders has been a key feature of the workload, and the firm has acted for The FA on corporate, commercial, broadcasting and IP matters. It has advised Microsoft on its appointment as official software supplier to the Manchester 2002 Commonwealth Games and on a range of sponsorship and endorsement issues. **Clients** ESPN; FLPTV; The FA; LTA; Microsoft; ProEvents; Sport+ (SPORTFIVE); Teamtalk; Welsh Rugby Union.

HAMMOND SUDDARDS EDGE The merger of the sports practices of Hammonds and Townleys was seen by our interviewees as a natural move for both firms, creating a pool of "*top seed*" individuals and a client list "*that touches every base.*" The "*tenacious and brilliant*" **Andy Korman** is regarded as "*the best in the country for sponsorship work*" and has had particular success in arranging sponsorship rights for the Heineken League. "*Expert and friendly*" **Peter Millichip** is recommended for his work in radio, television and new media, while **Jonathan Higton** has advised on media rights for a range of diverse events from The FA Cup to mountain biking. The team has been advising on the fallout of the ITV Digital collapse. **Clients** Australian Cricket Board; The Football League; International Tennis Federation; Octagon; Rugby World Cup; South African Cricket Board; Vodafone.

NICHOLSON GRAHAM & JONES (see firm details p.1083) This well-regarded firm was heavily endorsed by clients for its media-related advice. The focal point remains the "*enthusiastic*" **Warren Phelops** (see p.773) who has "*the right touch on commercial work.*" Highlights over the last 12 months include representing Sportscard in its acquisition by ukbetting for £4 million. The team is also busy on sponsorship, internet matters, fundraisings and securitisation. **Clients** AOL (UK); Association of Surfing Professionals; GBR Team Challenge Company; Leeds United plc; PGA European Tour; Ryder Cup; Sporting Index.

OLSWANG (see firm details p.1087) The group was recommended to our researchers for bringing its media expertise to the sports sector with such good effect. It has been involved recently on a number of key cases for UEFA, which included acting to counter complaints made by the European Commission that the sale of UEFA Champions League TV rights breached EU competition law, and offering advice on the development of a UEFA extranet project. The group has also gained plaudits for its work for Wimbledon FC in its mooted move to Milton Keynes. **Alasdair Bell** (see p.771) is praised "*as the doyen of competition law – regularly razor-sharp for UEFA,*" while **David Zeffman** (see p.592) is known by clients as "*the guru of TV work.*" **Clients** Channel 4; Granada Media Group; NIKE; RFU; Scottish Premier League; Tottenham Hotspur FC; Wimbledon FC; UEFA.

SJ BERWIN (see firm details p.867) The sports business group retains its buoyant profile, attracting recommendations across the market-

SPORT ■ LONDON

place. At its head remains **Jonathan Metliss** (see p.772), who "*knows how to pull in the big clients.*" The firm has recently represented ukbetting on its recommended offer for Sportscard Group (£4 million), and advised BBC Wales and S4C on their joint acquisition of Welsh rugby rights. **Clients** Arsenal FC; BBC Wales; British Ski Federation; Channel 4; England and Wales Cricket Board; ENIC; ITV Sport; S4C; Tottenham Hotspur FC.

FRESHFIELDS BRUCKHAUS DERINGER (see firm details p.964) The firm was commended by peers and clients for its success in building bridges across the sports market. The key name on the commercial side is the "*ever busy, ever ready*" senior associate **John Blain** (see p.771), who is perceived as "*a growing presence.*" Over the last year the team has acted on proposed listings and share offerings in a Premier League club and clubs in Italy, Spain and Portugal. The group's workload also encompasses IP and television issues. **Clients** Formula One racing team; football clubs.

HARBOTTLE & LEWIS (see firm details p.983) This firm is making a "*stronger and stronger impression*" in the sports market, handling an impressive array of work. Over the last year it has acted for International Sportsworld Communicators on its ongoing development of the World Rally Championship, and advised Philip Morris International on its motor sports sponsorship – including its highly valuable Ferrari deal. **Bob Mitchell** (see p.773) was described by commentators as "*undeniably top-notch.*" **Clients** International Sportsworld Communicators; PGA European Tour; Philip Morris International; QPR Football & Athletic Club; Ryder Cup; World Rally Championship; London Wasps RFC.

THE SIMKINS PARTNERSHIP (see firm details p.1136) The profile of this firm has risen in conjunction with that of leading light **Stephen Hornsby** (see p.772), described by clients as "*responsive with a willingness to get his hands dirty.*" The highlights of last year include advising Premier Rugby on its joint venture with the RFU, enabling the centralisation of broadcasting, sponsorship and other commercial rights. The firm also advised ITV on complications arising from the sale of UEFA Champions League rights. **Clients** IMG; MCC; Premier Rugby; TWI.

THEODORE GODDARD (see firm details p.1158) It has been a busy year for this highly regarded firm. Highlights include acting for BHB in the ground-breaking litigation against William Hill concerning copyright infringement for unauthorised use of racing fixture lists. The group also acted for Formula One after its removal from the Kirch empire. The key name of this firm remains the "*bright spark of sporting enthusiasm,*" **Fraser Reid** (see p.773). **Clients** BHB; Formula One Management; International Management Network; SFX; World Famous Group; World Squash Federation; WSM Sport.

ASHURST MORRIS CRISP (see firm details p.852) Acknowledged by peers to be a "*steady ship,*" the firm has a keen understanding of the sports market. Roger Finbow's team acted in the last year in the securitisation of gate receipts at Ipswich Town, which will be used in the development of Portman Road. It has also acted for TV Danmark 1 in its judicial review against the ITC's refusal to grant exclusive broadcast rights for the Danish national football team's away matches in the World Cup qualifying round. **Clients** 365 Corporation; Bayer 04 Leverkusen Football; IMG; Ipswich Town FC; SportingArena.

CLINTONS (see firm details p.912) This small but busy firm is recommended for its work with agents and media bodies, while "*key player*" **Philip Stinson** (see p.774) is famed for his sponsorship work. The team has acted for the global advertising agency of a major sporting company and advised on the restructuring of a popular sport. It has also handled various media issues for well-known sporting individuals. **Clients** Sports marketing agencies; high net worth individuals; manufacturers.

COLLYER-BRISTOW (see firm details p.917) This firm has found a healthy niche for itself in sponsorship work and remains well regarded for its advice to Sport England, which includes lottery grants, property, and planning issues and its undertakings with governing bodies. The team is described by clients as "*approachable, impressive and seeming to have efficiency on tap.*" The "*standout*" **Alan Burdon-Cooper** (see p.771) also acted for Fast Track in its renewed appointment as exclusive marketing agent for UK Athletics and organiser of the major televised athletic events in the UK. **Clients** Fast Track; Quink Music; Sport England.

FIELD FISHER WATERHOUSE (see firm details p.954) This well-regarded firm continues to perform a range of interesting work in the sports arena. Patrick Cannon's team advised Podia Group on its £2.8 million acquisition of TMG Worldwide – a company that exploits commercial sports rights primarily for Formula 1. It also advised London Irish Holdings (the ultimate owner of London Irish RFC) on a £2 million fundraising. **Clients** Dunlop Slazenger Group; Eurosport Consortium; GoalStriker; IMG; London Irish Holdings; Sport First.

HERBERT SMITH (see firm details p.992) This "*true heavy hitter*" of a firm is known across the industry for its highly recommended work for Sky – described by market experts a "*top quality sports-related work.*" The highly respected **Alan Watts** (see p.774) leads a team that has advised on a number of high-value deals and transactions, including Sky's joint venture with Ladbrokes to develop a betting business across its digital sports channels. The firm also acted for the FIA on the European Commission's review of rights for Formula 1 motor racing. **Clients** BSkyB; FIA; Motorsport Vision; West Ham United FC.

COUCHMAN HARRINGTON ASSOCIATES Although a smaller niche practice, the substantial profiles of ex-Townleys' men **Dan Harrington** (see p.772) and **Nicholas Couchman** (see p.771) mean that this firm punches well above its weight. Proclaimed as "*experts on IP rights,*" the duo has been active in a number of rights, sponsorship and new media matters in the last year. The team also works for companies developing youth sport skills. **Clients** Rights holders; governing bodies; sponsors.

MEMERY CRYSTAL (see firm details p.1067) Clients characterise the firm as wielding "*a repository of expertise which one can just dip into.*" The team, which includes David Hansel, approaches sporting matters with a commercial/corporate bent. The team has handled a number of rights' acquisitions over the last year and advised on football-related floats. **Clients** 24dogs; Britannic Asset Management; First Artist; Millwall FC; Watford FC.

OTHER NOTABLE PRACTITIONERS A new presence in our tables this year is Norton Rose partner **Richard Barratt** (see p.771). Praised by clients as a "*creative thinker,*" he is experienced in sponsorship and media issues.

THE REGIONS — SPORT

THE SOUTH

SPORT — THE SOUTH

1. Clarke Willmott & Clarke — Southampton

This book is the product of 6,582 1/2 hour interviews. See p.7 for BMRB audit. Within each band, firms are listed alphabetically.

CLARKE WILLMOTT & CLARKE (see firm details p.907) Even before its merger, the Southampton-based firm of Ensor Byfield was attracting plaudits during our research. Trevor Watkins' team brings a platter of good clients and experience to the table. It is particularly well known for its work in Formula 1, acting for both the drivers and the teams. This is complemented by a strong profile in football – acting for clubs and supporters' bodies – and racing. The much-respected John Byfield remains at the firm as a consultant. **Clients** Bournemouth AFC; Gillingham FC; various F1 clients.

SOUTH WEST

SPORT — SOUTH WEST

1. Clarke Willmott & Clarke — Bristol
2. Osborne Clarke — Bristol

LEADING INDIVIDUALS

1. SMITH Ian — Clarke Willmott & Clarke
2. BRAITHWAITE Andrew — Osborne Clarke

This book is the product of 6,582 1/2 hour interviews. See p.7 for BMRB audit. Within each band, firms are listed alphabetically.

CLARKE WILLMOTT & CLARKE (see firm details p.907) This long-established and well-respected sporting practice has recently supplemented its talent pool through a merger with Ensor Byfield. Leading light **Ian Smith** (see p.774) is commended by our interviewees as "*having a true empathy for sportsmen.*" This active team has advised the British Lions squad members in the negotiation of contracts, represented the Professional Rugby Players Association (PRA) in the establishment of England Rugby Ltd and worked with The Professional Cricketers' Association (PCA) in the setting up of cricnet.com. **Clients** cricnet.com Ltd; PCA; PRA; Springbok Supporters Club.

OSBORNE CLARKE (see firm details p.1090) This small Bristol team has maintained its strong reputation with a number of high-profile matters. It has been involved in the commercial consequences of the postponement of the Ryder Cup, and advised on venue arrangements for the Ryder Cup in 2010 and 2014. The team has also assisted on the commercial and regulatory aspects of rugby and motor sport. The admired **Andrew Braithwaite** leads a team that "*is always right on the money.*" **Clients** Bolton Wanderers FC; Bristol Rugby Ltd; Honda (UK); PGA; Ryder Cup; Wembley National Stadium.

WALES

SPORT — WALES

1. Hugh James — Cardiff

This book is the product of 6,582 1/2 hour interviews. See p.7 for BMRB audit. Within each band, firms are listed alphabetically.

HUGH JAMES (see firm details p.1004) Instruction from the Welsh Rugby Union (WRU) has helped raise the profile of this team, its principle advisor. Commentators UK-wide praised the team's skills in this field, handling such matters as corporate and property joint ventures, as well as broadcasting agreements for the WRU. It also acts on the more high-profile cases such as the sacking of Graham Henry. Bill Snowdon's team has handled the contracts for the staging of the FA Cup finals in Cardiff for the next five years, and the team advises the Special Olympics. **Clients** Cardiff Devils Ice Hockey Team; Merthyr Tydfil FC; Rhondda Rebels; Special Olympics; WRU.

MIDLANDS

SPORT — MIDLANDS

1. Hammond Suddards Edge — Birmingham

LEADING INDIVIDUALS

1. ALDERSON Richard — Hammond Suddards Edge

This book is the product of 6,582 1/2 hour interviews. See p.7 for BMRB audit. Within each band, firms are listed alphabetically. See individuals' profiles p.771

HAMMOND SUDDARDS EDGE The firm retains a strong brand name in the Midlands through the presence of **Richard Alderson**. He is described by peers and clients alike as "*the best out-of-London practitioner – a genius of sports law.*" Alderson and the team have been active over the last year on a number of high-profile matters for The Football League, including the repercussions of the collapse of ITV Digital.

THE NORTH

JAMES CHAPMAN & CO (see firm details p.1012) **Maurice Watkins** (see p.774) is acclaimed by both peers and clients as "*a legend*" in sports law, with a name that is recognisable from both media coverage and legal circles. He spearheads a firm that is still seen as one of the national front runners. He was a member of a FIFA working party drafting new world transfer regulations, and advised The FA Premier League on reaching a settlement with the PFA regarding a mooted strike. The firm also worked on the record-breaking transfers to Manchester United FC of Ruud van Nistelrooy and Juan Sebastian Veron, and sponsorship and merchandising deals worth £303 million. At the commercial forefront, **Jason Smith** (see p.774) remains "*an excellent and committed performer.*" **Clients** Amateur Swimming Association/Amateur Swimming Federation of Great Britain; The FA Premier League; Manchester United FC.

MCCORMICKS (see firm details p.1063) The team has been involved in a number of significant matters for The FA Premier League in the past year, including the high-profile dispute with the PFA and the arrangement of a new sponsorship deal with Barclaycard. Peter

SPORT ■ SCOTLAND

SPORT
■ THE NORTH

1. James Chapman & Co Manchester
   McCormicks Leeds
2. George Davies Manchester
3. Addleshaw Booth & Co Manchester
   Hill Dickinson Liverpool, Manchester
   Walker Morris Leeds
4. Zermansky & Partners Leeds

LEADING INDIVIDUALS

* WATKINS Maurice James Chapman & Co
1. MCCORMICK Peter McCormicks
2. HEWISON John George Davies
3. SMITH Jason James Chapman & Co
4. HOVELL Mark George Davies
   MORRISON Michael Hill Dickinson

This book is the product of 6,582 1/2 hour interviews. See p.7 for BMRB audit.
Within each band, firms are listed alphabetically See individuals' profiles p.771

McCormick (see p.772) is described by our interviewees as "*one of the main national players;*" he advised The FA Premier League in the European negotiations to change the football transfer system. **Clients** The FA Premier League; Leeds United FC; London Broncos RLFC; Wakefield Trinity Wildcats RLFC.

GEORGE DAVIES (see firm details p.968) The firm has been "*catapulted into the limelight*" in the last year, thanks to its high-profile work for the PFA, particularly concerning the increased TV revenue from the Premier and Nationwide leagues. **John Hewison** (see p.772) remains the figurehead of the firm and is praised for his "*passion and knowledge,*" while **Mark Hovell** (see p.772) is considered as "*experienced as any-one in the country.*" The firm has also acted in a number of disputes for well-known individuals. **Clients** Basketball Players' Association; Ice Hockey Players' Association; League Managers Association; PFA.

ADDLESHAW BOOTH & CO (see firm details p.838) The reputation of Robert Stoker's team remains largely tied up with its connections to the Manchester 2002 Commonwealth Games. The group has handled sponsorship agreements, broadcasting contracts, production agreements and trademark protection. However, its work for rugby league has also started to turn some heads, with commentators agreeing that they are "*impressed by the intelligence and imagination of this team.*" **Clients** Manchester 2002 Ltd; Manchester United plc; The Rugby Football League; Williams Grand Prix Engineering.

HILL DICKINSON (see firm details p.995) This small but efficient team is recommended for its work with sporting individuals, handling the traditional work of contract negotiation, breaches of contract, unfair dismissal and some disciplinary matters. The firm also takes care of image rights for high-profile individuals, as well as personal sponsorship and endorsements. **Michael Morrison** (see p.773) is praised highly by peers. **Clients** Individuals; some football clubs.

WALKER MORRIS (see firm details p.1178) The firm retains a profile through the size and scope of its profile as solicitors to Rugby Super League. Chris Caisley's team has advised it on trademark and sponsorship matters and negotiated broadcast contracts and internet agreements. The firm maintains its strong reputation acting for sporting individuals, and has advised on disputes for a number of football clubs. **Clients** Bradford Bulls; Bradford City FC; Grimsby Town AFC; Millwall FC; PCA; PRA; Rugby Super League; Sportsworld Media.

ZERMANSKY & PARTNERS (see firm details p.1200) Known throughout the region as a firm that "*can punch above its weight,*" its marquee client remains The Rugby Football League, and Richard Lindley's team has been active in the restructuring of that organisation. The firm also handles a variety of matters for the Rugby League Cup, and has been involved in a large case involving football agents. **Clients** The Rugby Football League.

SCOTLAND

SPORT
■ SCOTLAND

1. Anderson Strathern WS Edinburgh
   Harper Macleod Glasgow
2. Burness Glasgow
   Dundas & Wilson CS Edinburgh
   Henderson Boyd Jackson WS Edinburgh

LEADING INDIVIDUALS

1. KERR John Anderson Strathern WS
2. DUFF Alistair Henderson Boyd Jackson WS
   HENRY Graeme Dundas & Wilson CS
   MCKENZIE Rod Harper Macleod
   MILLER Stephen MacRoberts
   SLEIGH Andrew Burness

This book is the product of 6,582 1/2 hour interviews. See p.7 for BMRB audit.
Within each band, firms are listed alphabetically See individuals' profiles p.771

ANDERSON STRATHERN WS (see firm details p.844) This Edinburgh firm continues to attract the recommendations of peers and clients alike, bringing together a combination of "*sporting enthusiasm and a comfort with the law.*" It is endorsed primarily for its advice to the SRU, for which it has handled strategic, sponsorship and constitutional advice over the last year. The firm also boasts sportscotland as a client, giving it an expertise in lottery funding issues. **John Kerr** (see p.772) is praised as "*knowing this business inside and out.*" **Clients** Commonwealth Games Council for Scotland; sportscotland; SRU; Scottish Games Association.

HARPER MACLEOD (see firm details p.985) The firm has retained its strong reputation despite the loss of the well-regarded Stephen Miller to MacRoberts. **Rod McKenzie** (see p.772) is now seen as the force behind the practice, being both "*solidly sensible and forthright.*" The team has acted for Celtic FC on matters arising from the Champions League match against Juventus in Turin. It has also advised on issues arising from the SPL and TV contracts, and has carried out high-profile work for the SRU. **Clients** British Ice Hockey Association; Celtic; SPL; SRU.

BURNESS Football related matters see the firm at its best advantage, and peers regard it as "*a team of expert quality and depth.*" It has acted for The Scottish Football Association (SFA) litigation involving clubs and players. It has also been involved in a number of media matters, which include acting for Radio First and Gordon Smith (players' agent and broadcaster) in the merger with Prostar. **Andrew Sleigh** continues to be hailed as the "*safest pair of hands in Scotland.*" **Clients** Dunfermline Athletic FC; Radio First; SFA.

DUNDAS & WILSON CS (see firm details p.943) Although the firm has long been well regarded for the wide breadth of its sporting work, it has previously been perceived to lack a star individual. This has changed in the last year with the emergence of **Graeme Henry**, who is seen to be "*taking a dynamic lead*" in the market. The firm's representations at the top end of Scottish football have meant a greater involvement in the reorganisation of the TV contracts. The team also acted for the SRU on its sponsorship deal. **Clients** The Rangers FC; SRU.

HENDERSON BOYD JACKSON WS The "*sterling*" **Alistair Duff** (see p.771) continues to impress with his knowledge and enthusiasm for sporting issues. He has been active on contractual matters for Hibernian FC. The firm also advises sporting individuals. **Clients** Hastings International; Heart of Midlothian; Hibernian FC; various sports personalities and agents.

THE LEADERS ■ SPORT

OTHER NOTABLE PRACTITIONERS The former Harper Macleod man, **Stephen Miller** (see p.773), now resides at MacRoberts. Described by peers as "*one of the strongest leaders of sports work,*" he has recently been appointed a commissioner on the SPL panel and is taking instructions from Premier League clubs.

THE LEADERS IN SPORT

ALDERSON, Richard
Hammond Suddards Edge, Birmingham
(0121) 222 3000

BARRATT, Richard
Norton Rose, London
(020) 7283 6000
barrattrw@nortonrose.com
Specialisation: Over the last 18 years he has developed a substantial commercial IP/IT/media practice. He has advised on a wide range of arrangements for the acquisition and marketing of sponsorship and media rights relating to sports and other events. Recent deals include the complex $1.2 billion rights pending arrangements between the Teams Masters Series and ISL and subsequent restructuring following the collapse of ISL and a string of rights acquisition deals across a diverse range of sports, including football, rugby, surfing and polo.
Prof. Memberships: City of London Solicitors Company, Law Society Golf Club.
Career: Qualified in 1984. Joined *Norton Rose* in 1986 from *Rooks Rider*. Became a partner in *Norton Rose* in 1994. Head of *Norton Rose* Sports Group.
Personal: Educated at the Kings School, Chester and University of London, Kings College (LLB). Married with two children. Interests include golf, skiing and jogging. A keen Chelsea fan.

BARR-SMITH, Adrian
Denton Wilde Sapte, London
(020) 7320 6501
abs@dentonwildesapte.com
Specialisation: Main area of practice is sport, covering broadcasting contracts, licensing and merchandising, event regulation, official supplier contracts and disciplinary matters. Also covers media finance, film and TV production and distribution. Has acted for the FA Premier League, Commonwealth Games Federation, England and Wales Cricket Board and Rugby Football Union. Hon legal advisor to Sports Aid Foundation. Consulting Editor 'Law and the Business of Sport' (Butterworths, 1997). Specialist Editor 'Copinger and Skone James on Copyright' 14th Edition (Sweet & Maxwell, 1998). Member of the Arbitrators Panel of the American Film Marketing Association.
Career: Qualified in 1977. Solicitor at *Rubinstein Callingham* 1977-79. Legal Director of Artlaw Services 1980-81; Joined *Denton Wilde Sapte* in 1982, becoming a partner in 1986.
Personal: Born 1952. Emmanuel College, Cambridge, 1970-73. Governor of Sports Aid Trust. Leisure pursuits include cricket, golf and film. Lives in London.

BELL, Alasdair
Olswang, London
(020) 7290 7946
azb@olswang.com
Specialisation: EU and competition. Experienced in all aspects of EU and UK competition law and practised in Brussels for many years. Has been involved in many cases before the European Commission and the European Courts, including cartels, abuse of monopoly power and merger control. Particular experience in the areas of TV broadcasting and professional sport, and has represented the European governing body for football (UEFA) in relation to a wide range of EU legal issues, including player transfers, marketing of television rights, club-ownership rules, advertising and sponsorship, league governance issues and ticketing matters.
Prof. Memberships: Law Society of Scotland.
Career: Previous career: partner, *White & Case*, London and Brussels.

BITEL, Nicholas
Max Bitel, Greene, London
(020) 7354 2767
nick.bitel@mbg.co.uk
Specialisation: Partner in Sports and Entertainment Department of *Max Bitel, Greene*. Main area of practice is sports law. Acts for major sports events and sportsmen and women. Well known for acting for events such as the Ryder Cup, the London Marathon and the Wimbledon Championships. Author of articles in, amongst others, 'Sport and the Law Journal'.
Prof. Memberships: Chairman of British Association for Sport and Law, Member of Law Society, Sports Lawyers Association of America and of the UK Sports Major Events Committee. Chief Executive of the London Marathon since 1995.
Career: Qualified in 1983, having joined *Max Bitel, Greene* in 1981. Became a Partner in 1983.
Personal: Born 31 August 1959. Attended St Paul's School, London 1972-76; Davidson College, North Carolina 1976-77, and Manchester University 1977-80.

BLAIN, John
Freshfields Bruckhaus Deringer, London
(020) 7832 7482
john.blain@freshfields.com
Specialisation: Sport, energy, financial services. Acts for the Football Association on disciplinary matters, including Wenger, Grobbelaar and Seyers; the Betting Inquiry. Also acting in respect of OFT inquiry into replica shirt market. Also acted for English second division rugby clubs in dispute over promotion.
Prof. Memberships: British Association of Sports Law.
Career: *Freshfields Bruckhaus Deringer* (1992-).
Personal: Sport and music.

BRAITHWAITE, Andrew
Osborne Clarke, Bristol
(0117) 917 3000

BURDON-COOPER, Alan
Collyer-Bristow, London
(020) 7242 7363
alan.burdon-cooper@collyerbristow.com
Specialisation: Sponsorship in sports, arts and television; licensing and merchandising. Recent work has included advising on an appointment of Fast Track as the exclusive market agent and the organiser of the major televised events in this country for UK Athletics. Advice to Sport England on issues relating to grant aid to sport. Co-author of 'Vol. 39, Sports and Sponsorship: Encyclopaedia of Forms and Precedents' (Butterworths).
Prof. Memberships: Chairman of the Institute of Sports Sponsorship.
Career: Articled at *Collyer-Bristow*, qualified 1968, partner 1969.
Personal: Born 1942. Educated at Oundle School (1955-61), Emmanuel College, Cambridge (1964 MA LLB). Governor of the Rose Bruford College of Speech and Drama. Liveryman of the Worshipful Company of Dyers. Leisure pursuits include music, sport and gardening. Lives near Hemel Hempstead.

COUCHMAN, Nicholas
Couchman Harrington Associates, London
(020) 7611 9660
nic@chass.co.uk
Specialisation: Sports rights lawyer and Founding Partner of *Couchman Harrington Associates*. Former Partner and Head of intellectual property with the former leading sports law firm, *Townleys*, has extensive experience in sports contracts (sponsorship, licensing, interactive games, media), rights management/protection/exploitation and creating sports rights strategies. Clients include/have included major sports events rights owners (Formula One, Rugby World Cup 1999, Six Nations Championship, Royal Ascot), sponsors (Carlsberg/Tetley, Times Newspapers, Nationwide Building Society, Witan Investment Trust), sports organisations (the International Olympic Committee, International Rugby Board, Sport England), clubs (Fulham FC, Spartak Moscow, Saracens RFC) and several licensing/sponsorship agencies. Founder and Consultant Editor of 'Sports & Character Licensing' magazine.

DUFF, Alistair
Henderson Boyd Jackson WS, Edinburgh
(0131) 346 3617
a.duff@hbj.co.uk
Specialisation: Litigation/Sports Partner. Handles all types of sports work including damages actions between players, team contracts with players, commercial agreements regarding sponsorship/merchandising and other related matters.
Prof. Memberships: Law Society of Scotland, Writer to the Signet, committee member and on the Advisory Board for British Association for Sport and the Law. Scottish Arbiter for The Sports Dispute Resolution Panel Ltd.
Career: Qualified Solicitor since 1982. Joined *Henderson Boyd Jackson* as Litigation Partner in 1991; specialised in sports law since 1994.
Publications: Has published 34 articles for journals on sporting matters often lectures and is regularly quoted in the national press.
Personal: Married to a doctor, has two children and lives in Edinburgh. Has completed 13 marathons and has taken part in several climbing trips to the Himalayas.

FITZPATRICK, Nick
Denton Wilde Sapte, London
(020) 7242 1212
nef@dentonwildesapte.com
Specialisation: Partner with substantial media and intellectual property experience, including all aspects of the commercial exploitation of sport (eg disposal and acquisition of analogue/digital media rights, brand protection and licensing, agency appointments, event management, sponsorship/official supplier relationships, corporate hospitality, event management etc).
Prof. Memberships: Law Society.
Career: Educated at Jesus College Oxford (Exhibitioner). Qualified *Denton Wilde Sapte* 1993, 'Assistant Solicitor of the Year' ('Lawyer' awards 1998/9). Partner *Denton Wilde Sapte* 2001.
Publications: Co-author of 'Flint, Fitzpatrick and Thorne – A User's Guide to Copyright' (now in its 5th edition). Numerous articles in trade and legal publications.
Personal: Interest in the arts, film and music.

SPORT ■ THE LEADERS

GAY, Mark
Denton Wilde Sapte, London
(020) 7242 1212
meg@dentonwildesapte.com
Specialisation: Partner in technology, media and telecoms department. Has substantial experience in both the contentious and non-contentious aspects of sports law and advises various sporting bodies on constitutional media rights issues, disciplinary and contractual issues.
Career: Admitted 1989. Became a partner at *Herbert Smith* in 1995. Joined *Denton Wilde Sapte* 1 January 1999.
Personal: Educated at Lady Margaret Hall, Oxford.

GOLDBERG, Mel
Max Bitel, Greene, London
(020) 7354 2767
Specialisation: Partner in the Sports Division of *Max Bitel, Greene* in London. He has represented numerous international football players and clubs, Olympic gold medallists and several world champions in boxing, squash, tennis and athletics. He has arranged the transfers of several million pound football players from one club to another. He was the Legal Advisor of International Squash Players Association (IPSA) and was Vice-Chairman of the British Olympic Travel Association to the Moscow Olympic games in 1980. He represented Hans Segers in the successful defence of the footballer in the 'Match Fixing Trial' which was billed as the Football Trial of the Century. Regularly appears on CNN Sports News and Business, and Bloomberg Television.
Prof. Memberships: Sports Dispute Resolution Panel and an Associate Mediator of the Sports Dispute Resolution Panel of Mediators. Vice-Chairman of the British Association for Sport and Law.
Career: Educated at St John's College, Cambridge and founded his own firm under the style of *Douglas Goldberg & Co.*
Publications: Co-author of the book entitled 'The Final Score' published by Robson Books.
Personal: Educated at St. John's College, Cambridge.

HARRINGTON, Dan
Couchman Harrington Associates, London
(020) 7611 9660
Specialisation: Partner with *Couchman Harrington Associates*. Specialises in intellectual property with particular focus on sports rights, broadcasting, technology and new media. Advises a wide range of governing bodies, event rights holders, sport and media agencies, players, clubs, media companies and technology suppliers. Has advised on deals and legal issues across many different sports including (among others) FA Premier League, Rugby World Cup, Davis Cup Tennis, FA Cup, Horseracing, England football internationals, Eire football internationals, FIFA World Cup, Formula One, Olympic Games, Six Nations Rugby, European Rugby Cup, Australian Rules football, International Speedway events, Windsurfing World Championships, Ice Skating and English Cricket.

HENRY, Graeme
Dundas & Wilson CS, Edinburgh
(0131) 228 8000

HEWISON, John
George Davies, Manchester
(0161) 236 8992
Specialisation: Broad commercial background but now almost exclusively devoted to sports law principally in the football world representing many players as well as the Professional Footballers Association. Deals with player representation in disciplinary matters, contract negotiation and image exploitation. Represented the PFA in its dispute with the Leagues over television monies and dealt with the strike call and subsequent settlement negotiations. Is on the football bodies' working group to settle a new professional footballers' standard contract and has recently been appointed by the world governing body FIFA as a President of the Chamber of Presidents hearing appeals from the decisions of FIFA's Dispute Resolution Chamber.
Career: Manchester Grammar School and Nottingham University; Head of company at *George Davies* and now managing partner. Contributor of articles and speaker on all legal aspects of professional football.

HIGTON, Jonathan
Hammond Suddards Edge, London
(020) 7655 1000

HORNSBY, Stephen
The Simkins Partnership, London
(020) 7907 3023
stephen.hornsby@simkins.com
Specialisation: EU/competition, sport. Head of Sport Group which advises clubs, players, agents and representative bodies on the commercial and regulatory issues affecting sport – particularly rugby, football and cricket and their commercialisation. A competition lawyer by background ideally placed to deal with the increasing importance of competition law in sport. Promotion and relegation issues in Scotland, England and Wales in rugby have taken much of his time this year and the firm has added leading Welsh rugby clubs to its portfolio. Also advised the UK broadcaster in the EU Champions League broadcasting case.

HOVELL, Mark
George Davies, Manchester
(0161) 234 8810
mail@georgedavies.co.uk
Specialisation: Partner in the commercial department specialising in sports law. Acts for various professional footballers, rugby players, basketball players and other sports people on contractual, employment, taxation and insolvency-related matters. Advises the Professional Footballers Association and the Basketball Players Association on commercial and trade union-related matters. Recently developed a niche, acting with football and other sporting clubs in financial difficulties, most notably, Chesterfield, Bury, Halifax and Lincoln.
Prof. Memberships: British Association for Sport and Law. Licensed insolvency practitioner.
Personal: Lives in Manchester.

KERR, John
Anderson Strathern WS, Edinburgh
(0131) 220 2345
john.kerr@andersonstrathern.co.uk
Specialisation: Handles general corporate and commercial work, including acquisitions and disposals, corporate finance, banking law, general contract work, agency, distribution and EU law. Specialises in sports law. Acts as lead partner for Scottish Rugby Union and Sportscotland as well as other governing bodies and clubs; involved with constitutional issues, sport sponsorship and product endorsement, discipline and drug related issues as well as the provision of new facilities.
Prof. Memberships: Founder Member of Financial and Legal Advisory Panel of Sportscotland; Member of British Association of Sport and Law; Professional Member of Sports Dispute Resolution Panel; President of Napier University Sports Law Forum.
Career: LLB (Hons) Edinburgh 1978; qualified 1980, Partner in *Strathern & Blair* in 1984 and became Partner in merged *Anderson Strathern* in 1992.
Personal: Born 1956. Lives in Edinburgh. Married with young children. Enjoys sport at all levels.

KORMAN, Andy
Hammond Suddards Edge, London
(020) 7655 1000

MCCORMICK OBE, Peter
McCormicks, Leeds
(0113) 246 0622
p.mccormick@mccormicks-solicitors.com
Specialisation: Substantial area of practice is sports law (allied to portfolio of media and entertainment) with considerable experience in both contentious and non-contentious aspects. Member of the Legal Working Party of The FA Premier League and the lead laywer on commercial, media and broadcasting issues. Also advises Leeds United FC and a number of other sporting bodies, clubs and sports personalities. Handled the threatened strike by the PFA on behalf of The FA Premier League and the Football League and subsequent contractual negotiations. Also has expertise in horseracing, particularly disciplinary hearings and appeals; the only British lawyer to have appeared before the Jockey Club of Germany. Also handles matters relating to Rugby (Union and League), athletics, cricket, boxing, shooting (advises renowned Yorkshire Shoot) and motor racing. Other clients include The Football Association, Jenny Pitman, Freddie Trueman, Howard Wilkinson, Gordon Strachan, Gary Speed, Harry Kewell, Gary McAllister, David Batty, Castleford RLFC, Wakefield Trinity RLFC, Keighley Cougars RLFC, Otley RUFC and the Football Supporters Association. Negotiates contracts for personal benefits, corporate sponsorship and ancillary matters including broadcasting and deals with a substantial workload of intellectual property matters (registration, protection and enforcement). Advises on IP enforcement for The FA Premier League. Deals with litigation cases including defamation and complaints relating to broadcasting and the Press. Acted in the Leeds United/Stuttgart UEFA Disciplinary Hearing in Zurich. Also has 20 years experience of tax investigation and enquiry work, both Revenue and VAT and serious fraud cases. Addresses a substantial number of industry and legal conferences, including the Institute of Economic Affairs. Writes for a number of publications. Author of 'Sport, Business and the Law', published by Jordans. Awarded the Higher Courts (Criminal Proceedings) Qualification in 1994. Resident legal expert on Radio Leeds, Yorkshire Television and the Yorkshire Post. Inaugural Yorkshire Lawyer of the Year 2000.
Personal: Vice-President of the Outward Bound Trust. Chairman of the Yorkshire Young Achiever Awards. Member of the Advisory Board, Sports Law Centre, Anglia University; Solicitor to The Duke of Edinburgh's Award. Patron, Harrogate Junior Chamber of Commerce; Trustee, Friends of War Memorials.

MCKENZIE, Rod
Harper Macleod, Glasgow
(0141) 221 8888
rod.mckenzie@harpremacleod.co.uk
See under Employment, p.328

METLISS, Jonathan
SJ Berwin, London
(020) 7533 2220
jonathan.metliss@sjberwin.com
Specialisation: Is a senior partner in the corporate finance department and a founder member of the firm in 1982. He is actively involved in the property sector representing, inter alia, The British Land Company plc, and acted for them on the acquisition of the Broadgate Estate in the City of London and the Meadowhall Shopping Centre in Sheffield (the UK's largest single site property transaction at £1.17 billion) which won SJ Berwin 'The Property Team of the Year' at The Lawyer Awards 2000 as well as on joint ventures for them with a value of over £4 billion. He has also established and developed the Sports Business Group (of which he is head) within the firm dealing with all aspects of the business of sport which is now recognised as one of the leading dedicated sports practices in the UK. Has recently been described as one of the top sports lawyers in the country. Has been involved in sports and soccer-related

THE LEADERS ■ SPORT

businesses for a number of years. Has acted on numerous sports related transactions such as the takeover of the Tottenham Hotspur Football Club in the early 1980s, the acquisition by Pentland Group of the Speedo business and the investment by ENIC plc, of which he was a non-executive director for some five years, in Glasgow Rangers Football Club (the single largest investment in a UK football club), the acquisition by ENIC of interests in Vicenza Calcio, AEK Athens, Slavia Prague and FC Basel, the flotation and subsequent fund raisings by Birmingham City Football Club, the flotation of Sports Internet Group, and more recently, the flotation on AIM of First Artist Corporation Plc, the leading soccer agents. Has been involved in English Premier League clubs such as Arsenal, Chelsea, Derby County, Leeds United, Manchester United and West Ham and for nationwide football league clubs such as Birmingham City, Sheffield United, Swindon Town and Watford. Has advised companies in the sports and leisure area, such as Blacks Leisure, Claremont Garments, ENIC plc and Pentland. Has advised the England and Wales Cricket Board on the issue of central contracts and other related matters. Actively involved in South African sport, in particular the United Cricket Board of South Africa. Was a commercial adviser to the Football Taskforce, was a member of the government Working Group on Football Disorder (March 2001) and a member of the British Association of Sport and Law. His opinion is often sought on sporting issues and is widely quoted in the sports press and regularly speaks at sports related conferences and seminars. Is actively involved in the campaign to combat racism and hooliganism in sport.
Prof. Memberships: The executive committee of the Weizmann Institute Foundation; joint secretary and member of the executive of the Inter-Parliamentary Council against Anti-Semitism; member of Jewish Association of Business Ethics; vice-president of the Commonwealth Jewish Council; member of the board of the British Israel Public Affairs Centre (BIPAC); member Israel-Britain Business Council; member of the Executive of the British-Israel Chamber of Commerce and chairman of the British-Israel Chamber of Commerce Professional Services Committee; member of advisory board of Tel Aviv University Business School; member of the board of governors of Haifa University and chairman of the British Friends of Haifa University; member of UJIA (United Jewish Israel Appeal) Sports Committee, Jewish Care Sports Club, member of the Committee on South African Trade (COSAT) which provides commercial advice to the Department of Trade and Industry on Britain's trade promotion activities in South Africa; member of Government working group on Football Disorder; Law Society; Holborn Law Society;

member IoD; Lord's Taverner's; member of Trade Partners UK; Africa and Middle East Advisers; member of the Cricketers Club; Parkes Centre Development Board, University of Southampton.
Career: Articled *Nabarro Nathanson*, qualified 1973; assistant solicitor *Nabarro Nathanson* 1973-76; merchant banker, Capel Court Merchant Bank, Sydney 1976-78; assistant solicitor, *Berwin Leighton* 1978-82; senior corporate finance partner and founder member, *SJ Berwin* 1982; director of London Freeholds Plc; the Weizmann Institute Foundation; the Southern Africa Business Association; and the Parkes Centre Development Board (University of Southampton).
Publications: Articles for 'Sport Business'; 'Travel Trade Gazette'; 'Commercial Lawyer'; 'Law Society Gazette'.
Personal: Born 1949, resides London and Sussex. Education: Haberdashers' Aske's, Elstree; Southampton University (LLB Hons). Leisure: Squash, cricket, rugby, football, travel, Israel and South Africa. Clubs: Arundel CC, Middx CCC, Sussex CCC; RAC; Saracens RFC; Alcester RFC; MCC, Surrey CCC, Rugby Club Cricketers Club; Middlesex County Rugby Football Union, Broadgate Club, Marks Club, Primary Club - Lord Taverner's, Queen's Club.

MILLER, Stephen
MacRoberts, Glasgow
(0141) 332 9988
stephen.miller@macroberts.com
See under Employment, p.328

MILLICHIP, Peter
Hammond Suddards Edge, London
(020) 7655 1000

MITCHELL, Bob
Harbottle & Lewis, London
(020) 7667 5000
robert.mitchell@harbottle.com
Specialisation: Head of the Sports Group. Specialises in all aspects of sports law including constitutional and regulatory issues; sponsorship and endorsement agreements; merchandising agreements; brand management and protection. He is also involved in preparing agency, venue and groundshare agreements, terms and conditions of ticketing, as well as negotiating player, agent and management contracts.
Prof. Memberships: Law Society; British Association for Sport and Law.
Career: Trained *Keene Marsland*, qualified 1992; Assistant *Keene Marsland* 1992-93; Partner 1993-97; Senior Associate *Harbottle & Lewis* 1997-2000; Partner 2000 to date.
Personal: Born 1966; resides London. Hipperholme Grammar School, Halifax; Brunel University; College of Law, Chester. Enjoys golf, cricket, squash, watching all sports, films. Married with two children.

MORRISON, Michael
Hill Dickinson, Manchester
(0161) 817 7200
mjmorrison@hilldicks.com
Specialisation: Vast experience in a wide range of sport related business, including employment law (contentious and non-contentious); endorsement and sponsorship agreements; exploitation and protection of intellectual property rights, media law including publishing and defamation; administrative law. Involved principally in professional football, acting for clubs, players and agents, dealing with a variety of work including contracts, claims, commercial agreements, arbitrations and disciplinary tribunals. Other sports include rugby (both codes), swimming, golf and tennis.
Prof. Memberships: Law Society; British Association for Sport and Law; Manchester Law Society; Employment Lawyers Association.
Career: Educated at Cardinal Langley School and St Ambrose College. Joined *Gorna & Co* in July 1967, admitted 1974, Partner 1976. Partner, *Hill Dickinson*, January 2002.
Personal: Married 1971 with two sons. Enthusiastic but incompetent golfer, passionate Manchester United supporter, member of the Variety Club of Great Britain.

PARKER, Raj
Freshfields Bruckhaus Deringer, London
(020) 7936 4000
raj.parker@freshfields.com
See under Litigation, p.565

PHELOPS, Warren
Nicholson Graham & Jones, London
(020) 7360 8129
warren.phelops@ngj.co.uk
Specialisation: Business issues relating to sport, in particular rights ownership and exploitation, corporate structuring and strategy, company, commercial and media (including media, sponsorship, hospitality and merchandising).
Prof. Memberships: Director of Institute of Sports Sponsorship, City of London Solicitors Company, British Association of Sport and the Law.
Career: *Slaughter and May*: Trainee Solicitor, March 1990-92; Assistant Solicitor, March 1992-June 1993. *Nicholson, Graham and Jones*: Assistant Solicitor, June 1993 to Jan 1996. Partner and Head of Sports Group, January 1996 to date.
Personal: Fanatical sports player (rugby, football, cricket – for any teams that will have him, squash and tennis) and watcher, especially rugby (Wasps), football (Arsenal) and cricket (Middlesex).

REEVE, Felicity
Bird & Bird, London
(020) 7415 6000
Specialisation: Partner in Sports Group. Advises governing bodies, broadcasters, sports marketing agencies, sponsors and individuals on the creation, acquisition and exploitation of sports-related rights. Advises on new digital forms of rights

distribution and delivery including the acquisition of content for exploitation via the internet and via on demand services. Advises on the application of traditional legal principles to the internet including terms and conditions of sale, online gambling and jurisdiction and rights clearance issues. Author of a number of articles on sports related issues in the national, legal and sports industry press. Clients include The Football Association, Wembley National Stadium, Octagon.
Prof. Memberships: Law Society, British Association for Sport and Law.
Career: Qualified 1993. Joined *Bird & Bird* from *Macfarlanes* in 1994. Became a partner in 1998.
Personal: Educated at School of St Helen and St Katherine and Lady Margaret Hall, Oxford.

REID, Fraser
Theodore Goddard, London
(020) 7606 8855
fraserreid@theodoregoddard.co.uk
Specialisation: Sports law, entertainment/media law, commercial law, sports disciplinary proceedings. Specialising from 1997 in sports-related work. Provides advice on the protection and exploitation of commercial rights in sport including sponsorship, merchandising, broadcast new media and image rights. Also advises on players' contracts. Niche specialisation in disciplinary issues, particularly doping. Clients include individuals in sports and entertainment fields, sports marketing companies, sports governing bodies and sponsors. Represented the athletes Mark Richardson and Mark Hylton in disciplinary cases before UK Athletics and IAAF in 2000/2001.
Prof. Memberships: Committee member and Treasurer of the British Association for Sport and Law. Member of the Law Society, the International Bar Association – Sports and Gaming Group Member, and the Internationale Association Jeunes Advocats ('AIJA'). Sports group member.
Career: Qualified 1992 with *Beale & Co.* Advantage International (1997-98). Joined *Theodore Goddard* as head of sports group in June 2000.
Personal: Football, golf, rugby, squash, diving and travel. Member of Lancashire cricket club and Blackburn Rovers supporter.

RUSSELL, Patrick
Charles Russell, London
(020) 7203 5018
patrickr@cr-law.co.uk
Specialisation: Partner in Litigation Department. Acts for sporting regulatory authorities and clubs in the regulatory and disciplinary field. Experienced in public law, judicial review restraint of trade and including human rights. Also handles building and construction disputes and is Head of *Charles Russell's* Trust and Fidiciary Disputes Group. Acted in judicial review decisions for the

www.ChambersandPartners.com

SPORT ■ THE LEADERS

Jockey Club (including ex parte HH, Aga Khan), The Law Society and Swindon Town FC.
Prof. Memberships: Law Society, British Association for Sport and Law.
Career: Joined *Charles Russell* in 1976 and qualified in 1979. Became a Partner in 1980. Director of the Solicitors Indemnity Mutual Insurance Association Ltd. Contributing Editor, 'Cordery on Solicitors'.
Personal: Born 11 May 1952. Educated at Ampleforth College 1965-70 and University College, Oxford 1971-74. Recreations include golf, sailing and tennis. Lives near Towcester, Northants.

SLEIGH, Andrew
Burness, Glasgow
(0141) 248 4933

SMITH, Ian
Clarke Willmott & Clarke, Bristol
(0117) 941 6626
ismith@cw-c.co.uk
Specialisation: Partner with a background in employment law but more recently has been active at the highest level of sports governance, advising the Professional Cricketer's Association and the Professional Rugby Players Association on their respective relationships with the clubs and governing bodies in their sports. In particular, negotiating the standard players contracts in both sports and the England Rugby Limited deal. Ian is also active in sponsorship and licensing deals in motorsport. He is an advisor to the Springbok Supporters Club, various sports content websites including cricnet.com and many professional sportsmen on the protection and exploitation of their image rights. He is international legal advisor to the Federation of International Cricketers Associations and a trustee of SAINT, a charity for South African sportsmen, and is a non-executive director of various sports sector companies.
Prof. Memberships: Member of the British Association for Sport and Law.
Career: Articled with *Veale Wasbrough* 1992-94; admitted June 1994; *VW* Employment Team 1994-96; joined *Osborne Clarke* Employment Team 1996; joined as Partner with *CW&C* May 2001.
Personal: Attended University of West of England. Leisure interests includes a variety of sports in particular cricket and golf.

SMITH, Jason
James Chapman & Co, Manchester
(0161) 828 8000
jssport@james-chapman.co.uk
Specialisation: Specialises in the protection and exploitation of rights in the areas of event organisation, sponsorship, licensed products and services, broadcasting and online media for governing bodies, sports marketing companies, clubs and leading individuals. In particular, advises Manchester United Plc on all forms of rights protection and exploitation through sponsorship, promotions, licensing, broadcasting, online media and tours. Recent work includes Manchester United's 2003 USA Tour agreement, sponsorship deal with Anheuser-Busch, sponsorship, online and on-site betting agreements with Ladbrokes, and MU's global online alliance with Terra Lycos including arrangements for a Chinese language website, online rights exploitation, sponsorship and US online Tour partnership. Also works in the following sports: motor racing, rugby, aquatics, boxing, athletics and cycling. Increasingly advising on constitutional and disciplinary issues.

STINSON, Philip
Clintons, London
(020) 7395 8449
pjs@clintons.co.uk
Specialisation: Partner in Entertainment Department. The law as it applies to marketing, advertising and broadcasting with particular reference to the business of sport. Clients include sponsorship, advertising and other marketing consultants and agencies, international sportsmen and women, television production companies, sponsoring and sponsored organisations, governing bodies and organisers of major charitable and other events. Often advises in-house legal departments of sponsoring organisations. Author of articles in British Association for Sport and Law Journal and in numerous trade journals. Author of section of Sport in Practical Commercial Precedents.
Prof. Memberships: British Association for Sport and Law.
Career: Articled and qualified with *Richards Butler* 1988-91. Joined *Collyer-Bristow* in 1991, Partner 1995. Joined *Clintons* as Partner in 1996.
Personal: Born 16 May 1962. Educated at Oxford University. Enjoys football and the arts. Lives in London.

TAYLOR, Jonathan
Hammond Suddards Edge, London
(020) 7655 1000

VLECK, Karena
Farrer & Co, London
(020) 7242 2022
Specialisation: Partner in the commercial team. Principal area of practice is sports law providing specialist advice for sports governing and representative bodies, individual sports people, sports charities and sponsors. Areas of practice include sponsorship agreements, broadcasting agreements, disciplinary procedures and rules, sports doping cases, formations and advice on constitutions both corporate and unincorporated, merchandising and representation agreements. Other areas of practice are intellectual property generally, charity law and company and commercial law. A member of the Non-Executive Council of UK Athletics, the governing body for athletics in the UK. Clients include UK Athletics, Sport England, the British Olympic Association, the Lawn Tennis Association, the Football Association, the British Paralympic Association, the British Canoe Union, the Central Council of Physical Recreation and the All England Netball Association.
Prof. Memberships: Committee member of British Association for Sport and Law.
Career: Qualified in 1992 after articles at *Farrer & Co*. Partner 1998.
Personal: Born 10 March 1967. Educated at Millfield School, Street, Somerset 1983-85 and St John's College, Cambridge 1986-89. Lives in London.

WALKEY, Justin
Bird & Bird, London
(020) 7415 6000

WATKINS, Maurice
James Chapman & Co, Manchester
(0161) 828 8000
sport@james-chapman.co.uk
Specialisation: Senior Partner and Head of Commercial Department. Sports law specialist. Solicitor for Manchester United FC since 1976 and since flotation, Manchester United PLC. Advisor to the Football Association Premier League and other Premier and Football League clubs on various matters. Solicitor to a number of leading sportsmen and administrators. Has handled numerous high value soccer transfers at home and abroad. Represents clubs and players before UEFA and FA Disciplinary bodies and International and League Compensation Tribunals. Negotiates TV, sponsorship, licensing and advertising contracts in sport. Extensive media experience on football-related matters. Holds a number of key positions including: President of the British Association for Sport and Law; Member of the FA Premier League Legal Working Party; UEFA Panel of External Legal Experts; Premier League Representative on Association of European Union Premier Professional Football Leagues and Member of FIFA's new Dispute Resolution Chamber to deal with all disputes under the new FIFA world transfer regulations; Director of Manchester United Football Club and Manchester United PLC; Company Secretary of MUTV (MUFC TV) and Regional Director for Coutts Bank.
Prof. Memberships: President of the British Association for Sport and the Law Society.
Career: Qualified in 1966. Solicitor for the Co-operative Insurance Society 1966-68. Joined *James Chapman & Co* as a Partner in 1968. Senior Partner with effect from May 1999.
Personal: Educated at Manchester Grammar School and University College, London (LLB and LLM). Interests include cricket, soccer and tennis.

WATTS, Alan
Herbert Smith, London
(020) 7374 8000
alan.watts@herbertsmith.com
Specialisation: Partner with wide experience of all forms of dispute resolution including High Court litigation, arbitration and mediation, covering a wide area of different commercial disputes. Areas of expertise include sport law, partnership disputes, media and entertainment law, company and commercial disputes, professional negligence claims and defamation.
Career: LLB Hons, King's College, London, 1987. College of Law 1988, qualified 1990, Partner: 1998.

ZEFFMAN, David
Olswang, London
(020) 7208 8888
dcz@olswang.com
See under Media & Entertainment, p.592

TAX CORPORATE

London: 775; The Regions: 780; Scotland: 783; Profiles: 783

Research approved by BMRB For this edition, **Chambers'** researchers conducted 6,582 interviews – 3,900 with law firms, 511 with barristers and 2,171 with clients. The validity of the research was scrutinised by BMRB International, who audited both the methodology and the results at our offices in London. They interviewed **Chambers'** researchers and cross-checked sample interviews. Details of the audit appear on page 7.

OVERVIEW Increased sophistication in the marketplace has brought tax lawyers closer and closer to the heart of corporate deal-making. This is particularly true in the financial products arena where innovative, tax-efficient structures drive the deals. The *Chambers'* corporate tax section encompasses both contentious and advisory aspects of mergers and acquisitions, partnership agreements, finance and real estate transactions. London remains the hub for complex tax work, but there are pockets of excellence in the regions. Recent troubles within the accounting firms may provide an opportunity for firms to develop a stronger base of own-account tax planning and advisory work. The past few years have seen a rise in recruitment of accountants from the Big Five firms to develop an integrated legal and tax planning capacity. This edition features a new table incorporating all manner of indirect tax, including VAT, Customs & Excise and stamp duty. Onlookers await to see if the trend towards increasing specialisation in this area will continue.

LONDON

TAX: CORPORATE — LONDON

1
- Freshfields Bruckhaus Deringer
- Linklaters
- Slaughter and May

2
- Allen & Overy
- Clifford Chance

3
- Ashurst Morris Crisp
- Herbert Smith
- Norton Rose

4
- Berwin Leighton Paisner
- Denton Wilde Sapte
- Lovells
- Macfarlanes
- Simmons & Simmons
- SJ Berwin
- Travers Smith Braithwaite

5
- CMS Cameron McKenna
- Nabarro Nathanson
- Olswang

6
- Clyde & Co
- Field Fisher Waterhouse
- McDermott, Will & Emery
- Theodore Goddard
- Watson, Farley & Williams

This book is the product of 6,582 1/2 hour interviews. See p.7 for BMRB audit. Within each band, firms are listed alphabetically.

FRESHFIELDS BRUCKHAUS DERINGER (see firm details p.964) Singled out to our researchers as "*most integrated of all the international firms*," the group's greatest strength lies in its "*one stop shop*" service across European and Asian jurisdictions, which is also supported by a smaller US-based practice. "*Technical know-how, responsiveness and accessibility*" characterise the team, and the firm is said to "*pick only the brightest lawyers.*" The result is "*a phalanx of good people*" who "*cover the waterfront*" of corporate M&A, tax-based financing and tax planning.

The retirement of leading practitioner Ben Staveley, is but a minor setback for the group. An "*all-round intellectual guru,*" **David Taylor** (see p.789) heads the London practice and is recommended for "*difficult structured finance transactions*" ranging from debt and equity products, to derivatives and cross-border leasing arrangements. He recently advised National Express/Midland Mainline on the procurement, financing and maintenance of a new fleet of high-speed trains. Peers "*think highly of*" **Richard Ballard** (see p.784), a "*user friendly*" corporate finance specialist, who has been advising on the £7.28 billion demerger from BT of its wireless business, mm02. "*Bright*" **Sarah Falk** (see p.785) heads the corporate finance group, and in the past year has represented Prudential on the UK tax aspects of its proposed $46.5 billion merger with American General Corporation. Senior practitioner **Francis Sandison** (see p.789) offers "*wide ranging expertise,*" while rivals believe "*his name attracts work for the group.*" He advised Lehman Brothers on the pre-letting of one million sq ft of office space at Canary Wharf, and acted for Tempus Group on the £425 million recommended cash offer by Havas Advertising of France and the subsequent higher offer by WPP Group. His practice features primarily corporate matters, although he also manages the firm's VAT practice. **Michael Thompson** (see p.789) maintains a niche practice specialising in oil and gas taxation and recently advised joint venture company Telereal on the tax aspects of its acquisition of BT's £2.38 billion property portfolio. **Sue Porter** (see p.788) rates highly for her expertise in securitisation and capital markets transactions, while "*experienced player*" **Timothy Ling** (see p.787) has proved successful in advising Lattice Group in its recent appeal to the Special Commissioners concerning the tax treatment of pipeline replacement expenditure. Head of the tax finance practice, **Murray Clayson** (see p.784) is frequently associated with marquee client Lehman Brothers, which he advises on a range of international tax-based financings. He has also represented Land Securities Trillium on its property partnership with the BBC. **Colin Hargreaves** (see p.786) acts on a variety of leasing and project financings such as work for Angel Trains on its £750 million acquisition of 177 Desiro electric vehicles to be leased to South West Trains. Insurance tax specialist, **Stephen Hoyle** (see p.786) was commended by clients as "*sound and sensible*;" he recently advised Agilent Technologies in its $1.7 billion sale of Healthcare Solutions Group to Philips Electronics. Former accountant, **Alan Sinyor** (see p.789) enters the rankings as an up and coming practitioner for his adept handling of "*tricky VAT issues.*" **Clients** Goldman Sachs; Rolls Royce; Morgan Stanley; Ford; Kingfisher; Compass Group; Pearson; Royal Bank of Scotland; Lattice Group; Citibank; Amerada Hess; Six Continents; Lehman Brothers.

LINKLATERS (see firm details p.1043) This "*proactive*" team of specialists appears as advisors to large corporates and financial institutions on high grade tax work. Endorsed by our interviewees for its "*broad repertoire*" of tax work, the group provides "*a good all-round package*" for equities, stamp duty, VAT, personal and corporate tax. Practitioners are described as "*precise*" in approach and benefit from a "*depth of high-quality resources.*" Local law practitioners across Europe assist on cross-border transactions and the firm has recently added Spanish tax capacity to its armory.

Practice head **Guy Brannan** (see p.784) provides "*consistently high-quality*" advice whether involved in M&A work, IPOs or tax-based financings. He recently advised SSSB on the structuring of Tier 1 capital issues originating from Bank of Scotland and Halifax Bank of Scotland. "*Understated*" **Michael Hardwick** (see p.786) is highly regarded by peers for his "*analytic acumen*" and "*mastery of detail.*" He has acted on a number of PFI projects and real estate driven financings, and advised BBC in the BBC/Land Securities Trillium Property Partnership structure. Clients report that **Martin Lynchehan** (see p.787) "*adds value*" on structured finance transactions and he continues to

www.Chambersand Partners.com

TAX CORPORATE ■ LONDON

LEADING INDIVIDUALS

★ **EDGE Steve** Slaughter and May

1
- **FRENCH Douglas** Clifford Chance
- **NORFOLK Christopher** Norton Rose
- **TAYLOR David** Freshfields Bruckhaus Deringer
- **MEARS Patrick** Allen & Overy
- **NOWLAN Howard** Slaughter and May

2
- **AIRS Graham** Slaughter and May
- **BALLARD Richard** Freshfields Bruckhaus Deringer
- **ELMAN Jonathan** Clifford Chance
- **SANDISON Francis** Freshfields Bruckhaus Deringer
- **BALDWIN Mark** Macfarlanes
- **BEARE Tony** Slaughter and May
- **FALK Sarah** Freshfields Bruckhaus Deringer
- **WATSON John** Ashurst Morris Crisp

3
- **BALL Susan** Clyde & Co
- **FRASER Ross** Herbert Smith
- **HARDWICK Michael** Linklaters
- **LING Timothy** Freshfields Bruckhaus Deringer
- **NIAS Peter** McDermott, Will & Emery
- **RUPAL Yash** Linklaters
- **WALTON Miles** Allen & Overy
- **BRANNAN Guy** Linklaters
- **GETHING Heather** Herbert Smith
- **LEWIS David** Allen & Overy
- **LYNCHEHAN Martin** Linklaters
- **NOBLE Nicholas** Field Fisher Waterhouse
- **TROUP Edward** Simmons & Simmons

4
- **CRAWFORD Susan** Ashurst Morris Crisp
- **DOUGLAS Alasdair** Travers Smith Braithwaite
- **GREENBANK Ashley** Macfarlanes
- **LUDER Sara** Slaughter and May
- **MEHTA Nikhil** Cleary Gottlieb Steen & Hamilton
- **PORTER Sue** Freshfields Bruckhaus Deringer
- **SANDERS Tim** Skadden, Arps, Slate, Meagher & Flom
- **STRATTON Richard** Travers Smith Braithwaite
- **WHITTY Oonagh** Latham & Watkins
- **DORAN Nigel** Macfarlanes
- **ELLIOTT Peter** Clifford Chance
- **JACOBS Russel** Milbank, Tweed, Hadley & McCloy
- **MCGOWAN Michael** Shearman & Sterling
- **NORWOOD Andrew** Weil, Gotshal & Manges
- **PRESTON Christopher** Watson, Farley & Williams
- **SMITH Isla** Norton Rose
- **THOMPSON Michael** Freshfields Bruckhaus Deringer
- **WISTOW Michael** Clifford Chance

5
- **BUTLER Kay** Olswang
- **CLAYSON Murray** Freshfields Bruckhaus Deringer
- **FRIEL Daniel** Lovells
- **HARKNESS David** Clifford Chance
- **HOYLE Stephen** Freshfields Bruckhaus Deringer
- **KELLY Don** Lovells
- **SCOTT Tom** Linklaters
- **TRASK Michael** SJ Berwin
- **CHALLONER John** Norton Rose
- **COLEMAN Brenda** Allen & Overy
- **HARGREAVES Colin** Freshfields Bruckhaus Deringer
- **HIGGINBOTTOM Louise** Norton Rose
- **JOHNSON Ian** Ashurst Morris Crisp
- **OVERS John** Berwin Leighton Paisner
- **TAYLOR Stephen** Linklaters
- **WOODGATE Neil** White & Case

UP AND COMING
- **GREGORY Keith** CMS Cameron McKenna

ASSOCIATES TO WATCH
- **TAYLOR Isaac** Herbert Smith

LEADING INDIVIDUALS INDIRECT TAX (VAT, CUSTOMS & EXCISE, STAMP DUTY)

★ **SINFIELD Greg** Lovells

1
- **BALDWIN Mark** Macfarlanes
- **WONG Etienne** Clifford Chance
- **HUMPHREY Ann** Sole Practitioner

2
- **CANT Michael** Nabarro Nathanson
- **COLECLOUGH Stephen** PricewaterhouseCoopers
- **HALE Paul** Simmons & Simmons
- **MAINPRICE Hugh** Hutchinson Mainprice
- **WARRINER Neil** Herbert Smith
- **CLARK Simon** Linklaters
- **GARCIA Dario** Ernst & Young
- **LEWIS David** Allen & Overy
- **ROSE Simon** SJ Berwin
- **WOOLICH Richard** Nicholson Graham & Jones

3
- **CROKER Richard** CMS Cameron McKenna
- **PRESTON Christopher** Watson, Farley & Williams
- **STAPLETON Mark** Dechert
- **LYNCHEHAN Martin** Linklaters
- **SALTISSI Sally** Dechert

4
- **DUNCAN Susan** Baker & McKenzie
- **HODGKINSON Milly** Berwin Leighton Paisner

UP AND COMING
- **SALEH David** Clifford Chance
- **SINYOR Alan** Freshfields Bruckhaus Deringer

See individuals' profiles p.783

---

be respected by fellow practitioners for his expertise in VAT matters; he led the group's representation of Halifax in its acquisition of the Equitable Life Assurance Society's non-profit and unit-linked businesses. In addition, Lynchehan has been involved in the growth area of asset swap transactions; the team advised Compucenter in an asset swap in which the company purchased the French and UK business of GECITS (a subsidiary of GE Capital) in return for Compucenter's German business. **Yash Rupal** (see p.788) draws upon his in-house experience at Merrill Lynch in advising on financial products and other tax-driven financings. "*Demerger specialist*" **Tom Scott** (see p.789) elicits praise as a "*reliable and straightforward*" advisor. Expert in M&A and restructuring matters, he acted for BT on its £5.9 billion rights issue and subsequent demerger of its wireless business. Derivatives expert **Stephen Taylor** (see p.789) handles leasing and finance tax, and with his "*passion for property law*," **Simon Clark** (see p.727) fulfills a dual role as head of the firm's real estate department and primary VAT specialist. Interviewees report that his "*impressive mind*" makes Clark a "*formidable VAT advisor*." The departure of leading practitioner Nikhil Mehta to Cleary, Gottlieb, Steen & Hamilton is considered a blow to the firm's contentious tax practice. Clients ABN AMRO; Dixons; BBC; Rio Tinto; Sunlife & Provincial Holdings; JP Morgan Chase; Allied Domecq; Innogy; HSBC; BP Amoco; Centrica; Cookson; Le Group; Liberty International; BHP Biliton; BT; WHSmith; Lend Lease; Merrill Lynch.

SLAUGHTER AND MAY (see firm details p.1140) A "*phenomenal*" reputation for corporate M&A provides the tax department with a steady supply of high-level deals, even in a difficult transactional market. Less visible but equally strong are the firm's capacities in structured finance, asset finance and the development of financial products. Market sources proclaim that the firm is "*one of the few that get work in solely for its tax capacity.*" Practitioners possess a "*good line into clients*" and were endorsed for a "*non-point scoring*" approach to negotiation.

Although interviewees agreed the group offers a "*high level of consistency*" across the team, some felt the firm's reputation in the field was dependent on the profile of one or two key individuals. Of these, the most pre-eminent is clearly **Steve Edge** (see p.785), rated by rivals as "*in a class of his own.*" Edge's "*huge amount of experience*" contributes to his "*clear and consistent view of UK tax legislation*" and "*refined judgement.*" Clients appreciate his ability to "*cut through commercial transactions,*" and his immense popularity makes him both one of the busiest and sought after practitioners in the field. He recently advised Diageo on the tax aspects of its £9 billion joint acquisition with Pernod of Seagram drink assets. The "*grand old* *man*" of tax, **Howard Nowlan** (see p.788) has a leading reputation for corporate restructuring and transactional tax work. Known for his "*terrific client skills*," Nowlan "*gets straight to the point*" offering "*constructive advice*" to corporate clients. He recently counselled BHP in its £9 billion merger with Billiton and the establishment of a twin pillar structure in UK and Australia. Also focusing on corporate work, "*commercial*" **Graham Airs** (see p.783) is particularly rated for his experience in asset management and privatisation/PPP deals. He acted for Whitbread on the reconstruction, spin-off and sale of pubs to Morgan Grenfell Private Equity for £1.6 billion.

On the structured finance side, "*unflappable*" **Tony Beare** (see p.784) has made his name as an "*extremely good negotiator*" with "*exhaustive attention to detail.*" A "*quick-thinking*" practitioner, Beare acted for Unilever in its £1 billion multi-jurisdictional disposal of Diverseylever business to Johnsons. Junior partner **Sara Luder** (see p.787) is a "*clear communicator*" with particular experience in leasing and e-commerce matters. She recently assisted Adolph Coors Company in its acquisition of Carling from Interbrew. The group also handles contentious tax matters in conjunction with the litigation department and most notably represented Morgan Grenfell in an appeal to the House of Lords determining taxpayers' obligation to disclose to the Revenue documents subject to legal professional privilege. **Clients** Royal Caribbean; Unilever; Diageo; 3i; Du Pont; Coca-Cola Enterprises; General El; Whitbread; BHP; Adolph Coors Company.

ALLEN & OVERY (see firm details p.841) Viewed by some interviewees as "*the top firm for capital markets tax work in London*," the A&O practice has a leading profile for high-level financings, securitisations and repackaging transactions. Close institutional ties with major banks and finance houses see the group advising on a range of asset finance and leasing deals. Clients report that "*there are no weak partners there*" and praise the group for "*depth and quality*," at both the junior partner and associate levels. The presence of a US tax partner within the London team assists the group in providing seamless advice on US/UK cross-border transactions.

A large proportion of the practice's partners are recognised in the *Chambers*' tables. Best known is practice head, **Patrick Mears** (see p.787), described by peers as "*sensible and easy to work alongside.*" He advises on both corporate and structured finance matters, and has been instructed by Investcorp on the debt restructuring of independent printing company, The Polestar Group. Partner **David Lewis** (see p.787) undertakes international corporate tax work and was particularly commended by peers for his expertise in stamp duty issues. He has advised BT on the UK tax aspects of the £2.14 billion sale of Yell Group to a vehicle controlled by Apax Partners and Hicks, Muse, Tate & Furst. "*Commercial*" **Miles Walton** (see p.790) has a "*real presence which inspires confidence in clients.*" Seen most often in large leasing transactions, Walton recently acted for TXU on the lease of power stations at Peterborough and Kings Lynn to Centrica. **Brenda Coleman** (see p.784) handles a mix of corporate M&A and fund work; she led the firm's representation of United Business Media on the return of capital to its shareholders (by way of capital reorganisation) and advised TRW on its $6.7 billion hostile bid for Northrup Grumman. Although the move of Michael McGowan to Shearman & Sterling does not substantially weaken the firm's standing in the market, it is considered a loss for the practice. **Clients** Bank of America; ABN AMRO; ANZ; National Australia Bank; Royal & SunAlliance; ICI; DB Capital Partners; United Business Media; BT; Marks & Spencer; Dresdner Kleinwort Wasserstein; TXU; Citibank.

CLIFFORD CHANCE (see firm details p.911) A leading contender for its "*sheer size and might*," the firm boasts the biggest tax department in London with "*enormous resources at its disposal.*" The group's size has engendered an organisational structure that allows "*absolute specialists in a whole host of areas*" and many value the "*depth of knowledge*" available within the team. Noted for its "*global coverage*," the firm is especially strong in UK-US transactions and has recently expanded its European tax capacity to include a Brussels-based practice. This "*professional*" team receives accolades for its "*good documentation skills.*"

Practice head **Douglas French** (see p.785) is considered "*the first name at Clifford Chance.*" "*Terribly sensible*" and "*a pleasure to deal with*," he is a leading corporate finance specialist and recently acted for Duke Street Capital on its CDO fund. Partner **Jonathan Elman** (see p.785) is "*exceptionally clever*," he recently advised BAE Systems on the tax aspects of a $2.073 billion structured finance transaction. **Peter Elliott** (see p.785) advised JP Morgan Securities and ABN AMRO as joint-lead arrangers on tax aspects of the €214 billion real estate securitisation for ProLogis European Properties Fund. **Michael Wistow** (see p.790) "*burns the midnight oil*" on securitisation and structured finance deals, he has been active for Canary Wharf on its £875 billion lease rental securitisation. Partner **David Harkness** (see p.786) has a "*loyal client following*" and most notably acted for GKN on its demerger and merger in a dual listed company structure. The firm has a strong reputation on VAT matters under the leadership of **Etienne Wong** (see p.790), a "*worthy advisor*" commended for his "*impressive international practice.*" He and assistant **David Saleh** (see p.788) have advised on the VAT aspects of complex structures such as Lehman Brothers' £226 million senior and mezzanine debt financing for the acquisition of two UK property portfolios. Michael Ehrlich has retired but remains as a consultant to the tax practice. **Clients** Nomura Securities; CGNU; EADS; Energis; UBS; Xchanging; XL Insurance; Zurich Capital Markets; Commerzbank; Carlton Communications; BAE Systems; ABN AMRO; Citigroup; Zurich Capital Markets.

ASHURST MORRIS CRISP (see firm details p.852) This smaller practice offers "*good practical advice*" to corporate and financial institution clients. A highly developed private equity expertise sees the tax group advising on a large number of funds' PE investment. Practitioners are reported to "*inspire client confidence*" thanks to partners' "*long experience in the field.*" Department head **John Watson** (see p.790) focuses largely on tax aspects of equity funds and was commended for his "*analytic mind.*" "*Extremely sound*" **Susan Crawford** (see p.785) has a "*firm grasp of all the issues.*" Her practice has an emphasis on property tax work, although she also handles a full range of restructurings and corporate finance. **Ian Johnson** (see p.787) is well known for his work on derivatives and other highly structured financial products, and recently advised ABN AMRO on tax-structured derivative transactions and arbitrages which involved foreign exchange legislation. The group's work for Finmeccanica and AMS in a conditional agreement to form a missiles joint-venture to be owned by EADS, BAE Systems and Finmeccanica, demonstrates the practice's cross-border capabilities. Further highlights include acting for BT on the £2.38 billion outsourcing of its UK property portfolio to Telereal Holdings, and advising National Express Group on the tax-efficient structuring of the £241 million sale of its airport division. **Clients** ABN AMRO; Excel; BT; IBM; CapVest; Cinven; Swiss Reinsurance Company; National Express; Finmeccanica; Citigroup Investments; Royal & SunAlliance; West Private Equity; Imetal.

HERBERT SMITH (see firm details p.992) This "*strong, efficient department*" receives high-level tax work, with particular strength in the areas of insurance, energy, PFI and property tax. A large base of corporate clients keeps the group active with M&A, disposal and restructuring transactions. Market sources also pointed to a busy tax dispute practice, with practitioners acting on notable cases, such as representing Gerber Foods in the EC, including Court of First Instance on a back duty case concerning the import of tuna into the EC from Turkey. Four full time partners concentrate on a range of tax matters, led by "*proactive*" department head **Heather Gething** (see p.785). Recommended as someone able to "*get the job done*," Gething recently acted for Merrill Lynch in the unwind of £1.2 billion structured finance of the Edison Power's acquisition of the Fiddler's Ferry and Ferry Bridge Power Station. "*Accomplished*"

TAX CORPORATE ■ LONDON

Ross Fraser (see p.785) advised Friends Provident on a £4 billion demutualisation and flotation, and acted for the Royal National Pension Fund for Nurses on the £248 million transfer of its businesses to a wholly-owned subsidiary of Liverpool Victoria Friendly Society. Deputy head **Neil Warriner** (see p.790) was dubbed "*highly knowledgeable,*" particularly in relation to VAT and real estate transactions. His recent work includes advising Northern Electric on its £1.7 billion swap of electricity supply and distribution business with Innogy, and acting for AXA in its scheme for clarifying the £1.7 billion AXA Equity & Law inherited estate. **Clients** Bank of Scotland; De Beers; Eurotunnel; GE Capital; Severn Trent; Enterprise Oil; New Star; Lazard; Petrobras; Standard Life; Centrica; AXA; Time; First Choice Holidays; De La Rue; CSFB.

NORTON ROSE (see firm details p.1084) Highly prized for its strength in leasing and asset finance transactions, the group is a popular choice for aeroplane and shipping finance. Team members were praised by clients for providing "*clear explanations of complicated structures*" and their "*cautious consideration of all the angles.*" The firm has focused attention on developing its international tax capacity and is now able to call upon local law specialists in Paris and Frankfurt. "*Brilliant*" **Chris Norfolk** (see p.788) is a "*veteran in the field.*" Concentrating primarily on corporate M&A and joint-venture transactions, Norfolk recently advised TXU on the separation of its energy supply and distribution businesses and the sale of its distribution business to London Electricity Group. Department head **John Challoner** (see p.784) "*always comes up with the goods*" when advising on collective investment schemes and property transactions. Clients particularly praised his skill in drafting and documentation. "*Professional and tactful*" **Isla Smith** (see p.789) "*argues her client's corner in an effective manner.*" A tax-based leasing specialist, she has lately been acting for HSBC as the conduit sponsor to Regency on four consumer loans and one electricity receivables securitisation. Peers and clients report that **Louise Higgenbottom** (see p.786) "*brings a lot of experience to the table – she knows the law and how various issues will play themselves out.*" In the past year she represented P&O and its subsidiary North Sea Ferries in a £100 million lease financing of the cruise ferry Pride of Hull. **Clients** BMW; Emerson Electric; Harvey Nichols; AIG; KLM; Fox Kids Europe; HSBC; Chevron; P&O Princess Cruises; Northern Foods; Primark; TXU; Taylor Woodrow; Cathay Pacific; KLM; AXA.

BERWIN LEIGHTON PAISNER (see firm details p.866) Substantial expertise in property transactions attracts important developer and property fund clients to the group, while the practice is rounded out by a steady flow of general corporate and finance work. The corporate tax team also receives support from a strong personal tax department to provide clients with a "*tailored service.*" Department head **John Overs** (see p.788) maintains a generalist practice acting in both finance-driven tax work and VAT matters. He has recently been counselling a European industrial partnership on a tax-structured collective investment vehicle focused on real estate in Germany, Netherlands and France. Fellow practitioners specialise in VAT, corporate tax and asset finance: ex-Customs & Excise lawyer **Milly Hodgkinson** (see p.786) specialises in customs and VAT work, particularly compliance and liability issues with a strong cross-border flavour. Notable highlights for the firm include the representation of Royal Bank of Scotland on the principal financing of 12 hotels as part of the £1.9 billion acquisition of Le Meridien Hotels by Nomura, and advising City Academy Trust on the VAT aspects of the formation and construction of a new school. **Clients** Tesco; Royal Bank of Scotland; GUS; Prudential; Lex Service.

DENTON WILDE SAPTE (see firm details p.935) Especially commended for financing work, the group is acknowledged by peers to have "*an edge on asset finance*" and acts for a number of major UK lessors. The team has a strong following within the aviation industry for large aircraft and equipment leasing transactions. Additional strength exists in relation to energy and PFI projects and film finance. Department head Charlotte Sallabank led the team in representing London Electricity in its acquisition of Eastern Electricity. The group also acted for China National Offshore on international tax structuring issues in its acquisition of Indonesian oil interests from Repsol. **Clients** BMBF; London Electricity; MBNA; Rentokil Initial; Enel Power; Liberty Media; Energis; Pearson Television; Incepta; Encyclopaedia Britannica; Equitable Life; Ofreg.

LOVELLS (see firm details p.1045) The firm is widely acknowledged as the premier practice for VAT and indirect tax, thanks to the star reputation of "*leading light*" **Greg Sinfield** (see p.789), who has carved an impressive niche for himself as a "*VAT man, pure and simple.*" Distinguished by his litigation background, he has handled a number of headline cases in the UK and European courts, including representation of Trinity Mirror Group in an ECJ case concerning the VAT treatment of reverse premiums. On corporate tax, the group has been involved in recent PPP/PFI projects and retains close ties to the insurance industry. Practitioners **Daniel Friel** (see p.785) and **Don Kelly** (see p.787) received market commendation for their "*technical know-how.*" The group has acted for Ti Automotive Systems in its £940 million purchase by Smiths, and advised South African Breweries on the placing of £300 million of new ordinary shares. **Clients** Equitable Life Assurance Society; Granada; Tube Lines Consortium; JPMorgan; HJ Heinz; Nortel Networks; Consignia; Ford Motor Company; Barclays Bank; Abbey National.

MACFARLANES (see firm details p.1047) This smaller group of specialists "*covers it all,*" according to peers, who also agree that the firm "*stands out from the crowd for quality.*" The full-service practice assists the corporate department on a range of high-level transactions and also undertakes a large share of tax planning work. The corporate tax group acts together with the private client practice in advising high net worth individuals and owner-managed enterprises, and can draw upon related expertise in benefits and equity incentives. "*Outstanding*" partner **Mark Baldwin** handles both corporate and VAT matters. A "*personable*" individual, he is deemed to have the skills to "*move deals forward.*" He regularly advises clients Deutsche Asset Management, ISIS and Royal London/Scottish Life on fund structures and investments. Department head **Nigel Doran** is judged expert in his advice to investment trusts; he advised Royal Bank Private Equity on its acquisition of Britax. Doran also provides tax planning counsel to executives. Focusing primarily on corporate finance and cross-border M&A, **Ashley Greenbank** wins a following with his "*energy and enthusiasm.*" He acted for Pernod Ricard on its joint bid with Diageo to acquire the spirits and wine business of Seagram from Vivendi. **Clients** Vivendi; Pernod Ricard; HSBC; Deutsche Asset Management; ISI; 3i; Legal & General Ventures; Kingfisher; Cordiant Communications Group; Carlton Communication.

SIMMONS & SIMMONS (see firm details p.1136) An "*impressive deal list*" of corporate finance and M&A transactions sees this firm at its best advantage. Key figure **Edward Troup** (see p.790) is renowned throughout the market for his experience in acting for the Treasury Department, which interviewees believe gives him an "*insight into things no one else has.*" As head of tax strategy, Troup retains some of his policy advisory functions but devotes a large share of his practice to structured finance products. He led the firm's representation of British Land in its Meadowhall Centre securitisation programme, and advised Barclays Bank on a £1 billion US/UK financing. "*Creative thinker,*" **Paul Hale** (see p.786) is highly regarded as a VAT specialist. Also involved in corporate finance, he provided the tax advice to Gallaher Group on its acquisition of Austria Tabak for £1.14 billion. Highlights for the group include advising Interbrew on the £1.2 billion disposal of Carling Brewers to Adolph Coors Company, and acting for Geneva Technology on its $692 million merger with Convergys. **Clients** Interbrew; Gallaher Group; Geneva Technology; HFC Bank; CSFB; The British Land Company; Vivendi Environmental.

LONDON ■ TAX CORPORATE

SJ BERWIN (see firm details p.867) Adjudged the "*leading outfit on private equity*" transactions, this group of "*highly capable individuals*" has a particular niche in property funds and appears on a volume of deals for venture capital and investment funds and mid-market companies. Although the group itself covers a "*good spread*" of work, individual practitioners are felt to specialise heavily within certain sectors. Department head **Michael Trask** (see p.790) has expertise in international tax and double tax treaties, and advises a number of offshore funds on tax-efficient structures. High profile partner **Simon Rose** (see p.788) has an emphasis on VAT within corporate and property transactions. He recently advised Peabody Global Real Estate Partners on the £300 million acquisition of Cutlers Gardens, and acted for Sun Life Assurance on the £160 million sale of Premier Place. Other notable work includes advising Apax Europe V on the development of a pan-European structure to raise €4 billion, and representing Schroders on the establishment of the City of London Unit Trust. **Clients** Atlas Venture; Brixton Estates; The British Land Company; Gresham Trust; London & Regional; Schroder Ventures; J Sainsbury Developments; Delancey Group; Chelsfield; Rotch.

TRAVERS SMITH BRAITHWAITE (see firm details p.1166) These "*laid-back*" lawyers "*don't shout about themselves*" claim peers and clients, but the team is widely regarded as one that "*punches above their weight*." Known traditionally for the firm's corporate finance and private equity emphasis, the practice undertakes an increasing amount of fund work for the likes of Phoenix and Questor. Interviewees also highlighted the firm's strength in share schemes. Department head **Alasdair Douglas** (see p.785) contributes "*worldly wisdom*" to deal negotiations while partner **Richard Stratton** (see p.789) was praised by competitors as "*a joy to work with*." Significant work for the group includes acting for Barclays Capital on its acquisition of Nightfreight and representing Bridgepoint on the disposal on Lee Cooper for Matalan. **Clients** ntl Group; Peel Holdings; Phoenix Equity Partners; ProVen Private Equity; Apax Partners & Co Ventures; JPMorgan; Questor; Barclays Capital.

CMS CAMERON MCKENNA (see firm details p.914) This full-service practice is endowed with the "*critical mass*" to handle large and complex transactions. The group was particularly recommended to our researchers for property finance and leasing work and it scored a coup last year in strengthening its international network with the addition of French firm Bureau Francis Lefebvre. The team undertakes a growing share of international structured finance, with up-and-coming partner **Keith Gregory** (see p.786) particularly well thought of in the field. Gregory has played a key role in the development of hybrid loan structures used by Nomura in its £1.5 billion acquisition of the Le Meridien chain. VAT specialist **Richard Croker** (see p.785) brings to the table his "*relaxed manner*" and a tendency to "*think things through to the end.*" He is skilled in property tax and stamp duty. The group has advised National Australia Bank on a series of £175 million tax structured Gilt Repo transactions and acted for Enterprise Inns in a £525 million pub acquisition. **Clients** AIG; Delphi; J Sainsbury; Luminar; PRICOA; Legal & General Ventures; Lloyds Leasing; Camelot Group; BAA; Taylor Woodrow Property; Wellcome Trust; Angel Train Contracts.

NABARRO NATHANSON (see firm details p.1080) The group's forte in property finance is combined with support to the corporate departments on M&A and venture capital transactions. Individuals are experienced in tax controversy work and have been representing the Church Schools Foundation in a case against Customs & Excise in the Court of Appeal. Department head **Michael Cant** handles a mix of stamp duty and VAT matters. He has been advising on the £2.4 billion acquisition of BT's property portfolio by Telereal. The group has recently been strengthened by the recruitment of an additional lawyer from PricewaterhouseCoopers. In the past year the practice acted for O'Rourke in its acquisition of the construction division of John Laing and advised GE Capital in over £100 million of property transactions including Hendon Shopping Centre, Leeds and Moore House. **Clients** Alphameric; United Group; Westfield; Land Securities; Box Clever; Hammerson; GIC Real Estate; GE Capital; Pearl Assurance; Seascope Shipping Holdings; Church Schools Foundation.

OLSWANG (see firm details p.1087) The team is seen to have "*done well for itself*" under the direction of "*first-class*" partner **Kay Butler** (see p.784). The driving force behind the practice, Butler is acknowledged to have the support of a creditable team that clients feel "*makes a genuine effort to understand business concerns.*" In keeping with the firm's institutional client base, the practice has specialist expertise within the TMT sector. Niche strength exists in the area of film leasing. Practitioners handle a range of transactions including M&A, joint ventures, equity fundraisings, MBOs and corporate restructurings, and continue to advise a large number of property companies, most recently assisting Delancey Estates in its £686 million privatisation. Other notable matters include advising on the reorganisation of the BBC Worldwide and THL joint venture in beeb.com and representing Lloyds TSB Development Capital on its investment in the £31 million MCO of Transaction Technology. **Clients** Delancey Estates; Green Properties; Body Shop International; HIT Entertainment; Minerva; RTS Networks Group; Tiger Aspects; Creston; Akin Group; BBC Worldwide Limited.

CLYDE & CO (see firm details p.913) Although small, the practice retains its position in the market based on the "*enormous reputation*" of leading practitioner, **Susan Ball** (see p.783). A "*top quality technical person,*" Ball was praised by our interviewees as "*supremely clever and an excellent communicator.*" A noted "*intellectual figure,*" she is highly visible in the field for her work on company reorganisations. The group has strength in the insurance and shipping sectors and also undertakes a share of private client work. The group provided tax counsel to Alliance & Leicester on the £200 million outsourcing of cash handling system to Securicor and advised Microgen plc on the acquisition of OST Business Systems. **Clients** Swiss Re; Dell; Hewlett-Packard; Pacific Dunlop; ChevronTexaco; Microgen.

FIELD FISHER WATERHOUSE (see firm details p.954) Interviewees attribute the success of the team to the "*fantastic*" leadership of department head **Nick Noble** (see p.787). A "*talented technician,*" Noble has a loyal client following among venture capital and financial institutions. Financial instruments are a strong suit for the practice and it is further distinguished by its transfer pricing capability. Noble recently led the team in advising on the tax aspects of the merger between Thomas Cook Holidays and British Airways Holidays, and advised on the launch of a novel category of EIS fund. The firm advised Bradford & Bingley on transfers of PEP/ISA investments from an authorised unit trust to an OEIC, thereby saving £3.5 million of stamp duty reserve tax, and advised Delta Property Services on the VAT aspects of a major property development and its pre-letting to HSBC. **Clients** Bradford & Bingley; Skandia; Online Classics; Accenture; One2One; Oxford University; Whitbread; AstraZeneca; Deutsche Bank; Thomas Cook Holdings; Nomura International.

MCDERMOTT, WILL & EMERY (see firm details p.1064) One of the few American firms to successfully establish a significant UK tax practice, the firm is said to be attracting a number of important corporate, finance and property development clients. The firm recently lost Tim Sanders to Skadden, Arps, Slate, Meagher & Flom, but continues its progress under guidance of "*high-profile*" practitioner **Peter Nias** (see p.787). The workload has a decidedly international slant, advising on cross-border mergers and flotations. The group is handling increasing amounts of tax litigation and advises multinational corporations on transfer pricing. Highlights include acting for Kvaerner on the $100 million sale of its hydrocarbons and process technology divisions to Yukos Oil, and advising IAC Holdings on its proposed flotation on the London Stock Exchange by way of acquisition of AIM-listed investment vehicle, Advance Capital Invest. **Clients** Eli Lilly; Caterpillar; BAE Systems; Trinity Mir-

TAX CORPORATE ■ THE SOUTH & SOUTH WEST

ror; Zeus Technology Group; Dun & Bradstreet; Mirant; Kvaerner; Bank One; IAC Holdings; Abbott Laboratories; Telegraph Group; TXU.

THEODORE GODDARD (see firm details p.1158) This "*mainstream*" corporate tax practice is recommended by clients for offering "*sensible advice at sensible rates.*" The group has been able to attract a good share of own account advisory work and has a keen focus on the media and communications sectors. The department, headed by Peter Sayer, has been strengthened by the recent arrival of an additional partner and includes a full-time tax information lawyer. The firm has advised German media conglomerate, KirchGruppe, on its acquisition of a controlling interest in the Formula One World Championship Group and represented the Daily Mail and General Trust Group on its refinancing and acquisition of the Loot free ads papers from Scoot. The team also acts with various US and European firms in providing UK tax advice on cross-border transactions. **Clients** KirchGruppe; Associated British Foods; Gladstone; Royal Bank of Scotland; Daily Mail and General Trust Group; Bridgewell; Telcordia Technologies; Insinger; Entergy; Bayerische Landesbank; Signet; Greenpark Capital.

WATSON, FARLEY & WILLIAMS (see firm details p.1181) A market leader in ship leasing and asset finance, the group ably fills a specialist market niche. Long experience in shipping, aircraft and equipment leasing has engendered expertise in "*cutting-edge*" structured finance techniques. The group "*operates at the highest levels*" on "*big ticket*" leasing, international finance and tax planning, and competitors also rate "*well-rounded*" Christopher Preston (see p.788) for both corporate transactions and VAT issues. Praised for his "*depth of experience,*" he acts for both lessors and lessees on large transactions.

OTHER NOTABLE PRACTITIONERS US firms in London have successfully attracted high-profile UK tax practitioners, although many commentators continue to point to the issue of critical mass. Most recently Shearman & Sterling scored a coup by recruiting Michael McGowan from Allen & Overy, while Tim Sanders (see p.788) has left McDermott Will & Emery to join Skadden Arps Slate Meagher & Flom. Highly rated practitioner Nikhil Mehta (see p.787) has also jumped ship, moving from Linklaters to Cleary Gottlieb Steen & Hamilton. A solicitor advocate, Mehta is well known for his niche in tax litigation. Commentators await to see how each will develop the practice at these firms.   At Milbank, Tweed, Hadley & McCloy, Russel Jacobs (see p.786) is deemed "*popular with clients.*" He handles structured finance deals for the likes of CSFB and Deutsche Bank. Financial tax specialist Neil Woodgate (see p.790) has been establishing a market presence at White & Case. At Weil Gotshal & Manges, Andrew Norwood (see p.788) rates highly for his specialised knowledge of securitisation transactions and recently advised Bear Stearns on the £30 million securitisation of future ticket receipts at Everton Football Club. Oonagh Whitty (see p.790) maintains a solid reputation for asset and structured finance at Latham & Watkins. Mark Stapleton (see p.789) at Dechert covers a "*wide practice area*" but was particularly recommended for VAT issues. He recently acted in a VAT appeal on behalf of dispensing opticians whereby Customs sought to impose VAT at the standard rate on the exempt supplies of services provided by dispensing opticians. Here too, Sally Saltissi (see p.788) was commended for her "*practical attitude.*" She acted for a leading freight forwarding company in a customs duty appeal to the High Court. "*Careful*" Richard Woolich (see p.790) at Nicholson Graham & Jones has an established reputation in stamp duty and property tax. In the past year he advised Henderson Global Investors on VAT, stamp duty and corporate tax issues arising from the redevelopment of Moor House, London EC1. Susan Duncan (see p.785) of Baker & McKenzie is a former senior lawyer in the solicitors office of HM Customs & Excise, specialising now in the customs and VAT fields. She advised a Nasdaq listed company on the classification of imported hi-tech equipment, which resulted in the goods being listed under a duty free heading.   Sole practitioner Ann Humphrey is widely recognised as an "*incredibly good*" VAT specialist who "*deals at a high level .*" Although less visible than formerly, Hugh Mainprice at Hutchinson Mainprice still rates highly for "*long experience*" drawn from being "*involved in the most interesting VAT cases.*" Peers admire his "*conceptual approach to tax.*" Two solicitors at accounting firms were recommended for VAT advice: Stephen Coleclough (see p.784) at PricewaterhouseCoopers is an "*obvious choice*" for property and tax structuring, while Dario Garcia at Ernst & Young is involved in a number of high-profile VAT litigation matters.

THE SOUTH & SOUTH WEST

TAX: CORPORATE — THE SOUTH & SOUTH WEST

1. Burges Salmon Bristol
   Osborne Clarke Bristol
2. Blake Lapthorn Fareham
   Wiggin & Co Cheltenham

LEADING INDIVIDUALS
1. MOSS Philip Osborne Clarke
   MURPHY Niall Blake Lapthorn
   POPPLEWELL Nigel Burges Salmon
   UP AND COMING
   JUPE Erika Osborne Clarke

This book is the product of 6,582 1/2 hour interviews. See p.7 for BMRB audit. Within each band, firms are listed alphabetically. See individuals' profiles p. 783

BURGES SALMON (see firm details p.894) Adjudged a "*major player,*" this specialist tax practice is seen to be growing in size and status under the direction of Nigel Popplewell (see p.788). Peers credit him with "*building up a good team and getting involved in bigger deals.*" The team advises on all aspects of corporate tax from pre-sale tax planning and loan relationships to VAT and stamp duty. Respected for its experience in asset finance, the firm has also been handling increasing amounts of Customs & Excise investigations. Within the past year the practice acted for clients looking to regain tax and national insurance from former employees and provided advice and negotiation on tax issues arising out of leasing transactions in the transport sector. In addition, the group handles a share of international matters, including advising on cross-border syndicated debt and has counselled US investment funds on UK tax issues. **Clients** FirstGroup; Bristol & West; Orange; Tyco.

OSBORNE CLARKE (see firm details p.1090) Bristol remains the firm's hub for corporate tax matters, although the group receives additional support from tax specialists in London and Reading and is thought to succeed with "*strength in numbers.*" In addition to a large volume of transactional support, the practice handles an increasing share of tax consulting work. "*High calibre*" department head Philip Moss, has a wide practice that encompasses the tax aspects of M&A, project finance, fund work and debt and equity offerings. He recently represented ROK in an open offer for fresh capital, combined with the takeover of part of the Rockeagle Group. Partner   Erika Jupe was recommended as a "*bright*" up-and-coming practitioner. As head of the firm's international tax practice, she is active in co-ordinating tax advice with Osborne Clarke Alliance member firms on cross-border transactions. She has lately been involved in the sale of CIT Group's UK Technology Finance Business to GE Capital and the refinancing of Rotch Group's property portfolio. **Clients** 3i Group; Prudential; GATX; Invensys; ROK; Scottish & Newcastle; BG Group; Worldview; Churngold; Bristol Water; Marks & Spencer; Tribal Group.

BLAKE LAPTHORN (see firm details p.877) This sizeable Fareham-based tax team is headed by "*technically skilled*" **Niall Murphy**. His background as an accountant gives him a "*full view of the process*" according to competitors. The team handles corporate sales and reorganisations and is admired for its strength in property transactions. Clients range from private individuals to owner-managed businesses and large plcs. The group recently acted for Raytheon Systems on its $108 million sale of Raytheon Marine and recreational marine business and advised on the £22 million management buy-in of the ICS group of companies. **Clients** Raytheon Systems; Chelton; Templar Company; Graham Tatford & Co; ICS.

WIGGIN & CO (see firm details p.1186) Less visible in the local market, the practice is well known for its strength in international tax planning. Practitioners have particular expertise in arranging international tax structures for multinational corporations. The group benefits from the firm's niche in media and IT matters, and advises a concentration of clients in the technology sector. Private clients also provide instructions on trusts and personal tax planning. The firm's main practice is located in Cheltenham, but it has offices in both London and Los Angeles. Matthew Cain is the contact partner for the group.

MIDLANDS & EAST ANGLIA

TAX: CORPORATE
■ MIDLANDS & EAST ANGLIA

1 **Pinsent Curtis Biddle** Birmingham
  Wragge & Co Birmingham
2 **DLA** Birmingham
  Eversheds Norwich, Nottingham
3 **Mills & Reeve** Cambridge

LEADING INDIVIDUALS

1 **HYDE Ian** Pinsent Curtis Biddle
  LOWE Kevin Wragge & Co
  MORRIS Gregory DLA
2 **BURGESS Mark** DLA
  JONES Robert Eversheds
  POWELL Ted Mills & Reeve

This book is the product of 6,582 1/2 hour interviews. See p.7 for BMRB audit. Within each band, firms are listed alphabetically. See individuals' profiles p.783

PINSENT CURTIS BIDDLE (see firm details p.1102) Highly regarded across the Midlands, the practice is seen to have "*done a good job in attracting own account work*," thanks to "*good relationships with tax clients*." Nationally structured along specialist lines, interviewees believe that the "*strong Birmingham-Leeds axis*" works in its favour. The "*key figure*" here is **Ian Hyde** (see p.786), who concentrates on property tax for large plcs and foreign-controlled companies. He recently advised on a stamp duty saving scheme on a £23 million commercial and residential portfolio, and provided structural tax planning to Sunderland Housing Group on a large-scale voluntary transfer of housing stock. The firm also has separate employee share schemes and personal tax practices to complement its strength in corporate tax matters. **Clients** Pemberstone; New York Life LLC; IMI; Babcock; IM Properties; Avon Cosmetics.

WRAGGE & CO (see firm details p.1197) This large and "*excellent*" practice is perceived by commentators to have "*grown so fast to support a strong corporate department*." Clients appreciate the group's "*responsive*" attitude and ability to "*get things done in a commercial way*." The team has been developing its property tax capabilities and recently provided major property tax advice to Castlemore Securities on the restructuring of the Hampshire Centre (a £220 million retail development project) and on Temple Quay Bristol. **Kevin Lowe** is described as "*the face of Wragges for tax.*" He maintains a generalist practice, handling all aspects of corporate tax, advisory work and VAT, and has lately advised on a number of venture capital trust investments. Other highlights include advising a multinational IT consulting group and North American inward investors on cross-border planning. **Clients** AMEC; H.J. Heinz; BI Group; British Airways; 3i; Wilson Connolly; ProLogis; McAlpine Special Projects; Development Securities; Marconi; Westland Pension Fund; Powergen; RHM; MEPC.

DLA The firm's major corporate practice provides a steady flow of transactional work, particularly property deals. **Greg Morris** and **Mark Burgess** were recommended by both clients and peers.

EVERSHEDS (see firm details p.949) "*Always accessible,*" the practice was commended for its high standards of technical ability. Tax teams in Nottingham and Birmingham support the firm's busy corporate department. In addition, the practice has increased its tax advisory and indirect tax capacity through recruitment of a number of key individuals from accounting firms. "*Personable*" department head, **Robert Jones** (see p.787) co-ordinates the national property tax practice and is judged to have had success in developing strong client relationships. He advised Advantage West Midlands on the £140 million regeneration of Camp Hill and acted for Rover Group in the purchase of Rover Finance Services from BMW. **Clients** Rover Group; Advantage West Midlands; The Nottingham Trent University.

MILLS & REEVE (see firm details p.1071) The team has a strong market share throughout East Anglia, acting for owner-managed businesses, public and foreign-managed companies. **Ted Powell** (see p.788) heads an "*able*" team acting on a range of corporate, VAT and property tax matters. A "*thoughtful*" practitioner, he advises a number of educational institutions and charity clients. In the past year the firm acted on a major PFI project for development on a new university campus, and represented a partnership on the disposal of a telecoms business. The practice's Cambridge base sees the group advising a large number of local high-tech companies. **Clients** Corporates and institutions.

TAX CORPORATE ■ THE NORTH

THE NORTH

TAX: CORPORATE
■ THE NORTH

[1]
- **Addleshaw Booth & Co** Leeds, Manchester
- **Pinsent Curtis Biddle** Leeds

[2]
- **Eversheds** Leeds, Manchester
- **Hammond Suddards Edge** Leeds, Manchester

[3]
- **Dickinson Dees** Newcastle upon Tyne
- **Walker Morris** Leeds

LEADING INDIVIDUALS

[1]
- **CHRISTIAN John** Pinsent Curtis Biddle
- **JENKINS Edmund** Addleshaw Booth & Co
- **SIMPSON Mark** Hammond Suddards Edge

[2]
- **CONCANNON Simon** Walker Morris
- **GREAVES Judith** Pinsent Curtis Biddle
- **JERVIS David** Eversheds
- **TOON John** Addleshaw Booth & Co

[3]
- **HENNESSY Tony** Halliwell Landau
- **TOWNSEND Peter** Cobbetts

UP AND COMING
- **BRENNAN Sharon** Addleshaw Booth & Co
- **JARVIS Timothy** Hammond Suddards Edge

This book is the product of 6,582 1/2 hour interviews. See p.7 for BMRB audit. Within each band, firms are listed alphabetically. See individuals' profiles p.783

ADDLESHAW BOOTH & CO (see firm details p.838) "*Pre-eminent in the North,*" the firm is regarded by market sources as strong competition for corporate tax matters. Highly respected teams in both Leeds and Manchester "*operate at a national level.*" The "*well-balanced practice*" covers all aspects of corporate tax, but received particular commendation for its share of property transactions. A number of partners were singled out for their "*creative*" approach to tax issues. "*Top-drawer*" **Edmund Jenkins** (see p.786) heads the practice from Manchester. "*Extremely clever but tremendously practical,*" he is a key figure for M&A and corporate finance transactions. He led the group's representation of the vendors of Autowindscreens Group on the sale of the company to Lex/RAC for £120 million. In Leeds, **John Toon** (see p.789) is renowned as a property tax specialist. His "*commercial, can-do attitude,*" wins accolades from clients who also claim he "*makes deals work.*" He acted for the Whitehall Green Partnership and Whitehall Green Trading on the disposal of a substantial portfolio of properties to CRP and Carisbrooke Suon. Up-and-coming partner **Sharon Brennan** (see p.784) was endorsed as a "*sharp negotiator.*" Janet Jones has left the practice. **Clients** Aberdeen Murray Johnstone Private Equity; Airtours; Halifax; Oystertec; 3i Group; Standard Life; Barclays Private Equity; BT; Kingfisher.

PINSENT CURTIS BIDDLE (see firm details p.1102) The firm scores highly with clients for its "*national strength and organisation.*" The Leeds practice works closely with a strong Birmingham team and additional back-up in London to provide tax advice on high-quality corporate and property transactions. Its individuals are known to specialise within specific practice areas and interviewees pointed to the Leeds practice as the firm's locus for corporate-driven tax advice. National practice head, **John Christian** (see p.784) is an "*obvious name*" for corporate tax advice. In the past year he advised on the £35 million acquisition by Brown Shipley & Co of the Fairmount Group. **Judith Greaves** (see p.294) is renowned for her share schemes advice, but also handles a range of transactional and advisory tax work. The team has developed a strong practice in tax consulting and receives increasing amounts of cross-border work such as advising on the sale of BPT to Deutsche Bank Real Estate Private Equity Group and Grainger Trust for £477 million. **Clients** Brown Shipley & Co; Pace Micro Technology; SIG.

EVERSHEDS (see firm details p.949) A "*well-manned*" practice with the "*resources to support large transactions.*" Operating as a single, national unit, the firm has tax practitioners in Leeds, Manchester and Newcastle. It advises on corporate reorganisations and acquisitions, and fields a handful of dedicated share schemes specialists. **David Jervis** (see p.786) was singled out to researchers as a "*businesslike*" solicitor who "*knows his onions.*" He heads the department from the Leeds office and maintains a mixed practice, covering all aspects of tax law. Clients admire his ability to "*get through things quickly.*" Recently, Jervis has acted for Save Service stations on its acquisition of over 400 petrol stations and provided strategic advice on related stamp duty matters (a £50 million consideration). The team increasingly fills the roll of lead tax advisor to clients in the financial services and property sectors. The Manchester office led advice to HSBC on a disposal by HSBC/Caradon of Mira Showers Group, including pre- and post-sale restructuring. **Clients** HSBC; Save Service Stations; Thomson's Group; Next; Rutland Trust; Abbey National; AEA Technology; First National Bank.

HAMMOND SUDDARDS EDGE Market commentators perceive that the team "*draws upon a large national presence*" in advising property companies, local businesses and multinational plcs. A strong track record in corporate finance activity is noted, and interviewees consider the Leeds tax team to be the strongest in the national group. Practitioners work closely with other colleagues in the London, Manchester and Birmingham offices. "*Experienced*" department head **Mark Simpson** is deemed to be an "*effective*" force with a practice that covers M&A, property transactions and employee benefits. Up-and-coming partner **Timothy Jarvis** handles both direct and indirect tax and has particular expertise in advising on tax-efficient funding arrangements in relation to PFI and PPP projects. **Clients** Allied London Properties; Apax Partners; BPT; Findel; Compass Group; Kleinwort Benson Private Bank; MGM Mirage Online.

DICKINSON DEES (see firm details p.938) The departure of leading lawyer Tony Hennessey to Halliwell Landau is seen to have left a gap at the senior level; nevertheless, the group continues to receive positive endorsement under the direction of new practice head, Jeremy Smith. While predominantly corporate support work, the practice also handles a share of tax advisory and employee share scheme matters. Practitioners have experience advising on transfer-pricing issues, the establishment of BVCA limited partnerships and structuring investments to secure tax relief under the Enterprise Investment Scheme. Notable recent matters include acting for Govia on its acquisition of Connex South Central, and advising Northern Venture Managers on investments made by Northern VCT, including investments in Stainton Metal, Wests Engineering Design and Bowman Power Station. **Clients** The Go-Ahead Group; ARRIVA; Northern Venture Managers; Grainger Trust; Stadium Group.

WALKER MORRIS (see firm details p.1178) This smaller practice has a loyal following among local corporate clients, particularly within the property sector where the group is considered by peers to have particular expertise in stamp duty issues. Department head **Simon Concannon** (see p.784) is well respected for his "*constructive*" approach to negotiations. The team also includes a tax barrister focusing on employee share schemes. In the past year, the group advised on the demerger of part of Aquarius Group, and has acted for a major tour operator on both its VAT position, the application of EU directives to its business and its negotiation with HM Customs. **Clients** Debenhams Retail; Bradford City AFC; Aquarius Group; Homestyle Group; Stratagas.

OTHER NOTABLE PRACTITIONERS "*Personable*" **Peter Townsend** (see p.790) at Cobbetts acts for a number of significant clients. His academic background serves him well in advising The Welsh Assembly on taxation issues relating to the creation of a new corporate vehicle (to be registered under the Industrial Provident Societies Act) designed to receive and administer hundreds of thousands of council houses. **Tony Hennessey** (see p.786) has been building a tax practice at Halliwell Landau following his move from Dickinson Dees. He and his team focus on transactional corporate work and share schemes and recently advised Gamma NV on the acquisition of the Madison Filter Group.

SCOTLAND

TAX: CORPORATE
■ SCOTLAND

1
- Maclay Murray & Spens Glasgow
- MacRoberts Glasgow
- McGrigor Donald Glasgow

2
- Brodies Edinburgh
- Burness Edinburgh

LEADING INDIVIDUALS

1
- D'INVERNO Isobel MacRoberts
- GORDON Ian McGrigor Donald
- JONES Martyn Maclay Murray & Spens

2
- BARR Alan Brodies
- HOYLE Susan Dundas & Wilson CS

3
- TOSH Nial Dickson Minto WS

This book is the product of 6,582 1/2 hour interviews. See p.7 for BMRB audit.
Within each band, firms are listed alphabetically. See individuals' profiles p.783

MACLAY MURRAY & SPENS (see firm details p.1048) This strong corporate-based practice has recently been bolstered by the addition of a chartered accountant from Deloitte & Touche. The team advises on the structure of start-ups, mergers and acquisitions and undertakes a substantial amount of property transaction planning. Last year's merger with MacKay Simon has added employment expertise to the firm and the group handles employee taxation matters to complement its strength in corporate tax. Department head **Martyn Jones** (see p.787) is widely respected for his "*wealth of experience*" in the field. He focuses primarily on transactional advice, VAT and stamp duty matters, and also advises private clients on tax planning. The practice is increasingly moving towards tax advisory work but continues to support a busy corporate department. The group advised facilities maintenance company Steill on a joint-venture with Abbey National, and acted for Blairmhor and shareholders on the sale of the company to Pacific Spirits (UK). **Clients** Grampian Holdings; Steill; Scottish Enterprise; British Polythene Industries; Stagecoach Group; Clyde Bowers.

MACROBERTS (see firm details p.1049) This strong team is led by "*effective*" Isobel d'Inverno (see p.785). A chartered accountant by background, d'Inverno was noted for her "*extensive knowledge of tax law*." The group also benefits from healthy corporate and project finance departments in acting on a range of "*quality*" M&A and PFI transactions. The team includes a full time VAT specialist and has been receiving an increasing number of instructions on stamp duty planning in connection with property transactions. In addition, the group has devoted resources towards developing a tax litigation capacity. The team has provided tax advice to Johnston Press in its acquisition of the Trinity Mirror titles and Best Guide titles, and acted for Bridgepoint Equity and Hg Capital in the equity and capital refinancing of Worldmark Group. It was also instructed by the Royal Bank of Scotland in the MBO of Highland Fuels. **Clients** AHL Holdings; Braemore Estates; Devro; Ford Motor Company; GE Capital Commercial Finance; ISI Group; Royal Scottish Academy of Music & Drama; Railtrack; AMEC Group.

MCGRIGOR DONALD (see firm details p.1065) Market sources perceive that the team has been weakened by the departure of Susan Hoyle to Dundas & Wilson, although the practice has undergone an active recruitment programme. Additionally, many expect that the firm's linkup with KPMG through membership of Klegal International will provide the firm's tax practitioners with greater scope and access to corporate clients. The joint Tax & Pensions group is headed by high profile **Ian Gordon** (see p.785), who is recommended in *Chambers* in both areas of practice. He advises on the structuring of acquisitions and project financing and devises employee share scheme arrangements. Notable work for the group includes the negotiation of tax-based funding for the Edinburgh International Conference Centre, and acting for British Waterways on the development of a financing structure to fund the redevelopment of the Forth and Clyde canals, 'the Millennium Link'. **Clients** British Waterways; Vis Entertainment; C&B Publishing; Commerzbank; Wilson Connolly Holdings.

BRODIES (see firm details p.889) The growing practice was particularly endorsed by peers for its stamp duty expertise. **Alan Barr** (see p.784) ("*years of experience behind him*") remains highly visible within the market, both for his corporate tax advisory work and extensive writing on property tax. The team advised on stamp duty issues for the Scottish aspects of Telereal's acquisition of BT's UK property portfolio and counselled Corus/Ravenscraig on stamp duty, VAT and general tax issues in relation to a large property joint venture. **Clients** Corus; Land Securities Trillium; United Bank of Kuwait; The IFA Portfolio; Dawnay, Day Property Management.

BURNESS The departure of Victoria Nelson to KPMG is judged to be a setback to the practice, but the "*compact*" group soldiers on under the leadership of John Rafferty. He and chartered accountant John Finnick provide support to the corporate practice on commercial transactions, advising on all aspects of corporate tax, VAT and stamp duty. The client base ranges from private clients and family-owned businesses to larger plcs. Highlights of the past year include acting for Toronto-based Hummingbird on the acquisition of IT software company PeopleDoc, and advising Danish company Bodilsen on its restructuring. **Clients** GE Capital Bank; GE Capital Fleet Services; Ladbrokes; Ritchie & Co; Royal Bank of Scotland; Hummingbird.

OTHER NOTABLE PRACTITIONERS Highly rated practitioner, **Susan Hoyle** has moved to Dundas & Wilson to create a corporate tax team. Commentators anticipate her success in "*moving the firm forward.*" Nial Tosh (see p.789) at Dickson Minto continues to be recommended as an "*experienced*" corporate tax advisor.

THE LEADERS IN TAX

AIRS, Graham
Slaughter and May, London
(020) 7600 1200
graham.airs@slaughterandmay.com
Specialisation: Principal area of practice is corporate tax. Particular experience of privatisations, securitisations, mergers and acquisitions.
Prof. Memberships: Member of The Law Society's Revenue Law Committee, The Law Society, European American Taxation Institute.
Career: Qualified in 1978 after articles at *Slaughter and May* and stayed at firm until 1980. Partner in *Airs Dickinson* 1980-84. Returned to *Slaughter and May* 1984 and became a Partner in 1987.
Publications: Author of chapter on EC Direct Tax Measures in 'Tolley's Tax Planning'.
Personal: Born 8 August 1953. Married Stephanie 1981. Educated Newport (Essex) Grammar, Emmanuel College, Cambridge.

BALDWIN, Mark
Macfarlanes, London
(020) 7831 9222

BALL, Susan
Clyde & Co, London
(020) 7623 1244
Specialisation: Partner and Head of Tax Department. Main area of practice is corporate tax. Work covers tax aspects (including Stamp Duty) of corporate reorganisations, mergers, acquisitions and corporate disposals. Also handles taxation aspects of inward and outward investment for the UK and of new issues and flotations. Other area of practice is taxation of employees, including share schemes, ESOPs and employee benefits. Conducts occasional external and internal lecturing. Member of the Law Society Revenue Law Committee 1982-89 and Corporation Tax sub-committee 1995-. Co-Author of 'Gammie and Ball-Tax on Company Reorganisations.' Has written frequently on taxation topics.
Prof. Memberships: Law Society, City of London Solicitors Company, Law Society of New South Wales.
Career: Qualified in 1973. Worked at *Linklaters & Paines* 1971-89 (Partner 1981-89). Assistant Solicitor at *Blake Dawson Waldron* in Sydney 1989-91;

TAX CORPORATE — THE LEADERS

admitted in New South Wales in 1989. Joined *Clyde & Co.* as Deputy Head of Tax Department in 1993.
Personal: Born 3 November 1948. Holds an MA (Oxon) from St Hugh's College, Oxford 1967-70.

BALLARD, Richard
Freshfields Bruckhaus Deringer, London
(020) 7936 4000
richard.ballard@freshfields.com
Specialisation: Partner. Specialises in corporate finance (including mergers, demergers, reconstructions and cross border transactions); tax-based and structured financing of all types, including cross border transactions; capital markets work including structured bond issues, hybrid instruments, repackaging and securitisation; derivatives transactions of all types; experience in Inland Revenue enquiries and in Commissioners and court litigation. Contributor to 'Tolley's Tax Planning' and 'Tolley's Company Law' and frequent contributor to tax journals and to various *Freshfields Bruckhaus Deringer* publications.
Career: Qualified 1978. Became a Partner at *Freshfields* in 1984.
Personal: Born 1953. Attended Queens' College, Cambridge.

BARR, Alan
Brodies, Edinburgh
(0131) 228 3777
alan.barr@brodies.co.uk
Specialisation: Alan Barr is one of Scotland's leading authorities in the field of tax law. He has carried out substantial research on the subject and his papers and books have been published widely. He is a frequent speaker at professional seminars.
Prof. Memberships: Law Society of Scotland Tax Committee, Convenor of the VAT Sub-Committee.
Career: Admitted as a solicitor in Scotland in 1984, Alan has spent much of his career as a senior lecturer specialising in all areas of taxation, and is currently director of Edinburgh University's Legal Practice Unit (The Diploma Course). Joined *Brodies* as the firm's corporate tax and VAT consultant by agreement with Edinburgh University in 1997. Became a Partner at *Brodies* 2002. He consolidates *Brodies'* position as a leading legal firm in the field of taxation generally, and the aspect of tax on property in particular. When added to the specialist areas of environmental and planning law, Alan's expertise ensures full coverage in all disciplines.
Personal: Alan is married and, despite the fact that he lives in Edinburgh, keeps an optimistic eye on the progress of St Mirren Football Club. He enjoys watching rugby and cricket and collecting Marvel Comics.

BEARE, Tony
Slaughter and May, London
(020) 7600 1200
tony.beare@slaughterandmay.com
Specialisation: Corporate tax. Main area of practice is corporate tax and, in particular, structured finance, corporate finance and capital markets.
Prof. Memberships: The Law Society.
Career: Qualified 1987. Partner 1994.
Personal: Born 30 November 1959. Educated at Durban High School, Haberdashers' Aske's, Elstree, St. Catharine's College, Cambridge and St. Edmund Hall, Oxford.

BRANNAN, Guy C H
Linklaters, London
(020) 7456 5690
guy.brannan@linklaters.com
Specialisation: Specialises in corporate tax matters. Main areas of practice include mergers and acquisitions, international joint ventures, corporate finance, capital markets and finance transactions and contentious tax matters.
Career: Qualified 1981 *Linklaters*. 1981-1987 assistant solicitor, *Linklaters* London. Partner *Linklaters* since 1987, Tax Partner *Linklaters* New York office 1989-93. Head of *Linklaters'* Tax Department since 1998.

BRENNAN, Sharon
Addleshaw Booth & Co, Manchester
(0161) 934 6409
sharon.brennan@addleshawbooth.com
Specialisation: Senior solicitor in Commercial Tax Department. Advises upon all aspects of commercial tax and is primarily involved in advising on the tax aspects and structuring (including stamp duty planning) of disposals and acquisitions of companies and businesses, mergers and reorganisations, including stamp duty planning. Acts for a broad range of clients from individuals to listed companies and has a particular interest in advising institutional investors on investments in MBO vehicles and VCT investments generally.
Career: Qualified as a solicitor in 1995; joined *Addleshaw Booth & Co* in April 1997.

BURGESS, Mark
DLA, Birmingham
(08700) 111111

BUTLER, Kay
Olswang, London
(020) 7208 8888
kbb@olswang.com
Specialisation: Partner, head of tax unit. Spans the spectrum of tax work including corporate tax strategy, international group structuring, joint ventures (particularly in the property and media sectors) both domestic and cross-border, funds (for most asset classes but particularly property and private equity) limited partnerships, sale and lease backs, film investment, employee incentives and VAT and other tax disputes. She has lobbied the EC Commission, the Inland Revenue and HM Customs and Excise for changes in the law. She was also the only legal representative on the British Screen Advisory Counsel's committee which is negotiating with the Inland Revenue the extent of the changes introduced in the most recent budget and the new statement of practice concerning the relief for investment in film.
Prof. Memberships: Law Society; VAT Practitioners Group.
Career: Qualified 1987 at *Oppenheimers*; assistant solicitor *Richards Butler* 1988-90; *SJ Berwin & Co* 1990-95, becoming a partner in 1993. Joined *Olswang* in 1995 as head of tax.
Personal: Interests include horse racing and entertaining her young daughter.

CANT, Michael
Nabarro Nathanson, London
(020) 7524 6000

CHALLONER, John
Norton Rose, London
(020) 7283 6000
challonerj@nortonrose.com
Specialisation: Partner in Commercial Tax Department. Principal area of practice is corporate taxation. Extensive experience in relation to the taxation of company acquisitions; property developments; UK corporate restructurings; collective investment schemes; dealing with the complex VAT and other tax issues relating to international ventures.
Prof. Memberships: International Fiscal Association.
Career: Qualified 1977 while with *Nelson & Steele* in Stoke-on-Trent. HM Inspector of Taxes 1979-84. Joined *Norton Rose* in 1984 and became a partner in 1988.
Personal: Born 9 August 1952. Attended Wilmslow School and Exeter University. Lives in Saffron Walden.

CHRISTIAN, John
Pinsent Curtis Biddle, Leeds
(0113) 244 5000
john.christian@pinsents.com
Specialisation: Partner and head of corporate tax group. Corporate and property tax, including corporate finance, reconstructions and demergers, asset finance, treasury and financing, property taxation, employee incentives, VAT, collective investment schemes and public bodies.
Prof. Memberships: VAT Practitioners Group. Member of the Corporation Tax Sub-Committee of Law Society Revenue Law Committee. Fellow of the Chartered Institute of Taxation.
Career: Qualified 1985. *Freshfields* 1983-89. Joined *Simpson Curtis* in 1990 (now *Pinsent Curtis Biddle*). Partner in 1991.

CLARK, Simon
Linklaters, London
(020) 7456 4902
simon.clark@linklaters.com
See under Real Estate, p.727

CLAYSON, Murray
Freshfields Bruckhaus Deringer, London
(020) 7936 4000
murray.clayson@freshfields.com
Specialisation: International tax, corporate structuring especially cross-border, financing, banking, securities, capital markets, derivatives, structured finance.
Prof. Memberships: Chartered Institute of Taxation (FTII). Member of International Tax Sub-Committee. International Fiscal Association: Chairman of British Branch.
Career: Sidney Sussex College, Cambridge (MA, LL.M). Partner 1993.

COLECLOUGH, Stephen
PricewaterhouseCoopers, London
(020) 7212 4911
stephen.coleclough@uk.pwcglobal.com
Specialisation: VAT - banking and capital markets, especially securitisation and outsourcing. Recent deals, outsourcing cash processing for HSBC, Barclays and Securitas and securitisations for HFC Bank and Northern Rock.
Prof. Memberships: The Chartered Institute of Taxation, Council Member and Technical Committee; IBA; The Law Society; ICAEW.
Career: Currently Partner, Tax and Legal Services, Indirect Tax Solutions. Previously Head of Corporate and Indirect Taxes *Simmons & Simmons* (to 1996).
Publications: Various articles.
Personal: Married to Sarah Gillings, 2 daughters, Amy (3) and Poppy (1).

COLEMAN, Brenda
Allen & Overy, London
(020) 7330 3000
brenda.coleman@allenovery.com
Specialisation: Partner in the Tax Department specialising in all aspects of corporate tax with particular experience of advising on tax issues in relation to privatisations, mergers and acquisitions, takeovers, flotations, reorganisations, joint ventures and financial products as well as tax litigation. Experience of advising on tax issues to privatisations. She is a member of *Allen & Overy's* Tax Investigations Unit and Investment Funds Group.
Career: Qualified *Slaughter and May* (1984), assistant *Slaughter & May* (1984-89); assistant *Herbert Smith* (1989-91); Partner *Herbert Smith* (1991-98); Partner *Allen & Overy* (1998).
Personal: Born 1959. King's College London (LLB Hons 1st, 1981); College of Law (solicitors finals, 1982).

CONCANNON, Simon
Walker Morris, Leeds
(0113) 283 2500
stc@walkermorris.co.uk
Specialisation: Partner in Corporate Department, Head of Tax Unit. Principal area of practice is corporate and property tax. Work includes restructuring, leasing, structured bank financing, MBOs, venture capital funding, employee remuneration schemes and VAT planning. Also handles tax disputes including dealing with the Inland Revenue Special Compliance Office and the Special Investigation Section. Major clients include Redcats, Persimmon, Bank of Scotland, Royal Bank of Scotland, Homestyle, Selfridges, Aberdeen Murray Johnstone, Bradford City Football Club, Caterpillar and Debenhams.
Career: Educated at Hertford College, Oxford; qualified in 1990.

THE LEADERS ■ TAX CORPORATE

CRAWFORD, Susan
Ashurst Morris Crisp, London
(020) 7859 1293
susan.crawford@ashursts.com
Specialisation: Partner in tax department. Principal area of practice is corporate tax with particular emphasis on corporate reorganisations, mergers, demergers, and acquisitions including cross-border transactions. Also specialises in property taxation (including tax based structured financing, fund structures, and VAT and stamp duty on property matters).
Career: Articled *Coward Chance (Clifford Chance)*; qualified 1984. Partner *Ashurst Morris Crisp* since 1994.
Personal: Educated at Wycombe Abbey School; Girton College Cambridge University.

CROKER, Richard
CMS Cameron McKenna, London
(020) 7367 2149
radc@cmck.com
Specialisation: All aspects of corporate tax with particular emphasis on VAT and other indirect taxes, tax planning for property transactions, PPP, mergers/acquisitions and joint ventures.
Prof. Memberships: Member of City Chapter of VAT Practitioners Group; member of VAT and Duties Sub-Committee of Law Society's Revenue Law Committee.
Career: Qualified 1989. Partner *CMS Cameron McKenna* 1997.
Personal: Married with three sons. Lives Winchester.

D'INVERNO, Isobel
MacRoberts, Edinburgh
(0131) 229 5046
isobel.d'inverno@macroberts.com
Specialisation: Director - corporate tax and Head of Corporate Tax Group. Main area of practice is corporate taxation work. Includes corporate acquisitions, disposals, re-organisations, EIS and Reinvestment Relief issues, PFIs, stamp duty planning and VAT on commercial property and corporate transactions. Frequent speaker at seminars on PFI tax, VAT and Stamp Duty and company re-organisations. VAT examiner for Chartered Institute of Taxation.
Prof. Memberships: Institute of Chartered Accountants (England and Wales), Chartered Institute of Taxation, VAT Practitioners Group, Convenor of Tax Law Committee of Law Society of Scotland.
Career: Trained as chartered accountant with *Ernst & Whinney* in London. Practised with *Ernst & Young* as corporate tax specialist. Joined *Brodies WS* as VAT and corporate tax specialist in June 1991. Joined *MacRoberts* in August 1997.
Personal: Educated at St Andrew's University (MA Russian Language and Literature). Gained ACA, then ATII.

DORAN, Nigel
Macfarlanes, London
(020) 7831 9222

DOUGLAS, Alasdair
Travers Smith Braithwaite, London
(020) 7295 3000
Alasdair.Douglas@TraversSmith.com
Specialisation: Head of 18-strong Corporate Tax Department. Main areas of work are corporate finance, investment funds and tax investigation work.
Prof. Memberships: Member of the Law Societies of Scotland, England and Wales; Fellow of the Society for Advanced Legal Studies; member of the Executive Board of the Committee for Careers Service of Oxford University; member of the City of London Law Society Revenue Law sub-committee; member of the IBA and American Bar Association.

DUNCAN, Susan
Baker & McKenzie, London
(020) 7919 1000
susan.duncan@bakernet.com
Specialisation: Customs matters covering a variety of issues and procedures, e.g. valuation, inter-company pricing, classification, reliefs and warehousing. She also deals with VAT and Climate Change Levy. During the past year Susan has dealt with some contentious work. Classification disputes with customs and excise have been resolved in relation to a variety of products, including chemicals, electrical goods and computer equipment. Tribunal proceedings in one such case were successfully concluded before hearing, with a substantial proportion of costs recovered.
Prof. Memberships: Customs Practitioners' Group member, VAT Practitioners Group member.
Career: Called to the Bar (1987); HM Customs & Excise (1989 - 2000) - Susan spent four and half years in VAT Tribunal litigation section, one and a half in VAT advisory work and a further fifteen months in Customs litigation and advisory work; joined *Baker & McKenzie's* tax department (March 2000).
Publications: Regular contributor to the 'Customs Update' section in Butterworth's 'Volls Tax Intelligence' and has also written VAT planning articles for the same publication.
Personal: BA(Hons) Spanish & Latin American Studies from University of Newcastle upon Tyne (1982). Susan is married with three step-children. Her husband is a barrister and sits part time as a Recorder. Leisure interests include collecting antique silver and glass, playing the piano, travel, going to the theatre.

EDGE, Steve
Slaughter and May, London
(020) 7600 1200
steve.edge@slaughterandmay.com
Specialisation: Partner in corporate tax department. Principal area of practice is corporate taxation with a particular emphasis on corporate finance and structured asset finance. Expertise in investment funds, financial instruments, cross border financial transactions, securitisations and other capital markets work. Advises many UK and non-UK multinationals and banks on a wide range of tax matters. Contributes to a number of publications on corporate tax.
Career: Qualified in 1975 while with *Slaughter and May* and became a partner in 1982.
Personal: Born 29 November 1950. Attended Canon Slade Grammar School, Bolton 1962-69, then Exeter University 1969-72. Lives in London.

ELLIOTT, Peter
Clifford Chance, London
(020) 7600 1000
peter.elliott@cliffordchance.com
Specialisation: Tax, pensions and employment. Partner specialising in corporate and financial taxation including international cross-border structures and transactions.
Career: Partner since 1980.

ELMAN, Jonathan
Clifford Chance, London
(020) 7600 1000
jonathan.elman@cliffordchance.com
Specialisation: Tax, pensions and employment. Partner specialising in taxation of corporate and financing transactions.
Career: Qualified 1987; Partner since 1994.

FALK, Sarah
Freshfields Bruckhaus Deringer, London
(020) 936 4000
sarah.falk@freshfields.com
Specialisation: Partner and Head of the London Corporate Finance Tax Group. Main area of practice is corporate tax. Work covers corporate tax planning and corporate finance.
Prof. Memberships: Law Society.
Career: Qualified 1986, having joined *Freshfields* in 1984. Became a partner in 1994.
Personal: Born 1962. Attended Sidney Sussex College, Cambridge, 1980-83.

FRASER, Ross
Herbert Smith, London
(020) 7374 8000
ross.fraser@herbertsmith.com
Specialisation: Tax partner since 1982. Works extensively on the tax aspects of all corporate transactions, including structured finance. He has special expertise in tax planning for mergers and acquisitions, including mergers of insurance companies. He also specialises in tax and cross-border transactions and has particular expertise in the interaction between the European Union and UK tax law. Clients include Friends Provident, Iceland Group plc, Life Assurance Holding Corporation, Royal London, Moorfield Estates plc, Diageo, RJR Nabisco, Merrill Lynch, J Henry Schroder & Co and NPI.
Career: London School of Economics (LLM 1970). Qualified 1973. Partnership 1982.

FRENCH, Douglas
Clifford Chance, London
(020) 7600 1000
douglas.french@cliffordchance.com
Specialisation: Tax, pensions and employment. Partner and Head of the Tax Practice in London specialising in tax, particularly related to corporate and commercial transactions.
Career: Articled *Freshfields*; qualified 1981; Partner *Clifford Chance* since 1988.
Personal: Walbottle High School, Newcastle; Oxford (MA Law) ATII.

FRIEL, Daniel
Lovells, London
(020) 7296 5513
daniel.friel@lovells.com
Specialisation: All tax aspects of corporate transactions including mergers, demergers, acquisitions and disposals.
Career: Articled *Lovells*; qualified 1990; Partner 1996.

GARCIA, Dario
Ernst & Young, London
(020) 7951 2000

GETHING, Heather
Herbert Smith, London
(020) 7374 8000
heather.gething@herbertsmith.com
Specialisation: Head of Tax Group. Practice includes domestic and international tax planning for a variety of multinational companies, structuring and implementing a range of corporate transactions such as public and private mergers and acquisitions, reconstructions and amalgamations and joint ventures, structuring, advising on and implementing financing products and proposals, and tax disputes.
Prof. Memberships: International Bar Association and regular speaker at the Annual Meetings of the Tax Committee of the IBA.
Career: Qualified *Herbert Smith* 1984. Partner 1991.
Publications: Joint author of 'Demutualisation' published by FT Law & Tax, 1997.

GORDON, Ian
McGrigor Donald, Glasgow
(0141) 567 9269
ian.gordon@mcgrigors.com
Specialisation: Principal area of practice is employee benefits, including share incentive schemes, option schemes, and employee share ownership arrangements for listed and AIM and OFEX companies. Also advises on corporate acquisitions, reconstructions and tax driven financing arrangements. Frequent lecturer on taxation issues.
Prof. Memberships: Association of Pension Lawyers.
Career: Joined *McGrigor Donald* as a trainee in 1979. Qualified in July 1979. One year secondment to *Thomson McLintock CA* in 1983. Became a Partner at *McGrigor Donald* in the same year.
Personal: Educated at Edinburgh University 1975-79. Born 15 August 1957. Lives in Glasgow.

TAX CORPORATE ■ THE LEADERS

GREAVES, Judith
Pinsent Curtis Biddle, Leeds
(0113) 244 5000
judith.greaves@pinsents.com
See under Employee Share Schemes, p.294

GREENBANK, Ashley
Macfarlanes, London
(020) 7831 9222

GREGORY, Keith
CMS Cameron McKenna, London
(020) 7367 3000
keith.gregory@cmck.com
Specialisation: Specialises in corporate tax. Has a wide range of experience in the taxation aspects of mergers and acquisitions, company reconstructions and amalgamations, new issues, venture capital and joint ventures in the corporate, financial and property sectors, with particular expertise in acting for financial institutions including banks, building societies and insurance companies.
Career: Qualified in 1980. Became a partner in 1989.
Personal: Born 1955, of British nationality. Educated at Oxford University.

HALE, Paul
Simmons & Simmons, London
(020) 7628 2020
paul.hale@simmons-simmons.com
Specialisation: Partner in Corporate and Indirect Taxes Group. Main area of practice is corporate tax and value added tax. Work includes mergers and acquisitions, stock exchange listings, project finance, structured finance and property transactions. Also handles taxation of collective investment schemes, including unit trusts, investment trusts and offshore funds.
Prof. Memberships: Law Society, City of London Solicitors' Company (member of Revenue Law Sub-Committee), VAT Practitioners Group, International Bar Association.
Career: Qualified 1985, having joined *Simmons & Simmons* in 1983. Became a partner in 1990.

HARDWICK, Michael J
Linklaters, London
(020) 7456 5658
michael.hardwick@linklaters.com
Specialisation: Specialises in tax aspects of mergers, acquisitions, takeovers, joint ventures, flotations, privatisations and PFI transactions.
Prof. Memberships: Member, Revenue Law Committee of City of London Law Society; Member Tax Law Committee and International Tax Sub-Committee of The Law Society, Chairman, Corporation Tax Sub-Committee of the Law Society.
Career: 1991 to date: Partner, *Linklaters*; 1984-91: Assistant Solicitor, *Linklaters*. 1980-81: Gonville & Caius College, Cambridge, LLM (First Class); 1977-80: University College, Oxford. MA (First Class).

HARGREAVES, Colin
Freshfields Bruckhaus Deringer, London
(020) 7936 4000
colin.hargreaves@freshfields.com
Specialisation: Corporate tax.
Prof. Memberships: Law Society. City of London Law Society (member, CLLS Revenue Law Sub-Committee).
Career: Uppingham School; Leeds University; qualified 1988; partner *Freshfields* 1996.
Personal: Sailing (member, Burnham Overy Staithe Sailing Club).

HARKNESS, David
Clifford Chance, London
(020) 7600 1000
david.harkness@cliffordchance.com
Specialisation: Tax, pensions and employment. Partner specialising in corporate tax including mergers and acquisitions, corporate restructurings, joint ventures, international tax planning, financing transactions and securitisations.
Career: Articled *Clifford Chance*; qualified 1989; Partner since 1996.
Personal: Colchester Royal Grammar School; 1985 Sheffield University (LLB Law).

HENNESSY, Tony
Halliwell Landau, Sheffield
(0161) 835 3003
thennessy@halliwells.co.uk
Specialisation: A broad range of corporate tax work, including all tax aspects of mergers acquisitions, corporate reorganisations, flotations and corporate disposals together with employee share scheme and remuneration planning work, asset financing, leasing and VAT and stamp duty planning.
Career: Called to the bar in 1979. Practised corporate tax in both a City of London practice and in a major provincial practice; head of corporate tax group at *Dickinson Dees* in 1992-2001; head of corporate tax at *Halliwell Landau* 2001 to date.
Personal: Educated at St Mary's College, Crosby and University College Oxford (MA). Leisure interests include rugby, hill walking and 18th century music.

HIGGINBOTTOM, Louise
Norton Rose, London
(020) 7283 6000
higginbottomal@nortonrose.com
Specialisation: Partner in Tax Department. Corporate and asset finance.
Prof. Memberships: Law Society, Associate of Institute of Tax, member of Corporation Tax sub-committee of Revenue Law committee of Law Society, IBA, ABA.
Career: Joined *Norton Rose* 1981. Qualified 1983. Partner 1991.
Personal: Born 17 August 1958. Attended Southampton University 1977-80.

HODGKINSON, Milly
Berwin Leighton Paisner, London
(020) 7776 1000
milly.hodgkinson@berwinleightonpaisner.com
Specialisation: Cross-border, VAT, Customs & Excise duties. *Berwin Leighton Paisner* specialises in customs and excise advice for major international retailing clients. Has developed a particular specialisation in advising on cross-border VAT and Customs duties issues and Customs & Excise warehousing in Europe together with DTI licensing and export controls.
Prof. Memberships: The International Bar Association, The American Bar Association, World Trade Law Association, British Importers Association, United Kingdom Association for European Law, The CBI, The Enterprising Women Network.
Career: Qualified at *Kingsley Napley* in 1991, joined the Solicitors' Office of Customs & Excise in 1992 specialising in European law, customs duties, VAT and international advisory work. Seconded to MAFF in 1998 before joining City law firm *Berwin Leighton Paisner* as head of indirect tax at the beginning of 1999.
Publications: A regular contributor to journals including the 'Tax Journal', 'Tornado-Insider.com', 'Legal Week', 'The Institute of Indirect Taxation', 'The Evening Standard' and 'The Financial News'.
Personal: Educated at SOAS London University. Leisure interests include gardening and opera.

HOYLE, Stephen
Freshfields Bruckhaus Deringer, London
(020) 7936 4000
stephen.hoyle@freshfields.com
Specialisation: Partner 1988. Tax department. Main area of practice is the taxation of insurance business, financings and general corporate.
Personal: Born 17.9.1955. Attended St Catherine's College Oxford 1973-76, Gonville & Caius College Cambridge, 1976-77, and Northwestern Law School, Chicago, 1977-78.

HOYLE, Susan
Dundas & Wilson CS, Glasgow
(0141) 222 2200

HUMPHREY, Ann L
Ann L. Humphrey, London
(020) 7378 9370

HYDE, Ian
Pinsent Curtis Biddle, Birmingham
(0121) 625 3267
ian.hyde@pinsents.com
Specialisation: Partner specialising in corporate and property taxation including tax efficient structures for joint ventures, demergers, reconstructions and property development. Ian also advises on VAT planning, stamp duty, taxation of intellectual property and tax based investment structures.
Prof. Memberships: VAT Practitioners group.
Career: BA Oxford University (1987). *Rowe & Maw* (1988-1992). *Pinsent Curtis Biddle* (1992-date).
Publications: Consulting editor to Butterworth's 'Encyclopaedia of Forms and Precedents on VAT and Stamp Duty'.

JACOBS, Russel
Milbank, Tweed, Hadley & McCloy, London
(020) 7448 3009
rljacobs@milbank.com
Specialisation: Has significant expertise in the corporate and financial services sectors, focusing on the development and implementation of new financial cross-border products and the structuring of international consortia and joint ventures in mergers, acquisitions and corporate reconstructions.
Prof. Memberships: The Law Society of England & Wales. President, European - American Tax Institute, London.
Career: Trained *Slaughter & May*; qualified 1985; Partner, Tax Department, *Wilde Sapte* 1992-97, Partner, *Cadwalader Wickersham & Taft* 1997-2000.
Publications: Written articles for: Butterworths 'Finance Bill Handbook,' 'Tax Journal,' 'Financial Instrument Tax and Accounting Review.'

JARVIS, Timothy
Hammond Suddards Edge, Leeds
0113 284 7000

JENKINS, Edmund
Addleshaw Booth & Co, Manchester
(0161) 934 6420
ed.jenkins@addleshawbooth.com
Specialisation: Partner in Commercial Tax Department, Commercial Group. Practice covers all areas of business and property tax and includes advising upon the tax aspects of mergers and acquisitions, reorganisations and restructurings, exiting strategies for persons selling their business and MBOs and other venture capital transactions. Acts for a mixture of quoted and private companies, individuals and venture capital houses.
Career: Called to the bar 1985. Re-qualified as a Solicitor 1991. Joined the firm as a Partner in 1996.
Personal: Educated at Princethorpe College and Liverpool University. Interests include running, golf and family. Married with two daughters and a son. Lives in Hale, Cheshire.

JERVIS, David
Eversheds, Leeds
(0113) 243 0391
davidjervis@eversheds.com
Specialisation: Partner in the Corporate Tax and Employee Share Scheme Unit. Experience of a broad range of corporate transactions specialising in corporate acquisitions and disposals, all aspects of property taxation and employee share schemes and has set up both Inland Revenue approved schemes and long term incentive plans for both private and listed companies. Advised clients in the education and local authority sectors on stamp duty planning and tax efficient structures for their commercial operations.
Prof. Memberships: Member of the Institute of Taxation.
Career: Paralegal with *Minter Ellis Morris Fletcher* in Brisbane. Qualified 1992 with *McKenna & Co*. Joined *Eversheds* 1994.
Personal: Born 21 September 1966. Gar-

786   INDEX TO LEADING LAWYERS: PAGE 1693 ■ IN-HOUSE LAWYERS PROFILES: PAGE 1201

forth Comprehensive School in Leeds and University of Kent at Canterbury. Lives in Leeds. Interests include scuba diving and most sports.

JOHNSON, Ian
Ashurst Morris Crisp, London
(020) 7638 1111
ian.johnson@ashursts.com
Specialisation: Partner in tax department. Involved in advising on the taxation implications of a wide range of corporate transactions advising both overseas and UK clients.
Prof. Memberships: Associate of the Chartered Institute of Taxation.
Career: Graduated in law from Edinburgh University.
Publications: Co-author of Butterworth's 'Taxation of Loan Relationships, Financial Instruments and Foreign Exchange'.

JONES, Martyn
Maclay Murray & Spens, Glasgow
(0141) 248 5011
mhj@maclaymurrayspens.co.uk
Specialisation: Partner, Head of Corporate Tax Department and formerly senior tax lecturer at Glasgow University. Advises on VAT and property, company taxation, capital allowances, stamp duty and capital gains.
Prof. Memberships: Member of the Tax Law committee of the Law Society of Scotland and CBI Scotland's Economics and Taxation committee.
Career: Glasgow University (LLB 1974).
Personal: Born 1952.

JONES, Robert
Eversheds, Nottingham
(0115) 950 7000
robertjones@eversheds.com
Specialisation: Tax/property tax. Partner based in the *Eversheds* Midlands offices, qualified as a solicitor in 1991 and is now Head of Tax for the Midlands and National Head of Property Tax for *Eversheds*. Deals with many aspects of corporate tax with particular emphasis on all forms of property transactions including stamp duty structuring, VAT mitigation and maximising capital allowances. Is familiar with all manner of joint venture structures including special purpose companies, partnerships, trusts and urban regeneration companies. Has recently advised The Nottingham Trent University on the restructuring of its student residences and Advantage West Midlands on the structure for a major urban regeneration. Has also advised on a large number of corporate transactions including acting for MG Rover Group, Britax plc and Solectron Corporation.
Prof. Memberships: The Law Society, VAT Practitioners Group.

JUPE, Erika
Osborne Clarke, Bristol
(0117) 917 3000

KELLY, Don
Lovells, London
(020) 7296 2000
don.kelly@lovells.com
Specialisation: Corporate tax partner specialising in all aspects of business tax including taxation implications of mergers, acquisitions and joint ventures (particularly cross-border), UK equipment leasing and property transactions and North Sea oil tax.
Prof. Memberships: Law Society, City of London Solicitors' Company.
Career: Articled *Lovells*, qualified 1980; partner 1986; specialised in UK corporate tax since qualification.

LEWIS, David E
Allen & Overy, London
(020) 7330 3000
david.lewis@allenovery.com
Specialisation: Partner dealing with all aspects of UK and international corporate tax work, including both UK and cross-border mergers and acquisitions, disposals, reconstructions and group reorganisations. He also has wide experience of a range of banking and bond transactions and tax-based structured financing.
Prof. Memberships: Member Law Society Revenue Committee 1995, Chairman of the Stamp Duty Sub-Committee of the Law Society Revenue Law Committee 1995; Member Corporation Tax Sub-Committee of The Law Society Revenue Law Committee, 1988.
Career: Articled *Allen & Overy*, qualified 1976, Partner 1982.
Personal: Exeter University (1973, LLB).

LING, Timothy
Freshfields Bruckhaus Deringer, London
(020) 7936 4000
timothy.ling@freshfields.com
Specialisation: Partner in tax department. All aspects of corporate tax, and particularly UK and cross-border mergers and acquisitions, reconstructions, joint ventures, demergers, private company acquisitions and disposals, new issues.
Prof. Memberships: Law Society and City of London Law Society.
Career: Qualified in 1973. Became partner in *Freshfields* 1977. Head of tax department 1985-91. Member of Law Society Revenue Law Committee 1981-91.
Personal: Born 17th September 1948. Educated The King's School, Canterbury and The Queen's College, Oxford (MA). Leisure interests include sailing and music. Member of Royal Harwich Yacht Club.

LOWE, Kevin
Wragge & Co, Birmingham
0870 903 1000

LUDER, Sara
Slaughter and May, London
(020) 7600 1200
sara.luder@slaughterandmay.com
Specialisation: Sara's practice covers all direct taxes and value added tax, but, in particular, corporation tax. She has extensive experience of corporate transactions including acquisitions, disposals and flotations. She also has considerable experience in leasing and other structured finance transactions. Sara has a particular interest in e-commerce, and is a member of the firm's e-commerce group.
Career: Qualified 1991; joined *Slaughter and May* 1992; partner 1998.

LYNCHEHAN, Martin
Linklaters, London
(020) 7456 5716
martin.lynchehan@linklaters.com
Specialisation: Considerable experience of the taxation issues arising in corporate and corporate finance transactions including public and private company disposals and acquisitions and securities offerings as well as experience of structured finance transactions. Proven track record in building successful transactional working relationships with other tax professionals both from in-house tax departments and external accounting firms.
Career: 1998 to date: Partner, *Linklaters*; 1993-98: Assistant Solicitor, *Linklaters*; 1988: Trainee Solicitor/Assistant Solicitor, *Richards Butler*. Queen Mary College, London University, LLM (Tax); University of Nottingham BA (Law).

MAINPRICE, Hugh
Hutchinson Mainprice, London
(020) 7259 0121

MCGOWAN, Michael T
Shearman & Sterling, London
(020) 7655 5000

MEARS, Patrick
Allen & Overy, London
(020) 7330 3000
patrick.mears@allenovery.com
Specialisation: Managing Partner of *Allen & Overy* global tax practice. Advises on the corporate tax aspects of transactions in a wide range of areas including UK tax advice in the fields of domestic and cross-border acquisitions, corporate reorganisations, IPO's, transfer pricing and tax investigations, domestic and international banking, asset and tax structured financing, capital markets issues and securities trading and lending.
Prof. Memberships: City of London Law Society's Revenue Law Sub-committee.
Career: Articled *Allen & Overy*, qualified (1982), Partner (1988). Frequently lectures on topical corporate tax issues.
Personal: Born 1958. London School of Economics (1979, LLB).

MEHTA, Nikhil
Cleary Gottlieb Steen & Hamilton, London
(020) 7614 2330
nmehta@cgsh.com
Specialisation: Corporate tax. Specialises in corporate taxation with particular emphasis on international and structured finance, contentious tax, derivatives, mergers and acquisitions, cross-border structures and joint ventures.
Career: 2002: Joined *Cleary Gottlieb*. 1992 to 2002: Head of the India business group, *Linklaters*, 1989 to 2002: Partner, *Linklaters*, 1983-1989: Legal assistant/assistant solicitor, *Linklaters*; 1981-1983: Legal assistant, Inland Revenue Solicitor's Office; 1997-1980: Practising as tax advocate, India. Bristol University LLB (Hons).

MORRIS, Gregory
DLA, Birmingham
(08700) 111111

MOSS, Philip G S
Osborne Clarke, Bristol
(0117) 917 3000

MURPHY, Niall
Blake Lapthorn, Fareham
(01489) 579990

NIAS, Peter
McDermott, Will & Emery, London
(020) 7577 6920
pnias@europe.mwe.com
Specialisation: Main areas of practice are corporate, commercial and international taxation. Work includes cross border transactions (in particular, mergers, acquisitions, reorganisations), transfer pricing and thin capitalisation, finance leasing and structured finance transactions.
Prof. Memberships: Law Society. Chairman and Member of Law Society International Tax Sub-committee, and Chairman Chartered Institute of Taxation International Tax Sub-committee, member of ICC UK Tax Committee, International Fiscal Association, International Tax Planning Association, European-American Tax Institute.
Career: Qualified in 1979. Joined *Simmons & Simmons* in 1976, becoming a partner in 1982 and Head of Tax Department in 1992. Joined *McDermott, Will & Emery*, November 1998 as Head of Tax to set up full-service London office.
Publications: Author of the PLC Tax Manual - 'Tax Clearances' chapter; frequent speaker at conferences and seminars and regular contributor of articles on EU and international tax issues.
Personal: Born 24th November 1953. Attended Manchester University 1973-76. LLB. Leisure interests include family and outdoor life, clay and game shooting, music and skiing. Lives in Great Horkesley.

NOBLE, Nicholas
Field Fisher Waterhouse, London
(020) 7861 4000
nrn@ffwlaw.com
Specialisation: Partner and head of tax department. Practice covers the taxation of UK and international transactions, and in particular companies and company reorganisations, securities and transactions in securities.
Prof. Memberships: ATII.
Career: Qualified in 1979 having joined *Field Fisher Waterhouse* in 1977. Became a partner in 1984.
Publications: Co-author of 'Butterworths Company Reorganisations: Tax and Tax Planning' and 'Butterworths International Taxation of Financial Instruments and Transactions' and joint

TAX CORPORATE — THE LEADERS

editor of and contributor to 'Butterworths Tax Planning Service'.
Personal: Born 1 October 1953. Educated at Winchester College and Durham University. Recreations include fencing, walking and reading.

NORFOLK, Edward Christopher Dominic
Norton Rose, London
(020) 7283 6000
norfolkcd@nortonrose.com
Specialisation: Partner in commercial tax department. Principal area of work involves advising on tax aspects of mergers and acquisitions, corporate structuring (domestic and international), banking and energy. Author of 'Taxation Treatment of Interest and Loan Relationships' (Butterworths, 3rd edn 1997). Member of editorial committee 'Practical Law for Companies'. Frequent speaker at conferences and seminars.
Prof. Memberships: Law Society (member, Tax Law Committee); Chartered Institute of Taxation (FTII), International Bar Association, International Fiscal Association, American Bar Association (Foreign Lawyers Forum of the Section of Taxation).
Career: Articled at *Longmores* in Hertford, then joined *Gabb & Co* in Abergavenny. Joined *Norton Rose* in 1975 and became a partner in 1979.
Personal: Born 8 August 1948. Attended St. John's School, Leatherhead 1962-66, then Southampton University (LLB) 1966-69. Leisure pursuits include ski-ing and fishing. Lives Somerset and Wimbledon.

NORWOOD, Andrew
Weil, Gotshal & Manges, London
(020) 7903 1000
andrew.norwood@weil.com
Specialisation: Financial taxation partner specialising in the tax treatment of securitisation transactions. Has wide experience of all financial taxation matters and has been involved in advising both issuers and investors in respect of numerous capital markets and international equity offerings and in advising on all aspects of the taxation of derivative products. Specialises in advising on various UK and international innovative securitisation transactions involving a wide variety of asset types and has advised on numerous repackaging projects, and on receivables financings.
Career: Qualified in 1986. *Allen & Overy* 1986-96. *Weil, Gotshal & Manges* 1996, Partner 1999.
Personal: Born 1961. Educated at William Ellis School and Gonville & Caius College, Cambridge (BA, MA). Interests include skiing and gardening.

NOWLAN, Howard
Slaughter and May, London
(020) 7600 1200
howard.nowlan@slaughterandmay.com
Specialisation: Corporate tax - general, restructurings, demutualisations, transfer pricing.
Personal: MA Oxon.

OVERS, John
Berwin Leighton Paisner, London
(020) 7760 1000
john.overs@blplaw.com
Specialisation: Partner in Tax Department. Principal area of practice covers corporate taxation and VAT.
Prof. Memberships: Law Society.
Career: Qualified in 1978 while at *Berwin Leighton*. Became a Partner in 1981.
Personal: Born 15 August 1953. Attended Kilburn Grammar 1964-69, City of London School 1969-71, then St Peter's College, Oxford 1972-75. Leisure pursuits include music, photography and tennis. Lives in London.

POPPLEWELL, Nigel
Burges Salmon, Bristol
(0117) 902 2782
nigel.popplewell@burges-salmon.com
Specialisation: Head of Corporate Tax Unit, specialising in all aspects of corporate, commercial and property taxation (both direct and indirect), including cross border transactions, restructuring, inward investment, financing arrangements and property investment structures. Considerable experience in representing clients before the general and special commissioners and VAT tribunals. Further extensive experience in advising clients in investigations ranging from small scale enquiries to full-blown SCO investigations and subsequent criminal proceedings.
Prof. Memberships: Fellow, Chartered Institute of Taxation; Law Society.
Career: Natural Sciences degree at Cambridge, then seven years playing professional cricket for Somerset, teaching biology and chemistry during the winters. In 1985 retrained as a lawyer, joined *Clarke Wilmott & Clarke* in 1987, Partner 1993; joined *Burges Salmon* in 1999 as a Partner.

PORTER, Sue
Freshfields Bruckhaus Deringer, London
(020) 7936 4000
sue.porter@freshfields.com
Specialisation: Specialises in corporate taxation and corporate tax planning, particularly in the finance/capital markets area, including structured finance, securitisation, derivatives, banking and bond issues and general corporate tax advice. Acts for banks, building societies, consumer finance, media and corporates. Contributor, Tolley's 'Tax Planning'.
Career: Qualified 1984. Partner 1992 in tax department.

POWELL, Ted
Mills & Reeve, Cambridge
(01223) 222 297
tp@mills-reeve.com
Specialisation: All aspects of corporate and commercial tax including VAT and employee benefits. Specialist areas include tax planning for universities and other charities. Recent work - tax structuring for a major property development joint venture; advising buyout team on large utilities MBO; advising on sale of telecoms business from parent.
Prof. Memberships: Law Society; VAT Practitioners Group; Fellow of Royal Society of Arts.
Career: Merton College, Oxford 1973-76. Fellow in History, Downing College, Cambridge 1982-89; Trainee at *Freshfields* 1991-93; assistant Solicitor in Tax Department, 1993-95. Joined *Mills & Reeve* 1995. Became partner 1997. Currently Group Leader of Corporate Services Group.
Personal: Married with two children. Ex-professional interest in medieval history. Author of book on King Henry V.

PRESTON, Christopher
Watson, Farley & Williams, London
(020) 7814 8000
cpreston@wfw.com
Specialisation: Partner in international tax group. Main area of practice covers leasing and asset finance/structured finance, company taxation and international tax planning. Leasing work typically involves large sophisticated transactions. Also specialises in VAT and customs duties, including both contentious and non-contentious matters and appearing before the VAT tribunal.
Prof. Memberships: Law Society (member of Revenue Law Committee and VAT & Duties Sub-Committee), VAT Practitioners Group (founder member). Fellow of the Institute of Taxation. Lectures extensively on leasing topics.
Career: Admitted 1975. Joined *Watson, Farley & Williams* as a partner in 1982. Chairman 1999-
Personal: Born 9 October 1950.

ROSE, Simon
SJ Berwin, London
(020) 7533 2222
simon.rose@sjberwin.com
Specialisation: VAT, indirect and direct taxes in property and commercial transactions; structuring of property funds including limited partnerships; private equity and offshore funds, including venture capital trusts and investment trusts; property joint ventures and fund vehicles; VAT litigation in the UK and the EC.
Prof. Memberships: Law Society, Institute of Indirect Taxation, VAT Practitioners Group, Law Society Revenue Law Committee, Law Society VAT and Duties Sub Committee.
Career: Articled *Lovell White Durrant* 1990-92. Qualified 1992. Joined *SJ Berwin & Co* 1994.
Personal: Born 1968: Exeter University 1986-89 LLB (Law); London University 1996-98 LLM (Taxation).

RUPAL, Yash
Linklaters, London
(020) 7456 5646
yash.rupal@linklaters.com
Specialisation: Tax Partner. Specialises in general corporate tax with particular emphasis on structured finance/product development, derivatives and other financial instruments. Spent 18 months on secondment with *Merrill Lynch* (investment banking division) working on cross-border mergers and acquisitions and other corporate finance transactions.
Career: 1996 to date: Partner, *Linklaters*; 1988-96: Assistant Solicitor, *Linklaters*; 1986-88: Articled Clerk, *Linklaters*. 1995: Cambridge, LLM; 1984: East Anglia, LLB.

SALEH, David
Clifford Chance, London
(020) 7600 1000
Specialisation: Tax Department. Senior solicitor specialising in VAT and other indirect taxes and all aspects of UK real estate taxation (including, stamp duty planning, VAT, direct tax and capital allowances).
Career: Trained at *Clifford Chance*.
Personal: King's College, London (LLB - First Class Honours).

SALTISSI, Sally
Dechert, London
(020) 7775 7321
sally.saltissi@eu.dechert.com
Specialisation: Director of the international trade and customs practise in London. Negotiates and handles disputes with Customs and Excise and IBEA on all VAT, customs and excise duty matters. Work covers investigations cases, tariff classification, valuation and transfer pricing issues, origin, duty preference, export rebates, CAP questions, import and export licensing, anti-dumping duties, and appeals to and appearances before VAT and Duties Tribunal and the European Court. Cases have included agricultural levy dispute and CAP export refunds, tariff classification, origin disputes, customs duty panel, VAT liability and Single Market excise liabilities. Experienced Advocate intending to exercise full rights of audience in the Higher Courts.
Prof. Memberships: Law Society Revenue Law Committee, Customs Practitioners Group, Law Society representative on Joint Customs Consultative Committee, Honorary Legal Adviser to UKWA.
Career: Called to the Bar (Inner Temple) in July 1985 having studied law in London 1981-84. Worked for Crown Prosecution Service 1986-88 and the Solicitors Office of HM Customs & Excise from 1988 to 2000. Joined *Dechert* July 2000.
Personal: Qualified as a radiographer in 1970 and practised as such until qualifying in law. Lives in South London.

SANDERS, Tim
Skadden, Arps, Slate, Meagher & Flom LLP, London
(020) 7519 7039
tsanders@skadden.com
Specialisation: All corporate and banking related tax matters including cross-border financial structuring.
Prof. Memberships: Law Society; Fellow of the Chartered Institute of Taxation.
Career: Llandovery College (Thomas

THE LEADERS ■ TAX CORPORATE

Phillips Scholar), Thames Valley GS, London University (LLB). Head of the Corporate Tax Department at *Theodore Goddard* prior to joining *McDermott, Will & Emery*. Currently a Partner in the Tax Department of *Skadden, Arps, Slate, Meagher & Flom LLP*.
Publications: Co-author of Butterworths Tax Indemnities and Warranties. Contributor to Tolleys Company Law. Contributor to various tax journals.
Personal: Born 1959. Qualified 1984. Married with 2 children. Interests: golf, cinema, theatre, Buzkashi and gardening. Lives in Epsom.

SANDISON, Francis
Freshfields Bruckhaus Deringer, London
(020) 7936 4000
francis.sandison@freshfields.com
Specialisation: Partner. Main area of practice is corporate tax and VAT. Cases have included Collard v Mining and Industrial Holdings (H.L. 1989), R v HM Treasury, ex parte Daily Mail and General Trust (ECJ 1988). Worked on SmithKline Beckman's merger with Beecham, Varity's merger with Lucas, Amoco's merger with BP and Compass's merger with Granada. Co-author of 'Whiteman on Income Tax' (3rd edition, 1988). Member, Tax Law Review Committee.
Prof. Memberships: Law Society (Member, Tax Law Committee,) City of London Law Society (Distinguished Service Award 1997), Addington Society, VAT Practitioners' Group.
Career: Qualified in 1974. Partner 1980.
Personal: Born 1949. Educated Charterhouse and Magdalen College Oxford.

SCOTT, Tom
Linklaters, London
(020) 7456 5692
tom.scott@linklaters.com
Specialisation: Tax Department. Specialist in the corporate taxation aspects of mergers, acquisitions, reorganisations, capital restructurings and oil and gas tax.
Career: 1990 to date: Partner, *Linklaters*; 1983-90: Assistant Solicitor, *Linklaters*; 1981-83: Articled Clerk, *Linklaters*; 1980: Lecturer in Law, Lincoln College, Oxford. 1979: Magdalen College, Oxford University (MA Law, First Class Honours).

SIMPSON, Mark
Hammond Suddards Edge, Leeds
0113 284 7000

SINFIELD, Greg
Lovells, London
(020) 7296 2000
greg.sinfield@lovells.com
Specialisation: Head of Indirect Tax. VAT and other indirect taxes (customs/excise duty, insurance premium tax, landfill tax, climate change levy) relating to commercial, financial services and property sectors. Investigation and litigation regarding indirect taxes including judicial review, condemnation proceedings and appeals to the VAT and Duties Tribunal and the higher courts and judicial reviews. Represents clients in VAT Tribunals and has appeared in the High Court, Court of Appeal and European Court of Justice as a solicitor advocate. Writes articles on VAT matters and lectures in the UK and Europe on the above.
Prof. Memberships: Law Society, VAT Practitioners' Group.
Career: Called to the Bar 1981. Customs & Excise Solicitor's Office 1983-88. *Durrant Piesse* 1988. Qualified as a Solicitor 1989. Partner *Lovells* 1993. Solicitor advocate 1994.

SINYOR, Alan
Freshfields Bruckhaus Deringer, London
(020) 7936 4000
alan.sinyor@freshfields.com
Specialisation: UK and international VAT issues, and in particular property transactions, finance and e-commerce. Assistant Editor of De Voils Indirect Tax Intelligence.
Prof. Memberships: Institute of Chartered Accountants of England and Wales; Institute of Taxation; Deputy Chairman of the CIOT Indirect Taxes Sub-Committee; Member of the VAT Practitioners' Group.
Personal: Born 13 January 1961. Attended Balliol College, Oxford (BA, MA) and Wolfson College, Cambridge (PhD). Married with six children.

SMITH, Isla
Norton Rose, London
(020) 7283 6000
smithim@nortonrose.com
Specialisation: Partner in Taxation Department. Principal area of practice is the tax aspect of financing transactions, including leasing and asset finance, banking, structured finance and securitisation, project finance and international corporate tax structuring. Other main areas of practice are tax issues relevant to the insurance sector, corporate restructuring and company acquisitions and disposals. Has dealt with a substantial number of tax based aircraft, ship, rolling-stock and project financings and cross-border asset finance transactions. Clients include banks, bank leasing companies, airlines, shipping companies, rolling stock companies, multinational groups of companies, financial intermediaries and arrangers. Author of chapters in the ICAEW 'Taxation Service' and Longman's 'Practical Tax Planning'. Speaker at a number of conferences.
Prof. Memberships: Law Society, City of London Law Society, Chartered Institute of Taxation, International Fiscal Association, International Bar Association, Finance and Leasing Association.
Career: Admitted as an Attorney of the Supreme Court of S Africa in 1974. Qualified as a solicitor in England and Wales in 1980. Became a partner at *Norton Rose* in 1985.
Personal: Born 17 February 1952. Educated at Westville Girls' High School, Natal, SA 1960-68, the University of Pretoria and the University of Natal, Durban 1969-72. Leisure pursuits include keeping up with two children, aerobics, music, tennis and skiing. Lives in Wimbledon.

STAPLETON, Mark
Dechert, London
(020) 7775 7591
Mark.Stapleton@eu.dechert.com
Specialisation: Partner, tax, advises on UK and international direct and indirect taxation issues. Specialises in property sector work such as commercial property development, joint ventures and overseas aspects. Also, taxation of corporate mergers and acquisitions and onshore and offshore investment funds and collective investment schemes.
Prof. Memberships: Associate of the Institute of Taxation (1989-), Member of the VAT Practitioners Group and the International Fiscal Association.
Career: Articles at *Turner Kenneth Brown*. Qualified in 1988. Solicitors at *Turner Kenneth Brown* until 1993. Joined *Titmuss Sainer Webb* (now *Dechert*) 1993. Appointed partner at *Dechert* 1996-date.
Publications: Author of two chapters on close companies in the 'FT Law and Tax Publication', 'Practical Tax Planning with Precedents' and also co-author of a chapter on how to set up a hedge fund in the ISI publication 'Hedge Funds - A European Perspective'. Regular conference speaker.
Personal: Born 1964. Educated at King Edward VI Grammar School, Chelmsford. Graduated from Nottingham University (LLB). Resides in London. Interests include tennis, football, cinema and theatre.

STRATTON, Richard
Travers Smith Braithwaite, London
(020) 7295 3000
Specialisation: Partner in Corporate Tax Department. Handles corporate tax matters. Specialist in funds and investment structures including onshore and offshore funds, limited partnerships, venture capital trusts, property-based structures and structured finance.
Career: Qualified in 1983. Partner at *Travers Smith Braithwaite* since 1989.
Publications: Recent articles - Venture Capital Trusts chapter in Tolleys 'Tax Planning'; articles concerning CREST and SDRT in 'PLC' magazine.

TAYLOR, David
Freshfields Bruckhaus Deringer, London
(020) 7936 4000
david.taylor@freshfields.com
Specialisation: Partner in tax department. Main area of work is corporate tax including banking, asset and structured finance, and some corporate finance.
Prof. Memberships: Law Society, City of London Solicitors' Company.
Career: Qualified in 1984.
Personal: Born 26th July 1959. Attended Cambridge University 1977-80 and 1981-82. Lives in Hampshire.

TAYLOR, Isaac
Herbert Smith, London
(020) 7374 8000

TAYLOR, Stephen
Linklaters, London
(020) 7456 5722
Stephen.Taylor@linklaters.com
Specialisation: UK tax specialist dealing with all aspects of corporate tax, especially financial transactions including capital markets, structured finance, asset finance including leasing, derivatives, and securities transactions.
Career: Since 2000 Partner *Linklaters* London; 1991-2000 Assistant Solicitor *Linklaters* London; 1989-91 Trainee Solicitor *Linklaters* London.

THOMPSON, Michael
Freshfields Bruckhaus Deringer, London
(020) 7936 4000
michael.thompson@freshfields.com
Specialisation: Partner in tax department. Advises on most UK tax aspects of corporate transactions. Has a particular specialisation in oil and gas taxation and a second specialisation in structuring the financing of all types of receivable through securitisation techniques. Acts for a number of oil and gas companies and banks. Chairs the Law Society's sub-committee on oil taxation and was the first lawyer representative for professional firms on the Steering Group of the UK Oil Industry Taxation Committee.
Prof. Memberships: Law Society. UK Oil Industry Taxation Committee.
Career: Became a partner at *Freshfields* in 1985.
Personal: Educated at Bradford Grammar School and Trinity College, Cambridge.

TOON, John
Addleshaw Booth & Co, Leeds
(0113) 209 2380
john.toon@addleshawbooth.com
Specialisation: To a significant degree, his practice focuses on tax advice for property transactions and capital projects for a mix of retail, developer, institutional and public sector clients. Also heavily involved in the tax aspects of a broad range of corporate and commercial transactions.
Prof. Memberships: Law Society, Chartered Institute of Taxation, VAT Practitioners Group.
Career: Qualified as a solicitor in 1991; joined firm in January 1995; Partner 2000
Personal: Married with two children. Enjoys golf, theatre and gardening.

TOSH, Nial
Dickson Minto WS, Edinburgh
(0131) 225 4455
nial.tosh@dmws.com
Specialisation: Experienced in a wide range of corporate tax matters, with a particular focus on mergers and acquisitions work, MBOs and employee share schemes and benefits.
Prof. Memberships: Law Society of Scotland.

TAX CORPORATE ■ THE LEADERS

Career: Joined *Dickson Minto WS* in 1994.
Personal: Educated at Edinburgh University.

TOWNSEND, Peter
Cobbetts, Manchester
(0161) 833 7493
peter.townsend@cobbetts.co.uk
Specialisation: Corporate Tax Partner and Head of the Corporate Tax Team. Advises both public and private companies on a broad range of taxation issues including tax planning, employee share incentives, group reorganisations, disputes with taxation authorities and mergers/acquisitions. Joint draftsman of the Employee Share Scheme Bill 2002.
Prof. Memberships: Law Society; Manchester Law Society; AIIT; TEP; (Committee Member of the Manchester branch of STEP).
Career: Qualified in 1987. *Gorna & Co* 1987-88; London School of Economics; University of London (LLM Revenue Law 1989); *Slater Heelis* 1990-98 (Partner 1996). Joined *Cobbetts* as a Partner 1998 on *Slater Heelis* demerger. Formerly a lecturer in revenue law (part-time) at the University of Manchester (1990-94).
Personal: Leisure interests include skiing, football, tennis and walking. Lives in Sale, Cheshire.

TRASK, Michael
SJ Berwin, London
(020) 7533 2222
michael.trask@sjberwin.com
Specialisation: Structuring private equity funds, including the Barclays Private Equity European Fund, Innisfree M&G PPP LP fund, and carried interest plans for CSFB and JP Morgan.
Career: Called to the Bar 1971; *Slaughter & May* 1982-85; *SJ Berwin* 1985-present (Partner 1986).
Publications: 'SJ Berwin Guide to Going Offshore'.
Personal: Dulwich College 1958-67; Christ Church, Oxford 1967-70. Classical music, wine, rugby union.

TROUP, Edward
Simmons & Simmons, London
(020) 7628 2020
edward.troup@simmons-simmons.com
Specialisation: Head of the corporate tax group at *Simmons & Simmons* until 1995 when he was appointed Special Advisor on tax at the Treasury. Returned to the firm in 1997, since when he has advised on a wide range of corporate and financial transactions, and at the same time has remained active in tax policy, advising and commenting on numerous legislative changes, both in the UK and the EU. Corporate tax, including financing and corporate transactions. Advises on tax policy and strategic tax planning.
Prof. Memberships: Law Society (Chairman, Revenue Law Committee), Chartered Institute of Taxation, Institute for Fiscal Studies, International Fiscal Association, Chairman of British Branch.
Career: MA, MSc (Oxon).
Publications: Numerous articles in Financial Times and various professional journals.
Personal: Cinema, cycling, opera, Anglo-Saxon history, sleep.

WALTON, Miles
Allen & Overy, London
(020) 7330 3000
miles.walton@allenovery.com
Specialisation: Partner in Corporate Tax Department. Deals with all aspects of corporate tax with particular experience of bank taxation and tax-related financing transactions, including domestic and cross-border asset finance, project finance, structured finance, securitisation and capital markets.
Prof. Memberships: Law Society, Institution of Taxation (Associate).
Career: Qualified 1980. Associate *Slaughter and May*,1980-1983; Partner *Wilde Sapte*, 1984-87; Partner *Allen & Overy*, 1997.
Publications: Co-author of *Taxation and Banking* (Sweet & Maxwell).
Personal: Born 1955. Brasenose College, Oxford University (MA Jurisprudence).

WARRINER, Neil
Herbert Smith, London
(020) 7374 8000
neil.warriner@herbertsmith.com
Specialisation: Partner particularly experienced in all tax aspects of land and property transactions (construction and PFI projects, refurbishments and redevelopments, acquisitions and disposals, inward investment structures) and tax issues arising in the energy sector. Has also general expertise in corporate mergers, acquisitions and reorganisations and a special interest in indirect taxes (VAT, Stamp Duty).
Prof. Memberships: Law Society; UKOITC; UK Energy Lawyers Group.
Career: St Peter's College, Oxford 1981-84; qualified 1987; partner *Herbert Smith* 1994.

WATSON, John
Ashurst Morris Crisp, London
(020) 7638 1111
john.watson@ashursts.com
Specialisation: Partner in tax department. Fund work, enterprise zones, private equity, international tax, general corporate tax, tax litigation and property tax. Legal adviser to the EZPUTA. Leads IFMA Steering Committee on UK aspects of PFPVs. Contributor to Tolleys 'Tax Planning' and other textbooks.
Career: Christ's College, Cambridge (1970-73). Exhibition and MA in mathematics. Barrister 1975-78; *Neville Russell* 1978-83. Joined *Ashurst Morris Crisp* in 1983. Partner in 1989.
Personal: Born 23 April 1951.

WHITTY, Oonagh
Latham & Watkins, London
(020) 7710 1000
oonagh.whitty@lw.com
Specialisation: Partner, advises clients on tax matters and multi-jurisdictional tax transactions, as well as structured finance, high yield and mergers and acquisitions transactions. Extensive experience in tax-based financing both in financial instruments and asset finance and leasing.
Career: Qualified 1981; Partner *Watson, Farley & Williams* 1987-2000. Partner *Latham & Watkins* 2000.
Personal: Born 1954; resides London; attended Imperial College, London University (BSc).

WISTOW, Michael John
Clifford Chance, London
(020) 7600 1000
michael.wistow@cliffordchance.com
Specialisation: Tax, pensions and employment. Partner specialising in financing transactions including property finance, securitisation, leasing and tax-based structured financings.
Career: Trained at *Clifford Chance*; Partner since 1997.

WONG, Etienne
Clifford Chance, London
(020) 7956 0206
etienne.wong@cliffordchance.com
Specialisation: Tax, pensions and employment. Partner specialising in VAT and other indirect taxes, e-commerce, online services and the internet, financing transactions and property transactions.
Career: Trained at *Clifford Chance*.
Personal: Uppingham School; University of Bristol.

WOODGATE, Neil
White & Case, London
(020) 7397 3840
nwoodgate@whitecase.com
Specialisation: Partner in Corporate Tax Department with emphasis on international and cross-border asset finance and structured finance transactions.
Prof. Memberships: Law Society of England and Wales.
Career: Qualified 1988. Partner at *Wilde Sapte* before joining *White & Case* in 2001.

WOOLICH, Richard
Nicholson Graham & Jones, London
(020) 7360 8270
richard.woolwich@ngj.co.uk
Specialisation: Partner and Head of Corporate Tax and VAT Group. Advises on corporate tax generally, including corporate finance, reconstructions and mergers, but has a particular expertise in property tax and structuring joint ventures in the property sector, and VAT and stamp duty planning. Lectures for Henry Stewart and IIR.
Prof. Memberships: Associate member of Chartered Institute of Taxation and of Institute of Indirect Taxation; VAT Practitioners' Group; representative of Institute of Indirect Taxation on the VAT Land and Property Liaison Group; member of Technical Committee of Institute of Indirect Taxation; International Fiscal Association.
Career: Articled *Nabarro Nathanson*; qualified 1989; Partner *Nicholson Graham & Jones* 1997.
Publications: Stamp duty chapter in CCH's 'Indirect Tax Guide'. Tax section of FT's 'Practical lending and security precedents'.
Personal: Educated at St. Paul's School and St. John's College, Cambridge University. Married to Joanne, with children Maya and Samuel.

TELECOMMUNICATIONS

London: 791; The Regions: 793; Profiles: 793

Research approved by BMRB For this edition, **Chambers'** researchers conducted 6,582 interviews – 3,900 with law firms, 511 with barristers and 2,171 with clients. The validity of the research was scrutinised by BMRB International, who audited both the methodology and the results at our offices in London. They interviewed **Chambers'** researchers and cross-checked sample interviews. Details of the audit appear on page 7.

LONDON

TELECOMMUNICATIONS — LONDON

1
- Allen & Overy
- Bird & Bird
- Clifford Chance

2
- Baker & McKenzie
- Linklaters
- Olswang

3
- Denton Wilde Sapte
- Field Fisher Waterhouse
- Simmons & Simmons

4
- Ashurst Morris Crisp
- Freshfields Bruckhaus Deringer
- Taylor Wessing

5
- Charles Russell
- Mayer, Brown, Rowe & Maw
- Norton Rose
- Osborne Clarke

LEADING INDIVIDUALS

1
- HIESTER Elizabeth *Clifford Chance*
- LONG Colin *Olswang*

2
- BALLARD Tony *Field Fisher Waterhouse*
- KERR David *Bird & Bird*
- MERCER Edward *Taylor Wessing*
- SCHWARZ Tim *Clifford Chance*
- STRIVENS Peter *Baker & McKenzie*
- WATSON Chris *Allen & Overy*
- WHEADON Tom *Simmons & Simmons*

3
- EDWARDS John *Taylor Wessing*
- FERGUSON Ian *Allen & Overy*
- HIGHAM Nicholas *Denton Wilde Sapte*
- LISTON Stephanie *McDermott, Will & Emery*
- WILLIAMS Rhys *Simmons & Simmons*

4
- DICKINSON Peter *Mayer, Brown, Rowe & Maw*
- GILMOUR Moira *Field Fisher Waterhouse*
- MONCREIFFE Mark *Charles Russell*
- NICHOLSON Kim *Olswang*
- PREISKEL Daniel *Altheimer & Gray*

UP AND COMING
- GOOD Natasha *Freshfields Bruckhaus Deringer*
- HOBDAY Natasha *Olswang*

This book is the product of 6,582 1/2 hour interviews. See p.7 for BMRB audit. Within each band, firms are listed alphabetically. See individuals' profiles p.793

ALLEN & OVERY (see firm details p.841) Joining the ranks of the leaders in the field, this firm is praised by commentators not only for offering clients cutting-edge telecoms financing expertise, but for possessing "*all-round strength and depth.*" Rapidly becoming the first port of call for many leading telecom blue-chips, envious competitors describe it as "*a genuine telecoms practice, with first-class individuals, that appears in almost every large deal.*" "*Regulatory and competition expert*" Chris Watson (see p.795) wins notable plaudits from the market, while Ian Ferguson (see p.793) moves up the tables this year on the strength of his impressive finance expertise. Multinationals appreciate the integrated international service, which this year has been boosted by the strengthening of its team in Hamburg. The group represented Schroder Salomon Smith Barney in a £1.8 billion asset-backed securitisation of leasehold properties acquired from and leased back to BT by Telereal Securitisation, a deal involving complex regulatory elements. It was also instructed by BT on the large-scale disposal of Yell. **Clients** Cable & Wireless; Marconi; KPN; Morgan Stanley; Merrill Lynch.

BIRD & BIRD (see firm details p.874) The firm is "*still dominating the scene,*" according to competitors. Singled out for litigation and technology know-how, its determined move into Europe has reaped rewards for the UK practice. An example has been its success in winning work for Telefonica on the vendor financing of the build-out of its 3G network in Germany, one of only a handful of pure financing deals in a year of restructuring. The team has also advised BT on all the corporate and commercial unwinding, outside the US, regarding Concert, the £10 billion global joint venture between BT and AT&T. This included advice on global system separation and submarine cables. David Kerr (see p.794) is described by peers as "*impressive in action, with a fantastic brain.*" He recently acted for Interprovider on an £8 million venture capital funding, with the aim of establishing a worldwide off-net communications service provider. **Clients** BT; One2One; Standard Chartered Bank; Global Crossing; Japan Telecommunications; Storm Telecommunications.

CLIFFORD CHANCE (see firm details p.911) Pronounced "*the first amongst equals*" by peers, this team is the automatic choice of many top class clients, who enthuse "*we use them if we have something really off the wall or a massive project.*" Its cross-border capability, particularly its expansion into the US, is seen as a major selling point of the team, alongside its enormous resources and the calibre of the partners. Not only is Elizabeth Hiester (see p.794) "*the pre-eminent practitioner in the field, with superb industry expertise,*" according to one source, but she has stalwartly managed to "*maintain the commercial edge in a corporate firm.*" Tim Schwarz (see p.794) is respected for his regulatory background and his "*fine performance on foreign deals.*" The "*creative*" team has advised NTT DoCoMo on the licensing of the i-mode technology to a series of mobile telecoms operators in Europe and Asia. Litigation work has included advice to the Latvian Government on its dispute with Sonera, concerning the 20-year monopoly granted to Sonera by the Government in 1993. **Clients** France Telecom; Energis; Global Crossing; WorldCom; Nokia.

BAKER & MCKENZIE (see firm details p.855) This team is especially respected for its regulatory expertise and its global network. "*Technical expert*" Peter Strivens (see p.795) is the group's standout practitioner and is currently leading it in its substantial work for Hutchison 3G. Successfully weathering the downturn in network build-outs, the UK team has been involved in such ongoing cosmopolitan work as Dolphin Networks' establishment of Nava Networks, an $800 million fibre-optic cable system connecting Singapore and Sydney via Jakarta, Perth and Melbourne. Privatisation deals have also been to the fore, with the team assisting its Eastern European offices in representing the Republic of Croatia on its disposal of a 19% interest in Hrvatske Telecom. Finance work includes France Telecom's structured €400 million financing for the acquisition, with Kulczyk Holding, of a 12.5% stake in Polish national operator, TPSA. **Clients** Hutchison 3G; Pacific Century CyberWorks; ntl; Sony; Deutsche Bank.

LINKLATERS (see firm details p.1043) Competitors wait to see what effect the loss this year of Robyn Durie is going to have on the team. Despite this, however, the "*excellent combined finance and regulatory practice*" continues to be warmly recommended by clients as "*user-friendly, with good industry knowledge.*" The group, which includes Graeme Maguire, has been advising Citylink on innovative ways of utilising extra capacity. Corporate work has included such impressive transactions as BT's £5.9 billion rights issue and the demerger of its wireless business, involving the creation of BT plc and mmO2. In these the team represented BT, one top name among many operators and finance houses in its enviable client roster. Competition and regulatory activity has included a number of merger clearances, such as

www.ChambersandPartners.com

TELECOMMUNICATIONS ■ LONDON

TOP IN-HOUSE LAWYERS

Philip BRAMWELL, General Counsel and Company Secretary, mmO2

Robert BRATBY, Commercial Director, Colt Telecommunications

Tim COWEN, General Counsel, BT Ignite

J Daniel FITZ, Group General Counsel, Cable & Wireless

Anne FLETCHER, Group General Counsel, BT

Kate JARVIS, Chief Counsel, Content and Application, mmO2

Chris SMEDLEY, Legal Director, Colt Telecommunications

Stewart WHITE, Group Public Policy Director, Vodafone

Kate Jarvis has "*an excellent knowledge of the law*" *and represents mmO2 with her colleague, the highly recommended* **Philip Bramwell**. *The legal team at Colt Telecommunications is also respected:* **Chris Smedley** *and* **Robert Bratby**, *both with "impressive all-round skills", retain their places.* **Anne Fletcher** *and* **J Daniel Fitz** *continue to impress, each having "strong management skills".* **Stewart White** *continues to reap praise for "a good commercial understanding," while the "first-rate"* **Tim Cowen** *"must be on the list."*

In-house lawyers' profiles p.1201

---

advice to Vodafone on the acquisition of Eircell. **Clients** Vodafone Group; Tiscali; Kingston Communications; Bank of America; JP Morgan Chase & Co.

OLSWANG (see firm details p.1087) The team's reputation is built upon the presence of "*old school guru*" Colin Long (see p.794), whose "*unparalleled knowledge of the sector*" is marvelled at by commentators. Several interviewees raised questions about the level of support beneath him; however, these concerns would seem to be unfounded given that the team boasts several other leading names. Ex-barrister Natasha Hobday's (see p.794) experience in the sector gains her the respect of peers, while Kim Nicholson's (see p.437) "*distinctive style*" has impressed commentators, who point to her corporate expertise. Recent corporate work has included advising Radiant Networks on a £5.5 million issue of unsecured loan notes and subsequent venture capital financing. The group has also assisted key client Cable & Wireless with strategic advice on interconnect agreements and regulatory issues. **Clients** WorldCom; Thus; Belgacom; Offgem; Royal Bank Ventures; Cable & Wireless.

DENTON WILDE SAPTE (see firm details p.935) One client told researchers that "*the firm's real strength lies in regulatory frameworks and in the interpretation of EU directives*." This claim is borne out by its success in advising Nokia on the €750 million vendor financing of Orange's 3G network in France. The department's expertise within mobile and satellite systems has attracted some important clients, such as Virgin Mobile and has secured the team

a place on the Oftel panel. "*Remarkable all-rounder*" Nick Higham (see p.794) has advised the Government of Bulgaria's privatisation agency, alongside Deutsche Bank, on the privatisation of BTC and on the changes to the legislative and regulatory frameworks necessary to make Bulgarian telecoms law consistent with EC requirements. **Clients** Energis; Citibank; Europe Star; Radiocommunications Agency of Great Britain; Government of the Bahamas.

FIELD FISHER WATERHOUSE (see firm details p.954) The firm is perceived by competitors to be "*at the cutting edge of telecoms work.*" Clients admire the dexterity with which it handles all areas of telecoms law, particularly competition. This has included work for the A2B2 consortium, comprising WorldCom, Global Crossing, Cable & Wireless, KPNQwest and Telia, which it advised on the opening of BT's local telephone lines. The team assisted Orange on its challenge to the Government's re-regulation of the telecoms sector, successfully establishing that the new template licences were introduced unlawfully. Tony Ballard (see p.587) was described by clients as "*unusually knowledgeable and pragmatic,*" while Moira Gilmour (see p.793) was singled out for her "*excellent grasp*" of esoteric areas of telecoms property work. She has been appointed to support Hutchison 3G's network roll-out in the UK. **Clients** Cable & Wireless; COLT; Energis; BBC Technology; T-Mobile.

SIMMONS & SIMMONS (see firm details p.1136) Its work on large, complex deals has attracted the attention of the market this year, as has the "*vast competition expertise*" of the team. The department has also been bolstered by a new office in Japan with a strong telecoms presence. Financing work has included the issue by major client Pacific Century CyberWorks of 1% convertible bonds with a value of $450 million. The team has assisted various companies, including Global TeleSystems, WorldCom and Thus, with regulatory work such as the introduction of wholesale rates for partial private circuits in the UK. High-profile Tom Wheadon (see p.795) stands out for his skill and experience, while Rhys Williams (see p.795) rises in the tables this year following praise for his attention to detail and "*clear understanding of the commercial side.*" **Clients** WorldCom; Global Crossing; One2One; Radicall; Africa Lakes Corporation.

ASHURST MORRIS CRISP (see firm details p.852) A team respected for its work throughout the sector, it enjoys niche expertise in outsourcing. This has been especially busy of late as telecoms companies increasingly turn to outsourcing as a way of coping with their levels of debt. The team, which includes Tony Ghee, has been advising Quintel, the joint venture between Rotch Property and QinetiQ to develop and provide mast-sharing technology for 3G

mobile phone networks. This will allow 3G operators to provide a successful service with fewer masts. A good choice for corporate work, the firm was appointed by VANCO in one of the few telecoms flotations of the past year. It also advised Chelsfield and TrizecHahn on the sale of Global Switch SarL to Risanamento for €495 million. **Clients** BT; Deutsche Telekom; Atlantic Telecom; Virgin; Schlumberger Network Solutions.

FRESHFIELDS BRUCKHAUS DERINGER (see firm details p.964) While clients and competitors agree that this is a first-class corporate telecoms practice, some in the market are unsure as to how much standalone regulatory work it undertakes. Nevertheless, the expanding group has been involved in some of the most important commercial and regulatory projects of the past year. It assisted Hutchison 3G on the roll-out of its 3G service in the UK, advising on regulatory issues relating to its licence. It also advised Hutchison on 3G infrastructure sharing around Europe. Another highlight of the year has been the demerger of BT and mmO2, in which the team helped establish the framework for putting intragroup trading on an arm's length basis. Natasha Good (see p.794), who was involved in this deal, was described by competitors as "*on the ball.*" **Clients** BT; Cable & Wireless; France Telecom; Orange; Global Crossing.

TAYLOR WESSING (see firm details p.1156) This practice was singled out by competitors for its international regulatory expertise. With an impressive US and European client base, it is felt to be well placed to withstand the technology downturn. "*Sharp, massively experienced*" Ted Mercer (see p.794) acted for the founders and managers of start-up broadband company Eon Communications (now OMNE) on securing £265 million worth of funding to expand its cable network. Further work in the creation of telecoms companies has generally occurred abroad this year and the team has been especially active in the Czech Republic, where the extra resources it commands following its merger will prove invaluable. Another highlight has been advising on the reconstruction and administration of Dolphin Communications. "*Statesmanlike*" John Edwards (see p.793) maintains his impressive market profile. **Clients** AT&T; IDT; Lucent Technologies; 365/Symphony; Airspan.

CHARLES RUSSELL (see firm details p.904) Clients appreciate the "*good hold over quality*" this team possesses due to its relatively small size: "*you always get a genuine expert.*" A growing group, it is led by Mark Moncreiffe (see p.794) and has recently been acting for the management of Ericsson Enterprise Solutions on the $480 million sale of the company to Apax Partners. Litigation has included representing Cable & Wireless in a dispute with Excell, successfully defending an injunction allowing the termination of call centre contracts. The team has also assisted in drafting a communications bill for an overseas territory. **Clients** Cable & Wireless; ntl; Gamma Telecommunications; Alta Berkely Venture Partners.

MAYER, BROWN, ROWE & MAW (see firm details p.1060) Noted for its corporate slant on telecoms work, this team, led by the "*commercially savvy*" Peter Dickinson (see p.793) has advised Telia International Carrier on the purchase of a 1,500 kilometre UK fibre network, amongst other assets. Cable & Wireless is another key client, and the team has advised it on its construction contract with Alcatel for the new 'Apollo' transatlantic cable system. The group has also assisted second-tier carrier, Interoute, on its plan to construct the €1.2 billion i-21 network. **Clients** Telia International Carrier; Marconi; ETC; European Telecom; Equant NV.

NORTON ROSE (see firm details p.1084) This team is thought by peers to be heavily biased towards finance work. Led by Michael Ings, it advised JPMorgan, CIBC World Markets, The Bank of New York and TD Bank Europe on the £2.25 billion financing of Telewest Communications Networks and Telewest Finance. The structure will allow Telewest access to the institutional market on a *pari passu* basis. Another important finance deal, where the firm also advised the banks, was the £90 million facility taken by Thus, to finance its operations following its demerger from ScottishPower. **Clients** CIBC World Markets; Bank of America; JPMorgan Chase; Dolphin Telecommunications; Global TeleSystems Holdings.

OSBORNE CLARKE (see firm details p.1090) Its pan-European network and co-operative, pragmatic approach are viewed by clients as among the strengths of the team. Led by Simon Rendell, it recently advised Context Connect on its negotiations with UK mobile operators for the provision to mobile telephone subscribers of a directory assistance service. The team has also represented Viatel on IRU and co-location agreements with a major cable operator. It also boasts considerable telecoms-finance expertise and has advised several US banks. **Clients** OnStar; Orange; Xantic; 186K; Redstone.

OTHER NOTABLE PRACTITIONERS
Stephanie Liston (see p.794) of McDermott, Will & Emery has been praised for her client care and knowledge of the market, while "*leading light*" Danny Preiskel, formerly of Steptoe & Johnson Rakisons, created a stir in the market this year with his move to Altheimer & Gray. Competitors wait to see what success he will enjoy in building a team there.

THE REGIONS

TELECOMMUNICATIONS
■ THE REGIONS

1. **Eversheds** Leeds
Wragge & Co Birmingham

This book is the product of 6,582 1/2 hour interviews. See p.7 for BMRB audit. Within each band, firms are listed alphabetically.

EVERSHEDS (see firm details p.949) The firm offers a wide range of telecoms advice and justly enjoys a national reputation. Neil Brown led the team acting for Eurocall on the acquisition of a fixed wire indirect access customer base and network from RSL. A major recent client win has been BT Cellnet, for whom the team has handled a range of commercial and litigious matters. It has also advised the North West Development Agency on the regulatory issues surrounding a £40 million investment to facilitate broadband roll-out in Cumbria. **Clients** Eurocall; BT Cellnet; Kingston Communications; Via Networks; North West Development Agency.

WRAGGE & CO (see firm details p.1197) Newcomers to the tables, the team received recommendations from a range of interviewees, including international clients and City practitioners. It is recognised for "*working flexibly and productively with in-house counsel*" and is said by peers to possess "*real telecoms expertise.*" The group, led by Clive Douglas, has acted on one of the most important deals of the year, advising AT&T on the English law aspects of the unwind of its global joint venture with BT. Another highlight for the team has been advising 186K on a £25 million contract for the provision of dark fibre and managed services to a major telecoms company. **Clients** BT; AT&T; Vodafone; Telewest; Powergen.

THE LEADERS IN TELECOMMUNICATIONS

BALLARD, Tony
Field Fisher Waterhouse, London
(020) 7861 4000
jab@ffwlaw.com
See under Media & Entertainment, p.587

DICKINSON, Peter
Mayer, Brown, Rowe & Maw, London
(020) 7782 8747
pdickinson@eu.mayerbrownrowe.com
Specialisation: Partner, Corporate Department. Head of London's Communications Group. Main area of practice is corporate and commercial work involving transactions in the telecommunications and related converging industries, including mergers and acquisitions, disposals, joint ventures, network infrastructure projects and outsourcing. Also has considerable expertise in private equity matters
Prof. Memberships: Law Society.
Career: Articled Clerk *Clifford Turner* 1986-88; Assistant Solicitor 1988-93; Assistant Solicitor *Lovell White Durrant* 1993-94; Senior Legal Advisor Mercury Communications Limited 1994-95; *Rowe & Maw* 1995 to present.
Personal: Born 24 March 1962. Educated at Wells Cathedral School and Southampton University (LLB Hons). Leisure activities include sailing, cycling and skiing. Married to Sarah, they have three children, Ben, Ellen and James. Lives in London.

EDWARDS, John
Taylor Wessing, London
(020) 7300 7000
j.edwards@taylorwessing.com
Specialisation: Partner in IT/Telemunications Group. Telecommunications, broadcasting and information technology law including corporate and commercial transactions in the sector as well as regulatory advice including UK and EC competition law aspects.
Prof. Memberships: Law Society. City of London Solicitors' Company.

FERGUSON, Ian
Allen & Overy, London
(020) 7330 3000
ian.ferguson@allenovery.com
Specialisation: Partner specialising in telecommunications, advising on all aspects in the UK and internationally, including regulation, strategic investments, privatisations, mergers and acquisitions, joint ventures and on contracts for the supply of telecommunications systems, equipments and services. Also specialises in information technology, advising on all aspects including the acquisition and supply of computer and communications systems and software; outsourcing transactions, particularly in the financial services sector; e-commerce and internet-related projects; electronic banking for many major banks and other data transmission arrangements; acquisitions, disposals and joint ventures in the technology sector. Advising Mondex and MUCTOS, he is a member of the UK Government Taskforce on e-commerce. Clients include Swisscom, KPN, Unisource, Sprint, First Telecom, Mondex International, MULTOS, NatWest Electronic Markets, SWIFT and News Digital Systems.
Career: Articled *Allen & Overy*, qualified 1985, Partner 1992.
Personal: Educated at Southampton University 1982 (LLB). Born 1959.

GILMOUR, Moira
Field Fisher Waterhouse, London
(020) 7861 4115
mag@fflaw.com
Specialisation: Telecommunications infrastructure - major projects to support the roll-out of 3G Networks.
Career: MA, LLB (Glasgow University). Qualified Scotland 1981, England 1987. Partner *FFW* 1998 following merger with *Allison & Humphreys*.
Personal: Greenhall high school, Glasgow University. Reading, sailing, visiting art galleries.

TELECOMMUNICATIONS ■ THE LEADERS

GOOD, Natasha
Freshfields Bruckhaus Deringer, London
(020) 7936 4000
natasha.good@freshfields.com
Specialisation: Partner in the IP/IT Department, London. Specialising in commercial/corporate work in the telecoms and technology sectors.
Career: Joined *Freshfield Bruckhaus Deringer*, London 1993; spent six months training in Paris and completed a one-year secondment to the Office of Communications in 1996; practice development manager for the TMT group September 2000 to January 2001.
Personal: Bristol University; Rouen University. Languages: English and French.

HIESTER, Elizabeth
Clifford Chance, London
(020) 7006 8014
elizabeth.hiester@cliffordchance.com
Specialisation: Corporate Department. Partner specialising in telecommunications, computer, IT and media industry practice group, focusing on international and domestic projects, commercial contracts, joint ventures, regulatory advice and anti-trust and intellectual property law.
Career: Articled *Clifford Chance* 1980-82; qualified 1982; joined *Clifford Chance* 1982; Partner since 1988.
Personal: 1973 Manchester (LLB 1st Class Hons); 1974 Amsterdam (Diploma in European Integration).

HIGHAM, Nicholas
Denton Wilde Sapte, London
(020) 7242 1212
nach@dentonwildesapte.com
Specialisation: Main areas of practice are telecommunications, internet and digital media. Work includes telecoms regulation (20 countries), privatisations (six countries), market entry and acquisitions, network services and interconnection, internet start-ups, content and netcasting, data protection, systems development and outsourcing. Regular lecturer on telecommunications and internet.

HOBDAY, Natasha
Olswang, London
(020) 7290 7945
nah@olswang.com
Specialisation: Barrister, Media, Communications and Technology Group, focusing on regulatory law and policy in the utility sectors, including communications, and commercial work, including drafting and developing communications-related contracts. Regular speaker at legal and industry conferences in all areas of communications.
Prof. Memberships: Middle Temple.
Career: Exeter University, Bar School, called to the Bar in 1990; Department of Trade and Industry Legal Department; European Commission secondment; *Clifford Chance*; First Telecom (subsequently Atlantic Telecom).

KERR, David
Bird & Bird, London
(020) 7415 6000
david.kerr@twobirds.com
Specialisation: Joint Head of Communications Group and CEO of firm. Main area of practice is corporate and commercial work involving deals in the telecommunications, e-commerce, media and information technology sectors. Has extensive experience of major transactions in these areas, including acquisitions, joint ventures, project finance, privatisation and outsourcing agreements. Frequent speaker at conferences on the global issues relating to telecommunications, e-commerce and information technology.
Prof. Memberships: IBA, Law Society.
Career: Qualified in 1985. Joined *Bird & Bird* in 1985, becoming a Partner in 1987.
Personal: Born 1960. Attended Jesus College, Cambridge (MA Hons, 1982). Lives in London.

LISTON, Stephanie
McDermott, Will & Emery, London
(020) 7577 6985
sliston@europe.mwe.com
Specialisation: Partner, Corporate Department, leads the firm's European Communications and Technology Group. Communications work includes advising upon, drafting and negotiating communications related transactions and providing strategic, commercial and EU/UK regulatory advice in connection with telecommunications and broadcasting activities. Stephanie acts for numerous companies in the UK, European and international communications market, including investors, telecom operators, internet providers, equipment suppliers, cable operators and electricity companies. Regular guest speaker.
Prof. Memberships: Vice Chairman of the Communications Committee of the International Bar Association (IBA); Member of the Board of Directors of the European Competitive Telecommunications Association (ECTA).
Career: Qualified in England (1994); District of Columbia (1988) and Texas (1985). Associate with *Fulbright & Jaworski*, in London, Houston, Texas, and Washington, DC 1984-89. Senior attorney with MCI 1990-92. *Freshfields'* Company Department 1992-95. *Baker & McKenzie*, London 1995-99. Joined *McDermott, Will & Emery* in 1999.
Personal: Born 15 March 1958. Attended The Colorado College (BA in History/Political Science 1980), University of San Diego Law School 1980-82 and University of Notre Dame London Law Centre 1982-83 (Juris Doctor 1983). Attended Trinity Hall, Cambridge University (LLM in English Law - 1st Class - 1984). Lives in Hampstead.

LONG, Colin
Olswang, London
(020) 7208 8888
cdl@olswang.com
Specialisation: Partner and joint head of telecommunications in the UK law firm *Olswang*. Has guided many of the world's leading telecommunication companies over the years in a variety of deals related to fixed, mobile and satellite-based services. Work encompasses regulation and competition law, commercial legal issues, corporate transactions including privatisations, M&A, joint ventures and start-ups, as well as development funding in the communications, IT and general hi-tech sectors. Work in recent years includes acting for a bidder on the UK third generation mobile auction, advising an industry group of operators on DSL services, acting for a successful bidder in the UK broadband fixed wireless auction, advising on a global satellite-based internet service and advising various LLU operators and DSL services providers and generally UK public operators on competition-related issues and proceedings before the regulator OFTEL. He is author of the leading textbook 'Global Telecommunications Law and Practice' (pub. Sweet & Maxwell), a guest speaker at numerous conferences and a frequent writer of articles in the telecoms press.
Prof. Memberships: Former chairman of the Communications Law Committee of the International Bar Association and a member of the UK Parliamentary Information Technology Committee.
Career: A graduate of Bristol University, trained and worked at *Clifford Turner* before becoming a partner at *Bird & Bird* and later *Coudert Brothers*, before moving to *Olswang* in 1998.

MERCER, Edward
Taylor Wessing, London
(020) 7300 7000
t.mercer@taylorwessing.com
Specialisation: Head of Telecommunications Group. Main area of work covers the regulatory competition and commercial aspects of running telecommunications systems worldwide. Particular expertise in the regulatory field, interconnect, procurement agreements and in relation to the cable industry. Has worked extensively in the fields of submarine cable and high bandwidth pan-European networks. Does much work in development of 'telehouses' and IP protocol broadband wireless systems. Has particular knowledge of the regulation of conditional access and access control. Acted in a number of private placements and involved in regulatory aspects of flotation work associated with cable companies in the UK. Acts for cable and telecoms trade associations and operators' groups. Contributor to the 'Law Society Gazette', 'Annual Media Law Review' and trade magazines. Frequent lecturer at seminars on cable and telecommunication issues in the UK and Europe.
Prof. Memberships: Law Society, Association of Council Secretaries and solicitors.
Career: Qualified 1980. Head of Legal Section Adur District Council 1980-83, then Borough Solicitor, Rossendale Borough Council 1983-85. Secretary to Cable Authority 1985-89. Joined *Allison & Humphreys* in 1989, becoming a partner in 1990. Partner *Taylor Joynson Garrett* 1996.
Personal: Born 1 February 1956. Attended King Edward's Five-Ways School 1967-74, then Trinity College, Cambridge 1974-77. Leisure pursuits include clay pigeon shooting, acting and badminton. Lives in Lewes.

MONCREIFFE, Mark
Charles Russell, London
(020) 7203 5113
markm@cr-law.co.uk
Specialisation: Partner in Company/Commercial Department, Head of Media and Communications Group. Main area of specialisation is the corporate commercial and regulatory aspects of telecommunications, both in the UK and internationally. He heads *Charles Russell's* Telecommunications Unit which provides industry focused and multidisciplinary advice to clients in the telecommunications field. He speaks at conferences and contributes specialist articles to journals.
Prof. Memberships: Law Society.
Career: Qualified in 1978. Joined *Charles Russell* in 1984 and became a partner in 1985.
Personal: Born 23 March 1953. Attended Uppingham School 1966-70, Queens' College, Cambridge, 1971-74, and Université Libre de Bruxelles 1974-75, (licence en droit européen). Leisure interests include varied outdoor sports

NICHOLSON, Kim
Olswang, London
(020) 7208 8731
kan@olswang.com
See under Information Technology, p.437

PREISKEL, Daniel
Altheimer & Gray, London
(020) 7786 5700

SCHWARZ, Tim
Clifford Chance, London
(020) 7006 8206
tim.schwarz@cliffordchance.com
Specialisation: Corporate Department. Partner specialising in international telecoms, posts and IT.
Career: Trained *Clifford Chance* 1987-89; seconded to OFTEL's Legal Department 1989-90; Associate *Clifford Chance* 1989-95; main telecoms lawyer World Bank Legal Department 1995-97; Partner since 1997.
Personal: Oxford University (BA Jurisprudence); Oxford University (BCL); Université de Bruxelles (Première et deuxième licences en droit européen).

STRIVENS, Peter
Baker & McKenzie, London
(020) 7919 1000
peter.strivens@bakernet.com

Specialisation: Partner and head of the telecommunications practice group. Work includes advice on licensing and regulatory issues in the UK and other jurisdictions, investments and joint ventures in the telecommunications industry and advising on a wide range of industry issues, including contractual negotiations and disputes. Has extensive experience of cross-border transactions and telecoms privatisations. Gives frequent conference presentations on telecommunications issues and has written the UK and International Chapters of 'Baker & McKenzie - Telecommunications Laws in Europe', Butterworths 1998. Qualified in 1984 with *Baker & McKenzie* and became a partner in 1990.
Career: Educated at St Johns College, Johannesburg, University of Witwatersrand (1971-75) and Balliol College, Oxford (1979-81).
Personal: Born 15 December 1954. Leisure activities include painting, tennis and looking after a growing family. Lives in London.

WATSON, Chris
Allen & Overy, London
(020) 7330 3000
chris.watson@allenovery.com

Specialisation: Partner in communications and technology group. Recent deals include: prohibitions of BT/BKSkyB joint marketing campaign by OFTEL (1995); prohibition of BT Reconnect Offer (1996); acquisition of Imminus Limited by General Cable Plc (1997); issue of international facilities licences by Oftel (advice to 35-46 applicants); appointed as legal advisor to the panel of experts advising the National Audit Office on its review of Oftel's use of its competition regulation powers in the Licensing Regime (1997); advice to Viatel Inc on all European aspects of its US$1 billion debt and equity issues for its Circe project and on its implementation in eight separate European jurisdictions; advice on a similar project for Storm Telecommunications; recommended as legal advisor by the World Bank on international projects: Zimbabwe Telecoms Act review (1998); Powergrid Corporation of India diversification into telecoms (1999); advice to One2One on its successful judicial challenge, on community law grounds, to the arrangements for publication of the Monopolies and Mergers Commission Report into calls to mobile phones; advice to One2One on its successful bid for a UMTS 3g licence (1999); advice to Lebanese Government on its proposed new Telecommunications Law (2000); advice to One2One on its infrastructure deal with BT Cellnet; advice to T-Mobile in the Competition Commission inquiry into the termination charges of calls to mobile phones.
Career: Trained *Simmons & Simmons*; qualified 1983, admitted to the Paris Bar 1993; partner *Simmons & Simmons* 1989-99; partner *Allen & Overy* 2000.
Publications: General editor, Sweet & Maxwell 'Encyclopaedia of Telecommunications Laws'; joint author, 'Telecommunications - The EU Law'.

WHEADON, Tom
Simmons & Simmons, London
(020) 7825 3603
tom.wheadon@simmons-simmons.com

Specialisation: Specialisation is in the law, regulation and policy of telecommunications.
Prof. Memberships: Law Society and International Bar Association.
Career: Southampton University, Guildford Law School, admitted as a solicitor in England and Wales in 1989. 1987-89: Trainee solicitor, *Ashurst Morris Crisp*. 1989-95: Solicitor, *Ashurst Morris Crisp*. 1995-96: Corporate and regulatory affairs solicitor, Videotron Corporation Ltd. 1996 to date: Partner, communications practice at *Simmons & Simmons*.
Personal: Married to Kate with three sons, Fred, Henry and George.

WILLIAMS, Rhys
Simmons & Simmons, London
(020) 7628 2020
rhys.williams@simmons-simmons.com

Specialisation: Main area of specialisation is in commercial and regulatory aspects of communications law in the UK and internationally, in particular in respect of licensing, interconnection, and the introduction and implementation of new technologies in mobile telephony. He has advised several clients on the legal, regulatory and strategic issues involved in the planning and construction of submarine and inland telecommunications networks.
Prof. Memberships: Law Society.
Career: Educated at Emmanuel College, Cambridge; Manchester University and University of North Carolina, Chapel Hill. Qualified 1994. Joined *Simmons & Simmons* 1997, Partner 2002.
Personal: Born 29 October 1965. Married to Rachel. Interests include mountaineering; American literature and music; Welsh rugby.

TRANSPORT

Road: 796; Rail: 798; Profiles: 801

Research approved by BMRB For this edition, **Chambers'** researchers conducted 6,582 interviews – 3,900 with law firms, 511 with barristers and 2,171 with clients. The validity of the research was scrutinised by BMRB International, who audited both the methodology and the results at our offices in London. They interviewed **Chambers'** researchers and cross-checked sample interviews. Details of the audit appear on page 7.

OVERVIEW

ROAD (CARRIAGE/COMMERCIAL) The continued rationalisation of operators and insurers, combined with the downturn in global freight movement, allows little room for major changes in the market, and our tables remain relatively static. With an increasing emphasis on the alternative transference of risk there are fewer disputes, and those that do occur continue to be sent to mediation.

ROAD (REGULATORY) The lorry fines regime, whereby haulage companies were liable to a £2,000 fine for each clandestine entrant found in their vehicles, was declared disproportionate in 2002. However, enforcement by the Vehicle Inspectorate and Health and Safety Executive remains stringent and focused. Where previously the onus was on the operator alone, new guidelines apportion liability to individual drivers as well. Outside of the freight field, there has been a tightening up of the regulation of local bus services. Penalties for not running according to timetable can now include the loss of the operator's right to run services or of a portion of its fuel duty rebate. Clients increasingly appreciate those firms that can take a pre-emptive approach to these issues, and others, such as the Working Time Directive.

RAIL Although the industry has entered a period of upheaval, evidenced this year by the large amounts of one-off advisory work, the dominant view is sanguine. Longer franchise agreements and bigger asset finance and infrastructure deals are anticipated, with anxiety surrounding PPPs not generally felt to have impacted heavily on investment. Meanwhile, with public/private initiatives beginning to be replicated throughout Europe, continental projects like the Dutch High-Speed Line are expected to come to the fore.

NATIONWIDE

ROAD (CARRIAGE/COMMERCIAL)

TRANSPORT:
ROAD (CARRIAGE/COMMERCIAL)
■ NATIONWIDE

1. **Holmes Hardingham** London
2. **Hill Dickinson** London, Manchester
3. **Waltons & Morse** London
4. **Clyde & Co** London, Guildford
   Davies Lavery London
5. **Davies Arnold Cooper** London
   DLA London, Liverpool, Manchester
   John Weston & Co Felixstowe
   Prettys Ipswich

LEADING INDIVIDUALS

1. **HARDINGHAM Adrian** Holmes Hardingham
   KNIGHT Tim Holmes Hardingham
   MARSHALL Julia Hill Dickinson
   MESSENT Andrew Holmes Hardingham
2. **DUNN Chris** Waltons & Morse
   HILL Martin DLA
   JACKSON Peter Hill Dickinson
   PYSDEN Kay Davies Lavery
3. **HOBBS Jane** Holmes Hardingham
   SILK Ken Davies Arnold Cooper
   WARD Dominic Andrew M Jackson
4. **ARMSTRONG Stuart** Hill Dickinson
   MELBOURNE William Clyde & Co
   REYNOLDS Justin Hill Dickinson
   SHARP Roland Prettys
   THOMAS Tony Clyde & Co
   WESTON John John Weston & Co

UP AND COMING
CHATFIELD Christopher Waltons & Morse

This book is the product of 6,582 1/2 hour interviews. See p.7 for BMRB audit. Within each band, firms are listed alphabetically. See individuals' profiles p.801

HOLMES HARDINGHAM (see firm details p.1000) "*You could not do any better*" according to one competitor, reflecting a consensus that the firm's "*strength and depth*" now makes it pre-eminent in this field. Clients rate **Andrew Messent** (see p.803) for his "*all-round ability,*" and peers appreciate his academic capacities and detailed knowledge of the area. "*An excellent strategic lawyer,*" **Adrian Hardingham** (see p.802) is universally acknowledged for his expertise and experience, while **Tim Knight** (see p.803) also remains highly regarded in the market. Following hard on the heels of this all-star cast, **Jane Hobbs** (see p.802) was praised for "*arguing her corner straightforwardly and well.*" Acting for insurers – both as defendants and claimants – the group specialises in warehousing, freight forwarding, domestic road haulage work and CMR. It also has a proven track record in advising hauliers on immigration matters.

HILL DICKINSON (see firm details p.995) "*Good operators,*" the team retains its market position and continues to provide stalwart competition at the top of the table. London-based **Julia Marshall** (see p.803) has a strong reputation, and is considered by rivals to be central to the practice's continued success. Though his managerial commitments are felt to be making him less visible in the market, **Peter Jackson** (see p.802) continues to earn the respect of his peers. The team covers all aspects of the intermodal carriage of goods and has recognised contractual expertise. It assists an enviable national and international client base, including operators, brokers and insurance companies. A notable recent development has been its increasing emphasis on alternative risk transference. On the recoveries side, **Stuart Armstrong** (see p.801) is considered a player, while junior London partner **Justin Reynolds** (see p.804) boasts a growing reputation.

WALTONS & MORSE (see firm details p.1180) Clients and peers alike continue to praise this "*excellent specialist firm,*" with one client saying of practice head **Chris Dunn** that "*you could not find a better specialist for road carriage matters.*" Acting for a substantial number of underwriters and insurers, it covers road, rail and air transport issues. Assistant solicitor **Christopher Chatfield** was newly ranked this year, having received a weight of market recommendation, particularly for his advice on recoveries and liability issues.

CLYDE & CO (see firm details p.913) The firm fields a strong team in this area, and is active throughout the UK, Europe and beyond, acting for blue-chip insurers and some freight forwarders. The "*excellent*" **Tony Thomas** (see p.804) was warmly recommended to researchers for his knowledge of CMR and his specialist expertise in the Far Eastern markets. Praised as an "*impressive mediator,*" **William Melbourne** (see p.803) retains his firm market position. High-value theft claims have recently featured heavily in the team's workload.

DAVIES LAVERY This broad transport practice, covering cargo and carrier claims for defendants and claimants, transit damage and policy disputes, is considered by peers to enjoy a well-established position in the market. "*Tough negotiator*" **Kay Pysden** (see p.804) was praised for her track record on domestic cases and highly recommended for international freight

796 INDEX TO LEADING LAWYERS: PAGE 1693 ■ IN-HOUSE LAWYERS PROFILES: PAGE 1201

NATIONWIDE ■ TRANSPORT

disputes. As one of the key players in influencing the decision overturning the lorry fines regime, clients especially value the team's expertise in issues relating to clandestine entrants.

DAVIES ARNOLD COOPER (see firm details p.930) This low-profile operation acts for insurers, recovery agents and freight forwarders on matters relating to the carriage of goods. In line with its core strength in dispute resolution, the firm is involved in a lot of contentious transport questions. **Ken Silk** remains well regarded by peers, though he is thought to have been less visible in this field of late.

DLA The group remains well regarded for its advice on liabilities and cargo recovery. Most visible acting for insurers, the practice spans the firm's London, Liverpool and Manchester offices. Clients described well-known expert **Martin Hill** as "*an outstanding lawyer.*"

JOHN WESTON & CO Described by competitors as a "*thriving, smaller practice,*" it is best known for its UK advice, mostly for carrier and cargo insurers, hauliers and freight forwarders. Heading up the transport group, well-respected **John Weston** retains a high profile amongst clients and peers. Debt collection within the transport industry and niche expertise in the Italian transport market also feature among the group's strengths.

PRETTYS (see firm details p.1106) Active in CMR, particularly for Benelux and Scandinavian clients, and domestic haulage disputes, the firm retains its market position. Benefiting from its good location close to local ports, typical work includes drafting conditions of carriage and advising on logistical arrangements. It is also developing a transport-related insurance practice. **Roland Sharp** (see p.804) received high praise from peers for his mediation skills. Recent highlights include a successful challenge to a fine imposed on a haulier for breach of the Immigration and Asylum Act 1999.

OTHER NOTABLE PRACTITIONERS **Dominic Ward** (see p.804) of Andrew M. Jackson is considered by clients to be "*quite a star,*" and was strongly recommended for lien and transport-related advice in connection with local port matters. Said to possess "*a level of knowledge beyond his years,*" interviewees acknowledged his increasing profile on the shipping side.

NATIONWIDE — ROAD (REGULATORY)

TRANSPORT: ROAD (REGULATORY)
■ NATIONWIDE

1 Ford & Warren — Leeds
2 Backhouse Jones — Clitheroe
3 Barker Gotelee — Ipswich
Rothera Dowson — Nottingham
Wedlake Saint — London
4 Arthur Cox — Belfast
Bannister Preston — Sale
Bond Pearce — Bristol
Over Taylor Biggs — Exeter
Wake Dyne Lawton — Chester

This book is the product of 6,582 1/2 hour interviews. See p.7 for BMRB audit. Within each band, firms are listed alphabetically.

FORD & WARREN (see firm details p.959) The consensus amongst peers and clients remains that "*this firm is still out ahead.*" With wide-ranging PSV-related work taking up a considerable portion of **Stephen Kirkbright**'s (see p.803) time, he continues to attract heavy market endorsement, often as "*one of the few who are capable of top quality in both legal arguments and advocacy.*" Concentrating principally on haulage, younger partner **Gary Hodgson** (see p.802) was said to provide a similar level of service. Civil litigation, including CMR, goods in transit claims, haulage contracts and insurance claims, accounts for a majority of the team's workload.

BACKHOUSE JONES (see firm details p.853) This firm specialises in transport and boasts a high-profile, predominantly UK, client base, including passenger and goods elements. Transport tribunals and public inquiries continue to form a substantial portion of its workload, though it increasingly takes a proactive approach towards advising operators. Over the last year it has brought its landmark Court of Appeal case, Ribble Motor Services v Traffic Commission, to a close, resulting in a clarification of the law regarding the regulation of bus operators. Its team on this was led by **James Backhouse** (see p.801), praised by market sources as "*in control of his brief and extremely enthusiastic.*" It has also assisted in a death by dangerous driving case involving an Attorney General's Reference.

BARKER GOTELEE This remains the undisputed firm of choice in East Anglia. Said to "*instil confidence in his clients,*" **Michael Gotelee** (see p.802) remains a prominent practitioner, while interviewees noted that **Deborah Sharples** (see p.804) is increasingly coming to the fore. The group continues to represent defendants in the Magistrates' Court and operators at public inquiries. Involved in auditing operator systems, the team also boasts expertise in employment, health and safety issues and clandestine entrant cases. Other areas of expertise include issues surrounding waste haulage, CMR and liens.

ROTHERA DOWSON (see firm details p.1118) The firm received wide-ranging recommendations this year, leading to its promotion in *Chambers*' tables. Active in public inquiries, Magistrates' and Crown Court work, the firm also advises on employment, litigation, operator licensing, terms and conditions and acquisitions/disposals. Heading up the practice, **Ian Rothera** (see p.804) is highly respected and is said by competitors "*always to present well-balanced arguments.*" The firm had a lead role in a successful challenge to the Illegal Immigration Civil Penalty system in the High Court, which is now the subject of an appeal by the Home Office. "*Rising star*" **Jane George** (see p.801) was widely recognised for her part in this action.

WEDLAKE SAINT Though also active on the freight side, it is for its pioneering passenger vehicles work that this firm is best known. It provides a broad service, covering personal injury, health and safety and employers' liability, for a number of major operators. **Barry Prior** (see p.803), described to *Chambers*' researchers as an understated specialist, leads the practice.

ARTHUR COX (see firm details p.850) "*If anything came up that required advice in Northern Ireland,*" interviewees said without hesitation that they would go to **Amanda Wylie** (see p.804). She heads a small practice defending hauliers and warehouse operators, most recently advising on the environmental aspects of the maintenance of lorries and on an illegal immigrant case. The practice also covers PI litigation and tachograph offences and is supported by Dublin and London offices.

BANNISTER PRESTON Experienced in prosecuting for the Vehicle Inspectorate, **John Heaton** (see p.802) also defends police and trading standards prosecutions. He was described to researchers as a "*top quality prosecutor and a good advocate,*" with recognised expertise in driver hours, tachograph and construction and use regulations. Other work includes representing the Traffic Commissioner against appeals.

TRANSPORT ■ NATIONWIDE

LEADING INDIVIDUALS

1
- **BACKHOUSE James** Backhouse Jones
- **KIRKBRIGHT Stephen** Ford & Warren
- **ROTHERA Ian** Rothera Dowson
- **WHITEFORD Michael** Jeffrey Aitken Solicitors

2
- **HODGSON Gary** Ford & Warren
- **OVER Christopher** Over Taylor Biggs

3
- **FEAR Jeremy** Jeremy Fear & Co
- **GOTELEE Michael** Barker Gotelee
- **HEATON John** Bannister Preston
- **PRIOR Barry** Wedlake Saint

4
- **CARLESS Michael** Carless Davies & Co
- **HALLSWORTH Chris** Woodfine Foinette Quinn
- **JONES Geoffrey** Bond Pearce
- **WOOLFALL Andrew** Wake Dyne Lawton

5
- **ALLAN Michael** Allan, Burn & McGregor
- **BUTTERFIELD Christopher** Herbert Mallam Gowers
- **GEORGE Jane** Rothera Dowson
- **WYLIE Amanda** Arthur Cox

UP AND COMING
- **SHARPLES Deborah** Barker Gotelee

See individuals' profiles p.801

BOND PEARCE (see firm details p.879) The former Cartwrights' team, led by well-regarded Geoffrey Jones (see p.803), is considered by some market sources to have had a lower profile this year. It continues to be busy defending transport associations and bus, haulage and distribution companies, and has recently seen an upturn in public inquiry work relating to breaches of the Working Time Directive.

OVER TAYLOR BIGGS Covering the South West and Wales, the firm provides a comprehensive service, and has been heavily involved in defending hauliers against tachograph and overloading prosecutions. The team also recently acted in a death by dangerous driving case. Standout practitioner **Christopher Over** is rated by peers as an *"excellent advocate."*

WAKE DYNE LAWTON (see firm details p.1177) The practice covers a wide spectrum of industry sectors, acting primarily for utility and distribution companies, mobile crane operators and, to a lesser extent, owner drivers. Bringing its PI and health and safety expertise to bear in defence work, it is experienced in public inquiries, operator licensing, liens, conditions of carriage and CMR. *"Focused and enthusiastic,"* **Andrew Woolfall** (see p.804) spearheads the operation and is seen by market sources to enjoy a rising profile. Interviewees, however, wait to see whether the departure of consultant Jonathan Lawton to Hill Dickinson will have an effect on the firm.

OTHER NOTABLE PRACTITIONERS According to peers, **Michael Whiteford** (see p.804) of Jeffrey Aitken Solicitors is the natural first choice for referrals in Scotland. With a core practice defending hauliers and bus operators, he recently represented Reids Transport Company in a landmark tribunal appeal. Widely known for his niche transport practice, **Michael Carless** of Carless Davies & Co covers the Midlands and Wales, defending hauliers at Magistrates' Courts and public inquiries. A road haulage specialist, sole practitioner **Jeremy Fear** is best known for his advice on the London lorry ban. Covering the South East, East and Metropolitan traffic areas, he is often to be seen in the Magistrates' Court, public inquiries and appeals to transport tribunals. *"Cerebral"* **Chris Hallsworth** (see p.802) of Woodfine Foinette Quinn in Milton Keynes retains his market position and was particularly recommended for his qualities as an advocate, while **Michael Allan** of Allan, Burn & McGregor in Scotland is also well respected. **Chris Butterfield** at Oxford-based Herbert Mallam Gowers retains a strong reputation in this area, acting for operators.

NATIONWIDE — RAIL

TRANSPORT: RAIL
■ NATIONWIDE

1
- Freshfields Bruckhaus Deringer

2
- Denton Wilde Sapte
- Linklaters

3
- Clifford Chance
- **Eversheds** London, Birmingham, Leeds
- Hollingworth Bissell

4
- Allen & Overy
- Ashurst Morris Crisp
- **Burges Salmon** Bristol
- Herbert Smith
- Norton Rose
- Simmons & Simmons

5
- DLA
- Field Fisher Waterhouse
- Nabarro Nathanson
- Slaughter and May

6
- CMS Cameron McKenna
- **Dickinson Dees** Newcastle upon Tyne
- **Edwards Geldard** Derby
- **Lovells** London
- Mayer, Brown, Rowe & Maw
- **Osborne Clarke** Bristol
- **Wragge & Co** Birmingham

This book is the product of 6,582 1/2 hour interviews. See p.7 for BMRB audit.
Within each band, firms are listed alphabetically.

FRESHFIELDS BRUCKHAUS DERINGER (see firm details p.964) Though interviewees stressed how close the competition was, this *"first-rate practice"* retains its position at the top of our tables, providing an unmatched service across the corporate, financing and regulatory spheres of the industry. **Richard Phillips** (see p.803) continues to enjoy a huge reputation, providing advice *"of an extremely high standard"* to the government and London Underground in LU's PPP restructuring. *"A great character who is clearly a leader,"* he also advised EWS on renegotiating the freight track access regime with the rail regulator through the Railtrack periodic review process. *"Prepared to go the extra mile,"* **Bob Charlton** (see p.81) was described by one client as *"among the best lease lawyers in the country."* His talents were combined with those of **Andrew Littlejohns** (see p.83) (*"always a pleasure to work with"*) in advising Angel Trains on a £750 million purchase order for Desiro electric multiple units from Siemens, one of the largest single orders for new rolling stock in the UK since privatisation. Another highlight of the year was advising Midland Mainline on the procurement, financing and maintenance of a new fleet of high-speed trains, involving an innovative tripartite manufacturing and maintenance agreement that enables the company to become a 'pure operator'. **Clients** EWS; Angel Trains; Midland Mainline.

DENTON WILDE SAPTE (see firm details p.935) This impressive outfit clinched promotion to our second tier this year following warm market recommendation for its high-profile involvement with ATOC, who it advised on Railtrack's administration and industry restructuring, combined with the virtual doubling of its team size. This was achieved in part by the lateral hire of highly regarded **Naomi Horton** from Rowe & Maw. *"Hugely well-respected"* **Christopher McGee-Osborne** is particularly praised by peers for his part in advising ATOC, and individual TOCs, on post-Hatfield liabilities. Also contributing to this work, *"impressive, young guy"* **Matthew Hanslip Ward** was recently made up to partner. He has also acted for new clients such as GB Railfreight, advising them on a nationwide track access agreement for the creation of a new freight haulage business and deployment of a new fleet of trains. Other highlights include assisting Virgin and West Coast Trains in renegotiating the £2 billion upgrade of the West Coast Main Line and associated rolling stock procurement. **Clients** ATOC; Virgin and West Coast Trains; Thames Water.

NATIONWIDE ■ TRANSPORT

LEADING INDIVIDUALS

1
- **CHARLTON Bob** Freshfields Bruckhaus Deringer
- **ELLARD John** Linklaters
- **MCGEE-OSBORNE Christopher** Denton Wilde Sapte
- **PHILLIPS Richard** Freshfields Bruckhaus Deringer

2
- **BONAR Mary** Nabarro Nathanson
- **COPPEN Simon** Burges Salmon
- **HARRIS Anne** Eversheds

3
- **BEVEN Ray** Ashurst Morris Crisp
- **BISSELL Helen** Hollingworth Bissell
- **GWYNNE Simon** Linklaters
- **HOLLINGWORTH Sara** Hollingworth Bissell
- **HORTON Naomi** Denton Wilde Sapte
- **THOMPSELL Nicholas** Field Fisher Waterhouse

4
- **BEVAN Jonathan** Allen & Overy
- **HANSLIP WARD Matthew** Denton Wilde Sapte
- **LEIGH Robert** Simmons & Simmons
- **LITTLEJOHNS Andrew** Freshfields Bruckhaus Deringer
- **PREECE Andrew** Herbert Smith
- **WHITEHOUSE Michael** Wragge & Co

UP AND COMING
- **HERRING Andrew** Richards Butler

See individuals' profiles p.801

LINKLATERS (see firm details p.1043) With almost "*unrivalled depth and experience*" and its enviable position advising the SRA, this team enjoys one of the best positions in the sector. "*Strongly recommended and a long-standing figure in the rail industry,*" **John Ellard** (see p.801) retains his high profile. His team also includes **Simon Gwynne** (see p.802), who, having given "*a great deal of commitment,*" was praised to researchers for his "*excellent grasp of the regulatory environment.*" The firm continues to act for the SRA on the replacement of UK passenger rail franchises, advising recently on the replacement of the East Coast, South West Trains and TransPennine franchises. Other highlights include continuing advice to the SRA on the Thameslink 2000 and West Coast Main Line upgrades, as well as on the East London Line and Crossrail projects. The firm continues to advise on all financings and acquisitions of passenger rolling stock involving Mark 1 rolling stock replacements and new procurements. It also advised one of the consortia bidding on the JNP package of the London Underground PPP. Assistance abroad on privatisations in Zambia, Kenya and Pakistan also features in the team's workload. **Clients** SRA, SNCF; NS.

CLIFFORD CHANCE (see firm details p.911) A "*well-respected,*" cross-practice rail industry group, it boasts experience in the UK and internationally, and "*huge financing strength.*" Its profile is considered by market commentators to centre on train procurement. It advised GOVIA on the procurement of £1.2 billion of new passenger trains for the South Central franchise and GATX on the UK tax leasing to EWS of new rolling stock. New instructions for the team, which features Gavin Teague, include appointment to the SRA panel and assistance to the Amey/Skanska consortium in their bid for the East London Line PPP. **Clients** ATOC; Railtrack; ALSTOM Transport.

EVERSHEDS (see firm details p.949) The "*lynchpin of the practice*" is **Anne Harris** (see p.802), who is said by competitors to have "*excellent industry knowledge*" and to be "*a pleasure to work with.*" Covering infrastructure, franchise agreements, regulatory and employment elements within the rail industry, the team is best known for advising the SRA. Highlights include acting on the Chiltern franchise replacement process, the first to be completed since 1997, involving £371 million of investment. It also advised on the replacement of the South Central franchise, which involved setting up an SPV to undertake infrastructure improvements. **Clients** SRA; EWS; Jarvis.

HOLLINGWORTH BISSELL (see firm details p.998) Boasting "*under the fingernail experience difficult to match,*" this small but remarkably expert team retains an enviable position in the market. A former in-house lawyer at BR, **Helen Bissell** (see p.801) is "*steeped in industry knowledge.*" She recently advised Chiltern Railways on the replacement of its franchise. Also ex-BR, **Sara Hollingworth** (see p.802) received widespread recommendations. Competitors noted that she was "*receiving interesting instructions from the SRA*" on rail passenger partnership initiatives and advising ATOC on travel card product arrangements. Despite its size, the team is not limited to niche rail expertise, but has the capacity to deliver general commercial and commercial property advice to its rail sector clients. **Clients** SRA; ATOC; Rail Europe.

ALLEN & OVERY (see firm details p.841) The team provides the "*extremely impressive, commercial lawyers you would expect*" from a strong finance firm, and acts on rail sector transactions across Europe, Asia and the USA. Highlights include some of the year's biggest deals, such as advising Stagecoach Holdings on its £1 billion rolling stock and service provision order. It also advised the lenders on the Chiltern franchise and Railtrack, prior to its administration, in connection with SPV financings for rail infrastructure enhancements. **Jonathan Bevan** (see p.801), currently on secondment to the SRA, was felt by rivals to have raised his profile. **Clients** Stagecoach Holdings; Kreditanstalt für Wiederaufbau (KfW); Royal Bank of Scotland.

ASHURST MORRIS CRISP (see firm details p.852) According to market sources, this team is growing in strength and reputation. The practice group covers franchise agreements and infrastructure-related work, as well as rail privatisations abroad. Ongoing assistance to the National Express Group has recently included advising on its involvement in passenger refranchising and restructuring. Rated for his ability to offer "*detailed analysis of franchises and the regulatory regime,*" head of transport **Ray Beven** (see p.801) is part of the team advising Crossrail on two high-profile rail projects estimated to be worth up to £11 billion. The team also boasts expertise in international infrastructure projects and recently advised on a high-speed line between Amsterdam and the Belgian border. Its international privatisation experience includes that of the Tanzania Railways Corporation. **Clients** Crossrail; National Express Group; Railtrack Group.

BURGES SALMON (see firm details p.894) "*Pre-eminent in the regions,*" the rail practice covers franchise and regulatory matters, bringing extensive UK and EU competition expertise to bear on the latter. It has advised FirstGroup on new train procurements for three franchises and on joint ventures with NS and Keolis. "*Highly rated and heavily involved,*" **Simon Coppen** (see p.801) was characterised to Chambers' researchers as "*a thorough, no-nonsense practitioner.*" The practice provides ongoing advice to ATOC, including assistance on the development of systems authorities following recommendations made in the Cullen Report. The team received new instructions this year from EWS. **Clients** FirstGroup; ATOC.

HERBERT SMITH (see firm details p.992) Said by clients to "*excel in project-led work and all support functions,*" the team is seen as having further consolidated its industry connections, advising Stagecoach Group on its successful bid to retain the South West Trains franchise, and London & Continental Railways on stage two of the £5.2 billion Channel Tunnel Rail Link (CTRL). Leading the latter deal, "*co-operative*" **Andrew Preece** (see p.699) was praised by peers and clients for his ability to "*pull together all of the client's interests.*" Other highlights include advising Virgin on its bid for the East Coast Main Line franchise and assisting Zuid Rail Group on its tender for the Dutch High-Speed Line. The team is also experienced in rolling stock leasing and rail-related property advice. **Clients** Virgin Rail Group; Stagecoach Group; Zuid Rail Group; South West Trains.

NORTON ROSE (see firm details p.1084) The "*strongest firm in rolling stock finance,*" the rail group is headed by Gordon Hall. The team has acted for HSBC Rail on financing Midland Mainline's new fleet of Diesel Electric Multiple Units (DEMUs), and Porterbrook Leasing Company on negotiating operating leases with various operators in Germany, the Netherlands and Denmark. Another highlight was acting for WestLB in its bid to buy the Railtrack business, while its advice to Bechtel on the proposed SPV structure for rail network enhancements associ-

TRANSPORT ■ NATIONWIDE

ated with the South Central franchise signifies a strong infrastructure showing. New instructions from the rail regulator bolster the team's competition and regulatory profile. **Clients** Porterbrook Leasing Company; HSBC Rail (UK).

SIMMONS & SIMMONS (see firm details p.1136) There was consensus amongst interviewees that, despite the administration of Railtrack signalling a period of uncertainty for the practice, it retains "*significant nuts and bolts.*" Recent work for Railtrack has included ongoing advice on the West Coast Main Line at all levels (finance, dispute resolution, regulatory and construction), on the CTRL and on the major refranchising negotiations. The team also advised on 'Project Endeavour', the negotiations with the SRA and DTLR for the acceleration of grant funding to Railtrack. International work includes assisting on rail sector PPPs in Ireland, acting for Spanish company CAF on train procurement, and advising the government of New Zealand on privatisation models. **Robert Leigh** (see p.803), best known for his expertise on track access, enters our tables this year. **Clients** Rapid Transit International; Department of Public Enterprise, Ireland.

DLA An expanding team, which recently gained partner level recruits from, amongst others, Garretts and Pinsent Curtis Biddle. Under the leadership of Mark Swindell, the practice has cemented relations with existing clients as well as acting for other TOCs. It has advised Connex on the sale in separate transactions of the South Central business and rolling stock to GOVIA. **Clients** Connex; Merseytravel.

FIELD FISHER WATERHOUSE (see firm details p.954) **Nicholas Thompsell** (see p.804) and his team remain well regarded by competitors and clients alike. Best known for its advice to ARRIVA on, *inter alia*, bids for the TransPennine Express and Wales & Borders franchises, the firm has also consolidated relations with Transport for London, acting on the Crossrail and East London Line projects, amongst others. **Clients** ARRIVA; Transport for London; South West Trains.

NABARRO NATHANSON (see firm details p.1080) Interviewees noted that the practice's transactional strength has come to the fore, having acted for Siemens on a number of rolling stock deals, the highlight being the £1 billion procurement of Desiro trains for South West Trains. Said to have "*a way of holding the attention of the room,*" **Mary Bonar** (see p.801) heads up the group. It was recently appointed by Stagecoach as lawyers for the Main Line Station Co, to advise on the acquisition of a long lease of stations and their management under a 'sub-PFI' concession. **Clients** National Express Group; Siemens; Stagecoach.

SLAUGHTER AND MAY (see firm details p.1140) Advising Ernst & Young on the administration of Railtrack, a unique appointment involving many issues concerning railway infrastructure and the running of the network, exercises the firm's long-standing rail industry expertise to the full. Though as a result it has been conflicted out of advising the ORR, the firm clearly remains a force to be reckoned with. It also has a strong international rail sector project base. Its advice to the Infraspeed consortium (Siemens, Fluor Daniel, BAM NBM, Charterhouse and Innisfree) on the Dutch high-speed rail link HSL-Zuid project is led by Steve Edwards. **Clients** Central Railway; First-Group.

CMS CAMERON MCKENNA (see firm details p.914) Consistently praised by interviewees for its "*high-profile involvement*", the rail practice is based in projects and enters the tables following its advice to the DTLR on Railtrack's administration. Led by Ian Bendell, the team acts on a wide range of rail projects, most notably for the Dutch government on HSL-Zuid, the DTLR on the CTRL and Metronet on the London Underground PPP. It also advised Angel Trains on the lease financing for new rolling stock, to be leased to Great Western Trains Company and to First North Western Trains. **Clients** DTLR; Angel Trains; Kowloon-Canton Railway Corporation.

DICKINSON DEES (see firm details p.938) "*Immersed in all aspects of rail law,*" competitors have a high regard for this keen regional competitor in the sector. Now led by David Rewcastle, rail sector expertise is one element of a designated transport department. Recent highlights include acting for GOVIA on the £30 million purchase of South Central and the associated franchise replacement process. Rewcastle also advised GOVIA on an SPV, to be set up in co-operation with Railtrack and Bechtel, to deliver over £500 million worth of infrastructure enhancements to South Central. **Clients** GOVIA; Thameslink; The Go-Ahead Group.

EDWARDS GELDARD (see firm details p.944) Respected by market sources as providers of in-depth rail expertise, the team led by Roman Surma has had another active year. It advised Midland Mainline on track access agreements and Silverlink Trains on an appeal to the regulator over the possessions allowance for Railtrack on the West Coast Main Line. **Clients** National Express Group; Midland Mainline.

LOVELLS (see firm details p.1045) Increasingly influential in the industry, it is rated by solicitors and clients alike as a "*quality provider of rail expertise,*" which covers rolling stock and infrastructure as well as regulation, project and asset finance and litigation. Instructed by the Railtrack Shareholders Action Group and appointed recently to the ORR panel, it also advised the Rail Industry Association and ALSTOM Transport on the inauguration of the first System Authority. Other highlights include advising ALSTOM Group on the upgrade of the West Coast Mainline. Headed by Phillip Capper. **Clients** ALSTOM Transport, ORR; Railway Industry Association.fs17

MAYER, BROWN, ROWE & MAW (see firm details p.1060) Uncertain times ahead was the verdict returned by the market since the departure of Naomi Horton. Now headed by Neil Morrison, highlights for the group have included advising Grand Central on all aspects of its bid to become an open access operator, including extensive negotiations with Railtrack, SRA and ORR. It continues to advise Virgin Trains on the procurement of new rolling stock for the West Coast and CrossCountry franchises. **Clients** Hull Trains; Grand Central.

OSBORNE CLARKE (see firm details p.1090) This active team, led by Claire Wagner, continues to be heavily involved in the sector. It recently advised Wales & West Passenger Trains and the Cardiff Railway Company on the franchise migration to create Wales & Borders and Wessex Trains. It also advised c2c Rail on the handback to Railtrack of Fenchurch Street Station. **Clients** West Anglia and Great Northern Railway; c2c Rail; STVA UK.

WRAGGE & CO (see firm details p.1197) Rated highly by peers and clients for its "*responsive, commercial and objective*" approach, the rail practice covers freight, infrastructure, and overseas privatisation. "*Easy to work with,*" **Michael Whitehouse** led advice to BMW Group on the establishment, reconstruction and outsourcing of the rail operation and maintenance logistics for its new MINI plant. He also advises New Limpopo Projects Investments on its bid for the Zambian Railways privatisation. **Clients** Cummins Engine Company; BMW Group; Bombardier.

OTHER NOTABLE PRACTITIONERS Andrew Herring (see p.802) of Richards Butler, who was recently made up to partner, won praise for his advice to GNER on the successful extension of its East Coast Main Line franchise.

THE LEADERS IN TRANSPORT

ALLAN, Michael
Allan, Burn & McGregor, Aberdeen
(01224) 480890

ARMSTRONG, Stuart
Hill Dickinson, London
(020) 7695 1016
sarmstrong@hilldicks.com
Specialisation: Main areas of practice are cargo and goods in transit claims (charterparties, bills of lading, CMR and domestic road haulage, Warsaw Convention) and related cargo and G.I.T. liability insurance disputes. Acts for cargo underwriters, recovery agents, hauliers' liability underwriters, freight forwarders and hauliers.
Prof. Memberships: London Maritime Arbitrators' Association (supporting member).
Career: Articled with *Inglewed Brown Bennison & Garrett*, qualified in 1983 and became a partner in 1985. Joined *Hill Dickinson* in February 2001.
Personal: Born 1958. Educated at The King's School, Canterbury 1971-76 and Southampton University 1976-79 (LLB Hons). Leisure interests include golf and chess.

BACKHOUSE, James A
Backhouse Jones, Clitheroe
(01254) 828300
james@backhouses.co.uk
Specialisation: Commercial transport law including defending prosecutions brought by the Vehicle Inspectorate, Police and Trading Standards, Environment Agency, Health & Safety Executive; Operators and Vocational Licensing including inquiries, environmental, maintenance and financial; employment all issues; health and safety all issues. Recent cases include the successful defence in Nuttall v Wing in the House of Lords dealing with tachograph issues and R v Hennessey (Court of Appeal) an appeal against conviction of causing death by dangerous driving. Successfully dealt with eight cases of causing death by dangerous driving in the past four years, arising out of the passenger and goods transport industry. Has lectured on Article 177 references to the European Courts of Justice and involvement in two such references to the ECJ. Experience in rebated diesel cases, including Vat & Duties Tribunal. Successfully defended alleged illegal transportation of arms to Nigeria prosecution.

BEVAN, Jonathan
Allen & Overy, London
(020) 7330 3000
jonathan.bevan@allenovery.com
Specialisation: Partner in the banking and projects group specialising in project financing, telecoms financing, acquisition financing, asset financing, tax structured financing and rail; acting for arrangers, borrowers, equity and sponsors. Recent experience includes acting for Virgin Rail Group on the largest ever UK rolling stock procurement programme; the arrangers in connection with the financing of the acquisition of IPC Magazines and roll out of Bouygues Telecom's mobile phone network; and the arrangers on the acquisition of Drax Power Station which was awarded the IFR European Project Finance Loan of the Year.
Career: Qualified England and Wales, and Hong Kong, 1993; Partner 1999. Seconded to Skandinaviska Enskilda Banken.
Personal: Newcastle RGS; Cambridge University (1989, MA Law). Born 1976; resides London.

BEVEN, Raymond
Ashurst Morris Crisp, London
(020) 7859 1897
raymond.beven@ashursts.com
Specialisation: Partner in Energy, Transport and Infrastructure Department; Head of Transport Group. Extensively involved in privatisation, concessioning, corporate, commercial, regulatory and infrastructure project matters in transport, particularly in rail. Actively working in the UK passenger rail restructuring and re-franchising process, advising National Express and Govia. Involved in the CTRL London Underground PPP and Crossrail projects, and in corporate finance and M&A matters in transport. Internationally, involved in rail privatisation and rail projects in Africa.
Prof. Memberships: LLB (Hons) and MBA (Adelaide University). Admitted 1984 South Australia; 1999 England and Wales. Institute of Logistics and Transport, Law Society.
Career: Partner *Minter Ellison, Adelaide* 1992-1996. Partner *Kelly & Co, Adelaide* 1996-1998. With *Ashurst Morris Crisp* from 1998 (Partner 2001).
Personal: Born 1963, lives in London.

BISSELL, Helen
Hollingworth Bissell, London
(020) 7233 3300
hb@hollingworthbissell.co.uk
Specialisation: Provides wide ranging advice to the railway industry, including on replacement franchise agreements, franchise remapping, track, freight facility and station access, rail infrastructure development agreements, construction and bringing new stations into operational use, station trading and landlord and tenant matters.
Career: Born and educated in Nottingham and Sheffield University. Qualified 1990. From 1992 worked as an in-house lawyer for British Railways Board. Partner in *Hollingworth Bissell* in 1997.
Personal: Lives in London. Interests include food and wine, gardening, reading and the gym.

BONAR, Mary
Nabarro Nathanson, London
(020) 7524 6000
m.bonar@nabarro.com
Specialisation: Partner in the Projects Group and Head of Rail Sector Group. Main areas of practice are rail law, project finance and asset finance. Experience commercialisation of rail industry, financing of rail infrastructure including using Public Private Partnerships and rolling stock. In domestic market, specialises in track access, regulation and franchising. Clients include public sector, major banks, lessors, ECAs, governments, franchise groups and other corporates. Lectures and writes on rail industry and project finance.
Prof. Memberships: Liveryman, Worshipful Company of Carmen and City of London Solicitors Company; fellow of Institute of Logistics and Transport.
Career: LLB. London. Admitted in 1971. Partner *Wilde Sapte* Banking Department 1989-99.

BUTTERFIELD, Christopher
Herbert Mallam Gowers, Oxford
(01865) 244661

CARLESS, Michael Joseph
Carless Davies & Co, Halesowen
(0121) 550 2181

CHARLTON, Bob
Freshfields Bruckhaus Deringer, London
(020) 7936 4000
bob.charlton@freshfields.com
See under Asset Finance & Leasing, p.81

CHATFIELD, Christopher
Waltons & Morse, London
(020) 7623 4255

COPPEN, Simon
Burges Salmon, Bristol
(0117) 939 2291
simon.coppen@burges-salmon.com
Specialisation: Simon has particular experience of the application of UK and EU competition law in the field of commercial transactions, including intellectual property, technology transfer, agency, distribution and joint ventures. His specialist areas include the application of competition law within the UK rail industry.
Prof. Memberships: Law Society.
Career: 1985-89, *Allen & Overy*; 1989-date, *Burges Salmon*; 1993, Partner. Head of Commercial Unit.
Personal: Brasenose College, Oxford 1981-84.

DUNN, Chris
Waltons & Morse, London
(020) 7623 4255

ELLARD, John
Linklaters, London
(020) 7456 3324
john.ellard@linklaters.com
Specialisation: Privatisations, transport projects, international equity issues and corporate finance. Advisor to the Strategic Rail Authority on its franchise replacement programme; on the funding package for the Network Rail's bid for Railtrack plc; major rail investment projects. Extensive experience with Coca-Cola, including LSE listing of Coca-Cola Beverages plc, its merger with Hellenic Bottling SA and CCHBC's acquisitions. Advised on numerous utility privatisations including BT, KPN, Telecom Italia and Telecom Eireann.
Career: 1971-74 Trinity Hall Cambridge MA Law (First Class Honours). 1989 to date Partner *Linklaters* London, corporate; 1986-89 Partner *Linklaters* New York; 1983-86 Partner *Linklaters* London tax; 1977-83 Assistant Solicitor *Linklaters* tax; 1975-77 Articled Clerk *Linklaters*.

FEAR, Jeremy
Jeremy Fear & Co, Enfield
(020) 8367 4466

GEORGE, Jane
Rothera Dowson (Incorporating German and Soar), Nottingham
(0115) 910 6248
j.george@rotheradowson.co.uk
Specialisation: Transport, health and safety and environmental work. During the past two years has dealt mainly with the effects of the UK's Immigration Asylum Act of 1999 with particular reference to the implementation of its carrier's liability provisions. Regular appearances before Traffic Commissioner's Public Inquiries. Regularly appears before Traffic Commissioner's Public Inquiries, Magistrates Court and Vehicle Inspection prosecutions. Regularly deals with Tachographs, construction and use offences, and cases of dangerous or careless driving. Has been involved in advising the Road Haulage Association and the Freight Transport Association's members over many different aspects of transport law for the past 15 years. Is one of the founder members of the Association of Road Transport Lawyers. During the past 12 months clients have included P&O European Ferries, Giraud UK Limited and Denby Transport. Also represents Shanks Waste Services Limited, the largest UK waste disposal company. Has a practice which includes defending Health and Safety and Environmental prosecutions.
Career: Significant cases include: July 2001, representing a client on Health and Safety prosecution. Client was responsible for a site in which a fire and explosion occurred causing injury to a contractor; July 2000, defending a client at a seven day trial for breaching Health and Safety Act offences when the death of a non-employee was caused by one of the company's vehicles; July 2000, two day Environmental Public Inquiry before the Traffic Commissioner following appeal to the Traffic Tribunal and remission to the Traffic Commissioner for rehearing. Had a successful outcome for the client

TRANSPORT: THE LEADERS

who preserved their operating centre without further restrictions on use of site or operations.

GOTELEE, Michael
Barker Gotelee, Ipswich
(01473) 611211
michael.gotelee@barkergotelee.co.uk
Specialisation: Road haulage and public service vehicle licensing, vehicle operation, prosecutions, disciplinary and environmental public inquiries, accidents, drivers' hours, CMR and employment. The firm covers other commercial aspects for businesses, tax, land, planning, pollution and waste. Member of Institute of Transport Administration.
Career: Qualified 1963. Since 1966 has acted for a wide range of operators and RHA and FTA members.
Personal: Born 1938. Interests are old vehicles, sailing and walking.

GWYNNE, Simon
Linklaters, London
(020) 7456 5994
simon.gwynne@linklaters.com
Specialisation: Associate in the Asset Finance Group, with extensive experience in a broad range of structured financings involving aircraft, cable and telecommunications equipment, rolling stock and other big ticket assets.
Career: 1993-95, articles, *Linklaters*. 1995-date, Solicitor, *Linklaters*.

HALLSWORTH, Chris
Woodfine Foinette Quinn, Milton Keynes
(01908) 202150
Specialisation: Senior partner specialising in road transport law since 1983. Undertakes wide range of work and prosecutes for the Vehicle Inspectorate as well as defending operators and their employees. Specialises in HGV and PCV Law. Undertakes all types of public inquiries before Traffic Commissioners including environmental and disciplinary hearings. Represents clients at Crown Court as a Solicitor-Advocate. Represents FTA and RHA members and has been involved in advising and representing a number of well known UK and European companies. Also specialises in health and safety issues, environmental matters, planning appeals and defending complex criminal prosecutions. Contributes to 'Road Rescue Recovery Association Magazine' and to 'Commercial Motor Magazine'.
Career: Qualified July 1973. Prosecuted for Nottinghamshire and Sussex Police Authorities. Joined *Foinette Quinn* 1982. Solicitor-Advocate (Higher Courts Criminal) 1997. Deputy District Judge (Magistrates Courts).
Personal: Born 5 August 1948. LLB (Hons) London 1966-69.

HANSLIP WARD, Matthew
Denton Wilde Sapte, London
(020) 7242 1212

HARDINGHAM, Adrian
Holmes Hardingham, London
(020) 7280 3200
Adrian.Hardingham@HHLaw.co.uk
Specialisation: Principal areas of practice are transport and shipping law, encompassing international and domestic carriage of goods by road, sea and air. Other main areas of work are marine insurance, particularly cargo risks, and general commercial insurance. Major cases handled include Buchanan v Babco (H.L.) (1978), Silber v Islander Trucking (1985), ITT v Birkart (1988), the 'Rewia' (1991), and Spectra v Hayesoak (1997). Major clients include UK and overseas underwriters, traders, freight forwarders, hauliers and insurance recovery agents. Contributor of various articles on the CMR Convention in Lloyd's Maritime & Commercial Law Quarterly.
Career: Qualified 1978. Founding Partner of *Holmes Hardingham*.
Personal: Attended University College, Oxford. Holds private pilot's licence.

HARRIS, Anne
Eversheds, Birmingham
(0121) 232 1204
anneharris@eversheds.com
Specialisation: Specialises in commercial law and project work, in particular relating to railways. Has advised on railway facility access agreements, infrastructure developments, rolling stock and regulatory issues. Worked on the privatisation (pre-franchising) of West Coast Trains, and since 1997 for OPRAF/SRA, most recently on franchise replacement and development/SPV issues.
Prof. Memberships: Law Society; Railway Study Association.
Career: Qualified 1987 with *Eversheds*, Partner 1994. Head of *Eversheds* Rail Group.
Personal: BA English and American Literature. Married (to Simon) with one daughter (Kate). Has a keen interest in sport particularly Aston Villa FC. Friend of Barber Institute of Fine Arts.

HEATON, John Graham
Bannister Preston, Sale
(0161) 973 2434
info@bannisterpreston.co.uk
Specialisation: Road transport law (both prosecuting and defending), Magistrates Court and Crown Court advocacy, regulatory work before the Traffic Commissioners. Successfully acted for the prosecution in: Bird v Vehicle Inspectorate, case C235/94; Mahmood v Vehicle Inspectorate, 1998 (18WRTLB163, DC); Birkett & Naylor v Vehicle Inspectorate, (1998) RTR 264.
Career: 1967-75, William Hulmes Grammar School in Manchester. 1975-78, Liverpool University, LLB (Hons) Chester College of Law, qualified 1981. Partner, *Bannister Preston* in 1985
Publications: Articles and publications in legal journals and textbook on road transport and criminal law, lectures and seminars in these areas. Particular interest in jurisdiction issues and developments in the law on strict liability.
Personal: Married to Debbie (also a solicitor), two sons. Interests include travel, choral music, transport generally, family life.

HERRING, Andrew
Richards Butler, London
(020) 7772 5921
kah@richardsbutler.com
Specialisation: Partner in the Corporate Finance Group at *Richards Butler*. Acted for GNER Holdings in its bid for the South West Trains franchise and for a 20 year franchise on the East Coast Main Line and in the negotiation of the two year extension to its existing franchise agreed in 2002. Has also acted for a significant major European railway administrator and a number of other clients in the transport industry.
Prof. Memberships: Law Society of England and Wales.
Career: Joined *Richards Butler* as a trainee in 1993. Joined the partnership in 2001.
Personal: Educated at the Manchester Grammar School and Jesus College Oxford. Resident in London.

HILL, Martin
DLA, Liverpool
(08700) 111111

HOBBS, Jane
Holmes Hardingham, London
(020) 7280 3200
Jane.Hobbs@HHLaw.co.uk
Specialisation: Transport: Road-carriage/commercial. Main areas of practice are carriage of goods by road, sea and air and related insurance issues. Handles a wide range of cases involving domestic road haulage and CMR, including freight forwarding and warehousing. Insurance work includes advising on policy disputes and handling subrogated claims on behalf of underwriters. Experienced in pursuing and defending bill of lading and charterparty cargo claims.
Career: Attended Merton College, Oxford 1985-88. Qualified 1991. Joined *Holmes Hardingham* in 1992 and became a Partner in 1997. Contributor to 'Multi-modal Transport' and 'Insurance Disputes'.

HODGSON, Gary
Ford & Warren, Leeds
(0113) 243 6601
clientmail@forwarn.com
Specialisation: Partner in the Commercial Litigation Department. Main area of expertise – goods and passenger transport operations. Extensive experience in all aspects of operators licensing and other regulatory matters, regular appearances before Traffic Ommission on the Transport Tribunal. Defence expertise before Magistrates Courts and Crown Courts throughout England and Wales on a full range of road traffic matters. Experience in transport-related health and safety prosecutions including prosecutions of utmost seriousness. Regular appearance before Coroner's Court following fatal road traffic and transport related accidents. Particular specialisation in Environment Agency prosecutions and environmental problems generally, particularly waste disposal, transportation and storage of hazardous chemicals and environmental problems arising out of the use of the Operating Centres. Wide experience and particular specialisation in prosecutions arising from drivers hours, records offences, construction use offences and particularly prosecutions arising from the lost wheels mystery. Recommended Solicitor for the Road Haulage Association and the Freight Transport Association. Retained solicitor for many national and international transport logistic operators on regulatory transport matters. Heads team providing consultancy services on internal systems for monitoring safety and quality. Advises on and prepares documentation for applications for BS5750 and ISO9002 quality accreditations. Extensive experience in European Transport Law. Leading member of the Ford & Warren team, advising hauliers throughout Europe on 'flagging out'. Subsequently representing hauliers who are currently being prosecuted for flagging out unlawfully. Regularly lectures to trade associations on transport related matters. Co-author of the 'Commercial Motor Legal Bulletin'. Regular contributor to the Trade Press generally.
Career: Qualified 1977. Joined *Ford & Warren* in 1978. Became partner in 1985.
Personal: Bachelor of Laws; holder of the Certificate of Professional Competence in Freight and Passenger at national level and in freight at international level.

HOLLINGWORTH, Sara
Hollingworth Bissell, London
(020) 7233 3300
Specialisation: Provides a wide range of legal services to the railway industry, dealing with the negotiation and drafting of many types of commercial contracts; advises on foreign railway privatisations; joint ventures, station trading, sales promotion and advertising copy.
Career: Born and educated in Derbyshire and at Durham University. Trained at *Cameron Markby* and since 1985 has worked in the railway industry, initially as a lawyer with the British Railways Board (Head of Commercial within legal department 1993-96) and latterly as a partner in *Hollingworth Bissell*.
Personal: Married with two sons and lives in rural Kent. Interests include tennis, cookery, antique furniture and the theatre. Member of the English-Speaking Union.

HORTON, Naomi
Denton Wilde Sapte, London
(020) 7242 1212

JACKSON, Peter
Hill Dickinson, Manchester
(0161) 278 8800
Jacko@HillDicks.com
Specialisation: Main areas of practice are marine, goods in transit and insur-

ance litigation. Work includes cargo claims, for both cargo and liability insurers, particularly international and national road haulage claims; ship related cargo claims for cargo interests; salvage and monitoring foreign litigation. Also handles marine insurance work, particularly marine insurance policy interpretation for underwriters and transportation contract work. Acted in ICI plc v MAT Transport, ITT v Birkart, the Breydon Merchant F & W Freight, the Los Angeles, Microfine v Transferry Shipping, Inco Europe and Quantum v Plane Trucking.
Prof. Memberships: Liverpool Underwriters Association, Manchester Marine Insurance Association, London Maritime Arbitrators Association.
Career: Qualified in 1985, having joined *Hill Dickinson Davis Campbell* in 1983. Became a Partner in 1989.
Personal: Born 3 April 1961. Attended St Edward's College, Liverpool 1972-79, then Exeter College, Oxford 1979-82. Leisure interests include football, season ticket holder at Anfield. Former Chairman of Football Supporters Association. Cricket - member of Lancashire County Cricket Club. Lives in Liverpool.

JONES, Geoffrey
Bond Pearce, Bristol
(0117) 929 9197
gjones@bondpearce.com
Specialisation: Formerly with *Cartwrights*, Geoffrey is a consultant practising transport law with over 25 years experience in relation to all aspects of bus and lorry licensing and related public inquiries, road use public inquiries and judicial review challenges to local authorities. Also specialises in employment and industrial relations law with experience of all aspects of employment and industrial relations matters in contracts, service agreements and disciplinary procedures; multi-applicant employment tribunals; TUPE; commercial transactions and advice and legal action in relation to industrial action.
Career: Qualified in 1962 following articles with *Granville West Chivers & Dunford*. Joined *Cartwrights* 1964 becoming partner 1966. Joined *Bond Pearce* 2001 on merger.
Publications: Co-author of 'Basic Planning Law and Practice'.

KIRKBRIGHT, Stephen
Ford & Warren, Leeds
(0113) 243 6601
Specialisation: Main area of practice is transport. Experience since 1970 in all aspects of road transport law, particular specialisation in LGV and PCV, nationally and internationally. Regularly appears before traffic commissioners on public inquiries and Transport Tribunal on appeals. Extensive experience in all aspects of criminal defence work. Particular experience in cases of utmost severity, including HSE prosecutions, manslaughter and corporate manslaughter. Acted in inquests, criminal proceedings and public inquiries following Sowerby Bridge disaster. Acted in Bowles 'A2' manslaughter prosecution and subsequent public inquiries. Handled leading cases on 'causing and permitting' (Yorkshire Traction v Vehicle Inspectorate Kelly v Shulman, Redhead Freight v Shulman) and on using (Travel-gas Midlands Ltd v Reynolds and others). Acted in leading authorities before the Transport Tribunal on finance for HGV and PCV operators (Rosswood, RHA v John Dee Limited and JJ Adam Limited). Acts throughout the UK for PCV operators at public inquiries and Transport Tribunal in relation to PSV operator's licenses and registration of local bus services. Acted in leading authorities before the Transport Tribunal on local services and fuel duty rebate (Midland Bluebird, Yorkshire Rider Limited, First Bristol Buses Limited) and for operators in Manchester and Merseyside public inquiries. Acts as legal advisor to the Road Haulage Association and recommended solicitor for the Freight Transport Association, the Irish Road Haulage Association and is recommended solicitor to the FTA and Irish RHA. Acted in 500 plus claims against the French government following the French lorry drivers strike on behalf of Irish, UK, Dutch and Spanish hauliers. Co-ordinated the RHA 'flagging out scheme' following 1999 budget to assist hauliers to relocate to other EU member states. Currently lecturing extensively and advising clients and associations on implications of working time directive in the transport industry. Heads a department dealing with civil claims throughout Europe under CMR domestic conditions of carriage and GIT. Principal solicitor of 'Commercial Motor Legal Bulletin' and regular contributor to trade press.
Prof. Memberships: Fellow of the Chartered Institute of Logistics and Transport.
Career: Qualified in 1968. Joined *Ford & Warren* in 1966 becoming a partner in 1970. Currently Head of Business Law and member of managing board of *Ford & Warren*. Born 18 October 1941. Attended Sheffield University 1961-64 and College of Law 1965-66.
Personal: Leisure interests include music (plays guitar and piano) and painting. Lives in Wakefield.

KNIGHT, Tim
Holmes Hardingham, London
(020) 7280 3200
Tim.Knight@HHLaw.co.uk
Specialisation: Partner in transit and cargo claims department. Main area of practice is carriage of goods by road, covering national and international carriage by road, warehousekeeping, related insurance matters and terms and conditions of business. Also experienced in carriage by sea work, including bill of lading claims, and carriage by air and rail.
Career: Joined *Ingledew Brown* in 1986, qualifying in 1988. Joined *Holmes Hardingham* as a founding member in 1989. Became Partner in 1993.
Personal: Born 17 March 1964. Attended University of Kent 1983-85. Leisure pursuits include golf, motorsport and squash. Lives in Hertfordshire.

LEIGH, Robert
Simmons & Simmons, London
(020) 7628 2020
robert.leigh@simmons-simmons.com
Specialisation: Has advised on various major projects for Railtrack, including the Channel Tunnel Rail Link, the Thameslink 2000 Project, the upgrade of the West Coast Main Line and the £200m deal to upgrade the Cross Country part of the railway network. Has also advised Railtrack on all aspects of the Strategic Rail Authority's refranchising programme, the contractual implementation of the Rail regulator's five yearly review of Railtrack's access charges and on all aspects of track access, including the proposed introduction of model clauses.
Prof. Memberships: Law Society.
Career: Joined *Simmons & Simmons* in 1994 and became a partner in the corporate department in 1999, moving to the firm's commercial department in the same year. Admitted as a solicitor in England and Wales in July 1981.

LITTLEJOHNS, Andrew
Freshfields Bruckhaus Deringer, London
(020) 7936 4000
andrew.littlejohns@freshfields.com
See under Asset Finance & Leasing, p.83

MARSHALL, Julia
Hill Dickinson, London
(020) 7695 1000
jmm@hilldicks.com
Specialisation: Partner in Marine and Transit Department (London). Advice, litigation and dispute resolution in goods in transit liability and insurance issues. Is particularly interested in the emerging rail freight industry. Advises underwriters on policy wordings; advises merchants and carriers on contracts.
Prof. Memberships: LLB 1974; FCI Arb 1995; LMAA; European Intermodal Association; Director, Rail Freight Group; Freeman of the City of London Solicitors Company.
Career: Admitted 1977; proprietor of own firm 1981; May 1994 Partner in *Hill Dickinson*.
Personal: Resides London and Eastbourne. Married, one son. Leisure: creating order out of chaos.

MCGEE-OSBORNE, Christopher
Denton Wilde Sapte, London
(020) 7242 1212

MELBOURNE, William
Clyde & Co, Guildford
(01483) 555555
William.Melbourne@clyde.co.uk
Specialisation: In addition to road carriage, including GIT and removers block/warehousing related disputes, domestic and international road haulage and heavy haulage; also specialises in marine insurance (including rejection risks) and dry shipping/cargo claims, with particular experience of reefer cargoes (especially bananas and frozen meat), bulk ore, refractories (magnesite) and groundnuts (especially inherent vice-related issues). Also has experience of international sale of goods (especially steel), including ICC Arbitration.
Prof. Memberships: Solicitor (admitted 1985).
Career: BA (Hons) (C.N.A.A.) 1981; LLM (Lond) 1986.

MESSENT, Andrew
Holmes Hardingham, London
(020) 7280 3200
Andrew.Messent@HHLaw.co.uk
Specialisation: Partner in cargo claims department. Main area of practice is claims arising from the carriage of goods by sea, road and air, and other related areas, such as warehousing. Also advises on all related insurance issues. Co-author of 'CMR: Contracts for the International Carriage of Goods by Road' (3rd edition 2000). Contributor to 'International Carriage of Goods by Road (CMR)' (1987).
Career: Attended Gonville and Caius College, Cambridge. Qualified 1975, then took up a lecturing post in 1976 until 1985. Returned to marine practice in the City, and moved to *Holmes Hardingham* as one of the founding Partners in 1989.

OVER, Christopher
Over Taylor Biggs, Exeter
(01392) 823811

PHILLIPS, Richard
Freshfields Bruckhaus Deringer
London
(020) 7936 4000
richard.phillips@freshfields.com
Specialisation: Work includes asset and project finance, commercial and corporate law, mergers and acquisitions, joint ventures, disposals and privatisations. Specialist industry focus of railways, wide experience of high profile corporate, project and finance work within this industry.
Prof. Memberships: Law Society, Chartered Institute of Transport, City Solicitors' Company.
Career: Qualified in 1981. 1985 joined *Freshfields*, 1989 became partner.
Personal: Born 1955, lives in London.

PREECE, Andrew
Herbert Smith, London
(020) 7374 8000
andrew.preece@herbertsmith.com
See under Projects, p.699

PRIOR, Barry A
Wedlake Saint, London
(020) 7324 1870
barryp@wsch.co.uk
Specialisation: Senior Partner and head of firm's Transport Law Team of four fee-earners and para-legals. Main area of practice is road transport law for goods and passenger vehicles; work covers operators licensing, defence of prosecutions, personal injury (road traffic and employers' liability), contract drafting, and commercial litigation associated with the industry. Also handles carriage

TRANSPORT ■ THE LEADERS

of goods and passengers claims, including CMR/Domestic contracts and local authority tendering bus contracts. Cases have included litigation arising from many major motorway multi-vehicle accidents, public inquiries into operators licenses and major driver's hours/records prosecutions including a recent appeal to the House of Lords with reference to the powers of the Vehicle Inspectorate. Contributor to industry periodicals.
Prof. Memberships: Law Society, Chartered Institute of Transport, Institute of Logistics and Transport, Freight Transport Association, Confederation of Passenger Transport, Law Society Personal Injury Panel.
Career: Qualified in 1969. Joined *Wedlake Saint* as a Partner in 1985.
Personal: Born 24 October 1943. Attended Lawrence Sheriff School, Rugby, then Sheffield University. Fellow of the Chartered Institute of Transport; and of Institute of Logistics and Transport. Affiliate Member Institute of Road Transport Engineers; a sector of the Society of Operations Engineers, Council Member of CPT UK and FTA. Lives in Marlow, Bucks.

PYSDEN, Kay
Davies Lavery, London
(020) 7780 6868
fenchurch.street@davies-lavery.co.uk
Specialisation: Advice, litigation and arbitration in the fields of uni and multimodal transport including disputes of jurisdiction and law and ship arrest. Advising on appropriate terms and conditions of freight operators and insurers on policy wording. Has been involved in a number of leading decisions, such as: Spectra v Hayesoak on bailment and construction of limitation provisions under RHA 1991; Texas Instruments and Ors v Nason Europe & Ors, being one of the first High Court actions where the carriers right to limit liability was disallowed due to a finding of wilful default under article 29.1, CMR; Rhone Poulenc Rorer Ltd v TGA Ltd & Ors (CA) where due incorporation of terms was considered; and International Roth GmbH & Ors v Secretary of State for the Home Department (CA) where breaches of the Human Rights Convention and EC law were considered.
Prof. Memberships: Supporting member of the London Maritime Arbitrators Association, Panel Member of the Conciliation Panel of the London Maritime Arbitrators Association, Member of the Advisory Body of Legal Matters of FIATA and FIATA's representative at UNCITRAL's Working Group (III) Transport Law.
Career: Admitted 1987 having been educated at Tormead School, Guildford and gaining an LLB Hons Degree at University College London. Partner in three previous firms, having joined *Davies Lavery* as Partner and Head of Marine and Transit Department in 2001.

REYNOLDS, Justin
Hill Dickinson, London
(020) 7695 1000

Specialisation: Carriage of goods nationally and internationally and all related insurance and trade matters.
Prof. Memberships: London Solicitors Litigation Association. Law Society.
Career: Qualified with *Hill Dickinson* in 1995, becoming a partner in the firm in 2000.
Personal: Cinema and martial arts.

ROTHERA, Ian
Rothera Dowson (Incorporating German and Soar), Nottingham
(0115) 9100 600
i.rothera@rotheradowson.co.uk
Specialisation: Head of Transport Department. Since qualifying in 1973, has specialised in all aspects of road transport and traffic law. Acts for national and international HGV and PCV operators and drivers. Defence of prosecutions in Magistrates and Crown Courts throughout the UK, including construction and use offences and drivers' hours and tachograph cases. Defends Immigration Act carriers liability penalties in 'stowaway' cases. Handles Operator's Licence applications, disciplinary and environmental public inquiries before the Traffic Commissioners and appeals to the Transport Tribunal. Panel solicitor for the RHA and the FTA. Member of Nottinghamshire Chamber of Commerce Transport Committee. Deputy Coroner for Nottinghamshire.

SHARP, Roland
Prettys, Ipswich
(01473) 298234
rsharp@prettys.co.uk
Specialisation: Significant practice in carriage of goods by road – national and CMR. In addition to contentious work, advises on business terms, distribution, warehousing and logistics aspects and related transport matters.
Career: Attended Wellington College and Leeds University. Qualified 1986.

SHARPLES, Deborah
Barker Gotelee, Ipswich
(01473) 611211
Specialisation: Road Transport and Waste Management, including licensing, environmental and disciplinary public inquiries and prosecutions. Advocacy. Town and country planning and environmental law.
Prof. Memberships: Member of the Institute of Transport Administration and UKELA. The firm is a member of the RHA and FTA as panel solicitors.
Career: Qualified 1990. Trained at *Eversheds* in Birmingham and *Mills & Reeve* in Norwich before joining *Howes Percival* in 1991 (the Ipswich office later became *Barker Gotelee*).
Publications: Articles in the trade press including Croners Road Transport Briefing.
Personal: Graduated from Birmingham University 1987. Birmingham Law Society Medal 1988. Advanced Certificate in Planning and Environmental Law 1995. Certificate of Professional Competence (Freight National) 2000.

SILK, Ken
Davies Arnold Cooper, London
(020) 7936 2222

THOMAS, Tony
Clyde & Co, Guildford
(01483) 31161
Tony.Thomas@clyde.co.uk
Specialisation: In addition to road carriage, including GIT and removers block/warehousing related disputes, domestic and international road haulage and heavy haulage, also specialises in marine insurance and dry shipping/cargo claims.
Prof. Memberships: Law Society.
Career: Qualified in 1976, joining *Clyde & Co* the same year. Partner 1981.
Personal: Born 27 May 1952. Attended Leamington College 1963-70, then Manchester University 1970-73. Leisure interests include sport, art and architecture. Lives in Grayshott, Surrey.

THOMPSELL, Nicholas
Field Fisher Waterhouse, London
(020) 7861 4000
npt@ffwlaw.com
Specialisation: Corporate/commercial lawyer. Particular interests include transport/travel (especially rail) and privatisation/PFI. Acts for Arriva plc in relation to rail franchise and rail operational issues. Acts for Transport for London. Acted for British Railways in relation to numerous disposals. Acted for The Thomas Cook Group Limited in various transactions. Acted for an airline in relation to BA Franchise. Advised London Underground on its police accommodation PPP scheme and has advised on various other PFI schemes. Advised on the privatisation of HMSO and the Paymaster Agency.
Prof. Memberships: Law Society. City of London Law Society, Rail Study Association.
Career: School: Bablake School, Coventry. University: King's College, London (LLB, AKC). Law School: College of Law, Chester. Articled *Slaughter and May*. Assistant Solicitor *Slaughter and May* 1987-92. Assistant Solicitor *Field Fisher Waterhouse* 1992, becoming a partner in 1993.
Personal: Trying to keep up with daughters' interests in music and computers. Trustee London Suzuki Group.

WARD, Dominic
Andrew M. Jackson, Hull
(01482) 325242
djw@amj.co.uk
Specialisation: Partner in 1992. Disputes involving carriage of goods by sea and road including advising transport intermediaries. International trade disputes, other contractual disputes involving marine or transport-related matters.
Prof. Memberships: AIJA, SEG.
Career: Qualified 1987.
Personal: Born 30 March 1963 in London. Education to age 14 in Germany. Speaks German. Interests include rugby, golf, badminton, cinema, books and travel.

WESTON, John
John Weston & Co, Felixstowe
(01394) 282527

WHITEFORD, Michael G
Jeffrey Aitken Solicitors, Glasgow
(0141) 221 5983
m.whiteford@jeffrey-aitken.co.uk
Specialisation: Road transport law. Practice covers representation at operator licence public inquiries before the Traffic Commissioner and appeals to the Transport Tribunal, employment tribunals and defending in prosecutions in the Scottish courts. Acts for many leading haulage and bus operators.
Prof. Memberships: Law Society of Scotland. Panel Solicitor for the Freight Transport Association and the Road Haulage Association. The Royal Faculty of Procurators in Glasgow.
Career: Qualified 1971. Joined *Jeffrey Aitken* and has been a Partner since 1972.
Personal: Born 15 December 1946. Educated Glasgow University.

WHITEHOUSE, Michael
Wragge & Co, Birmingham
(0870) 903 1000

WOOLFALL, Andrew
Wake Dyne Lawton, Chester
(01829) 773106
aaw@wdl.co.uk
Specialisation: Road transport law, covering goods and passenger vehicles. Representing clients in Magistrates and Crown Courts as well as at Public Inquiries. Also been involved in cases before High Court and House of Lords. Appears at courts and tribunals throughout England and Wales. Provides consultancy advice to companies on internal systems for compliance with road transport law and operators' licensing requirements. Acted for companies and individuals in relation to drugs/smuggling seizures on the continent.
Prof. Memberships: The Law Society. Member of the Institute of Transport Administrators. Practice membership of HTA and RHA.
Career: Lancaster University. Early career in general practice before moving on to specialise in transport.

WYLIE, Amanda
Arthur Cox - Northern Ireland, Belfast
(028) 9023 0007
awylie@arthurcox.ie
Specialisation: Defence personal injury litigation, magistrates court work, Doe and Police Prosecutions, construction and use regulations, tachographs, speed limiters, vehicle excise – any transport-related matters.
Prof. Memberships: Freight Transport Association Panel Solicitor; Contentious Business Committee Member Law Society; Medico-Legal Society; Treasurer of FOIL Northern Ireland; Association of Road Transport Lawyers.
Career: Solicitor, FTA Panel Solicitor seven years.
Personal: Queens University, Belfast LLB Hons, 1993. Interests – cinema, theatre.

TRAVEL

London: 805; The Regions: 806; Hotels & Leisure:807; Timeshare:808; Profiles: 808

Research approved by BMRB For this edition, **Chambers'** researchers conducted 6,582 interviews – 3,900 with law firms, 511 with barristers and 2,171 with clients. The validity of the research was scrutinised by BMRB International, who audited both the methodology and the results at our offices in London. They interviewed **Chambers'** researchers and cross-checked sample interviews. Details of the audit appear on page 7.

OVERVIEW TRAVEL: The events of September 11th have sent a seismic shock through the travel industry, and have had particular impact on aviation costs, transport and insurance issues. Larger firms with cross-departmental expertise have proved themselves best able to meet the changing needs of the industry. New technologies have made their presence felt in the package industry, and there has been an increase in regulatory issues arising from the breakdown of traditional market segments. On the claimant side, there has been no abatement in class actions and claims, while public awareness is felt to have grown in response to media campaigns.

HOTELS & LEISURE: Hotels' occupancy rates have also been badly affected by the terrorist attacks, particularly at the high end of the market. Corporate transactions in this market have been quiet, and the emphasis has shifted onto restructuring and refinancing. Foreign companies and banks hoping to diversify their lending have been moving into the area, with a noticeable trend for securitisation and sale and leaseback.The two highlight transactions of the year were the Compass Group's sale of its hotel portfolio and the sale and leaseback by the Hilton Group.

TIMESHARE: Consolidation and globalisation in the timeshare sector saw RCI, the giant of timeshare exchange, move into development and the operational field. Suggestions of a second directive from Europe have been discussed, and the OTE has moved its base from London to Brussels.

LONDON

TRAVEL — LONDON

1
- Field Fisher Waterhouse
- Nicholson Graham & Jones

2
- Barlow Lyde & Gilbert
- Lane & Partners
- Norton Rose

3
- Badhams
- Davenport Lyons
- Vizards Wyeth

4
- Piper Smith & Basham

LEADING INDIVIDUALS

1
- BARBOR Cynthia Nicholson Graham & Jones
- STEWART Peter Field Fisher Waterhouse

2
- CHAMBERLAIN Simon Field Fisher Waterhouse
- GIMBLETT Richard Barlow Lyde & Gilbert
- ROBINSON Tim Nicholson Graham & Jones
- SEARS Trevor Davenport Lyons

3
- COOK John Norton Rose
- FARRELL Patrick Norton Rose
- GWILLIAM Michael Vizards Wyeth
- MULLIGAN Claire Badhams
- SKUSE Ian Piper Smith & Basham

UP AND COMING
- HARCOMBE Laura Nicholson Graham & Jones

This book is the product of 6,582 1/2 hour interviews. See p.7 for BMRB audit. Within each band, firms are listed alphabetically. See individuals' profiles p.808

FIELD FISHER WATERHOUSE (see firm details p.954) It has been another high-profile year for the team headed up by "*expert*" **Peter Stewart** (see p.811). The department handles corporate, commercial, regulatory and contentious work for tour operators and the travel industry. According to clients, the team "*really knows the industry and can cover all the bases.*" Stewart, described as "*tenacious, thorough and on the ball,*" has the ability to "*translate law into commercial issues – he pitches into battles, fights your corner and gives as good as he gets.*" **Simon Chamberlain** (see p.808) was also recommended as "*one of the most established*" players in the field. Last year the firm was involved in a number of important acquisitions and class actions in the travel sector and worked on Thomas Cook TV. **Clients** Thomas Cook; AITO; ITT.

NICHOLSON GRAHAM & JONES (see firm details p.1083) Peers consider that the group "*takes a more subtle approach to travel law*" and is particularly recommended for its judicial review, competition and litigation work. Clients agree that "*they understand the industry and are sensitive to the fact of costs,*" operating in a "*thorough and approachable*" manner. Team leader **Cynthia Barbor** (see p.808) is respected by clients for her "*practical advice,*" while competitors pointed to her handling of consumer legislation and contractual matters, particularly in "*highbrow industry issues requiring an in-depth knowledge and careful thought.*" Highlights for the firm include acting for ABTA in a landmark appeal to the Competition Commission Appeal Tribunal and lobbying on behalf of the FTO for regulatory changes in the light of the events of September 11th. The team has also been appointed lead solicitors in a group litigation order by ABTA against Ryanair. **Tim Robinson** (see p.810) is recommended for his "*unstuffy approach,*" while **Laura Harcombe** (see p.809) is considered to be "*highly professional.*" **Clients** ABTA; FTO; Thomson; Crystal Holidays.

BARLOW LYDE & GILBERT (see firm details p.858) Heading this regulatory practice is **Richard Gimblett** (see p.88), considered by peers and clients to provide "*excellent advice – an approachable guy.*" He specialises in aviation, travel law and commercial litigation, and has spent much of the year advising the tour operating industry on regulatory issues arising from the September 11th attacks. **Clients** FTO; Kuoni Travel; IATA.

LANE & PARTNERS (see firm details p.1028) Clients commend this team as "*reliable and prompt,*" although interviewees believe much of the firm's profile continues to lie with consultant Richard Venables. The firm advises on regulatory aviation issues, dealing primarily with tour operators and CAA licensing matters. **Clients** Trident Aviation; tour operators.

NORTON ROSE (see firm details p.1084) The travel, tourism and leisure group draws together lawyers from all areas of practice and is mainly engaged in corporate and competition law. It also advises tour operators and travel groups on contentious matters and contractual terms and conditions. **John Cook** (see p.808) is a "*competition specialist*" who is considered to be "*down-to-earth and practical,*" while **Patrick Farrell** (see p.809) is an expert on regulatory issues and commercial litigation. Highlights have included acting for Thomson Travel Group in relation to an OFT enquiry and acting for Hanover International on the disposal of businesses and assets. **Clients** Thomson; P&O; First Choice.

BADHAMS (see firm details p.853) Although our interviewees felt that the firm has had a "*quiet year,*" it continues to be well respected for its advice on travel insurance, policy and accident litigation. It also boasts a separate class action department for large claims. "*Fantastic*" **Claire Mulligan** (see p.810) is "*on the ball and willing to listen,*" and is rated particularly for personal injury, tour operator liability and claims issues. **Clients** Thomson Travel Group; First Choice Holidays.

www.ChambersandPartners.com

TRAVEL ■ LONDON/THE REGIONS

DAVENPORT LYONS (see firm details p.927) **Trevor Sears** (see p.810), UK Counsel to the IATA, is perceived to be the first line of defence for the organisation and is respected by our interviewees as "*knowledgeable and incisive*." He specialises in airline failure and problems with travel agencies. Highlights for the firm have included representing airlines in claims against Hamilton Travel and Flynow.com, and advising Swissair. **Clients** IATA.

VIZARDS WYETH Michael Gwilliam (see p.809) is respected for his reasonable approach and is considered by peers to be particularly experienced in class actions cases. In the past year the firm has mainly undertaken personal injury litigation on behalf of insurance and travel companies. **Clients** Airtours.

PIPER SMITH & BASHAM (see firm details p.1103) Adjudged a "*strong regulatory practice*" by our interviewees, its head, **Ian Skuse** (see p.810) ("*highly commercial*"), has spent much of the last year advising on employment law issues, as well as the corporate commercial and insolvency work within the sector. **Clients** Air France; Levy Gee.

THE REGIONS

TRAVEL
■ THE REGIONS

1 Mason Bond Leeds
2 Eversheds Newcastle upon Tyne
　 Irwin Mitchell Birmingham
3 Andrea & Co Guildford
　 Stones Exeter
4 asb law Croydon
　 Clairmonts Glasgow
　 Shakespeares Birmingham
　 Tozers Exeter

LEADING INDIVIDUALS

1 MASON Stephen Mason Bond
2 ANDREA Costas Andrea & Co
　 COURTENAY-STAMP Bronwen Stones
　 HENDERSON Stuart Irwin Mitchell
　 PEARS Melanie Eversheds
3 GARNER Clive Irwin Mitchell
　 INGLEBY Claire Mason Bond

This book is the product of 6,582 1/2 hour interviews. See p.7 for BMRB audit. Within each band, firms are listed alphabetically. See individuals' profiles p.808

MASON BOND (see firm details p.1057) Although based in Leeds, the firm is considered to rank alongside the London firms in terms of the quality and profile of its advice. Superlatives flow for team leader **Stephen Mason** (see p.810), who is considered by peers and clients alike to be "*tenacious and thorough – a real guru on contract and injury issues*." **Claire Ingleby** (see p.809) is commended for handling the "*nitty-gritty with ease*." The team can be "*aggressive when it needs to be*," and remains respected for its work with tour operators in regulatory, litigation, commercial and employment matters. **Clients** Thomson Holidays; JMC Holidays; Cosmos.

EVERSHEDS (see firm details p.949) The firm's work in the last year has encompassed contractual and employment issues. Clients requiring health checks on contracting arrangements, and insurance issues have come to the fore, particularly regarding the adequacy of airline protection against terrorism. Highlights of the year include advising on the sale of Newcastle International Airport, and issues arising from the collapse of Gill Airways. Partner **Melanie Pears** (see p.810) is deemed "*impressive*" and "*quick off the mark*" by rivals, while clients agree that she "*understands the commercial point of view*." **Clients** Center Parcs; Pontins; Euro Disney.

IRWIN MITCHELL (see firm details p.1009) The practice is judged to have "*cornered the market*" in claims against tour operators and foreign domiciled defendants for accident and group action illness claims arising abroad. Considered by some peers to be "*unnecessarily aggressive*," the firm is championed by many as the "*self-styled people's friend*," leading the market in terms of "*exposure, profile and ability*." **Stuart Henderson** (see p.809) "*knows his onions*" and is a "*hard negotiator*," while **Clive Garner** (see p.809) continues to attract a high level of recommendation. **Clients** FirstAssist; various groups and individuals.

ANDREA & CO This niche practice is headed by "*suave*" **Costas Andrea** (see p.808), who "*adopts a measured approach to litigation*." It undertakes claimant travel work involving personal injury in accidents abroad. Clients consider the firm to be "*responsive and reasonable*." The firm gained significant profile from the Madigan v Cooper & Airtours case, involving a swimming pool accident. **Clients** FirstAssist; individuals and groups.

STONES (see firm details p.1152) Bronwen Courtenay-Stamp (see p.808) is regarded by peers and clients as a "*constructive*" lawyer offering "*excellent advice*." The firm specialises in ski claims, but has also moved into insurance disputes and personal injury litigation for other types of accidents. **Clients** Fogg Travel Insurance Services; Europ Assist; T&C Adjusters.

ASB LAW (see firm details p.851) The offering at this multidisciplinary team encompasses corporate, travel and PI work, while aviation has been identified as a core area for development within the firm as a whole. Lee Hills heads up the litigation department, which acts on behalf of airlines, travel agencies and insurers. In the past year the firm has represented First Choice in its acquisition of Virgin Sun and advised the independent tour operator Titan Travel Group in its acquisitions. **Clients** First Choice; Unijet; Hayes & Jarvis; Virgin Holidays; JMC; Titan Travel Group.

CLAIRMONTS David Kaye and the team represent top UK agents and operators in Scotland, dealing with contract and trading standards issues in addition to property transactions. **Clients** UK operators and agents.

SHAKESPEARES (see firm details p.1127) This "*expert*" team is led by Mark Beesley and is respected for its involvement in waterways law. It is concerned mainly with continuous cruising and moorings issues. **Clients** The Inland Waterways Association; National Association of Boat Owners; individuals.

TOZERS (see firm details p.1165) Tony Beard heads the group, which acts for owners of holiday parks and park home estates. The foot-and-mouth crisis had an impact on the practice, which advised clients on the Government's rights regarding the closing of roads and footpaths. **Clients** Caravan park owners and developers.

HOTELS & LEISURE

TRAVEL: HOTELS & LEISURE
LONDON

1
- Berwin Leighton Paisner
- Clifford Chance

2
- Field Fisher Waterhouse
- Richards Butler
- SJ Berwin

3
- Denton Wilde Sapte
- Freshfields Bruckhaus Deringer
- Linklaters

4
- Allen & Overy
- Douglas Wignall & Co
- Lovells

5
- CMS Cameron McKenna
- Fladgate Fielder
- Taylor Wessing

LEADING INDIVIDUALS

1
- CARNEGIE Andrew Clifford Chance
- LEVY David Berwin Leighton Paisner
- PICKUP Bryan SJ Berwin
- RYLAND David SJ Berwin

2
- LITTLE Andrew Berwin Leighton Paisner
- PHILLIPS Rachel Berwin Leighton Paisner
- PLANT Patrick Linklaters

3
- HOUSTON Paul Field Fisher Waterhouse
- NICOLL Richard Richards Butler
- WIGNALL Douglas Douglas Wignall & Co

This book is the product of 6,582 1/2 hour interviews. See p.7 for BMRB audit.
Within each band, firms are listed alphabetically. See individuals' profiles p.808

BERWIN LEIGHTON PAISNER (see firm details p.866) Interviewees dubbed the firm "*an excellent one-stop shop.*" **David Levy** (see p.809) is "*user friendly and knows what the client wants,*" while **Rachel Phillips** (see p.810) is a "*good operator*" and considered by clients to be "*attentive, efficient and knowledgeable.*" The practice has been bolstered by the recent arrival of **Andrew Little** (see p.809) from Garretts, who specialises in operations and management agreements. The firm played a key role in Compass Group's sale of its portfolio, and a sale and leaseback transaction by Hilton Group. **Clients** Compass Group; Starwood Hotels & Resorts Worldwide; Le Méridien Hotels & Resorts; Royal Bank of Scotland.

CLIFFORD CHANCE (see firm details p.911) A prime choice for the larger transactions, **Andrew Carnegie** (see p.808) leads an experienced team that provides a full range of services including tax, financing, leasing, joint ventures and planning advice. Highlights for the firm included its involvement in the Thistle sale, as well as the sale of individual hotels such as the Hotel Arts in Barcelona. **Clients** Nomura; Thistle Hotels; Sol Meliá Hotels.

FIELD FISHER WATERHOUSE (see firm details p.954) **Paul Houston** (see p.809) leads this "*first-class*" one-stop leisure practice. The firm acts for hotel operators in the rolling out and development of their hotels, and has this year worked on the redevelopment of King's Cross St.Pancras. **Clients** MWB; Luminar; David Lloyd Leisure; Travel Inn.

RICHARDS BUTLER (see firm details p.1112) Drawing on cross-departmental expertise, the leisure and hotels team, led by **Richard Nicoll** (see p.810), is considered by clients to be "*commercial, technical and service-focused.*" Highlights included acting for Parkview International in the acquisition and funding of Battersea Power Station for a leisure, retail, entertainment and hotel development. **Clients** Parkview International; Marylebone Warwick Balfour (MWB); Coral; Orient-Express Hotels.

SJ BERWIN (see firm details p.867) "*Workaholic*" **David Ryland** (see p.810) was endorsed by peers for his efficiency in employing "*real industry knowledge,*" particularly of property finance with a particular expertise in lease structures. **Bryan Pickup** (see p.810) heads the firm's strong leisure practice and is recommended for his "*careful approach*" to property issues. The team handles hotel management contracts, financing and restructuring. The firm has acted on the Hilton Group leaseback for the Royal Bank of Scotland. **Clients** MWB; London & Regional; Hilton.

DENTON WILDE SAPTE (see firm details p.935) The firm remains best known for its hotel and stadium work, with an experienced team that includes Martin Quicke and Richard Budge. On the leisure front, the firm has acted for the Rugby Football Union (RFU) and Virgin Active, and has worked with Morgan Stanley on the financing of the Thistle deal. **Clients** Virgin Active; RFU; Novotel; Red Carnation Group.

FRESHFIELDS BRUCKHAUS DERINGER (see firm details p.964) It has been a busy year for Mark Wheelhouse and his "*excellent*" team, respected for its work on the corporate side of the travel market. The group advised Granada Compass on the disposal of the Granada/Forte hospitality business. **Clients** Compass Group; Starwood Hotels.

LINKLATERS (see firm details p.1043) **Patrick Plant** (see p.810) and his team handle corporate and commercial work in the leisure sector. The group derives advantage from the firm's top-flight property and corporate practices and has advised Six Continents on the acquisition of the Posthouse Hotel chain from Compass Group. **Clients** Six Continents; Jolly Hotels; Barclays Bank.

ALLEN & OVERY (see firm details p.841) This group has been pulled together from the corporate, banking and property departments by property partner Adam Cleal. The group has a particular strength in financing, and advised CIBC World Markets and Merrill Lynch on their funding of the acquisition by Nomura International's Principal Finance Group of the Le Méridien hotel chain. **Clients** CIBC World Markets; Merrill Lynch; Barclays.

DOUGLAS WIGNALL & CO (see firm details p.942) The firm was recommended to our researchers as a niche specialist outfit with expertise in management agreements. Peers agree that "*expert*" **Douglas Wignall** (see p.811) has a real understanding of the industry. **Clients** Six Senses Group; Sheraton; Luxury Hotel Group.

LOVELLS (see firm details p.1045) This "*highly experienced and professional*" team includes Bob Kidby and Jackie Newstead, bringing both corporate and property expertise to the table. Recent high-profile instructions include advising on an agreement to build a £40 million hotel at Stansted Airport. **Clients** BAA; Forte; Steinberger Hotels.

CMS CAMERON MCKENNA (see firm details p.914) Richard Price and Sally Badham sit within a team which is judged to be "*positive and helpful.*" The firm raised its travel profile this year by acting for Nomura in the Compass Group sale. A team of more than 80 of the UK firm's lawyers acted for Nomura International's Principal Finance Group in a £1.9 billion acquisition of the Le Méridien chain of 150 hotels located in more than 55 countries. **Clients** Six Continents; Nomura; Choice Hotels International.

FLADGATE FIELDER (see firm details p.957) A "*conscientious,*" cross-departmental hotels team, including Anthony Vaughan, has had a busy year advising on the flotation, acquisition, sale, funding and development of hotels and leisure facilities. Highlights include advising Orb Developments on its acquisition of a Thistle hotel. **Clients** Mövenpick Hotels & Resorts; Scotsman Hotel Group; Orb Developments.

TAYLOR WESSING (see firm details p.1156) The firm is judged particularly strong on development work. Adam Marks belongs to a team that is thought to be "*highly attentive*" to clients' needs. The group has recently advised the MWB Group on its business exchange expansion programme. **Clients** MWB; Kew Green Hotels.

TRAVEL ■ TIMESHARE/THE LEADERS

TIMESHARE

TRAVEL: TIMESHARE
■ NATIONWIDE

1 Tods Murray WS Edinburgh
2 Amhurst Brown Colombotti London
   Baker & McKenzie London
3 Stones Exeter

LEADING INDIVIDUALS

1 ANDERSON David Tods Murray WS
2 BOURNE Tim Stones
   GUMMERS Eric Amhurst Brown Colombotti

This book is the product of 6,582 1/2 hour interviews. See p.7 for BMRB audit. Within each band, firms are listed alphabetically. See individuals' profiles p.808

TODS MURRAY WS (see firm details p.1164) Department head **David Anderson** (see p.808) has been dubbed by our interviewees the "*godfather of timeshare.*" He and the team act for the timeshare industry on management agreements, trust deeds and marketing contracts. Clients consider him to be "*highly knowledgeable*" and "*a class act.*" **Clients** RCI; Barrett International Resorts; OTE.

AMHURST BROWN COLOMBOTTI Eric Gummers (see p.809) acts for corporate clients and is considered by peers to take a "*bright, pragmatic and commercial view.*" The group advises the hospitality sector in the UK and Spain. **Clients** RMI; Textron Financial; Interval International.

BAKER & MCKENZIE (see firm details p.855) Regarded as "*a good corporate team with gravitas*" by its peers, the team, which includes Mark Henrick, acts for timeshare developers, exchange organisations and financiers in the commercial and regulatory fields. The firm is particularly good on regulatory and purchasing issues. **Clients** RCI; Sunterra Corporation.

STONES (see firm details p.1152) Experience in corporate, development and trust company work affords "*energetic*" Tim Bourne (see p.808) a strong profile in the market. He and the team act for consumers, timeshare committees and clubs. The department has expanded with two partners and two assistants now working full-time. A greater focus on contentious work has appeared as a result of a downturn in the industry. **Clients** Timeshare funders; timeshare developers; owners' associations.

THE LEADERS IN TRAVEL

ANDERSON, David
Tods Murray WS, Edinburgh
(0131) 226 4771
david.anderson@todsmurray.com
Specialisation: All aspects of timeshare and leisure related work throughout the UK and Europe; 1975 devised legal structure for first UK timeshare project; advises developers, banks, management companies, trade bodies and other suppliers of services to timeshare industry; legal advisor and secretary to Timeshare Council; author of numerous articles.
Prof. Memberships: Law Society of Scotland.
Career: Qualified *Tods Murray* 1972; partner 1974.
Personal: Born 1948. Attended Perth Academy and Edinburgh University (1970 LLB). Leisure – golf.

ANDREA, Costas
Andrea & Co, Guildford
(01483) 889880
ca@andreaco.com
Specialisation: Senior Partner of the firm of *Andrea & Co*. Deals exclusively with travel and tourism law predominantly acting for claimants injured abroad. Currently pursuing personal injury claims in over 50 countries, as well as against UK defendants, primarily tour operators. Acted on higher profile claims such as Estonia ferry disaster and the Ethiopian airline hijacking.
Prof. Memberships: The Law Society Personal Injury Panel; Travel and Tourism Lawyers Association; Pan European Organisation of Personal Injury Lawyers. Founder member of the International Personal Injury Lawyers Association, being a network of personal injury lawyers throughout the world.
Career: Qualified in 1990 and set up the firm of *Andrea & Co* in 1997, which has doubled in size in each of its first five years.
Publications: The author of numerous articles and a consultant to the BBC and 'Holiday Which' magazine.
Personal: Born 28 December 1962. Travelled extensively prior to obtaining an LLB in 1987 and qualifying in 1990. Lives in Guildford, Surrey.

BARBOR, Cynthia
Nicholson Graham & Jones, London
(020) 7360 8170
cynthia.barbor@ngj.co.uk
Specialisation: Partner in Litigation Department and joint Head of Travel and Leisure Law Unit. Main area of practice is travel and leisure law. Has over twenty years experience in acting for major UK and international tour operators, travel agents, ground handlers, insurers, hotels, airlines, car hire companies and trade associations, advising on substantial litigation, commercial agreements and regulatory issues. Also handles general commercial litigation, including insurance and personal injury actions. Writes regularly for 'Travel Trade Gazette' and other travel publications. Speaks frequently on travel law at UK and international conferences.
Prof. Memberships: Fellow of the Institute of Travel and Tourism, Incentive Travel and Meetings Association. Law Society.

BOURNE, Tim
Stones, Exeter
(01392) 666777
timbourne@stones-solicitors.co.uk
Specialisation: Partner. All aspects of timeshare law. Acts for and has advised banks, developers, hotel groups, owners associations, the main timeshare exchange organisations and national timeshare organisations. Author of articles for the Law Society and 'Estates Gazette', 'International Banking and Financial Law Journal', 'New Law Journal' and travel magazines. Lectures on timeshare law to the Institute of Bankers and several universities.
Prof. Memberships: The Law Society, Institute of Management.
Career: Qualified 1981. Partner at *Stones*, 1983.
Personal: Born 22 March 1945. Educated Clifton College and HM Royal Marines. Lives in Exeter.

CARNEGIE, Andrew
Clifford Chance, London
(020) 7600 1000
andrew.carnegie@cliffordchance.com
Specialisation: Real estate. Partner specialising in real estate finance, hotels and insolvency.
Career: Articled *Cartmell Shepherd*, Carlisle; solicitor *Cameron Markby* 1986-88; Partner *Clifford Chance* since 1996.
Personal: Dollar Academy, Scotland; University of Newcastle upon Tyne.

CHAMBERLAIN, Simon
Field Fisher Waterhouse, London
(020) 7861 4000
stc@ffwlaw.com
Specialisation: Partner in the Aviation and Travel Department specialising in commercial, corporate and regulatory work within the aviation and travel industries.
Career: Qualified in 1977. *Richards Butler & Co* 1973-81. British Airways Plc 1981-90. *Rowe & Maw* 1990-94. Partner at *Field Fisher Waterhouse* since 1994.
Personal: Educated at Downside School. Born 8 August 1953. Lives in East Sussex.

COOK, John
Norton Rose, London
(020) 7444 3096
cookcj@nortonrose.com
Specialisation: Partner, competition and EC department. Competition law, EC law, (including international trade, public procurement and state aids) travel/transport and utilities regulation. A regular conference speaker and writer, he is the author, with CS Kerse, of 'EC Merger Control', the leading text book on EC merger control – published by Sweet & Maxwell – 3rd Ed December 1999.
Career: Called to the Bar of Grays Inn in 1975. Lectureship, Magdalen College, Oxford 1976-81. UK government legal service 1976-88. *Norton Rose* 1988-97 (headed competition and EC department). Rejoined *Norton Rose* in February 2000 after two years at *Macfarlanes*.

COURTENAY-STAMP, Bronwen
Stones, Exeter
(01392) 666777
bcs@stones-solicitors.co.uk
Specialisation: Heads the personal injury, travel and insurance team. Concentrates on travel and tourism litigation and sports law in connection with skiing. Provides an on-call 24 hour service for several client companies who may require immediate specialist advice. Organises attendance at the scene of ski accidents of a serious nature where necessary. Gives lectures and writes articles for both the travel industry and lawyers.
Prof. Memberships: A Member of the Law Society Personal Injury Panel and of the Association of Personal Injury Lawyers.
Career: Educated in the North East of England. Law Degree at Exeter University, First Class Honours in Law Society Finals. Trained at *Stones*, spending the majority of qualified career dealing with personal injury, travel, tourism and skiing law.
Personal: Married with two children. Enjoys foreign travel and watersports. A very keen snow skier.

THE LEADERS ■ TRAVEL

FARRELL, Patrick
Norton Rose, London
(020) 7283 6000
farrellpa@nortonrose.com
Specialisation: Advises tour operators, travel agents and airlines on claims handling, contractual disputes of all descriptions, brochure terms and conditions, bonding arrangements and regulatory matters. Also acts for airlines (including start-ups) and financiers advising on domestic and European regulatory matters. Acts regularly in aircraft finance litigation.
Prof. Memberships: MRAeS, Chairman of the Royal Aeronautical Society Air Law Group, Chairman of the UK ICC Commission on Air Transport, Member of Institute of Travel and Tourism, IBA, LSLA, CLLS (Chairman of the CLLS Aeronautical Law Sub-Committee).

GARNER, Clive
Irwin Mitchell, Birmingham
(0121) 212 1828
GarnerC@IrwinMitchell.co.uk
Specialisation: Partner heading *Irwin Mitchell*'s expanding International Travel Litigation Group. Acts for claimants in accident and illness claims arising abroad. Successfully acted in many high value head and spinal injury claims and coordinated a large number of multi-party claims against English tour operators arising from illness outbreaks, coach, aviation and maritime accidents. Acted in several reported and precedent setting cases, recovering many millions of pounds in damages for clients injured abroad. Lectured nationally and internationally on personal injury, foreign claims and multi-party issues.
Prof. Memberships: Law Society Personal Injury Panel; Association of Personal Injury Lawyers; Australian Plaintiff Lawyers Association; Pan European Organisation of Personal Injury Lawyers; Travel and Tourism Lawyers Association; Society for Advanced Legal Studies; Vice-Chair of the International Practice Section of the Association of Trial Lawyers of America.
Career: Education: LLB (1988), MA (1989), LLM (1997). Articled *Irwin Mitchell*. Qualified in 1992; Partner 1997.
Publications: Author of several published articles in various journals. Regular commentator on television, radio and in the press on travel and personal injury related issues.
Personal: Born 3 April 1966. Lives in Sheffield.

GIMBLETT, Richard
Barlow Lyde & Gilbert, London
(020) 7247 2277
rgimblett@blg.co.uk
See under Aviation, p.88

GUMMERS, Eric
Amhurst Brown Colombotti, London
(020) 7830 8234
eric.gummers@abc-solicitors.com
Specialisation: Corporate, M&A and corporate finance. Specialises in the proactive commercial advice on legal issues relevant to the leisure and travel industry. Particularly well-known for expertise in relation to innovative membership clubs, leisure, resort and timeshare developments.
Prof. Memberships: Member of State Legislative Committee of the American Resort Developers Association, Chair of ARDA International Committee, Commercial Law Sub-committee of City of London Solicitors and Legislative Council of the Organisation for Timeshare in Europe
Career: Cambridge University (Jesus College). Qualified with *Rowe & Maw* in 1985 where he became a partner in 1991. Head of *Rowe & Maw*'s Timeshare Group in 1997. Joined *Amhurst Brown Colombotti* in St James's during 1998 as a Partner. Focus on the leisure sector, working with a cross-departmental group at ABC which is very active in the travel, hotel, health, golf, restaurant and entertainment sectors across Europe.
Publications: Various publications and articles on matters relevant to the travel and leisure sector, UK chapter on 'Due Diligence on Corporate Acquisitions' (Kluwer).

GWILLIAM, Michael
Vizards Wyeth, London
(020) 7400 9999
mjg@vizardswyeth.com
Specialisation: Heads the Travel and Tourism Unit. Acts on behalf of tour operators and travel agents both directly and on the instruction of their liability insurers. Involved in litigation both in this jurisdiction and overseas in cross-border disputes. Acted on behalf of the Defendants in the cases of Brannan v Airtours Holiday Ltd, Hone v Going Places and Gallagher v Airtours Holiday Ltd. Involved in the defence of large multi-party actions brought against tour operators in relation to illness suffered abroad, as well as in relation to major incidents involving fatalities and serious injury.
Career: Articled *Vizards* 1989. Partner *Vizards Staples & Bannisters*. Partner *Vizards Wyeth* 1999.
Personal: Educated Leeds Grammar School and Exeter University. Interests include skiing, sailing and scuba-diving. Resides London.

HARCOMBE, Laura
Nicholson Graham & Jones, London
(020) 7360 8186
laura.harcombe@ngj.co.uk
Specialisation: Solicitor in the Travel and Leisure Law Group acting on a wide range of contentious and non-contentious matters for trade associations, tour operators, travel agents, hotels, car hire companies and their insurers. Acted for ABTA in its successful case against the OFT and the General Insurance Standards Council in the Competition Commission Appeals Tribunal, the first appeal to go before the Tribunal. Acting on behalf of travel agents in group litigation against Ryanair and defending class actions on behalf of tour operators.
Prof. Memberships: Law Society.
Career: Articled at *Nicholson Graham & Jones* and qualified in 1995.

HENDERSON, Stuart
Irwin Mitchell, Birmingham
(0121) 212 1828
See under Personal Injury, p.633

HOUSTON, Paul
Field Fisher Waterhouse, London
(020) 7861 4078
wph@ffwlaw.com
Specialisation: Paul has specialised in hotel and leisure property work since qualification. He has extensive experience of managing the roll-out of branded leisure concepts and franchise operations. In addition, he advises institutional investors in the acquisition, development, disposal and forward funding of properties in the hotel and leisure sector. His clients include Luminar PLC, Marriott, Travel Inn, David Lloyd Leisure and Deutsche Property Asset Management.
Prof. Memberships: Law Society.
Career: Qualified as a solicitor in Scotland in 1989 and in England and Wales in 1991. Paul was articled at *Ross Harper & Murphy* in Glasgow, joined *FFW* in 1989 and became a partner in 1995.
Personal: Born 3 April 1965. Chryston High School; University of Strathclyde. Married, two children. Leisure interests include golf, skiing and music.

INGLEBY, Claire
Mason Bond, Leeds
(0113) 242 4444
claire@masonbond.co.uk
Specialisation: Partner in Travel Law Department. Specialises in drafting and advising on contractual and other documentation of all descriptions for tour operators. Has drafted booking conditions for many major operators and prepares, amongst others, supplier's contracts, agency agreements, promotional agreements and conditions and brochure wording. Presently particularly involved in advising on 'unfair terms' in booking conditions. Also advises on regulatory matters. Conducts in-house seminars for tour operators on a number of subjects, including the Disability Discrimination Act. Provides advice on all areas of law affecting tour operators. Firm acts on behalf of more than 100 tour operators of varying sizes. Also represents travel agents, newspapers and a trade association.
Prof. Memberships: Law Society.
Career: Joined *Mason Bond* on qualification in 1990. Became a Partner in 1994.
Personal: Born 5 December 1965, married, two children. Exeter University 1984-87. Leisure activities include hill walking. Lives near Skipton, North Yorkshire.

LEVY, David N
Berwin Leighton Paisner, London
(020) 7760 1000
david.levy@blplaw.com
Specialisation: Partner in Property Department specialising in all types of commercial property work including planning. Acts in particular for the leading companies in the hotel and leisure fields, and over 20 years has dealt with the acquisition and disposal of many hundreds of hotels, restaurants and leisure properties of all types. Also has specialist involvement with motorway service areas. Most recent large transaction involvement in disposal of entire hotel portfolio by Compass Group plc for sums in excess of £3 billion.
Prof. Memberships: Law Society. Business In Sport & Leisure. British Israel Law Association.
Career: Educated at Wanstead County High School and Hertford College, Oxford. Qualified in 1972. Became a Partner at *Paisner & Co* in 1976 (now *Berwin Leighton Paisner*).
Publications: Author of several published articles in various legal and property journals.
Personal: Born 1948. Resides Finchley, London. Married with two children.

LITTLE, Andrew
Berwin Leighton Paisner, London
(020) 7760 4581
andrew.little@blplaw.com
Specialisation: Partner specialising in hotels and leisure industry related work. Work includes purchases and sales of hotel and leisure businesses, negotiating hotel management agreements and operating leases, advising on financing of hotels and leisure projects, negotiating joint venture and development agreements and advising on franchising and time-sharing arrangements. Also advises on restructuring schemes for hotels, and in negotiating loan and security documents. An adviser to the British Hospitality Association. Frequently lectures at seminars and conferences for the hotel industry.
Prof. Memberships: Law Society, International Bar Association, Hotel Catering & International Management Association, British Association of Hotel Accountants.
Career: Qualified in 1973. With *Lawrence Graham* 1971-76, then at *Fox & Gibbons*, Dubai and London 1976-84. Vice President and General Counsel, Holiday Inns International 1985-89. Partner at *Field Fisher Waterhouse* 1990-1997. *Garretts* 1997-2002. Joined *Berwin Leighton Paisner* 2002.
Personal: Born 25 November 1948. Educated at Uppingham School, Exeter University and Guildford College of Law. Leisure pursuits include sailing, golf, theatre, and travel. Lives in London W11. RAC, St. Mawes Sailing Club.

TRAVEL ■ THE LEADERS

MASON, Stephen
Mason Bond, Leeds
(0113) 242 4444
stephen@masonbond.co.uk
Specialisation: Partner in Travel Law Department. Advises tour operators and travel agents. Work includes defending claims brought by consumers, advocacy, dealing with trading standards departments, conducting seminars. Also handles commercial aspects of travel law, including commercial disputes and litigation, copyright, trademarks and passing off. Acted in Thomson Holidays v Birch 1999 DC, Mawdsley v Cosmosair 2002 CA and in many first instance travel law cases reported in 'Current Law'. Joint Editor of the 'International Travel Law Journal'. Has addressed numerous seminars on travel law topics including ABTA Convention 2001; and also teaches Civil Advocacy at the University of Northumbria. Higher Courts (Civil Proceedings) Qualification 1994. Used these Rights of Audience to defend a major tour operator successfully against a large claim in the High Court, January 1997 and to appear in the Court of Appeal in Carter v Lotus 2001. Joint Author 'Holiday Law' Sweet & Maxwell (3rd ed. due 2003), Member of the Law Society Civil Litigation Committee since 1997.
Prof. Memberships: Law Society, Travel and Tourism Lawyers Association (Deputy Chair).
Career: Qualified 1974, Senior Partner since 1986.
Personal: Married, three children. Attended Bradford Grammar School to 1967, and Cambridge University to 1971, Leisure interests include travel, theatre (Secretary of Ilkley Players) and supporting Leeds United FC. Lives in Ilkley, West Yorkshire.

MULLIGAN, Claire
Badhams, London
(020) 7242 4154
claire.mulligan@badhams.net
Specialisation: One of the firm's two partners specialising in travel litigation, as part of the firm's travel litigation unit. Advises tour operators, insurers, travel agents and hotels. Handles a variety of claims including class actions, diving accidents, substantial litigation and resort outbreaks. Recent court successes included the Court of Appeal case of Codd v Thomson Travel which confirmed that local regulations, not British standards, apply to Package Travel Litigation. Usually acts for tour operators or insurers as opposed to individuals. Regularly contributes to insurance press and many recent successes are reported in law reports. Provides in-house seminars to tour operators.
Prof. Memberships: Travel and Tourism Lawyers Association.
Career: Qualified in 1995, made Partner in 2000.

NICOLL, Richard
Richards Butler, London
(020) 7816 3725
rxn@richardsbutler.com
Specialisation: Has over 25 years experience of transactions of all kinds in the commercial property market. His practice covers mainstream corporate real estate, specialist leisure/hotel property and high value residential development. His recent high profile work includes the ongoing redevelopment of Battersea Power Station, advising Land Securities Trillium on various matters related to their property partnership with DSS (now DWP), the BBC and BT. He was also lead partner on the £250m sale of the Odeon cinema chain, the £90m purchase of retail/office investment in Central London; a £150m sale and leaseback transaction involving over 20 prime leisure properties; major multi-leisure developments. He also continues to act for a number of specialist residential developers.
Prof. Memberships: Law Society.
Career: Qualified 1974, joined *Richards Butler* in 1971. Appointed Partner in 1980. Headed property group between 1995-2000. Appointed to the partnership board in 2000.
Personal: Born 1950. Leisure interests include fishing, rugby and sports generally. Member of MCC.

PEARS, Melanie
Eversheds, Newcastle upon Tyne
(0191) 241 6056
melaniepears@eversheds.com
Specialisation: Partner. Acts as adviser to many household name travel sector clients. Work involves client compliance audits, agency contracts, promotions terms and conditions, consumer complaint handling, intellectual property disputes and general commercial matters. Member of the IBA Committee on Travel, has written for the Travel Law Journal and has presented papers at many recent IBA conferences.
Career: Qualified in 1994. Originally trained as a barrister, after which worked in industry for Shell and then in publishing, before joining *Eversheds* 1989.
Personal: Born 10 February 1965.

PHILLIPS, Rachel
Berwin Leighton Paisner, London
(020) 7760 1000
rachel.phillips@blplaw.com
Specialisation: All aspects of commercial real estate, especially in the hospitality and leisure sectors. 2000-01 acted on property aspects of the sale by Compass Hotels of its entire hotel portfolio for over £3 billion.
Prof. Memberships: Hotel Property Network (steering committee member since 1997).
Career: Articled *Paisner & Co*; qualified 1989. Assistant Solicitor *Paisner & Co* 1989-96. Assistant Solicitor *Wilde Sapte* 1996-99. Partner *Paisner & Co* 1999-2001. Partner *Berwin Leighton Paisner* 2001.
Personal: Born 1964. Educated North London Collegiate School and Cambridge University (Newnham College). Church organist/choirmaster.

PICKUP, Bryan
SJ Berwin, London
(020) 7533 2468
bryan.pickup@sjberwin.com
Specialisation: Head of Property Department. Covers a wide variety of property transactions for investors and developers. Also handles the sale, purchase and funding of office, retail and leisure businesses. Has acted on the funding and acquisition and disposal of leisure parks, the acquisition of the nightclubs and bars businesses of First Leisure and a number of restaurant transactions, and is currently primarily involved in major city centre retail development.
Prof. Memberships: British Property Federation.
Career: Qualified in 1981. Joined *SJ Berwin & Co* in 1988 as a Partner.
Personal: Born 15 April 1953. Attended Whitgift School, Croydon 1961-69 and Fitzwilliam College, Cambridge 1970-74. Leisure interests include golf and hockey. Lives in Wimbledon.

PLANT, Patrick
Linklaters, London
(020) 7456 4718
patrick.plant@linklaters.com
Specialisation: Specialist in UK commercial property advising investors, developers, lenders and tenants on all aspects of commercial property in the UK. Also a specialist in hotel and leisure with particular expertise in negotiating management and franchise agreements for hotel and leisure projects.
Career: 1994 to date: Partner in the Commercial Property Department of *Linklaters*. 1990-94: Assistant Solicitor, *Linklaters*. 1989-90: Assistant Solicitor, *Mallesons Stephen Jacques*, Sydney. 1986-89: Assistant Solicitor, *Linklaters*.

ROBINSON, Tim
Nicholson Graham & Jones, London
(020) 7360 8162
tim.robinson@ngj.co.uk
Specialisation: Consultant in Litigation Department, Joint Head Travel and Leisure Law Group. Travel, Tourism and Leisure law. Acts for tour operators, travel agents, hotel groups, insurers, airlines and trade associations. Also handles general commercial litigation, libel and media acting for newspaper and magazine publishers. Writes for 'Travel Trade Gazette' and major travel and tourism publications, the national press, TV and radio. Speaks at travel industry conferences in the UK and worldwide. Independent Member of Air Travel Insolvency Protection Advisory Committee.
Prof. Memberships: Institute of Travel and Tourism, Media Society, Incentive Travel and Meeting Association, Pacific Asia Travel Association (UK Chairman and Worldwide Board Director), European Tour Operators Association, International Hotel and Restaurant Association, African Travel & Tourism Association.
Career: Qualified 1977. Joined *Nicholson Graham & Jones* 1979. Partner 1982.
Personal: Born in 1953. Attended St Edmund Hall, Oxford 1971-73. Leisure interests include music, reading, and classic cars.

RYLAND, David
SJ Berwin, London
(020) 7533 2222
david.ryland@sjberwin.com
Specialisation: Hotel & leisure sales and purchases, structured finance transactions, management contracts, joint ventures and the establishment of collective investment schemes. Transactions dealt with in the last year relating to the hotel and leisure industry include the negotiation of forward funding agreements relating to substantial leisure parks the negotiation of new Mal Maison chain of hotels including the negotiation of the joint venture SAS, the sale and leaseback of 11 Hilton Hotels and regulatory agreements relating to a number of new Hilton Hotels, a portfolio of seven hotels for Hilton and the redevelopment of the Great Western Hotel. He has also been involved in the establishment of a wide range of tax efficient collective investment vehicles for property investment for an aggregate value of £5 billion.
Career: *Clifford Chance* 1981-88; *SJ Berwin & Co* 1988-date. Dulwich College 1965-72; Exeter College, Oxford University 1973-77 (double first in Mods and Greats). Frequent lecturer and writer of articles on property investment related matters.
Personal: Married. Interests include sport, music and cinema.

SEARS, Trevor
Davenport Lyons, London
(020) 7468 2600
tsears@davenportlyons.com
Specialisation: UK counsel to the International Air Transport Association (IATA) and consultant to airlines with particular regard to their relationship with travel agents. Licensed Insolvency Practitioner and speaker at airline and travel seminars, radio and TV.
Prof. Memberships: FABRP.
Career: Qualified 1972. Joined *Booth and Blackwell*. Partner 1974. Senior partner 1990.
Publications: Author of chapter 'Travel Insolvency' in Tolley's 'Insolvency Law'.
Personal: Born 1948. Educated at Epsom College. Lives in Surrey. Interests include travel, music and sport.

SKUSE, Ian
Piper Smith & Basham, London
(020) 7828 8685
Specialisation: Partner and Head of Travel and Commercial Law, and has specialised in travel law since 1983. Acts for large and small travel agents, tour operators, airlines, a substantial interna-

tional hotel chain, and for business travel agents. Practice covers claims, corporate and commercial work of all kinds including negotiations with Regulators including ABTA, CAA, IATA and Trading Standards Officers. Extensive experience in negotiating commercial agreements concerning all aspects of the travel business, both leisure and business. Excellent track record at managing litigation of all kinds in the Courts and with trade association and Regulators. Expert guidance offered through the regulatory framework of ATOL Licensing, Code of Conduct matters and Airline Regulation. The firm has recently acted in a number of major corporate acquisitions in both the leisure and business sector. A regular columnist for Business Travel World and founder member of the consultancy group, Travel Resources.

Prof. Memberships: Institute of Travel and Tourism, CIMTIG.

Career: Qualified in 1980. *Piper Smith & Basham* in 1983. Partner since 1987.

STEWART, Peter
Field Fisher Waterhouse, London
(020) 7861 4000

Specialisation: Partner and Head of Aviation Travel and Tourism Department. Practice covers commercial areas (contentious and non-contentious) concerning the travel industry. Non-contentious work includes contractual arrangements between travel companies and their suppliers, compliance with regulatory requirements, joint ventures and business sales/purchases. Contentious work includes disputes with suppliers, other travel companies and customers. Author of 'A Practical Guide to Package Holiday Law and Contracts' (third edition 1993) and regular articles for ITT journal and other trade papers. Regularly lectures for IBC and ITT at travel industry conferences.

Prof. Memberships: IFTTA, ITT.

Career: Qualified 1982, having joined *Field Fisher Waterhouse* in 1980. Became a Partner in 1985.

Personal: Born 3 February 1956. Attended Campbell College in Belfast 1969-73, then Pembroke College, Cambridge 1974-77. Leisure interests include golf, tennis and music. Lives near Sevenoaks, Kent.

WIGNALL, Douglas
Douglas Wignall & Co, London
(020) 7583 1362

Specialisation: Principal. Main area of practice is hotels and leisure. Special area of expertise is drafting and negotiating international hotel management contracts and related agreements involved in hotel developments such as joint venture/shareholder agreements. Work also includes negotiating hotel franchise agreements, acquisitions and disposal of hotels in the United Kingdom and advising on all aspects of hotel operational matters. Has been involved in hotel and/or resort projects primarily in the United Kingdom and Europe and also in Africa, Middle East, Russia and former CIS countries. Major clients include Starwood Hotels and Resorts Inc, Morrison International Developments Ltd, Blakes Hotel Ltd, Luxury Hotel Partners and the Six Senses Group. Has lectured and written articles on hotel management contracts. Individual charge out rate is £225.00 per hour.

Prof. Memberships: Law Society, International Bar Association, International Society of Hospitality Consultants, Member of British Middle East Law Council, Member of the Company of Scriveners.

Career: Qualified in 1974. Worked in industry for approximately 10 years including Legal Counsel with Sheraton Management Corporation between 1981-84. Set up *Douglas Wignall & Co* in 1984.

Personal: Born 15 April 1950. Attended Brentwood School 1957-68, Leeds University 1968-71, and Guildford Law College 1971-72. Leisure interests include squash and music; member of Hurlingham Club. Lives in London SW6.

TRUSTS & PERSONAL TAX

London: 812; The Regions: 815; Scotland: 821; Profiles: 822

Research approved by BMRB For this edition, **Chambers'** researchers conducted 6,582 interviews – 3,900 with law firms, 511 with barristers and 2,171 with clients. The validity of the research was scrutinised by BMRB International, who audited both the methodology and the results at our offices in London. They interviewed **Chambers'** researchers and cross-checked sample interviews. Details of the audit appear on page 7.

OVERVIEW The private client sector is booming despite the downturn in the economy. With the rise in property prices, more estates are going over the inheritance tax threshold, and calling upon tax lawyers as a result. Litigation is also on the rise, demanding increased specialisation on the part of lawyers in contentious trust and tax issues. A divide is emerging between the traditional firms handling core domestic estate and probate work, and firms building up broader cross-departmental practices integrated to advise on international corporate and commercial deals. Looking to the future, the taxation regime for non-domiciliaries in the UK is under threat of reform, while in Northern Ireland, the new Trustee Act, the first major piece of legislation since 1958, will bring it more into line with English law – imposing fresh duties of care on trustees and widening investment powers.

LONDON

TRUSTS & PERSONAL TAX
LONDON

1
Macfarlanes
Withers LLP

2
Allen & Overy
Charles Russell
Currey & Co
Lawrence Graham

3
Boodle Hatfield
Farrer & Co
Forsters
Speechly Bircham
Taylor Wessing

4
Baker & McKenzie
Bircham Dyson Bell
Payne Hicks Beach

5
Berwin Leighton Paisner
Hunters
Linklaters
May, May & Merrimans
Nicholson Graham & Jones
Simmons & Simmons
Wedlake Bell

6
Dawsons
Lee & Pembertons
Pemberton Greenish
RadcliffesLeBrasseur
Rooks Rider
Smyth Barkham
Trowers & Hamlins

This book is the product of 6,582 1/2 hour interviews. See p.7 for BMRB audit. Within each band, firms are listed alphabetically.

MACFARLANES (see firm details p.1047) "*The golden firm of London*" for trusts and personal tax, indeed rival firms confess that this is the department they seek to emulate. Commentators praised its "*stability, huge strength in depth, and cutting-edge lawyering*," skills shared by a large number of well-known players. Of this "*fantastic*" group and of the UK as a whole, head of department **John Rhodes** was endorsed as "*pre-eminent in the regulatory environment – always on top of his subject.*" Clients commend his "*massive international experience combined with one of the best intellects in the business.*" **Michael Hayes** is also at the pinnacle of the field, appreciated by peers for his "*capacity to think outside the box,*" while clients view him as "*pragmatic – he makes things simple.*" Observers described **Robin Vos** as "*cerebral and a legal talent,*" while **Ann Whitfield** is "*a commercial, first-rate practitioner.*" **Owen Clutton** impresses with his "*excellent technical skills,*" and **Matthew Pintus** is much sought after, "*superb with international private clients.*" The department operates under a strong team ethos. Its typical remit of personal tax planning and trust administration is mainly for new money clients, while its offshore expertise is particularly rated. Highlights in the past year include a complete review of the affairs of one of the wealthiest non-UK-domiciled families currently resident in the UK, leading to the establishment of a new offshore trust and company structure.

WITHERS LLP (see firm details p.1194) "*At the cutting edge and gearing up as a new competitor on the international scene,*" this firm's recent transatlantic merger with US firm Bergman, Horowitz & Reynolds has now created one of the largest private client departments in the world. It aims to provide an integrated service for high net worth individuals across the US and Europe. One client agreed "*these lawyers care about their customers, they think creatively and are technically strong.*" **Stephen Cooke** (see p.823), who specialises in landed estates, is "*held in universal respect by the profession.*" The "*sensible, academic*" **John Riches** (see p.828) is highly esteemed for his work as head of the entrepreneurs' team. **Murray Hallam** (see p.825) ("*pleasant to deal with*") is particularly endorsed for his work on American matters. The department's contentious work in international trust estate and charity litigation is led by **Dawn Goodman** (see p.825), while senior figure **Tony Thompson** (see p.829) continues to impress. Landed estates provide a steady flow of instructions. Recent highlights have included financial engineering, insurance wrappers and US-style remuneration packages, as well as all the traditional tax services for the wealthy. The firm recently acted for the executors in the administration of Lord Hamlyn's £450 million estate.

ALLEN & OVERY (see firm details p.841) The department has refocused this year to apply its trusts and tax expertise to corporate work, capital markets and securitisation deals. In this, it leads the way in placing the increasing commercial needs of an impressive international client base to the fore. The department is immensely respected as "*top quality,*" particularly for litigation and cross-border work. **Clare Maurice** (see p.827) takes over this year as head of department and is judged "*a real star,*" while **Richard Turnor** (see p.602) enjoys a "*wide base of experience.*" **Ceris Gardner** (see p.824) continues to draw accolades for her "*fiercely bright, commercial nous.*" The department specialises in unlocking offshore funds for its mostly non-UK-domiciled clients.

CHARLES RUSSELL (see firm details p.904) With a reputation for "*quality and courtesy,*" this firm remains a prime choice for the most complex trust structures, and both offshore and onshore advice. Observers agree that head of department **Catriona Syed** (see p.829) is "*on the ball, both intellectually and with clients.*" New additions to the table, **Michael MacFadyen** (see p.827) and the "*conscientious*" **Bart Peerless** (see p.828), both win acclaim from clients for their all-round skills and ability to communicate clearly. **David Long** (see p.826) continues to impress as one "*good at identifying the main point;*" he wins clients over with his "*cultured and quietly dynamic manner.*" Recent highlights have included acting for non-UK-based individuals, establishing asset-holding offshore structures for worldwide assets worth in excess of $750 million.

CURREY & CO At the opposite end of the spectrum from the corporate-focused private client teams sits this pre-eminent niche offering.

LONDON — TRUSTS & PERSONAL TAX

LEADING INDIVIDUALS

1
- GOWAR Martyn — Lawrence Graham
- HAYES Michael — Macfarlanes
- RHODES John — Macfarlanes

2
- BRIDGES Mark — Farrer & Co
- COOKE Stephen — Withers LLP
- MOYSE Richard — Boodle Hatfield
- POWELL Nicholas — Currey & Co
- STANFORD-TUCK Michael — Taylor Wessing
- WILLIS David — Forsters

3
- JARMAN Chris — Payne Hicks Beach
- MAURICE Clare — Allen & Overy
- REID Nigel — Linklaters
- RICHES John — Withers LLP
- STIBBARD Paul — Baker & McKenzie
- SYED Catriona — Charles Russell
- TURNOR Richard — Allen & Overy

4
- BLAKE-ROBERTS Philippa — Taylor Wessing
- CLUTTON Owen — Macfarlanes
- DOLMAN Robert — Wedlake Bell
- GARDNER Ceris — Allen & Overy
- GARNHAM Caroline — Simmons & Simmons
- GOODWIN Peter — Bircham Dyson Bell
- HALLAM Murray — Withers LLP
- HINE Andrew — Taylor Wessing
- JACOB Nicholas — Lawrence Graham
- PINTUS Matthew — Macfarlanes
- ROBINSON David — Forsters
- THOMPSON Tony — Withers LLP
- VOS Robin — Macfarlanes
- WHITFIELD Ann — Macfarlanes

5
- BROWN Graham — Payne Hicks Beach
- BRUCE-SMITH Keith — Harcus Sinclair
- BUZZONI Mark — Taylor Wessing
- FRYDENSON Henry — Berwin Leighton Paisner
- GOODMAN Dawn — Withers LLP
- HALL Brendan — Laytons
- JACOBS Michael — Nicholson Graham & Jones
- KENNEDY John — Hunters
- KIRBY Richard — Speechly Bircham
- LEWIS Michael — Finers Stephens Innocent
- LONG David — Charles Russell
- MACFADYEN Michael — Charles Russell
- MURDIE Alastair — Payne Hicks Beach
- OGILVIE Graham — Hunters
- PEERLESS Bart — Charles Russell
- PENNEY Andrew — Speechly Bircham
- RICHARDSON Joe — Dawsons
- WALSH Christopher — May, May & Merrimans
- YOUNG Andrew — Lawrence Graham

See individuals' profiles p.822

The firm has an outstanding reputation as a specialist adviser to its blue-blooded and often UK client base, and peers acknowledge that it is "*just superb — old-fashioned and heroically so.*" The "*civilised approach*" of its lawyers has created a low-key market profile. The "*straightforward and bright*" **Nicholas Powell** is the face of the firm – "*everyone thinks he is marvellous.*" In addition to the full range of advisory work, the firm is also active with heritage property trusts.

LAWRENCE GRAHAM (see firm details p.1031) International matters makes up 60% of this firm's workload and its thrust is very much towards global expansion. The practice is equally divided between direct instructions from multimillionaires and advising clients via private banks and trust companies. It possesses a "*market leader and key figure*" in **Martyn Gowar**, who is said to be "*extremely balanced in his opinions and intellectually brilliant.*" The recent high-profile acquisition of "*good brain*" **Nicholas Jacob** from Rooks Rider has been a coup for the firm. The "*charismatic*" and respected **Andrew Young** continues to head the private client team.

BOODLE HATFIELD (see firm details p.881) The firm has continued its steady growth, advising a wide range of private clients, trusts and charities on domestic and international projects. The "*intellectually outstanding*" **Richard Moyse** (see p.827) has won the admiration of his peers with his "*charisma and effective case management.*" The firm has a long-standing relationship with the Grosvenor estate and has played a substantial role in litigation surrounding the estate of Francis Bacon.

FARRER & CO (see firm details p.952) It is respected as the Queen's solicitors and seen by many sources as one of the pre-eminent London private client departments. It displays a depth of experience, catering for a good proportion of commercial clients as well as individuals in sports and the media. Much of its reputation derives from its longstanding work with the landed aristocracy. The "*dynamic, commercial and knowledgeable*" **Mark Bridges** (see p.823) heads the offshore side of the practice. The firm has a strong track record in the creation of tax-saving schemes and international structures to hold the assets of wealthy entrepreneurs.

FORSTERS (see firm details p.960) At the helm of these "*intelligent, serious players*" sits **David Robinson** (see p.828), respected in all quarters for his knowledge of complex trust structures. **David Willis** (see p.830), whose work centres on high net worth individuals, is described as a "*first-rate technical lawyer.*" The department's work includes creative capital gains tax (CGT) planning (sometimes using flip-flop schemes) and trust variations involving UK and offshore jurisdictions. The firm has recently advised trustees on a private company share sale and then restructured the trust. It also challenged the Inland Revenue on the conditions of taxation of chattels on behalf of clients.

SPEECHLY BIRCHAM (see firm details p.1141) "*Successful with a highly professional approach,*" this firm is seen by many as "*la crème de la crème.*" Its sometime reputation as a marketing and packaging machine for tax schemes is mistaken: 85% of the practice is bespoke work for individuals and of 31 fee-earners, only four work on these schemes. **Richard Kirby** (see p.826) heads the "*bright bunch*" now that star **John Avery Jones** has moved on to become a special commissioner. **Andrew Penney** (see p.828) ("*an experienced operator and commercially aware*"), has been recruited from the Rothschild Trust Corporation. The spread of work ranges from the ongoing restructuring of £100 million offshore trusts, including exporting a trust to New Zealand as a CGT 'wash' utilising a double tax treaty, to a particular involvement in taxation and trusts in the art world.

TAYLOR WESSING (see firm details p.1156) This straightforward department works closely with other practice areas in the firm, giving it a recognised "*broad base and a fine spread of people.*" Its "*lively*" head, **Philippa Blake-Roberts** (see p.822), "*understands issues quickly and can explain them to clients clearly.*" Clients find her "*absolutely superb on the international scene.*" **Michael Stanford-Tuck** (see p.829) ("*always good value*") is also commended for his work on international trust structures, while "*technical specialist*" **Andrew Hine** (see p.825) is dubbed "*honourable and user-friendly.*" **Mark Buzzoni** (see p.823) continues to draw respect from both peers and clients. The group deals with clients whose net worth reaches $6-7 billion dollars, and has expertise in cross-border work, bespoke investment structuring, intellectual property taxation and the intersection with matrimonial law. The firm's recent merger with German technology leader Wessing may indicate future growth in advising clients in the pan-European technology industry.

BAKER & MCKENZIE (see firm details p.855) Acknowledged as one of the market leaders in the field, this most international of firms is perceived to be less visible in the UK. The team has acted indirectly for the Government of Kuwait in ongoing litigation concerning offshore trust structures. It specialises in advising clients on cross-jurisdictional affairs and international concerns, in which area, it is judged by clients to have "*truly the best global private client capacity*" and by peers as possessing "*an absolutely cracking international client base.*" **Paul Stibbard** (see p.829), the head of department, holds the respect of the market.

BIRCHAM DYSON BELL (see firm details p.873) This expanding department has been gradually recruiting from RadcliffesLeBrasseur. It is respected, especially for its work in offshore trusts and the charity sector. The caseload here

TRUSTS & PERSONAL TAX ■ LONDON

includes contentious trusts and probate and heritage issues, while international succession projects and UK/US matters draw upon its substantial offshore practice. Members of the team of 11 partners recently advised on the restructuring of a group of Jersey settlements involving trust funds exceeding £30 million for an internationally based family. **Peter Goodwin** (see p.825) continues to be rated as "*an able and straightforward lawyer.*"

PAYNE HICKS BEACH (see firm details p.1097) The department has an emphasis on cross-border instructions, and continues to display strength in heritage matters and international trust litigation. The team also advises on and drafts terms for executorship and trustee services for major clearing banks. It has been instructed in the high-profile administration of the estate of the late Francis Bacon, the most highly-valued 20th-century artist in England. Possessed of "*good technical people and an in-depth experience of advising large and complicated families,*" the team is also commended for its long-standing commitment to the field. Former barrister, **Chris Jarman** (see p.826) is "*good with detail,*" while **Alastair Murdie** (see p.827) and head of department **Graham Brown** (see p.823) continue to be regarded as heavy-hitters in the firm.

BERWIN LEIGHTON PAISNER (see firm details p.866) Contentious trust and probate work forms one of this team's most respected planks. Founder and Chairman of the Association of Contentious Trusts and Probate Specialists, **Henry Frydenson**'s (see p.824) "*zeal earns him occasionally rueful recognition.*" He has recently drafted the merged pre-action protocol for the resolution of contentious trust and probate disputes, at the request of the Lord Chancellor's Department. The firm also practises tax investigation and planning for a majority of new money clients, with a respected offshore side to the practice. Its growing reputation for corporate tax and trust work complements that of its private client department.

HUNTERS (see firm details p.1006) This "*small, charming*" department specialises in landed estate work, in which field it is lauded as acting "*as a friend*" for 35 estates, both large and small. Heritage estate work is on the increase, and this portion of the practice is currently acting in around 20 cases. The offshore practice is also expanding, but the firm is noted primarily as being a traditional, UK-focused department. Senior Partner **John Kennedy** (see p.826) is esteemed as "*an old-style, tactful lawyer,*" while **Graham Ogilvie** (see p.828) "*doesn't waste time and always does the best for his clients.*"

LINKLATERS (see firm details p.1043) Endorsed for its "*meticulous*" approach, this small team is instructed by many non-UK-domiciled clients. Typical of its work is the assistance it provided in the reorganisation of a number of private trusts belonging to a European family on its relocation to France. The team has advised European organisations and individuals on setting up structured trusts in the UK. It also supports the firm's corporate practice, advising on trusts as part of commercial transactions. In addition the firm offers a traditional estate, probate and tax planning service for private clients, and also continues to advise charities. This "*boutique of high quality*" is led by the "*talented and pleasant*" Nigel Reid (see p.828).

MAY, MAY & MERRIMANS (see firm details p.1061) An "*impeccable blue-chip firm*" that specialises in private client work and within that category has a niche in trust creation, administration and restructuring for landed clients and in the related heritage estate work. It also offers probate and offshore expertise and often advises private companies. The practice is seen as "*careful and conscientious with a uniform standard of quality.*" **Christopher Walsh** (see p.830), who focuses on estate and financial planning and heritage property, is acclaimed for his "*sound judgement.*"

NICHOLSON GRAHAM & JONES (see firm details p.1083) The "*highly intelligent and experienced*" **Michael Jacobs** (see p.826) leads a team that has this year seen Eliza Mellor's move to a consultancy role. Recent work includes the major reorganisation of a life policy trust, capital gains tax planning for entrepreneurs' businesses and shares and the strategic review of offshore trusts worth a total of $100 million.

SIMMONS & SIMMONS (see firm details p.1136) The "*outstanding*" head of department, **Caroline Garnham** (see p.824), is respected for her "*smart ideas*" and strong presentation skills. Her practice includes working for banks on offshore trust schemes, advising on cross-border tax and succession matters and the reorganisation of family wealth structures in excess of £100 million. The group has also assisted in the development of tax products for institutions such as St James's Place. Contentious matters are handled in a dedicated litigation department.

WEDLAKE BELL (see firm details p.1182) The "*sound and sensible*" **Robert Dolman** (see p.824) is the recommended name in this practice. In addition to traditional estate and trust work for UK families, its ambit includes offshore trust litigation, private equity and unit trust creation worth £100 million. Offshore tax structuring for non-domiciliaries and overseas trust break-ups worth £25 million also feature in the workload.

DAWSONS (see firm details p.932) The practice is respected for its advice to wealthy landed estates, and it also has a matrimonial angle. The firm can boast "*quite a superb lawyer*" in **Joe Richardson** (see p.828), who is also rated by peers as "*thorough and learned.*" The department has become increasingly involved in advising on the tax aspects of company and business sales, and is receiving increasing instructions from entrepreneurs. It has formulated ways to enable clients to take advantage of the EIS Deferral Relief.

LEE & PEMBERTONS (see firm details p.1036) This firm, which underwent a demerger in 2000 has now acquired the private client team of Maples Teesdale, raising its tally by three partners. It handles tax planning, trust creation, administration and termination and probate matters. Senior partner and property specialist Julian Whately is the point of contact.

PEMBERTON GREENISH The other side of the demerger of Lee & Pembertons, here Andrew Stebbings leads a team of respected lawyers. Its practice focuses on London residential estates (it acts for the Cadogan Estate) and it also has an offshore operation advising on asset structures. In addition, the team boasts charity expertise. Peers and clients rate the firm's skills in handling property matters and traditional "*old money issues.*"

RADCLIFFESLEBRASSEUR (see firm details p.1107) Recommended to researchers as a "*traditional*" practice, the team is led by Clara Trounson. Its recent caseload includes advising on residency issues, capital gains tax liability and the creation of a charitable foundation.

ROOKS RIDER (see firm details p.1115) A firm of tax planning specialists, this "*superb practice*" is led by Chris Cooke. It advises on offshore trust and tax schemes such as schedule 4B schemes, performs reconstructions for non-domiciled assets and administrates family wealth, wills and probate matters. It has suffered a setback with the departure of well-known Nicholas Jacob to Lawrence Graham.

SMYTH BARKHAM A new addition to our rankings this year, this "*phenomenally good niche practice*" headed by Joyce Smyth and Caroline Barkham is known for representing high-profile entertainment stars. Best known for its tax structuring, the firm also undertakes all aspects of private client work, including litigation.

TROWERS & HAMLINS (see firm details p.1168) Its presence in the Gulf (half of its practice is overseas) ensures that this firm remains a presence in the marketplace. Luke Valner is head of this "*good, traditional*" department that has an increasing number of City clients on top of its usual old money base.

THE SOUTH — TRUSTS & PERSONAL TAX

OTHER NOTABLE PRACTITIONERS The prestigious **Keith Bruce-Smith** (see p.823) is rated by clients for his "*agile mind.*" He has this year decamped with colleagues from Withers and formed Harcus Sinclair; the market awaits the impact of this new firm. Newly recruited by Laytons, **Brendan Hall** (see p.825) has for some time been regarded as a top name in contentious trust and probate. At Finers Stephens Innocent, **Michael Lewis** (see p.826) is rated by clients as "*conscientious with good tax knowledge,*" and his practice caters for some high-profile artistic clients.

THE SOUTH

TRUSTS & PERSONAL TAX — THE SOUTH

1
- **Cripps Harries Hall** Tunbridge Wells

2
- **Adams & Remers** Lewes
- **Penningtons** Godalming
- **Stevens & Bolton** Guildford
- **Thomas Eggar** Chichester
- **Thomson Snell & Passmore** Tunbridge Wells

3
- **Blake Lapthorn** Portsmouth
- **Charles Russell** Guildford
- **Lester Aldridge** Bournemouth
- **Moore & Blatch** Lymington
- **Mundays** Cobham
- **Paris Smith & Randall** Southampton
- **White & Bowker** Winchester

4
- **Barlows** Guildford
- **Brachers** Maidstone

5
- **DMH** Brighton
- **George Ide, Phillips** Chichester
- **Godwins** Winchester
- **Griffith Smith** Brighton
- **Rawlison Butler** Crawley
- **Whitehead Monckton** Maidstone

LEADING INDIVIDUALS

1
- **LENEY Simon** Cripps Harries Hall
- **ROGERSON Gary** Cripps Harries Hall

2
- **ACOMB Nick** Stevens & Bolton
- **BROWN Simon** Thomson Snell & Passmore
- **FELLINGHAM Michael** Penningtons
- **GLAZIER Barry** Lester Aldridge
- **KING-JONES Amanda** Thomas Eggar
- **THORNELY Richard** Thomas Eggar
- **THURSTON Martyn** White & Bowker
- **WALLEY Ray** Mundays

This book is the product of 6,582 1/2 hour interviews. See p.7 for BMRB audit. Within each band, firms are listed alphabetically. See individuals' profiles p.822

CRIPPS HARRIES HALL (see firm details p.922) Judged as deserving of their "*top-tier*" rating, peers agree that this is "*a sound crew – it's a relief to see them on a deal.*" Its range is essentially domestic, and it has recently demerged its investment management arm. Head of department **Simon Leney** (see p.826) is widely esteemed, while **Gary Rogerson** is "*knowledgeable technically and academically.*" Discernibly high levels of growth have led to ongoing recruitment. The team's tax caseload is primarily inheritance-based, but it also advises on capital gains tax for owner-managers.

ADAMS & REMERS The department advises on both onshore and offshore work and has an expanding company commercial department acting for wealthy business people, alongside its traditional landed estates practice. The contact partner for trusts and personal tax at this respected firm is Paul Ardagh.

PENNINGTONS (see firm details p.1098) A reputation for consistently high-quality advice pushes this firm up the ranks this year. Its presence in London as well as in this Godalming office certainly adds to its clout. The widely acclaimed **Michael Fellingham** (see p.61) is the head of department and he is recognised as "*extremely practical and fiercely clever.*" Its traditional agricultural tax and trusts practice has been bolstered by new recruits.

STEVENS & BOLTON (see firm details p.1149) This expanding team is on the ascendancy as "*Surrey's premier private client practice.*" "*Tax-oriented*" **Nick Acomb** (see p.822) has impressed peers across the region. Most of the work undertaken by the firm comes from the business community and commercial institutions, including a recent instruction from an offshore trust company concerning assets of over £100 million. The practice also offers tax and trust planning such as flip-flop schemes and employee benefit trust work.

THOMAS EGGAR (see firm details p.1160) "*Intellectually switched-on,*" the firm is commended for its deep pool of talented lawyers. "*Level-headed, thoughtful*" **Richard Thornely** (see p.829) heads the department, which also includes the respected **Amanda King-Jones** (see p.826). The ten partners cover all the usual gamut of private client services, plus employee incentive schemes, international matters, contentious probate and estates and in-house investment advice. It also has a large tax and trust administration department with over 1,000 ongoing briefs.

THOMSON SNELL & PASSMORE (see firm details p.1161) The esteemed James Krafft has retired, but the practice has not diminished in its market profile. Providing onshore and offshore advice, estate administration, probate and tax planning, this firm is viewed as holding "*a confident place in the market and moving in the right direction.*" It also has the beginnings of a charities service. **Simon Brown** (see p.823), who specialises in capital tax planning, draws particular admiration for having "*a good understanding of the needs of private clients.*"

BLAKE LAPTHORN (see firm details p.877) This low-key operation continues to be "*pretty highly rated in the market,*" and is recognised as a competitor by many of its peers for its work, which centres on wills, probate and property issues. Michael Profit is the contact partner for private client instructions.

CHARLES RUSSELL (see firm details p.904) Certainly not hindered by its London sister's leading reputation, this Guildford branch has a low-key but well-respected presence in the area. Its services include estate planning, offshore trusts, wills and probate, deeds of variation and intestacy, trust and fiduciary disputes, trust formation and administration, tax planning and Court of Protection work. London partner David Long heads this team. Services provided include private capital (asset) management, estate planning, domicile and residence, offshore trusts, wills and probate, and deeds of variation and intestacy.

LESTER ALDRIDGE (see firm details p.1038) Peers are impressed that this firm has "*Bournemouth pretty well sewn up.*" Traditional in its approach, the firm advises on repatriation issues surrounding offshore trusts and the preparation of a tax saving scheme for terminally ill clients. Head of department **Barry Glazier** (see p.824) is well regarded in the local region.

MOORE & BLATCH (see firm details p.1074) The firm's services incorporate tax planning, probate and the creation, administration and breaking of trusts. Its fund management division has been demerged and is no longer part of the practice. David Rule leads the team, which has a strong track record in handling wealth management and tax and inheritance planning for its strong local client base.

MUNDAYS (see firm details p.1078) This small but highly regarded practice fields the respected **Ray Walley**. It offers offshore expertise amongst a range of services, including property and retirement relief and the creation of charitable trusts.

PARIS SMITH & RANDALL (see firm details p.1093) Crispin Jameson leads a team that advis-

815

TRUSTS & PERSONAL TAX ■ THAMES VALLEY

...es on tax planning, trust guidance and administration and Court of Protection work. Advice to Lottery winners is combined with its mix of old and new money clients. In addition, the team specialises in advising people who have been affected by unreliable tax avoidance schemes.

WHITE & BOWKER The firm offers a range of advisory work, as well as expertise with issues concerning the elderly. Observers claim it has "*the best client list in Winchester*" and a strong reputation on the agricultural angle. Head of department **Martyn Thurston** (see p.829) has "*a good pedigree*." The firm has had success of late in winning substantial new clients.

OTHER NOTABLE FIRMS Barlows continues to impress rivals as a small, "*decent*" firm worthy of referrals. **Brachers** has a well-valued department that has recently been involved in a leading test case on flip-flop schemes. **George Ide, Phillips** has a growing reputation among some top players. A new addition to the tables, "*traditional*" **Rawlison Butler** has a good name in this field.

DMH's commitment to the private client field has been reinforced with three new lawyers added to the team in the past year. The small department at **Godwins** is another new name in this table following commendation for its performance mostly on UK trusts. **Griffith Smith** is a "*good example of a good high-street firm*" that can offer "*all the traditional services you would expect*," while **Whitehead Monckton** was recommended for its involvement in this field.

THAMES VALLEY

TRUSTS & PERSONAL TAX
■ THAMES VALLEY

1. **Boodle Hatfield** Oxford
2. **Blandy & Blandy** Reading
   Boyes Turner Reading
   Henmans Oxford
   Iliffes Booth Bennett (IBB) Uxbridge
3. **BP Collins** Gerrards Cross
   Matthew Arnold & Baldwin Watford
4. **Pictons** Hemel Hempstead
5. **Stanley Tee** Bishop's Stortford

LEADING INDIVIDUALS
1. **LAING Sue** Boodle Hatfield
   WILKIN Ashley Boyes Turner

This book is the product of 6,582 1/2 hour interviews. See p.7 for BMRB audit. Within each band, firms are listed alphabetically. See individuals' profiles p.822

BOODLE HATFIELD (see firm details p.881) Spending a good proportion of her time in the London office, the fine **Sue Laing** (see p.826) brings the sophistication of the City to the Thames Valley. This office, which deals with the same complex international work and private client tax planning as its London sister, has a considerable reputation in the region. It acts for a large national and international client base, including landed estates and wealthy individuals.

BLANDY & BLANDY (see firm details p.878) Graham Benwell is the point of contact at this firm, which has a long-standing reputation in the private client field. It deals with tax compliance, trusts, wills, probate, and estate planning. Court of Protection work and enduring powers of attorney matters also feature in the caseload for a clientele that ranges from owner-managers to old money.

BOYES TURNER (see firm details p.883) The department has had a successful year and witnessed a high level of growth. It fields "*brilliant solutions man*" **Ashley Wilkin** (see p.830) who is described by a client as "*in a class of his own: proactive and used for the most complex of matters*," and rated by peers as "*full of energy and ideas*." The team has recently been involved in the establishment of private trusts for the disabled and worked on the Oli Bennett Trust in the wake of September 11th. It has also given seminars and advised a number of Lottery winners.

HENMANS (see firm details p.990) The firm has an impressive presence in the region. Zandra Houston heads this department, which offers the full panorama of largely onshore advice, including a dedicated contentious trust and probate practice. The team specialises in advising on the placing of personal injury and clinical negligence awards into trusts.

ILIFFES BOOTH BENNETT (IBB) (see firm details p.1007) The rising team is "*good at the high stuff*." Led by Gillian Murray, it covers general estate planning, probate, tax and trust work. An area of particular focus is on provision for the elderly and disabled through discretionary trusts and enduring powers of attorney. The team is instructed by a client base of estates, individuals and institutions.

BP COLLINS (see firm details p.884) Observers admired the firm's old money client base, and recommended the expanding practice for its "*charming manner.*" Its core focus is on discretionary, employee benefit and pension trusts and trusts structured for the disabled and charitable organisations. Inheritance and capital gains tax planning is also an area of expertise. The probate team dealt with 100 estates last year and the work often involved a foreign element. Court of Protection matters and litigation are on the increase for the team, which is headed by David Wilkinson.

MATTHEW ARNOLD & BALDWIN (see firm details p.1058) This low-profile firm has some eminent clients who rate its service as "*first class.*" Head of department Iain Donaldson and the team were praised by clients as proffering "*a different level of expertise from anyone else.*" The team handles a healthy stream of instructions from corporate and commercial clients, in addition to landed estate work. It has developed a niche in emergency practical assistance, called upon when there is a business to run or assets to protect during a crisis.

OTHER NOTABLE FIRMS At **Pictons**, Elizabeth Harrold leads a team that advises local business people, commercial clients and sporting celebrities. **Stanley Tee** continues to complement its strong agricultural practice with work in this arena.

SOUTH WEST

TRUSTS & PERSONAL TAX
SOUTH WEST

1
- Burges Salmon Bristol
- Wilsons Salisbury

2
- Osborne Clarke Bristol
- Wiggin & Co Cheltenham

3
- Bond Pearce Plymouth
- Charles Russell Cheltenham

4
- Clarke Willmott & Clarke Bristol
- Foot Anstey Sargent Plymouth
- Hooper & Wollen Torquay
- Veale Wasbrough Bristol

5
- Coodes St Austell
- Michelmores Exeter
- Rickerbys Cheltenham
- TLT Solicitors Bristol

LEADING INDIVIDUALS

1
- FITZGERALD Peter Wilsons
- MITCHELL Martin Burges Salmon
- WYLD Charles Burges Salmon

2
- BIRD David TLT Solicitors
- EMMERSON John Wilsons
- EVANS Michael Burges Salmon
- FULLERLOVE Michael Wiggin & Co
- MILLER Adrian Foot Anstey Sargent
- NICHOLSON Jonathan Bond Pearce
- WOLLEN Nigel Hooper & Wollen

3
- BROWN Sandra Osborne Clarke
- NELLIST Peter Clarke Willmott & Clarke
- VOREMBERG Rhoderick Wilsons

This book is the product of 6,582 1/2 hour interviews. See p.7 for BMRB audit.
Within each band, firms are listed alphabetically. See individuals' profiles p.822

BURGES SALMON (see firm details p.894) Peers believe that its "*cracking agricultural unit provides a great level of personal trusts and tax work*," although the private client team is rated for far more than traditional UK work: the offshore and international practice is also warmly commended. In addition, the firm advises executives on tax planning matters. Highlights of the past year include an application to the High Court for the variation of a complex £25 million family trust, and the formation of a family OEIC as the bespoke investment vehicle for a wealthy client. A trinity of outstanding lawyers raises it above other firms. **Charles Wyld** (see p.830) is head of the trusts and personal tax department and is hailed for his "*thorough mastery of technical issues.*" "*Elder statesman*" **Martin Mitchell** (see p.824) is "*a true specialist, and a robust opponent.*" "*Innovative*" **Michael Evans** (see p.824) has used his "*dry sense of humour, prudence and good technical skills*" to secure a following. The firm has been involved in substantial tax planning matters for its landed estates client base, including pool arrangements and offshore structures.

WILSONS (see firm details p.1191) City lawyers acknowledge that the firm's "*capabilities are far beyond what you would expect of a regional outfit,*" while its "*high-calibre*" lawyers keep it one of the most visible firms nationally. It enjoys "*strong roots in the landed gentry*" with a substantial landed estate, heritage and farming client base. The team also has a flourishing overseas tax planning practice. The possessor of "*integrity, gravitas and long experience,*" **Peter Fitzgerald** (see p.61), is also "*proactive and good with clients.*" "*Marvellous*" **John Emmerson** is credited by some peers and clients for growing the firm's profile, while **Roddy Voremberg** (see p.829), who focuses on landed estates, is "*a thorough lawyer, good with the complexities.*"

OSBORNE CLARKE (see firm details p.1090) This "*highly organised*" unit "*offers quality advice*" to its prestigious client list. It is recognised by interviewees as having a strong corporate/commercial bearing, and in particular, the department places an emphasis on tax planning for technology and communications entrepreneurs. Its skill in creating offshore structures is also commended. **Sandra Brown** is head of the department, which has recently advised trustees on the implications of the flotation of Marlborough Stirling and associated tax mitigation arrangements.

WIGGIN & CO (see firm details p.1186) The firm is renowned for its international work – 50% of its clients are derived from overseas, with a particular concentration of Americans. It offers the full range of tax and financial asset planning, trust work and litigation. "*Safe pair of hands*" **Michael Fullerlove** (see p.824) is "*quiet and analytical.*" He is praised for his commercial outlook and familiarity with offshore tax structures.

BOND PEARCE (see firm details p.879) This firm has a strong presence with its offices throughout the South and South West. The "*active*" head of department in Plymouth, **Jonathan Nicholson** (see p.131), has impressed with his "*breadth of knowledge.*" In addition to offering advice on the core areas of tax planning and wills, the firm specialises in substantial probates and corporate/commercial support, for institutions and high net worth individuals.

CHARLES RUSSELL (see firm details p.904) The Cheltenham office holds its "*strong profile*" and caters for a majority of landed clients, the business community and retired individuals. Christopher Page leads the respected team, which advises on VAT issues, tax structuring, inheritance and succession planning matters.

CLARKE WILLMOTT & CLARKE (see firm details p.907) The firm has a holistic approach, which combines legal and financial advice on issues such as annuities, property relief claims and inheritance income. **Peter Nellist** (see p.827), who has a particular interest in pensions, is recognised for his "*financial services expertise.*"

FOOT ANSTEY SARGENT (see firm details p.958) The firm's range of clients encompasses shareholders, business people and farmers. Its work includes tax planning, fund management and court of protection work, often approaching the sector from a company commercial angle. Sources valued the depth of experience offered by **Adrian Miller** (see p.827).

HOOPER & WOLLEN (see firm details p.1001) **Nigel Wollen** retains the market's approbation. The practice is engaged in the establishment of trusts for high net worth individuals, inheritance tax planning and landed estate work. It has seen an increasing amount of business with regard to charitable trusts.

VEALE WASBROUGH (see firm details p.1174) Clients enjoy instructing this firm, finding that "*they are able to apply their good knowledge of the field to our personal requirements.*" Mary McCartney is the head of department, which deals with mostly entrepreneurial clients and some landed estates. Its recent work has spanned the administration of 150 trusts, contentious probate and tax planning matters. The firm has also organised seminars for wealthy individuals and has advised on inheritance and capital gains tax issues.

OTHER NOTABLE FIRMS Coodes operates from several different offices, with the bulk of the work at St Austell, while head of department, David James, is based at Liskeard. Its work is split among trusts, probate and Court of Protection matters. At TLT, the "*reliable and up-to-date*" **David Bird** (see p.822) is highly valued for his "*good technical knowledge and practical approach.*" **Rickerbys** maintains its reputation this year, while **Michelmores** is an active member of the local market.

TRUSTS & PERSONAL TAX ■ WALES

WALES

TRUSTS & PERSONAL TAX
■ WALES

1 Edwards Geldard Cardiff
 Hugh James Cardiff
2 Margraves Llandrindod Wells

LEADING INDIVIDUALS

1 MARGRAVE-JONES Clive *Margraves*
2 WRIGHT Cherry *Hugh James*
3 WILLIAMS Sian *Edwards Geldard*

This book is the product of 6,582 1/2 hour interviews. See p.7 for BMRB audit.
Within each band, firms are listed alphabetically. See individuals' profiles p.822

EDWARDS GELDARD (see firm details p.944) This established local offering has 37 lottery winners on its books. Partner **Sian Williams'** (see p.830) "*empathetic*" bedside manner is praiseworthy: she "*doesn't just receive instructions; she actually gives caring advice.*" The department focuses on wills and inheritance tax planning for the wealthy and is heavily involved in the charities sector.

HUGH JAMES (see firm details p.1004) This firm has particular expertise in probate matters: it is currently advising on the systems to cover probate for over 7,000 deceased injured miners and their widows. In addition it advises on the structuring of tax planning, offshore trusts and employee benefit trusts. **Cherry Wright** (see p.830) is the respected head of department.

MARGRAVES **Clive Margrave-Jones** is the sole principal at this specialist trusts and personal tax outfit that "*goes well beyond the boundaries.*" 90% of its work is in this field, acting for a range of clients from substantial landowners to entrepreneurs. Recent work at this firm has included three rare strict settlements. Of Margrave-Jones, peers have claimed that "*people either use his precedence or have been taught by him – his skills are really worth mining.*"

MIDLANDS

TRUSTS & PERSONAL TAX
■ MIDLANDS

1 Martineau Johnson Birmingham
2 Browne Jacobson Nottingham
 Hewitson Becke + Shaw Northampton
 Lodders Stratford-upon-Avon
3 Higgs & Sons Brierley Hill
 Lee Crowder Birmingham
 Pinsent Curtis Biddle Birmingham
 Wragge & Co Birmingham
4 freethcartwright Nottingham
 Gateley Wareing Birmingham
 Shakespeares Birmingham

LEADING INDIVIDUALS

1 CARSLAKE Hugh *Martineau Johnson*
 COLACICCHI Clare *Hewitson Becke + Shaw*
 HANSELL Matthew *Martineau Johnson*
 LEEK Robert *Higgs & Sons*
 THOMPSON Wenna *Browne Jacobson*
2 COLACICCHI William *Browne Jacobson*
 GREEN Martin *Lodders*
 KERR Drummond *Lee Crowder*
 PALLISTER Stephen *Pinsent Curtis Biddle*
 ASSOCIATES TO WATCH
 WORWOOD Lucy *Browne Jacobson*

This book is the product of 6,582 1/2 hour interviews. See p.7 for BMRB audit.
Within each band, firms are listed alphabetically. See individuals' profiles p.822

MARTINEAU JOHNSON (see firm details p.1056) The clear market leader in the Midlands, thanks to its "*strength in depth, size and experience.*" It caters for a range of clients and enjoys a national profile. Recent highlights include the team's advice on the purchase of a £2.5 million offshore trust interest in order to obtain property for inheritance tax purposes. It has also advised on the use of home loan structures and discretionary trusts, Melville schemes, Section 4B tax planning for offshore trusts, and planning to wash out Section 87 chargeable gains in offshore trusts. **Matthew Hansell** (see p.825), head of department, is widely respected for his user-friendly approach and great technical skill, while **Hugh Carslake** (see p.823), ecclesiastical specialist, uses his "*sound judgement*" to good effect.

BROWNE JACOBSON (see firm details p.891) The department aims at the top end of the market, offering onshore and offshore advice. Its client base includes a number of lottery winners, landed estates, trustees and entrepreneurs. The well-known **William Colacicchi** (see p.823), newly acquired from Putsman.wlc, is "*building matters up*" and leads an "*innovative department,*" which has successfully managed the effects of Paul Jenkins' retirement. **Wenna Thompson** (see p.829) remains a respected member of this leading team.

HEWITSON BECKE + SHAW (see firm details p.993) This "*sophisticated*" practice handles mostly trust matters – especially for non-residents – and large landed estates. Recent instructions have included advice on maintenance funds and conditional exemptions. The team has also acted for clients whose wealth derives from both public and private company investment as well as agricultural or commercial property. The big draw here is **Clare Colacicchi** (see p.823), national deputy head of the Society of Trusts and Estates Practitioners. Observers agree that her technical prowess is backed up by a "*sensible manner borne from experience.*"

LODDERS (see firm details p.1044) The firm is thriving under "*safe pair of hands*" **Martin Green** (see p.825), whom interviewees credit as having "*built a big department from scratch.*" His expertise is in tax and financial planning. The group also offers advice on trusts administration and contentious matters and has a stable presence in the charities sector. A respected team offers financial advice. Green's "*all-round ability and technical knowledge*" typify the depth of talent at this firm.

HIGGS & SONS This "*small offering*" maintains a positive reputation throughout the region. "*Knowledgeable main man*" **Robert Leek** (see p.826) is on top of current trends in the sector and much respected for his technical skill. The firm handles discretionary, accumulation and maintenance lifetime trusts for clients including non-UK domiciliaries. Inheritance tax and capital gains tax planning also feature in the workload, as do deeds of variation.

LEE CROWDER (see firm details p.1035) This expanding group has won the respect of its peers for its increasing involvement in tax planning. A recent highlight was giving specialist tax advice to a major investment house and assisting it in the development of a unique offshore capital gains tax-saving financial product. **Drummond Kerr** (see p.826) is widely viewed as a "*sound and sensible lawyer.*"

PINSENT CURTIS BIDDLE (see firm details p.1102) Not quite viewed as a traditional private client practice, its focus is well rounded and has a corporate bent, advising technology clients and entrepreneurs on employee benefits, option schemes and corporate tax schemes. The group also advises on core trusts and tax matters. It recently provided estate planning advice to a family-owned trust possessing 75% of a publicly quoted media company. Clients and peers applaud the quality of service from both head of department **Stephen Pallister** (see p.828) ("*a good brain and knows his tax law well*") and the team.

WRAGGE & CO (see firm details p.1197) The firm is respected for its "*depth of knowledge*" and is acknowledged by peers to still be "*a force to be reckoned with*" despite the retirement of its

818   INDEX TO LEADING LAWYERS: PAGE 1693 ■ IN-HOUSE LAWYERS PROFILES: PAGE 1201

EAST ANGLIA/NORTH WEST ■ TRUSTS & PERSONAL TAX

previous head of department, Louise Woodhead. Gary Barber has taken on the role, and his team includes consultant Julie Fox. It is a traditional trust, tax and probate practice that also acts for charity and corporate trust matters. Recent work has included advising a bank in settling its trust deeds on the surrender of its banking licence. It has also been instructed on the establishment of a family trust to hold the majority of shares in a national company and in the trusts administration.

OTHER NOTABLE FIRMS A new team at **Gateley Wareing**, under Adrian Mabe (formerly of Lee Crowder), is establishing "*an important presence and a force to watch.*" **Shakespeares**, headed by Claire Laird, maintains its reputation for trusts management. At **freethcartwright**, Nigel Cullen heads a department that manages about 200 trusts.

EAST ANGLIA

TRUSTS & PERSONAL TAX — EAST ANGLIA

1 Mills & Reeve Norwich
2 Hewitson Becke + Shaw Cambridge
Taylor Vinters Cambridge
3 Greene & Greene Bury St Edmunds
Howes Percival Norwich
4 Cozens-Hardy & Jewson Norwich
Prettys Ipswich
Roythorne & Co Spalding
5 Ashton Graham Bury St Edmunds, Ipswich
Hood Vores & Allwood Dereham
Willcox & Lewis Norwich

LEADING INDIVIDUALS

1 RIPMAN Justin Mills & Reeve
2 BARCLAY Jonathan Mills & Reeve
FURNIVALL Peter Mills & Reeve
HEAL Jeremy Howes Percival
3 ALSTON Suzanne Greene & Greene
BRADLEY David Hewitson Becke + Shaw
EWART Peter Hewitson Becke + Shaw
HORWOOD-SMART Adrian Taylor Vinters

This book is the product of 6,582 1/2 hour interviews. See p.7 for BMRB audit. Within each band, firms are listed alphabetically. See individuals' profiles p.822

MILLS & REEVE (see firm details p.1071) A national reputation exists for this firm as a "*fine country estates practice*" attaining consistently "*high standards.*" It enjoys "*strength of numbers and deep experience.*" In addition to its range of trusts administration and probate matters, it advises on complex reorganisations of offshore trust structures and non-resident trusts. Although its clients tend to be landed estate owners, it also offers strategic tax advice to business people and other high net worth individuals. The head of department is the "*intelligent and able*" Justin Ripman (see p.828), and among those commanding respect are Peter Furnivall (see p.824) ("*first-class*") and Jonathan Barclay (see p.822).

HEWITSON BECKE + SHAW (see firm details p.993) The quality of advice at this firm has kept pace with its growth. It continues to work in conjunction with the Northampton office and under the leadership of Peter Ewart (see p.824) offers a similarly broad service. Its client base is drawn from the hi-tech and life sciences sector, landed estates and the local business community. David Bradley's (see p.823) experience continues to draw recommendation and the team not only advises on trust structuring and administration in the UK but also has offshore and international experience.

TAYLOR VINTERS (see firm details p.1156) The firm handles trusts and tax planning, wills and charity-related work. Contentious matters are a source of instruction, and the firm has recently been involved in business asset taper relief. Observers held it to be especially strong on work with an agricultural flavour, although many of its clients are entrepreneurs and economic migrants from London. Interviewees agree that "*experienced*" Adrian Horwood-Smart (see p.61) is "*clued-up on the agricultural interface*" with this sector.

GREENE & GREENE The firm has more than doubled its tax turnover in recent years and is successfully attracting new money clients, on top of its strong agricultural base. For some clients, this is the prime choice, especially for "*more sophisticated tax planning.*" Recent work has included offshore, setting up EMI and EIF schemes and advising on contentious investigations. The team has also helped trustees with the Trustee Act 2000 and drafted discretionary, accumulation and maintenance trusts. Head of the department Suzanne Alston (see p.822) is "*prompt, clear and thorough,*" and particularly respected for her handling of complex tax structures.

HOWES PERCIVAL (see firm details p.1003) The offering here is a comprehensive service of tax planning, investment and trust creation and management. Probate and estate administration is also a forte. The "*technically able*" practice acts mainly for landowners, particularly on issues of development land. Peers rate Jeremy Heal (see p.825), head of department, as "*clever and helpful.*"

OTHER NOTABLE FIRMS Cozens-Hardy & Jewson is judged to be a "*sensible practice.*" Under the leadership of Alistair Sursham, it has recently experienced an influx of professional clients on top of its landed gentry base. **Hood Vores & Allwood** retains its presence in the market. **Prettys** continues to be seen as a sound choice, with Carol Lockett leading a team that has a number of agricultural clients and a niche in French estate planning. In the heart of the Fens, Graham England heads a successful agriculturally orientated practice at **Roythorne & Co**. In Ipswich, David Hughes and the team at **Ashton Graham** are considered one of the best for contentious probate. The firm has offices in Ipswich and Bury St Edmunds and continues to be visible in the sector. **Willcox & Lewis** is repected in the offshore world as a "*niche practice*" handling sophisticated tax planning "*for a great client list of high net worth individuals.*"

NORTH WEST

HALLIWELL LANDAU (see firm details p.982) The redoubtable Geoffrey Shindler (see p.829) is "*the best-known name in Manchester,*" and his presence guarantees the firm a "*cracking*" profile. Possessed of "*more energy than five people put together,*" he is "*stunningly good*" on complex tax structuring matters. This is one of two firms nominated to advise high net worth individuals through St James's Place. It has also assisted Barclay's Bank with trust matters and continues to provide a range of estate planning services.

ADDLESHAW BOOTH & CO (see firm details p.838) This department maintains a strong presence, enjoying a degree of national recognition. This "*highly competent team*" is led across the North by Paul Howell, while peers have acknowledged its growth and commitment to this area. Instructions here range from landed estate work, tax planning for entrepreneurs and to assist the firm's respected corporate client base.

www.ChambersandPartners.com

TRUSTS & PERSONAL TAX ■ NORTH EAST

TRUSTS & PERSONAL TAX
■ NORTH WEST

1
- Halliwell Landau *Manchester*

2
- Addleshaw Booth & Co *Manchester*
- Birch Cullimore *Chester*
- Brabners Chaffe Street *Liverpool*
- Cuff Roberts *Liverpool*

3
- Cobbetts *Manchester*
- Pannone & Partners *Manchester*

LEADING INDIVIDUALS

1
- SHINDLER Geoffrey *Halliwell Landau*

2
- BISHOP David *David Bishop & Co*
- FEENY Mark *Brabners Chaffe Street*
- MASON Carol *Cuff Roberts*
- TAYLOR Philip *Bullivant Jones*

This book is the product of 6,582 1/2 hour interviews. See p.7 for BMRB audit. Within each band, firms are listed alphabetically. See individuals' profiles p.822

BIRCH CULLIMORE Over 200 years in existence, this department has a loyal following within its niche in Chester and North Wales. Headed by David Mason, it specialises in landed estates work and administers many family and charitable trusts. Probate matters also feature heavily.

BRABNERS CHAFFE STREET (see firm details p.885) The firm's merger with Chaffe Street has extended its geographical presence to the Manchester market. Mark Feeny (see p.824) is a pre-eminent figure in the tax market; he and the team act for owner-managed businesses, landed estates and old money clients. The firm has advised on chattels planning and reorganising estates to maximise inheritance tax relief on agricultural property, including profit-sharing arrangements.

CUFF ROBERTS Much of the firm's profile rests on the shoulders of Carol Mason, who also gives investment advice to a respected private client base. The team advises on the preparation and administration of trusts and foreign estates, wills and probate matters and inheritance tax planning.

OTHER NOTABLE PRACTITIONERS David Bishop (see p.822) at David Bishop & Co is said to be "*a good technician*" with a niche in pension-related trust work. At Bullivant Jones, Philip Taylor (see p.829) is held in high regard by peers. Cobbetts is reckoned to be a "*sound*" choice. It handles offshore as well as onshore matters, probate, trust creation and administration and personal estate planning, especially for owner-managers. The contact partner is Kathryn Graham. Also in Manchester, Pannone & Partners retains a healthy share of the market.

NORTH EAST

TRUSTS & PERSONAL TAX
■ NORTH EAST

1
- Dickinson Dees *Newcastle upon Tyne*
- Wrigleys *Leeds*

2
- Addleshaw Booth & Co *Leeds*

3
- Pinsent Curtis Biddle *Leeds*

4
- Andrew M Jackson *Hull*
- Grays *York*
- Irwin Mitchell *Sheffield*
- Lupton Fawcett *Leeds*
- Rollits *Hull*
- Ward Hadaway *Newcastle upon Tyne*

5
- Brooke North *Leeds*
- Gordons Cranswick Solicitors *Leeds*

LEADING INDIVIDUALS

1
- LYALL George *Dickinson Dees*
- WRIGLEY Matthew *Wrigleys*

2
- BINKS Nigel *Pinsent Curtis Biddle*
- CHADWICK Peter *Wrigleys*
- DICKINSON Alexander *Dickinson Dees*
- EATON John *Lupton Fawcett*
- HOWELL Paul *Addleshaw Booth & Co*

This book is the product of 6,582 1/2 hour interviews. See p.7 for BMRB audit. Within each band, firms are listed alphabetically. See individuals' profiles p.822

DICKINSON DEES (see firm details p.938) Blessed with "*high-quality staff and a fantastic client base*," the firm is thought to have "*an absolutely iron grip on big tracts of the North East and into Yorkshire.*" It draws national praise for its work on multidisciplinary trusts and personal tax. The much respected, "*competent and highly qualified*" George Lyall (see p.827) is head of the expanding team, which includes the highly respected Alexander Dickinson (see p.824) – a "*sensible private client lawyer whose sound judgement we trust.*" The firm makes considerable use of its other departments in providing a well-rounded service, encompassing capital gains tax planning, trust creation and administration, often with an offshore element, and property issues.

WRIGLEYS (see firm details p.1199) A clear leader, this firm wins national acclaim. Enjoying an "*excellent client base,*" peers acknowledge that it is "*growing like you wouldn't believe.*" The team is best known for its work with old money clients and charities. Clients rate its "*good rapport and clear correspondence.*" Recent highlights have included advising on inheritance tax home loan schemes and washing out stockpile gains in offshore trusts. Among the "*senior generation of stars*" whom the firm's younger lawyers have yet to supersede are Matthew Wrigley (see p.830), a "*class act*" who specialises in tax planning, and Peter Chadwick (see p.823), joint head of department. The team as a whole was commended in particular by London firms.

ADDLESHAW BOOTH & CO (see firm details p.838) The Leeds-based team is judged by sources to be an "*experienced and well-established outfit.*" The firm handles multimillion pound trusts and large estates as well as clients with corporate or entrepreneurial links. Work over the past year included obtaining a court order to vary a trust worth approximately £300-400 million, in order to update and modify its provisions. Peers are particularly envious of its "*fantastic*" client base. Paul Howell (see p.825) is said to be especially "*knowledgeable on tax planning*" and manages this and the Manchester-based unit.

PINSENT CURTIS BIDDLE (see firm details p.1102) As with the Birmingham offering, this is a practice with a definite corporate and commercial slant that advises estate owners, private banks and trust companies. Under the "*talented*" Nigel Binks (see p.822), recent matters have included advising an entrepreneurial client on his emigration to Jersey, restructuring onshore and offshore trusts and general inheritance and estate planning.

OTHER NOTABLE FIRMS In Hull, Andrew M. Jackson offers a range of services and sustains a respectable reputation, especially where agricultural matters are concerned. Grays in York is known for its charities practice, which crosses over into trusts and personal tax. The Sheffield office of Irwin Mitchell has a reasonable presence, and its Court of Protection work remains a particular forte. John Eaton at Lupton Fawcett in Leeds is well known for his investment management work. The firm undertakes financial planning together with personal tax. In Hull, Rollits is an "*up and coming*" smaller player, with an old money client base. Ward Hadaway in Newcastle has a quality practice with some enviable clients. Brooke North and Gordons Cranswick both received warm recommendation during our research.

SCOTLAND

TRUSTS & PERSONAL TAX
SCOTLAND

1 Turcan Connell *Edinburgh*
2 Maclay Murray & Spens *Glasgow*
3 Anderson Strathern WS *Edinburgh*
   Brodies *Edinburgh*
   MacRoberts *Glasgow*
   Morton Fraser, Solicitors *Edinburgh*
   Murray Beith Murray WS *Edinburgh*
   Tods Murray WS *Edinburgh*
4 Balfour & Manson *Edinburgh*
   Ledingham Chalmers *Aberdeen*
   Pagan Osborne *Cupar*
   Wright, Johnston & Mackenzie *Glasgow*

LEADING INDIVIDUALS

1 BIGGAR John *Tods Murray WS*
   MACKINTOSH Simon *Turcan Connell*
   MACROBERT David *MacRoberts*
   RAE Scott *Morton Fraser, Solicitors*
   STUBBS Ian *Maclay Murray & Spens*
2 CONNELL Douglas *Turcan Connell*
   DALGLEISH Andrew *Brodies*
   FULTON Robin *Turcan Connell*
   HENDERSON Colin *Anderson Strathern WS*
   PAGAN Bill *Pagan Osborne*

This book is the product of 6,582 1/2 hour interviews. See p.7 for BMRB audit.
Within each band, firms are listed alphabetically. See individuals' profiles p.822

TURCAN CONNELL (see firm details p.1170) Ahead of the chasing pack, the firm remains the leader in Scotland in terms of its size and expertise. It has over 20,000 trusts in hand. It also has a special heritage interest in advising the owners of over 150 historic properties. In addition, it advises on tax structuring and has recently been advising on the use of limited liability partnerships for overseas tax planning. Among this deep pool of talent sit **Simon Mackintosh** (see p.131), who is highly renowned for his "*intellectual abilities,*" while **Douglas Connell** (see p.129) is "*a mover and shaker*" and **Robin Fulton** (see p.824) is respected for his "*sharp intellect.*"

MACLAY MURRAY & SPENS (see firm details p.1048) Following its recruitment of the private client team at McGrigor Donald, the size of this highly recommended department has doubled. **Ian Stubbs** (see p.829), who is a chartered accountant as well as a solicitor, is rated for his "*common sense and practical approach;*" he is said to typify the team's commitment to technical excellence. The firm's workload includes estate planning, asset protection and the creation and administration of family, discretionary and charitable trusts.

ANDERSON STRATHERN WS (see firm details p.844) Peers are "*full of respect*" for this practice, which is particularly associated with its fine landed estates client base. It advises on litigation, trusts creation, administration and variation and succession planning. The team has advised on the variation of a trust for tax planning purposes and given tax advice to clients wishing to bring trusts to the UK from overseas. Peers agree that **Colin Henderson** (see p.825) is a "*great performer*" on complex tax matters.

BRODIES (see firm details p.889) A "*good, solid team*" that has a reputation for serving landed estates, but also advises general clients through financial advisers. **Andrew Dalgleish** (see p.823) ("*incredibly thorough*") has a broad specialism in estate planning and taxation. The team is also skilled in the preparation of wills, trusts administration and inheritance planning.

MACROBERTS (see firm details p.1049) Although smaller than its main competitors, this department has "*controlled its high level of quality well.*" Observers singled out **David MacRobert** (see p.827) for his strong technical abilities and long-standing experience in this sector. The practice has developed a focus on the provision of tax mitigation advice and it has been instructed by a number of company directors and shareholders of late.

MORTON FRASER, SOLICITORS (see firm details p.1077) Clients say they are "*extremely satisfied*" with the level-headed advice of this Edinburgh firm. **Scott Rae** (see p.828), who is seen specialising in trust matters, is praised as "*highly involved – he has won the respect of many.*" The firm operates both a traditional estate planning practice and a commercially linked service, advising bank trustee departments, IFAs and other law firms. It specialises in multi-jurisdictional issues, offers litigation advice and has over 200 trusts under its administration. Recent work includes a referral from an English law firm to advise on a protective trust for a Scottish family, following a large damages award in the US courts.

MURRAY BEITH MURRAY WS (see firm details p.1079) A long-standing presence in this sector and involvement with investment management secures this firm its reputation. Mark Stewart and the team advise on estate planning, trust management and tax compliance issues.

TODS MURRAY WS (see firm details p.1164) **John Biggar** (see p.822) continues to attract endorsement for his "*outstanding technical skills.*" The team this year bolstered its presence with the addition of a further partner. It advises on the creation and administration of trusts and general asset protection planning. The firm's client base includes landowners and farmers and high net worth individuals in the drawn from the local business community.

OTHER NOTABLE FIRMS Balfour & Manson has impressed its peers with its "*hard-working*" approach to the sector. Ledingham Chalmers retains a healthy presence in the Aberdeen market. In Cupar, the "*innovative*" Pagan Osborne attracts considerable instructions thanks to **Bill Pagan**, who "*belies the fact that he is in a non-central firm – he could hold his own with anybody.*" Wright, Johnston & Mackenzie is endorsed as a young, successful team.

NORTHERN IRELAND

TRUSTS & PERSONAL TAX
■ NORTHERN IRELAND

1 Cleaver Fulton Rankin Belfast
L'Estrange & Brett Belfast
2 C & J Black Belfast

LEADING INDIVIDUALS

1 HEWITT Alan L'Estrange & Brett
RANKIN Alastair Cleaver Fulton Rankin
2 MCCAW Elma C & J Black

This book is the product of 6,582 1/2 hour interviews. See p.7 for BMRB audit.
Within each band, firms are listed alphabetically. See individuals' profiles p.822

CLEAVER FULTON RANKIN (see firm details p.910) This first-class practice is led by the "*knowledgeable, calm and efficient*" Alastair Rankin (see p.828). It has seen an increase in trust work this year and its focus is mainly on discretionary trusts and general inheritance tax advice for an entrepreneurial client base.

L'ESTRANGE & BRETT (see firm details p.1039) Alongside Cleaver Fulton & Rankin, this firm clearly stands at the top of the market. At its foundations sit old money and charitable trust-related clients and it also advises Lotto winners and directors and shareholders of corporate clients. The "*conscientious*" head of department Alan Hewitt (see p.825), who is also seen in general company/commercial work, is "*one of a dying breed of experts – not gimmicky or flashy – someone with whom you can feel at ease.*"

C & J BLACK Elma McCaw (see p.827) is the respected head of the private client team, which has experience of inheritance tax planning, trusts creation and deeds of variation.

THE LEADERS IN TRUSTS & PERSONAL TAX

ACOMB, Nick
Stevens & Bolton, Guildford
(01483) 302264
nick.acomb@stevens-bolton.co.uk
Specialisation: Tax and trusts including offshore tax planning, tax planning for foreign domiciles, inheritance tax, capital gains tax, employee benefit trusts and employee share schemes, trust law advice to trustees.
Prof. Memberships: Law Society, Society of Trust and Estate Practitioners (STEP).
Career: Articles *Clifford Turner* 1982-84, solicitor tax department *Clifford Turner* (*Clifford Chance*) 1984-91, solicitor *Stevens and Bolton* 1991-92, partner *Stevens and Bolton* 1992 to date.
Personal: Education: Bramcote Hills Grammar School (Nottingham); Birmingham University LLB (Hons); Guildford College of Law (2nd class honours). Family: Married with two boys; lives in Guildford.

ALSTON, Suzanne
Greene & Greene, Bury St Edmunds
(01284) 762211
suzannealston@greene-greene.com
Specialisation: Retained directly by individual and corporate clients as well as on a consultancy basis by accountants and other professionals. Expertise and recent instructions include: capital tax and estate planning for individuals including tax planning through the incorporated and unincorporated business, business and agricultural reliefs, and inheritance tax; acting for management teams and shareholders on capital tax reduction strategies prior to sale, EIS deferral relief advice to entrepreneurs; Inland Revenue Special Compliance Division enquiries for executors where fraud was suspected; tax advice on professional negligence; repatriation of offshore investments post 1998 Finance Act.
Prof. Memberships: Law Society (President of Local Branch 2001-02); Associate of the Chartered Institute of Taxation 1996; Society of Trust and Estate Practitioners (Chairman of local branch 1996-97).

BARCLAY, Jonathan
Mills & Reeve, Norwich
(01603) 693211
jonathan.barclay@mills-reeve.com
Specialisation: Specialises in tax and estate planning with particular emphasis on trust and tax issues affecting landed estates.
Career: Articled *Whithers*, qualified 1971; partner *Mills & Reeve* 1976; managing partner 1987-90; chairman *Norton Rose* M5 Group 1990-94; senior partner 1995 to date. Other appointments director *Jarrold & Sons Ltd*; Invest East of England; Chairman Norwich Area Development Agency Ltd; Theatre Royal (Norwich) Trust Ltd; Britten Sinfonia Ltd.
Personal: Born 1947; resides Norfolk.

BIGGAR, John
Tods Murray WS, Edinburgh
(0131) 226 4771
john.biggar@todsmurray.com
Specialisation: Wills; tax and asset protection planning; trusts, formation and administration; probate; personal financial planning.
Prof. Memberships: Society of Trust and Estate Practitioners; Society for Computers and Law; Law Management Section; WS Society; Fellow of the Chartered Management Institute.
Career: Articled *Murray Beith & Murray* 1973-75; admitted solicitor 1975; assistant solicitor *Murray Beith & Murray* 1975-77; admitted *WS* 1976; partner *Murray Beith & Murray* 1977-91; partner *Tods Murray* 1991; managing partner 1998-date.
Publications: Co-author 'Drafting Wills in Scotland' (Butterworths 1994); occasional professional magazine contributions.
Personal: Oundle School; University of Edinburgh. Family; golf; music; married; four sons.

BINKS, Nigel
Pinsent Curtis Biddle, Leeds
(0113) 244 5000
nigel.binks@pinsents.com
Specialisation: Wide experience of tax and trust work with particular expertise in capital gains tax and inheritance tax planning for entrepreneurs and owner-managed businesses and estate planning, trusts and offshore structures.
Prof. Memberships: STEP.
Career: Born 1951. Educated at Repton School and Trinity College, Cambridge. Qualified in 1976. Partner in *Simpson Curtis* (now *Pinsent Curtis Biddle*) in 1978. Consultant with *Pinsent Curtis Biddle* from 1995.
Personal: Leisure interests include golf and skiing.

BIRD, David
TLT Solicitors, Bristol
(0117) 917 7866
dbird@TLTsolicitors.com
Specialisation: Tax and estate planning, specifically inheritance tax and capital gains tax planning for business clients, creating and advising on trusts and trust law, advising on taxation of group companies and VAT and stamp duty issues. Working alongside corporate finance team in drafting and negotiating the tax elements of documentation for business and share disposals.
Prof. Memberships: Fellow of the Chartered Insurance Institute; Associate of the Chartered Institute of Taxation; Chairman of Bristol Law Society Tax and Trusts Technical Committee.
Career: *Wilsons*, 1992-96; *Osborne Clarke*, 1996-98; *TLT* (formerly *Lawrence Tucketts*), 1998-present.
Personal: Interests include golf, cricket and football (spectator only).

BISHOP, David
David Bishop & Co, Liverpool
(01704) 878421
David_Bishop@compuserve.com
Specialisation: Main areas of specialisation are trusts and tax planning for individuals and private companies including offshore arrangements; all aspects of occupational pensions and charities. Notary Public.
Prof. Memberships: Law Society; chairman, Liverpool Branch Society of Trust and Estate Practitioners 1991-99; International Tax Planning Association; Association of Pension Lawyers.
Career: Qualified 1972. Partner *Laces & Co* (now *Berrymans Lace Mawer*) 1974. Head of private client department 1995-2000. 2000 principal, *David Bishop & Co*.
Personal: Born 6 April 1947. Educated Sedbergh School 1960-65, Caius College, Cambridge 1966-69. Lives in Formby.

BLAKE-ROBERTS, Philippa
Taylor Wessing, London
(020) 7300 7000
p.blake-roberts@taylorwessing.com
Specialisation: Non-solicitor and Head of *Taylor Wessing's* UK Private Client Department. Advises offshore and onshore trustees and individuals on tax planning and the preservation of wealth, particularly through the use of trusts and bespoke investment structures. Legal specialisations: private client – tusts and estates; tax – international; bespoke investment structures for trustees and individuals; the Family Office.
Prof. Memberships: Society of Trust and Estate Practitioners (Vice-President); Society of Authors.
Career: Joined *Parker Garrett & Co* in May 1978. Specialises in onshore and offshore trust and estate planning; bespoke investment structures and the Family Office, Deputy-Chairman Society of Trust and Estate Practitioners 1997-98, Chairman 1998-2000. Current Directorships: MT Fund Management Limited; Alta Advisers Limited; Society of Trust and Estate Practitioners; Medici Investments Limited; Townleigh Farm Limited; Ovenden Nominees Limited' Norby Investments Limited.
Personal: University of Wales (BA Hons); Trust and Estate Practitioner (TEP). In addition to being editor and co-author of 'Know-How for Trust and Estate Practitioners' (FT Law & Tax) Philippa has published four novels: 'Mzungu's Wife' and 'Looking Out' (both Bodley Head/Coronet), 'Waiting for the Sea to be Blue' and 'Heat of the Moment' (Orion). Another novel is on its way.

THE LEADERS ■ TRUSTS & PERSONAL TAX

BRADLEY, David
Hewitson Becke + Shaw, Cambridge
(01223) 461155
davidbradley@hewitsons.com
Specialisation: Probate, trusts, tax, charities.
Prof. Memberships: Law Society; STEP (past chairman Cambridge branch); Charity Law Association.
Career: Articles *Payne Hicks Beach*; admitted 1972; joined *Wild Hewitson & Shaw* now *Hewitson Becke + Shaw* 1975, partner 1977.
Personal: Kings School, Ely; Christ's College Cambridge (language/law). Married with three children. Leisure interests – garden, natural history, France.

BRIDGES, Mark
Farrer & Co, London
(020) 7242 2022
mtb@farrer.co.uk
Specialisation: Partner, head of international private client team. Handles tax and trust matters, particularly for non-domiciled and non-resident individuals.
Prof. Memberships: Law Society, Member of STAR Group, Trust Law committee, IBA, ITPA and STEP.
Career: Joined *Farrer & Co* in 1978. Qualified in 1980, became a partner in 1985. Solicitor to the Duchy of Lancaster 1998. Private Solicitor to HM The Queen 2002.
Personal: Born 25 July 1954. Educated at Cambridge University 1973-77. Special trustee of University College Hospital Charities. Treasurer of Bach Choir 1992-97. Governor of the Purcell School and of Sherborne School for girls. Treasurer of Music In Country Churches. Council member of Royal School of Church Music 1989-97. Recreations include sailing and music. Lives in London and Suffolk.

BROWN, Graham
Payne Hicks Beach, London
(020) 7465 4300
gbrown@paynehicksbeach.co.uk
Specialisation: Senior partner, and Head of Tax and Trust Department. Areas of practice include legal and fiscal advice to shareholders and boards of family and other private companies; landed estates and heritage property; international trusts, probates and family property; charities and educational institutions; French property and succession. Delivered papers on charities and non-profit organisations, trusts and estates at international conferences in London, Paris, Amsterdam, Munich and Taipei.
Prof. Memberships: Associate of Institute of Taxation in Ireland; sometime member of Law Society's Revenue Law Committee Capital Taxes Sub-Committee and of Law Society's Working Party on the Financial Services Act, Committee of Holborn Law Society; member: International Fiscal Association, Franco-British Lawyers' Association.
Personal: Born 1944. Educated at Bristol University (LLB, 1966), Catholic University of Louvain (Diploma, 1970), and King's College, London (LLM, 1975). Leisure interests include arts, heritage and music. Fellow of the Royal Society of Arts; Liveryman Clockmakers' Company. Lives in Bath.

BROWN, Sandra
Osborne Clarke, Bristol
(0117) 917 3000

BROWN, Simon
Thomson Snell & Passmore, Tunbridge Wells
(01892) 510000
sbrown@ts-p.co.uk
Specialisation: Personal tax planning, wills and onshore and offshore trusts.
Prof. Memberships: The Law Society; The Society of Trust and Estate Practitioners (ex-Chairman of the Kent Branch).
Career: 1982-87, *Stephenson Harwood*; 1988-89, *Boodle Hatfield*; 1989 to date *Thomson Snell & Passmore* (Partner).
Personal: Bradfield College, Oxford University (MA in Jurisprudence) and College of Law, Guildford, qualified solicitor. Interests include sport, travel and music. Married with three daughters.

BRUCE-SMITH, Keith
Harcus Sinclair, London
(020) 7583 7353
keith.bruce-smith@harcus-sinclair.co.uk
Specialisation: Private client trust and tax law with particular emphasis on capital tax planning for wealthy UK and foreign individuals and their families.
Prof. Memberships: Society of Trust and Estate Practitioners.
Career: Qualified December 1978. Assistant Solicitor (*Withers*) 1978-82; Partner (*Withers*) 1983-2001; Partner (*Harcus Sinclair*) 2002 to date
Publications: Co-author 'Practical Will Precedents' (Sweet & Maxwell); co-author 'Practical Trust Precedents' (Sweet & Maxwell); original co-editor 'International Trust Precedents' (Sweet & Maxwell).
Personal: Born 1953. Education Oundle School and Christ Church Oxford (MA (Hons) Modern History). Married with two daughters. Colonel in Territorial Army. Leisure: tennis and swimming

BUZZONI, Mark
Taylor Wessing, London
(020) 7300 4222
m.buzzoni@taylorwessing.com
Specialisation: Partner in *Taylor Wessing's* UK Private Client Department, Mark specialises in trust and tax planning advice and has wide experience of advising an international client base. Acting for individuals and their families, clients will usually have personal connections with more than one country. Main areas of work: advice in relation to the law and administration of trusts, whether or not the trustees, or family members, have significant connections with the UK; tax planning and mitigation for individuals and trustees; co-ordinating taxation advice in different countries where appropriate; structuring inward investment from overseas; implementing, or co-ordinating the implementation of, tax-driven restructuring or reorganisations.
Prof. Memberships: Chartered Institute of Taxation, STEP.
Career: Head of Private Client at *Baileys Shaw & Gillett* 1986-93; Tax Partner *Alexanders* 1994-99; Private Client.Tax Partner *Taylor Joynson Garrett* 2000.
Personal: Kings College Wimbledon and Bristol University. Married with three demanding daughters.

CARSLAKE, Hugh
Martineau Johnson, Birmingham
(0121) 678 1486
hugh.carslake@martjohn.com
Specialisation: Main area of practice covers tax planning, trusts and estate planning and ecclesiastical law. Acts for the owners of landed estates and private individuals in their personal and trustee capacities. Registrar for and legal advisor to the Diocese of Birmingham.
Prof. Memberships: Law Society, STEP. Ecclesiastical Law Association (ELA).
Career: Qualified in 1973, having joined *Martineau Johnson* in 1972. Became a partner in 1974, Notary Public in 1981, head of private client department in 1991 and Diocesan Registrar in 1992.
Personal: Born 15 November 1946. Attended Rugby School, 1960-65, then Trinity College, Dublin, 1966-70. Chairman of the Barber Institute of Fine Arts (University of Birmingham); Trustee of the Worcester Cathedral Appeal Trust. Leisure interests include family, music and gardening. Lives in Warwickshire.

CHADWICK, Peter
Wrigleys, Leeds
(0113) 244 6100
peter.chadwick@wrigleys.co.uk
Specialisation: Over 20 years specialising in trusts and estate planning, probate and wills, landed estates and charity law.
Prof. Memberships: Law Society, CLA, Charity Law Association.
Personal: Born 1951. Educated Oundle School and Newcastle-upon-Tyne University. Trustee various charities.

CLUTTON, Owen
Macfarlanes, London
(020) 7831 9222

COLACICCHI, Clare
Hewitson Becke + Shaw, Northampton
(01604) 233233
clarecolacicchi@hewitsons.com
Specialisation: Specialises in advice to individuals and trustees on estate planning, in particular as to the use of trusts with a view to alleviating capital taxation and advice to non-UK domiciliaries and non-UK residents.
Prof. Memberships: Deputy Chairman of the Society of Trust and Estate Practitioners. Member of Charity Law Association.
Career: Qualified 1983. *Macfarlanes* 1981-89. Joined *Hewitson Becke + Shaw* 1989. Became a partner in 1990.
Personal: Born 3 August 1958. Attended Somerville College, Oxford.

COLACICCHI, William
Browne Jacobson, Nottingham
(0115) 976 6281
wcolacicchi@brownej.co.uk
Specialisation: Specialising in private client work and charity law with particular emphasis on UK and offshore trust and tax planning, succession planning for businesses and landed estates and advising charity trustees on all aspects of charity law.
Prof. Memberships: STEP.
Career: Articled with *Colombotti & Partners* 1982; assistant solicitor at *Willcox Lane Clutterbuck* 1985, made partner 1987, Head of Private Client 1990, senior partner 1997; moved to *Browne Jacobson* 2002, appointed Head of Tax and Financial Planning Department.
Personal: Trustee of the Leadership Trust Foundation and Baron Davenport Foundation. Married with three children. Educated College of Law, Exeter University, Ampleforth College.

CONNELL, Douglas
Turcan Connell, Edinburgh
(0131) 228 8111
dac@turcanconnell.com
See under Charities, p.129

COOKE, Stephen
Withers LLP, London
(020) 7597 6062
stephen.cooke@withersworldwide.com
Specialisation: Principal in Private Client Department. Main area of practice is tax and asset management planning for the private client, both in the UK and offshore. Speaker at seminars on a wide range of trust, tax and related issues.
Prof. Memberships: City of London Law Society, International Fiscal Association, Society of Trust and Estate Practitioners.
Career: Qualified in 1971, having articled with *Clay Allison & Clark*, Nottinghamshire. Awarded the Law Society SH Clay prize. Joined *Withers* in 1971; partner in 1973.
Publications: Contributor to 'Tax Cases Analysis' and co-author of 'Inheritance Tax on Lifetime Gifts' (1987).
Personal: Born 30 July 1946. Attended Stamford School 1956-64 and Leicester School of Architecture. Chairman of the London Handel Society Ltd. Leisure interests include art, music, cricket, gardening and tennis. Lives in Well, Basingstoke.

DALGLEISH, Andrew
Brodies, Edinburgh
(0131) 228 3777
andrew.dalgleish@brodies.co.uk
Specialisation: Main areas of practice are capital tax planning, trusts (private client, commercial and public), wills and executries.
Prof. Memberships: Law Society of Scotland, Society of Trust and Estate Practitioners, Association of Pension Lawyers (associate); fellow of the Society of

TRUSTS & PERSONAL TAX ■ THE LEADERS

Advanced Legal Studies.
Career: Qualified 1975. Partner at *Brodies* since 1978.
Publications: Co-author Barr Biggar Dalgleish and Stevens, 'Drafting Wills in Scotland'; contributor to *Withers* 'International Trust Precedents'; Lawrence, 'International Personal Tax Planning Encyclopaedia'; Norrie & Scobbie, 'Trusts'; and George, 'International Charitable Giving'.
Personal: Born in 1951, resides in Edinburgh.

DICKINSON, Alexander
Dickinson Dees, Newcastle upon Tyne
(0191) 279 9615
alexander.dickinson@dickinson-dees.com
Specialisation: Partner in private client department advising wealthy individuals and their families across the UK, but particularly in the North of England, London and the home counties. Particular emphasis on capital taxation, heritage property, maintenance funds, trusts, wills and probates. Acts mainly for individuals with significant property interests (landed estates, commercial and residential portfolios) and entrepreneurs.
Prof. Memberships: Law Society; Society of Trust and Estates Practitioner.
Career: Qualified 1989. Joined *Dickinson Dees* in 1993 and appointed partner in 1997.
Personal: Born 1964 and lives in Northumberland. Keen sportsman and follower of Leeds United. School Governor and Charity Trustee. Travels extensively when time permits.

DOLMAN, Robert
Wedlake Bell, London
(020) 7395 3000
rdolman@wedlakebell.com
Specialisation: Specialises principally in private client personal tax and trusts both in UK and offshore.
Prof. Memberships: Law Society: STAR group.
Personal: Born 15 October 1945. Educated at Felsted and Oxford University. Chairman of Family Assurance Society. Chairman of the Jesters Club. Lives in West Sussex. Interests are court games and theatre.

EATON, John
Lupton Fawcett, Leeds
(0113) 280 2000

EMMERSON, John
Wilsons, Salisbury
(01722) 412412

EVANS, Michael
Burges Salmon, Bristol
(0117) 939 2249
michael.evans@burges-salmon.com
Specialisation: Head of international tax and trust unit, focusing on international work for both UK and non-UK based clients. Recent work includes: trust structures for South American clients; reviewing standard trust documentation for a major US bank for use by their customers worldwide; advice to private banks on UK and overseas real estate holding structures; tax and estate planning for substantial international families; advice on cross-transfer share schemes; capital gains tax planning for owner managers on company sales, including offshore trust schemes and non-residence.
Prof. Memberships: Law Society, STEP (member of International Committee).
Career: Joined *Burges Salmon* as a trainee in 1990 and became a partner in Tax and Trusts in 1999.
Personal: University of Bristol 1986-89. Enjoys golf and cricket.

EWART, Peter
Hewitson Becke + Shaw, Cambridge
(01223) 461155
peterewart@hewitsons.com
Prof. Memberships: Society of Trust & Estate Practitioners. Charity Law Association.

FEENY, Mark
Brabners Chaffe Street, Liverpool
(0151) 600 3000
mark.feeny@brabnerscs.com
Specialisation: Head of Probate and Trust Department. Deals with trusts, estate and tax planning and contentious probate and related matters.
Prof. Memberships: Law Society. Liverpool Law Society. Society of Trust and Estate Practitioners.
Career: Qualified in 1981. Partner 1983.
Personal: Chairman Merseyside branch STEP, Vice President of Liverpool Law Society. Deputy Sheriff for Counties of Merseyside, Lancashire and Greater Manchester. Born 16 October 1955.

FELLINGHAM, Michael
Penningtons, Godalming
(01483) 791800
fellinghammb@penningtons.co.uk
See under Agriculture, p.61

FITZGERALD, Peter R
Wilsons, Salisbury
(01722) 412412
See under Agriculture, p.61

FRYDENSON, Henry
Berwin Leighton Paisner, London
(020) 7427 1324
henry.frydenson@blplaw.com
Specialisation: Contentious trusts and probate and contentious tax matters. Multimillion pound probate dispute taken through to trial; undertaking complicated variation of trusts application; resolving by ADR complex matter turning on the decisions in Re Benham and Re Ratcliffe.
Prof. Memberships: Chairman Association of Contentious Trusts and Probate Specialists; member Society of Trusts and Estate Practitioners (STEP); member Medico-legal Society; member Charity Law Association; member Probate Section Law Society; Freeman of the City of London; member Public Guardianship Consultative Forum; chairman, PGO Standards Monitoring Subcommittee; member Trusts Law Committee.
Career: LLB, UCL (1978); partner *Paisner & Co* (1984); founder and chairman of the Association of Contentious Trusts and Probate Specialists (1987).
Publications: Chapter on contentious probate in the Law Society's 'Probate Practitioner's Handbook'; 'Trusts and Estates Law Journal' (September 2001 and January 2002); 'Solicitor's Journal' (18 August 2001); 'New Law Journal' (21 June 2002). Lectures widely on tax, trust and probate matters to practitioners and delivers law and ethics lectures at various hospitals for the UK Resuscitation Council.
Personal: Married with family. Interests include reading and chairing the Local Voluntary Ambulance First Aid Organisation.

FULLERLOVE, Michael
Wiggin & Co, Cheltenham
(01242) 224114
Specialisation: Private client work for high net worth individuals, both in the UK and elsewhere. A large part of his practice involves international asset and tax structuring on work inbound and outbound to and from the USA.
Prof. Memberships: The Law Society; International Tax Planning Association; STEP.
Career: University of Birmingham – LLB; Magdalen College, Oxford – BCL. Articles and assistant solicitor: *Freshfields*, City of London.
Personal: Born 1948. Gardening, genealogy and alpaca breeding.

FULTON, Robin
Turcan Connell, Edinburgh
(0131) 228 8111
rdf@turcanconnell.com
Specialisation: Partner. Specialist areas taxation, trusts and estates, partnerships and charity law.
Prof. Memberships: Qualified Solicitor Scotland 1979. Law Society of Scotland and Society of Writers to HM Signet. STEP.
Career: *Shepherd & Wedderburn*; qualified 1979; assistant solicitor 1979-82, partner 1982-99; partner *Turcan Connell WS* 1999. Senior tutor in wills, trusts and executries, Edinburgh University Diploma in Legal Education. Tutor GGSL/WS Society Professional Competency Course and regular contributor to courses run by the Law Society of Scotland, WS Society and others. Former member of Law Society of Scotland Revenue Committee. Accredited Specialist in Trust Law.
Publications: Scottish Editor 'Sergeant & Sims on Stamp Duties' 'Foster's Inheritance Tax' and 'Simon's Inheritance Tax'.
Personal: Born 1956; resides Edinburgh. Interests include sport generally but particularly squash, tennis, golf and skiing.

FURNIVALL, Peter
Mills & Reeve, Norwich
(01603) 660155
peter.furnivall@mills-reeve.com
Specialisation: Trusts and tax planning for shareholders and businessmen, UK and foreign domiciled, and for institutional industries.
Prof. Memberships: Law Society and STEP.
Career: Qualified 1981; *Rowe & Maw* 1978-84; *Mills & Reeve* 1984 to date, Partner.
Personal: Born 1954. Married with two daughters and lives in Norfolk.

GARDNER, Ceris
Allen & Overy, London
(020) 7330 3000
ceris.gardner@allenovery.com
Specialisation: Partner. Areas of expertise include tax and estate planning, advising UK and non-UK domiciled individuals, families, estates and trusts. Wide experience of advising banks and trust companies in relation to trust matters and advising on the use of trusts in a commercial context. Regularly advises on a wide range of issues affecting charities and gives advice to educational and non-profit organisations of every kind. Wide experience advising on immigration matters.
Prof. Memberships: IBA; Society of Trust and Estate Practitioners; Charity Law Association; European Association for Planned Giving and Immigration Law Practitioners Association.
Career: Assistant *Allen & Overy* (1988-91), Partner (1991). Director, First Combined Trust.
Personal: University of London (BA Hons Russian/German 1975).

GARNHAM, Caroline
Simmons & Simmons, London
(020) 7628 2020
caroline.garnham@simmons-simmons.com
Specialisation: Partner and head of the private capital, family office, and private banking group, providing a dedicated service to the high net worth client and the institutions which advise them. Wide experience of international and domestic tax and estate planning for private clients. Advises wealthy entrepreneurs, family offices and private banks.
Prof. Memberships: Awarded Fellowship of the Chartered Institute of Tax for thesis on tax planning for non-UK domiciliaries investing in commercial property. Member of the Technical Committee and the International Committee of the Society of Trusts and Estate Practitioners ('STEP'). Member of the editorial boards of Butterworths' 'Offshore Cases and Tax Havens' publication and STEP's publication of 'Wills and Trust Law Reports' published by Legalease Limited.
Career: BSc Exeter University. Solicitor, qualified in 1981.
Publications: Regular contributor to national newspapers, in particular the 'Financial Times', on trust and tax matters.

GLAZIER, Barry
Lester Aldridge, Bournemouth
(01202) 786 186
barry.glazier@lester-aldridge.co.uk
Specialisation: Trusts, tax and wills team leader. Corporate and personal tax, par-

ticularly for family-owned businesses, as well as landed estates, onshore and off-shore trusts, and charities. Managing partner 1994-2000.
Prof. Memberships: Articled *Penningtons*, London; qualified 1966; solicitor *Clifford Turner* 1966-71; partner *Lester Aldridge* since 1972; president of Dorset Chamber of Commerce and Industry 1992-93, president Bournemouth and Dorset District Law Society 1991-92; director and company secretary, Dorset Training and Enterprise Council 1989-2001; chairman of Eurolegal 1991-95; chairman of Hurstpierpoint Lawyers Society.
Personal: Born 1941; resides Wimborne Minster. Educated at Hurstpierpoint College (1950-60); St Peter's College, Oxford (1960-63 BA, 1968 MA Oxon); Notary Public. Recreations include concerts and opera, piano playing, walking, ornithology, gardening.

GOODMAN, Dawn
Withers LLP, London
(020) 7597 6014
dawn.goodman@withersworldwide.com
Specialisation: Head of Contentious Trust and Probate Group. Principal specialising in international and domestic trust litigation and contentious probate and succession; charity litigation. Major cases include Lemos v Coutts & Co 1992-93 CILR 460 (Cayman Islands); Hambro v Duke of Marlborough [1994] Ch158 (England); Bridge Trust Co Ltd v Attorney General 1996 CILR 52 (1997) 1 OFLR787 (Cayman Islands); T Choithram International & Ors v Pagarani [2001] 2 All ER 495 (British Virgin Islands).
Prof. Memberships: STEP; ACTAPS; Charity Law Association.
Career: Chester and Guildford Colleges of Law; joined *Withers* 1987; Partner at *Withers* 1989.
Publications: Co-author (with Brandon Hall) 'Probate Disputes and Remedies'. Contributor to Tolley's 'Administration of Trusts' and 'Administration of Onshore and Offshore Trusts'; contributor to 'Probate Practitioners Handbook'.
Personal: Married with three children. Interests are being with her children; opera; architecture; theatre; walking.

GOODWIN, Peter
Bircham Dyson Bell, London
(020) 7227 7000
petergoodwin@bdb-law.co.uk
Specialisation: Estate planning for UK families and non-UK domiciliaries; advice on UK and non-UK trusts.
Prof. Memberships: Law Society; Westminster Law Society; STAR Group; STEP.
Career: Qualified as solicitor (1968). Partner: *Freshfields* (1974-90). Partner: *Bircham Dyson Bell* (then *Bircham & Co*) (1990 to date).
Personal: Born October 1943. Shrewsbury School (1957-62). Worcester College, Oxford (1962-65). Member of Committee of 1930 Fund for District Nurses.

GOWAR, Martyn
Lawrence Graham, London
(020) 7379 0000

GREEN, Martin
Lodders, Stratford-upon-Avon
(01789) 293259
martin.green@lodders.co.uk
Specialisation: Trusts and tax planning with a special interest in all personal financial planning issues. A trustee of a large number of private and charitable trusts and has advised the elderly in connection with funding of care costs.
Prof. Memberships: Law Society Capital Taxes Sub-Committee (former chair of Birmingham Revenue Law Committee Birmingham Law Society); STEP. Associate member Securities Institute. A panel member of the PGO.
Career: Articled *Pinsent & Co* (later *Pinsent Curtis Biddle*) 1978-80. Partner in Private Client department of *Pinsent & Co* 1984-85. Partner in charge of Private Client department *Lodders* January 1986 to present day.
Publications: In the past contributed to CTT 'News and Reports' and articles in the 'Law Society Gazette'.
Personal: Married with four children. Interested in tennis, table tennis, golf and the countryside. Educated Cheltenham College and Birmingham University.

HALL, Brendan JC
Laytons, London
(020) 7842 8000
brendan.hall@laytons.com
Specialisation: As well as a range of non-contentious work, particularly expertise in will disputes, IH claims, trust variations, Order 85 and Court of Protection applications.
Prof. Memberships: STEP (London General Branch Committee), ACTAPS, Law Society.
Career: Qualified 1984. Partner *Wedlake Saint* 1988-2001. Partner *Laytons* 2001.
Publications: Tolley's 'Administration of Estates', 'Know-How for Trust and Estate Practitioners' (1995), 'Probate Disputes and Remedies' (1997).
Personal: Born 1958. Educated at Rendcomb College, Cirencester and Birmingham University (LLB). Resides London.

HALLAM, Murray
Withers LLP, London
(020) 7597 6000
murray.hallam@withersworldwide.com
Specialisation: Principal in the Private Client Department, specialising in trust and tax planning for the private client, partnership law, heritage property and charity law.
Prof. Memberships: Westminster Law Society, Society of Trusts & Estates Practitioners (STEP), Charity Law Association, The Fletchers Livery Company, The Historic Houses Association, The Hellenic Society.
Career: Articled at *Withers*. Qualified in 1970. Partner in 1977.
Publications: Co-author of 'Practical Trusts Precedents', 'Practical Will Precedents' and 'International Trust Precedents'. Contributor to 'Practical Tax Planning with Precedents'. Lectures on trusts and wills and charity matters.
Personal: Born 1946 and resides in London. Interests include theatre, classical civilisation, chess, cricket and tennis.

HANSELL, Matthew
Martineau Johnson, Birmingham
(0121) 678 1504
matthew.hansell@martjohn.com
Specialisation: Private client solicitor specialising in wills, trusts and estate planning for entrepreneurs and high net worth individuals.
Prof. Memberships: Member of the Society of Trust and Estate Practitioners (STEP), the Securities Institute and Capital Taxes sub-committee of the Tax Committee of the Law Society.
Career: Partner in *Martineau Johnson* since 1993. Former Chairman of the Birmingham branch of STEP and former secretary of the Revenue Law committee of Birmingham Law Society.
Personal: Married with two children. Interests include badminton and theatre.

HAYES, Michael
Macfarlanes, London
(020) 7831 9222

HEAL, Jeremy
Howes Percival, Norwich
(01603) 762103
jpwh@howes-percival.co.uk
Specialisation: Partner, Head of Estates Division. Acts for landowners and others in all areas of agricultural law, tax and land transactions, including agricultural tenancies and contracting agreements, minerals, farming partnerships, acquisition and disposal of farms and estates, town and country planning, landowners' consortia and joint ventures. Specialises in capital tax planning for landowners, and lectures on inheritance tax and trusts, valuation and other tax-related topics. Work also includes charity law; and is a trustee of a substantial grant-making charity.
Prof. Memberships: Agricultural Law Association; Chartered Institute of Arbitrators; Society of Trust and Estate Practitioners; Law Society; Country Land and Business Association; Royal Norfolk Agricultural Association.
Publications: Author of various articles in 'Farmers Weekly', 'Taxation', 'Personal Tax Planning Review', 'Private Client Business' and other periodicals.
Personal: Born 1942. Educated Marlborough College and Queens' College, Cambridge. MA, LLM (Cantab), ACIArb, TEP.

HENDERSON, Colin
Anderson Strathern WS, Edinburgh
(0131) 220 2345
colin.henderson@andersonstrathern.co.uk
Specialisation: Capital taxes planning for high net worth individuals and trusts, landowners, family businesses, non-domiciliaries.
Prof. Memberships: Society of Trust and Estate Practitioners. Chartered Institute of Taxation. Member of Law Society of Scotland Tax Law committee.
Career: Qualified in 1990 after army service; 1990-96 *Coopers & Lybrand* CA; partner *Anderson Strathern WS* 1997.
Publications: Articles on taxation subjects in trade press. Conference speaker.
Personal: Born 1960; resides Edinburgh. Interests: fishing, walking, military history and national heritage.

HEWITT, V Alan
L'Estrange & Brett, Belfast
(028) 9023 0426
alan.hewitt@lestrangeandbrett.com
Specialisation: Senior Partner and Head of Commercial Property Department. Main areas of work: commercial property and trusts.
Prof. Memberships: Law Society of Northern Ireland (Council Member 1991-, President 2001-02). Law Reform Advisory Committee for Northern Ireland 1997-2001.
Career: Qualified 1967. Partner in *L'Estrange & Brett* since 1969. Senior Partner since 1994.
Personal: Born 1941. Education: Queen's University, Belfast (LLB), University of Michigan (LLM).

HINE, Andrew
Taylor Wessing, London
(020) 7300 7000
a.hine@taylorwessing.com
Specialisation: Advises wide variety of clients, both resident and domiciled in the UK and overseas, on tax matters generally and has extensive experience in advising trustees and beneficiaries on all trust matters, both domestic and off-shore, and related issues; experienced in the areas of probate, succession, wills and contentious trusts including conflict of law issues; heritage property.
Prof. Memberships: STEP.
Career: Articled *Boodle Hatfield*; joined *Taylor Joynson Garrett* (now *Taylor Wessing*) in 1996; Partner in 1998.
Personal: Education: Repton School, Bristol University.

HORWOOD-SMART, Adrian
Taylor Vinters, Cambridge
(01223) 225209
adrian.horwood-smart@taylorvinters.com
See under Agriculture, p.61

HOWELL, Paul
Addleshaw Booth & Co, Leeds
(0113) 209 2000
paul.howell@addleshawbooth.com
Specialisation: Head of the firm's private client group. Main areas of expertise are in UK and offshore personal tax planning and trusts, and charities.
Prof. Memberships: Memberships: Society of Estate and Trust Practitioners. Country Land Owners Association. Law Society.
Career: Liverpool University 1974; admitted in 1977; joined the firm in 1990 as a partner.
Personal: Tennis, skiing, sailing, windsurfing and bridge.

TRUSTS & PERSONAL TAX ■ THE LEADERS

JACOB, Nicholas
Lawrence Graham, London
(020) 7379 0000

JACOBS, Michael
Nicholson Graham & Jones, London
(020) 7648 9000
michael.jacobs@ngj.co.uk

Specialisation: Tax; employee share schemes; international tax, trusts, charities and public sector bodies. Author of 'Tax on Take-overs' (7 editions) and 'Rewarding Leadership' (published by Quoted Companies Alliance, February 1998); contributor to 'Tolley's Tax Planning' and 'Tolley's VAT Planning'. Consultant editor of Tolley's 'Trust Law International'.
Prof. Memberships: Trust Law Committee (Founder Member and Secretary, 1994-97, Executive Committee member); Share Scheme Lawyers Group (Founder Member and Vice-Chairman); Executive Committee (member 1999-2002) and Employee Share Schemes Committee (Chairman 1996-2002) Quoted Companies Alliance; Deputy Chairman, The Young Committee on Corporate Governance and Investment of Charities (ACEVO); STEP; IFS; Charity Law Association; FRSA; Academician of (i) the Academy of the Learned Societies for the Social Sciences and (ii) International Academy of Estate & Trust Law; Fellow of The Society for Advanced Legal Studies.
Career: Articled at *Nicholson Graham & Jones* (1970). Partner 1976. Head of Private Client Department 1981.

JARMAN, Chris
Payne Hicks Beach, London
(020) 7465 4300
cjarman@paynehicksbeach.co.uk

Specialisation: Partner in tax, trust and probate department. Deals with a wide range of domestic and international trust, estate and tax planning for both old and new money clients, whether based in the UK or abroad; advice to 'private' and institutional charities; property-related VAT advice for charity, commercial and land-owning clients; commercial property advice to landowners seeking to realise potential development value. Member of Law Society's Tax Law Committee, and Income and Capital Taxes Sub-Committee.
Prof. Memberships: Law Society; City of Westminster & Holborn Law Society; STEP; Charity Law Association; Charities Property Association.
Career: Called to the Bar 1976, qualified as solicitor 1980. *Freshfields* 1978-84, *Payne Hicks Beach* 1984 to date. (Partner in 1986.)
Personal: Born 1954, educated at Sherborne School and Magdalene College, Cambridge. Leisure interests include singing and music generally, 'social' cricket, golf and cycling.

KENNEDY, John
Hunters, London
(020) 7412 0050
jmsk@hunters-solicitors.co.uk

Specialisation: Private client work including landed estates, national heritage property, inheritance tax planning, trusts and probate.
Prof. Memberships: Law Society, STEP.
Career: Sherborne School. Emmanuel College, Cambridge. Articled at *Hunters*, qualified in 1967, became a partner in 1970 and senior partner 2000.
Personal: Cricket, skiing, gardening.

KERR, Drummond
Lee Crowder, Birmingham
(0121) 237 2508
drummond.kerr@leecrowder.co.uk

Specialisation: Drummond Kerr is the head of the private client department at *Lee Crowder* Birmingham, comprising a team of 20 (including support staff) of whom seven lawyers are members of the Society of Trust and Estate Practitioners. It is one of the largest specialist private client teams outside London. Drummond specialises in estate planning and tax planning which will typically involve advising on inheritance tax and capital gains tax planning including structures to minimise tax exposure and maximise use of reliefs and tax shelters. His particular emphasis is on estate planning for owner managers, where the planning will also include advice on corporate wills, cross option agreements and share protection. A feature which distinguishes Drummond (and his department) from many other law firms is his commercial approach to the provision of private client services.
Prof. Memberships: Drummond is a trustee of numerous private and charitable trusts and is a member of the Society of Trust and Estate Practitioners and the Charity Law Association.
Personal: Born November 1960. Married with three children.

KING-JONES, Amanda
Thomas Eggar, Chichester
(01243) 786111
amanda.king-jones@thomaseggar.com

Specialisation: Partner. Main areas of practice are wills, personal tax planning, probate, trusts and the affairs of the elderly. Instructed as professional witness for probate related matters. Holding appointments as Judicial Trustee and Administrator appointed by the Court.
Prof. Memberships: Law Society. PGO Panel and Member of STEP and Solicitors for the Elderly.
Career: Joined *Thomas Eggar* in 1981. Qualified 1983. Partner since 1987.
Publications: Co-author of 'Probate Practice Manual' (Sweet & Maxwell).
Personal: Born 5 February 1959. Educated at Roedean School 1969-77. Exeter University (LLB) 1978-81.

KIRBY, Richard
Speechly Bircham, London
(020) 7427 6498
richard.kirby@speechlys.com

Specialisation: Partner 1973. Main area of practice is private client work, handling estate and tax planning for UK and non-UK domiciliaries and trusts. Has written numerous articles for national newspapers and specialist taxation periodicals.
Prof. Memberships: Law Society.
Career: Head Private Client and Charity Team 1980. Solicitor Worshipful Company of Pewterers 1981 (Hon. Freeman 1991, Liveryman 2000).
Personal: Born 18 September 1946. Educated Sevenoaks School 1960-65 and Jesus College, Oxford 1965-68 MA. Member Council Mental After Care Association 1982 (Hon. Treasurer 1987-). Member Carlton Club. Enjoys reading, theatre and cycling. Lives in Dulwich.

LAING, Sue
Boodle Hatfield, Oxford
(01865) 265101
slaing@boodlehatfield.co.uk

Specialisation: Handles UK capital, income and corporation tax planning for landed estates, individuals, trusts, partnerships and private companies; the creation, running and termination of UK and overseas trusts; the interaction of UK and foreign taxes via double tax treaties or UK unilateral relief; the taxation of land transactions within the UK or involving UK entities; UK and overseas taxation of complex trust/corporate structures; long-term planning for individuals, particularly with a foreign element.
Prof. Memberships: STEP (Society of Trust & Estate Practitioners).
Career: Qualified 1978. Trained at *Boodle Hatfield*, became a partner in 1981. Became the first resident partner in the Oxford office in 1994.
Publications: Regular contributor to various articles in tax publications and to 'Legal Network Television'.
Personal: Born 1954. MA (Oxon) 1978. Lives near Oxford.

LEEK, Robert
Higgs & Sons, Brierley Hill
(01384) 342100
rel@higgs-and-sons.co.uk

Specialisation: Inheritance tax and estate planning; capital gains tax advice; all aspects of onshore/offshore trust work. Probate and wills.
Prof. Memberships: Law Society; Society of Trust and Estate Practitioners. Member of Birmingham STEP Branch Technical Sub-committee (formerly branch technical officer); former member of Birmingham Law Society Revenue Law Committee.
Career: 1974-76: Lloyds Bank Trust Division; joined *Higgs & Sons* in 1978; qualified 1980 and became a partner in 1987.
Personal: Born 1952. BA (Hons); LLM (Lond). Interests include travel, sport and music. Married with three children. Lives in South Staffordshire.

LENEY, Simon
Cripps Harries Hall, Tunbridge Wells
(01892) 506221
sdl@crippslaw.com

Specialisation: Head of private client department and member of firm's private office group. Handles creation/use of settlements and will trusts; trusteeships and executorships; wills and administration of estates; powers of attorney and attorneyships; inheritance tax and estate planning; charity law; Inheritance (Provision for Family and Dependants) Act claims and other trust or inheritance disputes or claims; represents the Sovereign Harbour Trust (formed to manage public areas at Sovereign Harbour, Eastbourne, a major residential and commercial coastline development); advisor to a (charity-owned) private hospital.
Prof. Memberships: Member of Securities Institute, Director of Solicitors Benevolent Association, member of Society of Trust and Estate Practitioners (STEP), Notary Public.
Career: Articled at *Donne Mileham and Haddock*; qualified 1977; salaried partner 1979; equity partner 1982; head of private client department 1989; joined *Cripps Harries Hall* 1994; Educated at Sherborne School, Dorset. Head of private client department 1996 to date.
Personal: Married with two children. Interests include cricket, rugby, motoring, home and garden.

LEWIS, Michael
Finers Stephens Innocent, London
(020) 7323 4000

Specialisation: Partner and Head of Private Client Department. Main practice area is international tax and estate planning. Acts for high net worth families, many of whom are domiciled outside the UK. Clients include entrepreneurs, those running large and small businesses, musicians and others in the entertainment industry. Also deals with trust and probate litigation.
Prof. Memberships: STEP (Society of Trust and Estate Practitioners), Westminster Law Society.
Career: Barrister (Lincoln's Inn), called 1965. Qualified as Solicitor 1972. Partner and Head of Private Client Department: *Forsyte Kerman* (from 1994 *Forsyte Saunders Kerman*) 1976-98; *Edward Lewis* 1998-2000; *Finers Stephens Innocent* 2000 to date.
Personal: Born 1943. Interests include music (both listening and playing the piano badly), opera, watching football (Spurs) and family history.

LONG, David
Charles Russell, London
(020) 7203 5096

Specialisation: Head of Private Client Department. Handles a wide range of trusts, wills, probate, estate planning and charity law. Especially interested in international succession problems and contentious probate and trust litigation. Has broadcast on radio and television on wills and lectured on Powers of Attorney.
Prof. Memberships: Law Society, Holborn Law Society (President 1992-93, Chairman Trust Section), Charity Law Association, STEP. Member joint committee of The Law Society with the

826 INDEX TO LEADING LAWYERS: PAGE 1693 ■ IN-HOUSE LAWYERS PROFILES: PAGE 1201

THE LEADERS ■ TRUSTS & PERSONAL TAX

Court of Protection 1993-7.
Career: Joined *Charles Russell* 1972 and became partner in 1974. Hon. Solicitor Royal Philharmonic Society. Hon. Auditor the Law Society, 1994-98.
Personal: Born 3 March 1946. Educated at King Edward's School, Birmingham and Balliol College, Oxford 1964-67.

LYALL, George
Dickinson Dees, Newcastle upon Tyne
(0191) 279 9643
law@dickinson-dees.com
Specialisation: Personal tax partner and private/charitable trust specialist. Provides advice on domicile and related issues to UK expatriates in Northern Europe, including appeals of EC rulings and international estate planning.
Career: 1976-82 Edinburgh University – B.Com, LLB and Dip. LP; 1982-85 Scottish Court solicitor and Notary Public; 1985-94 chartered accountant and senior tax manager at *Arthur/Ernst and Young*, March 1994 joined *Dickinson Dees*. Qualifications: English and Scottish Solicitor, CA, NP and TEP.
Personal: Married to Roz with three sons.

MACFADYEN, Michael R
Charles Russell, London
(020) 7203 5000
Specialisation: Main areas of practice are private client (national and international), tax planning, charities, trusts, probate and Court of Protection.
Prof. Memberships: Law Society, City of London Solicitors Company, Society of Trusts and Estates Practitioners, Charity Law Association.
Career: Qualified in 1966. Joined *Norton Rose* in 1961, becoming a Partner in 1970. Joined *Charles Russell* 1997.
Personal: Born 1943. Attended Marlborough College 1956-61. Leisure interests include golf, cricket and walking. Lives in Henley-on-Thames.

MACKINTOSH, Simon
Turcan Connell, Edinburgh
(0131) 228 8111
sam@turcanconnell.com
See under Charities, p.131

MACROBERT, David
MacRoberts, Glasgow
(0141) 332 9988
david.macrobert@macroberts.com
Specialisation: Partner and Head of Private Client Group. Specialist areas include wills, trusts, inheritance tax, capital gains tax, income tax, executries, power of attorney, charities.
Prof. Memberships: Former member, Tax Law Committee Law Society of Scotland; Capital Taxes Sub-committee of Chartered Accountants of Scotland. Trustee of Scottish Civic Trust.
Career: Glenalmond College; Dundee University (1975 LLB). Trainee *Brechin Robb*; qualified 1977; Assistant Solicitor *MacRoberts* 1977-80; Partner 1980; former senior tutor Glasgow University; former external examiner in finance tax and investment Edinburgh University.

Diploma in Legal Practice; currently tutor in Finance and Investment Diploma in Legal Practice, Glasgow Graduate School of Law.
Personal: Born 1953; resides Paisley. Leisure: skiing, sailing, shooting, fishing, gardening. Member: Royal Gourock Yacht Club, Royal Western Yacht Club, Western Club, RSAC.

MARGRAVE-JONES, Clive
Margraves, Llandrindod Wells
(01597) 825565

MASON, Carol
Cuff Roberts, Liverpool
(0151) 237 7777

MAURICE, Clare M
Allen & Overy, London
(020) 7330 3000
clare.maurice@allenovery.com
Specialisation: Principal areas of practice involve advising on the creation and international structures through which to manage the wealth of both UK and non-UK domiciled individuals and families; has special experience in advising on the UK taxation of offshore structures and Inland Revenue investigations into such activities; lectures extensively on taxation of offshore trusts and cross-border estate planning; also acts for grant-making and operational charitable organisations advising on all aspects of their activities. Contributor to the Butterworths 'Encyclopaedia of Forms and Precedents' (Volumes 42(1) and 42(2) on 'Wills and Administration'.
Prof. Memberships: Charity Law association; Society of Trust and Estate Practitioners.
Career: Articled *Allen & Overy*; qualified 1978, partner 1985, Chairman of the St Bartholomew's and St Mary's Hospital, Director United Response in Business Limited. Director of English Touring Opera Ltd.
Personal: Educated Sherborne School for Girls. Birmingham University (1975 LL.B). Born 1954. Resides London.

MCCAW, Elma
C & J Black, Belfast
(028) 9032 1441
cjblack@dnet.co.uk
Specialisation: Probate, inheritance tax planning, discretionary trusts, wills, deeds of family arrangement.
Prof. Memberships: Member of the Incorporated Law Society of Northern Ireland, Belfast Solicitors' Association.
Career: LLB (2:1), Queens University, Belfast. Qualified as a solicitor in 1976. Partner in *C & J Black, Solicitors* since 1982.

MILLER, Adrian
Foot Anstey Sargent, Exeter
(01392) 411221
adrian.miller@foot-ansteys.co.uk
Specialisation: Senior partner working out of both Plymouth and Exeter offices. Family and financial planning for individuals, families, entrepreneurs, and landed estates; tax, trusts and attorney-

ship, equity and offshore, advance directives, charities and friendly society work.
Prof. Memberships: Law Society Probate Section Executive Committee, Vice Chairman and Secretary of STEP (West of England).
Career: Joined *Foot Anstey Sargent* in 1974 from *Gregory Rowcliffe & Co.*
Personal: Born 7 November 1947. Radley College and Corpus Christi College, Oxford (Jurisprudence). Chief personal interest is his family and their home and grounds in mid-Devon where he is church warden. His family Scottish estate and French holiday property absorb the rest of his leisure time.

MITCHELL, Martin
Burges Salmon, Bristol
(0117) 902 2792
martin.mitchell@burges-salmon.com
Specialisation: Tax and trusts. He advises on all aspects of UK and offshore trusts and probate, and on capital taxation. Clients are private individuals with commercial, agricultural and non-resident interests.
Prof. Memberships: Law Society, STEP.
Career: Joined *Burges Salmon* from *Macfarlanes* in 1981 and became a partner in 1983.

MOYSE, Richard
Boodle Hatfield, London
(020) 7318 8178
rmoyse@boodlehatfield.com
Specialisation: Senior partner of the firm. Has an international practice and reputation, and is one of the UK's leading specialists in tax and financial planning. Advises chiefly on taxation; succession; heritage property; trusts and probates, including contentious matters, often with an international focus. Also acts as an expert witness.
Prof. Memberships: Former member of the Revenue Law committee of the Law Society and member of the Capital Taxes sub-committee; president elect of the International Academy of Estate and Trust Law; member of STEP (Society of Trust & Estate Practitioners); founding member of the Solicitor's Tax and Revenue (STAR) group. Member of the Law Society.
Career: Qualified 1970. With *Lawrence Graham* from 1969-73. Joined *Boodle Hatfield* in 1973, became a partner in 1974 and elected senior partner in 1999.
Publications: Tolley's 'Administration of Estates Handbook' publication 1999. Extensive lecturing in the UK and abroad.
Personal: Born 1943. Educated at Oxford University. Married with four children. Enjoys choral singing, fly fishing, painting, cricket and travel. French speaker.

MURDIE, Alastair
Payne Hicks Beach, London
(020) 7465 4300
Specialisation: Partner in tax, trust and probate department. Deals with a wide range of trust, estate and tax planning for

old and new money clients, whether based in the UK or abroad. Particular interest in landed estate clients and tax and legal issues relevant to the farmer or other landowner
Prof. Memberships: STEP, professional member of CLA.
Career: Qualified as a solicitor in 1979. Senior lecturer at the College of Law 1979-84; assistant solicitor at *Leeds Day* 1984-86; *Payne Hicks Beach* 1986 to date (partner in 1987); consultant to *Leeds Day*.
Personal: Born 1954, educated at Bedford School. Leisure interests include classical music and golf.

NELLIST, Peter
Clarke Willmott & Clarke, Taunton
(01823) 445360
pnellist@cw-c.co.uk
Specialisation: Partner heading the Private Client Team which is authorised by the FSA for investment business advice. Qualified by examination under Law Society regulations to advise on all three heads of financial advice, namely securities and portfolio management, retail branded packaged products and corporate pensions. Passed the Chartered Insurance Institute's Advanced Financial Planning certificate G60 pension exam in 1999. In addition to investment and retirement planning, also specialises in wills, trusts and inheritance tax issues. Recent cases include negotiating on agricultural property relief with the CTO concerning the character appropriate, amenity value and occupied for agriculture arguments; using deeds of variation to create multiple bare trusts to reduce CGT liabilities during administration of estates; advising clients on retirement options including allocation of pension funds and other financial resources; and advising in depth on options available with personal pension death benefits. Has given four all day seminars on 'Inheritance tax in practice' on behalf of SOFA.
Prof. Memberships: Member of Society of Trusts and Estates Practitioners (STEP), chairman of the Association of Solicitor Investment Managers (ASIM), member of the Bristol Law society Tax Trust and Probate Committee (former chairman), a member (by examination) of the Society of Financial Advisers (SOFA).
Career: Guildford College of Law; Bristol University (LLB); articled with *Theodore Goddard*; admitted October 1973, associate partner from 1977; joined *Clarke Willmott & Clarke* July 1978; partner in 1980.
Personal: Winner of Money Management's Financial Planner of the Year competition in the categories of 'Investment Planner' 1999 and 'Retirement Planner' 2000. Runner up in the Estate Planning section of Planned Savings 2002 IFA of the Year competition and runner up in various investment categories in previous years.

TRUSTS & PERSONAL TAX ■ THE LEADERS

NICHOLSON, Jonathan
Bond Pearce, Plymouth
(01752) 266633
jnicholson@bondpearce.com
See under Charities, p.131

OGILVIE, Graham
Hunters, London
(020) 7412 0050
gdo@hunters-solicitors.co.uk
Specialisation: Trust issues, will drafting, capital tax planning, probate and general advice to a wide range of private clients.
Prof. Memberships: STEP, Law Society, Law Society Probate Group, City of Westminster and Holborn Law Society.
Career: Articled *Macfarlanes*. Qualified 1976. Became a partner with *Alexanders* in 1981 and Senior Partner from 1996-2001. Now a partner with *Hunters* following merger in 2001.
Personal: Born 1951. Educated at Cheltenham College, then Trinity College, Cambridge. Leisure interests include golf, cinephotography, travel and reading.

PAGAN, Bill
Pagan Osborne, Cupar
(01334) 653777

PALLISTER, Stephen
Pinsent Curtis Biddle, Birmingham
(0121) 200 1050
stephen.pallister@pinsents.com
Specialisation: Partner heading Personal Tax/Trust Team in the Birmingham office. Specialises in UK and international tax and estate planning, with a focus towards entrepreneurs and business clients especially within the technology field. Also specialises in advising charitable companies and trusts, and leads the charities group in the firm.
Prof. Memberships: Member, Law Society Wills and Equity Committee; Society of Trust and Estate Practitioners; International Tax Planning Association; Charity Law Association.
Career: Qualified 1989; *Macfarlanes*, 1987-93; *Osborne Clarke*, 1994-98; *Pinsent Curtis Biddle*, 1998 to date.
Publications: Co-author of 'International Taxation of Low-Tax Transactions'. Contributor to newspapers, legal journals and other publications.
Personal: Born 1963. Resides Cheltenham; educated Queen Elizabeth Grammar, Penrith, 1976-81; Downing College, Cambridge 1982-86.

PEERLESS, Bart
Charles Russell, London
(020) 7203 5000
Specialisation: Advising UK and international private clients and trustees on tax and estate planning. Also advises banks and trust companies or trustee issues. Charity formation and trusteeship issues. Trust disputes.
Prof. Memberships: Law Society, Society of Trust and Estate Practitioners, Charity Law Association, City of London Solicitors Company.
Career: Trained *Norton Rose*, qualified 1995. Joined *Charles Russell* 1997. Partner 1999.
Publications: Contributor to 'Private Client Business' and 'Trusts and Trustees'.
Personal: Born 1968. Educated: Durham University.

PENNEY, Andrew
Speechly Bircham, London
(020) 7427 6400
andrew.penney@speechlys.com
Specialisation: International tax and trust law for individuals, families and private companies. Structuring and ownership for families with international connections and resolving disputes; advice to private banks and trust companies on legal obligations.
Prof. Memberships: Law Society; Society of Trust & Estate Practitioners (TEP) – Member of International Committee.
Career: Qualified 1985. Assistant Solicitor *Lovells* 1985-86; *Wiggin and Co* 1986-91; Partner *Nabarro Nathanson* 1991-95; Director Rothschild Trust Corporation 1995-2001; Partner *Speechly Bircham* 2001 to date.
Publications: 'Tolley's International Tax Planning' 5th edn: 'Use of Trusts in International Tax Planning'; 'Journal of International Trusts & Companies' – Protector issues highlighted in the case of BTCL v Von Knieriem (Star Trust Case); 'Taxation & Financial Times': regular contributions include 'Belgravia Bombshell' case.
Personal: Born 1960. Educated London University and College of Law. Interests include opera, architecture, walking and history.

PINTUS, Matthew
Macfarlanes, London
(020) 7831 9222

POWELL, Nicholas R D
Currey & Co, London
(020) 7828 4091

RAE, Scott
Morton Fraser, Solicitors, Edinburgh
(0131) 247 1000
sar@morton-fraser.com
Specialisation: Tax, Trusts, Estate Planning, Charities.
Prof. Memberships: Solicitor, WS, NP, TEP.
Career: LLB (Hons 1st) Edinburgh University – 1966. Partner with *Morton Fraser* since 1970. Appointments: Member and past Convener Law Society of Scotland Tax Law Committee; Convener Law Society's Trust Law Committee; Council Member, The International Academy of Estate and Trust Law; Collector, WS Society; Member VAT and Duties Tribunal (Scotland); former National Co-ordinator, Wills Trust Course of Diploma in Legal Studies.
Personal: Born 17 December 1944.

RANKIN, Alastair
Cleaver Fulton Rankin, Belfast
(028) 9024 3141
Specialisation: Chancery and equity, probate, taxation, trusts and estates and wills.
Prof. Memberships: Member of Council The Law Society of Northern Ireland since 1985: treasurer 1991-95; junior vice-president 1995-96; president 1996-97. senior vice-president 1997-98.
Career: Qualified as solicitor 1977 (Northern Ireland 1977) (Republic of Ireland 1997). Partner 1980. Part-time lecturer on wills, revenue and administration of estates since 1988 at the Institute of Professional Legal Studies, Queens University of Belfast. General Commissioner of Income Tax. Part-time chairman Pensions Appeal Tribunals for Northern Ireland.
Publications: Consultant to 'Succession Law in Northern Ireland' by Sheena Grattan (SLS Publications); Northern Ireland editor, 'Which? Consumer Guides: Wills and Probate'.
Personal: Born 5 September 1951. Educated Trinity College Dublin (BA Dublin University). Member, Society of Trust and Estate Practitioners.

REID, Nigel
Linklaters, London
(020) 7456 5702
nigel.reid@linklaters.com
Specialisation: Head of Trust Department. Specialist in trusts and trust taxation in both commercial and family contexts; tax and estate planning for individuals; charities; Chancery litigation.
Career: 1994 to date: Head of Trust Department, *Linklaters*, 1987 to date: Partner, *Linklaters*, 1980-87: Assistant solicitor, *Linklaters*; 1978-80: Articled clerk, *Linklaters*. 1974-77: Christ Church, Oxford; 1963-73: Nottingham High School.

RHODES, John
Macfarlanes, London
(020) 7831 9222

RICHARDSON, Joe
Dawsons, London
(020) 7421 4836
j.richardson@dawsons-legal.com
Specialisation: Senior partner in private client department. Main area of specialisation is taxation. Covers all areas, particularly capital tax (CGT and IHT) and income tax planning, and has considerable experience on all aspects of settlements (offshore, variation, etc) and heritage property. Also deals with a range of general private client work for high net worth individuals and families, and some charity work. Acts for a number of major landed estates, entrepreneurs, and offshore clients.
Prof. Memberships: Law Society, Society of Trusts and Estates Practitioners, the Heritage Group, and the Revenue Law Committee of the City of Westminster and Holborn Law Society.
Career: Qualified in 1974. Partner at *Dawsons* since 1976. Senior Partner since 2000.
Personal: Born 21 October 1949. Educated at St Olave's and St Peter's Schools, York 1959-68, then Durham University 1968-71 (BA in law). Ex-squash international and former Chairman of Selectors, Squash Racket Association. Leisure interests include reading, walking, cricket, golf and squash. Married with three children and lives near Basingstoke, Hants.

RICHES, John
Withers LLP, London
(020) 7597 6000
john.riches@withersworldwide.com
Specialisation: Principal in Private Client Department leading Commercial Group. Main practice areas are estate and capital tax planning for UK and non UK domiciled individuals and use of derivative strategies/investment wrappers for wealthy families. Clients include entrepreneurs, private banks and offshore trustees. Has lectured at major conferences in UK and overseas and contributes to professional journals and professional training videos.
Prof. Memberships: Council Member of STEP, chairing UK Technical Committee.
Career: Qualified in 1985. Worked with two major regional firms before joining *Simpson Curtis* in 1990. Partner *Simpson Curtis/Pinsent Curtis* 1992-96, partner of *Withers* since May 1996.
Personal: Born 1961. Tennis, theatre, walking. Active member of local church.

RIPMAN, Justin
Mills & Reeve, Norwich
(01603) 693256
justin.ripman@mills-reeve.com
Specialisation: Partner specialising in tax and estate planning with particular emphasis on trust and tax issues affecting landed estates and offshore trusts.
Prof. Memberships: Member of CLA Tax committee and STEP Technical committee.
Publications: Contributor to Tolley's 'Administration of Trusts'.

ROBINSON, David
Forsters, London
(020) 7863 8333
djrrobinson@forsters.co.uk
Specialisation: Partner. Private client specialist, with particular expertise in estate planning, capital taxation and heritage property.
Prof. Memberships: City of Westminster and Holborn Law Society; City of London Law Society; Society of Trust and Estate Practitioners.
Career: Qualified in 1981. With *Glover & Co* 1982-85. Joined *Frere Cholmeley* in 1985 and became a partner in 1989. Founding partner of *Forsters* August 1998.
Personal: Born in 1955. Educated at Westminster School and Pembroke College, Cambridge. Leisure interests include collecting books, music, art and travel.

ROGERSON, Gary
Cripps Harries Hall, Tunbridge Wells
(01892) 515121

THE LEADERS — TRUSTS & PERSONAL TAX

SHINDLER, Geoffrey A
Halliwell Landau, Manchester
(0161) 831 2699
gas@halliwells.co.uk
Specialisation: Head of Trust and Estate Planning Department. Specialises in trusts, personal taxation with specific reference to inheritance tax, capital gains, wills and probate.
Prof. Memberships: Chairman Society of Trust and Estate Practitioners (STEP) 1994-98, now Vice President; American Bar Association Real Property, Probate and Trust Law Section; Institute for Fiscal Studies; Securities Institute; Trust Law Committee; Executive Committee International, Academy of Estate and Trust Law; Member Editorial Board Tolley's Trust Law International. Society of Legal Scholars.
Career: Qualified in 1969. Articled at *March Pearson*. Joined *Halliwell Landau* as a partner in 1986. Honorary Associate of Centre for Law and Business, Manchester University. Director of various local companies.
Publications: Consulting Editor of 'Trusts and Estates Law Journal', 'Trusts and Estates Tax Journal'. Member editorial board Wills and Trusts Law Reports. Regular conference speaker.
Personal: Born 1942. Attended Bury Grammar School and Cambridge University (MA LLM Cantab). Leisure interests include Marylebone Cricket Club, Lancashire CCC, Manchester United F.C, Manchester Literary and Philosophical Society and Portico Library; Royal Exchange Theatre. Manchester Chairman Development Committee, Manchester City Art Gallery, Member Development Trust. Lives in Prestwich, Manchester.

STANFORD-TUCK, Michael
Taylor Wessing, London
(020) 7300 4954
m.stanford-tuck@taylorwessing.com
Specialisation: Partner in and former head of private client department. Principal area of practice is international trust and tax planning, acting for high net worth individuals, mainly those who are non-UK domiciled. Work includes protection of assets, structuring cross-border investments, asset enhancement, diversification and protection. Also deals with domestic private client work, encompassing UK-based estate and tax planning, landed estates, heritage property, contentious and non-contentious probate and chancery litigation. Has administered a major multinational estate, principally in Japan involving detailed assessment of Japanese estate tax and capital gains tax law. Also undertakes trust restructuring for high net worth families relocating to or investing in the UK and has handled high profile contentious and non-contentious chancery proceedings under the Settled Land Act 1925. Experienced lecturer and author of various articles.
Prof. Memberships: Law Society, City of London Solicitors Company, Freeman of the City of London, Society of Trust and Estate Practitioners, Bermuda Society (Committee Member), Star Group.
Career: Qualified in 1972. With *Lovell White & King*, 1972-75. Partner with *Appleby Spurling & Kempe* (Bermuda), 1975-84. Admitted Barrister and Attorney Supreme Court of Bermuda 1978. Joined *Taylor Joynson Garrett* as a partner in 1985.
Personal: Born 3 November 1946. Educated at Radley College 1960-65 and Southampton University 1965-68. Leisure activities include golf, gardening, skiing and country sports. Lives in Newbury, Berks.

STIBBARD, Paul
Baker & McKenzie, London
(020) 7919 1000
paul.stibbard@bakernet.com
Specialisation: This includes advising on tax planning strategies for resident, non-resident and non-domiciled individuals, particular specialisation in offshore trust structures and effective tax planning for those coming to and leaving the UK, offshore trust litigation support and inheritance and probate matters involving an overseas aspect. Contributor to various legal journals. Has lectured at various conferences on tax and trust related issues with particular emphasis on international aspects.
Prof. Memberships: Law Society, STEP, ACTAPS, ITPA and member of the British Invisibles International Private Wealth Management Working Group.
Career: Qualified in 1972, partner *Baker & McKenzie* 1991 to date.
Publications: Author of chapter on Offshore Financial Centres in 'Tolley's Tax Havens', author of chapter on Succession Planning in 'Credit Suisse Guide to Managing your Wealth'.
Personal: Education: Marlborough College; Magdalene College, Cambridge; Insead Business School, France MBA (Deans List).

STUBBS, Ian
Maclay Murray & Spens, Glasgow
(0141) 248 5011
ims@maclaymurrayspens.co.uk
Specialisation: Tax and private capital partner specialising in personal tax planning, trusts, partnership law, agricultural property and forestry investment. Also a qualified chartered accountant.
Prof. Memberships: Member of Institute of Chartered Accountants of Scotland. Fellow of the Chartered Institute of Taxation. Sits on the Council of the Law Society of Scotland. Member of the Society of Trust and Estate Practitioners.
Career: Glasgow University, LLB 1965, CA 1968, FTII 1991.
Publications: 'The Interpretation of Cross Border Taxation Issues in Practice' (1991 Thesis & Chartered Institute of Tax Prize).
Personal: Born 1943.

SYED, Catriona
Charles Russell, London
(020) 7203 5000
catrions@cr-law.co.uk
Specialisation: International and domestic private client work, including tax and estate planning for UK and non-UK domiciliaries; trusts; charity law and practice; trust aspects of commercial transactions.
Prof. Memberships: STEP Technical Committee member; Charity Law Association; City of London Solicitors Company; Law Society; Fellow of the Society of Advanced Legal Studies.
Career: Practised at the Chancery Bar 1983-86. *Norton Rose* 1986-97. Joined *Charles Russell* (partner 1997).
Personal: Leisure interests include family, opera, fine wine, walking, travel and reading.

TAYLOR, Philip Greig
Bullivant Jones, Liverpool
(0151) 227 5671
pgt@bullivantjones.co.uk
Specialisation: Main area of practice in probate, wills and trusts.
Prof. Memberships: Law Society, STEP Membership, Liverpool Law Society.
Career: Qualified in 1973. Joined *Bullivant Jones* in 1986. Partner in 1994.
Personal: Golf, cricket and gardening.

THOMPSON, Tony
Withers LLP, London
(020) 7597 6070
tony.thompson@withersworldwide.com
Specialisation: Principal in Private Client Department. Main areas of practice are tax planning, asset structuring, trusts and probate. Clients include proprietors of landed estates, proprietors of businesses (particularly in the property industry) and trustees both onshore and offshore.
Prof. Memberships: Law Society, Society of Trust and Estate Practitioners. Member of Advisory Committee of FTSE International Private Client Indices. Board member of Royal National Theatre Development Council.
Career: Qualified in 1968. Partner of *Withers* since 1970. Head of Private Client Department 1980-87. Managing Partner 1987-93. Head of Private Client Department 2002 to date.
Publications: Editor of Trusts Section of Private Client Business.
Personal: Born 29 May 1943. Educated at Haberdashers Aske's School 1956-60 and Trinity College, Cambridge 1961-65. Chairman of Governors Glenesk School. President of Horsley & Send Cricket Club. Recreations include golf and amateur dramatics. Lives near Guildford.

THOMPSON, Wenna
Browne Jacobson, Nottingham
(0115) 976 6212
wthompson@brownej.co.uk
Specialisation: Trusts, tax and estate planning, charity law and practice.
Prof. Memberships: Society of trust and estate practitioners.
Career: Articled *Macfarlanes*; qualified 1986; *Macfarlanes* 1984-89; *Browne Jacobson* 1989; partner *Browne Jacobson* 1991.
Personal: Education: MA (Oxon).

THORNELY, Richard
Thomas Eggar, Horsham
(01403) 214500
richard.thornely@thomaseggar.com
Specialisation: Partner and head of private client department. Main areas of practice are personal tax planning, wills, probate and trusts, charities and the affairs of the elderly.
Prof. Memberships: Law Society, STEP.
Career: Qualified in 1981. After several years at *Slaughter and May*, joined current firm in 1992 and became a partner in 1993.
Personal: Born 20 January 1957. Educated at Rugby School 1969-74 and Trinity Hall, Cambridge 1975-78. Governor of Queen Alexandra Hospital Home, Worthing and honorary solicitor to various charities. Married with three sons. Recreations include mountaineering, skiing and music, particularly playing the piano. Lives near Horsham.

THURSTON, Martyn
White & Bowker, Winchester
(01962) 844440
martyn.thurston@wandb.co.uk
Specialisation: Partner and head of tax and trusts. Main areas of practice are tax planning for individuals and trusts, both UK and offshore, wills and succession planning.
Prof. Memberships: STEP, International Tax Planning Association.
Career: Partner *Woodham Smith* 1976-90; partner *Radcliffes* 1990-97; partner *White & Bowker* 1998 to present.
Personal: Born 1946. Interests include climbing and music. Lives in London.

TURNOR, Richard
Allen & Overy, London
(020) 7330 3000
richard.turnor@allenovery.com
See under Partnership, p.602

VOREMBERG, Rhoderick
Wilsons, Salisbury
(01722) 412412
rv@wilsonslaw.com
Specialisation: Partner specialising in general private client work and charity law; advises many substantial landowners and family trusts; also leads the firm's charity team (members of which include commercial, litigation, insolvency and property lawyers, all experienced in advising charities) providing advice on a wide range of legal issues affecting charities. He advises on most aspects of charity law, including the establishment and registration of new charities, the revision of their constitutions, restructuring mergers (particularly private schools and other educational charities), trustee powers and responsibilities, Charity Commission inquiries, trading by charities, commercial loans, property development and fund-raising. He advises

TRUSTS & PERSONAL TAX ■ THE LEADERS

both charities and private clients on trust law, taxation and heritage property matters. He is himself a trustee of several substantial charities and clients include many others such as the Royal Commonwealth Society, the Salisbury Diocesan Board of Finance, the Stanley Picker Trust and the National Motor Museum Trust.
Prof. Memberships: Member of STEP, Charity Law Association, Charities Property Association and Land Trusts Association.
Career: Qualified 1980; joined *Wilsons* 1982; partner from 1985. Head of Private Client services. Senior Partner 2002.
Personal: Married with 3 children (12-17). Amateur silversmith. Captain of the English Eight (Match Rifle) since 1993 and has represented England and Great Britain in match rifle competitions on numerous occasions since 1979.

VOS, Robin
Macfarlanes, London
(020) 7831 9222

WALLEY, Ray
Mundays, Cobham
(01932) 590500

WALSH, Christopher
May, May & Merrimans, London
(020) 7405 8932
mmm@elawuk.com
Specialisation: Estate and tax planning for landed estates/heritage property.
Prof. Memberships: STEP; Law Society.
Career: Trained *May, May, Merrimans*; qualified 1970; made Partner 1972, Senior Partner 1993.
Personal: Educated at Ampleforth College and Christ Church College, Oxford (1967 BA Law). Married with four sons. Enjoys cricket and gardening.

WHITFIELD, Ann
Macfarlanes, London
(020) 7831 9222

WILKIN, Ashley
Boyes Turner, Reading
(0118) 959 7711
awilkin@boyesturnerlegal.co.uk
Specialisation: Partner and head of group. Principal area of practice being capital tax planning for individuals and private shareholders through trusts, wills and financial products. Leads a team dedicated to all private client matters such as probate, Public Guardianship Office issues, trusts for the disabled, attorneyships, deeds of variation and living together agreements. Ashley has a reputation for his proactive practical approach to solving client issues and his clients include partners of the major law and accountancy firms. He lectures to financial advisors and accountants, has appeared in the College of Law training videos and is on the Lotto winner advisory panel.
Prof. Memberships: Law Society Probate section, Society of Trust and Estate practitioners.
Career: Admitted 1975. Partner from 1977 with *Fladgate Fielder*. Joined *Boyes Turner* in 1998 as partner.
Publications: Taxation and daily newspapers.
Personal: Born 1951. Married to Susan. He loves his labradors, theatre and travel. Ex Major in the Territorial Army.

WILLIAMS, Sian
Edwards Geldard, Cardiff
(029) 2023 8239
sian.williams@geldards.co.uk
Specialisation: Sian Williams is the head of *Edwards Geldard's* Trusts and Estates Team in Cardiff. She leads a team of four assistants specialising in inheritance tax and capital gains tax planning, all aspects of will drafting, trust matters, and probate and administration of estates. Sian has been a partner with *Edwards Geldard* since 1981, specialising in private client practice within the firm. She has an extensive background in property, particularly estate disposals. Since joining the Trusts and Estates Team in 1996, Sian has specialised in the preparation of wills, with particular emphasis on inheritance tax mitigation and will trusts, to address family problems; all aspects of trusts, including advising and preparing new trusts, advising on existing trusts and termination of trusts; administration of estates, including probate disputes; care for the elderly, enduring powers of attorney and Public Guardianship Receiverships. Sian's skills are tailored to the requirements of the wealthy private client, and she counts over 30 National Lottery winners amongst her clients.
Prof. Memberships: Sian is a member of the Public Guardianship Office's panel of receivers.
Career: 1979-81 Partner, *Athan Morgan & Shibko*, 1981 to date Partner at *Edwards Geldard*.
Personal: Food, gardening, floral art and family.

WILLIS, David
Forsters, London
(020) 7863 8333
dcwillis@forsters.co.uk
Specialisation: Partner. Trusts (UK and Offshore), estates and personal taxation together with some family law work.
Prof. Memberships: Society of Trusts and Estate Practitioners; Solicitors Family Law Association.
Career: Oxford University (MA). Qualified initially as a barrister before becoming a solicitor. Partner in *Frere Cholmeley Bischoff* 1978-98. Founding partner of *Forsters* August 1998.

WOLLEN, Nigel
Hooper & Wollen, Torquay
(01803) 213251

WORWOOD, Lucy
Browne Jacobson, Nottingham
(0115) 976 6000

WRIGHT, Cherry
Hugh James, Cardiff
(029) 2022 4871
cherry.wright@hughjames.com
Specialisation: Partner and head of wills, probate and trusts department. Handles all aspects of wills, probate, trusts, tax (especially capital tax) and Court of Protection receiverships, but in particular tax planning trusts for private clients, company directors and shareholders, special needs trusts for accident victims and those with learning difficulties; charitable trusts for both large and fledgling institutions and the constitutional aspects of registered social landlords with charitable rules.
Prof. Memberships: Law Society, STEP.
Career: Qualified in 1969. Became a partner in *Shaen, Roscoe and Bracewell* (London) in 1972. Lecturer UCL 1974-76. Lecturer University of Wales, Cardiff 1976-88. Consultant at *Hugh James* 1980-88. Became partner in *Hugh James* 1988.
Publications: 'Succession – Cases and Materials' (Butterworths 1986); Editor Butterworths 'Wills Probate and Administration Service' (loose-leaf).
Personal: Educated at Wolverhampton Girls High School and then at UCL. Graduated UCL LLB first class honours 1966. Obtained honours in Solicitors Finals. Leisure interests include tennis, opera, fell walking and reading. Lives in Vale of Glamorgan, one child.

WRIGLEY, Matthew
Wrigleys, Leeds
(0113) 244 6100
Specialisation: Partner. Private client and charities, particularly agricultural, and heritage property; educational, religious and conservation charities.
Career: Qualified 1972. Partner *Biddle & Co* 1975. Partner *Dibb Lupton Broomhead* 1978. Partner *Wrigleys* 1996.
Personal: Born 1947. Educated Westminster School (Queen's Scholar), King's College, Cambridge (Scholar).

WYLD, Charles
Burges Salmon, Bristol
(0117) 902 2773
charles.wyld@burges-salmon.com
Specialisation: Head of Tax and Trusts Department where his practice encompasses tax and estate planning for UK and overseas clients; advising on formation and ongoing legal requirements of charities, whether trusts or companies.
Prof. Memberships: Law Society; Capital Taxes Sub-committee of the Revenue Law Committee of the Law Society; International Tax Planning Association; Charity Law Association; STEP.
Career: Trained, qualified and practised at *Frere Cholmeley*, joining *Burges Salmon* in 1986, becoming a Partner in 1989. Qualified as financial planner in 1996.
Personal: New College, Oxford (MA) 1975-79.

YOUNG, Andrew
Lawrence Graham, London
(020) 7379 0000

OFFSHORE: CORPORATE/COMMERCIAL

Guernsey: 831; Isle of Man: 831; Jersey: 832; Profiles: 833

Research approved by BMRB For this edition, **Chambers'** researchers conducted 6,582 interviews – 3,900 with law firms, 511 with barristers and 2,171 with clients. The validity of the research was scrutinised by BMRB International, who audited both the methodology and the results at our offices in London. They interviewed **Chambers'** researchers and cross-checked sample interviews. Details of the audit appear on page 7.

GUERNSEY

OFFSHORE: CORPORATE/COMMERCIAL
■ GUERNSEY

1 Carey Langlois St Peter Port
2 Ozannes St Peter Port
3 Collas Day St Peter Port
   Ogier & Le Masurier St Peter Port
   Olsens St Peter Port

LEADING INDIVIDUALS

1
CAREY Nigel Carey Langlois
HALL Graham Carey Langlois
KIRK Ian Collas Day
SIMPSON William Ogier & Le Masurier

2
HARWOOD Peter Ozannes
LANGLOIS John Carey Langlois
MOORE David Ozannes

This book is the product of 6,552 1/2 hour interviews. See p.7 for BMRB audit.
Within each band, firms are listed alphabetically. See individuals' profiles p.833

CAREY LANGLOIS (see firm details p.901) There is consensus among *Chambers'* interviewees that the island's largest firm has the range of services on offer and strength in depth to make it the clear market leader. Investment funds form a major thrust of practice activity, and this is complemented by expertise in M&A, asset financing, insolvency and trusts. Banking and mutual funds expert **Nigel Carey** is a firm stalwart, and widely acknowledged by peers as a leading light. He is joined in a powerful team by **Graham Hall**, who handles banking, investment funds and M&A, and respected senior partner **John Langlois**. He continues to be active in trusts and captive insurance for corporate and private clients. Among its work for an international clientele, the team recently assisted Linklaters in advising on a new private equity business, and helped in the formation of a new closed-ended fund for JPMorgan to be listed on the Dublin stock exchange. **Clients** CSFB; Terra Firma; JPMorgan.

OZANNES (see firm details p.1091) This traditional heavyweight has recruited vigorously to maintain its position as a leading commercial firm. Litigation has proved to be a buoyant feature of a firm principally known for its strength in the commercial and financial spheres. Additional specialisms include investment funds, securitisations and tax. **Peter Harwood** (see p.833) heads up the corporate and commercial team, and is described by clients as an "*experienced old hand with a range of talents.*" **David Moore** (see p.834), who works as part of the same close-knit team, is noted for his hard-working approach in a broad spread of commercial work. The practice recently advised on the sale of Guernsey Telecoms to Cable & Wireless, and provided local assistance in respect of Vivendi's acquisition of Southern Water. It helped Scottish Widows set up a new property fund and has been involved in establishing platform funds for derivatives transactions. **Clients** Royal Bank of Scotland; Lloyds TSB; States of Guernsey; Rothschild.

COLLAS DAY Clients warmly endorsed the practice's ability to "*work to demanding timescales*" and commended its breadth of skills. Expertise takes in property, trusts and litigation in addition to core commercial work. Chief corporate lawyer **Ian Kirk** was the best recommended individual in a small but growing team, noted for its high quality levels. Banking, insurance and general commercial matters form the major chunk of his practice, and his style is said to "*combine knowledge and practicality to great effect.*" Deals of note include acting for Royal London Asset Management in its acquisition of the entire issued share capital of Union Fund Management (Guernsey) and related companies. The firm also represented NatWest Offshore and the Royal Bank of Scotland in connection with senior debt facilities, and advised Orange on the legal and regulatory aspects of its flotation. **Clients** Bank of Bermuda; Ernst & Young; Crédit Lyonnais.

OGIER & LE MASURIER (see firm details p.1085) The Guernsey office of this expanding Jersey firm was given a real boost with the arrival in 2002 of **William Simpson** (see p.834) from Ozannes. Making its debut in *Chambers'* tables, the practice is set to benefit from Simpson's "*substantial portfolio of clients*" and his "*high level of practicality.*" Clients warmed to the prospect of the firm's "*seamless pan-Channel Island service,*" and praised its skill in core corporate and commercial work. Further areas of expertise include banking, investment funds, securitisations and trusts. The practice recently advised on the restructuring of the Korea-Europe Fund as an open-ended Guernsey Class "B" Scheme and implemented a tender offer for the purchase of up to 40% of its shares. **Clients** Royal & Sun Alliance; QBE International Insurance; Channel Islands Stock Exchange.

OLSENS (see firm details p.1086) This is a new entry to our tables this year. Although its origins are as a litigation and private client-focused practice, clients and peers commended the firm for its success in developing corporate/commercial capability. Ben Morgan, the head of corporate, is the contact partner in a unit whose expertise now includes M&A, investment funds, banking and pensions. **Clients** Abacus; Royal Bank of Canada; United Bank of Kuwait.

ISLE OF MAN

CAINS ADVOCATES LIMITED (see firm details p.898) Clients were vocal in their praise for a firm now regarded as the island's premier choice. They say that "*despite being a big fish in a small pond, the service is as good as anywhere.*" Peers and international companies recommended the practice for its expertise in corporate/commercial, banking and associated litigation. **Andrew Corlett** heads the team and is highly regarded by financials for his "*great commercial instincts and wonderful communication skills.*" 2002 saw him take the lead on several large deals, including Barclay's £16 billion offshore reorganisation. **Richard Vanderplank**, described as a "*true heavyweight operator,*" has extensive experience, including collective investment schemes and project finance. He recently advised the Isle of Man Treasury on a £185 million bond issue. **Mike Pinson** continues to draw plaudits across the country for his expertise in complex finance structures, ship and aircraft finance. **Andrew Baker** enters the tables this year, and was recommended for mutual funds work. **Clients** Bank of Bermuda; Cathay Pacific; major shipping companies.

DICKINSON CRUICKSHANK & CO According to market commentators, the firm "*lacks the broad sweep of Cains,*" but is still considered an "*excellent choice*" by corporate and commercial

www.ChambersandPartners.com
831

OFFSHORE CORPORATE/COMMERCIAL ■ JERSEY

OFFSHORE: CORPORATE/ COMMERCIAL
■ ISLE OF MAN

1. **Cains Advocates Limited** Douglas
2. **Dickinson Cruickshank & Co** Douglas
3. **Maitland & Co** Douglas

LEADING INDIVIDUALS

1. **CORLETT Andrew** Cains Advocates Limited
   DOYLE David Dickinson Cruickshank & Co
   VANDERPLANK Richard Cains Advocates Limited
2. **BAKER Andrew** Cains Advocates Limited
   DOUGHERTY Paul Dougherty & Associates
   PINSON Mike Cains Advocates Limited
   RIMMER John Dickinson Cruickshank & Co
   WENTZEL Peter Maitland & Co

This book is the product of 6,552 1/2 hour interviews. See p.7 for BMRB audit. Within each band, firms are listed alphabetically. See individuals' profiles p.833

clients. Its expertise takes in banking, partnership, regulatory matters, e-commerce and M&A. **David Doyle** leads the team and is a "*large presence on the island.*" In tandem with a London firm, he recently acted for Friends Provident in its merger with Royal & SunAlliance. Although best known for his private client work, **John Rimmer**'s tax expertise remains a source of market recommendation. A team from the firm acted for the Financial Services Commission and the Government on a number of major matters. **Clients** Domestic and foreign companies; financial institutions; private clients.

MAITLAND & CO (see firm details p.1051) This niche practice continues to advise on Isle of Man interests for large South African companies and wealthy individuals. As part of the international network of Webber Wentzel Bowens, the office has access to an extensive client base of major companies and financial institutions. Its expertise lies primarily in cross-border transactions, tax structures and company reorganisations. **Peter Wentzel**, who handles corporate, trusts and tax planning work, is the group's leading name. **Clients** South African mining, banking and insurance companies.

OTHER NOTABLE PRACTITIONERS Paul Dougherty, of Dougherty & Associates is considered to have a "*neat little practice which always impresses*," and is recommended for his work in trusts and capital markets.

JERSEY

OFFSHORE: CORPORATE/ COMMERCIAL
■ JERSEY

1. **Mourant du Feu & Jeune** St Helier
   Ogier & Le Masurier St Helier
2. **Bedell Cristin** St Helier
3. **Olsens** St Helier

LEADING INDIVIDUALS

1. **BYRNE Chris** Ogier & Le Masurier
   JAMES Ian Mourant du Feu & Jeune
   RICHOMME Jacqueline Mourant du Feu & Jeune
   THOMAS Richard Ogier & Le Masurier
2. **GERWAT Richard** Bedell Cristin
   HERBERT Tim Mourant du Feu & Jeune
   HOWARD Simon Bedell Cristin
   KERSHAW Nick Ogier & Le Masurier
   LOMBARDI Michael Ogier & Le Masurier
   OHLSSON Alex Olsens
3. **BYRNE Peter** Bedell Cristin
   CHAPLIN Clive Ogier & Le Masurier
   DAVIES Nicola Mourant du Feu & Jeune
   SUGDEN Paul Olsens

This book is the product of 6,552 1/2 hour interviews. See p.7 for BMRB audit. Within each band, firms are listed alphabetically. See individuals' profiles p.833

MOURANT DU FEU & JEUNE (see firm details p.1077) This firm is considered by *Chambers*' interviewees to have "*come closest to achieving the aura of a City firm.*" The firm's international finance group benefits from a small London office practising Jersey law, while its Jersey base is said to possess some of the best lawyers on the island. Peers and clients agree that **Ian James** is one of the most prominent heavyweights. He is noted for a high level of visibility on finance deals. The team also contains **Jacqueline** Richomme, described by clients as "*energetic, powerful and quick.*" She was involved in a complex cross-border deal set up through Irish special purpose vehicle Prime Edge Capital – a novel private equity fund using securitisation. Another highlight for Richomme was advising on the enlargement of Hercules Unit Trust. It purchased the properties and units of another Jersey fund, The Retail Park Unit Trust, creating a portfolio of 28 retail parks valued at £1.5 billion. **Tim Herbert**, who heads up the commercial department, and **Nicola Davies**, who specialises in corporate finance and capital markets, retain their share of support among clients and peers. Herbert's team advised Standard Bank over the merging of Standard Bank Channel Islands and Standard Bank Jersey. The firm also provided substantial advice on the forthcoming amendment to the Companies Law in relation to redomiciliation and company mergers. **Clients** CSFB; Deutsche Bank; Royal Bank of Scotland; JP Morgan.

OGIER & LE MASURIER (see firm details p.1085) Partners with a "*professional approach and personal touch*" characterise this highly praised firm. Peers and clients believe it to be "*dominant in the offshore sector*" and it benefits from having an associated office in Guernsey. The firm has witnessed growth in its structured finance and securitisations practice, particularly collateralised debt obligation (CDOs).

Chris Byrne (see p.833) is regarded as an "*accomplished problem solver,*" whose recent deal highlights include advising Le Riche Group, the largest Channel Island retail group, on its application for a Stock Exchange (CISX) listing. He also acted for Morgan Stanley and ABN AMRO on securitisations worth almost $5 billion. **Richard Thomas** (see p.834) continues to enjoy a leading reputation, and was recently involved in FirstRand Bank's acquisition of shares in Jersey General Group to create FirstRand International Asset Management. "*Clear, quick-thinker*" **Nick Kershaw** (see p.833) focuses on investment funds and securitisations. Among a raft of recent M&A deals, he acted for Le Riche Group in its merger with Ann Street Group. **Michael Lombardi** (see p.834) is among the best-known lawyers at the firm, and led a team advising Cinven on the £400 million Foseco buyout from Burmah Castrol. **Clive Chaplin** (see p.833) acted for Ministry of Sound, the target of a £26 million investment by 3i, and for Phoenix Equity Partners in the buy out of Jimmy Choo Shoes' ready-to-wear business. **Clients** Standard Chartered; Morgan Stanley; CSFB; Abbey National.

BEDELL CRISTIN Although not considered as aggressive as its chief rivals, the firm is felt to have successfully "*preserved its niche position.*" It also profits from an association with Guernsey's Babbe Le Pelley Tostevin. **Simon Howard** (see p.833) is in charge of investment funds and pension schemes within the financial services group, and is admired by commentators for "*pulling in a tremendous volume of work.*" **Richard Gerwat** (see p.833) ("*intellectually and analytically strong*") is commended for helping to establish the firm's structured finance and securitisation practice. Together with Clifford Chance in Frankfurt, Gerwat advised Commerzbank on its first asset-backed ECP (European Commercial Paper) programme, a €5 billion transaction. **Peter Byrne**, head of banking and corporate finance, is a new addition to the tables this year. Described as "*meticulous in looking after his clients' interests,*" he formed part of the team advising C.I. Traders

THE LEADERS ■ OFFSHORE CORPORATE/COMMERCIAL

as bid company in the Ann Street Group/Le Riche Group merger. Alongside Allen & Overy in London, Byrne also advised a syndicate of banks on the €5 billion monetisation of a receivable due to a Jersey incorporated company. **Clients** Deutsche Bank; Aberdeen Asset Management.

OLSENS (see firm details p.1086) Interviewees say the firm possesses a "*keenness and an appetite*" that marks it out from more established rivals. A branch presence in Guernsey is also seen as an advantage. A vigorous recruitment drive aimed at growing the firm is felt to have raised its profile, notably in the areas of structured finance and property finance. Highly rated **Alex Ohlsson** (see p.834) has cemented his reputation as the "*lynchpin of the firm's international finance practice.*" His team was instructed by Lehman Brothers to assist on the £467 million securitisation of commercial mortgages originated by MABLE Commercial Funding. **Paul Sugden** (see p.834), widely regarded for his technical skills in the banking field, gains entry to the table this year. One of his transactional highlights was representing Tishman International in the sale of Hayes Park in London to the Challenger Group. **Clients** CSFB; Nomura; Sainsbury's.

THE LEADERS IN OFFSHORE CORPORATE/COMMERCIAL

BAKER, Andrew
Cains Advocates Limited, Douglas
(01624) 638300

BYRNE, Chris
Ogier & Le Masurier, St Helier
(01534) 504000
chris.byrne@ogier.com
Specialisation: Partner Business Law Group, *Ogier & Le Masurier*. Specialises in banking law, structured finance, investment funds, corporate law, commercial law, trusts and employee benefits.
Prof. Memberships: The Honourable Society of the Middle Temple; The English Law Society; The Law Society of Jersey; The International Bar Association.
Career: Trained *Allen & Overy*; qualified 1988; associate *Allen & Overy*; secondment from *Allen & Overy* to a London bank acting as bank's commercial in-house lawyer; posted to Asia to open *Allen & Overy's* Singapore office, 1992; admitted Jersey Bar 1996; Partner *Ogier & Le Masurier*, 1997.
Personal: Born 1965; resides St Clement, Jersey.

BYRNE, Peter
Bedell Cristin, St Helier
(01534) 814814

ANTHONY DESSAIN, Peter
Bedell Cristin, St Helier
(01534) 814814

CAREY, Nigel
Carey Langlois, St Peter Port
(01481) 727272

CHAPLIN, Clive
Ogier & Le Masurier, St Helier
(01534) 504000
clive.chaplin@ogier.com
Specialisation: Partner Business Law Group, *Ogier & Le Masurier* specialises in employee benefits, collective investment funds, limited partnerships, general commercial matters and trust law.
Prof. Memberships: The Law Society of England and Wales; The Law Society of Jersey; Member of the Jersey Law Commission.
Career: Admitted as an English Solicitor 1977, Jersey Solicitor 1986; became a partner at *Ogier & Le Masurier* 1994.
Personal: Born 1951. Resides in Trinity, Jersey. Leisure interests include tennis, choral singing and music. Language: English.

CORLETT, Andrew
Cains Advocates Limited, Douglas
(01624) 638300

DAVIES, Nicola
Mourant du Feu & Jeune, St Helier
(01534) 609000

DOUGHERTY, Paul
Dougherty & Associates, Douglas
(01624) 671 155

DOYLE, David
Dickinson Cruickshank & Co, Douglas
(01624) 647647

GERWAT, Richard
Bedell Cristin, St Helier
(01534) 814 814
richard.gerwat@bedellcristin.com
Specialisation: Partner and head of the structured finance practice area of the financial services law group. Extensive experience in banking and capital markets work with particular experience in securitisation. He has considerable experience in asset backed financing having acted as Jersey counsel in some of the most innovative securitisation transactions. *Bedell Cristin* is rated as a market leader in securitisation. He is frequently asked to write and speak on matters relating to the use of Jersey SPVs and regularly participates in initiatives with the Jersey regulatory authorities concerning matters relating to new legislation / codes of practice in this field.
Prof. Memberships: The Law Society of Jersey; The Law Society of England and Wales; Member of the Finance Industry Sub-Committee of the Law Society of Jersey.
Career: Became a partner of *Bedell Cristin* in 1994 after joining the firm in 1989. 1986/89 employed by *Clifford Chance*, London.
Personal: Born London, January 1965. 1992 Advocate of the Royal Court of Jersey. 1988 Solicitor of the Supreme Court of England and Wales. 1985 University of Buckingham (LLB(Hons)) 1985.

HALL, Graham
Carey Langlois, St Peter Port
(01481) 727272

HARWOOD, Peter
Ozannes, St Peter Port
(01481) 731436
p.harwood@ozannes.com
Specialisation: Senior Partner in the Corporate Department. Main areas of work include corporate and commercial law, banking and finance, investment funds, stock exchange listings, insurance, reinsurance and securitisations. Appointed as Director to a number of Guernsey companies, and the Channel Islands Stock Exchange.
Prof. Memberships: The Institute of Directors, Chairman of the Panel appointed by the States of Guernsey to Review the Machinery of Government in Guernsey.
Career: Qualified as an English solicitor in 1972 and a Guernsey advocate in 1982, Notary Public. Worked in London for *Coward Chance*, *Ziman & Co* and *Hill Samuel & Co*, before joining *Ozannes* in 1980 and becoming a Partner of the firm in 1983. Head of Corporate Department.

HERBERT, Tim
Mourant du Feu & Jeune, St Helier
(01534) 609000

HOWARD, Simon
Bedell Cristin, St Helier
(01534) 814 814
simon.howard@bedellcristin.com
Specialisation: Partner and head of the investment funds and pension schemes practice area of the financial services law group. Over a decade of experience in Jersey specialising in investment fund structures and general compliance law matters for corporate and institutional clients. Main area of work involves advising asset managers based around the world on the launch, restructuring and termination of funds and on other legal and regulatory issues relevant to the industry. With the growth of private equity, much of the current fund work is focussed on the use of Jersey limited partnership structures. Much time and effort has also been spent in the last year managing restructuring exercises for a number of Aberdeen Asset Management split capital funds based in Jersey. Participates on the Jersey Finance Industry Association sub-group and the related Jersey Financial Services Commission Working Group dealing with Jersey's response to the FATF consultation documentation on revisions to the 40 Recommendations and updating of Jersey's Anti-Money Laundering legislation and Guidance Notes. Significant training role with frequent participation as a speaker at conferences and seminars.
Prof. Memberships: The Law Society of Jersey, STEP, IBA.
Career: Became a partner of *Bedell Cristin* in 1994 after joining the firm in 1987. 1985 - 1987 employed by Macfarlanes in London.
Personal: Born 7th October, 1961 in Jersey. 1989 University of Oxford, Pembroke College (MA); 1985 Inns of Court School of Law London; 1984 University of Oxford, Pembroke College (BA Jurisprudence, First Class).

JAMES, Ian
Mourant du Feu & Jeune, St Helier
(01534) 609000

KERSHAW, Nick
Ogier & Le Masurier, St Helier
(01534) 504000
nick.kershaw@ogier.com
Specialisation: Partner Business Law Group, *Ogier & Le Masurier*. Head of Investment Funds Team. Also specialises in securitisation and structured finance, property holding structures, private company sales and acquisitions and general commercial matters.
Prof. Memberships: Chairman of the Legal and Regulatory Sub-Committee of the Jersey Fund Managers Association. Honourable Society of the Middle Temple; The Law Society of Jersey; International Bar Association.
Career: University of London (1986 LLB); Inns of Court School Law, Admitted English Bar 1988, New South Wales Bar 1989, Jersey Bar 1996; *UBS-Phillips & Drew* 1988-89; *Clifford Chance* 1990-93; *Ogier & Le Masurier* (1993-present), partner 1997.
Personal: Born 1963; resides in St Lawrence, Jersey. Interests include golf, tennis, sailing and skiing.

www.ChambersandPartners.com

833

OFFSHORE CORPORATE/COMMERCIAL ■ THE LEADERS

KIRK, Ian
Collas Day, St Peter Port
(01481) 723191

LANGLOIS, John
Carey Langlois, St Peter Port
(01481) 727272

LOMBARDI, Michael
Ogier & Le Masurier, St Helier
(01534) 504000
michael.lombardi@ogier.com
Specialisation: Partner Business Law Group, *Ogier & Le Masurier* and heads up the firm's securitisation practice. Has been engaged in structured finance work since the mid 1980s and has wide experience of international capital markets transactions with particular emphasis on asset-backed securities, collateralised bond offerings, structured debt instruments, securitisations and repackagings.
Prof. Memberships: The Law Society of Jersey; The Law Society of England and Wales; Law Society of Scotland; Society of Writers to Her Majesty's Signet; The International Bar Association; Executive Member of the European Securitisation Forum.
Career: Initially qualified as a solicitor in Scotland. Trained with *Dundas & Wilson* in Edinburgh. Also qualified as a lawyer in England, Hong Kong, Bermuda and Jersey.
Personal: Attended University of Dundee (LLB) and University of Exeter (LLM). Leisure interests include golf, skiing and field hockey.

MOORE, David
Ozannes, St Peter Port
(01481) 723466
d.moore@ozannes.com
Specialisation: Partner in the Corporate Department. Main areas of work include corporate, trust, banking and finance, insurance, mutual funds and e-commerce. Holds non-executive directorships of a number of investment and insurance business related companies.
Prof. Memberships: The Law Society.
Career: Qualified as an English solicitor in 1986 and a Guernsey advocate in 1995. Worked in London as a solicitor for *Ashurst Morris Crisp* and *Freshfields*, before joining *Ozannes* in 1993 and becoming a Partner of the firm in 1997.

OHLSSON, Alex
Olsens, St Helier
(01534) 822276
alex.ohlsson@olsenslaw.com
Specialisation: Partner specialising in finance and securities law, particular expertise in structured finance, securitisations and property finance. Regularly instructed by leading global law firms and financial institutions. Recent notable transactions include: White Pine Corporation Limited instructed by Bank One Capital Markets Limited in respect of a US$22,000,000,000 structured investment vehicle; Windermere CMBS Plc instructed by Lehman Brothers in respect of a £467,000,000 securitisation of commercial mortgages; MABLE Commercial Funding Limited in respect of a £290,000,000 loan; Stannifer Group in acquiring a portfolio of shopping centres for £235,000,000.
Prof. Memberships: Jersey Taxation Society; committee member of the Financial and Commercial Law sub-committee of the Jersey Law Society; Society of Trust and Estate Practitioners; States of Jersey Audit Commission.
Career: Joined *Olsens* 1991; Jersey Solicitor 1994; Advocate of the Royal Court of Jersey 1995; Partner at *Olsens* 1995; directorships with trust companies and offshore financing vehicles; advisory board member Structured Finance Management Limited.
Publications: 'International Company and Commercial Law Review'.
Personal: Educated at Victoria College, Jersey; Queens' College, Cambridge (MA Hons-Law). Born 1969; resides Jersey.

PINSON, Mike
Cains Advocates Limited, Douglas
(01624) 638300

RICHOMME, Jacqueline
Mourant du Feu & Jeune, St Helier
(01534) 609000

RIMMER, John
Dickinson Cruickshank & Co, Douglas
(01624) 647647

SIMPSON, William
Ogier & Le Masurier, St Peter Port
(01481) 721672
william.simpson@ogier.com
Specialisation: Partner Business Law Group, *Ogier & Le Masurier*. Finance, investment, corporate, trust and tax law.
Prof. Memberships: Honourable Society of Lincoln's Inn; Guernsey Bar; British Virgin Islands Bar; International Tax Planning Association.
Career: University of Leeds (1979 LLB); Inns of Court School Law, admitted English Bar 1980, British Virgin Islands 1989, Guernsey Bar 1996, 11 Kings Bench Walk 1983-87; Attorney General's Chambers, Cayman Islands 1987-88; *Harney Westwood & Riegels* 1988-90; *Ozannes*, Guernsey 1991-2002 (Partner 1996), Partner *Ogier & Le Masurier* 2002.
Personal: Born 1956; resides St Peter Port, Guernsey. Interests include sailing.

SUGDEN, Paul
Olsens, St Helier
(01534) 822261
paul.sugden@olsenslaw.com
Specialisation: Partner specialising in banking, regulation and compliance. He undertakes banking formations, restructurings and mergers in the Channel Islands. Significant instructions acted on in relation to regulatory and compliance issues, lending and security documentation and insolvency for leading banks and financial institutions in the Channel Islands, including: BNP Paribas; JP Morgan Chase; UBS AG; Gerrard Private Bank; Citibank; HSBC Plc; Bank of Scotland Offshore; CSFB; Rothschilds; Deutsche Bank International; BBVA Privanza.
Prof. Memberships: Associate of the Chartered Institute of Bankers.
Career: Formerly a banker with National Westminster from 1973-79. After qualifying at the English Bar in 1983, he worked as an in-house lawyer during which he gained experience in dealing with complex banking and regulatory issues, including those arising in connection with BCCI and Barlow Clowes. Since moving to Jersey in 1992, he has continued to work as a specialist banking and regulatory lawyer in private practice.

Became Partner at *Olsens* in 1998 heading the Channel Islands Banking and Regulation and Compliance Teams.
Personal: Educated at Scarisbrick Hall, BA Hons Law; ACIB 1977; Barrister of Lincoln's Inn 1983; Advocate of the Royal Court of Jersey 1996. Born 1956; resides Jersey with his family.

THOMAS, Richard
Ogier & Le Masurier, St Helier
(01534) 504000
richard.thomas@ogier.com
Specialisation: Partner Business Law Group, *Ogier & Le Masurier*, offshore funds, securitisation, commercial law, trust law, general commercial lawyer.
Prof. Memberships: The Law Society of Jersey; The Law Society of England and Wales.
Career: Trained College of Law, London; enrolled as English solicitor 1976; *Slaughter & May* 1974-78; in industry 1978-84; assistant commercial relations officer, financial regulation (mutual fund and banking supervisor) 1984-86; Joined *Ogier & Le Cornu* in 1986; became partner in 1990.
Personal: Born 1950; resides St Mary, Jersey. Education: Oundle School; St John's College, Oxford (MA Lierae Humaniores). Leisure: Jersey Symphony Orchestra and cycling

VANDERPLANK, Richard
Cains Advocates Limited, Douglas
(01624) 638300

WENTZEL, Peter
Maitland & Co, Douglas
(01624) 630000

SOLICITORS
A-Z OF LAW FIRMS

LAW FIRMS ■ A-Z

A & L Goodbody

Augustine House, Austin Friars, London, EC2N 2HA
Tel (020) 7382 0800 **Fax** (020) 7382 0810
Email info@algoodbody.com **Website** www.algoodbody.ie

THE FIRM A & L Goodbody's London office advises UK-based clients on matters of Irish corporate and commercial law and covers a wide range of services. The pivotal role of the London office reflects the international nature of the firm's business and its regard for London as a financial and commercial centre. The London office plays a central role in servicing the requirements of foreign entities establishing, acquiring or financing operations in Ireland, as well as local lawyers involved in transactions with an Irish dimension.

CLIENTELE The London office works on an integrated basis with the Dublin office to provide legal services to leading Irish and international institutions and organisations.

INTERNATIONAL The firm advises international companies seeking to invest in Ireland, as well as advising Irish companies on their overseas activities and offers the most extensive range of specialist business law services available in Ireland. These services are provided through a network of interdisciplinary units in key areas. The firm's healthcare and life sciences unit provides an industry-focused approach for the medical devices, pharmaceutical, life sciences, biotechnology and healthcare business sectors. The unit advises indigenous and international clients on the full range of healthcare and life sciences. The firm's commercial property department offers clients one of the most comprehensive services in Ireland, advising financial and investment institutions and developers on such issues as site acquisition and assembly, the negotiation and drafting of funding agreements, joint ventures, consortium and profit-sharing arrangements, and 'side by side' agreements. The firm's banking and financial services group advised on a number of key deals in 2001 which included advising the Bank of Scotland on the takeover of ICC for €350 million and advising the Irish Government's Minister for Finance Rabobank's €165 million takeover of ACC Bank. The firm also advised on the top five venture capital deals in 2001. M&A work in 2002 included advising Valentia Telecommunications Ltd. in relation to its successful bid for eircom, Ireland's major telecoms network. The firm also received a leading legal magazine's Private Equity Deal of the Year Award for its work on eircom. The deal was valued at €3.8bn and was one of the most complex and publicly contested bids for an Irish company.

RECRUITMENT Steve Rodgers, a Senior Associate in the firm's Dublin office, is to join the firm's team of lawyers in London.

Managing Partner	Paul Carroll
Number of partners	56

CONTACTS
Banking & Finance	Kevin Allen
	Steve Rogers
Capital Markets	Paul White
	Jack O'Farrell
EU & Competition	Vincent Power
Funds	Paul Dobbyn
	Brian McDermott
General Corporate & Commercial	Paul White
	Kevin Allen
Insurance	James Grennan
	Eithne Fitzgerald
Intellectual Property	David Sanfey
	Liam Kennedy
Inward Investment	Paul White
	Michael Greene
Litigation	Caroline Preston
	Marcus Beresford
Media & Entertainment	Paul White
	Geraldine East
Mergers & Acquisitions	Eithne Fitzgerald
	Paul Carroll
Private Finance	Kevin Feeney
Technology Law/E-commerce	David Sanfey
	John Olden

Aaron & Partners

Grosvenor Court, Foregate Street, Chester, CH1 1HG
Tel (01244) 405555 **Fax** (01244) 405566 **DX** 19990
Email enquiries@aaronandpartners.com **Website** www.aaronandpartners.com

THE FIRM This leading firm of commercial lawyers in Chester provides quality legal services to business clients.

PRINCIPAL AREAS OF WORK In addition to the traditional areas of commercial law such as litigation, corporate, commercial and property, other specialisms include planning, environmental, minerals and waste, transport and road haulage, warehousing, corporate finance, construction, insolvency and employment law, as well as serving clients with personal legal services.

CLIENTELE With a diverse client base, Aaron and Partners is able to offer a wide range of services to suit every type of business, both nationally and internationally.

Managing Partner	Simon Carter
Senior Partner	Simon Edwards
Number of partners	14
Assistant solicitors	11
Other fee-earners	9

CONTACTS
Commercial Litigation & Insolvency	
	John Devoy
Commercial Property	Christopher Tomkinson
Company/Commercial	Ben Quirk
Employment	Mark Ellis
Environmental & Agricultural Law	
	Richard Forrester
Insolvency & Litigation	Simon Edwards
Planning & Environmental Law	Simon Carter
Transport	Tim Culpin
Wills, Trusts & Probate	Clive Poynton

■ Actons
2 King Street, Nottingham, NG1 2AX **Tel** (0115) 910 0200 **Fax** (0115) 910 0290

■ Adams & Remers
Trinity House, School Hill, Lewes, BN7 2NN **Tel** (01273) 480616 **Fax** (01273) 480618

■ Adams Whyte
14/16 Frederick Street, Edinburgh, EH2 2HB **Tel** (0131) 225 8513 **Fax** (0131) 226 0949

A-Z ■ LAW FIRMS

Addleshaw Booth & Co

Sovereign House, P.O. Box 8, Sovereign Street, Leeds, LS1 1HQ
Tel (0113) 209 2000   **Fax** (0113) 209 2060   **DX** 12004 Leeds
Email info@addleshawbooth.com   **Website** www.addleshawbooth.com

25 Cannon Street, London, EC4M 5TB
Tel (020) 7788 5000   **Fax** (020) 7788 5060   **DX** 98948 Cheapside 2
Email info@addleshawbooth.com

100 Barbirolli Square, Manchester, M2 3AB
Tel (0161) 934 6000   **Fax** (0161) 934 6060   **DX** 14301 Manchester
Email info@addleshawbooth.com

Managing Partner	Mark Jones
Senior Partner	Paul Lee
Number of partners	127
Assistant solicitors	262
Other fee-earners	388

AREAS OF PRACTICE
Commercial Property	24%
Corporate Finance	22%
Commercial Services	19%
Banking & Finance	12%
Litigation & Dispute Resolution	10%
Housing	7%
Private Client	6%

CONTACTS
Banking & Finance	Richard Papworth
Commercial Property	John Pike
Commercial Services	Richard Kempner
Corporate Finance	Sean Lippell
Housing	Anthony Ruane
Litigation & Dispute Resolution	Simon Twigden
Private Client	Paul Howell

THE FIRM Addleshaw Booth & Co is a leading national law firm with an international capability offering a full range of commercial legal services. A business which works for business, the firm has developed quickly its national markets to provide commercial solutions to a wide range of clients in the corporate, financial, public and private sectors. With offices in Leeds, Manchester and London, the firm combines top level expertise and experience with strength in depth to provide clients with a range of legal services that their businesses need. Clients have a dedicated contact partner who creates a tailor-made team, drawing on the skills of the firm's many nationally recognised specialists. The wide range of clients from the corporate, financial, public and private sectors includes, amongst others, 3i plc, MyTravel plc, British Vita, BT plc, Trinity Mirror plc and GEHE (UK) plc, as well as over 169 UK based financial institutions. In the past year Addleshaw Booth & Co has further developed its capabilities and now has 127 partners, a further 262 lawyers and 388 other fee-earners firmwide.

PRINCIPAL AREAS OF WORK
Corporate Finance Addleshaw Booth & Co's corporate finance practice is one of the most significant in the UK. The practice has a tradition of deal-making, not just providing outstanding technical advice but also in making deals happen through extensive business and professional networks and by strategic input to deals at every stage. In 2001, the firm advised on corporate finance and banking deals with a total value in excess of £17 billion.
Banking During 2001, the firm's banking and finance practice acted on significant transactions involving total funding/facilities of over £8 billion.
Commercial Property In commercial property, the firm is recognised as one of the leading practices in volume and diversity of market sectors in the UK. It has a national reputation for work in retail and leisure.
Commercial Services Commercial services' expertise is provided in intellectual property, European and competition law, commercial contracts, employment law, pensions, share schemes and tax issues.
Litigation/Dispute Resolution The firm's litigation and dispute resolution group has widely respected practices in international litigation and arbitration, recognition and enforcement of foreign judgements and regularly provides corporate support advice on international and UK transactions on choice of law, jurisdiction and dispute resolution agreements.
Private Client The private client practice is regarded as a leading practice across the UK with an increasing number of national appointments and a strong national reputation in family law.
Housing Addleshaw Booth & Co's housing group incorporates arrears litigation, sales in possession, mortgage shortfall recovery.
Other In addition the firm has a number of cross-disciplinary units, including technology, media and telecommunications, together with pharmaceuticals, sport and entertainment and PFI, which bring together experts in a variety of legal disciplines.

CLIENTELE
The firm's clients include: 3i Group plc; Abbey National plc; MyTravel plc; ASDA Group Limited; British Aerospace plc; BT plc; GEHE UK plc; Halifax plc; HSBC Bank plc; J Sainsbury plc; Manchester 2002 Commonwealth Games; Ministry of Defence; Nationwide Building Society; Scapa Group plc; Stadium Group; Trinity Mirror plc; Yorkshire Bank; Yorkshire Electricity Group plc.

RECRUITMENT
In addition, the firm has invested substantially in state-of-the-art hardware, software, training and support across all offices. The firm continues to win significant new appointments through competitive tenders and client recommendations. For further information please visit Addleshaw Booth & Co's website (address given above) or contact Carolyn Roberson, Director of Marketing and Business Development, on (0161) 615 8520.

LAW FIRMS ■ A-Z

■ Agnew, Andress, Higgins
92 High Street, Belfast, BT1 2DG   **Tel** (028) 90320035   **Fax** (028) 90249380

Aitken Nairn WS

7 Abercromby Place, Edinburgh, EH3 6LA
Tel (0131) 556 6644   **Fax** (0131) 556 6509   **DX** 18 Edinburgh
Email reception@aitkennairn.co.uk   **Website** www.aitkennairn.co.uk

THE FIRM Aitken Nairn WS is a long established Scottish practice located in Edinburgh's New Town. It has two distinct areas of expertise for both of which it enjoys a strong reputation. Three partners and their staff deal with estate agency, property management, domestic and commercial conveyancing, domestic and commercial leasing, executries, trusts and private client advice. The emphasis is on a quality service at the top end of the market. Two partners and their litigation team handle personal injury, family law, commercial litigation, housing law, bankruptcies, judicial review and Industrial Tribunals. They will resolve disputes at whatever end of the market.

INTERNATIONAL Languages spoken include Spanish.

Managing Partner	Kenneth Stanley
Number of partners	5
Assistant solicitors	3
Other fee-earners	3

AREAS OF PRACTICE	
Residential Property	30%
Litigation	25%
Private Client	25%
Commercial Property	20%

CONTACTS	
Commercial Property	Kenneth Stanley
Litigation	Paul Harper
Private Client	Morag Yellowlees
Residential Property	Philip Harris

Alexander Harris

Ashley House, Ashley Road, Altrincham, WA14 2DW
Tel (0161) 925 5555   **Fax** (0161) 925 5500   **DX** 19866 Altrincham 1
Email info@alexharris.co.uk   **Website** www.alexharris.co.uk

1 Dyers Buildings, London, EC1N 2JT
Tel (020) 7430 5555   **Fax** (020) 7430 5500   **DX** 460 London Chancery Lane

Cheriton House, 51 Station Road, Solihull, B91 3RT
Tel (0121) 711 5111   **Fax** (0121) 711 5100   **DX** 720080

THE FIRM Specialises exclusively in health-related litigation work in the UK and abroad, including clinical and dental negligence, personal injury and pharmaceutical product liability. The firm's lawyers are amongst the leaders in the country in their chosen fields and the majority of its lawyers are members of the Law Society Clinical Negligence/Personal Injury and AVMA panels. The quality of service is confirmed by their being awarded a Legal Service Commission franchise in clinical negligence, personal injury, education and mental health. Alexander Harris is one of only 18 firms on the Legal Service Commission's Multi-party Action Panel.
Offices in the North West, London and Birmingham.

PRINCIPAL AREAS OF WORK
Clinical Negligence Cerebral palsy, birth injury, anaesthesia, misdiagnosis claims, surgical error, radiation damage, cancer, keyhole surgery and dental work. The team represented the parents of the victims of Beverley Allitt, and the families of the victims and alleged victims of Harold Shipman. Currently acting on behalf of the Leicester Epilepsy Concern Parents and Carers Group and individual parents in cases of alleged epilepsy misdiagnosis in children over a number of years. A team of medico-legal assistants supports the department, all of whom are qualified nurses and midwives.

Pharmaceutical Product Liability & Multi-party Actions The department is currently co-ordinating and jointly heading all generic Measles, Mumps and Rubella (MMR) vaccine claims. Work includes over 300 claims of over-treatment by Manchester orthodontist Melvyn Meggitt and representing women who have had their Trilucent breast implants explanted. The firm is also investigating claims of adverse effects after taking the anti-smoking drug Zyban, claims for Arsenic poisoning in Bangladesh, and receiving the meningitis C and DPT vaccine.

Personal Injury The department specialises in dealing with major cases, in particular brain, spinal and catastrophic injury in the UK and abroad. The firm acts for claimants in all areas of personal injury law – covering injuries on the road, at work, at home, through sporting activities, or as a result of industrial disease. The department also includes a specialist unit handling transatlantic compensation claims. Recently acted for the UK survivors of the Greek ferry disaster.

Education & Public Law The education and public law department represents children, disabled people and their families who may be experiencing difficulties with schools, local education authorities, colleges and other institutions. Appeals to and from the Special Educational Needs Tribunal and Judicial Reviews of local education authorities or other statutory bodies are a speciality. The Disability

Continued overleaf

Managing Partner	Ann Alexander
Senior Partner	David Harris
Number of partners	11
Assistant solicitors	13
Other fee-earners	38

AREAS OF PRACTICE	
Claimant Clinical Negligence	60%
Pharmaceutical Product Liability/Medical Devices/Disasters & Multi-party Actions	20%
Claimant Personal Injury	20%

CONTACTS	
Clinical Negligence	Lesley Herbertson
	Grainne Barton
Personal Injury	Jenny Kennedy
Pharmaceutical Product Liability & Multi-party Actions	David Harris
	Richard Barr
Education & Public Law	Douglas Silas

Alexander Harris
solicitors

A-Z LAW FIRMS

Rights Commission (DRC) has invited the firm to join its three specialist panels in education, civil litigation and employment.

CLIENTELE Clients are based throughout the UK and include UK citizens injured during visits to the US and Canada, and claimants against US-based manufacturers. The firm receives an increasing volume of referrals from non-specialist solicitors.

Alexiou Fisher Philipps

54 South Molton Street, London, W1K 5SG
Tel (020) 7409 1222 **Fax** (020) 7409 7222 **DX** 44610 Mayfair
Email mail@afp-law.co.uk **Website** www.afp-law.co.uk

Number of partners	4
Assistant solicitors	3

THE FIRM Alexiou Fisher Philipps is a specialist niche matrimonial and family law practice founded by Douglas Alexiou, Jeremy Fisher and Susan Philipps who are all very experienced family lawyers. Douglas Alexiou is the President of the International Academy of Matrimonial Lawyers which boasts an elected fellowship of over 300 of the best regarded specialist family lawyers from around the world. Jeremy Fisher is a fellow of the International Academy of Matrimonial Lawyers and lectures widely on the impact of divorce on international financial structures, trusts and business assets. Susan Philipps is an SFLA trained mediator and sits on the education committee of the Solicitors Family Law Association. Emma Harte joined them as a partner on formation of the practice. The firm has a wide ranging client base from the professional to the aristocracy, from entrepreneurs to entertainers, from the media to merchant bankers and their husbands and wives.

Alistair Meldrum & Co

8-9 Genotin Terrace, Enfield, EN1 2AF
Tel (020) 8367 0064 **Fax** (020) 8366 8578 **DX** 133180 Enfield 6

Abbey Chambers, 10 Bull Plain, Hertford, SG14 1DT
Tel (01992) 535866 **Fax** (01992) 535867 **DX** 57919 Hertford

Managing Partner	Richard Pugh
Senior Partner	Alistair Meldrum
Number of partners	4
Assistant solicitors	1
Other fee-earners	4

AREAS OF PRACTICE

Crime	100%

CONTACTS

Criminal	Alistair Meldrum (Hertford)
	Richard Pugh (Enfield)

THE FIRM Founded 12 years ago, Alistair Meldrum & Co has always specialised in criminal defence work and has become one of the foremost criminal firms in North London.

PRINCIPAL AREAS OF WORK The firm undertakes work in the areas of criminal law, including agency and legally aided work.

CLIENTELE The firm deals with both privately paying and legally aided clients.

Allan Janes
21-23 Easton Street, High Wycombe, HP11 1NU **Tel** (01494) 521301 **Fax** (01494) 442315

Allen, Burn & McGregor
Unit 5, Tillydrone Shopping Centre, Hayton Road, Aberdeen, AB24 2UY **Tel** (01224) 480 890 **Fax** (01224) 480 980

Allen & Overy

One New Change, London, EC4M 9QQ
Tel (020) 7330 3000 **Fax** (020) 7300 9999 **DX** 73
Email information@allenovery.com **Website** www.allenovery.com

THE FIRM Allen & Overy is a premier international law firm. Founded in 1930, it has 4,700 staff, including some 420 partners, working in 25 major centres on three continents serving businesses, financial institutions, governments and private individuals where there is a need for decisive legal advice on complex transactions.

PRINCIPAL AREAS OF WORK

Corporate The firm's corporate department advises on all aspects of company, corporate finance and commercial law. Lawyers in the department act extensively on public takeovers, international and cross-border mergers and acquisitions, Stock Exchange flotations, international equity offerings, private equity, joint ventures and strategic alliances, corporate restructuring, management buyouts and public private partnerships. In addition, the corporate department is actively involved in the work of specialist cross-departmental practice groups including energy, environmental law, insurance, media and communications (including telecommunications, new digital media, broadcasting and satellite), healthcare, financial services and compliance, international projects, construction, mining and metals, European anti-trust, intellectual property and information technology.

Banking The firm advises financial institutions and borrowers on all types of domestic and international financing transactions including acquisition finance, general bank lending, project finance, property finance, trade finance, restructurings and workouts, all forms of structured finance, asset finance (including aviation and shipping), telecommunications finance and securitisations. The practice acts for over 800 international banks worldwide in deals involving more than 100 jurisdictions.

International Capital Markets The firm advises in relation to capital markets transactions by issuers from all over the world (including developing countries as well as those with developed economies). These include eurobond issues, euro-equity offerings, equity linked issues, securitisations and derivatives. The firm also has a highly regarded US law practice which now numbers 29 partners and over 175 US qualified lawyers. The practice advises on a wide range of transactions with a significant or dominant US element. For example, Allen & Overy was the first non-US firm to advise the underwriters on a public securitisation deal in the US.

Litigation The firm's litigation and dispute resolution practice deals with all forms of commercial dispute including administrative and public law, banking and finance, business crime and corporate governance, civil fraud, communications and e-commerce, construction, defamation and media, employment and pensions, energy, environmental law, EU and competition, information technology, insolvency, insurance, intellectual property, investigations, inquiries and crisis management, product liability, professional negligence, projects, property, regulatory proceedings and trust litigation.

Private Client The firm's large practice provides comprehensive advice to wealthy individuals, entrepreneurs and senior directors, trustees, families, museums, universities and charities worldwide on trusts and estate planning, private capital and personal tax, professional partnerships, immigration, heritage property and private banking.

Project Finance The firm has one of the leading project finance practices advising all parties in major projects in the UK, Europe (including Western, Central and Eastern Europe), the Middle East, South East Asia and China, and Latin America, acting for sponsors, project companies, lenders and governments.

Property The firm provides a full commercial real estate service. Clients include leading national and international investors, landowners, institutions, property companies, developers, contractors, banks and government agencies. The group specialises in multi-real estate and structured transactions (including public to private deals for UK property companies and beneficial tax structures), as well as advising on building contracts, business rating, commercial leases and underlettings, compulsory purchase, construction law, development agreements, dilapidations, environmental audits, equity sharing leases, housing association law, joint ventures, letting and sale of completed developments, limited recourse funding, pension fund acquisitions, planning procedures and appeals, general property taxation and redevelopments. In conjunction with the firm's insolvency group, it has extensive experience of advising insolvency practitioners.

Taxation The firm provides a comprehensive corporate tax service including advice on employee benefits and share schemes, and VAT and other indirect taxation.

INTERNATIONAL The firm has offices in Amsterdam, Antwerp, Bangkok, Beijing, Bratislava, Brussels, Budapest, Dubai, Frankfurt, Hamburg, Hong Kong, Luxembourg, Madrid, Milan, Moscow, New York, Paris, Prague, Rome, Singapore, Tirana, Tokyo, Turin and Warsaw. Languages spoken include Afrikaans, Arabic, Bengali, Bulgarian, Byelorussian, Cantonese, Czech, Danish, Dutch, Finnish, French, German, Greek, Gujarati, Hebrew, Hindi, Hungarian, Italian, Japanese, Korean, Malay, Mandarin, Persian, Polish, Portuguese, Punjabi, Russian, Spanish, Swedish, Tamil and Urdu.

Managing Partner	John Rink
Senior Partner	Guy Beringer
UK: As of 30th April 2002	
Number of Partners	172
Assistant Solicitors	697
Other Fee Earners	312
International	
Number of Partners	216
Assistant Solicitors	696
Other Fee Earners	346

CONTACTS

Asset Finance	Graham Smith
Banking	David Morley
Bioscience	Robert Barry
Business Reconstruction & Insolvency	Gordon Stewart
Communications/Media/Technology	Ian Ferguson
Construction	John Scriven
Corporate/Commercial	Richard Cranfield
Derivative Products	Jeffrey Golden
Employment/Pensions & Incentives	Derek Sloan
Energy	Ian Elder
Environmental	Owen Lomas
European Anti-trust	John Wotton
Financial Services	Paul Phillips
Housing Association Finance	Richard Cranfield
Insurance	Ian Stanley
Intellectual Property	Colleen Keck
International Capital Markets	Boyan Wells
Leveraged Finance	Anthony Keal
Litigation	Peter Watson
MBOs	Alan Paul
Mergers/Acquisitions/Takeovers	Alan Paul
Private Clients	Richard Turnor
Projects & Project Finance	Graham Vinter
Property (Commercial)	Adam Cleal
Property (Finance)	Mark O'Neill
Public Private Partnerships	Anne Baldock
Securitisation	David Krischer
Tax (Corporate)	Patrick Mears
VAT & Indirect Tax	Peter Mendham

ALLEN & OVERY

A-Z ■ LAW FIRMS

■ Allington Hughes
10 Grosvenor Road, Wrexham, LL11 1SD **Tel** (01978) 291000 **Fax** (01978) 290493

■ Altheimer & Gray
7 Bishopsgate, London, EC2N 3AR **Tel** (020) 7786 5700 **Fax**

Ambrose Appelbe

7 New Square, Lincoln's Inn, London, WC2A 3RA
Tel (020) 7242 7000 **Fax** (020) 7242 0268 **DX** LDE 467
Email mailbox@ambrose.appelbe.co.uk **Website** www.ambrose.appelbe.co.uk

Managing Partner	Lisa Bolgar Smith
Senior Partner	Lisa Bolgar Smith

AREAS OF PRACTICE	
Trusts, Probate, Wills & Charities	30%
Family	30%
Conveyancing	25%
Litigation	15%

CONTACTS	
Conveyancing	Andrew Penfold
Family	Lisa Bolgar Smith
Trusts, Probate, Wills & Charities	Felix Appelbe

THE FIRM Based in Lincoln's Inn, the firm has notable expertise in family law, private client services and charity law. Litigation, property, company and commercial work are also handled, and there is a substantial agency department. Established in 1935 by Ambrose Appelbe, the practice maintains the principles by which he operated: personal attention, excellent service, and simple, innovative solutions to clients' needs. The firm is at the forefront of the legal world. It is a member of the Solicitors Family Law Association and the Relate Quality Partnership. Felix Appelbe is a member of the National Association of Estate Agents. The firm operates as a team, rather than being rigidly compartmentalised.

PRINCIPAL AREAS OF WORK
Family Law The department deals with all aspects of marriage and co-habitation breakdown. It enjoys a niche reputation in high finance issues, cases with an international element, property issues and arrangements concerning children. Child abduction is also handled, and advice is given on pre-marriage arrangements.

Litigation The litigation department handles a range of civil matters and has particular expertise in personal injury, including road traffic, workplace and leisure incidents. Professional negligence is a specialism, notably in cases concerning solicitors. Advice is given in partnership disputes, all aspects of employment law, including contracts, termination and tribunal cases, on behalf of both employers and employees, defamation cases are also handled. Alternative dispute resolution is offered wherever appropriate.

Private Client Extensive private client practice advises on all matters relating to wills and the administration of probates, estates and trusts. Advice is given on tax planning, and on the construction of trusts, in order to achieve significant tax savings. The firm has also helped to achieve excellent investment returns for clients. The practice has acted in the formation of many well-known national charities, and helps them in fundraising and sponsorship.

Conveyancing All types of residential and commercial conveyancing are dealt with, including landlord and tenant disputes. The firm has a property sales service and Ambrose Appelbe's agency services include actions before the Central London County Court, the High Court and the Privy Council.

CLIENTELE The large and diverse client base includes individuals and businesses worldwide, as well as charities. Solicitors around the UK, from small provincial firms to local authorities, instruct the firm in agency matters.

INTERNATIONAL There is an associate office in Vienna, Alex Frank Rechtsanwaelte KEG.

■ Amery-Parkes
Law Courts Chambers, 33 Chancery Lane, London, WC2A 1EN **Tel** (020) 7404 7100 **Fax** (020) 7404 6588

■ Amhurst Brown Colombotti
2 Duke Street, St. James's, London, SW1Y 6BJ **Tel** (020) 7930 2366 **Fax** (020) 7930 2250

■ Anderson Beaton Lamond
22 St John Street, Perth, PH1 5SP **Tel** (01738) 639 999 **Fax** (01738) 630 063

LAW FIRMS ■ A-Z

Anderson Fyfe

90 St. Vincent Street, Glasgow, G2 5UB
Tel (0141) 248 4381 **Fax** (0141) 204 1418 **DX** GW 138
Email mail@andersonfyfe.co.uk   **Website** www.andersonfyfe.co.uk

THE FIRM Anderson Fyfe provides services in business, company and employment law, while its private client division provides a comprehensive portfolio of services to individuals. The practice is responsive and flexible to the changing needs of its clients.

PRINCIPAL AREAS OF WORK

Business Law The firm's corporate division provides a range of services including company formation, finance, acquisitions and sales. The firm also advises on commercial contracts, intellectual property and trade protection, and has an expanding employment law division.

Private Client The private practice division looks after individual clients' investments, trusts, tax, wills and executry matters as well as residential conveyancing.

Commercial Property Services include land acquisition and development, house building developments, leasing, retail leasing, quarrying, security work, planning appeals and Housing Association work.

Litigation The firm has an extensive commercial and public sector litigation and recoveries department and has been instructed in a number of leading Scottish cases in the Court of Session and House of Lords. Roddy McIlvride is a solicitor advocate with rights of audience in the Court of Session and the House of Lords.

Public Sector The firm carries out work for public sector bodies in education, enterprise and housing.

Managing Partner	David Chaplin
Number of partners	7
Assistant solicitors	8
Other fee-earners	10

AREAS OF PRACTICE
Property	32%
Litigation & Recovery	29%
Corporate/Business Law/Insolvency	26%
Private Client/Trust/Executry	13%

CONTACTS
Private Client Services	Christopher Wilkin
Business Law	Derek Hamill
Public Sector	David Chaplin
Commercial Property	Kenneth Meldrum
Residential Property	Lesley Forrest
Litigation	Rhoderick McIlvride
Employment Law	Tom McEntegart

Anderson Partnership

125 West Regent Street, Glasgow, G2 2SA
Tel (0141) 248 6688 **Fax** (0141) 248 9697 **DX** 512403 Glasgow - Bath St
Email mailbox@anderson-partnership.co.uk

1 St Colme Street, Edinburgh, EH3 6AA
Tel (0131) 220 8242 **Fax** (0131) 220 8342 **DX** 551112 Edinburgh 7
Email edinburgh@anderson-partnership.co.uk

THE FIRM Established in 1994 under Gilbert Anderson & Partners, the practice has since more than doubled in size. At the end of 1999, the firm opened its Edinburgh office.

PRINCIPAL AREAS OF WORK

Insurance Law/Insurance Litigation & Claims Including advice on coverage, conduct of litigation in the Court of Session and in Sheriff Courts throughout Scotland, and representation at fatal accident inquiries. The firm provides advice on all aspects of road traffic claims/public/employers' liability, product liability and undertakes all related investigative work for insurers throughout Scotland. The firm has two members of FOIL.

Commercial/Commercial Property & Employment Law Work includes commercial leasing; security; business acquisition; disposal and start-ups for sole traders, partnerships and companies; contractual advice; employment law; commercial dispute resolution; asset recovery.

Private Client Including residential conveyancing; tax planning; wills and executries; financial services; matrimonial dispute resolution.

Senior Partner	Gilbert Anderson
Number of partners	9
Assistant solicitors	13
Other fee-earners	9

AREAS OF PRACTICE
Insurance/Insurance Litigation & Recoveries	70%
Company/Commercial Property	20%
Private Client	10%

CONTACTS
Administrative Law	Frank Hughes
Co/Comm Property	David Morris
	Alan Paton
Commercial Litigation	Andrew Ireland
Employment Law	James Herd
Ins/Ins Lit & Recoveries	Gilbert Anderson
	John Maillie
	Alan Taylor
Private Client	Morag Gibb

www.ChambersandPartners.com

843

A-Z ■ LAW FIRMS

Anderson Strathern WS

48 Castle Street, Edinburgh, EH2 3LX
Tel (0131) 220 2345   **Fax** (0131) 226 7788   **DX** 3 Edinburgh
Email forename.surname@andersonstrathern.co.uk   **Website** www.andersonstrathern.co.uk

Managing Partner	Robin Stimpson
Chairman	Alan Menzies
Number of partners	26
Assistant solicitors	45
Other fee-earners	34

CONTACTS	
Agriculture	James Drysdale
	Alasdair Fox
Banking	Ruari MacNeill
Charities	George Russell
Commercial Property	David Hunter
	Alan Menzies
	Andrew Morris
Construction	Neil Smith
Corporate	Simon Brown
	Jonathan MacQueen
Corporate/Sports	John Kerr
Employment	Alun Thomas
Entertainment/Media	Simon Brown
Family Law	Mac Rigg
	Fiona Stephen
Intellectual Property/IT	Simon Brown
Litigation	Robert Carr
	Robert Fife
	Ruari MacNeill
	Fiona Stephen
Parliamentary	Robert Carr
	Morag Ross
Personal Tax	Alex Gunn
	Colin Henderson
Planning	Alastair McKie
Private Client	John Blair
	Colin Henderson
	Lynda Pennell
	Robin Watt
Residential Property	Jean Broadwood
	Mike Keenan
Rural Property	James Drysdale
	Alasdair Fox
	Fiona Gibb
	Robin Stimpson

THE FIRM One of Scotland's leading commercial firms, complemented by its strong private client practice. Anderson Strathern's full service approach is combined with specialist skills in property, private client and corporate services. The firm is recognised for its reputation in niche practice areas including employment, intellectual property, entertainment and media, banking, and services to and for the Scottish Parliament. Anderson Strathern has grown, and continues to grow considerably reflecting a rapid growth in business primarily in the commercial sector, the last year saw a 15% increase in fee earners. Clients include national and international companies, public bodies, banks and property investors, developers and many substantial landowners. Anderson Strathern offers the resources of a large legal practice but features a high level of personal attention from genuine specialist advisors. The firm provides expertise in the Scottish aspects of cross-border transactions for both English and international legal firms. A member of the Association of European Lawyers, Anderson Strathern is strongly placed to provide advice on any European legal issue. The firm continues to introduce bespoke IT systems to support its commitment to client service. Anderson Strathern was the first large Scottish law firm to be awarded the Investors in People Standard.

PRINCIPAL AREAS OF WORK

Banking Specialising in providing service to banks in property, corporate and litigation work.

Commercial Property A growing team covers all aspects of commercial property law supported by specialists in landlord and tenant law, construction, and planning and environmental law. Two partners are accredited commercial leasing law specialists; one is accredited as a planning law specialist.

Agricultural/Rural Property Award winning team recognised as a leader in agricultural law and estates work. Two partners are accredited specialists in agricultural law.

Employment One of the largest dedicated employment teams in Scotland lead by an accredited specialist employment lawyer. All aspects of employment law for both employer and employee are undertaken.

Litigation With particular strengths in areas of liability insurance work and health service law, one partner is an accredited specialist in medical negligence. Three partners are admitted as solicitor advocates with rights of audience in the highest law courts in Scotland.

Private Client Recognised as one of the foremost private client practices in Scotland. The firm continues to develop with particular emphasis on providing investment and tax advice to high net worth individuals.

Parliamentary A specialist parliamentary team advises on all aspects of work in the Scottish Parliament and Anderson Strathern is the only law firm in Scotland to be appointed to the panel retained for the preparation of legislation on behalf of the Scottish Executive.

Corporate The corporate group houses many of the firm's key specialisms including media and entertainment, IP/IT and sports law work. Experienced in high value property funding work, M&A and corporate restructuring, the group covers the full spectrum of business law.

CLIENTELE Clients include The Royal College of Nursing, Napier University, The National Trust for Scotland, Scottish Rugby Union, The Coal Authority, The Crown Estate, Manor Kingdom, Bank of Scotland, The Royal Bank of Scotland, Scotmid, Stannifer and Bannatyne's.

LAW FIRMS A-Z

Andrea & Co
Triatha House, Millbrook, Guildford, GU1 3XJ **Tel** (01483) 889880 **Fax** (01483) 889881

Andrew Bryce & Co
7 Queen Street, Coggeshall, CO6 1UF **Tel** (01376) 563123 **Fax** (01376) 563336

Andrew Keenan & Co
Nickleby House, Charles Dickens Terrace, Maple Road, London, SE20 8RE **Tel** (020) 8659 0332 **Fax** (020) 8659 3689

Andrew M. Jackson

Essex House, Manor Street, Hull, HU1 1XH
Tel (01482) 325242 **Fax** (01482) 212974 **DX** 11920
Email lawyers@amj.co.uk   **Website** www.amj.co.uk

Managing Partner	John Hammersley
Number of partners	23
Assistant solicitors	32
Other fee-earners	22

AREAS OF PRACTICE	
Commercial Property	30%
Corporate	10%
Shipping	20%
Litigation	20%
Private Client	20%

CONTACTS	
Commercial Property	Bill Fisher
Corporate	Mark Warburton
Family	Andrew J Haines
Litigation	Hugh Smith
Private Client	Kevin Webster
Shipping	Silas Taylor

THE FIRM The firm's services are founded on committed and well-motivated lawyers delivering top quality advice and value for money.

PRINCIPAL AREAS OF WORK
Corporate M&A, corporate finance, partnership, franchise and agency agreements and joint ventures.
Shipping & Transport Ship sale, purchase and finance, collision, salvage, charterparty, and Bills of Lading disputes. Road and air transport, CMR.
Commercial Property Landlord and tenant, property development and planning.
Private Client Tax, trusts and tax planning.
Agency Work Undertaken in all local civil courts.
Legal Aid Family law and family mediation. Franchise holder.
Litigation Commercial, property, personal injury and employment.

CLIENTELE Local and national companies both public and private including MFI, Carpetright, Northern Foods, Express Dairies, Associated British Ports and P&O North Sea Ferries.

Anne Hall Dick & Co.
157 Kilmarnock Road, Shawlands, Glasgow, G41 3JE **Tel** (0141) 636 0003 **Fax** (0141) 636 0303

Ann L. Humphrey

The Boathouse Office, 57a Gainsford Street, London, SE1 2NB
Tel (020) 7378 9370 **Fax** (020) 7378 9360 **Email** annlhumphrey@dial.pipex.com
Contact Ann L Humphrey • Niche tax practice with substantial experience in VAT and corporate tax planning which operates from purpose-built offices at Tower Bridge. The firm provides a tax consultancy service for businesses and other professionals. Because the firm concentrates on what it does best, clients pay only for that dedicated expertise.

Anthony Collins Solicitors

St Philip's Gate, 5 Waterloo Street, Birmingham, B2 5PG
Tel (0121) 200 3242 **Fax** (0121) 212 7472 **DX** 13055 Birmingham 1
Email acs@anthonycollinssolicitors.com   **Website** www.anthonycollinssolicitors.com

Senior Partner	Anthony Collins
Number of partners	17
Assistant solicitors	35
Other fee-earners	26

AREAS OF PRACTICE	
Housing & Local Government	33%
Commercial Property	18%
Business Law/Licensing	16%
Litigation/PI/Medical Negligence	16%
Private Client (Family)	12%
Charities	5%

THE FIRM Founded in 1973, the Birmingham-based firm is a fast growing, niche law firm boasting the largest social housing, charities and community regeneration operations outside London, alongside strong commercial and private client teams.

PRINCIPAL AREAS OF WORK
Charities The team acts for over 100 clients, including Tearfund, Groundwork UK and Spring Harvest. It advises on strategic issues, and deals with the award of large-scale grants.
Clinical Negligence Dedicated specialists act for claimants in complex medical litigation including brain, spinal and birth injury cases, achieving multimillion pound settlements.
Construction The team advises clients operating especially in social housing and local government on procurement, partnering, adjudication and arbitration.

Continued overleaf

ANTHONY COLLINS SOLICITORS

Dispute Resolution The firm handles complex disputes and prides itself on a practical commercial approach. Particular successes have been achieved in claimant professional negligence work.

Employment The team advises Housing and Community Associations as well as the private sector. Clients include Maersk Air Limited and the United Kingdom Home Care Association. The firm is also well regarded for applicant work.

Family Balancing publicly funded and private work, the team undertakes matrimonial (including ancillary relief work), child contact and resident cases including social services. The firm has a number of multimillion pound high profile matters and the team has expanded in childcare law matters including Childrens Guardian work.

Licensing The team acts for many prominent names both nationally and at the forefront of the development of Birmingham, including bars and restaurants, theatres and cinemas, and hotels.

Projects & PFI Strong in PPP work, the team is involved in innovative funding projects for NE Derbyshire District Council and Stonebridge HAT and an IT procurement project for schools across Yorkshire and Humberside.

Commercial Property This team handles blue chip clients alongside social housing work such as a recent £210 million refinancing deal and a £65 million redevelopment.

Social Housing & Local Government The firm is a market leader in New Deal for Communities and social housing work, appointed by 15 NDC areas as legal advisors. The team conducts housing litigation work for social housing providers nationally and undertakes housing stock transfers and arms length arrangements for local authorities. Over 50 RSL clients, including Focus, Castle Vale HAT, Accord, HomeZone, West Wiltshire, Optima and Hanover.

Anthony Gold

New London Bridge House, 25 London Bridge Street, London, SE1 9TW
Tel (020) 7940 4000 **Fax** (020) 7378 8025 **DX** 39915 London Bridge South
Email mail@anthonygold.co.uk **Website** www.anthonygold.co.uk

43 Streatham Hill, London, SW2 4TP
Tel (020) 8678 5500 **Fax** (020) 8674 8004 **DX** 58604 Streatham
Email mail@anthonygold.co.uk

Managing Partner	David Marshall
Number of partners	10
Assistant solicitors	10
Other fee-earners	12

CONTACTS	
Admin/Public/Housing	Andrew Brookes
Clinical Negligence	Jon Nicholson
Commercial Disputes/Employment	Rajinder Mann
Commercial Property	Howard Lerman
Corporate & Commercial	David Marshall
Family Law/Mediation	Kim Beatson
	Caroline Bowden
Personal Injury	Jon Nicholson
Residential Property	Stephen Whitaker
Trusts & Estates	Christopher McNeill

THE FIRM Anthony Gold was founded in 1963. The firm is a progressive and expanding practice with specialist departments which represent both business and individual clients. Based at London Bridge, and also with offices in SW2, the firm excels at meeting the needs of both individual and business clients. The firm's highly regarded litigation practice is largely claimant-focused and aims to work in a way which matches clients' ability to pay its fees. In particular, it has been instrumental in the development of conditional fee agreements. David Marshall is co-author of *Conditional Fees: Law and Practice* (Sweet and Maxwell, 1999).

PRINCIPAL AREAS OF WORK

Company & Commercial The acquisition and disposal of companies and unincorporated businesses and all general commercial agreements.

Commercial Dispute Resolution General commercial contracts of both a national and international content with particular expertise in computer, engineering and construction disputes.

Employment Advising businesses and individuals on contracts of employment, redundancy, dismissal, European law, HR/employment policies at work and discrimination claims.

Family & Divorce Financial cases, maintenance and property, children's cases (including abductions), mediation and Inheritance Act cases. Kim Beatson is on the National Committee of the Solicitors' Family Law Association. Both Kim Beatson and partner, Caroline Bowden, are accredited family mediators. The firm has wide experience in international financial matters including high net worth individuals and freezing injunctions in multiple jurisdictions.

Housing/Property Litigation Residential and commercial landlord and tenant claims (for either party), disrepair, dilapidations, possession, forfeiture and lease renewals.

Clinical Negligence All categories of clinical negligence, with particular expertise in cerebral palsy and other brain injuries, obstetrics and gynaecology, infectious diseases, neurosurgery, orthopaedics, anaesthetics, accident and emergency medicine and general practice. Jon Nicholson and David Marshall are members of the Law Society's Clinical Negligence Panel.

Personal Injury A wide spectrum of personal injury claims for claimants, ranging from catastrophic brain and spinal injuries to road traffic accidents, accidents at work and tripping cases. All personal injury solicitors are members of APIL and on the Law Society's Personal Injury Panel.

Professional Negligence Acting for businesses and individuals in claims against solicitors, accountants, surveyors and financial advisors.

Public Law Judicial reviews of the decisions of local and public authorities in particular the housing, community care and education sectors. Andrew Brookes is Chair of the Housing Law Practitioners' Association.
Property Acquisitions, development and financial work for retailers, investors, landlords and home-buyers.
Trusts & Estates Specialising in tax planning, wills and the administration of estates and trusts.

Archibald Campbell & Harley WS

37 Queen Street, Edinburgh, EH2 1JX
Tel (0131) 220 3000 **Fax** (0131) 220 2288 **LP** 300 Edinburgh 2 **Email** admin@achws.co.uk
Website www.achws.co.uk

Ptnrs 15 **Asst solrs** 14 **Other fee-earners** 17 **Contact** Andrew Wallace • Known for innovative work in commercial property, corporate, planning, environment, debt recovery/insolvency, litigation and housing. Reputation for quality service, commercial flair and relevant, expert, practical advice.

AREAS OF PRACTICE	
Commercial Property	49%
Private Clients	25%
Litigation	12%
Corporate/Commercial	9%
Planning/Environmental	5%

Archon

Sun Court, 67 Cornhill, London, EC3V 3NB
Tel (020) 7397 9650 **Fax** (020) 7929 6316 **DX** 706 London/City
Email [nameoffeeearner]@archonlaw.co.uk

THE FIRM Archon was established in 1993 and specialises exclusively in employment law. Its principals are Jill Andrew, Nick Ralph and Susan Thompson, who between them have over 40 years' experience, and all of whom were previously with major City firms.

PRINCIPAL AREAS OF WORK The firm deals with all aspects of employment law for corporate clients including contentious and non-contentious matters and also acts for individuals in employment disputes. It aims to provide a highly personalised and responsive service geared to the needs of clients. It is pleased to offer competitive fee quotations and also has a range of fixed price services including the conduct of and representation at Employment Tribunals. Other services which the firm currently provides include bespoke employment law training courses for clients and the legal profession.

Number of partners	3
Assistant solicitors	4
Other fee-earners	4

AREAS OF PRACTICE	
Employment	90%
General Commercial Advice	10%

The inside view of the major UK law firms

Order the 2003 Student edition now:
www.ChambersandPartners.com

A-Z ■ LAW FIRMS

Arnold & Porter

Tower 42, 25 Old Broad Street, London, EC2N 1HQ
Tel (020) 7786 6100 **Fax** (020) 7786 6299
Website www.arnoldporter.com

THE FIRM Arnold & Porter was established in Washington, DC in 1946. The firm has a deserved reputation for providing high quality and efficient legal services. Central to the historic practice of the firm has been a focus on the intersection of law, business and public policy and an understanding of the industries in which clients operate. The firm's lawyers have frequently been retained by clients confronted with the most complex legal and business problems, often with a regulatory or governmental component, requiring innovative and practical solutions. Arnold & Porter provides a multi-disciplinary approach to client matters and works together across borders to develop international commercial and regulatory strategies for clients operating on a global basis.

London Office Arnold & Porter opened its London office in late 1997 to meet the increasing cross-border transactional and regulatory needs of its global clients. Since then, it has undergone immense change and growth. The office now has 34 attorneys and full transatlantic capabilities in competition, commercial transactions, intellectual property, product liability and regulatory matters. The year 2001 culminated with the acquisition of the leading UK/European product liability and pharmaceutical regulatory team of four partners: Ian Dodds-Smith, Dr Elizabeth Driver, Amanda Wearing and Alison Brown, and consultant Christine Bendall. Seven assistant solicitors joined as part of the team, including two medical doctors. The addition of this talented group, recognised for their legal expertise in the pharmaceutical, medical devices and cosmetics sectors, positions Arnold & Porter as the transatlantic law firm of choice for the pharmaceutical and medical technology industries.

PRINCIPAL AREAS OF WORK

Competition Arnold & Porter's London competition and EU team provides advice to clients undertaking national and international transactions, or who need to resolve competition issues at a European level or at a national level within Europe. The firm represents clients from a broad array of industries before the EC Commission, the Office of Fair Trading and the Competition Commission in relation to a range of competition concerns under EU and United Kingdom laws, including allegations of abuse of dominant position or anti-competitive prices. In addition, the team's lawyers have experience in dealing with major anti-trust inquiries, price fixing issues, distribution and licensing agreements, strategic alliances and joint ventures. Members of the London team undertake and co-ordinate work necessary to obtain competition clearances for mergers, acquisitions and joint ventures from the EC Commission and from national authorities in the EU, Central/Eastern Europe and beyond. The London team specialises in finding solutions to complex competition problems for large and multinational firms. In addition to competition work, the team advises on other aspects of EU law, particularly relating to the free movement of goods within the EU.

Intellectual Property The intellectual property team in London focuses on contentious and transactional intellectual property issues with a special emphasis on hi-tech matters. The firm's intellectual property specialists have comprehensive experience in the acquisition, protection, commercialisation and enforcement of all types of intellectual property rights. The team also has the ability to enforce or defend intellectual property rights, including patents, through litigation or arbitration when that proves necessary.

Information Technology London's information technology practice group understands the complex issues presented by transactions involving technology and provides advice on a wide range of information technology related transactions and regularly restructures, drafts and negotiates outsourcing and distribution of technology products and services. Other work involves issues relating to the protection of data, computer misuse, protection of know-how or confidential information, the transfer of software and rights in software. The London IT practice group also has considerable experience in outsourcing arrangements and in establishing strategic relationships. Group members all have a long track record of advising companies involved in outsourcing transactions, including some of the largest and most complex UK and global outsourcing deals undertaken to date.

Life Sciences The life sciences group in London is one of a very few groups in the world specialising exclusively in collaborative development and licensing agreements, strategic partnering agreements and other forms of licensing agreement between biotechs and large pharmaceutical companies, whether the biotech is a product company or a platform technology company. The group has unparalleled experience of these sorts of transactions. The London office life science practice is also able to offer an unparalleled service conducting mid-cap mergers and acquisitions for pharmaceutical and biotech companies in the European market either directly, in the UK, or as co-ordinating counsel in the case of other countries in Europe. With its knowledge of the business sector the firm is one of the leading groups in the UK for pharmaceutical and biotech sector transactions, whether commercial or corporate, with the exception of large, set-piece, industry headline, multibillion dollar mergers and acquisition transactions.

Telecommunications The telecommunications industry, with its wide array of existing and emerging

Chairman	Michael N Sohn
Managing Partner	James J Sandman
London Head Partner	Fern O'Brian
UK	
Number of partners	12
Assistant solicitors	22
UK total	34
International	
Number of partners	242
Associates	375
Of counsel	18
Special counsel	24
Staff attorneys	49
International total	690

CONTACTS
UK

Anti-trust, Competition & Trade Regulation	
	Tim Frazer
Corporate & Securities	Jeremy Willcocks
Life Sciences	Julian Thurston
Intellectual Property & Technology Litigation	
	Ian Kirby
Litigation	Fern O'Brian
Pharmaceutical & Medical Technology	
	Ian Dodds-Smith
Product Liability	Ian Dodds-Smith
Technology	Sarah Kirk
	Andrew Hooles
Telecommunications	Michael Ryan

US

Anti-trust, Competition & Trade Regulation	
	Bill Baer
Bankruptcy	Daniel Lewis
Benefits & Employment Law	Edward Bintz
Corporate & Securities	Steven Kaplan
Environmental	Thomas Milch
Financial Institutions	Patrick Doyle
Food, Drug & Medical Devices	William Vodra
Government Contracts	Joseph West
Healthcare	Grant Bagley
Intellectual Property & Technology	
	David Apatoff
	Joel Freed
International	Lawrence Schneider
Legislative/Public Policy	Jeffrey Smith
Life Sciences	Richard Johnson
Product Liability	Robert Weiner
	Ellen Reisman
Project Finance	Whitney Debevoise
Real Estate	George Covucci
Tax	Richard Hubbard
Telecommunications	Norman Sinel

ARNOLD & PORTER

technologies, poses complex problems and presents challenging opportunities that require effective legal strategies. Arnold & Porter has a broad and innovative practice representing entities grappling with telecommunications issues. Established more than 40 years ago by one of the firm's founding partners, a former chairman of the US Federal Communications Commission (FCC), the firm's practice covers the spectrum of activities that defines the telecommunications industry today, including traditional telephone, data and wireless communications; cable, satellite and broadcasting; internet and advanced technologies. The London practice provides commercial, regulatory, litigation and legislative counsel and strategic advice to corporations, government entities, institutions and individuals before the regulatory agencies, the courts and governments. Governments and international institutions also seek the firm's counsel on the domestic and international implications of existing and emerging technologies and in new regulatory and marketplace structures.

Corporate & Commercial The team of corporate lawyers in London has extensive experience in advising clients on a broad range of corporate transactions such as domestic and cross-border mergers and acquisitions, joint ventures, flotations/IPOs, secondary issues (such as placings or rights issues), private equity funding and venture capital investments. The corporate group also assists clients in establishing a wide range of commercial relationships, including asset acquisitions, distributorships and other sales relationships. For many relatively routine transactions, the firm strives to maximize value by closing quickly and cost-effectively. It also takes pride in its success in structuring complex and novel transactions. The lawyers in the London office work closely with lawyers in the firm's other offices to achieve client objectives in matters with cross-border implications.

Product Liability/Litigation Managing some of the largest and most complex product liability matters in the world, Arnold & Porter acts both as national counsel and as trial counsel in many individual cases in the US. For example, the firm serves as the US national co-ordinating counsel and trial counsel for Wyeth in its phen-fen diet drug litigation, which involves a wide range of issues, including compliance with Food and Drug Administration (FDA); new drug and adverse event reporting regulations; the development and evaluation of epidemiological and clinical data; and novel class action issues in both the litigation and settlement contexts. The firm has defended approximately 15,000 cases in 49 US states, as well as the 1,000 federal cases that have been consolidated in Philadelphia. The firm's lawyers have drafted most of the class action briefs and argued those motions. Arnold & Porter is also responsible for working with approximately 500 scientific and regulatory experts who have appeared in one or more of the cases. Most recently, the attorneys were the principal architects of a $4.75 billion settlement that should resolve much of that litigation. Arnold & Porter served as US national defence counsel for a large volunteer blood collector in cases concerning individuals who allegedly contracted the AIDS virus from blood transfusions. The firm obtained numerous rulings granting summary judgment on negligence, strict liability and breach of warranty claims and won favourable verdicts in four cases that have been tried before juries.

Pro Bono Work Arnold & Porter's distinguished 55 year tradition of pro bono service has established an exceptional reputation in the legal community as a whole. The firm has special ties with many important public interest organisations that provide critical legal services to the disadvantaged, and its pro bono work is characterised by diversity. There is a growing movement in US law firms in London to strengthen and enhance their pro bono programmes, with the overall view of promoting pro bono in a global environment. Arnold & Porter's recently established London office pro bono practice includes research on public defender schemes around the world for JUSTICE, a human rights charity project which involved its lawyers on both sides of the Atlantic; pro bono assistance to UK families affected by the US tragedy on September 11th in New York; assisting the international human rights organisation Interights on the application of UK data protection legislation; assisting the Lady Hoare Trust, a charitable company involved in providing social work support to the families and sufferers of juvenile chronic arthritis and limb deformities during childhood; and assisting Royal Albert Hall in establishing a US/UK not-for-profit organisation to foster US/UK cultural exchange.

CLIENTELE Arnold & Porter's clients are corporations from the *Fortune* 500. The firm's attorneys cover a broad spectrum of legal specialties and experience, and their approach to service is multidimensional.

INTERNATIONAL With 700 attorneys firmwide, the firm has a broad international practice, in addition to its Washington, DC and London offices, the firm maintains offices in New York, Los Angeles, Century City, Denver, and Northern Virginia, and an extensive network of working relationships with law firms throughout the world.

RECRUITMENT The firm's hiring standards are rigorous. It seeks candidates who have demonstrated academic excellence. Arnold & Porter's growing London office is located in the International Financial Centre in the City of London. The firm strives to foster a collegial and informal atmosphere, which is enhanced by twice weekly informal social gatherings and other events, casual dress, associate mentoring programmes and team based assignment policies. Arnold & Porter encourages attorneys at all levels to be involved in the administration of the office and the development of the firm's transatlantic practice. Associates are expected to work on several matters at once and to assume responsibility

Continued overleaf

A-Z ■ LAW FIRMS

quickly. The firm emphasises teamwork and exposure to a number of different partners and clients. It tries to accommodate associates' areas of interests. The firm's commitment to excellence ensures that training is a continuous process with a series of training programmes, seminars and discussion groups and on a day to day basis with partners, who are specialists in their own areas. There is an excellent mentoring programme, which is a continuous form of feedback with partners and associates. Associates receive evaluations on a yearly basis and at that time there is an opportunity to discuss his or her career with the firm's associate evaluation committee. Associates also provide feedback on a periodic basis to the partners with whom they work. Arnold & Porter is committed to equal employment opportunity and to a programme of affirmative action to fulfil that policy. The firm values diversity and affirmatively solicits applications from all qualified applicants, including women, minorities and individuals with disabilities.

■ Arnold Thomson

205 Watling Street West, Towcester, NN12 6BX
Tel (01327) 350266 **Fax** (01327) 353567 **DX** 16932 Towcester
Email enquiries@arnoldthomson.com **Website** www.arnoldthomson.com

AREAS OF PRACTICE	
Sales, Purchases & Development Work	35%
Trusts/Tax & Probate	25%
Agricultural Tenancies	15%
Civil Litigation	10%
Partnerships	10%
Quotas	5%

Contact Michael Thomson • Mike Thomson heads a team including several senior lawyers with extensive experience in areas of agricultural and commercial property work handled across England and Wales. The firm regularly deals with agricultural tenancy work for other solicitors.

■ Arthur Cox - Northern Ireland

Stokes House, 17-25 College Square East, Belfast, BT1 6HD
Tel (028) 9023 0007 **Fax** (028) 9026 2650 **DX** 2012 NR Belfast 2
Email bt@arthurcox.ie **Website** www.arthurcox.com

Contact Partner	Angus Creed
Number of partners	6
Assistant solicitors	7
Other fee-earners	5

AREAS OF PRACTICE	
Property	30%
Litigation (inc. Employment)	30%
Banking/Financial Services	20%
Company/Commercial Law	20%

THE FIRM Arthur Cox - Northern Ireland was established in 1996, following the merger of the Belfast office of Arthur Cox, one of the largest practices in the Republic of Ireland, with the long established law firm of Norman Wilson & Co which has particular strengths in the areas of corporate banking, commercial, property and employment law. The firm merged in December 1997 with Martin & Brownlie to give added strength to its employment and litigation departments. The firm is in a unique position to provide a range of cross-border services from its Belfast and Dublin offices.

PRINCIPAL AREAS OF WORK

Banking/Financial Services The firm is established as one of the leading practices in all aspects of banking and secured lending.
Company/Commercial Includes all types of company/commercial law matters, mergers and acquisitions, joint ventures, agency and distribution agreements with particular emphasis on cross-border transactions.
Competition/European Competition and EU regulatory advice with particular reference to cross-border transactions.
Commercial Property Covers a significant range of property and commercial property related transactions including commercial development for private and public companies and financial institutions.
Litigation/Employment A wide range of litigation services with particular reference to employment and commercial litigation.

INTERNATIONAL The firm has offices in Dublin, London and New York.

CONTACTS	
Banking/Financial Services	Angus Creed
	Judith Brown
Civil Litigation	Peter Martin
	Anna Beggan
	Angela Maguire
	Amanda Wylie
Commercial Property	Rowan White
	Patricia Lyons
	Anne Donnelly
Company/Commercial	Kerry Canavan
	Peter Stafford
Competition/European	John Meade

asb law

8 Ifield Road, Crawley, RH11 7YY
Tel (01293) 603603 **Fax** (01293) 603666 **DX** 57100 Crawley-1
Email enquiries@asb-law.com **Website** www.asb-law.com

Chief Executive	Christopher Honeyman Brown
Number of partners	45
Number of fee-earners	100
Total staff	327

AREAS OF PRACTICE

Commercial Property (inc. Planning)	17%
Commercial Litigation	15%
Corporate & Commercial	14%
Employment	12%
Residential Property	10%
Family	9%
Personal Injury	8%
Wills, Trusts & Probate	7%
Insolvency	7%

CONTACTS

Banking	Russell Bell
Claims	Francis Lacy-Scott
Commercial	Caroline Armitage
Commercial Contracts	Alina Nosek
Commercial Litigation & TeC Team	Andrew Clinton
Corporate Finance	Don Burstow
Corporate Reconstruction	Anne Kane
Employment	Rebecca Thornley-Gibson
Family	Fiona Wilson
Insolvency	Andrew Taylor
Insolvency & Litigation	Gary Player
IP	Karen Lord
Licensing	Stephen Thomas
M&A & Takeovers	Jonathan Grant
Private Client	Ursula Danagher
Property Litigation	Rex Cowell
Property Services	Michael Bailey
Residential Property	Robert Moyle
Town & Country Planning	Roger Curtis
Travel & Aviation	Lee Hills
Wills, Trusts & Probate	Raymond Harris

THE FIRM asb law continues to go from strength to strength across the South East. The recent merger with Keene Marsland has added significantly to both the commercial and private client sectors across Kent, Surrey, Sussex and South London. The firm's commercial and private client base demonstrates both breadth and depth. In the commercial sector, clients included airlines and travel companies, universities and colleges, blue-chip companies, local authorities, insurance companies, breweries, construction companies and accountants. The firm also acts for a wide range of substantial listed and privately owned companies with turnovers ranging from £500,000 to £100m. In the private client sector, the family, conveyancing, wills, trust, probate and personal injury groups are amongst the largest across the region.

Other Offices Brighton, Croydon, Horsham, Maidstone, Mitcham and Chatham.

PRINCIPAL AREAS OF WORK The firm continues its drive to develop services that focus on satisfying clients' needs.

Travel & Aviation The team has expanded and is ideally positioned to provide specialist legal advice to one of the world's most rapidly expanding industries.

Technology, E-Commerce & Computer (TEC) The team has built a substantial client base and been involved in a range of significant transactions.

Employment The employment group has further developed Praesidium, a service which offers employers 24 hour telephone helpline access to a solicitor specialising in employment law. Other features include employment tribunal representation with a protected guarantee that will meet up to £50,000 of legal fees and awards per claim.

Employment Benefit Scheme The Employee Benefit Scheme (EBS) has developed significantly during the last year. Under the scheme, employees receive a free initial consultation with a solicitor specialising in their area of concern, and a ten per cent discount on legal fees if further work is required.

Corporate Finance The corporate finance team handles a full range of high-value corporate finance, merger and acquisition and company restructuring work. The team has rapidly won a reputation as one of the largest and most experienced corporate groups in the region, and has won a series of high profile deals and banking clients.

Commercial Contracts The team deals regularly with high value procurement contracts which range from IT contracts to IPR licences and disposals in the private sector. Recent contracts have strengthened its reputation in the public sector.

Planning & Environment The team is a specialist unit dealing with planning, environmental and property litigation issues for a broad range of national clients, local authorities and representative groups.

Commercial Property The commercial property group provides advice on acquisitions, leasing, disposal of commercial property, agricultural interests, hotels, licensed premises, offices, shops, estate development and housing association law.

Insolvency The insolvency group is acknowledged to be a leader in their field in the South East and has won the DTI contract for handling directors' disqualification proceedings. The group has introduced the Insolvency Assist service, which is a joint venture with Greystoke Legal Services to cover the cost of litigation for insolvency practitioners.

Commercial Litigation The commercial litigation group has expertise in commercial disputes, professional negligence, construction, property and debt collection as well as High Court litigation for UK and overseas clients.

Family The expanding family group has brought in five highly experienced lawyers in the last year and continues to target high net worth clients.

Wills, Trusts & Probate The wills, trusts and probate group has further developed its long-standing relationships with City-based law firms and now receives regular London-based client referrals requiring technical guidance on personal tax and estate planning issues.

Personal Injury & Medical Negligence The personal injury and medical negligence group has expanded in relation to defendant work for insurance companies, plaintiff medical negligence and as a leading specialist in handling personal injury work for holiday companies and airlines.

Ashok Patel & Co

1 Crane Court, Fleet Street, London, EC4A 2EG **Tel** (020) 7797 6300 **Fax** (020) 7797 6315

Ashton Graham

Electric House, Lloyds Avenue, Ipswich, IP1 3HZ **Tel** (01473) 232425 **Fax** (01473) 230505

A-Z LAW FIRMS

Ashurst Morris Crisp

Broadwalk House, 5 Appold St, London, EC2A 2HA
Tel (020) 7638 1111 **Fax** (020) 7638 1112 **DX** 639 London
Email enquiries@ashursts.com **Website** www.ashursts.com

Senior Partner	Geoffrey Green
Managing Partner	Justin Spendlove

CONTACTS	
Buyouts/Private Equity	Charles Geffen
Commercial Contracts	Jeremy Hill
Commercial Litigation	Edward Sparrow
Construction & Engineering	Christopher Vigrass
Corporate	Chris Ashworth
E-commerce	Mark Lubbock
Employment & Benefits	Caroline Carter
Energy	Michael Johns
EU/Competition	Julian Ellison
	Nigel Parr
Financial Institutions	
Products & Services	Jeremy Hill
Information Technology	Mark Lubbock
Intellectual Property	Ian Starr
International Arbitration & Dispute Resolution	
	Ronnie King
International Finance	Nigel Ward
Investment Banking	Adrian Clark
Investment Funds	Roger Walsom
Life Sciences	Mark Lubbock
Media & Film	Tony Ghee
Planning	Tony Curnow
Product Liability	John Evans
Projects	Mark Elsey
Property Litigation & Licensing	Michael Madden
Public Sector	Tony Curnow
Real Estate	Simon Cookson
Reconstruction & Insolvency	Ben Tidswell
Tax	John Watson
Telecommunications	Clive Tucker
World Trade	Mark Clough QC

THE FIRM Ashurst Morris Crisp is a major international law firm with offices in Europe, Asia and America. Ashursts provides a high quality integrated legal service across all its offices, focused on all major aspects of business and financial law, with specialist sector knowledge and highly developed transaction management skills, supported by major investment in training and know-how infrastructure.

PRINCIPAL AREAS OF WORK Ashursts operates in all principal areas of commercial law including:
Company & Commercial The firm advises clients on cross-border mergers and acquisitions; joint ventures; private equity transactions; corporate finance; EU and competition law; reconstruction and insolvency; IP; IT; insurance and employment, incentives and pensions.
Energy, Transport & Infrastructure Ashursts offers a full service to both private and public sector clients in the infrastructure and transport businesses, energy and resources companies, and utilities, whether active or passive investors or intermediaries in those areas.
International Finance The firm advises lenders, issuers, borrowers and advisers in the fields of corporate debt derivatives, bond issues, acquisitions and project finance, leveraged finance transactions and trade finance.
Litigation Advice is given on construction and development issues, international arbitration and dispute resolution, EU and competition law, product liability, insolvency and professional negligence and property litigation.
Real Estate Ashursts works with landlords, developers, tenants and public authorities, offering general property, planning, environmental law and litigation advice.
Tax The firm handles all aspects of cross-border work including international buyouts, collective investment schemes, demergers, securitisations and debt trading.

INTERNATIONAL The firm has offices in Brussels, Frankfurt, London, Madrid, Milan, Munich, New York, Paris, Singapore and Tokyo. It also has a liaison office in New Delhi. All business and commercial languages are spoken.

RECRUITMENT The firm recruits both qualified and trainee solicitors to all areas of its practice. Applicants need not only to have achieved high academic standards, but also to possess individuality and commercial awareness that can be applied to issues, ensuring the most appropriate solution for the client. For more information, please visit the firm's website or contact Stuart Walker, HR manager.

■ Askews
4-6 West Terrace, Redcar, TS10 3BX **Tel** (01642) 475252 **Fax** (01642) 482793

■ A S Law
Myrtle Parade, Liverpool, L7 7EL **Tel** (0151) 707 1212 **Fax** (0151) 707 2458

■ Attwater & Liell
147 High Road, Loughton, IG10 4LY **Tel** 020 8508 2111 **Fax** 020 8508 8879

■ Avery Naylor
35-36 Walter Road, Swansea, SA1 5NW **Tel** (01792) 463 276 **Fax** (01792) 458 842

■ Babington & Croasdaile
9 Limavady Road, Waterside, Londonderry, BT47 1JV **Tel** (02871) 349631 **Fax** (02871) 345785

Backhouse Jones

The Printworks, Ribble Valley Enterprise Park, Clitheroe, BB7 9WD
Tel (01254) 828300 **Fax** (01254) 828301
Email enquiries@backhouses.co.uk **Website** www.backhouses.co.uk

THE FIRM Backhouse Jones is a specialist niche practice servicing the commercial road transport industry. The firm can trace its roots to 1825 and acted for its first transport clients in 1930 when the first Transport Act was introduced.

PRINCIPAL AREAS OF WORK Industry specific advice is dedicated to licensing, regulatory compliance law, and defendant insurance litigation. This technical specialism ensures outstanding solutions in employment, risk management, litigation, business structure and contractual issues.

CLIENTELE The client base ranges from large international plcs to owner operators whose one common characteristic is the transportation of goods or passengers

Number of partners	3
Assistant solicitors	3
Other fee-earners	3

AREAS OF PRACTICE	
Road Transport Law (Bus, Coach, Haulage Offences)	25%
Transport Licensing (Driver, Vehicle, Operator)	25%
Defendant Personal Injury	25%
Commercial Litigation	10%
Employment	10%
Other	5%

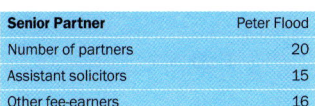

Badhams

95 Aldwych, London, WC2B 4JF
Tel (020) 7242 4154 **Fax** (020) 7404 0009 **DX** 14 Ch.Ln.
Email info@badhams.net **Website** www.badhams.net

8 Bedford Park, Croydon, CR02 2AP
Tel (020) 8688 3030 **Fax** (020) 8688 3166 **DX** 144481 Croydon 25
Email info@badhams.net

THE FIRM Badhams is a leading defendant insurance litigation firm and is on the panel of the four major insurers. Multi-track and fast track work, mainly personal injury, is carried out at the firm's Croydon offices. Large technical claims are handled at Aldwych. The firm has a substantial professional indemnity practice called plexus-Law, also at the Aldwych offices, which handles large and complex cases for the Lloyds and London company markets. Badhams was known as Badhams Thompson until 2001, when it was joined by Tim Oliver and a number of solicitors from a well established insurance law firm.

PRINCIPAL AREAS OF WORK Badhams has substantial fast track and multi-track teams. Motor, EL/PL form the bulk of this work. Technical claims, particularly related to subsidence are strengths of the firm. Professional indemnity work is handled by plexus-Law and comprises property, financial, disease, utilities, transport and subrogated property claims. Recent reported cases include Bybrook Barn, Court of Appeal; Codd v Thomson Holidays, Court of Appeal; Martin v Thomson Holidays; Anglian Water v Crawshaw Robbins; TSB Bank v Robert Irving & Burns; The Mortgage Corporation v Halifax; DSL Group v Unisys Intl.; UCB v Halifax; Capital & Counties v Hampshire Fire Brigade; MDIS Ltd v Swinbank; Kelly v London Transport Executive.

CLIENTELE The firm's client base comprises the major insurers and leading professional indemnity syndicates at Lloyds.

Senior Partner	Peter Flood
Number of partners	20
Assistant solicitors	15
Other fee-earners	16

A-Z LAW FIRMS

Baker Botts

99 Gresham Street, London, EC2V 7BA
Tel (020) 7726 3636 **Fax** (020) 7726 3637
Email tony.higginson@bakerbotts.com   **Website** www.bakerbotts.com

THE FIRM Founded in 1840 in Houston, Baker Botts is the legal and business advisor of choice to many of the world's leading companies. With over 650 lawyers in eight US and international offices, its business is global in scope, influence and perspective with leading practices in energy, high-tech, telecoms and life sciences. Baker Botts demonstrates an unwavering commitment to the highest professional standards in the service of its clients and its work has been acclaimed by *The Petroleum Economist* which ranked the firm in the top three global firms offering 'best overall value' to the worldwide energy sector in 2001 and the highest ranked US firm for 'best knowledge of English law'. Likewise, *IP Worldwide* ranked Baker Botts as one of the top four intellectual property litigation firms.

The London Office Since opening an office in London in 1998, Baker Botts has grown significantly and now handles from London market-leading energy, corporate, telecoms, chemicals and dispute resolution matters. Much of the office's work is cross-border in nature and examples of recent major assignments include advising on the $2.5bn SCP (Shah Deniz) gas pipeline from Azerbaijan to Turkey, and advising Liberty Media Corporation, a leading US media and broadband company, on its European expansion. The office has a successful dispute resolution practice, and in 2001 it advised on two multi-billion disputes in the UK and Europe.

INTERNATIONAL The London office is an integral part of the Baker Botts network of offices which includes Austin, Baku, Dallas, Houston, New York, Riyadh and Washington DC. The firm is a member of Lex Mundi and has a strategic alliance with Afridi & Angell, a law firm with offices in Abu Dhabi, Dubai, Islamabad and Sharjah.

Managing Partner (International)	
	Walter Smith
Partner-in-Charge (London)	Antony Higginson
London	
Number of partners	5
Number of associates	12
Number of other fee-earners	2
International	
Number of partners	242
Number of associates	409
Number of other fee-earners	195

CONTACTS	
Chemicals	Paul Landen
Corporate/M&A	Paul Landen
Electricity	Samantha Hampshire
Energy	Antony Higginson
	Samantha Hampshire
Litigation/Arbitration	Jennifer Smith
Oil & Gas	Antony Higginson
	Kevin Dent
Project Finance	Paul Landen
	Kevin Dent
TMT	Paul Landen

BAKER BOTTS

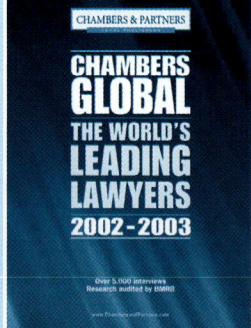

The world's leading lawyers
All 4,000 of them
All in one place

The 3rd edition: available now
www.ChambersandPartners.com

Baker & McKenzie

100 New Bridge Street, London, EC4V 6JA
Tel (020) 7919 1000   **Fax** (020) 7919 1999   **DX** 233 Chancery Lane, WC2
Email london.info@bakernet.com   **Website** www.bakernet.com

THE FIRM Baker & McKenzie, founded in 1949, is one of the world's leading law firms. The firm has grown by anticipating trade and capital flows around the world. Today Baker & McKenzie has 62 offices in 35 jurisdictions. Its strategy is to provide for its clients the best combination of local legal and commercial knowledge and international expertise and resources. Baker & McKenzie aims, above all, to provide commercially oriented advice of the highest quality which adds value to the client's business. The firm looks at the best method of service delivery in each case. It is sensitive to the need to provide not only legal excellence, but also a user friendly service which is efficient, transparent and value for money. To this end the firm implements a variety of client care and quality management programmes. Baker & McKenzie is uniquely placed to blend advice on the law and practice of a number of jurisdictions to help clients achieve their objectives; its lawyers work in national, European and international practice groups in their areas of expertise.

London Office The London office is an established City firm with a strong domestic and foreign client base. The London office has more than 390 legal professionals, the vast majority of whom are UK qualified, together with resident US admitted banking and securities specialists. Many lawyers have worked in other offices of the firm, enabling them to bring a fresh perspective even to purely domestic assignments. It provides a full range of legal services to corporations, financial institutions, governments and entrepreneurs. The office offers 'hot line' arrangements and secondments of its lawyers to major clients. As an integral part of its service, the firm offers to its clients regular seminars and workshops, newsletters and bulletins on legal developments, magazines and publications. The firm also offers access to its library services and to a number of commercial and legal databases, and rapid internal and external communications through its proprietary Bakernet email network and other networks.

PRINCIPAL AREAS OF WORK International and domestic banking and finance; derivatives and related markets; financial services; privatisations; domestic and cross-border corporate and commercial transactions; the structuring of multinational groups; domestic and international equity and debt offerings; corporate finance and flotations; venture capital; privately financed projects; international tax; VAT and import/export questions; litigation, arbitration and ADR; civil and commercial fraud; insolvency; European Union and competition law; trade law (WTO); energy; environmental; intellectual property; patents and trademarks; biotechnology; pharmaceuticals and healthcare; information technology; online services and e-commerce, telecommunications, entertainment and media; employment and pension matters; insurance and reinsurance; construction and engineering; commercial property; tax and trust planning; the legal aspects of lobbying.

INTERNATIONAL The firm has offices in Almaty, Amsterdam, Bahrain, Baku, Bangkok, Barcelona, Beijing, Berlin, Bogota, Brasilia, Brussels, Budapest, Buenos Aires, Cairo, Calgary, Caracas, Chicago, Dallas, Dusseldorf, Frankfurt, Geneva, Guadalajara, Hanoi, Ho Chi Minh City, Hong Kong, Houston, Juarez, Kyiv, Madrid, Manila, Melbourne, Mexico City, Miami, Milan, Monterrey, Moscow, Munich, New York, Palo Alto, Paris, Porto Alegre, Prague, Rio de Janeiro, Riyadh, Rome, St Petersburg, San Diego, San Francisco, Sao Paulo, Santiago, Singapore, Stockholm, Sydney, Taipei, Tijuana, Tokyo, Toronto, Valencia, Warsaw, Washington DC, Zurich. The firm conducts business in Afrikaans, Bulgarian, Cantonese, Czech, English, French, German, Greek, Hebrew, Hindi, Hungarian, Italian, Indonesian, Japanese, Kiswahili, Malay, Marathi, Polish, Portuguese, Punjabi, Russian, Spanish and Taiwanese.

RECRUITMENT For graduate recruitment opportunities, please contact Katie Allen on (020) 7919 1000 or email her at katie.allen@bakernet.com. Alternatively visit the firm's graduate website at www.ukgraduates.bakernet.com.

Managing Partner	Russell Lewin
UK	
Number of partners	73
Assistant solicitors	221
Other fee-earners	98
International	
Number of partners	605
Assistant solicitors	2,526
Other fee-earners	1,052

AREAS OF PRACTICE	
Corporate/Finance/EC/Tax/Commercial	53%
Employment/Pensions/Immigration	16%
Litigation/Construction	15%
Intellectual Property	11%
Commercial Property	5%

CONTACTS	
Banking & Finance	Chris Hogan
Capital Markets	Peter Magyar
Civil & Commercial Fraud	Nick Pearson
Commercial	Beatriz Araujo
Commercial Property	Stephen Turner
	Mike Smith
Construction	Jeremy Winter
Derivatives	Matthew Dening
Dispute Resolution	Nick Pearson
	Andrew Keltie
E-commerce	Robbie Downing
Employee Benefits	Michael Ingle
Employment	Christine O'Brien
Energy	Neil Donoghue
Environment	Alison Flood
EU, Competition & Trade	Lynda Martin Alegi
Financial Services	Marwan Al-Turki
Insolvency	Jeremy Goldring
Insurance	Peter Schwartz
Intellectual Property	Michael Hart
	Paul Rawlinson
IT	Michael Hart
	Harry Small
Pensions	Robert West
Pharmaceuticals & Healthcare	Beatriz Araujo
Projects	Mike Webster
Securities	Michael Caro
	Tim Gee
Structured & Project Finance	Annie Williams
Tax	James macLachlan
Telecommunications	Peter Strivens
VAT, Customs & Excise	Geoffrey Kay
Venture Capital	Charles Whitefoord

BAKER & MCKENZIE

A-Z ■ LAW FIRMS

Balfour & Manson

54-66 Frederick Street, Edinburgh, EH2 1LS
Tel (0131) 200 1200 **Fax** (0131) 200 1300 **DX** 4 Edinburgh **LP** 12 Edinburgh 2
Email enquiry@balfour-manson.co.uk **Website** www.balfour-manson.co.uk

THE FIRM One of the leading Scottish litigation practices, Balfour & Manson also has substantial commercial, private client and property client bases. The practice provides a comprehensive range of legal, financial and general advice, from a wide variety of departments with in-depth expertise, for Scottish, English and foreign clients and solicitors. The principal departments are litigation, commercial/corporate, private client and property.

PRINCIPAL AREAS OF WORK
Litigation Headed by Maggie Neilson, the firm has a strong litigation department which handles all aspects of litigation. It has particular expertise in acting in personal injury and has set up a dedicated Serious Injuries Unit. It also handles professional negligence and contractual claims; multi-party actions; and family law, with considerable experience in international child abduction. Additionally, this department handles commercial work, including insurance; intellectual property disputes; tribunal work; planning and building contracts.
Commercial/Commercial Property Led by John Hodge, this department handles purchase, lease, sale and security work for clients of all types and sizes and provides corporate services for medium-sized private companies.
Private Client Headed by Brenda Rennie, the department advises clients from within and without Scotland, providing wills, trusts and executries; tax work; finance and investment advice; and insurance services. This department offers unique support for elderly and infirm clients and their families.
Property Led by Kenneth Robertson, services include estate agency; mortgage advice; house purchase and sale and repossession work.

INTERNATIONAL Scottish Member of the PARLEX Group of European Lawyers. The firm handles work in French and German.

Chairman	Andrew Gibb
Number of partners	18
Assistant solicitors	15
Other fee-earners	25

AREAS OF PRACTICE
Litigation	50%
Private Client	20%
Property	20%
Commercial/Commercial Property	10%

CONTACTS
Commercial Property	John Hodge
Corporate	Alastair Keatinge
Domestic Property	Anne Pacey
	Kenneth Robertson
Employment	Katherine Taylor
Family	Andrew Gibb
Financial Services & Tax	Murray Burns
Litigation	A J Spencer Kennedy
	Elaine Motion
	Maggie Neilson
	Alfred Tyler
Private Client	Brenda Rennie

Band Hatton

1 Copthall House, Station Square, Coventry, CV1 2FY
Tel (024) 7663 2121 **Fax** (024) 7622 9038 **DX** 11207
Email law@bandhatton.co.uk **Website** www.bandhatton.co.uk

THE FIRM A well established practice, Band Hatton offers a high quality legal service to both business and private clients, utilising up-to-date working methods, while maintaining traditional values and a commitment to a personal and approachable service. The firm combines a thorough and accurate technical approach, with a commitment to providing a genuinely personal and responsive service, which offers good value for money. The firm enjoys a strong reputation in the commercial field, in particular for its commercial property work. The contentious side of the practice is expanding rapidly in the areas of commercial, employment and family law. Band Hatton is a member of LawNet, the Federation of Independent Law Firms and LawNet Europe, and has attained accreditation under ISO 9002 as well as holding a CLS Franchise.

Contact Partner	Philip Costigan
Number of partners	6
Assistant solicitors	4
Other fee-earners	6

CONTACTS
Commercial Litigation	Jon Wilby
Commercial Property	Philip Costigan
Other Commercial/Corporate	Haydn Jones
Private Client Litigation	Paul Wright
Private Client Non-contentious	Helen Dodd

■ Bannatyne, Kirkwood, France & Co

Exchange House, 16 Royal Exchange Square, Glasgow, G1 3AG
Tel (0141) 221 6020 **Fax** (0141) 221 5120
Email martin@b-k-f.demon.co.uk **Website** www.bkf.co.uk

Contact Martin B Smith • Established in 1785, the firm specialises in media law and defamation, representing several national newspaper companies. Other areas of expertise include employment law, reparation and trusts.

■ Banners Jones Middleton

Marsden Chambers, 2 Marsden Street, Saltergate, Chesterfield, S40 1JY **Tel** (01246) 560560 **Fax** (01246) 231188

Bannister Preston
30 Washway Road, Sale, M33 7QY **Tel** (0161) 973 2434 **Fax** (0161) 962 9562

Barbara Carter
117 Vicarage Road, King's Heath, Birmingham, B14 7QG **Tel** (0121) 441 3238 **Fax** (0121) 441 2191

Barcan Woodward
King William House, 13 Queen Square, Bristol, BS1 4NT **Tel** (0117) 925 8080 **Fax** (0117) 925 8081

Bark & Co
218 Strand, Temple Bar, London WC2R 1AT
Tel (020) 7353 1990 **Fax** (020) 7353 1880 **DX** 447 London Chancery Lane
Email office@barkco.com **Website** www.barkco.com

Senior Partner	Giles Bark-Jones
Number of partners	1
Assistant solicitors	22
Other fee-earners	18

AREAS OF PRACTICE	
White Collar Crime/Fraud	95%
General Crime	5%

CONTACTS	
White Collar Crime/Fraud	Giles Bark-Jones
General Crime	Claire Tyler
	Rifat Chowdhury
	Jonathan Wright

THE FIRM Bark and Co has established itself in recent years as a firm of solicitors offering many years experience of defending major fraud and other serious criminal cases. From the firm's foundation in 1997 to the present day, it has expanded, with turnover doubling in size annually to a firm of over 40 dedicated fee-earners specialising in defending all areas of major crime, including duty evasion, money laundering, internet fraud and all other areas of complex crime. The steady expansion of the firm has seen it move its offices in 2000 to the heart of the legal community on the Strand opposite the Royal Courts of Justice and, more recently, the opening of a second office on Fleet Street. As a member of the Serious Fraud Panel, the firm prides itself on the service to its clients and the standard of advice provided and, once instructed, assembles defence teams to deal with each individual case, bringing in specialist knowledge from across the firm whenever necessary. The firm only instructs barristers, both QCs and leading Juniors, who are well established within their field and brings them into the defence team as soon as is practicable. The firm being located so close to all the leading criminal Chambers allows the solicitors to easily keep in constant contact with the barristers instructed so they can deal with all matters that arise, even at short notice. The firm is experienced in dealing with work of an international nature and has associated offices in Spain with other links throughout Europe. General crime defence work is also handled by the firm with solicitors being members of local police station and court duty solicitor schemes. All types of general legal aid defence work is carried out for eligible clients.

PRINCIPAL AREAS OF WORK Bark and Co specialises in criminal defence work with particular expertise in defending in white collar crime and fraud cases, including all associated matters such as extradition, restraint and confiscation proceedings.

HM Customs & Excise Investigations/Prosecutions Extensive experience covering duty evasion, money laundering, missing trader, carousel and all other types of VAT fraud. Able to provide immediate assistance where allegations require attendance at premises of the client together with advice throughout investigation, negotiation or prosecution, with access to tax compliance experts to assist the defence team.

Inland Revenue Investigations/Prosecutions Experience in representing clients in negotiation with and prosecutions by the Special Compliance Office. Such matters can involve complex tax issues as well as alleged criminal conduct and use by the firm of specialist forensic accountants to assist the defence team is commonplace.

Serious Fraud Office Investigations/Prosecutions With the firm's emphasis on fraud and corporate crime, the firm has experience in defending cases brought by all major prosecuting authorities, including the Serious Fraud Office.

National Crime Squad Investigations/Prosecutions By defending cases that often involve police surveillance and undercover operations, the firm has accumulated vast knowledge of this type of defence work.

As specialists in defending large and complex cases, the firm also has a wealth of experience in dealing with matters ancillary to the criminal proceedings, such as:

Restraint Proceedings Offering expertise in all aspects of restraint proceedings, including applications to vary Restraint Orders, opposing the appointment of a receiver or liaising with receivers if appointed.

Confiscation Proceedings The firm has considerable experience in dealing with this specialised area of law in that it has a team of solicitors with wide-ranging knowledge of all aspects of confiscation who have successfully represented clients in opposing applications for multimillion pound confiscation orders.

Extradition The firm endeavours to provide the earliest possible advice to clients on all aspects of extradition proceedings with access to barristers who specialize in this area of the law.

A-Z LAW FIRMS

Barker Gotelee
41 Barrack Square, Martlesham Heath, Ipswich, IP5 3RF **Tel** (01473) 611211 **Fax** (01473) 610560

Barlow Lyde & Gilbert

Beaufort House, 15 St Botolph Street, London, EC3A 7NJ
Tel (020) 7247 2277 **Fax** (020) 7071 9000 **DX** 155 London CDE

Senior Partner	Richard Dedman
Managing Partner	Kennan Michel
Number of partners	68
Assistant solicitors	164
Other fee-earners	70

CONTACTS	
Aviation	Nicholas Hughes
Banking	Graham Wedlake
Commercial Litigation	David Arthur
Commercial Property	Malcolm Rogerson
Competition & EU	David Strang
Corporate & Finance	John Longdon
Corporate Insurance	Stephen Browning
Employment	Gary Freer
Environment	Valerie Fogleman
Information Technology/E-commerce	
	David Strang
Insolvency	Douglas Howie
Insurance Litigation	John Hanson
Medical Negligence	Kevin Bitmead
Personal Injury	Graham Dickinson
Professional Indemnity	David Arthur
Reinsurance	Colin Croly
Shipping	Nigel Wagland
Travel & Tourism	Richard Gimblett

THE FIRM Barlow Lyde & Gilbert is a major law firm with the main office located in the City of London. In addition, in the UK, BLG has a strategic presence in Oxford from where it advises clients in the technology sector, and a presence at Lloyd's to serve the insurance market. The firm also has an office in Hong Kong and has recently opened a second overseas office in Shanghai. BLG advises corporate organisations, government bodies, financial and other institutions in all spheres of business activity. The firm is recommended in all of its core areas – in commercial litigation, in insurance and reinsurance where the firm is regarded as pre-eminent, and in corporate and commercial work, especially in relation to e-business issues. The firm's long-term strategy is to build its strength in these chosen areas.

PRINCIPAL AREAS OF WORK
Litigation The firm has an outstanding reputation for its expertise in litigation and other forms of dispute resolution – it is the breadth and depth of the practice that distinguishes it from competitors. As well as acting for corporates in relation to a wide range of general commercial disputes, the firm is well known for several sector specialisms. Of particular note are the reinsurance, insurance, professional services and aerospace teams, which are all recognised as market leaders. Also highly regarded are the banking and financial institutions, employment, information technology and shipping teams. The firm's lawyers are geared to obtain the best possible result for the clients – alternative dispute resolution methods are used whenever appropriate and several partners are CEDR accredited mediators.
Corporate The corporate and finance practice handles the full range of corporate, finance and commercial work including buy-outs, joint ventures, flotations, reconstructions, corporate finance, corporate capital, banking regulatory investigations, taxation, insolvency, commercial property and EU and competition. The team has a particular focus on technology and e-business matters, containing one of the largest IT practices in the country. In this area BLG acts for a range of clients including banks lending to internet ventures, consultants advising on e-business strategy and applications, insurers providing internet based policies and manufacturers supplying essential companies for the transmission of data. BLG's corporate and finance skills combined with the pre-eminence in insurance and reinsurance work uniquely places the firm in a position to undertake corporate and corporate finance transactions for the insurance sector, and to remain at the forefront of alternative risk transfer and innovative bancassurance products.

INTERNATIONAL The firm also has offices in Hong Kong and Shanghai.

RECRUITMENT The provision of more than just legal services has always been at the heart of BLG's philosophy and this is demonstrated through the firm's impressive education and training programme. An extensive range of in-house publications and regular seminars on topical areas of aviation, banking, commercial, corporate finance, insurance, reinsurance, professional liability, employment and environmental law are provided for clients. Dedicated training programmes ensure that the firm's solicitors are completely up-to-date with all legal and practice developments and the firm puts great emphasis on effective commercial, as well as technically sound advice. The firm offers 16 training contracts each year. Prospective trainees should contact Caroline Walsh (grad.recruit@blg.co.uk) for details of the recruitment programme. Further information on Barlow Lyde & Gilbert is available at the firm's offices or can be viewed on the website.

Barlows
55 Quarry Street, Guildford, GU1 3UE **Tel** (01483) 562901 **Fax** (01483) 573725

LAW FIRMS ■ A-Z

Barnett Sampson

High Holborn House, 52-54 High Holborn, London, WC1V 6RL
Tel (020) 7831 7181 **Fax** (020) 7269 5141 **DX** 254 LDE
Email lawyers@barnett-sampson.co.uk

Number of partners	6
Assistant solicitors	5
Other fee-earners	3

THE FIRM Barnett Sampson is a niche firm able to 'punch above its weight'. It consistently works on transactions with leaders in the field. A hands-on approach by all fee-earners ensures a thorough, efficient and professional service to a range of clients.

CONTACTS
Commercial (inc. Company & Litigation)	Richard Barnett
Family	Ellie Chapman
	Camilla Fusco
	Julia Snow
Property	Ros Joseph

PRINCIPAL AREAS OF WORK

Commercial (inc. Company & Litigation) The firm deals with substantial value transactions and claims involving multijurisdictions, civil company fraud and financial services.

Family The expanded family team has substantial experience in all aspects of private family work, including high value ancillary relief; cohabitation cases; private childcare and adoption, including international aspects of these fields. All of the team are members of the Solicitors Family Law Association and partners are immediate past officers.

Property All types of commercial and residential property are dealt with, specialising in developments, franchises and shopping centre leases.

■ Barratt, Goff & Tomlinson
The Old Dairy, 67a Melton Road, West Bridgford, Nottingham, NG2 5GR **Tel** (0115) 981 5115 **Fax** (0115) 981 9409

■ Barrie Ward & Julian Griffiths
5 Clarendon Street, Nottingham, NG1 5HS **Tel** (0115) 941 2622 **Fax** (0115) 924 0485

■ Barry Shaw
13 Blackheath Village, London, SE3 9LA **Tel** (020) 8297 8899 **Fax** (020) 8297 2122

■ Bartram & Co
1st Floor, 302 Bath Road, Hounslow, TW4 7DN **Tel** (020) 8814 1414 **Fax** (020) 8814 1515

■ Bate Edmond Snape
6 The Quadrant, Coventry, CV1 2ED **Tel** (02476) 220 707 **Fax** (02476) 256 278

Bates, Wells & Braithwaite

Cheapside House, 138 Cheapside, London, EC2V 6BB
Tel (020) 7551 7777 **Fax** (020) 7551 7800 **DX** 42609 CHEAPSIDE 1
Email mail@bateswells.co.uk **Website** www.bateswells.co.uk

Number of partners	29
Assistant solicitors	23
Other fee-earners	24

THE FIRM Bates, Wells & Braithwaite was founded more than 100 years ago and the main office in London was opened in 1970. Originally handling the needs of smaller business clients the firm has developed a strong reputation for administrative, employment and immigration law as well as a pre-eminence in charity law. The firm is particularly notable for the large proportion of individuals, which actively participate in the sectors on which they advise in both a legal and non-legal capacity. Located in the City, Bates, Wells & Braithwaite is a unique firm combining a strong commercial and charity practice with a general emphasis on public interest work and the arts.

AREAS OF PRACTICE
Charity	25%
Employment	20%
Litigation	15%
Property	15%
Company/Commercial	10%
Immigration	5%
Media	5%
Private Client	5%

CONTACTS
Arts & Media	Sean Egan
Charity	Philip Kirkpatrick
	Stephen Lloyd
	Julian Blake
	Fiona Middleton
	Lord Phillips of Sudbury
	Rosamund Smith
	Alice Faure Walker
Commercial Litigation	Malcolm Robson
	Robert Oakley
Company/Commercial	Julian Blake
	Peter Bohm
	Hugh Craig

PRINCIPAL AREAS OF WORK

Charity Law The charity department has one of the largest charity law practices in the country and acts for many household names and international charities. It has particular expertise in obtaining charitable status for new groups and for initiatives within the charity sector. The firm provides a national advisory service to solicitors on charity matters and has been responsible through the years for many books, articles, and other publications.

Company & Commercial The company/commercial department undertakes work for a wide range of businesses and has developed considerable expertise. The work undertaken includes company takeovers, joint ventures, management buyouts, commercial contracts and tax advice.

Litigation The litigation department handles commercial litigation, mediation, and has a particular expertise in the field of administrative law/judicial review and human rights.

Property The property department handles all types of commercial property work and related financing and development work. There is particular expertise in advising charities.

Continued overleaf

A-Z ■ LAW FIRMS

Immigration The immigration department handles all aspects of immigration and nationality law including work permits, citizenship, residency and asylum work and human rights.
Employment The employment department advises on all aspects of employment law, including restrictive covenants, employee rights, discrimination, service agreements, dismissals and redundancies.
Arts & Media The arts and media department advises on all aspects of the theatre, film and television industries. The department deals with theatrical productions in the West End and throughout the UK, feature film production, all types of television production, and internet multimedia issues.
Private Client The private client department handles a wide range of tax and trust work.
Family Law The firm's family law department is the niche practice Hughes Fowler Carruthers. The two firms retain a close professional relationship.

INTERNATIONAL Bates, Wells & Braithwaite has significant involvement in international legal developments, being a co-founder of the Parlex Group of European Lawyers (EEIG No. 00001), which consists of a network of firms throughout western Europe.

CONTACTS (Continued)	
Employment	Martin Bunch
	William Garnett
Immigration	Emma Cohen
	Philip Trott
Private Client	Alice Faure Walker
Property	Tony Cartmell
	Nick Ivey
	Julius Wodzianski
Property Litigation	Eve Smith
Public Law	John Trotter
	Simon French

■ Batt Broadbent
Minster Chambers, 42-44 Castle Street, Salisbury, SP1 3TX   **Tel** (01722) 411 141   **Fax** (01722) 411 566

■ Battens (with Poole & Co)
Mansion House, Princes Street, Yeovil, BA20 1EP   **Tel** (01935) 846000   **Fax** (01935) 846001

Beachcroft Wansbroughs

100 Fetter Lane, London, EC4A 1BN
Tel (020) 7242 1011   **Fax** (020) 7831 6630   **DX** 45 London Chancery Lane WC2
Email info@bwlaw.co.uk   **Website** www.bwlaw.co.uk

30-40 Eastcheap, London, EC3M 1HD
Tel (020) 7208 6800   **Fax** (020) 7208 6801   **DX** 753 London City EC3

10-22 Victoria Street, Bristol, BS99 7UD
Tel (0117) 918 2000   **Fax** (0117) 918 2100   **DX** 7846 Bristol 1

9 Brindleyplace, Oozells Square, Birmingham, B1 2HE
Tel (0121) 698 5200   **Fax** (0121) 698 5290   **DX** 13057 Birmingham 1

7 Park Square East, Leeds, LS1 2LW
Tel (0113) 251 4700   **Fax** (0113) 251 4900   **DX** 14099 Leeds Park Square

St Ann's House, St Ann Street, Manchester, M2 7LP
Tel (0161) 934 3000   **Fax** (0161) 934 3288   **DX** 14341 Manchester 1

St Swithun's House, 1a St Cross Road, , Winchester, SO23 9WP
Tel (01962) 705500   **Fax** (01962) 705510   **DX** 2540 Winchester 1

Senior Partner	
The Rt Honourable The Lord Hunt of Wirral MBE	
Managing Partner	Robert Heslett
Number of partners	128
Number of associates	79
Other fee-earners	757

AREAS OF PRACTICE	
Commercial	45%
Litigation	45%
Mutual Law	10%

CONTACTS	
Commercial	Simon Hodson
Litigation	Paul Murray
Mutual Law	Christopher Charles
Corporate Services	Laurence Markham
Employment	Elizabeth Adams
Projects	Malcolm Austwick
Property	John Phelps
Public Law	Julian Gizzi

THE FIRM At Beachcroft Wansbroughs a different kind of law firm is being created. In 2001 changes were implemented to the way work is undertaken and the overall management of the firm. These changes enable the firm to work towards exceeding client expectations with innovative and cost effective solutions to business issues; a view supported by both client and feedback staff. The firm succeeds in combining the depth and spread of services that clients can expect from the UK's fourth largest national law firm, whilst maintaining an accessible and pragmatic business culture that is more often associated with single site or small law firms. The firm works with its clients extensively to anticipate, prevent and mediate as well as litigate. The firm's determination to understand the business issues and opportunities from a client's viewpoint demonstrates a distinct difference from many law firms who expect to work with clients only at times of difficulty. To meet the needs of sophisticated, risk aware clients, the firm has organised its practice areas to ensure that the focus is on delivering service and business solutions to clients, not just a set of highly expert professional skills. All three divisions focus on exceeding client expectations in terms of quality of advice, access to relevant expertise and responsiveness to the client's priorities, including timing, cost control and goals. Lawyers from all three divisions work together in interdisciplinary teams to continue to bridge the gap between convention and client needs. For many clients, the value of the firm's advice and services is not limited to a

single practice area. Client teams operate across practice areas and across divisions. The firm forms client teams on a national basis with access to partners and assistants in all or some of its offices in London, Birmingham, Bristol, Leeds, Manchester and Winchester. The firm's team in Brussels is an influential resource for the whole firm, ensuring that clients are fully aware of the opportunities available under EU and competition law. The firm is the first national law firm to achieve the Investor In People award in all its locations.

PRINCIPAL AREAS OF WORK

Commercial The firm's most widely regarded areas of expertise include corporate finance, employment, property, public law, IT/telecoms and public/private initiatives. Through these practices, the firm attracts work from existing and new clients from dynamic sectors of business including financial services, retail, property, health, technology, education, food, manufacturing and utilities as well as public bodies, local and central government. The strength of the firm's commercial practice can be seen in several ways:

Employment The firm's employment team is one of the largest national employment law teams in the UK.

Projects & PFI The firm's projects and PFI practice enjoys an enviable track record for completing deals during 2001 and 2002. The IT and telecom team attracts new partners and assistants, whilst the public law team continues to build a strong reputation for excellence.

Property The firm's property practice comprises specialist areas of commercial property, public sector property, planning, property litigation and property tax.

Corporate Services In the last year the firm's corporate services and banking practices have all attracted new partners and assistants from outside the firm.

Litigation Clients have access to dedicated, national teams with expert knowledge and experience across 16 specialist litigation services. The firm works closely with clients to take a planned and commercial approach to risk assessment. The firm has implemented team structures to complement the role of the lawyer as strategist, ensuring that its IT systems support its pro-active approach to case management and a consistent application of client protocols and high quality standards across all offices. The firm's specialist litigation teams have a unique depth of experience in dealing with landmark cases. The firm is one of the most active law firms in the Court of Appeal and handles a significant number of cases reaching the House of Lords. Landmark cases offer a decisive indication of future trends in business and risk. The firm's clients place a high value on the guidance its partners and assistants offer on both developing live issues as well as existing legal conventions. The firm's clients include most of the top 30 financial services and insurance companies, medium to large corporates, organisations in the public sector, particularly in health, education and utilities. The firm is a leader among law firms in its understanding of financial services legislation. Through the firm's senior partner, Lord Hunt, it takes a leading role in representing the interests of the financial services and insurance industries.

Mutual Law Volume claims management is one of the most competitive services and one of the most demanding of a conventional law firm. Changes in the way it works and the way Beachcroft Wansbroughs is managed, have given the firm the flexibility and focus needed to meet the needs of this challenging sector. Since the firm launched Mutual Law in October 2001, its insurance clients have confirmed that Beachcroft Wansbroughs has changed their expectations of how law firms can adapt to meet their business needs. A key feature of Mutual Law is its innovative team and IT infrastructure that allows its experienced lawyers to add value where it's needed most, determining strategy and negotiating claims settlement.

The firm has appointed over 12 new partners during the past year and is demonstrating a positive outlook for the year ahead.

A-Z ■ LAW FIRMS

Beale and Company

Garrick Hse, 27-32 King St, Covent Garden, London, WC2E 8JD
Tel (020) 7240 3474   **Fax** (020) 7240 9111   **DX** 51632 Covent Garden
Email reception@beale-law.com   **Website** www.beale-law.com

Managing & Senior Partner	John Ward
Number of partners	8
Associates	2
Assistant solicitors	6
Other fee-earners	9

AREAS OF PRACTICE	
Construction	30%
Professional Negligence/Insurance	30%
Company & Commercial/IT/Employment	30%
Other Commercial Litigation	5%
Private Client	5%

CONTACTS	
Company and Commercial	Michael Archer
Construction	John Ward
Employment	Tara Meagher
Engineers	Rachel Barnes
Insurance	Antony Smith
Litigation	Mark Jones
Private Client	Rachel Barnes
Professional Negligence	Antony Smith

THE FIRM Beale and Company is a long established firm (founded in 1837) which provides a comprehensive range of services to commercial clients. The main areas of the firm's practice are construction, professional negligence and IT. It has a strong international practice. Beale and Company provides high quality legal advice combined with a practical and commercial approach.

PRINCIPAL AREAS OF WORK

Professional Negligence The firm acts for insurers and their insureds in handling professional indemnity claims and advises on risk management and other ways of reducing or preventing claims. It also advises insurers on policy wording, coverage issues and disputes between insurer and insured.

Construction The firm provides legal advice and, where necessary, representation, in relation to projects in the UK and throughout the world, to employers, contractors and professionals, on all aspects of civil and structural engineering contracts; related insurance and bond provisions and collateral warranties; joint ventures; corporate structures; partnerships; DBFO forms of contract and other forms of contract; disputes and dispute resolution; on and in negotiations, litigation, arbitration and other alternative forms of dispute resolution.

Engineers This is a special section of the firm's construction practice. The firm is the solicitors for the Association of Consulting Engineers and has acted for more than 30 of the top 50 firms of consulting engineers in the UK. The firm acts for engineers and others prosecuted under Health and Safety legislation.

Litigation The firm handles a wide range of other commercial litigation, including disputes in the fields of banking, IT, intellectual property, supply of goods and services and employment. It also handles a large amount of international litigation and is a Privy Council agent.

Company & Commercial The firm advises on all aspects of company commercial transactions, including acquisitions and disposals of businesses; setting up joint ventures; corporate finance arrangements; restructuring of companies and partnerships; establishing commercial contractual relationships such as distribution, agency and licensing networks; intellectual property; directors' duties and liabilities; partnership disputes; corporate compliance. There is a strong emphasis on acting for clients in the IT and digital media industries. These range from dot com businesses (the firm having represented some of the first dot com enterprises in selling their businesses and raising finance) to national and multi-national companies including a number of technology companies quoted on Nasdaq.

Employment The firm also has a dedicated employment team advising on all aspects of employment law, both contentious and non-contentious, including employment policies and contracts, benefits, business reorganisations, redundancies and unfair dismissal and discrimination claims.

Private Client The firm advises private clients, domiciled and non-domiciled, on tax planning, formation of trusts, wills and probates.

INTERNATIONAL The firm is the founder member of a European network of correspondent law firms. The firm also has correspondent law firms in Bombay, Calcutta, Dhaka, Kampala, Karachi, Mombasa, Nairobi and Port Louis.

RECRUITMENT The firm recruits on average three graduate trainees each year. Currently there are six graduate trainees in the firm.

■ Beaumont and Son
Lloyds Chambers, 1 Portsoken St, London, E1 8AW   **Tel** (020) 7709 5000   **Fax** (020) 7481 3353

■ Beckford & Co
35A Prince of Wales Road, Norwich, NR1 1BG   **Tel** (01603) 660 000   **Fax** (01603) 660 010

■ Bedell Cristin
PO Box 75, 26 New Street, St Helier, JE4 8PP   **Tel** (01534) 814814   **Fax** (01534) 814815

■ Beecham Peacock
7 Collingwood Street, Newcastle upon Tyne, NE1 1JE   **Tel** (0191) 232 3048   **Fax** (0191) 261 7255

■ Bell & Buxton
Telegraph House, High Street, Sheffield, S1 2GA   **Tel** (0114) 249 5969   **Fax** (0114) 249 3804

■ Bell Lax Litigation
New Bank House, 21 Maney Corner, Sutton Coldfield, Birmingham, B72 1QL   **Tel** (0121) 355 0011   **Fax** (0121) 355 0099

Bell & Scott WS

16 Hill Street, Edinburgh, EH2 3LD
Tel (0131) 226 6703 **Fax** (0131) 226 7602 **DX** 114 Edinburgh
Email maildesk@bellscott.co.uk **Website** www.bellscott.co.uk

THE FIRM Bell & Scott WS is a niche firm servicing the Scottish property development sector. The firm delivers practical and innovative legal advice to commercial and residential property developers, complemented by litigation and private client services.

PRINCIPAL AREAS OF WORK

Commercial Property & Development The unit provides an integrated property service covering property development and management, sale and acquisition, contentious and non-contentious construction law, leasing, planning and joint ventures.

Residential Development Over thirty years of expertise has earned the firm a reputation for the provision of high quality legal services to the housebuilding industry.

Managing Partner	Iain MacDonald
Senior Partner	Simon Guest
Number of partners	8
Assistant solicitors	8
Other fee-earners	10

CONTACTS
Commercial Property & Development	Paul Jennings
Litigation & Employment	Colin Heggie
Private Client	Alan Sharp
Residential Conveyancing	Susan Calder
Residential Development	Simon Guest
	Iain MacDonald

Belmores

Goodchild House, 27 Castle Meadow, Norwich, NR1 3DS **Tel** (01603) 617947 **Fax** (01603) 630086

Beltrami & Co

93 West Nile Street, Glasgow, G1 2FH
Tel (0141) 221 0981 **Fax** (0141) 332 9892 **DX** GW8

Ptnrs 2 **Asst solrs** 3 **Other fee-earners** 1 **Contact** J D Murray Macara • Long-established and prominent criminal defence practice with substantial reputation in many high profile cases, specialising in all aspects of criminal defence work throughout Scotland.

AREAS OF PRACTICE
Criminal Litigation	95%
Other	5%

Ben Hoare Bell

47 John Street, Sunderland, SR1 1QU **Tel** (0191) 565 3112 **Fax** (0191) 510 9122

Benson Mazure & Co

22 Bentinck St, London, W1U 2AB
Tel (020) 7486 8091 **Fax** (020) 7935 8425 **DX** 9007 London West End
Email info@bensonmazure.co.uk

Ptnrs 2 **Asst solrs** 1 **Other fee-earners** 1 **Contact** Anthony Levy • Commercial and residential conveyancing; landlord and tenant; commercial litigation and company commercial; personal injuries, matrimonial and general litigation; probate and trusts.

AREAS OF PRACTICE
Conveyancing/Landlord & Tenant	50%
Litigation (inc. Commercial)	20%
Company Commercial	17%
Probate & Trusts	13%

Bentleys, Stokes & Lowless

International House, 1 St. Katharine's Way, London, E1 9YL
Tel (020) 7782 0990 **Fax** (020) 7782 0991 **DX** 1074
Email law@bentleys.co.uk

THE FIRM Bentleys, Stokes & Lowless is traditionally associated with the maritime and insurance sectors.

PRINCIPAL AREAS OF WORK

Admiralty Specialist advice and representation is offered in relation to salvage, pollution, total loss, groundings, unsafe port claims, damage claims, collisions and public, official and casualty inquiries and investigations.

Shipping, Insurance & Litigation The department advises on a wide range of marine and insurance related matters, including charterparty/bill of lading contracts, marine, cargo and aviation insurance, cargo claims, road transport, commodity contracts, commercial contracts, ship sale and purchase, construction, building and general litigation.

INTERNATIONAL The firm handles work in French, Greek, Italian, Japanese and Spanish.

Senior Partner	Andrew Bardot
Number of partners	12
Assistant solicitors	7
Other fee-earners	4

AREAS OF PRACTICE
Shipping, Marine & Non-Marine Insurance	100%

CONTACTS
Admiralty	J Quain
Charterparty/Marine Insurance	Andrew Bardot
	W J Chetwood

A-Z ■ LAW FIRMS

■ Benussi & Co

7th Floor, Newater House, 11 Newhall Street, Birmingham, B3 3NY **Tel** (0121) 248 4001 **Fax** (0121) 248 3990

Berg & Co

Scottish Mutual House, 35 Peter Street, Manchester, M2 5BG
Tel (0161) 833 9211 **Fax** (0161) 834 5566 **DX** MDX 14379
Email help@berg.co.uk **Website** www.berg.co.uk

THE FIRM Occupying modern offices at the heart of Manchester's commercial district, Berg & Co is a leading Manchester-based law firm, with a reputation for innovative and effective commercial problem-solving. The firm provides decisive, commercial advice to businesses of all sizes.

PRINCIPAL AREAS OF WORK

Corporate & Commercial Including choice of business structure, mergers and acquisitions, joint ventures and shareholders' agreements, directors' duties and responsibilities, banking and finance, stock exchange and other regulatory issues, insolvency procedures, commercial contracts, standard terms and conditions, internet law, agency and distribution agreements, intellectual property and information technology, EC law and competition law.

Litigation Including contractual claims, shareholders' actions, boardroom disputes and corporate fraud, professional negligence, insolvency, intellectual property, emergency applications.

Commercial Property Including sales and purchases, leases, development work, multi-let units and secured lending.

Human Resources Including employment contracts, contested dismissals and severance issues, business transfers, redundancy, discrimination, sickness and maternity, legislative changes and audit of employment practices.

Matrimonial Finance Concentrating upon high value financial cases.

Recoveries A bespoke debt recovery service equipped for volume collection work.

Intellectual Property Includes patents and registrability of inventions, designs, know-how and confidentiality, registered designs, copyright, trademarks, passing off, related competition issues, IT contracts, data protection and privacy.

CLIENTELE Clients include public (including listed) and private companies, education institutions, financial institutions, partnerships, innovative entrepreneurs seeking an innovative and practical approach to legal services.

INTERNATIONAL The firm has an extensive range of contacts in Europe, the USA and the Far East which enable it to progress its clients' affairs beyond UK boundaries. Languages spoken include French and German.

Senior Partner	Reuben Berg
Number of partners	9
Assistant solicitors	13
Other fee-earners	10

CONTACTS	
Commercial Litigation	Charles Khan
	Sydney Fulda
Commercial Property	Gabriel Rechnitzer
	Stephanie Klass
	Jonathan Dover
Corporate & Commercial	Reuben Berg
	Stephen Foster
Human Resources	Alison Loveday
	Stephanie Klass
Intellectual Property	Ian Morris
Matrimonial Finance & Professional Negligence	
	Peter Woolf
Recoveries	Sydney Fulda

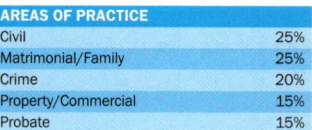

■ The Berkson Globe Partnership0

27 Dale Street, 4th Floor, Dale House, Liverpool, L2 2HD **Tel** (0151) 236 1234 **Fax** (0151) 236 5678

■ Bermans

Pioneer Buildings, 65-67 Dale St, Liverpool, L2 2NS **Tel** (0151) 227 3351 **Fax** (0151) 236 2107

■ Berry & Berry

11 Church Road, Tunbridge Wells, TN1 1JA
Tel (01892) 526344 **Fax** (01892) 511223 **DX** 3908 Tunbridge Wells **Email** mail@the-solicitors.co.uk

Ptnrs 8 **Asst solrs** 13 **Other fee-earners** 9 **Contact** Zai Koder • Branch offices in Tonbridge and Maidstone. General practice includes matrimonial, family, children, civil, personal injury, employment, criminal, commercial, conveyancing, tax and probate. Three Legal Aid franchises. Lawnet member.

AREAS OF PRACTICE	
Civil	25%
Matrimonial/Family	25%
Crime	20%
Property/Commercial	15%
Probate	15%

864   INDEX TO LEADING LAWYERS: PAGE 1693 ■ IN-HOUSE LAWYERS' PROFILES: PAGE 1201

LAW FIRMS ■ A-Z

■ Berryman Shacklock

Park House, Friar Lane, Nottingham, NG1 6DN **Tel** (0115) 945 3700 **Fax** (0115) 948 0234

Berrymans Lace Mawer

Salisbury House, London Wall, London, EC2M 5QN
Tel (020) 7638 2811 **Fax** (020) 7920 0361 **DX** 33861 Finsbury Sq.
Email info@blm-law.com **Website** www.blm-law.com

Castle Chambers, 43 Castle Street, Liverpool, L2 9SU
Tel (0151) 236 2002 **Fax** (0151) 236 2585 **DX** 14159 Liverpool 1
Email info@blm-law.com

King's House, 42 King Street West, Manchester, M3 2NU
Tel (0161) 236 2002 **Fax** (0161) 832 7956 **DX** 14302 Manchester 1
Email info@blm-law.com

National Senior Partner	Paul Taylor
Number of partners	73
Other fee-earners	280
Total staff	587

CONTACTS	
Birmingham	Christopher Wiggin
Leeds	Jonathan Clay
Liverpool	David Evans
London	Charlotte Capstick
Manchester	Nigel Roden
Southampton	Martin Bruffell
International	Paul Taylor

THE FIRM Berrymans Lace Mawer is a leading insurance law firm providing comprehensive legal and risk management services to its clients. Founded in the 18th century, today's national practice was created in 1997 with the merger of Berrymans and Lace Mawer to form a network of six offices in Birmingham, Leeds, Liverpool, London, Manchester and Southampton. Offices in the United Arab Emirates and associations with law firms in Europe and South East Asia provide its clients with an international service. The firm employs high calibre lawyers who are experts in their areas of practice, acting for a range of clients including insurance companies, brokers, loss adjusters, Lloyd's syndicates, professional service organisations, local authorities and public services, utility companies and blue-chip commercial firms from all industry sectors. The BLM approach to cases is client-focused providing fast, high quality commercial advice combining innovation with professionalism. The benefits of this approach are appreciated by many client organisations in both the UK and overseas, for whom Berrymans Lace Mawer is the preferred or nominated solicitors firm.

PRINCIPAL AREAS OF WORK The firm has distinct teams to serve specialist areas such as catastrophic injury, industrial disease, local authority claims, police, education, housing, motor, health and safety and medical law. BLM operates in more than 30 practice areas. In the areas listed below, BLM partners have established reputations as amongst the very best in their field: catastrophic injury, child abuse, clinical negligence, construction, education, employers' liability, employment, environmental, mediation, motor, occupational disease, personal injury, police and emergency services, professional indemnity, property insurance, public liability, stress. The firm has attracted a number of high-calibre individuals over the past 12 months including leading environmental barrister, Philip Vallance QC, experienced employment law specialists Michael Parr and John Stamper, and catastrophic injury specialist Jason Maley. For more information about the firm, please consult the website on www.blm-law.com or contact the marketing department.

■ Berry Smith

Brackla House, Brackla Street, Bridgend, CF31 1BZ **Tel** (01656) 645525 **Fax** (01656) 645174

865

A-Z ■ LAW FIRMS

Berwin Leighton Paisner

Adelaide House, London Bridge, London, EC4R 9HA
Tel (020) 7760 1000 **Fax** (020) 7760 1111 **DX** 92 London Chancery Lane WC2
Email firstname.surname@blplaw.com **Website** www.blplaw.com

Bouverie House, 154 Fleet Street, London, EC4A 2JD
Tel (020) 7760 1000 **Fax** (020) 7760 1111 **DX** 198 London
Email firstname.surname@blplaw.com

Senior Partner	Harold Paisner
Managing Partner	Neville Eisenberg
Number of partners	120
Number of other fee-earners	324
Total staff	924

AREAS OF PRACTICE

Real Estate	38%
Corporate	32%
Finance	18%
Litigation & Dispute Resolution	12%

CONTACTS

Banking & Capital Markets	Jennifer Mackerras
Charities	Moira Protani
Commercial	Jonathan Kropman
Construction & Engineering	Terry Fleet
Consumer Finance	Dennis Rosenthal
Corporate Finance	John Bennett
	David Collins
Corporate/International Tax	John Overs
Employment	Andrew Pipe
Environment	Andrew Waite
EU & Competition	Adrian Magnus
Insolvency & Regeneration	David Leibowitz
Insurance/Reinsurance	Jonathan Sacher
Licensing/Food Law/Health & Safety	
	Craig Baylis
Litigation & Dispute Resolution	
	Michael Goldmeier
	David Parkin
Pensions & Incentives	Norman Russell
PFI/Projects	Simon Allan
	Carol McCormack
Planning	Ian Trehearne
	Tim Pugh
Property Finance	Mark Waghorn
Real Estate	Philip Bretherton
Real Estate Disputes	Roger Cohen
Tech Media	Adam Rose
Trademarks	Debrett Lyons
Trusts & Estate Planning	Wynne Thomas

THE FIRM Berwin Leighton Paisner is a leading law firm based in the City of London. With a client base including many leading companies and financial institutions, the firm strives to lead the market in the excellence of its service delivery. The firm is well known for its success in developing market leadership positions within the real estate, corporate and finance areas. It distinguishes itself by working with its clients in creative and innovative ways to achieve commercial solutions. It is entrepreneurial, tenacious and responsive. Berwin Leighton Paisner represents UK and multinational institutions and companies across a wide range of industry sectors. A significant amount of the firm's work is international and it has established relationships with professional firms in many countries around the world. In addition to the firm's offices in the City of London, it has an office in Brussels and an association with Paris law firm Uettwiller, Grelon, Gout, Canat & Associes ('UGGC'). Berwin Leighton Paisner is committed to service innovation. It operates personalised client extranets, provides a free online legal briefing service via its website and has developed, with joint venture partner Deloitte & Touche, beprofessional, a web-based business solutions company.

PRINCIPAL AREAS OF WORK The firm's four core practice areas are corporate, real estate, finance and litigation and dispute resolution. These four core practice areas are complemented by specialist teams in employment, pensions and incentives, insurance and reinsurance, corporate tax, licensing and food law, trusts and estate planning and charities.

Corporate A broad range of corporate work is undertaken including corporate finance, M&A, flotations, private equity, corporate recovery and insolvency and on the commercial side, asset/consumer finance, retail banking, data protection, franchising and other commercial agreements. All aspects of EU and competition work are also undertaken. The TechMedia team is involved in the IT, IP, digital media and e-commerce fields. The firm also has a dedicated trademark unit.

Real Estate The firm's commercial real estate practice is one of the leading providers of high value services to the real estate sector. It undertakes work for institutions, investors, developers, retailers, banks, government bodies and major leisure operators. It includes one of the country's leading planning and environment teams and one of the largest combined contentious and non-contentious construction and engineering teams together with a team of specialist real estate litigators.

Finance The finance team advises lenders, issuers and borrowers on all principal financing techniques, specialising in project finance, property finance, banking and capital markets, asset finance and acquisition finance. It is one of the leaders in PFI/PPP work and has been involved in some of the UK's flagship schemes.

Dispute Resolution The litigation and dispute resolution team deals with a wide range of UK and international commercial disputes by means of negotiation, ADR, arbitration or through the courts.

RECRUITMENT The firm recruits around 35 trainee solicitors each year. A brochure and application details are available from the firm or via its website.

*berwin leighton paisner

SJ Berwin

222 Gray's Inn Road, London, WC1X 8XF
Tel (020) 7533 2222 **Fax** (020) 7533 2000 **DX** 255 London Chancery Lane WC2
Email info@sjberwin.com **Website** www.sjberwin.com

THE FIRM Founded in 1982, SJ Berwin's rapid growth and success is best explained by its ability to handle complex corporate and commercial transactions, coupled with a creative approach to clients' problems, a speedy response, and close involvement in their strategic decision making. SJ Berwin acts for clients ranging from major multinational business corporations and financial institutions, to internet entrepreneurs and to high net worth individuals. The firm is especially favoured by entrepreneurial business clients, who find the firm particularly well attuned to their outlook and needs. Increasingly, the firm is focusing on industry sectors including e-commerce, pharmaceuticals and biotechnology, media, communications and information technology, sport and leisure. SJ Berwin was named Law Firm of the Year at *The Lawyer* Awards 2000.

PRINCIPAL AREAS OF WORK

Corporate The firm is well known for its corporate work and offers a full range of corporate finance services, including mergers and acquisitions, capital markets, private equity, management buyouts, financial services and securities regulation, coupled with an active international banking practice. The firm was named Private Equity Law Firm of the Year (firm and fund work) by the *European Venture Capital Journal* in 2002.

Commercial Property Winner of *The Lawyer* Awards 2000 Property Team of the Year. All aspects of commercial property work are handled for a wide range of clients, including property companies, developers, institutions, retailers and hoteliers. Specialist groups advise on public and private funding programmes for major infrastructure projects, construction and local government finance issues. A highly regarded planning and environment team is an integral part of this growing and expanded practice. The property finance team is an established market leader in the development of innovative fund structures.

EU & Competition The firm has a strong European dimension. Its EU, competition and trade law practice is conducted principally through the London, Brussels, Madrid and Munich offices, and advises on domestic and EU mergers and acquisitions, competition, anti-trust and anti-dumping, regulatory work and judicial review proceedings. The firm was named Competition Team of the Year in the annual *Legal Business* Awards in 2001, following success in 1998.

Litigation The firm's litigation practice handles a broad range of substantial international and domestic commercial litigation as well as mediation and arbitration which is undertaken by the specialist ADR Services Unit. In addition, the practice includes groups specialising in property litigation, defamation, public law and judicial review, an employment and pensions group and an advocacy group.

Reconstruction & Insolvency An active insolvency group handles the whole spectrum of insolvency work, from corporate insolvency and bankruptcy to reconstructions.

Intellectual Property International trademark, copyright and patent litigation, international trademark registration and the identification, exploitation and protection of intellectual property rights are undertaken by a specialist intellectual property group.

Tax National and international taxation advice, including the structuring of international transactions and property development, is provided by the tax group. Estate planning and asset protection advice is given to private clients in the UK and overseas.

Other Areas E-commerce work is handled across the firm, with particular strengths in the venture capital, flotations, commercial, financial services, reconstruction and competition practices. Other leading areas of commercial work include film financing and animation production and also communications, as well as commercial contracts, frequently with an international dimension, including franchising, agency distributorship, joint venture and trading agreements, and information technology. The firm also handles pro bono work.

INTERNATIONAL Internationally, the firm operates through its own network of law firms in Europe and is also the English member of Interlaw.

Brussels Directly connected and working closely with the EU and competition department in London, the office comprises UK qualified solicitors, Spanish *abogados*, French and Belgian *avocats* and trainee solicitors. The office extends a multilingual environment to clients with fluency in several European languages. Key experience and strength lies in matters involving Article 81 (ex Article 85) and Article 82 (ex Article 86) of the EC Treaty and the EC merger control regulation and lobbying contact with various European institutions. Specific areas of practice include biotech regulation, agrifoods, institutional reform, tax law, environment, telecommunications and fishery law.

Madrid The firm provides corporate legal services with a strong focus on private equity, mergers and acquisitions and tax work. EU and competition law is also practised. Clients include major corporations acquiring top local companies or entering into joint venture agreements with local partners in

Continued overleaf

UK
Number of partners	86
Assistant solicitors	202
Other fee-earners	79

International
Number of partners	33
Assistant solicitors	71

AREAS OF PRACTICE
Company/Commercial	45%
Litigation	20%
Commercial Property	20%
EU/Competition	8%
Tax	7%

CONTACTS
ADR	David Shapiro
Advocacy	Richard Slowe
Banking	Gillian Smith
Commercial Litigation	Craig Pollack
	Tim Taylor
Company & Commercial	Andrew Shindler
Construction	Ian Insley
Corporate Finance	Jonathan Blake
	Robert Burrow
	Jonathan Metliss
Defamation	Hilton Mervis
E-commerce	Martin Bowen
	Simon Holmes
Employment	Nicola Kerr
Environment	Mark Brumwell
EU/Competition	Ralph Cohen
	Stephen Kon
Financial Services	Charles Abrams
	Tamasin Little
Hotels	David Ryland
Intellectual Property	Ray Black
	Jeremy Schrire
Investment Funds	Bruce Gardner
	Josyane Gold
IT	Tim Johnson
Leisure	Bryan Pickup
Media & Communications	Nigel Palmer
Music	Tom Usher
Parliamentary Lobbying	Simon Holmes
Pensions	Wyn Derbyshire
Pharmaceuticals & Biotechnology	
	Jeremy Schrire
Planning	Patricia Thomas
Projects/PFI	Simon McLeod
Property	Stephen Willson
Property Finance	David Ryland
Property Litigation	Michael Metliss
Public Law	Simon Ricketts
Reconstruction & Insolvency	Stephen Maffey
Sport	Peter McInerney
	Jonathan Metliss
Tax	Heather Corben
Trademark Litigation	Ray Black

the IT business. Specialisation covers advising investment services companies in matters related to setting up local branches, launching venture capital funds and co-operating in pan-European investment funds.

Frankfurt SJ Berwin in Germany has offices in Frankfurt, Munich and Berlin and consists of the law firm SJ Berwin Knopf Tulloch Steininger, the tax advising firm of Knopf, Tulloch & Partner GmbH and the auditing firm of GKT Industrie- und Handelstreuhand AG. They design tax-effective structures to accommodate mergers, acquisitions, sales, corporate divestitures and reorganisations. EU and competition law is also practised. The firm does not merely combine legal and tax expertise, it designs consistent business solutions which take all the relevant financial aspects into account.

Paris The office provides corporate legal services with a strong focus on private equity, mergers and acquisitions and tax work.

RECRUITMENT In order to maintain its commitment to organic growth and development, SJ Berwin will recruit up to 40 ambitious, commercially-minded individuals to begin training in September 2004. All trainees will be required to undertake two corporate seats as part of their training programme. Apply to Alison Archer, Recruitment Manager.

Betesh Fox & Co

Ralli Courts, West Riverside, Manchester, M3 5FT
Tel (0870) 998 9000 **Fax** (0870) 998 9100 **DX** 14579
Email chambers@beteshfox.co.uk   **Website** www.beteshfox.co.uk

Senior Partner	Stephen Fox
Managing Partner	Martin Coyne
Number of partners	9
Assistant solicitors	11
Other fee-earners	16

AREAS OF PRACTICE	
Personal Injury	45%
Commercial Litigation	20%
Corporate/Employment/Property	20%
Serious & Commercial Crime	15%

THE FIRM Betesh Fox & Co. was founded in 1973. Operating nationally and internationally from Manchester city centre and London, the firm is a progressive and developing practice. Specialist departments provide legal advice of the highest quality for a diverse portfolio of clients in private and commercial sectors. The firm is continually expanding in size, expertise and reputation, demonstrating a 'results driven' philosophy. The partners are acknowledged as experts in their chosen fields. Due to significant investment, the practice boasts a sophisticated IT system for case management and a stringent quality control protocol, thus demonstrating commitment to client care and service delivery. Business can be conducted in French, German, Spanish, Portuguese, Urdu, Hebrew and Russian.

PRINCIPAL AREAS OF WORK

Corporate Encompasses corporate, employment and property. The corporate lawyers act for private, public and listed companies advising on corporate and partnership matters, commercial contract and trading. The commercial property team handles commercial, industrial and residential property transactions. The employment team acts for both employers and employees on contracts, redundancy, tribunals, discrimination and severance packages. There is also a specialised unit handling wills, trusts and probate.

Commercial Litigation This department has a broad base of international experience across the range of commercial litigation and arbitration. Work includes environmental issues, construction disputes, debt recovery, contract claims, banking and finance.

Serious & Commercial Crime Well established as one of the country's leading firms dealing with commercial fraud and serious crime, handling substantial fraud cases in the UK and worldwide. Also representing company and individual clients in many other areas of serious crime. Work includes civil fraud, SFO, FSA, DTI, Inland Revenue, Customs and Excise matters, Extradition and Appeals.

Personal Injury The name Betesh has been associated with successful litigation in personal injury law in the UK, for over 55 years. The department has a solid team of skilled solicitors who deal with accident claims ranging from catastrophically injured clients to minor injuries – attracting quality referrers and quality personnel.

LAW FIRMS ■ A-Z

Bevan Ashford

35 Colston Avenue, Bristol BS1 4TT
Tel (0117) 923 0111   **Fax** (0117) 929 1865   **DX** 7828 Bristol 1
Email info@bevanashford.co.uk   **Website** www.bevanashford.co.uk

Alpha Tower, Suffolk Street, Queensway, Birmingham, B1 1TT
Tel (0121) 634 5000   **Fax** (0121) 634 5001   **DX** 715470 Birmingham 41
Email jean.sapeta@bevanashford.co.uk

1 Chancery Lane, London, WC2A 1LF
Tel (020) 7822 7822   **Fax** (020) 7822 7800   **DX** 1058 Chancery Lane
Email david.widdowson@bevanashford.co.uk

Curzon House, Southernhay West, Exeter, EX1 1AB
Tel (01392) 411111   **Fax** (01392) 250764   **DX** 8301 Exeter
Email info@bevan-ashford.com   **Website** www.beavan-ashford.com

1 Northumberland Avenue, Trafalgar Square, London, WC2N 5BW
Tel (020) 8938 6323   **Fax** (020) 8938 6995
Email info@bevan-ashford.com

Princess Court, 23 Princess Street, Plymouth, PL1 2EX
Tel (01752) 256888   **Fax** (01752) 250508   **DX** 8273 Plymouth 2
Email d.beadel@bevan-ashford.com

41 St James Street, Taunton, TA1 1JR
Tel (01823) 284444   **Fax** (01823) 270869   **DX** 32115 Taunton
Email p.fox@bevan-ashford.com

Gotham House, Tiverton, EX16 6LT
Tel (01884) 242111   **Fax** (01884) 259303   **DX** 49002 Tiverton
Email c.palmer@bevan-ashford.com

Chief Executive Bristol/Birmingham/London	
	Ann Conway-Hughes
Chief Executive Westcountry	Chris Hawkins
Managing Partner Westcountry	Simon Rous
Bristol/Birmingham/London	
Number of partners	57
Number of fee-earners	221
Total staff	393
Westcountry	
Number of partners	30
Number of fee-earners	184
Total staff	352

CONTACTS

Bristol, Birmingham, London

Head of Built Environment	Stephen Hughes
Head of Insurance & Recovery	Patricia Mitchell
Head of NHS Claims	Christian Dingwall
Head of Professional Services & Finance	
	Gordon Bon
Head of Public Sector	Bethan Evans
Head of Technology & Manufacturing	
	Stuart Whitfield

Westcountry

Head of Construction	John Birch
Head of Corporate & Banking	Simon Rous
Head of Corporate Recovery & Insolvency	
	David Pomeroy
Head of Commercial Litigation	Ian Daniells
Head of Commercial Property	Andrew Rothwell
Head of Employment	Rhiain Lewis
Head of Intellectual Property	Mark Lomas
Head of Matrimonial & Crime	John Smith
Head of Private Client	Judith Park
Head of Public Law	Malcolm Gilbert
Head of Tax, Trusts & Probate	James Pettit

THE FIRM Bevan Ashford is firmly established as a fast expanding, national law firm offering commercial legal services to clients across both the public and private sector. The firm operates in two distinct profit centres – Bristol/Birmingham/London (57 partners and 393 staff) and London and the Westcountry (30 partners and 352 staff).

Bristol/Birmingham/London Profit Centre Concentrates on a range of core practice areas across five distinct business sectors – insurance and recovery, public sector (including healthcare), the built environment, technology and manufacturing and professional services and finance. The firm operates in cross-departmental teams across these key industry sectors to harness the full range of skills and experience needed to meet clients' requirements. Bevan Ashford's approach is to keep an open mind in order to solve problems and deliver practical solutions to the business and legal issues faced by its clients. The firm is responsive to each client's own unique needs, flexible in the way it delivers its service and more than happy to challenge conventional thinking. This means a drive to achieve a detailed understanding of each client's requirements and a genuine commitment to deliver real value. It is through a combination of deep specialisms and breadth of expertise, along with a clear commercial focus, that enables Bevan Ashford to generate solutions that really work.

Westcountry Profit Centre This is the firm's corporate and banking core practice area, with the largest specialist team south of Bristol, dealing with both national and international clients through its office in Northumberland Avenue, Trafalgar Square. With a growing commercial reputation, the Westcountry Profit Centre encompasses corporate commercial and banking, commercial litigation, commercial property, corporate recovery and insolvency, employment, pensions and incentives, construction and a rapidly growing private client department. The firm ensures that its lawyers have a real understanding of clients' requirements and, using the best IT networking systems available, delivers a seamless service of City standards irrespective of location. It is the breadth and depth of the practice that distinguishes the firm from its competitors. The firm offers London quality at regional rates.

PRINCIPAL AREAS OF WORK
BRISTOL/BIRMINGHAM/LONDON PROFIT CENTRE Bevan Ashford's traditional reputation as a firm that excels in health and public sector work is increasingly balanced by its rapidly growing and nationally recognised private sector practice areas. In support of its five divisional sectors, the type of work undertaken can be divided into dispute resolution, public sector, built environment and commercial.

Continued overleaf

INVESTOR IN PEOPLE

www.ChambersandPartners.com

869

A-Z ■ LAW FIRMS

Dispute Resolution The range of litigation and dispute resolution work undertaken by Bevan Ashford – in areas such as insurance, clinical, personal injury, property, construction, IT/IP, and professional indemnity – places this cross-department practice area as one of the largest and most talented outside the City. In particular, Bevan Ashford's dedicated NHS Claims department is arguably the strongest team in the country. With 10 partners divided between Bristol, Birmingham and London, it is a member of the NHS Litigation Authority Panel for defendant clinical negligence work.

Public Sector (inc. Healthcare) Cross-departmental teams provide a comprehensive range of legal services to organisations responsible for regulating, delivering and supporting public services (such as healthcare, social care, local and central government, government agencies, higher and further education bodies). Bevan Ashford is widely regarded as a leading player in public law, regulatory, advisory and commercial services for the public sector, whilst its healthcare practice in particular is the dominant legal provider to NHS trusts, health authorities, PCGs/PCTs and local authorities in the Midlands and South of England.

Built Environment Encompassing the firm's PFI and projects, infrastructure, construction, real estate and planning practice groups, Bevan Ashford offers breadth and depth of expertise and a seamless end-to-end service. The firm is at the forefront of industry thinking and acts on a range of standard form documentation and Pathfinder schemes in conjunction with government departments. The projects team in particular has established a national reputation as one of the top three non City firms and has now advised on more than 200 schemes with a whole life value in excess of £25 billion, spanning the health, defence, leisure, waste and education sectors.

Commercial Bevan Ashford's commercial department specialises in corporate transactional work, including acquisition finance, joint ventures and venture capital work. The firm's dedicated insolvency department has grown to become the largest specialist group in Bristol. Other non-contentious business services are provided by experienced and highly regarded teams covering employment, health and safety, planning and environment and IT/IP.

WESTCOUNTRY PROFIT CENTRE The firm's corporate commercial and banking reputation is nationally recognised and is balanced by its rapidly growing other main areas of business which include commercial property, commercial litigation, public sector and private client, with each area being organised into specialist teams, according to their clients requirements.

Corporate Commercial & Banking Includes intellectual property, ICT business unit, corporate tax and corporate and recovery. The department has had a record year advising on transactions with an aggregate value of over £3.5 billion and has grown significantly in the last year, including the establishment of a banking and secured lending unit. The department acts for a number of established clients including Schlumberger.

Commercial Litigation Continues to expand rapidly. The team recently won the national tender to act as independent assessor in disputes between Equitable Life and its policyholders and regularly acts on multimillion pound disputes. The department, which includes construction, has added a further dimension with the appointment of Stephen Homer as an adjudicator; employment, pensions and incentives advise clients on a wide range of human resource issues, including representing clients at tribunals, with the team playing an active role in cross-department units brought together to deal with large transactions; and property litigation which has already been successful in winning new work and acts for numerous housing associations and local authorities.

Commercial Property Led by Andrew Rothwell, the Westcountry commercial property department has grown to 16 lawyers. Work is broad-based, ranging from high profile public sector developments to investment properties and the retail and leisure sectors. Major clients include the South West of England Regional Development Agency, Ivory Gate Limited, Hanson, Devon County Council and The English Brasserie Company plc.

Environment Focuses on environmental risk management for private and public sector clients, and offers practical, pragmatic, commercial and creative solutions matching clients needs. The team operates a multidisciplinary approach and is at the forefront of establishing partnership arrangements with other professionals in order to give clients a complete environmental risk management service.

Public Law, inc. Local Government, Planning & Education The public law team offers a unique blend of specialisms working together to cater for every aspect of the needs of local authorities and other public sector organisations for legal services. Services include ICT and e-business; local authority companies and public private sector partnerships; constitutional and governance; best value and legal audit; prosecutions; debt recovery; human rights; childcare, integrated social care, education and play; housing; CPOs.

Education Bevan Ashford provides cross-departmental advice to further education colleges, independent and maintained schools, LEAs, school organisation committees and private sector organisations working in the education market. The team's expertise encompasses specialist education knowledge, as well as experience of providing practical solutions in areas such as IT, intellectual property, employment and property, for institutions and organisations within the education sector.

Private Client, inc. Tax Trust & Probate & Institutional Conveyancing This area has large experienced teams that are quick to respond to clients' needs and changes in the law. The institutional conveyancing team, headed by Judith Park, continues to expand, acting for a number of major commercial organisations for relocation and re-mortgaging work on a national basis. Clients include Marks & Spencer, Barclays Bank and Abbey National.

Beviss & Beckingsale

Law Chambers, Holyrood Street, Chard, TA20 2AJ
Tel (01460) 61494 **Fax** (01460) 63821 **DX** 43701 Chard
Email enquiries@bevissandbeckingsale.co.uk   **Website** www.bevissandbeckingsale.co.uk

THE FIRM Established, progressive firm with a private and business client base practising from Axminster, Chard, Colyton, Honiton and Seaton. Unusually for a rural firm all staff are interconnected by dedicated broadband technology. In depth knowledge of rural matters, experts in supporting owners of agricultural and country property, smallholdings and estates. Substantial private client practice and innovative conveyancing team leading the way in local property matters. Litigation is particularly strong in matrimonial work, personal injury and licensing. One of only two firms in the area franchised by the Legal Services Commission.

Senior Partner	Nigel Cole
Number of partners	7
Assistant solicitors	8
Other fee-earners	6

CONTACTS	
Agricultural & Country Estates	Martin Hicks
Commercial/Conveyancing	Nigel Cole
Private Client, Wills, Trusts	Helen Clarke
Residential Conveyancing	Mark Ollier
Litigation, Licensing	Colin Chesterton
Matrimonial, Family	Sue Dowen
Personal Injury	Sara Saunders

Bhatt Murphy

23 Pitfield Street, London, N1 6HB   **Tel** (020) 7253 7744   **Fax** (020) 7253 7766

Biggart Baillie

Dalmore House, 310 St Vincent Street, Glasgow, G2 5QR
Tel (0141) 228 8000   **Fax** (0141) 228 8310   **DX** GW9
Email info@biggartbaillie.co.uk   **Website** www.biggartbaillie.co.uk

7 Castle Street, Edinburgh, EH2 3AP
Tel (0131) 226 5541   **Fax** (0131) 226 2278   **DX** ED15
Email info@biggartbaillie.co.uk

THE FIRM One of Scotland's leading law firms with a balance of quality work across the main practice areas of litigation, corporate and property. Biggart Baillie has reinforced its commitment to driving its business forward and enhance levels of service with the acquisition of Steedman Ramage. The enlarged Biggart Baillie has an even stronger body of expertise and the firm is better placed to provide clients with a high quality forward-looking service delivered by people who understand the business. The firm places particular emphasis on forming close working relationships with clients to ensure they receive the right service and value. Training and development of all its staff is regarded by the firm as vital to its future and the continuing provision of service which exceeds clients' expectations.

PRINCIPAL AREAS OF WORK Specialisms are in the areas of corporate finance, banking, PFI, IT/IP, mergers and acquisitions, pensions, construction and planning, retail and leisure, employment, energy and utilities, property, defender reparation (especially professional negligence and industrial disease cases), ADR and insolvency.

CLIENTELE The firm acts for major industrial, financial and commercial enterprises across Scotland and with its membership of the Euro-American Lawyers Group the firm has access to legal representation in many of the world's most important centres of commerce. With offices in both Edinburgh and Glasgow, the firm is able to serve a client base which ranges from small businesses to national and multinational companies, including banks, utilities, energy companies, retailers and property developers.

Managing Partner	Campbell Smith
Chairman	David Ross
Number of partners	36
Assistant solicitors	56
Other fee-earners	30

AREAS OF PRACTICE	
Commercial Property	30%
Litigation	30%
Corporate	29%
Private Client	11%

CONTACTS	
Banking	Derek Ellery
Charities	Gordon Wyllie
Construction/Planning	Murray Shaw
Corporate Finance	David Allan
Employment	Paul Brown
Aviation, Energy & Utilities/PFI	David Ross
Insurance Litigation	David Stevenson
IT/IP	Colin Miller
Litigation	Murray Shaw
Property/Projects	Peter Cruickshank

Bill Goyder - Sole Practitioner

42 Lowgreen, Gainford, Darlington, DL2 3DS   **Tel** (01325) 730 234

A-Z ■ LAW FIRMS

Bindman & Partners

275 Gray's Inn Rd, London, WC1X 8QB
Tel (020) 7833 4433 **Fax** (020) 7837 9792 **DX** 37904 King's Cross
Email info@bindmans.com **Website** www.bindmans.com

Senior Partner	Geoffrey Bindman
Number of partners	12
Assistant solicitors	19
Other fee-earners	10

THE FIRM The firm is prominent in human rights, crime, defamation, employment, family law, personal injury, clinical negligence, housing, mental health and immigration. The firm was founded in 1974 to specialise in civil liberties. This has remained the heart of the practice and emphasises the firm's continuing commitment to publicly funded legal work and to the improvement of the legal system in the interest of the ordinary citizen. The firm has broadened its practice over the years and is increasingly instructed by companies, organisations and institutions, as well as individuals. It remains a unique practice at the cutting edge of the law.

CONTACTS	
Defamation/Media	Tamsin Allen
Employment/Discrimination	Camilla Palmer
Housing	Saimo Chahal
Immigration	Alison Stanley
Medical Negligence	Claire Fazan
Civil Litigation	Robin Lewis
Family Law	Felicity Crowther
Children	Katherine Gieve
Criminal Law & Prisoners	Neil O'May
Mental Health	Saimo Chahal
Administrative Law	Stephen Grosz
Personal Injury	Terry Donovan

PRINCIPAL AREAS OF WORK

Criminal Criminal work includes theft, white collar fraud cases and terrorism, as well as street crime and homicide. The firm has a special interest in cases involving abuses of police powers as well as extradition and official secret act cases. It acts for journalists under investigation by the police, handles public order issues and is dedicated to uncovering miscarriages of justice.

Employment In employment cases the firm acts for both individuals and employers. Much of its work is for the non-profit sector including charities, colleges and local authorities. The firm is a leader in discrimination cases including disability and racial and sexual harassment.

Clinical Negligence The firm specialises in brain damage and other serious disabilities. The firm has regularly recovered awards of more than £1m. All types of personal injury are dealt with including road traffic and work place accidents and cases involving bullying and stress at work.

Defamation The practice is a leader in defamation and has brought and defended major libel actions. It also deals with copyright, confidentiality and contract claims and has wide experience of film production and media contractual work.

Other All aspects of immigration, nationality and refugee work are handled. The full range of matrimonial and family problems are also covered and the firm is known particularly for acting in care proceedings. Mental health is a specialism including lawfulness of detention and appropriateness of treatment. Advice is also given on education matters. The public law and human rights team has been at the forefront of the growth in judicial review work. Housing work includes homelessness, eviction and rent assessment. The firm has a particular expertise in cases concerning the European Convention on Human Rights, both in the National Courts and in the European Court of Human Rights in Strasbourg.

Bingham McCutchen LLP (Formerly Bingham Dana LLP)

8-10 Mansion House Place, London, EC4N 8LB
Tel (020) 7375 9770 **Fax** (020) 7220 7431
Email jroome@bingham.com **Website** www.bingham.com

Number of partners	4
Assistant solicitors	11
Other fee-earners	1

THE FIRM Bingham McCutchen's 100 lawyer financial restructuring group has been recognised by *The American Lawyer* as "the nation's preeminent international bankruptcy practice" and *Global Turnaround* as "one of the world's premier rescue and insolvency practices." The firm's London office has been recognised by *The Lawyer* as "the most credible transatlantic practice yet."

CLIENTELE The firm's London office represents a 'who's who' of institutional and distressed debt investors, funds, and financial institutions in public bond and private note restructurings throughout Europe and, together with its other offices, throughout the world.

Bircham Dyson Bell

50 Broadway, Westminster, London, SW1H 0BL
Tel (020) 7227 7000   **Fax** (020) 7222 3480   **DX** 2317 VICTORIA
Email reception@bdb-law.co.uk   **Website** www.bdb-law.co.uk

Senior Partner	Ian McCulloch
Executive Committee Chairman	
	Nicholas Brown
Number of partners	37
Assistant solicitors	30
Other fee-earners	46

AREAS OF PRACTICE

Private Client/Charities	32%
Property	20%
Company/Commercial	16%
Litigation	15%
Parliamentary & Public Law	14%
Investment Management	3%

CONTACTS

Agricultural Law	Christopher Findley
Charities	Simon Weil
Company/Commercial	Guy Vincent
Employment	Ian Adamson
Investment Management	Christopher Jones-Warner
Litigation	George Josselyn
Matrimonial	John Darnton
Parliamentary & Public Law	Robert Owen
Private Client	Sarah Stowell
Property	Michael Parker

THE FIRM Bircham Dyson Bell is highly regarded for its charities and private client work and has a leading parliamentary and public law practice. The firm also has strong company commercial, property, litigation and investment management teams. Established for many years in Westminster, the firm has experienced significant growth over recent years and outgrew its old premises. In 2001, the firm moved to new premises, bringing all members of the London office into one new building, a short distance from its previous location. Another significant change occurred in 2000, when Bircham & Co. combined its firm name with the name of its parliamentary and public law division, Dyson Bell Martin, to become Bircham Dyson Bell. The firm is continuing to expand and now has 250 people. By attracting partners and senior lawyers from other firms and maintaining a high percentage of internal partner promotions, the firm has grown to be the largest in Westminster. Other developments have included a significant expansion in the volume of corporate finance work undertaken. In addition, the private client department, one of the largest of any central London firm, is closely linked to a growing investment management division. The firm's leasehold reform and agricultural law practices have grown strongly as has the civil litigation practice. The charities group has expanded to become one of the largest teams in the country since the arrival of several senior practitioners. Because the firm places strong emphasis on maintaining a close working relationship between partners and clients, it is noted for the quality of the service it is able to provide.

PRINCIPAL AREAS OF WORK

Private Client Private client services include all aspects of financial planning for the individual including wills, trusts and tax compliance for individuals and trustees. In the area of tax planning, the firm acts increasingly for foreign nationals both within the UK and internationally. The department also includes a substantial probate practice.

Charities Charity clients range from major national charities to family charitable trusts, the firm advising on all aspects, including formation, administration and promotion. All commercial aspects of charities' activities are covered.

Investment Management The investment management team offers private clients a comprehensive investment management service. Bircham Dyson Bell is authorised by the Financial Services Authority to conduct investment business.

Property Commercial property expertise covers all the main areas, in particular investment, retail, landlord and tenant, development schemes, project management, funding loan arrangements and site acquisitions and disposals. Property activities for private clients include all aspects of landed estates, both urban and rural, such as estate management, agricultural and other tenancies and town and country planning. The firm also has a leading practice in the leasehold reform field.

Company & Commercial Services include corporate finance (in particular flotations on the Official List, AIM and OFEX), company acquisitions and disposals, partnerships and joint ventures and all types of commercial agreements. The department undertakes a substantial amount and variety of employment work and also gives advice on intellectual property matters.

Litigation All aspects of commercial litigation are handled, including building litigation, property disputes and insurance litigation. Matrimonial and family law matters are dealt with and civil litigation services are provided, covering such areas as personal injury, medical negligence and construction adjudications.

Parliamentary & Public Law This department advises on all aspects of the law-making process, whether at a European, national or local level. This includes advice on influencing government policy and resulting legislation, advice on transport infrastructure and other major public works, public enquiries and promoting and opposing private and local legislation.

INTERNATIONAL As a member of Lexwork International, an association of independent law firms, Bircham Dyson Bell has associated firms in other European cities.

Bircham Dyson Bell

■ Birch Cullimore

Friars, White Friars, Chester, CH1 1XS   **Tel** (01244) 321066   **Fax** (01244) 312582

A-Z LAW FIRMS

Bird & Bird

90 Fetter Lane, London, EC4A 1JP
Tel (020) 7415 6000 **Fax** (020) 7415 6111 **DX** 119 London
Email info@twobirds.com **Website** www.twobirds.com

THE FIRM Working with some of the world's most innovative and technologically advanced companies, Bird & Bird has established a formidable reputation for advice at the cutting edge of law. Yet the firm's approach is strongly commercial too, enabling its clients to capitalise on business opportunities and manage change effectively. Combining entrepreneurial ethos and hi-tech know-how in this way brings the firm's clients significant benefits. Sectoral focus has been pivotal to Bird & Bird's success, borne out by the fact that it is amongst the market leaders in the sectors in which it is active. As convergence issues increasingly affect every business, the firm's unrivalled expertise in communications, information technology, intellectual property, life sciences, e-commerce, media, sport and banking gives it a unique perspective. Across each of these sectors, the firm offers a fully comprehensive service. With offices in Brussels, Hong Kong, London, Paris, Stockholm and The Hague, Bird & Bird's lawyers are strategically placed to offer local expertise within a global context. That's how they've been successful in realising their clients' business goals, both domestically and internationally.

PRINCIPAL AREAS OF WORK By providing a full range of legal services within its principal industry sectors, Bird & Bird offers both breadth and depth of expertise, in the following areas:

Banking Working with leading banks and financial institutions, the firm advises on a full range of banking issues including e-banking, project finance, PFI, secured and syndicated lending, insolvency, corporate reconstruction and banking litigation.

Commercial Litigation The department offers specialist dispute resolution advice, both in the UK and internationally, focusing, in particular, on the communications, IT and sports sectors.

Commercial Property Advising telecoms providers, government departments and financial institutions, the firm's expertise ranges from PFI structures and commercial agreements to pan-European regulatory issues.

Communications The firm advises both telecoms users and suppliers on a variety of domestic and international issues including major infrastructure projects; regulatory issues; joint ventures and strategic alliances; M&A; interconnection agreements, outsourcing arrangements and 3G licences.

Corporate Offering a comprehensive range of corporate services, including tax, the firm's corporate lawyers undertake a wide variety of transactional work spanning M&A, joint ventures, strategic alliances, investment, equity financing, venture capital and public offerings.

E-commerce One of Europe's leading practices in e-commerce, expertise spans all the firm's principal departments and encompasses every aspect of e-commerce including: VC and Incubators funds; 'dotcom' start-ups; funding and IPOs; established businesses developing an internet presence and e-banking.

Employment Working with companies and individuals, the firm advises on both non-contentious and litigious issues, ranging from employee contracts and termination agreements to changes in employment regulation.

EU With substantial offices in both Brussels and Paris, the firm has a significant EU and competition capability, concentrating on anti-trust enforcement and legislative developments.

IP One the largest IP practices in Europe, the firm offers comprehensive expertise across all areas. Lawyers advise on brands and trademark strategy, advertising, media and internet domain name issues. They have established a strong reputation for conducting successful patent actions as well as providing transactional and litigation advice.

IT With considerable experience gained in-house within the IT industry and specialist technical backgrounds, the firm's lawyers advise both IT users and suppliers from the public, private and utilities sectors on a variety of major projects.

Media The firm's expertise spans all areas of media including music, film, TV, publishing and computer games, with a particular focus on negotiating and drafting finance and distribution agreements, publishing deals and issues of digital convergence.

Life Sciences The firm offers wide-ranging advice on IP, corporate and commercial issues, to diverse UK and multinational companies within these sectors.

Sport The firm's sports lawyers have extensive experience of advising governing bodies, rights purchasers, broadcasters, sponsors and leading sportsmen and women.

INTERNATIONAL The firm has offices in Brussels, Hong Kong, London, Paris, Stockholm and The Hague.

Chief Executive Officer	David Kerr
Non-Executive Chairman	Hamish Sandison
Number of partners	91
Assistant solicitors	216
Other fee-earners	62

AREAS OF PRACTICE	
Company	56%
Intellectual Property	23%
Litigation	12%
Property	8%
Private Client	1%

CONTACTS	
Banking	Trystan Tether
	Brett Israel
Brands & Trademarks	Morag Macdonald
Commercial	Justin Walkey
	Dominic Cook
Communications	David Kerr
	Frédérique Dupuis-Toubol
Corporate	Christopher Barrett
	Neil Blundell
Data Protection	Ruth Boardman
	Hazel Grant
E-commerce	Felicity Reeve
	Nicholas Perry
Employment	Ian Hunter
	Corinne Aldridge
EU & Competition	Jean Paul Hordies
	Olivier Freget
Intellectual Property	Trevor Cook
	Morag Macdonald
IT	Hamish Sandison
	Roger Bickerstaff
Life Sciences	Trevor Cook
	John Wilkinson
Litigation	Trevor Asserson
	Duncan Quinan
Media & Entertainment	Justin Walkey
PFI	Roger Bickerstaff
	Hamish Sandison
Real Estate	Jonathan Baker
	Robert Scott
Sport	Justin Walkey
	Felicity Reeve
Tax	Richard Ward

LAW FIRMS ■ A-Z

■ Birds Solicitors
1 Garratt Lane, Wandsworth, London, SW18 2PT **Tel** (020) 8874 7433 **Fax** (020) 8870 4770

■ Birkett Long
Essex House, 42 Crouch St, Colchester, CO3 3HH
Tel (01206) 217300 **Fax** (01206) 572393 **DX** 3603 Colchester
Email mail@birkettlong.co.uk **Website** www.birkettlong.co.uk

Ptnrs 17 **Asst solrs** 12 **Other fee-earners** 26 **Contact** Philip George • Birkett Long's team of specialist lawyers offers expertise, professionalism and cost effective solutions to both business and private clients.

AREAS OF PRACTICE	
Commercial Litigation	20%
Private Client, Family & Financial Services	32%
Property	24%
Company & Employment & Rural Business	24%

Birketts
24-26 Museum St, Ipswich, IP1 1HZ
Tel (01473) 232300 **Fax** (01473) 230524 **DX** 3206 Ipswich
Email mail@birketts.co.uk **Website** www.birketts.co.uk

THE FIRM Birketts is a long established independent law firm focused on East Anglia but with a reputation recognised much further afield. The firm is dedicated to both the commercial and private sector. Teams of industry experts provide the complete range of legal services and support to clients from one base in Ipswich, giving cost effective advice and efficient delivery of service.

PRINCIPAL AREAS OF WORK Corporate and intellectual property, commercial property and construction, wealth management and family law. Birketts is well known for its expertise in agriculture, particularly public rights of way.

Chief Executive	Alistair Lang
Senior Partner	Douglas Cotton

CONTACTS	
Corporate	Annette Whybrow
Property	Chris Schwer
Litigation	Bob Wright
Private Client	James Harbottle

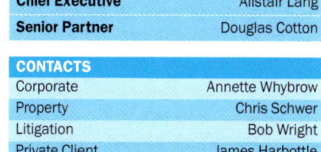

■ Birnberg Peirce & Partners
14 Inverness Street, Camden Town, London, NW1 7HJ **Tel** (020) 7284 4620 **Fax** (020) 7911 0170

Bishop & Sewell
32 Bloomsbury Street, London, WC1B 3QJ
Tel (020) 7631 4141 **Fax** (020) 7636 5369 **DX** 278 London/Chancery Lane
Email mail@bishopandsewell.co.uk **Website** www.bishopandsewell.co.uk

THE FIRM Established in 1979 to provide the quality and range of services with the seamless application of a larger City firm. The practice was founded on commercial and property work and has seen considerable growth in those areas.

PRINCIPAL AREAS OF WORK The firm has a strong commercial law practice that provides legal services to international banks, public and private companies, charities and high net worth clients and government corporate entities. The firm also has a formidable private client practice that provides legal services to high net worth individuals. The legal services provided include the following: banking; commercial litigation/dispute resolution (including arbitration, general commercial, construction, judicial review and private client litigation); commercial and residential property transactions; corporate/commercial (including franchising, mergers and acquisitions, and management buyouts); employment; insolvency; intellectual property; trusts; family, probate and private client work. The firm is committed to Solicitor Advocacy and has two qualified Solicitor Advocates.

Senior Partner	Stephen Bishop
Number of partners	5
Assistant solicitors	6
Other fee-earners	1

CONTACTS	
Commercial & Residential Property	
	Stephen Bishop
	Andrew Swain
Corporate/Commercial	Jill Sewell
	Richard Williams
Litigation/Dispute Resolution	
	Matthew Coleman
Private Client & Family	Michael Gillman

www.ChambersandPartners.com

875

A-Z ■ LAW FIRMS

Blackadders

30 & 34 Reform Street, Dundee, DD1 1RJ
Tel (01382) 229 222 **Fax** (01382) 342 220 **DX** LP-6
Email solicitors@blackadders.co.uk **Website** www.blackadders.co.uk

THE FIRM Blackadders is one of the foremost law firms in Tayside and Angus. The expertise of the firm's specialists is recognised at national as well as regional level.

PRINCIPAL AREAS OF WORK
Employment The firm's employment team is the only one North of Edinburgh and South of Aberdeen with two Law Society accredited employment law specialists.
Corporate & Commercial The corporate, commercial and litigation teams offer a full-function service in advising on matters from corporate finance and commercial contracts to licensing and intellectual property.

CLIENTELE Blackadders' substantial portfolio of private individuals, SME and large corporate clients includes businesses from start-up stage to multinationals.

Managing Partner	Johnston Clark
Chairman	Dennis Young
Number of partners	20
Assistant solicitors	8
Other fee-earners	33

CONTACTS	
Litigation	Ken Glass
Commercial	David Gow
Employment	Sandy Meiklejohn
Corporate	Campbell Clark
Corporate Recovery	Gregor Murray
Conveyancing	Donald Hutcheson
Private Client	Dennis Young
Estate Agency	Morton Simpson
Branches	Barbara Lovegrove
Financial Services	Keith Thomson

■ Blackett Hart & Pratt
11 Market Place, Durham, DH1 3NE **Tel** 0191 384 0840 **Fax** 0191 384 1523

Blacklock Thorley

89 Constitution Street, Leith, Edinburgh, EH6 7AS
Tel (0131) 555 7500 **Fax** (0131) 555 5535 **DX** 550863 Leith
Email bt@blackthor.co.uk

THE FIRM Blacklock Thorley was formed in 1992. The firm quickly established a reputation in the field of debt recovery both for the quality of service and for its cost effectiveness for clients. The firm does, however, offer a wide range of litigation services, both civil and criminal and in the Court of Session, Sheriff Courts and District Courts. With a wide range of commercial clients the firm also acts on instruction from debt collection agencies and from other legal firms both nationally and locally.

Managing Partner	Telfer Blacklock
Number of partners	4
Assistant solicitors	5
Other fee-earners	2

AREAS OF PRACTICE	
Debt Recovery	60%

CONTACTS	
Debt Recovery	Telfer Blacklock

■ Blair Allison & Co
Fountain Court, Steelhouse Lane, Birmingham, B4 6DR
Tel (0121) 233 2904 **Fax** (0121) 236 8913 **DX** 23534

Ptnrs 3 **Asst solrs** 2 **Other fee-earners** 4 **Contact** Grant Bird • Concentrates on family law. Nine fee-earners all highly specialist and experienced. Strong in finance, children, care and adoption. High level work, national reputation.

AREAS OF PRACTICE	
Family Law (inc. Care & Mediation)	98%
Conveyancing	2%

■ Blair & Bryden
27 Union Street, Greenock, PA16 8DD **Tel** (01475) 888777 **Fax** (01475) 781836

Blake Dawson Waldron

4th Floor, 90 Basinghall Street, London, EC2V 5AY
Tel (020) 7600 3030 **Fax** (020) 7600 3392
Email legal.info@bdw.co.uk **Website** www.bdw.com.au

THE FIRM Blake Dawson Waldron is a leading Australian law firm.

PRINCIPAL AREAS OF WORK
Banking & Finance Including advising major banks, clearing houses and issuers in capital markets transactions and on all aspects of commercial lending.
Corporate & Commercial Including advising on IPOs, M&A, privatisation, foreign investment, securities regulation, outsourcing, venture capital and funds management.
Other Including employment, insolvency, intellectual property and tax.

Chairman of Partners	Richard Fisher
London Resident Partner	Mary Padbury
Number of partners	184
Assistant solicitors	564
Other fee-earners	78

BLAKE DAWSON WALDRON
LAWYERS

CLIENTELE ANZ Bank, BAE Systems, BHP Billiton, BAT, BT Group plc, De Beers, ICI, National Express, Shell, Rio Tinto, Tate & Lyle and Telstra.

INTERNATIONAL The firm has offices in Australia, London, Jakarta, Shanghai and Port Moresby.

Blake Lapthorn

Holbrook House, 14 Great Queen Street, London, WC2B 5DG
Tel (020) 7430 1709 **Fax** (020) 7831 4441 **DX** 37957 Kingsway
Email post@blakelapthorn.co.uk

New Court, 1 Barnes Wallis Road, Segensworth, Fareham, PO15 5UA
Tel (01489) 579 990 **Fax** (01489) 579 126 **DX** 132290 Fareham 5

Harbour Court, Compass Road, North Harbour, Portsmouth, PO6 4ST
Tel (023) 9222 1122 **Fax** (023) 9222 1123 **DX** 124490 Portsmouth 9

Kings Court, 21 Brunswick Place, Southampton, SO15 2AQ
Tel (023) 8063 1823 **Fax** (023) 8022 6394 **DX** 38538 Southampton

Managing Partner	Walter Cha
Senior Partner	David Russell
Number of partners	59
Assistant solicitors	83
Other fee-earners	69

AREAS OF PRACTICE	
Property	32%
Commercial	30%
Litigation	30%
Private Client	8%

CONTACTS	
Aviation	Chris McClure
Banking	Kathryn Shimmin
Charities	Elizabeth Davis
Clinical Negligence	Alison McClure
Company/Commercial	Mark Shepherd
Competition	Mary Chant
Construction	Peter Barber
Debt Collection	Sadak Miah
Education	Sarah Palmer
Employment	Max Craft
Environment	David Rayner
Family	Michael Burridge
Franchising	Geoffrey Sturgess
Insolvency & Business Recovery	David Oliver
Intellectual Property	Chris McClure
IT	Chris McClure
Licensing	Phil Crier
Litigation	Stephen Murfitt
Pensions	Maria Riccio
Personal Injury	Alison McClure
Planning	Guthrie McGruer
Private Client	Michael Profit
Property (Commercial)	Carey Blake
Property (Residential)	Debbie Castle
Regulatory	John Mitchell
Tax	Niall Murphy

THE FIRM Established in 1869, and currently with almost 60 partners, 155 solicitors and executives and a total of 460 staff, Blake Lapthorn is one of the largest law firms based in the south of England. With a good proportion of its senior staff having joined the firm from major city law firms, Blake Lapthorn prides itself on being able to offer its clients a level of service comparable to most city-based firms. The firm acts for a wide variety of clients, both commercial and private. The recent growth in its commercial client base has attracted clients nationally and internationally. The firm also acts for many major commercial household names, as well as for a number of local authorities, educational establishments, government agencies and various other public bodies.

PRINCIPAL AREAS OF WORK
Commercial The firm has developed a high reputation for its corporate finance work in MBOs, MBIs, acquisitions, disposals and mergers as well as general advice to public and private companies. Within the firm there are specialist lawyers dealing with employment, pensions, intellectual property, IT, franchising, insolvency and corporate re-organisations, banking, aviation and tax. In addition, Blake Lapthorn has one of the country's leading licensing practices and a regulatory unit that handles all aspects of regulatory law for commercial clients.
Property The firm acts for a number of household names in connection with their property portfolios and undertakes a wide variety of property work including major office, retail and leisure developments. The property team is supported by highly expert environmental and planning teams. There is also a large residential conveyancing team servicing private clients, banks and building societies.
Litigation The firm acts as a resolver of disputes, whether by litigation, arbitration, mediation or negotiation. Specialist areas of expertise include all aspects of construction, engineering and property disputes, general contractual disputes, information technology and computer law, environmental law, foreign export insurance, professional negligence, and professional disciplinary tribunals. The firm also has a recognised specialism in personal injury and medical negligence work and a high-volume debt recovery team.
Private Client The firm offers its clients the full range of private client advice including inheritance and tax planning, wills and probate, matrimonial and family, including a particular specialism in handling cases involving children. It also has a niche expertise in handling the sale and purchase of properties in France.

INTERNATIONAL The firm has an associated office in Brussels.

RECRUITMENT The breadth of the firm's business offers both trainees and qualified lawyers all the challenges and opportunities of a big City firm, yet with all the advantages of a regional firm.

A-Z ■ LAW FIRMS

Blandy & Blandy

1 Friar St, Reading RG1 1DA
Tel (0118) 951 6800 **Fax** (0118) 958 3032 **DX** 4008 Reading
Email law@blandy.co.uk **Website** www.blandy.co.uk

THE FIRM Founded in 1733, Blandy & Blandy is the oldest established legal practice in Reading. Despite its longevity, the firm is modern and progressive in outlook, whilst remaining friendly and approachable. The firm's work is organised into specialist departments providing a full range of legal services to both business and individual clients.

PRINCIPAL AREAS OF WORK

Commercial The firm's commercial services are organised under the umbrella of the commercial group. Emphasis is placed on providing a practical and pro-active service and clients can expect a high degree of partner involvement.

Corporate & Commercial The department deals with a wide range of corporate and other non-contentious commercial work and has particular expertise in the area of mergers and acquisitions and other corporate transactional work, as well as in IT and intellectual property law.

Employment All aspects of employment law, both contentious and non-contentious are dealt with. One of the partners sits as a part-time chairman of employment tribunals and the firm is accordingly well placed to advise on industrial disputes and TUPE issues.

Litigation The firm has built a particularly strong reputation for litigation. Particular specialisms have been developed in relation to insurance litigation and betting, gaming and liquor licensing, and the department is regularly involved in heavy licensing work. A computerised debt collection service is offered and agency work is undertaken.

Commercial Property All aspects of commercial conveyancing work are handled including landlord and tenant, development and substantial planning applications and appeals.

Private Client The firm has an enviable reputation for its private client work and its clients range from private individuals and commercial entrepreneurs to large landed estates.

Trusts, Probate & Tax Planning The department specialises in all aspects of trusts and tax planning work, including the preparation of wills and has a substantial probate practice. The firm has particular expertise in handling the administration of large (including landed) estates.

Conveyancing The department's workload includes estate development, planning matters, work for housing associations as well as routine residential conveyancing.

Family The firm has an extensive and highly regarded matrimonial and family law practice. The firm is able to offer the services of trained mediators and has expertise in childcare and child support work. The firm's StepAhead initiative offers a 'one-stop' legal advice, mediation and counselling service.

Civil Litigation A full range of civil litigation work is dealt with including personal injury claims, probate litigation and bankruptcy.

Senior Partner	Richard Griffiths
Number of partners	12
Assistant solicitors	17
Other fee-earners	9

AREAS OF PRACTICE	
Litigation	21%
Family	20%
Private Client	16%
Corporate & Commercial	16%
Residential Property	14%
Commercial Property	13%

CONTACTS	
Child Care	Brenda Long
Commercial Property	Jane Gunnell
Corporate & Commercial	David Few
Employment	Richard Griffiths
Family	Andrew Don
Intellectual Property	David Few
Licensing	Susan Dowling
Litigation	Jacques Smith
Personal Injury	Philip D'Arcy
Planning	Simon Dimmick
Private Client	Graham Benwell
Residential Property	Nicholas Blandy

■ Blores Solicitors
Delegate House, 30A Hart St, Henley-on-Thames, RG9 2AL **Tel** (01491) 579 265 **Fax** (01491) 579 358

■ Blythe Liggins
Edmund House, Rugby Road, Leamington Spa, CV32 6EL **Tel** (01926) 831231 **Fax** (01926) 831331

■ B M Nyman & Co
181 Creighton Avenue, London, N2 9BN **Tel** (020) 8365 3060 **Fax** (020) 8883 5151

LAW FIRMS ■ A-Z

Bobbetts Mackan

17 Berkeley Square, Clifton, Bristol, BS8 1HB
Tel (0117) 929 9001 **Fax** (0117) 922 5697 **DX** 37011 Clifton (Bristol)
Email mail@bobbettsmackan.co.uk

THE FIRM Committed to providing quality, independent, efficient and cost-effective legal services. Provides a contemporary service based upon an established reputation. Organised in specialist teams, it aims to ensure that the service offered meets the clients' needs, be they 'lay clients' or referral and agency work for the profession. Advocacy services, including higher courts, are available. Member of LawGroup UK, an independent grouping of quality law firms subject to an annual and external quality audit. The firm undertakes franchised and contracted legal aid work.

PRINCIPAL AREAS OF WORK Civil litigation, including personal injury, employment, medical and professional negligence with expertise in judicial review and public law. Education and social welfare law, family and childcare including divorce, complex financial matters and children. Criminal defence including motoring matters, fraud and courts martial. Real property including conveyancing.
Agency Work Civil litigation; criminal defence; family and childcare.

Managing & Senior Partner	Anthony Miles
Number of partners	5
Assistant solicitors	14
Other fee-earners	17

AREAS OF PRACTICE	
Civil Litigation	35%
Criminal Defence	35%
Matrimonial, Care, Children	20%
Non-contentious	10%

CONTACTS	
Criminal Defence	Anthony Miles
Employment	Kevin Wood
Family & Childcare	Sally Mitchell
Non-contentious	Sara Marsh
Personal Injury	Jo Hillman

■ Bogue and McNulty
3 Carlisle Gardens, Belfast, BT14 6AT **Tel** (028) 9035 1502 **Fax** (028) 90742185

■ Bolt Burdon
16 Theberton Street, Islington, London, N1 0QX **Tel** (020) 7288 4700 **Fax** (020) 7288 4701

■ Bonar Mackenzie WS
9 Hill Street, Edinburgh, EH2 3JT **Tel** (0131) 225 8371 **Fax** (0131) 225 2048/240 0749

Bond Pearce

Bristol Bridge House, Redcliff Street, Bristol, BS1 6BJ
Tel (0117) 929 9197 **Fax** (0117) 929 9198 **DX** 200561 Bristol Temple Meads
Email info@bondpearce.com   **Website** www.bondpearce.com

Darwin House, Southernhay Gardens, Exeter, EX1 1LA
Tel (01392) 211185 **Fax** (01392) 435543 **DX** 8321 Exeter

1 City Square, Leeds, LS1 2ES
Tel (0113) 300 2026 **Fax** (0113) 300 2020

10 Fenchurch Avenue, London, EC3M 5BN
Tel (020) 7663 5607 **Fax** (020) 7663 5978

Ballard House, West Hoe Road, Plymouth, PL1 3AE
Tel (01752) 266633 **Fax** (01752) 225350 **DX** 8251 Plymouth

Town Quay House, 7 Town Quay, Southampton, SO14 2PT
Tel (023) 8063 2211 **Fax** (023) 8022 2480 **DX** 2005 Southampton

THE FIRM Bond Pearce's merger in 2001 with Bristol based Cartwrights consolidated its position as one of the UK's leading law firms and one of the fastest growing. Its sustained growth is based on strong client relationships and a national reputation for excellence. Commercially aware, progressive and innovative, Bond Pearce has the resources to deliver real expertise with people you will want to do business with – plain speaking, direct and open, clear about fees and fast on their feet. Advising commercial and institutional clients throughout the UK, the firm's legal teams work closely with clients to deliver fast and effective business solutions. Recognising that commercial clients need much more than just legal advice Bond Pearce provides a level of service, commitment and practical understanding one would expect from an in-house legal team. The firm's clients include a number of FTSE 100 companies, major UK leisure and brewery companies, supermarket chains, retailers, manufacturers, banks, financiers and insurance companies. Sectors in which the firm is highly regarded include: construction, education, energy, finance, insurance, IT and e-commerce, leisure, property, retail, transport, waste and the public sector. The firm's services are provided within the framework of modern office facilities and the latest technology.

Senior Partner	Richard Challands
Managing Partner	Simon Richardson
Number of partners	64
Assistant solicitors	141
Other fee-earners	93

AREAS OF PRACTICE	
Property	26%
Commercial, Banking & Insolvency	21%
Insurance	21%
Personal Injury & Private Client	13%
Litigation	13%
Employment	6%

CONTACTS	
Commercial	Nick Page
Compulsory Purchase & Local Government	Emrys Parry
Construction	Christine Hanley
Corporate Finance	Simon Hewes
Corporate Recovery & Banking	Victor Tettmar
Employment	Christina Tolvas-Vincent
Energy, Environment & Planning	Marcus Trinick
Health & Safety	Jon Cooper
Insurance & Professional Indemnity	Erik Salomonsen
IP & IT	Julian Hamblin
International	Nick Page
Licencing, Leisure & Gambling	Tim Davies
Dispute Resolution	Tony Askham
Mediation & ADR	Andrew Tobey
Personal Injury	Mark Thompson
Private Client	Jonathan Nicholson
Marine & Shipping	Nicholas Horton
Property	Luke Gabb
Technology & E-commerce	Nigel Williams
Transport	Peter Woodhouse

Continued overleaf

PRINCIPAL AREAS OF WORK

Banking & Corporate Recovery This team, including two licensed insolvency practitioners, has established a national reputation acting for financial institutions, on M&A work as well as corporate recovery.

Commercial This work is handled by a specialist team advising on the full spectrum of commercial agreements, often with an international element, which includes advice on intellectual property rights, trademarks, research and development agreements, licensing, joint ventures and competition law. The team advises on all forms of brand protection and identity and IP disputes.

Corporate The corporate team has built its reputation acting for management teams, lending institutions and investors in MBOs, MBIs, IBIs, acquisitions, disposals and mergers.

Commercial Property Bond Pearce undertakes a variety of property work, especially retail, commercial and industrial park developments, dealing with a wide range of investment, development, property litigation, project management, construction and H&S issues. A significant profile in the public sector arises from its work for Government departments on regional and national projects, and Bond Pearce's strong planning and environmental unit remains at the forefront of work relating to renewable energy and waste management. The firm is equally well known for its town centre regeneration, compulsory purchase expertise and port development work. Other specialisms include licensed premises and the education and transport sectors.

Dispute Resolution Bond Pearce is nationally regarded for its work in the fields of professional indemnity, insurance, personal injury, corporate recovery, construction, property, employment, insolvency, transport, intellectual property and e-commerce. The firm also acts for national and local retailers, advising in areas such as customer complaints, consumer credit, security issues, employment matters, food law, licensing, trading standards and Sunday trading. Recent cases include a number of cross-border matters and actions in the European Court of Justice. Bond Pearce accepts all types of agency work and is at the forefront of Alternative Dispute Resolution with trained and experienced mediators. A major provider of ADR experience to others, Bond Pearce acts regularly at mediations on behalf of clients.

Employment With in-house advocacy and mediation experts, this team has a strong national practice and provides a complete service to employers combining legal, human resources and industrial relations skills in a seamless package supplemented by practical training and HR consultancy services.

Leisure & Licensing A complete nationwide and EU-wide service to clients operating in the food and drink retailing, licensed trade, bingo, casino, cinema and leisure sectors, including many high street names. Further specialisation is also available in food hygiene, packaging and labelling matters.

INTERNATIONAL Bond Pearce continues to generate an increasing volume of cross-border work through overseas clients and contacts particularly in Europe, the USA, the Far East and Australia. It is a member of international organisations such as Euro Link for Lawyers.

Boodle Hatfield

61 Brook Street, London, W1K 4BL
Tel (020) 7629 7411   Fax (020) 7629 2621   DX 53 CHANCERY LANE
Email law@boodlehatfield.com   Website www.boodlehatfield.com

6 Worcester Street, Oxford, OX1 2BX
Tel (01865) 790744   Fax (01865) 798764   DX 4329 OXFORD 1
Email law@boodlehatfield.com

THE FIRM Boodle Hatfield is a leading central London practice with a well-established second office in Oxford. Known originally for representing wealthy individuals and landed estates, and while still outstanding in those fields, it now acts for a wide international, corporate, commercial and private client base. Services are tailored to the needs and methods of each client who can rely upon the close, continuing involvement of partners with a broad experience as well as specialist knowledge. Clients have commended the firm's high standard of advice, efficiency, commitment and ability to find practical solutions. The partnership has grown in recent years as the firm has invested in its core business and developed complementary skills. The firm has a private capital focus. It assists high net worth individuals and entrepreneurs with all aspects of their commercial transactions and personal affairs.

PRINCIPAL AREAS OF WORK

Property The highly rated property department is involved in major town centre and out-of-office retail and leisure developments, and in large urban estate transactions with associated landlord and tenant matters. It acts for developers, owners, occupiers, funders, and international and UK-based corporate and private investors. Skills include property finance and international corporate lending, property taxes, town and country planning, construction and environmental law.

Tax & Financial Planning The department is a leader in its field domestically and internationally and handles tax planning for large, complex estates, private companies, high net worth individuals and families, trustees, executors and charities. It advises on inheritance; capital gains and income tax planning; wills and probate; domicile and residence issues; VAT; property and corporate taxes; the establishment of UK overseas trusts; trust and probate disputes.

Corporate The expanding corporate department acts for entrepreneurs, public and private companies, partnerships and overseas businesses investing in the UK, and has many clients in IT-related sectors. It advises on mergers and acquisitions; MBOs and private equity transactions; joint ventures; banking transactions (especially property related); listings and the issue of securities; commercial agreements. The Anglo-German group consists of six German-speaking lawyers, including a bilingual, dual-qualified English partner.

Employment The expanding group is increasingly recognised for providing valuable solutions to all types of employment issues. It advises some of the largest companies and organisations in the UK, as well as high profile individuals.

Litigation The department is active in a broad range of commercial disputes and has substantial, well-regarded expertise in property, employment and agrochemicals litigation, acting for major property and commercial organisations.

Family The established and growing matrimonial and family law practice has notable international experience.

INTERNATIONAL Much of the firm's work is international, arising in particular from the USA, Germany, Switzerland, the Middle East and the Far East.

RECRUITMENT The firm has openings for assistant solicitors in each department. Four or five trainees are recruited each year; some spend six months on secondment to ICI. Application forms are available from the Graduate Recruitment department.

Senior Partner	Richard Moyse
Managing Partner	Chris Putt
Number of partners	32
Assistant solicitors	37
Other fee-earners	16

AREAS OF PRACTICE

Property	42%
Tax & Financial Planning	23%
Corporate & Employment	21%
Litigation	14%

CONTACTS

Anglo-German Group	Chris Putt
Banking	Nigel Stone
Charities	Andrew Farley (London)
	Nigel Roots (Oxford)
Commercial	Andrew Drake
Commercial Litigation	Simon Fitzpatrick
Commercial Property	Richard Maughan
Contentious Trust & Probate	Alison Meek
Corporate & Property Tax	Sara Maccallum
Corporate Finance/M&A	Jonathan Brooks
Employment	Russell Brimelow
	Warren Wayne
Family	Vivien Gifford
	Barbara Simpson
	Michael Tulloch
IT/E-commerce	Andrew Drake
	Jonathan Brooks
Partnership	Andrew Drake
Personal Tax	David Way
Private Client, Trusts	David Way (London)
	Sue Laing (Oxford)
Private Equity	Chris Putt
	Nigel Stone
Property Litigation	Michael Tulloch
Residential Property	Jane Littlejohn

BOODLE HATFIELD

A-Z ■ LAW FIRMS

Boyds

146 West Regent Street, Glasgow, G2 2RZ
Tel (0141) 221 8251   **Fax** (0141) 226 4799   **DX** GW120 - Glasgow
Email mail@boydslaw.com   **Website** www.boydslaw.com

Coates House, 13A Coates Crescent, Edinburgh, EH3 7AF
Tel (0131) 226 9230   **Fax** (0131) 226 6458   **DX** ED100 - Edinburgh

Managing Director	Martin Street
Senior Partner	David Boyce
Number of partners	11
Assistant solicitors	10
Other fee-earners	5

AREAS OF PRACTICE	
Commercial Property	42%
Corporate & Insolvency	32%
Litigation	22%
Private Client	4%

CONTACTS	
Commercial Property	David Boyce
	Brian Dennison
Corporate	Calum Jones
Debt Recovery	Michael Fleming
Employment	Robert Gall
Environment	Denise Loney
Insolvency	Calum Jones
IT/IP	Emily Wiewiorka
Liquor Licensing	Michael Fleming
Litigation	Denise Loney
Private Client	Robert Gall
Small Business Unit	Calum Jones

THE FIRM Boyds is one of Scotland's largest independent legal practices. With offices in Glasgow and Edinburgh, Boyds has become well established within Scotland's business community for its progressive commercial approach, which ensures that it is in tune with its clients' needs. Established for almost half a century, Boyds has advised many companies, their management and stakeholders on all types of corporate legal matters and wider business issues. A people-centred business, Boyds was one of the first law firms in Scotland to be accredited with Investor in People status. Additionally as members of Law Exchange International, an independent group of law practices in Europe and the United States, Boyds also provides readily accessible and informed legal advice for clients of member law firms. The firm is also qualified to handle both English and Scottish Law cases. Boyds has a solid reputation for excellence, quality and innovation. Staff operate in teams within and across departments, ensuring the firm is able to assist in all aspect of legal business.

PRINCIPAL AREAS OF WORK

Commercial Property Boyds assists with the purchase, sale and leasing of commercial property, property development, management and outsourcing, business parks and shopping centres, security work, environmental and planning issues and licensing.

Corporate & Insolvency The firm handles businesses in a variety of ways from starting a business to providing advice on expansion, mergers, buying out another business through to selling a business. In addition, the department provides advice to clients on corporate finance and venture capital, business terms and conditions, distribution/agency agreements, Competition Act issues and intellectual property rights. E-commerce is an increasingly significant part of every day business and Boyds' IP/IT team can support clients on matters across the e-commerce spectrum.

Litigation The firm provides advice at early stages with a view to avoiding disputes and difficulties designed to minimise conflict. The department handles employment law, environmental law, construction law, landlord and tenant disputes, IT disputes, international and cross-border disputes, debt recovery, matrimonial and personal injury claims.

Private Client Boyds provides advice and practical help in relation to house purchase and sale, remortgaging, wills and powers of attorney, trusts and executries.

CLIENTELE Boyds uses a practical consultative-led approach where clients, including Bank of Scotland, Safeway plc and Miller Homes, are assured the highest possible standard of pragmatic legal advice and representation.

RECRUITMENT Boyds' progressive business strategy has enabled the firm to attract some of the most talented lawyers in Scotland as well as a team of non-legal business experts. The practice continues to grow and looks to recruit lawyers in all disciplines who are commercially aware and client-focused.

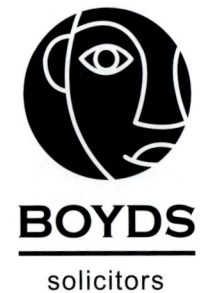

Boyes Turner

Abbots House, Abbey Street, Reading, RG1 3BD
Tel (0118) 959 7711 **Fax** (0118) 957 3257 **DX** 54741 Reading 2
Email mail@boyesturner.com / mail@boyesturnerlegal.co.uk **Website** www.boyesturner.com / www.boyesturnerlegal.co.uk

THE FIRM Boyes Turner is a leading law firm in the Thames Valley, successfully providing high quality commercial and individual client services. All of its lawyers specialise in their respective areas of law – from partners to legal executives – enabling the firm to offer clients a high degree of expertise and a rare depth of support and experience. The firm has achieved wide respect in commercial property, dispute resolution, employment, intellectual property, corporate recovery, clinical negligence, tax planning, and wills and probate, working in close contact with clients to achieve the right solution for them. In the course of the last year the firm has continued its strategy of controlled expansion and has strengthened its position in the marketplace enabling it to continue servicing the growing market while still meeting the needs of existing clients.

PRINCIPAL AREAS OF WORK

Banking & Corporate Recovery Headed by an LIP, the firm acts for all the major insolvency practices as well as for clearing banks and other financial institutions in both corporate and personal insolvency and securities work.

Corporate Business formations, acquisitions and disposals, partnerships and joint ventures, inward investment, and corporate restructuring.

Commercial The firm acts for many substantial businesses including UK subsidiaries of multinationals. Advice includes general business law, commercial and trading agreements, including distribution and licensing, competition law, EU issues and company secretarial work.

Debt Recovery A fully computerised system providing competitive rates and handling bulk recoveries for trading companies and financial institutions.

Employment Preparation of employment contracts, advice on disciplinary issues, industrial tribunal representation, restraint of trade, wrongful dismissal, and sex and race discrimination.

Family Divorce and separation, financial provision, children, emergency procedures, and education (members of SFLA).

Intellectual Property Ownership and exploitation of IPR, licensing, disputes, computer contracts (software and hardware) and product liability. Clients include engineering, electronics and computer companies as well as internet and software houses.

Litigation Contract disputes, shareholder and partnership disputes, negligence claims, property disputes, mortgage repossessions, and landlord and tenant. Agency work undertaken.

Clinical Negligence A specialist team acts exclusively for the victims of medical accidents (AVMA and Law Society referral solicitors, members of APIL).

Personal Injury RTAs, work related injuries, CICB/A, Personal Injury Panel, SIA referral panel and Headway, and maximum severity claims. (Members of APIL and Accident Line).

Private Client Wills, trusts, probate, personal tax planning and residential conveyancing.

Property Sales and leases of commercial property, commercial and residential development projects, commercial lending, and landlord and tenant.

Planning Planning advice for property development projects as well as for appeals and planning enforcement.

CLIENTELE Its clients in the Thames Valley and, increasingly, in London, range from multinationals to start-ups and growing businesses, many in the hi-tech sector. These include manufacturers and distributors of computers and peripherals, software houses and internet companies. Among the firm's other clients are white goods manufacturers, engineering companies and service organisations. Private client work continues to form an important part of the practice.

RECRUITMENT Recruitment targeted toward high quality specialist lawyers in growth areas of the practice. Key appointments over the last year include two new lawyers in technology and commerce, two new lawyers in employment, one new lawyer in commercial property and two new lawyers in corporate transactions. In addition the private client services team from the Thames Valley office of Nabarro Nathanson transferred to Boyes Turner in September 2001.

Partnership Chairman	William Gornall-King
Chief Executive	Andrew Chalkley
Number of partners	18
Assistant solicitors	19
Other fee-earners	17

AREAS OF PRACTICE

Commercial Property	21%
Dispute Resolution	14%
PI/Clinical Negligence	14%
Employment	11%
Corporate Recovery	10%
Corporate Transactions	9%
Technology & Commerce	8%
Private Client	8%
Family	5%

CONTACTS

Banking & Insolvency	Christopher Branson
Clinical Negligence	Susan Brown
	Adrian Desmond
Commercial	Mark Blunden
	William Gornall-King
Corporate	Roy Butler
	Robert Rice
Debt Recovery	Elaine Price
Dispute Resolution	Gary Parkinson
	Michael Robinson
Employment	Michael Farrier
	Barry Stanton
Family	Anthony Roe
Human Resources	Helen Barnett
Intellectual Property/IT	Mark Blunden
	William Gornall-King
Partnership Secretary	John Brunnen
Personal Injury	Kim Smerdon
Private Client	Ashley Wilkin
Property	Mark Appleton
	Peter Daniel
	Simon Doyle

A-Z ■ LAW FIRMS

■ BPC Business Lawyers

Sterling House, 20 Station Road, Gerrards Cross, SL9 8EL
Tel (01753) 279024 **Fax** (01753) 889870 **DX** 40256 Gerrards Cross
Email enquiries@bpcbusiness.co.uk **Website** www.bpcbusiness.co.uk

Contact David Stanning • The company commercial arm of the BP Collins Partnership has a team of experienced corporate lawyers, each with different individual specialist knowledge as well as a sound general background in commercial law, and each dedicated to provide a high degree of personal service to the firm's corporate clients.

■ B P Collins

Collins House, 32-38 Station Road, Gerrards Cross, SL9 8EL
Tel (01753) 889995 **Fax** (01753) 889851 **DX** 40256 Gerrards Cross
Email enquiries@bpcollins.co.uk **Website** www.bpcollins.co.uk

Ptnrs 17 **Asst solrs** 20 **Other fee-earners** 16 **Contact** Ian Johnson • Since 1996, now one of the largest law partnerships in the Thames Valley. Specialists that have the right blend of knowledge, experience, commitment and enthusiasm to achieve designated objectives in a professional, efficient and prompt manner.

BPE

St James's House, St James' Square, Cheltenham, GL50 3PR
Tel (01242) 224433 **Fax** (01242) 574285 **DX** 141660 Cheltenham 11
Email bpe@bpe.co.uk **Website** www.bpe.co.uk

11 Guilford Street, London, WC1N 1DH
Tel (020) 7421 1730 **Fax** (020) 7430 2300

Somerset House, 37 Temple Street, Birmingham, B2 5DP
Tel (0121) 6318400 **Fax** (0121) 6318402

Managing Partner	Malcolm Price
Senior Partner	David Oldham
Number of partners	16
Assistant solicitors	15
Other fee-earners	50

AREAS OF PRACTICE	
Commercial Property	19%
Corporate/Employment	17%
Personal Injury	14%
Commercial Litigation	9%
Residential Sales & Purchases	9%
Lender Services - Residential	32%

CONTACTS	
Commercial Litigation	Philip Radford
Commercial Property	Richard Handley
Corporate	John Workman
Employment	Matthew Jenkin
Lender Services	David Oldham
Personal Injury	Mark Ovington

THE FIRM Operating from modern, open-plan offices in Cheltenham and Birmingham, this practice offers a business services consultancy focused on corporate finance, 'niche' commercial disciplines (particularly IT and construction), commercial litigation and commercial property. BPE is innovative and entrepreneurial with an informal, friendly ethos. It has a strong commitment to technical excellence and has been praised by clients for its commercial acumen. BPE is now one of the largest law firms in Gloucestershire, and the firm has opened a new office in the heart of Birmingham. Led by David Billings (ex Irwin Mitchell & Rigbeys), the Birmingham office is focused on corporate and company commercial matters.

PRINCIPAL AREAS OF WORK

Corporate Advising on a wide range of corporate and company/commercial matters, the department is proactive in handling high value, high complexity M&A and funding work. Recommended for its strong commercial approach, the department has an excellent regional reputation for managing the sale of fast-growing owner-managed businesses. The firm recently acted for Summit Medical in a £17 million management buyout and successfully completed the £16 million re-financing of Quickmove Properties. Other national clients include Mears Group Plc and Jarvis International. The team also advises the Estonian Government and is associated with Heta, the leading law firm in Tallinn.

Employment A growing practice which deals with both contentious and non-contentious employment matters. The department also specialises in planning and implementation of preventative procedures.

Commercial Property The team regularly advises clients on property investment and development deals within the £5 million to £20 million range. It also has notable experience in acting for occupiers of B1/B8 space. The department continues to act for the Spanish arm of Rodamco in the development/acquisition of major Spanish shopping/leisure centres.

Commercial Litigation One of the largest commercial litigation teams in the South West, the department deals with commercial property litigation, intellectual property disputes, commercial contract disputes, and professional negligence. Renowned for having a commercial no-nonsense, pragmatic approach to litigation, the department offers a cost effective service for dispute resolution and, where appropriate, representation at trial.

Insolvency Paul Harris leads a new corporate rescue and recovery team based at the Birmingham office supported by a full debt recovery service.

Personal Injury Mark Ovington heads a large department acting for insurers and private clients on a

wide range of cases. The department also advises on claimant fraud, policy interpretation and other contractual insurance elements. The team has particular experience in handling successful asbestos related claims.

Lender Services The firm acts for financial institutions in remortgage and repossession sales transactions. The department deals with approximately 12,500 cases per annum for Cheltenham & Gloucester plc, Chelsea Building Society, and Eagle Star.

Residential Conveyancing The firm provides a high volume, customer focused residential conveyancing service to clients introduced by institutions, estate agency chains and property developers such as Bradford & Bingley, Your Move, and Bovis Homes.

Brabners Chaffe Street

1 Dale Street, Liverpool, L2 2ET
Tel (0151) 600 3000 **Fax** (0151) 227 3185 **DX** 14118 Liverpool
Email law@brabnerscs.com **Website** www.brabnerschaffestreet.com

Brook House, 77 Fountain Street, Manchester, M2 2EE
Tel (0161) 236 5800 **Fax** (0161) 228 6862 **DX** 14431 Manchester
Email robert.street@brabnerscs2.com

7 Chapel Street, Preston, PR1 8AN
Tel (01772) 823921 **Fax** (01772) 201918 **DX** 17118 Preston
Email john.boydell@brabnerscs1.com

Managing Partner	Michael Brabner
Number of partners	39
Assistant solicitors	44
Other fee-earners	39

AREAS OF PRACTICE	
Corporate	32%
Property	27%
Litigation & Dispute Resolution	16%
Private Client	15%
Employment	10%

CONTACTS	
Agency	Mark Manley
	Amanda Webster
Banking & Finance	Tony Harper
Charities	Stephen Brodie
Commercial/IP	Terry Montague
Construction	Daniel Brawn
Corporate	Denise Walker
	Robert Street
Debt Recovery	Jacqui Lloyd
Defamation	Mark Manley
Dispute Resolution	Mark Manley
	Amanda Webster
Employment	Andrew Cross
Environmental & Planning	Jeff Gillbanks
Housing Associations	Valerie Braide
Insolvency	Denise Walker
IT/New Media	Nik White
Matrimonial	Helen Richardson
Private Client & Wealth Protection	Mark Feeny
	George Erdozain
Property	Sandy Chapple Gill
	Ross Shine
	John Street

THE FIRM Brabners Chaffe Street is a leading corporate and commercial law firm serving the North West. Its business focus is on providing the full range of legal services to the OMB/SME sector; specialised services to the larger corporates; private client services to high net worth individuals. The firm has expanded by 85 percent in the 12 months following the merger with the commercial division of Berrymans Lace Mawer, and more recently with Manchester corporate boutique firm, Chaffe Street. Each client has a relationship manager whose role is to learn and understand the client's business objectives, preferences, priorities and concerns.

PRINCIPAL AREAS OF WORK

Corporate The firm is highly regarded for its corporate work, particularly on corporate finance, acquisitions, disposals, buyins and buyouts, banking and funding work. Commercial work includes considerable growth of activity in IP and IT particularly for the computer games software and multi-media markets.

Property The property team is one of the largest in the North West and is particularly experienced in the retail sector operating nationally for a number of clients and is heavily involved in urban regeneration projects. The social housing team enjoys a national reputation and the team is also strong on property development and finance work.

Litigation & Dispute Resolution The department's work includes contractual disputes; construction litigation; intellectual property actions; landlord and tenant and competition law. The team is nationally recognised for its media and defamation work (Lloyds Panel) and expertise in environmental issues and protestor problems. The team conducts mediations and is accredited by ADR and CEDR.

Employment The team is amongst the largest specialist departments in the North West and acts primarily for employers on the full spectrum of contentious and non-contentious employment issues. It also works on the employment aspects of corporate transactions including TUPE and pension issues.

Private Client/Charities Works closely with the firm's OMB/SME clients to provide tax planning, trust administration, matrimonial, probate and conveyancing services to an impressive base of high net worth clients. The firm also has an enviable reputation in the area of charity law.

INTERNATIONAL Brabners Chaffe Street is an active participant in Eurolegal and The Association of European Lawyers providing representations in 86 offices in 38 countries throughout Europe and elsewhere overseas.

RECRUITMENT Recruiting nine trainee solicitors annually, the firm is committed to a comprehensive personnel development programme for all staff.

■ Braby & Waller

Please see Irwin Mitchell, page 1009.

A-Z ■ LAW FIRMS

Bracher Rawlins

180 Fleet Street, London, EC4A 2HG
Tel (020) 7404 9400 **Fax** (020) 7404 9401 **DX** LDE 168
Email info@bracherrawlins.co.uk **Website** www.bracherrawlins.co.uk

THE FIRM Founded in April 1994, Bracher Rawlins is a commercial law practice based in the City. The firm is dedicated to servicing the needs of its clients in the business community.

PRINCIPAL AREAS OF WORK

Corporate/Commercial All areas of company and commercial matters are undertaken for both public and private companies and individuals.

Litigation The firm handles commercial litigation, insolvency and debt collection, professional negligence, medical negligence, auctioneering law and defamation.

Property Work includes retail, office and industrial property, development, investment/management and residential property.

Employment The firm deals with all aspects of contentious and non-contentious employment law for both employers and employees.

Senior Partner	Alan Bracher
Number of partners	6
Assistant solicitors	5
Other fee-earners	3

AREAS OF PRACTICE	
Corporate/Commercial	40%
Litigation	35%
Property	15%
Employment	10%

CONTACTS	
Corporate/Commercial	Alan Bracher
Litigation	Simon Rawlins
Property	John Gaymer
Employment	John Hayes

Brachers

Somerfield House, 59 London Road, Maidstone, ME16 8JH
Tel (01622) 690691 **Fax** (01622) 681430 **DX** 4806 Maidstone 1
Email name@brachers.co.uk **Website** www.brachers.co.uk

THE FIRM Brachers is a leading firm in the South East of England with an established City office at 12 New Fetter Lane, London EC4. With a staff of 240 and 22 partners the firm has taken strength from organic growth and continuous expansion over the last 15 years. The firm is predominantly involved in corporate and commercial work although it has built upon its roots as a leader serving the pre-eminent private client community in Kent. Many of the partners come from leading City firms. The private client practice is supported by Ashcourt Asset Management Limited, a separate company born out of the firm's investment management operation. The company, which now has in excess of £250m under management, provides leading investment management for private clients, trusts and pension funds in the City and in the South East.

PRINCIPAL AREAS OF WORK

Corporate & Commercial The firm has a strong and highly regarded corporate and commercial practice with an established track record in completing corporate finance deals from MBOs/MBIs, mergers and acquisitions to capital raising exercises for AIM listed companies. The transactional nature of the firm's work calls on the full range of support teams that corporate clients expect in a quality law firm including employment, commercial property, planning, environmental, IP and pension teams. From its Kent base, the firm is capitalising on its proximity both to Europe and London.

Healthcare The firm's prominence in the healthcare sector is reflected in its NHS Litigation Authority Panel appointment as one of 14 firms nationally acting for NHS Trusts in clinical negligence matters. Its 15 strong client list of NHS Trust and Authorities demonstrates the firm's strength and depth in this area.

Employment The firm's growing employment group based in London and in Maidstone provides proactive advice to employers and is increasingly involved in advice on corporate restructuring. The employment group provides interactive workshops for managerial staff of larger corporate clients involved in HR issues.

Debt Collection & Insolvency Brachers has one of the largest debt collection operations in the South East providing highly computerised services to national and international organisations.

Private Client The well established private client department provides a growing niche practice for directors, entrepreneurs, and high net worth individuals in the South East. The department provides a full range of services including specialist advice to the charity sector.

Managing Partner	Geoffrey Dearing
Number of partners	22
Assistant solicitors	24
Other fee-earners	44

AREAS OF PRACTICE	
Debt Recovery	21%
Commercial Property (inc. Planning)	16%
Corporate & Commercial	14%
Clinical Negligence	11%
Employment	10%
Commercial Litigation	10%
Personal Injury	8%
Wills, Trusts & Probate	7%
Family	3%

CONTACTS	
Corporate	Stuart Butler-Gallie
Commercial	Chris Holme
IT	Irfan Baluch
Litigation	John Sheath
Private Client	Simon Palmer
Commercial Property	Sue Hart
Employment	Alan Hannah
	Madeleine Thomson
Planning & Environmental	Henry Abraham
Debt Recovery	John Craig
Personal Injury	Henry Nydam
Property Litigation	Peter Burfoot

LAW FIRMS ■ A-Z

■ Bradley & Clarke
36 Clarence Rd, Chesterfield, S40 1XB **Tel** (01246) 211006 **Fax** (01246) 209786

■ Bray & Krais
70-71 New Bond Street, London, W1S 1DE **Tel** (020) 7493 8840 **Fax** (020) 7493 8841

■ Brechin Tindal Oatts
48 St. Vincent Street, Glasgow, G2 5HS **Tel** (0141) 221 8012 **Fax** (0141) 221 7803

■ Bremner Sons & Corlett
1 Crosshall Street, Liverpool, L1 6DH **Tel** (0151) 227 1301 **Fax** (0151) 227 1300

■ Brendan Kearney Kelly & Co
4 Clarendon Street, Derry, BT48 7EX **Tel** (028) 71266935 **Fax** (028) 7137 1845

■ Brethertons
16 Church St, Rugby, CV21 3PW **Tel** (01788) 579579 **Fax** (01788) 570949

■ Brian Koffman & Co
Queen's Chambers, 5 John Dalton Street, Manchester, M2 6ET **Tel** (0161) 832 3852 **Fax** (0161) 833 2547

■ Bridge McFarland Solicitors
19 South St. Mary's Gate, Grimsby, DN31 1JE **Tel** (01472) 311711 **Fax** (01472) 311500

Briffa

Business Design Centre, Upper Street, Islington, London, N1 0QH
Tel (020) 7288 6003 **Fax** (020) 7288 6004
Email mail@briffa.com **Website** www.briffa.com

THE FIRM Briffa is a leading and award winning intellectual property practice and new media practice. Its strength lies in offering the expertise of a specialist department within a large practice coupled with a personal service. Briffa lawyers are focused on getting results and creative problem solving. The team has experience across all media and is perfectly placed to undertake complex cross-media work. The service is genuinely different and refreshing. Fees are always fixed.

PRINCIPAL AREAS OF WORK Briffa undertakes a wide range of work within its specialist areas covering both contentious and non-contentious work and business affairs. Briffa competes with the largest city and national firms in its areas of expertise. It has a high level of success.

CLIENTELE Briffa has a diverse client base which spans most industry sectors. Notably, many clients are recognised innovators within their own industries.

Number of partners	2
Assistant solicitors	4
Other fee-earners	2

AREAS OF PRACTICE

Intellectual Property & New Media	100%

CONTACTS

Intellectual Property	Margaret Briffa
	Ralph Wehrle
	Clare Griffiths
	Alex Chapman
	Elizabeth Harding

887

A-Z LAW FIRMS

Bristows

3 Lincoln's Inn Fields, London, WC2A 3AA
Tel (020) 7400 8000 **Fax** (020) 7400 8050 **DX** 269 LONDON CHANCERY LANE WC2
Email info@bristows.com **Website** www.bristows.com

Senior Partner	David Brown
Number of partners	28
Assistant solicitors	46
Other fee-earners	39

AREAS OF PRACTICE	
Intellectual Property	50%
Company/Commercial	17%
IT	17%
Litigation/Employment	10%
Property/Environmental	4%
Partnership/Charities	2%

CONTACTS	
Charities	John Lace
Commercial	Laura Anderson
Partnership	John Lace
Commercial Litigation	Kevin Appleton
	Linda Farrell
Commercial Property	Michael Rowles
	Alexandra Lethbridge
Company	Paul Cooke, John Lace
Competition & Anti-trust	Patricia Treacy
Computer Games	Paul Cooke, Justin Watts
Corporate Finance	Paul Cooke
	Mark Hawes
Data Protection	Linda Farrell
E-business	Philip Westmacott, Rachel Burnett
Employment	Linda Farrell
Environmental	Alexandra Lethbridge
IP: Biotechnology	Tim Powell, Penny Gilbert
IP: Pharmaceuticals	Edward Nodder
	Simon Ayrton
IP: Brands/Trademk	Sally Field, Paul Walsh
IP: Commercial	Matthew Warren,
	Laura Anderson
IP: General	Alan Johnson
	Andrew Lykiardopoulos
IP: Patents	David Brown, Edward Nodder
IP: Regulatory	Alastair McCulloch
IT	Philip Westmacott, Rachel Burnett
Media	David Wilkinson
Publishing	David Wilkinson
Tax	Miranda Cass

THE FIRM Bristows is a firm dedicated to serving businesses with interests in technology or intellectual property, ranging from pharmaceuticals, electronics, IT and telecommunications to brands, media and e-business. The firm is a market leader in this area and acts for many FTSE 100 and Fortune 500 multinationals. With over 150 years of experience in this field, Bristows has earned an enviable international reputation and has developed one of the largest intellectual property law practices in Europe, and yet remains a friendly niche firm compatible with the needs of new, growing companies. Bristows is a young partnership in a long established firm committed to excellence in its chosen fields. With the continuing recruitment of lawyers and scientists of the highest quality, Bristows aims to stay at the forefront of specialist firms advising businesses with a strong technology or intellectual property base. The firm has an enviable staff retention rate and clients really do get to know their lawyers. The depth and breadth of expertise that its teams share keep Bristows at the forefront of scientific, technical and legal developments. Clients enjoy relationships that are built on competence, understanding, communication and compatibility and in many cases see Bristows as an extension of their own in-house team.

PRINCIPAL AREAS OF WORK The firm has a substantial number of lawyers who first trained as scientists and who are readily able to understand sophisticated technology. This factor sets it apart from its competitors and has generated unparalleled expertise in litigation and corporate/commercial transactions in which intellectual property or an understanding of technology plays a significant part. The firm's litigation expertise extends to commercial disputes of all kinds, including product liability and employment matters. Bristows is able to find teams of lawyers to handle litigation and transactions demanding multidisciplinary skills, often with an international or cross-border flavour. This is an increasingly important aspect of its business, particularly in the light of European integration and its effect on the development of intellectual property and competition law. Bristows has lawyers who are experienced in corporate and commercial law, and in all forms of transaction, from takeovers and mergers to joint ventures and technology spin-offs from universities. The firm also has significant complementary practices in commercial property, tax, competition, charity, employment and environmental law.

RECRUITMENT Bristows recruits outstanding trainee solicitors each year. The long term prospects are excellent; many of the firm's present partners trained with the firm. Applicants from all academic disciplines are encouraged to apply and scientific degrees are particularly relevant for certain areas of intellectual property. In-house training is comprehensive and many trainees and associates spend time on secondment at multinational companies, including IBM, Gillette and Guinness UDV. Fee earners are not set targets.

Brobeck Hale and Dorr

Alder Castle, 10 Noble Street, London, EC2V 7QJ
Tel (020) 7645 2400 **Fax** (020) 7645 2424
Email info@bhd.com **Website** www.bhd.com

25 Milton Park, Oxford, OX14 4SH
Tel (01235) 823 000 **Fax** (01235) 823 030
Email info@bhd.com

Managing Partner	Thomas Kellerman
Number of partners	12
Assistant solicitors	27
Other fee-earners	5

CONTACTS	
Biotechnology	Eric Doering
Brands & Trademarks	Pierre-Andre Dubois
Capital Markets	Trisha Johnson
Company Commercial	David Gent
Corporate Finance/Governance	
	Thomas Kellerman
Employment	Henry Clinton-Davis
Intellectual Property	Pierre-Andre Dubois
IT/Internet	Chris Grew
M&A	Richard Eaton
Tax	Simon Court
Venture Capital	Thomas Kellerman

THE FIRM Brobeck Hale and Dorr is a multinational partnership founded in 1990 by the independent law firms of Brobeck, Phleger & Harrison LLP and Hale and Dorr LLP. BHD is a leading international law firm dedicated to advising clients in the global technology industry. BHD's clients include a wide range of companies in the internet, information technology, computer software/hardware, biotechnology and life sciences industries, as well as the investment banks, venture capitalists and other financial intermediaries that serve technology companies.

PRINCIPAL AREAS OF WORK High technology, venture capital, biotechnology, mergers and acquisitions, public offerings, intellectual property, information technology, employment and human resources and tax.

INTERNATIONAL The firm has a branch office in Munich. Hale and Dorr LLP has offices in Boston, New York, Princeton, Reston, Waltham and Washington DC. Brobeck, Phleger & Harrison LLP has offices in Austin, Dallas, Denver, Irvine, Los Angeles, New York, Palo Alto, Reston, San Diego, San Francisco and Washington DC.

Brobeck Hale and Dorr

Brodies

15 Atholl Crescent, Edinburgh, EH3 8HA
Tel (0131) 228 3777 **Fax** (0131) 228 3878 **DX** ED10 Edinburgh-1
Email mailbox@brodies.co.uk **Website** www.brodies.co.uk

Managing Partner	William Drummond
Chairman	Alistair Campbell
Number of partners	34
Assistant solicitors	63
Other fee-earners	38

CONTACTS	
Banking & Finance	Bruce Stephen
	Linda Kinniburgh
Commercial Property	David Macartney
	Colin Morrison
Competition/Anti-Trust	Rodger Murray
Construction	Mark Finlay
Corporate & Commercial	Alistair Campbell
	Julian Voge
Corporate Tax	Alan Barr
Employment	Joan Cradden
Energy	Charles Smith
Environment	Charles Smith
Franchising	Julian Voge
IP/IT	Grant Campbell
Litigation	Joyce Cullen
	Robin Macpherson
Planning	Neil Collar
Private Business	Hew Dalrymple
	David Houldsworth
Projects	Dale Strachan
	Denis Garrity
Public Sector	Neil Collar
Trust, Tax & Charities	Andrew Dalgleish
	Hugh Stevens

THE FIRM Brodies stands out as a modern and powerful independent Scottish commercial law firm. The firm delivers client-focused, quality legal services to a strong UK public and private sector client base. Brodies offers legal advice in its core business areas of corporate and commercial, property, litigation, employment and trust and tax. It adds value through its specialist expertise in planning, environment, construction, banking, IP/IT and regulatory advice. The firm is widely recognised as the adviser of choice for significant private corporates and public bodies. Two important new banking appointments and significant tender wins in the public authority, transport, education and energy sectors have contributed to further success. The firm's property team continues to build its credentials in investment, retail and leisure, development and projects, and diversification/alternative land use strategies. Continuing to earn its place at the top of league tables, the commercial litigation team has recently appointed another solicitor advocate partner and the firm's employment team continues to grow as one of the largest in Scotland. Brodies provides significant expertise in the Scottish aspects of cross-border transactional work. Membership of European and global legal groups adds value to the advice the firm can offer in foreign jurisdictions.

PRINCIPAL AREAS OF WORK

Commercial Litigation The firm has an outstanding reputation in commercial, property, finance, professional negligence and employment litigation, adding value through specialist expertise in public law, human rights, and planning advocacy. In addition, it has an excellent practice in personal injury and family law. The firm has three solicitor advocates with extended rights of audience in the Court of Session, House of Lords and Judicial Committee of the Privy Council and a part-time Sheriff.

Corporate The corporate team has significant expertise in regulatory, privatisation and government work and has a strong reputation for mainstream corporate work. The firm has significantly grown its corporate finance and banking practices alongside its practice in mergers, acquisitions, corporate tax, IP/IT and franchising. The energy, technology and transport sectors are well-represented in its client base.

Employment The firm represents some of the largest employers and has one of the largest and strongest contentious and non-contentious employment law practices in Scotland with significant cross-border experience and expertise.

PROPERTY

Development The firm acts for major property developers active in the commercial, industrial and retail sectors and has established its niche in the growth areas of property related projects and real estate partnerships.

Investment The firm provides advice on acquisition, finance, development and disposals for private and institutional investors and continues to act in some of the most complex and highest value deals in Scotland.

Retail One of the largest retail practices in Scotland, the team has been involved in some of the highest profile deals in the Scottish retail market. There is hardly a prime retail shopping centre, High Street or out of town retail park development in which it has not been involved.

Countryside The team advises corporate and private business clients on a range of commercial legal issues including business diversification, renewable energy projects, agriculture, forestry and sporting law. The firm offers a comprehensive rural and high value residential property service incorporating legal and estate agency aspects. The firm's surveyors are experienced in valuation, purchase, sale and management of landed estates, farms and townhouse properties.

TRUST & TAX As tax and trust issues increasingly drive the structure of deals, Brodies can offer a considerable corporate tax, trust and VAT capability.

OTHER AREAS OF WORK

Private Business Brodies' private business department has considerable expertise in wills, trusts and executries and has a strong tax department able to advise the private client on business and personal taxation issues.

■ Brooke North

Crown House, Great George Street, Leeds, LS1 3BR **Tel** (0113) 283 2100 **Fax** (0113) 283 3999

A-Z ■ LAW FIRMS

BrookStreet Des Roches

1 Des Roches Square, Witan Way, Witney, OX8 6BE
Tel (01993) 771616 **Fax** (01993) 779030 **DX** 144160 Witney 2
Email bsdr@bsdr.com **Website** www.bsdr.com

Managing & Senior Partner	Nigel Street
AREAS OF PRACTICE	
Commercial Property	45%
Commercial Litigation	25%
Company	25%
Other	5%

THE FIRM BSDR was established in 1994. It is committed to delivering a responsive high quality and cost effective legal service in a relaxed atmosphere. The firm's primary objective is to provide pragmatic advice and solutions.

PRINCIPAL AREAS OF WORK BSDR is one of the leading law firms in the South East with particular expertise in commercial property and commercial litigation.
Property The group handles retail, warehouse, factory and office acquisitions advising on property finance and landlord and tenant matters.
Litigation The department continues to prosper and is seeking to expand. New clients include Arrows Grand Prix International Limited, McDonalds and Screen plc. In the last twelve months successful cases have included a judicial review for Oxford, Swindon and Gloucester Society Limited and a complex multi-party action concerning property rights at the new stadium site of Oxford United Football Club.
Corporate & Commercial The team advises on a range of business matters, particularly in the hi-tech and bioscience sectors. The technology group is very familiar with the OFEX market.

Browell Smith & Co

Pearl Assurance House, 7 New Bridge Street, Newcastle upon Tyne, NE1 8AQ
Tel (0191) 221 1611 **Fax** (0191) 241 8200 **DX** 61084 Newcastle
Email advice@browells.co.uk **Website** www.browells.co.uk

Number of partners	4
Assistant solicitors	24
Other fee-earners	67
AREAS OF PRACTICE	
Personal Injury	85%
Private Client	15%

THE FIRM Browell Smith & Co specialises in personal injury and industrial disease cases on behalf of trade union clients and their members, as well as for the general public. In particular, the firm undertakes work for the National Union of Mineworkers, GMB, NUM (COSA) and NACODS as well as an increasing volume of private client referrals including professional negligence. The firm continues to grow and develop in the plaintiff personal injury and industrial disease areas where expertise covers industrial deafness, chronic bronchitis and emphysema, vibration white finger, asbestos related diseases, industrial cancers, work-related upper limb disorders and stress cases. Product liability cases are handled and the firm also deals with a variety of personal injury cases with a foreign component. At its satellite offices, family law, probate, wills and trusts, domestic conveyancing and crime are undertaken on behalf of private clients of the firm. The practice has a well established immigration and asylum department under Katherine Henderson which continues to expand to include the associated areas of Judicial Review and Human Rights. Browell Smith & Co has also expanded its employment law department under partner Brian Freeman.

■ **AD Brown, Solicitors**
One Liverpool Street, London, EC2M 7QD **Tel** (020) 7956 2029 **Fax** (020) 7956 2229

LAW FIRMS ■ A-Z

Browne Jacobson

44 Castle Gate, Nottingham, NG1 7BJ
Tel (0115) 976 6000   **Fax** (0115) 947 5246   **DX** 718130
Email info@brownej.co.uk   **Website** www.brownej.co.uk

Aldwych House, 81 Aldwych, London, WC2B 4HN
Tel (020) 7404 1546   **Fax** (020) 7836 3882   **DX** 142420 Kingsway 3
Email lon@brownej.co.uk

102 Colmore Row, Birmingham, B3 3AG
Tel (0121) 237 3900   **Fax** (0121) 236 1291   **DX** 13009 Birmingham 1
Email birmingham@brownej.co.uk

Managing Partner	Brian Smith
Senior Partner	David Hibbert
Number of partners	42
Number of other fee-earners	156
Total Staff	416

AREAS OF PRACTICE	
Insurance & Public Sector	32%
Business Services	26%
Business & Professional Risk	25%
Property	17%

CONTACTS	
Banking	Duncan Murray
Biosciences	Sharon Jones
Clinical Negligence	Carole Ayre
Commercial Litigation	Peter Ellis
Commercial Property	David Hibbert
Company/Commercial	Iain Blatherwick
Construction	Peter Westlake
Corporate Finance	Rob Metcalfe
Debt Recovery	Paul Southby
Employment	Edward Benson
Environmental	Richard Barlow
Freight/Logistics	Caroline Green
Health Law	Gay Wilder
Intellectual Property	Peter Ellis
	Mark Snelgrove
IT/E-commerce	Mark Snelgrove
Pensions	Richard Davis
Personal Injury	Nick Parsons
Planning	Brian Smith
Professional Indemnity	Derek Bambury
Public Sector	Richard Barlow
Retail	Maggie O'Mahony
Social Housing	David Huddleston
Sport	David Hibbert
Taxation	William Colacicchi

THE FIRM Browne Jacobson is a substantial law firm, with a nationwide reputation for providing a first-class service to clients in the business, insurance and public sectors. Acknowledged as a leading regional and national practice with offices in Nottingham, Birmingham and London, the firm also has a growing international presence, driven primarily through its London commercial practice and its associated Paris office, which has bases elsewhere in Europe and the Far East. It also maintains key relationships with a number of US law firms.

PRINCIPAL AREAS OF WORK Browne Jacobson provides a broad spectrum of expertise to corporate and commercial clients, including acting on flotations and new issues, fund raising, M&A, MBO/MBI, IBO and private equity transactions. Sector focus groups provide services tailored to targeted industry sectors including IT and telecoms, freight and logistics, sport, retail, and biosciences. This division also offers commercial services such as franchising, competition law, joint ventures, intellectual property and regulatory work. It also provides property services to investors, developers, local authorities, housing associations and major retailers, including all planning, environmental and construction advice. Other areas of practice include high level corporate tax, personal financial planning, commercial litigation, dispute resolution and employment. For insurance and public authority clients Browne Jacobson provides services in the following specialist areas:

Personal Injury Litigation   The group defends personal injury, employers' liability, motor liability, industrial disease, public liability, and property and product liability claims on behalf of major insurers, and public and private institutions. It also provides risk management and post incident investigation services to clients, and has particular expertise in handling complex multi party personal injury claims.

Professional Indemnity   The group defends professional indemnity claims on behalf of the insurers of a broad range of professions including solicitors, accountants, and architects. It also specialises in policy drafting and risk management work. The team includes a chartered arbitrator.

Public Authority work   Acts for over 100 local authorities and their insurers. This team offers administrative and public law advice and has particular expertise in nature conservation and environmental work.

Medical Negligence Litigation   The firm is a National Health Service Litigation Authority panel member and provides risk management and litigation services to NHS trusts and health authorities. It also services all these clients' other legal requirements. Further information can be found at www.brownej.co.uk.

Brunton Miller

Herbert House, 22 Herbert Street, Glasgow, G20 6NB
Tel (0141) 337 1199   **Fax** (0141) 337 3300   **DX** GW21   **Email** info@bruntonmiller.com

Contact Archie MacIver • The firm is well known for its licensing expertise and also advises on criminal matters, debt collection, family/matrimonial law, and commercial and domestic conveyancing.

AREAS OF PRACTICE	
Licensing	42%
Conveyancing	24%
Court (Legal Aid & Non-Legal Aid)	20%
Commercial	14%

Brutton & Co

West End House, 288 West Street, Fareham, PO16 0AJ   **Tel** (01329) 236171   **Fax** (01329) 289915

A-Z ■ LAW FIRMS

Bryan Cave LLP

6th floor, 33 Cannon Street, London, EC4M 5TE
Tel (020) 7246 5800 **Fax** (020) 7246 5858
Email chattlee@bryancave.com **Website** www.bryancave.com

THE FIRM Founded in 1873, Bryan Cave is an international law firm with 18 offices around the world. A leader in corporate, transaction and litigation representation with a diversified international practice, the firm has over 700 fee-earners, ranking it among the 30 largest law firms in the United States and among the 50 largest worldwide. The firm acts for a variety of public and privately-held businesses: financial, institutional and individual clients. Bryan Cave's London office was established in 1982 and was reorganised in 1999 as a multinational partnership of US lawyers and English solicitors. The London office offers clients a distinct service advantage by combining the best practices of UK and US law firms. The office has grown substantially in the last three years and its UK and US qualified lawyers have broad multijurisdictional experience.

PRINCIPAL AREAS OF WORK The office advises on a wide range of corporate and commercial issues including cross-border transactions, mergers and acquisitions, investment funds, international trade, competition, regulatory work, conventional and Islamic finance, insolvency, intellectual property, telecommunications and technology work. The office has a growing UK commercial litigation capability as well as an international arbitration practice and international trust litigation expertise. In addition, there is a UK/EU employment practice and an international trade regulation and competition practice. The London office has one of the best known US private client practices outside the US representing US citizens residing in or investing in Europe and Europeans moving to or investing in the US. The practice has a strong US tax focus including ownership structures for closely held businesses and international trusts.

CLIENTELE The firm's clients include major publicly held multinational corporations, major and mid-sized publicly and privately held companies, financial institutions, partnerships, emerging enterprises, charities, private offices and high net worth individuals as well as governmental entities.

INTERNATIONAL The firm has 10 US offices located in Chicago, New York, Washington DC, St. Louis and Jefferson City, Missouri, two in the Kansas City area, Phoenix, Arizona, Santa Monica and Irvine, California. The firm has eight international offices located in London, Riyadh, Kuwait City, Dubai, Abu Dhabi, Hong Kong, Shanghai and Beijing. The firm has long standing links with other law firms around the world.

RECRUITMENT The London office has expanded rapidly. Lateral hires in 2001 included partners Rod Cowper who heads the UK commercial litigation practice and Peter Bond, a competition law expert. In the lateral hires it has made, the firm has aimed to attract professionals who are well experienced in their own right, comfortable in combining the best practices of UK and US law firms and who will support the firm's broad corporate/commercial and litigation practices. The London office has put in place a programme for trainee solicitors and recruits two trainees every year. Bryan Cave is keen to encourage lawyers to work in other offices for periods of time. This reflects Bryan Cave's 'one firm' approach and is of great benefit to the firm's culture and cohesion. The London office will be continuing its programme of recruitment throughout 2002/2003.

Lead Partner & Resident Manager	
	Charles Attlee
Number of partners	8
Counsel	2
Associates	14
Other fee-earners	4

CONTACTS	
Corporate/Commercial	Charles Attlee
	Anthony Fiducia
International Trade/Competition	Anita Esslinger
	Peter Bond
Banking & Finance	Richard Stewart
Investment Funds	Charles Attlee
Media & Entertainment	Anthony Fiducia
Islamic Finance	Richard Stewart
Middle East	David Pfeiffer
Employment	Sarah Linton
International Arbitration	Rod Cowper
	Paul E Hauser
Commercial Litigation	Rod Cowper
	Paul E Hauser
Private Client/Charities	Richard Cassell
International Tax	Paul E Hauser
	Dyke Davies
	Richard Cassell

BRYAN CAVE

■ Buckle Mellows

35/51 Priestgate, Peterborough, PE1 1LB **Tel** (01733) 888888 **Fax** (01733) 888999

■ Buller Jeffries

36 Bennetts Hill, Birmingham, B2 5SN
Tel (0121) 212 2620 **Fax** (0121) 212 2210 **DX** 13051 Birmingham 1 **Email** info@bullerjeffries.co.uk
Website www.bullerjeffries.co.uk

Ptnrs 8 **Asst solrs** 6 **Other fee-earners** 9 **Contact** Roger Coates • Specialist insurance practice: EL, motor, local authority, products, professional indemnity and construction. Volume personal injury and disease for leading insurers.

AREAS OF PRACTICE	
Civil Litigation	95%
Private Client/Commercial	5%

Bullivant Jones

State House, 22 Dale Street, Liverpool, L2 4UR
Tel (0151) 227 5671   **Fax** (0151) 227 5632   **DX** 14120 Liverpool
Email mail@bullivantjones.co.uk

Senior Partner	Pamela Jones
Number of partners	13
Assistant solicitors	22
Other fee-earners	8

AREAS OF PRACTICE	
Commercial Property	70%
Litigation & Employment Law	20%
Company/Commercial	5%
Probate, Trust & Residential Conveyancing	5%

THE FIRM Bullivant Jones has built on a long-standing reputation for excellence in the commercial property field to expand into other practice areas serving the commercial community. The firm has historically maintained a small but high quality client base in order to ensure that the provision of first rate client services is not compromised. Whilst not jeopardising this policy, in recent years the firm has strategically expanded its range of clients and developed the resources to meet their needs. The partners aim to be innovative and forward-looking in their approach to transactions and are equipped to advise where appropriate on all the commercial aspects of a client's business. At present the firm has 13 partners and 43 fee-earners in all, and is constantly seeking to enhance its level of service. In 1999 Bullivant Jones was among the first practices in the country to be awarded the Law Society's Lexcel badge of quality, which is reassessed annually, and the firm has been an accredited Investor in People since 1996.

PRINCIPAL AREAS OF WORK The firm concentrates largely on commercial conveyancing. It also has departments in general commercial work, litigation, employment, probate, trusts and residential conveyancing.

Commercial Conveyancing This department generates the largest portion of work carried out by the firm. Work includes sales, purchases and leases of offices, businesses and shops, and new developments such as out-of-town retail parks as well as high street premises. Clients include developers, retailers and investors.

Litigation The litigation department deals with a considerable volume of commercial and property-based matters, including building contract disputes. In addition it handles cases concerning food safety, health and safety litigation and liquor licensing.

Employment The firm's expanded resource in employment law deals with all aspects of both contentious and non-contentious employment law, including redundancy, unfair and wrongful dismissal, discrimination claims, and Employment Tribunal and Employment Appeal Tribunal cases, as well as drafting service agreements.

Private Client The firm has expanded its private client department from a sound base of considerable experience in wills, settlements, probate and trust work, in addition to residential conveyancing.

Company Commercial The department deals with acquisitions and disposals, joint ventures and general commercial transactions.

The inside view of the major UK law firms

Order the 2003 Student edition now:
www.ChambersandPartners.com

A-Z ■ LAW FIRMS

Burges Salmon

Narrow Quay House, Narrow Quay, Bristol, BS1 4AH
Tel (0117) 939 2000 **Fax** (0117) 902 4400 **DX** 7829 (Bristol)
Email email@burges-salmon.com **Website** www.burges-salmon.com

THE FIRM Burges Salmon is one of the UK's leading commercial law firms. Based in Bristol, with an office in London, the firm provides national and international clients with a full commercial service through four departments: company commercial, litigation, property and tax and trusts. Over recent years Burges Salmon has witnessed a high and sustainable rate of growth reflected by some 75% of the firm's clients being situated outside its South West base. This stems from a client-centric culture which pervades throughout the firm and is reflected in the acquisition of new clients and in the secure relationships maintained with them.

PRINCIPAL AREAS OF WORK

COMPANY COMMERCIAL The company commercial ('CoCo') department is the largest in the firm and covers a wide range of disciplines. In effect, the department is made up of five principal groups: corporate finance, finance, EPI (employment, pensions and incentives), corporate tax and commercial.

Corporate Finance The firm's highly regarded corporate finance unit provides a full service to corporate and business clients, ranging from emerging enterprises to multinational corporations. The core team covers the whole variety of corporate finance work including mergers and acquisitions, takeovers, flotations and equity financings, private equity and joint ventures.

Finance Burges Salmon's finance group provides a full range of services on all aspects of banking and finance including corporate banking, asset finance, structured finance, corporate rescue and restructuring, trade finance and property finance.

EPI The EPI unit provides advice to public and private sector clients on all aspects of employment, pensions law and employee benefits. Burges Salmon's team of corporate tax lawyers is recognised as having significant expertise and is able to advise on all aspects of corporate tax law.

Commercial The commercial unit has an outstanding reputation in advising on general commercial, competition, food law, technology and e-commerce, intellectual property and media, PFI and project finance and transport (including rail issues).

LITIGATION Burges Salmon's litigation department is one of the largest regional practices and covers a wide range of work including banking, rail, contracts, defamation and media, financial disputes, insurance, professional negligence and technical and engineering disputes.

Agriculture The litigation department is home to the firm's nationally respected agriculture unit. The unit provides expert legal advice and representation to commercial and private clients with businesses founded in agriculture, land use and the rural economy generally.

Property Litigation The firm's property litigation team specialises in commercial property disputes including landlord and tenant issues. The core work in this area is complex commercial disputes and flagship agricultural and commercial property cases.

PROPERTY The Burges Salmon property department enjoys a reputation for being a pre-eminent practice offering a first class service throughout the UK. The firm's geographical market for property services is truly national. The department consists of teams that cater for a number of specialist areas, including occupiers and portfolio management, brown land regeneration, property investment, rural property and agriculture, town and country planning and compulsory purchase, projects and construction, property development and property finance work.

TAX & TRUSTS Burges Salmon's tax and trusts department is one of the largest in the UK and provides an expanding national and international client base with a full range of services including tax and estate planning, international tax planning, trusts, trust administration, wills and probate, tax compliance and investigations, property taxation, matrimonial/co-habitation disputes and agriculture as well as specialist units focusing remuneration and charities.

RECRUITMENT The firm recruits law, non-law and mature graduates and offers both in-house training and residential courses. Vacation experience is also available – apply two years in advance to Lisa Head (lisa.head@burges-salmon.com).

Senior Partner	Richard Wynn-Jones
Managing Partner	Guy Stobart
Number of partners	49
Assistant solicitors	121
Other fee-earners	53

AREAS OF PRACTICE	
Corporate	25%
Property	25%
Agriculture	17%
Commercial Litigation	13%
Private Client	12%
Banking & Insolvency	8%

CONTACTS	
Agriculture	Roger Hawes
	William Neville
Arbitration	Adrian Llewelyn Evans
Asset Finance	Sandra Forbes
Construction	Marcus Harling
Corporate Banking	Sandra Forbes
Corporate Finance	Christopher Godfrey
Corporate Rescue	Guy Stobart
Corporate Tax	Nigel Popplewell
Dispute Resolution	Adrian Llewelyn Evans
Employment	Christopher Seaton
Environment/Land Use	Ian Salter
EU/Competition	Laura Claydon
Financial Services	Christopher Godfrey
Housing Associations	Stephen McNulty
Insurance	Christopher Jackson
Intellectual Property/IT	Simon Coppen
M&A	Alan Barr
Pensions	Tim Illston
PFI & Partnering	Richard Wynn-Jones
Planning	Patrick Robinson
Private Client	Martin Mitchell
Product Liability	Adrian Llewelyn Evans
Professional Indemnity	Paul Haggett
Property	Stephen McNulty
Property Development	David Gidney
Property Finance	Paul Browne
Property Litigation	Neil Ham
Rail	Nicholas Olley
Trade & Industry	Richard Wynn-Jones
Transport & Distribution	Philip Davey
Unit Trusts	Christopher Godfrey
Venture Capital	Richard Spink

■ **Burness**
50 Lothian Road, Festival Square, Edinburgh, EH3 9WJ **Tel** (0131) 473 6000 **Fax** (0131) 473 6006

■ **Burnett & Reid**
15 Golden Square, Aberdeen, AB10 1WF **Tel** (01224) 644333 **Fax** (01224) 632173

■ **Burnetts**
6 Victoria Place, Carlisle, CA1 1ES **Tel** (01228) 552222 **Fax** (01228) 522399

Burnside Kemp Fraser

48 Queens Road, Aberdeen, AB15 4YE
Tel (01224) 327500 **Fax** (01224) 327501 **DX** 78 Aberdeen
Email law@burnside-kemp-fraser.co.uk **Website** www.burnside-kemp-fraser.co.uk

Managing Partner	Sandy Kemp
Senior Partner	David M Burnside

AREAS OF PRACTICE	
Employment	35%
Personal Injury	35%
Matrimonial	20%
Other	10%

THE FIRM The firm specialises in all aspects of civil litigation. It has a particularly strong reputation in personal injury work and employment law, its work in employment law focusing on higher and further education and the offshore oil industry. The firm has two employment law specialists accredited by the Law Society of Scotland and is alone in the north east of Scotland in having that distinction.

Burroughs Day

14-16 Charlotte St, Bristol, BS1 5PT **Tel** (0117) 929 0333 **Fax** (0117) 927 2342

Burt Brill & Cardens

30 Old Steyne, Brighton, BN1 1FL
Tel (01273) 604123 **Fax** (01273) 570837 **DX** 2709 Brighton 1
Email help@bbc-law.co.uk **Website** www.bbc-law.co.uk

Senior Partner	J R Summers
Number of partners	5
Assistant solicitors	3
Other fee-earners	7

AREAS OF PRACTICE	
Private Client	45%
Litigation	40%
Corporate/Commercial	15%

CONTACTS	
Commercial	J R Summers
Litigation	K G Smyth
Private Client	D J Edwards

THE FIRM Burt Brill & Cardens was established in 1897. Offices in Brighton and Worthing serve both businesses and private clients. The firm's policy is to remain independent and objective, and to identify the best results desirable in each case. Members of the firm are approachable, understanding and courteous and provide a service that is both practical and reliable. Clients are regularly kept informed about the progress of their cases and about costs.

PRINCIPAL AREAS OF WORK Personal injury, clinical negligence, family, employment, professional negligence, commercial disputes, mediation, conveyancing, wills, trusts, probates, tax planning and company and commercial law. Dedicated conveyancing department, offering a friendly, quick and efficient service. Wherever possible the firm uses email, and an internet update service is available.

CLIENTELE The firm acts for a wide range of clients including the University of Brighton, a plc, businesses, charities, churches, trusts, schools, as well as numerous private clients.

Burton Copeland (London)

51 Lincoln's Inn Fields, London, WC2A 3LZ
Tel (020) 7430 2277 **Fax** (020) 7430 1101 **DX** 37981 Kingsway
Email law@burtoncopeland.co.uk **Website** www.burtoncopeland.co.uk

Senior Partner	Ian Burton
Number of partners	10
Assistant solicitors	7
Other fee-earners	4

AREAS OF PRACTICE	
Commercial/Tax Fraud Investigations/ Proceedings/Prosecutions	60%
Regulatory/Disciplinary Investigations/ Proceedings	25%
Serious Crime	15%

CONTACTS	
Commercial/Tax Fraud Investigations/ Prosecutions/Regulation	Ian Burton
	Harry Travers
	Jane Glass
General Crime	Mark Haslam

THE FIRM This specialist practice is widely regarded as one of the most prominent in the areas of commercial fraud, international financial regulation, investigation by the tax authorities, and serious crime. In 1991, Ian Burton, the founding partner of Burton Copeland, established the London office of the firm, which became a separate partnership in 2001. The firm is renowned for its dynamic approach to problem-solving and solution implementation in both national and international contexts, and for its expertise in acting for those who are the subject of, or affected by, the investigation and prosecution of commercial fraud, tax fraud and serious crime, and regulatory/disciplinary proceedings. Its partners and fee-earners have backgrounds in City law firms, the Bar, specialised criminal law practices and leading prosecuting authorities, and have been instructed in most of the largest commercial fraud prosecutions in the last 10-15 years. Its clients include large international organisations, foreign governments, major City law practices and individuals. For many years it has brought its experience to bear in protecting the rights and liberties of its clients in accordance with the European Convention on Human Rights and other international treaties.

PRINCIPAL AREAS OF WORK

Commercial Fraud The firm has one of the largest commercial fraud departments in the country and provides representation in commercial fraud prosecutions brought throughout the country. Its expertise, developed in major prosecutions brought by the SFO and the DTI such as Barlow Clowes, Maxwell and BCCI, has given it particular speciality in accountancy, banking, and international investment matters. In addition, it has substantial experience of large-scale prosecutions resulting from investigations brought by other authorities such as the Inland Revenue and HM Customs & Excise. This

Continued overleaf

expertise and experience is carried over into the related areas of confiscation, restraint, freezing, money laundering, international mutual assistance and extradition. The growing international dimension to the firm's practice involves complex matters in numerous jurisdictions and working alongside foreign governments and major legal practices in those jurisdictions.

Regulatory & Disciplinary The firm has substantial experience of advising organisations and individuals in respect of investigations and proceedings brought by the FSA, Lloyd's, the SFA, and other similar bodies responsible for the investigation and regulation of national and international financial markets. With its broad-based financial crime and regulation practice, it has been well placed to deal with the market abuse regime introduced by FSMA 2000. It also acts for professionals facing disciplinary enquiries/proceedings before tribunals such as the Bar Council, the Law Society, the General Medical Council and Courts Martial. Its work ranges from protecting individuals in an area where procedural safeguards are ill-defined to conducting internal investigations on behalf of organisations concerned about potential regulatory breaches.

Inland Revenue/HM Customs & Excise Investigations The firm has particular expertise in relation to Inland Revenue and HM Customs & Excise investigations and prosecutions as well as litigation concerning the tax authorities, an area where the client's best interests often lie in a negotiated settlement. Regularly working closely with eminent accountancy practices, Burton Copeland specialises in the protection of its clients' interests in the face of the exceptional powers of investigation exercised by the Inland Revenue and HM Customs & Excise. It has considerable expertise in securing negotiated financial settlements with the tax authorities and/or bringing judicial review proceedings in respect of their actions, particularly in relation to their extensive information gathering powers and the conduct of raids.

Health & Safety, Corporate Manslaughter/Killing & Environmental Investigations & Prosecutions The firm acts for individuals and organisations facing investigations and prosecutions relating to health and safety, corporate killing/manslaughter, trading standards and environmental matters. This area includes advising on orders for the compulsory provision of information. In keeping with the firm's commitment to being at the forefront of developing areas of legal practice, it has developed considerable expertise in the fast developing area of corporate killing/manslaughter and, in particular, in relation to the imminent new legislative regime.

Serious Crime Burton Copeland has an established reputation as market leader in the largest and most high-profile serious criminal cases, and a number of its partners are recognised as leading individuals in this field. It offers specialist advice across the whole spectrum from homicide to road traffic offences. Where relevant, this expertise is again carried over into the related areas of confiscation and restraint.

Civil Litigation The firm also acts in a range of civil proceedings ancillary to its core specialisms.

Burton Copeland (North)

Royal London House, 196 Deansgate, Manchester, M3 3NE
Tel (0161) 827 9500   **Fax** (0161) 832 2619   **DX** 14362 Manchester 1
Email crime@burtoncopeland.com   **Website** www.burtoncopeland.com

34 Castle Street, Liverpool, L2 0NR
Tel (0151) 243 7500   **Fax** (0151) 243 7501   **DX** 14117 Liverpool
Email liverpool@burtoncopeland.com

7-9 Bexley Square, Salford, M3 6DB
Tel (0161) 833 9398   **Fax** (0161) 833 9975   **DX** 14362 Manchester 1
Email salford@burtoncopeland.com

7 Washway Road, Sale, M33 7AD
Tel (0161) 905 8530   **Fax** (0161) 905 8531   **DX** 19271 Sale
Email trafford@burtoncopeland.com

Managing Partner	Michael Mackey
Number of partners	13
Assistant solicitors	11
Other fee-earners	23

AREAS OF PRACTICE	
General Crime/Road Traffic	55%
Commercial Fraud/Regulation	25%
Customs/VAT & Tax Controversy	20%

CONTACTS	
Manchester	Michael Mackey
Liverpool	Colin Downie
Salford	Tim Andrew
Sale	Martin Richardson
Regulation/Employee Representation (Manchester)	Louise Straw
Road Traffic (Manchester)	Gwyn Lewis

THE FIRM Burton Copeland enjoys long established recognition as one of the leading practitioners of criminal law, in all its spheres. During the past 25 years, the practice has developed in line with constant legislative change, coupled with the endless extension of those areas of business, professional and personal conduct, to which criminal sanctions might now apply. A member of the Serious Fraud Panel and Criminal Franchise Panel since their inception, Burton Copeland offers the traditional skills of presentation and advocacy, enhanced by the innovative deployment of the latest information technology, as a tool in the collation and analysis of complex evidence and data. Clients range from large international corporations to individuals and instructions are received from all areas of the UK and from clients abroad, who may have interests to protect in the UK.

PRINCIPAL AREAS OF WORK

Corporate & Commercial Fraud In this area of practice, the acknowledged strength of the firm derives from the fact that, however large or complex the transactions, the Crown has to prove its case in a criminal court, according to criminal standards. Success in the commercial fraud arena has been built on the application of the expertise in criminal practice, tactics and trial strategy.

Courts Martial The practice has undertaken many cases on behalf of service personnel, both here and abroad. Regular instructions are received on referral from recognised service organisations.

Customs Investigations Customs investigations focus on two major areas: the importation of contraband or prohibited materials and VAT or similar fraud irregularity, both coupled with the threat of proceedings for confiscation or forfeiture. The practice has been involved in many major customs prosecutions, from those involving allegations of minor infringement to those concerning many millions of pounds.

General Crime For some years, the practice has been a recognised market leader in an area which extends from handling to homicide, corruption to conspiracy, from simple theft to organised crime at the most serious level. Anyone might be the subject of an investigation and clients include members of the professions and celebrities from the worlds of sport and entertainment. A number of the firm's 21 advocates enjoy Higher Rights of Audience, enabling the provision of a seamless and cost-effective service, in appropriate cases. Particular expertise has been gained in the defence of cases involving forensic and medical issues, including a number of major investigations, in which medical malpractice has been alleged. The practice receives referrals from a number of professional bodies, including trade unions and is appointed to the referral panels of the Royal College of Nursing and the Police Federation.

Professional Disciplinary Proceedings The firm's advocates advise and appear on behalf of those reported to various professional disciplinary bodies, often in the context of referrals mentioned above.

Regulation & Employee Protection More and more of the sanctions of the criminal law are being applied to the conduct of everyday business. The practice provides advice and representation to corporate and individual clients, who face investigation by the proliferating number of regulatory and investigative authorities, in spheres such as health and safety, trading standards and environmental protection. The practice has been retained to represent the interest of major international corporations on issues ranging from so called corporate manslaughter through to simple breach of fire regulations.

Road Traffic Despite being at the lower end of the scale, a conviction for a road traffic offence can have far reaching consequences when licences are at risk. The firm has long had a significant reputation, especially in relation to drink driving and issues of disqualification.

Bury & Walkers

4 Butts Court, Leeds LS1 5JS
Tel (0113) 244 4227   **Fax** (0113) 246 5965   **DX** 12048 Leeds 1
Email leeds@burywalkers.com   **Website** www.burywalkers.com

THE FIRM Bury & Walkers was established over 150 years ago. Its property department is well respected and is currently expanding; it was recently involved with the Bolton Arena and the acquisition of a number of substantial retail and warehouse properties. It aims to provide sound practical advice on a cost-effective basis.

PRINCIPAL AREAS OF WORK

Commercial Company acquisitions; acts on behalf of national franchiser; Shareholder Agreements including television industry and professional practices.

Commercial Property Acquisitions and sales, development work, funding, construction and planning. National reputation in relation to residential landlord and tenant work.

Litigation Expanding department with international disputes and property disputes. Personal injury and general litigation in other offices.

Private Client Provides a full range of services to private individuals.

CLIENTELE
The firm acts on behalf of private individuals through to three Metropolitan Councils and large commercial organisations.

INTERNATIONAL
Members of Euro Link, an organisation of lawyers throughout Europe, USA and Asia.

Managing Partners	Michael Burke
	Simon Nuttall
Senior Partner	John Clark

AREAS OF PRACTICE	
Litigation	40%
Commercial Property	28%
Private Client	20%
Commercial	12%

CONTACTS	
Commercial	John Clark
Commercial Property	Michael Burke
Litigation	Simon Nuttall
Private Client	Alan Duffin

A-Z ■ LAW FIRMS

Cadwalader, Wickersham & Taft

265 Strand, London, WC2R 1BH
Tel (020) 7170 8700 **Fax** (020) 7170 8600 **DX** 238 Chancery Lane
Email cwtinfo@cwt.com **Website** www.cadwalader.com

THE FIRM Cadwalader Wickersham & Taft is one of the world's leading international law practices, providing financial institutions, Fortune 500 companies and other leading corporations, government entities, charitable and health care organisations, and private clients with innovative solutions to complex legal and business issues. Cadwalader's London office, staffed primarily with solicitors qualified in England and Wales, was established in 1997 to help clients capitalise on European and worldwide markets, as well as to serve those desiring US style services and access to American financial markets.

PRINCIPAL AREAS OF WORK Fully integrated with Cadwalader's US offices, the London group is renowned for expertise in financial restructuring, capital markets, energy, project finance and privatisation, litigation, real estate and tax matters.

Financial Restructuring The London office has substantial experience in contentious and non-contentious insolvency and insolvency litigation, with a particular focus on the insurance and reinsurance industry. In addition, the firm's London lawyers advise clients in all aspects of corporate and corporate finance transactions, including mergers and acquisitions and joint ventures. Members also specialise in debt and equity derivatives (including hedging transactions in relation to corporate mergers and acquisitions and ESOPs) and debt and equity offerings in both the private placement and capital markets. Cadwalader lawyers have extensive experience in both domestic and cross-border transactions and are adept at the co-ordination of foreign legal, regulatory and other professional advice.

Project Finance In the project finance sector, Cadwalader's London lawyers have experience in a wide variety of disciplines including energy and power, oil and gas, energy trading, rail, privatisation, telecoms and financing. The group has particular expertise in Europe, Africa, the Far East, the Indian sub-continent and the Middle East.

Capital Markets Cadwalader is a recognised market leader in the area of capital markets transactions, having assisted clients in over $1 trillion in residential mortgage, commercial mortgage and asset backed deals. The firm represents leading financial institutions in the full range of capital markets transactions, including all forms of bond and note issues, swaps, options, leasing deals and tax driven products and other OTC derivatives.

Real Estate The firm's leading real estate finance practice is complemented by a practice in London which employs the talents of US and UK lawyers to provide the complete spectrum of real estate representations, from financing, acquisitions, sales and exchanges to development, construction, joint ventures, management and leasing.

Litigation The litigation department handles significant disputes for a broad spectrum of financial institutions, as well as major commercial, industrial and service corporations and high net worth individuals. The firm also advises on both banking and corporate conflicts arising from the transactions carried out by the financial restructuring and capital markets departments.

Managing Partner	Robert Link Jr
UK	
Number of partners	8
Assistant solicitors	38
Other fee-earners	11
International	
Number of partners	89
Assistant solicitors	267
Other fee-earners	158

CONTACTS

UK Contacts

Financial Restructuring & Corporate	
	Andrew Wilkinson
	Lyndon Norley
Projects	Paul Biggs
Banking & Finance	Stephen RP Mostyn-Williams
Capital Markets	James Croke
	Jerry De Melo
Real Estate	Alan Lawrence
	Richard Streat
Litigation	Michelle Duncan
International Contacts	
Financial Restructuring	Bruce Zirinsky
Corporate & Litigation	Dennis Block
Capital Markets	Robert Link Jr
Real Estate	W Christopher White

■ Cains Advocates Limited

15-19 Athol Street, Douglas, IM1 1LB
Tel (01624) 638300 **Fax** (01624) 638333 **Email** law@cains.co.im **Website** www.cains.co.im

Directors 6 **Other lawyers** 16 **Contact** Andrew Corlett • The firm handles a comprehensive range of cross-border financial, corporate, commercial and property transactions and has considerable expertise in all areas of litigation and dispute resolution.

Campbell Hooper

35 Old Queen St, London, SW1H 9JD
Tel (020) 7222 9070 **Fax** (020) 7222 5591 **DX** 2364 Victoria
Email marketing@campbellhooper.com **Website** www.campbellhooper.com

Managing Partner	Martin Wright
Number of partners	20
Assistant solicitors	15
Other fee-earners	22

AREAS OF PRACTICE	
Corporate & Commercial	35%
Property	25%
Private Client	18%
Construction	16%
Employment	6%

CONTACTS	
Corporate/Commercial	Martin Wright
Litigation (Commercial)	Jonathan Whitehead
Media	Daniel Eilon
Litigation (Defamation)	Graham Atkins
Property	Stephen Siddall
Planning	Oliver Goodwin
Construction	Duncan Salmon
Private Client	Alex Cuppage
Charities	Brian Walsh
Employment	William Granger

THE FIRM Campbell Hooper's dual commitment to clients and people runs throughout the firm's systems and its recruitment methods. The firm's mission and vision are supported by clearly expressed values relating to dealings with clients and fellow members of the firm; Campbell Hooper has also implemented a modern and innovative system of skill-based development plans for partners, other fee-earners and supporting staff. The firm provides comprehensive commercial legal services to a range of clients that include international corporations, banks, construction companies, developers, publishers, IT companies, charities and individuals.

PRINCIPAL AREAS OF WORK

Corporate The practice deals with the complete range of commercial transactions including start-ups, joint ventures, project financing and corporate finance. It has particular expertise in mergers and acquisitions and management buyouts. Half of the corporate and commercial departments' work is for businesses based outside UK. The firm is a member of Proteus, the international network of independent law practices.

Media Whilst the media department has acknowledged expertise in theatre and other entertainment industries, they now find there is an increase in work in new media law in conjunction with the clients' needs for advice and support in this growing area. Campbell Hooper also offers a specialist defamation and media management team acting for individuals and corporations.

Property The firm's reputation in commercial and residential property development work continues to grow. The firm's extensive experience of mixed-use developments and urban regeneration schemes is equal to much larger city firms in this field of expertise. Other commercial property work undertaken includes commercial investment/occupier schemes, joint venture schemes, contaminated land issues and general landlord and tenant work. The firm represents a number of local authorities in town centre scheme developments as well as many retailers. Residential development is a particular specialism and the firm has recently set up the housebuilder team comprising specialists from property, planning and construction fields to support the firm's broad housebuilder clientele.

Planning The firm benefits from a specialist planning team which deals with a variety of work including property and corporate support, strategic planning on major developments, forward planning and local plan representations, appeals and high court challenges. This work is undertaken for a wide client base including local authorities as well as retail, housing and commercial developers. The planning team dovetails with the firm's construction team to form the urban regeneration group.

Construction Construction advice (for employers/developers, contractors and professionals) cover all kinds of traditionally structured development projects and the firm is increasingly handling specialist work such as urban regeneration, private finance initiative matters and public/private partnerships. Should disputes arise on a project, Campbell Hooper has a dedicated team of lawyers handling contentious work who have, this year, handled adjudications, mediations as well as arbitrations and High Court trials.

Private Client (inc. Charities, Estate Planning, Conveyancing & Family) The team offers a full range of services for domestic residential conveyancing which covers sales, purchases, leases, tenancies and mortgages. Through the estate planning section, the department advises both domestic and offshore clients on all aspects of wealth management including the creation and maintenance of both UK and offshore trusts, multijurisdictional administration and succession issues. The charities group acts for over 30 national charities.

Employment The firm advises on the drafting of contracts and procedures, day-to-day employee issues, the employment dimension to commercial transactions as well as on all aspects of contentious employment law in the Employment Tribunal, the High Court and Companies Court. Clients' businesses include banks, international corporations, charities, advertising and recruitment agencies

A-Z ■ LAW FIRMS

Capsticks

77-83 Upper Richmond Road, London, SW15 2TT
Tel (020) 8780 2211 **Fax** (020) 8780 1141 **DX** 59461 Putney
Email info@capsticks.co.uk **Website** www.capsticks.com

Senior Partner	Brian Capstick
Number of partners	27
Assistant solicitors	32
Other fee-earners	17

AREAS OF PRACTICE	
Clinical Law	54%
Property	14%
Dispute Resolution	13%
Employment	12%
Commercial	7%

CONTACTS	
Administrative Law	James Reynolds
Clinical Law	Janice Smith
Commercial	Christopher Brophy
Commercial Litigation & Regulatory	John Witt
Commercial Property	Suzanne Durey
Employment	Peter Edwards
PFI/PPP	Colin Lynch

THE FIRM CAPSTICKS is one of the UK's leading healthcare law firms, handling litigation, employment law and commercial and property work for healthcare bodies including the General Dental Council, the Commission for Health Improvement, United Response, the Terrence Higgins Trust and around 150 other NHS, regulatory, voluntary and private sector organisations. CAPSTICKS has developed an outstanding level of expertise through a modern infrastructure of research, training and data management. The firm has held the ISO 9001 standard of quality assurance since 1994, and was also in the first wave of firms to be awarded the Law Society's quality standard LEXCEL. Whilst CAPSTICKS has traditionally been well known for its work with Health Authorities and Acute NHS Trusts, the firm has recently made outstanding progress in areas such as mental health and primary care law. For example using its unique NHS experience and expertise, the firm has put together a package of facilities for PCTs to enable their board members to operate effectively within the new legislative framework. CAPSTICKS has also expanded into the private healthcare market, with an agreement with the Independent Healthcare Association to supply its members with healthcare advisory legal services. The firm's PFI practice has also expanded into the private sector, most recently advising Toshiba Medical Systems Ltd on a £45 million managed equipment PFI. Healthcare regulatory work is another of the firm's growth areas. Supporting all of this work is an expert system that provides online access to CAPSTICKS' database of previous advice articles and precedents derived from more than 30,000 NHS cases.

PRINCIPAL AREAS OF WORK The firm's work is divided between the clinical law, commercial, dispute resolution, employment and property departments.

Clinical Law This department deals with a large volume of clinical law advisory matters such as consent to treatment cases, and mental health issues in particular. It can field an exceptionally strong team able to provide a truly comprehensive service. The firm has an outstanding reputation for dealing safely with sensitive and high profile cases such as the Victoria Climbie Inquiry and the Ms B case on withdrawal of artificial ventilation. The department also deals with clinical negligence cases for the NHS Litigation Authority, including disasters arising from obstetric accidents, which comprise some of the largest PI claims in this country.

Commercial This department advises on the contractual aspects of major PFI and other projects. The work is carried out in multidisciplinary teams with members of the property and employment departments. The firm has already completed several major PFI schemes and is currently advising on two of the six government prioritised healthcare PFI schemes. The department has particular expertise in the procurement of electronic patient records and other IT systems for NHS clients.

Dispute Resolution This department specialises in the resolution of commercial and property disputes as well as working for healthcare regulatory bodies. The firm's commercial litigators continue to recover substantial sums of money lost through fraud on the NHS.

Employment This department provides employment law advice and representation to the NHS, which is the world's third largest employer, along with many other types of healthcare bodies including high profile charities such as United Response and the Terrence Higgins Trust.

Property This department carries out major healthcare property development work, including PFI. Innovative work is also carried out in conjunction with other departments, including development of new state-of-the-art primary care facilities and joint ventures between NHS bodies and local authorities.

CAPSTICKS
— SOLICITORS —

LAW FIRMS ■ A-Z

Carey Langlois

PO Box 98, 7 New Street, St Peter Port, GY1 4BZ
Tel (01481) 727272 **Fax** (01481) 711052
Email info@careylanglois.com **Website** www.careylanglois.com

THE FIRM Carey Langlois provides services to individuals in Guernsey's financial industry and a wide range of international corporations. Carey Langlois is Guernsey's largest law firm, with offices in London and Alderney. Carey Langlois prides itself on its innovative approach to client demands and its ability to manage major transactions on short notice. Carey Langlois is the only firm of Advocates in Guernsey with a training programme for solicitors and has recently received the Excellence in Training Award from the Institute of Directors. Carey Langlois is the Guernsey member firm of Lex Mundi and the Associate of European Lawyers.

Managing Partner	John Greenfield
Senior Partner	John Langlois
Number of partners	13
Assistants	22
Other fee-earners	9

AREAS OF PRACTICE	
Commercial Litigation	20%
Banking & Finance	25%
Commercial Property	15%
Private Client, Trust and Tax Planning	15%
Corporate & Commercial	25%

CAREY LANGLOIS
— ADVOCATES AND NOTARIES PUBLIC —

■ Carless Davies & Co
140 Stourbridge Road, Halesowen, B63 3UL **Tel** (0121) 550 2181 **Fax** (0121) 550 9954

■ Carnson Morrow Graham
80 Main Street, Bangor, BT20 5AE **Tel** (028) 9145 7911 **Fax** (028) 9145 0679

■ Carrick Read Insolvency
Trafalgar House, 29 Park Place, Leeds, LS1 2SP **Tel** (0113) 246 7123 **Fax** (0113) 244 2863

■ Carruthers Gemmill
81 Bath Street, Glasgow, G2 2EH **Tel** (0141) 333 0033 **Fax** (0141) 332 1072

Carson McDowell

Murray House, Murray Street, Belfast, BT1 6DN
Tel (028) 9024 4951 **Fax** (028) 9024 5768 **DX** 403 NR Belfast
Email law@carson-mcdowell.com **Website** www.carson-mcdowell.com

THE FIRM Founded in 1852, Carson McDowell has an outstanding reputation in Northern Ireland and beyond for its experience in all aspects of corporate and commercial practice, PFI, commercial property, corporate finance, employment, commercial contracts, insolvency, civil litigation and arbitration. It has strong relationships with leading firms in London and the regional centres and also in Scotland, often operating as the NI link in projects for inward investment. The firm's experience and reliability are complemented by the latest technology and by its commitment to achieving its client's business objectives. To this end Carson McDowell has formed a strategic alliance with leading Dublin firm Mason Hayes & Curran under the title 'i-law'. The firms remain independent, but are now able to offer a seamless and comprehensive legal service covering the whole of the island.

PRINCIPAL AREAS OF WORK

Company & Commercial The department offers a complete service, covering all areas of practice and involving close co-operation with other professionals. It has established links with a number of firms in the City of London through working alongside them on many transactions and has acted in the privatisation of Northern Ireland public utilities and in PFI projects. The department is also a leading practice in information and communication technology issues.

Commercial Property The department deals with the purchase, development, management and sale of business property, from the single shop unit to the city centre office building. It provides a complete package, including planning applications, site assembly, project management, developments by way of lease, mortgage and onward investment sale. This year the department acted as lead advisor to the purchaser in the largest ever single property transaction in Northern Ireland. It is equally experienced in residential development.

Commercial Security & Banking The firm has an established finance department which has built sound relationships with financial institutions in the province and beyond. It has extensive experience with the various forms of security which are available and will also deal with investigation of property title, land searches and enquiries, companies office file searches, property insurance cover and appropriate

Continued overleaf

Senior Partner	Brian Turtle
Number of partners	11
Assistant solicitors	15
Other fee-earners	10

AREAS OF PRACTICE	
Company/Commercial	30%
Commercial Property	30%
Civil Litigation	35%
Private Client	5%

CONTACTS	
Civil Litigation	Brian Turtle
Commercial Lit./Arbitration	Peter Davison
Commercial Property	Alan Reilly
Commercial Security	Tom Adair
Company/Commercial	Michael Johnston
Employment	Brian Turtle
PFI	Michael Johnston
Professional Negligence	Kenneth Gouk

A-Z ■ LAW FIRMS

legal registrations and statutory notices.

Litigation An experienced team, not only in the traditional court system but also in equal opportunity, employment and lands tribunal and building arbitrations. The firm also acts in more specialised fields of law such as professional negligence, marine law, defamation, carriage of goods and environment, as well as in areas which are unique to Northern Ireland such as the Criminal Damage Legislation, Fair Employment Law, and the licensing of the sale of intoxicating liquor and bookmakers' premises. In the business field it handles all types of commercial litigation, from simple debt collection (the firm's debt collection system has its own dedicated computer base) through normal contractual claims, intellectual property and employment problems to the major commercial dispute which may involve domestic and European law. In addition, the firm will deal with all aspects of corporate insolvency, both contentious and non-contentious.

■ Carter Lemon Camerons

11 Breams Building, London, EC4A 1DW **Tel** (020) 7405 7554 **Fax** (020) 7242 3926

■ Cartmell Shepherd

Viaduct House, Carlisle, CA3 8EZ **Tel** (01228) 516666 **Fax** (01228) 401490

■ Cartwright King

Norwich Union House, South Parade, Old Market Square, Nottingham, NG1 2LJ **Tel** (0115) 958 7444 **Fax** (0115) 958 8666

■ Cartwright & Lewis

100 Hagley Road, Edgbaston, Birmingham, B16 8LT
Tel (0121) 246 3000 **Fax** (0121) 246 3050 **DX** 707293 Edgbaston
Email legal@cartwrightlewis.co.uk **Website** www.cartwrightlewis.co.uk

AREAS OF PRACTICE	
Personal Injury	37%
Property	25%
Private Client	23%
Company/Commercial	9%
Commercial Litigation	6%

Ptnrs 8 **Asst solrs** 11 **Other fee-earners** 18 **Contact** Anthony Rich • The firm is one of the longest established solicitors in Birmingham with a large personal injury department. It is known for commercial litigation, commercial property, debt collection, employment and corporate law. The firm offers comprehensive private client services including personal injury, matrimonial and family law, conveyancing, wills, probate and trusts.

■ Cartwrights Adams & Black

36 West Bute Street, Cardiff, CF10 5UA **Tel** (029) 2046 5959 **Fax** (029) 2048 0006

■ Cartwrights Insurance Partners

2nd Floor, Netherton House, 23-29 Marsh St, Bristol, BS1 4AQ **Tel** (0117) 943 9960 **Fax** (0117) 929 8063

Cawdery Kaye Fireman & Taylor

25-26 Hampstead High Street, London, NW3 1QA
Tel (020) 7431 7262 **Fax** (020) 7431 7261 **DX** 57567 Hampstead
Email law@ckft.com **Website** www.ckft.com

Number of partners	10
Assistant solicitors	5
Other fee-earners	5
Total staff	37

THE FIRM This highly regarded firm has an established reputation for advising commercial clients and high net-worth individuals. Its focus and speciality is consistent with firms of a similar type in the West End and the City, whilst its location in Hampstead ensures a continuing emphasis on cost effectiveness. Founded in 1992 by three of its current partners, Graham Kaye, Daniel Fireman and Simon Taylor, the firm has expanded rapidly and now acts for substantial companies in London, nationally and abroad. It aims to offer clients success with an innovative approach to solving complex legal problems, and has invested heavily to ensure that its information technology is, and remains, at the cutting edge. Cawdery Kaye Fireman & Taylor strives continually to establish and maintain its close relationship with clients. Their needs are understood and their requirements dealt with quickly and effectively.

PRINCIPAL AREAS OF WORK The firm has particular strengths in commercial litigation, business and company transactions, landlord and tenant, property development and matrimonial work.
Litigation The litigation department, headed by Simon Taylor, handles commercial, contractual and negligence claims, shareholder disputes, banking litigation, insolvency, debt recovery and high value personal injury work.
Property The firm has a strong property group whose work includes development (from site acquisition through to individual plot sales), investment, all types of commercial property acquisitions and

disposals, and landlord and tenant matters.
Corporate The corporate department is regularly retained to deal with company purchases and sales, start-ups, partnerships and joint ventures.
Private Client The firm's traditional private client base has benefited from the recent expansion of the practice and the firm is able to advise on all aspects of wills, trusts, probate and inheritance tax planning.
Family & Matrimonial With a team of seven lawyers, this department handles all family law issues for high net-worth individuals, with many cases involving international elements such as property held offshore or by foreign trusts. Cawdery Kaye Fireman & Taylor provides its clients with the highest quality service. Further expansion in all areas is expected.

RECRUITMENT Although the firm is committed to organic growth, key appointments have been made from outside, with Pamela Collis joining the firm in 1999 to expand and head its highly regarded matrimonial department.

CCL

City Cloisters, 196 Old Street, London, EC1V 9FR
Tel (020) 7253 2277 **Fax** (020) 7253 2288
Email info@cclsolicitors.com **Website** www.cclsolicitors.com

Ptnrs 2 **Other fee-earners** 3 **Contact** Louis Charalambous • Founded in 2001, CCL has already established a reputation as a referral based practice providing both individuals and organisations (often in media based professions) with specialist expertise, particularly in the following: human rights litigation; breach of confidence issues; obscenity/freedom of expression; whistleblowing. Serious Fraud Panel member.

AREAS OF PRACTICE	
Criminal Litigation	30%
Employment	30%
Civil/Media Litigation	15%
Public Law	15%
Intellectual Property/Entertainment	10%

CEDR Solve
Exchange Tower, 1 Harbour Exchange Square, London, E14 9GB **Tel** (020) 7536 6060 **Fax** (020) 7536 6061

Challinors Lyon Clark
Guardian House, Cronehills Linkway, West Bromwich, B70 8SW **Tel** (0121) 553 3211 **Fax** (0121) 553 2079

Chambers & Co
Jonathan Scott Hall, Thorpe Road, Norwich, NR1 1UH **Tel** (01603) 616 155 **Fax** (01603) 616 156

Charles Dodson - Sole Practitioner
Lone Barn, Brown Candover, Alresford, SO24 9TW **Tel** 07802 389 127 **Fax** 01256 389 575

A-Z ■ LAW FIRMS

Charles Russell

8-10 New Fetter Lane, London, EC4A 1RS
Tel (020) 7203 5000   **Fax** (020) 7203 0200   **DX** 19 London/Chancery Lane
Email enquiry@cr-law.co.uk   **Website** www.charlesrussell.co.uk

Buryfields House, Bury Fields, Guildford, GU2 4AZ
Tel (01483) 252525   **Fax** (01483) 252550   **DX** 2436 Guildford 1
Email enquiry@cr-law.co.uk

Compass House, Lypiatt Road, Cheltenham, GL50 2QJ
Tel (01242) 221122   **Fax** (01242) 584700   **DX** 7442 Cheltenham 1
Email enquiry@cr-law.co.uk

Senior Partner	Laurence Watt
Managing Partner	Grant Howell
Number of partners	76
Assistant solicitors	94
Other fee-earners	98

AREAS OF PRACTICE
Private Capital/Family	27%
Commercial Property	17%
Media & Communications	16%
Litigation (Commercial)	15%
Other Corporate & Commercial/Employment	13%
Charities	8%
Insurance/Reinsurance	4%

CONTACTS
Charities	Michael Scott
Commercial Property	David Horner
Computer Law	David Berry
Corporate & Commercial	Simon Gilbert
Employment	David Green
Family	David Davidson
Insurance/Reinsurance	Stephen Carter
Intellectual Property	Robin Bynoe
Litigation	Richard Vallance
Media & Communications	Mark Moncreiffe
Pensions	Kris Weber
Planning	Geoffrey Jordan
Private Capital	Catriona Syed
Private Property	Ian Cooke
Sport	Patrick Russell
Tax	Tarl Lall

THE FIRM Charles Russell may have a long standing and highly regarded family and private client practice, but today around 70% of the firm's work is commercial, with major corporate clients in the media, telecoms, IT, employment and voluntary sectors. The firm and its staff are committed to the ambitious growth plans that they are following into the 21st century. It is not, however, just commercial and professional enthusiasm that motivates the firm. Unlike many of its competitors in the UK top 50 law firms, it manages to retain many of the more human traits that make is an invigorating place to work where individuals are recognised for their personality and integrity. This strong team spirit is proving a potent recipe for success across both the workforce and an unusually broad client base. The firm has five core areas spreading across the commercial and private sectors: mediacomms, employment, charities, private capital and family. The firm's single-minded determination to be in the top echelon for each of these areas is paying dividends. The services of the other practices are also highly regarded in their own right and the cross selling all of the firm's areas enables it to add significantly to the depth of the services it offers to clients. Charles Russell recognises that it is the clients who will be key to the success of this growing firm. As a result, it has implemented regular service reviews with clients, and sets great store by these. Reviews are designed to not only hear where work has gone well, but also to ascertain a client's wishes regarding future work. Issues are dealt with and clients receive feedback on how these have been dealt with.

PRINCIPAL AREAS OF WORK
Media & Communications This group provides an integrated service to the converging industries which include telecommunications, information technology, multimedia, film, music, entertainment and sport.

Employment The employment group is now one of the largest employment teams in the City and provides a comprehensive service.

Charity A long-established and expanding charity practice comprises a team of specialists who provide a wide range of legal services to the voluntary sector. The annual Charles Russell Charity Conference has become 'an institution' in the conference calendar for not-for-profit organisations.

Private Client & Family One of the UK's leading private client and family practices. The family team deals with all issues relating to marriage, its breakdown, separation and divorce, residence, adoption and child abduction, often involving legal and financial disputes in different jurisdictions. The private capital team advises individuals and institutions, both here and internationally, on tax, trusts, estate restructuring, probate, trust administration, agriculture and property transactions and management.

Corporate/Commercial The firm handles stock market flotations, mergers and acquisitions, venture capital financing, banking, institutional funding arrangements, management buyouts and buyins, business start-ups and corporate rescues, commercial contracts of all kinds, agency and distribution agreements, joint ventures and outsourcing, partnership matters and all aspects of corporate tax.

Dispute Resolution This team deals with litigation, arbitration and mediation both in the UK and overseas, with a special emphasis on commercial disputes, contentious IP, sports regulation, judicial review, pharmacy law and clinical and professional negligence.

Insurance The firm's specialist insurance group advises international insurance/reinsurance companies and consultants, Lloyd's syndicates, mutuals, brokers, underwriting agents and run-off managers on both contentious and non-contentious matters.

Commercial Property The commercial property group advises investors, developers and occupiers. In addition to handling the acquisition/disposal of industrial, commercial and retail property, the team devises and negotiates development and financing transactions. It also handles landlord and tenant agreements and all aspects of management for commercial property and planning matters.

LAW FIRMS ■ A-Z

Charsley Harrison

Madeira House, Madeira Walk, Windsor, SL4 1EU
Tel (01753) 851591 Fax (01753) 832550 DX 3800 Windsor
Email mail@charsleyharrison.com Website www.charsleyharrison.com

Notaries Public	Phillip Jones (01753) 851591
	Giles Shedden (01753) 496500
	Peter Beech (01753) 517600
Number of partners	6
Assistant solicitors	5
Other fee-earners	6

AREAS OF PRACTICE

Company/Commercial	35%
Property	40%
Litigation/Family Law	20%
Probate/Trust	5%

CONTACTS

Company/Commercial/Property	Phillip Jones
Litigation/Family Law	Kate McCulloch
Probate/Trust	Giles Shedden

THE FIRM Formed by the merger in 1973 of two long established and well respected Thames Valley practices, Charsley Harrison is a modern, forward-thinking firm geared to meet the needs of both commercial and private clients. The practice has developed rapidly in recent years to represent a wide range of business clients throughout the UK, the EC, the USA and the Pacific Basin and has established links with commercial lawyers in the major cities of the USA, Australia and throughout Europe. Two offices of the practice have recently joined forces in Windsor which will enable a high degree of partner involvement in the day-to-day matters of clients, together with a prompt, efficient and professional service. Other offices are located in Ascot and Slough.

PRINCIPAL AREAS OF WORK
Company/Commercial A comprehensive service both domestically and internationally encompassing corporate finance; competition; acquisitions and disposals; mergers; MBOs and joint ventures; distribution and agency agreements; intellectual property rights; taxation; insolvency and employment law matters.
Litigation All aspects of litigation for both corporate and private clients in the UK and abroad before a wide range of courts and tribunals. Work includes general contractual and commercial disputes; misrepresentation; employment matters; insolvency and banking-related litigation; personal injury; professional negligence and defamation.
Property Extensive experience of property transactions including purchase; sale; leasing and mortgaging of commercial and retail property; estate development; planning and environmental advice; licensing; site assembly; joint ventures and agricultural property.
Private Client The firm has a long tradition in providing a friendly and efficient service to individuals in all aspects of their private legal affairs. Work includes wills; tax and estate planning; personal and family finance; investment management; pensions; saving schemes and school fees planning; charity law and Court of Protection work. A full service is also provided in relation to matrimonial and family law including childcare and adoption.

INTERNATIONAL The firm works with an associate firm in the Netherlands.

Chiomenti Studio Legale

20 Berkeley Square, London, W1J 6HF
Tel (020) 7569 1500 Fax (020) 7569 1501
Email london@chiomenti.net

Managing Partner	Giorgio Cappelli
Senior Partner	Luigi Bendi
Number of partners	3
Assistant solicitors	10
Of-counsel	1

AREAS OF PRACTICE

Banking & Finance	40%
Securities & Capital Markets	30%
Taxation	20%
Corporate/M&A	10%

CONTACTS

Banking & Finance	Luigi Bendi
Corporate/M&A	Fillippo Domenico Vassalli
Securities & Capital Markets	Giorgio Cappelli
Taxation	Giulia Battaglia

THE FIRM Chiomenti Studio Legale continues the practice started by Avv. Pasquale Chiomenti in Rome in the mid 40s. The firm was established in England during 1993, has developed rapidly, particularly during the latter part of the 90s, and now has a strong presence in the market. It is currently composed of 14 fee-earners. In June 2001 Chiomenti Studio Legale announced an exclusive alliance with the US based international law firm Skadden, Arps, Slate, Meagher & Flom LLP, combining both firms' respective strengths in US, Italian and English law.

PRINCIPAL AREAS OF WORK The firm handles banking and finance; corporate, mergers and acquisitions; anti-trust and EU legislation; taxation; real estate; litigation and arbitration; telecommunications and IT.

CLIENTELE The firm's clients are predominantly Italian and foreign industrial corporations, banks, insurance companies, financial institutions and corporations. The firm has also acted for the Italian government and local authorities, foreign governments and public entities (including central banks), and international organisations (including the Commission of the European Communities).

INTERNATIONAL The firm has advised on a substantial number of Italy's major business transactions including IPOs, privatisations, mergers and acquisitions, structured finance and capital markets. The firm is associated with Lex Mundi. Languages spoken are English, Italian and French.

RECRUITMENT The firm is always looking for individuals who can make a contribution to its success. Recent growth provides opportunities for qualified solicitors across a range of specialisms. There are also vacancies for trainee solicitors. Candidates must have an Italian J.D. Long term prospects are excellent. Contact S. Djemili for application information.

A-Z ■ LAW FIRMS

Christian Fisher Khan

42 Museum Street, Bloomsbury, London, WC1A 1LY
Tel (020) 7831 1750   **Fax** (020) 7831 1726   **DX** 35737 Bloomsbury
Email info@christianf.co.uk   **Website** www.christianf.co.uk

Number of partners	8
Assistant solicitors	11
Other fee-earners	6

THE FIRM Christian Fisher, changing to Christian Fisher Khan in 2002, was set up in 1985 and specialises in civil liberties and human rights work. The firm has a long-standing reputation for undertaking high profile test cases in these areas and a commitment to delivering high quality legal aid work. A Legal Services Commission franchise is currently held in the categories of personal injury, clinical negligence, crime, housing, employment, immigration, actions against the police, family, mental health, education, community care and public law.

PRINCIPAL AREAS OF WORK

Human Rights Cases The firm has a particular commitment and expertise within this field and continues to bring test cases under the Human Rights Act. A large number of actions against the police, including many high profile cases, are undertaken. The firm has obtained funding from the Legal Services Commission for test cases arising out of the May Day 2001 protests. Past cases have included the lead Court of Appeal case on damages against the police (Hsu); cases on suing the police for negligence (Osman in the ECHR and Reeves in the House of Lords); the first successful challenge of an exclusion order (Farrakhan v UK).

Personal Injury The firm has a particular profile in the areas of construction, environmental and transport safety and a substantial caseload in the areas. It was the leading firm on the Steering Committees representing the victims of the Paddington and Southall train crashes and is dealing with a large number of the victims' claims. The firm acted for the family of Simon Jones in a successful judicial review over corporate manslaughter.

Clinical Negligence Wrongful birth and obstetric cases; accident and emergency cases; GP and hospital negligence; GMC prosecutions.

Crime Major criminal trials including fraud, political crime and miscarriages of justice. Emergency advice at police stations around the clock and court duty schemes are covered.

Family Care proceedings, contact and residence, ancillary relief and divorce.

Mental Health Publicly funded assistance at Manager's Hearings and Mental Health Review Tribunals.

Employment Particular areas of expertise in race and sex discrimination cases. Recent significant cases include the case of Bahl v Law Society, Bennett v Essex County Council and Murray v Newham Citizen Advice Bureau.

Housing Acts for claimants in disrepair and nuisance matters and homelessness matters. Also acts for defendants in possession proceedings.

Immigration The firm has an excellent reputation in acting for asylum seekers at all levels up to judicial review.

Public Law The firm conducts a large number of judicial review, in many areas, and a significant number of inquests (including a large number of deaths in custody) and actions against the police. The firm has held a franchise in public law since this was first available and has a number of cases before the ECtHR.

■ Churchers

12 High Street, Fareham, PO16 7BL
Tel (01329) 822333   **Fax** (01329) 822267   **DX** 40807 Fareham   **Email** solicitors@churchers.co.uk

Ptnrs 12   **Asst solrs** 2   **Other fee-earners** 15   **Contact** Duncan Johnson • A leading Hampshire firm with five offices. Partners specialise in personal injury, family, childcare, crime and employment, with a substantial volume of property work. Specialists in solicitor advocacy in civil litigation, also Law Society advanced panellists.

■ City Law Partnership

99 Charterhouse Street, London, EC1M 6NQ   **Tel** (020) 7253 5505   **Fax** (020) 7253 5525

■ C & J Black

Linenhall House, 13 Linenhall Street, Belfast, BT2 8AA   **Tel** (028) 90550060   **Fax** (028) 90234125

■ Clairmonts

9 Clairmont Gardens, Glasgow, G3 7LW   **Tel** (0141) 331 4000   **Fax** (0141) 221 0123

LAW FIRMS ■ A-Z

■ Claricoat Phillips
140 Barnsbury Road, London, N1 0ER **Tel** (020) 7226 7000 **Fax** (020) 7833 4408

■ Clark Holt
1 Sanford Street, Swindon, SN1 1HJ
Tel (01793) 617 444 **Fax** (01793) 617 436 **DX** 38606 Swindon (2) **Email** richardc@clarkholt.com
Website www.clarkholt.com

AREAS OF PRACTICE	
Corporate	45%
Commercial Property	35%
Commercial/Computer	20%

Ptnrs 5 **Asst solrs** 3 **Other fee-earners** 1 **Contact** Richard Clark • Specialises exclusively in commercial law in the area of corporate, commercial and computer law, and commercial property.

■ Clark Ricketts
Kingsway House, 103 Kingsway, London, WC2B 6QX
Tel (020) 7404 1551 **Fax** (020) 7404 2662 **Email** aviationlaw@clarkricketts.com

Ptnrs 2 **Asst solrs** 2 **Contact** Robert Ricketts • Clark Ricketts deals exclusively with aviation law matters and advises all sectors of the aviation industry. Between them the partners have over 30 years experience in aviation law and deal with all facets including finance, commercial matters, and regulatory and litigation aspects.

■ Clarke Willmott & Clarke
St James Court, St James Parade, Bristol, BS1 3LH
Tel (0117) 941 6600 **Fax** (0117) 941 6622 **DX** 78247 Bristol 1
Email information@cw-c.co.uk **Website** www.cw-c.co.u

Blackbrook Gate, Blackbrook Park Avenue, Taunton, TA1 2PG
Tel (01823) 442266 **Fax** (01823) 445800 **DX** 97175 Taunton Blackbrook

Equity Court, Millbrook Road East, Southampton, SO15 1RJ
Tel (023) 8048 3200 **Fax** (023) 8033 1376 **DX** 49665 Southampton 2

Number of partners	52
Assistant solicitors	74
Directors	4
Other fee-earners	96

CONTACTS	
Agriculture	Tim Russ
Asset Management	Peter Nellist
Clinical Negligence	Andrew Hannam
	Mervyn Fudge
Commercial Developers & Investors	
	Roger Seaton
	Stephen Rosser
Construction	Stephen Clarke
Corporate	Paul Hardman
	Nigel Lindsay
Dispute Resolution	Chris Taylor
	William Whiteley
Employment	Emma Ramsay
Environmental	Neil Baker
	Tim Hayden
Family	Felicity Shakespear
Financial Services	Robert Morfee
Food & Drink	Kevin Jones
Housebuilders	David Powell
Insolvency & Debt Collection	
	Stephen Allinson LIP
	Martin Askew
Insurance	Rod Evans
Intellectual Property	Huw Davey
Lender Services	Philip Tebbatt
Licensing	Tim Hayden
Personal Injury	Peter Livingstone
Planning	Neil Baker
Private Capital	Peter Nellist
	Stuart Thorne
Sport	Ian Smith
	Trevor Watkins

THE FIRM Clarke Willmott & Clarke has seen another year of dynamic growth and expansion. It is one of the leading regional South West and Southern law firms with a reputation and client base that extends far outside the region. Following the consolidation of its Somerset offices, the firm has trebled the size of its Taunton office which serves the entire South West peninsula. Through its recent merger with Ensor Byfield, Clarke Willmott & Clarke has enhanced its key sector strengths in insurance litigation and sports, and has established a new regional office in Southampton to better serve its clients across the South. The firm's Bristol headquarters has also seen dramatic growth resulting in the need to relocate in early 2003 to the centre of the commercial district. Client demand for greater specialisation has led to the firm concentrating on investing and expanding its vertical sector strengths in housebuilding, commercial developers and investors, food and drink, agriculture, private capital, volume personal injury and sports. Clarke Willmott & Clarke's client research shows that it is consistently regarded for its practical, results-orientated, commercial advice with an emphasis on cost-effective delivery. Clients acknowledge the firm's ability to grow and maintain long-term client relationships by concentrating on enhanced service delivery.

PRINCIPAL AREAS OF WORK

Property The property team continues to develop its three key areas of expertise: land development, planning and environmental, and commercial property. It has seen substantial growth in its client base both regionally and nationally, particularly serving the housebuilders, commercial developers and investors, and food and drink industry. The nationally recognised planning team has unrivalled expertise and is highly regarded for its advice regarding town and country planning, brown land issues, section 106 agreements and public inquiry representation. The environmental team offers a full range of advice, particularly in the areas of contaminated land, minerals and waste disposal. The commercial property team specialises in secured lending, licensed premises, project management of complex sites and commercial developments.

Litigation This remains a key part of the practice and CW&C is particularly regarded for its work in the areas of volume personal injury, clinical negligence, corporate recovery and insolvency, employment disputes, landlord and tenant, international contract disputes and specialist prosecution services, such as health and safety, environmental pollution offences, food and safety and fraud. The firm also has a

Continued overleaf

A-Z ■ LAW FIRMS

substantial insurance litigation practice, based primarily in Southampton, handling all types of cases relating to employer's liability, road traffic accidents, product liability, professional indemnity, public liability, industrial diseases, fire and disasters.

Commercial/Corporate This team provides transactional advice on M&As, joint ventures, share holder agreements, management restructures, acquisitions and sales, intellectual property and competition law.

Private Client CW&C is recognised as the South West's leading private client team. Services include personal tax planning, asset management, wills, trusts and probate, family and matrimonial law.

RECRUITMENT Training and personal development continue to be given high prominence and the firm has retained the Investor in People accreditation. The firm has a commitment to fast-tracking talented individuals.

INVESTOR IN PEOPLE

Clarks

Great Western House, Station Rd, Reading, RG1 1JX
Tel (0118) 958 5321 **Fax** (0118) 960 4611 **DX** 54700 Reading 2
Email inmail@clarks-solicitors.co.uk **Website** www.clarks-solicitors.co.uk

Managing Partner	Michael Sippitt
Number of partners	16
Assistant solicitors	38
Other fee-earners	21

CONTACTS	
Advertising	Peter James
Banking & Finance	David Clark
Commercial & European	Peter James
Commercial Dispute Resolution & Litigation	Antony Morris
Commercial Property	Derek Ching
Company & Corporate Finance	Richard Lee
Construction	David Rintoul
Corporate Recovery	David Clark
Debt Recovery	Kirstin Wells
Employment Services	Michael Sippitt
Environmental & Waste Management	Simon Thorne
Health & Medical Services	Derek Ching
Information Technology	Peter James
Intellectual Property	Peter James
Pensions	David Clark
Planning	David Corsellis
Public Sector	Derek Ching
Residential Property	Mary Robertson
Wills, Trusts & Tax Planning	Peter Clark

THE FIRM Clarks is a commercial law firm with a proven track record across the UK and overseas. Its clients range from small and medium sized enterprises to multinationals. Clarks is particularly recognised for the number of international and FTSE 250 clients who have chosen to use the firm. Clarks is committed to a strategy based on forging proactive relationships. Clients include listed companies, public sector bodies and non-profit organisations especially health, education and local government. Clarks is determined to stay one step ahead in the evolving market place by listening carefully to its clients and responding quickly to their needs, providing clear and constructive commercial advice. In over 85 years Clarks has built the practice its clients want. Clarks assigns a partner to each client providing a consistent personal contract and actively encourages the development of relationships with specialists from different disciplines, creating a known and trusted team of lawyers to help with more complex projects. The firm strongly believes in working in partnership with clients and has developed case plans and client protocols to facilitate this. Case plans provide a client with a project snapshot detailing timings, key events and estimated costs. Client protocols clearly define the basis of an ongoing relationship and the manner in which services are provided. Clarks' lawyers also devise and deliver highly successful training programmes geared to client and industrial sectors, enhancing management performance through greater knowledge of the relevant law and procedures. Whatever clients' legal needs, a specialist team at Clarks will work in partnership with the clients to meet its objectives. Clarks is part of TAGLaw, an international network of like-minded law firms providing clients with a safe pair of hands in numerous locations around the world. It operates on the principles of transparency of business terms, close client relationships, consistent quality and the provision of timely and cost-effective service.

PRINCIPAL AREAS OF WORK

Corporate Clarks has a long established and highly regarded corporate practice managing substantial and specialist transactions. It has a growing reputation for its work in finance related fields, particularly consumer finance and advertising and insolvency.

Commercial Litigation Clarks remains the principal regional commercial litigation practice offering unrivalled specialist expertise among many different practice areas and industries, including hands-on experience of successful ADR. The construction law service continues to grow from strength to strength, handling both contentious and non-contentious work.

Commercial Property A large commercial property team acts for owners, developers, investors and funders, providing a comprehensive service. A highly skilled planning and development consultancy handles planning applications and appeals. COMBAT (Clarks' Owner Managed Business Advisory Team) combines cross-departmental skills to offer a tailored team to meet the particular needs of owner managed businesses.

Employment The employment services unit is one of the fastest growing areas of business and enjoys an enviable national reputation. It also carries out extensive training and is particularly proactive in developing new employment related services including workshops, in-house seminars and human resources support.

IT & IP The firm's IT and intellectual property team, a specialist service within the firm's corporate and technology department, handles a varied portfolio of contentious and non-contentious work. Services include copyright, e-commerce, internet domain name issues, trademark, passing off, patents, licensing and infringement issues, computer system supply and software licence terms and IT outsourcing.

Environmental A new unit was established in 2002, focusing on pure environmental law with an

Clarks
Solicitors

emphasis on the waste management, timber, cement and construction industries.
Private Client The firm has busy private client and residential conveyancing teams, offering private client services to corporate quality standards.

RECRUITMENT The firm continues to seek individuals who can contribute to its success. Current growth provides opportunities for qualified solicitors across a range of specialisms.

Clarkson Wright & Jakes

Valiant House, 12 Knoll Rise, Orpington, BR6 0PG
Tel (01689) 887887 **Fax** (01689) 887888 **DX** 31603 Orpington
Email cwj@cwj.co.uk **Website** www.cwj.co.uk

THE FIRM Established in 1875, Clarkson Wright & Jakes is a substantial commercial practice whose aim is to offer a personal service tailored to clients' specific needs. The firm, a member of LawNet, undertakes a wide range of legal work, and offers notarial services and the expertise of units specialising in employment, partnership and doctors' matters. The firm advises French commercial clients and UK clients with interests in France. It has been recognised as an Investor in People and has achieved ISO 9002 accreditation.

PRINCIPAL AREAS OF WORK
Company & Commercial Company and business acquisitions and sales; MBOs and MBIs; franchise; agency; distribution and other commercial agreements; conditions of sale; terms of business; partnership especially for doctors; business start-ups.
Employment Contracts of employment and other employment documentation; claims in the industrial tribunals and civil courts for dismissal, discrimination and breach of contract.
Commercial Property Acquisition; mortgage and disposal of freehold and leasehold shops; factories and other properties; landlord and tenant matters (including lease renewals and surrenders).
Commercial Litigation Company and shareholder disputes; commercial and partnership disputes; construction disputes; arbitration; landlord and tenant matters; defamation; professional negligence; passing off actions and contractual disputes; licensing; debt collection.
Personal Injury Litigation Motor; employers' and public liability claims; industrial disease and professional indemnity claims; and medical negligence.
Private Client Residential property; wills and trusts; tax planning; enduring powers of attorney; winding-up of estates and executorships; Court of Protection; and matrimonial.

INTERNATIONAL Members of the firm also conduct business in French, German and Spanish.

Managing Partner	Claire Singleton
Senior Partner	Leslie Seldon
Number of partners	10
Assistant solicitors	10
Other fee-earners	16

AREAS OF PRACTICE	
Private Client	25%
Personal Injury Litigation	20%
Commercial Litigation	15%
Commercial Property	15%
Company/Commercial (inc. Notarial)	15%
Employment	10%

CONTACTS	
Commercial	Michael North
Commercial Litigation	Leslie Seldon
Personal Injury	David Greenhalgh
Private Client	Amanda Custis
	Peter Giblin

Claude Hornby & Cox

35-36 Great Marlborough Street, London, W1F 7JE
Tel (020) 7437 8873 **Fax** (020) 7494 3070 **DX** 37211 Piccadilly
Email law@claudehornbycox.fsnet.co.uk

THE FIRM A leading specialist criminal practice for over 70 years, providing all its clients, whether privately paying or legally aided, with high quality but reasonably priced advice and representation on any criminal matter.

PRINCIPAL AREAS OF WORK
Crime The firm defends clients in cases ranging from murder, terrorism, firearms and drug-related offences, and corporate fraud on a multimillion pound scale, to driving offences and shoplifting. The fraud work includes acting in major SFO, HM Customs and Excise, and Inland Revenue Investigations. The practice also prosecutes for individuals and corporate clients. The partners regularly represent defendants in Court Martial cases tried in the UK and abroad.
Other Areas General civil litigation, personal injury, and both commercial and residential conveyancing. The firm provides representation before Professional Disciplinary tribunals.

RECRUITMENT Two trainee solicitors are recruited each year. Applications to the training partner, Andrew Moxon.

Senior Partner	Richard Hallam
Number of partners	2
Assistant solicitors	6
Other fee-earners	4

CONTACTS	
Civil Litigation/Conveyancing	
	Mohammed Mir
Criminal Litigation/Disciplinary Proceedings	
	Richard Hallam

A-Z ■ LAW FIRMS

■ Claytons
PO Box 38, 22 Rothesay Rd, Luton, LU1 1PT **Tel** (01582) 724501 **Fax** (01582) 405815

Cleary Gottlieb Steen & Hamilton
City Place House, 55 Basinghall Street, London, EC2V 5EH
Tel (020) 7614 2200 **Fax** (020) 7600 1698
Website www.clearygottlieb.com

AREAS OF PRACTICE	
Corporate	100%

THE FIRM A leading US and international law firm with offices in New York, Washington DC, Paris, Brussels, London, Frankfurt, Rome, Tokyo and Hong Kong. The firm is well known for its expertise in finance, mergers and acquisitions, and for its tax, regulatory and litigation practice. The London office advises on all areas of international financial transactions, practising both English and US law.

Cleaver Fulton Rankin
50 Bedford Street, Belfast, BT2 7FW
Tel (028) 9024 3141 **Fax** (028) 9024 9096 **DX** 421 NR Belfast
Email info@cfrlaw.co.uk **Website** www.cfrlawonline.com

Contact Partner	Neil Faris
Number of partners	15
Assistant solicitors	11
Other fee-earners	16

AREAS OF PRACTICE	
Company/Commercial	25%
Litigation	25%
Commercial Property	25%
Private Client	15%
Employment	10%

CONTACTS	
Commercial Property	Kathryn Collie
	James Houston
Company/Commercial	Stephen Cross
	Jennifer Ebbage
Consultancy	Karen Blair
	Neil Faris
Employment	Alyn Hicks
	Rosalie Prytherch
Litigation	William Cross
	Brendan Fox
Private Client	Alastair Rankin
	Joy Scott

THE FIRM CFR is one of the largest and most dynamic law firms in Northern Ireland. Based in the heart of Belfast, its aim is to provide a world-class legal service to clients doing business in Northern Ireland. CFR focuses on helping clients to achieve their business objectives through the provision of legal advice that is imaginative and commercially aware. In addition to its core areas of work, CFR has developed recognised specialisms in many other areas of practice, including intellectual property, construction, planning, environment, IT law, employment law, public law and tax planning. CFR has enjoyed sustained growth and expansion in its areas of practice. As a result of this growth, five new partners were appointed in April 2001: Karen Blair, Kathryn Collie, William Cross, Stephen Cross and Alyn Hicks, together with seven new associates. CFR is a progressive and pro-active firm and all departments are regularly involved in carrying out training and giving talks in relevant areas to clients and potential clients.

PRINCIPAL AREAS OF WORK
Company & Commercial Including mergers and acquisitions, management buyouts, joint ventures, corporate finance, banking insecurities, company formation and secretarial services.
Commercial Property Including freehold and leasehold acquisitions and sales, development agreements, investment advice and landlord and tenant work.
Commercial Litigation Including insolvency, regulatory issues, financial services disputes, intellectual property, construction, competition and defamation.
Employment Services Including defence, litigation and unfair dismissal, all aspects of discrimination and general advice in all areas of employment, including TUPE matters and advice on executive service agreements and restrictive covenants.
Advice For Private Clients Including conveyancing, probate and family trusts, charities, administration of estates, succession and tax planning.
Consultancy & Advisory Work Including public law, environmental law (including contaminated land), planning law, human rights law and judicial review.
IT Including advising start-up web and technology companies.

RECRUITMENT The firm currently takes four trainee solicitors per year. Applications to commence in September of each year should be made, in writing, early in the year, to Patrick Cross. Details of our recruitment programme are available online at www.cfrlawonline.com.

LAW FIRMS A-Z

Clifford Chance

200 Aldersgate Street, London, EC1A 4JJ
Tel (020) 7600 1000 **Fax** (020) 7600 5555 **DX** 606 London
Email info@cliffordchance.com **Website** www.cliffordchance.com

CEO	Peter Cornell
London Managing Partner	Peter Charlton
Number of partners	231
Assistant solicitors	854
Other fee-earners	264

CONTACTS

Administration & Public Law	Michael Smyth
Alternative Dispute Resolution	Simon Davis
Arbitration (International)	John Beechey
Asset Finance	Geoffrey White
Banking	Mark Campbell, Stuart Popham
Banking Litigation	Roger Baggallay
Civil Fraud	Roger Best
Collective Investments	James Barlow
	Tim Herrington, Stephen Ross
Commercial	Raj Parkash
Commercial Litigation	John Potts
Commodities	Mark Morrison, Tim Plews
Construction & Engineering	John Beechey
	Tim Steadman
Contentious Trusts	Jeremy Kosky
	Jeremy Sandelson
Corporate Finance	David Childs
Corporate Immigration	Christopher Goodwill
Defamation	Michael Smyth
Derivatives	Habib Motani
E-commerce	David Griffiths
Employee Benefits	Kevin Thompson
	Robin Tremaine
Employment	Chris Osman
Energy & Natural Resources	Tony Bankes-Jones
	Peter Blake
Environment	Brian Hall
EU & Competition	Simon Baxter, Alex Nourry
Financial Services	Chris Bates
	Tim Herrington
Hotels	Andrew Carnegie
Housing Association Finance	Despina Pantelia
Insolvency & Restructuring	Mark Hyde
Insurance & Reinsurance	Katherine Coates
Insurance Litigation	Nicholas Munday
Intellectual Property	David Perkins
International Capital Markets	David Dunnigan
International Financial Markets	Tim Plews
Local Government	Brian Hall
M&A	David Childs
Marketing & Advertising	Richard Thomas
MBOs	James Baird
Media	Daniel Sandelson
Pensions	Helen Cox
Pharmaceuticals	Peter Dieners
Planning	Brian Hall
Product Liability	Andrew Edgar
Professional Negligence	Philip Rocher
Project Finance	Peter Blake
Public Policy/Sector	Richard Thomas
Real Estate	Robert MacGregor
	Cliff McAuley
Real Estate Finance	Andrew Carnegie
	Mark Rees-Jones
Real Estate Litigation	John Pickston
Retail	Neil Harvey, Vanessa Marsland
Securitisation	Chris Oakley, John Woodhall
Shipping	Mark Morrison, Tony Vlasto
Sovereign Debt Rescheduling	Cliff Godfrey
	Andrew Yianni
Tax	Douglas French
Technology	David Griffiths
Telecommunications	Joachim Fleury
	Elizabeth Hiester, Tim Schwarz
VAT	Etienne Wong

THE FIRM Clifford Chance is the world's only fully integrated global law firm. Our international reach means we can offer clients unified legal solutions on a worldwide basis. With a market-leading presence in London, New York, Asia and Continental Europe, Clifford Chance is able to provide multi-jurisdictional advice to the world's leading financial institutions and businesses. Unrivalled in terms of international resources, we have over 3,600 legal advisors, 688 of whom are partners, representing all nationalities and able to operate across all business cultures.

PRINCIPAL AREAS OF WORK Our practice is organised around six areas: Banking and Finance; Corporate (including M&A); Capital Markets; Litigation and Dispute Resolution; Real Estate; and Tax, Pensions and Employment.

Finance The firm has the world's largest Finance practice with over 1,000 partners and lawyers located in the world's major financial and commercial centres. The practice provides advice across the full spectrum of financial products, including banking, asset finance, derivative products, project finance, securitisation and structured finance.

Clifford Chance is the first firm to bring together lawyers in Europe, the Americas and Asia to advise on national and international regulatory issues and the relationship between regulatory systems. It acts for all the world's leading investment and commercial banks across all major jurisdictions as well as many corporates. The practice also advises regulatory authorities, supranational bodies, governments and government agencies.

Corporate The Corporate practice handles some of the world's largest and most complex M&A transactions, combining global transaction capability with a full service of English, US and civil law expertise in the key financial centres across Europe, the Americas and Asia. Apart from mainstream M&A, the firm also encompasses leading specialist practices: commercial contracts; competition/antitrust; communications; energy; financial institutions; funds; investment banking; insurance; media and technology; and private equity.

The practice focuses on providing practical and commercial legal advice. Clients include investment banks and financial institutions, multinationals and other public and private corporations, private equity providers and management teams, asset management clients, international partnerships and governments.

Capital Markets The Capital Markets practice comprises over 500 partners and lawyers. The practice is founded on a full-service US and UK securities law capability – the law of choice for the majority of international transactions – complemented by local securities law expertise in each of the key financial centres. This local/international perspective is brought to bear, for example, when helping to apply US disclosure standards to European, Asian, and Latin American issuers.

The firm acts on the whole range of securities offerings, whether public or private, where the proceeds may be used to finance mergers or acquisitions or for general capital. The firm is well known for its innovative approach to developing solutions. Clients include issuers, guarantors, arrangers, managers, investors, trustees, and regulatory bodies such as banks and financial institutions, specialised lenders, corporate originators, security and share trustees, rating agencies, monoline insurers and swap counterparties.

Litigation and Dispute Resolution The firm has an international team of more than 660 litigators – the world's largest and most comprehensive practice of its kind – and has experience in virtually all segments of the business and financial markets across multiple jurisdictions. The lawyers work with clients to resolve disputes efficiently and effectively – whether through arbitration, litigation or other techniques. They also work with clients to develop compliance programmes and other techniques to minimise future litigation risks.

The firm is currently representing clients in some of the largest and most significant actions underway, particularly in the areas of competition/antitrust law, white collar and regulatory, intellectual property, insurance, banking securities and international arbitration.

Real Estate The firm has one of the world's leading international Real Estate practices, which provides comprehensive domestic and cross-border advice on all transaction types where real estate is the core asset. This ranges from acquisition, development and construction work to joint ventures, tax structuring, debt and equity financing and securitisations, real estate investment banking, indirect investment, real estate funds, corporate outsourcing and PFI/PPP deals.

Continued overleaf

www.ChambersandPartners.com

A-Z ■ LAW FIRMS

The practice acts for market-leading clients in a broad range of sectors and has a client base that includes developers and investors, landowners, occupiers, lenders, hotwires/leisure operators, investment banks, commercial/mortgage banks, funds and major corporates, for whom it can act in both single and multiple jurisdictions.

Tax, Pensions & Employment Tax – the firm has the world's largest tax group providing advice on international and domestic taxation, covering a wide range of financing, investment, corporate and commercial issues, together with advice on tax, litigation, disputes and transfer pricing. Employment, Pensions and Employee Benefits – the firm has a leading pan-European employment group advising on all key employment issues and is a market leader in employee benefits and share schemes. Our international Pensions practice is also highly regarded and works jointly with the Litigation practice on pensions litigation matters.

INTERNATIONAL The firm has offices in Europe (Amsterdam, Barcelona, Berlin, Brussels, Budapest, Dsseldorf, Frankfurt, London, Luxembourg, Madrid, Milan, Moscow, Munich, Padua, Paris, Prague, Rome, Warsaw); the Americas (New York, Palo Alto, San Francisco, São Paulo, Washington DC); Asia (Bangkok, Beijing, Hong Kong, Singapore, Shanghai, Tokyo); and the Middle East (Dubai).

CLIFFORD CHANCE

Clintons

55 Drury Lane, London, WC2B 5RZ
Tel (020) 7379 6080 **Fax** (020) 7240 9310 **DX** 40021 Covent Gdn. 1
Email info@clintons.co.uk   **Website** www.clintons.co.uk

THE FIRM Clintons is widely recognised as one of the foremost media and entertainment law firms. The firm also has an extensive general commercial practice and has acknowledged strengths in litigation, family and property.

PRINCIPAL AREAS OF WORK

Media & Entertainment The firm acts for a wide range of clients, from high profile individuals to major corporations. Specialist advice is provided in the businesses of music, theatre, television, e-commerce, advertising and marketing, merchandising and sport, film and publishing and generally in the protection and exploitation of intellectual property rights.

Litigation Clintons is recognised for the strength of its practice in this area and for its ability to deal with heavyweight and high profile litigation. The firm advises on a wide range of contentious work in its core practice areas, as well as in banking, employment and personal injury.

Corporate & Commercial The firm provides advice in all aspects of the commercial world including new ventures, corporate restructuring, e-ventures, international taxation, employment, liquidation and receivership.

Family Clintons has a significant and highly regarded practice in family law and divorce, offering advice in all aspects, often for clients in the public eye. The family team is noted for its expertise in the detailed financial arrangements surrounding marriage breakdown and in advising on complex issues concerning children.

Property Clintons handles all types of property transaction, from commercial developments to residential conveyancing. The firm has special expertise in secured lending and includes banking and other lending institutions as its clients.

Private Client Clintons advises on all aspects of arrangements for private individuals, including offshore settlements, tax, wills, probate, trusts and matrimonial finance. The work undertaken includes advice relating to the links between the business and personal assets of private individuals. The firm works closely with other professional advisers in the establishment of tax-efficient and practical arrangements for the benefit of its clients.

INTERNATIONAL Clintons has considerable overseas connections, particularly in the USA, continental Europe, Ireland, Israel, the Channel Islands, Cayman and the Bahamas.

Senior Partner	John Cohen
Number of partners	17
Assistant solicitors	14
Other fee-earners	12

CONTACTS	
Advertising & Marketing	Philip Stinson
Corporate/Commercial & Employment	John Seigal
E-commerce	James Jones
Family	Maggie Rae
	Tim Bienias
	Elizabeth Vernon
Film & Television	David Landsman
Litigation	David Davis
	Tim Bienias
	Jacqueline Brown
	Andrew Sharland
	Stephen Joelson
Music	David Landsman
	Peter Button
	Andrew Myers
Property	Laurence Middleweek
	Michael Goldman
	David Benaim
Publishing	Sally Hamwee
Sport	Philip Stinson
	Jacqueline Brown
Tax, Trusts & Private Client	Sally Hamwee
Theatre	John Cohen
	James Jones

Clyde & Co

51 Eastcheap, London, EC3M 1JP
Tel (020) 7623 1244 **Fax** (020) 7623 5427 **DX** 1071
Email info@clyde.co.uk **Website** www.clydeco.com

12 Rue de Magellan, Paris, 75008
Tel +33 1 44 43 88 88 **Fax** +33 1 44 43 88 77
Email scp@hpmbc.com

Senior Partner	Michael Payton
Number of partners	114
Assistant solicitors	239
Other fee-earners	71

AREAS OF PRACTICE

Insurance/Reinsurance	28%
Banking/Corporate/Commercial & Tax	24%
Marine & Transport	20%
Commercial Litigation	10%
Energy & Natural Resources	8%
Property	6%
Employment	4%

CONTACTS

ADR	Jane Andrewartha
Arbitration	John Whittaker
Asset Finance & Leasing	Simon Poland
	Austen Hall
Aviation	Jane Andrewartha
Banking	David Page
Commercial Litigation	Jonathan Wood
	Stuart Macdonald
Commodities	John Whittaker
	Andrew Wells, Paul Turner
Corporate Finance	Gary Thorpe
	Tim Matthews
Corporate Insurance (Lloyds)	
	Andrew Holderness
Corporate Insurance (General)	James O'Shea
	David Salt
Corporate Litigation	Conrad Walker
Corporate & Commercial	David Salt
	Andrew Holderness
Construction	John Morris
EC & Competition Law	Stuart Macdonald
Employment	Chris Duffy
	Paul Newdick
Energy	Andrew Wells
Insolvency	Jonathan Wood
	Mark Fennessy
Insurance (Contentious)	Michael Payton
	Rod Smith, Nigel Chapman, John Dunt
IT, Telecoms & E-Commerce	Philip Hooley
	Sally Shorthose
IP	David Page, Sally Shorthose
Life Assurance	James O'Shea
Medical Negligence	John Mitchell
Personal Injury	Angela Horne
Product Liability	Chris Harris
Professional Indemnity	Peter Farthing
	Chris Harris
Property	Robert Pilcher, Aidan Heathcote
Reinsurance	Nigel Brook, Paul Bugden
Shipping	Brian Nash, Derek Hodgson
Tax	Susan Ball
Transport	Tony Thomas
WTO	Philippe Ruttley

THE FIRM Pre-eminent in shipping, insurance and reinsurance, Clyde & Co's reputation was established through facilitating international commerce. From this unique commercial perspective, the firm advises businesses in more than 130 countries. The dispute resolution practice, one of the largest in the UK, reflects the firm's strong contentious capability. With 400 lawyers in offices in Europe, the Middle East, South East Asia, the Far East and Latin America, Clyde & Co's professional resources include lawyers qualified in 17 jurisdictions and fluent in 25 languages.

PRINCIPAL AREAS OF WORK

Insurance/Reinsurance The firm's leading contentious insurance and reinsurance group advises on disputes in relation to aviation, general liability, insolvency and recovery, marine and energy, medical negligence, personal injury, political and credit risk, professional indemnity, property and construction.

Corporate Insurance The firm's non-contentious insurance group advises on transactions and regulatory matters including establishing insurance companies, alternative risk transfer projects, captives and captive syndicates, Lloyds underwriting vehicles and capacity offers.

Marine, Transport & Aviation The firm advises on all aspects of shipping, transport and aviation ranging from complex ship and aviation finance transactions, to disputes arising from salvage and collision, carriage of goods, charterparties, marine insurance policies, general average, pollution, ship repairs and disputes arising from the carriage of goods by air, road and rail.

Commodities & International Trade The firm advises on a full spectrum of commodities, including oil, gas, rice, sugar, grain, coffee, oil and fats, coals and metals. Areas of work range from preparing contracts, commodity financing, derivatives and credit enhancement, especially in emerging markets and turbulent jurisdictions, to resolving disputes of every kind, including trade arbitrations before GAFTA, FOSFA, RSA and the London Metal Exchange.

Commercial Litigation, Arbitration & Mediation The firm's extensive litigation practice encapsulates many of the work areas identified separately. Particular areas of expertise include UK and international arbitration, commodity and trade disputes, as well as dispute resolution through mediation.

Energy & Natural Resources The firm has a substantial contentious and non-contentious practice in energy and natural resources, advising on oil and gas transactions, asset, trade and ship finance, power and mining, mining finance and commodity trading. The practice has advised on the aftermath of many high profile casualties and clients include governments, state oil companies, regulatory bodies, privatised utilities, banks, global commodities traders, mining exploration and production companies.

Corporate, Commercial & Banking The firm advises on a wide range of corporate transactions including flotations, M&As, re-financings and restructurings, demergers, venture capital arrangements, MBOs, joint ventures and inward investment. Commercial advice spans commercial contracts, e-commerce and data protection as well as a broad range of IP, IT and telecommunications issues. UK and European regulatory and competition advice includes corporate transactions, financing arrangements and commercial contracts. The firm's banking group advises on diverse international and domestic financing arrangements.

Taxation The firm advises on all aspects of corporate and personal taxation including company reorganisations, financings, employee remuneration packages, equity incentive schemes, estate planning and settlements.

Property The firm advises a number of UK and international developers, contractors, consultants, investors and funders as well as advising on construction litigation.

Employment The firm advises companies and individuals, in the UK and internationally, on both non-contentious and litigious issues, ranging from employee contracts and termination agreements to changes in employment regulation.

INTERNATIONAL Clyde & Co has overseas offices in Caracas, Dubai, Hong Kong, Paris, Piraeus, Singapore and St Petersburg and Belgrade.

RECRUITMENT All enquiries should be made to Karen Jeffreys on (020) 7623 1244. For details of the firm's trainee solicitor recruitment programme, call Georgia de Saram on (020) 7648 1580.

A-Z ■ LAW FIRMS

CMS Cameron McKenna

Mitre House, 160 Aldersgate Street, London, EC1A 4DD
Tel (020) 7367 3000   Fax (020) 7367 2000   DX 135316 BARBICAN 2
Email info@cmck.com   Website www.law-now.com

THE FIRM CMS Cameron McKenna is an award-winning, full service international commercial law firm advising businesses, financial institutions, governments and public sector bodies. It is a founding member of CMS – the transnational legal services organisation. CMS member firms provide clients with access to integrated pan-European legal and tax services, managed by a single point of contact and with common high calibre service standards. The organisation has 40 offices, currently employs in excess of 1,700 lawyers, with a total staff of over 3,500 in 24 jurisdictions. In Europe, CMS Cameron McKenna is a top ten law firm in its own right, with over 150 partners and more than 800 fee earners. The firm has the resources and experience to advise clients on a wide range of transactions and projects both in the UK and internationally. It has offices and associated offices in various key business centres worldwide including the UK, Central and Eastern Europe, Central, East and South East Asia and North America.

PRINCIPAL AREAS OF WORK The firm's lawyers have strong specialist expertise in areas such as finance and financial services; corporate; utilities and natural resources; real estate and environment; insurance and reinsurance; cross-border investment; technology, life sciences and intellectual property; infrastructure and projects; human resources and pensions; competition and European law; arbitration and litigation. The firm is committed to providing the highest quality professional advice and building enduring relationships with its clients. It places great emphasis on the training and development of its partners and staff in both current legal and business issues. The firm's investment in know-how and information systems allows it to share its knowledge and experience throughout the firm, helping to ensure that all its lawyers add value to the services they provide. CMS Cameron McKenna works with its clients to identify their business needs and provide them with comprehensive, cost-effective commercial guidance. The firm offers a clear business lead – not just legal opinion.

INTERNATIONAL The locations of the firm's offices and associated offices are: Berlin, Brussels, London, Paris, Utrecht, Vienna, Zrich, Aberdeen, Amsterdam, Arnhem, Beijing, Belgrade, Bratislava, Bristol, Bucharest, Budapest, Buenos Aires, Casablanca, Chemnitz, Dresden, Düsseldorf, Frankfurt, Hamburg, Hilversum, Hong Kong, Leipzig, Lyon, Madrid, Milan, Montevideo, Moscow, Munich, New York, Prague, Rio de Janeiro, Rome, Shanghai, Stuttgart, Toronto, Warsaw and Washington DC. CMS member firms are CMS Bureau Francis Lefebvre, CMS Cameron McKenna, CMS Derks Star Busmann, CMS Hasche Sigle, CMS Adonnino Ascoli & Cavasola Scamoni, CMS Lexcelis and CMS Strommer Reich-Rohrwig Karasek Hainz.

Managing Partner	Dick Tyler
Senior Partner	Richard Price
Chief Executive	Robert Derry-Evans
UK	
Number of partners	127
Assistant solicitors	328
Other fee-earners	115
International	
Number of partners	22
Assistant solicitors	130

CONTACTS	
Aviation	Tim Brymer
Banking	Duncan Aldred
Charities	Andrew Crawford
Construction	John Uwins
Corporate Finance	Sean Watson
Corporate Tax	Mark Nichols
EC Law/Competition/Anti-trust	Sue Hankey
Employment	Simon Jeffreys
Energy	Mark Moseley
Environment	Paul Sheridan
Financial Services Regulation	Simon Morris
Health & Safety	Mark Tyler
Immigration	Julia Onslow-Cole
Infrastructure Projects/PFI	Robert Phillips
Insolvency	Dan Hamilton
Insurance & Reinsurance	Anthony Hobkinson
IP/Advertising & Mktg	Stephen Whybrow
IT/Telecoms	John Armstrong
Litigaton/Arbitrtation & Dispute Management	Tim Hardy
M&A	Richard Price
Media Complaints	Tim Hardy
Pensions	Nigel Moore
Planning	Chris Williams
Product Liability	Christopher Hodges
Project Finance	Andrew Ivison
Property	Edward Benzecry
Transport	Ian Bendell
Venture Capital	Andrew Sheach
Water	Richard Temple

C/M/S/ Cameron McKenna

Cobbetts

Ship Canal House, King Street, Manchester, M2 4WB
Tel (0161) 833 3333   Fax (0161) 833 3030   DX 14374 Manchester 1
Email lawyers@cobbetts.co.uk   Website www.cobbetts.co.uk

THE FIRM The new look Cobbetts now boasts offices on both sides of the Pennines following its merger in May 2002. The firm has always represented quality of work and high service standards and its strong independent stance, continues to impress its clients. Managing Partner, Michael Shaw, has been re-elected until 2005, a testament to the success of the programme of radical internal changes which has been effected under his direction. A drive for structured progression now places Cobbetts at the forefront of successful long-term relationship building with clients. The firm remains committed to further development of intranet and extranet technology and the application of e-commerce in order to better service client needs. It will also continue with its successful Client Relationship Management programme. Over recent years the firm has achieved an enviable record of controlled, sustained growth of around 20% pa through good management of the business as a whole and an emphasis on identifying and meeting the needs and expectations of clients, intermediaries and the firm's own personnel. Unlike many of its competitors, strong emphasis is placed on relationships, quality of environment and job satisfaction for all. Cobbetts continues to maintain its accreditation in both Investors in People and Lexcel (the Law Society's Quality Award), awards which the firm's partners consider to be vital in ensuring that it continues to deliver quality service to clients, whilst maintaining a work life balance for its staff. Cobbetts have two German qualified solicitors, an associated office

Managing Partner	Michael Shaw
Senior Partner	Stephen White
Number of partners	73
Assistant solicitors	70
Other fee-earners	69

AREAS OF PRACTICE	
Commercial Property	35%
Company/Commercial	29%
Litigation	26%
Private Client	10%

in Brussels, Renouf & Co, and are members of the US State Capital Global Law Firm Group. These affiliations, together with other close relationships around the world ensure that the firm can meet clients' needs for international legal services and enables it to offer proactive advice to clients in respect of international commerce and trade.

PRINCIPAL AREAS OF WORK Cobbetts operates through a number of flexible service teams based on work type and managed within two divisions: corporate and property.

Corporate The corporate division brings together all the non-property related business law services as well as private client services. The division is divided into teams covering Corporate Finance, Commercial (including IP & IT), Employment, Banking, Commercial Litigation, Tax & Pensions and Private Client. The firm's private client team is significantly larger than many of the major Northern commercial firms and also boasts an independent financial adviser, enabling Cobbetts to offer OMB clients in particular, a full range of legal and financial advice.

Property The property division is one of the largest in the North of England and incorporates the resources and expertise capable of handling commercial property work of any type and size from greenfield acquisitions through development, letting and general property management. The division has particular expertise in the retail and licensed trade sectors with the licensing and planning team in particular enjoying a national reputation. There is also a flourishing housing association client base.

CLIENTELE The firm's client base is extensive ranging from large multinational corporations, public sector, listed and private companies to family businesses. There is legal expertise across many industry sectors especially banking and finance, leisure, retail, public transport and information technology.

INTERNATIONAL Languages: French, German, Italian and Spanish.

RECRUITMENT The firm recruits ten to twelve trainee solicitors every year. The application form can be downloaded from the website and should be sent for the attention of Richard Webb.

Cobleys
19-23 Sir Thomas Street, Salford, L1 6BW **Tel** (0151) 242 9000 **Fax** (0151) 236 2911

Coffin Mew & Clover
17 Hampshire Terrace, Portsmouth, PO1 2PU **Tel** (023) 9281 2511 **Fax** (023) 9229 1847

Coker Vis Partnership
49 Broad Lane, Tottenham, London, N15 4DJ **Tel** (020) 8885 1415 **Fax** (020) 8885 2882

Cole & Co
St Andrew House, 141 West Nile Street, Glasgow, G1 2RN
Tel (0141) 353 0007 **Fax** (0141) 353 1110 **DX** GW15 Glasgow 1 **Email** ron@coleandco.co.uk

AREAS OF PRACTICE	
Commercial Property	98%
Residential Property	2%

Ptnrs: 1 **Associates:** 3 **Contact** Ron Cole • Commercial property practice established in 1996 by experienced former property partner of a large national firm.

Cole & Co
23 Tombland, Norwich, NR3 1RF **Tel** (01603) 617018 **Fax** (01603) 630050

A-Z ■ LAW FIRMS

Colemans-ctts

1-3 Union Street, Kingston, KT1 1RP
Tel (020) 8296 9966 **Fax** (020) 8546 1400 **DX** 84864 Kingston Upon Thames 1
Email ctts@ctts.co.uk **Website** www.colemans-ctts.co.uk

Elisabeth House, 16 St. Peter's Square, Manchester, M2 3DF
Tel (0161) 236 5623 **Fax** (0161) 228 7509 **DX** 14380 Manchester 1
Email info@colemans-sols.co.uk

Tameway Tower, Bridge St, Walsall, WS1 1JZ
Tel (01922) 431100 **Fax** (01922) 431105 **DX** 12124 Walsall 1
Email info@colemans-sols.co.uk

Joint Managing Partner	Roger Coleman
Joint Managing Partner	Janet Tilley
Number of Partners	11
Assistant solicitors	29
Other fee earners	65

CONTACTS

Agency	Paul Hennity
	Jason Slack
	Lorna Valcin
Clinical Negligence	Kerry Fifield
Commercial Litigation	Helen Hall
	Tony Sutton
Debt Recovery	Sue Paterson
	Tony Sutton
Employment	Helen Hall
	Lorna Valcin
Housing Disrepair	Steve Tonge
Immigration	Lorna Valcin
Insurance	Roger Coleman
Landlord & Tenant	Tony Sutton
Personal Injury	Sarah Barr
	David Stevenson
	Janet Tilley
Personal Legal Protection	Janet Tilley
Private Client	Nigel Tarrant
Property	Nigel Tarrant
Uninsured Loss Recovery	John Hesketh
	David Stevenson
	Janet Tilley

THE FIRM With offices spread across England, the firm has a particular specialism in legal expenses insurance work including personal injury and household legal protection. Commercial litigation, conveyancing, debt recovery and landlord and tenant work are among its other areas of expertise. The practice was established in 1983 in Manchester with a total of five staff. In 1988 it became known as Colemans Solicitors and the following year opened an office in Walsall. In January 2002, it merged with the Kingston-upon-Thames firm of Coleman Tilley Tarrant Sutton, to form colemans-ctts. The two firms had already enjoyed a close association and changes in some of their key markets presented significant opportunities for a new national firm. The merged practice has a staff of almost 200. It provides the resources to serve clients on a national basis, while retaining the high client service standards of a local firm. Core to the integration of the two firms has been the installation of a common case management system and a virtual private network linking all three offices, to enable work to be handled seamlessly throughout the organisation. The practice is willing to act as an agent for other solicitors in litigation matters through all its offices.

PRINCIPAL AREAS OF WORK

Personal Injury Colemans-ctts has one of the largest and most experienced personal injury departments in private practice. Cases handled on behalf of claimants include road traffic accidents, accidents at work, industrial diseases, sporting injuries and clinical negligence. The firm also has a substantial defendant insurance department, dealing mainly with personal injury claims but also providing a comprehensive recovery service from simple accident damage outlay to complex subrogated claims, and representation for motoring offenses. The firm also has one of the biggest personal legal expenses units in the country and acts for approximately 75% of the personal legal expenses insurers in England (as at April 2002) on a wide range of personal injury, property, consumer, employment and travel related disputes.

Commercial Litigation Commercial litigation is also a specialism, including commercial contract disputes, sale of goods actions, intellectual property cases and landlord and tenant disputes. All aspects of commercial property are dealt with and debt collection is also handled. Employment expertise includes dismissal, redundancy, restrictive covenants and part-time workers. Advice on housing disrepair is provided to both landlords and tenants regarding the private and public sectors.

Landlord & Tenant A dedicated team handles landlord and tenant issues such as arrears recovery, possession proceedings and planning issues. Advice on housing disrepair is provided to both landlords and tenants regarding the private and public sectors.

Private Client All aspects of residential conveyancing are dealt with, as well as wills and estate planning issues.

Immigration Immigration and nationality matters are dealt with including work permits, asylum applications and visa issues.

Colemans-ctts aims to develop further its position in its existing markets, focusing on its key specialisms.

colemans-ctts
SOLICITORS

Cole's Solicitors
4-5 Rigbys Court, St Giles Street, Norwich, NR2 1NT **Tel** (01603) 441 111 **Fax** (01603) 442 222

Colin Jones
17A Thompson Street, Barry, CF63 4JL **Tel** (01446) 420 043 **Fax** (01446) 420 045

Collas Day
PO Box 140, Manor Place, St Peter Port, GY1 4EW **Tel** (01481) 723191 **Fax** (01481) 711880

Collyer-Bristow
4 Bedford Row, London, WC1R 4DF
Tel (020) 7242 7363 **Fax** (020) 7405 0555 **DX** 163 Ch.Ln.
Email firstname.lastname@collyerbristow.com **Website** www.collyerbristow.com

Senior Partner	Roger Woolfe
Number of partners	26
Assistant solicitors	20
Other fee-earners	17

AREAS OF PRACTICE
Dispute Resolution	25%
Property (Commercial)	20%
Commercial	20%
Matrimonial & Family	15%
Private Client	15%
Sport, Music & Entertainment	5%

CONTACTS
Agency	Matthew Marsh
Banking	Stephen Rosen
Charity	Daniel Simon
Commercial Property	Janet Armstrong-Fox
Company/Commercial	John Bailey
Construction	Joanna Kennedy
Defamation	Joanna Kennedy
Dispute Resolution	Joanna Kennedy
E-commerce & IT	Paul Sillis
Employment	Keith Corkan
Entertainment/Music	Howard Ricklow
Family	Michael Drake
Immigration	Joe Cohen
Intellectual Property	Joe Cohen
Personal Injury	Peter Pratt
Residential Property	Janet Armstrong-Fox
Sport & Sponsorship	Alan Burdon-Cooper
Tax Planning & Trusts	Paul Clark
Wills & Probate	John Saner

THE FIRM Collyer-Bristow is a long established and innovative London firm that has been providing a complete service to commercial clients and individuals for over 250 years. It was established in 1760 but its environment and approach is progressive and friendly. The firm acts for a wide range of institutional clients; public and private companies; charities; businesses; professional partnerships; and private clients. An association with a group of European practices provides valuable continental links. The bright modernised offices contain a professionally run art gallery where regular and varied exhibitions are held.

PRINCIPAL AREAS OF WORK
Company/Commercial The department's work includes company formations; mergers; acquisitions; sales; buyouts; information technology and e-commerce; reorganisations and all the related range of contractual and commercial advice.

Commercial Property The work includes freehold and leasehold sales and disposals; residential and office development schemes; major shopping centre developments; agricultural matters; planning and other related work; residential and domestic transactions, including leasehold enfranchisement advice.

Dispute Resolution This strong team has experience in property-related and construction litigation and arbitration; judicial review work; commercial and contractual disputes; professional negligence; defamation; personal injury and in representation before professional tribunals.

Intellectual Property The firm has an excellent reputation for handling contentious trademark and patent disputes; and in the licensing of rights, publishing, franchising and technology transfer.

Private Client The firm has maintained and expanded its private client practice, for whom it handles tax planning; trusts; financial and investment advice within the UK and offshore; wills; and the administration of estates and charities.

Family This is one of the leading matrimonial practices in the country. Its work includes divorce; substantial financial disputes; children cases; cohabitation; international jurisdiction disputes and forum-shopping, and child abduction. It is one of the appointed firms on the Lord Chancellor's child abduction panel.

Employment The team handles a wide range of employment and boardroom disputes, industrial tribunal applications, executive service contract advice, and the preparation of employment terms and conditions and advice on business-related immigration.

Sport, Music & Entertainment The firm acts for sponsorship, promotions and merchandising consultancies; advertising and marketing agencies; governing bodies; sponsors; sports photographers and publishers; film and video producers; and distributors. In the music industry, the firm acts for artists, managers, record labels and publishers.

Agency Work The agency litigation department provides a service for more than 100 firms outside the capital and overseas.

RECRUITMENT For those candidates who do not believe that biggest necessarily means best, the firm offers a refreshing alternative. CV and references to John Saner.

COLLYER~BRISTOW
solicitors

A-Z ■ LAW FIRMS

■ Comerton & Hill

Murray House, 4 Murray Street, Belfast, BT1 6DN
Tel (028) 9023 4629 **Fax** (028) 9023 3908 **DX** 415 NR BELFAST 1
Email solicitors@comerton.co.uk **Website** www.comerton.com

Contact Mervyn H White • Comerton & Hill is a small niche market firm of solicitors based in Belfast but with a clientele throughout the British Isles. Comerton & Hill is the leading debt recovery practice in Northern Ireland with, in addition, a significant commercial/conveyancing practice.

AREAS OF PRACTICE	
Debt Recovery/Insolvency	60%
Commercial	15%
Conveyancying	15%
Employment	5%
Other	5%

■ Condies

2 Tay Street, Perth, PH1 5LJ **Tel** (01738) 440088 **Fax** (01738) 441131

■ Coningsbys

87-89 High Street, Croydon, CR9 1XE
Tel (020) 8680 5575 **Fax** (020) 8681 3941 **DX** 2611 Croydon 1 **Email** reception@coningsbys.co.uk
Website www.coningsbys.co.uk

Ptnrs 2 **Other fee-earners** 7 • A niche practice specialising in human rights, health, education and community care. Its client base is nationwide. Traditional high street work is undertaken, such as general litigation, residential conveyancy, and wills and probate.

AREAS OF PRACTICE	
Education	34%
Conveyancing	28%
Matrimonial	11%
Human Rights	8%
Personal Injury	5%
Probate	3%

■ Coodes

8 Market Street, St Austell, PL25 4BB **Tel** (01726) 75021 **Fax** (01726) 69103

Coole & Haddock

14 Carfax, Horsham, RH12 1DZ
Tel (01403) 210200 **Fax** (01403) 241275 **DX** 57600 Horsham

5 The Steyne, Worthing, BN11 3DT
Tel (01903) 213511 **Fax** (01903) 237053 **DX** 3717 Worthing

THE FIRM Established in Horsham in 1898 and Worthing in 1960, Coole & Haddock built its reputation initially on an extensive private client base mainly in Sussex. This is now complemented by expanding commercial and litigation departments which offer a comprehensive service to businesses over a wider area.

PRINCIPAL AREAS OF WORK Work handled includes company; commercial/commercial property; town and country planning; commercial and civil litigation/employment/personal injury; property litigation; residential conveyancing; probate and trusts; wills and estate planning; matrimonial/childcare; debt recovery; crime.

Managing Partner	Paul Burke
Senior Partner	Frank Haddock
Number of partners	10
Assistant solicitors	7
Other fee-earners	5

CONTACTS	
Commercial & Civil Litigation/Employment	Stephen Loosemore
Company/Commercial/Commercial Property	Iain Swalwell
Matrimonial/Childcare	Penelope Barker
Probate & Trusts	Jennifer Murphy
Residential Conveyancing	Paul Burke
	Peter Graves

Cooper Kenyon Burrows

Royal London House, 196 Deansgate, Manchester M3 3WF
Tel (0161) 834 7374 **Fax** (0161) 839 3299
Email commfraud@c-k-b.com **Website** www.c-k-b.com

Managing Partner	Michael Kenyon
Number of partners	5
Assistant solicitors	1
Other fee-earners	6

AREAS OF PRACTICE	
Commercial Fraud	50%
Customs & Excise	30%
Inland Revenue	10%
Regulation & Compliance	10%

CONTACTS	
All Areas of Practice	Michael Kenyon
	Lesley Burrows
	Ian Cooper
	Richard English

THE FIRM Cooper Kenyon Burrows is one of the leading firms nationally in the areas of commercial and corporate fraud, money laundering, regulatory proceedings and investigations and prosecutions by the Serious Fraud Office, DTI, FSA, Customs & Excise and Inland Revenue. Formerly the principals of the commercial fraud department of Burton Copeland in the North, Michael Kenyon, Lesley Burrows and Ian Cooper have long been recognised throughout the country as established leaders in commercial fraud investigation and defence, money laundering and Tax/VAT controversy cases. Together with their very experienced team they launched this already established practice, in May 2002. The simple strategy of the firm is to concentrate on providing the highest levels of service and expertise in these core disciplines. The firm is committed to the increasing use of information technology and has developed its own systems to assist in the preparation of financial fraud cases which grow ever more complex. Cooper Kenyon Burrows recognises that fraud and money laundering investigations have been crossing international borders for many years and with partners already qualified in the Republic of Ireland as well as England & Wales, the firm is actively building international associations to provide the high level of service that clients now require.

PRINCIPAL AREAS OF WORK

Corporate & Commercial Fraud: Cooper Kenyon Burrows has the largest and longest established commercial fraud and tax controversy practice outside London with five partners practising full-time in this area assisted by seven other experienced fee earners. The firm became a member of the Serious Fraud Panel at its inception and all the partners are accredited as supervisors of the most serious and complex cases. They are able to offer representation in commercial fraud and other similar prosecutions throughout the country. The firm is regarded as being amongst the leaders in the field with experience developed in many of the major prosecutions brought by the SFO and other agencies such as Barlow Clowes, Arrows, Butte Mining and Richmond Oil & Gas. Cooper Kenyon Burrows is at the forefront of cases involving stock market, accountancy, banking and international investment matters. This expertise and experience is carried over into the related areas of confiscation and civil restraint proceedings, money laundering and extradition.

Inland Revenue and Customs & Excise Investigations: The firm is an acknowledged leading practice in this area, where the client's best interests often lie in a negotiated settlement. Cooper Kenyon Burrows specialises in the protection of its clients' interests in the face of the exceptional powers of investigation which the Inland Revenue and Customs & Excise possess. Often working with expert accountancy practises it has substantial experience in securing negotiated financial settlements with the tax authorities as an alternative to prosecution. Nevertheless, if a prosecution is commenced the practice is able to bring to bear its long experience of the criminal law process in the defence of its clients interests.

Regulation & Employee Protection: Cooper Kenyon Burrows advises and represents both companies and individuals in respect of investigations and proceedings brought by the many other regulatory and investigatory bodies that have proliferated in recent years such as Trading Standards, the HSE and the Environment Agency. Apart from representation its work ranges from advising potential witnesses to conducting internal investigations on behalf of companies concerned with potential regulatory breaches.

CLIENTELE Clients range from large international corporations to individuals and instructions are received from all areas of the UK and from clients abroad who may have interests to protect within the UK.

Copleys

Red House, 10 Market Hill, St Ives, PE17 4AW **Tel** (01480) 464515 **Fax** (01480) 467171

Corbett & Co

Churcham House, 1 Bridgeman Road, Teddington, TW11 9AJ
Tel (020) 8943 9885 **Fax** (020) 8977 3122 **Email** mail@corbett.co.uk **Website** www.corbett.co.uk

AREAS OF PRACTICE	
International Construction Projects/Disputes	60%
UK Construction Projects/Disputes	40%

Contact Mr Edward Corbett • The firm has a growing reputation as a specialist in international and UK construction projects and disputes. Established in 1993, when Edward Corbett left the partnership of Masons, the firm has advised on a wide range of projects in the UK and all over the world. Dispute work includes TCC litigation, ICC arbitration and ADR including adjudication.

Continued overleaf

A-Z ■ LAW FIRMS

■ Corker Binning Solicitors
Natwest Bank Chambers, 218 Strand, London, WC2R 1AT **Tel** 0207 353 6007 **Fax** 0207 353 6008

SJ Cornish

Twyford House, Kennedy Way, Tiverton EX16 6RZ
Tel (01884) 243377 **Fax** (01884) 243388 **DX** 49014 Tiverton
Email solicitors@sjcornish.co.uk **Website** www.SJCornish.co.uk

Bankside House, 107/112 Leadenhall Street, London, EC3A 4AH
Tel (020) 7891 2470 **Fax** (020) 7891 2471 **DX** 528 London city

Senior Partner	Sarah Cornish
Number of partners	4
Assistant solicitors	2
Other fee-earners	1

AREAS OF PRACTICE	
Professional Indemnity	70%
Personal Injury	25%
Commercial Litigation/Debt Collection	5%

THE FIRM SJ Cornish is a niche insurance litigation practice dedicated to resolving claims against professionals for insurers. Established in 1991, the firm opened a London office in February 2001 with one resident partner.

PRINCIPAL AREAS OF WORK Work handled includes defendants' professional indemnity claims (valuers, surveyors, all construction professionals, accountants, insurance brokers, IFAs and solicitors); defendants' personal injury and liability claims ; commercial litigation; debt collection.

■ Couchman Harrington Associates
8 Bloomsbury Square, London, WC1A 2LQ **Tel** (020) 7611 9660 **Fax** (020) 7611 9611

Coudert Brothers

60 Cannon Street, London, EC4N 6JP
Tel (020) 7248 3000 **Fax** (020) 7248 3001 **DX** LDE 49
Email info@london.coudert.com **Website** www.coudert.com

Chairman	Steven Beharrell
Number of partners	8
Assistant solicitors	22
Other fee-earners	10

AREAS OF PRACTICE	
Corporate Finance	30%
Banking/Project/Structured Finance	15%
Litigation/Arbitration	15%
Capital Markets/Funds	10%
Energy/Telecoms/Multimedia	10%
Real Property	10%
Other	10%

CONTACTS	
Banking/Finance	Alexander Janes
Competition/Telecoms	Alastair Gorrie
Corporate Finance	Dean Poster
Energy	Steven Beharrell
Funds	Alasdair Gordon
Litigation/Arbitration	Maria Frangeskides
Project Finance	Peter O'Driscoll
Real Property	Anne O'Neill

THE FIRM Coudert Brothers in London is a multinational partnership of registered foreign lawyers and solicitors. It is part of a worldwide network of offices established in 33 cities in 19 countries around the world. Coudert Brothers is one global partnership and the London office provides the facilities of a full service London law firm as well as access to the international network of Coudert Brothers. The London office has eight partners, seven of whom are solicitors and one of whom is a US attorney. The London office specialises in international investment; trade and finance (with particular expertise in corporate finance); mergers and acquisitions; joint ventures; capital markets; banking and project finance; international tax and trust planning; telecommunications and IT law; energy privatisation and infrastructure projects; real estate; arbitration and litigation.

INTERNATIONAL Coudert Brothers has offices in the major financial centres in Europe, Central Asia, North America and the Asia Pacific region. In Europe, the firm has offices in London, Paris, Brussels, Antwerp, Ghent, Berlin, Frankfurt, Munich, Milan, Moscow, St. Petersburg and Almaty. The North American offices are established in New York, Washington, Los Angeles, San Francisco, San Jose, Palo Alto, Denver and Montreal and the Asia Pacific offices in Bangkok, Beijing, Hong Kong, Jakarta, Singapore, Shanghai, Sydney and Tokyo. Coudert Brothers has associated offices in Budapest, Stockholm, Prague, Rome and Mexico City. The firm's Moscow office was the first established by a foreign law firm (1988) and is now one of the largest in Moscow, servicing all the states of the former Soviet Union. Coudert Brothers opened an office in Kazakhstan in 1998.

COUDERT BROTHERS
INTERNATIONAL LAWYERS

Courts & Co

15 Wimpole St, London, W1G 9SY
Tel (020) 7637 1651 **Fax** (020) 7637 0205 **DX** 42722 Oxford Circus North
Email law@courtsandco.com **Website** www.courtsandco.com

THE FIRM Courts & Co is a niche firm, specialising in company and commercial work. The firm provides an in-depth, personal service to companies and their directors, working closely with their business advisers, particularly their accountants. The firm's policy is to combine the highest level of technical expertise with a close understanding of the client's business and commercial requirements.

PRINCIPAL AREAS OF WORK A large part of the firm's work consists of advising on the purchase and sale of businesses, corporate mergers and reorganisations, as well as a full range of business and commercial matters, including taxation and intellectual property work. The firm handles commercial conveyancing; heavy commercial litigation (including environmental and town and country planning matters); employment work (both litigious and non-litigious) mainly (but not exclusively) for employers; and estate planning, trusts and probate work.

CLIENTELE Clients include private and public companies, professional partnerships and individual entrepreneurs in all areas of business; charities and trusts. Much of the firm's work is for overseas clients.

Senior Partner	Bill Holmes
Number of partners	6
Assistant solicitors	4
Other fee-earners	1

AREAS OF PRACTICE

Company, Commercial & Tax	40%
Commercial Litigation	30%
Conveyancing/Trusts, Wills & Probate	30%

CONTACTS

Company/Commercial	Ian Paterson
	Patrick Gilmour
Conveyancing/Probate & Trusts	Bill Holmes
Employment	Frank Ryan
Intellectual Property	Michael Krantz
Litigation	Michael Krantz
	Frank Ryan

Covington & Burling

265 Strand, London, WC2R 1BH
Tel (020) 7067 2000 **Fax** (020) 7067 2222
Email kwimmer@cov.com **Website** www.cov.com

THE FIRM Covington & Burling is a leading international law firm with more than 500 lawyers and offices in London, Washington DC, New York, San Francisco and Brussels. The firm's major practices include mergers and acquisitions, venture capital and private equity transactions, securities and finance, licensing and strategic alliances, intellectual property, competition and regulatory law, tax and litigation. Covington & Burling is known for its expertise in cutting-edge industries, including information technology, e-commerce, life sciences and telecommunications.

PRINCIPAL AREAS OF WORK

Corporate The firm's corporate lawyers in London have particular expertise in mergers and acquisitions, venture capital and private equity transactions, securities, strategic investments and partnering, investment fund regulation and a broad range of licensing and commercial transactions. Covington is one of the only firms able to offer advice internationally with significant local resources in both the US and the UK. The transactional practice has a strong focus on the technology sector, including licensing and joint venture deals for leading software companies, and corporate partnering deals for pharmaceutical and biotechnology companies. The London office routinely works with networks of specialised corporate and tax local counsel in all major European jurisdictions. The firm's offices have co-ordinated advice from counsel in numerous countries worldwide in a variety of matters, including cross-border mergers and acquisitions, commercial expansion activity and securities offerings.

Intellectual Property The London office has notable expertise in intellectual property, acting for major technology and other clients in copyright and trademark infringement litigation and anti-piracy programmes in Europe. It handles litigation directly in the UK and co-ordinates it in other European, Middle East and African countries. The office has extensive legislative experience in IP matters, including regular work with the European Commission, WIPO, WTO and all member states. The office also advises extensively on internet regulatory and liability issues, and handles UK and EU trademark matters, patent licensing, and standard-setting.

Technology, Media & Telecommunications The firm also has deep expertise in technology, media and telecommunications, including data protection in the UK and throughout Europe. The London office also represents software, telecommunications and media clients on Internet and e-commerce policy issues in the UK and throughout Europe, including the current Telecommunications Directives and the UK Communications Bill. It is engaged in substantive law reform efforts relating to privacy, security, data retention and software copyright issues.

International Tax Law International tax law is a growing speciality in Europe, focusing on assisting US and non-US multinational companies to plan and implement tax-efficient corporate and operational structures. Clients also include start-up ventures and smaller companies that are developing strategies for entering Europe. The firm has particular expertise in transfer pricing associated with high-value intangible property, with new modes of business operations and with sophisticated trading structures.

Chairman of Managing Committee (Firm)	
	Stuart Stock
Managing Partner (London)	Kurt Wimmer
Number of resident lawyers	38
Total lawyers worldwide	Over 500

AREAS OF PRACTICE

Corporate & Commercial	40%
Intellectual Property	25%
Medicines & Consumer Product Regulation	20%
Litigation & Arbitration	10%
International Trade & Competition	5%

CONTACTS

Arbitration	Charles Lister
Corporate	Hilary Prescott
Corporate Finance	Simon Goodworth
EU & Competition	David Hull
Intellectual Property	Kurt Wimmer
IT & E-commerce	Kurt Wimmer
Litigation	Richard Mattick
Pharmaceuticals	Richard Kingham
Tax	David Hinds
Employment	Christopher Walter

Continued overleaf

COVINGTON & BURLING

A-Z ■ LAW FIRMS

The tax group also has significant practical experience with the tax incentive rules and practices available for European operations.

Consumer Products The regulation of pharmaceutical and biotech products, as well as food and other consumer products, is also an area of concentration. The firm provides multinational regulatory advice regarding foods, medicines, cosmetics, chemicals, packaging and other products. Clients include major pharmaceutical, cosmetic and food companies. Covington is one of the only firms able to offer advice internationally with significant local resources in both the US and the UK.

Litigation & Arbitration The London office handles international commercial arbitrations in London, The Hague and other locations in Europe. It deals with general commercial litigation in the English courts and advises policy holders on London insurance market issues.

Other Other regulatory areas include EU and other member state laws concerning advertising and privacy.

INTERNATIONAL Work is handled in all European languages as well as Japanese, Arabic, Cantonese, Mandarin and Korean.

■ Cozens-Hardy & Jewson
Castle Chambers, Opie Street, Norwich, NR1 3DP **Tel** (01603) 625231 **Fax** (01603) 627160

Cripps Harries Hall

Wallside House, 12 Mount Ephraim Road, Tunbridge Wells, TN1 1EG
Tel (01892) 515121 **Fax** (01892) 544878 **DX** 3954 Tunbridge Wells
Email reception@crippslaw.com **Website** www.crippslaw.com

14 Buckingham Street, London, WC2N 6DF
Tel (020) 7930 7879 **Fax** (020) 7839 9224
Email legal.london@crippslaw.com

Managing Partner	Jonathan Denny
Senior Partner	Andrew Fermor
Number of partners	35
Assistant solicitors	41
Other fee-earners	77

AREAS OF PRACTICE	
Commercial	42%
Dispute Resolution	31%
Private Client	27%

CONTACTS	
Agriculture	Andrew Fermor
Alternative Dispute Resolution	Peter Ashford
Charities	Peter Scott
Commercial Litigation	Peter Ashford
Commercial Property	Michael Stevens
Construction	Jane Ryland
Corporate Finance (inc. Buyouts)	Trevor Carney
Debt Recovery	Russell Simpson
Employment	Roger Byard
Environment	Jason Towell
Family/Matrimonial	Michael Rowlands
Information Technology	Larry Leporte
Insolvency	Ed Bible
Intellectual Property	Larry Leporte
Local Government	Michael Stevens
Partnership	Peter Garry
Personal Injury	Myles McIntosh
Planning	Jason Towell
Professional Negligence	Charles Broadie
Property Litigation	Carol Wakeford
Social Housing	Bill Mackie
Trusts & Personal Tax	Simon Leney

THE FIRM Cripps Harries Hall is a leading regional law firm with an excellent reputation for high standards and creating lasting client relationships. Although established for 150 years, the firm is recognised as being among the most progressive and innovative regional practices. It has focused commercial and private client divisions and is the natural first choice for many successful businesses and wealthy individuals. Cripps Harries Hall's strategy of concentrating its resources in one office has enabled it to provide a depth of expertise across a range of services which is not matched by other firms in the region. With its Tunbridge Wells headquarters 45 minutes out of London by rail, the firm's low overheads are reflected in charges which, typically, are at least one third less than those of comparable London firms. Dedicated to developing its team of expert legal advisors, the firm has attracted a number of high profile lawyers from leading City firms. Cripps Harries Hall was the first 'top 100' law firm to achieve accreditation to the Law Society's quality assurance standard for solicitors' firms known as 'Lexcel', designed to encourage excellence in law firms. The firm is committed to integrating the provision of legal advice with the effective use of IT, having invested over £1m on a new computer system. Among the benefits for clients are fast communications and a secure extranet.

PRINCIPAL AREAS OF WORK
Corporate A significant part of the firm's client base is mid-sized corporates, with the technology sector well represented. The firm regularly handles mergers, acquisitions and disposals, corporate finance, e-commerce, commercial contracts, employee benefits, limited liability partnerships, IT matters, intellectual property issues and corporate recovery. The firm is also respected for its employment work.

Commercial Property Among the firm's institutional property clients are government departments, utility companies, insurance companies, national pension funds, property portfolio companies and housing associations. The services provided cover planning and environmental law, as well as the full spectrum of commercial property work, PFI projects and property disputes. Also, the firm has a reputation for providing a cost-effective resource for major property projects, such as the Channel Tunnel High Speed Rail Link. A particular niche for the firm is property developers and house builders. The firm's clients include several household name companies in this sector.

Dispute Resolution The firm's dispute resolution practice is broad and includes mediation, arbitration, litigation and risk management. Two partners of the firm are accredited mediators. Substantial and complex claims, including some for eight figures and above, are handled on a regular basis. The specialist team defending professional liability claims acts for two of the major insurers of solicitors and continues to resolve existing claims on behalf of the Solicitors Indemnity Fund. Between them, the members of this team have also acted on behalf of insurers for surveyors, accountants, architects,

CRIPPS HARRIES HALL

valuers and management consultants.

Private Client Cripps Harries Hall has extensive private client experience and has developed a reputation in managing the affairs of wealthy private clients to rival the top London firms in this field. The firm is especially strong in providing integrated legal and tax advice.

INTERNATIONAL The firm is a member of a network of independent law firms in 18 European countries.

Croftons

Television House, Mount Street, Manchester, M2 5FA **Tel** (0161) 214 6180 **Fax** (0161) 839 1743

Crombie Wilkinson

Clifford House, 19 Clifford Street, York, YO1 9RJ **Tel** (01904) 624185 **Fax** (01904) 623078

Crosse & Crosse

14 Southernhay West, Exeter, EX1 1PL **Tel** (01392) 258451 **Fax** (01392) 278938

Crowell & Moring LLP

180 Fleet Street, London, EC4A 2HG
Tel (020) 7413 0011 **Fax** (020) 7413 0333 **DX** 91 London Chancery Lane
Website www.crowellmoring.com

THE FIRM Crowell & Moring is a leading international law firm with offices in London, Brussels, Washington DC and Irvine CA. It provides a full range of transactional, counselling, regulatory and litigation capabilities, with a particular emphasis within Europe on the technology, new media and communications sectors. The firm makes an effort to learn its clients' business and goals, and understands the importance of providing practical business advice clearly, concisely and quickly. Responsiveness and the accessibility of its lawyers are practice priorities.

PRINCIPAL AREAS OF WORK Crowell & Moring's offices in London and Brussels operate together as an integrated European practice group, offering advice on corporate and commercial transactions, competition law, communications/IT law, privacy, regulation employment law, international trade law, legislative counselling, health care regulation, litigation and international arbitration. The firm has extensive experience of mergers, acquisitions, and joint ventures – particularly those involving cross-border investments. It regularly assists clients with the establishment of new branches and subsidiaries, particularly for international businesses expanding into new European markets. The firm has expertise in the negotiation and drafting of all forms of corporate and commercial agreements commonly used in modern business. Its transactional capabilities are complemented by one of the leading international anti-trust practices in the world. Crowell & Moring provides competition law advice to some of the very largest international corporations and has obtained successful clearance of the full range of transactions requiring anti-trust approvals both in Brussels and in Washington.

CLIENTELE Clients range from major multinationals to New Economy start-ups and venture capital funds. Many clients are in the technology, new media and communications sectors. Lawyers combine a range of transactional, regulatory and litigation skills with an in depth understanding of the evolving legal, commercial and policy issues presented by the digital revolution and the convergence of the telecoms, broadcast and information technology industries. Many clients in these sectors are fast moving and innovative businesses with which the firm keeps pace in providing dynamic and creative legal solutions.

Managing Partner	Peter Teare
UK	
Number of partners	2
Assistant solicitors	6
Other fee-earners	1
International	
Number of partners	103
Senior counsel	7
Of counsel	40
Associates	107
Other fee-earners	48

CONTACTS	
Corporate/Commercial	Peter Teare
Competition	James Ashe-Taylor
Communications/IT	Peter Teare
Privacy	Rachael Wellby
International Trade	Gordon Mackenzie
Legislative	Peter Sellar
Litigation/Arbitration	Pippa Wheeler
Healthcare	Natasha Singarayer

A-Z LAW FIRMS

Crutes Law Firm

7 Osborne Terrace, Newcastle upon Tyne, NE2 1RQ
Tel (0191) 212 5600 **Fax** (0191) 212 5601 **DX** 62553 Jesmond
Email info@crutes.co.uk **Website** www.crutes.co.uk

28 Portland Square, Carlisle, CA1 1PE
Tel (01228) 525446 **Fax** (01228) 511517 **DX** 63000 Carlisle
Email info@crutes.co.uk

93 Borough Road, Middlesbrough, TS1 3YS
Tel (01642) 260470 **Fax** (01642) 231549 **DX** 60502 Middlesborough
Email info@crutes.co.uk

Senior Partner	Tim Wallis
Managing Partner	Stephen Crute
Number of partners	18
Assistant solicitors	16
Other fee-earners	21

AREAS OF PRACTICE	
Insurance/Personal Injury	59%
Insurance/Professional Indemnity	16%
Commercial	8%
Private Client	8%
Health Related Work	6%
Employment	3%

CONTACTS	
ADR/Mediation	Helen Ager
Commercial	Stuart Palmer
Employment	Tim Smith
Health Related Work	Tim Wallis
Insurance/Personal Injury	David Drewe
Insurance/Professional Indemnity	Helen Ager
Private Client	Stuart Palmer

THE FIRM Crutes Law Firm is a forward thinking law firm with three offices based in the North of England: the firm services clients on a national basis. Crutes is renowned for its insurance litigation, computer networked offices and case management systems. The firm is a leader in alternative dispute resolution and is committed to resolving disputes efficiently and speedily, which gives its clients a more cost-effective service. Paramount to the firm's ethos is the importance of listening to clients. The firm not only covers the principal areas listed below but now also has a reputable employment unit, which acts for the Treasury solicitors. Crutes has a specialist claims unit, a team of dedicated and experienced solicitors, dealing with the increasing number of stress related and abuse claims. With all the endorsements you expect from a professional law firm, including ISO 9001 and Investors in People, Crutes is proud of its 94 year history and excited by challenges, both in the legal and technological sense. The firm is dedicated to providing first class legal services.

PRINCIPAL AREAS OF WORK

Insurance Insurance work is a particular strength of Crutes, and the firm acts for a large number of the major insurance companies. Much of the work is personal injury. The firm has a reputation for providing a complete portfolio, including some of the more specialist work areas eg. physical and sexual abuse claims by children and stress claims.

Public Sector Services Across all offices, Crutes acts for virtually all of the local authorities in the North. The firm provides a complete range of services, including employment, commercial, property, health and insurance litigation.

Professional Indemnity Crutes has had a high profile professional indemnity practice for many years, and through its dedicated team not only continues to act in claims against solicitors, accountants, surveyors, and numerous other professionals.

Health Crutes has acted for the NHS since its inception, and now acts for many of the NHS Trusts in the North, for litigation, employment, property and commercial matters.

Commercial Crutes now boasts a range of services in this sector, ranging from commercial property and company commercial, to intellectual property, insolvency, debt recovery and housing management. The firm has seen a significant increase in the amount of cases they now handle.

Dispute Resolution Crutes is committed to ADR and has been pioneers of its development since 1992. All Crutes litigators are trained in ADR and the firm has gained a wealth of experience through its involvement in a substantial number of mediation whether as a party, mediator or trainee mediator.

Cuff Roberts
100 Old Hall Street, Liverpool, L3 9TD **Tel** (0151) 237 7777 **Fax** (0151) 237 7676

Culbert and Martin
7 Donegall Square West, Belfast, BT1 6JB **Tel** (028) 9032 5508 **Fax** (028) 90438669

Cumberland Ellis Peirs incorporating Barth & Partners

Columbia Hse, 69 Aldwych, London, WC2B 4RW
Tel (020) 7242 0422 **Fax** (020) 7831 9081 **DX** 250 Ch.Ln.
Email cep@cep-law.co.uk **Website** www.cep-law.co.uk

THE FIRM A merger of two long-established central London practices, the firm has attracted considerable company/commercial and commercial property work and has a substantial litigation department; it also continues to provide the full range of private client services. The firm's philosophy is to combine high quality advice with a positive, personal service, at reasonable cost.

PRINCIPAL AREAS OF WORK

Company/Commercial A wide variety of work is handled, including takeovers; buyouts; flotations; intellectual property; and employment law for businesses of all sizes.

Litigation The firm is active in High Court and County Court work (both commercial and private), including personal injury, landlord and tenant, and debt recovery. It is particularly strong in employment and family law.

Property The department acts for institutions and companies in a wide variety of commercial property work. A separate section deals with residential conveyancing.

Private Client The department handles all aspects of a client's personal affairs, including probate; wills; trusts; tax planning and landed estates. It also has expertise in charity law.

CLIENTELE The firm acts for public and private companies; institutions; charities (particularly City Livery companies); NGOs; sports associations; and a large number of private individuals.

Managing Partner	Suzanne Eva
Senior Partner	Lionel Judd
Number of partners	11
Assistant solicitors	9
Other fee-earners	7

CONTACTS	
Commercial Property	Rod Forsyth
Company/Commercial	Suzanne Eva
Employment	Barry Jameson
Family	Hazel Wright
Litigation	Neil Turner
Private Client	Nicola Waldman
Residential Conveyancing	Robert Maclean

Cunningham John

Fairstead House, 7 Bury Road, Thetford, IP24 3PL
Tel (01842) 752401 **Fax** (01842) 753555 **DX** 124810
Email postmaster@cunningham-john.co.uk **Website** www.cunningham-john.co.uk

THE FIRM Cunningham John's successful growth can be best explained by its extensive expertise and ability to handle high profile personal injury/clinical negligence actions and corporate and commercial transactions.

PRINCIPAL AREAS OF WORK

Company/Commercial Clients include plc and property companies. The innovative Legal4business concept provides instant legal access to a variety of commercial specialists including general and commercial litigation, property transactions, employment. Clients nationwide. A reputation as problem solvers.

Personal Injury/Clinical Negligence An accelerating national reputation for obtaining high damages. See 'Leaders in their Field', Simon John. Another new initiative from Cunningham John is the provision of a Fasttrack claim service for appropriate PI/CN matters.

Private Client An expanding department dealing with a full private client service, notably simple and complex wills and estates, personal legal and tax planning and trusts, family law, childcare and education law. Two PGO Panel Receivers are supported by innovative client funds management service. Fairstead Financial Services Ltd provides help and advice in the investment and use of funds recovered from court cases, to trustees and attorneys and generally.

Senior Partner	Simon John
Managing Partner	Tom Cook
Number of partners	11
Assistant solicitors	14
Other fee-earners	25

CONTACTS	
Commercial/Corporate	David Cunningham
Commercial/Corporate	Clive Wadham-Smith
Litigation & Employment	Donal Sheahan
	William Jackson
Conveyancing	Paul Dixon
Family	Amita Terry
Private Client	Robert Chalmers
	Helen Wingfield
PI/CN	Simon John, Tom Cook
Mark Flack, Graeme Peart, William Jackson	

CUNNINGHAM·JOHN
SOLICITORS

Cunninghams

Second Floor, Bridge Street Chambers, 72 Bridge Street, Manchester, M3 2RJ
Tel (0161) 833 1600 **Fax** (0161) 833 1060

Talbot House, 22 The Crescent, Salford, M50 4PF
Tel (0161) 745 9000 **Fax** (0161) 745 9500

THE FIRM The firm operates from offices in central Manchester and practises exclusively in criminal law. The firm now has a second office on The Crescent in Salford, dedicated to its serious crime, serious fraud and private client departments.

PRINCIPAL AREAS OF WORK Serious crime, serious fraud and private client are the main areas of work. The practice represents both private and publicly funded clients in all aspects of criminal law,

Continued overleaf

Number of partners	3
Assistant solicitors	5
Other fee-earners	12

AREAS OF PRACTICE	
Crime	90%
Prison Law	10%

CONTACTS	
Crime - Legal Aid	David Caplin
Prison Law	Urfan Mahmood
Private Client & Business Crime/Serious Fraud	
	Philip Lythgoe

A-Z LAW FIRMS

ranging from homicide to road traffic cases. A full criminal defence service is offered to all of the firm's clients including a specifically dedicated prison law department for advice and representation to the firm's clients held within the prison system. The practice has the privilege of being one of only a handful of firms in Greater Manchester who have been appointed to the Criminal Defence Services Serious Fraud Panel. The practice is willing to undertake agency work and to accept instructions from firms who are not themselves on the Serious Fraud Panel, and as a result unable to accept instructions for publicly funded serious fraud cases.

INTERNATIONAL The practice benefits from Punjabi and Urdu speaking lawyers and continues to expand with eight solicitors now within this three-partner practice.

Currey & Co
21 Buckingham Gate, London, SW1E 6LS **Tel** (020) 7828 4091 **Fax** (020) 7828 5049

Cuttle & Co
Bridge Street Chambers, 21 St John Street, Manchester, M3 4DT **Tel** (0161) 835 2050 **Fax** (0161) 831 7986

Dale & Co
10 Victoria Street, Felixstowe, IP11 7ER **Tel** 07074 794708 / 01394 284 118 **Fax** 07074 794709 / 01394 276 097

Dale Langley & Co
60 Lombard Street, London, EC3V 9EA **Tel** (020) 7464 8433 **Fax** (020) 7464 8659

Darbys

Sun Alliance House, 52 New Inn Hall Street, Oxford, OX1 2QD
Tel (01865) 811700 **Fax** (01865) 811777 **DX** 145840 Oxford 6
Email info@darbys.co.uk **Website** www.darbys.co.uk

THE FIRM The 18 partners and specialist client service teams provide a wide range of services to private and business clients.

PRINCIPAL AREAS OF WORK
Business Services Commercial litigation, commercial property, company and commercial and employment.
Private Client Services Clinical negligence, family, personal injury, residential conveyancing and probate and tax.
Crime & Immigration The criminal team is one of the largest in the Thames Valley. The immigration team enjoys a national standing.

CLIENTELE Multinational companies, University Colleges, start-up companies, partnerships and private individuals. Many partners enjoy an excellent professional standing with one qualified insolvency practitioner having a national reputation.

Senior Partner	Sturge Taylor
Number of partners	18
Assistant solicitors	17
Other fee-earners	21

CONTACTS	
Company, Commercial IP	Nick Hedges, Robert Bryan
Commercial Property & Conveyancing	Sturge Taylor, Mark Taylor
Litigation	Paul Lowe, Elizabeth Taylor
Criminal & Immigration	Jim Astle, Jennifer Harvey
Family	Catherine Eddy
Clinical Negligence & Personal Injury	Helen Niebuhr
Trusts & Probate	Sian Jeffrey, Nicholas Morgan

MC Darlington
Diocesan Registry, Church House, 90 Deansgate, Manchester, M3 2QH **Tel** (0161) 834 7545 **Fax** (0161) 839 0093

Darlington & Parkinson
78 Pitshanger Lane, Ealing, London, W5 1QX **Tel** 0208 998 4343 **Fax** (020) 8566 8285

Davenport Lyons

1 Old Burlington Street, London, W1S 3NL
Tel (020) 7468 2600 **Fax** (020) 7437 8216 **DX** 37233 Piccadilly 1
Email dl@davenportlyons.com **Website** www.davenportlyons.com

THE FIRM Davenport Lyons is a leading media and entertainment practice and combines this with strong company/commercial, property, litigation, tax, employment and private client departments. The firm adopts a commercial and practical partner-led approach focused on building long-term partnerships with its clients. The firm provides comprehensive legal services to corporate and commercial clients across a broad spectrum of market sectors, including media in all its forms (film, television, radio, music, theatre, publishing and the newspaper industry); information technology, e-commerce and new media; the retail sector; advertising; restaurants; hotels, the sport and leisure industries; the travel industry; property investment and development. The firm provides high quality legal expertise combined with commercial sensitivity to clients' needs. This service is provided in a timely and cost effective way, yet recognising the importance to clients of partner attention. The firm also enjoys close involvement with many US and EU businesses and lawyers and is the only English member of the international association of law firms, Globalaw. One of the firm's partners is admitted in New York.

PRINCIPAL AREAS OF WORK Specialised fields include:

Media The firm's media group is acknowledged as a leader in the field of film and TV finance, where it is heavily involved in advising on sale and leaseback partnerships and other tax-based financing arrangements and production/distribution, where it advises on British-based co-productions as well as international bilateral and multilateral co-productions. Clients include substantial film and television companies and personalities and the firm is the principal legal advisor to several banks and other financial institutions lending to the film and television sector.

Music, Entertainment & Theatre The firm has a strong reputation in the UK and US and acts for many leading music publishing corporations, producers, record companies and individual musicians, as well as clients in the film and TV industries, advising on recording contracts and copyright issues.

Defamation A leader in this field dealing with many high profile libel, privacy/confidentiality and other media related issues. Clients include a large number of national newspapers, book and magazine publishers including *Private Eye* magazine. The firm represents both plaintiffs and defendants.

Intellectual Property The firm's pre-eminent reputation in the media and entertainment and retail sectors has always been centred on its intellectual property expertise. Its IP group covers a full range of contentious and non-contentious IP matters as well as trademark expertise; advising on copyright; design right and trademark infringement disputes and the protection and exploitation of brands.

Company & Commercial With an excellent reputation in this area, providing an overall service normally associated with larger city firms, the department acts for growing companies up to and including Stock Exchange quotations. It provides advice on general company and commercial matters, corporate tax, insolvency and company restructuring, employment, and banking and finance issues. With a dedicated company secretarial service the department offers a full company secretarial function.

Property A strong commercial property department acts for major developers, property investors and lending institutions. It is particularly active in the retail and leisure/restaurant sectors in a broad range of substantial property and property related matters, and is supported by an experienced property litigation team. The department also provides a first class, specialist residential property service.

Liquor & Entertainment Licensing Boasting one of the largest and most successful licensing practices in London, the liquor and entertainment licensing group is the leading firm for West End operators of restaurant/pub and nightclub businesses.

Litigation Commercial litigation is a long-established, substantial and successful element of the practice, servicing not only the firm's media and entertainment, corporate, and property clients, but also businesses in a wide range of sectors.

Employment The department provides specialist and comprehensive advice in all areas of employment law. Advising both employers and employees, the department is particularly strong in representing and defending cases in the Employment Tribunal, the County Court and the High Court.

Private Client The department provides a full-service to both UK and overseas clients, including matrimonial matters, advice on tax planning, compliance and appeals, trust matters and charities, pensions, wills, the administration of estates and Court of Protection work.

Sport The firm has a well-established practice, advising promoters of sporting events and individuals in connection with protecting and enhancing their interests.

INTERNATIONAL The firm's membership of the international network of lawyers, Globalaw, has increased its volume of instructions from foreign businesses wishing to operate in the UK. The firm is also able to offer clients access to a network of over 70 firms worldwide, thereby enabling it to service clients beyond the UK.

Senior Partner	Leon Morgan
Number of partners	28
Assistant solicitors	40
Other fee-earners	18

AREAS OF PRACTICE	
Company/Commercial	25%
Litigation	23%
Entertainment/Media	22%
Commercial Property	20%
Private Client	10%

CONTACTS	
Banking & Finance	Alon Domb
Company/Commercial	Michael Hatchwell
	Alon Domb
	Robert Charlton
	Rebecca Ferguson
Competition	David Marchese
Copyright & Trademark Litigation	David Gore
	Stuart Lockyear
Corporate Tax	Leslie Powell
Defamation	Kevin Bays
	Philip Conway
	Robin Shaw
Employment	Kathryn Pavey
	Marie van der Zyl
Entertainment & Liquor Licensing	Philip Conway
	David Lavender
Insolvency	Trevor Sears
Intellectual Property & New Media	
	Stuart Lockyear
	Brian Miller
	David Marchese
International Coordinator	Michael Hatchwell
IT, Technology & E-commerce	David Marchese
	Brian Miller
Litigation (General)	Kevin Bays
	David Gore
	Robin Shaw
Litigation (Property)	Jonathan Aubrey
Media/Film/TV	Leon Morgan
	Richard Moxon
	Lawrence Brown
Music/Entertainment/Theatre	James Ware
	Jay Quatrini
Private Client (Matrimonial)	John Burrell
Private Client (Tax & Trusts)	Leslie Powell
Property	Graham Atkins
	John Downing
	Richard Kelsey
	Paul McCombie
	Marilyn Elstow
Publishing	Leon Morgan
	James Ware
Sport	Kevin Bays
Travel	Trevor Sears

A-Z ■ LAW FIRMS

■ David Richbell - Sole Practitioner
Church Cottage, Park Road, Melchbourne, MK44 1BB **Tel** (01234) 709 907 **Fax** (01234) 709 424

■ David Bishop & Co
14 Chapel Lane, Formby, Liverpool, L37 4DY
Tel (01704) 878421 **Fax** (01704) 878959 **Email** David_Bishop@compuserve.com

AREAS OF PRACTICE	
Wills & Probate	37%
Trusts	20%
Tax	20%
Pensions	10%
Company	8%
Charities	5%

Ptnrs 1 **Contact** David Bishop • Specialist practice in the areas of trusts (onshore and offshore), wills and estates and also capital tax planning for trusts, individuals and family companies both based in the UK and overseas. Other areas of work covered are charities and pensions and property ownership by cohabitants.

■ E David Brain & Co
8 Church Street, St Austell, PL25 4AT **Tel** (01726) 68111 **Fax** (01726) 61433

■ David Charnley & Co
Phoenix House, 102-106 South Street, Romford, RM1 1RX **Tel** (01708) 766155 **Fax** (01708) 730743

David du Pré & Co
90-92 Parkway, Regents Park, London, NW1 7AN
Tel (020) 7284 3040 **Fax** (020) 7485 1145 **DX** 57070
Email info@daviddupre.co.uk **Website** www.daviddupre.co.uk

Senior Partner	David du Pré
Number of partners	1
Assistant solicitors	1

AREAS OF PRACTICE	
Family/Matrimonial/Divorce	100%

CONTACTS	
Family/Matrimonial/Divorce	David du Pré

THE FIRM Established by David du Pré, a former matrimonial barrister, who later qualified as a solicitor in 1980 and held senior positions in leading City family departments before setting up his own specialist matrimonial practice in 1991. He is a member of the Solicitors Family Law Association and the International Society of Family Law.

PRINCIPAL AREAS OF WORK Matrimonial, family and co-habitation law including: separation and parental responsibility agreements; divorce petitions; financial applications, including complex and emergency applications, cases involving substantial assets/income or where there is an international dimension. Although both big and small cases are welcomed, a publicly funded service is not available.

■ David Gist Solicitors
21/23 Clare Street, Bristol, BS1 1TZ
Tel (0117) 927 9111 **Fax** (0117) 927 9101 **DX** 7880 Bristol **Email** info@davidgist.co.uk

Ptnrs 4 **Asst solrs** 8 **Associates** 1 • David Gist Solicitors deals mainly with claimant personal injury claims, predominantly those arising from motor accidents, and also an increasing number of clinical negligence and industrial accident claims.

■ David Gray Solicitors
Old County Court, 56 Westgate Road, Newcastle upon Tyne, NE1 5XU **Tel** (0191) 232 9547 **Fax** (0191) 230 4149

David Jeacock
16 Church St, Wootton Bassett, Swindon, SN4 7BQ
Tel (01793) 854111 **Fax** (01793) 853600
Email jeacock@lineone.net

Principal	David Jeacock
Number of partners	1

AREAS OF PRACTICE	
Company/Commercial	50%
Sports Law	30%
Private & General	20%

THE FIRM After 10 years personal experience as an in-house lawyer, David Jeacock established the practice in 1984 to provide practical commercial advice to business clients. Because of his involvement and experience in sports administration and doping control, the practice soon provided practical advice in those areas as well and is now well established in this field. Clients include three national governing bodies of sports. This is a small personal practice that clearly enjoys working with all its clients, to solve their problems.

David Price Solicitors & Advocates

5 Great James Street, London, WC1N 3DB **Tel** (020) 7916 9911 **Fax** (020) 7916 9910

Davidson Chalmers WS

12 Hope Street, Edinburgh, EH2 4DB
Tel (0131) 625 9191 **Fax** (0131) 625 9192 **DX** 408 Edinburgh
Email mailbox@davidsonchalmers.com

Chairman	Gordon Davidson
Managing Partner	Andrew Chalmers
Number of partners	7
CONTACTS	
Banking	Gordon Davidson
Commercial Property	Andrew Chalmers
Company/Commercial	Stuart Duncan
Litigation	Vannan McKellar
Mergers & Acquisitions	Michael Kane
Planning & Environmental	Caroline Court
Projects & Construction	Andrew Drane

THE FIRM Davidson Chalmers is one of the limited number of niche commercial firms in Scotland able to provide real depth of expertise in commercial property, corporate and construction. It is highly regarded for its legal expertise but more so its business like approach, getting the job done on time and within budget.

PRINCIPAL AREAS OF WORK

Corporate & Commercial General corporate advice but largely M&A and advice to North American corporations.
Commercial Property Main focus is on development and investment.
Projects & Construction Infrastructure, mining and environmental.

CLIENTELE Property developers and investors, housebuilders, large owner managed businesses, media clients, healthcare clients, shipowners, PCB sector and private equity investors.

Davies and Partners

135 Aztec West, Almondsbury, Bristol, BS32 4UB
Tel (01454) 619619 **Fax** (01454) 619696 **DX** 35007 Almondsbury

5 Highlands Court, Cranmore Avenue, Solihull, Birmingham, B90 4LE
Tel (0121) 711 7107 **Fax** (0121) 711 4851 **DX** 715358 Solihull 19

Rowan House, Barnett Way, Barnwood, Gloucester, GL4 3RT
Tel (01452) 612345 **Fax** (01452) 611922 **DX** 55253 Gloucester 2

Senior Partner	D Barrie Davies
Number of partners	18
Assistant solicitors	44
Other fee-earners	24
CONTACTS	
Commercial Litigation	Geoffrey Hand
Commercial Property	Peter Mitchell
Company/Commercial	Thomas Brennan
Land Development	D Barrie Davies
Personal Injury & Medical Negligence	Ewan Lockhart
Private Client	Richard Maisey

THE FIRM Davies and Partners is forward-thinking and objective in approach. The firm handles a large amount of commercial property, estate conveyancing, company and commercial, commercial litigation, and secured lending work and has also developed a strong personal injury and medical negligence practice.

PRINCIPAL AREAS OF WORK

Land Development The firm handles all aspects of development land, from initial site acquisition to individual unit transfers and ancillary documentation, planning applications and appeals, building contracts and freehold and leasehold matters.
Company/Commercial The firm has extensive experience in the whole range of company and commercial work, including corporate finance; mergers, acquisitions and restructuring; MBOs; publicly-quoted companies; company and partnership formation; joint ventures; shareholders' agreements; banking; financial services and franchising; intellectual property, including international, EU and UK competition implications.
Commercial Property The firm handles all aspects of commercial property including industrial, office and retail premises for both landlords and tenants and all associated funding, development and property management issues.
Commercial Litigation Work includes building contracts; judicial review; landlord and tenant; employment; insurance; professional negligence; public liability; economic torts; corporate insolvency; unlawful trading; licensing; debt collection and banking litigation.
Personal Injury & Medical Negligence The firm handles extensively both plaintiff and defendant personal injury work. Medical negligence work is plaintiff-orientated. Two fee-earners are members of the Law Society Personal Injury Panel.
Other Areas All aspects of corporate and personal tax and financial planning, agricultural law (including land acquisition and disposal, agricultural holdings, grazing agreements, share farming agreements, EU implications and business tenancies) and private client work (including residential conveyancing, re-mortgaging, wills, trusts and estate management, and distribution and winding-up of estates).

A-Z ■ LAW FIRMS

Davies Arnold Cooper

6-8 Bouverie Street, London, EC4Y 8DD
Tel (020) 7936 2222 **Fax** (020) 7936 2020 **DX** 172 London Chancery Lane WC2
Email daclon@dac.co.uk **Website** www.dac.co.uk

85 Gracechurch Street, London, EC3V 0AA
Tel (020) 7936 2222 **Fax** (020) 7410 7998 **DX** 172 London Chancery Lane WC2
Email daclon@dac.co.uk

60 Fountain Street, Manchester, M2 2FE
Tel (0161) 839 8396 **Fax** (0161) 839 8309 **DX** 14363 Manchester
Email dacman@dac.co.uk

Senior Partner	David McIntosh
Executive Partner	Daniel Gowan
Operations Partner	David Hertzell
UK	
Number of partners	43
Assistant solicitors	83
Other fee-earners	35

CONTACTS	
ADR	Michael Dobias
Banking/Commercial Litigation	Allan Reason
Banking/Property Finance	John Nelmes
Commercial Insurance	Stephen Gorman
Commercial Property	Robert Lee
Construction & Engineering	Daniel Gowan
Construction & Property	Nick Young
Corporate & Employment	David Smellie
Education	Pradeep Dandiker
Employers'/Public Liability	Allison Dias
	Lisa Collins, Deborah Broughton
Energy	Akbar Ali
Environment	Stephen Gorman
	Christopher Rees
E/Risk	Richard Highley
Fraud	Nick Young
Healthcare	Simon Pearl
Health & Safety	Richard Tovell
Insolvency	Bryan Green
Insurance	Kenneth McKenzie
International Transport/European/	
Competition	Marjorie Holmes
Medical Negligence	Simon Pearl
Motor	John Smith, Allison Dias
Occupational Health	Geoff Meyer
Planning	Christopher Rees
Product Liability/Group Actions	Anne Ware
Professional Indemnity/D&O	
	Kenneth McKenzie
Reinsurance	Michael Dobias
Sports Injuries	John Smith
Travel & Holiday	Allison Dias

THE FIRM The firm focuses on its core strengths of insurance, product liability, construction and energy, property and property finance, and transport and competition. It is a leading practice in its industry sectors and is noted for its commercial and pragmatic approach. The firm provides a comprehensive range of services in its chosen industry sectors demonstrating a genuine market commitment to its clients. The firm has collaborative relationships with its clients and focuses its resources on service delivery which adds value to their businesses. Davies Arnold Cooper's enthusiasm for its clients has led to its championing issues which affect clients' businesses. The firm looks at future issues and has recently been at the forefront of matters such as transnational litigation, rehabilitation, corporate governance and corporate accountability, and health and safety. The firm has a significant leaning towards international business through its clients in the insurance, construction and energy and international and transport and competition areas. Davies Arnold Coopers' office in Madrid is recognised as a leading practice in Spain and through it the firm acts for both UK and other clients in Spain and in Latin America. The firm is a leading practice in dispute resolution (including all forms of litigation, arbitration and alternative dispute resolution). It is a leading choice (in the UK and internationally) for defendants in multi-party actions relating to product liability and environmental issues, industrial disease and physical disasters and accidents. Examples of high profile litigation include transnational asbestos claims, MMR, Haemophilia, Benzodiazepine, Barings, Polly Peck, Banesto and Marconi. Davies Arnold Cooper has a thriving property department which has increased significantly in size over the past two years and is well-known for residential development, planning and increasingly property finance. Examples of its involvement in recent developments include Bedfont Lakes development, Portishead Quay, Hatfield Aerodrome, Repton Park and Napsbury Hospital.

CLIENTELE The firm works for major British and international companies, large UK and international insurers and reinsurers, Lloyd's and quoted property companies. The firm also acts for a number of banks, financial institutions and professional partnerships.

INTERNATIONAL The firm has an overseas office in Madrid, Spain.

■ Davies, Johnson & Co

The Old Harbour Office, Guy's Quay, Sutton Harbour, Plymouth, PL4 0ES
Tel (01752) 226020 **Fax** (01752) 225882 **DX** 8254 Plymouth 2 **Email** admin@djco.co.uk
Website www.djco.co.uk

Ptnrs 4 **Asst solrs** 1 **Other fee-earners** 3 **Contact** Jonathan Johnson • A niche practice providing a complete range of services to the commercial shipping industry and the international trading community. An extensive website provides full details.

■ Davies Lavery

ictoria Court, 17-21 Ashford Road, Maidstone, ME14 5FA **Tel** (01622) 625625 **Fax** (01622) 625600

■ Davis Blank Furniss

90 Deansgate, Manchester, M3 2QJ **Tel** (0161) 832 3304 **Fax** (0161) 834 3568

Davitt Jones Bould

15 The Crescent, Taunton, TA1 4EB
Tel (01823) 279279 **Fax** (01823) 279111 **DX** 32129 Taunton
Email general@djblaw.co.uk **Website** www.djblaw.co.uk

Managing Partner	Madeleine F Davitt
Chief Executive	Peter A Allinson
Number of partners	3
Assistant solicitors	6
Other fee-earners	4

AREAS OF PRACTICE

Commercial Property (including Planning, Environmental Law & Litigation)	100%

CONTACTS

Commercial Property	Madeleine F Davitt
Environmental Law	Tim Sylvester Jones
Public Law	Tim Sylvester Jones
Landlord & Tenant	Stuart Bould
Planning & Litigation	Peter A Allinson

THE FIRM Davitt Jones Bould was established in 1999 by a team of lawyers that had formerly worked within central government for the Government Property Lawyers. Since establishment the firm has expanded to include experienced commercial property lawyers from both the public and private sectors. The firm offers experience across the full breadth of commercial property transactions including major undertakings such as the property aspects of government privatisations, large scale developments and disposals. The firm's offices are based in Taunton but the firm acts for clients nationwide. Most of the firm's work currently centres on London and the South East of England.

PRINCIPAL AREAS OF WORK

Commercial Property All manner of commercial property work is undertaken ranging from small and large scale acquisitions, disposals, lettings and all aspects of property management through to development work and PFI/PPP transactions. In addition to transactional work the firm offers high quality technical legal advice on all matters involving property. Notable projects recently undertaken include the property aspects of the Ministry of Defence's privatisation of DERA and the refurbishment and reletting of high value office buildings in Central London. The firm deals with all associated areas of law relating to commercial property including planning and environmental law. The firm has particular experience in dealing with transactions involving clawback and overage, not only in the drafting and working of such provisions but also in their enforcement.

Property Litigation The firm has the ability to deal with all aspects of litigation involving commercial property.

Landlord & Tenant The firm handles all types of landlord and tenant work from the perspective of both landlord and tenant including the grant of and entry into leases, assignments, underlettings, lease renewals and termination of leases. Additionally, the full range of property management work is undertaken including licences for alterations and advice on rent review and other matters. Specialist work is also undertaken such as mobile phone aerial mast leases and wind farms.

CLIENTELE

Public Sector The practice has established a reputation and expertise in acting for the public sector. This includes administrative and public law aspects and the political dimensions of such work. Notably the firm is one of the four term commission lawyers for the Ministry of Defence undertaking all property related work on their behalf in London and the South East of England. Other government departments and local authorities are listed amongst the firm's clients. The firm is accustomed to accepting instructions of a most complex and sensitive nature.

Corporate The firm acts for a range of institutions and corporate clients including manufacturers, banks and small businesses.

Dawson Cornwell

15 Red Lion Square, Holborn, London, WC1R 4QT
Tel (020) 7242 2556 **Fax** (020) 7831 0478 **DX** 35725 Bloomsbury
Email mail@dawsoncornwell.co.uk **Website** www.dawsoncornwell.co.uk

Senior Partner	John Cornwell
Number of partners	9
Assistant solicitors	3
Other fee-earners	3

AREAS OF PRACTICE

Family & Matrimonial	73%
Conveyancing	12%
Wills, Trusts & Probate	10%
Litigation & Miscellaneous	4%

CONTACTS

Children's Issues	Anne-Marie Hutchinson
Family Law	Rhiannon Lewis

THE FIRM Dawson Cornwell is a specialist family firm dealing with all areas of matrimonial and family law. The firm is well known for its expertise in high value ancillary relief cases and for its award wining children's department. Dawson Cornwell provides a constructive and cost-effective approach and is committed to the principles of the Solicitors Family Law Association (founded by the firm's senior partner in 1982). The firm also offers expert advice in relation to property issues, conveyancing, wills, trust, estates and tax planning, enabling it to offer a complete service to clients in relation to their personal affairs. Dawson Cornwell's nine partners are able to offer an exceptional range of experience and expertise.

A-Z ■ LAW FIRMS

Dawsons

2 New Square, Lincoln's Inn, London, WC2A 3RZ
Tel (020) 7421 4800   **Fax** (020) 7421 4848   **DX** 38 LDE
Email info@dawsons-legal.com   **Website** www.dawsons-legal.com

Senior Partner	Joe Richardson
Managing Partner	Mathew Rea
Number of partners	21
Assistant solicitors	18
Other fee-earners	18

AREAS OF PRACTICE	
Property	28%
Private Client	27%
Litigation	21%
Corporate Commercial	14%
Matrimonial	10%

CONTACTS	
Commercial Litigation	Mathew Rea
Commercial Property	Andrew Harbourne
Corporate	Michael Edwards
Employment	Joanne Keddie
Family	Peter Alexander
Housing & Estates	Bill Smith
Partnerships & Insolvency	Stephen Ralph
Residential	Michael White
Tax	Joe Richardson
Wills & Trusts	Edward Martineau

THE FIRM Situated in Lincoln's Inn, this medium-sized practice offers a wide spectrum of services. In particular it carries out private client work and provides litigation, family, property, and corporate and commercial services for individuals, partnerships, businesses, charities and institutional clients. Over the course of the last five years the firm has expanded dynamically. It continues to grow in all departments in order to provide a specialist and full service to meet its clients' needs. The firm combines high professional and personal standards with a commercial approach to its work. Underpinning all its dealings with clients is the fundamental principle of the contact partner. That partner takes a personal responsibility for all the affairs of the clients in his or her care, irrespective of which department is dealing with a particular matter. It is part of the firm's philosophy to understand the nature of a client's business and broader concerns. For members of the firm the aim is to combine quality of work with quality of life.

PRINCIPAL AREAS OF WORK
Corporate & Commercial All aspects of work, both national and international, from the most complex e-commerce transaction to the most straightforward consultancy agreement. One partner is a licensed insolvency practitioner.
Employment A full service in contentious and non-contentious employment work to large and small companies and institutional employers, as well as to directors and other employees. Covering everything from urgent High Court applications to restrain competition, tribunal work and advising on redundancies.
Family Law All aspects of family law including divorce, judicial separation, disputes between cohabitees, financial provision, children and, where appropriate, mediation.
Litigation A proactive and commercial approach to resolving disputes, undertaking work in all courts (including the European Court of Justice) and a number of tribunals as well as engaging in alternative dispute resolution (arbitration and mediation). Particular areas of expertise include commercial contracts, commercial fraud, insolvency and asset tracing, defamation, contentious probate and trust disputes, contentious and non-contentious partnership law, shareholder and company disputes, property, professional negligence, agricultural disputes and quotas.
Private Client Services focus on all aspects of tax planning, including international tax, as well as wills, probate, settlements, trust administration and investment management.
Property Property services are a notable specialism, including commercial and residential conveyancing, acquisition, management and disposal of investment properties, and landlord and tenant matters. Expertise is also provided in agricultural law, farm quotas, property development, construction contracts, Settled Land Act and trust conveyancing, waste disposal, mineral extraction and housing association law.

CLIENTELE The practice acts for a broad range of commercial and private clients, for whom it aims to provide comprehensive expertise positively, imaginatively and cost-effectively. Clients include businesses of many types, landed estates, families and individuals, partnerships, charities, housing associations, educational institutions and professionals. Corporate work now has a strong international element. The firm's matrimonial team is renowned.

RECRUITMENT The firm expects to expand in all departments. Please contact Carmen Shemilt for more information. Dawsons offers four training contracts each year, please visit the website to download an application form.

DAWSONS
SOLICITORS

LAW FIRMS ■ A-Z

Dean Wilson Laing

96 Church Street, Brighton, BN1 1UJ
Tel (01273) 327241 **Fax** (01273) 770913 **DX** 2706 Brighton
Email thelawyers@deanwilson.co.uk

THE FIRM The firm offers high quality service to its clients over a comprehensive range of areas. The partners include a Recorder, a former local authority planning committee chairman, a former chairman of industrial tribunals, the holder of a High Courts Advocates Certificate, members of the Personal Injury Panel and the Family Law Panel, an accredited family law mediator and a member of the Society of Trust and Estate Practitioners. The firm also has the benefit of a public funding franchise in family and housing specialities.

PRINCIPAL AREAS OF WORK

Corporate & Commercial The firm can advise on all aspects of corporate, commercial and financial matters, including company and partnership formation, restructuring, acquisitions and disposals, and company and partnership disputes. A full range of commercial property work is undertaken including estate development, planning work, commercial leasing and commercial conveyancing.

Landlord & Tenant The firm specialises in all aspects of landlord and tenant law, both residential and commercial. A substantial amount of litigation for both landlords and tenants is dealt with. The firm are honorary solicitors to the Association of Residential Letting Agents and also to the Southern Private Landlords Association. Leasehold enfranchisement is fully covered.

Employment The firm is most experienced in all areas of this work, acting for both employers and employees.

Family Law The family law department covers all aspects of family law and has particular experience of substantial settlements.

Personal Injury The firm has wide experience acting for both claimants and defendants.

Sports Law The firm has experience acting for a number of this country's international sports persons before their sports disciplinary tribunals and also dealing with complex constitutional issues.

Litigation A range of civil litigation is undertaken including professional negligence actions, civil engineering and construction disputes, marine disputes, disputes including applications for restraint of trade and non-competition injunctions and debt recovery. Agency work for mortgage lenders and others is also undertaken.

Private Client Private client service includes wills, probate, administration of estates, trusts and tax planning, residential conveyancing and leases, charity law and immigration law.

Licensing The firm has specialist experience in licensing law relating to pubs, clubs, restaurants and gaming.

Financial Services The firm is authorised to carry out discrete investment business.

Managing Partner	Ian Wilson
Number of partners	6
Assistant solicitors	4
Other fee-earners	7

AREAS OF PRACTICE	
Domestic Conveyancing/Probate	21%
General Litigation	15%
Commercial Property	14%
Landlord & Tenant	14%
Employment	12%
Matrimonial	12%
Company Commercial	9%
Planning	3%

CONTACTS	
Children	Seema Roberts
Commercial, Commercial Property, Landlord & Tenant (Non-contentious)	David Barling
Domestic Conveyancing/Probate	Georgina James
Employment	Ian Wilson
Family	David Laing
Financial Services	John Atkinson
Landlord & Tenant Litigation	Claire Whiteman
Leasehold Enfranchisement	Jane Pritchard
Licensing	Nicholas Perkins
Planning	David Barling
Sport	David Laing

Debevoise & Plimpton

Tower 42, Old Broad Street, London, EC2N 1HQ
Tel (020) 7786 9000 **Fax** (020) 7588 4180
Website www.debevoise.com

THE FIRM Debevoise & Plimpton is a leading international firm practicing in the areas of corporate law, litigation, tax, real estate and trusts and estates.

PRINCIPAL AREAS OF WORK The London office, which advises on matters of US and English law, represents US, UK, and other clients in connection with mergers, acquisitions and joint ventures; global offerings and other securities transactions; telecommunications, including privatisations; acquisition, project and other financings; corporate restructuring; private investment funds, international tax planning; international commercial arbitration and dispute resolution. The office works closely with the firm's head office in New York and branch offices in Paris, Frankfurt, Moscow, Hong Kong and Washington DC.

INTERNATIONAL French, Spanish, Italian, Hungarian, German, Portuguese and Russian.

Managing Partner	Andrew Sommer
Number of partners	10
Assistant solicitors	32
Other fee-earners	6
Total lawyers worldwide	570

CONTACTS	
M&A	Colin Bogie
	James Kiernan
	Andrew Sommer
Corporate Finance	Katherine Ashton
	Robert Bruce
	James Scoville
Project Finance	Geoffrey Burgess
	Craig Bowman
Dispute Resolution	Arthur Marriott QC
	Mark W Friedman
Tax	Peter Schuur

A-Z ■ LAW FIRMS

Dechert

2 Serjeants' Inn, London, EC4Y 1LT
Tel (020) 7583 5353 **Fax** (020) 7775 7894 **DX** 30 London
Email advice@eu.dechert.com **Website** www.dechert.com

THE FIRM Dechert is a leading international law firm with a significant full-service practice in the City of London. With over 980 fee-earners working from 12 offices across the US and Europe, Dechert provides a full range of legal services to business, government and individual clients worldwide. 2002 saw the second anniversary of the merger between Titmuss Sainer Dechert and Dechert Price & Rhoads. The merger has greatly advanced the strategic aims of the practice, further strengthening Dechert's ability to compete at the highest level on an international stage. Property and construction, banking and securitisation, financial services, litigation and corporate finance are key areas of the practice that have fully capitalised on these developments. International offices in Boston, Brussels, Harrisburg, Hartford, London, Luxembourg, New York, Newport Beach, Paris, Philadelphia, Princeton and Washington.

PRINCIPAL AREAS OF WORK The London office of Dechert offers:
Corporate Services Core services include flotations, capital issues, transborder and domestic mergers, acquisitions and disposals and corporate reorganisations and recoveries. Specialist teams handle banking, securitisation and insolvency work.
Property A comprehensive range of property services including commercial, industrial and retail development, investment, planning, environment, property litigation and construction. Clients include investment funds, major retailers, property developers, large corporations and public authorities.
Financial Services Legal, regulatory and tax advice to financial service firms and advice on the legal aspects of operating an investment management business in Europe, North America and other markets around the globe.
Insurance Serves Lloyd's and non-Lloyd's insurance and reinsurance clients and deals with mergers and acquisitions in the insurance market, insurance litigation and arbitration.
Investigations The firm handles all civil and criminal aspects of corporate fraud, DTI inquiries, SFO investigations, Inland Revenue and Customs & Excise investigations, disciplinary proceedings, insider dealing, investigations by the SROs, money laundering and compliance.
Litigation A broad range of national and international commercial disputes in most areas of civil law with particular expertise in anti-trust, takeovers, fraud-related cross-border tracing, health and safety, corporate manslaughter, intellectual property and defamation. The firm also provides ADR services.
Commercial The firm handles intellectual property, UK and EU competition law, computer law, product liability, overseas joint ventures and general commercial contracts. The trademark practice offers a unified approach to the selection, requisition, exploitation and enforcement of intellectual property rights. Dechert also has specialist practices in employment, tax and private client, customs and excise and international trade.

CLIENTELE The firm's clients include substantial UK and international listed and private companies from a wide cross-section of industry and commerce.

RECRUITMENT In London, the firm recruits up to 20 trainees annually. Contact Lynn Muncey for a trainee solicitor recruitment brochure.

Senior Partner	Steven Fogel
Chief Executive	Peter Duffell
UK	
Number of partners	49
Assistant solicitors	110
Other fee-earners	56
International	
Number of partners	185
Assistant solicitors	447
Other fee-earners	133

CONTACTS	
Banking/Finance	Trevor Beadle
Commercial	Peter Crockford
Construction	Charles Brown
Corporate	David Vogel
Corporate Recovery	Ben Larkin
Customs & Excise/VAT	Sally Saltissi
Employment	Charles Wynn-Evans
EU & Competition	Peter Crockford
Financial Services	Peter Astleford
Insurance/Reinsurance	Robin Williams
Investigations & Fraud	David Byrne
IP/Defamation	Andrew Hearn
IT/E-commerce	Renzo Marchini
Litigation	David Byrne
Planning	Justin True
Property	Ciaran Carvalho
Property Litigation	Jeremy Grose
Retail	Paul Harding
Securitisation	Richard Ambery
Tax & VAT	Mark Stapleton
Trademarks	Paul Kavanagh

■ Deighton Guedalla
Top Floor, 30-31 Islington Green, London, N1 8DU **Tel** (020) 7359 5700 **Fax** (020) 7359 9909

■ Denison Till
Stamford House, Piccadilly, York, YO1 9PP **Tel** (01904) 611411 **Fax** (01904) 646972

Denton Wilde Sapte

5 Chancery Lane, Clifford's Inn, London, EC4A 1BU
Tel (020) 7242 1212 **Fax** (020) 7404 0087 **DX** 242
Email info@dentonwildesapte.com **Website** www.dentonwildesapte.com

One Fleet Place, London, EC4M 7WS
Tel (020) 7246 7000 **Fax** (020) 7246 7777 **DX** 242 EC4M 7WS

Bankside House, 107-112 Leadenhall Street, London, EC3A 4AA
Tel (020) 7246 7000 **Fax** (020) 7246 7722

Regency Court, 206/208 Upper Fifth Street, Milton Keynes, MK9 2HR
Tel (01908) 690260 **Fax** (01908) 668375 **DX** 31431

Chairman	James Dallas
Chief Executive	Virginia Glastonbury
UK	
Number of partners	154
Assistant solicitors	313
Other fee-earners	179
International	
Number of partners	43
Assistant solicitors	138
Other fee-earners	55

CONTACTS

Alternative Risk Transfer	George Sandars
Aviation	Hugh O'Donovan
Banking & Finance	Graham Paine
Construction	Julian Pope
Corporate & Commercial	Philip Goodwin
Dispute Resolution	Mark Gill
	Liz Tout
Employment	Stephanie Dale
Energy & Infrastructure	Michael Doble
Environmental	Jacqui O'Keeffe
EU & Competition	Polly Weitzman
Financial Markets	Robert Finney
Insurance & Reinsurance	Adrian Mecz
Intellectual Property	Simon Levine
IT & E-commerce	John Worthy
Leasing	Lisa Marks
Pensions	Alan Jarvis
PFI	Ian Hodgson
Project Finance	Howard Barrie
Rail	Christopher McGee-Osborne
Real Estate	Martin Quicke
Reconstruction & Insolvency	Mark Andrews
Sports	Adrian Barr-Smith
Tax	Charlotte Sallabank
Technology, Media & Telecoms	Tony Grant
Trade	Geoffrey Wynne

THE FIRM Denton Wilde Sapte is a leading international law firm based in the City of London. It offers a comprehensive range of the highest quality and affordable legal advice from 18 offices across Asia, Europe and the Middle East. A truly international organisation, it is heralded for its innovative and commercial approach. The firm's business is focused on a number of key sectors which ensures that its lawyers provide clients with a real understanding of the market as well as a comprehensive command of the law. Its network of offices is further strengthened by Denton international, a group of leading law firms that brings the firm's overall total to 35 offices in 23 jurisdictions around the world.

PRINCIPAL AREAS OF WORK Denton Wilde Sapte provides a wealth of contentious and non-contentious commercial legal advice. Its extensive knowledge and experience spans many jurisdictions and different business sectors, both public and private.

Banking & Finance The banking and finance department acts for banks and finance houses both on routine and complex ground-breaking transactions. It covers a wide range of work from corporate lending, project finance, PFI and leveraged finance through to general asset finance (including aviation, rail and shipping), trade finance, structured finance, capital markets, financial markets, regulation and rail insolvency, and workouts.

Corporate & Commercial Handling all aspects of corporate finance law, the department acts for many major public listed companies, advising on mergers and acquisitions, joint ventures, IPOs, employment law, regulatory and competition matters, EU law and corporate tax.

Energy & Infrastructure This leading practice brings together extensive international experience across a wide range of energy industries including oil and gas, electricity, water, mining, and minerals and construction.

International Projects Boasting an extensive international projects practice, the firm works in a wide range of sectors including electricity, oil and gas, water, mining and minerals, telecommunications infrastructure, transportation and environmental issues. The firm acts for banks, sponsors, governments and contractors.

Dispute Resolution The firm offers all forms of dispute resolution in areas including administrative law, insurance and reinsurance, banking, finance and financial services regulation, energy, fraud, construction disputes, environmental law, reconstruction and insolvency, judicial review, mergers and acquisitions, professional negligence, shipping, and tax.

Technology Media & Telecommunications Denton Wilde Sapte is a leader in telecommunications, media and technology. Its highly experienced department has worked extensively in broadcasting, publishing, IT, film, TV, sport, digital media, music and intellectual property.

Real Estate The Real Estate department advises on all aspects of commercial property and combines development, retail, institutional investment, property finance, planning and public sector.

Other In addition to these key areas, the firm has built up considerable expertise in a large number of specialist sectors such as insurance, aviation, rail, shipping and retail.

INTERNATIONAL The firm has offices in Abu Dhabi, Almaty, Beijing, Brussels, Cairo, Dubai, Gibraltar, Hong Kong, Istanbul, Moscow, Muscat, Paris, Singapore, Tashkent and Tokyo. The firm also has associated offices in Barcelona, Budapest, Chemnitz, Cologne, Copenhagen, Dar es Salaam, Düsseldorf, Frankfurt, Gothenburg, Hamburg, Lusaka, Madrid, Malmo, Potsdam, Prague, Stockholm and Vienna.

A-Z ■ LAW FIRMS

Devonshires

Salisbury House, London Wall, London, EC2M 5QY
Tel (020) 7628 7576 **Fax** (020) 7256 7318 **DX** 33856 Finsbury Square
Email info@devonshires.com **Website** www.devonshires.com

THE FIRM Devonshires is different. The focus is on clients and providing them with a genuine personal service – working in partnership with them and seeking to build long-term relationships, which benefit both the client and the firm. All fee-earners are encouraged to develop clients and share in the development of Devonshires. The firm actively seeks to support staff and to avoid the City tread-mill approach – weekend work is not encouraged. A balanced life leads to good advice. This approach has helped the firm grow five fold in the past five years. Devonshires is a City firm with a strong client focus towards business with a public/private dimension and recognised as a leading firm advising on social housing. Devonshires has a broad client base including registered social landlords, charities, companies, governments and individuals engaged in many different types of commercial activities. It deals with cases as diverse as securitising loans books to the Bloody Sunday Inquiry. Devonshires' lawyers offer practical and cutting-edge solutions to commercial problems. Staff training and personal development is given high priority to ensure staff retention and continuing strength in depth. Many professionals have joined the firm from larger City practices.

PRINCIPAL AREAS OF WORK Particular areas of expertise include all aspects of social housing including care, charities, contracts (including IT), commercial, employment, group structures, lending and securitisation; litigation, public-private partnership projects; outsourcing and PFI (especially in education, leisure, housing and municipal services); property acquisition, development and construction; public and administrative law (including EU law, Human Rights Act and judicial review).

RECRUITMENT Training at Devonshires is a challenge; new recruits will gain hands-on experience in many areas of law and develop the essential skills required to be a successful lawyer. From day one trainees will be valued fee-earners and will be fully integrated into the firm. All partners and fee earners operate an 'open-door' policy enabling trainees to benefit from their knowledge and experience. There will be plenty of opportunity for the new recruit to oversee their own files and develop relationships with clients.

Managing Partner	Julie Bradley
Senior Partner	Allan Hudson
Number of partners	15
Assistant solicitors	26
Other fee-earners	23

AREAS OF PRACTICE	
Property	30%
Litigation	25%
Banking & Corporate	20%
PPP/PFI	10%
Construction	5%
Employment	5%
Religious Charities	5%

CONTACTS	
Commercial Property	Allan Hudson
Company/Commercial	Gareth Hall
Development	David Brittain
Employment	Amanda Harvey
Finance/Corporate	Andrew Cowan
Housing Management	Nick Billingham
Litigation/Dispute Resolution	Philip Barden
Low Cost Home Ownership	Jane Nunnerley
PPP/PFI/Projects/Construction	Duncan Brown
	Paul Buckland
Religious Charities	Daniel Clifford
Securitisation/Local Authorities	Julie Bradley

Dewar Hogan

15 New Bridge St, London, EC4V 6AU
Tel (020) 7822 7400 **Fax** (020) 7822 7401 **DX** 98939 Cheapside 2
Email info@dewarhogan.co.uk

THE FIRM Dewar Hogan specialises exclusively in contentious property matters and property litigation in relation to commercial and residential property. The firm's clients include property companies, property funds, retailers, public authorities, banks and private investors. All of its solicitors were formerly with leading London firms.

PRINCIPAL AREAS OF WORK Contractual disputes, solicitors' negligence and landlord and tenant.

Managing & Senior Partner	Ronald Hogan
Number of partners	2
Assistant solicitors	3
Other fee-earners	2

AREAS OF PRACTICE	
Property Litigation	100%

CONTACTS	
Property Litigation	John Cox
	Ronald Hogan

936 INDEX TO LEADING LAWYERS: PAGE 1693 ■ IN-HOUSE LAWYERS' PROFILES: PAGE 1201

Dewey Ballantine

1 Undershaft, London, EC3A 8LP
Tel (020) 7456 6000 **Fax** (020) 7456 6001
Email fred.gander@deweyballantine.com **Website** www.deweyballantine.com

Managing Partner	Fred Gander
Number of partners	11
Other fee-earners	32

CONTACTS	
Capital Markets	Camille Abousleiman
	Louise Bernstein
	Alain Checri
Central & Eastern Europe	Stephen Jones
	James Simpson
Oil & Gas	Mark Saunders
	Adam Dann
M&A	Douglas Getter
	Stephen Jones
	Mark Saunders
Private Equity	James Simpson
Project Finance	James Simpson
	Jonathan Simpson
Securitisations	Alain Checri
Tax, Leasing	Stuart Odell
Tax, Structured Finance	Fred Gander

THE FIRM Dewey Ballantine LLP is an international law firm with more than 500 lawyers based in New York, Washington, DC, Los Angeles, Menlo Park, Houston, London, Hong Kong, Budapest, Prague and Warsaw. Founded in 1909, Dewey Ballantine's tradition of excellence has made it one of the world's pre-eminent law firms. It provides the highest quality legal representation with the utmost attention to client service. As the businesses of its clients have grown to encompass new types of matters in locations around the globe, so too has its practice. With offices in key financial centres around the world and a full complement of practice areas, clients regularly turn to Dewey Ballantine for creative solutions to their changing legal needs. The firm's London office opened in 1991 and is now a multinational practice of over 40 lawyers providing clients in Europe, the Middle East and Africa with advice under both English and US law.

PRINCIPAL AREAS OF WORK The London office advises on mergers and acquisitions, capital markets, private equity, project finance, securitisations, structured finance and international tax and has wide experience in the oil and gas, power, infrastructure, financial services, technology, telecom and transportation industries. Dewey Ballantine's client base includes a broad range of global financial institutions, multinational companies, FTSE 100, Fortune 100 companies and governmental institutions.

Capital Markets Winner of the *Legal Business* 2001 Capital Markets Team of the Year award, the London office has one of the leading practices in the emerging markets field and is a pioneer in developing capital market products for debt, equity and asset backed transactions. Recent representations include acting for the lead managers in the Arab Republic of Egypt's inaugural Eurobond issuance, acting for the Hellenic Telecommunications Organization (OTE) in the establishment of a Global Medium Term Note Programme and acting for the lead managers, JPMorgan and Morgan Stanley, on the first ever debt issue on the international market out of Kuwait.

Oil & Gas The London office has one of the UK's leading oil and gas practices. Work undertaken consists mainly of M&A, general corporate and commercial activity. Notable representations in 2001 include acting for TotalFinaElf in the sale of two of its gas pipeline businesses and acting for Premier Oil in the restructuring of its assets in Pakistan.

Mergers & Acquisitions Having participated as advisor in US deals totalling over $228 billion the firm was ranked number two in 2001 in terms of US announced transactions and 5th worldwide by *Thomson Financial*. The London practice has increased dramatically, in terms of personnel and workload, in the last few years resulting in a number of high profile transactions including representing the makers of Absolut Vodka in a four part cross-border transaction with the Jim Beam Brands Worldwide unit of Fortune Brands, Inc., and various acquisitions for South African Breweries plc, Riverdeep plc and MedImmune Inc.

Private Equity The London office regularly acts for leading financial institutions and institutional investors in equity investments throughout Europe. These transactions involve virtually all business sectors, ranging from infrastructure projects such as telecom (representative 2001 transactions included EON and Zone Vision) and power, to media and communications and real estate. The London office has five partners with considerable equity experience (two US qualified, three English qualified). The firm also regularly acts for participants in LBOs, private equity funds and structured financings in Western Europe.

Project Finance The firm is ranked second for power projects and eighth for all project finance transactions in Dealogic's 2001 global league tables. In addition, the projects group is ranked number two in Eastern Europe and number three in the power sector in the 2001 *Infrastructure Journal* league tables. Reflecting this ranking the London-based practice is strong in power, infrastructure, telecoms, petrochemicals and transportation and has a wealth of experience representing sponsors, lenders, international financial institutions and equity investors in projects throughout Europe, the Middle East and Africa. The only US firm to be nominated for the *Infrastructure Journal* Europe, Middle East and Africa (EMEA) award in 2001, the group is particularly well known for its work in Central and Eastern Europe including the former Soviet Union.

Tax The London office represents a substantial number of US and European financial institutions in connection with the structuring of complex, cross-border financial transactions, provides advice with respect to mergers and acquisitions and capital markets transactions and counsels multinational corporations on a wide range of international tax planning issues. One of the largest US tax practices in London, in 2001 the group was responsible for advising and closing on cross-border structured financing transactions with an aggregate value of over $9 billion.

DEWEY BALLANTINE

A-Z ■ LAW FIRMS

■ Diamond Heron
Corry House, 7-19 Royal Avenue, Belfast, BT1 1FB **Tel** (028) 9024 3726 **Fax** (028) 9023 0651

■ Dickinson Cruickshank & Co
PO Box 33, 33-37 Athol Street, Douglas, IM1 1LB **Tel** (01624) 647647 **Fax** (01624) 616448

Dickinson Dees
St Ann's Wharf, 112 Quayside, Newcastle upon Tyne, NE99 1SB
Tel (0191) 279 9000 **Fax** (0191) 279 9100 **DX** 61191
Email law@dickinson-dees.co.uk **Website** www.dickinson-dees.com

Senior Partner	Graham Wright
Managing Partner	Neil Braithwaite
UK	
Number of partners	62
Assistant solicitors	103
Other fee-earners	107
CONTACTS	
Commercial Property	Ian Ward
Company & Commercial	Nigel Bellis
Litigation	Glenn Calvert
Private Client	George Lyall

THE FIRM Dickinson Dees is the North East's largest law firm and one of the leading independent regional firms in the UK, providing a full range of services for corporate, public sector and private clients. The firm is a long-established practice with an impressive record in growth and staying power in recent years. It is one of the region's best connected professional services organisations with a national reputation for the quality of work undertaken for both public and private sector clients.

PRINCIPAL AREAS OF WORK The firm provides co-ordinated advice on a broad range of issues. It has an office in Brussels and associations with quality law firms in the major jurisdictions throughout the world. The firm offers a broad range of commercial and private client services. Traditionally strong in corporate mergers and acquisitions work and property development, it has a growing reputation for public sector work and also for PFI, transport and construction work where it has handled a range of projects of regional and national significance. The firm serves clients throughout the UK. Dickinson Dees has developed an innovative approach to delivery of services to clients, increasingly now involving the use of non-lawyer professionals. These include the online services 'Bizdocs' for cost-effective provision of documentation to clients and 'Web Wills' for provision of Wills. It has also established 'Remedy', a joint venture between the firm's nationally recognised human resources department and a leading human resources consultancy to provide a total outsourcing package to clients for all human resources/personnel requirements. The firm also has teams of non-lawyers specialising in financial planning, forensic accountancy, planning and pensions work, which complement the firm's specialised legal services. It has also developed a range of case management systems to support volume mortgage lending and conveyancing services. Dickinson Dees has developed a wide range of fully resourced specialist services supported by a substantial investment in IT and other support services.

Dickson Minto WS
11 Walker Street, Edinburgh, EH3 7NE
Tel (0131) 225 4455 **Fax** (0131) 225 2712

Royal London House, 22-25 Finsbury Square, , London, EC2A 1DX
Tel (020) 7628 4455 **Fax** (020) 7628 0027

Managing Partner	Bruce Minto
Senior Partner	Alastair Dickson
Number of partners	14
AREAS OF PRACTICE	
Company/Commercial/Corporate Finance	85%
Banking	15%
CONTACTS	
Banking	Michael Barron
Company/Commercial/Corporate Finance	Alastair Dickson

THE FIRM Established in 1985, the firm, through its offices in London, Edinburgh and Glasgow, has grown substantially and handles a full range of corporate transactions. The firm deals with transactions of all sizes and complexity for its wide range of clients, including private companies, listed companies and financial institutions. Dickson Minto has advised on some of the largest MBOs and MBIs in Europe, frequently involving numerous other jurisdictions in the USA, South America, Australasia and the Far East. The firm was lead advisor on the largest LBOs in Europe in each of the 1980s and 1990s.

PRINCIPAL AREAS OF WORK Although best known for its private equity work for financial institutions, the firm has specialist resources in the areas of investment funds, banking, financial services, EU and competition law, pensions law, information technology, intellectual property and taxation which enable it to advise its clients on a full range of corporate transactions. The firm has wide experience in dealing with and co-ordinating transactions involving other advisors, such as accountants, actuaries and environmental specialists and through its well established contacts with foreign lawyers in international transactions. The firm instructed lawyers in over 50 jurisdictions in the last year on behalf of its clients. Dickson Minto continues to expand and, through its emphasis on the recruitment and intensive training of high-quality staff, it has been able to maintain and continues to provide a flexible service, responsive and dedicated to the needs of all corporate clients, whether large, medium or small, private or public.

LAW FIRMS ■ A-Z

Digby Brown

The Savoy Tower, 77 Renfrew Street, Glasgow, G2 3BZ
Tel (0141) 566 9494 **Fax** (0141) 566 9500 **DX** GW17
Email maildesk@digbybrown.co.uk **Website** www.digbybrown.co.uk

7 Albyn Place, Edinburgh, EH2 4NG
Tel (0131) 225 8505 **Fax** (0131) 240 0949 **DX** ED 182
Email maildesk@digbybrown.co.uk

Royal Exchange, Panmure Street, Dundee, DD1 1DU
Tel (01382) 322197 **Fax** (01382) 205915 **DX** DD 26
Email maildesk@digbybrown.co.uk

Managing Partner	Graeme Garrett
Number of partners	12
Assistant solicitors	12
Other fee-earners	12

AREAS OF PRACTICE	
Pursuer Litigation	90%
Employment	4%
Conveyancing/Executry	6%

THE FIRM Digby Brown is one of the largest personal injury firms in Scotland with almost 90 years of experience in providing legal services. The firm has a strong geographical presence, with four offices across central Scotland. It specialises in pursuer reparation (approximately 90% of its work), where the firm has built up a reputation as a field leader in claims arising from accidents at work, industrial disease and road traffic accidents. The firm also covers employment law, conveyancing and welfare rights advice. It acts for Trade Union members as well as a large number of private clients on a no win no fee basis. The firm is also heavily committed to use of the latest technology in its everyday business, using permanent data link and digital voice lines between its offices, and constant desktop internet access for each fee-earner. All staff are well versed in the use of such technology to aide the progress of the case work. There are presently 12 partners in the firm, 12 assistant solicitors, three trainee solicitors and nine paralegals. The firm has expanded significantly over the last few years and continues to look towards further development. The firm is aware that the main strength of the firm lies in its personnel, and it remains committed to developing its talents and experience for the benefit of clients. Digby Brown's fee-earners work in litigation teams, representing clients in the Court of Session and the Sheriff Courts throughout the country. The firm has offices in Edinburgh, Glasgow, Dundee and Glenrothes.

Dixon, Coles & Gill

Bank House, Burton Street, Wakefield, WF1 2DA
Tel (01924) 373467 **Fax** (01924) 366234 **DX** 15030
Email box@dixon-coles-gill.co.uk **Website** www.dixon-coles-gill.co.uk

Ptnrs 4 **Other fee-earners** 2 **Contact** Linda M Box • The partners of the firm have been the Registrars to the Diocese of Wakefield since 1888.

D J Freeman

43 Fetter Lane, London, EC4A 1JU
Tel (020) 7583 4055 **Fax** (020) 7353 7377 **DX** 103 London Chancery Lane WC2
Email marketing@djfreeman.com **Website** www.djfreeman.com

Chief Executive	Laurence Harris
Senior Partner	Toby Greenbury
Number of partners	49
Assistant solicitors	84
Other fee-earners	38

CONTACTS	
Commercial Litigation	Kevin Perry
Commercial Property: Corporate & Joint Ventures	Graham Barber
Commercial Property: Development	Jonathan Lewis
Commercial Property: Investment	Susan Hall
Commercial Property: Litigation	Vivien King
Construction	David Johnson
E-commerce & IT	Clive Davies
Employment	David von Hagen
Insolvency & Restructuring	Colin Joseph
Insurance/Corporate & Regulatory	Richard Spiller
Insurance Insolvency	Vivien Tyrell
Insurance Litigation	David Kendall
IP, Branding & Trademarks	Alexander Carter-Silk

THE FIRM D J Freeman is a leading commercial practice focused on four broad business sectors: commercial property, insurance, technology and media, and commercial litigation. Within each business sector, multidisciplinary teams of lawyers take a commercial approach to providing clients with legal advice. Lawyers become familiar with the issues, opportunities and pressures their clients face and work to understand clients' businesses. The firm is acknowledged as an innovator in its use of technology and has won a reputation as a promoter of the use of plain English in legal documents.

PRINCIPAL AREAS OF WORK

Property The property services team deals with property development, leasing, acquisitions and disposals for some of the most important schemes in the UK. Corporate and tax lawyers advise on limited partnership structures, joint ventures, corporate acquisitions and restructuring work. A specialist property finance team advises banks, lending institutions and borrowers on all types of property finance and finance leasing transactions. Planning lawyers handle town planning appeals, local plan inquiries and frequently undertake advocacy work. Construction law specialists and property litigators deal with landlord and tenant disputes, rent reviews and arbitration.

Insurance The insurance team is one of the UK's leading insurance practices, specialising in coverage disputes, reinsurance, corporate finance and insolvency. Clients include major insurance companies, reinsurers, brokers, underwriting agents, P&I clubs and finance providers. Insurance litigators handle market and coverage disputes, third party and product liability claims and shipping contracts. A spe-

Continued overleaf

A-Z LAW FIRMS

cialist team handles all aspects of insurance company insolvency. Corporate and commercial lawyers deal with flotations, rights issues, the formation and authorisation of insurance and reinsurance companies, mergers and acquisitions, restructurings and joint ventures, including consortium and pool arrangements. D J Freeman is one of the leading firms advising on Lloyd's corporate capital and has particular expertise in insurance derivatives and other risk financing products.

Technology & Media The technology and media team's clients include three of the five leading terrestrial broadcasters, satellite channels, international publishing houses, and companies with interests in telecommunications, information technology and e-business. Media litigators handle high profile libel, copyright and contempt issues as well as contracts and other disputes. Corporate and commercial lawyers handle corporate finance transactions, provide regulatory advice to broadcasters, deal with programme acquisitions and advise on corporate contracts and joint ventures. The team includes a group of lawyers who specialise in IP, branding and trademark issues.

Commercial Litigation Commercial litigators act for major corporates, focusing on the requirements of in-house lawyers, in relation to a wide range of disputes. Lawyers handle some of the largest and most complex contractual disputes in the High Court as well as employment and insolvency matters. A public law team acts for a wide range of public sector and private bodies in administrative, regulatory, human rights and judicial review matters. International disputes are handled by the public international law team.

CONTACTS (Continued)	
Planning	Karen Howard
Property Finance	John Clark
Public International Law	Timothy Daniel
Public Law & Judicial Review	Laurence Harris
Taxation	Graham Chase
Technology & Media: Corporate	Tony Leifer
Technology & Media: Litigation	Susan Aslan

■ DJ Webb & Co
123 Commercial Road, London, EC1V 9HW **Tel** (020) 7247 9933 **Fax** (020) 7247 9444

■ DLA
3 Noble Street, London, EC2V 7EE **Tel** (08700) 111 111 **Fax** (020) 7796 6666

DMH

100 Queens Road, Brighton, BN1 3YB
Tel (01273) 329833 **Fax** (01273) 747500 **DX** 2703 Brighton 1
Email tim.aspinall@dmh.co.uk **Website** www.dmh.co.uk

Managing Partner	Tim Aspinall
Chairman	Derek Sparrow
Number of partners	33
Assistant solicitors	23
Other fee-earners	70

CONTACTS	
Commercial Litigation	Tim Aspinall
Commercial Property	Marion Wilcock
Corporate/Commercial	Ian Wilson
E-commerce	Justin Ellis
Employment	Rustom Tata
Innovation & Media	Tim Ashdown
Planning & Environment	Tony Allen
Private Client	Richard Pollins
Property Litigation	Tina George

THE FIRM DMH aims to be the law firm of choice throughout the South East; it operates from offices in Brighton, Gatwick and London. The firm's success has seen its continued growth and expansion. DMH's commercially astute lawyers offer specialist services structured around clients' markets, primarily in the technology, media and telecoms, land development, public service, retail, as well as arts and leisure sectors. Such a structure ensures that clients receive complete and creative solutions to the business challenges they face. In addition to this commercial practice a wide range of high quality private client services are offered, including onshore and offshore tax planning.

PRINCIPAL AREAS OF WORK

Corporate/Commercial The firm's corporate/commercial lawyers' skills go beyond putting together deals; they work closely with clients over several months, or more often years, to develop appropriate growth or exit strategies. This advice includes planning MBOs, takeovers, mergers and acquisitions and Stock Exchange flotations. In working towards these end goals DMH offers a combination of skills, including protecting and exploiting intellectual property rights, e-commerce and IT advice as well as reviewing commercial contracts.

Employment A distinguishing feature of DMH's employment team is its ability to do more than merely interpret current legislation; DMH offers creative solutions to practical problems faced by employers, employees and trade unions. The large team also conducts its own advocacy, appearing at Employment Tribunals and Employment Appeals throughout the UK.

Litigation The firm is well known for its litigation expertise and is skilled in handling large and complicated cases. The firm's litigators are particularly experienced in major commercial cases; trademark, domain name and IT disputes; professional negligence; property and construction cases; foreign litigation matters. DMH also has a dedicated debt recovery team handling large volumes of work.

Commercial Property Its ability to maximise the use of technology and handle large projects differentiates its large commercial property team from other regional players. DMH's team includes leading specialists in commercial conveyancing, planning and environmental law. The team works on all forms of freehold and leasehold transactions, with particular expertise in site assembly and development, development funding, joint ventures and institutional secured funding. In addition the firm has a team of in-house chartered town planners.

Other Areas The firm provides a wide range of private client services including onshore and offshore tax planning, residential conveyancing, wills, trusts and probate, family matters and personal injury claims.

INTERNATIONAL Clients with international interests benefit from the firm's membership of Law Europe and its associated offices in the USA.

Dolmans

17-20 Windsor Place, Cardiff, CF10 3DS
Tel (029) 2034 5531 **Fax** (029) 2039 8206 **DX** 33005 Cardiff 1

18A Merthyr Road, Whitchurch, Cardiff, CF4 1DG
Tel (029) 2069 2979 **Fax** (029) 2062 4415

Managing Partner	Adrian Oliver
Senior Partner	Jeffrey MacWilkinson
Number of partners	12
Assistant solicitors	20
Other fee-earners	12

CONTACTS	
Agency	John Wilkins
Company & Commercial	Johnathan Rees
Employment	Tracy Attwood
Insolvency	John Wilkins
Defendant Litigation	Jeffrey MacWilkinson
Landlord & Tenant	Claire Jones
Licensing	John Wilkins
Media	David Boobier
Motor Claims Litigation	Philip Bradley
Litigation	John Wilkins
Property	Simon Morgan
Sport	Hefin Archer-Williams
Wills, Trusts and Probate	Moy Lewis

THE FIRM Dolmans is a major Welsh firm providing commercial legal services to corporate, public sector and individual clients. Well known for its experience and expertise in litigation, property, commercial and private client work, the firm has an excellent relationship with a wide range of both public and private sector clients, ranging from local authorities and insurers to major Welsh businesses and SMEs.

PRINCIPAL AREAS OF WORK

Litigation The firm is dominant in the region for insurance and public sector defendant work, with the majority of instructions coming from local authorities and constabularies, either direct through insurers or others on both a regional and, increasingly, a national basis. Its workload covers employers' and public liability, personal injury, landlord and tenant work, and includes private sector work. The firm has a particular expertise and reputation in handling specialist areas of litigation, including occupational stress, sex abuse and harassment cases. Also well respected in the field of claimant litigation, Dolmans has a specialist motor claims litigation team which services claims on a national basis.

Corporate, Commercial & Employment Dolmans has a strong reputation for commercial and property work and is expanding its corporate, employment and property expertise. The business services team handles business start-ups, company formation, partnership agreements, takeovers, domestic conveyancing, property development, landlord and tenant, and institutional mortgages. The firm is also fast developing a reputation for its work in the field of media and entertainment and sports law.

Private Client Dolmans has a highly experienced private client team handling trusts, wills, probate and taxation, and complex estate planning.

Donald Rennie WS
7 Blinkbonny Cresent, Edinburgh, EH4 3NB **Tel** (0131) 476 7007 **Fax** (0131) 476 7008

Donnelly & Wall
Callender House, 58-60 Upper Arthur Street, Belfast, BT1 4GP **Tel** (028) 9023 3157 **Fax** (028) 9032 9743

Donns Solicitors
PO Box 41, The Observatory, Chapel Walks, Manchester, M60 1DZ **Tel** (0161) 834 3311 **Fax** (0161) 834 2317

Dorsey & Whitney

21 Wilson Street, London, EC2M 2TD
Tel (020) 7588 0800 **Fax** (020) 7588 0555 **DX** 33890 Finsbury Square
Email london@dorseylaw.com **Website** www.dorseylaw.com

Office Head	John Byrne
Number of partners	8
Assistant solicitors	15
Other fee-earners	3

CONTACTS	
Intellectual Property	Ian Craig, Niel Ackermann
Property	Nadeem Khan
Capital Markets	Jeffrey Hurlburt
Mergers & Acquisitions	John Byrne
	Andrew Rimmington
Private Equity	Jeffrey Hurlburt, Michael McFall
Media & Entertainment	Victoria Lockley
Employment Law	Steve Milne

THE FIRM Dorsey & Whitney is an international law firm with 21 offices throughout the world, with a strong international reputation in M&A, intellectual property and litigation/dispute resolution.

London Office Teams of UK & US lawyers specialise in international and cross-border mergers & acquisitions, capital markets, private equity (with particular TMT emphasis), general corporate advisory work, real estate and intellectual property (both contentious and non-contentious).

INTERNATIONAL In addition to offices throughout the USA, the firm has offices in London, Brussels, Tokyo, Hong Kong, Shanghai and Toronto.

A-Z LAW FIRMS

Dougherty & Associates
Ground Floor, Atlantic House, 4-8 Circular Road, Douglas, IM1 1AG
Tel (01624) 671155 **Fax** (01624) 610414
Email paul@doughertyassociates.com **Website** www.doughertyassociates.com

Contact Paul Dougherty • A niche practice dealing primarily with non-contentious trust and commercial work in the offshore environment. Involved in numerous transactions involving SPV's, complex trust structures in conjunction with tax advice given by experts in various jurisdictions. Has an adjunct corporate management company used to service the client base of the firm.

Douglas-Jones Mercer
147 St Helens Rd, Swansea, SA1 4DB
Tel (01792) 650000 **Fax** (01792) 656500 **DX** 39556 Swansea
Email post@djm.law.co.uk **Website** www.djm.law.co.uk

Contact T Marshall Phillips • A large provincal practice with specialist departments in conveyancing, probate, family, personal injury, insurance, crime, commercial and employment.

AREAS OF PRACTICE	
Defendant & Claimant PI	21%
Family	20%
Commercial	18%
Crime	16%
Conveyancing & Probate	15%
Civil	10%

Douglas & Partners
116 Grosvenor Road, St. Pauls, Bristol, BS2 8YA **Tel** (0117) 955 2663 **Fax** (0117) 954 0527

Douglas Wignall & Co
44 Essex Street, Strand, London, WC2R 3JF
Tel (020) 7583 1362 **Fax** (020) 7583 0532 **DX** 48 London/Chancery Lane
Email doug@easynet.co.uk

THE FIRM Douglas Wignall & Co specialises in hotels and leisure. Its niche is the drafting and negotiation of international management agreements mainly for hotels but also for other buildings such as arenas. Work also includes acquisitions and disposals of hotels, hotel franchise agreements and advising on all aspects of hotel operational matters. The practice also has experience in resort developments including timeshare and leaseback arrangements. The firm has been involved in many major hotel and resort projects in Europe (including the former CIS countries) as well as the UK and has many foreign clients. Douglas Wignall is a member of the International Society of Hospitality Consultants.

Sole Principal	Douglas Wignall

AREAS OF PRACTICE	
Hotels & Leisure	75%
Commercial & Residential Conveyancing	15%
Other Company/Commercial	10%

CONTACTS	
All Areas of Practice	Douglas Wignall

Doyle Clayton
69-70 Mark Lane, London, EC3R 7HS
Tel (020) 7702 3355 **Fax** (020) 7702 3322
Email pdoyle@doyleclayton.co.uk **Website** www.doyleclayton.co.uk

Ptnrs 4 **Asst solrs** 1 **Other fee-earners** 1 **Contact** Peter Doyle • Doyle Clayton is a leading niche employment practice based in the City of London. Clients include major plcs and private companies in particular within the retail and manufacturing sectors. The firm also acts for employees at all levels. The focus is upon providing a specialist service, giving clear, practical, and commercial advice.

AREAS OF PRACTICE	
Employment	90%
Company Commercial	10%

Draycott Browne
Peel Court, 45 Hardman Street, Manchester, M3 3PL **Tel** (0161) 833 1333 **Fax** (0161) 833 1444

Drummond Miller WS
32 Moray Place, Edinburgh, EH3 6BZ
Tel (0131) 226 5151 **Fax** (0131) 225 2608 **DX** 104 Edinburgh
Email reception@drummond-miller.co.uk **Website** www.drummondmiller.co.uk

Contact A Grant McCulloch • Litigation department handles a large volume of Court of Session actions on behalf of clients and correspondent solicitors. Also a substantial private client team and a large conveyancing department handling commercial and residential work.

AREAS OF PRACTICE	
Residential Conveyancing	24%
Sheriff Court (Civil)	23%
Court of Session (Reparation & Commercial Litigation)	22%
Trust/Executry	12%
Other	19%

LAW FIRMS ■ A-Z

Dundas & Wilson CS

Saltire Court, 20 Castle Terrace, Edinburgh, EH1 2EN
Tel (0131) 228 8000 **Fax** (0131) 228 8888 **Legal Post** LP2, EDINBURGH 6
Email dw-enquiries@dundas-wilson.com **Website** www.dundas-wilson.com

6th Floor Northwest Wing, Bush House, Aldwych, London, WC2B 4PA
Tel (020) 7240 2401 **Fax** (020) 7240 2448 **DX** 127 LDE

191 West George Street, Glasgow, G2 2LB
Tel (0141) 222 2200 **Fax** (0141) 222 2201 **Legal Post** LP1, GLASGOW 8

Chairman	Neil Cochran
Managing Partner	Chris Campbell
Number of partners	59
Assistant solicitors	163
Other fee-earners	54

CONTACTS
Industry Contacts

Financial Services	Michael Stoneham
Technology	Laurence Ward
Government Services	Michael McAuley
Real Estate	Donald Shaw
Energy & Utilities	Andrew Renton

Specialist Contacts

Banking	Stephen Phillips
Corporate	David Hardie
Employment, Pensions & Incentives	Eilidh Wiseman
IP/IT	Maureen Coutts
Litigation	Colin Macleod
Property	Iain Doran

THE FIRM Dundas & Wilson is a leading corporate and commercial law firm with a spread and depth of specialist skills largely unmatched in Scotland. The firm is one of the largest commercial law firms in Scotland. The operational structure is industry-focused, using teams of lawyers with different technical skills including banking, corporate, IP and IT, employment, pensions and incentives, property, litigation and infrastructure. Each team works closely together to service the needs of key industry sectors, with a particular focus on financial services, technology, government services, real estate and energy and utilities. Last year Chambers rated the firm top choice in 14 areas including financial services, banking, planning, insolvency, investment funds, local government, property and PFI.

PRINCIPAL AREAS OF WORK Dundas & Wilson has an exclusively corporate and commercial practice, providing the legal services listed in the specialist contacts box.

CLIENTELE Dundas & Wilson services a wide range of blue chip clients, including major corporates, financial institutions and public sector organisations, both at home and abroad.

DUNDAS & WILSON

■ Dundons

261 Lavender Hill, London, SW11 1JD **Tel** (020) 7228 2277 **Fax** (020) 7924 2759

DWF

5 Castle Street, Liverpool, L2 4XE
Tel (0151) 236 6226 **Fax** (0151) 236 3088 **DX** 14128 Liverpool
Email enquiries@dwf.co.uk **Website** www.dwf.co.uk

37 Peter Street, Manchester, M2 5GB
Tel (0161) 228 3702 **Fax** (0161) 835 2407 **DX** 14313 Manchester

Spencer House, 89 Dewhurst Road, Birchwood, Warrington, WA3 7PG
Tel (01925) 250800 **Fax** (01925) 250949 **DX** 719780 Birchwood, Warrington

Senior Partner	Jim Davies
Number of partners	55
Assistant solicitors	107
Other fee-earners	89

AREAS OF PRACTICE
Business Clients	65%
Insurance Clients	35%

CONTACTS
Asset Finance	Tony Bochenski
Banking	Tony Bochenski
Business Recovery	Andrew Gregory
Competition	Laurence Pritchard
Construction	Ross Wellman
Corporate	Andrew Needham
Debt Management	Sharon Williamson
Dispute Resolution	Graham Dagnall
Health, Safety & Environment	Andrew Leaitherland
Human Resources	Andrew Leaitherland
Insurance	Paul Berry
Intellectual Property	Laurence Pritchard
Internet & Technology	Laurence Pritchard
Licensing	Carl Bruder
Music, Media & Sport	Laurence Pritchard
Pensions	Mark Poulston
Planning	Marc Lovering
Property	Andy Green
Tax	Stan Blake
Training Services	Nigel Wallis
Wealthcare	Gary Donnellan

THE FIRM DWF (formerly Davies Wallis Foyster) has assembled an outstanding line up of specialist teams – including recognised market leaders – to deliver a comprehensive menu of world class services to its business clients and insurance clients. DWF acts for many active and growing companies in most business sectors – from high growth start-ups to multinational organisations – and has a proven track record of helping them achieve a genuine competitive edge. The firm has a reputation for the quality, style and energy of its people and its willingness to provide client references.

PRINCIPAL AREAS OF WORK Work handled for business clients includes asset finance, banking, business recovery, commercial agreements, competition, construction, corporate, debt management, dispute resolution, health safety and environment, human resources, insurance, intellectual property, internet and technology, licensing, music media and sport, pensions, planning, property, tax, training and wealthcare. Work handled for insurers includes accident and injury claims, legal expense insurance claims, commercial claims, policy documentation, recovery services and training. DWF delivers its services through a client team, selected to meet a client's particular needs, led by a Client Partner. DWF's constant drive to be in touch with the future for business has led to the development of innovative methods of service delivery. DWF HRhorizons, for example, is a unique 'single source' human resources package for HR professionals. DWF Maxima – the firm's purpose built centre for high volume, process driven legal services such as re-mortgaging, debt management and residential plot sales – is another example.

INTERNATIONAL DWF is a major player in the corporate finance market and cross-border work is a
Continued overleaf

www.ChambersandPartners.com

943

A-Z ■ LAW FIRMS

significant feature of the firm's capability. As well as having established relationships with many law firms around the world, DWF is also a member of EU-LEX International Practice Group, enabling the firm to co-ordinate legal work on behalf of clients wherever their business takes them.

RECRUITMENT DWF aims to attract and retain outstanding quality people across all its service areas to continue building on its success. The firm looks for employees who enjoy working as part of a busy team, who respond positively to a challenge and have what it takes to deliver results for clients. Contact Joanne Wright at the Manchester office.

■ Eamonn McEvoy & Co
22 Church Place, Lurgan, BT66 6EY **Tel** (028) 3832 7734 **Fax** (028) 3832 1760

■ Edmonds Bowen
4 Old Park Lane, London, W1K 1QW
Tel (020) 7629 8000 **Fax** (020) 7221 9334 **DX** 37217 Piccadilly
Email (name)@edmondsbowen.co.uk **Website** www.edmondsbowen.co.uk

AREAS OF PRACTICE	
Property/Private Client	35%
Media/Entertainment	25%
Company/Commercial	25%
Litigation/Dispute Resolution	15%

Ptnrs 4 **Other fee-earners** 5 • Provides client-orientated advice including corporate; employment; property; media/entertainment; sport; litigation and dispute resolution; and matrimonial.

Edward Fail Bradshaw & Waterson

402 Commercial Road, Stepney, London, E1 0LG
Tel (020) 7790 4032 **Fax** (020) 7790 2739 **DX** 300701 Tower Hamlets
Email main@efbw.co.uk

Managing Partner	John Lafferty
Senior Partner	Edward Preston
Number of partners	5
Assistant solicitors	6
Other fee-earners	9

CONTACTS	
Civil Litigation	John Lafferty
Criminal	Edward Preston
Family	Maeve O'Higgins

THE FIRM One of the oldest established firms in East London, Edward Fail have had a reputation as specialists in criminal law since the 1920s. A merger in 1961 with the general practice of Bradshaw & Waterson (founded in 1887) brought a wide range of legal services to the firm, and the merged practices have over a century of experience of dealing with the family and business problems of the area.

PRINCIPAL AREAS OF WORK The firm has a particularly strong reputation in the area of criminal law and deals with the whole spectrum of criminal offences, including serious crime, petty crime and white collar fraud. The firm also has thriving departments in family law and litigation.

■ Edwards & Co
28 Hill Street, Belfast, BT1 2LA **Tel** (028) 9032 1863 **Fax** (028) 9033 2723

■ Edwards Duthie
9-15 York Road, Ilford, IG1 3AD **Tel** (020) 8514 9000 **Fax** (020) 8514 9009

Edwards Geldard

Dumfries House, Dumfries Place, Cardiff, CF10 3ZF
Tel (029) 2023 8239 **Fax** (029) 2023 7268 **DX** 33001
Email info@geldards.co.uk **Website** www.geldards.com

44 The Ropewalk, Nottingham, NG1 5EL
Tel (0115) 840 4499 **Fax** (0115) 840 4500 **DX** 10010
Email info@geldards.co.uk

Number One Pride Place, Pride Park, Derby, DE24 8QR
Tel (01332) 331631 **Fax** (01332) 294295 **DX** 11509
Email info@geldards.co.uk

Senior Partner	Roderick Thurman
Number of partners	40
Assistant solicitors	60
Other fee-earners	72

AREAS OF PRACTICE	
Company/Commercial	40%
Property	25%
Litigation	20%
Other	15%

THE FIRM Edwards Geldard is one of the leading regional law firms. The firm's offices are located in Cardiff, Derby and Nottingham. Whilst continuing to expand the traditional areas of work in the company and commercial, commercial property, litigation and private client departments, the firm has acquired particular expertise in a variety of niche areas of legal work. These include mergers and acquisitions, corporate finance and banking, intellectual property, public law, planning and environmental law, energy law, rail and transport law, construction contracts and building arbitration, employment law, insolvency (in the UK and abroad), trusts and tax, secured lending, property litigation and clinical negligence. The firm's growth in recent years has been characterised by an expansion of its work for major Stock Exchange listed clients and for City of London based organisations and by the growing reputation of its work for public sector bodies and utilities. The firm also benefits from a strong core of work from the small to medium-size enterprise sector.

PRINCIPAL AREAS OF WORK The following services are offered from each office (initial enquiries can be directed to the most convenient office): company/corporate; intellectual property; EU law; environmental law; secured lending; construction and engineering; banking and insolvency; tax, trusts and estate administration; commercial contracts/utilities; employment; commercial property; property and development; planning and public law; commercial dispute resolution and clinical negligence; personal injury; private client.

INTERNATIONAL A variety of languages are spoken by members of the firm. These include French, German, Italian, Polish, Spanish, Ukrainian and Welsh.

Edwin Coe

2 Stone Buildings, Lincoln's Inn, London, WC2A 3TH
Tel (020) 7691 4000 **Fax** (020) 7691 4111 **DX** 191 London Chancery Lane WC2
Email law@edwincoe.com   **Website** www.edwincoe.com

THE FIRM The emphasis of this thriving London firm is on providing high quality advice on commercial and business issues to a worldwide client base. The firm is committed to providing a partner led service, which is responsive to clients' needs and achieves their objectives quickly and cost effectively.

PRINCIPAL AREAS OF WORK
Corporate The firm's corporate and commercial group acts for clients in all areas of business law and corporate activity including mergers, acquisitions, joint ventures and investments. Commercial work includes intellectual property, IT, sales and marketing activities. The group also has an acknowledged reputation in cross-border and international transactions, public offerings/flotations, banking work and new business start-ups.
Litigation The litigation group offers a complete dispute resolution service including arbitration and mediation, asset protection and recovery, banking, commercial litigation, factoring, fraud, insurance claims, intellectual property, landlord and tenant protection, professional and disciplinary tribunals and professional negligence claims.
Property The property group advises investors and developers, insurance companies, banks and retailers and undertakes all aspects of banking security work, property development, landlord and tenant, licensing, mortgages and debentures, planning, investment acquisitions, property portfolios and rent review advice.
Private Client The private client group specialises in the commercial development and management of the affairs of individuals and families and the creation and management of domestic and foreign trusts, charities, estate planning and administration, tax planning and wills.
Insolvency & Corporate Recovery The insolvency department is headed by a licensed practitioner and has strong connections with banks and accountants. It advises on all aspects of corporate reconstruction and recovery, on personal insolvency, company disqualification, professional licensing and disciplinary questions.
Employment The employment team advises on all contentious and non-contentious matters for employers and senior executives. Employment matters include drafting and reviewing service agreements, advising on transfer of undertakings on commercial transactions, how to handle disciplinary matters and representation at employment tribunals.

CLIENTELE Edwin Coe ensures that it understands the business of its clients and offers clear, practical advice. Clients include public and private companies, institutions, sovereign states, charities, unincorporated associations and private individuals. The firm receives instructions and referrals from other law firms. The firm has a seminar and briefing programme for clients and contacts, and partners have written standard works on several areas of law, including insolvency and the responsibility of directors.

INTERNATIONAL Instructions can be taken in Cantonese, French, German, Hebrew, Italian, Mandarin, Polish, Russian, Spanish and Urdu.

Senior Partner	John Tomlins
Number of partners	21
Assistant solicitors	10
Other fee-earners	12

AREAS OF PRACTICE	
Litigation	30%
Corporate	25%
Property	18%
Private Client	16%
Insolvency	6%
Employment	5%

CONTACTS	
Corporate	Russel Shear
Employment	Rachel Harrap
Insolvency	Christopher Berry
Litigation	David Greene
Private Client	John Shelford
Property	John Tomlins

A-Z ■ LAW FIRMS

■ Elaine Maxwell & Co
26 Sun Street, Lancaster, LA1 1EW
Tel (01524) 840810 **Fax** (01524) 840811
Email office@elainemaxwellsolicitors.co.uk **Website** www.elainemaxwellsolicitors.co.uk

AREAS OF PRACTICE	
Special Needs	70%
Student Cases	15%
Other Education, Disability & Community Care	15%

Contact Elaine Maxwell • Niche practice dealing solely with education law, community care for children, and disability discrimination in education. Acts nationwide for parents, students, schools and teachers, working closely with charities. Full Legal Aid franchise in education and community care.

Elborne Mitchell
One America Square, Crosswall, London, EC3N 2PR
Tel (020) 7320 9000 **Fax** (020) 7320 9111 **DX** 1063
Email lawyers@elbornes.com **Website** www.elbornes.com

Managing Partner	Alasdair Gillies
Senior Partner	Tim Brentnall

AREAS OF PRACTICE	
Insurance & Reinsurance	60%
Marine/Transport	20%
Commercial/Regulatory/ART	20%

CONTACTS	
ART	Andrew Pincott
Commercial	Chris Croft
Insurance	Tim Akeroyd
Marine/Transport	Peter Tribe
Professional Negligence	Timothy Goodger
Regulatory	Chris Croft
Reinsurance	Jolyon Patten

THE FIRM Elborne Mitchell is a specialist reinsurance, insurance and marine/transport law firm, which has a track record in acting in complex and high value cases within its particular areas of specialisation. In recent years the firm has widened its field to include engineering disputes and health and safety issues. The firm has also gained a reputation in the area of regulatory issues and alternative risk transfer. The firm is a forward-looking group of lawyers, ready to give constructive and independent advice to clients worldwide.

PRINCIPAL AREAS OF WORK Areas of specialism include insurance and reinsurance; marine and transport; commercial litigation; commercial, regulatory and alternative risk transfer.

■ Anselm Eldergill
Solicitors Chambers, 169 Malden Road, London, NW5 4HT **Tel** (020) 7284 1006 **Fax** (020) 7267 5113

■ Elizabeth McQuay - Sole Practitioner
The Old Rectory, Weston Road, Bletchingdon, Kidlington, OX5 3DH **Tel** (01869) 351229 **Fax** (01869) 350231

■ Elizabeth Cairns
Knowle Hill Farm, Ulcombe, Maidstone, ME17 1ES **Tel** (01622) 858191 **Fax** (01622) 858004

■ Elizabeth Rivers - Sole Practitioner
24 Diana Road, London, E17 5LF **Tel** (020) 8527 8654 **Fax** (020) 8523 4549

■ E & L Kennedy
72 High Street, Belfast, BT1 2BE **Tel** (028) 9023 2352 **Fax** (028) 9023 3118

■ Elliot Mather
The Courtyard, 49 Low Pavement, Chesterfield, S40 1PB **Tel** (01246) 231288 **Fax** (01246) 204081

Elliott Duffy Garrett

Royston House, 34 Upper Queen Street, Belfast, BT1 6FD
Tel (028) 9024 5034 **Fax** (028) 9024 1337 **DX** 400 NR Belfast
Email edg@edglegal.com **Website** www.edglegal.com

THE FIRM Elliott Duffy Garrett is a market leader in the provision of commercial legal services in Northern Ireland, offering expert legal advice to both the public and private sectors and to the local and international business communities. Underpinning this expertise is an understanding of the aspirations, objectives and business needs of clients and the recognition that they require a first class business service to the highest professional standards, care, quality and efficiency.

PRINCIPAL AREAS OF WORK

Company Law The firm advises on all aspects of banking and corporate finance; mergers and acquisitions; joint venture; management buyouts and buy-ins; secured lending; general banking law; inward investment; venture capital services; media and entertainment law.

Commercial Property & Planning This is a significant and widely recognised area of practice and includes commercial property development; institutional investment; investment acquisitions and disposals; planning and environmental law; landlord and tenant matters.

Employment Law Specialist advice is provided in relation to all aspects of employment and anti-discrimination law practice and human resources matters, to all types of public, private, commercial and other enterprises.

Litigation Work includes advice and representation, product liability, construction law, professional negligence, defamation, insurance, insolvency and general commercial litigation.

INTERNATIONAL The firm has links with leading law firms throughout the UK, Ireland, other EU countries, US and elsewhere in the world. Active membership of international groupings such as the IBA and Insol is encouraged. Languages spoken include French, German and Italian.

Managing Partner	Michael Lynch
Senior Partner	Harry Coll
Number of partners	12
Assistant solicitors	9
Other fee-earners	6

AREAS OF PRACTICE
Company Commercial	30%
Commercial Property	30%
Commercial Litigation	20%
Labour/Employment	15%
Insolvency	5%

CONTACTS
Commercial Property	W Laurence Mahood
Company Commercial	Kevin McVeigh
Employment Law	Harry Coll
Insolvency	Michael Wilson
Litigation	Michael Lynch

Elliotts

Centurion House, Deansgate, Manchester, M3 3WT
Tel (0161) 834 9933 **Fax** (0161) 832 3693 **DX** 14346
Email mail@elliott-law.co.uk

THE FIRM Manchester-based Elliotts Solicitors has been in the legal business for more than 30 years and during that time has built an enviable reputation for combining commercially aware advice with a personable, partner-led approach. Independent and offering a nationwide service, Elliotts puts a high value on teamwork and knows how important it is to be accessible to clients and to tailor legal advice to meet their particular needs.

PRINCIPAL AREAS OF WORK

Litigation Specialising in contentious work, the firm has particular experience in insurance law with niche expertise in personal injury, professional liability and employers liability. In the past year, the firm has established a specialist fraud department and a new division of the firm, Lincolns, which deals exclusively with the expanding claimant practice. The firm has also formalised its experience in construction claims, professional liability and high value commercial litigation with the creation of a commercial dispute resolution team.

Company/Commercial With extensive experience in the full range of company and commercial law, work includes advice on corporate finance matters and mergers and acquisitions.

Licensing Appearing in most of the 350 local licensing divisions, the department specialises in liquor, entertainment and gaming licences with niche expertise in applications for off licences in petrol station convenience stores.

Property Strengths include property advice to the retail and leisure sector complementing the firm's expertise in licensing and food safety, landlord and tenant advice, residential estate development and commercial property investment work.

Food Safety With Barry Holland as chairman of the food law group, the firm's national reputation as food safety experts continues.

Employment A specialist team provides advice both to employers and employees, including personal representation in employment tribunals.

INTERNATIONAL The firm is a founder member of the Euro-American Lawyers Group, which provides instant access to expert advice throughout Europe and America.

Senior Partner	Katharine Mellor
Number of partners	15
Assistant solicitors	15
Other fee-earners	8

CONTACTS
Aviation Law	Katharine Mellor
Commercial Litigation	Robert Jones
Commercial Property	David Walton
Company Commercial	Katharine Mellor
Construction	Michael Woolley
Employment Law	Fiona Miller
Insurance Litigation	Neal Samarji
	Graham Hughes
Intellectual Property	Robert Jones
Licensing	Barry Holland
Motor Litigation	Clare Edwards
Personal Injury	Julian Holt
	Sarah Temperley
Private Client	Tim Chapman
Professional Negligence	Sarah Naylor

A-Z ■ LAW FIRMS

■ Ellis Jones
Sandbourne House, 302 Charminster Road, Bournemouth, BH8 9RU **Tel** (01202) 525333 **Fax** (01202) 535935

■ Ellisons
Headgate Court, Head Street, Colchester, CO1 1NP **Tel** (01206) 764477 **Fax** (01206) 764455

■ Ellis Wood
Langdales, New Garden House, 78 Hatton Garden, London, EC1N 8LD **Tel** (020) 7242 1194 **Fax** (020) 7831 9480

■ Eric Robinson & Co
359 Bitterne Road, Bitterne, Southampton, SO18 1DN **Tel** (02380) 425000 **Fax** (02380) 446594

■ Ernst & Young
Becket House, 1 Lambeth Palace Road, London, SE1 7EU **Tel** (020) 7951 2000 **Fax** (020) 7951 1345

■ Erskine MacAskill & Co
21 Stafford Street, Edinburgh, EH3 7BJ
Tel (0131) 622 6062 **Fax** (0131) 622 6066 **DX** 191 Edinburgh

Ptnrs 2 **Associates** 2 **Asst solrs** 1 **Contact** Sarah Erskine • Specialist matrimonial and child law practice. Also undertakes conveyancing and criminal defence work.

AREAS OF PRACTICE	
Matrimonial/Child Law	53%
Criminal Defence Work	22%
Conveyancing	20%
Others	5%

■ Evans Butler Wade
165 Greenwich High Road, London, SE10 8JA **Tel** (020) 8858 8926 **Fax** (020) 8858 8131

Evans Dodd

5 Balfour Place, Mount Street, London, W1K 2AU
Tel (020) 7491 4729 **Fax** (020) 7499 2297 **DX** 44644 Mayfair
Email mail@evansdodd.co.uk

THE FIRM Established in 1975 as a commercial practice with a strong international bias.

PRINCIPAL AREAS OF WORK
Company & Commercial All aspects of company and commercial work including public and private corporate law; acquisitions; new issues; joint ventures; banking and finance; aircraft acquisitions; financing and tax planning.
Commercial Property Commercial property acquisitions, sales, leases and financing. Domestic property work also undertaken.
Litigation All types of claims, including commercial litigation, contractual disputes, employment and matrimonial matters, debt recovery and professional negligence.

Managing Partner	Geoffrey Dodd
Senior Partner	Geoffrey Dodd
Number of partners	5
Assistant solicitors	3
Other fee-earners	1

AREAS OF PRACTICE	
Company & Commercial	50%
Litigation	25%
Property	15%
Taxation	10%

CONTACTS	
Company & Commercial	Geoffrey Dodd
Litigation	Jeremy Hershkorn
Commercial Property	Joseph Hyde

Everatt & Company

101 High Street, Evesham, WR11 4DN
Tel (01386) 769160 **Fax** (01386) 769196 **DX** 16167 EVESHAM
Email post@everatt.co.uk

THE FIRM Specialists in defendant personal injury litigation since its foundation in 1970, Everatt & Company has earned a reputation within its field that is the envy of many a large legal firm. Its size and independence has played a significant part in this success, ensuring levels of flexibility, internal communication and access to partners that clients rarely see elsewhere. Its central location, too, has been a factor, placing the majority of UK courts within serviceable reach.

PRINCIPAL AREAS OF WORK
Defendant Personal Injury Litigation Work includes employers' liability; motor accident claims; industrial deafness; work-related upper limb disorders; asbestos-related claims; other respiratory claims; hand/arm vibration syndrome/VWF; catastrophic injury; work-related stress claims.

CLIENTELE The firm acts for insurance companies, both large and small, and various liability adjusters.

RECRUITMENT The firm has recruited individuals and trained them through to qualification. It is strongly committed to internal training.

Senior Partner	Catherine Arkell
Number of partners	5
Assistant solicitors	4
Other fee-earners	8

AREAS OF PRACTICE	
Defendant Personal Injury	90%
Other	10%

LAW FIRMS A-Z

Eversheds

Senator House, 85 Queen Victoria Street, London, EC4V 4JL
Tel (020) 7919 4500 **Fax** (020) 7919 4919 **DX** 83 Chancery Lane WC2
Email derby@eversheds.com   **Website** www.eversheds.com

115 Colmore Row, Birmingham, B3 3AL
Tel (0121) 232 1000 **Fax** (0121) 236 1900 **DX** 13004
Email birmingham@eversheds.com

Cloth Hall Court, Infirmary Street, Leeds, LS1 2JB
Tel (0113) 243 0391 **Fax** (0113) 245 6188 **DX** 12027 Leeds-27
Email leeds@eversheds.com

Kett House, 1 Station Road, Cambridge, CB1 2JY
Tel (01223) 443666 **Fax** (01223) 443777 **DX** 5807
Email eastofengland@eversheds.com

Fitzalan House, Fitzalan Road, Cardiff, CF24 0EE
Tel (029) 2047 1147 **Fax** (029) 2046 4347 **DX** 33016
Email cardiff@eversheds.com

1 Royal Standard Place, Nottingham, NG1 6FZ
Tel (0115) 950 7000 **Fax** (0115) 950 7111 **DX** 10031
Email nottingham@eversheds.com

Franciscan House, 51 Princes Street, Ipswich, IP1 1UR
Tel (01473) 284428 **Fax** (01473) 233666 **DX** 3249
Email eastofengland@eversheds.com

Holland Court, The Close, Norwich, NR1 4DX
Tel (01603) 272727 **Fax** (01603) 610535 **DX** 5206
Email eastofengland@eversheds.com

Eversheds House, 70 Great Bridgewater Street, Manchester, M1 5ES
Tel (0161) 831 8000 **Fax** (0161) 832 5337 **DX** 14344
Email manchester@eversheds.com

Central Square South, Orchard Street, Newcastle upon Tyne, NE1 3XX
Tel (0191) 241 6000 **Fax** (0191) 241 6499 **DX** 724321 Newcastle 24
Email newcastle@eversheds.com

Managing Partner	David Ansbro
Chairman	Keith James
Number of partners (UK)	332
Assistant solicitors (UK)	889
Other fee-earners (UK)	618
AREAS OF PRACTICE	
Corporate/Commercial	35%
Property	22%
Litigation/Dispute Management	19%
Human Resources	12%
Commoditised Services	12%

THE FIRM Eversheds has over 2000 legal and business advisors providing services to the private and public sector business and finance community. Access to all these services is provided through 17 European offices and three associated offices in Asia. Eversheds combines local market knowledge and access with the specialisms, resources and international capability of one of the world's largest law firms. Most commercial law firms offer clients the same core services, and Eversheds is no exception. Its difference, and its competitive advantage, lies in its strength and depth. It has vast resources and an unparalleled breadth of expertise and industry know-how.

PRINCIPAL AREAS OF WORK Alongside the five core areas of corporate, commercial, litigation and dispute management, property and human resources, Eversheds has established a sixth practice group, which consolidates volume conveyancing, mortgage enforcement, sales in possession, commercial recoveries, claims management, defendant personal injury and litigation support. Each Eversheds office provides expertise in a range of specialist legal services and market sectors. Specialist services are: business risk services; computer/IT; corporate tax; environment/health and safety; EU/competition; franchising; insolvency; intellectual property; international public law; licensing; PFI; planning; pensions; private capital/tax and venture capital. Market sectors include: banking; bioscience; chemicals; construction; education; energy; engineering; financial services; insurance and reinsurance; e-commerce; technology; media and communications; public sector and retail/leisure.

INTERNATIONAL The firm has overseas offices in Brussels, Monaco and Paris. Associated offices are located in Copenhagen, Milan, Rome and Sofia and three offices in Asia (Hong Kong, Kuala Lumpur and Singapore).

EVERSHEDS
Business Lawyers in Europe

A-Z ■ LAW FIRMS

■ Evill and Coleman

113 Upper Richmond Road, Putney, London, SW15 2TL
Tel (020) 8789 9221 **Fax** (020) 8789 7978 **DX** 59451 Putney
Email enquiries@evillandcoleman.co.uk **Website** www.evillandcoleman.co.uk

Ptnrs 4 **Asst solrs** 4 **Other fee-earners** 5 **Contact** Dominic Fairclough • Leading reputation in personal injury and clinical negligence claims. Legal Services Commission franchise in personal injury and clinical negligence. Conducted many ground breaking cases in these fields.

Faegre Benson Hobson Audley

7 Pilgrim Street, London, EC4V 6LB
Tel (020) 7450 4510 **Fax** (020) 7450 4544 **DX** 401 London
Email lawyers@faegre.com **Website** www.faegre.com

Joint Managing Partners	Gerald Hobson
	Gale Mellum

AREAS OF PRACTICE	
Corporate Finance/M&A	20%
Company/Commercial/Financial Services	25%
Employment & Labour Law	10%
Innovation & Technology	10%
Dispute Resolution	20%
Property	15%

THE FIRM Faegre Benson Hobson Audley is a multinational partnership of English and American lawyers in London, formed between Faegre & Benson LLP and Hobson Audley to provide English business law services to US clients and American business law services to English clients. Faegre & Benson LLP is a firm of more than 375 lawyers with offices in Frankfurt and Shanghai, and in the United States in Minnesota, Denver, Boulder and Des Moines. Hobson Audley is a firm of more than 35 solicitors in London. In the London office, English business law services are provided in corporate and commercial finance; intellectual property; innovation and technology; employment, dispute solution and real estate matters. American business law advice is provided in London and through the US offices of Faegre & Benson LLP, both on US corporate law and on commercial transactions, including acquisitions; incorporations; joint ventures; distribution agreements; product liability; employment and labour law and immigration.

INTERNATIONAL The firm handles transactions in French, German, Italian, Portuguese and Spanish.

■ Fairmays

10 Babmaes St, London, SW1Y 6HD
Tel (020) 7959 0202 **Fax** (020) 7959 0234 **DX** 37219 Piccadilly
Email advice@fairmays.com **Website** www.fairmays.com

Managing Partner	Andrew Miller
Number of partners	9
Assistant solicitors	8
Other fee-earners	8

AREAS OF PRACTICE	
Company/Commercial	30%
Litigation	30%
Property	30%
Private Client	10%

CONTACTS	
Company/Commercial	Robert Brooks
Litigation	Tony Guise
Private Client	Andrew Miller
Property	Nick Plaut

THE FIRM Founded in 1981 Fairmays is a progressive international commercial practice specialising in company/commercial, litigation, property and private client work. The firm has considerable experience of doing business in India and the Middle East. The firm's international clientele includes a significant proportion of high net worth individuals and SMEs. As a consequence it has developed the skills necessary to meet the demands of that particular market sector and handles a significant amount of new start-up, corporate finance and flotation work coupled with advice in the fields of IP/IT, employment and immigration (both individual and corporate). Its private client department offers a sophisticated tax planning service and works closely with the company/commercial department to provide strategic planning advice to the firm's clients both on an individual and on a corporate level. The firm also seeks to add value to its core commercial and business services by offering a discreet matrimonial service within the litigation department. Fairmays has established an infrastructure in its offices in St James' to augment the service which it provides to its clients both on and offline, including the availability of video conferencing facilities. The firm is proud of its ability to work closely with a discreet network of other service providers both in the UK and Europe to offer a depth of service which belies its size. Fairmays strives to offer a competitively priced yet high quality personal service to its clients, working in tandem with them to produce innovative solutions to their business problems.

LAW FIRMS ■ A-Z

The Family Law Consortium

2 Henrietta Street, London, WC2E 8PS
Tel (020) 7420 5000 **Fax** (020) 7420 5005 **DX** 40012 Covent Garden
Email flc@tflc.co.uk **Website** www.tflc.co.uk

Number of partners	7
Assistant solicitors	5
Other fee-earners	3

THE FIRM Based in Covent Garden this central London practice with its distinctive approach was formed in 1995 as (probably) England's first family law practice to combine lawyers, mediators and counsellors. It now comprises 12 lawyers (10 of whom are also mediators) who specialise exclusively in family law. Important members from the outset are two very experienced non-lawyer mediators and counsellors. Six lawyers were previously heads of family law departments in London practices.

Services The firm provides for all stages of relationship help: co-habitation and pre-marriage agreements and pre-relationship counselling; relationship counselling; resolutions on relationship breakdown, whether through law, mediation, counselling or ADR. Flexibility in charging rates results in covering low/medium finance work (two lawyers are top CSA specialists) to 'big money' complex finance cases, especially with an international element or family companies and trusts. Children work with specialisation in child abduction and voluntary taking abroad. Leading lawyers and mediators in co-habitation (finance and children) arrangements. Clients include entertainment and IT industries and the professions.

Focus Growth in six years from eight staff to over 30 is as a result, in part, of the distinctive approach adopted. The practice seeks conciliatory and constructive solutions, including beyond the formulaic. It focuses on wider needs and concerns of clients and their families. It brings mediation skills to legal work. Ancillary in-house professions are available to provide wider perspectives and solutions. There is accessibility for clients, in hours of work (within reason) but especially manner of communication. It works in partnership with clients to reduce cost and meet clients' styles. It tries to keep clients out of Court but will assertively represent at Court when needed for a fair outcome. More details at www.tflc.co.uk which has recently been voted one of the two top law firm websites for specialist and private client practices. Out of hours contact James Pirrie on (01727) 811478/mobile (07989) 303637.

Farleys

22-27 Richmond Terrace, Blackburn, BB1 7AQ
Tel (01254) 606000 **Fax** (01254) 583526 **DX** 13604 Blackburn 3
Email info@farleys.com **Website** www.farleys.com

Senior Partner	Michael Corrigan
Number of partners	13
Assistant solicitors	27
Other fee-earners	36

AREAS OF PRACTICE	
Civil Litigation	30%
Criminal	25%
Family	25%
Commercial & Property	15%
Probate/Private Client	5%

CONTACTS	
Actions Against the Police	Joanne Kearsley
Company/Commercial	Chris Porter
	Ian Liddle, Debbie King
Crime	Paul Schofield, Andrew Church-Taylor
	Bernard Horne, Kevin Preston
	Rachel Adamson
Matrimonial	Kathryn L Hughes
	Barbara Crook, Ann Bamford
	Anthony Rebello, Antonia Love
	Karen Frankland
Mental Health	Joseph Mulderig
Personal Injury/Litigation	Michael Corrigan
	Desmond Draper, Stephen McNeill
	Kieran O'Connor, Jonathan Bridge
	Beverley Jenkinson, Martin Thomas
Clinical Negligence	Kieran O'Connor
Property & Private Client	Peter Leyland
	Philip Taylor

THE FIRM Established in 1957, Farleys is a broad-based practice encompassing specialised departments in its offices in Blackburn, Accrington and Burnley. The firm has a strong and continually expanding client base built upon a reputation across the North West of England for providing a high level of service both to publicly funded and private clients together with an increasing number of well-known commercial clients. Farleys has Public Funding contracts for family, criminal, actions against the police and mental health.

PRINCIPAL AREAS OF WORK

Commercial This successful and expanding department covers all aspects of company and commercial work, with extensive expertise in entrepreneurial and manager-owned businesses.

Personal Injury/General Litigation The firm handles personal injury, professional negligence, employment matters and environmental disputes. Members of the Personal Injury Panel and the Mental Health Review Tribunal Panel.

Clinical Negligence The firm deals with all aspects of clinical negligence work.

Human Rights/Actions Against the Police Successful and developing areas of expertise particularly focused on actions against the police, police complaints and death in custody. The named contact is the northern co-ordinator for the police action lawyers group.

Family/Matrimonial The firm has one of the largest family law departments in the North West with considerable expertise in all aspects of family law, including care proceedings and substantial ancillary relief matters.

Criminal One of Lancashire's busiest and most effective criminal practices, dealing with all matters. The department has a special case work unit with extensive expertise in serious fraud/complex crime. Member of the Legal Services Commission's Serious Fraud Panel.

Property The firm handles all aspects of private client property transactions.

Private Client An extensive range of services is offered in the area of wills, probate, trustee and executorship.

A-Z ■ LAW FIRMS

Farrer & Co

66 Lincoln's Inn Fields, London, WC2A 3LH
Tel (020) 7242 2022   **Fax** (020) 7242 9899   **DX** 32 London Chancery Lane WC2
Email enquiries@farrer.co.uk   **Website** www.farrer.co.uk

THE FIRM Farrer & Co is one of the UK's leading law practices. It provides a range of specialist advice to private, institutional and corporate clients. The firm has long been recognised for the quality of its service, both technical and personal. This has been achieved by consistently recruiting team players possessing flair and intellect coupled with a desire to exceed clients' expectations. Their client base is worldwide and clients are frequently leaders in their fields. To meet the increasingly specialised demands of clients, the firm is divided into flexible, client-focused teams. Its breadth of expertise is reflected in the fact that it has an outstanding reputation in fields as diverse as family law, offshore tax planning, employment, heritage work, charity law and defamation.

PRINCIPAL AREAS OF WORK

Private Client The firm is recognised as an established leader in the services it provides to its private clients. Core work includes tax planning, heritage property, wills and the administration of estates, probate and trusts. Agricultural estates and private property specialists advise on property matters, while clients also benefit from the firm's strong reputation in management and employment practices. The family team is highly regarded and advises on family disputes arising from marriage breakdown or inheritance claims, family provision and child-related issues.

Institutional Work for institutions is focused on a highly successful and expanding charities team. In addition to charity law, teams advise these clients on taxation, employment, sponsorship and intellectual property issues. The firm has long had a reputation for advising sports industry clients and for its work for museums, galleries and educational organisations.

Commercial A full range of work is undertaken for commercial clients, with notable expertise in the media industry. Specialisations include employment and pensions, mergers and acquisitions, intellectual property, corporate tax, e-business, banking and FSA. The commercial property team manages all types of work for clients, while the litigation team has advised on almost every type of business dispute: contract, fraud, insolvency, construction, asset recovery, libel, government inspections and prosecutions.

INTERNATIONAL The firm handles work in French and German.

RECRUITMENT Six to eight trainee solicitors are recruited annually; a 2(1) degree is preferred, not necessarily in law. Applications to the Graduate Recruitment Manager.

Senior Partner	Robert Clinton
Chief Executive	Andrew Mills-Baker
Number of partners	52
Assistant solicitors	52
Other fee-earners	34

CONTACTS	
Agriculture	Simon Pring
Banking & FSA	Jonathan Bayliss
Charities	Judith Hill
	Anne-Marie Piper
Commercial Property	Raymond Cooper
Company/Commercial	James Thorne
E-commerce	Peter Wienand
Education	David Smellie
Employment & Pensions	David Smellie
Estates & Private Property	James Furber
Family	Richard Parry
Heritage Property	Judith Hill
	Michael Chantler
Intellectual Property	Peter Wienand
International Private Client	Mark Bridges
Litigation	Adrian Parkhouse
Media	Robert Clinton
	Rupert Grey
Private Client	Richard Powles
Sport	Karena Vleck

■ Fennemores

200 Silbury Boulevard, Central Milton Keynes, Milton Keynes, MK9 1LL   **Tel** (01908) 678241   **Fax** (01908) 665985

Fenners

15 New Bridge Street, London, EC4V 6AU
Tel (020) 7936 8000   **Fax** (020) 7936 8100   **DX** 256 Chancery Lane, London WC2
Email info@fenners.com   **Website** www.fenners.com

THE FIRM Fenners is a dynamic specialist City law firm, providing high quality legal services combining energy and innovation with senior level experience. Fenners specialises in corporate law, including corporate finance and mergers and acquisitions, commercial law, commercial property, banking and technology law, employment law, competition law, planning and residential development and offers a leading capability in urban regeneration. Fenners has a broad client base including public and private, domestic and overseas companies, financial advisors, banks and other institutions. The firm provides a wide range of legal services internationally through its associate law firms in the EU and the USA.

PRINCIPAL AREAS OF WORK

Corporate Work includes IPOs; rights issues and other secondary issues; venture capital funding; the raising of debt and private placings; public takeovers; share and asset sales; MBOs; MBIs; public to private transactions; joint venture arrangements; corporate reorganisations; investment funds.

Commercial Property The firm handles investment acquisitions and disposals; site assembly and development (retail, office, residential and industrial); regional and city centre schemes involving both the public and private sectors; institutional funding and forward sale agreements; commercial lettings for

Senior Partner	John Fenner
Managing Partner	Robert Fenner
Number of partners	6
Other fee-earners	9
Total staff	25

AREAS OF PRACTICE	
Corporate/Commercial	40%
Commercial Property	40%
Banking	20%

CONTACTS	
Banking	David Wisbey
Commercial Property	John Fenner
	Caroline Frampton
Corporate/Commercial	Robert Fenner
	Adam Fenner
Property Development	Caroline Frampton
	Jeremy Raj

Fenners

landlords and tenants; building agreements; environmental issues. The firm also has a dedicated residential investment team.

Commercial Work handled includes joint ventures; intellectual property; the laws relating to the internet and e-commerce; data protection; consumer credit; franchising; employment law; employee share option schemes; competition law.

Banking Including secured and unsecured lending; syndicated lending; mezzanine financing and reconstructions; property financing; limited partnerships and investment vehicles; securitisations.

Planning Fenners handles redevelopment schemes; urban regeneration schemes; planning agreements for infrastructure work; planning gain and use restrictions; planning appeals and inquiries.

Development Site assembly and acquisition; management schemes; sales; town planning and related matters are handled.

INTERNATIONAL The firm maintains associations with law firms throughout Europe, the USA and Israel. Languages spoken include French, German, Italian and Portuguese.

Fenwick Elliott

353 Strand, London, WC2R 0HS
Tel (020) 7956 9354 **Fax** (020) 7956 9355 **DX** 178 LDE
Email reception@fenwickelliott.co.uk **Website** www.fenwickelliott.co.uk

Number of partners	10
Assistant solicitors	8
Other fee-earners	3

AREAS OF PRACTICE	
Contentious Construction (inc. ADR & Arbitration)	60%
Non-contentious Construction	35%
Other Related Work	5%

THE FIRM Fenwick Elliott is a commercial law firm, which specialises exclusively in building, engineering and energy law. The firm provides a cost-effective service, drawing on a wealth of expertise to provide commercially aware and practical advice. The partners of the firm are members of the Technology and Construction Solicitors Association and the Society of Construction Law. Members of the firm are CEDR accredited mediators and are Fellows of the Chartered Institute of Arbitrators. All partners are TeCSA accredited adjudicators and several partners are on other industry panels. The partners speak regularly on construction law matters at conferences and contribute to Television Education Network and LNTV programmes on construction and dispute resolution. A member of the firm is a commissioner of the Foundation for International Arbitration. Another member is Chairman of the Society of Construction Law, President of the European Society of Construction Law, Master of the Worshipful Company of Arbitrators and a Fellow of the Chartered Institute of Building. Another member is editor of the Construction Industry Law Letter.

PRINCIPAL AREAS OF WORK

Contentious The firm handles large volumes of litigation, arbitration, adjudication and alternative dispute resolution. Defects claims, loss and expense claims, the securing of prompt payment, design liability, professional negligence and jurisdictional disputes are among the issues frequently dealt with. Particular regard is given to troubleshooting to assist the early resolution of any dispute.

Non-contentious The firm's burgeoning non-contentious practice includes pre-contract advice on terms and conditions of tender, negotiation and drafting of all types of contracts, from sub-contracts to joint venture agreements, including contracts for the engagement of professionals, bonds and warranties. Planning and environmental law considerations and insurance matters are also dealt with. The practice also has considerable experience of BOT type schemes in the areas of water and power and PFI schemes, in particular in the health and education sectors.

CLIENTELE The firm acts nationally and internationally for developers, institutional investors, local authorities, utilities, main contractors, specialist subcontractors, architects, engineers, surveyors, PFI consortia and private clients. Further, the firm acts for various foreign government corporations. Most of the firm's clients are well known in the construction industry.

INTERNATIONAL Work is also handled in French.

Few & Kester

Chequers House, 77-81 Newmarket Rd, Cambridge, CB5 8EU **Tel** (01223) 363111 **Fax** (01223) 323370

Fenwick Elliott
SOLICITORS

A-Z LAW FIRMS

Field Cunningham & Co

St. John's Court, 70 Quay St, Manchester, M3 3EJ
Tel (0161) 834 4734 **Fax** (0161) 834 1772 **DX** 728855 Manchester 4

Senior Partner	Peter Ashworth
Number of partners	3
Assistant solicitors	5
Other fee-earners	10

AREAS OF PRACTICE	
Commercial Property	78%
Commercial Litigation	15%
Company Commercial	5%
Private Client	2%

THE FIRM Established in 1867, Field Cunningham & Co is a successful niche commercial property practice specialising in development work and associated commercial and property litigation. It places much importance on providing a high level of personal service and commitment within a commercial environment.

PRINCIPAL AREAS OF WORK

Commercial Property The firm deals with all aspects of commercial property, with particular emphasis on development work in the retail, residential, office, leisure and commercial sectors, development funding, and joint ventures. Activities include work in associated planning, environmental and Lands Tribunal matters. An increasing volume of property secured lending work is being undertaken on behalf of banks. In addition to its commercial development and redevelopment work, the firm acts for national and local house-builders; the volume of new house sales undertaken is approximately one per cent annually of all UK private housing starts.

Commercial Litigation Especially in property and construction-related and environmental matters. Also intellectual property; employment and general commercial disputes.

Company/Commercial Private company sales and purchases; joint ventures; MBOs; business start-ups; partnerships; intellectual property and employment.

RECRUITMENT The firm normally takes one law graduate (2:1 required) annually. Applications by covering letter and CV.

Field Fisher Waterhouse

35 Vine Street, London, EC3N 2AA
Tel (020) 7861 4000 **Fax** (020) 7488 0084 **DX** 823 London City EC3
Email london@thealliancelaw.com **Website** www.thealliancelaw.com

Managing Partner	Colin McArthur
Senior Partner	John Wilson
Number of partners	77
Assistant solicitors	108
Other fee-earners	61

CONTACTS	
Anglo-French Trade	Marie-Caroline Frochot
Anglo-German/Austrian Trade	Babette Marzheuser-Wood
Aviation	Simon Chamberlain
Banking & Finance	Jon Fife, John Wilson
Capital Markets	Jon Fife, Guy Usher
Commercial Property	Howard Coffell, John Pedder
Competition	Charles Whiddington
Construction	Lawrence Bruce, Mark Lowe
Corporate	Tim Davies
Derivatives	Guy Usher, Jon Fife
E-commerce	Michael Chissick
Employee Benefits	Graeme Nuttall
Employment	Margaret Davis
Energy & Pipelines	Howard Coffell
Financial Services Regulation	Christopher Bond
Franchising & Licensing	Mark Abell
Hotels & Leisure	Paul Houston
Immigration	Alison Morris
Intellectual Property	Mark Abell
International Trade & Projects	John Wilson
Investment Funds & Products	Kirstene Baillie
IT	Michael Chissick, Nigel Wildish
Licensing	Peter Glazebrook
Litigation (Commercial)	Mark Lowe
Litigation (IP/IT)	Nick Rose
Media	Ellen Fleming
Medical Litigation	Paul McNeil
Partnership	Colin McArthur
Patents	Jonathan Radcliffe
Pensions	Belinda Benney
Personal Injury	Rodney Nelson-Jones
PFI/Projects	Nicholas Thompsell, Lawrence Bruce

THE FIRM Field Fisher Waterhouse has a substantial corporate and commercial practice. The firm has a reputation for providing an excellent all-round service to an impressive list of UK and international clients. In April 2002, the firm launched The European Legal Alliance with four other leading commercial law firms: Buse Heberer Fromm in Germany; Dubarry Le Douarin Veil in France; Beauchamps in Ireland; Harper Macleod in Scotland. The firms have worked together for some years and now operate under a single brand and on an exclusive basis with each other. The Alliance provides FFW with a full presence in 11 other key European business centres as well as London. The next stage in the Alliance's development is for Italian and Spanish firms to join, closely followed by establishing a presence in other key European jurisdictions. A distinctive feature of the firm is the number of close and long-standing relationships which it has developed with its clients, achieved by ensuring a high quality service and maintaining a high level of partner involvement in clients' affairs. The firm is well known for its commercial and practical approach and for its ability to create innovative solutions to legal problems.

PRINCIPAL AREAS OF WORK The firm's core practice areas are: corporate; brands, technology, media and telecommunications; banking and finance; commercial property. Other areas in which the firm has a leading reputation are: corporate tax; employment; employee share schemes; pensions; investment funds and products; commercial litigation and arbitration; partnership; personal injury and medical negligence. The firm has a substantial public sector practice, acting for many of the main government departments, several local authorities and other public bodies. The firm is also well known for its expertise in a number of industry sectors. They include: aviation; energy; financial services; franchising; health; hotels and leisure; rail; ship building and ship finance; sport; technology; travel and tourism.

CLIENTELE The firm has a wide-ranging UK and overseas client base. It includes listed and unlisted companies, commercial and industrial companies, multinationals, banks and other financial institutions. The firm has a substantial public sector practice, advising several central government departments, local authorities and other public bodies on their commercial arrangements.

INTERNATIONAL There is a strong international dimension to the firm's practice beyond Europe. The firm also acts for a substantial number of overseas clients and has particularly strong connections with China, Japan, Korea, Scandinavia and the US. The firm is experienced in managing overseas projects, including co-ordinating and interpreting local legal advice. Recent overseas projects on which the firm has advised have included chemical plants in a former Soviet Republic, a floating, production, storage and offloading platform in Vietnam, a privatised Polish steel project, a power station in South America, a major industrial complex in Pakistan and a precious metal mine in South Africa. Partners at the firm include French, German, American and Japanese qualified lawyers. The firm's lawyers speak a wide range of European languages, as well as Japanese, Korean and Mandarin.

RECRUITMENT The firm seeks to recruit high calibre individuals with varying levels of experience (both fee-earners and support staff) to support its continuing growth. All current vacancies are listed on the firm's website and email applications are welcomed. In addition, the firm recruits 10-12 trainee solicitors each year. Trainees benefit from a comprehensive training programme encompassing five seats across the firm's core and specialist practice areas. Prospects for retention upon qualification are excellent; many of the firm's partners trained with the firm. The firm's Equal Opportunities Policy applies to all stages of the recruitment process. Literature about the firm is available from the marketing department or from the firm's website. The firm also has several specialist websites at www.brandslaw.com (trademarks), www.ecomlex.com (European e-commerce lawyers' association); www.e-ploymentlaw.com (employment); www.europeanfranchising.com (franchising); www.equity-incentives.co.uk (employee benefits).

CONTACTS (Continued)	
Planning & Environmental	Richard Webber
Private Client	Penny Wotton
Private Equity & Venture Capital	Robert Wieder
Professional Regulation	Matthew Lohn
Rail	Nicholas Thompsell
Shipbuilding	John Wilson
Sports Business	Patrick Cannon
Telecommunications	Tony Ballard
Tax (Corporate)	Nicholas Noble
Trademarks	John Olsen
Travel & Tourism	Peter Stewart

FIELD FISHER WATERHOUSE

THE EUROPEAN LEGAL ALLIANCE

■ Fieldings Porter

Silverwell House, Silverwell Street, Bolton, BL1 1PT **Tel** (01204) 540900 **Fax** (01204) 362129

■ Field Seymour Parkes

The Old Coroner's Court, 1 London Street, PO Box 174, Reading, RG1 4QW **Tel** (01189) 951 6200 **Fax** (01189) 950 2704

Finers Stephens Innocent

179 Great Portland Street, London, W1W 5LF
Tel (020) 7323 4000 **Fax** (020) 7580 7069 **DX** 42739 Oxford Circus North
Email mralli@fsilaw.co.uk **Website** www.fsilaw.com

THE FIRM Finers Stephens Innocent is an expanding 90 lawyer practice based in Central London providing a range of high quality legal services to corporate and commercial clients. The firm offers a range of services focused to meet the requirements of its primarily commercial client base. The firm's philosophy includes close partner involvement and a commercial approach in all client matters. Dedicated teams create services that are supplied in a cost-effective manner with a working style which is personable, client supportive and informal. Services are offered through seven brands, FSI property, FSI corporate and commercial, FSI litigation and dispute resolution, FSI IP and media, FSI private client, FSI employment and FSI international.

PRINCIPAL AREAS OF WORK

Commercial Property The property department has seen a year of significant transactions for developers and investors as well as for major retailers. The niche retail practice Nathan Silman joined the firm to give a significant strengthening of the retail and leisure group and an enhancement of the group's client base. A highlight of the year has been the firm's appointment to the Virgin Group legal panel. In addition further recruitment in property funding and property development as well as a general recruitment at all levels in the department has added to the depth of resources for all commercial property work.

Corporate & Commercial This department has seen a year of rapid growth both in terms of the number and the size of transactions undertaken. The department handled the flotation and AIM listing of sportingbet.com plc (UK). Merger and acquisition deals included advice to LA Fitness on the purchase of four health and fitness clubs. FSI was advisor to Blueprint Audit Limited on the acquisition of the audit practices of seven accountancy practices and advisor to the shareholders of Mean Fiddler Holdings Limited on the company sale and reverse takeover of Mean Fiddler Music Group plc, an AIM listed company. The department also acted for Marylebone Warwick Balfour Group plc on the funding of a mixed use tower opposite Canary Wharf.

Litigation & Dispute Resolution Cases undertaken involve a wide variety of commercial actions, arbitrations and mediations both in the UK and other jurisdictions. The department has units specialising in finance, education, family law and personal injury/medical negligence.

IP & Media A particular feature has been the further development of an IP and media department in the firm. The department provides both contentious and non-contentious IP and media skills in defamation, IP, IT, film and TV work, financing and various other aspects of media law with a particular specialism in anti-piracy acting for a number of collection societies. The department has secured

Continued overleaf

Managing Partner	Anthony Barling
Senior Partner	Peter Jay
Number of partners	36
Assistant solicitors	27
Other fee-earners	8

AREAS OF PRACTICE	
Property	37%
Litigation	29%
Corporate/Commercial	24%
Private Client	10%

CONTACTS	
Commercial	Peter Carter
Commercial Litigation	Philip Rubens
Construction Law	James Harvey
Corporate	Peter Jay
Corporate Finance	Paul Millett
Defamation	Mark Stephens
Employment	Howard Goulden
Flotations	Ashley Reeback
Information Technology	Anthony Barling
Intellectual Property	Chris Parkinson
International	Mark Stephens
Litigation	Howard Zetter
Matrimonial	David Taylor
Media	Mark Stephens
Medical Negligence	Daniel Marks
Offshore Tax	Michael Lewis
Partnership	Michael Simmons
Personal Injury	Leon Marks
Planning	Nicola Armstrong
Property	David Battiscombe
Property Development	Michael Kutner
Property Funding	Martin Smith
Property Investment	Melvyn Orton
Property Litigation	John Hewitt
Property Retail	Julian Hindmarsh
Property Trading	Sam Charkham
Publishing	Nicola Solomon
Sports Law	Daniel Marks
Tax	Brian Slater
Trusts & Charities	Robert Craig

www.ChambersandPartners.com 955

A-Z LAW FIRMS

an increase in the number of US institutional clients for whom the firm now acts.

Employment A new stand alone employment department has been established to respond to the increasing number of employment related matters acting primarily for the employer but also for high profile employees/directors. The department also advises in employee benefit and other share option schemes.

Private Client The services of the private client department have continued to develop with an emphasis on complex, high value estate planning and offshore tax structuring which has continued to grow rapidly both for high net worth families and clients of offshore financial institutions.

INTERNATIONAL Internationally the firm continues to service the needs of its clients on both sides of the Atlantic and has seen an increasingly active profile in the US and Continental Europe.

Finers Stephens Innocent

Finn, Gledhill

1-4 Harrison Rd, Halifax, HX1 2AG
Tel (01422) 330000 **Fax** (01422) 342604 **DX** 16022 Halifax
Email marc.gledhill@finngledhill.co.uk **Website** www.finngledhill.co.uk

Ptnrs 12 **Asst solrs** 2 **Other fee-earners** 8 **Contact** Michael W Gledhill • By continually building on the foundations of a successful law practice spanning 200 years, Finn, Gledhill has become one of the most respected law firms in West Yorkshire.

Areas of Practice	
Commercial	35%
Civil Litigation (Commercial & Other)	18%
Conveyancing	12%
Crime	10%
Divorce & Matrimonial	10%
Probate & Trust	9%

Fishburn Morgan Cole

61 St Mary Axe, London, EC3A 8AA
Tel (020) 7743 7300 **Fax** (020) 7743 7301 **DX** 584 London **Email** info@fishburn-morgan-cole.co.uk

Ptnrs 11 **Asst solrs** 21 **Other fee-earners** 13 **Contact** John Cayton • Fishburn Morgan Cole is the specialist professional indemnity division of Morgan Cole. For further information, please refer to the main entry for Morgan Cole.

Fisher Meredith

2 Binfield Road, Stockwell, London SW4 6TA
Tel (020) 7622 4468 **Fax** (020) 7498 0415 **DX** 37050
Email mail@fishermeredith.co.uk **Website** www.fishermeredith.co.uk

THE FIRM Founded by Eileen Pembridge and another in 1975, Fisher Meredith now consists of 10 partners and 85 other staff. The firm remains firmly committed to personal litigation and state funded work but is increasingly obtaining instructions from organisations such as government agencies, charities, unions, local authorities and county councils. It is departmentalised for increased efficiency and to meet specialisation needs. There are departments specialising in family work of all types including a children's team dealing with children's advocacy and civil domestic violence; all aspects of criminal law; civil actions against the police; prison law; mental health work; conveyancing; community care and education; immigration; professional negligence; housing law; employment law. The senior partner is the Law Society Council member for London South, and a former Chair of the Law Society's Family Law Committee. The firm has Legal Aid franchises in family, crime, housing, immigration, mental health, civil actions against the police, employment, community care and education, prison law and public law.

PRINCIPAL AREAS OF WORK

Family A large team with an outstanding reputation in family matters where financial issues are complex.

Crime A large thriving department well known for expertise in acting for defendants across a range of offences including difficult human rights and civil liberties issues and complex appellate cases. A breadth of expertise including high calibre business crime specialists.

Police & Prison Law A cutting edge rights team.

Community Care & Education A high level specialist service.

Immigration The department covers all aspects from asylum to judicial review, including business immigration.

Residential & Commercial Conveyancing A friendly personalised service.

Mental Health Law A caring specialist service which includes Court of Protection work.

Housing Law A specialist service for tenants and residential occupiers.

Employment Law A specialist service for employers and employees with a particular specialism in dis-

Managing Partner	Stephen Hewitt
Senior Partner	Eileen Pembridge
Number of partners	10
Assistant solicitors	24
Other fee-earners	21

AREAS OF PRACTICE	
Civil	40%
Crime	29%
Family (inc. Children)	29%
Conveyancing	2%

CONTACTS	
Children	Judith Bishton
Community Care/Education	Patricia Wilkins
Conveyancing	Jason Halberstam
Crime	Stephen Hewitt
Employment	David Tyme
Family	Eileen Pembridge
Housing	David Foster
Immigration	Douglas Noble
Mental Health	Sally Hughes
Police Actions/Prison Law	David Tyme
Professional Negligence	Eleanor Wright

956 INDEX TO LEADING LAWYERS: PAGE 1693 IN-HOUSE LAWYERS' PROFILES: PAGE 1201

crimination claims.
Public Law This department is well known for expertise, in-house, in judicial review.
Agency Work Fisher Meredith accepts instructions in its areas of expertise.
Charges For Legal Aid work, the charges are as fixed by the LCD. For private clients, the firm charges between £120 and £200 per hour.

Fishers

9-13 Fenchurch Buildings, London, EC3M 5HR
Tel (020) 7709 7203 **Fax** (020) 7709 7204
Email info@fishcity.co.uk

Number of partners	3
Assistant solicitors	3

AREAS OF PRACTICE

Commercial Shipping & International Trade Litigation	70%
Professional Indemnity & Insurance Litigation	20%
Drafting Shipping & Insurance Documentation	10%

CONTACTS

General	Nicholas Fisher
	Graeme Lloyd
	Jamie Lyons

THE FIRM Founded in 1993. Small, independently minded, City firm specialising in commercial shipping and international trade litigation, also with significant practice in insurance and re-insurance disputes.

PRINCIPAL AREAS OF WORK

Shipping Commercial litigation work, predominantly for shipowners and charterers. Strong following of container and liner operators, tanker and gas carriers and reefer operators. The firm has close links with a number of P&I Clubs and Defence Associations. Experienced also in drafting charterparties and bills of lading.

International Trade Advises on disputes relating to buying and selling of hard and soft commodities and petroleum products, and on drafting sale contracts.

Insurance & Reinsurance Litigation, principally on behalf of Lloyd's brokers. Advises on GISC compliance and drafting of Brokers' Agreements.

Fisher Scoggins LLP

Hamilton House, 1 Temple Avenue, London, EC4Y 0HA **Tel** (020) 7489 2035

Fladgate Fielder

25 North Row, London, W1K 6DJ
Tel (020) 7323 4747 **Fax** (020) 7629 4414 **DX** 9057 West End
Email fladgate@fladgate.com **Website** www.fladgate.com

Number of partners	34
Assistants	30
Other fee-earners	17
Total	81

AREAS OF PRACTICE

Property	38%
Corporate/Commercial	37%
Litigation	20%
Tax	5%

CONTACTS

Anglo-American	Nicolas Greenstone
Anglo-French	Nicolas Greenstone
Anglo-Germanic	Andrew Kaufman
Anglo-Israeli	Avram Kelman
Commercial Contracts	Charles Boundy
Corporate	Nicolas Greenstone
Corporate Recovery	Rupert Connell
Employment	David Bickford
Libel	Simon Ekins
Litigation	Paul Leese
Property	Allen Cohen
Sports	Mark Buckley
Tax	Andrew McKenzie
Town Planning	Moira Fraser

THE FIRM Fladgate Fielder is one of the leading business law practices in the West End of London, providing legal advice of the highest quality for a diverse portfolio of clients. Pivotal to the firm's success are the following factors; namely its standard of excellence in client service, the calibre of its expertise, its innovative and commercial approach to the solution of problems and the combination of efficiency and cost-effectiveness to reach the optimum result.

PRINCIPAL AREAS OF WORK

Corporate The firm handles corporate; listings and flotations; AIM, NASDAQ Europe and OFEX quotations; mergers and acquisitions; venture capital; MBOs; UK and cross-border corporate and commercial transactions; employment; immigration; computer and intellectual property law; banking; partnership law; corporate restructuring; insolvency; company secretarial work.

Property Work includes acquisition and disposal; funding; construction and development; investment; secured lending; landlord and tenant; housing associations; joint ventures; portfolio management; residential estate conveyancing; town and country planning; environmental issues; enterprise zone development.

Litigation Work includes general commercial litigation; professional negligence; asset recovery; corporate recovery; landlord and tenant; intellectual property; libel; matrimonial; construction disputes; building and product liability; insurance litigation.

Tax All aspects of taxation are handled including corporate and business taxes as well as offshore and international aspects; personal tax planning; wills; probate; charities; land estate matters.

CLIENTELE The firm's client base has a strong commercial focus, comprising leading public and private companies, financial institutions and entrepreneurs in the UK and overseas.

INTERNATIONAL Fladgate Fielder has an expanding international dimension based on multilingual lawyers working in London. The firm has Anglo-American, Germanic, Israeli and French Desks. The firm is able to conduct business in French, German, Hebrew, Italian and Spanish.

A-Z ■ LAW FIRMS

■ Fleetwood & Robb
11 Queensgate, Inverness, IV1 1DF   **Tel** (01463) 226232   **Fax** (01463) 713447

■ Fletchers
111 Carrington Street, Nottingham, NG1 7FE   **Tel** (0115) 959 9550   **Fax** (0115) 959 9597

■ Flynn & McGettrick
9 Clarence Street, Belfast, BT2 8DX   **Tel** (028) 902 44212   **Fax** (028) 902 36490

■ Woodfine Foinette Quinn
125-131 Queensway, Milton Keynes, MK2 2DH   **Tel** (01908) 366333   **Fax** (01908)644096

■ Follett Stock
Malpas Road, Truro, TR1 1QH   **Tel** (01872) 241700   **Fax** (01872) 225052

Foot Anstey Sargent

21 Derry's Cross, Plymouth, PL1 2SW
Tel (01752) 675000   **Fax** (01752) 671802   **DX** 118102 Plymouth 2
Email info@foot-ansteys.co.uk   **Website** www.foot-ansteys.co.uk

4-6 Barnfield Crescent, Exeter, EX1 1RF
Tel (01392) 411221   **Fax** (01392) 218554   **DX** 8308 Exeter

Managing Partner	Jane Lister
Number of partners	26
Assistant solicitors	47
Other fee-earners	24

CONTACTS	
Advocacy	Nigel Lyons
Banking	Robin Brown
Childcare	Vanessa Priddis
Commercial Litigation	Angus McNicol
Commercial Property	Simon Gregory
Company & Commercial	Mark Lewis
E-commerce/IT	Edmund Probert
Employment	Jon Loney
Family Finance	Fiona Meadows
Insolvency	Gillian Smith
Marine	Charles Hattersley
Media	Tony Jaffa
Planning & Land Use	Isabel Diver
Private Client/Tax Planning	Louise Widley
Property Litigation	John Westwell

THE FIRM Foot Anstey Sargent is a major regional practice with a growing national and international client base. The firm offers a full range of services in commercial matters, private client work and litigation. Foot Anstey Sargent is highly committed to the region and the issues affecting those within it – but also has a strong client base further afield. The firm prides itself on providing a level of service and expertise which can be compared with the best in the country but from a South West base and at competitive regional rates. The firm, its partners and associates have a strong reputation and are well known within the region. Clients include Northcliffe Newspaper Group, The Wrigley Company Limited, Exeter Friendly Society Limited, University of Plymouth, UKRD Group Limited, Arbuthnot Latham & Co Limited, Bank of Scotland, The Wireless Group plc, local authorities and educational institutions.

PRINCIPAL AREAS OF WORK
Banking Over ten years of a growing national practice in claimant and defendant banking litigation, acting only for banks in MBOs, MBIs and other corporate transactions.
Commercial Property The team has strong links with local and national surveyors, agents, accountants and bankers, and is supported by the property litigation, licensing and planning niches within the firm.
Employment The employment team has established itself as a group of specialists providing employment law services to a growing number of corporate clients on all matters from complex reorganisations to everyday employment disputes.
Insolvency Deals with all aspects of insolvency, both personal and corporate, contentious and non-contentious. Key strengths lie in the team members' weight of experience, favourable costing rates and speed of response.
Media The team consists of recognised leaders in the field with substantial experience in defending defamation claims, pre-publication advice and challenges to Secrecy Orders in the Courts.
Property Litigation This expanding team possesses great depth of expertise in handling a continuing volume of high quality work. Works in partnership with other specialist teams within the firm's property group including commercial property and planning environmental and land use. Has close links with the private client division of the firm for residential matters.
Shipping The team prides itself as being the leading team in the west of England for legal services to the fishing industry. One of the leading provincial claimant marine teams with a growing reputation of non-contentious work. Is pioneering after-the-event insurance in obtaining substantial cover for own and opponents' costs. Work includes shipbuilding and finance contracts.

■ Forbes
Rutherford House, 4 Wellington Street, (St John's), Blackburn, BB1 8DD   **Tel** (01254) 54374   **Fax** (01254) 52347

Forbes Anderson

66 Chiltern Street, London W1U 4JT
Tel (020) 7535 1620 **Fax** (020) 7535 1630
Email aforbes@forbesanderson.com

Number of partners	2
Assistant solicitors	1
Other fee-earners	1

THE FIRM Forbes Anderson is a specialist litigation firm which was created in November 2001. The founding partners were previously partners in Statham Gill Davies, the leading music industry law firm.

PRINCIPAL AREAS OF WORK The firm advises on disputes relating to the media and entertainment industries, with a strong emphasis on the music industry. Expertise includes intellectual property, contract, tort, partnership issues, licensing disputes, brand issues and defamation.

CLIENTELE Clients include leading artistes, sports personalities, record companies, music publishers, merchandisers, managers, promoters, songwriters, advertising agencies, marketing services companies, brand owners, production companies and fashion designers.

FORBES ANDERSON

■ Ford Simey

8 Cathedral Close, Exeter, EX1 1EW **Tel** (01392) 274126 **Fax** (01392) 410933

Ford & Warren

Westgate Point, Westgate, Leeds, LS1 2AX
Tel (0113) 243 6601 **Fax** (0113) 242 0905 **DX** 706968 Leeds
Email clientmail@forwarn.com **Website** www.forwarn.com

Managing Partner	Keith Hearn
Number of partners	19
Assistant solicitors	33
Other fee-earners	25

THE FIRM Ford & Warren is a major commercial firm in the North of England. The size and strength of the firm enables expert teams of lawyers to be put together helping clients achieve their business objectives.

PRINCIPAL AREAS OF WORK
Business The business law department provides a full range of management advice to employers. The Managing Partner is in this department as head of employment law. The employment team deals with issues right across the board from tribunal claims, fraudulent directors, trade union disputes and injunctions. Corporate law encompasses mergers, acquisitions, MBOs, MBIs and commercial contracts along with intellectual property issues.
Commercial The commercial law department provides a full range of contentious and non-contentious services, from property litigation, planning and environment through to transport public inquiries. This department handles major commercial litigation in close liaison with the business law department. The head of department has enormous expertise in the transport industry.
Claims The claims department has strong teams acting for major insurance companies throughout the country. Litigation includes employers liability, road traffic, fire and insurance fraud claims. As well as the defendant claims team, the department has a plaintiff team who have unrivalled expertise in high profile multi-plaintiff claims, including Bradford stadium fire, Zeebrugge ferry sinking and the Hillsborough stadium disaster. The firm's medical negligence team goes from strength to strength.
Private Client This department caters for all the needs of the private client from matrimonial law to employee relocation. Residential conveyancing is also handled.

FORD & WARREN
Solicitors

Forsters

67 Grosvenor Street, London, W1K 3JN
Tel (020) 7863 8333   **Fax** (020) 7863 8444   **DX** 82 988 Mayfair
Email mail@forsters.co.uk   **Website** www.forsters.co.uk

Senior Partner	Sophie Hamilton
Managing Partner	Paul Roberts
Number of partners	22
Assistant solicitors	38
Other fee-earners	11

AREAS OF PRACTICE	
Property	55%
Private Client	20%
Corporate	12%
Commercial Litigation	8%
Property Litigation	5%

CONTACTS	
Commercial Property	Smita Edwards
Litigation	Caroline Bassett
Private Client	David Robinson
Residential Property	Paul Neville

THE FIRM Forsters is a leading commercial law firm, established in 1998. The 11 founding partners were previously partners in Frere Cholmeley Bischoff. They set up the business with the objective of offering clients a highly professional yet personal and tailor-made service. Since opening for business, the firm has gone from strength to strength and now comprises 22 partners and 38 assistants. The firm is committed to providing a wide range of legal service in its chosen areas of business: property (residential and commercial), private client, commercial and litigation. Forsters prides itself on the quality of its lawyers who are able to provide practical and cost-effective advice. The firm is particularly recognised as a leading firm in the areas of property and private client, punching well above its weight in these areas. Increasingly lawyers at Forsters have to think 'outside the box' and provide innovative approaches to transactions; this is particularly true in the commercial property field, where property transactions are becoming increasingly sophisticated and corporatised.

PRINCIPAL AREAS OF WORK

Commercial Property The department has a strong reputation for all aspects of commercial property work. Its principal strengths lie in investment work for both institutional clients and property companies, development work and occupier work, particularly in the leisure and retail sectors. Increasingly the commercial property department works with the commercial department on complex structuring of transactions, for example limited partnerships, joint ventures and stamp duty mitigation schemes. A specialist property finance partner advises banks, lending institutions and borrowers on all types of property finance. Within the commercial property department there are specialist planning lawyers who handle town planning appeals and enquiries, and frequently advise on large town centre developments. The firm is also able to offer advice on contentious and non-contentious construction work, an integral part of many property transactions. A specialist property litigation team handles landlord and tenant disputes, rent reviews and general property litigation.

Residential Property Forsters is one of the few leading London law firms with a specialist residential property group. The team acts for landlords and tenants, developers and investors, and high net worth individuals in purchasing and selling property. The team prides itself on its speed of service which is genuinely personal. The firm has particular expertise in leasehold reform and enfranchisement, acting for two estates and various residents associations.

Private Client The private client team is recognised as one of the leading players in the private client field in London. The client base comprises a broad range of individuals and trusts, as well as landed estates, charities and private banks. It advises on tax and estate planning for UK and offshore clients, as well as services relating to wills and probate, domicile and residence issues, and the establishment of trusts. The private client department also offers specialist advice on divorce and matrimonial matters.

Commercial The firm acts for listed and private companies, financial institutions, partnerships, sole traders and entrepreneurs. It has particular expertise in acquisitions and financing for technology, communications and media companies. In addition to its stand alone practice, the commercial department works regularly with the commercial property department in the structuring of property transactions, for example the establishment of limited and limited liability partnerships, joint venture agreements, and in connection with stamp duty mitigation. The commercial department has been involved with several high value property transactions involving such matters in the past year. Within the commercial department there is a specialist tax partner who is able to advise on tax planning for corporate vehicles.

Litigation The litigation team handles a wide variety of commercial litigation and arbitration. It has been involved in some high value and complex contractual disputes covering professional negligence, intellectual property, fraud recovery and insolvency.

Foster Baxter Cooksey

6-10 George Street, Snow Hill, Wolverhampton, WV2 4DN
Tel (01902) 311711 **Fax** (01902) 311102 **DX** 702433 Wolverhampton 5
Email solicitors@fbc-sol.co.uk

THE FIRM Formed by the merger of four well-established Midlands firms, Foster Baxter Cooksey now has over 100 staff and serves a broad spectrum of private and business clients. The firm has particular expertise in corporate work, commercial property, intellectual property, civil litigation, matrimonial and family. It has other offices in Telford and Willenhall.

PRINCIPAL AREAS OF WORK
Work includes commercial, property, corporate finance, building societies, civil litigation, family and trusts.

RECRUITMENT
The firm recruits two trainee solicitors (with at least a 2:1 degree) each year. Applicants should write to Guy Birkett, Training Partner, with a full CV.

Managing Partner	Graham Sower
Senior Partner	David Nixon
Number of partners	13
Assistant solicitors	12
Other fee-earners	27

CONTACTS	
Commercial Property	Simon Bowdler
Corporate Services	James Hayes
Employment	Tracy Worthington
Insolvency	Guy Birkett
Legal Audits	James Hayes
Litigation	Timothy Gray
Private Client	Kim Carr

Fosters

William House, 19 Bank Plain, Norwich, NR2 4FS
Tel (01603) 620508 **Fax** (01603) 624090 **DX** 5225 Norwich-1
Email enquiries@fosters-solicitors.co.uk

THE FIRM Fosters is a high street practice committed to the local community and excellent client care. Established in 1761, it merged with local firm Russell Steward in July 2001 and has won a number of national awards.

PRINCIPAL AREAS OF WORK
Family Law Substantial specialist family team with mixed client base.
Mediation This service is the biggest growth area and has been extended to cover five branch offices.
Commercial Advice is given on all aspects of company and commercial law.
Professional Negligence National client base with particular expertise in solicitors' negligence.

RECRUITMENT
Unique, award-winning contracts are offered to trainee solicitors.

Managing Partner	Andrew Saul

CONTACTS	
Commercial Litigation	Karim Mohamed
Commercial Property	Anne Kirby
Company Commercial	Alison Bignell
Matrimonial & Family	Iain McClay
Mediation	Catherine Iliff
Mental Health	Bruce Chilton
Personal Injury	Stephen Green
Professional Negligence	Karim Mohamed
Residential Property/Probate	Anne Kirby

Fox Brooks Marshall

Century House, St Peters Square, Manchester M2 3DN
Tel (0161) 236 7766 **Fax** (0161) 236 7794 **DX** 14452 Manchester 2
Email fbm@foxbrooks.co.uk

THE FIRM Fox Brooks Marshall, a leading presence in the Manchester legal scene for more than 150 years, has developed a sound reputation in the corporate commercial sector.

PRINCIPAL AREAS OF WORK
Corporate: Fox Brooks Marshall has gained a reputation for bringing companies to AIM and OFEX, developing particular expertise in mining companies.
Property: Fox Brooks Marshall advises on a range of issues, from simple acquisitions and disposals to complex site development; having recently advised Apollo Leisure on the £23 million acquisition of 11 cinemas and four bingo clubs.

CLIENTELE Fox Brooks Marshall's diverse client base includes: W H Ireland, Latin American Copper PLC, Virotec International Limited, Auiron Energy Limited and Goldmines of Sardinia.

INTERNATIONAL Fox Brooks Marshall has maintained strong links with the Australian Mining Federation.

Managing Partner	Heather Russell
Senior Partner	Andrew Wright
Number of partners	10
Assistant solicitors	10
Other fee-earners	22

A-Z ■ LAW FIRMS

Fox Williams

Ten Dominion Street, London, EC2M 2EE
Tel (020) 7628 2000   **Fax** (020) 7628 2100   **DX** 33873 Finsbury Sq.
Email mail@foxwilliams.com   **Website** www.foxwilliams.com

THE FIRM Fox Williams is a City firm handling a wide variety of business matters. The firm's core practice areas are mergers and acquisitions, corporate finance, employment, e-commerce and partnership law. Fox Williams adopts a particular approach to its work, involving a special effort to understand the business needs of its clients, a close relationship between clients and members of the Fox Williams team and a fast, responsive service. The firm pays meticulous attention to detail and to quality assurance, and strives to create a happy and efficient working environment for members of the firm.

PRINCIPAL AREAS OF WORK The firm is organised into departments focused on corporate law, e-commerce law, employment, commercial litigation and commercial property. A cross-departmental group advises on partnership law.

Corporate Corporate work includes international and domestic takeovers and mergers, company acquisitions and disposals, share issues, management buyins and buyouts, private placings, flotations, film financing and venture capital projects. General corporate matters such as business start-ups, restructurings and shareholder agreements are also handled.

E-commerce Fox Williams has specialist expertise in advising on legal issues arising from online commerce and the use of the internet. This expertise is based on its experience in advising on distribution and agency agreements, joint ventures, technology licensing and IT agreements, intellectual property and EU and UK competition law.

Employment The firm is well-known for its employment law expertise which includes service agreements, employee rights and restrictive covenants, share incentive and option schemes, golden handshakes, dismissals and redundancies. Employment litigation is handled by employment lawyers in the employment department.

Litigation A broad range of substantial UK and international litigation and arbitration is undertaken by the litigation department. It resolves disputes relating to intellectual property, trading, shareholder and joint venture arrangements. The litigation department also presents cases for mediation.

Partnership Fox Williams has an outstanding reputation for partnership work. Partners at Fox Williams have advised a number of professional firms on the implications of converting to a limited liability partnership structure. Fox Williams has specific expertise in helping US law firms with the development of their offices in London.

Property Commercial property work is concerned with a wide range of matters including land acquisitions and disposals, secured lending, business leases, and landlord and tenant issues.

CLIENTELE The firm's clients range from multinational corporations and major public companies to family businesses and individual entrepreneurs. They include banks, other financial institutions, regulatory authorities, accountants and other professionals (including overseas lawyers). Firms of solicitors often refer work to Fox Williams when City expertise is required.

Senior Partner	Ronnie Fox
Number of partners	14
Assistant solicitors	36
Other fee-earners	8

AREAS OF PRACTICE	
Employment	43%
Corporate	26%
Litigation	14%
E-commerce	12%
Property	5%

CONTACTS	
Commercial Agreements	Stephen Sidkin
Commercial Litigation	Tom Custance
Commercial Property	Bryan Emden
Corporate Finance	Paul Osborne
Corporate/Financial Services	Tina Williams
Discrimination & Business Immigration	
	Jane Mann
E-commerce & Internet Law	Nigel Miller
E-commerce & IT Law	Robin Baron
Employment (Executive Termination	
& International)	Clare Murray
Employment (UK & Corporate)	Mark Watson
M&A	Mark Tasker
Partnership	Ronnie Fox

Foy & Co

PO Box 111, 63 Hallgate, Doncaster, DN1 3DQ
Tel (01302) 327136   **Fax** (01302) 367656   **DX** 12563 Doncaster
Email info@foys.co.uk   **Website** www.foys.co.uk

Drakehouse Crescent, Waterthorpe, Sheffield, S20 7HT
Tel (0114) 251 1702   **Fax** (0114) 251 1750   **DX** 717230 Sheffield 28

Church Steps, All Saints Square, Rotherham, S60 1QD
Tel (01709) 375561   **Fax** (01709) 828479   **DX** 12601 Rotherham

102 Bridge Street, Worksop, S80 1HZ
Tel (01909) 473560   **Fax** (01909) 482760   **DX** 12207 Worksop

102/112 Burncross Road, Chapeltown, Sheffield, S35 1TG
Tel (0114) 246 7609   **Fax** (0114) 240 2625   **DX** 19836 Chapeltown

THE FIRM Established legal practice offering a wide range of domestic and commercial services including conveyancing, litigation, matrimonial and family, criminal and motoring, wills and probate, and all commercial matters.

Managing Partner	Paul Evans
Senior Partner	Stephen Paramore
Number of partners	8
Assistant solicitors	11
Other fee-earners	22

962   INDEX TO LEADING LAWYERS: PAGE 1693 ■ IN-HOUSE LAWYERS' PROFILES: PAGE 1201

Francis Hanna & Co
Central Chambers, 75-77 May Street, Belfast, BT1 3JL **Tel** (028) 9024 3901 **Fax** (028) 9024 4215

Freeman & Co
Rodesia House, 52 Princess Street, Manchester, M1 6JX **Tel** (0161) 236) 7007 **Fax** (0161) 236 0440

Freemans Solicitors
Stuart House, Lower Chepstow, NP16 5HH **Tel** (01291) 623225 **Fax** (01291) 628162

Freemans
7 St Mary's Place, Newcastle upon Tyne, NE1 7PG **Tel** (0191) 222 1030 **Fax** (0191) 222 1819

freethcartwright

Imperial House, 108-110 New Walk, Leicester, LE1 7EA
Tel (0116) 201 4000 **Fax** (0116) 201 4001 **DX** 715612 Leicester 2
Email postmaster@freethcartwright.co.uk

Willoughby House, 20 Low Pavement, Nottingham, NG1 7EA
Tel (0115) 936 9369 **Fax** (0115) 936 9358 **DX** 10039 Nottingham
Email postmaster@freethcartwright.co.uk

Norman House, Friargate, Derby, DE1 1NU
Tel (01332) 361000 **Fax** (01332) 207177 **DX** 11502 Derby 1
Email postmaster@freethcartwright.co.uk

Chief Executive	Peter Smith
Senior Partner	Ian Payne
Chairman	Colin S Flanagan
Number of partners	50
Assistant solicitors	72
Other fee-earners	60

AREAS OF PRACTICE	
Dispute Resolution	31%
Commercial Property	28%
Private Client	21%
Corporate & Commercial Services	20%

CONTACTS	
Admin/Public Law	Richard Beverley
Banking	Paul Thorogood
Charities	Nigel Cullen
Company/Commercial	Paul Thorogood
Competition	Phillip Raven
Construction	Guy Berwick
Corporate Finance	Karl Jansen
Employment	David Potter
Housing Associations	Gary Reynolds
Immigration	Sue Miles
Insolvency	Graham Greenfield
Internet	Andrew Margiotta-Mills
IP	Andrew Margiotta-Mills
IT	Andrew Margiotta-Mills
Licensing	Malcolm Radcliffe
Litigation (Commercial)	Philippa Dempster
Litigation (Property)	John Frith
Pensions	John Heaphy
Personal Injury	Jane Goulding
Planning	Ian Tempest
Private Client	Nigel Cullen
Product Liability	Paul Balen
Professional Negligence	Richard Beverley
Property (Commercial)	George Taylor
Risk Management	Philippa Dempster
Sports	Simon Taylor

THE FIRM freethcartwright is a major Midlands practice offering services to both commercial and private clients across the entire legal spectrum. Although based in Nottingham, Derby and Leicester, the firm has a wide range of clients throughout the UK and many of its clients have strong international connections. Freethcartwright has grown rapidly in recent years and now ranks as one of the leading East Midlands' firms offering comprehensive legal services in the public and private sectors. Whilst aiming to provide the very best service possible in all areas, the firm also prides itself on its wish and ability to understand the businesses of its clients and to demonstrate to them that with a properly developed relationship it can significantly add value. It believes that major legal practices should be in 'partnership' with their clients, not merely reacting to clients' specific instructions and dealing with problems after they have arisen. The firm aims to combine first-class legal expertise with a thorough knowledge of its clients' business. Its lawyers are encouraged and trained to be both practical and commercial in their approach to the provision of legal services.

PRINCIPAL AREAS OF WORK
Commercial The firm's commercial practice covers a broad spectrum of corporate, commercial and financial work from small day to day transactions to significant mergers and acquisitions, some with an international content.

Corporate & Commercial The corporate and commercial team provides the full range of services specialising in MBOs, MBIs, the reorganisation and financing of businesses, mergers, acquisitions and joint ventures. The firm also has a significant capability in specialist areas including pensions, competition, EU law, corporate tax and sport and entertainment law. It has a specialist intellectual property unit dealing with both contentious and non-contentious work including a comprehensive international trademark registration service and significant work in the telecommunications, internet and IT sectors.

Commercial Property With one of the largest commercial property departments in the Midlands, the firm acts for developers of industrial, residential and commercial property; institutional lenders and investors; privatised utilities; housing associations; and commercial landlords and tenants. The firm has dedicated units covering planning, environment issues and construction.

Dispute Resolution The emphasis in dispute resolution is on risk management and risk avoidance. The firm has specialist groups in employment, landlord and tenant, construction litigation, professional negligence and insurance. The firm also undertakes significant insolvency, recovery and litigation work for major banks and accountants. The firm acts for Lloyds underwriters, insurers and indemnity institutions. The firm has particular expertise in medical negligence and product liability under the leadership of Paul Balen who enjoys an established national reputation in the field. The group has significant experience in co-ordinating high profile group actions, both in the UK and overseas.

Private Client Emphasising the firm's range of services, the private client units provide expertise in family and childcare matters, housing litigation, immigration, personal injury, residential conveyancing and wills and probate. The firm plans to continue growth through organic development, by pursuing proactive strategic and marketing policies and by investing in high calibre people, from trainee solicitors to partners.

freethcartwright

A-Z LAW FIRMS

Freshfields Bruckhaus Deringer

65 Fleet Street, London, EC4Y 1HS
Tel (020) 7936 4000   Fax (020) 7832 7001   DX 23
Email email@freshfields.com   Website www.freshfields.com

THE FIRM Freshfields Bruckhaus Deringer is a leading international law firm providing a range of business legal services. It specialises in producing innovative, commercial solutions to the most complex issues based on its substantial business experience. The firm provides clients with exceptional advice that makes a real difference to their businesses. This approach demands the highest standards of intellectual rigour and service delivery as it strives to exceed the expectations of clients. The firm has a wealth of experience in its chosen practice areas and also invests in developing the specialist industry knowledge of its people so that they can combine their legal skills with genuine understanding of the markets in which their clients operate. Freshfields Bruckhaus Deringer lawyers think ahead – identifying the challenges of the future, and advising clients on how best to meet them.

PRINCIPAL AREAS OF WORK The firm is widely recognised as a world leader in a number of fields including arbitration, environment, competition, mergers and acquisitions, pensions, corporate tax, PFI and securitisation. It has thriving practices in the areas of IP/IT and e-commerce related issues. Overall, it specialises in providing a seamless service across practice areas and geographies.

CLIENTELE Freshfields Bruckhaus Deringer has advised most of the world's largest corporations and all of the leading investment banks. It frequently acts for governments and public bodies.

INTERNATIONAL Its international approach is founded on leading local capabilities and experience backed up by the knowledge and experience of the wider firm. With over 2300 lawyers in 19 countries across Europe, Asia and the US the firm has the resources to co-ordinate and execute even the largest and most complex matters involving numerous jurisdictions. The firm has offices in Amsterdam, Bangkok, Barcelona, Beijing, Berlin, Bratislava, Brussels, Budapest, Cologne, Düsseldorf, Frankfurt, Hamburg, Hanoi, Ho Chi Minh City, Hong Kong, Madrid, Milan, Moscow, Munich, New York, Paris, Prague, Rome, Singapore, Tokyo, Vienna, and Washington. It also has an associated office in Shanghai.

RECRUITMENT Great emphasis is placed on the training and development of the firm's lawyers to meet the changing needs of its clients. As well as the usual training tools, secondments to client organisations are actively encouraged. The firm has a range of state of the art e-services for clients to keep them up to date with progress on deals and legal developments of interest to them. Lawyers and trainees also have access to bespoke electronic databanks and services, ensuring that the combined sum of the firm's knowledge and experience can be applied to individual matters and the more routine parts of the job can be performed efficiently and cost-effectively.

UK	
Number of partners	162
Number of fee-earners	1091
International	
Number of partners	317
Number of fee-earners	1593
Total staff	5420

CONTACTS	
Arbitration	Nigel Rawding
Asset Finance	Tim Lintott
Banking	Edward Evans
Construction & Engineering	Sally Roe
Corporate/M&A	Barry O'Brien
Dispute Resolution	Josanne Rickard
Employment	Jocelyn Mitchell
Energy	Jonathan Rees
Environment	Paul Bowden
EU/Competition	Deirdre Trapp
Finance	Simon Hall
Financial Services	Guy Morton
Insolvency	Peter Bloxham
Insurance	Ian Poynton
Intellectual Property/IT	Avril Martindale
Investment Funds	Anthony McWhirter
Private Equity	Christopher Bown
Project Finance	Kent Rowey
Real Estate	Christopher Morris
Securities	Tom Joyce
	Tim Jones
Structured Finance	Ian Falconer
Tax	David Taylor
Telecoms, Media & Technology	Simon Marchant
Telecoms, Media & Technology - Regulatory	Rachel Brandenburger
Associate Recruitment	Judith Hesketh
Graduate Recruitment	Deborah Dalgleish

Fried, Frank, Harris, Shriver & Jacobson

99 City Road, London, EC1Y 1AX
Tel (020) 7972 9600   Fax (020) 7972 9602
Email info@ffhsj.com   Website www.ffhsj.com

THE FIRM An international law firm with approximately 550 attorneys, Fried Frank has offices in New York, Washington DC, Los Angeles, London and Paris. Firm practice includes a broad range of corporate and commercial matters including mergers, private equity, capital markets, anti-trust; bankruptcy and restructuring; benefits and compensation; litigation; real estate; securities regulation compliance and enforcement; tax; technology; trust and estates.

PRINCIPAL AREAS OF WORK The London office concentrates on complex corporate matters, including cross-border mergers and acquisitions, leveraged buyouts, joint ventures and private equity investments; global capital markets transactions; senior and mezzanine leveraged financings; structured finance and securitisation matters. The London office advises clients investing or raising capital outside of the United States, making acquisitions or investments, both public and private, or raising capital in the US, UK or internationally. The firm's London attorneys represent both underwriters and issuers in global, US and euro securities offerings involving equity and debt. They provide the full slate of acquisition finance legal services to capital providers and borrowers, including sourcing funds in senior, mezzanine and high yield markets. They also represent commercial and investment banks, insurance companies and other participants in complex structured finance securitisations. They provide US securities law advice and advise multinational professional services organisations, including

Managing Partner	Peter v.Z. Cobb
	Michael Rauch
International	
Number of partners worldwide	134
Number of other lawyers worldwide	426
UK	
Partners	6
Assistant solicitors	18
Other fee-earners	3
Total fee-earners	27
Total staff	49

AREAS OF PRACTICE	
Corporate	51%
Litigation	26%
Real Estate	6%
Bankruptcy	5%
Tax	5%
Anti-trust	3%
Benefits/Employment	3%
Trust & Estate	1%

the Big Five, on mergers and acquisitions and structural and regulatory issues.

INTERNATIONAL Fried Frank has an established international practice with a concentration in cross-border mergers, acquisitions and joint ventures; private equity investments; US registered and Rule 144A securities offerings; cross-border non-US debt and equity offerings, including high yield debt; commercial financing transactions; structured and securitised financings; establishment of LBO funds; international trade and investment; tax; trust and estate planning. The practice is conducted from the firm's US offices and its offices in London and Paris. Lawyers in its London office practise US, English and international law. Lawyers in the firm's Paris office practise French, US and international law. Recent international representations include Rouse Company, with two other property companies, in their $5.3 billion joint acquisition of Rodamco North America NV; Gallaher Group plc in its $2 billion acquisition of Austria Tabak; Invensys plc in the disposition of various divisions, including its Energy Storage Group; E.W. Blanch Holdings, Inc. in its $179 million acquisition by Benfield Greig Group plc; Goldman, Sachs & Co., financial advisor to Royal Caribbean Cruises, Ltd. in its $3 billion merger with P&O Princess Cruises, plc. Capital market transactions include KPNQwest NV in its €500 million issuance of 8 7/8% senior notes due February 1, 2008, and in its €525 million bank financing from a consortium of tier-one financial institutions to facilitate its acquisition of the Ebone and Central Europe businesses of Global TeleSystems, Inc.; GAL Finance SA in the issuance of €100 million of 11 1/2% senior notes due 2009 guaranteed by Global Automotive Logistics SAS; Pacific Century CyberWorks Limited and its wholly owned subsidiary PCCW-HKT Telephone Limited in connection with a $750 million global offering of notes and an immediate follow-on offering of an additional $250 million of notes; Gallaher Group, plc in its offering of £150 million ordinary shares; the Spanish government in the €527 million initial public offering of Iberia.

The Frith Partnership

53 The Calls, Leeds, LS2 7EY **Tel** (0113) 242 6633 **Fax** (0113) 242 6620

Furley Page

39 St Margaret's Street, Canterbury, CT1 2TX
Tel (01227) 763939 **Fax** (01227) 762829 **DX** 5301 Canterbury
Email enquiries@furleypage.co.uk **Website** www.furleypage.co.uk

52-54 High Street, Whitstable, CT5 1BG
Tel (01227) 274241 **Fax** (01227) 275704 **DX** 32352 Whitstable
Email enquiries@furleypage.co.uk

Senior Partner	Peter Hawkes
Number of partners	19
Assistant solicitors	6
Other fee-earners	21

AREAS OF PRACTICE	
Litigation	32%
Commercial Services	30%
Trust & Estates	25%
Residential	13%

CONTACTS	
Company/Commercial	Christopher Wacher
Employment	Jonathan Gauton
Litigation	Peter Hawkes
Private Client	Harvey Barrett

THE FIRM Furley Page is one of the largest practices in Kent. Lawyers are organised in specialist groups and offer a level of service that competes both regionally and nationally. The firm has associations with commercial practices in many countries to handle an increasing volume of overseas work.

PRINCIPAL AREAS OF WORK
Commercial Services Clients include national and international plcs, insurers and a wide range of private companies. Work includes company commercial, commercial property, intellectual property, competition, planning and environmental. There is a specialist e-business group.
Education & Charities The firm acts for charities, higher education institutions, colleges and schools.
Agriculture This is a long-standing and significant area of practice for the firm.
Litigation Groups specialise in personal injury, commercial and building, landlord and tenant and matrimonial. Agency work is regularly undertaken.
Employment A team of lawyers and specialist consultants advises nationally and internationally on employment, human resources, health and safety and commercial immigration.
Debt Recovery The firm offers a specialist computer-supported service operating debt recovery at fixed rates.
Private Client Work includes comprehensive tax planning, domestic conveyancing, probate, court of protection and wills.
Financial Services The firm advises on investment, life assurance, pensions and other financial matters.

A-Z LAW FIRMS

Fyfe Ireland WS

Orchard Brae House, 30 Queensferry Road, Edinburgh, EH4 2HG
Tel (0131) 343 2500 **Fax** (0131) 343 3166 **DX** ED 23
Email mail@fyfeireland.com **Website** www.fyfeireland.com

99 Charterhouse Street, London, EC1M 6NQ
Tel (020) 7253 5202 **Fax** (020) 7253 5525 **DX** 53346 Clerkenwell

Senior Partner	Alistair Wilson
Number of partners	13
Assistant solicitors	16
Other fee-earners	20

AREAS OF PRACTICE	
Commercial Property	39%
Private Client & Lender Services	28%
Corporate	25%
Litigation	8%

CONTACTS	
Commercial Property	James Roscoe
Corporate	David Lindgren
Litigation	Andrew Taylor
Private Client & Lender Services	
	Greig Honeyman

THE FIRM Based in Edinburgh, Fyfe Ireland is primarily a business-to-business law firm with a particular emphasis on commercial property. The firm has a strong client base across its many practice areas and is very well regarded in the market. Its major strength continues to be the provision of a personal, partner-led service. Fyfe Ireland, with its 13 partners, is often referred to as 'punching above its weight' and is well known in London. Clients include a significant number of substantial foreign and UK organisations, particularly banks, building societies, other financial institutions, educational establishments, retailers and IT companies.

PRINCIPAL AREAS OF WORK The principal focus of the firm continues to be on commercial law, the main work areas being commercial property, corporate and commercial and lender services.

Commercial Property The firm's commercial property expertise has been well established for many years and is provided to a significant number of financiers and investors, developers, retailers, and builders in both the private and public sectors. All aspects of work are undertaken but there is particular expertise in cross-border security transactions and an expanding construction practice.

Corporate & Commercial The corporate and commercial department has in-depth experience of public and private fundraisings, buyouts and other business acquisitions and disposals. Other practice areas include every aspect of private company work, contracts, joint ventures, intellectual property, banking, corporate finance and public/private partnerships. In addition, separate practice units have been established to provide employment advice and to service the specialised requirements of the technology sector.

Commercial Litigation The head of the commercial litigation department is accredited by the Law Society of Scotland as a specialist in construction law and is also on the Society's list of adjudicators. There is particular expertise in the areas of construction, commercial property and employment.

Private Client & Lender Services In the lender services division there is much experience in the provision of advice and services to financial institutions including Halifax plc, Yorkshire Building Society, Barclays Bank plc, HSBC and West Bromwich Building Society. The firm also retains a high quality private client base with core advice areas being wills, trusts and executries, tax planning and financial services. Owner-managed businesses, professional partnerships, agriculture and estates are also particular areas of expertise. A major practice area also exists in conveyancing on behalf of national housebuilders.

RECRUITMENT The firm is always keen to consider quality candidates. Any application with an appropriate CV should be sent to Steve Kerr (skerr@fyfeireland.com).

Gabb & Co

32 Monk Street, Abergavenny, NP7 5NW
Tel (01873) 852432 **Fax** (01873) 857589 **DX** 43752 Abergavenny
Email abergavenny@gabb.co.uk **Website** www.gabb.co.uk

AREAS OF PRACTICE	
Property & Agriculture	35%
Litigation	30%
Private Client & Tax & Probate	25%
Commercial	10%

Contact David Vaughan • A long established and high quality practice best known for company/commercial, employment, residential and commercial conveyancing, wills and tax planning.

LAW FIRMS ■ A-Z

Gadsby Wicks

91-99 New London Road, Chelmsford, CM2 0PP
Tel (01245) 494929 **Fax** (01245) 495347 **DX** 89707 Chelmsford 2
Email mail@gadsbywicks.co.uk

THE FIRM Gadsby Wicks was founded in 1993 as a specialist practice dealing with clinical negligence and medical products liability litigation on behalf of claimants. The firm now comprises eight lawyers, an in-house medical advisor and a dedicated team of support staff. The firm holds a clinical negligence legal aid franchise, is a member of the Legal Services Commission Multi Action Panel and has members of both the Law Society Clinical Negligence and AVMA Referral Panels. Gadsby Wicks has been at the leading edge of innovation in finding alternative methods of funding litigation and is able to offer affordable litigation to all clients with viable cases.

PRINCIPAL AREAS OF WORK

Clinical Negligence The firm is well known for its clinical negligence work obtaining several million pounds in compensation for its clients every year.

Medical Products Liability The firm has considerable experience and expertise in litigating successful claims on behalf of clients who have been injured by pharmaceutical or other medical products.

Managing Partner	Gillian Gadsby
Senior Partner	Roger Wicks
Number of partners	2
Assistant solicitors	5
Other fee-earners	1

AREAS OF PRACTICE	
Medical Negligence	83%
Medical Products Liability	15%
Personal Injury	2%

CONTACTS	
Clinical Negligence	Gillian Gadsby
Medical Products Liability	Roger Wicks

■ Gallen & Co
40 Carlton Place, 142 Queen Street, Glasgow, G5 9TW **Tel** (0141) 420 1441 **Fax** (0141) 420 8258

■ Gamlins
31-37 Russell Road, Rhyl, LL18 3DB **Tel** (01745) 343500 **Fax** (01745) 343616

■ Gamon Arden & Co
Church House, 1 Hanover Street, Liverpool, L1 3DW **Tel** (0151) 709 2222 **Fax** (0151) 709 3095

■ Garstangs
115A Chancery Lane, London, WC2A 1PP **Tel** (020) 7242 4324 **Fax** (020) 7242 4329

Gateley Wareing

Windsor House, 3 Temple Row, Birmingham, B2 5JR
Tel (0121) 234 0000 **Fax** (0121) 234 0001 **DX** 13033 B'ham 1
Email gw@gateleywareing.com **Website** www.gateleywareing.com

Knightsbridge House, Lower Brown Street, Leicester, LE1 5NL
Tel (0116) 285 9000 **Fax** (0116) 285 9001 **DX** 10829 Leicester 1

14 Regent Street, Nottingham, NG1 5BQ
Tel (0115) 983 8200 **Fax** (0115) 983 8201 **DX** 15491 Nottingham 2

THE FIRM Gateley Wareing is one of the leading firms of commercial solicitors in the Midlands. The firm is known for its innovative and practical approach, providing commercial advice and solutions to business clients, ranging from sole traders, partnerships and family ventures to fully quoted public companies and financial institutions. Gateley Wareing is the only law firm with offices in the three principal business centres of the Midlands: Birmingham, Leicester and Nottingham.

PRINCIPAL AREAS OF WORK

Corporate Services Gateley Wareing concentrates on the owner led business market and has a particular reputation for its private equity work, whether acting for management, vendors, equity or senior debt providers.

Banking & Recoveries The firm acts for a number of financial institutions, with a growing asset finance and invoice discounting practice.

Commercial Property This growing team acts for many commercial property owners and developers across the UK. The team also has a particular expertise advising housing associations and a growing practice advising banks and other lenders on property deals.

Construction Gateley Wareing has one of the most highly regarded construction teams in the country, acting for many leading developers and contractors on both non-contentious and contentious construction issues.

Dispute Resolution The firm advises a wide range of organisations on the resolution of commercial

Continued overleaf

Senior Partner	Michael Ward
Number of partners	19
Assistant solicitors	51
Other fee-earners	20

AREAS OF PRACTICE	
Corporate Finance	26%
Banking & Recoveries	18%
Construction	18%
Commercial Property	13%
Employment	9%
Dispute Resolution	7%
Commercial	6%
Private Client	3%

CONTACTS	
Asset Finance	Brendan McGeever
Banking	Andrew Madden
Commercial	Andrew Evans
Commercial Property	Tim Ledger
	Craig Mitchell
Construction	Peter Davies
Corporate Services	Michael Ward
Dispute Resolution	Stephen Goodrham
Employment	Ruth Armstrong
Housing Associations	Neil Handel
Private Client	Jonathan Howard
Recoveries	Brendan McGeever

A-Z ■ LAW FIRMS

disputes, including intellectual property disputes, whether through litigation, mediation or other forms of dispute resolution. The firm has two accredited mediators.

Employment In this fast changing area of law, Gateley Wareing provides hands on support for the human resource needs of businesses of all sizes, from large multi-national groups to small OMEs. The firm is also involved in guiding businesses through health and safety issues.

Commercial Gateley Wareing provides support to the contractual needs of owner-led businesses, with a particular emphasis on e-commerce and intellectual property.

Private Client Gateley Wareing is one of the few commercial firms operating in the Midlands to provide advice to high net worth clients in relation to capital taxes and estate planning.

GCL Solicitors

Connaught House, Alexandra Terrace, Guildford, GU1 3DA
Tel (01483) 577091 **Fax** (01483) 579252 **DX** 141450 Guildford 12
Email partners@gcl-solicitors.co.uk   **Website** www.gcl-solicitors.co.uk

Managing Partner	Chris Cooney
Number of partners	4
Other fee-earners	7

THE FIRM Guildford-based GCL solicitors (now 50 strong) focuses exclusively on property development principally residential but also mixed use schemes. GCL was restructured and reorganised in 1997 discarding other areas of work to focus totally on property development and it is now a leading niche firm in this field. The introduction of a bespoke case control system, a commitment to training with over 70% of all personnel activity involved in professional qualifications backed by high quality and innovative technology have kept GCL to the forefront in its field. ISO 9000 Accreditation was achieved in 1998. A prestigious Law Firm of the Year Award was achieved in 1999.

PRINCIPAL AREAS OF WORK Work includes land acquisition conditional or otherwise; options short term and strategic; consortium or collaboration agreements; land disposal; estate development set-up for sales; property exhibitions outside UK; unit sales.

CLIENTELE The firm has a wide client base including major UK volume housebuilders, leading publicly quoted developers, niche building companies and smaller traditional builders. The firm operates principally in Greater London and the Home Counties.

■ George Davies

Fountain Court, 68 Fountain Street, Manchester, M2 2FB
Tel (0161) 236 8992 **Fax** (0161) 228 0030 **DX** 14316 Manchester 1
Email mail@georgedavies.co.uk   **Website** www.georgedavies.co.uk

CONTACTS	
Healthcare	Claire Batchelor
Commercial Property	Anne Fairhurst
Wills & Tax	John Louden
Corporate	Mark Hovell
Sports	John Hewison
Litigation	Mak Lewis

Ptnrs 15 **Asst solrs** 25 **Other fee-earners** 9 **Contact** John Hewison • Specialists in healthcare, sports and insolvency law, acting for NHS trusts, health authorities, NHSLA panel member, as well as acting for the Professional Footballers' Association for over 40 years. A member of LawNet, it has a commitment to quality standards, demonstrated by its Investor in People and ISO 9002 accreditations.

George Green

195 High Street, Cradley Heath, West Midlands, B64 5HW
Tel (01384) 410410 **Fax** (01384) 634237 **DX** 20752 Cradley Heath
Email gg@georgegreen.co.uk   **Website** www.georgegreen.co.uk

Old Bank Chambers, 1 Summer Hill, Halesowen, West Midlands, B63 3BU
Tel (01384) 410410 **Fax** (0121) 585 5455 **DX** 14523 Halesowen
Email gg@georgegreen.co.uk

Senior Partner	Richard Havenhand
Number of partners	11
Assistant solicitors	6
Other fee-earners	13

CONTACTS	
Company/Commercial	Richard Cliff
Commercial Litigation	Neil Cutler
Commercial Property	Cheryl Leyser
Private Client	Neill Robb

THE FIRM Established in 1897 and based in the heart of the Black Country, George Green is recognised as a cost-effective alternative to City firms for the business community, whilst retaining its commitment to the provision of legal advice to its private clientele. Its strong reputation has attracted work from well beyond its Black Country base.

PRINCIPAL AREAS OF WORK

Company/Commercial Work includes start-ups, acquisition and mergers, reconstructions, corporate finance, MBOs, flotations, partnerships, commercial agreements, joint ventures and taxation.

Commercial Litigation Work includes contract disputes, debt collection, employment, intellectual property, building disputes, landlord and tenant, planning disputes, insolvency, defamation, European law and emergency injunctions and claims litigation. The work involves both High Court and County Court actions, in addition to arbitrations and industrial tribunal hearings.

Property Development/Planning The department undertakes and advises on acquisitions and disposals of land and buildings, leasing, building and development contracts, taxation, property finance, commercial/residential estate development and planning.

Private Client Work includes wills, probate, estate planning, trusts, charities, pensions, matrimonial law, residential conveyancing and personal taxation.

George Ide, Phillips

52 North Street, Chichester, PO19 1NQ
Tel (01243) 786668   **Fax** (01243) 831000   **DX** 30306 Chichester
Email maildesk@chi.georgeide.co.uk   **Website** www.georgeide.chi.co.uk

Lion House, 79 St Pancras, Chichester, PO19 4NL
Tel (01243) 786668   **Fax** (01243) 831300   **DX** 30306 Chichester
Email maildesk@chi.georgeide.co.uk

Belmont Lodge, Belmont Street, Bognor Regis, PO21 1LE
Tel (01243) 829231   **Fax** (01243) 825553   **DX** 31204 Bognor Regis
Email maildesk@bognor.georgeide.co.uk

Senior Partner	Jeffrey Hopkins
Number of partners	10
Assistant solicitors	9
Other fee-earners	16

AREAS OF PRACTICE	
Personal Injury/Clinical Negligence	50%
Private Client	30%
Other Litigation	20%

CONTACTS	
Clinical Negligence	Julian Bobak
Commercial Property	Jeffrey Hopkins
Commercial/Company	Robert Enticott
Crime	Ian Mellor
Employment	Julian Bobak
Family/Children	Fraser Poole
	Renella Squires
Mediation	Renella Squires
Mental Health	Ian Oliver
Personal Injury	Tony Goff
Trust & Probate	Ursula Watt
Civil Actions Against Police	Ian Oliver

THE FIRM George Ide, Phillips has become one of the leading firms in this part of the South East. With its niche areas of practice and broader specialities, the firm is well placed to serve both its business and private clientele. Each office has Lexcel accreditation.

PRINCIPAL AREAS OF WORK

Personal Injury This department concentrates on claimant work, and the firm represents many of the major legal costs insurers. The firm was a founder member of MASS (Motor Accident Solicitors Society). Much of the personal injury work is of a high value and profile. The firm has a specialist head injury department and an association with the charity Headway. Members of the department are on the Law Society's Personal Injury Panel and one is a fellow of the College of Personal Injury Lawyers.

Clinical Negligence This department specialises in medical and dental negligence with a strong emphasis on cerebral palsy cases. Law Society and AVMA referral panellists.

Other Litigation The firm has specialists dealing with landlord and tenant, clinical negligence and other mental health work, crime, building disputes, professional negligence, employment and civil actions against the police.

Commercial Property The firm has a substantial commercial property department with an established reputation and expertise in the range of commercial property issues and acts for a large national property company.

Business Services Flexible teams support business clients through advice on commercial activities of all types and related areas of finance and employment.

Family/Children A strong team with members of SFLA and Law Society Family and Children Panels.

Investment The firm has an investment department which specialises in private client Portfolio management.

Public Funding Franchises The firm holds current franchises and contracts in housing, clinical negligence, employment, mental health, family and personal injury and civil actions against the police.

George Mathers & Co

23 Adelphi, Aberdeen, AB1 2BL   **Tel** (01224) 588599   **Fax** (01224) 584147

Gepp & Sons

58 New London Rd, Chelmsford, CM2 0PA   **Tel** (01245) 493939   **Fax** (01245) 493940

A-Z ■ LAW FIRMS

Gherson & Co

1 Great Cumberland Place, London, W1H 7AL
Tel (020) 7724 4488 **Fax** (020) 7724 4888
Email roger@gherson.com **Website** www.gherson.com

Senior Partner	Roger Gherson
Number of partners	1
Assistant solicitors	2
Other fee-earners	6

AREAS OF PRACTICE
UK Immigration/ Nationality Law/ EU Freedom of Movement	98%

CONTACTS
Immigration & Nationality	Roger Gherson

THE FIRM Established in 1988 and now in its 14th year, Gherson & Co is a niche firm that specialises exclusively in providing in-depth advice and practical assistance with regard to UK immigration and nationality. The principal, Roger Gherson, has many years experience in all aspects of immigration law and is well known for his expertise in this area. The firm has extensive experience in providing practical immigration advice and in dealing with the resolution of complex immigration issues. In addition to its business clientele, the firm has an extensive private client base.

PRINCIPAL AREAS OF WORK Work covers the full spectrum of business/employment related immigration and personal immigration matters. Political asylum claims (private only) also covered. Expert in human rights law affecting all the firm's areas of practice. Business/employment expertise includes work permit applications and applications relating to visitors, sole representatives, business, investors, innovators, retired persons of independent means, ancestry, writers/composers/artists; as well as all free movement rights under European Community law, such as rights of establishment under the EC Association Agreements. The firm has dealt with a particularly large number of applications under the investor category and recently published government statistics suggest that in some years this firm handled a significant proportion of all such applications granted. In addition, the firm handles complex nationality matters, applications from EU and other citizens involving family reunion, student refusals and other issues. It advises start-up companies; multinational companies relocating employees to the UK; overseas companies seeking to establish a business in the UK for the first time; individual overseas nationals wishing to establish a UK business; a wide range of enterprises including e-commerce/IT businesses; and individuals in a number of capacities. Work also includes appeals before immigration adjudicators, the Immigration Appeals Tribunal and the Special Immigration Appeals Commission; and judicial review matters in the High Court.

CLIENTELE The firm has a wide corporate and private client base, including other firms of solicitors.

INTERNATIONAL Gherson & Co has extensive links overseas, particularly in China (including Hong Kong), FSU, South Africa and the USA. The firm has an associate office in Hong Kong.

Gibson, Dunn & Crutcher LLP

Telephone House, 2-4 Temple Avenue, London, EC4Y 0HB
Tel (020) 7071 4000 **Fax** (020) 7071 4244 **DX** 217 London/Chancery Lane
Website www.gibsondunn.com

Managing Partner	Wesley G Howell, Jr
Chairman of European Operations	
	Bernard Grinspan
Number of partners	12
Assistant solicitors	15
Other fee-earners	2

AREAS OF PRACTICE
Corporate	60%
Finance/Project Finance	20%
Real Estate	10%
Taxation	10%

CONTACTS
London Office	Paul Harter
	Judith Shepherd

THE FIRM Gibson, Dunn & Crutcher, with over 800 lawyers in 12 major cities across the US and in Europe, is known for its commitment to providing the highest quality legal services in a personal, responsive manner. The firm is a recognised leader in representing companies from start-up ventures to multinational corporations in industries ranging from high technology to financial services. The firm's offices are operated on an integrated basis so that clients may draw on the depth, expertise and resources provided by its multi-office structure. This ensures that specialists with expertise in appropriate legal disciplines are used, regardless of location. The London office, founded more than 20 years ago, has expanded significantly as the result of a strategic decision to bring on board English lawyers to enhance the firm's ability to provide high quality legal services to clients with national and international interests. In London, US and English lawyers work together to meet the complex international needs of the firm's clients.

PRINCIPAL AREAS OF WORK The firm provides the following services in the UK:
Corporate Top level UK and multijurisdictional mergers, acquisitions and joint ventures; international public offerings involving single or multiple listings on European and US stock exchanges; public and private takeovers; international and private equity offerings; corporate restructuring; management buy-outs; strategic alliances.
Finance/Project Finance Advice to investors and borrowers on a wide range of financial transactions including acquisition finance, debt finance, project finance, property finance, public bond offerings and private debt placement in the global markets.
Real Estate The firm advises clients from numerous jurisdictions on property and property finance transactions. Clients include financial institutions, investors, developers, retailers and opportunity funds. Transactions include joint ventures, portfolio acquisitions and sales, sale and leaseback financ-

GIBSON, DUNN & CRUTCHER

ings and outsourcing agreements, limited partnerships, development agreements, debt financing (including complex structured financing arrangements) site acquisition, planning procedures, building contracts and commercial leases.

Taxation The firm offers a full range of tax services to corporations, partnerships, financial institutions, foreign entities, high net worth individuals and others, as well as tax effective structuring on national and international transactions. The firm advises clients regarding their ongoing operations and domestic and international business transactions, both 'inbound' and 'outbound' and in connection with administrative proceedings, appeals and tax litigation.

INTERNATIONAL The firm has other offices in Century City, Dallas, Denver, Los Angeles, Munich, New York, Orange County, Palo Alto, Paris, San Francisco and Washington DC.

Gilfedder & McInnes
34 Leith Walk, Edinburgh, EH6 5AA **Tel** (0131) 553 4333 **Fax** (0131) 555 3712

Gill Akaster
25 Lockyer Street, Plymouth, PL1 2QW
Tel (01752) 203500 **Fax** (01752) 203503 **DX** 8284 Plymouth 2

Contact Jacqueline Ashley • Particular knowledge of commercial and property, employment, family and members of the Law Society Family Law, Children and Personal Injury panels. Three SFLA accredited specialists. SFLA mediator. Also offices at Scott Lodge, Milehouse, Plymouth.

AREAS OF PRACTICE	
Commercial & Property	27%
Residential Property	25%
Matrimonial & Family	20%
Civil Litigation	15%
Probate/Trusts/Tax	13%

Gill & Co
37 Grays Inn Road, London, WC1X 8PP **Tel** (020) 7242 0404 **Fax** (020) 7831 8537

Gillespie Macandrew WS
31 Melville Street, Edinburgh, EH3 7JQ
Tel (0131) 225 1677 **Fax** (0131) 225 4519 **DX** ED 113 Edinburgh-1
Email mail@gillespiemacandrew.co.uk **Website** www.gillespiemacandrew.co.uk

Managing Partner	Ian Turnbull
Senior Office Manager	David Macfarlane
Number of partners	8
Assistant solicitors	10
Other fee-earners	15

THE FIRM Gillespie Macandrew, with roots established for more than 300 years, has developed leading specialist disciplines for private and business clients and emphasis on high level partner/associate contact. Gillespie Macandrew's private client department is a leader in offering a fully integrated investment management, tax and financial planning service. The commercial department represents Scottish and European interests of both multinational companies and investors abroad. The firm's activities now also focus on charities, professional partnerships, farmers, and the developing SME business sectors of Scotland. Authorised by the Financial Services Authority for investment business.

AREAS OF PRACTICE	
Corporate/Commercial	30%
Private Client Tax & Trust	30%
Property (Commercial & Rural)	20%
Investment Management	20%

PRINCIPAL AREAS OF WORK

Agriculture & Farming This core specialist practice advises on partnerships, contract farming, crofting, landlord/tenant relations, quotas, mineral rights, fish farming and sporting estates. The firm is provider of NFU Scotland legal Helpline.

Charities Charities are a specialist focus of management and advice from the combined corporate, tax and investment teams. Clients include leading animal, disability, ex-service, arts and rural/environmental charities.

Corporate Client Company formation, acquisition and business support services include specific areas in technology, agribusiness, employment, and equity finance. Partners are experienced in providing general counsel to companies and assisting with negotiations. The firm supports Edinburgh Business Development with free consultancy for start-up and developing businesses and also Edinburgh International Trade.

Commercial Property/Lending Finance The firm is experienced in investment, leasing and development of property including leisure, brownfield, agribusiness, licensed property, construction, and planning and environmental law.

Energy & Electricity Energy and electricity is an area of specialist expertise and Gillespie Macandrew advises generators, industrial users and hydro/windpower SRO and NFFO projects.

Litigation & Employment Law Contentious and non-contentious cases are handled with specialist expertise in construction, employment, commercial and rural property, trust and family law disputes. The firm operates a debt recovery service.

Private Client/Tax Trust & Financial Planning This team of over 20 fee-earners combines tax, trust and

CONTACTS	
Agriculture/Estates	Simon Leslie
Charities	Thomas Murray
Commercial Property	Neil Wilson
Corporate/Commercial	Derek McCulloch
Corporate/Small Business	Christopher Smith
Employment	Ian Turnbull
Energy (Electricity)	Derek McCulloch
Executry/Probate	John McArthur
Investment/Fund Management	
	Charles Fotheringham
Litigation	Ian Turnbull
Residential Property	Tim Myles
Tax & Trust	Simon Leslie

Continued overleaf

A-Z ■ LAW FIRMS

financial planning advice with discretionary and advisory fund management and an execution-only dealing service.
Investment The investment department has six professionals from a wide range of investment disciplines with average experience of over 20 years each; and is an active participant in the Law Society of Scotland, ASIM and SIFA.
Residential Property The department maintains a full range of estate agency, conveyancing, relocation and letting services.

INTERNATIONAL The firm is the Scottish member of Lexwork International in Europe and maintains additional USA, Asian and other international contacts for both corporate and private client transactions.

■ Gills

Equity Chambers, 5 Hortus Road, Southall, UB2 4AJ
Tel (020) 8893 6869   **Fax** (020) 8893 6396   **DX** 52256 Southall 2
Email jgill@gills-solicitors.co.uk   **Website** www.gills-solicitors.co.uk

AREAS OF PRACTICE	
Education	55%
General Civil Litigation	45%

Ptnrs 2   **Other fee-earners** 1   **Contact** Jaswinder Gill • Specialises in education law.

■ Girlings
Crown Chambers, Broad Street, Margate, CT9 1BN   **Tel** (01843) 220274   **Fax** (01843) 297828

■ Glaisyers
10 Rowchester Court, Printing House Street, Birmingham, B4 6DZ   **Tel** (0121) 233 2971   **Fax** (0121) 236 1534

■ Glazer Delmar
223-229 Rye Lane, Peckham, London, SE15 4TZ   **Tel** (020) 7639 8801   **Fax** (020) 7358 0581

■ Glovers
115 Park Street, London, W1Y 4DY   **Tel** (020) 7629 5121   **Fax** (020) 7491 0930

■ Godwins
12 St Thomas Street, Winchester, SO23 9HF   **Tel** (01962) 841484   **Fax** (01962) 841554

Goldkorn Mathias

6 Coptic Street, Bloomsbury, London, WC1A 1NW
Tel (020) 7631 1811   **Fax** (020) 7631 0431   **DX** 35705 Bloomsbury
Email gmlaw@btinternet.com

Managing Partner	Roy Mathias
Number of partners	2
Other fee-earners	4

AREAS OF PRACTICE	
Litigation	30%
Criminal Work	25%
Conveyancing	15%
Probate	15%
Commercial	15%

CONTACTS	
Commercial	Roy Mathias
Crime	Tim Harries
Litigation	Geoffrey Goldkorn
Probate	Clive Bender
Conveyancing	Stewart Wiseman

THE FIRM Established in 1979 and reconstituted in its present form in March 2000. The Bloomsbury office is a niche practice specialising in civil litigation, commercial work and probate. The associated office at Camberwell practising under the name Goldkorns is an exclusively criminal practice.

PRINCIPAL AREAS OF WORK
Civil Litigation The partners are very experienced litigators, including a Deputy District Judge and solicitor with rights of audience in the High Court. The firm offers a comprehensive litigation service including in house advocacy in the County Court, the High Court and the Court of Appeal. The firm has an acknowledged reputation for handling complex legal disputes and for assimilating cases involving large volumes of documents. The firm has particular experience in a variety of commercial disputes, litigious probate, breach of trust, copyright, designright and passing off disputes, professional negligence (lawyers and accountants) and civil actions against the police. Agency work is regularly undertaken.
Crime The Camberwell office is a well run very substantial criminal practice with a legal aid franchise in crime and is one of the firms on the Serious Fraud Panel. The workload dealt with each year is very high - in excess of 1,000 individual cases.
Property Work includes commercial and residential conveyancing; landlord and tenant cases.
Probate Departmental work involves drafting wills and estate planning as well as winding-up estates.
Commercial Work includes employment contracts, partnerships, sports agreements.

Golds

8 Newton Terrace, Glasgow, G3 7PJ **Tel** (0141) 300 4300 **Fax** (0141) 300 4350

Goodman Derrick

90 Fetter Lane, London, EC4A 1PT
Tel (020) 7404 0606 **Fax** (020) 7831 6407 **DX** 122 Chancery Lane
Email law@goodmanderrick.co.uk **Website** www.goodmanderrick.co.uk

Managing Partner	Patrick Swaffer
Senior Partner	John Roberts
Number of partners	21
Assistant solicitors	9
Other fee-earners	8

CONTACTS

Charities/Private Client	Diana Rawstron
Commercial Litigation	Annabel Crumley
	Tim Langton
Company Commercial	David Edwards
Construction	Susan White
Corporate	John Roberts
Defamation	Patrick Swaffer
Employment	Belinda Copland
Film	Keith Northrop
Hotel & Leisure	Richard Gerstein
Insurance	Tim Langton
Media	Paul Herbert
	Patrick Swaffer
Property	Michael Collins
	Gregor Hamlen
Publishing	Nicholas Armstrong
Tax	Ian Montrose

THE FIRM Goodman Derrick is a progressive and dynamic City practice, founded in 1954 by Lord Goodman. It has a broad commercial practice focusing on commercial and corporate finance, property and litigation work and has a particularly strong reputation in media law.

PRINCIPAL AREAS OF WORK The main groups for Goodman Derrick are media, corporate, property, litigation, tax, employment, private client and charities.

Media This department advises both corporate and individual clients on the whole range of contentious and non-contentious matters in the fields of broadcasting, television, film and publishing, as well as other areas of the media and arts. These include film and television production and financing, cable and satellite, distribution, digital broadcasting, book and magazine publishing, sponsorship and licensing agreements. Notable experience has been developed in defamation and in other clearance advice relating to broadcast material, newspaper and magazine articles and book manuscripts.

Property Work includes all aspects of commercial property transactions, especially work for retail companies, investors, property development, funding, leases, planning, secured lending and landlord and tenant. In addition, the firm handles some high-quality residential work.

Commercial Litigation Work includes a broad range of commercial disputes, property litigation, professional negligence, insolvency, insurance, fraud, intellectual property and debt recovery.

Corporate Work includes mergers and acquisitions, flotations, banking and finance, joint ventures, business start-ups, shareholders' agreements, management buyouts, rights issues, share offers, mergers and reorganisations, commercial agreements, European law, intellectual property and IT law.

Private Client/Charities Work includes tax and estate planning, drafting of wills and trusts, administration of estates and probate work and registration of charities.

Employment This department offers the whole range of contentious and non-contentious advice and specialist advice to the recruitment industry.

CLIENTELE Goodman Derrick has an impressive client list acting for many public figures, public and private companies, charities, large retail chains, property companies and developers, television companies, broadcasters and independent producers, publishers and newspapers, and trade associations.

RECRUITMENT Applications by letter and CV to Mr Nicholas Armstrong, Recruitment Partner.

GOODMANDERRICK

Goodman Ray

450 Kingsland Road, Dalston, London, E8 4AE
Tel (020) 7254 8855 **Fax** (020) 7923 4345 **DX** 46807 Dalston **Email** mail@goodmanray.com

AREAS OF PRACTICE	
Family	100%

Ptnrs 4 **Asst solrs** 6 **Other fee-earners** 1 **Contact** Peggy Ray • Specialist family law. Strong reputation for child-related work. Expanding ancillary relief department. Three partners are members of the Law Society Children Panel. Legal Aid franchise.

Gordon & Smyth

Sovereign Centre, 153 Queen Street, Glasgow, G2 3BP **Tel** (0141) 275 4875 **Fax** (0141) 275 4800

A-Z ■ LAW FIRMS

Gordon Dadds

80 Brook Street, Mayfair, London, W1K 5DD
Tel (020) 7493 6151 **Fax** (020) 7491 1065 **DX** 131 Chancery Lane
Email info@gordondadds.com **Website** www.gordondadds.com

THE FIRM Gordon Dadds is a full-service law firm with a broad range of private and corporate clients. Founded in 1921, the firm has always been pre-eminent in the field of family and private client work. New joiners and the merger with City litigation and commercial firm Camillins in August 2001 have reinforced specialist skills in company and commercial law, property, litigation, media and privatised utilities, as well as extending the foreign reach of the firm. The employment law group draws on members of several departments to provide a total coverage of contentious and non-contentious issues in this area.

PRINCIPAL AREAS OF WORK

Company & Commercial This department handles a range of substantial corporate transactions, including national and international corporate tax planning, company acquisitions and sales in a broad range of business sectors, MBOs and corporate reorganisations. The firm advises on the full range of employment, pensions, intellectual property, environmental and regulatory matters, banking and commercial contracts, and has particular expertise in the utilities sector.

Family Law Combining determination with sensitivity, the family law team deals with complex financial cases, frequently with international elements, as well as all matters in relation to children, divorce, separation agreements and pre-nuptial contracts. Emergency procedures, injunction proceedings and problems arising from cohabitation are also specialist areas.

Litigation & Dispute Resolution The litigation department handles a wide range of litigation, including high profile cases, for commercial and private clients. The firm's expertise covers media, employment, breach of contract, commercial fraud, directors' disqualification, copyright and intellectual property, insolvency and asset recovery, defamation, health and safety, IT, inheritance disputes, insolvency, professional negligence, property (including landlord and tenant), road traffic (civil and criminal) and shareholder and partnership disputes. Where appropriate, disputes are resolved by arbitration and ADR techniques. Two members of the firm are accredited mediators.

Private Client Advice is given in the fields of tax and estate planning and administration, with particular regard to overall personal considerations as well as to strictly legal matters. Assignments include administration of estates and post death tax planning, advice on tax returns, drawing up and executing wills and financial management. The firm has a well established and growing charity law practice.

Property All kinds of commercial and domestic transactions are handled, from single buildings to large developments, from London flats to country estates. The firm has particular expertise in property finance.

INTERNATIONAL Languages spoken include Arabic, French, German, Greek, Italian and Spanish.

RECRUITMENT The firm recruits up to three high calibre graduates a year as trainee solicitors. Applications should be received by July, two years before training commences. Please address applications to Miss Sue Bland.

Senior Partner	Roger Peters
Managing Partner	David Goff
Number of partners	16
Assistant solicitors	11
Other fee-earners	8

AREAS OF PRACTICE	
Family	25%
Litigation	25%
Company & Commercial	20%
Private Client	15%
Property	15%

CONTACTS	
Company & Commercial	Michael Jepson
Family	Sue Bland
Litigation	Hugh Elder
Private Client	John Goodchild
Property	David Goff

GORDON DADDS
SOLICITORS

■ Gordons Cranswick Solicitors
14 Piccadilly, Bradford, BD1 3LX **Tel** (01274) 202202 **Fax** (01274) 202100

■ Gorman Hamilton Solicitors
Percy House, Percy Street, Newcastle upon Tyne, NE1 4PW **Tel** (0191) 232 1123 **Fax** (0191) 221 1689

Gorvin Smith Fort

6-14 Millgate, Stockport, SK1 2NN
Tel (0161) 930 5151 **Fax** (0161) 930 5252 **DX** 719421 Stockport 7
Email enquiries@gorvin.co.uk **Website** www.gorvin.co.uk

THE FIRM Based in Stockport, the firm is a substantial provider of services to both business and private clients. It has an emphasis on general transactional and commercial work, as well as accident and personal injury cases, high value divorce and private litigation. Gorvin Smith Fort is one of the largest practices in South Manchester, specialising in corporate and private client work. The firm acts for a wide variety of clients, from large companies to small businesses, partnerships and individuals. A major investment has been made in technology to maximise communication and efficiency. The firm has a programme of expansion and has dedicated professional negligence and corporate recovery departments. A strong commitment is made to recruiting high-calibre lawyers and other staff, as well as providing appropriate training for those already with the firm. The firm has the Investors in People award. The firm runs a popular series of seminars, and is actively involved in community life. Gorvin Smith Fort is willing to act as agent on behalf of other solicitors in litigation, debt collection and family matters.

PRINCIPAL AREAS OF WORK

Company & Commercial The Company and Commercial Department's expertise covers all aspects of business disposals, acquisitions and reconstruction; IT and other intellectual property protection; EU restrictive trade practices and commercial contract, health and safety; agency distribution and franchisee agreements; partnerships; pensions, share options and shareholder agreements, and venture capital funding.

Commercial Property Commercial and industrial retail property; building construction contracts and site developments; joint venture agreements, finance, funding and security documentation; landlord and tenant issues, including leases, lease renewals, sales or lease backs and options are all dealt with by our specialist Commercial Property Department.

Commercial Litigation The Commercial Litigation Department deals with contractual and commercial disputes, shareholder disputes and minority shareholder protection; partnership disputes and dissolutions, landlord and tenant and other property disputes; emergency order applications, licensing, unfair competition and intellectual property disputes. Specialist Higher Education and Healthcare units also fall under the remit of the department. The departmental head, Iain Campbell, is an ADR Group accredited mediator.

Employment The Employment Department undertakes work for employers, covering such areas as drafting contracts of employment, service agreements, business transfers; recruitment and unfair dismissal/wrongful dismissal/discrimination actions; advice on compromise agreements; and tribunal and court work. Areas of work undertaken on behalf of employees includes unfair dismissal and wrongful dismissal claims; deduction from wages claims; discrimination claims over race, sexuality, gender, disability or age; executive severance; tribunal representation, and health and safety issues.

Corporate Recovery Credit control, insolvency and debt collection are dealt with by the specialist Corporate Recovery Unit.

Probate, Wills & Estates In the Probate, Wills and Estates Planning department, Andrew Cusworth and Val Bown have been appointed to the panel of external receivers with The Public Guardianship Office. This confirms Gorvin Smith Fort's expertise in this area. The panel of external receivers has been established to manage the Public Trustee's existing and future appointments. Andrew Cusworth is a member of the Society of Trust and Estate Practitioners and Val Bown is a student member.

Industrial Disease Gorvin Smith Fort's Industrial Disease Department operates a case managed system for claims against British Coal and the team is now five strong.

Senior Partner	George Marriott
Managing Partner	P Andrew Callaghan
Number of partners	11
Assistant solicitors	24
Other fee-earners	22

AREAS OF PRACTICE

Company/Commercial	27%
Commercial Property	18%
Commercial Litigation	17%
Residential Conveyancing & Estate Planning	10%
Accident/Personal Injury	10%
Employment	5%
Professional Liability	5%
Family/Matrimonial	4%
Corporate Recovery	4%

CONTACTS

Accident/Personal Injury	Duncan Manners
Commercial Property	Ian Fletcher
	Lorraine Lockie
Company/Commercial	Tim Dennis
	Paul Lupton
Corporate Recovery	Mark Deverell
Employment	Guy Lightowler
	Nigel Crebbin
Estate Planning	Val Bown
	Andrew Cusworth
Family/Matrimonial	Amanda McAlister
Litigation	Iain Campbell
	Paul Humphreys
	Guy Lightowler
Professional Liability	Paul Humphreys
	George Marriott
Residential Conveyancing	P Andrew Callaghan

Gosschalks

Queens Gardens, Hull, HU1 3DZ **Tel** (01482) 324252 **Fax** (01482) 590290

Gotelee & Goldsmith

31-41 Elm St, Ipswich, IP1 2AY **Tel** (01473) 211121 **Fax** (01473) 230387

A-Z ■ LAW FIRMS

Gouldens

10 Old Bailey, London, EC4M 7NG
Tel (020) 7583 7777 **Fax** (020) 7583 6777 **DX** 67 City
Email info@gouldens.com **Website** www.gouldens.com

Senior Partner	Patrick Burgess
Managing Partners	Charters Macdonald-Brown
	Russell Carmedy
Number of partners	42
Assistant solicitors	67
Other fee-earners	37

AREAS OF PRACTICE
Company/Commercial (inc. Corporate Tax)	42%
Property (inc. Planning)	25%
Litigation (inc. IP)	20%
Banking/Capital Markets	12%
Personal/International Tax Planning	1%

CONTACTS
Banking	Tom Budd
CIS/Central Europe	James Campbell
Commercial Litigation	Charters Macdonald-Brown
Commercial Property	David Roberts
Communications, Media & IT	Simon Chalkley
Company/Commercial	Max Thorneycroft
Construction	Craig Shuttleworth
Corporate Finance	Russell Carmedy
Corporate Recovery & Insolvency	Barry Donnelly, Adrian Owen
Corporate Tax	Blaise Marin-Curtoud
Defamation	Barton Taylor
Employment	Richard Martin
	Martin Piers
EU & International	Charters Macdonald-Brown
Insurance/Reinsurance	Ian Lupson
Intellectual Property	Simon Chalkley
	Charters Macdonald-Brown
Pensions/Employee Benefits	John Papadakis
Personal/Int'l Tax Planning	Jennet Davies
Regulatory	Barry Donnelly

THE FIRM Gouldens is the eighth most profitable firm in the UK, has a policy of paying among the highest salaries of UK firms to its lawyers and, belying its size, is one of the few firms truly to 'punch above its weight'. The firm announced five new partners in 2002, bringing the total number of partners to 42. There are 146 lawyers and a total staff of 300. Gouldens is a commercial firm with leading practices and individuals in the traditional cornerstones of corporate, property and litigation as well as specialist teams which utilise the expertise of lawyers from these disciplines. Its dynamic and individual culture encourages innovation and a practical approach which achieves clients' objectives.

PRINCIPAL AREAS OF WORK Gouldens divides its work into the main practice areas described below. There are also a number of specialist areas staffed by multi-skilled teams such as construction, environment, insurance and reinsurance, communications, media and information technology, intellectual property, employment, employee benefits and pensions, and regulatory.

Company/Commercial The firm's company and commercial department has a strong reputation in the City and advises, amongst others, major public companies and investment banks, brokers and other City institutions on all aspects of commercial activity including corporate finance, public company takeovers and flotations, mergers and acquisitions, joint ventures, venture capital, management buy-outs, private equity, international agreements and trademark, patent, distribution agency and commercial agreements, as well as providing specialist support in areas such as EU and competition law, intellectual property and pensions and employee benefits.

Corporate Recovery & Insolvency The corporate recovery and insolvency group undertakes a wide range of assignments for insolvency practitioners, banks and other providers of debt and equity finance. Increasingly, this involves advising the full range of stakeholders in companies operating in dynamic business sectors where timely restructuring advice may avoid the need for formal insolvency procedures.

Banking The banking department has extensive experience in corporate lending and syndications, structured finance, trade finance, property finance, project finance, securitisation, capital markets and debt restructuring, acting for banks and financial institutions as well as borrowers.

Property & Planning The firm's property and planning departments advise developers, institutional investors, surveyors, and other professionals on the financing, planning implications, tax structuring, and implementation of major developments. The department is a market leader in respect of the establishment of unit trusts, limited partnerships and other co-ownership vehicles.

Litigation, Insurance & Reinsurance The firm handles a wide variety of domestic and international commercial disputes particularly in the banking and financial sector. It also has a strong reputation in intellectual property, construction and defamation. There is a dedicated recoveries group associated with the now well known practice that Gouldens has developed for asset based lenders. The insurance and reinsurance practice is broadly based with an increasing international bias. It also advises Lloyds syndicates and other London market insurers on many classes of risk including professional indemnity and directors' and officers' liability.

INTERNATIONAL As well as dealing with high profile EU legal and trade issues, the international practice includes advising major companies and institutions on infrastructure projects, privatisations and joint ventures as well as governments on a number of issues including the development of new banking, securities, and foreign investment-related legislation. Languages spoken include Czech, Dutch, German, Greek, Hebrew, Italian, Polish, Romanian, Russian, Spanish and Welsh.

RECRUITMENT The firm recruits solicitors and trainees who want the challenge of responsibility in an atmosphere where flair, originality and enthusiasm are highly regarded and rewarded. Its non-rotational training system is unique in the City and allows for freedom, flexibility and responsibility from the start. Up to 20 trainees are recruited each year and the firm aims to retain all trainees on qualification.

■ **Graeme Carmichael**
9 Paget Road, Ipswich, IP1 3RP **Tel** (01473) 252159 **Fax** (01473) 214778

LAW FIRMS ■ A-Z

■ Grahame Stowe, Bateson
5-7 Portland Street, Leeds, LS1 3DR **Tel** (0113) 246 8163 **Fax** (0113) 260 1749

■ Graham Evans & Partners
Moorgate House, 6 Christina Street, Swansea, SA1 4EP **Tel** (01792) 655822 **Fax** (01792) 645387

■ Grange Wintringham

St Mary's Chambers, Grimsby, DN31 1LD
Tel (01472) 253900 **Fax** (01472) 359904 **DX** 13505 Grimsby-1
Email juliet.savage@grangewintringham.com

Managing Partner	Juliet Savage
Senior Partners	David Overton
	Stephen Savage
Number of partners	9
Assistant solicitors	3
Other fee-earners	15
Other staff	50

THE FIRM Established in 1770 the practice has changed radically and is one of the largest corporate and commercial practices in the region.

PRINCIPAL AREAS OF WORK
Corporate/Commercial The firm has full corporate capability including e-commerce.
Commercial Property The firm has considerable expertise in advising national clients on all property and related funding matters. The firm has a particular speciality in the sale securitisation and development of properties within enterprise zones.
Employment The firm has a specialist employment department advising on all types of employment issues from tribunals to share options.
Agriculture The agricultural department is based at the Market Rasen office and advises agricultural clients on all matters appertaining to farming both contentious and non-contentious.
Litigation The firm provides a full range of litigation services.
Private Client The firm continues to have a strong private client department dealing with residential conveyancing, probate, tax and matrimonial.

CLIENTELE The firm handles work for the full range of clients, from private clients to national clearing banks.

RECRUITMENT Having made new partners in the last few years, the firm continues to recruit at all levels to accommodate its increasing client base. The firm recruits enthusiastic, well-qualified applicants and provides opportunities for progression in a friendly and supportive environment.

■ Grays

Duncombe Place, York, YO1 7DY
Tel (01904) 634771 **Fax** (01904) 610711 **DX** 61505
Email enquiries@grayssolicitors.co.uk **Website** www.grayssolicitors.co.uk

AREAS OF PRACTICE	
Private Client & Charity	46%
Agricultural, Commercial & Residential Property	28%
Litigation	12%
Family	6%
Employment	4%
Other	4%

Ptnrs 6 **Asst solrs** 1 **Other fee-earners** 4 **Contact** Helen Mellors • Best known for trusts and taxation, charities (Tony Lawton), agriculture and property work. Also specialism in employment and high value matrimonial financial disputes.

■ Green & Co
Alberton House, St Mary's Passage, Manchester, M3 2WJ **Tel** (0161) 834 8980 **Fax** (0161) 834 8981

■ Greene & Greene
80 Guildhall Street, Bury St Edmunds, IP33 1QB **Tel** (01284) 762211 **Fax** (01284) 705739

■ Greenland Houchen

38 Prince of Wales Road, Norwich, NR1 1HZ
Tel (01603) 660744 **Fax** (01603) 610700 **DX** 5217 Norwich
Email mail@ghlaw.co.uk **Website** greenland-houchen.co.uk

Senior Partner	Robert Plumbly
Number of partners	9
Assistant solicitors	3
Other fee-earners	7

THE FIRM A long established general practice which seeks to offer at its three offices a full range of legal services. The partners include in their clientele builders and developers, housing associations, members of the local farming community and other commercial and corporate enterprises, as well as the private client. All aspects of litigation are undertaken with a significant legal aid element.

A-Z ■ LAW FIRMS

Greenwoods

Monkstone House, City Road, Peterborough, PE1 1JE
Tel (01733) 887700 **Fax** (01733) 424900 **DX** 12599 Peterborough 4
Email mail@greenwoods.co.uk **Website** www.greenwoods.co.uk

THE FIRM One of the leading commercial law firms in East Anglia and the East Midlands. The Greenwoods' philosophy is simple, clients always come first. As the firm's growing client base demonstrates, it's an approach that clients appreciate. It's also an approach that attracts lawyers of the highest calibre, who understand commercial reality and deliver solutions. Through concentrating on its clients and on its people, Greenwoods' reputation for excellence has spread far beyond its Peterborough base.

PRINCIPAL AREAS OF WORK Greenwoods' legal services include commercial litigation, commercial property and planning, company and commercial, construction and engineering, employment and employee benefits, EU and competition law, health and safety, information technology, insolvency, intellectual property, property litigation and private client advice.

CLIENTELE Greenwoods' client base includes regional, national and international companies and organisations, whose operations are serviced nationally, throughout Europe and in some cases worldwide.

RECRUITMENT Greenwoods looks to recruit around four trainees each year, and may provide financial support in some circumstances. A minimum of 2:1 degree is required. To apply send a handwritten letter (plus typed CV) to Rosemary Gearing.

Managing Partner	Shelagh Smith
Senior Partner	Michael Taylor
Number of partners	14
Assistant solicitors	16
Other fee-earners	23

CONTACTS	
Agriculture	Nick Plumb
Commercial Litigation	James Maxey
Commercial Property	Stephen Illingworth
Company/Commercial	Shelagh Smith
Construction & Engineering	Martin Wood
Employment	Robert Dillarstone
Family	Jane Proctor
Property Litigation	Michael Taylor
IT/Telecoms	Nigel Moore
Insolvency	Theo Anderton
Intellectual Property	Philip Sloan
Probate, Wills & Trusts	Nick Monsell

■ Gregg Latchams Quinn

6 Queen Square, Bristol, BS1 4JE **Tel** (0117) 925 8123 **Fax** (0117) 925 5567

Gregory Rowcliffe Milners

1 Bedford Row, London, WC1R 4BZ
Tel (020) 7242 0631 **Fax** (020) 7242 6652 **DX** 95
Email law@grm.co.uk **Website** www.grm.co.uk

THE FIRM Gregory Rowcliffe Milners is a progressive firm with an established reputation in quality private client advice, litigation services, corporate and business law. The firm has its roots going back to 1784. It has particularly strongly developed Anglo-German connections, (with fluent German speakers at all levels throughout the firm); and long standing links with a number of organisations concerned with Anglo-German trade.

PRINCIPAL AREAS OF WORK
Company/Commercial The department has excellent international links with Europe, especially Germany, the USA and the Far East, and represents national and multinational concerns, providing practical legal and taxation solutions to business problems and objectives over a broad spectrum of commerce and industry.
Litigation The firm provides a full range of litigation services to institutional, business and private clients in respect of administrative law (especially judicial review applications against public bodies); commercial, employment and property disputes; family law, including matrimonial disputes with legal aid where appropriate; personal injury, clinical negligence and claims relating to trusts and wills. The firm is noted for the international (especially German) aspect of its commercial and family litigation. It also has an extensive and well regarded London agency practice.
Employment A strong employment group specialising in providing a range of employment and HR related services to business on employment contracts, negotiations on termination of senior executives, unfair dismissal, redundancy, discrimination claims and employment policies and structures with a legal framework.
Private Client The firm has expertise in inheritance and tax planning, including the preservation of listed buildings and works of art, the creation of charitable trusts, and the administration of estates, often with an international dimension.
Property All aspects of commercial, industrial, agricultural, residential and investment conveyancing including estate management, planning and tax planning.

Number of partners	18
Assistant solicitors	3
Other fee-earners	9

AREAS OF PRACTICE	
Litigation	27%
Property	27%
Company/Commercial	24%
Private Client	22%

CONTACTS	
Anglo German	Ingrid McKeown
Company/Commercial	Paul Holloway
	Adrian Mezzetti
Employment	Jane Laidler
	Ingrid McKeown
Family/Matrimonial	Lesley Pendlebury Cox
	Fenella Pringle
Litigation	Christopher Harper
	Timothy Moloney
Personal Injury/Clinical Negligence	
	Anthony Benbow
Private Client	Michael Parnell-King
Property	William Bennett
	David King
Tax	Michael Parnell-King

Griffith Smith

47 Old Steyne, Brighton, BN1 1NW
Tel (01273) 324041 **Fax** (01273) 384000 **DX** 2701 Brighton-1
Email brighton@griffithsmith.co.uk **Website** www.griffithsmith.co.uk

Contact Nicholas Evans • Company/commercial, civil litigation, and private client with specialist skills including planning and environmental law and charity services.

Gross & Co

84 Guildhall Street, Bury St Edmunds, IP33 1PR
Tel (01284) 763333 **Fax** (01284) 762207 **DX** 57203
Email gdk@gross.co.uk

23 Bentinck Street, London, W1M 6AB
Tel (020) 7935 5541 **Fax** (020) 7935 6638
Email gdk@gross.co.uk

Senior Partner	Graeme Kirk
Number of partners	5
Assistant solicitors	2
Other fee-earners	6

AREAS OF PRACTICE	
Immigration & Nationality Law	20%
Company/Commercial	15%
Wills & Probate	15%
Civil Litigation	12%
Residential Conveyancing	10%
Matrimonial	10%
Commercial Property & Agriculture	10%
Employment	8%

CONTACTS	
Civil Litigation	Susan Kerr
Commercial Property & Agriculture	Jonathan Cobbold
Company/Commercial	Graeme Kirk
Employment	Nick Amor
Immigration/Nationality Law	Graeme Kirk
Matrimonial	Liz Hodder
Wills & Probate	Jonathan Howe

THE FIRM Established in West Suffolk for over 150 years, this progressive firm offers a specialist immigration service and has a fast-expanding commercial practice as well as a traditional general practice. The firm has an unusually international clientele, as well as sizeable private companies, small businesses and private clients. It is a member of the NIS Group of Independent Solicitors. The firm has an office in London W1 to service its London and international clients.

PRINCIPAL AREAS OF WORK

Immigration & Nationality The majority of work handled is in the field of business immigration. Assistance is also given in international immigration law, and a consultancy service is offered to other solicitors through the ImmLaw service (brochure available).
Company/Commercial The firm has expertise in most areas of commercial practice, including commercial property, for a wide range of business clients. It acts for many doctors and dentists.
Litigation All types of litigation are handled, including commercial, civil, matrimonial and Legal Aid. Agency work is undertaken.
Private Client Work includes conveyancing and wills/estate planning.

INTERNATIONAL The firm has overseas associate offices in USA, Canada, South Africa, India, Spain, Russia and Hong Kong. Languages spoken include French, German and Russian.

GSC Solicitors

31-32 Ely Place, London, EC1N 6TD
Tel (020) 7822 2222 **Fax** (020) 7822 2211 **DX** 462 London/Chancery Lane
Email info@gscsolicitors.com **Website** www.gscsolicitors.com

Senior Partner	S R Sheikh
Number of partners	5
Other fee-earners	10

CONTACTS	
Commercial Litigation	P J Leathem
Commercial Property	Harvey Posener
	P L Belcher
Corporate Commercial/IT/Employment	
	S R Sheikh
	Clive Halperin
Media/Intellectual Property	P J Leathem
Private Client/Tax/Trusts/International	
	S R Sheikh

THE FIRM This City firm undertakes a broad range of legal work for business and private clients. It is known for its expertise in media and intellectual property, commercial property, corporate and international work. GSC Solicitors, previously Green David Conway & Co, was founded in 1972 and over the years has established a reputation for excellence in its chosen fields. Clients range from individuals, small businesses and family-owned companies to multinational plcs and industry bodies. Recent developments in the firm include an increase in international work, particularly in Asia, Africa and the Middle East.

A-Z ■ LAW FIRMS

Gulbenkian Harris Andonian

181 Kensington High Street, London W8 6SH
Tel (020) 7937 1542   **Fax** (020) 7938 2059   **DX** 47204 Kensington
Email PaulG@gulbenkian.co.uk

THE FIRM Whilst the firm engages in a wide range of commercial work (including litigation) it is best known for its expertise in immigration and nationality law which is undertaken for both commercial and private clients. In addition to the successful House of Lords Appeal on the case of Shah and Islam reported in *The Times* on 26th March 1999 under the heading 'Pakistan's Failure to Protect Women' a further notable success was the case of Rolet and Baumbast which was decided at the European Court of Justice on 1st July 2001. It was successful in making new law in Luxembourg where no High Court had previously decided on such a situation. This involved the immigration status of a foreign spouse previously married to an EU National who, during the marriage, had not regularised his/her stay in the UK through marriage, but who wanted to do so, based on the former relationship after divorce. The matter relating to the dependent children of such union was previously unclear. The firm won on both matters.

Number of partners	11
Assistant solicitors	5
Other fee-earners	3

AREAS OF PRACTICE	
Immigration	70%
Matrimonial	20%
General	10%

CONTACTS	
General	Paul Gulbenkian
Immigration	Peter Wyatt
	Bernard Andonian
Matrimonial	Paul Gulbenkian
	Bernard Andonian

PRINCIPAL AREAS OF WORK
Immigration & Nationality Law Work includes nationality applications, all aspects of UK immigration and advice (business and private), refugee and asylum work and obtaining work permits. The firm has experience in US immigration, Hong Kong, Eastern Europe (including Russia), Middle East, Sri Lanka, USA, South America and South Africa. The firm is a founder member of the European Immigration Lawyers Group of which the senior partner is the President. Two of the partners are part-time Immigration Adjudicators and have been appointed to the Law Society Immigration Law Panel.
Matrimonial & Family Law Comprehensive services are provided including advice on separation, divorce, wardship, custody, adoption and all related financial, property and taxation matters. The senior partner is one of the founder members of the Solicitors Family Law Association.

CLIENTELE A largely international client base including multinationals as well as small to medium sized companies and private individuals.

INTERNATIONAL The firm handles work in Armenian, Arabic, Danish, Farsi, French, Spanish and Swedish.

■ Gwynnes

Edgbaston House, Walker Street, Telford, Wellington, TF1 1HF   **Tel** (01952) 641651   **Fax** (01952) 247441

H₂O

The Media Centre, 3-8 Carburton Street, London, W1W 5AJ
Tel (020) 7886 0740   **Fax** (020) 7886 0741
Email forename.surname@h2o-law.com   **Website** www.h2o-law.com

THE FIRM H₂O is a niche media IP and human rights firm, with an international reputation. H₂O prides itself on the creativity of its lawyers and its flexible and responsive approach to client needs.

PRINCIPAL AREAS OF WORK H₂O has a media and human rights focus. It combines creative legal skills with expertise in PR and lobbying. H₂O has a worldwide reputation for legal campaigning and human rights actions. H₂O's lawyers are specialists in defamation, privacy and media disputes, employment issues, e-commerce (compliance), contentious intellectual property and human rights. H₂O has particular expertise in reputation management and advises on the legal aspects of public relations, media strategy and all forms of reputation protection, be it corporate or individual, name or brand. H₂O is an innovative and forward-thinking firm that offers a fast, reliable and cost-effective service for its clients.

AREAS OF PRACTICE	
Media/IP (Defamation)	35%
Defamation/Reputation Management	30%
Human Rights	20%
Litigation	10%
Employment	5%

CONTACTS	
Media	Paul Fox, Jason McCue
IP	Paul Fox
Litigation	David Greenhalgh, Paul Fox
Human Rights (Privacy)	Jason McCue, Paul Fox
Publishing	Jason McCue, Rose Alexander
Employment	David Greenhalgh

Haarmann Hemmelrath

Tower 42, 25 Old Broad Street, London, EC2N 1HQ
Tel (020) 7382 4800 **Fax** (020) 7382 4833
Email philip_newhouse@hhp.de **Website** www.haarmannhemmelrath.com

Number of partners	5
Assistant solicitors	12
Other fee-earners	6

AREAS OF PRACTICE

M&A	40%
International Tax & Tax Structuring	15%
Company & Corporate Law	10%
Capital Markets, Corporate Finance	10%
Private Equity	10%
IP & IT	10%
Turnaround & Reconstruction Finance	5%

CONTACTS

M&A	Jay Birch
	Philip Newhouse
Company & Corporate Law	Jay Birch
	Philip Newhouse
Turnaround & Reconstruction	Grant Jones
	David von Saucken
Capital Markets	Jay Birch
	David von Saucken
Corporate Finance	Jay Birch
	Philip Newhouse
	Anthony Webb
International Tax & Tax Structuring	Peter Vaines
	Adrian Murphy
Private Equity	Philip Newhouse
	Nicholas Foss-Pedersen
IP & IT	Michael Molineaux
	Chris Hubbard
	Martin Quinn

THE FIRM Haarmann Hemmelrath, the English arm of Haarmann Hemmelrath & Partner, opened its London office in spring 2000 in the heart of the City of London. Since then it has grown consistently. The London office comprises English solicitors, registered foreign lawyers and registered European lawyers. A speciality of Haarmann Hemmelrath & Partner is its integrated approach, which provides clients with legal and tax advice from a single source on domestic and cross-border issues. Through its close co-operation with all other Haarmann Hemmelrath offices, the firm ensures immediate access to the most recent legal and economic developments.

PRINCIPAL AREAS OF WORK The London office offers services across the spectrum of M&A; IPO; corporate and commercial law; IP; IT; e-commerce; capital markets; corporate finance; turnaround and reconstruction and international tax advice.

CLIENTELE The firm's clients include UK and German listed and private companies; leading multi-national corporations; high net worth individuals and government organisations.

INTERNATIONAL Founded in 1987, Haarmann Hemmelrath & Partner has 24 offices in Western, Central and Eastern Europe and Asia including seven offices in Germany's major business centres. An office in Rome will be opened during this year. The firm is a member of various international, professional and other associations and organisations, and regularly takes part in events organised by them. The result is a constant exchange of professional experience with recognised advisors on a worldwide basis. Further, the firm is a member of the RSM international network, an international association of independent firms of auditors with over 520 offices in more than 70 countries. The languages spoken are German, English, French, Italian, Polish, Czech, Romanian, Russian, Japanese, Mandarin, Cantonese, and many others according to the location of its offices.

RECRUITMENT The firm has set up a training contract scheme for trainee solicitors and provides funding for the vocational stage of the training. Candidates with first or upper second class degrees are preferred. Applications should be sent to Jane Hunter in London.

www.haarmannhemmelrath.com

Hadens (formerly Haden Stretton Slater Miller)

Leicester Buildings, Bridge Street, Walsall, WS1 1EL **Tel** (0121) 526 2626 **Fax** (01922) 720023

Hallett & Co

11 Bank Street, Ashford TN23 1DA
Tel (01233) 625711 **Fax** (01233) 643841 **DX** 30202 Ashford
Email info@hallettandco.co.uk

3 Upper Bridge Street, Wye, TN25 5AF
Tel (01233) 812353 **Fax** (01233) 813454

Senior Partner	Mark Skilbeck
Number of partners	8
Assistant solicitors	4
Other fee-earners	11

CONTACTS

Agriculture	Charles McDonald
Education	Mark Skilbeck
Employment	Martin Stevens
Tax & Trusts	Nicola Hopper
Wills & Estate Planning	Richard Rix

THE FIRM Hallett & Co has been serving the people of Ashord, Kent and beyond since 1830 and is one of the largest firms in East Kent. The firm is recognised as a local leader in a number of fields including advice to the agricultural community; employment; estate and residential conveyancing; private client work; wills, probate and the creation and management of trusts. Each client's work is supervised by a specific partner who can, if necessary, call on specialist support. Hallett & Co also has offices in Ashford Cattle Market, New Romney and Lydd.

A-Z ■ LAW FIRMS

■ Hall & Haughey
Ground Floor, 63 Carlton Place, Glasgow, G5 9TW **Tel** (0141) 418 0505 **Fax** (0141) 429 3131

■ Hallinan, Blackburn, Gittings & Nott
Suite 22, Westminster Palace Gardens, Artillery Row, London, SW1P 1RR
Tel (020) 7233 3999 **Fax** (020) 7233 3888 **Email** hallinans@btconnect.com

Ptnrs 2 **Asst solrs** 2 **Other fee-earners** 1 **Contact** Valerie Walsh • Specialises in crime, extradition, fraud, infanticide and road traffic offences. Legal Aid franchise/private client. Experienced and well respected in the defence of a broad spectrum of clients.

Halliwell Landau
St. James's Court, Brown St, Manchester, M2 2JF
Tel (0161) 835 3003 **Fax** (0161) 835 2994 **DX** 14317
Email info@halliwells.co.uk **Website** www.halliwells.co.uk

75 King William Street, London, EC4N 7BE
Tel (020) 7929 1900 **Fax** (020) 7929 4800

City Plaza, Pinfold Street, Sheffield, S1 2GU
Tel (0114) 229 8000 **Fax** (0114) 229 8001

Managing Partner	Paul Thomas
Senior Partner	Alec Craig
London Senior Partner	Clive Garston
Sheffield Managing Partner	
	Suzanne Liversidge
Number of partners	66
Assistant solicitors	121
Other fee-earners	85

CONTACTS	
Commercial Litigation	Ian Austin
Commercial Property	Mike Edge
Corporate	Mark Halliwell
Employment	Stephen Hills
Financial Institutions	Matthew Wightman
Insolvency	Andrew Buchanan
Insurance Litigation	Christopher Phillips
Intellectual Property	Jonathan Moakes
Planning	Roger Lancaster
Trusts & Estate Planning	Geoffrey Shindler

THE FIRM Halliwell Landau is one of the country's leading multidisciplinary law firms with over 550 people and offices in Manchester, London and Sheffield. The firm has enjoyed a prodigious 12 months with record turnover, significant national and international client gains, market leading lateral hires, innovative IT developments and a range of cutting edge management initiatives. Halliwell Landau is a fast growing entrepreneurial law firm providing legal business solutions to a wide range of commercial clients.

■ A Halsall & Co
47-48 Hamilton Square, Birkenhead, CH41 5BD **Tel** (0151) 647 6323 **Fax** (0151) 647 9818

■ Hamers
9-11 Scale Lane, Hull, HU1 1PH
Tel (01482) 326666 **Fax** (01482) 324432 **DX** 11933 Hull
Email info@hamers.com **Website** www.hamers.com

Ptnrs 6 **Asst solrs** 28 **Other fee-earners** 18 **Contact** Philip Hamer • One of Yorkshire's premier legal names with a growing network of offices throughout the Yorkshire region. The firm focuses on delivering specialist legal advice and prides itself on its levels of client care. Principal areas of practice are commercial, employment, personal injury, family law, conveyancing, probate and wills, and civil litigation.

LAW FIRMS ■ A-Z

Hamlins

Roxburghe House, 273-287 Regent St, London, W1B 2AD
Tel (020) 7355 6000 **Fax** (020) 7518 9100 **DX** 53803 Oxford Circus North
Email admin@hamlins.co.uk **Website** www.hamlins.co.uk

THE FIRM This medium-sized London practice, formerly known as Hamlin Slowe, is property-orientated with a substantial commercial client base. Founded in 1906, the firm undertakes a wide variety of work, but has particular expertise in commercial property, commercial, secured lending, intellectual property, entertainment and media matters. The firm's clients include several public companies and many large and well-known private companies.

PRINCIPAL AREAS OF WORK

Property The department has a long and established reputation in financing, acquisition, letting and disposal of shop, office and industrial property as well as handling development, town and country planning, compulsory purchase and landlord and tenant matters.

Secured Lending The department acts for lenders in professional negligence, possession, mortgage documentation, arrears, sales, insolvency, consumer credit and unsecured loss recovery matters. The department has developed on-line computer systems for mortgage and arrears recovery.

Litigation The firm is known for the strength of its litigation department which supports the non-litigious departments, handles heavy commercial litigation, matrimonial and personal injury matters and includes the entertainment, media and intellectual property department which has an outstanding reputation in the entertainment sector, particularly in the areas of copyright infringement. It handles all aspects of entertainment law for clients who include copyright societies, music publishers, record companies, record producers, composers, authors, recording artists, and film and video production companies. The department also advises on matters of defamation, libel, information technology, multimedia, trademarks, passing off and design right.

Company & Commercial The department deals with mergers, acquisitions, disposals, franchising, employment and partnership matters. The department also advises on share and rights issues, public flotations, corporate reorganisations, liquidations and joint ventures. This department encompasses a division which specialises in advising the leisure industry and has an asset planning division which handles personal taxation, inheritance tax planning, pensions, trusts, wills and probates. Hamlins has a strong client base of both large and small clients. The firm's brochure describing the services that the firm has to offer is available upon request.

Managing Partners	Brian Casey
	Laurence Gilmore
	Nigel Mason
Number of partners	18
Assistant solicitors	14
Other fee-earners	21

AREAS OF PRACTICE	
Property Services	36%
Company & Commercial	20%
Entertainment/Intellectual Property	20%
Litigation Services	12%
Secured Lending	12%

CONTACTS	
Company & Commercial	Gordon Oliver
Litigation (inc. Entertainment, Media & Intellectual Property)	Laurence Gilmore
Property Services	Brian Casey
Secured Lending	Keith Roffey

HAMLINS

■ Hammond Suddards Edge
7 Devonshire Square, Cutlers Gardens, London, EC2M 4YH **Tel** (020) 7655 1000 **Fax** (020) 7655 1001

■ Hansells
13 Cathedral Close, Norwich, NR1 4DS **Tel** (01603) 615731 **Fax** (01603) 633585

Harbottle & Lewis

Hanover House, 14 Hanover Square, London, W1S 1HP
Tel (020) 7667 5000 **Fax** (020) 7667 5100 **DX** 44617 Mayfair
Email info@harbottle.com **Website** www.harbottle.com

THE FIRM Harbottle & Lewis provides specialist advice to the media, entertainment and communications industries. It remains unique in having expertise right across these sectors and is consistently recognised as a leading firm by independent sources. Whilst its key practice areas continue to expand, the original values of the firm – to provide efficient legal advice, encourage originality and enjoy what it does – remain constant.

PRINCIPAL AREAS OF WORK The firm is well known for its knowledge of and interest in the industries in which it specialises, combined with its legal skills. The firm's work encompasses all areas of the media industry, including film, television, broadcasting, sports, music, publishing, advertising and theatre. The advent of new technologies has inevitably shaped its work and highly successful practices in complementary areas such as online, new media and interactive entertainment have emerged in recent years. The firm provides a complete range of commercial legal advice to its clients on corporate, technology, litigation, intellectual property, regulatory, defamation, property, employment, finance, tax issues. Clients of the firm range from actors, musicians and other celebrities to emerging growth companies, multinational rights-owners, entrepreneurs and charities. In undertaking any work, its aim is to understand its client's business and to add real value. Harbottle & Lewis shares clients'
Continued overleaf

Managing Partner	Samantha Phillips
Number of partners	17
Assistant solicitors	53
Other fee-earners	21

CONTACTS	
Advertising & Marketing	Gerrard Tyrrell
Aviation	Dermot Scully
Broadcasting	Medwyn Jones
Charities	Robert Porter
Company & Commercial	Colin Howes
Corporate Finance	Mark Bertram
Corporate Recovery & Insolvency	
	Samantha Phillips
E-commerce & New Media	Mark Phillips
Employment	Marian Derham, Dermot Scully
Film & TV Production	Robert Storer
Finance	Christopher Badham
Immigration	Anne Balcomb
Intellectual Property	Mark Owen
Interactive Entertainment	Sebastian Belcher
IT & Technology	Mark Owen
Leisure	Justin Dunlop

www.ChambersandPartners.com

A-Z LAW FIRMS

expectations of concise, commercial and strategic advice offered proactively but cost-effectively. The firm has around 100 lawyers of whom 17 are partners, two are consultants and 12 are senior associates, all based in London. The firm has no other offices but maintains a referral relationship with a number of law firms globally who are able to provide advice in the specialist areas required by the firm's clients.

CLIENTELE Harbottle & Lewis is big enough to handle virtually any transaction in its specialist sectors but also of a size which has enabled it to remain focused on those sectors and exploit the common factors between them. Recent highlights of its work include advising Chrysalis Group plc on the merger of internet sports businesses Rivals.net and 365.com and advising on arrangements for the World Rally Championship. Also advising Virgin Hotels on the disposal of two luxury properties and advising Marlborough Fine Arts regarding the Estate of Francis Bacon, one of the largest claims ever made in the art world.

CONTACTS (Continued)	
Litigation	Gerrard Tyrrell
Music	Ann Harrison
Property Development & Investment	Alan Patten
Publishing	Rachel Atkins
Sport & Sponsorship	Bob Mitchell
Tax	Glen Atchison
Theatre & Performing Arts	Colin Howes

Harbottle & Lewis

Harcus Sinclair
40 Victoria Embankment, London, EC4Y 0BA **Tel** (020) 7583 7353 **Fax** (020) 7583 7303

Harding Evans
Queen Chambers, 2 North Street, Newport, NP2 1TE **Tel** (01633) 244233 **Fax** (01633) 246453

Hardwick Stallards
Centurion House, 37 Jewry Street, London, EC3N 2ER
Tel (020) 7423 1000 **Fax** (020) 7481 3002 **DX** 822 London/City
Email mail@hardwickstallards.com **Website** www.hardwickstallards.com

PRINCIPAL AREAS OF WORK
Company & Commercial A broad range of corporate and commercial work, including intellectual property, partnerships, mergers and acquisitions, sales and other disposals, joint ventures, commercial contracts, share option arrangements and general commercial advice.
Corporate Finance Stock Exchange and regulatory advice, advising on issues, including official list, AIM and OFEX flotations, debt/equity issues, venture capital investment, institutional funding and secured lending, MBOs and MBIs, and corporate reconstructions.
Commercial Property Commercial development and investment work for private and public companies, overseas investors, financial institutions and individual entrepreneurs, together with all aspects of landlord and tenant work, estate management and work for local authorities.
Litigation Dealing with most kinds of commercial disputes, particular experience in the areas of landlord and tenant, construction contracts, factoring and banking, together with personal injury work.
Employment Contentious and non-contentious work.
Transportation Contentious and non-contentious shipping matters, multi-modal transport, containerisation, and trade finance and insurance.

CLIENTELE Clientele consists principally of entrepreneur-managed businesses and a number of listed companies. The partner-led approach provides an in-house style of service with an emphasis on business experience.

Senior Partner	Keith Robinson
Finance Partner	Alan Williams
Number of partners	13
Assistant solicitors	8
Other fee-earners	4

CONTACTS	
Commercial Property	Michael Pearson
Company & Commercial	Nick Roche
Corporate Finance	Keith Robinson
Employment	Tola Ogundimu
Litigation	Rhodri James
Transportation	Paul Bugden

Harold Benjamin Littlejohn

Hill House, 67-71 Lowlands Road, Harrow, HA1 3EQ
Tel (020) 8422 5678 **Fax** (020) 8864 7350 **DX** 4243 Harrow
Email hbl@hben.co.uk **Website** www.hben.co.uk

Senior Partner	Roger Lane
Managing Partner	Keith Flavell
Number of partners	11
Associates	4
Assistant solicitors	2
Other fee-earners	11

AREAS OF PRACTICE

Commercial Property	43%
Litigation	28%
Private Client, Family & Probate	19%
Corporate	10%

CONTACTS

Commercial Leases	Sarah Paul
Company/Commercial	Franklin Lavatta
Development	Chris Batty
Family	Keith Flavell
General Litigation	Keith Boddy
Personal Injury	Andrew Tilsiter
Private Client	Jonathan Dorman
Property Litigation	Richard Crowe

THE FIRM Known as Harold Benjamin & Collins until April 2000, the firm has undergone rapid growth in the past five years, investing in key people and information technology. Widely known for development and commercial conveyancing and property litigation, the firm is ideally located in central Harrow, which is increasingly convenient for a rapidly expanding base of property and other commercial clients, at regional and national levels. The increase in volume and quality of work has seen a series of expansions led by the property department but teams from all departments are fielded for multidisciplinary and high value transactions. The company/commercial and litigation departments continue to expand and attract new clients through recommendation. This year has seen a restructuring of the management team with the election of the first managing partner.

PRINCIPAL AREAS OF WORK
Property The firm handles development, commercial and residential conveyancing, including the acquisition and legal management of sites for residential and mixed commercial, leisure and residential development; town planning and environmental law; commercial leasehold premises work acting for both landlords and tenants, including the grant and renewal of leases of commercial property and the sale and purchase of tenanted commercial property for investment; retail premises; commercial mortgage work for institutional lenders.
Litigation Work includes building and property litigation with particular emphasis on the Landlord and Tenant Act 1954; personal injury and clinical negligence; employment law; general litigation; housing association tenant management.
Corporate/Commercial The firm has a wide range of corporate clients, dealing with a broad spread of work including acquisitions, joint ventures, intellectual property, partnership, general commercial contracts, agency distribution, finance and competition law.
Private Client The firm provides a full service of family law; wills and probate; residential conveyancing, especially substantial properties.
Family Recent expansion has led to the strengthening of the family department to include members of the Solicitors Family Law Association, Family Law panel and qualified mediators enabling the firm to offer a broad range of services in family law but particularly in high value ancillary relief work.

CLIENTELE The firm acts for a wide range of clients on a national basis including plcs, national house builders and private property developers engaged in both residential and commercial property development. The company commercial and litigation departments have national and local clients. The firm acts for a company with an excess of 1,500 retail units spread throughout the country. High value residential transactions are carried out for international clients, and the firm continues to value its associations with private clients, many of whom are local and have been with the firm for many years.

Harper Macleod

The Ca'd'oro, 45 Gordon Street, Glasgow, G1 3PE
Tel (0141) 221 8888 **Fax** (0141) 226 4198 **DX** GW86
Email info@harpermacleod.co.uk **Website** www.harpermacleod.co.uk

93 George Street, Edinburgh, EH2 3ES
Tel (0131) 240 1265 **Fax** (0131) 240 1266 **DX** ED167

Managing Partner	Lorne D Crerar
Number of partners	20
Assistant solicitors	20
Other fee-earners	11

CONTACTS

Banking	Lorne D Crerar
Commercial Litigation	Rod McKenzie
Commercial Property	David Bell
Construction	Michael Conroy
Corporate	Donald Munro
Employment	Claire McManus
Human Rights	Melanie Kerr
Insolvency	James Lloyd
Insurance	Richard Henderson
Intellectual Property & Technology	Tom Thomas
Licensing	Graeme Nisbet
Medical	Claire McManus
Private Client	Gordon Stoddart
Projects	Chris Kerr
Public Sector & Housing	Len Freedman
Recoveries	Dawn McKenzie
Sport	Rod McKenzie

THE FIRM Harper Macleod has a reputation for innovation and a progressive approach to law. The firm is well known for providing practical solutions to the demands of the corporate marketplace. The firm's practice group structure encourages the development of flexible and tailored legal services to meet the individual needs of clients. The firm is well-resourced to meet the needs of clients with European and international interests. In April 2002 Harper Macleod launched the European Legal Alliance with four other leading commercial law firms: Beauchamps in Ireland; Buse Heberer Fromm in Germany; Dubarry le Douarin Veil in France; and Field Fisher Waterhouse in England. The firms have worked together for some years and now operate under a single brand and on an exclusive basis with each other. The Alliance provides Harper Macleod with a full presence in 10 other key European business centres as well as Glasgow and Edinburgh. Along with the firm's other Alliance members, it is a Scottish member of Ecomlex, an association of leading European e-commerce lawyers set up to advise clients on issues such as cross-border internet ventures. A key feature of Harper Macleod is the long-standing relationships it develops with clients. The firm prides itself on getting to know clients'

Continued overleaf

A-Z ■ LAW FIRMS

businesses in the same way that clients are encouraged to become involved in Harper Macleod.

PRINCIPAL AREAS OF WORK The work undertaken by the firm is as wide ranging as its clients, from blue chip UK and multinational companies to entrepreneurs and small business start-ups, and from both private and public sectors. In addition to the six administrative departments of corporate, commercial property, housing, litigation, private client and recoveries, the firm operates 17 practice groups covering its main areas of specialism: banking; commercial property; construction; corporate and commercial; employment; insolvency; insurance; intellectual property and technology; human rights; medical; recoveries; licensing; planning and environmental; private client; projects; public sector and housing; sport. Membership of the practice groups is multidisciplinary and can draw upon the expertise of the firm as a whole.

Social Housing, Employment & Sports Law The firm is particularly well known and has a leading reputation in these areas. Harper Macleod's national conferences have a successful track record and the firm organised the sixth national housing, fifth national employment and second national football law and finance conferences in 2002.

E-commerce Harper Macleod is particularly active in the e-commerce sector and was the first firm in Scotland to launch a web-based legal package, dotcomstartup. The dotcom team acts for a wide range of online businesses and is ideally placed to provide a comprehensive business solutions package through the dotcom network (www.dotcomstartup.co.uk).

Commercial Property The firm is active in the commercial property market and clients range from institutional property owners and developers to retailers and other UK companies. The firm's banking expertise has previously been described as 'one of a few of any substantial size'. The firm's litigation expertise speaks for itself and it is quickly developing a speciality in pursuer defamation.

HARPER MACLEOD

THE EUROPEAN LEGAL
ALLIANCE

Harris Cartwright

Windsor Crown House, 7 Windsor Rd, Slough, SL1 2DX
Tel (01753) 810710 **Fax** (01753) 810720 **DX** 42268 Slough (West)
Email enquiries@hclaw.co.uk **Website** www.hclaw.co.uk

1 New Square, Lincoln's Inn, London, WC2A 3SA
Tel (0870) 043 3765 **Fax** (0870) 608 5393 **DX** 414 LDE

THE FIRM Established in 1922, Harris Cartwright is a progressive and enlightened firm, building on its accumulated knowledge and experience to provide a high quality, responsive and cost-effective service to all its clients. With two offices in Slough (one dedicated to company/commercial work) and one other in nearby Langley, the firm is one of the largest in the Thames Valley. The firm's London office trades as Harris Cartier and is operated in association with Cartier & Co.

PRINCIPAL AREAS OF WORK

Company & Commercial A rapidly expanding department, now accounting for approximately one third of total fee income, assists business clients across the full spectrum of problems faced from start-up to flotation and beyond. Services include commercial conveyancing, business sales, takeovers, mergers and acquisitions, partnership formations and agreements, commercial negotiations, company secretarial and administrative matters, commercial litigation, insolvency and receivership, employment, terms and conditions of sale, e-commerce, intellectual property, IT and data protection, service contracts and similar agreements. A growing niche market is advising organisations in the international context - British companies trading overseas and foreign companies wishing to operate in the UK.

Personal Injury & Clinical Negligence The firm has developed a specialisation for acting on behalf of severely disabled victims of accidents and clinical negligence. In recent years it has acted on behalf of the Claimants in the cases of Biesheuvel v Birrell (1998) where damages of £9.3 million were awarded at trial, Dashiell v Luttit (1999) where damages were agreed at £5.1 million, Owen v Brown with damages of £4.35 million, Penny v Southern Derbyshire Health Authority (2000) with damages in excess of £3.5 million awarded at trial and Lee v East Berkshire Health Authority (1999) – damages of £2.5 million. Personnel in the department are, variously, members of the Law Society's Personal Injury and Clinical Negligence Panels and of AVMA, Spinal Injuries Association and Headway.

Family All qualified staff are members of the Solicitors Family Law Association and are specialists in this field. They are also, variously, members of the Law Society's Family and Children panels. Matters dealt with include high profile ancillary relief, divorce, children and injunction proceedings.

Financial Services Headed by an independent financial advisor with 30 years industry experience, the department provides advice on investment, insurance and pensions to both individuals and organisations.

Residential Conveyancing Operating from offices in Slough and Langley, this department offers a full conveyancing service together with advice on development, planning and finance for residential properties.

Senior Partner	Paul Norris
Number of partners	9
Assistant solicitors	19
Other fee-earners	20

AREAS OF PRACTICE	
Civil Litigation	32%
Company/Commercial	31%
Conveyancing	25%
Family	6%
Wills, Probate, Trusts	6%

CONTACTS	
Clinical Negligence	Christopher Gooderidge
Commercial Litigation	Andrew Grant
Commercial Property	Paul Norris
Company/Commercial	Stephen Fuller
	Raj Dhokia
Debt Collection	Andrew Grant
E-commerce	Nick Burrows
Employment	Raj Dhokia
Family	Suzanne Allen
Financial Services	David McIntosh
Intellectual Property	Nick Burrows
Landlord & Tenant	Andrew Grant
Personal Injury	Kent Pattinson
Residential Conveyancing	Richard Palmer
Wills, Probate, Trusts	Ron Kerslake

Wills, Probate & Trusts Working closely with the financial services department, a full range of wills, probate, trusts and estate administration, tax and inheritance tax planning is provided.

INTERNATIONAL Languages spoken include Italian, French, Polish, Gujerati, Punjabi, Hindi and Urdu.

Harris & Harris

14 Market Place, Wells, BA5 2RE
Tel (01749) 674747 **Fax** (01749) 834060 **DX** 44900 Wells
Email enquiries@harris-harris.co.uk **Website** www.harris-harris.co.uk

Senior Partner	Timothy Berry

THE FIRM Established for over 150 years, the firm has a broad client base and prides itself on its commitment to client care. The firm also has an office in Frome and a consultant in France.

PRINCIPAL AREAS OF WORK Commercial, charity, ecclesiastical, education, employment, family, insolvency, mental health and personal injury law.

Harrison Bundey & Co.

219-223 Chapeltown Road, Leeds, LS7 3DX **Tel** (0113) 284 5000 **Fax** (0113) 237 4685

Harrison Curtis

8 Jockey's Fields, London, WC1R 4BF
Tel (020) 7611 1720 **Fax** (020) 7611 1721
Email mail@harrisoncurtis.co.uk **Website** www.harrisoncurtis.co.uk

Number of partners	3

CONTACTS	
Advertising & Marketing	Vanessa Hall-Smith
Film & Television	Tim Curtis
Immigration	Vanessa Hall-Smith
Music	Lawrence Harrison
Theatre	Lawrence Harrison

HARRISON CURTIS
Solicitors

THE FIRM A small niche practice set up in 1998 which is already established as a leading provider of legal services to the media, communication and entertainment industries. The firm's partners each have recognised expertise within their own practice areas. Emphasis is placed on providing a high quality and accessible service at competitive rates and on effectively meeting client needs and expectations within a friendly working environment.

PRINCIPAL AREAS OF WORK Areas covered include music, TV and film, theatre, advertising and marketing, e-commerce, sport, immigration.

Harrisons Solicitors

Victoria House, 54-58 Chichester Street, Belfast, BT1 4HN
Tel (028) 9032 3843 **Fax** (028) 9033 2644 **DX** 401 NR Belfast
Email Harrisonll@compuserve.com **Website** www.harrisonsni.com

Senior Partner	Ronnie Bowden

AREAS OF PRACTICE	
Litigation	40%
Property	25%
Company/Commercial/Employment	25%
Private Client/Other	10%

THE FIRM Harrisons (formerly Harrison Leitch & Logan) continues to build upon its expertise in litigation, borne initially out of a strong insurance base and its company and commercial work. In commercial property the firm is involved in many substantial and prestigious transactions. Quality assurance – ISO 9001. First private practice in Belfast to achieve Lexcel (Law Society Standard).

PRINCIPAL AREAS OF WORK
Litigation Represents a broad base of insurers, loss adjusters and travel companies, lending institutions and large UK listed companies, but places emphasis on personal injury and defence litigation.
Property PPP. Acquisition, disposal, development, financing and management of commercial (and residential) property.
Company/Commercial Company formations, sale and purchase of assets, acquisition of companies, licensing, partnership agreements and shareholder agreements.
Private client A large following to whom the firm provides advice on property, wills and probate, trusts and inheritance tax planning.

A-Z LAW FIRMS

Harrowell Shaftoe

1 St Saviourgate, York, YO1 2ZQ
Tel (01904) 558600 **Fax** (01904) 655855 **DX** 61506 York
Email jfy@harrowell-shaftoe.co.uk **Website** www.harrowells.co.uk

THE FIRM Harrowell Shaftoe is an expanding regional practice based in York. It is a major player in economically vibrant North Yorkshire and has eight specialist department serving both commercial and private clients.

PRINCIPAL AREAS OF WORK
Corporate/Commercial/IP Specialists in different aspects of business law, including IP for bioscience and IT businesses.
Employment Focuses on advising employers and senior employees.
Personal Injury Recognised as PI and clinical negligence specialists with a client base across the North of England.
Other Areas Significant conveyancing, private client, family and crime departments serving North and East Yorkshire.

Managing & Senior Partner	John Yeomans
Number of partners	15

CONTACTS	
Commercial Property	James Scott
Company/Commercial	Phillip Lewis Ogden
Crime	Jackie Knights
Employment	Simon Black
Family	John Reynard
Personal Injury	Mark Tempest
Probate & Trusts	William Miers
Residential Conveyancing	Robert Seaton

HARROWELL SHAFTOE SOLICITORS

Hartnells Family Law Practice
Oriel House, Southernay Gardens, Exeter, EX1 1NP **Tel** (01392) 421777 **Fax** (01392) 421237

Hartwig

15 William Mews, London, SW1X 9HF
Tel (020) 7235 1504 **Fax** (020) 8681 8183
Email hartwig@beeb.net

THE FIRM London's largest firm of solicitor-notaries, with English, European and US lawyers; Rechtsanwlte, licensed in Germany since 1978. London-based multinational commercial, industrial, corporate, finance and property practice. The firm handles international litigation and private clients work. A substantial part of the firm's work is at pre-arranged fees on counsel basis for law firms and in-house lawyers.

Senior Partner	H J Hartwig

Harvey Ingram Owston

20 New Walk, Leicester, LE1 6TX
Tel (0116) 254 5454 **Fax** (0116) 255 4559 **DX** 17014 Leicester 2
Email hio@hio.co.uk **Website** www.hio.co.uk

THE FIRM Harvey Ingram Owston is one of the East Midlands' largest law firms, acting for commercial and private clients regionally and nationally. This prominent Leicester practice makes client service a priority and has been accredited to ISO 9001 since 1995. Combining a long tradition with a modern approach to legal solutions, it lists total quality, reliability and ease of access as its key client-orientated objectives.

PRINCIPAL AREAS OF WORK The firm comprises the main departments of property, dispute resolution, company/commercial and private client, all of which contain various sub-departments. The firm's strength in such a wide range of legal disciplines enables it to provide clients with a fully comprehensive, cross-departmental service, offering specialist advice in myriad areas of law.
Company/Commercial The corporate team has a growing reputation for handling high profile, high value and often highly complex deals. In the past 12 months, for instance, it has advised on the acquisition of footwear retailer Jones Bootmaker from Prada, the takeover of Oliver Group by Shoe Zone and WR Group's purchase of a UK subsidiary from a large German company. The emergence of e-commerce and its increasing importance to business has led to a change of emphasis in the type of legal work undertaken by the department's e-commerce specialists. As well as advising internet start-ups, they have also seen demand for advice on specific technology-related issues such as intellectual property rights on the internet.
Commercial Property The department deals with all aspects of commercial property, including freehold

Managing Partner	Chris Finlay
Senior Partner	Stephen Woolfe
Number of partners	21
Assistant solicitors	27
Other fee-earners	44

AREAS OF PRACTICE	
Litigation	33%
Commercial Property	26%
Company/Commercial	18%
Residential Property	15%
Probate & Trusts	8%

Harvey Ingram Owston solicitors
THE SYMBOL FOR LEGAL EXCELLENCE

and leasehold transactions, site acquisition, landlord and tenant law, rent control, agricultural and environmental law. It has a particular strength in the areas of retail property and planning law.

Residential Property As well as private conveyancing, the firm's residential property team specialises in housing association work and repossessions sales for major institutions. The department also has a sports unit, advising the Leicester 'Tigers' Football Club, Leicestershire County Cricket Club and Nurishment Leicester Riders along with a number of players at Leicester City Football Club.

Dispute Resolution The department's expertise lies in a whole host of commercial matters such as employment law, insolvency, intellectual property, licensing and professional negligence. The firm also handles a wide range of general litigation work for private clients in the areas of personal injury, family law and debt collections.

Trusts The firm's trusts work includes estate planning, the drafting of trusts and wills, trust and estate administration as well as charity and Court of Protection work.

CLIENTELE
The firm provides legal services to national and regional companies as well as servicing the needs of small and medium-sized businesses. Clients include: Alliance & Leicester Plc, Everards Brewery, The BSS Group Plc, National Car Rentals, Stead & Simpson, Shoe Zone, Weetabix, Golden Wonder, Samworth Brothers, Vision Express (UK), De Montfort Housing Association and Leicester Housing Association. A network of overseas contacts enables Harvey Ingram Owston to advise on foreign matters, particularly in mainland Europe and the United States.

Hasties
51 South Bridge, Edinburgh, EH1 1PP **Tel** (0131) 556 7951 **Fax** (0131) 558 1596

Hatch Brenner
4 Theatre Street, Norwich, NR2 1QY
Tel (01603) 660811 **Fax** (01603) 619473 **DX** 5237 Norwich

Ptnrs 9 **Asst solrs** 4 **Other fee-earners** 12 **Contact** Richard Cassel • Property, commercial, civil litigation (including employment and personal injury), family and crime. Legal Aid Franchise, Personal Injury and Children Panels.

Hay & Kilner
Merchant House, 30 Cloth Market, Newcastle upon Tyne, NE1 1EE **Tel** (0191) 232 8345 **Fax** (0191) 221 0514

HBM Sayers
13 Bath Street, Glasgow, G2 1HY **Tel** (0141) 353 2121 **Fax** (0141) 353 2181

Hegarty & Co
48 Broadway, Peterborough, PE1 1YW **Tel** (01733) 346333 **Fax** (01733) 562338

Hempsons

Hempsons House, 40 Villiers Street, London, WC2N 6NJ
Tel (020) 7839 0278 **Fax** (020) 7839 8212 **DX** 138411 Charing Cross 1
Email London@hempsons.co.uk **Website** www.hempsons.co.uk

Clarendon House, 9 Victoria Avenue, Harrogate, HG1 1DY
Tel (01423) 522331 **Fax** (01423) 500733 **DX** 11965 Harrogate 1
Email Harrogate@hempsons.co.uk

Portland Tower, Portland Street, Manchester, M1 3LF
Tel (0161) 228 0011 **Fax** (0161) 236 6734 **DX** 14482 Manchester 2
Email Manchester@hempsons.co.uk

Managing Partner	Janice Barber
Senior Partner	Bertie Leigh
Number of partners	32
Assistant solicitors	85
Other fee-earners	22

CONTACTS

Charity	Ian Hempseed (London)
Clinical Litigation	Bertie Leigh (London)
	Frances Harrison (Manchester)
	Adrienne D'Arcy (Harrogate)
Commercial	Ian Hempseed (London)
Commercial Litigation	David Stone (London)
Commercial Property	Graham Lea (London)
	Jane Donnison (Manchester)
	Louise Holroyd (Harrogate)
Defamation	Mark Shaw (London)
Employment	Janice Barber (London)
	Kerry Devlin (Harrogate)
	Sean Reynolds (Manchester)

THE FIRM Hempsons is well known for its particular expertise in the field of medical and healthcare law, partnership work and charity law. The firm has long provided a comprehensive range of services to the NHS, the professions and charities.

PRINCIPAL AREAS OF WORK
Clinical Litigation The firm has long been renowned for its expertise in this field and handles matters relating to clinical and dental negligence (all areas of hospital and general practice). Also covered are class actions; disciplinary cases for NHS trusts, professional organisations and individual practition-

Continued overleaf

ers; codes of professional practice and medical crime. Hempsons is one of the national firms on the NHS Litigation Authority's panel of healthcare solicitors to act in defence of clinical negligence claims, and all three offices are represented.

Healthcare The firm advises a range of healthcare organisations on all aspects of law and ethics, mental health and community care law, administrative law, NHS regulatory law and the constitution and formation of Primary Care Trusts.

Partnership Advice is given to doctors and other professionals on the formation of partnerships and partnership agreements; the accession and retirement of partners; the dissolution of partnerships and partnership disputes.

Commercial Litigation/Defamation The firm advises on all forms of UK commercial disputes, including litigation in respect of employment, insurance, arbitration and ADR work. Defamation work is principally carried out for local authorities.

Commercial Property The department handles commercial, institutional, professional property, including acquisitions and developments, grant, renewal and termination of leases, rent reviews and the Cost Rent Scheme for general practitioners, including funding proposed surgery developments. Deals have included the funding of a large scale indoor real snow ski slope and leisure centre in West Yorkshire with a developed value of between £50 and £60 million; acting for one of the world's largest power suppliers on substantial sub-lettings at its headquarters building in the City of London; the acquisition of a new HQ for a newly established College for the Association of British Dispensing Opticians (ABDO) – The ABDO College of Education – and the funding and leasing of London Zoo.

Charity Law The firm provides a complete service to charities, large and small and currently numbering well in excess of 120. This includes: formation and restructuring of charities; advice to trustees and management on legal duties and powers; updating constitutions; employment issues; dealings with the Charity Commission and the Inland Revenue; financial and commercial activities; trading subsidiaries; fundraising and appeals; disputed legacies. The firm has been active in running seminars on topics of concern to charities and other 'not for profit' organisations.

Commercial Work The firm specialises in dealing with the commercial and contractual issues of NHS organisations, charities, membership bodies and professional clients.

Employment Hempsons has a lively and proactive team of employment lawyers providing solutions to HR problems in the NHS, for employers and professionals, and those of our charity and other clients. The firm has particular experience in all types of discrimination work and all the relevant NHS circulars.

CLIENTELE Clients include NHS trusts, health authorities, other healthcare organisations, professional bodies, Royal Colleges, learned societies and individual professionals.

CONTACTS (Continued)	
Healthcare	Bertie Leigh (London)
	Bill Leason (Manchester)
	John Taylor (Harrogate)
Medical Crime	Anne Ball (Manchester)
	Jill Crombie (London)
Partnership	Lynne Abbess (London)

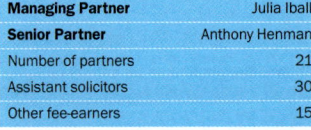

Henderson Boyd Jackson WS
19 Ainslie Place, Edinburgh, EH3 6AU **Tel** (0131) 226 6881 **Fax** (0131) 225 1103

Henmans
116 St. Aldates, Oxford, OX1 1HA
Tel (01865) 722181 **Fax** (01865) 792376 **DX** 4311 Oxford 1
Email welcome@henmans.co.uk **Website** www.henmans.co.uk

THE FIRM Henmans is an established Oxford-based practice with a national reputation, serving both corporate and private clients. Henmans' philosophy is to be extremely client focused to deliver exceptional levels of service. The firm achieves this through an emphasis on teamwork to ensure clients always have access to a specific partner with specialist support, and through an ongoing programme of recruitment and training to guarantee clients optimum advice and guidance. Henmans has invested heavily in IT and has implemented a case management system to enhance services and client care. Henmans' policy of bespoke services and controlled costs ensure that both corporate and private clients benefit from City level litigation standards at competitive regional prices.

PRINCIPAL AREAS OF WORK Henmans has continued to expand and further enhance its presence at national and regional scales.

Professional Negligence Henmans has greatly expanded its specialist professional indemnity work on behalf of solicitors and other professionals, and has assembled a large team of lawyers (including a higher courts solicitor-advocate) with expertise in professional negligence litigation. The firm also undertakes an increasing volume of insurance and commercial litigation and has the capacity to handle marine insurance disputes.

Personal Injury & Clinical Negligence The firm has a substantial insurance company client list. Both departments are particularly strong and have a number of AVMA and personal injury panelists.

Managing Partner	Julia Iball
Senior Partner	Anthony Henman
Number of partners	21
Assistant solicitors	30
Other fee-earners	15

AREAS OF PRACTICE	
Professional Negligence & Commercial Litigation	29%
Personal Injury	26%
Property	17%
Private Client (inc. Family)/Charities/Trusts	16%
Corporate/Employment	12%

Employment Employer and employee work undertaken across the spectrum, with a policy of in-house representation at Employment tribunals. The employer client base includes major national and international companies.

Corporate Henmans offers wide-ranging corporate work for both listed and private companies, including venture capital, sales and acquisitions. The corporate team is experienced in copyright, publishing and computer law, and the firm acts for several leading trade organisations. There is a strong commitment to the enterprise movement and to emergent businesses.

Commercial Property Specialist commercial property advice focuses on planning and development, option deals, management techniques, sales, purchases, landlord and tenant and employee relocation. Henmans' agricultural and land practice has developed to meet client needs both regionally and nationally. The firm represents a number of substantial estates, Oxford colleges and national charities.

Charities The firm's reputation for charity law continues to grow with a specialist department concentrating on legacy recovery work, charity start-ups, commercial ventures for charities, property matters and all types of advice to charity trustees.

Private Client There is a strong private client department providing tax planning for high net worth individuals and all types of trust and probate work, including contentious probate actions. Three members of the team belong to the Society of Trust and Estate Practitioners. Matrimonial and family work is undertaken (including a substantial amount of high quality financial work). Residential property work is also offered in the full range of services for private individuals. All the lawyers at Henmans are effective, hard negotiators, respected by competitors for their integrity, expertise and enthusiasm to obtain the best possible results for their clients.

Henry Hyams
7 South Parade, Leeds, LS1 5QX   **Tel** (0113) 243 2288   **Fax** (0113) 242 9714

Henry Milner & Co
County House, 14 Hatton Garden, London, EC1N 8AT   **Tel** (020) 7831 9944   **Fax** (020) 7831 9941

Heptonstalls

7-15 Gladstone Terrace, Goole, DN14 5AH
Tel (01405) 765661   **Fax** (01405) 764201   **DX** 28831 Goole
Email legal@heptonstalls.co.uk

1 Vicar Lane, Howden, DN14 7BP
Tel (01430) 430209   **Fax** (01430) 432101   **DX** 700844 Howden
Email legal@heptonstalls.co.uk

9-11 Ropergate End, Pontefract, WF8 1JU
Tel (01977) 602804   **Fax** (01977) 602805   **DX** 22255 Pontefract
Email legal@heptonstalls.co.uk

72 Mary Street, Scunthorpe, DN15 6LA
Tel (01724) 289959   **Fax** (01724) 289965   **DX** 14732 Scunthorpe
Email legal@heptonstalls.co.uk

Senior Partner	Roger Beattie
Assistant solicitors	14
Number of partners	8
Other fee-earners	23

AREAS OF PRACTICE	
PI/Clinical Negligence	55%
Property/Common Law/Civil	18%
Matrimonial	10%
Criminal	9%
Trusts, Probate & Tax	8%

CONTACTS	
Agriculture	Eileen J Godfrey
Clinical Negligence	John Burman
Commercial/Property	Roger Beattie
Criminal	Shaun A Pinchbeck
Employment	Shaun A Pinchbeck
Personal Injury	John Burman
Tax/Probate & Trust	John C H Gill
Welfare & Family	Colin Luckett

THE FIRM Heptonstalls, with its four offices in Goole, Pontefract, Scunthorpe and Howden, is a major provider of legal services in Yorkshire and North Lincolnshire. The firm aims to ensure that clients receive an efficient, personal and friendly service whatever their legal needs.

PRINCIPAL AREAS OF WORK

Personal Injury & Clinical Negligence This department has a leading regional reputation for claimant work arising from medical treatment, road traffic accidents, industrial accidents and disease, defective products and related matters. Special interests include obstetrics and gynaecology, head and spinal injuries, and traumatic brain injury. John Burman is one of two members of the AVMA and Law Society Clinical Negligence Panels and three members of the Personal Injury Panel. The department has both clinical negligence and personal injury franchises in Goole, Pontefract and Scunthorpe.

Commercial/Agriculture Advice on a wide range of business and commercial law including employment and commercial litigation. The firm has extensive experience in advising agricultural businesses on such areas as land law, conservation, agricultural tenancies and other aspects of land management.

Private Client The firm advises on property, tax and family finance, wills, probate and trusts, landlord and tenant disputes, family and matrimonial law, and welfare benefits.

A-Z ■ LAW FIRMS

■ **Herbert Mallam Gowers**
126 High St, Oxford, OX1 4DG **Tel** (01865) 244661 **Fax** (01865) 721263

Herbert Smith

Exchange House, Primrose Street, London, EC2A 2HS
Tel (020) 7374 8000 **Fax** (020) 7374 0888 **DX** 28
Email contact@herbertsmith.com **Website** www.herbertsmith.com

THE FIRM Founded in 1882, Herbert Smith is an international law firm with offices in Europe and Asia. With over 1,000 lawyers worldwide (including some 190 partners), the firm is committed to providing high quality and innovative legal services to major corporations, governments, financial institutions and all types of commercial organisations. Herbert Smith offers an unrivalled balance of corporate, commercial and dispute resolution advice to its clients worldwide. This is further enhanced by its formal alliance with the German firm Gleiss Lutz and the Dutch and Belgian firm Stibbe.

PRINCIPAL AREAS OF WORK
Corporate & Commercial Herbert Smith provides a comprehensive range of legal services across all areas of corporate and commercial life. Frequently, its role puts it at the centre of industries that are reshaping and the firm is well known for its innovative work on ground-breaking deals and restructurings. The firm has a long-standing reputation for advice on mergers, acquisitions and takeovers and is highly regarded for its expertise in corporate finance. Other areas of corporate expertise include: competition law; corporate recovery; employment; European law; insurance; investment funds; media; telecoms; pensions and share schemes; trusts and charities. The firm's expertise is reflected by its consistently high ranking in the major league tables of top law firms.

Finance & Banking Herbert Smith is known for the distinctive quality of its debt finance practice. The practice advises on international and domestic deals in the bank lending (including acquisition finance and property finance), securitisation and capital markets, asset finance and project finance markets as well as on corporate recovery matters. Its experience of acting for parties on all sides of transactions, and its reputation for innovation gives the firm a broad and original perspective when approaching transactions, particularly those that are complex.

Litigation & Arbitration Herbert Smith enjoys a formidable reputation for its expertise in both domestic and international litigation and arbitration – a pre-eminent position it has held for several decades. It has consistently been ranked as the leading UK and Asian firm for commercial litigation. In this, it is the breadth of the firm's practice and the experience and quality of its practitioners that distinguish it from its competitors. Areas of specialism include administrative and public law; banking; civil fraud; construction; defamation; employment; energy; environment; information technology; insurance and reinsurance; intellectual property; public and private international law; professional indemnity; regulatory and corporate compliance cases and sport. Herbert Smith has experience before every type of court and tribunal, and conducts arbitrations in all parts of the world. The firm uses ADR procedures in appropriate cases and several of the partners are accredited mediators.

CLIENTELE The firm's clients represent many of the world's leading companies including a significant proportion of the FTSE100.

INTERNATIONAL In addition to its network of international offices, the firm has a tripartite formal alliance with the German firm Gleiss Lutz and the Dutch and Belgian firm Stibbe. Its European capability is further enhanced by its strong relationships with Cuatrecasas in Spain and Pavia e Ansaldo in Italy. Herbert Smith also has an association with a leading team of commercial lawyers in Indonesia, Hiswara Bunjamin & Tundjung, and a formal alliance with the highly rated Singapore corporate law specialist firm, ASG Law Corporation. In the US, the firm has established close relationships with a small number of leading firms. All Herbert Smith offices co-operate closely with one another to ensure clients receive an integrated cross-border service. This is in accordance with the firm's stated objective of meeting the needs of its clients in the major financial and commercial centres of the world.

Senior Partner	Richard Bond
Worldwide Figures	
Number of partners	183
Assistant solicitors	568
Other fee-earners	287

CONTACTS	
Acquisition Finance	Clive Barnard
Administrative & Public Law	Andrew Lidbetter
Arbitration	Julian Lew
Construction & Engineering	Michael Davis
Corporate Recovery	Stephen Gale
Debt Capital Markets	Dina Albagli
Employee Incentives	Colin Chamberlain
Employment	John Farr
Energy, Natural Resources & Utilities	
	Ted Greeno
	Alan Jowett
Entertainment & Media	Charles Plant
	Stephen Wilkinson
Equity Capital Markets	Caroline Goodall
EU, Competition & Regulation	Jonathan Scott
Finance & Banking	Clive Barnard
Financial Institutions	David Willis
Financial Services	David Willis
Insurance & Reinsurance Litigation	
	David Higgins
	David Reston
Intellectual Property	Bill Moodie
International Law	Campbell McLachlan
Investment Funds	Nigel Farr
IT & E-commerce	Chris Rees
Leisure & Sport	Alan Watts
	Stephen Wilkinson
Life Sciences	Henry Raine
	Andrew Rich
Litigation	Harry Anderson
M&A	Michael Walter
Pensions	Ian Gault
PFI/PPP	Nick Tott
Planning & Environment	Sophie Quayle
	Patrick Robinson
Private Equity	Richard Lewis
Project Finance	Nick Tott
Real Estate	James Barnes
Securitisation	Jane Borrows
Tax	Heather Gething
Telecoms	Tim Bellis
	Philip Carrington
Trusts & Charities	John Wood
WTO/World Trade Law	Craig Pouncey

HERBERT SMITH

Hewitson Becke + Shaw

Shakespeare House, 42 Newmarket Road, Cambridge, CB5 8EP
Tel (01223) 461155 **Fax** (01223) 316511 **DX** 133155 Cambridge 8
Email mail@hewitsons.com   **Website** www.hbslaw.co.uk

7 Spencer Parade, Northampton, NN1 5AB
Tel (01604) 233233 **Fax** (01604) 627941 **DX** 12401 Northampton

53 High Street, Saffron Walden, CB10 1AR
Tel (01799) 522471 **Fax** (01799) 524742 **DX** 200300 Saffron Walden

Managing Partner	Alan Brett
Senior Partner	Ian Barnett
Number of partners	47
Assistant solicitors	48
Other fee-earners	40

AREAS OF PRACTICE	
Corporate	33%
Property	30%
Private	19%
Technology	18%

CONTACTS	
ADR	Dominic Hopkins
Agriculture	Ian Barnett
Bioscience	Simon Portman
Commercial Property	Elizabeth Jones
Construction	Tim Richards
Corporate/Commercial	John Dix
Debt Services	Clare Bangor-Jones
Employment	Nick Sayer
IT & IP	Bill Thatcher
Litigation	Dominic Hopkins
Pensions	Mary Legg
Planning & Environment	Peter Brady
Private Client	Clare Colacicchi
Property Funding	Alan Brett
Residential Property	Tim Middleton

THE FIRM Hewitson Becke + Shaw is one of the UK's leading corporate and commercial firms and also has a substantial private client practice. It has a record of substantial growth year on year, supported by its policy of investment in senior personnel. The firm is committed to maintaining its dynamic corporate management structure and quality care systems which provide flexibility and responsiveness to client needs. HB+S has a total of 110 lawyers, including 48 partners, who meet a growing demand for its services regionally, nationally and internationally. The firm has established a leading reputation in many specific areas of law, including corporate/commercial, bioscience, intellectual property, information and communications technology, commercial litigation, commercial property, construction, employment, competition law, planning and pensions. Its private client section is one of the largest outside London. HB+S has been closely associated over many years with the development of Cambridge and the 'Silicon Fen' region as a world-leading centre for information and technology-based businesses. The firm's legal expertise and professional approach matches that of major City of London firms and its strategic locations in East Anglia and the East Midlands add the benefits of cost-effectiveness combined with extensive local knowledge. A valuable international dimension to the firm's client services is provided through LawExchange International, a dynamic and growing network of like-minded firms across Europe, North America and the Pacific Rim, which HB+S co-founded in 1994.

PRINCIPAL AREAS OF WORK

Agriculture Work includes the granting of development options by landowners, joint venture and share farming agreements, farm partnerships, taxation and environmental matters, sales and tenancies and mineral exploitation. The firm has a significant number of landed estates and farming clients.

Bioscience The firm is an established player in the biotech field. It acts for clients of all types, from those engaged, at one extreme of the product development continuum, in fundamental academic biotechnical research, through to pharmaceutical companies, and HB+S members are active on industry committees

Charities HB+S advises public and private charities, with particular emphasis on service providing charities, for which a full range of services is provided.

Commercial Property The firm handles a large volume of work across the spectrum of areas including the acquisition, development and leasehold arrangements for all types of commercial property. It is increasingly used by major concerns abroad, especially in the hi-tech and biotech sectors, for pre-let and forward sale agreements. Its lawyers have particular expertise in complex funding mechanisms and joint ventures.

Construction HB+S advises on all contentious construction disputes (including building contract claims and claims for defects) as well as the non-contentious aspects of projects for employers and prospective occupiers. It has long-standing PFI experience.

Company/Commercial HB+S has strong, dedicated corporate transactions teams in Cambridge and Northampton. Work ranges over M&A, venture capital and private equity, buyouts, joint ventures and corporate restructurings. Specialists within the firm advise on competition/EU law, public markets listing and compliance, employee share schemes, pensions, insolvency, as well as general commercial contract work. Clients include a significant number of plcs, owner managed businesses, and technology start-ups and the workload frequently has an international, particularly transatlantic, element.

Debt Services The dedicated HB+S unit provides consultancy, outsourced credit control, pre-legal service and debt recovery, collecting in over 100 countries worldwide.

Employment Work includes injunctions, service contracts, pensions, dismissal, redundancy, compensation for unfair dismissal, profit sharing and share option schemes and general employee benefits. The firm is a member of the Employment Lawyers Association and the Industrial Law Society.

Intellectual Property The firm advises on all aspects of obtaining, exploiting and enforcing intellectual property rights, with particular expertise in computer hardware and software, biotechnology, pharmaceutical, film, music and book publishing industries.

Information & Communications Technology HB+S acts for users and suppliers including major IT companies, software houses and ISPs. The firm handles licensing, distribution, development, support and other procurement issues as well as disputes, data protection and e-commerce.

Investment Services The firm is the joint owner of Affinity Investment Management Ltd (AIM), which

Continued overleaf

looks after approximately £100m under management for around 500 clients who are private individuals, family trust funds, small charities and SIPPs.

Litigation The services are provided through groups, each consisting of lawyers dedicated to an area of specialisation including banking, intellectual property, personal injury, crime anily. The firm acts nationally for several major clearing banks.

Planning & Environment The firm, with two members of the Law Society's Specialist Planning Panel, provides a comprehensive service on all aspects of planning law and practice to public authorities, developers, landowners, investors and individuals. It has extensive expertise in environmental law.

Private Client The firm focuses on specialised tax and trust advice for individuals whose wealth derives from both public and private company investments as well as commercial and agricultural property.

Hextalls

28 Leman Street, London E1 8ER
Tel (020) 7488 1424 **Fax** (020) 7481 0232 **DX** 562 CITY
Email info@hextalls.com **Website** www.hextalls.com

3 Brindley Place, Birmingham, B1 2JB
Tel (0121) 698 8740 **Fax** (0121) 698 8703 **DX** 715473

118 High Street, Hurstpierpoint, BN6 9PX
Tel (01444) 462200 **Fax** (01444) 462007 **DX** 94803

Senior Partner	John Bundy
Number of partners	20
Other fee-earners	40

AREAS OF PRACTICE	
Liability/Personal Injury	50%
Insurance/Reinsurance	35%
Commercial/Property	7%
Employment	5%
Private Client	3%

CONTACTS	
Insurance/Reinsurance	John Startin
Liability/Personal Injury	Paul Connolly
Commercial/Property	John Castle
Employment	Anne Lumsden
Private Client	Branwen Castle

THE FIRM Hextalls has continued to strengthen its reputation as a leading insurance litigation practice. It has always been regarded as an excellent general insurance and personal injury firm. A steady change of emphasis over the last decade has rapidly accelerated and it is now firmly established as a strong presence in the international/London insurance and reinsurance markets. Through its multinational partnership, Clausen Miller Europe, the firm has immediate access to foreign law in many jurisdictions with partners in Chicago, New York, Paris and Rome. To improve access for its UK clients, it has opened an office in Birmingham. Hextalls is simultaneously developing its commercial and employment law expertise and has recently joined with Sussex practice, Castle & Co, to grow its commercial property and private client services. This is a firm that is, in the words of a client, 'forward thinking and focused'. Its broad client base includes major US and continental insurers, Lloyds syndicates, local authorities, public and private corporations. The firm is pro-active in the Forum of Insurance Lawyers (FOIL).

Clausen Miller Europe

PRINCIPAL AREAS OF WORK

Insurance/Reinsurance Market and reinsurance disputes, professional indemnity (construction, financial, legal), insurance coverage disputes, financial lines, casualty and property, construction and engineering, product liability, subrogated recoveries, and legal expenses.

Liability/Personal Injury Employers and public liability, industrial and occupational disease, product liability, health and safety, sport and leisure liability, travel and motor. The firm has a dedicated immediate response team for major incidents.

Commercial/Property Company commercial and commercial property.

Employment Acts for employers and employees. Family law.

Private Client Wills, trusts, probate and tax planning.

INTERNATIONAL The firm's London office is headquarters for the multinational law practice, Clausen Miller Europe. As such, it enjoys a close working relationship with the leading American law firm after whom CME takes its name and which has offices based in Chicago, New York, Newark, Newport Beach, Wheaton and White Plains. CME currently also has offices in Paris and Rome and is actively looking to expand into other European countries.

RECRUITMENT Hextalls is committed to the training and development of all staff and continues to hold the Investors in People award. This commitment extends to clients and the firm continues to provide regular update briefings, in-house training and well attended seminar programmes to help clients keep abreast of developments affecting their businesses. The firm recruits between four and five trainee solicitors a year. Applications by letter and CV to Andrew Nathan.

LAW FIRMS ■ A-Z

■ Hibbert Durrad Moxon

25 Barker Street, Nantwich, CW5 5EN
Tel (01270) 624225 **Fax** (01270) 628065 **DX** 22004 Nantwich

Ptnrs 10 **Asst solrs** 11 **Other fee-earners** 10 **Contact** Martyn Measures • The firm specialises in agriculture; commercial and domestic property; probate and trusts; licensing; litigation.

CONTACTS	
Agriculture	David Young
Commercial & Domesitc Property	
	Martin Measures
Company & Employment	Michael Bruce
Licensing	David Sayer
Litigation	Richard Lark
Probate & trusts	Derek Dale

Hickman & Rose

144 Liverpool Road, London, N1 1LA
Tel (020) 7700 2211 **Fax** (020) 7609 6044 **DX** 122234 Upper Islington
Email mail@hickmanandrose.co.uk

THE FIRM Hickman & Rose is a leading criminal law and human rights firm. It delivers a consistently high quality of work across the full spectrum of criminal justice issues. The firm has an excellent reputation in serious crime and commercial fraud and is renowned for its work on behalf of prisoners.

PRINCIPAL AREAS OF WORK

Crime A substantial criminal caseload is run with total commitment to quality and client care. A small group of highly experienced lawyers specialises in larger matters.
Serious Fraud Serious and international fraud work is backed by the commitment to hold prosecution authorities to the letter and the spirit of the law.
Police Actions This team has fought and won many cases involving police wrongdoing.
Prisoners Rights A tough and combative prison rights practice has succeeded on securing improvements in conditions for many prisoners.
Public Law/ECHR Specialist litigation in the UK and Strasbourg challenging human rights abuses across the criminal justice system.
Mental Health A growing team works for those detained under the Mental Health Act or affected by community care legislation.
Discrimination A small team specialises in sex, race and disability discrimination within the criminal justice and mental health systems.

Number of partners	6
Assistant solicitors	21
Other fee-earners	12

AREAS OF PRACTICE	
Crime	50%
Serious Fraud	15%
Police Actions	10%
Prisoners Rights	10%
Discrimination	5%
Mental Health	5%
Public Law	5%

CONTACTS	
Crime	Ross Dixon
Discrimination Law	Sarah Ricca
Mental Health	Ian Campbell
Police Actions	Hope Liebersohn
Prisoners Rights	Liz Sutcliffe
Public Law	Daniel Machover
Serious Fraud	Ben Rose

■ Higgs & Sons

Blythe House, 134 High Street, Brierley Hill, DY5 3BG **Tel** (01384) 342100 **Fax** (01384) 342000

■ R. & J. M. Hill Brown & Co

3 Newton Place, Glasgow, G3 7PU
Tel (0141) 332 3265/333 0286 **Fax** (0141) 332 2613/332 0514 **DX** 512207 Glasgow-Sandyford Place **Email** info@hillbrown.co.uk

Contact Jack Cummins • General practice specialising in licensing work for licensed trade and the entertainment industry.

AREAS OF PRACTICE	
Licensing	35%
Domestic/Commercial Conveyancing	25%
Trusts and Securities	21%
General Court	19%

Hill Dickinson

Pearl Assurance House, 2 Derby Square, Liverpool, L2 9XL
Tel (0151) 236 5400 **Fax** (0151) 236 2175 **DX** 14129 Liverpool 1
Email Law@HillDicks.com **Website** www.hilldickinson.com

34 Cuppin Street, Chester, CH1 2BN
Tel (01244) 896600 **Fax** (01244) 896601 **DX** 19991 Chester

50 Fountain Street, Manchester, M2 2AS
Tel (0161) 278 8800 **Fax** (0161) 278 8801 **DX** 14487 Manchester 2

Sun Court, 66/67 Cornhill, London, EC3V 3NB
Tel (020) 7695 1000 **Fax** (020) 7695 1001 **DX** 98940 Cheapside 2

THE FIRM Hill Dickinson is one of the UK's leading commercial-based law firms, with offices in Liverpool, London, Manchester and Chester, providing specialist legal advice to both the domestic and

Managing Partner	David Wareing
Senior Partner	Tony Wilson
Number of partners	85
Total number of Fee-earners	262
Total staff	470

AREAS OF PRACTICE	
Litigation	38%
Commercial Prop	17%
Shipping	13%
Clinical Negligence	16%
Company/Commercial/Pensions/Tax	16%

Continued overleaf

www.ChambersandPartners.com

995

A-Z ■ LAW FIRMS

international market. The practice has a strong and marked reputation in insurance, litigation, intellectual property, company commercial, commercial property, marine and goods in transit. The firm has over 470 staff, including more than 85 partners.

PRINCIPAL AREAS OF WORK With a wealth of specialist advisors, the firm undertakes a wide range of legal work in the commercial and private sectors broadly based around specialist groups of commercial, insurance, health, and marine and transit.

Commercial As one of the leading commercial litigation firms in the North West, the commercial/corporate group advises on a broad range of matters including all aspects of corporate law. The firm's intellectual property and technology department is one of the most highly rated outside of London, and the firm retains a strong private client base. The property and construction team provides legal advice across both development and construction areas. The firm acts for housebuilders, retailers, manufacturers, service providers, developers, investors, contractors and the public sector.

Insurance Having one of the largest insurance departments of its kind in the country, the team deals with a wide range of litigation issues including complex 'test' or multi-party actions. The 'one liability services' team provides corporate clients with a streamlined, value added claims and litigation management solution. Developed to reduce overall claims spend by bringing together legal expertise, claims management, investigation, IT and finance capabilities.

Health The firm has one of the UK's largest medico-legal practices, acting on behalf of health authorities, NHS trusts and other health service bodies and is a member of the panel of solicitors maintained by the National Health Service Litigation Authority.

Marine & Transit Recognised as one of the leading specialist shipping solicitors in the UK. The marine and transit department has well-established experts handling cargo and transit matters. The department also boasts a comprehensive yacht and small craft acquisition, liability and insurance team. The shipping team is recognised as a leader in its field both nationally and internationally.

CONTACTS	
Insurance	David Scott
Health	Allan Mowat
Construction	David Chinn
Commercial Property	David Swaffield (Liverpool)
	Michael Blakey (Manchester)
	Robin Jones (Chester)
Corporate	Glyn Dale-Jones
Marine & Transit	Peter Jackson
	Julia Marshall
Private Client	Mike Quinn
Intellectual Property	Philip Woods
Regulatory	Simon Parrington
Environmental	John Maxwell

Hill Taylor Dickinson

Irongate House, Duke's Place, London, EC3A 7HX
Tel (020) 7283 9033   **Fax** (020) 7283 1144   **DX** 550
Email enquiry@htd-london.com   **Website** www.htd-law.com

THE FIRM Hill Taylor Dickinson is a commercial firm servicing the business and financial community in the United Kingdom and internationally. The firm is based in the City of London, and also has offices in Dubai and Greece. The firm has expanded considerably with overseas offices being established and new areas of business being developed. This growth has been achieved by organic growth within the firm complemented by external recruitment (including at partner level). Clients range from major international corporations to owner managed businesses. Critical to the success of the firm's relationship with all of them is close partner involvement and understanding of their operations and markets. Hill Taylor Dickinson is a progressive and dynamic firm seeking to provide an effective personal service to both national and international clients and a commercial approach to legal problems and their resolution.

PRINCIPAL AREAS OF WORK Hill Taylor Dickinson's practice is entirely commercial.

Company/Commercial & Finance The firm's transactional work includes company/commercial and financing, including venture capital, leasing and asset finance, ship building and finance, corporate buy-outs and buy-ins, as well as commercial property. Its clients include banks and other financial institutions, both City-based and overseas, insurers, employers' organisations and a wide variety of corporate clients, notably in the leisure, manufacturing and publishing sectors.

Personal Injury, ITF & Employment This department acts mainly for employers, insurers, owners and P&I clubs in shipping and transport and a wide variety of industries. It deals with mass and individual claims. The department's work includes preventative and practical advice, including the drafting of accident reporting documents and procedures, drafting contractual clauses and employment contracts, safety policies and a whole spectrum of employment and personal injury claims.

Shipping Hill Taylor Dickinson's expertise in shipping, an area in which it acts for shipowners, P&I clubs, insurers, as well as major oil companies, makes it one of the foremost practices in this field. The shipping department handles the full range of commercial problems arising out of international trade and transport, including major maritime casualties, disaster litigation, pollution claims, charterparty disputes and cargo claims.

Commodities The firm has also significantly increased its practice in commodities disputes in recent years. Its clientele in this area includes trading houses and a number of trade associations.

Insurance & Reinsurance This division acts for underwriters, insurance companies, brokers and assureds. London - both Lloyd's and the companies market - is a major source of the division's work, but the firm derives its clients from all over the world. Hill Taylor Dickinson's reputation in marine insurance is well established.

Managing Partner	Rhys Clift
Chairman	Robert Wallis
UK	
Number of partners	22
Assistant solicitors	18
Other fee-earners	12
International	
Number of partners	5
Assistant solicitors	6

AREAS OF PRACTICE	
Shipping & Commodities	56%
Insurance	18%
Commercial Transactional	17%
Personal Injury	8%
Others	1%

CONTACTS	
Commercial Property	Richard Taylor
Commodities	Jeffrey Isaacs
Company/Commercial	Malcolm Entwistle
Insurance	Timothy Taylor
Personal Injury	Maria Pittordis
Shipping	John Evans
	Stephen Cropper
	Robert Wallis
	Andrew Johnson

Hill
Taylor
Dickinson
solicitors

996   INDEX TO LEADING LAWYERS: PAGE 1693 ■ IN-HOUSE LAWYERS' PROFILES: PAGE 1201

LAW FIRMS ■ A-Z

Hobson Audley

7 Pilgrim Street, London, EC4V 6LB
Tel (020) 7450 4500 **Fax** (020) 7450 4545 **DX** 401 London
Email lawyers@hobsonaudley.co.uk **Website** www.hobsonaudley.co.uk

THE FIRM Hobson Audley is a City firm specialising in business law with a broad range of international and UK clients and an emphasis on the corporate finance and technology sectors. The firm represents many leading companies in these sectors and also in more traditional areas of business such as energy, manufacturing, banking and finance and property. The firm's comprehensive range of legal skills is coupled with an international perspective and an awareness of business and commercial needs.

PRINCIPAL AREAS OF WORK Hobson Audley combines strength in corporate law, dispute solutions, commercial property with specialist areas such as innovation and technology, multimedia, electronic commerce, and employment.

CLIENTELE The firm's client base is drawn principally from the UK, continental Europe and North America. Clients are involved in innovation and technology, e-commerce, aviation, publishing, direct selling, healthcare, energy, manufacturing, banking and financial services and property investment and development.

INTERNATIONAL In 1997 Hobson Audley formed a multinational partnership with Faegre & Benson LLP under the name of Faegre Benson Hobson Audley. Faegre & Benson has offices in Frankfurt and Shanghai and in the United States, in Minnesota, Denver, Boulder and Des Moines. Association with Faegre & Benson LLP has enhanced the firm's international contacts with the introduction of a number of substantial US corporations whose UK interests are now represented by Faegre Benson Hobson Audley. Languages spoken include French, German, Italian, Spanish and Portuguese.

Managing Partner	Gerald Hobson
Number of partners	14
Assistant solicitors	22
Other fee-earners	6

AREAS OF PRACTICE	
Corporate Finance/Company Commercial	31%
Dispute Solution	22%
Innovation & Technology	20%
Property	18%
Employment	9%

CONTACTS	
Commercial Property	Malcolm Headley
	Simon Smith
	Godfrey Bruce-Radcliffe
Corporate Finance/Company Commercial	
	Max Audley
	Anthony Gordon
	Edward Hoare
	Donald Stewart
	Paul Taylor
Dispute Solution	Gerald Hobson
	Roger Hopkins
	Michael Cover
Employment	Caroline Whiteley
Innovation & Technology (inc. IP)	Robert Bond
	Nick Mallett

G.L. Hockfield & Co

41 Reedworth Street, Kennington Rd, London, SE11 4PQ
Tel (020) 7735 0489 **Fax** (020) 7820 1707 **DX** 33252 **Email** mail@hockfield.co.uk

Contact James Garvey • Principal areas of work are housing litigation, claimant personal injury and professional negligence work.

AREAS OF PRACTICE	
Housing	48%
Personal Injury	39%
Professional Negligence	7%
Miscellaneous Areas	6%

Hodge Jones & Allen

31-39 Camden Road, London, NW1 9LR
Tel (020) 7482 1974 **Fax** (020) 7267 3476 **Emergency** (01459) 111192
DX 57050 Camden Town
Email hja@hodgejonesallen.co.uk **Website** www.hodgejonesallen.co.uk

THE FIRM Hodge Jones & Allen was established in 1977 and has expanded rapidly, especially since moving to new premises in September 1997. The firm is led by one of the founding partners, Patrick Allen. It has been involved in a number of high profile cases including the King's Cross fire, Broadwater Farm, Greenham Common, the Marchioness disaster, the Sheep Dip litigation, MMR and Gulf War Syndrome. Good management and IT systems have played an important role in the firm's growth.

PRINCIPAL AREAS OF WORK
Crime The criminal team deals with a full range of offences from road traffic offences to serious crime. It can arrange representation at the police station, the magistrates' court and the crown court. The team includes solicitors who specialise in fraud and it is a member of the Serious Fraud Panel. Much of its work is funded by the Legal Services Commission and an initial free first appointment is available in most cases. All of its solicitors undertake their own advocacy and some of the team also have 'higher rights' to allow them to appear in the crown court. The firm has 14 solicitors who specialise in crime and cases include murder and manslaughter, drug related offences, youth work, mentally disordered offenders, extradition, sexual offences and public order offences. For people detained at a police station it offers 24 hour emergency cover on the number above.

Employment & Mental Health The employment team deals with all types of employment and discrimination claims for employees and employers as well as Mental Health tribunal work. All members of the team do their own advocacy. The team also provides non-contentious advice to employers. No win no fee contingency arrangements may be available.

Family The family team covers all aspects of family work including property disputes following sepa-

Continued overleaf

Senior Partner	Patrick Allen
Number of partners	20
Assistant solicitors	34
Other fee-earners	35
Total staff	155

AREAS OF PRACTICE	
Personal Injury & Clinical Negligence	33%
Crime	27%
Family	18%
Housing & Landlord & Tenant Litigation	10%
Residential & Commercial Property	6%
Employment & Mental Health	6%

CONTACTS	
Clinical Negligence	Nicola Mooney
Crime	Nigel Richardson
Employment/Discrimination	Robert Good
Family & Children	Simone McGrath
	Martin Ross
Housing Litigation	Wendy Backhouse
Mental Health Tribunals	Matthew Evans
Multi-party (PI/Med Neg/Product Liability)	
	Patrick Allen
Personal Injury	Louise Whitfield
Police Claims	Tina Salvidge
Property/Commercial	Elaine Morris
Property/Residential	Paul Browne

www.ChambersandPartners.com

ration or divorce, conflicts over children, care proceedings and applications for emergency injunctions. Five members of the team are on the child care panel and two on the Lord Chancellor's Department's Child Abduction panel. All solicitors belong to the Solicitor's Family Law Association. Mediation is offered by accredited family mediators.

Housing & Landlord & Tenant The housing team deals with disrepair, homelessness claims including applications for judicial review, possession cases and all aspects of landlord and tenant work, principally on behalf of tenants. The leader of the team, Wendy Backhouse, was Chair of the Housing Law Practitioner's Group for four years.

Personal Injury, Clinical Negligence & Actions Against the Police The personal injury team is led by Patrick Allen, Vice President and President-elect of the Association of Personal Injury Lawyers. The team acts for claimants, particularly those who have been injured in road accidents, tripping cases, accidents at work or as a result of medical negligence and claims against the police. The team has six solicitors on the personal injury panel and two on the clinical negligence panel. The multi-party unit is handling group actions - Gulf War Illness and the Kerrin Point explosion case. In each action the firm holds a generic contract with the Legal Services Commission. It also acts for large numbers of children with MMR claims and ex-servicemen with PTSD claims. The police claims unit deals with unlawful arrest, assault, malicious prosecution and false imprisonment. It is handling compensation claims for the Bridgewater Four and other notable miscarriage cases.

Property & Wills & Probate The property team handles residential and commercial property work for private individuals, local businesses and charities; as well as probate and wills.

RECRUITMENT The firm runs a structured and popular training scheme for trainee solicitors. The annual intake is presently five. Interviews take place in October for training places the following September.

Hodkinsons
42-43 Locks Heath Centre, Locks Heath, SO3 6DX **Tel** (01489) 885664 **Fax** (01489) 579149

Hollingworth Bissell
10 Storey's Gate, London, SW1P 3AY
Tel (020) 7233 3300 **Fax** (020) 7233 3336
Email info@hollingworthbissell.co.uk

AREAS OF PRACTICE	
Contracts	80%
Commercial Property	20%

THE FIRM Hollingworth Bissell provides legal services (both general and specialist rail related) to the railway industry.

PRINCIPAL AREAS OF WORK
Commercial – General Sales and acquisitions of companies and businesses, joint ventures, shareholders' agreements, reorganisations, procurement contracts, advice on foreign railway privatisations, intellectual property rights, computer contracts, agency contracts, conditions of trading and advice on the legal aspects of advertising, including the running of sales promotions.

Commercial – Rail Specific Advice on refranchising, railways legislation, licence conditions, station developments and project funding. Agreements for access to rail facilities, rail infrastructure projects, development agreements, connection agreements, agreements for railway services, traffic agreements and variations to Franchise Agreements.

Property Station trading and general commercial property advice.

LAW FIRMS ■ A-Z

Holman Fenwick & Willan

Marlow House, Lloyd's Avenue, London, EC3N 3AL
Tel (020) 7488 2300 **Fax** (020) 7481 0316 **DX** 1069 London City EC3
Email holmans@hfw.co.uk **Website** www.hfw.com

THE FIRM Holman Fenwick & Willan is an international law firm specialising in shipping and transportation, international trade and commodities, insurance and reinsurance, energy, information technology, banking and insolvency. The firm has a reputation worldwide for excellence and innovation and its international litigation, arbitration and dispute resolution practice is one of the largest and most specialist of its kind throughout the world.

PRINCIPAL AREAS OF WORK

Admiralty & Marine Litigation Holman Fenwick & Willan is pre-eminent in maritime work. It has one of the world's largest practices with a wealth of experience in the field. It is a recognised leader in dry shipping work including charter parties, bills of lading, other carriage contracts, marine insurance and related disputes. The firm is also renowned as a leader in admiralty and crisis management and operates a 24 hour emergency service geared to providing an immediate response to maritime casualties worldwide. Specialists deal with all forms of contractual disputes, marine insurance claims, collisions, fire and explosions, salvage, towage, wreck removal and recovery, personal injury, damage to oil terminals, rigs and offshore structures, pollution, environmental damage and clean up.

International Trade & Commodities The department complements the maritime practice. It provides the international trading and financial community with services including advising on sale, purchase and futures contracts, quality claims, damage and shortfall disputes, swaps and barter trade, trade finance, EU law, and transportation agreements.

Energy Energy is one of the firm's specialist work areas and covers power generation, oil and gas, coal and liquid natural gas.

Insurance & Reinsurance The firm's practice is recognised internationally as an industry leader. It advises on all aspects of insurance and reinsurance contentious and non-contentious matters including facultative insurance and reinsurance coverage issues and policy interpretation; captive insurance and reinsurance; errors and omissions and professional negligence; property damage, business interruption and liability insurance; insolvency and schemes of arrangement; contract drafting and regulatory issues.

Commercial Litigation, Arbitration & Disputes The firm has considerable strength in these practice areas, particularly in the areas of financial disputes, technology, coal, oil and gas, environmental claims, professional negligence, sovereign debt and fraud and asset recovery.

Fraud & Asset Recovery Work focuses on the civil side with an emphasis on asset tracing and recovery in overseas jurisdictions. Other methods of recovery are also pursued using constructive trust, negligence and fraud proceedings.

Insolvency The full spread of work is undertaken including voluntary arrangements, receiverships, provisional liquidations, liquidations and administrations. Much of the work focuses on international aspects, fraud related insolvency and the insurance industry (including schemes of arrangement).

Company & Finance The firm advises some of the world's largest ship owners and operators on a wide variety of contractual issues, ranging from shipbuilding, and other offshore and construction contracts, financing documentation, the raising of capital, corporate finance and acquisitions, project and asset finance and joint ventures, as well as advising banks and financial institutions. The department also advises clients on EC and competition law, intellectual property and commercial property matters.

Information Technology IT is a rapidly growing area for the firm and advice is given on every aspect of e-commerce and information technology.

Air, Road & Rail The firm advises operators, financiers and underwriters on transactions, litigation and regulatory issues.

Trusts, Succession & Taxation The practice provides private client services.

Employment The firm handles all aspects of employment law, both contentious and non-contentious.

INTERNATIONAL Holman Fenwick & Willan's international practice is founded upon its principal offices in London, Paris, Piraeus, Hong Kong, Singapore and Shanghai and over 120 years experience of working with other law firms in jurisdictions throughout the world. The firm also has other offices in Nantes and Rouen.

Senior Partner	Robert Wilson
UK	
Number of partners	57
Assistant solicitors	62
Trainee solicitors	18
Other fee-earners	23
International	
Number of partners	27
Assistant solicitors	35
Other fee-earners	8

CONTACTS	
Admiralty & Crisis Management	James Gosling
	Mike Stevens
Banking & Insolvency	Noel Campbell
Commercial Litigation & Arbitration	
	Peter Bennett
	Noel Campbell
Corporate & Financial	Nick Hutton
	Jay Tooker
Employment	Andrew Dekany
Energy	Keith Michel
	Diana France
Environmental	Hugh Brown
European Community Law & Competition Law	Phillip Wareham
Information Technology	George Eddings
Insurance & Reinsurance	Ian McKenna
	John Duff
International Trade & Commodities	Chris Swart
	Simon Blows
Marine Litigation	Hugh Livingstone
	Richard Crump
Marine Non-contentious	Stephen Drury
	Dan Tindall
Personal Injury	Alan Walls
Professional Negligence	Paul Wordley
Property	Nick Barr
Transport: Air, Rail & Road	Glenn Moore

HOLMAN FENWICK & WILLAN

A-Z LAW FIRMS

Holme Roberts & Owen

Heathcoat House, 20 Savile Row, London, W1S 3PR
Tel (020) 7494 5600 **Fax** (020) 7287 9344
Email thompsp@hro.com **Website** www.hro.com

Managing Partner	Paul Thompson
Number of partners	4
Assistant solicitors	4
Other fee-earners	2
CONTACTS	
Finance	Martha Collins Rolle
Securities	Thomas Laursen

THE FIRM Holme Roberts & Owen (HRO) was founded in Denver in 1898 and now has approximately 200 lawyers in Colorado, Utah and London. The firm's London office was established in 1991 to help its clients expand their businesses across Europe. With leading clients in the technology, telecommunications and media sectors, HRO's European practice has expanded rapidly, corresponding to the growth in those fields. The London office also represents clients in the breweries, entertainment/sports, and natural resources industries.

PRINCIPAL AREAS OF WORK HRO's London practice focuses on corporate finance, public and private securities offerings, complex multijurisdictional commercial transactions, market entry strategies, joint ventures and acquisitions as well as general corporate and commercial law matters. In particular, the office has substantial experience representing companies establishing or expanding European operations, assisting them with legal and regulatory requirements of multiple jurisdictions. The firm's experience includes acting in the UK and continental Europe, including Central and Eastern Europe.

INTERNATIONAL HRO's lawyers are qualified to practise in many jurisdictions including the UK, the US, Germany, and Belgium. In addition to English, the office has lawyers who are fluent in French, German and Spanish.

Holmes Hardingham

22-23 Great Tower Street, London, EC3R 5HE
Tel (020) 7280 3200 **Fax** (020) 7280 3201 **DX** 636
Email firstname.surname@HHlaw.co.uk **Website** www.HHlaw.co.uk

Managing Partner	David Johnston
Senior Partner	Glenn Winter
Number of partners	11
Assistant solicitors	10
Other fee-earners	7

THE FIRM Holmes Hardingham is a commercial and maritime law firm with an international practice, concentrating on litigation and arbitration related to shipping and transportation.

PRINCIPAL AREAS OF WORK The firm was founded in 1989 and has more than doubled in size in that time. Further expansion is expected in response to a growing workload. All 11 partners and 17 other fee-earners handle a variety of shipping and transport related matters including carriage of goods by sea, road and air; commercial and admiralty litigation and arbitration; marine and goods in transit insurance; collision and salvage; commodity sale disputes; ship sale and purchase; oil and gas exploration; yachts and pleasure craft.

Holmes Mackillop

109 Douglas Street, Glasgow, G2 4HB
Tel (0141) 226 4942 **Fax** (0141) 204 0136 **DX** GW50
Email general@homack.co.uk

Managing Partner	J Stuart McNeill
Contact	William Duffy
AREAS OF PRACTICE	
Commercial Property	40%
Private Client	20%
Corporate	20%
Litigation	20%

THE FIRM The firm was established over 200 years ago and now has a well established commercial and private client base.

PRINCIPAL AREAS OF WORK The firm has been involved in a number of major corporate transactions and commercial property deals within the last year. These are expanding areas of work together with the firm's specialist strengths in commercial litigation, agricultural law and charity law.

CLIENTELE The firm has acted in a number of major property developments and investment sales in the last year. It has also represented landlord and tenant in a number of major lettings. Clients include major developers, property companies, house builders and one of Scotland's leading motor retailers. The firm has also represented two of the major UK Banks in substantial security transactions as well as acting for vendors and purchasers in substantial corporate deals and is frequently handling transactions with a value in excess of £10 million.

RECRUITMENT The firm has expanded its commercial property department within the last year and is anxious to look at further expansion in personnel in this area and also in its corporate department.

Hood Vores & Allwood
The Priory, Church Street, Dereham, NR19 1DW **Tel** (01362) 692424 **Fax** (01362) 698858

Hooper & Wollen
Carlton House, 30 The Terrace, Torquay, TQ1 1BS
Tel (01803) 213251 **Fax** (01803) 296871 **DX** 59204 Torquay (2)
Email lawyers@hooperwollen.co.uk **Website** www.hooperwollen.co.uk

Ptnrs 10 **Asst solrs** 3 **Other fee-earners** 10 **Contact** Chris Hart • Specialising in conveyancing, family, child care, litigation, employment, PI, probate, trust, commercial, company, private client. Agency instructions accepted.

Horsey Lightly Fynn
20 West Mills, Newbury, RG14 5HG **Tel** (01635) 580858 **Fax** (01635) 582813

Howard Kennedy
19 Cavendish Square, London, W1A 2AW
Tel (020) 7636 1616 **Fax** (020) 7491 2899 **DX** 42748 Oxford Circus North
Email enquiries@howardkennedy.com **Website** www.howardkennedy.com

THE FIRM Howard Kennedy is a London-based law firm offering national and international clients a broad range of legal services. The firm combines the benefits of size and expertise with a high degree of personal care and attention. The firm's policy is to ensure that legal services are provided with a clear understanding of clients' general and specific commercial aspirations and the special requirements of their particular business. The firm has developed a range of services appropriate to the needs of business, from finance and set-up stage to maturity, acquisition and disposal. Howard Kennedy is a registered Sponsor on the London Stock Exchange. The firm has an international professional practice with connections worldwide, and is a member of Cercle Juridique European (CJE), Inter Counsel, Transnational Taxation Network, Euro Defi, and Lawyers Associated Worldwide (LAW). All principal European languages are spoken.

PRINCIPAL AREAS OF WORK
Banking & Property Finance Complex financing transactions including syndicated loans. Clients range from UK clearing banks and building societies to borrowers based in the UK and overseas.
Company & Commercial High quality corporate finance transactions including full Stock Exchange flotations, AIM and OFEX flotations, venture capital trusts, rights issues and unquoted public share offerings, (including those under the EIS), takeovers and acquisitions, both public and private. Other commercial services include employment law, IP/IT and tax.
Commercial Property A wide range of property work including the development and financing of retail, industrial and residential premises, with particular emphasis on the retail and leisure industries. The department has specialists in construction, secured lending and licensing.
Litigation A diverse range of disputes for both commercial and private clients, domestic and international, covering the areas of contract, negligence (including professional negligence), corporate and partnership disputes, property litigation, insolvency, banking, insurance, IP, personal injury, matrimonial and debt collecting. There are specialist groups dealing with construction, mediation and ADR.
International The team advises overseas clients investing in and conducting business in the UK and internationally. Areas of work covered include cross-border mergers and acquisitions, international project finance, international trade agreements, commodities, European Union Law, international property and hotel transactions, international corporate structures, cross-border disputes and international arbitration, agency and distribution agreements.
Trusts & Estate Planning Areas covered include personal tax planning (especially inheritance and capital gains tax), settlements and the administration of trusts and estates, complex family financial structures, shareholder and partnership relationships and charity law.
Media & Entertainment All aspects of entertainment, media and sports law are handled including film and television finance, production and distribution, music, theatre, publishing, merchandising and sponsorship.

Senior Partner	Trevor Newey
Number of partners	44
Number of fee-earners	89
Total staff	214

AREAS OF PRACTICE	
Property	42%
Company & Commercial	30%
Litigation	20%
Media & Entertainment	5%
Trusts & Estate Planning	3%

CONTACTS	
AIM	Keith Lassman
Aviation	Chris Gooding
Banking	Nigel Emerson
Company & Commercial	Alan Banes
Construction	James Stewart
Employment	Andrea Nicholls
IP/IT	John Fleming
Licensing	Allen Levene
Litigation	Craig Emden
Media & Entertainment	Brian Eagles
Property	Paul Springall
Property Finance	Jason Lewis
Trusts & Estate Planning	Roger Seaton

A-Z ■ LAW FIRMS

■ Howarth Goodman
8 King Street, Manchester, M60 8HG **Tel** (0161) 832 5068 **Fax** (0161) 819 7878

Howells

427-431 London Road, Sheffield, S2 4HJ
Tel (0114) 249 6666 **Fax** (0114) 250 0656 **DX** 10584

The Avery Buildings, 15-17 Bridge Street, Sheffield, S3 8NL
Tel (0114) 249 6666 **Fax** (0114) 249 1455 **DX** 10584

42 Spital Hill, Sheffield, S4 7LG
Tel (0114) 249 6666 **Fax** (0114) 249 6700 **DX** 10584

Managing Partner	John Gibson
Number of partners	13
Assistant solicitors	28
Other fee-earners	34

AREAS OF PRACTICE	
Civil & Community	33%
Crime	33%
Family	33%

CONTACTS	
Civil & Community	Guy Baddeley
Crime	Danny Simpson
Family	Jonathan Whybrow

THE FIRM Established in 1979 to specialise in protecting the rights of individuals, the firm has grown to be one of the country's largest legal aid practices with legal aid quality franchises in all available areas of work.

PRINCIPAL AREAS OF WORK
Crime The criminal department is now one of the largest in the country having four partners and a further 17 fee-earners. Work includes all criminal matters with particular expertise in public order offences, serious fraud, juveniles and youth, cases involving mentally disordered defendants and road traffic law. Increasing caseload in civil liberties/public law work including miscarriages of justice, prisoners' rights, actions against the police and judicial reviews. Head of department is Danny Simpson, recognised to be a 'leader in the field' for his civil liberties work.

Family Law The family department is the largest in Sheffield and one of the largest in the country. The department is divided into two teams covering children and matrimonial law. The children team consists of 11 fee-earners (including four partners) of whom six are members of the Law Society's Children's Panel. The team covers all areas of child law, including private and public law children cases, adoption and education advice and representation covering special educational needs, school admissions and exclusions appeals, grant disputes and higher and further education proceedings. Jonathan Whybrow (head of the department) is a co-author of *Emergency Remedies in Family Courts* and contributory editor to *Children Law and Practice*. A former civil servant, he worked on the Children Act 1989 as it was devised and enacted. The matrimonial team consists of 10 fee-earners (including two partners) of whom five are members of The Law Society's Family Law Panel. The team deals with all aspects of matrimonial law with particular expertise in domestic violence and financial relief of matrimonial breakdown.

Civil & Community The department provides a wide range of legal services for individuals through its litigation and community law teams.

Litigation Services include accident claims, industrial disease claims, clinical negligence and actions against the police. A strong team consists of three partners supported by a further seven fee-earners. The team has four Law Society personal injury panelists and one clinical negligence panelist.

Community Law The team provides specialist advice and representation in housing, employment and equal opportunities law, immigration, mental health and welfare benefits. The firm has one of the few specialist housing law teams in South Yorkshire and is a member of the South Yorkshire Housing Practitioners Group and deals with possession proceedings, disrepair, harassment by landlords etc. The employment team specialises in advising employees in the full range of employment problems and is a member of The Discrimination Law Association, Equal Opportunities Commission Equality Exchange, Stonewall and Lawyers for Liberty. The immigration team has been the leading team of immigration lawyers in the region for 20 years and deals with the full range of immigration cases. The team of five solicitors and five caseworkers is led by John Donkersley who has over 10 years immigration law experience and is South Yorkshire's leading immigration lawyer. The mental health team is a member of The Law Society Mental Health Review Tribunal Panel and specialises in representing patients before tribunals and provides general mental health law advice and help. An experienced welfare benefits and debt team is able to provide an in-depth service advising clients on all benefits administered by the government or the Local Authority together with judicial reviews, advocacy and representation.

Howes Percival

Oxford House, Cliftonville, Northampton, NN1 5PN
Tel (01604) 230400   **Fax** (01604) 620956   **DX** 12413 Northampton
Email law@howes-percival.co.uk   **Website** www.howes-percival.co.uk

Senior Partner	Michael Percival
Number of partners	32
Assistant solicitors	26
Other fee-earners	43

AREAS OF PRACTICE	
Company Commercial	30%
Commercial Property	25%
Commercial Litigation	20%
Insolvency	10%
Employment	10%
Private Client	5%

CONTACTS	
Company Commercial	Jit Singh
Commercial Litigation	Andrew Myers
Corporate Fraud	Ashwin Mody
Commercial Property	John Herd
Employment	Jon Taylor
Insolvency	Gerald Couldrake
Licensing	Alan Kefford
Motor Trade	Brandon Ransley
Private Client	Michael Percival

THE FIRM Howes Percival is a leading commercial firm with offices in Leicester, Milton Keynes, Northampton and Norwich. The firm aims to be the leading provider of commercial legal services in each of the locations that it has a presence. Personalities at the firm, the provision of commercially workable solutions to clients, and the standards of advice and services carried out across the four offices have won the firm the reputation of being a regional firm by location only. The firm has the expertise and resources that are usually associated with City firms.

PRINCIPAL AREAS OF WORK

Corporate Finance Howes Percival is a market leader in company and commercial services, and has particular expertise in corporate finance, acquisitions and disposals, and MBOs and MBIs. Outsourcing agreements are also handled. The firm has considerable experience in private equity transactions and is able to advise clients on listings to the Alternative Investment Market (this expertise is usually found only in City and Birmingham firms). All aspects of banking law are dealt with and insolvency is a particular specialism. Corporate tax advice is also given.

Commercial Property A broad range of commercial property work is carried out across the four offices and the firm also houses a specialist environmental law unit.

Commercial Litigation A variety of commercial litigation services are available, including specialised work handling Directors' Disqualifications for the Insolvency Service of the DTI. A debt recovery service is also provided. The firm has two partners who are accredited mediators.

Corporate Fraud Serious fraud office enquiries and HMCE Inland Revenue defence cases are undertaken by the firm's corporate fraud department in Leicester. White collar crime is another area of expertise.

Employment The firm has a large employment department. Contentious and non-contentious employment work is carried out for clients across the country and public sector work is a particular specialism. Employee relocation services are also available.

Licensing The liquor and entertainment licensing work that is carried out at the firm's Norwich office is highly regarded and the department hosts bespoke training courses, including the National Licensee Certificate to leisure industry clients.

Motor Trade The firm is particularly well known for its expertise in the automotive sector and acts for manufacturers, dealer groups and dealerships around the country.

CLIENTELE
The top quality work that is carried out by the firm means that it attracts instructions from major companies such as DaimlerChrysler UK Limited and Remington Consumer Products Ltd. The firm acts for both public and limited companies of varying sizes throughout the UK and features major UK financial institutions, manufacturers, retailers, drinks companies, transport companies, and leisure industry businesses in their client lists. When first instructed they will visit a client's business and invest time and resources into understanding the client, the industry in which they work and the expectations that the client has. To ensure that work is carried out efficiently, the firm operates a client partner system, enabling clients to have a regular and familiar point of contact. The vast proportion of new instructions received by the firm are from referrals or recommendations by banks, accountants, financial institutions and existing clients. The firm is also instructed by companies that it has previously acted against in corporate or commercial transactions. Breakfast and evening seminars are regularly given for clients and prospective clients, and in September the employment department hosts a day-long National Employment Seminar, with a guest speaker and a range of workshops, at an off site location.

RECRUITMENT
Through effective recruitment and development the firm is able to maintain its position as a forward thinking, top quality provider of legal services. Top quality lawyers are recruited at all levels (many of whom have City or industry-based backgrounds) in order to keep up with work-level demand. Trainee solicitors join the firm each year in September to begin their two year training contracts. Trainees complete four six month seats, each one in a different department. Trainees joining the Norwich office will remain there for the duration of their training contract. In order to gain exposure to as much of the firm as possible trainees in the East Midlands will, where possible, complete a seat in each of the three East Midland offices. The firm owns brand-new accommodation in the Northampton area which is rented out to trainees. The firm employs close to 300 people and aims to recruit at all levels those that share its desire to be the best.

A-Z ■ LAW FIRMS

Hughes Fowler Carruthers

Academy Court, 94 Chancery Lane, London, WC2A 1DT
Tel (020) 7421 8383   **Fax** (020) 7421 8384   **DX** 251 London/Chancery Lane
Email mail@hfclaw.com   **Website** www.hfclaw.com

Senior & Managing Partner	Frances Hughes
Number of partners	4
Number of fee-earners	8
Total staff	21

CONTACTS	
Matrimonial & Family Law	Frances Hughes
	Pauline Fowler
	Alex Carruthers
	John Nicholson

HUGHES FOWLER CARRUTHERS
SOLICITORS

THE FIRM This niche family law practice is based in Chancery Lane in Central London and specialises in all aspects of matrimonial and family law. It was established in July 2001 and incorporated the entire family department from the highly regarded City practice of Bates, Wells & Braithwaite. The founding partners are Frances Hughes who set up the Bates, Wells & Braithwaite department in 1983, Pauline Fowler and Alex Carruthers, all of whom worked at Bates, Wells & Braithwaite for many years. In January 2002 they were joined by John Nicholson from Manches. Hughes Fowler Carruthers is widely regarded as one of London's leading family law practices. All the partners share a considerable breadth of experience which enables them to offer a wide range of skills from skilful negotiation to complex litigation to suit the individual demands of each client. Work is conducted with a high degree of professionalism and dedication. All solicitors in the firm are members of the Solicitors Family Law Association. The firm is part of an extensive international family law network through memberships of associations such as the International Academy of Matrimonial Lawyers and the International Bar Association. This means Hughes Fowler Carruthers can provide a fully international service through the partners' close connections worldwide.

PRINCIPAL AREAS OF WORK The firm handles all kinds of family law work but puts a strong emphasis on work with financial complexity and international aspects. Fields of expertise also include defending and attacking trust structures, tracing hidden assets, jurisdictional disputes and pension issues. The partners also have special expertise in complex children and child abduction work. The firm's client base continues to cover a broad spectrum of UK and internationally based men and women including those in the city or in business elsewhere as well as those from the media, the arts and other professionals.

Hugh James

Arlbee House, Greyfriars Road, Cardiff, CF10 3QB
Tel (029) 2022 4871   **Fax** (029) 2038 8222   **DX** 33300 Cardiff
Email cardiff@hughjames.com   **Website** www.hughjames.com

Managing Partner	Matthew Tossell
Senior Partner	Russel Jenkins
Number of partners	44
Assistant solicitors	53
Other fee-earners	137

AREAS OF PRACTICE	
Business Services	30%
Business Litigation	26%
Claimant Litigation	28%
Public Funded	16%

CONTACTS	
Business Services	Geoffrey Adams
Business Litigation	Gareth Williams
Claimant Litigation	Peter Evans
Public Funded	Mark Powell

THE FIRM Hugh James is one of the leading regional law firms in the UK. It is a practice which provides a comprehensive range of commercial and private client services through its network of offices across South Wales and Bristol. Hugh James has experienced phenomenal growth and success since it was formed in 1960. It is a dynamic firm which has an enthusiastic and forward thinking approach to its work and the way in which its services are provided, without sacrificing service standards and quality. Its commitment to embracing new technology is reflected in the recent launch of the Hugh James gateway to the firm's online legal services websites, one of which is click2law.com. This site comprises automated document creation, client instruction questionnaires and fixed fee packages for the business community. The firm has a national reputation for its business and insurance litigation practice. It also has a strong reputation for its commercial property and insolvency work and has a rapidly growing commercial practice. The firm is proud of its commitment to private client work and the Community Legal Services scheme and continues to be involved in high profile claimant litigation.

PRINCIPAL AREAS OF WORK The practice is divided into four divisions: business litigation, business services, claimant litigation and public funded. Specialist teams have been established to serve niche areas of the law and the firm has a multidisciplinary approach to the provision of legal services. Teams comprise not only solicitors and barristers but also individuals with non-legal professional qualifications.

Business Litigation The business litigation division is recognised as a formidable force in the Wales and West region. The firm's insurance services department has expertise in all areas of insurance work acting for national and international insurers in cases including personal injury, product liability and professional negligence. The firm also has highly regarded construction and professional indemnity departments and specialist units dealing with property litigation and insolvency. In addition it provides a high quality and focused commercial litigation service to institutional and private clients.

Business Services The business services division provides a full range of services to its exceptionally wide client base which includes quoted companies, sports bodies, housing associations, charitable organisations and owner managed businesses (sole traders). The firm has a specialist media and technology department which offers advice on e-business start-ups and an e-business support package. The sports law department provides commercial advice to professional sports people and organisations, clubs, promoters and TV production companies in relation to the major sporting categories. The business services division incorporates a specialist employment team, which as well as providing clients with the full range of employment law advice and representation, offers a tailor-made employment services package at a fixed cost together with human resources consultancy services. The commercial property department is highly regarded and has achieved national recognition for its work. A full range of services is offered with particular expertise including planning, landlord and tenant, housing association law, acquisitions and disposals, building contracts and commercial and residential development. The firm's secured lending department has experienced a rapid expansion and due to advances in technology is able to service its clients' needs on a national basis from one location.

Claimant Litigation Division The firm has a national reputation for its work in the field of claimant personal injury litigation work, is appointed to the Community Legal Services Multi-party Actions Panel and represented claims in lead cases involving miners respiratory illnesses and vibration white finger. The firm undertakes union work and has a dedicated team dealing with catastrophic injury claims, in particular brain injury. Clinical negligence franchises are held in five of the firm's offices.

Public Funded Services The firm has the largest community legal service practice in South Wales. The service is provided in the firm's branch offices by specialist solicitors recognised by their various governing bodies and specialist support staff. Areas of work for which community legal service franchises have been awarded are consumer and contractual issues, debt, education, family, housing, mental health and welfare benefits.

INTERNATIONAL The firm also has informal associations with legal practices in Nantes, Madrid, Düsseldorf, Rome, Milan and Naples.

Languages Many partners are Welsh speakers and are delighted to conduct business in that language.

Hugh Potter & Company, Serious Injury Solicitors

14-32 Hewitt, Manchester, M15 4GB
Tel (0161) 237 5888 **Fax** (0161) 237 5999 **DX** Manchester 14342
Email hughpotterandcompany@hotmail.com **Website** www.hughpotter.com

The firm provides comprehensive advice to severely injured individuals particularly brain and spinal cord injured. It has franchises for Personal Injury, Clinical Negligence and Welfare Benefits and gives receivership and investment advice. Recently reported claims include Roebuck (£4.8 million) and Sullivan (duty owed by taxi driver to passengers). See website.

Humphreys & Co

14 King Street, Bristol, BS1 4EF
Tel (0117) 929 2662 **Fax** (0117) 929 2722 **DX** 78239
Email lawyers@humphreys.co.uk **Website** www.humphreys.co.uk

Contact Applicable Partner • Principal areas of work are company/commercial, litigation, employment, intellectual property, reinsurance, property, insurance, personal injury, entertainment, professional (including clinical) negligence, competition and insolvency.

Humphries Kirk

Glebe House, North Street, Wareham, BH20 4AN
Tel (01929) 552141 **Fax** (01929) 556701 **DX** 49700 WAREHAM
Email wareham@humphrieskirk.co.uk **Website** www.humphrieskirk.co.uk

Senior Partner	Felicity Hedger
Number of partners	9
Assistant solicitors	9
Other fee-earners	15

AREAS OF PRACTICE	
Conveyancing	31%
Trusts & Probate	27%
Commercial	23%
Matrimonial	12%
Litigation	5%
Personal Injury	2%

THE FIRM Humphries Kirk is one of the most innovative firms in the South, which manages to retain a successful balance between catering for substantial commercial clients and its traditional private client base. Humphries Kirk was one of the first firms to qualify for ISO 9001 in this region. Other offices are located at Bournemouth, Dorchester, London (consulting rooms), Poole and Swanage.

PRINCIPAL AREAS OF WORK

Company/Commercial Work includes intellectual property (Humphries Kirk acts for the Design Business Association), mergers and acquisitions (including international) and construction law (a rapidly growing specialisation within the firm).

Commercial Litigation All work from industrial, construction and lands tribunals to domestic and international litigation and arbitrations.

Banking & Financial Law The firm acts for a number of substantial German financial institutions and

Continued overleaf

A-Z LAW FIRMS

also for several German banks.

Other Areas Full range of private client services, including an in-house nominee company, trustee company and offshore client account. The firm has trained mediators, family mediators and arbitrators.

INTERNATIONAL Humphries Kirk has associated offices in Versailles, France and Cologne, Germany. It maintains a network of relationships with lawyers worldwide. Work is handled in French, German, Italian and Spanish.

Hunt & Morgan
46-48 Charles Street, Cardiff, CF10 2GE **Tel** (029) 2034 1234 **Fax** (029) 2034 2350

Hunt & Coombs
35 Thorpe Road, Peterborough, PE3 6AG **Tel** (01733) 565312 **Fax** (01733) 552748

Hunters
9 New Square, Lincoln's Inn, London, WC2A 3QN
Tel (020) 7412 0050 **Fax** (020) 7412 0049 **DX** 61 Chancery Lane.London
Email mail@hunters-solicitors.co.uk **Website** www.hunters-solicitors.co.uk

Senior Partner	John Kennedy
Number of partners	14
Assistant solicitors	4
Other fee-earners	11

THE FIRM Founded in the early 18th century, the firm is a thriving modern partnership, serving a broadly-based private and institutional clientele.

PRINCIPAL AREAS OF WORK The firm has a long-established reputation in private client, charity, banking security, and matrimonial work, with an increasing emphasis on commercial property, company/commercial law, employment and litigation.
Private Client A wide range of work includes trusts, tax planning, tax returns, heritage and agricultural property, wills, probate and residential conveyancing.
Charities Work includes acting for major charities, national and private, registrations, schemes, trading arrangements, and housing associations.
Matrimonial All aspects of work are covered, but particularly cases involving children, and those with a substantial financial element.
Commercial Property Work includes acquiring and selling property investments, and business tenancies.
Company/Commercial Law & Employment The firm advises private companies and partnerships on commercial contracts, acquisitions and disposals, and a full range of employment issues.
Litigation The firm undertakes a wide range of court work including personal injury, breach of contract, landlord and tenant disputes, debt recovery and enforcement of security.

INTERNATIONAL The firm has a close relationship with firms in Australia.

RECRUITMENT One trainee solicitor with a good degree is recruited annually. There is a wide spread of work and direct client contact.

Hunton & Williams
6th Floor, Fleetway House, 25 Farringdon Street, London, EC4A 4AB **Tel** (020) 7246 5700 **Fax** (020) 7246 5772

Kitson Hutchings
Hagley House, 38/40 The Terrace, Torquay, TQ1 1BN **Tel** (01803) 213513 **Fax** (01803) 213532

Hutchinson Mainprice
60 Ebury Street, London, SW1W 9QD **Tel** (020) 7259 0121 **Fax** (020) 7259 0051

LAW FIRMS ■ A-Z

Huttons

16 St Andrews Crescent, Cardiff, CF1 3DD
Tel (029) 2037 8621 **Fax** (029) 2038 8450 **DX** 33065 Cardiff
Email email@huttons-solicitors.co.uk

THE FIRM Huttons is a leading litigation practice in Wales, noted for plaintiff personal injury and medical negligence law, family and childcare law and criminal defence advocacy. The firm were ranked as 'leaders in their field' in clinical negligence (mainly claimant) and crime by Chambers (2000-2001). It has been awarded membership of several Law Society Panels, AVMA and Spinal Injuries Association and has been franchised by the Legal Aid Board. The firm is expanding its commercial division.

PRINCIPAL AREAS OF WORK The firm provides specialist litigation services.
Personal Injury & Medical Negligence Work ranges from RTA cases (including CFAs) to brain injury in children and multi-party actions.
Litigation Work done has an emphasis on miscarriages of justice including police actions and judicial review; employment disputes, libel, landlord and tenant and general contractual disputes.
Family & Child Care The firm handles divorce, children matters, high value ancillary relief applications and Court of Appeal work.
Criminal Advocacy High profile murder cases are handled, including the Lynette White murder trial and the Tooze murder and appeal case.
Commercial Work includes business formation, acquisitions and sales, partnership disputes, property matters, insolvency, employment, probate and wills.

Senior Partner	Stuart Hutton
Finance Partner	Clare Strowbridge
Number of partners	5
Associates	3
Assistant solicitors	3
Other fee-earners	3

AREAS OF PRACTICE	
Criminal Advocacy	35%
Family/Childcare	20%
PI/Medical Negligence	20%
Litigation	15%
Commercial	10%

CONTACTS	
Litigation	David Evans
Criminal Advocacy	Stuart Hutton
Commercial	Clare Strowbridge
PI/Medical Negligence	Tim Musgrave
Family/Childcare	Christine O'Brien

■ Iain Smith & Company

18-20 Queen's Road, Aberdeen, AB15 4ZT **Tel** (01224) 645454 **Fax** (01224) 646671

■ Ian Downing Family Law Practice

8 The Crescent, Plymouth, PL1 3AB **Tel** (01752) 226224 **Fax** (01752) 226213

Iliffes Booth Bennett (IBB)

Lovell House, 271 High Street, Uxbridge, UB8 1LQ
Tel (01895) 230941 **Fax** (01895) 207955 **DX** 45105 Uxbridge
Email Reception.lh@ibblaw.co.uk **Website** www.ibblaw.co.uk

THE FIRM With offices in Middlesex, Berkshire, Buckinghamshire and Essex, this firm is one of the largest practices in the South East outside central London. Its principal aim is to deliver efficient and effective legal services to an extensive business and private client community. IBB has a partner-led, team approach. Daily involvement from partners, who are specialists in their field, ensures clients receive a consistently high level of quality expertise. Strong emphasis is placed on problem solving and understanding a client's business to provide a tailor-made service. Many IBB lawyers are from City or heavyweight regional firms. ISO 9002 accredited and a member of LawNet – a federation of independent law firms.

PRINCIPAL AREAS OF WORK
Commercial Property The team is structured to reflect the key market sectors in which their clients operate: commercial development and construction, residential development, investment, finance and secured lending and occupational management. Clients range from major property developers, financial institutions, investors, charitable bodies, secured lenders to occupiers.
Commercial Dispute Resolution Commercial contract, e-commerce, shareholder, partnership and boardroom disputes, landlord and tenant, land and other commercial property disputes. The firm also advises on insurance and professional negligence claims, insolvency, debt collection, contentious probate, ADR, mediation and flexible funding arrangements. Acts for institutional insurers, property developers, construction companies, car manufacturers, national unions, charitable institutions and partnerships.
Corporate and Commercial Mergers and acquisitions, flotation and listings on recognised exchanges, project finance and investment, e-commerce, internet banking, employee share schemes and tax, IT, IP, franchising, offshore companies and trusts. Acts for large corporations, SME's, partnerships and start-ups.
Employment Employment contracts, staff handbooks, redundancy and restructuring programmes, preventing and defending claims, severance agreements, advice in the event of a sale or purchase of a business, protecting a business from competition, employee benefit schemes and trusts, phantom

Continued overleaf

Managing Partner	Steven Booth
Number of partners	21
Assistant solicitors	45
Other fee-earners	41

AREAS OF PRACTICE	
Commercial Property	26%
Crime & Fraud	22%
Private Client	17%
Commercial Dispute Resolution	15%
Family	13%
Corporate & Commercial	7%

CONTACTS	
Charities	Peter Burnett
Commercial Dispute Resolution	Andrew Olins
Commercial Property	Susan Mawson
Corporate & Commercial	David Jackson
Crime & Fraud	Tan Ikram
Employment	Victoria Harris
Family	Shôn Roberts
PI/Clinical Negligence	Anthony Wiseman
Residential Conveyancing	Gillian Outram
Wills, Probate, Tax & Trusts	Gillian Murray

A-Z ■ LAW FIRMS

equity schemes, share option schemes and taxation.
Charities Advises on charity law aspects of property, commercial and domestic conveyancing, charity law regulation and compliance, Charity Commission work, formations, mergers and incorporation of charities and personal liability of trustees.
Private Client High net worth private clients form a significant part of the client base. Services for individuals: wills, probate, tax, trusts and estate planning, crime and serious fraud, family including children's cases, residential conveyancing and property sales/lettings, independent financial advice, personal injury and clinical negligence. Please visit the Iliffes Booth Bennett website for details.

RECRUITMENT IBB has a full training programme for all professional and support staff, being fully aware of the need to maintain an appropriately skilled and motivated workforce. Trainee solicitors are offered a structured period of training with extensive professional supervision and maximum client contact.

■ Imran Khan & Partners
52-53 Russell Square, London, WC1B 4HP **Tel** (020) 7636 6314 **Fax** (020) 7636 6315

■ In Place of Strife
212 Piccadilly, London, W1V 9LD **Tel** (020) 7917 9449 **Fax** (020) 7917 9450

Ince & Co

Knollys House, 11 Byward Street, London, EC3R 5EN
Tel (020) 7623 2011 **Fax** (020) 7623 3225 **DX** 1070 London City EC3
Email firstname.lastname@ince.co.uk   **Website** www.ince.co.uk

Senior Partner	Peter Rogan
Recruitment Partner	Chris Sprague
UK	
Number of partners	49
Number of assistants	60
Other fee-earners	40
Total	149
CONTACTS	
Admiralty	Chris Beesley, Faz Peermohamed, James Wilson
ADR/Mediation	James Wilson
Asset Finance	Tony Suchy, Nick Gould
Asset Recovery	Bob Deering, Ben Horn
Aviation	Anthony Fitzsimmons, Ian Cranston
Commercial Insurance	Michael Jones, David Coupe
Commercial Litigation	Ben Horn, Steven Fox, Peter Rogan, Ben Ogden
Construction	Jeremy Farr, Nick Shepherd
Corporate	David Coupe, Nick Gould
Dry Shipping	Bob Deering, Chris Moore, Paul Herring
E-commerce	Nick Gould
EU & Competition	Anthony Fitzsimmons, Denys Hickey
Energy	Chris Sprague, David Steward, Andy Iyer
Environment & Pollution	Colin de la Rue, Ian Chetwood
Insurance & Reinsurance	Peter Rogan, Alan Weir, Allan Hepworth, Jan Heuvels
Insurance Fraud	Paul Arditti, Alan Weir
International Commercial Arbitration	Ben Horn, Steven Fox, Chris Jefferis
International Trade & Commodities	Tony George, Steven Fox, Stuart Shepherd
Marine Insurance	Simon Todd
P&I Clubs	Bob Deering, Graham Crane, Mike Volikas
Personal Injury	Gillie Belsham, Charlotte Davies, Chris Sprague
Political Risk Insurance	Tony George
Professional Indemnity	David Rutherford, Andrew Ottley, Charlotte Davies, Giles Adams
Project/Trade Finance	Tony Suchy, Tony George

THE FIRM Founded in 1870, and based in the City of London, the firm has offices in Hong Kong, Singapore, Piraeus and Shanghai, providing legal services to the shipping, insurance and business communities in the Pacific Rim and Mediterranean areas. In the past 12 months the firm has expanded its European operations with the opening of three new offices: Hamburg in October 2001, followed by Le Havre and Paris in January 2002. These offices practice German and French law respectively, as well as English law, and provide a comprehensive service to the firm's clients in all practice areas. The firm also has an international network of correspondent lawyers in collaboration with whom it can provide legal services at short notice wherever the need arises. The firm prides itself on the quality and dedication of its people and is unusual in that the majority of its partners and assistants are 'home-grown', many having been with the firm throughout their legal careers. The firm is acknowledged for clear legal analysis and tenacious, imaginative dispute resolution, deploying ADR, including mediation, arbitration and litigation. Underpinning this expertise is an understanding of clients' commercial needs. Another feature of the firm's service is continuity. Clients deal with the same partner or team from initial advice to resolution, be it settlement or trial.

PRINCIPAL AREAS OF WORK
Maritime Ince & Co handles every aspect of maritime law, including collisions, salvage, charterparty, carriage of goods, marine insurance, ship finance, general average, personal injury, pollution and clean-up, and has been involved in virtually every major maritime casualty from the Torrey Canyon in 1967 to the recent Stena King collision with British Vigilance. The firm represents all major P&I Clubs, shipowners, charterers and their underwriters. Ince & Co also operates a 24 hour emergency response service 365 days a year in respect of maritime, aviation and energy related casualties with a dedicated telephone number: (020) 7283 6999.
Insurance/Reinsurance In its long history Ince & Co has participated in the majority of the leading insurance cases which have contributed to the evolution of insurance law. The firm covers all aspects of insurance and reinsurance, including marine, aviation and non-marine insurance and reinsurance, regulatory and commercial insurance, political risks, personal injury and professional indemnity. The senior partner, considered by many to be the leading insurance practitioner in the London market, heads the insurance practice.
Energy Energy sector work, principally in the oil and gas fields, has been one of the firm's main practice areas for many years. The firm's expertise covers both contentious and non-contentious work including the drafting and negotiating of contracts; asset and project finance; insurance and dispute resolution (including ADR, arbitration and court proceedings). It has experience in all areas of the industry, including construction and operation of pipelines, offshore structures, rigs, FSPO's and other vessels for the industry; drilling and offshore services; transportation and refining of oil and gas. Its clients include construction firms, oil and gas companies, drilling and service contractors, brokers and insurers. The firm has acted on most of the significant cases arising from offshore operations in the

last 30 years, including Piper Alpha (in which it represented the operator).

International Trade & Commodities The firm has been a leader in the development of English law in this area, and is widely experienced in drafting contracts, joint venture, distribution and agency agreements, documentary aspects of trade finance and interpretation of standard contract wordings. The firm advises upon trading of oil and gas, metals and soft commodities and disputes relating thereto as well as political contingency credit and financial risk insurance.

Business & Finance Ince & Co has a thriving corporate group advising on general corporate and commercial issues ranging from employment to corporate finance through to international joint ventures.

Aviation The aviation team handles a wide range of aviation matters with particular emphasis on aviation insurance problems.

Other The firm also has significant practices in the areas of property and private client, asset recovery, EU and competition, sports and media, personal injury, and international commercial litigation and arbitration.

RECRUITMENT Ince & Co recruits in the region of 10 trainee solicitors annually. Full details of the firm's training regime and also of current vacancies for all legal staff are posted on the recruitment section of the firm's website.

CONTACTS (Continued)	
Property & Private Client	Albert Levy
Shipbuilding	David Steward
	Jeremy Farr, Chris Kidd
Ship Finance	Tony Suchy
Sale & Purchase	Patrick Shaw
	Paul Herring
Sports & Media	David Coupe
	Chris Jefferis
Transport	Simon Spark
	Louise Krenca
Total Loss Investigation	Paul Arditti
	Simon Todd, Jonathan Loftus
Yachts/Superyachts	Albert Levy
	Ben Horn

International Family Law Chambers

218 Strand, London, WC2R 1AP
Tel (020) 7583 5040   **Fax** (020) 7583 5151   **DX** 252 London/Chancery Lane
Email mail@internationalfamilylaw.com   **Website** www.internationalfamilylaw.com

Head of Chambers	David Truex
Number of principals	2
Other fee-earners	4
AREAS OF PRACTICE	
English & International Family Law (inc. Consultancy & Agency)	100%
CONTACTS	
England & Australia	David Truex
England	Lorna Samuels
England & Germany	Kerstin Beyer
England	Stephanie Wells
Sweden	Carin Thor
USA	Madeleine Dimitroff

THE FIRM Chambers specialising in international family law with principal members qualified in England and Wales, Australia, Germany, Sweden and the USA. Head of Chambers David Truex, also qualified as an Australian barrister and solicitor, is an SFLA accredited specialist family lawyer. He is Chairman of the SFLA International Committee and the UK Host Committee for the 2001 World Congress on Family Law and the Rights of Children and Youth. Members of the Chambers have expertise in dealing with multi-jurisdictional disputes in England and overseas.

PRINCIPAL AREAS OF WORK Most litigation is conducted in the English courts, generally involving international issues. Particular expertise is claimed in forum disputes, international enforcement, analysis of foreign laws, international treaties and complex financial matters where offshore assets are in issue. International consultancy and agency work for other lawyers is a substantial part of the practice. Most clients are referred by law societies, embassies and other lawyers.

Irwin Mitchell

St Peter's House, Hartshead, Sheffield, S1 2EL
Tel (0870) 1500 100   **Fax** (0114) 275 3306   **DX** 10513
Email enquiries@irwinmitchell.com   **Website** www.imonline.co.uk

Managing Partner	Howard Culley
Senior Partner	Michael Napier
Number of partners	84
Assistant solicitors	151
Other fee-earners	458
AREAS OF PRACTICE	
IM Insurance Service	34%
IM Business	27%
IM Personal Injury	26%
IM Private Client	11%
IM Investment	1%
Other	1%
CONTACTS	
Business	Kevin Cunningham
Business Crime	Kevin Robinson
Commercial Litigation	Peter Bellamy
Commercial Property	Kevin Docherty
Company/Commercial	Kevin Cunningham
Competition	Michael Jelly
Criminal	Michael Whitworth
Employment	Simon Coates
Family & Matrimonial	Martin Loxley
Insurance Service	Joe Simpson

THE FIRM IM is a broad-based national firm operating from four offices in Birmingham, Leeds, London and Sheffield. Now firmly established as one of the top national firms in the UK, IM offers a distinctive approach to its clients' needs. Whether acting for national or international companies, family businesses or private clients, the firm provides the highest levels of service delivery and customer care. Whatever the area of work, IM provides clear, direct and positive advice with a firm focus on the needs of the client. The firm has a strong customer service culture and a very high level of client retention. Widely regarded as a law firm with a difference, demand continues to grow for IM's services. The practice is accredited to ISO 9001 and is authorised by the Law Society to conduct investment business.

PRINCIPAL AREAS OF WORK The five practice areas provide a complete legal service for clients of the firm.

IM Business The department comprises four national groups. The commercial and transactions group handles mergers and acquisitions both in the UK and cross-border, buyouts, corporate finance, banking, public sector transactions and commercial contracts. The human resources group covers employment contracts, disputes and pensions and employee benefits. The commercial litigation group represents clients in national and international disputes, mediation and advises on risk management. Its activities include a debt recovery division; administrative and public law; business crime, professional

Continued overleaf

A-Z ■ LAW FIRMS

negligence; insolvency; commercial and property litigation. The property group handles property acquisition, disposal, leasing, site assembly, development and construction.

IM Personal Injury The firm also has an established national reputation for personal injury, clinical negligence and product liability work. It has successfully litigated in a number of multi-party cases as well as achieving substantial awards for individuals. Frequently working at the cutting edge of the law, it has won many significant cases that have often reshaped the law and set new precedents. Recent major victories have included the CJD human growth hormone litigation and the Vibration White Finger and Chest Disease cases against British Coal.

IM Insurance Service This practice area is arguably the largest supplier of motor-related legal services in England and Wales to an insurance-related client base. A one stop insurance service is provided to insurance companies and their policy holders. The practice area is able to deal with all claims whether they are for a claimant or defendant. There are over 450 employees in this practice area and claims are received on a truly national basis, where they are handled in customer focused teams utilising a sophisticated case management platform.

IM Private Client The private client practice area covers family, residential property, wills, trusts, probate and includes a Court of Protection unit. It acts for high net worth individuals particularly in ancillary relief disputes and the creation and administration of trusts. Commercial clients provide instructions in the volume areas of will writing and domestic property. In all areas the use of specialist IT has enhanced the firm's ability to obtain and retain work.

IM Investment Management The investment management division provides a full suite of financial and investment management services, which allows the firm to provide a fully holistic approach to its clients. It acts for a wide range of clients including high net worth individuals and personal injury claimants. It creates individually tailored solutions designed to match each client's particular needs, taking into account the degrees of flexibility and risks needed to deliver the results that the clients want.

CLIENTELE Clients range from the private individual and the family business to public companies and institutions on a national and international scale.

INTERNATIONAL IM has well-established links with lawyers in the USA and most other foreign jurisdictions. It has particular expertise in transatlantic and Far Eastern work.

CONTACTS (Continued)	
Intellectual Property	James Love
Investment Management	Ian Hale
Personal Injury	John Pickering
Police Prosecution	Michael Whitworth
Residential Conveyancing	Steven Martin
Wills & Trusts	Paul Hirst

■ **Isadore Goldman**
125 High Holborn, London, WC1V 6QF **Tel** (020) 7242 3000 **Fax** (020) 7242 9160

Ison Harrison

Duke House, 54 Wellington Street, Leeds, LS1 2EE
Tel (0113) 284 5000 **Fax** (0113) 284 5020 **DX** 713106 - Leeds Park Square
Email mail@isonharrison.co.uk   **Website** www.isonharrison.co.uk

THE FIRM Over the last year, Ison Harrison has doubled in size leading to the expansion of existing private client and corporate departments and the launch of a new commercial collections team called 'Equilibrium'. The firm has invested heavily in IT and case management systems. It has IIP accreditation and a LSC franchise and seeks Lexcel accreditation.

PRINCIPAL AREAS OF WORK

Business Client Specialisation in acquisition, disposals, property, employment, insolvency, partnership and debt recovery.
Private Client Specialisation in clinical negligence, personal injury, family, crime and immigration. The financial services team enhances the probate, wills, trust and conveyancing departments.

Senior Partner	Stephen Harrison
AREAS OF PRACTICE	
Personal Injury & Clinical Negligence	40%
Family/Crime	25%
Business Clients	20%
Conveyancing	15%

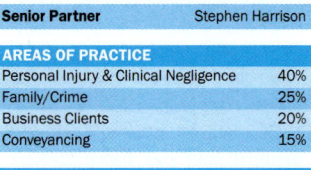

CONTACTS	
Business Clients	Richard Timperley
Clinical Negligence/PI	Neil Fearn
Family/Immigration	Jo Trythall

Jackson & Canter

32 Princes Road, Liverpool, L8 1TH
Tel (0151) 282 1732 **Fax** (0151) 282 1735 **DX** 14156
Email mailbox@jacksoncanter.co.uk **Website** jacksoncanter.co.uk

THE FIRM One of the leading civil rights firms in the North West undertaking a wide range of private client work both privately and publicly funded.

PRINCIPAL AREAS OF WORK The firm is strong in immigration including business; public law, particularly suing the police and sexual abuse litigation; mental health; children and family work; housing; welfare benefits; crime. The firm also has strong links with the ethnic minority communities on Merseyside and helps and advises new businesses in the community.

Senior Partner	Andrew Holroyd
AREAS OF PRACTICE	
Litigation	21%
Family	18%
Immigration	16%
Crime	14%
Welfare	7%

Jackson Parton

18 Mansell Street, London, E1 8AA
Tel (020) 7702 0085 **Fax** (020) 7702 0858
Email mail@jacksonparton.com **Website** www.jacksonparton.com

THE FIRM Jackson Parton is a medium-sized niche City practice specialising in shipping, commodity, insurance and related commercial litigation and arbitration. The firm was founded in 1992 and has flourished ever since.

PRINCIPAL AREAS OF WORK The firm offers expertise in the full range of P&I and FD&D work, including charter disputes, cargo claims, pollution and general average. Other work includes sale and purchase, shipbuilding, mortgage enforcement disputes, marine insurance matters, commodity disputes, grounding, collision and salvage cases.

INTERNATIONAL Work is handled in Arabic, Dutch, French, German, Greek, Italian, Japanese, Norwegian, Persian (Farsi) and Spanish.

Managing & Senior Partner	Graham Jackson
Number of partners	9
Assistant solicitors	5
Other fee-earners	6
AREAS OF PRACTICE	
Commercial Shipping: Owners, Charterers, Cargo Owners & Insurers	70%
Admiralty: Collision and Salvage	30%
CONTACTS	
Admiralty	Brian Roberts
Commercial Shipping	Nicholas Parton
Industrial Diseases & Injury	Brian Roberts

Jacksons

Innovation House, Yarm Road, Stockton on Tees, TS18 3TN
Tel (01642) 643643 **Fax** (01642) 873737 **DX** 715796 Stockton
Email genquiry@jacksons.law.co.uk **Website** www.jacksons.law.co.uk

Queens House, Wellington Street, Leeds, LS1 2DE
Tel (0113) 244 1666 **Fax** (0113) 386 0600 **DX** 706967 Leeds Park Square

Mayflower House, Fifth Avenue Business Park, Team Valley, Gateshead, NE11 0HF
Tel (0191) 497 7300 **Fax** (0191) 497 7301 **DX** 60407 Whickham

THE FIRM Jacksons was established over 125 years ago and has a strong reputation as an efficient and progressive firm. The firm's philosophy is based upon a modern approach to business, incorporating the most up to date technology and a commercial style management structure. Jacksons serves clients nationally in the field of both defendant insurance litigation and employment law and is renowned for providing high quality legal services to commercial clients in the North East. The firm has expanded over the last few years into Leeds and now has branches in Leeds and Tyneside.

PRINCIPAL AREAS OF WORK
Insurance Litigation With a client list which includes eight out of the UK's top 10 insurers, the firm's insurance litigation department offers expertise in disease work for defendants as well as traumatic injury, property damage and road traffic accidents.
Employment The firm has a national reputation for its experience in employment law and offers specialist representation at employment tribunals throughout the UK, as well as in the Employment Appeal Tribunal.
Company Commercial The firm covers the full range of services for the business client including sales and acquisitions, corporate finance and commercial contracts.
Commercial Property The commercial property team deals with all areas of commercial property including freehold, disposals and acquisitions, leasehold matters, development agreements and planning agreements.

Managing Partner	Richard Clarke
Senior Partner	Kevin Fletcher
Number of partners	16
Associates	7
Assistant solicitors	11
Other fee-earners	20
Total staff	133
AREAS OF PRACTICE	
Insurance Litigation	50%
Company/Commercial & Commercial Property	25%
Commercial Litigation	15%
Employment Law	10%
CONTACTS	
Agricultural	Adrienne Patterson
Commercial Litigation	Nigel Kidwell
Commercial Property	Geoffrey Skeoch
Company/Commercial	Anthony Wentworth
Employment	Kevin Fletcher
Insolvency	Stephen Wiles
Insurance Litigation	Richard Clarke

Continued overleaf

A-Z ■ LAW FIRMS

Commercial Litigation The firm offers expertise in contract disputes, debt recovery, insurance recovery and professional negligence. The firm additionally advises on all aspects of criminal and civil liability in connection with environmental issues. Jacksons has been at the forefront of alternative dispute resolution and has pioneered mediation techniques as founder members of ADR Net Limited.

Agriculture Jacksons is appointed by the NFU as its panel firm for the North East region, an area extending from the Humber River to the Scottish Border. The agricultural department covers areas of work such as agricultural property, litigation and other rural business matters.

Insolvency The expanding insolvency department acts for a number of insolvency practitioners, whilst advising companies, partnerships and individuals.

■ James & Co

99 Manningham Lane, Bradford, BD1 3BN
Tel (01274) 729900 **Fax** (01274) 721100 **DX** 712442 Bradford 8
Email jamesco@ukimmigration.co.uk **Website** www.ukimmigration.co.uk

AREAS OF PRACTICE	
Immigration	95%

Ptnrs 1 **Asst solrs** 2 **Other fee-earners** 5 **Contact** Charles James • Specialist immigration firm. Charles James is on the Law Society Immigration panel for business, general immigration and political asylum.

James Chapman & Co

76 King Street, Manchester, M2 4NH
Tel (0161) 828 8000 **Fax** (0161) 828 8018 **DX** 14492 Manchester 2
Email generalenquiries@james-chapman.co.uk **Website** www.james-chapman.co.uk

Managing Partner	Elisabeth Taylor
Senior Partner	Maurice Watkins
Number of partners	32
Assistant solicitors	26
Other fee-earners	15

AREAS OF PRACTICE	
Defendant Insurance/Indemnity	80%
Company Work	10%
Claimant Personal Injury	5%
Conveyancing Residential/Commercial & Probate	5%

CONTACTS	
Company/Commercial & Sports Law	Maurice Watkins
Personal Injury	Kevin Finnigan
Professional Negligence	Elisabeth Taylor
Property/Private Client	Peter Marsden

THE FIRM James Chapman & Co was established over 100 years ago and from its earliest days concentrated on insurance and professional negligence work. It has maintained this specialisation and also handles corporate and commercial work, commercial and residential conveyancing and private client work. The firm also has a European-wide recognised specialisation in sports and media law. Clients of the firm include many major insurance companies and substantial corporate entities. The firm is one of the leading practices in the insurance and professional negligence field in the North West. With 73 dedicated fee-earners, the firm can handle an individual claim or a series of claims, of any size and complexity. James Chapman & Co intends to sustain the high quality provision of insurance and professional negligence services, which has been its hallmark since the firm was founded, as well as developing its expertise in all other areas. In recent years, the practice has expanded steadily and has invested heavily in its office infrastructure and IT systems. The firm's policy is to increase the number of qualified staff, not only to meet the increase in demand for its services, but also to ensure all clients continue to receive a cost-efficient and quality service.

PRINCIPAL AREAS OF WORK The firm consists of four departments: personal injury work on behalf of defendants and insurers, insurance and professional negligence work on behalf of defendants, company/commercial work, including sports law, media and entertainment law, and property and private client work.

Personal Injury The department has dedicated specialists for cases of catastrophic injury, involving brain and spine injuries. The firm has been appointed as a member of restricted panels to several major insurers to deal with cases of the utmost severity and has a team of lawyers exclusively handling these cases. James Chapman & Co has pioneered a proactive consensual approach to the settlement of significant personal injury cases and the encouragement of negotiations between solicitors. The firm continues to handle an increasing number of motor claims, stress and other occupational disease claims.

Professional Negligence The department undertakes a wide range of high quality, complex claims on behalf of solicitors, surveyors, architects, barristers, valuers, insurance brokers, accountants and other professional groups. The firm has extensive experience in general litigation and handles a variety of actions in product liability, building and construction risks, policy disputes, property damage, subrogation recoveries, motor claims, environmental and employers' and public liability claims.

Company/Commercial The department provides services to a variety of clients from listed public companies to smaller owner-run businesses. The services include advice on general company law, including acquisition and sales of companies, commercial contracts, intellectual property law, employment law, commercial litigation and debt recovery, with a growing media and IT practice.

Commercial Property & Private Client The firm advises commercial property clients on property development, commercial leases, planning applications, estate management, landlord and tenant matters and secured lending. Private clients are advised on all aspects of financial planning, including personal

tax advice, inheritance tax and estate planning, probates and trusts including wills, estate administration and preparing and administering settlements, and residential conveyancing.

Sports Law James Chapman & Co's sports law team is led by partner Maurice Watkins, who is also a director of Manchester United plc and Manchester United Football Club. Maurice Watkins is a member of FIFA's new Dispute Resolution Chamber which deals with all disputes under the new FIFA world transfer regulations. The team's work also includes sponsorship, broadcasting and merchandising. It has been at the forefront in advising world-leaders in this sector for many years, acting for sporting bodies, event organisers, clubs and managers, as well as for individual sportsmen and women.

RECRUITMENT The firm recruits four trainees a year, as well as additional assistant solicitors.

Jameson & Hill
72-74 Fore Street, Hertford, SG14 1BY **Tel** (01992) 554881 **Fax** (01992) 551885

C & H Jefferson
Norwich Union House, 7 Fountain Street, Belfast, BT1 5EA
Tel (028) 9032 9545 **Fax** (028) 9024 4644 **DX** 439 NR.Belfast
Email law@chjefferson.co.uk **Website** www.chjefferson.co.uk

Number of partners	7
Assistant solicitors	16
Other fee-earners	5

AREAS OF PRACTICE
Litigation	65%
Commercial	20%
Employment	10%
Private Client	5%

CONTACTS
Commercial	Kenneth Rutherford
Employment	Mark Tinman
Litigation	Gareth Jones
Private Client	David G Lennon
Professional Indemnity	Gareth Jones

THE FIRM Established in 1898, C & H Jefferson is one of the leading practices in Northern Ireland with an excellent reputation for its comprehensive legal and agency services.

PRINCIPAL AREAS OF WORK
Litigation The firm is one of the largest litigation practices in Northern Ireland, specialising in all areas of defence and commercial litigation and has corporate membership of FOIL.

Commercial The firm has a strong commercial department embracing commercial property transactions; banking and securities, company formations, sales, acquisitions and reconstructions; partnerships; insolvency; debt recovery; agency work for leading firms in Great Britain and elsewhere, maritime law and defamation.

Employment The firm has a vibrant employment law practice with a dedicated team, acting for employers, with extensive expertise in discrimination law (sex, religion and disability), and advising on contracts of employment.

Private Client The firm provides a full range of services commensurate with a long-established practice including conveyancing; wills and administration of estates; tax planning and trusts and family law.

INTERNATIONAL Members of the firm are fluent in French, Italian and Spanish.

Jeffrey Aitken Solicitors
Fortune House, 74 Waterloo Street, Glasgow, G2 7DA **Tel** (0141) 221 5983 **Fax** (0141) 225 5750

Jeffrey Green Russell
Apollo House, 56 New Bond Street, London, W1S 1RG
Tel (020) 7339 7000 **Fax** (020) 7339 7001 **DX** 44627 Mayfair
Email jgr@jgrlaw.co.uk **Website** www.jgrweb.com

Managing Partner	Clive Whitfield-Jones
Senior Partner	Tony Coles
Number of partners	22
Assistant solicitors	18
Other fee-earners	15

CONTACTS
Company/Commercial	John O'Connell
Insurance Litigation	R Bryan Lincoln
Leisure & Licensing	Julian Skeens
Litigation	Philip Cohen
Private Client	Philip Harris
Property	Peter Johnson

THE FIRM Jeffrey Green Russell is a medium-sized commercial law firm based in Bond Street, London W1. The practice is committed to technology and human resources development, both of which have made a significant contribution to its success. The practice prides itself on being at the cutting edge in the use of technology to achieve its business goals.

PRINCIPAL AREAS OF WORK
Company/Commercial A broad spectrum of services focus on commercial and financial activity. Corporate work includes formations, mergers, acquisitions, MBOs, joint ventures, reorganisations and share issues. Other areas of expertise are commercial work (including computer contracts and the internet), banking and finance, intellectual property and franchising, and corporate taxation.

Litigation Rapid, positive, effective action is the hallmark of this department in general commercial litigation, insurance disputes including professional negligence and product liability, property litigation, employment matters, debt collection and insolvency, mortgage repossession and commercial fraud including computer and technology-related offences, and personal injury and legal expenses insurance.

Continued overleaf

A-Z ■ LAW FIRMS

Property The department offers a full range of services including planning, development work, property finance, investment, dealing (including portfolio break-ups and auction work) and landlord and tenant law.

Licensing & Leisure A strong department caters for the special demands of the leisure industry offering a comprehensive service representing clients in courts throughout the country. The firm deals with bingo, nightclubs and discos, pubs, off-licences, restaurants and catering, hotels, cinemas, amusement arcades and gaming.

Personal Finance The department provides a specialist service dedicated to the protection and enhancement of clients' personal wealth. The range of services includes wills and probate, estate and financial planning, trusts and settlements, administration of estates and overseas tax arrangements.

CLIENTELE Clients cover a spectrum of commerce, finance and industry, ranging from small businesses to multinational corporations. Activities include banking, finance, mortgage lenders, the internet, technology, leisure, restaurants, the licensed trade, brewers, insurance, airlines and property development.

INTERNATIONAL The firm is a member of ACL International, an association of commercial lawyers worldwide. For further information contact the senior partner.

■ Jenkins & Hand

Clutha House, 10 Storey's Gate, London, SW1P 3AY
Tel (020) 7222 5002   **Fax** (020) 7222 5004   **DX** 99924 Victoria

Ptnrs 3   **Contact** Keith Jenkins • Specialising in work for social landlords, local authorities and charities, including stock transfers, urban regeneration projects, local authority powers, care contracts and advice on all aspects of registered social landlord activities.

AREAS OF PRACTICE	
Housing Association	70%
Local Authority	30%

■ Jennifer Israel & Co

1346 High Road, London, N20 9HJ   **Tel** (020) 8445 3189   **Fax** (020) 8446 6608

■ Jeremy Fear & Co

5a St Onge Parade, Southbury Road, Enfield, EN1 1YU   **Tel** (020) 8367 4466   **Fax** (020) 8367 3481

■ JJ Rice

Law Society House, 94 Victoria House, Belfast,   **Tel** (028) 9028 8688   **Fax** (028) 9028 8588

Joelson Wilson & Co

70 New Cavendish Street, London, W1G 8AT
Tel (020) 7580 5721   **Fax** (020) 7580 2251   **Licensing Fax** (020) 7935 5167
Email info@joelson-wilson.co.uk   **Website** joelson-wilson.co.uk

THE FIRM Established in 1957, Joelson Wilson & Co provides a personal and individual approach and a highly commercial service to its clients. Known nationally and internationally for its work in the fields of corporate and company, and liquor, entertainment, betting and gaming licensing, the firm has a long-established reputation for its work in the leisure industry. Solicitors in its specialised licensing and leisure department appear in courts throughout the country, speak regularly at conferences and contribute to industry journals and legal textbooks. The corporate and company team has a strong international element to its practice and works closely with the firm's specialist employment law unit. The firm also provides a full range of services through its commercial property and litigation departments. Joelson Wilson & Co is the UK member of European Lawyers Network (EEIG), working closely with the other firms in Amsterdam, Brussels, Frankfurt and Paris, as well as the US associated firms in Pittsburgh PA and Sacramento CA. Partners in the firm are members of the International Association of Gaming Attorneys.

Managing Partner	Paul Baglee
Number of partners	5
Number of consultants	1
Assistant solicitors	6
Other fee-earners	6

AREAS OF PRACTICE	
Corporate & Company	34%
Licensing & Leisure (Liquor/Gaming/Betting/Entertainment)	34%
Commercial Litigation & Employment	20%
Property	12%

John Batters & Co
Craigie Hall, 6 Rowan Road, Glasgow, G41 5BS **Tel** (0141) 427 6884 **Fax** (0141) 427 7909

John Collins & Partners
Copper Court, Phoenix Way, Enterprise Park, Swansea, SA7 9EH **Tel** (01792) 773773 **Fax** (01792) 774775

John Ford Solicitors
3A Blackstock Road, London, N4 2JF **Tel** (020) 8800 6464 **Fax** (020) 8800 6066

John Gaunt & Partners
Omega Court, 372 Cemetery Road, Sheffield, S11 8FT
Tel (0114) 266 8664 **Fax** (0114) 266 0101 **DX** 717212 Sheffield 27
Email post@john-gaunt.co.uk **Website** www.john-gaunt.co.uk

AREAS OF PRACTICE	
Liquor Licensing	85%
Commercial Litigation	10%
Landlord & Tenant (Contentious/Non-contentious)	5%

Ptnrs: 3 **Associates:** 1 **Asst solrs:** 3 **Other fee-earners:** 3 **Contact** John R T Gaunt • Specialist commercial practice, particularly for the licensed and leisure industries, handling over 8,000 licence applications each year and exclusively retained by a number of leisure operatives.

John Hodge & Co
27/31 Boulevard, Weston-super-Mare, BS23 1NY **Tel** (01934) 623511 **Fax** (01934) 418210

John Kendall
The Manor House, St David's Street, Presteigne, LD8 2BP **Tel** (01544) 260019 **Fax** (01544) 260717

John McKee & Son
55 Royal Avenue, Belfast, BT1 1FD
Tel (028) 9023 2303 **Fax** (028) 9023 0081 **DX** 470 NR Belfast
Email info@jmckee.co.uk **Website** www.jmckee.co.uk

Senior Partner	Lex Ross
Number of partners	5
Assistant solicitors	5
Other fee-earners	4

AREAS OF PRACTICE	
Commercial	42%
Litigation	41%
Private client	14%
Other	3%

CONTACTS	
Corporate/Commercial	Avril McCammon
	Lex Ross
Litigation	Leonard Edgar
	Melanie Jones
Property	Albert Jordan

THE FIRM John McKee & Son is a major Belfast law firm, highly regarded for its corporate and litigation expertise. Founded in 1887, the firm is a progressive law firm which continues to enjoy rapid growth. The firm's lawyers have extensive experience in their fields, enabling them to serve the needs of both local and national clients.

PRINCIPAL AREAS OF WORK
Corporate/Commercial The firm advises business clients on all aspects of corporate and commercial law. Work includes advice on company acquisitions and disposals, corporate insolvency and personal insolvency acting in the main for insolvency practitioners, and banking and secured lending together with private finance initiative work, acting on behalf of the lending institutions.
Litigation The firm has an excellent reputation in insurance litigation, commercial and insolvency litigation, employment tribunals and debt recovery.
Property All aspects of commercial property transactions are undertaken together with building society repossession work.
Other Areas The firm also provides a full range of private client advice, including wills, tax planning, residential conveyancing and matrimonial matters.

John Morse Solicitors
St Helen's House, 156 St Helen's Road, Swansea, SA1 5DG
Tel (01792) 648111 **Fax** (01792) 648028 **Email** mail@johnmorse.co.uk

Contact John Morse • This is a commercial practice for commercial business and commercial properties. It has an extensive licensing practice for liquor licensing and betting and gambling licensing, acting for many large brewers and betting office operators. The practice is in South Wales and throughout the UK. Conveyancing probate and wills department.

John Pickering & Partners
9 Church Lane, Oldham, OL1 3AN **Tel** (0161) 834 1251 **Fax** (0161) 626 1671

Johns Elliot

40 Linenhall Street, Belfast, BT2 8BA
Tel (028) 9032 6881   **Fax** (028) 9024 8236   **DX** 419 NR Belfast
Email info@johnselliot.com   **Website** www.johnselliot.com

THE FIRM Johns Elliot is a leading City firm offering a wide range of legal services, with particular emphasis on commercial and corporate matters. The firm was established in 1837. Each client has contact with a single partner who bears responsibility for the conduct of that client's business, although individual aspects will be dealt with by specialist lawyers.

PRINCIPAL AREAS OF WORK

Company/Commercial Property Work includes company formations, reconstructions and acquisitions, and all aspects of commercial property, from initial planning applications to satisfying the requirements of the developers' financiers.

Employment An increasingly problematic area for commercial clients, legal advice is given at an early stage to assess the potential impact of legislation, evolve efficient working practices and ensure good industrial relations are established and maintained.

Litigation A major part of the firm's practice, this department deals with commercial litigation, building contract arbitrations, medical negligence, personal injury claims and debt collection, and is also involved in defamation actions for newspapers and local broadcasting networks.

Managing & Senior Partner	David A Leitch
Number of partners	7
Assistant solicitors	3
Other fee-earners	9

AREAS OF PRACTICE	
Company/Commercial	45%
Litigation & Employment	25%
Probate & Tax	15%
Other	15%

CONTACTS	
Company/Commercial	David A Leitch
Litigation	Ronald Robinson
Private Client	David A Leitch

The Johnson Partnership
Cannon Courtyard, Off Long Row, Nottingham, NG1 6JE   **Tel** (0115) 941 9141   **Fax** (0115) 947 0178

Johnsons

Johnson House, 50-56 Wellington Place, Belfast, BT1 6GF
Tel (028) 9024 0183   **Fax** (028) 9031 3300   **DX** 405 NR Belfast, 1
Email pt@johnsonslaw.co.uk

THE FIRM Johnsons offers a partner-driven, pragmatic and cost-effective legal service to commercial and private clients.

PRINCIPAL AREAS OF WORK

Johnsons has an extensive defence litigation practice representing many insurance companies. In addition, the firm has developed a recognised expertise in the fields of defamation and media-related law, and corporate law acting for, inter alia, the largest financial institution in Northern Ireland.

Senior Partners	John Marshall
	Paul Tweed
Number of partners	8
Assistant solicitors	10
Other fee-earners	1

AREAS OF PRACTICE	
Litigation	50%
Defamation/Media & Entertainment Law	25%
Company/Commercial/Employment	20%
Private Client	5%

John Weston & Co
10 Victoria Street, Felixstowe, IP11 7ER   **Tel** (01394) 282527   **Fax** (01394) 276097

John Winkworth-Smith
Churchdale Farm, Ashford-in-the-Water, Bakewell, DE45 1NX   **Tel** (01629) 640269   **Fax** (01629) 640608

Jonas Roy Bloom

Citadel, 190 Corporation Street, Birmingham, B4 6QD
Tel (0121) 212 4111   **Fax** (0121) 212 1770   **DX** 23540
Email info@jonasroybloom.co.uk   **Website** www.jonasroybloom.co.uk

THE FIRM The firm specialises in crime, personal injury, and civil actions against the police. Its longstanding reputation of dealing with the most serious criminal trials has been extended in recent years into white collar crime and fraud trials, and it is often instructed by professionals. The firm is on the Serious Fraud Panel and two of its partners have higher rights of audience. Agency commissions undertaken.

Number of partners	6
Assistant solicitors	2
Other fee-earners	12

AREAS OF PRACTICE	
Crime	75%
Personal Injury	25%

LAW FIRMS ■ A-Z

■ Jonathan Stephens & Co
Ty Cornel, 11 Castle Parade, Usk, NP15 1AA **Tel** (01291) 673344 **Fax** (01291) 673575

■ Jones & Cassidy
220 Ormeau Road, Belfast, BT7 2FY **Tel** (028) 9064 2290 **Fax** (028) 9064 2297

Jones, Day, Reavis & Pogue

Bucklersbury House, 3 Queen Victoria Street, London, EC4N 8NA
Tel (020) 7236 3939 **Fax** (020) 7236 1113 **DX** 98949 Cheapside 2
Email counsel@jonesday.com **Website** www.jonesday.com

Senior Partner	Robert L Thomson
Number of partners	11
Assistant solicitors	60
Other fee-earners	12

THE FIRM Founded in 1893, Jones Day is one of the world's largest law firms, employing more than 1,650 lawyers resident in 26 locations in major centres of business and finance around the globe. Established over 25 years ago, Jones Day London is a multinational partnership, providing UK and US legal advice through UK, US and dually qualified lawyers. The London office provides a full range of business legal services to UK and overseas clients, focusing principally on UK and cross-border M&A; corporate finance transactions; investment funds; private equity; corporate tax planning; banking, tax and tax-based structured finance; litigation/dispute resolution and arbitration; competition/anti-trust; commercial property and environmental law; share schemes, employment and pension matters; intellectual property and information technology. The London office is part of Jones Day Europe, which includes over 300 lawyers in Brussels, Frankfurt, Milan, Madrid and Paris. Jones Day Europe functions as an integrated organisation, with a wide range of skills and experience available to meet the needs of its clients.

PRINCIPAL AREAS OF WORK
Corporate, Corporate Finance & Commercial One of the strengths of the London office is its corporate practice and it is able to offer its clients the full range of high quality legal services required for all corporate transactions. The office has substantial expertise in public and private, domestic and cross-border mergers and acquisitions, reorganisations, auction sales, joint ventures and general commercial transactions. The corporate finance team advises companies, institutions, investment banks and funds on a wide variety of equity and debt issues, capital markets and securities work, funds structuring and financial services law. The private equity team advises a wide range of private equity providers, vendors and management teams. Members of the team have extensive experience in relation to all kinds of private equity transactions such as start-ups, second and subsequent round financings, buyouts and buy-ins (including 'take private' deals). The team also includes highly regarded acquisition finance, high yield and securitisation specialists and is able to draw upon the advice and experience of the worldwide Jones Day network. The breadth of all this expertise enables the firm to advise both UK and international clients from a broad range of industries and business sectors.

Taxation The London office tax group, one of the largest tax practices of any non-English firm in London, advises UK, US and other overseas enterprises on the tax aspects of international transactions and investments. It provides both UK and US tax expertise, with particular emphasis on the tax dimensions of cross-border mergers, acquisitions, post-acquisition restructurings, and other internal reorganisations and associated tax planning. The London office is a recognised leader in tax-based structured finance transactions.

Finance The London office handles a variety of financing and banking transactions, including leveraged acquisition financing, high-yield debt issues and other forms of capital market issues, tax-based structured finance, securitisations, and other secured and unsecured financial transactions.

Litigation & Arbitration The London office represents clients in English High Court litigation, English and other European arbitration proceedings, and alternative dispute resolutions in a broad range of substantive areas of law. The litigation group also frequently advises on the many complex issues that arise in cross-border litigation and arbitration, including questions of jurisdiction, conflicts of law, pre-trial investigations, disclosure, and enforcement of judgments. Jones Day's London-based lawyers have significant experience in matters that include fraud and white-collar crime, disputes arising out of international trade, commodities, shipping, energy, insurance, employment, product liability, tax, and other general contractual and tortious actions.

Property & Environmental Matters The London team advises on a full range of real estate transactions for both UK and overseas clients with a particular focus on maximising the value of the corporate real estate asset for clients. The team is also a key part of all corporate transactions providing advice on the liabilities relating to real estate and environmental issues, and in particular the negotiation of environmental indemnities. The environmental team also provides regulatory advice for clients on a wide range of environmental issues.

Continued overleaf

A-Z ■ LAW FIRMS

Employment, Pensions & Share Schemes The London office has a team of employment and pensions lawyers who advise on transactional and ongoing employee and pensions matters. They play a key role in the mergers and acquisitions practice and advise on all aspects of contentious and non-contentious employment and pensions issues. In addition, they work closely with members of the tax group in advising on and designing employment benefit schemes, such as profit sharing schemes and phantom share plans.

Competition The firm has a leading reputation in providing innovative competition law advice. As part of the Jones Day European competition team, the London office advises on merger control and the full range of EU and UK competition matters. Members of the team have significant experience in dealing with the European Commission and the UK regulatory authorities.

Intellectual Property & Information Technology The London office intellectual property/information technology group offers expertise on all aspects of patent, trademark, copyright, domain name and design right issues. The group also advises on software licensing and protection (having a number of leading technology clients for M&A and commercial work) and assists numerous hi-tec and industrial clients on e-commerce/internet issues. The group is equally experienced in offering sophisticated transactional and litigation support and is fully integrated into the firm's market leading practices in the US and Europe.

INTERNATIONAL The firm has other offices in Atlanta, Brussels, Chicago, Cleveland, Columbus, Dallas, Frankfurt, Hong Kong, Houston, Irvine, Los Angeles, Madrid, Milan, Menlo Park, New York, Paris, Pittsburgh, Shanghai, Singapore, Sydney, Taipei, Tokyo, Washington DC, New Delhi (associate office) and Mumbai (associate office). Work is handled in Cantonese, German, French, Italian and Turkish.

■ Jones Maidment Wilson
5 Byrom Street, Manchester, M3 4PF **Tel** (0161) 832 8087 **Fax** (0161) 835 3123

■ Jones Myers Gordon
The Pearl Building, 22 East Parade, Leeds, LS1 5BZ **Tel** (0113) 246 0055 **Fax** (0113) 246 7446

■ Joy Merriam & Co
67 Burdett Road, London, E3 4TN **Tel** (020) 8980 7171 **Fax** (020) 8981 7981

J R Jones

56A The Mall, Ealing W5 3TA
Tel (020) 8566 2595 **Fax** (020) 8579 4288 **DX** 5134 Ealing
Email Solicitors@jrjones.co.uk

Managing Partner	T Raza
Number of Partners	3
Assistant solicitors	11
Other fee-earners	7

THE FIRM Established in 1989 as a sole practice the firm now has three partners and a total staff of 35. The firm has Legal Aid franchises in the areas of personal injury, immigration, family, criminal, employment, housing, welfare and debt. The practice is organised into specialised departments providing full range of legal services to its clients. The firm has been involved in several high profile cases of recent times. It fought for justice on behalf of the parents of the black teenager Stephen Lawrence, culminating in a public inquiry set up by the Home Secretary under the Chairmanship of Sir William Macpherson. The firm also acted for the family of Dr Joan Francisco. This case made English legal history as the first case of civil murder in which there had been no previous criminal proceedings.

■ Julian Dobson Solicitors
6 Marllborough Place, Brighton, BN1 1UB **Tel** (01273) 693567 **Fax** (01273) 620742

■ Julian Holy

Emperor's Gate, 114A Cromwell Rd, London, SW7 4ES
Tel (020) 7370 5443 **Fax** (020) 7244 7371 **DX** 44106 Gloucester Road **Email** law@julianholy.co.uk

AREAS OF PRACTICE	
Commercial Property	60%
Commercial Litigation	25%
Company/Commercial	15%

Ptnrs 4 **Asst solrs** 5 **Other fee-earners** 3 **Contact** Nick Simpson • Specialises in commercial property and litigation, renowned for rapid reaction time. Provides clear incisive advice, high standard of service, personal attention, determined to achieve clients' needs.

■ Kaye Scholer LLP
Fifth Floor, 120 Aldersgate Street, London, EC1A 4JQ **Tel** (020) 7014 0550 **Fax** (020) 7014 0555

Keeble Hawson
Old Cathedral Vicarage, St. James' Row, Sheffield, S1 1XA **Tel** (0114) 272 2061 **Fax** (0114) 270 0813

Kelcey & Hall
Fosters Chambers, 17 Small Street, Bristol, BS1 1DE **Tel** (0117) 927 9604 **Fax** (0117) 925 0609

Kemp Little LLP
Saddlers House, Gutter Lane, London EC2V 6BR
Tel (020) 7600 8080 **Fax** (020) 7600 7878
Email info@comlegal.com **Website** www.comlegal.com

THE FIRM Kemp Little LLP is a City law firm dedicated to commercial, regulatory, corporate and employment work for business and technology clients. The firm has grown from one lawyer at inception in 1997 to nine partners and 20 lawyers in 2002, becoming Kemp Little LLP (the first UK law firm LLP) in July 2001. In December 2001 it was the only law firm and one of 50 firms named as the UK's most high potential young businesses in the annual survey carried out by *Real Business*, the UK's leading magazine for growing companies.

Managing Partner	Richard Kemp
Number of partners	9
Assistant solicitors	10
Other fee-earners	1

AREAS OF PRACTICE	
Commercial	50%
Corporate	24%
Employment	16%
Communications Regulation	10%

Kennedys
Longbow House, 14-20 Chiswell Street, London EC1Y 4TW
Tel (020) 7638 3688 **Fax** (020) 7638 2212 **DX** 46628 Barbican
Email mailbox@kennedys-law.com **Website** www.kennedys-law.com

50 Mark Lane, London, EC3R 7QT
Tel (020) 7638 3688 **Fax** (020) 7702 9757 **DX** 514 London/City

Ewing House, 130 Kings Road, Brentwood, CM14 4EA
Tel (01277) 233636 **Fax** (01277) 219175 **DX** 124462 Brentwood 5

Unit C, Evelyn House, Lanwades Business Park, Kentford, Newmarket, CB8 7PN

64-66 Upper Church Lane, Belfast, BT1 4QL
Tel (028) 9024 0067 **Fax** (028) 9031 5557 **DX** 490 NR Belfast 1

THE FIRM Kennedys is a leading dispute resolution firm known for its expertise both nationally and internationally. The firm's highly acclaimed logo 'Legal advice in black and white' reflects its approach to its work and its clients. The firm aims to offer clear, commercially aware and pragmatic advice, working in partnership with its clients, delivering services they need and offering value for money. The appointment of Kennedys' first Chief Executive further demonstrates the focused commercial outlook of the firm. Kennedys has 57 Partners and over 300 staff in five offices located in four different areas in the UK and three offices in the Asia-Pacific region. Throughout all the offices the firm provides a consistency of approach and clients of any office can draw upon the substantial body of expertise and resources within the whole of Kennedys. The firm also has a network of associated offices around the world. All of the firm's offices in England have been awarded ISO 9001 accreditation. Kennedys has been at the leading edge in its use of IT, not simply as a support function, but also to provide clients with access to information concerning their matters through its extranet.

PRINCIPAL AREAS OF WORK Kennedys provides a range of services to four key industry sectors: insurance, health, rail and construction. This ensures that its clients benefit not only from its legal skills but also from its deep industry knowledge.

Insurance Kennedys' insurance practice is divided into three areas; construction and engineering, financial lines and liability. The firm's two offices in London, its spread of offices in the Asia-Pacific region and its strong associations with firms in the US and across Europe reflect the importance of the London insurance and re-insurance market and the need for advice throughout the world in relation to that market. The majority of Kennedys' dispute resolution work involves complex and major issues, often involving several jurisdictions, on behalf of insurers and re-insurers. However, through its regional

Senior Partner	Nick Thomas
Chairman	Stephen Cantle
Number of partners	56
Assistant solicitors	68
Other fee-earners	62

AREAS OF PRACTICE	
Insurance Litigation	83%
Company/Commercial	6%
Employment	6%
Construction (Non-Contentious)	3%
Commercial Property	2%

CONTACTS	
Banking/Finance	John Harvey
Clinical Negligence	Janet Sayers
Commercial Property	Jeremy Palmer
Company/Commercial	James Shaw
Construction (Contentious)	Geoffrey Lord
	Nick Thomas
Construction (Non-Contentious)	James Shaw
Defamation	Philip Hartley
Employment	Marc Meryon
Financial Institutions Private Insurance	
	Chris Sharrock
Insolvency	Bernardino Paganuzzi
Insurance	Stephen Cantle
Motor	Richard West
	John Yates
Personal Injury	Jane Smith
	Timothy Wilson
Pharmaceutical/Product Liability	Shane Sayers
Professional Indemnity	Nick Thomas
Railway Litigation	Andrew Gilbert
Reinsurance	Nicholas Williams
Shipping	Eric Sumner

Continued overleaf

offices, the firm is also able to undertake less complex work at an acceptable cost.

Health Kennedys handles all types of clinical negligence and liability work for several NHS Trusts, the NHS Litigation Authority and for insurers of private clinics. Deep and detailed knowledge of this industry mean that the firm can provide employment, commercial property and general commercial advice appropriate to this sector.

Rail Kennedys' railway litigation team provides railway, health and safety and employment litigation services The team specialises in major accident response including inquiries, subsequent prosecutions and civil claims. It has considerable experience in acting for train operating companies, particularly on employment and industrial relations issues. Based on its experience in relation to the railway industry the team is able to advise clients in other industries on health and safety issues.

Construction The firm's construction team has been built on its successes in handling both contentious and non-contentious construction matters as well as dealing with professional indemnity issues for the insurance sector. Internationally the firm acts in relation to construction projects in Europe, the Indian sub-continent and the Middle and Far East. Kennedys' Commercial Unit not only supports clients from the key industry sectors, but also handles matters for multinational corporations, private companies, banks, financial institutions and partnerships. The Unit's range of expertise, comprising employment law, insolvency, banking, shipping, international arbitration, commercial property and a general commercial practice, ensures that all clients within all sectors are provided with a comprehensive service from lawyers who understand the industry.

Kennedys
Legal advice in black and white

RECRUITMENT The firm offers training contracts each year. Please contact Rob Hind, Personnel Director.

Kenneth Bush
Evershed House, 23/25 King Street, King's Lynn, PE30 1DU **Tel** (01553) 692737 **Fax** (01553) 691729

Kenneth Curtis & Co
88 Aldridge Road, Perry Barr, Birmingham, B42 2TP **Tel** (0121) 356 1161 **Fax** (0121) 356 2973

Kenneth Elliott & Rowe
162-166 South Street, Romford RM1 1SX
Tel (01708) 757575 **Fax** (01708) 766674 **DX** 4602 Romford
Email law@ker.co.uk **Website** www.ker.co.uk

24 Buckingham Gate, London, SW1E 6LB
Tel (020) 7834 6464 **Fax** (020) 7834 6470 **DX** 99921 Victoria

THE FIRM Whilst the firm's foundations were laid in the 1930s, its largely organic growth has taken place over the last 15 years, as the firm has evolved from its high street roots to one with offices in London's West End and Essex, serving an increasingly commercial and cosmopolitan client base with a substantial foreign element. The firm's administrative base remains in Essex, where it is known as a major player in the metropolitan Essex region, acting for local authorities, as well as major manufacturers, shipping companies and many others in addition to a burgeoning personal injury practice.

PRINCIPAL AREAS OF WORK
Commercial Property The firm's most recognised area of expertise is in the field of commercial property and it has added specialist property litigation to its range of services. Its property team is one of the largest in the region with six partners and five assistants and it continues to top the regional league tables for its work. The breadth of its work is extensive and highly respected, going beyond routine matters and frequently identifying deals for its domestic and international clients. It represents developers, retail chains, local authorities and overseas investment clients on complex property matters.
Insolvency The firm has its own licensed insolvency practitioner.
Company/Commercial The firm regularly acts on acquisitions, disposals, MBOs and MBIs of varying descriptions.
Personal Injury The personal injury department comprises two partners and three solicitors plus paralegal support, making it one of the largest plaintiff-only departments in the region.
Private Client The firm represents senior diplomats and forces personnel.
Planning Having left Parliament at the last election Keith Darvill is now concentrating on his planning practice.
Crime Since Richard Block and Barry Spanjar and their respective teams joined the practice, the firm has received a number of substantial instructions in high profile and high cost cases and has applied for membership of the Serious Fraud Panel. The crime department intends to concentrate on VHCC cases.

Managing Partner	Chris Dixon
Number of partners	11
Assistant solicitors	11
Other fee-earners	12

AREAS OF PRACTICE	
Commercial Property	30%
Common Law	25%
Employment	10%
Insolvency	10%
Private Client	10%
Crime	10%
Planning	5%

CONTACTS	
Commercial Property	Chris Dixon
Crime	Richard Block
Employment	Merwyn Emmanuel
Financial Services	David Rogers
Insolvency	Mark Dixon
Matrimonial	Rebecca Gardiner
Personal Injury Litigation	Neville Filar
Planning	Keith Darvill
Private Client	David Farr

LAW FIRMS ■ A-Z

INTERNATIONAL The firm is a founder member of LAWorld, an international law firm network and has close links with clients and lawyers in China, India and the Far and Middle East.

RECRUITMENT The firm takes three trainees a year and currently employs eight. It looks for plenty of brains and a sense of humour. Trainees may be sent on overseas work experience with other firms within the LAWorld network.

■ Kent Jones and Done

Churchill House, Regent Road, Stoke-on-Trent, ST1 3RQ
Tel (01782) 202020 **Fax** (01782) 202040 **DX** 20727 Hanley
Email mail@kjd.co.uk **Website** www.kjd.co.uk

Ptnrs 15 **Asst solrs** 15 **Other fee-earners** 14 **Contact** Adrian Ross • The dominant corporate practice in the region outside Birmingham, providing a range of specialist and general commercial advice. The firm has Lexcel and Investors in People accreditation.

AREAS OF PRACTICE	
Dispute Resolution	30%
Corporate	29%
Property	22%
Employment	8%
Planning & Environmental	7%
Personal	3%

■ Keoghs

2 The Parklands, Bolton BL6 4SE
Tel (01204) 677000 **Fax** (01204) 677111 **DX** 723540 Bolton (Lostock)
Email info@keoghs.co.uk **Website** www.keoghs.co.uk

1 Eastwood Business Village, Harry Weston Road, Binley, Coventry, CV3 2UB
Tel (024) 7665 8200 **Fax** (024) 7665 8208 **DX** 700127 Coventry 4
Email info@keoghs.co.uk

THE FIRM Sustained growth over recent years has seen Keoghs develop into one of the country's leading commercial law firms, specialising in insurance litigation and commercial business advice. The practice's success is based upon a combination of its no-nonsense, commercial outlook, the depth and variety of the legal services it provides, the approachability of its staff and, above all, its commitment to both high quality service delivery and competitive charges. Keoghs has full ISO quality accreditation and its clients range from national 'blue chip' organisations to small, growing businesses.

PRINCIPAL AREAS OF WORK

Defendant Litigation Keoghs is one of the country's leading advisors to the insurance industry, currently acting for more than 30 insurance organisations including the majority of the UK's top 10 composite insurers and many Lloyds syndicates. Working closely with clients to avoid costly, protracted disputes, Keoghs has the capacity and experience to handle not only large volume defendant personal injury litigation including RTA cases but also high-profile, specialist cases including catastrophic injury, disease and deafness. The firm has also developed a wide base of expertise in other insurance related areas ranging from employer's and public liability, product liability and negligence to insurance property work, subsidence claims and goods-in-transit cases.

Fraud Over recent years and to anticipate insurer clients' needs for specialist assistance Keoghs has established specific units to deal with both motor fraud and general fraud. The motor fraud unit now operates in tandem with many insurers' claims departments to identify fraud cases at an early stage and deal with them rapidly and effectively. The results have demonstrated substantial cost savings for clients.

Commercial Litigation Keoghs' commercial litigation team acts for both insurer and commercial business clients dealing with professional negligence claims, building and contractual disputes, injunctions, financial disputes and the recovery of outstanding debts. The team actively employs ADR methods wherever possible, saving clients both time and money.

Company/Commercial The company and commercial team provides advice to a wide variety of clients from national organisations to privately owned and managed businesses. It offers down-to-earth advisory services including corporate finance, company formation, disposals and acquisitions, contract drafting, buyouts and shareholders' agreements. In addition Keoghs offers a full range of commercial property advice and assistance. The commercial team specialises in providing assistance to small and medium-sized businesses.

Employment The firm deals with all aspects of contentious and non-contentious employment law both for employers and employees. One of the partners has considerable experience in dealing with all types of employment tribunal claims including advocacy before tribunals and other courts of higher jurisdiction.

Private Client The firm has a dedicated team dealing with trusts and estate planning and wills and domestic conveyancing for clients who require these specialist services.

Chief Executive Officer	Paul Smith
Head of Insurance Litigation	David Tyson
Head of Company & Commercial	Alan Robins
Number of partners	23
Assistant solicitors	16
Other fee-earners	151

AREAS OF PRACTICE	
Insurance Litigation	85%
Company/Commercial	15%

CONTACTS	
Commercial Litigation	Jonathan Lowe
Commercial Property	Rachel Senior
Company/Commercial	Alan Robins
Construction	Rachel Senior
Employment	Keith Cartmell
Fraud	Don Clarke
Insurance Litigation	David Tyson
Professional Indemnity	Nicola McLoughlin

A-Z ■ LAW FIRMS

■ Kerman & Co
5 St James's Square, London, SW1Y 4JU   **Tel** (020) 7451 9800   **Fax** (020) 7930 2532

Kershaw Abbott

Queen's Chambers, 5 John Dalton Street, Manchester M2 6FT
Tel (0161) 839 0998   **Fax** (0161) 839 1019   **DX** 14348 Manchester 1
Email mail@kershaw-abbott.co.uk   **Website** www.kershaw-abbott.co.uk

Contact Partners	Anne Kershaw
	Christopher Abbott
Number of partners	3
Assistant solicitors	1
Other fee-earners	3

THE FIRM Based in the centre of the Manchester business community, Kershaw Abbott is a modern and progressive practice serving commercial and insurance clients. Work of quality is handled in an effective and individual manner by partner-led teams, conscious always to provide a cost-effective service.

PRINCIPAL AREAS OF WORK The firm is best known for its work in the fields of construction, professional partnership disputes, commercial and insurance litigation and employment. Expertise is offered in alternative forms of dispute resolution including mediation, adjudication and arbitration. The firm undertakes agency work in the specialist courts of the North West.

Kidstons & Co

1 Royal Bank Place, Buchanan Street, Glasgow G1 3AA
Tel (0141) 221 6551   **Fax** (0141) 204 0507
Email mail@kidstons.co.uk   **Website** www.kidstons.co.uk

43 Milngavie Road, Bearsden, G61 2DW
Tel (0141) 943 1188   **Fax** (0141) 942 5886

Managing & Senior Partner	Iain F Atack
Number of partners	8
Assistant solicitors	3
Other fee-earners	9

AREAS OF PRACTICE	
Employment Law	20%
Commercial Property	20%
Business Law/Corporate	18%
Trusts & Probate	18%
Civil Litigation	14%
Residential Property	10%

CONTACTS	
Civil Litigation	Iain F Atack
Commercial Property	Kenneth Steven Gerber
Corporate/Business Law	
	Kenneth Steven Gerber
Employment	Iain F Atack
Insolvency	Sandy Reid
Residential Property	Alison Atack
Trusts	Douglas McKerrell

THE FIRM Established in Glasgow over 150 years ago, Kidstons & Co. has grown to provide expertise in employment law, commercial property, civil litigation, trusts, corporate and business law, insolvency law and residential property. The firm has two partners who are accredited by the Law Society of Scotland: Iain Atack, specialist in employment law and Kenneth Gerber, specialist in commercial leasing. The firm has nine partners and two associates with full support from assistant solicitors; the firm is a member of the Commercial Law Group. A significant part of the client base is from without Scotland.

CLIENTELE The firm has a varied client base of UK manufacturing and retail plcs, commercial private companies, medical and other partnerships, trusts and family owned property investment and other businesses, many of whom are based in England and Europe. The firm's philosophy is that transactions should be very much partner led with the emphasis on proactive and commercially orientated advice being given so as to enable clients to achieve their goals effectively.

■ Kieran Clarke Solicitors
36 Clarence Road, Chesterfield, S40 1XB   **Tel** (01246) 211006   **Fax** (01246) 209786

LAW FIRMS ■ A-Z

Kimbells

352 Silbury Court, Silbury Boulevard, Milton Keynes MK9 2AF
Tel (01908) 668555 **Fax** (01908) 674344 **DX** 31408
Email recep@kimbells.com **Website** www.kimbells.com

THE FIRM Kimbells' commercially focused services are driven by a concern for excellence in client care. Rigorous internal quality control procedures are combined with flexible service delivery tailored to meet identified client needs.

PRINCIPAL AREAS OF WORK
Corporate The firm has extensive experience of buyouts and mergers and acquisitions, with corporate finance capability.
Commercial Litigation Specific expertise in property-related matters, insolvency, recovery and EU/competition law is offered.
Commercial Property The firm's expertise covers acquisitions, disposals, landlord and tenant and large commercial developments, with particular experience in the retail and logistics sectors.
Employment Wide ranging issues handled include discrimination, disciplinary matters, TUPE and Employment Tribunals.
Information Technology Niche expertise is offered in e-commerce, software licensing, internet, data protection and competition.
Brewing/Licensed Trade A specialist knowledge of the UK regulatory regime has developed through working extensively with major national and regional brewers and pubcos.

Senior Partner	Stephen Kimbell
Number of partners	8
Assistant solicitors	11
Other fee-earners	7

AREAS OF PRACTICE	
Corporate	30%
Litigation	27%
Commercial Property	22%
Commercial/IT	21%

CONTACTS	
Brewing Services	Peter Holden
Commercial Litigation	Richard Brown
Commercial Property	Timothy Clark
Corporate	Jonathan Hambleton
IT	Robert Cain

Kingsley Napley

Knights Quarter, 14 St John's Lane, London EC1M 4AJ
Tel (020) 7814 1200 **Fax** (020) 7490 2288 **DX** 22 Ch.Ln.
Email mail@kingsleynapley.co.uk **Website** www.kingsleynapley.co.uk

THE FIRM Kingsley Napley is an internationally recognised commercial law firm based in the City of London. The firm has expertise in corporate and commercial work, criminal and commercial litigation, commercial property, employment, immigration, clinical negligence and family law. Kingsley Napley specialises in dealing with matters of particular complexity and difficulty in all branches of the law. The client base is wide and varied, ranging from large public companies to owner-managed businesses and individuals.

PRINCIPAL AREAS OF WORK
Litigation Work encompasses commercial and civil litigation and dispute resolution, professional negligence, construction disputes, landlord and tenant, and defamation. There is particular experience in asset tracing investigations.
Employment The department handles contentious and non-contentious employment law issues for companies and individuals.
Criminal Litigation Work covers a broad spectrum including corporate and City fraud, SFO, DTI and Inland Revenue investigations, money-laundering, asset tracing enquiries and mutual assistance. The department is internationally recognised for advising on extradition matters and crime. Members of the department appear regularly before various regulatory and professional bodies, both prosecuting and defending. Two of the partners also undertake licensing work.
Family All aspects of family and matrimonial work are undertaken, including issues concerning childcare, such as child abduction, surrogacy and adoption, through to cohabitation and complex financial matters on divorce.
Corporate & Commercial Advice on a wide range of business issues including joint ventures, corporate finance, taxation, flotations, rights issues, takeovers, insolvency and liquidation and partnerships.
Property All aspects of conveyancing of commercial freehold and leasehold property undertaken, together with a small amount of residential property work.
Clinical Negligence & Personal Injury Expertise in the management of all forms of serious personal injury claims including those arising out of medical negligence in the NHS as well as the private medical sector. It has particular interest in providing advice and assistance in relation to inquests and to complaints procedures, including General Medical Council. A range of funding options are available.
Immigration A highly personalised specialist business immigration service is provided to both corporate clients and individuals, advising on all aspects of UK and EU immigration and nationality issues.

INTERNATIONAL Work is handled in French, German and Spanish.

Senior Partner	David Speker
Number of partners	36
Assistant solicitors	33
Other fee-earners	9

AREAS OF PRACTICE	
Commercial Property	20%
Criminal Litigation	19%
Litigation	17%
Corporate & Commercial	14%
Family	10%
Business Immigration	10%
Clinical Negligence & Personal Injury	10%

CONTACTS	
Clinical Negligence & Personal Injury	Julia Cahill
Commercial Property	Francis Weaver
Construction	Michael Janney
Corporate & Commercial	David Walsh
Criminal Litigation	Christopher Murray
Employment	Richard Fox
Family	Jane Keir
Immigration	Hilary Belchak
Licensing	Michael Caplan
Litigation	Barry Samuels
Partnership	Tony Sacker

A-Z ■ LAW FIRMS

■ Kirbys
32 Victoria Avenue, Harrogate, HG1 5PR **Tel** (01423) 542 000 **Fax** (01423) 542 001

Kirkland & Ellis

Tower 42, 25 Old Broad Street, , London, EC2N 1HQ
Tel (020) 7816 8700 **Fax** (020) 7816 8800
Email stuart_mills@uk.kirkland.com **Website** www.kirkland.com

Office Administrator	Joan Batchen
CONTACTS	
Arbitration	Samuel Haubold
Capital Markets & Securities	Barbara Jones
German Practice	Thomas Verhoeven
Intellectual Property	Stephen Johnson
Private Equity/Venture Capital	James Learner
	Stuart Mills
UK Practice	Nigel Dunmore

THE FIRM Kirkland & Ellis handles complicated transactional, intellectual property, litigation and counselling matters for major US and international clients. The firm works with a base of long-standing clients engaged in varied industries such as hi-tech, manufacturing, computers, transportation, private equity, venture capital, oil and gas, healthcare, real estate, chemicals, food products, finance, insurance, advertising and accounting.

London Office The London office, with 30 lawyers focusing on private equity, mergers and acquisitions, capital markets, arbitration and intellectual property matters, has been serving UK, European and US clients since 1995.

PRINCIPAL AREAS OF WORK Kirkland is known for its ability to negotiate and close highly sophisticated transactions, representing private equity investors and public and private companies in mergers and acquisitions, securities, spin-off and split-off, and investment transactions.

Private Equity The firm has a premier private equity practice, having represented private investment funds, the private equity groups at several major money centre banks and other participants in this industry for over 25 years. During the last five years, Kirkland's private equity practice has represented more than 50 different clients in hundreds of leveraged acquisitions and other types of transactions and has been principal counsel in over US$50 billion in fund formations.

M&A & Securities In the mergers and acquisitions and securities area, Kirkland has recently represented clients ranging from some of the world's largest corporations through major banks and investment banks in some of the world's largest and most complex mergers and acquisitions transactions and securities offerings.

Litigation & Arbitration The firm has earned a reputation for successfully defending companies with business-threatening lawsuits and class actions in diverse legal areas such as commercial, intellectual property, product liability, insurance coverage, environmental, employment, securities law, mass torts, and anti-trust issues, handling the trial, appellate, and US Supreme Court phases. This trial-ready reputation has been the impetus for favourable and prompt results for the firm's clients through settlements as well as through the various Alternative Dispute Resolution mechanisms (ADRs) employed whenever practicable and desired by the client.

IP & IT Kirkland & Ellis advises some of the world's leading technology companies and handles all areas of intellectual property, including biotechnology, semiconductor processing, telecommunications, and internet and e-commerce technology. Kirkland & Ellis has adopted and adapted to the internet and e-commerce, and its 130 intellectual property lawyers specialise in the intricacies, implications, legal issues and arguments surrounding today's and tomorrow's communication and emerging technologies.

CLIENTELE Kirkland & Ellis bases its commitment to client service on developing an intimate knowledge of each client's needs and objectives. The firm seeks long term, partnering relationships with clients, to the end of providing the best total solution to the client's multidisciplined and industry-specific legal service needs. The firm's goal is to be an instrumental part of each client's success.

KIRKLAND & ELLIS
INTERNATIONAL

INTERNATIONAL The firm has other offices in Chicago, Los Angeles, New York and Washington DC. It handles work in English, French, German and Spanish.

LAW FIRMS A-Z

KLegal

1-2 Dorset Rise, London, EC4Y 8AE
Tel (020) 7694 2500 **Fax** (020) 7694 2501 **DX** 38053 BLACKFRIARS
Email firstname.surname@klegal.co.uk **Website** www.klegal.oc.uk

63 Queen Victoria Street, London, EC4N 4ST
Tel (020) 7329 3299 **Fax** (020) 7329 4000 **DX** 135180 CHEAPSIDE

Chairman, UK	Niall Scott
Managing Partner, UK	Nick Holt
Total staff	
London	268
UK (KLegal International)	636

CONTACTS	
Banking & Finance	Colin Mckay
Corporate & Commercial	Colin Fergusson
Dispute Resolution	Brandon Nolan
E-business & Digital Media	Mark Haftke
Employment (International)	Tim Johnson
Employment (UK)	Jim Young
IT	Chris Hoyle
IP	James Hodgson
Private Equity	Patrick Martin
Projects/PPP	Jim Smith
Real Estate	Philip Burroughs
Tax Litigation	James Bullock
Telecoms	Alan Whitfield

THE FIRM Founded in July 1999, KLegal is the UK law firm associated with KPMG and a founding member of KLegal International, a network of law firms associated with KPMG which has over 3000 lawyers in over 50 jurisdictions (with particular strength in Europe and Australasia). Since its formation, KLegal and associated firms have grown to be one of the top 30 law firms in the UK. In line with its growth strategy during 2001 and 2002, KLegal completed a deal with McGrigor Donald, the pre-eminent law firm in Scotland, and H20, the niche IP and media law firm. Together the firms have a total of over 70 partners and over 350 fee-earners.

PRINCIPAL AREAS OF WORK The firm's objective is to provide expert legal services both on a stand-alone basis and working with KPMG (assurance; consulting; corporate finance; forensic accounting; tax and transaction services), developing integrated solutions that address clients' business needs. The firm has focused on those areas which compliment KPMG's core business and has specific expertise in banking, corporate, dispute resolution, e-business and digital media, employment, intellectual property, IT and telecommunications, private equity, projects/PPP, real estate and tax litigation. These areas fall under three core practice areas: corporate, infrastructure and dispute resolution headed on a UK basis by Colin Gray, Colin McKay and Brandon Nolan respectively.

CLIENTELE Clients include national to multinational corporations, government bodies, banks and financial institutions, internet start-ups and entrepreneurs. They are introduced to the firm from a variety of sources, including KPMG, KLegal International member firms and external introductions. The firm's route to market is focused on four industry facing groups made up of lawyers from each of the firm's practice areas, namely: information, communications and entertainment (ICE); financial services (FS); consumer and industrial markets (CIM); infrastructure and government (I&G).

RECRUITMENT The firm is always interested in hearing from exceptional lawyers at all levels from recently qualified to partner. Applications are invited from ambitious and energetic lawyers with good academic backgrounds (min 2:1) and outstanding experience gained in either private practice or industry who are attracted by the prospect of working in a dynamic, cutting edge environment. Please apply to Rosalind Jamieson (Human Resources) or Kate Hedstrom (Graduate Recruitment).

Knights
Regency House, 25 High Street, Tunbridge Wells, TN1 1UT **Tel** (01892) 537311 **Fax** (01892) 526141

Knight & Sons
The Brampton, Newcastle-under-Lyme, ST5 0QW **Tel** (01782) 619225 **Fax** (01782) 620410

Kristina Harrison Solicitors
277-279 Chapel Street, Salford, M3 5JQ **Tel** (0161) 832 7766 **Fax** (0161) 832 3399

A-Z ■ LAW FIRMS

KSB Law

14 Old Square, Lincoln's Inn, London WC2A 3UB
Tel (020) 7447 1200   **Fax** (020) 7831 2915   **DX** 141 Chancery Lane
Email ksb@ksblaw.co.uk   **Website** www.ksblaw.co.uk

Elan House, 5-11 Fetter Lane, London, EC4A 1QD
Tel (020) 7822 7500   **Fax** (020) 7822 7600   **DX** 117 Chancery Lane

Lincoln House, 34 High Street, Harpenden, AL5 2SX
Tel (01582) 766866   **Fax** (01582) 712424   **DX** 80454 Harpenden

Senior Partner	Jonathan Wood
Number of partners	21
Assistant solicitors	15
Other fee-earners	67

AREAS OF PRACTICE	
Litigation & Personal Injury	52%
Property (Commercial & Residential)	21%
Company/Commercial	11%
Private Client	3%
Licensing	3%

CONTACTS	
Agency	Minhaj Saiyid
Commercial Litigation	Niki Olympitis
Commercial Property	Robert Sweet
Company/International	Anthony Lee
Employment	Niki Olympitis
Family	Andrew Hamilton
Insolvency & Factoring	Matthew Halton
Licensing	Robert Edney
Personal Injury	Simon Pinner
Private Client	Susan Floyd
Property Litigation	David White
Residential Property	Richard Martin

THE FIRM KSB Law is a pioneering legal practice with a solid history of service to major commercial clients for over 150 years. As a medium-sized London based law firm, KSB Law is big enough to have served some of the largest banks, brewers, retailers and property developers in the country and yet small enough to offer personalised service to a private client seeking discreet advice on inheritance planning or family disputes.

PRINCIPAL AREAS OF WORK Commercial litigation; insolvency; company/commercial; commercial property; licensing; defamation; employment; private client; factoring; landlord and tenant; family; residential property; competition law; personal injury. The firm offers a specialist London Agency Service and is able to provide notarial services. KSB Law has experienced rapid expansion over the last five years, particularly in its personal injury, commercial property, company/commercial, commercial litigation and family law departments.

INTERNATIONAL The firm is a founder member of Consulegis, a closely co-ordinated network of over 100 independent English speaking law firms throughout Europe, USA, Latin America and the Far East. Languages spoken by members of the firm include French, German, Greek, Italian and Spanish.

RECRUITMENT KSB Law is committed to continued expansion in its key departments. Lawyers with expertise and a following in these areas and who are considering a move are invited to contact the firm's personnel manager with details. For further information, visit the website.

Kuit Steinart Levy

3 St. Mary's Parsonage, Manchester M3 2RD
Tel (0161) 832 3434   **Fax** (0161) 832 6650   **DX** 14325
Email ksllaw@kuits.com   **Website** www.kuits.com

Executive Partner	Robert Levy
Managing Partner	Jonathan Marks
Number of partners	15
Assistant solicitors	15
Other fee-earners	11

AREAS OF PRACTICE	
Corporate	25%
Litigation/Employment	25%
Property	25%
Tax & Trusts	15%
Banking	10%

CONTACTS	
Corporate	Robert Levy
Litigation	Jeff Lewis
	Jai Ramsahoye
Employment	Lydia Edgar
Property	Jonathan Marks
Tax & Trusts	Jan Fidler
Banking	Steve Eccleston
IP/IT	Colin Hoffman
	Tracey Sheehan

THE FIRM Kuit Steinart Levy is securely established as a leading Manchester practice and continues to grow and develop its range of expertise to meet changing market needs. Its aim is to implement its dynamic growth strategy, while remaining committed to its client-focused approach to law. The firm is forward thinking and dynamic, and all clients receive a service that is professional and comprehensive. Direct access is provided to a partner who takes individual responsibility for work carried out on a client's behalf.

PRINCIPAL AREAS OF WORK
Corporate/Commercial The department has a strong corporate and corporate finance skill base, and advises on all aspects of company law and commercial matters, including corporate finance, mergers and acquisitions, management buyouts and buyins, reconstructions, insolvency, agency and distribution. Expertise also extends to terms of trading, commercial contracts, competition law, intellectual property and brand acquisitions, which is a particular specialism and all types of technology-related contracts.
Litigation A variety of litigation services are provided, including all commercial and contract disputes, landlord and tenant work, restraint of trade and competition disputes, professional negligence, personal injury, employment law and debt collection. In addition the firm has a CEDR-accredited mediator and provides a full dispute resolution service.
Property The commercial property team advises on a wide range of property matters, including acquisitions and disposals, development and planning, construction contracts, project finance, funding and joint ventures, leases, property investment and environmental law.
Tax & Trusts The firm specialises in tax and trust matters, including inheritance tax planning, estate planning, mitigation of taxation and Inland Revenue, Customs & Excise enquiries and investigations. All aspects of wills and probate are also handled.

Banking Kuits' cross departmental banking and secured lending team incorporates expertise in corporate, commercial property and securities law. Areas covered include loan syndication, acquisition banking, facility agreements, capital, mezzanine and asset finance, approval of security including inspection of title to real property.

CLIENTELE The client base ranges from large public companies through a broad base of small and medium-sized enterprises, to start-ups and vehicles for management buyouts and buyins. The firm also acts for a number of banks and financial institutions and high profile individuals.

RECRUITMENT Every member of the firm's legal staff has been recruited for their exceptional ability, expertise and knowledge. Several have trained and worked at national and international law firms in the City. The firm has six trainees, and places great emphasis on training and career development.

Lamport Bassitt

46 The Avenue, Southampton SO17 1AX
Tel (023) 8083 7777   **Fax** (023) 8083 7788   **DX** 38529 Southampton 3
Email e-mail@lamportbassitt.co.uk   **Website** www.lamportbassitt.co.uk

Sussex House, 6 The Forbury, Reading, RG1 3EJ
Tel (0118) 925 4242   **Fax** (0118) 925 3395

Senior Partner	Adrian Lightfoot
Number of partners	11
Assistant solicitors	18
Other fee-earners	14

AREAS OF PRACTICE	
Litigation	58%
Company/Commercial	29%
Private Client	13%

CONTACTS	
Commercial	Sean Kelly
Litigation	Robert Solomon
Private Client	John Excell

THE FIRM The firm operates an expanding and predominantly commercial practice, and places particular emphasis on technical ability and specialisation. The firm is a niche practice aiming to provide high quality services within specialist areas. The firm makes full use of modern technology. Most senior fee-earners are highly experienced in their chosen fields. The firm is ISO 9001 registered.

PRINCIPAL AREAS OF WORK
Commercial A wide range of corporate, employment, insolvency, planning, property, and liquor, betting and gaming licensing work.
Litigation The firm is involved in the full range of litigation work including building disputes, commercial contracts, debt collection, employment disputes, intellectual property matters, maritime law, property disputes, professional negligence, and has a large personal injury department. Agency work undertaken.
Private Client Residential property, personal tax, probate, trusts, wills and matrimonial.

CLIENTELE Clients include substantial UK and overseas-based listed and private companies from a wide area of industry and commerce, insurance companies, trade unions and trade associations.

RECRUITMENT A minimum of two trainee solicitors are recruited each year. Enquiries to Mr John Newton, partner.

Landwell

Southwark Towers, 32 London Bridge Street, London SE1 9AE
Tel (020) 7212 1616   **Fax** (020) 7212 1570   **DX** DX44303
Email firstname.lastname@uk.landwellglobal.com   **Website** www.landwell.co.uk

Senior Partner	Chris Arnheim
Number of partners	20
Assistant solicitors	44
Other fee-earners	20
Total	143

CONTACTS	
Mergers & Acquisitions	Leon Flavell
Corporate Restructuring	Sarah Holmes
E-business/IP/IT	Latika Sharma
Employment	Darryl Evans
Immigration	Julia Smye-Rumsby
Financial Services	Laura Cox
Banking	Celia Gardiner
Real Estate	Russell Dellar
Dispute Resolution	Simon Whitehead

THE FIRM Landwell is a multinational, multidisciplinary legal practice providing business orientated legal advice on domestic and cross-border deals. With 2,700 specialist lawyers in over 40 countries, it works closely with PricewaterhouseCoopers to provide seamless legal and consultancy expertise. Landwell in the UK advises a range of large national and multinational companies, governments and financial institutions. The firm works on both a stand-alone basis (often with other lawyers in the Landwell international network) and with consultants and other advisors in PricewaterhouseCoopers as part of a multidisciplinary team. Landwell's international network specialises in delivering national and international solutions to complex business problems. Acting for a large range of multinational and international clients, it has dedicated cross-border client service teams in the areas of M&A, corporate restructuring, intellectual property, financial services, e-business, employment and global mobility. Landwell's approach ensures that global teams are assembled quickly and effectively and that they work with the client through a single point of contact and to a single common standard.

PRINCIPAL AREAS OF WORK Leveraging off the strengths of PricewaterhouseCoopers, the key areas of specialisation at Landwell in the UK are M&A transactions, IPOs and private equity work, corporate

Continued overleaf

restructuring, e-business, intellectual property, IT, employment, immigration, financial services, banking, real estate and tax litigation. In the last year alone the firm has made a number of significant partner hires, including corporate lawyers Jonathan Wilson from Baker & McKenzie and Mark Satterly from Herbert Smith; financial services lawyer Deborah Sabalot from Lovells; technology expert Robert Carolina from Tarlo Lyons; and Noel Deans, who was formerly head of employment at Goodman Derrick. It has also recruited assistants from firms such as Clifford Chance, Denton Wilde Sapte, Shearman & Sterling, Herbert Smith and SJ Berwin. Through the international network and its links with PricewaterhouseCoopers, Landwell is able to continue to expand its practice throughout the economic cycle, thereby providing a dynamic and rewarding career platform for its lawyers, and a high quality service for its growing client database.

Correspondent law firms of PricewaterhouseCoopers

INTERNATIONAL Landwell has 100 offices across Europe, Australia and Asia Pacific, South America and Africa.

Lane & Partners

15 Bloomsbury Square, London WC1A 2LS
Tel (020) 7242 2626 **Fax** (020) 7242 0387 **DX** 134442 Bloomsbury
Email info@lane.co.uk **Website** www.lane.co.uk

Contact Partner	William Morton
Number of partners	13
Assistant solicitors	8
Other fee-earners	7

AREAS OF PRACTICE	
Litigation	32%
Company/Commercial	28%
Property (Commercial)	13%
Aviation & Travel	10%
Construction & Arbitration	10%
Intellectual Property & Marketing	7%

CONTACTS	
Aviation & Travel	Richard Venables
	William Morton
Company & Commercial	Keith Gallon
	William Morton
	Nicholas Sayers
Construction & Arbitration	Colin Hall
Intellectual Property & Marketing	
	Michael Varvill
Litigation	Ludovic de Walden
	Piers Lane
	Robin Springthorpe
	Peter Knight
Property	Richard Hardman
	Mark Barber
Insurance	Peter Knight

THE FIRM Lane & Partners concentrates on providing a partner-led service at competitive rates to commercial clients, covering all the main areas of law of relevance to them. It is well known for its work in the areas of international arbitration, construction, aviation and travel law.

PRINCIPAL AREAS OF WORK
Company & Commercial The firm advises clients on all aspects of company and commercial law, including mergers and acquisitions, joint ventures, listings, financial services, telecommunications, insolvency and employment and competition law.
Intellectual Property The firm advises in respect of patent, trademark and copyright matters, including licensing, franchising, merchandising, all aspects of infringement and on IT and e-commerce issues.
Litigation The firm is active in all aspects of commercial litigation, with particular emphasis on actions in the commercial court, and has a growing practice dealing with corporate, regulatory and fiscal investigations.
Arbitration The firm has an active international arbitration practice, with particular emphasis on major construction disputes.
Commercial Property The firm is involved on behalf of commercial clients in all aspects of property work including the acquisition of freehold and leasehold properties for occupation, investment or development, the sale and management of properties, planning law and appeals and environmental law.
Construction The firm advises on all aspects of construction law, including the negotiation and preparation of construction contracts, the interpretation of the standard forms used by the industry and the preparation and handling of claims. It has recently been joined by two senior construction law specialists.
Aviation & Travel The firm advises UK and foreign airlines and tour operators and travel agents. Advice is also given on aviation insurance and liability cases and on aircraft acquisition and leasing transactions.
Insurance The firm advises its corporate and insurance industry clients on insurance law. Typical work comprises coverage disputes and substantial, complex insurance and professional indemnity claims.

CLIENTELE As well as acting for UK companies, the firm has a considerable number of foreign clients, particularly Swedish, American and Japanese companies. In size, they range from well-known multinationals to small private companies. Their businesses are equally diverse, stretching from international construction and heavy engineering to cosmetics, computers and tour operating.

INTERNATIONAL The firm has associated offices in Europe, North America, Asia and the Far East. Languages spoken include French and Italian.

RECRUITMENT One to two trainees are taken on per annum.

Langleys

Queens House, Micklegate, York YO1 6WG
Tel (01904) 610886 **Fax** (01904) 611086 **DX** 720620 York 21
Email mike.williamson@langleys.co.uk **Website** www.langleys.co.uk

Newporte House, Doddington Road Business Park, Lincoln, LN6 3JY
Tel (01522) 888555 **Fax** (01522) 888556 **DX** 700678 North Hykeham-2
Email andrew.fearn@langleys.co.uk

34 Silver St, Lincoln, LN2 1ES
Tel (01522) 531461 **Fax** (01522) 510476 **DX** 11010 Lincoln
Email philip.cragg@langleys.co.uk

Managing Partners	Mike Williamson
	Philip Cragg
Senior Partner	John Morgan

CONTACTS	
Defendant Insurance Claims	David Thompson
Commercial	Roger Taylor
Claimant Personal Injury & Medical Negligence	Chris Jones
Family/Matrimonial	Philip Cragg
Residential Conveyancing	Mark Hodges
Criminal Defence	Jeremy Scott
Wills & Probate	Andrew Fearn
Agriculture	Andrew Fearn

THE FIRM Based in York and Lincoln, Langleys provides a comprehensive range of legal services to businesses, organisations and private clients with a focus on insurance claims work. Established in 1890, the firm has developed a thriving commercial practice whilst retaining and expanding its traditional private client services. Langleys is committed to the provision of a quality legal service, and continually strives to exceed clients' expectations.

PRINCIPAL AREAS OF WORK The firm's activities can be divided into three main areas: insurance claims, commercial and private client work.

Insurance Claims This is the single largest department at Langleys, offering specialist advice across the whole spectrum of insurance claims for a client base that includes major insurance companies, loss adjusters and local authorities. The insurance claims department has a long-established reputation for its work in this field.

Commercial This rapidly expanding department offers a comprehensive range of services to businesses including corporate, commercial property, commercial litigation, banking, employment, agriculture and debt recovery services. The team prides itself on its pro-active, cost-effective, commercial advice and its success is reflected in the department's diverse and growing client base.

Private Client Family law (including divorce/separation, childcare, domestic violence, adoption and mediation), clinical negligence and claimant personal injury, residential conveyancing, civil litigation, wills and probate, employment and crime. The firm has legal aid franchises for the majority of its private client specialisms and notably for clinical negligence work.

Lanyon Bowdler
Chapter House North, Abbey Lawn, Abbey Foregate, Shrewsbury, SY2 5DE **Tel** (01743) 280280 **Fax** (01743) 282340

Larby Williams
53 Mount Stuart Square, Cardiff, CF10 5LR **Tel** (029) 2047 2100 **Fax** (029) 2047 2011

Larcomes
168 London Rd, North End, Portsmouth, PO2 9DN **Tel** (023) 9266 1531 **Fax** (023) 9266 5701

Last Cawthra Feather
Airedale House, 128 Sunbridge Road, Bradford, BD1 2AT
Tel (01274) 848800 **Fax** (01274) 370552 **DX** 11723 Bradford 1
Email enquiries@lcf.co.uk **Website** www.lcf.co.uk

Ptnrs 14 **Asst solrs** 15 **Other fee-earners** 15 **Contact** Simon Stell • An expanding West Yorkshire practice with three offices and a total of 115 staff, undertaking work for businesses and private individuals.

AREAS OF PRACTICE	
Property	30%
Litigation (inc. Liquor Licensing)	25%
Company/Commercial	15%
Family	10%
Employment	10%
Wills/Probate/Trusts	10%

Latham & Co
15 High Street, Melton Mowbray, LE13 0TX **Tel** (01664) 563012 **Fax** (01664) 563014

A-Z ■ LAW FIRMS

Latham & Watkins

99 Bishopsgate, London EC2M 3XF
Tel (020) 7710 1000 **Fax** (020) 7374 4460
Email latham&watkins.london@lw.com **Website** www.lw.com

THE FIRM Latham & Watkins is a global law firm with 21 offices worldwide. The firm has over 240 lawyers in seven offices in Europe. The lawyers in the London office practice English and US law, focusing on capital markets, leveraged finance, mergers and acquisitions, project finance, restructuring, EU and competition law and tax. As client needs dictate, London-based lawyers can also call upon the collective expertise of over 1400 Latham & Watkins lawyers practising worldwide in disciplines encompassing virtually every aspect of business-related law.

London Office Latham's London office is well known for its expertise in debt and equity capital markets (including high yield), venture capital and investment funds, project finance, leveraged finance, mergers and acquisitions, private equity, EU and competition law, and tax. The office also has specific industry and regional focuses – media and telecoms, venture and technology, an Italian practice and a Scandinavian practice.

INTERNATIONAL The firm also has offices in Los Angeles, New York, Chicago, San Diego, Orange County, New Jersey, Washington DC, San Francisco, Silicon Valley, Brussels, Boston, New Jersey, Frankfurt, Hamburg, Hong Kong, Milan, Moscow, Paris, Singapore and Tokyo. The firm handles work in a number of languages including French, German, Italian, Spanish, Japanese and Urdu.

Managing Partner (office)	Joe Blum
Managing Partner (firm)	Robert M Dell
Number of partners	19
Assistant solicitors	50
Other fee-earners	7
AREAS OF PRACTICE	
Corporate Finance	35%
Company/Commercial	25%
Bank Finance	20%
Project Finance	10%
EU & Competition	10%

■ Latimer Hinks
5-8 Priestgate, Darlington, DL1 1NL **Tel** (01325) 341500 **Fax** (01325) 381072

■ Laurence Kaye
Wisley, Gills Hill Lane, Radlett, WD7 8DD **Tel** (07768) 190 59 **Fax** (01923) 853618

■ Lawford Kidd
12 Hill Street, Edinburgh, EH2 3LB
Tel (0131) 225 5214 **Fax** (0131) 226 2069 **DX** ED 159 EDINBURGH **Email** law@lawfordkidd.co.uk

Ptnrs 4 **Asst solrs** 6 **Other fee-earners** 1 **Contact** David R C Sandison • Specialises in personal injury litigation for trade union clients; medical negligence; aviation accidents; Court of Session litigation; relocation conveyancing. Associate office Lawfords, London.

AREAS OF PRACTICE	
Personal Injury	60%
Conveyancing/Estate Agency/General Business	25%
Litigation (General)/Employment	10%
Wills & Executries	5%

■ Lawfords
5 Richbell Place, London, WC1N 3LA **Tel** (020) 7871 8500 **Fax** (020) 7871 8511

The Law Offices of Marcus J. O'Leary

Anvil Court, Denmark Street, Wokingham RG40 2BB
Tel (0118) 989 7110 **Fax** (0118) 989 7189
Email moleary@mjol.co.uk **Website** www.mjol.co.uk

THE FIRM A well known and innovative practice specialising in information technology, e-commerce, intellectual property and related commercial matters. Comprising established practitioners in these fields, the practice is modern, progressive and provides an excellent cost-effective service to all of its clients.

PRINCIPAL AREAS OF WORK
Information Technology Experienced practitioners with in-house experience offer a full range of advice to high technology companies and other companies using high technology products.
Intellectual Property All copyright, design, patent, biotechnology, trademark, passing-off and confidential information issues handled quickly and efficiently with regard to the client's best interest.
Internet/E-commerce The firm acts for well known international companies active in this specialist area. Good quality leading edge advice on all web-related matters is assured.
Music, Media & Entertainment Advice and contracts for musicians and composers, particularly regarding rights maintenance and digital music delivery.
Advertising The firm has extensive experience in dealing with advertisements and promotions in different media formats both nationally, internationally and on the internet.

Number of partners	6
Assistant solicitors	3
Other fee-earners	1
AREAS OF PRACTICE	
IT/IP/Internet/Multimedia/E-commerce	75%
Company/Commercial/Commercial Property & Town Planning	10%
Litigation	5%
Advertising/Media/Entertainment	5%
Employment	5%
CONTACTS	
Advert/Media/Entertainment	Marcus O'Leary
	Celia Nortcliff
Commercial Property & Town Planning	Anthony Cooley
Company/Commercial	Rupert Wright
Employment	Andrew Fishleigh
IT/IP/Internet/Multimedia/E-commerce	Marcus O'Leary
	Paul Milton
	Celia Nortcliff
Litigation	Andrew Fishleigh

Competition Law Advice on UK and EU competition law is available in relation to all matters dealt with by the firm.

Company/Commercial The firm provides a full range of legal services including mergers and acquisitions, restructuring, joint ventures and MBOs and MBIs, particularly in connection with high technology companies.

Employment Advice on all aspects of employment law and human rights issues is available, tempered with down-to-earth practical advice relevant to the situation.

Commercial Property & Town Planning All freehold transactions and all lease/tenancy transactions or problems can be dealt with. Additionally there is extensive experience in town and country planning for either new developments or problems with existing planning permission.

Litigation Can be undertaken by the firm in connection with any of the matters listed above.

CLIENTELE Mainly well known international high technology companies.

INTERNATIONAL Languages spoken include French, German and Spanish.

RECRUITMENT A small number of very highly qualified and experienced assistant solicitors are needed each year.

Lawrence Graham

190 Strand, London WC2R 1JN
Tel (020) 7379 0000 **Fax** (020) 7379 6854 **DX** 39 Chancery Lane WC2
Email info@lawgram.com **Website** www.lawgram.com

61 St Mary Axe, London, EC3A 8JN
Tel (020) 7379 0000 **Fax** (020) 7480 5156 **DX** 1072 London City LDE
Email info@lawgram.com

Senior Partner	Bill Richards
Number of partners	85
Assistant solicitors	105
Other fee-earners	67

AREAS OF PRACTICE	
Property	34%
Corporate & Commercial	32%
Litigation	22%
Tax & Financial Management	12%

THE FIRM Lawrence Graham is a London based firm acting principally for UK and international public and private companies, pension funds, financial institutions, public authorities, shipping companies, small businesses and private individuals. The firm's business is divided into four principal practice areas; company and commercial, commercial property, litigation and tax and financial management. Each of these areas is organised into specialist teams according to clients' requirements or the services being provided. The firm has associations with many law firms throughout the world including North America, Europe, the Middle and Far East. It also has an office in the Ukraine, serving clients since the 1920s primarily, but not exclusively, involved in shipping. The firm works in partnership with clients to achieve their objectives in the most cost-effective and practical way. The aim is to add value to client's businesses.

PRINCIPAL AREAS OF WORK

Company/Commercial The department advises on a wide range of transactions including public company takeovers, mergers and acquisitions (both domestic and international) bank and other financings, new media/internet and EU/Competition related issues. It is organised into three main focus groups; corporate, finance and commerce/technology, with four other specialist teams supplying advice on employment/employee benefits, insolvency, energy and pensions/insurance. The firm's highly regarded public authority/housing association practice is also located in the company and commercial department.

Commercial Property The department acts for major institutions, corporate occupiers, pension funds, banks, developers and investors (both plc and private companies), retailers, local authorities and many other public bodies. The range of work undertaken is comprehensive. It includes acquisitions, disposals and financings, joint ventures, securitisation and telecommunications code powers. Construction, planning and property litigation teams are all located in this department.

Litigation The department is organised into teams advising on disputes relating to insurance, reinsurance, shipping and more general business disputes including, in particular, those arising out of banking and insolvency, financial services, intellectual property issues and employment rights. A feature of the firm's litigation practice is that much of its work has an international dimension to it. In addition to its extensive High Court practice, the department is actively engaged in arbitrations and other forms of dispute resolution.

Tax & Financial Management The department provides various specialist services. They include input as part of larger teams working on corporate property transactions, fiduciary risk management for both UK and international corporate trustees and a wide range of advice to private individuals. The latter includes tax, trust and estate planning work, much of which has an international element to it.

A-Z ■ LAW FIRMS

■ Lawson Coppock & Hart
18 Tib Lane, Cross Street, Manchester, M2 4JA **Tel** (0161) 832 5944 **Fax** (0161) 834 4409

Laytons

Saint Batholomews, Lewins Mead, Bristol BS1 2NH
Tel (0117) 930 9500 **Fax** (0117) 929 3369 **DX** 7895 Bristol-1
Email bristol@laytons.com **Website** www.laytons.com

Carmelite, 50 Victoria Embankment, Blackfriars, London, EC4Y 0LS
Tel (020) 7842 8000 **Fax** (020) 7842 8080 **DX** 253 Chancery Lane
Email london@laytons.com

Tempus Court, Onslow Street, Guildford, GU1 4SS
Tel (01483) 407000 **Fax** (01483) 407070 **DX** 2410 Guildford
Email guildford@laytons.com

22 St John Street, Manchester, M3 4EB
Tel (0161) 834 2100 **Fax** (0161) 834 6862 **DX** 14382 Manchester-1
Email manchester@laytons.com

Chief Executive Partner	Richard Kennett
Number of partners	38
Assistant solicitors	37
Other fee-earners	29

AREAS OF PRACTICE	
Company/Commercial	45%
Commercial Property/Land Development	17%
General Litigation	13%
Employment	10%
Technology & Media	10%
Trusts, Private Client & Private Tax	5%

THE FIRM Laytons is a commercial law firm whose primary focus is the mid-sized business sector. The firm's commitment is service to its clients, providing advice which combines technical excellence, practical effectiveness and timely service. Laytons assigns a core legal team to each client which knows its business and can advise directly or by deploying the specialist skills of colleagues. The approach to legal issues is practical, creative and energetic, providing high quality advice founded on a range of complementary specialist skills relevant to the firm's primary fields of focus. The firm is a single national team operating through its four offices, each of which draws on the strengths of the whole with the benefit of excellent IT and communications. Internally, the firm actively encourages a sharing and supportive environment where people can learn and contribute; Laytons pools its knowledge to the benefit of all.

LAYTONS
SOLICITORS

PRINCIPAL AREAS OF WORK
Corporate/Commercial The firm handles corporate finance (domestic and cross-border mergers, acquisitions and joint ventures, stock exchange work, regulatory compliance, venture capital, management buyouts, reconstructions, bank lending); commercial (commercial contracts, e-commerce, competition, product safety, international trade); human resources (employment contracts, share-related and other incentives, pensions, termination of employment, redundancy programmes, TUPE, health and safety); and insolvency and turnaround.

Intellectual Property & Technology Laytons has a substantial technology practice dealing with the acquisition, protection, exploitation and enforcement of intellectual property and having strong experience with the needs of technology-related businesses. The firm's technology and media group has several lawyers with degrees in science and engineering.

Property, Land Development & Construction Services The firm offers a range of skills serving these industries and the commercial property interests of clients generally. Laytons is project solicitor for a number of land development consortia (site acquisition, land warehousing, housebuilding, joint ventures, planning advice, hearings and infrastructure agreements). The firm also deals with environmental services (contaminated land projects, environmental claims, waste management, mineral extraction, contracts/tenders for environmental services); construction law (adjudication, arbitration, contract preparation, collateral warranty advice); and land portfolio management. Both fields of focus draw on the skills of each other and also on specialist teams working in both fields: corporate tax (corporation tax, employment taxation, capital taxation, value added tax, property taxation, customs duties); and regulatory compliance (environmental, transport, petroleum and other licensing, property misdescriptions). Strong dispute resolution skills are an integral part of the service provided, with specialist skills in particular fields of work, including UK and international mediation, litigation and arbitration; property disputes; insurance and professional negligence; product safety; land and environment; debt recovery; intellectual property; and employment-related issues.

Private Client This is an essential element of the firm's holistic approach and service to clients. A strong family law team is complemented by a comprehensive and specialist practice concentrating on the traditional areas of private client work. The firm provides practical advice focusing on the modern day needs and demands of its client base of high net worth individuals and trustees, covering tax and estate planning for UK resident and non-resident individuals and all aspects of charity law, including tax, fundraising and trading issues.

INTERNATIONAL International advice is a natural part of the commercial capability and is provided partly from the UK offices and partly through associated overseas law firms.

LAW FIRMS ■ A-Z

LCA - Legali Commercialisti Associati

16 Old Bailey, London EC4M 7EG
Tel (020) 7597 6491   **Fax** (020) 7329 2521   **DX** 160
Email r.crivellaro@studio-lca.com

London Partner	Roberta Crivellaro
Number of partners	1
Other fee-earners	1

THE FIRM LCA is a full-service, multidisciplinary Italian partnership based in Padua with branches in Milan, Venice, Munich and London. The London branch handles Italian-EU corporate law and international commercial transactions and litigation and assists Italian companies operating abroad and foreign companies with interests in Italy. Sports law, debt recovery, insolvency and property conveyancing are additional specialisations. Correspondents in Eastern Europe. LCA, formed as the result of the merger of Studio Legale Giordano, Studio Legale Camilotti Polettini Rolandi and Studio Commercialisti Bombassei Cerchiai Vidal, is the largest, independent practice in the North East of Italy.

■ Leathes Prior

74 The Close, Norwich, NR1 4DR   **Tel** (01603) 610911   **Fax** (01603) 610088

LeBoeuf, Lamb, Greene & MacRae

No 1 Minster Court, Mincing Lane, London, EC3R 7AA
Tel (020) 7459 5000   **Fax** (020) 7459 5099   **DX** 520 London/City
Website www.llgm.com

Managing Partner	Peter Sharp
Number of partners	12
Assistant solicitors	37
Other fee-earners	8

CONTACTS	
Aviation	Mitri Najjar
Capital Markets	Joseph Ferraro
Civil/Commercial Litigation	David Waldron
Commercial Property	Nick Shepherd
Corporate/Commercial	Tony Richmond
	Brian Zimbler
Energy/Utilities	Keith Hughes
Finance	Peter O'Flinn
	Tony Richmond
Intellectual Property	David Waldron
Insolvency	Peter Sharp
Insurance Litigation	David Wilkinson
Reinsurance Litigation	Nik Rochez
	Peter Sharp
Insurance Corporate	William Marcoux
	James Woods
Private Equity	Joseph Ferraro
	Tony Richmond
Project Finance	Bruce Johnston
Shipping & Marine	Andrew Bickley
Tax	Andrew Terry

THE FIRM LeBoeuf, Lamb, Greene & MacRae is a multinational partnership affiliated with LeBoeuf, Lamb, Greene & MacRae LLP, a United States law firm with over 750 lawyers in 14 US and 10 other international offices. The lawyers in the London office include English solicitors and US lawyers, as well as lawyers from other jurisdictions and represent a cross-section of the firm's clientele in corporate, finance, litigation and regulatory matters. Close co-ordination is maintained between the lawyers in the London office and those in other LeBoeuf offices so that the full resource of the firm may be called upon to assist clients in virtually every aspect of the law.

PRINCIPAL AREAS OF WORK

Insurance & Reinsurance London acts for insurers and reinsurers across Europe and globally. Locally the office acts for many of the major Lloyds syndicates. The team is well known for US, UK and EU corporate transactional and regulatory advice.

Corporate/Commercial A key strength of the London office is its cross-border mergers and acquisitions and joint ventures practice. The firm has the ability to structure and execute M&A transactions under both English and US law, in addition to its strong local M&A practices in France, Brussels and Moscow.

Private Equity & Capital Markets The office has a growing private equity and capital markets practice. It represents private equity sponsors in fund formations and in specific investments, as well as companies receiving such funding. The office has also represented both issuers and managers in European and global capital markets transactions, including listings on the London, Luxembourg and New York stock exchanges. It also specialises in obtaining US listings and completing US offerings for non-US companies wishing to tap the US capital markets and navigate the US securities laws.

Energy/Utilities The office advises globally on the regulatory, commercial and environmental aspects of oil and gas exploration and production and on international power projects.

Project Finance The office has a significant project finance capability with in-depth expertise advising projects developers and financial institutions on all aspects of structuring, negotiating, developing and financing major projects, across industry sectors.

International Litigation & Arbitration The London office has a team of dedicated litigators and arbitrators, the focus of both practices being on high-end, technical and international work. The team has been involved in some of the most major insurance and reinsurance cases around over the last two years.

Insolvency: The London office has substantial expertise in insolvency (both contentious and non-contentious) on a global basis, with a particular focus on the insurance and reinsurance industry.

Commercial Property All aspects of commercial property investment and transactions.

INTERNATIONAL LeBoeuf, Lamb, Greene & MacRae LLP has offices in the United States in New York, Washington DC, San Francisco, Albany, Boston, Denver, Harrisburg, Hartford, Houston, Jacksonville, Los Angeles, Newark, Pittsburgh, Salt Lake City, and elsewhere in Almaty, Bishkek, Beijing, Brussels, Johannesburg, Moscow, Paris, Riyadh and Tashkent together with working arrangements with local lawyers in numerous other jurisdictions.

A-Z LAW FIRMS

Ledingham Chalmers

5 Melville Crescent, Edinburgh, EH3 7JA
Tel (0131) 200 1000 **Fax** (0131) 200 1080 **DX** ED 275
Email mail@ledinghamchalmers.com **Website** www.ledinghamchalmers.com

Johnstone House, 52-54 Rose Street, Aberdeen, AB10 1HA
Tel (01224) 408408 **Fax** (01224) 408400 **DX** AB 15
Email mail@ledinghamchalmers.com

Kintail House, Beechwood Business Park, Inverness, IV2 3BW
Tel (01463) 667400 **Fax** (01463) 713755 **DX** 521009 Inverness – 3
Email mail@ledinghamchalmers.com

THE FIRM Ledingham Chalmers offers 'exportable skills' – skills and experience rooted in the rich Scottish legal tradition, developed in an enterprising economy and now offered to an international market. Now recognised as one of Scotland's leading oil and gas practices, Ledingham Chalmers provides a full range of legal services to the business community from offices in three Scottish centres – Edinburgh, Aberdeen and Inverness – and in three overseas locations – Baku (Azerbaijan), Istanbul (Turkey) and Stanley (Falkland Islands). The firm has been recognised for its entrepreneurial, 'can do' approach, giving clients the benefit of its own business experience. The firm encourages individual excellence within teams without suffering the extremes of rigid specialisation, with the aim of developing rounded business lawyers who can provide pragmatic solutions. There is also a focus on exportable skills which, while developed at home, can be applied to work overseas in both developed and developing jurisdictions.

PRINCIPAL AREAS OF WORK The firm has developed a particularly strong reputation within the oil and gas and oil services sectors; the land, leisure and construction sectors and more recently in social housing. Within the Scottish offices, the main services are corporate/commercial, corporate and project finance, oil and gas, commercial property (including planning and environmental), construction, employment, energy law and practice, intellectual property, information technology, insolvency, litigation and dispute resolution, agriculture and estates and private client (which in Scotland includes residential property) and social housing.

INTERNATIONAL The overseas offices have a special focus on oil and gas, transportation, infrastructure projects, banking and project finance in their respective regions and are supported by lawyers with international experience in the firm's Edinburgh office. The firm regularly works alongside lawyers in other jurisdictions sometimes as instructing counsel for UK clients or as part of a larger professional team.

Senior Partner	David Laing
UK	
Number of partners	36
Assistant solicitors	28
Other fee-earners	32
International	
Assistant solicitors	9
Other fee-earners	1

AREAS OF PRACTICE	
Company/Commercial (inc. Oil & Gas)	39%
Commercial Property (inc. Social Housing)	25%
Litigation (inc. Construction)	16%
Residential Property	14%
Private Client	6%

CONTACTS	
Agriculture	Allan Collie (Aberdeen)
Commercial Property	John Curran (Aberdeen)
Company/Commercial	Malcolm Laing (Aberdeen)
Construction	Jennifer Howitt (Aberdeen)
Corporate Finance	David Laing (Edinburgh)
Employment	Peter Sharp (Aberdeen)
International	Gavin Farquhar (Edinburgh)
Litigation	Marysia Lewis (Aberdeen)
Oil & Gas	Robert Ruddiman (Aberdeen)
Private Client	Daniel Stewart (Aberdeen)
Social Housing	Derek Hogg (Edinburgh)
Technology	Roger Connon (Aberdeen)

THE BUSINESS OF LAW

LEDINGHAM CHALMERS
SOLICITORS

Lee Bolton & Lee

1 The Sanctuary, Westminster, London, SW1P 3JT
Tel (020) 7222 5381 **Fax** (020) 7222 7502 **DX** 145940 Westminster 4
Email enquiries@1thesanctuary.com **Website** www.leeboltonlee.com

THE FIRM Established at 1 The Sanctuary in 1855, Lee Bolton & Lee is a well established Westminster practice, incorporating both commercial, charity, education and private client work. The firm offers extensive experience and advice across a wide spectrum of activities, and is associated with a firm of solicitors and parliamentary agents, Rees and Freres, to provide a specialist service in parliamentary, public and administrative law.

PRINCIPAL AREAS OF WORK

Private Client The firm provides expert advice on a full range of private client matters including domestic property, personal taxation and individual financial planning, wills, trusts, probate and the administration of estates. In addition, a separate department handles all aspects of family and matrimonial law.

Ecclesiastical, Education & Charities As well as general advice on ecclesiastical matters and disciplinary proceedings, the firm advises three diocesan bishops as Registrars. Advice is provided to independent schools on all matters from establishing a new school or hiving-off a school from a larger charity to day to day operational and employment issues. In the maintained sector the firm has considerable knowledge of the Education Acts and advises a number of diocese and many individual schools and trustees on education law and the law relating to school sites. The firm's charity practice is linked, but not confined to, its educational and ecclesiastical work and covers all aspects of charity creation,

Senior Partner	PF Beesley
Number of partners	12
Assistant solicitors	15
Other fee-earners	10

CONTACTS	
Charities	PF Beesley
	AC James
Commercial Property	GJ Fountain
Company/Commercial	JP Sergeant
Ecclesiastical/Education	PF Beesley
	NJ Richens
Litigation	JP Sergeant
Parliamentary	MAR Peto
Private Client	MJG Fletcher
Public Law	MAR Peto
Railway Property	P Robinson
	KE Wallace

registration and administration including trusts, tax and charitable property.

Corporate Services Advice is provided for clients ranging from established organisations to emerging businesses and entrepreneurs on every aspect of commercial life including company formations, reconstructions, mergers, MBOs, joint ventures, Stock Exchange work, employment law and pensions, banking and financial services. Funding, planning and development work is handled for banks, institutional clients, investors and developers.

Litigation A thriving litigation department handles a range of matters including general commercial contracts, employment disputes, professional and medical negligence, property building and landlord and tenant disputes, defamation, insurance and personal injury claims. The firm has long standing relations with numerous public bodies and has developed a considerable expertise in the area of judicial review proceedings.

Commercial Property This department acts for a wide variety of clients from small businesses to major companies, banks, institutional clients, housing associations, investors and developers. All types of commercial property transactions are undertaken including acquisitions and disposals, leasing of commercial property whether acting for Landlord or Tenant, renewal or termination of business lettings, Development Agreements and Joint Venture Agreements. The department draws on expertise elsewhere in the firm; for example where litigation or tax aspects arise. In addition, Rees & Freres have a large commercial property department currently handling work from the major rail transport providers and operators.

Lee Crowder

39 Newhall Street, Birmingham, B3 3DY
Tel (0121) 236 4477 **Fax** (0121) 236 4710 **DX** 13034
Email info@leecrowder.co.uk **Website** www.leecrowder.co.uk

THE FIRM Lee Crowder is a dynamic modern practice based in Birmingham city centre comprising eight specialist areas. In recent years the firm has expanded and developed at a great pace whilst still maintaining its established commitment to providing an excellent service. The firm has been at the forefront of developing new legal markets and now offers a full-service practice providing a greater range of services to a broader client base. The firm is committed to providing a first-rate client focused, partner led service, and is enhancing its reputation, both regionally and nationally.

PRINCIPAL AREAS OF WORK

Corporate Services The department deals with commercial as well as corporate and corporate finance matters. Principal activities involve acquisitions, mergers and disposals, AIM flotations, joint ventures and shareholder agreements, non-contentious insolvency, venture capital and commercial agreements. It is also recognised as a leading firm in e-commerce and media and entertainment on a regional and national basis. The department also has well-established expertise in corporate recovery and insolvency.

Property Services The department now has an extremely high profile and acts for commercial and residential property developers, institutions, retailers and landed estates. The firm has a logistics unit, which is recognised as a leader in its field, as well as dealing with acquisitions and disposals, major commercial and residential developments, landlord and tenant matters and joint ventures.

Commercial Dispute Resolution The department handles a broad range of disputes, specialising in professional negligence claims, particularly in the financial services sector, property litigation and IT disputes.

Private Client The firm is now a major player in the regional market dealing with all aspects of estate and tax planning and has particular expertise in financial services.

Housing With over 30 years experience as Housing Corporation panel solicitors, the firm currently acts for over 50 housing associations nationwide and assists several local authorities.

Construction & Engineering The department deals with the drafting of bespoke contracts and approval of special amendments produced in relation to standard forms. It advises national main contractors, major sub-contractors, developers and their insurers.

Employment The team advises on all aspects of employment problems including contracts, dismissals, discrimination, human rights and all issues arising out of employment legislation at home or in the EU.

Charities The department acts for over 100 charities across the UK, advising charitable trustees and assisting in dealings with the Charity Commission.

Senior Partner	Stephen Gilmore
Number of partners	22
Assistant solicitors	39
Other fee-earners	35

AREAS OF PRACTICE	
Corporate	25%
Property	24%
Construction & Engineering	14%
Commercial Dispute Resolution	13%
Housing	9%
Private Client	8%
Charity Services	4%
Employment	3%

CONTACTS	
Corporate	Graham Muth
	Stephen Gilmore
Property	Kevin Nagle
	Joel Kordan
Commercial Dispute Resolution	
	Richard Whittingham
	Bernard Singleton
Construction & Engineering	Jeffrey Brown
	Stephen Belshaw
Private Client	Drummond Kerr
Housing	Andy Ballard
	Simon Denslow
Charities	Martin Woodward
Employment	Michael Gillespie

LEE CROWDER
Solicitors

A-Z ■ LAW FIRMS

Lee & Pembertons

142 Buckingham Palace Road, London, SW1W 8TR
Tel (020) 7824 9111   **Fax** (020) 7824 8804
Email law@leepem.co.uk   **Website** www.leepem.co.uk

THE FIRM Established in the late eighteenth century, Lee & Pembertons recently moved to new offices in Victoria. The firm offers a full range of specialist services to private clients, a number of whom are owners of landed estates. The emphasis is on providing a partner led personal service backed up by a team structure.

PRINCIPAL AREAS OF WORK Agricultural, charities, commercial, dispute resolution, employment, matrimonial and family, property, wills, trusts, and tax planning including offshore structures.

CLIENTELE A wide range of private clients, including landowners and entrepreneurs, and their related companies and businesses.

RECRUITMENT Significant expansion of the private client team is planned for Summer 2002.

Senior Partner	Julian Whately
Number of partners	9
Assistant solicitors	4
Other fee-earners	8

AREAS OF PRACTICE	
Property (Agri, Res & Comm)	35%
Trusts, Probate & Tax Planning	25%
Dispute Resolution	20%
Company/Commercial	10%
Matrimonial & Family	10%

CONTACTS	
Property	Julian Whately
Agriculture	Anita Symington
Trusts & Tax Planning	Tristram Rae Smith
Dispute Resolution	John Roney
Company/Commercial	Richard Roney
Matrimonial & Family	Jacqueline Fitzgerald

■ Lees Lloyd Whitley
Castle Chambers, 43 Castle Street, Liverpool, L2 9TJ   **Tel** (0151) 227 3541   **Fax** (0151) 227 2460

■ Lee & Thompson
Greengarden House, 15-22 St Christopher's Place, London, W1U 1NL   **Tel** (020) 7935 4665   **Fax** (020) 7563 4949

Leigh, Day & Co

Priory House, 25 St John's Lane, London, EC1M 4LB
Tel (020) 7650 1200   **Fax** (020) 7253 4433   **DX** 53326 Clerkenwell
Email postbox@leighday.co.uk   **Website** www.leighday.co.uk

International House, 82-86 Deansgate, Manchester, M3 2ER
Tel (0161) 832 7722   **Fax** (0161) 839 2329   **DX** 718178 Manchester 3
Email postman@leighday.co.uk

Managing Partner	Martyn Day
Number of partners	17
Assistant solicitors	23
Other fee-earners	35

CONTACTS	
Accident & PI	Sally Moore
	Geraldine McCool (Manchester)
Administrative	Richard Stein
Clinical Negligence	Anne Winyard
	Russell Levy
	Frank Patterson (Manchester)
Environment	Martyn Day
Human Rights	Frances Swaine
Multi-party Actions	Martyn Day
Product Liability	Martyn Day
	Stephanie Hunter (Manchester)

THE FIRM Leigh Day & Co is a leading claimant-focused firm based in London and Manchester. The firm specialises in many aspects of complex personal injury and accident work, clinical negligence, human rights and multi-party actions. The specialised nature of the firm and shared sense of commitment has attracted a high quality group of lawyers to form a well resourced team dedicated to balancing the rights of victims against powerful corporations and large institutions. In reference to the settlement of a major international case, Afrika & 7,500 others v Cape plc, at the end of 2001, Leigh Day was commended in the House of Commons for working 'tirelessly to support the claimants'. Leigh Day & Co is the winner of the Lawyer/HIFAL Law Firm of the Year Award 1996.

PRINCIPAL AREAS OF WORK
Accident & Personal Injury The firm deals with a full range of complex personal injury claims including road traffic accidents and accidents at work. The firm has specialist legal expertise in actions against the MOD, aviation disasters, and asbestos-related disease.
Administrative & Public Law This department undertakes a large number of high profile judicial reviews of decisions taken by public bodies. Its clients include individuals, non-governmental groups and local authorities and objectors concerning plan making, development control, enforcement and appeals.
Clinical Negligence The firm has a leading reputation for specialist clinical negligence work, concentrating on cases involving serious disabilities and death. The firm also specialises in medical devices and product liability such as artificial heart valves, pacemakers and silicone breast implants and is well known for its work in the delayed diagnosis of cancer. The firm employs two qualified doctors, two nurses and two part-time forensic accountants.
Environment The firm is at the cutting edge of environmental law, specialising in supporting claims as a result of exposure to pollution (radiation, chemicals, pesticides, sewage in the sea) together with industrial disease and nuisance claims.
Human Rights A new department has been created which draws together aspects of human rights work across Leigh Day & Co. The department has handled high profile cases such as Ms B v NHS Trust and offers expertise in areas where human rights are of growing importance such as community care,

medical ethics, special needs education, child abuse, nuisance, confidentiality and planning.

Multi-party Actions Under Martyn Day and Richard Meeran, the firm has been at the forefront of legal developments in multi-party cases on behalf of claimants in the UK and overseas on a range of issues including asbestos-related disease, 3M Capital Hip replacements and the ongoing contraceptive pill litigation.

Product Liability: Leigh Day & Co has extensive experience in handling product liability cases, many of which are undertaken as class actions. Products include pharmaceutical products, medical devices and aircraft.

Lemon & Co

34 Regent Circus, Swindon, SN1 1PY
Tel (01793) 527141   **Fax** (01793) 614168   **DX** 400912 Swindon 6
Email enquiries@lemon-co.co.uk   **Website** www.lemon-co.co.uk

Chelsea House, 1 Little London Court, Albert Street, Swindon, SN1 3HY
Tel (01793) 496341   **Fax** (01793) 511639   **DX** 400912 Swindon 6
Email enquiries@lemon-co.co.uk

Senior Partner	Richard Fry
Number of partners	7
Assistant solicitors	9
Other fee-earners	7

AREAS OF PRACTICE	
Conveyancing	35%
Litigation	30%
Company/Commercial	20%
Trusts & Probate	15%

CONTACTS	
Commercial Litigation	Nita King
Commercial Property	Martin Evans
Company/Commercial	Nial Ledingham
Employment	Paul Archer
Family	Stephen Moss
Personal Injury	Timothy Dixon
Private Client	Deirdre Moss
Residential Property	David Halfhead

THE FIRM Founded in 1914, Lemon & Co is one of the largest and longest established firms in Swindon, providing an extensive range of services for businesses and private clients and is dedicated to client care. It is one of the few Swindon firms specialising in commercial law and has participated in several complex property and corporate transactions in recent years.

PRINCIPAL AREAS OF WORK

Company/Commercial Work includes company formations, acquisitions and disposals, MBO/MBI, employment contracts and conditions, shareholders and partnership agreements, jv agreements, intellectual property, franchise, agency and distribution agreements, commercial property and all aspects of landlord and tenant law.

Litigation All matters are undertaken. Specialists in commercial litigation, employment, personal injury, family, and childcare.

Private Client Work handled includes estate planning, wills, charity law, management of trusts and settlements, probate work, administration of estates and financial and tax advisory services. The firm's specialist residential conveyancing department is also widely acknowledged for providing a quality service.

Leo Abse & Cohen

40 Churchill Way, Cardiff, CF10 2SS   **Tel** (029) 2038 3252   **Fax** (029) 2034 5572

Leonard Gray

72-74 Duke Street, Chelmsford, CM1 1JY
Tel (01245) 504904   **Fax** (01245) 490728   **DX** 3309 Chelmsford 1
Email legal@leonardgray.co.uk   **Website** www.leonardgray.co.uk

Ptnrs 4   **Asst solrs** 2   **Other fee-earners** 9   **Contact** Barbara Morgan • Committed to providing quality, independent legal services with specialist departments. All aspects of family law with an emphasis on middle and higher income financial cases. Childcare, mediation and adoption.

A-Z ■ LAW FIRMS

Léonie Cowen & Associates

3A Loveridge Mews, London, NW6 2DP
Tel (020) 7604 5870   **Fax** (020) 7604 5871
Email leonie.cowen@lcowen.co.uk   **Website** www.lcowen.co.uk

THE FIRM Founded in 1989, the firm specialises in local government and administrative law. Léonie Cowen spent 15 years at senior level in local government.

PRINCIPAL AREAS OF WORK
Powers, Functions & Vires
Public Private Partnerships & Joint Ventures The firm advises on all types of public private partnerships, structures for service transfers (including sport and leisure, arts, culture and libraries, economic development, social services and housing companies), commercial and not-for-profit projects, and the Part V framework.
Leisure, Arts, Culture, Libraries & Heritage Includes reviews, service transfers and contracting.
Economic Development & Regeneration Projects Including enterprise hubs.
Local Authority Finance Including the capital finance regime, project funding, PFI, lottery, audit issues and relationships with external auditors.
Social Services Community care procurement, partnerships with health authorities, transfers of residential homes for older people/adults and securing capital funding for re-provisioning.
Best Value, Quality Systems & Benchmarking
Public Procurement Advice is given on the public procurement regime, safe procurement processes and drafting contracts.
Employment Including TUPE, local authority terms and conditions (including sensitive senior level cases), superannuation schemes and pensions.
Investigations & Inquiries
Education The firm works for LEAs and governors of schools, higher education establishments and private sector PPP partners.
Charities: Particularly the setting-up and management of charities and other non-profit bodies.
Municipal & Cross-Authority Trading
Corporate The firm handles business transfers, joint ventures, and shareholders agreements.
Commercial Property Work covered includes acquisition, funding, management and disposal of property for public authorities, housing associations, businesses and investors.

Principal	Léonie Cowen
Number of partners	1
Other fee-earners	1

AREAS OF PRACTICE	
Local Government Law	80%
Charities	10%
Corporate	5%
Commercial Property	5%

CONTACTS	
Charities	Léonie Cowen
	Andrew Riddell
Commercial Property	Andrew Riddell
Corporate	Léonie Cowen
	Andrew Riddell
Local Government Law	Léonie Cowen

Lester Aldridge

Russell House, Oxford Road, Bournemouth, BH8 8EX
Tel (01202) 786161   **Fax** (01202) 786110   **DX** 7623 Bournemouth 1
Email info@lester-aldridge.co.uk   **Website** www.lester-aldridge.co.uk

Alleyn House, Carlton Crescent, Southampton, SO15 2EU
Tel (023) 8082 0400   **Fax** (023) 8082 0410   **DX** 96882 Southampton 10

THE FIRM LA is a dynamic legal business. Based on the south coast, it aims to provide a one stop shop for its entrepreneurial client base and combines high quality commercial legal advice with wealth management. LA has a corporate structure with 15 legal teams reporting to a full time managing partner and lawyers are supported by directors of finance, personnel and marketing. The firm continues to invest heavily in tailored management training and in the last year has attracted the lead trainer from Bradenham Manor (Grant Thornton's national training centre) to work with them in-house. Warwick Business School has recognised the unique approach amongst professional firms and has featured LA in a national management training video. The exciting developments at LA have been much written about in the legal press and the firm continues to live up to its reputation for ambition, vigour and energy. Over the past 18 months the firm has grown by nearly 50%. This growth is partly due to the development of the Southampton office (opened in February 2001) which has firmly established itself as a leading player in the marketplace. LA's shockingly normal marketing campaign (based on a client response to a client satisfaction survey) has re-inforced LA's image of a very innovative law firm. Key appointments in early 2002 have included a highly rated corporate finance director to head the firm's one stop shop for legal and financial services.

RECRUITMENT LA continues its growth strategy and is actively seeking high calibre lawyers and other professionals. For more information contact Sarah Jones, head of personnel.

Managing Partner	Roger Woolley
Chairman	Jeremy Allin
Number of partners	34
Assistant solicitors	36
Other fee-earners	56

CONTACTS	
Asset Finance & Banking	Kevin Heath
Business Property	Bob Robertson
Commercial Litigation	Michael Giddins
	Richard Byrne
Corporate	David Ashplant
Corporate Recovery	Malcolm Niekirk
Employment	Susan Evans
Family Law	Stephen Foster
Health & Community Care	Peter Grose
Health & Safety	Richard Byrne
Intellectual Property	David Ashplant
Investment Services	Steve Dean
LA Fast Track (Corporate Claims)	Andrew Corke
LA Marine	Jonathan Hadley-Piggin
Personal Injury	Karen Thompson
Planning & Development	Andrew Hignett
Residential Property	Rachel Lapworth
Trusts, Tax & Wills	Barry Glazier

■ Lester Morrill

27 Park Square West, Leeds, LS1 2PL **Tel** (0113) 245 8549 **Fax** (0113) 242 1965

L'Estrange & Brett

Arnott House, 12-16 Bridge Street, Belfast, BT1 1LS
Tel (028) 9023 0426 **Fax** (028) 9024 6396 **DX** 424 NR Belfast 1
Email law@lestrangeandbrett.com **Website** www.lestrangeandbrett.com

Senior Partner	V Alan Hewitt
Number of partners	11
Assistant solicitors	19
Other fee-earners	7

AREAS OF PRACTICE

Corporate & Commercial Law	39%
Commercial Property	38%
Litigation (inc. Employment Law)	18%
Private Client	5%

CONTACTS

Banking & Financial Services/Insolvency	Brian Henderson
Commercial Law	Richard Gray
Commercial Property	V Alan Hewitt
Construction Law	Andrea McIlroy-Rose
Corporate Law	John Irvine
Employment	Adam Brett
Litigation	Sam Beckett
Private Client	Ian Huddleston
Projects & PFI	Richard Gray
Technology	Paul McBride

THE FIRM L'Estrange & Brett is one of the leading commercial firms in Northern Ireland and one of the oldest practices in Ireland, having been in existence since 1796. Today, it is a modern practice geared to the demands of a fast moving business environment and committed to giving clients the best professional advice and support available in the market. The firm has strong links with many City of London, national and regional firms in Great Britain. It also works on international transactions with firms in many parts of the world. Along with leading Dublin practice McCann FitzGerald, L'Estrange & Brett formed the North South Legal Alliance in 1999. The two firms retain their independence, but work together to provide clients with an integrated service in matters involving elements in both Northern Ireland and the Republic of Ireland.

PRINCIPAL AREAS OF WORK

Corporate Law The firm provides fast and effective legal advice across all types of work in the corporate sector, ranging from acquisitions, disposals and mergers to management buyouts, buyins, joint ventures and new inward investment projects.

Commercial Law The firm advises on diverse areas ranging from sales/distribution and competition law to intellectual property information.

Commercial Property L'Estrange & Brett has extensive experience across a full range of property related matters with an emphasis on commercial property. The firm's skills cover site acquisition and development, planning, building contracts and arbitration, landlord and tenant, housing developments and environmental law.

Construction Law The firm's construction unit advises contractors, employers and funders on all types of contentious and non-contentious construction matters.

Litigation The litigation department is focused on the requirements of commercial clients. Its work covers commercial actions, building contracts, litigation, professional negligence, administrative law and judicial review, as well as personal injury claims.

Banking & Financial Services/Insolvency The firm's cross-disciplinary unit advises on all aspects of borrowing, lending and corporate finance, including asset and project finance, corporate reconstructions and reorganisations. Its insolvency practice has wide experience of corporate rescue and recovery involving receivership, administration and liquidation.

Projects/PFI/PPP The firm has unrivalled experience of project finance and PFI/PPP transactions in Northern Ireland, acting for both public and private sector clients.

Employment The firm provides a comprehensive service for employers and employees advising on all aspects of litigious and non-litigious employment work.

Private Client The firm provides legal services to private clients across a wide range of matters, including domestic conveyancing, wills and trusts, probate and tax planning.

Technology The firm's business technology unit advises a range of clients, from dot.com start-ups to traditional businesses on all technology aspects of their businesses.

A-Z LAW FIRMS

Levenes

Ashley House, 235-239 High Road, Wood Green, London, N22 8HF
Tel (020) 8881 7777 **Fax** (020) 8889 6395 **DX** 135576 Wood Green 4
Email info@levenes.co.uk **Website** www.levenes.co.uk

The McLaren Building, 35 Dale End, Birmingham, B4 7LN
Tel (0121) 212 0000 **Fax** (0121) 233 1878 **DX** 23502 Birmingham 3
Email enquiries@levenes.co.uk

South Gate House, Wood Street, Cardiff, CF10 1EW
Tel (029) 2039 0777 **Fax** (029) 2023 0777 **DX** 122790 CARDIFF 13
Email contact@levenes.co.uk

Grove House, 140-142 The Grove, Stratford, London, E15 1NS
Tel (020) 8519 9515 **Fax** (020) 8522 0880 **DX** 92223 Stratford, London
Email info@levenes.co.uk

Bedford House, 125-133 Camden High Street, Camden, NW1 7JR
Tel (020) 7482 3555 **Fax** (020) 7482 3202 **DX** 57072 Camden Town
Email info@levenes.co.uk

Number of partners	14
Assistant solicitors	46
Other fee-earners	52

AREAS OF PRACTICE	
Personal Injury	55%
Employment	20%
Crime	10%
Education, Disability & Human Rights	10%
Family & Other Legal Aid	5%

CONTACTS	
Civil & Commercial Litigation	Geoffrey Morris
Crime	David Nicolls
Education/Disability & Human Rights	David Ruebain
Employment	Audrey Onwukwe
Family	Katy Rensten
Personal Injury	David Levene

THE FIRM Levenes is a socially aware firm providing a national service to both individual and commercial clients. The 250 staff are grouped in specialist teams at five locations across England and Wales (Birmingham, Cardiff and three offices in London). The firm has a particularly strong reputation for personal injury and employment. The innovative work undertaken by the education and disability department is nationally recognised and has an expanding human rights dimension.

PRINCIPAL AREAS OF WORK
Personal Injury A leading team of more than 50 lawyers handling all types of personal injury claims including spinal and head injury cases with several recent successful appeal decisions.
Employment: An expert team specialising in employment litigation for both employers and employees with particular expertise in race, sex and disability discrimination.
Education, Disability & Human Rights Law A specialist department offering a unique service in the areas of special educational needs, school and college matters, care assessments, and disability discrimination. The department is already one of the key advisors on human rights.
Family All types of family work, including the full range of children's cases, as well as property and financial matters following separation or divorce are handled.
Legal Aid Work includes family, crime, welfare benefits, education and community care.

Levi & Co
33 St Pauls Street, Leeds, LS1 2JJ **Tel** (0113) 244 9931 **Fax** (0113) 244 6789

Levison Meltzer Pigott

9-13 St Andrew Street, London, EC4A 3AE
Tel (020) 7556 2400 **Fax** (020) 7556 2401 **DX** 200 London Chancery Lane
Email LMP@LMPlaw.co.uk

Number of partners	3
Consultant	1
Assistant solicitors	3

AREAS OF PRACTICE	
Family/Matrimonial/Finance	60%
Children	30%
Cohabitation	10%

THE FIRM Levison Meltzer Pigott is a specialist divorce and family law firm formed on 1 June 1998. In April 2002 Alison Hayes joined the firm as a partner, and Claire Meltzer became a consultant. The firm deals with all areas of divorce and family law, including advising on pensions and the rights of unmarried couples. Jeremy Levison is a founder member of the International Academy of Matrimonial Lawyers and has been vice-president of its European section. His contact with family lawyers worldwide assists in the significant proportion of cases that have an international dimension. Claire Meltzer regularly broadcasts on television and radio, particularly on the subject of pensions and divorce, and has written numerous articles and papers on matters of divorce and family law. Simon Pigott is a member of the International Academy of Matrimonial Lawyers, has lectured for the College of Law, was one of the first family law mediators trained by the Family Mediators Association, was its Chair between 1995 and 1997, and was Vice-Chair of the United Kingdom College of Family Mediators between 1996 and 1998. Alison Hayes is familiar with and handles not only big money ancillary cases but also, having been a member of the Lord Chancellor's Child Abduction Panel, has specialist knowledge in international child abduction work. Jeremy, Claire and Simon are associates of the American Bar Association (Family Section) and all the firm's solicitors are members of the Solicitors Family Law Association.

Levy & McRae

266 St Vincent Street, Glasgow, G2 5RL
Tel (0141) 307 2311 **Fax** (0141) 307 6857/8 **DX** GW149 Glasgow
Email peterwatson@lemac.co.uk **Website** www.lemac.co.uk

Senior Partner	Peter Watson
Number of partners	4
Assistant solicitors	6
Other fee-earners	14

THE FIRM Levy & McRae is one of Scotland's leading law firms. The firm has a particularly strong reputation for litigation, media and personal injury.

PRINCIPAL AREAS OF WORK

Litigation All types of litigation work are handled.
Media One of the largest media law practices in the country providing advice to an extensive range of clients in the print and broadcast media.
Personal Injury Work handled includes claims resulting from car accidents, aircraft and shipping, wrongful death etc.

INTERNATIONAL Levy & McRae are involved in litigation around the world including in France, Spain, Turkey, Italy and the United States. As part of Legal Netlink, the firm offers worldwide access to local counsel.

Lewis Silkin

12 Gough Square, London, EC4A 3DW
Tel (020) 7074 8000 **Fax** (020) 7832 1200 **DX** 182 Chancery Lane
Email info@lewissilkin.com **Website** www.lewissilkin.com

Managing Partner	Trevor Watkins
Senior Partner	Roger Alexander
Number of partners	38
Assistant solicitors	48
Other fee-earners	20
Total	105

AREAS OF PRACTICE

Corporate Finance/Commercial	24%
Employment	21%
Property/Project Finance/Construction/Social Housing	21%
Advertising/Media/Defamation/IP/IT	17%
Litigation & Dispute Resolution	17%

CONTACTS

Advertising & Marketing Services	Roger Alexander
	Brinsley Dresden
Company Commercial	Trevor Watkins
Construction	Peter Morris
Corporate Finance	Clare Grayston
Defamation	Roderick Dadak
Employment	Michael Burd
	James Davies
Intellectual Property	Ian Jeffery
IT	Gillian Cordall
Litigation & Dispute Resolution	Thomas Coates
	Clive Greenwood
Project Finance	Lynne Murray
Property & Planning	Leonard Goodrich
Publishing	Simon Entwistle
Social Housing	Gillian Bastow

THE FIRM Lewis Silkin is a medium-sized commercial law firm which punches well above its weight, competing on equal terms with anyone in its chosen specialist areas. In tone as well as substance, it is distinctive; notably relaxed and unstuffy, it prides itself on friendly and productive working relationships.

PRINCIPAL AREAS OF WORK

Corporate Services The firm aims not just to come in at the tail-end of a transaction to document the deal, but to play a far more active role as a business advisor, helping clients to structure deals and conducting complex negotiations on their behalf. An impressive range of work includes flotations, employee benefits, shareholder agreements, project finance and regulatory advice, acting on behalf of venture capitalists and sponsors. Commercial work includes publishing, franchising and outsourcing.
Litigation & Dispute Resolution The firm is known for its success in winning disputes, as a result of a string of high profile victories. But, more broadly, Lewis Silkin takes the view that problems can be resolved with appropriate dispute resolution techniques. From highly sensitive mediation to High Court litigation, the firm works with clients to achieve their commercial objectives.
Property A 'seamless' approach enables the firm to take care of all a client's property-related needs, from leases to litigation, finance to planning issues, development to environmental issues.
Marketing Services From long-established advertising agencies to web marketing start-ups, clients value Lewis Silkin's understanding of the challenges they face, the result of over 30 years spent advising many of the industry's leading names. The firm's track record in this sector is second to none.
Employment The firm has one of the highest-rated teams in London, a group of outstanding lawyers with a reputation for straightforward practical advice when a sensitive and commercial approach is needed.
Housing & Project Finance A recognised leader in this field, Lewis Silkin's innovative thinking and long experience have resulted in a strong record of challenging work in the social housing sector, and the financing of grant-aided projects.
Technology & Communications In a field where moving quickly is not just desirable but essential, the firm helps drive projects forward, ensuring clients avoid the many pitfalls that await the unwary. The firm acts for IT and new media companies and advises on sales and development, procurement and outsourcing, intellectual property and regulatory issues.
Construction Highly regarded in this area, the firm works as part of the project team from the outset. A comprehensive service, covering everything from new-build property to heavyweight civil engineering.
Defamation Lewis Silkin offers expert and practical advice to corporations, firms or individuals whose reputation has been put at risk by libel, slander or malicious falsehood.
Sports Law Drawing upon Lewis Silkin's strength in employment, immigration, intellectual property and corporate finance, the sports law team advises on a wide range of issues, from player contracts to sponsorship, stadium construction to club ownership.

lewissilkin

Continued overleaf

A-Z LAW FIRMS

CLIENTELE The firm's clients range from large corporations and plcs to entrepreneurs, across a very wide range of sectors – from advertising and the internet to social housing and property, restaurants and retailers to government agencies and utilities.

INTERNATIONAL Lewis Silkin is the UK representative of the Global Advertising Lawyers' Alliance (GALA), an association of corporate communications lawyers.

Lightfoots

The Old Red Lion, 1-3 High Street, Thame, OX9 2BX
Tel (01844) 212305 **Fax** (01844) 214984 **DX** 80550 Thame
Website www.lightfoots.co.uk

Senior Partner	Martin Hector
Number of partners	5
Assistant solicitors	6
Other fee-earners	8

THE FIRM This progressive firm, the first nationally to gain and be re-awarded the Investors in People award, provides sound advice on most aspects of English corporate and private client law.

PRINCIPAL AREAS OF WORK
Commercial Services include company/commercial, commercial property, employment, tax, property litigation and specialist debt collection, mortgage repossession and asset management, professional negligence and pharmaceutical consulting departments.
Private Client Work includes wills, probate, trusts, residential conveyancing, other general civil litigation and a specialist family law and mediation department. The firm also has a thriving estate agency and a property letting and management business.

AREAS OF PRACTICE	
Commercial Litigation	28%
Domestic Conveyancing	16%
Trusts & Probate	16%
Commercial	14%
Family	13%
Pharmaceutical	8%
Commercial Conveyancing	3%
Employment	2%

INTERNATIONAL Members of the firm speak French, Hungarian and Spanish.

Linder Myers

Phoenix House, 45 Cross Street, Manchester, M2 4JF
Tel (0161) 832 6972 **Fax** (0161) 834 0718 **DX** 14360
Email law@lindermyers.co.uk **Website** www.lindermyers.co.uk

AREAS OF PRACTICE	
Company/Commercial	25%
Personal Injury	25%
General Litigation	15%
Medical Negligence	13%
Matrimonial	12%
Private Client	10%

Ptnrs 14 **Asst solrs** 17 **Other fee-earners** 19 **Contact** Bernard Seymour • Commercial and litigation practice carrying out services of all kinds for business clients. Strong employment department. Also well known for personal injury and clinical negligence ability.

Lindsay Ford Solicitors

93 Cardiff Road, Caerphilly, CF83 1WS **Tel** (029) 2088 2441 **Fax** (029) 2085 1386

Lindsays WS

11 Atholl Crescent, Edinburgh, EH3 8HE
Tel (0131) 229 1212 **Fax** (0131) 229 5611 **DX** 25 Edinburgh
Email mail@lindsays.co.uk **Website** www.lindsays.co.uk

201-203 Bruntsfield Place, Edinburgh, EH10 4DH
Tel (0131) 229 4040 **Fax** (0131) 466 7644 **DX** 25 Edinburgh **Email** mt@lindsays.co.uk

Barlas & Sharpe WS, 33a Westgate, North Berwick, EH39 4AG
Tel (01620) 893481 **Fax** (01620) 894442 **DX** ED 1245 **Email** rfm@lindsays.co.uk

Senior Partner	John Elliot
Number of partners	14
Assistant solicitors	11
Other fee-earners	39

AREAS OF PRACTICE	
Private Client	34%
Commercial	27%
Residential Conveyancing	21%
Litigation	18%

CONTACTS	
Asset Finance	Alasdair Cummings
Banking	Alasdair Cummings
Building Arbitration	Alan MacKay
Charitable Companies	Kathleen Preston
Commercial Contracts	William McIntosh
Commercial Property	David Reith
Corporate	Alasdair Cummings
Crofting/Agriculture	Roy Shearer
Education	Alasdair Cummings
Employment	Alasdair Cummings
Executry & Wills	Callum Kennedy
Intellectual Property	William McIntosh
Investments	Rodger Urquhart

THE FIRM Lindsays provides a partner-led personal service with an emphasis on quality. The firm has a substantial private client base as well as a strong commercial and litigation practice. To complement these legal services, Lindsays has developed a significant presence in the residential property market through its estate agency division, Lindsays Residential.

PRINCIPAL AREAS OF WORK
Company/Commercial All aspects of commercial property work are covered. This includes purchases, sales, leasing and secured lending, asset finance, asset recovery and building contracts, particularly in relation to disputes. Other more specialised areas of expertise are education, intellectual property (especially licensing agreements), road haulage and liquor licensing, including the purchase and sale of licensed premises. The department deals with company formations and secretarial services, takeovers and acquisitions and the formation and management of charitable trusts and companies.

Private Client In addition to traditional private client work involving the preparation of wills, acting for and as executors in winding up estates, setting up and administering trusts, this department now offers an in-house Investment Management service which has some £200,000,000 under management. Complementary income tax, tax planning and other independent financial advice is also available.

Litigation A comprehensive debt-recovery service is offered as is advice on employment law, contractual disputes, damages claims, arbitration and matters falling within the jurisdiction of the Scottish land courts. The members of the department are also experienced in dealing with personal litigation and can offer advice in connection with divorce and other family disputes and motoring offences.

Residential Conveyancing The department assists with all aspects of buying and selling residential property and is authorised to arrange mortgages.

CLIENTELE Lindsays has a wide range of clients including plcs, large and small companies, building societies, financial and educational institutions, charities, farmers and a broad spectrum of private individuals.

CONTACTS (Continued)	
Liquor Licensing	William McIntosh
Litigation	Alistair Mackie
Personal Financial Planning	John Elliot
Residential Property	Marjorie Townsend
Trusts & Tax Planning	John Elliot

Linklaters

One Silk Street, London, EC2Y 8HQ
Tel (020) 7456 2000 **Fax** (020) 7456 2222 **DX** 10 London City EC3
Website www.linklaters.com

Senior Partner	Anthony Cann
Managing Partner	Tony Angel
Worldwide figures	
Number of partners	460
Number of lawyers	2000

THE FIRM Linklaters advises the world's leading companies, financial institutions and governments on their most challenging transactions and assignments. With over 460 partners and 2,000 lawyers, and offices in major business and financial centres, its clients choose it for its distinctive combination of technical skill, commercial experience and outstanding service.

PRINCIPAL AREAS OF WORK

Asset Finance All principal financing techniques in the global asset finance industry, the financing of specific assets and the acquisition, disposal and financing of asset portfolios.

Banking Bank lending, telecom acquisition, trade, project and property finance, PFI and tax structured finance.

Capital Markets International capital markets and securities issues, debt and equity, structured and derivative products, project bonds and securitisations.

Construction & Engineering Domestic construction and engineering projects, major international projects, PFI/PPP work, construction finance, insolvencies, insurance contracts and claims analysis and negotiation.

Corporate & M&A Finance and commercial transactions including share offerings, M&A, restructurings and privatisations.

Corporate Tax Corporate tax advice including large international transactions, litigation and international tax planning.

Employment, Pensions & Incentives A comprehensive service covering disputes, remuneration, benefits and pensions.

Environment (inc. Planning) Environmental risks and liabilities; prepares, litigates and defends cases on risk assessment and crisis management; regulatory issues; development and planning law, policy and practice.

EU & Competition Law EU and competition/anti-trust issues: merger control, dominance and dealings with national, EU regulatory and WTO authorities.

Financial Markets Advises investment and commercial banks, securities houses and their affiliates.

Intellectual Property Exploitation and protection of patents, trademarks and other intellectual property rights.

Investment Management Structuring and organising offshore open and closed-ended investment companies, unit trusts, UCITS, limited partnerships, fonds communs de placement and other vehicles.

IT & Communications: Commercial and regulatory advice on e-commerce, telecoms and other forms of media.

Litigation & Arbitration Litigation and arbitration expertise, as well as ADR.

Projects: Power, infrastructure, oil and gas, petrochemical, telecommunications, water and PFI projects.

Real Estate Investment and funds; retail, leisure and headquarters projects; construction and engineering matters; tax and financing; planning and environmental issues; rent review and real estate-related litigation.

Restructuring & Insolvency Corporate recovery and workouts, including cross-border restructuring and insolvency.

Structured Finance Domestic and international expertise in securitisations, project bonds, high-yield debt and structured finance.

Trusts Trusts and estate planning are handled, both domestic and offshore.

INTERNATIONAL Work is handled in all commercial languages and local languages of countries in which Linklaters has offices.

RECRUITMENT In order to maintain Linklaters' premier position the firm actively recruits the highest calibre candidates. Undergraduates interested in making an application can visit the firm's website at www.linklaters.com or contact the firm at graduate.recruitment@linklaters.com.

CONTACTS	
Asset Finance	Ronald Gibbs
Banking	John C Tucker
Capital Markets	Michael Canby
Construction & Engineering	Marshall Levine
Corporate & M&A	David Cheyne
Corporate Tax	Guy CH Brannan
Employment, Pensions & Incentives	
	Janet Cooper
	Ruth Goldman
	Raymond Jeffers
Environment (inc. Planning)	Ray Jackson
EU & Competition	Bill Allan
Financial Markets	Paul Nelson
Intellectual Property	Jeremy Brown
Investment Management	Tim Shipton
IT & Communications	Ian Karet
Litigation & Arbitration	Christopher Style
Projects	Alan Black
Real Estate	Simon Clark
Restructuring & Insolvency	Robert Elliott
Structured Finance	Julian Davies
Trusts	Nigel Reid

A-Z ■ LAW FIRMS

Linnells

Greyfriars Court, Paradise Square, Oxford, OX1 1BB
Tel (01865) 248607 **Fax** (01865) 728445 **DX** 723000 Oxford 5
Email law@linnells.co.uk **Website** www.linnells.co.uk

THE FIRM Linnells is one of the South East's leading property and commercial firms. It has a national reputation for its work in the specialist sectors of charities, publishing, construction and asset finance litigation. The firm also has a strong private client practice. A successful refocus has brought rapid growth with new personnel at every level contributing to the breadth of services for the corporate client. Linnells has strong associations with the Oxford academic community, and is involved with many of the pioneering university spin-out ventures, assisting young entrepreneurs as well as serving established retail and technology businesses in the area. Intellectual property and IT, two major growth sectors in legal practice, are where the firm's Media and Technology team is at the forefront of developments with clients involved in e-commerce, mobile telephony, media and data management. More generally, the firm is attracting larger corporations and higher value transactions, many involving cross-border negotiations, as its reputation for high quality, professional, accessible advice becomes more widely recognised.

PRINCIPAL AREAS OF WORK

Commercial Property: The firm handles a high volume of property transactions ranging from large commercial residential developments to portfolio management for a number of large retail chains. This involves the acquisition, letting and development of major retail sites.

Corporate/Commercial The quality of Linnells' corporate work has increased steadily with the firm receiving regular instructions on larger multi-million pound deals. The firm has expertise in plc risk management, competition and EU law. Two partner appointments have increased depth in IT and funding expertise. The firm is actively forging links with international firms to assist its larger corporate clients engaged in cross-border commerce.

Commercial Dispute Resolution The Dispute Resolution team continues to grow and to attract work from across Southern England. In addition to the firm's strengths in claimant professional negligence disputes and (increasingly) IT-related disputes, there are specialist teams for construction, asset and credit finance, and intellectual property. Alternative dispute resolution, in its widest sense, remains core to the ethos of the department.

Private Client Tailoring services to high net worth individuals enables the firm to provide a high level, competitive service, with work feeding from its corporate practice and vice versa. The firm has specialists in high value ancillary relief, probate, tax and trust planning, as well as personal injury and clinical negligence.

Senior Partner	Jonathan Lloyd-Jones
Number of partners	21
Assistant solicitors	20
Other fee-earners	18

AREAS OF PRACTICE	
Residential Property/Development	25%
Commercial Property	16%
Corporate/Commercial	24%
Commercial Dispute Resolution	18%
Private Client	17%

CONTACTS	
Asset Finance	Richard Humphreys
Charities	Joss Saunders
Clinical Negligence	Jeremy Irwin-Singer
Commercial Litigation	Jonathan Lloyd-Jones
Commercial Property	John Deech
	Stanley Beckett
Construction	Richard Wade
Corporate Finance	Edward Lee
	Peter Elliott
Corporate/Commercial	Robert Foster
Education	Derek Elsey
Employment	James Whiter
Family	Christine Plews
Intellectual Property	Joss Saunders
Licensing	Carol Oster
Partnerships	Andrew Miscampbell
Publishing	Joss Saunders
Residential Property/Development	Anne Cowell
	Jamie Sutton

Livingstone Browne

84 Carlton Place, Glasgow, G5 9TD **Tel** (0141) 429 8166 **Fax** (0141) 420 1337

Lodders

10 Elm Court, Arden Street, Stratford-upon-Avon, CV37 6PA
Tel (01789) 293259 **Fax** (01789) 268093 **DX** 16201 Stratford-upon-Avon
Email lawyers@lodders.co.uk **Website** www.lodders.co.uk

THE FIRM Founded 150 years ago the firm has now developed into one of the leading firms covering Warwickshire and North Gloucestershire. The firm's traditional and substantial private client base includes proprietors of businesses, partnerships and large landowners, and has developed the capacity to professionally meet their business needs. A friendly atmosphere and the highest quality service are its hallmark.

PRINCIPAL AREAS OF WORK
The firm specialises in estate and tax planning together with probate, trust creation and administration and investment. Agriculture and charities are also specialities and the expanding corporate, commercial property and employment departments act for leading developers, banks and businesses.

Number of partners	10
Assistant solicitors	13
Other fee-earners	17

LAW FIRMS ■ A-Z

Loosemores

Alliance House, 18-19 High Street, Cardiff, CF10 1BP
Tel (029) 2022 4433 **Fax** (029) 2080 3100 **DX** 33008 CARDIFF 1
Email post@loosemores.co.uk **Website** www.loosemores.co.uk

Ptnrs 8 **Asst solrs** 7 **Other fee-earners** 14 **Contact** Linda A Jones • Loosemores specialises in the following areas of law: company management; mergers, acquisitions and disposals; finance; intellectual property; contracts; media matters; EU; commercial property management; residential property; court proceedings; credit control; employment; personal injury; clinical negligence; charities; wills, probate and trusts; powers of attorney and court of protection/receivers.

Lorenzo Zurbrugg

15-17 Jockey's Fields, London, WC1R 4BW
Tel (020) 7404 5641 **Fax** (020) 7831 8460 **DX** 0061 London/Chancery Lane
Email info@lorenzo-zurbrugg.co.uk **Website** www.lorenzo-zurbrugg.co.uk

Managing & Senior Partner	Michael Zurbrugg
Number of partners	2
Assistant solicitors	6
Other fee-earners	4

THE FIRM Lorenzo Zurbrugg specialises in insurance and personal injury litigation, both on behalf of insurers and private clients within the UK and other European countries. The firm also specialises in serious injury work particularly head injury. Clients include a number of Lloyd's syndicates and insurance companies, both UK and foreign, including legal expense insurers.

INTERNATIONAL Several languages are spoken fluently and the firm has established connections in most European countries with particular emphasis on France, Spain, Portugal, Belgium, Switzerland and Germany. The firm includes a Spanish partner whose main area of work consists of personal injury claims in Spain and giving evidence before English courts in relation to Spanish law. In addition, he deals with general litigation, property transactions, child abduction and custody cases.

Lovells

Atlantic House, Holborn Viaduct, London, EC1A 2FG
Tel (020) 7296 2000 **Fax** (020) 7296 2001 **DX** Box 57
Email information@lovells.com **Website** www.lovells.com

Managing Partner	Lesley MacDonagh
Senior Partner	Andrew Walker
Number of partners	147
Assistant solicitors	393
Other fee-earners	210

CONTACTS	
Advertising/Consumer Law	Andrew Skipper
Arbitration/ADR	Andrew Foyle
	Patrick Sherrington
Asset Finance	Robin Hallam
Banking	Matthew Cottis
	Andrew Gamble
Broadcasting	Lindy Golding
	Jennifer McDermott
Business Restructuring	Robin Spencer
Capital Markets	David Hudd
Commodities	David Moss
Computers/IT	Quentin Archer
Construction/Engineering	Phillip Capper
	Nicholas Gould
Corporate Finance/M&A	Hugh Nineham
Defamation	Jennifer McDermott
Employee Benefits	Louise Whitewright
Employment	David Harper
Energy	David Moss
	Michael Stanger
Environmental	Louise Moore
EU/Competition	Simon Polito
Financial Services	Richard Stones
Fraud/Asset Recovery	Keith Gaines
Insurance/Reinsurance	John Young
	John Powell
Litigation	Patrick Sherrington
Media Law	Jennifer McDermott
Pensions	Jane Samsworth
Planning	Michael Gallimore
Private Equity	Marco Compagnoni
Product Liability	John Meltzer

THE FIRM Lovells is one of the largest international law firms with some 3,000 people worldwide. In recent years, the firm has increased its European capabilities significantly and is now one of the few firms with cross-border expertise in a number of western, central and eastern European countries. Building upon strong and broadly based domestic practices, Lovells provides co-ordinated, multijurisdictional services from their offices around the world. Lovells places great emphasis on helping clients to achieve their business objectives by providing legal advice that is both imaginative and commercially aware. It is also known for nurturing its working relationships with clients both large and small and consistently achieves very high ratings for client satisfaction in independent research. The size and international strengths of the firm enable it to put together expert teams of lawyers with direct experience of advising on some of the largest and most complex transactions and cases of recent years, both in the UK and elsewhere in the world. Lovells' services are tailored to the needs of individual clients, drawing on the collective knowledge of the firm. Size, experience and international strengths enable the firm to assemble expert teams of lawyers to advise on transactions or issues that concern its clients. Lovells aims to add value at all stages of a project, from its initiation, through to planning and execution. Lawyers at Lovells are members of broad practice areas which work together closely. These practice areas operate internationally and are structured to facilitate the sharing of technical know-how and the development of a consistently high standard of legal advice across the firm.

INTERNATIONAL The practice of each of the firm's international offices reflects the requirements of clients and the nature of local and regional markets. London is the largest office and offers the full range of the firm's specialist services. The firm's German practice mirrors the decentralised structure of Germany in the heart of the 'Euro-zone', with offices in Frankfurt, Dusseldorf, Hamburg, Munich and Berlin from which it provides legal services in all business matters whether domestic or international. Elsewhere in Continental Europe, the Amsterdam, Brussels, Budapest, Milan, Moscow, Paris, Prague, Rome, Warsaw, Vienna and Zagreb offices offer a combination of local and cross-border legal services covering the areas of banking, corporate finance, private equity, project finance, capital markets, tax, IP, competition and trade regulation, financial services and property. The firm's office in Alicante specialises in trademark matters with the European Trademark Office. The Asia practice of Lovells is managed from the Hong Kong office and focuses on regional banking, project finance, capital markets,

Continued overleaf

A-Z ■ LAW FIRMS

corporate transactions, insolvency, construction, IP, litigation and property. The North America offices in New York, Chicago and Washington DC concentrate particularly on UK and EU advice on corporate transactions, US securities law advice, insurance and reinsurance litigation, insurance insolvency, consumer financial services including regulatory advice and product liability.

RECRUITMENT Prospective trainee solicitors should contact Clare Harris for details of the recruitment programme. Further information is available from any Lovells office or via the firm's website. A comprehensive selection of brochures, client notes and newsletters is available from Jan Frangs in the London office.

CONTACTS (Continued)	
Professional Indemnity	John Trotter
Project Finance	Gavin McQuater
Property	Robert Kidby
Property Litigation	Nicholas Cheffings
Public Policy	Neil Fagan
Shipping/International Trade	David Moss
Tax	Daniel Friel
Telecommunications	Heather Rowe
VAT	Greg Sinfield

■ Lovetts
Chertsey Court, 56-58 Chertsey Street, Guildford, GU1 4HL   **Tel** (01483) 306663   **Fax** (01483) 306664

Loyens & Loeff
26 Throgmorton Street, London, EC2N 2AN
Tel (020) 7826 3070   **Fax** (020) 7826 3080
Email marc.klerks@loyensloeff.com   **Website** www.loyensloeff.com

Number of partners	2
Other fee-earners	10

THE FIRM Loyens & Loeff is an independent law firm, which sets new standards in the field of tax and civil law services. The combination of tax, corporate and notarial law as equal components makes Loyens & Loeff unique in comparison to other domestic and international providers of legal services. Loyens & Loeff's multidisciplinary co-operation enables them to offer their specialisations as part of an integrated service. Characteristics of this dynamic firm are creativity and efficient service at the highest professional and legal standards.

PRINCIPAL AREAS OF WORK The firm advises on capital markets, banking and securities, commercial law and litigation, corporate law, M&A, joint ventures, economic regulatory law, structured finance, project finance, treaty laws, tax (including corporate tax, international tax, VAT, wage tax and social security, and individual income tax) and energy.

LOYENS LOEFF

INTERNATIONAL Other offices in Amsterdam, Arnhem, Eindhoven, Rotterdam, Antwerp (Loyens), Aruba, Brussels (Loyens), Curaao, Frankfurt, Geneva, Luxembourg, New York, Paris, Singapore and Tokyo. Languages spoken include English, French, German, Dutch.

■ Lucas & Wyllys
5 South Quay, Great Yarmouth, NR30 2QJ   **Tel** (01493) 855555   **Fax** (01493) 330055

■ Lupton Fawcett
Yorkshire House, Greek Street, Leeds, LS1 5SX   **Tel** (0113) 280 2000   **Fax** (0113) 245 6782

■ Luqmani Thompson
77-79 High Road, Wood Green, London, N22 6BB   **Tel** (020) 8365 7800   **Fax** (020) 8826 0169

Lyons Davidson
Victoria House, 51 Victoria Street, Bristol, BS1 6AD
Tel (0117) 904 6000   **Fax** (0117) 904 6006   **DX** 7834
Email info@lyonsdavidson.co.uk   **Website** www.lyonsdavidson.co.uk

Senior Partner	Richard Squire
Number of partners	20
Assistant solicitors	66
Other fee-earners	109

THE FIRM A group of exceptionally bright individuals working together as a team in partnership with their clients. The firm's specialist lawyers provide accurate information, guidance and advice in clear and understandable terms. 28 years of representing clients from individuals to large corporate entities has seen Lyons Davidson develop into one of the largest practices in the region. Whilst growing with, and utilising, the latest technology, the firm prides itself on providing practical advice to clients that answers their needs through a traditional level of personal care and the experience of specialists.

■ Macdonalds
1 Claremont Terrace, Glasgow, G3 7UQ   **Tel** (0141) 248 6221   **Fax** (0141) 333 0318

LAW FIRMS A-Z

Mace & Jones

Drury House, 19 Water Street, Liverpool, L2 0RP
Tel (0151) 236 8989 **Fax** (0151) 227 5010 **DX** 14166 Liverpool
Email law@maceandjones.co.uk **Website** www.maceandjones.co.uk

14 Oxford Court, Bishopsgate, Manchester, M2 3WQ
Tel (0161) 236 2244 **Fax** (0161) 228 7285 **DX** 18564 Manchester 7
Email law@maceandjones.co.uk

30 Sherborne Square, Huyton, L36 9UR
Tel (0151) 480 7000 **Fax** (0151) 449 1953 **DX** 15453 Huyton
Email law@maceandjones.co.uk

98 King Street, Knutsford, WA16 6EP
Tel (01565) 634234 **Fax** (01565) 652711 **DX** 22959 Knutsford
Email law@maceandjones.co.uk

Managing Partner	Lawrence Downey
Senior Partner	Graeme Jump
Number of partners	33
Assistant solicitors	42
Other fee-earners	13

AREAS OF PRACTICE

Commercial Property	20%
Employment	20%
Commercial Litigation/Insolvency	15%
Company/Commercial	15%
Construction	15%
PI/Private Client/Family	15%

CONTACTS

Commercial Litigation	Craig Blakemore
Commercial Property	Tim Williams
Company/Commercial	Alan Thompson
Construction	Ken Salmon
Employment	Martin Edwards
Insolvency	Graeme Jump
Personal Injury	Stewart McCulloch

THE FIRM A leading regional practice in the North West, Mace & Jones remains a full-service firm, while enjoying a national reputation for its commercial expertise, especially in employment, litigation/insolvency, corporate, construction and property, with the firm being voted Property Law Firm of the Year 2000 by Insider North West magazine. The firm's clients range from national and multinational companies and public sector bodies to owner-managed businesses and private individuals, reflecting the broad nature of the work undertaken. Sound practical advice is given always on a value-for-money basis. Today, nearly 100 lawyers deliver a service which is founded on an intimate understanding of the needs and objectives of their clients. Low staff turnover leads to a continuity of service which is rarely found in firms of this size. This in turn ensures an understanding of the client, whether in the business or private sector, which enables problems to be anticipated and a proactive approach adopted.

MACE & JONES SOLICITORS

Macfarlanes

10 Norwich Street, London, EC4A 1BD
Tel (020) 7831 9222 **Fax** (020) 7831 9607 **DX** 138
Email cpp@macfarlanes.com **Website** www.macfarlanes.com

Number of partners	56
Assistant solicitors	151
Other fee-earners	33

AREAS OF PRACTICE

Company/Commercial/Banking	52%
Property	22%
Private Client	13%
Litigation	13%

CONTACTS

Advertising & Marketing	Jeremy Courtenay-Stamp
Banking & Debt Finance	Julian Howard
Buy-outs/Private Equity	Charles Meek
Construction	Tony Blackler
Corporate Tax	Nigel Doran
Employment	Tony Thompson
Pensions	Hugh Arthur
Benefits	Douglas Shugar
EU/Competition	Jane Whittaker
Financial Services & Investment Funds	Bridget Barker
Intellectual Property	Jeremy Courtenay-Stamp
Litigation & Dispute Resolution	Willie Manners
M&A/Corporate	Robert Sutton
PFI	John Skelton
Tax & Financial Planning	John Rhodes

THE FIRM Macfarlanes offers a remarkable concentration of excellence. Its distinctive market position as a leading law firm is built on a reputation for the quality of its client service. Macfarlanes is widely recognised as one of a handful of high quality, unaligned law firms in the UK. The firm's focus on the practice of English law comes together with substantial experience of working on international transactions with equivalent law firms in other jurisdictions.

PRINCIPAL AREAS OF WORK

Corporate Macfarlanes is regarded particularly highly for its work in the areas of corporate finance and mergers and acquisitions, including private equity and takeovers. Together this represents over half the firm's work. The firm's related specialist areas such as intellectual property, corporate tax, banking and employee benefits mean that it can provide its broad range of commercial clients with high quality legal services both in relation to corporate transactional work and at the clients' operational level. The firm has a particularly strong reputation for advertising and marketing work as well as investment funds and financial services.

Property By City standards, Macfarlanes' property practice is substantial in size. The quality of the advice it provides is widely recognised. Property work accounts for over 20% of the firm's business – unusual for a successful City firm. Work for the property sector covers all transactions involving the ownership, development, investment in, and financing of land. Commercial property investment and development transactions are at the core of the firm's property practice.

Litigation & Dispute Resolution The wide range of business litigation and dispute resolution work includes: leading employment law cases; acting for insured and insurer, especially in advertising and surveying cases; IP cases and disputes over computer hardware and software; financial services regulatory issues and queries; Lloyd's related work; sovereign debt; securities and other banking disputes; judicial review; breach of contract and professional negligence claims; major shipping and construction arbitration and jurisdictional disputes and EU jurisdiction questions.

Private Client Macfarlanes' pre-eminent private client service commands a leading position. Combined with its strong corporate and property capability, the firm is in a particularly good position to advise the private client entrepreneur. The firm has a longstanding reputation for advising private clients and their

Continued overleaf

family trusts, both domestically and internationally. Tax planning, including the creation and administration of trusts, the preparation of wills and the administration of estates, is central to this work. The international element of its work is of special importance both for UK based families and for overseas taxpayers seeking advice on tax and trust law. The firm is frequently instructed at the request of many of the largest US firms and private banks for this work.

Mackinnons

21 Albert Street, Aberdeen, AB25 1XX
Tel (01224) 632464   **Fax** (01224) 632184   **DX** AB 34
Email admin@mackinnons.com   **Website** www.mackinnons.com

379 North Deeside Road, Cults, Aberdeen, AB15 9SX
Tel (01244) 868687   **Fax** (01224) 861012   **DX** AB 34
Email admin@mackinnons.com

Managing Partner	Charles M Scott
Senior Partner	Denis N Yule
Number of partners	6
Assistant solicitors	6
Other fee-earners	5

CONTACTS	
Commercial	Charles M Scott
	Graham E Jones
Marine & Litigation	Denis N Yule
	Keith MacRae
	Bruce Craig
Private Client & Property	Patricia J Gray

THE FIRM Progressive six-partner practice specialising in shipping and commercial law with substantial private client department providing a full range of legal services. The firm is very experienced in all aspects of marine and admiralty law including marine insurance, collisions, salvage, litigation and personal injury as well as acting in the defence of prosecutions under the full range of merchant shipping, pollution and fisheries legislation. The firm acts for numerous P&I clubs and fishing mutuals providing a hands-on service aboard ships, fishing boats and oil rigs. Mackinnons has a substantial marine and commercial practice dealing with purchase, sale, finance and chartering of fishing boats, offshore oil supply and stand-by vessels, and other vessels.

Mackintosh Duncan
103 Borough High Street, London, SE1 1NN   **Tel** (020) 7357 6464   **Fax** (020) 7357 8448

Maclay Murray & Spens

151 St. Vincent Street, Glasgow, G2 5NJ
Tel (0141) 248 5011   **Fax** (0141) 248 5819   **DX** GW 67
Email lawyer@maclaymurrayspens.co.uk   **Website** www.maclaymurrayspens.co.uk

3 Glenfinlas Street, Edinburgh, EH3 6AQ
Tel (0131) 226 5196   **Fax** (0131) 226 3174   **DX** ED137

10 Foster Lane, London, EC2V 6HR
Tel (020) 7606 6130   **Fax** (020) 7600 0992   **DX** 42616

Managing Partner	Michael Walker
Senior Partner	Bruce Patrick
Number of partners	63
Assistant solicitors	141
Other fee-earners	70

AREAS OF PRACTICE	
Company/Commercial	40%
Commercial Property	28%
Litigation	17%
Private Client	15%

CONTACTS	
Banking & Finance	Susan Kelly
Capital Projects	Alastair McEwan
Commercial Litigation & Advocacy	
	Alayne Swanson
Construction & Engineering	Mark Macaulay
Corporate	Kenneth Shand
Corporate Tax	Martyn Jones
Employment Pensions & Benefits	
	Malcolm Mackay
EU & Competition	Michael Dean
IP & Technology	Fiona Nicolson
Planning & Environmental	Chris Smylie
Property	Robin Garrett
Social Housing	Chris Smith
Tax & Private Capital	Andrew Biggart

THE FIRM Maclay Murray & Spens is a forward looking, practical, commercial legal firm which has a stated objective of providing its clients with the best possible service across the broad range of legal advice provided by the firm. Maclay Murray & Spens is well placed to offer clients throughout the UK and beyond commercial advice at competitive prices. The firm has a significant English, European and international client base, which can be serviced from any or all of the firm's four offices in Edinburgh, Glasgow, London and Brussels. These are linked by an integrated computer, video-conferencing and telephone network ensuring a fast, efficient service, and expert advice are delivered. The London office which offers a full English law service, provides an ideal platform both for Scottish clients doing business in the City and for London-based clients looking for a premier law firm without City overheads. The development and growth of the Brussels office reflects the firm's commitment to meet client needs.

PRINCIPAL AREAS OF WORK In the last year the firm's commitment to improving its service has resulted in an internal restructuring to create 13 departments. These are banking and finance, capital projects, commercial litigation and advocacy, construction and engineering, corporate, corporate tax, employment, pensions and benefits, EU and competition, IP and technology, planning and environmental, property, social housing and tax and private capital. The firm has exceptional quality in all of the departments listed and continues to strive for pre-eminence in these areas of work. The firm recognises that many transactions require hand-picked teams made up of lawyers with differing skills from differing departments if the specific needs of the client and the transaction are to be fully met. To this end, the firm ensures that all departments and units are closely linked to give the client the best possible service.

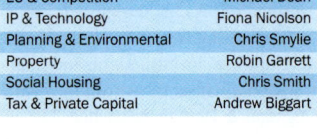

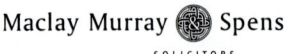

1048   INDEX TO LEADING LAWYERS: PAGE 1693   IN-HOUSE LAWYERS' PROFILES: PAGE 1201

INTERNATIONAL The firm has an overseas office in Brussels, and handles work in French, German, Italian, and Norwegian.

RECRUITMENT The firm is also committed to recruiting high quality assistant solicitors in all areas of work and takes on approximately 20 trainees every year. The growth of activity in the firm's London and Brussels offices and the firm's commitment to a policy of regular exchanges of lawyers with firms in other jurisdictions (both in Europe and further afield) ensure that those recruited receive the widest possible training. Maclay Murray & Spens is committed to investing in its people and their development, and continuing to improve its efficiency, quality and service.

■ Macleod & MacCallum

P.O. Box No.4, 28 Queensgate, Inverness, IV1 1YN **Tel** (01463) 239393 **Fax** (01463) 222879

MacRoberts

152 Bath Street, Glasgow, G2 4TB
Tel (0141) 332 9988 **Fax** (0141) 332 8886 **DX** GW70
Email maildesk@macroberts.com **Website** www.macroberts.com

Excel House, 30 Semple Street, Edinburgh, EH3 8BL
Tel (0131) 229 5046 **Fax** (0131) 229 0849 **DX** ED 207
Email maildesk@macroberts.com

Managing Partner	John Macmillan
Senior Partner	Raymond Williamson
Number of partners	31
Assistant solicitors	103
Other fee-earners	15

CONTACTS	
Banking	Norman M Martin
Charities	David MacRobert
Commercial Litigation	David Arnott
Commercial Property	Laurence Fraser
	Allan Mackenzie
Construction	Lindy A Patterson
Corporate	Neil Cunningham
Corporate Tax & VAT	Isobel d'Inverno
Employment	Raymond Williamson
Energy Law	Ian Dickson
Environmental & Planning	Jamie Grant
EU & Competition	David Flint
Intellectual Property/IT	David Flint
Pensions & Employee Benefits	Peter Trotter
PFI /PPP Projects	Michael Murphy
Private Client	David MacRobert

THE FIRM MacRoberts is a leading commercial law firm offering a comprehensive range of legal services to corporate, commercial, public sector and private clients. Established almost 150 years ago, MacRoberts, through its offices in Edinburgh and Glasgow, provides quality legal services in a prompt, efficient and friendly manner. The firm is committed to delivering the highest standards of professional advice and expertise.

PRINCIPAL AREAS OF WORK

Corporate All aspects of corporate and commercial law including incorporations, reorganisations, takeovers and mergers, management buyouts and joint ventures (UK and international); loan debenture and equity finance, syndications, consumer credit; banking flotations, Stock Exchange requirements, new issues, placings and other issues, employee share schemes and pension schemes; receivership, administration, liquidation and bankruptcy; partnership agreements; EU law; commercial contracts, including agency distribution and finance agreements; entertainment law; privatisations.

Commercial Property Corporate clients are advised on all aspects of property matters including acquisition, sale and leasing of commercial and industrial property; commercial, industrial and housing development, investment and finance; commercial secured loans; environmental law; agricultural law, including forestry; company relocation schemes; timeshare and leisure developments; planning law; licensing and gaming law.

Construction Advice in connection with drafting of construction contracts, professional appointments, collateral warranties; and building and engineering disputes and arbitration.

Corporate Tax & VAT Including tax and VAT aspects of corporate acquisitions, disposals and reorganisations, commercial property transactions and PFI/PPP projects.

Employment Employment and service contracts, disciplinary and grievance procedures, other procedural rules, employment policies including health and safety, sex race and disability discrimination, equal pay and trade union disputes are all covered.

Intellectual Property & IT Work includes franchising, patents and patent licensing, copyright, trademarks and know-how agreements, data protection and computer contracts.

Commercial Litigation The group acts for and advises on all aspects of civil litigation in both Sheriff Courts and the Court of Session; building and engineering disputes and arbitration; insurance and other commercial litigation; rating and valuation; planning; professional negligence; liquidation, administration, receivership and bankruptcy; product liability; debt recovery; reparation claims; intellectual property disputes; licensing.

PFI/PPP & Projects One of the largest practices in Scotland, clients include NHS Trusts, local authorities, bidding consortia and banks in a wide range of sectors including healthcare, education, roads, wastewater and office accommodation.

Private Client Specialist advice to individuals, trustees and executors in relation to tax planning and mitigation; preparation of tax returns; investment advice; establishment and administration of trusts; wills; administration of estates; preparation of Powers of Attorney; financial services; acquisition, sale and leasing of estate and domestic property; setting up and administration of curatories.

Continued overleaf

A-Z ■ LAW FIRMS

INTERNATIONAL Member of ADVOC, an international network of independent lawyers, providing access to legal services throughout Europe and Asia. Languages spoken include Dutch, French, German, Greek and Italian.

■ Madden & Finucane
88 Castle Street, Belfast, BT1 1HE
Tel (028) 9023 8007   **Fax** (028) 9043 9276   **DX** 434 NR Belfast
Email Enquiries@Madden-Finucane.com   **Website** www.Madden-Finucane.com

AREAS OF PRACTICE	
Criminal	30%
Civil	30%
Administrative Law/Human Rights	25%
General Practice	15%

Ptnrs 5   **Asst solrs** 9   **Other fee-earners** 35   **Contact** Peter Madden • Branch offices: Downpatrick, Armagh, Derry. Leading criminal/human rights practice with substantial civil law practice and speciality in judicial review. Main firm in Bloody Sunday Inquiry.

■ Madge Lloyd & Gibson
34 Brunswick Road, Gloucester, GL1 1JW   **Tel** (01452) 520224   **Fax** (01452) 306866

■ Magrath & Co
52-54 Maddox Street, London, W1S 1PA
Tel (020) 7495 3003   **Fax** (020) 7409 1745   **DX** 9009 West End
Email magrath@magrath.co.uk   **Website** www.magrath.co.uk

Senior Partner	Chris Magrath
Managing Partners	Rosalind Morris
	David Ashton
Number of partners	8
Assistant solicitors	18
Other fee-earners	12

AREAS OF PRACTICE	
Immigration	48%
Corporate Fraud/Crime	16%
Employment	12%
Civil Litigation	9%
Entertainment	8%
Property	4%
Commercial	3%

CONTACTS	
Civil Litigation	Nick Goldstone
Commercial	David Ashton
Corporate Fraud/Crime	Andrew Picken
	Chris Magrath
Entertainment	Alexis Grower
Immigration	Chris Magrath
Property	David Ashton

THE FIRM Founded in 1990, Magrath & Co has niche expertise in corporate immigration/employment, fraud and entertainment law, as well as providing general commercial and litigation services. The firm's lawyers have extensive experience in their fields, and are dedicated to providing prompt, expert advice which meets and anticipates their clients' requirements.

PRINCIPAL AREAS OF WORK
Immigration The firm's dedicated immigration department covers the full range of immigration issues but advises primarily on commercial immigration including global expatriation planning, work permits, applications and appeals. The firm has particular experience in US-UK immigration matters and produces a regular bulletin each quarter to provide legal updates on immigration and employment law.
Employment Law The firm's employment department deals with all aspects of employment law including contentious employment disputes, mass redundancies, consultation and industrial action, contract drafting and discrimination issues.
Corporate Fraud The firm is experienced in a wide variety of 'white collar' crime, and can also advise in cases of investigation by agencies such as the Serious Fraud Office, DTI, Inland Revenue and Customs & Excise. Additionally the firm handles a wide range of criminal allegations of a more general nature including confiscation and forfeiture matters.
Civil Litigation The firm is instructed by a wide range of clients on a variety of commercial and entertainment related issues. Although increasingly geared towards the corporate sector, the firm also welcomes private clients.
Entertainment Law Advice on music and literature publishing, recording, production and management agreements; financing, production, distribution and marketing of TV, film, theatre and commercials. Also: merchandising and sponsorship agreements; sports-related advice; and gaming and betting law.
Other Areas All aspects of company and commercial law and commercial property.

CLIENTELE The firm acts for a large number of major multinationals, together with other public companies, owner-managed businesses and private individuals throughout Britain, the US and Europe.

INTERNATIONAL The practice is affiliated to New York-based Gibney Anthony & Flaherty, and to Munich-based David Hole and has links with other legal and professional services firms throughout the rest of the world's major commercial centres. Chris Magrath is also a qualified US Attorney, admitted to the New York State Bar.

LAW FIRMS ■ A-Z

■ Maidments

St Johns Court, 74 Gartside Street, Manchester, M3 3EL
Tel (0161) 834 0008 **Fax** (0161) 832 4140 **DX** 14307 Manchester 1
Email law@amaidment.fsnet.co.uk **Website** www.maidments.com

AREAS OF PRACTICE	
Commercial Fraud	40%
Criminal	30%
Serious Crime	30%

Ptnrs 6 **Asst solrs** 21 **Other fee-earners** 38 **Contact** Allan Maidment • A national criminal law firm with an outstanding reputation in providing expert advice and representation in the most serious and high profile cases of serious crime and commercial fraud. Significant prison law, personal injury and family departments. Offices in Manchester, Birmingham, London, Liverpool, Leeds, Bolton, Sale and Salford.

Maitland & Co

5th Floor, 44-48 Dover Street, London, W1S 4NX
Tel (020) 7344 7500 **Fax** (020) 7344 7555
Email london@maitlandco.com **Website** www.maitlandco.com

Senior Partner	Eric Pfaff
Partners	5
Assistant solicitors	7

THE FIRM Maitland & Co is the European presence of Webber Wentzel Bowens, one of Southern Africa's largest law firms.

PRINCIPAL AREAS OF WORK Maitland & Co's main practice areas are corporate commercial; corporate and personal tax; private client; investment funds; commodities and trade.

INTERNATIONAL The firm has other offices in Paris, Luxembourg, the Isle of Man, Geneva, Dublin, Johannesburg and Cape Town.

■ Maitland Walker

22 The Parks, Minehead, TA24 8BT
Tel (01643) 707777 **Fax** (01643) 700020 **DX** 117408 Minehead
Email office@maitwalk.co.uk

Managing Partner	Julian H Maitland-Walker
Number of partners	2
Assistant solicitors	2
Other fee-earners	3

AREAS OF PRACTICE	
Competition/IP Law	40%
EC/Trade Law	20%
Commercial Litigation	20%
General Commercial	10%
Private Client	10%

THE FIRM Established in 1996 by Julian Maitland-Walker, the firm has expanded rapidly to become one of the leading niche EU and competition law practices. The firm acts for a wide range of commercial clients. In addition, a consultancy service is offered as a facility to other law firms in both the UK and abroad in specialist EU and competition law matters.

PRINCIPAL AREAS OF WORK
EU/Trade Law Including free movement of goods, persons and freedom of establishment, national and international trade, operational logistics, anti-dumping investigations, state aids and public procurement.
Competition/IP Law Advising EC & UK competition law, representing clients before the EU Commission and the UK Competition Authorities in anti-trust investigations. Advising on all aspects of intellectual property rights, registration, enforcement and licensing.
Commercial Litigation All aspects of commercial and property litigation, arbitration and employment law.
General Company & Commercial Advice on incorporations, mergers and acquisitions, joint ventures, commercial agreements and commercial property.
Private Client Residential property, matrimonial, wills, taxation and probate.
Consultancy Services The firm offers a unique consultancy service to other law firms both in the UK and abroad providing specialist advice on competition and trade law and other areas of EU law.

INTERNATIONAL Work is handled in French, German and Italian.

■ Mallesons Stephen Jaques

6th Floor, Alder Castle, 10 Noble Street, London, EC2V 7JX
Tel (020) 7778 7170 **Fax** (020) 7778 7199
Email lon@mallesons.com **Website** www.mallesons.com.au

AREAS OF PRACTICE	
Mergers & Acquisitions	30%
Securities Law	30%
Debt Finance & Capital Markets	20%
Foreign Investment	10%
General Commercial Work	10%

Ptnrs 2 **Asst solrs** 4 **Contact** Tim Blue • Mergers and acquisitions, foreign investment in Australia, banking and capital markets, international and domestic securities offerings, telecommunications law, general corporate/commercial, stamp duty and taxation, energy and resources law.

A-Z ■ LAW FIRMS

Manby & Steward

George House, St John's Square, Wolverhampton, WV2 4BZ
Tel (01902) 578000 **Fax** (01902) 311886 **DX** 702431 Wolverhampton 5
Email info@manbys.co.uk **Website** www.manbys.co.uk

Senior & Managing Partner	Clive Williams
Number of partners	15
Assistant solicitors	10
Other fee-earners	21

CONTACTS	
Agricultural	Steven Corfield
Commercial Litigation	Peter Taylor
Commercial Property	Kevin Styles
Company Commercial	Gavin Southall
Ecclesiastic	John Thorneycroft
Employment	Sue Massey
Planning	Niall Blackie

THE FIRM Established in Wolverhampton for more than 175 years and with offices in Telford and Bridgnorth, Manby & Steward provides an extensive range of services for business and the private client. The firm has a structure of specialist groups, which are partner led. It has invested extensively in information technology (to ensure it is an efficient and competitive operation) and has achieved IIP and ISO 9002 status. Manby & Steward aims to provide practical, responsive advice in accordance with its clients' requirements.

PRINCIPAL AREAS OF WORK All aspects of commercial property; company and commercial; commercial litigation; town and country planning; employment; agricultural; private client; family and childcare; residential conveyancing.

INTERNATIONAL The firm is a founder member of LAWNET and a member of Eurojuris.

Manches

Aldwych House, 81 Aldwych, London, WC2B 4RP
Tel (020) 7404 4433 **Fax** (020) 7430 1133 **DX** 76
Email manches@manches.co.uk **Website** www.manches.com

3 Worcester Street, Oxford, OX1 2PZ
Tel (01865) 722106 **Fax** (01865) 201012 **DX** 4322

Senior Partner	Alasdair Simpson
Chief Executive	Alun Lamerton
Number of partners	53
Assistant solicitors	71
Other fee-earners	23

AREAS OF PRACTICE	
Corporate	25%
Commercial Property	20%
Commercial Litigation	16%
Employment	11%
Family Law	10%
Construction	10%
Intellectual Property	8%

CONTACTS	
Biotechnology	Christopher Shelley
Commercial Property	Louis Manches
Commercial Tax	Stephen Goldstraw
Commercial/IT	Christine Reid
	Peter Stevens
Construction	James Foster
Corporate & Technology	Melvin Pedro
Employment	Alasdair Simpson
Environment/Planning	Paul Manning
	Richard Smith
Family Law	Jane Simpson
Insolvency	Vernon Dennis
Intellectual Property	John Rubinstein
Litigation	John Roebuck
Personal Estate Planning	Alan Poulter
Publishing	John Rubinstein
Social Housing	Paul Butterworth

THE FIRM Manches continues to provide a broad spectrum of services to its clients. However, strategically there is now a greater concentration and focus on its four core commercial sectors of technology, property, construction and retail. This strategy, which largely reflects the existing business mix, is geared to establish it firmly as a market leader in these sectors, whilst retaining that standing in family law. Manches commits itself to innovative problem solving. It offers a level of service and support which reflects the immediacy of its commercial clients' requirements.

PRINCIPAL AREAS OF WORK

Corporate & Technology The firm handles mergers and acquisitions, venture capital, corporate reorganisations, AIM flotations, IPOs, joint ventures and partnerships, Enterprise Investment Schemes, Private Finance Initiatives, competition law and franchising.
Property All aspects of commercial property are handled, including investment and development work for institutions and property companies; retail property; secured lending and joint ventures; social housing.
Construction A wide range of domestic and international instructions, including contentious and non-contentious work in Europe, the Far East, India and Africa. Work is handled in the areas of litigation; arbitration; adjudication; mediation; PFI and PPP project work; contract drafting and negotiation; advisory work.
Litigation Commercial dispute resolution with particular expertise in construction, property, banking, insolvency, product liability, breach of contract and intellectual property.
Intellectual Property IT; computer law; biotechnology; advertising; sales promotions; marketing and trade description law is handled, including copyrights; film; television and entertainment products and services; multimedia exploitation; passing off; publishing; defamation; UK and EU competition.
Family Work includes divorce, children, financial provision, separation agreements, adoption, guardianship, affiliation proceedings and jurisdiction crossing.
Employment The firm deals with executive renumeration and benefits; service agreements; share options and other executive incentive schemes; termination packages; staff manuals; discrimination policies; unfair and wrongful dismissal claims in the Employment Tribunal, County and High Court.
Tax Areas covered include mergers and acquisitions; joint ventures; flotation planning; profit extraction; leasing; management buyouts; employee benefits; property tax; VAT planning; stamp duty planning; partnership tax; offshore trading agreements; insurance and tax; company pension schemes; tax appeals.
Personal Estate Planning The firm covers estate planning, preparation of wills, establishment of trusts, and the administration of estates and charities.

RECRUITMENT There are currently 17 trainee solicitors. The firm's Director of Education and Training has responsibility for directing and monitoring each individual's training. Application forms can be obtained by telephoning the recruitment line (020) 7872 8690 or by e-mailing sheona.boldero@manches.co.uk.

LAW FIRMS A-Z

M and A Solicitors

Kenneth Pollard House, 5-19 Cowbridge Road East, Cardiff, CF11 9AB
Tel (029) 2066 5793 **Fax** (029) 2066 5798
Email enquiries@manda.uk.com **Website** www.mandasolicitors.co.uk

Managing Partner	Stephen Berry
Senior Partner	Alan Whiteley
Number of partners	4
Associates	1
Assistant solicitors	2
Other fee-earners	1

THE FIRM M and A Solicitors is recognised as one of the leading corporate and commercial legal practices in Wales and the South West. Its niche specialist practice focuses on corporate, commercial and property transactions and projects. Recent successes have included advising on public funding raisings, joint ventures, management buyouts and large commercial property transactions. M and A Solicitors is able to offer an integrated legal and financial service in association with Gambit Corporate Finance.

Maples and Calder Europe

7 Princes Street, London, EC2R 8AQ
Tel (020) 7466 1600 **Fax** (020) 7466 1700
Email ukinfo@maplesandcalder.com **Website** www.maplesandcalder.com

Senior Partner	Anthony Travers
Number of partners	5
Associates	7
Other fee-earners	1
Number of partners (other offices)	19
Number of associates (other offices)	49

THE FIRM Maples and Calder Europe is a full execution office opened in 1997 as an affiliated office of Maples and Calder, the largest law firm in the Cayman Islands, to provide greater proximity to the firm's client base and enable the firm to provide time zone sensitive advice. Maples and Calder now has over 275 lawyers and staff worldwide. Advice is given to leading international and domestic law firms, major financial institutions and high net worth clients in relation to Cayman Islands law. The firm also offers a highly specialised management service to structured finance transactions through its controlling interest in QSPV Limited and QSPV (Jersey) Limited, licensed trust company administrators of Cayman Islands structured debt special purpose vehicles.

PRINCIPAL AREAS OF WORK Specialisations include banking, capital markets, structured debt, securitisation, asset financing, captive insurance, international equity offerings and listings, mutual and hedge funds, venture capital, commercial and private trusts and commercial and trust litigation.

MAPLES and CALDER Europe
Cayman Islands Attorneys-at-Law

INTERNATIONAL Maples and Calder in the Cayman Islands is based in George Town, Grand Cayman, and Maples and Calder Asia is based in Hong Kong.

Maples Teesdale

21 Lincoln's Inn Fields, London, WC2A 3DU
Tel (020) 7831 6501 **Fax** (020) 7405 3867 **DX** 192 London
Email enq@maplesteesdale.co.uk **Website** www.maplesteesdale.co.uk

AREAS OF PRACTICE	
Commercial Property	43%
Private Client	35%
Commercial Property Litigation	8%
Construction	7%
General Commercial	7%

Ptnrs 10 **Asst solrs** 7 **Other fee-earners** 10 **Contact** Andrew Whittaker • The firm's principal areas of work are commercial property and private client. The commercial property department includes a strong property litigation and construction team and deals with all aspects of property acquisition, disposal, development, funding and portfolio management. The private client department advises on all contentious and non-contentious aspects of family and private business affairs.

Margaret Bennett

Charlton House, 5A Bloomsbury Square, London, WC1A 2LX
Tel (020) 7404 6465 **Fax** (020) 7240 5492 **DX** 35740 Bloomsbury 1
Email exclusive@divorce.uk.com

Senior Partner	Margaret H Bennett
Number of partners	3
Assistant solicitors	4
Other fee-earners	2
AREAS OF PRACTICE	
Family Law	100%
CONTACTS	
Family Law	Margaret H Bennett

THE FIRM Established in 1990, as the first law firm practising exclusively in family law (uniquely with in-house divorce counselling as well), Margaret Bennett Solicitors provides outstanding experience in this specialist field. The principal, Margaret Bennett, is a former chairman of the Family Law committee of the International Bar Association and now chairman of its Hague Child Abduction Task Force; founder member and former vice-president of the International Academy of Matrimonial Lawyers; founder of the Institute of Family Mediation and Arbitration and a Deputy District Judge, Principal Registry of the Family Division, High Court, London. The consultant, John D Bieber is a former partner of Price Bieber and author of *If Divorce is the Only Way*, published by Penguin Books. The consultant counsellor, The Countess of Minto is former chairman of Marie Curie Cancer Care and Cruse Bereavement Care and a personal coach with Therapist U. In addition to counselling, Caroline Minto also deals with family mediation.

Continued overleaf

A-Z ■ LAW FIRMS

PRINCIPAL AREAS OF WORK
Family: Practising exclusively in family law, the firm's focus is on helping clients with the emotional burden of marital breakdown creating better awareness of client needs and how their problems may best be resolved. Selective with its clientele, Margaret Bennett Solicitors can devote the time and attention to each matter that it deserves. In complex international cases, the firm's work is facilitated by a close connection with family lawyers and other specialists around the world.

INTERNATIONAL Languages spoken include French, German and Italian.

■ Margetts & Ritchie
Coleridge Chambers, 177 Corporation Street, Birmingham, B4 6RL **Tel** (0121) 236 5517 **Fax** (0121) 236 5520

■ Margraves
Old Court Chambers, Llandrindod Wells, LD1 5EY **Tel** (01597) 825565 **Fax** (01597) 825220

Marriott Harrison
12 Great James Street, London, WC1N 3DR
Tel (020) 7209 2000 **Fax** (020) 7209 2001 **DX** 0001 London Chancery Lane
Email email@marriottharrison.co.uk **Website** www.marriottharrison.com

Managing Partner	Tony Morris
Number of partners	12
Assistant solicitors	8
Other fee-earners	5

AREAS OF PRACTICE	
Company & Commercial	50%
Commercial Media	30%
Litigation	15%
Property	5%

CONTACTS	
Company	Jon Sweet
Venture Capital	Duncan Innes
Media/Entertainment	Tony Morris
IT/Commercial	Mark Halama
Litigation	Peter Curnock
Property	Vivienne Elson

THE FIRM With the rapid growth of its corporate finance practice, the firm has now successfully repositioned itself as a leading corporate/media specialist law firm. Most of the partners have backgrounds with major City firms which they left with a commitment to provide a high quality personalised service to clients. Marriott Harrison's traditional client base of television and film production companies and broadcasters continues to generate significant corporate finance work. In addition to servicing the requirements of the media clients, the corporate department now has a significant client base of its own which includes, banks, venture capitalists, VCT's, financial institutions, private equity providers and new technology companies. The media group has broadened the range of its clientele beyond the film and television sectors to include all aspects of new media and e-commerce, information technology, the music industry, entertainment software and computer games, the internet, publishing, the visual and performing arts and other activities in which intellectual property rights play a key role. Regular referral work is received from overseas lawyers, particularly leading firms in the US, Canada and the EU. The firm has also significantly strengthened its litigation department through the appointment of two new partners with particular reference to intellectual property and its protection.

MARRIOTT HARRISON
SOLICITORS

PRINCIPAL AREAS OF WORK
Company & Commercial Company and commercial expertise is provided in such areas as mergers, acquisitions and disposals, management buyouts and venture capital, restructuring, banking and financial services, share option schemes, OFEX and AIM Listings. Recent projects include advising on the establishment of new funds such as VCT's and extensive work with those involved in the new technology sectors. The group is particularly strong in venture capital and corporate acquisitions both within and without the firm's media industry clients, which it increasingly supports in a broad range of complex commercial transactions, including the acquisition and disposal of companies whose assets include extensive portfolios of IP assets, such as sound recordings, software, computer games, films and TV programmes. Major projects undertaken in 2001 included the £107 million MBO of Albion Chemicals acting for Newco and management, the sale of Robertson Research Holdings Limited to Fugro N.V. for £70 million acting for vendors and representing management in the £34 million MBO of Eagle Rock Limited.
Commercial Media The commercial media team deals with all aspects of the creation and exploitation of content including films, television, music and sound recordings, computer games and software programs. In addition to negotiating contracts and advising on copyright and intellectual property rights and regulatory matters, the team applies its knowledge and experience of the way in which the business of the sectors function. The group has also developed an expertise in advising on large scale IT procurement contracts in respect of which it is generally retained by two major banks and one of the major record companies. Clients include multinational media corporations, cable channels and operators, television and film production companies, record companies and music publishers, computer games publishers and developers, software developers and IT providers, book and magazine publishers, photographers, website designers, authors, composers and performers, internet service providers and website designers.

Litigation The litigation group is widely experienced in commercial litigation with particular expertise in media-related cases and general intellectual property matters. Considerable work is undertaken in co-operation with US lawyers in international litigation involving intellectual property rights. There is a substantial proportion of interlocutory work seeking injunctive relief.

Property The property group supports the activities of the corporate and media teams, advising on a wide range of freehold and leasehold acquisitions and disposals.

Marrons

1 Meridian South, Meridian Business Park, Leicester, LE19 1WY
Tel (0116) 289 2200 **Fax** (0116) 289 3733 **DX** 710910 Leicester Meridian
Email enquiries@marrons.net **Website** www.marrons.net

Number of partners	7
Assistant solicitors	5
Other fee-earners	5

CONTACTS	
Commercial Property	Kevin Sumner
Planning	Morag Thomson
Judicial Review	Simon Stanion

THE FIRM Marrons is a niche practice with an excellent reputation for planning, public law, environmental law and development for which the firm has unrivalled depth of expertise. As advisors to Alconbury Developments Ltd, both at the planning inquiry and in the House of Lords human rights proceedings, Marrons has enhanced its considerable reputation throughout the UK. The RTPI publication *Planning* recently published a league table showing three of the partners as being amongst the highest rated individual planning solicitors as chosen by leading solicitors and planners. Marrons also has a thriving commercial property department and also provides commercial litigation support for its clients. The firm is deliberately located on junction 21 of the M1 motorway to allow national accessibility.

CLIENTELE Marrons acts on behalf of most of the major national house builders, a large number of prominent developers and local authorities.

Marrons
58 Jesmond Road West, Newcastle upon Tyne, NE2 4PQ **Tel** (0191) 281 1304 **Fax** (0191) 212 0080

Marshall Ross & Prevezer

4 Frederick's Place, London, EC2R 8AB
Tel (020) 7367 9000 **Fax** (020) 7367 9001 **DX** 133107 CHEAPSIDE 2
Email mail@mrp-law.co.uk

Senior Partner	Mark Prevezer
Managing Partner	Richard Marshall
Number of partners	8
Assistant solicitors	3
Consultants	4
Other fee-earners	8

THE FIRM Established in the early 1980s, Marshall Ross & Prevezer is a well-regarded City firm, which has attracted a strong property, corporate, commercial and private client base. The firm is best known for commercial property, company/commercial, commercial litigation (including insolvency and large debt recoveries), white collar crime, insurance litigation, franchise and trade finance. The firm also has strong overseas connections in India, China, Hong Kong, Africa, the United States, as well as most European countries. Acting for a number of household names Marshall Ross & Prevezer has grown on its reputation of being one of the youngest firms in the City, and for being able, as a result of its size, to give a personal and individual service to its clients at partner level.

Marsons Solicitors
Amadeus House, 33-39 Elmfield Road, Bromley, BR1 1LT **Tel** (020) 8313 1300 **Fax** (020) 8466 7920

A-Z ■ LAW FIRMS

Martineau Johnson

St Philips House, St Philips Place, Birmingham, B3 2PP
Tel (0121) 200 3300 **Fax** (0121) 200 3330 **DX** 721090 Birmingham 50
Email marketing@martjohn.com **Website** www.martineau-johnson.co.uk

78 Cannon Street, London, EC4N 6NQ
Tel (020) 7618 6610 **Fax** (020) 7618 8130 **DX** 42 London Chancery Lane
Email marketing@martjohn.com

Managing Partner	David Gwyther
Senior Partner	William Barker
Number of partners	46
Assistant solicitors	63
Other fee-earners	45

CONTACTS	
ADR	Andrew Spooner
Automotive	Geraldine Tickle
Banking & Insolvency	Ian Baker
Charities	Keith Dudley
Commercial	Roger Blears
Commercial Litigation	Andrew Spooner
Commercial Property	Simon Arrowsmith
Construction	Paul Mountain
Corporate Finance	Richard Wrigley
Debt Recovery	Andrew Adams
Education	Nicola Hart
Employment	Ian Marshall
Energy & Projects	Andrew Whitehead
Environmental	Simon Arrowsmith
EU & Competition	Geraldine Tickle
Financial Services	Enid Armstrong
Inheritance & Estates	Matthew Hansell
Intellectual Property	William Barker
IT/Computers	Tom McGuire
Licensing	Andrew Spooner
Life Sciences	Niall Head-Rapson
Pensions	Simon Laight
PFI	Andrew Whitehead
Professional Indemnity	David Gwyther
Property Litigation	Martin Edwards
Tax (Corporate)	Richard Pincher
Wills, Tax & Trusts	Matthew Hansell

THE FIRM As a full-service commercial law firm, Martineau Johnson's practice dates back to the early 19th century, but is now divided into teams operating in specialist focused areas of law. The firm's approach to business encourages continuity and the development of long-term relationships. This has formed the basis of the firm's expansion into new areas of activity. The firm is large enough to offer the specialist skills that clients demand and small enough to maintain partner contact at every level, whilst looking to introduce the lawyer into the bloodstream of the client's organisation and to become part of the decision-making process at the earliest stage. It has invested substantially in information technology and systems to ensure efficiency and more accessibility. It has recruited carefully to assemble teams which are experts not only in the law, but in the business and activities of the clients they represent. It has responded both to the needs of its clients and anticipated them. It does not pay lip service to the fashionable concept of partnership with clients. The firm's lawyers are business professionals who understand the importance of being part of their clients' team. What all their clients have in common is a need for solutions which address the key issues directly and solve their problems. Its service is based on people. They are team players and clients respond to this personal involvement; they know who they are dealing with. It is committed to working long-term with all clients. Whatever the nature of the case, it explores every angle in order to achieve the best possible result for clients. It has combined modern expertise with personal service and maintained the continuing contact for clients with the individual partner. Martineau Johnson addresses legal affairs via the know-how of specialist teams, works on behalf of its clients with passion and prides itself on its practicality and plain speaking. It's the way that Martineau Johnson conducts its business that distinguishes it, a method which has resulted in an impressive portfolio of done deals and a client list which is the envy of many other law firms.

INTERNATIONAL The firm is a founder member of MultiLaw, an international association of independent law firms, which has more than 55 members worldwide and enables it to deliver legal services internationally.

RECRUITMENT Committed to the personal supervision and training of trainees, the firm takes on 14 trainees per year. Each trainee has a mentor and benefits from a unique system of seat rotation. There is also a formal structured training programme. The majority of trainees stay with the firm after qualification. Those interested in applying for an open day or training contract should visit the firm's graduate website www.graduates4law.co.uk or email Emily Dean at emily.dean@martjohn.com.

Martin-Kaye

Hazledine House, Central Square, Telford Centre, Telford, TF3 4JL
Tel (01952) 291757 **Fax** (01952) 291759 **DX** 28073
Email law@martinkaye.co.uk **Website** www.martinkaye.co.uk

Ptnrs 6 **Asst solrs** 12 **Other fee-earners** 40 **Contact** Andrew Green • A progressive practice in the expanding new town of Telford dealing with all aspects of commercial, corporate, intellectual property, employment, litigation and property. Agency work is undertaken.

AREAS OF PRACTICE	
Commercial	40%
Bulk Conveyancing	20%
Bulk PI	20%
Trusts & Probate	10%
Family	10%

Martyn Prowel Solicitors

Hallinans House, 3rd Floor, 22 Newport Road, Cardiff, CF24 0TD
Tel (029) 2047 0909 **Fax** (029) 2049 8566 **DX** Cardiff 33037 **Email** enquiries@martynprowel.co.uk

Ptnrs 7 **Asst solrs** 6 **Other fee-earners** 5 **Contact** Martyn Prowel • Established in 1996 by three partners of the demerged Hallinans. Remaining at the same location, the new practice undertakes criminal, civil litigation, employment, family and conveyancing work.

AREAS OF PRACTICE	
Crime	30%
Civil Litigation	30%
Conveyancing	15%
Family	15%
Other	10%

LAW FIRMS ■ A-Z

■ Mason Bond

King Charles House, King Charles Croft, Leeds, LS1 6LA
Tel (0113) 242 4444 **Fax** (0113) 246 7542 **DX** 12064 Leeds 1
Email stephen@masonbond.co.uk **Website** www.masonbond.co.uk

Ptnrs 6 **Asst solrs** 3 **Other fee-earners** 5 **Contact** Stephen Mason • A leading young practice working nationwide in the holiday and travel industries including litigation, commercial and employment, plus family and childcare department.

■ Mason and Co

Bridge Street, Bakewell, DE45 1DS **Tel** (01629) 815175 **Fax** (01629) 815176

■ Mason & Moore Dutton

Kirkton House, 4 Hunter Street, Chester, CH1 2AS **Tel** (01244) 348881 **Fax** (01244) 351513

Masons

30 Aylesbury Street, London, EC1R 0ER
Tel (020) 7490 4000 **Fax** (020) 7490 2545 **DX** 53313 Clerkenwell
Website www.masons.com

1-4 Portland Square, Bristol, BS2 8RR
Tel (0117) 924 5678 **Fax** (0117) 924 6699 **DX** 78154 BRISTOL

18-22 Melville Street, Edinburgh, EH3 7NS (Regulated by the Law Society of Scotland)
Tel (0131) 225 0000 **Fax** (0131) 225 0099

33 Bothwell Street, Glasgow, G2 6NL (Regulated by the Law Society of Scotland)
Tel (0141) 248 4858 **Fax** (0141) 248 6655 **DX** GW74 Glasgow

Springfield House, 76 Wellington Street, Leeds, LS1 2AY
Tel (0113) 233 8905 **Fax** (0113) 245 4285 **DX** 706955 Leeds Park Square

100 Barbirolli Square, Manchester, M2 3SS
Tel (0161) 234 8234 **Fax** (0161) 234 8235 **DX** 14490 Manchester 2

Senior Partner	John Bishop
UK & Republic of Ireland Managing Partner	
	Peter Wood
Worldwide	
Number of partners	98
Assistant solicitors	209
Other fee-earners	85
Total staff	693

CONTACTS	
Commercial Dispute Resolution	
	Raymond Werbicki
Commercial Property & Development	
	Guy Jordan
Construction & Engineering	Martin Roberts
Corporate & Commercial	Russell Booker
Data Protection	Shelagh Gaskill
E-commerce & New Media	Jon Fell
	John Salmon
Employment	Michael Ryley
Energy	Peter Cassidy
Facilities Management	Joanna Higgins
Health & Safety	Karen Cooksley
Information & Technology	Robert McCallough
	Clive Seddon
Infrastructure	Ron Nobbs
Insolvency	Richard Williams
International Arbitration	Mark Roe
Pensions	Patrick Kennedy
Planning & Environment	Karen Cooksley
Projects & Finance	Chris Brown
Property Litigation	Siobhan Cross
Taxation	Stephen Lane

THE FIRM Masons is one of the most highly regarded specialist law firms in Europe and the Asia Pacific region. The firm's aim is to be recognised as pre-eminent advisors providing a complete range of legal services to businesses operating in the construction and engineering, energy, projects and infrastructure industries and to users and suppliers of information and technology. Masons lawyers are based in offices located in six prominent UK business regions in England and Scotland as well as elsewhere in Europe and Asia. The firm operates its UK practice on a 'one firm' approach with each office offering a national service. Resources can be provided from any office as necessary giving clients access to the widest possible range of knowledge available within the firm. International matters are handled by the firm's offices in Dublin, Brussels, Hong Kong, PRC and Singapore, as well as by the firm's UK based lawyers who work regularly in Continental and Central Europe, Scandinavia, the Middle East, the Pacific Rim, Latin America, Africa and the Indian subcontinent. Clients appoint Masons because of the depth of its industry knowledge and because of its commitment to provide legal and commercial advice of the highest quality. The firm is extremely proud to have worked on a number of the most exciting and innovative projects and feels privileged to have played a part in some of its clients' greatest achievements.

PRINCIPAL AREAS OF WORK

Masons provides a full legal service to businesses operating in the construction and engineering, energy, projects and infrastructure industries, to users and suppliers of information and technology and to any other clients wishing to draw on the skills of its specialist lawyers. Its range of services includes capital projects; commercial property and development, construction and engineering; corporate and commercial, e-commerce/new media; employment, data protection, dispute resolution (property and commercial), environment, facilities management, freedom of information; health and safety; information technology, insolvency, pensions, planning, project finance and taxation. Masons' Projects and Finance Group was awarded the accolade of 'Best Law Firm' at the Public Private Finance Awards 2001, as voted for by the Industry. Out-Law.com, the firm's innovative specialist e-commerce and new media service continues to win industry praise and has attracted in excess of 10,000 registered users.

MASONS

A-Z ■ LAW FIRMS

Matthew Arnold & Baldwin

21 Station Road, Watford, WD17 1HT
Tel (01923) 202020 **Fax** (01923) 215050 **DX** 4508 Watford
Email info@mablaw.co.uk **Website** www.mablaw.co.uk

Senior Partner	Richard Hanney
Number of partners	16
Assistant solicitors	22
Other fee-earners	32
AREAS OF PRACTICE	
Company Commercial	24%
Commercial Litigation/Banking/Debt Recovery	20%
Commercial Property & Estate Development	18%
Residential Conveyancing	12%
Tax, Trusts & Probate	10%
Insolvency	9%
Family & Childcare	6%
Intellectual Property & IT	4%
CONTACTS	
Commercial Litigation/Banking	Steven Mills
Commercial Property	Richard Hanney
Corporate	Richard A Phillips
Debt Collection	Laura Seaman
Employment	Alan Piper
Family	Richard J Phillips
Commercial & IT/E-commerce	Christopher Green
Insolvency & Corporate Reconstruction	Alistair Bacon
	Adrian Hyde
Intellectual Property	Clare Stothard
Licensing	Alan Piper
Residential Conveyancing & Estate Development	David Marsden
Tax, Trusts & Probate	Iain Donaldson

THE FIRM Based in Watford since its foundation in 1900, the firm's client base is now national and international. Matthew Arnold & Baldwin is recognised as the major firm in the region, and has established a considerable reputation for its commercial and private client services. As a member of both LawNet and Eurojuris International, the firm has developed strong links throughout Europe and in particular Scandinavia. The firm's commitment to quality and continuous improvement has been recognised by the award of the LawNet Quality Standard/ISO9002. The firm prides itself on forming strong relationships with its clients.

PRINCIPAL AREAS OF WORK

Commercial The commercial team is one of the largest in the region. The size and background of the team gives it the strength and depth to handle multiple, complex, commercial transactions. Some of the team has worked in-house and is widely respected for its commercial awareness. Specialist units dealing with employment, insolvency, IP, IT, commercial property and company secretarial support the team.

Information Technology Building on its long experience of the computer industry, the IT team has developed a reputation for its support of the e-commerce sector.

Commercial Litigation/Banking/Debt Recovery The commercial litigation, banking and debt recovery team is particularly well known for its recovery work for Barclays Bank and defence of other financial institutions. This large team has the depth and experience to handle all types of major commercial disputes, especially pre-emptive remedies.

Insolvency & Corporate Recovery As well as servicing the firm's banking and financial sector clients, the team is well regarded by corporate recovery specialists.

Commercial Property The commercial property team deals with all aspects of the acquisition, financing and disposal of freehold and leasehold property, from shops to large residential and industrial developments.

Intellectual Property The intellectual property team has created an enviable and much reported reputation for its contentious IP work. It advises both listed and small businesses in all areas of IP law. Clients include those in the media, healthcare and e-commerce sectors.

Employment & Employee Benefits The team supports the needs of personnel departments, and is noted for its work on restraints, on TUPE and in tribunals. Services for senior executives also feature in its workload, as does the creation of share and other employee benefit plans. The team includes HR professionals and an Employment Tribunal Chairman.

Private Client A full range of private client services is offered including residential conveyancing, family, and advice on personal tax, trusts and related financial planning.

■ Max Barford & Co

16 Mount Pleasant Road, Tunbridge Wells, TN1 1QU **Tel** (01892) 539379 **Fax** (01892) 521874

Max Bitel, Greene

1 Canonbury Place, London, N1 2NG
Tel (020) 7354 2767 **Fax** (020) 7226 1210 **DX** 51852 Highbury
Email office@mbg.co.uk **Website** www.mbg.co.uk

Managing Partner	Ean Reid
Senior Partner	Max Bitel
Number of partners	7
Assistant solicitors	2
Other fee-earners	3
CONTACTS	
Commercial Property	Colin Ledward
Company/Commercial	Brian Levy
Insolvency	Nicholas Bitel
Matrimonial/Litigation	Ean Reid
Private Client	Ean Reid
Sports Law	Mel Goldberg

THE FIRM Founded in 1954 moving from High Holborn to Canonbury in 1981 this seven partner firm has a growing commercial and private client practice including commercial property, company, commercial litigation and matrimonial work. The firm has niche specialisations in insolvency law and sports law and has been recently joined by leading sports lawyer Mel Goldberg. Clients include Wimbledon All England Lawn Tennis & Croquet Club, P.G.A. European Tour and London Marathon, and well known sporting and media personalities. The firm recruits one trainee per year.

■ The Max Gold Partnership

Suffolk House, 21 Silver Street, Hull, HU1 1JG **Tel** (01482) 224900 **Fax** (01482) 216068

Maxwell Batley

27 Chancery Lane, London, WC2A 1PA
Tel (020) 7440 4400 **Fax** (020) 7440 4444 **DX** 190 London Chancery Lane WC2
Email mailroom@maxwellbatley.com **Website** www.maxwellbatley.com

Senior Partner	Raymond Levine
Number of partners	17
Assistant solicitors	7
Other fee-earners	9

AREAS OF PRACTICE	
Property & Construction	40%
Company/Commercial	20%
Banking	12%
Litigation & Employment	20%
Private Client	8%

CONTACTS	
Banking	Fraser McColl
Commercial Property	Nigel Wilson
Company/Commercial	Ian McIntyre
Construction & Property Development	Raymond Levine
Employment	Philip Wood
Litigation	Philip Knights
Private Client	Frank O'Shea

THE FIRM Maxwell Batley is a multidisciplinary City law firm with highly regarded commercial property expertise and a strong reputation in corporate, banking, litigation and private client work. The firm is known for working in partnership with clients and for providing a partner-led service, using the latest technology. Maxwell Batley takes a business-like approach to the law, by offering practical, innovative advice, good value for money and prompt service.

PRINCIPAL AREAS OF WORK

Property & Construction The firm's largest discipline is recognised as a real alternative to the large international firms. Advice is based on the assessment of risk in a competitive and commercial context – not merely legal analysis. The group has substantial experience in acquisitions and sales, property finance and development, joint ventures, landlord and tenant matters and portfolio management. A key expertise is construction work. Clients include leading pension funds, institutional investors, and blue chip property companies, developers and occupiers of all types of property. A wide range of innovative transactions is handled, including development finance transactions and setting up of creative structures to deal with the joint ownership of property. The group advises on the use of various types of corporate and non-corporate vehicles, ensuring that the right balance between risk, control and taxation is achieved in the structure adopted. The group also acts extensively for smaller investors and occupiers. The commercial property group includes a retail unit, which specialises in the acquisition, management and disposal of shopping centres and retail premises and acts for occupiers.

Banking & Finance The group works extensively with both UK and international banks and financial institutions, as well as their clients in all types of banking and financial transactions. It provides an expert, cost-effective service, enabling clients to achieve their commercial objectives with their interests being fully protected. Transactions handled include secured and unsecured lending, project finance, structured finance, acquisition finance, portfolio acquisitions and securitisations.

Company & Commercial The group adopts a practical approach, working closely with its clients to achieve their commercial aims. It advises on mergers and acquisitions, venture capital, loan capital, management buyouts, PFI, local authority and competitive tendering, distribution and marketing agreements, information technology and insolvency. The corporate finance team advises companies and their financial advisors on flotations, takeovers, placings and rights issues. The group also advises on joint ventures, shareholder agreements and the resolution of corporate disputes.

Litigation & Dispute Resolution The aim is to prevent contentious situations arising. Where they do arise, expert representation in tribunal or court applications is provided. The group acts for institutional, corporate and private clients and particularly strong on property-related litigation, including construction disputes. It also handles banking, commercial disputes, insolvency, partnership disputes, professional negligence and general insurance work (including employers and product liability claims).

Employment The employment group provides comprehensive, pragmatic advice to business and private clients on the whole range of employment-related law. It advises on service and consultancy agreements, recruitment and all areas of remuneration, including changes in terms of conditions. The group's expertise extends to intellectual property matters, restrictive covenants, maternity and discrimination issues.

Private Client The group provides a comprehensive service for private capital and family affairs. It deals with estate planning, trusts, probate and wills, both UK and offshore, and capital tax planning; charities; residential conveyancing for offshore buyers, sellers and lenders as well as UK based.

Maxwell MacLaurin
100 West Regent Street, Glasgow, G2 2QB **Tel** (0141) 332 5566 **Fax** (0141) 332 6757

A-Z ■ LAW FIRMS

Mayer, Brown, Rowe & Maw

11 Pilgrim Street, London EC4V 6RW
Tel (020) 7248 4282 **Fax** (020) 7248 2009 **DX** 93
Email london@eu.mayerbrownrowe.com **Website** www.mayerbrownrowe.com

Canada House, 3 Chepstow Street, Manchester, M1 5FW
Tel (0161) 236 1612 **Fax** (0161) 236 9712

Suite 892-894, Lloyds, One Lime Street, London, EC3M 7QD
Tel (020) 7327 4144 **Fax** (020) 7623 7965

Senior Partner	Stuart James
UK	
Number of partners	91
Assistant solicitors	168
Other fee-earners	82
International	
Number of partners	330
Assistant solicitors	700
Other fee-earners	2300

CONTACTS	
Aviation & Transport	Paul Maher
Construction Litigation	Michael Regan
Corporate Finance	Stephanie Bates
Employment	Julian Roskill
Environment	Cate Sharp
EU/Competition	Kiran Desai
Finance	Ian Coles
Insolvency	David Allen
Insurance	Sean Connolly
Intellectual Property	Stephen Gare
Litigation & Dispute Resolution	David Allen
	Sean Connolly
Mergers & Acquisitions	Paul Maher
Partnership	Richard Linsell
Pensions	Stuart James
Public & Administrative	Tony Child
Tax	Peter Steiner

THE FIRM Mayer, Brown Rowe & Maw is a leading international law firm. With over 400 partners and 1300 lawyers globally, the firm serves its international client-base from 13 international offices including representation in the world's major financial centres; London, Paris, Frankfurt and New York. The London office consists of 90 partners, over 300 lawyers in total and 600 staff. On the 1st February, leading UK law firm Rowe & Maw and top 10 American law firm Mayer, Brown & Platt joined forces to create Mayer, Brown, Rowe & Maw, a top 10 international law firm by size and revenue. The firm has an excellent reputation in a diverse range of practice areas, receiving recognition in numerous prestigious legal awards, which have included, Insurance Team of the Year 2001 (*The Lawyer*) for its innovative use of web technology and cutting edge service to the insurance and reinsurance markets, nomination for Corporate Team of the Year 2001 (*The Lawyer*), nomination for Law Firm of the Year 2001 (The Chambers Directory) and runners-up for Litigation Team of the Year 2002 (*Legal Business*).

PRINCIPAL AREAS OF WORK Major practice groups in the firm's London office include: corporate and securities, litigation and arbitration, finance and banking, IP, IT and outsourcing, real estate, construction, employment, insurance and reinsurance, anti-trust and trade, tax, environment and securitisation.

Corporate & Securities The corporate and securities group is one of the largest in London with 31 partners and over 100 lawyers and is highly regarded by independent commentators. In recognition of its ability to advise clients on complex cross-border transactions, it was short-listed for the 2001 Corporate Team of the Year Award. In addition to all aspects of corporate, private equity and securities work, the group is known to be a leader in the chemicals and telecommunications sectors. Major clients include Reuters, Marconi, ICI, AstraZeneca, Syngenta, and Cable & Wireless.

Litigation & Dispute Resolution The litigation and dispute resolution group has over 100 lawyers in the London office. In addition to general litigation, arbitration and mediation, the group offers specialist teams in insolvency and corporate restructuring, insurance and reinsurance, public law, property litigation, construction and professional indemnity. Clients include AIG, Bank of America, GEC, NBC and AXA.

Real Estate The real estate group comprises over 30 lawyers and deals with all aspects of property-related work including planning, property finance, investment, development, retail and industrial, commercial and environmental. Major clients include Unilever, British Gas, Nationwide Building Society, EMI, The Football Association, Rolls Royce and HMV.

Pensions, Employment & Construction The pensions, employment and construction practices have long been regarded as top tier within the UK legal market place. Other teams such as the environment and public law are enjoying a similar status. Intellectual property and IT are growing strengths within the London office, as the team has doubled in 18 months to approximately 30 lawyers. Trademarks, patents and the transfer of rights in M&A work are specialties, as is the clearance of advertising copy. Advertising, music and publishing are also industry sectors of focus. Mayer, Brown, Rowe & Maw is also a member of the *Ius Laboris International Alliance*, which is based in Brussels. This membership enables the firm to offer a pan-European advisory service to clients on employment, pensions and employee benefits. It currently comprises leading law firms in France, Germany, Italy, Belgium, Holland, Spain, Denmark and Luxembourg and consists of almost 400 employment and pensions lawyers based in nearly 40 cities throughout Europe.

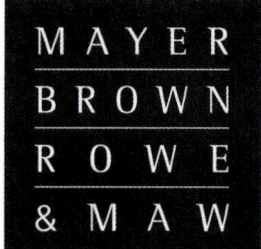

CLIENTELE Mayer, Brown, Rowe & Maw represents major multinational corporations. The London client base includes numerous FTSE 250 companies including Cable & Wireless, General Electric, ICI, Reuters, Unilever, EMI, BP, NBC, Marconi, Ernst & Young, Bank of America and AstraZeneca. The firm also advises a wide range of companies including business start-ups, joint ventures, partnerships and major financial institutions. Much of the work is cross-border and multijurisdictional. In addition to the other Mayer, Brown, Rowe & Maw offices in Brussels, Paris, Frankfurt and Cologne, the firm's London team has a network of well-established contacts throughout Europe to assist in regional matters.

LAW FIRMS ■ A-Z

May, May & Merrimans

12 South Square, Gray's Inn, London, WC1R 5HH
Tel (020) 7405 8932 **Fax** (020) 7831 0011 **DX** 225 London
Email mmm@elawuk.com

THE FIRM Founded in 1786, May, May & Merrimans is best known for its private client work, offering a high quality personal service to individuals and families, some of whom are the owners of substantial residential and agricultural estates, including heritage property. The firm brings the same quality of service to its corporate clients and undertakes a broad range of company and commercial business.

PRINCIPAL AREAS OF WORK

Private Client Specialist advice includes estate planning, will drafting, the creation and variation of all types of settlements including offshore and charitable trusts, and personal and estate taxation. A considerable volume of probate work is handled, often involving large estates which may include overseas property.

Property A full range of property work is undertaken, ranging from new town sites to mineral excavations, office and shop leases, agricultural tenancies, estate sales and substantial domestic conveyancing transactions.

Litigation The litigation element of the practice deals with most types of contentious civil law, including landlord and tenant issues, negligence claims, employment, defamation and general commercial disputes.

Matrimonial This department handles all aspects of family law, including marriage breakdown and related financial issues, disputes involving children and Inheritance Act claims.

Company & Commercial The firm can assist in the formation of companies and partnerships, in the sale and acquisition of existing enterprises and in all matters which arise in the course of running a business or private company, including share issues, the drafting of contracts and employment questions.

Senior Partner	Christopher Walsh
Number of partners	12
Assistant solicitors	5
Other fee-earners	2

AREAS OF PRACTICE	
Private Client (Tax, Trust & Probate)	50%
Property (Domestic, Agricultural & Commercial)	30%
Litigation/Matrimonial	15%
Company/Commercial	5%

CONTACTS	
Civil Litigation	Sarah Gillette
Company/Commercial	Alexandra Sarkis
Family/Matrimonial	Susan Black
Private Client	Giles Gostwick
Property	Sandy Schofield

McClenahan Crossey & Co

41 New Row, Coleraine, BT52 1AE **Tel** (028) 7034 3491 **Fax** (028) 7034 2377

McCloskeys

Rochester Building, 28 Adelaide Street, Belfast, BT2 8GD
Tel (028) 9024 0310 **Fax** (028) 9024 0312 **DX** 495 NR Belfast 1
Email mccloskeys@mccloskeys.co.uk

THE FIRM McCloskeys is a long established and predominantly defendant-focused litigation practice. Litigation clients include UK insurers, Lloyds syndicates and government bodies.

PRINCIPAL AREAS OF WORK The firm is one of Northern Ireland's leading insurance litigation practices. It has expertise in professional negligence, public liability, employers' liability, product liability, road traffic claims, and all other areas of insurance litigation. It has developed a particular expertise in dealing with the defence of fraudulent fire claims.

Senior Partner	Joseph McGuigan
Number of partners	2
Assistant solicitors	3

AREAS OF PRACTICE	
Professional Negligence	40%
Other Defence Negligence	40%
General	20%

CONTACTS	
Other Defence Litigation	Hugh McGrattan
Professional Negligence	Joseph McGuigan

A-Z ■ LAW FIRMS

McClure Naismith

49 Queen Street, Edinburgh, EH2 3NH
Tel (0131) 220 1002   **Fax** (0131) 220 1003   **DX** 135 Edinburgh
Email Edinburgh@McClureNaismith.com   **Website** www.mcclurenaismith.com

Pountney Hill House, 6 Laurence Pountney Hill, London, EC4R OBL
Tel (020) 7623 9155   **Fax** (020) 7623 9154   **DX** 764 CDE London
Email London@McClureNaismith.com

292 St Vincent Street, Glasgow, G2 5TQ
Tel (0141) 204 2700   **Fax** (0141) 248 3998   **DX** 64 Glasgow
Email Glasgow@McClureNaismith.com

Senior Partner	Kenneth Chrystie
Number of partners	24
Assistant solicitors	42
Other fee-earners	22

AREAS OF PRACTICE	
Litigation	25%
Commercial Property	25%
Corporate/Commercial	25%
Banking/Finance	10%
Private Client	10%
Intellectual Property	5%

CONTACTS	
Banking/Asset Finance	John Blackwood
Commercial Property	Wilson Aitken
Consumer Credit/Debt	Frank Johnstone
Corporate/Commercial	Kenneth Chrystie
Employment	Alan Thomson
Intellectual Property	Kenneth Chrystie
Litigation	William Walker
Private Client	Gordon Shearer
Project Finance/PFI	Steven Brown

THE FIRM McClure Naismith is a commercial law firm providing a wide range of legal services to its clients in Scotland, England and overseas. Through its membership of the World Law Group the firm accesses a worldwide network covering all major jurisdictions in the Americas, Europe and the Far East. McClure Naismith continues to develop its range of specialist commercial services and its reputation for a determined approach to achieve results for clients. All of its offices have grown substantially in the last three years including the London office, which provides a full range of English law advice in the fields of corporate, banking, commercial property and commercial litigation.

PRINCIPAL AREAS OF WORK

Corporate/Commercial The firm advises on all aspects of corporate and commercial law. It has a particularly strong reputation for handling complex commercial negotiations and commercial contracts. Specialist advice is offered on corporate finance; MBOs and MBIs; mergers, acquisitions and joint ventures; shareholder disputes; agency distribution and licensing contracts; insolvency; competition law; and oil and gas developments. Industrial expertise handles mining, transport, pharmaceuticals, distilling and electronic sectors.

Project Finance & PFI Project finance advice is given to companies promoting infrastructure projects principally in the energy and water industries in the UK and overseas, as well as a range of public sector organisations, construction consortia and banks in PFI projects, mainly in the health, water and education sectors.

Commercial Property The firm handles property development work for institutional, corporate and private clients including site acquisition; sale and leasing; secured lending and funding; factory, shop and office developments; private sector rented housing contracts; housing associations; joint venture agreements. The firm advises landlords and tenants on commercial, agricultural and residential leasing and environmental law.

Litigation Litigation work of all types is undertaken in all courts, tribunals and inquiries throughout Scotland and in the High Court and county courts in England. The firm is well regarded for its personal injury/reparation practice acting for many leading defence insurers. It also covers property planning and construction litigation, intellectual property disputes and matrimonial and family litigation.

Consumer Credit/Debt Recovery The group handles mainly UK leading finance houses, leasing companies and banks and advises the Consumer Credit Trade Association. The firm is a member of the Finance and Leasing Association. It gives advice on drafting credit documentation and increasingly on data protection issues and also provides volume debt and asset recovery services to a wide range of commercial and financial companies.

Banking & Asset Finance The firm acts for many UK and overseas banks, including all of the Scottish clearing banks, on secured lending, corporate lending and asset finance as well as in relation to PFI projects. Contentious banking/recovery work is also carried out for leading banks and building societies.

Employment In this growing area of practice the firm principally advises employers on all aspects of employment law, contentious and non-contentious, including drafting terms and conditions of employment, advice on individual employment rights, claims for unfair and wrongful dismissal and common law claims before employment tribunals and courts throughout the UK.

Intellectual Property The firm has considerable expertise in negotiating licence agreements for client companies worldwide and for its handling of IP disputes including patent infringement, breach of copyright or trademark and passing off. It has a growing practice in computer contracts and e-commerce.

Private Client The firm offers advice on estate planning, wills, trusts and executries, insurance, pensions, investments and the purchase sale and leasing of residential property.

LAW FIRMS ■ A-Z

McCormacks

122 Mile End Road, London, E1 4UN
Tel (020) 7791 2000   Fax (020) 7790 5846   DX 300704 Tower Hamlets
Email lawyers@mccormacks.co.uk   Website www.mccormacks.co.uk

86 Long Lane, London, EC1 9ET

49 Queen Victoria Street, London, EC4N 4SE

74-76 Town Square, Basildon, SS14 1DT

10 Stepney Green, London, E1 3JU

Senior Partner	Ugo Palazzo
Number of partners	4
Assistant solicitors	16
Other fee-earners	7

AREAS OF PRACTICE	
Criminal Litigation	85%
Family Litigation	15%

CONTACTS	
Serious Fraud	Ugo Palazzo
Crime	Andrew Palazzo
Advocacy Unit	Hugh Mullan
Employment Law	Tayab Ali
Mental Health	Richard Conley
Barristers	Gary Pons

THE FIRM An outstanding reputation in crime. The founding office is still based in the heart of London's east end. The firm specialises in high-end advocacy and complex casework with six higher courts advocates.

PRINCIPAL AREAS OF WORK
Criminal Law All areas, with particular expertise in serious and complex crime casework including defence in serial murder, importation of drugs, major fraud, terrorism, extradition.
Family Law Childcare, adoption, injunctions.
Employment Tayab Ali is the firm's rising star in this rapidly expanding department.

McCormicks

Britannia Chambers, 4 Oxford Place, Leeds, LS1 3AX
Tel (0113) 246 0622   Fax (0113) 246 7488   DX 26527 Leeds Park Square
Email enquiries@mccormicks-solicitors.com   Website www.mccormicks-solicitors.com

Wharfedale House, 37 East Parade, Harrogate, HG1 5LQ
Tel (01423) 530630   Fax (01423) 530709   DX 11974 Harrogate 1
Email d.ezard@mccormicks-solicitors.com   Website www.mccormicks-solicitors.com

Managing & Senior Partner	Peter McCormick OBE
Number of partners	11
Assistant solicitors	13
Other fee-earners	13

AREAS OF PRACTICE	
Company/Commercial & Litigation	75%
Matrimonial, Private Client & Conveyancing	15%
Criminal (Fraud & Tax)	10%

CONTACTS	
Charity	Peter McCormick OBE
Commercial Litigation	Roger Hutton
Company/Commercial (inc. Property)	Clive Lawrence
	Richard Moran
Debt Collection	David Arundel
Defamation	Peter McCormick OBE
	Clive Lawrence
Employment	Neil Goodrum
European Law	Richard Moran
Family/Matrimonial	Mark Burns
	Geoffrey Rogers
Insolvency	Roger Hutton
	David Arundel
Intellectual Property & IT	Clive Lawrence
	Richard Moran
Media & Entertainment Law	
	Peter McCormick OBE
	Clive Lawrence
Partnership	Peter McCormick OBE
Personal Injury	Neil Goodrum
Serious Fraud	Geoffrey Rogers
	Robert Rode
Sports Law	Peter McCormick OBE
	Clive Lawrence
Wills & Trusts	Sara Rogers

THE FIRM McCormicks is a high-profile, progressive and highly regarded firm, which has expanded by planned organic growth to attain a reputation for expertise in a number of fields. It has offices in Leeds and Harrogate and associated offices throughout Europe. It offers a comprehensive range of legal services, both to its national and international corporate clients as well as to many notable private clients. It has been described in a survey of the law firms in Yorkshire and Humberside by the *Yorkshire Post* as 'a law firm in the top rank' and by Yorkshire Television as 'one of the region's top law firms'. The firm is admired for its continued ability to operate successfully in the company and commercial field, whilst at the same time maintaining its commitment to the private client. The average age of the partners is 35, and the firm has a reputation for a vibrant and dynamic atmosphere. Currently, company/commercial and litigation account for 75% of the fee income, criminal (serious fraud, tax cases and complex criminal matters) 10% and matrimonial, private client and conveyancing 15%. Partners hold the Higher Courts Qualification, memberships of the Law Society's Personal Injury, Family and Childcare panels and Fellowship of the Chartered Institute of Arbitrators; partners are also trained and experienced in mediation and alternative dispute resolution. The firm is a member of the Law Society's Accident Line scheme. Both the Leeds and Harrogate practices were the first in the region to be awarded Legal Aid franchises and membership of the Law Society's Family Law Scheme. The firm has strengthened its corporate recovery department dealing with all aspects of insolvency work with personnel having worked on the Maxwell and BCCI cases.

PRINCIPAL AREAS OF WORK Commercial litigation, company and commercial, corporate and white collar crime including VAT and Inland Revenue investigation work and tribunals, debt collection and mortgage repossession, employment, European law, family law, intellectual property, IT, media and entertainment, partnership, property, sports law (one of the premier practices in the country), insolvency, personal injury, general crime (especially road traffic), private client, defamation, charity law. Agency instructions welcomed.

INTERNATIONAL Associated offices in France, Germany, The Netherlands, Belgium, Eire, Spain, Italy, Portugal and Gibraltar. Fluent French, German, Italian and Spanish spoken.

www.ChambersandPartners.com

A-Z ■ LAW FIRMS

■ McCourts
53 George IV Bridge, Edinburgh, EH1 1EJ **Tel** (0131) 225 6555 **Fax** (0131) 225 5054

■ McDermott, Will & Emery
7 Bishopsgate, London, EC2N 3AR
Tel (020) 7577 6900 **Fax** (020) 7577 6950 **DX** 42619 Cheapside
Website www.mwe.com/london

THE FIRM McDermott, Will & Emery is one of the largest international law firms, with more than 900 lawyers in 10 offices worldwide. The global practice is founded on the calibre of the firm's lawyers and its practical, integrated and responsive approach.

PRINCIPAL AREAS OF WORK The London office, which has a full service commercial capability, provides cutting edge legal advice to multinational and national corporates, financial institutions, investment banks and private clients.

Banking, Capital Markets & Finance Eurobond issues, MTN and ECP programmes, syndicated and bilateral loans, acquisition and venture capital finance, asset and project finance, structured finance, swaps, derivatives and other treasury products, treasury management and electronic banking, and the regulation of the UK's banking and financial services sectors.

Communications Communications-related contracts and commercial transactions. The firm provides strategic and regulatory advice on telecommunications and broadcasting activities. Extensive experience acting for numerous companies entering the UK, European and international communications markets, including international telecoms operators, internet providers, equipment suppliers and electricity companies.

Corporate Finance/Mergers & Acquisitions/Securities General corporate issues; domestic and cross-border mergers and acquisitions, international equity offerings, flotations, corporate restructurings, private equity investments, joint ventures and strategic alliances and takeover bids (including taking companies private). Advice on the full range of securities law issues which may arise in the UK or in cross-border contexts. The firm provides effective cross-border and multijurisdictional transaction management with full service US and English law expertise.

E-Business B2C and B2B advice spanning multinational corporates, ISPs, dot.coms, media, marketing and IT companies. Advice covering data protection, "e"-law, portal set up, PKI security, website audits, trading exchanges and cross-border advice on e-business issues.

Employment Wrongful and unfair dismissal, executive severance, breach of contract, confidentiality and restrictive covenants, breaches of fiduciary duty, fraud by employees, sex/race/disability discrimination, union recognition and works councils, industrial disputes, EU employment law, corporate governance, TUPE and the employment, employee benefits and data protection aspects of acquisitions.

EU Competition Full range of competition law representation in Brussels, the EU and US. The firm's service includes counselling, merger control, transaction structuring arrangements and representation in contentious matters.

Intellectual Property/Information Technology Expertise in IP litigation, especially patents and trademarks, acting across EU competition law, patent and trademark prosecution and oppositions, general IP and IT advisory and commercial work with special expertise in finance and banking, data protection, advertising/marketing, e-Business and internet trading advice, UK and EU pharmaceuticals and agrochemicals substantive and regulatory law.

Litigation Commercial disputes, both in the UK and internationally and in public international law. The firm litigates in all UK courts and is also involved in international arbitrations. Presently, the firm is advising in disputes concerning international trade, complex contracts, shareholder/boardroom issues, environmental issues, fraud, technology and media.

Pensions Pensions aspects of mergers, acquisitions, disposals, flotations, MBOs and MBIs; litigation and Pensions Ombudsman disputes; investment management and custody agreements; issues affecting internationally mobile employees; mergers, reorganisations and terminations; design and establishment of new plans; best practice audits; outsourcing from the public sector to the private sector.

Taxation Multidisciplinary service on all UK and international tax especially in relation to corporate and commercial business matters, including mergers and acquisitions, spin-offs, flotations, corporate structuring, asset and structured finance, treasury management, cross-border transactions, and transfer pricing.

INTERNATIONAL The firm has global reach. From its extensive network of offices in the US and growing number of offices in Europe, the firm advises on numerous transjurisdictional transactions, assignments and cases.

Senior Partner	William Charnley
Managing Partner	John Reynolds
UK	
Number of partners	21
Associate lawyers	45
Other fee-earners	7
Total	73
International	
Number of partners	532
Associate lawyers and other fee-earners	551
Total	1083

CONTACTS

Banking & International Capital Markets	
	Graham Rowbotham
	Andrew Watson
	Chris Forrest
Communications/Media & Technology	
	Stephanie Liston
Corporate/Corporate Finance/Commercial	
	William Charnley
	Rick Mitchell
E-Business/Marketing & Advertising	
	Rafi Azim-Khan
Employment	Fraser Younson
	David Dalgarno
	Alison Wetherfield
EU Competition	Scott Megregian
Financial Markets Technology	Phillip Rees
Information Technology	Phillip Rees
Intellectual Property/Biotech & Pharmaceuticals	Larry J Cohen
Insolvency	Graham Rowbotham
	Rick Mitchell
	Chris Forrest
Litigation	John Reynolds
Mergers & Acquisitions	William Charnley
MBOs	William Charnley
Pensions & Employee Benefits	Steven Hull
Projects & Project Finance	Andrew Watson
US Securities	Rick Mitchell
	Daniel Rabinowitz
Taxation	Peter Nias

McDermott, Will & Emery

LAW FIRMS ■ A-Z

■ McGrath & Co
4th Floor, King Edward House, 135a New Street, Birmingham, B2 4QJ **Tel** (0121) 643 4121 **Fax** (0121) 624 1060

■ McGrigor Donald
Pacific House, 70 Wellington Street, Glasgow, G2 6SB
Tel (0141) 248 6677 **Fax** (0141) 248 1301 **DX** GW135 Glasgow 1
Email enquiries@mcgrigors.com **Website** www.mcgrigors.com

Princes Exchange, 1 Earl Grey Street, Edinburgh, EH3 9AQ
Tel (0131) 777 7000 **Fax** (0131) 777 7003 **DX** ED723301 Edinburgh43

2 Donegall Square East, Belfast, BT1 5HB
Tel (028) 9027 8800 **Fax** (028) 9027 8811 **DX** 539NR

Senior Partner, Scotland	Shonaig Macpherson
Managing Partner, Scotland	Kirk Murdoch
Total Staff	
Scotland	346
UK (KLegal International)	636

CONTACTS

Banking & Finance	Colin McKay
Commercial Litigation	Craig Connal QC
Construction	Brandon Nolan
Corporate & Commercial	Morag McNeill
Employment	Jim Young
IP	Shonaig Macpherson
MDr (Human Rights)	Professor Alan Miller
MDTS (Training Services)	Stuart Neilson
Projects/PPP	Jim Smith
Project Finance	Colin McKay
Real Estate	Philip Burroughs
Public Law	Alan Boyd
MDPP (Public Policy)	Adam Bruce
Tax & Pensions	Ian Gordon
Technology	Shonaig Macpherson

THE FIRM McGrigor Donald is one of the top legal firms in Scotland and since opening in Belfast in January 2000 it has become a significant practice in Northern Ireland. The firm provides a complete range of corporate legal services for a wide client base and has a reputation for providing excellent technical legal service. The firm's success can be attributed to the business and commercial acumen of its lawyers allied to a strong commitment to working alongside its clients to help them achieve their business objectives. In March 2002, the McGrigor Donald London practice merged with KLegal and the McGrigor Donald practices in Scotland and Northern Ireland became members of KLegal International. KLegal and McGrigor Donald have an executive body in the UK that will ensure consistency of approach and quality standards. The firm feels this to be very important considering the majority of clients operate throughout the UK and beyond and want a level and depth of service to match. The practice in England operates as KLegal and the practices in Scotland and Northern Ireland as McGrigor Donald. KLegal International operates with over 3000 lawyers in over 50 jurisdictions including Europe, Australasia, South America, and the Far East. In turn this gives the firm's clients access to international services and, through the association of KLegal International with KPMG, the firm can offer its clients the benefit of extra knowledge and skills as appropriate to the development of their businesses. It also gives McGrigor Donald employees an opportunity to develop their careers in an international environment. On a UK level the combined firm has a total of 72 partners and over 350 fee-earners. The provision of legal services is changing and the firm is at the forefront of new electronic delivery systems. Using document management systems and through the firm's internet based extranet system (MDeX) it provides secure deal rooms and knowledge databases and is working in partnership with many key clients to provide more efficient and effective services.

PRINCIPAL AREAS OF WORK
Current practice areas split into three practice groups: corporate, infrastructure and dispute resolution managed on a UK basis by Coin Gray, Colin McKay and Brandon Nolan respectively. Practice areas operating under these heading specialities include banking and finance; company and commercial; employment; financial regulation; intellectual property; IT and telecoms; planning and environment; project finance/PPP; public law and human rights; and tax litigation. Clients include national to multinational corporations, government bodies, banks and financial institutions, internet start-ups and entrepreneurs. Clients are introduced to the firm from a variety of sources, predominantly through external sources but also via KPMG and KLegal International member firms.

RECRUITMENT The firm is actively seeking exceptional lawyers at all levels from partner to recently qualified. Applications are invited from ambitious and energetic lawyers with good academic backgrounds (min 2:1) and outstanding experience gained in either private practice or industry who are attracted by the prospect of working in a dynamic, cutting-edge environment. Please apply to Rosalind Jamieson (Human Resources) or Kate Hedstrom (Graduate Recruitment).

McGrigor Donald

■ McKay Norwell WS
5 Rutland Square, Edinburgh, EH1 2AS **Tel** (0131) 222 8000 **Fax** (0131) 222 8008

A-Z ■ LAW FIRMS

McKenzie Bell

19 John St, Sunderland, SR1 1JG
Tel (0191) 567 4857   **Fax** (0191) 510 9347   **DX** 60719
Email mckbell@dial.pipex.com

Managing Partner	Paul Heron
Senior Partner	William Temperley
Number of partners	8
Assistant solicitors	2
Other fee-earners	5

THE FIRM McKenzie Bell has been established in Sunderland for well over 100 years, providing legal services throughout the North East. Other offices: Washington.

PRINCIPAL AREAS OF WORK

Company/Commercial: Work undertaken by the department includes commercial leases, partnerships, limited companies, business transfers and contracts.
Property: A full range of residential and commercial property services are offered.
Litigation: Full range of civil and criminal work undertaken. The firm has a Legal Aid franchise.
Private Client: Advice includes matters relating to family/matrimonial law, childcare, landlord and tenant, employment, wills, trusts and probate.
Licensing: The firm undertakes work regarding all aspects of the application for, or opposition to, liquor, betting and public entertainment licences.

McKinty and Wright

5-7 Upper Queen Street, Belfast, BT1 6FS
Tel (028) 9024 6751   **Fax** (028) 9023 1432   **DX** 510 NR Belfast 1
Email post@mckinty-wright.co.uk   **Website** www.mckinty-wright.co.uk

Senior Partner	John Cross
Number of partners	11
Assistant solicitors	11
Other fee-earners	7
CONTACTS	
Commercial Property	Ivan Frazer
Company/Commercial	Eric Boyd
Litigation	Paul J Johnston

THE FIRM McKinty and Wright is a Belfast-based firm with a client-oriented, commercial and litigation practice. Although the firm offers specialist expertise on matters peculiar to Northern Ireland, it has a wide client base outside the province, including international and multinational companies. It is also pleased to include amongst its clients many leading insurance companies, Lloyds syndicates and insurance intermediaries. McKinty and Wright strives to provide an efficient and cost-effective service to all its clients and to maintain a close working relationship.

PRINCIPAL AREAS OF WORK McKinty and Wright offers a wide range of services to the commercial and insurance client, from routine advice to insolvency, property, insurance matters and litigation. The firm's litigation department has extensive experience in all aspects of commercial litigation with specialised expertise in personal injury, construction, professional negligence, defamation, insurance and general commercial litigation. The firm also has departments handling employment, licensing, corporate finance, property and general commercial advice.

■ McLean & Stewart
51/53 High Street, Dunblane, FK15 0EG   **Tel** (01786) 823217   **Fax** (01786) 822575

McLellans

Old Cross House, Old Cross, Hertford, SG14 1RB
Tel (01992) 532000   **Fax** (01992) 534020   **DX** 57921 Hertford
Email mclellans@mclellans.co.uk   **Website** www.mclellans.co.uk

Senior Partner	Simon Locke
Number of partners	4
Assistant solicitors	4
Other fee-earners	1
AREAS OF PRACTICE	
Commercial Property	45%
Licensing	25%
Employment	15%
Property Litigation	10%
Civil Litigation	5%
CONTACTS	
Commercial Property	Sylvia Goulding
Employment	Shital Pandya
Licensing	Clare Eames
Property Litigation	Martin Miller

THE FIRM McLellans is a niche commercial practice specialising in commercial property, licensing and employment law and is one of the leading leisure practices in the northern home counties. Four fee-earners are experienced advocates.

PRINCIPAL AREAS OF WORK

Commercial Property The firm provides a comprehensive commercial property service, including planning, development work, landlord and tenant, complex property acquisitions, disposals and the specialist aspects of licensed premises.
Licensing The firm has a dedicated liquor licensing department which handles advocacy from within its own ranks throughout England and Wales.
Employment The firm advises on all aspects of employment and disciplinary matters and handles advocacy in the Employment Tribunal and Employment Appeal Tribunal, particularly in relation to licensed trade employment matters.
Property Litigation The firm advises and assists in resolving a variety of commercial and landlord and tenant disputes.

LAW FIRMS ■ **A-Z**

CLIENTELE Clients include two national pub chains, a regional brewer, a national airline and other leisure, travel, manufacturing and property investment companies.

■ McManus Kearney
Law Society House, 106 Victoria Street, Belfast, BT1 3JZ **Tel** (028) 9024 3658 **Fax** (028) 9033 2151

■ McNeive Solicitors
26 Cowper Street, London, EC2A 4AP **Tel** (020) 7253 0535 **Fax** (020) 7253 0537

■ Meade-King
11/12 Queen Square, Bristol, BS1 4NT **Tel** (0117) 926 4121 **Fax** (0117) 929 7578

Memery Crystal
31 Southampton Row, London, WC1B 5HT
Tel (020) 7242 5905 **Fax** (020) 7242 2058 **DX** 156 Chancery Lane
Email info@memerycrystal.com **Website** www.memerycrystal.com

Managing Partner	Jonathan Davies
Senior Partner	Peter Crystal
Number of partners	15
Assistant solicitors	14
Other fee-earners	11

THE FIRM The emphasis at Memery Crystal is commercial business and corporate issues. The firm focuses on providing its clients with practical, commercially viable advice with an entrepreneurial flair and strong sense of commitment.

PRINCIPAL AREAS OF WORK Memery Crystal operates in corporate finance, commercial litigation and property. Within these areas, specialist groups deal with company/commercial, intellectual property, digital technology, sport, tax, insolvency, construction, insurance, corporate crime and regulatory law, employment and property litigation.

CLIENTELE Memery Crystal deals with all requirements of smaller companies and specialist requirements of larger companies.

CONTACTS	
Corporate Finance	Lesley Gregory
Employment	Merrill April
Litigation	Harvey Rands
Property & Property Litigation	
	Douglas Robertson
Intellectual Property	David Hansel
Sport	Peter Crystal

■ Mercy Messenger – Sole Practitioner
1683B High Street, Knowle, Solihull, B93 0LL **Tel** (01564) 779 427 **Fax** (01564) 778 732

■ Merricks Solicitors LLP
207-208 Moulsham Street, Chelmsford, CM2 0LG
Tel (01245) 491414 **Fax** (01245) 263829 **DX** 89702 Chelmsford 2
Email chelmsford@merricks.co.uk **Website** www.merricks.co.uk

AREAS OF PRACTICE	
Commercial Litigation (& Construction)	30%
Personal Injury	30%
Commercial Property	20%
Employment	10%
International Trade and Transport	10%

Number of members 12 **Assistant solicitors** 10 **Other fee-earners** 31 **Contact** Anthony Sheppard • Merricks Solicitors is a specialist practice with particular expertise in commercial litigation (including insurance); construction; employment; international trade and transport; property (private, commercial and residential); personal injury; and private client. Also located in Birmingham, London and Ipswich, Merricks aim to ensure a commercial and practical approach to all client needs.

A-Z ■ LAW FIRMS

Merriman White

3 King's Bench Walk, Inner Temple, London, EC4Y 7DJ
Tel (020) 7936 2050 **Fax** (020) 7353 0914 **DX** 1015 London Chancery Lane
Email info@merrimanwhite.com **Website** www.merrimanwhite.com

Merlaw House, 12 The Mount, Guildford, GU2 4HN
Tel (01483) 574466 **Fax** (01483) 306184 **DX** 2457 GUILDFORD
Email j.wolff@merrimanwhite.co.uk

61 Fleet Street, London, EC4Y 1JU
Tel (020) 7936 2050 **Fax** (020) 7583 1783 **DX** 1015 London Chancery Lane
Email info@merrimanwhite.com

Managing Partner	Jeremy M Wolff
Senior Partner	Raymond Murphy
Number of partners	2
Assistant solicitors	14
Other fee-earners	24

AREAS OF PRACTICE	
Litigation	60%
Property	20%
Commercial	10%
Private Client	10%

THE FIRM A long established City firm acting on behalf of UK and overseas clients. Merriman White are Privy Council agents.

PRINCIPAL AREAS OF WORK Merriman White carries out litigation, property and commercial work for business clients of all sizes including major companies in house building, contracting and publishing. It does adjudication and arbitration work in both the construction and commodities fields. It provides a wide spectrum of property, estate, tax and matrimonial services for private clients, as well as specialising in insurance and personal injury work, handling claims from minor through to major injuries. The firm advises individuals and companies facing criminal investigation and prosecution and has acted for defendants in prosecutions brought by the Inland Revenue, Customs and Excise and by the SFO. The firm also advises individuals and companies facing prosecution for breaches of health and safety and environmental protection legislation. The firm advises and acts for both employers and employees on contentious and non-contentious employment matters.

INTERNATIONAL The firm benefits from staff who are able to speak a variety of languages including French, Spanish, Italian, German, Yoruba and Farsi.

■ Michael Hutchings

Sandhayes, Corsley, Warminster, BA12 7QQ
Tel (07768) 105777 **Fax** (01373) 832785 **Email** mbh@dircon.co.uk

Michael Hutchings specialises in EU law and advises on competition cases before the Office of Fair Trading, Competition Commission, European Commission and European Court.

Michelmores

18 Cathedral Yard, Exeter, EX1 1HE
Tel (01392) 436244 **Fax** (01392) 215579 **DX** 8304
Email enquiries@michelmores.com **Website** www.michelmores.com

Managing & Senior Partner	Andrew Maynard
Number of partners	20
Assistant solicitors	25
Other fee-earners	27

CONTACTS	
ADR	Tim Richards
Charities	Richard Wheeler
Commercial Property	Peter Lowless
Company/Commercial	Malcolm Dickinson
Construction	Patrick Power
Employment	Nick Benson
Family	Simon Thomas
Litigation	Simon Barnett
Medical Negligence	Laurence Vick
Private Client	Will Michelmore
Private Equity	Stephen Morse

THE FIRM Michelmores is a dynamic law practice which takes a practical approach to providing a first class service to a wide range of clients comprising major institutions, large companies and public bodies throughout the country, as well as offering a full range of professional services to corporate and private clients in the South West. Following a period of considerable investment, the firm has experienced all round growth including the introduction of new services, the rationalisation of the headquarters offices on to a single city centre site and the appointment of a senior former banking executive as Practice Director. The firm can trace its history over 100 years, acting for many of the major institutions of the South West including the Diocese of Exeter, Exeter University and regionally based charities as well as looking after the interests of large numbers of high net worth individuals. Michelmores also has a history of attracting top quality lawyers from leading City firms, who are drawn both by the quality of work the firm can offer and the quality of life the location affords. Michelmores is a progressive and expanding firm and one of the leading legal advisors to the business community, being seen as a viable alternative for national and international corporate clients looking for service, intellectual quality and value for money. During the course of the year the firm's company commercial department has been involved in some of the largest corporate deals in the South West. It has recently established a corporate recovery and turnaround service and offers specialist information technology and e-business advice. Michelmores also plays a leading role in commercial property with the largest department of its kind in the South West. With a team of over 20 lawyers including specialist planning lawyers, the firm acts for

many public bodies and government departments, as well as some of the most significant regional institutions, developers and investors. The firm also has a thriving litigation department where alternative dispute resolution, licensing and construction are the latest areas to attract new and highly experienced lawyers with specialist abilities.

Middleton Potts

3 Cloth Street, Barbican, London, EC1A 7NP
Tel (020) 7600 2333 **Fax** (020) 7600 0108 **DX** 46621
Email mail@middletonpotts.co.uk   **Website** www.middletonpotts.co.uk

Senior Partner	David Lucas
Number of partners	17
Assistant solicitors	9
Other fee-earners	9

CONTACTS	
Commercial Litigation	Patrick Hann
	Edwin Cheyney
Corporate/Commercial/Banking/ Insurance/Employment	David Godfrey
	David Rabagliati
	Stephen Morrall
	Lindsey Hemingway
Property	Richard Schmidt
	Howard Lupton
Commodities/Trade/Finance/ Shipping/International Trade	Christopher Potts
	David Lucas
	Andrew Donoghue
	Anthony Hall-Jones
	Andrew Ridings
	Petra Leseberg
	Faye Doherty
	Frederick Konynenburg
	Andrew Meads

THE FIRM Founded in 1976 by six partners, all of whom had previously been with a well-established City practice, Middleton Potts has grown steadily over the past two and a half decades. Middleton Potts' specialist expertise and size enable it to offer very competitively, highly personal, partner led service.

PRINCIPAL AREAS OF WORK

Commodities/Trade Finance/Shipping/International Trade The firm's commodities practice has long been one of the most respected in the City, led by several of the best known names in this field. Cases handled involve all types of commodities, the main clients being international trading houses and trade finance banks. The shipping practice also has a long-established and solid reputation with 14 partners and assistants conducting primarily charterparty and bill of lading disputes, as well as salvage, wreck removal and pollution cases. The main clients are P&I and defence clubs, shipowners, charterers and their insurers, and companies in the offshore energy field.

Corporate/Commercial/Banking/Insurance/Employment Partners specialising in these fields have also achieved considerable success, enjoy work of the highest calibre and often act in transactions where counterparties are represented by the largest City firms. The department handles international and domestic banking and financial matters of all kinds (including ship and project finance transactions); insurance and reinsurance; the establishment by foreign entities of UK branches and subsidiaries; regulatory and compliance work; acquisitions and disposals of shares and assets; corporate reorganisations; joint ventures; ship sales and purchases; international construction contracts and other major industrial, commercial and infrastructure projects (including PFI schemes); tax and a very broad spectrum of corporate and commercial matters (including employment, pensions, insolvency and intellectual property).

Commercial Litigation This expanding group handles commercial disputes of all kinds and conducts both High Court litigation and domestic and international arbitration proceedings concerning: insurance and reinsurance; construction and technical disputes; banking and financial services; insolvency; commercial fraud; tracing and cross-border actions and disputes regarding real estate, intellectual property, employment and corporate matters.

Property Work handled includes the acquisition, funding, development and disposal of freehold and leasehold office and residential premises, industrial sites and other commercial property units and portfolios, planning matters, the general management of property interests, and general commercial transactions related to property.

CLIENTELE The clientele from all over the world is very broadly based, and includes: commodity trading houses and trade finance banks; shipowners and charterers; P&I clubs; oil majors and traders; major international banks, insurance companies and other financial institutions; freight forwarders and transportation companies; airlines; multinational manufacturing and trading corporations; property companies; international engineering and construction companies and project joint ventures; foreign state enterprises.

INTERNATIONAL With its strongly international focus, the firm has developed close contacts with clients, lawyers and other professionals from different jurisdictions throughout the world. Many of its lawyers speak at least one (some speak several) of the following languages: Arabic, Bengali, Cantonese, French, German, Greek, Italian, Mandarin, Portuguese, Spanish and Turkish.

MIDDLETON POTTS
SOLICITORS

A-Z ■ LAW FIRMS

Milbank, Tweed, Hadley & McCloy

Dashwood House, 69 Old Broad Street, London, EC2M 1QS
Tel (020) 7448 3000 **Fax** (020) 7448 3029
Website www.milbank.com

Managing Partner	Phillip Fletcher
Worldwide fee-earners	480
Number of UK partners	7
Number of UK associates	29
Total UK staff	60

AREAS OF PRACTICE	
M&A, Corporate & Acquisition Finance	40%
Project Finance	35%
Banking & Structured Finance	25%

CONTACTS	
Project Finance	John Dewar
Acquisition Finance	Kevin Muzilla
Banking	Patrick Holmes
Capital Markets	Tom Siebens
M&A	Michael Goroff
Securitisations	John Walker
Tax	Russel Jacobs

THE FIRM The roots of the practice can be traced back to 1866, with the establishment of the firm that acquired its present name in 1962. It was one of the first US practices to expand internationally and it opened in London more than twenty years ago. The firm has offices throughout Asia and the United States and during 2001, it broadened its European base by opening in Frankfurt. The London office of this prominent international law firm offers a range of services in cross-border transactions under English and New York law. These include private equity, banking, capital markets, project finance, securitisation, M&A and acquisition finance. A leading legal business journal recently recognised the firm's prominence by naming its London office the 'Banking and Finance Team of the Year' for 2001.

PRINCIPAL AREAS OF WORK Milbank is a global leader in complex cross-border transactions. Its London lawyers apply their expertise across a range of sophisticated legal products under both English and New York law. They act for the world's leading commercial and investment banks and many of Europe's most prominent corporations and utilities. Over the last decade, Milbank's London lawyers have been ranked among the market leaders in Europe in the area of project finance. Their experience has included acting on the largest project bond in Europe (Drax); the largest petrochemical financing in the Middle East (Yanpet); the largest power project in the Gulf (Taweelah A1); the first IPPs in Italy (Rosen), Spain (Tortosa), Portugal (Tapada), Morocco (Jorf Lasfar), Oman (Al Manah) and Turkey (Birecik). The firm has a leading practice in private equity and leveraged buyouts, drawing on its expertise in acquisitions and sophisticated financings. Milbank lawyers advised sponsors on the structuring and financing of the two largest LBOs executed in Europe last year: Messer Griesheim and Cognis. The firm's acquisition finance and high yield lawyers also acted on a broad range of other transactions, including the buyout of United Biscuits, one of the largest European leveraged finance transactions of the year. The London office has recognised expertise in securitisations and structured financings involving collateralised debt obligations, vendor financings, aircraft portfolios and natural resource receivables. The practice has advised on a number of the most complex CDO and CLO transactions executed to date in Europe. Milbank regularly acts on cross-border mergers and acquisitions; for example, it advised Scottish Power on its groundbreaking acquisition of a regulated electric utility company in the United States. It also acts on restructurings, most recently advising bondholders in relation to the administration of Global Telesystems (Europe) Limited and the creditors committee in the Enron bankruptcy. The London office offers tax advice in cross-border deals, adding significant value to its tax-driven structured products as well as to M&A transactions.

CLIENTELE Clients of the London office include major European, US and Japanese financial institutions as well as prominent multinational corporations and international utilities.

INTERNATIONAL Milbank has other offices in Frankfurt, New York, Los Angeles, Washington, Palo Alto, Singapore, Hong Kong and Tokyo.

Miles Preston & Co

10 Bolt Court, London EC4A 3DQ
Tel (020) 7583 0583 **Fax** (020) 7583 0128
Email miles.preston@milespreston.co.uk

Managing & Senior Partner	Miles Preston
Number of partners	4
Assistant solicitors	3

AREAS OF PRACTICE	
Family & Matrimonial	90%
Cohabitation/Paternity Disputes	10%

THE FIRM Miles Preston & Co is a specialist matrimonial and family law practice formed in May 1994, the three founding partners having previously worked together for over 10 years in a large central London general practice.

PRINCIPAL AREAS OF WORK
Family The firm deals with all aspects of matrimonial and family law including divorce and separation, cohabitation and pre-marriage agreements, all issues relating to children and the full range of emergency procedures. Many of the cases involve the resolution of complex financial issues usually concerning substantial assets, some with an international dimension. The practice aims to adopt a firm, effective and fair approach to the conduct of its cases and to offer a high quality and cost efficient service to its clients. All its solicitors are members of the Solicitors' Family Law Association.

CLIENTELE The firm acts for UK and foreign individuals from a wide variety of backgrounds including business people, professionals and those in the entertainment world and the media.

INTERNATIONAL The practice has close contacts with a number of other family lawyers worldwide. In addition, two of the partners are members of the International Academy of Matrimonial Lawyers, an association of over 300 prominent international family lawyers practising in various countries around the world.

Millar Shearer & Black

40 Molesworth Street, Cookstown, BT80 8PH   **Tel** (028) 8676 2346   **Fax** (028) 8676 6761

Miller Samuel & Co

RWF House, 5 Renfield Street, Glasgow, G2 5EZ
Tel (0141) 221 1919   **Fax** (0141) 221 3796   **DX** 161 Glasgow
Email email@millersamuel.co.uk   **Website** www.millersamuel.co.uk

THE FIRM Founded in 1973, Miller Samuel is a well established city centre firm, which provides a comprehensive legal service to commercial clients, with particular expertise in property development and leasing. The firm has developed a thriving litigation practice which complements the commercial work, including landlord and tenant litigation and employment law. It also handles a substantial amount of debt recovery, personal injury and matrimonial work. Its range of services include all private client fields.

PRINCIPAL AREAS OF WORK

Commercial Work handled includes corporate property development; commercial leasing; investment; funding; construction etc, service with specialist rent review arbitration/expert services. Private company work and general commercial contracts also handled.

Litigation Work includes contract disputes; employment; reparation; debt collection; recovery of possession of heritable property; finance leasing; consumer credit; arbitration; road traffic accident claims; matrimonial.

Private Client A comprehensive service is provided, offering clients advice on the administration of estates, tax planning, charities and wills. This department also deals with the purchase and sale of residential property.

Managing & Senior Partner	Michael Samuel
Number of partners	14
Assistant solicitors	8
Other fee-earners	12

AREAS OF PRACTICE	
Commercial Litigation, Employment & Reparation	50%
Commercial Property & Corporate	40%
Personal (inc. Residential, Conveyancing, Wills, Trusts)	10%

CONTACTS	
Commercial	Douglas Lamb
Commercial Litigation	Robert Kerr
Employment Law	Laura Doherty
Motor Claims	Diane Cairney
Personal Injury	Marie MacDonald
Private Client	Michael Samuel

Miller Sands

75-79 Regent Street, Cambridge, CB2 1BE   **Tel** (01223) 366741   **Fax** (01223) 227300

Mills & Co

Milburn House, Dean Street, Newcastle upon Tyne, NE1 1LE   **Tel** (0191) 233 2222   **Fax** (0191) 233 2220

Mills & Reeve

Francis House, 112 Hills Road, Cambridge, CB2 1PH
Tel (01223) 364422   **Fax** (01223) 355848   **DX** 122891 Cambridge 4
Email mark.jeffries@mills-reeve.com   **Website** www.mills-reeve.com

Ptnrs 59 **Asst solrs** 112 **Other fee-earners** 85 **Contact** Mark Jeffries • One of the UK's largest law firms with offices in Birmingham, Cambridge, London and Norwich. Mills & Reeve focuses on advising businesses, entrepreneurs and their financiers, especially in the technology sector; commercial property owners and developers; education institutions; the NHS and local authorities; professional indemnity insurers; and owners and occupiers of agricultural land.

AREAS OF PRACTICE	
Corporate	25%
Property	20%
Health	15%
Land & Agriculture	10%
Education	10%
Insurance	10%
Private Client	5%
Local Authorities	5%

A-Z ■ LAW FIRMS

Mills Selig

21 Arthur Street, Belfast, BT1 4GA
Tel (028) 9024 3878   **Fax** (028) 9023 1956   **DX** 459 NR BELFAST
Email info@nilaw.com   **Website** www.millsselig.com

THE FIRM Founded in 1959, Mills Selig has since developed to become a major force both in Northern Ireland and beyond, providing a comprehensive range of services to its predominantly corporate clientele. The firm's traditional strengths are in commercial property and corporate/corporate finance work but it has also developed a strong presence in litigation, particularly defamation, commercial litigation, product liability, intellectual property and employment law. Placing a strong emphasis on high quality service and developing close working relationships with clients, each client has an assigned partner to act as a contact point with overall knowledge of the client's affairs.

PRINCIPAL AREAS OF WORK

Commercial Property Acting for developers of retail, industrial, commercial and residential property, institutional lenders and investors and commercial landlords and tenants.

Company & Commercial Complete range of company and commercial services with particular expertise in merger and acquisition of companies and businesses, joint ventures both locally and internationally, corporate finance, distribution and agency agreements. Specialist knowledge of retail, pharmaceuticals, energy, textiles, food industries, agrichemicals and franchising.

Litigation Full range of civil litigation and tribunal services, with particular expertise in commercial litigation (including injunction work), defamation, product liability, intellectual property, professional indemnity, employment, construction, criminal damage and property litigation.

Private Client Residential conveyancing, wills, trusts, estate planning and probate.

Managing Partner	Richard Fulton
Senior Partner	Brian Ham
Number of partners	7
Assistant solicitors	5
Consultants	2
Other fee-earners	4

AREAS OF PRACTICE

Commercial Property	40%
Company & Commercial	30%
Litigation	25%
Private Client	5%

CONTACTS

Commercial Litigation	Paul Spring
	Adam Curry
Commercial Property	Brian Ham
	Jeremy Mills
Company & Commercial	Richard Fulton
	Bill McCann
Corporate Finance	Richard Fulton
Defamation	Paul Spring
Employment	Bill McCann
	Adam Curry
Insolvency	John Kearns
Intellectual Property	Paul Spring
	Adam Curry
Private Client	Jeremy Mills
Product Liability	Paul Spring

■ Mincoffs

Kensington House, 4-6 Osborne Road, Newcastle upon Tyne, NE2 2AA   **Tel** (0191) 281 6151   **Fax** (0191) 281 8069

Mishcon de Reya

Summit House, 12 Red Lion Square, London, WC1R 4QD
Tel (020) 7440 7000   **Fax** (020) 7404 5982   **DX** 37954 Kingsway
Email feedback@mishcon.co.uk   **Website** www.mishcon.co.uk

THE FIRM Mishcon de Reya is a unique law firm chaired by John Jackson, a senior business figure. It is an unconventional commercial law firm, run by lawyers who understand the needs of their business clients. It is an energetic and innovative practice committed to providing intelligent and creative legal advice. The practice has an open culture and many of its partners are young.

PRINCIPAL AREAS OF WORK
Organised internally into litigation, corporate and commercial, property and family departments, the firm has also developed specialist groups to meet the demands and opportunities of a constantly evolving commercial world.

Corporate & Commercial The corporate and commercial group advises on mergers, acquisitions and disposals, MBOs, flotations, joint ventures and venture capital, as well as providing general commercial advice including contracts, strategic alliances and distribution agreements.

Technology & Media The technology and media group focuses on e-commerce, convergence, digital delivery, publishing, music, advertising and marketing, television and radio carriage, film and TV production, theatre and computer games. Other areas of work include competition and EU law, non-contentious employment, media, IP and information technology.

Financial Service This group specialises in transactional work in this sector, and in the US and European regulation of financial institutions with expertise in derivatives, hedge funds, secured lending, cross-border transactions and structured products.

Business Immigration The business immigration group provides strategic and individual advice on business immigration issues and the establishment of business in the UK.

Commercial Litigation This department is internationally respected for its work, which includes defamation, corporate disputes, employment law, fraud and all contentious media. The department also acts for high profile individuals and institutions. Other niche contentious practices include art, design, financial services and sport. Consideration is always given to alternative dispute resolution.

Property The property department acts for a broad range of clients. Among them are publicly quoted companies, developers, pension funds, banks, house builders, as well as private investors and occupiers. It has a growing reputation in the retail and leisure sector and in urban regeneration. Work ranges from

Chairman	John Jackson
Joint Managing Partners	Kevin Gold
	Philip Freedman
Number of partners	38
Number of fee-earners	120
Total staff	233

AREAS OF PRACTICE

Litigation	32%
Corporate & Commercial	32%
Property	27%
Family	9%

CONTACTS

Banking & Finance	Richard Tyler
Betting & Gaming	Grant Gordon
Commercial Property	Nick Doffman
Corporate & Commercial	Larry Nathan
Corporate Tax	Patrick Harrison
Defamation	Karen Sanig
Employment	James Libson
	Rowena Herdman-Smith
Family	Sandra Davis
Film & TV Production	Andrew Millett
Financial Services	Adam Epstein
	Richard Tyler
Fraud	Gary Miller
	Kasra Nouroozi
Immigration	Kamal Rahman
	Philip Barth
Insolvency	Danny Davis
Intellectual Property	Grant Gordon
Litigation	Tony Morton-Hooper
Media (Contentious)	Karen Sanig
Media & Communications	Andrew Millett
Mergers & Acquisitions	Larry Nathan
Music	Martin Dacre

major site assemblies, sale and purchase of investment portfolios, joint venture structuring, secured lending, planning and environment, construction, pre-lets and plot sales.

Family One of the leading practices in this field, the family department advises on all family law matters, including on complex money and tax issues emanating from both domestic and international divorce and separation, together with conflicts arising over children which require sensitive and creative solutions. Other key areas of expertise range from advising on co-habitation disputes, pre-nuptial contracts and international child abduction cases. The firm has established particular expertise in acting for high net worth, high profile individuals who are under the media spotlight. The partners are trained mediators and use these skills to enhance the practice.

CONTACTS (Continued)

Personal Tax, Trusts & Probate	David Collins
Planning & Environmental	Gordon Campbell
Property Litigation	Kevin Steele
Property inc. Retail & Leisure	Nick Doffman
	Monica Blake
Sport	Tony Morton-Hooper
	Grant Gordon
Technology & E-commerce	Grant Gordon

CLIENTELE Mishcon de Reya provides legal services to a wide range of corporate, entrepreneurial and individual clients and has a continuing commitment to a range of pro bono causes. Further details of the firm's services are available from its main website.

MLM

Waterloo House, Fitzalan Court, Newport Road, Cardiff, CF24 0BA
Tel (029) 2046 2562 **Fax** (029) 2049 1118 **DX** 33011 Cardiff 1
Email info@mlmsolicitors.com **Website** www.mlmsolicitors.com

THE FIRM Founded in 2001 by three of the four partners and an associate of Bevan Ashford's Cardiff office to acquire that office, the firm continues to provide a principally commercial legal service built around the core practice areas of commercial property, corporate and commercial, litigation, healthcare and employment.

CLIENTELE The firm's clients include public companies, NHS trusts, government agencies, private venture capital funds and many owner-managed businesses operating in many sectors including manufacturing, mobile telecommunications, investment property, venture capital, healthcare, environmental, media and leisure.

Senior Partner	Nigel Morgan
Managing Partner	Jon Fernandez Lewis
Number of partners	4
Assistant solicitors	9
Other fee-earners	8

CONTACTS

Corporate	Jon Fernandez Lewis
Employment	Chris Mayers
Litigation	Chris Mayers
Commercial Property	Nigel Morgan

H. Montlake & Co

197 High Rd, Ilford, IG1 1LX
Tel (020) 8553 1311 **Fax** (020) 8553 3066 **DX** 124842 Ilford 7
Email mail@montlake.co.uk

THE FIRM H Montlake & Co has been established since 1953 and has always specialised in carrying out property, company and commercial work and litigation for business clients of all sizes. A wide spectrum of property, tax, estate and matrimonial services is also available to private clients. The practice also has substantial experience in the sporting field where its clients include two football league clubs. Michael Bonehill, the managing partner, also has extensive experience in relation to theatrical work and charitable work and is the chairman of the National Youth Theatre of Great Britain and a Life Governor of the Imperial Cancer Research Fund. The practice has formed and acted for a large number of charities including theatrical, musical and medical charities.

Senior Partner	Michael Bonehill
Number of partners	5

CONTACTS

Commercial Property	Michael Bonehill
Company & Commercial	Andrew Montlake
Litigation	Daniel Hockman
Probate & Trusts	Jeremy Davies
Residential Conveyancing	Jacqueline Joseph

Moon Beever

24-26 Bloomsbury Square, London, WC1A 2PL **Tel** (020) 7637 0661 **Fax** (020) 7436 4663

A-Z ■ LAW FIRMS

Moore & Blatch

11 The Avenue, Southampton SO17 1XF
Tel (023) 8071 8000   **Fax** (023) 8033 2205   **DX** 38507 Southampton 3
Email marketing@m-b.co.uk   **Website** www.mooreandblatch.co.uk

London Court, 64 London Road, Southampton, SO15 2EH
Tel 023 8071 8000   **Fax** 023 8033 3104   **DX** 38524 Southampton 3

48 High Street, Lymington, SO41 9ZQ
Tel (01590) 625800   **Fax** (01590) 672371   **DX** 34050 Lymington

5 High Street, Milford-on-Sea, Lymington, SO41 0QG
Tel (01590) 642172   **Fax** (01590) 644905

Managing Partner	Michael Caton
Senior Partner	David Thompson
Number of partners	13
Assistant solicitors	26
Other fee-earners	46

AREAS OF PRACTICE	
Insurance & Personal Injury	36%
Property	28%
Corporate	19%
Private Client	17%

CONTACTS	
Commercial Property	Stephen Ingram
Corporate	Roger Bailey
Insurance & Personal Injury	David Thompson
Litigation	Dinshaw Printer
Private Client	Jessica Wiltshire

THE FIRM Moore & Blatch is a leading South Coast firm delivering excellence in legal solutions for both business and private clients. Moore & Blatch seeks to understand its clients' needs before providing high quality advice and practical outcomes across a comprehensive range of services including corporate and commercial work, employment, property, land development, litigation, personal injury and wealth management. Moore & Blatch is forward thinking and proactive delivering its service in a way the client understands.

PRINCIPAL AREAS OF WORK Corporate and Commercial; Personal Injury and Insurance; Litigation; Property; Planning and Development; Private Client; Health and Safety; Transport.

Moorhead James

21 New Fetter Lane, London, EC4A 1AW
Tel (020) 7831 8888   **Fax** (020) 7936 3635   **DX** 288 London/Chancery Lane
Email mail@moorheadjames.com

Senior Partner	Ben Moorhead
Number of partners	7
Assistant solicitors	1
Other fee-earners	8

THE FIRM Moorhead James is a commercial practice offering a comprehensive range of services to clients ranging from private individuals to multinational businesses.

PRINCIPAL AREAS OF WORK
Corporate & Commercial Work includes formations, flotations, corporate restructuring, franchising and licensing, sports and leisure, banking, corporate finance, education, EU law and aviation.
Property The department advises on all aspects of commercial and residential conveyancing; environmental law; construction and development; oil and gas; landlord and tenant.
Litigation This includes High Court and County Court actions, landlord and tenant and other property disputes, employment matters, debt collection, professional negligence and insolvency.
Matrimonial All aspects of divorce, financial settlements and cohabitation are handled.
Private Client Work includes tax planning, charities, wills and probate.

INTERNATIONAL The firm has offices in Frankfurt, Rome, Milan, Paris, Hong Kong, Beijing, Prague and Budapest. Work is handled in Cantonese, French and German.

CONTACTS	
Company/Commercial	David James
	Ben Moorhead
Corporate Finance	David James
	Ben Moorhead
Employment	Christine Bowyer-Jones
	Wayne de Nicolo
	Edward Wheen
Insolvency	Edward Wheen
Litigation	Christine Bowyer-Jones
	Wayne de Nicolo
	Edward Wheen
Matrimonial/Family	Susan Leon
Offshore Tax Planning	Rachael Moorhead
Oil & Gas	Julian Bishop
Property	Julian Bishop
	Susan Leon
Sports & Leisure	Ben Moorhead

Moran & Co

40 Upper Gungate, Tamworth, B79 8AA
Tel (01827) 54631   **Fax** (01827) 68905   **DX** 12659 Tamworth
Email info@moranlaw.co.uk

Senior Partner	Patrick Moran
Number of partners	3
Other fee-earners	2

CONTACTS	
Banking, Finance & Professional Negligence	
	Patrick Moran
Personal Injury	Paul Isherwood
Commercial Litigation/ADR	Tim Lawrence

THE FIRM Moran & Co. is a niche commercial litigation firm established in 1983. The firm's approach combines technical expertise with commercial awareness and a strong commitment to the client's best interests.

PRINCIPAL AREAS OF WORK The firm specialises and enjoys an excellent reputation in banking and finance litigation. The firm also handles heavyweight commercial disputes on behalf of UK and multinational companies, ADR, professional negligence and claimant and defendant personal injury.

CLIENTELE The firm's client base includes AIB Group (UK) PLC and a number of major UK financial institutions as well as prominent multinational corporations such as Vauxhall Motors Limited, Factoring Companies and UK Public Limited Companies.

More & Co
19 Dublin Street, Edinburgh, EH1 3PG **Tel** (0131) 557 1110 **Fax** (0131) 557 8882

Morecroft Urquhart
8 Dale Street, Liverpool, L2 4TQ **Tel** (0151) 236 8871 **Fax** (0151) 236 8109

More Fisher Brown
1 Norton Folgate, London, E1 6DA **Tel** (020) 7247 0438 **Fax** (020) 7247 0649

Morgan Cole

167 Fleet Street, London, EC4A 2JB
Tel (020) 7822 8000 **Fax** (020) 7822 8222 **DX** 261 London
Email info@morgan-cole.com **Website** www.morgan-cole.com

Bradley Court, Park Place, Cardiff, CF10 3DP
Tel (029) 2038 5385 **Fax** (029) 2038 5300 **DX** 33014 Cardiff
Email info@morgan-cole.com

Buxton Court, 3 West Way, Oxford, OX2 0SZ
Tel (01865) 262600 **Fax** (01865) 721367 **DX** 96200 Oxford West
Email info@morgan-cole.com

Apex Plaza, Forbury Road, Reading, RG1 1AX
Tel (0118) 955 3000 **Fax** (0118) 939 3210 **DX** 117878 Reading Apex Plaza
Email info@morgan-cole.com

Chairman	John Cole
Chief Executive	David Main
Number of partners	83
Assistant solicitors	162
Other fee-earners	135

AREAS OF PRACTICE	
Insurance Litigation	31%
Business Services	26%
Commercial Litigation	21%
Property	17%
Private Client	5%

CONTACTS	
Commercial Litigation	Allan Wilson
Commercial Property	Philip Jardine
Company/Commercial	Graeme Guthrie
	Bruce Potter
Construction	Andrew Campbell
Corporate Finance	Duncan Macintosh
Dispute Resolution	Phillip Howell-Richardson
Employment	Anthony Rees
Energy	Oliver Drennan
Health	Graham Miles
Insurance	Robin Havard
IT & IP	Alison Sarsfield-Hall
Landlord & Tenant	Jonathan Cantor
Public Law & PFI/Projects	Alun Cole

THE FIRM Morgan Cole is a major law firm holding an unrivalled position across the southern half of the UK. With eight offices in London, Thames Valley and South Wales the firm provides a comprehensive service to commercial clients throughout the UK. Morgan Cole is a forward-looking firm committed to providing its clients with legal services to the highest possible standards. The firm enjoys a reputation for being both commercially aware and progressive and for giving strong and practical advice. Its aim is to be one of the UK's leading business law firms providing services to clients in the UK, Europe and beyond. It is committed to investment in clients, staff, IT and training, and to innovation and the continual pursuit of excellence. Partnership is key to the firm's approach and the reason for its commitment to gaining a real understanding of clients' businesses and building relationships. Lawyers work cross-office providing clients with access to greater resources and skills from all offices. A number of industry-focused groups are set up within the firm to ensure that specialised knowledge is always the basis on which advice is given. These groups include banking, construction, energy, health, insurance and technology.

PRINCIPAL AREAS OF WORK The firm services a wide range of organisations in a variety of sectors. Main areas of work include ADR; agriculture; banking; charities; commercial litigation; construction; corporate and commercial; debt recovery; EU and competition law; employment; energy; health; insolvency; insurance litigation; intellectual property; information technology; landlord and tenant; leisure and licensing; PFI and projects; professional negligence; property, planning and environmental; public law.

ADR At the forefront of alternative dispute resolution for many years, the firm has 27 trained mediators who have experience in mediating a wide range of cases.

Insurance Fishburn Morgan Cole is the firm's specialist insurance division, dealing with professional indemnity litigation, Lloyds and the London market, financial services and reinsurance. It has a strong track record in the defence of claims against professionals such as architects, engineers, surveyors, brokers, accountants and financial advisors. The specialist claims department is staffed by a unique mixture of personnel qualified in law and insurance and currently administers a number of individually designed schemes where a full claims service is provided. Additional services include pre-risk surveys and claims audits.

INTERNATIONAL Enjoying strong international links, Morgan Cole is a founder member of the Association of European Lawyers and has established connections with law firms in North America and the Far East.

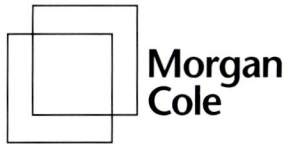

A-Z ■ LAW FIRMS

■ **Morgan Jones & Pett**
95 St Georges Road, Great Yarmouth, NR30 2NR **Tel** (01493) 334700 **Fax** (01493) 334710

Morgan, Lewis & Bockius

2 Gresham Street, London, EC2V 7PE
Tel (020) 7710 5500 **Fax** (020) 7710 5600 **DX** 42603 Cheapside 1
Website www.morganlewis.com

THE FIRM Founded in Philadelphia in 1873, Morgan Lewis & Bockius LLP is one of the oldest and largest law firms in the US with over 300 partners and more than 1,000 lawyers. Morgan Lewis ranks among the top ten US law firms in the world. Every area of the firm's practice – from anti-trust to litigation – has a strong international component. Morgan Lewis represents clients in mergers and acquisitions, technology and emerging business all over the world, resolving differing and sometimes conflicting laws in a number of jurisdictions to produce the optimum results. Additionally, the firm's lawyers understand the problems and complexities of transnational litigation and can advise on US and EU regulatory matters. Morgan Lewis' clients are diverse and include Fortune 250 companies, leading financial services and investment banking organisations, as well as pioneers in the e-commerce and internet sector. All of the firm's clients receive the same high level of care and the firm recognises why they chose Morgan Lewis – because they want a professional firm with experienced, quality people who are as internationally minded as they are.

London Office The London office of Morgan Lewis, which was founded in 1981, is fully integrated with the firm's other offices and works closely not only with the US offices, but also with the offices located outside the US, in particular Brussels and Frankfurt. In addition, the lawyers in the London office frequently act as liaison with clients who seek to have their legal representation co-ordinated with local counsel in countries where the firm does not have offices. In this regard, the firm has developed a comprehensive network of contacts and leading law firms in such countries.

PRINCIPAL AREAS OF WORK The firm handles a vast diversity of legal work including: anti-trust, business and commercial litigation, business and finance, corporate transactions, employment, labour and benefits, energy and utilities, intellectual property, investment management, life sciences, personal law, mergers and acquisitions, real estate, securities, tax and technology.

INTERNATIONAL The firm has other offices in Brussels, Frankfurt, Tokyo, New York, Harrisburg, Los Angeles, Philadelphia, Pittsburgh, Princeton, Miami, Washington, Northern Virginia.

UK	
Number of partners	8
Assistant solicitors	14
Other fee-earners	2
International	
Number of partners	344
Other fee-earners	over 1000

AREAS OF PRACTICE	
Corporate/Commercial	40%
Litigation	33%
Tax	20%
Pharmaceutical	5%
Other	2%

CONTACTS	
Corporate/Commercial	Thomas Benz
	Peter Wallace
	Zoë Ashcroft
Litigation	Robert Goldspink
	Neville Byford
Pharmaceutical	Anthony Warnock-Smith
Trust & Tax	Charles Lubar
	Michael Cashman

Morison Bishop

2 Blythswood Square, Glasgow, G2 4AD
Tel (0141) 248 4672 **Fax** (0141) 221 9270 **DX** GW 11
Email mail@morisonbishop.co.uk **Website** www.morisonbishop.co.uk

Erskine House, 68 Queen Street, Edinburgh, EH2 4NN
Tel (0131) 226 6541 **Fax** (0131) 226 3156 **DX** ED 38
Email mail@morisonbishop.co.uk

THE FIRM Morison Bishop is a leading Scottish commercial law firm with offices in Glasgow and Edinburgh, enabling the firm to provide a personal, fast service to suit its clients' requirements. The firm's success is a result of the strong relationships it builds with clients and its understanding of their business objectives and goals. The depth of knowledge and breadth of experience within the firm provides Morison Bishop with the ability to assist clients on legal matters ranging from one to one advice for a business start-up to a specialist team working with a large corporate client. Morison Bishop has particular strengths and abilities in commercial property and litigation, with dedicated units for asset recovery, reparation, corporate law, employment law, debt recovery, environmental law, house builders and developers and construction. As a member of the IAG (Integrated Advisory Group), a unique worldwide association of independent professional firms including lawyers, accountants, tax advisors and actuaries, the firm is able to assist clients with international matters.

Managing Partner	Ewen Dyce
Chairman	John Welsh
Number of partners	22
Assistant solicitors	29
Other fee-earners	31

PRINCIPAL AREAS OF WORK
Litigation Specialist areas of work within this division include reparation, family law, debt recovery, alternative dispute resolution, personal injury, professional negligence, health and safety, and general civil litigation.

Commercial Property Specialist advice includes purchase and sale, leasing property investment, shopping and retail centres, environmental law, licensing and franchising. This division also includes a house builders unit that deals with land acquisition and disposals, leasing, re-development and managing the sale of plots.

Corporate Specialist areas of work within this division include business purchase, business start-up, corporate finance, intellectual property, e-commerce, education, constitutional law, general corporate, insolvency, media and sports law.

Asset Recovery Specialist services within this division include repossessions, recovery of mortgage arrears, property management, estate agency service and financial advice.

Private Client Specialist advice includes wills, tax, administration of trusts and executries, financial and investment advice and services for elderly clients.

Employment The employment unit provides a wide range of employment-related advice on both contentious and non-contentious issues including unfair dismissal, redundancy, transfer of undertakings, contracts of employment and employment policies.

Construction The construction unit act on behalf of developers, major house builders, joint ventures, housing associations, funders, contractors, consultants and sub-contractors, advising on both contentious and non-contentious issues.

Residential Property The unit offers estate agency services, conveyancing and mortgage advice.

CLIENTELE Clients include, BP Oils, Alliance and Leicester, Persimmon PLC including Persimmon Homes Limited and Beazer Homes Limited, Motorola, ICI, Royal Bank of Scotland, BT, Arnold Clark, Capability Scotland, Equity Red Star Motor Policies at Lloyds, Westminster Motor Insurance Association Limited, Hastings Direct, Wren Motor Policies at Lloyds, NIG.

Morrish & Co
Oxford House, Oxford Row, Leeds, LS1 3BE **Tel** (0113) 245 0733 **Fax** (0113) 242 5168

Morton Fisher
Carlton House, Worcester Street, Kidderminster, DY10 1BA **Tel** (01562) 820181 **Fax** (01562) 820066

Morton Fraser, Solicitors
30-31 Queen Street, Edinburgh, EH2 1JX
Tel (0131) 247 1000 **Fax** (0131) 247 1007 **DX** ED119
Email infodesk@morton-fraser.com **Website** www.morton-fraser.com

AREAS OF PRACTICE	
Commercial Property	34%
Litigation	27%
Private Client	14%
Residential Property	13%
Corporate	12%

Ptnrs 24 **Asst solrs** 28 **Other fee-earners** 100 **Contact** Debbie Entwistle • Commercial firm with a strong private clients practice – specialisms in banking and asset finance, family, employment, e-business and online legal services the firm deals with a growing number of cross-border transactions.

Mourant du Feu & Jeune
PO Box 87, 22 Grenville Street, St Helier JE4 8PX
Tel (01534) 609000 **Fax** (01534) 609333
Email enquiry@mourant.com **Website** www.mourant.com

4th Floor, 35 New Bridge Street, Blackfriars, London, EC4V 6BW
Tel (020) 7332 6161 **Fax** (020) 7332 6199
Email enquiry@mourant.com

Managing Partner	Richard Jeune
Senior Partner	Conrad Coutanche
Jersey	
Number of partners	21
Assistant solicitors	5
Other fee-earners	40

CONTACTS	
Capital Markets	Ian James
	Moz Scott
Structured Finance	Alastair Syvret
	Jacqueline Richomme
Collective Investment Funds	Tim Herbert
	Edward Devenport
Banking	Ian James
	Rob Hickling
Trusts	Cyman Davies
	Nicole Hamel
Corporate & Business Law	Tim Herbert
	Wendy Malorey
Commercial Litigation	Jonathan Speck
	Beverley Lacey
Commercial Property	Liz Breen
	Gio Pollano

THE FIRM Mourant du Feu & Jeune is part of Mourant, the largest Channel Islands-based legal and specialist administration provider, with 24 partners heading 500 staff in offices in Jersey and the UK. It specialises in offshore legal services and has been active in the development of Jersey's financial services industry. Areas of expertise include capital markets, structured finance, securitisation, funds, property holding and finance, employee benefits and commercial litigation. Recognising the importance of its City client base, the firm opened a London branch office in April 2000, the first in the Channel Islands to do so. The firm acts for global financial institutions in international finance, and advises City lawyers and investment banks on the Jersey aspects of securitisation and structured finance transactions. Work for collective investment funds includes advising the largest management buyout of a private equity fund in Europe and several other major European funds. In 2001, Mourant acted for 68% of the FTSE100 companies and 30% of the top 100 companies in *Business Week's* Global 1000.

Continued overleaf

A-Z ■ LAW FIRMS

PRINCIPAL AREAS OF WORK

International Finance The firm advises global financial institutions on the Jersey legal aspects of securitisation, capital markets transactions, structured and corporate finance and banking. Recent transactions include Prospect 6 (Jersey) Limited, Chaves Funding No 1 Limited, Granite, Trident Securities Limited, Indigo Funding Limited and Portland Capital Limited.

Funds The firm has advised on almost 50% of Jersey-domiciled collective investment funds, and specialises in particular in private equity and venture capital funds. Clients include the largest management buyout private equity fund in Europe.

Commercial The commercial team specialises in advising businesses on Jersey commercial and corporate law, in particular trust and company law, collective investments, financial services regulation, M&A and employment law.

Commercial Litigation The practice focuses on banking and trust litigation, asset tracing and fraud.

SPECIALIST ADMINISTRATION SERVICES Mourant also provides the following services:

Employee Share Plans Mourant Equity Compensation Solutions is a specialist administrator of complex global, UK domestic and offshore employee share plans. It acts for 43% of the UK FTSE100 index, while the largest of its 100+ global share plans has over 42,000 active participants.

Private Wealth Management Mourant Private Wealth Management provides lawyer-led independent wealth management for clients with the most exacting standards.

Funds Mourant International Finance Administration offers highly skilled lawyer-led administration for complex international private funds. It administers some of the chief European private equity funds including CVC European Equity Partners II, and has fund assets of over US$16 billion under administration.

Corporate Property Structures Mourant International Finance Administration advises on the establishment and administration of onshore and offshore financing and holding structures for property assets. Its services include off balance sheet financing arrangements, securitisation of property assets and joint venture structures for property co-ownership and property holding structures.

INTERNATIONAL Languages spoken include English, French, German, Italian, Portuguese and Spanish.

CONTACTS (Continued)	
Private Wealth Management	Richard Jeune
	Conrad Coutanche
Securitisation	Alastair Syvret
	Jonathan Walker
Private Funds	Julia Chapman
	Jacqueline Richomme
Mergers & Acquisitions	Wendy Malorey
	Nigel Weston
SPV Structures	Nicola Davies
Employee Benefits	James Crill

■ Mowat Dean WS
45 Queen Charlotte Street, Leith, Edinburgh, EH6 7HD **Tel** (0131) 555 0616 **Fax** (0131) 553 1523

■ Mullis & Peake
8-10 Eastern Road, Romford, RM1 3PJ
Tel (01708) 784000 **Fax** (01708) 784099 **DX** 138126 Romford 4
Email office@mplaw.co.uk **Website** www.mplaw.co.uk

AREAS OF PRACTICE	
Private Client	60%
Commercial	25%
Probate	15%

Ptnrs 10 **Asst solrs** 6 **Other fee-earners** 6 **Contact** John Poulten • Well known locally for commercial development conveyancing, commercial and probate work. The firm also specialises in both gaming and liquor licensing.

■ Mundays
Cedar House, 78, Portsmouth Road, Cobham KT11 1AN
Tel (01932) 590 500 **Fax** (01932) 590 220 **DX** 36300 ESHER
Email hub@mundays.co.uk **Website** www.mundays.co.uk

Chief Executive	Roger Formby
Senior Partner	Peter Munday
Number of partners	17
Other fee-earners	8
Assistant solicitors	13
Notaries public	3

AREAS OF PRACTICE	
Corporate/Commercial	35%
Commercial Property	23%
Dispute Resolution/Litigation	13%
Residential Conveyancing	10%
Private Wealth	10%
Family	9%

CONTACTS	
Commercial Agreements	David Irving
Property	Simon Withers
Corporate Finance	Richard Powell
Dispute Resolution	Fiona McAllister
Intellectual Property	Valerie Toon
Mergers & Acquisitions	Peter Munday
Private Wealth & Tax	Ray Walley

THE FIRM Mundays is a leading regional practice that is particularly strong in the corporate and commercial fields. Established in 1960, Mundays has a diverse client base that includes major international and national companies as well as small local businesses and individuals.

PRINCIPAL AREAS OF WORK

Corporate/Commercial Mergers and acquisitions (takeovers, share and asset sales, MBOs, MBIs, public to private transactions, joint ventures and corporate reorganisations); corporate finance (fundraising including IPOs, rights issues, venture capital funding and private placings); IP (copyright, trademarks, know-how, IT law); franchising (agreements, disputes, international franchising and property transactions); employment (from employers and employee perspectives); partnership agreements and advice; all forms of general commercial agreements.

Commercial Property The complete range of transactions is handled by this department, including drafting and negotiating all forms of freehold and leasehold documentation, renewal of leases, sale and purchase of incorporated businesses, and town and country planning matters.

Dispute Resolution Advice on disputes concerning commercial matters, franchising, property, employment, IP/IT and software and private client services.

Private Client Private wealth and tax planning, probate, family and residential conveyancing.

LAW FIRMS ■ A-Z

■ Murphy & O'Rawe
Scottish Provident Building, 7 Donegall Square West, Belfast, BT1 6JF **Tel** (028) 9032 6636 **Fax** (028) 9024 3777

Murray Beith Murray WS
39 Castle Street, Edinburgh, EH2 3BH
Tel (0131) 225 1200 **Fax** (0131) 225 4412 **DX** ED40 Edinburgh
Email mbm@murraybeith.co.uk **Website** www.murraybeith.co.uk

Managing Partner	John K Scott Moncrieff
Chairman	William Berry
Number of partners	10
Assistant solicitors	18
Other fee-earners	34
AREAS OF PRACTICE	
Legal Services	67%
Asset Management	33%
CONTACTS	
Asset Management	Ruthven Gemmell
Legal Services	Hugh Younger
	Sandy Finlayson

THE FIRM Murray Beith Murray is a progressive Edinburgh-based practice, which offers an extensive range of services to private and business clients, with specialities including asset management and tax planning, agricultural law and land purchase and advising companies at all stages in their life cycles. Established in 1849, Murray Beith Murray actively seeks to combine its traditional strength of a dedicated client service with modern management and innovative use of technology. The firm's aim is to create, enhance and protect the wealth of its clients. The client base includes national and international companies, property investors and developers, financial institutions and private investors and a significant number of land owning interests. Murray Beith Murray provides its services through two departments; legal services and asset management, both of which have a number of dedicated groups to provide specialist advice in a wide range of legal and financial areas.

PRINCIPAL AREAS OF WORK
Legal Services Murray Beith Murray's core business is private client work and the firm is regarded as one of Scotland's leading firms in this field. It provides a comprehensive range of legal, financial and administrative services, including wills and estate planning, trusts, taxation and executries. In the area of property law it offers a full service on agricultural law and rural property matters alongside a residential estate agency and conveyancing service. The firm's legal services department also offers commercial advice to assist companies from start-up, through the early years, to flotation and beyond. An efficient, competitive and personal service is combined with excellent financial contacts and deal-making skills. The commercial service also includes the acquisition, development and realisation of commercial property of all kinds, together with advice on regulatory planning and environmental issues. These are supported by a litigation service, which works in the areas of employment law, professional negligence claims, property and commercial disputes.

Asset Management The award-winning asset management team offers a full financial planning service, including a comprehensive, independent overview of a client's investment and financial needs. Advice is given on a wide range of financial planning issues, including protection of the family, school fees planning, insurance, pensions advice for retirement planning and investment. Measured by funds under management, Murray Beith Murray is one of the largest solicitor investment managers in the UK. It provides a full range of investment management and administration services on both a discretionary and advisory basis.

■ M.W. Cornish, Solicitors
Gainsborough House, 33 Throgmorton Street, London, EC2N 2BR
Tel (020) 7397 3400 **Fax** (020) 7397 3401
Email martin.cornish@mwcornish.com **Website** www.mwcornish.com

Ptnrs 1 **Asst solrs** 2 **Contact** Martin Cornish • Specialist in financial services regulation – FSA authorisations and related documentation; exchange rules and regulations; market abuse; insider dealing and money laundering. Also specialist in asset management – structuring all forms of onshore and offshore funds, related contractual documentation and the marketing of investment funds and other products and services.

A-Z ■ LAW FIRMS

Nabarro Nathanson

Lacon House, Theobald's Road, London, WC1X 8RW
Tel (020) 7524 6000 **Fax** (020) 7524 6524 **DX** 77 London/Chancery
Email info@nabarro.com **Website** www.nabarro.com

The Anchorage, 34 Bridge Street, Reading, RG1 2LU
Tel (0118) 950 4700 **Fax** (0118) 950 5640 **DX** 4068 Reading
Email info@nabarro.com

1 South Quay, Victoria Quays, Wharf Street, Sheffield, S2 5SY
Tel (0114) 279 4000 **Fax** (0114) 278 6123 **DX** 712550 Sheffield 20
Email info@nabarro.com

Senior Partner	Simon Johnston
Managing Partner	Nicole Paradise
Number of partners	102
Assistant solicitors	288
Other fee-earners	73

CONTACTS

Administrative & Public Law	Malcolm Iley
Banking	Andrew McLean
Charities	Jonathan Burchfield
Commercial Litigation & Dispute Resolution	Jonathan Warne
Corporate/Commercial	Gareth Jones
Construction	Roger Wakefield
Corporate Finance	Iain Newman
Corporate Recovery & Insolvency	Patricia Godfrey
Employment	Sue Ashtiany
Energy & Infrastructure	Robert Tudway
Environment	Mike Renger
EU/Competition	Cyrus Mehta
Health & Safety	Gareth Watkins
TMT	Tony Bailes
Intellectual Property	Guy Heath
Pensions	John Quarrell
Planning	Norna Hughes
Projects, Project Finance & PFI	Norna Hughes
Real Estate	Kevin Stimpson / Nick Collins
Property Finance	Amanda Howard
Property Litigation	Iain Travers
Tax	Michael Cant
Telecoms	Robert Bell
Venture Capital	Andrew Inkester

THE FIRM Nabarro Nathanson is one of the UK's foremost commercial law firms. It has 102 partners leading more than 350 lawyers offering a broad range of legal services to major national and international corporate, government, institutional and public sector clients. The firm's headquarters are in central London, with additional offices in Reading, Sheffield and Brussels. More than 25 per cent of its work is with clients based overseas. Nabarro Nathanson provides a cross-disciplinary, business-focused and pragmatic approach to meeting the legal challenges facing clients today. The firm offers clients in-depth technical expertise from experienced partners and associates.

PRINCIPAL AREAS OF WORK The firm's industry groupings, including real estate, projects and TMT, and its practice areas, including a large corporate/commercial group, match the needs of the industries it serves.
Real Estate Nabarro Nathanson has one of the UK's largest and most active commercial property departments handling some of the most complex and technically demanding commercial and legal challenges in the industry. The group advises on all aspects of commercial property law representing developers, owners and investors as well as corporate occupiers.
Projects The projects group brings together specialists in infrastructure, construction, energy, planning, public sector and oil and gas. The firm has built a reputation in the PFI, energy and railways sectors having successfully completed a large number of PFI projects in the UK.
Technology, Media & Telecommunications The firm is at the heart of the UK's technology industry and is one of the leading law firms in this fast evolving area. It has a blue chip client base. The firm represents multinationals and IT corporates, together with many UK and US fast growth technology companies.
Corporate/Commercial The corporate/commercial department covers mergers and acquisitions, flotations, venture capital, and management buyouts, joint ventures, EU and competition law, intellectual property and tax. The firm's banking group is very active in representing domestic and international banks and other major financial institutions.
Other Areas The firm has significant strengths in charity, commercial litigation, employment, environment, H&S, insolvency and pensions.

INTERNATIONAL Nabarro Nathanson has an office in Brussels and associations with leading firms in France and Germany. It also has well established relationships with leading law firms in Europe, the USA and other regions around the world.

RECRUITMENT The firm is always looking for individuals who can make a contribution to its success. Recent growth provides opportunities for qualified solicitors across a range of specialisms. There are also a number of vacancies for trainee solicitors, mostly in London, but also in the firm's Reading and Sheffield offices. Candidates must have an upper second degree, although not necessarily in law. Long term prospects are excellent. Contact Jane Drew for application information.

NabarroNathanson

■ Napier & Sons

1/9 Castle Arcade, Belfast, BT1 5DF **Tel** (028) 9024 4602 **Fax** (028) 9033 0330

Napthens

7 Winckley Square, Preston, PR1 3JD
Tel (01772) 883883 **Fax** (01772) 257805 **DX** 714572 Preston 14
Email Reception@nhc-sol.co.uk

Senior Partner	PJ Hosker
Number of partners	12
Assistant solicitors	6
Other fee-earners	14

THE FIRM Formerly Napthen Houghton Craven, Napthens is based in Preston although it has a client base spread throughout the country and which includes offshore companies and trusts. The firm continues to expand by concentrating on the development of specialist departments providing quality services to clients. The firm is partner managed and led and is structured to provide efficient services for all clients.

PRINCIPAL AREAS OF WORK

Commercial The firm provides a wide range of legal services for commerce, industry and investor clients. Best known for its commercial property (including planning and compensation) and corporate work, the firm has developed a thriving employment law department and a burgeoning commercial litigation department. The firm deals extensively in agricultural legal work throughout the North West region and was appointed in 1999 as the sole Panel Solicitors for the National Farmers Union for the region.

Private Client Napthen Houghton Craven has a highly developed residential conveyancing department and undertakes tax planning, wills and estates work as well as offering a discreet family law department. A specialist department handles personal injury work with particular emphasis on road traffic accidents. The firm has a long established strong dedicated probate and trusts department.

NautaDutilh

Bowman House, 29 Wilson Street, London, EC2M 2SJ
Tel (020) 7786 9100 **Fax** (020) 7588 6888
Email ndlondon@nautadutilh.com **Website** www.nautadutilh.com

Resident Partners	Gijs Gerretsen
	Joanne Kellermann
Number of fee-earners	9

THE FIRM NautaDutilh is one of continental Europe's leading law firms. With close to 500 attorneys, civil law notaries and tax advisors, the firm operates from three main offices in Amsterdam, Brussels and Rotterdam, from substantial and growing offices in London and New York, as well as from offices in Madrid and Paris.

PRINCIPAL AREAS OF WORK The London office specialises in the following types of work: corporate, corporate finance, mergers and acquisitions, banking and structured finance and tax.

CLIENTELE Clients include financial institutions, corporates and referrals from other firms.

INTERNATIONAL Despite the increasingly global nature of the firm's practice and intensive ties with many law firms in other jurisdictions, NautaDutilh has clearly and publicly chosen to remain independent.

Needham & James

25 Meer Street, Stratford-upon-Avon, CV37 6QB **Tel** (01789) 414444 **Fax** (0121) 633 4450

Neil Myerson Solicitors

The Cottages, Regent Road, Altrincham, WA14 1RX
Tel (0161) 941 4000 **Fax** (0161) 941 4411
Email lawyers@neil-myerson.co.uk **Website** www.neil-myerson.co.uk

AREAS OF PRACTICE	
Company Commercial	70%
Personal Injury/Housing	20%
Private Client	10%

Ptnrs 5 **Asst solrs** 17 **Other fee-earners** 3 **Contact** Neil Myerson • Established in 1982, Neil Myerson Solicitors is a company/commercial law firm which also offers specialist expertise in IT, internet and motor law.

A-Z LAW FIRMS

Nelsons

Pennine House, 8 Stanford Street, Nottingham, NG1 7BQ
Tel (0115) 958 6262 **Fax** (0115) 958 4702 **DX** 179462 Nottingham 35
Email mailbox@nelsons-solicitors.co.uk **Website** www.nelsonsonline.com

THE FIRM With headquarters in Nottingham and other offices in Derby, Leicester and Grantham, Nelsons is a prominent broad-based practice for commercial, private and Legal Aid clients. Nelsons is one of the few firms in the region to offer strength and depth in all areas.

PRINCIPAL AREAS OF WORK The firm has a national reputation in business defence work and has recently been appointed to the Serious Fraud Panel. Company and commercial expertise includes corporate finance, venture capital work and all forms of agreements. All aspects of litigation are handled, including cross-border cases. Liquor, gaming and bingo licensing are also dealt with. Construction and employment are both rapidly expanding specialisms. The personal injury department has particular expertise in asbestos-related cases and group actions. The firm has been accepted onto the Multi-party Action Panel. Family law, crime, immigration and mental health are also areas of strength. All forms of property work are undertaken, including acting for major property developer clients. The firm has a thriving private client department, which also provides tax advice.

RECRUITMENT Recent developments include the recruitment of personnel from Warren & Allen, the Nottingham firm, which ceased practice on 15th February. Partners John Atkinson and Tim Quincey join the Family department. Christopher and Peter Allen, members of the founding family of Warren & Allen join as consultants in the Private Client department. The Leicester corporate team has been strengthened by the recruitment of partner Phillipa Dawkins and associate Melanie Oswin.

Managing Partner	Tim Hastings
Senior Partner	Richard Nelson
Number of partners	52
Assistant solicitors	56
Other fee-earners	97

CONTACTS	
Advocacy & Higher Court	Simon Chaplin
Business Defence	Richard Nelson
Corporate	Duncan Taylor
Family	Hilary Freeman
Immigration	David Smith
Licensing	David Lucas
Litigation	Chris Adams
PI	Bruce Williams
Private Client	Richard Grosberg
Property	Noel Tornbohm

Ness Gallagher
95 Stewarton Street, Wishaw, ML2 8AG **Tel** (01698) 355525 **Fax** (01698) 262012

Newsome Vaughan

Greyfriars House, Greyfriars Lane, Coventry, CV1 2GW
Tel (024) 7663 3433 **Fax** (024) 7625 6496 **DX** 18,854 Coventry 2
Email pauls@n-v.co.uk **Website** www.n-v.co.uk

THE FIRM Newsome Vaughan is a leading practice in Coventry and Warwickshire, enjoying a strong reputation in personal injury litigation. The firm continues to attract high quality instructions in corporate and commercial property work, and acts for a large Midlands housing association. It also represents a large American corporation, acting as their UK lawyers and assisting the in-house European Legal Office. The firm has attained the ISO 9001 Quality Standard.

PRINCIPAL AREAS OF WORK The firm specialises in civil litigation; claimant personal injury litigation; commercial property; company and commercial; employment law; housing association law; private client work; mortgage repossessions; mortgage lending law; professional negligence.

Senior Partner	Rupert M B Griffiths
Number of partners	4
Assistant solicitors	14
Other fee-earners	11

AREAS OF PRACTICE	
Litigation	50%
Private Clients	25%
Commercial/Business	25%

Nicholas Pryor – Panel of Independent Mediators
19 Sotheby Rd, Highbury, London, N5 2UP **Tel** (020) 7359 2819 **Fax** (020) 7359 4984

Nicholson Graham & Jones

110 Cannon Street, London, EC4N 6AR
Tel (020) 7648 9000 **Fax** (020) 7648 9001 **DX** 58 London Chancery Lane
Email info@ngj.co.uk **Website** www.ngj.co.uk

Managing Partner	Michael Johns
Number of partners	52
Assistant solicitors	54
Other fee-earners	29

CONTACTS	
Banking	Paul Salsbury
Charities	Carole Cook
Corporate & Commercial	Richard Talbot
Commercial Litigation	John Magnin
Competition	Neil Baylis
Construction & Engineering	David Race
Corporate Finance	Richard Herbert
Corporate & Property Tax	Richard Woolich
E-commerce	Peter McBride
Election Law	Piers Coleman
Employee Share Schemes	Michael Jacobs
Employment	Jane Liddington
Healthcare & Pharmaceuticals	Owen Waft
Insolvency	Tony Griffiths
	Robin Tutty
Intellectual Property	Peter McBride
New Technologies	Michael Webster
Planning & Environment	Michael Broughton
Private Client & Tax	Michael Jacobs
Projects/PFI/PPP	Christopher Causer
Property	Piers Coleman
Property Finance	Paul Salsbury
Property Litigation	Jane Harte-Lovelace
Public Sector	David Race
Sport & Sponsorship	Warren Phelops
Travel & Leisure	Cynthia Barbor
	Tim Robinson

THE FIRM The firm aims to deliver a better partnership with, and for, its clients. It does this by creating and developing close, integrated and professional relationships amongst all partners and staff. This helps to deliver to clients consistent, cost-effective and commercial legal advice. It also provides its lawyers with a stimulating and satisfying career, and staff with an enjoyable working environment. Over the past 10 years the firm has doubled in size, enabling it to undertake an increasingly complex workload, extending its specialist capabilities.

PRINCIPAL AREAS OF WORK The six main departments provide the combination of legal expertise necessary to provide relevant high quality advice to a range of industry and service sectors. Cross-departmental groups bring a commercial understanding of all areas such as sport, travel and leisure, employment and media.

Corporate Commercial The firm is well known for its corporate work, including flotations, mergers and acquisitions, corporate finance, joint venture structures and all UK, EU and international business transactions. It has specialist expertise in banking, insolvency, venture capital, UK and EC competition, corporate tax, property tax, employee share schemes, sport and sponsorship.

Litigation The firm has extensive experience in commercial dispute resolution, both domestic and internationally, through ADR, arbitration and the courts. It specialises in financial services and banking, insolvency, employment, travel and leisure. The firm also covers a wide range of general commercial, corporate and property litigation.

Property The 25 strong experienced team covers property development, property investment, finance, planning and environment law. The department has been involved in some of the largest and most complex property projects of recent times.

Construction & Engineering This department is one of the largest and strongest in the country, advising on contentious and non-contentious matters. It offers a wide range of services. This covers project and contract work through to litigation, arbitration and alternative dispute resolution, which includes adjudication, mediation and conciliation.

Intellectual Property, Technologies & Sport This expanding department includes recognised leaders in their field, and acts for some household names. It has a strong commercial understanding of companies and individuals in these areas, combined with wide experience and in-depth legal expertise.

Private Client & Tax There are few City firms that still have a strong private client department. This firm is one. It advises on all aspects of estate and individual tax planning, frequently with an international element. It specialises in international trust and tax advice, probate and acting for charities.

CLIENTELE The firm acts for a wide range of clients, ranging from listed companies to individual entrepreneurs; from financial institutions to charities; from public sector bodies to sports and media companies.

INTERNATIONAL The firm is a founder member of GlobaLex, an international alliance of law firms with offices across the USA, Europe and the Far East, and a representative office in Brussels.

RECRUITMENT Always keen to consider applications from qualified lawyers who are confident and commercially driven, the firm also recruits up to ten trainee solicitors each year. For more information contact Gail Harcus or visit the firm's website.

NICHOLSON GRAHAM & JONES
a better partnership

■ **Nicholsons**
23 Alexandra Rd, Lowestoft, NR32 1PP **Tel** (01502) 532300 **Fax** (01502) 568814

■ **Nicol, Denvir & Purnell**
798 Newport Road, Rumney, Cardiff, CF5 8DH **Tel** (029) 2079 6311 **Fax** (029) 2077 9261

■ **Nigel Davis Solicitors**
The Sheepfold, Carr Hall Farm, Turnditch, Belper, DE56 2LW **Tel** (01335) 372889 **Fax** (01335) 372891

A-Z ■ LAW FIRMS

■ Nigel Dewar Gibb & Co
43 St John Street, London, EC1M 4AN
Tel (020) 7608 1091   **Fax** (020) 7608 1092
Email ndg@e-legaluk.co.uk   **Website** www.e-legaluk.co.uk

Areas of Practice	
Music	40%
Commercial	25%
Copyright/IP	25%
Film/TV/Advertising	10%

Ptnrs 1   **Other fee-earners** 2   **Contact** Nigel Gibb • Since 1998 this independent firm has provided commercial/media IP, legal services (including artist management services) to creative and media industries supported by network of specialist advisors. Client base comprises recording artists, DJs, club operators, performers, record labels, publishers, audio and audio-visual production companies, management companies, agencies, fashion designers and related commercial operations.

■ NJ Goodman & Co
14 Market Street, Altrincham, WA14 1QB   **Tel** (0161) 928 0990   **Fax** (0161) 941 6254

■ Nolan Macleod
Donaldson House, 39 Donaldson Street, Kirkintilloch, Glasgow, G66 1XE
Tel (0141) 777 6366   **Fax** (0141) 777 8639   **Email** mail@nolmac.co.uk

Ptnrs 3   **Asst solrs** 1   **Other fee-earners** 16 • Nolan Macleod is a long established Scottish legal firm specialising solely in commercial debt collection and insolvency for blue chip companies. A genuine one stop service covering all stages of recovery from telephone collections, pre-sues, tracing, instigating and concluding court actions, enforcement, cash and asset collection through to company and personal insolvencies.

Norton Rose
Kempson House, Camomile Street, London, EC3A 7AN
Tel (020) 7283 6000   **Fax** (020) 7283 6500   **DX** 85 London/1064 City
Website www.nortonrose.com

Managing Partner	Roger Birkby
Senior Partner	David Lewis
UK	
Number of partners:	121
Assistant solicitors:	359
Other fee-earners:	176
International	
Number of partners:	75
Assistant solicitors:	238
Other fee-earners:	48

AREAS OF PRACTICE	
Banking & Asset Finance	31%
Litigation	24%
Corporate Finance	23%
Technology	15%
Property, Planning & Environmental	8%

CONTACTS	
Aviation	Jeremy Edwards
Banking	Stephen Parish
Capital Markets	Jonathan Walsh
Commercial Litigation & Arbitration	
	Juliet Blanch
	Peter Rees
Construction	Peter Hall
Corporate Finance	Barbara Stephenson
Energy	Michael Taylor
EU & Competition	Martin Coleman
Human Resources	Timothy Russell
Insolvency	Hamish Anderson
Insurance	Francis Mackie
Intellectual Property	Chris Ryan
Media & Telecommunications	Richard Barratt
Project Finance	Jeffery Barratt
Property Planning & Environmental	
	Robin Mitchell
Railways	Gordon Hall
Shipping	Jeremy Gibb
Taxation	John Challoner

THE FIRM Norton Rose continues to excel as a finance and business firm uppermost in its chosen markets – corporate finance, asset finance, project finance, acquisition finance, development finance and financial litigation. The firm has continued its international expansion with the opening of offices in Hong Kong and Amsterdam in early 2002. It provides an international service from offices in Athens, Amsterdam, Bahrain, Bangkok, Brussels, Cologne, Frankfurt, Hong Kong, London, Milan, Moscow, Munich, Paris, Piraeus, Singapore and Warsaw and associated offices in Beijing, Jakarta and Prague. In addition Norton Rose has significant experience in advising clients in Scandinavia, Central, Eastern and Southern Europe and throughout the Middle East, East Asia and Sub-Saharan Africa. Norton Rose provides expert services to leading players in a select number of international industry and market sectors. The firm is clearly established as a leading advisor in banking, insurance, shipping, aviation, railways, construction, energy, media and telecoms. Clients rely upon Norton Rose's in-depth understanding of industry issues, commitment to industrial expansion and ability to develop new techniques to accelerate commercial advance. For each sector, Norton Rose provides banking and corporate clients with asset finance, equity and structured financial advice, development, acquisition, consolidation and restructuring services, contractual, tax and employee relations advice, regulatory and competition advice, real and intellectual property services, and, where necessary, risk management, arbitration, litigation, workouts and insolvency advice. The firm's specialist teams build long term relations with clients at an international level and in their various domestic markets.

PRINCIPAL AREAS OF WORK
Corporate Finance The firm's corporate finance teams advise on public and private company mergers and acquisitions, privatisations, international joint ventures, inward investments, collective investment media, venture capital and general commercial work.

Capital Markets The capital markets teams advise banks and other financial institutions on international and domestic equity issues, securities trading, bonds, convertibles, derivatives, swaps, options, and asset, property and development finance securitisations. Norton Rose also offers its clients fully integrated UK/US securities law advice. This adds an important dimension to an already thriving capital markets practice and enables the firm to advise on a full range of US securities matters.

Project Finance The firm's project finance teams act for banks, contractors, sponsors, ECAs and mezzanine finance interests. They advise on all financial issues, inter-creditor agreements, risk management, receivables and trading issues, securitisation and restructuring, land, environmental, property and construction matters. Projects include energy, oil and gas, water, telecoms, infrastructure and transportation.

Commercial Litigation The commercial litigation teams undertake a high proportion of multijurisdictional and international disputes. Clients are advised on risk management, arbitration and alternative dispute resolution, litigation, regulatory disputes, workouts and insolvency.

Other Areas Other specialist teams cover intellectual property; competition and EC law, state aid, public procurement and international trade and utilities regulation; employment law, employee benefits, pension and employment-related immigration matters; international, corporate and commercial taxation; property development, investment and management, planning and the environment.

CLIENTELE The firm's clients are international banks, financial institutions and funds, multinational corporate businesses, major public and private companies in the firm's various domestic markets, government departments and agencies, statutory undertakings and sovereign states.

RECRUITMENT The firm's team structure enables partners and assistants to work closely together on related types of work. This provides a more in-depth and proactive level of service to clients, improves know-how and quality of training, and gives better support and career development for trainee solicitors and junior assistants. As the firm expands it creates excellent career prospects, including opportunities to work overseas both before and after qualification. Norton Rose recruits 85 trainee solicitors every year. It encourages high quality graduates of any discipline to apply: intellectual ability, personality, determination, and the ability to get on with others are more highly prized than degree subject matter. The firm has always been a pioneer of training and personal development. It has a training programme dedicated specifically to trainee solicitors. Highly competitive salaries are offered, as well as other benefits including sports club, regular social events, and a staff restaurant. Recruitment brochures and application forms are available from Brendan Monaghan, Graduate Recruitment Manager. Norton Rose remains one of the most genuinely pleasant places to work. There is a cohesiveness and camaraderie in the firm that is hard to find elsewhere. This provides real benefits for the firm's clients. The ability to field teams of lawyers who work effectively together and who enjoy the development and achievement of long term relationships with their clients is clearly welcomed.

■ Nunn Rickard Solicitor Advocates
24 Southern Hay East, Exeter, EX1 1QL **Tel** (01392) 200888

■ Ogier & Le Masurier

Whiteley Chambers, Don Street, St Helier, JE4 9WG
Tel (01534) 504000 **Fax** (01534) 504444
Email legal@ogier.com **Website** www.ogier.com

Chairman	Jonathan White
Managing Partner	Sarah Fitz

AREAS OF PRACTICE	
Litigation	20%
Banking	15%
Investment Funds	15%
Structured Finance	15%
Trust	15%
Corporate & Commercial	10%
Property	10%

THE FIRM Ogier & Le Masurier is one of the largest practices in the Channel Islands and has a presence in both jurisdictions of Jersey and Guernsey, through associated offices. The firm now has more than 65 lawyers and some 230 professional and support staff across both Islands. The firm provides a specialised range of legal services to financial institutions and business clients with banking and finance work, securitisation, investment funds and commercial litigation forming the core of its practice. All the work done by the firm is undertaken by teams of specialists, led by a partner, selected to achieve the commercial objectives of the client. A large proportion of qualified lawyers have worked in major financial centres outside Jersey and bring to the firm the international experience and commercial awareness sought by today's clients. The firm places a great importance on the referral of work to them by professional advisors in other jurisdictions, and seeks to work closely with those advisors not only to meet client requirements but to exceed their expectations.

CONTACTS	
Banking & Finance	Chris Byrne (St Helier)
	Roger Le Tissier (St Peter Port)
	William Simpson (St Peter Port)
Employment Benefits	Clive Chaplin (St Helier)
	Marcus Leese (St Peter Port)
Investment Funds	Nick Kershaw (St Helier)
	Roger Le Tissier (St Peter Port)
	William Simpson (St Peter Port)
Litigation	Matthew Thompson (St Helier)
	Timothy Le Cocq (St Helier)
Securitisation	Michael Lombardi (St Helier)
	Chris Byrne (St Helier)
	Roger Le Tissier (St Peter Port)
	William Simpson (St Peter Port)
Trusts	Steven Meiklejohn (St Helier)
	Jonathan White (St Helier)
	Marcus Leese (St Peter Port)

PRINCIPAL AREAS OF WORK
Banking & Finance Ogier & Le Masurier is particularly respected for banking and international finance work in Jersey. The banking team specialises in advising on all areas of banking, security and banking regulation and on structured finance transactions.

Securitisation Securitisation of assets is a particular strength of the firm. With particular expertise in asset-backed securities, CP conduits and structured debt instruments, the firm is able to add value to the structuring process.

Investment Funds The firm has a large well respected investment funds team advising on the establishment and structuring of funds, as well as on regulatory and compliance aspects. The firm also advises on listings on the Channel Islands Stock Exchange.

Trusts The trust and estate planning group has one of the largest teams of lawyers in the Channel Islands exclusively dedicated to advising trust companies, intermediaries and individuals in matters of trust law. The group has particular expertise in the commercial application of trusts in structured financing and the employee benefits sphere.

Litigation The litigation group is the sole litigation practice in the Island specialising exclusively in

Continued overleaf

commercial litigation. Its areas of expertise include trust disputes, shareholder remedies and asset tracing and freezing orders.

CLIENTELE Clients for whom the firm acts on a regular basis include Abbey National, ANZ, Bank of America, Bank of Scotland, Barclays Private Bank, BNP, Cazenove, JP Morgan, Chase, Citibank, Deutsche Bank, Dresdner, Hill Samuel, HSBC, ING, Lloyds/TSB, Lazards, Merrill Lynch, Morgan, Guaranty, Schroders, UBS and Zurich Financial Services. The firm's client list also includes many private clients worldwide who use Jersey structures to preserve and manage their wealth as well as trust companies providing trustee services.

Oglethorpe Sturton & Gillibrand

16 Castle Park, Lancaster, LA1 1YG
Tel (01524) 67171   **Fax** (01524) 382247   **DX** 63500 Lancaster   **Email** sales@osgr.co.uk

Ptnrs 7   **Asst solrs** 7   **Other fee-earners** 6   **Contact** Philip Oglethorpe • The firm has significant expertise in agricultural, farming and property law; strong private client department; niche company commercial practice (both contentious and non-contentious).

AREAS OF PRACTICE	
Agricultural Law	23%
Litigation	22%
Private Client (Wills, Probate)	19%
Property (Commercial & Residential)	14%
Commercial	13%
Family	9%

Olsens

47 Esplanade, St Helier, JE1 0BD
Tel (01534) 888900   **Fax** (01534) 887744
Email enquiry@olsenslaw.com   **Website** www.olsensgroup.com

PO Box 212, Hadsley House, Lefebvre Street, St Peter Port, GY1 4JE
Tel (01481) 712277   **Fax** (01481) 701435
Email enquiry@ofmlaw.com

THE FIRM With offices in Jersey and Guernsey, Olsens is a leading law firm which provides legal services across the Channel Islands. The firm has 12 partners in Jersey and 4 in Guernsey and a total of 68 lawyers. Olsens is part of The Olsens Group that provides a range of associated services with a total of 180 staff. The firm provides specialist knowledge to law firms, financial institutions and other specialist advisors in the UK and worldwide. Much of the work undertaken by the firm is on a referral basis. Olsens' lawyers have a reputation for innovation, approachability, practicality and identification with client objectives. The partners have acted in many high profile cases and high value transactions earning them excellent reputations. The firm divides itself into partner-led practice teams drawing on specialist know-how and the resources of both islands to provide the client with a seamless service through a single contact partner.

PRINCIPAL AREAS OF WORK

Structured Finance & Securitisation With a reputation for innovation and quality, the team acts for issuers, arrangers, originators and trustees on ABS and MBS transactions, CDO's, SIVs, repackagings and conduits. Transactions with an aggregate value of several billion $US have been undertaken.

Banking & Finance The team has extensive experience of bank start-ups, mergers and reorganisations in the Channel Islands. It undertakes a wide range of work in support of lending, the taking and protection of security, and in customer relationship and product-related documentation.

Investment Funds & Private Equity The team has a strong reputation for its commercial client-driven approach. A leading Jersey Funds Encyclopedia ranked Olsens number one for new business in the investment funds sector. In private equity and venture capital the firm continues to attract significant new instructions from major financial institutions and business clients.

Corporate Transactions The team has wide company and commercial experience and advises major clients on Jersey and Guernsey company law and transactions in general. It provides a company and trust formation service to private and institutional clients.

Trusts The trust and fiduciary law team advises financial institutions and intermediaries on the creation of trusts and other fiduciary structures. Advice is given on international tax and estate planning, fiduciary compliance legislation and trust related disputes.

Pensions & Employee Benefits The team has considerable experience in setting up and acting for private and public sector and employee benefit share schemes. Dominion Fiduciary Services Group, recently created within the Olsens Group, provides corporate clients and financial institutions with a comprehensive trustee and administration service in employee benefits, pensions and share schemes.

Regulation & Compliance The firm provides legal support to clients in regulation and compliance. It works alongside Keldon Consultants Limited for the provision of client reviews, the production of

Senior Partner	Anthony Olsen
Number of partners	16
Assistant solicitors	41
Other fee-earners	11
Notaries public	2

CONTACTS	
Structured Finance & Securitisation	
	Alex Ohlsson (St Helier)
	Nicholas Crocker (St Helier)
	Eve Kosofsky (St Helier)
Banking	Paul Sugden (St Helier)
	Alex Ohlsson (St Helier)
	Ben Morgan (St Peter Port)
Investment Funds & Private Equity	
	Edward Quinn (St Helier)
	Eve Kosofsky (St Helier)
	Ben Morgan (St Peter Port)
Corporate Transactions	
	Nicholas Crocker (St Helier)
	Alex Ohlsson (St Helier)
Regulation & Compliance	Paul Sugden (St Helier)
	Eve Kosofsky (St Helier)
Property Finance	Alex Ohlsson (St Helier)
	Edward Quinn (St Helier)
	Nicholas Crocker (St Helier)
Pensions & Employee Benefits	
	Nicholas Crocker (St Helier)
	Paul Matthams (St Helier)
	Paul Buckle (St Peter Port)
Trusts	Edward Quinn (St Helier)
	Paul Matthams (St Helier)
	Paul Buckle (St Peter Port)
Commercial Litigation	Anthony Olsen (St Helier)
	Nicolas Journeaux (St Helier)
	Christopher Lakeman (St Helier)
	Jason Morgan (St Peter Port)
Trust Disputes	John Kelleher (St Helier)
	Nicolas Journeaux (St Helier)
	Jason Morgan (St Peter Port)
Regulatory Disputes	John Kelleher (St Helier)
Commercial Property	John Kelleher (St Helier)
Private Wealth Management	
	Anthony Olsen (St Helier)

operational and compliance procedure manuals and the provision of training in areas such as anti-money laundering awareness. Keldon also undertakes forensic investigation work and litigation support.
Commercial Litigation Olsens has the largest litigation practice in the Channel Islands. The team deals with all areas of client litigation, specialising in contentious and non-contentious trust litigation, multi-jurisdictional disputes, asset tracing, freezing orders, professional negligence claims, and insurance and related claims. Notable cases include Grupo Torras and In Re: Esteem Settlement.
Commercial Property The team acts for several of the Island's leading property developers and has been acting in Jersey's biggest ever land dispute.
Private Wealth Management The team provides a high degree of personal attention. It undertakes private trusts, wills, residential property and probate.

CLIENTELE The firm's clients include law firms, international banks, financial institutions and funds, governments, heads of state, companies and private clients from all over the world. Clients for whom the firm acts regularly include: Nomura, Merrill Lynch, CSFB, DKW, JP Morgan Chase, Barclays, Citibank, Deutsche Bank AG, Bank of Scotland Offshore, Gerrard Private Bank, BNP Paribas, UBS AG, HSBC Plc, The Royal Bank of Scotland International, Rothschilds, West Deutsche Landesbank LB, Newton Mellon.

INTERNATIONAL Olsens is a member of Legalink, International Grouping of Lawyers, STEP, International Bar Association, ACTAPS. Between the offices languages spoken include English, French, Italian, Spanish, German, Dutch, Flemish and Afrikaans.

RECRUITMENT Olsens attracts senior lawyers from the Channel Islands and overseas, believing its appeal lies in its dynamic approach, career opportunities and range of work. The firm is held in high regard, not only for the quality of lawyers it attracts, but also the quality of work it undertakes.

Olswang

90 Long Acre, London, WC2E 9TT
Tel (020) 7208 8888 **Fax** (020) 7208 8800 **DX** 37972 London Kingsway
Email olsmail@olswang.com **Website** www.olswang.com

Abbots House, Abbey Street, Reading, RG1 3BD
Tel (0118) 949 0000 **Fax** (0118) 949 0049 **DX** 54711 Reading 2

Chief Executive	Jonathan Goldstein
Senior Partner	Mark Devereux
Number of partners	67
Assistant solicitors	139
Other fee-earners	49

CONTACTS	
Advertising	Jonathan Goldstein
	Louise Quinn
Banking	Graeme Levy
	Moni Mannings
Biosciences	Michael Burdon
Commercial Litigation	David Stewart
	Martin Davies
	Steven Baker
	Tim Clark
Construction	Richard Wilson
Corporate	Moni Mannings
	Simon Morgan
	Stephen Hermer
	Richard Hildebrand
	Paul Blackmore
	Marshall Leopold
Defamation	Geraldine Proudler
	Julia Palca
E-commerce	Kim Nicholson
	John Enser
	Matthew Cowan
	Clive Gringras
Employment Benefits	Nicky Griffin
Employment	Catherine Taylor
	Julia Palca
	Sarah Keeble
	Gary Henderson
	Daniel Aherne
EU & Competition	Howard Cartlidge
	Dirk van Liedekerke
	Alasdair Bell
Film & TV Finance	Mark Devereux
	Jacqueline Hurt
	Jane Moore
	Charles Moore
	Lisbeth Savill

THE FIRM Olswang is a full-service law firm that has been focusing primarily on clients in the media, communications and technology sectors for over 20 years. Olswang has a commanding reputation as a forward-thinking, dynamic and innovative firm, and it is these characteristics that have enabled the firm to keep its edge despite the turbulent times of 2001. In Spring 2002 the firm was boosted by the establishment of a new Thames Valley office, created when the firm hired the partners and staff of the Garretts Reading office, and providing a crucial M4 corridor stronghold.

Lawyers at Olswang provide an unparalleled understanding of the key strategic and commercial issues driving clients in the firm's chosen sectors, delivering innovative business solutions through legal excellence. Frequently one step ahead of its competitors, the firm has been involved in a number of ground-breaking cases in recent times, including Dyson's high profile patent litigation victory over Hoover, the attheraces media rights deal with the Racehorse Association and British Horseracing Board and the Eddie Irvine/TalkSport case.

The firm's collection of awards keeps on growing, including in the last year the Legal Business award for Media, Entertainment and Sport for their work advising Channel 4/attheraces on the acquisition of media rights for horseracing. The firm's reputation in the business of sport has grown in stature this year with the team working on a number of newsworthy cases for high profile organisations, including acting for Wimbledon Football in relation to their proposed move to Milton Keynes.

The Olswang ethos has always focused on realising potential: the potential of our clients and of our people. The firm is proud to work with some of the most successful companies in the media, communications and technology industries, and the Olswang partnership boasts one of the highest percentages of 'leading lawyers' in their fields. Established in 1981, the firm has a total staff of more than 460 and has offices in London, the Thames Valley and Brussels.

PRINCIPAL AREAS OF WORK
Advertising Corporate structure, brand protection, agency services, sponsorship, taxation and clearance, defamation.
Banking All aspects of corporate debt financing, secured lending and insolvency.
Biosciences Offers a range of legal and regulatory advice (especially IP, corporate, private equity/venture capital, UK and EU regulation, tax) to the pharmaceutical, biotechnology and medical service industry.
Commercial Litigation Claims for breach of contracts and warranties, shareholder/boardroom disputes,

Continued overleaf

A-Z ■ LAW FIRMS

negligence claims, film and television production disputes, fraud claims.
Corporate & Commercial Flotations, private fund raisings, MBOs, MBIs, start-ups, acquisitions and disposals, takeovers, share option schemes.
Defamation Libel and content-related litigation, pre-publication/broadcast advice, challenging reporting restrictions by courts, internet libel and content.
E-commerce ISP terms and conditions, finance raising, start-ups, www advice, online trading.
Employment Employee packages, incentive schemes, disciplinary issues, unfair dismissal, redundancy, discrimination, restrictive covenants, High Court and tribunal work, industrial relations, team moves, data protection and other employee information issues, European employment law issues.
EU & Competition Competition and regulatory complaints, investigations and litigation, merger control clearances and interventions, commercial agreements, special rules for businesses with market power, licensing and regulatory compliance, public procurement, state aids, general EU law.
Film & TV (Finance/Production) Production finance, talent agreements, assessing UK and international benefits, tax-based finance, co-productions, sales and distribution, dispute resolution and risk avoidance, corporate finance.
IT Hardware/software procurement and maintenance, systems integration, outsourcing agreements, development, implementation and maintenance of e-commerce systems, website development.
Intellectual Property IP protection, acquisition strategy, IP rights, trade secrets, copyright, cross-border IP litigation including multijurisdictional internet/e-commerce patent issues, trademark and patent filings.
Music M&A, competition law, IP, e-commerce, digital distribution, copyright, anti-piracy and artist disputes.
Private Equity/Venture Capital MBOs, MBIs, development capital, start-ups, corporate reconstructions, debt and mezzanine financing.
Property Investment, development, funding, planning, construction, property litigation, tax efficient and transparent structures.
Publishing Pre-publication, negotiating, commercial contracts, contractual and IP disputes.
Sport: Broadcasting rights, sports finance, regulation, IP rights, sponsorship, online business, dispute resolution, risk avoidance.
Tax Acquisitions and disposals, corporate reorganisations, partnerships, joint ventures, structured finance arrangements, property, employee incentives, designing new financial products, VAT.
Technology Investments research and development, exploitation, protection and enforcement, both internationally and domestically.
Telecommunications Global telecom projects, investments in network infrastructure, terrestrial and satellite, ISPs, M&A, financings, commercial contracts, regulation, competition, litigation.
TV/broadcasting The entire spectrum of broadcasting issues including carriage agreements, uplinking, transmission and transponder facilities, conditional access technology, all aspects of interactive TV deals, electronic programme guides, rights acquisitions, competition and regulatory issues.

CONTACTS (Continued)	
Film & TV Production	Mark Devereux
	Lisbeth Savill
	Jacqueline Hurt
	Jane Moore
	Charles Moore
Information Technology	Simon Briskman
	Kim Nicholson
	Kim Walker
	Clive Gringras
	Alison Harrington
Insolvency	Graeme Levy
Intellectual Property	Andrew Inglis
	Paul Stevens
	Kim Walker
	Michael Burdon
	Alison Harrington
Music	John Enser
	Stephen Hermer
Planning	Richard Max
Private Equity/Venture Capital	Tina Cowen
	Fabrizio Carpanini
	Chris Mackie
Property	Tim Westhead
	Martyn Needham
	Philip Olmer
	David Kustow
	John Castell
	Debra Kent
Property Litigation	Marcus Barclay
Publishing	Kim Walker
	Selina Potter
	Geraldine Proudler
Sport	Michael Brader
	David Zeffman
	Claire Harvey
Tax	Kay Butler
	Mark Joscelyne
Technology	Andrew Inglis
	Kim Nicholson
Telecommunications	Colin Long
	Kim Nicholson
TV/Broadcasting	David Zeffman
	Selina Potter
	John Enser
	Jane Moore

O'Melveny & Myers

3 Finsbury Square, London, EC2A 1LA
Tel (020) 7256 8451 **Fax** (020) 7638 8205
Email omminfo@omm.com **Website** www.omm.com

Managing & Senior Partner	Stephen J Stern
Number of partners	4
Assistant solicitors	4

THE FIRM O'Melveny was founded in 1885 in Los Angeles. The firm now has over 800 lawyers with offices in thirteen US and international locations. Many of its lawyers have distinguished themselves through their leadership in public service and other organisations. In the US, the firm ranks include a former US Secretary of State, a former Secretary of Transportation, a former Counsel to the President, and a former Acting Solicitor General, among other Executive Branch and Capitol Hill policy makers, in addition to some of the most respected litigators and transactional lawyers. The firm's London office was founded in 1986 and is a multinational partnership of US attorneys and English solicitors with experience in areas including acquisition and leveraged financing facilities, international securities offerings, corporate recovery, insolvency and restructuring work, project finance, securitisation, venture capital/private equity, joint ventures, mergers and acquisitions, and general banking matters.

PRINCIPAL AREAS OF WORK O'Melveny & Myers engages in a broad and diversified US and international practice with several areas of specialisation for which it has established distinct departments within the firm: litigation, transactions, tax, labour and employment, intellectual property, and business restructuring and reorganisation. The London office works closely with the firm's other offices and has ready access to the resources of the entire firm. It has been involved in acquisitions, disposals, project developments, insolvencies and restructurings, joint ventures and/or financings in various western European countries, and in recent years has been increasingly involved in the firm's emerging markets practice, both in eastern Europe and Latin America, and the firm's emerging companies practice (particularly in the technology and internet areas). The London office's most significant areas of activity, however, are in complex, structured multijurisdictional financings (often related to acquisitions, film financing or projects) and corporate recovery, insolvency and restructuring work. The London office advises on English Law as well as US and international law, and believes it is unique among international law firms in offering recognised financing experts as well as insolvency and reorganisation experts in the UK and the US on both the east coast (New York) and the west coast (Los Angeles).

INTERNATIONAL Other Offices: Century City (California); Hong Kong; Irvine Spectrum (California); Los Angeles; New York; Newport Beach (California); San Francisco; Shanghai; Silicon Valley (California); Tokyo; Tysons Corner (Virginia); Washington DC.

O'Reilly Stewart

O'Reilly Stewart House, 114-116 Royal Avenue, Belfast, BT1 1DL
Tel (028) 9032 1000   **Fax** (028) 9032 3003   **DX** 3700 NR Belfast
Email oreillystewart@dnet.co.uk   **Website** www.oreilly-stewart.co.uk

Number of partners	3
Assistant solicitors	12
Other fee-earners	7

THE FIRM O'Reilly Stewart can trace its roots back to 1920 and combines a wealth of experience with a steadily increasing number of young highly qualified solicitors familiar with all the latest developments in law, business and technology.

PRINCIPAL AREAS OF WORK

Litigation One of the senior partners has practised in the province since 1980 and now deals primarily with defence work. He is a member of the International Association of Defence Counsel and Chairman of the Legal Aid Committee. He leads a team of six solicitors with emphasis on insurance defence work, multijurisdictional class actions, product liability, plaintiff personal injury, medical negligence, uninsured loss recovery and defamation.

Commercial/Licensing One of the senior partners has a long established reputation in relation to licensing and commercial property work. He leads a team of five solicitors with emphasis on all aspects of commercial conveyancing and property work including acquisition of freehold and leasehold properties for investment or development, planning law and appeals, multinational property transactions, agency work for English firms, Building Society panel work, mortgage portfolio acquisitions and all aspects of liquor licensing, gaming and entertainment law.

General Within the firm there are also individual solicitors who practice in employment law, industrial tribunals law, discrimination law, criminal law, domestic conveyancing, matrimonial law and probate law.

AREAS OF PRACTICE	
Litigation	45%
Company/Commercial	20%
Conveyancing	15%
Criminal	5%
Family	5%
Licensing & Gaming	5%
Building Society Work	5%

CONTACTS	
Commercial	Linus Murray
Conveyancing	Janet McMillan
Litigation	Joseph Moore

CLIENTELE Direct Line Insurance, Hastings Hotels, Bradford & Bingley PLC, Privilege Insurance, Amazon.com, Green Flag, C.N.A. Insurance, The Queen's University of Belfast, the Planning Appeals Commission, and the Equality Commission for Northern Ireland.

Orrick, Herrington & Sutcliffe

4 Broadgate, London, EC2M 2DA
Tel (020) 7562 5000   **Fax** (020) 7628 0078
Email mbacon@orrick.com   **Website** www.orrick.com

Managing Partner	Michael Bacon
Chairman (Firmwide)	Ralph H Baxter, Jr
Number of partners	4
Assistant solicitors	7
Other fee-earners	4
Total staff (worldwide)	1364

THE FIRM Orrick is a leading international finance and technology law firm, with headquarters in San Francisco and over 570 lawyers worldwide. The firm's core strategic practices are securitisation, structured finance, global energy, communications and infrastructure, technology and corporate. These are also the focus of the London office. Orrick, Herrington & Sutcliffe was founded in 1863 in California, where it assisted in the formation of some of the state's oldest institutions and industrial corporations and the financing of much of its infrastructure. The firm expanded to New York, now its largest office, and other key commercial centres in the United States, Asia and Europe, including London and Tokyo. The London office was established in September 1998 and comprises 15 lawyers providing advice under English, German and US law. The practice is organised to provide integrated international legal services, and Orrick's extensive use of the latest technologies enables it to deal with matters originating virtually anywhere in the world.

AREAS OF PRACTICE	
Corporate & Technology	19%
Public Finance	15%
Intellectual Property	12%
Litigation	12%
Structured Finance	11%
Real Estate	7%
Global Infrastructure	7%
Private Finance	7%
Employment	6%
Compensation & Benefits	2%
Tax	2%

PRINCIPAL AREAS OF WORK The London office has particular expertise in structured finance capital markets transactions, with notable emphasis on securitisation of all kinds, and project finance including privatisations, infrastructure projects and energy-related work. In the United States, and internationally, the firm has earned leading rankings in structured finance, municipal finance, project finance and

Continued overleaf

representation in initial public offerings. In addition, many of its litigators are recognised as leaders in their fields. Other key areas include intellectual property, employment, taxation, real estate, bankruptcy and restructuring derivatives, market regulation and financial services.

CLIENTELE US and international clients include major industrial and financial corporations, city, state and other governmental entities, universities, charities and public service organisations.

INTERNATIONAL Orrick has offices in London, New York, Los Angeles, Seattle, Sacramento, San Francisco, Silicon Valley, Washington DC, Singapore and Tokyo. Orrick, Herrington & Sutcliffe plans to further strengthen and expand in London, in Europe and in its other international offices in Singapore and Tokyo.

CONTACTS	
Structured Finance/Capital Markets/ Securitisation	Paul Weiffenbach
Project Finance/Debt Restructuring	Martin Stewart-Smith
Corporate & Technology	Paul Stock

Osborne Clarke

Hillgate House, 26 Old Bailey, London, EC4M 7HW
Tel (020) 7809 1000 **Fax** (020) 7809 1005 **DX** 466 LONDON CHANCERY LANE WC2
Email info@osborneclarke.com **Website** www.osborneclarke.com

2 Temple Back East, Temple Quay, Bristol, BS1 6EG
Tel (0117) 917 3000 **Fax** (0117) 917 3005 **DX** 7818 Bristol – 1
Email info@osborneclarke.com

Apex Plaza, Forbury Road, Reading, RG1 1AX
Tel (0118) 925 2000 **Fax** (0118) 925 0038 **DX** 117882 – Reading Apex Plaza
Email info@osborneclarke.com

THE FIRM Osborne Clarke: one firm operating across Europe as leading advisors in its chosen fields, principally technology, media and communications; banking and financial services; and real estate, retail and construction. Considered one of the UK's most dynamic and enterprising firms, Osborne Clarke is a dominant commercial force across the south of England, advising both key corporate and institutional clients – including 17 FTSE 100 companies. It also has a unique geographical reach. Across Europe the firm fields 550 lawyers in 14 cities, where its reputation in key corporate and commercial areas sees it compete head on with the largest City, national and international firms. It is also still the only pan-European law firm to open an office in Silicon Valley, California, where it provides exclusively European law advice to many leading US companies.

PRINCIPAL AREAS OF WORK Osborne Clarke is well known for its services in corporate and commercial, property and construction, employment, pensions and incentives, technology, dispute resolution and tax. Internationally, the firm is active principally in those sectors it represents in the UK, namely technology, media and communications, banking and financial services, real estate, retail and construction. The firm's technology, media and communications focus is widely recognised and partnering and investment in the technology sector is at the heart of what Osborne Clarke does, working with technology and finance companies on both sides of the Atlantic to develop significant opportunities for growth. In March 2002 the European Technology Forum named Osborne Clarke 'UK Law Firm of the Year' for its international vision and long-term commitment to the sector. Banking and finance is also an integral part of Osborne Clarke's European practice. In the UK, the firm acts on a regular basis for over 30 financial institutions, including high street banks, foreign banks, venture capital houses and other finance providers. The firm's private equity practice is one of the largest in the UK and Germany and acts for 15 venture capital houses. In 2002, the firm's property practice grew by 55%. Following its merger with property specialist McGuinness Finch, the firm offers the complete range of property services including investment, development, planning, finance, construction, environmental, landlord and tenant, leisure and retail, litigation and tax. Clients include UK and overseas investors, developers, retailers, corporate occupiers, house-builders, contractors and landowners.

INTERNATIONAL The firm also has offices in Barcelona, Brussels, Copenhagen, Helsinki, Madrid, Paris, Rotterdam, St Petersburg and Tallinn.

Managing Partner	Leslie Perrin
Senior Partner	Chris Curling
Number of partners	114
Assistant solicitors	255
Other fee-earners	132
Total staff	897

AREAS OF PRACTICE	
Corporate & Commercial	30%
Real Estate & Construction	20%
Employment, Pensions & Incentives	15%
Dispute Resolution	15%
IT	10%
Tax	5%
Banking	5%

CONTACTS	
Advertising & Marketing	Tim Birt
	Stephen Groom
Anglo-Danish Matters	Roy Lambert
	Per Troen
Anglo-German Matters	Adrian Taylor
Competition	Claire Wagner
Corporate Banking	Chris Sykes
	Jeremy Cross
	Hugh Jones
Corporate Finance	Andrew Saul
	Patrick Graves
	Andrew Gowans
Corporate Tax	Philip G S Moss
Dispute Resolution	Clare Robinson
	Irene Dallas
	Adrian Lifely
Employment	Julian Hemming
	Nicholas Moore
	Ralph Nathan
	Danielle Kingdon
Insolvency	Patrick Cook
Pensions & Incentives	Mark Womersley
Private Capital & Personal Trusts	Sandra Brown
Private Equity	Kieran O'Connor
	Alisdair Livingstone
	Greg Leyshon
	Simon Beswick
Real Estate & Construction	Simon Speirs
	Nadine Strahl
TMT	Simon Rendell
	Andrew Braithwaite
	Russell Bowyer

Osborne Morris & Morgan
Danbury House, West Street, Leighton Buzzard, LU7 7DD **Tel** (01525) 378177 **Fax** (01525) 851006

Osbornes
68 Parkway, London, NW1 7AH **Tel** (020) 7485 8811 **Fax** (020) 7485 5660

Oswald Goodier & Co
10 Chapel St, Preston, PR1 8AY
Tel (01772) 253841 **Fax** (01772) 201713 **DX** 714571 Preston 14
Email oswgoodier@aol.com

Senior Partner	Mark Belderbos
Number of partners	3
Other fee-earners	1

AREAS OF PRACTICE	
Charity, Trust & Probate	35%
Residential Property & Landlord & Tenant	35%
Commercial Property/Company	18%
Personal Injury & Other Litigation	5%
Matrimonial & Family	3%
Other	4%

THE FIRM Established in 1897 in central Preston, the firm has a substantial charity, trust, property and private client practice in the North West and further afield. For very many years, Oswald Goodier & Co has represented numerous charities, both religious and secular, involving much work in the fields of trusts, property, educational and ecclesiastical law. Highlights include regular substantial property transactions, and continuous involvement in charity law matters. The firm is highly regarded as experienced in all aspects of private client work, as well as being much involved in civil litigation, licensing, employment and elderly client work.

CLIENTELE Substantial connections in private client work and several religious, diocesan and secular charities, schools and colleges and long-established trust and estate clients.

Oury Clark Solicitors
5 Arlington Street, London, SW1A 1RA
Tel (020) 7629 8844 **Fax** (020) 7629 8855 **DX** 140543 Piccadilly 5
Email james.oury@ouryclarksolicitors.com **Website** www.ouryclark.com

Ptnrs 2 **Asst solrs** 5 **Other fee-earners** 4 **Contact** James Oury LLB ACA • Specialists in criminal defence work (particularly white-collar crime) providing advice and representation to individuals facing fraud proceedings, DTI/FSA/Inland Revenue/HM Customs & Excise investigations, providing regulatory advice to members of professional bodies, human rights and commercial inward investment adopting a multidisciplinary legal/accountancy approach.

Overbury Steward Eaton & Woolsey
3 Upper King St, Norwich, NR3 1RL **Tel** (01603) 610481 **Fax** (01603) 632460

Over Taylor Biggs
1 Oak Tree Place, Manaton Close, Matford Business Park, Exeter, EX2 8WA **Tel** (01392) 823811 **Fax** (01392) 823812

Owen White
Senate House, 62-70 Bath Road, Slough, SL2 3SR **Tel** (01753) 876800 **Fax** (01753) 876876

Ozannes
PO Box 186, 1 Le Marchant Street, St Peter Port, GY1 4HP
Tel (01481) 723466 **Fax** (01481) 727935
Email advocates@ozannes.com **Website** www.ozannes.com

Contact Peter Harwood • Ozannes is one of Guernsey's leading law firms, specialising in offshore commercial and corporate work, in particular mutual funds, company and trust law, banking, finance, securitisations, insurance, tax, listings and litigation. Ozannes has a large team of established lawyers with experience gained in London and other major financial centres.

Pagan Osborne
12 St. Catherine Street, Cupar, KY15 4HN **Tel** (01334) 653777 **Fax** (01334) 655063

Palser Grossman
Discovery House, Scott Harbour, Cardiff Bay, CF10 4HA **Tel** (029) 2045 2770 **Fax** (029) 2045 2328

Panel of Independent Mediators
Panel of Independent Mediators, 47 Campden Hill Square, London, W8 7JR **Tel** (020) 7221 5893 **Fax** (020) 7727 6321

A-Z LAW FIRMS

Pannone & Partners

123 Deansgate, Manchester, M3 2BU
Tel (0161) 909 3000   **Fax** (0161) 909 4444   **DX** 14314 Manchester 1
Email law@pannone.co.uk   **Website** www.pannone.com

Managing Partner	Joy Kingsley
Senior Partner	Rodger Pannone
Number of partners	63
Assistant solicitors	71
Other fee-earners	76

AREAS OF PRACTICE	
Personal Injury	26%
Commercial Litigation	19%
Corporate	14%
Commercial Property	12%
Family	8%
Clinical Negligence	8%
Private Client	8%
Employment	5%

CONTACTS	
Business Crime	Paul Taylor
Clinical Negligence	John Kitchingman
Commercial Litigation	Vincent O'Farrell
Commercial Property	Andrew Simpkin
Construction	Tom Ellis
Corporate & Commercial	Søren Tattam
Debt Collection	Paul Johnson
Employment	Christine Bradley
Family	Catherine Jones
Financial Services	Tony Ashton
French Property	Lindsay Kinnealy
Insolvency	Paul Johnson
Intellectual Property	John McMuldroch
Licensing	Nick Dickinson
Personal Injury	Carol Jackson
Private Client	Hugh Jones
Public Sector	Steven Grant

THE FIRM Pannone & Partners is the largest single-site practice in Manchester. It has strengths not shared by firms of a similar size in its ability to service all types of work for both commercial and personal clients, with the firm's strength and size being split evenly between the two. Pannone & Partners was the first law firm to achieve BS5750 accreditation, now ISO 9001, and has held this quality mark for the last 11 years. The firm prides itself on its ability to work in partnership with its clients and to offer practical and cost-effective solutions to meet clients' needs.

PRINCIPAL AREAS OF WORK

Corporate & Commercial A comprehensive range of corporate services is available including all aspects of business start-up and formation, banking and finance, commercial contracts, company law and competition law. The department also has a number of specialist teams offering particular expertise in public sector, intellectual property and media law.

Commercial Property This department provides a full range of advice on commercial property transactions including purchases, sales, mortgages, planning, development, leases, joint ventures and portfolio management.

Commercial Litigation This progressive and successful department is acknowledged by its competitors to be tough, knowledgeable and effective. Experienced in litigating in all courts and tribunals, its watchword is commerciality. It also houses the debt recovery unit.

Employment This specialist department handles its own tribunal advocacy and provides quality advice nationally and locally, predominantly for employers, but also for employees, dealing with all aspects of the employment relationship.

Business Crime An experienced, highly-regarded team advising on white collar, serious and complex criminal/regulatory cases and investigations.

Construction A dedicated team of construction specialists who carry out work of both a contentious and non-contentious nature.

Insolvency This team aims to give prompt considered practical advice from which clients, who include banks, receivers, creditors and debtors, can derive financial commercial benefit.

Licensing This department provides a full range of liquor licensing services with a particular specialism in licensed forecourts. It is the only accredited training provider for the British Innkeepers' Institute National Licensing Course in central Manchester (with Grade 1 status) and offers on-site training and examinations.

Personal Injury This department is consistently accredited as the strongest personal injury team in the North West, with a demonstrable national and international reputation for the quality of its work, the size of settlements obtained and expertise in handling multi-party and complex claims. The department also handles many hundreds of claims each year arising out of less serious accidents. As with clinical negligence, a significant amount of work is referred from other non-specialist solicitors.

Clinical Negligence This dedicated team of medical negligence specialists acts for clients throughout the country seeking redress for sometimes catastrophic injuries received during medical treatment. Members of this department do not undertake any other form of personal injury work thereby guaranteeing a high degree of specialism.

Family This is one of the pre-eminent family law departments in the country, handling divorce and all that goes with it. Its specialities include substantial and complex financial cases acting for high net worth individuals and contested adoption.

Private Client A large department dealing with residential conveyancing, tax planning, wills and estates and Court of Protection work. This department also includes the hugely successful re-mortgaging team, which provides a specialist service to most major lenders.

INTERNATIONAL The firm is a founder member of the Pannone Law Group, Europe's first integrated international law group taking the form of a European Economic Interest Grouping. Its lawyers recognised the need to offer creative, imaginative and practical advice on a pan-European basis. PLG maintains offices in Andorra, Belgium, Brazil, Canada, France, Germany, Italy, Luxembourg, Netherlands, Portugal, Spain, Switzerland and the UK. The firm recognises the importance of communication between different cultures and often transacts business in French, German, Swedish and Danish.

RECRUITMENT The firm recruits eight trainee solicitors each year. LPC course fees are fully sponsored. There is a structured training and development programme and the majority of the firm's trainees remain with the firm on qualification. Full details and applications are on the firm's website.

Pardoes

6-9 King Square, Bridgwater, TA6 3YB **Tel** (01278) 457891 **Fax** (01278) 429249

Paris Smith & Randall

Number 1 London Road, Southampton, SO15 2AE
Tel (023) 8048 2482 **Fax** (023) 8063 1835 **DX** 38534 Southampton 3
Email info@parissmith.co.uk **Website** www.parissmith.co.uk

Number of partners	15
Assistant solicitors	28
Other fee-earners	20

AREAS OF PRACTICE	
Company & Commercial	21%
Commercial Property	20%
Family	14%
Tax & Estate Planning	14%
Residential Property	13%
Litigation	13%
Employment	5%

CONTACTS	
Child Care	Justin Belcher
Company & Commercial	Andrew Heathcock
Employment	Mary Siddall
Family & Mediation	Neil Davies
Insolvency	Malcolm Le Bas
Litigation	Clive Thomson
Personal Injury	Peter Taylor
Probate/Tax/Trusts	Crispin Jameson
Property (Commercial)	Mark Howarth
Property (Residential)	Peter Gammie

THE FIRM Client feedback is of primary importance at Paris Smith and Randall, and is sought at the end of every case. The responses provide the key requirements that the firm is always striving to meet: a quality service, a fast response, good, practical advice from professional advisors who understand clients' business. Paris Smith and Randall has been in practice in Southampton since 1818. The firm prides itself on having deep roots in, and an extensive knowledge of, the Solent area, currently one of the most vibrant regions of the UK economy. The firm's main client base (covering the Central Southern Area and South Coast from Chichester to Basingstoke and Bournemouth) reflects the changes that have taken place around the Solent in recent years – traditional industries associated with the docks and shipbuilding alongside software houses and businesses within the telecommunications industry. The firm has other national and international clients including property work for two London local authorities. Paris Smith and Randall has doubled in size since 1995, requiring a move in 1997 to modern, prestigious premises overlooking the City's parks and the Civic Centre.

PRINCIPAL AREAS OF WORK Paris Smith and Randall's company commercial and commercial property team has a broad portfolio of clients including quoted companies, UK subsidiaries of multi-nationals and SME's, local authorities, educational institutions, banks and lending institutions, developers and large estates. There is a planning unit within the commercial property team, and other teams within the firm specialise in corporate recovery, and sports law. The litigation department deals with various matters including large-scale commercial disputes, personal injury and medical negligence, landlord and tenant and debt collection. The firm's employment team represent both employers and employees, as well as providing support to the other commercial departments. Paris Smith and Randall has a large and respected practice in family and childcare matters, and members of the firm's tax and estate planning team are recognised experts in trust and tax law.

RECRUITMENT A position in Paris Smith and Randall offers excellent prospects in this fast-growing practice, and the firm welcomes applicants from lawyers, trainees and support staff (which should be addressed to the Practice Manager).

PARIS SMITH & RANDALL
SOLICITORS

Park Nelson

1 Bell Yard, London, WC2A 2JP
Tel (020) 7539 2000 **Fax** (020) 7405 4266 **DX** 186 Chancery Lane WC2
Email law@parknelson.co.uk **Website** www.parknelson.co.uk

Senior Partner	Eugene O'Keeffe
Number of partners	13
Assistant solicitors	10
Other fee-earners	11

AREAS OF PRACTICE	
Commercial Property	46%
Resolution/Construction/Insurance	31%
Private Client Services	12%
Corporate	11%

CONTACTS	
Commercial Property	Eugene O'Keeffe
Corporate	Timothy Ford
Employment	Joce Rickard
Litigation/Construction	John Kings
Mediation	David Herbert
Private Client Services	Richard Fairbairn

THE FIRM Park Nelson is one of the oldest firms of solicitors having celebrated its 200th birthday in 1996. It is now continuing its development with the most advanced technology pursuing controlled growth through strong management and a determination that services will be partner-led. Clients always have immediate access to partners who supervise the provision of services day to day and control the work of the firm to ensure constant excellence of standards.

PRINCIPAL AREAS OF WORK
Commercial Property The firm believes that its considerable strengths in commercial property are equal to those of much larger practices. It is particularly well known for its expertise in handling developments, funding agreements and commercial leases in the retail and other fields. Special areas of property expertise include negotiating and advising on retail licensing and franchising agreements, as well as advice on all aspects of town and country planning, compulsory purchase negotiations, and public inquiries and appeals.
Litigation, Dispute Resolution & Insurance The firm is prominent in construction litigation, dispute resolution and mediation as well as in non-contentious construction law and contract matters. The firm has three certified mediators. The litigation department handles specialist professional indemnity work for leading underwriters and professional firms, personal injury and medical negligence cases, landlord and tenant disputes, commercial and contractual matters, intellectual property litigation and judicial review proceedings.

Continued overleaf

A-Z ■ LAW FIRMS

Employment The firm has specialist and extensive skills in all aspects of employment law matters.

Corporate & Business Services Includes acquisitions and disposals of companies and their businesses, advice on drafting and negotiating commercial agreements, handling joint venture and marketing agreements and preparing financing, banking and loan, funding agreements and insolvency, as well as extensive skills in consumer and consumer credit matters. With its strong international connections, UK and Irish business operations for overseas companies is an important feature and there is a rapidly growing expertise and client base in e-commerce ventures.

Private Client Services The work of the private client department involves trust management, probate, estate and tax planning, tax returns and the preparation of wills, with particular expertise in French, South African and Italian cases.

CLIENTELE The firm's clients include substantial UK companies, as well as private, professional, institutional and commercial firms in Europe and internationally. A number of French, Belgian and Dutch governmental, cultural and educational institutions in London are also clients. Many of the firm's lawyers are fluent in foreign languages.

INTERNATIONAL The firm has strong international connections and conducts work throughout the world, in the United States, southern Africa, the Far East and Australia. These connections include eastern Europe, but are particularly strong in the European Union member states and neighbouring territories, especially France and Ireland. Three of the partners are also admitted as solicitors in the Republic of Ireland and two partners are admitted as solicitors in Northern Ireland. The firm's associated practice, Park Nelson Ireland, has its office in Dublin. The firm is a member of Groupe Monassier and the ACEE, a European Economic Interest Grouping.

Parker Bullen

45 Castle Street, Salisbury, SP1 3SS
Tel (01722) 412000 **Fax** (01722) 411822 **DX** Salisbury 58001
Email law@parkerbullen.com **Website** www.parkerbullen.co.uk

8 Newbury Street, Andover, SP10 1DW
Tel (01264) 400500 **Fax** (01264) 355957 **DX** Andover 90304
Email law@parkerbullen.com

THE FIRM This firm based in the South of England is a responsive and up to date provider of comprehensive legal services, recruiting mainly from London firms. It has particular strengths in company commercial (including employment), commercial property, commercial litigation and probate, trusts and charity work. Each of the offices of the firm is an affiliate member of the British Franchise Association. Notarial services are available.

PRINCIPAL AREAS OF WORK The firm offers the complete range of commercial and private client services from its offices situated in Salisbury, Wiltshire and Andover, Hampshire. Particular areas of expansion at present are company and commercial services to local and regional businesses including acquisitions and disposals, commercial contracts of all kinds, employment matters, trademark registration and franchising, and commercial property work for pension fund managers. The firm's private client department services local and national charities and has also developed teams dealing with the military, rural business and care of the elderly. In litigation the firm has accumulated a wealth of experience on insolvency and bank recovery work.

CLIENTELE Includes Lloyds TSB Bank plc, Cheltenham & Gloucester plc, Enterprise Inns plc, Icon Clinical Research (UK) Ltd, The Hop Back Brewery plc, Bryanston School, Clayesmore School, RNIB, Dean & Chapter of Salisbury, Civil Service Pensioners Alliance, Civil Service Benevolent Fund and JJ Fox International Ltd.

RECRUITMENT The firm is always looking for additional personnel of high calibre at all levels to support its policy of managed growth.

Senior Partner	Robert Sykes
Managing Partner	Tim Crarer
Number of partners	11
Assistant solicitors	11
Other fee-earners	9

CONTACTS	
Commercial Litigation	Andrew Breckenridge
Commercial Property	Chris Nichols
Company & Commercial	Mark Lello
Domestic Property	Giles Bevan-Thomas
Employment	Richard Le Masurier
Family	Tricia Gower
Licensed Trade	Tim Crarer
Personal Injury	Peter Hatvany
Private Client	Robert Sykes

■ Parker & Grego

18-19 Freeman Street, Birmingham, B5 5H2 **Tel** (0121) 633 3031 **Fax** 0121 633 3029

Parlett Kent

Signet House, 49-51 Farringdon Rd, London, EC1M 3PP
Tel (020) 7430 0712 **Fax** (020) 7430 1796 **DX** 53308 Clerkenwell
Email enquiries@parlettkent.co.uk

Portland House, Longbrook Street, Exeter, EX4 6AB
Tel (01392) 494455 **Fax** (01392) 491199 **DX** 134052 – Exeter 15
Email enquiries@exeter.parlettkent.co.uk

Senior Partner	Caroline Jenkins
Number of partners	5
Assistant solicitors	2
Other fee-earners	4

AREAS OF PRACTICE

Clinical Negligence	80%
Personal Injury	15%
Professional Negligence	5%

CONTACTS

Clinical Negligence	Caroline Jenkins (London)
	Magi Young (Exeter)
Personal Injury	Mary Hassell

THE FIRM Established in the 1950s, Parlett Kent is a firm noted in particular for its expertise in a wide range of complex, clinical negligence and personal injury litigation. The firm has in-house paramedical support and is committed to applying its expertise to cases of merit regardless of venue or quantum of case. The firm has Legal Aid franchises for personal injury and clinical negligence litigation and undertakes private work including conditional fee agreement cases. Partners are members of the Law Society's Medical Negligence Panel, the Association of Personal Injury Lawyers; the AVMA Referral Panel; the Law Society's Personal Injury Panel; and the Association of Trial Lawyers of America. The firm has an office in Exeter where lawyers specialise in clinical negligence and personal injury litigation.

PRINCIPAL AREAS OF WORK
Clinical Negligence This department deals with cases of the utmost severity (accidents at birth, brain injuries and spinal injuries) as well as a wide range of both High Court and County Court claims. The firm has particular expertise in cases of obstetric and psychiatric negligence as well as cases arising out of failures to diagnose and treat cancer. It also specialises in claims against the legal profession arising out of mishandling of clinical negligence claims. Members of the practice regularly lecture lawyers, doctors, nurses, health service managers and social workers on medical negligence and risk management.
Personal Injury This department deals with a full range of claimant personal injury claims, including road traffic accidents and accidents at work.

INTERNATIONAL Business is handled in French, Gujarati, Singhalese, Basic Sign Language.

RECRUITMENT At least one trainee solicitor is recruited annually. The firm has an equal opportunities policy and all posts are advertised.

O.H. Parsons & Partners

Sovereign Hse, 212-224 Shaftesbury Avenue, London, WC2H 8PR **Tel** (020) 7379 7277 **Fax** (020) 7240 1577

Patience & Buchan

13 Bon Accord Square, Aberdeen, AB11 6DJ **Tel** (01224) 588333 **Fax** (01224) 588555

Pattinson & Brewer

30 Great James Street, London, WC1N 3HA
Tel (020) 7400 5100 **Fax** (020) 7400 5101 **DX** 394 London
Email enquiries@pattinsonbrewer.co.uk **Website** www.pattinsonbrewer.co.uk

Managing Partner	John Davies
Number of partners	18
Assistant solicitors	9
Other fee-earners	28

AREAS OF PRACTICE

Personal Injury	59%
Employment/Labour Law	18%
Medical Negligence	10%
General Litigation	6%
Conveyancing/Commercial	5%
Criminal	2%

THE FIRM The firm of Pattinson & Brewer was founded in about 1893. It has long been a leading trade union practice, having connections going back to the Taff Vale case in 1901 and the formation of the TGWU in 1921. It has a proud commitment to claimant personal injury and disease work, and a well-established reputation in the fields of equal opportunities, and clinical and professional negligence. It has developed a leading profile in the field of employment law and acts frequently for directors and senior executives on their personal employment issues. It has a strong team of general litigators and a very experienced property department. The firm also has offices in Chatham, Bristol, York and Kingsway WC2.

RECRUITMENT The firm presently recruits one or two trainee solicitors each year, and looks for an interest in claimant-orientated work.

A-Z LAW FIRMS

Paul Davidson Taylor
Chancery Court, Queen Street, Horsham, RH13 5AD **Tel** (01403) 262333 **Fax** (01403) 262444

The Paul Rooney Partnership
19-23 Stanley Street, Liverpool, L1 6AA
Tel (0151) 227 2851 **Fax** (0151) 255 0455 **DX** 14183

Ptnrs 5 **Asst solrs** 13 **Other fee-earners** 15 **Contact** Paul Rooney • Established in 1977. Specialist civil and criminal litigation firm dealing mainly with personal injury claims including factory accidents, industrial diseases, medical and professional negligence, sports injuries and road traffic accidents.

AREAS OF PRACTICE	
Road Traffic Accidents/Personal Injury	85%
Crime	10%

Paull & Williamsons

Investment House, 6 Union Row, Aberdeen, AB10 1DQ
Tel (01224) 621621 **Fax** (01224) 640446 **DX** 35 Aberdeen
Email info@paull-williamsons.co.uk   **Website** www.paull-williamsons.co.uk

New Investment House, 214 Union Street, Aberdeen, AB10 8QY
Tel (01224) 621621 **Fax** (01224) 627437 **DX** 82 Aberdeen
Email info@paull-williamsons.co.uk

13 North Bank Street, Edinburgh, EH1 2LP
Tel (0131) 226 6180 **Fax** (0131) 226 6797 **DX** ED 261 Edinburgh
Email info@paull-williamsons.co.uk

Senior Partner	Bruce Smith
Number of partners	30
Assistant solicitors	42
Other fee-earners	14

CONTACTS	
Commercial Property	Leslie Dalgarno
Corporate	Sidney Barrie
Litigation	Sean Saluja
Oil & Gas	Gordon Buchan
Planning & Environment	Bruce Smith
Private Client	George Alpine
	David Geddie

THE FIRM One of the largest firms in Aberdeen, Paull & Williamsons has enhanced its legal services to meet the increased pace of economic activity in the North East of Scotland in recent years. Moreover, clients benefit from an efficient cross referral system, which provides immediate access to other departments on other areas of the law. The firm also conducts seminars for clients on matters of concern to them, including employment, industrial relations and the effects of new legislation.

PRINCIPAL AREAS OF WORK
Corporate Services The firm has an established reputation for serving commercial clients in the North East and has close links with the local financial community. The department handles all types of corporate and commercial transactions including business start-ups, partnerships and incorporations; company administration; takeovers and acquisitions; disposals; management buyouts; insolvency, receivership, liquidation and administration; commercial contracts, licensing and intellectual property; shipping and vessel finance; venture capital financing and investment. The oil and gas unit has acquired a specialist reputation for upstream North Sea work.

Commercial Property Services The department has recently expanded its operations and now has considerable experience in commercial property developments throughout Scotland. Valuable connections are maintained with other professionals in the commercial property field, such as surveyors, architects and project managers. The firm offers a comprehensive service covering the acquisition and development, leasing and funding of both office and industrial developments. In addition, proven experience has been demonstrated in the fields of retail development, major residential development, licensed premises, agricultural and sporting estates, and woodland and aquacultural development. The planning and environmental unit is active throughout Scotland and is gaining in its profile of resource and expertise.

Private Client Services The first practice in Aberdeen to open a separate estate agency office, the department now operates from large premises in the heart of the city. The service includes advice on valuation, marketing strategy, mortgages, insurance, contracts of sale and purchase and the handling of enquiries prior to sale. The firm also meets the client's personal financial requirements in the areas of tax planning, succession, trusts, insurance and personal financial management. This expertise extends to cover agricultural partnerships and estate work.

Litigation The firm has the experience to deal with all areas of contentious work either prior to formal litigation or arbitration or through representation in the courts and tribunals. The department's work ranges from matters which might face the commercial client, including commercial contracts, employment matters, credit control, health and safety at work, and insolvency, to matters of personal concern, such as employment problems. Having developed expertise in the negotiation, pursuit and defence of personal injury claims, the firm has also recently achieved a significant reputation in advising clients and their insurers following major disasters and representing them at subsequent public inquiries.

1096 INDEX TO LEADING LAWYERS: PAGE 1693 IN-HOUSE LAWYERS' PROFILES: PAGE 1201

Payne Hicks Beach

10 New Square, Lincoln's Inn, London, WC2A 3QG
Tel (020) 7465 4300 **Fax** (020) 7465 4400 **DX** 40 Ch.Ln.
Email mail@paynehicksbeach.co.uk

THE FIRM A well-known and respected Inns of Court firm, Payne Hicks Beach was established in the early eighteenth century. Although the firm draws strength from its long traditions, the character of the firm is an entirely modern one which has been created by the present partners' own chosen specialisations, several of which have been the object of favourable comment in journals in the last few years.

PRINCIPAL AREAS OF WORK The firm is organised into seven work areas.
Tax, Trust & Probate These are areas of specialisation for which the firm has a reputation as one of the best in London. The range of work undertaken is wider than traditionally associated with private client work, and extends from heritage and agricultural work and property development taxation, to advising entrepreneurs and senior directors, charities, and to offshore and continental transactions.
Corporate/Commercial This department deals with the full range of corporate and business law, acting for public and private companies and a range of individual entrepreneurs. The international section deals with many clients and correspondents abroad, and has strong connections both within the European Community and elsewhere, including North America and Japan. Work includes acquisitions and mergers; banking; competition law; employment law; EC law; intellectual property including computers and franchising; management buyouts; marketing and sale of goods law; new issues and partnership agreements.
Commercial Litigation The firm has a strong commercial litigation department handling a broad range of work including commercial disputes requiring urgent injunctive relief, arbitration, intellectual property, commercial, landlord and tenant and town and country planning. There is also particular experience in representing clients before regulatory enquiries. Specialised areas of work include advising clients in yacht racing and design and construction, building contract work, partnership disputes and all other aspects of insolvency for both corporate and individual clients.
Family Law This department is well known for its specialisation in all aspects of family law including divorce and separation, adoption, custody and wardship, and financial claims.
Commercial Property This section deals with all aspects of property transactions, leases, secured lending, management of investment property, development work including joint ventures and planning agreements.
Residential & Agricultural Conveyancing This section deals with residential conveyancing, farm and forestry transactions and agricultural property.
Employment The firm has recently set up a unit specialising in employment matters. The work includes both contentious and non-contentious matters.

INTERNATIONAL The firm has associates in Paris with a network of other correspondents internationally. Several of the partners conduct legal work in French, German or Danish.

RECRUITMENT There are usually two or three vacancies for trainee solicitors every year. The minimum educational requirement is a good degree, but emphasis is placed on personality as well as academic achievements. Applications should be made by letter (with CV and references) to the recruitment partner. The firm is also always interested to receive applications from high quality solicitors seeking to move from the City.

Senior Partner	Graham Brown
Managing Partner	Guy Green
Number of partners	26
Assistant solicitors	18
Other fee-earners	21

AREAS OF PRACTICE	
Private Client	33%
Commerical Litigation	13%
Commercial Property	12%
Matrimonial & Family Law	12%
Residential/Agricultural Property	10%
Tax (Business & Corporate)	10%
Corporate/Commercial	10%

CONTACTS	
Commercial Litgation	Richard Butcher
Commercial Property	David FitzGerald
Corporate/Commercial	Guy Green
	Max Hudson
Employment	Peter McRobert
Family/Matrimonial	Ian Airey
	Fiona Shackleton
General Conveyancing	Peter Black
Intellectual Property	Richard Butcher
Probate	Alastair Murdie
Sports	Richard Butcher
Tax/Trust	Graham Brown

Payne Marsh Stillwell

6 Carlton Crescent, Southampton, SO15 2EY
Tel (023) 8022 3957 **Fax** (023) 8022 5261 **DX** 96886 Southampton 10
Email enquiries@pms.gs **Website** www.pms.gs

Ptnrs 5 **Other fee-earners** 5 **Contact** Chris Marsh • Formed in 1990 following the demerger of a large South Coast practice, the firm is renowned for its commercial litigation (dispute resolution), especially in the fields of intellectual property and defamation, and medical partnership work.

AREAS OF PRACTICE	
Litigation	68%
Non-contentious	32%

A-Z ■ LAW FIRMS

Peden & Reid

22 Callender Street, Belfast, BT1 5BU
Tel (028) 9032 5617 **Fax** (028) 9024 7343 **DX** 389 NR Belfast
Email peden-reid@dnet.co.uk

Senior Partner	Niall Browne
Number of partners	4
Assistant solicitors	4

CONTACTS	
Commercial Property	Richard Palmer
Company/Employment	Niall Browne
Family	Simon Crawford
Litigation	Nicholas Harvey

THE FIRM The firm acts in a general advisory capacity for a number of large public and private companies, public sector and statutory bodies, agricultural and marketing organisations, lending institutions, insurers and property developers.

PRINCIPAL AREAS OF WORK

Company & Commercial Property Formation and structuring of companies and inter-shareholder arrangements; preparation of vending and purchase agreements; partnerships and joint venture agreements relating to business acquisitions and disposals; capital and other finance sourcing; commercial mortgages and secured lending.

Employment Advising on drafting of complex service agreements and in disputes arising out of employment contracts including fair employment, discrimination and Industrial Tribunal cases.

Family Marriage breakdown and divorce. The firm has a large and successful family law practice often involving complex and substantial financial settlements.

Litigation Wide experience in prosecuting and defending all types of civil actions including personal injuries, professional negligence, employer's and public liability, breach of contract, repossession proceedings, defamation, disputes relating to property rights and product liability including representation of insurers and the interests of other parties.

■ Pemberton Greenish

45 Pont St, London, SW1X 0BX **Tel** (020) 7591 3333 **Fax** (020) 7591 3300

Penningtons

Bucklersbury House, 83 Cannon Street, London, EC4N 8PE
Tel (020) 7457 3000 **Fax** (020) 7457 3240 **DX** 98946 Cheapside 2
Email info@penningtons.co.uk   **Website** www.penningtons.co.uk

de Vinci House, Basing View, Basingstoke, RG21 4EQ
Tel (01256) 407100 **Fax** (01256) 479425 **DX** 122362 Basingstoke 8
Email info@penningtons.co.uk

Phoenix House, 9 London Road, Newbury, RG14 1DH
Tel (01635) 571000 **Fax** (01635) 523444 **DX** 30801 Newbury
Email info@penningtons.co.uk

Highfield, Brighton Road, Godalming, GU7 1NS
Tel (01483) 791800 **Fax** (01483) 424177 **DX** 58300 Godalming 1
Email info@penningtons.co.uk

Managing Partner	Lesley Lintott
Number of partners	54
Assistant solicitors	80
Other fee-earners	40

AREAS OF PRACTICE	
Property	35%
Litigation	32%
Corporate	20%
Private Client	13%

CONTACTS	
ADR	Henry Brown
	Sue Dixon
Agricultural	Michael Fellingham
	Julian Chadwick
Banking	Richard Tyson
	Noel McMichael
Clinical Negligence	David Raine
Commercial Property	Catriona Smith
	Anthony Bussy
	Tom Rossiter
	Tim Rafter
Construction	Jessica Taylor
	Sue Dixon
Corporate & Commercial	Ron Allsopp
	Charles Brooks
	Robin Peile
	John Riddick
Corporate Recovery & Insolvency	
	Noel McMichael
	Abraham Ezekiel
Employment	Paul Hadow
	Mike Cole
	Simon Fenton
	Jacqueline McDermott
Environmental	John Mathé
Family	Richard Price
Immigration	Henry Brown
	Gülay Mehmet

THE FIRM Penningtons is a commercial law firm which provides legal services tailored to individual requirements. Specialist teams address the specific objectives of each client and provide a partner led service with an emphasis on team working. The firm's aims are to match client expectations in the areas of quality, time of delivery and cost of service and to add value. The firm's principal office is in the City of London. There are further UK offices in Basingstoke, Godalming and Newbury and an office in Paris. In addition, Penningtons has close links with law firms in jurisdictions throughout the world. It is therefore able to offer flexibility in the scope of the specialist commercial and private client services it delivers to a wide range of clients with differing requirements.

PRINCIPAL AREAS OF WORK The main areas of legal services provided are property, litigation, corporate and commercial (including intellectual property), and private client (including immigration). The firm also has several specialist teams providing focused and co-ordinated services to specific industry sectors, often on a cross departmental basis.

Corporate & Commercial The department offers a full range of legal skills and experience in corporate finance, management buyouts and buyins, mergers and acquisitions and joint ventures. Multi-disciplinary and cross-border transactions are regularly undertaken. Advice is also given on most aspects of commercial law, including intellectual property (where there is a particular expertise in information technology, especially e-commerce and computer law) publishing, trademarks and technology transfer, distribution, agency and supply, competition law, inward investment and establishment in the UK, banking, pensions and employees' benefits schemes. The department can provide taxation support in relation to all aspects of its corporate and commercial work.

Litigation The department handles a broad range of national and international work, including banking; construction disputes; employment matters; insolvency work; insurance; partnership disputes; personal injury and clinical negligence claims (for which community legal services quality marks are held in the firm's Godalming and Basingstoke offices); professional indemnity claims; secured lending recoveries; share sale and purchase disputes; trade arbitrations; all aspects of commercial property and landlord and tenant matters. Agency work is also carried out. Members of the department are familiar with ADR techniques in addition to litigation and arbitration. The professional regulation group acts for a number of professional bodies, not only investigating and presenting cases for hearing by their disciplinary committees, but also advising on rules, procedures and codes of conduct and conducting appeals and applications for judicial review.

Property The department has wide experience in dealing with a range of property related transactions including investment sales and purchases, funding agreements, development schemes, landlord and tenant matters, portfolio management, agricultural investments, as well as general commercial property work and high value residential sales and purchases. Specialist town and country planning, environmental and construction law advice is also available.

Private Client A wide range of services is provided, including, in particular, all aspects of personal tax planning (including offshore), wills, trusts, charities and the administration of estates. All aspects of immigration and nationality law are covered, including investors, work permits, business applications and sole representatives of overseas companies.

INTERNATIONAL A full international service is provided by Penningtons in association with the member firms of MULTILAW and the European Law Group (ELG). The firm, through its merger with Walker Martineau, is a founder member of MULTILAW, a multinational association of over 50 law firms in more than 40 countries, and is also a founder member of ELG, an association of business law firms in the EU, Norway and Switzerland. It is also a member of the Law Society Solicitors European Group. Penningtons has in-house lawyers qualified in several overseas jurisdictions. Overseas activity includes specialist knowledge of, and experience in, many different jurisdictions, particularly France, Hong Kong and the Far East, India, Italy, South Africa and the USA. Work is handled in Chinese, French, German, Gujerati, Italian, Spanish and Turkish.

RECRUITMENT For training placements and recruitment enquiries contact Lesley Lintott at our London office or visit our website. Penningtons is always interested to hear from first class individuals who wish to advance their careers within a progressive and entrepreneurial firm.

CONTACTS (Continued)

Intellectual Property	Geoffrey Walkley
Litigation	Paul Hadow
	Jonathan Rouse
	John Sommerville
	Michael Felce
Personal Injury	David Raine
Planning	Roger Bullworthy
Private Client	Lesley Lintott
	Richard Underwood
	Michael Fellingham
	Julian Chadwick
Professional Negligence	Michael Felce
Professional Regulation	Katrina Wingfield
	Geoffrey Hudson
Relocation/Housing Associations	
	Andrew Templeman
	Jonathan Rouse
Residential Property	Paul Collard
	Anthony Bussy
	Tim Rafter
	Richard Hornsby
Tax	Paul Eaton

Peter Carter-Ruck and Partners

International Press Centre, 76 Shoe Lane, London, EC4A 3JB
Tel (020) 7353 5005 **Fax** (020) 7353 5553 **DX** 333 Ch.Ln.
Email lawyers@carter-ruck.com **Website** www.carter-ruck.com

THE FIRM Peter Carter-Ruck and Partners sees itself as a young and progressive partnership. It is committed to retaining, and indeed expanding upon, its undoubted predominance in the field of defamation, whilst at the same time building upon its name and client base to develop a higher profile and presence on the part of its intellectual property and entertainment media practice. The firm runs a Conditional Fee Agreement ('no win no fee') scheme for actions involving defamation, intellectual property and other media related matters.

PRINCIPAL AREAS OF WORK The firm handles both contentious and non-contentious media work. The media litigation group, offers both pre and post publication advice on libel, slander, contempt, breach of confidence, privacy and advertising law and regulatory and Official Secrets Act issues. The intellectual property and media group advises both in relation to contentious matters, including infringement of copyright, passing off and trademark disputes, and non-contentious matters, including licensing, commercial and internet content agreements.

CLIENTELE The firm's clients are drawn equally from the media and from those seeking advice on dealing with the media.

Senior Partner	Andrew Stephenson
Number of partners	9
Assistant solicitors	5
Other fee-earners	4

CONTACTS

Employment	Nigel Tait
Intellectual Property	Guy Martin
	Mark Thomson
Media Litigation	Ruth Collard, Cameron Doley
	Claire Gill, Alasdair Pepper
	Andrew Stephenson, Nigel Tait
	Mark Thomson, Charlotte Watson

Peter Carter-Ruck

■ **Peter Edwards Law**
Ventura, 8 Market Street, Hoylake, CH47 2AE **Tel** (0151) 632 6699 **Fax** (0151) 632 0090

A-Z ■ LAW FIRMS

Peterkins

100 Union Street, Aberdeen, AB10 1QR
Tel (01224) 428000 **Fax** (01224) 626123 **DX** AB3
Email maildesk@peterkins.com **Website** www.peterkins.com

Senior Partner	Philip Anderson
Number of partners	17
Assistant solicitors	8
Other fee-earners	16

THE FIRM Peterkins is a progressive Aberdeen firm with an office in Glasgow. The firm combines traditional skills with new methods and is committed to making full use of technology to provide high quality, cost effective solutions for clients.

PRINCIPAL AREAS OF WORK Commercial work includes IP/IT, oil and gas, sea fishing industry and commercial property. The banking group carries out high-volume, case-managed security work as well as higher value corporate lending transactions.

INTERNATIONAL North Sea Group member, with associated offices in Belgium, Denmark, England and Germany. Oil industry clients include companies based in Russia and the firm has Russian speakers.

CONTACTS	
Corporate & Commercial	Neil Hunter
Banking	Brian Aitken
Oil & Gas/Sea Fishing	Duncan MacNiven
IP/IT	Thomas Rennie
Commercial Property	Philip Anderson
Litigation	Colin Forbes
Private Client	Hartley Lumsden

PETERKINS

■ Peter Maughan & Co
15A Walker Terrace, Gateshead, NE8 1EB **Tel** (0191) 477 9779 **Fax** (0191) 477 7997

Peters & Peters

2 Harewood Place, Hanover Square, London, W1S 1BX
Tel (020) 7629 7991 **Fax** (020) 7499 6792 **DX** 44625 Mayfair
Email law@petersandpeters.co.uk **Website** www.petersandpeters.co.uk

Managing Partner	Julia Balfour-Lynn
AREAS OF PRACTICE	
Fraud/Regulatory	51%
Commercial Litigation	46%
Commercial Conveyancing	3%

THE FIRM This specialist practice is best known as a leading firm in the areas of financial regulation fraud and commercial litigation involving fraud. The firm has particular experience in dealing with civil and criminal litigation with an international flavour, including extradition and mutual legal assistance matters. In addition, the firm offers high quality services in employment law, anti money laundering and prevention of corruption advice. Peters & Peters concentrates not only on the quality of the service it provides but also on technical expertise and practical know-how. It aims to be innovative and to provide solutions to problems that cut across traditional boundaries separating the criminal and civil law practitioner. The firm believes it is one of the first practices to develop such a multidisciplinary approach; consequently both partners and assistants at the firm have built up a considerable level of expertise acting for companies, institutions and regulators as well as individual clients. Much of the practice's work is high profile and is frequently international in scope. The firm has built up a close working relationship with law firms overseas. Partners often receive invitations to speak at international conferences and seminars, as well as to contribute to business and legal journals throughout the world. Members of the firm have received requests to work with government committees and to advise foreign regulators and international organisations. Members also contribute to law reform and human rights initiatives both here and overseas.

CONTACTS	
Fraud/Regulatory	Monty Raphael
	Louise Delahunty
	Jo Rickards
	Claire Lipworth
	Helen McDowell
	Elizabeth Robertson
Commercial Conveyancing	Geoffrey Herman
Commercial Litigation	Keith Oliver
	Kathryn Garbett
	Sarah Gabriel
	Lisa McMillan
	Jonathan Tickner
Customs & Excise	Monty Raphael
	Louise Delahunty
	Jo Rickards
Financial Regulation	Monty Raphael
	Keith Oliver
	Jo Rickards
Tax	Monty Raphael
	Louise Delahunty
	Sarah Gabriel

PRINCIPAL AREAS OF WORK Areas in which the firm's practice has expanded rapidly include money laundering compliance, commercial litigation and financial regulation, which complement the firm's traditional strengths in tax, customs and commercial fraud.

Commercial Litigation Peters & Peters' depth of expertise has been put to good use in a number of cases involving substantial litigation both here and overseas, including asset tracing aided by freezing orders and search orders. The firm has acted both for claimants and defendants, as well as performing the supervisory role in search orders. The firm's expertise covers the whole range of contentious work including civil fraud, contractual disputes, employment law and defamation, together with personal and corporate bankruptcy and related insolvency matters. Due to the firm's particular mixture of expertise, it is often asked to deal with civil litigation matters where criminal and/or regulatory proceedings are also contemplated, with all the complications of parallel litigation. Such cases often include the further complexities of private or public international law.

Fraud/Regulatory Matters The practice's long-standing experience and pre-eminence in fraud and regulatory matters is universally recognised. It has been built up over a huge variety of cases in which it has acted for large organisations in both an investigative and preventative role, as well as for many private clients. Case loads encompass all forms of corporate fraud, cross-border issues including extradition and mutual assistance, as well as forensic tax and revenue work. Expertise includes VAT and customs infractions, insolvency crimes, securities offences and all examples of business delinquency. Money laundering has become of universal concern and the firm is pre-eminent in dealing with compliance issues, crisis

management and defence, not only for financial firms, but also for the professions. It has co-operated with the Law Society of England and Wales in developing a CD rom based training programme for the legal profession.

Financial Regulation The firm has been instructed in most of the high profile cases involving alleged financial mismanagement in the last two decades. As a result, it has built up a group of fee-earners with an in-depth knowledge of the domestic and international regulation of the markets. Their work has contributed significantly to legal developments in this area. Cases have regularly involved the DTI, the FSA and other regulators.

Other The firm undertakes many other corporate criminal matters as well as regulatory prosecutions and professional disciplinary work. The firm also provides a service to corporate and private clients in commercial conveyancing and conducts agency work in all its specialist areas.

Pettman Smith

79 Knightsbridge, London, SW1X 7RB
Tel (020) 7235 1288 **Fax** (020) 7235 2683 **DX** 38168 Knightsbridge
Email ps@pslaw.co.uk

Managing Partner	Ann Glaves-Smith
Senior Partner	Michael Pettman
Number of partners	9
Assistant solicitors	2
Other fee-earners	3

AREAS OF PRACTICE

Litigation	33%
Company & Commercial	33%
Property	33%

CONTACTS

Commercial Litigation	Jonathan Sachs
	Duncan McNair
	Richard Homewood
Commercial Property	Ann Glaves-Smith
	Marie-Garrard Newton
Company & Commercial	Michael Pettman
Intellectual Property	Richard Homewood

THE FIRM A modern commercial practice, established in 1982, which has since grown considerably. The firm seeks to provide practical and commercially viable solutions to legal and business problems in a friendly, professional manner. The practice is particularly noted for its work in intellectual property.

PRINCIPAL AREAS OF WORK

Commercial Litigation A comprehensive service includes commercial fraud, employment disputes and property and building contract litigation.

Commercial Property The firm handles development work from acquisition to sale, mortgage and other bank security work.

Intellectual Property Both contentious and non-contentious work is handled. Actions include copyright and designs, patents, trademarks, passing-off and confidential information. The firm has particular experience in interlocutory proceedings. Non-contentious work includes software licensing and character merchandising.

Company/Commercial Company acquisitions and mergers, joint ventures and shareholders' agreements. Venture capital funding and technology-related work. Company reorganisations and restructuring. Business acquisitions and disposals. Management buyouts and investments. Financial services work including disciplinary and regulatory work. Shareholder and partnership disputes. Insolvency advice, personal and corporate. Company formation and administration. Commercial agreements in particular intellectual property licensing agreements. Software licensing and development and hardware contracts. Service and consultancy agreements. Other commercial advice.

Taxation International tax planning is a particular strength, and immigration and nationality questions are also handled.

CLIENTELE Clients include major public companies, small businesses and entrepreneurs. There is a substantial client base in America and the Middle East.

Pickworths

55 Marlowes, Hemel Hempstead, HP1 1LE
Tel (01442) 261731 **Fax** (01442) 230356 **DX** 8809 Hemel Hempstead
Email hemel@pickworths.co.uk **Website** www.pickworths.co.uk

6 Victoria Street, St Albans, AL1 3JB
Tel (01727) 844511 **DX** 6143 St Albans

Senior Partner	David Forbes

CONTACTS

Civil Litigation (inc. Personal Injury)	David White
Commercial Property & Company	Glenda Ferneyhough
Company Commercial & Litigation	Belinda Walkinshaw
Employment	Ian Tottman
Property (inc. Planning)	David Forbes

THE FIRM Pickworths' teams offer a comprehensive range of services to private and commercial clients. Specialists lead each team with recognised experts heading the employment and planning law teams.

PRINCIPAL AREAS OF WORK Commercial teams offer full range of advice on employment law, property (including planning/environment/agriculture law), company/commercial matters and litigation. Private client teams advise on residential property matters, family and child law, civil litigation including personal injury, planning for the future - wills, trusts, enduring powers of attorney and probate matters.

A-Z ■ LAW FIRMS

■ Pictons

28 Dunstable Road, Luton, LU1 1DY **Tel** (01582) 870870 **Fax** (01582) 870871

■ Pillsbury Winthrop LLP

2 George Yard, 54 Lombard Street, London, EC3B 9DH
Tel (020) 7648 9200 **Fax** (020) 7283 1656

Ptnrs 3 **Asst solrs** 2 **Other fee-earners** 1 **Contact** Peter S Brown • As a full-service firm based in the US, Pillsbury Winthrop has over 800 attorneys and 15 offices worldwide. Pillsbury Winthrop's London practice focuses on international corporate, project and financial transactions. The firm represents UK, Scandinavian and other European clients as well as US, Latin American and Asian clients with European interests.

Areas of Practice	
Energy & Projects	30%
Mergers & Acquisitions	25%
Finance	15%
Securities	15%
Corporate, Commercial & Employment	15%

Pinsent Curtis Biddle

Dashwood House, 69 Old Broad Street, London, EC2M 1NR
Tel (020) 7418 7000 **Fax** (020) 7418 7050 **DX** 119516 Finsbury Square
Email martin.lane@pinsents.com **Website** www.pinsents.com

1 Gresham Street, London, EC2 7BU
Tel (020) 7606 9301 **Fax** (020) 7606 3305 **DX** 1008 London
Email martin.lane@pinsents.com

3 Colmore Circus, Birmingham, B4 6BH
Tel (0121) 200 1050 **Fax** (0121) 626 1040 **DX** 703167 Birmingham-12
Email greg.lowson@pinsents.com

1 Park Row, Leeds, LS1 5AB
Tel (0113) 244 5000 **Fax** (0113) 244 8000 **DX** 26440 Leeds-28
Email nigel.kissack@pinsents.com

The Chancery, 58 Spring Gardens, Manchester, M2 1EW
Tel (0161) 247 8282 **Fax** (0161) 247 8283 **DX** 709040 Manchester 7
Email chris.lumsden@pinsents.com

Senior Partner	Julian Tonks
National Managing Partner	David Ryan
Number of partners	169
Assistant solicitors	297
Other fee-earners	120

THE FIRM Pinsent Curtis Biddle is a fast growing, dynamic law firm striving to deepen its service to clients whilst maintaining standards of the highest quality. In the past 18 months the firm has doubled the size of its London office through the merger of Pinsent Curtis and Biddle, and opened an office in Manchester. The firm has also extended its international capability, notably in France, Germany and Sweden. The firm is one of the UK's leading legal advisors to public listed companies, consistently ranked in the top 10, and has been ranked in the top five nationally, for client service by in-house lawyers in the UK. The firm acts extensively for UK and foreign controlled companies in addition to a wide range of financial institutions and public sector organisations. Pinsent Curtis Biddle has a reputation for the depth of its expertise across a range of specialist areas with more than 60 of its lawyers independently rated by clients, competitors and peers for their knowledge, experience and ability. In 2002, the firm was voted the 'Most Enterprising Law Firm of the Year' by a leading legal publication. The firm has more than 160 partners, a full legal team of more than 550 and total UK staff of over 1,000.

PRINCIPAL AREAS OF WORK Pinsent Curtis Biddle is committed to strategic growth through a number of carefully selected chosen markets, aiming to achieve a leading position in the next three to five years in financial institutions, foreign controlled companies, insurance and reinsurance, major projects, pensions, private equity, property, public companies, and technology and media. Within the public companies and foreign controlled companies markets the firm is further focusing its business on a sector basis targeting automotive, food, manufacturing and engineering, retail and leisure, and transport and distribution. The firm's strategy is driven forward by specialist cross-discipline teams drawn from its core areas of legal expertise in corporate, employment, dispute resolution and litigation, insurance and reinsurance, pensions, projects and commercial, property, tax, and technology and media.

INTERNATIONAL Pinsent Curtis Biddle is committed to developing its international profile, building on its extensive overseas experience and long standing relationships. To this end, the firm has formed strategic alliances with progressive top 10 Swedish firm Magnusson Wahlin, Granrut in France and Hoffmann, Liebs Fritsch Ruhe in Germany. Pinsent Curtis Biddle also has a dedicated in-house German desk bringing together dual qualified lawyers, UK German speaking lawyers and German lawyers who have a range of specialist legal expertise. The firm's US group is responsible for developing relationships with US corporations, including its 18 Fortune 500 clients, and US law firms.

Piper Smith & Basham

31 Warwick Square, London, SW1V 2AF
Tel (020) 7828 8685 **Fax** (020) 7630 6976 **DX** 110 Ch.Ln.
Email postmaster@pipersmith.co.uk **Website** www.pipersmith.co.uk

THE FIRM A long established firm based in Westminster since 1875. The firm still retains its Pimlico roots, but has developed into a number of areas of property, commercial, travel and tour operating work, commercial litigation, company commercial, and employment advice and litigation.

PRINCIPAL AREAS OF WORK

Tour Operating & Travel The firm acts for many companies in this industry both large and small.
Commercial & Other Real Property Development and investment property, landlord and tenant, housing association and local authority work together with residential conveyancing.
Other Areas Private client, corporate, and general litigation, company, immigration and employment.

Managing Partner	Mark Spash
Senior Partner	Richard Berns
Number of partners	6
Assistant solicitors	4
Other fee-earners	4

CONTACTS	
Commercial & Other Real Property	Richard Berns
Private Client	Mark Spash
Tour Operating & Travel	Ian Skuse
Litigation	Richard Twyman

Pitmans

47 Castle Street, Reading, RG1 7SR
Tel (0118) 958 0224 **Fax** (0118) 958 5097 **DX** 40102 Reading (Castle Street)
Email cavery@pitmans.com **Website** www.pitmans.com

THE FIRM Pitmans is one of Thames Valley's leading commercial practices, offering a comprehensive legal service to local, national and international businesses. In recent years the partnership has grown and with it, the breadth of skills and specialisations offered. Pitmans' membership of InterAct Europe 1993 EEIG has proved to be invaluable to the success and growth of the practice.

PRINCIPAL AREAS OF WORK

Company/Commercial The company/commercial department is one of the largest in the South East, outside London. It handles a wide variety of work including company formations, mergers and acquisitions, management buyouts, institutional investment agreements, trading agreements, employment issues, share option schemes and financial services. It advises overseas clients on questions of location and handles work overseas for British clients. The department also offers specialist reports tailored to the needs of individual clients on developing European law affecting them, and is able to review legal frameworks in other countries.
Corporate Security & Insolvency A specialist department is dedicated to corporate security and insolvency work.
Intellectual Property The intellectual property department has gone from strength to strength and acts for a large number of the international computer and software companies both in the Thames Valley and overseas. The department offers a wide range of services both of a contentious and non-contentious nature in the patent, copyright, trademark, know-how and entertainment sectors.
Commercial Property A significant percentage of Pitmans' work is in the commercial property sector. The firm is renowned for its work in land acquisitions, joint venture arrangements and particularly for its expertise in planning and public enquiries. The department's clients include some of the largest housebuilders in the country, a number of substantial plcs, and local authorities. It also has a department specialising in the sale of new homes for residential developers.
Environmental Law The environmental law department integrates well with the existing commercial property, general commercial and planning work. This department offers a wide range of services within this complex area of law with particular emphasis on the new laws developing in the European Union.
Litigation The litigation department has wide experience in all areas of commercial litigation, especially in the hi-tech, construction and finance industries and in international trade. It regularly works with other departments to provide a team approach for larger litigation matters. A debt collection service is available to clients. Criminal and matrimonial litigation is not undertaken.

Managing Partner	Christopher Avery
Senior Partner	Tony Jones
Number of partners	15
Assistant solicitors	46
Other fee-earners	49

AREAS OF PRACTICE	
Property (Commercial)	24%
Company/Commercial	23%
Commercial Litigation	21%
Residential Development	10%
Employment	7%
Planning & Environmental	6%
Corporate Recovery	5%
Intellectual Property	3%
Private Client	1%

CONTACTS	
Commercial Property	Christopher Avery
Company Commercial	John Hutchinson
Corporate Recovery	David Archer
Employment	Mark Symons
Environmental	Daniel Drukarz
Intellectual Property	Philip Weaver
Litigation	Sue O'Brien
Planning	Daniel Drukarz
Private Client	Tony Jones

Continued overleaf

A-Z ■ LAW FIRMS

Planning Nearly all the commercial property partners have specialist knowledge of planning law, and a broad range of expertise covers: development strategy, agreements with highway and planning authorities, major planning appeals and judicial reviews of planning decisions.

CLIENTELE Clients include both public and private companies, banks and local authorities throughout the UK, as well as an increasing number of organisations in Europe.

INTERNATIONAL Pitmans is a founder member of an EEIG, with associated law firms in Amsterdam, Berlin, Copenhagen, Finland, Hamburg, Leipzig, Lisbon, London, Madrid, Malmo, Moscow, Munich, New York, Oslo and Paris.

plexus Law

95 Aldwych, London, WC2B 4JF
Tel (020) 7242 4154 **Fax** (020) 7404 0009 **DX** 14 Ch. Ln
Email mail@plexus-law.com

Managing Partner	Tim Oliver
Number of fee-earners	20

THE FIRM plexus Law is a specialist professional indemnity and high value defendant liability firm. The firm was formed in 2001 by the merger of the technical risks team of Badhams with Lloyd's specialist firm Williams Davies Meltzer. plexus Law has quickly flourished and expanded and now handles high value technical claims and advises on professional indemnity and insurance related matters. The firm acts for a number of leading Lloyd's professional indemnity syndicates and major insurers in the London market.

PRINCIPAL AREAS OF WORK plexus Law handles a substantial amount of complex professional indemnity cases covering property, professionals, education, IT, financial and medical malpractice. Its team of experienced practitioners also include specialists in transport, employment, utilities, reinsurance and policy interpretation. plexus Law aims to provide a very pro-active and commercial approach to its clients' needs. Other multi-track and fast-track work is handled by the Croydon offices of Badhams. Major reported cases are: Kelly v London Transport Executive; Anglian Water v Cranshaw Robbins; Farley - Skinner, House Of Lords (2001); The Mortgage Corp. v Halifax; Camphill v Conoco (Uk) Ltd; Dsl Group v Unisys Intl. Services; Bybrook Garden Centre v Kent County Council; Ucb v Halifax; Platform Homeloans Ltd v Oyston Shipway & Orrs.

CLIENTELE The firm's client base comprises leading professional indemnity syndicates at Lloyd's and the major insurers.

Poppleston Allen

37 Stoney Street, The Lace Market, Nottingham, NG1 1LS
Tel (0115) 953 8500 **Fax** (0115) 953 8501 **DX** 10100 Nottingham
Email mail@popall.co.uk **Website** www.popall.co.uk

Number of partners	5
Assistant solicitors	1
Other fee-earners	12

AREAS OF PRACTICE	
Licensing (Liquor, Public Entertainment, Betting & Gaming)	100%

THE FIRM Poppleston Allen is a niche licensing practice dedicated to the leisure industry. Established in 1994 by renowned licensing advocates Jeremy Allen and Susanna Poppleston, and a previous winner of Law Firm of the Year at The Lawyer Awards, it has achieved a high national profile with a focus on client care, staff training and information technology. The firm offers an award-winning website and email newswire service.

PRINCIPAL AREAS OF WORK

Licensing Specialists in liquor, public entertainment, betting and gaming licensing and regulatory crime, especially late-night licensing, with administration and planning services to provide for all the needs of the leisure industry.

CLIENTELE The firm's client base reflects its leading national position, ranging from large leisure operators to independent licensees, throughout England and Wales. Clients include Butlins/Bourne Leisure, Carluccios, Henry J Beans, Ladbrokes, Luminar Leisure, PizzaExpress, Scottish & Newcastle, Signature Restaurants, Spirit Group, Urbium (formerly Chorion plc), Wilson Bowden, Yo!Sushi, various developers and more student unions than any other solicitor.

Porter Dodson

Central House, Church Street, Yeovil, BA20 1HH
Tel (01935) 424581 **Fax** (01935) 706063 **DX** 100501 Yeovil
Email porterdodson@porterdodson.co.uk   **Website** www.porterdodson.co.uk

THE FIRM Porter Dodson is a substantial high street practice with specialist departments offering a wide range of specialist advice with the philosophy of total client care. There are six offices across Somerset and Dorset.

PRINCIPAL AREAS OF WORK The firm's core areas of practice are litigation, probate, tax and trusts, commercial law and conveyancing.

CLIENTELE The firm has a substantial commercial and private client base across a broad spectrum, together with insurance companies, county and local authorities and substantial corporations. There is strong representation of the farming and land owning community.

RECRUITMENT Porter Dodson has a very healthy recruitment policy. It appoints three trainee solicitors each year and is currently recruiting strongly due to continuing expansion and development of services.

Managing Partner	David Perratt
Senior Partner	Michael Lloyd-Davies
Number of partners	24
Assistant solicitors	18
Other fee-earners	44

AREAS OF PRACTICE	
Litigation	41%
Conveyancing	28%
Probate	19%
Commercial	12%

CONTACTS	
Litigation	Mike Pitt
Conveyancing	Steve Mahoney
Commercial	David Perratt
Probate	Bill Morris

Portrait Solicitors in Association with Denton Wilde Sapte

1 Chancery Lane, London, WC2A 1LF
Tel (020) 7320 3888 **Fax** (020) 7430 1242 **DX** 69
Email dbf@dentonwildesapte.com

Contact Judith Portrait or Dominic Flynn • Specialist private client and charity practice.

Pothecary & Barratt

Talbot Hse, Talbot Court, Gracechurch St, London, EC3V 0BS **Tel** (020) 7623 7520 **Fax** (020) 7623 9815

Powell & Co

77 Woolwich New Road, Woolwich, London, SE18 6ED
Tel (020) 8854 9131 **Fax** (020) 8855 4174

A community-based firm providing a high quality, specialist service in clinical negligence, personal injury, housing for tenants, immigration and family. Franchised in seven areas.

Powell Spencer & Partners

290 Kilburn High Rd, London, NW6 2DD
Tel (020) 7624 8888 **Fax** (020) 7328 1221 **DX** 123862 Kilburn 2
Email enquiries@psplaw.co.uk

THE FIRM Powell Spencer & Partners is one of London's foremost legal aid practices, with a strong reputation for its work in the areas of criminal, family, matrimonial, personal injury, clinical negligence, political asylum and human rights litigation. The firm offers a community-based service, has adapted its offices to meet the requirements of clients with disabilities and undertakes home visits.

PRINCIPAL AREAS OF WORK
Litigation A specialist range of litigation is undertaken, namely criminal defence, personal injury and medical negligence, child care, family and matrimonial work, and welfare benefits advice.

Managing & Senior Partner	Greg Powell
Number of partners	5
Assistant solicitors	18
Other fee-earners	14

AREAS OF PRACTICE	
Criminal Defence	60%
Civil Family	18%
Personal Injury	18%
Welfare Benefits	4%

Praxis Partners

2 Park Lane, Leeds, LS3 1ES **Tel** (0113) 207 6700 **Fax** (0113) 207 6701

Preston Goldburn

The Old Brewery Yard, High Street, Falmouth, TR11 2BY **Tel** (01326) 318900 **Fax** (01326) 311275

A-Z ■ LAW FIRMS

Prettys

Elm House, 25 Elm Street, Ipswich, IP1 2AD
Tel (01473) 232121 Fax (01473) 230002 DX 3218
Email mail@prettys.co.uk Website www.prettys.co.uk

THE FIRM Prettys is one of the largest practices in East Anglia, with an established private client base and a comprehensive commercial law service. The majority of its commercial clients are small to medium sized companies key to the regional economy. The firm's insurance clients are large composite insurers for whom it operates internationally.

PRINCIPAL AREAS OF WORK Company, commercial property, litigation, alternative dispute resolution, construction, employment, insolvency, credit management, intellectual property, health and safety, estates, financial services, family, French property, personal injury, clinical negligence, transport, shipping, agriculture and insurance.

RECRUITMENT Four to five high calibre graduates gain training contracts each year. Brochure available.

Managing Partner	Jonathan Gorst
Senior Partner	Clive Brynley-Jones
Number of partners	16
Assistant solicitors	20
Other fee-earners	29

CONTACTS	
Agriculture	Toby Pound
Clinical Negligence	Stephen Skinner
Commercial Litigation	Peter Blake
Commercial Property	David Clark
Company/Commercial	Ian Waine
Employment	Richard Stace
Insurance	Clive Brynley-Jones
IT/IP	Roland Sharp
Personal Law	Carol Lockett
Shipping	Paul Dickie
Transport	Roland Sharp

■ PricewaterhouseCoopers

10-18 Union Street, London, SE1 1SZ Tel (020) 7939 3000 Fax (020) 7804 1200

Prince Evans

77 Uxbridge Rd, Ealing, London, W5 5ST
Tel (020) 8567 3477 Fax (020) 8840 7457 DX 5100 Ealing
Email rjennings@prince-evans.co.uk

THE FIRM This broad-based West London firm has an enviable reputation in housing and public sector work but has also built strong specialisms in banking/finance, litigation, company/commercial, personal injury and private client work. Prince Evans has one of the largest dedicated housing and public sector departments in the UK, acting for over 100 registered social landlords and numerous local authorities. The firm prides itself on its innovative and energetic approach to work with the highest commitment to client care. The partners hold regular seminars and have forged a significant client base of public/private limited companies together with residential/commercial landlords.

PRINCIPAL AREAS OF WORK

Housing & The Public Sector This is the largest area of the firm's practice, for which it has developed a reputation for innovation. It involves: constitutional development of Registered Social Landlords; land acquisition and development for individual/consortium Registered Social Landlords; stock transfers of rundown estates using ERCF Funding; HAT succession projects; Pathfinder PFI projects with social services/health authorities; reprovision schemes involving PFI; residential care home transfers with VAT and capital finance efficiency; regeneration and on estate planning gain schemes; foyer schemes; mixed tenure, multi-tenure and flexible tenure projects; joint venture company/off-balance sheet transactions using special purpose vehicles. The department is involved in the development of the next generation PFI and quasi-PFI Schemes utilising housing revenue account assets and has the largest Low Cost Home Ownership Unit in the UK. The department is at the forefront of high profile estate regeneration involving mixed tenure, Trowbridge Estate, London Borough of Hackney. It has also acquired Lovell Partnerships Limited and Botes Building Limited as clients.

Banking/Finance This continues to be an expanding area of practice, acting for both lenders and borrowers of housing and public sector finance on a range of transactions, from bilateral and syndicated loans to group borrowing arrangements and capital market issues and large scale security based transactions. Advice is provided on all aspects of banking law, including treasury management.

Litigation & Arbitration In litigation and arbitration, Prince Evans has a strong reputation for conducting all types of commercial disputes. The firm has developed one of the largest dedicated landlord and tenant litigation functions in London, providing a variety of housing management advice. Recently, the department has advised the National Housing Federation and its members nationwide on the high profile issue of rent increases and during the last year, has successfully brought three Court of Appeal cases. The litigation department has also received recognition for its growth in contentious/non-contentious construction work, acting for building contractors as well as Registered Social Landlords. In the last year, the department successfully acted for the claimant in the lead case of Austin Hall Building Limited v Buckland Securities Limited. Commercial litigation has acquired new prestigious pharma-

Managing Partner	Trevor Morley
Senior Partner	Louis Robert
Number of partners	6
Assistant solicitors	28
Other fee-earners	18

AREAS OF PRACTICE	
Housing & Public Sector (inc. Banking & Finance)	50%
Litigation	25%
Personal Injury	10%
Private Client (inc. Company/Commercial)	10%
Crime (inc. Childcare)	5%

CONTACTS	
Banking & Finance	Trevor Morley
Company/Commercial	Tom Lemon
Crime/Childcare	Philip Eldin-Taylor
Housing & Public Sector	Louis Robert
Litigation	Robert Jennings
Personal Injury	Bryan Neill
Private Client	Tom Lemon

ceutical/chemical manufacturing Plc clients. The firm is also recommended by the Law Society for contentious and non-contentious employment advice, including employment contracts, discipline, matters before the Employment Tribunal and the transfer of undertakings. In the last year, the department has successfully undertaken multi-witness sex/race/disability discrimination cases.

Company/Commercial The firm has considerable expertise in company/commercial transactions, including formation M&As, takeovers together with partnership matters; service/commercial agreements; lettings/disposals both for occupation and investment companies.

Personal Injury/Medical Negligence All aspects of personal injury/medical negligence are handled. Particular specialisms include severe spinal injury (tetraplegic and paraplegic) and head injury claims. The firm has a pioneering reputation in cases involving major catastrophic injury/disability, obtaining UK record damages on several occasions.

Private Client Private client work is also undertaken, such as tax, trusts, wills/probate childcare and crime. Residential conveyancing has been expanded to three fee-earners.

Pryce Collard Chamberlain
6 East Saint Helen Street, Abingdon, OX14 5EW   **Tel** (01235) 523411   **Fax** (01235) 533283

Public Interest Lawyers
Centre Court, 50-54 St Paul's Square, Birmingham, B3 1QS   **Tel** (0121) 702 2110   **Fax** (0121) 702 2206

Pullig & Co
Bridewell House, 9 Bridewell Place, London, EC4V 6AZ   **Tel** (020) 7353 0505   **Fax** (020) 7936 2548

Purcell Parker
204-206 Corporation Street, Birmingham, B4 6QB   **Tel** (0121) 236 9781   **Fax** (0121) 236 8218

Putsman.wlc
50 Great Charles Street, Birmingham, B3 2LT   **Tel** (0121) 236 9441   **Fax** (0121) 236 4733

RadcliffesLeBrasseur

5 Great College Street, Westminster, London, SW1P 3SJ
Tel (020) 7222 7040   **Fax** (020) 7222 6208   **DX** 113 London Chancery Lane WC2
Email info@rlb-law.com   **Website** www.rlb-law.com

6-7 Park Place, Leeds, LS1 2RU
Tel (0113) 234 1220   **Fax** (0113) 234 1573   **DX** 14086 Leeds Park Square
Email info@rlb-law.com

25 Park Place, Cardiff, CF10 3BA
Tel (029) 2034 3035   **Fax** (029) 2034 3045   **DX** 33063 CARDIFF 1
Email info@rlb-law.com

Senior Partner	Robert Vallings
Chief Executive	Vincent Denham
Number of partners	59
Assistant solicitors	41
Other fee-earners	45

AREAS OF PRACTICE	
Healthcare (inc. Crime)	24%
Private client (inc. Family)	22%
Property	18%
Litigation	16%
Corporate/Commercial	13%
Employment	5%

CONTACTS	
Charities	Jean Dollimore
Commercial	Roland Gillott
	Stephen Everett
Corporate	Phillip Peacock
Corporate Finance	Rupert Lescher
Employment	Michael Elks
	Kate Williams
Family	Roger Cobden-Ramsay
Health: Advisory, Professional Regulation & Employment	Simon Dinnick
	Nick Rawson
Health: Mental Health	Andrew Parsons
Health: NHS & Personal Injury	Stephen Janisch
Health: Professional Parnership	Robert Sumerling
Immigration	Tim Newsome
Insolvency	Gillian Benning
Insurance	Michael Scanlan
International - Italy	Michael Nathanson
International - Other	Phillip Peacock
International - South Africa	Tim Newsome
International - USA/Canada	Paul Clements
IT	Roland Gillott
Litigation & Dispute Resolution	Michael Elks

THE FIRM RadcliffesLeBrasseur is a full service top 70 law firm formed in 2001 out of a merger between Radcliffes and Le Brasseur J. Tickle. It has a wide and varied client base which includes healthcare services providers, public and private companies, property companies, charities, banks, institutions, public authorities and private individuals. RadcliffesLeBrasseur is dedicated to providing clients with the very highest standards of service. It strives to build strong relationships with its clients through accessibility, responsiveness, and by delivering a consistently high quality legal service.

PRINCIPAL AREAS OF WORK The firm offers expertise in focused areas of law with particular strengths in the following sectors:

Healthcare Over 40 specialist lawyers provide premier services to the healthcare sector. Mental health law, clinical negligence, personal injury, NHS constitutional law, judicial review, the defence of doctors, dentists and other healthcare professionals, employment and disciplinary issues, crime, inquests, together with commercial contracts, property matters, and all issues specific to the sector are covered. Clients include medical defence organisations, NHS trusts, health authorities, medical and dental practitioners, primary care groups and trusts, nursing homes, healthcare professionals, the Royal Colleges, associated healthcare professions, private sector healthcare providers, and insurers.

Corporate The firm provides high quality advice to a wide range of industries and businesses. Specific areas of work include corporate issues such as acquisitions, mergers and disposals, management buy-outs and buyins, company restructuring, joint ventures, corporate finance, capital issues, and listings on the AIM and the Stock Exchange.

Continued overleaf

A-Z ■ LAW FIRMS

CONTACTS (Continued)	
Property	Roger Thornton
	Michael Thorniley-Walker
Residential Property	Karen Mayne
Tax & Private Client	Clara Trounson

Commercial Advice includes: insolvency; information technology issues such as supply, procurement and licensing; data protection; intellectual property; distribution and agency agreements; competition law; and dispute resolution in domestic and overseas markets by negotiation, arbitration, mediation or litigation. Specialist lawyers provide expert advice on all aspects of employment law.

Property Acting for property investors, developers and occupiers - including institutions, livery companies, and landed estates - the firm's specialist property group handles mainstream property work as well as advising on property dispute resolution, planning (including consultancy and advocacy), environmental law, advice on property VAT and secured lending.

Private Client The firm serves private clients with advice on tax, family law and residential conveyancing. UK and international tax advice is provided to business owners, senior executives, professionals, individuals, executors, and trustees. Advice includes estate planning, tax compliance and investigation, trusts, wills, estates, receivership, and elderly care. Specialists deal with family law issues including matrimonial problems involving substantial financial and property matters, and issues concerning children. Residential property conveyancing is also undertaken.

Charity The firm is a recognised name in the field of charity law, acting for more than 150 charities and not-for-profit organisations, schools and colleges. The Dresdner RCM Global Investors Charity Directory ranks the firm in the top 15 charity legal advisors (recommended by number of charity clients). It has a particular strength in advising health, mental health, and welfare charities.

RadcliffesLeBrasseur

INTERNATIONAL RadcliffesLeBrasseur is a member of State Capital Global Law Firm Group, a global network enabling clients to have access to high quality legal advice from reliable, like-minded lawyers around the world. RadcliffesLeBrasseur offers offshore trust and company management services from both Geneva and Jersey. The firm has a representative office in Singapore.

RECRUITMENT Five trainees are recruited each year. A recruitment brochure is available on request and application is by CV or the firm's application form with covering letter to the Human Resources Department.

■ Raeburn Christie & Co
16 Albyn Place, Aberdeen, AB9 1PS **Tel** (01224) 640101 **Fax** (01224) 638434

■ Rawlison Butler
Griffin House, 135 High Street, Crawley, RH10 1DQ **Tel** (01293) 527744 **Fax** (01293) 520202

■ Rayfield Mills
3 Collingwood Street, Newcastle upon Tyne, NE1 1JE **Tel** (0191) 261 2333 **Fax** (0191) 261 2444

■ Ray Hemingway - Sole Practitioner
4 Holywell Way, Longthorpe, Peterborough, PE3 6SS **Tel** (01733) 262523 **Fax** (01733) 330280

■ RD Black & Co.
31 Old Jewry, London, EC2R 8DQ
Tel (020) 7600 8282 **Fax** (020) 7600 8228

AREAS OF PRACTICE	
Commodities	40%
Shipping	40%
Commercial Litigation	20%

Established in 1996 by Richard Black, formerly of Middleton Potts, this niche practice is renowned for its expertise in handling commodity, shipping and commercial disputes.

Reed Smith Warner Cranston LLP

Minerva House, 5 Montague Close, London, SE1 9BB
Tel (020) 7403 2900 **Fax** (020) 7403 4221 **DX** 39904 LONDON BRIDGE SOUTH
Email marketing@reedsmith.co.uk **Website** www.reedsmith.com

Park House, Station Square, Coventry, CV1 2FL
Tel (024) 7629 3000 **Fax** (024) 7629 3030 **DX** 11203
Email marketing@reedsmith.co.uk

Senior Partner UK	Ian Fagelson
Managing Partner UK	Tim Foster
Number of partners (UK)	30
Number of fee earners (UK)	89
Total staff (UK)	186

CONTACTS

Business & Finance	Peter Borrowdale (London)
	Christopher Hill (Coventry)
Business Immigration	Peter Alfandary (London)
Debt Recovery	Larry Coltman (Coventry)
Employment	Geoffrey Mead (London)
	Jane Hobson (Coventry)
European Litigation	Paul Fallon (London)
	Jonathan Hofstetter (Coventry)
Healthcare	Jerry Mansmann (London)
	John Muolo (London)
Insurance & Reinsurance	Ian Fagelson (London)
Real Estate	Peter Davis (London)
	David Hayes (Coventry)
Risk & Liability	Darren Smith (Coventry)
Tax	Charles Elphicke (London)
Technology, Media & Communications	Jeff Rodwell (London)
	Jonathan Hofstetter (Coventry)

THE FIRM Reed Smith Warner Cranston is the UK arm of Reed Smith, a leading global law firm with more than 700 lawyers located in 11 US and 2 UK cities. Clients include financial institutions, technology companies and innovators, healthcare providers and insurers, communications companies, manufacturers, universities, real estate developers, and municipalities on both sides of the Atlantic. Reed Smith Warner Cranston prides itself on big firm expertise coupled with a long standing commitment to quality, teamwork and professionalism.

Offices Reed Smith joined forces with Warner Cranston in January 2001 to form Reed Smith Warner Cranston. Warner Cranston itself was founded in 1979 in London and in 1986 opened in Coventry to service clients in the Midlands. The UK head office in London is located in the heart of the London Bridge area and the office in the Midlands is one of the largest commercial practices in the region. The 11 offices in the US are located in Pennsylvania, New York, New Jersey, Washington DC, Virginia and Delaware regions.

PRINCIPAL AREAS OF WORK The firm's core areas of expertise in the UK are business and finance, business immigration, employment, litigation and real estate. The firm also offers highly comprehensive advice in other specialist areas, including tax, technology, media and communications, debt recovery and risk and liability. The firm has developed particular expertise in representing financial institutions across all areas of its business and now counts five top banks, four major insurance companies and two investment advisors within its client base. The UK practice is also building up an expertise in healthcare and technology which are both well established industry focus areas in the USA. New lateral hires in both areas aim to develop a strong presence in the market within the next year. The firm also has a particularly strong reputation in advising French corporate clients doing business in the UK and has a growing practice in advising German corporations.

Business & Finance The firm's largest department handles a wide variety of corporate and commercial domestic and cross-border transactions for an international client base including in particular clients in the US and continental Europe. Areas of work include mergers and acquisitions, joint ventures, asset and corporate finance, public offerings, banking and all aspects of English and EU competition law. The department also deals with corporate taxation, insurance, reinsurance, IT contracts, e-commerce including data protection and housing association work. Although the department has grown largely through its representation of the corporate client, it also has particular expertise in advising both UK and US financial institutions.

Litigation The department handles substantial commercial, technical and financial services disputes and is well known for its work in international asset recovery, financial regulation and multijurisdictional claims. The firm boasts a unique team of French-speaking litigators and a team of four qualified advocates who regularly appear in the High Court. Areas of expertise also include intellectual property, international and domestic arbitration, product liability claims and international trade, banking, agency, distribution and licensing arrangements.

Real Estate The department handles transactions for corporate clients in the retail, media, financial services and manufacturing industries, as well as for major developers and investors. The department regularly advises on town centre and out-of-town developments and handles all aspects of landlord and tenant litigation. The department has also developed a specialist area focusing on inward investment particularly from the US and France.

Employment The department offers a full employment law service covering not only the areas of service agreements and employment contracts, pensions, share options, dismissals, redundancy, discrimination and trade union law but also 'best practice' training and the development of human resource strategies. The firm also advises on all EU aspects of employment law. The department runs a comprehensive series of free seminars to its clients and contacts on current employment issues.

Business Immigration The department has established an excellent reputation for providing advice on UK work permits to major corporate clients. Areas of expertise also cover the rules relating to personal investors, business investments and nationality and naturalisation applications.

Specialist Areas The firm provides high level legal advice in tax, technology, media and communications and risk and liability, which provides corporate clients with comprehensive investigation, reporting and claim handling and directors liability issues. The Midlands office has a debt recovery department which handles claims in excess of £40m per annum.

ReedSmith
WarnerCranston

A-Z ■ LAW FIRMS

■ Rees & Freres

1 The Sanctuary, Westminster, London, SW1P 3JT
Tel (020) 7222 5381 **Fax** (020) 7222 4646 **DX** 145940 Westminster 4
Email enquiries@1thesanctuary.com **Website** www.reesandfreres.com

Ptnrs 11 **Asst solrs** 12 **Other fee-earners** 13 **Contact** Monica Peto • Specialists in commercial property, public, parliamentary and local government law, transport infrastructure projects, planning, compulsory acquisition and commercial litigation.

Reid Minty

14 Grosvenor Street, Mayfair, London, W1K 4PS
Tel (020) 7318 4444 **Fax** (020) 7318 4445 **DX** 44615 Mayfair
Email lawyers@reidminty.co.uk **Website** www.reidminty.co.uk

Managing Partner	Stephen Moss
Senior Partner	Andrew Reid
Number of partners	12
Assistant solicitors	11
Other fee-earners	56

AREAS OF PRACTICE	
Commercial Litigation	50%
Personal Injury	30%
Healthcare	10%
Other	10%

CONTACTS	
Banking	Ian Searle
	David Pacey
Commercial Litigation	Stephen Moss
	Simon Goldhill
	Andrew Reid
Commercial Property	Martin Gunson
Corporate/Sports	Jonathan Ebsworth
Costs Consultancy	Andrew Reid
Health Authority	Ashley Irons
Employment	Nick Neocleous
Horseracing	Andrew Reid
Insolvency	Ian Searle
Insurance	Simon Edwards
Personal Injury	Sue Brown
	Andrew Reid
Property Litigation	Michael Pulford

THE FIRM Reid Minty is renowned for its ability to successfully handle substantial commercial litigation matters. The firm handles City work with a lower cost base and no difference in quality, and is recognised as an expert in this field.

PRINCIPAL AREAS OF WORK The firm advises on major domestic and international commercial disputes, banking and insolvency matters, and covers the full range of commercial litigation from the House of Lords, and Privy Council, through to the Commercial Court, High Court and County Courts. Recent reported cases include Dubai Aluminium v Salaam, Dardana v Yukos Oil and Ashworth v MGN. The firm advises specialist hospitals on sensitive issues concerning secure unit patients (Ian Brady v Ashworth Hospital, R v Broadmoor SHSA ex p S), on local authority healthcare regulations and on a wide range of specialist employment matters. It also provides supporting commercial and property advice. The firm carries out a number of insurance related services including risk and cost assessment, and volume personal injury work.

CLIENTELE Prominent clients include domestic and international banks, financial institutions, international insurers, plcs, substantial multinational corporations, health authorities, international transport and container leasing companies, private companies and individuals.

RECRUITMENT Reid Minty has a comprehensive programme for trainee solicitors, and recruits five to six trainees per year, as well as taking on a number of paralegals.

Reynolds Dawson

34 John Adam Street, Charing Cross, London, WC2N 6HW
Tel (020) 7839 2373 **Fax** (020) 7839 2344
24-hour Emergency Number (08457) 056767 (code: 9571) **DX** 40040 Covent Garden 1
Email inquiries@reynoldsdawson.co.uk **Website** www.reynoldsdawson.co.uk

Partner	Colin Reynolds
Salaried Partners	Elizabeth Fox
	Catherine Ridley

THE FIRM Reynolds Dawson was established in 1982 by Colin Reynolds and Stephen Dawson, who is now a District Judge (Crime) and Recorder. Colin Reynolds is a well established and highly respected criminal practitioner and former President of the LCCSA. The practice, which holds a Legal Aid franchise, specialises in crime and is a member of the Serious Fraud Panel. The practice also undertakes Extradition work. Reynolds Dawson enjoys a long established private client base that extends to Personal Injury and Employment Tribunal work. The partners specialising in criminal law, have both been involved in high profile criminal cases as well as participating in the Stephen Lawrence, Marchioness and Victoria Climbié Inquiries.

Reynolds Porter Chamberlain

Chichester House, 278-282 High Holborn, London, WC1V 7HA
Tel (020) 7242 2877 **Fax** (020) 7242 1431 **DX** 81 London Chancery Lane WC2
Email rpc@rpc.co.uk **Website** www.rpc.co.uk

38 Leadenhall Street, London, EC3A 1AT
Tel (020) 7242 2877 **Fax** (020) 7335 9000 **DX** 81 Chancery Lane WC2

Senior Partner	Alan Toulson
Number of partners	56
Assistant solicitors	94
Other fee-earners	71

CONTACTS	
Commercial Property	David Haywood
Construction	Robert Hogarth
Corporate Finance	Jonathan Watmough
Corporate/Commercial	Alan Toulson
Defamation	Liz Hartley
Dispute Resolution	Stephen Mayer
Education	Geraldine Elliott
Employment	Geraldine Elliott
Family	James Stewart
Insolvency	Justin Westhead
Insurance & Reinsurance	Simon Greenley
Intellectual Property	Andrew Hobson
Media & Technology	Tim Anderson
Pensions/Tax	Jonathan Davies
	Charles Suchett-Kaye
Personal Injury	Duncan Harman-Wilson
Professional Indemnity	Barney Micklem
Trusts & Estates	Colin Russell

THE FIRM Reynolds Porter Chamberlain (RPC) is a substantial commercial firm and one of the country's leading insurance and media and technology practices. RPC has two offices, one in central London, the other in Leadenhall Street in the heart of the insurance market. The firm has well established overseas connections and is a founder member of Terralex, one of the largest international organisations of law firms stretching across over 100 jurisdictions.

PRINCIPAL AREAS OF WORK The firm offers a wide range of legal services and is particularly well adapted to handle the legal requirements of the insurance and media and technology industries.
Insurance Most classes of insurance businesses are dealt with. RPC is particularly noted for its professional indemnity work, acting for insurers of the legal professions, accountants, architects, brokers, engineers and financial advisors. It also has a substantial practice acting for the insurers of directors and officers, banks and financial institutions, as well as claims handling and loss adjusting divisions. In addition, RPC advises on policy wording, corporate and regulatory matters. As a member of the National Health Service Litigation Authority solicitors panel, RPC also acts for the NHS trusts, health authorities and the insurers of private clinics.
Media & Technology The media and technology practice embraces publishing, e-commerce, IT and internet law, defamation, media-related litigation, intellectual property and commercial agreements. Media clients include national newspapers, broadcasters, IT companies and insurers. This group specialises in both contentious and non-contentious media and IT-related work.
Corporate The corporate department acts for publicly quoted companies, multinational corporations, private companies, trade associations and partnerships. Work includes acquisitions and mergers, corporate finance, banking, Yellow Book work, corporate rescue, franchising and distribution, competition law, tax, VAT and pensions.
Dispute Resolution The firm also handles all areas of dispute resolution with specialist teams providing advice on construction law, property disputes, personal injury claims and employment issues.
Education The firm has a wide experience in education, acting for several professional associations in this area as well as for universities, colleges and schools.
Commercial Property The commercial property department acts for publicly quoted property companies and investment funds as well as general trading companies. Areas of work include property investment, site acquisitions, joint ventures, development, town and country planning and landlord and tenant law.
Construction The construction department offers a complete dispute resolution service from mediation to the largest scale computer aided litigation. It also advises on risk management through careful structuring of project documentation.
Family The well regarded family department handles all aspects of matrimonial work and is especially noted for its high profile child abduction work as well as wardship cases on behalf of local authorities, foreign embassies and the Lord Chancellor's Department.
Trusts & Estates The trusts and estates department offers the full spectrum of trust, tax, tax planning, wills, probate and estate administration services for UK and foreign clients. It also undertakes charity formation and administration.

Richard Buxton
40 Clarendon Street, Cambridge, CB1 1JX **Tel** (01223) 328933 **Fax** (01223) 301308

Richard Monteith
34 Portmore Street, Portadown, BT62 3NG
Tel (028) 3833 0780 **Fax** (028) 3835 0271

Ptnrs 1 **Asst solrs** 2 **Contact** Richard Monteith • Specialisation in criminal law in addition to general practice of conveyancing, wills and probate, matrimonial and civil litigation.

A-Z LAW FIRMS

Richards Butler

Beaufort House, 15 St Botolph Street, London, EC3A 7EE
Tel (020) 7247 6555 Fax (020) 7247 5091 DX 1066 City/18 London
Email law@richardsbutler.com Website www.richardsbutler.com

Chairman	Andrew Taylor
Managing Partner	Roger Parker
Worldwide	
Number of partners	116
Number of fee-earners	433
Total staff	815

CONTACTS

Admiralty & Casualty (Wet)	Richard Harvey
ADR	John Hull
Anti-piracy	Mike Northern
Aviation & Aircraft Finance	Adam Morgan
Banking & Financial Services	Gordon Stewart
Commercial	Stephen Sayer
Commercial Disputes	Charles Hewetson
Competition & EU	Katherine Holmes
Corporate Finance	David Boutcher
Defamation	Michael Skrein
E-commerce	Alan Hawley
Employment	Robin Jeffcott
Energy	Stephen Sayer
Financial Services Regulation & Compliance	Richard Parlour
Insolvency	Jon Yorke
Insurance & Reinsurance	Mark Connoley
Intellectual Property	Graham Simkin
International Arbitration (Commercial)	Charles Hewetson
International Arbitration (Shipping)	Andrew Hughes
International Banking	Gordon Stewart
International Trade & Commodities	Richard Swinburn
IT & Telecommunications	Graham Simkin
Licensing	Elizabeth Southorn
Litigation	Charles Hewetson
Marine Casualty Response	Richard Harvey
Media & Entertainment	Stephen Edwards
Pensions	Simon Hartley
Planning, Environment & Construction	John Aylwin
Professional Negligence	Charles Hewetson
Property	Jon Pike
Ship Finance	Adam Morgan
Shipping	Adam Morgan
Tax	Huw Witty
Unit Trusts & Investment Funds	Simon Hartley

THE FIRM Richards Butler is one of the country's pre-eminent medium to large law firms. Its core strategy is to invest in key practice areas, enabling it to establish renowned capabilities that appeal to significant international concerns. This year Richards Butler received a Queen's Award for Enterprise 2002 for International Trade, for its achievements in the international market and for making a significant contribution to British invisible earnings. The firm's principal practice areas are corporate finance, litigation, finance and banking, media/entertainment/leisure, shipping, insurance, commodities, telecommunications, IT and commercial property. Its rated corporate finance team acted for Direct Line in its purchase of the Italian direct insurance business of Royal Insurance, and its acquisition of Allstates subsidiaries in Germany and Italy; for MTV in the restructuring of its Italian operations; Salton on its successful offer to acquire the entire share capital of Pifco and Cordiant in relation to its agreement with Publicis for the transfer of units Optimedia and Zenith media to a new holding company, creating the fourth largest media organisation in the world. Its specialist finance practice recently acted on what is believed to be the world's largest financial restructuring. The disputes group has continued to represent City financial institutions on investigatory and regulatory work and, in the area of media, has represented the BBC and was named as the Litigation Team of the Year at the 2001 Lawyer Awards. The property group acted for LandSecuritiesTrillium on the service partner agreement to develop and manage the BBC's London and Scottish estates. The property group also acted for Microsoft on the lease of its new laboratory building in Cambridge. Over two thirds of Richards Butler's work contains an international dimension, a fact reflected in its long-held belief of investing in overseas offices. Its Hong Kong office alone is rightly regarded as the leading British law firm in the region and, with a physical presence in not less than three of the Gulf states, the firm has been providing advice to the Gulf region for a quarter of a century. The European offices continue to expand - the Paris branch moving to larger premises and a new office opening in Athens. Richard Butler's aim is to provide the best advice in the areas it specialises in to all clients, irrespective of their size, and to ensure each of them receives the same quality of service and care. The rigorous control of costs is just another pleasant surprise.

PRINCIPAL AREAS OF WORK Richards Butler advises in all major areas of commercial law, including:
Corporate & Commercial The firm advises clients on domestic and international mergers and acquisitions; IPOs and stock exchange listings; management buyouts and buyins; corporate and government debt restructuring; joint ventures and inward investment; regulatory environments; project finance including asset financing; venture capital; cross-border leasing and PFI; unit trusts; EU and competition law; intellectual property and IT; insurance; media and entertainment law; anti-piracy and copyright protection; pensions; employment and industrial relations; energy.
Dispute Resolution Advice is given on all matters requiring dispute resolution skills including litigation at all court levels. As one of the largest litigation practices in the UK, the group has expertise in all major litigation areas including financial services/regulatory and banking, all aspects of media and information technology, insurance, employment and general corporate litigation. It also has substantial experience in arbitration and mediation techniques. The firm has acted in many of the major commercial disputes in the City.
Property The firm advises on all aspects of property, environment and planning law, including investment and financing of land and commercial property; VAT; planning requirements for local authorities; construction and contract negotiations; financing and claim preparation; advice related to licensing of hotels and leisure premises, including liquor licensing, betting, gaming, late-night licensing and multi-leisure site licensing.
Shipping The group advises on all aspects of shipping, including charterparty disputes; bill of lading claims; ship sale and purchase; drafting of and disputes concerning shipbuilding contracts; marine insurance and reinsurance (such as P&I and defence clubs); salvage; collision and major casualties (the firm has a 24 hour casualty response line); all aspects of ship finance acting both for banks and borrowers; trade and commodities including buying and selling of hard and soft commodities; trade finance.

INTERNATIONAL The firm has offices in Abu Dhabi, Athens, Beijing, Brussels, Hong Kong, Paris, Piraeus and São Paulo, and associated offices in Doha and Muscat.

LAW FIRMS A-Z

Richard Whish - Sole Practitioner
School of Law, King's College, The Strand, London, WC2R 2LS **Tel** (020) 7848 2237 **Fax** (020) 7848 2211

Rickerbys
Ellenborough House, Wellington Street, Cheltenham, GL50 1YD
Tel (01242) 224422 **Fax** (01242) 518428 **DX** 7415 Cheltenham
Email info@rickerby.co.uk **Website** www.rickerby.co.uk

Ptnrs 17 **Asst solrs** 18 **Other fee-earners** 21 **Contact** Mark Fabian • Rickerbys, formerly Rickerby Watterson. An innovative, progressive and client-focused firm. It has a reputation for delivering city expertise and value for money. Areas of work include agriculture, asset management, commercial litigation, commercial property, company commercial, education, employment, EU and competition, family, insolvency, IT and e-commerce, private client, residential property.

Ricksons
6 Winckley Square, Preston, PR1 3JJ **Tel** (01772) 556677 **Fax** (01772) 562030

RM Broudie & Co
1-3 Sir Thomas St, Liverpool, L1 8BW **Tel** (0151) 227 1429 **Fax** (0151) 236 5161

Roberta McDonald - Sole Practitioner
12 Wake Green Road, Moseley, Birmingham, B13 9EZ **Tel** (0121) 449 6821 **Fax** (0121) 449 5160

Robert Lizar
159 Princess Road, Moss Side, Manchester, M14 4RE **Tel** (0161) 226 2319 **Fax** (0161) 226 7985

Robert Muckle
Norham House, 12 New Bridge Street West, Newcastle upon Tyne, NE1 8AS **Tel** (0191) 232 4402 **Fax** (0191) 261 6954

Robertson & Co, Technology Law Practice
18 Broomhouse Road, London, SW6 3QX
Tel (020) 7731 4626 **Fax** (020) 7731 4598
Email drcr@techlaw.co.uk

Contact Ranald Robertson • Specialist legal support to users and suppliers on computing, software and e-business/internet issues. Benefits include speedy access to senior IT/computer law experience at a reasonable and affordable cost and genuine pan-European capability through membership of IT LAW EUROPE network.

Robertsons
6 Park Place, Cardiff, CF1 3DP **Tel** (029) 2023 7777 **Fax** (029) 2034 0219

Robson McLean WS
28 Abercromby Place, Edinburgh, EH3 6QF
Tel (0131) 556 0556 **Fax** (0131) 556 9939 **DX** LP11-Edin 2
Email info@robson-mclean.co.uk **Website** www.robson-mclean.co.uk

Senior Partner	Walter N J Thomson
Number of partners	10
Assistant solicitors	9
Other fee-earners	10

AREAS OF PRACTICE	
Litigation	50%
Commercial/Corporate	25%
Private Client	25%

CONTACTS	
Business	Walter Thomson
Commercial Property	Nick Atkins
Litigation	Duncan Murray
Private Client	Neil Paterson

THE FIRM This leading Scottish firm, operating from Edinburgh's city centre, continues to see growth in its commercial litigation and commercial/business departments. It has a strong client focus offering value-for-money services tailored to individual client needs. The firm is approved to ISO 9001 and is the only Scottish member of LawGroup UK.

PRINCIPAL AREAS OF WORK Specialisms include commercial litigation, corporate, employment, environmental/planning, IP/technology, personal injury, matrimonial, PFI, commercial property and private client.

CLIENTELE Major clients include government bodies, local authorities, leading insurers and financial institutions, property companies, charities and special interest groups, trade unions and associations.

A-Z ■ LAW FIRMS

Rochman Landau

45 Mortimer Street, London, W1W 8HJ
Tel (020) 7544 2424 Fax (020) 7544 2400 DX 42700 Oxford Circus North
Email mail@rochmanlandau.co.uk Website www.rochmanlandau.co.uk

THE FIRM This West End law firm provides a high quality, cost effective legal service to clients, both in the UK and overseas. It combines technical expertise with a commercial approach.

PRINCIPAL AREAS OF WORK Rochman Landau has considerable expertise in the following areas: business; property; litigation; family matters; wills and probate; trusts - UK and overseas; tax; employment; landlord and tenant, both commercial and residential; licensing; insolvency and immigration. The firm can also offer mediation and ADR services.

CLIENTELE Corporate clients, banks, PLCs, mid-sized companies, entrepreneurs and professionals. Clients are both within the UK and overseas.

INTERNATIONAL The firm has strong links with the Far East, Australia and America. It also has French speaking fee-earners.

RECRUITMENT The firm continues to recruit to support its expansion programme with the addition of a further three fee-earners. The firm takes pride in the fact that a number of its former trainees have remained with the firm, and are represented amongst the partners.

Managing Partners	Teresa Cullen
	John Rochman
Number of partners	9
Assistant solicitors	2
Other fee-earners	4

AREAS OF PRACTICE	
Property	40%
Litigation	30%
Company/Commercial	20%
Private Client/Other	10%

CONTACTS	
Property	John Rochman, Edward Landau
Litigation	David Liebeck, Alan Langleben
Employment	Teresa Cullen, Arthur Fernandes
Insolvency	David Liebeck
Company/Commercial	Arthur Fernandes
	John Rochman
Private Client	John Rochman, Edward Landau
Licencing	Patricia Negus-Fancy
Matrimonial	Teresa Cullen, Philippa Dolan

Rodgers & Burton

15-17 Church Rd, Barnes, London, SW13 9HG
Tel (020) 8939 6300 Fax (020) 8876 8228 DX 59702 Barnes
Email info@randb.law.co.uk

THE FIRM The firm was founded in 1835, and has had a presence in Barnes since 1952. The firm occupies offices overlooking Barnes Common and incorporated another local firm, Messrs Ashbys, in 1998.

PRINCIPAL AREAS OF WORK Whilst being a general High Street practice, Rodgers & Burton offers certain specialist advice in servicing landlords and Housing Associations. In particular, the firm offers experience in landlord and tenant litigation, housing association law and finance, disposals and acquisitions of property, lease back financing of acquisitions, shared ownership schemes, construction contracts and disputes.

Other Areas Rodgers & Burton also has fee-earners with experience in employment law, personal injury, debt recovery, contractual disputes, commercial litigation and a busy matrimonial department. Conditional fee arrangements are available if appropriate. The firm will draft wills, where no tax planning or will trust advice is required, for a fixed fee. The firm has obtained a franchise for community legal service specialist help in family. The firm offers an Agency Service in Wandsworth, West London and Brentford County Courts. Rodgers & Burton has a well respected residential conveyancing department and, following the incorporation of Messrs Ashbys, has considerable expertise in commercial conveyancing.

Senior Partner	David Moore
Number of partners	5
Other fee-earners	4

AREAS OF PRACTICE	
Private & Commercial Conveyancing	52%
Civil Litigation	33%
Matrimonial	10%
Wills & Probate	5%

CONTACTS	
Conveyancing/Wills & Probate	Kathryn Kinnear
Landlord & Tenant	David Moore
Matrimonial	Gillian Tyndall
Personal Injury/Employment/ Debt Recovery	Mark Woloshak

■ Roebucks
12 Richmond Terrace, Blackburn, BB1 7BG Tel (01254) 274000 Fax (01254) 274002

■ Roger Tabakin - Sole Practitioner
61 Onslow Gardens, London, N10 3JY Tel (020) 8374 2562 Fax (020) 8883 8352

Roiter Zucker

5-7 Broadhurst Gardens, Swiss Cottage, London, NW6 3RZ
Tel (020) 7328 9111   Fax (020) 7644 8953   DX 38850 Swiss Cottage
Email mail@roiterzucker.co.uk   Website www.roiterzucker.co.uk

THE FIRM Roiter Zucker is well known for its intellectual property and competition law work. The firm has an excellent reputation for litigation, having acted in many of the leading IP and competition law cases, including the terfenadine and paclitaxel patent cases, the Glaxo/Dowelhurst case concerning parallel imports and the extent of the free movement of goods, and judicial review cases, most recently for parallel importers in connection with their claim of illegality of the 1999 PPRS governing reimbursement for pharmaceutical products. As well as its high profile litigation, RZ does a full range of non-contentious IP work for clients in various fields, including leading biotech companies and generic pharmaceutical companies, media and an increasing amount of brand work. RZ is small, but highly skilled. It is used to working in the international arena and can draw on expert advice worldwide.

Number of partners	8
Assistant solicitors	6
Other fee-earners	1

AREAS OF PRACTICE	
Intellectual Property (inc. Pharmaceutical)	50%
Commercial	20%
Private Client	15%
Litigation Non IP	5%

CONTACTS	
General Contact	Anna McKay

Rollits

Wilberforce Court, High Street, Hull, HU1 1YJ
Tel (01482) 323259   Fax (01482) 326239   DX 715756 Hull 15
Email info@rollits.com   Website www.rollits.com

Rowntree Wharf, Navigation Road, York, YO1 9WE
Tel (01904) 625790   Fax (01904) 625807   DX 61534 York

THE FIRM One of the principal firms in the Yorkshire region offering a comprehensive commercial legal service. Expertise in corporate and commercial law is unrivalled in East Yorkshire.

PRINCIPAL AREAS OF WORK

Company Work includes acquisitions and disposals, flotations, share issues, fund raising, joint ventures, MBOs, finance and credit agreements, corporate recovery, employment law and telecommunications.
Commercial Including e-commerce, intellectual property, trading agreements, franchising, and competition law.
Commercial & Residential Property Work includes commercial conveyancing, planning and development, environmental law, landlord and tenant, housing association work and agriculture.
Litigation Work undertaken includes commercial litigation, intellectual property disputes, building and construction, mediation debt recovery, insurance litigation, professional indemnity, licensing and matrimonial.
Private Capital Including tax and estate planning, settlements, asset protection, wills, estate administration, education and charity law.

Managing Partner	Stephen Trynka
Senior Partner	James Brennand
Number of partners	30
Assistant solicitors	18
Other fee-earners	25

AREAS OF PRACTICE	
Company & Commercial	26%
Litigation	22%
Property	22%
Private Capital	14%
Planning & Development	10%
Employment	6%

CONTACTS	
Charity	Ros Harwood
Commercial	Keith Benton
Commercial Litigation	George Coyle
Company	Richard Field
Employment	Neil Maidment
Planning	Steve Hawkins
Private Capital	John Lane
Property	Martyn Justice

Rooks Rider

Challoner House, 19 Clerkenwell Close, London EC1R 0RR
Tel (020) 7689 7000   Fax (020) 7689 7001   DX 53324 Clerkenwell
Email nblackledge@rooksrider.co.uk   Website www.rooksrider.co.uk

THE FIRM Established in 1761 (making Rooks Rider one of the oldest law firms in the country) it has a tradition of offering a high quality service to individuals and businesses. Building from this foundation, the partnership is continually expanding the breadth of its expertise to respond to the needs of its clients and the changing business environment. It has a friendly and informal atmosphere and prides itself on finding creative and practical solutions to its clients' needs. The firm is committed to the continued development of both the private client and commercial sides of its practice. It achieved Investors in People accreditation in 1999. In addition to offering a comprehensive, high quality service to businesses and individuals Rooks Rider has developed an international reputation for its tax planning skills both in the UK and offshore. It has particular expertise in serving growing businesses (from start-up to major listed company). It is a leading firm in the private client field.

PRINCIPAL AREAS OF WORK
The firm has growing practices in a broad spread of commercial and private client areas.
Commercial Rooks Rider commercial clients range from substantial listed companies to family

Managing Partner	Clare Foinette
Senior Partner	Christopher Cooke
Number of partners	13
Assistant solicitors	19
Other fee-earners	14

AREAS OF PRACTICE	
Company/Commercial	40%
Private Client	23%
Litigation	19%
Property	18%

CONTACTS	
Banking	Christopher Cooke
Company & Commercial	Christopher Cooke
Commercial Litigation	Paul Whitaker
	Scott Farnsworth
Employment	Paul Whitaker
Insolvency	Christopher Cooke
Intellectual Property	Scott Farnsworth

Continued overleaf

A-Z LAW FIRMS

businesses and in a diverse array of market sectors. The firm offers clients a full service in handling transactions, managing disputes and providing advice on commercial issues. The firm's commercial practice is dovetailed with its international tax practice, and within the commercial practice, solicitors are encouraged to develop a broad legal knowledge. This structure has allowed the firm to provide balanced, practical advice to entrepreneurs and entrepreneurial business in a seamless manner and to create a stimulating working environment. The approach has worked particularly well for inward investment into the UK, business start-ups and company sales. Existing strengths in advising start-ups, intellectual property and corporate sales have been applied to good effect to the growing group of e-commerce clients.

International Tax The international tax practice has particular strengths in the fields of offshore trusts and international corporate structures for companies and individuals. It is instructed by professional trustees, banks and individuals around the world and partners visit virtually all of the major low tax jurisdictions each year. Team members regularly contribute to conferences and journals in this area and are invited to lecture as far afield as Hong Kong and New Zealand.

Private Client Its traditional private client base has expanded considerably, advising in relation to landed estates, wills, trusts, probate, and tax planning. This enables the firm to provide an extensive service to wealthy individuals be they UK residents, foreign nationals or expatriates. It works closely with the matrimonial practice which has dedicated specialists dealing with family law issues including complex financial cases.

Property The property team handles all types of commercial and residential property transactions, and landlord and tenant matters. It has developed a particular expertise on leasehold reform and is a founder member of the Leasehold Advisory Group. It counts developers and investment funds amongst its regular clients and has built a major specialisation in designing tax efficient structures for property purchases in the UK by foreign nationals and residents.

Litigation The litigation department has an excellent track record of resolving disputes to its clients' advantage through negotiation, arbitration and mediation. However, if litigation proves necessary it will always fight very hard for its clients through skilful use of court procedures and a sound knowledge of the law. It has a high success rate in cases taken to trial. The department's core practice areas include commercial litigation, property litigation, family law issues and trust and probate disputes.

Other Cross-departmental teams deal with employment and intellectual property. The intellectual property group (IPG) has a significant IP practice and advises a complete range of clients from individuals and small businesses to multinational brand and patent owners on both the contentious and non-contentious aspects of intellectual property. The IPG has a particularly strong reputation for its multinational work in the fields of trademark and patent litigation. The employment law group (ELG) advises employers and employees on all aspects of employment law, including the drafting of employment contracts, the consequences of the acquisition and disposal of businesses, including TUPE, severance and compromise agreements, and court and employment tribunal proceedings.

RECRUITMENT The firm is always seeking to recruit high calibre qualified staff, and recruits at least two trainee solicitors each year. All areas of practice are expanding. Enquiries should be sent to Ros Ehren (Head of Personnel).

CONTACTS (Continued)	
International Tax	Christopher Cooke
	Gerald Chappell
	Karen Methold
Matrimonial	Paul Whitaker
	Emma Morris
Private Client	Christopher Wright
	Nicholas Jenkins
	Charlotte Simm
	Claire Archer
Property	Clare Foinette
	John Spencer-Silver
	James John
	Anthony Shalet

Rosling King

2-3 Hind Court, Fleet St, London, EC4A 3DL
Tel (020) 7353 2353 **Fax** (020) 7583 2035 **DX** 154
Email info@roslingking.co.uk **Website** www.roslingking.co.uk

THE FIRM Rosling King is a dynamic commercial firm based in Fleet Street. It also has a London insurance office in the City. Rosling King offers an imaginative and practical approach to working with clients and is unique in having developed a client care programme. The firm's clientele include a significant number of UK banks, building societies and financial institutions, insurance and reinsurance companies, Lloyds syndicates, insurance professionals, property companies, developers and investors. This niche firm provides advice in: banking/finance; commercial property; company and commercial; insurance and reinsurance; litigation and dispute resolution; construction; employment; health and safety.

Senior Partner	Owen Rafferty
Number of partners	10
Assistant solicitors	27
Other fee-earners	21

Ross & Connel
10 Viewfield Terrace, Dunfermline, KY12 7JH **Tel** (01383) 721156 **Fax** (01383) 721150

Ross & Craig

12A Upper Berkeley Street, London, W1H 7PE
Tel (020) 7262 3077 **Fax** (020) 7724 6427 **DX** 44416 Marble Arch
Email reception@rosscraig.com **Website** www.rosscraig.com

THE FIRM Established in the 1950s with an emphasis on commercial client work, acting for public and private companies, businesses and individual entrepreneurs and with distinctive employment, family, personal injury, litigation and media expertise.

PRINCIPAL AREAS OF WORK

Commercial Property Work includes development projects, portfolio acquisitions and break-ups, structuring joint venture schemes of varying complexity with associated planning and funding requirements conducted through SPV and other tax efficient procedures. Clients number major traders, developers, retailers and hotel operators.

Company/Commercial/Media Encompasses a full range of corporate and commercial transactions, acting for purchasers, vendors and joint venturers and drafting consequential employment, shareholder and director agreements. Some of the firm's specialist areas include intellectual property, media, entertainment, film and TV, defamation and sports law.

Litigation Work handled includes commercial disputes, landlord and tenant litigation and property disputes, employment issues, intellectual property, complex personal injury work, professional negligence, insolvency and liquidations. The firm actively encourages mediation to resolve disputes where appropriate.

Environmental Law The specialist land regeneration unit enjoys high level connections with relevant professionals and government departments. It provides services in a consultancy capacity and as a principal advisor on legal and risk management.

Family Law As well as usual areas of advice, this team has special expertise in dealing with cohabiting partners and in advising on the financial issues of matrimonial problems in a practical way.

Employment The firm advises employers and employees in respect of both contentious and non-contentious work.

CLIENTELE Clients range in size from internationally known companies to small businesses and individuals.

INTERNATIONAL The firm has close links with lawyers in Europe and America. Work is handled in French, Italian and German.

RECRUITMENT Two trainees a year. Applications to the Recruitment Partner for 2004/5.

Managing Partner	David Leadercramer
Senior Partner	Leonard Ross
Number of partners	9
Assistant solicitors	8
Other fee-earners	5

AREAS OF PRACTICE	
Property	30%
Company/Commercial/Media	25%
Litigation	20%
Family	13%
Employment	10%
Private Client	2%

CONTACTS	
Company/Commercial/Media	Ian Bloom
Employment	Stephen ten Hove
Environmental	Hugh Barrett
Family/Private Client	Simone Katzenberg
Litigation	David Leadercramer
Property	Stephen Gilbert
Sport	Colin Barr

Ross Harper

58 West Regent Street, Glasgow, G2 2QZ
Tel (0141) 333 6333 **Fax** (0141) 333 6334 **DX** 519242 GLW 12
Email westregentstreet@rossharper.com **Website** www.rossharper.com

Ptnrs 9 **Asst solrs** 16 **Other fee-earners** 15 • Multi-practice firm specialising in commercial and domestic conveyancing, wills and executries, family law, compensation claims, employment matters, sports and media, white collar and all other crime.

Areas of Practice	
Criminal	30%
Family	23%
Litigation & Employment	17%
Residential Conveyancing	15%
Claims	8%
Commercial Conveyancing	6%
Sports & Media	1%

A-Z LAW FIRMS

Rothera Dowson (Incorporating German and Soar)

2 Kayes Walk, Stoney Street, The Lace Market, Nottingham, NG1 1PZ
Tel (0115) 9100 600 **Fax** (0115) 9100 800 **DX** 10028 Nottingham
Email enquiries@rotheradowson.co.uk **Website** www.rotheradowson.co.uk

THE FIRM The firm has strong connections in the City of Nottingham and has several offices based in and around the city. The firm serves a wide and varied client base including large institutions, commercial businesses, small companies and individuals. A number of the partners hold judicial positions including Deputy Coroner, Deputy District Judge, Clerk to the Commissioners of Income Taxes and Southwell Diocesan Registrar. Two partners have higher rights of audience. Rothera Dowson has longstanding links with the Road Haulage Association and the Freight Transport Association. Through its work this year, in connection with the High Court/Court of Appeal victories for lorry drivers against stowaway fines, the firm has expanded its European client base. Although the firm has a long history, its philosophy and approach is very much up-to-date, having invested heavily in technology and modern city offices.

PRINCIPAL AREAS OF WORK
Corporate & Commercial Company formations, share issues, acquisitions, commercial agreements, commercial property, employment contracts, intellectual property, commercial property including landlord and tenant, compulsory purchase, leases, town and country planning.
Litigation Civil litigation of all kinds, including a significant personal injury department with PI Panel members, contentious intellectual property matters, employment disputes, contractual disputes including construction, debt recovery for large companies and also work for housing associations. This department also includes a number of specialist road transport lawyers, experienced criminal practitioners and a sports law interest.
Private Client All aspects of personal taxation, trusts, wills, probate and administration. Family and matrimonial solicitors covering all kinds of family work including advice upon divorce, financial disputes, cohabitation, child abduction etc. Family solicitors are Law Society Children and Family Panel members and include a qualified SFLA mediator. Advocacy in mental health law is undertaken by an MHRT Panel member.
Independent Financial Advice In-house independent advisor for all kinds of investment advice.
Agency Work Undertaken General civil contract in family and mental health.

Managing Partner	Jane George
Senior Partner	Christopher Hodson
Number of partners	20
Assistant solicitors	10
Other fee-earners	16

AREAS OF PRACTICE	
Litigation	25%
Probate, Trusts & Tax	20%
Property	20%
Company Commercial & Employment	15%
Family	15%
Other	5%

CONTACTS	
Company, Commercial & Planning	Christopher Hodson
Commercial Litigation	Richard Hammond
Commercial Property	Amanda Redgate
Crime & Motoring	Tony Priest
Ecclesiastical/Education	Christopher Hodson
Employment	James Collard
Family & Matrimonial	Christine Doughty
Financial Advice	Beryl Morgan
Personal Injury	Anton Balkitis
Residential Conveyancing/ Landlord & Tenant	Carole Fox
Sports Law	John Gardiner
Transport	Ian Rothera
Wills, Trusts, Probate & Tax	Jeremy Allen
White Collar Crime	David Colyer

Rowe Cohen

Quay House, Quay Street, Manchester, M3 3JE
Tel (0161) 830 4600 **Fax** (0161) 831 7436
Email info@rowecohen.com **Website** www.rowecohen.com

THE FIRM Rowe Cohen is a leading law firm, with offices in London and Manchester and a national client base. Its strengths lie in its commercial and personal legal expenses work and its litigation and dispute resolution, acting for many of the UK's largest national associations and trade organisations. Its success has been through identifying trends in the market place and being innovative, especially in the small business sector.

PRINCIPAL AREAS OF WORK Include commercial and corporate, commercial litigation, carriage of goods, regulatory defence, insurance, legal expenses, employment, personal injury, police discipline, private client, commercial property.

Managing Partner	Simon Cohen
Number of partners	15
Assistant solicitors	29
Other fee-earners	31

CONTACTS	
Commercial Litigation	Graham Small
Corporate & Commercial	Ian Lewis
Insurance	David Horwich
Personal Injury	Ivor Rowe
Property	Mike Hymanson

Rowlands
3 York Street, Manchester, M2 2RW **Tel** (0161) 835 2020 **Fax** (0161) 835 2525

Rowley Ashworth
247 The Broadway, Wimbledon, London, SW19 1SE **Tel** (020) 8543 2277 **Fax** (020) 8543 0143

Roy Morgan & Co
Norfolk House, 57-59 Charles Street, Cardiff, CF1 4ED **Tel** (029) 2039 8511

LAW FIRMS A-Z

Roythorne & Co
10 Pinchbeck Rd, Spalding, PE11 1PZ **Tel** (01775) 724141 **Fax** (01775) 725736

Rudlings & Wakelam
1 Woolhall Street, Bury St Edmunds, IP33 1LA **Tel** (01284) 755771 **Fax** (01284) 762436

Rupert Bear Murray Davies
Union Chambers, 11 Weekday Cross, Nottingham, NG1 2GB
Tel (0115) 924 3333 **Fax** (0115) 924 2255 **DX** 10015 Nottingham
Email rbmdlaw@aol.com

Senior Partner	Murray Davies
Number of partners	3
Assistant solicitors	3
AREAS OF PRACTICE	
Matrimonial/Public Child Law	95%
Conveyancing	5%
CONTACTS	
Matrimonial	Murray Davies
	Isobel England
	Sarah Heathcote
Mediation	Sarah Heathcote
	Catherine Stevens
Public Child Law	Isobel England
	Russell Tolley

THE FIRM A specialist family law practice founded in 1992, by Rupert Bear, an established Nottingham family solicitor. The firm encompassed the family law practice of Eversheds, Nottingham and in 1996, was supplemented by the arrival of Murray Davies as partner, bringing with him in excess of 16 years experience in the field. Sarah Heathcote became a partner in the same year, having been with the firm since its inception. Upon Rupert Bear's retirement in 1999, Isobel England, with some 20 years experience, joined the firm, bringing a particular interest in the law relating to children, adoption and matrimonial finance. The firm has established contacts with accountants, pensions advisors, insurance brokers and other professionals, to assist in resolving financial matters resulting from the breakdown of relationships.

PRINCIPAL AREAS OF WORK Work includes separation and divorce and the financial agreements relating to all aspects of family relationships, the resolution of disputes involving children, their legal status, and adoption. The firm has considerable experience in co-habitation issues and pre-marriage arrangements. Mediation work, conveyancing, wills and the legal requirements of the elderly are also catered for.

Russel & Aitken
22 & 24 Stirling Street, Denny, FK6 6AZ **Tel** (01324) 822194 **Fax** (01324) 824560

Russell-Cooke
2 Putney Hill, Putney, London, SW15 6AB
Tel (020) 8789 9111 **Fax** (020) 8780 1194 **DX** 59456 Putney
Email advice@russell-cooke.co.uk

8 Bedford Row, London, WC1R 4BX
Tel (020) 7405 6566 **Fax** (020) 7831 2565 **DX** 112 London
Email advice@russell-cooke.co.uk

Bishop's Palace House, Kingston Bridge, Kingston-upon-Thames, KT1 1QN
Tel (020) 8546 6111 **Fax** (020) 8541 4404 **DX** 31546 Kingston
Email advice@russell-cooke.co.uk

Senior Partner	Michael Maskey
Managing Partner	John Gould
Number of partners	26
Assistant solicitors	36
Other fee-earners	25
AREAS OF PRACTICE	
Property	35%
Family/Child Care/PI Litigation/other	22%
Probate Wills & Trusts	15%
Commercial Litigation	10%
Company/Commercial	10%
Criminal Law	8%
CONTACTS	
Administrative Law/Solicitors	John Gould
Child Care	John Hackett
Commercial & Construction Litigation/ADR	Francesca Kaye
Commercial Property	Peter Dawson
Company/Commercial	Jonathan Thornton
Conveyancing	Nigel Coates
Criminal Matters	Ian Ryan
Employment	Anthony Sakrouge
Family Law	Fiona Read
French Property & Law	Dawn Alderson
Insolvency	Lee Ranford
Medical Negligence & Personal Injury	Janice Gardner
Probate & Wills	Richard Frimston
Professional Regulation	Peter Cadman
Property Litigation	Jason Hunter
Trusts	Michael Best

THE FIRM Russell-Cooke is an energetic, professionally managed firm with over 170 solicitors and staff. The firm has its headquarters in a historic Grade II* building in Bedford Row, Central London. It also has flourishing offices in Putney, SW15; Kingston-upon-Thames, Surrey; and in Bordeaux, where its French law and property department is based.

PRINCIPAL AREAS OF WORK The firm offers a sophisticated and cost-effective service to corporate and institutional clients, with close-knit, specialist teams encouraged to match the best competing expertise in each area. It has well-respected commercial property, company and commercial and property litigation departments, and a professional regulation department which acts both for regulatory authorities and individuals. A specialist employment law team acts for both employers and employees. Other departments handle probate, wills and trusts; personal injury and medical negligence; conveyancing; and French law and property matters. The firm's criminal litigation department is regarded as one of London's leading criminal defence teams. An area of growing expertise is administrative law; the firm has handled a number of high-profile judicial reviews. The firm has specialist departments dealing with family law, including international abduction, and with issues relating to children in care. A number of the firm's senior lawyers are trained mediators.

CLIENTELE Clients range from major plcs, public bodies, regulatory bodies and institutions to smaller companies and professional and creative partnerships. The firm also has a large and loyal private client base.

www.ChambersandPartners.com

A-Z LAW FIRMS

Russell Jones & Walker

Swinton House, 324 Gray's Inn Road, London, WC1X 8DH
Tel (020) 7837 2808 **Fax** (020) 7837 2941 **DX** 202 London Chancery Lane
Email enquiries@rjw.co.uk **Website** www.rjw.co.uk

THE FIRM Russell Jones and Walker, founded in London in the 1920s, has grown rapidly in the last 10 years expanding from 100 to over 600 staff and partners, and establishing offices in Newcastle, Sheffield, Leeds, Manchester, Birmingham, Bristol, Cardiff, Northampton, and an associated office in Edinburgh. The firm's emphasis on people has enabled it to develop an impressive range of specialist services of particular value to individuals and those who represent them.

PRINCIPAL AREAS OF WORK

Personal Injury The firm is one of the leading claimant personal injury practices. A total of over 100 lawyers deal with a wide range of claimant personal injury work including compensation for industrial injury, disasters, chemical poisoning and environmental pollution, road traffic accidents, disease and disablement and criminal assault.

Employment The firm has a large specialist employment department with a highly respected reputation within the industry. It deals with all aspects of individual and collective claimant employment law, both litigious and non-litigious, including contracts, discrimination, dismissal issues, transfers and pensions and human rights issues.

Criminal Law & Investigations The firm has a reputation as one of the leading criminal law practices within the UK, advising and representing clients on all aspects of criminal law with a particular focus on white collar crime, tax investigations and commercial fraud.

Litigation The commercial litigation department advises on all aspects of commercial litigation including professional negligence, defamation, intellectual property and insolvency. The department is particularly well regarded for its libel expertise having successfully acted against all national daily and Sunday newspapers and most radio and TV companies.

Healthcare The firm has a first class reputation for resolving clinical negligence cases. The department is a rapidly expanding area of the practice with an exceptional success rate. All types of claimant clinical negligence work is undertaken with particular expertise in claims involving young children, representation at inquests and alternative dispute resolution in litigation including mediation.

Other Areas In addition to the specialist areas of work listed above the firm has expertise in the following areas: commercial and residential conveyancing; landlord and tenant contracts; public and administrative law; public inquiries; family and matrimonial law; and other private client services including wills, probate and trusts and financial services.

Senior Partner	John Webber
Number of partners	56
Assistant solicitors	101
Other fee-earners	106

AREAS OF PRACTICE	
Personal Injury	64%
Crime & Fraud	9%
Defamation	8%
Employment	8%
Healthcare	5%
Professional Negligence, Commercial Litigation, Property & Probate	2%

CONTACTS	
Business Services	Simone Kilka
Commercial Litigation	Sue Thackeray
Crime, Business Investigations & Fraud	Rod Fletcher
	Scott Ingram
Defamation	Sarah Webb
	Jeremy Clarke-Williams
Employment	Edward Cooper
Family, Wills, Probate & Trusts	Oliver Gravell
Financial Services	Peter Haywood
Healthcare	Rosamund Rhodes-Kemp
Personal Injury	Neil Kinsella
	Ian Walker
	Fraser Whitehead
Professional Negligence, Commercial Litigation & General Commercial	Sarah Webb
	Jeremy Clarke-Williams
Property	Peter Klim

Russell & Russell
Churchill House, Wood Street, Bolton, BL1 1EE **Tel** (01204) 399299 **Fax** (01204) 389223

Russells

Regency House, 1-4 Warwick St, London, W1R 6LJ
Tel (020) 7439 8692 **Fax** (020) 7494 3582 **DX** 37249 Piccadilly 1
Email media@russells.co.uk

THE FIRM Founded by its present senior partner in 1974, Russells is best known for its experience and reputation in the entertainment industry.

PRINCIPAL AREAS OF WORK Although recognised as one of the leading firms in the entertainment industry, with eight commercial partners, the firm also advises on general commercial matters. Three litigation partners also handle all types of litigation including breach of copyright, defamation, property disputes and divorce. It is also active in commercial and residential property, wills and probate.

Managing Partners	CD Organ
	BK Howard
Senior Partner	AD Russell
Number of partners	11
Assistant solicitors	5
Other fee-earners	2

Russells Gibson McCaffrey
13 Bath Street, Glasgow, G2 1HY **Tel** (0141) 332 4176 **Fax** (0141) 332 7908

Rustemeyer & Co
49 The Droveway, Hove, BN3 6P3 **Tel** (01273) 241807

Sach Solicitors
24 Alie Street, Second Floor, London, E1 8DE **Tel** (020) 7680 1133 **Fax** (020) 7680 1144

LAW FIRMS ■ A-Z

Sacker & Partners

29 Ludgate Hill, London, EC4M 7NX
Tel (020) 7329 6699 **Fax** (020) 7248 0552 **DX** 63 Ch.Ln.
Email enquiries@sacker-partners.co.uk **Website** www.sacker-partners.co.uk

THE FIRM Sacker & Partners is known as the principal specialist UK law firm practising exclusively in the pensions field. The practice has been known for pensions since its establishment in 1966, and since 1990 has concentrated solely on pensions work and related areas. The firm is well represented in the pensions industry. Its partners serve on the committees of various professional bodies which comment on proposals for changes in pensions law and practice. Several are known through books, specialist articles and speeches to pensions conferences. Clients are employers (including leading public companies), trustees (including independent trustees) and trade unions. Referral work from other law firms (such as pensions advice on transactions) is an important area of the practice. The firm provides an independent trusteeship service through Independent Trustee Ltd, the leading law firm-based independent trustee company in the UK. Sackers attaches particular importance to client care through partner supervision. The firm's technical expertise is complemented by its practical approach and its ability to produce innovative solutions when needed.

PRINCIPAL AREAS OF WORK The workload consists entirely of pensions work and related activities such as employment work, pensions litigation and pensions advice on commercial transactions. Specialist expertise includes the establishment, variation and winding-up of pension schemes (including unapproved arrangements) in the UK and Ireland. The firm sets up stakeholder and personal schemes for insurers and other providers. Other matters handled routinely include acquisitions, disposals, scheme mergers and reorganisations and dispute resolution/litigation on a variety of subjects, such as transfer values and equal treatment claims. Advice is given on international transfers and multinational pension provision. Expertise is also provided concerning privatisations, the contracting-out of central and local government operations (including the impact of TUPE), tax, documentation, powers and duties of employers and trustees, and investment management agreements.

Senior Partner	Mark Greenlees
Number of partners	20
Assistant solicitors	20
Other fee-earners	1
AREAS OF PRACTICE	
Pensions	100%
CONTACTS	
Pensions	Ian Pittaway
	Jonathan Seres
	Peter Lester
	Chris Close
	Jonathan Berman
	Monica Coombs

Salans

Clements House, 14-18 Gresham Street, London, EC2V 7NN
Tel (020) 7509 6000 **Fax** (020) 7726 6191 **DX** 196
Email london@salans.com **Website** www.salans.com

THE FIRM Salans is an international law firm with substantial offices in London, Paris, New York and Warsaw, together with further full-service offices in St Petersburg, Moscow, Kyiv, Almaty and Baku. The firm currently has approximately 450 fee-earners, including about 110 partners. The firm's London office is situated in the City and provides a full range of services to both domestic and international clients. It is particularly well known for its work in the banking/finance sector and the motor vehicle industry. Its employment department enjoys a strong reputation. Founded just over 20 years ago as a general law practice, the firm's growth has been continuous and rapid. On 1 January 1998, Salans merged with London-based Harris Rosenblatt & Kramer and now has a London presence of 65 fee earners, including 18 partners. On 1 January 1999, Salans merged with New York-based Christy & Viener, in the first transatlantic law firm merger. The merged firm is a multinational partnership which includes lawyers of more than a dozen nationalities. The diverse skills, professional qualifications, national backgrounds and linguistic abilities of its lawyers enable the firm to handle matters requiring local expertise as well as skill in cross-border transactions.

PRINCIPAL AREAS OF WORK The London office acts for a wide range of domestic and international businesses, including UK and foreign banks, finance houses, building societies, international financial institutions and investment funds.

Banking The firm has a well-deserved reputation for its work both in UK and overseas financing (including the emerging markets of Eastern Europe and the former Soviet Union). Its services include advising upon a wide variety of loans (including syndicated loans), lease and security documentation, and terms and conditions for trade, asset-based and project financings and arrangements for development capital and investment funds in the UK and overseas. The department has specialist knowledge of motor vehicle stocking finance, lease and hire-purchase arrangements, consumer credit-related documentation, portfolio securitisations and insolvency-related issues.

Litigation The firm has extensive expertise in banking and recoveries litigation and professional negligence claims, acting for clearing banks and major institutional lenders. In addition, the firm is experienced in all aspects of general commercial litigation including contractual disputes, insolvency, fraud, asset tracing and breach of trust claims. The firm's work encompasses landlord and tenant disputes,

Continued overleaf

Senior Partner	Lionel Rosenblatt
UK	
Number of partners	18
Assistant solicitors	22
Other fee-earners	20
International	
Number of partners	113
Other fee-earners	340
AREAS OF PRACTICE	
Banking & Finance/Corporate	35%
Company & Commercial/High-tech	25%
Litigation	20%
Employment	10%
Commercial Property	10%
CONTACTS	
Banking & Finance	Stephen Finch
	Howard Cohen
Banking Recoveries	Caroline Havers
Commercial Arbitration	Lionel Rosenblatt
Commercial Property	Roger Abrahams
Corporate & Commercial	Philip Enoch
	Richard Thomas
Emerging Markets	Robert Starr
	Mira Davidovski
	Joel McDonald
Employment	Barry Mordsley
	Michael Bronstein
General Commercial Litigation	Jeffrey Elton
High-Tech & E-commerce	Richard Thomas
Insolvency	Alison Gaines
International Banking & Finance	Stephen Finch
	Philip Prowse
Professional Negligence	Lionel Rosenblatt

www.ChambersandPartners.com

1121

consumer credit claims, LPA receiverships and an expanding domestic and international arbitration practice. The litigators have experience in mediation and ADR.

Corporate The firm offers a full domestic and international corporate and commercial service and advice on corporate structuring and privatisation in emerging markets. This includes structuring, documenting and negotiating domestic and cross-border mergers and acquisitions, subscription and funding agreements, agency, distribution and franchise arrangements and joint venture agreements.

High-tech & E-commerce The department represents numerous software, communications and services suppliers, content providers, website designers and users. Its services include: advice, drafting and negotiating on all IT-related transactions, such as licensing, support and maintenance, consultancy; reseller and channels-related contracts; databases and content provision; Internet software and services supply; application service provider master and end-user licences; mobile communications, advice in respect of interception and encryption obligations; outsourcing.

Property The firm acts for developers, contractors, financiers, operators and investors on projects in the UK and abroad. The work embraces all aspects of acquisitions, disposals, development and financing of commercial properties.

Employment The firm is widely recognised as a leader in its practice area. It is headed by Barry Mordsley, who sits as a part-time chairman of Employment Tribunals, is a member of the Employment Lawyers' Association and was on the Law Society Employment Law Committee. The department deals with both contentious and non-contentious work, providing advice on such matters as restrictive covenants, employee benefits, unfair dismissals, redundancies and discrimination cases.

Bromley Office A dedicated out-of-town office in Bromley deals with volume recoveries and title perfection for leading banks, finance houses and building societies.

INTERNATIONAL The firm has other offices in Paris, New York, Warsaw, Moscow, St Petersburg, Kyiv, Almaty and Baku.

Samuel Phillips & Co

Gibb Chambers, 52 Westgate Road, Newcastle upon Tyne, NE1 5XU
Tel (0191) 232 8451 **Fax** (0191) 232 7664 **DX** 61028
Email admin@samuelphillips.co.uk **Website** www.samuelphillips.co.uk

THE FIRM Samuel Phillips & Co is a long-established firm offering a comprehensive range of legal services to private and business clients. In particular, it has many years' experience in medico-legal matters, and acts for a number of NHS trusts. Members of the firm sit on Law Society panels, which include Clinical Negligence, Personal Injury, Children and Family. It has a Legal Aid franchise, covering areas that include clinical negligence, crime, family, employment and personal injury.

PRINCIPAL AREAS OF WORK

Litigation Clinical negligence, employment, commercial disputes, building contract disputes, debt collection, employment and other tribunal representation, crime, immigration and personal injury.

Company & Commercial Includes partnerships and joint ventures, acquisitions, formations, reconstructions, commercial contracts, intellectual property, advising on funding, tax and insurance requirements, licensing and services to overseas companies.

Property Partnership agreements for GP practices and other professionals. All aspects of commercial and residential property including investment, funding, planning, residential building estates and inward investment.

Other Areas All family and matrimonial matters, particularly in relation to divorce, childcare and adoption, as well as wills, probate and tax planning, and a large criminal department. Specialist in Chinese businesses.

Managing & Senior Partner	Barry Speker
Number of partners	5
Assistant solicitors	8
Other fee-earners	7

AREAS OF PRACTICE	
Clinical Negligence & Related Medico-Legal Work	30%
Crime	20%
Family & Childcare	20%
Property	15%
Civil Litigation	10%
Employment	5%

CONTACTS	
Childcare	Robert Gibson
	Barry Speker
	Jenny Goldstein
Clinical Negligence	Rod Findlay
	Barry Speker
Company/Commercial	Stephen Doberman
Crime	Stuart Grant
Employment	Robert Gibson
	Barry Speker
Family Law	Jenny Goldstein
Immigration	Barry Speker
Personal Injury	Rex Winter
Property	Stephen Doberman

■ **Sansbury Campbell**
6 Unity Street, Bristol, BS1 5HH **Tel** (0117) 926 5341 **Fax** (0117) 922 5625

LAW FIRMS ■ A-Z

Saunders & Co

71 Kingsway, London, WC2B 6ST
Tel (020) 7404 2828   **Fax** (020) 7404 2929   **DX** 37995 Kingsway
Email rcp@saunders.co.uk   **Website** www.saunders.co.uk

THE FIRM Since 1974, a litigation practice with particular expertise in fraud and crime. Client base from Fortune 500 to private client. Investors in People.

PRINCIPAL AREAS OF WORK
Crime An unusually broad central London crime department. Serious Fraud Panel member dealing with SFO prosecutions, money laundering, tax and international cases. Renowned for high profile criminal trial and appellate work. Exceptional forensic science and medico/legal experience. 24 hour crash team for police station emergencies (Tel (07699) 705988). Legal aid work undertaken.
Civil/Crime Restraint and confiscation proceedings, civil actions against the police, directors' disqualification, human rights.
Civil Major tax and insolvency cases. General commercial litigation. International disputes. Privy Council agents. Telecommunications work.

Managing & Senior Partner	James Saunders
AREAS OF PRACTICE	
Crime	47%
Civil Litigation	30%
Fraud	23%
CONTACTS	
Non-Contentious	Robert Fleischmann
Crime	James Saunders
Civil	Robin Lloyds

Savage Crangle

15 High Street, Skipton, BD23 1AJ
Tel (01756) 794611   **Fax** (01756) 791395   **DX** 21751
Email mail@savagecrangle.co.uk   **Website** www.savagecrangle.co.uk

Ptnrs 5   **Other fee-earners** 5   **Contact** Peter Crangle • General practice known for private client, agricultural, housing, PFI, PI and commercial work.

AREAS OF PRACTICE	
Commercial (including PFI)	40%
Private Client/Agricultural	30%
Housing	15%
Personal Injury	15%

Savery Pennington

11, Moira Terrace, Adamsdown, Cardiff, CF24 0EJ   **Tel** 02920 457222   **Fax** 02920 452211

Schillings

Royalty House, 72-74 Dean St, London, W1D 3TL
Tel (020) 7453 2500   **Fax** (020) 7453 2600   **DX** 89265 (Soho Square 1)
Email legal@schillings.co.uk   **Website** www.schillings.co.uk

THE FIRM Schillings is a dynamic leading specialist in libel, privacy and the protection of image and reputation from commercial exploitation without consent. It has unrivalled expertise in all areas of media law. It also has a burgeoning sports department, it specialises in high net worth matrimonial work and it services its clients' commercial needs. It has been involved in a number of successful, groundbreaking cases, including libel actions for leading restauranteur, Marco Pierre White against The New York Times and the International Herald Tribune and the award winning composer Monty Norman against the Sunday Times over the composition of the James Bond Theme tune. It is renowned for its creative and innovative use of the laws of breach of confidence, and the Data Protection Act and the Human Rights Act, to protect the rights of its clients. At the time of writing it represents celebrities Naomi Campbell, Sara Cox and Jamie Theakston in their actions in privacy. The firm also acts in substantial commercial litigation, intellectual property and sports-related cases and acts for organisations including Formula One, MG Rover and the architects Foster & Partners. Schillings has a flexible approach and is often able to achieve highly competitive commercial solutions in a short timescale. It is renowned for its media management and media intervention for individual personalities, corporations and broadcast clients. The firm works with overseas lawyers in Europe, the USA and worldwide, talent agents, public relations advisors, literary agents, managers, business advisors, publishers and in-house counsel to provide an uncompromising legal service. Clients range from international media corporations, broadcasters, film producers and distributors to celebrities and sports personalities. Partners and other members of the firm are acknowledged industry experts, regularly writing articles for legal publications and national newspapers and often give legal and industry seminars on topical subjects.

Emergency Number A weekend number is available for out of hours emergencies and injunctions: (07711) 715345.

PRINCIPAL AREAS OF WORK Schillings specialises in all aspects of media work including confidence;
Continued overleaf

Senior Partner	Keith Schilling
Managing Partner	Simon Smith
Number of partners	7
Assistant solicitors	5
Other fee-earners	6
AREAS OF PRACTICE	
Libel, Privacy, Confidence & Contempt	50%
IP & Sport	20%
Matrimonial	10%
Commercial Litigation	10%
Film, TV, Music & New Media	10%
CONTACTS	
Commercial Litigation	Simon Smith
Company Commercial	Peter Goodman
Contempt	Martin Cruddace
False Endorsement/ Protection of Image	Simon Smith
	Eddie Parladorio
Film, TV Music & New Media	Eddie Parladorio
Intellectual Property	Eddie Parladorio
Libel & Privacy (Claimant/Corporate)	
	Simon Smith
	Susan Heller
Libel & Privacy (Defendant, Pre-publication/ Broadcast) (Corporate)	Amber Melville-Brown
Libel & Privacy	Martin Cruddace
Matrimonial	Keith Schilling
	Shazia Imtiaz
Media Management	Keith Schilling
	Martin Cruddace
	Peter Goodman
	Amber Melville-Brown

A-Z ■ LAW FIRMS

contempt; copyright; cyber squatting; defamation; intellectual property; internet; matrimonial; media management; passing off; privacy; racing and betting; trademark; trade name and domain names; and all media matters. It is structured into two areas (1) litigation and dispute resolutions and (2) company and commercial. The firm is dedicated to, and at the cutting edge of, the protection of reputation and brand image. This is achieved through the firm's creative vision and innovative use of the law of libel, privacy, confidence, copyright, data protection, domain ownership, passing off and trademark. It is effective in obtaining prompt and prominent apologies and corrections from publishers and obtained the first front-page apology in a national newspaper. In relation to the internet, it can quickly identify offending material by the use of advanced search engines and will often obtain its removal within hours of being published. The firm is committed to a proper balance between freedom of expression and an individual's right to reputation and privacy. The acquisition of partners Martin Cruddace, formerly of the Mirror and Amber Melville-Brown, also specialising in defendant work, adds depth to the services available to corporate defendants in the publishing industry and beyond. The sports department has also recently acquired Peter Goodman, formerly a director of CSS Stellar Management Limited, a leading international sports and entertainment agency, who has been involved in Formula One since the early 1970s and who has advised Lotus, Arrows, Jordan, McLaren and Williams F1 as well as drivers including David Coulthard. The firm is well known for its in-depth knowledge and understanding of the various media industries in which it works, which enables it to provide legal advice and solutions that properly further the clients' interests.

CONTACTS (Continued)	
Racing & Betting	Martin Cruddace
Sport	Peter Goodman
	Eddie Parladorio
	Martin Cruddace

■ Scott-Moncrieff, Harbour & Sinclair
19 Greenwood Place, London, NW5 1LB **Tel** (020) 7485 5588 **Fax** (020) 7485 5577

■ Scrivenger Seabrook
26 New Street, St Neots, PE19 1XB
Tel (01480) 214900 **Fax** (01480) 474833 **DX** 100315 St Neots
Email email@sslaw.co.uk

Ptnrs 4 **Asst solrs** 1 • The firm deals exclusively in claimant clinical negligence and general healthcare work, and claimant personal injury.

■ Searles
The Chapel, 26A Munster Road, London, SW6 4EN
Tel (020) 7371 0555 **Fax** (020) 7371 7722 **Email** searles@searles-solicitors.co.uk

Areas of Practice	
Music Industry (both Classical & Popular)	70%
Film & Television	20%
Sponsorship, Merchandising & Advertising	10%

Ptnrs 2 **Asst solrs** 2 • Specialising in intellectual property with particular emphasis on entertainment law. Specialist in the music, multimedia and design industries (contentious and non-contentious), merchandising, and literary publishing. Sponsorship advice is also given.

■ Sears Tooth
50 Upper Brook Street, London, W1Y 1PG
Tel (020) 7499 5599 **Fax** (020) 7495 2970 **DX** 44643 Mayfair

THE FIRM Sears Tooth is a specialist matrimonial and family law niche practice, with a commercial and residential property department. The firm is headed by Raymond Tooth, and is supported by three other partners specialising in matrimonial law, namely Elaine Williams, David Lister and Ann Ison. The firm handles all aspects of matrimonial and family law, predominantly dealing with financial issues arising on separation or breakdown of marriage, but also some private child work. The financial issues handled by the firm are usually complex, involving significant assets and frequently have an international aspect. The firm has a reputation for a forthright approach, and the often difficult nature of the cases it routinely tackles is reflected in the quantity of citations the firm enjoys in Family Law Reports, notwithstanding the relatively small size of the practice. Most of the members of the firm are members of the Solicitors Family Law Association. Raymond Tooth is a member of the International Academy of Matrimonial Lawyers.

Senior Partner	Ray Tooth
Number of partners	5
Assistant solicitors	3
Other fee-earners	3
AREAS OF PRACTICE	
Divorce & Matrimonial	95%
Conveyancing (Commercial & Residential)	5%
CONTACTS	
Conveyancing	JFW Wilson
Matrimonial	Ray Tooth

LAW FIRMS ■ A-Z

Semple Fraser

10 Melville Crescent, Edinburgh, EH3 7LU
Tel (0131) 273 3771 **Fax** (0131) 273 3776 **DX** ED 447
Email info@semplefraser.co.uk

130 St Vincent Street, Glasgow, G2 5HF
Tel (0141) 221 3771 **Fax** (0141) 221 3776/3859 **DX** GW 337
Email info@semplefraser.co.uk

Managing Partner	Alister Fraser
Number of partners	21
Associate partners	10
Assistant solicitors	17
Consultants	1

AREAS OF PRACTICE	
Commercial Property	45%
Company/Commercial	20%
Litigation	15%
Banking	10%
Planning	5%
Construction	5%

CONTACTS	
Banking	Angus MacRae
Commercial Property	Elspeth Carson
Company/Commercial	Stuart Russell
Construction	Stuart Macfarlane
Employment	Alison Gow
Environmental	Vincent Brown
Insolvency	Rachel Grant
IP/IT	Scott Kerr
Landlord & Tenant	Paul Haniford
Litigation	Alison Gow
Planning	Kenneth Carruthers
Property Tax	Heather Nisbet
Venture Capital	David Deane

THE FIRM Established in 1990, Semple Fraser is a specialist commercial law practice with a very strong reputation built on commercialism, innovation and cohesion. A focused practice, the firm believes in doing what it does extremely well, so as to maximise the clients' benefit. With one of the largest commercial property teams in Scotland the firm has developed highly regarded experts in areas such as construction, planning, property tax and property litigation. The firm is also well recognised for its expertise in corporate transactions including MBOs, MBIs and mergers and acquisitions. Semple Fraser's approach is to develop close relationships with clients so as to have a full understanding and appreciation of their individual circumstances and business objectives. The firm is organised on the basis of special sector groups made up of lawyers who share expertise in different and complementary areas of law and industry. These groups keep abreast of business and legal developments in their sector in order to develop optimum and innovative responses to complex commercial transactions. The firm continues to invest heavily in IT, and is committed to maintaining business advantages derived from that investment and enabling the client to receive better value from a faster and better service. The firm believes strongly in the continuous training and development of all its staff. The team spirit at Semple Fraser is the result of this investment and the benefit is recognised by its clients.

PRINCIPAL AREAS OF WORK

Company & Commercial Business start-up, acquisition and disposal, takeovers, M&A, corporate finance, MBOs and MBIs, institutional investment, banking, insolvency and reconstruction, taxation, interactive media law, IP, PFI, leisure and recreation matters.

Commercial Property All matters relating, including property development and investment, leasing, retail, offices, industrial, leisure and recreation and property finance.

Commercial Litigation A wide range of commercial litigation in both the Court of Session and Sheriff Court with particular strength on property litigation, employment, construction and alternative dispute resolution.

Planning & Environmental Law Pre-application negotiations, drafting S 75 agreements and planning conditions, representations at planning appeals and other inquiries, statutory challenges in the Court of Session and judicial review.

Construction Representing a broad cross-section of employers, funders, contractors and design team members; drafting and negotiating building and engineering contracts, professional appointments and warranties; construction related litigation including disputes in the commercial court; arbitration, adjudication and insurance claims.

SEMPLE FRASER W.S.
THE BUSINESS LAW PARTNERSHIP

■ Senior Calveley & Hardy

8 Hastings Place, Lytham St Annes, FY8 5NA
Tel (01253) 733333 **Fax** (01253) 794430 **DX** 28440 Lytham
Email lawyers@seniorslaw.co.uk **Website** www.seniorslaw.co.uk

AREAS OF PRACTICE	
Private Client	65%
Commercial	20%
Litigation	15%

Contact Richard Hardy • Best known for private client work, particularly probate and trust, tax and charity law work. Provides a comprehensive service to elderly clients and deals with commercial, development and agricultural matters. Two Partners are STEP members.

A-Z ■ LAW FIRMS

Shadbolt & Co

Chatham Court, Lesbourne Road, Reigate RH2 7LD
Tel (01737) 226277 **Fax** (01737) 226165 **DX** 30402 Reigate 1
Email mail@shadboltlaw.com **Website** www.shadboltlaw.com

One Creed Court, 5 Ludgate Court, London, EC4M 7AA
Tel (020) 7332 5750 **Fax** (020) 7332 5799 **DX** 98937 Cheapside 2
Email mail@shadboltlaw.com

Ibex House, Minories, London, EC3N 1DY
Tel (020) 7702 1156 **Fax** (020) 7702 1160 **DX** 568 London/City
Email mail@shadboltlaw.com

Managing & Senior Partner	Richard Shadbolt
Number of partners	26
Assistant solicitors	21
Other fee-earners	14

AREAS OF PRACTICE	
Disputes	50%
Construction & Engineering (Non-contentious/Major Projects)	20%
Corporate/Other	30%

CONTACTS	
Aviation	Tim Unmack
Construction & Engineering	Simon Delves
Corporate	Andrew Trotter
Disputes Resolution/Litigation	Peter Sheridan
Employment	Helen Boddy
IT/IP/E-commerce	John Warchus
Marine	Hugh Bryant
Projects	Joe Bellhouse
	Liz Jenkins
Property	Sean Ryan

THE FIRM Shadbolt & Co is a specialist commercial law practice providing a high quality service to business clients in the United Kingdom and internationally. As well as its office in Reigate, it has two offices in the City of London, one in Hong Kong, Athens and an associated office in Paris and Dar es Salaam. The firm originally acquired its outstanding reputation advising clients in the field of major projects and in the construction and engineering industries. It now works in a wide range of practice areas including corporate, property, IT, IP and e-commerce, employment and aviation. The firm offers a cost-effective and imaginative commercial service backed by an unusual degree of experience. The firm's clients range from multinational quoted companies to entrepreneurial family businesses. The firm's clientele has a strong international bias.

PRINCIPAL AREAS OF WORK

Construction & Engineering The firm handles a wide range of contentious and non-contentious work relating to the construction, engineering and facilities management industries in the UK and internationally. Recent disputes have been handled in Uganda, China, Hong Kong, Egypt, Ethiopia and Tanzania.

Projects The firm advises a variety of clients on the commercial and legal aspects of PFI, PPP, concession and BOT schemes and other major projects including reviewing and drafting contract documentation. The firm is used to working in collaboration with financial and other advisors on major projects both in the United Kingdom and elsewhere in the world.

Corporate The firm has particular expertise in company sales and purchases, corporate finance, reorganisations and joint ventures. The firm also undertakes a wide variety of other high quality commercial work including intellectual property, franchising, European law, competition law and advice on general commercial agreements of all kinds.

Commercial Dispute Resolution The firm's work includes litigation, arbitration and other forms of dispute resolution in relation to international and domestic business disputes. The firm is experienced in ADR techniques.

Commercial Property The firm's commercial property practice is able to provide specialist advice on development and commercial property matters of all kinds, particularly in the fields of sales and purchases, property financing and landlord and tenant law.

Employment The firm acts for many substantial employers as well as for employees. The firm represents clients in the courts and employment tribunals and deals with employment and related matters such as health and safety. Clients are kept up to date with developments under both European and UK law.

IT, IP & E-commerce The firm provides specialist advice to a growing client base on all aspects of IT, new media and e-commerce law including advice on IT agreements and disputes, software licences and development issues, major IT procurement, web design issues, e-commerce trading terms and the protection of intellectual property rights.

Aviation The firm's work covers all aspects of international aviation operations including liabilities, insurance, airport planning, air traffic control and environmental and regulatory questions.

RECRUITMENT
The firm has an ongoing recruitment programme for trainee solicitors and for qualified candidates. Considerable importance is attached to in-house training and the continuing education programme for its solicitors.

LAW FIRMS ■ A-Z

Shakespeares

Somerset House, Temple Street, Birmingham, B2 5DJ
Tel (0121) 632 4199 **Fax** (0121) 643 2257 **DX** 13015 Birmingham - 1
Email info@shakespeares.co.uk **Website** www.shakespeares.co.uk

Managing Partner	Gary Christianson
Senior Partner	Tony Jones
Number of partners	20
Assistant solicitors	14
Other fee-earners	57

AREAS OF PRACTICE	
Business Services	41%
Insurance, Institutional, Banking Litigation; Personal Injury & Medical Negligence	39%
Private Client	20%

CONTACTS	
Banking Litigation	Stephen Jones
Business Litigation	Mark Beesley
Charities	Tony Jones
Company & Commercial	Richard Baizley
Corporate Finance	Richard Baizley
Crime	Stephen Daly
Debt Collection	Rohit Deepak
Education	Tony Jones
Employment	Michael Hibbs
Family Law	Nicola Walker
Insurance Litigation	Tony Hannington
Medical Negligence	Gary Christianson
Private Client	Clare Laird
Professional Indemnity	Diana Wareing
Property	Richard Bolton
Property Litigation	Julie Russell

THE FIRM Shakespeares is a well established and forward thinking law firm, located in the heart of the Midlands. The firm has a long and successful history of delivering thoughtful and timely legal advice to business owners, directors and managers throughout the region as well as nationally and internationally. With a strong commitment to delivering consistently high levels of service to clients, the firm continues to make substantial investment in key aspects of the business namely: business processes; people and IT support systems. Shakespeares delivers its services through three key departments: business services; insurance, institutional and banking litigation; and private client. In addition, the firm also provides legal services relating to personal injury, medical negligence claims and criminal matters.

PRINCIPAL AREAS OF WORK

Business Services The business services department offers knowledge and skills in all areas of business law. The department works across many different sectors including traditional and hi-tech manufacturing, financial and professional services, education and charities. Specialist teams include corporate, commercial, commercial property, business litigation, debt recovery and employment as well as education and charities.

Private Client The private client department handles wills, trusts, probate and tax advice connected with the administration of estates as well as family and matrimonial work and investment management.

Insurance, Institutional & Banking Litigation The insurance, institutional and banking litigation department delivers services to a range of clients including high street banks, insurance companies, self-insured organisations, local authorities, adjusters and claims handling organisations. The team also has significant experience in defending claims.

Personal Injury & Medical Negligence The personal injury and medical negligence team handles a range of personal injury work on behalf of claimants, as well as specialist medical negligence work.

Crime Fully franchised, the crime team is able to deal with all crimes including 'white collar' crimes such as serious fraud, conspiracy, fraud, money laundering and motor offences.

Sharpe Pritchard

Elizabeth House, Fulwood Place, London, WC1V 6HG
Tel (020) 7405 4600 **Fax** (020) 7242 2210 **DX** 353
Email planning@sharpepritchard.co.uk **Website** www.sharpepritchard.co.uk

Senior Partner	A Badcock
Number of partners	14
Assistant solicitors	10
Other fee-earners	14

AREAS OF PRACTICE	
Civil Litigation	37%
Contracts/PPP	29%
Planning	15%
Property	11%
Parliamentary	8%

CONTACTS	
Civil Litigation	A Badcock
Contracts	S Millen
Parliamentary	Alastair Lewis
Planning	John Sharland
Property	J Pickering

THE FIRM A well established practice in the fields of litigation, projects and commercial work mainly for the public sector, with property and some company and commercial. Also well known parliamentary agents.

PRINCIPAL AREAS OF WORK

General Description A general practice with a strong emphasis on litigation for a wide variety of clients, particularly public and local authorities and professional clients. Undertakes joint ventures, development agreements, public/private partnerships and PFIs for the public authorities. Expanding town and country planning practice.

Litigation All areas covered particularly construction, environmental and property related litigation, personal injury including medical negligence; local and public authority related litigation - judicial review; commercial and defamation; employment; insolvency and debt collection; Chancery, childcare and family.

Parliamentary A substantial practice for public and local authorities, promotion and opposition of bills for a variety of clients.

Property & Commercial A wide variety of property-related work, conveyancing and some company/commercial.

Contracts The firm undertakes drafting and negotiation of contracts for works, services and supplies and advises on EU and UK public procurement, and joint ventures, private finance transactions and public/private partnerships.

Planning All aspects of town and country planning, mainly for local authorities.

Agency Work Substantial agency practice in all areas; urgent work. Charges on application.

CLIENTELE Public and local authorities, professional, private and small corporate, registered social landlords, charities etc.

Continued overleaf

A-Z ■ LAW FIRMS

INTERNATIONAL Work is handled in Italian and French.

RECRUITMENT Four trainee solicitors a year are taken on. They should have good academic qualifications and the ability to work as part of a well-knit team. Applications with a CV should be made in September of each year to Ashley Badcock.

■ Sharratts
1 The Old Yard, 1 Rectory Lane, Brasted, Westerham, TN16 1JP **Tel** (01959) 568000 **Fax** (01959) 568001

Shaw and Croft
115 Houndsditch, London, EC3A 7BR
Tel (020) 7645 9000 **Fax** (020) 7645 9001 **DX** 824
Email shawandcroft@btinternet.com **Website** shawandcroft.com

Number of partners	10
Assistant solicitors	9
Other fee-earners	8

AREAS OF PRACTICE

Shipping Litigation	25%
Admiralty	25%
Commercial Litigation (& Fraud)	20%
Ship Finance, Corporate & Other Non-contentious	16%
Insurance (Marine & Non-Marine)	9%
Commodities	5%

CONTACTS

Admiralty	Ben Browne
	Hamish Edgar
Commercial Litigation	Nicholas Taylor
Commodities	Robert McCunn
Fraud	Mark Aspinall
	Robert McCunn
Insurance	Jonathan Kenyon
Personal Injury	Hamish Edgar
Property	Roger Colton
Ship Finance/Corporate	Richard Coles
Shipping Litigation	Mark Aspinall
	Ben Browne
	Roland Jackson

THE FIRM Established in 1980 as a specialist shipping and commercial law practice, the firm has grown steadily in these fields, while developing expertise in related areas.

PRINCIPAL AREAS OF WORK
Shipping & Maritime Law The firm handles every aspect of contentious shipping work, including collisions, salvage, charterparties, bills of lading, cargo damage, pollution, and shipbuilding disputes.
Ship Finance & Corporate Sale and purchase, finance and registration of ships, yachts and fishing vessels, company acquisitions and disposals, joint ventures, agency and employment law.
Commercial Litigation and Fraud Work includes commercial fraud, international asset tracings and intellectual property and other commercial disputes.
Commodities Work handled includes international sale of goods (particularly oil, grain and other commodities), together with other international commercial transactions.
Insurance Litigation and advice on all aspects of the insurance markets in London and abroad, particularly marine insurance, P&I, Brokers E and O, reinsurance.
Property Acquisition and disposal of commercial and residential property, landlord and tenant, probate.

CLIENTELE Shipowners, charterers, P&I clubs and insurers, salvage companies, banks, commodity traders, oil companies, ship managers, shipbuilders, insolvency practitioners, property developers and investors.

INTERNATIONAL The firm has an office in Greece as well as strong connections with France, Eastern Europe, North Africa and the Middle East. A worldwide network of correspondent lawyers in all major shipping and commercial centres is actively maintained. Work is handled in French, German, Greek, Italian and Spanish.

Shaw Pittman
Tower 42, Level 23, 25 Old Broad Street, London, EC2N 1HQ
Tel (020) 7847 9500 **Fax** (020) 7847 9501
website www.shawpittman.com

Managing Partner (US)	Paul Mickey
Managing Partners (UK)	Alistair Maughan
	Andrew Moyle
Number of partners	6
Assistant solicitors	14
Other fee-earners	4

AREAS OF PRACTICE

Technology	75%
Corporate	20%
Employment	5%

THE FIRM Shaw Pittman is an international firm, based in the USA, with a major specialisation in technology law. The London office opened in 1998 to reinforce Shaw Pittman's global reputation for technology law work, and handles significant UK, EU and global technology transactions.

PRINCIPAL AREAS OF WORK Shaw Pittman's London office focuses on technology and outsourcing projects, including IT, business process outsourcing, e-commerce and telecoms. The office also has a dedicated corporate and commercial practice and provides employment law advice in the technology sector.

CLIENTELE UK office clients include government departments, major banks, multinational plcs, e-commerce companies and other users and vendors of technology and services.

ShawPittman

Shean Dickson Merrick

14/16 High Street, Belfast, BT1 2BS
Tel (028) 9032 6878   **Fax** (028) 9032 3473   **DX** 460 Nr Belfast
Email law@shean-dickson-merrick.com

THE FIRM A long established firm providing a full range of services to corporate commercial and private clients. The firm is renowned for its constructive and pragmatic approach to servicing its clients' needs.

Senior Partner	David Moffett
Number of partners	3
Assistant solicitors	2
Other fee-earners	3

CONTACTS	
Commercial/Corporate	David Moffett
Liquor Licensing	Maura McKay

PRINCIPAL AREAS OF WORK

Commercial All aspects of commercial work are undertaken. The firm has an expanding practice in the area of mergers and acquisitions and has earned an excellent reputation in that field.

Licensing The firm is highly regarded for its expertise in licensing and acts for major players in the drinks industry in Northern Ireland. It recently obtained (uniquely for Northern Ireland) four new public house licences for the Odyssey Pavilion, a landmark millennium site.

Shearman & Sterling

Broadgate West, 9 Appold Street, London, EC2A 2AP
Tel (020) 7655 5000   **Fax** (020) 7655 5500
Email kmacritchie@shearman.com   **Website** www.shearman.com

THE FIRM Shearman & Sterling is one of the world's leading law firms with more than 1,100 lawyers in 18 major financial centres worldwide. Its substantial European practice has over 350 lawyers based in the UK, France, Germany, Belgium and Italy. Over half of the firm's lawyers in Europe are admitted to practice locally, with the balance qualified in the US. The firm's London office, with over 130 lawyers, provides English and US law advice to major international companies and financial institutions. It is a recognised market leader in the areas of work which it undertakes under both English and US law.

Other Offices Abu Dhabi, Beijing, Brussels, Düsseldorf, Frankfurt, Hong Kong, Mannheim, Menlo Park, Munich, New York, Paris, Rome, San Francisco, Singapore, Tokyo, Toronto, Washington DC.

Senior Partner	David W Heleniak
Managing Partner	Kenneth MacRitchie
Resident lawyers	139
Total lawyers in firm	1066

AREAS OF PRACTICE	
Banking, Leveraged Finance & Securitisation	25%
Project Finance	25%
Capital Markets	25%
M&A/Competition	15%
International Arbitration & Litigation	5%
Tax	5%

CONTACTS	
Banking & Leveraged Finance	Anthony Ward
Capital Markets	Pamela M Gibson (US)
	Clifford Atkins (UK)
Competition	Christopher Bright
International Arbitration & Litigation	
	Christopher Colbridge
Mergers & Acquisitions	Bonnie Greaves (US)
	Adrian Knigh (UK)
Project Finance	Nicholas Buckworth
	Kenneth MacRitchie
Securitisation	Marke Raines
Tax	Michael T McGowan (UK)
	Bernie Pistillo (US)

PRINCIPAL AREAS OF WORK

M&A A main strength of the firm is its cross-border mergers and acquisitions and joint ventures practice. The London office handles public and private, intra-European and Europe/US cross-border acquisitions, divestitures, mergers and LBOs. It has the ability to structure and execute M&A transactions under both English and US law, in addition to its strong local M&A practices in France and Germany.

EU & Competition Law The firm's European anti-trust practice is based in London, Brussels, Düsseldorf and Paris. The offices handle all aspects of competition law, particularly EU, national and multi-jurisdictional mergers, cartel, restrictive practice and abuse of dominance issues, state aid and public procurement as well as competition matters before the European and national courts. The London practice also covers utility regulation. The European anti-trust practice complements and works closely with the firm's US anti-trust practice.

Tax The London office provides English and US law tax advice and structuring and works closely with the firm's French and German tax lawyers on European tax products and structuring.

Equity Capital Markets Shearman & Sterling has one of the leading capital markets practices in Europe for international equity offerings by European companies and provides multijurisdictional expertise under US, French, German and English law. The London office specialises in US-registered offerings and Rule 144A and other private placements of equity-linked, tracking and other derivative stocks, as well as in ADR facilities and listings and corporate advisory and compliance work.

Debt Capital Markets The London office has a dedicated team of US and English lawyers specialising in the structuring and execution of high-yield and investment-grade debt as well as asset-backed, hybrid and derivative debt financings, either US registered or privately placed in the US and internationally. Shearman & Sterling has a leading market share for high-yield debt offerings for European issuers.

Banking & Leveraged Finance The London office is a focal point of the firm's European banking and leveraged finance practices, providing structured senior and subordinated debt, bridge facilities, debt trading and restructuring capability.

Project Finance The office has one of the leading project development and finance practices with in-depth expertise advising projects developers and financial institutions on all aspects of structuring, negotiation, development and financing of major projects, particularly in the sectors of power, oil and gas, telecommunications, mining and transport infrastructure.

Continued overleaf

A-Z ■ LAW FIRMS

Securitisation The London office has more than a dozen English and US lawyers specialising in securitisation and other rated structured finance, supported by UK and US tax and derivatives specialists.
International Arbitration & Litigation The London office has a dedicated team of English and US lawyers handling a broad range of international arbitration and litigation matters. Shearman & Sterling's international arbitration practice group is one of the few specialist teams operating in this field on a global basis.

Shepherd+ Wedderburn

Saltire Court, 20 Castle Terrace, Edinburgh, EH1 2ET
Tel: (0131) 228 9900 **Fax:** (0131) 228 1222 **DX:** 553049 Edinburgh 18
Email: edinburgh@shepwedd.co.uk **Website:** www.shepwedd.co.uk

155 St Vincent Street, Glasgow, G2 5NR
Tel: (0141) 566 9900 **Fax:** (0141) 565 1222 **DX:** GW 409 Glasgow 1
Email: glasgow@shepwedd.co.uk

Bucklersbury House, 83 Cannon Street, London, EC4N 8SW
Tel: (020) 7763 3200 **Fax:** (020) 7763 3250 **DX:** 98945 Cheapside 2
Email: london@shepwedd.co.uk

Chief Executive	Paul Hally
Number of partners	44
Assistant/Associate solicitors	97
Other fee-earners	73

CONTACTS	
Banking	Shona Sanders
Charities	Andrew Holehouse
Commercial	James Saunders
Commercial Litigation	Kenny Cumming
Competition & Regulation	Gordon Downie
Construction	Kevin Taylor
Corporate Finance	James Will
Corporate Recovery	Gillian Carty
Debt Recovery	Gillian Carty
Employment	Sheila Gunn
Energy	James Saunders
Funds & Financial Services	Marian Glen
Leisure & Hospitality	Hugh Smith
IT/IP	Joanna Boag-Thomson
Medical Negligence	Hugh Donald
Public Law & Policy	Hazel Moffat
Pensions	Andrew Holehouse
Personal Injury	Hugh Donald
PFI/PPP	David Nash
Planning & Environment	Colin Innes
Private Client	Malcolm Rust
Property	Dorothy Boyd
Public Sector	Alistair Robertson
Tax	Malcolm Rust

THE FIRM Shepherd+ Wedderburn is a leading UK law firm. It has offices in Edinburgh, Glasgow and London, and its lawyers are able to work for clients and intermediaries from any other location due to its advanced remote access and communications technology. Client relationship management is an integral part of the firm's approach, with an emphasis on long term, mutually beneficial client relationships. Shepherd+ Wedderburn's approach is to acquire an in-depth understanding of its clients' businesses and the legal issues they face and to employ this knowledge in developing solutions-led business advice. All its lawyers understand that delivering an excellent legal service in today's environment demands not only high quality legal advice but also a thorough understanding of the client's business, its environment and its commercial objectives. The firm's lawyers are able to concentrate on client service delivery thanks to excellent internal support services in terms of management, training, technology, knowledge management, administration and communications. Shepherd+ Wedderburn's desire to provide excellent career and personal development opportunities for its people, as well as to improve its understanding of its clients' businesses and its ability to meet their needs, means it always has several staff on secondment to client organisations.

PRINCIPAL AREAS OF WORK Shepherd+ Wedderburn provides clients with a full range of legal services, including property, construction, planning and environment, corporate finance, funds and financial services, PFI/PPP, banking, intellectual property, information technology, competition and regulation, energy, employment, pensions, litigation, insolvency, debt recovery and private client services. In addition, the firm's public law and policy division, Saltire, uses its legal expertise and knowledge of government to advise clients on legislation that will affect them now and in the future. The firm's London office focuses on corporate, technology and projects work. The German desk focuses on addressing the needs of inward investing German companies and UK companies looking to locate or seek business in Germany.

CLIENTELE The firm acts for corporate, commercial, public sector and private clients throughout the UK and abroad. Its impressive and expanding client base includes not only large, well-known organisations, but also small and medium-sized enterprises based both in Scotland and increasingly further afield.

Sheridans

14 Red Lion Square, London, WC1R 4QL
Tel (020) 7404 0444 **Fax** (020) 7831 1982 **DX** 270
Email info@sheridans.co.uk

3000 Hillswood Drive, Hillswood Business Park, Chertsey, KT16 0RS
Tel (01932) 796016 **Fax** (01932) 796816 **DX** 144103 Chertsey 5
Email info@sheridans.co.uk

Managing Partner	Howard Jones
Number of partners	17
Assistant solicitors	10
Other fee-earners	7

AREAS OF PRACTICE	
Entertainment & Media	40%
Commercial & Other Litigation	35%
Property & Planning	15%
Company/Commercial	10%

CONTACTS	
Commercial Litigation	Stephen Taylor
Company/Commercial	Murray Wells
Computers/IT/Internet/E-commerce	Michael Thomas
Entertainment & Media	Russell Roberts
Matrimonial & Immigration	Richard Gifford
Property/Planning/Probate	Jay Soneji
	Gregory Stafford
Residential Conveyancing	Jay Soneji

THE FIRM This central London firm has notable expertise in the entertainment and media and litigation fields both within the UK and abroad. Related to those activities, the firm specialises in many complementary areas including e-commerce and IT-related work, employment, licensing, funding of businesses and sales and purchases. The company/commercial department has a general practice but also specialises in entertainment and media-related businesses and their requirements. The firm has substantial property and private client expertise. In 2001 Sheridans opened an office in Chertsey to provide a high quality and personalised service aimed at local, corporate and private clients. The Chertsey office offers corporate, commercial litigation, property and employment services. All of the resources of the London office are available at the Chertsey office.

PRINCIPAL AREAS OF WORK

Entertainment & Media The entertainment and media department spans several departments and includes an e-commerce unit. It offers a comprehensive service covering recording artists, recording and management companies, popular and classical music publishing, contract negotiation and renegotiations and merchandising and sponsorship. Work relating to licensing, franchising, television and video, the theatre, sport, books and magazines, the press, general copyright, trademarks and domain names is also handled. Other specialisms include international entertainment law involving European Union law, royalty audits, computer games, online music delivery and general internet, e-commerce and multimedia-related issues. The department has a substantial employment practice specialising in senior executives in the media and entertainment industry. The department has also been involved in a number of securitisations and other secured lendings, acting in a number of high profile transactions in the last few years.

Litigation The litigation department handles a wide range of proceedings in many courts and tribunals (often with an international element), including appellate courts and the Privy Council. It is especially strong in commercial litigation and the entertainment and media field, including defamation and the press. Specialisms include audit and copyright, trademark and passing off disputes; banking and insolvency work including asset recovery, securitisations and fraud; IT disputes including computer hardware and software cases; employment cases. Immigration and work permits are also dealt with together with non Legal Aid matrimonial and private client disputes, including divorce, maintenance and children. Other areas include restraint of trade, competition law and some specialist criminal work.

Company/Commercial Company and commercial work undertaken involves mergers, acquisitions and disposals, management buyouts and buyins, corporate finance, joint ventures and corporate reorganisations. General company/commercial work is also undertaken including employment matters, insolvency and winding up, company formations and company taxation.

Property & Planning Services in the property and planning department include sale and purchase of commercial property involving investment, acquisitions and sales, leasehold work, planning matters, granting of leases, secured lending, building and development schemes, property financing and licensing. Domestic conveyancing is also undertaken as are trusts, wills and probate cases.

CLIENTELE The clientele includes major recording artistes and companies, sports personalities, theatre production companies, classical music composers and publishers, computer software companies, online music distribution companies, book publishers and banks.

INTERNATIONAL The work undertaken in the entertainment, media and communications field and the commercial field generally, requires extensive overseas contact, with the result that the firm is well versed in dealing with foreign lawyers and professional advisors.

RECRUITMENT The firm recruits three trainee solicitors every year. Applications should be made with a CV and an accompanying letter to Cyril Glasser during August 2003 only (for September 2005).

A-Z ■ LAW FIRMS

Sherrards

45 Grosvenor Road, St Albans, AL1 3AW
Tel (01727) 832830 **Fax** (01727) 832833 **DX** 141853 St Albans 17
Email law@sherrards.co.uk   **Website** www.sherrards.co.uk

THE FIRM Sherrards is one of the major providers of commercial property and corporate advice in the area, and a growing force in the South East. The firm acts for a number of major retailers and restaurateurs, both quoted and private. It also acts as preferred commercial property sub-contractor to a major US law firm in London. Two years ago, Sherrards established a European commercial unit, recruiting a former partner from an international law firm. The department deals with all types of inward investment and dispute resolution for clients from Europe, and regularly assists UK and US companies establishing a presence in European countries. The firm has a thriving commercial litigation department, with particular expertise in employment law. A further niche area on the litigation side is the firm's unit specialising in anti-social tenant work acting for housing associations and local authorities. Also established two years ago was a specialist direct conveyancing and remortgaging department, acting principally for a major lender and as a panel member for a nationwide estate agency chain. This expanding part of the business is housed in its own building in a large open plan environment suited to the needs and growth of the operation.

PRINCIPAL AREAS OF WORK Work includes commercial property; corporate/commercial; commercial litigation; employment; housing association/local authority anti-social tenant work; direct conveyancing; European.

Managing Partner	Alasdair McMillin
Number of partners	10
Assistant solicitors	14
Other fee-earners	16

AREAS OF PRACTICE
Commercial Property	26%
Litigation	20%
Direct Conveyancing/Remortgaging	20%
Company Commercial	12%
Residential Conveyancing & Development	12%
Employment	6%
Private Client	4%

CONTACTS
Commercial Litigation	Simon Braun
Commercial Property	Mark Peters
Company/Commercial	Daniel Gardener
Direct Conveyancing/Remortgaging	John Brian
Employment	Joan Page
European	Stuart Miller

■ Sherrards

Grosvenor Hall, Bolnore Road, Haywards Heath, RH16 4BX
Tel (01444) 473344 **Fax** (01444) 473249
Email advice@harrysherrard.com   **Website** www.harrysherrard.com

Sherrards is a specialist employment law practice and has an impressive client base, ranging from international airlines through to well known charities. The firm is a multidisciplinary practice, offering a range of Human Resource consultancy services alongside its core employment law work, and operates an executive recruitment division.

Shook, Hardy & Bacon

25 Cannon Street, London, EC4M 5SE
Tel (020) 7332 4500 **Fax** (020) 7332 4600
Website www.shb.com

THE FIRM Shook, Hardy & Bacon is one of the largest litigation practices in the United States of America, where it has offices in seven major centres (Houston, Kansas City, Miami, New Orleans, San Francisco, Tampa and Washington DC). In Europe, it has offices in London and Geneva. It is particularly well known for its handling of very large product liability and commercial litigation cases. Notable features of the firm are its extensive internal analysis resources and its very significant investment in technology to support its business. In London, Shook, Hardy & Bacon specialises in the resolution of commercial disputes and in the law of intellectual property. Its commercial litigation department focuses on fraud, banking and financial services, professional negligence, shipping, commerce and manufacturing (including employment) and product liability. The intellectual property department deals with all aspects of contentious and non-contentious intellectual property rights, including their acquisition, exploitation, protection and enforcement. In London and in the rest of the world, the firm is a specialist practice and does not practise other than in its areas of expertise, which are primarily in litigation. SHB's practice having a strong international bias, the firm is conversant with the laws and procedures of a large number of foreign jurisdictions. In London, French, German and Italian are spoken and the partners and staff include lawyers admitted to practice in the UK, Scotland, the USA, Canada, New Zealand, Australia and Hong Kong.

PRINCIPAL AREAS OF WORK

Commercial Commercial disputes of all kinds are covered. The firm's practice includes banking (enforcement of securities, actions on letters of credit), professional negligence, insolvency and restructuring, financial services, shipping, employment, manufacturing and product liability. SHB has significant expertise in the tracing and recovery of assets, both domestically and internationally, and extensive practical experience in the application of the Brussels and Lugano Conventions and in the conduct of multijurisdictional proceedings and international arbitration. It has very wide experience

Managing Partners London	Laurel Harbour
	Ian MacDonald
Number of partners	17
Assistant solicitors	17
Other fee-earners	17

AREAS OF PRACTICE
Commercial Litigation	70%
Intellectual Property	30%

CONTACTS
Banking Litigation	Geoffrey Gauci
Brand Protection	Andrew Shaw
Commercial	Ian MacDonald
Commercial Litigation	Clive Zietman
	John Bramhall
Defamation	Geoffrey Gauci
E-commerce	Lorna Robertson
Employment	Andrew Shaw
Financial Services Regulation	Clive Zietman
Fraud	Clive Zietman
Information Technology	Ian MacDonald
Insolvency Litigation	Charles Pugh
International Commercial Arbitration	
	Geoffrey Gauci
Patents, Design & Copyright	James Irvine
	Conrad Arnander
	Gerard Cronin
Product Liability	Robert Northrip
	Laurel Harbour
Shipping	Geoffrey Gauci
Trademarks	Andrew Shaw

in product liability, where it is highly regarded.

Fraud The firm advises on all aspects of fraud, including its prevention and investigation as well as the recovery of monies, and has considerable experience in dealing with the Serious Fraud Office and the DTI. Clive Zietman is an acknowledged expert in the field.

Intellectual Property SHB's practice in London extends to all aspects of non-contentious and contentious intellectual property law in relation to patents, trademarks and service marks, copyright, unregistered and registered designs and breach of confidence. James Irvine is particularly well known in this area.

Patents & Trademarks The firm in London has particular expertise in European patent litigation, especially in relation to the areas of chemistry, biochemistry, pharmaceuticals, telecommunications, software and engineering. Scientific and engineering qualifications are held by members of the firm in London.

CLIENTELE The firm's clients are predominantly international corporations. A substantial and growing part of its practice in London is in referral work from major US and UK law firms, both for reasons of conflict and otherwise.

Shoosmiths

The Lakes, Bedford Road, Northampton, NN4 7SH
Tel (01604) 543000 **Fax** (01604) 543543 **DX** 712280 Northampton-12
Email northampton@shoosmiths.co.uk **Website** www.shoosmiths.co.uk

Regents Gate, Crown Street, Reading, RG1 2PQ
Tel (0118) 965 8765 **Fax** (0118) 965 8700 **DX** 4009 Reading-1
Email reading@shoosmiths.co.uk

Russell House, 1550 Parkway, Solent Business Park, Whiteley, Fareham, PO15 7AG
Tel (01489) 881010 **Fax** (01489) 881000 **DX** 124693 Whiteley
Email solent@shoosmiths.co.uk

Quantum House, Basing View, Basingstoke, RG21 4EX
Tel (01256) 696200 **Fax** (01256) 696201 **DX** 98574 BASINGSTOKE
Email basingstoke@shoosmiths.co.uk

Lock House, Castle Meadow Road, Nottingham, NG2 1AG
Tel (0115) 906 5000 **Fax** (0115) 906 5001 **DX** 10104 Nottingham-1
Email nottingham@shoosmiths.co.uk

Exchange House, 482 Midsummer Boulevard, Milton Keynes, MK9 2SH
Tel (01908) 488300 **Fax** (01908) 488488 **DX** 3140 Central Milton Keynes
Email miltonkeynes@shoosmiths.co.uk

Property Direct, Rushmills, Northampton, NN4 7PD
Tel (01604) 543000 **Fax** (01604) 542245 **DX** 712280 Northampton-12
Email northampton@shoosmiths.co.uk

Chairman	Andrew Tubbs
Chief Executive	Paul Stothard
Number of partners	58
Number of fee-earners	323
Total Staff	981

AREAS OF PRACTICE	
Commercial	47%
Personal Injury	38%
Financial Institutions	15%

CONTACTS	
Commercial Property	Nigel Haynes
Corporate & Commercial	Oliver Brookshaw
Dispute Resolution	Claire Rowe
Employment	Susan Mallalieu
Financial Institutions	Andrew Tubbs
IP	Gary Assim
IT	Sebastian Price
Pensions	Jill Lehman
Personal Injury	John Spencer
Planning	Iain Gilbey
Private Capital	Trevor George
Property Direct	David Parton

THE FIRM Depth of resource and quality, combined with geographic accessibility and value make national law firm Shoosmiths a first-choice alternative to City law firms. Renowned for excellent client service, Shoosmiths delivers quality advice and pragmatic business solutions to clients. The quality of Shoosmiths' clients evidences the firm's ability to meet the exacting requirements of some of the world's most successful and demanding businesses. Shoosmiths advises listed companies and large, rapid-growth or technology based private companies.

PRINCIPAL AREAS OF WORK Shoosmiths operates at the top end of a number of related markets and industry sectors.

Commercial Shoosmiths is tuned to the needs of commercial companies and regarded by its clients as a commercial 'ally' and trusted advisor. The firm's proactive yet personal approach is evidenced by areas such as tailored email knowledge updates, client manager scheme and CRM programme. Shoosmiths continually introduces services in anticipation of client needs - for example legal skills and management training courses and an in-house lawyer forum programme, designed to improve clients' skills and their understanding of the legal process. Shoosmiths has in-depth teams in commercial, corporate, real estate, dispute resolution and employment law, in addition to specialist teams in pensions, IP/IT, planning, debt recovery, competition law and banking. Industry sectors where the firm is particularly active include food, retail, property regeneration and housebuilding, technology, financial institutions and science research parks.

Continued overleaf

A-Z ■ LAW FIRMS

Financial Institutions The firm possesses a detailed understanding of the FI market and acts for many of the UK's top lenders. Its dedicated recoveries operation is regarded as a market leader with one of the largest and most experienced teams of lawyers specialising in risk management services to lenders in the UK. This service is focused upon cost transparency and commercial benefit.

Personal Injury Shoosmiths has one of the largest PI practices in the country, based at dedicated offices in Basingstoke. Acting for major legal expense insurers and other institutional work providers, the firm is recognised for its excellence in service delivery. The personal injury division continues to lead the way in personal injury case handling innovations. A state of the art information technology system design to provide fee-earners with on-line information and case handling provides the capability for immediate research and knowledge gathering facilities to gain faster and better awards for claimants.

Private Capital The financial planning needs of directors, executives and high net worth individuals are dealt with by a dedicated private client unit.

Property Direct Shoosmiths is the leader in e-conveyancing with its Property Direct online operation, launched in 1997. Property Direct is a radical alternative to the traditional conveyancing model and has achieved high profile and market penetration with estate agency chains and lenders.

CLIENTELE Clients include eight major banks and three of the top ten building societies as well as fully listed and AIM quoted companies ranging from pharmaceutical and technology companies to manufacturing and distribution companies, major insurance companies and motoring organisations.

■ Short Richardson & Forth
4 Mosley St, Newcastle upon Tyne, NE1 1SR **Tel** (0191) 232 0283 **Fax** (0191) 261 6956

■ Sibley & Co
1 Heathcock Court, 415 Strand, London, WC2R 0NT **Tel** (020) 7395 9790 **Fax** (020) 7379 3371

Ptnrs 3 **Asst solrs** 1 **Contact** Edward Sibley • The firm provides a range of specialist services in international and domestic dispute resolution, primarily in financial services, commercial contract, employment and professional negligence disputes; in commercial property, particularly the acquisition, disposal and letting of retail property; and in commercial work, including agency, distribution, franchising and competition law.

Areas of Practice	
Dispute Resolution	50%
Commercial Property	40%
Commercial	10%

Sidley Austin Brown & Wood

1 Threadneedle Street, London, EC2R 8AW
Tel (020) 7360 3600 **Fax** (020) 7626 7937 **DX** 580 LONDON CITY
Email ukinfo@sidley.com **Website** www.sidley.com

Princes Court, 7 Princes Street, London, EC2R 8AQ
Tel (020) 7778 1800 **Fax** (020) 7796 1807 **DX** 580 LONDON CITY
Email ukinfo@sidley.com

THE FIRM Sidley Austin Brown & Wood gives advice in all major areas of financial and commercial activity. Its London practice comprising joint teams of English and US qualified lawyers focuses particularly on securitisation and structured finance, debt/equity capital markets, mergers and acquisitions, corporate, banking, taxation, property and investment funds. Clients include many of the world's leading institutions, banks and businesses. The London practice aims to maintain the firm's tradition of furnishing high quality, cross practice, innovative advice in a collegiate environment. The firm has adopted a strategy of matching its clients' requirements with focused advice, emphasising excellence, experience, market awareness and product knowledge. Its reputation is based on the quality, innovation and client driven focus of its practice. All lawyers in the London office have extensive European practice experience and can assist clients with matters within the European Union and elsewhere. Teams of lawyers are quickly mobilised, and carefully managed, to assist clients wherever their needs arise. The London office liaises with the other offices of the firm and by relationships with leading independent law practices around the world.

PRINCIPAL AREAS OF WORK
Securitisation & Structured Finance Securitisation is an area of excellence and work in this field is carried out for originators, underwriters, credit enhancers, liquidity banks and credit rating agencies. The London office works closely with lawyers in the firm's US offices in adapting US financing techniques to European and other non-US assets and markets. The firm's structured finance work covers all aspects of structured derivatives, synthetics and capital markets.

Managing Partner	Drew Scott
Resident partners	28
Resident fee-earners	105
Total resident staff	194

CONTACTS	
Banking Regulation	Sarah Smith
Banking Regulation (US)	John Casanova
Banking, Export & Project Finance	Nicholas Brittain
	Graham Penn
	Robin Parsons
	Howard Waterman
Corporate Securities (US)	Scott Cameron
	Hugh Frame
	Christopher Mead
	Mark Walsh
Corporate Securities (England)	Michael Doran
	John Russell
Corporate/Commercial (England)	Struan Oliver
Corporate/Commercial (US)	Robert Asher
	Tom Thesing
Derivatives & Synthetics	Elizabeth Uwaifo
	Howard Waterman
IP/Technology	Struan Oliver
Property	Julian Goodman
Securitisation & Structured Finance (England)	Andrew Bliss
	Nicholas Brittain
	Colin Mercer
	Graham Penn
	Sarah Smith
	Jenifer Williams

Corporate Advice is given on corporate and commercial matters including mergers, acquisitions and takeovers, joint ventures, flotations, inward investment and company formations. The group's expertise extends to IT/IP and commerce generally and employment law. The group provides expert advice across a broad range of transactions and industries, with an emphasis on cross-border transactions.

Corporate Securities The firm's corporate securities group regularly represents the principal participants in the European debt and equity capital markets. These include sovereign, agency and private sector issuers and guarantors as well as financial intermediaries such as investment banks, sponsors, financial advisors and trustees. It specialises in structuring and developing new, innovative financial products and execute a broad range of financial transactions in the capital markets.

Banking The firm's expertise in banking and structured finance covers such areas as banking regulation, domestic and international lending, export and project finance and trade finance.

Taxation Advice is given on domestic and international transactions, including mergers and acquisitions, corporate structuring, joint ventures, corporate finance, capital markets, banking and structured finance, commercial property, oil and gas and tax litigation.

Property & Property Finance The firm's expertise includes debt and equity based financing, development arrangements, acquisitions and disposals and institutional investment work.

Investment Funds Offshore investment funds, including umbrella and single fund structures. Advice is offered on hedged, structured and guaranteed products for sale to institutional and retail investors in the US, Europe and Asia, including Japan.

INTERNATIONAL Other offices are located in Beijing, Chicago, Dallas, Geneva, Hong Kong, Los Angeles, New York, San Francisco, Shanghai, Singapore, Tokyo and Washington DC.

CONTACTS (Continued)	
Securitisation & Structured Finance (US)	Scott Cameron
	Dennis Dillon
	Michael Durrer
	Jenna Janss
	Robert Torch
	Marc Wassermann
Tax (England)	Graeme Harrower
	Drew Scott
Tax (US)	R J Ruble
US Matters	Robert Asher
	Christopher Mead

Silks

Barclays Bank Chambers, 27 Birmingham St, Oldbury, B69 4EZ
Tel (0121) 511 2233 **Fax** (0121) 552 6322 **DX** 20876 Oldbury 2
Email info@silks-solicitors.co.uk **Website** www.silks-solicitors.co.uk

Managing Partner	J B Burn
Senior Partner	J G Silk

THE FIRM This long-established reputable practice offers both its commercial and individual clients a professional, efficient and cost-effective service. The firm has other offices in Netherton and Smethwick.

PRINCIPAL AREAS OF WORK

Company/Commercial Work includes small business to plcs, company formations, mergers and acquisitions, partnerships and joint ventures.

Employment The firm advises on all aspects of employment law.

Licensing Work handled includes application for, or opposition to, betting, liquor and entertainment licences.

Other The firm also handles domestic/commercial property, family, criminal, personal injury and probate and wills work.

Silver Fitzgerald

15-17 Castle Street, Cambridge, CB3 0AH
Tel (01223) 562001 **Fax** (01223) 518310 **DX** 88009 Cambridge 1

Managing Partner	Suzanne Fitzgerald
Senior Partner	Raphael Silver
Number of partners	4
Assistant solicitors	3
Other fee-earners	2
Consultants	2

CONTACTS	
Childcare	Raphael Silver
Civil	Victoria Davey
Crime	Jason Coulter
Matrimonial	Karen Anker

THE FIRM This successful firm offers a specialist range of legal services and is widely recognised as a leading advocacy practice. The firm was one of the first in Cambridge to obtain a Legal Aid franchise. The firm is a niche litigation practice specialising in family law and childcare, crime and civil litigation. The family department is one of the largest in Cambridge, having two solicitors on the Children Panel, three solicitors on the Family Law Panel, three solicitors on the SFLA Panel and a trained mediator. The firm is situated close to both the County Court and Magistrates Court and so is ideally located to undertake agency instructions.

A-Z ■ LAW FIRMS

The Simkins Partnership

45-51 Whitfield Street, London, W1T 4HB
Tel (020) 7907 3000 **Fax** (020) 7907 3111 **DX** 7 Ch.Ln
Email info@simkins.com **Website** www.simkins.com

THE FIRM The Simkins Partnership is one of the leading media and entertainment law firms in Europe. The firm has a large, dedicated and well established team of solicitors, an extensive depth and range of experience and an impressive client list. The firm's aim is to provide a full range of top quality, good value legal services to people and businesses in the media, entertainment and leisure sectors. Acting across all sectors for both talent and corporates as well as trade bodies, the firm has a balanced view of each marketplace. Expertise in the media area was recognised by the firm's appointment to the EC Commission's list of experts on competition law and new media. The firm formed the Advertising Law International network and has close contact with numerous law firms specialising in media and entertainment throughout the world. The Simkins Partnership selects foreign firms on a case by case basis, picking those which are best suited to the job. The firm provides a highly acclaimed email bulletin service covering developments in specialist industry sectors. Registration details can be found on the website.

PRINCIPAL AREAS OF WORK The firm is organised into industry focus groups which include film and TV, music, sport, theatre, media litigation (including defamation and privacy), advertising and marketing, photography, publishing and e-commerce. In addition to the industry focus groups the firm also has corporate, property, litigation, competition, family and employment groups, all of whom work regularly with companies and individuals in the media sector. The firm provides focused legal and commercial advice to clients operating in these sectors. Its size and breadth of expertise ensure that clients receive a partner-led service with full access to experienced lawyers at competitive rates. Specialist understanding of all industry sectors adds value by providing legal solutions that are practical, innovative and commercial.

RECRUITMENT The firm takes on two trainees a year and particularly welcomes applications from people with experience in the world of media.

Number of partners	20
Assistant solicitors	10
Other fee-earners	8

AREAS OF PRACTICE	
Media, Entertainment & Sport	70%
Other	30%

CONTACTS	
Advertising/Marketing	Charles Swan
Competition	Stephen Hornsby
Corporate	Sebastian Briggs
Defamation & Privacy	Jonathan Coad
E-commerce	Robin Hilton
Employment	Roger Billins
Family	Howard Stacey
Film	Nigel Bennett
Litigation (General)	Roger Billins
Litigation (Media)	Dominic Free
Music	Julian Turton
Photography	Charles Swan
Private Client	Robert Rutteman
Property	Cyrus Fatemi
Publishing	Julian Turton
Radio	Nigel Bennett
Sport	Stephen Hornsby
Television & Video	Antony Gostyn
Theatre	David Franks

THE SIMKINS PARTNERSHIP
SOLICITORS

Simmons & Simmons

CityPoint, One Ropemaker Street, London EC2Y 9SS
Tel (020) 7628 2020 **Fax** (020) 7628 2070 **DX** 12
Email enquiries@simmons-simmons.com **Website** www.simmons-simmons.com

THE FIRM Simmons & Simmons is a world-class law firm providing advice to financial institutions, corporates, public and international bodies, and private individuals through its international network of offices. Simmons & Simmons has over 200 partners, of which 90 are based in its international offices outside the UK, and a total staff worldwide of more than 1800. It provides a comprehensive range of legal services with strength and depth. It applies considerable expertise to all business sectors but focuses on those key to its clients. These include financial markets, energy and utilities, TMT, real estate and construction, aerospace and defence, pharmaceuticals and biotechnology, transport and consumer goods. In the past two years, four independent studies into job satisfaction (research conducted by and published in The Sunday Times (February 2001 and March 2002)) and a leading legal publication (August 2001 and 2002) have credited Simmons & Simmons with being a good place to work; in these publications Simmons & Simmons is consistently ranked higher than its competitors.

In September 2001, Simmons & Simmons' office in Japan was opened in conjunction with the creation of a qualified joint venture with TMI associates. Based in Tokyo, TMI Associates is one of Japan's leading law firms with 17 partners and a legal staff of over 80 of which 44 are qualified Japanese lawyers (bengoshi). The joint venture allows clients to access both international and Japanese legal advice on a scale greater than other UK firms can offer. In May 2002, Simmons & Simmons merged with one the Netherlands' leading law firms, Nolst Trenité. Based in Rotterdam, the Dutch practice has been named Simmons & Simmons Trenité. This merger gives Simmons & Simmons a presence in all the major EU jurisdictions. In July 2002, the firm opened its second German office in Frankfurt which will focus on financial markets and corporate finance work.

PRINCIPAL AREAS OF WORK As a leading international law firm, Simmons & Simmons focuses on the needs of its international financial markets and corporate clients. It has particular expertise in mergers and acquisitions, privatisations, venture capital, international securities, corporate finance, financial services, capital markets, securitisations, repackagings, bank lending, asset management,

Managing Partner	David Dickinson
Senior Partner	Janet Gaymer
Number of partners	113
Assistant solicitors	273
Other fee-earners	144

AREAS OF PRACTICE	
Corporate/Corporate Finance/M&A	40%
Banking & Capital Markets	15%
Commercial/Intellectual Property/EU	14%
Litigation	11%
Property	10%
Tax	6%
Employment	3%
Environmental	1%

CONTACTS	
Aviation/Asset Finance	Kim Walkling
Banking	Nicholas Fisher
Capital Markets	Tony Smith
Commercial	Richard Armitage
	Edwin Godfrey
Communications	Tom Wheadon
Construction	Robert Bryan
Corporate Finance	Stuart Evans
	Charles Fuller
Corporate Recovery	John Houghton
Corporate/M&A	Jerry Walter
	Ken Woffenden
Dispute Resolution	Philip Vaughan
Employment	William Dawson
Energy	Jerry Walter
Environmental	Kathy Mylrea
EU/Competition Law	Peter Freeman

1136 INDEX TO LEADING LAWYERS: PAGE 1693 ■ IN-HOUSE LAWYERS' PROFILES: PAGE 1201

major projects, PFI and PPP. The firm is also able to provide a strength and depth of quality advice in commercial law, EU and competition, intellectual property, communications and media law, development and construction work, property and planning, environmental law, energy, biotechnology, railways, all forms of dispute resolution, employment and pensions advice, and taxation. Other areas of expertise include corporate recovery, unit trusts, insurance, commodities, asset finance and aviation and advice on private capital to individuals.

INTERNATIONAL Languages spoken in the firm include English, French, German, Spanish, Italian, Swedish, Portuguese, Dutch, Greek, Mandarin, Japanese, Russian, Czech, Slovakian, Polish, Cantonese, Afrikaans, Hungarian, Latvian, Hindi, Arabic and Vietnamese.

RECRUITMENT The recruitment of the very best candidates that are interested in a career in a leading international law firm is a priority for Simmons & Simmons. For further information, please see the firm's website www.simmons-simmons.com

CONTACTS (Continued)	
Financial Services	Iain Cullen
	Richard Slater
Insurance	Christopher Braithwaite
IP	Kevin Mooney
	Helen Newman
IT	David Barrett
Pensions	Michael Wyman
Pharmaceuticals/Biotech	Gerry Kamstra
Private Client	Caroline Garnham
Project Finance/PFI	Edwin Godfrey
Property (Commercial)	Alan Butler
Securitisation	James Bresslaw
Tax	Paul Hale
Transport	Charles Mayo
	Jerry Walter
Venture Capital	Alan Karter
	Chris Wilkinson

Simmons & Simmons

Simons Muirhead & Burton

50 Broadwick Street, Soho, London, W1V 7AG
Tel (020) 7734 4499 **Fax** (020) 7734 3263 **DX** 144060 Soho Sq 5
Email rec@smab.co.uk **Website** www.smab.co.uk

THE FIRM Simons Muirhead & Burton is a media, corporate fraud and commercial practice in the heart of Soho. The firm also has an expanding commercial property and construction department, and an award-winning pro bono human section. All these areas have been strengthened by the recent arrival of the two senior partners of Soho neighbours Offenbachs and Nic Lom from Schilling & Lom. Most assignments are undertaken by partners, and the firm aims to provide a high-quality, hands-on service at competitive rates for commercial and private clients.

PRINCIPAL AREAS OF WORK

Non-contentious Media & Entertainment Contract advice for independent film and television production companies, theatres and publishers. Clients include Natural Nylon, Brook Lapping, Royal Court Theatre and Dennis Publishing.

Media Litigation Defamation, intellectual property and media litigation for broadcasters, book and magazine publishers, national/local newspapers, including internet-related matters; employment and general litigation.

Commercial Property & Construction Commercial property transactions, development projects, funding, building contracts, licensing, large-scale development residential conveyancing.

Company/Commercial Company commercial work, with a particular emphasis on media-related companies.

Commercial Fraud All fraud investigations (SFO, DTI, CPS, Inland Revenue, Customs & Excise, FSA), including commercial fraud, insider dealing, corruption, money laundering, back duty and regulatory proceedings. Advice is provided on international police enquiries and extradition. The firm is a member of the Very High Cost Cases Panel and has a Legal Aid franchise.

Investigations Investigations carried out, and reports prepared, for commercial clients with fraud and compliance problems.

General Crime Serious criminal cases are undertaken for private and legally aided clients.

Civil Liberties & Human Rights The long-established work of the firm in its commitment to providing pro bono advice and representation in death row cases in the Caribbean has won awards and wide media recognition. The firm provides advice on Civil Liberties and Human Rights issues in the UK and Europe.

Privy Council Private civil and criminal cases undertaken.

Agency Work The firm acts as London agents in all courts and tribunals.

Managing Partner	David Kirk
Senior Partner	Anthony Burton
Number of partners	8
Assistant solicitors	2
Other fee-earners	11
Consultants	6

AREAS OF PRACTICE	
Criminal Litigation	35%
Civil Litigation	20%
Media Law	20%
Conveyancing	15%
Company & Commercial Law	10%

CONTACTS	
Civil Liberties	Anthony Burton
Civil Litigation	Razi Mireskandari
Commercial Fraud	Anthony Burton
	David Kirk
Company & Commercial	Martin Smith
Employment	Martin Smith
General Crime	Anthony Burton
Investigations	David Kirk
Media/Entertainment	Simon Goldberg
Privy Council	Razi Mireskandari
Property & Construction	David Michaels

simons muirhead & burton

A-Z ■ LAW FIRMS

Simpson & Marwick

Albany House, 58 Albany Street, Edinburgh, EH1 3QR
Tel (0131) 557 1545 **Fax** (0131) 557 4409 **DX** 161 Edinburgh
Email email@simpmar.com **Website** www.simpmar.com

15 South Tay Street, Dundee, DD1 1NU
Tel (01382) 200373 **Fax** (01382) 200370 **DX** DD52
Email email@simpmar.com

93 West George Street, Glasgow, G2 1PB
Tel (0141) 248 2666 **Fax** (0141) 248 9590 **DX** GW377
Email email@simpmar.com

1 Carden Place, Aberdeen, AB10 1UT
Tel (01224) 624924 **Fax** (01224) 626590 **DX** AB6
Email email@simpmar.com

Senior Partner	John Miller
Management Board	Douglas Russell
	Paul Wade
	Pamela Abernethy
Number of partners	16
Assistant solicitors	28
Other fee-earners	17

AREAS OF PRACTICE	
Personal Injury	40%
Professional & Clinical Negligence	35%
Commercial Litigation	10%
Property/Private Client	10%
Employment Law	5%

CONTACTS	
Commercial	Peter Anderson
	Charles McGregor
Employment Law	Alan Cowan
Family	John Thomson
Health & Safety	Robert Leith
	Gordon Keyden
Insurance Law	Paul Wade
Local Government	Kate Shaw
Oil Industry	Douglas Russell
	Robert Leith
Personal Injury	Gordon Keyden
	Michael Wood
Private Client	John Miller
Professional & Clinical Negligence	Pamela Abernethy
	Peter Anderson
Property	Richard Loudon

THE FIRM Simpson & Marwick is a dispute resolution practice providing a range of expert services to clients from offices in Edinburgh, Glasgow, Aberdeen and Dundee. The firm has particular expertise in defender reparation work and provides a partner-led service to a wide range of clients involved in the insurance industry throughout the UK. Oil companies, aerospace companies and several prominent professional bodies are also numbered amongst the firm's corporate clients. In recent years the firm has grown considerably, particularly in Glasgow and Aberdeen, and has developed new areas of practice including healthcare law, employment law and commercial and contractual disputes. The firm's team of litigators is one of the largest and most experienced in the country. In addition, the firm boasts a thriving conveyancing department, which operates in the Edinburgh market and beyond, and handles all aspects of purchasing, selling and leasing residential and commercial property. Website address: www.edinburghprimeproperty.com.

PRINCIPAL AREAS OF WORK Personal injury, professional and medical negligence, major accident actions, commercial litigation, public/employers' liability, health and safety, healthcare law, employment law and property.

■ Sinclair Roche & Temperley

In May 2002 Sinclair Roche & Temperley and Stephenson Harwood combined to form an enlarged firm, practising under the name Stephenson Harwood. Please see page 1147 for details.

■ Sinclairs

Windsor Chambers, Stanwell Road, Penarth, CF64 2AA **Tel** (0131) 225 8800 **Fax** (0131) 220 2677

■ Sinclair Taylor & Martin

9 Thorpe Close, Portobello Road, London, W10 5XL **Tel** (020) 8969 3667 **Fax** (020) 8969 7044

Singletons

The Ridge, South View Road, Pinner, London, HA5 3YD
Tel (020) 8866 1934 **Fax** (020) 8429 9212
Email susan@singlelaw.com **Website** www.singlelaw.com

Managing Partner	Susan Singleton
Number of partners	1

AREAS OF PRACTICE	
Competition	30%
Commercial	30%
Intellectual Property	25%
Computer/Internet	15%

CONTACTS	
All Categories	Susan Singleton

THE FIRM Founded in 1994 by well known competition/intellectual property solicitor, Susan Singleton, Singletons provides highly specialised advice on EU/UK competition law, intellectual property, computer/e-commerce and commercial and EU law to over 360 well known public companies and others at £200 per hour. The firm also advises other solicitors' firms and provides in-house training to clients and solicitors. Both contentious and non-contentious work is undertaken. Susan Singleton is author of 20 books including: *Commercial Agency*; *Competition Act 1998*; *Data Protection Handbook*; *Business, The Internet & the Law*; *E-Commerce: A Practical Guide* and edits *Comparative Law of Monopolies*.

Sinton & Co

5 Osborne Terrace, Newcastle upon Tyne, NE2 1SQ
Tel (0191) 212 7800 **Fax** (0191) 281 3675 **DX** 62551 Jesmond
Email law@sinton.co.uk **Website** www.sinton.co.uk

Ptnrs 13 **Asst solrs** 9 **Other fee-earners** 19 **Contact** W Murray Magowan • Sinton & Co is a long established and multi-skilled practice. The firm's recognised pedigrees in litigation and private client are now supplemented by a burgeoning commercial department.

AREAS OF PRACTICE	
Litigation	60%
Private Client	27%
Commercial	13%

Skadden, Arps, Slate, Meagher & Flom LLP

One Canada Square, Canary Wharf, London, E14 5DS
Tel (020) 7519 7000 **Fax** (020) 7519 7070
Wbsite www.skadden.com

Executive Partner	Robert C Sheehan
Senior Partner	Joseph H Flom
European Practice Leader	Bruce M Buck
Number of partners worldwide	355
Number of lawyers worldwide	1698

THE FIRM With approximately 1,700 attorneys in 23 offices, Skadden, Arps, Slate, Meagher & Flom LLP & Affiliates is one of the largest law firms in the world. The firm provides a wide array of legal services in the US, Europe and Asia to the corporate, financial, industrial and governmental communities.

PRINCIPAL AREAS OF WORK

Corporate Skadden, Arps handles a wide variety of international M&A transactions, from some of the largest deals in corporate history to transactions involving middle-market and emerging companies. The firm represents US and non-US clients in negotiated transactions, including mergers, stock or asset purchases, leveraged buyouts and post-buyout transactions, as well as contested transactions such as tender offers, proxy fights and other transactions involving changes in corporate control.

Competition/European Union The firm advises clients regarding the rapidly evolving areas of European Union law, including a full range of competition issues related to mergers, acquisitions and joint ventures; various industry sectors; and intellectual property issues.

International Arbitration & Litigation Skadden, Arps's international litigation practice encompasses a wide range of general commercial litigation, arbitrations, trade cases and merger and acquisition transactions. The firm has experience in the full scope of international dispute proceedings and has handled arbitrations under all major rules systems and before every major international arbitral institution.

Finance Skadden, Arps advises underwriters, issuers and purchasers in public and private financings via all types of debt and equity instruments, including offerings of Eurodollar issues and American Depositary Receipts; structured finance, lease and project financing; public finance; commodities; futures and derivative products; investment companies, advisors and broker-dealers; and private investment funds. The firm also has a diversified international privatisation practice that is active across a range of industries.

Corporate Restructuring The firm represents debtors, creditors, acquirors, investors and others in Chapter 11 reorganisation cases, Chapter 11 filings and other debtor/creditor matters, both in the US and internationally.

International Trade Skadden, Arps represents US and non-US clients in international trade cases, including issues of market access, anti-dumping and countervailing duty, and provides advice on matters of US embargoes, anti-boycott laws, customs matters and the Foreign Corrupt Practices Act.

CLIENTELE The firm represents a broad spectrum of clients, from small start-up companies to nearly 50% of the Fortune 250 industrial and service corporations, in addition to many financial and governmental entities.

INTERNATIONAL Since its first non-US office opened in 1987, Skadden, Arps has expanded into major financial centres and emerging market economies around the globe. The firm has six offices in Europe, six offices in Asia, Australia and Canada, and 11 US offices, and has substantial practices in Israel and Latin America.

RECRUITMENT Recent lateral hires include London private equity partner Allan Murray-Jones, September 2001; London litigation and arbitration partner Paul Mitchard, October 2001; London tax partner Tim Sanders, November 2001; London banking partner Mark Darley, April 2002.

A-Z ■ LAW FIRMS

Slaughter and May

One Bunhill Row, London, EC1Y 8YY
Tel (020) 7600 1200 **Fax** (020) 7090 5000 **DX** LDE and CDE Box No. 11
Email mail@slaughterandmay.com **Website** www.slaughterandmay.com

Senior Partner	Tim Clark
Number of partners	105
Assistant solicitors	372
Other fee-earners	132

AREAS OF PRACTICE	
Corporate & Financial	65%
Litigation	11%
Tax	6%
Property	6%
Pensions/ Employment	5%
EC/Competition	4%
Intellectual Property	3%

CONTACTS	
Competition	Malcolm Nicholson
Corporate/M&A	Nigel Boardman
	Stephen Cooke
Environment	Dermot Rice
Financial Regulation	Ruth Fox
Insurance/Financial Institutions	Glen James
Intellectual Property	Nigel Swycher
Investment Funds	James Cripps
Litigation & Arbitration	Richard Grandison
Pensions & Employment	Eddie Codrington
Property	Graham White
Taxation	Steve Edge
Technology, Media & Telecoms	William Underhill
Financing:	
General	Richard Slater
Acquisition/Leveraged Finance	Andrew Balfour
Asset Finance/Leasing	Tom Kinnersley
Banking	Andrew Balfour
Debt Capital Markets	Sanjev Warna-kula-suriya
Derivatives	Sanjev Warna-kula-suriya
Insolvency & Restructuring	Jonathan Rushworth
Project Finance	Christopher Saunders
Securitisation	Christopher Smith
Structured Finance	David Frank

THE FIRM Slaughter and May is one of the pre-eminent law firms in the world. It has a diverse and extensive international practice dealing with a wide range of corporate, commercial and financial work for UK and international clients. The firm has a distinctive approach to the practice of law and encourages all its lawyers to gain a wide experience in commercial and financial matters so that they offer not only a depth of legal expertise but also versatility and a breadth of commercial experience. Slaughter and May is noted for its positive approach combining technical excellence, commercial awareness and an ability to provide practical, constructive solutions. Every client receives a personal service tailored to requirements; special emphasis is placed on Partner involvement, approachability and continuity of client services.

PRINCIPAL AREAS OF WORK Slaughter and May's practice covers a broad spectrum of corporate, commercial and financial work. Clients include industrial and commercial companies from all business sectors, banks, financial institutions and professional firms as well as governments, public bodies and other organisations. The principal areas of practice comprise:

Corporate & M&A Securities issues, flotations, mergers and acquisitions and corporate and commercial transactions generally, including privatisation-related work.

Financing International debt and equities issues and derivatives; international and domestic lending, structured finance and project and asset finance; and insolvency and asset-tracing work.

Financial Regulation The regulatory aspects of corporate finance, fund management, securities and derivatives as well as supervision and regulation of banks, building societies, insurance companies and the Lloyd's market.

Litigation & Arbitration A wide range of commercial proceedings and disputes including hearings before the High Court, the House of Lords and the Privy Council, domestic and international arbitrations, formal enquiries, investigations and inter-jurisdictional disputes.

Intellectual Property All aspects of the creation, acquisition, exploitation and protection of intellectual property rights.

Property All types of commercial property transactions as well as advice on construction and engineering projects in the UK and overseas.

Environment Specialist advice on a broad spectrum of environmental issues.

Tax The tax aspects of corporate transactions and activities, including the development of tax-efficient structures and instruments.

Competition Advice from London and Brussels on competition law, particularly in relation to acquisitions and mergers and joint ventures.

Pensions & Employment Employee share benefit schemes, industrial conflicts, sex discrimination and equal pay problems and pensions and employment aspects of company acquisitions, disposals and takeovers.

INTERNATIONAL International work is fundamental to the firm's practice both in London and in its overseas offices and Slaughter and May's lawyers travel widely. The firm has close working relations with leading independent law firms in the major jurisdictions so that the best local advice and service is available to each client wherever this is required.

RECRUITMENT Approximately 85 trainee solicitors are recruited every year. Financial assistance is available for the PgDL/CPE and LPC in the form of a maintenance grant plus tuition and examination fees. For further information on recruitment, please write to Charlotte Houghton, Personnel Manager, or email grad.recruit

SLAUGHTER AND MAY

LAW FIRMS A-Z

AE Smith & Son

Frome House, London Road, Stroud, GL5 2AF
Tel (01453) 757444 **Fax** (01453) 757586 **DX** 58801 Stroud
Email stroudenquiries@aesmith.co.uk **Website** www.aesmith.co.uk

Stokescroft, Cossack Square, Nailsworth, GL6 0DZ
Tel (01453) 832566 **Fax** (01453) 835441 **DX** 123329 Nailsworth
Email nailsworthenquiries@aesmith.co.uk

Number of partners	4
Assistant solicitors	6
Other fee-earners	2

CONTACTS	
Nailsworth Office	Caroline James
Stroud Office	John C Bridges

THE FIRM Founded about 1835, the firm operates from offices in Stroud and Nailsworth. As well as dealing with a very wide range of commercial and private client work, the firm has particular experience in the fields of trusts and probate, property and estate development, advocacy, mental health and education (particularly special educational needs). The firm has Legal Aid franchises in family, mental health, crime and education. Members of the firm are on the Law Society Family Law and Mental Health Review Tribunal panels. The firm also has connections with European lawyers.

The Smith Partnership

6th Floor, Celtic House, Heritage Gate, Friary Street, Derby, DE1 1LS **Tel** (01332) 225225 **Fax** (01332) 225444

Smith Roddam

56 North Bondgate, Bishop Auckland, Durham, DL14 7PG **Tel** (01388) 603073 **Fax** (01388) 450483

Smyth Barkham

29 Fleet Street, London, EC4Y 1AA **Tel** (020) 7353 4777 **Fax** (020) 7353 4666

Speechly Bircham

6 St Andrew Street, London, EC4A 3LX
Tel (020) 7427 6400 **Fax** (020) 7427 6600 **DX** 54 Chancery Lane
Email information@speechlys.com **Website** www.speechlys.com

Senior Partner	Mervyn Couve
Managing Partner	Michael Lingens
Number of partners	39
Assistant solicitors	62
Other fee-earners	21

CONTACTS	
Commercial Dispute Resolution	
	Stephen Dobson
Construction & Engineering	Tim Raper
Corporate	Michael Lingens
Corporate Tax	James Carter
Employment & Pensions	Alan Julyan
Financial Services	Mervyn Couve
Private Clients & Charities	Richard Kirby
Property	Charles Palmer
Property Litigation	Graham Ling
Technology & Commerce	Tom Shaw

THE FIRM Speechly Bircham is a medium-sized City law firm with an excellent client base that includes a number of well known corporate and institutional clients. Its strong commercial focus is complemented by a highly regarded private client practice. The firm handles major transactions as well as commercial disputes, and has a good reputation for several specialist advisory areas, notably personal and corporate tax. There are several discreet practice groups, in many of which the firm has an acknowledged reputation and where its performance is competitive with that of larger firms. The structure of the firm and its ability to provide partner time and attention to 'mid-market' transactions and disputes mean that it is a good alternative to the very large City firms for many clients. The legal affairs of each client are managed by a single partner, responsible for ensuring that the service is delivered quickly and cost-effectively. Much of the firm's work has an international dimension. It acts for UK clients doing business overseas, supervising and co-ordinating the work of foreign law firms, as well as advising non-UK clients on legal issues and transactions in this country. Long standing relationships with law firms in many countries enable it to refer clients to professional advisors who are best suited to assist them.

PRINCIPAL AREAS OF WORK

Corporate Within the corporate practice, merger and acquisitions work ranges from corporate acquisitions and divestments (often cross-border) to buyouts, joint ventures and the sale of family companies. Finance work includes a full range of debt and equity transactions, including private equity financings, banking and capital markets work as well as stock exchange flotations. The financial services group advises on an extensive range of transactions in the financial services and insurance sectors (including the demutualisation of Scottish Life) as well as regulatory and funds work. The technology and commerce practice acts on corporate and commercial IT/IP projects for hi-tech, internet, media, telecoms and biotech companies.

Corporate Tax Tax is offered as an integral part of the firm's transactional and advisory service and the group often advises on company restructurings, reorganisations and M&As. There is a strong emphasis on property sector work, involving the use of collective investment schemes and stamp duty planning. Share scheme work is also a significant part of the corporate tax practice. Much of the tax work has an international dimension.

Private Clients & Charities The private client practice is recognised as a leader in the field of advising indi-
Continued overleaf

www.ChambersandPartners.com

1141

viduals and families on wealth management issues. Its members have considerable expertise in planning and implementing tax strategies, including setting up offshore trusts and investment vehicles to protect assets in the UK and abroad. The charities team has a strong market reputation and acts for a broad range of charities.

Employment & Pensions The employment practice works closely with the firm's corporate and tax lawyers to help businesses develop appropriate employment strategies in the face of increasing legislative complexity. It advises on the negotiation of employment contracts and termination packages and handles individual and collective employment disputes. The firm also advises on the setting up, running, selling or closing of all types of pension scheme.

Dispute Resolution For clients seeking a cost-effective and commercially satisfactory outcome, the firm advises clients on UK and international dispute resolution methods, including litigation, arbitration, mediation and other forms of Alternative Dispute Resolution (ADR). A particular area of specialisation is handling disputes for financial institutions.

Property The property practice has an established reputation in advising property investors (including a number of blue chip life companies, property companies, urban estate owners, developers and local authorities) on all aspects of commercial and industrial property. The practice includes a strong property litigation team which advises on management issues, such as possession orders, dilapidation claims, renewals, rent reviews and recovery of arrears. For complex projects the practice draws on a range of internal specialists in tax, corporate structuring, planning and environmental law.

Construction & Engineering The construction and engineering practice works with investors, developers and contractors to assist them with their development and construction projects (including contractual disputes involving arbitration, mediation or litigation). The practice works with a range of mainly international engineering groups on contractual disputes on major projects in the oil, utility and chemical sectors.

Spiro Grech & Harding-Roberts Solicitors
Clifton House, 8 Four Elms Road, Roath, Cardiff, CF2 1LE **Tel** (029) 2022 2255 **Fax** (029) 2045 0162

Spraggon Stennett Brabyn
225 Kensington High Street, London, W8 6SA **Tel** (020) 7938 2223 **Fax** (020) 7938 2224

Sprecher Grier Halberstam LLP
30 Farringdon Street, London, EC4A 4HJ **Tel** (020) 7544 5555 **Fax** (020) 7544 5565

Squire & Co

49/50 St. Johns Square, London, EC1V 4RF
Tel (020) 7490 3444 **Fax** (020) 7250 4087/4115 **DX** 46617 Barbican
Email squire@squireandco.co.uk

THE FIRM The firm specialises in all types of professional indemnity insurance claims including accountants, solicitors, barristers, insurance brokers, surveyors, independent financial advisors and construction related risks such as engineers, architects, quantity surveyors and project managers. In addition, the firm deals with all classes of liability insurance business, as well as insurance and reinsurance disputes; insurance investigations; construction and civil fraud and is regularly involved in arbitrations and mediations as well as commercial litigation at all levels.

Senior Partner	Nicholas Squire
Partners	8
Assistant solicitors	18
Other staff	14
Total	40

Squire, Sanders & Dempsey LLP

Royex House, Aldermanbury Square, London, EC2V 7HR
Tel (020) 7776 5200 **Fax** (020) 7776 5233
Email ssdinfo_london@ssd.com **Website** www.ssd.com

THE FIRM Founded in the United States in 1890, Squire Sanders is a full service global law firm with more than 750 attorneys in 28 offices worldwide. Offices are located throughout the US (14 offices), Europe (nine offices) and Asia (five offices). The firm also has associations with legal firms in Bucharest, Dublin, Rio de Janeiro and São Paulo and a 'Renaissance' network of 18 law firms in China. The firm's attorneys are fluent in more than 50 languages, have been admitted to practice in more than 150 courts and jurisdictions worldwide and counsel nearly 20,000 clients involved in almost every industry segment.

London Office: An important centre of the firm's international practice, the London office serves the needs of clients with businesses spanning the globe as well as UK companies and UK operations of companies headquartered in the US, Europe and Asia. Lawyers in the London office take advantage of their position in Europe's largest financial and business market to counsel clients on complex corporate, communications, technology and real estate transactions, as well as employment law matters, international disputes and a host of other issues. Opened in 1992, the London office has grown rapidly to offer a full set of legal services. International transactions frequently require English or US law to govern key contractual relationships. Both legal systems are served from the London office. London is a strategic locale for generating capital and advising, facilitating, negotiating, documenting and executing deals. Most of Squire Sanders' London office lawyers were trained in the UK and are admitted to practice as solicitors in England and Wales. In addition, a number of experienced US educated international transaction lawyers are resident in the London office. Collectively, the London lawyers fluently speak nine languages.

PRINCIPAL AREAS OF WORK

Corporate: Lawyers in the London office advise corporate and investment banking clients on transactional and commercial matters including cross-border international mergers and acquisitions, privatisations, joint ventures, project finance, real estate and hospitality, securitisations, international capital markets, due diligence, company restructuring and reorganisations and management buyouts, infrastructure, international dispute resolution and employment - often in multiple jurisdictions around the UK, Europe and the world.

Communications: Lawyers in the London office have contributed significantly to the firm's communications practice. The London office of Squire Sanders' telecommunications group provides advice on regulatory and transactional matters to cable broadband and telephony companies, satellite service providers, GSM and other wireless operators, data service and network companies, internet service providers, private equity investors and investment banks, government agencies and multinational development organisations. The London group is particularly active in telecommunications M&A transactions in Europe, having led the acquisition and related equity financings of several large European cable telephony companies, including a controlling interest in the largest-ever leveraged buy-out in Germany.

Employment: The London employment group counsels clients on all aspects of UK and European employment law. Areas of particular concentration include transactional due diligence, domestic and international employment contracts, company handbooks, TUPE issues, secondment arrangements, large-scale redundancy programs, stock options, pensions and other incentives. Squire Sanders offers considerable experience in the issues surrounding employee conduct at work, including email and internet use, and has represented employers in disciplinary matters involving improper computer downloads. The employment team also resolves discrimination and disability matters, handles working time and collective bargaining issues, structures termination arrangements and represents employment clients in tribunal claims.

Information Technology/E-business: The London office has a particular focus on information technology and e-business and represents a number of sophisticated global vendors and purchasers of hardware, software, systems integration services, networking systems and outsourcing and IT services. Squire Sanders has a cutting-edge approach to advising technology clients - an interlocking service platform that combines the firm's leading resources in business, finance and technology. The IT team handles cross-border IT mergers and acquisitions, systems integration, network management and project outsourcings, as well as other IT and e-business related contracts and arrangements.

Property & Tourism: The London property and tourism group represents global and European corporate and financial groups, private equity investors and governments in a wide variety of multi-jurisdictional transactions, project development and finance projects involving resort facilities, stadiums and transport.

UK	
Number of partners	11
Assistant solicitors	15
Other fee earners	1
Worldwide	
Number of partners	285
Assistant solicitors	420
Other fee earners	107
Counsel/Of counsel	79

CONTACTS	
Commercial	Andrew Wilkinson
Communications	Mara Babin
	James Nimmo
	Richard Sterling Surrey
	Martin Walsh
	Carol Welu
Corporate	Mara Babin
	Paul Lewis
	Stephen Nelson
	James Nimmo
	Richard Sterling Surrey
	Martin Walsh
	Carol Welu
Dispute Resolution	Carol Welu
Employment	Fiona McLaren
Information Technology/E-commerce	
	Andrew Wilkinson
Privatisation	James Nimmo
	Richard Sterling Surrey
Project Finance	Daniel Larkin
	Richard Sterling Surrey
Property & Tourism	Daniel Larkin
	Stephen Law
Securities	James Nimmo
	Martin Walsh

Continued overleaf

A-Z ■ LAW FIRMS

INTERNATIONAL Offices abroad: Asia: Almaty, Beijing, Hong Kong, Taipei, Tokyo. Europe: Bratislava, Brussels, Budapest, Kyiv, London, Madrid, Milan, Moscow, Prague. US: Cincinnati, Cleveland, Columbus, Houston, Jacksonville, Los Angeles, Miami, New York, Palo Alto, Phoenix, San Francisco, Tampa, Tysons Corner, Washington DC. The firm also has associations with legal firms in Bucharest, Dublin, Rio de Janeiro and São Paulo.

■ St James Solicitors
St James Road, Exeter, EX4 6LD **Tel** (01392) 204205

Stafford Young Jones
The Old Rectory, 29 Martin Lane, London, EC4R 0AU
Tel (020) 7623 9490 **Fax** (020) 7929 5704 **DX** 176 London
Email postmaster@s-yj.co.uk

Managing Partner	Helen Wenham
Senior Partner	Paul Adams
Number of partners	11
Assistant solicitors	5
Other fee-earners	6

CONTACTS	
Company/Commercial	Terry Chandler
Employment	Paul Adams
Family	Paul Adams
Housing Litigation	Pamela Yelland
Litigation (General)	Andrew Strong
Property (Commercial)	Martin Gaston
Property (Residential)	Francis Backman
Tax & Personal Planning	Neil Fulton
Wills & Probate	Christopher Munday

THE FIRM Stafford Young Jones is a very long established general practice particularly geared to the needs of individuals living/working in and around the City of London, who will find a friendly and personal service in a convenient location at a cost comparable to similar provincial firms. The firm also provides legal services in some niche areas, as below.

PRINCIPAL AREAS OF WORK
Family Law Paul Adams heads a small specialist team of family lawyers all of whom are members of the Solicitors Family Law Association. The firm is a member of the Relate Quality Partnership. The team deals with all aspects of family breakdown including divorce, cohabitation, financial and property disputes and private childrens' disputes involving contact and residence.
Housing Litigation The firm acts for a considerable number of registered social landlords in the area of housing litigation.
Employment Law Advice given to both employer and employee on a full range of employment issues, including Employment Tribunal work.
General Litigation The firm has a computerised and cost-effective debt recovery system and acts in this area for both individual and corporate clients. The firm is also experienced in other claims, including contractual and consumer disputes, personal injury, commercial and property litigation, acting for both claimants and defendants.
Wills & Probate Preparation of wills and living will; enduring powers of attorney; inheritance tax planning; administration of estates; advice to executors and beneficiaries on probate and succession laws; variation of estates and the obtaining of grants of representation in England to the estates of foreign nationals.
Trusts & Personal Tax Planning Formation, management and administration of trusts; asset management and financial planning; Court of Protection work. The firm offers a Nominee Company service which is a sponsored member of CREST.
Residential Property A fast and efficient service in the purchase and sale of freehold and leasehold property, short term letting and re-mortgages with specialist advice in the area of insolvency.
Commercial Property A comprehensive service acting for corporate and individual clients advising buyers and sellers, landlords and tenants and borrowers and lenders in the acquisition, disposal and management of commercial property with specialist advice in the area of insolvency.
Company & Commercial Advice on the formation, acquisition and disposal of commercial ventures and associated matters. Acting for financial institutions in the areas of lending and borrowing.

INTERNATIONAL Work can be handled in French, German and Portuguese.

RECRUITMENT The firm has a maximum number of three trainee solicitors. Prospective trainees should write to Paul Adams enclosing a CV.

■ Stamp Jackson and Procter
5 Parliament Street, Hull, HU1 2AZ **Tel** (01482) 324591 **Fax** (01482) 224048

Stanley Tee

High Street, Bishop's Stortford, CM23 2LU
Tel (01279) 755200 **Fax** (01279) 758400 **DX** 50404 Bishop's Stortford
Email law@stanleytee.co.uk **Website** www.stanleytee.co.uk

42 High Street, Great Dunmow, CM6 1AH
Tel (01371) 872166 **Fax** (01371) 875747 **DX** 89803 Great Dunmow
Email law@stanleytee.co.uk

Star House, 38 Rayne Road, Braintree, CM7 2QP
Tel (01376) 552277 **Fax** (01376) 551919 **DX** 56203 Braintree
Email law@stanleytee.co.uk

Senior Partner	Rodney Stock
Number of partners	14
Assistant solicitors	15
Other fee-earners	15

AREAS OF PRACTICE	
Litigation (incl. Family Law)	40%
Private Client	20%
Residential Property	17%
Commercial Property	12%
Company Commercial	7%
Criminal & Regulatory	4%

CONTACTS	
Agricultural & Estates	Caroline Metcalf
	Richard Tee
Commercial Litigation/Personal Injury	
	John Donovan, David Jacobs
	Caroline Metcalf, David Redfern
Commercial Property	Govan Bramley
	Bob Elms, Jeremy Gillham, Rodney Stock
Company & Commercial	Govan Bramley
	Michael Kirby, Rodney Stock
Employment	Helena Myska
Family	David Jacobs, David Redfern
Private Client, Personal Tax, Trusts & Probate	Richard Tee
Residential Property	Bob Elms

THE FIRM A well-established, yet highly progressive firm which has substantially increased its business in the last two years; the most tangible evidence of this being the opening of two additional premises in Bishop's Stortford. These openings have increased the area of its existing office complex by almost 50% and have been built to accommodate the latest technology and streamline working methods, which are in turn serving to generate new business. The firm benefits from a strategic location close to the City of London, Stansted Airport and the M11/M25 motorway network.

PRINCIPAL AREAS OF WORK The main focus of the firm's business is in commercial litigation and defendant personal injury cases - frequently of a complex, high value and widely publicised nature. Private client work also features strongly, particularly in the agriculture business, with tax and trust advice an area of specialist expertise. Assets dealt with on behalf of clients in the region of £80 million, of which £20 million is held in the firm's nominee companies enabling clients to participate in the CREST system. At the time of submitting these details, the firm was in the process of acquiring an IFA business to operate in conjunction with the asset management and investment advice service, all within one FSA controlled entity. The firm continues to act for some of the largest insurers in Europe and, despite consolidation of the market, has retained its niche advisor role with an emphasis on personal service. The firm has a growing reputation for its work in the health and educational sectors. Bringing land forward for property development, the letting and management of retail and other schemes and the sale and acquisition of agricultural property for development are other areas of expertise.

Steele & Co

2 Norwich Business Park, Whiting Rd, Norwich, NR4 6DJ
Tel (01603) 274700 **Fax** (01603) 625890 **DX** 5218 Norwich
Email ca@steele.co.uk **Website** www.steele.co.uk

10 Park Place, Lawn Lane, London, SW8 1UD
Tel (020) 7735 9006 **Fax** (020) 7735 7875 **DX** 33265 Kennington London
Email lbc@steele.co.uk

11 Guilford Street, London, WC1N 1DH
Tel (020) 7421 1720 **Fax** (020) 7421 1749
Email lonemp@steele.co.uk

2 Mount Street, Diss, IP22 4QE
Tel (01379) 652141 **Fax** (01379) 650150 **DX** 42507 Diss
Email ca@steele.co.uk

Managing Partner	Philip Hyde

CONTACTS	
Commercial Disputes/ Arbitration/Construction	Chris Gilbert
Commercial	Nigel Lubbock
Commercial Property	Ron Clare
Corporate	Nigel Lubbock
Criminal	Jamieson Plummer
Debt Recovery	Stephen Drake
Employment	Oliver Brabbins
	Carmel Sunley
Family	Neale Grearson
Personal Injury Litigation	Samantha Kemp
Private Client	Karen Bacon
Public Sector	Richard Hewitt
Tax	Alan Skeates

THE FIRM Steele & Co is a substantial, independent, commercial law firm and a leader in local authority, public sector and employment practice work. The firm provides a wide range of legal and business services to both UK and international businesses and institutions. One of the first and largest firms to be accredited to both ISO 9001 and Investor in People standards, Steele & Co places a great emphasis on quality and is committed to continuous improvement. Steele & Co has developed a portfolio of services for business which it either provides directly or through associated companies. Services involved include an interactive online business support service e-business one stop, a human resource consultancy, web and database design services and a commercial insurance brokerage. This approach provides clients with comprehensive solutions to their legal and business problems at all levels and ensures

Continued overleaf

A-Z ■ LAW FIRMS

appropriate expertise and continuity of service.

PRINCIPAL AREAS OF WORK Steele & Co offers a full range of business services to an established and growing national portfolio of corporate clients. The firm's employment team has a national reputation and is one of the largest and most successful employment teams for a firm of this size. In 2002, the firm handled the disposal of a bottled water business for a US client with a consideration of c.$124 million. Steele & Co enjoys a well established, national reputation in local authority and public sector work. From becoming the first firm in the country to take over responsibility for running an entire local authority's legal department (which it still runs), it has become a market leader for the provision of local authority services in London and is contracted to provide such services to 13 authorities within the capital. The firm also has particular expertise in relation to alternative dispute resolution and construction law. Steele & Co is growing not only in size but, perhaps more significantly, in influence too, due to its provision of legal and business support services.

Steele Raymond

Richmond Point, 43 Richmond Hill, Bournemouth, BH2 6LR
Tel (01202) 294566 **Fax** (01202) 552285 **DX** 7643 Bournemouth 1
Email mail@steeleraymond.co.uk **Website** steeleraymond.co.uk

31 West Street, Wimborne, BH21 1JT
Tel (01202) 885211 **Fax** (01202) 887746 **DX** 45303 Wimborne
Email mail@steeleraymond.co.uk

THE FIRM Steele Raymond was formed in 1979 and has expanded rapidly since that date, building up a wide range of business clients both in this country and abroad. The firm advises on all areas of company, commercial and business law, with a niche speciality in education law. It also has a substantial private client practice. Steele Raymond has achieved ISO 9001 accreditation for the complete range of its services. The Wimborne office undertakes all areas of work other than criminal matters.

PRINCIPAL AREAS OF WORK Company and business sales and purchases, company formations and reorganisations, partnership matters, intellectual property, EC law, competition law, commercial contracts (including computer contracts), aviation, commercial property matters, town and country planning, environmental law, insolvency and commercial litigation, personal injury, professional and medical negligence, education law and high level tax planning and advice. Unusually, the firm has a partner with a particular interest in canine law.
Agency Work The firm undertakes work, other than criminal work, on an agency basis.

CLIENTELE The firm advises a wide range of clients including individuals, partnerships, housing associations, higher, further and other educational bodies, insolvency practitioners, private and public companies and insurance companies.

INTERNATIONAL Increasingly the firm's work involves an overseas element, and it works with legal firms in Europe and the USA.

RECRUITMENT The firm aims to take on one or two trainee solicitors per year and normally has opportunities for specialist staff in various parts of its practice. Strong emphasis is placed on training at all levels.

Managing Partner	John Raymond
Senior Partner	David Steele
Number of partners	13
Assistant solicitors	9
Other fee-earners	8

AREAS OF PRACTICE	
Litigation	30%
Company Commercial	27%
Commercial Property	26%
Private Client	10%
Education	7%

CONTACTS	
Aviation/Medical Negligence	John Andrews
Commercial Litigation	Simon Outten
Commercial Property	John Raymond
	Bill Oliver
Company & Commercial	Paul Longland
	David Steele
Education	Peter Rolph
Employment	Simon Outten
Insolvency, Landlord & Tenant	Julian Fenn
Partnership	John Raymond
Personal Injury	John Andrews
Private Client	Paul Causton
Residential Developments	Sue Middleton
Taxation	Paul Causton

LAW FIRMS A-Z

Stephenson Harwood

One St Paul's Churchyard, London, EC4M 8SH
Tel (020) 7329 4422 **Fax** (020) 7606 0822 **DX** 64 Chancery Lane
Email info@shlegal.com **Website** www.shlegal.com

Chief Executive	John Pike
Senior Partner	Tony Scales
UK	
Number of partners	84
Assistant solicitors	126
Other fee-earners	66
International	
Number of partners	16
Assistant solicitors	74
Other fee-earners	17

CONTACTS	
Banking & Asset Finance	Mark Russell
Business Technology	James Robertson
Commercial Litigation	John Fordham
Commercial Property	Richard Light
Company/Commercial	James Robertson
Corporate Finance	Sharon White
Corporate Tax	Hugo Jenney
Construction	Steven Wait
Corporate Investigations/Asset-Tracing	John Fordham
Employment, Pensions & Benefits	Kate Brearley / Tom Flanagan
Environment	David Cuckson
Family & Matrimonial	Jonathan Walsh
Funds & Financial Services	William Saunders
Fraud & Regulation/Business Crime	Tony Woodcock
Insolvency	Paul Gordon-Saker
Insurance Insolvency	Rod Baker
Insurance/Reinsurance	Paul Howick
International Arbitration	Richard Gwynne
IP	Adrienne Seaman / Sunil Gadhia
Private Client	Robert Partridge
PFI/PPP	Peter Walters / David Cuckson
Professional Indemnity	Roland Foord
Property Development	Marcel Haniff
Property Finance	Richard Light
Property Litigation	Ken Duncan
Shipping Finance	Mark Russell
Shipping Litigation	Paolo Ghirardani
Town & Country Planning	Barry Jeeps
Trade & Project Finance	Tony Stockwell

THE FIRM Stephenson Harwood is an international law firm with an established position in chosen sectors of the international financial markets. In May 2002 Stephenson Harwood combined with Sinclair Roche & Temperley to create an enlarged firm with around 100 partners, 625 employees and revenue of £70m worldwide. Stephenson Harwood has refined its market focus and concentrates its business development on four key sectors where the firm has great competitive strength: the financial industry, maritime services and the property market together with opportunities arising from today's information and technology driven economy. Internationalism and teamwork lie at the heart of the firm's business. Stephenson Harwood has offices in seven countries in Europe and Asia; in London, Bucharest, Madrid, Paris, Piraeus, Singapore and, in the People's Republic of China, in Guangzhou and Hong Kong with an associated office in Shanghai. Nearly a quarter of the firm's revenue is earned from offices outside the UK. In London, some 40% of revenue is earned from clients abroad.

PRINCIPAL AREAS OF WORK Stephenson Harwood offers legal services through eight practice areas: banking and asset finance; commercial litigation; corporate; employment, pensions and benefits; insurance/reinsurance; private capital (including matrimonial and family); property and shipping litigation.

Banking & Asset Finance In direct response to the substantial growth of complex structured financings, often tax driven, the firm recently brought together its long established commercial banking and ship finance practices into one team. This is a key step in the firm's strategy to extend its asset finance expertise across a wider range of assets.

Commercial Litigation The firm is widely recognised for its expertise in handling disputes, acting for clients across a broad spectrum of business sectors in all aspects of litigation, arbitration and other forms of dispute resolution. Work extends across complex fraud and asset tracing, insolvency, professional indemnity, investigation and regulation, intellectual property and property litigation.

Corporate The firm has a well-established corporate practice with expertise in M&A and corporate finance; fund management; business technology, e-commerce and intellectual property; general corporate and commercial transactions and corporate tax.

Employment, Pensions & Benefits The firm provides a comprehensive range of advice on employment law and practice, pensions, employee benefits, tax and immigration. It is familiar not only with the ever increasing volume of legislation and case law, but also the practical problems that arise in these areas.

Insurance/Reinsurance The firm advises on every aspect of contentious and non-contentious insurance and reinsurance business, all classes, marine and non-marine, including liability, coverage, and recovery issues. It represents the full range of industry players including UK and international insurers, reinsurers, Lloyd's underwriters, P&I Clubs, run-off organisations, intermediaries and consultants.

Private Capital (including Family & Matrimonial) Stephenson Harwood is strongly committed to acting for individuals and trustees giving practical advice on tax, trusts and estates; heritage property and trust litigation. The firm is unusual among City-based firms in having a comprehensive matrimonial practice.

Property The firm regularly advises on all aspects of commercial property, with particular expertise in property investment, planning, property finance, development, landlord and tenant, environmental law and private finance initiative transactions for clients which include property companies, institutional investors, banks, developers, local authorities, hotel groups, public bodies and professional service companies.

Shipping Litigation Stephenson Harwood frequently acts in high profile disputes reported in the shipping press involving complex legal and commercial problems. The firm often has to advise on cross-border and jurisdictional disputes which has resulted in a considerable pool of experience relating to the majority of important maritime jurisdictions.

INTERNATIONAL The firm has offices in Bucharest, Guangzhou, Hong Kong, Madrid, Paris, Piraeus, Shanghai and an associated office in Singapore. It is also associated with Zuric i Partneri, Croatia; Barb Carpentier Thibault Groener, France; Elias Sp. Paraskevas Attorneys at Law 1933, Greece; Al Sarraf & Al Ruwayeh, Kuwait and Routledge-Modise, South Africa.

STEPHENSON HARWOOD

A-Z LAW FIRMS

Stephensons
The Pound, 230 Chapel Street, Salford, M3 5LE **Tel** (0161) 832 8844 **Fax** (0161) 832 8912

Stephens & Scown
25-28 Southernhay East, Exeter, EX1 1RS **Tel** (01392) 210700 **Fax** (01392) 274010

Stepien Lake Gilbert & Paling
8-14 Vine Hill, London, EC1R 5DX
Tel (020) 7812 0900 **Fax** (020) 7812 0999 **DX** 9 Chancery Lane

Senior Partner	Kaz Stepien
Number of partners	4
Other fee-earners	2

CONTACTS	
Banking/Funding	Kaz Stepien
Development	Tim Lake
	Mark Thomas
Investment	Paul Paling
	Kaz Stepien
Retail/Offices	Paul Paling

THE FIRM The firm was founded in April 1991. Its major activities are in the commercial property field, and this covers all aspects of commercial and residential development, banking, secured lending, investment, property finance and joint ventures.

CLIENTELE The firm acts for a number of banks, major commercial and residential developers, and a number of UK and overseas investors. It also acts for a number of UK property investment funds and high net worth individuals.

RECRUITMENT The recruitment partner is MW Thomas.

Steptoe & Johnson LLP
Clements House, 14/18 Gresham Street, London, EC2V 7JE
Tel (020) 7367 8000 **Fax** (020) 7367 8001 **DX** 206 London
Email mshenk@steptoe.com **Website** www.steptoe.com

Managing Partner	Maury Shenk
Number of partners	14
Assistant solicitors	17
Other fee-earners	9
Total lawyers worldwide	368

AREAS OF PRACTICE	
Telecommunications/Technology	30%
Corporate/Commercial	25%
Commercial Arbitration & Litigation	25%
Property	15%
Employment	5%

CONTACTS	
International Commercial Arbitration & Litigation	Ian Meredith
Commercial Property	Brendan Patterson
Corporate/Commercial	Jonathan Polin
Employment	Neil Adams
Gaming & Betting	Tony Wollenberg
International Trade/EU Law	Iain MacVay
Intellectual Property	Christopher Gibson
Technology/Telecommunications	David Judah

THE FIRM The London office of Steptoe & Johnson LLP provides large-city firm experience in a smaller environment. The firm has a strong international emphasis and provides a comprehensive range of legal services to market-leading businesses throughout the world. Clients range in size from the largest international conglomerates to individual entrepreneurs. Steptoe & Johnson LLP has gained a national and international reputation for vigorous representation of clients before governmental agencies, exceptional advocacy in litigation and arbitration, and creative and practical advice in guiding business transactions. With nearly 400 lawyers, the firm has offices in Washington, D.C., Phoenix, Los Angeles, London and Brussels.

PRINCIPAL AREAS OF WORK The London office of Steptoe & Johnson LLP is a world leader in providing legal services to clients in the telecommunications, technology and electronic commerce sectors. In the London market it is also a forceful presence in the more traditional areas of corporate law, commercial dispute resolution encompassing ADR, arbitration and litigation and property and has experienced partners in employment, international trade and intellectual property law, complementing Steptoe & Johnson LLP in those fields.

International Commercial Arbitration & Litigation Steptoe lawyers are actively engaged in the resolution of disputes involving ADR techniques, arbitration before the ICC, LCIA, LMAA and AAA as well as disputes before a range of domestic and international first instance and appellate courts. Steptoe has experience in issues as diverse as Islamic financing, fraud within emerging markets and digital television and theme park financing.

Commercial Property Steptoe's experience includes issues relating to industrial and residential development, investment, acquisitions and disposals, property finance, portfolio management, planning and environmental law.

Corporate/Commercial Steptoe handles takeovers and mergers, joint ventures (UK and cross-border), shareholder agreements, agency, distribution, licensing and franchising agreements, venture capital finance and international corporate structures with a focus on technology and telecommunications transactions.

Employment Steptoe's employment lawyers are well versed in employee/employer relations, employment documentation, redundancy, termination packages, maternity, discrimination, TUPE and advocacy at tribunals.

EU Law Steptoe has experience in many aspects of EU law, including anti-dumping and anti-subsidy proceedings, EU trade barriers regulation and EU competition law, and represents parties before the European Commission and the European courts.

Gaming & Betting Steptoe handles credit betting, in particular enforcement of contracts for differences worldwide, casino licensing and regulatory law and internet gaming.

International Law & Trade Steptoe has broad experience on regional and multilateral trade negotiations

and disputes, US and EU trade policy, customs matters and regulatory requirements are handled.
Intellectual Property Steptoe lawyers provide IP advice in transactional matters, particularly licensing and act also in IP contentious matters.
Technology Steptoe has extensive experience concerning hardware and software licensing, e-commerce, internet and ISP issues, co-location, domain name disputes and film and video on demand technology.
Telecommunications Steptoe provides pan-European regulatory and commercial advice on a wide variety of issues in the fixed, wireless and satellite sectors, including interconnection, IP service equipment agreements, privatisations and mergers and acquisitions.

Stevens & Bolton

The Billings, Guildford, GU1 4YD
Tel (01483) 302264 **Fax** (01483) 302254 **DX** 2423 Guildford 1
Email mail@stevens-bolton.co.uk   **Website** www.stevens-bolton.co.uk

Managing Partner	Michael Laver
Number of partners	20
Assistant solicitors	29
Other fee-earners	8

AREAS OF PRACTICE

Company/Commercial	29%
Litigation	23%
Commercial Property	19%
Tax, Trust, Will & Probate	14%
Other Property	6%
Employment	5%
Family/Matrimonial	4%

CONTACTS

Charities & Schools	Richard King
Commercial	Tudor Alexander
Commercial Litigation	Richard King
Commercial Property	James Mitchell
Commercial Recovery Service	Michael Frisby
Competition	Rebecca Homes-Siedle
Corporate	Richard Baxter
E-commerce, IT & IP	Nick Fieldhouse
Employment	Paul Lambdin
Family/Matrimonial	Caroline Gordon-Smith
Insolvency	Paul Lambdin
Personal Tax & Trusts	Nick Acomb
	Peter Snowden
Planning & Environment	Catherine Davey
Property Litigation	Janet Waine
Residential Property	Andrew Bussy
Sales & Marketing	Beverley Whittaker
Wills & Probate	Michael Hunter

THE FIRM One of the South East's leading law firms, Stevens & Bolton has grown rapidly in the past five years and is one of the major firms in the region. Located in Guildford, the firm provides a high quality service to commercial and private clients across the UK and further afield. In 2001, the firm's expertise was consolidated under one roof, enhancing team co-ordination and management. Stevens & Bolton's main areas of expertise are corporate and commercial (including IT and intellectual property), commercial property (including planning and environment), business litigation and dispute resolution, employment and private client services. Commercial clients range from fully listed plcs and major subsidiaries of international groups, to privately owned companies and an increasing number of e-commerce businesses. Private clients are typically medium to high net worth individuals. Particular features of its approach include a high level of specialist skill; the strength in depth and individual discipline to respond swiftly; an emphasis on sound, practical advice aimed at achieving clients' commercial objectives; open, collaborative and friendly relationships with clients and a constructive approach with other lawyers; a continuing investment in technology, know-how and training to enhance the quality, effectiveness and value of its services.

PRINCIPAL AREAS OF WORK

Company & Commercial This department, described as 'a strong team' in *Chambers Guide to the Legal Profession 2001-2002*, is experienced in corporate finance and transactional work, including acquisitions and disposals of companies and businesses, management buyouts, company restructurings, venture and development capital and other business finance. A broad range of commercial matters is handled and the group has significant expertise in outsourcing, franchising, asset finance (including aviation), competition law and trading agreements. The intellectual property, IT and e-business practice is also flourishing, benefiting from the firm's location in the heart of this hi-tech region.

Commercial Property Work handled includes acquisitions and disposals of freehold and leasehold properties, landlord and tenant work, and the department represents European and overseas property investors, handling associated funding, development and security issues. 'Clearly punching above its weight, with a service which goes down well with clients' was how the department was described in a recent commercial property directory. The firm also enjoys an excellent reputation in the areas of planning and environment.

Commercial Litigation Work involves predominantly UK and international contract disputes, including complex litigation in the IT and finance and leasing sectors. The commercial litigation department is also experienced in handling professional negligence claims; intellectual property disputes (primarily trademark and copyright infringement); insurance matters; construction and civil engineering disputes; shareholder and partnership disputes; property related litigation (including landlord and tenant). The department uses ADR and arbitration to resolve disputes.

Debt Recovery This is undertaken by the commercial recovery service and a specific cross-departmental team handles insolvency work.

Employment This dedicated department handles a full range of contentious and non-contentious employment work.

Private Client As well as advising on wills, probate and personal tax planning, the private client department handles a wide range of trust matters, both UK and offshore. These include employee benefit trusts and work for insurance and trust companies, as well as family trusts. A dedicated team handles family law matters, particularly complex financial cases with an international element. The department also deals with charities work for individuals and commercial organisations.

INTERNATIONAL Work undertaken often includes an international dimension. Stevens & Bolton is a member of Eurolink, a major global network of associated law firms.

RECRUITMENT Stevens & Bolton is always seeking to recruit high quality lawyers for varying roles in the firm. Those interested in applying should contact Michael Laver on (01483) 734230.

A-Z ■ LAW FIRMS

Stewarts

63 Lincoln's Inn Fields, London, WC2A 3LW
Tel (020) 7242 6462   **Fax** (020) 7831 6843   **DX** 369 London
Email info@stewarts-solicitors.co.uk   **Website** www.stewarts-solicitors.co.uk

Managing Partner	John Cahill
Number of partners	11
Assistant solicitors	10
Other fee-earners	16

AREAS OF PRACTICE	
Personal Injury & Clinical Negligence	75%
Commercial Litigation	20%
Non-Contentious	5%

CONTACTS	
Commercial Litigation	Jack Leonard
Non-Contentious	Chris Horspool
Personal Injury & Clinical Negligence	
	John Cahill
	Kevin Grealis

THE FIRM This medium-sized London-based firm was founded in 1989. Whilst being well known for its litigation practice (personal injury, clinical negligence, commercial litigation, professional negligence and insolvency), it is also active in non-contentious matters for a wide range of clients. The firm's philosophy has been to develop focused teams in specialist areas. It provides the quality of service commonly associated with much larger firms at a cost which is highly competitive. All client matters are handled or supervised by a partner with the relevant expertise. The partners seek pragmatic and cost effective solutions to their clients' problems. It is a forward thinking, expanding firm with international contacts delivering a high quality of service to clients.

PRINCIPAL AREAS OF WORK
Personal Injury/Clinical Negligence In the past twelve months there has been significant growth in the personal injury and clinical negligence departments, both of which have legal aid franchises and are acknowledged leaders in their fields. The focus on claims of the utmost severity (particularly brain and spinal injuries) continues although further niche areas are developing, including abuse litigation, US travel claims, child injury and aviation claims. Multi-party work is also undertaken by the personal injury department which was awarded a multi-party franchise in March 2000. Claims currently being undertaken include Ladbroke Grove, Kenya Airways, Nwala coach crash, Trilucent breast implants and Ford USA.
Commercial Litigation The commercial litigation department handles a broad range of work including commercial disputes requiring urgent interim relief. The partners have particular expertise in professional negligence claims, insolvency and regulatory work, banking (including the enforcement of securities) and insurance litigation on behalf of Lloyds syndicates.
Non-contentious The firm maintains a non-contentious client following acting for individuals, private companies, charities, banks and other financial institutions.
Alternative Dispute Resolution Stewarts are committed to alternative dispute resolution procedures and four partners are now accredited mediators.

INTERNATIONAL The firm is a founder member of a worldwide network of lawyers and regularly instructs foreign lawyers.

Stibbe

Exchange House, Primrose Street, London, EC2A 2ST
Tel (020) 7466 6300   **Fax** (020) 7466 6311
Email info@stibbe.co.uk   **Website** www.stibbe.com

Senior Partner	Jeroen Fleming

AREAS OF PRACTICE	
Banking, Finance & Securities	35%
Mergers & Acquisitions	35%
Tax Law	30%

CONTACTS	
Corporate	Jeroen Fleming
Tax Law	Michael Molenaars

THE FIRM Stibbe is a leading international law firm with offices in Amsterdam, Brussels, London and New York. Among the firm's international clients are some of the world's foremost companies listed on one or more stock exchanges in continental Europe, London and New York. The firm has 371 fee-earners, of which 88 are partners.

PRINCIPAL AREAS OF WORK Stibbe's internationally orientated practice places special emphasis on the following areas: banking, capital markets, competition, constitutional law, construction, corporate and structured finance, corporate restructuring, distribution and franchising, e-commerce, energy, environment, European law, fraud and white-collar crime, ICT, industrial projects, intellectual property, labour, media, mergers and acquisitions, planning, project finance, public private partnership, public procurement, real estate, regulatory matters, securities, tax, telecommunications, trade practices, transport, venture capital, WTO, as well as having expertise in litigation and arbitration.

INTERNATIONAL Stibbe is co-operating intensively with British law firm Herbert Smith and German law firm Gleiss Lutz. The three firms work together in project teams and exchange associates and knowledge on a larger scale. Herbert Smith has over 1,000 lawyers, of which nearly 200 are partners, in 10 offices throughout Europe and Asia. Gleiss Lutz has 47 partners and a total of around 180 lawyers and notaries in eight offices throughout Europe and Asia. Both Herbert Smith and Gleiss Lutz are firms with broad-based expertise in corporate law.

Stikeman Elliott

Regis House, 45 King William Street, London, EC4R 9AN
Tel (020) 7648 1300 **Fax** (020) 7648 1400
Email smiller@lon.stikeman.com **Website** www.stikeman.com

Managing Partner (London)	Shawna M Miller
Number of partners (London)	4
Number of lawyers (London)	10

CONTACTS	
London	Shawna M Miller

THE FIRM Stikeman Elliott is a leading international law firm based in Canada with an established and active practice in the City of London that offers the services of a number of senior practitioners collectively covering a wide range of legal expertise. The London office was established in 1969 and currently has over 20 staff, including 10 lawyers of Canadian and English qualification. The firm maintains offices in Montreal, Toronto, Ottawa, Calgary and Vancouver and, outside Canada, in London, New York, Hong Kong and Sydney.

PRINCIPAL AREAS OF WORK International corporate finance; capital markets including CDO transactions, banking and derivative products; securitisation, securities, mergers and acquisitions; privatisation; infrastructure and project finance; international taxation, private client and political risk planning.

CLIENTELE Banks; investment banks; multinational corporations; investment managers; pension funds and private equity investors.

STIKEMAN ELLIOTT

Stokoe Partnership

646-648 High Road, Leytonstone, London, E11 3AA **Tel** (020) 8558 8884 **Fax** (020) 8539 9007

Stone King

13 Queen Square, Bath, BA1 2HJ
Tel (01225) 337599 **Fax** (01225) 335437 **DX** 8001 Bath
Email admin@stoneking.co.uk **Website** www.stoneking.co.uk

39 Cloth Fair, London, EC1A 7JQ
Tel (020) 7796 1007 **Fax** (020) 7796 1017

Senior Partner	Michael King
Number of partners	11
Assistant solicitors	17
Other fee-earners	13

AREAS OF PRACTICE	
Commercial & Charities	48%
Private Client Litigation	35%
Private Client	17%

THE FIRM Established in 1785, Stone King has a substantial commercial and private client practice in the West Country, where its strengths are in the fields of commercial property, employment and commercial litigation, family and matrimonial, crime and trusts. It has a leading national reputation for its charity and education work, and has a London office to service clients in those sectors as well as its London-based commercial clients.

CLIENTELE The firm's work is divided between private clients and, in the commercial sphere, medium-sized businesses, schools, colleges, other large charities, and landed estates. It also provides specialist assistance in commercial litigation and employment to major national and international companies.

A-Z ■ LAW FIRMS

Stones

Linacre House, Southernhay Gardens, Exeter, EX1 1UG
Tel (01392) 666777 **Fax** (01392) 666770 **DX** 8306 Exeter
Email mail@stones-solicitors.co.uk **Website** www.stones-solicitors.co.uk

21 Fore Street, Okehampton, EX20 1AJ
Tel (01837) 650200 **Fax** (01837) 650201 **DX** 82500 Okehampton
Email mail@stones-solicitors.co.uk

14 South Street, Torrington, EX38 8AF
Tel (01805) 623725 **Fax** (01805) 624040 **DX** 140192 Great Torrington
Email mail@stones-solicitors.co.uk

13 Bampton Street, Tiverton, EX16 6AA
Tel (01884) 259660 **Fax** (01884) 259661 **DX** 49015 Tiverton
Email mail@stones-solicitors.co.uk

12 Middle Street, Taunton, TA1 1SH
Tel (01823) 323440 **Fax** (01823) 335206
Email mail@stones-solicitors.co.uk

Cosmopolitan House, Fore Street, Sidmouth, EX10 8AQ
Tel (01395) 516531 **Fax** (01395) 578964 **DX** 48702 Sidmouth
Email mail@stones-solicitors.co.uk

Senior Partner	Hugh Winterbotham
Managing Partner	Bronwen Courtenay-Stamp
Number of partners	23
Associates	4
Assistant solicitors	19
Other fee-earners	22
Total number of staff in 6 offices	144

AREAS OF PRACTICE
Property	21%
Commercial	19%
Trusts & Probate	18%
PI	18%
Family inc. Crime	15%
Commercial Litigation	9%

CONTACTS
Agricultural	Paul Tucker
Charity Law	Helen Honeyball
Commercial Litigation	Paul Keeling
Commercial Property	Christopher Rundle
Company/Commercial	Tony Lloyd
Crime	Peter Seigne
Defence Insurers	Robin Challans
E-commerce	Peter Cox
Employment	Kate Gardner
Childcare & Family	David Howell-Richardson
Insolvency	Paul Keeling
Leisure/Timeshare	Tim Bourne
Matrimonial	Lynn Henderson
Plaintiff Personal Injury	James Browne
Planning & Development	Hugh Winterbotham
Residential Property	Mike Giles
	Shirley Parsons
Skiing & Travel Personal Injury	
	Bronwen Courtenay-Stamp
	Heloise Marlow
Social Housing	Nick Dyer
Wills/Trusts/Probate/Tax	Helen Honeyball
	Mike Harris
OKEHAMPTON & TORRINGTON	
Property Landlord/Tenant	Philip Bailey
	John Dobie
TIVERTON & TAUNTON	
Mental Health	Jim Elliott
SIDMOUTH	
Wills/Trusts/Conveyancing/Contracts	
	Brad Thorpe

THE FIRM Stones is one of the largest practices in Exeter with a strong presence in Okehampton and offices in Torrington, Tiverton, Taunton and Sidmouth. Stones merged with Thorpes of Sidmouth in August 2001, bringing the total number of offices to six across the region. Established c. 1917, the firm provides a range of services to both private and corporate clients, and has a progressive outlook with all offices linked by modern communications systems. It has a Community Legal Service franchise and has been awarded the Law Society's Family Lawyers scheme. In its newly refurbished offices at Linacre House, Southernhay Gardens, Stones is excellently situated in the heart of the Exeter business community. Stones holds Lexcel accreditation, becoming the first firm in Okehampton, Torrington, Sidmouth and Tiverton to receive this and one of only three firms in Exeter.

PRINCIPAL AREAS OF WORK The firm has a particularly strong private client and commercial base in the West Country covering private client property, commercial, commercial litigation, personal injury, employment law, family, trust and probate, criminal and mental health work. The firm is known regionally and nationally for its timeshare, social housing and personal injury claims with a speciality in international ski law and holiday claims. The firm's niche areas are:

Social Housing Expertise in site acquisition throughout the South and South West; shared ownership schemes; HAMA and Care in the Community schemes with local authorities and health trusts; funding of housing schemes and repossession work.

Personal Injury With four members on the Personal Injury Panel and Robin Challans also a member of FOIL (The Forum of Insurance Lawyers), the department has long standing experience of this type of work with particular specialisation in international skiing law, holiday claims and defence litigation for major insurers.

Timeshare This department acts for some of the leading timeshare development companies, Owners' Committees, funders, and advises other countries on compliance with international regulations.

Family A strong, growing family team with skills and experience in handling divorce, Children Act and cohabitation cases. The firm has specialists in ancillary relief including cases involving substantial value assets. It also has specialists in issues of domestic violence. The partner heading the family team leads three solicitors specialising in childcare and adoption. The firm holds a family law franchise. The team has Family Law Panel members and supports the Solicitors Family Law Association Code of Practice. There are representatives on the Children Panel. The firm supports mediation and has staff qualified as mediators.

Development & Planning This department acts for a number of developers dealing with site acquisition, planning, service agreements and site sales. The senior partner acts on a regular basis for landowners looking to co-operate in promoting their land for development. This involves option agreements with development companies, joint venture agreements between the land owners and the schemes involved in both residential and retail development.

Mental Health A new niche area for Stones. The partner responsible has been a member of the Law Society Mental Health Review Tribunal Panel since 1988. This has enabled him to conduct applications to the Tribunal and before Parole Board Discretionary Lifer Panels. As a rule he will either see or, as a last resort advise over the telephone, any client within 24 hours of a referral.

E-commerce Law Another new area of law to Stones. The partner responsible has a wealth of experience and expertise in the area of technology and e-commerce law, having had hands-on experience and knowledge of setting up both his own dot.com business and an online law firm.

INTERNATIONAL Stones is a member of OTE, with one partner being a committee member. Work is handled in French, German, Spanish, Maltese and Tagalog (Philippines).

RECRUITMENT The past year has seen the addition of three new partners. Following the merger with Thorpes of Sidmouth in August, Brad Thorpe joined the team bringing many years of experience and an established client base to the Stones team, having run his practice in Sidmouth since 1985. Peter Cox, of Peter Cox Associates, also merged with the firm and became a new partner in July. Peter brings with him a wealth of experience and expertise in the area of technology and e-commerce law. Heloise Marlow, having been an associate for a number of years, became a partner in November, working within the personal injury team and specialising in foreign personal injury. New Stones associates include Nick Emson, working in the family and criminal departments; Clive Williamson, who covers general litigation at the Okehampton office; Robert Mitchell, from trust and probate; Lynn Henderson, who heads the matrimonial team.

Stringer Saul

17 Hanover Square, London, W1S 1HU
Tel (020) 7917 8500 **Fax** (020) 7917 8555 **DX** 82984 Mayfair
Email law@stringersaul.co.uk **Website** www.stringersaul.co.uk

THE FIRM Stringer Saul is a general commercial law firm with a number of specialisms. A major focus is advising 'knowledge-based' businesses. As such it acts for many clients involved in intellectual property, for example in the pharma/biotech, publishing and IT sectors. Work conducted for these organisations however, is much broader than IP advice alone; well over one third of the firm's business is company/commercial work, 15% is litigation and 11% property.

PRINCIPAL AREAS OF WORK The main areas of work are commercial property and planning; corporate advice including insolvency, reconstruction and recovery; corporate finance; mergers and acquisitions; employment; general commercial litigation; e-commerce; intellectual property and information technology (contentious and non-contentious); pharmaceuticals and biotechnology; publishing; secured lending; taxation.

CLIENTELE The firm's clients range from multinational public companies to small owner managed businesses, including companies in the pharmaceutical and biotechnology sectors, e-commerce, finance, leisure, publishing, the media, property and mining. It currently acts for around 20 plcs across a range of business sectors, including: Celltech, e-capital investments, The Evolution Group, Antisoma, ML Laboratories, Probus Estates, SmithKline Beecham, SkyePharma and Wolters Kluwer. The firm typically has very long-standing relationships with clients - many reaching back to its very beginnings. Because the firm is committed to its focus on knowledge-based businesses, there is true value to clients in the advice they receive across the full range of commercial legal disciplines - from corporate finance to patents.

INTERNATIONAL Stringer Saul regularly acts for clients overseas and has long standing relationships with a number of European and US lawyers and accountants with whom the partners work on a regular basis. Work is also handled in German, Russian and Hebrew.

Managing Partner	Norman Ziman
Number of partners	13
Assistant solicitors	14
Other fee-earners	1

AREAS OF PRACTICE	
Company/Commercial	37%
Intellectual Property	23%
General Commercial Litigation	15%
Property	11%
Employment	9%
Tax	5%

CONTACTS	
Commercial Property & Planning	Bill Harrup
Company/Commercial	June Paddock
	David Smith
E-commerce	Allistair Booth
Employment	Ruth Hickling
General Commercial Litigation	Justin Ede
IP/IT	Gary Howes (IP)
	Roger Loosely (IT)
Mergers & Acquisitions	David Smith
Pharmaceuticals & Biotechnology	Gary Howes
Publishing	Norman Ziman
Reconstruction & Recovery	David Smith
Secured Lending	Martin Ackland
Taxation	Paul Yerbury

 STRINGER SAUL

Stronachs

34 Albyn Place, Aberdeen, AB10 1FW **Tel** (01224) 845845 **Fax** (01224) 845800

A-Z ■ LAW FIRMS

Sturtivant & Co

54 Welbeck Street, London, W1G 9XS
Tel (020) 7486 9524   **Fax** (020) 7224 3164
Email visas@sturtivant.co.uk

THE FIRM Established in 1985, and well-known as a specialist practice which is devoted exclusively to UK immigration law. The principal, Karen Sturtivant, is an active member of various professional associations concerned with immigration law and she regularly lectures and gives seminars on this subject.

PRINCIPAL AREAS OF WORK All types of immigration work undertaken; primarily client representation for work permits, business residence, investor status, innovator status, highly skilled migrant programme and other residence categories. Also settlement; extension of stay; visitors, students and temporary stay. Appeals to Adjudicators and Tribunals; Judicial Review and deportation and removal cases.
Additional Areas Nationality and citizenship problems.

CLIENTELE Wide corporate and private client base.

INTERNATIONAL Contacts with immigration lawyers in many other jurisdictions.

Number of partners	1
Assistant solicitors	1
AREAS OF PRACTICE	
UK Immigration, Nationality Law & Work Permits	100%

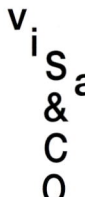

■ Sugaré & Co

36 Park Square, Leeds, LS1 2NY   **Tel** (0113) 244 6978   **Fax** (0113) 245 5708

■ Susan Holmes - Sole Practitioner

Woodside, Great Corby, Carlisle, CA4 8LL   **Tel** (01228) 560617   **Fax** (01228) 562372

Studio Legale Sutti

19 Princes St, London, W1B 2LW
Tel (020) 7409 1384   **Fax** (020) 7409 1384
Email london@sutti.com   **Website** www.sutti.com

THE FIRM Studio Legale Sutti was established in Milan in 1953 and its activity is organised across three main departments: commercial and company law, intellectual property and competition, and employment law.
London Office The aim of Studio Legale Sutti's presence in London is that of offering a full range of prompt and efficient on-site legal services regarding Italian, Yugoslavian and Bulgarian laws and jurisdictions. In this respect, the SLS operation in the UK would like to be viewed as a barrister-like practice - fully backed by the combined resources and know-how of its domestic offices to which it is connected through a high-speed encrypted link - with the purpose of serving British law firms, patent and trademarks agents and corporate counsel for their clients' and employers' needs related to Italy and south-eastern Europe.

PRINCIPAL AREAS OF WORK The firm covers the following areas of specialisation: company law; commercial contracts; international contracts; international tax law; M&A; joint ventures; foreign investments; agency and franchise arrangements; EU law; competition law; financial and banking law; debt collection; insolvency; environmental law; construction law; product liability; IT and TLC law; entertainment law; maritime law; commercial litigation and arbitration; white collar crime; administrative law; intellectual property advice and litigation; industrial models and design; licence negotiation; technology transfer; advertising law; pharmaceuticals; patent and trade mark agency service; labour law; employment law; employer's liability; industrial relations and pensions law.

INTERNATIONAL The firm's main office is situated in Milan. Other offices are located in Rome, Genoa, Sofia, Belgrade and Tokyo.

Managing Partner	Stefano Sutti
Office Contact	Livia Oglio
Worldwide	
Number of partners	12
Assistant solicitors	62
AREAS OF PRACTICE	
Commercial/Company	45%
Intellectual Property/Competition	35%
Employment	20%

1154   INDEX TO LEADING LAWYERS: PAGE 1693 ■ IN-HOUSE LAWYERS' PROFILES: PAGE 1201

LAW FIRMS ■ A-Z

Tarlo Lyons

Watchmaker Court, 33 St. John's Lane, London, EC1M 4DB
Tel (020) 7405 2000   **Fax** (020) 7814 9421   **DX** 53323 Clerkenwell
Email info@tarlolyons.com   **Website** www.tarlolyons.com

THE FIRM Tarlo Lyons is a leading London firm focused on delivering commercial solutions for technology driven business. Having developed one of the largest teams of dedicated technology lawyers in the UK, the firm believes in leveraging the expertise and talent it has assembled to provide real benefits for clients. The firm's success is measured by the contribution it makes to clients' objectives, for which the ability to understand and work with technology is central. The development of an intelligent document generation system, DealMaker®, and a leading role as a founder member of euroIT-counsel® (an association of technology focused law firms covering 11 jurisdictions), demonstrate the firms ability to innovate in order to optimise return for clients. With an increasing number of partners skilled in project and risk management, the firm aims to deliver its services in a way which is efficient, leading edge and relevant to its clients. The firm's clients span global corporates, UK-listed and unlisted corporates, entrepreneurial businesses and individuals, all of whom value the firm's dedication to excellence in service delivery.

PRINCIPAL AREAS OF WORK

Technology Projects Global IT procurement and supply arrangements for suppliers and end-users; software and data licensing; risk management.

E-commerce & Digital Media Information security, encrypted communications regulations, data protection, web hosting and connectivity agreements, website terms and conditions, online email mandates and indemnities, content management and web policy documents.

Outsourcing Advising end-users and suppliers, with particular expertise in IT outsourcing in the regulated financial markets, HR outsourcing, structuring of outsourcing SPV's, and cross-border and multi-jurisdictional outsourcings

Corporate & Commercial Flotations, MBO/MBI's, acquisition and disposals, secured lending, financial services, joint ventures and commercial arrangements.

Private Equity/Venture Capital Fundraisings, development capital, restructurings and mezzanine finance.

Commercial Litigation Contractual and shareholder disputes, negligence, fraud, engineering disputes, international arbitration and dispute resolution.

Technology Disputes Hardware supply and software development disputes, licensing disputes, service level disputes.

Intellectual Property Patent; trademark; design right; copyright and other IP issues, including disputes and domain name ownership; art and copyright.

Tax Investigations The firm deals with the entire range of enquiries by the Inland Revenue and HM Customs & Excise and acts mainly for clients being investigated by these bodies.

Restraint & Confiscation The firm acts both for receivers and defendants generally.

Hotel & Leisure Hotel and restaurant acquisitions and sales, hotel and restaurant development and funding, management contracts, shop and restaurant leases, HR issues, technology systems, liquor licensing and amusement arcades.

Entertainment Film and theatre production, film finance, rights acquisition and exploitation, licensing and copyright protection, contract drafting and negotiation, and company structure and tax advice.

IT Personnel Advising users and suppliers of IT personnel on all aspects of HR outsourcing including, employment rights of contractors and IR35, contractor service management agreements, preferred supplier arrangements and the Temporary Workers Directive.

Employment & Resourcing Employment contracts, service agreements, EU and UK employment law, collective agreements, discrimination, TUPE and unfair or constructive dismissals.

Commercial Property Investment acquisitions and disposals, site assembly, development and planning, landlord and tenant, portfolio acquisitions and disposals, finance and funding, joint ventures, environmental and construction issues, and tax saving schemes.

Senior Partner	Maurice Martin
Managing Partner	Nigel McEwen
Number of partners	28
Other fee-earners	38
Total staff	122

AREAS OF PRACTICE

Technology Disputes	15%
Technology Projects	14%
Commercial Litigation	10%
Commercial Property	9%
Corporate & Commercial	7%
Outsourcing	7%
Tax Investigations	7%
Hotel & Leisure	7%
E-commerce & Digital Media	4%
Employment & Resourcing	4%
IT Personnel	4%
Intellectual Property	3%
Restraint & Confiscation	3%
Entertainment	3%
Private Equity/Venture Capital	3%

CONTACTS

Technology Projects	John Mawhood
E-commerce & Digital Media	Simon Stokes
Outsourcing	Tim Couldrick
Corporate & Commercial	Lawrence Phillips
Private Equity/Venture Capital	Sarah Collins
Commercial Litigation	Patrick Pennal
Technology Disputes	Peter Moody
Intellectual Property	Nick Arnold
Tax Investigations	Maurice Martin
Restraint & Confiscation	Warren Foot
Hotel & Leisure	Philip Diamond
Entertainment	Simon Meadon
IT Personnel	Kevin Barrow
Employment & Resourcing	Warren Foot
Commercial Property	Philip Diamond

tarlo lyons

■ Taylor Nichol

3 Station Place, London, N4 2DH   **Tel** (020) 7272 8336   **Fax** (020) 7281 9148

■ Taylors

Rawlings House, Exchange Street, Blackburn, BB1 7JN   **Tel** (01254) 563333   **Fax** (01254) 682146

A-Z ■ LAW FIRMS

Taylor Vinters

Merlin Place, Milton Rd, Cambridge, CB4 0DP
Tel (01223) 423444 **Fax** (01223) 423486 **DX** 724560 Cambridge 12
Email info@taylorvinters.com **Website** www.taylorvinters.com

THE FIRM As one of the largest law firms in East Anglia, Taylor Vinters has a reputation for quality legal services to the commercial sector. The University of Cambridge is just one of a number of substantial institutional clients. Taylor Vinters' main strength lies in the firm's extensive experience with high-technology industries.

PRINCIPAL AREAS OF WORK

Corporate & Commercial Acquisitions; disposals; MBOs; joint ventures; venture capital funding; construction; employment; insolvency; intellectual property; and commercial litigation.

Commercial Property Investment sales and purchases; landlord and tenant; large scale sales and purchases; development planning; agricultural and environmental law.

Rural Business Services Encompasses the wide range of rural-based business activity undertaken for food processors, farmers, estates, institutions and related organisations. The firm has a national reputation for bloodstock and equestrian work.

Other Specialisms Claimant personal injury, charities and private client.

Managing Partner	Christine Berry
Number of partners	27
Assistant solicitors	35
Other fee-earners	14

CONTACTS	
Commercial Litigation	Edward Perrott
Commercial Property	Steven Beach
Company & Commercial	John Short
Corporate Finance	John Short
Family & Matrimonial	Jackie Wells
Innovation & Technology	David Rainford
Personal Injury	Paul Tapner
Planning, Development & Construction	Philip Kratz
Private Client	Jocelyn Fox
Rural Services	Adrian Horwood-Smart

Taylor Wessing

Carmelite, 50 Victoria Embankment, Blackfriars, London, EC4Y 0DX
Tel (020) 7300 7000 **Fax** (020) 7300 7100 **DX** 41 London
Email enquiries@taylorwessing.com **Website** www.taylorwessing.com

THE FIRM Taylor Wessing came into existence on 1 September 2002 through a combination of the practices of Taylor Joynson Garrett and German law firm Wessing to provide a pan European legal service in the two largest economies in Europe. The firm provides a full range of legal services to major corporations and growing enterprises, with a particularly strong track record in serving knowledge-based businesses in sectors such as information technology, telecommunications and life sciences. A market leader in many of its practice areas such as intellectual property, corporate finance and inward investment from the US, Taylor Wessing offers constructive, commercial advice through a partner-led service with a total, long-term commitment to its clients around the world. Taylor Wessing has offices in Berlin, Brussels, Cambridge, Dusseldorf, Frankfurt, Hamburg, London, Munich and associated offices in Alicante and Shanghai.

PRINCIPAL AREAS OF WORK

Corporate This highly regarded department deals with international and domestic work, with particular expertise in mergers and acquisitions, tax, inward investment, PFI and EU law issues. It acts for a varied client base including public companies, banks and other financial institutions, management teams, private companies and venture capitalists.

Intellectual Property TJG's IP department is one of the largest in Europe and is recognised as a leader in this field. It deals with contentious and non-contentious work, including patent litigation, trade marks, industrial design, passing off and trade libel. An experienced and respected sector-focused group, forged from the firm's IP and corporate departments, deals with the advances in digital media, e-commerce, internet, IT and telecoms, advising and protecting inventors, investors, manufacturers, suppliers and users.

Finance & Projects Lawyers in this department provide an integrated service acting for banks and sponsors in relation to all types of debt financing and in particular international project finance transactions. The department's product range includes all types of debt, security, trade finance and securitisation instruments. Industry specialisations include property, transport, telecoms and energy.

Commercial Property The firm offers a range of services incorporating specialist planning, property management and environmental teams, meeting the differing needs of trading companies, developers, finance institutions and national and international investors. The firm's dedicated rail practice group adopts a multidisciplinary approach to meet the needs of businesses active in the rail industry, including development companies.

Dispute Resolution This department handles a wide variety of commercial litigation and arbitration matters and incorporates particular strengths in construction, banking, fraud, property, insolvency and

UK Managing Partner	Gary Moss
UK Senior Partner	Richard Marsh
Number of partners	181
Other fee-earners (inc. assistants and paralegals)	307
Trainees	103
Support	540
Total	1131

AREAS OF PRACTICE	
Corporate	25%
Intellectual Property	19%
Dispute Resolution	17%
Commercial Property	13%
Finance & Projects	11%
Private Client	7%
Employment	7%

CONTACTS	
Banking	Rodney Dukes
Commercial Property	John Whitfield
Construction	Christopher Bourgeois
	Peter Shaw
Corporate Finance	Gordon Jackson
	Tim Stocks
Corporate Tax	Peter Jackson
Corporate/Commercial	Tim Eyles
Dispute Resolution	Neil White
Employment	Andrew Granger
Entertainment/Multimedia	Paul Mitchell
Environment & Planning	Alison Askwith
European Union/Competition	Martin Baker
Insolvency	Michael Frawley
Insurance/Reinsurance	Peter Kempe
Intellectual Property	Charles Lloyd
Inward Investment	David Kent
IT/E-commerce/Internet	Glyn Morgan
Life Sciences	Simon Cohen
	David Kent
London Stock Exchange	Tim Eyles
	Tim Stocks
Pharmaceutical	Mark Hodgson
Professional Indemnity	Clare Ferguson
Projects & PFI	Declan Tarpey

insurance. In particular the specialised construction and engineering group assists clients to achieve their commercial objectives through drafting of documents to protect their interests, support and assistance in maintaining the smooth running of projects, and if necessary the pursuit or defence of claims in court or arbitration.

Employment This specialist department handles a wide variety of employment-related matters including pensions and employee benefits together with increasingly complex legal relationships both domestically and internationally.

Private Client The firm's long standing and well respected private client department provides advice on taxation, wills and settlements (including trusts and estates), matrimonial law and residential property.

CONTACTS (Continued)	
Shipping	James Sleightholme
Tax & Personal Planning	Philippa Blake-Roberts
	Michael Stanford-Tuck
Telecommunications/Broadcast	John Edwards
	Edward Mercer
Transport	Jane McKee

Teacher Stern Selby

37-41 Bedford Row, London, WC1R 4JH
Tel (020) 7242 3191 **Fax** (020) 7242 1156 **DX** 177 Ch.Ln.
Email contact@tsslaw.com **Website** www.tsslaw.com

THE FIRM A central London-based general commercial firm, with clientele and caseload normally attributed to much larger firms. It has a wide range of contacts overseas. A higly commercial firm, driving deals through for clients, adopting creative problem-solving approaches and adding value to clients by providing commercial advice and options.

PRINCIPAL AREAS OF WORK

Commercial Property Work includes acquisitions and disposals for developers, investors, landlords and tenants. Secured lending and the drafting of security documentation (acting for banks and building societies) are also handled, as is every aspect of landlord and tenant work.

Company/Commercial The department is active in the corporate sector, handling takeovers, mergers, joint ventures, MBOs and disposals, demergers, reconstructions and asset sales. Work for AIM listed companies, including listings, placings and raising capital. The firm also deals with employment law, intellectual property licences and confidentiality agreements. The firm has particular experience in IT, e-commerce and telecommunications contracts, oil exploration agreements and financing, PR and media law, entertainment law (music, film, TV, cable and multimedia), and in the pharmaceutical industry.

Litigation Primarily in the commercial field, especially banking, insolvency and finance house matters and in particular commodities-related litigation and arbitration, together with commercial property litigation. The firm also specialises in clinical negligence and personal injury cases, and has a national reputation in the field of education law. The firm has considerable experience in media and entertainment litigation.

Other Areas The firm gives specialist tax planning advice and has substantial experience in the formation and use of foreign trusts and offshore corporate entities to produce the most efficient tax structure to suit individual circumstances. A full range of private client services from residential conveyancing to wills, trusts, probate and estate administration is also provided.

CLIENTELE Primarily from the finance, commercial property, IT, corporate and entertainment fields, and also corporate and business clients from Canada, Israel and Eastern Europe. The firm also has excellent links with accountants, banks, financial institutions, and surveyors and has wide-ranging legal contacts overseas.

INTERNATIONAL Languages spoken include Afrikaans, Arabic, Chinese (Mandarin), French, German, Hebrew, Italian, Russian, Serbo-Croat and Spanish.

Managing Partner	Graham Shear
Number of partners	17
Assistant solicitors	19
Other fee-earners	7

AREAS OF PRACTICE	
Commercial Property	37%
Commercial Litigation	30%
Company & Commercial	20%
Secured Lending	8%
Personal Injury/Education/Judicial Review	3%
Residential Conveyancing/Probate	2%

CONTACTS	
Commercial Litigation	Jack Rabinowicz
Commercial Property	Stuart Stern
	Russell Raphael
Corporate/Investment	David Salisbury
Education	Jack Rabinowicz
Entertainment	Graham Shear
General Commercial	David Salisbury
	Martine Nathan
IT/IP E-commerce	Martine Nathan
IT/IP Litigation	Colin Richman
Media Companies	David Teacher
Media Litigation	Graham Shear
Clinical Negligence	Jack Rabinowicz
Secured Lending	Philip Berry

A-Z ■ LAW FIRMS

Thanki Novy Taube

Imperial Works, Perren Street, London, NW5 3ED
Tel (020) 7485 5558 **Fax** (020) 7485 5556 **DX** 46475 Kentish Town
Email info@tntlaw.co.uk **Website** www.tntlaw.co.uk

Number of partners	7
Assistant solicitors	10
Other fee-earners	11

CONTACTS	
Civil Actions	Harriet Wistrich
General Crime & Appellate	Martin Taube
Inquests	Marcia Willis-Stewart
International Crime/Extraditions	Girish Thanki
Prison Law	Vicky King
White Collar Crime	Kenneth Carr
	(Higher Court Advocate)

THE FIRM The firm specialises in criminal litigation, serious fraud, civil liberties and human rights. The firm has considerable experience of handling complex and weighty cases, often with forensic elements. Recent work includes a number of homicide cases (including appellate work in slow-burn provocation cases); extraditions, assisting a war crimes defendant at ICTY in The Hague; serious frauds, Privy Council cases for death-row prisoners. Martin Taube appears regularly on the radio to advise on legal matters. Girish Thanki is a member of the Law Society's Task Force on implementation of the Human Rights Act 1998. Ken Carr is approved by the UNO to represent war crimes defendants before the ICTY in The Hague. The firm has a strong commitment to excellence and a quality-driven approach. It has a state of the art IT system for file management, costing and management controls. The firm provides high quality training to its own staff and to others. It arranges legal conferences. It undertakes a large amount of publicly funded work. For private clients charges vary from 150 per hour upwards depending on the degree of expertise required. The firm also has an office at Harlow.

PRINCIPAL AREAS OF WORK Work includes criminal litigation, serious fraud, civil liberties, Customs & Excise cases, drug trafficking, asset confiscation cases and public law. It has specialist knowledge of extradition law and international criminal law. The firm has substantial experience of appellate work and public law. The firm has expertise in civil actions against detaining authorities, coroner's inquests and prison law. The firm provides seamless representation from the police station to the appellate courts. It has substantial experience of advocacy and media relations.

CLIENTELE A large amount of publicly funded work with a growing private client base.

Theodore Goddard

150 Aldersgate Street, London, EC1A 4EJ
Tel (020) 7606 8855 **Fax** (020) 7606 4390 **DX** 47 London Chancery Lane WC2
Email info@theodoregoddard.co.uk **Website** www.theodoregoddard.com

Chief Operating Officer	Nigel West
Senior Partner	Paddy Grafton Green
Number of partners	69
Assistant solicitors	116
Other fee-earners	25
Total staff	353

AREAS OF PRACTICE	
Corporate & Corporate Finance	26%
Property	20%
Media/IP	18%
Banking & Projects	15%
Litigation	10%
Employment	6%
Corporate Tax	5%

CONTACTS	
Advertising	Rupert Earle
Arbitration	Peter Fitzpatrick
Asset Finance	James Ballingall
Aviation	Rory MacCarthy
Banking & Projects	Michael Black
Commercial Litigation	John Kelleher
Commercial Property	Mark Gilbert
Corporate	Graham Stedman
Construction	Clive Lovatt
Corporate Tax	Peter Sayer
E-commerce	Paul Renney
EC/Competition	Guy Leigh
Employment	Jane Bullen
Entertainment	Paddy Grafton Green
Environment	Claire Sheppard
Film/TV	Peter Armstrong
Insolvency	Louise Wilkinson
Insurance	Jennifer Donahue
Intellectual Property	Hamish Porter
IT	Graham Stedman
Media Litigation	Martin Kramer
Music	Paddy Grafton Green
Pensions	Mark Catchpole

THE FIRM Theodore Goddard is a London-based law firm, with strengths in banking and projects, commercial, corporate, dispute resolution, media and communications and property law. The firm's clients like its modern approach and the commercial and innovative way in which it delivers its services. Theodore Goddard has provided businesses with a full range of legal services and advice since 1902. This long tradition of client care continues today, combined with up-to-date skills and technological innovation. The firm prides itself on understanding its clients' markets and fitting in with the way they work so that it can add value by offering relevant business advice as well as legal services. Theodore Goddard has over 200 lawyers and operates from offices in London, Brussels, and through a network of law firms worldwide.

PRINCIPAL AREAS OF WORK

Banking & Projects The group has succeeded in establishing itself as one of the City's leading practices. The group acts for a number of leading banks, financial institutions and corporates on a range of transactions. Similarly, the group enjoys an enviable reputation in the PFI sector where the group acts for a number of the firm's banking clients and for project sponsors. The group also has a dedicated insolvency and corporate recovery unit handling work for a portfolio of blue-chip clients.

Commercial Theodore Goddard's commercial group encompasses a wide range of legal services. From aviation, competition and regulation, data protection and IT, to employment, employee benefits, pensions and tax. The group pools the expertise of various areas of the firm, advising a high quality client base with a service to match.

Corporate The group has significant experience of domestic and international mergers and acquisitions, disposals, joint ventures, group reconstructions, flotations and all forms of equity and debt financing. It also has a strong reputation for handling a wide range of domestic and international securities and capital markets transactions for banks, brokers, institutional investors and corporate clients. Work includes advising on initial public offerings, listings, placings and secondary issues; international securities offerings; public takeovers; corporate trustees; debt issues and capital markets transactions. The group is particularly strong on advising sponsors of domestic flotations and underwriters of equity issues, both on the main market and AIM.

Dispute Resolution Considerable expertise in relation to the banking and securities sector; fraud and asset recovery; major contractual disputes; insurance and reinsurance, product liability, especially in the healthcare industry and in arbitration and ADR.

Media & Communications Led by Paddy Grafton Green, Theodore Goddard's media and communications group is recognised as one of the leading practices in the world. Together with strengths in the traditional areas of music, film, television, advertising and publishing, the group also advises extensively on issues relating to new media and information technology. Clients range from household name superstars, major record and film producers to individuals taking their first steps in the industry.

Property The group advises household names, developers, institutions, retailers and leisure clients on all aspects commercial property. Its specialist practitioners enable it to offer a true one-stop service, with experts in the fields of property acquisition and disposal, construction, planning, environmental law, tax and property litigation.

INTERNATIONAL The firm has an office in Brussels and its associated offices are TG Jersey and Klein Goddard in Paris. Work is handled in Cantonese, French, German, Hebrew, Italian, Japanese and Spanish.

CONTACTS (Continued)	
PFI	James Ballingall
Planning	Douglas Evans
Property Finance	Dave Wilson
Sport	Fraser Reid
Telecommunications	Edward Pitt
Trade	Dan Horovitz

THEODORE GODDARD

The Law Offices of Richard Hemmings LLM Solicitor
Sandy Lane, Barham, Ipswich, IP6 0PB **Tel** (01473) 833844 **Fax** (01473) 833230

Thomas A. Higgins & Co
Capital Buildings, 10 Seaview Road, Wallasey, L45 4LA **Tel** (0151) 691 1211 **Fax** (0151) 630 8007

Thomas Cooper & Stibbard
Ibex House, 42-47 Minories, London, EC3N 1HA
Tel (020) 7481 8851 **Fax** (020) 7480 6097 **DX** 548
Email tcs@tcssol.com **Website** www.tcssol.com

THE FIRM Thomas Cooper & Stibbard was established in 1825 and specialises in commercial law, with a particular emphasis towards shipping, aviation and international trade. The firm offers advice to industrial, commercial and financial clients worldwide. Thomas Cooper & Stibbard has built strong, long lasting relationships with clients, through a thorough understanding of the demands and developments of their different market places. The firm's client base is broadly international, with many of its multilingual lawyers travelling widely on client business. The firm has a branch office in Singapore which opened in 1996 and is led by Paul Barfield, covering both admiralty and dry shipping work. The firm also has a strong presence in Greece, led by Douglas Bateson, where it opened a branch office in March 1999, undertaking both contentious and non-contentious work. In October 2001 the firm opened an office in Vancouver which is headed by Mark Sachs, who spent the previous five years successfully developing the practice in Singapore. With dual qualified Canadian and English practitioners the firm is able to offer an international focus to shipping and international trade clients located in Vancouver and those trading with Canada. The firm also has greatly expanded its involvement with the Spanish and Latin American markets, with increasing instructions from shipowners, underwriters, oil companies and financial institutions. The firm was joined by a team practising aviation law late in 2001.
Overseas Offices Athens, Singapore and Vancouver.

PRINCIPAL AREAS OF WORK
Maritime The firm's international reputation in shipping and marine insurance embraces the full range of P&I, FD&D and hull and machinery work covering charterparties, bills of lading, carriage of goods, cargo claims, containers, ship building and repair contracts, terminal and jetty damage, personal injuries, management disputes, multimodal carriage, sale and purchase, electronic shipping and trade documentation. The firm's admiralty specialists also handle casualties, salvage and towage, general average, fires and explosions, pollution, wreck removal and all areas of marine insurance and reinsurance. The firm has been instructed in connection with many of the major casualties of recent years and David Hebden is particularly well known for work on crisis management. The firm operates a 24 hour emergency response service in respect of maritime related casualties. Thomas Cooper & Stibbard keeps close links with specialist maritime lawyers in all major maritime centres worldwide with special emphasis in the Far East, Spain and South America, Scandinavia and Greece.

Aviation The team can assist insurers and the wider aviation industry with a comprehensive range of UK and international issues including: claims and litigation handling involving Carriage by Air (passenger and cargo); general aviation, industrial aid; sports aviation; product liability and professional negligence; airports and ground handling; regulation infringements; surface damage and collision; as well as aviation-related commercial litigation and contractual issues, inquests and inquiries.

Personal Injury The firm is very well known for marine personal injury work, acting in the main for P&I clubs and shipowners.

Senior Partner	Stephen Swabey
Managing Partner	Tim Goode
Number of partners	19
Assistant solicitors	15
Other fee-earners	14

AREAS OF PRACTICE	
Shipping (Admiralty, Maritime & Carriage)	50%
Aviation	10%
Business Finance & Insurance	20%
Commercial Litigation & International Arbitration	10%
Personal Injury	10%

CONTACTS	
Aviation Litigation	Tim Scorer
	John Korzeniowski
Aviation Finance	Alfred Merckx
Banking	Grant Eldred
Commercial Litigation	Nick Green
Company Law	Stephen Swabey
EU Competition Law	Alfred Merckx
	Stephen Swabey
Personal Injury	John Strange
Property	Kate Harrison
Shipping & Maritime Law	John Strange
	Tim Kelleher

THOMAS COOPER & STIBBARD

Continued overleaf

A-Z ■ LAW FIRMS

Company/Commercial The firm's company and commercial department advises all types of UK and international businesses including public and private companies, partnerships and individuals. Particular areas of expertise include business start-ups, reorganisations, mergers and acquisitions, management buyouts, corporate recovery, restructuring, Stock Exchange listings, venture capital commercial contracts, employment law, financial services, insolvency, property and commercial litigation.

CLIENTELE The client base is strongly international and covers a broad spectrum including shipowners, charterers, banks, insurance companies, foreign governments and ministries, major oil companies, commodity traders and manufacturers.

INTERNATIONAL Many of the firm's lawyers are fluent in several languages including Arabic, Bahasa, Dutch, French, German, Greek, Italian, Mandarin, Portuguese and Spanish.

Thomas Eggar

76 Shoe Lane, London, EC4A 3JB
Tel (020) 7842 0000 **Fax** (020) 7842 3900 **DX** 183 Chancery Lane
Email info@thomaseggar.com **Website** www.thomaseggar.com

The Corn Exchange, Baffins Lane, Chichester, PO19 1GE
Tel (01243) 786111 **Fax** (01243) 775640 **DX** 30300 Chichester
Email info@thomaseggar.com

Sussex House, North Street, Horsham, RH12 1BJ
Tel (01403) 214500 **Fax** (01403) 241457 **DX** 57608 Horsham
Email info@thomaseggar.com

1 Liverpool Gardens, Worthing, BN11 1SL
Tel (01903) 234211 **Fax** (01903) 207641 **DX** 3704 Worthing
Email info@thomaseggar.com

Chatham Court, Lesbourne Road, Reigate, RH2 7FN
Tel (01737) 240111 **Fax** (01737) 248249 **DX** 30400 Reigate 1
Email info@thomaseggar.com

Managing Partner	John Stapleton
Chairman	Neil Hart
Number of partners/partner status	59
Other fee-earners (inc. partners/partner status)	209

CONTACTS	
Agriculture	Richard Kyrke
Banking & Finance	Steven Clifford
Commercial Property	Chris Baker
Company & Commercial	Tony Edwards
Construction	Tina Webster
Debt Recovery	Paula James
E-commerce	Philip Krauss
Employment	Peter Stevens
Financial Services	Anthony Wands
Franchising	Michael Crooks
Insolvency	Martin Cross
Intellectual Property	Tracey Rose
Litigation	Tom McKeown
Mediation/Family	Jill Goldman
Personal Injury	Stephen Richards
Private Client	Patricia Woolgar

THE FIRM Thomas Eggar is one of the country's leading regional law firms. It has over 400 staff with offices across the South East. Thomas Eggar has recently been endorsed as the leading law firm in the South East region by a leading legal magazine. The firm represents a diversified range of clients. It supports some of the largest corporations in the United Kingdom with its leading edge, specialist litigation, commercial property, company commercial, banking and e-commerce expertise. Additionally, the firm has continued to build its pre-eminent private practice, and has the largest solicitor-owned financial services and investment management firm - Thesis Asset Management plc. Recent energies have gone towards building the strength of its commercial practice. The firm offers City-based specialisms through its London office and across all of its regional offices. The firm has built its business around exceptional customer service and this underpins all of its activities. It is the foundation of the firm and assures long-term commitment to its clients. The firm has been accredited with the Law Society's quality mark, Lexcel.

PRINCIPAL AREAS OF WORK Thomas Eggar offers specialist, industry-specific legal expertise that is relied upon by national and international clients.
Commercial Property Work includes property development and investment, environmental issues, construction law, commercial leases and under-leases and station trading lettings. Within the division there is an unparalleled depth of experience and expertise covering the whole of the spectrum of railway property work.
Company Commercial The firm handles acquisitions, mergers and disposals, management buyouts and buyins, terms and conditions of trading and company formations.
Financial The firm handles banking and finance matters. Its associated specialist financial services and investment management firm, Thesis Asset Management plc, has in excess of 600m of client funds under advisory and discretionary management, offering corporate finance services to a range of companies as well as financial planning and investment advice to a large number of private clients.
Litigation Work includes intellectual property, banking, construction, commercial property, professional negligence and e-commerce.
Private Client Services focus on taxation and trusts but also cover residential property, family law, pensions and wills.

Other Areas The firm has also expertise in franchising, insolvency, e-commerce, agriculture, personal injury and employment.

CLIENTELE Thomas Eggar serves a diverse range of clients from local, regional, national and international businesses to well-known personalities and private clients. All clients receive a partner-led, comprehensive service in all areas of legal advice. Major clients include the Alliance & Leicester Group Union Staff, Alliance & Unichem plc, Britannia Pharmaceuticals, British Railways Board in property matters, Brighton & Hove Council, Gleeson, Hamptons Estates Ltd, Maplin plc, Marshall-Tufflex Ltd on the corporate side, Nationwide Building Society, Perfect Pizza, Railtrack plc in property and litigation, as well as Southern Water, The Glanmore Property Fund, West Bromwich Building Society, Wyndeham Press Group plc and Woolwich. The firm is also a leading advisor to the Church of England and various other charities.

INTERNATIONAL Growth has continued through 2001/2002 and the firm has built up its international links that enables the firm's clients to have access to advice in the majority of the American states, and AvrioAdvocati, a formal network of European law firms. It is the result of a merger of two organisations. The organisation provides legal advice for its members and their clients in foreign jurisdictions. It has developed significant legal expertise on a group basis in the areas of sports law, international fraud and telecommunications.

Thompsons

Congress House, Great Russell Street, London, WC1B 3LW **Tel** (020) 7290 0000 **Fax** (020) 7637 0000

Thompson Smith & Puxon

4-5 North Hill, Colchester, CO1 1EB
Tel (01206) 574431 **Fax** (01206) 563174 **DX** 3617 Colchester
Email info@tsplegal.com **Website** www.tsplegal.com

Contact Lindsay Brydson • General practice with two offices. Members of Law Society Family Panel and Childcare, Clinical Negligence and Personal Injury Panels; two solicitors accredited by SFLA. Legal Aid franchise holders.

Thomson Snell & Passmore

3 Lonsdale Gardens, Tunbridge Wells, TN1 1NX
Tel (01892) 510000 **Fax** (01892) 549884 **DX** 3914 Tunbridge Wells 1
Email solicitors@ts-p.co.uk **Website** www.ts-p.co.uk

Stafford House, East Street, Tonbridge, TN9 1HG
Tel (01732) 771211 **Fax** (01732) 770445 **DX** 5502 Tonbridge 1
Email solicitors@ts-p.co.uk

THE FIRM This large regional law firm whose head office is located in Tunbridge Wells is renowned for providing a high quality service, focusing on approachability and friendliness. Thomson Snell & Passmore is an organisation of talented, energetic and efficient lawyers. Founded in 1570 and founder member of The Law South Group, TS&P holds the highly regarded 'Lexcel' award, the Law Society's quality assurance standard. During the last 3 years, the firm has grown substantially in all areas and has a long standing reputation for its expertise, with many of the partners being recognised in the legal press as leaders in their particular area of practice.

PRINCIPAL AREAS OF WORK The extensive range of legal services offered to commercial and private clients can be viewed at the firm's website.

INTERNATIONAL The firm is a founder member of INTERLEGAL with associate offices throughout Europe, the USA and Canada.

Senior Partner	Trevor May
Number of partners	31
Assistant solicitors	24
Other fee-earners	23

CONTACTS	
Charities	Jeremy Passmore
Construction Litigation	David Brown
Commercial Litigation	Peter Radula-Scott
Company & Commercial	James Partridge
Commercial Property	David White
Clinical Negligence	Andrew Watson
E-commerce & Intellectual Property	Henar Dyson
Employment	Nick Hobden
Estate Planning & Trusts	Jeremy Passmore
Family Law	Barbara Wright
Personal Injury	Julie Reynolds
Professional Negligence	Trevor May
Probate	Edward Fardell
Property Development	Gilbert Green
Residential Property	Michael Sugden

Thomson Snell & Passmore

A-Z ■ LAW FIRMS

■ Thomson Webb & Corfield
94 Regent Street, Cambridge, CB2 1DP **Tel** (01223) 578088 **Fax** (01223) 578050

■ Thornhill Ince
Suite 3, Third Floor, Grampian House, 144 Deansgate, Manchester, M3 3ED **Tel** (0161) 839 2550 **Fax** (0161) 819 5005

■ Thorntons WS
50 Castle Street, Dundee, DD1 3RU
Tel (01382) 229111 **Fax** (01382) 202288 **DX** LP29
Email enquiries@thorntonsws.co.uk **Website** www.thorntonsws.co.uk

Ptnrs 25 **Asst solrs** 27 **Other fee-earners** 30 **Contact** Lindsay Wood • Full range of legal services to a wide range of clients, from private individuals to large commercial concerns. Client profile embraces commercial and industrial companies, institutions, public authorities, Higher and Further educational institutions, research institutes, private developers, housing associations, farmers, landowners and private individuals, across Scotland and beyond.

■ Thring Townsend

6 Drakes Meadow, Penny Lane, Swindon, SN3 3LL
Tel (01793) 410200 **Fax** (01793) 539040
Email solicitors@ttuk.com **Website** www.ttuk.com

Midland Bridge, Bath, BA1 2HQ
Tel (01225) 340000 **Fax** (01225) 319735 **DX** 8002 Bath
Email solicitors@ttuk.com

18 London Road, Newbury, RG14 1JX
Tel (01635) 264400 **Fax** (01635) 32877 **DX** 30810 Newbury
Email solicitors@ttuk.com

Senior Partner	Jeremy Thring
Chairman of Management Board	
	Julian George
Number of partners	37
Total staff	294

AREAS OF PRACTICE	
Litigation	32%
Commercial	28%
Private Client	20%
Conveyancing	19%

CONTACTS	
Agriculture	Jonathan Cheal
Banking Law	Brian Jacomb
Building & Construction	David Patterson
Charities	Samantha O'Sullivan
Commercial Litigation	Peter Cusick
Commercial Property	Thomas Sheppard
Company Law	Jonathan Wyld
Education	Stephen Roberts
Employment (Contentious)	Mike Nield
Employment (Non-contentious)	Jonathan Payne
Family	Richard Sharp
Industrial Diseases	Brigitte Chandler
Insolvency	Brian Jacomb
Internet Law	John Forshaw
Investment Management	Adrian Cantwell
IP/IT	John Davies
Options	Alan Goulding
Personal Injury	Huw Ponting
Private Client	Helen Starkie
Probate	Liz Evans
Relocation	William Power
Residential Property	Yvette Morcombe
Sports Law	Stephen Roberts
Tax Planning	Jeremy Thring
Traded Endowment	William Power
Trusts & Tax	Michael Young

THE FIRM Thring Townsend is one of central southern England's leading law firms, providing a focused range of commercial and private client services. With 294 staff and offices in Swindon, Bath and Newbury, the current practice resulted from the merger of Thrings & Long and Townsends in November 2000. Thring Townsend has already acquired a high profile and reputation for results. The new firm offers greater strength and diversity of legal work and has been appointed legal advisor to the largest provider of post secondary education in the region. The firm's client base is impressive, ranging from local subsidiaries of multinational companies to government bodies, charities and family owned enterprises, through to internet start-ups and entrepreneurs. Clients are provided with strong, partner led teams that look for innovative solutions and help provide a value added service. Private client services are tailored to meet specific clients' needs and the private client department is renowned for its high level of personal service. Thring Townsend has achieved IIP accreditation, has a Community Legal Service franchise for personal injury and family work and holds the highly regarded 'Lexcel' award. The firm makes considerable investment in both the skills and welfare of its staff and six trainees are recruited annually.

PRINCIPAL AREAS OF WORK

Company/Commercial An extensive range of corporate work is handled by one of the largest commercial teams in the region. Services include advice on most aspects of company and commercial matters from start-ups to mergers and acquisitions, MBOs, MBIs, Purple Book work, franchising and partnership agreements.

Commercial Property The team offers a broad range of expertise covering landlord and tenant work, specialist options, infrastructure agreements, development and associated pensions work. Clients include a national telecommunications company, a major institutional landlord and many of the region's top companies.

Employment The firm's employment law expertise is well recognised. The team advises on both contentious and non-contentious employment law and handles all employment matters including redundancy, contracts, discrimination, health and safety, equal pay, and employment tribunals.

Agriculture This is an area of key strength and the firm has won the contract for the provision of legal services to NFU members covering central England.

Commercial Litigation The team deals with commercial and construction disputes, licensing, debt recovery, defamation, product liability, landlord and tenant and professional negligence.

Family The renowned family team is one of the largest in central southern England. All lawyers are

members of the SFLA and the Law Society's Children and Family Law panels. Two lawyers are also accredited family mediators.

Personal Injury The reputation of the team is outstanding and the firm has a national reputation in asbestosis, deafness, spinal injuries and serious head injuries for plaintiffs. Sports law is a particular strength and continues to grow in importance.

Private Client Services include all aspects of wills and probate, estate planning and administration as well as tax planning, wealth management, advice for retirement, private self-assessment and investment management.

Traded Endowment The firm has a national reputation for dealing with traded endowment work, covering acquisition, gearing and disposal of policies. Clients include market-makers, banks, funds and corporate investors.

TLT Solicitors

One Redcliff Street, Bristol, BS99 7JZ
Tel (0117) 917 7777   **Fax** (0117) 917 7778   **DX** 7815 Bristol
Website www.tltsolicitors.com

THE FIRM TLT aims to distinguish itself in the minds of its clients as a powerful 'business ally'. Its reputation has been built on an eagerness to understand its clients' businesses and to provide practical, commercial legal solutions. The firm takes the time to understand the needs and aspirations of its clients and its staff. As a leading commercial law firm, TLT's clients include financial institutions, public and private companies as well as family businesses and private individuals. TLT is the UK member of European Law Firm (ELF), which has member firms in over 20 European countries. Although the firm advises a broad spread of clients, it has particular sector expertise in financial services, technology and media, retail and leisure and construction and development. As a modern and dynamic firm, TLT attracts and retains specialist lawyers who understand commercial priorities and have specialist sector knowledge. The firm utilises new technology wherever possible and is continually developing its IT systems in order to deliver a highly efficient and cost effective service.

PRINCIPAL AREAS OF WORK

Corporate Corporate work is handled by one of the largest corporate groups in the region, including corporate finance, acquisitions, disposals, JVs, stock exchange and a substantial amount of AIM and OFEX work. Specialist teams handle tax, IP and partnership issues. The firm has set up one of the first UK Corporate Venturing agencies, TLT Venturing.

Banking TLT is one of the few firms who act for three clearing banks and for six of the top 10 mortgage lenders. The firm provides a comprehensive service to this sector including advising on corporate lending, all types of banking litigation, mortgage documentation, insolvency, in addition to volume recoveries and conveyancing. A specialist unit handles compliance and regulation issues.

Employment Strategic employment work, HR consultancy services and management training is carried out for an impressive national client base, and is complemented by specialist pensions expertise.

Property The firm's property group is particularly strong, with specialist expertise in investment and finance including secured lending, development, planning, landlord and tenant, dispute resolution, management of property portfolios and estates and project based activity. The group includes a number of nationally rated individuals.

Dispute Resolution TLT is renowned for dispute resolution expertise, handling a wide range of heavyweight domestic and international litigation, as well as a substantial amount of ADR work, particularly mediation and arbitration.

Other TLT's client list also includes high net worth individuals whom it advises on both commercial and private issues including family matters, tax and trusts. The firm's family team is widely regarded as the best in the region.

RECRUITMENT
The firm is always looking for individuals who can contribute to its success. See its website for more information on the firm's activities and its ethos.

Managing Partner	David Pester
Senior Partner	Robert Bourns
Number of partners	32
Assistant solicitors	50
Other fee-earners	64

AREAS OF PRACTICE

Banking & Lender Services	29%
Commercial & Corporate	22%
Property	21%
Dispute Resolution	11%
Employment	10%
Family	7%

CONTACTS

Banking & Lender Services	Richard Waller
Commercial	William Hull
Commercial Dispute Resolution	Philip May
Commercial Property	Andrew Glynn
Corporate	Nicole Little
Employment	Alana Weeks
Family	David Woodward
Insolvency	Judith Brown
Planning	Katherine Evans
Tax & Estate Planning	David Bird
	Olivia Kendall
Technology & Media	James Touzel

A-Z ■ LAW FIRMS

TMK Solicitors

County Chambers, 25-27 Weston Road, Southend-on-Sea, SS1 1BB
Tel (01702) 339222 **Fax** (01702) 331563 **DX** 2821 Southend
Email tmk@tmksols.co.uk **Website** www.tmksols.co.uk

Contact Partner	Patrick Musters
Number of partners	9
Assistant solicitors	13
Other fee-earners	18

AREAS OF PRACTICE	
Crime	50%
Family	30%
Civil Litigation	20%

THE FIRM The largest criminal practice and the largest legal aid firm in Essex. The firm holds LSC and CDS contracts covering 10 categories of work including membership of the Serious Fraud Panel. The firm is a litigation specialist with individual solicitors concentrating on a single field of work within crime, family (including childcare) and civil litigation. The firm prides itself on its speed of response and attention to clients' needs. Partners and solicitors are Law Society panel members in their respective fields.

PRINCIPAL AREAS OF WORK Crime, personal injury and civil litigation, social welfare law and immigration, family and childcare. Agency work welcomed.

Tods Murray WS

66 Queen Street, Edinburgh, EH2 4NE
Tel (0131) 226 4771 **Fax** (0131) 225 3676 **DX** ED58
Email maildesk@todsmurray.com **Website** www.todsmurray.com

33 Bothwell Street, Glasgow, G2 6NL
Tel (0141) 275 4771 **Fax** (0141) 275 4781 **DX** 512815 Glasgow Central
Email maildesk@todsmurray.com

Chairman	Peter Misselbrook
Managing Partner	John Biggar
Number of partners	37
Number of fee-earners	114
Total staff	232

AREAS OF PRACTICE	
Corporate	38%
Commercial Property	34%
Private Client	20%
Litigation	8%

CONTACTS	
Agriculture, Landed Estates & Forestry	John Fulton
	Neil King
Banking	Graham Burnside
	Hamish Patrick
Capital Projects/PFI/PPP	William Simmons
	Ian McPake
Charities	Peter Ryden
Commercial Property	Douglas Moffat
	Sandy McEwen
Construction	Ross Campbell
Corporate & Commercial	David Dunsire
	Alistair Burrow
Corporate Finance	Granger Brash
Corporate Financial Services	Chris Athanas
	Martin Thurston Smith
Employment Law	Robert Dobie
	Peter Paterson
Entertainment & Media	Richard Findlay
Hotels & Leisure	Angus McIntyre
Information Technology	Lynn Beaumont
Insolvency	Robert Dobie
Intellectual Property	Lynn Beaumont
Investment Funds	Chris Athanas
Litigation	Michael Simpson
Pensions	Martin Thurston Smith
Planning & Environment	Ian McPake
Residential Property	Gordon Cunningham
Securitisation	Graham Burnside
	Hamish Patrick
Timeshare	David Anderson
Wills, Tax & Trusts	John Biggar

THE FIRM Tods Murray is one of Scotland's leading all service law firms with offices in Edinburgh and Glasgow. It provides specialist advice in corporate, banking, commercial and employment law; capital projects and commercial property law; construction law and commercial litigation; private clients; agriculture and estate law; investment funds and corporate financial services; e-commerce, IT and IP; media and entertainment law; leisure and timeshare. Tods Murray takes a commercial approach to the changing needs of all its clients, building and maintaining close client relationships and establishing trust and confidence. Access to information and the delivery of the firm's service is supported by investment in the latest IT systems. Tods Murray provides the highest quality of professional advice and expertise in a competitive market.

PRINCIPAL AREAS OF WORK
Corporate The corporate team is recognised for its experience in corporate finance including public issues, acquisitions, placings and buyouts, and expertise in pension schemes.
Banking The banking team has extensive experience in corporate and public sector lending, project finance, property finance and securitisation.
Capital Projects The capital projects team deals with all capital and infrastructure projects including PFI/PPP with particular expertise in healthcare, water, waste to energy, social housing and local authority projects.
Commercial Property The commercial property team, which specialises in major developments and funding agreements, acts for insurers, pension funds and property companies in relation to their property portfolios. The team also offers advice on planning, construction and environmental projects.
Litigation The litigation team handles all types of commercial and civil litigation and employment issues across the firm for both commercial and private clients.
Private Client The private client team, with a renowned reputation, undertakes all legal work associated with landed estates and farms. The team deals with wills, trusts and executries, charities, tax and estate planning, financial management (for both individuals and trusts) and the purchase and sale of residential property.
Other Areas T2M is an integrated team of experts in e-commerce, intellectual property, information technology, and media and entertainment. Tods Murray has an investment funds and corporate financial services team which is recognised as having a leading reputation, and a specialist hotels and leisure team with significant expertise including timeshare.

CLIENTELE Tods Murray's clients include banks and financial institutions, listed and private companies, public sector organisations, property investors and developers, large and small businesses, land owners and private individuals.

INTERNATIONAL On an international level, membership of Multilaw provides the firm with a network of associated law firms located in the world's major commercial centres.

RECRUITMENT The firm is committed to the recruitment and continued training and development of high quality staff.

Toller Beattie
Queens House, Queen Street, Barnstaple, EX32 8TS **Tel** (01271) 375821 **Fax** (01271) 374762

Toller Hales & Collcutt
Castilian Chambers, 2 Castilian Street, Northampton, NN1 1JX **Tel** (01604) 258558 **Fax** (01604) 258500

Tozers

Broadwalk House, Southernhay West, Exeter, EX1 1UA
Tel (01392) 207020 **Fax** (01392) 207019 **DX** 8322
Email enquiries@tozers.co.uk **Website** www.tozers.co.uk

Strand Chambers, Dawlish, EX7 9EZ
Tel (01626) 862323 **Fax** (01626) 866851 **DX** 82100 Dawlish

2-3 Orchard Gardens, Teignmouth, TQ14 8DR
Tel (01626) 772376 **Fax** (01626) 770317 **DX** 82051 Teignmouth

8-10 St Paul's Road, Newton Abbot, TQ12 4PR
Tel (01626) 207020 **Fax** (01626) 207019 **DX** 59102 Newton Abbot

73 Abbey Road, Torquay, TQ2 5NN
Tel (01803) 407020 **Fax** (01803) 407021 **DX** 59023 Torquay 1

9 The Crescent, Plymouth, PL1 3AB
Tel (01752) 206460 **Fax** (01752) 301662 **DX** 118106 Plymouth

Managing Partner	Peter Edwards
Chairman	Graham Bond
Number of partners	18
Assistant solicitors	16
Other fee-earners	21

AREAS OF PRACTICE

Litigation	32%
Commercial	30%
Property	21%
Probate	17%

CONTACTS

Charities & Schools	Richard King
Children & Family	Patrick Towey
Clinical Negligence	Tim Dyde
Commercial Lending	Richard Thorneycroft
Employment	Jill Headford
Leisure, Planning & Mobile Home Law	Tony Beard
Litigation	Jill Headford
Private Client	Vernon Clarke
Property	Richard Thorneycroft

THE FIRM Tozers has a long and distinguished history of service to clients. Established in Devon over 200 years ago, the firm has adapted and continues to adapt to the rapidly changing environment for legal services.

PRINCIPAL AREAS OF WORK Specialist teams have been developed to ensure expertise in these niche areas:

Leisure & Environmental Law The firm's expertise includes licensing and caravan parks and mobile homes law.

Charities & Schools The team advises religious, educational, health/disability and other charities, as well as schools in both the private and state sectors.

Property & Planning In both the commercial and residential sectors, with a member on the Law Society's Planning Panel.

Employment The team continues to expand and the emphasis remains on employer advice and representation.

Litigation Work includes professional negligence, business and property disputes and debt recovery.

Family & Childcare One of the strongest teams in the South West, dealing with all aspects of family law. Six Law Society Children Panel members, including a panel assessor and interviewer.

Clinical Negligence & Personal Injury The firm's reputation has grown in the areas of birth injury, gynaecology and cardiac surgery, with members on the Law Society's Clinical Negligence and Personal Injury Panels.

Private Client The team covers wills, probate, tax and trusts, including tax planning and investment management for trusts and individuals.

Commercial Lending & Recovery The team acts on behalf of banks and financial institutions.

Additional Areas All agency work.

A-Z LAW FIRMS

Travers Smith Braithwaite

10 Snow Hill, London, EC1A 2AL
Tel (020) 7295 3000 **Fax** (020) 7295 3500 **DX** 79
Email Travers.Smith@TraversSmith.com **Website** www.traverssmith.com

THE FIRM Travers Smith Braithwaite is a leading corporate, financial and commercial law firm with the expertise and capability to advise on a wide range of business activities. Today's clients include regulatory, financial, trade and industrial organisations throughout the UK and from all over the world. Travers Smith Braithwaite prides itself on not being so large as to have an impersonal atmosphere but enjoys a quality of work and a range of clients normally associated with larger firms. By resisting rapid growth and focusing on quality, the firm has been able to maintain the high standards of service it provides to clients. Closely-knit and consistent teams of lawyers will provide advice to a client year in year out, ensuring a clear understanding of the client's business and an effective working relationship. Central to the firm's approach is the philosophy that partners should be closely involved in most of the matters undertaken and that delegation should not be automatic but considered in every case in the light of both effectiveness and cost.

PRINCIPAL AREAS OF WORK The firm's business comprises eight main areas:

Corporate Law Takeovers, mergers and acquisitions, new issues, company law, financial services and regulatory law, private equity and venture capital.

Commercial Law Joint ventures, EU and competition law, intellectual property, information technology, multi-media, privatisations and broadcasting.

Banking/Corporate Recovery Secured and unsecured lending, finance leasing, acquisition finance, trade and project finance, property finance, capital markets, banking regulations, rescheduling and insolvency.

Employment Executive service agreements, restrictive covenants, health and safety, works councils and employee consultation, industrial disputes and employment litigation, employment aspects of mergers, acquisitions and reorganisations (including transfers of undertakings).

Dispute Resolution Domestic and international, commercial litigation, arbitration and ADR.

Property Investment, acquisition, disposal and development of industrial, retail and office property, planning and construction law.

Pensions Establishment, administration and winding up of pension funds and pension litigation.

Tax Domestic and international corporate tax planning, acquisition and structured finance, employee share (and other) incentive schemes, private client tax planning.

INTERNATIONAL The firm enjoys a close working relationship with leading law firms in each of the main foreign jurisdictions. The firm believes that generally its clients' best interests are served by the firm having access to, and the ability to select, established overseas firms which have the necessary expertise and experience. This approach also allows the firm the flexibility to work with a client's existing advisors in different jurisdictions or to select alternative advisors where conflicts of interest arise. Travers Smith Braithwaite opened a Paris liaison office in April 1999. The office sources and manages the provision of French legal services to the firm and its UK and overseas clients. In addition, the office acts as a liaison between French clients (including French law firms) and the London office. In November 2001, due to the contraction of independent German legal practices, Travers Smith Braithwaite opened a Berlin office when Dr Karl Pilny and his team joined the firm. The office advises on all aspects of German law and is of particular help to the various practice areas in London where their clients or work involves a German dimension. The firm can handle work in French, German, Italian, and Spanish.

RECRUITMENT Travers Smith Braithwaite continues to develop and is always looking to recruit at both assistant and trainee level, people of academic excellence and sound judgement who are able to take their careers, but not themselves, seriously. The firm's training philosophy is that skill and expertise are best acquired through practical experience complemented by carefully targeted formal instruction. Great emphasis is placed on ensuring that trainees are actively involved in a broad range of work. Applications for traineeships should be made in writing to Germaine Vangeyzel (Graduate Recruitment Coordinator) enclosing a full CV together with the names and addresses of academic and personal referees.

Managing Partner	Christopher Carroll
Senior Partner	Christopher Bell
UK	
Number of partners	51
Assistant solicitors	111
Other fee-earners	41
International	
Number of partners	2
Assistant solicitors	5

AREAS OF PRACTICE	
Corporate	38%
Litigation	15%
Property	15%
Finance	14%
Tax	8%
Pensions	5%
Employment	5%

CONTACTS	
Banking	Neil Murray
Commercial	Margaret Moore
Competition & EU law	Margaret Moore
Construction	Peter Hill
Corporate	Oliver Barnes
Corporate Recovery	Jeremy Walsh
Dispute Resolution	John Kingston
Employment	Andrew Lilley
Environment	Alison Lea
Financial Services	Margaret Chamberlain
Insurance/Reinsurance	Stephen Paget-Brown
Pensions	Paul Stannard
Planning	Alison Lea
Private Equity	Chris Hale
Property	Robert Harman
Tax	Alasdair Douglas

Trethowans

College Chambers, New Street, Salisbury, SP1 2LY
Tel (01722) 412512 **Fax** (01722) 411300 **DX** 58004 SALISBURY
Email info@trethowans.com **Website** www.trethowans.com

The Director General's House, Rockstone Place, Southampton, SO15 2EP
Tel (023) 8032 1000 **Fax** (023) 8032 1001 **DX** 49678 SOUTHAMPTON 2

Managing Partner	Miles Brown
Number of partners	17
Assistant solicitors	19
Other fee-earners	25

AREAS OF PRACTICE	
Commercial	19%
Commercial Property	18%
Personal Injury	22%
Residential Property	14%
Licensing	7%
Private Client	13%
Family	7%

CONTACTS	
Company/Commercial	Catherine MacRae
Property	Miles Brown
	John Fletcher
Commercial Litigation	Phil Banks-Welsh
Employment	James Humphery
Personal Injury	Neil Elliott
	Chris Whiteley
Licensing	Michael Messent
Private Client	Michael Ricketts
	Elizabeth Webbe
IP/E-business	Owen Santry

THE FIRM One of the largest and strongest general law firms in the South of England, this expanding firm provides a complete range of legal services for both commercial and private clients. Genuine expertise and increasing reputations in key areas are a feature of the firm. Its commercial client expertise is increasingly focused on the Southampton office. The private client expertise is spread across the firm but the Salisbury office is at its core. Teams of specialists work as client needs dictate, either individually or, particularly on corporate work and larger litigation cases, in team groups. The firm places an unusually high emphasis on 'knowing its clients' and their objectives. The firm regards its commercial services as providing large London law firm expertise but with more competitive cost structures, and with close direct partner involvement in the work in hand.

PRINCIPAL AREAS OF WORK

Commercial Client Work Licensing Services The firm has an unrivalled reputation in betting, gaming and liquor licensing. Work is undertaken nationwide for Ladbrokes, Pizza Hut, Bacardi-Martini and other household names.

Commercial Property Services A strong client base involving all types of commercial property and significant project work, including insolvency. Again, the firm acts for major national companies in this area.

Commercial & Business Services An experienced team dealing with major clients shared with other groups within the firm, as well as its own client base. A wide range of corporate work including acquisitions, disposals, management-led transactions, share options and commercial contracts of various kinds. Specialist areas include e-business, business recovery, intellectual property, IT and employment.

Commercial Litigation Services This includes advisory as well as straightforward representational work in all areas including credit management, general claims and liability cases, IP and employment.

Private Client Work Litigation Services This group has a strong reputation for its personal injury and medical negligence work. It acts for both claimants and defendants.

Family Services An experienced team of accredited family law specialists dealing with all aspects of marriage/relationship breakdown.

Property Services, Tax, Trusts & Agricultural/Estates Services These areas remain an important part of the practice. The firm has an established and strong client base requiring these services.

CLIENTELE The firm's clients range from major quoted public companies to start-up businesses, and from private individuals to large landed estates.

Trevor Smyth & Co
13 Chichester Street, Belfast, BT1 4JB **Tel** (028) 9032 0360 **Fax** (028) 9032 5636

A-Z LAW FIRMS

Trowers & Hamlins

Sceptre Court, 40 Tower Hill, London, EC3N 4DX
Tel (020) 7423 8000   **Fax** (020) 7423 8001   **DX** 774 CDE Lon/City
Email marketing@trowers.com   **Website** www.trowers.com

Heron House, Albert Square, Manchester, M2 5HD
Tel (0161) 211 0000   **Fax** (0161) 211 0001   **DX** 14323 Manchester 1
Email marketing@trowers.com

Portland House, Longbrook Street, Exeter, EX4 6AB
Tel (01392) 217466   **Fax** (01392) 221047   **DX** 134051 Exeter 15
Email marketing@trowers.com

Senior Partner	Jonathan Adlington
UK	
Number of partners	54
Assistant solicitors	72
Other fee-earners	40
International	
Number of partners	10
Assistant solicitors	9
Other fee-earners	7

AREAS OF PRACTICE	
Property (Housing, Public Sector, Commercial Property)	39%
Company/Commercial & Construction	37%
Litigation	19%
Private Client	5%

CONTACTS	
Banking	Ralph Picken
Charities	Ian Davis
Commercial Property	Elizabeth McKibbin
Construction	David Mosey
Corporate	Jennie Gubbins
Corporate Finance	Jennie Gubbins
Employment	Emma Burrows
Environmental	Ian Doolittle
Health	Joanne Easterbrook
Housing (General)	Ian Graham
Housing Finance	Sarah Hayes
Housing Projects (General)	Jonathan Adlington
International Projects	Martin Amison
Litigation	John Linwood
	Don Moorhouse
Private Client	Luke Valner
Projects/PFI	Ian Graham
	Jonh Holden-Ross
Public Sector	Ian Doolittle
Tax	Neil Cohen

THE FIRM City and international law firm Trowers & Hamlins continues to flourish through successful specialisations developed across a broadly-based commercial, property, litigation and private client practice. Particular strengths include housing and housing finance, local government, UK and international projects, company commercial, construction, commercial property and public/private sector initiatives including private finance. Other specialisations include the health sector, environmental law, employment and charities. Trowers & Hamlins provides clear, practical solutions to achieve its clients' objectives. In all matters a client partner will call on appropriate lawyers and resources within the firm to fulfil the particular requirements of the client's brief. The firm's clients include banks, public and private companies, national and local government departments, NHS Trusts, housing bodies, partnerships, charities and individuals.

PRINCIPAL AREAS OF WORK Through its UK offices and internationally, the firm has developed a dynamic corporate and commercial practice. Particular strengths are recognised in its UK and international finance and project work, including PFI and other DBFO schemes. As leading lawyers to the housing movement, the firm's London, Manchester and Exeter offices advise government bodies, lenders and some 250 housing associations. In addition, the firm has an impressive commercial litigation reputation and a highly regarded private client practice.
Corporate The department is a substantial team with a growing City profile. It advises public and private companies and individuals operating in the financial, property, industrial and commercial sectors.
Projects & Construction This department advises UK and international clients in a variety of sectors, spanning innovative PFI/DBFO project structures and joint venture/partnering initiatives.
Property The department covers commercial, housing, local authority, residential, estate and institutional law. It has a substantial team and has established a reputation for innovation, working in the forefront of changing legislation. It provides a wide range of services to corporate clients, international businesses and individuals. Clients include investment institutions, developers, housing associations and local authorities.
Litigation This department deals with a wide range of commercial civil litigation, arbitration and ADR both nationally and internationally, with a particular profile in professional and negligence cases. It is also involved in banking, property, insolvency, employment and personal injury work. The department has a high reputation for its construction work, including mediation and adjudication.
Private Client The department provides legal advice to individuals with industrial or commercial wealth, invested assets or landed estates. It is concerned particularly with tax planning, trusts, wills, probate, charities and the administration of trusts and estates.

INTERNATIONAL The firm has a strong international practice, particularly in the Middle East, where it has offices in Abu Dhabi, Bahrain, Cairo, Dubai and Oman. It is particularly well known for its energy and infrastructure projects.

RECRUITMENT The firm is always happy to hear from lawyers interested in working in a commercial environment. It recruits at least 12-15 trainee solicitors each year.

TROWERS & HAMLINS

Tuckers
39 Warren Street, London, W1T 6AF   **Tel** (020) 7388 8333   **Fax** (020) 7388 7333

LAW FIRMS A-Z

Tughans

Marlborough House, 30 Victoria Street, Belfast, BT1 3GS
Tel (028) 9055 3300 **Fax** (028) 9055 0096 **DX** 433NR Belfast 1
Email law@tughans.com **Website** www.tughans.com

Number of partners	13
Assistant solicitors	15
Other fee-earners	12

AREAS OF PRACTICE

Corporate	30%
Litigation	30%
Property	30%
Banking	10%

CONTACTS

Banking & Finance	John Mills
Commercial Litigation	Michael McCord
Commercial Property	Phyllis Agnew
Conveyancing/Building Estates	John Mills
Corporate	John-George Willis
	Ian Coulter
Employment & Labour Law	Grahame Loughlin
Environmental Law	Deirdre Magill
Litigation & Insurance	Michael Gibson
M&A	John-George Willis
	Ian Coulter
Private Client	John Irwin

THE FIRM Tughans was established in 1896 and has developed over the years into one of the largest firms of solicitors in Northern Ireland. The firm provides clear, sound advice to its clients supported by the latest technological developments. The principal practice areas within the firm are defence litigation, commercial property and corporate work. Tughans has a formal association with one of the leading Dublin corporate law firms, William Fry, enabling both firms to offer an all-Ireland service. A significant number of new instructions are received on the recommendations of other law firms principally in the City of London with whom Tughans has, over the years, developed strong links. These relationships mean that Tughans is regularly involved in the Northern Ireland element of multijurisdictional transactions.

PRINCIPAL AREAS OF WORK

Litigation The firm handles a broad range of litigation and arbitration and is particularly active in insurance defence work.

Employment Tughans acts for many of Northern Ireland's larger employers in both the public and private sector. The firm deals with contentious matters including unfair dismissal, discrimination, restrictive covenants and breach of contract and non-contentious matters including advice on service agreements, policies and procedures and employment aspects of mergers and acquisitions.

Commercial Property The firm acts for a broad range of Irish and UK-based property developers, institutions, investors and national retail chains in connection with developments, town centre regeneration, joint ventures, PFI projects, sales and purchases and leases of commercial and industrial property in Northern Ireland.

Corporate The firm has been involved in a number of high profile corporate transactions in Northern Ireland in recent years. Principal activities include acquisitions, mergers, share issues in public and private companies, inward investments, joint ventures and shareholder agreements.

Banking The firm acts for a heavyweight client list of national and international banks and financial institutions requiring assets and securitisation advice.

Tunnard & Co

Cathedral Chambers, 4 Kirkgate, Ripon, HG4 1PA **Tel** (01765) 600421 **Fax** (01765) 690523

Turbervilles with Nelson Cuff

122 High Street, Uxbridge, UB8 1JT
Tel (01895) 201700 **Fax** (01895) 273519 **DX** 45116 Uxbridge
Email solicitors@turbervilles.co.uk **Website** www.turbervilles.co.uk

Senior Partner	Sess Sigré
Managing Partner	Russell Hallam
Number of partners	11
Total staff	90

CONTACTS

Corporate/Commercial	Sess Sigré
Commercial Property	Tim Sellers
Licensing	David Smith
Civil Litigation	Robert Dixon
Family	Annabel O'Sullivan
Private Client	Russell Hallam

THE FIRM Turbervilles with Nelson Cuff is one of the leading commercial firms situated within the outer West London sector with main offices easily accessible from the M25, M40, and M1 at Uxbridge and Harrow. It is a broad-based practice offering a comprehensive range of legal services to both commercial and private clients. The practice prides itself on a dynamic, flexible and pragmatic approach in the provision of service whilst at the same time being mindful of giving excellent value for money which is based on a clear charging structure. The practice has an impressive range of clients within its portfolio including many plcs, blue chip and multinational companies and often finds itself working with the much larger City of London practices. It also has a very strong local client following within the West London sector and also often benefits from the referral of more complex cases from other practices. Emphasis is placed on building long term relations with every one of the firm's clients, and developing a complete understanding of their requirements. Staff are encouraged whenever possible to provide comprehensive business advice and take a wider view of all matters consulted on. The practice is looking towards the future and in doing so continues to invest heavily, not only in both the skills and welfare of its staff, but also in information technology where the aim is to improve efficiency for all and develop scales of economy for the benefits of its clients. In order to provide clients with the best possible service, Turbervilles with Nelson Cuff has organised itself into a clearly defined departmental structure with specialist teams. This grouping of expertise, which can be flexible to meet individual clients needs, ensures the provision of the highest quality service and standards at all times. Turbervilles with Nelson Cuff will continue to expand its commercial expertise. To do this it will increase the number of high-grade lawyers it employs so that the service it gives to its clients remains at the very highest level.

Other Offices Harrow, Hillingdon, and Uxbridge.

Continued overleaf

A-Z ■ LAW FIRMS

PRINCIPAL AREAS OF WORK

Commercial Practice The firm's commercial practice covers commercial contracts, competition law, mergers and acquisitions and all aspects of finance, funding and commercial credit. It also handles franchising, private finance initiative work (National Health Service Trusts) and health sector law and has expertise in telecommunications law. In addition it deals with agency and distribution agreements.

Civil Litigation Department Deals with general commercial litigation in the High Court and lower Courts. It covers all employment matters (which is a speciality) including health and safety, data protection, general civil litigation, insolvency and debt recovery including volume recovery work. In addition it is building up a niche area practice on all aspects of mobile homes.

Commercial Property Commercial property is a particular area of expertise with the department handling all areas of land development and construction, mineral rights and planning and environmental law. Considerable work is undertaken in the landlord and tenant field.

Licensing The firm has a niche department, which specialises almost exclusively with liquor licensing work. It also has expertise in and deals with, for historical reason, animal welfare issues.

Private Client Services to private clients include finance and estate planning - trusts both general and charitable, wills and probate, tax planning, inheritance arrangements, asset protection. In particular the department provides a tailored range of planning services for the elderly. The financial services arm of the practice is linked to this department and through a team of Independent Financial Advisors provides advice on a wide range of matters.

Residential Conveyancing All aspects of residential conveyancing are dealt with including the sale and purchase of properties through the firm's estate agencies.

Family & Matrimonial Department Handles separations and divorces, ancillary relief and childcare matters.

Criminal Criminal matters are dealt with for both prosecution and defence. In addition, the firm has a Legal Aid franchise for the family and matrimonial department and offers to carry out work as agents to other solicitors.

Turcan Connell

Princes Exchange, 1 Earl Grey Street, Edinburgh, EH3 9EE
Tel (0131) 228 8111 **Fax** (0131) 228 8118 **DX** 723300 Edin 43
Email enquiries@turcanconnell.com **Website** www.turcanconnell.com

THE FIRM Turcan Connell is the leading Scottish private client practice. It concentrates exclusively on the needs of private clients, trusts, charities and those involved with rural property. As well as a strong team of lawyers, the firm has a large number of other professionals, including an investment management team, a consulting actuary, a life assurance expert, a tax compliance and a trust accounting team. The Guernsey office specialises in the management of offshore trusts and companies, Turcan Connell being the only Scottish firm to offer such a facility, which is a unique and integral part of the service provided to its clients.

PRINCIPAL AREAS OF WORK

Personal Tax & Financial Planning The firm acts for a wide range of clients including entrepreneurs, estate owners, expatriates and professionals. The work includes inheritance tax and capital gains tax planning, the handling of large and complex estates, and advice to shareholders on corporate transactions. Tax and financial planning and asset protection involve extensive use of trusts, including their establishment, variation and termination. The firm has one of the largest trust management practices in the UK with over 2000 trusts under management. Offshore trusts are used where appropriate.

Financial Services This service is seen as integral to the all-round service provided to private clients, trusts and charities, incorporating an investment management team and pensions and life assurance advice.

Agriculture & Estates The firm advises on all aspects of rural property throughout Scotland, including purchase and sale of estates and their commercial development; farming and agricultural law; fishing and sporting law; and the commercial exploitation of rural property including wind farm developments. The firm is active in the residential and small estate market particularly in Edinburgh, Lothian, the Borders, Fife and Perthshire.

Family & Litigation Advice is given in relation to separation and divorce and the negotiation of financial settlements; and employment and related matters. The arrival of Alasdair Loudon has greatly strengthened this area of the firm's work.

Charity Law & Heritage Property Charity law is an area of great importance to the firm. The range of charitable clients advised by the firm covers all types of charity from small privately established bodies to major national institutions, and includes grant giving and grant receiving bodies. The firm has a particular expertise in heritage property, acting for the owners of over 150 historic houses.

Joint Senior Partners	Robert Turcan
	Douglas Connell
Number of partners	15
Assistant solicitors	30
Other fee-earners	48

AREAS OF PRACTICE	
Tax & Trusts	35%
Agriculture & Estates	35%
Pensions & Investment	15%
Charity	10%
Family Law	5%

CONTACTS	
Agriculture & Estates	Robert Turcan
	Malcolm Strang Steel
	Jonathan Robertson
	Adam Gillingham
Charities	Robin Fulton
	Neil MacLeod
	Simon Mackintosh
Heritage Property	Douglas Connell
Litigation/Family	Alasdair Loudon
Private Client/Trusts	Douglas Connell
	Simon Mackintosh
	Robin Fulton
Tax	Ian Clark
	Heather Thompson

TURCAN CONNELL
SOLICITORS

LAW FIRMS ■ A-Z

■ Turnbull, Simson & Sturrock WS

26 High Street, Jedburgh, TD8 6AE
Tel (01835) 862391   **Fax** (01835) 862017   **DX** 581223 Jedburgh
Email mail@tssjed.co.uk

Ptnrs 2   **Other fee-earners** 4   **Contact** David Sturrock • Offers a broad range of services. Expertise in relation to agricultural law.

Turner Parkinson

Hollins Chambers, 64a Bridge Street, Manchester, M3 3BA
Tel (0161) 833 1212   **Fax** (0161) 834 9098   **DX** 14373 Manchester
Email tp@tp.co.uk   **Website** www.tp.co.uk

THE FIRM This Manchester-based firm of commercial law specialists has deliberately developed a broad portfolio of services that focuses on the needs of owner-managed businesses, providing them with the very best partner-led legal advice at a highly competitive price. Its results-driven philosophy and highly competitive fee structure is particularly appealing to entrepreneurs, although clients also include larger corporations and institutions.

PRINCIPAL AREAS OF WORK

Company/Commercial Work includes company formation, company restructuring, directors' duties, partnership law, franchising, agency and distribution, contract negotiations and drafting, competition law and pensions.

Corporate Finance The team handles raising finance, venture capital, share, business and asset sales and purchases, joint ventures and shareholders' agreements.

Intellectual Property Trademarks, passing off, copyright, design right and registered design, patents and confidentiality are handled. Computer contracts and entertainment law are other niche areas of excellence.

Commercial Litigation The firm handles breach of contract, defective goods, financial claims, construction disputes and defamation. Professional negligence and insolvency are particular specialisms.

Employment Work includes terms of employment, service agreements, restraint of trade, transfer of undertakings, discrimination, termination of employment, redundancy and unfair or wrongful dismissal.

Commercial Property Sales, purchases and exchanges, options, auctions and tenders, commercial leases, residential tenancies, mortgages and planning applications are handled.

Private Client The firm handles divorce and family matters; residential property matters.

Managing Partner	Mark Openshaw-Blower
Senior Partner	Nick Davenport
Number of partners	7
Assistant solicitors	16
Other fee-earners	5

AREAS OF PRACTICE	
Company Commercial	40%
Litigation	35%
Property	20%
Private Client	5%

CONTACTS	
Company/Commercial	Nick Davenport
	Richard Parkinson
	Mark Openshaw-Blower
	Andrew Booth
Litigation	Malcolm Hunnisett
	Phil Turner
	Mark Lund
Private Client	Janet Fleming
	Sharon Lund
Property	David Blackburn
	Mike Livesey
	Colette Johnson

turnerparkinson
solicitors

■ Turpin & Miller

2nd Floor, Kennett House, London Road, Headington, Oxford, OX3 9AW   **Tel** (01865) 308200

■ TV Edwards

Park House, 29 Mile End Road, London, E1 4TP
Tel (020) 7790 7000   **Fax** (020) 7702 7178   **DX** 300700 Tower Hamlets
Email enquiries@tvedwards.com

AREAS OF PRACTICE	
Criminal	38%
Civil	34%
Family	28%

Contact Anthony Edwards • TV Edwards is a substantial legal aid practice using its specialist skills to develop a growing private practice. The criminal department belongs to the serious fraud panel. There is an active family department. The civil department undertake personal injury, employment, housing, mental health, community care and welfare benefit cases.

A-Z ■ LAW FIRMS

Tweedie & Prideaux (incorporating Wood, Nash Kimber)

5 Lincoln's Inn Fields, London, WC2A 3BT
Tel (020) 7405 1234 **Fax** (020) 7831 1525 **DX** 6 London/Ch.Ln
Email enquiry@tweedieandprideaux.co.uk **Website** www.tweedieandprideaux.co.uk

Number of partners	11
Assistant solicitors	1
Other fee-earners	12

AREAS OF PRACTICE	
Probate & Trusts	33%
Residential Conveyancing	17%
Litigation	16%
Commercial Conveyancing	14%
Commercial	12%
Other Private Client Work	4%
Charities	4%

THE FIRM Tweedie & Prideaux was joined in September 1998 by the firm of Wood Nash Kimber which had previously been in Raymond Buildings, Gray's Inn since 1826, and which brought with it a greater international dimension. Both are long-established practices with Tweedie & Prideaux being at the same address since 1864. The firm undertakes commercial and company work; banking law; foreign and UK commercial and residential property; agricultural property; town and country planning; landlord and tenant; UK and offshore wills, trusts, and probate; business and personal taxation; matrimonial and family; commercial and general civil litigation and work for charities.

INTERNATIONAL The firm has connections in France, Germany, Zimbabwe and Albania. Work is handled in French, German, and Spanish.

RECRUITMENT In September 2000, Michael Fowler joined the firm as a consultant from Scott Fowler, and in January 2001 David Eldridge joined as a consultant from Lee & Pembertons.

Tyndallwoods

Windsor House, Temple Row, Birmingham, B2 5TS
Tel (0121) 624 1111 **Fax** (0121) 624 8401 **DX** 13039 Birmingham 1
Email Mike_Dyer@tyndallwoods.co.uk

Areas of Practice	
Legal Aid	80%
Private Client	20%

Contact Mike Dyer • Undertakes a wide range of contracted work within the Community Legal Service and private client work.

Underwood & Co (incorporating Corbould Rigby & Co)

40 Welbeck Street, London, W1G 8LN
Tel (020) 7526 6000 **Fax** (020) 7526 6001 **DX** 9074 West End
Email enquiries@underwoodco.com

Managing Partner	Peter Hughes
Senior Partner	Hilary Guest
Number of partners	8
Assistant solicitors	9
Other fee-earners	3

CONTACTS	
Commercial	Peter Hughes
Commercial Property	Leona Mason
Employment	Roger Digby
Litigation	James Baird
	Paul Redfern
Private Client	Hilary Guest
Property Development	Louise Reid
Property Finance	Justin Roche

THE FIRM Founded in 1845, Underwood & Co is a forward-looking firm with a broad client base including banks, partnerships, public and private companies and private clients.

PRINCIPAL AREAS OF WORK All aspects of property, property finance, healthcare, banking and commercial litigation, professional negligence litigation, insolvency, company/commercial, employment law and private client work.

LAW FIRMS A-Z

Underwoods

83/85 Marlowes, Hemel Hempstead, HP1 1LF
Tel (01442) 430900 Fax (01442) 239861
Email underwoods@compuserve.com Website www.underwoods-solicitors.com

Managing Partner	Robert Males
Number of partners	3
Assistant solicitors	8
Other fee-earners	8

AREAS OF PRACTICE

Employment	30%
Personal Injury	25%
Litigation	15%
Local Governt/Administrative & Public Law	10%
Human Rights	10%
Other	10%

CONTACTS

Administrative/Public Law	Kerry Underwood
Clinical Negligence	Joanna McGlew
Employment	Marc Jones
Human Rights	Kerry Underwood
Litigation	Fiona Hewitt
Personal Injury	Nichola Pitman
Private Client	Robert Males

THE FIRM Underwoods is a flagship firm and a model for other law firms. It has pioneered contingency and conditional fees, menu pricing and fixed fees and is one of the very few secretary-free law firms. The firm prides itself on its innovative approach. The firm specialises in civil litigation and is particularly well-known for its employment, personal injury and public and administrative law work. It provides a distinctive high-quality service and with its unparalleled standards of client care, Underwoods' glowing reputation is fully deserved. It is one of the best firms of its size. Kerry Underwood leads a team of talented specialist solicitors. Three solicitors are on the Law Society Personal Injury Panel and Marc Jones and Kerry Underwood are members of the Employment Law Advisers Appeal Scheme (formerly the Employment Appeal Tribunal Advice Scheme) and on the Equal Opportunities Commission Panel of Solicitors. The firm undertakes agency advocacy in the Employment Appeal Tribunal as well as Employment Tribunals. The firm has no Legal Aid franchises or contracts and offers a genuinely independent service. The firm's senior partner is a leading authority on conditional fees and author of the best-seller No Win No Fee No Worries first published to huge critical acclaim in 1998. He is editor of the Costs Products section of Butterworths Personal Injury Litigation Service, on the editorial board of the Law Society's Litigation Funding, and editor of Employment Litigation; he also conducts seminars for the Univeristy of Cambridge, the Law Society and contributes to radio, television and to legal journals. He is a former Chairman of Employment Tribunals and a fellow of the Chartered Institute of Arbitrators. Robert Males lectures for a number of concerns. Marc Jones is joint editor of Employment Litigation. The firm is a consultant to Commonwealth Governments, government departments, local authorities and law firms large and small. Dominic Regan is now associated with the firm in this capacity.

PRINCIPAL AREAS OF WORK

Employment Work includes pensions, human rights, transfer of undertakings regulations, sex, race and disability discrimination, maternity law, EU law, Employment Tribunal and Employment Appeal Tribunal advocacy, redundancy and contract, and severance.

Litigation Work includes personal injury, claimant and defendant (Law Society's Personal Injury Panel), clinical negligence, intellectual property matters, debt recovery and contractual disputes.

Administrative/Public Law Work includes judicial review, education, civil liberty matters, discrimination, human rights and local authority work.

Local Government Law Work includes education law, judicial reviews, joint ventures, leasing and funding, transfers of undertakings and human rights.

CLIENTELE Includes major companies (including many plcs), local authorities and employees. Kerry Underwood and Marc Jones are members of the Employment Law Advisers Appeal Scheme (formerly the Employment Appeal Tribunal Advice Scheme), and are both on the Equal Opportunities Commission Panel.

Uría & Menéndez

Royex House, Aldermanbury Square, London, EC2V 7NJ
Tel (020) 7367 0080 Fax (020) 7600 1718
Email rmn@uria.com Website www.uria.com

Managing Partner	Rodrigo Uría Meruéndano
Number of partners	56
Assistant solicitors	199

AREAS OF PRACTICE

Banking & Securities	40%
Energy & Project Finance	30%
Corporate & M&A	30%

CONTACTS

London Office	Rafael Molina
Madrid Office	Charles Coward
	José Pérez Santos
	Rafael Sebastián
	José María Segovia

THE FIRM Founded in the 1940s, Uría & Menéndez established itself as a partnership in 1973. Faithful to the tradition begun by Professor Uria, the firm combines the day-to-day practice of law with its scientific and scholarly study. Uría & Menéndez prides itself on the quality of its legal advice, attention to clients, professional objectivity and enduring professional relationships with clients. Currently, the firm comprises 56 partners, 199 associates and over 50 trainee lawyers. A considerable number of Uría & Menéndez's members are actively involved in academic and university life and are authors of numerous legal publications. The London office provides advice on Spanish law to international clients operating from the UK who have interests in Spain or who wish to offer their banking or investment services, make acquisitions or engage in business in Spain. The office also advises Spanish companies already established in the UK or that wish to become established or otherwise engage in business there.

PRINCIPAL AREAS OF WORK Banking, corporate and commercial, energy law, mergers and acquisitions, foreign investment, project finance and securities.

Continued overleaf

A-Z ■ LAW FIRMS

INTERNATIONAL With its head office in Madrid, Uría & Menéndez also has offices throughout Spain (in Barcelona, Valencia and Bilbao), the rest of Europe (in Brussels, Lisbon and London), the USA (in New York) and in Latin America (in Buenos Aires, Santiago de Chile, Lima, São Paulo and Mexico City). A variety of languages are spoken throughout its various offices including Catalan, English, Finnish, French, German, Italian, Polish, Portuguese, Russian, Spanish and Swedish.

■ Varley Hadley Siddall
3rd Floor, 66-72 Houndsgate, Nottingham, NG1 6BA   **Tel** (0115) 958 3737   **Fax** (0115) 958 3434

Varley Hibbs

Kirby House, Little Park Street, Coventry, CV1 2JZ
Tel (024) 7663 1000   **Fax** (024) 7663 0808   **DX** 18892
Email comm@varleyhibbs.co.uk

16 Hamilton Terrace, Leamington Spa, CV32 4LY
Tel (01926) 881251   **Fax** (01926) 831900   **DX** 11870

Senior Partner	Edward Bayliss
Number of partners	6
Assistant solicitors	12
Other fee-earners	6

AREAS OF PRACTICE	
Civil & Commercial Litigation	18%
Company & Commercial	23%
Advocacy	15%
Conveyancing	23%
Family	12%
Probate & Miscellaneous	9%

THE FIRM Varley Hibbs is a leading Midlands firm with offices in Coventry and Leamington Spa. Established for over 60 years, the firm offers a wide range of services to a variety of businesses including public and private companies, banks and building societies, along with company directors and private individuals. The practice is committed to being not only a dominant force in commercial law in its own region, but also to providing a real alternative to the major Birmingham practices. The practice is large enough to offer the specialist advice needed by large companies, yet retains the key elements of providing a personal service at competitive rates.

Veale Wasbrough

Orchard Court, Orchard Lane, Bristol, BS1 5WS
Tel (0117) 925 2020   **Fax** (0117) 925 2025   **DX** 7831 Bristol
Email aguise-tucker@vwl.co.uk   **Website** www.vwl.co.uk

Managing Partner	Simon Pizzey
Number of partners	24
Assistant solicitors	52
Other fee-earners	40

AREAS OF PRACTICE	
Business (Non-contentious)	42%
Business (Contentious)	29%
Personal Legal Services	29%

THE FIRM Veale Wasbrough is a Bristol-based firm with a regional and national profile. It is recognised as being a young, dynamic, people centred firm with a commitment to success and excellence. The team of partners, lawyers and support staff achieve this by providing a professional and personalised service, underpinned by a team culture founded on the principles of partnership and support. The firm is enjoying significant expansion.

PRINCIPAL AREAS OF WORK

Company & Commercial The focus of much of the firm's work is in the provision of specialist services to the mid-sized business sector in Bristol and the South West. The firm advises its clients on a wide range of issues including MBOs, joint ventures, acquisitions, mergers, sales, company start-ups, partnerships and commercial transactions. Project finance and banking are both growing areas.

Property Services With one of the biggest and fastest growing property teams in the region, Veale Wasbrough has the breadth of experience and expertise to advise on a whole range of property-related matters including property development, property management, property investment and property litigation. Specialist areas include energy and environment, planning, urban regeneration and pipelines.

Education The nationally recognised education team advises on a whole range of matters affecting schools and colleges around the UK including crisis management.

Construction The construction team builds on the industry experience of its lawyers and handles all aspects of construction law including contract formation and procurement advice as well as dispute management.

Employment The full spectrum of issues affecting employment and the workplace is covered: employee benefits and rights, discrimination, grievance procedures, dismissal and transfers of undertakings.

Commercial Litigation Well known for its strength in commercial litigation, the firm is active in alternative dispute resolution and has a number of qualified mediators.

Technology & E-commerce The technology and e-commerce team provides advice on all aspects of this growing area, including intellectual property (particularly in the context of technology), computer systems, procurement and e-commerce.

Personal Injury The extremely successful personal injury team acts for claimants and handles accidents at work, RTAs, sports injuries and clinical negligence claims.

Estates & Tax Planning Trusts and personal planning requirements are handled by a dedicated team that

CONTACTS	
Alternative Dispute Resolution	Mike Davies
Central Government	David Worthington
Charities	Gary De'Ath
Clinical Negligence	Gary McFarlane
Commercial Litigation	Simon Heald
Company Commercial	David Worthington
Construction	Roger Hoyle
Education	Robert Boyd
Employment	Mike Davies
Energy/Environment	Tim Smithers
Estates & Tax Planning	Mary McCartney
Family	Janet Forbes
Insolvency	Simon Heald
International Trade	David Worthington
Local Authorities	Simon Baker
Partnership: Medical Practices	Derek Bellew
Personal Injury	John Webster
Pipeline Projects	Tim Smithers
Planning	Tim Smithers
Property Services	Gary Philpott
Public Sector & Utilities	Simon Baker
Residential Conveyancing	Mike Rendell
Retail	Michelle Rose
Technology & E-commerce	Paul Sampson
Wastes Management	Tim Smithers

LAW FIRMS ■ A-Z

provide advice and assistance to the business sector as well as to the private client.

INTERNATIONAL Veale Wasbrough is a founder member of the Association of European Lawyers, which provides a valuable network of lawyers in 27 countries. The firm has a growing client base in Europe, the Far East and the US.

RECRUITMENT The firm offers seven training contracts each year. Information and an application form are available on the firm's website.

Veitch Penny

1 Manor Court, Dix's Field, Exeter, EX1 1UP
Tel (01392) 278381 **Fax** (01392) 410247 **DX** 8309 Exeter 1
Email law@veitchpenny.co.uk **Website** www.veitchpenny.co.uk

2 Market Street, Crediton, EX17 2AL
Tel (01363) 772244 **Fax** (01363) 775874 **DX** 54201 Crediton
Email credlaw@veitchpenny.co.uk

THE FIRM Dedicated to providing a high quality service, encouraging a team ethos, and approachability, Veitch Penny became the first law firm in the South West to achieve the LEXCEL award in recognition of its efficiency, quality and client care; as well as the Investors in People in 1998.

PRINCIPAL AREAS OF WORK
Insurance Department Regarded as one of the leading insurance advisors in the country, handling work on behalf of district and county councils across the South and West of England, and over 20 national insurers. Committed to the robust but economical disposal of claims, wide experience is held in motor, employment, public and professional indemnity work, with particular expertise in dyslexia, abuse and stress.
Claimant Department Considered one of the largest claimant practices in the South West specialising in accident work, the department undertakes personal injury and bulk insured/uninsured loss recovery work for legal expense insurers, listing amongst its clients a major motoring organisation.
Other Areas Company/commercial; insolvency; employment; commercial and residential property; wills, probate, tax and trusts; matrimonial.

Managing Partner	Peter Taylor
Number of partners	10
Assistant solicitors	7
Other fee-earners	10

AREAS OF PRACTICE	
Defendant Litigation	49%
Plaintiff Litigation	28%
Conveyancing	12%
General Litigation	5%
Commercial	3%
Trust & Probate	3%

CONTACTS	
Claimant PI	Andrew Harris
	Alan Crawford
Commercial, Insolvency & Employment	Peter Taylor
Conveyancing, Probate & Trusts	Charles Dowell
	Ian Penny
Defendant PI	Mark Fowles
	Mark Hammerton
	Michael Penny
	Jessica Ross
	James Ruttledge

Venters Solicitors

1-6 Camberwell Green, London, SE5 7AD
Tel (020) 7277 0110 **Fax** (020) 7277 0132/(020) 7252 6889 **DX** 35310-Camberwell
Email info@venters.co.uk **Website** www.venters.co.uk

THE FIRM Venters & Co. was established in 1991 by June Venters. June Venters is a solicitor/advocate who is President of the London Criminal Courts Solicitors Association. She is an accredited assessor for the children panel and sits as a Recorder of the Crown Court. In 1996 she was the subject of a BBC TV documentary entitled Law Women. The firm specialises in crime, family and welfare benefits. It undertakes both legal aid and privately funded cases. June Venters, as Managing Partner, heads a strong and committed team which comprises Robin Brown, Practice Director and Alison Todd and Sean Longley, salaried partners, along with associate solicitors and support staff. The firm has a recognised and established reputation and is well known for its representation of high profile cases. Including: The Dome Robbery, the Euston handbag Murder and the Damilola Taylor Murder.

Partners	June Venters
	Alison Todd
	Sean Longley
Number of partners	3
Assistant solicitors	7
Other fee-earners	6

■ Victor Lissack & Roscoe

8 Bow Street, Covent Garden, London, WC2E 7AJ
Tel (020) 7240 2010 **Fax** (020) 7379 4420 **DX** 40026 Covent Garden
Email law@victorlissack.co.uk

Ptnrs 3 **Asst solrs** 3 **Other fee-earners** 2 **Contact** Richard Almond • Specialists in white collar and all other crime including extradition and courts martial.

AREAS OF PRACTICE	
Criminal Law	75%
Private Client	25%

www.ChambersandPartners.com   1175

A-Z ■ LAW FIRMS

Vinson & Elkins LLP

CityPoint, 33rd Floor, One Ropemaker Street, London, EC2Y 9UE
Tel (020) 7065 6000 **Fax** (020) 7065 6001
Email jlamaster@velaw.com

Administrative Partner	John LaMaster
Managing Partner	Joe Dilg

THE FIRM Vinson & Elkins is one of the largest international law firms and one of the world's leading energy practices. Its London office has developed a successful practice providing an integrated legal service on a wide variety of transactions. In 1917, Vinson & Elkins was founded in Houston, Texas and has grown into a worldwide operation with a diverse corporate, finance and business practice comprising of more than 860 lawyers in nine offices around the globe. Vinson & Elkins is regarded as a leading firm in America as well as being the premier firm in the south western United States. It has topped the Petroleum Economist international survey of law firms offering the best overall service to the energy sector for five of the last six years and regularly achieves high survey rankings in other sectors including, mergers and acquisitions, corporate finance and privately financed infrastructure projects.

The London Office Vinson & Elkins has been committed to London since 1972 and, in 1994, was one of the first US-based law firms to establish a multinational partnership in order to practice English as well as US law. The London office is primarily comprised of solicitors and US attorneys, but has a number of lawyers qualified in other jurisdictions. The London office acts for clients based in Europe, the US or elsewhere in the world, ranging from start-ups and joint ventures to financial institutions, private companies and listed global corporations. In the last year, the London office has been involved in transactions in countries as far apart as the UK, the Netherlands, Portugal, Italy, Czech Republic, Hungary, the former Soviet Union, Lithuania, Romania, Mexico, the USA, Japan and India.

PRINCIPAL AREAS OF WORK The practice in London is focused on six core areas: mergers and acquisitions and other corporate transactions; project development and finance; international energy transactions; corporate finance, securities and capital markets; banking and international finance; and international arbitration and dispute resolution. In addition to these main areas, the firm advises on matters including joint ventures and other strategic alliances; construction contracts; commercial agreements of all types, and employment matters. The London office acts as a centre for Vinson & Elkins' work in Europe, the Middle East, Africa, the former Soviet Union and the Indian sub-continent. The firm has received worldwide recognition including Power Legal Adviser of the Year by Infrastructure Journal 2001 and Best Overall Service in the energy industry in the 2001 Petroleum Economist Energy Finance Survey. Three London partners were named in Euromoney's 2001 Guide to the World's Leading Energy and Natural Resource Lawyers, and two in Euromoney's 2001 Guide to the World's Leading Project Finance Lawyers. The London practice is of strategic importance to Vinson & Elkins and, as well as being an integral part of the wider firm, operates as an independent, international practice. Vinson & Elkins' London office will continue to build on its established practice in its core, targeted areas, serving clients wherever they do business.

INTERNATIONAL Other offices: Austin, Beijing, Dallas, Houston, Moscow, New York, Singapore, Washington DC.

■ Vizards Wyeth

Rivers Ridge House, Anchor Boulevard, Crossways, Dartford, DA2 0SL **Tel** (020) 7400 9999 **Fax** (020) 7903 5555

■ v-lex ltd

Ivy House, Gateford Rd, Gateford, Worksop, S81 8AE
Tel (01909) 544000 **Fax** (01909) 544001
Website www.v-lex.com

Contact John Yates • V-lex is an incorporated law firm with an overwhelming focus on the technology sector. The foundations of the business are industry knowledge, account management, transparent pricing and award-winning training. Services include legal advice and training in risk management and IT procurement.

■ Wace Morgan

2 Belmont, Shrewsbury, SY1 1TD **Tel** (01743) 280100 **Fax** (01743) 280111

Wacks Caller

Steam Packet House, 76 Cross Street, Manchester, M2 4JU
Tel (0161) 957 8888 **Fax** (0161) 957 8899 **DX** 14383 Manchester 1
Email law@wackscaller.com **Website** www.wackscaller.com

THE FIRM Wacks Caller occupies a unique position in the Manchester commercial legal market place: a medium sized city firm with 18 partners, it regularly advises clients and works on deals of the size and complexity that may traditionally have been the preserve of the larger regional firms. The policy of 'playing with the big boys' has seen the firm strengthen its position as a leading specialist corporate finance player, which also provides the full range of services required by the corporate client.

PRINCIPAL AREAS OF WORK

Company/Commercial This is the firm's flagship department with seven partners supported by associates and assistants. The department provides experienced expert advice to the business community in relation to all types of corporate finance and commercial transactions including full Stock Exchange flotations, corporate sales and acquisitions, joint venture agreements and MBOs/MBIs and the like. During the past 12 months the firm has advised in numerous multi-million pound transactions bearing a total value of approximately 500m.

Commercial Litigation The firm's second largest department continues to grow rapidly under the leadership of Kit Sorrell and Michael Kennedy. The department is known for a no-nonsense commercial approach to litigation, being very results-driven, and yet with an overriding commercial attitude. The department specialises in high value complex commercial cases. Recent high profile cases include Liverpool and Lancashire Properties Limited v B&Q Plc (defining commercial Landlords' rights over common parts), Union Music Limited & Arias Limited v Russell Watson (a case in which the world famous opera star's former management is suing for sums running into millions).

Commercial Property A careful recruitment policy in this department has produced, and will develop, a closely-knit team who are principally commercial lawyers skilled in property matters - not conveyancers who aspire to the commercial arena. Major property investment and development clients provide a full range of high value work and the department is now embarking on specialist funding work, acting for institutions. The department consists of three partners, four solicitors and three support fee earners. Led by Elizabeth Mackay and Robert Harris, the team aspires to take the pain (for the client at least) from even the most complicated property transaction, without sacrificing the quality of technical input.

Insolvency Working closely with the commercial litigation team, the insolvency department now consists of two partners and four assistant solicitors. Greatly strengthened by the recruitment of a new partner, Gareth Dodds from DLA, the department acts for leading insolvency practitioners and financial institutions. The last 12 months have been categorised by a steady growth in the quality of the nature of instructions received by this rapidly expanding department.

Employment The emphasis on the service provided by this department is that it aspires to be proactive rather than simply reactive. It advises the firm's commercial client base in both contentious and non-contentious matters including planning for redundancy, dealing with sensitive senior employee/director issues and providing support to the corporate finance department on issues arising out of corporate transactions generally. The department consists of two partners, an associate and an assistant solicitor and is very much on the expansion trail.

Managing Partner	Martin Caller
Head of Corporate Finance	Kevin Philbin
Head of Litigation & Insolvency	Kit Sorrell
Head of Commercial Property	Elizabeth Mackay
Head of Employment	Tony Dempsey
Number of partners	18
Assistant solicitors	40
Other fee-earners	4

AREAS OF PRACTICE	
Company/Commercial	40%
Litigation	30%
Commercial Property	20%
Employment	5%
Intellectual Property	5%

CONTACTS	
Corporate Finance	Kevin Philbin
	Phil Barry
Commercial Litigation/Insolvency	Kit Sorrell
Commercial Property	Elizabeth Mackay
Employment	Tony Dempsey
Information Technology	Simon Wallwork

Wake Dyne Lawton

Worley Bank House, Bolesworth Road, Tattenhall, Chester, CH3 9HL
Tel (01829) 773100 **Fax** (01829) 773109
Email bdw@wdl.co.uk **Website** www.wdl.co.uk

Ptnrs 4 **Asst solrs** 1 **Other fee-earners** 5 **Contact** Brian Wake • Specialist practice dealing on a national basis exclusively with minerals, waste, planning, environmental, road haulage law and health and safety law.

Areas of Practice	
Minerals & Energy	30%
Planning/Environmental	25%
Transport	25%
Waste	15%
Health & Safety	5%

Wake Smith

68 Clarkehouse Road, Sheffield, S10 2LJ **Tel** (0114) 266 6560 **Fax** (0114) 267 1253

Walker Charlesworth & Foster

26 Park Square, Leeds, LS1 2PL
Tel (0113) 245 3594 **Fax** (0113) 244 4312 **DX** 26415 Leeds Park Square
Email mail@walkercharlesworth.co.uk **Website** www.walkercharlesworth.co.uk

Ptnrs 8 **Asst solrs** 4 **Other fee-earners** 6 **Contact** Colin Birtwistle • A long established practice specialising in registered social landlord and charitable work.

A-Z ■ LAW FIRMS

Walker Morris

Kings Court, 12 King Street, Leeds, LS1 2HL
Tel (0113) 283 2500   **Fax** (0113) 245 9412   **DX** 12051 LEEDS-1
Email info@walkermorris.co.uk   **Website** www.walkermorris.co.uk

Managing Partner	Michael Taylor
Number of partners	40
Assistant solicitors	86
Other fee-earners	226

AREAS OF PRACTICE

Commercial Litigation	30%
Commercial Property	25%
Company & Commercial	25%
Building Societies	16%
Private Clients	2%
Tax	2%

CONTACTS

Banking & Finance	Michael Taylor
Building Societies	David Duckworth
Commercial Dispute Resolution	Gwendoline Davies
Commercial Property	Paul Walker
Competition	Jeremy Scholes
Construction	Simon Anderson
	Martin Scott
Corporate & Commercial	Peter Smart
Corporate Finance	Ian Gilbert
Corporate Tax	Simon Concannon
Employment	David Smedley
Information Technology/E-commerce	Patrick Cantrill
Insolvency	Philip Mudd
Insurance Litigation	Christopher Caisley
Intellectual Property	Patrick Cantrill
	Alison Murphy
Media & Entertainment	Ralph Coyle
Pensions	Andrew Turnbull
Planning & Environment	Andrew Williamson
Private Client	Richard Manning
Professional Negligence	Andrew Beck
Public Sector & PFI	David Kilduff
Sports Law	Christopher Caisley

THE FIRM Walker Morris is one of the leading independent law firms in the country. Recent recognition includes the Regional Law Firm of the Year award and the Most Successful Regional Law Firm accolade from leading legal magazines. Walker Morris has achieved its success by always placing clients first. The firm's strong and innovative client service was recognised recently in a weekly legal magazine's marketing awards. In 2001 the firm was awarded Best Use of Information Technology by the Legal IT Forum, highlighting its development of an impressive range of fee-earner productivity tools and innovative use of automation. Speed, commerciality, value and approachability have been cited by clients as major attributes of the firm. Walker Morris has an extensive and impressive client list including substantial public companies, banks, insurers, venture capitalists, fund managers, multinational corporations and private companies operating in all sectors. The firm's major strength is its ability to recruit, train and motivate top quality lawyers. Walker Morris was the first firm to give clients direct access to its time recording systems to ensure complete transparency on billing and its innovative approach to client service includes sharing its knowhow and providing legal training via its ground-breaking online service reach...™

PRINCIPAL AREAS OF WORK

Corporate The corporate department acts for corporate clients, institutions and management teams. Its work includes the full range of corporate finance, flotations, acquisitions, disposals, joint ventures and innovative private deals, with specialists dealing with areas such as competition law and pensions advice.

Commercial Property & Planning The property department is one of the largest outside London, with great strength in depth to deal with transactions involving large portfolios. Clients turn to specialist partners for advice on all aspects of development, including major town centre redevelopments and large-scale residential sites. Its retail team acts for many of the best known national and international high street names and its town and country planning and environmental group includes more nationally ranked partners than any other. The department has a growing institutional client base and its property management service is supported by specialist property litigators.

Commercial Dispute Resolution Commercial dispute resolution is an important part of Walker Morris' practice. The team deals with a broad range of major dispute work both within the UK and internationally, and has had a number of notable successes in the Court of Appeal during 2000. walkermorriscollect™ is a specialist unit within the group that acts for institutional clients collecting commercial debt, using the latest systems with online access.

Banking & Finance Banking and finance are particular strengths of the firm. Clients include the major banks, asset based lenders and insolvency practitioners and the team's work includes advising on structured finance, acquisition and project finance, property finance, turnaround and insolvency. Specialist litigators and property lawyers complete the picture to provide a complete service to the finance sector.

Employment & Human Resources These issues are critical to all large clients and the firm's employment group is held in the highest regard. The group offers a complete service to human resources departments, including helplines and consultancy services.

Construction The construction sector is well catered for at Walker Morris. It is one of the strongest groups in the region acting for main contractors, sub-contractors and employers on both contentious and non-contentious matters.

Intellectual Property & Information Technology Walker Morris has a highly regarded intellectual property and information technology group, which ranks amongst the largest outside London. Offering a truly one stop practice covering all aspects of contentious and non contentious work, it has achieved a number of successes in patent and other IP/IT actions and been engaged in some high profile licensing, procurement and joint venture projects. In accordance with this full service, the group includes one of the UK's most active and fast growing trademark management practices. Recently, it has strengthened its new media practice and has carried out some groundbreaking work in the areas of interactive TV and e-commerce.

Public Sector & PFI The firm's public sector and PFI group provides a full service to public sector clients, including health authorities and trusts, local government, the education sector, utilities and others.

Commercial Commercial contracting work is a major focus of Walker Morris' development. In both the private and public sectors, the firm provides advice on procurement contracts, joint ventures, agency and distribution agreements, outsourcing and the full range of commercial agreements.

Sports Law The sports law unit acts for sports personalities, clubs and associations working within this industry and work includes contract negotiations and disputes, personality merchandising and licensing agreements.

LAW FIRMS ■ A-Z

Additional Areas Walker Morris is one of few firms able to provide advocacy and advisory services to directors, corporations and other bodies in connection with commercial fraud, corporate killing, health and safety and other areas where the criminal law touches on corporate or public life. The advocacy group has had outstanding successes in coroners' courts, public enquiries and the criminal courts. Walker Morris has developed a service called Walker Morris OnLine which is now a market leader in providing volume mortgage lending services. This has added to the firm's long-standing services to the building society and domestic finance sector which includes mortgage recovery and professional negligence services.

CLIENTELE Clients are drawn from the whole spectrum of commerce and industry including manufacturing, construction and development, high technology, the financial services industry, banking and finance, and the retail and service industries.

INTERNATIONAL The firm advises on European and EU issues and has a growing international practice and has developed very close and mutually beneficial relationships with law firms in the EU and around the world. The consistent element in those relationships is a common philosophy and approach.

RECRUITMENT The firm's year-on-year expansion has resulted in always having a continuing recruitment policy for motivated young solicitors in all major disciplines. The firm recruits around 10 trainee solicitors every year. Discretionary grants are provided. Career prospects are excellent (most of the partners were articled within the firm). Application forms and recruitment brochures are available from Nick Bates, Recruitment Partner. A training scheme is available to keep its lawyers up-to-date, consisting of in-house seminars, external conferences, and information updates.

■ **Walker Smith & Way**
26 Nicholas Street, Chester, CH1 2PQ **Tel** (01244) 357 400 **Fax** (01244) 357 444

Wallace & Partners

One Portland Place, London, W1B 1PN
Tel (020) 7636 4422 **Fax** (020) 7636 3736 **DX** 82990 Mayfair
Email lawyers@wallace.co.uk **Website** www.wallace.co.uk

Managing Partner	Rex Newman
Number of partners	5
Assistant solicitors	7
Other fee-earners	7

CONTACTS	
Company/Commercial	Rex Newman
Employment	Nicholas Yapp
Litigation	Simon Serota
Private Client	Barry Shaw
Property	Martin Otvos
	Barry Shaw

THE FIRM Wallace & Partners is a niche commercial practice based in Portland Place, London. The firm has developed a strong client base and established a reputation for conducting the transactional work more commonly associated with much larger practices. Wallace & Partners prides itself on close team-work generated in a smaller, more collegial environment.

PRINCIPAL AREAS OF WORK
Company/Commercial Work includes Stock Exchange advice including public issues, commercial contracts, venture capital, joint ventures, management buyouts and buyins, mergers and acquisitions, loan arrangements, advice on the responsibilities of directors; shareholder agreements; tax planning, franchising and general commercial matters.
Litigation The firm is strong in property-related litigation as well as professional negligence, shareholder and boardroom disputes, leasehold enfranchisement and general commercial litigation. One partner is a Deputy Costs Judge.
Employment This department deals with all aspects of employment law both contentious and non-contentious.
Property Work includes development, investment, acquisition and funding, planning and environmental, business leases, rent reviews, estate management and general landlord and tenant work.
Private Client This department deals with personal financial planning including wills, capital taxes advice, trusts and probate, as well as employment-related immigration work.
ADR & Mediation The firm also handles ADR and mediation work, one partner being a registered mediator, and another fee-earner being an Associate Member of the Chartered Institute of Arbitrators.

CLIENTELE The firm acts for a diverse spread of clients including listed companies, family businesses, entrepreneurs and overseas investors.

INTERNATIONAL Wallace & Partners has developed a network of contacts throughout Europe and provides advice on many aspects of international commerce. One partner is a member of the New York Bar, and another fee-earner is a member of the Illinois Bar.

RECRUITMENT Apply in writing, enclosing your CV to Samantha Bone.

A-Z LAW FIRMS

Waltons & Morse

Birchin Court, 20 Birchin Lane, London, EC3V 9ER
Tel (020) 7623 4255   **Fax** (020) 7626 4153   **DX** City 1065
Email waltons@wamlaw.co.uk   **Website** www.waltonsandmorse.com

THE FIRM Waltons & Morse is a long-established City firm serving the marine insurance market, and with an international reputation in the areas of shipping, transport and international trade.

PRINCIPAL AREAS OF WORK
General Description All aspects of marine insurance, shipping and transit law including international trade.

CLIENTELE Lloyd's, London and overseas insurance companies, ship operators (particularly from the Far East) and salvors.

Managing Partner	Ian Charles-Jones
Senior Partner	David Perry
Number of partners	7
Assistant solicitors	3
Other fee-earners	7

AREAS OF PRACTICE	
Shipping & Transit	78%
Marine Insurance	10%
International Trade	10%
Reinsurance	2%

CONTACTS	
Shipping	David Perry

Ward Gethin

8-12 Tuesday Market Place, King's Lynn, PE30 1JT   **Tel** (01553) 660033   **Fax** (01553) 766857

Ward Hadaway

Sandgate House, 102 Quayside, Newcastle upon Tyne, NE1 3DX
Tel (0191) 204 4000   **Fax** (0191) 204 4001   **DX** 61265 Newcastle Upon Tyne
Email legal@wardhadaway.com   **Website** www.wardhadaway.com

THE FIRM Ward Hadaway is one of the most progressive commercial law firms in the north of England. The firm's services are structured around market sector groups with multi-disciplined teams serving client needs. Known for its fresh and innovative approach, Ward delivers a comprehensive range of legal services to the highest quality standards.

PRINCIPAL AREAS OF WORK Ward Hadaway has a substantial client base from both the public and private sectors, and is particularly strong in technology (IT/IP), corporate finance, healthcare, commercial litigation, commercial property, construction and employment.

Senior Partner	George Scott
Managing Partner	Jamie Martin
Number of partners	44
Assistant solicitors	51
Other fee-earners	59

AREAS OF PRACTICE	
Litigation	39%
Property	30%
Commercial	25%
Private Client Services	6%

Warner Goodman & Streat

66 West Street, Fareham, PO16 0JR   **Tel** (01329) 288121   **Fax** (01329) 822714

Waterson Hicks

140 Fenchurch Street, London, EC3M 6BL
Tel (020) 7929 6060   **Fax** (020) 7929 3748
Email law@waterson-hicks.com

THE FIRM Waterson Hicks is a commercial practice specialising in all aspects of maritime law and commodity litigation. The firm's work and clientele are largely international.

PRINCIPAL AREAS OF WORK Shipping work covers all areas of commercial and admiralty litigation and arbitration, particularly including charterparty and trading disputes, sale and purchase disputes, and total losses.

CLIENTELE Clients include major ship owners, oil companies, charterers, commodity traders, P&I clubs, insurance companies and shipyards for whom primarily contentious work is carried out.

INTERNATIONAL The firm has strong overseas connections particularly in Greece, the United States, Spanish-speaking countries and the Indian subcontinent. French, Spanish and Portuguese are spoken within the firm.

Managing Partner	Martin J Wisdom
Number of partners	3
Assistant solicitors	4
Other fee-earners	2

CONTACTS	
Admiralty	Stuart Parkin
Commodities & Commercial	Martin J Wisdom
Insurance	John Hicks
Shipping	John Hicks
	Brian Isola

Watson Burton
20 Collingwood Street, Newcastle upon Tyne, NE99 1YQ **Tel** (0191) 244 4444 **Fax** (0191) 244 4500

Watson, Farley & Williams
15 Appold Street, London, EC2A 2HB
Tel (020) 7814 8000 **Fax** (020) 7814 8141 **DX** 530 London City EC3
Email inquiries@wfw.com **Website** www.wfw.com

Chairman	Christopher Preston
Chief Executive	Michael Reid
Managing Partner	Michael Greville
Number of partners worldwide	55
Number of lawyers worldwide	218

CONTACTS
International Corporate	Jan Mellmann
International Finance	Michael Vernell
International Litigation	David Kavanagh
International Tax	Stéphane Salou

THE FIRM Established in 1982, Watson, Farley & Williams is an international corporate and commercial finance law firm recognised for its excellence in banking and asset financing, particularly ship finance and leasing. The firm also advises in a number of specialist areas in corporate law, litigation and arbitration and tax law. Through its spread of international offices and contacts, the firm offers an integrated multijurisdictional service to clients. A key feature is the firm's division into four international practice groups - corporate, finance, litigation and tax. These groups are not divided by location. They work together internationally to serve clients. With its broad base of clients, the international experience of the firm is comprehensive and has been acknowledged through a number of awards. In November 2000 the firm was voted by the international shipping industry as the world's leading firm for ship finance and in the same year received international recognition for its asset finance and leasing work. In 2001, the firm's commercial litigation team was short-listed for litigation team of the year award in London.

PRINCIPAL AREAS OF WORK
International Corporate Group Public and private company clients have access to a wide range of domestic and international expertise covering all aspects of international corporate law, including acquisitions, disposals and mergers, public offerings of securities, management buyouts and buyins, business and asset sales, debt structuring, equity financings, corporate restructurings, international privatisations, and a wide range of commercial agreements such as distributorship, outsourcing purchase and agency agreements, and joint ventures and partnerships. In addition, the group offers specialist advice on real property, intellectual property, employment, service agreements, share option and incentive schemes, executive immigration, and all aspects of European Union competition law. The group focuses particularly on the provision of advice to clients in the transportation, power, telecommunication and e-commerce sectors.

International Finance Group Lawyers advise all project participants, covering areas such as general banking finance, structured finance, securities and capital markets, derivatives, trade finance, asset finance, project finance, cross-border tax leverage lending and leasing, and workouts and insolvencies. The group has particular expertise and experience in a number of industry sectors heavily dependent on the financing of large capital assets, including shipping, aviation, telecommunications, power and energy.

International Litigation Group Large scale litigation, arbitration and dispute resolution matters are handled by the group on a worldwide basis. Lawyers have represented clients involved in international disputes in the areas of shipping (wet and dry), banking, offshore oil and gas, international trade, and aviation. The group also advises on the enforcement of security over vessels, marine pollution, marine insurance, shipbuilding, charterparties, and offshore oil and gas contracting.

International Tax Group Lawyers advise on domestic and cross-border tax leasing, non-asset based structured finance, international tax planning, investigations and litigation, and indirect tax. They also give advice generally on all types of transactions. The indirect tax team specialists have considerable VAT experience.

CLIENTELE The firm's client base spans the world, and includes international banks, financial institutions, quoted and private companies, shipping companies, airlines, offshore oil and gas companies, and governments and government agencies.

INTERNATIONAL With offices in Piraeus, Paris, New York, Bangkok and Singapore, and a network of correspondent specialist lawyers, the firm's reach is truly international. Lawyers are able to advise on English, French, Russian, Thai, New York and US Federal law. All offices have expertise in the laws of the local jurisdiction and an understanding of local business customs and culture. Languages spoken at the firm include Cantonese, Dutch, English, French, Greek, Italian, Mandarin, Malay, Norwegian, Russian, Spanish, Swahili and Swedish.

A-Z LAW FIRMS

Wedlake Bell

16 Bedford Street, Covent Garden, London, WC2E 9HF
Tel (020) 7395 3000   Fax (020) 7836 9966   DX 40009 Covent Gdn.
Email legal@wedlakebell.com   Website www.wedlakebell.com

Managing Partner	Julian Cuppage
Senior Partner	Robert Dolman
Number of partners	35
Assistant solicitors	33
Other fee-earners	24

AREAS OF PRACTICE	
Property & Construction	30%
Corporate Finance & Banking	25%
Tax & Trusts	20%
Commercial/IP/Internet	15%
Employment, Pensions & Share Schemes	10%

CONTACTS	
Banking	Hilary Platt
Commercial	Jonathan Cornthwaite
Commercial Property	Peter Day
Construction	Suzanne Reeves
Corporate Finance	Adam Walker
E-business/IT	Jonathan Cornthwaite
Employment	Richard Isham
Intellectual Property	Jonathan Cornthwaite
Litigation	Richard Hewitt
Pensions & Share Schemes	Clive Weber
Tax & Trusts	Peter Watts

THE FIRM Wedlake Bell serves business and the owners, managers and inheritors of business and their families. It is recognised as having the transaction experience, skills and back up support of much larger firms from whom it consistently wins business. Its size and approach enables clients to build long-term personal relationships with the individual lawyers of their choice. Its informal, creative culture has resulted in very low staff turnover and has made it an attractive alternative for top class lawyers who wish to escape the big law firm environment. During the last year Wedlake Bell advised clients in the following sectors: banking, computing and software; dot.com start-ups; construction and engineering; consumer goods manufacturing; food manufacturing; healthcare; hotel and catering; information technology; marketing and branding; offshore trusts; oil, gas and mineral extraction; pharmaceuticals; property; publishing and printing; sport and leisure; support services; private wealth planning.

PRINCIPAL AREAS OF WORK

Corporate Finance & Banking The corporate finance team advises on mergers and acquisitions, flotations, placings and rights issues, venture capital, asset transactions, joint ventures, inward investment and investment funds. The banking team advises on transaction and project finance, secured, syndicated and bilateral lending for both borrowers and lenders and on asset finance.

Commercial Property & Construction The commercial property team acts for developers, investors, banks, landlords and tenants in relation to trading, developing, funding, occupying or investing in land. The construction team advises on construction contracts and disputes.

IP/IT, Commercial & Internet This team advises on e-business issues, intellectual property, data protection, internet law, IT contracts, commercial agreements such as franchises, merchandising and outsourcing and competition law.

Employment, Pensions & Share Schemes This team advises on both contentious and non-contentious employment law. It acts for the trustees, employers and members of a wide range of occupational pensions schemes, and advise on share schemes and long-term incentive plans.

Private Clients, Tax & Wealth Protection This team advises on tax planning, trusts, offshore tax jurisdictions, wills and inheritance, asset protection, landed estates, probate, heritage and agricultural properties. It acts for entrepreneurs, business managers and new enterprise investors as well as long established family wealth. The team also provides residential conveyancing and matrimonial dispute services.

Dispute Resolution Specialists in dispute resolution provide support for all the firm's core practice areas whether by litigation, arbitration, mediation or adjudication (in construction).

INTERNATIONAL Wedlake Bell has affiliate law firms in most European jurisdictions and in the USA. A significant part of its annual turnover derives from overseas business and clients. The firm has an office in Guernsey, which operates Breams Trustees Limited, a Guernsey trust company and handles UK investment property transactions for offshore investment funds.

RECRUITMENT The firm recruits up to six trainees each year. It also runs a summer student placement programme every July for three weeks. Trainees consistently report that the quality of training received far exceeds the experiences of those in much larger firms. CVs should be addressed to the HR and Training Manager.

WEDLAKE BELL

Wedlake Saint
140 - 142 Saint John Street, London, EC1 V4UB   Tel (020) 7324 1870

LAW FIRMS ■ A-Z

Weightman Vizards

India Buildings, Water Street, Liverpool, L2 0GA
Tel (0870) 241 3512   **Fax** (0151) 227 3223   **DX** 14201 Liverpool
Email enquiries@weightmanvizards.com   **Website** www.weightmanvizards.com

3rd Floor, 60 Charles Street, Leicester, LE1 1FB
Tel (0116) 253 9747   **Fax** (0116) 253 6101   **DX** 721641 Leicester 18

41 Spring Gardens, Manchester, M2 2BG
Tel (0161) 833 2601   **Fax** (0161) 833 1199   **DX** 14427 Manchester 2

79-83 Colmore Row, Birmingham, B3 2AP
Tel (0121) 233 2601   **Fax** (0121) 233 2600   **DX** 13035 Birmingham 1

High Holborn House, 52-54 High Holborn, London, WC1V 6RL
Tel (020) 7067 4506   **Fax** (020) 7067 4501   **DX** 310 London/Chancery Lane

Senior Partner	Ian Evans
Managing Partner	Mike Radcliffe
Deputy Managing Partner	David Lewis
Number of partners	73
Assistant solicitors	152
Other fee-earners	84

THE FIRM With 73 partners supported by more than 550 staff across Birmingham, Leicester, Liverpool, London and Manchester, Weightman Vizards has the resources to meet the most demanding legal needs. The firm combines a rapidly growing commercial team serving all areas of public and private business with an unrivalled presence in the insurance market. Specialist teams operate across all five offices in workplace litigation, transport and large loss. In addition, Weightman Vizards' police team is recognised as the largest specialist department of its kind in private practice in the UK. Other niche practice areas include healthcare, local authority and professional indemnity. Weightman Vizards is the only UK firm to provide a partner dedicated to promoting best practice and knowledge management.

Weil, Gotshal & Manges

Head Office - Europe, One South Place, London, EC2M 2WG
Tel (020) 7903 1000   **Fax** (020) 7903 0990   **DX** 124402
Email weil.london@weil.com   **Website** www.weil.com

UK	
Number of partners	28
Associates	83
Other fee-earners	22
Total legal staff	133

THE FIRM Weil, Gotshal & Manges is a premier international law firm, with over 950 lawyers worldwide and a reputation for providing first-class US and European legal advice that meets the commercial needs of its international corporate and finance clients. Established in New York in 1931, the firm has successfully pursued a strategy of expansion across Europe through organic growth, in response to client demand. The London office, established in 1996, has grown rapidly to become the second largest of the firms' 13 offices and is now the hub of the European practice. With more than 135 corporate and finance lawyers, it is one of the largest US-based international law firms in London, with one of the widest ranging practices.

PRINCIPAL AREAS OF WORK The firm's practice in London bridges the traditional divides between US and UK corporate and finance law, encompassing acquisition finance, asset finance and leasing, banking, biotechnology and pharmaceuticals, business finance and restructuring, capital markets, commercial litigation and arbitration, competition, consumer finance, corporate, environmental, financial services, mergers and acquisitions, pensions, private equity, project finance, real estate, securitisation, structured finance, taxation and technology.
Business Finance & Restructuring Weil Gotshal has an unrivalled reputation in bankruptcy and restructuring in the United States, which the firm is building on with the creation of a team in Europe led from London. The London practice was established in October 2001 and its current focus is on transactional restructurings and insolvencies of multinational companies. It is representing both Enron and Global Crossing on the UK and other non-US aspects of their restructurings.
Biotechnology & Pharmaceuticals The firm's biotechnology and pharmaceutical group, based in its London, Silicon Valley and New York offices, comprises lawyers of the highest calibre and technical excellence with a detailed understanding of the pharmaceutical and biotechnology industries across Europe and the US. Their combined European/US experience in these sectors means that they can provide clients and their investors with legal advice on all aspects of their businesses, from mergers and acquisitions and fundraising transactions through to commercial contracts, IPR licensing and regulatory compliance on a worldwide basis.
Capital Markets Weil, Gotshal & Manges has established a capital markets practice with a track record for innovative and ground-breaking debt and equity offerings, high yield debt issues and structured

Continued overleaf

and derivative capital markets transactions.

Corporate The firm has an established corporate team of over 50 lawyers, which has a high profile in London through its work on major public mergers and acquisitions. Its capability in UK and US law is a key reason for its appeal to clients seeking advisors on multi-billion pound cross-border deals. Client demand has led to the development of core ancillary areas such as corporate tax, competition, property, pensions, litigation and environmental law.

Finance The broad-based finance team has significant expertise in highly leveraged financings, acquisitions financings and asset-backed financings. London is especially well suited to act on financings governed by UK law and US law because of the office's ability to advise in both jurisdictions.

Securitisation The securitisation team at Weil, Gotshal & Manges has earned a reputation for advising not only on innovative and highly complex transactions but also on transactions involving more mainstream UK consumer assets, such as residential mortgages. The team has extensive CBO/CLO and conduit expertise and are recognised as experts with respect to the establishment of CDOs, structured investment vehicles and ABCP/MTN conduits. The team has been involved in a wide range of transactions in Europe and the US.

Technology The Weil, Gotshal & Manges' technology practice provides integrated UK and US corporate, commercial and finance advice to hi-tech businesses and investors. The firm offers clients the advantage of a significant Silicon Valley presence and lawyers with experience in advising both online companies and investors in relation to venture capital/private equity funding matters and all other aspects of corporate and finance legal issues. Its lawyers are experienced in advising suppliers/vendors and customers on the supply, licensing and exploitation of technology and telecommunications related products and services.

CLIENTELE The London office represents major corporations and financial institutions including Apax Partners, Bank of America, Barclays Capital, Bear Stearns, CeNeS Pharmaceuticals plc, Coca Cola, Credit Suisse First Boston, Deutsche Bank, Dresdner Kleinwort Benson, Enron, Estée Lauder, GE Capital, Global Crossing, Hicks, Muse, Tate and Furst, JP Morgan Chase & Co, Lehman Brothers, Matsushita, Merrill Lynch, Morgan Stanley, Netia, Nomura International, Oxford BioMedica plc, Acambis plc, Pirelli, Schroder Salomon Smith Barney, Simply Internet, Telewest, Wit Capital and Yell Limited.

INTERNATIONAL The firm also has offices in Brussels, Budapest, Dallas, Frankfurt, Houston, Miami, Prague, New York, Silicon Valley, Singapore, Warsaw and Washington DC.

RECRUITMENT The firm is looking for flexible, highly motivated people who will be expected to take advantage of the wide-ranging legal and business training provided and develop the requisite skills to provide their clients with commercially-driven legal solutions.

■ Wellman & Brown
23 West Parade, Lincoln, LN1 1NW **Tel** (01522) 525463 **Fax** (01522) 513199

■ Wendy Hopkins & Co
26 Windsor Place, Cardiff, CF1 3BZ **Tel** (029) 2034 2233 **Fax** (029) 2034 3828

■ Wesley Gryk
140 Lower Marsh, London, SE1 7AE
Tel (020) 7401 6887 **Fax** (020) 7261 9985 **DX** 36517 Lambeth
Email wesley@gryklaw.com **Website** www.gryklaw.com

Ptnrs 1 **Asst solrs** 5 **Other fee-earners** 8 • A niche immigration practice.

■ White & Bowker
19 St Peter Street, Winchester, SO23 8BU **Tel** (01962) 844440 **Fax** (01962) 842300

White & Case

7-11 Moorgate, London, EC2R 6HH
Tel (020) 7600 7300   **Fax** (020) 7600 7030

THE FIRM White & Case is an internationally recognised name in the provision of finance and corporate law with 1600 lawyers in 40 offices across 27 countries. The London office was founded in 1971 to provide top-flight international legal advice to the world's leading institutions and corporations and now has over 120 lawyers, with a unique mix of UK and US law capability. White & Case is a full-service law firm and clients include public and private corporations, financial institutions, governments and state-owned entities. In two years the firm has doubled the size of its corporate and finance law operations in Europe and in total now has more than 670 lawyers in the region. The firm was recently named Best US Law Firm in London, independently placed in the Top Five Global Law Firms, and named Global Law Firm of the Year.

INTERNATIONAL The firm has other offices in Almaty, Ankara, Bahrain, Bangkok, Berlin, Bratislava, Brussels, Budapest, Dresden, Düsseldorf, Frankfurt, Hamburg, Helsinki, Ho Chi Minh City, Hong Kong, Istanbul, Jakarta, Jeddah, Johannesburg, Los Angeles, Mexico City, Miami, Milan, Moscow, Mumbai, New York, Palo Alto, Paris, Prague, Riyadh, Rome, San Francisco, São Paulo, Shanghai, Singapore, Stockholm, Tokyo, Warsaw and Washington DC.

Executive Partners	John Bellhouse
	Mike Goetz
Number of partners	32
Associates	74

CONTACTS	
Asset Finance	Mark Western
Bank Finance	Maurice Allen
Capital Markets	Francis Fitzherbert-Brockholes
Construction	John Bellhouse
Disputes	Margaret R Cole
Employment	Oliver Brettle
Energy, Infrastructure & Project Finance	Philip Stopford
IP	David Llewelyn
M&A	Peter Finlay
Private Equity	Mats Sacklén
Securitisation & Structured Finance	Rich Reilly
Sovereign Debt	Martin Hughes
Taxation	Neil Woodgate
TMT	David Eisenberg

Whitehead Monckton

Monckton House, 72 King Street, Maidstone, ME14 1BL
Tel (01622) 698000   **Fax** (01622) 690050   **DX** 4807
Email enquiries@whitehead-monckton.co.uk

THE FIRM Whitehead Monckton is a well established Kent firm serving both corporate and private clients - dealing with their commercial, property, investment and personal affairs in an integrated manner.

PRINCIPAL AREAS OF WORK
Commercial Acquisitions and disposals of companies, commercial agreements, director and shareholder advice, employment law, commercial property, debt collection and dispute resolution.
Private Client Wills, probate, trusts, tax law and planning, charities. Investment management and financial services. Family and matrimonial work. Residential property.
Personal Injury Claimant personal injury work including both pre and post event legal expenses insurance.

Chairman/Senior Partner	Richard Stogdon
Chief Executive	Ron Voden MBA
Number of partners	14
Assistant solicitors	9
Other fee-earners	15

Whitelock & Storr

5 Bloomsbury Square, London, WC1A 2LX
Tel (020) 7242 8612   **Fax** (020) 7404 4131   **DX** 35739

THE FIRM Well-established and highly respected firm with specialisation in serious fraud, major crime, extradition, drugs and smuggling cases, revenue and duty matters. Additionally, immigration, civil litigation (including agency work), conveyancing, and landlord and tenant work. Legal Aid franchise holder in crime and extradition, contract holder in immigration and VHCC/serious fraud panel (Autumn 2000).

PRINCIPAL AREAS OF WORK The senior criminal litigation partner has 11 years experience and specialises in general crime, serious fraud, substantial drug cases, extradition and immigration. The firm also practices civil litigation, conveyancing, and landlord and tenant.

INTERNATIONAL The firm has associated offices in Italy, Ireland and USA. Members of the firm speak Italian, French, Turkish, German, Spanish, Hebrew, Arabic and Punjabi.

Senior Partner	Anthony Bloom
Number of partners	4
Assistant solicitors	3
Other fee-earners	8

A-Z ■ LAW FIRMS

Whittles

Pearl Assurance House, 23 Princess Street, Manchester, M2 4ER
Tel (0161) 228 2061   Fax (0161) 236 1046
Website www.whittles.com

Suite 9C, Josephs Well, Park Lane, Leeds, LS3 1AB
Tel (0113) 244 2216   Fax (0113) 242 1214

First Floor, Four Oaks House, Lichfield Road, Birmingham, B74 2TZ
Tel (0121) 308 1331   Fax (0121) 323 4846

Second Floor, Northumberland House, Princess Square, Newcastle, NE1 8ER
Tel (0191) 261 4992   Fax (0191) 261 4887

Managing Partner	David Towler
Senior Partner	Charles Hantom
Number of partners	19
Assistant solicitors	24
Other fee-earners	36

AREAS OF PRACTICE	
Personal Injury Litigation	80%
Employment	16%
Private Client	4%

CONTACTS	
Employment	Charles Hantom
	Helen Parkinson
	David Towler
Personal Injury Litigation	David Rogers

THE FIRM Whittles is a strong and growing trade union and staff association niche practice specialising in plaintiff personal injury work with a growing caseload in wider aspects of employment law. Founded in the 1930s by Preston solicitor John Whittle, the practice's offices currently cover the whole of England and Wales from bases in Manchester, Leeds, the West Midlands and Newcastle upon Tyne. The firm prides itself on its long tradition of working for union members and sees itself as an integral element of the services the unions provide for their members. A high level of client retention and long-term working relationships are borne out of the firm's commitment to plain speaking, openness and listening to their clients needs. Through the adoption of a partnership approach, founded on quality legal advice and built on personal and responsive service, Whittles aims to promote the best interests of union members at all times.

PRINCIPAL AREAS OF WORK
Personal Injury Litigation Whittles is committed to using the firm's experience and specialist skills to protect the interests of union members at work. The firm specialises in personal injury litigation. The majority of this work is made up of claims arising from workplace accidents and diseases with an increasingly growing number of high profile, high value and complex claims. In response to this, Whittles has adopted a modern, client led approach to its services. Specialist teams offering expertise on traumatic and fatal accidents through to minor workplace injuries and post-traumatic shock handle accidents in the workplace. Similarly, through the establishment of specialist industrial disease departments at each of its offices, they are able to offer expertise in asbestosis, asthma, dermatitis, vibration white finger, upper limb disorder, repetitive back strain, industrial deafness, stress and industrial cancer cases.
Employment The firm also has extensive experience in all aspects of employment and labour law including tribunal claims for dismissal, unfair selection for redundancy, sex, race and disability discrimination, equal pay, transfer of undertakings and all aspects of trade union law and human rights.
Other Additional services for trade union clients and their members include discounted conveyancing and wills services together with free initial legal advice on any aspect of law.

CLIENTELE Whittles acts mainly for employees and injured claimants, the majority of whom are trade union and staff association members.

Wiggin & Co

95 The Promenade, Cheltenham, GL50 1WG
Tel (01242) 224114   Fax (01242) 224223   DX 7427
Email law@wiggin.co.uk   Website www.wiggin.co.uk

Senior Partner	Tim Osborne
Managing Partner	Mike Turner
Number of partners	13
Assistant solicitors	13
Other fee-earners	5

AREAS OF PRACTICE	
Media, Entertainment & Commercial	50%
Private Client	28%
Litigation	13%
Property	9%

CONTACTS	
Media & Entertainment	Tim Osborne
	Sean James
Company/Commercial	Mike Turner
Litigation/Defamation	Caroline Kean
IP/IT	Shaun Lowde
Private Client	Michael Fullerlove
Property	Matthew Bullock

THE FIRM Founded in 1973, Wiggin & Co has for many years been known for the high quality of its practice and has a national and international reputation for its expertise, with several of the partners being regarded as leaders in their field. Wiggin & Co is recognised as a major player in many areas of the law including private client, broadcast media and entertainment, corporate/commercial and commercial litigation. Based in Cheltenham, the majority of the partners and assistant solicitors have joined the firm from well-known London practices. The firm continues to expand and today many assistant solicitors are retained on qualification. Three trainees are recruited annually. Since the majority of clients are based in London or overseas the firm has a London office as well as a base in Los Angeles. This was set up to advise clients on the west coast of America wishing to do business in the UK and Europe and to assist European clients with US investment and business activities.

PRINCIPAL AREAS OF WORK The principal areas of work are media and private client.
Media, Entertainment & Commercial The firm handles all aspects of entertainment and media law,

LAW FIRMS ■ A-Z

whether contentious or non-contentious, including terrestrial, satellite and cable TV, multi-media, publishing, music and defamation. The firm also has particular expertise in intellectual property and the internet. The firm offers the full range of commercial and corporate services including joint ventures, acquisitions and mergers, buyouts, reorganisations and financing, insolvency, financial services compliance, employment, immigration and advice in European law.

Private Client, Trusts & Estate Planning The firm has considerable experience and expertise in tax management and protection of worldwide privately owned wealth, where it continues to be an international leader in the field. Work in this area includes income tax and capital planning work for individuals and for companies, their shareholders and executives. There is a strong international emphasis with particular skills in the establishment and restructuring of UK and overseas trusts. Asset protection, in the UK and internationally, is another area of expertise.

Property There is a strong commercial property department dealing with development structuring, sales and leaseback funding, secured loan transactions, sale and purchase of agricultural land and private estates in the UK and EU countries.

RECRUITMENT Due to continuing expansion the firm is always seeking to recruit good quality solicitors. A brochure is available on request.

Wikborg, Rein & Co

One Knightrider Court, London, EC4V 5JP
Tel (020) 7236 4598 **Fax** (020) 7236 4599
Email wrco@wrco.co.uk **Website** www.wr.no

THE FIRM Wikborg, Rein & Co is an international law firm founded in 1923 with offices in Oslo, Bergen, London, Singapore and Japan. The two founding partners set the early course of the firm, establishing its reputation as a commercial firm and attracting clients from the world of shipping and other industries. Although one of the largest law firms in Norway with some 145 lawyers, Wikborg, Rein & Co continues to operate on the basis of a close working relationship with each client. The firm is prepared, if required, to take on management responsibility for the detailed handling of transactions. The London office is staffed by four Norwegian lawyers. In addition to providing liaison services for the firm's international clients on Norwegian business and Norwegian clients on international business, the office has particular expertise in the areas of shipping, mergers and acquisitions, finance and securities.

London Partner	Morten Lund Mathisen
Associate lawyers	3

AREAS OF PRACTICE - LONDON	
Shipping/Admiralty	50%
Company/Commercial/Securities	20%
Finance	30%

PRINCIPAL AREAS OF WORK

Company & Corporate Work includes company formation, corporate acquisitions and disposals, demergers, joint ventures, partnerships, registration services, share issues and voting rights.

Shipping Work includes agency, arrest, building contracts, broking, cargo claims, charters, collisions, finance, flag changes, insurance, management, mortgages, pollution, protection and indemnity claims, sales, salvage and terminals.

Securities Work includes private placings, public offers, acquisitions, bonds, capital reorganisations, convertible issues, demergers, investor protection, mergers, registration services, Stock Exchange listings, trading disputes, underwriting agreements and venture capital.

Finance Work includes ship and other asset finance, project finance, debt rescheduling, guarantees, leases, loan agreements, security documentation, and off-balance sheet instruments.

General Commercial Including agency and distribution, employment and natural resources.

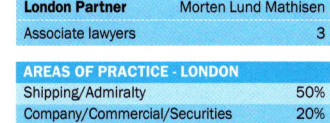

Wilbraham & Co

Minerva House, East Parade, Leeds, LS1 5PS
Tel (0113) 243 2200 **Fax** (0113) 244 9777
Email wilbraham@wilbraham.co.uk **Website** www.wilbraham.co.uk

THE FIRM Wilbraham & Co is a niche practice specialising in planning, environmental, highways, compulsory purchase/compensation and administrative law. The firm's philosophy is to provide its clients with the highest quality of advice on planning and environmental matters, and to produce a cost effective service in a commercial context.

PRINCIPAL AREAS OF WORK The firm handles infrastructure and commercial development projects throughout the UK and has recently advised on a number of high profile residential and employment schemes. In addition to mainstream commercial work it specialises in utility projects for water companies, electricity generators and waste management companies. Further areas of technical expertise

Continued overleaf

Joint Managing Partners	Peter Wilbraham
	Richard Wade-Smith
Number of partners	5
Assistant solicitors	2
Other fee-earners	6

AREAS OF PRACTICE	
Planning	85%
Environmental	15%

CONTACTS	
Partners	David Walton
	Kate Butterfield
	Robert Waite

www.ChambersandPartners.com

1187

include renewable energy, quarrying, waste disposal and regeneration. Public sector work includes advising local authorities, health trusts and educational institutions. The firm increasingly works alongside other legal practices to provide specialist planning advice within property law transactions including the advocacy services of in-house counsel.

The Wilkes Partnership

41 Church Street, Birmingham, B3 2RT
Tel (0121) 233 4333   **Fax** (0121) 233 4546   **DX** 13047
Email law@wilkes.co.uk   **Website** www.wilkes.co.uk

Managing Partner	Anna Dunford
Senior Partner	Nigel Wood
Number of partners	18
Assistant solicitors	31
Other fee-earners	34

THE FIRM Established over 60 years ago, The Wilkes Partnership has developed into a modern commercial practice offering a wide range of legal services to business, industry and private individuals.

PRINCIPAL AREAS OF WORK
Company & Commercial The department handles all aspects of company formation, acquisitions and disposal, corporate finance, management buyouts and corporate restructuring.
Litigation The firm deals with the full range of commercial litigation services including High Court, County Court and matters arising from EU legislation. It also provides a specialised commercial debt collection service. Other work includes commercial contract disputes, personal injury, employment matters and health and safety at work.
Property The practice undertakes and advises on domestic and commercial conveyancing, property development, shops, offices, factories, leases, planning matters, joint ventures and landlord and tenant matters.
Private Client The firm offers advice to individuals regarding wills, settlements, probate, inheritance tax, personal taxation and pensions. The firm also provides a service to private clients on matters of employment, personal injury, consumer legislation, family matters and divorce, criminal work and licensing.

AREAS OF PRACTICE	
Litigation (inc. Insolvency)	48%
Corporate & Commercial	18%
Conveyancing	15%
PI	10%
Tax/Trust/Probate	7%
Other	2%

CONTACTS	
Building Contracts	Peter Tugwell
Civil Litigation	Nigel Wood
Commercial Conveyancing	Adele McDermott
Corporate/Commercial	Gareth O'Hara
Debt Recovery	David Cleary
Employment	Andrew Yendole
Insolvency	John Cooper
Large Scale Voluntary Transfer	Mark Colder
Personal Injury	Maxine Kelly
Public Authority & Housing Associations	Adele McDermott
Tax/Trust	Anna Dunford

CLIENTELE Business and industrial clients nationally as well as long-standing private clients.

INTERNATIONAL The firm has professional links in the major European cities particularly in relation to property buying in Europe. Links with France and Germany are particularly strong. The firm has an associate office in Munich - Messrs Kantenwein von Bechtolsheim.

■ Wilkin Chapman
PO Box 16, Town Hall Square, Grimsby, DN31 1HE   **Tel** (01472) 358234   **Fax** (01472) 360198

Willcox & Lewis

The Old Coach House, Bergh Apton, Norwich, NR15 1DD
Tel (01508) 480100   **Fax** (01508) 480001

Lincoln House, 1 Berrycroft, Willingham, Cambridge, CB4 5JX
Tel (01954) 261444   **Fax** (01954) 261777

Senior Partners	Michael Willcox
	Ian Lewis
Number of partners	2
Assistant solicitors	3

AREAS OF PRACTICE	
Tax Planning	25%
Trust Work	25%
Probate	25%
Charity	20%
Conveyancing	5%

CONTACTS	
Cambridge	Ian Lewis
Norwich	Michael Willcox

THE FIRM Willcox & Lewis is a niche private client law firm, with offices at Cambridge and Norwich, established by two leading specialists in trusts and personal tax. The senior partners are both elected to The International Academy of Estate and Trust Law based in San Francisco, California, and members of the firm belong to the Society of Trust and Estate Practitioners.

PRINCIPAL AREAS OF WORK The firm advises high net worth individuals, trustees and charities, and specialises in complex trusts and estates containing international and commercial elements. Parallel and complementary to the legal practice, separate corporate structures provide advice on substantial general insurance risk assessment and investment advice. Contentious and commercial work is outsourced, and the firm acts regularly with and for other professionals.

■ William Marsh - Sole Practitioner
Tel (020) 7917 6040   **Fax** (020) 7917 6041

■ Williamsons Solicitors
Lowgate, Hull, HU1 1EN   **Tel** (01482) 323697   **Fax** (01482) 328132

Williamson & Soden

Stanton House, 54 Stratford Road, Shirley, Solihull B90 3LS
Tel (0121) 733 8000   **Fax** (0121) 733 3322   **DX** 20652
Email law@williamsonandsoden.co.uk

Citadel, 190 Corporation Street, Birmingham, B4 6QB
Tel (0121) 212 1155   **Fax** (0121) 212 4961

THE FIRM The practice was founded by Ian Williamson and John Soden in 1979. Williamson & Soden has grown significantly and now operates from its own purpose-built premises at Stanton House, Shirley, Solihull and from offices in the centre of Birmingham, adjacent to the law courts.

PRINCIPAL AREAS OF WORK
Crime A large and respected department deals with police matters for clients charged with anything from a motoring offence to a murder. Specialists also deal with Customs & Excise and Inland Revenue Investigations.
Company/Commercial Work includes company/business sales and purchases, trading agreements, mergers and acquisitions and insolvencies.
Litigation All types of commercial disputes with particular experience in Directors Disqualification and landlord and tenant.
Private Client A full range of services covers all aspects of family and matrimonial law, personal injury compensation, wills, probate and trusts.
Property Commercial and residential conveyancing.

Managing Partner	Ian Williamson
Number of partners	9
Assistant solicitors	6
Other fee-earners	9

CONTACTS	
Business Clients	John Soden
	Jeremy Briars
Disputes (General & Commercial)	Stephen Rowe
	Kevin Reilly
Family Law	Clare Fletcher
Motor Racing	John Soden
Personal Injury	Gerard Cusack
Planning Law	Ian Williamson
Police Matters (inc. Motoring)	Alan Bryce
	Fiona Warman
	Colin Doyle
	Vanessa Brown
Property	Lynne Goldsby
Wills & Inheritance	Angela Beck

LG Williams & Prichard
22 St Andrews Crescent, Cardiff, CF10 3DD   **Tel** (029) 2022 9716   **Fax** (029) 2037 7761

Willoughby & Partners

The Isis Building, Thames Quay, 193 Marsh Wall, London, E14 9SG
Tel (020) 7345 8888   **Fax** (020) 7345 4555   **DX** 42577 Isle of Dogs
Email rouse@iprights.com   **Website** www.iprights.com

Pembroke House, Pembroke Street, Oxford, OX1 1BP
Tel (01865) 791990   **Fax** (01865) 791772
Email rouse@iprights.com

THE FIRM Willoughby & Partners is a specialist firm which practises exclusively in the areas of intellectual property (IP) and information technology (IT). It offers a comprehensive service covering all IP rights, as well as IT and e-commerce. It prides itself on being accessible and responsive and providing high quality and competitively priced legal services that take account of commercial objectives and budgets. It has a well respected and dynamic team of lawyers who are supported by the latest technology and a first rate research capability.

PRINCIPAL AREAS OF WORK The firm has a proven track record in relation to all aspects of intellectual property litigation. Recent cases include Asprey & Garrard Ltd v WRA (Guns) Ltd & Another; Impact Plus Plc v Impact Executives Ltd, and Manton & Others v Van Day & Others. The firms associated business, Rouse & Co International, provides a full trade mark agency service in the UK and internationally. Willoughby & Partners develops, co-ordinates and executes enforcement strategies and also advises in relation to the exploitation, acquisition, transfer and financing of IP and IT rights. It can assist in negotiating and structuring deals and drafting agreements - whether as part of a transactional support programme or licensing, distribution or other commercial arrangements. It has developed a strategic IP management service to assist clients in carrying out IP audits and implementing recommendations. The firm offers its services as a 'virtual IP department' for other firms without an IP/IT capability.
Agency Work The firm acts as London agent for other firms in litigation and has five solicitors with experience of supervising Search Orders on behalf of other firms. It also acts as UK agent for foreign law firms in both contentious and non contentious matters.

CLIENTELE Clients include multinational and domestic companies across a wide range of industries (including pharmaceuticals, biotechnology and consumer healthcare, luxury goods, motor vehicle manufacturing, food and drink, publishing and entertainment, clothing and footwear, IT and the internet, sports and telecommunications); international and domestic law firms; accountants and financial institutions.

Continued overleaf

Managing Partner	Shireen Peermohamed
Senior Partner	Tony Willoughby
Number of partners	10
Assistant solicitors	13
Other fee-earners	23

AREAS OF PRACTICE	
Intellectual Property Protection, Enforcement & Exploitation	100%

CONTACTS	
Intellectual Property	Anna Booy (Oxford)
	Ben Goodger (Oxford)
	Shireen Peermohamed (London)
	Rupert Ross-Macdonald (London)
	Diana Sternfeld (London)
	Tony Willoughby (London)

INTERNATIONAL Willoughby & Partners is associated with the Rouse & Co International Group of companies which provides IP consultancy services throughout the world from offices in Europe, the Middle East, Asia Pacific and the Americas. Investigation services throughout the world are provided by the group's in-house investigation unit. The unit also constantly monitors clients' brands worldwide through its 'spotter' service.

RECRUITMENT The firm runs regular training programmes for clients as well as staff on a range of IP and IT related issues. Its lawyers also regularly attend and speak at external seminars and industry meetings. The firm also offers a current awareness and research service to clients.

Wilmer, Cutler & Pickering

4 Carlton Gardens, London, SW1Y 5AA
Tel (020) 7872 1000   **Fax** (020) 7839 3537
Email law@wilmer.com   **Website** www.wilmer.com

Managing Partner	Michael Holter
Number of partners	9
Assistant solicitors	20
Other fee-earners	8

AREAS OF PRACTICE

International Arbitration & Litigation	40%
Financial Services & Venture Capital	20%
Aviation	15%
Telecommunications	15%
Company & Commercial	10%

CONTACTS

International Arbitration & Litigation	Gary Born
	Tom Connell
Company & Commercial	Michael Holter
	James Greig
Telecommunications	Michael Holter
	Paul Von Hehn
Aviation	Dieter Lange
	Michael Holter
Financial Services	Simon Firth
	James Greig
Venture Capital/Private Equity	Gerry Cater
	Simon Firth

THE FIRM Wilmer, Cutler & Pickering is an international law firm with offices in London, Brussels, Berlin, Washington DC, New York, Baltimore and Northern Virginia. Founded in 1962, WCP has over 500 lawyers engaged in a broadly diversified practice.

PRINCIPAL AREAS OF WORK

International Arbitration & Litigation The firm has one of the world's leading international arbitration and dispute resolution practices. The firm handles complex international disputes under rules of all leading arbitral institutions as well as ad hoc arbitrations, and advises clients on disputes under numerous national laws in disputes located throughout the world. The firm has successfully represented clients in several of the largest institutional arbitrations in recent decades, including the largest ICC arbitrations in history. The firm also represents clients in international litigation, particularly in the UK and US, as well as in ADR proceedings. Clients include multinational, European, and US corporations in manufacturing, energy, telecommunications, financial services, and construction sectors.

Company & Commercial The firm has an international commercial and corporate transactions practice, including: cross-border mergers and acquisitions; venture capital; joint venture and partnership arrangements and international corporate alliances; equity and debt financing; distribution arrangements, technology and licensing matters. Particular strengths in cross-border transactions, competition law and UK/US - German issues.

Telecommunications The firm provides specialist advice in multijurisdictional, including internet-related, transactions and international joint ventures. The firm covers all related trade, investment and global information infrastructure issues. The firm guides clients through the regulatory environment of individual European countries, the EU and the US. The firm advises telecoms entrants seeking access to liberalised telecoms markets (especially Germany).

Aviation One of WCP's main practice areas. The aviation team comprises more than 30 lawyers and experts in economic, transport and infrastructure issues involved in multijurisdictional transactions. The firm provides advice on high-level strategy, legal and policy guidance. Clients include airlines, airports, governments, and international agencies in the aviation sector.

Financial Services The firm advises investment businesses on all aspects of regulation by the Financial Services Authority (FSA) and on EU financial services legislation. Clients include asset managers, securities and derivatives broker-dealers, commodity traders, private equity advisors and corporate financiers. Transactional work includes establishing, structuring and marketing offshore and onshore funds.

Private Equity/Venture Capital The firm represents venture capital and private equity funds in a variety of transactions, including early stage financings, mezzanine financings, leveraged buyouts and exits. The firm also represents start-ups and management teams. The firm structures and forms private equity and hedge funds.

INTERNATIONAL The firm has offices in Brussels, Berlin, Washington DC, New York, Baltimore and Northern Virginia. Languages spoken by members of the firm include French, German, Italian, Swedish and Spanish.

Wilson & Co

697 High Road, London, N17 8AD
Tel (020) 8808 7535 **Fax** (020) 8880 3393 **DX** 52200 Tottenham 2
Website www.wilsonandco.co.uk

Ptnrs 5 **Asst solrs** 18 **Other fee-earners** 16 • Legal Aid firm serving the community since in 1990 - specialising in immigration and asylum, criminal defence, family/children and mental health. Members of: The Serious Fraud Panel and the Law Society Immigration Law Panel, Mental Health Review Tribunal Panel, Children Panel and Family Law Panel.

Wilson, Elser, Moskowitz, Edelman & Dicker

65 Fenchurch Street, London, EC3M 4BE
Tel (020) 7553 8383 **Fax** (020) 7553 8399 **DX** 858 City
Email cherryt@wemed.com **Website** www.wemed.com

Number of partners	1
Assistant solicitors	2
Other fee-earners	1

AREAS OF PRACTICE	
US Defence Litigation	50%
Insurance Coverage Disputes	10%
Arbitration	10%
Creditors' Rights	10%
E&O Brokers (US & UK)	10%
D&O	10%

THE FIRM The firm is one of the largest in the United States, and has been serving clients for more than a quarter of a century. It has grown considerably during this period and now has offices in 16 major cities in the US. The London office of Wilson, Elser, Moskowitz, Edelman & Dicker is a multi-national partnership associated with the US firm. The office concentrates on insurance and reinsurance work including product liability, insurance broker errors and omissions and international arbitration. Mr Cherry is both a US lawyer and a solicitor. Mr Cherry is also a Fellow of the Chartered Institute of Arbitrators. The London office conducts litigation in English courts.

PRINCIPAL AREAS OF WORK Initially, the practice was insurance-related, and the firm maintains a pre-eminent position with regard to all aspects of insurance law and the insurance industry. However, it has broadened its services and expertise to meet the needs of clients in the following areas: corporate organisation, negotiation, rendering business advice for both domestic and international clients on acquisitions, mergers, regulatory matters, financing, real estate and leasing transactions, contract negotiations and drafting, employment law and tax advice. The firm maintains close relationships with insurance specialist law firms in Europe.

INTERNATIONAL Members of the firm speak French, German, Spanish, Japanese and Korean. There are additional offices in New York, Albany, Baltimore, Boston, Chicago, Dallas, Houston, Los Angeles, Miami, Newark, Philadelphia, San Diego, San Francisco, Washington DC, White Plains and Garden City.

Wilson Nesbitt

Citylink Business Park, Albert Street, Belfast, BT12 4HB **Tel** (028) 9032 3864 **Fax** (028) 9033 3707

Wilsons

Steynings House, Fisherton Street, Salisbury, SP2 7RJ
Tel (01722) 412412 **Fax** (01722) 411500 **DX** 58003 Salisbury 1
Email info@wilsonslaw.com **Website** www.wilsonslaw.com

Number of partners	19
Assistant solicitors	16
Other fee-earners	26

THE FIRM Wilsons is one of the best known firms in the South of England, with a nationwide reputation for private client work. Specialist practitioners provide all the legal services required by wealthy individuals and owner managed companies. The firm is structured so that differing specialisations can, when appropriate, work together as teams so as to provide the client with a comprehensive service. The firm is well known for acting for landed estates and its skills in agriculture, but it is increasingly also acting for people and companies whose assets are not represented by rural land holdings. The firm also acts for a substantial number of private schools and an increasing number of charities. It has acquired both Lexcel and IiP accreditation.

PRINCIPAL AREAS OF WORK

Private Client The firm is believed to have one of the highest net worth of private client practices outside London. Three partners principally specialise in advising owners of landed estates whilst three other partners deal with all aspects of tax planning including offshore work. There are also partners specialising in property and agriculture within the private client sector as well as two litigators.

Commercial The firm deals with all types of company-related and business transactions. It also has experienced teams advising on employment matters and commercial property. It also undertakes substantial commercial litigation. Wilsons also provides company secretarial services to its corporate

Continued overleaf

A-Z ■ LAW FIRMS

clients. The commercial sector frequently works closely with the private client sector.

Family Law This is led by a member of the Family Law Association, who trained at Withers; this department deals with top drawer High Court family work.

Schools Wilsons acts for a growing number of independent schools. Typical issues dealt with are governors' liabilities, insurance issues, employment problems, charitable appeals, mergers and school/parent contracts.

Charities Wilsons' charity team is headed by Alison McKenna who was formerly an assistant commissioner with the Charities Commission. Wilsons is taking positive steps to alert charities to the increasing demands placed on them by changes in the regulatory framework.

Winckworth Sherwood

35 Great Peter Street, Westminster, London, SW1P 3LR
Tel (020) 7593 5000 **Fax** (020) 7593 5099 **DX** 2312 Victoria
Email wandp@winckworths.co.uk

THE FIRM Began in the 1780's in Westminster and is very much still there but maintains a notional 'Westminster Practice' also in the City of London, Chelmsford and Oxford.

Niche Areas Public sector, parliamentary, housing, ecclesiastical law, local government, education, charities, health, retail, licensing and services to the police. The original private client practice remains strong.

Client-led Approach Teams of lawyers led by partners, dedicated to their clients' business areas, make up the firm's departments. Most departments boast a 'one-stop' service for all their clients' needs. This means that the client's problems are dealt with by the same team and responded to by people who know the client and what the client is trying to achieve.

Typical Clients Leading commercial, institutional and public sector clients who are publicly accountable and business-like in their approach but whose raison-d'être is the provision of a service for public benefit rather than the generation of a profit.

Normal Legal Portfolio There is a lot of activity around the Public/Private interface. The firm also has a growing commercial litigation group and a lively construction law practice.

New Opportunities Lead to new specialist departments. Lawyers share professional experiences across the firm and form cross-departmental teams to respond to particular challenges. Because the firm is client-led, the expertise demanded probably already exists in the firm and when a new client approaches the firm with an old problem or an old client approaches it with a new problem, the firm will be able to produce the client-led team to address it. It is these teams that, in the firm's philosophy, become the departments of the future.

PRINCIPAL AREAS OF WORK

Litigation Work in this area is conducted on a client-led basis, whenever possible, with a dedicated team following each particular client sector.

Public Law & Parliamentary Work handled includes matters relating to legislation and legislative drafting, constitutional law, infrastructure projects (particularly in relation to all forms of transport, ports and other utilities), statutory and other companies, financial institutions, local authorities and professional bodies. Areas of law also include town planning, compulsory purchase and compensation.

Police Advice to the police covers governance and accountability issues and links between forces. National police organisations are provided for and strategic partnerships.

Ecclesiastical, Education & Charity These are traditional areas of practice and developing client sectors. The firm acts for the Church of England, the Roman Catholic Church and the Archbishop of Canterbury and many charities. Education clients include primary and secondary schools and institutions of further and higher education both with and without church connections.

Social Housing The full range of constitutional, property, finance and litigation services are provided to the firm's many housing association clients and to lenders in the housing sector, housebuilders and local authorities.

Licensing The firm has extensive experience in commercial and licensed property, and licensing generally, including the licensing of petrol stations.

Medical There is a growing health and medical practice which is being nurtured in the firm's client-led culture.

Employment This area of law covers all the firm's client sectors.

Costs The firm provides a specialised costs service to its clients to ensure they maximise their recovery of costs from other parties.

Public Inquiries This multi-niche public sector practice has led to the firm's involvement in a number of high profile inquiries and investigations. The Bristol Babies inquiry, the Hillsborough scrutiny and the Marchioness investigation represent three recent cases.

Number of partners	20
Assistant solicitors	32
Other fee-earners	29

AREAS OF PRACTICE

Litigation	26%
Parliamentary & Planning	20%
Housing & Local Government	19%
Ecclesiastical, Education & Charities	16%
Private Client	15%
Licensed Property	4%

CONTACTS

Charities	Owen Carew-Jones
Commercial Property	Robert Botkai
Commercial	Ronald Farrants
Commercial Litigation	Jim Rai
Construction	Jim Rai
Costs	Malcolm Goodwin
Disciplinary Proceedings	Tim Watts
	Peter Williams
Ecclesiastical	Paul Morris
	John Rees
	Michael Thatcher
	Brian Hood
Education	Michael Thatcher
	Owen Carew-Jones
Employment	Owen Carew-Jones
	Tim Watts
Family	Lorna Grosse
Healthcare	Simon Eastwood
Housing Finance & Governance	Anna Clark
Human Rights	Tim Watts
Licensing	Robert Botkai
Local Government	Andrew Murray
Parliamentary	Alison Gorlov
Police	Nick Owston
	Tim Watts
Public/Private Sector Partnerships	Nick Owston
Public Inquiries	Simon Eastwood
Public Law	Alison Gorlov
	Paul Irving
Private Client	Hugh MacDougall
Property Litigation	Jim Rai
	Peter Williams
Residential Development	Roger Fitton
Residential Conveyancing	John Plummer
Social Housing	Andrew Murray
Town Planning	Chris Vine
Transport, Docks & Harbours	Paul Irving
	Stephen Wiggs
Urban Regeneration	Roger Fitton

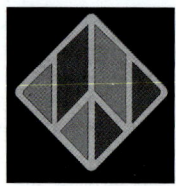

INTERNATIONAL The firm is a founder member of an international network of law firms called Eurseau.

RECRUITMENT Qualified staff should apply in the first instance to the Partnership Secretary, Mr TF Vesey. The firm recruits three trainee solicitors each year - a 2:2 law or 2:1 non-law degree is usually required and applications should be made by handwritten letter (and typed CV) to Mr RHA Mac-Dougald.

Winstanley-Burgess

378 City Road, London, EC1V 2TQ
Tel (020) 7278 7911   **Fax** (020) 7833 2135   **DX** 58253 Islington
Email law@winstanley-burgess.co.uk

Contact Bridget Taylor • Established 1975. Handles probate and property. Best known for immigration and public interest law.

AREAS OF PRACTICE	
Immigration & Nationality	90%
Non-contentious	10%

Winward Fearon

35 Bow Street, London, WC2E 7AU
Tel (020) 7420 2800   **Fax** (020) 7420 2801   **DX** 37959 Kingsway
Email enquiries@winwardfearon.co.uk   **Website** www.winwardfearon.co.uk

THE FIRM This central London firm is one of the UK's top construction law practices. It has also established a significant reputation in infrastructure project work, litigation and property. Winward Fearon was founded in 1986. As a matter of policy it concentrates its development around an expanding number of niche areas, rather than professing to expertise across the board. Those niche areas are carefully chosen to facilitate the creation of cross-departmental teams which specialise in industry sectors, rather than technical legal disciplines. In addition to their litigation and arbitration work, the firm's construction and commercial litigation departments increasingly make use of alternative dispute resolution procedures. The firm above all seeks to provide a top-quality and cost-effective service. It has an established and enviable client base, including large plcs, owner-managed businesses, and developers. The firm's international links have been strengthened by its membership of Eurolegal, which is a European Economic Interest Group of law firms in EU jurisdictions.

PRINCIPAL AREAS OF WORK

Construction Construction law forms a large part of the firm's practice and is carried out for national and international clients in building, civil engineering, and the professions. Typical issues may concern defective building, formation of contracts, liquidated damages, extension of time, and critical-path analysis, as well as payment. In addition, the department deals with bonds and insurance-related matters, certificates, statutory obligations, variations in construction work, indemnities and warranties, together with product liability. The work of the department is both contentious and non-contentious, including very large cases in the High Court and in ICC, LCIA and UNCITRAL arbitrations. Mediation continues to increase.

Commercial & Property Litigation Winward Fearon's commercial litigation team handles a wide variety of commercial claims, including employment disputes for UK and international clients. Part of the team specialises in property and landlord and tenant litigation, including dilapidation claims, lease renewals, rent review problems, easement and right of way actions, service charge disputes, and franchises. The team often works closely with the firm's property team.

Infrastructure Projects, PFI & Corporate Finance The infrastructure project, PFI and corporate finance team has handled a number of high profile transactions in the past five years. Adrian Luto has established a reputation in infrastructure projects, particularly in the independent power plant section both in the UK and overseas. The Company/Commercial Department focuses on the purchase and sale of private companies and businesses, management buyouts, other venture capital transactions, joint ventures and partnership agreements.

Property The property team, headed by Guy Fearon, one of the firm's four founding partners, focuses on commercial property and residential development. Work includes the acquisition and sale of development sites, industrial estates, offices, and other commercial and investment property. The department advises on redevelopment projects, auction contracts, joint ventures, and partnership developments, including taxation, property finance, and landlord and tenant work. The team also provides a service in high quality residential property.

Senior Partner	David Cornes
Partnership Secretary	Adrian Luto
Number of partners	10
Assistant solicitors	6
Other fee-earners	3

AREAS OF PRACTICE	
Construction	59%
Infrastructure Projects, PFI & Corporate Finance	19%
Property	8%
Commercial & Property Litigation	14%

CONTACTS	
Commercial & Property Litigation	Clive Levontine
Construction	Richard Winward
Infrastructure Projects, PFI & Corporate Finance	Adrian Luto
Property	Guy Fearon

A-Z ■ LAW FIRMS

Witham Weld

70 St George's Square, London, SW1V 3RD
Tel (020) 7821 8211 **Fax** (020) 7630 6484 **DX** 86164 Victoria 2
Email postmaster@wwlaw.co.uk

Number of partners	7
Assistant solicitors	3
Other fee-earners	3

THE FIRM Established for over 200 years, Witham Weld has a long-standing reputation in its work for every kind of client, including religious and civil institutions, charities and trusts, commercial and private clients. Today, the aim remains the same; to provide the highest quality legal services, founded on experience and expertise and supported by innovation and the use of modern working methods.

PRINCIPAL AREAS OF WORK The firm provides advice and assistance in a wide range of areas including charity law, property, revenue and tax planning, wills and probates, company/commercial, contracts, education, employment, copyright, and all forms of litigation.

Withers LLP

16 Old Bailey, London, EC4M 7EG
Tel (020) 7597 6000 **Fax** (020) 7597 6543 **DX** 160 Chancery Lane
Email claire.o'connor@withersworldwide.com **Website** www.withersworldwide.com

Number of principals	50
Assistant solicitors	61
Other fee-earners	46

AREAS OF PRACTICE

Private Client & Charities	38%
Family	15%
Litigation	20%
Corporate	14%
Property	13%

CONTACTS

Agricultural Property	Penelope Elliott
Banking	David Dannreuther
Charities	Alison Paines
Commercial Litigation & Dispute Resolution	Christopher Coffin
Commercial Property	Claudia D'Ambrosio
Corporate Finance	Hugh Devlin
Employment	Meriel Schindler
Family	Gill Doran
Fraud Litigation	Margaret Robertson
Healthcare, Pharmaceutical & Bioscience	Anthony Indaimo
Information Technology	Riccardo Abbate
Insolvency	Roberto Moruzzi
Intellectual Property	John Maycock
Personal Tax, Trust & Probate	Tony Thompson
Professional Negligence	Christopher Coffin
Residential Property	Henry Stuart
Trust & Probate Litigation	Dawn Goodman

THE FIRM Withers' transatlantic merger with US firm Bergman, Horowitz & Reynolds has created the first international law firm dedicated to the business, personal and philanthropic interests of successful people, their families and advisors.

PRINCIPAL AREAS OF WORK

Private Client In the private client field, Withers has over 100 tax and trust specialists in the UK and US, by far the largest and most comprehensive private client practice in the world. The firm responds to client needs by forming dedicated teams which service particular types of private client - entrepreneurs, families, investment and private banks, trust companies, landed estates and the globally wealthy. Other professionals use standard textbooks written and edited by the firm's lawyers.

Family Withers is a leading firm in the UK for family law and has an established reputation for international work in the sector. It has one of the largest family law teams comprising six principals, ten assistant lawyers and one consultant. All aspects of family work are covered and many of the cases involve foreign dimensions and complex issues and trust/financial structures. The team works closely with the private client groups in London and in the US.

Corporate On the corporate side the firm acts for listed and private companies, financial institutions, partnerships, sole traders and entrepreneurs. Specialist areas of practice include corporate finance (in particular AIM), intellectual property, banking and employment. Areas of particular industry expertise include fashion, motor racing, technology and media.

Litigation Withers is one of the very few firms that has a specialist practice in litigation relating to trusts and probate. This has been further enhanced by the firm's merger since the beneficiaries of most major trusts will have either a US or UK link. It is also well known for its litigation expertise in fraud (particularly tracing assets through trusts), employment, insolvency and professional negligence.

Charities The firm's charities practice continues to grow and it is now ideally suited to deal with the establishment of US charities. It is supported by a range of linked specialisms from across the firm.

Property Withers' property practice encompasses all aspects of residential, commercial and agricultural property. The firm is particularly renowned for its expertise in agricultural law and in handling international property transactions, particularly for US purchasers.

INTERNATIONAL In another pioneering move, Withers is the first top 100 law firm to convert to a UK limited liability partnership (LLP) taking advantage of the new legislation which came into force last year. With offices in London, New York, New Haven (Connecticut) and Milan, the merged firm is known as Withers LLP in the UK and internationally and as Withers Bergman in the US. The firm provides integrated answers to the US, UK and international legal and tax needs of its clients whether this means restructuring their own assets, buying or selling businesses and properties, coping with divorce, termination of their employment or setting up charitable foundations. Clients can deal directly with US lawyers in London, providing US advice in London time and UK lawyers in New York providing UK advice in US time. Withers LLP has the largest team of specialist US private client lawyers in Europe and more Italian speakers than any other City law firm. This year the firm is extending its presence in Milan, opening a new office there. For more than two decades, the firm has been assisting Italians investing and doing business in the UK and beyond.

RECRUITMENT The firm recruits 12 trainees each year many of whom stay with the firm on qualification. A significant proportion of the principals (the LLP equivalent of 'partners') trained with the firm.

Withy King

5-6 Northumberland Buildings, Queen Square, Bath, BA1 2JE
Tel (01225) 425731 Fax (01225) 315562 DX 8014 Bath
Email mail@withyking.co.uk Website www.withyking.co.uk

THE FIRM Withy King was founded in 1883, and has developed a number of specialist practice areas as well as two separate brands. Complete, its conveyancing brand and Accrue - stockbroking and financial planning.

PRINCIPAL AREAS OF WORK Commercial property, personal injury, clinical negligence, construction, employment, corporate and private client.

RECRUITMENT There have been six main additions to Withy King with solicitors joining the corporate, construction and CDR departments from Wragge & Co., Fussel Wright, Wilsons and Thring Townsend. The personal injury department has grown and opened new premises in Wiltshire.

Managing Partner	Martin Powell
Number of partners	17
Assistant solicitors	16
Other fee-earners	35

CONTACTS	
Clinical Negligence	Simon Elliman
Commercial	Chris Kane
Construction	Graham Street
Personal Injury	Muiris Lyons

Wolferstans

Deptford Chambers, 60-66 North Hill, Plymouth, PL4 8EP
Tel (01752) 663195 Fax (01752) 672021 DX 8206 Plymouth -1
Email info@wolferstans.com Website www.wolferstans.com

THE FIRM Wolferstans is a major regional practice with three offices in Plymouth and another in Taunton. Founded in 1812, it is committed to excellence whilst providing a comprehensive personal service. A number of partners are chairmen of various tribunals.

PRINCIPAL AREAS OF WORK
Company/Commercial Work handled includes company formations, acquisitions and sales, funding arrangements, management buyouts, employment matters, licensing, commercial conveyancing and a wide range of commercial litigation. One member of the team is a licensed insolvency practitioner.
Personal Injury This division of the practice operates from all major offices. The specialist motorcycle division is operated only from the Taunton office. The medical specialist division is headed by an assessor and member of the panel and a referral panel member for AVMA. The firm is involved in a number of group actions. Clinical negligence franchises are held at Plymouth and Taunton.
Crime The leader of the team is well known for his courts martial work. In addition to defence criminal work, the practice also acts for government agencies in prosecutions and provides advocates for inquests, inquiries, disciplinary hearings and tribunals.
Sport Clients include Somerset County Cricket Club, Plymouth Argyle Football Club and Plymouth Basketball Club.
Matrimonial & Family Work handled by this division includes separation and divorce, mediation, custody and access, adoption, child welfare, financial settlements and maintenance agreements. There are three members of the Children's panel and two accredited specialist family lawyers.
Private Client Work includes wills, probate and trusts and residential conveyancing.
Additional Areas The firm regularly appears on behalf of accused persons at courts martial and has extensive experience in inquests and inquiries.

INTERNATIONAL Languages spoken include French, German, Greek and Spanish.

Senior Partner	Paul Woods
Number of partners	26
Assistant solicitors	13
Other fee-earners	13

AREAS OF PRACTICE	
Personal Injury/Clinical Negligence	45%
Matrimonial & Children	20%
Commercial	10%
Insurance	10%
Private	10%
Crime	5%

CONTACTS	
Clinical Negligence	Simon Parford
Commercial	Nick Roper
Crime	David Teague
Insurance	Colin Brazier
Litigation	Bill Duncan
Matrimonial/Family	Phil Thorneycroft
Personal Injury	Colin Brazier
Private	John Chapman
Probate	Gill Hollinshead
Sport	Nick Roper

A-Z ■ LAW FIRMS

Wollastons

Brierly Place, New London, Road, Chelmsford, CM2 0AP
Tel (01245) 211211 **Fax** (01245) 354764 **DX** 89703 Chelmsford 2
Email enquiries@wollastons.co.uk   **Website** www.wollastons.co.uk

Number of partners	12
Assistant solicitors	11
Other fee-earners	17

AREAS OF PRACTICE	
Corporate/Commercial	39%
Litigation	28%
Property/Planning	19%
Employment	8%
Private Client	6%

CONTACTS	
Commercial	Nicholas Burnett
Corporate	Richard Wollaston
	Richard Payne
Employment	Kevin Palmer
Intellectual Property	Nigel Thompson
Landlord & Tenant	Nicholas Cook
Litigation	Bruce Bowler
Planning	Jim Little
Property Development	Alan Wyatt
Property Litigation	Michael Callaghan
Trusts & Tax	Patrick Penny

THE FIRM Wollastons provides high levels of expertise and service to business clients based mainly in Essex, London and surrounding counties, as well as foreign companies and their UK subsidiaries. It also advises private individuals and families, including some who are resident abroad. The firm is located in Chelmsford, only 35 minutes by train from central London, with easy access to the motorway network and Stansted airport. It is exceptionally well resourced and well organised with first-rate IT and communications.

PRINCIPAL AREAS OF WORK
Corporate & Commercial Work includes corporate finance; company sales and acquisitions; MBOs and MBIs; insolvency and reconstructions; European law; intellectual property; commercial agreements; business immigration. The firm has considerable international experience.
Employment The firm handles employment contracts; unfair and wrongful dismissal; redundancy; race and sex discrimination; business transfers; frequent advocacy in the Employment Tribunal.
Property Work handled includes commercial development, investment and agricultural property; landlord and tenant.
Litigation The firm handles commercial disputes; professional negligence claims; debt recovery; insolvency; property and inheritance disputes; personal injury.
Private Client Work includes wills; trusts; capital tax planning; probate; family property and finance.

INTERNATIONAL Wollastons is an active member of IAG International, an association of independent professional firms represented throughout Europe and beyond.

RECRUITMENT Wollastons welcomes enquiries from outgoing candidates with a strong academic record. The firm takes two or three trainees annually, and is prepared to fund LPC course fees in some cases.

■ Woodford-Robinson

4 Castilian Terrace, Northampton, NN1 1LE **Tel** (01604) 624926 **Fax** (01604) 231457

Woodroffes

36 Ebury Street, London, SW1W 0LU
Tel (020) 7730 0001 **Fax** (020) 7730 7900 **DX** 99923 Victoria
Email enquiries@woodroffes.org.uk

Senior Partner	Peter Woodroffe
Number of partners	2
Assistant solicitors	4

CONTACTS	
Banking & Project Finance	Roger Brown
Conveyancing	Roger Brown
Education & Art	Peter Woodroffe
Licensing	Howard Timms
Litigation & Other	Philip Gordon-Smith
Probate	Richard Wheatcroft

THE FIRM Founded by CG Woodroffe in 1877, it is a general practice with emphasis on individual attention. The office is situated in Belgravia and is close to Victoria Station.

PRINCIPAL AREAS OF WORK Known for problem solving in the company/commercial field, private client, education, charities and foreign work. A specialist department handles commercial conveyancing including development, hotels, nightclubs and restaurants and licensing for the same. Work also includes the transfer of works of art, residential conveyancing, employment, probate, matrimonial, litigation, European Court, fraud recovery, insurance claims, insolvency and most legal matters.

CLIENTELE The firm acts for private clients in UK and abroad, public companies, banks and charities.

■ Woollcombe Beer Watts

Church House, Queen Street, Newton Abbot, TQ12 2QP **Tel** (01626) 202404 **Fax** (01626) 202420

LAW FIRMS A-Z

Wragge & Co

55 Colmore Row, Birmingham, B3 2AS
Tel (0870) 903 1000 **Fax** (0870) 904 1099 **DX** 13036
Email mail@wragge.com **Website** www.wragge.com

Managing Partner	Quentin Poole
Senior Partner	John Crabtree

CONTACTS	
ADR	Paul Howard
Automotive	Bob Gilbert
Aviation	Jane Pittaway
Banking	Julian Pallett
Biopharmaceuticals	Patrick Duxbury
Building Societies	Jonathan Denton
Charities	Gary Barber
Commercial Litigation	Paul Howard
Commercial Property	Gerald Bland
Construction	Simon Baylis
Corporate Finance	Jeremy Millington
Employees' Benefit/ Share Schemes	Kevin Poole
Employment	Andrew Hodge
Energy/Utilities	Neil Upton
Environmental	Lee McBride
EU/Competition	Guy Lougher
Financial Services	Jonathan Denton
Food	Richard Haywood
Insurance	Mark Hick
Intellectual Property	Gordon Harris
International	Jane Pittaway
Local Government	Peter Keith-Lucas
Media & Entertainment	Conan Chitham-Mosley
Outsourcing	David Hamlett
Pensions	Vivien Cockerill
PFI	Stephen Kenny
Planning	Dan Hemming
Property Litigation	Suzanne Lloyd Holt
Retail & Leisure	Jack Jacovou
Tax	Kevin Poole
Technology	David Vaughan
Transport	Michael Whitehouse
Travel	Jane Pittaway

THE FIRM Wragge & Co is a major UK law firm based in Birmingham with a substantial national and international client base including over 250 listed companies and 60 local authorities. Over 70% of the firm's turnover is generated from outside the Midlands. Wragge & Co has built its business on four strategic building blocks - clients, quality, people and profits - a focus which has fuelled the firm's national profile and growth. There is real strength and depth across a fully comprehensive range of services combined with the development of leading practices. Investment in IT has maximised efficiency while a focus on 'people culture' has secured staff retention and high profile appointments. And always there is devotion to providing the highest quality work and client service - Wragge & Co prides itself on being a 'relationship' firm. In recognition of its progressive personnel policies the firm was placed 19th in The Sunday Times 100 Best Companies to Work For 2002. In recognition of its commitment to the community, Wragge & Co has a dedicated pro-bono and community support co-ordinator. Other offices are located in Brussels and London.

PRINCIPAL AREAS OF WORK Wragge & Co is organised into six groups each comprising several teams many of which are leading UK practices.

Technology The technology group is a national heavyweight with 18 partners and 60 lawyers bringing together the firm's top technology players in corporate, IP, dispute resolution, IT outsourcing, e-commerce and telecoms. In the last three years Wragge & Co's technology related work has increased by over 250% and clients include AT&T, British Airways, BT, Cap Gemini, Ernst & Young and Ordnance Survey.

Dispute Resolution The dispute resolution group includes Wragge & Co's leading construction practice and a 32 partner commercial litigation team equal to City firms in size, depth of dedicated commercial litigation resource and quality of work.

Property Development The property development group and the retail and property services group represent the UK's third largest property group providing a full range of services - including planning, litigation, environmental, tax and management - to landlords and tenants, property developers, contractors, funding institutions, investors and public authorities. This includes a team dedicated to residential development.

Corporate The corporate group, the largest of its kind outside London and number one in the Midlands, competes on a national platform. Acknowledged to be 'a competitor to all but the largest City firms', the group works in client-facing teams for PLC, private equity and major corporates.

Human Resources The human resources group covers employment, employee benefits, pensions, personal tax, trusts and charities. This group enjoys a reputation for workable solutions to business problems.

Finance & Projects The finance and projects group offers a range of top specialists in the core areas of energy and utilities - working on an international scale - banking, EU and competition, financial services, insolvency, outsourcing, PFI, regulation and transport.

Other Wragge & Co also operates a number of industry focused teams in aerospace and aviation, automotive, bio-pharmaceutical, food, media and entertainment and travel. For more information and the latest news on Wragge & Co please visit www.wragge.com.

Wright Hassall

9 Clarendon Place, Leamington Spa, CV32 5QP
Tel (01926) 886688 **Fax** (0871) 871 2071 **DX** 11863 Leamington Spa
Email email@wrighthassall.co.uk **Website** www.wrighthassall.co.uk

Managing Partner	Peter Beddoes
Number of partners	22
Assistant solicitors	16
Other fee-earners	34

CONTACTS	
Agriculture	Graham Davies
Commercial Litigation	Richard Lane
Commercial Property	Tim Rowe
Construction	Philip Harris
Corporate/Commercial	Peter Beddoes
	Mark Lewis
Employment	Ian Besant
Family	Julia Bunting
Housing	Carol Matthews
Insolvency	Robin Koolhoven

THE FIRM Wright Hassall has an enviable portfolio of clients that value the firm's quality of advice, high standard of service and the location. The firm continues to attract high quality lawyers from leading firms who enhance the firm's reputation as a major player in the region. 'Regional Firm, City League' sums up Wright Hassall.

PRINCIPAL AREAS OF WORK

Agriculture The agricultural team advises local landowners, farmers and major agricultural organisations on all aspects of agricultural law.

Construction The team advises on all aspects of contentious and non-contentious work, including PFI projects. The firm also offers an effective dispute resolution service.

Commercial Property The firm advises a number of blue chip plcs on their property matters as well as

1197

advising on leases, the sale and purchase of commercial property and building development work.

Corporate/Commercial Work includes the sale and purchase of companies and business assets, MBOs and joint ventures. The firm is also strong in employment law, commercial contracts, partnerships, business formations and intellectual property.

Housing Associations The department, which has doubled in size within the last year, boasts two of the leading practitioners in the country. The team deals with every legal requirement of social housing providers.

Litigation The department covers a number of disciplines: commercial, property, including landlord and tenant, construction, professional negligence, defendant insurance and personal and corporate insolvency. The firm also has a matrimonial department with a formidable reputation.

Private Client Work includes advising on trusts, estates and probate as well as residential property transactions.

CONTACTS (Continued)	
Insurance	Richard Lane
Intellectual Property	Laurie Heizler
Private Client	Charles McKenzie
Property Litigation	Jane Senior
Residential Property	Chris Meredith

Wright, Johnston & Mackenzie
302 St Vincent Street, Glasgow, G2 5RZ **Tel** (0141) 248 3434 **Fax** (0141) 221 1226

Wright Son & Pepper

9 Gray's Inn Square, London, WC1R 5JF
Tel (020) 7242 5473 **Fax** (020) 7831 7454 **DX** 35 London/Chancery Lane
Email wsp@wrightsonandpepper.co.uk **Website** www.wrightsonandpepper.co.uk

THE FIRM Wright Son & Pepper has been established in Gray's Inn Square since 1800. Its clients range from public companies, institutions and regulators through to small businesses and professional and private individuals. The firm is highly regarded for its work in professional and partnership matters.

PRINCIPAL AREAS OF WORK

Professional Regulation The firm has an extensive practice in advising regulators of professionals in relation to both regulatory and disciplinary matters.

Partnership The firm advises on the formation and dissolution of partnerships and on disputes in which partnerships or their members are involved as well as on problems which may arise on the admission or retirement of partners.

Litigation The firm has extensive experience in general commercial and private litigation including professional negligence claims. High Court agency work is also undertaken.

Property All aspects are covered, with the main emphasis on offices, shop and factory/warehouse leases and developments, planning and funding arrangements.

Company/Commercial The firm deals with the normal range of company and commercial work and has considerable experience in dealing with all forms of computer-related contracts and restraint of trade covenants.

Family Law All aspects of matrimonial, family, welfare and childcare law are covered with special emphasis on ancillary relief in matrimonial proceedings.

Private Client & Tax The firm deals with wills, settlements, trust formation and administration, powers of attorney, Court of Protection, investment advice, personal tax, estate planning, probates and the administration of estates.

Other Areas The firm also undertakes work in debt recovery, intellectual property, building contract disputes, employment, landlord and tenant, transport, and consumer law.

INTERNATIONAL The firm has professional connections in Belgium and the USA.

Number of partners	8
Assistant solicitors	3
Other fee-earners	2

AREAS OF PRACTICE	
Company/Commercial/Partnership	22%
Litigation	16%
Property	16%
Family	16%
Regulation	15%
Private Client	15%

CONTACTS	
Company/Commercial	Steven Alais
Family	Paul Butner
Litigation	John Kenneally
Partnership	Nicholas Wright
Private Client	Brian Wates
Property	Hilary Palmer
Regulatory/Disciplinary	Iain Miller

LAW FIRMS ■ A-Z

Wrigleys

19 Cookridge Street, Leeds, LS2 3AG
Tel (0113) 244 6100 **Fax** (0113) 244 6101 **DX** 12020 Leeds 1
Email thepartners@wrigleys.co.uk

Managing Partner	Richard Sutton
Senior Partners	Peter Chadwick
	Annabel Duchart
	Matthew Wrigley
Number of partners	12
Assistant solicitors	16
Other fee-earners	4

THE FIRM Wrigleys was formed as a specialist private client practice in May 1996. It combines the private client departments of DLA, Hammond Suddards and the Leeds and Manchester offices of Eversheds. In August 2000 it was joined by the specialist charities firm of Malcolm Lynch. The department has also seen substantial organic growth and now has 12 partners and a total of 70 staff. The main office is in Leeds and the firm has benefited from the remarkable rise of the city as a professional centre. There is a smaller but thriving office in Sheffield. As a specialist practice with relatively low overheads, the firm presents itself as a logical alternative to London practices.

PRINCIPAL AREAS OF WORK Wrigleys advises wealthy individuals, charities, foundations, social economy clients and trustees. A great deal of the work is tax and trust based, with a growing property department serving the same clientele. Originally best known for its strength in the heritage and landed areas, the firm now serves a wide spectrum of old and new money. In addition the pensions team advises sponsoring employers, trustees and members of occupational pension schemes and has a particular strength in advising on unapproved and personal pension schemes. Contentious or commercial work is referred elsewhere, and the firm regularly acts with and for other professionals. Recent developments have included the strengthening of the pensions department with the arrival of two experienced pensions lawyers. The department now includes four of the region's best known lawyers.

CLIENTELE The firm acts for a large number of charities, foundations and well-known families, with most of the individual clients being rich enough to face serious tax problems. Historically, most clients were northern based, but, latterly, the firm has begun to attract clients nationally and internationally, since some offshore clients perceive a cost benefit in using a regional practice for work that has traditionally gone to London. The firm acts for a wide range of charities, particularly in the religious, educational and conservation areas. The firm's pension clients include a number of substantial occupational pension schemes, IFAs and independent trustees.

■ Wynne Baxter
Century House, 15-19 Dyke Road, Brighton, BN1 3FE **Tel** (01273) 775533 **Fax** (01273) 207744

■ Young & Partners
New Law House, Saltire Centre, Glenrothes, KY6 2DA **Tel** (01592) 630890 **Fax** (01592) 631052

■ Young & Lee
No 6 The Wharf, Bridge Street, Birmingham, B1 2JS **Tel** (0121) 633 3233 **Fax** (0121) 632 5292

■ Young & Pearce
58 Talbot Street, Nottingham, NG1 5GL **Tel** (0115) 959 8888 **Fax** (0115) 947 5572

TC Young

30 George Square, Glasgow, G2 1LH
Tel (0141) 221 5562 **Fax** (0141) 221 5024 **DX** GW 78
Email mail@tcyoung.co.uk

Managing Partner	Andrew Cowan
CONTACTS	
Charities/Structures	Mark Ewing
Corporate/Stock Transfers	Stephen MacGregor
Litigation	Andrew Cowan
Private Client	Andrew Robertson
Property	Isabel Ewing

THE FIRM TC Young provides a wide range of legal services to housing organisations, lenders, charities, general commercial organisations and private clients. The firm has seen significant growth in the last year, with particular emphasis in the fields of social housing and charities and is now the leading player in the Scottish social housing scene. TC Young has strength in depth in all aspects of social housing law.

PRINCIPAL AREAS OF WORK
Social Housing & Charities A recognised leader in the field, TC Young currently acts for more than 120 social housing organisations. It provides a full range of legal services to its social housing and charity clients, including corporate structures, funding, stock transfers, development services and housing management.
Business & Commercial The firm advises in a wide range of general business and commercial/corporate matters, including corporate structures, funding, commercial property, contracts and employment.
Private Clients The firm has a significant private client base and offers a full range of personal client legal services.

A-Z ■ LAW FIRMS

Yuill & Kyle
79 West Regent Street, Glasgow, G2 2AR **Tel** (0141) 331 2332 **Fax** (0141) 332 4223

Zermansky & Partners
10 Butts Court, Leeds, LS1 5JS
Tel (0113) 245 9766 **Fax** (0113) 246 7465 **DX** 12061

THE FIRM Zermansky & Partners is an expanding firm combining private client work and a strong commitment to Legal Aid work (franchised in seven areas), with a comprehensive range of services to small to medium sized businesses and not-for-profit organisations.

PRINCIPAL AREAS OF WORK The firm is particularly known for its large family department, including matrimonial finance, child abduction, emergency and childcare work. The litigation department has specialised employment, housing and personal injury/clinical negligence sections. Insolvency work is a new area of development. It has substantial experience in sports law, particularly with governing bodies.

INTERNATIONAL Languages spoken include Hindi, Polish and Punjabi.

Managing Partner	Lindsay Ward
Senior Partner	Norman Taylor
Number of partners	11
Assistant solicitors	8
Other fee-earners	6

CONTACTS	
Childcare	Lynn McFadyen
Company & Commercial	David Honeybone
Insolvency	Neil Lieberman
Litigation	Richard Lindley
Matrimonial & Family	Norman Taylor
Personal Injury	Gurchan Jandu
Probate	Christopher Dudzinski
Property	Russell Graham
Sports	Richard Lindley

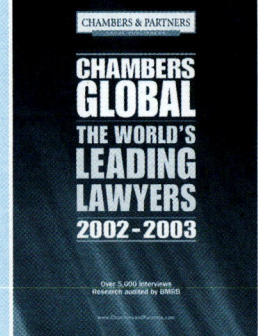

The world's leading lawyers
All 4,000 of them
All in one place

The 3rd edition: available now
www.ChambersandPartners.com

IN-HOUSE LAWYERS AND COMPANY SECRETARIES

INDEX OF IN HOUSE LAWYERS & COMPANY SECRETARIES

List by name. For full details see the alphabetical listing of firms on pages 1206-1224

Abdoo, David
Carlton Communications PLC

Adams, Laurie
ABN Amro Equities Holdings (UK) Limited

Ainger, Roy
Croda International PLC

Allen, Paul A
Aggreko PLC

Allison, Austin
TT International

Allnut, Richard
Fujitsu Services

Allnutt, Robert E B
Amersham plc

Alway, Jackie
BMG Music Publishing Limited

Applegarth, Chris
Arriva PLC

Armour, Robert M
British Energy PLC

Aron, Jeremy
DS Smith plc

Ashcroft, Charles P
EMI Group PLC

Ashcroft, Clive
Land Securities PLC

Ashley, Juliet
Omnicom Europe Limited

Ashley-Brown, Michael
Canary Wharf Group plc

Atkinson, Richard
Merrill Lynch Europe PLC

Atkinson, Richard
Yule Catto & Co PLC

Austin, Keith
Tibbett & Britten Group PLC

Bailey, Christopher S
Aggregate Industries PLC

Bailey, John PC
Kingston Communications PLC

Baker, Brian
Rolls-Royce PLC

Baker, Martin
CarltonTelevision plc

Barma, Hussein
Antofagasta PLC

Barratt, Simon
Whitbread Group PLC

Bartlett, Stephen
Bear Stearns International Limited

Bate, David
Enterprise Energy Ireland Ltd

Bates, Deanna
British Sky Broadcasting Group PLC (Sky Digital)

Battle, John
Independent Television News Ltd (ITN)

Bellhouse, Robin
Greene King PLC

Bennett, Richard
HSBC Holdings plc

Berry, John G
Matalan PLC

Bestmann, Jay
Bank One Corporation

Beswitherick, David
Manchester United PLC

Bevan, Peter B P
BP plc

Bicheno, Janet
Arab Bank PLC

Bickell, Brian
Shaftesbury PLC

Birch, Karen
Bank of New York

Blacker, Michael
AMEC Group Limited

Bloom, David
HSBC Holdings plc

Bloom, Jonathan
Woolworths Group plc

Blum, Barbara
Shell International Ltd

Boad, Robert
BP plc

Bondy, Rupert
GlaxoSmithKline

Bowden, Mike
Innogy Holdings PLC

Bowley, Bill
Mersey Docks & Harbour Company

Boyd, Justin
Hess Energy Trading

Braine, Anthony
British Land Company PLC

Braithwaite, Nick
Associated Newspapers Limited

Bramwell, Phillip
mmO2 plc

Brett, Alastair
Times Newspapers Ltd

Brierley, Tony
3i Group plc

Brimacombe, David
Standard Chartered Bank

Brinley-Codd, Peter
Sir Robert McAlpine (Holdings) Ltd

Britton, Bob
Hiscox Syndicate 33

Britton, Rupert J
Civil Aviation Authority (CAA)

Brown, Elizabeth
Acambis PLC

Brown, Leonie
Bank of America

Buchanan, Alan
British Airways plc

Budd, Geoffrey
Dixons Group PLC

Budge, Duncan
RIT Capital Partners PLC

Burchill, Jeremy
Aberdeen Asset Management PLC

Burge, Patricia
Times Newspapers Ltd

Burke, Jonathan
Wm Morrison Supermarkets PLC

Burnett, Louis
Euromoney Institutional Investors PLC

Bush, Daniel
Interserve plc

Butterworth, Siobhain
Guardian Newspapers Limited

Bye, Tim
British Midland Airways Ltd

Byrne, Stephen G
Bank of Cyprus (London) Limited

Cadd, Susan
Fitness First PLC

Caller, Mitchell B
JP Morgan Chase

Calow, David
WPP Group PLC

Cameron, Alex
Barclays Capital

Campbell, Colin
Channel 5 Broadcasting Limited

Carfora, Carmelina
Electrocomponents PLC

Carr, Chalmers
Coutts & Co

Cavanagh, Julia
Serco Group plc

Chadwick, Peter
Bovis Construction Ltd

Chain, Julia
T-Mobile (UK)

Chambers, Martin
Kingfisher PLC

Chambers, Paul
Smith & Nephew PLC

Chandler, Neil
Westbury PLC

Chapman, Claire
Reuters Group PLC

Charnock, Stephen
Hays PLC

Chase, Suzanne
The Big Food Group PLC

Chelsom, Paul
Credit Suisse First Boston (CFSB)

Chesney, Carol
Halma PLC

Chester, J Geoffrey
Hilton Group PLC

Chidley, Mark
The Royal Bank of Scotland Group plc

Chinnery, Paul
Channel 5 Broadcasting Limited

Chitty, Ian
BG Group PLC

Churchill-Coleman, Richard
TUI UK Ltd

Circus, Philip
Institute of Sales Promotion (ISP)

Clarke, Peter
Man Group PLC

Clayton, Neil
First Technology PLC

Clifton, Roger C
TBI PLC

Cohen, Yehuda
Dynegy Europe

Coker, David J
The Morgan Crucible Company plc

Coles, Pamela
RAC plc

Collier-Wright, Charles
Trinity Mirror PLC

Collins, John
ABN Amro Equities Holdings (UK) Limited

Collins, Michael
RMC (UK) Ltd

Cook, Rosemary
International Power plc

Cooper, Nick
JD Wetherspoon PLC

Cooper, Richard
Johnston Press PLC

Cormick, Charles
The Rank Group PLC

Cox, Alan
GlaxoSmithKline

Crone, Tom
News International PLC

Curtin, Edmond
Credit Suisse First Boston (CFSB)

Curtis, John E
Intermediate Capital Group PLC

da Cunha, Maria
British Airways plc

Dalby, Marc
Merck Sharp & Dohme Limited

Dand, Anthony
Expro International Group plc

Davison, Andrew
Greggs PLC

Dawes, Peter G
VT Group plc

Dawson, Grant
Centrica plc

de Laperouse, Marc
Bank of America

Deeming, Nick
BOC Group Plc

Denham, Grey
GKN plc

Denison, Graeme
Caledonia Investments plc

Dennis, Will
Lazard

Dent, Laurence
Barratt Developments PLC

Dhillon, Marla
ING Baring Asset Management Holdings

Dodds, Simon
Deutsche Bank AG

Doherty, Patrick
Cattles PLC

Doherty, Stephen P
Singer & Friedlander Group PLC

Downey, Antonia S
Jim Henson Company Ltd

Dransfield, Graham
Hanson PLC

Dregent, Patricia
Carpetright PLC

Dryden, Patricia
London Underground Limited

Dunlop, Alan
Amerada Hess Limited

Durant, Ian
Thistle Hotels PLC

Durrant, Dawn
Geest PLC

Dyball, Jane
Warner Chappell Music Ltd

Dyke, Philip
Electra Investment Trust PLC

Eardley, Paul
Spirent plc

East, Anna
Britannic Group PLC

Edwards, Pamela
Fidelity Investments International

Elliot, William
Goldman Sachs International

Ellis, Gerald
Safeway Stores PLC

Elmore-Jones, Michael
Friends Provident Life

Ezekiel, Ivan
Minerva PLC

Ezekiel, Marcus
EGG PLC

Farrant, Simon
Johnson Matthey PLC

Firth, Patrick
awg plc

Fitz, Daniel
Cable & Wireless

Fletcher, Anne
BT Group PLC

Flinn, David
Viridian Group PLC

Fluker, Louise
De La Rue plc

Folland, Nick
EMAP plc

Forster, Garry
Alfred McAlpine PLC

Foulkes Shaw, Sarah M
BBA Group PLC

Fowkes, Nigel
Innogy Holdings PLC

Foye, Anthony
Taylor & Francis Group PLC

Francis, Neil
Persimmon PLC

Francis, Richard
CMG PLC

French, Julian
EMI Recorded Music UK & Eire

INDEX OF COMPANIES

Friedrich, William
BG Group PLC

Fritchie, Andrew
Marlborough Stirling PLC

Fulton, Kate
Young & Rubicam Group Ltd

Garner, Margaret
Credit Agricole Indosuez

Garratt-Frost, Stephen
HSBC Holdings plc

Geen, David
Goldman Sachs International

Geissmar, Svenja
MTV Networks

Gemmell, John
Paragon Group of Companies PLC

George, Alastair
Sony Music Entertainment (UK) Ltd

Gibber, Robert
Tate & Lyle PLC

Gibbons, Duncan
Royal Bank of Canada

Gibson, David William
Rexam PLC

Gibson, Graham D
John Laing plc

Gladman, Hugh
St James's Place Capital PLC

Gledhill, James
Citibank

Goddard, Ian
The Alliance Trust PLC

Goodenough, Adrian J
Alliance UniChem Plc

Gorman, Jeremy
The Game Group PLC

Goulbourne, Sarah-Jane
Stanley Leisure plc

Goulden, Ian
Exel plc

Gradon, Michael
Peninsular & Oriental Steam Navigation Company (P & O)

Graham, Alan
N M Rothschild & Sons Limited

Grantham, Helen
Chubb plc

Green, Philip E
Meggitt PLC

Green, Trevor L
McCarthy & Stone PLC

Greenwood, David
JJB Sports PLC

Gregory, Janet
GE Capital Equipment Finance

Greig, Kenneth J
Scottish Widows Investment Partnership

Griffiths, Nigel E
Securicor plc

Grime, John
Bodycote International PLC

Guedes, Lawrence
Logica PLC

Haig, David
UFJ International plc

Harding, Iain M
Scottish Investment Trust PLC

Hardman, Steven
Waste Recycling Group PLC (WRG)

Harland, Philip
N Brown Group PLC

Harman, Ian
Brambles Industries plc

Harris, Mark
Next PLC

Harris, Philip
St Ives PLC

Hartrey, Patrick
PizzaExpress PLC

Haydon, Stuart
Hammerson PLC

Healy, Christopher
Coats plc

Heard, Robert
BPB PLC

Heath, Richard
Unilever plc

Heather, Christopher
Vizzavi Europe Limited

Henderson, David
Northgate PLC

Henderson, Sheila
Reckitt Benckiser plc

Hendrie-Liano, Jessica
Freeserve PLC

Herga, Robert
BAA plc

Herlihy, Michael H C
Imperial Chemical Industries PLC (ICI)

Hicks, Jeremy
Aegis Group PLC

Highley, Owen
British Airways plc

Higson, Robert Ian
London Electricity Group plc

Hildebrand, Andrew
FilmFour

Hodges, Simon
Millennium & Copthorne Hotels PLC

Holland, Anthony
Novar plc

Horn, Nigel D
Torex PLC

Horner, Elizabeth
Rothschild Asset Management Limited

Hosker, David
United Utilities Water plc

Hoskin, Malcolm C
Davis Service Group plc

Houghton, Ian
WH Smith PLC

House, Richard
Tokyo-Mitsubishi International PLC

Huddle, Stephen
Premier Oil plc

Hughes, Kathrine
Alliance & Leicester PLC

Hui, Carol
Amey plc

Hull, Jonathan
Really Useful Group Limited (The)

Hull, Victoria
Invensys plc

Humphries, Gordon
British Assets Trust PLC

Hunt, Simon A
Anite Group PLC

Hussey, Paul
Bunzl plc

Ivens, Robert
Marks and Spencer plc

Jackman, Ian
Arcadia Group

Jameson, Ian
Lehman Brothers International (Europe)

Jenkins, Mark
COLT Telecom Group plc

Jepson, Susy
Somerfield plc

John, Andrew
First Choice Holidays PLC

Johnson, Catherine
London Stock Exchange

Johnson, Geoffrey
Lloyds TSB Group PLC

Johnson, Guy
Debenhams plc

Johnson, Simon
ITV Network Limited

Jones, Clare
Citibank

Jones, Sarah
BBC

Jordan, James
George Wimpey PLC

Jordan, Paul
Bradford & Bingley plc

Jowett, Jonathan D
SSL International PLC

Joy, Larissa
Ogilvy & Mather

Kanter, Andrew
Autonomy Corporation PLC

Kass, Harvey
Daily Mail & General Trust PLC

Kaufman, Anthony
P & O Princess Cruises

Kaye, Paul
Shanks Group PLC

Keating, Michael
Cadbury Schweppes PLC

Keevil, Tom
Gallaher Group plc

Keisler, Ben
Anglo American PLC

Kelloe, Jane
American Express Bank Ltd

Kelly, Fiona
Capita Group plc

Kilbee, Michael
Lloyds TSB

Kite, Timothy
Derwent Valley Holdings PLC

Knight, Michael R
Severn Trent Water Ltd

Kyriakides, Evie
Mars Incorporated

Lanaghan, Brian
Mizuho International plc

Lawton, Charles
Rio Tinto PLC

Le Marchant, Piers
Lehman Brothers International (Europe)

Leff, Clyde M
Pilkington plc

Lenihan, Martin
Skanska Construction Group Ltd

Lester, Michael
BAE Systems plc

Levin, Sarah
Universal Music Publishing Group

Lewis, David A
JP Morgan & Co

Lilley, Charles E
Xansa PLC

Lister, Paul
Associated British Foods PLC

Lynch, Lucy
Morgan Stanley Investment Management Ltd

Ma, Joan
Morgan Stanley International & Co Limited

MacKernan, Colm P
ARM Holdings plc

Mahoney, Lee
PHS Group plc

Malkin, Gwyn
Abbey National PLC

Manning, Richard
GWR Group plc

Manson, Ian
Scottish & Southern Energy plc

Marcus, Robert
IBM UK Ltd

Marshall, Alexander
Goldman Sachs International

Marshall, Bridget
Scottish Environmental Protection Agency (SEPA)

Martin, Desna
Great Portland Estates PLC

Martin, Graham
Tullow Oil PLC

Martin, Philip J
Pillar Property PLC

Martin, Simon
Gartmore Investment Management PLC

Mason, Geoff
Jarvis PLC

Massey, Roger
Daiwa Securities SMBC Europe Limited

Maurice, Emmanuel
European Bank for Reconstruction & Development (EBRD)

May, Robert G
Slough Estates PLC

May, Tatjana
Shire Pharmaceuticals Group plc

Maynard, Peter
Prudential PLC

McBride, Richard A
Michael Page Group PLC

McClenan, Michael S
Bank of Scotland

McCormack, Frank
Balfour Beatty PLC

McCracken, Cameron
Pathé Pictures Limited

McDonald, Tony
National Express Group PLC

McElhatton, Jane
Cable & Wireless PLC

McFarlane, Stuart
Kelda Group plc

McKeown, Mark
William M Mercer Limited

McMahon, Greg
MyTravel Group plc

McQuoid, Christopher
TTP Communications plc

Mee, David
Nomura International PLC

Mellett, Diane
Cambridge Antibody Technology Group PLC

Milburn, Lucian
Westdeutsche Landesbank Girozentrale (London)

Mileson, Chris
EMI Music Publishing Ltd

Miller, Therese L
Goldman Sachs International

Mitchelson, Alan
The Weir Group PLC

Moore, Lawrence
Innovation Group PLC

Morley, Ronald M
Compass Group PLC

Morris, David
GUS plc

Morris, Philip
Balfour Beatty Civil Engineering Limited

Morris, Tim
The Carphone Warehouse Group

Morrison, Angela
Working Title Films Ltd

Mostert, Frederick
Richemont

Murphy, Finbarr
Bank of Ireland

Murray, Kenneth
Edinburgh Fund Managers Group PLC

Murray, Martin
Old Mutual plc

Musker, Graeme H R
AstraZeneca PLC

Neate, Francis W
Schroders PLC

Nicholson, Judith A
Avis Europe PLC

Nimmo, Mark
Société Générale

Nunn, Carol
Wilson Connolly Holdings PLC

Oakes, Andy
Misys plc

INDEX OF COMPANIES

Ogden, Jeremy
Barclays Bank PLC (Barclays Private Clients)

Ogilvie Smals, Rufus
GKN plc

O'Hara, Simon
Cookson Group plc

Oliver, Michael J
The Boots Company PLC

Olsen, Peter
Dairy Crest Group plc

Ormond, Jon
Deutsche Bank AG

O'Shea, John
IMI PLC

Owen, Jane
Aon Limited

Page, Adrian
South Staffordshire Group PLC

Page, Ann
Co-Operative Bank PLC

Paget-Brown, Edward
Credit Lyonnais

Palmer, Martin
Bovis Homes Group PLC

Pank, Edward
ICAP plc

Partington, Marcus
Trinity Mirror PLC

Patterson-Brown, Ian
Friends Ivory & Sime PLC

Pearce, Julia
Credit Suisse First Boston (Europe) Ltd

Pearce, Michael
Lonmin plc

Pearce, Simon
P & O Princess Cruises PLC

Perrot, Robin
Chelsfield PLC

Pethybridge, Eldon
Centrica plc

Petty, Chris
AstraZeneca International

Pike, Andrew S
Travis Perkins PLC

Pool, Fiona
Omnicom Europe Limited

Poole, James
Enterprise Inns PLC

Pope, John
Cobham PLC

Porter, Alan
Imperial Tobacco Group PLC

Porter, Leslie
The Wolverhampton & Dudley Breweries PLC

Porter, Norman
Tomkins PLC

Potterell, Clive
Chrysalis Group PLC

Pottinger, Alan
Computacenter PLC

Price, Philip
UBS Warburg Group

Primer, Daniel
Catlin Underwriting Agencies Limited

Pritchard, Wendy
Berkeley Group PLC

Proctor, Timothy
Diageo plc

Purvis, Martin
Brake Bros PLC

Pybus, Mark
Company Pictures

Quaranto, Leonard A
Allied Domecq plc

Quinlan, Diane
Kidde PLC

Radice, James
Polydor Ltd

Rayner, Timothy
United Utilities PLC

Rees, David
Provident Financial plc

Reeves, Jane
Thomson Financial

Reid, Marijke
Sky Interactive Limited

Rhys-Jones, Steven
Rotork PLC

Rice, Geoffrey
City of London Investment Trust PLC

Rigby, Victoria
Vivendi

Roberts, Allen C G
Renishaw plc

Roberts, David
GlaxoSmithKline

Robinson, Deborah
WS Atkins PLC

Robinson, Michael
The Sage Group plc

Rosenthal, Richard
Morgan Stanley International & Co Limited

Ross, Corina K
MITIE Group PLC

Ross-Stewart, Charles
UBS AG

Ruppel, Louise
FirstGroup plc

Ryan, Bill
Deutsche Bank AG

Salt, Kirsten
The Merchants Trust PLC

Sampson, Jeremy
Taylor Woodrow plc

Sanghvi, Rakesh
Sony Music Entertainment (UK) Ltd

Saphra, Robin
BTG PLC

Schofield, Christopher
Filtronic PLC

Schwarz, Nathalie
Capital Radio PLC

Scott, Derek
Stagecoach Group PLC

Scott, Stephen
Vodafone Group Plc

Sellers, Robin
Close Brothers Group plc

Shah, Sheeraz
Working Title Films Ltd

Shepherd, Clare
Smiths Group plc

Sher, Farrell
Liberty International PLC

Shirran, Jane L
National Australia Group Europe Limited

Shirras, James
Film Finances Limited

Slater, John
Celltech Group PLC

Smethurst, Edward G
Ultraframe PLC

Smith, Fiona
National Grid Company PLC

Smith, Peter
Spirax-Sarco Engineering PLC

Smith, William
BHP Billiton Plc

Smyth, Rodney
Invesco UK Limited

Soley, Martin
Le Meridien Hotels & Resorts Limited

Solomon, Deryck J
AGA Foodservice Group plc

Sowerbutts, Kevin
BNP Paribas

Stables, Jane
United Business Media plc

Stanley, James
Scottish Power PLC

Stark, Fiona
Powergen UK plc

Stemmons, Robert
Citigroup Wealth Management

Stephens, Roger
Spectris plc

Stephenson, Mandy
New Look Group PLC

Stevinson, Jenny
ABN Amro Equities Holdings (UK) Limited

Stirzaker, Mark
British Vita plc

Stoker, Peter J
Bellway PLC

Stride, Andrew
Luminar PLC

Studd, Kevin
Credit Suisse First Boston (CFSB)

Sugrue, Claire
Universal/Island Records Limited

Swingland, Charles
PowderJect Pharmaceuticals

Swynnerton, John
SIG PLC

Sykes, Stephen
Certa (UK) Ltd

Tames, Jane
Scottish Radio Holdings PLC

Tang, Norma
Renishaw plc

Tapp, Richard
Carillion plc

Taylor, Colin
Northern Rock PLC

Taylor, Simon
HIT Entertainment PLC

Thomas, Emma
Nestor Healthcare Group PLC

Thomas, Jonathan
Goldman Sachs International

Thornton, Jane
Gartmore Investment Management PLC

Thurston, David
J Sainsbury PLC

Timms, Geoffrey
Legal & General Group plc

Tingay, Sarah
FremantleMedia Ltd

Todhunter, Barry
DFS Furniture Company PLC

Tomalin, Jan
Channel Four Television Corporation

Tomlinson, Humphrey
Royal & Sun Alliance Insurance Group Plc

Tonkinson, Andrew OC
SABMiller PLC

Tothill, John
Forth Ports PLC

Toubkin, Michael
BNP Banque Nationale de Paris PLC

Townsend, Nicolas J
Wilson Bowden PLC

Trust, Howard B
Barclays PLC

Tubbs, Josephine
Framlington Group Ltd

Vardy, Val
Towers Perrin

Vaughan, Chris
Six Continents PLC

Vellani, H Andrew S
Scottish & Newcastle PLC

Ventrella, Tony
FKI PLC

Vickers, Paul
Trinity Mirror PLC

Virelli Jr, Louis J
Unilever plc

Wade, Vyvienne
Jardine Lloyd Thompson Group plc (JLT)

Walford, Justin
Express Newspapers Ltd / Express Sunday

Walker, Rhiannon E
Redrow PLC

Wallace, Lindsay
SMG PLC

Walsh, Stephen
Associated British Ports (ABP)

Ward-Jones, Robert
Rentokil Initial PLC

Watkins, Eric
London Bridge Software Holdings PLC

Watson, John
Warner Music UK Ltd

Watts, Nigel
Brixton PLC

Webb, Robert
British Airways plc

Webb, Steven
Premier Farnell PLC

Whiston, Tim
iSOFT Group PLC

White, Mark J
Wolseley PLC

Whittaker, Andrew
The Financial Services Authority (FSA)

Willey, Stuart
The Financial Services Authority (FSA)

Williams, Carol
Northern Foods PLC

Williams, Gareth
Countrywide Assured Group plc

Williams, Kathryn
Channel 4

Williams, Roy
Inchcape PLC

Williams, Simon
Taylor Woodrow Construction Ltd

Williams, Stephen G
Unilever plc

Wilson, Andrea
Informa Group plc

Wilson, Hilary
Skanska Construction Group Ltd

Withington, Neil
British American Tobacco PLC

Witt, David
IBM UK Ltd

Wood, Duncan
Cairn Energy PLC

Woodcock, Ian
The Royal Bank of Scotland Group plc

Woodier, Kenneth D
Pennon Group PLC

Woodward, Deborah
easyJet Airlines

Woodward, Keith
John Mowlem & Company PLC

Wrangles, Kay
Collins Stewart Holdings PLC

Wright, Paul
Taylor Nelson Sofres plc

Wyatt, Marina
Psion PLC

Wyn-Davies, Arthur
Telegraph Group Limited

Young, Eddie
Associated Newspapers Limited

IN-HOUSE LAWYERS ■ COMPANY SECRETARIES

3i Group plc
91 Waterloo Road London SE1 8XP
Tel: (020) 7928 3131 **Fax:** (020) 7928 0058
Tony Brierley, Company Secretary & Head of Legal Services

Abbey National PLC
Legal Department Genesis House 301-349 Midsummer Boulevard Milton Keynes MK9 2JE
Tel: (01908) 348076 **Fax:** (01908) 348282
Email: gwyn.malkin@abbeynational.co.uk
Website: www.jobsatabbeynational.co.uk
No of lawyers in dept: 35 (including legal executives)
Gwyn Malkin, Secretary & Counsel
Specialisation: Handles commercial and corporate law matters and management of the legal function. Member of Legal Committee of British Bankers Association.
Career: Qualified 1975. Became Head of Legal Services at Abbey National in July 1992. Appointed Secretary and Counsel of Abbey National plc in January 2002.
Other lawyers: Corporate and Regulatory Law Team : Simon Goldburn, Richenda Kullar, Sally Hopwood, Alan Squires, Jane Stolberger , Kevin Plaskitt, Katrina Wild . Commercial Law Team : Desmond Pettit, Katie Ward, Ian Wallbank, Jane Hayden, Geoffrey Pope, John Candlish , Inderjeet Hohal, Alan Cufaude, Lisa Hattersley, Mike Willoughby . Banking and Lending Law Team: Carole Jones, John Hamilton, Jacqueline Neblett, Pauline Fone, Damask Smith, Sara Mayes, Tina Gohil, Gillian Macey . Life Division and Offshore Law Team : Colin Browning, Gwynedd Miller, John Laing, Dawn Adshead, Joanna Morton, John Forsyth , Helen Nellist . Intellectual and Real Property Law Team : Alison Greene , Ben Raybould .

Aberdeen Asset Management PLC
One Albyn Place Aberdeen AB10 1YG
Tel: (01224) 631999 **Fax:** (01224) 647010
Email: jeremy.burchill@aberdeen-asset.com
Website: www.aberdeen-asset.com
No of lawyers in dept: 8
Work outsourced: 50% - Aquisitions: overseas.
Jeremy Burchill, Head of Legal & Compliance
Specialisation: Financial services, compliance in UK and Europe.
Career: Barrister in Northern Ireland 1979-1984; Financial Services (in-house) since 1984; Educated: Campbell College, Belfast and Queens University, Belfast.
Personal: Married with two children.
Other lawyers: John Brett - Corporate; Paul Campbell - Closed Ended Funds; Elizabeth Moxham - Open Ended Funds; Colin Forbes; Lisa Brown; William Drummond; David Bryson; Joanne Carle.

ABN Amro Equities Holdings (UK) Limited
250 Bishopsgate London EC2M 4AA
Tel: (020) 7678 8000 **Fax:** (020) 7678 7612
Jenny Stevinson, General Legal & Company Administration Director
250 Bishopsgate London EC2M 4AA
Tel: (020) 7678 8000 **Fax:** (020) 7678 7612
Laurie Adams, Head of Legal and Compliance
250 Bishopsgate London EC2M 4AA
Tel: (020) 7678 8000 **Fax:** (020) 7678 7612
John Collins, Deputy Head of Legal Products

Acambis PLC
Peterhouse Technology Park 100 Fulbourn Road Cambridge CB1 9PT
Tel: (01223) 275300 **Fax:** (01223) 416300
Website: www.acambis.com
Work outsourced: All.
Elizabeth Brown, Director of Finance and Planning & Company Secretary

Aegis Group PLC
43-45 Portman Square London W1H 6LY
Tel: (020) 7070 7700 **Fax:** (020) 7070 7800
Jeremy Hicks, Chief Financial Officer & Company Secretary

AGA Foodservice Group plc
Headland House New Coventry Road Sheldon Birmingham B26 3AZ
Tel: (0121) 722 7618 **Fax:** (0121) 722 7611
Email: d.solomon@glynwed.com
Website: www.agafoodservice.com
No of lawyers in dept: 2
Work outsourced: Variable - All litigation. A proportion of other work.
Deryck J Solomon, Group Company Secretary
Specialisation: Company/Commercial, Property and Company Secretarial.
Career: Education: Keble College, Oxford (1972 - 1975) M.A. (Oxon) Career: joined Glynwed as Solicitor in 1984 moved to Group Legal Manager 1993, in 1996 moved to Group Secretary 1996 to date.
Other lawyers: Mr. Deryck J Solomon: group secretary, company/commercial/property. Mrs. F. Wheeler: solicitor, property.

Aggregate Industries PLC
Bardon Hall Copt Oak Road Markfield LE67 9PJ
Tel: (01530) 816600 **Fax:** (01530) 816666
Christopher S Bailey, Group Finance Director

Aggreko PLC
Ailsa Court 121 West Regent Street Glasgow G2 2SD
Tel: (0141) 225 5900 **Fax:** (0141) 225 5949
Paul A Allen, Company Secretary

Alfred McAlpine PLC
8-10 Suffolk Street London SW1Y 4HG
Tel: (020) 7930 6255 **Fax:** (020) 7839 6902
Website: www.alfred-mcalpine.com
No of lawyers in dept: 3
Work outsourced: 80% + - All types
Garry Forster, Group Company Secretary

Alliance & Leicester PLC
Group Legal Services Building 3 Floor 2 Carlton Park Narborough LE19 0AL
Tel: (0116) 200 4559 **Fax:** (0116) 200 4995
Email: kathrine.hughes@alliance-leicester.co.uk
Website: www.alliance-leicester.co.uk
No of lawyers in dept: 14
Kathrine Hughes, Head of Group Legal Services

The Alliance Trust PLC
Meadow House 64 Reform Street Dundee DD1 1TJ
Tel: (01382) 201700 **Fax:** (01382) 225133
Website: www.alliancetrusts.com
No of lawyers in dept: 1
Ian Goddard, Company Secretary
Specialisation: Company law, corporate governance, contracts , employment.
Career: Rugby School; Brasenose College, Oxford; Bar (Midland & Oxford Circuit) 1974-1984; 3i plc (Manager, Legal Department) 1984-1998; The Alliance Trust (Company Secretary) 1998- to date.

Alliance UniChem Plc
Alliance House 2 Heath Road Weybridge KT13 8AP
Tel: (01932) 870550 **Fax:** (01932) 870551
Email: adrian_goodenough@alliance-unichem.com
Website: www.alliance-unichem.com
Work outsourced: 95%
Adrian J Goodenough, Company Secretary

Allied Domecq plc
The Pavilions Bridgwater Road Bedminster Down Bristol BS13 8AR
Tel: (0117) 978 5000 **Fax:** (0117) 978 5300
Email: leonard.quaranto@adsweu.com
Website: www.allieddomecqplc.com
No of lawyers in dept: 27
Work outsourced: 50% - M&A, litigation, conveyancing, employee share schemes.
Leonard A Quaranto, General Counsel & Company Secretary
Specialisation: Mergers/Acquisitions/Joint Ventures; Major corporate transactions; Company Secretarial Matters - UKLA, NYSE, Board
Career: BS Languages 1969, Georgetown University; JD International Commercial Law, George Washington National Law Centre 1977; Member District of Columbia Bar. Assistant International counsel - ralston Purina Company 1978-1980. Assistant International counsel - Chrysler Corporation 1980-1984. General Counsel - Boles Trade Corp 1984. Private Practice - Washington D.C. 1984-1985. Chief Counsel, Europe/Africa/Middle East - Kimberly Clark Corp 1985-2001.
Personal: Married to Nancy (nee Burns) Quaranto, one son Paul (12). Resides Cotswolds - Naunton, Cheltenham and London
Other lawyers: Maria Reay - Deputy Group General Counsel General Counsel - Wines Harold Gorman - General Counsel - North America Stephen Horn - General Counsel - Quick Service Restaurants Marcos Taracon - General Counsel - Europe Agustin Lopez Padilla - General Counsel - Latin America Simon Reeves - Head of Trademarks Tom Mains - Senior Legal Adviser

AMEC Group Limited
76-78 Old Street London EC1V 9RU
Tel: (020) 7539 5839 & 077 68 554 698 **Fax:** (020) 7539 6952
Email: michael.blacker@amec.com
Website: www.amec.com
No of lawyers in dept: 9
Work outsourced: Some corporate and commercial work, some commercial property and conveyancing litigation and any litigation requiring specialist expertise.
Michael Blacker, Head of Legal Services
Specialisation: Providing legal services to AMEC Group and AMEC Asia Pacific, including drafting and negotiating agreements for construction and engineering related projects. Also handles dispute resolution and supervises external solicitors . Manages AMEC plc's corporate legal work.
Career: Attended Nottingham University, BA (Hons) Barrister (1978). Has worked in-house for Taylor Woodrow Group, BP Minerals, George Wimpey Plc (1982-1997) and joined AMEC in 1997.
Personal: Leisure interests include cricket, rugby and gardening.
Other lawyers: AMEC Capital Projects Limited - Michael Blacker, Kevin Smith (Senior Legal Adviser), Andrew Taylor , Christine Kiernan, George Andronicou . In Addition: AMEC Project Investments Limited - Tony Rogers (Legal Services Director), Alison Sandle, Pascal Fel; AMEC Developments Limited - Sarah-Anne Shankland.

Amerada Hess Limited
33 Grosvenor Place London SW1X 7HY
Tel: (020) 7823 2626 **Fax:** (020) 7887 2199
Alan Dunlop, Associate General Counsel, Exploration and Production

American Express Bank Ltd.
60 Buckingham Palace Road London SW1W 0RR
Tel: (020) 7824 6387 **Fax:** (020) 7730 5067
Email: jane.b.kelloe@aexp.com
Website: www.aexp.com
No of lawyers in dept: 2 + 1 paralegal
Work outsourced: 20% - Litigation, real property, complex transactions, FSA Rules queries.
Jane Kelloe, Group Counsel
Specialisation: Responsible for legal services for American Express Bank Ltd . and its subsidiaries in Europe, Africa , the Middle East and American Express Asset Management outside the USA . Principal areas of work - banking, regulatory, employment and litigation management.
Career: Solicitor 1976 . LLB University of Southampton 1973 Coward Chance 1974-1979 . American Express Bank Ltd . 1980 to date.

Amersham plc
Amersham Place Little Chalfont HP7 9NA
Tel: (01494) 544000 **Fax:** (01494) 542242
Email: robert.allnutt@amersham.com
Website: www.amersham.com
No of lawyers in dept: 7
Work outsourced: 20% - Property, litigation, corporate acquisitions, employment.
Robert E B Allnutt, Company Secretary & Group Legal Adviser
Specialisation: Responsible for provision of legal advice on general commercial matters, intellectual property and product liability.
Career: Qualified 1979.
Other lawyers: Kevin Kissane, Tom Kilroy, Sheena Ginnings, Sara Lovick , Paresh Jasani, Henry Parkinson.

Amey plc
24 Hanover Square London W1S 1JD
Tel: (020) 7659 1900 **Fax:** (020) 7659 1901
Email: carol.hui@amey.co.uk
Website: www.amey.co.uk
No of lawyers in dept: 2
Carol Hui, Group Company Secretary & Director of Legal Affairs
Other lawyers: Mr Paolo Stefferini, Ms Louisa Reay.

Anglo American PLC
20 Carlton House Terrace St James's London SW1Y 5AN
Tel: (020) 7698 8888 **Fax:** (020) 7698 8570
Website: www.angloamerican.co.uk
No of lawyers in dept: 3
Ben Keisler, Executive Vice President, General Counsel and Head of Legal Services
Specialisation: Corporate transactions, commercial, corporate finance, competition/antitrust.
Career: Senior Vice President, General Counsel, Minono, 1997-1999; Vice president and General Counsel, Minono (USA) Inc., 1993-97; Vice President and General Counsel,

IN-HOUSE LAWYERS ■ COMPANY SECRETARIES

Terra Industries Inc.
Other lawyers: Paul Roebuck - acquisitions, general corporate, competition.

Anite Group PLC
100 Longwater Avenue Green Park Reading RG2 6GP
Tel: (0118) 945 0121 **Fax:** (0118) 945 0131
Simon A Hunt, Finance Director & Company Secretary

Antofagasta PLC
Park House 16 Finsbury Circus London EC2M 7AH
Tel: (020) 7374 8091 **Fax:** (020) 7628 3773
Hussein Barma, Chief Financial Officer

Aon Limited
8 Devonshire Square London EC2M 4PL
Tel: (020) 7623 5500 **Fax:** (020) 7621 1511
Jane Owen, Senior Lawyer

Arab Bank PLC
PO Box 138 15 Moorgate London EC2R 6LP
Tel: (020) 7315 8500 **Fax:** (020) 7600 7620
Email: webmaster@arabbank.com.jo
Website: www.arabbank.com
No of lawyers in dept: 1
Janet Bicheno, Legal Adviser
Specialisation: All aspects of banking law and management of external legal advisers, where necessary.
Career: Felsted School, Dunmow, Essex . LLB (Hons) Leicester University . Guildford Law College.
Other lawyers: Banking, Property.

Arcadia Group
Colegrave House 70 Berners Street London W1T 3NL
Tel: (020) 7636 8040 **Fax:** (020) 7927 7651
Website: www.arcadiagroup.co.uk
No of lawyers in dept: 3
Ian Jackman, Director of Legal Services & Company Secretary
Other lawyers: Adam Goldman - Commercial, Trade Marks ; Julie Crossland - Commercial.

ARM Holdings plc
110 Fulbourn Road Cambridge CB1 4NJ
Tel: (01223) 400400 **Fax:** (01223) 400410
Email: colm.mackernan@arm.com
Website: www.arm.com
No of lawyers in dept: 12
Work outsourced: 1% - Litigation / corporate.
Colm P MacKernan, Executive Vice President & General Counsel
Specialisation: Major transactions, intellectual property, corporate strategy, litigation.
Career: 1988: BA Physics, University of Dublin, Trinity College.1992: JD, Georgetown University Law Center.Admitted: New York, Washington DC, United States Court of Appeals for the Federal Circuit, US Supreme Court, United States International Trade Commission, CAFC, etc; Solicitor - England and Wales, Republic of Ireland.Private Practice: Tokyo, Washington DC.
Personal: Sailing, travel, reading.
Other lawyers: Colm P MacKernan, Executive Vice President and General Counsel, Chief Legal Officer, Major Litigations and Transactions.Ehab Youssef, General Manager and Vice President Legal, Head of America.Philip David, Vice President Legal, responsible for EMEA.Amy Pullen, Senior Corporate Counsel, responsible for IP Licensing and Transactions, America.Suzannah Gozna, Senior Corporate Counsel, IP Licensing and Transactions, Asia.Amy Miller, Corporate Counsel, IP Licensing.Lindsey White, Corporate Counsel, IP Licensing.Kristie Ranney, Paralegal, IP Licensing/Corporate Filings.Andrew Barling, Corporate Counsel, EMEA.Judith Kirkpatrick, Corporate Counsel, EMEA.Melinda Jackson, Paralegal, Contracts Manager.Samantha Funnell, Patent Attorney, managing patent applications worldwide.

Arriva PLC
Admiral Way Doxford International Business Park Sunderland SR3 3XP
Tel: (0191) 520 4000 **Fax:** (0191) 520 4001
Chris Applegarth, Director of Group Legal Services & Company Solicitor

Associated British Foods PLC
Weston Centre Bowater House 68 Knightsbridge London SW1X 7LR
Tel: (020) 7589 6363 **Fax:** (020) 7584 8560
Paul Lister, Director or Legal Services & Company Secretary

Associated British Ports (ABP)
150 Holborn London EC1N 2LR
Tel: (020) 7430 1177 **Fax:** (020) 7430 1456
Website: www.abports.co.uk
Stephen Walsh, General Counsel
Specialisation: Corporate, alliances, joint ventures.
Career: Ashurst Morris Crisp - 1986-199 1. Joined British Airways - 1991 . Head Legal Adviser - 1996 . Legal Director - 1999.

Associated Newspapers Limited
Northcliffe House 2 Derry Street Kensington London W8 5TT
Tel: (020) 7938 7224 **Fax:** (020) 7938 6020
Email: nick.braithwaite@assocnews.co.uk
Website: www.associatednewspapers.com
Nick Braithwaite, Group Legal Adviser
Specialisation: Newspaper Lawyer.
Career: St Paul's School, Barnes.Queen's College, Cambridge.Admitted Solicitor 1985.
Personal: Born 1959.
Northcliffe House 2 Derry Street Kensington London W8 5TT
Tel: (020) 7938 6000 **Fax:** (020) 7938 6020
Eddie Young, Group Legal Adviser

AstraZeneca PLC
15 Stanhope Gate London W1Y 6LN
Tel: (020) 7304 5000 **Fax:** (020) 7304 5151
Email: graeme.musker@astrazeneca.com
Website: www.astrazeneca.com
No of lawyers in dept: 14
Graeme H R Musker, Company Secretary & Solicitor
Alderley House Alderley Park Macclesfield SK10 4TF
Tel: (01625) 582828 **Fax:** (01625) 585022
Email: chris.petty@astrazeneca.com
Website: www.astrazeneca.co.uk
Chris Petty, Assistant General Counsel
Specialisation: Responsible for management of legal Department at Alderley Park (10 lawyers). Commercial law, competition law, medical legal, etc. Also responsible for External Relations, AstraZeneca in the North West.
Career: Cambridge University (Selwyn College) MA.Called to Bar 1976.Joined ICI Pharmaceuticals 1977.Advanced Management Programme INSEAD 1994.Legal Director, Zeneca Pharmaceuticals 1994-1999.Member, ABPI Legal Committee.

Autonomy Corporation PLC
Cambridge Business Park Cowley Road Cambridge CB4 0WZ
Tel: (01223) 448000 **Fax:** (01223) 448001
Andrew Kanter, Head of Legal & Company Secretary

Avis Europe PLC
Avis House Park Road Bracknell RG12 2EW
Tel: (01344) 426644 **Fax:** (01344) 485616
Judith A Nicholson, Company Secretary, Director of Legal Services

awg plc
Anglian House Ambury Road Huntingdon PE29 3NZ
Tel: (01480) 323140 **Fax:** (01480) 323918
Email: info@anglianwater.co.uk
Website: www.awg.com
No of lawyers in dept: 2
Work outsourced: 60% - Work where in-house expertise is lacking e.g major corporate transactions.
Patrick Firth, Group Legal Counsel
Specialisation: Responsible for providing legal services to the Group using the in-house team wherever possible but outsourcing where specialisations are lacking or volume of work is too great. Personal responsibilities include corporate and commercial work both in the UK and internationally.
Career: Education - Nottingham High School and Sheffield University; Career - Leicestershire and Surrey County Councils before joining Anglian Water (now awg plc) in 1988.
Personal: Leisure interests include Environmental Development, Lepidoptery, Nottingham Forest FC.
Other lawyers: Patrick Firth - Corporate Commercial ; Roger Sudbury.

BAA plc
130 Wilton Road London SW1V 1LQ
Tel: (020) 7834 9449 **Fax:** (020) 7932 6699
Robert Herga, Group Legal Director

BAE Systems plc
Stirling Square 6 Carlton Gardens London SW1Y 5AD
Tel: (01252) 373232 **Fax:** (01252) 383991
Email: michael.lester@baesystems.com
Website: www.baesystems.com
No of lawyers in dept: 50
Work outsourced: Varies - Litigation, conveyancing, major M&A.
Michael Lester, Group Legal Director
Specialisation: Overall responsibility for all legal matters within the BAE Systems Group companies.
Career: Coopers Company's School, New College; Teaching Fellow University of Chicago Law School 1962-64; Articled Solicitor in private practice 1964-80; The General Electric Company plc 1980-99; Director 1983, Vice-chairman, 1994; BAE Systems plc - director, 1999; Premier Farnell plc - non-executive director, 1998.
Personal: Married with one daughter and one son.
Other lawyers: We do not organise by relevance to specialist areas.

Balfour Beatty Civil Engineering Limited
7 Mayday Road Thornton Heath CR7 7XA
Tel: (020) 8684 6922 **Fax:** (020) 8710 5158
Philip Morris, Solicitor

Balfour Beatty PLC
130 Wilton Road London SW1V 1LQ
Tel: (020) 7216 6840 **Fax:** (020) 7216 6940
Email: info@balfourbeatty.com
Website: www.balfourbeatty.com
Work outsourced: 90% - Litigation, property, large projects.
Frank McCormack, Head of Legal Services
Specialisation: Corporate law, general counsel.
Career: Finchley Catholic Grammar School 1965-1974; Liverpool University 1975-1978, BA (Hons), Philosophy; College of Law, London W2, 1978-1980, Common Professional Examination, Solicitors Final Examination; Admitted as solicitor of the Supreme Court April 1983. Articled Clerk 1981-1983, Assistant Solicitor 1983-1984 - Gregory Rowcliffe & Co, London; Assistant Solicitor 1984-1985, Partner 1985-1987 - Bucher, Williams & Harrup, London; Senior Legal Adviser 1987, Head of Legal Services 1988 to 1999, Company Secretary 1993 to date - Balfour Beatty Group Limited, London; Head of Legal Services 1999 to date - BICC plc, London (now Balfour Beatty plc). Seminar/courses attended: Cranfield 1989; Project finance 1988 (Balfour Beatty); Managing Corporate Legal Services 1992 (Nottingham University). Papers/presentations: Managing Corporate Legal Services; Managing External Lawyers. Associations: Society of Construction Law; Holborn Law Society.
Personal: Rugby (spectator and mini rugby), sailing (RTYC, Bosham SC; Law Society YC). Opera, theatre, film, horse racing and most other sports as spectator. Govenor, St Cuthbert Mayne Catholic Primary School, Cranleigh; Trustee, Surrey Alcohol and Drug Advisory Service.
Other lawyers: Company commercial, M&A, banking.

Bank of America
PO Box 407 Bank of America House 1 Alie Street London E1 8DE
Tel: (020) 7634 4000 **Fax:** (020) 7634 4374
Marc de Laperouse, Head of EMEA Legal & Assistant General Counsel
PO Box 407 Bank of America House 1 Alie Street London E1 8DE
Tel: (020) 7634 4000 **Fax:** (020) 7634 4374
Leonie Brown, Head of Global Markets Legal & Assistant General Counsel

Bank of Cyprus (London) Limited
87-93 Chaseside Southgate London N14 5BU
Tel: (020) 8267 7330 **Fax:** (020) 8447 8066
Email: sbyrne@bankofcyprus.co.uk
Website: www.bankofcyprus.co.uk
No of lawyers in dept: 1
Work outsourced: Approximately one third. - Some litigation, large contracts, property.
Stephen G Byrne, Legal Adviser & Company Secretary
Specialisation: Banking, compliance, company/commercial, employment, property , litigation.
Career: University of Reading - BA (Hons) Modern History and German 1979-1983 . College of Law, York 1991-1994. Admitted as a solicitor in July 1994 . Worked in Legal Dept, Alliance & Leicester Building Society 1992-1996 . Company Solicitor & Company Secretary for Lombard Bank 1996-2001 . Bank of Cyprus (London) Ltd May 2001 to date.
Other lawyers: Company/Commercial, Litigation, Banking, Employment, Property.

Bank of Ireland
2 College Green Dublin 2
Tel: +353 1 677 6801 **Fax:** +353 1 670 3602
Finbarr Murphy, Group Legal Adviser

1207

IN-HOUSE LAWYERS ■ COMPANY SECRETARIES

Bank of New York
1 Canada Square London E14 5AL
Tel: (020) 7570 1784 **Fax:** (020) 7893 6030
Karen Birch, Head of Legal Services

Bank of Scotland
Thistle House City Road Chester CH88 3AN
Tel: (01244) 690000 **Fax:** (01244) 311373
Michael S McClenan, Legal Director

Bank One Corporation
Bank One 1 Triton Square London NW1 3FN
Tel: (020) 7388 3456 **Fax:** (020) 7388 4747
Jay Bestmann, Senior Vice President & Regional Counsel

Barclays Bank PLC (Barclays Private Clients)
5th floor Murray House 1 Royal Mint Court London EC3N 4HH
Tel: (020) 7977 4088 **Fax:** (020) 7977 4648
Email: jeremy.ogden@barclays.co.uk
Website: www.barclays.co.uk
Jeremy Ogden, Deputy Group General Counsel, General Counsel Barclays Private Clients
Specialisation: General Advice to Senior Executives; New Product Development; Private Banking.
Career: Boodle Hatfield, 1981-1984; Wilde Sapte 1984-1987.
Personal: Two children aged 12 and 14.

Barclays Capital
5 The North Colonnade Canary Wharf London E14 4BB
Tel: (020) 7623 2323 **Fax:**(020) 7773 6827
Alex Cameron, Director of Legal for London & Europe

Barclays PLC
54 Lombard Street London EC3P 3AH
Tel: (020) 7699 2957 **Fax:** (020) 7699 3414
Email: GGCO@barclays.co.uk
Website: www.barclays.co.uk
No of lawyers in dept: 165
Work outsourced: 50% - General advisory, commoditised products, business banking, HR, litigation, Barclays Capital Securitisations, structured tax, tax planning/private client, private equity, corporate bank debt recovery, corporate & regulatory.
Howard B Trust, Group General Counsel & Company Secretary
Specialisation: Howard Trust is Group General Counsel and Secretary at Barclays PLC providing advice to the main Board and senior management on legal risk issues as it affects the Barclays Group and its businesses as a whole. As the head of the Barclays Group Legal Function which has some 200 staff world-wide, he chairs the Legal Function Executive and is responsible for the provision of advice on key issues of legal risk affecting the Group including banking and capital markets transactions and dispute resolution. He also lectures regularly to external audiences on a variety of topics. Also secretary to the Group Board and responsible for corporate governance.
Career: Solicitor, Lovell White & King 1980-85. Solicitor, Morgan Grenfell 1985-87 and Company Secretary 1987-89. Group Legal Director, BZW 1989-95. Group General Counsel and Group Secretary Barclays plc since 1995.
Other lawyers: Howard Trust - Group General Counsel; Jeremy Ogden - Deputy Group General Counsel, General Counsel Barclays Private Clients ; John Featherstone - General Counsel Litigation & Disputes and Barclays Africa; Bjarnie Anderson - Projects and Operations Director; Frances Spencer - General Counsel Human Resources; Joanne Medero - Managing Director and General Counsel BGI; Guy Dempsey - Managing Director and General Counsel Barclays Capital (Americas); Michael Webber - General Counsel Personal Financial Services; Rachel Harris - General Counsel Barclaycard; Penny Bruce - General Counsel Business Banking; Neil Hodges - Deputy General Counsel, Corporate & Commercial.

Barratt Developments PLC
Wingrove House Ponteland Road Newcastle upon Tyne NE5 3DP
Tel: (0191) 286 6811 **Fax:** (0191) 271 2242
Website: www.barratthomes.co.uk
No of lawyers in dept: 1
Laurence Dent, Company Secretary
Specialisation: Company, commercial, employment and pensions.

BBA Group PLC
70 Fleet Street London EC4Y 1EU
Tel: (020) 7842 4900 **Fax:** (020) 7353 1757
Email: sshaw@bbagroup.com
Website: www.bbagroup.com

No of lawyers in dept: 9
Work outsourced: 50% - Corporate, commercial, litigation, property.
Sarah M Foulkes Shaw, Company Secretary
Specialisation: Corporate, commercial, regulatory, compliance.
Career: Trainee solicitor 1980-82 Freshfields, Solicitor 1982-85 Freshfields, Corporate Lawyer 1986-89 Cadbury Schweppes plc, Corporate Lawyer 1989-92 Reed International plc, Group Secretary and Legal Advisor 1992-95 Signet Group plc, Group Secretary 1997 to date BBA Group plc.
Personal: Born 1958. Lives in London. Married with 2 daughters.

BBC
White City Building 201 Wood Lane London W12 7TS
Tel: (020) 8752 4339 **Fax:** (020) 8752 5080
Email: sarah.jones@bbc.co.uk
Sarah Jones, Head of Litigation
Specialisation: Resoponsible for litigation brought by or against the BBC.
Career: Head of Litigation BBC 1996-to date; Solicitor, Allen & Overy 1985-1996.

Bear Stearns International Limited
One Canada Square London E14 5AD
Tel: (020) 7516 6000 **Fax:** (020) 7516 6621
Email: sbartlett@bear.com
Website: www.bearstearns.com
No of lawyers in dept: 5
Stephen Bartlett, Senior Managing Director and Head of Legal
Specialisation: Responsible for all legal matters for firm's investment banking European franchise. Primarily: investment banking, capital markets; OTC derivatives; structured debt & equity; regulatory; employment ; litigation.
Career: 19 85-88, BA Jurisprudence (Oxon); LSF 1989; 1989-94 Slaughter and May; qualified as solicitor 1991. July 1994 Bear Stearns International Limited.

Bellway PLC
Seaton Burn House Dudley Lane Seaton Burn Newcastle upon Tyne NE13 6BE
Tel: (0191) 217 0717 **Fax:** (0191) 236 6230
Website: www.bellway.co.uk
No of lawyers in dept: 1
Peter J Stoker, Director

Berkeley Group PLC
Berkeley House 19 Portsmouth Road Cobham KT11 1JG
Tel: (01932) 868555 **Fax:** (01932) 860661
Website: www.berekleygroup.com
No of lawyers in dept: 1
Wendy Pritchard, Group Solicitor

BG Group PLC
100 Thames Valley Park Drive Reading RG6 1PT
Tel: (0118) 935 3222 **Fax:** (0118) 935 3484
William Friedrich, Deputy Chief Executive & General Counsel Legal Department 100 Thames Valley Park Drive Reading RG6 1PT
Tel: (0118) 935 3222 **Fax:** (0118) 929 2854
Email: ian.chitty@bg-group.com
Website: www.bg-group.com
Ian Chitty, In-house Solicitor
Specialisation: Corporate: specialism - upstream, mainly UK
Career: 1986-1989 Cambridge University; 1989-1990 Guildford College of Law; 1990-1996 Allen & Overy; 1996-to date BG Group.

BHP Billiton Plc
1-3 Strand London WC2N 5HA
Tel: (020) 7747 3800 **Fax:** (020) 7747 3900
William Smith, Legal Counsel

The Big Food Group PLC
Equity House Irthlingborough Road Wellingborough NN8 1LT
Tel: (01933) 371827 **Fax:** (01933) 371058
Email: suzanne.chase@thebigfoodgroup.co.uk
Website: www.thebigfoodgroup.co.uk
No of lawyers in dept: 3
Work outsourced: 80% - Conveyancing, litigation, corporate tax.
Suzanne Chase, Company Secretary
Specialisation: Corporate/commercial / property / corporate governance
Career: BA(Hons) Leicester University; College of Law Chancery Lane London; DJ Freeman; Wickes plc; The Big Food Group since 2001.
Other lawyers: Company/commercial, corporate finance, litigation, employment, property.

BMG Music Publishing Limited
Bedford House 69-79 Fulham High Street London SW6 3JW
Tel: (020) 7384 7806 **Fax:** (020) 7384 8163
Jackie Alway, Director of Legal and Business affairs

BNP Banque Nationale de Paris PLC
BNP Paribas London Branch 10 Harewood Avenue London NW1 6AA
Tel: (020) 7595 2000 **Fax:** (020) 7929 0310
Michael Toubkin, Head of Legal

BNP Paribas
10 Harewood Avenue London NW1 6AA
Tel: (020) 7595 2000 **Fax:** (020) 7595 2555
Kevin Sowerbutts, Head of Legal

BOC Group Plc
Chertsey Road Windlesham GU20 6HJ
Tel: (01276) 477222 **Fax:** (01276) 471333
Email: nick.deeming@group.boc.com
Website: www.boc.com
No of lawyers in dept: 40
Work outsourced: Nick Deeming, Group Legal Director & Company Secretary
Specialisation: Head of global corporate in-house legal department, Corporate/Commercial law specialist, Company Secretary.
Career: Law Degree - Guildhall University.MBA - Cranfield University.Qualified in 1980.
Personal: Board Member - Diabilities Trust.
Other lawyers: Percentage of people globally utilised in each area: Corporate/Commercial 70%, Litigation 5%, Health & Safety 5%, Employment 5%, Competition/Code of Conduct, Intellectual Property 10%.

Bodycote International PLC
Hulley Road Hurdsfield Macclesfield SK10 2SG
Tel: (01625) 505300/340 **Fax:** (01625) 505 313
Email: jgrime@bodycote.co.uk
Website: www.bodycote.com
No of lawyers in dept: 1
Work outsourced: 95% - Corporate finance, M&A, property , employment.
John Grime, Company Secretary
Specialisation: Stock Exchange, regulatory and compliance. Executive share option schemes. Service of board's requirements for meetings. Investor relations, pensions.
Career: 1975-82 & 1996-97 Private practice in Manchester. 1982-70 Principal solicitor (commercial and property) Co-operative Wholesale Society Ltd. 1997-to date Bodycote International plc. London University LLB (external via Trent Polytechnic). Qualified 1977.
Personal: Aged 48, married with 1 daughter. Lives Bramhall, Cheshire. 3 cats. Enjoys golf, walking and entertaining.
Other lawyers: Company law, share option schemes, pensions, corporate governance, stock exchange compliance.

The Boots Company PLC
Group Headquarters 1 Thane Road Beeston Nottingham NG2 3AA
Tel: (0115) 950 6111 **Fax:** (0115) 959 2727
Michael J Oliver, Company Secretary

Bovis Construction Ltd
Bovis House 142 Northolt Road Harrow Harrow HA2 OEE
Tel: (020) 8271 8000
Peter Chadwick, Company Secretary

Bovis Homes Group PLC
Cleeve Hall Cheltenham Road Bishops Cleeve Cheltenham GL52 8GD
Tel: (01242) 662400 **Fax:** (01242) 662997
Martin Palmer, Company Secretary

BP plc
International Headquarters 1 St James's Square London SW1Y 4PD
Tel: (020) 7496 4013 **Fax:** (020) 7496 4242
Email: bevanpb@bp.com
Website: www.bp.com
No of lawyers in dept: 375 (worldwide)
Work outsourced: 10-20% - Litigation, local employment and land matters.
Peter B P Bevan, Group General Counsel
Specialisation: Corporate, M&A, Finance
Career: Peter joined the BP Group in 1970 after qualifying as a solicitor with a City of London firm. He worked initially in the Law Department of BP Chemicals and then of the Parent Company. Subsequently he became Manager of the Legal func-

IN-HOUSE LAWYERS ■ COMPANY SECRETARIES

tion within BP Exploration and then Assistant Company Secretary, followed by the Deputy Group Legal Adviser of The British Petroleum Company plc. In September 1992 he became Group General Counsel. His main areas of expertise are corporate and company law, mergers and acquisitions, finance, and cross-jurisdictional and cross-business issues.
Personal: Leisure interests include sailing, walking, cycling, golf, music, local history and travel.
Other lawyers: Associate General Counsel: Robert Moore, Robin Morris and Colin Saunders(UK) Jack Lynch and Steve Winters (USA)Peter Ling (Singapore).
Corporate Headquarters Britannic House 1 Finsbury Circus London EC2M 7BA
Tel: (020) 7496 5510 **Fax:** (020) 7496 5800
Email: boadrw@bp.com
Website: www.bp.com
Robert Boad, Assistant Head of Group Trade Marks
Specialisation: Protection of trade marks for BP Group of companies, together with some work on copyright, design and domain name internet issues. Emphasis recently on retail-related issues including registration of BP's green service station livery as a trade mark and enforcement actions against lookalike service stations.
Career: Formerly Assistant Trade Marks Manager, The Wellcome Foundation Ltd (until July 1983). Registered Trade Mark Attorney (UK) and Professional Representative Before The Office for Harmonisation in the Internal Market. BA (Hons) Business Studies. Diploma in Marketing.
Personal: Keen writer in spare time: co-editor (with Tom Blackett, Interbrand) of 'Co-branding: the science of alliance' (published by Macmillan/Palgrave) and author of numerous articles on brand-related matters.

BPB PLC
Park House 15 Bath Road Slough SL1 3UF
Tel: (01753) 898800 **Fax:** (01753) 898888
Website: www.bpb.com
Work outsourced: Company/Commercial/Corporate Finance/Litigation/Property
Robert Heard, Company Secretary

Bradford & Bingley plc
PO Box 88 Crossflatts Bingley BD16 2UA
Tel: (01274) 554186 **Fax:** (01274) 554967
Paul Jordan, Head of Group Legal

Brake Bros PLC
Enterprise House Eureka Business Park Ashford TN25 4AG
Tel: (01233) 206000 **Fax:** (01233) 206159
Martin Purvis, Group Company Secretary

Brambles Industries plc
Cassini House 57-59 St James's Street London SW1A 1LD
Tel: (020) 7659 6000 **Fax:** (020) 7659 6001
Email: info@brambles.com
Website: ww.brambles.com
Ian Harman, General Counsel

Britannic Group PLC
1 Wythall Green Way Wythall Birmingham B47 6WG
Tel: (0870) 887 0001 **Fax:** (0870) 887 0002
Website: www.britannic.co.uk
No of lawyers in dept: 3
Work outsourced: 40% - Various.
Anna East, Company Secretary & Solicitor
Specialisation: Company Secretarial work including listed and board plc responsibilities, administration of savings related share option scheme and executive schemes. Management of Legal issues and Chairman of Britannic Group Pension Scheme.
Career: Rugby High School. Nottingham University (BA hons). Trent Polytechnic (Law Society Finals). Talbots (articles), 1982-84. Eversheds, 1984-88. Britannic plc 1988 to date.
Personal: Interests: family, tennis, travel.
Other lawyers: Liz Riley - Senior Solicitor , Employment Law; James Bird - Solicitor, Commercial Contracts and IT.

British Airways plc
Waterside PO Box 365 Harmondsworth UB7 0GB
Tel: (020) 8738 5330 **Fax:** (020) 8738 9362
Website: www.britishairways.com
No of lawyers in dept: 19
Work outsourced: Various.
Maria da Cunha, Legal Director
Other lawyers: Jim Blaney (US Law), Caroline Boone (IP, Data Protection), Maria da Cunha (Competition), Julia Harrison (Employment), Chris Haynes (Corporate Commercial), Owen Highley (Air Law Commercial), Paul Jasinski (US Law), Claire Large (Employment), Iben McCracken (Commercial),

Paul Nichols (IP), Jo Pawley (Employment), Tina Smith (Commercial), Peter Watson (Aircraft Finance), Roger Whipp (Commercial, Litigation).
Waterside PO Box 365 Harmondsworth UB7 0GB
Tel: (020) 8738 6870 **Fax:** (020) 8738 9647
Website: www.britishairways.com
Robert Webb, General Counsel
Specialisation: Government and industry affairs, safety, security, the enviroment, risk management, legal, compliance.
Career: Wycliffe College 1959-1967; Exeter University 1967-1970; Barrister 1971-1998 (Q.C. 1988. Barrister, Inner Temple 1997).
Waterside PO Box 365 Harmondsworth UB7 0GB
Tel: (020) 8738 5050 **Fax:** (020) 8738 9602
Alan Buchanan, Company Secretary
Waterside PO Box 365 Harmondsworth UB7 0GB
Tel: (020) 8738 5050 **Fax:** (020) 8738 9602
Owen Highley, In-house Solicitor

British American Tobacco PLC
Globe House 4 Temple Place London WC2R 2PG
Tel: (020) 7845 1000 **Fax:** (020) 7240 0555
Website: www.bat.com
No of lawyers in dept: 40 (UK), 166 (worldwide)
Work outsourced: Specialist advice, property , pensions.
Neil Withington, Legal Director & General Counsel
Other lawyers: Aileen McDonald - Company Secretary; Stephen Walzer - Competition and European law; Philip Scourfield - Litigation & Regulation ; Robert Casey - Corporate and Treasury ; Mark Biss - Commercial.

British Assets Trust PLC
One Charlotte Square Edinburgh EH2 4DZ
Tel: (0131) 225 1357 **Fax:** (0131) 225 2375
Gordon Humphries, Company Secretary, British Assets Trust PLC

British Energy PLC
3 Redwood Crescent Peel Park East Kilbride G74 5PR
Tel: (01355) 594020 **Fax:** (01355) 594022
Email: robert.armour@british-energy.com
Website: www.british-energy.com
No of lawyers in dept: 6
Work outsourced: 60+% - Project support, overseas ventures, litigation, competitions, corporate, conveyancing, employment, E.U .
Robert M Armour, Company Secretary & Director of Corporate Affairs
Specialisation: Deals with corporate legal issues, corporate governance, regulation and compliance, environmental issues, European Scottish and UK parliamentary matters. Also responsible for planning and estates, and private shareholder issues.
Career: Assistant solicitor - Wright Johnston & McKenzie - Edinburgh 1983-85, and Partner 1986-90. Scottish Nuclear's Company Secretary from 1990-1995. Company Secretary of British Energy plc - 1995 to date. Also Director of Corporate Affairs and General Counsel for British Energy plc.
Other lawyers: Dr Jean MacDonald, John Young, Andrew McMillan, Sue Challenger, Peter McCall , Anne Bodkin.

British Land Company PLC
10 Cornwall Terrace Regent's Park London NW1 4QP
Tel: (020) 7486 4466 **Fax:** (020) 7935 5552
Anthony Braine, Company Secretary

British Midland Airways Ltd
Donington Hall Castle Donington Derby DE74 2SB
Tel: (01332) 854089 **Fax:** (01332) 850301
Email: tim.bye@flybmi.com
Website: www.iflybritishmidland.co.uk
No of lawyers in dept: 8
Work outsourced: Approx 25% - Property, employment, major corporate transactions, EC.
Tim Bye, Legal Director & Company Secretary
Specialisation: Responsible for all legal issues principally focused on major commercial and corporate transactions. Also Company Secretary and responsible for property, insurance , personnel , guvernment affairs, corporate comunications and member of Star Alliance Management Board.
Career: Watford Grammer School; 1971-74 Leicester University (2:1); 1975 College of Law Guildford; 1989 London Business Scholl MBA (Distinction). Articles - Lawrence Messer & Co 1975-1977; 1977-1983 - John Laing plc Legal Adviser; 1983-1998 - TNT Group Vice President Corporate Affairs.
Personal: Married, 3 children. Lives in Nottingham. Hobbies: golf, skiing and tennis.

British Sky Broadcasting Group PLC
6 Centaurs Business Park Grant Way Isleworth TW7 5QD
Tel: (020) 7705 3000 **Fax:** (020) 7705 3030
Deanna Bates, Head of Legal & Business Affairs

British Vita plc
Oldham Road Middleton Manchester M24 2DB
Tel: (0161) 643 1133 **Fax:** (0161) 653 5411
Website: www.britishvita.com
No of lawyers in dept: 2
Work outsourced: 30% - Public issues, heavyweight litigation, some M&A.
Mark Stirzaker, Company Secretary & Solicitor
Specialisation: f1Principal areas of work are mergers and acquisitions and commercial property. Also provides general commercial advice and all company secretarial duties.
Career: Qualified 1980.
Other lawyers: Catherine Parry - Assistant Solicitor.

Brixton PLC
50 Berkeley Street London W1J 8BX
Tel: (020) 7400 4504 **Fax:** (020) 7399 4550
Email: nigelwatts@brixton.plc.uk
Website: www.brixton.plc.uk
Work outsourced: All - Property and corporate
Nigel Watts, Company Secretary
Specialisation: Company secretarial, employment, share schemes, pension arrangements.
Career: Professionally qualified accountant with extensive UK and International experience in handling complex corporate, secretarial and treasury matters in the context of corporate restructuring and take-overs of leading publicly quoted Groups. Bourner Bullock 1968-1975 - Audit Senior from Junior. Coopers & Lybrand 1975-1976 - Audit Senior. United Kingdom Property Company Ltd (British Land plc) 1976-1980 Secretary and Group Accountant. John Brown plc (Kvaerner plc Trafalgar House plc) 1980-1984 Group Financial Accountant, 1984-1987 Treasury Manager, 1986-1996 Secretary. Nigel Watts Consultancy Ltd Financial and Secretarial Consultant 1996 to 1999.
Personal: Aged 52 , married with 2 sons.
Other lawyers: Company/commercial, employee benefit schemes, pension schemes, employment law.

BT Group PLC
BT Centre 81 Newgate Street London EC1A 7AJ
Tel: (020) 7356 5000 **Fax:** (020) 7356 6638
Email: anne.fletcher@bt.com
Website: www.bt.com
No of lawyers in dept: 130
Anne Fletcher, Group General Counsel
Career: Education: Bolton School Girls Division; Newham College, Cambridge; College of Law, Chester. Career: Foysters Manchester (1981-1984); Freshfields (1984-1986); BT (1986 to date) - mainly in legal department has also role of Director, Regulatory Compliance.
Personal: Married, two sons.
Other lawyers: Miles Jobling: Director Legal and Business Services, BT Wholesale ; Christine Moore: Head of Employment Law and Business Services ; Tim Cowen: General Counsel, Ignite; Andrew Parker: General Counsel & Head of Business Affairs for BT Openworld; Sarah Betteley: General Counsel, BT Retail; Kevin Purell: Head of Intellectual Property Department; Rupert Orchard: Head of Transactions ; Jeff Fisher: Head of Corporate Law .

BTG PLC
10 Fleet Place Limeburner Lane London EC4M 7SB
Tel: (020) 7575 0000 **Fax:** (020) 7575 0010
Website: www.btgplc.com
No of lawyers in dept: 15
Work outsourced: 10% - Litigation.
Robin Saphra, General Counsel & Company Secretary
Career: University of Cape Town - BA (Hons) 1981. Solicitor 1992. Trained: Allison & Humphreys. Career: Partner, Allison & Humphreys. Director, Public Policy & Legal Affairs, One-2-One. Executive Director Strategic Development, T-Mobile.
Personal: Born 1960. Resides in London.
Other lawyers: London Office: R Davison, G Georgiou, Z Ali, A Sekhri, E Simpson, P Mussenden , M Frankel - compliance and corporate, intellectual property, commercial and litigation. US Office Lawyers: Larry Schroepfer, A Burt, M Rosen, C Egolf, B Ditty, B Bernstein, M Malkani.

Bunzl plc
110 Park Street London W1K 6NX
Tel: (020) 7495 4950 **Fax:** (020) 7495 2527
Website: www.bunzl.com
No of lawyers in dept: 2
Work outsourced: 50% - Large corporate transactions, litigation, property.
Paul Hussey, Company Secretary & Group Legal Adviser
Specialisation: Provides legal services and advice on company/commercial and general corporate matters, and a full company secretarial service including compliance.

IN-HOUSE LAWYERS ■ COMPANY SECRETARIES

Career: Qualified 1983 while with Addleshaw Sons & Latham. Commercial solicitor, Grand Metropolitan Retailing Division 1985-86 and Senior Solicitor, Contract Services Division 1986-87. Company Secretary and Group Legal Adviser, Compass Group 1987-88. Legal Adviser, Bunzl plc 1988-92 and then took up present position.
Personal: Educated at Woking Grammar School 1970-77, University College, Cardiff 1977-80 and College of Law 1980-81. Leisure pursuits include walking, tennis, music and golf. Born 11 January 1959. Lives in London.

Cable & Wireless
124 Theobalds Road London WC1X 8RX
Tel: (020) 7315 4000 **Fax:** (020) 7315 5000
Daniel Fitz, Group General Counsel

Cable & Wireless PLC
26 Red Lion Square London WC1R 4HQ
Tel: (020) 7315 3493 **Fax:** (020) 7315 6242
Email: jane.mcelhatton@cw.com
Website: www.cw.com
Jane McElhatton, Senior Corporate Counsel
Specialisation: Commercial IT, operational transaction support, product development/marketing, outsourcing, legal training.
Career: Barrister (called 1989); Cable & Wireless Group (1989 to date).
Personal: Married, 2 children.

Cadbury Schweppes PLC
Legal Department Franklin House PO Box 2138 Bournville Birmingham B30 2NB
Tel: (0121) 625 7000 **Fax:** (0121) 459 0383
Michael Keating, Legal Director

Cairn Energy PLC
50 Lothian Road Edinburgh EH3 9BY
Tel: (0131) 475 3000 **Fax:** (0131) 475 3030
Email: dwood@cairn-energy.plc.uk
Website: www.cairn-energy.plc.uk
No of lawyers in dept: 3
Work outsourced: 0-20% Depending on type - Potentially from all areas.
Duncan Wood, Company Secretary & Group Legal Adviser
Specialisation: Company/commercial, corporate finance, litigation, pensions, employment.
Career: Aberdeen University 1981-1985; Blackadder Reid Johnston 1985-1987; Linklaters & Paines 1987-1989; Bird Semple Fyfe Ireland 1989-1993; Cairn Energy PLC 1993 - present.
Other lawyers: Pensions, employment.

Caledonia Investments plc
Cayzer House 30 Buckingham Gate London SW1E 6NN
Tel: (020) 7802 8080 **Fax:** (020) 7802 8090
Graeme Denison, Company Secretary

Cambridge Antibody Technology Group PLC
The Science Park   Melbourn SG8 6JJ
Tel: (01763) 263233 **Fax:** (01763) 263413
Email: info@cambridgeantibody.com
Website: www.cambridgeantibody.com
No of lawyers in dept: 2
Work outsourced: 40% - Property, litigation, corporate finance, tax, IP/commercial contracts.
Diane Mellett, General Counsel & Company Secretary
Specialisation: Intellectual property; commercial agreements.
Career: University of Birmingham LLB (Hons) 1983; Chicago IIT-Kent J.D. 1991; Law Society 1986; Admitted to Illinois Bar, United States & 7th Circuit, 1992.
Other lawyers: Alistair Moodie - Assistant General Counsel.

Canary Wharf Group plc
One Canada Square Canary Wharf London E14 5AB
Tel: (020) 7418 2000 **Fax:** (020) 7418 2195
Email: webmaster@canarywharf.com
Website: www.canarywharf.com
No of lawyers in dept: 5
Work outsourced: 99% - Litigation/commercial property/IP.
Michael Ashley-Brown, Head of Legal
Specialisation: Commercial property.
Career: Cranleigh School, Surrey; Millbrook School, New York; College of Law.
Personal: Interests: Motor racing, skiing.
Other lawyers: Commercial property, construction, IP and facilities management.

Capita Group plc
71 Victoria Street Westminster London SW1H 0XA
Tel: (020) 7799 1525 **Fax:** (020) 7799 1526
Fiona Kelly, Legal Director

Capital Radio PLC
30 Leicester Square London WC2H 7LA
Tel: (020) 7766 6000 **Fax:** (020) 7766 6008
Email: capitalradio.plc.uk
Website: www.capitalradio.co.uk
No of lawyers in dept: 4
Work outsourced: 25% - Corporate finance transactions, property.
Nathalie Schwarz, Director oF Strategy and Development & Company Secretary
Specialisation: As Company Secretary and responsible for group legal affairs, provide corporate support to the Plc Board and Sub-Committees. Heads a department of four lawyers and one company secretary assistant. The department advises the group across various pertinent business matters including corporate affairs, joint ventures, acquisitions, disposals, rights clearances, distribution, digital licensing matters and commercial agreements.
Career: The North London Collegiate School; University of Manchester 1988-91; College of Law 1991-92; Degrees/qualifications: Law (LLB, Honours) - 2:1 (1991); Law Society Final Professional Examination - First Class Honours (1992); Articled at Clifford Chance . Qualified as a solicitor in the Corporate Department in 1995, specialising in corporate finance, M&A and general corporate/commercial matters. Joined Capital Radio plc as Company Secretary and Head of Legal Affairs in 1998. Promoted to Director of Strategy and Development in 2001.
Personal: Born 1970, resides in London. Enjoys theatre, cinema, travelling.

Carillion plc
Construction House 24 Birch Street
Wolverhampton WV1 4HY
Tel: (01902) 422431 **Fax:** (01902) 316165
Email: rtapp@carillionplc.com
Website: www.carillionplc.com
No of lawyers in dept: 9
Richard Tapp, Company Secretary & Director of Legal Services
Specialisation: Responsible for provision of legal services worldwide, in consultation with overseas subsidiaries, and for company secretarial work in the UK. Principal areas of work are acquisitions and disposals, contract and commercial law, competition law and property. Responsible also for risk management and insurance.
Career: 1981-84 National Coal Board. 1985-86 Imperial Foods Ltd, part of Imperial Group plc. Joined Blue Circle as Commercial Solicitor 1986, Principal Solicitor 1992, Company Secretary and Legal Adviser 1996. LLB (Sheffield), LLM (Leicester) FCIS, MCI Arb. MBA (Nottingham Law School).
Other lawyers: Building: Alan Foster (Head of Dept of 3); PFI: David Anderson ; Services: Alison Shepley (Head of Dept of 2); CHE (Crown House Engineering): Jennifer Charlson; Capital Projects/Infrastructure Management: Kim Humphreys.

Carlton Communications PLC
25 Knightsbridge London SW1X 7RZ
Tel: (020) 7663 6312 **Fax:** (020) 7663 6370
Email: david.abdoo@carlton.com
Website: www.carlton.com
No of lawyers in dept: 4
Work outsourced: 90%
David Abdoo, Company Secretary
Career: Mill Hill School 1974-1979; Kings College London 1979-1982; Clifford Chance (Clifford Turner) 1984-1988; Carlton Communications PLC 1988 - to date.
Other lawyers: Richard Ray ; Dianne Denmead - Corporate transactions; Julie Medal-Johnsen - IP.

CarltonTelevision plc
35-38 Portman Square   London W1H 0NU
Tel: (020) 7612 7292 **Fax:** (020) 7612 7403
Martin Baker, Commercial Director, Content

Carpetright PLC
Amberley House New Road Rainham RM13 8QN
Tel: (01708) 525522 **Fax:** (01708) 559361
Email: companysecretarial@carpetright.co.uk
Website: www.carpetright.co.uk
Work outsourced: All
Patricia Dregent, Company Secretary

The Carphone Warehouse Group
North Acton Business Park Wales Farm Road
London W3 6RS
Tel: (020) 8896 5000 **Fax:** (020) 8896 5179
Website: www.carphonewarehouse.com
No of lawyers in dept: 6

Work outsourced: 1% - Property
Tim Morris, Company Secretary
Specialisation: Corporate Finance and General Corporate
Career: LLB (Hons) Leeds University; Chester College of Law; DLA Partner
Personal: Entrepreneurism, Current Affairs, Golf
Other lawyers: Corporate Finance, Company/Commercial, Litigation, Employment.

Catlin Underwriting Agencies Limited
6th Floor 3 Minster Court Mincing Lane
London EC3R 7DD
Tel: (020) 7626 0486 **Fax:** (020) 7623 9101
Website: www.catlin.com
Daniel Primer, Corporate Counsel
Specialisation: Insurance
Career: Admitted to practice in New York and California. BA University of Pennsylvania. JD Boston University.

Cattles PLC
Kingston House Centre 27 Business Park Woodhead Road Birstall Batley WF17 9TD
Tel: (01924) 444 466 **Fax:** (01924) 442 255
Patrick Doherty, Company Secretary

Celltech Group PLC
208 Bath Road Slough SL1 3WE
Tel: (01753) 534655 **Fax:** (01753) 447859
Website: www.celltech.co.uk
John Slater, Director of Legal Services & Company Secretary
Specialisation: Responsible for the provision of legal and company secretarial services. Main areas of work are general company/commercial matters, intellectual property, licensing, corporate affairs and Yellow Book.
Career: Qualified as a solicitor 1978.

Centrica plc
Millstream Maidenhead Road Windsor SL4 5GD
Tel: (01753) 494601 **Fax:** (01753) 494602
Website: www.centrica.co.uk
No of lawyers in dept: 30
Work outsourced: Vast majority undertaken by in-house legal team - Litigation and property.
Grant Dawson, Group General Counsel & Company Secretary
Specialisation: General Counsel & Company Secretary of Centrica plc. Responsible for the provision of legal, regulatory and company secretarial services to the Centrica Group of Companies.
Career: Educated in Leicester and London. Called to the Bar in 1982. A member of Lincolns Inn. Practised at the Bar for a period of two years before joining the legal department of Racal Electronics plc in 1984. Joined STC plc as Legal Adviser in 1986 until they were taken over in 1991 by Northern Telecom Limited. 1992 appointed Associate General Counsel with Northern Telecom Europe Limited. Appointed General Counsel and Company Secretary of Centrica plc in October 1996.
Personal: L ives in Windsor. Enjoys golf, scuba diving, sailing and opera.
Other lawyers: Company commercial; corporate finance; utility regulation; and litigation.
3 The Square Stockley Park Uxbridge UB11 1TD
Website: www.centrica.co.uk
Eldon Pethybridge, General Counsel, British Gas

Certa (UK) Ltd
America House 2 America Square London EC3N 2LU
Tel: (020) 7903 6522 **Fax:** (020) 7903 6588
Email: stephen.sykes@certa.com
Website: www.certa.com
No of lawyers in dept: 3
Work outsourced: 2% - Specialist commercial and claims related work.
Stephen Sykes, Legal Director
Specialisation: Legal Director dealing with all legal matters relating to underwriting long term environmental risks for leading global insurers; analysis of liability in property and corporate deals; insurance structures and policy design; negotiating bespoke policies with leading city lawyers for FTSE 100 companies, major property developers, companies in chemical, water and waste, engineering, retail.
Career: Buxton College, Derbyshire; University of Lancaster (1986); University of Oxford (1987-9); De Montfort University (1995 -MA). Addleshaw Sons & Latham 1990-92; Booth & Co 1992-95; Thomas Miller & Co Ltd 1995-8; Co-founder of Certa (UK) Ltd, City of London.
Personal: Born 1965. Resides London. Married with one son and one daughter.
Other lawyers: Andrea Muirhead MA - Environmental, Waste Management, Insurance, Commercial ; Jo Bain - Enviromental, Planning, Commercial.

IN-HOUSE LAWYERS ■ COMPANY SECRETARIES

Channel 5 Broadcasting Limited
22 Long Acre London WC2E 9LY
Tel: (020) 7550 5505 **Fax:** (020) 7497 5618
Email: dutyoffice@channel5.co.uk
Website: www.channel5.co.uk
No of lawyers in dept: 10
Work outsourced: 10-20% - Corporate finance, employment, some litigation.
Colin Campbell, Director of Legal & Business Affairs
Specialisation: Delivering a high quality legal and business affairs service to Channel 5. Implementing a focussed business affairs strategy. Managing a department of 15 staff. Providing authoritative advice on legal regulatory and commercial issues including programme commissions, programme and rights acquisitions (including sports and films) compliance, arranging for external advice when required.
Career: Educated Royal Russell School and College of Law. 1997 to date - Director of Legal and Business Affairs, Channel 5; 1996-7 Head of Business Affairs, BBC Broadcasting; 1994-6 Head of Rights Group, BBC Network (Television & Radio); 1981-1994 Group Director of Legal and Business Affairs / Company Secretary, Central Independent Television Plc; 1974-1981 Solicitor, Associated Communications Corporation Plc.
Personal: Married with two children. Interests: the Arts generally, most sports, reading, cycling. fine food and wine.
Other lawyers: Company / commercial, media and entertainment, intellectual property.
22 Long Acre London WC2E 9LY
Tel: (020) 7421 7137 **Fax:** (020) 7550 5521
Email: chinneryp@channel5.co.uk
Website: www.channel5.co.uk
Paul Chinnery, Head of Legal & Regulatory Compliance
Specialisation: The law and regulation as it relates to the media and in particular broadcasting. Litigation.
Career: McKenna & Co - Articuled Clerk & Assistant Solicitor; Stephens Innocent - Assistant Solicitor; Channel 5 - Head of Legal & regulatory Compliance; The Wavell School, Farnborough, Hampshire; Farnborough Sixth Form College; Nottingham Univesity - BA History; Trent Polytechnic CPE & LSF

Channel Four Television Corporation
124 Horseferry Road London SW1P 2TX
Tel: (020) 7306 4444 **Fax:** (020) 7306 8366
Jan Tomalin, Head of Legal & Compliance
124 Horseferry Road London SW1P 2TX
Tel: (020) 7306 8495 **Fax:** (020) 7306 8116
Kathryn Williams, Senior Business Affairs
Specialisation: Television and Film
Career: Birmingham University; Lawrence Graham; Cinema Verity Productions; BBC.

Chelsfield PLC
67 Brook Street London W1K 4NJ
Tel: (020) 7493 3977 **Fax:** (020) 7493 1444
Email: rperrot@chelsfield.co.uk
Website: www.chelsfield.co.uk
No of lawyers in dept: 1
Robin Perrot, Company Solicitor

Chrysalis Group PLC
Chrysalis Building 13 Bramley Road London W10 6SP
Tel: (020) 7221 2213 **Fax:** (020) 7221 6355
Clive Potterell, Company Secretary

Chubb plc
Cleveland House 33 King Street London SW1Y 6RJ
Tel: (020) 7766 4800 **Fax:** (020) 7766 4803
Email: info@chubbplc.com
Website: www.chubbplc.com
No of lawyers in dept: 2
Helen Grantham, Company Secretary

Citibank
1 Canada Square Canary Wharf London E14 5AA
Tel: (020) 7500 5000 **Fax:** (020) 7500 0635
Email: james.gledhill@citigroup.com
James Gledhill, Senior Vice President & Co-head of Corporate Finance Legal
Specialisation: Corporate Lending, Project Finance, Structured Trade Finance, Asset Finance, Restructuring & Workouts.
Career: BSc (economics) International Relations First Class Honours, London School of Economics.Solicitor Clifford Chance 1992-1998.
Personal: Family, Northampton rugby team, History, Travel
1 Canada Square Canary Wharf London E14 5AA
Tel: (020) 7500 5000 **Fax:** (020) 7500 0635
Clare Jones, Senior Vice President & Co-head of Corporate Finance Legal

Citigroup Wealth Management
41 Berkeley Square London W1J 5NA
Tel: (020) 7508 8000 **Fax:** (020) 7508 8472
Email: robert.stemmons@citigroup.com
Website: www.citigroup.com
Robert Stemmons, General Counsel

City of London Investment Trust PLC
3 Finsbury Avenue London EC2M 2PA
Tel: (020) 7638 5757 **Fax:** (020) 7377 5742
Geoffrey Rice, Company Secretary, City of London Investment Trust

Civil Aviation Authority (CAA)
CAA House 45-59 Kingsway London WC2B 6TE
Tel: (020) 7453 6160 **Fax:** (020) 7453 6163
Email: rupert.britton@caa.co.uk
Website: www.caa.co.uk
No of lawyers in dept: 6
Work outsourced: 10% - Commercial, pensions.
Rupert J Britton, Secretary & Legal Adviser
Specialisation: Aviation, litigation, prosecutions, employment, competition, EC and public international.
Career: Bedford School, Bedford; Lincoln College, Oxford.

Close Brothers Group plc
10 Crown Place London EC2A 4FT
Tel: (020) 7426 4000 **Fax:** (020) 7426 4044
Robin Sellers, Company Secretary

CMG PLC
Parnell House 25 Wilton Road London SW1V 1LW
Tel: (020) 7592 4000 **Fax:** (020) 7592 4804
Website: www.cmg.com
No of lawyers in dept: 9 (accross the group)
Work outsourced: 20% - Litigation, conveyancing, acquisitions
Richard Francis, Company Secretary
Specialisation: Company secretarial, company commercial, acquisitions & disposals, joint ventures, information technology.
Career: City of London.Honours degree in law from University of London.Legal Adviser to Thorn EMI plc 1989-1991.Company Secretary Thom Software/Data Sciencies 1991-1995.Legal Adviser/Company Secretary CMG 1995 to date.
Personal: Hobbies include climbing and vintage cars.
Other lawyers: Company/Commercial, Information Technology.

Coats plc
1 The Square Stockley Park Uxbridge UB11 1TB
Tel: (020) 8210 5053 **Fax:** (020) 8210 5025
Email: chris.healy@coats.com
Website: www.coats.com
No of lawyers in dept: 1
Work outsourced: 70 % - Corporate/Employment/Property
Christopher Healy, Legal Director & Company Secretary
Specialisation: Corporate/Commercial
Career: Kent University, Chancery Lane Law School, Articled at Lee Bolton & Lee, Qualified February 1987.
Other lawyers: Gemma Aldridge - Assistant Company Secretary, David Younger - Intellectual Property Manager.

Cobham PLC
Brook Road Wimborne BH21 2BJ
Tel: (01202) 882020 **Fax:** (01202) 840523
John Pope, Company Secretary

Collins Stewart Holdings PLC
9th Floor 88 Wood Street London EC2V 7QR
Tel: (020) 7283 1133 **Fax:** (020) 7283 8031
Kay Wrangles, Assistant Company Secretary

COLT Telecom Group plc
International Headquarters 15 Marylebone Road London NW1 5JD
Tel: (020) 7863 5476 **Fax:** (020) 7390 3701
Email: majenkins@colt-telecom.com
Website: www.colt-telecom.com
No of lawyers in dept: 1
Work outsourced: 50% - Litigation, property, employment.
Mark Jenkins, Legal Services Director & Company Secretary
Specialisation: Management of all of the legal and secretarial requirements of the group. Corporate/commercial, M&A, employment.
Career: Chelmer. Bar School. M.K. Electric plc/SKF (UK) Ltd/Peek plc.
Personal: Married. 3 children.

Company Pictures
Suffolk House 1-8 Whitfield Place London W1T 5JU
Tel: (020) 7389 8555 **Fax:** (020) 7380 1166
Email: mark.pybus@companypictures.co.uk
Website: www.companypictures.co.uk
Mark Pybus, Head of Business Affairs
Specialisation: Film & TV Production.
Career: Cambridge, Harvard.

Compass Group PLC
Cowley House Guildford Street Chertsey KT16 9BA
Tel: (01932) 573000 **Fax:** (01932) 569956
Ronald M Morley, Group Company Secretary

Computacenter PLC
Hatfield Avenue Hatfield AL10 9TW
Tel: (01707) 631 000 **Fax:** (01707) 639 966
Alan Pottinger, Company Secretary

Cookson Group plc
The Adelphi 1-11 John Adam Street London WC2N 6HJ
Tel: (020) 7766 4500 **Fax:** (020) 7747 6600
Website: www.cooksongroup.co.uk
No of lawyers in dept: 1
Simon O'Hara, Group Legal Adviser
Specialisation: Banking and corporate finance, acquisitions, disposals and joint ventures. General commercial contracts and intellectual property . Management of property portfolio. Responsible also for risk management.
Career: Qualified in 1992. Previously Solicitor/Team Leader with Lloyd's (1994-2000). Joined Cookson Group in 2000.
Other lawyers: Responsible for the provision of legal services. General company/commercial matters.

Co-Operative Bank PLC
1 Balloon Street PO Box 101 Manchester M60 4EP
Tel: (0161) 829 5599 **Fax:** (0161) 839 8471
Website: www.co-operativebank.co.uk
No of lawyers in dept: 6
Work outsourced: Predominantly in-house, contracts, litigation, property
Ann Page, Head of Legal Services
Other lawyers: Company/Commercial, Marketing/Financial ServicesProducts, Supplier Contracts, Litigation, Brand/Intellectual Property, Employment.

Countrywide Assured Group plc
Countrywide House Perry Way Witham CM8 3SX
Tel: (01376) 533700 **Fax:** (01376) 520758
Email: info@countrywideassured.co.uk
Website: www.countrywideassured.co.uk
No of lawyers in dept: 5
Work outsourced: 25% - Company/Commercial, Litigation
Gareth Williams, Head of Legal & Company Secretary
Specialisation: All areas of legal work relevant to the group and its business units including company/commercial, compliance, litigation and employment. Also group insurances and occupational pension scheme.
Career: Educated at Leicester University. Qualifying as a solicitor in 1990. Private practice in Berg & Co, Manchester (1990-1994) and Reynolds Porter Chamberlain (1994-5). In-house with Thorn EMI Plc from 1996. Head of Legal of demerged Thorn Group in 1999 and joining Countrywide Assured Group Plc as Head of Group Legal in 2000.
Personal: Born 1964. Lives in Essex with wife and two children. Enjoys family, sport and socialising.
Other lawyers: Gareth Williams-Company/Comercial, Litigation; Shirley Low-Company Secretrarial; Glenn Quodros-Company/Commercial; Khosrow Varnous-Employment/Litigation; Jonathon Angell-Litigation/Insurance.

Coutts & Co
2 Lower Sloane Street London SW1W 8BJ
Tel: (020) 7753 1000 **Fax:** (020) 7753 1999
Website: www.coutts.com
No of lawyers in dept: 8
Work outsourced: 50% - Litigation, specialist advice, commercial transactions.
Chalmers Carr, Chief Legal Officer
Specialisation: Banking, investment and trusts.
Career: February 1998 to date Chief Legal Officer, Coutts Group Legal Services . 1989-1997 HSBC Holdings plc, General Manager and Group Legal Adviser . 1983-1989 Central Electricity Generating Board, Head of Legal Services .1980-1983 Capsticks, helped set up law practice. 1973-1980 Bridon plc, Contracts Director . 1967-1973 Guest Keen & Nettlefolds plc, Assistant Secretary . 1962-1967 Elliott Automation Ltd, Deputy Legal Adviser. 1961-1962 Rolls Royce Ltd, Legal Adviser.

IN-HOUSE LAWYERS ■ COMPANY SECRETARIES

Personal: Married to Julia, 2 sons.
Other lawyers: Sarah Chidgey, Gloria Glennie, Ian Levene, Julie Teuten, Neil Cave, Merrilie McLeod, Simon Amer.

Credit Agricole Indosuez
122 Leadenhall Street London EC3V 4QH
Tel: (020) 7971 4000 **Fax:** (020) 7628 4724
Margaret Garner, Head of Group Legal Services (London)

Credit Lyonnais
Broadwalk House 5 Appold Street London EC2A 2DA
Tel: (020) 7214 7080 **Fax:** (020) 7214 7007
Website: www.creditlyonnais.com
No of lawyers in dept: 10
Edward Paget-Brown, General Counsel
Specialisation: The entire range of legal work emanating from UK Business activities of Credit Lyonnais includ ing transaction support, drafting and negotiation of agreements, advice on banking, capital markets, regulatory, corporate, employment and IT matters as well as all aspects of litigation.
Career: Bristol University (LLB). Kingston University (MBA). Barrister at law. Credit Lyonnais Rouse Ltd 1987-1997. Credit Lyonnais 1997 to date.
Personal: Married, with 2 children
Other lawyers: Joseph Crowley - Banking, Derivatives; James Denham - Litigation.

Credit Suisse First Boston (CFSB)
One Cabot Square London E14 4QJ
Tel: (020) 7888 8888 **Fax:** (020) 7888 4251
Kevin Studd, General Counsel - Europe
One Cabot Square London E14 4QJ
Tel: (020) 7888 8888 **Fax:** (020) 7888 4251
Paul Chelsom, Director in Legal & Compliance
One Cabot Square London E14 4QJ
Tel: (020) 7888 8888 **Fax:** (020) 7888 4251
Edmond Curtin, Managing Director and European Deputy General Counsel, Credit Suisse First Boston

Credit Suisse First Boston (Europe) Ltd
One Cabot Square London E14 4QJ
Tel: (020) 7888 4337 **Fax:** (020) 7890 2394
Email: julia.pearce@csfb.com
Website: www.credit-suisse.com
Julia Pearce, Director - Head of Transaction Management Group
Specialisation: debt capital markets

Croda International PLC
Cowick Hall Snaith Goole DN14 9AA
Tel: (01405) 860551 **Fax:** (01405) 861767
Roy Ainger, Company Secretary

Daily Mail & General Trust PLC
Northcliffe House 2 Derry Street Kensington London W8 5TT
Tel: (020) 7938 6000 **Fax:** (020) 7937 3251
Harvey Kass, Legal Director, Associated Newspapers

Dairy Crest Group plc
Dairy Crest House Portsmouth Road Surbiton KT6 5QL
Tel: (020) 8910 4000 **Fax:** (020) 8910 4111
Peter Olsen, Company Legal Adviser

Daiwa Securities SMBC Europe Limited
5 King William Street London EC4N 7AX
Tel: (020) 7597 8000 **Fax:** (020) 7597 8600
Roger Massey, Executive Director of Legal and Transaction Management Department

Davis Service Group plc
4 Grosvenor Place London SW1X 7DL
Tel: (020) 7259 6663 **Fax:** (020) 7259 6948
Malcolm C Hoskin, Company Secretary

De La Rue plc
De La Rue House Jays Close Viables Basingstoke RG22 4BS
Tel: (01256) 605311 **Fax:** (01256) 605336
Email: louise.fluker@uk.delarue.com
Website: www.delarue.com
No of lawyers in dept: 4
Work outsourced: 30% in UK: Varies according to specialist projects - Conveyancing, litigation, pensions, major transactions, work requiring foreign jurisdiction advice.
Louise Fluker, General Counsel & Company Secretary
Career: MA (Cantab); LLB (Cantab).
Other lawyers: Douglas Denham, Elizabeth Joyce, Hector Martin: Each lawyer concentrates on particular divisions and in addition may have specialist areas across the group.

Debenhams plc
1 Welbeck Street London W1G 0AA
Tel: (020) 7408 4444 **Fax:** (020) 7408 3765
Website: www.debenhams.co.uk
No of lawyers in dept: 3
Guy Johnson, Company Secretary & General Counsel
Other lawyers: Pat Skinner; Sam Khandpur

Derwent Valley Holdings PLC
Head Office 25 Saville Row London W1S 2ER
Tel: (020) 7659 3000 **Fax:** (020) 7659 3100
Timothy Kite, Company Secretary

Deutsche Bank AG
Winchester House 1 Great Winchester Street London EC2N 2DB
Tel: (020) 7547 4538 **Fax:** (020) 7547 3102
Email: simon.dodds@db.com
Website: www.deutsche-bank.de
No of lawyers in dept: 70
Simon Dodds, General Counsel UK & Western Europe
Specialisation: Responsible for providing and supervising the provision of legal services to Deutsche Bank in the UK & Western Europe.
Career: 1 976-79: MA, Downing College, Cambridge; 1981-84: JD North Western University School of Law, Chicago; 1984-91: Associate, Cleary Gottlieb Steen and Hamilton, New York & London; 1991-99: Managing Director, Bankers Trust Company, London.
Personal: Born 27.8.1957.
Winchester House 1 Great Winchester Street London EC2N 2DB
Tel: (020) 7545 8000 **Fax:** (020) 7545 1481
Jon Ormond, Legal Counsel
Winchester House 1 Great Winchester Street London EC2N 2DB
Tel: (020) 7545 8000 **Fax:** (020) 7545 1481
Bill Ryan, Legal Counsel

DFS Furniture Company PLC
Bentley Moor Lane Adwick-Le-Street Doncaster DN6 7BD
Tel: (01302) 330365 **Fax:** (01302) 330880
Barry Todhunter, Company Secretary

Diageo plc
Kingsley House 1A Wimpole Street London W1M 8DB
Tel: (020) 7927 5300 **Fax:** (020) 7927 4600
Timothy Proctor, Group General Counsel

Dixons Group PLC
Dixons House Maylands Avenue Hemel Hempstead HP2 7TG
Tel: (01442) 353000 **Fax:** (01442) 233218
Geoffrey Budd, Company Secretary

DS Smith plc
4-16 Artillery Row London SW1P 1RZ
Tel: (020) 7932 5000 **Fax:** (020) 7932 5003
Email: jeremy.aron@dssmith.co.uk
Website: www.dssmith.co.uk
Jeremy Aron, Head of Group Legal
Specialisation: Responsible for managing all legal risks and the provision of legal services throughout the group. Key areas of expertise include cross-border M&A, joint ventures and commerical contracts.
Career: Solicitor - Winward Fearon & Co - 09/89 to 06/92. Region Legal Counsel - Baker Hughes - 07/92 to 07/98. Senior Counsel - Halliburton Brown & Root - 08/98 to 03/99. Legal Manager - Siemens PLC - 04/99 to 06/02.
Personal: Born 17 August 1964.

Dynegy Europe
Dynegy House 28 The Quadrant Richmond TW9 1DN
Tel: (020) 8403 1000 **Fax:** (020) 8403 1001
Yehuda Cohen, Head of Legal

easyJet Airlines
easyLand London-Luton Airport Luton LU2 9LS
Tel: (01582) 443 330 **Fax:** (01582) 443 355
Deborah Woodward, Company Secretary

Edinburgh Fund Managers Group PLC
Donaldson House 97 Haymarket Terrace Edinburgh EH12 5HD
Tel: (0131) 313 1000 **Fax:** (0131) 313 6300
Kenneth Murray, Head of Legal / Deputy client administrator

EGG PLC
1 Waterhouse Square 142 Holborn Bars London EC1N 2ST
Tel: (020) 7526 2500 **Fax:** (020) 7526 2665
Marcus Ezekiel, Chief Legal Officer & Company Secretary

Electra Investment Trust PLC
65 Kingsway London WC2B 6QT
Tel: (020) 7831 6464 **Fax:** (020) 7404 5388
Philip Dyke, Company Secretary

Electrocomponents PLC
International Management Centre 5000 Oxford Business Park South Oxford OX4 2BH
Tel: (01865) 204000 **Fax:** (01865) 207400
Carmelina Carfora, Group Company Secretary

EMAP plc
40 Bernard Street London WC1N 1LW
Tel: (020) 7278 1452 **Fax:** (020) 7278 6941
Email: nick.folland@emap.com
Website: www.emap.com
No of lawyers in dept: 1
Nick Folland, Group Legal Director & Company Secretary
Specialisation: Mergers and Acquisitions, Finance, Commercial, Media, Employment.
Career: Bristol University; Law Society Finals: First Class; Linklaters and Paines: 5.5 years (including Singapore and Hong Kong offices); Cable and Wireless: 3.5 years ; 365 Corporation plc (1 year).

EMI Group PLC
4 Tenterden Street Hanover Square London W1A 2AY
Tel: (020) 7355 4848 **Fax:** (020) 7495 1308
Charles P Ashcroft, Company Secretary & Group General Counsel

EMI Music Publishing Ltd
Publishing House 127 Charing Cross Road London WC2H 0QY
Tel: (020) 7434 2131 **Fax:** (020) 7434 3531
Chris Mileson, Director of Legal and Business Affairs

EMI Recorded Music UK & Eire
43 Brook Green London W6 7EF
Tel: (020) 7605 5000 **Fax:** (020) 7605 5220
Email: julian.french@emimusic.com
Website: www.emigroup.com
Julian French, Director of Business Affairs, EMI Recorded Music UK & Eire

Enterprise Energy Ireland Ltd
Corrib House 52 Lower Leeson Street Dublin 2
Tel: +353 1 669 4100 **Fax:** +353 1 669 4101
David Bate, Legal Manager

Enterprise Inns PLC
Head Office 3 Monkspath Hall Road Shirley Solihull B90 4SJ
Tel: (0121) 733 7700 **Fax:** (0121) 733 6447
Email: james.poole@enterpriseinns.com
Website: www.enterpriseinns.com
No of lawyers in dept: 1
Work outsourced: all
James Poole, Assistant Company Secretary
Other lawyers: James Poole - Company/Commercial/Company Secretarial/Property

Euromoney Institutional Investors PLC
Nestor House Playhouse Yard London EC4V 5EX
Tel: (020) 7779 8888 **Fax:** (020) 7779 8656
Louis Burnett, Company Secretary

European Bank for Reconstruction & Development (EBRD)
One Exchange Square Primrose Street London EC2A 2JN
Tel: (020) 7338 6000 **Fax:** (020) 7388 6100
Emmanuel Maurice, General Counsel

Exel plc
Ocean House The Ring Bracknell RG12 1AN
Tel: (01344) 744310 **Fax:** (01344) 710031
Email: ian.goulden@exel.com
Website: www.exel.com
No of lawyers in dept: 23
Work outsourced: 40% - Major acquisitions and disposals, litigation, property, overseas work, construction, pensions, environmental, competition, IT/IP.
Ian Goulden, Director of Legal Services
Specialisation: Responsible for all commercial matters affecting Exel's operational divisions, with particular emphasis on contractual matters. Manages in-house department compris-

IN-HOUSE LAWYERS ■ COMPANY SECRETARIES

ing twenty-three lawyers and seven paralegals worldwide.
Career: Hull University. Partner with Carter Hodge (private practice). Joined Ocean Group PLC in 1990. Appointed Head of Legal 1996. Appointed Director of Legal Services, Exel, following the merger of Ocean Group plc and NFC plc in 2000.
Other lawyers: By Region: 10 in UK, 6 in US, 2 in Holland, 2 in Singapore and 2 in Beijing.

Express Newspapers Ltd / Express Sunday
Ludgate House 245 Blackfriars Road Blackfriars London SE1 9UX
Tel: (020) 7928 8000 **Fax:** (020) 7620 1654
Justin Walford, Legal Manager

Expro International Group plc
Reading Bridge House Reading RG1 8PL
Tel: (0118) 959 1341 **Fax:** (0118) 958 9000
Anthony Dand, Company Secretary

Fidelity Investments International
Kingswood Fields Millfield Lane Lower Kingswood Tadworth KT20 6RB
Tel: (01737) 836 000 **Fax:** (01737) 838 886
Pamela Edwards, Executive Director, Legal Services, Europe

Film Finances Limited
14-15 Conduit Street London W1S 2XJ
Tel: (020) 7629 6557 **Fax:** (020) 7491 7530
No of lawyers in dept: 2
Work outsourced: 10% - Litigation.
James Shirras, Director Legal & Business Affairs
Specialisation: Contractual work in relation to the financing of film and television productiona, relating in particular to completion guarantees and reinsurance arrangements.
Career: Film Finances Limited, Director, Legal & Business Affairs 1992 to date. Harbottle & Lewis: Partner 1988-1992 Assistant Solicitor 1983-1988. Assistant Solicitor 1982-1983. Articled Clerk 1980-1982. College of Law, Lancaster Gate 1979-1980. Christ Church, Oxford: Law Degree 1976-1979.
Personal: Born 1957.
Other lawyers: James Shirras, David Lewison.

FilmFour
76-78 Charlotte Street London W1P 1LY
Tel: (020) 7868 7700 **Fax:** (020) 7868 7773
Andrew Hildebrand, Director of Business Affairs

Filtronic PLC
The Waterfront Salts Mill Road Saltaire Shipley BD18 3TT
Tel: (01274) 530622 **Fax:** (01274) 531561
Christopher Schofield, Company Secretary

The Financial Services Authority (FSA)
25 The North Colonnade Canary Wharf London E14 5HS
Tel: (020) 7676 1000 **Fax:** (020) 7676 1099
Email: andrew.whittaker@fsa.gov.uk
Website: www.fsa.gov.uk
No of lawyers in dept: 45
Andrew Whittaker, General Counsel to the Board
Specialisation: Responsible for legal advice to FSA Board and Senior Management of FSA on UK and European law, overall management and organisation of FSA legal function, quality control of legal advice in FSA, input into proposals for legislative change. Member of FSA Directors Committee; Chairman, FSA Lawyers Consultative Group.
Career: Torquay Boys Grammar School; Balliol College, Oxford, BA 1977, MA 1980, College of Law, Lancaster Gatey 1978. Qualified 1980. DTI 1982-1985. Securities and Investments Board, Deputy Legal Director 1987-1992; Head of Department for International policy and relations; markets policy, supervision of securities markets (1992-1997); Financial Services Authority - Deputy General Counsel 1997-2000, General Counsel 2000 - to date.
Personal: Travel, photography, family.
Other lawyers: Greg Choyce - Deposit Taking; Stuart Willey - Investment Business; Robin Ford - Insurance; Megan Butler - Markets.
25 The North Colonnade Canary Wharf London E14 5HS
Tel: (020) 7676 1000 **Fax:** (020) 7676 1099
Email: fsa@fsa.gov.uk
Website: www.fsa.gov.uk
Stuart Willey, Chief Counsel - Investment Business

First Choice Holidays PLC
First Choice House London Road Crawley RH10 2GX
Tel: (01293) 560777 **Fax:** (01293) 539039
Website: www.firstchoiceholidays.com
No of lawyers in dept: 4
Work outsourced: 30% - large corporate finance transactions and M&A work; major banking transactions; property; large scale commercial litigation and aviation finance.
Andrew John, Director of Legal Affairs & Company Secretary
Specialisation: Mergers & Acquisitions, Company/Commercial, Risk & Insurance, Company Secretarial, Corporate Governance.Member of First Choice Executive Committee.
Career: LLB 1st Class Honors Manchester University.1975 - 1978 Assistant Solicitor.1978 - 1981 European Legal Adviser, Coward Chance.1981 - 1989 Staff Director, Legal & Contracts, Vickers PLC.1989 - 1991 Director Legal Affairs, Unisys Limited.1991 - 2000 Commercial Director & Company Secretary, Vickers PLC.

First Technology PLC
9 High Street Egham TW20 9EA
Tel: (01784) 221500 **Fax:** (01784) 221525
Neil Clayton, Company Secretary

FirstGroup plc
E Block 3rd Floor Macmillan House Paddington Station London W2 1FG
Tel: (020) 7291 0505 **Fax:** (020) 7636 1338
Email: louise.ruppel@firstgroup.com
Website: www.firstgroup.com
Louise Ruppel, Group Legal Adviser & Company Secretary
Specialisation: Company, commercial law, corporate finance.
Career: University of Liverpool (LL.B. First Class Hons) 1985-1988; Guildford College of Law 1988-1989; Slaughter and May 1990-1997; Merrill Lynch (UK Counsel) 1997-1998; FirstGroup plc 1998-present.

Fitness First PLC
58 Fleets Lane Fleetsbridge Poole BH15 3BT
Tel: (01202) 845000 **Fax:** (01202) 683510
Susan Cadd, Company Secretary

FKI PLC
15-19 New Fetter Lane London EC4A 1LY
Tel: (020) 7832 0000 **Fax:** (020) 7832 0001
Tony Ventrella, Director, Legal Services

Forth Ports PLC
Tower Place Leith Edinburgh EH6 7DB
Tel: (0131) 555 8700 **Fax:** (0131) 555 9000
Website: www.forthports.co.uk
No of lawyers in dept: 2
Work outsourced: 60% - Property/Construction.
John Tothill, Legal Adviser & Company Secretary
Specialisation: Corporate, commercial property, construction, contracts.
Career: LLB, Dip LP 1982 (Scots Law).Qualified Solicitor 1984.ACIS 1992.Qualified English Law 2000.

Framlington Group Ltd
155 Bishopsgate London EC2M 3XJ
Tel: (020) 7330 6433 **Fax:** (020) 7660 6406
Email: contact@framlington.co.uk
Website: www.framlington.co.uk
No of lawyers in dept: 1
Work outsourced: 50% - Investment trusts, pensions, employment, IP, litigation, incentive schemes, unit trust authorisation and amendments, offshore funds.
Josephine Tubbs, Head of Legal & Company Secretariat
Specialisation: Financial sevices (funds, investment trusts, investment management), commercial, IT, company secretarial, IP.
Career: Clarendon School, Felsted School, Bristol University (1989 LLB 2:1), Chester College of Law (1990 LSF, Hons); Simmons & Simmons (articles); Association of Unit Trusts & Investment Funds; Burges Salmon; Eversheds (then Frere Cholmeley Bischoff); Gartmore.
Personal: Sport, horseracing, cinema, reading, travel.
Other lawyers: Commercial,financial services,funds and investment management,IT,datafraction,litigation,pensions,IP.

Freeserve PLC
500 The Campus Maylands Avenue Hemel Hempstead HP2 7TG
Tel: 0870 909 0666
Jessica Hendrie-Liano, Company Lawyer

FremantleMedia Ltd
1 Stephen Street London W1T 1AL
Tel: (020) 7691 6000 **Fax:** (020) 7691 6100
Sarah Tingay, Director of Legal & Business Affairs

Friends Ivory & Sime PLC
1 Charlotte Square Edinburgh EH2 4DZ
Tel: (0131) 465 1000 **Fax:** (0131) 225 2375
Ian Patterson-Brown, Head of Compliance & Company Secretary

Friends Provident Life
Pixham End Pixham Lane Dorking RH4 1QA
Tel: (0870) 608 3678 **Fax:** (01306) 740150
Michael Elmore-Jones, Head of Legal

Fujitsu Services
26 Finsbury Square London EC2A 1SL
Tel: (020) 7614 4532 **Fax:** (020) 7614 4521
Richard Allnut, Group Counsel

Gallaher Group plc
Members Hill Brooklands Road Weybridge KT13 0QU
Tel: (01932) 859777 **Fax:** (01932) 832792
Tom Keevil, Group Legal Counsel

The Game Group PLC
Link House Ellesfield Avenue Bracknell RG12 8TB
Tel: (01344) 464000 **Fax:** (01344) 464054
Email: headoffice@eb.uk.com
Website: www.electronicsboutique.plc.uk
Jeremy Gorman, Company Secretary

Gartmore Investment Management PLC
Fenchurch Exchange 8 Fenchurch Place London EC3M 4BH
Tel: (020) 7782 2000 **Fax:** (020) 7374 3075
Email: helpline@gartmore.com
Website: www.gartmore.com
No of lawyers in dept: 8
Work outsourced: 30% - Non UK law; significant corporate transactions; new products.
Jane Thornton, Head of Legal Department & Company Secretary
Specialisation: Strategic support to the Board; corporate transactions; Director of the trustee of the company's pension scheme; Ad hoc significant corporate projects.
Career: 1st class Hons (LL.B) from University of Southampton in 1988; 2nd class Hons in Law Society Final Examinations (1989); Trained at and spent five years past qualification with Clifford Chance specialising in financial services and corporate matters (1989-1996), became Head of Legal and Company Secretary later that year.
Other lawyers: Sade Kilaso; Simon Martin; Katy Ruddell; Rachel Wheeler; Sandeep Bandesha; Liz Jemenetts; Ines Balay Fenchurch Exchange 8 Fenchurch Place London EC3M 4BH
Tel: (020) 7782 2000 **Fax:** (020) 7374 3075
Simon Martin, Legal Manager

GE Capital Equipment Finance
Capital House Bond Street Bristol BS1 3LA
Tel: (0117) 929 8899 **Fax:** (0117) 946 3450
Janet Gregory, UK Legal Director

Geest PLC
Midgate House Midgate Peterborough PE1 1TN
Tel: (01775) 761111 **Fax:** (01775) 763098
No of lawyers in dept: 2
Work outsourced: 25% - Litigation, property, banking, M&A.
Dawn Durrant, Company Secretary
Specialisation: Company secretarial, company and commercial, corporate finance, insurance and risk management.
Career: Nottingham University - LLB Hons Class 2:1; College of Law, Chester - Solicitor Hons; Alan Overy, London 1988-94; Geest plc - 1994 to date.
Personal: Interests: Travel, theatre, cookery.
Other lawyers: Fiona Spencer - Company/Commercial.

George Wimpey PLC
Manning House 22 Carlisle Place Victoria London SW1P 1JA
Tel: (020) 7963 6351 **Fax:** (020) 7963 6355
Email: jjordan@georgewimpey.co.uk
Website: www.georgewimpey.co.uk
Work outsourced: Corporate.
James Jordan, Company Secretary
Specialisation: Corporate, Competition, M&A, Litgation. Group Company Secretary.
Career: BA Law (Hons) - Nottingham Trent.Counsel Europe/Pacific - The Rugby Group PLC.Group Secretary and Director of Legal Affairs - Molins PLC.Group Secretary - George Wimpey PLC.
Personal: Date of Birth: 4/11/1961. Married with three children. Solicitor.
Other lawyers: Company/Commercial, Litigation.

IN-HOUSE LAWYERS ■ COMPANY SECRETARIES

GKN plc
Ipsley House Ipsley Church Lane PO Box 55
Redditch B98 0TL
Tel: (01527) 533253 **Fax:** (01527) 533470
Email: Rufus.OgilvieSmals@gknplc.com
Website: www.gknplc.com
No of lawyers in dept: 5
Work outsourced: Litigation, conveyancing, minor matters, public offers, pensions work, tax, regulatory, employment.
Rufus Ogilvie Smals, Head of Legal Department
Career: Read Law at Emmanuel College, Cambridge University. Attended Inns of Court School of Law. Called to the Bar (Middle Temple) 1973. Studied at Europa Institute, University of Amsterdam. Joined GKN in 1975, from Deputy Head of the Legal Department to Head of the Group Legal Department in 1995. Chairman of CBI Competition Panel.
Personal: Interests include sailing, skiing, military history and current affairs.
Other lawyers: Deputy Head of Legal Department: David Radford ; Principal Legal Adviser: Sarah Eddowes ; Senior Legal Advis er : Martin Brostoff ; Legal Adviser: A N Other.
Ipsley House Ipsley Church Lane PO Box 55
Redditch B98 0TL
Tel: (01527) 533255 **Fax:** (01527) 516981
Email: information@gknplc.com
Website: www.gknplc.com
Grey Denham, Company Secretary
Specialisation: The Group Secretary has overall responsibilty for all Secretarial and Governance services provided to the listed parent company and other central companies and for compliance and legal services to the Group worldwide. The Group Legal Department specialises in M&A, joint ventures, finance, strategic contracts (including helicopter and other defence contracts) litigation management, competition law and general company and commercial work, including e-commerce.
Career: 1972 - Lecturer in Law, Leicester Polytechnic; 1974 - Senior Lecturer in Legal Philosophy, Nottingham Law School; 1978 - Company Legal Officer, Alfred Herbert Limited; 1980 - Company Lawyer, GKN plc; 1983 Deputy Head of Legal, GKN plc; 1986 - Head of Legal, GKN plc; 1995 - Chairman, GKN Group Services Limited; 1996 - Company Secretary, GKN plc, Director GKN (United Kingdom) plc, President GKN North America Inc. Member of London Stock Exchange Regional Advisory Group, Council of Birmingham Chamber of Commerce and Industry, West Midlands Council of CBI.
Personal: Educated - Handsworth Grammar School; Brooklyn Technical College; Bristol College of Commerce; London University (LL.B.); Inns of Court Law School (called 1972); Columbia University Graduate School of Business (CSEP 1995).

GlaxoSmithKline
980 Great West Road Brentford TW8 9GS
Tel: (020) 8047 5000 **Fax:** (020) 8047 0679
Website: www.gsk.com
No of lawyers in dept: 231 Worldwide
Work outsourced: 10% approx - Where additional resource or specialist knowledge required.
Rupert Bondy, Senior Vice President & General Counsel
Other lawyers: Departments: Corporate Legal & Secretarial; Corporate Compliance; Legal Operations International; Legal Operations USA inclduing Corporate Guardianship & Dispute Resolution & Strategic Transactions; Corporate Intellectual Property; Legal Operations Europe ; Corporate Environment & Safety; Corporate Security; Corporate Insurance & Risk Management.
980 Great West Road Brentford TW8 9GS
Tel: (020) 8047 4396 **Fax:** (020) 8047 6891
Email: Alan.s.cox@gsk.com
Website: www.gsk.com
Alan Cox, Global Head - Trade Marks
980 Great West Road Brentford TW8 9GS
Tel: (020) 8047 5000 **Fax:** (020) 8047 7807
David Roberts, Director & Senior Vice-President, Corporate Intellectual Property

Goldman Sachs International
Peterborough Court 133 Fleet Street London EC4A 2BB
Tel: (020) 7774 1000 **Fax:** (020) 7774 1989
Therese L Miller, Managing Director & General Counsel
Daniel House 140 Fleet Street London EC4A 2BB
Tel: (020) 7774 1000 **Fax:** (020) 7774 1989
William Elliot, Executive Legal Director
Peterborough Court 133 Fleet Street London EC4A 2BB
Tel: (020) 7774 1000 **Fax:** (020) 7774 1989
David Geen, Executive Director & Senior Counsel
Daniel House 140 Fleet Street London EC4A 2BB
Tel: (020) 7774 1000 **Fax:** (020) 7774 1989
Alexander Marshall, Executive Director & Senior Counsel
Daniel House 140 Fleet Street London EC4A 2BB
Tel: (020) 7774 1000 **Fax:** (020) 7774 1989

Jonathan Thomas, Executive Director & Counsel

Great Portland Estates PLC
Knighton House 56 Mortimer Street London W1W 7RT
Tel: (020) 7580 3040 **Fax:** (020) 7631 5169
Desna Martin, Company Secretary

Greene King PLC
Westgate Brewery Westgate Street
Bury St Edmunds IP33 1QT
Tel: (01284) 714212 **Fax:** (01284) 723719
Website: www.greeneking.co.uk
Work outsourced: 95% - General Corporate, Property, Licensing , Employment.
Robin Bellhouse, Company Secretary

Greggs PLC
Fernwood House Clayton Road Jesmond
Newcastle upon Tyne NE2 1TL
Tel: (0191) 281 7721 **Fax:** (0191) 281 1444
Andrew Davison, Company Secretary

Guardian Newspapers Limited
119 Farringdon Road London EC1R 3ER
Tel: (020) 7278 2332 **Fax:** (020) 7713 4481
Email: siobhain.butterworth@guardian.co.uk
Website: www.guardianunlimited.co.uk
No of lawyers in dept: 5
Work outsourced: 30% - Libel, litigation and contracts.
Siobhain Butterworth, Head of Legal Affairs
Specialisation: Responsible for providing legal services to Guardian Newspapers Ltd, publishers of the Guardian and the Observer newspapers and the Guardian unlimited network of websites. Responsible for all contentious and non-contentious matters; pre-publication, libel and media related litigation, intellectual property and commercial work.
Career: St. Leonards RC Comprehensive School, Durham; Newcastle University 1984. Articled Stephens Innocent, Qualified 1991; Stephens & Scown 1992; Solicitor Stephens Innocent 1993-1997; Head of Legal Affairs, Guardian Newspaper Ltd 1997-present.
Personal: Born 1963; Resides London.
Other lawyers: Libel and media related litigation, intellectual property, commercial.

GUS plc
One Stanhope Gate London W1K 1AF
Tel: (020) 7495 0070 **Fax:** (020) 7495 1567
Website: www.gusplc.com
David Morris, Company Secretary

GWR Group plc
One Passage Street Bristol BS2 OJF
Tel: (0117) 900 5316 **Fax:** (0117) 900 5306
Email: richard.manning@musicradio.com
Website: www.gwrgroup.com
No of lawyers in dept: 1
Work outsourced: 50% - All types.
Richard Manning, Group Solicitor
Specialisation: All aspects of legal work for GWR Group plc, from corporate/M&A to local radio station issues and everything in between.
Career: Law degree at Leeds University (1983-86) followed by MBA at Bradford Management Centre (1987). After a spell in non-legal roles, articles at Swainson Son & Reynolds, Lancaster followed by 7 years in-house with Burmah Castrol plc. Commenced current head of legal role with GWR Group plc in January 2001.
Personal: Married with 3 children. Interests: music, squash, golf.
Other lawyers: Company/ Commercial, Corporate/M&A, Corporate Finance, Litigation, Property, Intellectual Property.

Halma PLC
Misbourne Court Rectory Way Amersham HP7 0DE
Tel: (01494) 721111 **Fax:** (01494) 728032
Email: carol.chesney@halma.com
Website: www.halma.com
Carol Chesney, Company Secretary

Hammerson PLC
100 Park Lane London W1Y 4AR
Tel: (020) 7887 1000 **Fax:** (020) 7887 1010
Email: shaydon@hammerson.co.uk
Website: www.hammerson.co.uk
Stuart Haydon, Company Secretary

Hanson PLC
1 Grosvenor Place London SW1X 7JH
Tel: (020) 7245 1245 **Fax:** (020) 7245 9939

Email: graham.dansfield@hansonplc.com
Website: www.hansonplc.com
No of lawyers in dept: 2
Work outsourced: Varies by division. - Property, litigation.
Graham Dransfield, Legal Director
Specialisation: Company/commercial, corporate finance. Acting for the UK head office companies and UK subsidiaries in corporate and commercial activities. Property and litigation not dealt with in-house; legal structure operates on decentralised basis.
Career: Colne Valley High School; St Catherine's College, Oxford. Articled Slaughter and May 1974-82; Joined Hanson plc 1982, Legal Director since 1992.
Personal: Beckenham Tennis and Squash Club; The Addington Golf Club.
Other lawyers: Elliot Laurie - Company / commerical, corporate finance, finance general.

Hays PLC
Hays House Millmead Guildford GU2 4HJ
Tel: (01483) 302203 **Fax:** (01483) 302226
Email: stephen.charnock@hays.com
Website: www.hays.com
No of lawyers in dept: 8
Work outsourced: 60% - Acquisitions/disposals of companies/businesses, major commercial contracts, employment, litigation, property, pensions.
Stephen Charnock, Company Secretary & Head of Legal
Specialisation: Acquisitions, joint ventures, major contracts, company secretarial, share options, pensions.
Other lawyers: Paul Dungate - Senior Solicitor. Jon Webourne-Green - Solicitor (Head Office). Plus 2 in Milton Keynes, 2 in New Malden and 2 in Paris.

Hess Energy Trading
33 Grosvenor Place London SW1X 7HY
Tel: (020) 7201 7101 **Fax:** (020) 7887 0191
Website: www.hess.com
Justin Boyd, Head of Legal
Specialisation: Energy commodity trading relating to oil, gas and power primarily in European markets.
Career: Enron: 1992-2001; TotalFinaElf: 1991-1992; Private Practice: 1987-1991; LLB(Hons)

Hilton Group PLC
Maple Court Central Park Reeds Crescent
Watford WD24 4QQ
Tel: (020) 7856 8299 **Fax:** (01923) 202024
Website: www.hiltongroup.com
No of lawyers in dept: 5
Work outsourced: 20% - Various.
J Geoffrey Chester, Solicitor, General Counsel & Secretary
Specialisation: Responsible for all legal and company secretarial work for Hilton Group plcs Hotel division including all Hilton International Co's Hotels with particular emphasis in development (new hotels).
Career: Articed Lloyd Raymond & Co / Edward Thompson & Co; qualified 1976; company commercial solicitor National Coal Board 1981-1985; head of company / commercial section of the legal department Ladbroke Group plc 1985-1988; transferred in 1988 from Ladbroke to head up Hilton International Co's legal department (solicitor, general counsel and secretary). Univeristy College, Cardiff (1973, BSc); City of London Polytechnic (1977, MA Business Law); City University (1986, MBA).
Personal: Born 1951; resides Kew Gardens.

Hiscox Syndicate 33
1 Great Street Helen's London EC3A 6HX
Tel: (020) 7448 6000 **Fax:** (020) 7448 6901
Email: robert.britton@hiscox.com
Website: www.hiscox.com
Bob Britton, In-house Lawyer

HIT Entertainment PLC
Maple House 5th Floor 149 Tottenham Court Road
London W1T 7NF
Tel: (020) 7224 2500 **Fax:** (020) 7388 9744
No of lawyers in dept: 4
Work outsourced: 10% - Corporate finance, trademarks.
Simon Taylor, Director of Legal and Business Affairs
Specialisation: Media and entertainment law, intellectual property, employment, property, company/commercial.
Career: 1994-2000 - BBC Programme Aquisition - Head of Business and Legal Affairs; 1991-1994 - Copyright and Artists Rights - Lawyer; 1989-1991 - Mishcon de Reya - Trainee Solicitor. Joined HIT in July 2000.
Other lawyers: Intellectual property, media law, employment, property, company/commercial.

IN-HOUSE LAWYERS ■ COMPANY SECRETARIES

HSBC Holdings plc
Level 41 Canada Square London E14 5HQ
Tel: (020) 7991 0205 **Fax:** (020) 7991 4608
Email: richard.bennett@hsbc.com
Website: www.hsbc.com
No of lawyers in dept: 60 UK, more than 300 worldwide.
Work outsourced: 60% - Major transactions, litigation.
Richard Bennett, Group General Counsel, Legal and Compliance
Specialisation: Responsible for the Legal & Compliance function of the HSBC Holdings Group.
Career: Bristol University (LLB), graduated 1973. Qualified with Stephenson Harwood, 1976. Assistant Solicitor with Harwood until 1979 (seconded to the East Asiatic Company, Denmark 1977). Appointed Assistant Group Legal Adviser with The Hong Kong and Shanghai Banking Corporation 1979. Deputy Group Legal Adviser 1988. Head of Legal & Compliance of The Hong Kong and Shanghai Banking Corporation Ltd 1993 with responsibility for legal, compliance and secretarial functions in Asia Pacific. Appointed to present position 1 January 1998.
Personal: Born 20th September 1951. Leisure pursuits include; all sports, particularly rugby and golf. Lives in Surrey, London.

Vintners Place 68 Upper Thames Street London EC4V 3BJ
Tel: (020) 7260 9000 **Fax:** (020) 7623 5768
Email: David.Bloom@hsbcgroup.com
Website: www.hsbc.com
David Bloom, Head of Legal Corporate, Investment Banking and Markets

Regent Court 16 George Road Edgbaston Birmingham B15 1NT
Tel: (0121) 455 2710 **Fax:** (0121) 455 2770
Email: stephen.garratt-frost@hsbc.com
Website: www.hsbc.com
Stephen Garratt-Frost, Head of Legal Services, Birmingham
Specialisation: Responsible for providing legal advice and support to HSBC Bank plc and it's subsidiaries comprising the Retail Branch Network, Personal Financial Services and Asset/Invoice Finance businesses.
Career: Joined the former Midland Bank plc in 1984 to do general banking work, after 15 years in private practice in Kent. Became Head of Legal Services, Birmingham 1st January 1999.
Personal: Born 9th December 1952. Inveterate traveller who also enjoy cinema, antiques, history and archaeology.

IBM UK Ltd
PO Box 41 North Harbour Portsmouth PO6 3AU
Tel: (0990) 727272 **Fax:** (0990) 426329
Robert Marcus, Senior Counsel
South Bank 76 Upper Ground London SE1 9PZ
Tel: (020) 7202 3000 **Fax:** (020) 7202 5935
David Witt, Senior Counsel, Europe Middle East and Africa, Litigation and Intellectual Property

ICAP plc
Park House 16 Finsbury Circus London EC2M 7UR
Tel: (020) 7463 4367 **Fax:** (020) 7463 4345
Email: edward.pank@icap.com
Website: www.icap.com
No of lawyers in dept: 3
Work outsourced: 30% - Property, tax, some corporate finance.
Edward Pank, Company Secretary & Global Head of Legal Services
Specialisation: Company commercial, share/venture schemes, information technology.
Career: Framlington College 1958-62; Trinity Hall, Cambridge 1963-66; St Thomas's Hospital Medical School 1977-82; Herbert Smith 1969-70; Slater Walker Ltd 1970-76; ICAP plc 1986-present.
Other lawyers: Mark Schreiber - General; Laura Georgulas - General.

IMI PLC
Kynoch Works PO Box 216 Witton Birmingham B6 7BA
Tel: (0121) 356 4848 **Fax:** (0121) 356 3526
Website: www.imi.plc.uk
No of lawyers in dept: 3
Work outsourced: Corporate, litigation and conveyancing.
John O'Shea, Company Secretary
Other lawyers: Paul Boulton : General Corporate and Commercial; Joanne Bower : General Corporate and Commercial.

Imperial Chemical Industries PLC (ICI)
20 Manchester Square London W1U 3AN
Tel: (020) 7009 5000 **Fax:** (020) 7009 5727
Email: michael_herlihy@ici.com
Website: www.ici.com
Michael H C Herlihy, General Counsel & Executive Vice President, Mergers and Acquisitions
Specialisation: Oversees the lawyers in the Group and responsible for provision of legal advice to the ICI Board and all members of the ICI Group.
Career: Qualified in 1977. University - St. Catherine's College, Oxford. Joined ICI 1979; 1985-1992 Manager of Legal Affairs Department, ICI Agrochemicals; 1992-1995 Group Taxation Controller; 1996 to date General Counsel.

Imperial Tobacco Group PLC
PO Box 244 Upton Road Southville Bristol BS99 7UJ
Tel: (0117) 963 6636 **Fax:** (0117) 966 7405
Alan Porter, Legal Manager

Inchcape PLC
22A St James Square London SW1Y 5LP
Tel: (020) 7546 0022 **Fax:** (020) 7546 0010
Roy Williams, Group Company Secretary

Independent Television News Ltd (ITN)
200 Gray's Inn Road London WC1X 8XZ
Tel: (020) 7833 3000 **Fax:** (020) 7430 4868
Email: contact@itn.co.uk
Website: www.itn.co.uk
John Battle, Head of Compliance ITN
Specialisation: Libel, contempt, copyright and any media law issues. Industry regulatory advice (ITC and BSC codes), data protection.
Career: 2001 Head of Compliance, ITN; 1996-2001 Group Legal Adviser, Associated Newspapers Ltd; 1990-1996 Legal Adviser, News International. Education: Warwick University LLB (Hons) 1984; Kings College, University of London, 2000, Postgraduate Diploma in UK and European Copyright Law and Related Rights; Institute of Chartered Secretaries, Post Qualification Certificate; Advanced Company Secretarial Practice, 1999.

Informa Group plc
19 Portland Place London W1B 1PX
Tel: (020) 7453 2222 **Fax:** (020) 7453 2450
Andrea Wilson, Company Secretary

ING Baring Asset Management Holdings
155 Bishopsgate London EC2M 3XY
Tel: (020) 7628 6000
Marla Dhillon, Global Head of Compliance & Head of Legal

Innogy Holdings PLC
Windmill Hill Business Park Whitehill Way Swindon SN5 6PB
Tel: (01793) 877777 **Fax:** (01793) 892525
Mike Bowden, Company Secretary; Director of Legal & Regulatory Affairs
Windmill Hill Business Park Whitehill Way Swindon SN5 6PB
Tel: (01793) 877777 **Fax:** (01793) 892525
Nigel Fowkes, Solicitor

Innovation Group PLC
Yarmouth House 1300 Parkway Solent Business Park Whiteley PO15 7AE
Tel: (01489) 898300 **Fax:** (01489) 579181
Lawrence Moore, Company Secretary

Institute of Sales Promotion (ISP)
Arena House 66-68 Pentonville Road Islington London N1 9HS
Tel: (020) 7837 5340 **Fax:** (020) 7837 5326
Email: philip.circus@virgin.net
Website: www.isp.co.uk
Philip Circus, Director of Legal Affairs
Specialisation: Providing advice on marketing law in general and sales promotions and direct marketing law in particular. Also, government affairs work both in the UK and EU.
Career: MA (London), M.Phil. (Southampton), Diploma in Consumer Affairs (Prize winner) and Postgraduate diploma in European Community Law. Called to the Bar by the Inner Temple, July 1975. Several legal posts in trade associations over 25 years, including the Confederation of British Industry (CBI)

Intermediate Capital Group PLC
20 Old Broad Street London EC2N 1DP
Tel: (020) 7628 9898 **Fax:** (020) 7628 2268
Website: www.icgplc.com
Work outsourced: 100%
John E Curtis, Company Secretary

International Power plc
Senator House 85 Queen Victoria Street London EC4V 4DP
Tel: (020) 7320 8600 **Fax:** (020) 7320 8705
Website: www.internationalpowerplc.com
No of lawyers in dept: 8
Work outsourced: Less than 35-40% - Project Finance (part outsourced, rest done in-house), Pensions, Real Property, Intellectual Property, Employment, Litigation.
Rosemary Cook, General Counsel
Specialisation: Project Finance, M&A, Asset Management (legal support).
Career: 1981 LLB (Hons) University of Southampton, England.1984 Admitted as a solicitor New South Wales, Australia.1985-1989 Law at Milne, Sydney, NSW, Australia.1990-1994 Freshfields, London.1991 Admitted as a solicitor, England & Wales.1996 to date National Power PLC / International Power plc.
Other lawyers: Stephen Ramsay - Company Secretary & Corporate Counsel, Rosemary Cook - General Counsel. Kian Min Low, Kristi Massie, Graham Methold, Roger Simpson, Clint Steyn, David Waldham, Kimio Yamasaki.

Interserve plc
Interserve House Ruscombe Park Twyford Reading RG10 9JU
Tel: (01189) 320123 **Fax:** (01189) 320206
Daniel Bush, Group Solicitor

Invensys plc
Carlisle Place London SW1P 1BX
Tel: (020) 7834 3848 **Fax:** (020) 7834 3879
Victoria Hull, Senior Vice President & General Counsel

Invesco UK Limited
11 Devonshire Square London EC2M 4YR
Tel: (020) 7626 3434 **Fax:** (020) 7929 5888
Rodney Smyth, General Counsel Invesco UK

iSOFT Group PLC
Bridgewater House 58-60 Whitworth Street Manchester M1 6LT
Tel: (0161) 233 8800 **Fax:** (0161) 233 8899
Tim Whiston, Financial Director & Company Secretary

ITV Network Limited
200 Grays Inn Road London WC1X 8HF
Tel: (020) 7843 8000 **Fax:** (020) 7843 8158
Simon Johnson, Head of Legal

J Sainsbury PLC
33 Holborn London EC1N 2HT
Tel: (020) 7695 7468 **Fax:** (020) 7695 7610
Email: David.Thurston@sainsburys.co.uk
Website: www.j-sainsbury.co.uk
No of lawyers in dept: 8
David Thurston, Head of Group Legal Services
Other lawyers: George Robertson : Deputy Head / Litigation; Nicholas Grant : Commercial and Competition; Su Jenkins : Employment; Sue Redding : Trading and Marketing.

Jardine Lloyd Thompson Group plc (JLT)
6 Crutched Friars London EC3N 2PH
Tel: (020) 7528 4444 **Fax:** (020) 7528 4432
Website: www.jltgroup.com
No of lawyers in dept: 4
Work outsourced: 10% or less - Litigation only.
Vyvienne Wade, Group Legal Director
Specialisation: Acquisitions, corporate, insurance and reinsurance.
Career: Joined JIB in 1987 and has remained with the group after its merger with Lloyd Thompson Group plc to form Jardine Lloyd Thompson Group plc. Recent announcement of appointment to main board w.e.f. 01/01/2002.
Other lawyers: M&A; Insurance and Reinsurance (contentious and non-contentious), employment, litigation.

Jarvis PLC
Frogmore Park Watton-at-Stone Hertford SG14 3RU
Tel: (01920) 832800 **Fax:** (01920) 832832
Geoff Mason, Group Company Secretary

JD Wetherspoon PLC
Wetherspoon House Central Park Reeds Crescent PO Box 616 Watford WD1 1YN
Tel: (01923) 477777 **Fax:** (01923) 219810
Nick Cooper, Company Secretary

Jim Henson Company Ltd
30 Oval Road Camden Town London NW1 7DE
Tel: (020) 7428 4000 **Fax:** (020) 7267 3817
Email: adowney@henson.com

IN-HOUSE LAWYERS ■ COMPANY SECRETARIES

No of lawyers in dept: 2
Work outsourced: 25-30% - Employment, litigation, property.
Antonia S Downey, Senior Vice President, International Business & Legal Affairs
Specialisation: Film and television production, licensing and publishing , TV and video distribution, special effects and post production.
Career: LLB (Hons 2:1) - University College, London; 5 years as trainee and assistant solicitor in media department of Denton Wilde Sapte (formerly Denton Hall).
Personal: Travel, art, films, theatre.

JJB Sports PLC
Martland Park Challenge Way Wigan WN5 0LD
Tel: (01942) 221400 **Fax:** (01942) 629809
David Greenwood, Finance Director & Company Secretary

John Laing plc
Nations House 103 Wigmore St London W1U 1RR
Tel: (020) 7647 8800 **Fax:** (020) 7647 8811
Graham D Gibson, Manager Group Legal Services & Group Solicitor

John Mowlem & Company PLC
White Lion Court Swan Street Isleworth TW7 6RN
Tel: (020) 8568 9111 **Fax:** (020) 8847 4802
Keith Woodward, Company Secretary & Group Chief Legal Officer

Johnson Matthey PLC
2-4 Cockspur Street Trafalgar Square London SW1Y 5BQ
Tel: (020) 7269 8400 **Fax:** (020) 7269 8476
Simon Farrant, Company Secretary & Head of Legal

Johnston Press PLC
53 Manor Place Edinburgh EH3 7EG
Tel: (0131) 225 3361 **Fax:** (0131) 225 4580
Richard Cooper, Company Secretary

JP Morgan & Co
60 Victoria Embankment London EC4Y 0JP
Tel: (020) 7600 2300 **Fax:** (020) 7325 8150
David A Lewis, Managing Director and Associate General Counsel

JP Morgan Chase
125 London Wall London EC2Y 5AJ
Tel: 020 7777 2000 **Fax:** (020) 7777 3141
Mitchell B Caller, Senior Vice President & Associate General Counsel.

Kelda Group plc
Western House Halifax Road Bradford BD6 2SZ
Tel: (01274) 804159 **Fax:** (01274) 804165
Email: stuart_mcfarlane@keldagroup.com
Website: www.keldagroup.com
No of lawyers in dept: 12
Work outsourced: 5% - Regulatory, commercial, litigation, employment, construction litigation, planning.
Stuart McFarlane, Head of Legal Services
Specialisation: Principal areas of work for the department include conveyancing, company/commercial, litigation (civil and criminal) and environmental.
Career: Articled Ian Gillis and Co 1982-84, Solicitor 1984 to date. Joined Yorkshire Water plc 1989, Head of Legal Services since 1994.
Other lawyers: Ann Chapman ; Andrew Newton - company/commercial; Peter Cockburn ; Matthew Stevens ; Perminder Kaur; Michelle Parlett ; Kate Hartland-Westwood - property; Shona Flood ; Graeme Stonehouse ; Jill Sowden ; Deborah Stirling - litigation.

Kidde PLC
Mathisen Way Colnbrook Slough SL3 0HB
Tel: (01753) 766338 **Fax:** (01753) 689309
Email: diane.quinlan@kidde.com
Website: www.kidde.com
No of lawyers in dept: 2 in USA
Work outsourced: 80% - Major corporate.
Diane Quinlan, Company Secretary
Other lawyers: Corporate, litigation, company/commercial.

Kingfisher PLC
North West House 119 Marylebone Road
London NW1 5PX
Tel: (020) 7725 2948 **Fax:** (020) 7724 0355
Email: martin.chambers@kingfisher.co.uk
Website: www.kingfisher.co.uk
No of lawyers in dept: 1
Work outsourced: 90% - M&A, Employment, Litigation, Property.
Martin Chambers, Director of Legal Affairs
Specialisation: M&A, IP, Joint Ventures, Competition.
Career: Bristol University (German and French).Qualified 1975. Articled at Clifford-Turner. Assistant Solicitor at McKennas. European Legal Counsel at Eaton Corporation 1977. Group Legal Controller at Guiness PLC 1983. House of Fraser Holdings plc 1988. European Legal Controller at Albert Fisher Group PLC 1991. Group Legal Adviser and Company Secretary at Hillsdown Holdings plc 1993. Director of Legal Affairs at Kingfisher plc 2001.
Personal: Married with 3 children. Lives in Wendover.Interests: Tennis, cricket, golf.Languages: Trilingual in German and French.

Kingston Communications PLC
Telephone House 37 Carr Lane
Kingston-upon-Hull HU1 3RE
Tel: (01482) 602576 **Fax:** (01482) 320652
Email: John_Bailey@kingston-comm.co.uk
Website: www.kcom.com
No of lawyers in dept: 4
Work outsourced: 30% - Property matters, litigation, transactions involving foreign law, planning, acquisitions, pensions, some commercial and regulatory work.
John PC Bailey, Company Secretary & Head of Legal Affairs
Specialisation: Company Secretarial and Admin; Commercial Contracts; Competition and Regulatory.
Career: Birmingham University 2.1 LL.B; Liverpool Polytechnic Law Society Finals; Daniel Ashworth and Booth Macclesfield Articles; Ernest Scragg and Sons Ltd. - Assistant Legal Adviser; Nickerson Plant Breeders Ltd. - Legal Adviser; GEC Telecommunications Ltd - Legal Adviser; Plessy Office Systems Ltd - Legal Adviser.
Personal: Married with four children. Interests include sailing and classic car maintenance.
Other lawyers: John Bailey; Matthew Pearson; Melanie Hall; Lindy Campbell .

Land Securities PLC
5 The Strand London WC2N 5AF
Tel: (020) 7413 9000 **Fax:** (020) 7925 0202
Email: clive.ashcroft@landsecurities.com
Website: www.landsecurities.co.uk
No of lawyers in dept: 7 (non-qualified)
Work outsourced: 80-85% - Some property - all corporate.
Clive Ashcroft, Head of Legal Services - Portfolio Management
Specialisation: All areas of property investment development and management.
Career: 1974-1978 University of Kent, Degree in Law [BA] ; 1982 - present Land Securities Group, Legal Services Department. Membership of various trade committees and focus groups.
Personal: Lives in Calfont St Peter, wife and two children. Hobbies: travel, walking, camping and reading.
Other lawyers: Keith Weston, Ian Petts: all areas.

Lazard
21 Moorfields London EC2P 2HT
Tel: (020) 7588 2721 **Fax:** (020) 7920 0670
Website: www.lazard.com
No of lawyers in dept: 4
Will Dennis, Company Secretary & General Counsel
Specialisation: Corporate finance, asset management, capital markets, alternative investment.
Career: Cambridge University 1971-74, MA LLM. Foreign & Commonwealth Office 1977-86. Cliford Chance 1987-91. Partner Denton Hall 1991-93. Director N M Rothchild & Sons (Hong Kong) Ltd 1993-96. Lazard since 1996.

Le Meridien Hotels & Resorts Limited
166 High Holborn London WC1V 6TT
Tel: (020) 7301 2270 **Fax:** (020) 7301 2288
Email: martin.soley@lemeridien.com
Website: www.lemeridien.com
No of lawyers in dept: 1
Work outsourced: 50% - Employment, property, M&A, litigation.
Martin Soley, UK Legal Director
Specialisation: Commercial - contracts, dispute resolution, sales and marketing (loyalty programme, promotions etc.) joint ventures, franchising, general advice to hotels, construction contract advice , overseeing litigation.
Career: Jesus College, Cambridge (M&A in Law); Articled Herbert Oppenheimer, Nathan & Vandyk; Assistant Solicitor Ziman & Co; Legal Adviser Humphreys & Glasgow Ltd, Vickers plc; Company Solicitor 14 years with Forte Hotel Group. Now with Le Meridien Hotels, formely part of Forte.
Personal: Rowed for Jesus College; Chairman of Churchyard Committee (St Marys, N.Mymms, Hertfordshire); Hobbies: Driving MGB Roadster, athletics, reading, travel, gardening.
Other lawyers: David Mandefield - General Counsel - Overseas Work. Martin Soley - Corporate /Commercial - UK Work.

Legal & General Group plc
Temple Court 11 Queen Victoria Street London EC4N 4TP
Tel: (020) 7528 6200 **Fax:** (020) 7528 6222
Geoffrey Timms, Group Head of Legal

Lehman Brothers International (Europe)
European Headquarters One Broadgate
London EC2M 7HA
Tel: (020) 7601 0011 **Fax:** (020) 7260 2999
Piers Le Marchant, European Legal Director
European Headquarters One Broadgate London EC2M 7HA
Tel: (020) 7601 0011 **Fax:** (020) 7260 2999
Ian Jameson, European Corporate Counsel

Liberty International PLC
40 Broadway London SW1H 0BT
Tel: (020) 7960 1200 **Fax:** (020) 7960 1333
Farrell Sher, Legal Director

Lloyds TSB
51 Holdenhurst Road Bournemouth BH8 8EP
Tel: (01202) 522077
Michael Kilbee, Legal Director, Lloyds TSB Asset Finance Division

Lloyds TSB Group PLC
71 Lombard Street PO Box 215 London EC3P 3BS
Tel: (020) 7626 1500 **Fax:** (020) 7929 1654
Website: www.lloydstsb.co.uk
No of lawyers in dept: 10
Geoffrey Johnson, Group Chief Legal Adviser

Logica PLC
Stephenson House 75 Hampstead Road London NW1 2PL
Tel: (020) 7446 1771 **Fax:** (020) 7446 1937
Email: guedesl@logica.com
Website: www.logica.com
No of lawyers in dept: 5
Work outsourced: Various
Lawrence Guedes, Legal Director
Specialisation: Merger and acquisition and related commercial work. IT/IP related work. General C orporate/ C ommercial matters , Competition, Employment, Regulatory, Insurance, Outsource Contracts.
Career: LL.M, LL.B.

London Bridge Software Holdings PLC
New London Bridge House 16th Floor 25 London Bridge Street London SE1 9SG
Tel: (020) 7403 1333 **Fax:** (020) 7403 8981
Eric Watkins, Legal Counsel

London Electricity Group plc
Templar House 81-87 High Holborn London WC1V 6NU
Tel: (020) 7242 9050 **Fax:** (020) 7242 2815
Robert Ian Higson, Group Solicitor & Company Secretary

London Stock Exchange
Old Broad Street London EC2N 1HP
Tel: (020) 7797 1000 **Fax:** (020) 7334 8921
Email: cjohnson@londonstockexchange.com
Website: www.londonstockex.co.uk
No of lawyers in dept: 9
Work outsourced: 10% - Transactional, Various - depending on risk profile
Catherine Johnson, Head of Legal
Specialisation: Financial services / Regulation; General commercial/corporate.
Career: Cambridge University 1986-1989 - Law and Economics degree, MA. Guildford College of Law 1990-1991 Hons. Articled at Herbert Smith, worked at Herbert Smith to 1996. 1996-2001 worked in regulatory area of London stock Exchange (Head of Market Supervision 1997-2000, Head of Regulatory Policy 2000-2001). January 2001 to date Head of Legal.
Personal: Married. Three children - 5, 3, 1 years.
Other lawyers: Jennifer Croxford, Lisa Condron (Company Secretary), Natasha George, Stephanie McGillian, Ginny Tegner, William Courtenay, Daniel Marcus, Lorna Barrington, Kylie Martens, Jo Riedy (Paralegal).

London Underground Limited
London Underground Legal Services 55 Broadway London SW1H 0BD

IN-HOUSE LAWYERS ■ COMPANY SECRETARIES

Tel: (020) 7918 3112 **Fax:** (020) 7918 3071
Email: drydenpa@email.lul.co.uk
Website: www.londontransport.co.uk
Patricia Dryden, Head of Litigation
Specialisation: Commercial Litigation.
Career: LLB Hons Birmingham University; M.Sc Bristol University.
Personal: Married. 1 daughter

Lonmin plc
4 Grosvenor Place London SW1X 7YL
Tel: (020) 7201 6000 **Fax:** (020) 7201 6100
Email: contact@lonmin.com
Website: www.lonmin.com
Michael Pearce, Company Secretary

Luminar PLC
1 Primrose Hill Preston PR1 4BX
Tel: (01582) 589400 **Fax:** (01582) 589303
Email: mailbox@luminar.co.uk
Website: www.luminar.co.uk
No of lawyers in dept: 1
Work outsourced: 75% - All.
Andrew Stride, Company Secretary
Specialisation: Company commercial, property, contracts, litigation, IP.
Career: LL B (Hons) - Qualified ICSA 1998. Qualified as solicitor in 1991, spent five years in Private Practice (Goodger, Auden, Miles & Cash) 2 years in house before joining Boots 1997-2000 legal dept. Joined Luminar in May 2000.
Personal: Born 10 November 196 6 .
Other lawyers: Andrew Stride: Company commercial, property, litigation, IP.

Man Group PLC
Sugar Quay Lower Thames Street London EC3R 6DU
Tel: (020) 7285 3000 **Fax:** (020) 7285 3838
Peter Clarke, Finance Director & Company Secretary

Manchester United PLC
Sir Matt Busby Way Old Trafford Manchester M16 0RA
Tel: (0161) 868 8000 **Fax:** (0161) 868 8818
David Beswitherick, Assistant Company Secretary

Marks and Spencer plc
Michael House 47-67 Baker Street London W1U 8EP
Tel: (020) 7935 4422 **Fax:** (020) 7487 2679
Email: robert.ivens@marks-and-spencer.com
Website: www.marksandspencer.com
No of lawyers in dept: 9
Robert Ivens, Head of Legal

Marlborough Stirling PLC
Allen Jones House Jessop Avenue Cheltenham GL50 3SH
Tel: (01242) 547000 **Fax:** (01242) 547100
Website: www.marlborough-stirling.com
No of lawyers in dept: 5
Work outsourced: 10% - Litigation and some acquisitions.
Andrew Fritchie, Legal & Commercial Director
Specialisation: Company/Commercial, Intellectual Property, Technology.
Career: Law degree LLB (Hons).Called for Bar 1988 (InnerTemple).Executive Management - London Business School.Practical in Chambers 1988-1997.Also worked in California & Sydney.
Other lawyers: Liz Jenkin - Commercial/Company; Stephen Thomas - Commercial; Alison Jones - Employment.

Mars Incorporated
c/o Dundee Road Slough SL1 4JX
Tel: (01753) 550055 **Fax:** (01753) 550111
Website: www.mars.com
Evie Kyriakides, Market Property Manager

Matalan PLC
Gillibrands Road Skelmersdale WN8 9TB
Tel: (01695) 552400 **Fax:** (01695) 552622
Website: www.matalan.co.uk
No of lawyers in dept: 2
John G Berry, Group Company Secretary

McCarthy & Stone PLC
Homelife House 26-32 Oxford Road Bournemouth BH8 8EZ
Tel: (01202) 292180 **Fax:** (01202) 557261
Email: trevor.green@mccarthyandstone.co.uk
Website: www.mccarthyandstone
No of lawyers in dept: 3
Work outsourced: 40% - Land Aquisition, Litigation, Major corporate

Trevor L Green, Company Secretary
Other lawyers: Mr Julian Heath - Land Acquisition; Mrs Beverley Chase - Litigation

Meggitt PLC
Farrs House Cowgrove Wimborne BH21 4EL
Tel: (01202) 847847 **Fax:** (01202) 842478
Website: www.meggitt.com
Work outsourced: 100% - All.
Philip E Green, Group Corporate Affairs Director
Specialisation: Company secretarial, legal, mergers & acquisitions, commercial, pensions, insurance, property, administration.
Career: Fellow: Institute of Chartered Secretaries and Administrators - admitted 1988; B.A. (Law) Durham University, gained 1979.

The Merchants Trust PLC
10 Fenchurch Street London EC3M 3LB
Tel: (020) 7475 2700 **Fax:** (020) 7956 7161
Kirsten Salt, Deputy Company Secretary

Merck Sharp & Dohme Limited
West Hill Hertford Road Hoddesdon EN11 9BU
Tel: (01992) 452289 **Fax:** (01992) 470189
Website: www.merck.com
Marc Dalby, Legal Director

Merrill Lynch Europe PLC
Merrill Lynch Financial Centre 2 King Edward Street London EC1A 1HQ
Tel: (020) 7995 8563 **Fax:** (020) 7995 1998
Email: richard_atkinson@ml.com
Website: www.ml.com
Richard Atkinson, Director of Law & Compliance & Senior Counsel
Specialisation: Debt markets, structured drivatives and other financial products.
Career: 1974-1981 - Kingston GS.1987-1994 - Allen & Overy.1994-1997 - DKB Financial Products. 1997 to date - Merrill Lynch.

Mersey Docks & Harbour Company
Maritime Centre Port of Liverpool Liverpool L21 1LA
Tel: (0151) 949 6340 **Fax:** (0151) 949 6300
Website: www.merseydocks.co.uk
No of lawyers in dept: 3
Work outsourced: 20% - Litigation, major corporate, joint ventures.
Bill Bowley, Director of Legal Services
Specialisation: Responsible for all the Company's legal affairs and aspects of the company secretarial, insurance, claims and share registration sections. Principal areas of work are general company/commercial matters. Also handles shipping, property and environmental law and advises on litigation. Member of Law Society Commerce and Industry Group.
Career: Articled with J. Frodsham & Sons, St. Helens 1971-72 and solicitor 1973-74. Joined The Mersey Docks and Harbour Company in 1974 as an assistant solicitor. Became PA to the MD 1979, Principal assistant solicitor 1981, Company Secretary and Solicitor 1982 and Director of Legal Services 1991.
Personal: Educated at Prescot Grammar School, University of Bristol (LLB) and Guildford Law School. Born 6 October 1947.
Other lawyers: Henry Hrynkiewicz - property; Geoff Chadwick - commercial.

Michael Page Group PLC
Page House 39-41 Parker Street London WC2B 5LN
Tel: (020) 7831 2000 **Fax:** (020) 7269 2280
Richard A McBride, Company Secretary

Millennium & Copthorne Hotels PLC
Victoria House Victoria Road Horley RH6 7AF
Tel: (01293) 772288 **Fax:** (01293) 772345
Simon Hodges, Company Secretary

Minerva PLC
10 Gloucester Place London W1U 8EZ
Tel: (020) 7535 1000 **Fax:** (020) 7535 1001
Ivan Ezekiel, Company Secretary

Misys plc
Burleigh House Chapel Oak Salford Priors Evesham WR11 8SP
Tel: (01386) 871373 **Fax:** (01386) 871045
Andy Oakes, Commercial Director

MITIE Group PLC
The Stable Block Barley Wood Wrington Bristol BS40 5SA
Tel: (01934) 862050 **Fax:** (01934) 862239

Website: www.MITIE.co.uk
Work outsourced: Various - Acquisitions, property, litigation, employment.
Corina K Ross, Company Secretary

Mizuho International plc
Bracken House One Friday Street London EC4M 9JA
Tel: (020) 7236 1090 **Fax:** (020) 7236 0484
Brian Lanaghan, Legal Director

mmO2 plc
Wellington Street Slough SL1 1YP
Tel: (01753) 628143 **Fax:** (01753) 628142
Email: phillip.bramwell@O2.com
Website: www.mmo2.com
No of lawyers in dept: 40 across UK, NL, Germany & Ireland.
Work outsourced: Aproximately 20% - Commercial, Litigation, Pensions.
Phillip Bramwell, General Counsel & Company Secretary
Specialisation: Responsible for legal department, company secretariat, regulatory affairs department, security and risk management.
Career: BA (Hons) Law 1982. Called to Bar 1983, Lincoln's Inn. Secretary and Legal Adviser to Smithkline Beecham Pharmaceuticles International 1985-89, Vice President and General Counsel, Bellsouth Europe 1989-94, Partner DDV Group 1994-98; Chief Counsel, Corporate Development, BT plc 1998-2001.
Personal: Family, reading and old boats.
Other lawyers: Corporate, Corporate Finance, Commercial, Procurement, Regulatory & Competition.

The Morgan Crucible Company plc
Morgan House Madeira Walk Windsor SL4 1EP
Tel: (01753) 837000 **Fax:** (01753) 850872
David J Coker, Company Secretary

Morgan Stanley International & Co Limited
20 Cabot Square Canary Wharf London E14 4QW
Tel: (020) 7677 7299 **Fax:** (020) 7677 7125
Email: Joan.Ma@morganstanley.com
Website: www.morganstanley.co.uk
Joan Ma, Executive Director
20 Cabot Square Canary Wharf London E14 4QW
Tel: (020) 7677 2400 **Fax:** (020) 7677 2500
Email: enquiries@morganstanley.co.uk
Website: www.morganstanley.co.uk
Richard Rosenthal, European General Counsel

Morgan Stanley Investment Management Limited
20 Cabot Square Canary Wharf London E14 4QW
Tel: (020) 7425 8000 **Fax:** (020) 7425 4848
Email: enquiries@morganstanley.co.uk
Website: www.morganstanley.co.uk
Lucy Lynch, International Counsel

MTV Networks
United Kingdom House 180 Oxford Street London W1N 0DS
Tel: (020) 7478 6240 **Fax:** (020) 7284 7788
Svenja Geissmar, Senior Vice President & General Counsel

MyTravel Group plc
Parkway One Parkway Business Centre 300 Princess Road Manchester M14 7QU
Tel: (0161) 232 6515 **Fax:** (0161) 232 6524
Email: gjm@mytravel.com
Website: www.mytravelgroup.com
No of lawyers in dept: 7
Work outsourced: 40% - Large UK claims, Asset finance, corporate financee, Overseas litigation, major contractual work, IT contracts, serious personal injury, selected property issues.
Greg McMahon, Company Secretary & Head of Legal Services
Specialisation: Company Secretarial support for PLC Board, Board Committees, Group Management Board. Corporate governance. Head of legal for entire worldwide group. Principal legal adviser to Board and individual executive and non-executive directors.
Career: Xaveira College, Manchester.Manchester University, LLB (Hons) 1982.College Law, Chester.Addler, Shaw, Sons & Latham 1983 to 1995 (Trainee, Solicitor, Associate Partner, Partner (1991-1995)).Gomett & Co, Manchester 1993 to 1998 (Partner).Company Secretary and head of legal services. Airtours plc (now My Travel Group plc) 1998 to date.
Personal: Married with two children. Lives in Saddleworth. Interests: Walking, cooking, travel, cricket, spending time with family.

www.ChambersandPartners.com 1217

IN-HOUSE LAWYERS ■ COMPANY SECRETARIES

Other lawyers: Sam Plant, Dominic Kay, Mike Bowers, Mike Vaux, Joanna Edwards, Rebecca Gilder.

N Brown Group PLC
53 Dale Street Manchester M60 6ES
Tel: (0161) 236 2298 **Fax:** (0161) 236 2918
Website: www.nbrown.co.uk
No of lawyers in dept: 2
Philip Harland, Head of Legal & Company Secretary

N M Rothschild & Sons Limited
New Court St Swithins Lane London EC4P 4DU
Tel: (020) 7280 5000 **Fax:** (020) 7929 1643
Alan Graham, Company Secretary

National Australia Group Europe Limited
Group Legal, Great Britain PO Box 43 40 St Vincent Place Glasgow G1 2HL
Tel: (0141) 223 2802 **Fax:** (0141) 223 2887
Website: www.cbonline.co.uk
No of lawyers in dept: 8
Jane L Shirran, Senior General Counsel
Specialisation: Company/ Commercial, Corporate Financial Litigation and Management of the Legal function.
Career: Present: Senior General Counsel and Secretary, National Australia Group Europe Limited, Clydesdale Bank PLC, Yorkshire Bank PLC. 1996-June 1998 Principal Solicitor with Clydesdale Bank PLC, Legal Services, Glasgow; Responsible for provision of legal advice to Corporate, Business Banking and Head Office areas of Bank.1995-1996 Senior Solicitor with Bank of Scotland, Legal Services, Edinburgh; Provision of corporate and general advice to the Bank's Head Office, Structured Finance and Investment Banking Departments.1988-1995 McGrigor Donald, Solicitors, Associate - 1992-1995; General Corporate, Banking and Insolvency; Worked in Glasgow, London and Edinburgh offices.1987-1988 Tods Murray, Edinburgh, Assistant.1985-1987 Allan Dawson Simpson & Hampton (now Henderson Boyd Jackson), Trainee.
Personal: Nationality: British. Date of Birth: 27/6/63. Driving Licence: Full/Clean.Education: Pre 1975 Schooling in Malaysia, Malawi, Zimbabwe. 1975-1978 Cults Acadamy, Aberdeen. 1980-1985 Aberdeen University. LL.B Honours (2:1); Diploma in Legal Practice.

National Express Group PLC
75 Davies Street London W1K 5HT
Tel: (020) 7529 2000 **Fax:** (020) 7529 2100
Website: www.nationalexpressgroup.com
No of lawyers in dept: 3
Work outsourced: 60% - Mergers and acquisitions, commercial, IT, IP.
Tony McDonald, Company Secretary & Group Legal Adviser
Specialisation: Corporate/commercial.
Career: University of Nottingham, 1979-82; Slaughter and May, 1983-88; The British Petroleum Company plc, 1988-95; Guardian Royal Exchange plc, 1995 - 2000.
Other lawyers: Tony McDonald - Company Secretary and Group Legal Adviser; Jenny Casson - Deputy Company Secretary; James Meldrum - Legal Adviser ; Alex Gibbs - Legal Adviser.

National Grid Company PLC
National Grid House Kirby Corner Road Coventry CV4 8JY
Tel: (024) 7653 7777 **Fax:** (024) 7642 3620
Fiona Smith, Company Secretary

Nestor Healthcare Group PLC
The Colonnades Beaconsfield Close Hatfield AL10 8YD
Tel: (01707) 255636 **Fax:** (01707) 255633
Email: emma.thomas@nestorplc.co.uk
Website: www.nestor-healthcare.co.uk
No of lawyers in dept: 2
Work outsourced: 80%
Emma Thomas, Group Company Secretary
Specialisation: Cambridge (Law); Richards Butler (qualified 1993); Company Secretary, Hazlewood Foods plc 1994-1996; Assistant Company Secretary, Kingfisher plc 1997-1998; Company Secretary, Nestor Healthcare Group plc 1998 -present.
Other lawyers: Corporate, IT, litigation, property.

New Look Group PLC
New Look House Mercery Road Weymouth DT3 5HJ
Tel: (01305) 765000 **Fax:** (01305) 765001
Mandy Stephenson, Company Secretary

News International PLC
1 Virginia Street Wapping London E1 9BD
Tel: (020) 7782 4000 **Fax:** (020) 7782 4090
Tom Crone, Head of Legal

Next PLC
Desford Road Enderby Leicester LE9 5AT
Tel: (0116) 284 4167 **Fax:** (0116) 284 2642
Email: mark_harris@next.co.uk
Website: www.next.co.uk
No of lawyers in dept: 7
Work outsourced: 20% - Major corporate deals. Specialist litigation areas.
Mark Harris, Head of Legal Department & Company Secretary
Specialisation: Commercial Property
Career: LSE LLB; University of Virginia USA LLM; Partner Hammond Suddards Edge, Birmingham; Head of Legal at Next plc since 2002
Personal: Walking, cinema, travel, sport.
Other lawyers: Ms S. Noble - Commercial; Ms C. Moody - Commercial; Mr T. Birch - Commercial Property; Ms Lorraine Emery - Commercial; Ms E. Burdett - Data Protection and Mr M. Davis - Property.

Nomura International PLC
Nomura House 1 St Martins-le-Grand London EC1A 4NP
Tel: (020) 7521 2000 **Fax:** (020) 7521 3565
David Mee, General Counsel

Northern Foods PLC
Beverley House St Stephen's Square Hull HU1 3XG
Tel: (01482) 325432 **Fax:** (01482) 598355
Email: carol.williams@northern-foods.co.uk
Website: www.northern-foods.co.uk
No of lawyers in dept: 4
Work outsourced: 40% - Commercial conveyancing, corporate finance, litigation, intellectual.
Carol Williams, Head of Legal
Specialisation: Employment, litigation, commercial.
Career: Qualified, 1985. 1985-87 Booth & Co (Leeds). 1987-90 Asda plc. 1990 to date Northern Foods.
Personal: 1998 to date: Chair North East Commerce and Industry Group.
Other lawyers: Jennifer Groves - Commercial conveyancing, Andrew Lindley - Company commercial; Mark Davis - Employment

Northern Rock PLC
Northern Rock House Regent Centre Newcastle upon Tyne NE3 4PL
Tel: (0191) 285 7191 **Fax:** (0191) 284 8470
Website: www.northernrock.co.uk
No of lawyers in dept: 6
Work outsourced: All mortgage possession, some treasury, commercial litigation and commercial conveyancing.
Colin Taylor, Director Compliance & Legal Services
Other lawyers: Peter Millican - litigation and employment; Jasan Fitzpatrick - consumer credit, commercial conveyancing and contracts ; Gwilym Williams - commercial conveyancing and contracts, e-commerce; Colin Greener - conveyancing, consumer credit and general work ; Andrew Soulsby - conveyancing, title queries and general work.

Northgate PLC
Northgate House 6th Floor St Augustine's Way Darlington DL1 1XA
Tel: (01325) 467 558 **Fax:** (01325) 363 204
David Henderson, Company Secretary

Novar plc
Novar House 24 Queens Road Weybridge KT13 9UX
Tel: (01932) 850850 **Fax:** (01932) 823365
Website: www.novar.com
No of lawyers in dept: 2
Anthony Holland, Group Legal Adviser
Other lawyers: Helen Leckey - Legal adviser.

Ogilvy & Mather
10 Cabot Square Canary Wharf London E14 4QB
Tel: (020) 7345 3000
Larissa Joy, Vice Chairman

Old Mutual plc
3rd Floor Lansdowne House 57 Berkeley Square London W1J 6ER
Tel: (020) 7569 0100 **Fax:** (020) 7569 0209
Email: martin.murray@omg.co.uk
Website: www.oldmutual.com
No of lawyers in dept: 1
Work outsourced: 75% - Corporate finance, property, employment.
Martin Murray, Company Secretary
Specialisation: Responsible for company / commercial matters at plc level and corporate governance.
Career: 1999 to date: Company Secretary, Old Mutual plc;

1997 - 1999: General Counsel and Secretary, The Energy Group plc; 1986 - 1997: Solicitor, Hanson plc. MA, LL.B. (Cantab) , LL.M. (Harvard). Admitted as a solicitor in 1979.

Omnicom Europe Limited
239 Old Marylebone Road London NW1 5QT
Tel: (020) 7298 7007 **Fax:** (020) 7298 7085
Juliet Ashley, Group Solicitor
239 Old Marylebone Road London NW1 5QT
Tel: (020) 7298 7007 **Fax:** (020) 7298 7085
Fiona Pool, General Counsel

P & O Princess Cruises
11-12 Charles II Street London SW1Y 4QU
Anthony Kaufman, General Counsel

P & O Princess Cruises PLC
77 New Oxford Street London WC1A 1PP
Tel: (020) 7805 1200 **Fax:** (020) 7805 1240
Simon Pearce, Company Secretary

Paragon Group of Companies PLC
St Catherine's Court Herbert Road Solihull B91 3QE
Tel: (0121) 712 2323 **Fax:** (0121) 711 1330
John Gemmell, Company Secretary

Pathé Pictures Limited
Kent House Market Place London W1N 8AR
Tel: (020) 7323 5151 **Fax:** (020) 7462 4417
Email: cameron.mccracken@pathe-uk.com
Website: www.pathe.co.uk
Cameron McCracken, Deputy Managing Director
Specialisation: Film production, finance & distribution.
Career: Balliol College, Oxford.
Personal: Chairman, First Film Foundation,.Council Member, British Screen Advisory Council.

Peninsular & Oriental Steam Navigation Company (P & O)
79 Pall Mall London SW1Y 5EJ
Tel: (020) 7321 4515 **Fax:** (020) 7930 6042
Email: michael.gradon@pogroup.com
Website: www.p-and-o.com
No of lawyers in dept: 3
Work outsourced: Major corporate and banking.
Michael Gradon, Executive Director, Commercial & Legal Affairs
Specialisation: Deals with acquisitions, disposals, joint ventures, financing and other major group matters.
Career: Qualified in 1983. With Slaughter and May 1981-86. Became P&O Group Legal Director in 1991 and Company Secretary in 1996. Appointed Board Director in 1998, Appointed Director, Commercial & Legal Affairs in 2001.
Personal: Educated at Haileybury 1972-76 and Downing College, Cambridge 1977-80. Leisure interests include tennis and golf. Born 7th April 1959. Lives in Oxted, Surrey.
Other lawyers: Mark Wandless; Iain Simm.

Pennon Group PLC
Peninsula House Rydon Lane Exeter EX2 7HR
Tel: (01392) 443150 **Fax:** (01392) 443939
Email: kwoodier@pennon-group.co.uk
Website: www.pennon-group.co.uk
No of lawyers in dept: 7
Work outsourced: 10% - Specialist banking and major litigation.
Kenneth D Woodier, Group General Counsel & Company Secretary
Specialisation: Company/commercial, litigation, competition, property, contract/procurement, environmental and employment.
Career: Management (business) prior to qualifying as a solicitor. Articles with Severn Trent Water. Legal Adviser with Investors in Industry plc (3i). Group legal manager with HP Bulmer Holdings plc and Group Legal Adviser with South West Water PLC. 16 years in legal practice.
Other lawyers: John Jelley, Alan Roberts, Alan Podger, Dr Buckingham, Simon Pugsley, Richard Abbot.

Persimmon PLC
Persimmon House Fulford York YO19 4FE
Tel: (01904) 642199 **Fax:** (01904) 610014
Website: www.persimmon.plc.co.uk
No of lawyers in dept: 17
Work outsourced: 40% - Corporate, property, litigation.
Neil Francis, Legal Director & Company Secretary
Specialisation: Residential housing land development, planning, employment.
Career: Kingston G.S.; College of Law; Partner Fennemores Milton Keynes 1983-95.
Personal: Interests: Cricket, hockey, golf, football, skiing.

IN-HOUSE LAWYERS ■ COMPANY SECRETARIES

Other lawyers: N.P. Knight, G.K.E. Hale, J.Baird, P. Bowen, C. Balderstone, S. McGuinness, C. Cantoni, Ms J. Dempster, Mrs J. Gibson.

PHS Group plc
Western Industrial Estate Caerphilly CF83 1XH
Tel: (029) 2085 1000 **Fax:** (029) 2086 3288
Lee Mahoney, Head of Legal

Pilkington plc
Prescot Road St Helens WA10 3TT
Tel: (01744) 28882 **Fax:** (01744) 692960
Website: www.pilkington.com
No of lawyers in dept: 4
Work outsourced: 50% - Major litigation, international, large scale acquisitions and divestments, specialist counsel advice.
Clyde M Leff, Group General Counsel
Specialisation: Principal areas of work are antitrust/competition law, acquisitions and disposals, major litigation, senior level service contracts and related matters, and corporate compliance programmes. The majority of work involves international aspects and the necessary management of external legal resources in a number of jurisdictions.
Career: Graduated Law School 1980, University of Chicago, J.D. Numerous U.S. positions, both in private practice (Mayer, Brown and Platt; Reuben and Proctor) and Corporate Legal Departments (Ameritech; Owens Corning). Officer level position at Owens Corning before joining Pilkington plc as Group Legal Adviser/General Counsel in 2000.
Personal: Married, two children.
Other lawyers: Miss J. P. Halligan; C. M. Leff; C.R. Bayley; I.J. McKillop. Specialism: Manages the provision of legal advice to an international Group (80% of turnover overseas).

Pillar Property PLC
Lansdowne House Berkeley Square London W1X 6HQ
Tel: (020) 7915 8000 **Fax:** (020) 7915 8001
Philip J Martin, Company Secretary

PizzaExpress PLC
1 Union Business Park Florence Way Uxbridge UB8 2LS
Tel: (01895) 618 618 **Fax:** (01895) 618 600
Patrick Hartrey, Company Secretary

Polydor Ltd
72-80 Black Lion Lane Hammersmith London W6 9BE
Tel: (020) 8910 4800 **Fax:** (020) 8910 4801
No of lawyers in dept: 2 plus 1 legal executive
Work outsourced: 10% - Litigation, commercial.
James Radice, Senior Director, Legal and Business Affairs
Specialisation: Artist contracts. Label Joint Ventures. Litigation Management.
Career: Latimer Upper School. Bristol University. College of Law. Norton Rose Solicitors. EMI Music International.EMI Records Limited. Polydor Limited.
Other lawyers: Contracts with Artists, labels, etc. Management of litigation.

PowderJect Pharmaceuticals
Florey House Robert Robinson Avenue Oxford Science Park Oxford OX4 4GA
Tel: (01865) 332600 **Fax:** (01865) 332601
Charles Swingland, General Counsel & Company Secretary

Powergen UK plc
Westwood Way Westwood Business Park Coventry CV4 8LG
Tel: (024) 7642 4000 **Fax:** (024) 7642 5432
Website: www.pgen.com
No of lawyers in dept: 7
Fiona Stark, Director UK Legal & General Counsel
Specialisation: Responsible forprovision of Legal and Company Secretarial services to Powergen UK plc and its operational businesses.
Career: Birmingham University; Chester College of Law.
Personal: Leisure pursuits include most sports, bridge and fine food and wine.
Other lawyers: James Jones - Retail Counsel, Henry Loweth - Energy Trading Counsel, Ian Fairclough - Generation Counsel, Stephanie Hammond - Distribution Counsel, Graham Line - Services Counsel

Premier Farnell PLC
150 Armley Road Leeds LS12 2QQ
Tel: (08701) 298608 **Fax:** (08701) 298610
Email: information@premierfarnell.com
Website: www.premierfarnell.com
No of lawyers in dept: 5
Work outsourced: 30% - Broad spectrum, share schemes, employment litigation, major corporate.

Steven Webb, Group Company Secretary & General Counsel
Specialisation: Corporate/commercial.
Career: King's College, London LLB (Hons); Norton Rose 1987-1990; Walker Morris 1990-1994; Kalon Group plc 1994-1997, Company Secretary; Kelda Group plc 1997-2000, Company Secretary and General Counsel.
Other lawyers: UK- Mark Sanford, Dorcas Murray. US- Joe Daprice, Tim Leslie, Amy Malloy. All lawyers carry out general legal work, mainly Company/Commercial.

Premier Oil plc
23 Lower Belgrave Street London SW1W 0NR
Tel: (020) 7824 1104 **Fax:** (020) 7824 8874
Email: premier@premier-oil.com
Website: www.premier-oil.com
No of lawyers in dept: 4
Work outsourced: 5% - Litigation, some Corporate Finance.
Stephen Huddle, Group Legal Manager & Company Secretary
Specialisation: Joint Venture Agreements, general Company/Commercial, Company secretarial.
Career: Elf UK to 1996.Hardy Oil & Gas/British Borneo to 2000.Premier Oil since 2000.
Other lawyers: Joint Ventures, Company/Commercial, Corporate Finance.

Provident Financial plc
Colonnade Sunbridge Road Bradford BD1 2LQ
Tel: (01274) 731111 **Fax:** (01274) 727300
David Rees, Group Legal Advisor

Prudential PLC
Laurence Pountney Hill London EC4R 0HH
Tel: (020) 7548 3737 **Fax:** (020) 7548 3191
Email: peter.maynard@prudential.co.uk
Website: www.prudential.co.uk
No of lawyers in dept: 4
Work outsourced: 90% - Property, employment, venture capital, corporate financing.
Peter Maynard, Company Secretary & Group Legal Services Director
Specialisation: Heads a small team of commercial lawyers providing legal services to the Corporation and its subsidiaries.
Career: 1971-74 University of Cambridge. 1975-82 Slaughter and May. 1982-84 Clifford-Turner. 1984-98 Hong Kong Bank Group. (1984-92 Legal Adviser Europe, 1992 Compliance Director, James Capel, 1993-95 President & CEO, James Capel Inc, New York, 1996-98 Deputy Group Legal Adviser, HSBC Group). 1998 Director, Group Legal Services, Prudential Corporation plc.
Other lawyers: D. Higgins - company/commercial ; J. O'Keefe; D. Green.

Psion PLC
12 Park Cresent London W1B 1PH
Tel: (020) 7317 4207 **Fax:** (020) 7317 4193
Website: www.psion.com
Marina Wyatt, Finance Director & Company Secretary

RAC plc
Boston Drive Bourne End SL8 5YS
Tel: (01628) 843588 **Fax:** (01628) 810294
Email: lex@lex.co.uk
Website: www.lex.co.uk
No of lawyers in dept: 8
Work outsourced: 60% - Major acquisition-divestments, litigation, property, employment.
Pamela Coles, Head of Corporate Legal & Company Secretary
Specialisation: Corporate finance, company Law.
Career: BA, FCIS.

The Rank Group PLC
6 Connaught Place London W2 2EZ
Tel: (020) 7706 1111 **Fax:** (020) 7262 9886
Charles Cormick, Company Secretary

The Really Useful Group Limited (The)
22 Tower Street London WC2H 9NS
Tel: (020) 7240 0880 **Fax:** (020) 7240 1204
Jonathan Hull, Legal and Business Affairs Manager

Reckitt Benckiser plc
103-105 Bath Road Slough SL1 3UH
Tel: (01753) 217800 **Fax:** (01753) 217899
Website: www.reckittbenckiser.com
Sheila Henderson, Trade Marks Director
Specialisation: Trade Marks, Copyright, Unfair Competition.
Career: LLB (Hons)Qualified Solicitor in 1990.

Redrow PLC
Redrow House St David's Park Flintshire CH5 3RX
Tel: (01244) 520044 **Fax:** (01244) 520720
Rhiannon E Walker, Company Secretary & Head of Legal Department

Renishaw plc
New Mills Wotton-under-Edge GL12 8JR
Tel: (01453) 524524 **Fax:** (01453) 524001
Norma Tang, Corporate Lawyer & Assistant Company Secretary
New Mills Wotton-under-Edge GL12 8JR
Tel: (01453) 524524 **Fax:** (01453) 524001
Allen C G Roberts, Group Finance Director & Company Secretary

Rentokil Initial PLC
Felcourt East Grinstead RH19 2JY
Tel: (01342) 833022 **Fax:** (01342) 835672
Robert Ward-Jones, Company Secretary & Legal Director

Reuters Group PLC
Corporate Headquarters 85 Fleet Street London EC4P 4AJ
Tel: (020) 7250 1122 **Fax:** (020) 7542 5896
Claire Chapman, Area General Counsel - United Kingdom & Ireland

Rexam PLC
4 Millbank London SW1P 3XR
Tel: (020) 7227 4100 **Fax:** (020) 7227 4109
Email: david.gibson@rexam.com
Website: www.rexam.com
No of lawyers in dept: 2
Work outsourced: 50% - Large M&A transactions, litigation, conveyancing.
David William Gibson, Company Secretary & Director of Legal Affairs
Specialisation: Company and commercial law , company secretarial, intellectual property, insurance, risk management, property and h ead o ffice human resources .
Career: Qualified as a Solicitor in 1987. Assistant Solicitor with Alsop Wilkinson 1987-1989. Company Solicitor with Rexam PLC (formerly Bowater plc) 1989-1995. Member of the Law Society.

Richemont
15 Hill Street London W1J 5QT
Tel: (020) 7499 2539 **Fax:** (020) 7493 1018
Frederick Mostert, Chief Intellectual Property Counsel

Rio Tinto PLC
6 St James's Square London SW1Y 4LD
Tel: (020) 7753 2345 **Fax:** (020) 7753 2197
Email: Charles.Lawton@riotinto.com
Website: www.riotinto.com
No of lawyers in dept: 6
Work outsourced: 15% - Litigation, property, public issues.
Charles Lawton, Head of Legal
Specialisation: Mergers and acquisitions, competition.
Career: Westminster School; Articled Clark then Solicitor, Slaughter & May, 1965-1972; Lovell White Durrant, 1972; Rio Tinto, 1972- Present.
Other lawyers: M&A, competition, litigation.

RIT Capital Partners PLC
27 St James's Place London SW1A 1NR
Tel: (020) 7493 8111 **Fax:** (020) 7493 5765
Duncan Budge, Chief Operating Officer

RMC (UK) Ltd
RMC House Coldharbour Lane Thorpe Egham TW20 8TD
Tel: (01932) 568833 **Fax:** (01932) 568933
Email: michaelcollins@rmc.co.uk
Website: www.rmc-group.com
No of lawyers in dept: 6
Work outsourced: Work outside specialisms of Department and high volume work.
Michael Collins, Head of UK Legal Department
Specialisation: Conducting advisory and transactional work over a broad spectrum.
Career: LL.B (Birmingham University), Solicitor, Prior to RMC, extensive County Council experience.
Personal: Married.
Other lawyers: Property:, Stephen Bottle, Andrew Smith, James Harrison ; Litigation: Jason Smailey; Environmental/Planning: Stephen Gardiner.

Rolls-Royce PLC
65 Buckingham Gate London SW1E 6AT
Tel: (020) 7222 9020 **Fax:** (020) 7227 9170
Brian Baker, General Counsel

IN-HOUSE LAWYERS ■ COMPANY SECRETARIES

Rothschild Asset Management Limited
1 King William Street London EC4N 7AR
Tel: (020) 7623 1000 **Fax:** 020 7634 2555
Elizabeth Horner, Director

Rotork PLC
Rotork House Brassmill Lane Bath BA1 3JQ
Tel: (01225) 733200 **Fax:** (01225) 733381
Steven Rhys-Jones, Company Secretary

Royal & Sun Alliance Insurance Group Plc
Worldwide Group Office 30 Berkeley Square
London W1J 6EW
Tel: (020) 7569 4034 **Fax:** (020) 7569 6294
Email: humphrey.tomlinson@wgo.royalsun.com
Website: www.royalsunalliance.com
No of lawyers in dept: 3
Humphrey Tomlinson, Legal Director
Other lawyers: George Scott; Kiron Farooki

Royal Bank of Canada
71 Queen Victoria Street London EC4V 4DE
Tel: (020) 7489 1188 **Fax:** (020) 7329 6138
Email: duncan.gibbon@rbccm.com
Website: www.royalbank.com
No of lawyers in dept: 2
Work outsourced: 30% - Litigation, Mergers and Acquisitions, Structured Finance and Capital Markets including International bonds.
Duncan Gibbons, Legal Counsel Capital Markets, Europe
Specialisation: Responsible for all legal aspects of the activities of Royal Bank of Canada London branch and Royal Bank of Canada Europe Limited including debt capital markets, banking and structured finance activities.
Career: 1982-1989 Commissioned Officer, Royal Army Ordenance Corps.1990-1993 London Guildhall University (LLB).1994-2002 Allen Avery, Capital Markets.2002 to date Royal Bank of Canada, London, Legal Counsel Capital Markets, Europe.
Other lawyers: Katherine Petcher - Global Custody.

The Royal Bank of Scotland Group plc
Group Legal Department 42 St Andrew Square
Edinburgh EH2 2YE
Tel: (0131) 556 8555 **Fax:** (0131) 557 6565
Mark Chidley, Head of Group Legal Services
6th Floor 27 Leadenhall Street London EC3A 1DD
Tel: (020) 7726 1000 **Fax:** (020) 7454 2807
Ian Woodcock, Group Legal

SABMiller PLC
One Stanhope Gate London W1K 1AF
Tel: (020) 7659 0100 **Fax:** (020) 7659 0111
Email: atonkinson@sab.co.za
Website: www.sabplc.com
No of lawyers in dept: 4
Work outsourced: 40% - Conveyancing, registration, opinions, litigation.
Andrew OC Tonkinson, Group Company Secretary
Specialisation: Company Secretarial, remuneration, benefits, corporate law, commercial law, intellectual property law, taxation.
Career: BA (Law and Economics) University of Natal, South Africa - 1996; B. Juris, University of South Africa - 1970 Trust Manager - Syfrets Trust Ltd. - 1968-1975; Company Secretary and Administration Director - The Lion Match Company Ltd. 1975-1991; Group Company Secretary, South African Breweries, 1991-Present.
Personal: Lecturer part-time in company/commercial and banking law, Natal Technicon, 1970-1973.
Other lawyers: A.O.C. Tonkinson - Company/commercial, corporate finance; J. Romein - Company intellectual property; Ms J. Taylor - General commercial.

Safeway Stores PLC
Safeway House 6 Millington Road Hayes UB3 4AY
Tel: (020) 8848 8744 **Fax:** (020) 8756 1069
Gerald Ellis, Deputy Company Secretary & Head of Legal

The Sage Group plc
Sage House Benton Park Road
Newcastle upon Tyne NE7 7LZ
Tel: (0191) 255 3000 **Fax:** (0191) 255 0306
Website: www.sage.com
No of lawyers in dept: 8
Work outsourced: 60% - Acquisitions, major litigation.
Michael Robinson, Head of Legal & Group Secretary

Schroders PLC
31 Gresham Street London EC2V 7QA
Tel: (020) 7658 6000 **Fax:** (020) 7658 6669
Email: francis.neate@schroders.com
Website: www.schroders.com
Francis W Neate, Group Legal Adviser
Career: Formerly a partner in Slaughter and May.

Scottish & Newcastle PLC
33 Ellersly Road Edinburgh EH12 6HX
Tel: (0131) 528 2110 **Fax:** (0131) 528 2311
Email: andrew.vellani@scottish-newcastle.co.uk
Website: www.scottish-newcastle.com
No of lawyers in dept: 4 plus 1 paralegal
Work outsourced: Not disclosed
H Andrew S Vellani, Group Legal Director
Specialisation: The Group Legal Director is responsible for the provision of legal services to the Scottish & Newcastle plc group of companies. Work includes company/commercial, EEC and domestic competition law. International joint ventures; intellectual property; acquisitions and disposals; beer supply agreements; brewing, packaging and distribution agreements; trading law (including food labelling, advertising and promotion).
Career: Kings College, Cardiff; Staffordshire University (LLB Hons); the Inns of Court School of Law, London; called to the Bar (Middle Temple) 1981. Admitted as solicitor 1991. Assistant commercial and legal adviser - Heating and Ventilating Contractors Association 1982; Assistant Group Secretary/Group Legal Adviser - The Kenneth Wilson Group 1984; Group Legal Adviser - Scottish & Newcastle plc 1986. Other positions held include: Company Secretary and Member of the Board Executive Committee: Scottish Courage Ltd 1986. Secretary: The Fosters European Partnership (an Anglo Australian Joint Venture).
Personal: Born 1957, resides in Edinburgh. Interests include overseas travel, music and reading.

Scottish & Southern Energy plc
200 Dunkeld Road Perth PH1 3AQ
Tel: (01738) 455151 **Fax:** (01738) 455281
Email: ian.manson@scottish-southern.co.uk
Website: www.scottish-southern.co.uk
No of lawyers in dept: 10
Work outsourced: 25% - Litigation, major projects, acquisitions, employment law, competition law.
Ian Manson, Director of Legal Services
Specialisation: All legal areas including commercial, litigation, property and projects.
Career: LL.B - 1979.
Personal: Married, 3 children, resides Dundee.
Other lawyers: Corporate, Commercial, P property, Litigation.

Scottish Environmental Protection Agency (SEPA)
15-17 SAPA Stirling Office Erskine Court Castle Business Park Stirling FK9 4TR
Tel: (01786) 457700 **Fax:** (01786) 446885
Bridget Marshall, In-house Lawyer

Scottish Investment Trust PLC
6 Albyn Place Edinburgh EH2 4NL
Tel: (0131) 225 7781 **Fax:** (0131) 226 3663
Email: iharding@sit.co.uk
Website: www.sit.co.uk
Work outsourced: 100% - All
Iain M Harding, Company Secretary

Scottish Power PLC
1 Atlantic Quay Glasgow G2 8SP
Tel: (0141) 566 4594 **Fax:** (0141) 566 4687
James Stanley, Group Director, Legal & Commercial

Scottish Radio Holdings PLC
Clydebank Business Park Clydebank Glasgow G81 2RX
Tel: (0141) 565 2200 **Fax:** (0141) 565 2322
Jane Tames, In-house counsel and Company Secretary

Scottish Widows Investment Partnership
Edinburgh One Morrison Street Edinburgh EH3 8BE
Tel: (0131) 655 8146 **Fax:** (0131) 655 6385
Website: www.swipartnership.com
No of lawyers in dept: 4
Work outsourced: 15% - Public funds, litigation / contentious, IT/IP
Kenneth J Greig, Director of Legal & Technical Services
Specialisation: Asset management and investment funds; corporate and commercial; regulatory.
Career: BA (Jurisprudence) Balliol College, Oxford. Admitted as a solicitor 1986, articled Norton Rose (London); Legal Director, Templeton International (Edinburgh); Legal Adviser, Bankers Trust Global Funds Management (London); Head of Legal & Compliance (Europe), Morgan Stanley Asset Management; Global Head of Legal Services. AXA Investment Managers.
Personal: Married, four children. Member Leven Golfing Society, Islay Golf Club, London Scottish Football Club. Interests: rugby, golf, skiing, ornithology, literature.
Other lawyers: Financial services, investment funds, asset management, company, commercial

Securicor plc
Sutton Park House 15 Carshalton Road Sutton SM1 4LD
Tel: (020) 8770 7000 **Fax:** (020) 8770 1145
Email: nigel.griffiths@plc.securicor.com
Website: www.securicor.co.uk
No of lawyers in dept: 5
Work outsourced: 15% - Litigation, property, major corporate mergers and acquisitions.
Nigel E Griffiths, Group Legal Director & Company Secretary
Specialisation: Contract, insurance, employment, commercial, international, mergers and acquisitons.
Career: Educated at Whitgift School and Liverpool University LLB (Hons) 1968. Qualified as a solicitor in 1971. Securicor since 1973.
Other lawyers: Peter David - company and commercial; Stephen Lyell - commercial and international; Roger Whetnall - employment; Amanda Wolfe - employment.

Serco Group plc
Palm Court 4 Heron Square Richmond-upon-Thames TW9 1EW
Tel: (020) 8334 4335 **Fax:** (020) 8334 4320
Julia Cavanagh, Company Secretary

Severn Trent Water Ltd
2297 Coventry Road Sheldon Birmingham B26 3PU
Tel: (0121) 722 4000 **Fax:** (0121) 722 4800
Michael R Knight, Company Solicitor

Shaftesbury PLC
Pegasus House 37-43 Sackville Street London W1S 3DL
Tel: (020) 7333 8118 **Fax:** (020) 7333 0660
Email: shaftesbury@shaftesbury.co.uk
Website: www.shaftesbury.co.uk
Work outsourced: 100% - Corporate, property and general matters.
Brian Bickell, Finance Director & Company Secretary
Specialisation: Finance and accounting.
Career: Chartered Accountant (FCA).

Shanks Group PLC
Astor House Station Road Bourne End SL8 5YP
Tel: (01628) 524523 **Fax:** (01628) 524114
Paul Kaye, Company Secretary

Shell International Services Ltd
Legal Services Shell Centre York Road London SE1 7NA
Tel: (020) 7934 1234 **Fax:** (020) 7934 5354
Email: Barbara.B.Blum@SI.Shell.com
Website: www.shell.com
Barbara Blum, Legal Counsel

Shire Pharmaceuticals Group plc
Hampshire International Business Park Chineham Basingstoke RG24 8EP
Tel: (01256) 894117 **Fax:** (01256) 894710
Email: tmay@uk.shire.com
Website: www.shiregroup.com
No of lawyers in dept: 10 (In UK, USA & Canada) plus 6 in IP
Work outsourced: 10% - Complex M&A, Property, Litigation.
Tatjana May, General Counsel & Company Secretary
Specialisation: Corporate, Commercial, M&A, IP, Licensing, Empoyment, Anti-Trust, Litigation Mangement.
Career: Southampton University - Law LLB - 1987. Slaughter & May (Corporate/Commercial) 1988-1994. AstraZeneca Plc 1995-2001. Shire Pharmaceuticals Group Plc 2001 to date.
Personal: Interests: Skiing, tennis, theatre.

SIG PLC
Hillsborough Works Langsett Road Sheffield S6 2LW
Tel: (0114) 285 6300 **Fax:** (0114) 285 6385
John Swynnerton, Company Secretary

Singer & Friedlander Group PLC
21 New Street Bishopsgate London EC2M 4HR
Tel: (020) 7623 3000 **Fax:** (020) 7623 2122
Stephen P Doherty, Company Secretary

Sir Robert McAlpine (Holdings) Ltd
Eaton Court Maylands Avenue Hemel Hempstead
HP2 7TR

IN-HOUSE LAWYERS ■ COMPANY SECRETARIES

Tel: (01442) 412897 **Fax:** (01442) 248393
Email: p.brinley-codd@sir-robert-mcalpine.com
Website: www.sir-robert-mcalpine.com
Peter Brinley-Codd, Solicitor & Legal Services Manager

Six Continents PLC
20 North Audley Street London W1K 6WN
Tel: (020) 7409 8145 **Fax:** (020) 7409 8526
Email: chris.vaughan@sixcontinents.com
Website: www.sixcontinents.com
No of lawyers in dept: 4
Work outsourced: 60% - Corporate (major projects), litigation, property.
Chris Vaughan, Director of Group Legal
Specialisation: General company and commercial matters, with a particular specialisation in M&A transactions. General commercial agreements, joint ventures, employment, IP, antitrust and management of litigation. Member of CBI Competition Law Panel.
Career: Qualified 1991 with Freshfields. Corporate assistant with Freshfields until 1994, when moved to Cameron McKenna. Joined Bass PLC (now Six Continents PLC) in 1995. Education: Leicester University (LLB Law with French), College of Law (Chester).
Personal: Born 1964. Married with three children. Interests include golf, tennis and skiing.
Other lawyers: M&A, commercial, banking, litigation, IT, intellectual property.

Skanska Construction Group Ltd
Maple Cross House Denham Way Maples Cross Rickmansworth WD3 9AS
Tel: (01923) 423966 **Fax:** (01923) 423864
Email: martin.Lenihan@skanska.co.uk
Website: www.skanska.co.uk
Martin Lenihan, Legal Advisor
Specialisation: All aspects of law relating to Major Construction Projects - Non-Contentious (including PFI and PPP), commercial development projects, tunnelling & mining, LNG and general corporate/commercial law advice.
Career: Previous career, included 11 years at John Laing Construction (Group Legal Adviser) and spells at Nabarro Nathanson Solicitors, Taylor Woodrow Construction and James R Knowles (Construction Consultants). Education included Kentish Town comprehensive school and other institutions including Bar School, (Middle-Temple Barrister) and London School of Economics, (L.L.M.) - Master of Laws (Commercial Law).
Personal: Manchester United, sports and good food/wine.
Maple Cross House Denham Way Maples Cross Rickmansworth WD3 9AS
Tel: (01923) 776666 **Fax:** (01923) 423864
Email: hilary.wilson@skanska.co.uk
Website: www.skanska.co.uk
Hilary Wilson, Legal Adviser
Specialisation: Major projects in the UK and Overseas. Civil engineering and construction, commercial, PFI. Adviser to civil and engineering and construction companies within the Skanska Construction Group.
Career: Howell's School, Denbigh. Newnham College, Cambridge. Called to bar Gray's Inn 1974. In-house adviser since 1977.

Sky Interactive Limited
Grantway Isleworth Middlesex TW7 5QD
Tel: (020) 7941 5300 **Fax:** (020) 7941 5929
Marijke Reid, Legal/Compliance Manager

Slough Estates PLC
Slough Estates House 234 Bath Road Slough SL1 4EE
Tel: (01753) 537171 **Fax:** (01753) 820585
Robert G May, Legal Supervisor

SMG PLC
200 Renfield Street Glasgow G2 3PR
Tel: (0141) 300 3300 **Fax:** (0141) 300 3030
Email: Lindsay.Wallace@smg.plc.uk
Website: www.smg.plc.uk
No of lawyers in dept: 5
Work outsourced: 60% - Corporate Finance.
Lindsay Wallace, Group Legal Director
Other lawyers: Corporate Finance, Company/Commercial.

Smith & Nephew PLC
Heron House 15 Adam Street London WC2N 6LA
Tel: (020) 7401 7646 **Fax:** (020) 7930 3353
Paul Chambers, Group Company Secretary & Legal Adviser

Smiths Group plc
765 Finchley Road London NW11 8DS
Tel: (020) 8457 8283 **Fax:** (020) 8201 8041
Website: www.smiths-group.com
No of lawyers in dept: 4
Work outsourced: 30% - M&A, Litigation.
Clare Shepherd, Director of Legal Affairs
Other lawyers: M&A, Company/Commercial, Litigation, Employment.

Sociètè Gènèrale
SG House 41 Tower Hill London EC3N 4SG
Tel: (020) 7676 6000 **Fax:** (020) 7676 8888
Mark Nimmo, Executive Director, Group Legal & Company Secretary

Somerfield plc
Somerfield House Whitchurch Lane Whitchurch Bristol BS14 0TJ
Tel: (0117) 935 9359 **Fax:** (0117) 978 0629
Email: susy.jepson@somerfield.co.uk
Website: www.somerfield.co.uk
No of lawyers in dept: 4
Work outsourced: 75% - Health and safety, property, commercial, corporate, litigation.
Susy Jepson, Head of Group Legal
Specialisation: Company commercial; including IT/IP, advertising and promotional law, data protection, competition.
Other lawyers: Company commercial, employment, property, IP/IT, liquor licensing, litigation, company secretarial.

Sony Music Entertainment (UK) Ltd
10 Great Marlborough Street London W1F 7LP
Tel: (020) 7911 8200 **Fax:** (020) 7911 8600
Alastair George, Vice President of Legal & Business Affairs
10 Great Marlborough Street London W1F 7LP
Tel: (020) 7911 8875 **Fax:** (020) 7911 8233
Email: rakesh_sanghvi@uk.sonymusic.com
Website: www.sonymusic.co.uk
Rakesh Sanghvi, General Manager
Specialisation: All aspects of music publishing for Sony/ATV Music Publishing (UK) Limited and Sony Music Entertainment(UK) Limited trading as Sony Music Publishing
Career: Haberdasher's Aske's School; University College London - LLB; College of Law, Lancaster Gate; Nicholson, Graham & Jones, London

South Staffordshire Group PLC
Green Lane Walsall WS2 7PD
Tel: (01922) 638282 **Fax:** (01922) 723631
Adrian Page, Finance Director & Company Secretary

Spectris plc
Station Road Egham TW20 9NP
Tel: (01784) 470470 **Fax:** (01784) 470848
Roger Stephens, Head of Commercial & Company Secretary

Spirax-Sarco Engineering PLC
Charlton House Cirencester Road Cheltenham GL53 8ER
Tel: (01242) 521361 **Fax:** (01242) 581470
Peter Smith, Company Secretary

Spirent plc
Spirent House Crawley Business Quarter Fleming Way Crawley RH10 9QL
Tel: (01293) 767676 **Fax:** (01293) 767929
Email: paul.eardley@spirent.com
Website: www.spirent.com
No of lawyers in dept: 3
Work outsourced: 70% - Most types.
Paul Eardley, Company Secretary & General Counsel
Specialisation: Company/Commercial, Compliance/Regulatory, M&A, Litigation, IP.
Career: LLB (Hons) Manchester University.Admitted as a solicitor 1986.Linklaters 1987-1993.DLA Manchester (Corporate partner) 1993-1998.Joined Spirent 1998.
Other lawyers: Company/commercial, Litigalia, IP, regulatory/compliance.

SSL International PLC
Toft Hall Toft Knutsford WA16 9PD
Tel: (020) 7367 5760 **Fax:** (020) 7367 5790
Email: Jonathan.Jowett@ssl-International.com
Website: www.ssl-international.com
No of lawyers in dept: 5
Work outsourced: 70% - All.
Jonathan D Jowett, Group Secretary & Legal Director
Specialisation: The provision of legal and administration services to the UK-listed parent company and its subsidiaries. Main legal focus in M&A and general commercial.

Career: LL.B. Business Law 1985; Solicitor 1989; LL.M. European Union Law 1999.

St Ives PLC
St Ives House Lavington Street London SE1 0NX
Tel: (020) 7928 8844 **Fax:** (020) 7902 6436
Philip Harris, Company Secretary

St James's Place Capital PLC
St James's Place House Dollar Street Cirencester GL7 2AQ
Tel: (01285) 640302 **Fax:** (01285) 653 993
Email: hugh.gladman@sjp.co.uk
Website: www.sjpc.co.uk
No of lawyers in dept: 4
Work outsourced: 15-20% - Property, litigation, debt collection, major transactions.
Hugh Gladman, Group Risk Director
Specialisation: Director in charge of the legal and compliance and risk departments of the St James's Place Group.
Career: LLB Southampton University. 1986-93 Herbert Smith (including articles). 1993-94 Hammond Suddards . 1994 Head of Legal Department - J.Rothschild Assurance. 1997 - Legal and Compliance Director for the St James's Place Group. 2002 Group Risk Director.
Personal: Hobbies include tennis, hockey and other sports, film, theatre and family.
Other lawyers: Catherine Thearle, Simon Titterton and Helen Pearne - company/commercial; Carmen Chapple - debt collection.

Stagecoach Group PLC
10 Dunkeld Road Perth PH1 5TW
Tel: (01738) 442111 **Fax:** (01738) 643648
Email: derek.scott@stagecoachgroup.com
Website: www.stagecoachgroup.com
Work outsourced: 80% - Opinions, drafting, commercial, banking.
Derek Scott, Company Secretary
Specialisation: Company Secretary. Chairman of Group Pension Trustees. Director of Group ESOP Trustee. Director of Railways Pension Scheme Trustee.
Career: University of Glasgow 1971-75. Chartered Accountant 1978. Arthur Andersen 1975-86. Stagecoach Group (Previous Holdings) plc 1987 to date. Director of Railways Pension Trustee Company Ltd 1997 to date. Member of NAPF Investment Council 1998 to date.
Other lawyers: Pensions, ESOP's.

Standard Chartered Bank
1 Aldermanbury Square London EC2V 7SB
Tel: (020) 7280 7106 **Fax:** (020) 7280 7112
Website: www.standardchartered.com
No of lawyers in dept: 7
David Brimacombe, Head of Group Legal
Other lawyers: Helen Dodds - litigation, banking, commercial, employment; Susan Adams - litigation, banking commercial, employment; Martin Rowlands - litigation, banking, commercial; Rowan Gillies - M&A, corporate; Mark Thomas - IT/IS; Christian Gordon-Pullar - I.T., ebusiness.

Stanley Leisure plc
Stanley House 151 Dale Street Liverpool L2 2JW
Tel: (0151) 237 6000 **Fax:** (0151) 237 6197
Website: www.stanleyleisure.com
No of lawyers in dept: 1
Work outsourced: Property, Employment, Licensing.
Sarah-Jane Goulbourne, Group Company Secretary & Director of Legal Services
Other lawyers: Company/Commercial.

Tate & Lyle PLC
Sugar Quay Lower Thames Street London EC3R 6DQ
Tel: (020) 7626 6525 **Fax:** (020) 7623 5213
Robert Gibber, Company Secretary & General Counsel

Taylor & Francis Group PLC
11 New Fetter Lane London EC4P 4EE
Tel: (020) 7583 9855 **Fax:** (020) 7842 2298
Anthony Foye, Finance Director & Company Secretary

Taylor Nelson Sofres plc
Westgate London W5 1UA
Tel: (020) 8967 0007 **Fax:** (020) 8967 4060
Website: www.tnsofres.com
No of lawyers in dept: 4
Work outsourced: 25% - Excess workload, property, litigation.
Paul Wright, Group General Counsel
Specialisation: M&A, Corporate Finance, Company/Commercial.
Career: MA (Oxon) Qualified 1984. Articles at Nabarro,

IN-HOUSE LAWYERS ■ COMPANY SECRETARIES

Nathanson and worked in city law firms prior to joining TNS in 1994.
Other lawyers: Paul Wright - Corporate Finance ; Raj Afghan - Intellectual Property ; Ellora Ahmed; Mike Slotznick - U.S.A.; Trevor Braman - General; David Stanley - General.

Taylor Woodrow Construction Ltd
Taywood House 345 Ruislip Road Southall UB1 2QX
Tel: (020) 8578 2366 **Fax:** (020) 8575 4701
Simon Williams, Chief Solicitor

Taylor Woodrow plc
Venture House 42-54 London Road Staines TW18 4HF
Tel: (01784) 428650 **Fax:** (01784) 428797
Website: www.taylorwoodrow.com
No of lawyers in dept: 9
Work outsourced: Variable. - Construction, litigation, property, corporate finance, PFI.
Jeremy Sampson, Group General Counsel
Specialisation: Responsible for the provision of legal services of Taylor Woodrow plc and assists the subsidiary companies and their legal functions where appropriate. Principle area of work is company/commercial work.
Career: Chesham High School-1980-1986. Leicester Polytechnic-1986-1989. College of Law, Chester-1989-1990. Prudential Corporation (Trainee Solicitor)-1990-1991. Richards Butler (Trainee Solicitor)-1991-1992. Taylor Woodrow-1993 to date .
Personal: Age 3 4 . Married living in West London. Interests include: Sailing, sport and the theatre.
Other lawyers: Jeremy Sampson-Company/Commercial; Simon Williams - Construction; Bill Bidder - Housing.

TBI PLC
159 New Bond Street 4th Floor London W1S 2UD
Tel: (020) 7408 7300 **Fax:** (020) 7408 7321
Email: tbi@tbiplc.co.uk
Website: www.tbiplc.com / www.tbiplc.co.uk
No of lawyers in dept: 1
Roger C Clifton, Group Company Secretary
Career: FCIS; Barrister.

Telegraph Group Limited
1 Canada Square Canary Wharf London E14 5DT
Tel: (020) 7538 5000 **Fax:** (020) 7538 6242
Arthur Wyn-Davies, Legal Manager

Thistle Hotels PLC
2 The Calls Leeds LS2 7JU
Tel: (0113) 243 9111 **Fax:** (0113) 244 5555
Ian Durant, Finance Director & Company Secretary

Thomson Financial
Aldgate House 33 Aldgate High Street London EC3N 1DL
Tel: (020) 7369 7000 **Fax:** (020) 7369 7278
Email: jane.reeves@tfeurope.com
Website: www.thomson.com
Jane Reeves, European Counsel
Specialisation: Data, information technology and intellectual property.
Career: Wadham College, Oxford and Guildhall University. Qualified in 1992 with Clifford Chance, associate in the Intellectual Property Group of Linklates. Joined Thomson Financial in 1996.
Personal: Company Secretary to National Charity (Big Brothers and Sisters); school governor.

Tibbett & Britten Group PLC
Ross House 1 Shirley Road Windmill Hill Enfield EN2 6SB
Tel: (020) 8367 9955 **Fax:** (020) 8366 7042
Keith Austin, Company Secreaty & Head of Legal Services

Times Newspapers Ltd
Times House 1 Pennington Street London E98 1LG
Tel: (020) 7782 5858 **Fax:** (020) 7782 5860
Email: alastair.brett@newsint.co.uk
Website: www.the-times.co.uk / www.sunday-times.co.uk
Alastair Brett, Legal Manager
Times House 1 Pennington Street London E98 1LG
Tel: (020) 7782 5857 **Fax:** (020) 7782 5860
Website: www.the-times.co.uk / www.sunday-times.co.uk
Patricia Burge, Company Solicitor
Specialisation: Contracts, Libel, defamation, copyright, trademark.

T-Mobile (UK)
Imperial Place Maxwell Road Borehamwood WD6 1EA
Tel: (020) 8214 2751 **Fax:** (020) 8214 3441
Email: julia.chain@t-mobile.co.uk
Work outsourced: 20% - Large corporate contracts, some property, competition, same regulatory, employment, litigation, banking.
Julia Chain, General Counsel
Career: Educated at Gurton College, Cambridge, Julia spent 2 years at Shearman and Sterling and then returned to qualify at Herbert Smith. In 1993 she became managing partner of Garretts the law firm associated with Arthur Anderson. She remained as managing partner for 5 years and then joined T-Mobile (UK) as a Director and General Counsel.
Personal: Married with 4 children ages between 11 and 20.
Other lawyers: Commercial, Property, Corporate, IP/IT, Telecoms, Regulatory.

Tokyo-Mitsubishi International PLC
6 Broadgate London EC2M 2AA
Tel: (020) 7577 2804 **Fax:** (020) 7577 2872
Email: richard.house@t-mi.com
Website: www.t-mi.com
No of lawyers in dept: 9 (Inclusive of Richard House)
Work outsourced: 40% - Capital markets, securitisation, banking.
Richard House, Director, Legal, Company Secretary
Specialisation: Responsible for all new issue business, bonds, MTNs and warrants; equity linked structures, securitisations and structured transactions. All forms of general legal advice to the company.
Career: Articled Simmons Church Smiles; Qualified 1990; Articled and one year qualified at Simmons Church Smiles; moved to Mitsubishi Finance International plc (a wholly owned subsidiary of the Mitsubushi Bank) in March 1991. Following the global merger of Mitsubishi Bank with the Bank of Tokyo, the parent bank has changed its name to the Bank of Tokyo-Mitsubishi Ltd, and Mitsubishi Finance International has changed its name to Tokyo-Mitsubishi International plc. Education: University of Nottingham (1986 LL.B. Hons)
Personal: Born 1964, resides Fulham. Leisure: theatre, sport, sailing, impractical cars, sloth.
Other lawyers: Transaction Mangement: Chris O'Hara, Jamie Flynn, Michael Pithey, Pierre Alvernhe, Reiko Masada.General Legal: Georgiana Davidson, Olivier Begoin, Mitsue Miyajima.

Tomkins PLC
East Putney House 84 Upper Richmond Road London SW15 2ST
Tel: (020) 8871 4544 **Fax:** (020) 8877 9700
Norman Porter, Company Secretary

Torex PLC
PO Box 74 Banbury OX15 5YS
Nigel D Horn, Company Secretary

Towers Perrin
Castlewood House 77-91 New Oxford Street London WC1A 1PX
Tel: (020) 7379 4000 **Fax:** (020) 8895 7478
Val Vardy, Principal

Travis Perkins PLC
Lodge Way House Lodge Way Harlestone Road Northampton NN5 7UG
Tel: (01604) 683040 **Fax:** (01604) 683160
Email: apike@travisperkins.co.uk
Website: www.travisperkins.co.uk
No of lawyers in dept: 1
Work outsourced: 80% - Property, litigation, major acquisitions, disposals.
Andrew S Pike, Company Secretary & Lawyer
Specialisation: General responsibility for groups legal affairs. Also responsible as Company Secretary for pensions, insurance and risk management, and share schemes. General contract and commercial advice, employment law, acquisitions and disposals.
Career: University of Birmingham LL.B 1973; Costain Group 1981-1989; Alfred McAlpine 1989-1994; Ibstock plc 1994-1999; Travis Perkins plc 1999 - date.

Trinity Mirror PLC
1 Canada Square Canary Wharf London E14 5AP
Tel: (020) 7293 3000 **Fax:** (020) 7293 0435
Paul Vickers, Company Secretary & Group Legal Director
1 Canada Square Canary Wharf London E14 5AP
Tel: (020) 7293 3000 **Fax:** (020) 7293 3613
Website: www.trinity-mirror.co.uk
Marcus Partington, Head of the Editorial Legal Department Legal Affairs 24th Floor One Canada Square Canary Wharf London E14 5DJ
Tel: (020) 7293 3000
Charles Collier-Wright, Group Legal Manager

TT International
Martin House 5 Martin Lane London EC4R 0DP
Tel: (020) 7410 3500 **Fax:** (020) 7410 3539
Austin Allison, Compliance and Legal Partner

TTP Communications plc
Melbourn Science Park Cambridge Road Melbourn Royston SG8 6EE
Tel: (01763) 266266 **Fax:** (01763) 261216
Christopher McQuoid, General Counsel

TUI UK Ltd
Greater London House Hampstead Road London NW1 7SD
Tel: (020) 7387 9321 **Fax:** (020) 7383 1485
No of lawyers in dept: 6
Work outsourced: 50% - Finance, competition, employment.
Richard Churchill-Coleman, Group Legall Counsel
Other lawyers: Henry Banks - Commercial / Litigation; Thomas Schmid - Aviation; Nigel Vickery - Property ; Karen Goh - IT/IP.

Tullow Oil PLC
30 Old Burlington Street 5th Floor London W1S 3AR
Tel: (020) 7333 6800 **Fax:** (020) 7333 6830
Email: grahammartin@tullowoil.co.uk
Website: www.tullowoil.com
No of lawyers in dept: 3
Work outsourced: 25% - Corporate Finance, Litigation, Property. Foreign Jurisdictions
Graham Martin, Legal & Commercial Director
Specialisation: International Oil & Gas, UK Corporate & Commercial
Career: Partners Dickson Minto WS; Partner Vinson & Elkins LLP.
Other lawyers: Michael Comber - UK & International Oil & Gas, Company & Commercial; Angela Evans - UK Oil & Gas, Commercial

UBS AG
100 Liverpool Street London EC2M 2RH
Tel: (020) 7568 7221 **Fax:** (020) 7568 9247
Email: charles.ross-stewart@ubsw.com
Website: www.ubsw.com
Charles Ross-Stewart, Executive Director
Specialisation: Fixed Income, equity and credit derivatives. Structured finance, CDOs, securitisation.
Career: Edinburgh University LL.B (1982-1987); Dundas & Wilson, Edinburgh (1987-1989); Freshfields, London (1989-1994); Citibank, London (1994-1998); UBS Warburg (1998 to date).

UBS Warburg Group
100 Liverpool Street London EC2M 2RH
Tel: (020) 7568 8000 **Fax:** (020) 7568 4800
Email: philip.price@ubsw.com
Website: www.ubsw.com
No of lawyers in dept: 8
Philip Price, Head of Corporate Legal Services
Other lawyers: Corporate Secretarial, Litigation, Regulatory, Employments and Benefits, IP/IT/e-Commerce

UFJ International plc
1 Exchange Square London EC2A 2JL
Tel: (020) 7638 6030 **Fax:** (020) 7588 5875
Website: www.ufji.com
No of lawyers in dept: 6
Work outsourced: 10% - MTN programme updates, repackagings, leases.
David Haig, Head of Legal & Compliance Depts.
Other lawyers: Peter Rice, Julie Vamberto, Debra Coltman, Richard Williams, Ronald Laugat.

Ultraframe PLC
Enterprise Works Salthill Road Clitheroe BB7 1PE
Tel: (01200) 414622 **Fax:** (01200) 452231
Email: edward.smethurst@ultraframe.co.uk
Website: www.ultraframe.com
No of lawyers in dept: 2
Work outsourced: 100% - Litigation, mergers and acquisitions, corporate.
Edward G Smethurst, Group Company Solicitor & Group Company Secretary
Specialisation: Company Secretary to plc board and all subsidiaries. Responsible for commercial and contract drafting. Major litigation to include IP related litigation, contract litigations. Responsible for pensions and insurance matters. Company Solicitor to the group.
Career: Oulder Hill School, Rochdale; Leeds University LL.B (Hons) 2:1; Halliwell Landau 1990-1993; British Nuclear plc

IN-HOUSE LAWYERS ■ COMPANY SECRETARIES

1993-2000 - Senior Legal Advisor; 2000 to date - Ultraframe plc - Company Secretary and Solicitor.
Personal: Chairman Law Society C&I Group Nationally June 1999 to June 2000 and January 2001 to March 2001. Chief Executive of this group June 2000 to date. Chairman Law Society C&I Northwest Group from 1994 to date. European Company Lawyers Association - UK. Director to European Board 2000 to date. Interests: Football, cricket and rugby.

Unilever plc
Unilever House Blackfriars PO Box 68 London EC4P 4BQ
Tel: (020) 7822 5441 **Fax:** (020) 7822 6108
Email: steve.williams@unilever.com
Website: www.unilever.com
No of lawyers in dept: Over 30 in London & Rotterdam Corporate centres.
Stephen G Williams, General Counsel & Joint Secretary
Specialisation: Responsible for all legal, intellectual property and secretarial departments in the head offices in London and Rotterdam and is also responsible for Unilever legal services worldwide.
Career: Educated at Brentwood School, Essex and King's College, University of London where gained Bachelor of Law Degree (LLB) Hons. Following Law School, joined Slaughter and May and spent time in their tax planning and commercial departments. In 1975 joined the legal department of Imperial Chemical Industries plc. In 1984 he transferred to ICI's company secretary's department, becoming one of two assistant company secretaries in 1985. Appointed Joint Secretary of Unilever on 1st January 1986 and General Counsel of Unilever in 1993.
Personal: Admitted as a Solicitor and member of the Law Society in April 1972. Member of the Company Law Committee of the Law Society and of the Companies Committee of the CBI. Non-executive director of Bunzl plc.
Other lawyers: Mr R Leek - Overseas legal services; Ms T Dougal-Biggs - Uk legal services; Mr R Heath - Trade mark legal services; Mr L Virelli - Patents legal services; Mrs S Franklin- Marketing legal services; Mr J Moolenburgh - European legal services (based in Rotterdam); Mrs SBM Andnessen Netherlands legal services (based in Rotterdam)
Unilever House Blackfriars PO Box 68 London EC4P 4BQ
Tel: (020) 7822 6188 **Fax:** (020) 7822 5951
Website: www.unilever.com
Richard Heath, Head of Corporate Trade Marks & General Trade Mark Counsel
Specialisation: Responsible for all aspects of trade mark and brand protection worldwide, including related Intellectual Property Rights. Portfolio size: 135,000. Departmental size: 54 including 11 lawyers based in London & Rotterdam head offices.
Career: Joined Unilever in 1992, formerley Head of Trade Marks at Smitt & Nephew PLC. Also held positions in Hoffman La Roche in Basel, Switzerland and Amersham International, in 1981 & 1980. Educated at Reading Grammer School & Brunel University of West London, BSc. (Hons)
Personal: Director of International Trade Mark Association (INTA); Director of Pharmaceurical Trade Mark Group (PTMG); Member of the Institute of Trade Mark Attorneys (ITMA) & Chartered Institute of Patent Agents (CIPA); Registered Trade Mark Attorney (RTMA)
Unilever House Blackfriars PO Box 68 London EC4P 4BQ
Tel: (020) 7822 5252 **Fax:** (020) 7822 5464
Email: louis.verelli@unilever.com
Website: www.unilever.com
Louis J Virelli Jr, Senior Vice President, General Patent Counsel
Specialisation: Responsible for Unilever patent services worldwide
Career: Educated at Villanova University, Philadelphia, PA, Bachelor of Engineering in 1970, and University of Tennessee where he gained his Law Degree (JD with distinction) in 1972. Joined Sperry New Holland Co, as a patent attorney in 1973. In 1974 he went to Westinghouse to join its litigation department. In 1976 he joined law firm of Paul & Pal and became a partner specialising in intellectual property litigation. In 1984 he joined National Starch & Chemical Co. as its General Counsel of Intellectual Property. In 1988, became Assistant General Counsel Patents for Unilever US and in 1996 Senior Vice President General Patent Counsel Unilever NV and PLC.
Personal: Admitted to the Bar of the State of Pennsylvania and the United States Patent and Trademark Office in 1973. Also admitted to practice before the US Supreme Court, and various State, District and Appellate Courts in the United States. Member of Association of Corporate Patent Counsel (Vice President), American Bar Association, New Jersey and Phiadelphia Patent Law Associations, and the American Intellectual Property Law Association.

United Business Media plc
Ludgate House 245 Blackfriars Road Blackfriars London SE1 9UY
Tel: (020) 7921 5000 **Fax:** (020) 7921 5047
Email: stablesj@unitedbusinessmedia.com
Website: www.unitedbusinessmedia.com
No of lawyers in dept: 11
Work outsourced: 60% - Corporate, litigation, employment.
Jane Stables, Group Legal & Personnel Director
Specialisation: M&A, commercial, litigation, employment practices, strategy/development.
Career: Qualified as a lawyer in 1985 and worked in the city firm of Freshfields doing mainly mergers and acquisitions but always retaining an employment law specialism. Moved into industry to be company secretary and legal adviser to a retailing plc, prior to joining MAI in 1994. She took over the personnel function at MAI in 1995 and became Legal & Personnel Director on the United/MAI merger. Responsible for the United News & Media plc group legal and personnel issues.

United Utilities PLC
Dawson House Liverpool Road Great Sankey Warrington WA5 3LW
Tel: (01925) 237062 **Fax:** (01925) 237066
Email: info@uuplc.co.uk
Website: www.unitedutilities.com
No of lawyers in dept: 20
Work outsourced: 50% - Major transactions, litigation, property, employment.
Timothy Rayner, Head of Legal & Company Secretary
Specialisation: Company/Comercial, Corporate Finance, Corporate Governance.
Career: 1998 to date Company Secretary United Utilities Plc.1995 - 1998 Legal Manager United Utilities Plc.1985 - 1995 Solicitor/Associate/Partner Addleshaw, Booth & Co.1983 - 1985 Trainee Solicitor Eversheds.1979 - 1982 King's College, London (LLB)1968 - 1978 Russell School\sb100\sa100
Personal: Married. Resides Lower Withington, Cheshire.Interests - Showing horses, France, motor sport.

United Utilities Water plc
Dawson House Liverpool Road Great Sankey Warrington WA5 3LW
Tel: (01925) 234000 **Fax:** (01925) 233360
David Hosker, Head of Legal Services

Universal Music Publishing Group
Elsinore House 77 Fulham Palace Road London W6 8JA
Tel: (020) 8752 2600 **Fax:** (020) 8752 2601
Sarah Levin, Head of Legal and Business Affairs

Universal/Island Records Limited
22 St Peter's Square London W6 9NW
Tel: (020) 8910 3333 **Fax:** (020) 8910 3218
No of lawyers in dept: 2
Work outsourced: Less than 5% - Litigation, Contracts.
Claire Sugrue, Director of Legal & Business Affairs

Viridian Group PLC
Danesfort House 120 Malone Road Belfast BT9 5HT
Tel: (028) 9066 1100 **Fax:** (028) 9068 9269
Email: legal@nie.co.uk
Website: www.viridiangroup.co.uk
No of lawyers in dept: 2
Work outsourced: Acquisitions, joint venture, commercial.
David Flinn, Group Solicitor
Specialisation: Electricity law, employment law, joint ventures, acquisitions, general commercial.
Career: Educated Rossall School and Queens University Belfast. Qualified Solicitor Northern Ireland 1975. Qualified Solicitor England and Wales 1981. Chairman Belfast Solicitors Association 1993. Chairman Employment Lawyers Group (NI) 1995 to 1999. Chairman Belfast Civic Trust 1999.
Personal: Interests: Skiing and hill walking.
Other lawyers: N Macdougall: Property law, employment, contract, general commercial.

Vivendi
37-41 Old Queen Street London SW1H 9JA
Tel: (020) 7393 2700 **Fax:** (020) 7393 2748
Victoria Rigby, International Counsel

Vizzavi Europe Limited
80 Strand London WC2R 0RJ
Tel: (020) 7212 0271 **Fax:** (020) 7212 0720
Email: chris.heather@corp.vizzavi.net
Website: www.vizzavi.net
No of lawyers in dept: 4
Work outsourced: 10% - Corporate, employment, property.
Christopher Heather, Group Legal Counsel
Specialisation: Non-contentious intellectual property, information technology, corporate and company/commercial.
Career: Articles and 3 years PQE at Herbert Smith (IP/IT group), 18 months at Olswang (multimedia group), 14 months at Freshfields (IP/IT group) and 14 months at boo.com (Group Legal Counsel). 2 years at Vizzavi Europe Ltd (Group Legal Counsel).
Personal: Current affairs, tennis and reading.
Other lawyers: Matthew Wisbey, Legal Counsel - Information Technology, Intellectual Property, E-Commerce, Insurance, Internet Law and Regulation, Data Protection and litigation. James Maxwell, Legal Counsel - Corporate, Commercial, IT, Litigation. Mark Britt, Legal Counsel - Outsourcing and IT

Vodafone Group Plc
The Courtyard 2-4 London Road Newbury RG14 1JX
Tel: (01635) 33251 **Fax:** (01635) 580857
Email: stephen.scott@vodafone.com
Website: www.vodafone.com
No of lawyers in dept: 19
Work outsourced: 10% - Major M&A, litigation and regulatory, complex tax and finance.
Stephen Scott, Company Secretary & Group Legal Director
Specialisation: Corporate
Career: Manchester Grammer School & St. Catherine's College, Cambridge; Qualified Solicitor 1978 - Payne Hicks Beach & Co; Racal Electronics Plc 1980-1991; Vodafone Group Plc 1991 to date.
Personal: Interests: Golf, Football (Manchester United), theatre, gardening.
Other lawyers: Nick Godwin - Legal Director, Group Operations; Jacqueline Barratt - Intellectual Property; Sarah Goodwin - Competition Law; Helen Drake - Corporate; Clare Moulder - Banking and Treasury; Claire Carless - Company & Commercial; Ian Gardener - Litigation; John Loughrey - Company/Commercial

VT Group plc
Victoria Road Woolston Southampton SO19 9RR
Tel: (023) 8042 6000 **Fax:** (023) 8042 6040
Website: www.vosperthornycroft.co.uk
Work outsourced: 100% - corporate, commercial, employment benefits, property
Peter G Dawes, Company Secretary

Warner Chappell Music Ltd
Griffin House 161 Hammersmith Road London W6 8BS
Tel: (020) 8563 5800 **Fax:** (020) 8563 5801
Website: www.warnerchappell.com
No of lawyers in dept: 3
Work outsourced: 5% - Litigation, employment.
Jane Dyball, Director of Legal and Business Affairs
Specialisation: Music copyright, contracts, litigation, licencing, employment.
Career: Culford School, Suffolk 1972-1980; Bristol University (LLB Hons) 1984; Virgin Music Publishers Ltd 1986-1992; Warner/Chappell Music Ltd 1992 - current. Music Publishers Association Board Member; MCPS Commercial Committee; Pop Bureau; International Confederation of Music Publishers , Director of Performing Rights Society. Director of Mechanical Copyright Protection Society.

Warner Music UK Ltd
The Warner Building 28 Kensington Church Street London W8 4EP
Tel: (020) 7368 2500 **Fax:** (020) 7938 3901
John Watson, Commercial and Business Affairs Director

Waste Recycling Group PLC (WRG)
Group Executive Office Riverside Court Bowling Hill Chipping Sodbury Bristol BS37 6JX
Tel: (01454) 333975 **Fax:** (01454) 320300
Email: info@wrg.co.uk
Website: www.wrg.co.uk
No of lawyers in dept: 1
Work outsourced: Variable.
Steven Hardman, Group Legal Director
Specialisation: All.
Career: BA Joint Hons French, Russian, Bussines Studies (2:1) University College Swansea 1986-1990.CPE/LSF. Newcastle-upon-Tyne Polythechnic 1990-1992.Articles - Gouldens 1992-1994.Corporate/Commercial department, Gouldens 1994-1999.In-house legal department, Harlon plc 1999-2001.Head of legal, Waste Recycling Group PLC, 2001 to date.
Other lawyers: All areas.

IN-HOUSE LAWYERS ■ COMPANY SECRETARIES

The Weir Group PLC
149 Newlands Road Cathcart Glasgow G44 4EX
Tel: (0141) 637 7111 **Fax:** (0141) 637 2221
Alan Mitchelson, Group Company Secretary

Westbury PLC
Westbury House Lansdown Road Cheltenham GL50 2WH
Tel: (01242) 236191 **Fax:** (01242) 584281
Neil Chandler, Company Secretary

Westdeutsche Landesbank Girozentrale (London)
Woolgate Exchange 25 Basinghall Street
London EC2V 5HA
Tel: (020) 7020 2000 **Fax:** (020) 7020 2320
Lucian Milburn, Head of Legal

WH Smith PLC
Nations House 103 Wigmore Street London W1U 1WH
Tel: (020) 7409 3222 **Fax:** (020) 7514 9633
Ian Houghton, Group Legal Director

Whitbread Group PLC
Citypoint One Ropemaker Street London EC2Y 9HX
Tel: (020) 7806 5400 **Fax:** (020) 7806 5456
Email: simon.barratt1@whitbread.com
Website: www.whitbread.co.uk
No of lawyers in dept: 3
Work outsourced: 80% - Litigation, property, debt collection, licensing, environmental health and food safety issues.
Simon Barratt, Legal Affairs Director & Company Secretary
Career: Educated at Sevenoaks School; St. Johns College, Oxford (Jurisprudence 1982); Law Society finals 1983). Articled Slaughter and May; qualified 1985; assistant solicitor, Slaughter and May; solicitor RTZ Legal department, 1987-1989; corporate counsel, Heron Corporation 1989-1991, group legal adviser, Whitbread July 1991-March 1997. Appointed Legal Affairs Director, Company Secretary Whitbread PLC March 1997.
Personal: Born 1959; resides Tunbridge Wells. Leisure pursuits include keeping fit, gardening, keeping the children occupied.
Other lawyers: Russell Fairhurst - Group Legal Advisor (M&A, commercial); Tanya Msimang - Solicitor (commercial).

William M Mercer Limited
Mercer Legal Unit 1 Grosvenor Place London SW1P 4LZ
Tel: (020) 7488 4949 **Fax:** (020) 7201 0800
Mark McKeown, Litigation Counsel UK & Europe

Wilson Bowden PLC
Wilson Bowden House 207 Leicester Road Ibstock Leicester LE67 6WB
Tel: (01530) 260777 **Fax:** (01530) 262805
Email: ewilson@wilsonbowden.plc.uk
Website: www.wilsonbowden.co.uk
No of lawyers in dept: 7
Work outsourced: 80% - Land acquisitions, land sales, plot sales, litigation.
Nicolas J Townsend, Group Legal Director
Specialisation: Responsible for monitoring and supervision of all major contracts for land acquisition/sale, troubleshooting, strategic land acquisition and the provision of external legal services for the group.
Career: Qualified in January 1970. Previously a Partner with Gardiner & Millhouse 1976-78, Marron Townsend 1978-80, Nicolas Townsend & Co 1980-87, Staunton Townsend 1987-89 Edge and & Ellison 1989-93.
Other lawyers: Owen Hill, Peter Carr, Wendy Satchwell, Verina Wenham, Liz Bailey, Juliette Gallagher - planning and property development.

Wilson Connolly Holdings PLC
Thomas Wilson House Tenter Road Moulton Park PO Box 39 Northampton NN3 6QJ
Tel: (01604) 790909 **Fax:** (01604) 499154
Email: wilcon@wilcon.co.uk
Website: www.wilcon.co.uk
Work outsourced: 1
Carol Nunn, Group Company Secretary
Specialisation: All Company Secretarial services. Corporate & Stock Exchange Complinace, commercial/contract/hand/insurance, pensions.
Career: Warwick University: LLB (Hons).A.C.I.S. [Associate of the Chartered Institute of Company Secretaries].
Other lawyers: Company Secretarial Department.

Wm Morrison Supermarkets PLC
Hilmore House Thornton Road Bradford BD8 9AX
Tel: (01274) 494166 **Fax:** (01274) 494831
Jonathan Burke, Company Secretary

Wolseley PLC
Parkview 1220 Arlington Business Park Theale Reading RG7 4GA
Tel: (0118) 929 8700 **Fax:** (0118) 929 8701
Email: mark.white@wolseley.com
Website: www.wolseley.com
Mark J White, Group Company Secretary

The Wolverhampton & Dudley Breweries PLC
Park Brewery Bath Road PO Box 26
Wolverhampton WV1 4NY
Tel: (01902) 711811 **Fax:** (01902) 429136
Leslie Porter, Company Secretary

Woolworths Group plc
Woolworth House 242-246 Marylebone Road
London NW1 6JL
Tel: (020) 7262 1222 **Fax:** (020) 7706 5416
Website: www.woolworths.co.uk
No of lawyers in dept: 2 out of 10
Work outsourced: Less than 20% - Property, litigation, material acquisition/disposal.
Jonathan Bloom, Company Secretary & General Counsel
Specialisation: Company/commercial, Entertainment, Corporate Finance, Risk, Corporate social responsibility.
Career: LLB (Hons)Norton Rose London, Hong Kong 1992-1996.VCI plc 1996-2001.Woolworths Group plc 2001 to date.
Other lawyers: Company/Commercial, Consumer Affairs, Corporate Finance, Litigation, Risk/Insurance.

Working Title Films Ltd
Oxford House 76 Oxford Street London W1D 1BS
Tel: (020) 7307 3000 **Fax:** (020) 7307 3003
Angela Morrison, Chief Operating Officer
Oxford House 76 Oxford Street London W1D 1BS
Tel: (020) 7307 3000 **Fax:** (020) 7307 3003
Email: sheeraz.shah@unistudios.com
Sheeraz Shah, Head of Legal & Business Affairs
Specialisation: All aspects of feature film production.
Career: Joined WTF in January 2000 as Vice President of Legal and Business Affairs. Promoted to Head of department in August 2002. Formely assistant solicitor at SJ Berwi's Media and Communication Group (1998-2000) and at Slaughter and May (1994-1998).Educated at Christ's College, Cambridge (First Class, Law) and the Manchester Grammar School, Manchester.
Personal: Hobbies include: film (naturally), music, exterior sports, reading. Keen gardener.

WPP Group PLC
27 Farm Street London W1J 5RJ
Tel: (020) 7318 0014 **Fax:** (020) 7495 0484
Email: dcalow@wpp.com
Website: www.wpp.com
Work outsourced:
David Calow, Group Chief Counsel
Other lawyers: Company/commercial, corporate finance, corporate governance, employment, international.

WS Atkins PLC
Woodcote Grove Ashley Road Epsom KT18 5BW
Tel: (01372) 726140 **Fax:** (01372) 740055
Email: info@atkinsglobal.com
Website: www.wsatkins.co.uk
No of lawyers in dept: 4
Work outsourced: 5% - Commercial conveyancing, litigation, major acquisition.
Deborah Robinson, Legal Director
Specialisation: Responsible for legal risk and insurance issues affecting the Atkins Group, both in the UK and overseas.
Career: Articled Macfarlanes 1988-90; Assistant Solicitor Macfarlanes 1990-94; Assistant Legal Adviser WS Atkins 1994-99; Group Legal Adviser 1999 to date. Sutton High School. University of Bristol (LLB 1986). Kings College London (MSc 1992).
Personal: Born 1964. Resides in Kingston-Upon-Thames.

Xansa PLC
Legal Department Campus 300 Maylands Avenue Hemel Hempstead HP2 7TQ
Tel: (08705) 416181 **Fax:** (01442) 434248
Charles E Lilley, Senior Legal Adviser

Young & Rubicam Group Ltd
Greater London House Hampstead Road
London NW1 7QP
Tel: (020) 7611 6374 **Fax:** (020) 7611 6743
Email: kathryn_fulton@eu-yr.com
No of lawyers in dept: 2 plus paralegal
Work outsourced: 10% - Corporate; Company/Commercial
Kate Fulton, Chief Counsel
Specialisation: Advising the Young & Rubicam Group of companies on advertising and related areas (copyright, talent agreements etc.), direct marketing and sales promotion. Company related issues including employment advice.
Career: 1973-83 Manchester High School for Girls; 1983-86 Queen Mary College, University of London; 1987 Bar School; 1988-89 Pupillages.
Personal: Run a legal surgery for a cancer charity. Married with 3 children.
Other lawyers: Advertising and medialaw; Public relations

Yule Catto & Co PLC
Central Road Temple Fields Harlow CM20 2BH
Tel: (0127) 9442791 **Fax:** (0127) 9641360
Email: richard.atkinson@yulecatto.com
Website: www.yulecatto.com
No of lawyers in dept: 1
Work outsourced: 80-90% - All
Richard Atkinson, Company Secretary
Specialisation: Company/Commercial
Other lawyers: IP, Employment, Company/Commercial, Corporate Finance, Litigation.

SUPPORT SERVICES

Accountants page 1227
Consultants 1238
Investigators 1239

ACCOUNTANTS

Alexanders

Redhill Chambers, High Street, Redhill, RH1 1RJ
Tel (01737) 779500 **Fax** (01737) 779548
Email Alex@Alexanders.uk.co

Contact Partner	J Donoghue

THE FIRM For a number of years, Alexanders has been helping lawyers and their clients by providing forensic accounting, litigation support and expert witness services whenever financial issues are involved. The firm has worked closely with insurance companies, lawyers, leading counsel and their clients, in such areas as the production of high quality reports, graphs and financial summaries of a clear, concise nature for presentation at court; litigation strategies; the examination and appraisal of documents through Disclosure and assessing the quantum of claims or exposure. Alexanders has a firm grasp of the laws of evidence and understands the necessity of providing reliable evidence. It also has first hand courtroom experience of both the Royal Courts of Justice and the Central Criminal Courts.

Litigation Support Partners The Litigation Support Partners have all held senior positions within the top four accountancy firms and have worked in public practice for a number of years. All partners are members of the Academy of Experts and are qualified accountants with a wide range of business experience.

Litigation Support Services Alexanders has assisted in a wide variety of cases involving loss of earnings; professional negligence; negligence of Investment Managers; fraud; conspiracy to defraud; family and marital disputes; compliance with Investor Protection regulations; insurance claims; breach of contract claims; and offences under the Companies Acts.

BDO Stoy Hayward

8 Baker Street, London, W1U 3LL
Tel (020) 7486 5888 **Fax** (020) 7487 3686 **DX** 0925 West End W1
Email gervase.macgregor@bdo.co.uk **Website** www.bdo.co.uk

Contact	Gervase MacGregor
Number of partners	270
Number of staff	2,500

THE FIRM BDO Stoy Hayward has an established national forensic accounting unit in recognition of the need for sophisticated accountancy input into trials and potential proceedings. The unit offers a cost effective approach based on a high level of partner involvement and backed by professional staff familiar with legal concepts and procedures. Through the BDO worldwide network BDO Stoy Hayward is also able to offer forensic services on an international basis.

Litigation Support Services
Pre-trial Detailed investigation and analysis of documents including prime accounting records; advice on technical accountancy matters; evaluation of economic loss; tracing of assets.
Trial Provision of expert witnesses; analysis of opposition's financial evidence; provision of detailed support during cross examination. Available to act as experts in determinations, as arbitrators, mediators and SJES. The firm's partners have considerable witness box experience.
Settlement Support Assistance with settlement negotiations; evaluation of taxation implications; evaluation of business implications.
IT Advanced computer software and graphics are used to present complex financial and quantitative data with clarity and precision. The firm is also able to offer sophisticated computer forensic techniques for the purposes of data imaging and retrieval.
PRACTICE AREA Types of work undertaken includes breach of warranty; expert determination; fraud; general commercial disputes; loss of profit/earnings including personal injury; mediation; partnership disputes; professional negligence; share purchase agreements; valuations of professional goodwill; wrongful dismissal.

SUPPORT SERVICES ■ ACCOUNTANTS

Carter Backer Winter Chartered Accountants

Hill House, Highgate Hill, London, N19 5UU
Tel (020) 7263 7111 **Fax** (020) 7281 2166 **DX** 54760 Archway
Email peter_luscombe@cbw.co.uk **Website** www.cbw.co.uk

Contacts	
	Peter Luscombe
	Arthur D Harverd

THE FIRM Carter Backer Winter is a long established, major independent London firm with over 70 personnel. Its litigation specialists have a sound understanding of legal concepts and procedures derived from over 30 years experience of litigation work, including many leading cases. They are able to analyse complex financial data quickly and present their findings in a clear, non-technical manner, both in written form and in oral evidence. The litigation team is led by Peter Luscombe, a CEDR accredited mediator, and Arthur Harverd, a registered arbitrator and a past chairman of The Chartered Institute of Arbitrators. Both are members of the Academy of Experts and have given evidence as expert witnesses on numerous occasions. Their experience covers both civil and criminal cases in the areas of commercial, insurance, fraud, tax, personal injury and matrimonial disputes and professional and medical negligence. Their team also includes experts in the fields of insolvency and banking.

Deloitte & Touche

Hill House, 1 Little New Street, London, EC4A 3TR
Tel (020) 7936 3000 **Fax** (020) 7936 2638 **DX** 599
Website http://forensic.deloitte.co.uk

Contact Partners	
	Mike Barford
	Gerry Boon
	Humphry Hatton
	Will Inglis
	Patrick Maher
	Angus Pollock
	Mark Tantam

THE FIRM Deloitte & Touche has a dedicated team of forensic specialists in offices throughout the country. The firm's forensic partners have significant experience as expert witnesses, both in the UK and overseas. Where a case requires specific sector or industry expertise the firm is able to provide the appropriate expert from one of its dedicated industry or technical groups. As a leading member of Deloitte Touche Tohmatsu, the firm is also able to call upon the assistance of its 95,000 staff located in over 140 countries throughout the world.

Litigation Support Services

Commercial Disputes The firm has extensive experience in general commercial disputes including claims for business interruption and loss of profits, product liability, breach of contract, intellectual property, fidelity and warranty breaches and also valuations. As one of the leading firms providing services to the public sector, Deloitte & Touche has also assisted local authorities and government bodies in a wide range of such disputes.
Determinations, Mediations & Arbitration The firm has developed considerable expertise in the role of expert in determinations as well as acting for clients during arbitrations and mediations.
Personal Claims The firm has a significant reputation in personal injury, fatal accident and medical negligence claims. It also provides quantum reports in matrimonial disputes and libel actions.
Professional Negligence The firm provides expert opinion on negligence claims involving accountancy firms as well as quantum reports in claims against other professionals.
Insurance Claims The firm provides expert accountancy services to insurance companies, loss adjusters and commercial clients and has a significant record in acting for Lloyd's Syndicates involved in disputes.
Fraud & Criminal Work The firm conducts fraud investigations, traces and recovers assets and carries out reviews to identify the risk of fraud or money laundering in both the public and private sectors. The firm's investigators have access to the most advanced data recovery and computer investigation tools.
Business Intelligence Services The firm can undertake detailed research into individual's backgrounds, connections and other business activities, whether as part of a commercial dispute or fraud investigation or as a prelude to a new business opportunity or joint venture.
Computerised Litigation Systems The firm's involvement in several major liquidations has led it to develop a computerised database document management and retrieval system for large cases.

ACCOUNTANTS ■ SUPPORT SERVICES

Fisher Forensic, A Division of H. W. Fisher & Company, Chartered Accountants

Acre House, 11-15 William Road, London, NW1 3ER
Tel (020) 7388 7000 **Fax** (020) 7380 4900
Email forens@hwfisher.co.uk **Website** www.hwfisher.co.uk

Contact Partner	Stuart Burns
Number of partners	24
Number of staff	320

THE FIRM Fisher Forensic is the specialist forensic practice within H W Fisher & Company, a medium-sized accountancy firm comprising 24 partners and approximately 320 staff. Fisher Forensic offers a level of expertise rarely found outside the ranks of the largest international firms, combined with a commitment to a prompt, effective and personal service. Its effectiveness is enhanced by experience of acting for both claimants and defendants. The firm has in-depth skills in all aspects of litigation support, including professional negligence, breach of contract, business interruption, fraud and criminal investigations, licensing and royalty recovery, matrimonial, share valuations, expert determinations, medical negligence and personal injury.

Litigation Support Partners

Stuart Burns Stuart heads Fisher Forensic and is a member of the Academy of Experts and the Association of Certified Fraud Examiners. He has considerable court experience and writes regularly on forensic issues for a range of professional publications. He is an experienced expert witness with a number of single joint expert appointments, and expert determination appointments by the Presidents Appointments Scheme, ICAEW.

David Selwyn A forensic partner, David is also a former UK Governor of the Association of Certified Fraud Examiners. He has particular expertise in share valuations, a subject on which he has written and lectured widely.

Grant Thornton

Grant Thornton House, Melton Street, Euston Square, London, NW1 2EP
Tel (020) 7383 5100 **Fax** (020) 7383 4715 **DX** 2100 Euston
Website www.grant-thornton.co.uk

Contacts	
London	Philip Kabraji
Leeds	Robin Hall
Birmingham	Robert Kess
Manchester	Mike Glancy
Cardiff	Will Davies
Bristol	Will Davies
Number of partners	245
Number of staff	2,800

THE FIRM Grant Thornton is a leading national and international accounting firm providing a comprehensive range of business advisory services to a wide variety of clients from private individuals to major companies. The firm operates from over 40 offices in the UK and has an international network spanning nearly 100 countries. A team of specialist forensic partners and staff offers extensive experience of commercial litigation, complex insurance claims, fraud and personal injury. Investigative financial, accounting and taxation services are provided to assist in the building of a case, obtaining settlement or the giving of expert evidence in court. The insurance claims solutions team offers an insurance claims support service ranging from an overview including strategic and tactical advice as well as assistance with the preparation, presentation and negotiation of an insurance claim.

Forensic & Investigations Services The partners in the firm have experience in a wide number of business sectors, including construction, manufacturing, motor dealers, engineering, banking, financial, oil and gas, hotel and leisure, defence and professional services. Partners with appropriate expertise and witness box experience are available to act in contractual and commercial disputes, consequential loss of profit claims, breach of warranty, business and share valuations, fraud, computer disputes, professional negligence claims, shareholder disputes, directors' disqualification hearings, personal injury, medical negligence and fatal accident claims, structured settlements, intellectual property disputes, matrimonial disputes and libel claims.

SUPPORT SERVICES ■ ACCOUNTANTS

Horwath Clark Whitehill

25 New Street Square, London, EC4A 3LN
Tel (020) 7353 1577   **Fax** (020) 7353 6435   **DX** London Chancery Lane 0014
Email enquiry@horwathcw.co.uk   **Website** www.horwathcw.co.uk

Contacts	
London	Richard Freeman
	Humphrey Creed
	Daniel Djanogly
	James Gemmell
	Keith Warner
	Howard Williams
Thames Valley	Humphrey Creed
West Midlands	Chris Bicknell
Leeds	Ross MacLaverty
	David Baxter
Number of partners	72
Number of staff	532

THE FIRM Horwath Clark Whitehill is a leading national firm of chartered accountants and business advisors in the UK.

FORENSIC ACCOUNTING Horwath Clark Whitehill provides forensic accounting services on a national and international basis. Principals act as advisor or expert witness, including single joint expert, in personal and in corporate disputes, supported by a dedicated team of forensic accounting specialists and other experts from within the firm as required. Full use is made of the latest technology including data interrogation software. Dispute resolution services are also provided: arbitration (including London Scheme); mediation; expert determination. The firm is a corporate member of the Academy of Experts and quality control procedures are employed to ensure the high standards of the Code of Practice of the Academy are met. Principals are experienced in giving evidence in court and have undertaken in excess of 1,000 cases, many high profile.

Kingston Smith

Devonshire House, 60 Goswell Road, London, EC1M 7AD
Tel (020) 7566 4000   **Fax** (020) 7566 4010
Email ks@kingstonsmith.co.uk   **Website** www.kingstonsmith.co.uk

Contact Partner	Emile Woolf
Number of partners	43
Number of staff	400

THE FIRM The Kingston Smith litigation support facility was established in 1980, and all members of the service team have many years of professional and commercial experience to complement their legal and regulatory knowledge and skills. The team undertakes a wide range of specialist assignments for lawyers, insurers, loss adjusters, professional and regulatory bodies and government agencies, acting for either defendants or claimants. Civil and criminal assignments undertaken, including legally aided cases.

Litigation Support Partners
Emile Woolf FCA, FCCA, MAE, FInstM, FIIA. Has for many years been Chairman of the Professional Indemnity Insurance Panel of the Institute of Chartered Accountants in England and Wales (ICAEW) and represents the Institute on the Joint Advisory Panel of Participating Insurers, of which he is Chairman. Is widely known throughout the profession for his lectures and frequent contributions to the professional press on litigation issues. He is the author of several leading texts including *Professional Liability of Accountants* (ICAEW), *Risk Management for Auditors* (ICAEW), *Preserving Your Right to Audit* (CCH Editions), *Auditing Today* (Prentice Hall), *Emile Woolf on Audit Exemption* (CCH Editions), and *The Legal Liabilities of Practising Accountants* (Butterworths). He is a member of the Academy of Experts and is a CEDR-accredited mediator. He was the founder in 1975 of one of the largest listed accountancy training groups in the UK.
Moira Hindson BA, ACA. Is in the Litigation Support and Dispute Resolution department of Kingston Smith. Over the past 12 years has been involved in a wide range of litigation support work, including professional negligence cases involving auditors and accountants, business interruption, loss of profits and breach of contract. Has been instructed to act as expert accountant in a number of cases involving the quantification of lost earnings, lost pensions and other benefits arising as a consequence of personal injury and medical negligence. Has also acted as expert in a defamation action and in matrimonial proceedings.
Peter Holgate FCA, MSI, TEP. Is a member of Kingston Smith's forensic accountancy and litigation services team and has undertaken or assisted on a wide range of assignments including: expert witness and forensic reporting work in civil liability cases involving professional negligence of auditors and other professionals, with special emphasis on technical tax issues; assisting individuals and firms in establishing a defence following complaints by professional bodies and clients in respect of offences, including misconduct and criminal defence issues; measurement of loss and damage in commercial cases arising from breach of contract; reports for solicitors in matrimonial cases; business and share valuation reports; acting as expert in a variety of assignments involving fee disputes, technical accounting and tax issues. Is an elected member of the Council of the Institute of Chartered Accountants in England and Wales (ICAEW) and has been a member of its Investigation Committee.
Adrian Houstoun FCA, ACIArb. Is a Chartered Accountant and a member of the Chartered Institute of Arbitrators. Specialises in matters where knowledge of the law of contract, tort and evidence can be combined with extensive business experience, including public company acquisitions and VAT services.

ACCOUNTANTS ■ SUPPORT SERVICES

Litigation Support Services Include professional negligence, consequential loss and business interruption including personal injury. Matrimonial, white collar crime, fraud, regulatory and compliance matters including directors' disqualification. Commercial disputes, breach of contract and defamation. Forensic accounting including fraud investigations, asset tracing, modelling in insurance and commercial cases. Inland Revenue and Customs investigations, settlements and related disputes. Business and share valuations. Sectors include financial and investment business. Specialist insolvency division.

KPMG Forensic

20 Farringdon Street, London, EC4A 4PP
Tel (020) 7311 1000   **Fax** (020) 7311 3672
Website www.kpmg.co.uk

Contacts	
Expert Witness	Nick Andrews
Fraud Investigations	Alex Plavsic
Fraud Risk Management	David Davies
Regulatory Investigations	Karen Briggs
Birmingham	David Alexander (0121) 232 3000
Edinburgh	Judith Scott (0131) 527 6619
Manchester	Richard Powell (0161) 838 4000
Reading	Yvonne Craggs (0117) 905 4000

THE FIRM KPMG Forensic is a member of KPMG's international Forensic network of over 300 partners and staff providing forensic advice and services worldwide. KPMG is the global network of professional services firms whose aim is to turn understanding of information, industries and business trends into value. With more than 100,000 people worldwide, KPMG member firms provide assurance, tax and legal, financial advisory and consulting services from more than 750 cities in 152 countries.

Litigation Support Services KPMG Forensic has a dedicated team of more than 150 partners and professional staff throughout the UK, and a global co-ordinated forensic service. The provision of these services is enhanced by expert knowledge of various industry sectors including banking; insurance; commodities; information technology; telecommunications; shipping and transportation; construction; manufacturing; oil and gas; infrastructure and government; leasing; retailing; healthcare and pharmaceutical; intellectual property. The firm provides specialist services in seven broad areas:
Commercial Disputes Loss of profits claims; international and national arbitrations; breach of contract and warranty claims; purchase and sale disputes and agreement vetting; shareholder and partnership disputes; libel and slander actions; intellectual property; e-business disputes; business and share valuations; insurance claims; security for costs applications.
Professional Negligence Accounting; auditing; corporate finance and IT implementation (liability and quantum); other professions (quantum).
Fraud Investigation KPMG Forensic has developed particular expertise in handling investigations into fraud. Numerous assignments for government, police, companies and public bodies bear witness to the firm's reputation in this area. The firm uses a refined investigation methodology which, when combined with advanced technology, allows KPMG Forensic to investigate suspected frauds of all sizes effectively and efficiently.
Fraud Risk Management Including fraud risk profiling; procurement diagnostic review; manipulation diagnostic review (including assessing e-business risk); fraud response planning and fraud awareness training.
Personal Disputes Personal injury claims; fatal accidents; clinical negligence; family and matrimonial disputes; employment; pension disputes.
Regulatory Investigations Investigations and accounting assistance for regulatory authorities and those under investigation. Also assistance in statutory and disciplinary enquiries.
Determinations & Arbitrations Expert determinations; arbitrations; mediations; valuations.

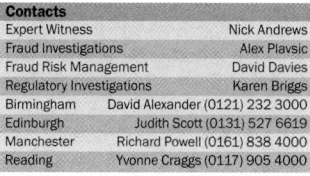

SUPPORT SERVICES ■ ACCOUNTANTS

Littlejohn Frazer

1 Park Place, Canary Wharf, London, E14 4HJ
Tel (020) 7987 5030 **Fax** (020) 7987 9707 **DX** 42660
Email info@littlejohnfrazer.com **Website** www.littlejohnfrazer.com

Contact Partner	Ian Hobbs
Number of partners	19
Number of staff	120

THE FIRM Partners at Littlejohn Frazer now have over 15 years' experience of providing litigation support services to the legal profession. Of the firm's 23 partners, 12 have relevant experience and the lead partners (Ian Hobbs and Alastair Campbell) have considerable experience of justifying their expert opinions in the witness box. Ian Hobbs is the co-author of *Expert Accounting Evidence – A Guide for Litigation Support* published by the ICAEW in 1998. Lord Woolf wrote the preface and said: "*I welcome the publication of this book and congratulate the authors on a job well done. I do so, because while I welcome the greater involvement of accountants in the court process, this welcome is conditional. It is conditional on the involvement being constructive. It can only be constructive if the involvement is knowledgeable and proportionate. Unfortunately, sometimes it is not and this is all too often due to ignorance or a lack of professionalism for which this book provides the remedy. The authors rightly stress the need to keep costs under control and echo the messages which are contained in my report in Access to Justice...* Partners have experience of investigations for the DTI, and the firm has undertaken a number of assignments for the Serious Fraud Office. Legally aided work is undertaken, in both civil and criminal matters. The firm has extensive experience of the insurance sector and in particular the Lloyd's market.

LITTLEJOHN FRAZER
CHARTERED ACCOUNTANTS

Litigation Support Partners
I.C. Hobbs (FCA) Member of Academy of Experts; CEDR Accredited Mediator. Specialises in accountants' negligence; quantification of loss, particularly consequential loss in construction disputes and fire claims; share valuations; tax as a non-specialist; serious fraud; personal injury; matrimonial.
A.H.F. Campbell (FCA) Serious fraud, regulatory, Lloyd's, accountants' negligence, breach of financial warranties.
R.L. Green (FCCA) Solicitors' Accounts Rules.
D.R.M. Frame (FCA) Serious fraud, forensic.
M.T. Stenson (FCA) Serious fraud, regulatory.
D.W. Roberts (FCA) Regulatory, Lloyd's.

Litigation Support Services
Civil Accountants professional negligence; financial consequences of: personal injury; consequential loss, particularly in construction and fire-damage claims; insurance and re-insurance disputes; purchase and sales disputes; matrimonial disputes; intellectual property disputes. Experience as single joint expert.
Criminal Serious fraud; crime with financial motive; Companies Act offences.
Investigations Computer consultancy; forensic accounting.
Regulatory ICAEW; FSA; Law Society; RICS; DTI; SFO; Lloyd's.
ADR Mediations as expert and as mediator.

Martin Greene Ravden

55 Loudoun Road, St. Johns Wood, London, NW8 0DL
Tel (020) 7625 4545 **Fax** (020) 7625 5265
Email mgr@mgr.co.uk **Website** www.mgr.co.uk

Contact Partners	
	David Greene
	David Ravden
	Robert Braham

THE FIRM Martin Greene Ravden is a medium-size firm of chartered accountants with 10 partners and over 70 staff. It represents a broad range of clients and is best known as one of the leading specialists in the media, entertainment and sports industries. The firm has a highly experienced forensic accounting and litigation support group, with an excellent track record in helping solicitors achieve very favourable results in contentious cases.

Litigation Support Services
Matrimonial Disputes Valuation of businesses and shares in private companies; investigating the completeness of disclosures; clarifying income and capital positions; assessment of income requirement; tax efficient structuring of settlements.
Commercial Disputes Entertainment industry and intellectual property disputes; quantification of loss in commercial disputes and claims for damages; shareholder and partnership disputes; claims for consequential loss and loss of earnings; fraud investigations.

ACCOUNTANTS ■ SUPPORT SERVICES

Mazars

24 Bevis Marks, London, EC3A 7NR
Tel (020) 7377 1000 **Fax** (020) 7377 8931
Email peter.hyatt@mazars.co.uk **Website** www.mazars.co.uk

THE FIRM Mazars is an international firm delivering high quality professional accounting and advisory services across the world. Mazars has a team of dedicated forensic and investigation specialists with extensive experience in providing evidence in court and arbitration proceedings, both in the UK and overseas. In addition to bringing all the resources that might be expected from an international firm, the emphasis of the service is on ensuring work is undertaken on a timely, effective and efficient basis. This is achieved through a high level of proactive contribution and personal partner involvement at all stages. The firm is among the top 10 firms (by size) of accountants and business advisors in most European countries. It operates in 24 countries in Europe and in 51 countries worldwide. Services offered include forensic and investigation, corporate finance, corporate recovery, tax, audit and consultancy. The partners in the firm have extensive experience in a wide number of business sectors including insurance, government, regulators, education, housing, and in the large corporate and large OMB market place.

Contacts Partners	
London	Gly Williams
	Peter Hyatt
	Paul Smethurst
	Philip Chamberlain
Midlands	Nigel Grummitt
North	Alastair Smith
South	Graham Platts
Number of partners	90
Number of staff	1,000

Moore Stephens

St Paul's House, Warwick Lane, London, EC4P 4BN
Tel (020) 7334 9211 **Fax** (020) 7248 3408 **DX** 15 London
Email postmaster@moorestephens.com **Website** www.moorestephens.co.uk

Litigation Support Partners
Julian Wilkinson FCA, MAE Shipping-related matters including alleged scuttling claims and joint venture disputes and also loss of profits and other commercial and contractual disputes. Has given evidence in Court in UK and overseas.
Charles Lazarevic BSc, MBA, FCA, MAE Most types of commercial and contractual disputes, forensic investigations, individual and family disputes and valuations. Has acted as single joint expert and given evidence in Court in UK and overseas.
James A Smart FCA Non-life insurance and reinsurance business. Has conducted confidential inquiries, reviews and investigations for regulators and others and acts as expert in insurance and reinsurance related litigation. Has given evidence in Court in UK.
Phillip Sykes MA, ACA Corporate recovery, insolvency and fraud investigation. Has acted for the Fraud Squad and for defendants. Directors' disqualification proceedings and wrongful and fraudulent trading actions.

Litigation Support Services
Commercial & Contractual Business interruption, loss of profits, business and share valuations, professional negligence, breach of warranty claims, disputes over royalties, expert determinations, mediations and ADR and appointments as arbitrator.
Forensic Investigations Fraud, tax investigations, FSA, DTI and other regulatory investigations, money laundering, conduct of directors and asset tracing.
Individual & Family Disputes Personal injury and fatal accident claims, medical negligence, matrimonial disputes and libel claims
Valuations Business valuations, partnership disputes, security for costs and share valuation disputes

Contact Partners	
	Julian Wilkinson
	Charles Lazarevic
Number of partners	144
Number of staff	1,238

SUPPORT SERVICES ■ ACCOUNTANTS

Morley and Scott

Lynton House, 7-12 Tavistock Square, London, WC1H 9LT
Tel (020) 7387 5868   **Fax** (020) 7388 3978   **DX** 2112 Euston
Email ms@morley-scott.co.uk   **Website** www.morley-scott.co.uk

THE FIRM Morley & Scott is a medium-sized firm of chartered accountants providing an outstanding service that is both highly professional and highly personal, to an impressive list of corporate and private clients in the South East of England. It is dedicated to delivering the highest level of professional competence and expertise, and knows that the basic key to achieving this is personal client relationship. The firm has links internationally through the GMN network.

Litigation Support Partners
Kay Linnell (FCA, MBA) Member of the Expert Witness Institute, a certified fraud examiner, a member of the ICAEW London Police Liaison Panel, fellow of the Chartered Institute of Arbitrators, a liveryman of the Worshipful Company of Arbitrators and CEDR accredited mediator. Before joining Morley & Scott, she was head of the Joint Insolvency Monitoring Unit at the DTI and also an advisor in the Special Compliance Office at the Inland Revenue. She is the author of Tolley's Tax Appeals (published 2001) and co-author of Tolley's Accountancy Litigation Support (published since 1998).
Simon Howard (FCCA) Member of the Expert Witness Institute.

Contacts	
Contact Partners	Kay Linnell
	Simon Howard
London	Malcolm Bolton, John Clay
	Gerry Collins, Stuart Cumberland
	Taha Dharsi, Geoff Elwell
	Philip King, Kay Linnell
	Kathryn Moran, Martin Payne
	Vanessa Rush, Stanley Salter
	Dick Watson
Portsmouth	Bill Arnold, Adrian Price
	Andrew Sainsbury
TVO	Stephen Garland, Linda Richardson
Winchester	Alistair Cole, Simon Howard
Number of partners	20
Number of staff	135

Numerica Forensic Accounting & Dispute Resolution Ltd, A Division of The Numerica Group plc

66 Wigmore Street, London, W1U 2HQ
Tel (020) 7467 4000   **Fax** (020) 7467 4040
Email investigations@numerica.biz   **Website** www.numerica.biz

THE FIRM Numerica Forensic Accounting & Dispute Resolution Ltd comprises the former forensic accounting and dispute resolution practices of Levy Gee, NMGW, Pole Arnold and Burnett Swayne, creating an enhanced national team of specialists operating from offices in London, Birmingham, Bristol, Leicester, Manchester and Southampton. The team comprises dedicated experts and advisors who assist the legal profession, insurers, regulatory and prosecuting bodies in the pursuance and defence of claims by providing expert opinions in the quantum of loss.

Litigation Support Services The team comprises specialists who can advise on breach of warranty claims; business interruption and consequential loss claims; contractual disputes; due diligence; family and matrimonial disputes; fraud investigations; personal injury and clinical negligence claim; professional negligence claims; shareholder and partnership disputes and share valuations. The directors have considerable experience of giving evidence in Court in both civil and criminal proceedings. In addition the directors accept appoints in the areas of arbitration, mediation and expert determination.

Contacts	
London (020) 7467 4000	David Epstein
London (020) 7467 4000	David Stern
London (020) 7467 4000	Gail Rifkind
Birmingham (0121) 456 2525	Alan Thompson
Bristol (0117) 927 7702	David Cook
Leicester (0116) 272 8200	Ian Monk
Manchester (0161) 833 8300	David Rabinowitz
Southampton (023) 8070 2345	Mike Mason
Number of directors nationwide	91
Number of staff nationwide	462

Peter Lobbenberg & Co

74 Chancery Lane, London, WC2A 1AD
Tel (020) 7430 9300   **Fax** (020) 7430 9315   **DX** 204 London/Chancery Lane

THE FIRM A niche practice well known as specialists in matrimonial litigation support throughout the country; its clients include over 80% of the leading London family law firms listed in Chambers. The firm also specialises in share valuations, and operates a caring tax service for private clients and trusts. As a member of Horwath Clark Whitehill Associates, the firm has access to a wide range of facilities and specialisms. The contact partner is a Fellow of the Academy of Experts.

International Work is handled in German and French.

Contact Partner	Peter Lobbenberg
Number of partners	1
Number of staff	2

ACCOUNTANTS ■ SUPPORT SERVICES

Pinders Professional & Consultancy Services Limited

Pinder House, Central Milton Keynes, MK9 1DS
Tel (01908) 350500 **Fax** (01908) 350501 **DX** 84752 Milton Keynes 3
Email pcs@pinders.co.uk **Website** www.pinders.co.uk

Contacts
Contact Director	Mark Ellis BSc FRICS MCIArb MAE
Directors	Jon Chapman BA Hons QDR
	Simon Bird BSc ARICS MCIArb
Senior Chartered Surveyor	Graham Coulter FRICS
Consultants	Marek Bilecki FRICS
	Justin Cain MRICS
Senior Chartered Building Surveyor	
	Ray Chamberlain ARICS

THE FIRM The Pinders name has become synonymous with the appraisal and valuation of businesses since 1969, providing specialist professional services to the legal and banking professions on the healthcare, retail, licensed and leisure sectors. Particular areas of expertise include business valuations (both current and retrospective), loss of profits claims, expert witness evidence and professional negligence. Pinders can call upon a database containing detailed trading and valuation information on over 160,000 businesses throughout the United Kingdom, together with continually updated records of sale transactions.

Litigation Support Partners

Mark Ellis (BSc FRICS MCIArb MAE), previously a member of The RICS Skills Panel on Trading Related Valuations, heads up the professional services and litigation support team based at the head office in Milton Keynes and a team of regional valuers who combine knowledge of local values, trade sources, legislation and competition with the wider accumulation of centralised information and expertise. The team includes a QDR and Arbitrators.

PKF

New Garden House, 78 Hatton Garden, London, EC1N 8JA
Tel (020) 7831 7393 **Fax** (020) 7405 6736 **DX** 479 Chancery Lane
Email forename.surname@uk.pkf.com **Website** www.pkf.co.uk

Contacts
London	(020) 7831 7393
	Richard Bolton, Roger Claxton
	Hugh Mathew-Jones, Nick Whitaker
Birmingham	David Liddell (0121) 212 2222
Edinburgh	Jim Riddell (0131) 225 3688
Glasgow	Frank Paterson (0141) 429 5900
Great Yarmouth	Jon Dodge (01493) 842281
Guildford	Valerie Martin (01483) 564646
Ipswich	Marilyn Martin (01473) 217691
Leicester	Tim Aspell (0116) 250 4400
Leeds	Liesel Annible (0113) 228 0000
Lincoln	Jeff Kirkham (01522) 531441
Liverpool	Mark Fairhurst (0151) 708 8232
Manchester	John Grogan (0161) 832 5481
Norwich	Roger Walton (01603) 615914
Nottingham	Simon Bold (0115) 960 8171
Sheffield	Jeremy Lai (0114) 276 7991
Worcester	Mick Maton (01905) 24437
Number of partners	113
Number of staff	1,414

THE FIRM PKF is an international grouping with offices in 94 countries. The UK firm of accountants and business advisors was established in 1869 and offers the full range of corporate finance, business advisory, risk management, assurance and taxation skills together with important specialisms such as the international management consultancy and the hotels division. The nationally organised forensic services group provides a partner led service, backed by experienced professional staff with a grounding in commercial and professional life.

Litigation Support Services The PKF approach to helping clients extends throughout the practice. Multidisciplinary teams can be assembled to handle the largest corporate actions. Those consulting PKF's forensic accounting section can rely on careful analysis of the issues and clear presentation of the findings by experts in the particular area concerned. PKF gives timely and positive advice whether as advisors or as independent experts.

Forensic Work Work undertaken includes the quantifying of: breach of contract and warranty claims; commercial business interruption and consequential loss claims; loss of profit from public or product liability issues; reinsurance claims; third party damage and other financial loss claims; professional negligence; personal injury, dependency and clinical negligence claims. Many of these involve valuations of businesses or shares of businesses. PKF also has a specialist fraud unit able to respond quickly and appropriately and conduct sensitive investigations. PKF forensic accountants are experienced in providing evidence across the spectrum of the Courts and in various arbitral tribunals. PKF assists clients in their mediation and other ADR endeavours.

SUPPORT SERVICES ■ ACCOUNTANTS

PricewaterhouseCoopers

Plumtree Court, London, EC4A 4HT
Tel (020) 7583 5000 **Fax** (020) 7212 4863
Website www.pwcglobal.com/uk/forensics

Contacts	
London	
(020) 7583 5000	Chris Lemar
	(Head of Forensic Services)
Birmingham	
(0121) 265 5000	Tony Parton
Leeds	
(0113) 289 4000	Andrew Palmer
Manchester	
(0161) 245 2000	Simon Cuerden
Edinburgh	
(0131) 226 4488	Peter Graham
Belfast	
(028) 90 245454	Paul Kinney
Channel Islands	
(01534) 602000	Peter Feeney

THE FIRM The firm's forensic specialists provide solutions and support for clients throughout Europe. The firm provides expert evidence and advice in legal proceedings and the firm's investigators provide a unique approach incorporating the use of forensic technology. Time and again Pricewaterhouse-Coopers' expertise has made a real difference in the outcome of an investigation, claim or dispute.

LITIGATION SUPPORT SERVICES Specialists have experience in many areas including commercial, acquisition and shareholder, construction and intellectual property disputes. Services offered, amongst others, are forensic accounting/financial investigations, litigation and arbitration support, expert witness services, forensic due diligence, construction audit, dispute prevention, project management oversight, account of profit, copyright tribunal disputes, IP valuation disputes and licence right of actions.
Insurance Claims Services The firm's insurance specialists have expertise in property, loss of profits and liability insurance amongst others, combined with key industry sector knowledge the firm can help management achieve effective claims handling solutions.
Corporate Investigations The investigations team conducts fraud, corruption and regulatory investigations and advises on fraud risk management and business ethics matters.
Financial Services Investigations & Computer Forensics The firm's specialists carry out investigations into, amongst others, fraud, impropriety, regulatory compliance, money laundering and cybercrime. In addition computer investigations and data capture services are offered.
Licensing Advisory Services Services offered include management of licensing agreements, negotiation and litigation consulting services on royalty related issues, contract disputes and anti-trust matters.
Industry Expertise Forensic Services has a strong focus on industry specialisation and the firm has experts in the fields of automotive, financial services, energy, mining, pharmaceuticals, retail, manufacturing, technology, government, telecommunications, entertainment and media.

Quintana & Lewis Ltd

78 Cannon Street, London, EC4N 6NQ
Tel (020) 7618 8475 **Fax** (020) 7618 8161
Email edward.rossmacnairn@qandl.com **Fax** www.qandl.com

Contact	Edward Ross-McNairn

THE FIRM Quintana & Lewis Ltd is the UK arm of Quintana & Lewis LLP, an international accounting and consultancy group. The forensic accounting group undertakes a wide range of assignments for lawyers, insurers, loss adjusters and professional bodies, in the areas of commercial litigation, medical and professional negligence, criminal litigation and fraud, partnership disputes, insurance, share valuations, fatal accidents claims, forensic accountancy and regulatory investigations. The emphasis of the service is to provide objective practical cost-effective advice.

ACCOUNTANTS ■ SUPPORT SERVICES

RGL – Forensic Accountants and Consultants

17 Devonshire Square, London, EC2M 4SQ
Tel (020) 7247 4804   **Fax** (020) 7247 4970
Email expert@rgl.com   **Website** www.rgl.com

Contact Partners	
	Anthony Levitt
	Edward Leighton
	Keith Tuffin
	Catherine Rawlin
	James Stanbury

THE FIRM RGL is a worldwide firm of Forensic Accountants and Consultants. They quantify claims in insurance and litigation, determine business value and advise on related issues. They establish the true facts and the correct figures, wherever they are hidden and whatever is being claimed. They assist lawyers in disputes, both in settling them before they go to court, and in providing expert testimony in court. They help with pre-trial conferences, meetings of experts, provide accounting support and give specialist evidence as expert witnesses. RGL's forensic accountants are fully conversant with the Rules of Civil Procedure issued by the Lord Chancellor's Department. They can identify exactly which documents should be made available for discovery, whether internal or external. The high quality reports they provide for use in litigation or negotiations identify a claim's strengths and weaknesses and draw attention to any errors or omissions. In court, RGL's forensic accountants can clearly and succinctly explain evidence included in the accounting expert's report, both under examination-in-chief and cross-examination. Areas of expertise include: business interruption and loss of profits; stock losses; product liability; fatal accident and personal injury; commercial litigation; fraud; breach of contract; third party disputes; insurance claims; reinsurance disputes; subrogation; general quantification of damages. As a specialist firm, RGL very seldom has a conflict of interest, always dedicates a partner and team to every investigation, ensures fees are cost-effective and reasonable and utilises expertise from its forensic accountants worldwide.
Offices Atlanta, Charlotte, Chicago, Denver, Indianapolis, London, Los Angeles, Nashville, New York, Orange County, Orlando, Portland, Sacramento, St Louis, Salt Lake City, San Diego, San Francisco, Seattle, Sydney, Tokyo

Saffery Champness

Lion House, Red Lion Street, London, WC1R 4GB
Tel (020) 7841 4000   **Fax** (020) 7841 4100   **DX** 287-Chancery Lane, London
Email info@saffery.com   **Website** www.saffery.com

THE FIRM The Saffery Champness litigation team works with lawyers throughout the country on a wide variety of cases. As accountants and business advisors, the firm's expertise in and understanding of the business environment means that it can offer valuable forensic accounting advice. The team includes partners Stewart Garrard, David Macey and Nick Kelsey for general financial issues, Peter Horsman, Jason Lane and Clare Cromwell for matrimonial and tax issues and Mike Di Leto for share valuations. Saffery Champness is a top twenty accountancy practice with nine offices in the UK and one in Guernsey. The firm has over a century's experience of advising private clients, business owners, their businesses and landed estates and their owners.

Litigation Support Services Areas covered include e-commerce related business and taxation issues; personal injury and fatal accident; matrimonial issues; medical negligence; loss of profits or earnings; professional negligence; valuation of shares and businesses; fraud; Inland Revenue and Customs & Excise investigations.

Smith & Williamson

No 1 Riding House Street, London, W1A 3AS
Tel (020) 7637 5237   **Fax** (020) 7631 07410
Email <recipient>@williamson.co.uk   **Website** www.smith.williamson.co.uk

Contact Partners	
	Douglas J Hall
	Iain J Allan
	Frank A M Akers-Douglas
Number of partners	130
Number of staff	160

THE FIRM Smith & Williamson combines a firm of chartered accountants and an investment management house. Its full range of accountancy services covers accountancy, auditing, corporate finance, corporate recovery, corporate taxation, investigations, litigation support and personal taxation.

Litigation Support Services Smith & Williamson has a dedicated litigation support team whose expertise covers the full range of forensic accounting, including assistance for regulatory bodies, civil litigation, investigations of fraud and personal injury. The firm has experience in acting for either the claimant or the defendant and its objective is always to understand the wider implications of a case in order to provide a flexible and constructive approach to every assignment.

▼ CONSULTANTS

Grandfield

69 Wilson Street, London, EC2A 2BB
Tel (020) 7417 4170 **Fax** (020) 7417 9180
Email enquiries@grandfield.com **Website** www.grandfield.com

Contact Directors
Paul Jaffa
Clare Abbot

THE FIRM Grandfield is an independent corporate communications consultancy and one of the UK's leading public relations specialists advising the professional services sector. The firm's work also encompasses corporate and financial public relations, analyst and investor relations, professional and financial services, PR and marketing, and e-commerce. Grandfield has a specialist team dedicated to advising legal and professional clients, creating communications strategies to manage profile and reputation whilst supporting and adding value to business development activities. The team includes former lawyers, accountants, business managers, journalists, analysts and in-house marketing and communications experts. This experience produces exceptional results linked directly to clients' business objectives. The firm acts for major law firms in the UK, US and Europe, as well as leading professional firms in accountancy, surveying, management consultancy, recruitment and insurance. Grandfield's services include corporate positioning; crisis and issues management; marketing and business development strategies; media relations planning and execution; mergers and acquisitions; communications; opinion research audits; strategic and tactical advice; interview and presentation training; and website and internet communications analysis.

INTERNATIONAL Grandfield is a founder member of Advisor Group, an international alliance of independent communication consultancies in leading commercial centres throughout Europe, with established links across the US and the Far East.

Litigation Support Services Grandfield has a dedicated litigation support unit and has extensive experience in creating communications strategies to support high profile legal actions in the UK and worldwide. Pre-trial support includes the development of key messages, communications planning, reputation management and media training; whilst support at trial includes the provision of offline and online press office services, media monitoring, evaluation, perceptions research and post-trial review.

Lehmann Communications plc

Lloyds Avenue House, 6 Lloyds Avenue, London, EC3N 3EH
Tel (020) 7266 3020 **Fax** (020) 7266 3060
Email pr@lehmanncommunications.com
Website www.lehmanncommunications.com

Contacts
Chief Executive — Ronel Lehmann MIPR
Corporate & Financial — Adrian Lithgow MIPR
Account Manager — Darshna Patel
Consumer — Anthony Poppleton MIPR
Business Development — Grenville Burn MIPR
James Meek
Kevin Hibbert

THE FIRM International agency Lehmann Communications is one of the City's most experienced legal services PR consultancies. The firm is a full service consultancy resourced to provide the best people offering the highest levels of service with clear, innovative, imaginative thinking across the whole spectrum of communications. Since the firm's foundation in 1988 its professional services division has raised the profile of some of the leading firms in Britain and has been at the forefront of the wave of American firms establishing themselves in London and Europe. As well as working for leading solicitors and barristers the firm is strongly established in the corporate and financial sectors where it acts for accountants, banks and fund managers, insurance brokers, management and recruitment consultants and technology businesses. The firm's account directors include senior journalists on national newspapers and entrepreneurial marketing specialists who together bring a unique focus to the way the firm operates its clients' accounts.

International The firm also has an office at 730 Fifth Avenue, New York, NY 10019, USA. Tel +1 212 333 8780 Fax +1 212 307 3221.

Litigation Support Partners The firm considers its staff and their expertise to be its greatest asset and its best resource. The firm continually invests in recruiting and training people to provide leading edge thinking and advice. The firm focuses on developing long-term relationships with its clients and most fall into this category even if it is instructed on a project basis. The firm invests time and effort in getting to know clients' organisations and their culture.

CONSULTANTS/INVESTIGATORS ■ SUPPORT SERVICES

Litigation Support Services The firm's services include public relations advice and implementation; public affairs, political and parliamentary consultancy; design and print management; advertising and copywriting; new business presentation; media training; project and event management; sponsorship; crisis management; internal communications; website and e-commerce development. The firm provides comprehensive marketing and public relations strategy for law firms; implements energetic media relations programmes; takes pride in understanding partners' practice areas; takes pride in the firm's knowledge of the legal press; projects legal clients to a wide range of prospects through the press they read; uses new technology to create innovative round table events; develops a proprietary media management system for clients; regularly positions clients as commentators on breaking news; acts for many US law firms who have moved into the London market; launches offices and new practices for City and regional firms; represents law firms during mergers and takeovers; sponsors a major legal award. The firm is respected for the work it produces on behalf of leading law firms. The firm is the number one legal services PR specialist in London.

Other Areas of Work Work handled: accountancy 10%; charity 5%; finance 25%; insurance 10%; law 25%; technology 15%; recruitment 5%; property 5%.

▼INVESTIGATORS

1st Call Investigations

27 Old Gloucester Street, London, WC1N 3XX
Tel (020) 7531 6666   **Fax** (020) 7987 1625
Email sebastiancrispin@yahoo.co.uk   **Website** www.privatedetectiveslondon.co.uk

Contacts	
	Sebastian Crispin
	Marcus Adams
	Sarah Henderson
Number of staff	21

THE FIRM 1st Call Private Investigations was founded in 1986 and has a vast wealth of experience in dealing with all aspects of surveillance and private investigation throughout the UK and overseas. The firm operates a 24 hour control room and same-day response service for legal firms. The firm has four offices with a network of local agents in the UK and experienced and fully trained staff use the latest digital technology and equipment for hi-tech surveillance and covert filming and also counter surveillance/de-bugging work. Overseas agents are supervised from the firm's control room (near Canary Wharf).

Litigation Support Services All types of investigation dealing with criminal and civil cases, matrimonial matters, tracing witnesses and assets/shares/liabilities. Investigation of property transactions and development projects. Acquisitions, mergers and takeovers. Corporate and professional conflict matters. Due diligence, intellectual property, corporate governance, counter surveillance, undercover work. Crisis management, security consulting work. Electronic sweeps using latest de-bugging equipment. Sale and hire of surveillance and monitoring equipment for commercial/domestic cases. Detailed management schemes, plans and staff-watch assignments prepared and monitored. Accident/disability/sickness, compensation claims verified. Employment and pilfering, fraud and deception enquiries. Staff screening and CV verification, checking of public record information. Company/business enquiries. Contract issues, breach of contract/damages. Family, custody and maintenance matters. Domestic violence, blackmail and libel cases. Wills, oaths and probate enquiries. Property issues, insurance matters/fraudulent claims verified. Tracing of witnesses, beneficiaries, debt recovery; information gathering. Anti-stalking and protection situations. VIP/celebrities service with secure chauffeurs. Initial consultation 24 hour on (020) 7531 6666 or faxed enquiries on (020) 7987 1625.

SUPPORT SERVICES ■ INVESTIGATORS

CLB

Aldwych House, 81 Aldwych, London, WC2B 4HP
Tel (020) 7242 2444   **Fax** (020) 7242 1117
Email info@clb.co.uk   **Website** www.clb.co.uk

Contact Partners
Mark Ling (London)
Mike Garratt (Bolton)

14 Wood Street, Bolton, BL1 1DZ
Tel (01204) 531573   **Fax** (01204) 361552
Email bolton@clb.co.uk

THE FIRM CLB has provided support to the legal profession for over 120 years. The CLB legal support team produces reports that are clear, comprehensive, detailed and accurate. Confident in their investigative abilities, senior members of the team are comfortable appearing in court to defend a client's interests. As one of the UK's larger firms of chartered accountants, CLB serves the needs of clients and legal professionals throughout the country. CLB is active in one of the top global networks of independent accountancy firms, Polaris International. CLB can, therefore, deal with disputes on an international level, drawing on the expertise of their affiliates around the world – accountants whom they know and trust.

Other Offices The firm has other offices in Lancaster, Manchester, Reigate and Sheffield.

THE BAR

CHAMBERS
UK
2002–2003

STARS AT THE BAR

This section is devoted to those members of the Bar who have been ranked in five sections or more in this year's *Chambers Guide*. Omitting, as it does, those practitioners who display their prowess in a single discipline, it does not purport to be a definitive rundown of the top performers. From the most battle-hardened silk to those juniors who are superstars of the future, these are some of the most prolific and well-respected faces at today's Bar.

STARS AT THE BAR (ranked in 5 or more sections of this book)

1 RANKED IN 9 AREAS

Michael Briggs QC - *Serle Court*
Banking & Finance (5); Chancery: Commercial (1); Chancery: Traditional (1); Commercial (Litigation) (1); Company (2); Financial Services (2); Fraud: Civil (3); Insolvency/Corporate Recovery (5); Partnership (1); Professional Negligence (3).

2 RANKED IN 8 AREAS

Gordon Pollock QC - *Essex Court Chambers*
Arbitration (International) (1); Banking & Finance (2); Commercial (Litigation) (*); Energy & Natural Resources (*); Fraud: Civil (3); Insurance (2); Media & Entertainment (1); Shipping (1).

Jonathan Sumption QC - *Brick Court Chambers*
Administrative & Public Law: General (1); Banking & Finance (1); Commercial (Litigation) (*); Energy & Natural Resources (*); Financial Services (1); Fraud: Civil (2); Insurance (1); Professional Negligence (1).

3 RANKED IN 6 AREAS

Christopher Butcher QC - *7 King's Bench Walk*
Arbitration (International) (4); Banking & Finance (5); Commercial (Litigation) (5); Insurance (3); Professional Negligence (4); Shipping (s).

Elizabeth Gloster QC - *One Essex Court*
Chancery: Commercial (1); Commercial (Litigation) (1); Company (2); Energy & Natural Resources (2); Fraud: Civil (3); Insolvency/Corporate Recovery (1).

Joe Smouha - *Essex Court Chambers*
Arbitration (International) (2); Banking & Finance (3); Commercial (Litigation) (*); Fraud: Civil (2); Shipping (4); Tax: Indirect Tax (VAT, Customs & Excise, Stamp Duty) (2).

Bankim Thanki - *Fountain Court*
Aviation (2); Banking & Finance (1); Commercial (Litigation) (1); Fraud: Civil (1); Professional Negligence (1); Sport (2).

4 RANKED IN 5 AREAS

Mark Barnes QC - *One Essex Court*
Arbitration (International) (3); Banking & Finance (5); Commercial (Litigation) (2); Energy & Natural Resources (1); Fraud: Civil (4).

Anthony Boswood QC - *Fountain Court*
Banking & Finance (3); Commercial (Litigation) (1); Energy & Natural Resources (2); Fraud: Civil (3); Insurance (3).

Michael Brindle QC - *Fountain Court*
Banking & Finance (*); Commercial (Litigation) (1); Financial Services (2); Fraud: Civil (1); Professional Negligence (1).

John Brisby QC - *4 Stone Buildings*
Chancery: Commercial (3); Company (3); Financial Services (3); Fraud: Civil (4); Insolvency/Corporate Recovery (5).

Robin Dicker QC - *3-4 South Square*
Banking & Finance (3); Company (3); Energy & Natural Resources (3); Fraud: Civil (s); Insolvency/Corporate Recovery (2).

Barbara Dohmann QC - *Blackstone Chambers*
Commercial (Litigation) (1); Financial Services (2); Fraud: Civil (3); Insurance (3); Media & Entertainment (3).

Charles Flint QC - *Blackstone Chambers*
Administrative & Public Law: General (2); Commercial (Litigation) (4); Financial Services (1); Fraud: Civil (1); Sport (2).

Anthony Grabiner QC - *One Essex Court*
Arbitration (International) (1); Banking & Finance (2); Commercial (Litigation) (*); Energy & Natural Resources (*); Fraud: Civil (2).

Robert Hildyard QC - *4 Stone Buildings*
Chancery: Commercial (2); Company (2); Energy & Natural Resources (3); Financial Services (3); Insurance (3).

Mark Howard QC - *Brick Court Chambers*
Banking & Finance (2); Commercial (Litigation) (1); Energy & Natural Resources (3); Insurance (2); Professional Negligence (3).

Anthony Mann QC - *Enterprise Chambers*
Chancery: Commercial (2); Commercial (Litigation) (5); Company (4); Insolvency/Corporate Recovery (1); Professional Negligence (4).

Robert Miles QC - *4 Stone Buildings*
Banking & Finance (s); Chancery: Commercial (s); Company (s); Energy & Natural Resources (s); Insolvency/Corporate Recovery (s).

Richard Millett - *Essex Court Chambers*
Arbitration (International) (4); Banking & Finance (2); Commercial (Litigation) (4); Insolvency/Corporate Recovery (3); Media & Entertainment (2).

David Pannick QC - *Blackstone Chambers*
Administrative & Public Law: General (*); Employment (1); Human Rights (1); Immigration (2); Sport (1).

Laurence Rabinowitz QC - *One Essex Court*
Banking & Finance (s); Commercial (Litigation) (s); Company (s); Energy & Natural Resources (s); Fraud: Civil (s).

Alan Steinfeld QC - *24 Old Buildings*
Chancery: Commercial (2); Company (4); Insolvency/Corporate Recovery (5); Partnership (2); Pensions (4).

Ranked in 9 practice areas

Michael Briggs QC - Serle Court

Banking & Finance (5); Chancery: Commercial (1); Chancery: Traditional (1); Commercial (Litigation) (1); Company (2); Financial Services (2); Fraud: Civil (3); Insolvency/Corporate Recovery (5); Partnership (1); Professional Negligence (3).

Michael Briggs QC cuts a swathe through the opposition in a number of fields. At heart a chancery practitioner of both the traditional and commercial varieties, his repertoire extends as far as insolvency, professional negligence and fraud. He is happiest in court where he "outflanks his opponents through subtlety rather than attacking head-down and running." A popular figure within the Inns, he is constantly importuned, but finds time to indulge his love of sailing whenever possible.

STARS AT THE BAR

Ranked in 8 practice areas

Gordon Pollock QC - Essex Court Chambers

Arbitration (International) (1); Banking & Finance (2); Commercial (Litigation) (*); Energy & Natural Resources (*); Fraud: Civil (3); Insurance (2); Media & Entertainment (1); Shipping (1).

Gordon Pollock QC built his legendary reputation in shipping law where he remains a great draw. He has, however, demonstrated a versatility, which "means he can crash the party in any number of legal areas with devastating consequences." Commercial litigation and energy cases have showcased his "gunslinger's attitude" to best effect although media, banking, insurance and fraud matters also feature prominently in his caseload. "A real courtroom star," his strength emanates from "a physical and intellectual presence, which has left many a judge charmed and many a hardened opponent reaching for the smelling salts." Described by one observer as having "an oratory command that would have made Demosthenes green," his recent highlights have included appearing in Three Rivers District Council v HM Treasury.

Jonathan Sumption QC - Brick Court Chambers

Administrative & Public Law: General (1); Banking & Finance (1); Commercial (Litigation) (*); Energy & Natural Resources (*); Financial Services (1); Fraud: Civil (2); Insurance (1); Professional Negligence (1).

"One runs out of superlatives when extolling the praises of Jonathan Sumption QC." Quite simply a phenomenon, he has a reputation of the finest standing in a host of areas, while somehow finding the time to be a respected medieval historian in his own right. *Chambers UK* rates him in the starred category for commercial litigation and energy matters but his effortless handling of cases in the spheres of banking, administrative and public law, insurance and professional negligence law is well documented. Set apart by the power of his intellect, he has "a surgical precision in cross-examination" and "a mind incisive enough to anticipate the arguments of his opponents," gifts that have regularly laid waste the best defences of his finest rivals. Continuing a remarkable career, his most recent headline appearance has been in the Unilever v Mercury Asset Management case.

Ranked in 6 practice areas

Christopher Butcher QC - 7 King's Bench Walk

Arbitration (International) (4); Banking & Finance (5); Commercial (Litigation) (5); Insurance (3); Professional Negligence (4); Shipping (s).

Christopher Butcher QC's brief tenure as a silk has already confirmed his reputation as "one of the more exciting performers of his generation." Although most at home on insurance and professional negligence work, he is often pressed into service in banking and straight commercial litigation. A key player in the recent spate of film financing disputes, contemporaries admire him for his sound judgement and nerveless performances. "Cooler headed," he is "a good man to have around when the flak is flying."

Elizabeth Gloster QC - One Essex Court

Chancery: Commercial (1); Commercial (Litigation) (1); Company (2); Energy & Natural Resources (2); Fraud: Civil (3); Insolvency/Corporate Recovery (1).

A solicitor's dream, Elizabeth Gloster QC "amalgamates inexhaustible reserves of energy with a furious will to win." Always on the go and often working into the night, she "makes the other man look like a slothful scrimshanker," impressing as being almost constantly available and ready to put up the dukes at any time. A real commercial animal, she appears in the juiciest fraud, insolvency and insurance-related matters, winning the respect of the judges through her "clean, direct advice" across a number of jurisdictions. Recent years have seen her called to the Bars of Bermuda, Gibraltar and the Isle of Man for specific cases and she has been appointed a judge of the Courts of Appeal of Jersey and Guernsey. Closer to home, another frantically busy year has seen her acting for the institutional Railtrack Shareholders' Action Group in relation to claims for compensation arising out of the administration of Railtrack.

Joe Smouha - Essex Court Chambers

Arbitration (International) (2); Banking & Finance (3); Commercial (Litigation) (*); Fraud: Civil (2); Shipping (4); Tax: Indirect Tax (VAT, Customs & Excise, Stamp Duty) (2).

Commercial litigation, arbitration, banking, shipping, fraud and taxation matters have all felt the force of Joe Smouha's "considerable drive and intellect." Considered by many to be the best at the junior Bar, it is his advocacy above all that sets him apart. Not content to go through the motions he "brings real artistry to his addresses," producing "a wit, sparkle and invention" that makes his offerings "as much entertainment as legal enlightenment." Widely tipped to be one of the brightest stars in the firmament, his recent cases include Richard Drake v Thomas Agnew and Sons.

Bankim Thanki - Fountain Court

Aviation (2); Banking & Finance (1); Commercial (Litigation) (1); Fraud: Civil (1); Professional Negligence (1); Sport (2).

"Oozing charm from every pore," Bankim Thanki is prized by solicitors for his "ability to tame the most liverish of clients." He radiates calm before dropping the mask in court and revealing himself as "a cold tactician, ruthless in his execution of the master plan." This, however, is no triumph of style over substance. His vast knowledge of matters as diverse as banking and aviation, can be pressed into service in the largest and most byzantine cases, such as the BCCI litigation, where he has played a full role.

STARS AT THE BAR

Ranked in 5 practice areas

Mark Barnes QC - One Essex Court
Arbitration (International) (3); Banking & Finance (5); Commercial (Litigation) (2); Energy & Natural Resources (1); Fraud: Civil (4).

Like many of his versatile contemporaries in this list, Mark Barnes QC founds his success on effective time management. Putting himself out to meet tight deadlines, he possesses "an uncanny skill for hoovering up dense clumps of information in no time at all," a facility that allows him to "beard the finest specialist practitioners in their own lairs." Not for him the whizz-bang theatricals of some of his more colourful rivals, he produces "an almost mesmeric performance, enervating his opponents through calm, reasoned logic." Energy remains his first love, but arbitration and general commercial litigation also feature prominently in his portfolio. One recent appearance has been on behalf of the defendant in Getmapping v Ordnance Survey, an action alleging breach of the Competition Act.

Anthony Boswood QC - Fountain Court
Banking & Finance (3); Commercial (Litigation) (1); Energy & Natural Resources (2); Fraud: Civil (3); Insurance (3).

A giant of the commercial Bar, Anthony Boswood QC is recommended for his expertise in banking, insurance, fraud and professional negligence cases. Owner of a villa in Tuscany, he marries the learning of a true Renaissance man with a tough courtroom technique. A hard fighter, "he stoops over his prey," swatting the opposition aside through forceful cross-examination. Popular among solicitors for his ability to drill large litigation teams, he has conducted a number of important cases in the recent past including Steamship Mutual Underwriting Association v Feasey et al.

Michael Brindle QC - Fountain Court
Banking & Finance (*); Commercial (Litigation) (1); Financial Services (2); Fraud: Civil (1); Professional Negligence (1).

"Everyone's first choice for banking litigation," Michael Brindle QC practises on a broader canvas than most, demonstrating superior skills in fields such as professional negligence, financial services and fraud. His "first-class mind" is regularly commandeered for the biggest litigation, with solicitors particularly prizing his advice on public policy issues and his ability to come at tangled problems from a fresh perspective. "Restrained but purposeful," he "fillets evasive witnesses with an unswerving, dead-eyed calm that borders on the unsettling." Undoubtedly approaching the very summit of the profession, he has devoted much of his time of late to appearing with the very best in the Barings litigation.

John Brisby QC - 4 Stone Buildings
Chancery: Commercial (3); Company (3); Financial Services (3); Fraud: Civil (4); Insolvency/Corporate Recovery (5).

Over the years John Brisby QC has been seen sifting through the rubble of many a large-scale corporate collapse, including those of Barlow Clowes, BCCI and SASEA. Practising from a company and commercial law background, he seems drawn like a magnet to the heavier litigation, offering a brand of "abrasive advocacy" which, while not to everybody's tastes, is undoubtedly effective. Financial services work continues to form a substantial part of a practice that has seen him appear in Morris v Bank of America, and Hamilton et al v Law Debenture Trustees et al, a matter arising out of the Barings litigation.

Robin Dicker QC - 3-4 South Square
Banking & Finance (3); Company (3); Energy & Natural Resources (3); Fraud: Civil (s); Insolvency/Corporate Recovery (2).

Touted as a future star from early in his career, Robin Dicker QC has fulfilled his promise in the short time he has been a silk. A heavy hitter in the world of insolvency, he is no mean performer on banking, company, energy and fraud matters. A veteran of all the major cases relating to corporate collapses of the last few years, he has a depth of experience which belies his relative youth, and has won the trust of a number of leading City solicitors. "Circumspect, analytical and precise," he "puts his shoulder to the wheel with unfailing good humour," winning over both clients and lawyers alike in cases of the importance of Bellmex International v British American Tobacco.

Barbara Dohmann QC - Blackstone Chambers
Commercial (Litigation) (1); Financial Services (2); Fraud: Civil (3); Insurance (3); Media & Entertainment (3).

The multilingual Barbara Dohmann QC is known for her "rigorously schooled intellectual grasp" and a reach that extends into commercial litigation, fraud, media, insurance and financial services. It is, however, the impression she makes in the courtroom that is strongest. Part of the instructing solicitor's heavy ordnance, she "enters the fray like Ate hot from hell, locking her jaws round the opposition and refusing to let go." Such single-minded drive, allied to "palpitation-inducing cross-examination," led one solicitor to peg her as first choice "for her sheer blood and guts approach." A regular in the Court of Appeal, she acted for the claimant in Lubbe v Cape and has been involved in a number of keynote matters such as PIA v National Westminster Bank.

STARS AT THE BAR

Charles Flint QC - Blackstone Chambers
Administrative & Public Law: General (2); Commercial (Litigation) (4); Financial Services (1); Fraud: Civil (1); Sport (2).

Action man Charles Flint QC, a former member of the Armed Services, is proof incarnate of the old saw: mens sana in corpore sano. Climber, stunt pilot and yomper extraordinaire he shows up the rest of his colleagues at the Bar as a positive shower of malingering sluggards. Tackling a varied legal assault course, he comfortably straddles the worlds of commercial litigation, financial services and fraud but is perhaps best known for his efforts on judicial review cases in the arenas of sport and administrative and public law. "Confidence-inspiring and tactically shrewd," our man Flint's illustrious campaigns include appearances in the Prince Jefri litigation and on the Abacha case. More recently he acted on behalf of the plaintiff in British Waterways Board v Severn Trent Water, a case dealing with the definition and construction of statutory powers.

Anthony Grabiner QC - One Essex Court
Arbitration (International) (1); Banking & Finance (2); Commercial (Litigation) (*); Energy & Natural Resources (*); Fraud: Civil (2).

Eternally busy, Anthony Grabiner QC is something of a "plate spinner extraordinaire," for when not politicking in the Upper Chamber he is addressing the knottiest of legal problems across a number of disciplines. A key figure in the London Court of International Arbitration, his practice further embraces major commercial litigation, banking and fraud cases, all of which are conducted with tireless spirit. Steeped in experience at the highest level, he "assists judges in navigating the most tortuous of legal pathways, often reducing them to the level of simpering cat's paws" and "has an aura of self-possession which undoes many an opponent." Reservations persist among some solicitors as to his lack of availability but this by-product of his own success has not prevented him from securing top billing in recent causes célèbres such as the £315 million Granada Media v The Football League television rights dispute.

Robert Hildyard QC - 4 Stone Buildings
Chancery: Commercial (2); Company (2); Energy & Natural Resources (3); Financial Services (3); Insurance (3).

Company and commercial law expert Robert Hildyard QC has built a reputation as a "gun for hire on the international scene." Orbiting the globe on a regular basis, this is one celestial body in the legal firmament whose wanderlust shows no sign of abating. Called to the Bars of Bermuda, the Cayman Islands, the Turks and Caicos Islands and Hong Kong for specific cases, he has "a confident style that plays well wherever he washes up." He allies "assurance with comprehensibility" and is regularly instructed by insurance companies and regulatory bodies. He has featured in the largest matters, such as the Grupo Torras litigation. Of late he has been seen in a substantial case in The Bahamas: Oracle Fund et al v Fortis Fund Services (Bahamas) et al.

Mark Howard QC - Brick Court Chambers
Banking & Finance (2); Commercial (Litigation) (1); Energy & Natural Resources (3); Insurance (2); Professional Negligence (3).

"A paragon of the modern silk" with "an amazing success rate," Mark Howard QC is a commercial litigator rapidly assuming a reputation to rival that of his esteemed stablemate Jonathan Sumption QC. Solicitors appreciate his progressive approach, citing him as "a team player par excellence" who assumes no airs and graces. Most at home on the technically complicated case, he has further specialisms in banking, insurance and professional negligence, areas where he deploys his "cool logic" to good effect. Testament to his reputation, he was chosen to replace Gordon Pollock QC in acting for Sir Elton John v PwC.

Anthony Mann QC - Enterprise Chambers
Chancery: Commercial (2); Commercial (Litigation) (5); Company (4); Insolvency/Corporate Recovery (1); Professional Negligence (4).

"Heavyweight" Anthony Mann QC earned his spurs in general company and commercial work, but it is as an insolvency practitioner that he has hit the heights. Appearing in cases of the highest calibre, such as Money Markets International v London Stock Exchange, he regularly confounds the best in the business through his "forceful submissions." A prime weapon in his armoury is his "limitless self-confidence," an infectious property, which allows him to catch the ear of the most resistant of judges, and to bend the courtroom to his will. In full flow he can be "disarmingly down-to-earth," a characteristic that plays well with those juniors who are led by him. Both poacher and gamekeeper, he sits as a deputy High Court Judge, a deputy Bankruptcy Registrar and an arbitrator, while also finding time to edit the Lloyds Publication on Professional Negligence.

Robert Miles QC - 4 Stone Buildings
Banking & Finance; Chancery: Commercial; Company; Energy & Natural Resources; Insolvency/Corporate Recovery (New Silk).

Robert Miles QC's "generous, understanding and sympathetic manner" has won over many clients and solicitors. With a practice revolving around insolvency and commercial chancery, he has developed an "aptitude for devouring paperwork," which leaves him free to pursue cases in other areas such as banking and energy. As a junior he featured in a vast array of high-profile cases such as Maxwell, BCCI and Bermuda Fire and Marine Insurance, and is set fair to assume roles of this magnitude as a leader in his own right. Combining "a pellucid oratorical style" with "well-reasoned points," he has been seen to good effect recently in Morris v Bank of America and Konamaneni et al v Rolls-Royce Industrial Power (India) et al.

STARS AT THE BAR

Richard Millett - Essex Court Chambers
Arbitration (International) (4); Banking & Finance (2); Commercial (Litigation) (4); Insolvency/Corporate Recovery (3); Media & Entertainment (2).

Richard Millett has over the years nimbly negotiated some of the largest pieces of litigation spread right across the globe. A specialist in banking and media work, he adds a strong insolvency element to a widely respected commercial litigation practice, which has made him "the toast of many a leading solicitor." "Dauntingly bright" with a background as an Oxford law lecturer, he combines undoubted wisdom with a "cheerful countenance and sanguine outlook." Cases on which he has sprung into action of late include Papamichael v NatWest Bank.

David Pannick QC - Blackstone Chambers
Administrative & Public Law: General (*); Employment (1); Human Rights (1); Immigration (2); Sport (1).

In a set noted for its expertise on human rights and judicial review, David Pannick QC is the embodiment of its ethos. Hugely popular amongst solicitors, he is the best in the business when it comes to administrative and public law and brings his unparalleled knowledge of EC and human rights to the areas of immigration and employment law. A Fellow of All Souls, he draws his life force from his "profound intelligence and complete devotion to his subject," to the extent of citing legal literature as one of his outside interests. His involvement in matters of great moment and public interest has been confirmed again with his representation on behalf of the Home Secretary in Anderson and Taylor v Secretary of State for the Home Department, a case establishing that the Secretary of State is entitled to set his own tariff for a mandatory life prisoner. Further appearances have been on behalf of a Saudi Arabian citizen whose assets have been frozen on suspicion of his involvement in sponsoring terrorism. An interest in and undoubted flair for sports law has also been ratified by his successful challenge to The Football League against its refusal to allow Wimbledon FC to move to Milton Keynes.

Laurence Rabinowitz QC - One Essex Court
Banking & Finance; Commercial (Litigation); Company; Energy & Natural Resources; Fraud: Civil (New Silk).

After what many bamboozled peers felt to be an unconscionable delay, Laurence Rabinowitz QC has been elevated to silk. His reputation as a Treasury Junior and impressive achievements in the energy and commercial litigation spheres led many to believe that he had "outstripped the majority of his rivals" and deserved the nod. Over the years, this "absolute star" with his "outstanding technical expertise" has been led on many headline cases by the very best around and "a bright future as a silk lies ahead of him." A recent highlight has been his appearance in NM Rothschild & Sons (CI) v Equitable Life et al.

Alan Steinfeld QC - 24 Old Buildings
Chancery: Commercial (2); Company (4); Insolvency/Corporate Recovery (5); Partnership (2); Pensions (4).

Keen yachtsman Alan Steinfeld QC has clearly travelled the seven seas in a long and distinguished legal career. A "highly respected operator around the Inns" he is often out of port conducting cases in locations as far-flung as The Bahamas, Bermuda and Hong Kong. Company and commercial work form the stuffing of his practice, but he also has a noted specialism in partnership law where he is seen as "a big draw." "Punchy and confident in an unpompous way," he is retained by the large City firms in cases of the magnitude of the Picasso litigation where he acted for the settlor's former husband in relation to paintings held in an Isle of Man trust.

BARRISTERS' CHARGES AND REMUNERATION

THE MILLION-A-YEAR CLUB

Those few barristers who can claim a place in the millionaire's club really are the élite, with proven track records in cases where big-name clients play for the biggest stakes. Clients' willingness to pay such large fees shows no sign of abating, and there are some new names on the list this year. Such reputations are hard-won, and reflect both commitment and consummate ability. It is no surprise to see the heavy tax and commercial guns so well represented. A top-flight commercial silk may charge the earth, but then they will win or save the client many times their own fee.

THE MILLION-A-YEAR CLUB

Graham Aaronson QC	Julian Flaux QC	Robert Ham QC	Gordon Pollock QC
Charles Aldous QC	Michael Flesch QC	Mark Hapgood QC	Robin Potts QC
Michael Bloch QC	Jonathan Gaisman QC	Mark Howard QC	Jules Sher QC
Rex Bretten QC	John Gardiner QC	Gavin Kealey QC	Nicholas Stadlen QC
Christopher Carr QC	Elizabeth Gloster QC	George Leggatt QC	Jonathan Sumption QC
Roderick Cordara QC	David Goldberg QC	Iain Milligan QC	Peter Trevett QC
Ian Croxford QC	Anthony Grabiner QC	Terence Mowschenson QC	Robert Venables QC
Michael Crystal QC	Brian Green QC	David Oliver QC	
Barbara Dohmann QC	Nicholas Green QC	David Pannick QC	

BARRISTERS' CHARGES

The range of fees that barristers can command remains pretty static, although those commanded by the very best commercial and tax lawyers have edged up, merely reflecting their value to many. The figures given represent gross income, which can vary between consultations, advisory and court work. Different sets have different charging methods, and some do not charge by the hour at all. Charges may also vary according to estimates of complexity and risk.

HOURLY CHARGE RATES

Seniority	Commercial	Tax	Chancery	Common law	Criminal
QC	£300-£1,000	£600-£2,000	£250-£750	£150-£400	£125-400
10 yrs call	£100-£350	£200-£500	£150-£300	£100-£200	£75-£300
4-9 yrs call	£75-£250	£175-£350	£100-£200	£50-£150	£50-£150
1-3 yrs call	£50-£150	£75-£150	£60-£125	£40-£100	£25-£75

All figures represent gross earnings before deduction of expenses.

BARRISTERS' REMUNERATION

The figures depict a range, in which average earnings tend towards the bottom. The upper figures are the preserve of those outstanding in their field. Inevitably, perhaps, practitioners in criminal and common law will earn significantly less than their banking, tax and company counterparts. All barristers will pay approximately 20% of their earnings to chambers for expenses including rent, and another 20% will go towards individual expenses like pensions, insurance, travel fees and accountancy. Furthermore, given the amount of delay common between completion of work and payment, earnings on paper may vary widely from year to year.

ANNUAL EARNINGS (THOUSANDS)

Seniority	Commercial	Tax	Chancery	Common law	Criminal
QC	£200-£2,000	£300-£2,000	£250-£2,000	£150-£425	£125-550
10 yrs call	£100-£750	£200-£500	£100-£350	£75-£300	£40-£400
4-9 yrs call	£60-£350	£175-£350	£75-£300	£30-£200	£30-£165
1-3 yrs call	£25-£125	£75-£150	£25-£125	£20-£100	£10-£75

All figures represent gross earnings before deduction of expenses.

SET OVERVIEWS

OVERVIEWS TO BARRISTERS' CHAMBERS RANKED IN FIVE OR MORE PRACTICE AREAS

The criterion for entry into this section is a ranking in five or more disciplines in this year's Chambers Guide. Of necessity, this militates against common law sets which may have fewer strings to their bow but maintain an excellence in their chosen field. Instead, commercial and chancery practices proliferate, many of which house some of the leading luminaries at the Bar.

Ranked in 12 practice areas

Brick Court Chambers

Administrative & Public Law: General (3); Arbitration (International) (3); Aviation (1); Banking & Finance (2); Commercial (Litigation) (1); Competition/European Law (1); Energy & Natural Resources (3); Environment (4); Fraud: Civil (2); Insurance (1); Professional Negligence (4); Sport (2).

This 'super-set' specialises in commercial, European and public law, with particular emphasis on insurance, banking and administrative law. Its premises, opposite the High Court, reflect its standing at the very hub of the legal world. It can count amongst its number some of the big box office draws at the Bar such as Jonathan Sumption QC. Strengths in international trade, finance and commerce are complemented by a number of European Union lawyers specialising in EU and competition litigation. Some of these spend much of their time in Brussels where the set has an annexe. Members also have expertise in human rights and in commercial and regulatory judicial review, as well as in professional negligence, takeovers and mergers, and media and entertainment, employment, sports and public international law. Instructions stem from private and commercial clients, as well as the UK and other Governments, and international institutions such as the European Commission. Barristers were involved in the high-value House of Lords appeal, Fairchild & Fox et al v Spousal et al, which determined the issue of payments to the sufferers of inhalation of asbestos.

Ranked in 11 practice areas

Blackstone Chambers

Administrative & Public Law: General (1); Commercial (Litigation) (2); Employment (3); Environment (4); Financial Services (1); Fraud: Civil (2); Human Rights (2); Immigration (4); Media & Entertainment (1); Public International Law (1); Sport (1).

Over half a century after its formation this set continues to attract the finest minds. 28 of its 60-plus members have taken silk and the recent arrival of Michael Beloff QC speaks volumes. Its hugely cerebral barristers display first-rate skills across an astonishing range of subjects, and have virtually made heavyweight public law cases their own. Ranked in no fewer than 11 of our tables this year, the set is top tier not just in administrative and public law but also in financial services, media and entertainment, public international law and sport. It further puts in a respected performance in commercial litigation, civil fraud and human rights, as well as employment, environment and immigration. Amongst the commercial niches that members have made their own are international trade, conflict of laws, regulatory tribunals, defamation and intellectual property. The flagship public law and human rights work, however, takes centre stage, with the set undertaking judicial review cases, both for and against public bodies and regulatory authorities, touching on areas as diverse as freedom of expression, immigration, social security and housing. Its undoubted expertise and the rich resource of so many talented individuals makes it a popular choice for those magic circle firms looking for a crack team to handle the larger litigation. No clearer evidence of this can be provided than the set's participation in the Sultan of Brunei/Prince Jefri litigation.

Ranked in 9 practice areas

Essex Court Chambers

Arbitration (International) (1); Aviation (2); Banking & Finance (4); Commercial (Litigation) (1); Energy & Natural Resources (2); Insurance (1); Media & Entertainment (3); Public International Law (2); Shipping (1).

Founded in the 1960s by an elite cadre of four barristers, all of whom went on to be respected judicial figures, this set has grown considerably over time. Now accommodating more than 65 tenants, it is particularly strong in international commercial arbitrations and litigation, insurance and reinsurance, and wet and dry shipping. Expertise also covers banking, international trade, energy and media and entertainment. In public international law, it can rightly claim to offer some of the finest practitioners in what is a very narrow field. Barristers act for clients ranging from institutions and multinational corporations to private companies and individuals. The set has especially strong international capabilities in terms of barristers' linguistic skills and jurisdictional qualifications. In Europe, barristers have appeared as advocates before the Commission, Court of Justice and Court of Human Rights, and International Court of Justice. Many travel further afield and have appeared in courts from Hong Kong to Kenya. Barristers have been involved in the ongoing Commercial Court case of Three Rivers District Council v HM Treasury.

SET OVERVIEWS

Ranked in 8 practice areas

Fountain Court

Aviation (1); Banking & Finance (1); Commercial (Litigation) (1); Energy & Natural Resources (4); Fraud: Civil (1); Insurance (2); Product Liability (3); Professional Negligence (3).

Acclaimed as part of the magic circle, this set has, in the past, had its problems. The turn of the century, for example, heralded a number of high-profile departures, the effect of which was ameliorated by the arrival of new blood. Added to that, the set has removed its chambers director and returned to a traditional clerking system. However, it remains one of the most celebrated commercial sets in London. Based in the Temple, its members are recognised as leaders in commercial disputes, offering a high-quality and efficient service to business clients. We rank them in the top tier for banking and finance, commercial litigation, civil fraud and aviation. The set also boasts impressive practitioners in energy, insurance, product liability and professional negligence. Barristers have made appearances before courts at every level, and many are experienced as sitters or advocates in arbitrations. An ethos of generalism means that the set can field well-balanced teams to meet the needs of just about any commercial client. The set's highlight case of the year is the Barings case in the High Court, where it is acting for the Singaporeans.

Maitland Chambers

Chancery: Commercial (1); Chancery: Traditional (3); Charities (1); Company (3); Insolvency/Corporate Recovery (3); Media & Entertainment (3); Professional Negligence (4); Property Litigation (3).

In January 2001 13 Old Square and 7 Stone Buildings, two well-established and respected chancery sets, combined to form Maitland Chambers, now the largest set of its kind in the country. Highly esteemed and a great favourite of Herbert Smith, it handles a wide range of cases with aplomb, ranging from international litigation for multinational companies to County Court disputes. Acknowledged strengths lie in company law, charity law, insolvency and media. The barristers provide advocacy and advice for every level of civil tribunal in England and Wales, and several have been called to the Bars of Hong Kong, Singapore, the Cayman Islands and the Isle of Man. Members are being increasingly instructed by overseas lawyers seeking advice on English law or on related common law problems, accountants, surveyors and other professionals with access under the Direct Professional Access (DPA) scheme. Barristers have acted, and continue to be involved in, the fallout from Barings' collapse.

Matrix Chambers

Administrative & Public Law: General (2); Crime (3); Education (2); Employment (4); Environment (3); Human Rights (1); Immigration (2); Public International Law (2).

This set was created in part to anticipate a future increasingly dominated by Europe and human rights issues. Perhaps there is some way to go. It has, however, demonstrated an avowed commitment to the protection of individuals' rights and enjoys a correspondingly high profile in our human rights, public law and immigration tables. It acts for a great diversity of public and private individuals and bodies in the areas of UK public and private law, the law of the European Union and European Convention on Human Rights, and public international law. It has acknowledged depth and strength in crime, education, employment and environmental law, and has cut a sophisticated dash in EU competition law. These barristers display a commitment to a public service ethos, including publicly funded work, public interest litigation and pro bono work. In a high-profile representation at the Special Immigration Appeals Commission, barristers acted for seven of nine individuals detained under current anti-terrorism legislation.

3 Verulam Buildings

Arbitration (International) (3); Banking & Finance (1); Commercial (Litigation) (2); Financial Services (1); Fraud: Civil (1); Insurance (3); Media & Entertainment (3); Professional Negligence (4).

Despite losing some manpower to Matrix Chambers, this leading commercial set based in Gray's Inn continues to live up to its long and distinguished history in all aspects of commercial law. Its main strengths lie in banking and financial services, and barristers are also recognised as specialists in insolvency, insurance and reinsurance, professional negligence, media and entertainment, IT, public international and environmental law. Members are as at home giving short advice as they are appearing before the Privy Council or House of Lords. The set is known for its strong and fluent teams, especially in banking, where an effective practice management ensures efficiency and cohesion. Clients include many high-profile litigation firms both in London and nationally, in-house legal departments and international law firms. In addition, many lay clients instruct their professional advisors to retain counsel from the set, though it generally does not accept instructions from lay clients directly. Leading cases over the past year include involvement in Royal Bank of Scotland v Etridge.

Ranked in 7 practice areas

One Essex Court

Arbitration (International) (2); Banking & Finance (3); Commercial (Litigation) (1); Energy & Natural Resources (1); Fraud: Civil (1); Intellectual Property (2); Tax: Corporate (3).

This is a high-powered commercial set, which embraces domestic and international commerce and finance. The set is recognised as being at the very top both in terms of quality of practitioner and financial turnover. Ranked by Chambers Guide in the first tier for commercial litigation, energy and civil fraud, it also wins approbation for its deft handling of arbitrations and expertise in IP, banking and finance, and tax. Fine advocacy skills are something of a tradition at the set, and barristers employ them to the full in a range of court and tribunal settings. Barristers were involved on both sides of Unilever Superannuation Trustees v Mercury Asset Management, concerning standards to be applied to City fund managers.

SET OVERVIEWS

Ranked in 6 practice areas

Doughty Street Chambers
Administrative & Public Law: General (3); Clinical Negligence (4); Crime (1); Human Rights (1) Immigration (2) Product Liability (2).

This large set with its emphasis on civil liberties and human rights has always shown an interest in the redress of abuses across the globe. Its head of chambers, Geoffrey Robertson QC, is a committed proponent of the International Criminal Court, and an appeal judge for the new UN Special Court in Sierra Leone. Members include specialists in criminal law, public law, prisoners' rights, discrimination and immigration. More than half of the work is in criminal practice, with most of it for legally aided defendants. Barristers specialise in public order, drugs, commercial fraud and clients with mental health problems. They are experienced in representing appellants at the European Court of Human Rights and in appeals before the Privy Council on behalf of Caribbean appellants awaiting execution. Experience also covers anti-terrorist legislation and the security services, and representing defendants in political public order cases such as the miners' dispute, the poll tax riots and demonstrations by animal rights activists, road protesters and other interest groups.

Ranked in 5 practice areas

4 Breams Buildings
Administrative & Public Law: General (3); Environment (2); Local Government (1); Planning (1); Property Litigation (3).

One third of this set's members are silks, many at the top of the profession. Home to the respective chairmen of the Planning & Environment Bar Association and the Administrative Law Bar Association, it is a planning and local government powerhouse with complementary expertise in environmental and property law. Members have varied litigious and advisory experience in these fields, including European law aspects and matters concerning human rights and professional negligence. The set acts for a wide variety of clients both in the public and private sectors, and appears at inquiries and in the courts. Property work comprises all aspects of landlord and tenant issues such as property-related torts. Public law work is carried out not only for central and local government and for a variety of public and regulatory bodies, but also for those challenging the exercise of executive power. The set was involved in the notorious local government gerrymandering case, Magill v Dame Shirley Porter.

Crown Office Chambers
Clinical Negligence (4); Construction (2); Personal Injury (2); Product Liability (2); Professional Negligence (3).

Issuing forth from the union of One Paper Buildings and 2 Crown Office Row, this is one of the largest and most highly regarded civil common law sets in London. Its 70 members specialise variously in professional and clinical negligence, product liability, personal injury, insurance and reinsurance and construction work. The set fields specialist advocates and advisors at all levels, working together as appropriate in high-calibre teams of counsel for large and complex disputes, whether in litigation or arbitration. A team of barristers acted for the pharmaceuticals in the Oral Contraceptive Group Litigation in the High Court.

39 Essex Street
Administrative & Public Law: General (3); Construction (4); Environment (4); Immigration (4); Personal Injury (1).

There are over 50 barristers here, and between them they have expertise in commercial, public and common law. The set is particularly rated for environmental, personal injury, construction, administrative and immigration matters, and boasts a wide experience in courts and tribunals from the House of Lords, Privy Council, Court of Appeal and international and domestic arbitrations, through to public inquiries and industrial and VAT tribunals. Members also participate in investigations before parliamentary select committees, and are known for undertaking pro bono work for public interest organisations. The set has a corporate outlook and a modern management structure, and accepts instructions from established international clients, particularly, but not exclusively, in Hong Kong, Singapore and India. A successful year has seen five of its members newly appointed to silk and its ranks swelled by the arrival of five specialists in environmental and planning law. Barristers were involved in Ashworth Security Hospital v MGN.

Serle Court
Chancery: Commercial (2); Company (4); Fraud: Civil (2); Insolvency/Corporate Recovery (3); Partnership (1).

Drawing on the best traditions of the commercial and Chancery Bar, more than 40 tenants offer outstanding service in administrative and public law, civil fraud, insolvency and company commercial law. Barristers are experienced in litigation, advisory work and arbitrations, and have been at the forefront of the ADR revolution. A number of gifted individuals have particular expertise in Arab, charities, public international, sports and telecom law, and a significant proportion of work originates overseas.

4 Stone Buildings
Chancery: Commercial (2); Company (2); Energy & Natural Resources (4); Financial Services (1); Insolvency/Corporate Recovery (2).

This is a medium-sized, forward-thinking set specialising in company and commercial law. Members' work covers all aspects of company law, commercial and general business law and corporate insolvency, as well as financial services and regulatory work, with a particular emphasis on litigation. The set is noted for its work in corporate fraud and asset recovery, and shareholder disputes. Barristers are credited with a highly commercial approach and fluid case management. Members have close ties to the US, the Far East and Europe, and particularly strong connections with Hong Kong, Bermuda, the Turks & Caicos Islands, Trinidad and the Cayman Islands. A team of barristers is involved for the Bank of America in its fight against Morris, arising out of the collapse of BCCI.

SET OVERVIEWS

Wilberforce Chambers

Chancery: Commercial (2); Chancery: Traditional (1); Pensions (1); Professional Negligence (4); Property Litigation (2).

A tremendously respected traditional and commercial chancery set, which offers services across a range of specialist fields that includes property, professional negligence, tax and trusts. Following the loss of its status as the largest chancery set following the creation of Maitland Chambers, it recruited wisely and can claim to offer depth and breadth across a range of services. Its 35 members, of whom 15 are QCs, are noted experts in occupational and personal pensions with barristers appearing in jurisdictions outside the UK including Bermuda, the Cayman Islands, Singapore, Hong Kong and The Bahamas. It was one of the first to pursue, and appears to be one of the last to abandon, the strategy of employing a chambers director.

Two Garden Court

Administrative & Public Law: General (4); Crime (2); Human Rights (3); Immigration (1); Local Government: Social Housing (2).

Hatched in the liberal dreamscape of the early 1970s these chambers have made good their promise to undertake morally and socially progressive work, to fight test cases and to challenge injustice. Exhibiting zeal, the members' motto is 'Do right, fear no one', and as the adoption of such a creed might suggest, these barristers are certain that they know what is right. Their battle cry is a call for greater sexual and racial justice allied to a belief in human rights that has been present long before it was fashionable. It is fitting, therefore, that the set should be ranked so highly in our directory in areas like immigration, social housing and human rights while also being an acknowledged heavyweight in crime and public law. There are nearly 70 tenants, in comparison to the six who set off on the missionary trail in 1974, and between them they have tended the flame at this shrine to liberal ideals with great care. Often undertaking pro bono work, they continue to appear in cases of great public interest and enjoyed a recent highlight acting for the appellants in the Sepet and Bulbul case.

ADMINISTRATIVE & PUBLIC LAW

Research The rankings are based on in-depth interviews with 6,582 solicitors, barristers and clients in the UK. **Chambers'** research is audited by the British Market Research Bureau (see page 7)

BARRISTERS' PROFILES ▶ See pages 1353-1504

OVERVIEW: There has been little change in the tables this year, which continues to feature barristers who are often at the forefront of public affairs as well as the profession.

LONDON

ADMINISTRATIVE & PUBLIC LAW • London

	QCs	Jnrs
1. Blackstone Chambers (Baxendale/Flint)	8	6
2. Matrix Chambers	4	3
3. 4 Breams Buildings (Christopher Lockhart-Mummery QC)	2	2
Brick Court Chambers (Christopher Clarke QC)	4	1
Doughty Street Chambers (Geoffrey Robertson QC)	3	2
39 Essex Street (Nigel Pleming QC)	4	3
11 King's Bench Walk Chambers (Tabachnik/Goudie)	3	2
4. 1 Crown Office Row (Robert Seabrook QC)	2	-
Two Garden Court (Davies/Griffiths)	1	2

Numbers show recommended barristers in this practice area

BLACKSTONE CHAMBERS (see full details p.1515) In terms of "pure fire power," the set is "unassailable." A "highly professional outfit," it is serviced by clerks who solicitors find to be "up there with the best." Receiving an enormous volume of applause, **David Pannick** QC (see p.1458) emerges from our research as the top public law silk in the country. Described by peers as "a leader in every respect," he acted for the Home Secretary in Anderson and Taylor. **Michael Beloff** QC (see p.1364) remains respected as a "practitioner of the highest calibre," who solicitors say will never suffer from a shortage of instructions for as long as he is available to take them. "Intellectually brilliant," **John Howell** QC (see p.1420) is "adept and supple" as an advocate, recently taking a lead role in Magill v Porter. With proven judicial review ability of the highest order, the practice of **Charles Flint** QC (see p.1398) has its origins in the commercial and regulatory sphere, within which interviewees consider him to have a "superb reputation" as a public and administrative lawyer. **Anthony Lester** QC (see p.1434) has appeared in a plethora of recent high-profile cases, notably for the respondents in Roth. A "brilliant and persuasive advocate," he is said to "excel on human rights issues," an area to which he has contributed much pioneering work. "Bright, client friendly and practical," **Monica Carss-Frisk** QC (see p.1377) has established herself quickly as a leading silk, according to competitors, having acted on weighty commercial matters as well as on high-profile cases such as Farrakhan. Highly respected **Beverley Lang** QC (see p.1431) completes an awe-inspiring catalogue of established silks, while **Mark Shaw** QC (see p.1477) ("thorough and hard-working") takes his place amongst the new QCs. He has acted for the BBC, most recently in Regina (Quintavalle) v British Broadcasting Corporation, concerning whether its refusal to transmit the ProLife Alliance's party political broadcast was lawful. Presiley Baxendale QC is now working as a mediator. As well as boasting the stellar silk, the set also boasts the stellar junior in **Michael Fordham** (see p.1399). A "sophisticated writer and thinker" on the specialty, his "compendious knowledge" has led to his involvement in cases of international significance, most recently in relation to nuclear weapons and power, and the detention of asylum seekers. Also very close to the star category, **Dinah Rose** (see p.1470) is said to be "approaching the pinnacle of her career as a junior," acting for both applicants and respondents. **Javan Herberg** (see p.1415) provides "balanced advice" and attracts accolades from traditional and commercial solicitors alike, while "diligent and clever," **Pushpinder Saini** (see p.1473) has principally been involved in human rights cases, particularly those with an asylum bent, including one at the

LEADING SILKS • London

1
- PANNICK David — Blackstone Chambers

1
- BELOFF Michael — Blackstone Chambers
- DRABBLE Richard — 4 Breams Buildings
- GORDON Richard — Brick Court Chambers
- HOWELL John — Blackstone Chambers
- PLEMING Nigel — 39 Essex Street
- SUMPTION Jonathan — Brick Court Chambers

2
- BLAKE Nicholas — Matrix Chambers
- FLINT Charles — Blackstone Chambers
- GOUDIE James — 11 King's Bench Walk Chambers
- HAVERS Philip — 1 Crown Office Row
- LESTER Anthony — Blackstone Chambers
- NICOL Andrew — Doughty Street Chambers

3
- BOOTH Cherie — Matrix Chambers
- CARSS-FRISK Monica — Blackstone Chambers
- FITZGERALD Edward — Doughty Street Chambers
- KENTRIDGE Sydney — Brick Court Chambers
- LUBA Jan — Two Garden Court

4
- ANDERSON David — Brick Court Chambers
- JAY Robert — 39 Essex Street
- KATKOWSKI Christopher — 4 Breams Buildings
- KERR Tim — 11 King's Bench Walk Chambers
- LANG Beverley — Blackstone Chambers
- LOWE Mark — 2-3 Gray's Inn Square
- OWEN Tim — Matrix Chambers
- SUPPERSTONE Michael — 11 King's Bench Walk Chambers

NEW SILKS
- CATCHPOLE Stuart — 39 Essex Street
- CLAYTON Richard — 39 Essex Street
- CORNER Timothy — 4-5 Gray's Inn Square
- GARNHAM Neil — 1 Crown Office Row
- SHAW Mark — Blackstone Chambers
- SINGH Rabinder — Matrix Chambers
- STARMER Keir — Doughty Street Chambers

For details of these leading barristers see Profiles on page 1353

LEADING JUNIORS • London

★
- FORDHAM Michael — Blackstone Chambers

1
- LEWIS Clive — 11 King's Bench Walk Chambers
- ROSE Dinah — Blackstone Chambers
- WOLFE David — Matrix Chambers

2
- GIFFIN Nigel — 11 King's Bench Walk Chambers
- GRIFFITHS Alan — One Essex Court
- HERBERG Javan — Blackstone Chambers
- HUNT Murray — Matrix Chambers
- LIEVEN Nathalie — 4 Breams Buildings
- MOUNTFIELD Helen — Matrix Chambers
- SAINI Pushpinder — Blackstone Chambers

3
- HARRISON Stephanie — Two Garden Court
- RICHARDS Jennifer — 39 Essex Street

4
- KNAFLER Stephen — Two Garden Court
- KOVATS Steven — 39 Essex Street
- LEWIS Adam — Blackstone Chambers
- MACLEAN Alan — Brick Court Chambers
- MARKUS Kate — Doughty Street Chambers
- MORRIS Fenella — 39 Essex Street
- TAM Robin — 1 Temple Gardens

UP AND COMING
- CRAGG Stephen — Doughty Street Chambers
- DE LA MARE Thomas — Blackstone Chambers
- MAURICI James — 4 Breams Buildings

For details of these leading barristers see Profiles on page 1353

ECHR. "Details man" **Adam Lewis** (see p.1435) is rated both in court and for his expansive regulatory advice. He enters the tables following warm

www.ChambersandPartners.com   1253

ADMINISTRATIVE & PUBLIC LAW

Research The rankings are based on in-depth interviews with 6,582 solicitors, barristers and clients in the UK. **Chambers'** research is audited by the British Market Research Bureau (see page 7)

BARRISTERS' PROFILES ▶ See pages 1353-1504

endorsement from solicitors, while "exceptionally talented young barrister" **Thomas de la Mare** (see p.1389) is building a brilliant reputation, especially among City practitioners.

MATRIX CHAMBERS (see full details p.1573) The set won considerable praise for the broad range of its expertise and the approachability of its members, whose "commitment to sticking their necks out in any given case" particularly impressed the traditional solicitors. **Nicholas Blake QC** (see p.1367) was praised for his ability to "explain the most difficult of concepts so that anyone can understand them." "A pleasure to work with," **Cherie Booth QC** (see p.1368) continues to act both for claimants and companies in a wide range of domestic and international cases. **Tim Owen QC** (see p.1457) impressed interviewees, particularly with regard to his representation of claimants in civil rights cases, recently including prisoners' rights and police powers. Everyone agreed that **Rabinder Singh QC** (see p.1479) would "do terribly well" as a new silk. Solicitors praised him for "striking a balance between being a brilliant, talented lawyer and having a social conscience." **David Wolfe** (see p.1501) ("bright and inventive in every way") has enjoyed a meteoric rise to prominence in the tables, and was heavily tipped as next in line for a starred ranking. Said to "prepare and present arguments beautifully," recent cases have involved appeals on behalf of claimants in the community care and education sectors, as well as on behalf of public bodies. **Murray Hunt** (see p.1421) is regarded as a "fantastic author and a knock out advocate" and is well known for his human rights expertise, while **Helen Mountfield** (see p.1451) received strong market commendation, particularly for the education aspects of her expansive public law practice.

4 BREAMS BUILDINGS (see full details p.1516) The set caters especially for the considerable volume of public law and judicial review work arising from its traditional areas of specialisation, namely planning and local government. The "quality of advice and extensive experience" on offer has given it a loyal following, with some interviewees vowing that they "would never go outside the set." A "fearsome opponent," **Richard Drabble QC** (see p.1391) is deemed to have "mastered the administrative arena, civil liberties and planning" while also possessing a sound knowledge of European law. Another "excellent advocate," **Christopher Katkowski QC** (see p.1426) has retained his market share, while the set's star junior **Nathalie Lieven** (see p.1436) combines a "clear, crisp style" with an "astonishing ability to grasp the issues quickly and become fluent in them." Lieven's expertise in social security matters was particularly well received by interviewees, and she has also appeared in judicial reviews in the health, mental health and education sectors. "Undoubtedly a rising star," according to solicitors, **James Maurici** (see p.1443) accordingly enters the tables.

BRICK COURT CHAMBERS (see full details p.1517) Fielding "a raft of incredibly able lawyers," it was felt by interviewees to be "especially expert on European competition law." The market particularly values this overlap in expertise, and the set moves up the tables accordingly. **Richard Gordon QC** (see p.1407) is the "barrister of choice if you have an unarguable case to argue," as he "is willing to challenge and develop the law where necessary." **Jonathan Sumption QC** "convincingly straddles the commercial and public spheres." Indeed, he is such a powerful advocate that one solicitor felt moved to claim: "he is brilliant at everything." **Sydney Kentridge QC** (see p.1428), whose "gravitas" wins admirers, continues to enjoy his place as "one of the sector's great names," while **David Anderson QC** (see p.1356) gains a foothold in the tables as the "practitioner who jumps out for having successfully bridged the gap between EU competition law and public law." Together with his colleagues at the set, **Alan Maclean** (see p.1440) continues to be involved in an impressive number of ground-breaking cases.

DOUGHTY STREET CHAMBERS (see full details p.1526)The Pantheon of civil liberties and human rights, the set also enjoys a large immigration practice. In the public law sphere, it continues to be fêted by the traditional solicitors. "A pre-eminent applicant lawyer," **Andrew Nicol QC** (see p.1455) was described by interviewees as "meticulous in arguing his case." He recently appeared in high-profile challenges concerning data protection and police actions. **Edward Fitzgerald QC** has been lead counsel in high profile life sentencing cases, including those of Anderson and Taylor. His formidable success as a barrister is said by peers to be "derived from his imaginative understanding of human rights law," particularly in the criminal context, where his profile is highest. Maintaining an extraordinarily wide practice, the "reliable and creative" **Kate Markus** has recently been involved, *inter alia*, in community care, education, and prisoners' rights cases. An "absolutely excellent human rights lawyer," much of new silk **Keir Starmer QC**'s considerable caseload involves public law, including judicial reviews. **Stephen Cragg** (see p.1385) has also "worked tremendously hard" to build up "respectable public law credentials."

39 ESSEX STREET (see full details p.1537) Typically described by market sources as "a dynamic chambers," researchers were persuaded by the praise lavished upon it that this set poses the strongest challenge to the top two. Rated as being "the most engaging of advocates," **Nigel Pleming QC** (see p.1461) is "vigorously analytical" to boot and is considered a major asset for the set. **Robert Jay QC** (see p.1424) has built up a large practice in the area, while, as a new silk this year, **Stuart Catchpole QC** (see p.1378) is deemed by interviewees to be "capable of going a long way." Newly advanced **Richard Clayton QC** (see p.1381), "a well established and highly rated public lawyer," has particular expertise in human rights. The set's top ranking junior **Jennifer Richards** (see p.1468) enjoys a "rising profile" and is especially admired for her community care expertise. **Steven Kovats** (see p.1431) has a "great capacity for absorbing complex principles," and **Fenella Morris** (see p.1450) was described by sources as providing "excellent strategic advice." Entering the tables for the first time, her high-profile recent cases have included that of Diane Pretty.

11 KING'S BENCH WALK CHAMBERS (see full details p.1566) "Some fantastic practitioners" are supported here by "a traditional clerking service that's nothing but helpful." Its all-round local authorities prowess makes the set well qualified for judicial reviews at both local and central government level. Interviewees also discern "steady growth," especially in terms of its education expertise. "A mental heavyweight," it was the versatility of **James Goudie QC** (see p.1408) that interviewees most admired. "Aggressive when necessary," **Tim Kerr QC** (see p.1428) is believed to have a promising career ahead of him, while solicitors also continue to call upon the services of highly respected **Michael Supperstone QC** (see p.1485). "Intellectually as sharp as mustard," **Clive Lewis**'s (see p.1435) high level of peer recommendation guarantees him a ranking amongst the best juniors. "Academically talented," his capacity for advising on policy and legislation, based on his extensive knowledge of local government through to EC law, particularly impressed interviewees. "Stylish, thoughtful and clever" **Nigel Giffin** (see p.1404) is also rated as "one of the brightest juniors," often receiving instructions on "cases with a twist" involving EC law, or where local government issues overlap with commercial law.

ADMINISTRATIVE & PUBLIC LAW

Research The rankings are based on in-depth interviews with 6,582 solicitors, barristers and clients in the UK. **Chambers'** research is audited by the British Market Research Bureau (see page 7)

BARRISTERS' PROFILES ▶ See pages 1353-1504

1 CROWN OFFICE ROW (see full details p.1524) The set offers a range of expertise and boasts two notable silks. Attracting praise for the breadth of his practice, **Philip Havers QC** (see p.1413) is described by solicitors as "succinct and clever while simultaneously possessing a human touch" in court. He has been involved in some high-profile right to life and right to die cases, acting as counsel to Diane Pretty and to 'Miss B'. **Neil Garnham QC** (see p.1402) is also felt to have consolidated his reputation, having devoted considerable time as lead counsel to the Climbié inquiry.

TWO GARDEN COURT (see full details p.1544) Immigration, housing and crime continue to be the core strengths of this set, whose supporters are drawn predominantly from the ranks of the traditional solicitors. When it comes to social housing and human rights law, **Jan Luba QC** is said to be "on the cutting edge." Interviewees were adamant that he is "certain to progress up the table," while the "stubborn persistence" of **Stephanie Harrison** won the admiration of lawyers working both with and against her. **Stephen Knafler** (see p.1430) also won plaudits from solicitors.

AGRICULTURE

Research The rankings are based on in-depth interviews with 6,582 solicitors, barristers and clients in the UK. **Chambers'** research is audited by the British Market Research Bureau (see page 7)

BARRISTERS' PROFILES ▶ See pages 1353-1504

OVERVIEW: By consensus, the enervated state of the industry has produced another quiet year at the agricultural Bar. Falcon Chambers remains the only true agricultural chambers, with a depth of knowledge and experience that none can match. In Scotland, advocates Gordon Reid of Simpson Stable ("pre-eminent") and Crispin Agnew of Westwater Stable ("innovative, high-profile") won special mention from solicitors.

LONDON

AGRICULTURE • London	QCs	Jnrs
[1] Falcon Chambers (Gaunt/Lewison)	4	6

Numbers show recommended barristers in this practice area

LEADING SILKS • London	
[1] MORGAN Paul	Falcon Chambers
WOOD Derek	Falcon Chambers
[2] BROCK Jonathan	Falcon Chambers
GAUNT Jonathan	Falcon Chambers

For details of these leading barristers see Profiles on page 1353

LEADING JUNIORS • London	
[1] MOSS Joanne	Falcon Chambers
RODGER Martin	Falcon Chambers
[2] HUTTON Caroline	Enterprise Chambers
JOURDAN Stephen	Falcon Chambers
[3] DE FREITAS Anthony	4 Paper Buildings
FANCOURT Timothy	Falcon Chambers
MCALLISTER Ann	Serle Court
MERCER Hugh	Essex Court Chambers
THOMAS Nigel	Maitland Chambers
WINDSOR Emily	Falcon Chambers
UP AND COMING	
SHEA Caroline	Falcon Chambers

For details of these leading barristers see Profiles on page 1353

FALCON CHAMBERS (see full details p.1539) Recognised as the UK's premier agricultural chambers; one solicitor enthused, "I can call up their clerk and not care who I get – they're all terrific." Top silks **Paul Morgan QC** (see p.1449) ("an agile mind") and **Derek Wood QC** (see p.1501) ("none wiser") combine presentation skills with a genuine interest in agricultural affairs, while **Jonathan Brock QC**'s (see p.1372) strong reputation is based on his courtroom muscle. "Calm and effective" **Jonathan Gaunt QC** won plaudits for his knowledge of landlord and tenant matters. The set is also home to a raft of juniors equally rich and vibrant. **Joanne Moss** and **Martin Rodger** (see p.1470) remain favourites among solicitors and clients on a national basis. Moss is both "flamboyant and academic," while "rights of way master" Rodger has a "mind like a steel trap." **Stephen Jourdan** (see p.1426) and **Timothy Fancourt** (see p.1396) also draw strong recommendations from both solicitors and members of the Bar. "Doughty fighter" **Emily Windsor** (see p.1500) moves up through our rankings this year, and "energetic" **Caroline Shea** (see p.1477) continues to be viewed as a barrister in the ascendant.

OTHER NOTABLE PRACTITIONERS At Enterprise Chambers, the "robust and practical" **Caroline Hutton** (see p.1372) handles agricultural cases with aplomb. **Anthony De Freitas** (see p.1372) of **4 Paper Buildings** was held up by solicitors as an example of a "safe pair of hands," while **Ann McAllister** (see p.1372) at **Serle Court** also wins many votes of confidence. **Hugh Mercer** (see p.1372) of **Essex Court Chambers** ("charming, effective") has a strong profile for agricultural cases that connect directly with human rights or the EU. **Nigel Thomas** (see p.1372) from **Maitland Chambers** was envied by peers for his client care skills.

ARBITRATION

Research The rankings are based on in-depth interviews with 6,582 solicitors, barristers and clients in the UK. Chambers' research is audited by the British Market Research Bureau (see page 7)

BARRISTERS' PROFILES ▶ See pages 1353-1504

LONDON

ESSEX COURT CHAMBERS (see full details p.1530) "Unbeatable for breadth and experience," this set remains "a byword for quality arbitration." It also boasts "the one name known everywhere outside England," **V.V. Veeder QC** (see p.1495), whose "great sensitivity, incredible talent and astounding knowledge" place him "in a league of his own" for commercial arbitrations. Praised for his "sensitivity to other cultures and ways," his linguistic skills and perceptiveness make him "the first and best" name that springs to mind for many of our interviewees. His duties at the FSA do not appear to affect the visibility of "robust character" **Stewart Boyd QC** (see p.1369). He is "a real heavyweight," and "top of the tree" for insurance work. His "cerebral" style notwithstanding, he "goes for the throat" and "gets things sorted." The "dependable" **Ian Hunter QC** (see p.1421) is also best known for his insurance/reinsurance work. His is a "direct style" and observers commended his "thoroughness." When he turns his hand to arbitration **Gordon Pollock QC** (see p.1461) is "terribly impressive" and a "real fighter." He is sought after as "ideal in any situation where the courtroom style suits." **Michael Collins QC** (see p.1382) is a "stalwart" of the arbitration sphere, and despite commitments in the US, is still professionally active in London. **Michael Thomas QC** (see p.1490) retains the "highest regard" of the market, whilst **Graham Dunning QC** (see p.1392) is "outstanding" and "in big demand." Peers proclaim that **Jeffrey Gruder QC** (see p.1410) is "damned good" in any commercial arbitration, with a style that is "highly versatile." "First amongst juniors" is the "super-smart and committed" **Toby Landau** (see p.1431) who offers "a happy marriage of common sense and intelligence." "A future Veeder," claimed one solicitor, he is considered "immensely articulate and charming," with that all important internationalism, and has achieved "immense stature for his work on the Arbitration Act." Commentators praise **Joe Smouha**'s (see p.1480) clarity and regard him as "an essentially brilliant advocate." **Richard Millett** (see p.1447) continues to build a name in this sphere.

ATKIN CHAMBERS (see full details p.1508) Rated highly for its engineering work across a range of sectors, including power projects, this is a "top-flight construction set." **Robert Akenhead QC** (see p.1355) is a "trusted advocate," and **John Blackburn QC**'s (see p.1366) reputation in civil engineering is recognised in all quarters. **Colin Reese QC** is a "tenacious operator," and a "brilliant writer" who is "unstoppable once the bit's between his teeth." The market also offered a resounding endorsement of **Andrew White QC** (see p.1499).

ONE ESSEX COURT (see full details p.1531) A highly regarded set with some first-rate silks doing commercial arbitrations in areas such as banking, oil and gas, insurance and joint ventures. "Golden-tongued" **Tony Grabiner QC** is "sensitive to the issues, yet always decisive." Sources conclude that his "classic silky smoothness" and "even-handed" style "get results out of difficult cases." **Ian Glick QC** (see p.1405) has both a "powerful yet low-key style" and **Mark Barnes QC** (see p.1362) impresses colleagues and tribunals alike with his "highly subtle but effective informality."

20 ESSEX STREET (see full details p.1534) In this admired set most barristers spend more than half their time in arbitrations. Following Peter Gross's move to the Bench, the spotlight is on "quietly persuasive" head of chambers, **Iain Milligan QC** (see p.1447), whom observers commend for being "careful and well prepared," and "non-theatrical."

ARBITRATION (INTERNATIONAL) • London

		QCs	Jnrs
1	Essex Court Chambers (Gordon Pollock QC)	8	3
2	Atkin Chambers (Robert Akenhead QC)	4	-
	One Essex Court (Anthony Grabiner QC)	3	-
	20 Essex Street (Iain Milligan QC)	1	-
	Keating Chambers	8	-
3	Brick Court Chambers (Christopher Clarke QC)	1	1
	4 Essex Court (Nigel Teare QC)	5	-
	7 King's Bench Walk (Kealey/Flaux)	4	-
	3 Verulam Buildings (Symons/Jarvis)	2	-

Numbers show recommended barristers in this practice area

LEADING SILKS • London

★	VEEDER V V	Essex Court Chambers
1	BOYD Stewart	Essex Court Chambers
	GLICK Ian	One Essex Court
	GRABINER Anthony	One Essex Court
	HUNTER Ian	Essex Court Chambers
	POLLOCK Gordon	Essex Court Chambers
	RAMSEY Vivian	Keating Chambers
2	AKENHEAD Robert	Atkin Chambers
	BLACKBURN John	Atkin Chambers
	COLLINS Michael	Essex Court Chambers
	FERNYHOUGH Richard	Keating Chambers
	MALEK Ali	3 Verulam Buildings
	UFF John	Keating Chambers
3	BARNES Mark	One Essex Court
	ELLIOTT Timothy	Keating Chambers
	GEE Steven	Stone Chambers
	HADDON-CAVE Charles	4 Essex Court
	HEILBRON Hilary	Brick Court Chambers
	KEALEY Gavin	7 King's Bench Walk
	MILLIGAN Iain	20 Essex Street
	REESE Colin	Atkin Chambers
	TACKABERRY John	Arbitration Chambers
	THOMAS Michael	Essex Court Chambers
4	BRENTON Timothy	7 King's Bench Walk
	BUCKNALL Belinda	4 Essex Court
	BUTCHER Christopher	7 King's Bench Walk
	DARLING Paul	Keating Chambers
	DUNNING Graham	Essex Court Chambers
	FURST Stephen	Keating Chambers
	GRUDER Jeffrey	Essex Court Chambers
	HOWARD M N	4 Essex Court
	SCHAFF Alistair	7 King's Bench Walk
	TEARE Nigel	4 Essex Court
	THOMAS Christopher	Keating Chambers
	WHITE Andrew	Atkin Chambers
5	JARVIS John	3 Verulam Buildings
	RUSSELL Jeremy	4 Essex Court
	TAVERNER Marcus	Keating Chambers

For details of these leading barristers see Profiles on page 1353

LEADING JUNIORS • London

1	LANDAU Toby	Essex Court Chambers
2	SMOUHA Joe	Essex Court Chambers
3	DAVIES Helen	Brick Court Chambers
	PLANTEROSE Rowan	Littman Chambers
4	MILLETT Richard	Essex Court Chambers

For details of these leading barristers see Profiles on page 1353

www.ChambersandPartners.com

ARBITRATION

Research The rankings are based on in-depth interviews with 6,582 solicitors, barristers and clients in the UK. **Chambers'** research is audited by the British Market Research Bureau (see page 7)

BARRISTERS' PROFILES ▶ See pages 1353-1504

KEATING CHAMBERS (see full details p.1560) Many agree it remains "first choice for construction arbitrations," and much of the set's work comes from the Far East, especially Hong Kong. Interviewees report that **Vivian Ramsey QC** (see p.1466) is "amenable, effective and very much in demand," while **Richard Fernyhough QC** (see p.1397) retains "a reputation of the first order" for large-scale domestic and international disputes. **John Uff QC** (see p.1494) is "at the forefront" of the construction arbitrations field despite being so occupied as chairman of the Southall Rail Inquiry. **Timothy Elliott QC**'s (see p.1394) reputation for infrastructure projects is "richly deserved," which is true also of **Paul Darling QC** (see p.1387), who is "going from strength to strength." Observers praise **Stephen Furst QC**'s (see p.1402) "wide-ranging competence" and **Christopher Thomas QC**'s (see p.1489) advocacy on the Tsung Ma Bridge arbitration. **Marcus Taverner QC** (see p.1387) offers energy and natural resources expertise.

BRICK COURT CHAMBERS (see full details p.1517) Experienced set with expertise in film finance and insurance. **Hilary Heilbron QC** (see p.1387) maintains an "outstanding reputation as an arbitrator and an attorney." **Helen Davies** (see p.1387) has a growing practice in high-value arbitrations and is acknowledged as a "highly impressive writer," who has a clear sight of all the issues.

4 ESSEX COURT (see full details p.1532) Commercial matters, shipping and international trade are at the foundations of this set. The diplomatic skills of **Charles Haddon-Cave QC** (see p.1410) are "highly prized," and his "first-class advocacy" is often deployed on aviation arbitrations. Chambers head **Nigel Teare QC** (see p.1489) is considered a favourite for shipping matters, in particular shipbuilding, while **Jeremy Russell QC** (see p.1472) was commended for his "astute" handling of matters ranging from insurance to aviation and wet and dry shipping. Admired as a skilled adviser, **M N Howard QC** (see p.1420) also sits as an ICC arbitrator and an LCIA arbitrator. **Belinda Bucknall QC** (see p.1374) secured the admiration of her peers, especially as one who has "a nice line in shipping."

7 KING'S BENCH WALK (see full details p.1564) The "always impressive" **Gavin Kealey QC** (see p.1371) has reinsurance expertise and admired advocacy skills. "Able and articulate - in French if need be," with a "delightful sense of humour," he is considered "a star." **Timothy Brenton QC** (see p.1371) scores well for his "clarity of expression" and "straightforwardness." A "rising star" is "tenacious advocate" **Christopher Butcher QC** (see p.1375), while **Alistair Schaff QC** (see p.1474) is "gifted and sensitive."

3 VERULAM BUILDINGS (see full details p.1615) A "fine choice for finance," this set boasts the "generally underrated" **Ali Malek QC** (see p.1440). Making deep inroads into arbitration, he wields "impressive court skills" and a "fluid manner" to great effect, often on behalf of Iranian clients. **John Jarvis QC** (see p.1424) also has the approbation of the market.

OTHER NOTABLE PRACTITIONERS "Prolific" **Steven Gee QC** (see p.1403) of Stone Chambers is valued for his "encyclopaedic knowledge." Head of Arbitration Chambers, **John Tackaberry QC** has a strong profile in the field and earns the respect of his peers. "Solid and persistent" **Rowan Planterose** (see p.1355) from Littman Chambers is valued for his "unassuming manner," and is considered "just right for very technical matters."

AVIATION

Research The rankings are based on in-depth interviews with 6,582 solicitors, barristers and clients in the UK. **Chambers'** research is audited by the British Market Research Bureau (see page 7)

BARRISTERS' PROFILES ▶ See pages 1353-1504

OVERVIEW: The former 5 Bell Yard members continue to dominate the Bar from their respective chambers, owing to long experience within the sector. Several barristers acquire aviation expertise in the course of other specialisms, such as insurance or finance. Increasingly important to the aviation industry is competition law, by which regulatory issues are becoming subsumed.

LONDON

AVIATION • London	QCs	Jnrs
1. Brick Court Chambers (Christopher Clarke QC)	1	1
4 Essex Court (Nigel Teare QC)	1	1
Fountain Court (Anthony Boswood QC)	1	2
2. Essex Court Chambers (Gordon Pollock QC)	1	1

Numbers show recommended barristers in this practice area

LEADING SILKS • London	
1. CRANE Michael	Fountain Court
2. HADDON-CAVE Charles	4 Essex Court
WOOD William	Brick Court Chambers
3. HUNTER Ian	Essex Court Chambers
MCMANUS Richard	4-5 Gray's Inn Square

For details of these leading barristers see Profiles on page 1353

LEADING JUNIORS • London	
1. LYDIARD Andrew	Brick Court Chambers
SHAH Akhil	Fountain Court
SHEPHERD Philip	24 Old Buildings
2. LAWSON Robert	4 Essex Court
THANKI Bankim	Fountain Court
3. JOSEPH David	Essex Court Chambers
OWEN Tudor	9-12 Bell Yard

For details of these leading barristers see Profiles on page 1353

BRICK COURT CHAMBERS (see full details p.1517) Respected commercial chambers populated by "highly individual practitioners." A much admired aviation practice has produced "two outstanding barristers" recommended to Chambers. "Youthful and impressive" **William Wood QC** (see p.1502) has acted extensively in drafting and advisory work for major carriers on commercial and Warsaw Convention issues. He also has expertise in private arbitrations of leasing disputes, and he acted in the Southend Airport licensing dispute. "Intellectual powerhouse" **Andrew Lydiard** (see p.1439) is much admired in the sector, particularly for his work on the insurance side, and is said to be "knocking on the doors of QC." He also has considerable experience in arbitrations.

4 ESSEX COURT (see full details p.1532) Together with shipping, aviation is a key specialism of this "well-run" chambers. It remains the first choice for many in matters across the board in aviation, from cargo to disasters. The "ever-excellent" **Charles Haddon-Cave QC** (see p.1410) is the name of choice here. A "first-rate, classy pair of hands," he has a broad commercial, aviation, shipping and insurance practice, and is regarded as "the authority in air disaster work." He acted for KLM in Morris v KLM, a crucial case to clarify the meanings of the terms 'bodily injury' and 'accident' under the Warsaw Convention. **Robert Lawson** (see p.1433) is widely respected for his grasp of civil and commercial law, especially in relation to aviation, and he is considered an expert on the Warsaw Convention.

FOUNTAIN COURT (see full details p.1541) A respected set that is established in this area, and that boasts some of the top names in the business, acting in related commercial, regulatory and insurance matters. The market is virtually unanimous in its crowning of **Michael Crane QC** as "undisputed king of the hill." An "imaginative and stylish advocate," he is praised for his "ability to absorb hugely demanding technical problems at short notice." He acted in R v Civil Aviation Authority exp Jet Services Ltd, upholding a public law challenge to the CAA's ruling on Air Travel Organisers' Licence. Also singled out was "gifted and rising" **Akhil Shah** (see p.1476), commended for his technical grasp. He represented Royal Brunei Airlines in the cargo claim brought by Aspreys on the loss of jewellery. **Bankim Thanki** (see p.1489) has admirers who consider him "bright and thorough, responsive and understated." Solicitors, won over by his "great intellect and tactics," are using him more and more in this field. He acted for Boeing in the Commercial Court in the case of the repossession of a 747 aircraft.

ESSEX COURT CHAMBERS (see full details p.1530) A full-service commercial litigation set where much of its aviation work is generated by an expertise in insurance. **Ian Hunter QC** (see p.1421) is a "sharp commercial silk," who specialises in insurance/reinsurance. He acted in the case of the Gerona air crash, and is widely admired for his work in arbitration. **David Joseph** (see p.1426) also comes from the insurance angle and acted in Quantum v Air France. He also has expertise in space-related matters.

OTHER NOTABLE PRACTITIONERS Considered in some quarters to be "by far the best in the business," **Philip Shepherd** of 24 Old Buildings impresses as "dedicated, reliable and enthusiastic." He boasts "a QCs practice," without the initials. Respected **Richard McManus QC** at 4-5 Gray's Inn Square acted on the R v CAA exp Jet Services matter. 9-12 Bell Yard's **Tudor Owen** is renowned for his work in criminal matters, and receives the recognition of the marketplace for his specialist aviation knowledge.

BANKING

Research The rankings are based on in-depth interviews with 6,582 solicitors, barristers and clients in the UK. **Chambers'** research is audited by the British Market Research Bureau (see page 7).

BARRISTERS' PROFILES ▶ See pages 1353-1504

OVERVIEW: Leading City banking practices aim to remove the transactional advisory role from the Bar, resulting in its remit being increasingly restricted to second opinions and matters that are client-driven or that involve high stakes where solicitors seek to share the risk. Swelling numbers of in-house advocates and dedicated provincial practices have decreased law firms' need for junior counsel on contentious regulatory matters. However, the scope for leaders within this context remains broad, not least because "Olympian figures are needed on Olympian cases." Industry players agree that there are "fewer giants about" with the departure of Goldsmith, Hoffman, Millet and Scott leaving a slight void - "there are but a few who can fill the gap."

LONDON

FOUNTAIN COURT (see full details p.1541) "Pre-eminent for pure banking work," according to market sources who acknowledge the set's "mark of quality" on significant cases that include the Barings litigation, Morgan Grenfell v SACE, RBS v Etridge and Three Rivers District Council v Bank of England. Plaudits abound for "outstanding all-rounder" **Michael Brindle QC** (see p.1372) whose clients appreciate his "broader perspective on commercial issues." A barrister with "real authority and great conviction," he is "always well prepared and looks at all angles for a positive answer." Head of chambers **Anthony Boswood QC** (see p.1368) is recommended for his expertise across banking regulatory matters, particularly within the contexts of insurance, professional negligence, judicial review and administrative law. Described as "direct, often bullish" in court, his clients endorse his ability to "see the wood for the trees." Those who instruct **David Railton QC** (see p.1466) enthuse about his "colossally thorough" approach and "conversational, relaxed, modern advocacy" that appeals to both judges and tribunals. "Brainbox" **Nicholas Stadlen QC** (see p.1482) gains strong recognition for championing high-profile matters on behalf of the Bank of England. Among the new silks, **Raymond Cox QC** (see p.1385) gains his peers' admiration for his "calm, straightforward" advocacy and "skilful" writing of leading texts, while clients report that **David Waksman QC** (see p.1496) is "well prepared and responsive" to their needs. "Everyone loves" leading junior **Bankim Thanki** (see p.1489) who continues to garner "universally good press," while **Timothy Howe** (see p.1420) is popular with City firms as one who will "produce the goodies" and is "incredibly diligent – no stone gets left unturned." Solicitors endorse **Andrew Mitchell** (see p.1448) as a "striking courtroom presence" who, along with **Richard Handyside** (see p.1411), is a "strong team player who rolls up his sleeves and gets stuck in."

3 VERULAM BUILDINGS (see full details p.1615) A set of "extremely able specialists," it is favoured by City firms for its technical advice on general and domestic banking matters, although its "low-key" style leads some to opine that it "hides its light under a bushel." Leading practitioners endorse "the undisputed technical guru" **William Blair QC** (see p.1367) for his "sound, user-friendly" advice on regulatory and derivatives matters. Clients repeatedly instruct "top-notch" **Ali Malek QC** (see p.1440) for his "self-assured ability to see which way the wind is blowing." Described as "enormously engaging," he handles complex matters "with consummate ease." Market commentators endorse **Richard Salter QC** (see p.1473) as "an effective and highly industrious" advocate, writer and lecturer, who "knows a lot about the subject." Still regarded by many as "first-rate," **Neville Thomas QC** (see p.1490) gains recognition for his work in the Far East, while **John Jarvis QC** (see p.1424) is commended, particularly in an advisory context. Popular among retail banking clients, new silk **Andrew Onslow QC** (see p.1457) impresses with his "extreme articulacy on complex matters that makes things sound simple." "Brilliant cross-examiner" **Stephen Phillips QC** (see p.1460) has also taken silk this year and receives peer endorsement as a "hard-working, safe pair of hands" on general commercial matters. Among the juniors, solicitors recommend "sharp, smooth" **Adrian Beltrami** (see p.1364) for his broad-ranging skills in banking, transactional and derivatives work, while they endorse "softly spoken, low-key" **Jonathan Nash** (see p.1453) as a "penetrating, thorough" practitioner. His peers commend "quiet, clever" junior **Jonathan Davies-Jones** (see p.1388), while "sensible, bright" **Ewan McQuater** (see p.1445) is noted for his ability to "get quickly to the point." "Leading solicitors have "great hopes for" **Sonia Tolaney** (see p.1491), endorsing her "confident, determined" approach on general commercial banking matters.

BANKING & FINANCE • London

	QCs	Jnrs
1 Fountain Court (Anthony Boswood QC)	6	4
3 Verulam Buildings (Symons/Jarvis)	7	5
2 Brick Court Chambers (Christopher Clarke QC)	3	-
3 One Essex Court (Lord Grabiner QC)	4	2
4 Erskine Chambers (Robin Potts QC)	3	-
Essex Court Chambers (Gordon Pollock QC)	2	2
20 Essex Street (Iain Milligan QC)	1	-
3-4 South Square (Crystal/Alexander)	4	-

Numbers show recommended barristers in this practice area

LEADING SILKS • London

★ BRINDLE Michael	Fountain Court
HAPGOOD Mark	Brick Court Chambers
1 SUMPTION Jonathan	Brick Court Chambers
2 BLAIR William	3 Verulam Buildings
GRABINER Anthony	One Essex Court
HOWARD Mark	Brick Court Chambers
MALEK Ali	3 Verulam Buildings
MILLIGAN Iain	20 Essex Street
POLLOCK Gordon	Essex Court Chambers
POTTS Robin	Erskine Chambers
3 BOSWOOD Anthony	Fountain Court
DICKER Robin	3-4 South Square
RAILTON David	Fountain Court
SALTER Richard	3 Verulam Buildings
4 ANDREWS Geraldine	Essex Court Chambers
HACKER Richard	3-4 South Square
JARVIS John	3 Verulam Buildings
KNOWLES Robin	3-4 South Square
MALEK Hodge	4-5 Gray's Inn Square
PHILLIPS Mark	3-4 South Square
STADLEN Nicholas	Fountain Court
5 BARNES Mark	One Essex Court
BRIGGS Michael	Serle Court
BUTCHER Christopher	7 King's Bench Walk
DAVIES Rhodri	One Essex Court
OLIVER David	Erskine Chambers
RICHARDS David	Erskine Chambers
THOMAS R Neville	3 Verulam Buildings
WATERS Malcolm	11 Old Square
NEW SILKS	
COX Raymond	Fountain Court
MILES Robert	4 Stone Buildings
ONSLOW Andrew	3 Verulam Buildings
PHILLIPS Stephen	3 Verulam Buildings
RABINOWITZ Laurence	One Essex Court
WAKSMAN David	Fountain Court

For details of these leading barristers see Profiles on page 1353

BANKING

Research The rankings are based on in-depth interviews with 6,582 solicitors, barristers and clients in the UK. **Chambers'** research is audited by the British Market Research Bureau (see page 7)

BARRISTERS' PROFILES ▶ See pages 1353-1504

LEADING JUNIORS • London

1
THANKI Bankim	Fountain Court

2
BELTRAMI Adrian	3 Verulam Buildings
HOWE Timothy	Fountain Court
MILLETT Richard	Essex Court Chambers
NASH Jonathan	3 Verulam Buildings
WOLFSON David	One Essex Court

3
DAVIES-JONES Jonathan	3 Verulam Buildings
MCCAUGHRAN John	One Essex Court
MCQUATER Ewan	3 Verulam Buildings
MITCHELL Andrew	Fountain Court
SMOUHA Joe	Essex Court Chambers
TOLANEY Sonia	3 Verulam Buildings

UP AND COMING
HANDYSIDE Richard	Fountain Court

For details of these leading barristers see Profiles on page 1353

BRICK COURT CHAMBERS (see full details p.1517) Not regarded as a traditional banking name, this "high-quality" commercial set nevertheless features strongly on financial and regulatory matters, and is a popular choice among City practices for construction of "slender, fine decisions." "Top of the class" **Mark Hapgood QC** is widely regarded as a "leading authority and genuine specialist" with "succinct" advocacy skills. He is said to be the City's "first port of call" for advice on letters of credit and SWAPs matters. **Jonathan Sumption QC**'s stellar reputation "just gets better and better," according to leading practitioners. A "first-class cross-examiner with a brilliant brain," he has maintained his high profile within the sector with major cases such as Unilever. Witnesses of his performance marvel : "Unbelievably good – he doesn't appear to draw breath." Both leaders appeared for opposing parties in Emerald Properties v Allied Irish Bank. **Mark Howard QC** (see p.1420) also receives high praise from leading solicitors for his "excellent" ability to get on top of technically complicated cases. He is described as an "articulate, formidable opponent" who is "incredibly credible and has the ear of the judge."

ONE ESSEX COURT (see full details p.1531) Providing a broad mix of specialist and commercial expertise, the set enjoys "cosy" long term relationships with leading City practices. "Great commercial heavyweight" head of chambers **Anthony Grabiner QC** continues to be "in high demand" with a reputation that is "off the end of the scale." A "favourite" with premier law firms, **Mark Barnes QC** (see p.1362) is described as an "immensely clever and engaging" silk who puts himself out to meet tight deadlines. Leading solicitors commend "incredibly industrious, well-organised" **Rhodri Davies QC** (see p.1387) for his expertise on SWAPs matters, and enthuse that new silk **Laurence Rabinowitz QC** (see p.1465) has "outstanding" technical expertise that renders him "an absolute delight to work with" and "effective in everything he does." His peers describe **David Wolfson** (see p.1501) as "a charming advocate" whose clients are "taken by his hard - working, perceptive approach and enormous enthusiasm. "Newly ranked **John McCaughran** (see p.1444) receives solid endorsement as an "experienced, measured" advocate.

ERSKINE CHAMBERS (see full details p.1529) Firms gravitate towards this set for "skilled examination" of banking matters that often cross into corporate aspects. Leading lawyers report that head of chambers **Robin Potts QC** (see p.1462) has a "guru-like quality, so people always listen to him." An "outstandingly practical" silk, he has been advising on lending and company debt matters. Commentators are also "really impressed by top-class advocate" **David Richards QC** (see p.1468), while **David Oliver QC**'s (see p.1456) ability to "read the commercial situation and the other side with such impressive clarity" makes him an "ideal choice for discussing matters with before taking them to court."

ESSEX COURT CHAMBERS (see full details p.1530)This set is home to a number of leaders who have considerable reputations in the field. Head of chambers **Gordon Pollock QC** (see p.1461) continues to display the "measure of his reputation" as "an absolutely fearless, formidable opponent" who "can be counted on to fight a difficult case successfully." **Geraldine Andrews QC** (see p.1357) has a strong reputation in undue influence and security guarantee work. "A cerebral, original thinker, " she is said by solicitors to apply her "purist banking credentials" with an "amazingly thorough and vigorous approach." In a similar vein, leading junior **Richard Millett** (see p.1447) appeals to solicitors for his "human" qualities and "novel approach," while "superb" **Joe Smouha** (see p.1480) has widely impressed with his busy, broad-based practice.

20 ESSEX STREET (see full details p.1534) Clients praise the "excellent service" they receive from this set, allotting strong commendation to the strength among its juniors. Famed for his expertise in derivatives and SWAPs matters, head of chambers **Iain Milligan QC** (see p.1447) continues to impress his peers with his "accurate grasp and attention to detail" on "conspicuous cases," which have included advising Equitable Life on its scheme of arrangement and Shanning in the House of Lords. As regards his advocacy, he "cross-examines with a nice tempo that judges like" and has "a great ability to express complicated things simply and clearly."

3-4 SOUTH SQUARE (see full details p.1603) This "talent-packed set" has a strong profile in finance and insolvency-based matters. Recent highlights include Three Rivers District Council v Bank of England and National Westminster Bank v Utrecht-America Finance Company. Leading lawyers wax lyrical about "shooting star" **Robin Dicker QC** (see p.1390) , who stands out as having "fulfilled all the promise he showed at an early stage." An "unflappable" silk, he "cuts everything right down to the bone." **Richard Hacker QC** (see p.1410) remains highly rated, despite his decreased profile while advising in Hong Kong, on matters that include letters of credit, derivatives and jurisdictional disputes. Instructing solicitors also rate "quietly effective, smooth operator" **Robin Knowles QC** (see p.1430), and **Mark Phillips QC** (see p.1460) who is "extremely approachable and user-friendly" and "a real bruiser in court."

OTHER NOTABLE PRACTITIONERS An acknowledged expert on discovery disclosure and regulatory matters, **Hodge Malek QC** (see p.1440) of 4-5 Gray's Inn Square is "diligent, entertaining and superb with clients," according to those who instruct him. Newly ranked, **Michael Briggs QC** (see p.1371) of Serle Court is endorsed by solicitors as a "reliable, commercial" silk who benefits from his traditional chancery background. His peers admire "desperately clever" insurance specialist **Christopher Butcher QC** (see p.1375) of 7 King's Bench Walk for his "sensible judgement and nerves of steel." **Malcolm Waters QC** (see p.1498) of 11 Old Square is best known for his "substantial" work for building societies and banks on mortgage and other retail products, while instructing solicitors report that **Robert Miles QC** (see p.1447) of 4 Stone Buildings "adds value" with his "enormously careful, imaginative" input on a broad range of work that includes banking and financial services-related disputes.

CHANCERY

Research The rankings are based on in-depth interviews with 6,582 solicitors, barristers and clients in the UK. Chambers' research is audited by the British Market Research Bureau (see page 7)

BARRISTERS' PROFILES ▶ See pages 1353-1504

LONDON — COMMERCIAL

CHANCERY: COMMERCIAL • London	QCs	Jnrs
1 Maitland Chambers (Lyndon-Stanford/Aldous)	7	4
2 Serle Court (Lord Neill of Bladen QC)	4	4
3-4 South Square (Crystal/Alexander)	4	2
4 Stone Buildings (Philip Heslop QC)	5	3
Wilberforce Chambers (Edward Nugee QC)	3	4
3 New Square Chambers (Charles Purle QC)	2	-
24 Old Buildings (Mann/Steinfeld)	2	-
3 Stone Buildings (Geoffrey Vos QC)	2	-
11 Stone Buildings (Murray Rosen QC)	2	1

Numbers show recommended barristers in this practice area

MAITLAND CHAMBERS (see full details p.1572) Firmly established as a set with "a number of eye-catching leaders and juniors," **Charles Aldous QC** continues to generate admiration for his work in the Barings litigation and on a host of leading cases where he shows himself to be "a real thinker, coming at questions from every conceivable angle." Vice-chairman of the Chancery Bar Association **Anthony Trace QC** (see p.1492) has appeared in Shalson v Russo, a £20 million fraud case, and "combines complaisance with vigour," while **Guy Newey QC**'s (see p.1453) "indubitable intellect" leads some observers to peg him as "destined for the Bench." **Christopher Pymont QC** (see p.1465) is lauded for his property-related work, whereas **Paul Girolami QC** (see p.1405) is viewed as "formidable on company commercial matters." **Mark Cunningham QC** (see p.1387), who handled an abundance of work for the Government as a junior, is also recommended, alongside **Catherine Newman QC** (see p.1453), whose "imposing stance proves effective." Solicitors and barristers alike were full of enthusiasm for **John Nicholls**' "low-key efficiency" and identified him as "undoubtedly a barrister one would not like to be against," an epithet also applied to **Matthew Collings** (see p.1382), whose "appealing and confident manner" is regularly deployed on DTI disqualification matters. Rounding out the picture here are two barristers of differing seniority. **Alastair Walton** (see p.1497) is a seasoned junior, "reserved in manner, but with a classy practice that stretches from insolvency to construction," while the comparative parvenu, **Rebecca Stubbs** (see p.1485), shines as "an academically gifted performer who can exploit a weakness well."

SERLE COURT (see full details p.1602) **Michael Briggs QC** (see p.1371) is the star performer here, handling commercial and traditional chancery with his "customary spark of brilliance." Rivalling him is **Alan Boyle QC** (see p.1370), back from his exertions in Bermuda on the Thyssen case, and respected for his "understated but meticulous style." Further buttressing the sound reputation for leaders in this set are **Patrick Talbot QC** and **Victor Joffe QC**, who are both viewed as "decent and thorough." Leading juniors include **Douglas Close** (see p.1381), who is "humorous and engaging, with a clear grasp of the commercialities of a situation," and **Philip Marshall** (see p.1442), "one of the toughest advocates around" who can "collapse the house round the feet of evasive witnesses." At the more junior end, **Philip Jones** (see p.1426) displays "wells of common sense," while **Daniel Lightman** (see p.1436) "continues to show every indication of one day matching the achievements of his illustrious father."

3-4 SOUTH SQUARE (see full details p.1603) Renowned within the Inns for its insolvency expertise, this set also offers general chancery advice to a high standard. **Michael Crystal QC** (see p.1386) has finished his stint on Thyssen and is a "leading light" in areas including banking, company and professional negligence. **Gabriel Moss QC** (see p.1450) has a similar com-

LEADING SILKS • London

1	ALDOUS Charles	Maitland Chambers
	BRIGGS Michael	Serle Court
	GLOSTER Elizabeth	One Essex Court
	HESLOP Philip	4 Stone Buildings
	SHER Jules	Wilberforce Chambers
	VOS Geoffrey	3 Stone Buildings
2	BOYLE Alan	Serle Court
	CRYSTAL Michael	3-4 South Square
	HILDYARD Robert	4 Stone Buildings
	MANN Anthony	Enterprise Chambers
	MOSS Gabriel	3-4 South Square
	OLIVER David	Erskine Chambers
	STEINFELD Alan	24 Old Buildings
3	BANNISTER Edward	3 Stone Buildings
	BOMPAS Anthony	4 Stone Buildings
	BRISBY John	4 Stone Buildings
	MOWSCHENSON Terence	Wilberforce Chambers
	PURLE Charles	New Square Chambers
	ROSEN Murray	11 Stone Buildings
	TRACE Anthony	Maitland Chambers
4	CROXFORD Ian	Wilberforce Chambers
	KAYE Roger	24 Old Buildings
	MCDONNELL John	9 Stone Buildings
	NEWEY Guy	Maitland Chambers
	NEWMAN Catherine	Maitland Chambers
	PYMONT Christopher	Maitland Chambers
	SMITH Stephen	New Square Chambers
	TALBOT Patrick	Serle Court
	TROWER William	3-4 South Square
NEW SILKS		
	CUNNINGHAM Mark	Maitland Chambers
	GIRET Jane	11 Stone Buildings
	GIROLAMI Paul	Maitland Chambers
	JOFFE Victor	Serle Court
	MILES Robert	4 Stone Buildings
	PASCOE Martin	3-4 South Square

For details of these leading barristers see Profiles on page 1353

LEADING JUNIORS • London

1	NICHOLLS John	Maitland Chambers
2	CLOSE Douglas	Serle Court
	COLLINGS Matthew	Maitland Chambers
	MARSHALL Philip	Serle Court
	WALTON Alastair	Maitland Chambers
3	AYLIFFE James	Wilberforce Chambers
	COHEN Edward	11 Stone Buildings
	GRIFFITHS Peter	4 Stone Buildings
	HARRISON Christopher	4 Stone Buildings
	HOCHBERG Daniel	Wilberforce Chambers
	JONES Philip	Serle Court
4	ARDEN Peter	Enterprise Chambers
	ATHERTON Stephen	3-4 South Square
	FURZE Caroline	Wilberforce Chambers
	LEECH Thomas	9 Old Square
	ZACAROLI Antony	3-4 South Square
UP AND COMING		
	CAMPBELL Emily	Wilberforce Chambers
	HILL Richard	4 Stone Buildings
	LIGHTMAN Daniel	Serle Court
	STUBBS Rebecca	Maitland Chambers

For details of these leading barristers see Profiles on page 1353

CHANCERY

Research The rankings are based on in-depth interviews with 6,582 solicitors, barristers and clients in the UK. **Chambers'** research is audited by the British Market Research Bureau (see page 7)

BARRISTERS' PROFILES ▶ See pages 1353-1504

pass to his practice and is "one of the first in there on the bigger matters," along with **William Trower QC** (see p.1493), who can count the Maxwell, BCCI, Polly Peck, and Bermuda Fire & Marine Insurance cases as feathers in his cap. They have recently been joined in silk by **Martin Pascoe QC** (see p.1458), who has been involved in the Government of Brunei v Prince Jefri case and acted for the English administrators of Enron. Talented juniors include **Stephen Atherton** (see p.1359), who worked on the Barings litigation, and **Antony Zacaroli** (see p.1503), who proved himself "hot stuff" in the Brunei case.

4 STONE BUILDINGS (see full details p.1606) **Philip Heslop QC** remains "a towering presence" despite being slightly out of sight recently due to work on the Abacha case and on a major derivatives trial in Hong Kong. Negotiating a practice that includes insolvency, financial services, commercial chancery and banking, he is "very much the totem of the set." His colleagues include the "lyrical" **Anthony Bompas QC** (see p.1368) and **John Brisby QC** (see p.1372) who, despite eliciting differing reactions from our researchers, was generally seen to have "undoubted acumen in this field." **Robert Hildyard QC** (see p.1415) is "enormously respected as an advocate." He is now joined in silk, to the consternation of none, by **Robert Miles QC** (see p.1447), "a real star of the future." Prominent among the juniors are **Peter Griffiths** (see p.1410), "good at unravelling the more esoteric aspects of the law," and **Christopher Harrison** (see p.1412), a regular presence in the Interim Applications Court, who is "well thought of by solicitors." Solicitors were also agreed that **Richard Hill** (see p.1416) was a name for the future, citing in support his "acute intelligence, commercial awareness and ability to devour papers."

WILBERFORCE CHAMBERS (see full details p.1616) Our researchers detected great affection towards **Jules Sher QC** (see p.1478) from those juniors who had been led by him. Possessed of "peerless knowledge, a tremendously sharp brain and an appealing manner," observers felt that he is "expensive but ultimately more than worth his salt." **Ian Croxford QC** and **Terence Mowschenson QC** (see p.1451) also received praise. The former is known for his "booming court delivery," and the latter for "a measured and cerebral approach." The most high-profile juniors are **James Ayliffe** (see p.1359), "a good, straight up and down lawyer," **Caroline Furze** (see p.1402) and **Emily Campbell** (see p.1376), who both retain the support of the market. **Daniel Hochberg** (see p.1417) is respected for his work in trusts (offshore and onshore) and professional negligence.

NEW SQUARE CHAMBERS (see full details p.1580) Described by one leading solicitor as "the best I've ever seen," **Charles Purle QC** (see p.1465) is "clever, inventive and committed." His "impeccable preparation" belies an outward impression of occasional disorganisation. Younger silk **Stephen Smith QC** (see p.1480) is touted as a name with a starry future.

24 OLD BUILDINGS (see full details p.1582) At this set, interviewees endorsed the "highly authoritative" **Alan Steinfeld QC**. "Punchy and confident in an unpompous way," he handles a broad practice that embraces a good deal of offshore work. Fellow silk **Roger Kaye QC** spends a proportion of his time sitting as a deputy judge and is regarded as "wholly unflappable."

3 STONE BUILDINGS (see full details p.1605) Proud holder of one of the largest practices at the Chancery Bar, **Geoffrey Vos QC** (see p.1496) is "a daunting and extremely honourable opponent." Similarly lauded, **Edward Bannister QC** (see p.1361) is "a consummate court performer, especially good at disarming hostile tribunals."

11 STONE BUILDINGS (see full details p.1608) **Murray Rosen QC** (see p.1471) has a broad caseload and is "well versed in the lore of legal niceties," while junior **Edward Cohen** (see p.1382) and new silk **Jane Giret QC** (see p.1405) are both known for their "forceful approach."

OTHER NOTABLE PRACTITIONERS Elizabeth Gloster QC (see p.1406) of One Essex Court is "a real commercial animal" who is "effective on her feet and able to pitch her case at the correct level." Her commercial awareness is shared by **Anthony Mann QC** (see p.1441) of Enterprise Chambers, who "is fantastic and presents as down to earth." At the same set **Peter Arden** received the backing of a number of his peers. **David Oliver QC** (see p.1456) of Erskine Chambers is "an interesting character with a fantastic legal brain." "Brilliant on his day" he has "a carefree approach," often dispensing with the use of notes in court and relying on his "exceptional advocacy skills." **John McDonnell QC** (see p.1444) of 9 Stone Buildings is "extremely learned, with "a dogged attitude," which sees him "fight everything up hill and down dale." **Thomas Leech** (see p.1433) of 9 Old Square, a veteran of the Thyssen case, is recommended as "a busy bee around the Inns" who undertakes a fair proportion of professional negligence work.

LONDON — TRADITIONAL

CHANCERY: TRADITIONAL • London	QCs	Jnrs
1. **Wilberforce Chambers** (Edward Nugee QC)	7	3
2. **5 Stone Buildings** (Henry Harrod)	5	3
3. **Maitland Chambers** (Lyndon-Stanford/Aldous)	2	1
11 New Square (Sonia Proudman QC)	1	2
New Square Chambers (Charles Purle QC)	2	2
10 Old Square (Leolin Price QC)	1	4

Numbers show recommended barristers in this practice area

WILBERFORCE CHAMBERS (see full details p.1616) Rightfully heading our tables, this set has a clutch of respected minds in this most cerebral of legal disciplines. **Brian Green QC** (see p.1408) "goes from strength to strength," applying his "not inconsiderable brain" to a caseload rich in pensions work. He offers a "costly but unparalleled service" in common with **Jules Sher QC** (see p.1478), another "great trusts expert with peerless knowledge." The set further boasts the chairman of the Chancery Bar Association **Nick Warren QC** (see p.1497), "a wonderfully clever and painstaking practitioner" heavily involved in tax and private client work. **Robert Ham QC** (see p.1411) is celebrated for his "extensive knowledge," as is **John Martin QC**, who is seen in the larger cases, many of which concern liquidation and receivership issues. Completing the silks line-up are **Edward Nugee QC** (see p.1455), "extremely senior and something of a demigod," and his son **Christopher Nugee QC** (see p.1455), who "always gives the opposition a real headache." Those in waiting among the juniors include "accomplished draftsman" **John Child** (see p.1379), "veteran of many a campaign" **Anthony Taussig** (see p.1488) and "classic trusts and private client practitioner" **Judith Bryant** (see p.1373).

5 STONE BUILDINGS (see full details p.1607) Interviewees commented upon **Mark Herbert QC**'s (see p.1415) "logical and thoughtful" approach to a practice that straddles tax and trusts work. "Happier on the advisory side," he is a skilled draftsman with a "wonderful conceptual grasp." He shares an interest in revenue work with **Launcelot Henderson QC** (see p.1414), a Fellow of All Souls, who "has appeared in the House of Lords

CHANCERY

Research The rankings are based on in-depth interviews with 6,582 solicitors, barristers and clients in the UK. Chambers' research is audited by the British Market Research Bureau (see page 7)

BARRISTERS' PROFILES ▶ See pages 1353-1504

LEADING SILKS • London

1
BRIGGS Michael	Serle Court
GREEN Brian	Wilberforce Chambers
MCCALL Christopher	Maitland Chambers
SHER Jules	Wilberforce Chambers
WARREN Nicholas	Wilberforce Chambers

2
HAM Robert	Wilberforce Chambers
HERBERT Mark	5 Stone Buildings
MOWBRAY John	New Square Chambers
NUGEE Christopher	Wilberforce Chambers
NUGEE Edward	Wilberforce Chambers
PROUDMAN Sonia	11 New Square
TAUBE Simon	10 Old Square

3
HENDERSON Launcelot	5 Stone Buildings
LAURENCE George	New Square Chambers
MARTIN John	Wilberforce Chambers
NEWMAN Catherine	Maitland Chambers
SIMMONDS Andrew	5 Stone Buildings

4
| BERRY Simon | 9 Old Square |
| DRISCOLL Michael | 9 Old Square |

NEW SILKS
HINKS Frank	Serle Court
TIDMARSH Christopher	5 Stone Buildings
WARNOCK-SMITH Shân	5 Stone Buildings

For details of these leading barristers see Profiles on page 1353

LEADING JUNIORS • London

1
AINGER David	10 Old Square
BARLOW Francis	10 Old Square
MASON Alexandra	3 Stone Buildings

2
CHAPMAN Vivian	9 Stone Buildings
CHILD John	Wilberforce Chambers
HARROD Henry	5 Stone Buildings
MARTEN Hedley	11 New Square
MEADWAY Susannah	10 Old Square
ROGERS Beverly-Ann	Serle Court
TUCKER Lynton	New Square Chambers

3
BRYANT Judith	Wilberforce Chambers
HAYES Josephine	Gough Square Chambers
LEGGE Henry	5 Stone Buildings
MULLIS Roger	11 New Square
RICH Barbara	5 Stone Buildings
ROWELL David	9 Stone Buildings
RUSSEN Jonathan	Maitland Chambers
STEWART SMITH Rodney	New Square Chambers
TAUSSIG Anthony	Wilberforce Chambers
TOPHAM Geoffrey	3 Stone Buildings
WALLINGTON Richard	10 Old Square

For details of these leading barristers see Profiles on page 1353

more than most." **Andrew Simmonds QC** (see p.1478) concentrates largely on pensions and professional negligence work and has "made a good start as a silk," something which both **Christopher Tidmarsh QC** (see p.1491) and **Shân Warnock-Smith QC** (see p.1497) will be keen to do, having taken silk this year. Both are highly recommended, with Tidmarsh, in particular, being "a big favourite of the Inland Revenue." Following their appointment to silk, **Henry Harrod** (see p.1412) carries the torch as the leading junior here and is respected for his "mature advice and heavyweight practice." **Henry Legge** (see p.1434) continues to be widely instructed by an impressive roster of solicitors and is joined in the tables this year by **Barbara Rich** (see p.1468), who marshals a contentious trusts and inheritance practice. Her work in the Court of Protection was generously praised across the market.

MAITLAND CHAMBERS (see full details p.1572) **Christopher McCall QC** (see p.1443) "tackles a number of red blood breach of trust cases" and is popular among clients for his "inventive, free-flowing style." **Catherine Newman QC** (see p.1453) allies skills in the traditional field to her undoubted competence as a commercial chancery practitioner and is known for her "imperious delivery" – "she bats the opposition away with lordly disdain." More low-key, but well liked by clients and solicitors alike, **Jonathan Russen**'s (see p.1472) charm was brought to the attention of our researchers.

11 NEW SQUARE (see full details p.1579) Leading the pack in this strong set is **Sonia Proudman QC** (see p.1464), who possesses "exquisite judgement and knows exactly the point at which to ram home her case." Talented juniors include **Roger Mullis** (see p.1452), who is highly rated for his landlord and tenant work, and **Hedley Marten** (see p.1442), a senior junior who "loves court work and excels in contested probate matters."

NEW SQUARE CHAMBERS (see full details p.1580) **John Mowbray QC** (see p.1451) has "accumulated many friends and admirers" during a lengthy career at the Chancery Bar. Holder of "an offshore trusts practice to die for," he is an editor of Lewin on Trusts and can also point to a large following in the Caribbean. **George Laurence QC** (see p.1432), meanwhile, has an altogether more specialist practice focusing on highways, while **Lynton Tucker** and **Rodney Stewart Smith** (see p.1483) both received warm endorsement from peers and solicitors.

10 OLD SQUARE (see full details p.1585) The "frighteningly impressive" **Simon Taube QC** (see p.1488) is deemed by many commentators to be "destined to be a High Court Judge." In the interim he negotiates a heavy trusts and tax caseload with "lashings of tactical nous" and is supported by a crew of immensely talented juniors. **David Ainger** (see p.1355) "undertakes the most convoluted and protracted of cases with distinction," while **Francis Barlow** is "much venerated as a pillar of the establishment." Observers singled out **Susannah Meadway**'s (see p.1446) "attractive presentation and back-room skills," making mention also of **Richard Wallington**'s (see p.1496) "wide-ranging knowledge and academic flair." Author of a number of texts, he has produced an edition of Foster's Inheritance Tax.

OTHER NOTABLE PRACTITIONERS Serle Court accommodates a number of well-known characters. **Michael Briggs QC**'s (see p.1371) commercial chancery prowess has in the past somewhat overshadowed his efforts in the traditional field. He is, however, proficient in Inheritance Act and international trusts work and reportedly "has no side to him at all." **Frank Hinks QC** (see p.1417) in comparison is more understated but "a real gentleman who shines on the technical side." **Beverly-Ann Rogers** (see p.1470) was endorsed as "tenacious and hard-working." Distinguished among the juniors is **Alexandra Mason** (see p.1442) of 3 Stone Buildings who specialises in trusts and estate planning. Quite a bit younger than her rivals she is nevertheless "a natural candidate for the top" due to "her trenchant advice and ability to work tremendously quickly." **Geoffrey Topham** (see p.1492) "has been around so long he knows practically everything." **Josephine Hayes** (see p.1413), newly moved to Gough Square Chambers, continues to be recommended for her pensions and financial services work. **Vivian Chapman** (see p.1378) of 9 Stone Buildings is "no stranger to the House of Lords" where he conducts himself with "quiet authority." At the same set is "gifted draftsman" **David Rowell** (see p.1471). **Simon Berry QC** (see p.1365) of 9 Old Square shines in the banking and professional negligence sphere, and shares a set with **Michael Driscoll QC** (see p.1391)

CHANCERY

> **Research** The rankings are based on in-depth interviews with 6,582 solicitors, barristers and clients in the UK. **Chambers'** research is audited by the British Market Research Bureau (see page 7)

> **BARRISTERS' PROFILES** ▶ See pages 1353-1504

whose "knowledge of land law and landlord and tenant matters is up with the best."

WESTERN, WALES & CHESTER CIRCUITS

LEADING SILKS • Western & Wales & Chester

1	DAVIES Stephen	Guildhall Chambers
2	COOKE Nicholas	9 Park Place
3	JARMAN Milwyn	9 Park Place

For details of these leading barristers see Profiles on page 1353

LEADING JUNIORS • Western & Wales & Chester

1	BAMFORD Jeremy	Guildhall Chambers
	BLOHM Leslie	St John's Chambers
	KEYSER Andrew	9 Park Place
2	MAHER Martha	Guildhall Chambers
	SHARPLES John	St John's Chambers

For details of these leading barristers see Profiles on page 1353

Stephen Davies QC of Guildhall Chambers has a practice on an old-fashioned chancery footing and is known for "standing his ground but never unreasonably so." Similarly forceful is fellow tenant **Jeremy Bamford**, whose "keen intellect pares down a case to its essentials," while also at the same set **Martha Maher** (see p.1440) is a "fearless" advocate particularly effective at partnership matters. Rival Bristol set, St John's Chambers, fields comparable juniors in the "professional and thoroughly committed" **Leslie Blohm** (see p.1367) and **John Sharples** (see p.1476), who "is relentless in battle." In Wales, 9 Park Place continues to house a number of key individuals. **Nicholas Cooke QC** (see p.1383) is rated as "perceptive and penetrating in his reading of a case" and has a "commercial flair" matched by fellow silk **Milwyn Jarman QC** (see p.1424). **Andrew Keyser** (see p.1429) often acts as junior to the pair of them, bringing his "quiet confidence" to bear, often on professional negligence matters.

MIDLANDS CIRCUIT

LEADING SILKS • Midlands

1	RANDALL John	St Philips Chambers
2	CORBETT James	St Philips Chambers

For details of these leading barristers see Profiles on page 1353

LEADING JUNIORS • Midlands

1	ASHWORTH Lance	St Philips Chambers
	CHARMAN Andrew	St Philips Chambers
	STOCKILL David	No5 Chambers

For details of these leading barristers see Profiles on page 1353

Our table is again largely saturated with individuals from St Philips Chambers. **John Randall QC** (see p.1466) is widely accepted as "the best commercial silk on circuit" and a strong contender for the best in the provinces as a whole. Running him close is **James Corbett QC** (see p.1384), who has a more "tigerish" style, and was involved in the Dunkin' Donuts franchise dispute where he led ex-Freshfields solicitor **Andrew Charman** (see p.1379). Instructing solicitors appreciate that **Lance Ashworth** (see p.1358) is "totally relaxed in high-cost cases," a characteristic shared by **David Stockill** of No5 Chambers.

NORTHERN & NORTH EASTERN CIRCUITS

LEADING SILKS • Northern & North Eastern

1	ALLEN James	No.6 Barristers Chambers
	BARTLEY JONES Edward	Exchange Chambers
	BOOTH Michael	40 King St
	ELLERAY Anthony	Exchange Chambers
2	CAWSON Mark	Exchange Chambers
	CHAISTY Paul	40 King St
	LEEMING Ian	St. James's Chambers

For details of these leading barristers see Profiles on page 1353

LEADING JUNIORS • Northern & North Eastern

1	ANDERSON Lesley	40 King St
	BERRAGAN Neil	40 King St
2	DUNN Katherine	40 King St
	JOHNSON Michael	9 St. John Street
	RIDDLE Nicholas	14 Castle Street
	STERLING Robert	St. James's Chambers
	TERRY Jeffrey	8 King St
3	CASEMENT David	Exchange Chambers
	HALLIWELL Mark	40 King St
	HARPER Mark	40 King St
	ORR Nicholas	14 Castle Street
	UP AND COMING	
	CLARK Andrew	8 King St
	DOYLE Louis	40 King St

For details of these leading barristers see Profiles on page 1353

James Allen QC of No.6 Barristers Chambers sits as a Deputy High Court Judge and with his "highly capable and considered" approach he remains the highest profile chancery silk on the circuit. Over the Pennines, however, 40 King St, in particular, can lay claim to a considerable corpus of talented silks and juniors. As denotes an ex-Cambridge boxing blue, **Michael Booth QC** (see p.1368) is "a bit of a bruiser in the courtroom," while **Paul Chaisty QC**'s (see p.1378) "academic brain and tenacious style" win him plaudits. Rich in juniors, the set houses the top two in **Lesley Anderson** (see p.1357), "fierce, and always on the front foot," and the "urbane" **Neil Berragan** (see p.1365), who is a recent arrival from Merchant Chambers. **Louis Doyle** (see p.1390) is seen as "a good drafter" whose "name crops up more and more." **Katherine Dunn** (see p.1392) takes a similarly "hard-headed" approach as Anderson and is popular with solicitors for her "ability to work at speed," while **Mark Harper** (see p.1412) is seen as "bullish but pleasant to work with." "Measured but humane," **Mark Halliwell** (see p.1411) is a new addition to the tables following peer recommendation. At Exchange Chambers, **Edward Bartley Jones QC** (see p.1362) is an "ebullient patrician, fast on his feet," who is complemented by the "sober and deep-thinking" **David Casement** (see p.1377). Other respected silks here include "sturdy and dogged" **Anthony Elleray QC** (see p.1394) and **Mark Cawson QC** (see p.1378), a "smooth character" with a particularly fine paper practice. **Ian Leeming QC** (see p.1433) of St. James's Chambers is exclusively dispute-based, handling bankruptcy and company, partnership and land disputes, while the recommended junior at the same set, **Robert Sterling** (see p.1483), is "quiet and persistent both in court and in negotiation." **Jeffrey Terry** (see p.1489) of 8 King St is "cerebrally strong" on commercial chancery matters, while ex-solicitor **Andrew Clark** (see p.1380), at the same set, is "at the cream of the younger end, successfully threshing the good points from difficult cases." **Michael Johnson** (see p.1425) of 9 St. John Street is also a well-known name in the city. "Humble but highly talented," he handles a significant amount of VAT and income tax work, "slicing

CHANCERY

Research The rankings are based on in-depth interviews with 6,582 solicitors, barristers and clients in the UK. **Chambers'** research is audited by the British Market Research Bureau (see page 7)

BARRISTERS' PROFILES ▶ See pages 1353-1504

through masses of detail with ease." Liverpool's representatives in the table, **Nicholas Riddle** (see p.1468) and **Nicholas Orr** (see p.1457), are both from 14 Castle Street and are "highly dependable senior juniors."

CHARITIES

Research The rankings are based on in-depth interviews with 6,582 solicitors, barristers and clients in the UK. **Chambers'** research is audited by the British Market Research Bureau (see page 7)

BARRISTERS' PROFILES ▶ See pages 1353-1504

LONDON

CHARITIES • London	QCs	Jnrs
1 Maitland Chambers (Lyndon-Stanford/Aldous)	2	-
11 New Square (Sonia Proudman QC)	2	2
11 Old Square (Crawford/Simpkiss)	1	2

Numbers show recommended barristers in this practice area

LEADING SILKS • London	
1 MCCALL Christopher	Maitland Chambers
PICARDA Hubert	Sole Practitioner
2 CRAMPIN Peter	11 New Square
NEWEY Guy	Maitland Chambers
NUGEE Edward	Wilberforce Chambers
PROUDMAN Sonia	11 New Square
3 HERBERT Mark	5 Stone Buildings
WATERS Malcolm	11 Old Square

For details of these leading barristers see Profiles on page 1353

LEADING JUNIORS • London	
★ QUINT Francesca	11 Old Square
1 DUMONT Thomas	11 New Square
MACLENNAN Alison	11 Old Square
PEARCE Robert	11 New Square
2 KESSLER James	24 Old Buildings

For details of these leading barristers see Profiles on page 1353

MAITLAND CHAMBERS (see full details p.1572) **Christopher McCall QC** (see p.1443) is described as a "silk of epic proportions." He is especially recommended for his tax work, and his name is said to carry "a lot of weight in disputes." A former counsel to the Charity Commission, **Guy Newey QC** (see p.1453) was said by one source to be "much more practical than most people at the Bar."

11 NEW SQUARE (see full details p.1579) The "excellent" **Peter Crampin QC** (see p.1386) wins considerable praise this year, with clients drawing particular attention to his impressive courtroom manner. **Sonia Proudman QC** (see p.1464), meanwhile, is admired for her "superb mind." Sources find her "sense and understanding" particularly valuable on the commercial aspects of the sector. Amongst the juniors, **Thomas Dumont** (see p.1391) wins plaudits for his "good, common sense advice," while the "outstanding" **Robert Pearce** (see p.1459) has recently been appointed standing counsel to the Charity Commission.

11 OLD SQUARE (see full details p.1586) **Francesca Quint** (see p.1465) won more recommendations than any other charities barrister in the country. "Approachable, efficient, thoughtful, swift, calm" and even "saintly" are some of the adjectives applied to her by grateful clients. She moved set this year from 11 Old Square (J Simeon Thrower), as did **Alison MacLennan** (see p.1440) who has a growing reputation and is praised for her "excellent commercial sense." Also active in this sector is **Malcolm Waters QC** (see p.1498), who peers consider "a smart, intelligent, practical man."

OTHER NOTABLE PRACTITIONERS Sole practitioner the "legendary" **Hubert Picarda QC** (see p.1460) retains a top-flight reputation, especially for his academic ability. Some sources claim that "his name alone attached to a document can swing some transactions." **James Kessler** (see p.1429) at 24 Old Buildings remains highly recommended amongst the juniors, particularly for his work on the interface of charities with tax and trusts. At 5 Stone Buildings, chancery expert **Mark Herbert QC** (see p.1415) is praised for the quality of his work, particularly on the trust side, while at Wilberforce Chambers head of chambers **Edward Nugee QC** (see p.1455) retains his "historic high profile."

CHURCH LAW

Research The rankings are based on in-depth interviews with 6,582 solicitors, barristers and clients in the UK. **Chambers'** research is audited by the British Market Research Bureau (see page 7)

BARRISTERS' PROFILES ▶ See pages 1353-1504

LONDON

CHURCH LAW • London	QCs	Jnrs
1 2 Harcourt Buildings (Robin Purchas QC)	1	2
2 Pump Court Chambers (Christopher Harvey Clark QC)	1	1

Numbers show recommended barristers in this practice area

LEADING SILKS • London
1 GEORGE Charles	2 Harcourt Buildings
2 CLARK Christopher	Pump Court Chambers
KAYE Roger	24 Old Buildings
SEED Nigel	3 Paper Buildings

For details of these leading barristers see Profiles on page 1353

LEADING JUNIORS • London
1 BRIDEN Timothy	8 Stone Buildings
HILL Mark	Pump Court Chambers
2 BEHRENS James	Serle Court
MYNORS Charles	2 Harcourt Buildings
PETCHEY Philip	2 Harcourt Buildings
RODGERS June	Harcourt Chambers

For details of these leading barristers see Profiles on page 1353

2 HARCOURT BUILDINGS (see full details p.1554) The planning expertise, for which this set is justly famed, places it in a strong position to act in the disputes between religious heritage and practicality inherent in much ecclesiastical controversy. **Charles George QC** (see p.1403), Chancellor of the Diocese of Southwark, was described as a planning expert whose style is "learned and thoughtful, wise and pastoral." Since Sheila Cameron QC became Dean of the Arches, he has stepped into her shoes as "undoubtedly the leading silk." The admired **Charles Mynors** (see p.1452) is the Chancellor of the Worcester Diocese. He also boasts planning expertise and has written a "highly relevant" book on listed buildings. "Leading junior" **Philip Petchey**, currently deputy Chancellor of Southwark Diocese, has a busy practice, including recent Court of Appeal work. Peers consider him "knowledgeable" and draw attention to his writing on graveyard matters.

PUMP COURT CHAMBERS (see full details p.1594) **Christopher Clark QC** (see p.1380) plays an active part in this field and recently sat in the Court of Arches on an exhumation case. He is said to have "come to some thoughtful and sound judgments." "Front-runner" **Mark Hill** (see p.1416) is an extremely prominent barrister with a special interest in human rights law as it affects the church. He was recently appointed editor of the *Ecclesiastical Law Journal* and is considered by peers to be "learned, experienced, able to take the more unusual point, and capable of dispensing good judgments and advice."

OTHER NOTABLE PRACTITIONERS **Roger Kaye QC** of **24 Old Buildings** is Chancellor of the Dioceses of Hereford and St Albans. Possessing "real presence," he is highly recommended by solicitors, especially for advice on how difficult points of chancery law affect the church. Grave spaces and stones, faculty jurisdiction, reorganisations and "stroppy church wardens" are some of his areas of interest. At **3 Paper Buildings**, "sensible and knowledgeable" **Nigel Seed QC** is Chancellor of the Diocese of London and is seen as particularly useful if criminal issues are involved. **Timothy Briden** (see p.1371) of **8 Stone Buildings** is another "leading junior and front-runner." Praised by peers for his "brilliant" book, he is "knowledgeable, careful and precise." **James Behrens** (see p.1364) of **Serle Court** is Chancellor of the Diocese of Leicester and is "definitely a rising star" who rivals acknowledge is "going places." Active in judicial reviews, he has a special interest in the mediation of ecclesiastical disputes. "Good speaker" **June Rodgers** (see p.1470) of **Harcourt Chambers** is described as "robust and no-nonsense" with a "nice manner."

REGIONAL CIRCUITS

LEADING SILKS • Regional Circuits
1 COLLIER Peter	30 Park Square

For details of these leading barristers see Profiles on page 1353

LEADING JUNIORS • Regional Circuits
1 GARDEN Ian	Derby Square Chambers
2 NEWSOM George	St John's Chambers

For details of these leading barristers see Profiles on page 1353

Chancellor of the Dioceses of Lincoln and Wakefield, **Peter Collier QC** of **30 Park Square** is "increasingly encountered." Solicitors praise his "good brain." **Ian Garden** of **Derby Square Chambers**, deputy Chancellor of the Diocese of Sheffield, is on the General Synod, spends much of his time as a member of the Archbishop's Council and is heavily involved in ecclesiastical and employment issues. At **St John's Chambers**, property specialist **George Newsom** (see p.1454) also maintains his reputation in this field.

CLINICAL NEGLIGENCE

Research The rankings are based on in-depth interviews with 6,582 solicitors, barristers and clients in the UK. **Chambers'** research is audited by the British Market Research Bureau (see page 7)

BARRISTERS' PROFILES ▶ See pages 1353-1504

OVERVIEW: Falcon Chambers maintains its apparently unassailable lead over other sets. As mediations slowly gain in popularity and solicitors become more adept at pre-emptive planning when drawing up deals, competition at the bar is turned up a notch or two.

LONDON

CLINICAL NEGLIGENCE • London	QCs	Jnrs
1 3 Serjeants' Inn (Francis/Grace)	5	8
2 1 Crown Office Row (Robert Seabrook QC)	8	3
3 6 Pump Court (Kieran Coonan QC)	1	7
4 Cloisters (Laura Cox QC)	2	1
Crown Office Chambers (Spencer/Purchas)	1	2
Doughty Street Chambers (Geoffrey Robertson QC)	1	4
4 Paper Buildings (Jean Ritchie QC)	1	2
No. 1 Serjeants' Inn (Edward Faulks QC)	1	1

Numbers show recommended barristers in this practice area

3 SERJEANTS' INN (see full details p.1600) The solicitors' favourite, this set is able to provide top-level silks and juniors across a broad spectrum of specialist areas. There is a consensus among interviewees that the set can always find someone to meet their requirements; one instructing solicitor claimed " it's useful to instruct members of a Chambers that is so immersed in both defendant and claimant work." "Feisty and hard-working" **John Grace QC** continues to live up to the "high standards" ascribed to him. **Adrian Whitfield QC** (see p.1499) draws a variety of accolades from instructing solicitors and those at the Bar. A "fantastic court man," he is said to "argue consistently and coherently for the party instructing him," enjoying, as he does, the advantage of a "sharp legal mind." "Old master" **Robert Francis QC** (see p.1400) is another favourite. When called upon, he can "smooth his way through court with all the sensitivity it takes." As part of her high-profile crime practice, **Nicola Davies QC** (see p.1387) takes an interest in clinical negligence and has recently appeared in the Royal Devon and Exeter Breast Screening Case. She also defended a gynaecologist against thirty one indictments of assault. "Bright and able" **James Watson QC** is making strides as a new silk. The set's depth is evident by the raft of talent at junior level. Leading light **Adrian Hopkins** (see p.1419) is deemed "effective and thorough," while solicitors appreciate **Mary O'Rourke** for the way that she "gets straight to the point" and avow to counting themselves lucky if they can get hold of her. **Angus Moon** (see p.1449) focuses particularly on European convention work and human fertilisation cases; solicitors describe him as "the standout figure in this sphere." "Effective" **Christopher Johnston** (see p.1425) is instructed by both claimant and defendant solicitors. **Fiona Neale** (see p.1453) is "certainly busy; a thoroughly talented barrister," whilst **Michael Horne** (see p.1419) and **Huw Lloyd** (see p.1437) are both popular juniors. **Richard Partridge** has secured a national profile in clinical negligence.

1 CROWN OFFICE ROW (see full details p.1524) Rated by NHS Trusts, solicitors and other barristers alike, this set has the resources to cover the full range of claimant and defendant work. "Superb advocate" **Philip Havers QC** (see p.1413) has a roughly 50/50 split practice and is clearly at the top of his game. He is rated by a large number of solicitors who say "his co-operation is unstinting." **Stephen Miller QC** (see p.1359) has particular focus on brain-damaged baby claims and a practice slightly biased towards defendant work. He is described as "an extremely impressive advocate" and recommended by solicitors across the UK. The "highly skilled" **James Badenoch QC** (see p.1359) is endorsed by peers as one who takes on board "challenging legal issues." His "extremely thorough preparation" also wins him a following. **Paul Rees QC** has made a favourable impression nationally over the past 12 months. "One of the stars," he is praised for his "ferocious brain" and "extremely helpful" approach to cases. A solicitor described him as "completely first rate" and

LEADING SILKS • London

1
GRACE John	3 Serjeants' Inn
HAVERS Philip	1 Crown Office Row
IRWIN Stephen	Doughty Street Chambers
MASKREY Simeon	7 Bedford Row
MILLER Stephen	1 Crown Office Row
WHITFIELD Adrian	3 Serjeants' Inn

2
BADENOCH James	1 Crown Office Row
COONAN Kieran	6 Pump Court
COX Laura	Cloisters
FRANCIS Robert	3 Serjeants' Inn
REES Paul	1 Crown Office Row
RITCHIE Jean	4 Paper Buildings

3
BOWRON Margaret	1 Crown Office Row
BROOKE Michael	Four New Square
BROWNE Benjamin	2 Temple Gardens
COGHLAN Terence	1 Crown Office Row
DAVIES Nicola	3 Serjeants' Inn
FAULKS Edward	No. 1 Serjeants' Inn
FOSKETT David	1 Crown Office Row
GIBSON Christopher	Four New Square
LANGSTAFF Brian	Cloisters
SMITH Sally	1 Crown Office Row
SPENCER Michael	Crown Office Chambers
WATSON James	3 Serjeants' Inn

NEW SILKS
BLOCK Neil	39 Essex Street

For details of these leading barristers see Profiles on page 1353

LEADING JUNIORS • London

1
HOPKINS Adrian	3 Serjeants' Inn
LAMBERT Christina	6 Pump Court
MOON Angus	3 Serjeants' Inn
OPPENHEIM Robin	Doughty Street Chambers
O'ROURKE Mary	3 Serjeants' Inn
SPINK Andrew	35 Essex Street
TAYLOR Simon	Cloisters

2
GARRETT Annalissa	6 Pump Court
HOCKTON Andrew	6 Pump Court
JOHNSTON Christopher	3 Serjeants' Inn
JONES Charlotte	Crown Office Chambers
MATTHEWS Dennis	Crown Office Chambers
NEALE Fiona	3 Serjeants' Inn
PRATT Duncan	6 Pump Court
READHEAD Simon	No. 1 Serjeants' Inn
SPENCER Martin	4 Paper Buildings

3
EVANS David	1 Crown Office Row
FOSTER Charles	6 Pump Court
HORNE Michael	3 Serjeants' Inn
KENNEDY Andrew	6 Pump Court
LLOYD Huw	3 Serjeants' Inn
MCCULLOUGH Angus	1 Crown Office Row
PARTRIDGE Richard	3 Serjeants' Inn
TRACY FORSTER Jane	4 Paper Buildings

UP AND COMING
GLASSON Jonathan	Doughty Street Chambers
HERMER Richard	Doughty Street Chambers
MANGAT Tejina	6 Pump Court
SPARKS Paula	Doughty Street Chambers
WHIPPLE Philippa	1 Crown Office Row

For details of these leading barristers see Profiles on page 1353

CLINICAL NEGLIGENCE

> **Research** The rankings are based on in-depth interviews with 6,582 solicitors, barristers and clients in the UK. **Chambers'** research is audited by the British Market Research Bureau (see page 7)

BARRISTERS' PROFILES ▶ See pages 1353-1504

said "if he applied for a High Court appointment it would be a sad loss." **Margaret Bowron QC** has an "increasing profile" in this area and **Terence Coghlan QC** (see p.1382) remains a favourite of London solicitors. **David Foskett QC** (see p.1399) and **Sally Smith QC** (see p.1480) were both endorsed for their commitment to this field. Three newly ranked juniors typify the set's broad scope. **David Evans** was recommended as a "good up-and-coming junior," while **Angus McCullough** garnered a variety of plaudits, typically portraying him as "bright and user-friendly." **Philippa Whipple** (see p.1499) has been instructed by solicitors throughout the UK and described as "an incredibly talented junior."

6 PUMP COURT (see full details p.1593) Althought this set only has a single silk, it remains a powerful force with a deeply talented pool of juniors. **Kieran Coonan QC** (see p.1383) is a "brilliant exponent" of healthcare law, including clinical negligence and personal injury. He has been involved in inquiries relating to care and treatment and acted on issues such as confidence, and a claim made for a disabled child. "Liked by clients," **Christina Lambert** was described by interviewees as "outstanding - always thorough in her preparation." **Annalissa Garrett** has "a keen understanding of the issues at stake." Solicitors judged **Andrew Hockton** as "consistently excellent," while **Charles Foster** (see p.1400) has secured a following with his practical, straightforward style. **Duncan Pratt** (see p.1463) received resounding praise from interviewees; he is "an extremely gifted barrister with an immense knowledge of medico-legal issues." He is also prime choice as one who is "good with clients, sympathetic in the extreme." **Andrew Kennedy** (see p.1428) is popular with solicitors and ex-doctor **Tejina Mangat** was singled out as an increasing favourite among solicitors.

CLOISTERS (see full details p.1521) When **Laura Cox QC** (see p.1385) turns her hand to clinical negligence, she is felt to be "an extremely strong operator." Her recent work incudes cerebral palsy and brain-damaged baby claims and she has an interest in gynaecological and obstetric cases. According to solicitors, **Brian Langstaff QC** (see p.1432) is "loved by clients." He has a broad practice on both the claimant and defendant side. **Simon Taylor** (see p.1488) has been involved in heavyweight cases relating to foetal medicine, congenital dislocation of the hip and cerebral palsy. He appeared in the high-profile Touche and Peet cases. Solicitors spoke of him as "reliable; he indicates realistic deadlines" as well as being "bright, committed and efficient." His ability to communicate effectively with client families and particularly children, was noted.

CROWN OFFICE CHAMBERS (see full details p.1522) **Michael Spencer QC** is well known for his work on behalf of NHS health authorities and Trusts, advising on a broad spectrum of claims brought against them. Peers agree his is a "definite presence in the market," employing his "constructive manner" to good effect. Senior junior **Charlotte Jones** was described as "an impressive performer," and **Dennis Matthews** has a longstanding reputation amongst solicitors.

DOUGHTY STREET CHAMBERS (see full details p.1526) Researchers were impressed by the level of support for this set's tranche of young juniors. At the senior level it fields the talents of **Stephen Irwin QC** (see p.1422); a "brilliant" barrister, who for some solicitors is their "first port of call." Author of a leading text on the area, much of his workload is in the medico-legal field. **Robin Oppenheim** (see p.1457) is considered "impressive" across the board, while some interviewees singled out his fine advocacy skills. **Jonathan Glasson** (see p.1405) is newly ranked, following commendation of him as an "exceptionally clever barrister and quick with his paperwork." **Richard Hermer** is "always busy" and an "extremely good trial barrister," while **Paula Sparks** (see p.1481) was endorsed by solicitors across the country.

4 PAPER BUILDINGS (see full details p.1588) **Jean Ritchie QC's** (see p.1469) clinical negligence practice continues to be rated at the highest level. Her aptitude for client care is noted and she is characterised as "intelligent, efficient and ferocious with the other side." At junior level, **Martin Spencer** (see p.1481) is "extremely technically competent" and "pleasant to deal with." Newly arrived at the set from 13 King's Bench Walk, **Jane Tracy Forster** (see p.1492) retains a strong market following.

NO. 1 SERJEANTS' INN (see full details p.1599) "Superb" **Edward Faulks QC** (see p.1397) has a longstanding reputation in clinical negligence. He acts for health authorities and trusts and has been involved in a number of group actions. Solicitors singled out **Simon Readhead** (see p.1467) for his "excellent attention to detail" and "brilliant understanding of medical issues."

OTHER NOTABLE PRACTITIONERS Interviewees commended "fearless, tenacious advocate" **Simeon Maskrey QC** (see p.1442) of 7 Bedford Row. He has "an analytical approach" and is felt to be "a great communicator." Solicitors describe him as "feisty, he pushes and pushes where others give up" and they appreciate his "unusual spin on cases." The increasing clinical negligence practice of **Benjamin Browne QC** (see p.1373) at 2 Temple Gardens has impressed peers, while new silk **Neil Block QC** (see p.1367) of 39 Essex Street is a "star in the making." At 35 Essex Street **Andrew Spink** was applauded by his contemporaries, as "incisive and particularly good with clients." At Four New Square, **Michael Brooke QC** (see p.1372) retains a strong solicitor following and **Christopher Gibson QC** (see p.1404) is "personable and approachable."

MIDLANDS CIRCUIT

LEADING SILKS • Midlands

1	LEWIS Ralph	No 5 Chambers
	NEW SILKS	
	HUNJAN Satinder	No 5 Chambers

For details of these leading barristers see Profiles on page 1353

LEADING JUNIORS • Midlands

1	BRIGHT Christopher	3 Fountain Court
2	GREGORY Philip	No.6 Fountain Court

For details of these leading barristers see Profiles on page 1353

Ralph Lewis QC (see p.1435) of No 5 Chambers retains an enviable reputation for his clinical negligence work. He generally undertakes high-value claims relating to orthopaedic surgery, general surgery, obstetrics, cerebral palsy and other birth injury claims. New silk **Satinder Hunjan QC** of the same chambers undertakes both claimant and defendant work. At 3 Fountain Court, **Christopher Bright** (see p.1372) is "a bright and busy" barrister, and **Philip Gregory** of 6 Fountain Court received endorsement from both members of the Bar and instructing solicitors.

CLINICAL NEGLIGENCE

Research The rankings are based on in-depth interviews with 6,582 solicitors, barristers and clients in the UK. **Chambers'** research is audited by the British Market Research Bureau (see page 7)

BARRISTERS' PROFILES ▶ See pages 1353-1504

NORTH EASTERN & NORTHERN CIRCUITS

LEADING SILKS • Northern & North Eastern

[1]
REDFERN Michael	28 St John St
SWIFT Caroline	Byrom Street Chambers
WINGATE-SAUL Giles	Byrom Street Chambers

[2]
GOLDREIN Iain	7 Harrington Street Chambers
GRIME Stephen	Deans Court Chambers
MELTON Christopher	Byrom Street Chambers

[3]
BRASLAVSKY Nicholas	40 King St
MORAN Andrew	Byrom Street Chambers

For details of these leading barristers see Profiles on page 1353

LEADING JUNIORS • Northern & North Eastern

[1]
HEATON David	18 St John Street

[2]
ECCLES David	8 King St
FREEDMAN Jeremy	Plowden Buildings
PRITCHARD Sarah	40 King St
ROWLEY James	28 St John St
RUCK Mary	Peel Court Chambers

For details of these leading barristers see Profiles on page 1353

At 28 St John Street, **Michael Redfern QC** (see p.1467) remains first port of call for complex matters. **Caroline Swift QC** (see p.1486) of Byrom Street Chambers has been detained on the Shipman inquiry, although this has done nothing to dampen her popularity among instructing solicitors. At the same set, **Giles Wingate-Saul QC** (see p.1501) has a "high-quality" clinical negligence practice, **Christopher Melton QC** is "extremely talented and committed" and **Andrew Moran QC** was described by interviewees as a "remarkable advocate." At 7 Harrington Street Chambers **Iain Goldrein QC** (see p.1407) is deemed "thorough and on the ball" while **Stephen Grime QC** (see p.1410) of Deans Court Chambers is widely considered "a leader in his field." **Nicholas Braslavsky QC** (see p.1370) and **Sarah Pritchard** (see p.1464) of 40 King Street are newly ranked following the endorsement of solicitors across the region. **David Heaton** (see p.1413) at 18 St John Street is "fantastic, lovely with clients - his preparation is second to none." **David Eccles** (see p.1393) of 8 King Street is a "consistently high-calibre performer" and **Jeremy Freedman** (see p.1401) at Plowden Buildings is respected for his broad practice. **James Rowley** (see p.1471) of 28 St John Street is a favourite of some of the larger law firms. At Peel Court, **Mary Ruck** (see p.1472) has drawn accolades after her involvement in high-value, complex clinical negligence claims, including cerebral palsy, neurological, gynaecological and psychiatric matters.

www.ChambersandPartners.com

COMMERCIAL LITIGATION

Research The rankings are based on in-depth interviews with 6,582 solicitors, barristers and clients in the UK. **Chambers'** research is audited by the British Market Research Bureau (see page 7)

BARRISTERS' PROFILES ▶ See pages 1353-1504

LONDON

COMMERCIAL LITIGATION • London	QCs	Jnrs
1 Brick Court Chambers (Christopher Clarke QC)	10	3
Essex Court Chambers (Gordon Pollock QC)	6	9
One Essex Court (Anthony Grabiner QC)	9	6
Fountain Court (Anthony Boswood QC)	7	2
2 Blackstone Chambers (Baxendale/Flint)	4	3
3 Verulam Buildings (Symons/Jarvis)	5	5

Numbers show recommended barristers in this practice area

BRICK COURT CHAMBERS (see full details p.1517) "A veritable pantheon of superstars," this set accommodates one of the brightest of them all: **Jonathan Sumption QC**. "Quite simply remarkable," he has "a depth of understanding, intuition and commercial awareness virtually unparalleled at the Bar." Stalking the very largest stages, he is hugely in demand and "a true polymath." Similarly busy, **Mark Howard QC** (see p.1420) is "a paragon of the modern silk," "cold and unyielding in court" but outside, "a team player always prepared to roll up his sleeves and get stuck in." **Mark Hapgood QC** is prized for his "acuity and trenchant, logical mind," in common with **Jonathan Hirst QC** (see p.1417) whose "fluent advocacy and surgical cross-examination skills" regularly "squeeze the pips out of the opposition." In an often combative world, the set possesses some of the more amenable players in the field. **Charles Hollander QC** (see p.1418) is seen as "approachable and clever," qualities shared by the "ingenious and dignified" **Andrew Popplewell QC** (see p.1462). Both have doubtless learned from the model of **Sydney Kentridge QC** (see p.1428), "a byword for fair play, integrity and civilised conduct," who is now taking on more of a consultative role. Extremely senior, he complements nicely the younger silks of the likes of **George Leggatt QC** (see p.1434), "big-hitter" **Richard Lord QC** (see p.1438), and "incisive" **Michael Swainston QC** (see p.1486). Juniors include **Neil Calver** (see p.1375), popular with solicitors for being "switched-on and responsive," and "super-bright" **Andrew Lydiard** (see p.1439). **Simon Salzedo** (see p.1473) is a new entrant to our table following recommendations from leading solicitors, who dubbed him "an exceptional talent."

ESSEX COURT CHAMBERS (see full details p.1530) "Headline-grabber" **Gordon Pollock QC's** (see p.1461) reputation is unassailable. "Immensely impressive in the largest matters," he is "never afraid to take on the weakest cases" and "often turns the opposition's spines to jelly." His popularity with solicitors mirrors that of **Bernard Eder QC** (see p.1393) whose "stiletto mind" and willingness to be "a team player" go down well. To some commentators, **Andrew Hochhauser QC** (see p.1417) "comes across as prickly," a symptom of the fact that he "takes great pride in his work," exhibiting thoroughness in all he does. **Geraldine Andrews QC** (see p.1357) was celebrated by solicitors as being "pragmatic and client-friendly," particularly in banking litigation, while **Jeffrey Gruder QC** (see p.1410) and **Richard Jacobs QC** (see p.1423) also score well in that area in the context of wide general commercial practices. Outstanding amidst a phalanx of top juniors, **Joe Smouha** (see p.1480) is "unquestionably excellent" and "infuses his case with a wit and verve few can match." **Vernon Flynn's** (see p.1399) salient features are "speed of response and splendid extemporisation in the courtroom," while **David Joseph's** (see p.1423) reputation rests on his "charm, intelligence and sureness of touch" especially in shipping, insurance and banking cases. Another with "preternatural brainpower" is **David Foxton** (see p.1400), who matches **Richard Millett** (see p.1447) and **Paul Stanley** (see p.1482) in having the "facility to absorb daunting amounts of information in a short space of time." Also recommended for their "straightforward approach and knack of getting results" are **Claire Blanchard** (see p.1367), **John Lockey** (see p.1437) ("gets great results") and **Paul McGrath** (see p.1444) ("a straightforward operator").

LEADING SILKS • London

★	GRABINER Anthony	One Essex Court
	POLLOCK Gordon	Essex Court Chambers
	SUMPTION Jonathan	Brick Court Chambers
1	BOSWOOD Anthony	Fountain Court
	BRIGGS Michael	Serle Court
	BRINDLE Michael	Fountain Court
	CARR Christopher	One Essex Court
	DOHMANN Barbara	Blackstone Chambers
	GLOSTER Elizabeth	One Essex Court
	HOWARD Mark	Brick Court Chambers
2	BARNES Mark	One Essex Court
	EDER Bernard	Essex Court Chambers
	HAPGOOD Mark	Brick Court Chambers
	MILL Ian	Blackstone Chambers
	ROSEN Murray	11 Stone Buildings
	VOS Geoffrey	3 Stone Buildings
3	HIRST Jonathan	Brick Court Chambers
	HOCHHAUSER Andrew	Essex Court Chambers
	MALEK Ali	3 Verulam Buildings
	MILLIGAN Iain	20 Essex Street
	ONIONS Jeffery	One Essex Court
4	BEAZLEY Thomas	Blackstone Chambers
	CRANE Michael	Fountain Court
	FLAUX Julian	7 King's Bench Walk
	FLINT Charles	Blackstone Chambers
	GLASGOW Edwin	39 Essex Street
	HOLLANDER Charles	Brick Court Chambers
	IVORY Thomas	One Essex Court
	JARVIS John	3 Verulam Buildings
	KENTRIDGE Sydney	Brick Court Chambers
	POPPLEWELL Andrew	Brick Court Chambers
	RAILTON David	Fountain Court
	STADLEN Nicholas	Fountain Court
	TEMPLE Anthony	4 Pump Court
	TOZZI Nigel	4 Pump Court
5	ANDREWS Geraldine	Essex Court Chambers
	BUTCHER Christopher	7 King's Bench Walk
	DAVIES Rhodri	One Essex Court
	FREEDMAN Clive	Littleton Chambers
	GEERING Ian	3 Verulam Buildings
	GLICK Ian	One Essex Court
	GRUDER Jeffrey	Essex Court Chambers
	ISAACS Stuart	3-4 South Square
	JACOBS Richard	Essex Court Chambers
	JONES Elizabeth	Serle Court
	KEALEY Gavin	7 King's Bench Walk
	LEGGATT George	Brick Court Chambers
	MANN Anthony	Enterprise Chambers
	MOWSCHENSON Terence	Wilberforce Chambers
	RUBIN Stephen	Fountain Court
	SMITH Stephen	New Square Chambers
	SYMONS Christopher	3 Verulam Buildings
	TUGENDHAT Michael	5 Raymond Buildings
	NEW SILKS	
	CHIVERS David	Erskine Chambers
	DOWLEY Dominic	Serle Court
	LORD Richard	Brick Court Chambers
	ONSLOW Andrew	3 Verulam Buildings
	RABINOWITZ Laurence	One Essex Court
	SWAINSTON Michael	Brick Court Chambers
	WAKSMAN David	Fountain Court

For details of these leading barristers see Profiles on page 1353

COMMERCIAL LITIGATION

Research The rankings are based on in-depth interviews with 6,582 solicitors, barristers and clients in the UK. **Chambers'** research is audited by the British Market Research Bureau (see page 7)

BARRISTERS' PROFILES ▶ See pages 1353-1504

LEADING JUNIORS • London

★	MCCAUGHRAN John	One Essex Court
	SMOUHA Joe	Essex Court Chambers
1	MCQUATER Ewan	3 Verulam Buildings
	ORR Craig	Fountain Court
	THANKI Bankim	Fountain Court
2	ANDERSON Robert	Blackstone Chambers
	DE GARR ROBINSON Anthony	One Essex Court
	HOWE Robert	Blackstone Chambers
3	CALVER Neil	Brick Court Chambers
	FLYNN Vernon	Essex Court Chambers
	LYDIARD Andrew	Brick Court Chambers
4	BAKER Andrew	20 Essex Street
	CHOO CHOY Alain	One Essex Court
	FOXTON David	Essex Court Chambers
	JOSEPH David	Essex Court Chambers
	MILLETT Richard	Essex Court Chambers
	STANLEY Paul	Essex Court Chambers
	TOLEDANO Daniel	One Essex Court
	WEITZMAN Tom	3 Verulam Buildings
	WOLFSON David	One Essex Court
5	AYLIFFE James	Wilberforce Chambers
	BELTRAMI Adrian	3 Verulam Buildings
	BLANCHARD Claire	Essex Court Chambers
	CAVENDER David	One Essex Court
	CHAMBERS Dominic	Maitland Chambers
	FLETCHER Andrew	3 Verulam Buildings
	LOCKEY John	Essex Court Chambers
	MCGRATH Paul	Essex Court Chambers
	UP AND COMING	
	DAVIES-JONES Jonathan	3 Verulam Buildings
	HILL Richard	4 Stone Buildings
	HUNTER Andrew	Blackstone Chambers
	SALZEDO Simon	Brick Court Chambers

For details of these leading barristers see Profiles on page 1353

ONE ESSEX COURT (see full details p.1531) Anthony Grabiner QC's "heightened strength of character and gravitas" are such that "judges often defer to him." "A true heavyweight," his fellow barristers believe that his arrival in siege-like situations is "the equivalent of wheeling up a trebuchet to the castle walls." Equally "authoritative and commanding," **Christopher Carr QC** (see p.1377) "explains cases clearly and precisely," being seen by many interviewees as "a front runner to take up Grabiner's mantle." In a set renowned for the robust nature of its performers, **Liz Gloster QC** (see p.1406) "tells it like it is, in a solidly down-to-earth manner" and, like **Jeffery Onions QC** (see p.1457), is "best in the heat of battle." **Mark Barnes QC** (see p.1362) is more of "a thorough and calm performer," particularly strong in technical cases, while **Ian Glick QC** (see p.1405) has a "circumspect and cerebral approach." **Thomas Ivory QC** (see p.1423) and **Rhodri Davies QC** (see p.1387) also received substantial backing from peers, along with **Laurence Rabinowitz QC** (see p.1465) whose "appointment as silk shows there is some justice in the world." An "absolute star as a junior," there is a settled expectation that "a bright future as a silk lies ahead of him." Filling his shoes as the outstanding junior in the set is **John McCaughran** (see p.1444) whose fans are legion, praising his "wise and considered advice" and "happy knack of never putting a foot wrong." **Anthony de Garr Robinson** (see p.1388) was not short of endorsement for his "client skills and commercial nous," while **Alain Choo Choy** (see p.1379) continues to increase his profile through appearances in the larger contractual disputes such as Railtrack. Also rated are **David Cavender** (see p.1378), the "punctilious" **David Wolfson** (see p.1501) and **Daniel Toledano** (see p.1492), "a star in the making whose name crops up all the time," particularly with his expertise in the energy field.

FOUNTAIN COURT (see full details p.1541) Head of chambers **Anthony Boswood QC** (see p.1368) is "a hard fighter who can savage opponents through intensive cross-examination." Receptive to solicitors' needs, he is "adept at providing leadership within a team dynamic." Almost on a par, **Michael Brindle QC** (see p.1372) is "appearing in the choicest litigation" as is **Nicholas Stadlen QC** (see p.1482), who was able to demonstrate his "rapier-like advocacy" and "ability to synthesise masses of paperwork" in the BCCI-related Three Rivers v Bank of England case. **Michael Crane QC** "exudes suavity and intelligence" and "has masterful courtcraft," while **David Railton QC** (see p.1466) exhibited his "stamina and stickability" in the lengthy Abache litigation, where he acted successfully on behalf of the Nigerian government. Other respected silks include **Stephen Rubin QC** (see p.1471), "a brawler, with a great intellect" and **David Waksman QC** (see p.1496), an expert on IT who "relishes a challenge." Necessarily dependent upon good juniors, these silks are not disappointed. **Craig Orr** (see p.1457), hailed as "a supreme draftsman," has assisted Brindle in the Barings litigation, while **Bankim Thanki** (see p.1489) appeared with Stadlen in the Three Rivers case, displaying his brand of "smooth persuasion."

BLACKSTONE CHAMBERS (see full details p.1515) **Barbara Dohmann QC** (see p.1390) was commended to researchers as "utterly self-possessed" and "a daunting presence in her natural habitat, the courtroom." Equally effective, **Charles Flint QC** (see p.1398) "endears himself to client and solicitor alike" through his "patient and solicitous bearing;" he recently acted on British Waterways Board v Severn Trent Water Ltd in a case dealing with the definition and construction of statutory powers. **Ian Mill QC** (see p.1447) is a similarly attractive figure, giving off "a spirit of joie de vivre that can be infectious." Clients were especially complimentary about **Thomas Beazley QC's** (see p.1363) style. "Unstuffy and prepared to give advice in anti-social hours," his "quiet judgement and vast experience" were much appreciated by solicitors. He has been heavily involved in cases concerning Prince Jefri. Among the juniors, **Robert Anderson** (see p.1357) "goes his own way" and is "skilled both in court and on paper," while **Robert Howe** (see p.1420) "works well with all levels of the team and looks at problems in the round." New to the tables on the back of a raft of recommendations, **Andrew Hunter** (see p.1421) is a "hyper-bright member of the new breed who combines bookish intelligence with creativity."

3 VERULAM BUILDINGS (see full details p.1615) Receiving strong recommendations from clients, **Ali Malek QC** (see p.1440) is "outwardly relaxed but with an inner strength of purpose," while **Ian Geering QC** (see p.1403) "has an incisive mind and speaks with authority." **John Jarvis QC's** (see p.1424) "well-regulated mind" produces "draftsmanship of the first water" while "forthright and strong" **Christopher Symons QC** (see p.1486) scores well particularly in professional negligence cases. Also recommended is **Andrew Onslow QC** (see p.1457) whose "friendly approach" and "trenchant advice" is much appreciated. Lively juniors include **Ewan McQuater** (see p.1445), who solicitors appreciated as "no prima donna and always adds value." **Tom Weitzman** (see p.1498) possesses "a quicksilver mind" and is highly rated on insurance matters. Also much sought after are **Andrew Fletcher** (see p.1398), veteran of the Elton John v PwC litigation, and **Adrian Beltrami** (see p.1364). **Jonathan Davies-Jones** (see p.1388) enters the tables in recognition of his skills as "a sensible litigator who gives it his all."

OTHER NOTABLE PRACTITIONERS "A top performer who can turn his hand to anything," **Michael Briggs QC** (see p.1371) of Serle Court has recently been seen in the Francis Bacon litigation. Although in a

COMMERCIAL LITIGATION

Research The rankings are based on in-depth interviews with 6,582 solicitors, barristers and clients in the UK. *Chambers'* research is audited by the British Market Research Bureau (see page 7)

BARRISTERS' PROFILES ▶ See pages 1353-1504

Chancery set, he has "undoubted pedigree in commercial litigation" and delights solicitors through his "willingness to work round the clock." Fellow silk **Elizabeth Jones QC** (see p.1425) is noted for her "speed of thought and rapid turnaround of paperwork," while new silk at the set **Dominic Dowley QC** (see p.1390)"has a fine academic mind and never drowns in detail." At 3 Stone Buildings, **Geoffrey Vos QC** (see p.1496) is "full of insight and always assured," sharing a similarly high profile with **Murray Rosen QC** (see p.1471) of 11 Stone Buildings who is "tactically flawless." 20 Essex Court has a pair of fine practitioners in **Iain Milligan QC** (see p.1447), who "allies a serious mind to an outgoing personality," and **Andrew Baker** (see p.1359), who "never flags even on the most interminable of cases." **Julian Flaux QC** (see p.1398) of 7 King's Bench Walk comes from a shipping and insurance background but has won applause for his role in the recent, well-publicised film finance litigation. "Most able and accommodating," his fellow head of chambers **Gavin Kealey QC** (see p.1427) is "a fluent off-the-wall thinker with boundless energy." **Christopher Butcher QC** (see p.1375) is "never intimidated, whether by client, judge or opponent." At 4 Pump Court, **Anthony Temple QC** proves most industrious handling a heavyweight commercial and insurance practice alongside **Nigel Tozzi QC** (see p.1492) whose "preparation and pleasing manner with the judges" catch the eye. "Unflappability" is the besetting characteristic of **Terence Mowschenson QC** (see p.1451) of Wilberforce Chambers, a set that also houses **James Ayliffe** (see p.1359), "a talented practitioner who takes the client through his case at a pace he is comfortable with." **Edwin Glasgow QC** (see p.1405) of 39 Essex Street was endorsed for his broad practice, while **Clive Freedman QC** of Littleton Chambers has impressed solicitors both on paper and in court, where his style is "analytical and ordered," providing the judge with "an fine framework." **Stuart Isaacs QC** (see p.1422) ("an expensive animal but worth it – he gets results that others only dream of") has a broad-based practice at 3-4 South Square. Elsewhere, **Anthony Mann QC** (see p.1441) of Enterprise Chambers has "proved himself more than just a Chancery barrister." **Stephen Smith QC** (see p.1480) of New Square Chambers is seen as "bright and disarmingly robust," and **David Chivers QC** (see p.1379) of Erskine Chambers has impressed as "quick to get on the client's wavelength." Completing the line-up, **Michael Tugendhat QC** (see p.1494) of 5 Raymond Buildings retains the support of the market as does **Dominic Chambers** (see p.1378), a recent recruit at Maitland Chambers.

WESTERN CIRCUIT

LEADING SILKS • Western

1	DAVIES Stephen	Guildhall Chambers
2	PALMER Adrian	Guildhall Chambers

For details of these leading barristers see Profiles on page 1353

LEADING JUNIORS • Western

1	BAMFORD Jeremy	Guildhall Chambers
	MAHER Martha	Guildhall Chambers
	VIRGO John	Guildhall Chambers
2	BLOHM Leslie	St John's Chambers
	LEVY Neil	St John's Chambers
	STEAD Richard	St John's Chambers
	UP AND COMING	
	PATON Ewan	Guildhall Chambers

For details of these leading barristers see Profiles on page 1353

Guildhall Chambers fields the highest number of leading barristers in this area, and has a reputation for the quality of its insolvency-related work.

Stephen Davies QC is particularly highly rated in this field. Solicitors characterise him as "extremely commercial and practical." Fellow silk **Adrian Palmer QC** (see p.1458) was described to researchers as "a strong all-rounder." Amongst the juniors, "thorough" **Jeremy Bamford** was commended for his "good grasp of contractual disputes" and rises in the rankings this year. **Martha Maher** (see p.1440) is also popular amongst local solicitors, while **John Virgo** (see p.1495) is widely recognised as a quality practitioner. New to *Chambers'* tables, **Ewan Paton** (see p.1458) was recommended by local solicitors and barristers as an up-and-coming junior with a sure touch. At rival St John's Chambers, strength in this area is felt to lie at the junior level. "Forthright" **Leslie Blohm** (see p.1367) won plaudits from the local legal community, while "excellent" **Neil Levy** (see p.1435) was described by one major client as "the only barrister I'd use outside London," and **Richard Stead** (see p.1482) was praised for his "knowledgeable" advice.

MIDLANDS CIRCUIT

LEADING SILKS • Midlands

1	RANDALL John	St Philips Chambers
2	CORBETT James	St Philips Chambers
	COUSINS Jeremy	St Philips Chambers

For details of these leading barristers see Profiles on page 1353

LEADING JUNIORS • Midlands

1	ANDERSON Mark	3 Fountain Court
	ASHWORTH Lance	St Philips Chambers
	KHANGURE Avtar	St Philips Chambers
	WYVILL Alistair	St Philips Chambers
2	CAMPBELL Stephen	St Philips Chambers
	CHARMAN Andrew	St Philips Chambers
	EYRE Stephen	1 Fountain Court
	HITCHING Isabel	No 5 Chambers

For details of these leading barristers see Profiles on page 1353

St Philips Chambers is so far ahead in the region that its competitors have almost lost sight of it. **John Randall QC** (see p.1466) "the best," is rated for his "expertise in company matters." Solicitors love him, and according to one: "He's immensely bright and extremely thorough; in court his advocacy is immaculate." **James Corbett QC** (see p.1384) is also highly esteemed and his work on the Dunkin' Donuts litigation won him particular approval in the market, while **Jeremy Cousins QC** (see p.1384) is commended for the breadth of his commercial knowledge and "skill in court." At the junior level, **Lance Ashworth** (see p.1358) is considered "approachable" as well as "bright and extremely thorough." **Avtar Khangure** (see p.1429) is well respected, particularly for his expertise in insolvency matters, and **Alistair Wyvill** (see p.1503) is a consistent favourite with a number of local solicitors. **Stephen Campbell**'s (see p.1376) "authoritative" style brings him consistent market applause. They are joined in the tables by **Andrew Charman** (see p.1379) who was recommended by a number of solicitors. At 1 Fountain Court, **Stephen Eyre** is deemed a "thorough and well-prepared" barrister, while **Mark Anderson** (see p.1357) at 3 Fountain Court was praised for his positive commercial attitude and was described by one solicitor as "the best barrister outside St Philips." **Isabel Hitching** of No 5 Chambers is newly ranked after a convincing array of commendations. A "class act", she is said to have "a first-rate analytical mind."

COMMERCIAL LITIGATION

Research The rankings are based on in-depth interviews with 6,582 solicitors, barristers and clients in the UK. **Chambers'** research is audited by the British Market Research Bureau (see page 7)

BARRISTERS' PROFILES ▶ See pages 1353-1504

NORTH EASTERN CIRCUIT

LEADING SILKS • North Eastern

1	ALLEN James	No.6 Barristers Chambers

For details of these leading barristers see Profiles on page 1353

LEADING JUNIORS • North Eastern

1	JORY Hugh	Enterprise Chambers
2	GROVES Hugo	Enterprise Chambers
	JAMES Michael	Enterprise Chambers
3	CAMERON Neil	Wilberforce Chambers
	PIPE Gregory	Chancery House Chambers

For details of these leading barristers see Profiles on page 1353

LEADING JUNIORS • Northern

1	ANDERSON Lesley	40 King St
2	BERRAGAN Neil	40 King St
	CASEMENT David	Exchange Chambers
	DAVIES Stephen	8 King St
	TERRY Jeffrey	8 King St
3	COGLEY Stephen	Merchant Chambers
	DOYLE Louis	40 King St
	DUNN Katherine	40 King St
	UP AND COMING	
	HARPER Mark	40 King St
	LATIMER Andrew	40 King St

For details of these leading barristers see Profiles on page 1353

The only silk to be recommended by the market continues to be **James Allen QC** of No.6 Barristers Chambers, whose "gravitas and vast experience earns him the respect of the judges." Enterprise Chambers can boast a "rising star" in **Hugh Jory**, whose impressive courtroom performances, one peer admitted, "induce fear into his opponents." **Michael James** (see p.1424) is "particularly strong on jurisdictional points;" his previous experience as a solicitor lends him "practical sense" to which other barristers may aspire. **Hugo Groves** (see p.1410) is respected for his expertise within insolvency. He is viewed as an "academic, good on paper, and a safe pair of hands in the courtroom." Wilberforce Chambers offers the talents of **Neil Cameron** (see p.1376), whose "detailed cross-examination will never let you down," while Chancery House Chambers houses the "assertive" and "client-friendly" style of **Gregory Pipe** (see p.1460).

NORTHERN CIRCUIT

COMMERCIAL LITIGATION • Northern

		QCs	Jnrs
1	40 King St	2	6
2	Exchange Chambers (Turner/Braithwaite/Globe)	3	1
3	Byrom Street Chambers	1	-
	8 King St (Gerard McDermott QC)	-	2

Numbers show recommended barristers in this practice area

LEADING SILKS • Northern

1	BARTLEY JONES Edward	Exchange Chambers
	WINGATE-SAUL Giles	Byrom Street Chambers
2	BOOTH Michael	40 King St
	CHAISTY Paul	40 King St
	ELLERAY Anthony	Exchange Chambers
3	CAWSON Mark	Exchange Chambers

For details of these leading barristers see Profiles on page 1353

40 KING ST (see full details p.1645) "The first port of call in Manchester" for many solicitors, this set retains "the lion's share of the work here." The departure of Peter Smith QC to the bench has been lamented; however, the "outstanding advocate," **Michael Booth QC** (see p.1368) has been highly praised by the market: "He will fight on to the end for his client." He is supported by **Paul Chaisty QC** (see p.1378), who is described by solicitors as "bright and thorough." Amongst the juniors, **Lesley Anderson** (see p.1357) pulls away from the pack - the one barrister who solicitors claim they would use as readily as the London Bar; she "delivers the goods time after time." She is joined by **Neil Berragan** (see p.1365), formerly of Merchant Chambers, "a sensible opponent, with great depth of knowledge." The "conscientious" **Louis Doyle** (see p.1390) provides "an excellent service" to clients, and is also a regular feature in the North Eastern Circuit. **Katherine Dunn** (see p.1392) makes an entrance into the tables following endorsement of her as a "high-flyer, with an excellent brain." The set also boasts two up-and-coming juniors: **Mark Harper** (see p.1412), whose "measured presence" is making its mark on the Northern Circuit; and **Andrew Latimer** (see p.1432), whose "quiet but devastating advocacy" has impressed peers and clients alike.

EXCHANGE CHAMBERS (see full details p.1638) This set enjoys a substantial presence both in Manchester and Liverpool: "It brings in fantastic cases, and supplies quality barristers." **Edward Bartley Jones QC** (see p.1362) rises up the tables this year. Celebrated for being "able to win the unwinnable," he is a "commercially astute ally" on any case. **Anthony Elleray QC** (see p.1394) is noted for his expertise in mediation, while peers agree that "silk suits" **Mark Cawson QC** (see p.1378). **David Casement** (see p.1377) is a good advert for the juniors at this set, rising up the tables due to his "eye for detail" and his "understated, yet commercial and effective advocacy."

BYROM STREET CHAMBERS The set lays claim to the "inimitable" **Giles Wingate-Saul QC** (see p.1501) whose "incredibly thorough, capable presence resonates throughout the courtroom."

8 KING ST (see full details p.1644) The set is renowned for its "commercial juniors and loyal clients." **Stephen Davies** (see p.1388) is a "good cross-examiner and great team player," while **Jeffrey Terry** (see p.1489) is noted by solicitors for his experience in the London courts and thorough preparation.

OTHER NOTABLE PRACTITIONERS **Stephen Cogley** (see p.1382) of Merchant Chambers was endorsed by peers as "a tough opponent," who "relishes a challenge" and whose powerful advocacy renders him "consistently effective."

www.ChambersandPartners.com
1275

COMPANY

Research The rankings are based on in-depth interviews with 6,582 solicitors, barristers and clients in the UK. **Chambers'** research is audited by the British Market Research Bureau (see page 7)

BARRISTERS' PROFILES ▶ See pages 1353-1504

LONDON

COMPANY • London	QCs	Jnrs
[1] **Erskine Chambers** (Robin Potts QC)	8	8
[2] **4 Stone Buildings** (Philip Heslop QC)	5	4
[3] **Maitland Chambers** (Lyndon-Stanford/Aldous)	5	2
3-4 South Square (Crystal/Alexander)	4	-
[4] **Enterprise Chambers** (Anthony Mann QC)	1	3
24 Old Buildings (Mann/Steinfeld)	2	1
Serle Court (Patrick Neill QC)	2	1

Numbers show recommended barristers in this practice area

ERSKINE CHAMBERS (see full details p.1529) The set remains in a class of its own. Prized for its unparalleled degree of specialisation in the field and the "reassuring consistency" on offer, this dedicated company set continues to prevail. Loyalty is fostered through its "user-friendly approach" and devotees consider it "the only chambers" claiming that "nobody there is weak – if you don't get your first choice, you know your second or third will be equally as good." Solicitors also point to advice that is "technically excellent." Solicitors were keen to declare their "huge respect" for **Robin Potts QC** (see p.1462). "Responsive and an extraordinary advocate," "his acutely tuned legal brain" is regularly sought out for the "most difficult points." Fans describe his style as "combative – he takes strong views and fights for them." **David Richards QC**'s (see p.1379) popularity continues to flourish. Clients insist he is "wonderful to work with" and are awed by his "skilfully coaxing" courtroom style. "Always clear in advice and advocacy," he is endorsed for his "practical nature" and his "willingness to listen and debate." **Leslie Kosmin QC**'s (see p.1431) "brilliance" is underpinned by a "sensible and helpful" manner. Peers believe he strikes a good balance with an approach that is "commercial enough, but not overly so that he misses the point." Firms appreciate the fact that "there is no ceremony" with **David Oliver QC** (see p.1456). His "ease, intelligence and good sense" earn him continued respect and popularity, whilst "strong and inventive" **Michael Todd QC** (see p.1491) is distinguished by an "unstuffy approach to technical advice." "A talented intellectual who is great for difficult questions," **David Mabb QC** is widely admired for his "meticulous mind." New silk **David Chivers QC** (see p.1379) has acquired an enthusiastic following. According to one client, he "cuts through the morass of detail and gets quickly to the nub of the matter," while another declares: "I couldn't go to anyone better, he is clear, and will give you an answer with no ifs or buts." **Martin Moore QC** (see p.1449) also took silk this year and is particularly recommended as an "excellent choice for schemes of arrangement." The set is home to a raft of talented and creative juniors. "On the ball" **John Cone** (see p.1383) "has his feet on the ground" and is recommended for proffering a "sensible view on a topic," whilst **Richard Snowden** (see p.1480) was endorsed for his knowledge of company law, insolvency and financial services matters. Immensely respected by City firms, **Thomas Stockdale** (see p.1484) is reputed to "know as much about schemes of arrangement as anybody." Characterised by some as the "incarnation of Richard Sykes," clients rely on his "clear, forthright" advice. When called upon, **Mary Stokes** (see p.1484) gives an "instant reaction." Lauded as "helpful in every way and utterly practical," she is treasured for her ability to "always provide the additional dimension to a matter under discussion." **Catherine Roberts** (see p.1469) and **Andrew Thompson** (see p.1490) are both singled out as "strong performers." **Dan Pretince** (see p.1463) manages his company law practice in combination with his academic commitments, while **Philip Gillyon** (see p.1404) is respected both for directors' disqualifications and insolvency-related matters.

4 STONE BUILDINGS (see full details p.1606) A host of stars sit within its ranks, and the set is undisputedly "right up there for company law." Head of chambers **Philip Heslop QC** is viewed as a "man of considerable mettle." "Ferociously bright," he remains one of the area's premier names. **Robert Hildyard QC** (see p.1415) was described as a "real star" whose interpretation of company law "inspires huge confidence." Heaped with praise by clients, **Anthony Bompas QC** (see p.1368) has a strong reputation in the field. "Sensible and sure-footed" in court with a "combative" style, his views on company and financial services law are "always clear and helpful." **John Brisby QC**'s (see p.1372) "hawkish" approach polarises opinion, though no one disputes his "excellent mind." New silk **Robert Miles QC** (see p.1447) "provides good commercial analysis" and it is expected that he "will certainly do well" following his elevation. Interviewees pointed to the considerable reputation of **Malcolm Davis-White** (see p.1388), who is "rock solid for reductions and schemes." Both solicitors and barristers were quick to commend the technical skill of **Jonathan Crow** (see p.1386), although, as Treasury Counsel, his instructions are restricted to the Government and certain public bodies. "A creative thinker," **Peter Griffiths** (see p.1410) enjoys a broad company/commercial practice, while **Sarah Harman** continues to impress with her "pragmatic and effective" handling of directors' disqualification issues, company and insolvency law.

MAITLAND CHAMBERS (see full details p.1572) Best known for the chancery side of company law, this set has cemented its reputation as a leading force in the market. **Michael Lyndon-Stanford QC** (see p.1439) is reputed to have a "wider range than many," whilst **Charles Aldous QC** remains "brilliant on his feet." "A tough, but likeable litigator," **Catherine Newman QC**'s (see p.1453) soaring reputation is attributed as much to her "dedication to company work" as to her "charmingly ferocious" style. **Guy Newey QC** (see p.1453) has a following amongst both solicitors and barristers who appreciate his "easy-going approach coupled with a sharp, technical mind." **Rebecca Stubbs** (see p.1485) is recommended for her expertise in disqualification matters. **Matthew Collings** (see p.1382) "gets hold of a problem and analyses it expertly." Chancery lies at the heart of **Paul Girolami QC**'s (see p.1405) practice, while **Christopher Parker** handles disputes relating to insolvency, company and professional negligence.

3-4 SOUTH SQUARE (see full details p.1603) Rightly regarded as the first port of call for insolvency, the set maintains a robust profile for company matters. Head of chambers **Michael Crystal QC** (see p.1386) is back in the UK following his presence on the Thyssen litigation in Bermuda. Rivals express considerable admiration for "intellectually impressive" **Robin Knowles QC** (see p.1430), whilst of **Robin Dicker QC** (see p.1390) it has been said "he is better than his years and experience." **Mark Phillips QC** (see p.1460) wins commendations for his "in-depth experience."

ENTERPRISE CHAMBERS (see full details p.1529) This lower profile but popular set is headed up by **Anthony Mann QC** (see p.1441). "Level-headed" and a "great client-charmer," he specialises in all areas of commercial chancery work and company law. "Redoubtable" **Geoffrey Zelin** (see p.1503) has particular experience in shareholder disputes, enforcement of directors' duties and share sale agreements, whilst commercial litigator **Linden Ife** (see p.1422) is regarded as a "tough cookie." **Peter Arden** is warmly praised for insolvency and company work.

24 OLD BUILDINGS (see full details p.1582) The set is recommended for both international and UK company law. "Piercingly intelligent" **Alan Steinfeld QC** is commended for "taking the bull by the horns." Often visible on large-scale, long-running cases, **Lawrence Cohen QC** excels in

COMPANY

Research The rankings are based on in-depth interviews with 6,582 solicitors, barristers and clients in the UK. **Chambers'** research is audited by the British Market Research Bureau (see page 7)

BARRISTERS' PROFILES ▶ See pages 1353-1504

LEADING SILKS • London

1
POTTS Robin	Erskine Chambers
RICHARDS David	Erskine Chambers

2
ALDOUS Charles	Maitland Chambers
BOMPAS Anthony	4 Stone Buildings
BRIGGS Michael	Serle Court
CRYSTAL Michael	3-4 South Square
GLOSTER Elizabeth	One Essex Court
HESLOP Philip	4 Stone Buildings
HILDYARD Robert	4 Stone Buildings
KOSMIN Leslie	Erskine Chambers
OLIVER David	Erskine Chambers
TODD Michael	Erskine Chambers

3
BRISBY John	4 Stone Buildings
DICKER Robin	3-4 South Square
KNOWLES Robin	3-4 South Square
MOWSCHENSON Terence	Wilberforce Chambers
NEWMAN Catherine	Maitland Chambers
PURLE Charles	New Square Chambers
VOS Geoffrey	3 Stone Buildings

4
BANNISTER Edward	3 Stone Buildings
BOYLE Alan	Serle Court
COHEN Lawrence	24 Old Buildings
GIRET Jane	11 Stone Buildings
HAPGOOD Mark	Brick Court Chambers
HOLLINGTON Robin	New Square Chambers
LYNDON-STANFORD Michael	Maitland Chambers
MABB David	Erskine Chambers
MANN Anthony	Enterprise Chambers
NEWEY Guy	Maitland Chambers
PHILLIPS Mark	3-4 South Square
SMITH Stephen	New Square Chambers
STEINFELD Alan	24 Old Buildings

NEW SILKS
CHIVERS David	Erskine Chambers
GIROLAMI Paul	Maitland Chambers
MILES Robert	4 Stone Buildings
MOORE Martin	Erskine Chambers
RABINOWITZ Laurence	One Essex Court

For details of these leading barristers see Profiles on page 1353

LEADING JUNIORS • London

1
CONE John	Erskine Chambers
STOCKDALE Thomas	Erskine Chambers
STOKES Mary	Erskine Chambers

2
DAVIS-WHITE Malcolm	4 Stone Buildings
SNOWDEN Richard	Erskine Chambers

3
COLLINGS Matthew	Maitland Chambers
MARSHALL Philip	Serle Court
ROBERTS Catherine	Erskine Chambers
STUBBS Rebecca	Maitland Chambers

4
ARDEN Peter	Enterprise Chambers
CROW Jonathan	4 Stone Buildings
GILLYON Philip	Erskine Chambers
GREEN Michael	Fountain Court
GRIFFITHS Peter	4 Stone Buildings
HARMAN Sarah	4 Stone Buildings
IFE Linden	Enterprise Chambers
PRENTICE Dan	Erskine Chambers
RITCHIE Richard	24 Old Buildings
SHEKERDEMIAN Marcia	11 Stone Buildings
THOMPSON Andrew	Erskine Chambers
ZELIN Geoffrey	Enterprise Chambers

For details of these leading barristers see Profiles on page 1353

---

disputes relating to finance. In addition to company law, **Richard Ritchie** handles property, business and insolvency matters.

SERLE COURT (see full details p.1602) Enhanced by its merger with One Hare Court in 2000, the set is excellent for all aspects of general business law. Clients turn to "top-notch advocate" **Michael Briggs QC** (see p.1371) for his depth of knowledge in both the company and insolvency field, whilst **Alan Boyle QC** (see p.1370) is noted for his "immense experience" of insolvency and civil fraud matters. Market commentators respect **Philip Marshall** (see p.1442); his experience encompasses commercial litigation and insolvency.

OTHER NOTABLE PRACTITIONERS Tremendously popular **Elizabeth Gloster QC** (see p.1406) of One Essex Court is "forceful and effective." Clients appreciate her "support and hard work" as well as her "intricate knowledge" of contract, insolvency and insurance law. New silk **Laurence Rabinowitz QC** (see p.1465) of One Essex Court has many strings to his bow. A company and commercial lawyer, his practice encompasses banking and insurance expertise. **Terence Mowschenson QC** (see p.1451) of Wilberforce Chambers is renowned for his "razor-sharp, brilliant mind," whilst **Mark Hapgood QC** of Brick Court Chambers "leaves no stone unturned" and can be relied upon for "strong, clear opinions." **Robin Hollington QC** (see p.1418) of New Square Chambers has carved a niche within shareholder disputes. "Extremely effective" **Charles Purle QC** (see p.1465) is valued by solicitors who agree that he "seems to present his case effortlessly whilst remaining completely on top of the details." The set is also home to high-profile litigator **Stephen Smith QC** (see p.1480), who wins peer admiration for his wide-ranging company and commercial practice. "Extraordinarily bright and aware" head of chambers **Geoffrey Vos QC** (see p.1496) of 3 Stone Buildings is endorsed for his ability to handle "the heavy cases." Here also **Edward Bannister QC** (see p.1361) is sought out for his "reliability and focus." **Jane Giret QC** (see p.1405) of 11 Stone Buildings continues to impress with her "focused and pragmatic" advice. She is recommended in particular for insolvency and investment fund work. At the same set, **Marcia Shekerdemian** (see p.1477) was endorsed for her "reliable and intuitive advice," and **Michael Green** (see p.1408) of Fountain Court maintains a following among solicitors.

COMPETITION/EUROPEAN LAW

Research The rankings are based on in-depth interviews with 6,582 solicitors, barristers and clients in the UK. **Chambers'** research is audited by the British Market Research Bureau (see page 7)

BARRISTERS' PROFILES ▶ See pages 1353-1504

OVERVIEW: This section covers expertise in all spheres of competition law including merger notification, anti-dumping and behavioural issues. Included also are those barristers adept in pure European law reflecting the integral role played by Brussels in this particular field.

LONDON

COMPETITION/EUROPEAN LAW ■ London	QCs	Jnrs
1 Brick Court Chambers (Christopher Clarke QC)	6	4
Monckton Chambers (Parker/Lasok)	8	4

Numbers show recommended barristers in this practice area

LEADING SILKS ■ London

1
ANDERSON David	Brick Court Chambers
FOWLER Richard	Monckton Chambers
GREEN Nicholas	Brick Court Chambers
PARKER Kenneth	Monckton Chambers

2
LASOK Paul	Monckton Chambers
LEVER Jeremy	Monckton Chambers
ROTH Peter	Monckton Chambers
SHARPE Thomas	One Essex Court
SWIFT John	Monckton Chambers
VAJDA Christopher	Monckton Chambers

3
BARLING Gerald	Brick Court Chambers
LLOYD JONES David	Brick Court Chambers
PAINES Nicholas	Monckton Chambers
PLENDER Richard	20 Essex Street
SHARPSTON Eleanor	4 Paper Buildings
VAUGHAN David	Brick Court Chambers

NEW SILKS
BREALEY Mark	Brick Court Chambers
MORRIS Stephen	20 Essex Street
THOMPSON Rhodri	Matrix Chambers

For details of these leading barristers see Profiles on page 1353

LEADING JUNIORS ■ London

1
ANDERSON Rupert	Monckton Chambers
ROBERTSON Aidan	Brick Court Chambers
TURNER Jon	Monckton Chambers

2
FLYNN James	Brick Court Chambers

3
BEARD Daniel	Monckton Chambers
HOSKINS Mark	Brick Court Chambers
PERETZ George	Monckton Chambers
STRATFORD Jemima	Brick Court Chambers

For details of these leading barristers see Profiles on page 1353

BRICK COURT CHAMBERS (see full details p.1517) Housing some of the very best names in the field, Brick Court maintains its credentials as a "formidable fighting force." Its silks with their "lengthy record of success" are complemented by the type of junior that has led a number of solicitors to confidently predict an assured future for a set which sits at the forefront of developments in EU law. **David Anderson QC** (see p.1356), a relatively youthful silk, was consistently commended as "accessible and clever" and was praised for the "selective and thoughtful approach he brings to his cases." He has been heavily involved in pharmaceutical pricing issues. Equally lauded was **Nicholas Green QC** (see p.1409) who "has exactly the sort of quality practice that reflects his standing." "A highly entertaining court performer," he is a Competition Act and regulatory expert often to be seen appearing before the Competition Appeal Tribunal. Although not a pure competition specialist, the "bright and knowledgeable" **David Lloyd Jones QC** (see p.1437) was recommended alongside **David Vaughan QC** (see p.1495), "one of the senior statesmen of the competition world," and **Gerald Barling QC** (see p.1361), "a quiet, intellectual man who brings a studious air to the courtroom." New silk **Mark Brealey QC** (see p.1370) possesses "excellent court craft" and "a priceless ability to think laterally." Of the juniors, **Aidan Robertson** (see p.1469) shone in the eyes of the majority of solicitors due to his "rare combination of intellectual ability and commercial pragmatism." Other juniors strongly tipped for the very top include the "level and persuasive" **James Flynn** (see p.1399), who is something of an EC expert. **Mark Hoskins** (see p.1419) rounds off the picture here, being feted as a "fine EC lawyer who piledrives through the paperwork." **Jemima Stratford** (see p.1485) is a new addition to the tables following endorsement from solicitors and fellow barristers for her "intelligent and enthusiastic approach."

MONCKTON CHAMBERS (see full details p.1574) A great friend of governmental bodies, Monckton Chambers again provides a substantial number of entrants to our tables. The set is perceived by our interviewees as leading the charge as a pure competition offering. **Richard Fowler QC** (see p.1400) is a pivotal figure, "100% at the top of the tree," who possesses "the skill and determination to pursue a matter." An expert at both competition and EC law he was consistently praised by solicitors for his organisation of a brief and his track record on meeting deadlines. **Kenneth Parker QC** has an "enviable knowledge of UK, US and EU law." "Technically excellent," he is "without a trace of arrogance" and "someone the client really warms to." Fellow silk **Paul Lasok QC** (see p.1432) is recommended for all EC law-related matters and is felt to have "a securer grasp than most on state aid and procurement matters," areas in which **Jeremy Lever QC** (see p.1434) also "applies innovative thinking." The set houses two silks back in practice: **John Swift QC** (see p.1486) "has picked up the reins effortlessly since returning to practice from the rail regulator" while **Peter Roth QC** (see p.1471) returns to the tables this year following a stint editing Bellamy & Child. Counsel to the OFT in the highly publicised Napp case, he is a "disconcertingly good advocate" who "always gives fantastic support in a crisis situation." **Christopher Vajda QC** (see p.1471), meanwhile, "has instinctive understanding coupled with a creative prowess" that makes him "the man to go to for a difficult point of European constitutional law." **Nicholas Paines QC** (see p.1458) is also recommended for his "dependability and clarity of thought." Leading practitioner **Rupert Anderson** (see p.1357) was described to our researchers as "one of the most experienced juniors at the Bar." A veteran of a number of Monopolies and Mergers Commission cases, his is "a fine mind and a sought-after talent." Similarly popular is **Jon Turner** (see p.1494), standing counsel to the OFT, and "a really serious player with the makings of a future Treasury devil." Other respected juniors include **George Peretz** (see p.1459), who is "strong and to the point" in his OFT work, and **Daniel Beard** (see p.1363), who, despite his relative youth, "appears in the most impressive cases and has an intuitive feel for the business side of things."

OTHER NOTABLE PRACTITIONERS **Thomas Sharpe QC** (see p.1476) of **One Essex Court**, an expert on both procurement and pure competition matters, is widely admired for his breadth of knowledge and the ability to "infuse his cases with passion." At **20 Essex Street** **Richard Plender QC** (see p.1461) combines EC work with human rights and public law to good effect, receiving support for his "well prepared, analytical approach," while new silk **Stephen Morris QC** (see p.1450) is "famed for knowing the Competition Act inside out." **Eleanor Sharpston QC** (see p.1476) of **4 Paper Buildings** is "a favourite of the government" on EU cases. **Rhodri Thompson QC** (see p.1490) at **Matrix Chambers** has taken silk this year, and is considered "approachable and straight to the point."

CONSTRUCTION

Research The rankings are based on in-depth interviews with 6,582 solicitors, barristers and clients in the UK. **Chambers'** research is audited by the British Market Research Bureau (see page 7)

BARRISTERS' PROFILES ▶ See pages 1353-1504

LONDON

CONSTRUCTION • London	QCs	Jnrs
1 Atkin Chambers (Robert Akenhead QC)	10	11
Keating Chambers	13	9
2 Crown Office Chambers (Spencer/Purchas)	4	1
4 Pump Court	3	3
3 2 Temple Gardens (Dermod O'Brien QC)	2	2
4 39 Essex Street (Nigel Pleming QC)	3	-
Four New Square (Justin Fenwick QC)	2	-

Numbers show recommended barristers in this practice area

LEADING SILKS • London

★ BLACKBURN John	Atkin Chambers	
RAMSEY Vivian	Keating Chambers	
1 AKENHEAD Robert	Atkin Chambers	
DARLING Paul	Keating Chambers	
FERNYHOUGH Richard	Keating Chambers	
FURST Stephen	Keating Chambers	
SLATER John	Crown Office Chambers	
TAVERNER Marcus	Keating Chambers	
WHITE Andrew	Atkin Chambers	
2 BAATZ Nicholas	Atkin Chambers	
DENNYS Nicholas	Atkin Chambers	
FRIEDMAN David	4 Pump Court	
MARRIN John	Keating Chambers	
TER HAAR Roger	Crown Office Chambers	
UFF John	Keating Chambers	
WILMOT-SMITH Richard	39 Essex Street	
3 BARTLETT Andrew	Crown Office Chambers	
BOWDERY Martin	Atkin Chambers	
COULSON Peter	Keating Chambers	
ELLIOTT Timothy	Keating Chambers	
GRAY Richard	39 Essex Street	
STREATFEILD-JAMES David	Atkin Chambers	
4 ACTON DAVIS Jonathan	Atkin Chambers	
BLACK Michael	2 Temple Gardens	
BOULDING Philip	Keating Chambers	
DENNISON Stephen	Atkin Chambers	
EDWARDS-STUART Antony	Crown Office Chambers	
FENWICK Justin	Four New Square	
NICHOLSON Jeremy	4 Pump Court	
SPEAIGHT Anthony	4 Pump Court	
STEWART Roger	Four New Square	
THOMAS Christopher	Keating Chambers	
NEW SILKS		
CATCHPOLE Stuart	39 Essex Street	
O'FARRELL Finola	Keating Chambers	
RAESIDE Mark	Atkin Chambers	
THOMAS David	2 Temple Gardens	
WILLIAMSON Adrian	Keating Chambers	

For details of these leading barristers see Profiles on page 1353

ATKIN CHAMBERS (see full details p.1508) Still neck and neck with Keating Chambers for its consistency of quality and considerably ahead of its competitors. The number of direct instructions from overseas is increasing. "Able to relate to clients and work in teams," the set is considered to have taken further steps to enhance its efficiency and a more flexible response to instructions. Solicitors reported "you can be confident that the timetable stated will be adhered to." Its silks were particularly singled out during our research this year. Possessing "a brain like no one else, immensely quick and extremely practical," **John Blackburn QC** (see p.1366) sits at the top of his game as both an arbitrator and advocate. He is involved in several matters overseas and is a lead advisor to London Underground. Interviewees attributed his success to his approach which "gets to the kernel of any argument;" he is "one of the finest advocates for thinking on his feet and getting results where others wouldn't go." **Robert Akenhead QC** (see p.1355) has "the rare combination of detail and strategic planning, and is enormously good at communicating with clients." His ability to digest large quantities of documents and expertise in PPC 2000 contracts was commended. **Andrew White QC**'s (see p.1499) "forensic approach" has been utilised in matters concerning the Channel Tunnel and the House of Commons' new parliamentary building. This, combined with " an array of weapons from charm to fight" ensured he retains his position in the top flight. **Nicholas Baatz QC** (see p.1359) was deemed "thorough, intelligent and reassuring to have in the team," while **Nicholas Dennys QC**'s (see p.1389) "lovely appellate style" and charming demeanour enable him to be "good at making something grisly seem quite sweet." The latter is also respected for his IT expertise. Viewed as "an excellent advocate," **Jonathan Acton Davis QC** (see p.1355) has expertise in energy matters, particularly power stations and has been involved in arbitrations in Singapore. **Martin Bowdery QC** is " highly valued if a case requires a hard fight" and is also experienced on the energy-related side of construction. Peers point to the meticulous **Stephen Dennison QC** (see p.1389) as "one of the best advocates – judges adore him." **David Streatfeild-James QC** (see p.1485) received accolades for his hard-working approach and cross-examination skills. Interviewees rate new silk **Mark Raeside QC** (see p.1466) as "a real street fighter" with an " ability to marshal facts and turn papers around in a short time." The set also has good breadth with its stock of juniors. **Stephanie Barwise**'s (see p.1362) profile is judged to have increased over the last year – she is "good to have by your side." Well-respected, **Chantal-Aimée Doerries** (see p.1390) enjoys the ear of the court with a client-friendly manner – "she can handle big litigation and has what it takes." "Well-prepared and with a gravitas beyond his years," **Peter Fraser** (see p.1400) has a no-nonsense style. Solicitors described the client feedback on arbitration specialist **Manus McMullan** (see p.1445) as universally positive. **Delia Dumaresq** (see p.1391) has carved out a name as a specialist construction adjudicator, although she keeps her hand in more mainstream advocacy. **Andrew Goddard** (see p.1406) is particularly noted for his ADR experience. **James Howells** (see p.1421) offers sound arguments and "complete advice," while **Simon Lofthouse** (see p.1438) has been instructed on disputes relating to large commercial developments, airport terminals and computer installations. Instructing solicitors agreed "he worked hard for us – he is talented both on paper and in cross examination." **Fiona Parkin**'s (see p.1458) "spirited" approach has impressed both solicitors and peers. **Andrew Burr** (see p.1375) impressed with his "phenomenal hard work" and advocacy skills as well as his "masterly attention to detail." **Dominique Rawley**'s (see p.1466) energetic approach and "tenacious, determined" style also found favour with interviewees.

KEATING CHAMBERS (see full details p.1560) Excelling at "getting the right people for the right jobs," solicitors also highlighted the set's strength and depth of its juniors. The set has "notably improved its client care and its response times over the last year." The "exceptional" reputation of dual-qualified **Vivian Ramsey QC** (see p.1466) is second to none. Some solicitors reflected that "our dream team comprises him and (if needs be) a junior of his choice." Active both domestically and extensively on overseas matters, "his client service is marvellous – he is not afraid of giving a view." He combines a genuine all-round ability and "an unrivalled knowledge of the industry" and yet he remains accessible to clients. Adjudged "heavily committed" to the sector, **Paul Darling QC** (see p.1387) has

CONSTRUCTION

Research The rankings are based on in-depth interviews with 6,582 solicitors, barristers and clients in the UK. **Chambers'** research is audited by the British Market Research Bureau (see page 7)

BARRISTERS' PROFILES ▶ See pages 1353-1504

LEADING JUNIORS • London

1
BARWISE Stephanie	Atkin Chambers
HARGREAVES Simon	Keating Chambers
JEFFORD Nerys	Keating Chambers
NISSEN Alexander	Keating Chambers
SEARS David	4 Pump Court

2
BRANNIGAN Sean	4 Pump Court
DOERRIES Chantal-Aimée	Atkin Chambers
FRASER Peter	Atkin Chambers
MCMULLAN Manus	Atkin Chambers

3
BOWSHER Michael	Monckton Chambers
BURR Andrew	Atkin Chambers
CONSTABLE Adam	2 Temple Gardens
DAVIES Jane	Crown Office Chambers
DUMARESQ Delia	Atkin Chambers
GODDARD Andrew	Atkin Chambers
HANNAFORD Sarah	Keating Chambers
HOWELLS James	Atkin Chambers
HUGHES Adrian	4 Pump Court
HUGHES Simon	Keating Chambers
LOFTHOUSE Simon	Atkin Chambers
MORT Justin	2 Temple Gardens
PARKIN Fiona	Atkin Chambers
PENNICOTT Ian	Keating Chambers
PLANTEROSE Rowan	Littman Chambers
RANDALL Louise	Keating Chambers
RAWLEY Dominique	Atkin Chambers
ROWLANDS Marc	Keating Chambers

UP AND COMING
LEMON Jane	Keating Chambers

For details of these leading barristers see Profiles on page 1353

spent much of the last year on the huge Panatown v McAlpine case. His is "effective and practical with a good sense of humour," and was endorsed for his "imagination and drive." Cross-examination specialist **Richard Fernyhough QC** (see p.1397) has spent much of his time on a major arbitration in Hong Kong. He has "gravitas as an advocate" and "a superb bedside manner." Peers believe that **Stephen Furst QC** (see p.1402) is "a great predictor of the case outcomes and judges like his quiet and persuasive style." **Marcus Taverner QC** (see p.1488) has acted in a series of cases connected to the long-running Brompton litigation. While "clients warm to his pugnacious style," he " can temper his aggressiveness according to the judge." An accomplished mediator, **John Marrin QC** (see p.1442) was commended for his measured approach and attention to details. Dual qualified **John Uff QC**'s (see p.1494) technical ability is outstanding – "he has a quiet style but few judges will debate a point with him." Uff has spent the majority of the last year as chairman of the Southall Rail Inquiry. "Hard-working" **Peter Coulson QC** (see p.1384) is promoted in our tables this year following endorsement of his "constructive attitude – he is persuasive on his feet." **Timothy Elliott QC** (see p.1394) is "a good cerebral lawyer with an effective approach in court," while the "extremely reliable" and "client-friendly" **Philip Boulding QC** (see p.1368) has been particularly busy on international arbitrations. **Christopher Thomas QC** (see p.1489) has etched a reputation among interviewees as the man to turn to with a difficult matter, employing his "responsive and tenacious" approach. The set has two new silks this year. The "extremely efficient" **Finola O'Farrell QC** (see p.1368) has a broad practice and is "excellent on detail," while **Adrian Williamson QC** (see p.1500)("intellectually bright and technically shrewd,") has been active on the Royal Brompton Hospital case. The set has a good stable of juniors. **Simon Hargreaves**'s (see p.1412) attention to detail in advising on and drafting pleadings has won him a following among solicitors. "Smooth," **Nerys Jefford**'s (see p.1424)

practice is weighted towards international arbitration, tempered by work on UK matters such as a dispute arising out of the Greenwich Millennium Village. The robust **Alexander Nissen** (see p.1455) has "impressed with the extent and depth of his knowledge." He has been involved in a number of cases concerning the jurisdictional and enforcement issues of adjudications. New to our table this year, **Simon Hughes** (see p.1421) arrives with " no airs and graces – efficiency and style personified." Senior junior **Ian Pennicott** (see p.1459) is dual-qualified in Hong Kong and solicitors say he fits in well as part of a team. **Louise Randall** (see p.1466) deals with a broad base of matters, from offshore oil production disputes to architects' negligence, solicitors appreciate that **Marc Rowlands** (see p.1471) "rolls his sleeves up and gets stuck in." **Jane Lemon** (see p.1434) spent much of last year on an ICC arbitration abroad and is "continuing to mature into a top-notch advocate." New to our tables this year, **Sarah Hannaford** (see p.1412) also received warm market recommendation.

CROWN OFFICE CHAMBERS (see full details p.1522) Considered by some interviewees to be "the third building set" after the clear leaders, it has a broad litigation base with a focus on the insurance side. This "cohesive unit" has been involved in contested enforcement applications and insurance-based work. **John Slater QC** (see p.1479) is "a classic silk in the best traditions: erudite, eloquent and with unshakeable self-confidence." Peers believe that he "combines razor sharp advocacy with excellent technical analysis." **Roger ter Haar QC** (see p.1489) has "impressed with his tremendous strategic thinking and his handling of witnesses." Interviewees endorsed **Andrew Bartlett QC**'s (see p.1362) "relentless" approach, while **Antony Edwards-Stuart QC** (see p.1393) has been busy on the landmark case Royal Brompton Hospital v Hammon and others for most of the year. The "flamboyant and dedicated" **Jane Davies** (see p.1387) is the set's most high-profile junior in this field.

4 PUMP COURT (see full details p.1592) The set has committed resources to building up its construction practice and the wider market is beginning to see the results. It has won a healthy share of instructions, with the emphasis on adjudication and resultant claims. Formerly chairman of TECBAR, much of **David Friedman QC**'s (see p.1401) time has been taken up with the Factortame litigation on behalf of the government. His "crystal clear analysis" and "technical excellence" have been well noted. **Jeremy Nicholson QC** (see p.1454) "gets stuck into the details," and has been involved on the continuing McAlpine v Panatown litigation on behalf of the employer. **Anthony Speaight QC** (see p.1481) has arrived at the set from 12 King's Bench Walk. Of the juniors available, **David Sears** (see p.1475) has "a great deal of rounded experience" and the ability to " gradually manoeuvre people into a corner." "Articulate," **Sean Brannigan** (see p.1370) is considered by some to be "an outstanding prospect and cool as you like." **Adrian Hughes** (see p.1421) was also recommended for his growing practice.

2 TEMPLE GARDENS (see full details p.1612) Considered by solicitors to be making a push for this area, the set's smaller size was said by solicitors to make it more competitive in the market. Instructions from the USA and the Far East have also helped build its profile. "An extremely good mediator and arbitrator," the hugely experienced **Michael Black QC** (see p.1366) has a knack for picking up big cases. He led on the £2 billion liquidation of Prince Jefri of Brunei's construction company. New and, in the eyes of many interviewees, long overdue silk **David Thomas QC** (see p.1490) marries a "hard-working, straightforward" approach with "a mature, sensible style." He has acted on adjudicator jurisdiction matters and on the Ladbroke Grove railway inquiry. Many eyes are on **Adam Constable** (see p.1383); his "clever and capable" approach is "as good as it

CONSTRUCTION

Research The rankings are based on in-depth interviews with 6,582 solicitors, barristers and clients in the UK. **Chambers'** research is audited by the British Market Research Bureau (see page 7)

BARRISTERS' PROFILES ▶ See pages 1353-1504

gets." **Justin Mort** (see p.1450) was identified by solicitors and clients alike as analytically sharp with a willingness to work as part of a team.

39 ESSEX STREET (see full details p.1537) Although the set is thought to lack high-profile construction juniors, the impression made of its well-respected silks goes some way to redressing the balance. "A good, punchy cross-examiner," **Richard Wilmott-Smith QC** (see p.1500) has considerable experience in all aspects of the construction sector in many jurisdictions – he "knows it all backwards." The "understated" **Richard Gray QC** (see p.1408) was recommended for his ability to put forward an argument simply, while new silk **Stuart Catchpole QC** (see p.1378) drew plaudits "for his absolute dedication to a case, calm authority and personal charm." Respected also for his work in administrative and public law, he is "able to give sensible, commercially sound advice promptly."

FOUR NEW SQUARE (see full details p.1576) These long-time professional liability specialists can bring this and other elements to construction cases. The "outstanding" **Justin Fenwick QC** (see p.1397) is respected as a commercial and insurance litigation specialist, alongside his extensive construction experience. Observers consider his colleague, professional negligence expert **Roger Stewart QC** (see p.1483) to be "a persuasive advocate."

OTHER NOTABLE PRACTITIONERS **Michael Bowsher** (see p.1369) at **Monckton Chambers** has a focus on EC procurement law and leading solicitors consider him to be "receptive to ideas, thorough and approachable." Proving to be a strong alternative, **Rowan Planterose** (see p.1461) at **Littman Chambers** was particularly recommended for his arbitration work.

CONSUMER LAW

Research The rankings are based on in-depth interviews with 6,582 solicitors, barristers and clients in the UK. **Chambers'** research is audited by the British Market Research Bureau (see page 7)

BARRISTERS' PROFILES ▶ See pages 1353-1504

OVERVIEW: Food, consumer credit, trade descriptions and travel law all come under the remit of practitioners featured in this section, for whom business has largely continued as usual. Exceptions include local authority trading standards' departments becoming more stringent, while the increasing profile of the Food Standards Agency, only established in 2000, is felt to have contributed to wider enforcement of food regulations. The Human Rights Act has also had some impact, particularly on consumer credit law.

LONDON

CONSUMER LAW • London	QCs	Jnrs
1 Gough Square Chambers (Fred Philpott)	1	6
2 2-3 Gray's Inn Square (Porten/Scrivener)	1	1

Numbers show recommended barristers in this practice area

LEADING SILKS • London	
1 GOODE Roy	Blackstone Chambers
SCRIVENER Anthony	2-3 Gray's Inn Square
2 DE HAAN Kevin	3 Raymond Buildings
GOODHART William	Gough Square Chambers
3 WATERS Malcolm	11 Old Square

For details of these leading barristers see Profiles on page 1353

LEADING JUNIORS • London	
1 PHILPOTT Fred	Gough Square Chambers
2 TRAVERS David	6 Pump Court
3 ANDREWS Claire	Gough Square Chambers
GOULDING Jonathan	Gough Square Chambers
HIBBERT William	Gough Square Chambers
STEPHENSON Geoffrey	2-3 Gray's Inn Square
4 SAGGERSON Alan	No. 1 Serjeants' Inn
SAYER Peter	Gough Square Chambers
SMITH Julia	Gough Square Chambers

For details of these leading barristers see Profiles on page 1353

GOUGH SQUARE CHAMBERS (see full details p.1545) Widely regarded as pre-eminent in its field, the set continues to be valued for the "co-operative spirit" shown by its members. Adding to its already considerable weight of expertise, the arrival of highly regarded consumer credit specialist **William Goodhart QC** (see p.1407) (formerly 3 New Square) is perceived to provide as much benefit to the set as to himself: "it will give him scope to develop his practice still further." Head of chambers **Fred Philpott** (see p.1460) has a "terrific" reputation, is swift in "striking up a rapport with clients," who appreciate his "down-to-earth approach to advocacy." Together with "resourceful advocate" **William Hibbert** (see p.1415), Goodhart and Philpott appeared in the appeal to the House of Lords in Director General of Fair Trading v First National Bank, the first case to have been brought under the Unfair Terms in Consumer Contracts Regulations. **Claire Andrews** (see p.1357) remains well regarded for her wide ranging regulatory practice, and is recommended for both her trading standards and food law advice. Entering the tables for the first time this year, **Jonathan Goulding** (see p.1408) covers many aspects of consumer protection and was commended for the "useful reservoir of technical knowledge" he has built up in relation to food law, laying the foundation for a "refreshing approach." **Julia Smith** (see p.1479) also retains a strong consumer law practice acting for both lending institutions and consumers, covering credit agreements, advertising, licensing and consumer contracts. **Peter Sayer** (see p.1474) is best known for advisory work on behalf of financial institutions in consumer credit matters, and has also been involved in issues surrounding pricing and trade descriptions.

2-3 GRAY'S INN SQUARE (see full details p.1548) "High-profile and high-powered," **Anthony Scrivener QC** (see p.1475) continues to be viewed by solicitors as the "final authority on difficult cases." His specialist knowledge covers consumer law and consumer credit as well as food law. Also "extremely experienced and analytical," **Geoffrey Stephenson** (see p.1475) continues to be active in the sphere.

OTHER NOTABLE PRACTITIONERS A "leading light academically," **Roy Goode QC** (see p.1407) of Blackstone Chambers possesses a "fantastic breadth and depth of knowledge," particularly with regard to consumer credit. Observers conclude that **Kevin de Haan QC** (see p.1388) of 3 Raymond Buildings "knows the regulatory regime inside out." He regularly advises a wide range of companies on trading, consumer, and food law matters under domestic and EU legislation. Interviewees continue to show appreciation of the "fine intellect" of **Malcolm Waters QC** (see p.1498) at 11 Old Square. Another eminent consumer credit specialist, Waters also appeared in the First National Bank case. **David Travers** (see p.1492) of 6 Pump Court has had a sustained impact on the London market, described by interviewees as "an excellent, client friendly advocate backed by a considerable depth of knowledge." His significant profile in this area of law comes about as part of an expansive regulatory practice, which includes advice on trading standards and food law matters. **Alan Saggerson** (see p.1473) of No. 1 Serjeant's Inn provides the first port of call for often high profile consumer law cases originating in the travel industry, advising both tour operators and individuals.

WESTERN CIRCUIT

LEADING JUNIORS • Western	
1 GIBNEY Malcolm	17 Carlton Crescent
HAGGAN Nicholas	17 Carlton Crescent

For details of these leading barristers see Profiles on page 1353

17 CARLTON CRESCENT possesses two outstanding practitioners in the field. "Tenacious" **Malcolm Gibney** and **Nicholas Haggan**, who combine "specialist expertise with a smooth advocacy style," remain key regional players.

WALES & CHESTER CIRCUIT

LEADING JUNIORS • Wales & Chester	
1 SCHOLZ Karl	Nicholas Street Chambers

For details of these leading barristers see Profiles on page 1353

Acting for local authorities on an advisory basis and in court, **Karl Scholz** of Nicholas Street Chambers is a "terrier-like opponent."

CONSUMER LAW

Research The rankings are based on in-depth interviews with 6,582 solicitors, barristers and clients in the UK. **Chambers'** research is audited by the British Market Research Bureau (see page 7)

BARRISTERS' PROFILES ▶ See pages 1353-1504

MIDLANDS CIRCUIT

LEADING SILKS • Midlands

[1]	TREACY Colman	3 Fountain Court

For details of these leading barristers see Profiles on page 1353

LEADING JUNIORS • Midlands

BERLIN Barry	St Philips Chambers

For details of these leading barristers see Profiles on page 1353

Colman Treacy QC (see p.1493) of 3 Fountain Court "always conducts cases extremely effectively" and continues to enjoy praise of the highest order. "Thorough and forceful," peers consider **Barry Berlin** (see p.1365) of St. Philips Chambers to be a formidable opponent. Specialising in consumer protection, trading standards and food law, he can also bring health and safety and environmental health expertise to bear when acting both for and against local authorities. He recently appeared at the Court of Appeal in a trading standards case concerning a fraudulent mortgage pricing statement.

CRIME

Research The rankings are based on in-depth interviews with 6,582 solicitors, barristers and clients in the UK. **Chambers'** research is audited by the British Market Research Bureau (see page 7)

BARRISTERS' PROFILES ▶ See pages 1353-1504

LONDON

CRIME • London	QCs	Jnrs
1 2 Bedford Row (William Clegg QC)	8	7
Doughty Street Chambers (Geoffrey Robertson QC)	11	3
Hollis Whiteman Chambers (Bevan/Whiteman)	7	4
6 King's Bench Walk (Roy Amlot QC)	11	6
3 Raymond Buildings (Clive Nicholls QC)	7	3
2 23 Essex Street (Michael Lawson QC)	6	1
Two Garden Court (Davies/Griffiths)	4	3
3 Gray's Inn Square (Rock Tansey QC)	5	5
2 Hare Court (Stephen Kramer QC)	5	5
18 Red Lion Court (Anthony Arlidge QC)	7	1
3 7 Bedford Row (David Farrer QC)	4	-
9-12 Bell Yard (D Anthony Evans QC)	3	3
Furnival Chambers (Andrew Mitchell QC)	3	3
2 Harcourt Buildings, Atkinson Bevan Chambers (Atkinson/Bevan)	3	2
Matrix Chambers	5	1
Tooks Court Chambers (Michael Mansfield QC)	3	3
2-4 Tudor Street (Richard Ferguson QC)	2	5
4 10 King's Bench Walk (David Nathan QC)	1	1
187 Fleet Street (Andrew Trollope QC)	2	2
5 Paper Buildings (Carey/Caplan)	2	1
3 Temple Gardens (Jonathan Goldberg QC)	2	2

Numbers show recommended barristers in this practice area

2 BEDFORD ROW (see full details p.1509) This specialist criminal set retains its strong reputation in the criminal arena. Head of chambers **William Clegg QC** (see p.1381) possesses "forensic expertise" while always having "all his contingencies worked out." Peers described "exceptionally bright" **Trevor Burke QC** (see p.1374) as "an incisive practitioner who is great on his feet," while fellow silk **Peter Lodder QC** (see p.1438) is a favourite for heavyweight crime matters. "Professional and down-to-earth," new silk **Jim Sturman QC** (see p.1485) received enthusiastic support for his "charisma in court, unique presence and his ability to communicate with clients." "Strong and hard-working" **Mark Milliken-Smith** (see p.1448) has enjoyed a high profile this year, as has **Brian Altman** (see p.1356), who made headlines with his work on the Damilola case.

DOUGHTY STREET CHAMBERS (see full details p.1526) This heavyweight human rights set includes such star silks as **Geoffrey Robertson QC** (see p.1469) who retains his reputation as "a master of words, a real craftsman." "Instantly likeable" **Peter Thornton QC** (see p.1490) is praised by competition for the moderation and fairness in the way he presents arguments. Renowned for his work in prisoners' rights, **Edward Fitzgerald QC** is "a good cross-examiner and an intellectual giant." One peer even went so far as to say "he is wonderful in everything he touches." "Masterful with jurors" **Christopher Sallon QC** is also said to be "a superb raconteur." The highly individual **Patrick O'Connor QC** is a man of immense talent, a real fighter, while competitors also noted that **Michael Grieve QC** is "absolutely brilliant on homicide." **Keir Starmer QC** (see p.1368) also enjoys "a tip top reputation." **Jill Evans** (see p.1396) was applauded by solicitors for "always getting good results."

HOLLIS WHITEMAN CHAMBERS (see full details p.1559) A top-class crime set wih a healthy contingent of leading criminal barristers, it includes **Julian Bevan QC** (see p.1365), who has a reputation as "an excellent cross-examiner." **Anthony Glass QC** (see p.1363) was praised by solicitors for his superb courtroom manner, while "devastating cross-examiner" **Timothy Langdale QC** (see p.1431) is reputed to be "organised and professional; a good barrister for difficult clients." "Intellectually very quick" **John Kelsey-Fry QC** (see p.1428) "has a superb reputation as a tactical defender," while possessing "great charm." Treasury Counsel **Richard Horwell** (see p.1419) and fellow junior **Mark Ellison** (see p.1395) were both also highly commended by the marketplace.

6 KING'S BENCH WALK (see full details p.1563) "Cool as a cucumber" **Roy Amlot QC** (see p.1356) provoked a slightly mixed reaction from solicitors although fellow barristers "would completely endorse him as at the top of the tree." **Ann Mallalieu QC** is said to be "a superb advocate with a honeyed voice," while fellow silk **Joanna Korner QC** retains commendation for her commitment to a case, and now spends much of her time in The Hague. **Bruce Houlder QC**, who was applauded by peers as "stylish and effective in the finest traditions of the Bar," was said to "cross-examine like a knife between the ribs." Researchers were also struck by the volume of praise for "the outstanding junior at the criminal Bar," **David Perry**, who does a lot of work in the Court of Appeal. **Mark Dennis** (see p.1389) and **Nicholas Hilliard** (see p.1416) impressed solicitors, who would also trust **Jonathan Turner** (see p.1494) "to do whatever is necessary with a case."

3 RAYMOND BUILDINGS (see full details p.1596) A strong offering from this set includes barristers with substantial extradition expertise. **Stephen Batten QC** (see p.1363) is "a good all-rounder who gives the jury the facts and not unnecessary, complex details." Equally adept at crime and fraud, **Alun Jones QC** (see p.1425) possesses "great enthusiasm for clients and cases" while being "good for complex technical issues." **Clive Nicholls QC** (see p.1454) is said to be "great on extradition" and to "work 26 hours a day to achieve results." Highly regarded **John Nutting QC** (see p.1456) is "a true gent" who continues to act on heavyweight criminal cases, while **Nicholas Price QC** (see p.1463) is good on the "academic side." **James Lewis QC** (see p.1435) is known in some quarters simply as "the extradition specialist," while **David Whitehouse QC** (see p.1499) was also commended for his work. Solicitors praised "first-rate" and "intellectually brilliant" **Helen Malcolm** (see p.1363).

23 ESSEX STREET (see full details p.1535) Solicitors queued up to declare themselves members of the **Nicholas Purnell QC** (see p.1465) fan club. "A smooth operator with a great memory," he is great on his feet and with clients. **Michael Hill QC** (see p.1416) also drew praise from all quarters as "an experienced and aggressive practitioner."

TWO GARDEN COURT (see full details p.1544) "Star" **Courtenay Griffiths QC** (see p.1409) was praised for his commitment to clients and his confident advocacy. He represented one of the defendants on the case of Damilola Taylor. New silk **Icah Peart QC** (see p.1459) "has a lovely way with the jury and is a delight to be with on a case: there is no side to him." **Henry Blaxland QC** is "a great lawyer and good on the paperwork." A specialist criminal barrister, he is especially experienced in miscarriage of justice cases.

3 GRAY'S INN SQUARE (see full details p.1549) A specialist defence set, it is bolstered by the reassuring presence of founder **Rock Tansey QC** (see p.1488). Reputed to be "a great defender," he is "immensely experienced" and a man whose "quality of work justifies his ranking." Solicitors rate **George Carter-Stephenson QC** (see p.1377) "as an extremely solid defence practitioner." **Jeremy Dein** (see p.1389) retains his reputation as a top junior, while **Penelope Barrett** (see p.1362) was lauded for being "hard-working and focused."

CRIME

Research The rankings are based on in-depth interviews with 6,582 solicitors, barristers and clients in the UK. **Chambers'** research is audited by the British Market Research Bureau (see page 7)

BARRISTERS' PROFILES ▶ See pages 1353-1504

Recent High Profile Criminal Cases (Jul 2001 – Jul 2002)

Case	Parties for the plaintiff	Parties for the defence	Comments
Murder of Damilola Taylor	Mark Dennis, 6 King's Bench Walk (Roy Amlot QC); Brian Altman, Navaz Daruwalla, 2 Bedford Row (William Clegg QC)	**Defendant 1:** Courtenay Griffiths QC, Two Garden Court (Owen Davies QC & Courtenay Griffiths QC); Michael Magarian, 2 Dyers Buildings (Nadine Radford QC); **Defendant 2:** Baroness Ann Mallalieu QC, 6 King's Bench Walk (Roy Amlot QC); Gregory Fishwick, 2 Dyers Buildings (Nadine Radford QC); **Defendant 3:** George Carter-Stephenson, 3 Gray's Inn Square (Rock Tansey QC); Simon Gedge, 15-19 Devereux Court; **Defendant 4:** John Ryder QC, 6 King's Bench Walk (Roy Amlot QC); Kerim Fuad, 15-19 Devereux Court. **Solicitors – Defendant 1 and 2:** Christopher Hartnell, Hartnells; **Defendant 3:** Greg Stewart, Brady Eastwood Pierce & Stewart; **Defendant 4:** Sean Longley, Venters Solicitors.	April 2002. All four defendants acquitted after the testimony of the leading crown witness was branded unsafe by the judge.
Trial of Jonathan Woodgate and Lee Bowyer	Nicholas Campbell QC, Adrian Waterman 11 King's Bench Walk (FJ Muller QC)	**Jonathon Woodgate:** David Fish QC, Deans Court Chambers (Stephen Grime QC). Instructed by Nick Freeman, Freeman & Co. **Lee Bowyer:** Desmond de Silva QC, Steven Berrick, 2 Paper Buildings (Desmond de Silva QC); Ben Emmerson QC, Matrix Chambers. Instructed by Barker Gillette.	Judgment December 2001. Jonathan Woodgate, was convicted of affray and given 100 hours' community service for the assault on Safraz Najeib. Lee Bowyer and the other defendants were acquitted.
Trial of Nicholas van Hoogstraten	David Waters, QC, 2 Hare Court (Stephen Kramer QC)	Richard Ferguson QC, Peter Binder, 2-4 Tudor Street. Instructed by Danny Solomon, Hughmans	Central Criminal Court July 2002. Nicholas van Hoogstraten convicted of manslaughter for hiring contract killers Robert Knapp and David Croke to murder business rival Mohammed Raja.
Dome Jewellery Heist	Martin Heslop QC, 2 Hare Court (Stephen Kramer QC); Ed Brown, Hollis Whiteman Chambers (Julian Bevan QC & Peter Whiteman QC)	**Robert Adams:** George A Carter-Stephenson QC, 3 Gray's Inn Square (Rock Tansey QC); Samuel Stein, 2 Dyers Buildings (Nadine Radford QC); **Raymond Betson:** Andrew Mitchell QC, Furnival Chambers (Andrew Mitchell QC); Charles Benson, 2 Paper Buildings (Desmond de Silva QC); **Aldo Ciarrocchi:** John Ryder QC, 6 King's Bench Walk (Roy Amlot QC). Instructed by June Venters, Venters Solicitors; **William Cockram:** Oliver Blunt QC, Charles Sherrard, Furnival Chambers (Andrew Mitchell QC)	Central Criminal Court, 17 February 2002. Gang convicted for the attempted robbery of the Millenium Star and 11 Millenium Blue Diamonds worth £200m from the Millenium Dome. Martin Heslop QC said it would have been the greatest robbery ever in terms of value.
The Barry George appeal	Orlando Pownall QC, Jonathan Laidlaw QC, 2 Hare Court (Stephen Kramer QC)	Michael Mansfield QC, Tooks Court Chambers (Michael Mansfield QC); Miss Maryam Syed, 7 Bedford Row (David Farrer QC). Instructed by Marilyn Etienne, Kean Etienne	Court of Appeal 16 July 2002. Barry George lost his appeal against his conviction for the murder of Jill Dando despite widespread misgivings about the initial verdict
Clydach Murder Trial	Patrick Harrington QC, Farrar's Building (John Leighton Williams QC); Tom Glanville Jones, Jim Davis, Angel Chambers.	Peter Rouch QC, 9-12 Bell Yard (D Anthony Evans QC)	July 2002 – David Morris convicted of murdering three generations of the same family at their home in the Swansea Valley.
Tony Martin Appeal	Rosamund Horwood-Smart QC, 18 Red Lion Court (Anthony Aldridge QC), Ian James, Octagon House (Guy Ayers & Andrew Lindquist)	Michael Wolkind QC, Michael Edmonds (now based at Furnival Chambers), 2 Bedford Row (William Clegg QC). Instructed by James Saunders, Saunders & Co.	Royal Courts of Justice, 30 October 2001. Tony Martin lost his appeal against his conviction for the murder of Freddie Barras and wounding with intent.
James Hanratty Appeal	Nigel Sweeney QC, Mark Dennis, David Perry, 6 King's Bench Walk (Roy Amlot QC)	Michael Mansfield QC, Tooks Court Chambers; Henry Blaxland QC, Two Garden Court (Owen Davies QC & Courtenay Griffiths QC). Instructed by Bindman & Partners.	Court of Appeal, May 2002. Hanratty's 1962 conviction for the fatal shooting of scientist Michael Gregsten upheld on the basis of DNA evidence
Murder of William Moseley	Victor Temple QC, Sarah Whitehouse, Alison Foulkes, 6 King's Bench Walk (Roy Amlot QC)	P O'Connor QC, CH Blaxland QC for **Maynard**; M Mansfield QC, Mr CH Blaxland QC for **Dudley**; Instructed by James Saunders, Saunders and Co. J Goldberg QC, Mr CH Blaxland QC for **Bailey**; J Goldberg QC, MH Curtis for **Clarke**.	Court of Appeal 16 July 2002. 1977 convictions quashed against Robert Maynard, Reginald Dudley, Kathleen Bailey and Charles Clarke for murder and conspiracy to murder. Maynard and Dudley between them served 46 years for murder.
Angela Cannings, "cot deaths" case	Paul Dunkels QC, Sean Brunton, Walnut House	Michael Mansfield QC, Tooks Court Chambers (Michael Mansfield QC). Instructed by Pye-Smiths, Salisbury.	16 April 2002. Winchester Crown Court. In an echo of the Sally Clark case, Angela Cannings was convicted of murdering her two baby children in 1991 and 1999.
Murder of Sarah Payne	Tim Langdale QC, Hollis Whiteman Chambers; Crispin Aylett, 3 Raymond Bldgs	Sally O'Neill QC, Furnival Chambers (Andrew Mitchell QC), Iain Morley, 23 Essex Street (Michael Lawson QC)	December 2001. Roy Whiting convicted of the murder of Sarah Payne.
Ian Thomas Appeal	Andrew Edis QC, Anne Whyte, 14 Castle Street (Andrew Edis QC)	Michael Mansfield QC, Tooks Court Chambers (Michael Mansfield QC), James Gregory, Lincoln House Chambers (Mukhtar Hussain QC). Instructed by Stephensons	Court of Appeal 13 March 2002. Ian Thomas lost his appeal against his conviction for the murder of Julie Christian in 1990.
Murder of Marion Crofts	Michael Bowes QC, James Leonard, 2 King's Bench Walk	Andrew Bright QC, Antony Chinn, 9 Bedford Row (Anthony Berry QC). Instructed by Foster Wells.	10 May 2002 Winchester Crown Court. Tony Jasinsky, a former army chef, was convicted of the 1981 rape and murder of schoolgirl Marion Crofts on the basis of DNA evidence.
Allegation of Rape against Quinten Hann	Irena Ray-Crosby, 6 King's Bench Walk (Roy Amlot QC)	Ivan Lawrence QC, Rachel Lawrence; 2 Paper Buildings (Desmond de Silva QC). Instructed by Ugo Palazzo, McCormacks.	Central Criminal Court, July 2002. Controversial Australian snooker player Quinten Hann cleared of raping a 21-year old South African student. Unusually the defence counsels were father and daughter.

www.ChambersandPartners.com

CRIME

Research The rankings are based on in-depth interviews with 6,582 solicitors, barristers and clients in the UK. Chambers' research is audited by the British Market Research Bureau (see page 7)

BARRISTERS' PROFILES ▶ See pages 1353-1504

LEADING SILKS • London

★
- **AMLOT Roy** 6 King's Bench Walk
- **FULFORD Adrian** Tooks Court Chambers
- **MONTGOMERY Clare** Matrix Chambers
- **ARLIDGE Anthony** 18 Red Lion Court
- **LAWSON Edmund** 9-12 Bell Yard
- **BATTEN Stephen** 3 Raymond Buildings
- **MACDONALD Ken** Matrix Chambers
- **CLEGG William** 2 Bedford Row
- **MANSFIELD Michael** Tooks Court

1
- **FITZGERALD Edward** Doughty Street
- **ROBERTSON Geoffrey** Doughty Street
- **JONES Alun** 3 Raymond Buildings
- **TANSEY Rock** 3 Gray's Inn Square
- **PRICE Nicholas** 3 Raymond Buildings
- **THORNTON Peter** Doughty Street Chambers
- **PURNELL Nicholas** 23 Essex Street
- **TROLLOPE Andrew** 187 Fleet Street

2
- **BEVAN Julian** Hollis Whiteman Chambers
- **GLASS Anthony** Hollis Whiteman Chambers
- **NUTTING John** 3 Raymond Buildings
- **SCRIVENER Anthony** 2-3 Gray's Inn Square
- **BLUNT Oliver** Furnival Chambers
- **HESLOP Martin** 2 Hare Court
- **O'CONNOR Patrick** Doughty Street
- **SEABROOK Robert** 1 Crown Office Row
- **ESCOTT-COX Brian** 36 Bedford Row
- **LANGDALE Timothy** Hollis Whiteman
- **RUMFITT Nigel** 7 Bedford Row
- **WHITEHOUSE David** 3 Raymond Buildings
- **NICHOLLS Clive** 3 Raymond Buildings
- **SALLON Christopher** Doughty Street

3
- **ATKINSON Nicholas** 2 Harcourt Buildings
- **FERGUSON Richard** 2-4 Tudor Street
- **HOULDER Bruce** 6 King's Bench Walk
- **SHAW Antony** 18 Red Lion Court
- **COWARD Stephen** 7 Bedford Row
- **GOLDBERG Jonathan** 3 Temple Gardens
- **LOVELL-PANK Dorian** 6 King's Bench Walk
- **TEMPLE Victor** 6 King's Bench Walk
- **EVANS Anthony** 9-12 Bell Yard
- **GREENBERG Joanna** 3 Temple Gardens
- **MALLALIEU Ann** 6 King's Bench Walk
- **WOLKIND Michael** 2 Bedford Row
- **FEINBERG Peter** 2-4 Tudor Street
- **HILL Michael** 23 Essex Street
- **RAGGATT Timothy** 4 King's Bench Walk

4
- **AUSTIN-SMITH Michael** 23 Essex Street
- **FARRER David** 7 Bedford Row
- **HACKETT Philip** 6 Bedford Row
- **LAWSON Michael** 23 Essex Street
- **BARNES Timothy** 7 Bedford Row
- **FISHER David** 6 King's Bench Walk
- **KAY Steven** 3 Gray's Inn Square
- **LEDERMAN David** 18 Red Lion Court
- **CAPLAN Jonathan** 5 Paper Buildings
- **GRIEVE Michael** Doughty Street Chambers
- **KELSEY-FRY John** Hollis Whiteman Chambers
- **MACDONALD Ian** Two Garden Court
- **DE SILVA Desmond** 2 Paper Buildings
- **GRIFFITHS Courtenay** Two Garden Court
- **KENNEDY Helena** Doughty Street
- **MUNDAY Andrew** 2 Bedford Row

5
- **BATE David** Hollis Whiteman Chambers
- **ETHERINGTON David** 18 Red Lion Court
- **LISSACK Richard** 35 Essex Street
- **RYDER John** 6 King's Bench Walk
- **BURKE Trevor** 2 Bedford Row
- **JENNINGS Anthony** Matrix Chambers
- **LITHMAN Nigel** 2 Bedford Row
- **SOLLEY Stephen** Charter Chambers
- **CASSEL Timothy** 5 Paper Buildings
- **KORNER Joanna** 6 King's Bench Walk
- **PERRY John** 3 Gray's Inn Square
- **SWEENEY Nigel** 6 King's Bench Walk
- **EMMERSON Ben** Matrix Chambers
- **LESLIE Stephen** Furnival Chambers
- **REES Edward** Doughty Street

6
- **BEVAN John** 2 Harcourt Buildings
- **EDWARDS Susan** 23 Essex Street
- **LODDER Peter** 2 Bedford Row
- **OWEN Tim** Matrix Chambers
- **WATERS David** 2 Hare Court
- **BORRELLI Michael** 187 Fleet Street
- **GREY Robin** Hollis Whiteman Chambers
- **LYNCH Patricia** 18 Red Lion Court
- **SAYERS Michael** 2 King's Bench Walk
- **WOOD James** Doughty Street Chambers
- **CARTER Peter** 18 Red Lion Court
- **KRAMER Stephen** 2 Hare Court
- **MITCHELL Andrew** Furnival Chambers
- **SUTTON Richard** 18 Red Lion Court
- **CARTER-STEPHENSON** 3 Gray's Inn Sq
- **LEONARD Anthony** 6 King's Bench Walk
- **MYLNE Nigel** 2 Harcourt Buildings
- **WASS Sasha** 6 King's Bench Walk

NEW SILKS
- **BENSON Jeremy** 2 Hare Court
- **ELLIS Diana** 3 Gray's Inn Square
- **MORRISON Howard** 36 Bedford Row
- **STARMER Keir** Doughty Street Chambers
- **BLAXLAND Henry** Two Garden Court
- **HALL Andrew** Doughty Street Chambers
- **NATHAN David** 10 King's Bench Walk
- **STURMAN Jim** 2 Bedford Row
- **BOYCE William** Hollis Whiteman Chambers
- **JANNER Daniel** 23 Essex Street
- **PEART Icah** Two Garden Court
- **TURNER Michael** Tooks Court Chambers
- **CHAWLA Mukul** 9-12 Bell Yard
- **LEWIS James** 3 Raymond Buildings
- **POWNALL Orlando** 2 Hare Court

For details of these leading barristers see Profiles on page 1353

LEADING JUNIORS • London

★
- **DEIN Jeremy** 3 Gray's Inn Square
- **DENNIS Mark** 6 King's Bench Walk
- **LAIDLAW Jonathan** 2 Hare Court
- **PERRY David** 6 King's Bench Walk

1
- **ALTMAN Brian** 2 Bedford Row
- **MILLIKEN-SMITH Mark** 2 Bedford Row
- **ELLISON Mark** Hollis Whiteman Chambers
- **WHITTAM Richard** Furnival Chambers
- **GIBBS Patrick** 2 Harcourt Buildings
- **HILLIARD Nicholas** 6 King's Bench Walk

2
- **BARRETT Penelope** 3 Gray's Inn Square
- **MARTIN-SPERRY David** Charter Chambers
- **EVANS Jill** Doughty Street Chambers
- **TURNER Jonathan** 6 King's Bench Walk
- **HORWELL Richard** Hollis Whiteman Chambers
- **KHALIL Karim** 1 Paper Buildings

3
- **BANKS Robert** 100E Great Portland Street
- **LUCAS Noel** 187 Fleet Street
- **TAYLOR Martin** 2-4 Tudor Street
- **FEDER Ami** Lamb Building
- **MALCOLM Helen** 3 Raymond Buildings
- **WINBERG Stephen** 2-4 Tudor Street
- **GARDINER Nicholas** 187 Fleet Street
- **PRICE Roderick** Tooks Court Chambers
- **JAFFERJEE Aftab** 2 Harcourt Buildings
- **REES Gareth** Hollis Whiteman

4
- **ABELL Anthony** 2 Bedford Row
- **EISSA Adrian** Two Garden Court
- **MOORE Miranda** 5 Paper Buildings
- **BOURNE Ian** 3 Temple Gardens
- **FORTSON Rudi** 3 Gray's Inn Square
- **OWEN Tudor** 9-12 Bell Yard
- **CAUDLE John** 2 Bedford Row
- **JAFFA Ronald** 3 Gray's Inn Square
- **SAUNDERS Neil** 3 Raymond Buildings
- **CONWAY Charles** 2 Bedford Row
- **MILLETT Kenneth** 2 Hare Court

5
- **ARMSTRONG Dean** 6 King's Bench Walk
- **FARRELL Simon** 3 Raymond Buildings
- **LEVY Michael** 2 Bedford Row
- **REILLY John** Tooks Court Chambers
- **BECK James** 2-4 Tudor Street
- **JOYCE Michael** 9 Gough Square
- **LLOYD-ELEY Andrew** 2 Hare Court
- **ROWLANDS Peter** 18 Red Lion Court
- **BENNETT-JENKINS Sallie** 2 Hare Court
- **KAMLISH Stephen** Tooks Court Chambers
- **MAIDMENT Kieran** Doughty Street Chambers
- **BOGAN Paul** Doughty Street
- **LEIST Ian** 2 Hare Court
- **MATTHEWS Richard** 2 Bedford Row

6
- **BRISCOE Constance** 9-12 Bell Yard
- **COOPER John** 3 Gray's Inn Square
- **ENGLAND William** 2-4 Tudor Street
- **OWEN-JONES David** 3 Temple Gardens
- **SCOBIE James** Two Garden Court
- **VINE James** Hardwicke Building
- **BRYANT-HERON Mark** 9-12 Bell Yard
- **CORRIGAN Peter** 2-4 Tudor Street
- **GOWER Peter** 6 Pump Court
- **PEARCE Ivan** Furnival Chambers
- **SHEPHERD Nigel** 2 Paper Buildings
- **CAUSER John** 23 Essex Street
- **DUNN-SHAW Jason** 6 King's Bench Walk
- **HENRY Annette** 10 King's Bench Walk
- **REED Piers** 3 Temple Gardens
- **STRUDWICK Linda** Hollis Whiteman Chambers
- **CHRISTIE Richard** 2 Pump Court
- **EDIE Alastair** Two Garden Court
- **LANDSBURY Alan** 6 Gray's Inn Sq
- **RYDER Matthew** Matrix Chambers
- **SWAIN Jon** Furnival Chambers

For details of these leading barristers see Profiles on page 1353

---

2 HARE COURT (see full details p.1557) This generalist crime set is bolstered by the presence of a number of esteemed practitioners. **Martin Heslop QC** (see p.1415) acted as prosecution counsel on the Dome jewellery heist case, while "exceptionally gifted" new silk **Orlando Pownall QC** also received numerous market plaudits. He acted as prosecution counsel on the Jill Dando murder case. Completing a triumvirate of top-quality silks, **David Waters QC** (see p.1498) was described by solicitors as "a self-effacing advocate with an eye for detail." **Jonathan Laidlaw** (see p.1431) has been busy on a number of high-profile cases and also acted for the prosecution in the Jill Dando murder trial.

CRIME

Research The rankings are based on in-depth interviews with 6,582 solicitors, barristers and clients in the UK. **Chambers'** research is audited by the British Market Research Bureau (see page 7)

BARRISTERS' PROFILES ▶ See pages 1353-1504

18 RED LION COURT (see full details p.1598) Head of chambers **Anthony Arlidge QC** (see p.1358) remains highly esteemed by peers for his intelligence and abilities as a cross-examiner. Also "tremendous at cross-examination," fellow silk **David Lederman QC** (see p.1433) is "hugely attentive to the client and the job." "Advocate's advocate" **David Etherington QC** (see p.1395) won praise from peers for his "lovely manner with the court."

7 BEDFORD ROW (see full details p.1510) This set boasts an impressive team of criminal specialists, which includes **Nigel Rumfitt QC** (see p.1472). Active in prosecution and defence, he retains the admiration of peers. Instructed by a number of prosecution agencies, **Stephen Coward QC** (see p.1385) is active on the Midlands and Oxford circuits as well as in London, while **Timothy Barnes QC** (see p.1362) also prosecutes and defends in the criminal and fraud arenas.

9-12 BELL YARD (see full details p.1514) This leading criminal set boasts the presence of several high-profile barristers. "Polished all-rounder" **Ed Lawson QC** was praised by lawyers and peers for his commitment and approachability. Although well known in the fraud arena, he also "deserves top billing for his general criminal practice," according to peers. He has been instructed by the Treasury Solicitors on behalf of a number of soldiers in the Bloody Sunday Inquiry. **Mukul Chawla QC** (see p.1379) is said to be "an attractive advocate" with "a commanding presence in court."

FURNIVAL CHAMBERS (see full details p.1542) **Oliver Blunt QC** (see p.1367) retains his reputation for assured advocacy on heavyweight criminal matters. Lawyers applauded **Stephen Leslie QC** (see p.1434) "for working like a Trojan, but still being great fun." Among the set's juniors, **Richard Whittam** (see p.1499) is praised for his "attention to detail."

2 HARCOURT BUILDINGS, ATKINSON BEVAN CHAMBERS (see full details p.1553) A set boasting a number of well-known individuals, it includes "popular and well-liked" **Nicholas Atkinson QC** (see p.1359), who possesses "a wonderful way with clients and judges alike." **Patrick Gibbs** (see p.1403) was applauded as "an excellent advocate" and in the words of one silk "the most thorough junior I have ever met."

MATRIX CHAMBERS (see full details p.1573) This astonishingly accomplished public law and human rights set is also acclaimed for its stable of "good, young criminal silks." In particular it boasts the presence of "top bracket" **Clare Montgomery QC**. She "slaughters everyone by a long shot," according to more than one source, and is widely considered "the brightest of the bright but not full of her own self-regard." Fellow silk **Ken Macdonald QC** (see p.1439) is said to be "a force to be reckoned with" and adept at wielding the "iron fist in the velvet glove."

TOOKS COURT CHAMBERS Adrian Fulford QC is "a brilliant advocate who gives the jury everything it needs in a clear, concise way." "Media savvy" **Michael Mansfield QC** (see p.1441) was praised highly by solicitors, who agreed that "he listens carefully and talks to you rather than at you." So popular is he, however, that several interviewees claimed "he could take on too much."

2-4 TUDOR STREET This specialist criminal defence set is headed by **Richard Ferguson QC** (see p.1397), who won wide acclaim for his "immense experience," while fellow silk **Peter Feinberg QC** (see p.1397) also retains a strong market presence.

OTHER NOTABLE PRACTITIONERS According to one interviewee, **Andrew Trollope QC** (see p.1493) of 187 Fleet Street, "is astounding; he seems to control a case." He also "has guts and is very thorough." **Brian Escott-Cox QC** of 36 Bedford Row continues to act on heavyweight crime matters as part of his extensive practice, while "attractive and distinguished advocate" **Anthony Scrivener QC** (see p.1475) of 2-3 Gray's Inn Square continues to include crime as part of his wide common law practice. Head of chambers at 1 Crown Office Row, **Robert Seabrook QC** (see p.1475) retains a strong position in the marketplace. "Smooth, debonair and a supreme lawyer," **Karim Khalil QC** (see p.1429) is at 1 Paper Buildings. **David Martin-Sperry** of Charter Chambers also received warm recommendations from solicitors.

SOUTH EASTERN & EAST ANGLIAN CIRCUITS

LEADING JUNIORS • South Eastern & East Anglian	
1 AYERS Guy	Octagon House Chambers
CLARE Michael	Octagon House Chambers
MOORE Katherine	Octagon House Chambers
2 JAMES Ian	Octagon House Chambers
MORGANS John	Octagon House Chambers
OLIVER Andrew	Octagon House Chambers
POTTS Richard	Octagon House Chambers

For details of these leading barristers see Profiles on page 1353

Octagon House Chambers retains its monopoly in the region. **Guy Ayers QC** brings a "technical ability and an enthusiasm to the cause," making him the first port of call for many. **Michael Clare QC** possesses a "geniality and practicality," making him a popular choice with clients and lawyers alike, while **Katherine Moore QC** boasts "a commitment to the cause that knows no bounds." **Ian James** impressed with his work on the Tony Martin case, while **Richard Potts** enters the tables this year. An ex-solicitor, market sources claim "he is good on appeals and magistrates work."

WESTERN CIRCUIT

LEADING SILKS • Western	
1 ROYCE John	Guildhall Chambers
2 DUNKELS Paul	Walnut House
PASCOE Nigel	Pump Court Chambers
TABOR James	Albion Chambers
3 FORD Neil	Albion Chambers
GLEN Ian	Guildhall Chambers
JENKINS Alun	Queen Square Chambers
MEEKE Martin	Colleton Chambers
NEW SILKS	
MERCER Geoffrey	Walnut House
MUNRO Sarah	Walnut House
SMITH Richard	Guildhall Chambers

For details of these leading barristers see Profiles on page 1353

John Royce QC (see p.1471) of Guildhall Chambers possesses "a huge presence and wealth of knowledge; he can turn his hand to anything." At Albion Chambers, **Neil Ford QC** enjoys a sound profile; "the finished product is very polished" said peers. **Julian Lambert** (see p.1431) has an "excellent" reputation, while "solid generalist" **Stephen Mooney** is "good at communicating with clients, clear in his explanations, and will also give you a fight." **Martin Picton** (see p.1460) continues to enjoy the wholehearted backing of his contemporaries. **Mike Fitton** (see p.1398) was described by one source as "highly impressive with clients and the judge." St John's Chambers is bolstered by the presence of "first-rate" **Simon**

CRIME

> **Research** The rankings are based on in-depth interviews with 6,582 solicitors, barristers and clients in the UK. **Chambers'** research is audited by the British Market Research Bureau (see page 7)
>
> **BARRISTERS' PROFILES ▶** See pages 1353-1504

LEADING JUNIORS • Western

1	LAMBERT Julian	Albion Chambers
	MOONEY Stephen	Albion Chambers
	MORGAN Simon	St John's Chambers
	PICTON Martin	Albion Chambers
2	DIXEY Ian	St John's Chambers
	FITTON Michael	Albion Chambers
	HORTON Mark	**St John's Chambers**
3	CULLUM Michael	Albion Chambers
	DUVAL Robert	St John's Chambers
	EVANS Susan	Pump Court Chambers
	HART William	Albion Chambers
	LANGDON Andrew	Guildhall Chambers
	LETT Brian	South Western Chambers
	LONGMAN Michael	St John's Chambers
	WHITEHALL Mark	Colleton Chambers

For details of these leading barristers see Profiles on page 1353

Morgan, while **Ian Dixey** and **Mark Horton** won plaudits from local solicitors as "good trial lawyers." **Robert Duval** is "very bright and conscientious." **Susan Evans** of Pump Court Chambers was praised for being "highly organised, great fun and able to achieve great results." Over at Colleton Chambers **Martin Meeke QC** (see p.1446) remains a favourite with solicitors, while **Mark Whitehall** enjoys a reputation for "rarely losing."

WALES & CHESTER CIRCUIT

LEADING SILKS • Wales & Chester

1	REES John Charles	33 Park Place
2	AUBREY David	Temple Chambers
	ELIAS Gerard	Farrar's Building
	MURPHY Ian	9 Park Place
	THOMAS Roger	9 Park Place
	NEW SILKS	
	DAVIES Huw	30 Park Place
	EVANS Elwen Mair	Iscoed Chambers
	LEWIS Paul	30 Park Place
	MURPHY Peter	30 Park Place
	TAYLOR Gregg	9 Park Place

For details of these leading barristers see Profiles on page 1353

LEADING JUNIORS • Wales & Chester

1	DAVIES Trefor	Iscoed Chambers
	FERRIER Susan	9 Park Place
	THOMAS Keith	9 Park Place
	TWOMLOW Richard	9 Park Place
2	BULL Gregory	30 Park Place
	JEARY Stephen	Temple Chambers
	LEWIS Marian	30 Park Place
	RIORDAN Kevin	Iscoed Chambers
	THOMAS Paul	Iscoed Chambers
3	TREHARNE Jennet	33 Park Place

For details of these leading barristers see Profiles on page 1353

John Charles Rees QC (see p.1467) of 33 Park Place retains his reputation as the best in Wales: "if you haven't called him for a case by 9.30 on Monday morning, the other side will have him already," said one solicitor. At 9 Park Place, **Roger Thomas QC** (see p.1490) remains a favourite, and is said to be "laid-back and a pleasure to deal with." **Susan Ferrier** also received commendation from solicitors as "extremely capable and good on her feet." **Gerard Elias QC** (see p. 1349) of Farrar's Building is "quiet, well respected and an excellent advocate."

MIDLANDS CIRCUIT

LEADING SILKS • Midlands

1	BARKER Anthony	No 5 Chambers
	CRIGMAN David	1 Fountain Court
	JOYCE Peter	No.1 High Pavement
	SAUNDERS John	4 Fountain Court
	TREACY Colman	3 Fountain Court
	WAKERLEY Richard	4 Fountain Court
2	INMAN Melbourne	1 Fountain Court
	SMITH Roger	No.6 Fountain Court
	TEDD Rex	St Philips Chambers
	NEW SILKS	
	MANN Paul	No.1 High Pavement

For details of these leading barristers see Profiles on page 1353

LEADING JUNIORS • Midlands

1	DUCK Michael	3 Fountain Court
	EVERARD William	King Charles House Chambers
	JACKSON Andrew	3 Fountain Court
	STOBART John	King Charles House Chambers
	THOMAS Sybil	3 Fountain Court
2	BRAND Simon	Coleridge Chambers
	BURBIDGE James	St Philips Chambers
	CARR Peter	St Ive's Chambers
	ELWICK Martin	No.1 High Pavement
	EVANS John	1 Fountain Court
	EVANS Michael	No.1 High Pavement
	FARRER Paul	1 Fountain Court
	NAWAZ Amjad	Coleridge Chambers
	REYNOLDS Adrian	No.1 High Pavement
	SMITH Shaun	No.1 High Pavement
	THOROGOOD Bernard	No 5 Chambers
3	BARTON Roger	No.1 High Pavement
	EASTEAL Andrew	No.1 High Pavement
	HEGARTY Kevin	St Philips Chambers
	LOCKHART Andrew	St Philips Chambers
	NICHOLLS Benjamin	1 Fountain Court
	SHANT Nirmal	No.1 High Pavement
	WALL Mark	4 Fountain Court

For details of these leading barristers see Profiles on page 1353

Anthony Barker QC (see p.1361) of No5 Chambers and **David Crigman QC** of 1 Fountain Court retain strong market profiles. No.1 High Pavement boasts a number of highly regarded individuals. **Peter Joyce QC** (see p.1426) is a "prominent figure in the region." **Paul Mann QC** (see p.1441) is a new silk who is expected to do well. **Michael Evans** (see p.1396) is applauded as "a strong multi-litigator and trial lawyer," while stablemate **Adrian Reynolds** (see p.1468) is "top notch." One local solicitor described **Shaun Smith** (see p.1480) as "the one I would call if in trouble." 4 Fountain Court boasts the presence of **John Saunders QC**, who acted on the Court of Appeal case of R v Cotter and others, as well as **Richard Wakerley QC**, who retains his position in the marketplace. **Colman Treacy QC** (see p.1493) of 3 Fountain Court was lauded for his "safe pair of hands." King Charles House Chambers is a set deemed to be "growing in stature for its crime representation." **William Everard** has a good name there.

CRIME

Research The rankings are based on in-depth interviews with 6,582 solicitors, barristers and clients in the UK. **Chambers'** research is audited by the British Market Research Bureau (see page 7)

BARRISTERS' PROFILES ▶ See pages 1353-1504

NORTH EASTERN CIRCUIT

LEADING SILKS • North Eastern

1
BOURNE-ARTON Simon	Park Court Chambers
SMITH Robert	Park Court Chambers

2
COSGROVE Patrick	Broad Chare Chambers
HARRISON Michael	Park Court Chambers
MARSON Geoffrey	Sovereign Chambers
SWIFT Malcolm	Park Court Chambers

3
HEDWORTH Toby	Trinity Chambers
HYLAND Graham	Broadway House
KERSHAW Jennifer	No.6 Barristers Chambers

For details of these leading barristers see Profiles on page 1353

LEADING JUNIORS • North Eastern

1
BARNETT Jeremy	St. Paul's Chambers
HARVEY Colin	St. Paul's Chambers
PALMER Patrick	Sovereign Chambers

2
BATTY Christopher	St. Paul's Chambers
BUBB Tim	39 Park Square
JAMESON Rodney	No.6 Barristers Chambers
LEES Andrew	St. Paul's Chambers
MYERSON Simon	Park Court Chambers
PRINCE Christopher	New Court Chambers
ROSE Jonathan	St. Paul's Chambers
STUBBS Andrew	St. Paul's Chambers

3
STANISTREET Penelope	Paradise Chambers

For details of these leading barristers see Profiles on page 1353

Simon Bourne-Arton QC (see p.1369) of Park Court Chambers retains the commendation of the marketplace for his "hard-working, thorough and committed approach to cases." Fellow silk **Robert Smith QC** (see p.1480), at the same set, was applauded as "fantastic" by solicitors who instruct him on heavyweight crime. Silk **Patrick Cosgrove QC** of Broad Chare Chambers is "human, hard-working and excellent both in court and in conference with often difficult clients." St Paul's Chambers has a fine roster of heavyweight juniors which includes **Jeremy Barnett** (see p.1362). He has "a huge wealth of experience," while colleague **Colin Harvey** (see p.1413) offers an expertise in handling criminal cases as part of a wider repertoire that extends to complex frauds.

NORTHERN CIRCUIT

Henry Globe QC of Exchange Chambers retains his heavyweight reputation in the arena, while **Tim Holroyde QC** (see p.1418) of the same chambers is "gimlet-eyed in determining the kernel of a case." **Stephen Riordan QC** of 25-27 Castle Street is seen by some as "the best QC in the North." Fellow silk **Michael Shorrock QC** (see p.1478) of Peel Court Chambers is another popular choice for instructions, while **David Turner QC** (see p.1494) of Exchange Chambers is lauded as "popular, down-to-earth and bright." **Peter Wright QC** of Lincoln House Chambers has a "tenacious, no-nonsense manner." Interviewees praised him for building "an excellent rapport with clients and commanding a huge

LEADING SILKS • Northern

1
GLOBE Henry	Exchange Chambers
HOLROYDE Tim	Exchange Chambers
RIORDAN Stephen	25-27 Castle Street
SHORROCK Michael	Peel Court Chambers
STEER David	7 Harrington Street Chambers
TURNER David	Exchange Chambers
WRIGHT Peter	Lincoln House Chambers

2
BIRKETT Peter	18 St John Street
CARUS Roderick	9 St John Street
GEE Anthony	28 St John St
GOLDSTONE Clement	28 St John St
MARKS Richard	Peel Court Chambers

3
BENTHAM Howard	Peel Court Chambers
CHRUSZCZ Charles	Exchange Chambers
EDIS Andrew	14 Castle Street
FISH David	Deans Court Chambers
GARSIDE Charles	9 St John Street
MORRIS Anthony	Peel Court Chambers
PICKUP James	Lincoln House Chambers

NEW SILKS
REID Paul	Lincoln House Chambers

For details of these leading barristers see Profiles on page 1353

LEADING JUNIORS • Northern

1
ANDREWS Philip	Young Street Chambers
DENNEY Stuart	Deans Court Chambers
GREGORY James	Lincoln House Chambers
HERMAN Ray	India Buildings Chambers
LLOYD Heather	Chavasse Court Chambers
MCDERMOTT John	Chavasse Court Chambers
MCMEEKIN Ian	Kingsgate Chambers
MEADOWCROFT Stephen	Peel Court Chambers
STOUT Roger	18 St John Street
WILLIAMS David	Chavasse Court Chambers

2
BERKSON Simon	Exchange Chambers
CATTAN Philip	28 St John St
CLARKE Nicholas	9 St John Street
FORSYTH Julie	Chavasse Court Chambers
HARRISON Keith	24A St John Street
O'BYRNE Andrew	Peel Court Chambers

3
BLACKWELL Kate	Lincoln House Chambers
BRENNAND Timothy	Manchester House Chambers
GOODE Rowena	28 St John St
LONG Andrew	Peel Court Chambers
MYERS Benjamin	Young Street Chambers
ROBERTS Lisa	Lincoln House Chambers
SAVILL Mark	Deans Court Chambers
WATSON David	14 Castle Street

For details of these leading barristers see Profiles on page 1353

presence in court" while 7 Harrington Street Chambers sees **David Steer QC** continuing to command the respcet of his peers. **Ian McMeekin** of Kingsgate Chambers is commended for being "incredibly hard-working and well informed."

DEFAMATION

Research The rankings are based on in-depth interviews with 6,582 solicitors, barristers and clients in the UK. **Chambers'** research is audited by the British Market Research Bureau (see page 7)

BARRISTERS' PROFILES ▶ See pages 1353-1504

OVERVIEW: Although other chambers house star individuals, none can claim the critical mass of expertise assembled in 1 Brick Court and 5 Raymond Buildings. With "commercial acumen and the skills to charm juries," these sets continue to dominate the defamation Bar. This year libel actions, although they have dwindled in number, have became lengthier and more complex. Another trend was the increasing amount of work produced by the budding field of privacy and data protection law with several of the barristers in our table leading the charge in this niche

LONDON

1 BRICK COURT (see full details p.1518) "Calm, lateral thinker" **Andrew Caldecott QC** (see p.1375) was held up by interviewees as proof that brains and diligence can coexist with courtroom flair and jury skills. Head of chambers **Richard Rampton QC** (see p.1466), a "superb cross-examiner and master strategist" has returned from his sabbatical, lecturing on Irving v Penguin Books. Boasting a "fabulous subtle touch with a jury," **Thomas Shields QC** (see p.1478) can "outmanoeuvre anyone." Similarly dynamic is **Patrick Moloney QC** (see p.1448), who boasts a broad practice and a "capacity to fashion unexpected solutions to seemingly intractable problems." **Victoria Sharp QC** (see p.1476), who took silk last year, moves up our rankings thanks to praise that portrayed her as a "charming, persuasive, and clear-headed" operator. **Geoffrey Shaw QC** (see p.1476) won praise for his "behind the scenes ingenuity." Among the juniors, the "smart, smooth" **Manuel Barca** (see p.1361) was said to "relish the cut and thrust, while one peer said **Rupert Elliot** (see p.1394) was the "paragon of lawyerly virtue – honest, precise and economical with his words." **Benjamin Hinchliff**, "busy and affable", also continues to command respect among his peers, while "academic and realistic" **Stephen Suttle** (see p.1486) is well known for his expertise at complex defamation work on a large canvas; for instance, pharmaceutical trade libel. Of **Caroline Addy** (see p.1355) one interviewee's comment was typical of many: "when she's up against a tough opponent, she's a superstar." "Cool customer" **Catrin Evans** (see p.1395) was in great demand thanks to an "unflappable intellect," while the "tireless" **Jane Phillips** (see p.1460) won acclaim for the thoroughness of her preparation. The name of "hard-headed and practical" **Harvey Starte** also emerged during the research interviews.

5 RAYMOND BUILDINGS (see full details p.1597) "Phenomenal advocate" **Desmond Browne QC** (see p.1373) is a "quick thinker and a bruiser." "If he's on your side, you can relax," claimed one solicitor. Accorded the same respect is "jury charmer" **James Price QC** (see p.1463), who cross-examines with "panache and focused intensity." **Adrienne Page QC** (see p.1457) puts in a "frankly stupendous effort" according to rivals; she "rolls her sleeves up and is a pleasure to work with." The head of chambers is "veteran" **Patrick Milmo QC** (see p.1448) who other barristers said provides a "sterling example" to those under him. **Michael Tugendhat QC** (see p.1494), "possibly a genius," has had a "spectacular" year carving out a niche for himself in the nascent field of privacy law. **Mark Warby QC** (see p.1497) takes his "very much deserved" silk this year. If our interviewees are right he will "make a significant mark." Amid a fine raft of juniors, **Justin Rushbrooke** (see p.1472) is "really going places," with a special aptitude for online defamation, while **David Sherborne** was described by one solicitor as "quick, personable, thoughtful and open-minded." **Alexandra Marzec** has "determination" and "some well-won skirmishes under her belt," while the "industrious" **Godwin Busuttil** (see p.1375) makes an entrance in our rankings for the first time this year. **Matthew Nicklin** (see p.1454) was acclaimed as a "pragmatic and committed team player," and solicitors continue to endorse the "approachable" **Adam Wolanski** (see p.1501). This year, the "prodigious" **Sara Mansoori** (see p.1441) joins the ranks as an up-and-comer; she is "keen and diligent" in her approach to cases.

OTHER NOTABLE PRACTITIONERS Ronald Thwaites QC (see p.1491) of Ely Place Chambers has firmly established his reputation in the libel field. An outstanding "bruising advocate," he is a "real contender" and a favourite of certain newspaper clients. At Doughty Street Chambers, polymath **Geoffrey Robertson QC** (see p.1469) is said to have "the US market sewn up." This set also fields a "fine academic" in the shape of **Andrew Nicol QC** (see p.1455). **Richard Spearman QC** (see p.1481) of 4-5 Gray's Inn Square joins our defamation rankings this year. Exercising "the soundest judgement," he is "pre-eminent" in the field of confidence and privacy. **Hugh Tomlinson QC** (see p.1492) of Matrix Chambers took his silk this year, while stablemate **Heather Rogers** retains star status among the juniors. "No one can touch her," said a peer, while a client proclaimed, "she gets her teeth into things and goes the extra mile."

DEFAMATION • London

	QCs	Jnrs
1 Brick Court (Richard Rampton QC)	6	8
5 Raymond Buildings (Patrick Milmo QC)	6	7

Numbers show recommended barristers in this practice area

LEADING SILKS • London

1 BROWNE Desmond	5 Raymond Buildings
CALDECOTT Andrew	1 Brick Court
PRICE James	5 Raymond Buildings
2 PAGE Adrienne	5 Raymond Buildings
RAMPTON Richard	1 Brick Court
3 MILMO Patrick	5 Raymond Buildings
SHIELDS Thomas	1 Brick Court
TUGENDHAT Michael	5 Raymond Buildings
4 MOLONEY Patrick	1 Brick Court
SHARP Victoria	1 Brick Court
THWAITES Ronald	Ely Place Chambers
5 NICOL Andrew	Doughty Street Chambers
ROBERTSON Geoffrey	Doughty Street Chambers
SHAW Geoffrey	1 Brick Court
SPEARMAN Richard	4-5 Gray's Inn Square
NEW SILKS	
TOMLINSON Hugh	Matrix Chambers
WARBY Mark	5 Raymond Buildings

For details of these leading barristers see Profiles on page 1353

LEADING JUNIORS • London

★ ROGERS Heather	Matrix Chambers
1 BARCA Manuel	1 Brick Court
2 RUSHBROOKE Justin	5 Raymond Buildings
SHERBORNE David	5 Raymond Buildings
3 ELLIOTT Rupert	1 Brick Court
HINCHLIFF Benjamin	1 Brick Court
MARZEC Alexandra	5 Raymond Buildings
SUTTLE Stephen	1 Brick Court
4 ADDY Caroline	1 Brick Court
BUSUTTIL Godwin	5 Raymond Buildings
EVANS Catrin	1 Brick Court
NICKLIN Matthew	5 Raymond Buildings
PHILLIPS Jane	1 Brick Court
STARTE Harvey	1 Brick Court
WOLANSKI Adam	5 Raymond Buildings
UP AND COMING	
MANSOORI Sara	5 Raymond Buildings

For details of these leading barristers see Profiles on page 1353

EDUCATION

Research The rankings are based on in-depth interviews with 6,582 solicitors, barristers and clients in the UK. **Chambers'** research is audited by the British Market Research Bureau (see page 7)

BARRISTERS' PROFILES ▶ See pages 1353-1504

OVERVIEW: As described in the overview for solicitors, educational negligence litigation is opening up so fast it is almost out of control. Many of the barristers below are famous for having pioneered the educational negligence Bar from the start; others have recognised the field more recently as a salient area of practice.

LONDON

EDUCATION • London

		QCs	Jnrs
1	11 King's Bench Walk Chambers (Tabachnik/Goudie)	3	5
2	Goldsmith Building (Christopher Llewellyn-Jones QC)	-	5
	Matrix Chambers	2	4
3	4-5 Gray's Inn Square (Elizabeth Appleby QC)	1	1

Numbers show recommended barristers in this practice area

LEADING SILKS • London

1	KERR Tim	11 King's Bench Walk Chambers
	MCMANUS Richard	4-5 Gray's Inn Square
2	BOOTH Cherie	Matrix Chambers
3	BEAN David	Matrix Chambers
	CAVANAGH John	11 King's Bench Walk Chambers
	GOUDIE James	11 King's Bench Walk Chambers
	LANG Beverley	Blackstone Chambers

For details of these leading barristers see Profiles on page 1353

LEADING JUNIORS • London

1	FRIEL John	Goldsmith Building
	GIFFIN Nigel	11 King's Bench Walk Chambers
	HAY Deborah	Goldsmith Building
2	CALLMAN Tanya	2 King's Bench Walk
	LEWIS Clive	11 King's Bench Walk Chambers
	MOUNTFIELD Helen	Matrix Chambers
	RAWLINGS Clive	Goldsmith Building
3	HUNT Murray	Matrix Chambers
	HYAMS Oliver	5 Paper Buildings
	OLDHAM Peter	11 King's Bench Walk Chambers
4	BOWEN Nicholas	29 Bedford Row Chambers
	BRADLEY Anthony	Cloisters
	LIEVEN Nathalie	4 Breams Buildings
	SHELDON Clive	11 King's Bench Walk Chambers
	WISE Ian	Doughty Street Chambers
	WOLFE David	Matrix Chambers
	UP AND COMING	
	MCKENDRICK John	Goldsmith Building
	SCOLDING Fiona	Goldsmith Building
	SHARLAND Andrew	4-5 Gray's Inn Square
	SQUIRES Dan	Matrix Chambers
	STEYN Karen	11 King's Bench Walk Chambers

For details of these leading barristers see Profiles on page 1353

11 KING'S BENCH WALK CHAMBERS (see full details p.1566) The set of choice for education work; its skills are considered of the highest quality and it boasts a number of eminent practitioners who are respected "for their sheer intellectual ability and academic excellence." Most renowned on the defendant side, barristers from this set represent local education authorities, central government and HE and FE institutions, as well as doing a large amount of claimant work. The range of specialisms includes exclusions, admissions, employment, school reorganisations and industrial action. At once a "thinker" and a "performer," combining "excellent paperwork and presentation," **Tim Kerr QC** (see p.1428) is "top of our list," according to one solicitor, for his knowledge of the sector and ability to advise on contractual, human rights and special needs issues. He has a particular reputation for educational negligence cases and is described by admirers as "thorough, efficient and conscientious," and "well-liked by the judiciary." **James Goudie QC** (see p.1408) is highly rated by many and combines his top reputation for local government with education expertise, while **John Cavanagh QC** (see p.1378) is considered "fantastic, brilliant and pragmatic." Amongst the juniors, **Nigel Giffin**'s (see p.1404) work has impressed many: "meticulous, with excellent preparation, he'll work like a Trojan on a case." His dealings with local authorities were particularly noted. **Clive Lewis** (see p.1435), admired for his applicant work, is "intelligent, incredibly good with clients and understands education institutions." Also widely respected is **Karen Steyn** (see p.1483), while **Peter Oldham** (see p.1456) was praised by solicitors for his sound advice. According to one, "he has given me opinions I didn't like but had to accept." **Clive Sheldon** (see p.1477) is praised by clients as "effective, productive, concise and clear in his arguments."

GOLDSMITH BUILDING Acting in the main for individual claimants, barristers from this set have been visible on high-profile cases relating to admissions and exclusions, and special educational needs. **Deborah Hay** enjoys a huge following as "one of the leading lights," and is especially noted for her work with parents. Clients find her "effective and approachable." According to one solicitor, "you would be hard pushed to get anyone better" than **John Friel** (see p.1401). "Mr Special Needs," he was described by peers as "an excellent barrister with great integrity." One source considered him "the most knowledgeable senior junior at the education Bar." **Clive Rawlings**, who used to be a teacher, is "personable, able and liked by clients," as well as being "a persuasive advocate with cutting-edge ideas." Amongst younger juniors, "excellent" **Fiona Scolding** is said to be "showing great promise," while, according to one admiring solicitor, **John McKendrick** "has pulled out some phenomenal results in cases where I thought there was no way we would get a result."

MATRIX CHAMBERS (see full details p.1573) The set's high standards were much valued on the claimant side, but it is also active for institutions. Barristers from the set have recently appeared in some of the sector's most high-profile actions, including the Alperton School case concerning exclusions in the light of human rights. "Able and committed" **Cherie Booth QC** (see p.1368) is highly respected, her excellent paperwork meriting special note. **David Bean QC** (see p.1363) is "one of the safest pairs of hands in the business," according to solicitors, as well as being "easy to deal with," while **Helen Mountfield** (see p.1451), who edits the *Education Law Report*, is held in high esteem for her "good mind." **Murray Hunt** (see p.1421) was praised by peers for his academic brilliance and for "thinking ahead of the judges." **David Wolfe** (see p.1501) won wide praise as "an excellent advocate with a good intellect" and plenty of gusto. One to watch is **Dan Squires** (see p.1482), who has a developing reputation.

4-5 GRAY'S INN SQUARE (see full details p.1550) Despite having a lower market profile in recent years, the continued presence of **Richard McManus QC** – "the leading specialist there" – has sustained this set's reputation in education. "A good advocate," he "knows the sector" and is enormously respected. **Andrew Sharland** (see p.1476) also flies high as "bright, hard-working and conscientious."

OTHER NOTABLE PRACTITIONERS At Blackstone Chambers, **Beverley Lang QC** (see p.1431) works on special educational needs negligence claims and advises Oxbridge colleges on individual disputes. At 2 King's Bench Walk, **Tanya Callman** (see p.1375) "has built a very successful

www.ChambersandPartners.com

EDUCATION

Research The rankings are based on in-depth interviews with 6,582 solicitors, barristers and clients in the UK. **Chambers'** research is audited by the British Market Research Bureau (see page 7)

BARRISTERS' PROFILES ▶ See pages 1353-1504

practice." Representing local authorities and parents, she does special educational needs work, and admissions and exclusions. Interviewees say she has "considerable presence" in court, is "super to deal with" and "gets straight to the point." At 5 Paper Buildings is the "thorough, academic and innovative" **Oliver Hyams** (see p.1422). **Nicholas Bowen**, at 29 Bedford Row, is "a very good litigator, very attentive to detail, first class with a great brain," while at Doughty Street Chambers **Ian Wise** (see p.1501) is said to be "immersed in the field and cares about what he's doing."

Anthony Bradley (see p.1370) at Cloisters is "extremely well respected" for his academic grasp of education law, and especially the implications of human rights legislation on it. Peers say that he is a great choice to "untangle a knotty problem." At 4 Breams Buildings, "clear and calm" **Nathalie Lieven** (see p.1436) has earned a reputation for her "steady judgement" in special educational needs cases.

EMPLOYMENT

Research The rankings are based on in-depth interviews with 6,582 solicitors, barristers and clients in the UK. **Chambers'** research is audited by the British Market Research Bureau (see page 7)

BARRISTERS' PROFILES ▶ See pages 1353-1504

LONDON

EMPLOYMENT • London	QCs	Jnrs
1 11 King's Bench Walk Chambers (Tabachnik/Goudie)	8	13
2 Old Square Chambers (John Hendy QC)	4	10
3 Blackstone Chambers (Baxendale/Flint)	4	5
Cloisters (Laura Cox QC)	3	6
Littleton Chambers (Michel Kallipetis QC)	5	4
4 Devereux Chambers (Colin Edelman QC)	2	4
Matrix Chambers	2	2

Numbers show recommended barristers in this practice area

LEADING SILKS • London

★	JEANS Christopher	11 King's Bench Walk Chambers
1	COX Laura	Cloisters
	LANGSTAFF Brian	Cloisters
	PANNICK David	Blackstone Chambers
2	BEAN David	Matrix Chambers
	BOWERS John	Littleton Chambers
	GOULDING Paul	Blackstone Chambers
	HOCHHAUSER Andrew	Essex Court Chambers
	UNDERHILL Nicholas	Fountain Court
3	ALLEN Robin	Cloisters
	BLOCH Selwyn	Littleton Chambers
	CAVANAGH John	11 King's Bench Walk Chambers
	CLARKE Andrew	Littleton Chambers
	MCGREGOR Alistair	11 King's Bench Walk Chambers
	SLADE Elizabeth	11 King's Bench Walk Chambers
4	BELOFF Michael	Blackstone Chambers
	BOOTH Cherie	Matrix Chambers
	GOUDIE James	11 King's Bench Walk Chambers
	GRIFFITH-JONES David	Devereux Chambers
	HAND John	Old Square Chambers
	HENDY John	Old Square Chambers
	LYNCH Adrian	11 King's Bench Walk Chambers
	STAFFORD Andrew	Littleton Chambers
	TABACHNIK Eldred	11 King's Bench Walk Chambers
	NEW SILKS	
	BRENNAN Timothy	Devereux Chambers
	CARSS-FRISK Monica	Blackstone Chambers
	GATT Ian	Littleton Chambers
	HILLIER Andrew	11 King's Bench Walk Chambers
	MCNEILL Jane	Old Square Chambers
	ROSE Paul	Old Square Chambers

For details of these leading barristers see Profiles on page 1353

11 KING'S BENCH WALK CHAMBERS (see full details p.1566) The pre-eminent employment law set, the chambers is reported to be "bursting with talent" and possesses unusual strength at the junior level. Its top ranking QCs command hefty fees, but many solicitors feel their advice is "worth every penny." Barristers were uniformly praised for their "academic" grasp and enjoy the support of a "helpful group of clerks." "Tremendously hard-working," **Christopher Jeans QC** (see p.1424) emerged as the "favourite" among the solicitors for his "overwhelming intellectual capacity" and ability to "communicate well with clients." Particularly recommended for opinion work and tricky multi-applicant cases, he "cuts to the chase" and "finds his way out of difficult legal problems." He has recently appeared in the Julie Bower equal pay tribunal case. An "extremely bright" silk with a "great future ahead of him," **John Cavanagh QC** (see p.1378) is seen to be the chamber's "next big star." Commended for his "feel for strategy," Cavanagh handles a large number of TUPE and discrimination cases, including a recent disability discrimination case concerning imaginary injuries. **Alistair McGregor QC** (see p.1445) is known as a "tough guy advocate" with expertise in whistleblowing and injunction work. Sources describe him as a "fearsome cross examiner" and "someone you want on your side." "Calm and collected" **Elizabeth Slade QC** (see p.1479) was recommended for cases with "real legal complexity." She applies a "cautious" manner to a mix of employment and pensions work. "Tremendously persuasive" **James Goudie QC** (see p.1408) is reported to be "on the judicial wavelength." A "gifted generalist," he maintains a combined public law and employment practice. He heads the chambers with senior silk **Eldred Tabachnik QC** (see p.1487), the "undisputed king of hard work." Although less visible than formerly, Tabachnik is widely esteemed as a "giant." Another standout name is **Adrian Lynch QC** (see p.1439), a "user friendly" practitioner "utterly lacking in pomposity." Solicitors appreciate his attentive service and quick response time. "Versatile" new silk **Andrew Hillier QC** (see p.1416) was mentioned as "good on his feet." **Seán Jones** (see p.1426) attracted a wealth of comment as a "rumbustious personality" with a "good grasp of detail." Highly sought after as a "junior of choice," he has lately been active in a number of whistleblowing cases. Fans praised him as a "sparkling advocate" who impresses both clients and the judiciary. "Extroverted" **Jonathan Swift** (see p.1486) "wins by diplomacy rather than aggression." His "idiosyncratic" approach combines "flamboyant personal flair" with a "can-do attitude." Clients also noted his "willingness to use technology." "Clear thinking" **Paul Nicholls** can "master a brief in seconds." Commentators report that he is "intelligent and persuasive without being bullying." **Timothy Pitt-Payne** (see p.1461) wins praise as a "fluent advocate" who "absorbs material quickly and puts it across well." "Charming, clever and practical," **Dan Stilitz** (see p.1484) is considered a "star in the making." Particularly good on paper, he was singled out for his work on discrimination issues. Highly rated junior, **Charles Béar** (see p.1363) takes an "aggressive" stance in employment litigation. "Outstanding" **Nigel Giffin** (see p.1404) acts in a mix of employment, education and public law work. "Young and bright" **Akhlaq Choudhury** (see p.1379) has solid experience representing NHS trusts, City institutions and local authorities in multiparty employment litigation. "Academic" **Peter Wallington** (see p.1496) elicits praise from clients for his "in-depth consideration of the issues" and expertise in complex cases. **Simon Devonshire** (see p.1390) is "good at spotting the other side's weaknesses." Interviewees report that he "combines a pugnacious advocacy style with extremely thorough preparation." Up-and-coming **Cecilia Ivimy** (see p.1423) rates as a "promising" young practitioner. **Richard Leiper** (see p.1434) has been visible on a number of breach of contract issues and enters the rankings as a popular young barrister. "Charming" **Jane McCafferty** (see p.1443) demonstrates a good knowledge of employment law issues and "provides polished service."

OLD SQUARE CHAMBERS (see full details p.1583) With an annex in Bristol, the set is popular among practitioners in the regions who appreciate its "affordable fees" and "relaxed" atmosphere. Head of chambers **John Hendy QC** (see p.1414) is frequently seen acting for trade union applicants. A "vigorous" advocate, he "really throws himself into cases." He was mentioned to researchers as knowledgeable both on union recognition legislation and international law. "Skillful" **John Hand QC** (see p.1411) handles a mix of employment, personal injury and environmental law. His expertise extends from collective redundancy and transfer of undertakings to strike and picketing action. New silk **Jane McNeill QC** (see p.1445) was recommended for her work on part-time pensions and retirement age regulation. "Down-to-earth" **Paul Rose QC** (see p.1470), another new silk, possesses "across the board" expertise in discrimination, wrongful dismissal and restraint of trade issues. "Trustworthy"

www.ChambersandPartners.com 1293

EMPLOYMENT

Research The rankings are based on in-depth interviews with 6,582 solicitors, barristers and clients in the UK. **Chambers'** research is audited by the British Market Research Bureau (see page 7)

BARRISTERS' PROFILES ▶ See pages 1353-1504

LEADING JUNIORS • London

★	LINDEN Thomas	Matrix Chambers
	ROSE Dinah	Blackstone Chambers
1	CARR Bruce	Devereux Chambers
	EADY Jennifer	Old Square Chambers
	GRIFFITHS Martin	Essex Court Chambers
	JONES Seán	11 King's Bench Walk Chambers
	KIBLING Thomas	Cloisters
	SIMLER Ingrid	Devereux Chambers
	SWIFT Jonathan	11 King's Bench Walk Chambers
2	MOOR Sarah	Old Square Chambers
	NICHOLLS Paul	11 King's Bench Walk Chambers
	PITT-PAYNE Timothy	11 King's Bench Walk Chambers
	RANDALL Nicholas	Devereux Chambers
	STILITZ Daniel	11 King's Bench Walk Chambers
	TETHER Melanie	Old Square Chambers
3	BÉAR Charles	11 King's Bench Walk Chambers
	BOTHROYD Shirley	Littleton Chambers
	CIUMEI Charles	Essex Court Chambers
	CLARKE Gerard	Blackstone Chambers
	CROXFORD Thomas	Blackstone Chambers
	GIFFIN Nigel	11 King's Bench Walk Chambers
	GILL Tess	Old Square Chambers
	NAPIER Brian	Fountain Court
	ROMNEY Daphne	Cloisters
	SENDALL Antony	Littleton Chambers
	TAYLER James	Devereux Chambers
4	BROWN Damian	Old Square Chambers
	CHOUDHURY Akhlaq	11 King's Bench Walk Chambers
	CHUDLEIGH Louise	Old Square Chambers
	DUGGAN Michael	Littleton Chambers
	KORN Anthony	199 Strand
	MOUNTFIELD Helen	Matrix Chambers
	OMAMBALA Ijeoma	Old Square Chambers
	WALLINGTON Peter	11 King's Bench Walk Chambers
5	DEVONSHIRE Simon	11 King's Bench Walk Chambers
	EPSTEIN Paul	Cloisters
	GALBRAITH-MARTEN Jason	Cloisters
	GALLAFENT Kate	Blackstone Chambers
	NEAMAN Sam	Littleton Chambers
	O'DEMPSEY Declan	Cloisters
	SCOTT Ian	Old Square Chambers
	SEGAL Oliver	Old Square Chambers
UP AND COMING		
	CRASNOW Rachel	Cloisters
	IVIMY Cecilia	11 King's Bench Walk Chambers
	LEIPER Richard	11 King's Bench Walk Chambers
	MCCAFFERTY Jane	11 King's Bench Walk Chambers
	MULCAHY Jane	Blackstone Chambers
	SMITH Emma	Old Square Chambers

For details of these leading barristers see Profiles on page 1353

Jennifer Eady (see p.1392) "maintains good relations with the opposition." As a member of the treasury panel, she undertakes a lot of government equal pay cases. Clients appreciate her "conscientious" attitude and "clear communication." She has recently been acting in the European Court of Human Rights on a trade union case regarding the fundamental right of freedom of association. "Feisty" Sarah Moor (see p.1449) "walks the line between assertiveness and aggressiveness well." "Quietly assured" Melanie Tether (see p.1489) has a "great rapport with solicitors" who warmly recommend her for TUPE matters. A former solicitor, she takes a "progressive, stage by stage approach" to advocacy and "always gets results." Trade union advocate, Tess Gill (see p.1404) "hits all the right buttons." She recently acted in the House of Lords on a sex discrimination and maternity case, IGE Medical Systems Ltd v Halfpenny. Louise Chudleigh (see p.1380) has significant experience in discrimination and equal pay claims. Damian Brown (see p.1373) takes a "comforting approach with clients" but "doesn't lose his commercial edge." A "real star" Ijeoma Omambala (see p.1456) brings a "relaxed" and "friendly" manner to race and sex discrimination cases. Ian Scott (see p.1474) rates highly for his experience in collective employment matters. He is able to draw upon knowledge of industrial diseases in advising on stress at work claims and trade union disputes. Oliver Segal (see p.1475) has wide experience of most aspects of employment law, including negligent reference claims and restrictive covenant litigation. "Sensible" Emma Smith (see p.1479) handles a mix of employment and personal injury/clinical negligence work.

BLACKSTONE CHAMBERS (see full details p.1515) This distinguished public law set is noted for high standards and consistent quality. It is said to contain a high number of "intimidatingly bright people" and is considered particularly strong at the junior level. "Phenomenal" David Pannick QC (see p.1458) is a "glamorous all-rounder." "Everyone's first choice on public law cases," he draws upon comprehensive knowledge of human rights issues in advising on complicated employment cases. His popularity makes him a rare commodity, but interviewees agree he's "great if you can get him." In the past year he successfully represented a group of workers against Wolverhampton Healthcare in a House of Lords sex discrimination case involving pension benefits for female workers. A "class act," Paul Goulding QC (see p.1408) can "master a large volume of material" and provide "incisive commentary" on difficult problems. Said to possess a "great range of technical skills," he was recommended for his excellent written advice and friendly manner. A "superb" advocate, Michael Beloff QC (see p.1364) is considered equally adept at many areas. Although also occupied with his position as president of Trinity College, Oxford, he draws widespread commendation as a "lion of the Bar." New silk Monica Carss-Frisk QC (see p.1377) is "always impressive" both in court and on written advice. "Feisty" junior Dinah Rose (see p.1470) "shines" on discrimination cases. "Punchy and straightforward" she has established a leading reputation for important race and sex discrimination matters. She represented Kamlesh Bahl in an EAT sex discrimination and victimisation case against the Law Society. "Approachable" Gerard Clarke (see p.1380) is strong on restrictive covenant matters and has recently been acting on behalf of AMCO in a case dealing with the EC Directive and Transfer of Undertakings. "Well-prepared" Thomas Croxford (see p.1386) is "exactly what you want in a barrister." Solicitors particularly recommend him for "messy cases" because he "doesn't blink if you have a bad case on paper – he looks tactically at how to win it." Up-and-coming junior Kate Gallafent (see p.1402) is a popular choice for tribunal cases while "user friendly" Jane Mulcahy (see p.1452) is able to "explain difficult messages to clients."

CLOISTERS (see full details p.1521) Chambers head Laura Cox QC (see p.1385) is a preferred choice for discrimination cases. A "top-drawer" advocate, she is currently acting in the ECJ on a challenge to the Working Time Regulations. Brian Langstaff QC (see p.1432) "gets along with everyone" and has experience ranging from rule books to TUPE cases. He frequently acts for applicants and, say competitors, has the ability to "make even unattractive submissions sound perfectly attractive and logical." "Effective" Robin Allen QC (see p.1356) brings a "thorough understanding of European and human rights law" to applicant representation. He has recently been acting in the House of Lords on claims of aiding discrimination. Thomas Kibling (see p.1429) is "always prepared to the nth degree." Noted for his "good bedside manner," he "sways clients

EMPLOYMENT

Research The rankings are based on in-depth interviews with 6,582 solicitors, barristers and clients in the UK. *Chambers*' research is audited by the British Market Research Bureau (see page 7)

BARRISTERS' PROFILES ▶ See pages 1353-1504

with an intelligent charm and sense of fun." He is currently acting in the House of Lords on a post-termination discrimination case brought under the Disability Discrimination Act. **Daphne Romney** (see p.1470) has recently joined the chambers. Interviewees describe her as a "fearsome cross examiner" able to "mince the opposition." A new addition to the tables, **Paul Epstein** has experience in whistleblowing and unfair dismissal cases. "Extremely responsive" **Jason Galbraith-Marten** (see p.1402) has recently been involved in Henry v London General Transport Services regarding the incorporation of collective agreements into individual contracts. Junior **Rachel Crasnow** (see p.1386) is an employment and discrimination law specialist with "all-round" experience. **Declan O'Dempsey** (see p.1456) has moved to Cloisters and retains a good reputation in the field.

LITTLETON CHAMBERS (see full details p.1570) Appearing frequently on high-profile cases, the set is reported to offer "good value for money" and a "willingness to accommodate" solicitors' needs. "Heavyweight" silk **John Bowers QC** (see p.1369) is recommended for restrictive covenants and tricky TUPE matters, and it said by peers to possess an "exceptional legal knowledge." Clients appreciate his "personable" manner and quick turnaround of documents. **Selwyn Bloch QC** (see p.1367) is a "guru on restrictive covenants and injunction cases." His "sharp mind" and "eye for detail" make him particularly suited to complex cases. **Andrew Clarke QC** (see p.1380) has the "weight of experience behind him." Although "cerebral" in style, he "doesn't intimidate the clients" and "fits in well as part of a team." He handles a mix of company and employment law. "Mild mannered" **Andrew Stafford QC** (see p.1482) "speaks the client's language." Particularly noted for cases involving pensions issues in connection with employment, Stafford takes a "modern" approach to cases and is "capable of giving a fresh insight or angle." "Terribly debonair and charming," **Ian Gatt QC** (see p.1403) combines knowledge of professional negligence and employment law. Interviewees describe him as an "old-style" barrister who "reads every document at length." A "skilled mediator," he employs an "arm around the shoulder approach" to dealing with clients. "Forthright" **Shirley Bothroyd** (see p.1368) applies "tremendous energy" to cases and rates highly for her expertise in injunctions. Experienced advocate **Antony Sendall** (see p.1475) is "good on his feet." Solicitors report that he "asks the right questions in cross-examination." According to one source **Michael Duggan** (see p.1391) "looks innocuous" but "turns into a Rottweiler" in court. He is well known for his writing on unfair dismissal issues. A "safe pair of hands," **Sam Neaman** (see p.1453) received warm praise from solicitors, one of whom attested that "he worked hard and turned a case around when we thought we'd be mauled."

DEVEREUX CHAMBERS (see full details p.1525) **David Griffith-Jones QC** (see p.1410) is described by peers as an "impressive opponent," who is "absolutely committed to his client's cause." His practice is a mix of employment, pensions and sports law. Highly rated **Timothy Brennan QC** (see p.1371) maintains a similarly mixed practice, focusing on the overlap between tax and employment law. At the junior level, **Bruce Carr** (see p.1377) was recommended for his "ability to summarise issues quickly." With a "brain the size of a planet," solicitors report that "even difficult clients respect him." His recent work includes a case dealing with bias in employment tribunals and another concerning the taxation of termination payments. "Everyone speaks highly of" **Ingrid Simler** (see p.1478), a "tenacious advocate" who "gets to grips with the papers quickly and easily." She has been involved in a race discrimination claim for a senior bank employee against a Japanese bank and is well known for her representation of the Law Society in the Kamlesh Bahl case. "Industrious" **Nicholas Randall** (see p.1466) has a "deceptively easy-going manner" in tribunal. "Always on top of his stuff," he rates highly with both solicitors and clients. "Thoughtful" **James Tayler** (see p.1488) is "not afraid to venture forth into difficult areas."

MATRIX CHAMBERS (see full details p.1573) The human rights set boasts of a number of big-name employment specialists. Chairman of the Bar **David Bean QC** (see p.1363) specialises in employment, discrimination and education law. He recently acted for the NASUWT in an industrial dispute in which members refused to teach an unruly pupil. "Innovative thinker" **Cherie Booth QC** (see p.1368) "produces quality opinions." She represents both applicants and respondents in individual and collective disputes. Top ranking junior **Thomas Linden** (see p.1436) stands out for his "intellectual ability and forensic approach." A "courteous opponent" he "gets to the nitty-gritty in cross-examination but manages to look nice about it." With a "low-key" presentation style, he is said to "pitch his case well" in tribunals. Linden recently acted in the ECJ in Bowden v Tuffnells Parcels concerning the scope of the road transport sector exclusion under the Working Time Directive. Better known for human rights work, **Helen Mountfield** (see p.1451) also has an impressive reputation at the employment Bar. A "personable" negotiator, she is "good at getting people to agree." Mountfield and Booth acted for the TUC on parental leave case R v Secretary of State for Trade and Industry ex parte Trade Union Congress.

OTHER NOTABLE PRACTITIONERS At Essex Court Chambers, "fierce" **Andrew Hochauser QC** (see p.1417) is "one of the best cross-examiners around." He comes across as "urbane and civilised until you unleash him – then he becomes a rotweiler" and is said to be "good for cases where you want to rough up the opposition." Often appearing with him is **Martin Griffiths** (see p.1410), an "on the ball" advocate who "has it all." "User friendly" and "very very clever" he is reported to be a "good foil to Hochauser." He has been acting in an EAT case relating to automatic disqualification of tribunal members as shareholders. "Professional" **Charles Ciumei** (see p.1380) has a "reassuring, measured style." Known for his "practical advice," he "puts the client's case well." He recently acted for the Royal Shakespeare Company in relation to a potential injunction to prevent industrial action and TUPE claims. "Classy" **Nicholas Underhill QC** (see p.1494) of Fountain Court is both "brilliantly clever" and "receptive to client input." He recently appeared in the Court of Appeal on a race discrimination case, Anya v University of Oxford, and has been involved in a number of City employment disputes. At the same chambers, **Brian Napier** (see p.1452) combines an academic background with a "commercial focus." He has recently been appointed silk at the Scottish Bar and was warmly recommended by solicitors across the UK for his TUPE advice. **Anthony Korn** (see p.1430) at 199 Strand has a "flair for the showmanship of an industrial tribunal." Skilled in all areas of employment, his practice focuses on TUPE and discrimination cases.

EMPLOYMENT

Research The rankings are based on in-depth interviews with 6,582 solicitors, barristers and clients in the UK. **Chambers'** research is audited by the British Market Research Bureau (see page 7)

BARRISTERS' PROFILES ▶ See pages 1353-1504

WESTERN CIRCUIT

LEADING JUNIORS • Western

[1]	KEMPSTER Toby	Old Square Chambers
	SMITH Nicholas	Queen Square Chambers
[2]	DRACASS Timothy	Eighteen Carlton Crescent
	PIRANI Rohan	Old Square Chambers

For details of these leading barristers see Profiles on page 1353

Toby Kempster (see p.1428) at Old Square Chambers was commended for "making a real effort with clients." A "user friendly" barrister, he handles all aspects of discrimination, TUPE, restrictive covenants and collective agreements. He and **Rohan Pirani** (see p.1460) practice from both the London and Bristol chambers. Pirani received warm recommendation from local solicitors as someone who "always knows his stuff" but remains "nice to work with." At Queens Square Chambers, **Nicholas Smith** (see p.1480) has "built up a good local employment practice" and attracted a specialist team in Bristol. He acts principally in employment law matters and has particular expertise in relation to sports contracts. At Eighteen Carlton Crescent, **Tim Dracass** (see p.1391) is admired for his "adept handling of difficult cases."

MIDLANDS CIRCUIT

LEADING JUNIORS • Midlands

[1]	JONES Jennifer	No 5 Chambers
[2]	GEORGE Sarah	St Philips Chambers
	TUCKER Katherine	St Philips Chambers

For details of these leading barristers see Profiles on page 1353

At No 5 Chambers, "down-to-earth" **Jennifer Jones** (see p.1426) "gives it to you straight." She specialises in race, sex and disability discrimination cases for both employers and employees. At St Philips Chambers, **Katherine Tucker** (see p.1493) has comprehensive knowledge of UK and European employment law. Her colleague **Sarah George** was also recommended.

NORTH EASTERN CIRCUIT

LEADING JUNIORS • North Eastern

[1]	CAPE Paul	Milburn House Chambers
	SWEENEY Seamus	Plowden Buildings
[2]	WOODWARK Jane	Plowden Buildings
	UP AND COMING	
	FALKENSTEIN John	Plowden Buildings

For details of these leading barristers see Profiles on page 1353

Paul Cape (see p.1376) at Milburn House Chambers appears frequently in the tribunal and EAT where he is considered a "formidable opponent" and a leader at the local bar. A number of younger practitioners have recently left Milburn House Chambers for Plowden Buildings. These include highly rated employment specialists **Jane Woodwark** (see p.1502), **Seamus Sweeney** (see p.1486) and **John Falkenstein** (see p.1396).

NORTHERN CIRCUIT

LEADING SILKS • Northern

[1]	BENSON John	14 Castle Street
	HAND John	9 St. John Street

For details of these leading barristers see Profiles on page 1353

LEADING JUNIORS • Northern

[1]	GILROY Paul	9 St. John Street
	GRUNDY Nigel	9 St. John Street
[2]	BRADLEY Richard	Oriel Chambers
	BREEN Carlo	9 St. John Street
	CONNOLLY Joanne	8 King St
	SADIQ Tariq	9 St. John Street
	WEDDERSPOON Rachel	9 St. John Street

For details of these leading barristers see Profiles on page 1353

Manchester chambers 9 St John Street contains a number of specialist practitioners. John Hand QC (see p. 1411) is popular locally for being both "very approachable" and "technically skilled." He recently acted in Middlebrook Mushroom v TGWU concerning whether a boycott as part of an industrial dispute constituted an economic tort. He operates from both the London and Manchester chambers. "Personable" **Paul Gilroy** (see p.1404) maintains a "generalist" practice encompassing multi-applicant tribunal cases, disciplinary inquiries and equal pay claims. "Bright" **Nigel Grundy** (see p.1410) is "very good with paperwork." **Carlo Breen** (see p.1371) "goes in fully prepared" while **Tariq Sadiq** (see p.1473) was recommended for "good client care." **Rachel Wedderspoon** (see p.1498) advises local authorities, companies and trade unions on industrial relations problems and contributes a knowledge of personal injury law to employment cases. At 14 Castle Street in Liverpool, **John Benson QC** (see p.1364) offers "pragmatic advice." Richard Bradley of Oriel Chambers retains a strong following among local practitioners, while **Joanne Connolly** (see p.1383) at 8 King Street was praised as "well prepared" and "easy to get on with."

ENERGY & NATURAL RESOURCES

Research The rankings are based on in-depth interviews with 6,582 solicitors, barristers and clients in the UK. **Chambers'** research is audited by the British Market Research Bureau (see page 7)

BARRISTERS' PROFILES ▶ See pages 1353-1504

OVERVIEW: The porous boundary between Projects and Energy resists any attempt at clear demarcation at the Bar. One of the year's biggest cases exemplifies this. The Rowan Gorilla V case, involving contracts, world markets and rigs, was a real hybrid. Dragged through the Commercial Courts for 25 weeks, it involved the great and the good of the energy Bar. On display were the talents of energy stars such as Mark Barnes, Lord Goldsmith, Richard Siberry and David Unwin. And behind the leaders came a plethora of quality juniors, including three from construction experts Atkin Chambers. Enron's ability to generate quantities of litigation appears undiminished by its collapse, and the market awaits the final impact of this event.

LONDON

ENERGY & NATURAL RESOURCES • London

		QCs	Jnrs
1	One Essex Court (Lord Grabiner QC)	7	2
2	Essex Court Chambers (Gordon Pollock QC)	4	-
3	Brick Court Chambers (Christopher Clarke QC)	2	-
4	Fountain Court (Anthony Boswood QC)	1	-
	4 Stone Buildings (Philip Heslop QC)	2	-

Numbers show recommended barristers in this practice area

LEADING SILKS • London

★	GRABINER Anthony	One Essex Court
	POLLOCK Gordon	Essex Court Chambers
	SUMPTION Jonathan	Brick Court Chambers
1	ALDOUS Charles	Maitland Chambers
	BARNES Mark	One Essex Court
	CARR Christopher	One Essex Court
	GLICK Ian	One Essex Court
2	BOSWOOD Anthony	Fountain Court
	GLOSTER Elizabeth	One Essex Court
	SHER Jules	Wilberforce Chambers
3	DICKER Robin	3-4 South Square
	EDER Bernard	Essex Court Chambers
	HILDYARD Robert	4 Stone Buildings
	HOWARD Mark	Brick Court Chambers
	ONIONS Jeffery	One Essex Court
	SIBERRY Richard	Essex Court Chambers
4	CROOKENDEN Simon	Essex Court Chambers
	MALES Stephen	20 Essex Street
	NEW SILKS	
	MILES Robert	4 Stone Buildings
	RABINOWITZ Laurence	One Essex Court

For details of these leading barristers see Profiles on page 1353

LEADING JUNIORS • London

1	GRIFFITHS Alan	One Essex Court
2	TOLEDANO Daniel	One Essex Court

For details of these leading barristers see Profiles on page 1353

ONE ESSEX COURT (see full details p.1531) Still "indisputably the best" thanks to the "sheer quantity of real quality," the set acts on the full gamut of oil and gas and electricity matters. Such is the wide scope of **Anthony Grabiner QC**'s expertise, solicitors endorse him as "good for anything." The Gorilla case has enhanced the "great credibility" of **Mark Barnes QC** (see p.1362) and he is thought to have the ear of major industry clients. **Christopher Carr QC** (see p.1377) has a "fabulous oil and gas track record" and continues to employ his "first-rate judgement" to good effect. "Superb generalist" **Ian Glick QC** (see p.1405) is experienced in utilities and is "quite simply a brain on legs." Clients find the "incredibly bright" **Elizabeth Gloster QC** (see p.1406) "a charm to work with: explain once and she's away." **Jeffery Onions QC** (see p.1457) impresses clients with his "sound and thorough commercial awareness." At long last the "frighteningly intelligent" **Laurence Rabinowitz QC** (see p.1469) has made it to well-deserved silk. Clients value his "great judgement" and "willingness to analyse critically and also to provide solutions." Solicitors talk of their "deepest admiration" for the intelligence of **Alan Griffiths** (see p.1409), and **Daniel Toledano** (see p.1492) is "a definite future star." "Bright and thorough with excellent analysis," he employs "outstanding tactics" and strong advocacy skills to his cases.

ESSEX COURT CHAMBERS (see full details p.1530) The set retains its strong position among solicitors who commend it as "a trusted favourite, offering some bright stars." The "clearly outstanding advocate and advisor," **Gordon Pollock QC** (see p.1461), is regarded with something approaching awe by colleagues and clients alike. **Bernard Eder QC** (see p.1393) is a "confidence-inspiring" performer and has been active in a number of domestic and overseas matters. **Richard Siberry QC**'s (see p.1478) involvement in the Amoco (UK) Exploration Co v British American Offshore tussle sees his profile bolstered, whilst **Simon Crookenden QC** (see p.1386) receives plaudits for his work on Enron Oil & Gas v Oil & Natural Gas Corporation & Reliance Industries Group.

BRICK COURT CHAMBERS (see full details p.1517) A devoted solicitor following declared its allegiance for this "incredibly efficient" chambers. Clients reported that these barristers are "unusually responsive" and "the juniors are first class." Of course, the set fields **Jonathan Sumption QC**, "the sharpest in the box," whose "stunning" skills have been enlisted to take the Gorilla case to appeal. The "thoughtful and helpful" **Mark Howard QC** (see p.1420) acted in the BHP v Dalmine pipeline dispute.

FOUNTAIN COURT (see full details p.1541) The set garners praise from market sources for its "definite quality and style." "Analytical" **Anthony Boswood QC** (see p.1368) remains the principal here for energy and related matters, and is admired by peers as "a good bruising battler."

4 STONE BUILDINGS (see full details p.1606) This highly commercial set is acknowledged as possessing a "fine energy profile riding on the shoulders of **Robert Hildyard QC** (see p.1415) and **Robert Miles QC** (see p.1447)." The latter has this year taken silk. In recent years the energy practices of both QCs have been primarily advisory in nature.

OTHER NOTABLE PRACTITIONERS **Charles Aldous QC** is the most notable energy barrister at Maitland Chambers and widely regarded as "a figure of distinction." Wilberforce Chambers is home to **Jules Sher QC** (see p.1478) ("sharp and penetrating"), who has a reputation as an expert in electricity-related matters. The career of 3-4 South Square's **Robin Dicker QC** (see p.1390) ("excellent, rigorous, hard-working and accurate") provokes intense interest as he gets more experience under his belt, and **Stephen Males QC** (see p.1440) of 20 Essex Street continues to be a favourite of solicitors.

ENVIRONMENT

Research The rankings are based on in-depth interviews with 6,582 solicitors, barristers and clients in the UK. **Chambers'** research is audited by the British Market Research Bureau (see page 7)

BARRISTERS' PROFILES ▶ See pages 1353-1504

LONDON

OLD SQUARE CHAMBERS (see full details p.1583) Solicitors commend the "huge effort of these committed barristers," which has been focused on establishing an "excellent environmental practice." The set is particularly well received for its claimants work, approaching environmental law, for the most part, from a common law angle. Leading silks **John Hand QC** (see p.1411) and **John Melville Williams QC** (see p.1500) continue to occupy the vanguard, though it is the substantial weight of expertise supplied by its juniors that gives the set its critical mass and guarantees the top slot in our tables. Interviewees point to **John Bates**'s (see p.1391) intimate knowledge of English and Scottish regulations and their interplay with EU law. He is best known for his opinions on waste and water pollution. Embracing the personal injury/environment divide, **Charles Pugh** (see p.1464) is said to excel in major pollution cases. He displays specialist knowledge in toxic tort issues and is a "truly flamboyant advocate." **William Birtles** (see p.1366) was categorised by solicitors as an "environmental common law expert," with the "capacity of a workhorse." **Philip Mead** (see p.1445) was consistently praised for the "rapport he is quick to establish with both clients and magistrates."

4 BREAMS BUILDINGS (see full details p.1516) The depth of knowledge possessed by the set's "extremely capable" practitioners has gone some way to compensating against the departure of Christopher Kingsland to 2 Harcourt Buildings. It retains three highly regarded silks generally, though not exclusively, approaching environmental issues via their planning workload. "Extremely well-respected and highly specialised" **David Elvin QC** (see p.1395) recently appeared for the RSPB in the Dibden Terminal inquiry, and receives wide-ranging recommendation. "Full of ideas," **David Holgate QC** (see p.1418) has "total mastery of a brief" and has also had a busy year appearing in public inquiries, including one concerning the granting of planning permission for a waste to energy plant. **Christopher Katkowski QC** (see p.1426) has appeared in inquiries involving port developments with implications under the European protected habitats directive, and several high-profile projects in both the City and the regions.

ELDON CHAMBERS (see full details p.1527) Though sorely tested by the departure of a group of five barristers to 39 Essex Street, including environmental specialist Stephen Tromans, this set nevertheless retains practitioners of considerable stature. **Lionel Read QC** (see p.1467) is still felt to be "as good as ever – devastating in cross-examination." Judged by peers to have achieved early success as a silk, **Rhodri Price Lewis QC** (see p.1435) is a highly regarded advocate, best known for his understanding of the waste business. Solicitors also report that his criminal expertise is especially helpful. **Russell Harris** (see p.1412) also remains well regarded.

2 HARCOURT BUILDINGS (see full details p.1554) The clerks at this set attracted a high level of praise ("the best clerking of the specialist sets"), and interviewees typically commented that "overall, it provides an outstanding service," with some noting the willingness of practitioners to give "generous informal advice." Possessor of "everything you need for big projects," it was the strongest challenger to the leaders, with environmental expertise that often combines with wide-ranging planning work. The retirement of former head of chambers Gerard Ryan QC is countered by the arrival of **Christopher Kingsland QC** (see p.1429), who is particularly respected for his expertise in waste law. **Charles George QC** (see p.1403) received plaudits for his broad environmental practice, which often crosses over into planning matters. **Greg Jones** is best known for his European experience and was described to researchers as the "real emerging talent on judicial reviews." "Trailblazer" **Robert McCracken** (see p.1444) is considered an expert in statutory nuisance issues.

1 CROWN OFFICE ROW (see full details p.1524) Consistently endorsed by solicitors, the set is particularly respected for acting in environmental

ENVIRONMENT • London

		QCs	Jnrs
1	Old Square Chambers (John Hendy QC)	2	4
2	4 Breams Buildings (Christopher Lockhart-Mummery QC)	3	-
	Eldon Chambers (Lionel Read QC)	2	1
	2 Harcourt Buildings (Robin Purchas QC)	2	2
3	1 Crown Office Row (Robert Seabrook QC)	1	2
	Matrix Chambers	1	3
4	Blackstone Chambers (Baxendale/Flint)	1	1
	Brick Court Chambers (Christopher Clarke QC)	1	1
	39 Essex Street (Nigel Pleming QC)	1	2
	4-5 Gray's Inn Square (Elizabeth Appleby QC)	-	2
	6 Pump Court (Stephen Hockman QC)	1	2

Numbers show recommended barristers in this practice area

LEADING SILKS • London

1	BRENNAN Daniel	Matrix Chambers
	HAND John	Old Square Chambers
	KINGSLAND Christopher	2 Harcourt Buildings
2	ELVIN David	4 Breams Buildings
	GEORGE Charles	2 Harcourt Buildings
	GORDON Richard	Brick Court Chambers
	HAVERS Philip	1 Crown Office Row
	HOCKMAN Stephen	6 Pump Court
	HOLGATE David	4 Breams Buildings
	HOWELL John	Blackstone Chambers
	KATKOWSKI Christopher	4 Breams Buildings
	KING Neil	2 Mitre Court Buildings
	LEWIS Rhodri Price	Eldon Chambers
	PLEMING Nigel	39 Essex Street
	READ Lionel	Eldon Chambers
	WILLIAMS John Melville	Old Square Chambers

For details of these leading barristers see Profiles on page 1353

LEADING JUNIORS • London

★	HART David	1 Crown Office Row
1	BATES John	Old Square Chambers
	MCCRACKEN Robert	2 Harcourt Buildings
	PUGH Charles	Old Square Chambers
	TROMANS Stephen	39 Essex Street
2	BIRTLES William	Old Square Chambers
	FORDHAM Michael	Blackstone Chambers
	JONES Gregory	2 Harcourt Buildings
	SANDS Philippe	Matrix Chambers
3	BYRNE Garrett	4-5 Gray's Inn Square
	MEAD Philip	Old Square Chambers
	READ Graham	Devereux Chambers
	SHERIDAN Maurice	Matrix Chambers
	UPTON William	6 Pump Court
	WOLFE David	Matrix Chambers
4	EDIS William	1 Crown Office Row
	HARRIS Russell	Eldon Chambers
	HILL Thomas	4-5 Gray's Inn Square
	LEWIS Robert	11 New Square
	MACRORY Richard	Brick Court Chambers
	PUGH-SMITH John	39 Essex Street
	TRAVERS David	6 Pump Court
	WEST Lawrence	2 Harcourt Buildings

For details of these leading barristers see Profiles on page 1353

> **Research** The rankings are based on in-depth interviews with 6,582 solicitors, barristers and clients in the UK. **Chambers'** research is audited by the British Market Research Bureau (see page 7)
>
> **BARRISTERS' PROFILES** ▶ See pages 1353-1504

prosecutions and advising on the impact of the Human Rights Act. Best known for his public law practice, **Philip Havers QC** (see p.1413) is nevertheless regarded by environmental specialists as a "definite leader in the field." But it was "legally and mentally rigorous" **David Hart** (see p.1412) who excelled in this year's research, impressing with the level of commendation for toxic tort prosecutions in particular. His technical ability, common law and human rights expertise and his skills as an advocate received accolades, and in the view of one interviewee he is deemed "indispensable." **William Edis** also retains a good reputation among the higher echelons of this field.

MATRIX CHAMBERS (see full details p.1573) Although opinion was divided as to the level of the set's overall environmental profile, its individual practitioners elicited consistent endorsement from diverse sources. High-profile **Dan Brennan QC** is especially rated for his approach to environmental matters via personal injury, while **David Wolfe** (see p.1501) retains his profile as a public lawyer who is also "an emerging environmental talent." The set has a well-defined international dimension in the practice of **Philippe Sands** (see p.1473). He recently appeared in Ireland v United Kingdom at the International Tribunal for the Law of the Sea, the MOX plant case. **Maurice Sheridan** (see p.1478) was highly praised for his ability to work "closely with his client and as part of a team." An "incredibly hard worker," he is best known for advice on extensive landfill sites and general regulatory work, and has recognised expertise on GM crops and nuclear issues.

BLACKSTONE CHAMBERS (see full details p.1515) The set attracts many instructions on environmental matters via its strength in public law. Deriving an advantage from the crossover, **John Howell QC** (see p.1420) is seen as having been "fantastically successful." He and **Michael Fordham** (see p.1399) ("frighteningly bright") are felt to have consolidated their positions in the environmental sphere. Howell has acted for the Environment Agency in a case concerning whether substitute liquid fuels derived from waste materials remained waste for the purpose of the Waste Framework Directive, while Fordham acted for the appellant in the Marchiori case.

BRICK COURT CHAMBERS (see full details p.1517) "A delight to work with," **Richard Gordon QC** (see p.1407) is best known for his judicial review appearances involving weighty environmental matters. When it comes to opinions, "you could not expect to go to anyone better than" **Richard Macrory**, claim solicitors. He recently appeared in the Court of Appeal for Severn Trent Water against the British Waterways Board.

39 ESSEX STREET (see full details p.1537) It has leapt into the limelight this year as far as having an environmental practice is concerned, with a swathe of barristers from Eldon Chambers arriving to build on the set's already thriving public practice. **Nigel Pleming QC** (see p.1461) has also been recognised in his own right. Said by clients to possess a "gift for grappling with the multifarious elements of environmental cases under pressure," he acted for the Treasury Solicitors in Marchiori. Known ubiquitously, **Stephen Tromans** (see p.1493) has successfully adapted his "knowledge and authority" to following a career at the Bar, with one solicitor interviewee claiming "no-one has even come close to his depth and vision in the area." Unanimous in their praise for his written opinions and regulatory advice, interviewees maintain that the former Simmons & Simmons' star solicitor remains essentially an "unknown quantity as an advocate." Also a recognised specialist in the field, **John Pugh-Smith** (see p.1464) recently acted in cases concerning the compatibility of the CPO process with Article 6 of the Human Rights Act, and the timing of environmental impact assessment.

4-5 GRAY'S INN SQUARE (see full details p.1550) The environmental track record of this set stems from its public authority expertise. Interviewees applauded its "first-rate environmental capabilities," although the set's profile is diminished by the departure of Philip Vallance QC to Berrymans Lace Mawer. Boasting an "excellent grasp of regulatory matters," **Garrett Byrne** (see p.1375) is best known for his prosecution work, while **Tom Hill** (see p.1416) continues to elicit favourable commendation.

6 PUMP COURT (see full details p.1594) A new addition to the tables this year, the chambers is seen as steadily building a profile in this specialist area. "Adept at common law points and human rights issues," **Stephen Hockman QC** (see p.1417) has been involved in a number of high-profile environmental cases this year. He successfully represented Mr Marcic at the Court of Appeal in a claim against Thames Water Utilities under the Human Rights Act, for failing to prevent sewage flooding his home. **David Travers**' (see p.1492) wide-ranging regulatory practice also continues to attract praise among environment practitioners. Holding a strong reputation with solicitors nationally, **William Upton** (see p.1495) acted for the RSPB in the Chardon LL public hearing, on the application by Aventis to place its GM maize on the National Seed List. Typically acting for local authorities, he recently acted for one in a case where English Nature and the RSPB contested a proposed residential development on the grounds that it would affect land protected under European conservation laws. Upton has recently joined the set from Eldon Chambers.

MIDLANDS CIRCUIT

LEADING SILKS • Midlands

NEW SILKS

CAHILL Jeremy	No 5 Chambers

For details of these leading barristers see Profiles on page 1353

LEADING JUNIORS • Midlands

1	KIMBLIN Richard	3 Fountain Court
2	DIGGINS Martin	Claremont Chambers

For details of these leading barristers see Profiles on page 1353

"An accomplished big-hitter," **Jeremy Cahill QC** of No 5 Chambers retains a high environmental profile, with waste planning matters thought to be his forte. **Richard Kimblin** (see p.1429) of 3 Fountain Court received several plaudits for "devoting real time and effort to developing true environmental expertise." He recently appeared for English Nature in a public inquiry concerning sand extraction from the Ribble Estuary area. Solicitors recognised that his scientific background contributed to an informed judgment. The "economical and thorough" **Martin Diggins** of Claremont Chambers enjoyed sufficient commendation to enter the tables. He is often seen acting for public authorities, and interviewees identified his strengths in statutory nuisance, water pollution and habitats.

ENVIRONMENT

Research The rankings are based on in-depth interviews with 6,582 solicitors, barristers and clients in the UK. **Chambers'** research is audited by the British Market Research Bureau (see page 7)

BARRISTERS' PROFILES ▶ See pages 1353-1504

NORTHERN & NORTH EASTERN CIRCUITS

LEADING SILKS • Northern & North Eastern

[1]	PATTERSON Frances	40 King St

For details of these leading barristers see Profiles on page 1353

LEADING JUNIORS • Northern & North Eastern

BARRETT John	40 King St
CAMERON Neil	Wilberforce Chambers

For details of these leading barristers see Profiles on page 1353

Frances Patterson QC (see p.1459) of 40 King Street continues to further the chambers' reputation for environmental expertise via its planning core, while **John Barrett** (see p.1362) is considered "excellent on environmental prosecutions." He has recently focused, although not exclusively, on waste management matters. **Neil Cameron** (see p.1376) of Wilberforce Chambers is highly rated for his criminal defence work, often appearing on behalf of chemical companies.

FAMILY

Research The rankings are based on in-depth interviews with 6,582 solicitors, barristers and clients in the UK. **Chambers'** research is audited by the British Market Research Bureau (see page 7)

BARRISTERS' PROFILES ▶ See pages 1353-1504

LONDON

ONE KING'S BENCH WALK (see full details p.1561) Home to a raft of experts across the family divide, the set is popular with solicitors both in London and nationally for being "well clerked and extremely helpful." **Barry Singleton QC** is "one of the kings of finance," known for his "blunt approach and tactical aperçu." There is clear water between **Judith Parker QC** (see p.1458) and her contemporaries in the children sphere. "A tremendously vivacious performer," she combines well on many a complex case with **Deborah Eaton** (see p.1392), who is "outstandingly knowledgeable" and also "a dab hand at financial matters." Similarly versatile is **James Turner QC** (see p.1494), "a great cross-examiner" and "a top finance practitioner" who has carved out a further specialism in child abduction. A couple of years into silk, **Charles Howard QC** (see p.1419) "continues to make strides" and is appearing in increasingly high-profile cases while **Rodger Hayward Smith QC** (see p.1413) has demonstrated his "academic bent" by writing extensively on family law. The set boasts two more experienced child practitioners in **Andrew McFarlane QC** (see p.1444), who combines his work in this field with advice on human rights, and **Anthony Kirk QC** (see p.1430), who "brings a light touch to his cases." Completing this impressive stable of silks are **Richard Anelay QC** (see p.1357), the "immovable" **Camden Pratt QC** (see p.1463) and **Clive Newton QC** (see p.1454) whose elevation to silk was widely welcomed. Prominent juniors include **Christopher Pocock** (see p.1461), "one of the most numerate around," and **Richard Harrison** (see p.1412) who is "coming to the fore in better and better cases." Commentators spoke of his comfortable approach to international matters, a trait he shares with **Ian Cook** (see p.1383). Of the younger crop, **Philip Marshall** (see p.1442) and **James Roberts** (see p.1469) were viewed as "real names for the future," the latter being praised fulsomely for his "confidence, energy and unwillingness to give ground easily." **Caroline Lister** (see p.1437) and **Caroline Budden** (see p.1374) retain the confidence of the market.

1 HARE COURT (see full details p.1556) Purveyors of "fine all-round ability at every level." Head of chambers **Bruce Blair QC** is an "old school gentleman advocate" who is "intellectually in the top bracket." Of a different kidney, **Nicholas Mostyn QC** adopts a more "colourful and creative approach," presenting as both "a classy advocate and a bullish gambler," while **Jeremy Posnansky QC** (see p.1462) similarly "adds a bit of spark and fire" to his delivery. The latter has a mixed practice in common with **Michael Horowitz QC** (see p.1419) who is deemed by commentators to have "tremendous judgement." **Martin Pointer QC** (see p.1461) demonstrates "the courage of a lion" in the courtroom, an arena in which **Philip Moor QC** (see p.1449) displays his "quick-witted thinking when on his feet," whereas **Mark Everall QC**'s (see p.1396) "true forte lies on the advisory side." Joining this august troupe of silks is **Valentine Le Grice QC** (see p.1433), another deemed to be "one to go to for sound written advice." An already strong band of juniors has been fortified by the arrival of a couple of refugees from 29 Bedford Row: **Ann Hussey** (see p.1421), popular with solicitors as "a good team player who backs up well," and **Deborah Bangay** (see p.1360), "who really believes in her cause and is a good one to set on difficult husbands." They join a talented group that includes **Michael Nicholls** (see p.1454) who "has an interesting practice and specialist knowledge in child abduction." **Nicholas Cusworth** (see p.1387) is "excellent at contested hearings, being able to take the heat out of volatile situations," while "big-hitter" **Nigel Dyer** (see p.1392) is "utterly fair-minded but nobody's pussy cat." Also recommended were **Catriona Murfitt** (see p.1452), **Tim Bishop** (see p.1366), ("an advocate with skills beyond his years") and **Christopher Wood** (see p.1501) who "has an amazing grasp of the facts and is never fazed."

FAMILY/MATRIMONIAL • London

	QCs	Jnrs
1 One King's Bench Walk (Anthony Hacking QC)	10	6
1 Hare Court (Bruce Blair QC)	8	8
Queen Elizabeth Building (Florence Baron QC)	4	7
2 29 Bedford Row Chambers (Nicholas Francis QC)	4	5
One Garden Court Family Law Chambers (Platt/Ball)	3	4
4 Paper Buildings (Lionel Swift QC)	3	4
3 14 Gray's Inn Square (Joanna Dodson QC)	1	3
Renaissance Chambers (Jubb/Setright)	1	2

Numbers show recommended barristers in this practice area

LEADING SILKS • MATRIMONIAL FINANCE • London

1	BARON Florence	Queen Elizabeth Building
	BLAIR Bruce	1 Hare Court
	MOSTYN Nicholas	1 Hare Court
	POSNANSKY Jeremy	1 Hare Court
	SINGLETON Barry	One King's Bench Walk
2	POINTER Martin	1 Hare Court
	SCOTT Timothy	29 Bedford Row Chambers
	STONE Lucy	Queen Elizabeth Building
	TURNER James	One King's Bench Walk
3	ANELAY Richard	One King's Bench Walk
	COHEN Jonathan	4 Paper Buildings
	HAYWARD SMITH Rodger	One King's Bench Walk
	HOROWITZ Michael	1 Hare Court
	HOWARD Charles	One King's Bench Walk
	MOOR Philip	1 Hare Court
	MOYLAN Andrew	Queen Elizabeth Building
	PRATT Camden	One King's Bench Walk
	SEABROOK Robert	1 Crown Office Row
NEW SILKS		
	BALCOMBE David	1 Crown Office Row
	CAYFORD Philip	29 Bedford Row Chambers
	FRANCIS Nicholas	29 Bedford Row Chambers
	LE GRICE Valentine	1 Hare Court
	MARKS Lewis	Queen Elizabeth Building
	NEWTON Clive	One King's Bench Walk
	STOREY Paul	29 Bedford Row Chambers

For details of these leading barristers see Profiles on page 1353

LEADING JUNIORS • MATRIMONIAL FINANCE • London

1	AMOS Tim	Queen Elizabeth Building
	CLARKE Elizabeth	Queen Elizabeth Building
	CUSWORTH Nicholas	1 Hare Court
	DYER Nigel	1 Hare Court
	POCOCK Christopher	One King's Bench Walk
	ROBERTS Jennifer	Queen Elizabeth Building
2	BANGAY Deborah	1 Hare Court
	EATON Deborah	One King's Bench Walk
	HARRISON Richard	One King's Bench Walk
	SANDERS Neil	29 Bedford Row Chambers
	WOOD Christopher	1 Hare Court
3	BISHOP Timothy	1 Hare Court
	BRASSE Gillian	14 Gray's Inn Square
	BRUDENELL Thomas	Queen Elizabeth Building
	COOK Ian	One King's Bench Walk
	HUSSEY Ann	1 Hare Court
	LEECH Stewart	Queen Elizabeth Building
	MARSHALL Philip	One King's Bench Walk
	MOLYNEUX Brenton	29 Bedford Row Chambers
	NATHAN Peter	One Garden Court Family Law Chambers
	PEEL Robert	29 Bedford Row Chambers
	ROBERTS James	One King's Bench Walk
	SHAW Howard	29 Bedford Row Chambers
	TIDBURY Andrew	Queen Elizabeth Building
UP AND COMING		
	COWTON Catherine	Queen Elizabeth Building

For details of these leading barristers see Profiles on page 1353

www.ChambersandPartners.com

FAMILY

Research The rankings are based on in-depth interviews with 6,582 solicitors, barristers and clients in the UK. **Chambers'** research is audited by the British Market Research Bureau (see page 7)

BARRISTERS' PROFILES ▶ See pages 1353-1504

QUEEN ELIZABETH BUILDING (see full details p.1596) This long-standing set has a fine tradition of producing the very best financial barristers. With a claim to being perhaps the best of them all, **Florence Baron QC** (see p.1356) was uniformly eulogised by interviewees as "sharp, commercial and meticulously prepared." Her ability to "effectively distil complex issues with a dash of humour" makes her "a great favourite among clients." **Lucy Stone QC** (see p.1484) is "rapidly scaling the heights" despite her relatively recent appointment to silk. Perceived by sources to be "ace judge material," she "sees the full picture." Solicitors agree that **Andrew Moylan QC** (see p.1452) is "a reassuring presence," while new silk **Lewis Marks QC** (see p.1441) has justified his elevation by impressing as "a ball of energy," who is "thorough, supportive and particularly skilled in international cases." Blessed with some of the finest members of the junior bar, the set can call upon the likes of the "bright and extremely well-organised" **Tim Amos** (see p.1356). **Elizabeth Clarke** commands the respect of the very best solicitors for her "superb, no-frills performances," while **Jennifer Roberts**, one of the few at the set to straddle finance and children, brings "maturity and a commanding presence" to a practice that involves much international and forum shopping work. Two characters particularly praised for their court craft were **Thomas Brudenell** (see p.1373), "who can shrink the opposition down to size," and **Stewart Leech**, a former Eton master and latecomer to the Bar, who has "great confidence and delivery." **Andrew Tidbury** maintains the respect of his peers. Joining them in the tables this year is **Catherine Cowton**, commended to our researchers as "spectacularly efficient."

29 BEDFORD ROW CHAMBERS (see full details p.1512) The set is deemed to have a more modern approach than many of its rivals and is home to a panoply of talented financial practitioners. **Timothy Scott QC** (see p.1474) "evinces an equal sureness of touch in both children and big money cases," while **Philip Cayford QC** is "a brilliant advocate, well known to judges." In what has been a bonanza year for **Nicholas Francis QC** (see p.1400), he has become both a silk and the new head of chambers. "Charming and intelligent," his "easy manner and fight-until-you-drop attitude" plays particularly well with clients, who also appreciate **Paul Storey QC's** (see p.1484) "even-handedness and indomitable spirit." Of the juniors, **Neil Sanders** (see p.1473) "always finds a way through and doesn't get bogged down in the technicalities," while **Brenton Molyneux's** (see p.1448) "trenchant advice and direct style" scores well with solicitors. Also commended are **Robert Peel** (see p.1459) for his "good judgement," and **Howard Shaw** (see p.1476) for his "pleasing personality and constructive approach." The set has enjoyed the good fortune this year of obtaining the services of **Debbie Taylor** (see p.1488), formerly of Hardwicke Building.

ONE GARDEN COURT FAMILY LAW CHAMBERS (see full details p.1543) A set to go to for advice on all child-related matters but also one that can handle matrimonial finance cases. **Eleanor Platt QC** (see p.1461) is applauded by solicitors as "a consummate court performer who often blasts the opposition." She shares the role of head of chambers with **Alison Ball QC** (see p.1360), who is also known for a "resolute" approach. **Ian Peddie QC's** (see p.1459) role is that of a "steady hand," while **Stephen Cobb** (see p.1381) is "a name that immediately springs to mind for complex contested matters." Other rated juniors include **Judith Rowe** (see p.1471) and **Peter Horrocks** (see p.1419), both seen as "unflappable in a crisis." In this set so heavily dominated by children practitioners, **Peter Nathan** (see p.1453) is recommended as "understated but rigorous in his preparation" in finance matters.

LEADING SILKS • CHILDREN • London

★	PARKER Judith	One King's Bench Walk
1	HOROWITZ Michael	1 Hare Court
	LEVY Allan	17 Bedford Row
	MCFARLANE Andrew	One King's Bench Walk
	PAUFFLEY Anna	4 Paper Buildings
	POSNANSKY Jeremy	1 Hare Court
	SETRIGHT Henry	Renaissance Chambers
2	EVERALL Mark	1 Hare Court
	JACKSON Peter	4 Paper Buildings
	KIRK Anthony	One King's Bench Walk
	PLATT Eleanor	One Garden Court Family Law Chambers
	SCOTT Timothy	29 Bedford Row Chambers
	TURNER James	One King's Bench Walk
3	BALL Alison	One Garden Court Family Law Chambers
	DODSON Joanna	14 Gray's Inn Square
	HAYWARD SMITH Rodger	One King's Bench Walk
	PEDDIE Ian	One Garden Court Family Law Chambers
NEW SILKS		
	NEWTON Clive	One King's Bench Walk

For details of these leading barristers see Profiles on page 1353

LEADING JUNIORS • CHILDREN • London

1	COBB Stephen	One Garden Court Family Law Chambers
	EATON Deborah	One King's Bench Walk
2	BRASSE Gillian	14 Gray's Inn Square
	HALL Joanna	14 Gray's Inn Square
	LISTER Caroline	One King's Bench Walk
	NICHOLLS Michael	1 Hare Court
	ROWE Judith	One Garden Court Family Law Chambers
	SCOTT-MANDERSON Marcus	4 Paper Buildings
	SLOMNICKA Barbara	14 Gray's Inn Square
	STERNBERG Michael	4 Paper Buildings
	TAYLOR Debbie	29 Bedford Row Chambers
3	BARDA Robin	4 Paper Buildings
	BUDDEN Caroline	One King's Bench Walk
	DREW Jane	Coram Chambers
	HARDING Cherry	Renaissance Chambers
	HARRISON Richard	One King's Bench Walk
	HORROCKS Peter	One Garden Court Family Law Chambers
	JUBB Brian	Renaissance Chambers
	MITCHELL Janet	4 Brick Court
	MOLYNEUX Brenton	29 Bedford Row Chambers
	MURFITT Catriona	1 Hare Court
	ROBERTS Jennifer	Queen Elizabeth Building
	ROSENBLATT Jeremy	4 Paper Buildings

For details of these leading barristers see Profiles on page 1353

4 PAPER BUILDINGS (see full details p.1589) Despite Gordon Murdoch's move to the bench, this set continues to be peopled by strong individuals, especially on the children side. **Anna Pauffley QC** (see p.1459) is "a dyed-in-the-wool children expert who has nothing left to prove," while **Peter Jackson QC** (see p.1423) shines due to "his quick and well-organised mind." Enjoying a mixed practice, **Jonathan Cohen QC** (see p.1382) was lauded particularly for his work on ancillary relief. Effective leaders, they can look to their own set for talented juniors of the ilk of **Robin Barda** (see p.1361) and "child abduction expert" **Marcus Scott-Manderson** (see p.1474). **Michael Sternberg** (see p.1483) was recommended by solicitors for his "long-standing mastery" of the field, while **Jeremy Rosenblatt** (see p.1471) maintains his following.

14 GRAY'S INN SQUARE (see full details p.1551) A set with a strong children law bias, it is led by head of chambers "leading public law advo-

FAMILY

> **Research** The rankings are based on in-depth interviews with 6,582 solicitors, barristers and clients in the UK. **Chambers'** research is audited by the British Market Research Bureau (see page 7)

BARRISTERS' PROFILES ▶ See pages 1353-1504

cate" **Joanna Dodson QC** (see p.1390). Stablemates include **Barbara Slomnicka**, "feisty but thoughtful" **Gillian Brasse** (see p.1370) and "forceful and effective" **Joanna Hall**.

RENAISSANCE CHAMBERS Contemporaries feel the set has found its feet in the child law sphere. **Henry Setright QC** prompted encomia from leading solicitors who believe him to be "phenomenal on child abduction cases." **Brian Jubb** (see p.1426) and **Cherry Harding** (see p.1412), "a cross-examiner of some distinction," are noted names amongst the juniors.

OTHER NOTABLE PRACTITIONERS At 1 Crown Office Row, criminal expert **Robert Seabrook QC** (see p.1475) turns his hand to family law on a relatively regular basis and is "a quietly confident advocate who works well in front of the Court of Appeal." Similarly versatile is fellow tenant **David Balcombe QC** who is "outstanding as a cross-examiner." On the children front, **Allan Levy QC** (see p.1434) of 17 Bedford Row "bursts with self confidence" and frequently appears in the more important cases. **Janet Mitchell** (see p.1448) of 4 Brick Court has "an eye for both the legal and human side of things," while **Jane Drew** (see p.1391) at Coram Chambers is "beginning to convince as a top-class performer."

SOUTH EASTERN & EAST ANGLIAN CIRCUIT

LEADING SILKS • South Eastern & East Anglia

1	BAKER Jonathan	Harcourt Chambers

For details of these leading barristers see Profiles on page 1353

LEADING JUNIORS • South Eastern & East Anglian

1	KEFFORD Anthony	East Anglian Chambers
	MCLOUGHLIN Timothy	East Anglian Chambers
	TATTERSALL Simon	Fenners Chambers
2	DAVIES Lindsay	Fenners Chambers
	ELLIOTT Margot	Regency Chambers
	ESPLEY Susan	Fenners Chambers
	MILLER Celia	East Anglian Chambers
	NEWTON Roderick	East Anglian Chambers
	WAIN Peter	East Anglian Chambers
3	JUDD Frances	Harcourt Chambers
	PARNELL Graham	East Anglian Chambers
	RICHARDS Jeremy	Octagon House Chambers

For details of these leading barristers see Profiles on page 1353

East Anglian Chambers is a set rich in quality juniors of the calibre of **Anthony Kefford**, who "gives no quarter" and is "an ideal choice in a heated contest." **Timothy McLoughlin** "knows the local courts inside out" and enjoys a healthy child care practice while **Celia Miller** displays "sympathy and clear-headedness in equal measure." **Peter Wain** "retains the confidence of local authorities," and, with **Graham Parnell**, shares a talent for "drawing the sting out of emotional situations." Their head of chambers **Roderick Newton** continues to "add a dash of brio in the courtroom." Rival Fenners Chambers has unearthed a "star performer" in **Simon Tattersall**. "A robust advocate," he is "a whizz at digesting complex financial documents." **Susan Espley**'s (see p.1395) "sense of humour" and "never-say-die spirit" have endeared her to local solicitors, while **Lindsay Davies** (see p.1387) has her supporters due to her "knack of nipping at the heels of the opposition." Recommended individuals in other sets include **Margot Elliott** (see p.1394) of Regency Chambers, "a proficient child care specialist," and **Jeremy Richards** of Octagon House Chambers who has a similar practice. Completing the picture is **Frances Judd** (see p.1426) of Harcourt Chambers who has "calmed the nerves of

many a jittery client" whilst handling children cases. She has the good fortune to be in the set that contains **Jonathan Baker QC** (see p.1360), the only silk featured in our list. His "indefatigable nature and all-round knowledge" set him apart.

WESTERN CIRCUIT

LEADING SILKS • Western

1	SHARP Christopher	St John's Chambers
	WILDBLOOD Stephen	Albion Chambers

For details of these leading barristers see Profiles on page 1353

LEADING JUNIORS • Western

1	BROMILOW Richard	St John's Chambers
	DIXON Ralph	2HG Chambers
	DUTHIE Catriona	St John's Chambers
	HYDE Charles	Albion Chambers
	JACKLIN Susan	St John's Chambers
	MILLER Nicholas	Guildhall Chambers
	WILLS-GOLDINGHAM Claire	Albion Chambers
2	CORFIELD Sheelagh	St John's Chambers
	HORTON Mark	Colleton Chambers
	KER-REID John	Pump Court Chambers
	MEREDITH George	King's Bench Chambers
3	ALLARDICE Miranda	Pump Court Chambers
	BOYDELL Edward	Pump Court Chambers
	CAMPBELL Susan	Southernhay Chambers
	DASHWOOD Robert	17 Carlton Crescent
	DINAN-HAYWARD Deborah	Albion Chambers
	NAISH Christopher	Southernhay Chambers

For details of these leading barristers see Profiles on page 1353

Billeted at Albion Chambers, **Stephen Wildblood QC** is rated as "top of the tree" and lauded as "brilliant in conference with clients." Juniors at the set include **Charles Hyde**, who "wins over the court with his eloquence and detailed preparation," care expert **Claire Wills-Goldingham** (see p.1500) ("a tough nut to crack") and **Deborah Dinan-Hayward** whose "fluent address" has not gone unnoticed among both solicitors and clients. At St John's Chambers, **Christopher Sharp QC** (see p.1476) "rivals the very best" and has "superb attention to detail," while **Richard Bromilow** is "a tidy performer much in demand." **Susan Jacklin** (see p.1423) has a catholic practice embracing children issues, Inheritance Act cases and ancillary relief, and "rarely if ever takes a weak point." Children specialist **Sheelagh Corfield** is typical of other gifted juniors at a set that has received a boost with the arrival of **Catriona Duthie**, "a punchy advocate who always infuses her cases with a bit of oomph." Southernhay Chambers houses **Susan Campbell** (see p.1376), "a master of diplomacy in difficult cases," and **Chris Naish** (see p.1452), who has fostered strong links with local authorities. The set has recently lost the services of **George Meredith** in the child care world; he has gone to King's Bench Chambers in Plymouth. In Winchester, Pump Court Chambers has a trio of effective juniors, recommended by both peers and instructing solicitors: **John Ker-Reid** (see p.1428) is a "serious worker" heavily instructed by guardians but with a mixed practice similar to that of the "doughty" **Miranda Allardice** (see p.1356); while **Edward Boydell** (see p.1370) is more finance-based, often acting for clients from the agricultural community. Rounding out the picture, at Guildhall Chambers **Nicholas Miller** is "a financial expert any set would be proud to call its own" whilst at Colleton Chambers the respected **Mark Horton**'s (see p.1419) field of endeavour is predominantly child care. In an interesting twist, **Ralph Dixon** (see p.1390), has moved to 2HG Chambers, a modern set based on new technology, and retains his reputation as "a barrister who presents excellently

FAMILY

Research The rankings are based on in-depth interviews with 6,582 solicitors, barristers and clients in the UK. **Chambers'** research is audited by the British Market Research Bureau (see page 7).

BARRISTERS' PROFILES ▶ See pages 1353-1504

and has climbed up the ladder on pure merit." **Robert Dashwood** of 17 Carlton Crescent remains respected; he has close ties to the London set, Renaissance Chambers.

WALES & CHESTER CIRCUIT

LEADING SILKS • Wales & Chester

1	CROWLEY Jane	30 Park Place
2	BISHOP Malcolm	30 Park Place
	EVANS Mark	Temple Chambers
	NEW SILKS	
	TILLYARD James	30 Park Place

For details of these leading barristers see Profiles on page 1353

LEADING JUNIORS • Wales & Chester

1	FURNESS Jonathan	30 Park Place
	MIFFLIN Helen	30 Park Place
2	ALLEN Mark	30 Park Place
3	HENKE Ruth	30 Park Place
	MORGAN Lynne	Temple Chambers
	WALTERS Jill	30 Park Place

For details of these leading barristers see Profiles on page 1353

30 Park Place continues to dominate the scene and is proving an irresistible draw for those barristers anxious to establish a heavyweight family practice. Its leading luminaries are **Jane Crowley QC**, a children expert "who has the full confidence of many a local authority," and **Malcolm Bishop QC**, who has a sound name in wardship. Newly elevated to silk, **James Tillyard QC** shines in finance cases where he exhibits his "direct, penetrating analysis." Among the juniors, the "excellent preparation" of **Jonathan Furness** and **Helen Mifflin**'s (see p.1447) "tact and compassion" in care work were commended to researchers, as were **Mark Allen**'s client-handling skills. Indicative of the set's appeal, two barristers have made the pilgrimage from rival sets in the past year. **Ruth Henke** (see p.1414) has brought her "enviable mixed practice" from Iscoed Chambers, whilst **Jill Walters** has arrived from 33 Park Place and continues to be engaged with work on behalf of the Official Solicitor. Temple Chambers is now home to **Mark Evans QC** (see p.1396), formerly active on the Western Circuit. "Laid back, his relaxed manner disguises a powerhouse of effort and determination." He shares chambers with **Lynne Morgan**, similarly "easy-going" but "with the results to justify a top billing."

MIDLANDS CIRCUIT

LEADING SILKS • Midlands

1	MACUR Julia	St. Ive's Chambers
	NEW SILKS	
	HERSHMAN David	St Philips Chambers
	KEEHAN Michael	St. Ive's Chambers

For details of these leading barristers see Profiles on page 1353

St. Ive's Chambers has a pair of headline practitioners in **Julia Macur QC** whose "mixed practice is unrivalled by most," and **Michael Keehan QC** (see p.1427), "a practitioner of steely resolve." Observers singled out child care expert **Margaret Hodgson** (see p.1418) as its leading junior. At No 5 Chambers, **Stephanie Brown** "goes through fat briefs like a hot knife through butter," while **Ros Bush** "never turns her care cases into fee-building exercises." **Robin Rowland** has a firm grasp of figures and "takes a tough negotiating stance," displaying a tenacity shared by the "helpful and grimly determined" **Anne Smallwood**. **Christopher James** continues

LEADING JUNIORS • Midlands

1	BROWN Stephanie	No 5 Chambers
	BUSH Rosalind	No 5 Chambers
	HODGSON Margaret	St. Ive's Chambers
	ROGERS Mark	St. Mary's Chambers
	ROWLAND Robin	No 5 Chambers
	SMALLWOOD Anne	No 5 Chambers
	THOMAS Sybil	3 Fountain Court
2	CASEY Mairin	St. Mary's Chambers
	FARQUHAR Stuart	St. Mary's Chambers
	JAMES Christopher	No 5 Chambers
3	BUCHANAN Vivien	St. Mary's Chambers
	BUTLER Christopher	St. Mary's Chambers
	GILEAD Beryl	St. Mary's Chambers
	MEYER Lorna	No 5 Chambers
	PAGE Nigel	St. Mary's Chambers
	SOMERVILLE Bryce	No.6 Fountain Court
	UP AND COMING	
	DUFFY Joanne	No 5 Chambers

For details of these leading barristers see Profiles on page 1353

to receive praise for his ancillary relief practice, while **Joanne Duffy** and **Lorna Meyer** both show "great promise" in handling their respective finance and children practices. In Nottingham, St Mary's Chambers has juniors to match the best in the region: **Mark Rogers** approaches finance and children cases in a "consistently resolute" fashion; **Mairin Casey** has "just the right blend of sensitivity and dispassion" for her child care cases; and **Stuart Farquhar** has "an economy of expression that goes down well with the judges." **Vivien Buchanan**'s mixed public and private law practice wins her many admirers among the local solicitors who further favour **Christopher Butler** as he is "no stranger to the big-ticket financial cases." Also present are **Beryl Gilead**, highly rated for her expertise in children work, and **Nigel Page** who appears on the finance side. At St Philips Chambers, **David Hershman QC** (see p.1415) is an expert on child care and abduction who "has been on the target list of other sets of chambers for many years." At 3 Fountain Court, **Sybil Thomas** (see p.1490) is lauded as "single-minded and intensive," while at No.6 Fountain Court, **Bryce Somerville** merits inclusion in our tables for being "sensible, calm and yet tough in negotiation."

NORTH EASTERN CIRCUIT

LEADING SILKS • North Eastern

1	BRADLEY Sally	York Chambers
	HAMILTON Eleanor	No.6 Barristers Chambers

For details of these leading barristers see Profiles on page 1353

In Newcastle, doyenne of the local bar, **Sally Bradley QC** is "a great thinker," strong on public law matters. Trinity Chambers is home to **Christopher Knox** (see p.1430), who is "great for ancillary relief where large assets are involved," the "assiduous and dogged" **James Richardson** (see p.1468) and the "energetic" **Rachel Hudson** (see p.1421). Rival Broad Chare Chambers is represented by **Ian Kennerley**, a barrister "well clued-up and always ready to take on a complex case," and finance and child care specialist **Kester Armstrong**. In Leeds, **Eleanor Hamilton QC** continues to be "head and shoulders above the rest" on the big financial matters, where she exhibits "real vivacity and a genuine interest." She is occasionally seen in tandem with respected junior **Adam Wilson**. **Paul Isaacs** (see p.1422) of Mercury Chambers leads the way among the juniors, as "a silk in everything but name whose swashbuckling style has unmanned many a potential rival." Such is his reputation that he gener-

FAMILY

Research The rankings are based on in-depth interviews with 6,582 solicitors, barristers and clients in the UK. **Chambers'** research is audited by the British Market Research Bureau (see page 7)

BARRISTERS' PROFILES ▶ See pages 1353-1504

LEADING JUNIORS • North Eastern

★	ISAACS Paul	Mercury Chambers
1	CAHILL Sally	Park Lane Chambers
	KENNERLEY Ian	Broad Chare Chambers
	KNOX Christopher	Trinity Chambers
2	BICKERDIKE Roger	Zenith Chambers
	COHEN Raphael	Mercury Chambers
	GLOVER Stephen	37 Park Square
	HAJIMITSIS Anthony	Zenith Chambers
	WOOD Martin	Broadway House
3	ARMSTRONG Kester	Broad Chare Chambers
	HUDSON Rachel	Trinity Chambers
	LIGHTWING Stuart	Counsel's Chambers
	PYE Jayne	Sovereign Chambers
	RICHARDSON James	Trinity Chambers
	SHELTON Gordon	Broadway House
	THORNTON Rebecca	Zenith Chambers
	WILSON Adam	No.6 Barristers Chambers

For details of these leading barristers see Profiles on page 1353

ates enormous amounts of work. **Raphael Cohen** (see p.1382) is considered by solicitors to be "a hit with judges and clients alike." At Park Lane Chambers, **Sally Cahill**'s "address to the court is never frivolous," while **Stephen Glover** (see p.1406) of 37 Park Square "isn't frightened to square up to the opposition." Zenith Chambers calls upon the undoubted talents of **Roger Bickerdike** (see p.1365), "a breath of fresh air" who is "often led by the best in care proceedings." Also in situ here are "wise counsel" **Anthony Hajimitsis** and **Rebecca Thornton** (see p.1491), "a venerated character who never takes duff points." Completing the picture is **Jayne Pye** of Sovereign Chambers who "understands the day-to-day needs of the client." Elsewhere, **Stuart Lightwing** (see p.1436) of Counsel's Chambers in Middlesbrough does well on the finance front, while **Gordon Shelton** of Broadway House in Bradford retains market support. His colleague **Martin Wood** (see p.1502) is further commended as being "an excellent choice for a fight."

NORTHERN CIRCUIT

LEADING SILKS • Northern

1	RYDER Ernest	Deans Court Chambers
2	DE HAAS Margaret	7 Harrington Street Chambers

For details of these leading barristers see Profiles on page 1353

LEADING JUNIORS • Northern

1	BOOTH Alan	Deans Court Chambers
2	BANCROFT Louise	Deans Court Chambers
	DODDS Stephen	15 Winckley Square
	GAL Sonia	28 St John St
	HARRISON Sally	28 St John St
	SANDER Andrew	Oriel Chambers
	WALLWORK Bernard	28 St John St
3	ASHWORTH Fiona	40 King St
	BENNETT Martyn	Oriel Chambers
	DUGGAN Ross	India Buildings Chambers
	EDGE Timothy	Deans Court Chambers
	HEATON Frances	Deans Court Chambers
	JOHNSON Christine	14 Castle Street
	KENNEDY Michael	India Buildings Chambers
	OWEN Gail	India Buildings Chambers
	READE Kevin	7 Harrington Street Chambers
	SINGLETON Sarah	28 St John St
	WALKER Jane	28 St John St

For details of these leading barristers see Profiles on page 1353

Liverpool's India Buildings Chambers contains a number of gifted juniors, especially in the children area. Famed for its connections with local authorities, it fields **Gail Owen**, "veteran of media-worthy children cases," "guardian's choice" **Michael Kennedy** and part-time Recorder **Ross Duggan**. The city also contains Oriel Chambers, home to "financial expert and good numbers man" **Andrew Sander** and **Martyn Bennett**, "a great choice for the high-value cases." Other renowned figures include "personable" **Christine Johnson** (see p.1425) of 14 Castle Street and the much more senior **Margaret de Haas QC** (see p.1389) of 7 Harrington Street Chambers, "a barrister to instruct if your life depends on it." She is a stablemate of the respected **Kevin Reade**. In Manchester, **Ernest Ryder QC** (see p.1472) of Deans Court Chambers is the "clear pick of the bunch." "A strong character," he "pushes the issues through" and is recommended both for finance and children cases. He has the luxury of being in a set blessed with fine juniors of the likes of **Alan Booth** (see p.1368) whose "preparation and conference technique are second to none," and **Louise Bancroft** (see p.1360) who is "a great battler." **Tim Edge** and children expert **Frances Heaton** (see p.1413) also enjoy the backing of local solicitors. The set is matched in terms of quality by local rival 28 St John St where **Sonia Gal** is "good at looking at the wider picture" and has, in common with the "unsinkable" **Sally Harrison**, "considerable commercial acumen." **Bernard Wallwork**'s "sweet and gentle bedside manner" was alluded to by commentators, as was the "calmness under fire" of both **Jane Walker** and **Sarah Singleton**. **Fiona Ashworth** (see p.1358) of 40 King St and **Stephen Dodds** of 15 Winckley Square ("an amazing force") were also commended to our researchers.

www.ChambersandPartners.com

FINANCIAL SERVICES

Research The rankings are based on in-depth interviews with 6,582 solicitors, barristers and clients in the UK. **Chambers'** research is audited by the British Market Research Bureau (see page 7)

BARRISTERS' PROFILES ▶ See pages 1353-1504

FINANCIAL SERVICES • London

		QCs	Jnrs
1	Blackstone Chambers (Baxendale/Flint)	2	-
	Erskine Chambers (Robin Potts QC)	2	1
	Four New Square (Justin Fenwick QC)	1	1
	4 Stone Buildings (Philip Heslop QC)	4	1
	3 Verulam Buildings (Symons/Jarvis)	2	-

Numbers show recommended barristers in this practice area

LEADING SILKS • London

1	BLAIR Michael	3 Verulam Buildings
	BLAIR William	3 Verulam Buildings
	FLINT Charles	Blackstone Chambers
	POTTS Robin	Erskine Chambers
	POWELL John	Four New Square
	SUMPTION Jonathan	Brick Court Chambers
2	BRIGGS Michael	Serle Court
	BRINDLE Michael	Fountain Court
	DOHMANN Barbara	Blackstone Chambers
3	BOMPAS Anthony	4 Stone Buildings
	BRISBY John	4 Stone Buildings
	HESLOP Philip	4 Stone Buildings
	HILDYARD Robert	4 Stone Buildings
	RICHARDS David	Erskine Chambers

For details of these leading barristers see Profiles on page 1353

LEADING JUNIORS • London

1	LOMNICKA Eva	Four New Square
2	MARQUAND Charles	4 Stone Buildings
	SNOWDEN Richard	Erskine Chambers

For details of these leading barristers see Profiles on page 1353

OVERVIEW: Financial services related matters continue to pepper the typically corporate-based workloads of counsel, who feature as specialists in this sector. Advisory work at the Bar remains limited and is generally restricted to discrete aspects or situations involving high stakes, or where secondary or confirmatory opinion is required. There is, however, prevailing demand at the highest level for advice on the CCA and consumer-related financial products. In the climate of a general lull in contested regulatory decisions, solicitors seek specialist counsel in disciplinary actions relating to the conduct of litigation and tactical issues. Within the low-key environment of a tribunal, their utility attaches principally to those that involve witnesses and or esoteric areas of law, such as further rights under human rights legislation. Junior counsel is favoured for advocacy work on retail-oriented claims such as demutualisation, pensions mis-selling and endowment mortgage disputes, although the Ombudsman's involvement renders a large proportion of potential disputes "courts and JR-proof."

LONDON

BLACKSTONE CHAMBERS (see full details p.1515) "A favourite" with City practices because its leaders have a "sensible, down-to-earth" approach. Joint head of chambers **Charles Flint QC** (see p.1398) enjoys a "well-established reputation" in acting for and against self-regulating organisations on judicial review, disciplinary proceedings and Companies Act investigations. Solicitors extol his "thorough, confidence-inspiring advice" and "intelligent approach on tactics," while opponents describe him as a "hard fighting litigator." "A real fighter who's been at it for ages," **Barbara Dohmann QC** (see p.1390) is endorsed by her peers for displaying "enormous commitment" to her clients, which include regulators on disciplinary matters. She acted for the claimant in Personal Investment Authority v National Westminster Bank.

ERSKINE CHAMBERS (see full details p.1529) This set "always provides excellent opinions and top service," according to leading solicitors. Endorsing chambers head **Robin Potts QC** (see p.1462) as "your man if you want confident, robust advice," they point to his company law expertise as "added value for understanding the dynamics of the problem." Peers also describe his advocacy skills as "superb." Solicitors also approve of **David Richards QC**'s (see p.1468) "cautious, detailed analysis of issues" and "strongly practical approach," while singling out **Richard Snowden** (see p.1480) as a "knowledgeable, industrious" junior with whom they can "chat through the issues."

FOUR NEW SQUARE (see full details p.1576) Co-authors of the *Encyclopaedia of Financial Services Law*, **John Powell QC** (see p.1462) and his wife, **Eva Lomnicka** (see p.1438), are the best-known FS experts in this set. Equally regarded as a "supreme professional negligence exponent," Powell QC primarily advises on tax-driven collective investment schemes and regulatory aspects of limited partnership schemes. Describing him as "well-prepared and client-friendly," solicitors value his ability to provide "detailed analysis with a practical dimension." Others enthuse that "academically rigorous" Lomnicka "knows so much more about the legislation than anyone in the universe", which enables her to "think ahead and bring to bear changes in the pipeline in her response."

4 STONE BUILDINGS (see full details p.1606) Adjudged by market sources as an "impressive stable" of general company law specialists, with broad practices covering financial services and contractual matters. Clients describe head of chambers **Philip Heslop QC** as "extremely user-friendly and knowledgeable," and one who retains a "highly respected" reputation in the field. "Tenacious to the nth degree," **John Brisby QC** (see p.1372) is admired for his ability to "get up to speed rapidly" and dispense "gritty" advice. Interviewees also endorsed **Anthony Bompas QC** (see p.1368) and **Robert Hildyard QC** (see p.1415) as "respected counsel with in-depth knowledge," despite having lower focus on the area. Enjoying a strong following among leading US law firms, former Treasury Solicitor **Charles Marquand** (see p.1442) wins accolades from solicitors for his user-friendly approach and possessing the "benefit of the inside track."

3 VERULAM BUILDINGS (see full details p.1615) The set handles financial services work as an integral part of its "well-recognised" banking expertise. **Michael Blair QC** (see p.1367) has been "at the hub of it all" as former general counsel of the Financial Services Authority. He is leading practitioners' "prime choice for a technical answer to a tricky problem" – not least because he "knows the regulations backwards!" Part-time Chair of the Financial Services and Markets Association Tribunal, **William Blair QC** (see p.1367) is "immensely bright on regulatory matters" and "extremely constructive in looking for solutions," according to solicitors. One confided "it's great if he's on your side because you can be pretty sure the FSA will listen."

OTHER NOTABLE PRACTITIONERS Perennially regarded as being "in a class of his own" because he can apparently "do anything," **Jonathan Sumption QC** at Brick Court Chambers is well known for his involvement in major disciplinary actions. "Top client advisor" **Michael Briggs QC** (see p.1371) at Serle Court Chambers receives solicitors' endorsement for being "extremely good at whatever you involve him in." He acted on the directors' disqualification following the Barings collapse. Leading lawyers commend **Michael Brindle QC** (see p.1372) at Fountain Court for his "first-class judgement on public policy issues" and "sterling" advice on money laundering and insider dealing matters.

FRAUD

Research The rankings are based on in-depth interviews with 6,582 solicitors, barristers and clients in the UK. **Chambers'** research is audited by the British Market Research Bureau (see page 7)

BARRISTERS' PROFILES ▶ See pages 1353-1504

LONDON — CRIMINAL

FRAUD: CRIMINAL • London	QCs	Jnrs
1 Hollis Whiteman Chambers (Bevan/Whiteman)	9	5
2 3 Raymond Buildings (Clive Nicholls QC)	5	3
3 2 Bedford Row (William Clegg QC)	4	5
9-12 Bell Yard (D Anthony Evans QC)	2	3
23 Essex Street (Michael Lawson QC)	3	-
18 Red Lion Court (Anthony Arlidge QC)	4	-
4 6 King's Bench Walk (Roy Amlot QC)	1	1
5 Paper Buildings (Carey/Caplan)	2	-

Numbers show recommended barristers in this practice area

HOLLIS WHITEMAN CHAMBERS (see full details p.1559) "One of the best jury advocates around," **Julian Bevan QC** (see p.1365) elicits praise for his "knack of being incredibly friendly and leading you by the hand in a non-patronising way." Possessed of "real personality," **John Kelsey-Fry QC** (see p.1428) was described as "an advocate in the mould of George Carman QC." The bulk of his practice is defence, and it has included representation of Andrew Regan. **Anthony Glass QC** (see p.1405) is a "tenacious and thorough operator." "Much underrated" **Timothy Langdale QC** (see p.1431) "has all the assets to deal with a wide range of cases" and is "a devastating cross-examiner." **David Evans QC** (see p.1395) is a favourite for the most complex cases, while **William Boyce QC** (see p.1369) possesses "a great eye for detail." "Hard-working and meticulous," both barristers and solicitors agreed "you can guarantee every angle will be well thought out." "Tough" **Vivian Robinson QC** (see p.1469) "will go the extra mile." **Peter Kyte QC** (see p.1431) is best known for his pure criminal expertise, but remains popular for fraud cases. **Alan Suckling QC** (see p.1485) retains the respect of his peers. Solicitors lauded **Ian Winter** (see p.1501) as a "superstar" for his lateral thinking and great presence in court, a trait also shared by **Mark Ellison** (see p.1395). Esteemed **Tom Kark** (see p.1426) is now standing counsel to HM Customs and Excise. Sources singled out **Gareth Rees** (see p.1467) as "one of the top advocates for fraud." He also undertakes advisory work for companies, and is continuing his representation of Moore on the Jubilee Line fraud. **Ian Stern** (see p.1483) remains a respected junior for fraud matters.

3 RAYMOND BUILDINGS (see full details p.1596) Renowned for his work in straight crime, **Stephen Batten QC** (see p.1363) retains the respect of leading fraud solicitors as "a powerful cross-examiner with a hypnotic presence in court." Some sources find **Alun Jones QC** (see p.1425) on occasion "irascible," but to all quarters he remains "immensely dedicated and exceptionally talented on complex technical cases." **Clive Nicholls QC** (see p.1454) is "the crème de la crème in extradition matters," which has seen him acting on the Pinochet case. His multi-jurisdictional abilities encompass mutual assistance, money laundering and confiscations. **David Whitehouse QC** (see p.1499) brings a broad base of skills to fraud matters. **Colin Nicholls QC** (see p.1454) maintains his excellent reputation for his work in the mutual assistance arena. **Alex Cameron** (see p.1375) possesses "an impressive court and client manner," while **Simon Farrell** (see p.1396) "always spots the unusual points and will get stuck in and argue well." Interviewees also commended the "incredibly bright" **Helen Malcolm**.

2 BEDFORD ROW (see full details p.1509) **William Clegg QC** (see p.1381) is "a good all-rounder," who enjoys "one of the best track records in the business." Solicitors appreciate that he is "not intimidated by judges." **Jonathan Ashley-Norman** (see p.1358) employs an approach

LEADING SILKS • London

★	BEVAN Julian	Hollis Whiteman Chambers
	LAWSON Edmund	9-12 Bell Yard
	MONTGOMERY Clare	Matrix Chambers
	PURNELL Nicholas	23 Essex Street
1	ARLIDGE Anthony	18 Red Lion Court
	BATTEN Stephen	3 Raymond Buildings
	GLASS Anthony	Hollis Whiteman Chambers
	JONES Alun	3 Raymond Buildings
	KELSEY-FRY John	Hollis Whiteman Chambers
	LANGDALE Timothy	Hollis Whiteman Chambers
	NICHOLLS Clive	3 Raymond Buildings
	TROLLOPE Andrew	187 Fleet Street
2	AMLOT Roy	6 King's Bench Walk
	CLEGG William	2 Bedford Row
	EVANS David	Hollis Whiteman Chambers
	HILL Michael	23 Essex Street
	MACDONALD Ken	Matrix Chambers
	MITCHELL Andrew	Furnival Chambers
3	GRIEVE Michael	Doughty Street Chambers
	HACKETT Philip	2 Bedford Row
	LISSACK Richard	35 Essex Street
	NICHOLLS Colin	3 Raymond Buildings
	ROBINSON Vivian	Hollis Whiteman Chambers
	ROOK Peter	18 Red Lion Court
	SINGH Kuldip	5 Paper Buildings
	SOLLEY Stephen	Charter Chambers
	WHITEHOUSE David	3 Raymond Buildings
4	BOWES Michael	2 King's Bench Walk
	BOYCE William	Hollis Whiteman Chambers
	CAPLAN Jonathan	5 Paper Buildings
	CHAWLA Mukul	9-12 Bell Yard
	ETHERINGTON David	18 Red Lion Court
	GODFREY Howard	2 Bedford Row
	KYTE Peter	Hollis Whiteman Chambers
	LATHAM Richard	7 Bedford Row
	LYNCH Jerome	Charter Chambers
	MISKIN Charles	23 Essex Street
	SHAW Antony	18 Red Lion Court
	SUCKLING Alan	Hollis Whiteman Chambers
	NEW SILKS	
	STURMAN Jim	2 Bedford Row

For details of these leading barristers see Profiles on page 1353

LEADING JUNIORS • London

1	CAMERON Alexander	3 Raymond Buildings
	PERRY David	6 King's Bench Walk
	WINTER Ian	Hollis Whiteman Chambers
2	ELLISON Mark	Hollis Whiteman Chambers
	STAFFORD-MICHAEL Simon	4 King's Bench Walk
3	KARK Tom	Hollis Whiteman Chambers
	REES Gareth	Hollis Whiteman Chambers
4	ALTMAN Brian	2 Bedford Row
	ASHLEY-NORMAN Jonathan	2 Bedford Row
	EGAN Michael	9-12 Bell Yard
	FARRELL Simon	3 Raymond Buildings
	INGRAM Nigel	2 Bedford Row
	LUCAS Noel	187 Fleet Street
	MALCOLM Helen	3 Raymond Buildings
5	HEALY Alexandra	9-12 Bell Yard
	MATTHEWS Richard	2 Bedford Row
	POPLE Alison	2 Bedford Row
	RUSSELL Christina	9-12 Bell Yard
	STERN Ian	Hollis Whiteman Chambers
	WINBERG Stephen	2-4 Tudor Street

For details of these leading barristers see Profiles on page 1353

FRAUD

Research The rankings are based on in-depth interviews with 6,582 solicitors, barristers and clients in the UK. **Chambers'** research is audited by the British Market Research Bureau (see page 7)

BARRISTERS' PROFILES ▶ See pages 1353-1504

that is "honest and straightforward," impressing many as a "thorough and dedicated practitioner." **Philip Hackett QC** (see p.1410) is a "tough cross-examiner," and one "never overwhelmed by the detail." **Howard Godfrey QC** (see p.1406) combines "courtroom skills with a technical understanding of the issues." New silk **Jim Sturman QC** (see p.1485) peppers his fine criminal practice with complex fraud matters. Amongst the juniors, **Brian Altman** (see p.1356) stands out for his "confidence" in the courtroom, while **Nigel Ingram**'s "calming influence" is admired by all, and **Richard Matthews** (see p.1443) is a "highly competent performer." **Alison Pople** (see p.1462) makes an entry to the tables this year, commended by solicitors as "a star of the future."

9-12 BELL YARD (see full details p.1514) Interviewees commended **Ed Lawson QC** as "head and shoulders above the market" for fraud, while remaining "completely approachable." He is defending the chief executive of Wickes. **Mukul Chawla QC** (see p.1379) has "an attractive advocacy style," which "commands the attention of all." **Alexandra Healy** (see p.1413) is a new entrant to our tables this year; she "keeps in tune with every matter," with a tough advocacy style that "never once is pompous." **Michael Egan** has attracted "some interesting cases," while fraud defence junior **Christina Russell** joins him in the tables following commendations portraying her as "incredibly clever on paper as well as a fine advocate."

23 ESSEX STREET (see full details p.1535) The set enjoys the skills of **Nick Purnell QC** (see p.1465), a barrister blessed with a "phenomenal memory." Solicitors pegged him as the man for the most complex cases: he is "the master and he knows it." **Charles Miskin QC** is thought to be "courageous in battle," while **Michael Hill QC**'s (see p.1416) style takes an "aggressive tone," which has attracted a number of supporters.

18 RED LION COURT (see full details p.1598) This set remains home to a raft of "talented criminal barristers," many of whom incorporate fraud into their remit. Among a clutch of respected silks, **Anthony Arlidge QC** (see p.1358) received unanimous support as "an exceptionally skilled advocate." "Jury-friendly," he has strong communication skills and "always knows which issues to pursue." **Antony Shaw QC** (see p.1476) is a familiar sight on the biggest of cases. **Peter Rook QC** (see p.1470) has won a following for his "utter thoroughness; his preparation is second to none," while **David Etherington QC** (see p.1395) retains a high profile in the marketplace.

6 KING'S BENCH WALK (see full details p.1563) A criminal barrister of stellar repute, it is no surprise to find **Roy Amlot QC** (see p.1356) is a popular choice for fraud matters. "Immensely able," his absolute dedication lead some to perceive him as "rather stern," although they praise his capacity to handle heavyweight cases. Researchers were impressed with the level of commendation for the "absolute star" **David Perry**; his broad-based skills have led many to consider him a "first port of call."

5 PAPER BUILDINGS (see full details p.1589) The set remains commended for its understanding of HM Customs and Excise matters. Head of chambers **Jonathan Caplan QC** (see p.1376) is a leading figure "blessed with eloquence and an analytical mind." **Kuldip Singh** is a popular criminal barrister, respected for his "ablity to explain things in layman's terms."

OTHER NOTABLE PRACTITIONERS Richard Latham QC (see p.1432) of 7 Bedford Row has impressed solicitors with his "good brain and excellent delivery." At 35 Essex Street, **Richard Lissack QC** (see p.1436) is respected for his commercial nous. **Andrew Trollope QC** (see p.1493)of 187 Fleet Street "controls the fattest brief with consummate ease," while at the same set **Noel Lucas** (see p.1439) is respected as standing counsel to HM Customs and Excise. **Andrew Mitchell QC** (see p.1448) of Furnival Chambers is respected for his knowledge of customs-related frauds. At Doughty Street Chambers, **Michael Grieve QC** is thought to display a "mastery of the courtroom," an asset shared by the "quick-witted" **Stephen Solley QC** of Charter Chambers. At the same set, **Jerome Lynch QC** brings "authority to a brief," while solicitors believe that **Michael Bowes QC** (see p.1369) of 2 King's Bench Walk has taken well to silk. Interviewees enthused about the work of **Clare Montgomery QC** of Matrix Chambers: she is "one of the crème de la crème," whose advocacy skills "overwhelm all before her." Her fraud expertise encompasses both criminal and civil matters. **Ken Macdonald QC** (see p.1439) at this set is a "force to be reckoned with" and one who "lends himself to the detail." At 2-4 Tudor Street, **Stephen Winberg**'s "robust advocacy" has won him many fans. **Simon Stafford-Michael** (see p.1482) of 4 King's Bench Walk is a "fantastic lateral thinker with a fiery personality."

LONDON — CIVIL

FRAUD: CIVIL • London	QCs	Jnrs
1 One Essex Court (Anthony Grabiner QC)	5	2
Fountain Court (Anthony Boswood QC)	3	1
3 Verulam Buildings (Symons/Jarvis)	3	2
2 Blackstone Chambers (Baxendale/Flint)	2	-
Brick Court Chambers (Christopher Clarke QC)	2	-
Serle Court (Patrick Neill QC)	2	-

Numbers show recommended barristers in this practice area

ONE ESSEX COURT (see full details p.1531) **Anthony Grabiner QC** was praised for his "ability to lead the judge through a morass of conflicting evidence," a trait shared by **Elizabeth Gloster QC** (see p.1406). With an "absolutely stunning intellect," she is described as "luminary" of her chambers, while fraud and asset tracing are part of her wider commercial repertoire. "Brain of Britain" **Mark Barnes QC** (see p.1362) possesses "an ability to absorb matters quickly; he really knows the law." **Christopher Carr QC** (see p.1377) is "a flamboyant advocate with an instinctive flair for strategy." New silk **Laurence Rabinowitz QC** (see p.1465) was also deemed a strong performer, both in court and on paper, while **Anthony de Garr Robinson** (see p.1388) "is a delight to work with as well as being technically very able." Solicitors appreciate that **John McCaughran** (see p.1444) brings his "immense efficiency and clear head" to each case.

FOUNTAIN COURT (see full details p.1541) This strongly commercial set boasts a roster of barristers who encompass fraud as part of their wider practice. "At the heart of the commercial Bar" sits **Michael Brindle QC** (see p.1372), who is said to be "everyone's first choice" thanks to his "first-class mind and good judgement on public policy issues." **Anthony Boswood QC** (see p.1368) retains the commendation of solicitors as "practical and commercial," while **Nicholas Stadlen QC** (see p.1482) is "a tenacious litigator," who wins a following with his "calming presence." He represents both claimants and defendants and is acting on Prince Mohamad Bin Fahad Bin Abdulaziz Al Saud v Said Ayas, and First Union National Bank v Arab Banking Corporation. Many solicitors predict that **Bankim Thanki** (see p.1489) is "soon for silk," endowed as he is with the qualities of "great intellect and gravitas."

3 VERULAM BUILDINGS (see full details p.1615) "Hugley experienced and an excellent strategist," **Ian Geering QC** (see p.1403) possesses "an

FRAUD

Research The rankings are based on in-depth interviews with 6,582 solicitors, barristers and clients in the UK. **Chambers'** research is audited by the British Market Research Bureau (see page 7)

BARRISTERS' PROFILES ▶ See pages 1353-1504

LEADING SILKS • London

1
BRINDLE Michael	Fountain Court
FLINT Charles	Blackstone Chambers

2
COHEN Lawrence	24 Old Buildings
GEERING Ian	3 Verulam Buildings
GRABINER Anthony	One Essex Court
SUMPTION Jonathan	Brick Court Chambers

3
BOSWOOD Anthony	Fountain Court
BRIGGS Michael	Serle Court
BROWNE-WILKINSON Simon	Serle Court
DOHMANN Barbara	Blackstone Chambers
GLOSTER Elizabeth	One Essex Court
MALEK Ali	3 Verulam Buildings
MONTGOMERY Clare	Matrix Chambers
POLLOCK Gordon	Essex Court Chambers
PURLE Charles	New Square Chambers
STADLEN Nicholas	Fountain Court

4
BARNES Mark	One Essex Court
BRISBY John	4 Stone Buildings
CARR Christopher	One Essex Court
POPPLEWELL Andrew	Brick Court Chambers
ROSEN Murray	11 Stone Buildings

5
CROXFORD Ian	Wilberforce Chambers
JARVIS John	3 Verulam Buildings
SINGH Kuldip	5 Paper Buildings
SMITH Stephen	New Square Chambers

NEW SILKS
DICKER Robin	3-4 South Square
RABINOWITZ Laurence	One Essex Court

For details of these leading barristers see Profiles on page 1353

LEADING JUNIORS • London

1
DE GARR ROBINSON Anthony	One Essex Court
MCCAUGHRAN John	One Essex Court
MCQUATER Ewan	3 Verulam Buildings
THANKI Bankim	Fountain Court

2
BELTRAMI Adrian	3 Verulam Buildings
SMOUHA Joe	Essex Court Chambers

For details of these leading barristers see Profiles on page 1353

---

done." Focusing on commercial fraud, including asset recovery and interlocutory relief, he represented the beneficiaries of the trust of Grupo Torras.

BLACKSTONE CHAMBERS (see full details p.1515) **Charles Flint QC** (see p.1398) "does a lot and deserves his position." The Prince Jefri of Brunei and Abacha cases have occupied a lot of his time of late. The "practical and straightforward" **Barbara Dohmann QC** (see p.1390) retains a reputation for being "straight-talking and effective."

BRICK COURT CHAMBERS (see full details p.1517) The set boasts the presence of **Jonathan Sumption QC**, who solicitors like "because of the size of his brain, pure and simple," but many opine "he's so busy it's hard to get hold of him." **Andrew Popplewell QC** (see p.1462) impresses as "both practical and commercial."

SERLE COURT (see full details p.1602) A "powerful" commercial silk, **Michael Briggs QC**'s (see p.1371) "smooth approach" to the most complex of cases has afforded him a reputation for fraud amid his chancery and general commercial litigation expertise. Solicitors applauded **Simon Browne-Wilkinson QC** as "a pleasure to deal with."

OTHER NOTABLE PRACTITIONERS Essex Court Chambers houses "a powerful advocate" in **Gordon Pollock QC** (see p.1461). He "can lecture to the court and get away with it," and he is also endowed with a unique presence that ensures that "judges listen to him." **Joe Smouha** (see p.1480) of the same chambers is "hard-working and is set to be one of the stars." "Tenacious and determined" **Lawrence Cohen QC** of 24 Old Buildings "has a good eye for detail and gets stuck in without prompting." New Square Chambers plays host to **Charles Purle QC** (see p.1465), who possesses "an extraordinary ability to perform without notes;" he is "incredibly witty with a deep knowledge and understanding of the law." Also at this set, **Stephen Smith QC** (see p.1480) was appreciated by peers and lawyers for being "clever, determined, focused and ferocious in that he never gives up." Banking is also a substantial part of his practice. **Clare Montgomery QC** of Matrix Chambers is one of the few who "successfully crosses over between civil and criminal." She has "a sharp mind and first-rate cross-examination skills." **Murray Rosen QC** (see p.1471) of 11 Stone Buildings was applauded for being "inventive and a fighter with a profound knowledge of his field." At 3-4 South Square, **Robin Dicker QC** (see p.1390) specialises in civil fraud as part of his commercial, business and financial law expertise. Although previously a mainstay in our criminal fraud tables, **Kuldip Singh QC** of 5 Paper Buildings makes an appearance in civil this year as an "industrious and intense advocate" who "understands difficult business concepts." **Ian Croxford QC** of Wilberforce Chambers retains market recommendation, while **John Brisby QC** (see p.1372) of 4 Stone Buildings was praised for his commitment to clients; "he is so determined and never gives up."

awesome knowledge and understanding in fraud matters," while some solicitors feel that "his depth of judgement in the field is unparalleled." **Ali Malek QC** (see p.1440) was deemed "always entertaining and deeply knowledgeable - a clear favourite with clients." He handles a wide range of work for claimants and defendants including the recent case of Montrod v Grundkotter. **John Jarvis QC** (see p.1424) is "a good team leader and a tough advocate." "Experience beyond his years" is a key attribute belonging to **Ewan McQuater** (see p.1445), whose "user-friendly approach" has proved most popular. Stablemate **Adrian Beltrami** (see p.1364) is "a fine draftsman and good on his feet - he rolls up his sleeves and gets the job

HEALTH & SAFETY

Research The rankings are based on in-depth interviews with 6,582 solicitors, barristers and clients in the UK. **Chambers'** research is audited by the British Market Research Bureau (see page 7)

BARRISTERS' PROFILES ▶ See pages 1353-1504

OVERVIEW: The area has seen a high level of activity due in part to a new-style Health & Safety Executive. New entries this year reflect the fact that health and safety is becoming an area of law in its own right with increasing numbers of juniors specialising in this field.

LONDON

1 TEMPLE GARDENS (see full details p.1612) At this general common law practice, which specialises in prosecutions, "old-style advocate" **Hugh Carlisle QC** (see p.1376) has acted on a number of inquiries, including Southall. He remains at the helm of the set, which enjoys the presence of **Ian Burnett QC** (see p.1374), also counsel to the inquiry into Southall. Peers stated "he is first class in whatever he does," while **Dominic Grieve** (see p.1409) is "a good performer, and you can trust him and deal sensibly with him." His practice combines health and safety and pollution prosecutions. A noted expert, **Geoffrey Nice QC** (see p.1454) has been occupied with the Milosevic trial, while the "charming" **Keith Morton** (see p.1450) was also commended by the market; his specialist criminal experience in the field of health and safety is put to good use in defence and prosecution.

2-3 GRAY'S INN SQUARE (see full details p.1548) "A pleasant voice to listen to," **Anthony Scrivener QC** (see p.1475) is renowned for tackling matters from "the union route." **Gerard Forlin** (see p.1399) meanwhile was noted by market experts as "one of the very few workplace manslaughter specialists," who combines a "flamboyant manner" with an "astute and tactically sound" approach.

OLD SQUARE CHAMBERS (see full details p.1583) Our interviewees described **John Hendy QC** (see p.1414) as "a man of the people" who is "a skilled and accomplished practitioner." He acted on behalf of the victims of the Ladbroke Grove Train Crash Inquiry. **Charles Pugh** (see p.1464) has "quite a reputation" in both the defence and prosecution of cases. Adjudged "a class act" by peers, **Michael Ford** (see p.1399) has joined the set from Doughty Street Chambers.

OTHER NOTABLE PRACTITIONERS Kevin de Haan QC (see p.1388) of 3 Raymond Buildings received strong recommendation across the board as "a smooth advocate – brilliant on his feet." He acts for commerce, industry and local authorities in defence and prosecution matters. **Michael de Navarro QC** (see p.1389), head of the personal injury group at 2 Temple Gardens can "cross-examine like a rottweiler." At 2-4 Tudor Street, the "robust and charming" head of chambers **Richard Ferguson QC** (see p.1397), stands out as "a charming advocate." He was counsel to the engineers in the prosecution arising out of the collapse of the gantry under the Severn Bridge. **Neil Garnham QC** (see p.1402) at 1 Crown Office Row and **Richard Lissack QC** (see p.1436) of 35 Essex Street continue to attract the commendation of solicitors, while at the latter set **Stephen Climie** (see p.1381) is "a lightning quick advocate, steeped in health and safety." Focusing on 2 Bedford Row, researchers were struck by the warmth of recommendation for **James Ageros**, who is "a straight operator; his gentle way of prosecuting cuts right through things and is a delight to all." His experience in health and safety matters includes scaffolding collapse, agricultural accidents and construction matters. **Richard Matthews** (see p.1443) also came to the fore; "his paperwork is excellent and he is a great advocate who communicates well with clients." Devereux Chambers boasts **Stephen Killalea** (see p.1429), "a real star" in the eyes of both barristers and solicitors. **David Travers** (see p.1492) of 6 Pump Court is noted as "an expert in the area," while the "Churchillian"

HEALTH & SAFETY • London	QCs	Jnrs
1 1 Temple Gardens (Geoffrey Nice QC)	3	2
2 2-3 Gray's Inn Square (Porten/Scrivener)	1	1
Old Square Chambers (John Hendy QC)	1	2

Numbers show recommended barristers in this practice area

LEADING SILKS • London

1	BURNETT Ian	1 Temple Gardens
2	CARLISLE Hugh	1 Temple Gardens
	DE HAAN Kevin	3 Raymond Buildings
	HENDY John	Old Square Chambers
3	DE NAVARRO Michael	2 Temple Gardens
	FERGUSON Richard	2-4 Tudor Street
	GARNHAM Neil	1 Crown Office Row
	LISSACK Richard	35 Essex Street
	NICE Geoffrey	1 Temple Gardens
	SCRIVENER Anthony	2-3 Gray's Inn Square
	NEW SILKS	
	WAITE Jonathan	Crown Office Chambers

For details of these leading barristers see Profiles on page 1353

LEADING JUNIORS • London

1	AGEROS James	2 Bedford Row
	KILLALEA Stephen	Devereux Chambers
2	GRIEVE Dominic	1 Temple Gardens
	MORTON Keith	1 Temple Gardens
3	CLIMIE Stephen	35 Essex Street
	FORLIN Gerard	2-3 Gray's Inn Square
	MATTHEWS Richard	2 Bedford Row
	TRAVERS David	6 Pump Court
	WOOD Nicholas	5 Paper Buildings
4	EASTMAN Roger	2 Harcourt Buildings
	FORD Michael	Old Square Chambers
	POPAT Prashant	2 Harcourt Buildings
	PUGH Charles	Old Square Chambers

For details of these leading barristers see Profiles on page 1353

Nicholas Wood (see p.1502) of 5 Paper Buildings is respected as "a good competitor and an experienced prosecutor." 2 Harcourt Buildings makes a much deserved entry this year, particularly on the strength of its work in the rail sector. Enjoying what clients described as "a good track record," **Roger Eastman** (see p.1392) was noted as having his "finger on the pulse - he is skilled in the strategy of a case." **Prashant Popat** (see p.1461) was also noted as "superbly bright," while his work on the Ladbroke Grove inquiry has impressed many. New silk at Crown Office Chambers **Jonathan Waite QC** (see p.1496) is known for his focus on industrial accidents and health and safety.

REGIONAL CIRCUITS

"Immaculate preparation, measured advocacy and thorough case preparation" are the attributes ascribed by solicitors to **Henry Globe QC** at Exchange Chambers. **Timothy Horlock QC** (see p.1419) of 9 St. John Street remains a favourite, while at Park Court Chambers, **Robert Smith QC** (see p.1480) was described as "first choice - superb." Making his entrance into the rankings this year, **Oba Nsugbe QC** (see p.1455) at Pump Court Chambers is "thorough, good with clients, positive in attitude; he provides a seamless service." **Neil Cameron** (see p.1376) at Wilberforce Chambers "has the technical grasp; he has always prepared his papers thoroughly and has an excellent argument at the ready." **Barry**

HEALTH & SAFETY

Research The rankings are based on in-depth interviews with 6,582 solicitors, barristers and clients in the UK. **Chambers'** research is audited by the British Market Research Bureau (see page 7)

BARRISTERS' PROFILES ▶ See pages 1353-1504

LEADING SILKS • Regional Circuits

1
GLOBE Henry	Exchange Chambers
HORLOCK Timothy	9 St. John Street

2
SMITH Robert	Park Court Chambers

NEW SILKS
NSUGBE Oba	Pump Court Chambers

For details of these leading barristers see Profiles on page 1353

LEADING JUNIORS • Regional Circuits

1
CAMERON Neil	Wilberforce Chambers
COTTER Barry	Old Square Chambers
LAMBERT Julian	Albion Chambers
LANGDON Andrew	Guildhall Chambers

2
ANTROBUS Simon	40 King St
COOPER John	40 King St
LAWRENCE Nigel	7 Harrington Street Chambers

For details of these leading barristers see Profiles on page 1353

Cotter (see p.1384) at Old Square Chambers maintains his following among solicitors. **Julian Lambert** (see p.1431) at Albion Chambers remains "a walking textbook on corporate manslaughter issues." Guildhall Chambers boasts "a polished performer with an eye for detail" in the form of **Andrew Langdon** (see p.1432). He is "robust, will take a point and stick with it, but is sensible at the same time." New to the tables this year, 40 King Street was noted by clients as "a good regional set providing senior and junior health and safety specialists." A "man to watch," **Simon Antrobus** (see p.1357) has a "client friendly manner" and provides "succinct advice." **John Cooper** (see p.1383) "will muck in as part of the team and always prepares thoroughly." At 7 Harrington Street Chambers, **Nigel Lawrence** (see p.1433) is "an absolute master, he absorbs huge chunks of technical issues quickly and can translate them all into English."

HUMAN RIGHTS

Research The rankings are based on in-depth interviews with 6,582 solicitors, barristers and clients in the UK. **Chambers'** research is audited by the British Market Research Bureau (see page 7)

BARRISTERS' PROFILES ▶ See pages 1353-1504

LONDON

DOUGHTY STREET CHAMBERS (see full details p.1526) The set is felt by market sources to be a well-coordinated and accessible operation with a balanced spread of expertise throughout silk and junior levels. Although "prominent across the board," **Edward Fitzgerald QC** has particular expertise in prisoners' rights and has been involved in the recent death penalty proceedings in the Eastern Caribbean. His other main areas of focus are extradition and mental health, and he has recently been involved in litigation following on from September 11th. Clients rate him as "approachable and extremely sharp." **Andrew Nicol QC** (see p.1455) has been highly visible acting in the appeal of a group apprehended under the new anti-terrorism legislation, and is known for his immigration-related practice. He is characterised by peers as "a bright and original barrister" with a vast legal knowledge. "Imaginative" **Patrick O'Connor QC** has noted expertise in death in custody, judicial review, actions against the police and criminal appeals, while "old warhorse" **Geoffrey Robertson QC** (see p.1469) has been representing journalists in the Derry inquiry. **Peter Thornton QC** (see p.1490) also retains a high degree of respect in the market. "Exceptional" new silk **Keir Starmer QC** is consistently praised by peers who consider him "an authority on human rights." He has acted in several major recent human rights proceedings, including the Caribbean death penalty proceedings. **Phillippa Kaufmann** (see p.1427) is widely praised for her "effective" court presence and high-profile prison work, while **Heather Williams** (see p.1499) retains a strong reputation for police cases and **Kate Markus** won plaudits for her strong all-round knowledge. Mental health specialist **Paul Bowen** (see p.1369) has been involved in a lot of high-profile cases of late, winning consistent praise from his peers, while **Ian Wise** (see p.1501) received glowing recommendations from solicitors, who especially appreciated his fast turnaround. "A pleasure to instruct," one solicitor claimed, adding that "if you give him instructions one day, the next you'll be in court getting bail."

MATRIX CHAMBERS (see full details p.1573) According to interviewees, **Nicholas Blake QC** (see p.1367) "continues to shine." Rivals admire the "imagination and creativity" he brings to his practice. He represented Louis Farrakhan in connection with his exclusion from the UK. Peers rave that **Ben Emmerson QC** (see p.1395) is "a superstar with a fantastically wide knowledge" and characterise him as "an extremely clear, lucid and intelligent advocate." **Tim Owen QC** (see p.1457) is felt to have "really carved out a niche in human rights appeal work" and his judicial review work is roundly praised. The "brilliant, stunningly good" **Clare Montgomery QC** wins consistent plaudits, while new silk **Rabinder Singh QC** (see p.1479) is said by clients to be "extremely authoritative." He has recently been involved in advising on the new anti-terrorism act and assisting a number of organisations affected by it. He has also handled a right-to-life case in the European Court of Human Rights. Amongst the juniors, **Murray Hunt** (see p.1421) is perceived as "good on interpretation of the European Convention and the Human Rights Act" and "much in demand." **Raza Husain** (see p.1421) has made a big impression on the human rights field. His immigration and asylum work is particularly admired and he is described as having "the makings of a star of the future." **Helen Mountfield** (see p.1451) is said by clients to be "strong on employment human rights" and her style is deemed "wise, measured and thoughtful." **Julian Knowles** (see p.1430) has undertaken a sizeable amount of extradition and death penalty work whilst **Matthew Ryder** (see p.1472) is described as a "dedicated" newcomer. "Tremendous" **Danny Friedman** (see p.1401) also enters the tables this year. He specialises in criminal defence and due process cases as well as actions against state authorities.

BLACKSTONE CHAMBERS (see full details p.1515) "Phenomenally good advocate" **David Pannick QC** (see p.1458) is thought by competitors to "know human rights inside out." He is currently representing a Saudi Arabian citizen who has had his assets frozen following allegations of supporting terrorism. **Anthony Lester QC** (see p.1434) is valued for his

HUMAN RIGHTS • London	QCs	Jnrs
1 Doughty Street Chambers (Geoffrey Robertson QC)	6	5
Matrix Chambers	5	6
2 Blackstone Chambers (Baxendale/Flint)	3	2
3 Cloisters (Laura Cox QC)	2	-
Two Garden Court (Davies/Griffiths)	2	1
Tooks Court Chambers (Michael Mansfield QC)	1	1

Numbers show recommended barristers in this practice area

LEADING SILKS • London

★ BLAKE Nicholas	Matrix Chambers	
FITZGERALD Edward	Doughty Street Chambers	
1 EMMERSON Ben	Matrix Chambers	
OWEN Tim	Matrix Chambers	
PANNICK David	Blackstone Chambers	
2 LESTER Anthony	Blackstone Chambers	
NICOL Andrew	Doughty Street Chambers	
3 COX Laura	Cloisters	
GORDON Richard	Brick Court Chambers	
4 ALLEN Robin	Cloisters	
BELOFF Michael	Blackstone Chambers	
MANSFIELD Michael	Tooks Court Chambers	
MONTGOMERY Clare	Matrix Chambers	
O'CONNOR Patrick	Doughty Street Chambers	
PLEMING Nigel	39 Essex Street	
ROBERTSON Geoffrey	Doughty Street Chambers	
5 DAVIES Owen	Two Garden Court	
HAVERS Philip	1 Crown Office Row	
THORNTON Peter	Doughty Street Chambers	
NEW SILKS		
BLAXLAND Henry	Two Garden Court	
SINGH Rabinder	Matrix Chambers	
STARMER Keir	Doughty Street Chambers	

For details of these leading barristers see Profiles on page 1353

LEADING JUNIORS • London

1 HUNT Murray	Matrix Chambers	
KAUFMANN Phillippa	Doughty Street Chambers	
ROSE Dinah	Blackstone Chambers	
2 HUSAIN Raza	Matrix Chambers	
MOUNTFIELD Helen	Matrix Chambers	
3 THOMAS Leslie	Two Garden Court	
WILLIAMS Heather	Doughty Street Chambers	
4 KNOWLES Julian	Matrix Chambers	
MARKUS Kate	Doughty Street Chambers	
SOUTHEY Hugh	Tooks Court Chambers	
UP AND COMING		
BOWEN Paul	Doughty Street Chambers	
DE LA MARE Thomas	Blackstone Chambers	
FRIEDMAN Daniel	Matrix Chambers	
RYDER Matthew	Matrix Chambers	
WISE Ian	Doughty Street Chambers	

For details of these leading barristers see Profiles on page 1353

HUMAN RIGHTS

> **Research** The rankings are based on in-depth interviews with 6,582 solicitors, barristers and clients in the UK. **Chambers'** research is audited by the British Market Research Bureau (see page 7)

> **BARRISTERS' PROFILES** ▶ See pages 1353-1504

vast experience in this field and has particular interest in freedom of speech and discrimination cases. All-round star **Michael Beloff QC** (see p.1364) is not thought to be very visible in this area, but competitors acknowledge that he is "brilliant" when he turns his hand to it. "Frighteningly good" **Dinah Rose** (see p.1470) was consistently commended by peers and rated for her clarity. She has been involved in the Bloody Sunday Inquiry judicial review. Competitors admire **Thomas De La Mare**'s (see p.1389) ability to produce "an awful lot of high-quality work" and respect his commitment to pro bono work.

CLOISTERS (see full details p.1521) Well known for her top-quality employment and discrimination practice, **Laura Cox QC** (see p.1385) is considered "excellent" for the nexus of employment law and human rights. **Robin Allen QC** (see p.1356) also won respect from competitors and clients for his work in this field.

TWO GARDEN COURT (see full details p.1544) Known for its immigration and inquiry expertise, the set includes extradition specialist **Owen Davies QC**, whose talent for combining law with campaigning is well appreciated. The set is bolstered by the presence of "hard-working and conscientious" **Leslie Thomas** (see p.1490). Another new silk, **Henry Blaxland QC** is also popular with solicitors for his knowledge and enthusiasm.

TOOKS COURT CHAMBERS Perhaps less visible in the sector than in the past, "big-name silk" **Michael Mansfield QC** (see p.1441) boasts a strong name for civil liberties flowing from his superb crime-based practice. Respected across the sector, **Hugh Southey** (see p.1481) was particularly recommended for his work in Strasbourg. Competitors characterised him as "thoughtful, helpful and sharp."

OTHER NOTABLE PRACTITIONERS At Brick Court Chambers, the "creative" **Richard Gordon QC** (see p.1407) maintains a highly reputed judicial review practice and "really gets involved." He regularly works for the Society for the Protection of Unborn Children and in mental health cases. "Really excellent" **Nigel Pleming QC** (see p.1461) at 39 Essex Street is newly ranked following glowing reports of his frequent work on behalf of the Government, and expertise in discrimination and mental health. **Philip Havers QC** (see p.1413) at 1 Crown Office Row was also strongly recommended for his work on the Diane Pretty case.

IMMIGRATION

Research The rankings are based on in-depth interviews with 6,582 solicitors, barristers and clients in the UK. *Chambers'* research is audited by the British Market Research Bureau (see page 7)

BARRISTERS' PROFILES ▶ See pages 1353-1504

OVERVIEW: An explosion of complex legislation and an increase in the political sensitivity and profile of the sector has channelled a great deal of work towards the Bar. As a result, asylum is becoming a particularly large subsector within immigration.

LONDON

TWO GARDEN COURT (see full details p.1544) This is the leading set by some distance in terms of both size and expertise, according to the majority of interviewees. Praised for its efforts to bring test cases for claimants on specific matters, the set runs advice and training courses on immigration under contract from the Legal Service Commission (LSC) and also operates a daily advice line for LSC franchise firms. Although **Laurie Fransman QC** (see p.1400) was frequently recommended to *Chambers* for his sterling work on naturalisation matters, he spends the majority of his time on issues of national security and exclusion cases before SIAC (Special Immigration Appeals Commission). He has an "approachable and generous" manner both with clients and in court. Peers thought that he has the ability to "strike up a rapport with the Home Office and adjudicators." He is a well-known academic and author and was dubbed "the guru and greatest brain" in this sector. **Ian Macdonald QC** led in the Court of Appeal for the appellants in the Sepet and Bulbul case. His long experience of the sector remains well respected among his peers. **Rick Scannell** (see p.1474) is said to possess the winning formula of "legal rigour combined with human compassion." Thought of as "an original thinker who understands the big picture," he acted for the respondents in the Saadi and Osman case, concerning the Home Secretary's decision on asylum seekers detained at the Oakington Reception Centre. In the eyes of many interviewees, he remains the leading junior in the field and a future silk. **Frances Webber** (see p.1498) has taken great strides in establishing herself in this sector. She is said to command the court's respect with a "deftness of hand" and by "discriminating correctly between the most meritorious points and those which are less important." **Nadine Finch** (see p.1397) was recommended in particular for her work on human rights cases and those with a slant towards family and children's matters. "Tenacious and clear-headed," **Stephanie Harrison**'s creative advice won plaudits from solicitors, while **Duran Seddon**'s thorough preparation and strong advocacy skills proved equally popular. He has worked with Scannell on the Oakington case.

DOUGHTY STREET CHAMBERS (see full details p.1526) A claimant-only set, it can call on a number of personnel with additional expertise in related civil liberties and human rights law. An "authoritative, precise and strategic thinker," **Andrew Nicol QC** (see p.1455) was considered by commentators to be "a powerful and persuasive advocate" with an attractive, fluent court style. He is working on the Sepet and Bulbul case in the House of Lords. "A good tactician," **Simon Cox** (see p.1385) was recommended for bringing to bear his overlapping knowledge between immigration law and associated community care and welfare matters: "in this combination, he is probably unmatched," agreed one solicitor. Peers and solicitors alike commented on **Mark Henderson**'s (see p.1414) hard-working ethos and effective advocacy, he also respected for his "creative mind." **Shahram Taghavi** (see p.1487) "brings a dynamic touch to his work – his knowledge shines through," and **John Walsh** (see p.1496) was noted for his commitment and tenacious argument.

MATRIX CHAMBERS (see full details p.1573) The set was considered to have made some ground on the leaders over the past year, and has been involved in some high profile matters applying the ECHR to expulsion and exclusion cases. These have included the ongoing Louis Farrakhan immigration dispute and the case of Saad, Diriye and Osorio, concerning a challenge to the continuing refugee status of refugees granted exceptional leave to remain. **Nicholas Blake QC**'s (see p.1367) expertise and intellect come well recommended. Interviewees believe that he has "the clout to affect the view of the Home Office." His immense tactical awareness and light-footed court manner is a favourite among both solicitors and barristers. He is "still the sharpest mind in this field - he dissects matters and identifies the issues." **Raza Husain** (see p.1421) has broadened his scope to include judicial review and public law matters, as well as core immigration and asylum concerns. "A gifted lawyer," personable and effective in court, he is said to fight for his clients to the bitter end.

6 KING'S BENCH WALK Interviewees appreciated that **Manjit Gill QC** is prepared to "take up and move forward difficult issues." He was singled out by solicitors for his expertise in anti-terrorist and third country cases. "Good with clients and able to explain himself clearly," the proliferation of his leading case law has seen his personal sector profile increase. Of the set's juniors, "excellent all-rounder" **Rambert De Mello**'s patient and occasionally "adventurous" approach is said to be popular with clients.

IMMIGRATION • London

		QCs	Jnrs
1	Two Garden Court (Davies/Griffiths)	2	5
2	Doughty Street Chambers (Geoffrey Robertson QC)	1	4
	Matrix Chambers	1	1
3	6 King's Bench Walk (Sibghat Kadri QC)	1	1
4	Blackstone Chambers (Baxendale/Flint)	1	-
	39 Essex Street (Nigel Pleming QC)	-	1
	Renaissance Chambers (Jubb/Setright)	-	2
	Tooks Court Chambers (Michael Mansfield QC)	-	3

Numbers show recommended barristers in this practice area

LEADING SILKS • London

1	BLAKE Nicholas	Matrix Chambers
	FRANSMAN Laurie	Two Garden Court
	NICOL Andrew	Doughty Street Chambers
2	GILL Manjit	6 King's Bench Walk
	MACDONALD Ian	Two Garden Court
	PANNICK David	Blackstone Chambers

For details of these leading barristers see Profiles on page 1353

LEADING JUNIORS • London

1	SCANNELL Rick	Two Garden Court
	WEBBER Frances	Two Garden Court
2	COX Simon	Doughty Street Chambers
	EICKE Tim	Essex Court Chambers
	FARBEY Judith	Tooks Court Chambers
	GILLESPIE James	Renaissance Chambers
3	FINCH Nadine	Two Garden Court
	HARRISON Stephanie	Two Garden Court
	HENDERSON Mark	Doughty Street Chambers
	HUSAIN Raza	Matrix Chambers
	SEDDON Duran	Two Garden Court
	SOORJOO Martin	Tooks Court Chambers
	SOUTHEY Hugh	Tooks Court Chambers
4	COX Buster	Renaissance Chambers
	DE MELLO Rambert	6 King's Bench Walk
	KOVATS Steven	39 Essex Street
	TAGHAVI Shahram	Doughty Street Chambers
	WALSH John	Doughty Street Chambers

For details of these leading barristers see Profiles on page 1353

IMMIGRATION

Research The rankings are based on in-depth interviews with 6,582 solicitors, barristers and clients in the UK. *Chambers*' research is audited by the British Market Research Bureau (see page 7)

BARRISTERS' PROFILES ▶ See pages 1353-1504

BLACKSTONE CHAMBERS (see full details p.1515) Predominantly a respondent set working on behalf of the Home Office and Government, the majority of its caseload is taken up by asylum work. Highlights from the past year have included a Court of Appeal victory in the Sepet and Bulbul case, now going to the House of Lords. It has also been involved in the International Transport Roth case, concerning the automatic civil fining of lorry drivers whose vehicles contained asylum-seekers. "An amazing ability to simplify complex arguments" has made **David Pannick QC** (see p.1458) a leading name at the Bar. "A formidable opponent" in court, he is involved in a host of leading and related public law and human rights cases. He has worked on the Campsfield Detention Centre case in the House of Lords, represented the Home Office in the Louis Farrakhan case, and acted in the Oakington Reception Centre case in the Court of Appeal.

39 ESSEX STREET (see full details p.1537) Predominantly a Home Office set, it can boast leading names in related public law matters, including European law and human rights issues. Peers considered **Steven Kovats'** (see p.1431) pugnacious style to be a favourite of the Government. He acted on the case for the Government in the R (Farrakhan) v Home Secretary case, concerning the exclusion of the black Muslim leader Louis Farrakhan on public good grounds.

RENAISSANCE CHAMBERS New to our tables this year and said to be building up a notable team, the set's approachable and practical style has won a healthy following. **James Gillespie** brings years of experience to this sector. Formerly of Enfield Chambers and the JCWI, his "exceptional knowledge" and careful presentation in court was popular among instructing solicitors. A "tenacious barrister," **Buster Cox** was said to be willing to share initiatives with others.

TOOKS COURT CHAMBERS Recommended for its efficient and helpful clerking, the set has expanded during the last year. **Judith Farbey** (see p.1396) was praised for her "overall vision" of the sector, commitment and "meticulous preparation." "An approachable and human barrister," **Martin Soorjoo** (see p.1481) applies his sharp mind confidently in court, "struggling hard in the interest of his clients." **Hugh Southey**'s (see p.1481) "innovative and well-received" arguments have been heard in a number of Court of Appeal cases. He is respected for his knowledge of human rights.

OTHER NOTABLE PRACTITIONERS **Tim Eicke** (see p.1394) of **Essex Court Chambers** was frequently recommended to *Chambers* for his firm grasp of European and related human rights matters. Peers considered him "a skilful opponent with good care and knowledge."

NORTHERN CIRCUIT

IMMIGRATION • Northern	QCs	Jnrs
1 Garden Court North (Ian MacDonald QC) Manchester	-	2

Numbers show recommended barristers in this practice area

LEADING JUNIORS • Northern	
1 WESTON Amanda	Garden Court North
2 PLIMMER Melanie	Garden Court North

For details of these leading barristers see Profiles on page 1353

GARDEN COURT NORTH has seen the increased use of dispersement for asylum seekers contributed to its caseload. This set is comprised of "experienced people with a bit of courage," according to law firms. **Melanie Plimmer**'s "up-to-the-minute knowledge" and substantial High Court experience in asylum and employment work was well received, while **Amanda Weston** was considered on a par with some of the best in London. Her professional approach and positive style was popular with firms – "she won't shy away from mixing it with the adjudicator."

INFORMATION TECHNOLOGY

Research The rankings are based on in-depth interviews with 6,582 solicitors, barristers and clients in the UK. **Chambers'** research is audited by the British Market Research Bureau (see page 7)

BARRISTERS' PROFILES ▶ See pages 1353-1504

LONDON

INFORMATION TECHNOLOGY • London	QCs	Jnrs
1 11 South Square (Christopher Floyd QC)	3	2
2 Atkin Chambers (Robert Akenhead QC)	3	-
Three New Square (David Young QC)	1	1
8 New Square (Mark Platts-Mills QC)	1	2
4 Pump Court	1	2

Numbers show recommended barristers in this practice area

11 SOUTH SQUARE (see full details p.1604) Housing the undisputed star of the IT Bar, and many of the established players, the set emerged from this year's research as the clear leader in the field. **Henry Carr QC** (see p.1377) received a wealth of recommendations. Solicitors describe him as "one of the few real IT specialists," and he is the "first port of call" for the majority of interviewees. "Providing a balance of legal expertise and practical advice," **Michael Silverleaf QC** is highly-rated by peers, especially for cases spanning IP and IT, while **Richard Arnold QC** (see p.1358) is noted for his software copyright experience. The set boasts niche expertise in data protection, something on which **Heather Lawrence** (see p.1432) excels. **Mark Vanhegan** (see p.1495) also receives plaudits from solicitors across the country for his skill in the sector.

ATKIN CHAMBERS (see full details p.1508) A set predominantly known for its top-flight construction work, it also provides a host of IT specialists, such as **Nicholas Baatz QC** (see p.1359), whose expertise in microchip quality disputes is widely admired by market sources. **Nicholas Dennys QC** (see p.1389) enters the tables this year on the strength of his "great track record" and "powerful courtroom style." **David Streatfeild-James QC** (see p.1485) is regularly involved in software supply and development disputes.

THREE NEW SQUARE (see full details p.1575) The set continues to be better known for its work on IP cases; however, it retains a foothold in the IT sphere. New silk **Guy Burkill QC** (see p.1374) is singled out for his focus and attention to detail in IT, while **Colin Birss** (see p.1366) is noted for his IP slant on IT work.

8 NEW SQUARE (see full details p.1578) This set's skills are perceived to lie within IP and the crossover between IP and IT. **Martin Howe QC** (see p.1420) remains a noted presence for technology work, while **Richard Meade** (see p.1446) is lauded by clients and competitors alike for his technical expertise. He heads the ranks of the juniors alongside fellow IT specialist, **Adrian Speck** (see p.1481).

4 PUMP COURT (see full details p.1592) Felt by peers to be "really focusing on IT work," this newly ranked set is developing its expertise in construction cases to build a reputation for all-round excellence in all the technical sectors. "Brilliant strategist" **Jeremy Storey QC** (see p.1484) stands out among the silks, while of the juniors **Alex Charlton** (see

LEADING SILKS • London

1 CARR Henry	11 South Square
2 SILVERLEAF Michael	11 South Square
STOREY Jeremy	4 Pump Court
WILSON Alastair	19 Old Buildings
3 ARNOLD Richard	11 South Square
BAATZ Nicholas	Atkin Chambers
DENNYS Nicholas	Atkin Chambers
HOWE Martin	8 New Square
NEW SILKS	
BURKILL Guy	Three New Square
STREATFEILD-JAMES David	Atkin Chambers

For details of these leading barristers see Profiles on page 1353

LEADING JUNIORS • London

1 MEADE Richard	8 New Square
SPECK Adrian	8 New Square
2 BIRSS Colin	Three New Square
CHARLTON Alex	4 Pump Court
FREEDMAN Clive	3 Verulam Buildings
LAWRENCE Heather	11 South Square
MCCALL Duncan	4 Pump Court
SHIPLEY Graham	19 Old Buildings
VANHEGAN Mark	11 South Square

For details of these leading barristers see Profiles on page 1353

p.1378) has impressed interviewees with his experience and pragmatism. **Duncan McCall** (see p.1444) is also highly rated for his intimate industry knowledge.

OTHER NOTABLE PRACTITIONERS 19 Old Buildings boasts two highly respected tenants, the "specialised" **Alastair Wilson QC** (see p.1500) and "pragmatic" **Graham Shipley** (see p.1478). **Clive Freedman** (see p.1401) of 3 Verulam Buildings has been active in technology-related mediation work according to market sources.

INSOLVENCY/CORPORATE RECOVERY

Research The rankings are based on in-depth interviews with 6,582 solicitors, barristers and clients in the UK. Chambers' research is audited by the British Market Research Bureau (see page 7)

BARRISTERS' PROFILES ▶ See pages 1353-1504

LONDON

3-4 SOUTH SQUARE (see full details p.1603) The set dominates this sector with its "sheer depth of talent." Solicitors report that "if my first choice isn't available, the clerks know exactly who is right for the case." These barristers attain "consistently high standards" in insolvency and corporate restructuring, winning a following with their "creative minds and lateral thinking." All quarters of the market agreed that **Gabriel Moss QC** (see p.1450) remains "unchallengeable - a true star." The "ultimate heavyweight court performer," he "intuitively spots the essential points to a case" and can "apply his extensive knowledge" to arrive at solutions that many find "come at you from left field and are absolutely brilliant." He has recently been in action advising the Royal Bank of Scotland on matters concerning Independent Insurance, representing the Special Railway Administrators of Railtrack, and advising the European operations of Enron. Solicitors expressed relief that **Michael Crystal QC** (see p.1386) had returned from the Thyssen case in Bermuda. "A favourite for the most complex matters," he is "fleet of foot" in court, and on paper "has a clarity of expression that makes life so much easier." The set houses two younger stars, who are clearly stepping up to challenge the Moss/Crystal hegemony. **Robin Dicker QC** (see p.1390) is "fantastically intelligent and analytical;" a "great all-rounder - he can turn his hand to anything." Although deemed prime choice if you need a "heavy hitter," his "user-friendly" approach wins him fans and is an attribute shared by **Mark Phillips QC** (see p.1460). The latter's "breezy and positive demeanour" is combined with a "polished courtroom manner." He is "always listening" and relays the issues in a "most persuasive" fashion. **Robin Knowles QC** (see p.1430) is a "highly honourable" barrister, deemed "a safe pair of hands for the difficult questions" and "quick in his turnaround of papers." **Simon Mortimore QC**'s (see p.1450) advice is "utterly commercial;" he has recently acted in Barings, Hamilton et al v Law Debenture Trustees et al. **Richard Adkins QC** (see p.1355) is an "exceptionally intelligent individual" and one who "takes a sensible approach" to his cases. **Christopher Brougham QC**'s (see p.1373) "rich eloquence" is combined with "his attention to detail," while **Richard Hacker QC** (see p.1410) continues to impress with his "pragmatism" and "deep understanding of the law." **Richard Sheldon QC** (see p.1477) applies his "sharp intellect" to matters such as Banca Carige v Banco Nacional de Cuba. Many find that **William Trower QC** (see p.1493) adopts a "practical approach - he's not stand-offish," and has been visible in a number of significant cases of late. He acted on Optimum Solutions v Yorkshire Electricity, a matter concerning material disclosed in 'without prejudice' correspondence. **Martin Pascoe QC** (see p.1458) is a "popular new silk," whose "long-standing experience" makes him "knowledgeable across the board." Amongst a deep pool of juniors, **John Briggs** (see p.1371) stands out for his "top-flight advice" and ability to "lead a team." **Lexa Hilliard** (see p.1416) is a favourite of leading solicitors, who appreciate her "keen eye for details" and her "mastery of administrative exits." **Antony Zacaroli** (see p.1503) inspires trepidation in some peers who are "more concerned when he is on the other side," while instructing solicitors value his "smooth handling of complex matters." **Stephen Atherton** (see p.1359) is "thoroughly prepared" and "technically astute." **Andreas Gledhill**'s (see p.1405) manner is "thoughtful and careful," while solicitors appreciate that he "keeps clear lines of communication open at all times." **Adam Goodison** (see p.1407) has "an incisive knowledge of the law" that helps him "track down the right points to play." Senior junior **David Marks** (see p.1441) "parries with the best of them," employing his "long track record" and "broad base of expertise." **Fidelis Oditah** has a "huge brain" and "what he doesn't know probably isn't worth knowing." **Lloyd Tamlyn** (see p.1487) enjoys an "eclectic knowledge of the law." Solicitors agree that **Felicity Toube** (see p.1492) "devours the fattest briefs," while **Mark Arnold** (see p.1358) is a "tenacious and committed" practitioner. **Glen Davis** (see p.1388) is "user-friendly and highly intelligent." "Practical" **Barry Isaacs** (see p.1422) gives that "extra dimension needed for the more complex cases," while **Hilary Stonefrost** (see p.1484) has a "detailed understanding of the law." The picture is rounded out with new entrant to the tables **Jeremy Goldring** (see p.1407). A "favourite" among leading solicitors, he has recently impressed with his advice (alongside Mark Phillips QC and Glen

INSOLVENCY/CORPORATE RECOVERY • London

		QCs	Jnrs
1	3-4 South Square (Crystal/Alexander)	12	15
2	Erskine Chambers (Robin Potts QC)	5	2
	4 Stone Buildings (Philip Heslop QC)	4	2
3	Maitland Chambers (Lyndon-Stanford/Aldous)	3	1
	24 Old Buildings (Mann/Steinfeld)	4	1
	Serle Court (Lord Neill of Bladen QC)	3	1
	11 Stone Buildings (Murray Rosen QC)	1	4

Numbers show recommended barristers in this practice area

LEADING SILKS • London

★	MOSS Gabriel	3-4 South Square
1	CRYSTAL Michael	3-4 South Square
	GLOSTER Elizabeth	One Essex Court
	MANN Anthony	Enterprise Chambers
	POTTS Robin	Erskine Chambers
2	DICKER Robin	3-4 South Square
	PHILLIPS Mark	3-4 South Square
3	KNOWLES Robin	3-4 South Square
	KOSMIN Leslie	Erskine Chambers
	MORTIMORE Simon	3-4 South Square
	OLIVER David	Erskine Chambers
4	ADKINS Richard	3-4 South Square
	BROUGHAM Christopher	3-4 South Square
	HACKER Richard	3-4 South Square
	NEWMAN Catherine	Maitland Chambers
	PREVEZER Susan	Essex Court Chambers
	SHELDON Richard	3-4 South Square
	TROWER William	3-4 South Square
5	BANNISTER Edward	3 Stone Buildings
	BOMPAS Anthony	4 Stone Buildings
	BOYLE Alan	Serle Court
	BRIGGS Michael	Serle Court
	BRISBY John	4 Stone Buildings
	COHEN Lawrence	24 Old Buildings
	DE LACY Richard	3 Verulam Buildings
	GIRET Jane	11 Stone Buildings
	HAMILTON Eben	New Square Chambers
	HESLOP Philip	4 Stone Buildings
	HOLLINGTON Robin	New Square Chambers
	JOFFE Victor	Serle Court
	KAYE Roger	24 Old Buildings
	NEWEY Guy	Maitland Chambers
	RICHARDS David	Erskine Chambers
	STEINFELD Alan	24 Old Buildings
	VOS Geoffrey	3 Stone Buildings
	NEW SILKS	
	CHIVERS David	Erskine Chambers
	GIROLAMI Paul	Maitland Chambers
	MILES Robert	4 Stone Buildings
	MOVERLEY SMITH Stephen	24 Old Buildings
	PASCOE Martin	3-4 South Square

For details of these leading barristers see Profiles on page 1353

INSOLVENCY/CORPORATE RECOVERY

Research The rankings are based on in-depth interviews with 6,582 solicitors, barristers and clients in the UK. **Chambers'** research is audited by the British Market Research Bureau (see page 7)

BARRISTERS' PROFILES ▶ See pages 1353-1504

LEADING JUNIORS • London

★	SNOWDEN Richard	Erskine Chambers
1	AGNELLO Raquel	11 Stone Buildings
	ARDEN Peter	Enterprise Chambers
	BRIGGS John	3-4 South Square
	HILLIARD Lexa	3-4 South Square
	ZACAROLI Antony	3-4 South Square
2	ATHERTON Stephen	3-4 South Square
	COLLINGS Matthew	Maitland Chambers
	DAVIS-WHITE Malcolm	4 Stone Buildings
	GLEDHILL Andreas	3-4 South Square
	GOODISON Adam	3-4 South Square
	MARKS David	3-4 South Square
	MARSHALL Philip	Serle Court
	MCQUATER Ewan	3 Verulam Buildings
	ODITAH Fidelis	3-4 South Square
	SHEKERDEMIAN Marcia	11 Stone Buildings
	TAMLYN Lloyd	3-4 South Square
	TOUBE Felicity	3-4 South Square
3	ARNOLD Mark	3-4 South Square
	DAVIS Glen	3-4 South Square
	DE GARR ROBINSON Anthony	One Essex Court
	GRIFFITHS Peter	4 Stone Buildings
	IFE Linden	Enterprise Chambers
	ISAACS Barry	3-4 South Square
	KYRIAKIDES Tina	11 Stone Buildings
	MILLETT Richard	Essex Court Chambers
	RITCHIE Richard	24 Old Buildings
	STOCKDALE Thomas	Erskine Chambers
	STONEFROST Hilary	3-4 South Square
UP AND COMING		
	BOARDMAN Christopher	11 Stone Buildings
	GOLDRING Jeremy	3-4 South Square

For details of these leading barristers see Profiles on page 1353

Davis) to the English provisional liquidators of HIH Group, the second largest general insurer in Australia.

ERSKINE CHAMBERS (see full details p.1529) Better known for its outstanding pure company work, the set is also a repository for expertise on corporate restructurings and insolvency. **Robin Potts QC** (see p.1462) is "one of the most senior figures in the marketplace;" he has the ability to "digest the complicated briefs" and wins the court with "eloquence on his feet and on paper." He appeared for the appellant in the Court of Appeal in Leyland Daf, Butcher & Hughes v Talbot & McKillop et al, a case concerning a liquidator's rights to recover expenses. **Leslie Kosmin QC** (see p.1431) has an "astute understanding of the issues" and a "bright, practical" approach that makes him "popular" with many solicitors. **David Oliver QC** (see p.1456) is a "highly talented" barrister whose intelligence "takes the case to that next level," while **David Richards QC** (see p.1468) is another company star with a "varied base of knowledge - brilliant in everything he touches." The latter advised the Government on the application to put Railtrack into administration, and appeared for the administrator in Ciro Citterio Menswear (In Administration). New silk **David Chivers QC** (see p.1379) remains well respected for his corporate restructuring advice, and it is predicted that he "will go far in silk." **Richard Snowden** (see p.1480) "stands head and shoulders above" the market, claim solicitors. He is a "real star" whose "attention to detail" and "strong drafting skills" have generated a healthy following. He appeared for the respondent liquidator in the Leyland Daf Court of Appeal case. Senior junior **Thomas Stockdale** (see p.1484) continues to be well respected for his mixed company/corporate restructuring expertise.

4 STONE BUILDINGS (see full details p.1606) This "user-friendly" set bridges the fields of company and insolvency law. Solicitors value the "practical, pragmatic and utterly sensible" approach of **Anthony Bompas QC** (see p.1368). He is "a great lateral thinker" and can "see the solutions that others overlook." Some find **John Brisby QC** (see p.1372) "abrasive" but there is no doubting his "mastery of the technical issues" and "dedication to his clients." Respected as a "hugely senior figure" **Philip Heslop QC** is most often seen on the larger complex cases, where his "technical nous" and "commercial awareness" combine effectively. New silk **Robert Miles QC** (see p.1447) is viewed as "a great generalist, who can turn his hand to any matter." Among the juniors, **Malcolm Davis-White** (see p.1388) is an "established figure" with "an enormous sense of what will work in a case," while **Peter Griffiths** (see p.1410) is respected for his "authority in court."

MAITLAND CHAMBERS (see full details p.1572) Traditionally known as a chancery set, it fields a good level of expertise in insolvency and restructuring matters. **Catherine Newman QC** (see p.1453) possesses a "steely manner in court," while solicitors find her "a delight to brief - she has an almost instantaneous grasp of the issues." **Guy Newey QC** (see p.1453) is "highly personable," and "thoroughly prepared for court." New silk **Paul Girolami QC** (see p.1405) "can find solutions to seemingly intractable problems." A "highly focused technical barrister," he is well known for his broad practice that encompasses corporate insolvency. **Matthew Collings** (see p.1382) is "strong on his feet" and not afraid to "bounce ideas off the wall."

24 OLD BUILDINGS (see full details p.1582) The set is home to a number of well-known corporate recovery specialists. **Lawrence Cohen QC** "works hard for his clients" and can be relied upon as "a good source of expertise" in this field. "Seasoned" **Roger Kaye QC** has "a straightforward" approach to major cases; "he rolls his sleeves up and gets on with the job at hand." **Alan Steinfeld QC** remains popular among barristers and solicitors for his "clear thinking and astute examination of the issues." **Stephen Moverley Smith QC** has taken silk this year; he is respected for his strong litigation skills. **Richard Ritchie** is praised for his long experience in insolvency matters.

SERLE COURT (see full details p.1602) **Alan Boyle QC** (see p.1370) has returned from the Thyssen case in Bermuda. His varied expertise encompasses corporate insolvency, and his increased presence is viewed by solicitors as a major boost for the set. **Michael Briggs QC** (see p.1371) brings "gravitas" to each matter he handles. A "a proactive and intuitive" barrister, he remains popular for the "heavyweight cases." **Victor Joffe QC** possesses a "quieter temperament" but has won the loyalty of solicitors who appreciate that "he just gets on with it and brings home the result." **Philip Marshall** (see p.1442) was endorsed for his "personable and practical" manner.

11 STONE BUILDINGS (see full details p.1608) A thorough knowledge of the whole scale of insolvency matters is on offer here. **Jane Giret QC** (see p.1405) is the set's most high-profile silk in this field. She is "intelligent and level-headed" and is "committed to achieving the right results for her clients." **Raquel Agnello** (see p.1355) is a popular junior, described by interviewees as "aggressive but in the right way" and "a sensible courtroom operator," an attribute shared by **Marcia Sherkerdemian** (see p.1477) whose "sound judgement" means that she "always takes the right points in court." **Tina Kyriakides** (see p.1431) is a "strong all-round litigator," while **Christopher Boardman** (see p.1368) has won market approval for his "clear understanding of the law."

INSOLVENCY/CORPORATE RECOVERY

Research The rankings are based on in-depth interviews with 6,582 solicitors, barristers and clients in the UK. **Chambers'** research is audited by the British Market Research Bureau (see page 7)

BARRISTERS' PROFILES ▶ See pages 1353-1504

OTHER NOTABLE PRACTITIONERS Although One Essex Court is not well known for its insolvency expertise, it does field two general commercial litigators, who have proved popular with instructing solicitors. **Elizabeth Gloster QC** (see p.1406) is a "formidable opponent" whose "gravitas and courtroom presence has found favour with many a judge." **Anthony de Garr Robinson**'s (see p.1388) "solid technical knowledge" and "great advocacy skills" combine effectively. At Enterprise Chambers **Anthony Mann QC** (see p.1441) is respected for his "confident courtroom style;" "serious but user-friendly with it," he is recommended for those matters "where you do need a heavy hitter." He is often seen in action with junior **Peter Arden** whose "clear advice" and "ordered paperwork" have won him a number of fans. The set also houses **Linden Ife** (see p.1422), a "seasoned" company/commercial barrister. **Susan Prevezer QC** (see p.1463) of Essex Court Chambers is "making her name in a number of interesting cases." A "true specialist," she is "blessed with get-up-and-go." Also at this set is **Richard Millett** (see p.1447), respected for his strong advocacy skills. At 3 Stone Buildings, **Edward Bannister QC** (see p.1361) ("deeply experienced") and **Geoffrey Vos QC** (see p.1496) ("a great legal mind") have attracted warm commendation. **Richard de Lacy QC** (see p.1389) has an "understanding of what will work well in court," while also at 3 Verulam Buildings, **Ewan McQuater** (see p.1445) remains a favourite of leading solicitors. New Square Chambers is home to **Eben Hamilton QC** and **Robin Hollington QC** (see p.1418) who continue to command the respect of their peers.

WESTERN CIRCUIT

LEADING SILKS • Western

1	DAVIES Stephen	Guildhall Chambers

For details of these leading barristers see Profiles on page 1353

LEADING JUNIORS • Western

1	BAMFORD Jeremy	Guildhall Chambers
	BRIGGS Nicholas	Guildhall Chambers
2	ASCROFT Richard	Guildhall Chambers
	FRENCH Paul	Guildhall Chambers
	MAHER Martha	Guildhall Chambers

For details of these leading barristers see Profiles on page 1353

GUILDHALL CHAMBERS continues to dominate the Western Circuit, with its talented barristers and commitment to the sector. **Stephen Davies QC** is "clearly the best silk in the South West." He employs his "amazing brain to good effect" and supplies advice that is always "innovative - he never fails to see the bigger picture." **Jeremy Bamford** "goes from strength to strength" and, like **Nicholas Briggs** (see p.1371), is "devoted to his clients' best interests." The latter was also commended for his "hands-on approach to problem solving." **Richard Ascroft** (see p.1358), **Paul French** (see p.1401) and **Martha Maher** (see p.1440) were all deemed typical of the user-friendly, commercially astute juniors available at this set.

MIDLANDS CIRCUIT

LEADING SILKS • Midlands

1	RANDALL John	St Philips Chambers
2	CORBETT James	St Philips Chambers

For details of these leading barristers see Profiles on page 1353

LEADING JUNIORS • Midlands

1	ASHWORTH Lance	St Philips Chambers
	KHANGURE Avtar	St Philips Chambers

For details of these leading barristers see Profiles on page 1353

In this region, the "go-to set" remains St Philips Chambers. Solicitors valued it as a "progressive set" that has raised its profile through "clever marketing and some highly personable individuals." **John Randall QC** (see p.1466) is a "real favourite" as one of the "most high-profile silks in the region." He is joined in the tables this year by the "more understated but always reliable" **James Corbett QC** (see p.1384). Observers endorsed **Lance Ashworth** (see p.1358) for his "measured and gentle persuasion," while **Avtar Khangure** (see p.1429) has impressed with his "bright intelligence" and is "comfortable handling the bigger issues."

NORTH EASTERN CIRCUIT

LEADING SILKS • North Eastern

1	ALLEN James	No.6 Barristers Chambers

For details of these leading barristers see Profiles on page 1353

LEADING JUNIORS • North Eastern

1	GROVES Hugo	Enterprise Chambers
	JORY Hugh	Enterprise Chambers
2	COOPER Mark	5 Park Place

For details of these leading barristers see Profiles on page 1353

James Allen QC of No.6 Barristers Chambers "wins over the court with the strength of his technical knowledge." He remains the highest profile insolvency silk in the region. At Enterprise Chambers, **Hugo Groves** (see p.1410) has won a following as one who is "open and approachable" and who will "go to all ends for his client." **Hugh Jory** is a "quick-witted" barrister whose "off the cuff" advice has pleased many. **Mark Cooper** (see p.1384) of 5 Park Place is a "strong player with a great manner and a sure technical touch."

INSOLVENCY/CORPORATE RECOVERY

Research The rankings are based on in-depth interviews with 6,582 solicitors, barristers and clients in the UK. **Chambers'** research is audited by the British Market Research Bureau (see page 7)

BARRISTERS' PROFILES ▶ See pages 1353-1504

NORTHERN CIRCUIT

LEADING SILKS • Northern

1	BARTLEY JONES Edward	Exchange Chambers
	BOOTH Michael	40 King St
2	CAWSON Mark	Exchange Chambers
	CHAISTY Paul	40 King St

For details of these leading barristers see Profiles on page 1353

LEADING JUNIORS • Northern

1	ANDERSON Lesley	40 King St
	MAYNARD-CONNOR Giles	Exchange Chambers
2	DOYLE Louis	40 King St
	STERLING Robert	St. James's Chambers

For details of these leading barristers see Profiles on page 1353

40 King Street in Manchester retains its reputation for fielding high-profile insolvency silks and juniors. **Michael Booth QC** (see p.1368) is a senior figure, respected as "a hard act to follow" in court, while **Paul Chaisty QC** (see p.1355) is similarly respected for his advocacy skills. **Lesley Anderson** (see p.1357) is "experienced and knows the local judges well," while solicitors value that **Louis Doyle** (see p.1390) ensures "a quick turnaround of papers." At Exchange Chambers, **Edward Bartley Jones QC** (see p.1362) was strongly recommended for his "gravitas and command of the courtroom." **Giles Maynard-Connor** (see p.1443) was endorsed as a "light performer on his feet" and for his "good level of experience in insolvency matters." **Mark Cawson QC** (see p.1378) was also recommended. **Robert Sterling** (see p.1483) of St James's Chambers continues to be a popular choice amongst local solicitors.

INSURANCE

Research The rankings are based on in-depth interviews with 6,582 solicitors, barristers and clients in the UK. **Chambers'** research is audited by the British Market Research Bureau (see page 7)

BARRISTERS' PROFILES ▶ See pages 1353-1504

LONDON

BRICK COURT CHAMBERS (see full details p.1517) Widely regarded as one of the leading sets for insurance matters, it is home to silks and juniors who are proclaimed by solicitors as "the experts amongst experts." **Jonathan Sumption QC** "brings gravitas into any room he enters," and has "a surgeon's touch" on the most complex of matters. **Mark Howard QC** (see p.1420) commands a large following as one who "scores an amazing success rate," although he may be suffering from his own success with an extremely busy workload. **Stephen Ruttle QC** (see p.1472) "conducts himself without an inch of pomposity or condescension;" he is highly regarded for his work as a mediator. **Sydney Kentridge QC** (see p.1428) remains a legendary name in the insurance world. He is said to be still "the doyen of the Bar - he has no equal." **William Wood QC** (see p.1502) is praised by solicitors as "intelligent, articulate and brilliant to work with," while **George Leggatt QC** (see p.1434) is known as "sharp-witted" and blessed with an understanding of the need for "swift response." **Andrew Popplewell QC** (see p.1462) "stands out high" in the insurance market, while of the new silks, **Michael Swainston QC** (see p.1486) is praised as "one of the best up-and-coming names on the scene." The top-rated junior here is **Helen Davies** (see p.1387), who possesses "logic and astute understanding."

ESSEX COURT CHAMBERS (see full details p.1530) Seen as cutting a busy swathe through insurance work, this chambers "deserves its placing at the top of the heap." It rises up with a "mountain of gifted individuals." **Gordon Pollock QC** (see p.1461) is rated in the market as "a first-rate gunslinger," with "experience ready for any situation." **VV Veeder QC** (see p.1495) is "a knowledgeable, approachable guy" with a truly outstanding reputation for his arbitration prowess. Solicitors believe that **Bernard Eder QC** (see p.1393) is "a damned fine choice on jurisdictional issues," while **Ian Hunter QC** (see p.1421) is "a shooting star in the insurance firmament." **Richard Jacobs QC** (see p.1423) is said by peers to be "currently bringing his technical know-how and user-friendly style to film finance," while new silk **Steven Berry QC** (see p.1365) is seen to be "making the jump with aplomb." Of the juniors both **David Foxton** (see p.1400) and **Mark Templeman** (see p.1489) are "people we can expect good things from." "Highly prominent" **John Lockey** (see p.1437) has impressed both barristers and solicitors as "an imaginative thinker, who comes up with the most fantastic arguments."

7 KING'S BENCH WALK (see full details p.1564) Clearly one of the major sets, one commentator thought it to "offer the full orchestra and chorus line for quality insurance work." **Julian Flaux QC** (see p.1398) is described as a man whose "name is above the lights," on the most complex of cases. He is particularly picked out in court for his "razor-sharp skills." **Gavin Kealey QC** (see p.1427) possesses "charm, tenacity and flair in the courtroom." **Dominic Kendrick QC** is praised by members of the Bar for his skills on his feet; it is said by solicitors that "clients love him." **Christopher Butcher QC** (see p.1375) is "a star performer" much praised by clients and peers. **Jonathan Gaisman QC** is known to be "desperately busy at the present time - a top-class advocate," while **Alistair Schaff QC** (see p.1474) remains a "thorough, competent performer." Of the juniors, **David Edwards** (see p.1393) is a "brilliant, supportive lawyer whose knowledge shines through," while **Adam Fenton** (see p.1397) is successfully "moving his way up."

FOUNTAIN COURT (see full details p.1541) This well-regarded chambers is home to a "crew of sharp intellects." **Michael Crane QC** retains a strong following in the market, described as having "enviable skills; he's a true handful for the opposition." "Heavyweight" **Anthony Boswood QC** (see p.1368) is praised as being "effortlessly practical and extremely hard-working." **David Railton QC** (see p.1466) is "rated for anything that is intellectually challenging, a cracker of a man to have on your side," while solicitors appreciated that **Timothy Howe** (see p.1420) is "fun to work with" and "superbly proficient."

INSURANCE • London

		QCs	Jnrs
1	Brick Court Chambers (Christopher Clarke QC)	8	1
	Essex Court Chambers (Gordon Pollock QC)	6	3
	7 King's Bench Walk (Kealey/Flaux)	6	2
2	Fountain Court (Anthony Boswood QC)	3	1
3	4 Pump Court	2	-
	3 Verulam Buildings (Symons/Jarvis)	2	-

Numbers show recommended barristers in this practice area

LEADING SILKS • London

1	FLAUX Julian	7 King's Bench Walk
	KEALEY Gavin	7 King's Bench Walk
	SUMPTION Jonathan	Brick Court Chambers
2	CRANE Michael	Fountain Court
	EDELMAN Colin	Devereux Chambers
	HOWARD Mark	Brick Court Chambers
	KENDRICK Dominic	7 King's Bench Walk
	POLLOCK Gordon	Essex Court Chambers
	RUTTLE Stephen	Brick Court Chambers
	VEEDER V V	Essex Court Chambers
3	BOSWOOD Anthony	Fountain Court
	BUTCHER Christopher	7 King's Bench Walk
	DOHMANN Barbara	Blackstone Chambers
	EDER Bernard	Essex Court Chambers
	GAISMAN Jonathan	7 King's Bench Walk
	HILDYARD Robert	4 Stone Buildings
	HUNTER Ian	Essex Court Chambers
	KENTRIDGE Sydney	Brick Court Chambers
	ROWLAND John	4 Pump Court
4	JACOBS Richard	Essex Court Chambers
	LEGGATT George	Brick Court Chambers
	POPPLEWELL Andrew	Brick Court Chambers
	RAILTON David	Fountain Court
	SCHAFF Alistair	7 King's Bench Walk
	SYMONS Christopher	3 Verulam Buildings
	WOOD William	Brick Court Chambers
NEW SILKS		
	BERRY Steven	Essex Court Chambers
	PHILLIPS Rory	3 Verulam Buildings
	SWAINSTON Michael	Brick Court Chambers
	TOZZI Nigel	4 Pump Court

For details of these leading barristers see Profiles on page 1353

LEADING JUNIORS • London

1	EDWARDS David	7 King's Bench Walk
	LOCKEY John	Essex Court Chambers
2	EDEY Philip	20 Essex Street
	FOXTON David	Essex Court Chambers
	HOWE Timothy	Fountain Court
	TEMPLEMAN Mark	Essex Court Chambers
3	DAVIES Helen	Brick Court Chambers
	FENTON Adam	7 King's Bench Walk
	WYNTER Colin	Devereux Chambers

For details of these leading barristers see Profiles on page 1353

INSURANCE

Research The rankings are based on in-depth interviews with 6,582 solicitors, barristers and clients in the UK. **Chambers'** research is audited by the British Market Research Bureau (see page 7)

BARRISTERS' PROFILES ▶ See pages 1353-1504

4 PUMP COURT (see full details p.1592) **John Rowland QC** (see p.1471) was described by one commentator as "tough stuff; he handles rigorous, demanding cases with the utmost ease," while new silk **Nigel Tozzi QC** (see p.1492) is settling into his elevation; he is said to be "handling insurance issues with aplomb."

3 VERULAM BUILDINGS (see full details p.1615) A favourite among solicitors, **Christopher Symons QC** (see p.1486) ("one supremely clever guy") has been involved over the past year in a couple of cases relating to engineers. New silk **Rory Phillips QC** (see p.1460) employs his "well-honed intellect" and is perceived to be one "definitely on the rise."

OTHER NOTABLE PRACTITIONERS **Colin Edelman QC** (see p.1393) of Devereux Chambers is recommended for his courtroom presence; he is "an impressively formidable opponent." At the same set **Colin Wynter** (see p.1503) is "clued up" on all aspects of insurance and is appreciated for his ability to "crunch through piles of documents." Some solicitors perceive **Barbara Dohmann QC** (see p.1390) of Blackstone Chambers to be "virtually omnipresent." She remains a "tower of strength" in the insurance world and is described as "beautifully forthright." **Robert Hildyard QC** (see p.1415) of 4 Stone Buildings has "a tremendous knowledge of corporate insurance matters." Among the juniors, **Philip Edey** (see p.1393) of 20 Essex Street is strongly tipped "to survive and thrive in this arena."

INTELLECTUAL PROPERTY

Research The rankings are based on in-depth interviews with 6,582 solicitors, barristers and clients in the UK. **Chambers'** research is audited by the British Market Research Bureau (see page 7)

BARRISTERS' PROFILES ▶ See pages 1353-1504

OVERVIEW: Victories for brand owners have been highlighted this year, due to the ECJ rulings on Levi Strauss v Tesco, closely followed by Davidoff v A&G Imports. Brand owners can now influence who sells their products, with ramifications extending across the retail sector to the pharmaceuticals market. Brand enforcement will now be easier; however, the issue of grey market importation continues to provide a wealth of instruction for the Bar.

LONDON

INTELLECTUAL PROPERTY ■ London

		QCs	Jnrs
1	Three New Square (David Young QC)	6	5
	8 New Square (Mark Platts-Mills QC)	6	9
	11 South Square (Christopher Floyd QC)	3	7
2	One Essex Court (Lord Grabiner QC)	1	1
	Hogarth Chambers (Rayner James/Morcom)	2	1
	19 Old Buildings (Alastair Wilson QC)	1	1

Numbers show recommended barristers in this practice area

LEADING SILKS ■ London

★	CARR Henry	11 South Square
	KITCHIN David	8 New Square
	THORLEY Simon	Three New Square
1	ARNOLD Richard	11 South Square
	BALDWIN John	8 New Square
	FLOYD Christopher	11 South Square
	HOBBS Geoffrey	One Essex Court
	PRESCOTT Peter	8 New Square
	WAUGH Andrew	Three New Square
2	HOWE Martin	8 New Square
	MILLER Richard	Three New Square
	MORCOM Christopher	Hogarth Chambers
	PLATTS-MILLS Mark	8 New Square
	SILVERLEAF Michael	11 South Square
	VITORIA Mary	8 New Square
	WATSON Antony	Three New Square
	WILSON Alastair	19 Old Buildings
	WYAND Roger	Hogarth Chambers
	YOUNG David	Three New Square
	NEW SILKS	
	BURKILL Guy	Three New Square

For details of these leading barristers see Profiles on page 1353

LEADING JUNIORS ■ London

1	ALEXANDER Daniel	8 New Square
	MEADE Richard	8 New Square
	MELLOR James	8 New Square
2	BIRSS Colin	Three New Square
	PURVIS Iain	11 South Square
	TAPPIN Michael	8 New Square
	VANHEGAN Mark	11 South Square
3	ACLAND Piers	11 South Square
	CAMPBELL Douglas	Three New Square
	CLARK Fiona	8 New Square
	HACON Richard	11 South Square
	HICKS Michael	19 Old Buildings
	LAWRENCE Heather	11 South Square
	SPECK Adrian	8 New Square
	TRITTON Guy	Hogarth Chambers
4	HAMER George	8 New Square
	HIMSWORTH Emma	One Essex Court
	MAY Charlotte	8 New Square
	MCFARLAND Denise	Three New Square
	MITCHESON Thomas	Three New Square
	MOODY-STUART Thomas	8 New Square
	TURNER Justin	Three New Square
	WHITTLE Henry	11 South Square
	UP AND COMING	
	CUDDIGAN Hugo	11 South Square

For details of these leading barristers see Profiles on page 1353

THREE NEW SQUARE (see full details p.1575) A set characterised by its depth, encouraging the growth of its younger barristers; it "successfully passes down the top-end work to the juniors." "The first port of call for a meaty case," Simon Thorley QC (see p.1490) is prime choice for solicitors due to his formidable reputation at the Court of Appeal and "unparalleled preparation for a case." The "cerebral" Andrew Waugh QC (see p.1498) has been singled out as one of the leaders in the field, and has impressed clients by "considering every angle on a patent case." The "authoritarian" David Young QC (see p.1503) is celebrated by solicitors for a "low-key delivery, which pays off in the end." Richard Miller QC (see p.1447) impresses clients, who describe him as "meticulous; he thinks of every angle on a case." Antony Watson QC "gets on and does a good job." New silk Guy Burkill QC (see p.1374) is "creative and tenacious," and is particularly recommended for software work. Of the juniors, "all-rounder" Colin Birss (see p.1366) is supported by Douglas Campbell (see p.1376), who is renowned for his paperwork and "gets stuck in to his cases." The "experienced" Denise McFarland (see p.1444) is supported by the "bright, hard-working" Thomas Mitcheson (see p.1448), while Justin Turner (see p.1494) stands out as "good with difficult cases and clients."

8 NEW SQUARE (see full details p.1578) An expanding set "packed with heavyweights and hungry juniors;" however, commentators lament the loss of Michael Fysh QC to the bench. "The star of IP, almost impossible to get hold of," David Kitchin QC (see p.1430) is a "brilliant strategist" according to various commentators. John Baldwin QC (see p.1360) has a significant reputation for trademark work, gratifying solicitors by "annihilating the opposition." The "eccentric" Peter Prescott QC (see p.1463) is described by one peer as "a font of ideas, one of the cleverest members of the Bar." The "underrated" Martin Howe QC (see p.1420) gets to the heart of the matter," while Mark Platts-Mills QC (see p.1461) is deemed a "fierce cross-examiner" by his peers. "Copyright expert" Mary Vitoria QC (see p.1496) is "quick to grasp the details." The set boasts all three top ranking juniors: Daniel Alexander (see p.1356) is known for his "tactical vision and creative strategies," while Richard Meade (see p.1446) is "on top of the game." James Mellor (see p.1446) joins them at the top of the tables; he is pronounced the best junior at the bar, possessor of "an outstanding knowledge of the law." "First-class" Michael Tappin (see p.1488) is acclaimed as a "brainbox," whilst also being user-friendly. Fiona Clark (see p.1380) moves up the tables this year; she is perceived not only to be "creative" but also "extremely sharp." Adrian Speck (see p.1481) is favoured by various specialist firms, while Charlotte May (see p.1443) is perceived as "hard-working, a good team player." Thomas Moody-Stuart (see p.1449) has been recommended for his trademark work; he is perceived to possess "authority beyond his years." George Hamer (see p.1411) is highly rated by the market for his experience.

11 SOUTH SQUARE (see full details p.1604) The set moves up in the tables following heavy endorsement for the quality of work it produces. Covering media and entertainment IP alongside the harder elements, this "diverse" set is "prepared to muck in, with good team members who are

www.ChambersandPartners.com

1323

INTELLECTUAL PROPERTY

Research The rankings are based on in-depth interviews with 6,582 solicitors, barristers and clients in the UK. **Chambers'** research is audited by the British Market Research Bureau (see page 7)

BARRISTERS' PROFILES ▶ See pages 1353-1504

excellent calibre barristers." The "exceptional" **Henry Carr QC** (see p.1377) gains a starred ranking, for being not only "unflappable and lucid," but also a great fighter in court. **Christopher Floyd QC** (see p.1398) "has a phenomenal brain; one of the best patent lawyers around," while **Richard Arnold QC** (see p.1358) moves up this year; he is perceived as "staggeringly fast, uncompromising, with a measured courtroom presence." Popular with clients, **Michael Silverleaf QC** is "bullish in court; he will fight hard for you." The set enjoys high quality juniors, including the "creative, lateral thinker," **Iain Purvis** (see p.1465), and **Mark Vanhegan** (see p.1495), of whom peers claim "he has had a storming run." **Piers Acland** (see p.1355) is lauded for his "first-class examination and use of pace," while **Richard Hacon** gains praise for his performance on Glaxo Wellcome v Dowelhurst. **Heather Lawrence** (see p.1432) is singled out as "scarily bright, a tough player." **Henry Whittle** possesses "real gravitas," and is joined in the tables by up-and-comer **Hugo Cuddigan**, who is perceived as "a rising star on copyright and trademarks."

ONE ESSEX COURT (see full details p.1531) The set impresses solicitors for its high quality advice on commercial cases with an IP angle. It boasts "everyone's first choice for trademark work," **Geoffrey Hobbs QC**, who employs his "phenomenal brainpower" to the most complex cases. "Punching above her weight," **Emma Himsworth** (see p.1416) is "terrific in preparation work."

HOGARTH CHAMBERS (see full details p.1558) Adjudged an "intellectual set," it is headed by the "academic" **Christopher Morcom QC** (see p.1449), whom solicitors perceive to be "the name in these chambers." **Roger Wyand QC** (see p.1502) attracted a raft of recommendations from leading City solicitors, who regard him as "a delight to work with, superb on his feet." **Guy Tritton** (see p.1493) moves up the tables, impressing solicitors with his bullish presence in court and "excellent delivery."

19 OLD BUILDINGS (see full details p.1581) **Alastair Wilson QC** (see p.1500) was recommended by solicitors as "inventive; he can fight a poor case," while the "enthusiastic, commercial" **Michael Hicks** (see p.1415) is best known for his slant on the media side of IP.

LICENSING

Research The rankings are based on in-depth interviews with 6,582 solicitors, barristers and clients in the UK. **Chambers'** research is audited by the British Market Research Bureau (see page 7)

BARRISTERS' PROFILES ▶ See pages 1353-1504

OVERVIEW: There is no shortage of work in this specialism and a favourable environment for gaming and betting licence applications has been created. The Budd report has recommended liberalisation of the industry, and changes to the General Betting Duty made in the 2001 Budget were designed to attract bookmakers onshore. Liquor licensing practitioners are seeing the effects of over-licensing and a counter-reaction by the police and authorities to consequent public order problems. Alongside work on contested licence applications, there continues to be a demand for regulatory advice in relation to online gaming and betting schemes.

LONDON

LICENSING • London

		QCs	Jnrs
1	3 Raymond Buildings (Clive Nicholls QC)	4	4

Numbers show recommended barristers in this practice area

LEADING SILKS • London

1	BECKETT Richard	3 Raymond Buildings
2	DE HAAN Kevin	3 Raymond Buildings
	FITZGERALD Susanna	One Essex Court
3	GRAY Gilbert	3 Raymond Buildings
	MEHIGAN Simon	5 Paper Buildings
	MOGER Christopher	4 Pump Court
	NEW SILKS	
	BROMLEY-MARTIN Michael	3 Raymond Buildings

For details of these leading barristers see Profiles on page 1353

LEADING JUNIORS • London

1	GOURIET Gerald	3 Raymond Buildings
	RANKIN James	3 Raymond Buildings
2	WALSH Stephen	3 Raymond Buildings
3	MONKCOM Stephen	Tanfield Chambers
	MUIR Andrew	3 Raymond Buildings

For details of these leading barristers see Profiles on page 1353

3 RAYMOND BUILDINGS (see full details p.1596) The consensus is that this set "continues to dominate," possessing as it does "the licensing doyens." A "formidable advocate" with an "appealing court manner," **Richard Beckett QC** (see p.1364) applies a "thoroughly detailed approach when necessary," and remains best known for casino and liquor licensing work. He has also acted for most major bookmakers in the past year on contested licence applications. **Kevin de Haan QC** (see p.1388) is respected for covering the full spectrum of licensing work as part of a sophisticated regulatory practice that includes internet gaming issues. He received wide-ranging praise for his "charming, clever, ordered and enthusiastic" approach. Although **Gilbert Gray QC** has been less visible in licensing than during previous years, interviewees admitted he "always was a great name and certainly still is." An "effective and pleasant opponent," **Michael Bromley-Martin QC** (see p.1372) joins some select company at his set in receiving silk this year. Many interviewees singled out **Gerald Gouriet** (see p.1408) as the "best junior at the licensing Bar," while one peer described him as a "skilful performer against whom you have to be on your toes." Gouriet is often seen acting for, and against, local authorities. Solicitors appreciate that **James Rankin** (see p.1466) is "always a fighter for our cause," and they also value his "rare depth of knowledge of the specialist area." **Stephen Walsh** (see p.1497) "hotly pursues the lead juniors" with interviewees remarking he is "always thorough and well-prepared." **Andrew Muir** (see p.1452) attracts compelling commendation from City and regional solicitors alike, one of whom said he is "extremely able and rolls his sleeves up more than most."

OTHER NOTABLE PRACTITIONERS **Susanna FitzGerald QC** of One Essex Court advises on all aspects of licensing and is considered an "obvious candidate for inclusion in the upper echelons." Interviewees portrayed her as "a well-prepared and concise advocate with a good deal of charm." **Simon Mehigan QC** of 5 Paper Buildings has recently concentrated on contractual disputes with a licensing bent that are often cross-border in scope and have involved major nightclub operators. Despite being less visible in court recently, **Christopher Moger QC** (see p.1448) of 4 Pump Court has secured a following for his "formidable advocacy skills," and continues to provide regulatory advice on licensing matters that often have a multi-jurisdictional dimension, including internet gaming. The author of a standard work on gaming and betting, **Stephen Monkcom** (see p.1449) of Tanfield Chambers is best known for his outstanding academic ability, being "most impressive on paper."

WESTERN CIRCUIT

LEADING SILKS • Western

1	GLEN Ian	Guildhall Chambers

For details of these leading barristers see Profiles on page 1353

LEADING JUNIORS • Western

1	BARKER Kerry	Guildhall Chambers
2	WADSLEY Peter	St John's Chambers

For details of these leading barristers see Profiles on page 1353

While licensing is not the highest profile work undertaken by "effective performer" **Ian Glen QC** (see p.1405) of Guildhall Chambers, he remains active as the leading silk in his region, attracting a preponderance of gaming and betting work while also more than able to cover liquor licensing cases. At the same chambers, "worthy opponent" **Kerry Barker** (see p.1361) is a senior junior, highly respected for a wide licensing practice. Acting for both public bodies and commercial and private clients, **Peter Wadsley** remains well respected.

WALES & CHESTER CIRCUIT

LEADING JUNIORS • Wales & Chester

1	WALTERS Graham	33 Park Place
	WALTERS Jonathan	33 Park Place

For details of these leading barristers see Profiles on page 1353

While **Graham Walters** (see p.1497) of 33 Park Place acts predominantly for commercial clients trading in liquor, he is best known for advising local authorities and sustains a respected licensing practice. He has most recently provided advice on the impact of the Human Rights Act on procedural aspects of the betting industry. Also an acknowledged specialist at the same chambers, **Jonathan Walters** (see p.1497) retains a strong reputation.

LICENSING

> **Research** The rankings are based on in-depth interviews with 6,582 solicitors, barristers and clients in the UK. **Chambers'** research is audited by the British Market Research Bureau (see page 7)

BARRISTERS' PROFILES ▶ See pages 1353-1504

MIDLANDS CIRCUIT

LEADING SILKS • Midlands
★ SAUNDERS John	4 Fountain Court

For details of these leading barristers see Profiles on page 1353

LEADING JUNIORS • Midlands
1 GOSLING Jonathan	4 Fountain Court

For details of these leading barristers see Profiles on page 1353

There was broad-based agreement that **John Saunders QC** of 4 Fountain Court is now "one of the leading licensing figures in the country," with the volume and quality of praise he elicited often outweighing that for his London competitors. "Technically superb, he gets the best out of everyone," and recently acted for Martin Gough, the Bristol pub landlord, in setting the precedent for the right to serve drinks being extended to early morning World Cup matches. **Jonathan Gosling** at the same chambers has also carved a name in this field for his "effective" approach.

NORTH EASTERN CIRCUIT

LEADING SILKS • North Eastern
NEW SILKS
SLOAN Paul	Trinity Chambers

For details of these leading barristers see Profiles on page xxxx

LEADING JUNIORS • North Eastern
1 HOLLAND Charles	Trinity Chambers

For details of these leading barristers see Profiles on page xxxx

"Straightforward in dealing with the issues," **Paul Sloan QC** (see p.1479) of Trinity Chambers continues to attract commendation as the leading silk in the region. Solicitors note that **Charles Holland** (see p.1418) "shows a depth of knowledge and valuable research" and is gradually developing a practice at the same chambers.

NORTHERN CIRCUIT

LEADING JUNIORS • Northern
1 WALSH Martin	Peel Court Chambers

For details of these leading barristers see Profiles on page 1353

With the appointment of Clement Goldstone QC to the bench, **Martin Walsh** of Peel Court Chambers becomes the leading licensing barrister on the Northern circuit, and the first port of call for a number of solicitor referees who commended his "great expertise."

LOCAL GOVERNMENT

Research The rankings are based on in-depth interviews with 6,582 solicitors, barristers and clients in the UK. **Chambers'** research is audited by the British Market Research Bureau (see page 7)

BARRISTERS' PROFILES ▶ See pages 1353-1504

OVERVIEW: Responding to demands from the market to highlight those lawyers with specific social housing expertise, we have this year introduced it as a subsection within Local Government. Although it seems insufficiently developed to warrant a full, standalone section at this stage, we will continue to monitor market demand.

LOCAL GOVERNMENT • London	QCs	Jnrs
1 4 Breams Buildings (Christopher Lockhart-Mummery QC)	5	2
4-5 Gray's Inn Square (Elizabeth Appleby QC)	4	1
11 King's Bench Walk Chambers (Tabachnik/Goudie)	3	2
2 2-3 Gray's Inn Square (Porten/Scrivener)	2	2
3 2 Harcourt Buildings (Robin Purchas QC)	2	-

Numbers show recommended barristers in this practice area

LEADING SILKS • London

1	GOUDIE James	11 King's Bench Walk Chambers
	HOWELL John	Blackstone Chambers
2	DRABBLE Richard	4 Breams Buildings
	STRAKER Timothy	4-5 Gray's Inn Square
3	ARDEN Andrew	Arden Chambers
	GEORGE Charles	2 Harcourt Buildings
	SUPPERSTONE Michael	11 King's Bench Walk Chambers
4	ELVIN David	4 Breams Buildings
	HENDERSON Roger	2 Harcourt Buildings
	HOLGATE David	4 Breams Buildings
	TABACHNIK Eldred	11 King's Bench Walk Chambers
5	HOBSON John	4-5 Gray's Inn Square
	KATKOWSKI Christopher	4 Breams Buildings
	LOCKHART-MUMMERY Christopher	4 Breams Buildings
	LOWE Mark	2-3 Gray's Inn Square
	PORTEN Anthony	2-3 Gray's Inn Square
	PURCHAS Robin	2 Harcourt Buildings
	READ Lionel	Eldon Chambers
	STEEL John	4-5 Gray's Inn Square
NEW SILKS		
	CORNER Timothy	4-5 Gray's Inn Square
	SINGH Rabinder	Matrix Chambers

For details of these leading barristers see Profiles on page 1353

LEADING JUNIORS • London

1	BÉAR Charles	11 King's Bench Walk Chambers
	FINDLAY James	2-3 Gray's Inn Square
	GIFFIN Nigel	11 King's Bench Walk Chambers
	LIEVEN Nathalie	4 Breams Buildings
2	BAKER Christopher	Arden Chambers
	COOK Mary	2-3 Gray's Inn Square
3	BROWN Paul	4-5 Gray's Inn Square
	MOULD Timothy	4 Breams Buildings

For details of these leading barristers see Profiles on page 1353

LONDON — LOCAL GOVERNMENT

4 BREAMS BUILDINGS (see full details p.1516) Most of the barristers at this set also have strong planning practices, and their expertise is widely used by local authorities. "Outstanding and always helpful," **Richard Drabble QC** (see p.1391) is known particularly for his auditing work. **David Elvin QC** (see p.1391) has impressed solicitors with his deep knowledge of local government law. He has expertise in planning, compulsory purchase, environment and highways law. "Star" **David Holgate QC** (see p.1418) has a varied and renowned practice. **Christopher Katkowski QC** (see p.1426) spends the majority of his time on planning matters, although when he undertakes local government work, solicitors judge the results as "incredibly thorough." **Christopher Lockhart-Mummery QC** (see p.1438) is similarly focused on planning, while the "forceful and articulate" **Nathalie Lieven** (see p.1436) is considered by solicitors to be "a real local government specialist." She is respected for the counselling she does on behalf of local authorities and her High Court judicial review work. **Timothy Mould** (see p.1451) is experienced in compulsory purchase and compensation and highways matters, and related land law.

4-5 GRAY'S INN SQUARE (see full details p.1550) This set is home to a number of respected specialists. Among them, **Timothy Straker QC** (see p.1484) is known as a "strong performer" and is described by peers as "impressive and thorough - a man with a laser-like brain." **John Hobson QC** (see p.1417) undertakes a substantial amount of advisory work and counsels local authorities on their powers and duties. **John Steel QC** (see p.1482) handles a great deal of urban regeneration and town development work; he has a broad-ranging planning practice that is often of use to local authorities. "Man of the moment" **Timothy Corner QC** (see p.1384) has been in a number of high-profile cases of late, resulting in one interviewee describing him as "the highest flyer amongst the new silks and rightly so." **Paul Brown** (see p.1373) is characterised as "a committed local government lawyer".

11 KING'S BENCH WALK CHAMBERS (see full details p.1566) Solicitors claim they are attracted to this set because of its expertise in "pure local government" matters. Its barristers are considered "reliable and thorough," quick in the turnaround of papers and distinctly user-friendly. Called a "guru" by some, **James Goudie QC** (see p.1408) is said to be "good for complicated local government finance." He is a regular advisor to several local authorities, and is "a favourite on vires and procurement issues," giving advice in "a clear and client-friendly way." **Eldred Tabachnik QC** (see p.1487) is popular among solicitors and is praised for his "precise and quick opinion." **Michael Supperstone QC** (see p.1485) has impressed many interviewees, who described him as a "creative thinker" and a "practical lawyer." **Charles Béar** (see p.1363) is roundly praised as an "impressive" advocate, while **Nigel Giffin** (see p.1404) is said to have "made some big strides" in the past year. Offering "focused and practical advice," solicitors find him "constructive and helpful."

2-3 GRAY'S INN SQUARE (see full details p.1548) "Able" silk **Mark Lowe QC** (see p.1438) turns his hand to a variety of cases for local authorities in the areas of housing, planning and local government finance and powers. He recently represented the London Borough of Southwark as it extricated itself from an unwanted £200 million contract. **Anthony Porten QC** (see p.1462) does a lot of highly rated planning-related local government work. He often acts in an advisory capacity and advised English Partnerships and the Commission for the New Towns on disposing with the Millennium Dome. He has also been instructed by Wandsworth Council regarding a public nuisance case against Railtrack. **James Findlay** (see p.1398) is respected by solicitors for his "focused" local government practice. He takes on a variety of cases for local authorities in areas such as licensing, planning, environment and compulsory purchase/compensation matters. His understanding of local government issues at the cutting edge is highly rated by solicitors. **Mary Cook** (see p.1383) ("an able advocate") has recently been occupied by advising authorities on issues relating to the Local Government Act 2000.

2 HARCOURT BUILDINGS (see full details p.1554) Although the set has a planning slant, it is nevertheless involved in a substantial level of local government matters. "Careful and thorough" **Charles George QC** (see p.1403) is admired for his "sound grasp of local government and admin-

LOCAL GOVERNMENT

> **Research** The rankings are based on in-depth interviews with 6,582 solicitors, barristers and clients in the UK. **Chambers'** research is audited by the British Market Research Bureau (see page 7)
>
> **BARRISTERS' PROFILES ▶** See pages 1353-1504

istration law." Fellow barristers have "a lot of time for" **Roger Henderson QC** (see p.1414). He is particularly well known for advisory work and "doing a lot behind the scenes". **Robin Purchas QC** (see p.1465) is widely respected, although his emphasis falls on planning.

OTHER NOTABLE PRACTITIONERS A "formidable intellect," **John Howell QC** (see p.1420) of Blackstone Chambers received accolades from all quarters. A "foremost authority on local government finance," he was described as "one of the leading lights" at the Bar. **Andrew Arden QC** (see p.1358) ("able and expert") and **Christopher Baker** (see p.1360) of Arden Chambers were respected for their local government and housing-based practice. **Lionel Read QC** (see p.1467) of Eldon Chambers remains highly regarded in this field. New silk **Rabinder Singh QC** (see p.1479) of Matrix Chambers was widely commended for his work in this area, and was described as "an able performer."

WALES & CHESTER CIRCUIT

"Proficient practitioner" **Nicholas Cooke QC** (see p.1383) of 9 Park Place

LEADING SILKS • Wales & Chester

1	COOKE Nicholas	9 Park Place

For details of these leading barristers see Profiles on page 1353

LEADING JUNIORS • Wales & Chester

1	WALTERS Graham	33 Park Place
	WILLIAMS Rhodri	30 Park Place

For details of these leading barristers see Profiles on page 1353

is widely praised by clients, and felt by peers to "shine in Wales." **Graham Walters** (see p.1497) of 33 Park Place is "a real fighter" in court, and **Rhodri Williams** (see p.1500) of 30 Park Place is considered a "focused and effective" performer.

LONDON — SOCIAL HOUSING

SOCIAL HOUSING • London

		QCs	Jnrs
1	Arden Chambers (Andrew Arden QC)	1	2
2	Two Garden Court (Davies/Griffiths)	1	-

Numbers show recommended barristers in this practice area

LEADING SILKS • London

1	ARDEN Andrew	Arden Chambers
	LUBA Jan	Two Garden Court

For details of these leading barristers see Profiles on page 1353

LEADING JUNIORS • London

1	OKOYA William	Arden Chambers
2	BHOSE Ranjit	2-3 Gray's Inn Square
	DYMOND Andrew	Arden Chambers

For details of these leading barristers see Profiles on page 1353

ARDEN CHAMBERS (see full details p.1507) Undeniably the set with the best overall reputation and experience, it is the natural first choice of a wide variety of instructing solicitors. They were particularly impressed by the speed and efficiency of barristers like leading silk **Andrew Arden QC** (see p.1358), whose "clear and direct advice" is especially valued. Peers claim that "the court will listen to his opinions and probably act on them – the weight of his presence moves things forward." Many commented on **William Okoya**'s (see p.1456) experience and knowledge of the market and his amenable style, while the practical **Andrew Dymond** (see p.1392) was commended for his advocacy skills and "thorough, well thought out advice."

TWO GARDEN COURT (see full details p.1544) Increasing in strength and numbers, the set's social housing expertise was well noted by both solicitors and barristers. The undoubted star of the show is **Jan Luba QC**. "A great orator," he is one of the best known names in the field, with a particular name for tenant cases.

OTHER NOTABLE PRACTITIONERS **Ranjit Bhose** (see p.1365) of 2-3 Gray's Inn Square is said by solicitors to have a thorough understanding of the whole field and a particular talent for the "practical application of the law."

MEDIA & ENTERTAINMENT

Research The rankings are based on in-depth interviews with 6,582 solicitors, barristers and clients in the UK. **Chambers'** research is audited by the British Market Research Bureau (see page 7)

BARRISTERS' PROFILES ▶ See pages 1353-1504

LONDON

BLACKSTONE CHAMBERS (see full details p.1515) "An unstuffy set," according to solicitors, it retains poll position with its group of top-calibre barristers who "possess an unparalleled knowledge of the industry." **Ian Mill QC** (see p.1447) has been universally praised as the leading entertainment silk. He is "absorbed in the industry, and will put up a great fight for his client." The "cerebral" **Robert Englehart QC** (see p.1395) is highly respected for his experience, while **Barbara Dohmann QC** (see p.1390) was described as a "tough advocate with faultless judgement." "Indubitably the star of the juniors," **Pushpinder Saini** (see p.1473) is admired by barristers and solicitors alike for "rarely making a bad point." The only other junior who comes close to challenging his supremacy is **Robert Howe** (see p.1420), who solicitors describe as "a top-flight, cut-and-thrust advocate with the ability to get to the nub of things."

HOGARTH CHAMBERS (see full details p.1558) This "academic set" boasts the talents of "smooth performer" **Kevin Garnett QC** (see p.1402), who is said to bring "a real specialism in copyright law" to the sector. **Jonathan Rayner James QC** (see p.1466) is another authority on copyright matters, whose clients praise his "persistent and effective advocacy." "Trained musician" **Paul Dickens** "won't give up when the going gets tough," while **Amanda Michaels** (see p.1446) has a respected profile, especially for cases that involve a trademark element.

8 NEW SQUARE (see full details p.1578) A leading set for IP, it brings that IP expertise to bear in media work. **John Baldwin QC** (see p.1360) is viewed as "a good, plain-speaking advocate," while **Peter Prescott QC** (see p.1463) was lauded by peers for his technical copyright knowledge. **Mary Vitoria QC** (see p.1496) is not only admired for her copyright expertise, but also for "technical brilliance in court." While more focused on IP cases, **Daniel Alexander** (see p.1356) is highly rated for his publishing knowledge, and was described by one interviewee as "one of the brightest juniors at the Bar." Fellow junior **James Mellor** is also recommended for bringing IP expertise to media work.

ESSEX COURT CHAMBERS (see full details p.1530) Although unlikely to appear on run-of-the-mill media cases, rivals confirm that this commercial set pops up on some of the biggest cases within the sector. When it does, the silk of choice is likely to be "brilliant" **Gordon Pollock QC** (see p.1461), who is "a superb advocate who can turn his hand to anything." On the junior side, **Vernon Flynn** (see p.1399) is said by solicitors to be "good with clients," while **Richard Millett** (see p.1447) is described as "engaging, robust and excellent on his feet."

MAITLAND CHAMBERS (see full details p.1572) With David Unwin QC retired and Nigel Davies QC headed for the bench, the set is felt to have a lower profile in this area. However, amongst the juniors, **Edmund Cullen** (see p.1387) is recognised for his prowess in music-related cases, and was tipped to do well by several silks. **Simon Barker** (see p.1361) also gains his share of market approval.

3 VERULAM BUILDINGS (see full details p.1615) Although the set's juniors have a low profile in this area, solicitors acknowledge that it has a strong reputation as "the top two silks are a popular pair." **Nicholas Merriman QC** (see p.1446) is highly regarded for his expertise within entertainment law, while **Andrew Sutcliffe QC** (see p.1485) has "a fantastic practice."

OTHER NOTABLE PRACTITIONERS **Richard Price QC** (see p.1463) of Littleton Chambers is recommended for his courtroom style, while **Vincent Nelson QC** (see p.1453) of 39 Essex Street has been active on cases involving written media. At Fountain Court, **David Waksman QC** (see p.1496) is viewed by peers as "a redoubtable opponent who takes good points." **Stephen Bate** (see p.1363) of 5 Raymond Buildings was described by one interviewee as being "as good as it gets for understanding the industry."

MEDIA & ENTERTAINMENT • London

		QCs	Jnrs
1	Blackstone Chambers (Baxendale/Flint)	3	2
2	Hogarth Chambers (Rayner James/Morcom)	2	2
	8 New Square (Mark Platts-Mills QC)	3	2
3	Essex Court Chambers (Gordon Pollock QC)	1	2
	Maitland Chambers (Lyndon-Stanford/Aldous)	-	2
	3 Verulam Buildings (Symons/Jarvis)	2	-

Numbers show recommended barristers in this practice area

LEADING SILKS • London

1	MILL Ian	Blackstone Chambers
	POLLOCK Gordon	Essex Court Chambers
2	ENGLEHART Robert	Blackstone Chambers
	RAYNER JAMES Jonathan	Hogarth Chambers
3	DOHMANN Barbara	Blackstone Chambers
	GARNETT Kevin	Hogarth Chambers
	SUTCLIFFE Andrew	3 Verulam Buildings
4	BALDWIN John	8 New Square
	MERRIMAN Nicholas	3 Verulam Buildings
	PRESCOTT Peter	8 New Square
	PRICE Richard	Littleton Chambers
	VITORIA Mary	8 New Square
NEW SILKS		
	NELSON Vincent	39 Essex Street
	WAKSMAN David	Fountain Court

For details of these leading barristers see Profiles on page 1353

LEADING JUNIORS • London

★	SAINI Pushpinder	Blackstone Chambers
1	HOWE Robert	Blackstone Chambers
2	ALEXANDER Daniel	8 New Square
	BATE Stephen	5 Raymond Buildings
	CULLEN Edmund	Maitland Chambers
	DICKENS Paul	Hogarth Chambers
	MILLETT Richard	Essex Court Chambers
3	BARKER Simon	Maitland Chambers
	FLYNN Vernon	Essex Court Chambers
	MELLOR James	8 New Square
	MICHAELS Amanda	Hogarth Chambers

For details of these leading barristers see Profiles on page 1353

PARTNERSHIP

Research The rankings are based on in-depth interviews with 6,582 solicitors, barristers and clients in the UK. **Chambers'** research is audited by the British Market Research Bureau (see page 7)

BARRISTERS' PROFILES ▶ See pages 1353-1504

LONDON

48 BEDFORD ROW (see full details p.1513) This bijou set houses the only two barristers to devote themselves solely to partnership law. **Roderick I'Anson Banks** (see p.1361) is so synonymous with this area of the law that potential clients go to him directly. "Outstandingly well prepared" and with "encyclopaedic knowledge dating back to the very origins of the subject," he remains a leading authority. **Simon Jelf** (see p.1424) is felt to be "following in his steps nicely." An "excellent draftsman," he is seen by solicitors as being "particularly good at bringing a case to a close."

SERLE COURT (see full details p.1602) Healthily represented in our tables, this set boasts practitioners of the calibre of **Michael Briggs QC** (see p.1371), "a cut and thrust litigator" who is "a tough beast in court." Fellow silk **Frank Hinks QC** (see p.1417) is also making a name for himself in the field. **John Machell** (see p.1439) brings "youthful vigour to the discipline" and is "sought out by the top firms for difficult drafting on partnership agreements." Similarly accomplished on the drafting side is **John Whittaker** (see p.1499) who is widely published on the subject of LLPs.

OTHER NOTABLE PRACTITIONERS Hazel Williamson QC (see p.1500) of Maitland Chambers is "a heavyweight advocate" seen by many solicitors as "a fine alternative if Briggs isn't available" while **Alan Steinfeld QC** of 24 Old Buildings is a "meticulous performer with finely tuned advocacy skills," as demonstrated in many of the more prominent cases.

PARTNERSHIP • London

		QCs	Jnrs
1	48 Bedford Row (Roderick I'Anson Banks)	-	2
	Serle Court (Lord Neill of Bladen QC)	2	2

Numbers show recommended barristers in this practice area

LEADING SILKS • London

1	BRIGGS Michael	Serle Court
2	STEINFELD Alan	24 Old Buildings
	WILLIAMSON Hazel	Maitland Chambers
3	HINKS Frank	Serle Court

For details of these leading barristers see Profiles on page 1353

LEADING JUNIORS • London

1	BANKS Roderick I'Anson	48 Bedford Row
2	BLACKETT-ORD Mark	5 Stone Buildings
	MACHELL John	Serle Court
	WHITTAKER John	Serle Court
	UP AND COMING	
	JELF Simon	48 Bedford Row

For details of these leading barristers see Profiles on page 1353

Author of *Partnership*, published by Butterworths **Mark Blackett-Ord** (see p.1367) of 5 Stone Buildings is "well clued up on the law," and possesses "a bubbly courtroom presence."

PENSIONS

Research The rankings are based on in-depth interviews with 6,582 solicitors, barristers and clients in the UK. **Chambers'** research is audited by the British Market Research Bureau (see page 7)

BARRISTERS' PROFILES ▶ See pages 1353-1504

LONDON

WILBERFORCE CHAMBERS (see full details p.1616) "More or less a monopoly," said one interviewee, expressing what remains a consensus. Although exceptional individuals practise elsewhere, no other chambers can match either the concentration of star barristers or the mass of technical knowledge. **Brian Green QC** (see p.1408) has built up a substantial fan club amongst pensions solicitors, with interviewees typically attributing his popularity to "silky" witness-handling skills and "confidence inspiring thoroughness." "Smooth-talking" **Christopher Nugee QC** (see p.1455) has also won a large number of admirers. His "persuasive style and intellect" make him the automatic choice for many interviewees. Researchers were also impressed with the level of support for "innovative, clear and responsive" **Nicholas Warren QC** (see p.1497) who earned accolades for his activities in the academy as well as at the coal face. **Jules Sher QC** (see p.1478) is another "born advocate," whose "intelligence, class and experience" can make the world of difference in court. **Michael Furness QC** (see p.1401) ("understated, confident and determined") wins applause for his work both on his feet and on paper, while **Edward Nugee QC** (see p.1455) is said by peers to retain a "commanding, paternal presence" at the pensions bar. Alongside its superb array of top silks, the set also boasts the leading junior in "energetic" **Paul Newman** (see p.1453). He won particular praise from solicitors for his "logical and clear-sighted" style of advocacy. Rising in the tables, "aggressive" **Michael Tennet** (see p.1489) is said to be as "meticulous as he is swift to grasp issues." The "commercially literate and incredibly intelligent" **Caroline Furze** (see p.1402) rounds off the Wilberforce contingent.

35 ESSEX STREET (see full details p.1536) Although it doesn't possess the depth of top pensions silks on offer at Wilberforce, it does have, in **Nigel Inglis-Jones QC** (see p.1422) an impressive practitioner who interviewees admire for his clear and insightful advice. The set's real strength, however, is felt to lie in its "well-stocked" ranks of juniors. **Richard Hitchcock** is known for his ability to "get to the crux of the issue," while **John Stephens** (see p.1483) won respect for his "boundless enthusiasm" and for "seeing the big picture." "Client-friendly" **Nicholas Stallworthy** (see p.1482) rises in this year's rankings after warm praise from solicitors who describe him as "full of promise."

3 STONE BUILDINGS (see full details p.1605) "Robust, clear and bright," **Sarah Asplin QC** (see p.1359) is said to be popular with clients for her "sensible, practical advice" and intelligent analysis. A good choice for big pensions cases, competitors are in no doubt that she will be a huge success as a silk. The same chambers also boasts "academic, experienced and bright" **Geoffrey Topham** (see p.1492).

5 STONE BUILDINGS (see full details p.1607) The set boasts a top silk in "bright and practical" **Andrew Simmonds QC** (see p.1478), who interviewees commend for his ability to "cut through to the issues" and for being "never less than thoroughly prepared." Joining him in the silks list this year is the impressive **Christopher Tidmarsh QC** (see p.1491), praised by solicitors for his intelligence and responsiveness. At the junior end, the set boasts **Barbara Rich** (see p.1468), commended as a potential future leader.

OTHER NOTABLE PRACTITIONERS At 24 Old Buildings, **Alan Steinfeld QC** is prized by solicitors for his "brilliant advocacy," and is especially in demand for cases that involve a mix of pensions and professional negligence issues. At chancery set Maitland Chambers, **James Clifford** (see p.1381) is said to be popular with clients for his ability to "grasp difficult issues quickly."

PENSIONS • London

		QCs	Jnrs
1	Wilberforce Chambers (Edward Nugee QC)	6	3
2	35 Essex Street (Christopher Wilson-Smith QC)	1	3
3	3 Stone Buildings (Geoffrey Vos QC)	1	1
3	5 Stone Buildings (Henry Harrod)	2	1

Numbers show recommended barristers in this practice area

LEADING SILKS • London

1	GREEN Brian	Wilberforce Chambers
	NUGEE Christopher	Wilberforce Chambers
	WARREN Nicholas	Wilberforce Chambers
2	SIMMONDS Andrew	5 Stone Buildings
3	INGLIS-JONES Nigel	35 Essex Street
	SHER Jules	Wilberforce Chambers
4	FURNESS Michael	Wilberforce Chambers
	NUGEE Edward	Wilberforce Chambers
	STEINFELD Alan	24 Old Buildings
NEW SILKS		
	ASPLIN Sarah	3 Stone Buildings
	TIDMARSH Christopher	5 Stone Buildings

For details of these leading barristers see Profiles on page 1353

LEADING JUNIORS • London

1	NEWMAN Paul	Wilberforce Chambers
2	HITCHCOCK Richard	35 Essex Street
	STEPHENS John	35 Essex Street
	TENNET Michael	Wilberforce Chambers
	TOPHAM Geoffrey	3 Stone Buildings
3	CLIFFORD James	Maitland Chambers
	FURZE Caroline	Wilberforce Chambers
	STALLWORTHY Nicolas	35 Essex Street
UP AND COMING		
	RICH Barbara	5 Stone Buildings

For details of these leading barristers see Profiles on page 1353

www.ChambersandPartners.com

PERSONAL INJURY

Research The rankings are based on in-depth interviews with 6,582 solicitors, barristers and clients in the UK. Chambers' research is audited by the British Market Research Bureau (see page 7)

BARRISTERS' PROFILES ▶ See pages 1353-1504

LONDON

PERSONAL INJURY • London	QCs	Jnrs
1 39 Essex Street (Nigel Pleming QC)	3	4
12 King's Bench Walk (Richard Methuen QC)	4	4
2 Temple Gardens (Dermod O'Brien QC)	4	3
2 Crown Office Chambers (Spencer/Purchas)	3	1
Devereux Chambers (Colin Edelman QC)	2	3
3 Farrar's Building (John Leighton Williams QC)	3	1
9 Gough Square (John Foy QC)	1	4
4 7 Bedford Row (David Farrer QC)	1	1
Cloisters (Laura Cox QC)	1	1
Old Square Chambers (John Hendy QC)	3	-

Numbers show recommended barristers in this practice area

39 ESSEX STREET (see full details p.1537) This set remains the top choice of many solicitors and is able to boast "class act" **Edwin Glasgow QC** (see p.1405), still considered one of the leaders in the field. **Richard Davies QC** (see p.1388) wins the respect of fellow barristers and solicitors alike, not only due to his fine client handling skills but also for his "pragmatic approach; he's a fighter when it's needed." Taking silk this year is **Neil Block QC** (see p.1367), rated for his "impeccable judgement." A strong base of juniors adds to the set's prowess; **Charles Brown** (see p.1373) is considered a "strong performer" in court and **Charles Cory-Wright**'s (see p.1384) style is characterised by solicitors as "alert, crisp and clear." **Christian Du Cann** (see p.1391) is a favourite of defendant solicitors and **Geoffrey Brown** (see p.1373) is judged to be a reliable advocate.

12 KING'S BENCH WALK (see full details p.1567) An established name for personal injury, the set is led by "calm and collected" **Richard Methuen QC** (see p.1446). "Impressive" **Frank Burton QC** (see p.1375) is rated by defendant and claimant solicitors, while our researchers were told that **Ronald Walker QC** is "good with judges and experienced in court." **Susan Rodway QC** (see p.1470) takes silk this year and is felt to be a "perceptive" advocate. She leaves behind her a convincing array of top-notch juniors including the darling of claimant solicitors, **Allan Gore** (see p.1408), whose expertise in disease claims is widely acknowledged. "Extremely clever" **Stephen Worthington** (see p.1502) is admired for his staunch advocacy and is considered by some solicitors, "one of the best juniors around." **Stephen Archer** (see p.1357) is felt to be a "rising star" and has recently been involved in a number of stress cases. **William Featherby** also attracts market commendation.

2 TEMPLE GARDENS (see full details p.1612) Instructing solicitors appreciate that this set "always has someone that fits the bill." **Ben Browne QC** (see p.1373) is a "good operator" who is often "used on the top end stuff to good effect," whilst **Andrew Collender QC** (see p.1382) is well respected by both barristers and solicitors. **Dermod O'Brien QC** (see p.1456) is considered "extremely thorough in his preparation" and **Jeremy Stuart-Smith QC** (see p.1485) is endorsed as "a tough cookie." **Tim Lord** (see p.1438) is a popular junior and **Christopher Russell** (see p.1472) is newly ranked following solicitor commendation; he is an "excellent senior junior who knows his stuff," while **Martin Porter** (see p.1462) continues to be well regarded.

CROWN OFFICE CHAMBERS (see full details p.1522) The set's "commercial understanding" and ability to relate to clients is highly prized by law firms. The presence of star personal injury silk **Christopher Purchas QC** (see p.1464) is a considerable feather in its cap. He attracts the highest praise from all sides, described variously as "confident in court," "intellectually brilliant" and "extremely bright and clever." **William Stevenson QC**

LEADING SILKS • London

1 LANGSTAFF Brian	Cloisters
PURCHAS Christopher	Crown Office Chambers
2 BROWNE Benjamin	2 Temple Gardens
BURKE Jeffrey	Devereux Chambers
BURTON Frank	12 King's Bench Walk
DAVIES Richard	39 Essex Street
FAULKS Edward	No. 1 Serjeants' Inn
FOY John	9 Gough Square
GLANCY Robert	Devereux Chambers
GLASGOW Edwin	39 Essex Street
IRWIN Stephen	Doughty Street Chambers
JEFFREYS Alan	Farrar's Building
NORRIS William	Farrar's Building
3 BADENOCH James	1 Crown Office Row
BURNETT Ian	1 Temple Gardens
COLLENDER Andrew	2 Temple Gardens
FOSKETT David	1 Crown Office Row
HENDY John	Old Square Chambers
KELLY Matthias	Old Square Chambers
LEIGHTON WILLIAMS John	Farrar's Building
LISSACK Richard	35 Essex Street
LIVESEY Bernard	Four New Square
MASKREY Simeon	7 Bedford Row
METHUEN Richard	12 King's Bench Walk
O'BRIEN Dermod	2 Temple Gardens
PULMAN George	Hardwicke Building
SPENCER Michael	Crown Office Chambers
STEVENSON William	Crown Office Chambers
STUART-SMITH Jeremy	2 Temple Gardens
WALKER Ronald	12 King's Bench Walk
NEW SILKS	
BLOCK Neil	39 Essex Street
COOKSLEY Nigel	Old Square Chambers
RODWAY Susan	12 King's Bench Walk

For details of these leading barristers see Profiles on page 1353

LEADING JUNIORS • London

1 GORE Allan	12 King's Bench Walk
KILLALEA Stephen	Devereux Chambers
KING Simon	7 Bedford Row
WORTHINGTON Stephen	12 King's Bench Walk
2 ARCHER Stephen	12 King's Bench Walk
BROWN Charles	39 Essex Street
CORY-WRIGHT Charles	39 Essex Street
DU CANN Christian	39 Essex Street
HILLIER Nicolas	9 Gough Square
TUDOR-EVANS Quintin	199 Strand
3 BROWN Geoffrey	39 Essex Street
GODDARD Christopher	Devereux Chambers
HIORNS Roger	9 Gough Square
MATTHEWS Dennis	Crown Office Chambers
4 BUCHAN Andrew	Cloisters
FEATHERBY William	12 King's Bench Walk
LEVY Jacob	9 Gough Square
LORD Tim	2 Temple Gardens
PORTER Martin	2 Temple Gardens
RITCHIE Andrew	9 Gough Square
RUSSELL Christopher	2 Temple Gardens
SEYS LLEWELLYN Anthony	Farrar's Building
TRUSTED Harry	35 Essex Street
WEIR Robert	Devereux Chambers

For details of these leading barristers see Profiles on page 1353

PERSONAL INJURY

Research The rankings are based on in-depth interviews with 6,582 solicitors, barristers and clients in the UK. **Chambers'** research is audited by the British Market Research Bureau (see page 7)

BARRISTERS' PROFILES ▶ See pages 1353-1504

(see p.1483) and **Michael Spencer QC** are held in high esteem by solicitors, while junior **Dennis Matthews** is considered a "strong operator."

DEVEREUX CHAMBERS (see full details p.1525) A strong offering of silks and juniors at every level makes this an impressive personal injury outfit. "Fabulous advocate" **Jeffrey Burke QC** (see p.1374) is clearly a favourite of solicitors, who enthuse about his "unbelievable knowledge of the law" and describe him as "hugely experienced in heavyweight personal injury." **Robert Glancy QC** (see p.1405) is a popular silk, not only "a good fighter" but "incisive." At junior level, **Stephen Killalea** (see p.1429) is a "confident, decisive advocate" and **Christopher Goddard** (see p.1406) attracted commendation, while solicitors deemed **Robert Weir** (see p.1498) "someone to watch;" he "turns stuff around incredibly fast."

FARRAR'S BUILDING (see full details p.1539) Solicitors agree that head of chambers **John Leighton Williams QC** (see p.1434) has the "full command of his subject," and he is rated for his ability to think laterally. **Alan Jeffreys QC** (see p.1424) has a strong profile and, like **William Norris QC** (see p.1455), he is admired for his understanding of the market. Peers describe Norris' style as "capable, open and steady," whilst intellectually he is "pragmatic" and "sharp." **Anthony Seys Llewellyn** (see p.1475) is an active junior, with his "pleasant manner" winning many fans.

9 GOUGH SQUARE (see full details p.1545) One solicitor said of this set: "all the barristers give high-quality service" and it remains well known for its accessible approach and forte in disease. Head of chambers **John Foy QC** (see p.1400) is "excellent" on high-value claims and occupational disease litigation. **Roger Hiorns**' (see p.1417) RSI work is particularly highly rated and **Nicolas Hillier**'s (see p.1416) expertise is such that he is retained as specialist counsel by one of the leading personal injury law firms for police hearing loss cases. "Upbeat and enthusiastic" **Jacob Levy** (see p.1434) handles a large number of RTA claims, while **Andrew Ritchie** (see p.1469) received glowing recommendations from interviewees; "he doesn't have his head in the clouds and has the right mixture of pragmatism and knowledge of the law."

7 BEDFORD ROW (see full details p.1510) Amongst the set's deep resources in personal injury, "top-notch" **Simeon Maskrey QC** (see p.1442) stands out with his keen solicitor following. **Simon King** (see p.1429) reinforces the set's strength and has been described by one solicitor as "sound, trustworthy and co-operative."

CLOISTERS (see full details p.1521) "Leading union claimant's silk" **Brian Langstaff QC** (see p.1432) evokes praise from all sides. "A calm performer," he is said to prepare cases well and possess "a good grasp of detail," while solicitors appreciate his "wonderful way with clients." **Andrew Buchan** (see p.1374) is considered a sound operator.

OLD SQUARE CHAMBERS (see full details p.1583) Our interviewees endorsed this "approachable" set that fields the high-profile **John Hendy QC** (see p.1414), admired for his "large claimant practice" and involvement in "heavy cases". **Matthias Kelly QC** (see p.1427) is popular amongst solicitors, whilst new silk **Nigel Cooksley QC** (see p.1383) is "good for industrial disease, particularly loss of hearing."

OTHER NOTABLE PRACTITIONERS **Stephen Irwin QC** (see p.1422) of Doughty Street Chambers is highly rated for his activity in group actions involving Falkland and Gulf war veterans; he also played a key role in the Callery v Gray and Sarwar cases. At 1 Crown Office Row, **James Badenoch QC** (see p.1359) and **David Foskett QC** (see p.1399) were described to researchers as "good news." **Edward Faulks QC** (see p.1397) of No. 1 Serjeants' Inn is a "clever" silk with "a good manner in court;" his work in establishing duty of care regulations is praised by peers. At 1 Temple Gardens **Ian Burnett QC** (see p.1374) is deemed by peers to be "extremely good quality," while **Bernard Livesey QC** (see p.1437) of Four New Square is "doing the complex work." **George Pulman QC** (see p.1464) of Hardwicke Building is perceived by solicitors to have "an imaginative approach to difficult cases." "Clever" **Quintin Tudor-Evans** (see p.1493) of 199 Strand brings an even-handed approach to his cases. At 35 Essex Street, **Richard Lissack QC** (see p.1436) is felt to be "really excellent" in multiparty actions and **Harry Trusted** (see p.1493) can always be counted on to deliver in brain injury matters, often on the "more difficult cases."

WALES & CHESTER

PERSONAL INJURY • Wales & Chester	QCs	Jnrs
1 9 Park Place (Ian Murphy QC) Cardiff	1	1
30 Park Place (John Jenkins QC) Cardiff	-	3
33 Park Place (Neil Bidder QC) Cardiff	2	-

Numbers show recommended barristers in this practice area

LEADING SILKS • Wales & Chester	
1 BIDDER Neil	33 Park Place
MURPHY Ian	9 Park Place
2 REES John	33 Park Place

For details of these leading barristers see Profiles on page 1353

LEADING JUNIORS • Wales & Chester	
1 HARRISON Robert	30 Park Place
REES Philip	9 Park Place
VENMORE John	30 Park Place
WILLIAMS Lloyd	30 Park Place

For details of these leading barristers see Profiles on page 1353

9 PARK PLACE (see full details p.1625) At this experienced set, **Ian Murphy QC** (see p.1452) is "a polished operator" with a large defendant caseload and "strong performer" **Philip Rees** (see p.1468) provides the set with greater PI expertise.

30 PARK PLACE Solicitors commend **Robert Harrison**'s ability to "get to the nub of a situation quickly" and consider him an "articulate advocate." The set's experienced juniors include **John Venmore** (see p.1495) and **Lloyd Williams**, both of whom are reputedly "consistently thorough."

33 PARK PLACE (see full details p.1626) Possessor of a large claimant practice, **Neil Bidder QC** (see p.1365) is deemed "a safe pair of hands," while the "sound counsel" of **John Rees QC** (see p.1467) commands respect amongst solicitors.

PERSONAL INJURY

Research The rankings are based on in-depth interviews with 6,582 solicitors, barristers and clients in the UK. **Chambers'** research is audited by the British Market Research Bureau (see page 7)

BARRISTERS' PROFILES ▶ See pages 1353-1504

WESTERN

PERSONAL INJURY • Western	QCs	Jnrs
1 St John's Chambers (Christopher Sharp QC) Bristol	1	4
2 Guildhall Chambers (Adrian Palmer QC) Bristol	-	2

Numbers show recommended barristers in this practice area

LEADING SILKS • Western	
1 SHARP Christopher	St John's Chambers

For details of these leading barristers see Profiles on page 1353

LEADING JUNIORS • Western	
1 COTTER Barry	Old Square Chambers
EDWARDS Glyn	St John's Chambers
2 BARRIE Peter	Guildhall Chambers
BULLOCK Ian	St John's Chambers
CHIPPINDALL Adam	Guildhall Chambers
MCLAUGHLIN Andrew	St John's Chambers
STEAD Richard	St John's Chambers

For details of these leading barristers see Profiles on page 1353

ST JOHN'S CHAMBERS (see full details p.1623) This "good all-round chambers" offers strength at all levels. Head of chambers **Christopher Sharp QC** (see p.1476) continues to stand out in this region, described by solicitors as "an excellent performer." **Glyn Edwards** (see p.1393) is an extremely popular junior, "as good on paper as he is on his feet," while colleague **Ian Bullock** retains a following amongst solicitors. **Andrew McLaughlin** (see p.1445) is a "rising star" and has had an impressive string of wins over the past year. **Richard Stead** (see p.1482) is characterised as "a good trial barrister."

GUILDHALL CHAMBERS (see full details p.1622) The teaming of "strong advocate" **Peter Barrie** (see p.1362) and "conscientious" **Adam Chippindall** gives the set significant personal injury strength.

OTHER NOTABLE PRACTITIONERS Barry Cotter (see p.1384) of Old Square Chambers also works in the London annex. He is widely considered "down-to-earth" and "good in court," and has a particular strength in stress and product liability claims.

MIDLANDS

PERSONAL INJURY • Midlands	QCs	Jnrs
1 Ropewalk Chambers (Ian McLaren QC) Nottingham	4	5
2 No 5 Chambers (Gareth Evans QC) Birmingham	3	-

Numbers show recommended barristers in this practice area

LEADING SILKS • Midlands	
1 EVANS Gareth	No 5 Chambers
LEWIS Ralph	No 5 Chambers
MCLAREN Ian	Ropewalk Chambers
WOODWARD William	Ropewalk Chambers
2 BLEASDALE Paul	No 5 Chambers
MAXWELL Richard	Ropewalk Chambers
OWEN Robert	Ropewalk Chambers

For details of these leading barristers see Profiles on page 1353

ROPEWALK CHAMBERS (see full details p.1654) This comprehensive PI set dominates in the East Midlands with its plethora of technically skilled and high-profile individuals. **Ian McLaren QC** (see p.1445) and **William Woodward QC** (see p.1502) were both described to researchers

LEADING JUNIORS • Midlands	
1 LIMB Patrick	Ropewalk Chambers
NOLAN Dominic	Ropewalk Chambers
2 ADAMS Jayne	Ropewalk Chambers
ASHWORTH Lance	St Philip's Chambers
COE Rosalind	Ropewalk Chambers
HERBERT Douglas	Ropewalk Chambers

For details of these leading barristers see Profiles on page 1353

as "first-rate" silks. **Robert Owen QC** (see p.1457) is noted for his expertise in multiparty actions and **Richard Maxwell QC** (see p.1443) is regarded as "an urbane performer". "Capable" **Patrick Limb** (see p.1436) and "efficient" **Dominic Nolan** (see p.1455) form part of the set's strong junior base, while **Jayne Adams** (see p.1355) and **Rosalind Coe** (see p.1382) maintain significant local presences. **Douglas Herbert** (see p.1415) also comes recommended.

NO 5 CHAMBERS (see full details p.1618) A trio of top quality silks give the leading West Midlands set strength at the highest level. "First-rate" **Gareth Evans QC** works alongside **Paul Bleasdale QC** (see p.1367), admired by solicitors for having an "exceptionally good nose for work" and the ability to "pick things up and run with them." "Golden boy of the bar" **Ralph Lewis QC** (see p.1435) secured an impressive haul of compliments; he is considered by many solicitors in the region to be "the best" for serious cases.

OTHER NOTABLE PRACTITIONERS Lance Ashworth (see p.1358) of St Philip's Chambers mixes his personal injury practice with commercial law and retains his following among local solicitors.

NORTH EASTERN

PERSONAL INJURY • North Eastern	QCs	Jnrs
1 Plowden Buildings (William Lowe QC) Newcastle upon Tyne	-	3
2 Park Court Chambers (Robert Smith QC) Leeds	-	1
Park Lane Chambers (Stuart Brown QC) Leeds	-	2

Numbers show recommended barristers in this practice area

LEADING SILKS • North Eastern	

For details of these leading barristers see Profiles on page 1353

LEADING JUNIORS • North Eastern	
1 ELGOT Howard	Park Lane Chambers
FOSTER Catherine	Plowden Buildings
FREEDMAN Jeremy	Plowden Buildings
WOOD Simon	Plowden Buildings
2 JACKSON Simon	Park Court Chambers
THORP Simon	Park Lane Chambers

For details of these leading barristers see Profiles on page 1353

PLOWDEN BUILDINGS (see full details p.1651) The set possesses an extremely strong profile on the North Eastern circuit for personal injury cases. It includes the talents of **Catherine Foster** (see p.1400), the "adaptable" **Jeremy Freedman** (see p.1401) and "incisive" **Simon Wood** (see p.1502).

PARK COURT CHAMBERS (see full details p.1633) **Simon Jackson** (see p.1423) is respected for his personal injury and medical negligence expertise.

PERSONAL INJURY

Research The rankings are based on in-depth interviews with 6,582 solicitors, barristers and clients in the UK. **Chambers'** research is audited by the British Market Research Bureau (see page 7)

BARRISTERS' PROFILES ▶ See pages 1353-1504

PARK LANE CHAMBERS (see full details p.1634) **Howard Elgot** (see p.1394) and **Simon Thorp** (see p.1491) are favourites of solicitors in the region due to their depth of experience and seniority in the field.

NORTHERN

PERSONAL INJURY • Northern

		QCs	Jnrs
1	Byrom Street Chambers Manchester	5	-
	Deans Court Chambers (Stephen Grime QC) Manchester	3	-
2	Exchange Chambers (Turner/ Braithwaite/Globe) Liverpool	2	-
	9 St John Street (John Hand QC) Manchester	2	1
	18 St John Street (Jonathan Foster QC) Manchester	-	3
	28 St John St Manchester	1	1

Numbers show recommended barristers in this practice area

LEADING SILKS • Northern

1	MACHELL Raymond	Byrom Street Chambers
	WINGATE-SAUL Giles	Byrom Street Chambers
2	ALLAN David	Byrom Street Chambers
	HINCHLIFFE Nicholas	9 St John Street
	STOCKDALE David	Deans Court Chambers
	SWIFT Caroline	Byrom Street Chambers
	TURNER Mark	Deans Court Chambers
3	BRAITHWAITE Bill	Exchange Chambers
	EDIS Andrew	14 Castle Street
	HORLOCK Timothy	9 St John Street
	REDFERN Michael	28 St John St
	SEPHTON Craig	Deans Court Chambers
	TATTERSALL Geoffrey	Byrom Street Chambers
	NEW SILKS	
	WOOD Graham	Exchange Chambers

For details of these leading barristers see Profiles on page 1353

LEADING JUNIORS • Northern

1	HEATON David	18 St John Street
	ROWLEY James	28 St John St
2	KILVINGTON Simon	18 St John Street
	LAPRELL Mark	18 St John Street
	LITTLE Ian	9 St John Street

For details of these leading barristers see Profiles on page 1353

BYROM STREET CHAMBERS This is an impressive personal injury outfit including the region's two leading personal injury silks. The acquisition from Deans Court Chambers of "outstanding defendant" Raymond Machell QC is a considerable boost for the set; he is praised for his "incisive attention to detail." A solicitor fan of **Giles Wingate-Saul QC** (see p.1501) said, " if I got knocked over by a bus I'd want him," while others pointed to his "impressive recall of detail." "Experienced" **David Allan QC** has established a "formidable" reputation for disease work. He is described as "unfailingly courteous" and "an excellent opponent who can win courts round." **Caroline Swift QC** (see p.1486) is a respected practitioner and **Geoffrey Tattersall Q**'s (see p.1488) approachable manner has won him a healthy following amongst solicitors.

DEANS COURT CHAMBERS (see full details p.1642) The set provides advice on a range of PI matters including catastrophic injury, industrial disease and class actions. "Top negotiator" **David Stockdale QC** (see p.1484) works alongside the popular **Mark Turner QC** (see p.1494) and **Craig Sephton QC** (see p.1475).

EXCHANGE CHAMBERS (see full details p.1638) Devotees of **Bill Braithwaite QC** (see p.1370) describe him as "an aggressive fighter who doesn't give an inch," while other solicitors point to the depth of resources within the set. **Graham Wood QC** (see p.1502) is applauded by peers as "perceptive and effective."

9 ST JOHN STREET (see full details p.1647) "Tenacious" **Nicholas Hinchliffe QC** (see p.1416) is widely recommended by peers and solicitors, whilst **Timothy Horlock QC**'s (see p.1419) significant defendant practice is also admired. **Ian Little** is regularly used by a stable of Northern law firms.

18 ST JOHN STREET (see full details p.1648) This set fields a formidable collection of juniors, including **David Heaton** (see p.1413), who is said to "cream up the market as one of the most experienced senior juniors." **Mark Laprell** (see p.1432) is "a highly visible presence" and **Simon Kilvington** (see p.1429) is a popular choice for local solicitors.

28 ST JOHN ST (see full details p.1649) The set possesses a winning combination with **Michael Redfern QC** (see p.1467), whom solicitors rate as "particularly good on his feet," and **James Rowley** (see p.1471). The latter is endorsed for his "good eye for detail and great recollection."

OTHER NOTABLE PRACTITIONERS **Andrew Edis QC** (see p.1393) of 14 Castle Street has a broad practice and is characterised by solicitors as a "robust performer."

PLANNING

Research The rankings are based on in-depth interviews with 6,582 solicitors, barristers and clients in the UK. *Chambers'* research is audited by the British Market Research Bureau (see page 7)

BARRISTERS' PROFILES ▶ See pages 1353-1504

OVERVIEW: Interviewees applauded the general high quality of specialist planning counsel. *Chambers'* tables remain dominated by the top six sets.

LONDON

PLANNING • London	QCs	Jnrs
1 4 Breams Buildings (Christopher Lockhart-Mummery QC)	5	3
4-5 Gray's Inn Square (Elizabeth Appleby QC)	6	2
2 Harcourt Buildings (Robin Purchas QC)	5	2
2 Eldon Chambers (Clarkson/Hicks)	4	5
2-3 Gray's Inn Square (Porten/Scrivener)	5	5
2 Mitre Court Buildings (Guy Roots QC)	3	5

Numbers show recommended barristers in this practice area

4 BREAMS BUILDINGS (see full details p.1516) Clearly one of the premier sets for court and inquiry advocacy, its "user-friendly and exceptionally brainy" barristers maintain a tight grip on the area. Proclaimed by some as "the brightest star of the planning firmament," **Christopher Katkowski QC** (see p.1426) possesses "incredible intelligence" whilst remaining a "down-to-earth team player." His practice includes judicial review, compulsory purchase and highways. "Soothing, diligent and extremely bright" **Christopher Lockhart-Mummery QC** (see p.1438) specialises in planning, compulsory purchase and compensation. "High-flyer" **Richard Drabble QC** (see p.1391) maintains a powerful profile for court and judicial review matters, whilst clients applaud "ingenious" judicial review expert **David Elvin QC** (see p.1395) on his "eagle-eyed approach to detail." **David Holgate QC**'s (see p.1418) wide-ranging practice incorporates planning and local authority work. He is rated as a "forceful, tenacious advocate" and an "inquisitive and testing legal advisor." "Absolutely excellent" **Nathalie Lieven** (see p.1436) is said by solicitors to possess "first rate knowledge" of planning, local government and general public law, and has built up an impressive level of High Court experience. **Timothy Mould** (see p.1451) is on the Treasury aid panel, and is a respected ratings specialist. "Team player" **Daniel Kolinsky** (see p.1430) is "extremely able, but wears it lightly." He was strongly endorsed by interviewees this year.

4-5 GRAY'S INN SQUARE (see full details p.1550) Despite losing a number of its brightest stars to the bench, with David Mole QC to join Duncan Ouseley QC and Gregory Stone QC, this set is singled out for its "enviable spread of experience." **Brian Ash QC** (see p.1358) is recognised as one of the most established advocates in the field, whose manner with clients ensures continued success. "User-friendly" **John Hobson QC** (see p.1417) is also highly rated, with recent work including an appeal by Mercia Waste Management in Worcestershire. "Creative thinker" **Timothy Straker QC** (see p.1484) is "excellent" for judicial review issues, whilst "dynamic" **John Steel QC** (see p.1482) has had an active year with cases including the Brett Waste Management appeal and the Derby County FC Training Ground. New silk **Timothy Corner QC** (see p.1384) is immensely popular. A "top-notch brain," he is said to "work with humour." Clients rate **Peter Village QC** (see p.1495) for "pushing cases as far as they can go," while leading junior **Thomas Hill** (see p.1416) was described as a "consummate advocate" who "can build a team impressively." **Richard Humphreys** also received recommendations as an impressive advocate who "makes points punchily."

2 HARCOURT BUILDINGS (see full details p.1554) The set was commended to researchers for its "pool of talent in terms of both silks

LEADING SILKS • London

★ KATKOWSKI Christopher	4 Breams Buildings
LINDBLOM Keith	2 Harcourt Buildings
1 HICKS William	Eldon Chambers
LOCKHART-MUMMERY Christopher	4 Breams Buildings
PURCHAS Robin	2 Harcourt Buildings
2 DRABBLE Richard	4 Breams Buildings
ELVIN David	4 Breams Buildings
HOWELL John	Blackstone Chambers
PHILLIPS Richard	2 Harcourt Buildings
READ Lionel	Eldon Chambers
3 ASH Brian	4-5 Gray's Inn Square
CLARKSON Patrick	Eldon Chambers
DINKIN Anthony	2-3 Gray's Inn Square
GEORGE Charles	2 Harcourt Buildings
HOBSON John	4-5 Gray's Inn Square
HORTON Matthew	2 Mitre Court Buildings
KING Neil	2 Mitre Court Buildings
PORTEN Anthony	2-3 Gray's Inn Square
ROOTS Guy	2 Mitre Court Buildings
STRAKER Timothy	4-5 Gray's Inn Square
4 HOLGATE David	4 Breams Buildings
KELLY Andrew	2 Harcourt Buildings
LEWIS Rhodri Price	Eldon Chambers
LOWE Mark	2-3 Gray's Inn Square
PUGH Vernon	2-3 Gray's Inn Square
STEEL John	4-5 Gray's Inn Square
WOLTON Harry	2-3 Gray's Inn Square
NEW SILKS	
CORNER Timothy	4-5 Gray's Inn Square
SINGH Rabinder	Matrix Chambers
VILLAGE Peter	4-5 Gray's Inn Square

For details of these leading barristers see Profiles on page 1353

LEADING JUNIORS • London

1 HARRIS Russell	Eldon Chambers
HILL Thomas	4-5 Gray's Inn Square
WHITE Sasha	Eldon Chambers
2 COOK Mary	2-3 Gray's Inn Square
DRUCE Michael	2 Mitre Court Buildings
ELLIS Morag	2-3 Gray's Inn Square
HOWELL WILLIAMS Craig	2 Harcourt Buildings
LIEVEN Nathalie	4 Breams Buildings
3 BIRD Simon	2-3 Gray's Inn Square
CAMERON Neil	Eldon Chambers
HUMPHREYS Richard	4-5 Gray's Inn Square
HUMPHRIES Michael	2 Mitre Court Buildings
MORGAN Stephen	Eldon Chambers
MOULD Timothy	4 Breams Buildings
ORNSBY Suzanne	2 Harcourt Buildings
4 ALBUTT Ian	2-3 Gray's Inn Square
GLOVER Richard	2 Mitre Court Buildings
LYNESS Scott	Eldon Chambers
STEPHENSON Geoffrey	2-3 Gray's Inn Square
UP AND COMING	
BOYLE Christopher	2 Mitre Court Buildings
KOLINSKY Daniel	4 Breams Buildings
WARREN Rupert	2 Mitre Court Buildings

For details of these leading barristers see Profiles on page 1353

and juniors." Hugely sought-after **Keith Lindblom QC**'s (see p.1436) meteoric rise through the ranks is attributed to "excellent advocacy skills" and "strategic, lateral thinking." Often described by solicitors as "a joy to work with," his style is "economical and urbane." **Robin Purchas QC**'s (see p.1465) deputy judge status gives him kudos, and he

PLANNING

Research The rankings are based on in-depth interviews with 6,582 solicitors, barristers and clients in the UK. **Chambers'** research is audited by the British Market Research Bureau (see page 7)

BARRISTERS' PROFILES ▶ See pages 1353-1504

is universally acknowledged as an "excellent lawyer and advocate." **Richard Phillips QC** (see p.1460) appeared for English Heritage on the Heron case. Renowned for his forensic skills, he has an "amazing capacity for work and tremendous presentational skills." **Charles George QC** (see p.1403) is thought to be "extremely good, especially on paper," whilst researchers found "slightly reserved and cerebral" **Andrew Kelly QC**'s (see p.1427) advice to be widely respected. Among the juniors, **Craig Howell Williams** (see p.1420) is best known for his work on the T5 Inquiry. **Suzanne Ornsby** (see p.1457) received spontaneous recommendation from an array of clients.

ELDON CHAMBERS (see full details p.1527) Five defections appear to have done little to dent this set's buoyant reputation for planning. In addition to several classic names among the silks, it fields some of the area's most promising juniors. "Commercial, energetic and imaginative" **William Hicks QC** (see p.1415) is lauded by peers as "somebody who swiftly reaches the heart of a matter." He is particularly noted for his proficiency with figures and his "rigorous style." Eminent **Lionel Read QC** (see p.1467) enjoys a reputation as one of the most experienced silks, and **Patrick Clarkson QC** (see p.1380) is regarded as an "excellent inquiry advocate." "Sociable" **Rhodri Price Lewis QC** (see p.1435) is felt by solicitors to provide "first-class advice," and has a thorough knowledge of environmental matters. A "team player," clients say that "you can go out for a beer with him." **Russell Harris** (see p.1412) has many fans. According to clients, he is "extremely able, user-friendly and so good." Star of the future **Sasha White** is heavily in demand. He counts Tesco among his clients, and is considered "phenomenally impressive." "Astute" **Neil Cameron** (see p.1376) displays "solid advocacy skills," while **Stephen Morgan** (see p.1450) and **Scott Lyness** were both rated by interviewees as "thoroughly sound."

2-3 GRAY'S INN SQUARE (see full details p.1548) A large set housing some of the area's most colourful juniors, it is rated for its high level of technical proficiency. "Thorough, effective" **Anthony Dinkin QC**'s (see p.1390) recent cases include Polhill Garden Centre v Secretary of State for the Environment. **Anthony Porten QC** (see p.1462) is noted for his "excellent tactics" and has recently appeared in Waters v The Welsh Development Agency. Clients applaud **Mark Lowe QC** (see p.1438) for his "sharp mind," while **Vernon Pugh QC** (see p.1464) continues to be strongly endorsed by solicitors for his planning, environmental and local government expertise. Recommended for inquiry advocacy, **Harry Wolton QC** (see p.1501) attracts a high volume of work from in-house solicitors for building and development companies, planning consultants and architects around the country. "Star personality" **Mary Cook** (see p.1383) boasts an impressive and wide client base, whilst **Morag Ellis** (see p.1395) is particularly rated for compensation and CPOs. "Careful and thorough on opinions," she is said to have a "nice touch." **Simon Bird**'s (see p.1366) "gentle sense of humour" serves him well. "Bright, with a lovely manner," he is praised for his ability to build strong teams. "Genuinely charming" **Ian Albutt** (see p.1355) has a thorough knowledge of planning, administrative, environmental and local government law. "Quite a veteran" **Geoffrey Stephenson** (see p.1483) has a reputation for possessing a "tremendously versatile and independent mind" with "nous and judgement."

2 MITRE COURT BUILDINGS (see full details p.1573) This year sees further retirements for the set, to add to those of Anthony Anderson QC and John Taylor QC last year, with the departures of David Silsoe QC and Michael Fitzgerald QC. Fortunately, some seasoned silks remain and the set boasts a crop of younger talent. "Thorough and analytical" **Matthew Horton QC** (see p.1419) "has a grand style and is great if you need finely expressed arguments." Clients appreciate him for his "user-friendliness and fantastically dry sense of humour." Respected for his "superb skills as a team leader," **Neil King QC** (see p.1429) apparently shares a dry sense of humour, and his direct style in court also wins him praise. **Guy Roots QC** (see p.1470) is felt to provide "concise analysis of complex issues," whilst, among the juniors, **Michael Druce** (see p.1391) is said to possess an old school "forthright" advocacy style. "Good on detail" **Michael Humphries** (see p.1421) continues to be recommended, along with "capable" **Richard Glover** (see p.1406). "Stars of the future," **Christopher Boyle** (see p.1370) and **Rupert Warren** (see p.1497) are new to *Chambers'* rankings this year following substantial market endorsement. Rivals say that they "deserve to be mentioned for their sheer ability."

OTHER NOTABLE PRACTITIONERS **John Howell QC** (see p.1420) of Blackstone Chambers is building up a following for public law and continues to be rated by his planning peers. New silk **Rabinder Singh QC** (see p.1479) of Matrix Chambers also continues to be active in the area, and is handling an increasing volume of public law as well.

MIDLANDS

PLANNING • Midlands		QCs	Jnrs
1 No 5 Chambers (Gareth Evans QC) Birmingham		2	2

Numbers show recommended barristers in this practice area

LEADING SILKS • Midlands	
★ KINGSTON Martin	No 5 Chambers
NEW SILKS	
CAHILL Jeremy	No 5 Chambers

For details of these leading barristers see Profiles on page 1353

LEADING JUNIORS • Midlands	
1 DOVE Ian	No 5 Chambers
UP AND COMING	
CREAN Anthony	No 5 Chambers

For details of these leading barristers see Profiles on page 1353

NO 5 CHAMBERS (see full details p.1618) Clients enthuse that **Martin Kingston QC** is "wonderful." One declared: "He makes me think twice about going to London." A "capable inquiry advocate," he possesses the quality of "not overcomplicating matters, whilst giving a strong argument." Immensely respected **Ian Dove** has built a reputation as a "skilful, solid" advocate, while new silk **Jeremy Cahill QC** is also felt to be doing well. All agree that "stylish performer" **Anthony Crean** will go far.

PLANNING

Research The rankings are based on in-depth interviews with 6,582 solicitors, barristers and clients in the UK. **Chambers'** research is audited by the British Market Research Bureau (see page 7)

BARRISTERS' PROFILES ▶ See pages 1353-1504

NORTHERN

PLANNING • Northern	QCs	Jnrs
[1] 40 King St Manchester	5	2

Numbers show recommended barristers in this practice area

LEADING SILKS • Northern	
[1] GILBART Andrew	40 King St
[2] FRASER Vincent	40 King St
HOGGETT John	40 King St
PATTERSON Frances	40 King St
SAUVAIN Stephen	40 King St

For details of these leading barristers see Profiles on page 1353

LEADING JUNIORS • Northern	
[1] BARRETT John	40 King St
[2] TUCKER Paul	40 King St

For details of these leading barristers see Profiles on page 1353

40 KING ST (see full details p.1645) Acknowledged by solicitors to have a near monopoly on the Northern planning market, the set is said to offer an accessible, convenient service with a wealth of expertise and experience. "Excellent advocate" **Andrew Gilbart QC** (see p.1404) continues to foster a formidable reputation. **John Hoggett QC** (see p.1418) is warmly recommended, along with **Frances Patterson QC** (see p.1459), who clients described as "extremely user-friendly with an impressive intellectual grasp." Rounded lawyer **Stephen Sauvain QC** (see p.1474) is rated as "good on paper and good on his feet." A new addition to *Chambers*' rankings this year, **Vincent Fraser QC** (see p.1401) is said by solicitors to "go quietly about his business" but always to be "much in demand." **John Barrett** (see p.1362) is continuing to establish himself in the area, and **Paul Tucker** (see p.1493) is known as an "up-and-coming mainstream planning junior."

PRODUCT LIABILITY

Research The rankings are based on in-depth interviews with 6,582 solicitors, barristers and clients in the UK. *Chambers'* research is audited by the British Market Research Bureau (see page 7)

BARRISTERS' PROFILES ▶ See pages 1353-1504

OVERVIEW: Use of the Consumer Protection Act continues to develop. The group actions that do come to fruition demand greater strategic planning and more commercially-minded case leadership than ever; as well as an earlier specialisation in a barristers career given their multifaceted complexity. Liaising at board level prior to trial is now commonplace.

LONDON

PRODUCT LIABILITY • London

		QCs	Jnrs
1	2 Harcourt Buildings (Roger Henderson QC)	2	4
2	Crown Office Chambers (Spencer/Purchas)	2	-
	Doughty Street Chambers (Geoffrey Robertson QC)	1	4
3	Fountain Court (Anthony Boswood QC)	2	-
	Four New Square (Justin Fenwick QC)	2	1
	2 Temple Gardens (Dermod O'Brien QC)	1	1

Numbers show recommended barristers in this practice area

LEADING SILKS • London

1	BRENNAN Dan	Matrix Chambers
	FENWICK Justin	Four New Square
	PRYNNE Andrew	2 Harcourt Buildings
	SPENCER Michael	Crown Office Chambers
2	GIBSON Charles	2 Harcourt Buildings
	IRWIN Stephen	Doughty Street Chambers
	LANGSTAFF Brian	Cloisters
	STUART-SMITH Jeremy	2 Temple Gardens
	UNDERHILL Nicholas	Fountain Court
3	BROOKE Michael	Four New Square
	MASKREY Simeon	7 Bedford Row
	ULLSTEIN Augustus	29 Bedford Row Chambers
	NEW SILKS	
	BROOK SMITH Philip	Fountain Court
	WAITE Jonathan	Crown Office Chambers

For details of these leading barristers see Profiles on page 1353

LEADING JUNIORS • London

1	OPPENHEIM Robin	Doughty Street Chambers
2	COTTER Barry	Old Square Chambers
	POPAT Prashant	2 Harcourt Buildings
3	ASIF Jalil	Four New Square
	BOURNE Charles	2 Harcourt Buildings
	HERMER Richard	Doughty Street Chambers
	LYDIARD Andrew	Brick Court Chambers
	RILEY-SMITH Toby	2 Harcourt Buildings
	THOROLD Oliver	Doughty Street Chambers
	TURNER David	2 Temple Gardens
	UP AND COMING	
	GLASSON Jonathan	Doughty Street Chambers
	WEBB Geraint	2 Harcourt Buildings

For details of these leading barristers see Profiles on page 1353

2 HARCOURT BUILDINGS (see full details p.1553) Described as a "dynasty with an outstanding tradition" by one rival barrister, it principally acts for defendants and their insurers across a broad spectrum of group action litigation, and remains the first port of call for many solicitors. Its top silks have taken lead roles in the major cases of late, including the Cape, MMR and benzene litigation. "Clear and cogent advocate" **Andrew Prynne QC** (see p.1464) was considered by many interviewees this year as being "up there with the best," and therefore has risen in our tables. The volume of commendation for **Charles Gibson QC** (see p.1403) impressed researchers; "the brightest young star of all" and assurances of a spectacular career ahead were widespread, while it was also noted he had "retained the thoroughness of a junior in the transition to silk." **Prashant Popat** (see p.1461) is a "formidable opponent," while **Toby Riley-Smith** (see p.1468) was commended as a "team player carving out a niche tobacco and pharmaceutical practice." Two juniors new to the tables also feature this year. Following his appearance in the Cape litigation, **Charles Bourne** (see p.1369) has impressed City solicitors and is increasingly focusing on the specialism, while **Geraint Webb** (see p.1498) also attracted praise from senior litigators, having played a key role in the benzene litigation among others. Webb was applauded for producing "clear and thoughtful work of the highest quality."

CROWN OFFICE CHAMBERS (see full details p.1522) This set is "able to give even the lead set a run for its money" in terms of quality; it is not to be underestimated. The "most experienced barrister" **Michael Spencer QC** possesses "exceptional ability as an advocate," and also benefits from having a medical background. He is currently involved in tobacco, oral contraceptives and the MMR litigation. Distinguished for the "unparalleled clarity of his arguments" and described as a "doughty opponent," **Jonathan Waite QC** (see p.1496) is considered by interviewees to be in line for a promising career upon receiving silk this year.

DOUGHTY STREET CHAMBERS (see full details p.1526) The pre-eminent claimant set, interviewees applaud the development of expertise outside its core civil liberties and medical negligence activity, proven this year by market recognition of two juniors new to *Chambers'* tables. Known for his "shining advocacy" and "swift assimilation of information," **Stephen Irwin QC** (see p.1422) would be the first choice of counsel for many claimant solicitors. There was little dissent from the position that **Robin Oppenheim** (see p.1457) was "now unrivalled as a junior," both in terms of experience and through possessing "the ideal combination of intellect and advocacy." **Oliver Thorold** (see p.1491) retains his market position, making a specialism out of pharmaceutical product liability derived from his core clinical negligence practice. He is joined in the tables by "skilful and bright" **Richard Hermer** who is involved in several group actions including the oral contraceptives litigation, and "tactically adept" **Jonathan Glasson** (see p.1405). The latter has attracted praise early in his career, "displaying a depth of expertise comparable with that of the leading juniors," particularly in pharmaceutical product liability actions.

FOUNTAIN COURT (see full details p.1541) "Cerebral but approachable," **Nicholas Underhill QC** (see p.1494) is held in "enormously high regard." Receiving silk this year, **Philip Brook Smith QC** (see p.1372) impressed *Chambers'* researchers with the level of recommendation he elicited. "Accomplished at getting under the skin of technical matters" according to solicitor referees; opposing barristers commented that he was a "pleasure to be against." Having combined forces in the Hepatitis C litigation, the two appear together for the defendants in the oral contraceptive group litigation. Brook Smith is also involved in the Persona litigation, involving pregnancy testing kits.

FOUR NEW SQUARE (see full details p.1576) The set's long-standing product liability figurehead with wide-ranging group action experience is **Justin Fenwick QC** (see p.1397). Widely considered to be a "top bracket advocate," he is often seen acting for Government, public authorities and manufacturers, especially on cases of scientific and technical complexity. Catching the attention of interviewees as key players in the Hepatitis C litigation, "incredibly hard worker" **Michael Brooke QC** (see p.1372) was

PRODUCT LIABILITY

Research The rankings are based on in-depth interviews with 6,582 solicitors, barristers and clients in the UK. **Chambers'** research is audited by the British Market Research Bureau (see page 7)

BARRISTERS' PROFILES ▶ See pages 1353-1504

praised for his "ground-breaking performance." His junior for the case, **Jalil Asif** (see p.1359), spends a majority of his time on professional negligence, but is nevertheless regarded as "something of a rising star" among practitioners in this field. Both continue to be involved in product liability group actions of a medical nature for claimants and defendants.

2 TEMPLE GARDENS (see full details p.1612) **Jeremy Stuart-Smith QC** (see p.1485) is "thorough in mastering the detail" and an "economical advocate." He continues his involvement in the Sodium Valproate litigation, and has most recently contributed to the claimant side in the MMR litigation. **David Turner** (see p.1494) remains a respected commercial product liability dispute specialist, often acting for manufacturers.

OTHER NOTABLE PRACTITIONERS Among the best claimant silks, **Dan Brennan QC** of Matrix leads in the oral contraceptives case, and continues to be rated as the "shrewdest of tacticians." **Brian Langstaff QC** (see p.1432) of Cloisters garners praise for his "considerable forensic powers." A "flamboyant performer," **Simeon Maskrey QC** (see p.1442) of 7 Bedford Row enters the tables following his expansion into the practice area, most recently instructed on behalf of the claimants in the MMR litigation. Rated as an "imaginative performer," the inclusion of claimant barrister **Augustus Ullstein QC** of 29 Bedford Row Chambers is warmly endorsed by peers. **Barry Cotter** (see p.1384) of Old Square Chambers "always shows enthusiasm in getting to grips with cases," while **Andrew Lydiard** (see p.1439) of Brick Court Chambers continues to enjoy an "excellent reputation" in the field.

PROFESSIONAL NEGLIGENCE

Research The rankings are based on in-depth interviews with 6,582 solicitors, barristers and clients in the UK. **Chambers'** research is audited by the British Market Research Bureau (see page 7)

BARRISTERS' PROFILES ▶ See pages 1353-1504

LONDON

FOUR NEW SQUARE (see full details p.1576) "Packed to the rafters with talented individuals," this set scores highly in terms of both silks and juniors. **Nicholas Davidson QC**'s (see p.1387) "terrifying intellect and precision" confirm what a coup it was to secure him from 4 Paper Buildings. Rated in our highest category, he is joined by "smooth" **Justin Fenwick QC** (see p.1397), whose "tremendous case management and client skills" were widely commented on, and **John Powell QC** (see p.1462), "a fine, confidence-inspiring barrister," who is co-author of the standard textbook on professional negligence. Seemingly destined to join this august company in the near future is **Roger Stewart QC** (see p.1483), who was widely seen as "a star in the ascendant." His "youth, bravery and self-reliance mark him out as likely to go to the very top." Completing the picture is **Bernard Livesey QC** (see p.1437), whose background in PI and criminal law has allowed him to mature into a "devastating cross-examiner." Of the juniors, **Sue Carr** (see p.1377) stands alone. Solicitors talked constantly of her "superb client skills," as well as her "technical ability and bloody-minded refusal to lay down and die." Equally "committed to the cause" is **David Halpern** (see p.1411), who "makes points forcefully but never arrogantly," while **Graeme McPherson**'s (see p.1445) "directness of manner and cordiality" were also highlighted by interviewees. **Fiona Sinclair** (see p.1479) is "a very competent courtroom performer who can make a difference." She shares "a certain personability" with the "endlessly helpful" **Ben Hubble** (see p.1421). Other respected individuals include **Mark Cannon** (see p.1376), **Andrew Nicol** (see p.1455) ("a fantastic proactive advocate with a quick turnaround") and **Paul Sutherland** (see p.1486) ("approachable and hard-working"), who all offer "sensible, practical advice." Indicative of the set's strength in depth and promise for the future are the presence in our up and coming category of **Anneliese Day** (see p.1388) and **Jamie Smith** (see p.1479), whose "tenacity never fails to lift the morale of the client."

4 PAPER BUILDINGS (see full details p.1588) "One of the real stars," **Michael Pooles QC** (see p.1461) is a youngish silk who is "extremely smart" and a favourite of new insurers. His fellow silk **Patrick Lawrence QC** (see p.1433) embodies the spirit of the set as a whole by being "sensible, competitively priced and very approachable." Amongst the juniors, **Francis Bacon** (see p.1359) is said by solicitors to have "flexibility and knowledge in a wide number of areas," while **Derek Holwill** (see p.1418) impresses as "a genuinely bright bloke who is very down-to-earth." **William Flenley** (see p.1398) wins support from solicitors as "excellent in court and good on paper." Providing academic authority is **Mark Simpson** (see p.1478), who has written on the subject but "doesn't have his head in the clouds." **Spike Charlwood** (see p.1378) continues to maintain his share of market support.

4 PUMP COURT (see full details p.1592) With its fine reputation sustained by the presence of a number of high-quality silks and juniors, this set remains a popular choice amongst those in the know. **Christopher Moger QC** (see p.1448) gained market plaudits for his "ability to make the courtroom his own through unflappable advocacy," while **Anthony Temple QC** was noted as having "a brain so agile it can turn on a sixpence." **Nigel Tozzi QC**'s (see p.1492) "elevation to silk came as no surprise," according to commentators, leaving the mantle of leading junior to be picked up by the "incredibly bright" **Andrew Neish** (see p.1453). **James Cross** (see p.1386), "an exceptionally thorough advocate," is commonly felt to be on the rise.

PROFESSIONAL NEGLIGENCE • London

		QCs	Jnrs
1	Four New Square (Justin Fenwick QC)	5	10
2	4 Paper Buildings (Jean Ritchie QC)	2	5
	4 Pump Court	3	2
	2 Temple Gardens (Dermod O'Brien QC)	3	3
3	Crown Office Chambers (Spencer/Purchas)	4	-
	Fountain Court (Anthony Boswood QC)	2	2
4	Atkin Chambers (Robert Akenhead QC)	2	-
	Brick Court Chambers (Christopher Clarke QC)	3	-
	Keating Chambers	3	1
	Maitland Chambers (Lyndon-Stanford/Aldous)	2	-
	9 Old Square (Michael Driscoll QC)	2	1
	3 Verulam Buildings (Symons/Jarvis)	2	1
	Wilberforce Chambers (Edward Nugee QC)	2	2

Numbers show recommended barristers in this practice area

LEADING SILKS • London

1	BRINDLE Michael	Fountain Court
	DAVIDSON Nicholas	Four New Square
	FENWICK Justin	Four New Square
	POWELL John	Four New Square
	SUMPTION Jonathan	Brick Court Chambers
2	EDELMAN Colin	Devereux Chambers
	HARVEY Michael	Crown Office Chambers
	POOLES Michael	4 Paper Buildings
	STEWART Roger	Four New Square
	SYMONS Christopher	3 Verulam Buildings
	TER HAAR Roger	Crown Office Chambers
3	BARTLETT Andrew	Crown Office Chambers
	BRIGGS Michael	Serle Court
	HODGE David	9 Old Square
	HOWARD Mark	Brick Court Chambers
4	BUTCHER Christopher	7 King's Bench Walk
	DRISCOLL Michael	9 Old Square
	MANN Anthony	Enterprise Chambers
	MOGER Christopher	4 Pump Court
	MOXON-BROWNE Robert	2 Temple Gardens
	SIMMONDS Andrew	5 Stone Buildings
	STUART-SMITH Jeremy	2 Temple Gardens
	TAVERNER Marcus	Keating Chambers
	TEMPLE Anthony	4 Pump Court
5	AKENHEAD Robert	Atkin Chambers
	COULSON Peter	Keating Chambers
	CROXFORD Ian	Wilberforce Chambers
	ELLIOTT Timothy	Keating Chambers
	LIVESEY Bernard	Four New Square
	MANSFIELD Guy	1 Crown Office Row
	PYMONT Christopher	Maitland Chambers
	SLATER John	Crown Office Chambers
	TRACE Anthony	Maitland Chambers
	TROWER William	3-4 South Square
NEW SILKS		
	EKLUND Graham	2 Temple Gardens
	GATT Ian	Littleton Chambers
	LAWRENCE Patrick	4 Paper Buildings
	PHILIPPS Guy	Fountain Court
	PHILLIPS Rory	3 Verulam Buildings
	RAESIDE Mark	Atkin Chambers
	SWAINSTON Michael	Brick Court Chambers
	TOZZI Nigel	4 Pump Court
	WARDELL John	Wilberforce Chambers

For details of these leading barristers see Profiles on page 1353

PROFESSIONAL NEGLIGENCE

Research The rankings are based on in-depth interviews with 6,582 solicitors, barristers and clients in the UK. **Chambers'** research is audited by the British Market Research Bureau (see page 7)

BARRISTERS' PROFILES ▶ See pages 1353-1504

LEADING JUNIORS • London

★	CARR Sue	Four New Square
1	BACON Francis	4 Paper Buildings
	HALPERN David	Four New Square
	HOLWILL Derek	4 Paper Buildings
	NEISH Andrew	4 Pump Court
	THANKI Bankim	Fountain Court
2	FLENLEY William	4 Paper Buildings
	LOMAS Mark	Littleton Chambers
	MCPHERSON Graeme	Four New Square
	NEWMAN Paul	Wilberforce Chambers
	SIMPSON Mark	4 Paper Buildings
	SINCLAIR Fiona	Four New Square
3	CANNON Mark	Four New Square
	CHARLWOOD Spike	4 Paper Buildings
	CROSS James	4 Pump Court
	HARGREAVES Simon	Keating Chambers
	HUBBLE Ben	Four New Square
	MOODY Neil	2 Temple Gardens
	NICOL Andrew	Four New Square
	PRYOR Michael	9 Old Square
	ROBERTSON Patricia	Fountain Court
	RUSSELL Christopher	2 Temple Gardens
	SEITLER Jonathan	Wilberforce Chambers
	SUTHERLAND Paul	Four New Square
	TURNER David	2 Temple Gardens
	WEITZMAN Tom	3 Verulam Buildings
	UP AND COMING	
	DAY Anneliese	Four New Square
	SMITH Jamie	Four New Square

For details of these leading barristers see Profiles on page 1353

2 TEMPLE GARDENS (see full details p.1612) This set of commercial specialists offers a plethora of barristers skilled in professional negligence. **Robert Moxon-Browne QC** (see p.1451) is "underrated at your peril," while **Jeremy Stuart-Smith QC** (see p.1485) is noted for his "lack of havering in the courtroom." They are now joined in silk by **Graham Eklund QC** (see p.1394), hailed as both "personable and analytical." Of the juniors **Neil Moody** (see p.1449), **Christopher Russell** (see p.1472) and **David Turner** (see p.1494) are all recommended as being "to the point in their advice."

CROWN OFFICE CHAMBERS (see full details p.1522) This set has a solid showing in our tables by virtue of the presence of a phalanx of respected silks. **Michael Harvey QC** (see p.1413) is said by peers to be "somewhat bookish and cerebral, with a fantastic facility for making complicated matters sound very simple." **Roger ter Haar QC** (see p.1489), meanwhile, is "both formidable and highly articulate," while fellow silk **Andrew Bartlett QC** (see p.1362) was described by competitors as "analytically impressive." Also recommended is **John Slater QC** (see p.1479), "a good, old-fashioned, knockabout leader who consistently provides entertaining cross-examinations."

FOUNTAIN COURT (see full details p.1541) **Michael Brindle QC** (see p.1372) is "at the very top of the profession" and is "your man for heavyweight professional negligence with a strong commercial flavour." He remains embroiled in the Barings litigation, acting for the liquidators of the Singapore-based claimant company in its multimillion pound claim against its auditors. Colleague **Guy Philipps QC** (see p.1459) again received commendation for his efforts for Deloittes in resisting a $650 million claim by Dubai Aluminium Company, and has recently been made silk. As in so many areas, "star junior" **Bankim Thanki** (see p.1489) is making a huge mark, while **Patricia Robertson** (see p.1469) also received warm support from the market.

ATKIN CHAMBERS (see full details p.1508) Experts in construction-related negligence, the host of highly rated practitioners at this set can as easily employ their expertise in a range of negligence claims, particularly those with a technology angle. According to one solicitor, "any of the barristers here can do it, but these are not easy claims so you tend to go to the senior end." This often means **Robert Akenhead QC** (see p.1355), particularly "if you need to go the charm route." Newly ranked this year, he joins his set mate **Mark Raeside QC** (see p.1466), who has a particularly long-standing reputation in this field.

BRICK COURT CHAMBERS (see full details p.1517) "Brain on a stick" **Jonathan Sumption QC** displays the same model assurance in this field as in his many other pursuits. Combining "a brilliant intellect with thorough preparation," his "abundant experience allows him to anticipate the arguments of his opponents." His chambers also houses "Sumption's heir apparent" **Mark Howard QC** (see p.1420) and **Michael Swainston QC** (see p.1486), who is described as an "effective advocate."

KEATING CHAMBERS (see full details p.1560) Its three representatives in the silks table are said by peers to "illustrate the strength in depth at this set." "Bright and robust" **Marcus Taverner QC** (see p.1488) is described as "commercially astute and quick to identify weaknesses." **Timothy Elliott QC** (see p.1394) stood out for many with his "ability to assimilate difficult issues quickly and give realistic advice," while **Peter Coulson QC** (see p.1384) is said by solicitors to be "excellent for claims against construction professionals – a superb tactician and advocate, and good with clients." They are complemented by "a good, reliable junior" in **Simon Hargreaves** (see p.1412), who wins praise from solicitors for his "fun, friendly and supportive" manner with clients.

MAITLAND CHAMBERS (see full details p.1572) Making their debut this year following enthusiastic peer recommendations are **Christopher Pymont QC** (see p.1465) and **Anthony Trace QC** (see p.1492), two talented members of this renowned chancery set. Solicitors appreciate Pymont because "clients like him, he's intelligent and he doesn't panic," while Trace is said to be a good man for a tricky situation: "he will fight to the death and can turn around a seemingly hopeless case."

9 OLD SQUARE (see full details p.1584) Handling professional negligence as it relates to his general chancery and professional litigation practice, **Michael Driscoll QC** (see p.1391) is again rated as excellent, while his colleague **David Hodge QC** (see p.1417) "continues to pull in reams of the highest quality work." **Michael Pryor** (see p.1464) remains "junior most likely to" within this set.

3 VERULAM BUILDINGS (see full details p.1615) Known for its finance expertise, the set boasts a number of superb advocates with experience in professional negligence. **Christopher Symons QC** (see p.1486) has appeared in Somatra v Sinclair Roche and Temperley, one of the biggest negligence actions of recent times in the Commercial Court. Handling similarly high-profile work is **Rory Phillips QC** (see p.1460), who is "unstuffy and never unduly aggressive," while **Tom Weitzman** (see p.1498) has garnered praise for his practice, which encompasses negligence and the crossover with insurance.

PROFESSIONAL NEGLIGENCE

Research The rankings are based on in-depth interviews with 6,582 solicitors, barristers and clients in the UK. **Chambers'** research is audited by the British Market Research Bureau (see page 7)

BARRISTERS' PROFILES ▶ See pages 1353-1504

WILBERFORCE CHAMBERS (see full details p.1616) This commercial chancery set has a broad strand of professional negligence expertise running through it. **Ian Croxford QC** handles a number of insurance and accountancy-related cases and is "one of the best of the bunch on his feet." **John Wardell QC** (see p.1497) is described as "one of the top people for Bar-related work" and displayed his credentials recently in a pioneering High Court case dealing with advocates' immunity. Talented juniors include **Paul Newman** (see p.1453), who has a strong pensions bias, and **Jonathan Seitler** (see p.1475), who handles commercial and property-linked matters.

OTHER NOTABLE PRACTITIONERS For some time now **Colin Edelman QC** (see p.1393) of Devereux Chambers has had "a stunning practice" and is known amongst peers for his "razor-sharp cross-examination." More than one barrister described **Christopher Butcher QC** (see p.1375) of 7 King's Bench Walk as an "exciting" barrister who "can vividly bring a case alive," whereas **Andrew Simmonds QC** (see p.1478) of 5 Stone Buildings has more of an air of "sober assurance." **Michael Briggs QC** (see p.1371) of Serle Court brings his "flowing and finely honed courtroom skills" to the discipline, while at Enterprise Chambers, **Anthony Mann QC**'s (see p.1441) "persuasive charm" continues to win admirers. "Popular with the judges," **Guy Mansfield QC** (see p.1441) of 1 Crown Office Row has been active on behalf of SIF and Bar Mutual, while **William Trower QC** (see p.1493) of 3-4 South Square impresses as "an attractive advocate." Finally, Littleton Chambers lays claim to both a talented silk and junior in the form of **Ian Gatt QC** (see p.1403), who "always lives up to expectations," and the "self-confident" **Mark Lomas** (see p.1438).

PROPERTY LITIGATION

Research The rankings are based on in-depth interviews with 6,582 solicitors, barristers and clients in the UK. **Chambers'** research is audited by the British Market Research Bureau (see page 7)

BARRISTERS' PROFILES ▶ See pages 1353-1504

OVERVIEW: Falcon Chambers maintains its apparently unassailable lead over other sets. As mediations slowly gain in popularity and solicitors become more adept at pre-emptive planning when drawing up deals, competition at the bar is turned up a notch or two.

LONDON

FALCON CHAMBERS (see full details p.1539) This "fast and efficient" set is pre-eminent thanks to "a winning formula combining great brains and real characters." Clients are spoilt for choice: "the silks are all brilliant" and there are "hordes of unmatchable specialists." "All-round outstanding," according to competitors, **Kim Lewison QC** (see p.1435) has "an amazing mega-brain; possibly two." He acted recently in Pye v Graham, in the House of Lords, opposite "wonderfully calm and authoritative" **Jonathan Gaunt QC**, who solicitors admire for his "phenomenal ability to absorb the facts of a case." **Paul Morgan QC** (see p.1449) is described as "super clever and a delight to work with." Admired as a "fighter," he nevertheless "knows when to stop." "Awe-inspiring" **Nicholas Dowding QC** (see p.1390) "delivers a dream service" according to peers, and is praised for his ability with clients, who respond well to his "meticulous preparation and approachable, friendly manner." **Jonathan Brock QC** (see p.1372) is recommended for his aggressive advocacy and "brilliant, empassioned style," while **Kirk Reynolds QC** (see p.1468) is "creative, rational, calm," and popular with clients, who appreciate his sharp commercial brain. Amongst the juniors, **Timothy Fancourt** (see p.1396) is rated highly for his "proactive instinct." Visible recently in Bland v Ingrams Estates, competitors acknowledge that he "can look after himself in a fight." "Thorough and technical," **Wayne Clark** (see p.1380) has niche expertise in business tenancies, while "scholarly" **Stephen Jourdan** (see p.1426) also won market applause. **Edward Cole** (see p.1382) is a "pragmatic commercial all-rounder," regarded by solicitors as "unassuming and straightforward." For Lands Tribunal work, clients beat a path to ex-surveyor **Barry Denyer-Green** (see p.1389), who is "brilliant on evaluations" and specialises in CPO matters. "Forceful and charming" **Guy Fetherstonhaugh** (see p.1397) is said to have "grown in presence and authority," and to be particularly adept at cross-examination. Known for "whirlwind stuff," clients say that he can "win the unwinnable." Best known for his focus on leasehold enfranchisement, **Anthony Radevsky** (see p.1465) is regarded as "top of his class". "Sensible and to the point," **Martin Rodger** (see p.1470) is praised by peers for his "great delivery" and superb grasp of both fact and law, especially in the field of agricultural property. "Sparky and enthusiastic" **Caroline Shea** (see p.1477) and **Catherine Taskis** (see p.1488) both receive enthusiastic peer endorsement, while commentators also note that **Anthony Tanney** (see p.1487) ("personable, with good analytic skills") has been busy lately.

9 OLD SQUARE (see full details p.1584) This "traditional style" set contains a host of "serious quality people." The "stellar" **Simon Berry QC** (see p.1365) is a "fantastic lateral thinker" and "an inventive arguer." Known for his good judgement, law and presentation, competitors say that he "can win both client and court in seconds." "Incisive and reliable" **Michael Driscoll QC** (see p.1391) is "fantastically calm and good at sorting out messes." Commentators report that **David Hodge QC** (see p.1417) is an "excellent advocate and performer," with a punchy, well-organised style and "one of the best brains around." An "old-school chancery litigator," **John Dagnall QC** (see p.1387) has strong property experience, while **Judith Jackson QC** (see p.1423) ("quite the specialist") is winning respect for her work in development and leasehold enfranchisement. "Persuasive and thorough," **John McGhee** (see p.1444) offers a useful mix of property and insolvency. "Not afraid to roll up his sleeves,"

he is described by solicitors to be "a good man for a tight spot." "Client-friendly and incisive" **Timothy Harry**, (see p.1412) is said to have a "calming" effect on clients, much like "solid, safe" **Edwin Johnson** (see p.1425), who "grinds small but relentlessly." **Katherine Holland** (see p.1418) is "good with witnesses," while **Alan Johns** (see p.1425) is also

PROPERTY LITIGATION • London

		QCs	Jnrs
1	Falcon Chambers (Gaunt/Lewison)	6	11
2	9 Old Square (Michael Driscoll QC)	5	6
	Wilberforce Chambers (Edward Nugee QC)	4	2
3	4 Breams Buildings (Christopher Lockhart-Mummery QC)	2	2
	Maitland Chambers (Lyndon-Stanford/Aldous)	1	2

Numbers show recommended barristers in this practice area

LEADING SILKS • London

	LEWISON Kim	Falcon Chambers
	MORGAN Paul	Falcon Chambers
1	BERRY Simon	9 Old Square
	DOWDING Nicholas	Falcon Chambers
	DRISCOLL Michael	9 Old Square
	GAUNT Jonathan	Falcon Chambers
2	BARNES Michael	Wilberforce Chambers
	MALE John	4 Breams Buildings
	WILLIAMSON Hazel	Maitland Chambers
3	BROCK Jonathan	Falcon Chambers
	FURBER John	Wilberforce Chambers
	HODGE David	9 Old Square
	NUGEE Christopher	Wilberforce Chambers
	REYNOLDS Kirk	Falcon Chambers
4	CHERRYMAN John	4 Breams Buildings
	DAGNALL John	9 Old Square
	JACKSON Judith	9 Old Square
	MARTIN John	Wilberforce Chambers

For details of these leading barristers see Profiles on page 1353

LEADING JUNIORS • London

1	FANCOURT Timothy	Falcon Chambers
	SEITLER Jonathan	Wilberforce Chambers
2	CLARK Wayne	Falcon Chambers
	DUTTON Timothy	No. 1 Serjeants' Inn
	JOURDAN Stephen	Falcon Chambers
	KARAS Jonathan	Wilberforce Chambers
	MCGHEE John	9 Old Square
	TAGGART Nicholas	4 Breams Buildings
3	COLE Edward	Falcon Chambers
	DENYER-GREEN Barry	Falcon Chambers
	FETHERSTONHAUGH Guy	Falcon Chambers
	HARRY Timothy	9 Old Square
	JOHNSON Edwin	9 Old Square
	RADEVSKY Anthony	Falcon Chambers
	RODGER Martin	Falcon Chambers
	TIPPLES Amanda	Maitland Chambers
	WONNACOTT Mark	Maitland Chambers
4	HOLLAND Katharine	9 Old Square
	HUTTON Caroline	Enterprise Chambers
	JOHNS Alan	9 Old Square
	MCALLISTER Ann	Serle Court
	MORSHEAD Timothy	4 Breams Buildings
	SHEA Caroline	Falcon Chambers
	TASKIS Catherine	Falcon Chambers
	THOM James	New Square Chambers
	WALKER Andrew	9 Old Square
UP AND COMING		
	TANNEY Anthony	Falcon Chambers

For details of these leading barristers see Profiles on page 1353

1344

PROPERTY LITIGATION

Research The rankings are based on in-depth interviews with 6,582 solicitors, barristers and clients in the UK. **Chambers'** research is audited by the British Market Research Bureau (see page 7)

BARRISTERS' PROFILES ▶ See pages 1353-1504

widely respected by peers and **Andrew Walker** (see p.1496) is said to be "a solid, hard worker."

WILBERFORCE CHAMBERS (see full details p.1616) Described as "a Rolls-Royce chambers – expensive and polished," this set fields a number of fine quality barristers in the "all round chancery mould," who appear on a broad range of cases. Best-known name here is the "fearsome and brilliant" **Michael Barnes QC**, who is renowned for his rent review work. "As good as anyone when he's on song," opponents admit that they "have to think long and hard about who to send up against him." **John Furber QC** (see p.1401) is a "gentlemanly advocate," while one solicitor described **Christopher Nugee QC** (see p.1455) as "a treasure; a secret I'd like to keep." **John Martin QC** wins plaudits as "a super all-rounder." Amongst the juniors, "feisty" **Jonathan Karas** (see p.1426) maintains the respect of his peers, while "fantastically smooth" **Jonathan Seitler** (see p.1475) is said to "win instructions on both personality and ability," and can "make a good job of a bad case."

4 BREAMS BUILDINGS (see full details p.1516) A "user-friendly" set with a reputation for planning and public law, it is also "really good for straight property." The star here is "diligent, meticulous, and hugely capable" **John Male QC** (see p.1440), who solicitors say is "perfect for cautious work," thanks to his "ability to see around corners." The "avuncular, experienced, and highly analytic" **John Cherryman QC** (see p.1379) inspires confidence in clients by being "super in delicate situations." Junior **Nicholas Taggart** (see p.1487) is described by peers as "a details man, but very creative." Good with paperwork, his "infectious and off-the-wall sense of humour" can help in relations with solicitors and clients. Peers rate **Timothy Morshead** (see p.1450) as "an excellent analyst."

MAITLAND CHAMBERS (see full details p.1572) Possessing "impressive and experienced practitioners at every level," this respected chancery set derives much of its property strength from the 13 Old Square part of the amalgam. **Hazel Williamson QC** (see p.1500) is a "rent review star," and is highly recommended for her "careful and painstaking" approach and "good courtroom style." Rivals say **Mark Wonnacott** is "just so damned good!" that he is "tipped for the top, once he has the necessary experience." Praised for his fertile mind, he "often takes on unusual points and handles them well." The market was also warm in its praise for the "persuasive" **Amanda Tipples** (see p.1491).

OTHER NOTABLE PRACTITIONERS At No 1 Serjeants' Inn "responsive and intelligent" **Timothy Dutton** (see p.1392) wins approval from peers for his "colourful advocacy," while **Caroline Hutton** (see p.1422) of Enterprise Chambers attracts clients with her "energy and enthusiasm." **Ann McAllister** (see p.1443) is the name to go to at Serle Court for her "level-headed and thorough" approach to cases. Interviewees were warm in their praise for New Square Chambers' **James Thom**.

PUBLIC INTERNATIONAL LAW

Research The rankings are based on in-depth interviews with 6,582 solicitors, barristers and clients in the UK. **Chambers'** research is audited by the British Market Research Bureau (see page 7))

BARRISTERS' PROFILES ▶ See pages 1353-1504

OVERVIEW: In acknowledgement of its increasing prevalence, this is the first year in which we have introduced a discrete section on Public International Law (PIL). The major centre, worldwide, for this area of law remains London. The capital's travel links, libraries and close proximity to Oxford and Cambridge (major centres of research into this most academic of legal fields) conspire to make it the obvious choice. The fact that it is home to the UK government, historically a major player on the international stage, further adds to its allure. Traditionally, PIL cases were handled by a coterie of distinguished, senior barristers. Governments were, not surprisingly, loathe to put their affairs in the hands of anybody other than the most learned experts in their field and accordingly cherry-picked the cream of academia to represent them, a situation which to some extent persists today. However, recent times have seen a mini-explosion in work. The number of international tribunals multiplies year-on-year, and international law itself is increasingly being invoked before the domestic courts.

SOLICITORS

As it touches on more and more areas, it has resulted in solicitors becoming alive to its importance. The consequence has been the emergence of specialist PIL departments in a handful of firms. Rodman Bundy at **Eversheds** in Paris, for example, has built up an excellent state to state practice, and regularly appears before the International Court of Justice (ICJ). **D J Freeman**, under the stewardship of Alan Perry and Tim Daniel, has similarly made strides, undertaking, *inter alia*, a significant amount of boundary disputes on behalf of Nigeria. Not to be outdone, magic circle firms have staked their claim. **Freshfields Bruckhaus Deringer**, now headed by Malcolm Forster, has had one of the longest associations with this area, while Jeremy Carver at **Clifford Chance** is widely acknowledged as having flown the flag for many years. The importance to such firms of this type of work is, however, perhaps best illustrated by a firm such as **Herbert Smith**. Now housing two experts in this area it epitomises a slightly more youthful thrust and eagerness to specialise in the form of 37-year-old Robert Volterra, who runs the practice in tandem with Campbell McLachlan. Yet it is still the barristers who hold sway. As our table will reveal, the leading figures continue to be largely associated with government and the groves of academia. As PIL washes over the rest of the legal world in years to come, the mix may well become more diverse.

LONDON

BLACKSTONE CHAMBERS (see full details p.1515) Former Chichele Professor of Public International Law at the University of Oxford, **Ian Brownlie QC** (see p.1373) is considered by his peers to be "a brilliant figure at the summit of his profession." Author of many of the major publications in this area, he is "a regular in the highest fora," with a raft of major cases under his belt. These include acting on the Pinochet appeal for Amnesty International, advising on the claims of Japanese POWs and advising Cyprus on its fourth inter-state application filed against Turkey. **Maurice Mendelson QC** (see p.1446) has also dabbled in the Cyprus question, having advised the Turkish government on the former's entitlement to join the EU. Possessor of "a first-class legal mind," he has appeared in the ICJ in the Cameroon/Nigeria case, and is known for "his exhaustive submissions." These two carry on a tradition for excellence in this sphere in a set of chambers which is also home to Ian Sinclair QC, a redoubtable practitioner who is set to retire after a highly successful career.

PUBLIC INTERNATIONAL LAW • London

		QCs	Jnrs
1	Blackstone Chambers (Baxendale/Flint)	2	-
	20 Essex Street (Iain Milligan QC)	3	1
2	Essex Court Chambers (Gordon Pollock QC)	3	2
	Matrix Chambers (Tim Owen QC)	-	2

Numbers show recommended barristers in this practice area

LEADING SILKS • London

1	BROWNLIE Ian	Blackstone Chambers
	LAUTERPACHT Elihu	20 Essex Street
	WATTS Arthur	20 Essex Street
2	GREENWOOD Christopher	Essex Court Chambers
3	BERMAN Franklin	Essex Court Chambers
	MENDELSON Maurice	Blackstone Chambers
	PLENDER Richard	20 Essex Street
	NEW SILKS	
	SHAW Malcolm	Essex Court Chambers

For details of these leading barristers see Profiles on page 1353

LEADING JUNIORS • London

1	BETHLEHEM Daniel	20 Essex Street
	CRAWFORD James	Matrix Chambers
	LOWE Vaughan	Essex Court Chambers
2	SANDS Philippe	Matrix Chambers
3	QURESHI Khawar	Serle Court
	UP AND COMING	
	WORDSWORTH Sam	Essex Court Chambers

For details of these leading barristers see Profiles on page 1353

20 ESSEX STREET (see full details p.1534) Professor **Elihu Lauterpacht QC** (see p.1432) carries over 50 years of experience into the courtroom. "Never frightened and always willing to take on new areas," he advises on territorial and boundary problems, fisheries and expropriation claims. His reputation is such that he sat as Commission President on the Ethiopia/Eritrea boundary dispute and also appeared in the Qatar v Bahrain maritime delineation and territorial question. **Arthur Watts QC** (see p.1498) enjoyed a distinguished career as legal advisor to the Foreign & Commonwealth Office before moving into PIL. His "decades of practical experience" there have been translated into cases such as the Nigeria/Cameroon border dispute, where he displayed "a realistic sense of the role of the PIL lawyer." Adjudged by our interviewees an "intensely charming man," he has committed much of his efforts to PIL. **Richard Plender QC** (see p.1461) mixes PIL work in with his EU/competition practice. "A fine advocate with a broader legal sweep than most," he appeared for the British against Ireland in the recent International Tribunal for the Law of the Sea case to determine the validity of the UK's plans to expand operations at its Sellafield nuclear plant. Also present in this case was leading junior **Daniel Bethlehem** (see p.1365). Mainly, but not exclusively, active on behalf of the UK government, he is "fantastically rigorous," has a "wonderful breadth of knowledge" and produces "excellent written work." A recent highlight for him was appearing in the ICJ for Belgium against the Congo, concerning a dispute over the issue of an international warrant for the arrest of the latter's foreign minister.

ESSEX COURT CHAMBERS (see full details p.1530) This set is increasingly featuring in the bigger cases. Its main player is **Christopher Greenwood QC** (see p.1409), Professor of International Law at the LSE. Hailed as "a marvellous court performer and superb communicator of ideas," he distinguishes himself in an area of the law associated more with analytical rather than advocacy skills. An eclectic caseload has seen him

PUBLIC INTERNATIONAL LAW

Research The rankings are based on in-depth interviews with 6,582 solicitors, barristers and clients in the UK. **Chambers'** research is audited by the British Market Research Bureau (see page 7)

BARRISTERS' PROFILES ▶ See pages 1353-1504

acting for Kuwait Airways v Iraqi Airways, advising the UK government on the Bankovic v Belgium case in the European Court of Human Rights and appearing in the Honduras/Nicaragua boundary dispute case before the ICJ. His colleague, **Franklin Berman QC**, has not enjoyed quite as much exposure, but is strongly fancied to play a key role in the future. Having succeeded Arthur Watts QC as legal advisor to the Foreign & Commonwealth Office, he has only recently come into private practice. "Learned and considered," he appeared with Greenwood in the Lockerbie proceedings in the ICJ and in the Yugoslavia v United Kingdom 'legality of the use of force' case. Lauded for his "scholarly approach" is new silk **Malcolm Shaw QC** (see p.1477), Sir Robert Jennings Professor of International Law at the University of Leicester, and described by many as "a pleasure to work with." The set also boasts talented juniors. **Vaughan Lowe** (see p.1439) is the sitting Chichele Professor of Public International Law at the University of Oxford and consequently in demand for his academic skills. An "understated performer," he appeared for Ireland against the UK in the International Tribunal for the Law of the Sea case regarding Sellafield. **Sam Wordsworth** (see p.1502), a former solicitor with Eversheds in Paris, is a possessor of "excellent analytical skills" who acted for Slovakia in the Gabcikovo-Nagymaros Project case.

MATRIX CHAMBERS (see full details p.1573) Australian silk **James Crawford SC** (see p.1386) can lay a fair claim to being the busiest of all the current silks in this area. The Whewell Professor of International Law at the University of Cambridge, he is the youngest of those featured in our top band, and is recognised for the "vibrancy of his argument." As a mark of distinction, he has previously been a Member of the International Law Commission, and is described by peers as "one of the most creative PIL lawyers around," who is "brilliant at thinking laterally." He is joined at the set by leading junior **Philippe Sands** (see p.1473), another of the new breed. Although largely focused on environmental law, he has applied his "great enthusiasm and self-belief" to a wide range of matters. His portfolio includes appearing before the ICJ as counsel for Honduras in its boundary dispute with Nicaragua and acting as a mediator in the Belize v Guatemala maritime boundary dispute.

OTHER NOTABLE PRACTITIONERS Treasury Counsel **Khawar Qureshi** (see p.1465) of Serle Court undertakes occasional PIL work. He is an advisor on treaty drafting and interpretation, and state and diplomatic immunity, and has also advised the Bosnian government in the Dayton peace talks and on ICJ cases against Yugoslavia concerning genocide. He recently appeared for the US government in the Kenyan Embassy bombing case of Al-Fawwaz in seeking to determine whether a state can seek extradition for crimes not actually committed on its own soil.

SHIPPING & COMMODITIES

Research The rankings are based on in-depth interviews with 6,582 solicitors, barristers and clients in the UK. Chambers' research is audited by the British Market Research Bureau (see page 7)

BARRISTERS' PROFILES ▶ See pages 1353-1504

LONDON

ESSEX COURT CHAMBERS (see full details p.1530) Described by solicitors as "truly living up to its billing of 'first port of call' on any shipping matter," this set is home to "any number of truly excellent individuals." High among these is, of course, "the legendary" **Gordon Pollock QC** (see p.1461) who "made his reputation in shipping, and remains a name to turn to for that touch of gravitas" although "you can only win his attention with the most complex of cases." **Bernard Eder QC** (see p.1393) has his praises sung by solicitors in both the fields of shipping and commodities. A "creative, imaginative barrister," he employs his "first-class brain to good effect." Peers appreciate that **Graham Dunning QC** (see p.1392) is "like a terrier – he will never give up on you," while **Jonathan Gilman QC** (see p.1404) is described as "the oracle on insurance shipping work." The highly commercial **Jeffrey Gruder QC** (see p.1410) stands out from the crowd as "conscientious and clever." His precise understanding of the law ensures that "he can always find the good points to highlight in the papers." **Richard Jacobs QC** (see p.1423) is a new addition to the table, thanks to his "sharp and incisive" approach to commodities work. Peers rate him as "truly outstanding in tribunals." New silk **Steven Berry QC** (see p.1365) was described to researchers as "consolidating those skills that made him an expert shipping junior." Amongst a raft of talented juniors, **Claire Blanchard** (see p.1367) continues to stand out as "a tough opponent you have to be watchful of," while **David Foxton** (see p.1400) is recommended as having "a first-class mind." **Philippa Hopkins** (see p.1419) earns plaudits for her "expert dry skills," and **David Joseph** (see p.1426) continues to be a force in marine insurance matters. Some sources credited **Paul McGrath** (see p.1444) as "the brains behind a lot of the innovative ideas out there," and the "superb and commercially aware" **Joe Smouha** (see p.1480) continues to be recommended by all quarters.

4 ESSEX COURT (see full details p.1532) This chambers is recommended nationwide for its "notable individuals and a rigorous approach." **Simon Rainey QC** (see p.1466) is a familiar figure on the horizon, commended by solicitors as "user-friendly and incisive." He "can turn his hand to every aspect and is knowledgeable about them all;" for many, he is "a definite favourite." **Nigel Teare QC** (see p.1489) was praised as "a stunning advocate – one of the best silks in the country for wet work." Sources admired **Belinda Bucknall QC**'s (see p.1374) "genuine enthusiasm;" she "considers every matter, and is utterly responsive." **Lionel Persey QC** (see p.1459) is one of the "top dogs in the field;" he is "sharp and precise" in his advice, and solicitors value his constructive approach to problem solving. **Charles Macdonald QC** (see p.1439) "operates on cases with a surgeon's touch" and **Jeremy Russell QC** (see p.1472) has "a cracking courtroom presence." Of the new silks, **Simon Kverndal QC** (see p.1431) is "highly impressive in his advice – a wonderful all-rounder," while peers rate **Nigel Meeson QC** (see p.1446) as "bright, practical and likeable." In the ranks of the juniors, **Luke Parsons** (see p.1458) continues to stand above all others. Described by many as an "absolutely outstanding operator, whose only possible flaw is that he's so busy because he's so popular." **David Goldstone**'s (see p.1407) "intellectual capacity impresses" and he retains the ability to talk in layman's terms. **Nigel Jacobs** (see p.1423) is "a gentleman and a scholar through and through," and **Michael Davey** has "a practical sea-faring background and a clear sight of what is important in a case."

20 ESSEX STREET (see full details p.1534) This set attracts the commendation of solicitors nationally for its "fantastic range of skills and deep pool of talented individuals." Described by **Nicholas Hamblen QC** (see p.1411) is

SHIPPING & COMMODITIES • London

		QCs	Jnrs
1	Essex Court Chambers (Gordon Pollock QC)	7	6
	4 Essex Court (Nigel Teare QC)	8	4
	20 Essex Street (Iain Milligan QC)	6	3
	7 King's Bench Walk (Kealey/Flaux)	7	4
2	Stone Chambers (Steven Gee QC)	2	1

Numbers show recommended barristers in this practice area

LEADING SILKS • London

1	POLLOCK Gordon	Essex Court Chambers
	SCHAFF Alistair	7 King's Bench Walk
2	BRENTON Timothy	7 King's Bench Walk
	EDER Bernard	Essex Court Chambers
	HAMBLEN Nicholas	20 Essex Street
	RAINEY Simon	4 Essex Court
	TEARE Nigel	4 Essex Court
3	BUCKNALL Belinda	4 Essex Court
	FLAUX Julian	7 King's Bench Walk
	GAISMAN Jonathan	7 King's Bench Walk
	MILLIGAN Iain	20 Essex Street
	PERSEY Lionel	4 Essex Court
	YOUNG Timothy	20 Essex Street
4	DUNNING Graham	Essex Court Chambers
	GILMAN Jonathan	Essex Court Chambers
	GLENNIE Angus	20 Essex Street
	GRUDER Jeffrey	Essex Court Chambers
	HOFMEYR Stephen	7 King's Bench Walk
	JACOBS Richard	Essex Court Chambers
	KAY Jervis	Stone Chambers
	KEALEY Gavin	7 King's Bench Walk
	MACDONALD Charles	4 Essex Court
	MALES Stephen	20 Essex Street
	RUSSELL Jeremy	4 Essex Court
NEW SILKS		
	BERRY Steven	Essex Court Chambers
	BUTCHER Christopher	7 King's Bench Walk
	KVERNDAL Simon	4 Essex Court
	LORD Richard	Brick Court Chambers
	MATTHEWS Duncan	20 Essex Street
	MEESON Nigel	4 Essex Court
	SELVARATNAM Vasanti	Stone Chambers

For details of these leading barristers see Profiles on page 1353

LEADING JUNIORS • London

1	PARSONS Luke	4 Essex Court
2	BAKER Andrew	20 Essex Street
	BLANCHARD Claire	Essex Court Chambers
	GOLDSTONE David	4 Essex Court
	JACOBS Nigel	4 Essex Court
	PRIDAY Charles	7 King's Bench Walk
3	COBURN Michael	20 Essex Street
	DAVEY Michael	4 Essex Court
	EDEY Philip	20 Essex Street
	SOUTHERN Richard	7 King's Bench Walk
4	BRIGHT Robert	7 King's Bench Walk
	EDWARDS David	7 King's Bench Walk
	FOXTON David	Essex Court Chambers
	HILL Timothy	Stone Chambers
	HOPKINS Philippa	Essex Court Chambers
	JOSEPH David	Essex Court Chambers
	MCGRATH Paul	Essex Court Chambers
	SAUNDERS Nicholas	199 Strand
	SMOUHA Joe	Essex Court Chambers

For details of these leading barristers see Profiles on page 1353

SHIPPING & COMMODITIES

Research The rankings are based on in-depth interviews with 6,582 solicitors, barristers and clients in the UK. **Chambers'** research is audited by the British Market Research Bureau (see page 7)

BARRISTERS' PROFILES ▶ See pages 1353-1504

described "as a great team player." A "superb intellect, trained on the real issues," he impresses as one "receptive to new ideas." **Iain Milligan QC** (see p.1447) is "an outstanding commercial silk;" sources perceive that he "features prominently in this type of work." **Timothy Young QC** (see p.1503) employs his "vigorous mind" and "quick wit" on the most involved cases. An "advocate in the 'street fighter' mould," **Angus Glennie QC** (see p.1405) divides his time between briefs in England and Scotland. He is regarded as "thorough in his preparation" and an "intelligent, hard-working barrister – a truly respectable choice." **Stephen Males QC** (see p.1440) joins the list this year, following endorsement for his "expert knowledge, sound advice and unwavering enthusiasm." New silk **Duncan Matthews QC** (see p.1442) has maintained his "straightforward" approach that, combined with his "clever mind," makes him a "doughty opponent." Amongst the juniors, **Andrew Baker** (see p.1359) brings a "dynamic approach" to his work and "has the uncanny ability to see the result of the case at the beginning." **Michael Coburn** (see p.1381) is a "prime choice for major cases," while **Philip Edey**'s (see p.1393) star is "definitely on the rise."

7 KING'S BENCH WALK (see full details p.1564) Observers commended this set for its "consistently high-quality shipping and commodities skills," found across a range of silks and juniors. **Alistair Schaff QC** (see p.1474) is "an absolutely outstanding choice." "A formidable court performer," he employs clear lines of communication with both solicitors and clients and is "not frightened of difficult points." **Timothy Brenton QC** (see p.1371) takes an approach that is "utterly sensible and knowledgeable," which he delivers with "a human touch." **Julian Flaux QC** (see p.1398) is "a star – without doubt a first-class operator." Interviewees respect "busy" **Jonathan Gaisman QC** as a "formidable advocate, and a true expert." Solicitors reported that it is "always rewarding" to instruct **Stephen Hofmeyr QC** (see p.1418), appreciating that he is "thorough in his preparation." Opposing counsel concur: "You know you have a fight on your hands if he's on the other side." **Gavin Kealey QC** (see p.1427) is "an amusing, effervescent presence" who "plies his trade with an expert hand." **Christopher Butcher QC** (see p.1375) brings "fresh ideas, and clear thought" to his cases. Among the juniors, **Charles Priday** (see p.1464) is an "asset to any team" and one who is "light on his feet" in court. Solicitors find that **Richard Southern** (see p.1481) is "excellent at putting forward complex ideas in a simple way." **Robert Bright** is "one of the best up-and-coming juniors," while **David Edwards** (see p.1393) is "truly intelligent and diligent."

STONE CHAMBERS (see full details p.1609) Following the dissolution of 4 Field Court, this chambers, which has been adopted by a number of the former's tenants, was described as the "phoenix rising from the flames." **Jervis Kay QC** (see p.1427) has a "good head on his shoulders," and for some solicitors is "our first port of call on admiralty work." New silk **Vasanti Selvaratnam QC** (see p.1475) is "remarkably skilled," while junior **Timothy Hill** (see p.1416) is recommended for his experience across the shipping sphere.

OTHER NOTABLE PRACTITIONERS At Brick Court Chambers, **Richard Lord QC** (see p.1438) is respected by solicitors, who trust that "he'll provide a top class service every time." Junior **Nicholas Saunders** (see p.1474) of 199 Strand is described as "absolutely on the ball."

SPORT

Research The rankings are based on in-depth interviews with 6,582 solicitors, barristers and clients in the UK. **Chambers'** research is audited by the British Market Research Bureau (see page 7)

BARRISTERS' PROFILES ▶ See pages 1353-1504

LONDON

BLACKSTONE CHAMBERS (see full details p.1515) Clear favourites among solicitors, it draws together an admired team of top-flight practitioners. **Michael Beloff QC** (see p.1364) retains his "fiefdom" in sports law, preferring "an inherent understanding and a mind that races ahead of everyone else's." He recently served as an arbitrator for the 2002 FIFA World Cup. **David Pannick QC** (see p.1458) is described as having "one of the most able brains of anyone in the sporting world" while colleague **Charles Flint QC** (see p.1398) is hailed along with Pannick and Beloff as being "one of the three wise men of sports' law." He recently represented the Football league in its claim against Carlton and Granada. **Ian Mill QC** (see p.1447) is commended by solicitors for the depth of his experience across a range of sports, while **Paul Goulding QC** (see p.1408) is "an exciting option" for any law firm with a difficult case. At the junior level, **Adam Lewis** (see p.1435) is known as "the top junior in the country; a good carrier of the Blackstone torch," while **Michael Fordham** (see p.1399) and **Robert Howe** (see p.1420) were both recommended to researchers as "expert technicians."

BRICK COURT CHAMBERS (see full details p.1517) Home to "the cream outside Blackstone," the set fields **Charles Hollander QC** (see p.1418), who is recommended by different parties for his "crack mind on both disciplinary and commercial." His colleague, **Nicholas Green QC** (see p.1409), is praised for his "encyclopaedic knowledge of broadcasting and European issues," while junior **Mark Hoskins** (see p.1419) is praised as "an individual whose future is bright."

OTHER NOTABLE PRACTITIONERS At 11 King's Bench Walk Chambers the much-admired **Tim Kerr QC** (see p.1428) rises through our tables this year. Noted for his work on a number of prominent cases, he is praised for his "sharpness" and his "serious but always approachable manner." **Murray Rosen QC** (see p.1471) of 11 Stone Buildings is another figure of import, commended for his pragmatism. **David Griffith-Jones QC** (see p.1410) of Devereux Chambers has attracted a following among solicitors, while **Peter Leaver QC** (see p.1433) of One Essex Court is "an expert whose skills and interests coincide." At 5 Paper Buildings **Kuldip Singh QC** remains a true force, while **Richard Spearman QC** (see p.1481) of 4-5 Gray's Inn Square is regarded by peers as "massively popular on the media side." At the junior level, **Jonathan Crystal** (see p.1386) at Cloisters is rated as a lawyer "who will leap through flaming hoops in the interests of a case." **Christopher Stoner** (see p.1484) of Serle Court impresses as a "powerful litigator;" he has recently moved from 9 Old Square. **Bankim Thanki** (see p.1489) of Fountain Court "attracts a steady flow of classy work," and **Paul Harris** (see p.1412) of Monckton Chambers is a man "most definitely on the rise."

SPORT • London

		QCs	Jnrs
1	Blackstone Chambers (Baxendale/Flint)	5	3
2	Brick Court Chambers (Christopher Clarke QC)	2	1

Numbers show recommended barristers in this practice area

LEADING SILKS • London

1	BELOFF Michael	Blackstone Chambers
	PANNICK David	Blackstone Chambers
2	FLINT Charles	Blackstone Chambers
	HOLLANDER Charles	Brick Court Chambers
	KERR Tim	11 King's Bench Walk Chambers
	ROSEN Murray	11 Stone Buildings
3	GREEN Nicholas	Brick Court Chambers
	GRIFFITH-JONES David	Devereux Chambers
	LEAVER Peter	One Essex Court
	MILL Ian	Blackstone Chambers
	SINGH Kuldip	5 Paper Buildings
4	GOULDING Paul	Blackstone Chambers
	SPEARMAN Richard	4-5 Gray's Inn Square

For details of these leading barristers see Profiles on page 1353

LEADING JUNIORS • London

1	LEWIS Adam	Blackstone Chambers
2	CRYSTAL Jonathan	Cloisters
	STONER Christopher	Serle Court
	THANKI Bankim	Fountain Court
3	FORDHAM Michael	Blackstone Chambers
	HARRIS Paul	Monckton Chambers
	HOSKINS Mark	Brick Court Chambers
	HOWE Robert	Blackstone Chambers

For details of these leading barristers see Profiles on page 1353

TAX

Research The rankings are based on in-depth interviews with 6,582 solicitors, barristers and clients in the UK. **Chambers'** research is audited by the British Market Research Bureau (see page 7)

BARRISTERS' PROFILES ▶ See pages 1353-1504

LONDON

TAX • London	QCs	Jnrs
1 Gray's Inn Tax Chambers (Milton Grundy)	4	3
Pump Court Tax Chambers	4	4
2 11 New Square (John Gardiner QC)	3	-
3 One Essex Court (Lord Grabiner QC)	1	-
24 Old Buildings (Rex Bretten QC)	1	1
3 Temple Gardens Tax Chambers (Richard Bramwell QC)	1	1

Numbers show recommended barristers in this practice area

LEADING SILKS • Corporate Tax • London

1	AARONSON Graham	Pump Court Tax Chambers
	GARDINER John	11 New Square
	GOLDBERG David	Gray's Inn Tax Chambers
	MILNE David	Pump Court Tax Chambers
2	BRETTEN Rex	24 Old Buildings
	PROSSER Kevin	Pump Court Tax Chambers
3	BRAMWELL Richard	3 Temple Gardens Tax Chambers
	FLESCH Michael	Gray's Inn Tax Chambers
	GOY David	Gray's Inn Tax Chambers
	THORNHILL Andrew	Pump Court Tax Chambers
	TREVETT Peter	11 New Square
NEW SILKS		
	BAKER Philip	Gray's Inn Tax Chambers
	GAMMIE Malcolm	One Essex Court
	PEACOCK Jonathan	11 New Square

LEADING JUNIORS • Corporate Tax • London

1	GHOSH Julian	Pump Court Tax Chambers
2	EWART David	Pump Court Tax Chambers
	NOCK Reginald	24 Old Buildings
	SHIPWRIGHT Adrian	Pump Court Tax Chambers
3	CULLEN Felicity	Gray's Inn Tax Chambers
	JAMES Alun	3 Temple Gardens Tax Chambers
	MCKAY Hugh	Gray's Inn Tax Chambers
	THOMAS Roger	Pump Court Tax Chambers
UP AND COMING		
	MCDONNELL Conrad	Gray's Inn Tax Chambers

LEADING SILKS • Inland Revenue • London

1	HENDERSON Launcelot	5 Stone Buildings
2	FURNESS Michael	Wilberforce Chambers
	GLICK Ian	One Essex Court
	MCCALL Christopher	Maitland Chambers
NEW SILKS		
	BRENNAN Timothy	Devereux Chambers
	TIDMARSH Christopher	5 Stone Buildings

LEADING SILKS • VAT • London

1	CORDARA Roderick	Essex Court Chambers
	MILNE David	Pump Court Tax Chambers
2	GOY David	Gray's Inn Tax Chambers
	LASOK Paul	Monckton Chambers
	PARKER Kenneth	Monckton Chambers
	PROSSER Kevin	Pump Court Tax Chambers
NEW SILKS		
	CONLON Michael	Pump Court Tax Chambers

LEADING JUNIORS • VAT • London

1	BALDRY Rupert	Pump Court Tax Chambers
	BARLOW Richard	11 King's Bench Walk
	CARGILL-THOMPSON Perdita	Essex Court Chambers
	HITCHMOUGH Andrew	Pump Court Tax Chambers
2	SMOUHA Joe	Essex Court Chambers

For details of these leading barristers see Profiles on page 1353

GRAY'S INN TAX CHAMBERS (see full details p.1552) Renowned for corporate work, the set also handles private client matters and is said to attract "choice work" through its members' "reputation for excellence." For many interviewees, **David Goldberg QC** (see p.1406) is the "counsel of choice for complex, technical structured finance issues." Solicitors describe him as a "man who can;" his "wide range of analytical skills" allows him to "think round a problem and always come up with an answer." Goldberg appeared for the appellant in Acorn Management Services v Commissioners of Customs and Excise arguing whether the student accommodation provider was an exempt supply of land. "Approachable" **Michael Flesch QC** (see p.1398) was named "brilliant on heavyweight structuring." His practice covers all aspects of planning, Revenue disputes and related tax appeals. Clients have "complete and total trust" in **David Goy QC** (see p.1408), a "fantastic analyst" with the skills to "anticipate the other side's arguments." Singled out as "good on everything to do with property," Goy was recommended for both corporate tax and VAT matters and is considered a "heavy hitter" in both areas. "Shrewd" **Philip Baker QC** (see p.1360) is considered another "star performer" at the Bar. Interviewees report that double taxation treaties "are his thing." Senior junior **Hugh McKay** (see p.1445) has had a busy year, appearing in a number of cases both for corporate clients and Customs & Excise. "Easy to work with," his "practical" approach to developing projects and tax products is a hit with solicitors. He recently represented West Devon Borough Council in an attempt to recover input tax in connection with a large improvement works at the Tavistock Wharf. "Quick-thinking" **Felicity Cullen** (see p.1387) was commended for her advocacy skills in corporate tax litigation, while up-and-coming practitioner **Conrad McDonnell** (see p.1444) was commended as "ferociously bright."

PUMP COURT TAX CHAMBERS (see full details p.1595) Recommended for both contentious and advisory work, this "commercial" set is felt to "understand business concerns" and receives abundant praise from peers and solicitors for its "readiness to handle any issue." "Strong at all levels," the chambers include a number of highly recommended silks and juniors. "At the top of the profession" is **David Milne QC** (see p.1448), ranked for impressive expertise in both corporate tax and VAT. A "relaxed and persuasive" manner in court is coupled with a "good instinct for the course and outcome of litigation." He "cross-examines sympathetically" with a "softly spoken" style that charms the bench. An accountant by training, he is for many the preferred choice for difficult VAT cases. He recently appeared in the Court of Appeal in connection with a case determining if an agreement to install a cigarette vending machine in a pub constituted a license to occupy land and as such a supply exempt from VAT (Commissioners of Customs and Excise v Sinclair Collins Ltd). Courtroom litigation is a "real strength" for **Graham Aaronson QC** (see p.1355), an esteemed force in the structured finance market. "Serene" in tax counseling, Aaronson is said to "approach things positively," while his "phenomenal brain" allows him to "distill complex information into easy language." "Bright and sparky" **Kevin Prosser QC** (see p.1464) displays "great confidence" in VAT and corporate taxation cases. "Bold," he takes a "bullish" approach to litigation and is distinguished by an "astonishing ability to think quickly on his feet." Clients appreciate his "commercial outlook" and "clear advice" and frequently instruct him in connection

www.ChambersandPartners.com

1351

TAX

> **Research** The rankings are based on in-depth interviews with 6,582 solicitors, barristers and clients in the UK. **Chambers'** research is audited by the British Market Research Bureau (see page 7)
>
> **BARRISTERS' PROFILES** ▶ See pages 1353-1504

with offshore unit trusts and exit tax planning matters. "Innovative thinker" **Andrew Thornhill QC** (see p.1490) is reputed to be "brilliant at dealing with business people and explaining difficult answers to them." He handles all aspects of corporate and private client tax advice and litigation with particular expertise in corporate reconstructions and employee remuneration. Solicitors agree that new silk **Michael Conlon QC** (see p.1383) "comes to mind immediately for VAT." A former solicitor himself, he relates well to lawyers who value his "experience and enthusiasm." "Iconoclastic" **Julian Ghosh** (see p.1403) is reputed to be a "treasure" of the junior Bar. He is highly regarded for his knowledge of financial instruments and EC tax. Commended as "friendly and accessible," clients report "you can ring him up and he'll give you five minutes at a moment's notice." Junior counsel to the Inland Revenue, **David Ewart** (see p.1396) is endorsed as "impressive" on share scheme and tax planning work. "Technically able and practically minded," senior junior **Adrian Shipwright** (see p.1478) commands a "huge amount of experience" encompassing stamp duty, corporate reconstruction, financings and the taxation of intellectual property. An ex-solicitor, Shipwright is noted for taking a "commercial view" on tax matters. Interviewees rated **Roger Thomas** (see p.1490) as a "precise and responsive" barrister; he received widespread praise for his stamp duty work. **Rupert Baldry** (see p.1360) and **Andrew Hitchmough** (see p.1471) were commended to researchers as "absolutely excellent" on VAT cases.

11 NEW SQUARE (see full details p.1578) This smaller set has a long history of handling landmark tax cases. The chambers contains a number of "heavy hitting" practitioners and was singled out by solicitors for the clerks who "go out of their way to help." Head of chambers, **John Gardiner QC** (see p.1402) has been described as "the ultimate tax QC." "Charming" and "hugely intelligent" he "reads all the papers and has all the angles figured out in advance." Widely admired for his "keen analytical judgement" he is reported to be "the number one QC to use if you've got a blank cheque." "Well-organised" **Peter Trevett QC** (see p.1493) was endorsed for both his private client and corporate tax work, and received accolades for his knowledge of stamp duty. New silk **Jonathan Peacock QC** (see p.1459) is "the first port of call" for many, and described as an "entirely modern barrister" who takes a "friendly and approachable" line with clients. Peacock acts for both corporate taxpayers and tax authorities and is therefore judged to have "a balanced view of the process."

ONE ESSEX COURT (see full details p.1531) As a former City solicitor, new silk **Malcolm Gammie QC** (see p.1402) has "experience far beyond his calling" and is a popular choice for many London firms. With an "encyclopaedic knowledge of tax" he advises on all aspects of commercial, European and international taxation. A "careful" practitioner, he is "pragmatic" in his approach to commercial matters and is highly regarded for his work on the taxation of company reorganisations. **Ian Glick QC** (see p.1405) acts regularly for the Crown and taxpayers in Revenue cases. Notable recent work includes appearing on behalf of the Inland Revenue in an appeal by a bank against the refusal to allow it to set off bad loans. He also acted in DTE Financial Services v Anthony Francis Wilson involving the receipt of a bonus by an employee through a scheme used by the employer to avoid national insurance contributions.

24 OLD BUILDINGS Although better known for private client work, the set has its share of talented corporate tax advisors. Most prominent is **Rex Bretten QC** (see p.1371) whose practice has a focus on merger and reconstruction work as well as international and double taxation treaty matters. A "robust and clinical" advocate, he is extremely popular with solicitors who claim his "deep knowledge of tax law" and "quick response time" make him "suited for anything." Another "favourite" at the Bar, **Reginald Nock** has established a reputation as the practitioner for stamp duty. A well-liked figure who "shoots from the hip," Nock rates highly for his "encyclopaedic knowledge of stamp duty."

3 TEMPLE GARDENS TAX CHAMBERS (see full details p.1614) This "user-friendly" set was applauded by sources for developing close relationships with clients. It is also thought to "make a real effort to accommodate business needs." A "sharp thinker," **Richard Bramwell QC** (see p.1370) maintains a broad-based practice, advising plcs and owner-managed businesses on tax compliance and disputes with Revenue or Customs. "Hard-working" junior **Alun James** (see p.1423) continues to be recommended for corporate tax matters. He recently appeared in Longson v Baker determining the extent to which grounds and gardens are exempt from capital gains tax under the principal private residence exemption.

OTHER NOTABLE PRACTITIONERS At **Monckton Chambers**, "incisive" **Paul Lasok QC** (see p.1432) is highly rated for VAT advice and said to be "excellent on European law." Noted for his advocacy skills, this "clever" practitioner is "difficult to throw off his stride." At the same chambers, **Kenneth Parker QC** "cuts straight to the chase" and is regularly instructed by Customs & Excise in VAT cases. A "clear and concise communicator," peers are "impressed by the quality of his arguments." Interviewees agree "there's no one like" **Roderick Cordara QC** (see p.1384) at **Essex Court Chambers** for complex VAT litigation. A "compelling advocate" he was lauded for his ability to "think outside the box" and "find innovative solutions." He is often accompanied by "excellent" junior **Perdita Cargill-Thompson** (see p.1376), a "shrewd operator" praised for her thorough preparation. In the same chambers, the "energetic" **Joe Smouha** (see p.1480) retains a high profile for VAT litigation; his recent cases have dealt with partial exemption issues in property and financial services, telecommunications, including place of supply issues. Described as the "IR's primary choice" **Launcelot Henderson QC** (see p.1414) at **5 Stone Buildings** appears regularly for the Inland Revenue in tax cases at all levels. A "formidable" opponent, fellow advocates admit to being "wary of having an argument with him." He recently appeared for the Inland Revenue against Sema Group Pension Scheme Trustees in relation to tax-exempt share "buy-back" schemes. His colleague **Christopher Tidmarsh QC** (see p.1491) has recently taken silk. Reckoned to be "exceedingly able," Tidmarsh was formerly standing junior counsel to the Inland Revenue and will continue work on VAT cases as a QC. Active in the London and Northern Circuits, **Richard Barlow** (see p.1362) at **11 Kings Bench Walk** received market commendation for his "wealth of experience" in corporate taxation. Both **Michael Furness QC** (see p.1401) at **Wilberforce Chambers** and **Timothy Brennan QC** (see p.1371) of **Devereux Chambers** appear regularly for Inland Revenue on tax cases, as does **Christopher McCall QC** (see p.1443) at **Maitland Chambers** who was singled out for his "impeccable judgement."

BARRISTERS' PROFILES

CHAMBERS
UK
2002–2003

LEADERS AT THE BAR

AARONSON, Graham QC
Pump Court Tax Chambers, London
(020) 7414 8080
Recommended in Tax
Specialisation: Principal area of practice is commercial taxation, covering all aspects (including the impact of EU law); in particular: mergers and acquisitions; structured finance; asset-based finance; corporate reorganisations; life insurance taxation; oil taxation. Acted in Scorer v. Olin Energy Systems; Elliss v BP Oil, BMI (No. 3) v Melluish; Unigate v McGregor; Nuclear Electric v Bradley; Prudential v Bibby; Citibank v Griffin, Hoechst v IRC and A-G; HSBC Life v Stubbs; Transco v Dyall. Clients include most of the UK's leading companies, the leading city solicitors and the 'Big 5' accountancy firms.
Prof. Memberships: Chairman Revenue Bar Association 1994-98; Chairman, Tax Law Review Committee 1994-98. Bencher of Middle Temple since 1991.
Career: Educated at City of London School and Trinity Hall, Cambridge 1963-66 (Waraker Law Scholar). Called to the Bar 1966 and practised commercial law before joining 4 Pump Court to specialise in taxation, 1968-73. Managing Director of Worldwide Plastics Development Ltd 1973-77. Director Bridgend Group Plc 1973-92. Tenant at Queen Elizabeth Building 1978-91 and 1 Essex Court 1991-2000. Took Silk 1982. Rejoined current Chambers in 2000. Advisor on tax reform to Israel Treasury 1986-89 as part of the team brought in to tackle Israel's hyperinflation.
Personal: Founder, Standford Grange Rehabilitation Centre for Offenders. Born 31 December 1944. Lives in Stanmore, Middlesex.

ABELL, Anthony
2 Bedford Row (William Clegg QC), London
(020) 7440 8888
Recommended in Crime

ACLAND, Piers
11 South Square (Christopher Floyd QC), London
(020) 7405 1222
piers@acland.net
Recommended in Intellectual Property
Specialisation: All aspects of intellectual property law with particular interest in chemical and pharmaceutical patents. Recent reported cases include: American Home Products v Novartis [2001] – patent, infringement, sufficiency; Instance v Denny [2002] – patent, obviousness; Inhale Therapeutics v Quadrant [2002] – patent, anticipation, obviousness; Rohm and Haas v Collag [2002] – patent, preliminary issue, infringement; Instance v CCL [2002] – patent, amendment proceedings; EasyJet v Dainty [2002] – domain name, summary judgment; Luk Leamington v Whitnash [2002] – rectification of patent agreement.
Prof. Memberships: Intellectual Property Bar Association; Lincoln's Inn – Mansfield Scholar, Denning Scholar.
Career: Called to the Bar and joined Chambers in 1993.
Personal: Born 1965. Educated at Bristol Grammar School; University College London 1984-87, 1st Class Hons Biochemistry; Imperial Cancer Research Fund 1987-91 – PhD Molecular Virology.

ACTON DAVIS, Jonathan QC
Atkin Chambers (Robert Akenhead QC), London
(020) 7404 0102
jadavis@atkinchambers.law.co.uk
Recommended in Construction
Specialisation: Practice covers international arbitration, construction law work and professional negligence, also general common law matters. Clients include most large construction companies, insurers and other commercial bodies.
Prof. Memberships: Tec Bar, Professional Negligence Bar Association, COMBAR, London Common Law Bar Association, Association des Juristes-Franco-Brittaniques.
Career: Called the Bar 1977, Member of Bar Council 1993-98, Bencher of Inner Temple 1995; Queens Counsel, 1996. Assistant Recorder 1997, Recorder 2000. Chairman of Professional Conduct Committee of Bar Council 2001 and 2002; (Vice-Chairman 1999-2000).
Personal: Born 15 January 1953. Educated at Harrow School and P.C.L. LLB (Lond.).

ADAMS, Jayne
Ropewalk Chambers (Ian McLaren QC), Nottingham
(0115) 947 2581
clerks@ropewalk.co.uk
Recommended in Personal Injury
Specialisation: Personal injury, industrial disease and clinical negligence. Junior Counsel in both the Leicestershire and North Wales abuse in care multi-party litigation.
Prof. Memberships: Personal Injury Bar Association.
Career: Birmingham University LLB (Hons); called 1982; Chairman of the James Stemp inquiry for Leicestershire Health Authority; Chairman of the Care Ethics Committee (fertility services); Member of the Legal Services Commission Committee.
Personal: Married, three children.

ADDY, Caroline
1 Brick Court (Richard Rampton QC), London
(020) 7353 8845
clerks@1brickcourt.co.uk
Recommended in Defamation
Specialisation: Defamation, confidence, advertising, contempt of court and media related law generally.
Career: LLB (Euro) Exon 1990. Called 1991, joined chambers 1992. Cases include: Upjohn v Oswald, A-G v Limbrick, McPhilemcy v Times Newspapers Limited, Tancic v Times Newspapers Ltd.
Personal: Born 1968. Lives in London. Languages French and German.

ADKINS, Richard QC
3-4 South Square (Michael Crystal QC & Lord Alexander of Weedon QC), London
(020) 7696 9900
clerks@southsquare.com
Recommended in Insolvency
Specialisation: A business and financial law practice, including both domestic and international disputes with particular specialisations in corporate insolvency law and reconstructions, in takeover litigation and professional negligence cases. Advisory work in relation to banking, securities, receivables financing, chattel leasing, debt issues, securitisation and general corporate law issues.
Prof. Memberships: Middle Temple.
Career: MA (Oxon). Called to the Bar 1982; took Silk 1995.
Publications: Contributor, 'Gore Browne on Companies' and a member of the Editorial Board of the 'Insolvency Lawyer' and the 'Company Financial and Insolvency Law Review'.
Personal: Keen tennis player and opera-goer.

AEBERLI, Peter
46 Essex Street (Geoffrey Hawker), London
(020) 7583 8899
Recommended in ADR

AGEROS, James
2 Bedford Row (William Clegg QC), London
(020) 7440 8888
Recommended in Health & Safety

AGNELLO, Raquel
11 Stone Buildings (Murray Rosen QC), London
(020) 7831 6381
agnello@11stonebuildings.com
Recommended in Insolvency
Specialisation: Specialises in corporate and personal insolvency and general company law. Is well known for her involvement in the field of voluntary arrangements, both corporate and individual. It is an area in which she has lectured extensively and has many reported cases. She also practises in commercial litigation, such as contract, banking, guarantees and other securities whilst retaining an interest in private international litigation.

AINGER, David
10 Old Square (Leolin Price CBE QC), London
(020) 7405 0758
Recommended in Chancery
Specialisation: Principal area of specialisation is Chancery; general Chancery practitioner with both an advisory and litigation practice. In addition to work in real property, professional negligence, fraud, partnership, trusts (including breach of trust), pensions, probate, banking and insurance, has experience of public inquiries, local government, water, waterways and highways, ecclesiastical law, commons, village greens and similar matters. Has conducted litigation in Hong Kong and the Isle of Man and advised on Chancery matters in other jurisdictions.
Career: Appointed to the Conveyancing Counsel of the Supreme Court in November 1991.

AKENHEAD, Robert QC
Atkin Chambers (Robert Akenhead QC), London
(020) 7404 0120
Recommended in Arbitration, Construction, Professional Negligence
Specialisation: Practising Barrister specialising in the field of Construction law – Arbitration and Litigation. Has practised continually and exclusively since 1972 in Construction Law. Practice has been in the English Courts and in British and international arbitrations. International work has involved arbitrations and contracts inter alia in Europe, Africa, Middle East, Asia, Australia, Fiji, W. Indies and USA. Work has frequently included claims relating to final account, defects, delay and disruption and measurement. Has lectured and given seminars on all legal aspects of building and civil engineering. Recent publication: 'Site Investigation and the Law' (Thomas Telford Ltd – 1984). Joint Editor – Building Law Reports.
Career: Called to Bar July 1972; Queen's Counsel 1989; Recorder 1994; Bencher Inner Temple 1997.
Personal: Born 15 September 1949. Educated Exeter University (LLB Hons). Bar Final 1972 (8th out of 700).

ALBUTT, Ian
2-3 Gray's Inn Square (Anthony Porten QC & Anthony Scrivener QC), London
(020) 7242 4986
Recommended in Planning
Specialisation: Planning and local government. Practice encompasses all aspects of planning, administrative and local government law. This includes planning inquiries, local plans, CPO, housing and retail development. Extensive recent experience in green belt, conservation and listed building issues including large scale MSA provision on M4 and M40 including the M25 and M40 reopened inquiries, s.288 s.289 appeals, judicial review and High Court challenges. Recent planning inquiries include major motorway service area provision on M40 and M25. Birmingham Bull Ring development CPO 2 and 3. Thames Water Utilities v London Borough of Bromley. Leisure Great Britain plc v Isle of Wight Council 2000 PLCR88. Rossington Hall Investments Ltd v Doncaster Metropolitan Borough Council 2000 PLCR 222 (and in CA). Michael Shanley Group Limited v Secretary of State for the Environment Transport and Regions

www.ChambersandPartners.com

1355

LEADERS AT THE BAR

of Windsor and Maidenhead Royal Borough Council 2000 PLCR 136 CA. South Bucks District Council v Porter 2002 1 WLR 135 GCP (leave to petition HL granted).
Prof. Memberships: Planning and Environmental Bar Association; Legal Assessor for the RICS; Member of the Bar Disciplinary Tribunal.
Career: Called to the Bar in 1981 by Gray's Inn. Member of the President of the Bar Council's list of approved counsel to act as an arbitrator in planning disputes.

ALDOUS, Charles QC
Maitland Chambers (Michael Lyndon-Stanford QC & Charles Aldous QC), London
(020) 7406 1200
Recommended in Chancery, Company, Energy

ALEXANDER, Daniel
8 New Square (Mark Platts-Mills QC), London
(020) 7405 4321
daniel.alexander@8newsquare.co.uk
Recommended in Intellectual Property, Media & Entertainment
Specialisation: Barrister specialising principally in intellectual property, media and entertainment, EC and scientific commercial law. Practice regularly involves cases with international aspects, advocacy and advisory work in a wide variety of cases, many with EC and international aspects. For comprehensive CV and list of recent cases, visit our website at www.8newsquare.co.uk.
Prof. Memberships: Intellectual Property Bar Association (IPBA); Bar Council Policy Committee.
Career: Called 1988. Junior counsel to the crown in patent cases (treasury junior).
Publications: Joint author of 'Guidebook to Intellectual Property Law'; joint editor 'Clerk & Lindsell on Torts' (17th edn). 'Encyclopaedia of UK & European Patent Law'.
Personal: Born 1963. Educated at University College Oxford (1985 BA Physics and Philosophy); Central London Polytechnic (1986 Dip Law); Harvard Law School (1987 LLM).

ALLAN, David QC
Byrom Street Chambers, Manchester
(0161) 829 2100
Recommended in Personal Injury

ALLARDICE, Miranda
Pump Court Chambers (Christopher Harvey Clark QC), Winchester
(020) 7353 0711
Recommended in Family
Specialisation: Inheritance Act and associated probate issues. Ancillary relief with a particular interest and expertise in pension issues. Cohabitants' property disputes constructive trust/Trust of Land and Appointment of Trustees Act 1996. Professional negligence cases in above area of law. Lectures and contributes articles regularly for outside organisations.
Prof. Memberships: Committee member of Family Law Bar Association; United Kingdom Environmental Law Association.
Career: Called to the Bar 1982. Joined present chambers 1984.
Personal: Educated at Somerville College, Oxford 1978-81 (BA Jurisprudence), Kings College London 1995, LLM Merit. Born 5 March 1959. Lives in London. Chair of IVF Ethics Committee Chelsea and Westminster Hospital.

ALLEN, James H QC
No.6 Barristers Chambers (Jennifer Kershaw QC), Leeds
(0113) 245 9763
Recommended in Chancery, Commercial (Litigation), Insolvency

ALLEN, Mark
30 Park Place (John Jenkins QC), Cardiff
(029) 2039 8421
Recommended in Family

ALLEN, Robin QC
Cloisters (Laura Cox QC), London
(020) 7827 4000
Recommended in Employment, Human Rights
Specialisation: Public, Employment, European, Discrimination and Human Rights law.
Prof. Memberships: Chair of the Employment Law Bar Association 1997-99, committee member of the Discrimination Law Association, member of the Administrative Law Bar Association.
Career: Recorder, Chairman of the Bar Pro Bono Unit, and Bar in the Community, Chairman of the Bar Conference 2002 and special advisor to the Disability Rights Commission. Formerly member of the Bar Council 1999-2001, Bar Council representative on the Home Office Human Rights Act Task Force 1999-2001, Chair of the Employment Law Bar Association from 1997-99, the Brandon Centre for Psychotherapy 1991-93 and the London Youth Advisory Centre 1984-90. Chair of the Publicity Sub-Group of the Home Office Human Rights Task Force which arranged for the publicity in relation to the implementation of the Human Rights Act in October 2000. Member of the Executive of the European Circuit of the Bar. May 2000 addressed the European Parliament in relation to Article 13 (the power to make anti-discrimination legislation). December 1998 key note address at the European Commission's first international conference on Article 13 EC. Most important cases include: Coker v Lord Chancellor (Special Political Advisors), Bahl v Law Society, Chagos Islanders (Tort of exile), Rutherford v Harvest Town Circle (Age discrimination), Triesman v Ali (discrimination and political parties), Hallam v Cheltenham HL (Aiding discrimination), BCCI v Ali HL (Compromise agreements), Williams v Cowell (Welsh language), Waters v Met Police HL (Bullying and Police), Smith v Secretary of State for Trade and Industry (Article 6 and Employment Tribunals), R v Secretary of State for Employment, ex parte Seymour-Smith HL and ECJ (Unfair dismissal and European law), Kaba v Home Office ECJ (Free movement and discrimination and Advocate General and Article 6), R v Lord Chancellor, ex p. Lightfoot (Insolvency and ECHRR), Edmonds v Lawson (Pupil barrister and minimum wage) Burton v Camden London Borough Council HL (Secure tenancy Assignment), London Underground Ltd v Edwards (No. 2), (Single Mothers and shiftwork), Goodwin v Patent Office (Definition of disability), Clark v Novacold (Disability discrimination), Bossa v Nordstresse (Race Relations Act and Community law), Post Office v Adekeye (Post-termination discrimination), Jones v Tower Boot (Harassment), R v Mid Glamorgan Family Health Services Authority, ex p. Martin (access to medical records), R v Secretary of State for Education, ex parte Prior (Duties of school Governing bodies), Balfour v FCO (PII), Delaney v Staples HL (Wages), Pickering v Liverpool Daily Post (Mental health review tribunal publicity), Hampson v DES HL (justification and indirect discrimination), R v Bradford City Metropolitan Council, ex p. Wilson and Corris (Mayor's casting vote), R v Kensington and Chelsea Royal London (Injunctions and JR), Alexander v Home Office (Discrimination Damages), Polkey v A.E. Dayton Services Ltd HL (Unfair Dismissal), Puhlhofer v Hillingdon HL (Homelessness), Notcutt v Universal Equipment (Frustration).
Publications: Publications include 'Employment Law and Human Rights' 2002, writes and lectures widely, also contributed to the following books: 'The Legal Framework and Social Consequence of Free Movement of Persons in the European Union', 'Women Work and Inequality', 'New Routes to Equality', 'Bullen and Leake and Jacob's Precedents of Pleading' (the Human Rights section), 'Legal Regulation of the Employment Relation'. Edited the 'Study Guide to the Human Rights Act' published jointly by the Bar Council and Home Office.

ALTMAN, Brian
2 Bedford Row (William Clegg QC), London
(020) 7440 8888
baltman@2bedfordrow.co.uk
Recommended in Crime, Fraud
Specialisation: Crime.
Prof. Memberships: Criminal Bar Association.
Career: Treasury Counsel at CCC from 1997.

AMLOT, Roy QC
6 King's Bench Walk (Roy Amlot QC), London
(020) 7583 0410
Recommended in Crime, Fraud
Specialisation: Principal area of practice is criminal law with an emphasis on high profile, serious crime cases and commercial fraud. Defence work includes Barlow Clowes, Blue Arrow, Brent Walker, Fiona Jones MP and Lord Archer and Francis. Prosecution work includes the Brighton bombing, Guildford Four (on appeal) and Clive Ponting cases. Editor, 'Phipson on Evidence' (11th Edition).
Career: Called to the Bar 1963 and became a tenant of King's Bench Walk in 1964. Treasury Counsel 1977-89. Took Silk 1989. Chairman of the Bar, 2001.
Personal: Educated at Dulwich College 1953-60. School Governor, Dulwich College. Leisure pursuits include skiing, music, squash, and windsurfing. Born 22 September 1942. Lives in London.

AMOS, Tim
Queen Elizabeth Building (Florence Baron QC), London
(020) 7797 7837
Recommended in Family
Specialisation: All aspects of family law and related professional negligence, but predominantly family finance, married or unmarried, alive or dead. Specially interested in Anglo-German cases and those with a foreign or international element. Fluent in German (including legal German). Work experience in German Courts and German law firms. Standing Counsel to the Queen's Proctor.
Prof. Memberships: Family Law Bar Association and British German Jurists Association.
Publications: Contributor to 'Essential Family Practice' (Butterworths).

ANDERSON, David QC
Brick Court Chambers (Christopher Clarke QC), London
(020) 7379 3550
anderson@brickcourt.co.uk
Recommended in Administrative & Public Law, Competition/European Law
Specialisation: European Union law, human rights law, public law, competition law. Over 70 cases in the European Court of Justice and 35 before the European Commission/Court of Human Rights. Involved at all stages of Factortame and Sunday Trading litigation; ICI v Commission (Article 81); Rees Mogg (Maastricht Treaty); Generics (pharmaceutical licensing); Orange (telecoms regulation); Iberian Trading (effect of Commission decision); UK v Commission and Commission v France (BSE); Grant v SW Trains (sexual orientation discrimination); Building Societies (retrospective legislation); Easyjet v BA (Article 82); Imperial Tobacco (advertising ban); McGonnell v UK (separation of powers); A (conjoined twins); Hatton (night flights); Z v UK

(access to court); Interbrew (mergers); Levi v Tesco (trademarks); Three Rivers (BCCI); ProLife v BBC (political speech).
Career: Called 1985; Lawyer from Abroad, Covington & Burling, Washington DC, 1985-86; Cabinet of Lord Cockfield, EC Commission, 1987-88; Junior Counsel to the Crown, 1995-99; Visiting Professor, King's College London, 1999; QC 1999.
Publications: 'References to the European Court' (1995, 2nd ed 2002).

ANDERSON, Lesley
40 King St, Manchester
(0161) 832 9082
landerson@40kingstreet.co.uk
Recommended in Chancery, Commercial (Litigation), Insolvency
Specialisation: Corporate and personal insolvency including directors' disqualifications; banking; commercial landlord and tenant; professional negligence; commercial litigation including shareholders disputes, business and share sale agreements and joint ventures.
Prof. Memberships: Chancery Bar Association; Northern Chancery Bar Association; Northern Circuit Commercial Bar Association.
Career: Lecturer in law at University of Manchester 1984-89; Training Manager, Norton Rose M5 Group of Solicitors 1989-91;on Attorney General's Provincial Panel of Counsel.
Personal: CEDR Accredited Mediator.

ANDERSON, Mark
3 Fountain Court (Robert Juckes QC), Birmingham
(0121) 236 5854
clerks@3fc.co.uk
Recommended in Commercial (Litigation)
Specialisation: Professional negligence and commercial law including banking, employment, restraint of trade and construction. Mortgages and other securities. Personal injury and clinical negligence.
Prof. Memberships: Midland Chancery & Commercial Bar Association. Professional Negligence Bar Association. Personal Injuries Bar Association.
Career: Educated at King Edward's School, Birmingham and Exeter College, Oxford.

ANDERSON, Robert
Blackstone Chambers (Presiley Baxendale QC & Charles Flint QC), London
(020) 7583 1770
robertanderson@blackstonechambers.com
Recommended in Commercial (Litigation)
Specialisation: Commercial (in particular, commercial fraud), insurance/reinsurance, entertainment and sports law. Recent reported cases include Pangood v Barclay Brown [1999] Lloyd's Rep IR 405, Brown v Bennett [1999] 1 BCLC 649, Merrill Lynch v Raffa ('The Times', 14/6/00), and Pride Valley Foods v Hall and Partners [2001] 76 Con LR 1.
Prof. Memberships: COMBAR, TECBAR, Bar Sports Law Group.
Career: Called 1986 (Gray's Inn & Middle Temple). Teaches advocacy and trains advocacy teachers on behalf of Gray's Inn.
Publications: The Impact of Human Rights Act on Sports Tribunals [2000] ISLR 65.
Personal: Educated at Oundle School and Pembroke College, Cambridge.

ANDERSON, Rupert
Monckton Chambers (Kenneth Parker QC & Paul Lasok QC), London
(020) 7405 7211
randerson@monckton.co.uk
Recommended in Competition/European Law
Specialisation: Practice includes all aspects of EU and domestic competition law including OFT, Competition Commission and EC Commission investigations, EU law generally, VAT and customs and excise, utilities regulation, administration law, judicial review and broadcasting. Recent cases include Competition Commission inquiries into BSkyB/Manchester United; Mobile Telephones; case T-342/99 Airtours v EC Commission; case T-67/01 JCB v EC Commission; IIB and ABTA v DGFT and GISC (CCAT); Morgan Stanley Dean Witter v Visa International (High Court and EC Commission); Sinclair Collis v CCE; F&I Services v CCE [2001] STC 939 (Court of Appeal); Lex v CCE [2001] STC 1568 (Court of Appeal); Kingfisher v CCE [2000] STC 992.
Prof. Memberships: Member of the Bar European Group.
Career: Called 1981. MA (CANTAB); Treasury Panel A List.
Publications: Weinberg and Blank on 'Take-Overs and Mergers'; Copinger on 'Copyright'; PLC Handbook on 'Competition Law'.

ANDREWS, Claire
Gough Square Chambers (Fred Philpott), London
(020) 7353 0924
Recommended in Consumer Law
Specialisation: Consumer law – experienced in civil litigation and prosecuting and defending regulatory offences, and advising on interpretation of statutes. Cases include: R v Warwickshire CC [1993] AC 583 (misleading prices); LB Bexley v Gardner Merchant [1991] COD (improvement notices); Birmingham City Council v Asda Stores. Clients have included food and other wholesalers and retailers and enforcement authorities. Author 'The Enforcement of Regulatory Offences' and 'Atkins Court Forms on Consumer Protection'. Other main areas of practice include landlord and tenant, employment and commercial fraud.
Prof. Memberships: Food Law Group, MSOFHT, FCIArb, ALBA, EBA, London Common Law and Commercial Bar Association.

ANDREWS, Geraldine QC
Essex Court Chambers (Gordon Pollock QC), London
(020) 7813 8000
gandrews@essexcourt-chambers.co.uk
Recommended in Banking & Finance, Commercial (Litigation)
Specialisation: Broad-based commercial practice. In particular shipping, insurance and reinsurance, banking law, asset tracing and preservation, international commodity transactions, company law, insolvency, EC law, entertainment, intellectual property (excluding patents) and general commercial and Chancery matters.
Prof. Memberships: Member of COMBAR; the Chancery Bar Association; the London Common Law and Commercial Bar Association; the Bar European Group; supporting member of the London Maritime Arbitrators' Association.
Career: King's College, University of London: LLB (1st Class Hons), 1980. LLM (1982). Recorder Midland Circuit 2000. Silk 2001.
Publications: Co-author of Andrews and Millett, 'The Law of Guarantees' (3rd edn 2000).
Personal: Born 1959. Languages spoken: French, German, Italian.

ANDREWS, Philip
Young Street Chambers (John Jackson & David Hernandez), Manchester
(0161) 833 0489
Recommended in Crime
Specialisation: Practice encompasses all aspects of criminal law.
Prof. Memberships: Criminal Bar Association.
Career: Called to Bar (Inner Temple) February 1977 thereafter practising on Northern Circuit. Visiting lecturer law, University of Manchester 1979-82.
Personal: Born 24 July 1950. Educated at Blackpool Grammar School and University of Hull (LLB) (Hons).

ANELAY, Richard QC
One King's Bench Walk (Anthony Hacking QC), London
(020) 7936 1500
Recommended in Family
Specialisation: All areas of family and criminal law. Has undertaken leading work in matrimonial finance, child care, Inheritance Act provision, international child abduction, serious fraud, murder, manslaughter and rape. Election law: acted in Tower Hamlets Election. Case (1990) - 22 day hearing before Commissioner. In public law children cases has undertaken leading work for local authorities, parents and guardians ad litem in complex medical, Munchaussen syndrome by proxy, sexual, physical and emotional abuse cases. Reported cases: Re KDT (Minor) [1994] 2 FCR 721CA; Re G [1994] 2 FCR 216. Re D (care: Natural Parent Presumption) 1999 1 FLR 134 CA.
Career: Called 1970. QC 1993. Recorder 1992. Deputy High Court Judge (Family Division) 1995.
Publications: Consulting editor, 'Encyclopedia of Financial Provision in Family Matters' (General editors Wildblood and Eaton, Sweet & Maxwell, 1998).
Personal: Born 1946. Educated at Queen Elizabeth Grammar School, Darlington and Bristol University (BA Hons Classics and Philosophy). Enjoys golf.

ANTROBUS, Simon
40 King St, Manchester
(0161) 832 9082
santrobus@40kingstreet.co.uk
Recommended in Health & Safety
Specialisation: Specialises in all areas of regulatory, corporate criminal and consumer law, predominantly those involving health and safety at work, trade descriptions, fair trading and trading standards, food safety, licensing, building regulations, housing, environmental pollution law and regulation of financial services and service industries. Has particular experience of the leisure and construction industries. Practice is predominantly defence-based, representing in criminal prosecutions, disciplinary proceedings and associated judicial reviews on behalf of substantial FTSE 100 companies, insurers and individual directors or employers. During the last five years has also represented the Department of Trade & Industry in the largest group litigation experienced in the United Kingdom (Griffiths & Others v British Coal Corporation 'The British Coal Respiratory Disease Litigation') representing at trial of lead actions and advising in relation to the drafting of the resulting Compensation Scheme. Has been retained in order to represent the Department in relation to the recent Group Litigation Order relating to contribution proceedings against mining contractors.
Prof. Memberships: Professional Negligence Bar Association.
Career: Law LLB First Class (Sheffield), called to the Bar October 1995.
Publications: Series of four articles in the 'Solicitors' Journal', Prosecution of Regulatory Offences (2001) SJ Vol 145 pp 520-521, 552-553, 574-575, 594-595.

ARCHER, Stephen
12 King's Bench Walk (Richard Methuen QC), London
(020) 7583 0811
Recommended in Personal Injury
Specialisation: Industrial disease (with increasing emphasis on multi-party test actions); brain damage, quadriplegia, paraplegia; personal injury work generally with long experience of disputes involving on medical causation; clinical negligence. Recent cases: Abbott and others v Rockware Glass plc (2000 BLC 73); Makepeace v Evans Brothers (2000 BLR 73), Hatton v Sutherland 2002 PIQR P21, Davis v Balfour Kilpatrick and ors CA 23/5/2002.

LEADERS AT THE BAR

Prof. Memberships: PIBA; ELA.
Career: By 1985 practised almost exclusively in personal injury work. Following Mountenay v Bernard Matthews plc [1994] 5 Med LR 293 has acted increasingly for defendants in a wide range of industrial disease actions including upper limb disorders, asbestos related conditions, vibration white finger, respiratory disease occupational stress claims and injuries from electromagnetic radiation.
Personal: Education: Sherborne School; Oxford (Pembroke College); Inner Temple. Leisure/family: cycling; joint research (with wife) into African-American music; large model association.

ARDEN, Andrew QC
Arden Chambers (Andrew Arden QC), London
(020) 7242 4244
clerks@ardenchambers.com
Recommended in Local Government
Specialisation: Principal areas of practice are housing and landlord and tenant law (including homelessness, right to buy/acquire and enfranchisement, leases and service charges, rents and security of tenure, disrepair and environmental health, business tenancies, housing association law (including finance, disposals, status, powers and procedures, committee membership, mixed-funding arrangements, stock acquisition) local government (including finance, constitution, asset disposals, local authority companies, powers and procedures, best value, access to information, data protection, PFI, public/private partnerships, pensions, waste disposal), and miscellaneous aspects of public and administrative law. Has conducted five local government inquiries/reviews; appeared for the Objectors at the Westminster Audit Hearing (1994). Author/Co-Author: Housing Law, Local Government Constitutional and Administrative Law, Local Government Finance Law, Assured Tenancies (Vol. 3, The Rent Acts, 11th ed.), Manual of Housing Law, Homelessness and Allocation, Annotated Statutes (including Housing Acts 1980, 1985, 1988, 1996, Local Government and Housing Act 1989, Housing Grants, Construction and Regeneration Act 1996). General Editor: Housing Encyclopaedia, Housing Law Reports, Journal of Housing Law, Arden's Housing Library. Editorial Board Member: Journal of Local Government Law.
Prof. Memberships: Administrative Law Bar Association; Local Government, Planning and Environmental Bar Association; Bar European Group, Property Bar Association, Housing Law Practitioners' Association.
Career: Called to the Bar 1974. Director, Small Heath Community Law Centre 1976-78. Silk 1991. Founded Arden Chambers in 1993.
Publications: 'Local Government Constitutional and Administrative Law'.
Personal: Educated at University College London 1969-72 (LLB). Writes novels and thrillers. Born 20 April 1948. Lives in London.

ARDEN, Peter
Enterprise Chambers (Anthony Mann QC), London
(020) 7405 9471
Recommended in Chancery, Company, Insolvency

ARLIDGE, Anthony QC
18 Red Lion Court (Anthony Arlidge QC), London
(020) 7520 6000
anthony.arlidge@18rlc.co.uk
Recommended in Crime, Fraud
Specialisation: Serious fraud from Griffiths and Others in 1965 to Blue Arrow. Author of Arlidge and Parry on Fraud 2nd edn. Revenue cases including Carmel College and more recently Stannard and Nelson (two barristers charged with tax fraud). Prosecuted Jeremy Bamber and defended Baroness De Stempel. Past clients include Michael Allcock (defended for corruption in relation to the Revenue), Terence Ramsden (derivatives), Dr Crockett (alleged purchase of kidneys for transplant) and Dr Bichan (Butte Mining). Appeared in Graham and Ords, the post-Preddy appeals. Disciplinary tribunals including General Medical Council, Stock Exchange, Lloyds, Fimbra.
Career: Double first class degree in law, Cambridge.

ARMSTRONG, Dean
6 King's Bench Walk (Roy Amlot QC), London
(020) 7583 0410
Recommended in Crime
Specialisation: Prosecutes and defends in all forms of crime and commercial fraud.
Career: MA (Cantab).

ARMSTRONG, Kester
Broad Chare Chambers (Patrick Cosgrove QC), Newcastle upon Tyne
(0191) 232 0541
Recommended in Family

ARNOLD, Mark
3-4 South Square (Michael Crystal QC & Lord Alexander of Weedon QC), London
(020) 7696 9900
markarnold@southsquare.com
Recommended in Insolvency
Specialisation: Business and financial law, including in particular: insolvency (corporate and individual), banking, company, chancery and professional negligence.
Prof. Memberships: COMBAR, Chancery Bar Association, Insolvency Lawyers Association.
Career: MA Cantab. (Downing College, Cambridge).

ARNOLD, Richard QC
11 South Square (Christopher Floyd QC), London
(020) 7405 1222
Recommended in Information Technology, Intellectual Property
Specialisation: Patents, trademarks, passing off, copyright, design right, registered designs, performers' rights, database right, confidential information, entertainment and media law, computer contract disputes, data protection, restraint of trade, trade libel, trade descriptions, related EU law. Recent cases include Norowzian v Arks [2000] EMLR 67, Fulton v Grant Barnett [2001] RPC 257, Rugby Football Union v Cotton Traders [2002] EWHC 467 (Ch) and Stena Rederi v Irish Ferries [2002] EWHC 737 (Ch).
Prof. Memberships: IP Bar Association, Chancery Bar Association, CIPA (Associate).
Career: Called 1985, QC 2000.
Publications: 'Performers' Rights' (2nd ed, Sweet & Maxwell, 1997); 'Computer Software: Legal Protection in the United Kingdom' (2nd edn, Sweet & Maxwell, 1992) (co-author); 'Entertainment and Media Law Reports' (Sweet & Maxwell, 1993-) (editor); articles in 'European Intellectual Property Review', 'Entertainment Law Review', 'Intellectual Property Quarterly' and 'Yearbook of Copyright and Media Law'.

ASCROFT, Richard
Guildhall Chambers (Adrian Palmer QC), Bristol
(0117) 930 9000
richard.ascroft@guildhallchambers.co.uk
Recommended in Insolvency
Specialisation: Insolvency: bankruptcy; directors' disqualification; corporate insolvency. Company: shareholders' disputes; directors' duties. Commercial litigation: contractual disputes including sale of goods. Banking: bills of exchange; bank payments; enforcement of securities.
Prof. Memberships: Chancery Bar Association; R3.
Career: Called to Bar 1995. Barrister and Solicitor High Court of NZ 1990.
Personal: Born 9 August 1966, Wellington, NZ. Educated NZ (LLB Hons) and Oxford University (BCL).

ASH, Brian QC
4-5 Gray's Inn Square (Elizabeth Appleby QC), London
(020) 7404 5252
Recommended in Planning
Specialisation: Principal area of practice is planning and local government. Work involves public inquiries concerning all forms of development, compulsory purchase and compensation, including references to the Lands Tribunal, and High Court proceedings including statutory appeals and judicial review. Involved in public inquiries concerning development of Stansted, Heathrow, Doncaster and Finningley airports, sub-regional and other major shopping proposals, road development including motorway service areas and large scale commercial, industrial and housing proposals. Clients include Rolls Royce Plc, Safeway Stores Plc, Peel Holdings, BP Oil, Guiness Plc, London Underground Ltd, The Civil Aviation Authority, major insurance companies, The Commission for Local Administration, County, Metropolitan Borough and District Councils.
Prof. Memberships: Local Government Planning and Environmental Bar Association.
Career: TV Producer, Reporter and Programme Presenter 1967-73. Called to the Bar 1975 and joined current chambers 1977. Took Silk 1990.
Personal: Educated at New Collge, Oxford 1960-64. Leisure pursuits include golf, cricket, sailing and skiing. Born January 31 1941. Lives in London.

ASHLEY-NORMAN, Jonathan
2 Bedford Row (William Clegg QC), London
(020) 7440 8888
Recommended in Fraud
Specialisation: Criminal law specialist in fraud, restraint and confiscation, and drugs related offences. On the approved prosecutors list for Customs and Excise, Department of Trade and Industry, Inland Revenue and DSS. Regularly prosecutes in substantial cases, especially fraud and drugs importation offences. Instructed to defend in major SFO cases including Alpine Windows, concerning the collapse of the double glazing company and Richmond Oil and Gas, concerning a fraudulent company flotation. Undertakes specialist Customs defence work, including anti-dumping duty cases and High Court restraint work. Some Company Directors Disqualification Act work undertaken.
Prof. Memberships: Member of Criminal Bar Association.

ASHWORTH, Fiona
40 King St, Manchester
(0161) 832 9082
fashworth@40kingstreet.co.uk
Recommended in Family
Specialisation: Personal injury (employer's and public liability), industrial disease including deafness and asbestosis, road traffic and sporting injuries); clinical and PI related professional negligence (including obstetrics, gynaecological, orthopaedic and dental); family and matrimonial provision; ancillary relief cases.
Prof. Memberships: PIBA; FLBA; Clinical Negligence Association; Northern Circuit Medical Law Association; also sits on the Legal Services Commission Appeal Tribunal.
Career: Bolton School (Girl's Division). Leeds University (LLB). Called 1988 (Lincoln's Inn) (Hardwicke Scholar).
Personal: Married with two children and lives in Cheshire.

ASHWORTH, Lance
St Philips Chambers (John Randall QC), Birmingham
(0121) 246 7000
Recommended in Chancery, Commercial

LEADERS AT THE BAR

(Litigation), Insolvency, Personal Injury
Specialisation: Commercial Law. Group Actions. Insolvency, corporate recovery and directors disqualification – Junior Counsel to the Crown. Personal Injury.
Prof. Memberships: P.I.B.A. Midland Chancery and Commercial Bar Association, COMBAR.
Career: Oundle School. Pembroke College Cambridge. MA (Cantab).
Personal: Married, three children.

ASIF, Jalil
Four New Square (Justin Fenwick QC), London
(020) 7822 2000
j.asif@4newsquare.com
Recommended in Product Liability
Specialisation: Practice is mainly professional liability (lawyers, architects, valuers and accountants) and clinical negligence/product liability, but with other significant strands (general commercial, insurance, construction and property law). Extensive experience of multi-party clinical negligence/product liability actions; HIV, benzodiazepines, Hepatitis C and fetal anti-convulsant litigations.
Prof. Memberships: Professional Negligence Bar Association, London Common Law and Commercial Bar Association, COMBAR.
Career: Called to the Bar 1988.
Publications: Editor of the 'Professional Negligence & Liability Reports' and of 'Jackson & Powell's Professional Liability Precedents'.
Personal: Born 1965. Educated at Twyford High School, Acton, and St Paul's School, then Peterhouse, Cambridge. Leisure pursuits include scuba diving, music and cinema.

ASPLIN, Sarah J QC
3 Stone Buildings (Geoffrey Vos QC), London
(020) 7242 4937
sasplin@3sb.law.co.uk
Recommended in Pensions
Specialisation: Principal area of practice pensions litigation, advice and drafting and professional including actuarial negligence. Acts for principal employers, trustees and beneficiaries in relation to questions of rectification construction, winding-up, merger, general administration of pension schemes and appeals from the Pensions Ombudsman. Also general Chancery matters including trusts and probate advice and litigation. Cases include Imperial Tobacco, British Coal, Hillsdown Holdings Plc, Spooner & Ors v British Telecommunications plc, Equitable Life v Hyman, Needler v Taber and Bestrustees v Stuart.
Prof. Memberships: Chancery Bar Association, Association of Pension Lawyers.
Career: Called 1984. Silk: 2002.
Personal: Educated at Fitzwilliam College, Cambridge 1979-82 (MA Law) St Edmund Hall, Oxford 1982-83 (BCL).

ATHERTON, Stephen
3-4 South Square (Michael Crystal QC & Lord Alexander of Weedon QC), London
(020) 7696 9900
clerks@southsquare.com
Recommended in Chancery, Insolvency
Specialisation: Main area of practice: insolvency, general commercial and civil fraud. Major cases: junior counsel to the administrators of Railtrack plc and ITV Digital, junior counsel to the Brunei Government, junior counsel to majority share holders of BCCI, junior counsel to Mirror Group Pensioners, advising 1986 bond holders in relation to Barings. Highlights of the past year have included major involvement in many of the recent high profile insolvencies and restructurings such as Railtrack, ITV Digital, ntl, Enron, Marconi, Energis, Global Crossing and Cammell Laird. In addition, the last 12 months has seen a continuation in the receipt of instructions from law firms in the UK and overseas relating to insolvencies and commercial disputes around the world, in particular in the United States, Hong Kong, Taiwan, Europe and a number of off-shore jurisdictions.
Prof. Memberships: Middle Temple, Gray's Inn, Chancery Bar Association, Commercial Bar Association, Insolvency Lawyers' Association.
Career: LLB (Hons) Lancaster. LLM (Cantab). Secondee to the Fraud Investigation Group (CPS).
Personal: Rugby, cricket. Player/member Old Emanuel RFC and CC. Married 1992 Lucy Atherton (neé Coppock) BBC news correspondent.

ATKINSON, Nicholas QC
2 Harcourt Buildings, Atkinson Bevan Chambers (Nicholas Atkinson QC & John Bevan QC), London
(020) 7353 2112
clerks@2hb.co.uk
Recommended in Crime
Specialisation: Criminal law specialist. In last two years has defended in cases of murder, rape, child sexual abuse, drugs, corruption and commercial fraud.
Prof. Memberships: Criminal Bar Association and served on Bar Council on three occasions in 70s, 80s and 90s.
Career: Practice in London and upon Western Circuit. Called to the Bar in 1971. Appointed Recorder of Crown and County Court in 1987. Took Silk in 1991.
Personal: Patron of Road Peace, the national charity for road traffic victims.

AUBREY, David J M QC
Temple Chambers (David J M Aubrey QC), Cardiff
(029) 2039 7364
Recommended in Crime

AUSTIN-SMITH, Michael QC
23 Essex Street (Michael Lawson QC), London
(020) 7413 0353
michaelaustin-smith@23essexstreet.co.uk
Recommended in Crime
Specialisation: Fraud, major crime of all types, crime-related civil, including civil jury actions, and police law. Appellate work includes R v Gomez [House of Lords] and Darker v West Midlands Police [House of Lords].
Career: Educated at Hampton Grammar School and Exeter University. Called to the Bar 1969; a Crown Court Recorder since 1986; DTI Inspector 1988 and 1989; Silk 1990. Formerly chairman of the Surrey and South London Bar Mess and member of the South East Area Criminal Justice Consultative Committee.
Personal: Married with two children. Leisure interests include sailing and rugby football.

AYERS, Guy
Octagon House Chambers (Guy Ayers & Andrew Lindquist), Norwich
(01603) 623186
Recommended in Crime

AYLIFFE, James
Wilberforce Chambers (Edward Nugee QC), London
(020) 7306 0102
Recommended in Chancery, Commercial (Litigation)
Specialisation: Commercial/chancery litigation with an emphasis on asset finance, banking, company, financial services, insolvency, property and related professional negligence.
Prof. Memberships: COMBAR, Chancery Bar Association.
Career: BA (Hons) Politics, Philosophy and Economics from New College, Oxford (1985) (First). Diploma in Law from City University, London (1986) (Distinction).

BAATZ, Nicholas QC
Atkin Chambers (Robert Akenhead QC), London
(020) 7404 0102
Recommended in Construction, Information Technology
Specialisation: Specialist in technology and construction and related commercial disputes. Acted in UK and internationally in a wide variety of cases with a scientific or technical content. Recent cases include disputes as to energy conversion plant productivity; biomedical process plant design; oil pipeline and associated plant design; steelworks plant fitness for purpose and productivity; industrial; commercial and institutional buildings; railways; motorways; power stations; sea defence works; bespoke software disputes in commercial, financial and industrial applications, including disputes as to software design and construction.
Career: Editor of 'Building Law Reports' (1986-98); Editor 'Technology and Construction Law Reports' (1999-2002).

BACON, Francis
4 Paper Buildings (Jean Ritchie QC), London
(020) 7643 5000
Recommended in Professional Negligence
Specialisation: All areas of professional negligence and commercial litigation with particular emphasis on civil fraud. Acted for the defendant Solicitors in the Nationwide Managed Litigation (Nationwide Building Society v Balmer Radmore [1999] Lloyd's Rep PN 241; the Nat West home loans and the Halifax Building Society managed mediations. Recent reported cases include Egan Lawson Limited v Standard Life [2001] 08 EG 168; Sharif v Garrett & Co [2001] Lloyd's Rep PN 751.
Prof. Memberships: PNBA.
Career: Called to the Bar in 1989 (Karmel Scholar – Commercial) Gray's Inn.
Personal: Educated Keele and Loughborough. Married with three children.

BADENOCH, James QC
1 Crown Office Row (Robert Seabrook QC), London
(020) 7797 7500
james.badenoch@1cor.com
Recommended in Clinical Negligence, Personal Injury
Specialisation: Principal area of practice is clinical negligence, medical discipline and all medically-related work. Also handles personal injury matters. Major cases include Wilsher v Essex Area Health Authority 1998 AC 1074 (HL); medical negligence, causation principles. The Wendy Savage enquiry, (1986); NHS disciplinary tribunal. Dobbie v Medway Health Authority (1994) 5 Med LR 160 (CA); medical injury limitation, principles. Hossack v General Dental Council (1998), 40 BMLR 97 (PC); appeal to Privy Council, principles. GMC v Rodney Leonard (1999); disciplinary proceedings. Penney & others v East Kent Health Authority (2000) Lloyds Rep Med 41 (CA); applications and limits of 'Bolam Test'. Heil v Rankin (2000) 2 WLR 1173 (CA); Landmark case on general damages. Preiss v General Dental Council [2001] Lloyds Rep Med 491 (PC); human rights and professional discipline.
Prof. Memberships: Professional Negligence Bar Association, London Common Law Bar Association, Association of Regulatory & Disciplinary Lawyers.
Career: Called to the Bar in 1968 and joined current chambers in 1968. Appointed Recorder 1987. Took silk 1989. Deputy High Court Judge from 1994 onwards. Admitted to the Hong Kong Bar (ad eundem).
Publications: 'Medical Negligence', Powers and Harris, Butterworths (contrib) 1990, 1994, 2000.
Personal: Educated at Dragon School, Rugby School 1959-63 and Magdalen College, Oxford (MA) 1964-67. Born 24 July 1945. Lives in London.

BAKER, Andrew
20 Essex Street (Iain Milligan QC), London
(020) 7842 1200
clerks@20essexst.com
Recommended in Commercial (Litigation), Shipping
Specialisation: Main areas of practice are dry shipping, arbitration, banking

LEADERS AT THE BAR

(principally international trade financing and foreign exchange trading/derivatives), international trade/commodities, conflict of laws, insurance and reinsurance (including in particular marine, mortgage indemnity insurance and LMX reinsurance). Experience as arbitrator. Reported cases include Honam Jade [1991] 1 Lloyd's Rep 38 (C/A); PNB v de Boinville [1992] 1 Lloyd's Rep 7 (C/A); Banque Paribas v Cargill [1992] 2 Lloyd's Rep 19 (C/A); Nissho Iwai v Cargill [1993] 1 Lloyd's Rep 80 (Comm Ct); Angelic Grace [1995] 1 Lloyd's Rep 87 (C/A); Orjula [1995] 2 Lloyd's Rep 395 (Comm Ct); Nicholas H [1995] 2 Lloyd's Rep 299 (H/L); Atlas [1996] 1 Lloyd's Rep 642 (Comm Ct); Roar Marine v Bimeh Iran [1998] 1 Lloyd's Rep 423 (Comm Ct); Trade Nomad [1998] 1 Lloyd's Rep 57 (Comm Ct) [1999] 1 Lloyd's Rep 723 (C/A); Morgan Stanley v Puglisi [1998] CLC 481 (Comm Ct); Den Danske Bank v Skipton Building Society [1998] 1 EGLR 155 (Comm Ct); Deepak v ICI [1998] 2 Lloyd's Rep 139 (Comm Ct) [1999] 1 Lloyd's Rep 387 (C/A). CSFB Europe v Seagate [1999] 1 Lloyd's Rep 784 (Comm Ct); Mira Oil v Bocimar [1999] 2 Lloyd's Rep (Comm Ct); Rustal Trading v Gills Duffus [2000] 1Lloyd's Rep 14 (Comm Ct).
Prof. Memberships: Lincoln's Inn, COMBAR.
Career: Born 21 December 1965. Educated at Lenzie Academy, Merton College, Oxford (reading Mathematics 1983-86) and The City University (Diploma in Law, 1987). Called to the Bar 1988. Joined 3 Essex Court (now 20 Essex Street) in 1989.
Personal: Married with three sons. Keen golfer.

BAKER, Christopher
Arden Chambers (Andrew Arden QC), London
(020) 7242 4244
Christopher.Baker@ArdenChambers.com
Recommended in Local Government
Specialisation: Principal areas (both contentious and advisory) are all aspects of housing (public, social and private), landlord and tenant, and local government, including human rights.
Prof. Memberships: Administrative Law Bar Association; Property Bar Association.
Career: Called to the Bar 1984. Founder member of Arden Chambers in 1993. Clients include very many local authorities and RSLs, together with work in offshore jurisdictions. Examples of advisory work include the Channel Tunnel link, the Barbican estate, major regeneration schemes, allocations schemes, human rights compliance, and RSL rent increases. Principal recent cases include: Baxter v Camden L.B.C. (No 2) [2001] 1 A.C. 1, HL (noise nuisance); Ingle v Scarborough B.C. [2002] EWCA Civ 290 (home loss payments); R (Mohammed) v Birmingham C.C. (2002) May 30, Admin Ct (community care, children, human rights); Lee v Leeds C.C. [2002] EWCA Civ 06 (human rights, dampness, disrepair, defective premises); Reigate & Banstead B.C. v Forrest [2001] EWCA Civ 16 (human rights, introductory tenancies); R. v Broadland D.C. ex p. Lashley [2001] B.L.G.R. 264, CA (standards committee); R. v Greenwich L.B.C. ex p. Glen International Ltd (2001) 33 H.L.R. 87, CA (renovation grants); Bath & N.E. Somerset D.C. v Nicolson [2002] EWHC 674 (Ch) (adverse possession); Lambeth L.B.C. v Henry (2000) 32 H.L.R. 874, CA (possession orders); R. v Birmingham City Council ex p. Mohammed [1999] 1 W.L.R. 33, QBD (disabled facilities grants); R. v Camden L.B.C. ex p. Mohammed (1998) 30 H.L.R. 315, QBD (homelessness policy).
Publications: 'Encyclopedia of Local Government Law' (Sweet & Maxwell - editor); 'Housing and Human Rights Law' (LAG, 2001 – co-author); 'Human Rights Act 1998: A Practitioner's Guide' (Sweet & Maxwell, 1998 – general editor); 'Housing Law: Pleadings in Practice' (Sweet & Maxwell, 1994 – co-author); regular column in 'Solicitors Journal' on local government.

BAKER, Jonathan QC
Harcourt Chambers (June Rodgers), Oxford
(020) 7353 6961 (London)
(01865) 791559 (Oxford)
jbaker@harcourtchambers.law.co.uk
Recommended in Family
Specialisation: All aspects of family law with particular expertise in children's law.
Prof. Memberships: Midland Circuit and South-Eastern Circuit, Family Law Bar Association, Association of Lawyers for Children.
Career: Called to the Bar in 1978, Middle Temple. Member of Harcourt Chambers since 1979, based in Oxford since 1991. Appointed assistant recorder 1998, recorder 2000. Took silk in 2001.
Personal: Born 6 August 1955. MA in Law St John's College, Cambridge. Married with two children. Chair of Oxfordshire Relate.

BAKER, Philip QC
Gray's Inn Tax Chambers (Milton Grundy), London
(020) 7242 2642
pb@taxbar.com
Recommended in Tax
Specialisation: All forms of revenue law, with particular specialisation in international taxation (issues of residence and domicile, double taxation agreements, foreign tax credit and transfer pricing) also taxation and human rights.
Prof. Memberships: Barrister, Grays Inn (1979) QC (2002); Visiting professorial fellow, Centre for Commercial Law Studies, Queen Mary, London University. Member, Addington Society; Committee Member, International Fiscal Association (UK Branch).
Career: 1979-87, Lecturer in Law, School of Oriental and African Studies, London University. 1987-present, Barrister, Grays Inn Tax Chambers.
Publications: 'Double Taxation Conventions and International Tax Law' (3rd edn, 2001).
Personal: Educated: Emmanuel College, Cambridge (MA); Balliol College, Oxford (BCL); University College, London (LLM); SOAS, London (PhD); London Business School (MBA). Married, three children. Awarded OBE, July 1997.

BALCOMBE, David QC
1 Crown Office Row (Robert Seabrook QC), London
(020) 7797 7500
Recommended in Family

BALDRY, Rupert
Pump Court Tax Chambers, London
(020) 7414 8080
Recommended in Tax
Specialisation: VAT and customs duties; trusts; corporate and EU tax law. Recent reported cases: CCE v Sinclair Collis; CCE v Continuum; Higher Education Statistics Agency v CCE; R v CCE ex p Bosworth Beverages; CCE v University of Leicester Students Union; R v Dimsey; R v Allen; CCE v JDL.
Prof. Memberships: Revenue Bar Association; Attorney General's Panel of Junior Counsel, VAT Practitioners' Group.
Career: Specialist tax barrister at Pump Court since 1993.
Publications: Co-author 'Trusts and UK Taxation' (Keyhaven). Editor 'Potter and Monroe's Tax Planning' (Sweet & Maxwell). Editor 'The Use of Offshore Jurisdictions' (Gee). Tax editor Jacksons 'Matrimonial Finance and Taxation'. Editor 'International Trusts and Estates Law Reports' (Butterworths).
Personal: Marlborough College; London and City Universities.

BALDWIN, John QC
8 New Square (Mark Platts-Mills QC), London
(020) 7405 4321
clerks@8newsquare.co.uk
Recommended in Intellectual Property, Media & Entertainment
Specialisation: Barrister specialising in all aspects of intellectual property law, including patents, trademarks, copyrights, confidential information, computer law, passing off, trade libel, EC law, data protection, restrictive covenants and restraint of trade. For comprehensive CV and list of recent cases, visit our website at www.8newsquare.co.uk.
Prof. Memberships: Intellectual Property Bar Association (IPBA); The Intellectual Property Lawyers Organisation (TIPLO).
Career: Called 1977, Gray's Inn; QC 1991.
Publications: Co-editor 'Patent Law of Europe & UK'.
Personal: Born 1947. Educated at Nelson Grammar School; University of Leeds (1968 BSc Agricultural Chemistry); St John's College, Oxford (1972 D.Phil 1972 Research Fellowship).

BALL, Alison QC
One Garden Court Family Law Chambers (Eleanor F Platt QC & Alison Ball QC), London
(020) 7797 7900
a.ball@onegardencourt.co.uk
Recommended in Family
Specialisation: All aspects of family law.
Prof. Memberships: Family Law Bar Association, South Eastern Circuit.
Career: Called 1972. Founder member and Head of Chambers of One Garden Court (Family Law Chambers) 1989. Mediator (FMA) 1993. Took silk in 1995. Assistant Recorder 1993. Recorder 1998.
Personal: Educated at Bedales School, 1955-66 and Kings College, London University 1967-71. Lives in London and Sussex.

BAMFORD, Jeremy
Guildhall Chambers (Adrian Palmer QC), Bristol
(0117) 930 9000
Recommended in Chancery, Commercial (Litigation), Insolvency

BANCROFT, Louise
Deans Court Chambers (Stephen Grime QC), Manchester
(0161) 214 6000
bancroft@deanscourt.co.uk
Recommended in Family
Specialisation: Practises solely in the field of family law. Private law including matrimonial finance, residence and contact. Representation on behalf of local authorities, parents and guardians in adoption and care proceedings. International child abduction. Mediation.
Prof. Memberships: Family Mediator Member of the Family Law Bar Association and Child Concern.
Career: MA Hons (Oxon) St Anne's College, Oxford. Diploma in Law, University of Westminster. Called to the Bar in 1985 (Inner Temple).

BANGAY, Deborah
1 Hare Court (Bruce Blair QC), London
(020) 7797 7070
Recommended in Family
Specialisation: Family law especially matrimonial finance (Re P CA 1991 FLR 1 286 – wordship contempt); private children (GV J CA 1993 FLR 1 1008 - ouster); public law children work (Re H CAA 1994 1 FLR CA 3); H v J MHV (costs: residence proceedings) 2000 IFLR 394; Rose v Rose 2002 1 FLR 845; Wells v Wells 2002 2 FLR 1; A v A; and B v B 2000 1 FLR 701.
Prof. Memberships: Family Law Bar Association.
Career: 1972-76, Wycombe High School; 1976-79, Exeter University LLB Hons; 1970-80, Council of Legal Education; 1982-92, 13 Kings Bench Walk/Hardwicke Building; 1992, 29 Bedford Row.
Personal: Football, swimming and cooking.

LEADERS AT THE BAR

BANKS, Robert
100E Great Portland Street (Robert Banks), London
(020) 7636 6323
Recommended in Crime

BANKS, Roderick I'Anson
48 Bedford Row (Roderick I'Anson Banks), London
(020) 7430 2005
rciab@partnershipcounsel.co.uk
Recommended in Partnership
Specialisation: Exclusively partnership law. Has specialised in this area since 1977. Handles all aspects of partnership law from the drafting and review of agreements to advice and representation in partnership disputes, arbitrations and mediations. Acts for solicitors, accountants, and other professional firms, as well as various financial and commercial institutions. Acted as a consultant to the Law Commission on its reviews of partnership law and limited partnership law.
Prof. Memberships: Lincoln's Inn.
Career: Called to the Bar 1974 and joined Stone Buildings, (Chambers of DR Stanford). Set up 48 Bedford Row in 1991, as the only chambers specialising exclusively in partnership law. CEDR Accredited Mediator, 1993. Hon. Associate of British Veterinary Association. Founder member of the Association of Partnership Practitioners.
Publications: Editor of 'Lindley & Banks on Partnership'; author and editor of 'The Encyclopedia of Professional Partnerships'.
Personal: Educated at Westminster School 1965-69 and University College London 1970-73. Leisure pursuits include reading and films. Born 5 December 1951. Lives in Beare Green, Surrey.

BANNISTER, Edward Alexander QC
3 Stone Buildings (Geoffrey Vos QC), London
(020) 7242 4937
ebannister@3sb.law.co.uk
Recommended in Chancery, Company, Insolvency
Specialisation: Specialises in company/insolvency and commercial litigation and all related matters, including property and contract; extensive professional negligence litigation practice. Recent cases include Stein v Blake [1996] AC 243 (set off in insolvency); re Duckwari plc [1997] Ch 201 (measure of compensation on breach of 320 Companies Act 1985); Swindle v Harrison [1997] 4 All ER 705 (causation and fiduciary duty claims); Paragon Finance v Thakerar [1999] 1 All ER 400 (limitation and constructive trusts); Worby v Rosser[1999] Lloyd's Rep PN 974 (CA) (whether White v Jones applies to costs of beneficiaries under earlier will); Triffitt Nurseries v Salads Etcetera [2000] 1 All ER Comm 737 (CA) (insolvent agent's right to retain proceeds of sale against principal); re Greenhaven Motors Limited [1999] BCLC 635 (court control over liquidator's discretion); North Holdings Limited v Southern Tropics Limited [1999] 2 BCLC 625 (unfair prejudice petitions and CPR); Garrow v Society of Lloyds [2000] Lloyds Rep IR 38 (effect of sue now pay later clause in bankruptcy proceedings); Jones v Society of Lloyds, Times 2 February 2000 (penalty clauses); Society of Lloyds v Twinn, (2000) 97 (15) LSG 40 (whether acceptance of offer qualified by side letter); Motor Crown Petroleum v *SJ Berwin* [2000] Lloyd's Rep PN 438 (CA) (whether Allied Maples to be applied in case involving failed planning appeal); Barings Plc v Coopers & Lybrand, [2000] 1 WLR 2352 (CA) (Banking Act 1987 - when exhibits to affidavits available to the public); Mamidoil-Jetoil Greek Petroleum Co SA v OKTA Crude Oil Refinery AD [2000] 1 Lloyd's Rep 554 (Arbitration Act 1996; construction of oil importation contract; Sale of Goods Act 1979); Clef Aquitaine SARL v Laporte Materials (Barrow) [2001] QB 488 (CA) (measure of damages for fraudulent misrepresentation); Paragon Finance v Nash [2002] 1 WLR 685 (implied terms in variable interest rate mortgages).
Prof. Memberships: Bencher, Honourable Society of Lincoln's Inn; Member Management Committee, Bar Pro Bono Unit.
Career: Called to the Bar 1974, Silk 1991.

BARCA, Manuel
1 Brick Court (Richard Rampton QC), London
(020) 7353 8845
Recommended in Defamation
Specialisation: Media and information law, principally defamation, malicious falsehood, confidence/privacy, contempt of court etc, but also media/literary copyright and passing off.
Career: Graduate trainee, Reuters 1984-85. Called to Bar 1986 (Lincoln's Inn, Levitt Scholar). Joined 1 Brick Court in 1987. Cases include A-G v Associated Newspapers; Cambridge Nutrition v BBC; Pickering v Liverpool Daily Post; Cumming v Scottish Daily Record; Major v New Statesman; Oyston v Blaker; Berkoff v Burchill; Stern v Piper; Watts v Times Newspapers; GMC v BBC; Adams v Associated Newspapers; Godfrey v Demon Internet; Beta Construction v Channel 4; Upjohn v BBC; Walker Wingsail Systems v IPC; Bottomley v Express Newspapers; British Coal v NUM; Barclay Brothers v BBC; Howarth v Guardian Newspapers; Newton v Express Newspapers; Clunes v Express Newspapers; Home Secretary v BBC; Loucas v Channel 4; Dick v Times Newspapers; Marks & Spencer v Granada TV; City of London Police v BBC & Ors; Rondel v BBC; Merciar v BBC; ITN v Living Marxism; Khalili v Associated Newspapers; Trimble v Amazon; Walker v Newcastle Chronicle; R v Shilibier ex p HTV; Multigroup v Oxford Analytica; Rahamim v ITN; Elite Model Management v BBC; Skrine & Co v Euromoney Publications; Austin v Newcastle Chronicle; Steedman v BBC; Green v Times Newspapers; MacIntyre v Chief Constable of Kent.
Personal: Educated at Wimbledon College and Cambridge University (Law Tripos, MA). Bilingual in English and Spanish. Fluent French. Working Italian and Portuguese.

BARDA, Robin
4 Paper Buildings (Lionel Swift QC), London
(020) 7583 0816
rb@4pb.com
Recommended in Family
Specialisation: All aspects of family and matrimonial work, including residence and contact disputes, adoptions, child abductions, public law applications, matrimonial finance, disputes between unmarried couples and Inheritance Act applications. A considerable amount of work for local authorities and guardians, in particular the official solicitor, most in the High Court at the Principal and other district registries, but also in County Courts around London and elsewhere in the Court of Appeal. Cases have involved clients across a broad spectrum of wealth, including well-known personalities, and cases which have received media attention. Recently reported cases include P v P (Abduction: Acquiescence) [1998] 1 FLR 630, Re R (Adoption: Disclosure) [1999] 2 FLR 1123; Re Z and A (Contact: Supervision Order) [2000] 2FLR 406; Re JS (Private International Adoption) [2000] 2 FLR 638; B v H (Habitual Residence; Wardship) [2002] 1 FLR 388.
Prof. Memberships: Family Law Bar Association. London Common Law and Commercial Bar Association.
Career: B.A. Oxon. Called to the Bar 1975, Gray's Inn. Joined Chambers of John Byrt QC, 4 Paper Buildings, Temple as a pupil in 1975, taken on as a tenant in 1976.
Personal: Education: Bryanston School 1960-66. Academical Clerk (Choral scholar) Magdalen College, Oxford 1967-70 – BA in Philosophy, Politics and Economics. Hobbies: Freelance musician/singer 1970-74. Chairman of The Sixteen Ltd. Director of Singcircle Ltd. Singing with The Sixteen (occasionally) and the Choir of St Clement Danes, including concerts. Music generally. Squash. Clubs: Savage Club.

BARKER, Anthony QC
No5 Chambers (Gareth Evans QC), Birmingham
(0121) 606 0500
Recommended in Crime
Specialisation: Criminal law, in particular substantial cases involving expert scientific, accounting and direct expert evidence.
Career: Called 1966, Silk 1985, Bencher 1999.

BARKER, Kerry
Guildhall Chambers (Adrian Palmer QC), Bristol
(0117) 930 9000
kerry.barker@guildhallchambers.co.uk
Recommended in Licensing
Specialisation: All aspects of licensing law including: liquor licensing, public entertainments and local authority licensing (sex establishments, taxis, street trading etc) acting for applicants, objectors, police authorities, licencing justices and local authorities. Has expertise in betting, gaming and lotteries (casinos, bingo clubs, gaming machines, bookmakers and betting offices, lotteries, competitions and fundraising). Related appeals, judicial review and cases stated. Former Justices' Clerk.
Publications: Publications include 'Betting Gaming and Lotteries' (Fourmat Publishing 1992). Editor of 'Licensing Law Reports' [2001] and [2002] LLR (Jordans Publishing). Contributor to 'Paterson's Licensing Acts'.

BARKER, Simon
Maitland Chambers (Michael Lyndon-Stanford QC & Charles Aldous QC), London
(020) 7406 1200
Recommended in Media & Entertainment
Specialisation: Media and entertainment litigation (including copyright, passing off, breach of confidence, format rights); Copyright Tribunal references; commercial litigation and arbitration including warranty and contract claims on sale of businesses and shares, company law; partnership disputes; professional negligence; committal; disciplinary tribunals.
Prof. Memberships: Fellow of Institute of Chartered Accountants. Member of Chartered Institute of Arbitrators.
Career: Qualified as chartered accountant 1976. Called to the Bar 1979 (Lincoln's Inn). Chartered Accountant and Fellow ICAEW 1982. Assistant Recorder 1995. Recorder 2000.

BARLING, Gerald QC
Brick Court Chambers (Christopher Clarke QC), London
(020) 7379 3550
Recommended in Competition/European Law
Specialisation: EC law, UK competition and administrative law.
Prof. Memberships: Chairman Bar European Group (1994-96); Chairman EC Sub-Ctee, IPC Bar Council (1991-92).
Career: Called 1972, took silk 1991, Recorder 1993. Bencher Middle Temple 2001. Important cases include: R v Secretary of State for Transport ex p: Factortame I, II, III & IV; R v SS for Trade & Industry ex p Greenpeace; R v Customs & Excise ex p Lunn Poly; R v IRC ex p Commerzbank; R v Licensing Authority ex p Generics & R v MAFF ex p Monsanto; R v Treasury ex p BT; R v IRC ex p Professional Contractors Group; International Transport Roth v Home Office; numerous appearances in

LEADERS AT THE BAR

ECJ Luxembourg.
Publications: Co-editor: 'Practitioners Handbook of E.C Law' (1998).
Personal: Born 18 September 1949 in Preston. Educated at St Mary's College, Blackburn and New College, Oxford. Degree in Law (First Class Hons). Scholarships include Peel Foundation (USA), Burnett Open Exhibition (Oxford), Harmsworth Entrance Exhibition (Middle Temple) and Astbury Law Scholarship (Middle Temple). Languages: French.

BARLOW, Francis
10 Old Square (Leolin Price CBE QC), London
(020) 7405 0758
Recommended in Chancery

BARLOW, Richard
11 King's Bench Walk (FJ Muller QC), London
(020) 7353 3337
clerks@11kbw.co.uk
Recommended in Tax
Specialisation: Value Added Tax, Customs and Excise and criminal fraud.
Prof. Memberships: Revenue Bar Association, Chartered Institute of Arbitrators, Institute of Indirect Tax.
Career: Called to the Bar 1970. Customs and Excise Solicitor's Office 1973-88. Private Practice 1988 to present. Chairman (part-time) Social Security and Disability Appeals Tribunal, VAT and Duties Tribunal and Deputy Special Commissioner.
Publications: Contributor to Tax Journals.
Personal: LLB (LSE) 1969. MSc, Fellow Chartered Institute of Arbitrators 1999, Accredited Mediator, RIIT.

BARNES, Mark QC
One Essex Court (Lord Grabiner QC), London
(020) 7583 2000
mbarnes@oeclaw.co.uk
Recommended in Arbitration, Banking & Finance, Commercial (Litigation), Energy, Fraud
Specialisation: Commercial law and litigation, with experience of company and insolvency law; European Community law and administrative law, where these touch upon commercial disputes. In the commercial field, practice includes banking, commodities, oil and gas, energy supply and option contracts, IT and telecommunications outsourcing and supply contracts, sale of commercial goods, share sales and professional negligence. Has acted and advised in arbitrations (under ICC and LME rules, and ad hoc) and in or in connection with expert determinations and redeterminations in the gas and construction industries.

BARNES, Michael QC
Wilberforce Chambers (Edward Nugee QC), London
(020) 7306 0102
Recommended in Property Litigation

BARNES, Timothy QC
7 Bedford Row (David Farrer QC), London
(020) 7242 3555
Recommended in Crime
Specialisation: Commercial fraud and other serious criminal work. Clients include SFO, CPS, HQ and CPS areas on Midland and Oxford Circuit, and major defence solicitors in London and on circuit. Acted for the prosecution in Wallace Smith and Durnford Ford cases (SFO) and in the de Stempel fraud (CPS West Mercia). Prosecuted 'R v Kellard and others (Britannia Park Ltd)' (1990). Acted for the defence in Swithland Motors (Howes Percival, Northampton) and in Pearce (Lloyds Re-Insurance Fraud) (*Kingsley Napley*). R v Cheung (Fraudulent Foreign Exchange Dealing) (Kingsley Napley) and R v Sawtell (conspiracy to defraud) (Burton Copeland). Assists in teaching at seminars for accountants and lawyers on techniques of expert evidence and advocacy.
Prof. Memberships: Criminal Bar Association.
Career: Called to Bar, Gray's Inn 1968. Queen's Counsel 1986. Recorder 1987.
Personal: Educated at Bradfield College and Christ's College, Cambridge. Married with 4 children. Interests include music and gardening.

BARNETT, Jeremy
St. Paul's Chambers (Nigel Sangster QC), Leeds
(0113) 245 5866
Recommended in Crime
Specialisation: Specialist in white collar crime. Fraud: defended in numerous recent high profile SFO and CPSHQ prosecutions. Regulatory breach: wide ranging experience in nursery and toy industries, with emphasis on the defence of due diligence and quality management, also health and safety prosecutions. Director of 'Court 21' project, UK Centre of Courtroom Technology at Leeds University.
Prof. Memberships: Criminal Bar Association and North Eastern Circuit elected member of Bar Council. Chair of Bar Council IT Panel.
Career: Called to Bar 1980. Founder member of St Paul's Chambers in 1982.
Personal: Educated Leeds Grammar School, Liverpool University. Keen interest in computers. Leisure pursuits include golf, football and music.

BARON, Florence QC
Queen Elizabeth Building (Florence Baron QC), London
(020) 7797 7837
Recommended in Family
Specialisation: All aspects of family law and related professional negligence - with a particular emphasis on "Big Money" cases. Appeared in several high profile cases, including F v F 1995 2 FLR 45, Cowan v Cowan (2001) 2 FLR 1999 192, Rose v Rose 1 FLR 978 and advised the Prince of Wales in his divorce. Also specialises in cases with an international

element.
Prof. Memberships: FLBA.
Career: BA (Oxon). QC (1995). Recorder and Deputy High Court Judge.

BARRETT, John
40 King St, Manchester
(0161) 832 9082
jbarrett@40kingstreet.co.uk
Recommended in Environment, Planning
Specialisation: Town and country planning; environment; compulsory purchase; highways; local government; judicial review; waste disposal; retail; minerals; housing.
Prof. Memberships: Planning and Environment Bar Association; member of Northern Circuit and Administrative Law Bar Association.
Career: Called 1982; elected member of Northern Circuit 1983. Occasional lecturer at University of Newcastle-upon-Tyne.
Publications: Former assistant editor of the Encyclopaedia of Environmental Health.
Personal: Married with two children.

BARRETT, Penelope
3 Gray's Inn Square (Rock Tansey QC), London
(020) 7520 5600
Recommended in Crime
Specialisation: Criminal defence advocate instructed in leading work. Her recent caseload reflects her practice, including as it does murder, attempted murder and kidnap, large-scale cocaine importations, armed robbery and substantial offences of dishonesty. Has considerable experience in representing children and young people accused of serious crime and is currently engaged in representing one such young person accused of attempted murder. Retains her expertise in defending mentally disordered and vulnerable offenders and those accused of serious sexual offences. She lectures on a number of aspects of criminal law/evidence.
Prof. Memberships: Criminal Bar Association, Liberty, British Academy of Forensic Sciences.
Career: Called to the Bar 1982.
Personal: Educated through state schools – Haygrove Comprehensive and Bridgwater College – and Trinity Hall, Cambridge (BA Hons 1981). Friend of the Tate and Hayward Galleries, and of the Royal Academy.

BARRIE, Peter
Guildhall Chambers (Adrian Palmer QC), Bristol
(0117) 930 9000
peter.barrie@guildhallchambers.co.uk
Recommended in Personal Injury
Specialisation: Personal injury and clinical negligence.
Prof. Memberships: PIBA.
Publications: 'Compensation for Personal Injuries' (OUP 2002).

BARTLETT, Andrew QC
Crown Office Chambers (Michael Spencer QC & Christopher Purchas QC), London

(020) 7797 8100
bartlett@crownofficechambers.com
Recommended in Construction, Professional Negligence
Specialisation: Professional negligence, construction, insurance/reinsurance, product liability, commercial contracts. Frequently instructed in major claims and appeals involving complex legal or technical issues. Cases of note include Group Josi Re v Walbrook Insurance Co Ltd (CA), Royal Brompton Hospital v Hammond (CA), Hammersmith Hospitals v Troup Bywaters & Anders (CA), Albright & Wilson UK v Biachem Ltd (CA), Co-operative Retail Services v Taylor Young Partnership (HL). Chartered Arbitrator. TECSA and TECBAR accredited adjudicator. Panel member of Chartered Institute of Arbitrators. Member of London Court of International Arbitration.
Prof. Memberships: COMBAR, PNBA, TECBAR, LCLCBA, Society of Construction Law.
Career: Called 1974, FCI Arb 1988, QC 1993, Chairman of Financial Services and Markets Tribunal.
Publications: General Editor of 'Emden's Construction Law'.

BARTLEY JONES, Edward QC
Exchange Chambers (David Turner QC & Bill Braithwaite QC & Henry Globe QC), Liverpool
(0151) 236 7747/(0161) 833 2722
jonesqc@exchangechambers.co.uk
Recommended in Chancery, Commercial (Litigation), Insolvency
Specialisation: Commercial, professional negligence, insolvency, banking, chancery, companies, commercial property and landlord and tenant, commercial arbitration, intellectual property.
Prof. Memberships: Northern Circuit Chancery Bar Association; Chancery Bar Association; Northern Circuit Commercial Bar Association.
Career: BA (Oxon) 1973 called 1975. Practised in Liverpool from 1976. Head of Commercial Department, Exchange Chambers, Liverpool and Manchester, since 1994. Formerly part-time tutor in law at Liverpool University. Recorder. QC (1997).

BARTON, Roger
No.1 High Pavement (John B Milmo QC), Nottingham
(0115) 941 8218
Recommended in Crime

BARWISE, Stephanie
Atkin Chambers (Robert Akenhead QC), London
(020) 7404 0102
clerks@atkinchambers.law.co.uk
Recommended in Construction
Specialisation: General commercial including all aspects of the law relating to the construction and civil engineering industry both in litigation and arbitration. Experience includes major road and tunnel construction (e.g. Conway Crossing), ship refurbishment (Q.E.2), North Sea oil rig construction

LEADERS AT THE BAR

and Ladbroke Grove Rail Inquiry. Practice also involves professional negligence in general and in particular of architects, engineers and surveyors. A further area of specialisation is rights appurtenant to land and property: party wall disputes, easements including interference with rights of support, e.g. Midland Bank plc v Bardgrove Property Services 60 BLR 1 (Court of Appeal 1992).
Career: Called to the Bar 1988. Joined Atkin Building in 1989.
Personal: Educated at Bolton School and Cambridge University (Downing College). Fluent in French and German.

BATE, David QC
Hollis Whiteman Chambers (QEB) (Julian Bevan QC & Peter Whiteman QC), London
(020) 7583 5766
barristers@holliswhiteman.co.uk
Recommended in Crime
Specialisation: All forms of criminal work. Since 1990 he has concentrated mainly on defence work. Many of his cases involve organised crime; gangland murder, major drug importations, armed robbery, police corruption, blackmail etc. He has appeared in many notorious cases involving members of the Arif, Frazer, Raymond, Reeves, Blundell and Joyce families. Notable cases include R v Doran, R v McAvoy (Brinks Mat bullion robbery), R v Relton (Brinks Mat money laundering), R v Buck (REM air rage), R v Bayfield (baby shaking murder), R v Knott & Others (gangland assassinations), R v Lydiate (gangland torture). He also specialises in Serious Fraud Office cases representing solicitors, accountants and businessmen charged with white collar fraud of all kinds: corporate, revenue, VAT, etc.
Prof. Memberships: Criminal Bar Association.
Career: Called 1969. Silk 1994. Recorder.
Personal: Hendon Grammar School. Manchester University (LLB). Running, singing and drinking wine.

BATE, Stephen
5 Raymond Buildings (Patrick Milmo QC), London
(020) 7242 2902
Recommended in Media & Entertainment
Specialisation: Television, music, film, publishing, new media and telecommunications, dealing with contractual, intellectual property (including Copyright Tribunal), regulatory, judicial review, competition, passing off, breach of confidence, privacy and defamation. Major cases include BBC Enterprises v Hi-Tech Xtravision (rights in encrypted transmissions), Island Records v Tring (election between remedies), R v ITC ex p TVNI (judicial review of C3 licences), MMC Report on Channel 3 Networking, BBC World Service v Star TV (termination of satellite broadcasting service), Enigma v Godlcrest (film rights), Nicholl v Ryder (artist/manager dispute), Candy Rock v PPL (Copyright Tribunal), Ludlow v Williams (music publishing), Allason v Random House (book publishing), A v B & C (privacy), A v B & Anr sub nom Flitcroft v MGN (privacy), Co-author of 'The Law of Privacy & Media'. See further www.5rb.co.uk.
Career: Called 1981.

BATES, John H
Old Square Chambers (John Hendy QC), London
(020) 7269 0300
read@oldsquarechambers.co.uk
Recommended in Environment
Specialisation: An experienced environmental law practitioner in both civil and criminal courts and in statutory inquiries. Has particular expertise in water pollution and waste management cases and has been involved in a number of appeals against noise related abatement notices. In addition has acted in judicial review actions on environmental matters, advised in such areas as nature conservation, contaminated land, transfrontier shipment of waste, toxic torts, water abstraction licensing, land drainage and flooding disputes and fishing rights.
Prof. Memberships: Chairman UK Environment Law Association 1991-93.
Career: Author: 'Water and Drainage Law', 'Marine Environment Law', 'UK Waste Law'.

BATTEN, Stephen QC
3 Raymond Buildings (Clive Nicholls QC), London
(020) 7400 6400
chambers@3raymondbuildings.com
Recommended in Crime, Fraud
Specialisation: All forms of crime: white collar (First Defendant R v Blackspur Leasing; R Szjraber for SFO; R v Judge Gee); murder: Kenneth Noye (the M25 Road Rage murder), First Defendant in private prosecution for murder of Stephen Lawrence; dishonesty (Brinks Matt); professional tribunals: health and safety (Port Ramsgate Walkway Collapse).
Career: BA (Oxon). Call 1968. QC 1989. Recorder of the Crown Court.

BATTY, Christopher
St. Paul's Chambers (Nigel Sangster QC), Leeds
(0113) 245 5866
Recommended in Crime

BAXENDALE, Presiley QC
Blackstone Chambers (Presiley Baxendale QC & Charles Flint QC), London
(020) 75831770
presileybaxendale@blackstonechambers.com
Recommended in ADR
Specialisation: Principal area of practice is mediation. Has specialised in commercial/public law, local government, human rights, education, employment and financial services. Counsel to the Inquiry into Exports of Defence Equipment and Dual Use of Goods to Iraq, CEDR registered Mediator, member of Sports Dispute Resolution Panel.
Prof. Memberships: London Common Law and Commercial Bar Association, Administrative Law Bar Association, Qualified Mediator accredited by CEDR.
Career: Called to the Bar and joined 2 Hare Court in 1974. Appointed Junior Counsel to Crown (Common Law). Took silk in 1992. Joint Head of Chambers since 1998.
Personal: Educated at Oxford University (MA). Governor of the LSE. Executive Committee: Justice.

BEAN, David QC
Matrix Chambers, London
(020) 7404 3447
Recommended in Education, Employment
Specialisation: Principal area of practice is employment law. Also deals with administrative and education law. Major cases include P v NASUWT (trade dispute); Foley v Post Office (unfair dismissal); Carver v Saudi Arabian Airlines (overseas employment); Re Leyland DAF (employees' rights in insolvency); London Underground v Edwards (indirect discrimination); South Bank University v Anyanwu ('aiding' discrimination); Meade v British Fuels (transfer of undertakings); Chief Constable of West Yorkshire v Khan (victimisation). Clients include major employers and trade unions.
Prof. Memberships: Employment Law Bar Association (Chairman 1999-2001), Employment Lawyers' Association, ALBA.
Career: Called to the Bar 1976. Recorder 1996. QC 1997. Chairman Bar Council 2002.
Publications: 'Injunctions' (7th edn 1997). Editor 'Law Reform for All (1996).

BEAR, Charles
11 King's Bench Walk Chambers (Eldred Tabachnik QC & James Goudie QC), London
(020) 7632 8500
bear@11kbw.com
Recommended in Employment, Local Government
Specialisation: Specialises in commercial, employment and public law. Notable commercial work includes claims arising on business sales, commercial fraud and restitutionary claims. In the employment field, specialises in the protection of business interests after termination of employment, including the enforcement of anti-competition clauses, protection of confidential information and related freezing and search and seizure orders. Other main area of practice is judicial review and public law, with a particular interest in local authority powers and financing.
Prof. Memberships: COMBAR, ALBA.
Career: Called to the Bar in 1986 and joined current chambers in 1988.
Personal: Educated at Oxford University (scholar of Magdalen College) 1982-85 (1st Class Hons). Fluent in French. Born 1963. Lives in London.

BEARD, Daniel
Monckton Chambers (Kenneth Parker QC & Paul Lasok QC), London
(020) 7405 7211
dbeard@monckton.co.uk
Recommended in Competition/European Law
Specialisation: Competition law: UK and EU litigation, regulatory and merger control. Also EU state aid and free movement of goods/services (in particular, relationship between IP and competition/free movement rules). Administrative law and human rights: including judicial review of competition, immigration, health and licensing decisions. Recent cases include R(Interbrew) v Competition Commission – JR of CC report re Bass acquisition; Birds Eye Wall's v Coldstream – competition damages action; P&O Ferries (Vizcaya) v EC Commission – annulment of state aid recovery order; UFC/Pointing – CC merger inquiry; Scottish Power v Elexon – competition in the electricity industry; R (Quark Fishing) v Foreign Secretary – judicial review of licensing allocation; Pembroke County Cricket Club v Lovell (nature of sports disciplinary rules).
Prof. Memberships: Bar European Group; Administrative Law Bar Association; Competition Lawyers' Association.
Publications: Editor 'Competition Law Journal; Competition Law and the Internet in 'Laws of the Internet' ed Gringras 2nd ed (forthcoming); Butterworths 'Competition Law', contributing editor.

BEAZLEY, Thomas QC
Blackstone Chambers (Presiley Baxendale QC & Charles Flint QC), London
(020) 7583 1770
clerks@blackstonechambers.com
Recommended in Commercial (Litigation)
Specialisation: Practice involves substantial commercial (including insurance/reinsurance) and financial service cases, frequently with a significant foreign or fraud element, both in court, arbitration and regulatory proceedings. Cases include: the State of Brunei v Prince Jefri, Brunei HC and CA 2000, and related cases; Hyundai Engineering and Construction Co v Prince Jefri Ch D, 9 March 2001; Guild (Claims) Ltd v *Eversheds* (a firm) [2001] L1 R PN 910; In re Q's Estate [1999] 1 L1 R 424; Phoenix Finance v Formula One Management, V-C 22.5.02; Republic of Nauru v Allen, Allen and Hemsley; BFG Bank AG v Brown and Mumford 30.10.96; SFA disciplinary proceedings; including SFA v Nomura, SFA v Reed and Murch, SFA v BZW, SFA v Dootson; Kleinwort Benson Ltd v Glasgow City Council [1996] QB 57 ECJ, 678 CA and [1994] QB 404; Marinari v Lloyds Bank [1993] All ER (EC) 84; the

LEADERS AT THE BAR

Morgan Grenfell/Peter Young cases; the News International v Clinger litigation; the Dobb White cases; DTI investigations, including the Atlantic Computers DTI investigation; Berezovsky v Michaels [2000] 1 WLR 1004; Sheldon v Outhwaite [1996] 1 AC 102 and insurance/reinsurance arbitrations; Continental Bank v Aeakos [1994] 1 L1 R 505; Owens Bank Bracco [1992] 2 AC 443; Kurz v Stella Musical [1992] Ch 196; Re Polly Peck International Plc (in administration) [1998] 2 BCLC 185; Henry Ansbacher v Binks Stern 141 SJLB 151.
Prof. Memberships: COMBAR.
Career: Called to the Bar 1979 (MT), Queen's Counsel 2001.
Personal: Working knowledge of Dutch, French and German.

BECK, James
2-4 Tudor Street (Richard Ferguson QC), London
(020) 7797 7111
Recommended in Crime

BECKETT, Richard QC
3 Raymond Buildings (Clive Nicholls QC), London
(020) 74006400
chambers@3raymondbuildings.com
Recommended in Licensing
Specialisation: Licensing. Work includes preparation and advice relating to applications and objections in all licensing matters, such as liquor, gaming, betting and amusement centres, representing parties at all levels from local committees to Administrative Court. Advises on lotteries and other related activities. Clients include the Rank Organisation, Ladbrokes and JD Wetherspoon plc.
Career: Called to the Bar 1965 and joined present chambers 1967. Took silk 1988.

BEHRENS, James
Serle Court (Lord Neill of Bladen QC), London
(020) 7242 6105
jbehrens@serlecourt.co.uk
Recommended in Church
Specialisation: Commercial disputes, computer law, company law, church law, partnerships, property law, probate and trusts, arbitration and mediation.
Prof. Memberships: Chancery Bar Association; Property Bar Association; Association of Contentious Trust and Probate Specialists; Society for Computers and Law; Ecclesiastical Law Society; Associate tenant of Zenith Chambers, Leeds.
Career: Called to the Bar in 1979; member of the Bar Council 1992-94; CEDR accredited mediator 1998; deputy chancery master 2000; director of Mediation UK, 2000; chartered arbitrator 2001; Chancellor of the diocese of Leicester 2002.
Publications: 'Practical Church Management' (1998); 'Confirmation, Sacrament of Grace' (1995); 'Word Perfect for the Legal Profession' (1991).

Contributor to 'Researching the Legal Web' by Nick Holmes and Delia Venables (1999), and 'Case Preparation' by the Inns of Court School of Law (1997).
Personal: Born 22 December 1956, educated Eton College; Trinity College, Cambridge (MA); Cardiff University (LLM and PhD). Married with three children. Lives in Kensington and Yorkshire.

BELOFF, Michael QC
Blackstone Chambers (Presiley Baxendale QC & Charles Flint QC), London
(020) 7583 1770
clerks@blackstonechambers.com
Recommended in Administrative & Public Law, Employment, Human Rights, Sport
Specialisation: Extremely wide ranging practice encompasses litigation and arbitration, covering a large number of areas including judicial review, commercial, EU law, employment, libel, insurance, sport, immigration, civil liberties and aviation. Has appeared in more than 375 reported cases in House of Lords, Privy Council, European Court of Justice, European Court of Human Rights and courts in Hong Kong, Singapore, Kuala Lumpur, Kuching, Bermuda, Trinidad, Brunei, Gibraltar and Belfast. In three major public inquiries: Crown Agents 1980-82; Brixton Disorders 1981 (Scarman Inquiry) and Sentosa Collision (Singapore, 1983). Chaired inquiry into academic plagiarism for University of Oxford 1987, and into 'The Connection' for Carlton TV 1998. 'Racism in Rugby Football' for the Rugby Football Union in 2002. Women's Legal Defence Award 1991. Clients have included governments, local authorities, regulators, unions, national newspapers, television channels, banks, insurance companies, major ports, corporations, universities, statutory bodies, pressure groups, sporting organisations, and leading individuals and personalities from all fields of achievement including The Chief Rabbi, the Aga Khan, L. Ron Hubbard, Robert Maxwell, Ernest Saunders, The Al-Fayeds, Prime Ministers of three countries, Lennox Lewis, George Best, Sebastian Coe, and David Coulthard. Author of numerous articles for legal periodicals. Books include Butterworths 'The Sex Discrimination Act 1976'. Halsbury's Laws 'Time' (1999). Conference addresses include Sweet and Maxwell Conference on Judicial Review (Chairman 1990-91 and 1993-96); ECHR Salzburg (1988). IAAF Monte Carlo (1991) Singapore Law Academy (1992), Hong Kong Bar Association (1994), FCO-arranged 'Human Rights in the UK' (for Mayor of Moscow [1991]). McCarthy - Tetrault – Vancouver (1996) Institute of Human Rights: Moscow (1996), Auckland (1997), Beijing (1997), Berlin (1997), Tokyo, University of Virginia, Tulane University, Commonwealth Law Conference (all 1999). Annual Lectures: ALBA (1994) Statute Law Society (1994) UC Dublin (1997), Lasok Exeter U (1998), Atkin (Reform) 1999, Ramamani (Madras) 1999. Consultant Editor: Judicial Review Bulletin.
Prof. Memberships: COMBAR, Administrative Law Bar Association (First Chairman, now Emeritus Chairman and Vice-President), Bar European Group. Environmental Law Foundation (Advisory Council). Honorary Fellow, Institute of Advanced Legal Studies.
Career: Called to the Bar 1967. QC 1981. Recorder of the Crown Court 1984-95. Master of the Bench, Grays Inn 1988. Deputy High Court Judge (QBD) 1989-96. Nominated to sit in Divisional Court of QBD 1992. Joint Head of Chambers at 4-5 Gray's Inn Square from 1992-2000. Judge of the Court of Appeal of Guernsey and Jersey 1995. Member Court of Arbitration for Sport (Lausanne) 1995; Steward of the Royal Automobile Club 1998-; Deputy Chairman, Data Protection (National Security) Tribunal 2000-; Chairman, International Cricket Council Code of Conduct Commission 2002; CAS Ad Hoc Panel Atlanta Olympics 1996; Sydney Olympics 2000; Kuala Lumpa Commonwealth Games 1998; Manchester Commonwealth Games 2002. Ad Hoc Legal Advisor to British team, World Athletics Championship Seville (1990). President Trinity College, Oxford 1996-.
Personal: Born 18 April 1942. Educated at Dragon School, Oxford 1950-54, Eton College 1954-60 (King's Scholar and Captain of School 1960) and Magdalen College, Oxford 1960-65 (BA History Class 1, 1963; Jurisprudence 1965, MA 1967). Moved motion which procured admission of women to full membership of the Oxford Union 1964. Five marathons, including London marathon (twice). Honorary member of International Athletics Club. Member of Gridiron (Oxford), Vincents (Oxford) Achilles, Reform Club (on Political Committee), FRSA, FICPD. Lives in London and Oxford. Married to Judith Beloff, Barrister JP, IS, ID.

BELTRAMI, Adrian
3 Verulam Buildings (Christopher Symons QC & John Jarvis QC), London
(020) 7831 8441
chambers@3vb.com
Recommended in Banking & Finance, Commercial (Litigation), Fraud
Specialisation: All aspects of commercial litigation, in particular domestic and international banking, insolvency, commercial fraud and professional negligence. Cases include: BCCI v Price Waterhouse (1996, 1997 and 1998) (Banking Act, auditors' duties and liabilities), Box v Barclays Bank (1998) (banking Act, constructive trusts), Electra v KPMG (1999) (auditors' duty of care), Middle Temple v Lloyds Bank (1999) (cheque collection), Thyssen v Thyssen (undue influence), Grupo Torras v Al-Sabah (fraud, tracing). Principal contributor to Banking Litigation (1999).
Prof. Memberships: COMBAR.
Career: Called to the Bar 1989. Admitted to the Bar of the Cayman Islands on several individual cases.
Personal: Stonyhurst, Downing College, Cambridge and Harvard Law School. MA (1st class) LLM. Born 8 November 1964. Lives in London. Married with one son and one daughter.

BENNETT, M
Oriel Chambers (Andrew Sander), Liverpool
(0151) 236 7191/236 4321
Recommended in Family

BENNETT-JENKINS, Sallie
2 Hare Court (Stephen Kramer QC), London
(020) 7353 5324
salliebennett-jenkins@2harecourt.com
Recommended in Crime
Specialisation: Criminal law specialist. Work undertaken includes the prosecution of high profile murder cases. Defence work includes acting for multinational companies in HSE matters and investment banks in an advisory capacity, defending in murders, representing sports personalities including Jeremy Guscott.
Career: Called 1984; Assistant Recorder 1998; Junior Treasury Counsel 1998; Recorder 2000.
Personal: Educated at University College London.

BENSON, Jeremy QC
2 Hare Court (Stephen Kramer QC), London
(020) 7353 5324
jeremybenson@2harecourt.com
Recommended in Crime
Specialisation: Principal area of practice is criminal law. In last year dealt with murder, money laundering and commercial computer fraud.
Prof. Memberships: Criminal Bar Association: Committee Member since 1996. British Academy of Forensic Science.
Career: Called 1978. Assistant Recorder 1993-97. Recorder 1997-. Appointed QC 2001.
Personal: Essex University 1970-73 (BA in Economics).

BENSON, John QC
14 Castle Street (Andrew Edis QC), Liverpool
(0151) 236 4421
johntbenson@hotmail.com
Recommended in Employment
Specialisation: Specialist practitioner in all aspects of employment law inc interlocutory relief, restrictive covenants, personal injuries, clinical negligence.
Prof. Memberships: Employment Law Bar Association, Personal Injuries Bar Association. Medical Law Association. Northern Circuit.

Career: LL.B (Hons). Called to the Bar in 1978. Northern Circuit. Part-time chairman of employment tribunals 1995. Recorder 1998, Silk 2001.
Personal: Age 46.

BENTHAM, Howard QC
Peel Court Chambers (Michael Shorrock QC), Manchester
(0161) 832 3791
Recommended in Crime

BERKSON, Simon
Exchange Chambers (David Turner QC & Bill Braithwaite QC & Henry Globe QC), Liverpool
(0151) 236 7747
Recommended in Crime

BERLIN, Barry
St Philips Chambers (John Randall QC), Birmingham
(0121) 246 7000
barry@berlin.fsnet.co.uk
Recommended in Consumer Law
Specialisation: Trading standards, health and safety at work, environmental health, food safety, Formula One Autotraders v Birmingham City Council (1998) 163 JP 234, Davenport v Walsall MBC (1996) 28 HLR 754, Sterling Homes v Birmingham CC (1996) L.R. 121, Toys R Us v Gloucestershire CC (1994) 158 JP 338, Whirlpool (UK) Ltd & Magnet Ltd v Gloucestershire CC (1993) 259 S.P. 123, R v Newcastle Upon Tyne M.C. ox P. Poundstretcher Ltd (1998) co/3282/97 D.C.
Prof. Memberships: Crim. Bar Ass., Midland and Oxford circuit.
Career: BSc. Hons (1980). Call 1981 Gray's Inn. Provincial Treasury Council (civil) appointed to att gov list in 1995.
Personal: Hon. Lecturer MSc environmental health. Birmingham University. Lecture to local authorities. Enjoys racing, theatre.

BERMAN, Franklin QC
Essex Court Chambers (Gordon Pollock QC), London
(020) 7813 8000
Recommended in Public International Law

BERRAGAN, Neil
40 King St, Manchester
(0161) 832 9082
Recommended in Chancery, Commercial (Litigation)
Specialisation: Commercial and property litigation; general commercial disputes, banking, corporate insolvency, and insurance related professional indemnity work; shareholder disputes, directors disqualification.
Career: Educated Pocklington School, York and Pembroke College, Oxford. Call 1982.
Personal: Lives in Alderley Edge. Married, three children. Travels in Ireland.

BERRY, Simon QC
9 Old Square (Michael Driscoll QC), London
(020) 7405 4682
chambers@9oldsquare.co.uk
Recommended in Property Litigation
Specialisation: Property and chancery commercial litigation.
Prof. Memberships: Chancery Bar Association, Professional Negligence Bar Association, Property Bar Association, Anglo-American Rent Property Institute.
Career: Called to Bar 1977. Silk 1990. Recorder 2000. Deputy High Court Judge 2001.
Publications: Contributor to 'Professional Negligence and Liability'.

BERRY, Steven QC
Essex Court Chambers (Gordon Pollock QC), London
(020) 7813 8000
Recommended in Insurance, Shipping
Specialisation: Broad-based practice, in particular the associated fields of insurance and reinsurance, shipping, international banking, international sale of goods and arbitration.
Career: Exeter College, Oxford BA (Jurisprudence) (1st Class Hons); BCL (1st Class Hons) 1983. Astbury scholar, Middle Temple. Eldon Law scholar. Called to the Bar 1984.
Personal: Born 1961.

BETHLEHEM, Daniel
20 Essex Street (Iain Milligan QC), London
(020) 7842 1200
clerks@20essexst.com
Recommended in Public International Law
Specialisation: Specialist in public international law, including WTO law and aspects of EC/EU law (notably external relations). Notable cases include: Case C-55/94, Gebhard (ECJ; counsel to the UK); Nuclear Weapons Advisory Opinions (ICJ; counsel to the UK); Lockerbie (Libya v UK) (ICJ; counsel to the UK); US v Canada (Agricultural tariffs) (NAFTA; Assistant to the Chair of the Panel); EC – Restrictions on Butter Products (WTO; counsel to New Zealand); US v Canada (Softwood Lumber) (Ad hoc US/Canada; Assistant to the Chair of the Panel); Advisory Opinion on the Immunity of the Special Rapporteur on Human Rights (ICJ; counsel to Malaysia); Legality of Use of Force (Yugoslavia v Belgium) (ICJ; counsel to Belgium); Mitchell Committee of Inquiry (Inquiry into Middle East violence; counsel to Israel); Emin v Yeldag (High Court; counsel to the HM Foreign Secretary and Attorney-General); Arrest Warrant Case (DRC v Belgium); (ICJ; counsel to Belgium); Ireland v UK (ITLOS; counsel to the UK).
Career: Investment banking with Barclays de Zoete Wedd Ltd and Nikko Securities 1985-89; called 1988.
Personal: University of the Witwatersrand (1981 BA); Bristol University (1985 LLB Hons); Cambridge University (1990 LLM).

BEVAN, John QC
2 Harcourt Buildings, Atkinson Bevan Chambers (Nicholas Atkinson QC & John Bevan QC), London
(020) 7353 2112
clerks@2hb.co.uk
Recommended in Crime
Specialisation: General criminal law, emphasis on high-profile serious cases. Prosecutions include child abuse – Jasmine Beckford, Heidi Koseda; terrorism – Sidhu and others (1994: 98 Criminal Appeal Reports 59), Hayes and Taylor (Harrods bombing), Patrick Kelly, McArdle and McKinley (South Quay bombing 1996); murder – Kenneth Erskine (Stockwell Strangler), Morss and Tyler (Child Victim Daniel Handley), Miah and others (Victim, Richard Everitt), Chindamo (Headmaster, Philip Lawrence), Eades and others (Police Sergeant Robertson); Also – McLean (Notting Hill Rapist), Evans, Whitby and Burrell (death of illegal immigrant, Joy Gardner); Ricky Reel inquest.
Prof. Memberships: Criminal Bar Association. South Eastern Circuit.
Career: Called 1970. Treasury Counsel 1983-97. Took Silk 1997.

BEVAN, Julian QC
Hollis Whiteman Chambers (QEB) (Julian Bevan QC & Peter Whiteman QC), London
(020) 7583 5766
barristers@holliswhiteman.co.uk
Recommended in Crime, Fraud
Specialisation: High profile general crime with emphasis on white collar fraud. Involved in Maxwell case; Gokal; sanction busting cases. Other cases include M25 Murder Appeal and the Bakewell Cemetery Appeal. Is currently involved in the Jubilee Line extension fraud. Has also advised on matters concerning health and safety and corporate manslaughter.
Career: Former 1st Senior Treasury Counsel.

BHOSE, Ranjit
2-3 Gray's Inn Square (Anthony Porten QC & Anthony Scrivener QC), London
(020) 7242 4986
Recommended in Local Government
Specialisation: Most aspects of public and local government, housing, commercial property, and housing association law. Extensive experience both in judicial review and in trial and appellate work at all levels, most recently including: (R) L&D v L.B. Lambeth (CA, 2002); Barnet L.B.C. v Hurst (CA, 2002); O'Connor v Old Etonian Housing Association (CA, 2002); L.B. Wandsworth v Railtrack plc (CA, 2001); Notting Hill Housing Trust v Brackley (CA, 2001); Mowam v L.B. Wandsworth (CA, 2000); Begum v L.B. Tower Hamlets (CA, 2000); R v Bristol C.C. ex p Everett (CA, 1999). Also instructed on public law issues in the Thyssen litigation.
Career: Called 1989.
Publications: Joint editor of 'Human Rights and Judicial Review: Case Studies in Context' (Butterworths, 2001) and contributor to Vol.35 'Halsbury's Laws of England (Protection of Environment & Public Health)'.
Personal: Born 1965. Educated at Haberdashers' Aske's, Elstree, and University College, Oxford.

BICKERDIKE, Roger
Zenith Chambers (Andrew Campbell QC & John Collins), Leeds
(0113) 245 5438
Recommended in Family
Specialisation: Highly noted junior specialising in family/matrimonial work with particular emphasis on public law children cases and ancillary relief work. Considerable experience in appellate work both in the High Court and in the Court of Appeal. Involved in numerous reported cases, some of them landmark. Busy matrimonial practice, with an emphasis on cases where there are substantial assets.
Prof. Memberships: Member of the Family Bar Association, and Association of Lawyers for Children.
Career: Called to the Bar in 1986.

BIDDER, Neil QC
33 Park Place (Neil Bidder QC), Cardiff
(029) 2023 3313
Recommended in Personal Injury
Specialisation: Personal Injury, Criminal Law.
Prof. Memberships: Personal Injury Bar Association, Criminal Bar Association, Welsh Personal Injury Lawyers Association (Founder Chairman).
Career: MA (Cantab), LLM (Dalhousie University Canada). Recorder since 1994. Queen's Counsel since 1998.

BIRCH, Elizabeth
3 Verulam Buildings (Christopher Symons QC & John Jarvis QC), London
(020) 7831 8441
chambers@3vb.com
Recommended in ADR
Specialisation: Specialist in international and domestic commercial arbitration, mediation, commercial and maritime law including banking and financial services, commodities, conflict of laws and jurisdiction disputes, information technology (IT), injunctions, insurance (marine, non-marine and Lloyds Market), international sale of goods, joint ventures, oil and gas, shipping, transportation and all types of contractual and professional disputes. Tribunal emphasis: Commercial Court, Admiralty Court, arbitration and mediation. Appears as advocate and receives appointments to sit as arbitrator and mediator in general commercial and shipping disputes. Arbitration tribunals include LMAA, LCIA, ICC, ACI and ad hoc. Has sat as arbitrator and published awards in numerous Lloyd's Market disputes and in other commercial cases within fields of expertise. Founding Director of ACI (A Commercial Initiative for dispute resolution), an administered arbitration and mediation group offering a distinguished lawyer panel of commercial arbitrators and

LEADERS AT THE BAR

mediators to determine and/or assist in the settlement of commercial disputes. Regularly mediates commercial disputes including high value, cross-border and multi-party disputes.
Prof. Memberships: Chartered Arbitrator and Fellow of the Chartered Institute of Arbitrators (FCIArb), Qualified Mediator (QDR) accredited by CEDR and The Academy of Experts. Appointed to the Panels of the Lloyds's Arbitration Schemes (LAS) from 1992 to date. On the ACI Panel of Arbitrators, Panel member of CIA for arbitration and mediation and on the CIA Maritime Panel. On the list of supporting members of LMAA available to sit as arbitrator and mediator. Panel member of FEPA's Representative Committee (receives appoints to sit as Legal Chairman in appeals against decisions by MAFF in relation to licenses to deposit articles or substances in the sea or under the seabed). Member of the Commercial Bar Association (COMBAR) – secretary 1993-96. Member of the London Common Law and Commercial Bar Association (LCLCBA).
Career: Called to Gray's Inn 1978; joined 3 Essex Court in 1980 (later to become 20 Essex Street); joined 3 Verulam Buildings in 1998; Fellow Chartered Institute of Arbitrators (FCIArb) 1993; Accredited mediator (CEDR and Academy of Experts) 1995; Diploma in International Commercial Arbitration 1998.
Personal: Member of the Commercial Court ADR Working Party chaired by Mr Justice Colman. Member of the ADR Service Providers working party chaired by Sir Brian Neill. Member of the Bar Council ADR sub-committee.

BIRD, Simon
2-3 Gray's Inn Square (Anthony Porten QC & Anthony Scrivener QC), London
020 7242 4986
sbird@2-3graysinnsquare.co.uk
Recommended in Planning
Specialisation: A wide range of planning, local government and environmental work. Planning work includes inquiries throughout the country dealing with housing, retail, leisure, waste, industrial, commercial, hospital and other developments. Major inquiry work includes the Cambridge Hinxton Hall and Arbury Park Inquiries and many development plan inquiries, the most recent being the North East Lincolnshire Local Plan Inquiry. Environmental and local government work includes Court and advisory covering all aspects of the work of public bodies. A particular specialism is waste management licensing.
Prof. Memberships: Planning and Environment Bar Association; South Eastern Circuit; United Kingdom Environmental Law Association.
Career: Called to the Bar in 1987.
Personal: University of Reading.

BIRKETT, Peter QC
18 St John Street (Jonathan Foster QC), Manchester
(0161) 278 1800
Recommended in Crime
Specialisation: Criminal law, both prosecution and defence. Has been involved in many high profile and notable trials on circuit over the past 10 years. If he has a specialisation, it is in the field of commercial fraud.
Prof. Memberships: Criminal Bar Association. Leader of the Northern Circuit 1999-.
Career: Called 1972. Q.C. 1989. Recorder of the Crown Court 1989. Acting deemster (Isle of Man). Governing member of the Inns of Court Advocacy Training Committee.
Personal: Married, 2 sons, hobbies include sport, political biography, music (keyboard player in 'The Prestons'). Education: Sedbergh School, Yorkshire. University of Leicester LL.B. Master of the Bench (Inner Temple 1996-).

BIRSS, Colin
Three New Square (David Young QC), London
(020) 7405 1111
colinbirss@compuserve.com
Recommended in Information Technology, Intellectual Property
Specialisation: Intellectual property, information technology. Cases before United Kingdom courts include: Merrell Dow v Norton (terfenadine – Patents Court, CA and HL), Harrods v Harrodian School (passing off – High Court and CA), Kirin – Amgen v Boehringer Mannheim (erythropoietin – Patents Court and CA), Fujitsu (computer software patent – CA), PCME v Goyen (electronics – Patents Court) NAD Electronics v NAD Computer Systems (trademark and passing off – High Court), Chocosuisse v Cadbury (passing off – High Court and CA), Lilly Icos v Pfizer (sidenfil – Patents Court, CA and EPO). Cases before the European Patent Office include: Berlex Biosciences (E Coli inclusion bodies), Net 1 Corp. (smart cards), G4/97 (straw man oppositions).
Career: Called 1990; joined chambers 1991.
Personal: Educated at Downing College, Cambridge 1983-86 (MA 1st Class Natural Sciences); City University 1988-89 (Dip Law). Born 28 December 1964.

BIRTLES, William
Old Square Chambers (John Hendy QC), London
(020) 7269 0300
birtles@oldsquarechambers.co.uk
Recommended in Environment
Specialisation: Principal areas of practice are environmental, planning and local government law. Has had considerable experience in both civil and criminal aspects of pollution claims including land contamination (arising from oil, toxic waste and industrial waste disposal), water (eg Barry Docks, Cardiff), air (particularly industrial smells and noise). Major inquiries include the Sizewell B Nuclear Power Station Inquiry (1984-86), the second Part I Environmental Protection Act Inquiry (Cumbria 1994), the Westminster Council District Audit Inquiry (1994-95) and various internal inquiries for local authorities.
Prof. Memberships: Planning and Local Government Bar Association; Administrative Law Bar Association; Environmental Law Foundation. Senior Associate Member St Antony's College Oxford.
Career: Academic lawyer 1968-74. Called to the Bar 1970. Joined Old Square Chambers 1986. Recorder 1993. Frequent speaker at legal conferences.
Publications: Co-author of 'Planning and Environmental Law' (Longman 1994 with Richard Stein); co-author of 'Local Government Finance Law' (Butterworths 2000 with Anna Forge and Tony Child). Numerous articles and chapters in books.
Personal: Opera, classical music and travel.

BISHOP, Malcolm QC
30 Park Place (John Jenkins QC), Cardiff
(029) 2039 8421
Recommended in Family

BISHOP, Timothy
1 Hare Court (Bruce Blair QC), London
(020) 7797 7070
Recommended in Family
Specialisation: Ancillary relief; agreements; enforcement; private law Children Act.
Prof. Memberships: Inner Temple; Family Law Bar Association.
Career: Called 1991. Pupil and tenant 1 Mitre Court Buildings.
Publications: 'Smith & Bishop: Enforcement of Financial Orders in Matrimonial Proceedings at a Glance 1993-2002'; Halsbury Volume 29(3) – Joint contribution.
Personal: Maidstone Grammar School; Trinity College, Cambridge. Married; one son, one daughter.

BLACK, Michael QC
2 Temple Gardens (Dermod O'Brien QC), London
(020) 7822 1200
mblack@2tg.co.uk
Recommended in Construction
Specialisation: The resolution of disputes arising out of commercially and technically complex contracts principally concerning building, engineering and other high-technology projects, including those involving the professional liability of parties' advisors. Within the last year he has advised or represented the Liquidators of a Far Eastern development corporation in relation to claims of excess of US$4 billion; software manufacturers in a US$50 million dispute in Hong Kong; Canadian wireless telesystems operators in a US$400 million dispute concerning part of the Brazilian cellular telephone network and parties involved in various forms of private dispute resolution procedures relating to claims each in excess of US$100 million for defective works and cost overruns under EPC and EPCM contracts in the UK, USA and Far East. He has also appeared recently in the following reported cases: Tameside MBC v Barlows [2001] BLR 113, Henry Boot Construction (UK) Limited v Malmaison Hotel (Manchester) Limited, [2000] 2 Lloyds Rep 625 and Al-Naimi v Islamic Press, [2001] 1 Lloyds Rep 522. Regularly acts as an Arbitrator and Mediator.
Prof. Memberships: American Bar Association's Forum on the Construction Industry; Conseil International du batiment pour la Recherche l'Etude et la documentation (CIB) (Rotterdam, The Netherlands); London Court of International Arbitration; Fellow of the Chartered Institute of Arbitrators; Fellow of the Institution of Civil Engineering Surveyors; TECBAR; COMBAR.
Career: Member of the Civil Procedure Rule Committee; Deputy Judge of the Technology and Construction Court; Accredited mediator (Harvard Law School and Chartered Institue of Arbitrators); member of Court of Appeal panel of mediators; Visiting Research Fellow, Civil and Construction Engineering Department, UMIST.
Publications: Written and spoken extensively in the UK, Europe and USA. Currently writing chapters on Arbitration and Construction for 5th edition of the 'Law and Practice of Compromise'.

BLACKBURN, John QC
Atkin Chambers (Robert Akenhead QC), London
(020) 7404 0102
clerks@atkinchambers.law.co.uk
Recommended in Arbitration, Construction
Specialisation: In the fields of building and civil engineering disputes, professional negligence actions involving contractors and engineers and arbitration, including international arbitration. Has conducted several heavy disputes under rules of the International Chamber of Commerce in Paris. Has been appointed Arbitrator in disputes arising out of construction contracts under the International Chamber of Commerce, also acts as arbitrator over disputes arising in England. Has been admitted to the bar in Hong Kong and Singapore to conduct cases arising out of building and civil engineering contracts. Construction Law experience has involved him in advising upon, presenting and defending all kinds of building and civil engineering claims worldwide. Advises and acts for numerous Public Corporations. Advises on and drafts various kinds of building and different types of engineering contracts. Work undertaken generally involves substantial projects involving sophisticated plan, and building and

engineering structures including tunnels, dams and hydro-electric schemes.
Career: Called to the Bar 1969. Took silk 1984.

BLACKETT-ORD, Mark
5 Stone Buildings (Henry Harrod), London
(020) 7242 6201
Recommended in Partnership
Specialisation: Well-known for his experience in advice and litigation in Chancery matters especially those concerning partnerships and other quasi-corporate bodies, from unincorporated associations to family trusts (Murphy v Murphy [1999] 1 WLR 1P2) and bodies alleged to be carrying on the business of insurance (Re a company No 007816 of 1994) (1997) 2 BCLC 685 and non-incorporated companies (Bragmist v Wise Finance (2002) 2 AER 333). Has appeared in cases at all levels from the County Court to the House of Lords and European Court (Webb v Webb (1994) QB 696). Co-edited the original 4th edition of 'Partnership' in Halsbury Laws of England, and wrote the major new book 'Partnership' (Butterworths, 1997), and its second edition (2002).
Prof. Memberships: ACTAPS; STEP; APP. Chairman of the Chancery Bar Association Working Party on Partnership Law.

BLACKWELL, Kate
Lincoln House Chambers (Mukhtar Hussain QC), Manchester
(0161) 832 5701
Recommended in Crime

BLAIR, Bruce QC
1 Hare Court (Bruce Blair QC), London
(020) 7797 7070
Recommended in Family

BLAIR, Michael QC
3 Verulam Buildings (Christopher Symons QC & John Jarvis QC), London
(020) 7831 8441
mblair@3vb.com
Recommended in Financial Services
Specialisation: Financial services. Advised the Financial Services Authority on content and quality of the FSA Handbook. Also appointed Chairman of the three self-regulating organisations (SFA, IMRO, PIA, 2000-02).
Prof. Memberships: COMBAR. Bencher, Middle Temple.
Career: Under secretary Lord Chancellor's Department 1982-87, general counsel (later Acting Chief Executive) Securities and Investments Board 1987-98, General Counsel, FSA 1998-2000. Member, Competition Commission (Appeals Panel) 2000-, Chairman, Review Body on Doctors' and Dentists' Remuneration 2001-.
Publications: Recently, Blackstone's Guides to the Financial Services and Markets Act 2000 (2001) and Bank of England Act 1998 (1998); general editor, Butterworths Financial Regulation Service (2001-).

BLAIR, William QC
3 Verulam Buildings (Christopher Symons QC & John Jarvis QC), London
(020) 7831 8441
chambers@3vb.com
Recommended in Banking & Finance, Financial Services
Specialisation: Commercial work, domestic and international banking, arbitration, business law, commercial fraud, company law, financial services, international trade, insolvency, private international law.Cases include: Esal v Oriental Credit 1985; LAFB v Bankers Trust 1988; LAFB v Manufacturers Hanover 1989; IE Contractors v Lloyds Bank 1990; Barclays Bank v O'Brien 1993; Macmillan v Bishopsgate 1994; Polly Peck v Citibank 1994; TSB v Camfield 1995; Macmillan v Bishopsgate 1996; Wahda Bank v Arab Bank 1998; MCC Proceeds v Bishopsgate 1998, Middle Temple v Lloyds 1999. Struggles v Lloyds Bank.
Career: Called to the Bar 1972, Silk 1994. Visiting professor of law (London School of Economics), member of the International Monetary Law committee of the International Law Association, member of FLP working party on Single European Currency, recorder. Co-editor 'Encyclopaedia of Banking Law', co-author 'Banking and Financial Services Regulation' (2nd Ed) 1998, editor 'Banks and Remedies' (2nd Ed) 1999.

BLAKE, Nicholas QC
Matrix Chambers, London
(020) 7404 3447
Recommended in Administrative & Public Law, Human Rights, Immigration
Specialisation: Immigration asylum free movement law, public law: education, environmental, data protection, inquests, social welfare, human rights law, miscarriages of justice, constitutional law. Recent cases 2001-02: Javed and Ali (quashing delegated legislation), Robertson (privacy and electoral registers), Farrakhan (free speech and aliens), Mills and Poole (reviewing the CCRC), Plumb (family life and child support), Baumbast (family life and free movement), Barkoci (business movement and the Europe Agreements), Alder (right to life and inquests), Hilaire v Trinidad (mandatory death penalty).
Prof. Memberships: ALBA, ILPA (Chair 1993-97), JUSTICE (Council 1996-date).
Career: MT (1974), QC (1994), Asst Recorder (1999), Recorder (2000) Master of the Bench 2002.
Publications: 'Immigration Law and Practice' with Ian Macdonald (1991 3rd Edn) 1995 (4th Edition); 'Immigration Asylum and Human Rights Law' (2002) with Raza Husain.
Personal: Cranleigh School, Magdalene College, Cambridge. Married with 3 children.

BLANCHARD, Claire
Essex Court Chambers (Gordon Pollock QC), London
(020) 7813 8000
Recommended in Commercial (Litigation), Shipping
Specialisation: Broad-based commercial practice. In particular shipping, insurance, banking, conflicts.
Career: Liverpool Polytechnic LLB (Hons) 1991. Inns of Court School of Law. Called to the Bar 1992.
Personal: Born 1969.

BLAXLAND, Henry QC
Two Garden Court (Owen Davies QC & Courtenay Griffiths QC), London
(020) 7353 1633
Recommended in Crime, Human Rights

BLEASDALE, Paul QC
No5 Chambers (Gareth Evans QC), Birmingham
(0121) 606 0500
Recommended in Personal Injury
Specialisation: Personal Injury Litigation; Claimants and Defendants. In particular industrial disease claims and also medical negligence. Planning and Environment; Developers and Local Authorities. Appeals and Local Plan, UDP and Compulsory Purchase Inquiries.
Prof. Memberships: Personal Injuries Bar Association, Planning Environment Bar Association.
Career: London University, Recorder of the Crown Court, Deputy Chairman of the Agricultural Lands Tribunal. Queen's Counsel.

BLOCH, Selwyn QC
Littleton Chambers (Michel Kallipetis QC), London
(020) 7797 8600
Recommended in Employment
Specialisation: Practice encompasses business law and employment law. Work includes general commercial litigation, restraint of trade, garden leave and other interlocutory injunctions, confidential information, wrongful and unfair dismissal, discrimination, entertainment and sports law. Contributor to conferences on employment law.
Prof. Memberships: ELBA, COMBAR, ELA.
Career: Attorney, South Africa 1976. Called to the Bar 1982 and joined current chambers in the same year.
Publications: Co-author, 'Employment Covenants and Confidential Information' (Butterworths, 2nd edition 1999).
Personal: Educated at Stellenbosch and Witwatersrand Universities, South Africa. (BA, LL.B). Born 23 February 1952. Lives in London.

BLOCK, Neil QC
39 Essex Street (Nigel Pleming QC), London
(020) 7832 1111
Recommended in Clinical Negligence, Personal Injury
Specialisation: A contract and tort based practice. Insurance (including policy avoidance/fraud and material loss claims eg McGregor v Prudential Assurance Co 1998 Lloyds). Personal injury (including sporting cases eg Smolden v Whitworth & Nolan, O'Neill v Wimbledon & Fashanu, Watson v British Boxing Board of Control), catastrophic injury claims, medical negligence (in particular paediatric brain damage), professional negligence (including solicitors, accountants, surveyors and valuers, architects, stockbrokers and insurance brokers), group actions (Hepatitis C, Supertram, shipyards, organo-phosphates), disaster litigation (eg Selby rail crash) and product liability.
Prof. Memberships: Professional Negligence Bar Association, Personal Injury Bar Association, London Common Law and Commercial Bar Association, Bar Sports Law Group.
Career: Called to the Bar in 1980; took Silk 2002.
Personal: BA (Hons), LLM (Exon).

BLOHM, Leslie
St John's Chambers (Christopher Sharp QC), Bristol
(0117) 921 3456
clerks@stjohnschambers.co.uk
Recommended in Chancery, Commercial (Litigation)
Specialisation: Commercial landlord and tenant; real property; equity and trusts. Counsel for respondent in Bettison v Langton & Penter [2000] Ch.54 (CA) and [2002] IAC 27 (HL) on profits à prendre and rights of common; Brown v Gloucester City Council [1998] 1 EGLR 95 (CA) on construction of rent review clauses.
Prof. Memberships: Chancery Bar Association, Bristol and Cardiff Chancery Bar Association.
Career: Christ's Hospital Horsham & Keble College, Oxford; BA 1981. Lincoln's Inn 1982. Hardwicke & Jenkins scholar of Lincoln's Inn 1981-82. St John's Chambers Bristol 1984. Head of Chancery Department 1992.
Personal: Family, cycling and chess.

BLUNT, Oliver QC
Furnival Chambers (Andrew Mitchell QC), London
(020) 7405 3232
Recommended in Crime
Specialisation: Entirely defence-based practice with a substantial emphasis on murder, terrorism, fraud and drugs cases. Murder and violent crime: recently conducted Regina v William Cockram and Others (the Millenium Dome robbery trial CCC 2002). Has also represented such clients as John Taft ('Beauty in the Bath' murder trial, Liverpool Crown Court, 1999), Maria Hnautik (murder, Norwich CC, 1996), Ngarimu (female contract killer, CCC, 1995), Syd Owen ('Ricky' of 'Eastenders', wounding, Snaresbrook CC, 1995), Michael Sams (kidnapping, blackmail, murder, Nottingham CC, 1993), also the trial and successful appeal of the 'Chelsea Headhunters' (Regina v Drake and Others). Sexual crime: including

LEADERS AT THE BAR

high profile cases such as Richard Baker (DJ Rapist, CCC, 1999). Drugs: represented such clients as Jason Fitzgibbon (Birmingham CC, 2000), Thomas Adams and Others (Woolwich CC, 1998). Successfully defended the first defendant in a £150 million cocaine importation (Regina v Hillier and Others, 1993). Terrorism: has acted on behalf of the Iranian Embassy and represented two members of the Consular Staff in separate terrorist trials at the CCC (Tabari Abcou/Fouladi). Appeared for the second defendant in Regina v Canning and Lamb (IRA trial, CC, 1993). Fraud: including William Casey, acquitted in a multimillion pound arson/insurance fraud, (CCC 1997), and Chananya Gross, acquitted in Hackney electoral fraud trial (Wood Green CC 2001).
Prof. Memberships: SE Circuit. Criminal Bar Association.
Career: Called to Bar 1974. Queen's Counsel 1994. Recorder 1995.
Personal: Born 8 March 1951. Married with four children. Member of Roehampton Club, Rosslyn Park Rugby Club and Barnes Cricket Club.

BOARDMAN, Christopher
11 Stone Buildings (Murray Rosen QC), London
(020) 7831 6381
boardman@11stonebuildings.com
Recommended in Insolvency
Specialisation: Christopher is a company and insolvency specialist with a practice that extends to partnerships, financial services, asset-tracing and commercial disputes. On the insolvency side, he has particular expertise in voluntary arrangements, administrations, liquidations and directors' disqualification. His company law practice embraces shareholders disputes, claims against directors and security instruments. It also encompasses more technical aspects such as meetings, articles of association and reductions of capital. He has also been involved in several recently reported decisions and is retained by R3 (formerly SPI) to advise on voluntary arrangement terms.

BOGAN, Paul
Doughty Street Chambers (Geoffrey Robertson QC), London
(020) 7404 1313
Recommended in Crime
Specialisation: Criminal defence, leading work regularly undertaken. Specialist: fraud, including company/insolvency cases; large scale drug offences and money laundering; serious violence. Experienced in appellate work, including Privy Council, and High Court restraint/confiscation proceedings. Recent reported cases: R v Forsyth, R v Vasiliou.
Prof. Memberships: Criminal Bar Association, South Eastern Circuit.
Career: Called to the Bar in 1983. Council member and ex-treasurer of Liberty, for whom drafted several responses to government and Law Commission papers.

BOMPAS, Anthony George QC
4 Stone Buildings (Philip Heslop QC), London
(020) 7242 5524
clerks@4stonebuildings.com
Recommended in Chancery, Company, Financial Services, Insolvency
Specialisation: Principal area of practice is company law (all aspects, including minority shareholders proceedings and insolvency) and financial services. Other main area of practice is professional negligence work. Has been instructed in many of the major, widely publicised, company matters in recent years, including the Guinness affair, the Blue Arrow, the Barlow Clowes, the Brent Walker and the BCCI affairs. Author of 'Investigations by the DTI' in Tolley's 'Company Law' (3rd Ed.).
Prof. Memberships: Chancery Bar Association, Insolvency Lawyers' Association and Commercial Bar Association (COMBAR). Called to the Bar of the British Virgin Islands and, for specific cases, to the Bar of Trinidad and Tobago.
Career: Called to the Bar 1975 and joined present chambers in 1976. Junior Counsel to the DTI 1989-94. Took Silk in 1994.
Personal: Educated at Merchant Taylors' School, Northwood 1964-69 and Oriel College, Oxford 1970-74. Born 6 November 1951.

BOOTH, Alan
Deans Court Chambers (Stephen Grime QC), Manchester
(0161) 214 6000
booth@deanscourt.co.uk
Recommended in Family
Specialisation: Ancillary relief and professional negligence arising out of ancillary relief.
Prof. Memberships: FLBA, PNBA.
Career: Bolton School (Boy's Division). Selwyn College Cambridge.
Personal: Married, two children.

BOOTH, Cherie QC
Matrix Chambers, London
(020) 7404 3447
Recommended in Administrative & Public Law, Education, Employment
Specialisation: Specialist in all aspects of employment law and administrative and public law. Notable public law cases include E v Dorset County Council and Others [1995]; Phelps v LB of Hillingdon [1998] (dyslexia); White and Others v Ealing LBC (SEN); R v Law Society ex p Dalton [1999]; B v Chief Constable of Avon and Somerset (5/4/2000 Human Rights). Notable employment cases are Grant v SW Trains (sexual orientation discrimination); Preston v Wolverhampton NHS Trusts ECJ 2000; Barry v Midland Bank HL 22/77/99; BCCI v Ali 1999 and Wilson v St Helens Borough Council [1997] IRLR 505; Pearce v Governing Body of Mayfield School (April 2000).

BOOTH, Michael QC
40 King St, Manchester
(0161) 832 9082
mbooth@40kingstreet.co.uk
Recommended in Chancery, Commercial (Litigation), Insolvency
Specialisation: Chancery and commercial, including company, insolvency, property, computer related litigation (hardware and software including copyright ownership), commercial contracts, banking, professional negligence and competition aspects relating to the above.
Career: Scholarship to Manchester Grammar School. Open scholarship to Trinity College, Cambridge. President Cambridge Union Society, Michaelmas 1979. Appointed Queen's Counsel 1999.
Personal: Married, three young children. Hobbies include walking, swimming, tennis, reading (literature and history), theatre, wine and antiques. Avid football fan.

BORRELLI, Michael QC
187 Fleet Street (Andrew Trollope QC), London
(020) 7430 7430
Chambers@187fleetstreet.com
Recommended in Crime
Specialisation: Specialist defence practice in serious and complex crime. Wide experience in defending SFO and HM Customs & Excise prosecutions, and extensive experience in cases of professional crime, including homicide, drugs trafficking, robbery and corruption, as well as in serious sexual offences involving children. Fraud cases include R v Desoura (VAT), R v Weston (banking), R v Cosker (VAT), R v Milsom (Harrovian Properties). Other cases include R v Angus Diggle (solicitor rapist), R v Mainstone (£60 million forger), R v Newton (£1 billion cocaine import cartel), R v Lutfi (Stansted Airport Hijack). In October 2002, due to defend in R v Campbell (Danielle Jones, missing Essex schoolgirl, abduction and murder).
Prof. Memberships: Criminal Bar Association (Committee Member 1986-91), International Relations Committee Bar Council (1991-98), European Criminal Bar Association, Anglo-Italian Law Association.
Career: Called to the Bar 1977 (Middle Temple), QC 2000. South Eastern Circuit since 1978 and also Western Circuit since 1999.

BOSWOOD, Anthony QC
Fountain Court (Anthony Boswood QC), London
(020) 7583 3335
Recommended in Banking & Finance, Commercial (Litigation), Energy, Fraud, Insurance
Specialisation: A broad based commercial practice with particular experience in insurance/reinsurance (including Lloyds litigation); mergers and acquisitions (including actions against merchant banks and others arising out of public bids); energy law (including litigation arising out of long term North Sea gas supply and gas transportation contracts); banking and international trade; international civil procedure; professional negligence (solicitors and accountants); computer law; civil fraud; media and entertainment. Notable cases include Outhwaite (Lloyds insurance); SAIL v Farex [1995] LRLR 116 (international property reinsurance); Napier v Hunter [1993] AC 718 and Henderson v Merrett [1995] 2AC 1451 (both Lloyds insurance); Yeoman v Warburgs (breach of duty by merchant bank); GE v Bankers Trust, Arthur Andersen and others (proceedings arising out of an MBO; negligence of lead bank/accountants); Bank Negara v Lariza [1998] AC 583 (letters of credit); Philips Petroleum and Enron Amoco and J Block (oil and gas litigation); EDS v Standard Chartered Bank (computer software; bank message switching system); Dubai Aluminium Company v Salaam & Ors [1999] Lloyds Rep 415 (international fraud); Grupo Torras v Fahad & Ors [1999] (international fraud); Re State of Norway [1990] 1 AC 723 (letters rogatory) Barclays Bank v Broad (film completion guarantees); Arab Bank v Zurich Insurance [1999] 1 Lloyds Rep 262 (construction of composite E&O Policy); Britvic v Messer [2000]: product liability; Grecia Express [2001]: shipping; Morgan Grenfell v SACE [2002]: Italian insurance law. Also very considerable experience of national and international arbitration both as counsel and as arbitrator.
Career: Called to Bar 1970; took Silk in 1986. Bencher of Middle Temple. Deputy High Court Judge.
Personal: Italian speaker.

BOTHROYD, Shirley
Littleton Chambers (Michel Kallipetis QC), London
(020) 7797 8600
Recommended in Employment
Specialisation: Principal areas of practice: employment law: appearing in employment tribunals and employment appeal. Tribunal: unfair dismissal, sex and race discrimination. High Court: restrictive covenants – all injunctive matters. General commercial and contract, commercial fraud. Cited as a Leading Employment Junior in 'Chambers & Partners Directory'. Frequently instructed in sensitive race and discrimination cases. Has reputation for being a tough litigator, instructed by leading employment solicitors.
Prof. Memberships: COMBAR, ELBAR, South Eastern Circuit, Counsel for Inland Revenue.
Career: Called to the Bar and joined present chambers in 1982.
Personal: Born 23 July 1958.

BOULDING, Philip QC
Keating Chambers, London
(020) 7544 2600

pboulding@keatingchambers.com
Recommended in Construction
Specialisation: Construction and civil engineering law, including arbitration and professional negligence. Clients in this field include local authorities, major PLCs, international joint ventures, governments and professionals from all the construction and engineering disciplines. Current instructions relate to various infrastructure projects in Hong Kong, various power stations as well as nuclear processing plants, disputes and ICC Arbitrations relating inter alia to oil projects in Sudan.
Career: Qualified 1979; Gray's Inn; Queen's Counsel 1996. Admitted to Hong Kong Bar 1997.
Personal: Downing College, Cambridge (1976) BA Law 1st class Hons, (1977) postgraduate LLB (now LLM), 1979 MA; 1976 elected to title of Scholar of Downing College, 1976 Harris Scholar, 1976 Pilley Scholar, 1977 Senior Harris Scholar, 1976 Rebecca Flowers Squire Scholar. Gray's Inn Holker Entrance Award (1978) and Gray's Inn Senior Holker Award (1979). Born 1954.

BOURNE, Charles
2 Harcourt Buildings (Roger Henderson QC), London
(020) 7583 9020
clerks@harcourt.co.uk
Recommended in Product Liability
Specialisation: Product liability and group actions (Afrika v Cape plc; America v Meggitt Properties plc); Public law and human rights; Telecommunications (R v Director General of Telecommunications ex p BT plc).
Prof. Memberships: ALBA, London CLCBA, Bar European Group, Association of Regulatory and Disciplinary Lawyers.
Career: Called 1991 Middle Temple. CEDR Accredited mediator.
Publications: Contributing Editor 'Halsbury's Laws, Practice and Procedure' (2001). Contributor 'Halsbury's Laws, Consumer Credit' (1998). Co-author 'Civil Advocacy' (Cavendish, 2001).
Personal: Born 1964. Educated Trinity College Cambridge (MA Hons), Paris-Sorbonne (Maîtrise en Lettres). Speaks French and Italian. Married, two children.

BOURNE, Ian
3 Temple Gardens (Jonathan Goldberg QC), London
(020) 7583 1155
Recommended in Crime

BOURNE-ARTON, Simon QC
Park Court Chambers (Robert Smith QC), Leeds
(0113) 243 3277
Recommended in Crime
Specialisation: Fraud: In the last year defended in two cases brought by the SFO. Defended in R v Boid at Hull Crown Court, a case involving supply of unfit meat into the human food chain. R v Claridge & Ors, Liverpool Crown Court (extensive paedophile ring case), R v Smart (government land grant fraud). Homicide: In particular cases involving joint enterprise. See R v Mitchell & King 163 JP75 CA. Other cases: R v Hedworth 1997 1 Cr.App.R.421; R v Klineberg 1999 1 Cr.App.R.427.
Prof. Memberships: CBA.
Career: Called 1975; Recorder 1993; Q.C 1994.

BOWDERY, Martin QC
Atkin Chambers (Robert Akenhead QC), London
(020) 7404 0102
Emergency Tel: (020) 7242 4703
Recommended in Construction

BOWEN, Nicholas
29 Bedford Row Chambers (Nicholas Francis QC), London
(020) 7404 1044
Recommended in Education

BOWEN, Paul
Doughty Street Chambers (Geoffrey Robertson QC), London
(020) 7404 1313
p.bowen@doughtystreet.co.uk
Recommended in Human Rights
Specialisation: Public law and human rights law in the following main areas: healthcare, mental health, local authorities, community care and social welfare, education, crime, police, prisoners, criminal injuries compensation and inquests. Particular interest in the rights of children and adults with disabilities in public law cases, also in cases engaging issues of capacity and consent to treatment, crime, education (particularly special educational needs) and claims under Part III of the Disability Discrimination Act. Reported cases include R (Wilkinson) v Broadmoor RMO (1) MHAC (2), [2002] 1 WLR 419 (Court of Appeal, lawfulness of compulsory treatment of detained patient under Articles 3, 6 & 8), R (H) v Mental Health Review Tribunal, [2002] Q.B. 1 (Court of Appeal, declaration of incompatibility made in respect of 'reverse burden of proof' requirement in Mental Health Review Tribunals under Mental Health Act 1983; R (Von Brandenburg) v East London and the City Mental Health NHS Trust [2001] QB 235 (Court of Appeal, lawfulness under Article 5(1) of compulsory detention immediately after discharge by Mental Health Review Tribunal); Re F (Adult Patient: Court's jurisdiction) [2001] Fam 38 (Court of Appeal, considering extent of the High Court's inherent 'best interests' jurisdiction in relation to incapacitated adults); Broadmoor v R [2000] QB 775 (Court of Appeal, jurisdiction of Court to grant injunctions restraining publication of book by detained patient); R v Bournewood Community Mental Health NHS Trust ex p L [1999] 1 AC 458 (House of Lords, 'de facto' detention and treatment of incapacitated adult).
Prof. Memberships: Constitutional and Administrative Law Bar Association; Committee member of the Law Society of Mental Health and Disability Committee.
Career: Called to the Bar October 1993 (former solicitor, qualified September 1993).
Publications: Editor, 'Judicial Review and Crown Office Practice' by Richard Gordon QC (December 1998) (Sweet & Maxwell); editor, 'Administrative Court Digest', (Sweet & Maxwell) since July 1998.

BOWERS, John QC
Littleton Chambers (Michel Kallipetis QC), London
(020) 7797 8600
Bowersjohnsimon@aol.com
Recommended in Employment
Specialisation: Employment law, pensions, judicial review, discrimination. Recent cases have included Associated British Ports v TGWU (injunctions to prevent national dock strike); McLaren v Home Office (role of judicial review in employment); News Group Newspapers Ltd v SOGAT and Others ('the Wapping cases'); Porter & Nanayakkara v Queens Medical Centre (dismissal of Consultant Paediatricians following Allitt murders); Saatchi & Saatchi plc v M. Saatchi and C. Saatchi and Others (garden leave case); Sibson v UK (application to European Court of Human Rights on remedies for disadvantages caused to employees who are not members of trade unions in 'closed shops'); Smith v UK (gay servicemen's case in European Court of Human Rights); Gibson v East Riding of Yorkshire Council (direct effect of Working Time Directive); De Keyser v Wilson (first EAT case on human rights); Celtec v Astley (Court of Appeal, Time of Transfer under Tupe); Clingham v Royal Borough of Kensington & Chelsea (House of Lords case on anti-racial behaviour order and human rights).
Prof. Memberships: Chair of ELBA, member ALBA, ELA. Home Office Task Force on Human Rights; Bar Council Race Relations Committee; Legal advisor, Public Concern at Work; Coordinator of Workplace Mediation Services; member Standards Board of England; Hon Prof University of Hull.
Publications: Author of many publications including 'Bowers on Employment Law', 'Textbook of Labour Law', 'Transfer of Undertakings', 'Employment Tribunal Practice', 'The New Law Employment Law and Human Rights', 'The Employment Law Manual' (chapter on Tribunals) and 'Basic Procedure in Courts and Tribunals'. Atkins Court Form, (Employment).

BOWES, Michael QC
2 King's Bench Walk, London
(020) 7353 1746
Recommended in Fraud
Specialisation: Criminal law, specialising in commercial fraud. Financial services regulatory work.
Prof. Memberships: Criminal Bar Association, Western Circuit.
Career: Called to the Bar in 1980. Joined 2 King's Bench Walk in 1996. Recorder (2000). Queen's Counsel (2001).
Personal: Educated at St George's College, Weybridge (1969-75), Manchester University (LL.B) 1976-79. Born on 22 December 1956.

BOWRON, Margaret QC
1 Crown Office Row (Robert Seabrook QC), London
(020) 7797 7500
Recommended in Clinical Negligence

BOWSHER, Michael
Monckton Chambers (Kenneth Parker QC & Paul Lasok QC), London
(020) 7405 7211
mbowsher@monckton.co.uk
Recommended in Construction
Specialisation: Technology, construction and commercial law; International Arbitration; European law, especially procurement and competition; environmental law.
Career: Qualified 1985; Middle Temple; tenant Keating Chambers 1986-2001; now tenant at Monckton Chambers. Associate, based full-time in offices of *Cleary, Gottlieb, Steen & Hamilton* in Brussels 1988-92; member of editorial team 'Keating on Building Contracts'; Fellow of the Chartered Institute of Arbitrators; Member of the Northern Ireland Bar. Involved in numerous procurement disputes, notably acting for the successful claimant in Harmon v House of Commons. Wide experience of international arbitration involving construction claims under English and various foreign laws. Most of his foreign arbitration experience has been for major non-UK contractors. Also active in a broad range of construction and technology matters in court, adjudication and arbitration, including judicial review and environmental disputes. For full details see website entry on www.monckton.co.uk.
Personal: Born 1963; Brasenose College, Oxford (1984 BA Hons).

BOYCE, William QC
Hollis Whiteman Chambers (QEB) (Julian Bevan QC & Peter Whiteman QC), London
(020) 7583 5766
barristers@holliswhiteman.co.uk
Recommended in Crime, Fraud
Specialisation: Crime and regulatory and disciplinary proceedings – especially high profile, grave and complex matters from homicide to serious fraud.
Prof. Memberships: Criminal Bar Association.
Career: Called to the Bar in 1976. Senior Treasury Counsel at the Central Criminal Court. Recorder.

BOYD, Stewart QC
Essex Court Chambers (Gordon Pollock QC), London

LEADERS AT THE BAR

(020) 7813 8000
Recommended in Arbitration
Specialisation: Construction, EC law, financial services and markets, international commercial transactions, insurance and reinsurance, oil and gas, private international law, shipping and aviation. Has been appointed an arbitrator in international commercial disputes in many fields, such as advertising, banking, commercial agency, computer software, construction, electricity generation and transmission, insurance and reinsurance, intellectual property, oil and gas, shipping.
Career: Trinity College, Cambridge: MA. Called to the Bar 1967. Queen's Counsel 1981. Deputy Chairman Financial Services Authority (non-exec) 1999.
Personal: Born 1943.

BOYDELL, Edward
Pump Court Chambers (Christopher Harvey Clark QC), Winchester
(020) 73530711
epb@3pumpcourt.com
Recommended in Family
Specialisation: Family, particularly financial provision, also equitable co-ownership and public and private children cases. Civil: personal injury (particularly accidents in the workplace and complex road traffic accidents) and professional negligence concerning solicitors, predominantly as to matrimonial finance matters. Appeared in Hill v Hill [1998] 1 FLR 198, CA; [1997] 1 FLR 730.
Prof. Memberships: FLBA, PNBA, Western Circuit.
Career: Called 1989. Tenant at 3 Pump Court since 1990; Western Circuit London Junior; Qualified Teacher (1987).
Personal: B.Ed.(Hons) (Cantab), Dip. Law (PCL). Married with one son. Leisure interests include sport, theatre and travel.

BOYLE, Alan QC
Serle Court (Lord Neill of Bladen QC), London
(020) 7242 6105
clerks@serlecourt.co.uk
Recommended in Chancery, Company, Insolvency
Specialisation: Commercial and chancery litigation, financial services and entertainment. Case during the last year: Thyssen-Bornemisza v Thyssen-Bornemisza Trust-litigation in Bermuda (undue influence).
Prof. Memberships: Chancery Bar Association, Commerical Bar Association. Deputy High Court Judge.
Career: Royal Shrewsbury School, St Catherine's College Oxford (MA). Called to the Bar 1972. Silk 1991.
Publications: Editor and contributor, 'The Practice and Procedure of the Companies Court', Lloyds of London Press.
Personal: Married, two daughters.

BOYLE, Christopher
2 Mitre Court Buildings (Guy Roots QC), London
(020) 7583 1380
clerks@2mcb.co.uk
Recommended in Planning
Specialisation: Planning; compulsory purchase; environmental; rating. Cases include: London City Racecourse; Nottingham Clearzone; Mansfield Ashfield Regiment Route; Gatwick Express; William Sinclair v English Nature; BT Cellnet v SSETR; R v Staffordshire Moorlands ex p Bartlam.
Prof. Memberships: PEBA.
Career: Called Lincoln's Inn 1994; joined chambers 1995.
Publications: 'Butterworths Local Government Law (Rating)', Joint Editor; contributor to 'Journal of Planning Law'.
Personal: Sedberg School; Merton College, Oxford (BA (Hons) Jurisprudence). Married, two sons. Resident: London and Cumbria.

BRADLEY, Anthony
Cloisters (Laura Cox QC), London
(020) 7827 4000
Recommended in Education
Specialisation: Public law, including judicial review, education law, and constitutional issues. Important cases include M v Home Office [1994], R v Devon County Council ex p. Baker [1995] and R (Bancoult) v Foreign Secretary [2001]. Publications include Bradley and Ewing, 'Constitutional and Administrative Law' (13th ed. 2002) and 'European Human Rights Law: Text and Materials' (2nd edn. 2000 - with M. Janis and R. Kay).
Prof. Memberships: Professor. Administrative Law Bar Association, Education Law Association.
Career: Formerly a solicitor. Professor of Constitutional Law, University of Edinburgh 1968-89. Called to the Bar in 1989.
Personal: Hon LLD, Staffordshire University (1993) and Edinburgh University (1998).

BRADLEY, R
Oriel Chambers (Andrew Sander), Liverpool
(0151) 236 7191/236 4321
Recommended in Employment

BRADLEY, Sally QC
York Chambers (Aidan Marron QC), York
(01904) 620048
Recommended in Family

BRAITHWAITE, Bill QC
Exchange Chambers (David Turner QC & Bill Braithwaite QC & Henry Globe QC), Liverpool
(0151) 236 7747
Recommended in Personal Injury
Specialisation: Personal injury litigation, including medical negligence, with a particular interest in injury to the brain and spine. The consultant editor of Kemp & Kemp on ' The Quantum of Damages'. Joint editor of 'Medical Aspects of Personal Injury Litigation' (1997).
Prof. Memberships: European Brain Injury Society; International Medical Society of Paraplegia; Spinal Injuries Association; Association of Personal Injury Lawyers; Headway.
Career: Called 1970, QC 1992.
Publications: 'Brain & Spine Injuries - The Fight for Justice'.
Personal: Gordonstoun School, Liverpool University. Class 1 Heavy Goods Vehicle Licence. Motor Racing Competition Licence.

BRAMWELL, Richard QC
3 Temple Gardens Tax Chambers (Richard Bramwell QC), London
(020) 7353 7884
clerks@taxcounsel.co.uk
Recommended in Tax
Specialisation: Corporate and personal tax planning and tax disputes. Examples of advisory work: apportionment of losses in corporate film leasing partnership; VAT on securitisation costs; 'trading group' requirement for sale of substantial shareholdings; complex partitions; stock-lending schemes; EBT's in the football industry; section 260 hold-over schemes; section 703 and company reorganisations; relevance of accounting principles.
Career: Took Silk in 1989.
Publications: 'Taxation of Companies and Company Reconstructions' (8th Edition, 2002).

BRAND, Simon
Coleridge Chambers (Simon Brand), Birmingham
(0121) 233 8500
Recommended in Crime

BRANNIGAN, Sean
4 Pump Court, London
(020) 7842 5555
sbrannigan@4pumpcourt.com
Recommended in Construction
Specialisation: Construction and civil engineering: acts for employers, contractors and professionals in a wide variety of disputes, including large international arbitrations. Very significant practice in relation to adjudication (where he has appeared in many of the reported cases) and mediation. Professional negligence: deals especially with cases involving allegations of negligence against valuers, engineers, accountants and solicitors. Instructed by many lending institutions, Professional Indemnity Insurers and the Solicitors Indemnity Fund. Media: acts for artists and management companies in relation to contractual and financial disputes.
Prof. Memberships: Dually called to the Northern Irish Bar. Member of COMBAR, Technology and Construction Bar Association, London Common Law and Commercial Bar Association.
Career: BA (Oxon) in Jurisprudence. Called in 1994.

BRASLAVSKY, Nicholas QC
40 King St, Manchester
(0161) 832 9082
nbraslavsky@40kingstreet.co.uk
Recommended in Clinical Negligence
Specialisation: Clinical negligence (including orthopaedic, obstetric, gynaecological, intensive care, anaesthetics, vascular, accident and emergency, opthalmic, ENT and neurology) and personal injury, industrial diseases, employers' liability, product liability, and public liability; professional disciplinary matters.
Prof. Memberships: Personal Injuries Bar Association, Professional Negligence Bar Association, Northern Circuit Executive Committee; Committee member of the Northern Circuit Medical Law Association.
Career: Called 1983 (Inner Temple). Recorder 2001.
Personal: Married with children.

BRASSE, Gillian
14 Gray's Inn Square (Joanna Dodson QC), London
(020) 7242 0858
clerks@14graysinnsquare.co.uk
Recommended in Family
Specialisation: Practice covers all aspects of family work including public and private law cases under the Children Act, wardship, adoption and child abduction, as well as ancillary relief matters, and Inheritance Act cases. Reported cases include O v Berkshire CC (Education Procedure) (1992) 2 FLR 7; Re B Contact (1994) 2 FLR 1; Re W (arrangements to place for adoption) (1995) 1 FLR 163; Conran v Conran [1997] 2 FLR 615 (Money – wife's contribution); Re J (adoption: appointment of Guardian ad Litem) 1999 2 FU 86.
Prof. Memberships: Family Law Bar Association, Association of Lawyers for Children, committee member, Bar Benevolent Association.
Career: Called 1977. Appointed Deputy District Judge September 1995. Appointed Recorder 2001.
Personal: Educated at Varndean School for Girls, Brighton, and Liverpool University. Leisure pursuits include: travel, concerts, theatre, eating out, keep fit, my two daughters.

BREALEY, Mark QC
Brick Court Chambers (Christopher Clarke QC), London
(020) 7379 3550
brealey@brickcourt.co.uk
Recommended in Competition/European Law
Specialisation: European Community Law, UK Competition Law. Recently reported cases: Passmore v Morland [1999] 3 All ER 1005 (CA); Matra Communications S.A.S. v Home Office [1999] 1 WLR 1646 (CA); Inntrepreneur Beer Supply Company v Byrne The Times Law Reports 14 June 1999 (CA); Case T-110/98 RJB Mining v Commission [1999] 3 CMLR 445 (CFI); Case C-124/97 Laara [1999] ECR1-60657 The Times Law Reports 20 October 1999 (ECJ); Glaxo Group v

Dowelhurst (No 1) [2000] EuLR 493 (Laddie J); Glaxo Group v Dowelhurst (No 2) [2000] FSR 529: The Times Law Reports 14 March 2000 (Laddie J); Case T-25/95 Blue Circle Industries v Commission 15 March 2000 (CFI); Severn Trent Plc v Dwr Cymru (Welsh Water) 10 October 2000 (Langley J); Synstar Computer Service (UK) Ltd v ICL (Sorbus) Ltd The Times Law Reports 1 May 2001 (Lightman J); Case 156/98 RJB Mining v EC Commission [2001] 3 CMLR 308; Cases T12 & 63/99 UK Coal v Commission [2001] 3 CMLR 332; Case C-453/99 Courage v Crehan The Times Law Reports 4 October 2001; R (on the application of BT 3G and others) v Secretary of State For Trade and Industry [2001] 3 CMLR 1588; World Wide Fund for Nature v World Wrestling Federation The Times Law Reports 13 November 2001: [2001] IP&T 1320: The Times Law Reports 12 March 2002 (CA); Consignia v Hays The Times Law Reports 24 January 2002; Secretary of State for the Environment (acting by the Pesticides Directorate) v Crop Protection Association [2002] 1 CMLR 178; Case C-143/00 Boehringer v Swingward The Times Law Reports 23 May 2002; Getmapping v Ordnance Survey The Times Law Reports 25 June 2002.
Prof. Memberships: Bar European Group.
Career: Called 1984.
Publications: Publications: co-author of 'Remedies in EC Law' (1998 Sweet & Maxwell); co-editor of Butterworths Encyclopedia on Competition Law; co-editor of 'Practitioners Handbook of EC Law' (1998 Bar Council); co-author of 'Civil Procedure The White Book Service' (section on references to the Court of Justice).
Personal: LLB, LLM, DEA.

BREEN, Carlo
9 St. John Street (John Hand QC), Manchester
(0161) 955 9000
clerks@9stjohnstreet.co.uk
Recommended in Employment
Specialisation: Practices exclusively in employment law and has very wide experience of Tribunal work including unfair dismissal and breach of contract applications, group redundancy applications and transfer of undertakings. He has extensive experience of advising/drafting work and advocacy. He regularly appears in the Employment Tribunal, the Employment Appeal Tribunal and the High Court and is highly regarded amongst the Judiciary and Chairman of Employment Tribunals. He has a particular interest in disability discrimination, maternity rights and the Working Time Regulations. His specialist interest led to him gaining a Masters Degree from Queensland University in Australia where he completed a thesis on Civil Rights from a European perspective. He has acted for a variety of public institutions including various National Health Trust Hospitals throughout the country and numerous local authorities. He has conducted many multi-party actions involving equal pay cases and has handled cases with as many as 5000 employees involving issues on the Transfer of Undertakings Regulations and the Working Time Regulations. He has also acted for and against the Chief Constable of various constabularies in very serious sex discrimination and race discrimination cases. He is not averse to conducting these cases unassisted by Leading Counsel and frequently appears against eminent Leading Counsel in the employment law field in these and other cases. He is approved by the Commission for Racial Equality and the Equal Opportunities Commission to act in these discrimination cases. In addition, he acted for numerous applicants in the Armed Forces pregnancy dismissal litigation conducted in Industrial Tribunals across the United Kingdom in 1994 and 1995. He is a frequent speaker on employment law and is highly committed to providing the best possible service for his clients whilst still maintaining a personal and professional approach.
Prof. Memberships: Employment Law Bar Association, Employment Lawyers Association, Personal Injury Bar Association, Professional Negligence Bar Association. Member of the Association of American Trial Lawyers.
Career: LLB Hons, MA, Queensland University. Called to the Bar of Queensland, Australia, 1993. Called to the Bar (Middle Temple), 1987.

BRENNAN, Lord QC
Matrix Chambers, London
(020) 7404 3447
Recommended in Environment, Product Liability

BRENNAN, Timothy QC
Devereux Chambers (Colin Edelman QC), London
(020) 7353 7534
brennan@devchambers.co.uk
Recommended in Employment, Tax
Specialisation: Public and commercial law, particularly judicial review, tax litigation, employment, discrimination and pensions. Has appeared in scores of reported cases in those fields. Contributing editor to 'Harvey: Industrial Relations and Employment Law' (Butterworths).
Prof. Memberships: Revenue, Employment and Administrative Law Bar Associations.
Career: Called 1981. QC 2001. Recorder. Junior Counsel to the Inland Revenue (Common Law) 1997-2001.
Personal: Balliol College, Oxford (1976-80). BCL MA. Atkin Scholar of Gray's Inn.

BRENNAND, Timothy
Manchester House Chambers (J D S Wishart), Manchester
(0161) 834 7007
Recommended in Crime

BRENTON, Timothy QC
7 King's Bench Walk (Gavin Kealey QC & Julian Flaux QC), London
(020) 7910 8300
clerks@7kbw.law.co.uk
Recommended in Arbitration, Shipping
Specialisation: Principal areas of practice are shipping, international trade, commercial contracts, insurance (marine and non-marine) and reinsurance, sale and carriage of goods (international and domestic) and commercial fraud. Appointed QC 1998.
Prof. Memberships: COMBAR, supporting member of London Maritime Arbitration Association.
Career: Royal Navy 1975-79. Lecturer in law at King's College, London 1979-80. Called to the Bar 1981 and joined 4 Essex Court. Moved to 7 King's Bench Walk in 2001.
Personal: Educated at King's School, Rochester to 1975; Bristol University 1976-79 (LLB) and Bar School 1980-81. Born 4 November 1957.

BRETTEN, Rex QC
24 Old Buildings (Rex Bretten QC), London
(020) 7242 2744
taxchambers@compuserve.com
Recommended in Tax
Specialisation: All aspects of United Kingdom taxation, with special emphasis on multinational corporate work, the interaction of United Kingdom and foreign taxes, and the operation of double taxation treaties; tax litigation.
Prof. Memberships: Revenue Bar Association.
Career: Commenced practice at the Bar in 1971. Appointed Queen's Counsel in 1980. Elected a Bencher of Lincoln's Inn in 1989.

BRIDEN, Timothy J
8 Stone Buildings (John M Cherry QC), London
(020) 7831 9881
barristers@8stonebuildings.co.uk
Recommended in Church
Specialisation: Principal area of practice is ecclesiastical law. Editor, 'Macmorran's Handbook for Churchwardens and Parochial Church Councillors' and 'Moore's Introduction to English Canon Law'. Also handles personal injury and health and safety cases.
Prof. Memberships: Inner Temple, Ecclesiastical Law Society.
Career: Called to the Bar 1976; joined 1 Temple Gardens 1977 and moved to 8 Stone Buildings 1996. Appointed Chancellor of the Diocese of Bath and Wells 1993 and Chancellor of the Diocese of Truro 1998. Secretary of Ecclesiastical Judges Association since 1996.
Personal: Educated at Ipswich School 1958-70 and Downing College Cambridge (BA 1974; LL.B 1975; MA 1978). Born 29 October 1951. Lives in South London.

BRIGGS, John
3-4 South Square (Michael Crystal QC & Lord Alexander of Weedon QC), London
(020) 7696 9900
clerks@southsquare.com
Recommended in Insolvency
Specialisation: All personal and corporate insolvency related work, including representing insolvency practitioners before Recognised Professional Bodies and Insolvency Practitioners Tribunal.
Prof. Memberships: Insolvency Lawyers' Association. British Italian Law Association (Committee Member). COMBAR. Chancery Bar Association.
Career: LLB (London). Ex Du Doc d'Univ (Nancy, France). 1973: Called to the Bar. 1973-75: Jurist Linguist, European Court of Justice. Deputy Bankruptcy Registrar of the High Court.
Publications: Joint Senior Author, 'Muir Hunter on Personal Insolvency' (Stevens, 1987). Joint Author, 'Asset Protection Trusts' (Keyhaven, 1997). Consultant Editor of 'Bankruptcy and Personal Insolvency Reports' (Jordans, 1996-date).

BRIGGS, Michael QC
Serle Court (Lord Neill of Bladen QC), London
(020) 7242 6105
clerks@serlecourt.co.uk
Recommended in Banking & Finance, Chancery, Commercial (Litigation), Company, Financial Services, Fraud, Insolvency, Partnership, Professional Negligence
Specialisation: Main fields of chancery and commercial litigation including banking, corporate insolvency, property, commercial fraud, professional negligence and regulation and partnership disputes.
Prof. Memberships: Commercial Bar Association; Chancery Bar Association; Association of Partnership Practitioners; Association of Contentious Trust and Probate Specialists.
Career: Called to Bar in 1978, Lincolns Inn. Pupil to Patrick Talbot and John Jarvis. Joined Serle Court in 1979. One of the Junior Counsel to the Crown, Chancery (1990-94). Took Silk in 1994. Attorney General to the Duchy of Lancaster, from 2001.
Personal: Married with four children. Leisure activities include sailing, solo and choral singing, member of Bar Yacht Club and Emsworth sailing club.

BRIGGS, Nicholas
Guildhall Chambers (Adrian Palmer QC), Bristol
(0117) 930 9049
nicholas.briggs@guildhallchambers.co.uk
Recommended in Insolvency
Specialisation: Corporate and personal insolvency; directors' disqualification; shareholder disputes. Commercial litigation including enforcement of securities; bank payments. Recent cases: Re Purvis [2001] 4 A11ER 749; Royal

LEADERS AT THE BAR

Bank of Scotland v Etridge no 2 [2001] 4 ALLER 449 HL; Re Westmead Consultants [2002] 1BCLC 384; Hicks v Gulliver [2002] BPIR 518; Vooght v Hoath [2002] BPIR.
Prof. Memberships: Chancery Bar Association; R3.
Career: Called to Bar 1994 (Lincoln's Inn); appointed to Attorney General's panel of Junior Counsel to the Crown.

BRIGHT, Christopher
3 Fountain Court (Robert Juckes QC), Birmingham
(0121) 236 5854
chris.bright@3fc.co.uk
Recommended in Clinical Negligence
Specialisation: All aspects of clinical negligence. Over 80 per cent of Chris Bright's work consists of clinical negligence litigation, handling cases of moderate valuation to severe damage claims in excess of £4 million. An award of £4.55m in November 1999 was said by the Treasury and NHSLA to be the largest to that date in a clinical negligence claim.
Prof. Memberships: AVMA/APIL. Birmingham Medico-Legal Society.
Career: Durham University BA Hons. Malcolm Hilberry Award, Gray's Inn. Medical Negligence Litigation Pilot Group, Birmingham. Lecturer upon AVMA regional and national courses and to health service professionals/clinicians.
Personal: Interests: Tuscany and Gloucester RFC.

BRIGHT, Robert
7 King's Bench Walk (Gavin Kealey QC & Julian Flaux QC), London
(020) 7910 8300
Recommended in Shipping

BRINDLE, Michael QC
Fountain Court (Anthony Boswood QC), London
(020) 7583 3335
Recommended in Banking & Finance, Commercial (Litigation), Financial Services, Fraud, Professional Negligence
Specialisation: Practice encompasses a variety of work in the commercial and corporate sphere as well as employment law. Emphasis is on banking and financial services, company law, professional negligence in financial and commercial matters, insurance and international trade. Experienced in city related matters, including litigation arising out of audits, takeovers and rights issues. Practises in chancery as well as commercial and common law courts. Important cases include Caparo v Dickman [1989] (auditors' negligence); Morgan Crucible v Hill Samuel [1990] (merchant banker's and auditor's negligence and takeover code); G & H Montage v Irvani [1990] (bills of exchange); Deposit Protection Board v Dalia [1993] (depositor compensation); Shah v Bank of England [1994] (banking supervision); Camdex v Bank of Zambia [1997] (liabilities of central banks); BCCI v Price Waterhouse [1997] (Banking Act 1987); Nuova Safim v Sakura Bank [1998] (ISDA standard agreement); Barclays Bank v Boulter [1999] (banking and securities) and Marks & Spencer Plc v Baird [2001] (contractual certainty). Currently involved in the litigation between Barings and its former auditors. Author of journal articles and of 'Law of Bank Payments' [1999] (with Raymond Cox).
Prof. Memberships: Midland & Oxford Circuit.
Career: Called to the Bar in 1975 and joined Fountain Court Chambers in 1976. Took silk in 1992. Recorder since 2000. Chairman of Commercial Bar Association.
Personal: Educated at Westminster School 1965-69 and New College, Oxford (double first in classics and jurisprudence). Chairman of Trustees: Public Concern at Work. Member of Financial Reporting Review Panel. Born 23 June 1952. Lives in London.

BRISBY, John QC
4 Stone Buildings (Philip Heslop QC), London
(020) 7242 5524
clerks@4stonebuildings.law.co.uk
Recommended in Chancery, Company, Financial Services, Fraud, Insolvency
Specialisation: Litigation and advice in the fields of company law, corporate insolvency and financial services. Emphasis on heavy corporate litigation, mainly in the Chancery Division and Court of Appeal. Cases: Instructed in a number of actions resulting out of the Maxwell affair with a view to locating and recovering assets on behalf of the Maxwell pensioners, and in other high profile fraud or asset recovery situations such as DPR Futures, Barlow Clowes and BCCI. Has also acted for and against various regulatory bodies such as SIB, IMRO and LAUTRO. Has appeared in well over 80 reported cases, well-known examples being Re Cloverbay [1991] Ch 90, Re Bishopsgate Investment Management [1993] Ch 1 Re British & Commonwealth Holdings plc [1993] AC 426, Ispahani v Bank Melli Iran [1998] Lloyds Rep 133, Morris v Bank of America National Trust & Others [2000] 1 AER 954, Sasea Finance Ltd v KPMG [2000] 1AER 676, UPC v Deutsche Bank AG [2000] 2 BCLC 461, Re Barings plc [2001] 2 BCLC 159.
Prof. Memberships: Member of the Commercial Bar Association (COMBAR) and Chancery Bar Association.
Career: Call 1978. QC 1996.
Publications: Former Contributor: 'Encyclopaedia of Forms and Precedents' (4th edn) Vol 9 Companies.
Personal: Educated at Westminster School 1969-73 and Scholar of Christ Church, Oxford 1974-77. Born 8 May 1956. Lives in London and Northamptonshire.

BRISCOE, Constance
9-12 Bell Yard (D Anthony Evans QC), London
(020) 7400 1800
Recommended in Crime

BROCK, Jonathan QC
Falcon Chambers (Jonathan Gaunt QC & Kim Lewison QC), London
(020) 7353 2484
Recommended in Agriculture, Property Litigation
Specialisation: Commercial property litigation and advice; overseas work particularly in commonwealth jurisdictions; has appeared in Jamaica, Brunei, Jordan, Bermuda etc; agriculture; arbitration; ecclesiastical law. Recent cases include Amec v Jury's Hotel [2001] 1 EGLR 81; Ibrahim v Dovecorn [2001] 2 EGLR 46; Fluor Daniel v Shortlands [2001] 2 EGLR 103; Batt v Adams [2001] 2 EGLR 92; Plummer v TIBSCO [2002] 12 EG 137; Bisichi v Bass [2002] 18 EG 159; Saeed v Plustrade [2002] 25 EG 154; First Property Growth v Sun Alliance [2002] 22 EG 140.
Prof. Memberships: Chairman London Common Law and Commercial Bar Association; member Bar Council; member Court of Appeal Users Committee; Bar permanent representative UK Inter-Professional Group; chairman working party on Bar Joint Arbitration Scheme; Western Circuit; member Chancery Bar Association.
Career: St Pauls School; Corpus Christi College, Cambridge; called 1977; Silk 1997; fellow Chartered Institute of Arbitrators; Recorder; Church Commissioner; editor 'Woodfall on Landlord and Tenant'; Blundell Lecturer 1992 and 1998.
Personal: Married with five children. Lives in London and Devon. Captain Snakepit Strollers FC.

BRODIE, Bruce
39 Essex Street (Nigel Pleming QC), London
(020) 7832 1111
bb@39essex.co.uk
Recommended in ADR
Specialisation: Practises as arbitrator and advocate in arbitration with emphasis on international commercial disputes. Also serves as mediator (CEDR accredited mediator). Before transfer to Bar in 1993 was *Frere Cholmeley* senior litigation partner.
Personal: Called 1993.

BROMILOW, Richard
St John's Chambers (Christopher Sharp QC), Bristol
(0117) 921 3456
Recommended in Family

BROMLEY-MARTIN, Michael QC
3 Raymond Buildings (Clive Nicholls QC), London
(020) 7400 6400
chambers@3raymondbuildings.com
Recommended in Licensing
Specialisation: Criminal Law, including extradition and mutual assistance. Particularly commercial and investment fraud, both prosecuting and defending. Notable cases include Blue Arrow, BCCI, Norton, Landhurst Leasing, Facia Group, Bhutto/Zardari and advising in Nissan and Maxwell. Police Discipline, Inquests, Food Safety, Health and Safety, Trade Descriptions. All forms of Licensing, including liquor, public entertainment, betting, gaming and lotteries.
Career: Call 1979. Department of Trade and Industry Inspector 1989, 1990. Advisor to the Police Complaints Authority 1996 -.

BROOK SMITH, Philip QC
Fountain Court (Anthony Boswood QC), London
(020) 7583 3335
Recommended in Product Liability
Specialisation: Wide-ranging practice covers a broad spread of commercial and common law work with considerable experience of product liability issues. Instructed in (for example) HIV Haemophilia, Hepatitis C, and Oral Contraceptives group litigation. Wider commercial and general civil work undertaken includes banking disputes (e.g. National Westminster Bank v Morgan, and numerous cases since), insurance/reinsurance – with experience extending back to the Howden affair of the early 1980s, oil and gas (eg Texaco v Arco), arbitration work, employment, professional negligence claims – particularly accountants' and solicitors' (eg ADT v Binder Hamlyn; Summit Properties v Pitmans), and all commercial fraud (eg Dubai Aluminium v Salaam). Other notable cases include In re a Solicitor (confidentiality) and Sarwar v Alam (costs arrangements). Extensive experience of offshore jurisdictions (particularly as regards financial services), and also practises as a member of the Gibraltar Bar.
Prof. Memberships: Common Law and Commercial Bar Association; South Eastern Circuit.
Career: Called to the Bar in 1982, joined Fountain Court Chambers in 1983, appointed QC in 2002.
Personal: Educated at the London School of Economics (BSc Mathematics 1st Class Hons) and London University (MSc Mathematics - distinction). Born 6 March 1957. Lives in London.

BROOKE, Michael QC
Four New Square (Justin Fenwick QC), London
(020) 7822 2000
barristers@4newsquare.com
Recommended in Clinical Negligence, Product Liability
Specialisation: Clinical negligence; product liability; NHS Tribunals; cases with French connections; HIV haemophiliac litigation; Ratcliffe v E Devon HA (1998) 4 Lloyd's Rep Med 162; Roberts v Winbow (1998) 2 Lloyds Rep Med 31; Bristol Royal Infirmary Inquiry; Hepatitis Litigation (2001) 5 Lloyds Rep Med 187; Henderson v Jaoven [2002] 2 All ER 705.

Prof. Memberships: PNBA, BEG, PIBA, COMBAR, LCCLBA, UIA.
Career: Called 1968. Silk 1994. Assistant Recorder 1997. Recorder 2000. Admitted to Paris Bar 1987. Member SE Circuit.
Personal: Lycée Français de Londres; LLB (Edin).

BROUGHAM, Christopher QC
3-4 South Square (Michael Crystal QC & Lord Alexander of Weedon QC), London
(020) 7696 9900
christopherbrougham@southsquare.com
Recommended in Insolvency
Specialisation: Insolvency, individual and corporate – matrimonial financial provision/insolvency – litigation arising out of insolvencies (security disputes, disqualification of directors, professional negligence etc). Krasner v Dennison [2001] Ch 76, CA.
Prof. Memberships: ILA, ChBA, FLBA, COMBAR.
Career: 1969: called to the Bar (IT). 1984-date: Deputy Bankruptcy Registrar. 1988: Appointed Queen's Counsel. 1990-91: Inspector appointed under Companies Act 1985 s.432(2) to investigate the affairs of BOM Holdings PLC.
Publications: Joint senior author of 'Muir Hunter on Personal Insolvency' (Sweet & Maxwell). Author of Personal Insolvency chapter of 'Encyclopedia of Financial Provision in Family Matters' (Sweet & Maxwell).
Personal: BA (Jurisprudence) Worcester College, Oxford. Music; crossword puzzles (solving and setting); theatre. Married with a family.

BROWN, Charles
39 Essex Street (Nigel Pleming QC), London
(020) 7832 1111
Recommended in Personal Injury
Specialisation: Has extensive experience and undertakes a comprehensive range of employers liability, public liability, product liability and road traffic claims which include multi-party actions, disaster claims and inquiries and group, industrial and environmental disease claims. His practice also includes a variety of local authority tortious liability claims, sports injuries, accidents in foreign jurisdictions, CICB/CICA applications, health and safety prosecutions and insurance contract and coverage disputes. He has a particular interest in the analysis and application of expert evidence to issues of medical causation, especially in high value quantum disputes.

BROWN, Damian
Old Square Chambers (John Hendy QC), London
(020) 7269 0300
dbrown@oldsquarechambers.co.uk
Recommended in Employment
Specialisation: Leading cases: Bowden v Tuffnells Parcel Express Ltd [2001] IRLR 838; Westminster City Council v Unison [2001] IRLR 524; UCLH NHS Trust v Unison [1999] 204; Greaves v Kwiksave [1998] IRLR 245; PLA v Payne [1994] IRLR9. All employment areas: discrimination, restraint of trade, wrongful dismissal, trade union law and strikes. International labour law (including EU and ILO) and human rights.
Prof. Memberships: Employment Law Bar Association; Industrial Law Society; Employment Lawyers Association; Haldane Society.
Career: Called to Bar 1989.
Publications: Tolleys 'Employment Law' – contributor; 'Employment Tribunal Practice and Procedure' – co-author; 'Employment Law Precedents' – co-author (Gee); numerous pamphlets. Editor 'UK and EU Employee Consultation' (Sweet & Maxwell) 2000.
Personal: Interests include politics, trade union history, Arsenal Football Club and cinema.

BROWN, Geoffrey
39 Essex Street (Nigel Pleming QC), London
(020) 7832 1111
Recommended in Personal Injury
Specialisation: Personal injury and related work (including health insurance, clinical negligence and health and safety). Property damage claims (including fire, subsidence, crop and livestock claims, etc). Professional negligence. Insurance and general commercial work.
Career: MA Cantab.

BROWN, Paul
4-5 Gray's Inn Square (Elizabeth Appleby QC), London
(020) 7404 5252
Recommended in Local Government
Specialisation: Town and country planning, environmental law, education law, local government and employment.
Prof. Memberships: PEBA, ALBA, ELBA.
Career: Called to the Bar 1991. LL.B (Hons) (NZ) Ph.D (Cantab). Appointed to the Treasury 'B' Panel (1999).

BROWN, Stephanie
No5 Chambers (Gareth Evans QC), Birmingham
(0121) 606 0500
Recommended in Family

BROWNE, Benjamin QC
2 Temple Gardens (Dermod O'Brien QC), London
(020) 7822 1200
Recommended in Clinical Negligence, Personal Injury
Specialisation: Personal injury, including many paraplegic, tetraplegic and brain damage claims. Disaster litigation, including Clapham Disaster and M1 air crash and Chechnya hostage taking. Clinical negligence including many cerebral palsy cases. Professional negligence, engineers/architects, barristers, solicitors, surveyors, valuers, insurance brokers etc. Insurance and insurance related litigation. Product liability. Environmental exposure cases. Horse and farming cases.
Career: Christ Church, Oxford. MA Jurisprudence.
Personal: Country and family pursuits, gardening.

BROWNE, Desmond QC
5 Raymond Buildings (Patrick Milmo QC), London
(020) 7242 2902
Recommended in Defamation
Specialisation: Defamation and media law. Campbell v MGN: CA: July 2002: public interest and Data Protection Act. McManus v Beckham: CA: Times 11 July 2002: damages for repetition. Ashworth Hospital v MGN: HL: Times 1 July 2002: journalistic confidentiality for source. Kiam v MGN: CA: (2002) EMLR 475: jury award above judge's bracket. Persey v Environment Secretary: DC (2002) WLR: foot and mouth enquiry. Loutchansky v Times: CA (2002) 2 WLR 640: ambit of Reynolds qualified privilege. Thomas v News Group: CA (2002) EMLR 78: harassment in media. Berezovsky v Forbes: CA (2001) 1 WLR 292: public inquiry into Shipman murders. Venables v News Group: (2001) 2 WLR 1038: privacy injunction in Bulger case. Hamilton v Fayed: HL (2001) 1 AC 395: libel and parliamentary privilege. Berezovsky v Michaels: HL: (2000) 1 WLR 1004: forum conveniens and foreign publication. Nicholls v BBC: (1999) EMLR 791: privacy in supergrass's identity. Shah v Standard Chartered: CA (1999) QB 650: repetition rule. Watts v Times: CA (1997) QB 650: qualified privilege for solicitors. John v MGN: CA (1997) QB 586: quantum and exemplary damages. Barrymore v News Group: (1997) FSR 600: kiss and tell injunction. Also acted for successful defendants in Graham v Rechem (1994), a 15 month trial toxic nuisance action.
Prof. Memberships: Western Circuit.
Career: Called to the Bar 1969. Legal correspondent for 'British Medical Journal' 1970-79. Silk 1990. Recorder 1994.
Personal: Educated: Eton and New College, Oxford (Scholar). Born 5 April 1947.

BROWNE-WILKINSON, Simon QC
Serle Court (Lord Neill of Bladen QC), London
(020) 7242 6105
Recommended in Fraud

BROWNLIE, Ian QC
Blackstone Chambers (Presiley Baxendale QC & Charles Flint QC), London
(020) 7583 1770
Recommended in Public International Law
Specialisation: International Court of Justice; arbitration; European Court of Human Rights; territorial disputes; maritime delimitation; damage to the environment. 2001 Cases: Ethiopia/Eritrea Boundary; Cameroon v Nigeria; Nicaragua v Honduras.
Prof. Memberships: The English Bar; Institute of Int. Law (Vice-President).
Career: Called to the Bar 1958; practice begins 1967; CBE for services to International Law 1993; Chichele Professor of Public International Law, Oxford, 1980-99; London School of Economics, Chair of Int. Law, 1976-80; Fellow of British Academy, 1979; QC, 1979; Editor, British Year Book of Int. Law, 1974-99; Director of Studies, International Law Association, 1982-91; Member of the International Law Commission, 1997 (re-elected 2001); Ad Hoc Judge, International Court of Justice, 2001-2.
Publications: 'Principles of Public International Law', 5th ed, 1998 (Eds in Portuguese, Russian, Korean, Japanese and Chinese).
Personal: Oxford, MA, D.Phil.

BRUDENELL, Thomas
Queen Elizabeth Building (Florence Baron QC), London
(020) 7797 7837
tom.brudenell@supanet.com
Recommended in Family
Specialisation: Principal area of practice is family law.
Prof. Memberships: Family Law Bar Association.
Career: Called to the Bar 1977 and joined current chambers in 1978.
Personal: Educated at Eton College 1969-74. Born 12 August 1956. Lives in London.

BRYANT, Judith
Wilberforce Chambers (Edward Nugee QC), London
(020) 7306 0102
Recommended in Chancery
Specialisation: Practice covers a wide range of advisory and litigation work in chancery/commercial matters, with particular emphasis on: trusts and their taxation, including advice on the creation and administration of trusts, the duties of trustees and breaches of trust, contentious trust matters, conflicts of laws, the variation of trusts, and the drafting of trust deeds and related instruments; pension schemes, including advice in relation to the construction of trust deeds and rules of pension schemes, the duties of pension scheme trustees and breaches of those duties, applications to Court in relation to pension schemes, and complaints to the Pensions Ombudsman; wills and probate, including advice on the construction of wills, conflicts of laws, the variation of wills, the administration of estates, the duties of executors, and contentious probate matters; professional negligence relating to trusts and pension schemes.
Prof. Memberships: Society of Trust and Estate Practitioners (STEP) and Chancery Bar Association.
Career: Called to the Bar: 1987. Jesus College, Cambridge 1982-86. BA 1st Class Hons (1985), LLM (1986).

LEADERS AT THE BAR

BRYANT-HERON, Mark
9-12 Bell Yard (D Anthony Evans QC), London
(020) 7400 1800
clerks@bellyard.co.uk
Recommended in Crime
Specialisation: Specialist in criminal law with a wide-ranging practice. Instructed as leading junior for prosecution and defence. Particular areas of practice are fraud; DTI prosecutions and insolvency-related crime; money-laundering and asset confiscation; serious drug trafficking and specialist customs and excise work; judicial review of criminal matters and High Court Appeal cases.
Prof. Memberships: Criminal Bar Association, South Eastern Circuit.
Career: Called to the Bar in 1986.
Personal: Educated at Cambridge University 1981-84.

BUBB, Tim
39 Park Square (Tim Bubb), Leeds
(0113) 245 6633
Recommended in Crime

BUCHAN, Andrew
Cloisters (Laura Cox QC), London
(020) 7827 4000
abu@cloisters.com
Recommended in Personal Injury
Specialisation: Serious personal injury cases involving mental health issues. In particular stress and bullying at work. Brain damage. Clinical negligence. Professional negligence work in these fields. Employment law discrimination cases involving psychiatric injury. Has a special interest in mental health law. Recent reported cases include Walker v Northumberland County Council (first successful stress induced breakdown (second) caused by work case); Sheriff v Klyne Tugs Lowestoft Ltd CA (jurisdiction of the Employment Tribunal for personal injury cases), Waters v Metropolitan Police Commissioner HL (duty of care of police for bullying within the force); Long v Mercury Mobile Communications (successful first breakdown claim for bullying: award of £327,500).
Prof. Memberships: PIBA; PNBA; ELBA; APIL; AVMA; ELF; accredited mediator with CEDR.
Career: Called to the Bar 1981.
Publications: Co-author: 'Personal Injury Practice and Procedure the Guide to Litigation in the County Court and High Court' (2000) Butterworths 3rd edn. Co-author of the chapter on Psychological Injuries for Munkman, 'Employers Liability', 2001 in print, Butterworths. Article, Stress: Forseeability and Breach, 'JPIL', March 2001. Co-author 'Personal Injury Schedules: Calculating Damages,' Butterworths, 1st edition, 2001.
Personal: Born 6 December 1956.

BUCHANAN, Vivien
St. Mary's Chambers Family Law Chambers (Nigel B Page), Nottingham
(0115) 950 3503
Recommended in Family

BUCKNALL, Belinda QC
4 Essex Court (Nigel Teare QC), London
020 7653 5653
bbucknall@4sx.co.uk
Recommended in Arbitration, Shipping
Specialisation: Admiralty practitioner specialising in marine insurance (hull and yacht); collision; salvage; maritime pollution; dry shipping work; P.I.; fatal accident claims (arising from shipboard incidents). Also land based building and construction disputes and air law (in particular limitation of liability).
Prof. Memberships: Western Circuit; Combar.
Career: Education: The School of St. Helen and St. Katherine (Abingdon); Oxford University (MA). Appointments: QC – 1988; Lloyd's panel of Salvage Arbitrators; Master of Middle Temple – 1996; Recorder – 1997. Deputy High Court Judge. Languages: French and Italian.
Personal: A longstanding interest in the RNLI. Ice skating and canoeing.

BUDDEN, Caroline
One King's Bench Walk (Anthony Hacking QC), London
(020) 7936 1500
cbudden@1kbw.co.uk
Recommended in Family
Specialisation: Principal area of practice is family law, including public and private law aspects of the Children Act, adoption, wardship and related social services law, child abduction. South Eastern Circuit. Cases of interest include: Re V (Jurisdiction: Habitual Residence) [2001] 1 FLR 253; Re H (minors) (Care proceedings: Intervenor) [2000] 1 FLR 775; Re G (interim care order) [1992] 2FLR 839 CA; Re H (a minor) (parental responsiblity) [1993] 1FLR 484 CA; Re W (a minor) [1992] 3WLR 758 CA (medical treatment of an anorexic teenager/court's jurisdiction); Re C (adoption by relative) [1989] 1 WLR 61 CA; R v North Yorkshire CC ex p. M [1988] 3WLR 1344 (judicial review of local authority's conduct in care proceedings).
Prof. Memberships: Family Law Bar Association, Professional Negligence Bar Association.
Career: Called to the Bar 1977. Assistant Recorder 1998. Recorder 2000.
Personal: Educated at Alfred Colfox School, Bridport, Dorset, and Bristol University (LL.B 1976). Born 30 July 1954. Lives in London.

BULL, Gregory
30 Park Place (John Jenkins QC), Cardiff
(02920) 398421
Recommended in Crime
Specialisation: Fraud; all areas of serious crime.
Prof. Memberships: Criminal Bar Association.
Career: Called 1976; Recorder 1995.
Personal: Aberdare Boys Grammar School; Birmingham University.

BULLOCK, Ian
St John's Chambers (Christopher Sharp QC), Bristol
(0117) 921 3456
Recommended in Personal Injury

BURBIDGE, James
St Philips Chambers (John Randall QC), Birmingham
(0121) 246 7000
Recommended in Crime

BURKE, Jeffrey QC
Devereux Chambers (Colin Edelman QC), London
(020) 7353 7534
Recommended in Personal Injury
Specialisation: Principal areas of practice are: commercial and common law, employment law, discrimination, personal injury, medical negligence, professional negligence, insurance, public and administrative law. Recent cases include: Green v British Aerospace (1995) CA – discovery in mass redundancy case; Burgess v Bass Taverns (1995) CA – dismissal for trade union reasons. A substantial number of cases involving brain damage or other serious injuries in excess of £1 million. Blue Circle v West Midlands CC (1995) CA – Lands Tribunal award of compensation for compulsory purchase; Wandsworth BC v NAS/UWT (1993) CA – industrial action - teachers; R. v Hull University ex p Page (1992) CA, HL – security of tenure, university lecturers; BT v Ticehurst (1992) CA – deductions from pay during industrial action; London Underground v RMT (1985) CA industrial action – underground workers; Palmer v Associated British Ports (1994) HL – action short of dismissal – dock workers; Hunt v Douglas (1991) HL – interest on costs; D'Souza v LB of Lambeth [1997] IRLR 677 race discrimination (CA); [1999] R v West Yorkshire Fire and Civil Defence Authority ex p McCalman & Lockwood [June 2000] CA – pensions and employment; N&K Kowlessur v Suffolk Health Authority [December 2000] CA – registered homes/administrative; D'Souza v LB of Lambeth [2001] CA – race discrimination; House of Lords – discrimination against gypsies.
Prof. Memberships: Committee Member Personal Injuries Bar Association. Employment Law Bar Association.
Career: Called, 1964 (Major Scholarship: Middle Temple). QC: 1984. Recorder: 1983. Legal Member Mental Health Independent Review Tribunal (1993). Since 1993 appointed by Lord Chancellor to sit as a Deputy High Court Judge and since 2000 as a Judge of the Employment Appeal Tribunal.
Personal: Educated Shrewsbury School. Open Exhibition in Classics to Brasenose College, Oxford MA (Oxon) Jurisprudence. Interests, football, cricket and wine.

BURKE, Trevor QC
2 Bedford Row (William Clegg QC), London
(020) 7440 8888
tburke@2bedfordrow.co.uk
Recommended in Crime
Specialisation: Has previously defended John Fashanu in the football corruption trial. Sol Campbell on an alleged assault. Nigel Benn on a serious assault. Terry Marsh on a student grant fraud and the Taylor sisters. Also defended Gary Glitter. Extensive experience in defending white collar fraud, recently defended Dr Padelis in a large fraud on the NHS. Also undertakes consumer protection/trade description work, particularly experienced representing solicitors before the OSS.
Prof. Memberships: CBA, Member of South Eastern Circuit.

BURKILL, Guy QC
Three New Square (David Young QC), London
(020) 7405 1111
clerks@3newsqaure.co.uk
Recommended in Information Technology, Intellectual Property
Specialisation: All intellectual property, mainly patent with particular interest in computer hardware and software and electronics. Has acted for many leading multinational companies in the computer, electronics, paper, chemical, pharmaceutical, aviation and other fields. Notable cases include Pavel v Sony (Walkman case); Lubrizol v Exxon (oil additives); Hoechst v British Petroleum (chemical manufacture, account of profits); Discovision v Disctronics (CD mastering); Texas Instruments v Hyundai (integrated circuitry); Dyson v Hoover (vacuum cleaners, post expiry injunction).
Prof. Memberships: Intellectual Property Bar Association; Chancery Bar Association.
Career: Winchester College; Corpus Christi College Cambridge – MA Degree, 1st Class Hons in Engineering (Electrical Option); called to Bar 1981; QC 2002.
Publications: Co-author of 'Terrell on the Law of Patents' (15th edition)
Personal: Leisure interests include violin, opera and travel.

BURNETT, Ian QC
1 Temple Gardens (Geoffrey Nice QC), London
(020) 7583 0808
clerks@1templegardens.co.uk
Recommended in Health & Safety, Personal Injury
Specialisation: Public law, coroners, health and safety, personal injury. Public inquiries (King's Cross, Clapham Junction, Guildford Four, Bloody Sunday, Southall Rail, Joint Rail). Representative cases: R v Associated Octel (HL) [1996] 1 WLR 1543; Boddington v British Transport Police (HL) [1999] 2 AC 143; R v Home Secretary ex p Daly (HL) [2001] 2 WLR 1622; R v North London Coroner ex p

Touche (CA) [2001] 2 ALLER 752; R v Home Secretary ex p Saleem (CA) [2001] IWLR 443.
Prof. Memberships: ALBA, PIBA.
Career: MA (Oxon). Called MT 1980. Junior Counsel to the Crown (Common Law) 1992-98; QC 1998. Recorder.

BURR, Andrew
Atkin Chambers (Robert Akenhead QC), London
(020) 7404 0102
clerks@atkinchambers.law.co.uk
Recommended in Construction
Specialisation: Practises primarily in domestic and international construction and technology disputes. Acts as advocate in litigation and arbitration, as a TECSA adjudicator and in an advisory capacity regarding ADR. Experienced in all aspects of construction and technology law and professional negligence, particularly of architects, engineers and surveyors. General and articles editor 'Construction Law Journal' (Sweet and Maxwell).
Prof. Memberships: ACI Arb. (Committee member European Branch), Swiss Arbitration Association, TECBAR, COMBAR, BILA.
Career: Called November 1981. Joined chambers in 1983. Speaks Italian and French.
Personal: Educated at Barclay School, Stevenage and Trinity Hall, Cambridge. Lives in London.

BURTON, Frank QC
12 King's Bench Walk (Richard Methuen QC), London
(020) 7583 0811
Recommended in Personal Injury
Specialisation: Principal area of practice is personal injury work with an emphasis on industrial diseases and clinical negligence.
Prof. Memberships: Personal Injury Bar Association, Member of Executive.
Career: University lecturer 1974-83. Called to the Bar and joined present chambers 1982. QC 1998. 1999 Assistant Recorder, Recorder 2000.
Publications: Co-author of 'Medical Negligence Case Law' and 'Personal Injury Limitation Law', both published by Butterworths. Author on medical practitioners chapter in Butterworths Professional Negligence Service.
Personal: BA Hons 1st Class and PhD. Born 19 June 1950. Lives in London.

BUSH, Rosalind
No5 Chambers (Gareth Evans QC), Birmingham
(0121) 606 0500
Recommended in Family

BUSUTTIL, Godwin
5 Raymond Buildings (Patrick Milmo QC), London
(020) 7242 2902
godwinbusuttil@5rb.co.uk
Recommended in Defamation
Specialisation: Defamation, media law generally including breach of confidence/privacy, copyright and reporting restrictions. Re G (minors) (celebrities: publicity) (reporting restrictions) reporting custody proceedings CA [1999] 1 FLR 409; Nicholls v BBC (confidence) injunction to restrain broadcast where alleged that it would increase risk of physical harm to claimant CA [1999] EMLR 791; Gaddafi v Telegraph Group (libel) media qualified privilege CA [2000] EMLR 431; Medway Council v BBC (reporting restrictions) injunction to restrain broadcast of interview with child subject to ASBO [2002] 1 FLR 104; Carlton Communications plc v News Group Newspapers (libel) meaning CA [2002] EMLR 299.
Career: 1988-92 Jesus College, Cambridge MA, MPhil; 1992-3 City University, Dip Law; 1993-4 ICSL, London; 1994 called to the Bar (Lincoln's Inn; Mansfield and Hardwick Scholar).

BUTCHER, Christopher QC
7 King's Bench Walk (Gavin Kealey QC & Julian Flaux QC), London
(020) 7910 8300
clerks@7kbw.law.co.uk
Recommended in Arbitration, Banking & Finance, Commercial (Litigation), Insurance, Professional Negligence, Shipping
Specialisation: Insurance and reinsurance, commercial agreements, banking, agency, shipping, international trade, arbitration, and professional negligence.
Career: Called to the Bar 1986. Took Silk 2001. Recent cases include: Vale de Rio v Bao Steel (2000) 2 Lloyd's Rep (arbitration – jurisdiction); HIH Casualty v Chase Manhattan Bank (2001) Lloyd's Rep. IR 191 (insurance, duty of brokers). Barings Plc v Coopers & Lybrand [1997] 1 BCLC 427 (auditors – duty of care), Denby v English and Scottish Maritime Insurance Co. [1998] Lloyd's Rep. IR 343 (reinsurance), Credit Suisse First Boston v MLC [1999] 1 Lloyd's Rep. 767 (practice – anti-suit injunction).
Personal: Born 1962. MA (Oxon), Dip L (City University), Dip Eur Law (King's College, London). Has a working knowledge of French and Italian.

BUTLER, Christopher M
St. Mary's Chambers Family Law Chambers (Nigel B Page), Nottingham
(0115) 950 3503
Recommended in Family

BYRNE, Garrett
4-5 Gray's Inn Square (Elizabeth Appleby QC), London
(020) 7404 5252
clerks@4-5graysinnsquare.co.uk
Recommended in Environment
Specialisation: Environmental law and planning. Instructed by major city solicitors to advise and represent substantial industrial concerns and major developers. Regular speaker at conferences.
Prof. Memberships: United Kingdom Environmental Law Association; Environmental Law Foundation, founding member of 'EarthRights', environmental rights charity and public interest law firm.
Career: Called to the Bar in 1986, Masters degree in Environmental Law in 1993.

CAHILL, Jeremy QC
No5 Chambers (Gareth Evans QC), Birmingham
(0121) 606 0500
Recommended in Environment, Planning

CAHILL, Sally
Park Lane Chambers (Stuart Brown QC), Leeds
(0113) 228 5000
Recommended in Family

CALDECOTT, Andrew QC
1 Brick Court (Richard Rampton QC), London
(020) 7353 8845
Recommended in Defamation
Specialisation: Defamation, confidence, contempt of court and media related law generally.
Career: Called to the Bar 1975.
Personal: Educated Eton College and New College, Oxford. Lives in London.

CALLMAN, Tanya
2 King's Bench Walk (Philip Rueff), London
(020) 7353 9276
Recommended in Education
Specialisation: MA (Cantab), Exhibitioner, Peterhouse. Harmsworth Major Scholar, Middle Temple. Appears regularly before all types of Court and Tribunal. Advises local authorities on varied aspects of education law/policy and related matters. Also acts for parents/children and independent schools. Frequently lectures/provides training on education law, in particular to local authorities. Chair, Universities and College Education Law Network conferences. Reported cases include: represented Westminster in S v Special Educational Needs Tribunal and the City of Westminster CA [1996] 1 WLR 382 – first case of appeal from decision of Special Educational Needs Tribunal to Court of Appeal. L v Kent County Council and the Special Educational Needs Tribunal [1998] ELR140. Sage v South Gloucestershire County Council and Confrey [1998] ELR 525 and Glasner v South Gloucestershire Council and Special Educational Needs Tribunal [2000] ELR 136. Gregory v Frensham Heights Educational Trust [1997] 8 C.L. 242.
Prof. Memberships: Executive Committee, Administrative Law Bar Association. Advisory Group, National Autistic Society's Advocacy Service. Education Law Association.
Publications: Founder Editor Education, Public Law and the Individual (Hart). Has written for 'Judicial Review'. Course material for Open University. Paper WG Hart Human Rights Seminar, Institute Advanced Legal Studies. Appeared on Legal Network Television discussing education negligence claims.

CALVER, Neil
Brick Court Chambers (Christopher Clarke QC), London
(020) 7379 3550
Recommended in Commercial (Litigation)
Specialisation: Commercial law, in particular insurance, reinsurance, commercial arbitration, contractual disputes, professional negligence, EC law, sports law. Major cases this year so far include Heaton v AXA [2001] 1 WLR 111 (House of Lords: effect of settling claim against one concurrent contract breaker upon claim against other contract breaker); Odyssey Re v OIC Run Off Ltd (Court of Appeal: setting aside judgment on grounds of fraud of witness) and acting for Sir Elton John in professional negligence action against his former accountants (Court of Appeal). Important previous cases include: Stoke CC v B&Q [1993] AC 900 [HL and ECJ: whether Sunday trading ban contrary to EC law]; Kirklees BC v Wickes [1993] AC 227 [HL: whether public authorities should give cross-undertakings in damages as price of injunctive relief]; Ernst & Young v Butte Mining [1996] 1 LLR 91 and 104 [striking out of accountant's negligence claim]; Wurttembergische v Home Insurance [1999] LRLR 397 [CA: Pool reinsurance dispute]; Junior Counsel for Williams Grand Prix Motor Racing team. Acted for reinsurers in major insurance market arbitration concerning Eastern European shipbuilding losses after collapse of communism (1999).
Prof. Memberships: COMBAR.
Career: LLM, Christ's College, Cambridge University (Double First Class Honours). Elected Life Scholar, Squire Scholar and De Hart Scholar, Christ's College Cambridge University. Gray's Inn Entrance Scholar; David Karmel Scholarship prize winner (Commercial Law, Gray's Inn).
Publications: Contributing author to the Bar Council's European Law Handbook' (1998); Contributing author to 'TUPE and the Acquired Rights Directive' (1996).

CAMERON, Alexander
3 Raymond Buildings (Clive Nicholls QC), London
(020) 7400 6400
chambers@3raymondbuildings.com
Recommended in Fraud
Specialisation: Substantial experience in all areas of criminal law. A specialist in commercial crime/fraud. Has defended solicitors and accountants, businessmen and financiers in matters ranging from conspiracy to defraud, through theft, fraudulent trading, cheating the Revenue, insider dealing and corruption. Recently defended in one of the first prosecutions brought by OPRA. Has advised in money laundering investigations and appeared in the commercial court in relation to criminal and extradition matters. Has prosecuted and defended in many cases of serious crime including murder, attempted

LEADERS AT THE BAR

murder, robbery, rape and perjury. Has appeared in licensing matters including recently the application to restrict liquor licensing at Twickenham RFC. Notable cases include Peter (known as Beth) Young (fraud, fitness to plead); Jeffrey Archer (perjury); Augusto Pinochet Ugarte (extradition); Jonathan Aitken (perjury); Susan Goddard (extradition); Marquis of Bath (assault); Blackspur Leasing (fraud); Blue Arrow (fraud).
Prof. Memberships: Criminal Bar Association, International Bar Association.
Career: Called 1986. At *3 Raymond Buildings* (formerly QEB) throughout.
Personal: Bristol University (LL.B Hons).

CAMERON, Neil
Wilberforce Chambers (Bernard Gateshill), Hull
(01482) 323264
clerks@hullbar.demon.co.uk
Recommended in Commercial (Litigation), Environment, Health & Safety
Specialisation: Civil: cases relating to the conveyancing and use of land (in particular boundaries; restrictive covenants; easements; public rights of way; landlord and tenant and nuisance); commercial litigation. Criminal: health and safety, environmental and local authority prosecutions.
Prof. Memberships: North Eastern Circuit; Professional Negligence Bar Association; Property Bar Association.
Career: Called 1984, Junior Counsel to the Crown (Provincial Panel) 2000.

CAMERON, Neil
Eldon Chambers (Patrick Clarkson QC & William Hicks QC), London
(020) 7583 1355
clerks@eldonchambers.com
Recommended in Planning
Specialisation: Planning and environmental. Recent work includes: UK Nirex RCF appeal, Barnsley MBC CPO Special Parliamentary Procedure, Medway Cement Works Inquiry, Kent & Medway Bills (2000), Heron Tower.
Prof. Memberships: Planning and Environment Bar Association, Parliamentary Bar Mess.
Career: Called 1982. Recorder 2002.
Personal: Educated at Eton College and Durham University.

CAMPBELL, Douglas James
Three New Square (David Young QC), London
(020) 7405 1111
clerks@3newsquare.co.uk
Recommended in Intellectual Property
Specialisation: All intellectual property matters especially chemistry, computers. Notable cases: Thermos v Aladdin [2000] FSR 402, [2002] FSR 11 (CA); Marshalltown Trowel v CEKA Works [2001] FSR 633; MedGen v Passion for Life Products [2001] FSR 496, Decon Laboratories v Fred Baker Scientific [2001] RPC 293; Playhut v Spring Form [2000] FSR 327, Texas Instruments v Hyundai Electronics [2000] FSR 86,

Union Carbide v BP [1998] RPC 1, [1999] RPC 409 (CA); Discovision Associates v Disctronics [1999] FSR 196; Demel v Jefferson [1999] FSR 204; Lubrizol v Exxon [1997] RPC 195, [1998] RPC 727 (CA).
Prof. Memberships: Intellectual Property Bar Assn; Chancery Bar Assn.
Career: Dollar Academy, Scotland 1976-84; (Scholarship to) Hertford College, Oxford 1984-88 1st Class Hons, Chemistry with Distinction in Quantum Chemistry. 1989-90 employed by Andersen Consulting in Information Technology 1990-91 Teaching English in Kagoshima, Japan. Fluent in Japanese. Called to Bar 1993, Pegasus Scholarship to Melbourne, Australia 1997.
Publications: Contributor to 'European Patent Litigation Handbook'; 'Terrell on Patents' (both Sweet & Maxwell).

CAMPBELL, Emily
Wilberforce Chambers (Edward Nugee QC), London
(020) 7306 0102
Recommended in Chancery
Specialisation: All areas of general chancery work with an emphasis on trust, tax and estate planning and pensions litigation.
Prof. Memberships: Revenue Bar Assoc., Association of Pensions Lawyers, Chancery Bar Assoc.
Career: Lecturer in law of trusts, King's College, London (1994-95). Judicial Assistant to Court of Appeal (1997).
Publications: Halsburys Laws – Settlements title. International Trust Laws (Ed G Lasson) – contributor. Various articles: PCB; Sol. J.; Trusts & Estates LJ; Christies Bulletin. Author of 'Changing the Term of Trusts', Butterworths.
Personal: Classical music

CAMPBELL, Stephen
St Philips Chambers (John Randall QC), Birmingham
(0121) 246 7000
Recommended in Commercial (Litigation)
Specialisation: Commercial law, building, personal injury.
Prof. Memberships: Midland Chancery and Commercial Bar Association; Personal Injury Bar Association; Birmingham Technology and Construction Court Users Group; Assistant Deputy Coroner to Birmingham and Solihull. Recorder.
Career: King Edward VI School, Birmingham. Liverpool University.
Personal: Married, three children. Tennis. School Governor.

CAMPBELL, Susan
Southernhay Chambers (Anthony Ward), Exeter
(01392) 255777
southernhay.chambers@lineone.net
Recommended in Family
Specialisation: Family law. Practice covers all areas of family law: ancillary relief and all aspects of law relating to children, particularly care proceedings.
Prof. Memberships: Family Law Bar

Association.
Career: Called 1986. Spent seven years as an employed barrister in local government, specialising in care proceedings.
Personal: Born 29 April 1964. Two children. Enjoys swimming and walking.

CANNON, Mark
Four New Square (Justin Fenwick QC), London
(020) 7822 2000
m.cannon@4newsquare.com
Recommended in Professional Negligence
Specialisation: Professional negligence (accountants, architects, engineers, financial advisors, insurance brokers, lawyers, Lloyd's agents and surveyors); construction and engineering; insurance and reinsurance; general commercial law. Editor 'Jackson & Powell on Professional Negligence' (chapters 2 to 5 in 5th edition (2001) – duties, defences etc; chapters 7 and 9 in 4th edition (1996) – insurance brokers and members' and managing agents at Lloyd's; chapter 7 in 3rd edition (1991) – insurance brokers). Recent interesting cases include ICS v West Bromwich Building Society [1998] 1 WLR and [1999] Lloyd's PN 496, Somatra v Sinclair Roche & Temperley [2000] 1 WLR 2453 and Royal Brompton Hospital v Hammond [2002] 1 WLR 1397.
Prof. Memberships: COMBAR; Professional Negligence Bar Association; London Common Law and Commercial Bar Association.
Career: Educated at Lincoln College, Oxford 1980-83 (BA in Modern History) and Robinson College, Cambridge 1983-84 (Part 1B of Law Tripos). Called to the Bar in 1985.

CAPE, Paul
Milburn House Chambers (Paul Cape), Newcastle upon Tyne
(0191) 2305511
Recommended in Employment
Specialisation: Almost exclusively employment and discrimination work, mainly factually complex discrimination, sensitive and/or high value dismissals, restraint of trade and all aspects of the police as an employer. Acts mainly for employers (primarily police and local authorities) as well as employees.
Career: Obtained a 'First' in Law at Newcastle Polytechnic following a career as a trade union official. Co-founder and Head of Chambers, Milburn House Chambers, a set specialising in all aspects of employment and discrimination law. Appointed a part-time Chairman of the Employment Tribunal 2000 and, hence is unable to accept instructions to appear in the Employment Tribunal in the Manchester Region.
Personal: Interests include theatre, reading and watching cricket. Born 5 March 1955.

CAPLAN, Jonathan QC
5 Paper Buildings (Godfrey Carey QC &

Jonathan Caplan QC), London
(020) 7583 6117
Recommended in Crime, Fraud
Specialisation: Criminal fraud; corporate liability; media law and contempt; health and safety; disciplinary tribunals; gross negligence manslaughter; public inquiries. Recent reported cases include AG's Reference No 2 of 1999 (2000) QB 796; Boddington v BTP (1999) 2 AC 143; AG v Associated Newspapers Ltd (1998) EMLR 711; HKSAR v Lee Ming Tee (Hong Kong Court of Final Appeal) (2001) 1 HKLRD 599. Cases include the defences of P&O Ferries in the Herald of Free Enterprise disaster and of Great Western trains in the Southall rail crash; appearing in the Guinness (1996) 1 Cr.App.Rep. 463, Maxwell and Blue Arrow fraud trials; representing the Attorney General in the Barings/Leeson case; the defence of a medical practitioner for alleged euthanasia; the defence in Hong Kong of the Chairman of the Allied Group in long running proceedings concerning an alleged Stock Exchange fraud; and representing newspapers and television companies in contempt and libel cases.
Career: Recorder of the Crown Court; Master of the Bench of Gray's Inn; Co-head of chambers; former Chairman of the Public Affairs Committee of the Bar Council.
Publications: Member of the Editorial Board of 'Journal of Criminal Law'.
Personal: MA (Cantab). Married with three children.

CARGILL-THOMPSON, Perdita
Essex Court Chambers (Gordon Pollock QC), London
(020) 7813 8000
Recommended in Tax
Specialisation: VAT and Customs & Excise litigation and advisory work; judicial review and human rights; EC litigation and advisory work; Brussels Convention and Rome Convention; UK commercial disputes; broking disputes; banking, guarantee and insolvency work.
Career: Jesus College, Oxford: BA 1984 (Jurisprudence). College of Law: Solicitors' Professional Examinations 1984-85. London School of Economics: Masters in Human Rights and International Law 1991-92. British Academy Scholarship 1991-92. Bar Council: Conversion examinations 1992. Called to the Bar 1993. Treasury Panel (B List).
Personal: Born 1964. Speaks French.

CARLISLE, Hugh QC
1 Temple Gardens (Geoffrey Nice QC), London
(020) 7583 1315
clerks@1templegardens.co.uk
Recommended in Health & Safety
Specialisation: Health and safety at work: R v Board of Trustees of Science Museum [1993] IWLR 1171 CA; R v Associated Octel Co Ltd [1996] 4 All ER 846, [1996] 1 WLR 1543 HL; R v British

LEADERS AT THE BAR

Steel plc [1995] I WLR 1356 CA; R v Nuclear Electric plc [Sept 1995]; R v Coalite Products Ltd [Feb 1996]; HSE v Howletts Zoo [Oct 1995]; R v Port Ramsgate and others [Jan-Feb 1997]; Harris v Evans [1998] 3 All ER 522 CA; R v FH Howe Ltd [1999] 2 All ER 249 CA; R v Balfour Beatty and Geoconsult [Jan-Feb 1999]; Counsel for Department of Health in BSE Inquiry 1999-2000; Counsel for HSC/E in the Ladbroke Grove Railway Inquiry 2000; R v Yarm Row Ltd and Costain Ltd [Nov 2001] etc. Personal injuries: Fields v Hereford Health Authority [1992] etc.
Career: Called to Bar Middle Temple 1961; Junior Treasury Counsel, personal injuries cases, 1975-78; QC 1978; DTI Inspector into Ramor Investments Ltd 1979-85 and into Milbury plc 1982-85; Bencher, Middle Temple 1985.
Personal: Married with two children. Interests include fly fishing, woodworking and croquet.

CARR, Bruce
Devereux Chambers (Colin Edelman QC), London
(020) 7353 7534
Recommended in Employment
Specialisation: Employment law, commercial law, personal injury. Regularly instructed on behalf of both employers and trade unions, in particular in the EAT. Also frequently appears in interlocutory injunction applications, ranging from restrictive covenants to trade disputes. Substantial practice in discrimination, transfer of undertakings and large scale redundancy matters. Junior Counsel to the Crown (Panel A).
Prof. Memberships: Employment Law Bar Association; Employment Lawyers Association; ILS, Recorder; Member - EAT User Group.
Career: Called 1986. Inner Temple.
Personal: Cambs High School for Boys, Cambridge. Hills Road Sixth Form College, Cambridge. LSE (BSc Economics) 1983, Central London Polytechnic (Dip. Law) 1985.

CARR, Christopher QC
One Essex Court (Lord Grabiner QC), London
(020) 7583 2000
Recommended in Commercial (Litigation), Energy, Fraud
Specialisation: A general commercial law advisor and advocate, he is particularly experienced in international finance based legal work and in financial, banking and commercial transactions. Also does a substantial amount of competition and European law and international and jurisdictional matters. Has frequently acted either as an advocate or an arbitrator in international commercial arbitrations. Is reasonably fluent in French and has a working knowledge of German.
Prof. Memberships: Member and Bencher of Lincoln's Inn.
Career: Called to Bar in 1968. Took silk in 1983.

CARR, Henry QC
11 South Square (Christopher Floyd QC), London
(020) 7405 1222
clerks@11southsquare.com
Recommended in Information Technology, Intellectual Property
Specialisation: Principal areas of practice are patents, copyrights, designs and trademarks. Leading cases include Philips v Remington, Levis v Tesco, Glaxo and others v Dowelhurst and others, all of which were referred to the ECJ and concern the Trade Marks Directive. Also AHP v Novartis (patents); R v Registrar of Designs ex p Ford Motor Company (House of Lords) R v Licensing Authority ex p Smith Kline & French (House of Lords) and Scotia v Norgine (European Court). Also has a substantial practice in computer contracts (including negligence claims); and judicial review relating to the grant of product licences. In addition, has appeared in numerous cases in the Data Protection Tribunal on behalf of the registrar.
Career: Called to the Bar 1982. Joined South Square in 1983. Took Silk 1998. Educated at Hertford College, Oxford and the University of British Columbia. Lives in London.
Publications: Computer software: 'Legal Protection in the United Kingdom'.

CARR, Peter
St. Ive's Chambers (Julia Macur QC), Birmingham
(0121) 236 0863
Recommended in Crime

CARR, Sue
Four New Square (Justin Fenwick QC), London
(020) 7822 2000
s.carr@4newsquare.com
Recommended in Professional Negligence
Specialisation: Principal area of practice is professional negligence: in particular, solicitors, barristers, accountants, clinical, surveyors, architects and engineers. Also handles civil fraud, employment, general contract and insurance work. Important cases include Biggs v Sotnicks [2002] (s.32 limitation); Donsland Ltd v Van Hoogstraten [2002] (professional's implied authority); Quorum SA v Schramm [2002] (policy cover and depreciation valuation); BDG Roof Bond Ltd v Douglas and others [1999] (company/solicitors' negligence); Twinsectra Ltd v Yardley and others [2002] (constructive trusts/accessory liability); Mortgage Express v Newman v SIF [1999] [2001] (solicitors' dishonesty), Broadley v Guy Clapham [1993], Hopkins & MacKenzie [1995] (both concerning limitation); Interdesco S.A v Nullifire Ltd [1992] (registration of foreign judgement) and Morley v Heritage Plc [1993] (employment), Hipwood v Gloucestershire HA [1995] (Disclosure), Halifax plc v Gould & Swayne [1999] (solicitor's duties); Interdesco SA v Nullifire [1992] (registration of foreign judgments).
Prof. Memberships: Committee Member Professional Negligence Bar Association, Professional Conduct Committee, Commercial and Common Law Bar Association. Member of New South Wales Bar. The General Editor and contributing author to 'Jackson & Powell: Professional Liability Precedents'.
Career: Called to the Bar 1987 and joined Crown Office Row in 1988.
Personal: Born 1 September 1964. Educated at Wycombe Abbey School 1976-82 and Trinity College, Cambridge 1983-86 (MA). Leisure pursuits include sports, music and acting. Fluent in French and German.

CARSS-FRISK, Monica QC
Blackstone Chambers (Presiley Baxendale QC & Charles Flint QC), London
(020) 7583 1770
clerks@blackstonechambers.com
Recommended in Administrative & Public Law, Employment
Specialisation: Judicial review, employment law, with a particular emphasis on discrimination in both domestic and EU law, and the European Convention on Human Rights (particularly in the commercial context). Also handles general commercial contract disputes (including conflict of laws issues) and commercial fraud.
Prof. Memberships: Administrative Law Bar Association, Employment Lawyers Association, COMBAR.
Career: Called to the Bar 1985 and joined current chambers in 1986; member of the Treasury Solicitor's Supplementary Common Law Panel 1997-99; Junior Counsel to the Crown (A Panel) 1999-2001; Queen's Counsel 2001.
Publications: Contributor to 'Halsbury's Laws on Constitutional Law and Human Rights', 'Butterworths' Human Rights Law and Practice' and 'European Employment Law and the UK' (Sweet and Maxwell).
Personal: Educated at London University (LLB, 1983) and Oxford University (BCL, 1984). Speaks Swedish and has a working knowledge of Finnish. Member of Board of Interights.

CARTER, Peter QC
18 Red Lion Court (Anthony Arlidge QC), London
(020) 7520 6000
Peter.Carter@18rlc.co.uk
Recommended in Crime
Specialisation: Principal area of practice is criminal law, both prosecution and defence work. Particular focus on fraud cases, but also handles drugs cases, offences of violence and sexual offences. Acted in BCCI and DPR litigation and has defended in a number of murder cases. Also deals with human rights, local authority and pollution cases. Clients include CPS headquarters, SFO and Customs and Excise. Regular seminar speaker.
Prof. Memberships: Criminal Bar Association, South Eastern Circuit.
Career: Called to the Bar 1974 and joined current chambers in 1975. Secretary of Criminal Bar Association 1987-90. Took Silk 1995. Undertakes pro bono work, especially capital cases.
Publications: 'Offences of Violence' (with Ruth Harrison), Sweet & Maxwell.
Personal: Educated at University College, London 1970-73 (LLB). Governor of British Institute of Human Rights. Leisure pursuits include poetry, cricket and walking. Born 8 August 1952. Lives in Enfield, Middlesex.

CARTER-STEPHENSON, George QC
3 Gray's Inn Square (Rock Tansey QC), London
(020) 7520 5600
Recommended in Crime
Specialisation: Experience in the conduct of the most serious and complex criminal cases including murder, serious fraud, organised crime and drug trafficking. A specialist in the field of criminal defence.
Prof. Memberships: South Eastern Circuit, Criminal Bar Association.
Career: Called to the Bar in 1975 and joined current chambers in 1977.
Personal: Leeds University 1971-74 (LLB Hons).

CARUS, Roderick QC
9 St. John Street (John Hand QC), Manchester
(0161) 955 9000
Recommended in Crime
Specialisation: Fraud and related crime involving banking and accountancy disciplines but very experienced in all areas of criminal advocacy from corporate manslaughter to the Trade Marks Act 1994.
Career: 1964: Law degree University College Oxford. 1965: Postgraduate Diploma in Advanced Business Studies (specialising in Finance and Accountancy). 1966-70: Investment Controller for leading merchant bank. 1971: Called to the Bar (Gray's). 1986: Assistant Recorder. 1990: Queen's Counsel and Recorder.

CASEMENT, David
Exchange Chambers (David Turner QC & Bill Braithwaite QC & Henry Globe QC), Liverpool
(0151) 236 7747
casement@exchangechambers.co.uk
Recommended in Chancery, Commercial (Litigation)
Specialisation: Company and insolvency; commercial landlord and tenant; professional negligence; banking and finance; insurance; technology and construction in particular product liability disputes; sale of goods as well as intellectual property in particular media and entertainment law disputes.
Prof. Memberships: Chancery Bar Association; Northern Circuit Commercial Bar Association; Northern Chancery Bar Association.

LEADERS AT THE BAR

Career: BA (Oxon). Called to the Bar by Middle Temple (1992) and King's Inns, Dublin (1997).
Personal: Sports and interests include swimming, tennis, flying light aircraft and playing saxophone. Educated at Methodist College, Belfast and St. Hugh's College, Oxford.

CASEY, Mairin
St. Mary's Chambers Family Law Chambers (Nigel B Page), Nottingham
(0115) 950 3503
Recommended in Family

CASSEL, Timothy QC
5 Paper Buildings (Godfrey Carey QC & Jonathan Caplan QC), London
(020) 7583 6117
Recommended in Crime

CATCHPOLE, Stuart QC
39 Essex Street (Nigel Pleming QC), London
(020) 7832 1111
Recommended in Administrative & Public Law, Construction
Specialisation: Construction and civil engineering. Professional negligence. Public law. Commercial law. Cases: Counsel to the Ministry of Agriculture Fisheries and Food in the BSE Inquiry; counsel for Sheffield Wednesday FC at the Hillsborough public inquiry and inquests. Details of reported cases and experience in any of areas of practice can be provided on request.
Prof. Memberships: TecBar. Administrative Law Bar Association. Until being appointed to silk was Junior Counsel to the Crown ('A' Panel), appointed by the Attorney General in July 1999. Formerly a member of the Supplementary Panel of Treasury Counsel Common Law (appointed May 1992), transferred to the Treasury 'B' Panel on its creation in November 1998.
Career: Durham University 1983-86: First Class Honours Degree in Law (Maxwell Law Prize). Colchester Royal Grammar School 1975-82: A-Level History, English & Classical Civilisation (all Grade A). Judicial appointments: part-time legal member of the Proscribed Organisations Appeal Commission (31 July 2001).
Personal: Married. Six year old son and two daughters (aged three and six months). Speaks French. Enjoys theatre, cinema, wine.

CATTAN, Philip
28 St John St, Manchester
(0161) 834 8418
Recommended in Crime

CAUDLE, John
2 Bedford Row (William Clegg QC), London
(020) 7440 8888
Recommended in Crime

CAUSER, John
23 Essex Street (Michael Lawson QC), London
(020) 7413 0353
johncauser@23essexstreet.co.uk
Recommended in Crime

Specialisation: Commercial fraud and related areas of civil and criminal law including disqualification of directors, actions against the police etc. Recent clients include Lord Brocket and Roger Levitt. Legal and other disciplinary proceedings.
Prof. Memberships: Gambian Bar [1982]. Gibraltar Bar [1998].
Career: BA English Literature 1977. Called (Inner Temple) 1979.
Personal: Puzzle setting and solving, toy making, bicycling, photography, Babylonian cuneiform.

CAVANAGH, John QC
11 King's Bench Walk Chambers (Eldred Tabachnik QC & James Goudie QC), London
(020) 7632 8500
cavanagh@11kbw.com
Recommended in Education, Employment
Specialisation: Principal areas of practice are employment law, local government law and judicial review and commercial law. In employment law particular emphasis on discrimination and equal pay, TUPE, the European aspects of employment law, restraint of trade, wrongful dismissal, industrial disputes and large-scale redundancies. Has recently acted in Preston v Wolverhampton Healthcare (part-timers pensions); Gregory v Wallace (breach of contract); Jepson v Labour Party (all-women shortlists); Abbey Life v Tansell (disability discrimination); R v Portsmouth CC, ex p Coles (public procurement); Gregory v Portsmouth CC (malicious prosecution); Arthurworrey v Haringey (judicial review); Rugamer v Sony (disability discrimination).
Prof. Memberships: Treasurer of Employment Law Bar Association, Member of the Employment Lawyers Association, ALBA and COMBAR. Junior Counsel to the Crown – B Panel (1997-2001).
Career: Called 1985. Joined 11 King's Bench Walk 1985, QC 2001.
Publications: Contributor to Harvey, Tolley's 'Employment Law', Butterworths 'Local Government Law'.
Personal: Educated: Warwick School; New College, Oxford (MA); Clare College, Cambridge (LLM) and University of Illinois. Lives in Harpenden.

CAVENDER, David
One Essex Court (Lord Grabiner QC), London
(020) 7583 2000
Recommended in Commercial (Litigation)
Specialisation: Commercial litigation.
Prof. Memberships: COMBAR.
Career: Called to Bar and joined 1 Essex Court in 1993.
Personal: Educated at Kings College, London 1986-89 (LLB 1st class Hons). Born 1964.

CAWSON, Mark QC
Exchange Chambers (David Turner QC & Bill Braithwaite QC & Henry Globe QC), Manchester
(0161) 833 2722
cawsonqc@exchangechambers.co.uk
Recommended in Commercial (Litigation)
Specialisation: General chancery/commercial with emphasis on contentious insolvency and company work, commercial litigation and professional negligence. Recent cases include A.F Budge directors' disqualification (1996), Home Income Scheme litigation, Secretary of State for Trade and Industry v Ashcroft [1998] Ch 71, Barakot v Epiette [1998] 1BCLC 283, Lombard North Central v Brook [1999] BPIR 701, Cammel Laird Receivership (2001) and work in connection with the administrations of Phone People Plc (2001) and Enron (UK) (Ltd) (2001) and Chesterfield Football Club (2002)..
Prof. Memberships: Northern Circuit, Chancery Bar Association, Northern Chancery Bar Association, Northern Circuit Commercial Bar Association, Professional Negligence Bar Association.
Career: Wrekin College. Liverpool University. Called 1982 (Lincoln's Inn). Junior Counsel to Treasury (Charity/Manchester) 1990-2001. Recorder (2000). QC (2001).

CAYFORD, Philip QC
29 Bedford Row Chambers (Nicholas Francis QC), London
(020) 7404 1044
Recommended in Family

CHAISTY, Paul QC
40 King St, Manchester
(0161) 832 9082
pchaisty@40kingstreet.co.uk
Recommended in Chancery, Commercial (Litigation), Insolvency
Specialisation: Insolvency; administration; receivership; director disqualification; banking; commercial landlord and tenant; partnership; commercial litigation.
Prof. Memberships: Northern Chancery Bar Association, Chancery Bar.
Career: Recorder 2000, QC 2001. Recent reported cases CIS v Argyle Stores (Holdings) Ltd. [1996] AC 1, Re Sutton Times November 3 1999, Michael Gerson (Leasing) Ltd. v Wilkinson [2000] 3WLR 1645. Lincoln's Inn called 1982 (Hardwicke and Cassell Scholar).

CHAMBERS, Dominic
Maitland Chambers (Michael Lyndon-Stanford QC & Charles Aldous QC), London
(020) 7406 1200
dchambers@maitlandchambers.com
Recommended in Commercial (Litigation)
Specialisation: Principal area of practice is commercial law, including banking, conflicts, negotiable instruments, insurance and reinsurance, guarantees and indemnities. Also handles commercial fraud, partnership, restitution and professional negligence. Professional clients predominantly major City and international law firms and law firms in the Channel Islands. Extensive experience of cross-border litigation, and of international commercial arbitrations (as Counsel and as arbitrator).
Prof. Memberships: COMBAR, Chancery Bar Association, Professional Negligence Bar Association.
Career: Called to the Bar and joined 1 Hare Court in 1987. Joined the Chambers of Christopher Clarke QC in September 1997. Joined Maitland Chambers in July 2002.
Personal: Educated at Harrow School 1976-81 and King's College, London 1983-86. Born 28 February 1963. Lives in Surrey.

CHAPMAN, Vivian R
9 Stone Buildings (Michael Ashe QC), London
(020) 7404 5055
vchapman@9stonebuildings.com
Recommended in Chancery
Specialisation: Property litigation with particular interest in Law of Commons and Greens. Described as 'a barrister with great experience of this branch of the law' by Lord Hoffmann in R v Oxfordshire CC ex p Sunningwell PC [2000] 1 AC 335 at p. 348g. Recent reported cases: Fitzpatrick v Sterling Housing Association Ltd [2001] 1AC 27 (Landlord and Tenant); R v National Assembly of Wales ex p Robinson [2000] 80 P+CR 348 (rights of way); Bettison v Langton [2002] I AC 27 (Commons); Re Good, The Times, May 22 2002 (Costs; probate action) Price Meats Ltd v Barclays Bank plc, The Times 19 January 2000 (forgery of cheques); Fraser v Canterbury Diocesan Board of Finance [2001] Ch 669 (School Sites Act 1841).
Prof. Memberships: Lincoln's Inn: Middle Temple.

CHARLTON, Alex
4 Pump Court, London
(020) 7842 5555
acharlton@4pumpcourt.com
Recommended in Information Technology
Specialisation: Predominantly in commercial cases of a technical nature, information technology and computer law, construction and professional negligence. All cases that require cross-examination.
Prof. Memberships: Society for Computers & Law, Professional Negligence Bar Association, London Common Law & Commercial Bar Association, TECBAR, COMBAR.
Career: Called to the Bar 1983.
Publications: Contributing editor to 'Professional Negligence & Liability' published by LLP in 2000; co-author of Chapter 18 'Computer Consultants'.
Personal: Born 13 March 1958. Education: Tonbridge School; University of St Andrews; City University. Leisure interests: sailing, rugby, golf and tennis. Family details: Married with young children.

CHARLWOOD, Spike
4 Paper Buildings (Jean Ritchie QC), London
(020) 7353 3366
spike.charlwood@4paperbuildings.com

LEADERS AT THE BAR

Recommended in Professional Negligence
Specialisation: Main areas of practice: professional negligence (especially claims against solicitors, barristers, surveyors, valuers, accountants and brokers) and insurance law (including recovery actions and policy disputes). Reported cases: Farley v Skinner [2001] 3 WLR 899, HL; Brocklesby v Armitage & Guest [2001] 1 All ER 172, CA; UCB v Carr [2000] Lloyd's Rep PN 754, QBD; Abbey National v Sayer Moore [1999] EGCS 114, ChD; Nationwide v Various Solicitors [1999] Lloyd's Rep PN 241, ChD; Miller v Eyo [1998] NPC 95, CA; City Electrical Factors v Hardingham [1996] BPIR 541, ChD. He has experience of managed litigation (claims by Nationwide and Abbey National) and large-scale mediation and has lectured widely on professional negligence.
Prof. Memberships: Professional Negligence Bar Association; London Common Law and Commercial Bar Association.
Career: Called to the Bar 1994; supervisor in Tort, Queens' College, Cambridge 1993-95.
Publications: 'Professional Negligence and Liability' (LLP, 2000): assistant editor and joint author of the chapter on barristers' negligence; 'Lloyds Law Reports: Professional Negligence', contributing editor; 'Cordery on Solicitors' (9th edition, looseleaf): contributing editor; articles in the 'Solicitors' Journal' on Platform Home Loans and Twinsectra.
Personal: Education: Queens' College, Cambridge (MA (Hons) 1st Class). Leisure interests include hill walking, travel, wine, reading.

CHARMAN, Andrew
St Philips Chambers (John Randall QC), Birmingham
(0121) 246 7000
acharman@st-philips.co.uk
Recommended in Chancery, Commercial (Litigation)
Specialisation: Company law, commercial law, insolvency, financial services, franchising, professional negligence, real property, trusts, wills and probate, litigation, advisory and drafting.
Prof. Memberships: Member of the Chancery Bar Association and the Midland Chancery and Commercial Bar Association. Member of the Chartered Institute of Arbitrators.
Career: Educated at Imberhorne School, East Grinstead and Clare College, Cambridge. Worked as a researcher at The House of Commons then articles with *Freshfields* in London and Tokyo followed by practice as a solicitor in *Freshfields*' corporate department (company and financing transactions).

CHAWLA, Mukul QC
9-12 Bell Yard (D Anthony Evans QC), London
(020) 7400 1800
mchawlaqc@aol.com
Recommended in Crime, Fraud

Specialisation: Defending and prosecuting criminal cases particularly commercial fraud, Customs and Excise prosecutions and cases involving restraint and confiscation issues. Practice also covers general crime and in particular defending Police Officers in criminal and disciplinary proceedings. Recently acted for a police officer charged with the unlawful killing of Christopher Alder. Has previously acted (as junior) for the police officers charged in relation to the 'Guildford Four', the 'Birmingham Six' and officers charged with the unlawful killings of Joy Gardner and Richard O'Brien. Currently instructed to prosecute fraud cases on behalf of the Serious Fraud Office, Customs and Excise and the Crown Prosecution Service and to defend in, inter alia, the Jubilee Line Extension corruption and fraud trial.
Prof. Memberships: Criminal Bar Association.
Career: Called 1983. Standing counsel to HM Customs and Excise 1996-2001.
Personal: Born 31 May 1961. Educated at Eton College and University College, London.

CHERRYMAN, John QC
4 Breams Buildings (Christopher Lockhart-Mummery QC), London
(020) 7430 1221
Recommended in Property Litigation
Specialisation: Moved from Lincolns Inn to Breams Buildings in 1992 to concentrate on property related litigation and advice, including mining, professional negligence, mortgage securities, contaminated land and rating as well as mainstream landlord and tenant and vendor and purchaser work. A Bencher of Grays Inn and a member of the Chancery Bar and Property Bar Associations. Recent cases include TSB Bank v Camfield 1995 CA and Dunbar Bank v Nadeem 1998 CA (variants of O'Brien); Bentley v Gaisford 1996 CA (solicitors undertaking); Mannai Investment Co. v Eagle Star 1997 HL (validity of break notice); Shimizu (UK) v Westminster City Council 1997 HL (listed building: demolition or alteration); Attwell v Michael Perry & Co 1998 V-C (barristers immunity from suit for alleged negligence in property litigation). Sabah Foundation v Dat Syed Kechik 1999 Borneo H Ct and 2001 CA of Malaysia (breaches of fiduciary duty); Prudential Assurance v Eden Restaurants 1999 CA (curative effect of registration) SCB v PNSC 2002 HL (fraud) Morrells of Oxford v Oxford Utd FC 2000 CA (LPA 1925, s 79); Broderick v Alcoa of Jamaica 2000 PC (Leisbosch distinguished); Holding & Barnes plc v Hill House Hammond 2000 ChD, 2001 CA (construction of repairing obligation); Jury's Inn Management v Amec Investments 2001 Ch.D. (equitable damages).

CHILD, John
Wilberforce Chambers (Edward Nugee QC), London
(020) 7306 0102
jchild@wilberforce.co.uk
Recommended in Chancery
Specialisation: Heavy trust work – advice and drafting and some litigation. In part this is private client work dealing with family trusts and landed estates. The remaining part is commercial trust work, mostly relating to the Society of Lloyd's.
Prof. Memberships: Chancery Bar Association; Revenue Bar Association. Books – main contributor vol 19 (Sale of land) Encyclopaedia of Forms and Precedents (4th edn). Forms of accumulation and maintenance Settlements for Encyclopaedia of Forms and Precedents (5th edn) Vol 40 (2002 reissue).
Career: Firsts in Law at University of Southampton and Sidney Sussex College Cambridge. BA Scholar Sidney Sussex College. Droop Scholar and Tancred Common Law Student, Hon Soc of Lincoln's Inn. Supervisor in Law at Sidney Sussex and other Cambridge colleges 1966-78.

CHIPPINDALL, Adam
Guildhall Chambers (Adrian Palmer QC), Bristol
(0117) 930 9000
Recommended in Personal Injury

CHIVERS, David QC
Erskine Chambers (Robin Potts QC), London
(020) 7242 5532
clerks@erskine-chambers.co.uk
Recommended in Commercial (Litigation), Company, Insolvency
Specialisation: Principal area of practice is company law, including corporate insolvency.
Prof. Memberships: Chancery Bar Association, COMBAR, Insolvency Lawyers Association.
Career: Called to the Bar 1983 and joined *Erskine Chambers* 1984.
Publications: Contributor to 'Gore-Brown on Companies', 'Practice and Procedure in the Companies Court' and 'Co-Operatives That Work'.
Personal: Born 1960. Educated at Downing College, Cambridge 1979-82.

CHOO CHOY, Alain
One Essex Court (Lord Grabiner QC), London
(020) 7583 2000
achoochoy@oeclaw.co.uk
Recommended in Commercial (Litigation)
Specialisation: Broad range of commercial litigation including banking and financial services. Recent cases include: Sumitomo Corporation v Credit Lyonnais Rouse ltd (first case before the Commercial Court concerning the privileged nature of foreign language translations obtained for litigious purposes in a US$250 million claim); Montrod ltd v Grundkoetter (first case before the Commercial Court regarding whether there is a 'nullity' exception to payment against documents under letters of credit), both of which are due to be heard in the Court of Appeal in the second half of 2001 and also acting for Railtrack in connection with disputes with train companies resulting from the Hatfield crash.
Prof. Memberships: Member of COMBAR.
Career: LLB Hons (Queen Mary College, University of London).
Personal: Married with two children, enjoys classical music, badminton and also table tennis in which he appeared in the 1988 Seoul Olympics.

CHOUDHURY, Akhlaq
11 King's Bench Walk Chambers (Eldred Tabachnik QC & James Goudie QC), London
(020) 7632 8500
choudhury@11kbw.com
Recommended in Employment
Specialisation: Employment and public/administrative law including human rights. Recently reported cases: Wincanton v Cranny [2000] IRLR 716, CA (restrictive covenants); Kapfunde v Abbey National [1999] ICR 1, CA (duty of care owed by company doctor).
Prof. Memberships: ELBA, ALBA.
Career: Called 1992.
Publications: Tolley's 'Employment Handbook' (1996-date), contributor. Butterworths 'Local Government Law', contributor. 'Local Authorities and The Human Rights Act', contributor.
Personal: BSc Hons, Physics (Glasgow); LLB Hons (1st Class) (London). Governor of Tower Hamlets FE College.

CHRISTIE, Richard
2 Pump Court (Philip Singer QC), London
(020) 7353 5597
rchristie@2pumpcourt.co.uk
Recommended in Crime
Specialisation: All areas of criminal work but especially fraud and cases requiring substantial client care. Also general common law and family work. (i) R v Johnson (Aldin) [1995] 2 Cr. App. R. I (Albi and severance); (ii) Martin v Watson [1994] Q.B.425 and [1995] A.C.74 (malicious prosecution); (iii) R v Bosson [1999] Crim. L.R. 596 (Handling/theft: Multiple Appropriations); (iv) R v Mian [1997] (£1.5million cannabis importation by high ranking Pakistani, said to have been framed by Pakistani Regime); (v) R v Parr [1997] (Money laundering following cross-jurisdictional Eurobond fraud); (vi) R v Phipps [1998] (Murder: educationally subnormal defendant, cut-throat defences); (vii) R v Butler [1999] (Leading junior – major local government corruption fraud: stayed for abuse of process); (viii) R v Alkadiki [1999] ($3.5 million international banking fraud: stayed for abuse of process); (ix) R v Robinson [2000] (Paedophile family: allegations of rape etc); R v Rodrigues [2001] (Leading Junior – banking/computer fraud: Stayed for abuse of process). R v Wheeler

LEADERS AT THE BAR

[2001] (Murder – drugs gang killing). R v Stapleton [2001-02] (£12m VAT carousel fraud and confiscation proceedings). R v Smith [2001-02] (Murder – appeal involving new evidence). CC of Essex v R [2001] sex offender order: admin. court: re CC's authorisation of the court process. R v Dixon [2002] (assault: automatism brought on by a combination of ADHD, bipolar mood disorder and wrongly administered prescription drugs).
Career: Clifton College; Manchester University; Touche Ross & Co (Accountants).
Personal: Cinema and reading. Wife (Solicitor) and three children.

CHRUSZCZ, Charles
Exchange Chambers (David Turner QC & Bill Braithwaite QC & Henry Globe QC), Manchester
(0161) 833 2722
Recommended in Crime

CHUDLEIGH, Louise
Old Square Chambers (John Hendy QC), London
(020) 7269 0300
chudleigh@oldsquarechambers.co.uk
Recommended in Employment
Specialisation: Principal area of practice is employment law including all areas of discrimination, equal pay, internal disciplinary disputes, all post termination difficulties including unfair and wrongful dismissal and injunctive proceedings related to confidential information and restrictive covenants. Also practices in sports law, particularly disciplinary and contractual disputes.
Prof. Memberships: Employment Lawyers Association; Industrial Law Society. Employment Law Bar Association.
Career: Called to the Bar 1987 (England and Wales), 1989 (Bermuda); member of Old Square Chambers since 1988; Honorary lecturer in Labour Law at University of Kent at Canterbury. Part-time Employment Tribunal Chairman.

CIUMEI, Charles
Essex Court Chambers (Gordon Pollock QC), London
(020) 7813 8000
Recommended in Employment
Specialisation: All areas of employment law including sex, race and disability discrimination, transfers of undertakings (TUPE), industrial relations/strikes, breach of confidence and restrictive covenants. Recent cases include Morse v Wiltshire County Council (disability discrimination); Credit Suisse v Padiachy (restrictive covenants/TUPE); Wandsworth v D'Silva (collective agreements/terms of employment); UCLH v UNISON (strike action); Hall v Woolston Hall Leisure Ltd (discrimination/illegal contracts).

CLARE, Michael
Octagon House Chambers (Guy Ayers & Andrew Lindquist), Norwich
(01603) 623186
Recommended in Crime

CLARK, Andrew
8 King St (Gerard McDermott QC), Manchester
(0161) 834 9560
andrew.clark@8ks.co.uk
Recommended in Chancery
Specialisation: Chancery including real property litigation, business tenancies, insolvency, partnership, wills and inheritance. Also commercial and employment work.
Prof. Memberships: Northern Chancery Bar Association. NCCBA.
Career: Admitted as Solicitor: 1998. Called to Bar: 1994.
Personal: New College, Oxford. Keen film enthusiast; walking; travelling.

CLARK, Christopher Harvey QC
Pump Court Chambers (Christopher Harvey Clark QC), London
(020) 7353 0711
clerks@3pumpcourt.com
Recommended in Church
Specialisation: Western Circuit common law practice in both criminal and civil work. Particular experience in complex fraud cases, and other serious criminal matters. Prosecuting/defending regularly in murder trials, both on and off Circuit.
Prof. Memberships: Chancellor of the Diocese of Winchester since 1993. Deputy Chancellor of the Dioceses of Salisbury, Portsmouth and Chichester. Member of the Ecclesiastical Judges Association Standing Committee.
Career: Called 1969. Recorder of the Crown Court since 1986 Q.C. 1989. Bencher of Gray's Inn. 2001, Head of Chambers.
Personal: Church of England Reader. Extensive social and sporting interests, including golf and amateur dramatics.

CLARK, Fiona
8 New Square (Mark Platts-Mills QC), London
(020) 7405 4321
clerks@8newsquare.co.uk
Recommended in Intellectual Property
Specialisation: Barrister specialising in all aspects of intellectual property law including related contractual and EC matters, breach of confidence and trade libel. Has a particular interest in copyright and designs (both registered and unregistered). Trademarks and service marks are a particular speciality with extensive experience of product branding and media and entertainment law. For comprehensive CV and list of recent cases, visit our website at www.8newsquare.co.uk.
Prof. Memberships: Chancery Bar Association; Intellectual Property Bar Association (IPBA); The Intellectual Property Lawyers Organisation (TIPLO).
Career: Called 1982.
Publications: 'Encyclopedia of United Kingdom and European Patent Law' (senior editor).
Personal: Educated at Trinity College, Cambridge, MA.

CLARK, Wayne
Falcon Chambers (Jonathan Gaunt QC & Kim Lewison QC), London
(020) 7353 2484
Recommended in Property Litigation
Specialisation: Property litigation, including commercial leases, vendor and purchaser disputes, easements, restrictive covenants, mortgages and property related professional negligence.
Prof. Memberships: Chancery Bar Association, COMBAR.
Career: LLB (Lon), BCL (Oxon), former lecturer in law at QMC, London University. Contributor to Halsbury's Laws of England, Vol 27 (i), 4th edn, 'Landlord and Tenant'. Contributor to Hill and Redman, 'Law of Landlord and Tenant', Standing Counsel (civil) to Attorney General; co-Author, 'Renewal of Business Tenancies Law Practice', 2nd edn (Sweet & Maxwell 2002); co-author 'Tenant's Rights of First Refusal' (2001) (Butterworths); co-ordinating editor and contributor, Fisher and Lightwood 'Law of Morgage' (2001) (Butterworths).
Personal: Keen chess player.

CLARKE, Andrew QC
Littleton Chambers (Michel Kallipetis QC), London
(020) 7797 8600
Recommended in Employment
Specialisation: Experienced commercial and employment lawyer, having appeared in these areas before all relevant courts and tribunals. Particular specialism in disputes relating to garden leave, restrictive covenants and confidential information. Also handles company law and sport related matters, both relating to employment (including directors' duties) and generally. Appeared in numerous high profile cases on individual employment rights (wrongful dismissal, bonus issues, unfair dismissal and TUPE cases), sex and race discrimination, restrictive covenants and garden leave injunctions (including Bruce v Crystal Place). Clients include major UK companies, solicitors' firms and senior employees, as well as leading sporting bodies, clubs and players.
Prof. Memberships: Employment Law Bar Association; Employment Lawyers Association; COMBAR (Committee Member).
Career: Called to the Bar 1980, QC 1997, joined Littleton Chambers in 1981.
Personal: Educated at Crewe County Grammar School, King's College London 1974-77 (LL.B) and Lincoln College, Oxford 1977-79 (BCL). Leisure pursuits include playing and watching cricket and football. Lives in Cheshunt. Born 23 August 1956.

CLARKE, Elizabeth
Queen Elizabeth Building (Florence Baron QC), London
(020) 7797 7837
Recommended in Family

CLARKE, Gerard
Blackstone Chambers (Presiley Baxendale QC & Charles Flint QC), London
(020) 7583 1770
clerks@blackstonechambers.com
Recommended in Employment
Specialisation: Public, employment, broadcasting, sports, and media law. Member of the Attorney General's A Panel of Counsel. Interesting cases include Premier League v Professional Footballers Association (2001); R v Two Police Forces ex p A ('Times' October 2000); Allen & Others v AMCO [2000] IRLR; R v North West Lancs; Health Authority ex p A,B,G 1999 TLR, Scully UK v Lee 1998 IRLR, R v Rhonda Cynon Taf DC ex p Evans [1999]; Wallace v Gregory 1998 IRLR, R v Riverside Mental Health NHS Trust ex p London [1999] 3 WLR, Holly v Smyth 1998 IWLR, R v Cobham Hall School ex p G [1998] ELR, Credit Suisse v Armstrong [1996] IRLR 450, Spring v Guardian Assurance PLC [1995] 2 AC 296 and Meade Hill v British Council [1995] 1CR 847.
Prof. Memberships: Employment Lawyers' Association, Employment Law Bar Association, Administrative Law Bar Association.
Career: Called to the Bar 1986.
Publications: Author of TUPE section in 'New Law Online Employment Law Service'.
Personal: Born 1962. Educated in Solihull and at Wadham College, Oxford (MA).

CLARKE, Nicholas
9 St. John Street (John Hand QC), Manchester
(0161) 955 9000
clerks@9stjohnstreet.co.uk
Recommended in Crime
Specialisation: Defending cases of homicide; drug importation, production and distribution; sexual and physical abuse of children. Particular interest in cases with medical or psychiatric background and has extensive experience cross-examining expert witnesses including pathologists, neuroradiologists and paediatric specialists in various disciplines. Defended the first trial in this country where the Crown relied solely on an earprint identification and also the first murder trial to rely on earprints. Recently defended a consultant orthopaedic surgeon charged with indecently assaulting patients over 25 years.
Prof. Memberships: Criminal Bar Association, Northern Circuit.
Career: Sheffield University, LLB. Called to the Bar, 1981. Assistant Recorder, 1999. Recorder 2000.
Personal: Married, two children. Chairman 3rd Hazel Grove Scout Group. Enjoys snooker, football and cycling.

CLARKSON, Patrick QC
Eldon Chambers (Patrick Clarkson QC & William Hicks QC), London
(020) 7583 1355
clerks@eldonchambers.com

LEADERS AT THE BAR

Recommended in Planning
Specialisation: Planning, local government, environmental and Parliamentary.
Prof. Memberships: Planning & Environmental Bar Association.
Career: Called 1972, Silk 1991, Recorder 1996.

CLAYTON, Richard QC
39 Essex Street (Nigel Pleming QC), London
(020) 7832 1111
Recommended in Administrative & Public Law
Specialisation: Principal areas of practice are public law and human rights/civil liberties. Public law covers education, environmental, health care, regulatory and disciplinary matters, local government law and prisoners' rights. (Visiting Fellow, Centre for Public Law, University of Cambridge). Also handles employment law (both individual and collective), discrimination law, European law and civil actions against the police. Acted in R (Greenfield) v Home Secretary [2002] 1 WLR 545 (CA-human rights); Rossiter v Pendragon The Times, 28 May 2002 (CA-TUPE); R(Green) v Police Complaints Authority, The Times, 6 May 2002 (CA- human rights); Attorney General v Blake [2001] AC 268 (HL-confiscation of royalties); Derby Specialist Engineering v Burton [2001] 2 All ER 840 (race discrimination); R(Wirral Health Authority) v Mental Health Review Tribunal The Times, 26th November 2001 (CA-mental health); R(Lemonland) v Hackney LBC (2001) LGR 555 (land disposal); R v NE Devon Health Authority ex p Bowhey [2001] ACD 159 (closure of residential care home); R(Addinell) v Sheffield City Council [2001] ACD 331 (human rights); R v Broadcasting Standards Commission ex p BBC [2000] 3 WLR 1327 (privacy); R v Wirral ex p B (2001) 1 LGR 1 (special educational needs); R v CICA ex p Leatherhead, The Times 12 October 2000; RICS v Fryer The Times, 17 May 2000 (CA) R v School Adjudicator ex p Wirral [2000] ELR 620 (school admissions); Saga Oil v Bourgeois EAT June 2000 (discrimination claim settled £1.8m); R v Swale BC ex p Marchant 1 FLR 1087 (CA-housing benefit); R v Lincolnshire Crown Court ex p Jude [1998] 1 WLR 24; Steward-Brady v United Kingdom (1998) 27 EHRR CD 284 (European Convention) and R v Press Complaints Commission, ex p Stewart-Brady (1997) 9 Admin LR 274 (privacy rights); R v Northamptonshire County Council ex p W [1998] ELR 314 (school expulsion); Bamber v United Kingdom [1998] EHRLR 110 (European Convention); R v Chief Constable of West Midlands Police ex p Wiley [1995] 1 AC 274 (public interest immunity). Clients include local authorities, PLCs, pressure groups and private individuals.
Prof. Memberships: Administrative Law Bar Association (Committee since 1996); Employment Law Bar Association; Liberty.
Career: Called to Bar 1977; QC 2002; South Islington Law Centre 1980/82; Osler Hoskin Harcourt (Toronto) 1983; Returned to practice 1984; joined 39 Essex Street, 2001.
Publications: Co-author 'Law of Human Rights' Oxford University Press (2000); 'Judicial Review Procedure' (Wiley) (2nd edition 1997); 'Civil Actions against the Police' (Sweet & Maxwell). Author of 'Practice and Procedure at Industrial Tribunals' (LAG) (1986).
Personal: Educated New College, Oxford. Leisure pursuits include reading, cinema, theatre and travel. Born 25 May 1954. Lives in London.

CLEGG, William QC
2 Bedford Row (William Clegg QC), London
(020) 7440 8888
wclegg@2bedfordrow.co.uk
Recommended in Crime, Fraud
Specialisation: Specialist in defending cases of alleged fraud. Cases include Brent Walker PLC; Alliance Resources PLC; Bute Mining PLC; R v Smith (£100m bank fraud); R v Khan (income tax fraud); R v Smithson (The Arrows fraud); R v De Vandiere (VAT fraud); R v Alder (international bank fraud); R v Morley (fraudulent trading); R v Hales (solicitors legal aid fraud). Cases of a more general nature include Serafinowicz (war crimes); R v Stone (Chillingden murders); R v Wardell (Nuneaton Building Society murder); R v Stagg (Wimbledon Common murder); R v Varathadasan (Tamil Tigers); R v McMahon (UDA terrorists); R v Sawoniuk (war crimes); Prosecutor v Jelisic (war crimes the Hague); Prosecutor v Tadic (war crimes, The Hague); R v Duckenfield (Hillsborough Disaster). Has also been instructed in a lengthy public enquiry by the Medical Protection Society and many cases in the Court of Appeal Criminal Division and Divisional Court. Was a member of the standing committee of Justice on fraud trials and prepared submissions to the Fraud Trials Committee chaired by Roskill (HMSO 1986).
Prof. Memberships: Criminal Bar Association (Committee Members); South Eastern Circuit (Committee Member). Chairman Essex Bar Mess, 1997-2000.
Career: Called to the Bar 1972 and joined present chambers in 1973. Took silk 1991. Appointed Recorder 1992. Head of chambers 1995.
Personal: Educated at Bristol University (LLB). Leisure pursuits include squash, cricket and wine. Born 5 September 1949.

CLIFFORD, James
Maitland Chambers (Michael Lyndon-Stanford QC & Charles Aldous QC), London
(020) 7406 1200
jclifford@maitlandchambers.com
Recommended in Pensions
Specialisation: Specialises in pensions and trusts and has general commercial chancery litigation practice. Reported cases handled include Barclays Bank v Holmes, ITS v Rowe, Polly Peck v Henry, Re Scientific Investment Pension Plan, Edge v The Pensions Ombudsman, Hood Sailmakers Ltd v Axford, Miller v Scorey, Process Developments Ltd v Hogg, Coloroll Pension Trustees Limited v Russell, Thrells Ltd v Lomas Nestle v National Westminster Bank, LRT v Hatt, Mettoy Pensions Trustees v Evans.
Prof. Memberships: Association of Pension Lawyers, COMBAR and the Chancery Bar Association.
Career: Called to the Bar in 1984.
Publications: Contributor to 'Trust Law International', 'British Pensions Lawyer', and author of 'Pensions Title', 'Atkins Court Forms'.
Personal: Educated at Oxford University.

CLIMIE, Stephen
35 Essex Street (Christopher Wilson-Smith QC), London
(020) 7353 6381
rsclimie@msn.com
Recommended in Health & Safety
Specialisation: Corporate crime (especially health and safety, manslaughter by negligence and serious fraud); clinical negligence; personal injury. His experience as an advocate and attention to detailed preparation have enabled him to command instructions from prosecuting authorities and defendants' representatives alike, including CPS Policy Directorate, Serious Fraud Office, Health and Safety Executive and HM Customs and Excise. In civil jurisdictions he has a similar combination of claimant and defendant work. Within 35 Essex Street he is a leading junior in a strong Crime Work Group led by C Wilson-Smith QC, Philip Mott QC and Richard Lissack QC. He is always receptive to group preparation and expects to involve both professional and lay clients throughout the decision making processes leading to trial. Recent cases include Crime: Gross Negligence Manslaughter, CPS Policy Directorate, Advice re Hatfield Rail Crash; R v Great Western Trains (Southall Rail Crash); R v IMCO Plastics and Lewis (legionnaires disease outbreak): Foot Anstey Sargent: R v De Vey & others (death at fairground) Health and Safety: HSE: R v Costain & Kavaerner (Avonmouth gantry collapse); R v Junttan Oy (pile driver death); R v Raven Cornwall & others (first major CDM Regulations prosecution); R v Magnox plc Fraud: SFO: R v Young & others (Morgan Grenfell Fraud £300m). Recent professional lectures include: corporate manslaughter and directors' responsibilities: Electricity Association Health and Safety Conference 2001. Fitness to plead and be tried: Serious Fraud Office Prosecutors Forum 2002.
Career: Called Lincoln's Inn 1982, Recorder 1998 onwards, Member Western Circuit, Member AVMA, 35 Essex Street Treasurer.

CLOSE, Douglas
Serle Court (Lord Neill of Bladen QC), London
(020) 7242 6105
clerks@serlecourt.co.uk
Recommended in Chancery
Specialisation: General commercial chancery litigation, in particular commercial fraud and international trust litigation. Cases include: The Thyssen-Bornemisza litigation in Bermuda, Don King Productions Inc v Frank Warren & Ors, the Palumbo litigation and the Wahr-Hansen litigation in the Cayman Islands.
Prof. Memberships: Chancery Bar Association, COMBAR.
Career: Called 1991. Pupil to Michael Briggs QC and Frank Hinks QC.
Personal: Born 1966. Educated at Berkhamsted School; Jesus College, Oxford (MA, BCL). Interests include theatre, restaurants, abstract art.

COBB, Stephen
One Garden Court Family Law Chambers (Eleanor F Platt QC & Alison Ball QC), London
(020) 7797 7900
stephen.cobb@onegardencourt.co.uk
Recommended in Family
Specialisation: Family law, including public and private law aspects of the Children Act 1989; adoption; child abduction (convention and non-convention) and children cases with an international element including 'leave to remove'; applications with Human Rights Act 1998 element; matrimonial finance, judicial review (mainly family law related); applications/appeals under Part X Children Act 1989 and Care Standards Act 2000.
Prof. Memberships: FLBA; Elected Committee member FLBA.
Career: Called to the Bar in 1985.
Publications: General Editor of 'Essential Family Practice 2001' (Butterworths).
Personal: Winchester College. Liverpool University (LLB Hons 1984). Born 12 April 1962. Lives in London. Married, three children.

COBURN, Michael
20 Essex Street (Iain Milligan QC), London
(020) 7842 1200
clerks@20essexst.com
Recommended in Shipping
Specialisation: Commercial law, including in particular shipping, international sale of goods and insurance and reinsurance. Recent reported cases include 'Grecia Express' Stive Shipping v Hellenic Mutual War Risks [2002] EWHC 203; 'ELPA' [2001] 2 Lloyd's Rep 596 Charterparty; 'Baltic Flame' [2001] 2 Lloyds Rep 203.

LEADERS AT THE BAR

Career: Called 1990.
Personal: Educated at Charterhouse; Worcester College, Oxford; City University.

COE, Rosalind
Ropewalk Chambers (Ian McLaren QC), Nottingham
(0115) 947 2581
clerks@ropewalk.co.uk
Recommended in Personal Injury
Specialisation: Personal injury; clinical negligence; industrial disease; solicitor's negligence. Currently junior Counsel for Claimants in cases arising from physical and sexual abuse in childrens' homes in the North West of England and Cambridgeshire. Notable cases include Lister v Hesley Hall Limited [2001] UKHL 22 [2001] 2 WLR 1311 (vicarious liability).
Prof. Memberships: Personal Injuries Bar Association; Nottinghamshire Medico-Legal Society.
Career: Called 1983. Circuit Junior (Midland and Oxford Circuit) 1991-92.
Personal: Family, friends and saxaphone.

COGHLAN, Terence QC
1 Crown Office Row (Robert Seabrook QC), London
(020) 7797 7500
terence.coghlan@1cor.com
Recommended in Clinical Negligence
Specialisation: Covers all aspects of medical work including medical negligence. Has appeared for both plaintiffs and defendants in numerous medical negligence actions and arbitrations as well as regularly appearing in the GMC, GDC and other disciplinary bodies. Represented all the health authorities involved in the "Myodil" litigation and the defendant in Bolitho v City & Hackney HA (House of Lords). Clients have included the Medical Defence Union, Medical Protection Society and leading medical negligence solicitors. Has lectured and written on personal injury and medical negligence matters and has appeared on television. Has acted as mediator on CA Panel and privately. President, Mental Health Review Tribunal.
Prof. Memberships: Professional Negligence Bar Association.
Career: Called in 1968. Recorder of the Crown Court 1989. QC 1993.
Personal: Education: New College, Oxford (BA, MA).

COGLEY, Stephen
Merchant Chambers (David Berkley QC), Manchester
(0161) 839 7070
Recommended in Commercial (Litigation)
Specialisation: Banking, commercial law, consumer credit, finance, company, partnership, insolvency, sale of goods, professional negligence. Various reported cases in the fields of insolvency, shareholder disputes, banking, consumer credit/licensing and contract. Instructed frequently in banking and finance leasing cases by banks and finance houses and building societies. Clients include most of the major banks, several major finance houses. Acts in company disputes/shareholder disputes. Has been involved in many high profile cases involving prominent individuals. Has acted on behalf of academics, UK Rich List individuals, Barristers Chambers and football clubs (for and against). Is frequently instructed on behalf of solicitors in personal matters. Lectures solicitors for the Law Society – in commercial matters and directors' duties and director disqualification. Lives in Lancashire and Scotland.
Prof. Memberships: Founder member of Northern Circuit Commercial Bar Association. Member of COMBAR and the Northern Chancery Bar Association.
Career: Called to the bar in 1984.
Publications: Has appeared in Chambers Guide to the Legal Profession – consistently ranked as a leading barrister in the field of Commercial Law (six consecutive years).
Personal: Aged 41 years. Educated at Spalding and Ripon Grammar Schools and Newcastle University. Hobbies: fell running, mountaineering, rock climbing and anything with a hint of danger.

COHEN, Edward
11 Stone Buildings (Murray Rosen QC), London
(020) 7831 6381
Recommended in Chancery
Specialisation: He practises in commercial and Chancery litigation and advisory work, including contract, sale of goods, banking, professional negligence, partnership, libel, media and entertainment, real property, company and insolvency, commercial fraud, insurance, arbitration, intellectual property, telecoms and e-commerce. An experienced practitioner and forceful advocate, he has appeared in reported decisions ranging from the House of Lords through the Court of Appeal and courts of first instance involving diverse legal issues. His wide-ranging practice enables him to advise and act in individual cases involving simultaneously different areas of law. He is known for his meticulous approach towards preparation, paperwork and advocacy and for his dedicated support of Newcastle United FC.

COHEN, Jonathan QC
4 Paper Buildings (Lionel Swift QC), London
(020) 7583 0816
jc@4pb.com
Recommended in Family
Specialisation: Practice encompasses all areas of family law, in particular matrimonial finance, professional negligence arising out of family law matters and childcare. Recent cases include G v G (care proceedings: split trials) [2001] 1 FLR 872 and (Standard of proof) [2001] 1 FCR 97; Westbury v Sampson (professional negligence in ancillary relief proceedings) [2002] 1 FLR 166; Piglowska (House of Lords: ancillary relief [1999] 2 FLR 763); N v N (ante nuptial contract: enforceability [1999] 2 FLR 745; and C v C [1997] 2 FLR 26 (financial provision: short marriage).
Prof. Memberships: Family Law Bar Association; Professional Negligence Bar Association.
Career: Called to the Bar 1974. Recorder and Silk 1997. Member, Mental Health Review Tribunal 2000.
Publications: Contributing editor of family law chapters in 5th edition of 'Foskett on Compromise' (2002).
Personal: School Governor.

COHEN, Lawrence QC
24 Old Buildings (Martin Mann QC & Alan Steinfeld QC), London
(020) 7404 0946
Recommended in Company, Fraud, Insolvency

COHEN, Raphael
Mercury Chambers (Benjamin Nolan QC), Leeds
(0113) 234 2265
Recommended in Family
Specialisation: Specialist in matrimonial property work. Involved in cases with substantial assets and with a commercial bias including company accounts and contracts.
Career: Called to the Bar in 1981. A founder member of Mercury Chambers which is a specialist civil and commercial set.

COLE, Edward
Falcon Chambers (Jonathan Gaunt QC & Kim Lewison QC), London
(020) 7353 2484
cole@falcon-chambers.com
Recommended in Property Litigation
Specialisation: Real property.
Prof. Memberships: Gray's Inn .
Career: Called to the Bar in 1980.
Personal: Contributor to 'Megarry on the Rents Act', 11th edn; specialist editor Hill & Redman 'Law of Landlord and Tenant'. Contributor Halsbury's Laws, vol 27, title 'Landlord and Tenant'. Atkin's Court Forms: title 'Agriculture'.

COLLENDER, Andrew QC
2 Temple Gardens (Dermod O'Brien QC), London
(020) 7822 1200
acollender@2templegardens.co.uk
Recommended in Personal Injury
Specialisation: Specialises in serious personal injury and clinical negligence cases and disaster litigation, appearing for both claimants and defendants. Has in-depth experience of the conduct of substantial and multi-party actions especially in cases involving recognisable psychiatric injury caused (for example) by stress or witnessing shocking events, industrially caused diseases, musculo-skeletal disorders, and vicarious liability for sexual abuse. Recent important cases include Frost v South Yorkshire Police [1999] (H of Ls); Lister v Hesley Hall [2001] (H of Ls); Hatton v Sutherland [2002] C of A.
Prof. Memberships: London Common Law Bar Association. Professional Negligence Bar Association. Personal Injuries Bar Association.
Career: University of Bristol – LLB (Hons) 1968. Called Lincoln's Inn July 1969. Silk April 1991. Recorder January 1993. Deputy High Court Judge 1998. Bencher of Lincoln's Inn 2000.
Publications: A member of the editorial team of the 13th edition of Munkman on Employer's Liability and a co-author of the second edition of the 'Personal Injuries Bar Association Handbook'.
Personal: Married, two sons. Interests: violin, sailing.

COLLIER, Peter QC
30 Park Square (Peter Collier QC), Leeds
(0113) 243 6388
Recommended in Church

COLLINGS, Matthew
Maitland Chambers (Michael Lyndon-Stanford QC & Charles Aldous QC), London
(020) 7406 1200
clerks@maitlandchambers.com
Recommended in Chancery, Company, Insolvency
Specialisation: Company law (litigation and advisory work) including corporate reconstructions, takeovers and mergers, shareholders disputes, directors duties and disqualification; reported cases include British & Commonwealth, Leeds United, Carecraft, Manlon, Barings, UMB v Doherty, Nottingham Forest and Astec. Corporate insolvency; reported cases include Arrows, BCCI, Harris Simons, Wallace Smith, Charnley Davies, Galileo Group, Vanilla Accumulation, Hamlet International, Atlantic Computers and Trading Partners (versailles). Personal insolvency and bankruptcy; reported cases include Naeem, Murjani and Hadkinson. Regulatory work and financial services including extensive appearances in tribunals (including SIB v Lancs and Yorks and the 'Flaming Ferraris' case), public law (ex p Clegg: DTI inspection) and human rights (ex p McCormick and ex p Eastaway), company and insolvency investigations (including Banking Act and criminal), the use of compelled evidence, and competition law. Commercial Chancery including guarantees and securities, banking, share sale warranties and professional negligence; reported cases include The Law Society v KPMG, and Phillips v Symes.
Prof. Memberships: Chancery Bar Association, COMBAR and Insolvency Lawyers' Association. Member, Insolvency Rules Advisory Committee.

COLLINS, Michael QC
Essex Court Chambers (Gordon Pollock QC), London
(020) 7813 8000
mcollins@essexcourt-chambers.law.co.uk
Recommended in Arbitration
Specialisation: International and

LEADERS AT THE BAR

commercial arbitration, insurance, shipping, conflict of laws, commercial and technical contract and tort disputes generally, arbitration.
Prof. Memberships: American Bar Association, International Bar Association, Commercial Bar Association.
Career: University of Exeter LLB (First Class Hons). Called to the Bar 1971. Queen's Counsel 1988. Recorder 1997-2000.
Personal: Born 1948.

CONE, John
Erskine Chambers (Robin Potts QC), London
(020) 7242 5532
clerks@erskine-chambers.co.uk
Recommended in Company
Specialisation: Corporate reorganisations and reconstructions including reduction of capital and schemes of arrangement. Takeovers and mergers. Schemes of arrangement in insolvencies.
Prof. Memberships: Chancery Bar Association. COMBAR. A Bar Representative on the Law Society Company Law Committee, Member of the Law Reform Committee of the Bar Council.

CONLON, Michael QC
Pump Court Tax Chambers, London
(020) 7414 8080
Recommended in Tax
Specialisation: All areas of indirect taxation, including investigations and litigation.
Prof. Memberships: COMBAR; Revenue Bar Association; Chancery Bar Association; Bar European Group; National President, VAT Practitioners Group; President, Institute of Indirect Taxation; Fellow, Chartered Institute of Taxation; Tax Law Review Committee.
Career: Called to the Bar (1974); government legal service (1976-86); international accountancy and law firms (1986-97); solicitor (1992-97); returned to the Bar 1997; QC (2002).
Publications: On educational boards of De Voil Indirect Taxation Service, 'The Tax Journal', 'Butterworths Education Law Manual'. Numerous technical articles.
Personal: Educated: Enfield Grammar School; Queen's College, Cambridge. Recreations: art, music, literature, badminton. Married; one son, one daughter. Resides Wimbledon SW19 and east Sussex.

CONNOLLY, Joanne
8 King St (Gerard McDermott QC), Manchester
(0161) 834 9560
joanne.connolly@8ks.co.uk
Recommended in Employment
Specialisation: All aspects of employment work from simple unfair dismissal and redundancy to the more complex sexual, racial and disability discrimination cases and group actions under the Transfer of Undertakings, Working Time or Minimum Wage legislation both before the Employment Tribunal and at the Employment Appeal Tribunal. Also personal injury, including stress at work and bullying claims. Reported cases include: Mediguard v Thane [1994] 1RLR 504, EAT Staffordshire County Council v Barber [1996] 1RLR 379, CA. RCO Support Services and Aintree Hospital Trust v UNISON and others [2002] EWCA Civ 464 leave to the House of Lords pending.
Prof. Memberships: The Employment Law Bar Association, the Employment Lawyers Association and the Professional Negligence Bar Association.
Career: LLB (Nottingham.) Called to the Bar in 1992. Awarded Council of Legal Education Studentship and Jules Thorn scholarship.

CONSTABLE, Adam
2 Temple Gardens (Dermod O'Brien QC), London
(020) 7822 1200
Recommended in Construction
Specialisation: Construction, and engineering disputes and associated professional negligence. Recent instructions include a broad range of projects, including FPSOs, process engineering plant and complex M&E services. Particular experience of high value, international arbitration, having acted in a number of substantial disputes in the UK, Europe and the Far East. He has been involved in a number of insurance-related construction disputes arising out of CAR policy disputes, and related matters. Recent cases also include adjudication enforcement: C&B Scene v Isobars (CA) and Shimizu v Automajor.
Prof. Memberships: TECBAR, Society of Construction Lawyers, PNBA.
Personal: Balliol College, Oxford (MA, 1st Class Honours in Jurisprudence). Called to Bar in 1995. Resides in Putney. Interests include rugby, scuba diving and wine.

CONWAY, Charles
2 Bedford Row (William Clegg QC), London
(020) 7440 8888
Recommended in Crime

COOK, Ian
One King's Bench Walk (Anthony Hacking QC), London
(020) 7936 1500
Recommended in Family
Specialisation: Main areas of practice: matrimonial finance including recent experience involving UK and overseas based family run businesses and domestic and offshore trusts, public law children cases, child abduction, crime. Reported cases include Re H (Abduction: Acquiescence) [1998] AC 72, Re S (Care Proceedings: Split Hearing) [1996] 2 FLR 773, FD, Re M and R (Child Abuse: Evidence) [1996] 2 FLR 195, CA.
Prof. Memberships: FLBA.
Career: BA (Hons) 1st Class Philosophy, King's College London. CPE City of London Polytechnic.

COOK, Mary
2-3 Gray's Inn Square (Anthony Porten QC & Anthony Scrivener QC), London
(020) 7242 4986
mcook@2-3graysinnsquare.co.uk
Recommended in Local Government, Planning
Specialisation: Planning and local government work. Wide planning inquiry experience, both promoting and resisting development, called-in applications and Local Plan appearances, the promotion of CPO particularly town centre schemes, footpath and road closures. Court experience includes judicial review and high court challenges involving environmental, planning, property and vires issues and Lands Tribunal work.
Prof. Memberships: Planning and Environmental Bar Association.
Career: Called 1982, commenced practice from these chambers in 1985.

COOKE, Nicholas QC
9 Park Place (Ian Murphy QC), Cardiff
(029) 2038 2731
clerks@9parkplace.co.uk
Recommended in Chancery, Local Government
Prof. Memberships: Wales and Chester circuit; Planning and Environmental Bar Association; Bristol and Cardiff Chancery Bar Association; Wales Public Law and Human Rights Association.
Career: King Edward's School, Birmingham. UCW Aberystwyth (1st Class Hons LLB). Recorder. Appointed Queen's Counsel in 1998. Deputy President Mental Health Review Tribunal for Wales.
Personal: Hockey, theatre.

COOKSLEY, Nigel QC
Old Square Chambers (John Hendy QC), London
(020) 7269 0300
cooksley@oldsquarechambers.co.uk
Recommended in Personal Injury
Specialisation: Principal area of practice for many years has been personal injury litigation and has a widespread practice throughout the country. Other areas of practice include professional negligence, product liability and sporting injuries.
Prof. Memberships: Personal Injury Bar Association, Association of Personal Injury Lawyers, Professional Negligence Bar Association.
Career: Called to the Bar in 1975.
Personal: Educated at Felsted School and Cambridge University. Lives in North Hertfordshire. Outside interests include sport.

COONAN, Kieran QC
6 Pump Court (Kieran Coonan QC), London
(020) 7583 6013
Recommended in Clinical Negligence
Specialisation: Specialises in health care law; clinical negligence; solicitors' negligence; product liability; personal injury; professional conduct matters (GMC/GDC/Privy Council); mental health law and criminal law.
Prof. Memberships: Professional Negligence Bar Association; Personal Injury Bar Association; Criminal Bar Association.
Career: Called 1971; Commenced practice in 1974; Silk 1990; Head of Chambers 1991; Recorder 1996.

COOPER, John
40 King St, Manchester
(0161) 832 9082
jcooper@40kingstreet.co.uk
Recommended in Health & Safety
Specialisation: Specialises in regulatory law, predominantly concerning health and safety at work, food safety, trading standards, licensing and the regulation of financial services. Represents corporate defendants and company directors in respect of such proceedings at Courts and tribunals. During past seven years has represented the DTI as First Junior Counsel in (Griffiths & Others v British Coal Corporation 'The British Coal Respiratory Disease Litigation') initially as trial counsel to deal with the engineering and apportionment aspect of the case and thereafter to advise and assist in drafting the Compensation Scheme. Has been retained to represent the DTI in the Contribution Proceedings against Mining Contractors. Appeared on behalf of the appellant in Friskies Petcare (UK) PLC (2000) 2 Cr. App Rep (S) 400. Regularly conducts lectures and seminars to companies and professional bodies for training purposes. Has represented a number of FTSE 100 companies.
Prof. Memberships: Professional Negligence Bar Association.
Career: Law (LLB) Reading University. Called to the Bar 1985.
Publications: Series of four articles in the 'Solicitors Journal' The prosecution of Regulatory Offences (2001) SJ Vol 145 pp 520-521, 552-553, 574-575, 594-595.

COOPER, John
3 Gray's Inn Square (Rock Tansey QC), London
(020) 7520 5600
Recommended in Crime
Specialisation: Specialist in serious criminal law. Also deals with media law and human rights.
Prof. Memberships: Criminal Bar Association; Bar Council Public Affairs Committee; Bar Human Rights Committee; Standing Counsel to Statute Law Revision Society.
Career: Call 1983. Butterworths' Law Prizeman. Member, New South Wales Bar. Represented British employees in BCCI litigation. Successfully represented defendant in the Leah Betts Ecstasy drug trials. Leading authority in Master of Rolls court on the criminality of wheel clamping (Arthur v Anker), indictment rules (R v Wrench), R v Ward & Baker (Duress), R v Plummer & Simpkins (Juveniles). Represented Lord Ahmed in privacy claim against Government.

LEADERS AT THE BAR

Instructed for Louise Woodward by campaign committee, Columnist for The Times. Advisor to the emerging democracies in Eastern Europe upon criminal law and justice. Judicial Commissioner in Lambeth Childcare enquiry. Entry in Debretts People of Today. Had led in serious trial including murder for both prosecution and defence. Undertakes serious junior work. Health and Safety Executive Approved Counsel. Leading brief in Blackpool Pleasure Beach case. Environment Agency Approved Council.
Publications: 'Police Interviews' (Sweet & Maxwell); Judicial Review from the 'Magistrates Court' (Sweet & Maxwell); Jutis (Context); 'Torture, Inhuman and Degrading Treatment' (Sweet & Maxwell).
Personal: Commended as Barrister of the Year 1998 (The Lawyer). Writer: screenplays include The Law Lord (BBC Screen 2), The Advocate (ITV)' The Cure (Royal Court Theatre).

COOPER, Mark
5 Park Place, Leeds
(0113) 242 1123
mcooper@40kingstreet.co.uk
Recommended in Insolvency
Specialisation: Business, commercial and financial law, in particular corporate restructuring, insolvency (personal and corporate) banking and commercial disputes involving contractual, restitutionary and professional negligence claims. Recent reported cases include Rye v Ashfield Nominees Limited, New Law Online 2010815901. Addressed R3 Legal Forum on Legal and Practical Implications of European Insolvency Regulations.
Prof. Memberships: Chancery Bar Association, R3, Insolvency Lawyers Association, Northern Chancery Bar Association.
Career: Called 1998 (Middle Temple), (Harmsworth Exhibitioner). Previous Career as an investment banker in London and New York (1989-95). Joined 40 King Street Chambers in 2002 after a previous tenancy at Chancery House Chambers, Leeds.
Personal: Educated at Dame Allans Boys School, Newcastle upon Tyne 1979-86 and Exeter College, Oxford 1986-89 (MA in 1995). Married. Lives outside Bingley, West Yorkshire. Interests include local history, travel and sports cars.

CORBETT, James QC
St Philips Chambers (John Randall QC), Birmingham
(0121) 246 7000
jcorbett@st-phillips.co.uk
Recommended in Chancery, Commercial (Litigation), Insolvency
Specialisation: Also at Serle Court (Lord Neill of Bladen QC) Lincoln's Inn (020) 7242 6105. Practises in commercial, company, insolvency, trusts and probate.
Prof. Memberships: Fellow of Chartered Institute of Arbitrators and Chartered Arbitrator; CEDR registered mediator; member of Chancery Bar Association; Employment Law Bar Association; Professional Negligence Bar Association; COMBAR.
Career: LLB and LLM (European Legal Studies), University of Exeter. Called in 1975. Irish Bar (1981) and Northern Irish Bar (1994). Legal practitioner NSW (2002). Joined present chambers in 1983. Lecturer in European and commercial law, 1975-77 (Leicester University). QC, 1999. Recorder, 2000 (Asst Recorder 1996-2000).

CORDARA, Roderick QC
Essex Court Chambers (Gordon Pollock QC), London
(020) 7813 8000
cordara@aol.com
Recommended in Tax
Specialisation: Indirect tax and duties law and VAT planning; insurance and reinsurance litigation; shipping and shipbuilding work; banking; film industry litigation; oil and gas disputes; general business litigation.
Prof. Memberships: Revenue Bar Association; COMBAR; LMAA.
Career: Trinity Hall, Cambridge: BA (Law) (1st class) 1974. Called to the Bar 1975. Queen's Counsel 1994. Senior Counsel (NSW) 2000.
Publications: Editor, 'Indirect Tax Intelligence'.
Personal: Born 1953.

CORFIELD, Sheelagh
St John's Chambers (Christopher Sharp QC), Bristol
(0117) 921 3456
Recommended in Family

CORNER, Timothy QC
4-5 Gray's Inn Square (Elizabeth Appleby QC), London
(020) 7404 5252
Recommended in Administrative & Public Law, Local Government, Planning
Specialisation: Major part of practice is in the fields of town and country planning and compulsory purchase, and public law including education, local government and environmental law. Planning work includes appeals throughout the country relating to housing, retail, employment, minerals, waste, listed buildings and conservation areas. Recent court cases include R v North Warwickshire DC ex p. Jones and Howe [2001] 2 PLR 59, Court of Appeal, planning, material considerations, City Logistics v Northamptonshire Fire Officer [2002] 1 WLR 1124, Court of Appeal, public law, duties of a fire authority, W v Special Educational Needs Tribunal, Times, 12th December 2000, Court of Appeal, education, duties of a SENT, and Taylor Lawrence [2002] 2 All ER 353, Court of Appeal, whether the Court can re-open its own decisions.
Prof. Memberships: Member [and former Committee member] of Planning and Environment Bar Association, Administrative Law Bar Association, United Kingdom Environmental Law Association, and South Eastern Circuit.
Career: Called to the Bar 1981, Silk 2002. Junior Counsel to the Crown, A Panel, 1999-2002. Member, Advisory Panel on Standards for the Planning Inspectorate, 2001-. Member, Joint Oxford Planning Law Conference Committee, 2001-.
Publications: Publications include articles at [1998] JPL 201 and [2002] JPL 661 on planning and environment law and the European Convention on Human Rights.
Personal: Educated at Bolton School 1966-76, Magdalen College, Oxford 1976-80 (MA Jurisprudence, and BCL, and Demy of the College). Languages: French, Italian and Spanish. Leisure: singing (studying with Prof. Ian Kennedy at Guildhall, London), walking, gardens. Born 25 July 1958. Lives in London.

CORRIGAN, Peter A
2-4 Tudor Street (Richard Ferguson QC), London
(020) 7797 7111
Recommended in Crime

CORY-WRIGHT, Charles
39 Essex Street (Nigel Pleming QC), London
(020) 7832 1111
Recommended in Personal Injury
Specialisation: Main areas of practice: professional negligence, personal injury, insurance, construction. Reported cases: personal injury – Biesheuvel v Birrell (enhanced multiplier for foreign claimant), Nicholls v Rushton (no recovery of damages for shock), Giles v Thompson (CA, HL) (legality of credit hire agreements), Campbell v Mylchreest, Sharp v Pereira (jurisdiction re interim payments), Cutter v Eagle Star (CA, HL) (a car park is not a 'road' for the purpose of the RTA); construction – Barclays v Fairclough (contributory negligence and contract), SAS v John Laing (retention of title clauses); insurance - Banque Financiere v Skandia (insurers duty of utmost good faith).
Prof. Memberships: COMBAR.
Career: Appointed to the Treasury A Panel in 2001.

COSGROVE, Patrick QC
Broad Chare Chambers (Patrick Cosgrove QC), Newcastle upon Tyne
(0191) 232 0541
Recommended in Crime

COTTER, Barry
Old Square Chambers (John Hendy QC), Bristol
(0117) 9277 1111
cotter@oldsquarechambers.co.uk
Recommended in Health & Safety, Personal Injury, Product Liability
Specialisation: All aspects of product liability law, personal injury and clinical negligence, health and safety at work, public inquiries and multi-party actions. Appeared in Clapham Junction Rail Inquiry, Strangeways (Woolf) Inquiry, Ashworth Hospital Inquiry, Severn Tunnel Inquiry, Cowden, Southall and Ladbroke Grove Train Crash Inquiries. Cases include Richardson v LRC [2001] PIQR; Williams v BOC 2000 [PIQR] Q 253; MRS Environmental Service Ltd v Marsh [1997] 1 All ER 92; Coventry City Council v Ackerman [1995] Crim. LR 140; P&M Supplies v Walsall [1994] Crim LR 590; Deane v Ealing [1993] ICR 329; R v Secretary of State ex p POA; 'The Times' 28 October 1991. Counsel in the Guards and Shunters multi-party deafness action, larium, organophosphate and persona actions.
Prof. Memberships: Personal Injury Bar Association; Committee Member 1995-99 and 2002 onwards.
Career: LLB; called to Bar in 1985.
Publications: Author 'Defective and Unsafe Products'; 'Law and Practice' (Butterworths 1996).
Personal: LLB University College, Lincoln's Inn, scholarship. Based in London and Bristol.

COULSON, Peter QC
Keating Chambers, London
(020) 7544 2600
pcoulson@keatingchambers.com
Recommended in Construction, Professional Negligence
Specialisation: Involved in all types of engineering, construction and related disputes, in the TCC and in arbitration in the UK, Hong Kong, USA and the West Indies; reported cases include: Ashville v Elmer; Ben Barrett v Boot; Barker v Leyden; British Airways v PDP and McAlpine; Copthorne v Bovis; Design 5 v Keniston; Kruger Tissues v Frank Galliers; McAlpine Humbrook v McDermott; Marston v Barnard; Regalian v LDDC; Wates v Bredero; Wessex v HLM; Woodspring v Venn.
Career: Qualified 1982; Gray's Inn; Member of Keating Chambers since 1984; associate of the Chartered Institute of Arbitrators 1990; contributor to 'Construction Law Yearbook'; contributing editor of 'Lloyds Law Reports'; co-author of 'Professional Negligence and Liability' (LLP).
Personal: Lord Wandsworth College; University of Keele (BA Hons Law, English 2:1). Born 1958; resides London. Interests: British art, architecture, music, comedy, cricket. Working knowledge of French.

COUSINS, Jeremy QC
St Philips Chambers (John Randall QC), Birmingham
(0121) 246 7000
Recommended in Commercial (Litigation)
Specialisation: Banking, commercial, and professional negligence litigation. AIB v Martin [2002] 1 WLR 94 (HL) (construction of mortgage deeds); Shogun Finance v Hudson [2001] Times LR 4th July (CA) (leased goods/passing of title). Barry v Alberex [2001] Times LR 3rd April (CA), (future loss multipliers); Acton v Graham Pearce [1997] 3 All ER 909 (solicitors' negligent preparation for criminal trial). State Bank of India v Kaur [1996] 5 Bank LR

158 (CA) (Statute of Frauds/guarantees). Midland Chancery & Commercial Bar Association.
Career: Call 1977; Assistant Recorder 1996; Silk 1999; Recorder 2000.
Personal: Oxford School; Warwick University LIB (Hons); Married with three children; sidesman and PCC member St Anne's, Moseley. Interests include France and Italy; their languages, wine and food.

COWARD, Stephen QC
7 Bedford Row (David Farrer QC), London
(020) 7242 3555
Recommended in Crime
Specialisation: Specialist in all aspects of serious crime from murder to fraud. Appeared in the following cases: 1. R v Stanley – assistant bosun Herald of Free Enterprise. 2. R v Nedrick and R v Slack – the liability of secondary parties in murder. 3. R v Ivor Jones and others the leading authority on section 16 Firearms Act 1968. 4. R v Prime – espionage. 5. R v John Tanner – the murder of Rachel McLean, the Oxford undergraduate. 6. R v Leslie Jones – murder allegation turning on the cooling rate of dead bodies. 7. R v Hayes and others – acted for the SFO. 8. R v Cheung - acted for the SFO. 9. R v Robinson – the 'Yardie' trial. 10. R v Baroness de Stempel – acted for the Defendant. 11. R v Winzar – murder of husband who was a paraplegic by administering insulin injection (CPS). 12. R v Postill and Ors - murder/manslaughter of elderly residents in care home – administering excess fluids by injection (CPS). 13. Advising CPS HQ on corporate manslaughter Dreamland Leisure.
Career: Educated at King James Grammar School, Huddersfield and University College, London (LLB). 1962: Lecturer in Law and Constitutional History, University College, London and Bramshill Police College. 1964: Called to the Bar (Inner Temple). 1980: Appointed Recorder. 1984: Took Silk. 1997: High Court Examiner (The State of New York v Don King Boxing Promotions).
Personal: Born 1937, lives in Northampton. Leisure pursuits: gardening, wine, singing.

COWTON, Catherine
Queen Elizabeth Building (Florence Baron QC), London
(020) 7797 7837
Recommended in Family

COX, Buster
Renaissance Chambers (Brian Patrick Jubb & Henry Setright QC), London
(020) 7404 1111
Recommended in Immigration

COX, Laura QC
Cloisters (Laura Cox QC), London
(020) 7827 4000
lc@cloisters.com
Recommended in Clinical Negligence, Employment, Human Rights
Specialisation: Laura Cox specialises, writes and lectures in discrimination, equal pay, employment, European and human rights law and in clinical negligence. She has been named for several years in the 'Chambers Directory' as one of the leading silks at the Bar in her specialist fields. She has been involved in many of the leading employment and discrimination cases, often instructed by the Equal Opportunities Commission or the Commission for Racial Equality. She speaks and writes regularly on subjects in her specialist areas and was recently a member of the panel of experts advising the Independent Review of the Enforcement of UK Anti-Discrimination Legislation, Cambridge University. A Vice-President of the Institute of Employment Rights and member of the Industrial Law Society, Laura Cox is one of the founding lawyers for LIBERTY, for whom she has advised and lectured extensively on equality and human rights. She is also on the Council of JUSTICE, the independent legal and human rights organisation, and is currently a member of their working group on socio-economic rights. As one of the leading silks in the field of clinical negligence Laura Cox has long been interested in medical ethics and the practice of medicine. She is regularly instructed in catastrophic injury claims and invited to chair or speak at conferences on medical issues, often for Action for Victims of Medical Accidents and often on human rights issues. She was recently instructed in the Norplant contraceptive implant product liability litigation. Laura Cox has been extensively involved in human rights training since the arrival of the Human Rights Act. In particular she assisted in the development and delivery of the human rights training programme for all Employment Tribunal Chairmen and was invited to lecture on the Act and the Convention at training seminars, devised by the Judicial Studies Board, for all members of the judiciary. She is currently a member of the LIBERTY human rights expert counsel panel. Recent cases in which Laura Cox has been instructed include Webb v EMO Air Cargo (pregnancy discrimination), R v MOD ex parte Smith and Others (gays in the armed forces), Burton and Rhule v De Vere Hotels (the "Bernard Manning" case), Harrods v Elmi (employers' liability for acts of discrimination by third parties), FBU v Knowles and Johnson (meaning of "industrial action"), Crees v Royal London Insurance/Greaves v Kwiksave (the right to return from maternity leave), Halfpenny v IGE Medical Systems Ltd. (maternity discrimination), Smith v Gardner Merchant (sexual orientation discrimination), Sheffield and Horsham v UK (ECHR, transsexual rights), Aydin v Turkey (ECHR, human rights of women prisoners, amicus submissions for Amnesty) Enderby v Frenchay HA (speech therapists-equal pay), R v Secretary of State for Trade and Industry ex parte BECTU (Working Time qualifying period), KB v NHS Pensions Agency (transsexual pension entitlements), Pearce v Governors of Mayfield School (discrimination against gay school teacher), Whiffen v Milham Girls School (discrimination against fixed-term contract teachers), Anyanwu and Ebuzome v South Bank University (aiding race discrimination), Mahmood v Siggins (GP's negligence), Bowler v Walker (negligent treatment of psychiatric patient), Tredget v Bexley Health Authority (recovery for "nervous shock" in clinical negligence cases), Bellinger v Bellinger (validity of transsexual marriage), Goodwin v UK (ECHR, status of transsexuals), Alabaster v Woolwich plc (maternity pay discrimination), Liversidge v Bedfordshire Police (liability of chief constables for race discrimination), Sykes v JP Morgan (City sex discrimination), Wilding v BT (mitigation of loss in disability discrimination case), Masterman-Lister v Home Counties Dairies and Anr. (meaning of "capacity" and patient status for Court of Protection). Clients include trade unions and individual members, major organisations, applicants and respondents in employment and discrimination litigation, claimants and defendants in clinical negligence litigation.
Career: Head of Chambers at Cloisters since 1995. Queen's Counsel since 1994. Recorder and Part-Time Judge of the Employment Appeal Tribunal. Bencher of the Inner Temple. Current Chairman of the Bar Council Equal Opportunities Committee and past Chairman of the Sex Discrimination Committee. Past executive committee member of the Employment Law Bar Association. Appointed in 1998 as the United Kingdom representative on the International Labour Organisation Committee of Experts meeting in Geneva, monitoring UN member states' compliance with international labour standards. Appointed in 2002 as Chair of the Board of Interights, the international human rights organisation based in London providing human rights expertise and training for lawyers and members of the judiciary throughout the world.
Personal: Educated at Wolverhampton High School for Girls 1963-70 and London University (1970- 75, LLB and LLM). Married with three sons. Leisure pursuits include music, theatre, cinema, cooking and watching the beautiful game!

COX, Raymond QC
Fountain Court (Anthony Boswood QC), London
(020) 7583 3335
Recommended in Banking & Finance
Specialisation: Principal areas of practice are all aspects of reinsurance and insurance, banking (including documentary credits, bills, financial services and credit security) professional negligence (including valuers, accountants, solicitors and banks) and commercial law generally.
Career: Raymond Cox is co-editor of 'Commercial Court Procedure', Cox and Moriarty (Sweet & Maxwell, 1999) and 'Law of Bank Payments', Brindle and Cox (2nd ed, Sweet & Maxwell, 1999) and has lectured on insurance and banking.

COX, Simon
Doughty Street Chambers (Geoffrey Robertson QC), London
(020) 7404 1313
s.cox@doughtystreet.co.uk
Recommended in Immigration
Specialisation: Immigration, social security and public law. Particular expertise in welfare support for immigrants. Instructed in test cases by Child Poverty Action Group (CPAG), Joint Council for Welfare of Immigrants and British Union for the Abolition of Vivisection (Home Office interpretation of animal experiments law). Also experience before child support commissioners. Reported cases include: M v Secretary of State, HL [disability benefits for immigrants]; Westminster v Mehanne, HL [housing benefit]; Kadhim v Brent, CA [housing benefit]; Megarry v Secretary of State, CA [disability benefit: IQ tests for autistic child]; ex p Restrepo, CA [child benefit for asylum seeker]; ex p Jeyeanthan, CA [validity of immigration appeal]; Aramide v Secretary of State, CA [deportation]; ex p Akpre, CA [appeal procedure]. Co-author "Migration and Social Security Handbook," CPAG, since 1997. Co-author "Child Support Handbook" 1996-2000, CPAG. Regular lecturer to solicitors.
Prof. Memberships: ILPA, ALBA, Bar European Group, Liberty and Justice.
Career: Called to Bar 1992. Social Security and immigration caseworker at Free Representation Unit 1993-95.

CRAGG, Stephen
Doughty Street Chambers (Geoffrey Robertson QC), London
(020) 7404 1313
s.cragg@doughtystreet.co.uk
Recommended in Administrative & Public Law
Specialisation: Public law in social welfare and human rights areas, especially community care, mental health, education, travellers' rights, coroners' inquests and policing. Reported cases include: Rexworthy v Secretary of State [1998] JPL (human rights, planning decisions and travellers); R v Gloucestershire County Council ex p Barry [1998] AC 581 (taking resources into account when assessing need for services for disabled people); R v Powys CC ex p Hambidge (1998) 1 FLR 643, CA (power to charge for services to disabled persons); Monsanto v Tilly (2000) Env LR 313, CA (defence of necessity and destruction of

LEADERS AT THE BAR

GM crops); R(A) v Lambeth LBC (2002) 2 FLR 353, CA (nature of duty under section 17 Children Act 1989); R (Howard) v Secretary of State for Health (2002) Times 28 March (Art 10 rights to public enquiry); R (Green) v Police Complaints Authority (2002) UKHRR 293 (Art 2 and investigation of police complaints); R (Marper) v South Yorkshire Police (2002) Times 4 April (Art 8 and retention of DNA samples).
Prof. Memberships: Administrative Law Bar Association; Lawyers for Liberty; Police Actions Lawyers Group.
Career: Called to the Bar 1996. Project Solicitor to the Public Law Project (1993-96). Fellow in Public Law Essex University 1997-99; and a member of the Civil Justice Council (1998-2000).
Publications: Co- author 'Police Misconduct: Legal Remedies'; Consultant Editor 'UK Human Rights Reports'; legal update editor for the 'Community Care Law Reports'; co-author of 'An Applicant's Guide to Judicial Review', Sweet and Maxwell (1995).
Personal: LLB (Hons) Kings College, London; MA Sociology and Law (Brunel): Interests: travel; cinema; two young children.

CRAMPIN, Peter QC
11 New Square (Sonia Proudman QC), London
(020) 7831 0081
Recommended in Charities
Specialisation: Chancery:- property litigation and advice, trusts, charities, pensions, insolvency, professional negligence, Court of Protection.
Career: Called 1976. 2nd Junior Counsel to the A-G in charity matters 1988-93. Took silk 1993. Recorder.
Personal: Born 7 July 1946.

CRANE, Michael QC
Fountain Court (Anthony Boswood QC), London
(020) 7583 3335
Recommended in Aviation, Commercial (Litigation), Insurance

CRASNOW, Rachel
Cloisters (Laura Cox QC), London
(020) 7827 4000
rc@cloisters.com
Recommended in Employment
Specialisation: Employment law, with a particular emphasis on discrimination and human rights. Practices in all areas of the employment law field from equal pay to individual and collective rights. Also undertakes range of medical law work, public law, civil actions against the police and inquests.
Prof. Memberships: ELBA, ELA, PIBA, DLA, Bar Pro-Bono Unit, ELAAS.
Career: Represents both applicants and respondents in wide variety of courts/tribunals. Notable work in the last year includes Gridquest Ltd v Blackburn [2002] ICR 682, Rutherford & Bentley v Harvest Town Circle and Secretary of State, acting for Liberty in ECHR cases including Goodwin v UK and Counsel in the Climbié Inquiry.

Standing Junior Counsel for the BPS. Member of Liberty's specialist Human Rights Litigation Unit Panel and DRC Litigation Panel. Counsel to the 1999-2000 Turner Inquiry. Lectures for organisations including JUSTICE, IRS and the Law Society. Advisor at Camden Law Centre 1996-2000. On Employment Panel of Legal Network Television.
Publications: Co-author of 'Employment Law and Human Rights', OUP, 2002; editor of the Educational Law Journal's Case Commentaries. Writes for range of legal periodicals; has written responses to many Government Consultation Papers on issues including terrorism, flexible hours and transsexuals' rights.
Personal: Educated at Pembroke College Oxford and City University London. Middle Temple Diplock Scholarship 1993; Pegasus Scholarship 1999 (based at Human Rights and Equal Opportunities Commission, Sydney).

CRAWFORD SC, James
Matrix Chambers, London
(020) 7404 3447
Recommended in Public International Law
Specialisation: International law/State Contract Arbitration.
Prof. Memberships: UK and NSW Bars.
Career: Professor of Law, University of Adelaide 1983-86; Challis Professor of International Law, University of Sydney, 1986-92; Whewell Professor of International Law, University of Cambridge 1992-.
Publications: 'The Creation of States in International Law' (1977), 'Australian Courts of Law' (1993), 'The ILC's Articles on State Responsibility' (2002).
Personal: LLB, BA (Adel), DPhil (Oxon). Married with five children.

CREAN, Anthony
No5 Chambers (Gareth Evans QC), Birmingham
(0121) 606 0500
Recommended in Planning

CRIGMAN, David QC
1 Fountain Court (Melbourne Inman QC), Birmingham
(0121) 236 5721
Recommended in Crime

CROOKENDEN, Simon QC
Essex Court Chambers (Gordon Pollock QC), London
(020) 7813 8000
clerksroom@essexcourt-chambers.co.uk
Recommended in Energy
Specialisation: Shipping. Insurance and Reinsurance: policies; proportional and excess of loss involving both Lloyd's of London and the company market. Building/Engineering. Commodity sales. Arbitration. Energy and Utilities
Prof. Memberships: Fellow of the Chartered Institute of Arbitrators. Panel member, Lloyd's of London Arbitration Panel. Accredited mediator.
Career: Corpus Christi College, Cambridge MA (Mechanical Sciences). Called to the Bar 1975. Queen's Counsel 1996.

Personal: Born 1946.

CROSS, James
4 Pump Court, London
(020) 7842 5555
chambers@4pumpcourt.com
Recommended in Professional Negligence
Specialisation: A general and varied practice in common law and commercial litigation/arbitration, but with particular experience of professional negligence (architects, engineers, the medical profession, solicitors, surveyors and valuers), construction and civil engineering (including adjudication), insurance and reinsurance, product liability, sale of goods and commodities and contractual disputes.
Prof. Memberships: COMBAR, London Common Law and Commercial Bar Association, TECBAR.
Career: Called to the Bar in 1985 and joined 4 Pump Court in 1986.
Personal: Educated at Shrewsbury and Magdalen College, Oxford.

CROW, Jonathan
4 Stone Buildings (Philip Heslop QC), London
(020) 7242 5524
clerks@4stonebuildings.com
Recommended in Company
Specialisation: First Treasury Junior (Chancery).

CROWLEY, Jane QC
30 Park Place (John Jenkins QC), Cardiff
(029) 2039 8421
Recommended in Family

CROXFORD, Ian QC
Wilberforce Chambers (Edward Nugee QC), London
(020) 7306 0102
Recommended in Chancery, Fraud, Professional Negligence

CROXFORD, Thomas
Blackstone Chambers (Presiley Baxendale QC & Charles Flint QC), London
(020) 7583 1770
clerks@blackstonechambers.com
Recommended in Employment
Specialisation: Specialist in employment, financial services and commercial law. Particular interests in employment law-restraint of trade, confidentiality, fiduciary duties, whistleblowing and discrimination. Recent cases: Gerrard v Read, TLR, 17/1/02; CMS Dolphin Ltd v Simonet [2001] 2BCLC704. Others: Blue Circle v MOD [1999] Ch 289 CA; Christmas v Hampshire [1995] 2 AC 633.
Prof. Memberships: COMBAR, ELA (committee member).
Career: Call: 1992.
Personal: Clare College, Cambridge (MA).

CRYSTAL, Jonathan
Cloisters (Laura Cox QC), London
(020) 7827 4000
jonathancrystal@cloisters.com
Recommended in Sport
Specialisation: Sport. Advisory work

including: (boxing) Prince Naseem Hamed, Audley Harrison and Danny Williams; (football clubs) Liverpool, Leeds United, Cardiff City and Chesterfield; (footballers) Stan Collymore, Steve McManaman, Magnus Hedman, Phil Thompson, Michael Ricketts and Robbie Fowler; (cricket) Brian Lara, West Indies Cricket Board and Queen's Park CC; (rugby) Dean Ryan, Bristol RFU, Ellery Hanley, Andy Farrell, ARL and Wakefield Wildcats; also numerous football agents, athletes, motor racing drivers and teams, the ASA, venues, sponsors, broadcasters and clothing (Puma). Notable cases: (contract) Duffy v Newcastle United FC, ISL v Mars, Don King v Frank Warren and Redman v British Lions; (discipline) FAW v Cardiff City, FL v Chesterfield, FA v Margate Town, RFU v Ryan and RFL v Jason Stevens; (injury) McCord v Swansea City, Watson and Bradford City v Gray and Huddersfield Town, Bayfield v Eagle Star and Hinchcliffe v BSMA. Numerous libel claims. Drafting: Broadcast contracts (HBO, BBC); Association rules (Premier League). Players' contracts and commercial agreements.
Prof. Memberships: BSLG, BASL and NSPCC Sports Steering Group
Career: Called 1972. Cloisters since 1992.
Personal: Leeds GS and QMC, University of London. Director Tottenham Hotspur 1991-93, Cardiff City 2000-. Married to Trinidadian lawyer with three children living in central London.

CRYSTAL, Michael QC
3-4 South Square (Michael Crystal QC & Lord Alexander of Weedon QC), London
(020) 7696 9900
clerks@southsquare.com
Recommended in Chancery, Company, Insolvency
Specialisation: Commercial and financial law.
Career: Called to the Bar, Middle Temple, 1970; Queen's Counsel, 1984; Bencher Middle Temple, 1993; Deputy High Court Judge, since 1995; Admitted to the Bars of the Bahamas, Bermuda, the British Virgin Islands, the Cayman Islands, Gibraltar, Hong Kong and the Isle of Man for specific cases; Senior Visiting Fellow Centre for Commercial Law Studies, University of London since 1987; DTI Inspector 1988-89, 1992; Member Insolvency Rules Advisory Committee 1993-97; Member Financial Law Panel 1996-2002; Member Advisory Council, University of Oxford Law Foundation since 1998; Honorary Fellow, Queen Mary, University of London 1996; Honorary Fellow, Society for Advanced Legal Studies 1997.

CUDDIGAN, Hugo
11 South Square (Christopher Floyd QC), London
(020) 7405 1222
Recommended in Intellectual Property

LEADERS AT THE BAR

CULLEN, Edmund
Maitland Chambers (Michael Lyndon-Stanford QC & Charles Aldous QC), London
(020) 7406 1200
ecullen@maitlandchambers.com
Recommended in Media & Entertainment
Specialisation: A broad range of chancery and commercial work including media and entertainment, professional negligence (in particular involving solicitors and accountants), company and insolvency litigation.
Prof. Memberships: Chancery Bar Association and COMBAR.
Career: Called to the Bar 1990.
Personal: Educated at Winchester, University of Bristol.

CULLEN, Felicity
Gray's Inn Tax Chambers (Milton Grundy), London
(020) 7242 2642
fe@taxbar.com
Recommended in Tax
Specialisation: All aspects of revenue law including in particular commercial and corporate tax, capital gains tax, stamp duty, taxation of individuals and tax litigation.
Prof. Memberships: Revenue Bar Association. Chancery Bar Association. Called to the Bar 1985. Joined Gray's Inn Tax Chambers 1986.
Career: LLB Birmingham (1st Class Hons), LLM Cantab.

CULLUM, Michael
Albion Chambers (Neil Ford QC), Bristol
(0117) 927 2144
Recommended in Crime

CUNNINGHAM, Mark QC
Maitland Chambers (Michael Lyndon-Stanford QC & Charles Aldous QC), London
(020) 7406 1200
mcunningham@maitlandchambers.com
Recommended in Chancery
Specialisation: General chancery practitioner, with a bias towards commercially orientated litigation. He has appeared in over 40 reported cases concerning: company law, directors' disqualification, personal insolvency, sale of land, landlord and tenant, rent reviews, easements, land registration, copyright, passing off, entertainment law, the Inheritance Act, subrogation, the Court of Protection, the Copyright Tribunal and betting and gaming. He has also been appointed as a DTI Inspector in relation to insider dealing matters.
Prof. Memberships: Chancery Bar Association, Patent Bar Association, COMBAR.
Career: Called 1980. Appointed Junior Counsel to the Crown (Chancery), February 1992. Appointed Junior Counsel to the Crown 'A' Panel, 1999. Appointed Queens Counsel, 2001.
Publications: Contributor to 'Mithani: Directors' Disqualification'.
Personal: Educated at Stonyhurst College and Magdalen College Oxford (BA History). Born 6 June 1956. Lives in Buckinghamshire. Four children.

CUSWORTH, Nicholas
1 Hare Court (Bruce Blair QC), London
(020) 7797 7070
cusworth@1hc.com
Recommended in Family
Specialisation: Ancillary relief; Children Act 1989, Schedule 1 applications; cohabitees; private law Children Act applications.
Prof. Memberships: Family Law Bar Association. Committee member elected 1998.
Career: MA (Oxon). Called to the Bar 1986. Occasional lecturer for Professional Conferences.
Publications: Contributor to 'Essential Family Practice' and 'Financial Provision in Family Matters'.
Personal: St. Paul's School, London and Christ Church, Oxford. Married (to Rachel Platts of Counsel), one daughter.

DAGNALL, John QC
9 Old Square (Michael Driscoll QC), London
(020) 7405 4682
Recommended in Property Litigation
Specialisation: Specialisations are chancery, commercial and property litigation; including banking, trusts, civil fraud, insolvency, property (including mortgages and landlord and tenant) and professional negligence.
Prof. Memberships: Member of Chancery Bar Association, Professional Negligence Bar Association and Parliamentary Bar Mess.
Career: Bristol Grammar School, St John's College, Oxford (BA (Jurisprudence – 1st Class), BCL). Called Nov 1983, tenant Mar 1985.
Personal: Family, church, real tennis, bridge. Further details on application.

DARLING, Paul QC
Keating Chambers, London
(020) 7544 2600
pdarling@keatingchambers.com
Recommended in Arbitration, Construction
Specialisation: Building and engineering cases in the UK and abroad. Important cases include: Temloc v Errill; Richard Roberts v Douglas Smith; Wyatt v Gleeson; Yeandle v Wynn Realisations; Vascroft v Seeboard; Mooney v Boot; PLC v McAlpine; McAlpine v Unex; Hunt v Paul Sykes; Chatbrown v McAlpine; Barking & Dagenham v Stamford Asphalt; Holbeck Hall Hotel v Scarborough; Flannery v Halifax; BHP v British Steel; Kelston Sparkes v Balfour Beatty.
Career: Qualified 1983. Middle Temple. Queens Counsel 1999. Director Family Pharmaceutical Company; Editor 'Construction Law Newsletter'; member of editorial team 'Keating on Building Contracts'.
Personal: Winchester College; St Edmund Hall, Oxford (1981 BA, 1982 BCL). Horseracing, Newcastle United.

DASHWOOD, Robert
17 Carlton Crescent (Jeremy S Gibbons QC), Southampton
(023) 8032 0320/2003
Recommended in Family

DAVEY, Michael
4 Essex Court (Nigel Teare QC), London
(020) 7653 5653
Recommended in Shipping

DAVIDSON, Nicholas QC
Four New Square (Justin Fenwick QC), London
(020) 7822 2000
n.davidson@4newsquare.com
Recommended in Professional Negligence
Specialisation: Solicitors' and financial negligence. Other main areas of work cover general commercial cases, including insurance disputes and computer litigation.
Prof. Memberships: Professional Negligence Bar Association (Chairman 1997-99), Bar European Group, COMBAR, Chancery Bar Association, Society for Computers and Law.
Career: Called 1974; joined present Chambers 1999. Silk 1993.
Personal: Educated at Winchester 1964-69 (Scholar) and Trinity College Cambridge (Exhibitioner in Economics) 1969-72. Certificate of Honour, Bar Finals.

DAVIES, Helen
Brick Court Chambers (Christopher Clarke QC), London
(020) 7379 3550
davies@brickcourt.co.uk
Recommended in Arbitration, Insurance
Specialisation: All aspects of Commercial and EU law, including professional negligence, insurance/reinsurance, banking, oil and gas disputes, competition and human rights.
Career: Called November 1991. Brick Court Chambers (1992-present). Stage in European Commission, DGIV (Transport) 1993. Member of the B Panel to the Crown.

DAVIES, Huw QC
30 Park Place (John Jenkins QC), Cardiff
(029) 2039 8421
Recommended in Crime

DAVIES, Jane
Crown Office Chambers (Michael Spencer QC & Christopher Purchas QC), London
(020) 7797 8100
davies@crownofficechambers.com
Recommended in Construction
Specialisation: Professional negligence in a building context (architects, engineers, quantity surveyors, project administrators) as well as accountants and solicitors; insurance policy disputes, contract and commercial disputes. Numerous large claims in the building industry, including contractual disputes.
Prof. Memberships: Tec Bar, Combar.
Career: Read English at Lady Margaret Hall, Oxford, entrance scholarship; diploma in Arts Administration, Arts Council of Great Britain, worked as arts administrator and stage designer before coming to the Bar. Jules Thorn Scholar (Middle Temple).
Personal: Second home in France: fluent French.

DAVIES, Lindsay
Fenners Chambers (Paul Hollow), Cambridge
(01223) 368761
clerks@fennerschambers.co.uk
Recommended in Family
Specialisation: Her practice covers the whole range of family work. Children's cases include public law applications involving parents and/or children with psychiatric illness or personality disorders. Private law cases include applications under the Hague Convention and other cross-border issues. Financial cases include applications relating to family companies and farming divorces, unmarried parties property disputes. She advises under the Fenners Chambers Suggested Settlement Scheme. Other family disputes including cases of forced marriages, injunctions to restrain publicity and termination of medical treatment. Recently reported cases: Re AK (Medical treatment: Consent) [2001] 1 FLR 129.
Prof. Memberships: FLBA.

DAVIES, Nicola QC
3 Serjeants' Inn (Robert Francis QC & John Grace QC), London
(020) 7427 5000
Recommended in Clinical Negligence
Specialisation: Medical law including inquiries, professional disciplinary tribunals and crime. Cases include GMC & Dr John Brennan (Royal Devon and Exeter Breast Cancer Screening), Re A (children), Conjoined Twins, R v Doctor Harold Shipman, BSE Inquiry, GMC - case of Bristol heart surgeons. Chairman of the Committee of Inquiry into the death of Jonathan Newby (Mental Health).
Career: Called to the Bar in 1976. Silk 1992. Recorder 1998.
Personal: Birmingham University (LL.B).

DAVIES, Owen QC
Two Garden Court (Owen Davies QC & Courtenay Griffiths QC), London
(020) 7353 1633
Recommended in Human Rights

DAVIES, Rhodri QC
One Essex Court (Lord Grabiner QC), London
(020) 7583 2000
Recommended in Banking & Finance, Commercial (Litigation)
Specialisation: Principal area of practice is banking and professional negligence including disputes over derivatives. Acted in swaps litigation, representing various banks in Hazell v London Borough of Hammersmith & Fulham and in restitution claims in Kleinwort Benson v Birmingham and Kleinwort Benson v Lincoln. Acted for KPMG in

LEADERS AT THE BAR

Law Society v KPMG and for the liquidator in the litigation against the auditor of Barings Europe. Also handles general commercial work, encompassing contractual disputes, sale of goods, arbitration, insurance and reinsurance.
Prof. Memberships: South Eastern Circuit, LCLCBA.
Career: Called to the Bar in 1979 and joined 1 Essex Court in 1980. QC 1999.
Personal: Educated at Winchester College 1970-74 and Downing College, Cambridge 1975-78. Leisure pursuits include running, walking and sailing. Born 29 January 1957. Lives in Harpenden, Herts.

DAVIES, Richard QC
39 Essex Street (Nigel Pleming QC), London
(020) 7832 1111
Recommended in Personal Injury
Specialisation: Personal injuries, professional negligence, insurance, construction.
Prof. Memberships: LCLCBA.

DAVIES, Stephen
8 King St (Gerard McDermott QC), Manchester
(0161) 834 9560
stephen.davies@8ks.co.uk
Recommended in Commercial (Litigation)
Specialisation: Practice: commercial litigation; construction (including arbitration and adjudication), professional negligence; banking; property; insolvency, predominantly in North West.
Prof. Memberships: Northern Circuit Commercial Bar Association; Tec Bar; Professional Negligence Bar Association.
Career: Educated at Baines' School, Poulton-le-Fylde and Downing College, Cambridge. Called to the Bar in 1985. Practised at current chambers since 1987. Recent notable cases: Transco v Stockport MBC [2001] EWCA Civ 212 (nuisance); Queen Elizabeth's Grammar School v Banks Wilson (2001) EWCA Civ 1360 (professional negligence).

DAVIES, Stephen QC
Guildhall Chambers (Adrian Palmer QC), Bristol
(0117) 930 9000
Recommended in Chancery, Commercial (Litigation), Insolvency

DAVIES, Trefor
Iscoed Chambers (Elwen Mair Evans QC), Swansea
(01792) 652988/9
Recommended in Crime

DAVIES-JONES, Jonathan
3 Verulam Buildings (Christopher Symons QC & John Jarvis QC), London
(020) 7831 8441
chambers@3vb.com
Recommended in Banking & Finance, Commercial (Litigation)
Specialisation: General commercial work, including banking, insurance and reinsurance, fraud, professional negligence, sale of goods and commercial agency.
Career: MA (Cantab). Worked as an investment banker 1988-92. Called to the Bar in 1994 and joined 3 Verulam Buildings. In 1995 spent six months as a judicial assistant in the Commercial Court.

DAVIS, Glen
3-4 South Square (Michael Crystal QC & Lord Alexander of Weedon QC), London
(020) 7696 9900
glendavis@southsquare.com
Recommended in Insolvency
Specialisation: Business, commercial and financial law, in particular banking, corporate restructuring and insolvency. E-commerce, e-banking and internet law, and related aspects of computer and intellectual property law. Regulatory aspects of UK websites and financial restructuring of dot.com companies. Injunctive relief. Fraud, tracing claims and recovery of assets. Duties of directors and insolvency practitioners. Insolvent partnerships and limited partnerships. Company law. Professional negligence and general corporate disputes and advice. Recent cases have included Gwembe Valley Development Co v Koshy (Court of Appeal: construction of debentures); FJL Realisations Ltd (Court of Appeal: priority of payments in Administration); Re Brelec Installations Ltd (Blackburne J: effects of termination on funds in voluntary arrangement); Re Double S Printers (Jonathan Parker J: fixed charge over book debts); advising in connection with numerous provisional liquidations including HIH and Rafidain Bank, and numerous Administrations including Teleglobe.
Prof. Memberships: Member, Insolvency Lawyers Association; associate member, R3; member, Insol Europe; member, International Bar Association; member, International Chamber of Commerce; member, Justice; member, Society for Computers and Law.
Career: Previously television producer/director (BBC, Channel 4, satellite television). Called to Bar 1992, member of Chambers at 3/4 South Square since 1993. Member, Insolvency Courts Users Committee (2001-). Trustee/Directors (2002-) and Chair, Media Board (2002-), Society for Computers and Law.
Publications: Editor, Butterworths 'Insolvency Law Handbook'; consultant editor, Butterworths 'Insolvency Law Manual' (prospective). Co-author, 'Insolvent Partnerships' (Jordans, 1996). Contributing editor, 'Totty & Moss on Insolvency'.
Personal: Educated University College School, Hampstead, and Balliol College, Oxford (Goldsmith Scholar, 1st Class Hons). MA (Oxon), Dip Law (City). Diploma in Investment Management from London Business School. Interests include contemporary art and garden design.

DAVIS-WHITE, Malcolm
4 Stone Buildings (Philip Heslop QC), London
(020) 7242 5524
clerks@4stonebuildings.law.co.uk
Recommended in Company, Insolvency
Specialisation: Principal area of practice encompasses company, insolvency and financial services law.
Prof. Memberships: Member of the Chancery Bar Association, Commercial Bar Association (COMBAR), Society of Advanced Legal Studies and Insolvency Lawyers Association.
Career: Called to the Bar in 1984 and joined present chambers in 1985. Appointed Junior Counsel to the Crown (Chancery) in 1994.
Publications: Co-author (with Adrian Walters) on 'Directors' Disqualification and Practice'. Contributor to 'Atkin' Vol. 9 (Companies), and Vol. 10 (Companies winding up) and Butterworths' 'Practical Insolvency'.
Personal: Educated at St Edmund's College, Old Hall Green, Ware 1969-78 and Hertford College, Oxford 1979-83. Born 18 September 1960.

DAY, Anneliese
Four New Square (Justin Fenwick QC), London
(020) 7822 2000
a.day@4newsquare.com
Recommended in Professional Negligence
Specialisation: Principal areas of practice are professional negligence (in particular, claims involving solicitors and barristers, accountants and auditors, surveyors, construction professionals, insurance brokers, healthcare professionals and financial service professionals); commercial and insurance litigation; employment and human rights. Important cases include: Balfron Trustees v Peterson [2002] (solicitor's liability to pension fund); Trybuild Ltd v Invicta Leisure Tennis Ltd [1997] (design duties of engineers); Simba-Tola v Elizabeth Fry Hospital [2001] (disclosure and duties of bail hostel); Blatchford v Berger [2001] (unfair dismissal and redundancy).
Prof. Memberships: Professional Negligence Bar Association, COMBAR, Society of Construction Lawyers, TECBAR.
Career: MA (Cantab). Kennedy Scholar. Called to Bar (Inner Temple) 1996 (Princess Royal Scholarship). Joined Four New Square (formerly 2 Crown Office Row) in 1997.
Publications: Assistant editor of 'Jackson and Powell on Professional Negligence' and contributor to 'Civil Practice and Human Rights'.
Personal: Educated at the Edinburgh Academy, Clare College, Cambridge and Harvard University. Leisure interests: travel, running and triathlons. Speaks French and Spanish.

DE FREITAS, Anthony
4 Paper Buildings (Jean Ritchie QC), London
(020) 7643 5000
anthony.defreitas@4paperbuildings.com
Recommended in Agriculture
Specialisation: Sporting and entertainment contracts, professional negligence. Agricultural holdings. Warren v Mendy 1989 IWLR 853, Featherstone v Staples 1986 IWLR 861, John v George 1996 EGLR 1, Greenbank v Pickles 2001 1EGLR 1, Trustees of St John's Hospital v Keevil 2001 EWCA CIV 1730.
Prof. Memberships: Professional Negligence Bar Association. Agricultural Law Association.
Career: Stonyhurst College, St. John's College Oxford. MA Oxon, Recorder.
Personal: Married, cricket, bridge, horse racing, reading.

DE GARR ROBINSON, Anthony
One Essex Court (Lord Grabiner QC), London
(020) 7583 2000
Recommended in Commercial (Litigation), Fraud, Insolvency
Specialisation: Tony de Garr Robinson's practice includes a broad range of substantial commercial litigation. He has expertise in a wide variety of fields, including (in no particular order) arbitration, company law, corporate and business acquisition, insolvency, transnational fraud, media and sport. He has considerable experience of international asset tracing, including in the United States, Switzerland, Bermuda, the Channel Islands, the Cayman Islands and the British Virgin Islands.
Prof. Memberships: Commercial Bar Association and Chancery Bar Association.
Career: He was called to the English Bar in 1987. He is also a member of the Bar of the Eastern Caribbean Supreme Court in the Territory of the Virgin Islands.
Personal: He was born in 1963 and was educated at University College and at Harvard University (where he held a Kennedy Scholarship).

DE HAAN, Kevin QC
3 Raymond Buildings (Clive Nicholls QC), London
(020) 7400 6400
chambers@3raymondbuildings.com
Recommended in Consumer Law, Health & Safety, Licensing
Specialisation: Specialises in all areas of environmental law, consumer protection and licensing. Environmental practice includes all relevant aspects of EC law and covers pollution control, waste regulation, statutory nuisances and environmental issues arising in road transport licensing and health and safety regulation. Experience includes conducting proceedings before various regulatory bodies, associated judicial reviews, defending criminal prosecutions. Contributor to 'Pollution in the UK' (Sweet & Maxwell 1995). Clients have included a number of public corporations and institutions. Consumer protection practice includes

all aspects of regulation under the Fair Trading Act 1973, Trade Description Act 1968, the Medicines Act 1968, the Consumer Credit Act 1974, the Consumer Protection Act 1987, the Weights and Measures Act 1985, the Food Safety Act 1990 and the relevant EC law. Has particular expertise in the regulation of e-commerce at national, European and International level. Contributor to 'Food Safety, Law and Practice' (Sweet & Maxwell 1994). Clients have included a number of major public companies, former nationalised industries, banks, building societies and other institutions. Licensing practice includes all aspects, particularly betting, gaming and lotteries. Has considerable experience of proceedings before various regulatory bodies, appeals and associated judicial reviews. Clients have included major casino operators, bookmaking concerns and promoters of lotteries and competitions. Has particular expertise and experience in all aspects of internet gambling. Other areas of practice include some extradition and commercial fraud work.
Prof. Memberships: Local Government, Environmental and Planning Bar Association.
Career: Called to the Bar 1976.
Personal: Educated at the Universities of London and Brussels (VUB).

DE HAAS, Margaret QC
7 Harrington Street Chambers (David Steer QC & Robert Fordham QC & Iain Goldrein QC), Liverpool
(0151) 242 0707
goldhaas@netcom.co.uk
Recommended in Family
Specialisation: Ancillary relief; child care; medical negligence, personal injury.
Prof. Memberships: Family Law Bar Association; Professional Negligence Bar Association.
Career: LL.B (Hons) (Bristol). Author of several books on personal injury litigation and ancillary relief. Recorder. Sits as Deputy High Court Judge, member of Criminal Injuries Compensation Board.
Personal: Theatre; reading; her children.

DE LA MARE, Thomas
Blackstone Chambers (Presiley Baxendale QC & Charles Flint QC), London
(020) 75831770
tod@blackstonechambers.com
Recommended in Administrative & Public Law, Human Rights
Specialisation: Public law; EC law; human rights; commercial; IP and entertainment; employment.
Prof. Memberships: ALBA (Committee); BEG (Committee); ELA.
Publications: Lester & Pannick (Contributor).

DE LACY, Richard QC
3 Verulam Buildings (Christopher Symons QC & John Jarvis QC), London
(020) 7831 8441
rdelacy@3vb.com
Recommended in Insolvency
Specialisation: Principal area of practice is commercial law, particularly banking, finance, financial services, accountants', solicitors' and barristers' professional indemnity, insolvency, company law, property law and arbitration. Acts for clearing banks, major accountancy firms and leading insolvency practitioners.
Prof. Memberships: Fellow of The Chartered Institute of Arbitrators, COMBAR, Chancery Bar Association; Institute of Chartered Accountants Practice Regulation Review Committee; CEDR Accredited Mediator.
Career: Called to the Bar 1976. Bencher, Middle Temple. QC 2000.
Personal: Educated at Hymers College, Hull and Clare College, Cambridge (MA 1979).

DE MELLO, Rambert
6 King's Bench Walk (Sibghat Kadri QC), London
(020) 7583 0695 / 7353 4931
Recommended in Immigration

DE NAVARRO, Michael QC
2 Temple Gardens (Dermod O'Brien QC), London
(020) 7822 1200
Recommended in Health & Safety
Specialisation: Personal injury, professional and clinical negligence, insurance and health and safety at work. Reported personal injury cases include Adams v SEB [1993] (CA), Green v Building Scene [1994] (CA), O'Shea v Kingston-upon-Thames [1995] (CA), Hunter v Butler [1995] (CA), Jolley v LB of Sutton [1998] (CA). [2001] (HL). Other reported cases include Wentworth v Wiltshire CC [1992] (CA), Nykredit Mortgage Bank v Edward Erdman [1996] (HL), John Monroe (Acrylics) v LFCDA [1997] (CA), Day v Cook [2000], Royal Victoria Infirmary v B [2002].
Prof. Memberships: PIBA (Committee member 1995, Chairman 1997-99). Western Circuit.
Career: Called 1968, QC 1990, Recorder 1990. Bencher Inner Temple 2000.

DE SILVA, Desmond QC
2 Paper Buildings (Desmond de Silva QC), London
(020) 7556 5500
clerks@2pb.co.uk
Recommended in Crime
Specialisation: Crime, commercial fraud, extradition, constitutional law, international law. R v Levitt and others (City Fraud); R v Jaqui Oliver (Fraud - Britain's foremost female National Hunt Jockey); R v Lord Brocket (Insurance Fraud); R v Ghizzelli (EEC Fraud); R v Segers (Football match fixing/corruption); R v Ron Atkinson (road rage); R v Nagi (aircraft highjacking); R v Bowyer (Leeds Footballer Trial).
Prof. Memberships: Criminal Bar Association; British Academy of Forensic Sciences.
Career: Middle Temple – called to the Bar of England and Wales 1964. QC 1984. Deputy Circuit Judge 1976-84. Apart from the UK, has practised in many other countries and is a member of many foreign Bars. Has appeared abroad in many cases involving high treason and the death penalty. Deputy Prosecutor, Special Court for Sierra Leone 2002.
Personal: Married, one daughter. Leisure interests: travelling, politics.

DEIN, Jeremy
3 Gray's Inn Square (Rock Tansey QC), London
(020) 7520 5600
Recommended in Crime
Specialisation: Specialises in criminal defence work. Leading junior practice in serious crime of all types. Has led in several high profile cases and numerous murder cases. Keen interest in points of law. Wide experience in the Court of Appeal. Author of various articles, including 'Police Misconduct Revisited' (Criminal Law Review, October 2000): a detailed analysis of authorities concerning the Court of Appeal's approach in cases where police officers face outstanding allegations at the time of a defendant's trial. Has also acted as legal advisor to BBC's Rough Justice programme, Channel Four News and other media outlets.
Prof. Memberships: South Eastern Circuit, Criminal Bar Association, Bar Race Relations Committee, Bar Human Rights Committee, Foreign Office Pro Bono Lawyers Panel (representation of British subjects imprisoned abroad), Middle Temple.
Career: 2:1 (Hons), University of London. Former lecturer in the law of evidence and criminal procedure.
Personal: Married with four children. Interests include salsa dance, travel, politics, history and football.

DENNEY, Stuart
Deans Court Chambers (Stephen Grime QC), Manchester
(0161) 214 600
denney@deanscourt.co.uk
Recommended in Crime
Specialisation: Crime, including fraud. Actions against the Police.
Prof. Memberships: Criminal Bar Association.
Career: St. Johns School, Leatherhead. Gonville & Caius College Cambridge 1977-80. MA.
Personal: Married, one son. Interests: Rugby Union, Malt Whisky.

DENNIS, Mark
6 King's Bench Walk (Roy Amlot QC), London
(020) 7583 0410
clerks@bkbw.com
Recommended in Crime
Specialisation: Crime.
Prof. Memberships: CBA.
Career: Call: 1977. Senior Treasury Counsel. (Treasury Counsel since 1993).

DENNISON, Stephen QC
Atkin Chambers (Robert Akenhead QC), London
(020) 7404 0102
Emergency Tel: (020) 7242 4703
Recommended in Construction
Specialisation: Specialist practitioner in the fields of civil engineering, construction, professional negligence, information technology, oil, telecommunication, water and power generation industries. Substantial experience in the preparation and conduct of proceedings in the Courts of England and Wales and in domestic and international arbitrations.
Career: Called to Bar 1985.
Personal: Born 26 February 1958. Educated Manchester University (LLB).

DENNYS, Nicholas QC
Atkin Chambers (Robert Akenhead QC), London
(020) 7404 0102
Recommended in Construction, Information Technology
Specialisation: Building and Civil Engineering disputes and related matters including Professional Negligence, Insurance, Conflict of Laws, Information Technology, Energy and general commercial work. Extensive arbitration experience as advocate, before both international and domestic tribunals. International disputes usually involving large multinational corporations or Governmental Agencies in many parts of the world. Appointed to act as sole arbitrator under the Common and Commercial Bar Association Scheme and as Chairman by the London Court of International arbitration.
Career: Admitted to Middle Temple August 1973; Called to the Bar November 1975; Queen's Counsel May 1991.
Personal: Born 14 July 1951. Educated Eton College and Brasenose College, Oxford (PPE).

DENYER-GREEN, Barry
Falcon Chambers (Jonathan Gaunt QC & Kim Lewison QC), London
(020) 7353 2484
clerks@falcon-chambers.com
Recommended in Property Litigation
Specialisation: Compulsory purchase and compensation; planning; agricultural tenancies. Member DETR compulsory purchase working party 1998-2000.
Prof. Memberships: Fellow, Royal Institution of Chartered Surveyors. Honorary fellow, College of Estate Management. Honorary Member of Central Association of Agricultural Valuers.
Career: LLM, PhD (London University).
Publications: Author 'Compulsory Purchase and Compensation' (edn 2000). Joint author 'Development and Planning Law' (3rd edn 1999). Editor 'Estates Gazette Law Reports'. Joint editor 'Planning Law Reports'.

LEADERS AT THE BAR

DEVONSHIRE, Simon
11 King's Bench Walk Chambers (Eldred Tabachnik QC & James Goudie QC), London
(020) 7632 8500
devonshire@11kbw.com
Recommended in Employment
Specialisation: All aspects of employment and entertainment law, including wrongful and unfair dismissal, discrimination, restrictive covenants and confidential information, agency, recording, publishing and management disputes, copyright and intellectual property.
Prof. Memberships: Employment Law Bar Association. LCLCBA.
Career: Called 1988.

DICKENS, Paul
Hogarth Chambers (Jonathan Rayner James QC & Christopher Morcom QC), London
(020) 7404 0404
Recommended in Media & Entertainment

DICKER, Robin QC
3-4 South Square (Michael Crystal QC & Lord Alexander of Weedon QC), London
(020) 7696 9900
clerks@southsquare.com
Recommended in Banking & Finance, Company, Energy, Fraud, Insolvency
Specialisation: Specialises in business, commercial and financial law and litigation, in particular banking, corporate restructuring and insolvency. He has acted in relation to almost all of the major corporate collapses. Recent reported cases include: Three Rivers District Council v Bank of England (No 3) [2001] 2 All ER 513 (House of Lords) and (No 2) [2000] 2 WLR 1220 (House of Lords); National Westminster Bank v Utrecht-America [2001] 3 All ER 733 (Court of Appeal); Morris v Bank of America [2000] 1 All ER 954 (Court of Appeal); Sea Assets v Garuda [2000] 4 All ER 371 (Longmore J).
Prof. Memberships: Commercial Bar Association; Chancery Bar Association; ICC and LCIA.
Career: Exhibitioner at Brasenose College, Oxford (BA and BCL). Called to the Bar (Middle Temple) in 1986 and a Harmsworth Exhibitioner. Appointed Queen's Counsel in 2000. Practises at 3-4 South Square.
Publications: Contributing Editor to 'Totty & Moss on Insolvency' (Sweet & Maxwell). Contributing Editor to 'Professional Negligence and Liability (LLP).

DIGGINS, Martin
Claremont Chambers (J.G Mendas Edwards), Wolverhampton
(01902) 426222
Recommended in Environment

DINAN-HAYWARD, Deborah
Albion Chambers (Neil Ford QC), Bristol
(0117) 927 2144
Recommended in Family

DINKIN, Anthony QC
2-3 Gray's Inn Square (Anthony Porten QC & Anthony Scrivener QC), London
(020) 7242 4986
chambers@2-3graysinnsquare.co.uk
Recommended in Planning
Specialisation: Specialises in town and country planning, local government, valuation and compensation, landlord and tenant, restrictive covenants. With extensive experience in conducting planning inquiries concerning all aspects of planning including major food and non-food retailing developments, housing, conservation, pollution control and hazardous substances, local plans, CPO's and enforcement. Court experience includes legal challenges/judicial review of Secretary of State/Inspector and local government decisions and appearances in the Lands Tribunal.
Career: College of Estate Management (BscEst Management) 1966; Called to the Bar 1968; QC 1991; Recorder 1989; past Lecturer and External Examiner in Law, Reading University. Legal Member of Lands Tribunal 1998-99. President, Mental Health Review Tribunal 2000-present.

DIXEY, Ian
St John's Chambers (Christopher Sharp QC), Bristol
(0117) 921 3456
Recommended in Crime

DIXON, Ralph
2HG Chambers (Jonathan Dingle & Harry Hodgkin), Taunton
(0845) 083 3000
dixon@clerksroom.com
Recommended in Family
Specialisation: Higher value matrimonial finance cases, in particular business and farming.
Prof. Memberships: Family Law Bar Association.
Career: BA Hons, University of York, Called to the Bar 1980.

DODDS, R Stephen
15 Winckley Square (R Stephen Dodds), Preston
(01772) 252828
Recommended in Family

DODSON, Joanna QC
14 Gray's Inn Square (Joanna Dodson QC), London
(020) 7242 0858
Recommended in Family
Specialisation: Practice encompasses all aspects of family law.
Prof. Memberships: Family Law Bar Association.
Career: Called to the Bar 1971. Joined 14 Gray's Inn Square in 1991 and took Silk in 1993.
Personal: Educated at James Allen's Girls School 1956-63 and Newnham College, Cambridge (BA 1967, MA 1971). Born 5 September 1945. Lives in London.

DOERRIES, Chantal-AimEe
Atkin Chambers (Robert Akenhead QC), London
(020) 7404 0102
clerks@atkinchambers.law.co.uk
Recommended in Construction
Specialisation: All stages of disputes from court proceedings, domestic and international arbitration to mediation and adjudication, in respect of construction and engineering, information technology, oil and gas, professional negligence and associated areas of commercial and property law. Recent cases: Floods of Queensferry Ltd. and Anor v Shand Construction Ltd. and Ors (2000) BLR 81, TCC; QPS Consultants Ltd. v Kruger Tissue (Manufacturing) Ltd. (1999) BLR 366, CA; RTZ Pension Trust v ARC and Others (1999) 1 All ER 532, CA; David Flood v Shand Construction Ltd. and Os (1996) 81 BLR 31, CA; Floods of Queensferry Ltd. v Shand Construction Ltd. and Os (1997) 81 BLR 31, TCC.
Prof. Memberships: TECBAR (Bar Council Representative 2000 to date; Secretary 1997-2000). Society for Computers and Law. Society of Construction Lawyers.
Career: Called to the Bar 1992. Major Harmsworth Entrance Exhibition and Diplock Scholar, Middle Temple. Gertrude de Gallaix Achievement Award for Study of Law, FAWCO. Editor of the Building Law Reports 1999 to date.
Personal: Educated at Roedean School (1982-86), University of Pennsylvania (1986-87) and New Hall, Cambridge (1987-91). Fluent in German and working knowledge of French.

DOHMANN, Barbara QC
Blackstone Chambers (Presiley Baxendale QC & Charles Flint QC), London
(020) 7583 1770
clerks@blackstonechambers.com
Recommended in Commercial (Litigation), Financial Services, Fraud, Insurance, Media & Entertainment
Specialisation: Insurance and reinsurance; financial services; banking; private international law; commercial fraud (civil); commercial arbitration; entertainment and media/intellectual property; disciplinary tribunals; regulatory tribunals.
Prof. Memberships: Chairman of the Commercial Bar Association 1999-2001, committee member; member London Common Law and Commercial Bar Association, Learned Society for International Civil Procedure Law, Bar European Group.
Career: Called 1971; Queen's Counsel 1987; Recorder (1990-) and Deputy High Court Judge (1994-2002).
Personal: Educated in German and American schools, Universities of Erlangen, Mainz and Paris. Languages: German, French, Spanish, Italian.

DOVE, Ian
No5 Chambers (Gareth Evans QC), Birmingham
(0121) 606 0500
Recommended in Planning

DOWDING, Nicholas QC
Falcon Chambers (Jonathan Gaunt QC & Kim Lewison QC), London
(020) 7353 2484
dowding@falcon-chambers.com
Recommended in Property Litigation
Specialisation: All aspects of Chancery and real property law, commercial property litigation and arbitration.
Prof. Memberships: Chancery Bar Association; London Common Law and Commercial Bar Association; Property Bar Association.
Career: Called to the Bar 1979. Silk 1997. Corresponding member of Royal Institution of Chartered Surveyors Dilapidations Practice Panel. Member of Falcon Chambers since 1980. Blundell memorial lecturer 1992 and 1997.
Publications: Joint author 'Dilapidations - The Modern Law and Practice'. Joint editor 'Woodfall on Landlord and Tenant'. General editor of 'Landlord and Tenant Reports'.

DOWLEY, Dominic QC
Serle Court (Lord Neill of Bladen QC), London
(020) 7242 6105
clerks@serlecourt.co.uk
Recommended in Commercial (Litigation)
Specialisation: Commercial fraud, insurance/reinsurance, arbitration, banking and financial services/regulation specialist.
Career: Called to the Bar and joined One Hare Court in 1983 (merged with Serle Court in 2000). QC 2002.
Personal: Educated at Oxford University 1977-80. Bacon Scholar of Gray's Inn; Barstow Law Scholar. Born 25 March 1958.

DOYLE, Louis
40 King St, Manchester
(0161) 832 9082
ldoyle@40kingstreet.co.uk
Recommended in Chancery, Commercial (Litigation), Insolvency
Specialisation: All aspects of corporate and personal insolvency (predominantly but not exclusively for office-holders under the insolvency legislation), company law (in particular shareholder disputes), director disqualification, credit, security, banking (in particular mortgages, recoveries and guarantees), partnerships, commercial contracts, financial disputes and related litigation including indemnity insurance work relating to solicitors' professional negligence in areas of specialism. Recently instructed in relation to the administration of Chesterfield Football Club and Fads, proceedings in the bankruptcy of the actor William Roache and claims against businessman Amer Al Midani. Has appeared in nine reported first instance and Court of Appeal decisions over the last three years.
Prof. Memberships: Insolvency Lawyers' Association, R3, Chancery Bar Association, Northern Chancery Bar Association, Professional Negligence Bar Association.
Career: Lecturer in Law 1989-92. Admitted as a solicitor 1994. Called to

LEADERS AT THE BAR

the Bar, Lincoln's Inn, 1996. Joined present Chambers 1999. Appointed to Treasury Solicitor's Civil Litigation Provincial Panel 2000.
Publications: Author 'Administrative Receivership: Law and Practice' (1995, 2nd edn forthcoming 2002) and 'Insolvency Litigation' (1998). Also a member of the editorial board of Sweet & Maxwells 'Insolvency Lawyer' and has written numerous articles in professional and academic journals.
Personal: Born Liverpool, 23 August 1966. Educated St Anselm's College, Birkenhead. LLB 1987, LLM 1990.

DRABBLE, Richard QC
4 Breams Buildings (Christopher Lockhart-Mummery QC), London
(020) 7430 1221
Recommended in Administrative & Public Law, Local Government, Planning
Specialisation: Specialises in public law, planning, local government and social security.
Prof. Memberships: Former Chairman of the Administrative Law Bar Association, member of the Planning and Environmental Bar Association.
Career: Member of the Panel of Junior Counsel to the Crown (Common Law) 1992-95, took Silk 1995, contributor to Goudie and Supperstone Judicial Review.

DRACASS, Timothy
Eighteen Carlton Crescent (Martin Blount), Southampton
(023) 8063 9001
Recommended in Employment
Specialisation: Principal area of practice is employment. Wide variety of employee and employer work undertaken, ranging from unfair dismissal and contractual claims to more complex discrimination and equal pay matters and trade union based actions. A number of recent appearances in the EAT. Also practices in civil (in particular personal injury) and family law.
Prof. Memberships: Western Circuit; Employment Law Bar Association.
Career: Called to the Bar in 1998, Inner Temple.
Personal: Passions include football, supporting Southampton FC, golf, snow-boarding and theatre.

DREW, Jane
Coram Chambers (Roger McCarthy QC), London
(020) 7797 7766
Recommended in Family
Specialisation: Family law. Handles all types of work concerning children with a special emphasis on children in local authority care, care proceedings, adoption, private children law, divorce, matrimonial property, family provision and inheritance. Also deals with cohabitees covering real property disputes, cases under Section 14 of the Trusts of Land and Trustees Act 1996. Has dealt with numerous cases of sexual abuse and non-accidental injury. Regular lecturer and provider of seminars on cohabitees and public law children's work.
Prof. Memberships: Family Law Bar Association.
Career: Called to the Bar 1976. Tenant at Francis Taylor Building 1977-82, then joined current chambers.
Personal: Educated at Stevenage Girls Grammar School 1963-70, Trevelyan College, Durham 1971-74 and Inns of Court School 1974-76. Leisure pursuits include swimming, tennis and badminton. Born 6 June 1952. Lives in Knebworth.

DRISCOLL, Michael QC
9 Old Square (Michael Driscoll QC), London
(020) 7405 4682
Recommended in Professional Negligence, Property Litigation
Specialisation: General Chancery (advisory and litigation) but in particular property related, partnership and company law matters.
Career: Rugby and Cambridge (BA LLB).

DRUCE, Michael
2 Mitre Court Buildings (Guy Roots QC), London
(020) 7583 1380
michael.druce@2mcb.co.uk
Recommended in Planning
Specialisation: Main areas of practice are town and country planning, compulsory purchase and compensation, rating, local government, environmental and administrative law. Recent cases include the major retail proposals for the Westgate Centre, Oxford and MetroCentre, Gateshead; the redevelopments of Gloucester Docks and Spitalfields Market; Park and Ride schemes; Croft motor racing circuit; the development of a registered battlefield site; Battersea Heliport; and numerous MSA proposals. Has also appeared before the Grand Court of the Cayman Islands.
Prof. Memberships: Planning and Environment Bar Association. Justice.
Career: Called to Bar 1988 and joined current chambers 1990.
Publications: Contributing editor to Butterworths 'Local Government Law'.
Personal: Educated at Repton School and Sidney Sussex College, Cambridge. Born 23 March 1964. Married with two children. Lives in London.

DU CANN, Christian
39 Essex Street (Nigel Pleming QC), London
(020) 7832 1111
cdc@39essex.co.uk
Recommended in Personal Injury
Specialisation: Catastrophic injury. Occupational disease (especially asbestos ULD and stress claims). Disaster claims. Health and safety law (including criminal prosecution). Sports injury claims. Also specialises in medical and professional negligence.
Prof. Memberships: Member of Gray's Inn (member of its Continuing Education Committee and Advocacy teacher). Member of PIBA. Member of London Common Law and Commercial Bar Association. Member of Bar Council.
Career: Called to the Bar 1982. Practised at 39 Essex Street since 1991.
Personal: Speaks French and Spanish.

DUCK, Michael
3 Fountain Court (Robert Juckes QC), Birmingham
(0121) 236 5854
Recommended in Crime

DUFFY, Joanne
No5 Chambers (Gareth Evans QC), Birmingham
(0121) 606 0500
Recommended in Family

DUGGAN, Michael
Littleton Chambers (Michel Kallipetis QC), London
(07957) 365 302 (Mobile)
mdugg@aol.com
Recommended in Employment
Specialisation: The main area of practice is in the field of employment law, covering all areas of discrimination (particularly disability discrimination and harassment), wrongful and unfair dismissal, redundancies and dismissals/variation of employment contracts arising out of reorganisations, restrictive covenants, trade union law including labour disputes, whistle blowing and the emerging interface of the European Convention on European Rights with employment issues. Other areas of practice include building and construction law, health and safety and professional negligence and general commercial law including applications for interim injunctions and freezing orders.
Career: Called to the Bar 1984. Regular writer and lecturer on employment and commercial law, human rights law and civil procedure in the light of the Woolf reforms.
Publications: Author: 'The Modern Law of Strikes'; 'Business Re-Organisations and Employment Law (FT Law & Tax)'; 'Termination of Employment of Directors (FT Law & Tax June 1997)'. 'Unfair Dismissal'; 'Law, Practice and Guidance'; 'Wrongful Dismissal'; 'Law Practice and Precedents and Contracts of Employment'; 'Law Practice and Precedents'. EMIS Publishing. Editor in Chief of the 'Civil Practice Law Reports'.
Personal: BA. BCL. LLM (First Class, Sidney Sussex College, Cambridge University). Holt Scholar of Gray's Inn. Lives in Coton, Cambridgeshire and Gray's Inn. Married with three boys. Interests: music, guitar.

DUGGAN, Ross
India Buildings Chambers (Ray Herman), Liverpool
(0151) 243 6000
Recommended in Family

DUMARESQ, Delia
Atkin Chambers (Robert Akenhead QC), London
(020) 7404 0102
Emergency Tel: (020) 7242 4703
Recommended in Construction
Specialisation: All aspects of construction, building and engineering dispute resolution including international and domestic arbitration, mediation and adjudication. Advocate, mediator, writer and lecturer in ADR. Counsel in leading adjudication cases – Macob v Morrison; Project Consultancy v Gray's Trustees; Bloor Construction; Bridgeway v Tolent; Cameron v Mowlem; Gibson Lea v Makro.
Prof. Memberships: New South Wales Bar (Australia), TECBAR and CEDR Mediator and panel of adjudicators. Fellow of Chartered Institute of Arbitrators. Inter Mediation (Mediator). Adjudication Society.
Career: 1967- BA - Australia. Prior to reading law, worked in Southeast Asia (as an archaeologist) and Europe. 1973 - MA (Hons) - London (Work and research on disadvantaged groups and communities) 1983 - Dip Law (Hons); 1984 - called; Inner Temple.
Personal: One son. Interests include music, modern art, Italian culture and Language.

DUMONT, Thomas
11 New Square (Sonia Proudman QC), London
(020) 7831 0081
Recommended in Charities
Specialisation: Professional negligence principally solicitors and accountants: Paragon Finance v Thakerar & Co (1999); Gibbons v Nelsons (2000). Charity and private client advice and litigation, including trusts, wills and probate, re Ratcliffe (1999), re Anker-Petersen (2002). Commercial property: landlord and tenant. Restrictive covenants and mortgages: Mortgage Corporation v Nationwide Credit Corporation (1994). Rutland House Textiles v Mace (1999).
Prof. Memberships: Charity Law Association; Society of Trust & Estate Practitioners; Professional Negligence Bar Association; ACTAPS.
Career: MA (Cantab) Exhibitioner in Law, Trinity Hall. Called 1979, Gray's Inn. Lecturer in trusts and revenue, University of Westminster 1981-85.
Personal: Married with two children. Fellow of the Zoological Society of London. Plays cricket whenever possible.

DUNKELS, Paul QC
Walnut House (Paul Dunkels QC), Exeter
(01392) 279751
clerks@walnuthouse.co.uk
Recommended in Crime
Specialisation: Prosecutes and defends in all types of serious crime. Prosecuted cases on behalf of the Serious Fraud Office. Prosecuted a five month series of trials of members of a paedophile ring (R v M and others [2000] Cr.App.R.266). Frequently involved in trials concerning the abuse and deaths of

LEADERS AT THE BAR

babies including Munchausen Syndrome by Proxy and allegations of smothering by a parent.
Prof. Memberships: Criminal Bar Association.
Career: Called 1972. Recorder 1988. Silk 1993.

DUNN, Katherine
40 King St, Manchester
(0161) 832 9082
kdunn@40kingstreet.co.uk
Recommended in Chancery, Commercial (Litigation)
Specialisation: General chancery (with a litigation bias) and commercial litigation, including personal and corporate insolvency, company law, landlord and tenant, professional negligence, mortgages and land law generally, non-contentious work, including wills, trusts and probate also undertaken.
Prof. Memberships: Northern Circuit, Northern Chancery Bar Association, Chancery Bar Association.
Career: On DTI Panel for Directors' Disqualifications.

DUNNING, Graham QC
Essex Court Chambers (Gordon Pollock QC), London
(020) 7813 8000
gdunning@essexcourt-chambers.co.uk
Recommended in Arbitration, Shipping
Specialisation: Specialist in all aspects of international and commercial law, particularly arbitration (both as arbitrator and as counsel), banking and finance, commodities and trade, insurance and reinsurance, professional negligence and shipping and transport. In the international field practice covers jurisdictional and private international law disputes, arbitrations, injunctions, forum conveniens and applicable law. Commodities and trade work covers cases involving oil, metals, foodstuffs and futures. Practice encompasses all aspects of insurance and reinsurance litigation. Professional negligence experience covers cases involving insurance brokers, actuaries, accountants and solicitors. Shipping and transport practice covers charterparty disputes and bill of lading claims, ship sale and shipbuiding, aviation.
Prof. Memberships: Commercial Bar Association; British Insurance Law Association; British Maritime Law Association; London Maritime Arbitrators Association; London Court of International Arbitration.
Career: Called to the Bar 1982. QC 2001.
Personal: Educated at Cambridge University (BA Hons 1st Class) 1977-80, and at Harvard Law School (LLM) 1980-81. Scholarships: Emmanuel College Entrance Scholarship (1977); University of Cambridge Squire Law Scholarship (1978 and 1979); Lincoln's Inn Hardwicke Scholarship (1979); Kennedy Scholar, Harvard Law School (1980); Lincoln's Inn Denning Scholarship (1981). Born 13 March 1958. Lives in London.

DUNN-SHAW, Jason
6 King's Bench Walk (Roy Amlot QC), London
(020) 7583 0410
jason.dunn-shaw@6kbw.com
Recommended in Crime
Specialisation: Crime, including courts martial and appellate proceedings. Extradition. Available for advisory and regulatory work.
Prof. Memberships: Criminal Bar Association; Committee of the Central London Courts Bar mess; Junior of the Old Bailey Bar mess.
Career: Called to the Bar by Lincoln's Inn in 1992. Wide-ranging practice has included cases of murder, hijack, major drugs importations, sexual offences, money-laundering and fraud.
Personal: Born 18 September 1964. Malvern College; Manchester University; University of Westminster.

DUTHIE, Catriona
St John's Chambers (Christopher Sharp QC), Bristol
(0117) 921 3456
Recommended in Family

DUTTON, Timothy
No. 1 Serjeants' Inn (Edward Faulks QC), London
(020) 7415 6666
clerks@no1serjeantsinn.com
Recommended in Property Litigation
Specialisation: Property-related litigation, with a strong landlord and tenant bias: rent reviews and lease renewals; breaches of covenant and other disputes in respect of commercial property; long leases of residential property (including leasehold enfranchisement); Rent Act and Housing Act tenancies. Recent cases include Gilje and Others v Charlegrove Securities Ltd [2002] 1EGLR 41 (CA); Forrester v UYCF [2001] EGCS 2 (CA); Wallis Fashions Group Ltd v CGU Life Assurance Ltd [2000] 2 EGLR 49; West Sussex Properties v Chichester DC [2000] NPC 74 (CA); Hallissey v Petmoor Developments Ltd [2000] NPC 114 (ChD).
Prof. Memberships: Chancery Bar Association.
Career: Called to the Bar in 1985. Employed for several years (post-call) in the property litigation departments of *Speechly Bircham* and *Lovells*.
Personal: Born 1962. Educated at Godalming Grammar School (1972-80) and Durham University (1981-84).

DUVAL, Robert
St John's Chambers (Christopher Sharp QC), Bristol
(0117) 921 3456
Recommended in Crime

DYER, Nigel
1 Hare Court (Bruce Blair QC), London
(020) 7797 7070
Recommended in Family
Specialisation: Family law, principally ancillary relief often involving 'big money cases' where assets are held in companies, trusts and farms in the UK and abroad.
Prof. Memberships: Family Law Bar Association. Co-editor of 'Rayden and Jackson on Divorce and Family Matters'.
Career: Called to the Bar by Inner Temple 1982.
Personal: Married with two children and lives in London.

DYMOND, Andrew
Arden Chambers (Andrew Arden QC), London
(020) 7242 4244
andrew.dymond@ardenchambers.com
Recommended in Local Government
Specialisation: All areas of housing, landlord and tenant and local government law. Founder member of Arden Chambers in 1993. He advises and represents both public and private sector clients, including local authorities, RSLs, leaseholders, tenants and the homeless. He lectures and provides training in all aspects of housing law. He has contributed articles on housing and local government law to numerous publications and provides the Legal Update on Housing Law in the Law Society Gazette. Reported cases include Lambeth L.B.C. v Blackburn (2001) 82 P.&C.R. 494, CA; Lambeth L.B.C. v Bigden [2001] 33 H.L.R. 43, Lambeth L.B.C. v Archangel [2000] 33 H.L.R. 44, CA; R. v Islington L.B.C., ex p Bibi (1996) 29 H.L.R. 74, CA.
Prof. Memberships: Housing Law Practitioners Association, Property Bar Association.
Career: Called to the Bar in 1991
Publications: Author: 'Security of Tenure' (1st and 2nd Eds.); 'Presenting Possession Proceedings'; 'Houses in Multiple Occupation' (all Lemos & Crane); 'Arden & Partington's Quiet Enjoyment' (LAG, co-author with David Carter of 5th and 6th Eds). Contributor: 'Housing and Human Rights in Human Rights Act 1998: A Practitioner's Guide' (Sweet & Maxwell). Editor: 'Housing Law Reports' (1997-date); 'Journal of Housing Law' (1997-date); 'Arden & Partington's Housing Law' (1997-2001) (all Sweet & Maxwell).

EADY, Jennifer
Old Square Chambers (John Hendy QC), London
(020) 7269 0300
eady@oldsquarechambers.co.uk
Recommended in Employment
Specialisation: All aspects employment law (collective and individual), discrimination and restraint of trade. Cases of significance: R v BCC ex p Vardy 1993 (pit-closures JR); R v BCC ex p Price 1993 (collective redundancies); Associated Newspapers v Wilson 1995 HL (trade union); RJB v NUM 1995 CA (strike ballot); MRS v Marsh 1996 CA (TUPE); RMT v Intercity 1996 CA (strike ballot); Smith v BCC 1996 HL (equal pay); BRS v Loughran 1997 NICA (equal pay); NACODS v Gluchowski 1996 EAT (trade union); Halford v UK 1997 ECHR (Human Rights); BBC v Kelly-Phillips 1998 CA (employment contracts); England v Magill (1997) (Westminster 'gerrymandering') Div Ct; Brookes and ors v BCS 1998 EAT (TUPE); Gibson v E Riding Yorks 2000 CA (working time); SoS Trade & Industry v Bottirll 1999 CA (employee status); Cheesman v Brewer 2001 EAT (TUPE). Inquiries: The UCATT Inquiry (1992), the Westminster Audit Hearing (1994/5).
Prof. Memberships: Former Chair ILS, Committee member ELBA, Bar representative London ET and EAT users' group, ELA, DLA.
Career: 1986 BA Hons PPE (Oxon), 1988 Dip Law. Called 1989, Northern Ireland Bar 1994. Standing junior counsel to NUJ and NUM, appointed to the Treasury A panel. Part-time Chairman of Employment Tribunal.
Publications: 'Discrimination Law: Remedies and Quantum of Damages' (Sweet & Maxwell) (1998); 'Employment Tribunal Procedure' (LAG) (2001); 'Employment Law Review' (IER); contributor: Bullen & Leake, ICSL 'Employment Law Manual' (Blackstone), 'Employment Law Precedents' (Sweet & Maxwell), ILJ.

EASTEAL, Andrew
No.1 High Pavement (John B Milmo QC), Nottingham
(0115) 941 8218
Recommended in Crime
Specialisation: Practising exclusively in crime for the last 11 years (excluding fraud): sexual offences including child abuse; human rights; high profile drugs cases; attempted murder and manslaughter cases (single counsel) involving complex fitness to plead issues.
Personal: Long-suffering Villa fan.

EASTMAN, Roger
2 Harcourt Buildings (Roger Henderson QC), London
(020) 7583 9020
Recommended in Health & Safety
Specialisation: Predominantly common law practice with a particular emphasis on personal injury matters, health and safety (civil and criminal prosecution and defence work) and professional negligence (especially clinical negligence). Specialises in railway law in general. Represented Railtrack upon the Southall Rail Crash Inquiry. Also deals with the law relating to markets.
Prof. Memberships: Criminal Bar Association, COMBAR, Professional Negligence Bar Association, Official Referees' Bar Association, Personal Injury Bar Association.
Career: Called to the Bar 1978 and joined current chambers in 1981.
Personal: Educated at Maidstone Grammar School 1964-72; St. John's College, Durham 1972-75; and Council of Legal Education 1976-78. Born 23 May 1953. Lives in London.

EATON, Deborah
One King's Bench Walk (Anthony Hacking QC), London
(020) 7936 1500

LEADERS AT THE BAR

Recommended in Family
Specialisation: All aspects of family law including matrimonial finance and children (private and public law), inter country adoption and professional negligence. Latest case of interest; Re W (minors) (care order: adequacy of care plan) [2002] 1 FLR 815. Co-Author: 'Wildblood and Eaton: Financial Provision In Family Matters' published by Sweet and Maxwell 1998. Author Sweet and Maxwell Practical Research Papers. Contributor to Family Law. General editor: 'Essential Family Practice' published by Butterworths 2000.
Prof. Memberships: Family Law Bar Association. Intercountry Adoption Lawyers Association.
Career: Called to the Bar in 1985.
Personal: Born 28 March 1962, BSc (Hons) Psychology and Anthropology, Diploma in Law. Leisure pursuits include travel, opera, theatre and cinema.

ECCLES, David
8 King St (Gerard McDermott QC), Manchester
(0161) 834 9560
Recommended in Clinical Negligence
Specialisation: Clinical negligence, personal injury, civil actions for malicious prosecution and wrongful arrest. Ancillary Relief. Cases include: Smith v West Lancs Health A [1995] PIQP P514; Wagstaffe v Wagstaffe [1992] IWLR 320; Wilding v Chief Constable of Lancashire (March); Hyland v Chief Constable of Lancs – Times 7/2/96.
Prof. Memberships: PIBA, PNBA.
Career: Wilmslow Grammar School and Clare College, Cambridge.
Personal: Theatre, cinema, playing bridge, reading, travel and playing squash.

EDELMAN, Colin QC
Devereux Chambers (Colin Edelman QC), London
(020) 7353 7534
Recommended in Insurance, Professional Negligence
Specialisation: Principal areas of practice are insurance and reinsurance, professional negligence and commercial law. Recent reported cases include Killick v Rendall (insurance), Kennecott v Cornhill (insurance/reinsurance), Gan Insurance v Tai Ping (reinsurance), HIH v Chase Manhattan (insurance).
Prof. Memberships: Commercial Bar Association, member of Middle Temple and Midlands & Oxford Circuit.
Career: Called to the Bar in 1977 and has been a tenant at Devereux Chambers since 1979. Appointed Assistant Recorder in 1993. Took Silk in 1995. Appointed Recorder 1996. Appointed Head of Chambers 2002.
Publications: Has written articles for 'International Insurance Law Review', 'Commercial Liability Law Review' and the 'British Insurance Law Association Journal'. Contributor to 'Insurance Disputes' (LLP). Speaker/chairman at conferences on insurance and reinsurance topics.
Personal: Educated at Haberdashers' Aske's School, Elstree 1961-72 and Clare College, Cambridge 1973-76. Leisure pursuits include skiing, walking, badminton. Born 2 March 1954. Lives in London.

EDER, Bernard QC
Essex Court Chambers (Gordon Pollock QC), London
(020) 7813 8000
clerksroom@essexcourt-chambers.co.uk
Recommended in Commercial (Litigation), Energy, Insurance, Shipping
Specialisation: Most work of a litigious nature involving appearances in arbitration and the Commercial Court, Court of Appeal and House of Lords. All aspects of commercial law, including insurance and reinsurance, shipping and banking, international sale of goods, oil and gas.
Career: Downing College, Cambridge BA (Law) (1st Class Hons). Called to the Bar 1975. Queen's Counsel 1990. Visiting Professor in the Faculty of Law, University College London.
Personal: Born 1952.

EDEY, Philip
20 Essex Street (Iain Milligan QC), London
(020) 7842 1200
clerks@20essexst.com
Recommended in Insurance, Shipping
Specialisation: Commercial litigation including arbitration, commodities, insurance and reinsurance, international sale of goods and shipping. Cases include shipping – 'The Jalagouri' [1999] 1 Lloyd's Rep 903; Cory Brothers Limited v Baldan Limited [1997] 2 Lloyd's Rep 58; The Laconian Confidence [1997] 1 Lloyd's Rep 139. Insurance/Reinsurance – HIM v New Hampshire [2001] 1 Lloyds Rep 378 (film finance reinsurance); Kingscroft v Nissan [1999] LLR 18R 603; Imperio v Heath [1999] LLR I&R 571 and [2001] 1 WLR 112 (CH). One of the junior counsel for the Wellington Names in their action against their managing agents, members agents and auditors.
Prof. Memberships: COMBAR.
Career: Eton College, Oxford University (BA Hons 1st Class). Gray's Inn Queen Elizabeth Scholar. Called 1994.
Personal: Tennis; squash; real tennis; bridge; opera; theatre.

EDGE, Timothy
Deans Court Chambers (Stephen Grime QC), Manchester
(0161) 214 6000
Recommended in Family

EDIE, Alastair
Two Garden Court (Owen Davies QC & Courtenay Griffiths QC), London
(020) 7353 1633
Recommended in Crime

EDIS, Andrew QC
14 Castle Street (Andrew Edis QC), Liverpool
(0151) 236 4421
andrew.edis@rapid.co.uk
Recommended in Crime, Personal Injury
Specialisation: Personal injury, including disease and product liability. Professional negligence, in particular legal and clinical negligence. Serious crime including disciplinary tribunals. Police law and human rights. Civil cases involving fraud. Recent cases include: Arthur JS Hall v Simons [2002] 1 AC 615, House of Lords (abolition of advocates, immunity); LR v Witherspoon & Others [2000] 1 FLR CA; L & B v Reading Borough Council, and The Chief Constable of the Thames Valley Police [2001] 1 WLR 1575, (striking out negligence claims). Vellino v Chief Constable of Manchester [2002] 1 WLR 218 (duty of care owed by police to suspect). Webb v Chief Constable of Merseyside Police [2000] QB 427 CA. Norman v Aziz & Ali [2000] PIQR P72 CA. Nunnerley & Nunnerley v Warrington Health Authority & Liverpool Health Authority [2000] PIQR Q69 (Clinical Negligence). Timmins v Gormley (reported with Locabail v Bayfield Properties Ltd) [2000] QB 451 CA (Judicial Bias). In crime: R v Bruce Grobbelaar; R v Taft (Beauty in the Bath murder); R v Allan (Death on the Nile murder); R v Dietschmann [2002] Crim LR 132 (drink in diminished responsibility); R v Elmore Davies, Bray & Ahearne (Police Corruption), R v Abedin and Mostafa (terrorism), R v Ian Thomas Archbold News, Issue 5 2002 (powers of CA after CCRC referral).
Prof. Memberships: Northern Circuit, Professional Negligence Bar Association, Bar Sports Law Group, Northern Circuit Medical Law Group, Personal Injury Bar Association.
Career: Educated Liverpool College and University College, Oxford. Called 1980, Silk 1997. Assistant Recorder 1994-99, Recorder 1999 to date. Deputy High Court Judge (QBD) 2001. Head of Chambers 2000 to date.

EDIS, William
1 Crown Office Row (Robert Seabrook QC), London
(020) 7797 7500
Recommended in Environment

EDWARDS, David
7 King's Bench Walk (Gavin Kealey QC & Julian Flaux QC), London
(020) 7910 8300
clerks@7kbw.law.co.uk
Recommended in Insurance, Shipping
Specialisation: Commercial law predominantly insurance and reinsurance, international sale of goods, banking and finance, shipping.
Career: Called to the Bar 1989. Recent cases include: The 'Nicholas H' [1996] AC 211 (shipping – duty of care owed by Classification Society); New Hampshire v MGN [1997] RLR 24 (fidelity insurance – joint or composite); Glencore v Portman [1996] 1 Lloyd's Rep. 430 and [1997] 1 Lloyd's Rep. 225 (insurance – non-disclosure); The 'Bergen' [1997] 1 Lloyd's Rep. 380 (Clarke J) (jurisdiction – Brussels Convention); The 'Lendoudis Evangelos II' [1997] 1 Lloyd's Rep. 404 (charterparty – duration expressed 'without guarantee'); The Sumitomo Bank, Limited v Banque Bruxelles Lambert SA [1997] 1 Lloyd's Rep. 487 (syndicated lending – duty owed by arranger to syndicate members); Source v TUV [1997] 3 WLR 364 (jurisdiction – Brussels Convention); HMH v Cecar [2000] 1 Lloyd's Rep 316 (political risks insurance-brokers commission); The 'Seta Maru' [2000] 1 Lloyd's Rep 367 (Shipbuilding exemption clauses); HIH v Chase Manhattan Bank [2001] 1 Lloyd's Rep 30 (insurance-backed film finance); Deutsche Ruck v La Fondiaria [2001] 2 Lloyd's Rep 621 (pool reinsurance – jurisdiction).
Personal: Born 1966. King's School, Chester and Peterhouse, Cambridge, M.A. (Cantab). Member of Commercial Bar Association.

EDWARDS, Glyn
St John's Chambers (Christopher Sharp QC), Bristol
(0117) 921 3456
clerks@stjohnschambers.co.uk
Recommended in Personal Injury
Specialisation: Personal Injury. Appointed with effect from July 2000 onto Provincial Panel of Treasury Counsel.
Prof. Memberships: Personal Injury Bar Association.
Career: Formerly lecturer at Oxford Brookes University.
Personal: Married with three children. Welsh-speaking. Education: Penglais Comprehensive and Emmanuel College, Cambridge.

EDWARDS, Susan QC
23 Essex Street (Michael Lawson QC), London
(020) 7413 0353
susanedwards@23essexstreet.co.uk
Recommended in Crime
Specialisation: Serious crime including homicide, drugs, robbery, child abuse, vulnerable witnesses, fraud.
Prof. Memberships: CBA.
Career: Parkstone Grammar School, Poole. Southampton University – LLB (1971). Recorder. QC 1993.
Personal: Tennis, hill walking, travel, gardening.

EDWARDS-STUART, Antony QC
Crown Office Chambers (Michael Spencer QC & Christopher Purchas QC), London
(020) 7797 8100
edwards-stuart@crownofficechambers.com
Recommended in Construction
Specialisation: Principal area of practice is insurance, reinsurance and general commercial litigation and advice. Considerable experience of major

LEADERS AT THE BAR

insurance and reinsurance disputes, both marine and non-marine, together with highly complicated technical commercial cases including radioactive contamination (Merlins v BNFL, Blue Circle Industries plc v MOD, leading test cases), microbiology and chemistry (AKZO v Cyprus, contaminated paint) and electron beam welding (Burnley Engineering v Cambridge Vacuum Engineering). Other main areas of practice involve professional negligence work particularly concerning architects and engineers, but also insurance brokers, Lloyd's agents, solicitors, accountants and surveyors, both for plaintiffs and defendants, and major construction cases (Royal Brompton Hospital v Hammond, Plant Construction v Clive Adams) and arbitrations. Clients have included major insurance companies, BNFL, leading professional practices and large construction firms.
Prof. Memberships: COMBAR, London Common Law and Commercial Bar Association, TECBAR.
Career: Called to the Bar 1976 and joined 2 Crown Office Row in 1977. Took Silk in 1991. Appointed Recorder in 1997. Chairman, Home Office Advisory Committee on Service Candidates, 1995-98.
Personal: Education: Sherborne School, Dorset 1960-64, RMA Sandhurst 1965-66, St. Catharine's College, Cambridge 1969-72. Married with four children. Leisure pursuits include woodwork, restoring property in France, theatre, fishing and shooting. Born 2 November 1946. Lives in London.

EGAN, Michael
9-12 Bell Yard (D Anthony Evans QC), London
(020) 7400 1800
Recommended in Fraud

EICKE, Tim
Essex Court Chambers (Gordon Pollock QC), London
(020) 7813 8000
Recommended in Immigration
Specialisation: Specialises inter alia in human rights law (including discrimination law), EC law (including free movement and EC Association Agreements) and all aspects of public law, acting both for applicants and for respondents. Appears regularly in both the European Court of Human Rights and the ECJ. Important recent cases include El-Ali v SSHD (pending in CA), Kaba v SSHD (No 2) (pending before ECJ), Bosphorus Airways v Ireland (pending), P, C and S v UK (16 July 2002), Goodwin v UK (11 July 2002), Gora et al v Commissioners of Customs and Excise (VAT Tribunal, 20 June 2002), Sadak v Turkey (11 June 2002), Kingsley v UK (No 2) (28 May 2002)(amicus submissions), Pellegrini v Italy (2002) 35 EHRR 33 (amicus submissions), B v United Kingdom (2002) 34 EHRR 529, Sepet and Bulbul (for UNHCR) [2001] ImmAR 452, R (Alconbury Developments Ltd) v SSETR [2001] 2 WLR 1389, Kondova v SSHD [2001] ECR I-6247, Barkoci and Malik v SSHD [2001] ECR I-6557, Beard v UK (2001) 33 EHRR 442, Kaba v SSHD [2000] ECR I-2623, Yiadom [2000] ECR I-9265, Nabadda v Westminster CC [2000] ICR 951, KB v NHS Pensions Agency [1999] ICR 1192 (pending before ECJ).
Prof. Memberships: ILPA; Bar European Group; Lawyers for Liberty; Employment Law Bar Association; Administrative Law Bar Association; British German Jurists Association. Member of the Justice Expert Panel on Human Rights in the EU.
Career: Called 1993; LLB (Hons) Dundee University; Junior Council to the Crown (B Panel).
Publications: Joint editor, 'European Human Rights Reports' (Sweet & Maxwell), co-author of 'Human Rights Damages' (Sweet & Maxwell) and 'Strasbourg Caselaw: Leading Cases from the European Human Rights Reports' (Sweet & Maxwell), contributor Grosz, Beatson and Duffy 'Human Rights – the 1998 Act and the European Convention' (Sweet & Maxwell), co-author of 'Human Rights in the Workplace' (NATFHE/Liberty 1999), one of original authors of 'Study Guide Human Rights Act 1998' (Home Office and Bar Council 2000), consultant editor to Hershman and McFarlane 'Children Law and Practice' (Jordans), contributing editor second edition of 'Smith & Monkcom's - The Law of Betting, Gaming and Lotteries' (Butterworths).
Personal: Bi-lingual German-English, advanced French.

EISSA, Adrian
Two Garden Court (Owen Davies QC & Courtenay Griffiths QC), London
(020) 7353 1633
Recommended in Crime

EKLUND, Graham QC
2 Temple Gardens (Dermod O'Brien QC), London
(020) 7822 1200
Recommended in Professional Negligence
Specialisation: Professional negligence, particularly surveyors, solicitors, accountants and insurance brokers. Insurance related matters, particularly fraudulent claims, policy construction points, fire and disaster claims, including pollution and contamination claims. Personal injury, particularly serious injuries (including tetraplegic and paraplegic cases). Computer and IT. Reported cases include Jones & Marsh McLennan v Crowley Colosso (1996); Yorkshire Water v Sun Alliance (1996); John Munroe (Acrylics) Limited v London Fire and Civil Defence Authority (1997); Chapman v Christopher (1998); Greatorex v Greatorex (2000); Beckett and others v Midland Electricity PLC (2001). James v CGU Insurance (2002).
Prof. Memberships: PNBA, PIBA.
Career: Educated at Auckland University (1969-74) BA; LLB (Hons). Barrister and Solicitor of the High Court of New Zealand (1975-78). Solicitor of the Supreme Court of England and Wales (1979-84). Called 1984.
Personal: Married, two children. Interests include music, particularly opera and piano, cricket and wine.

ELGOT, Howard
Park Lane Chambers (Stuart Brown QC), Leeds
(0113) 228 5000
helgot@parklanechambers.co.uk
Recommended in Personal Injury
Specialisation: Personal injury (including claims of maximum severity), industrial disease litigation, clinical and professional negligence, insurance and commercial litigation. Many reported cases at first instance, Court of Appeal and House of Lords. Examples of well-known reported cases are Hatton v Sutherland CA (stress at work); Clarke v Kato HL (extent of RTA/MIB liability;) Roebuck v Mungovin HL (want of prosecution,) Liddell v Middleton CA (role of expert witnesses) and D and D v Donald QB (risk of breakdown of marriage in Fatal Accident Claim).
Prof. Memberships: PIBA; PNBA.
Career: BA BCL New College, Oxford. 3 Paper Buildings, Temple 1974-86, present chambers since 1986. Chairman, Park Lane Chambers Management Committee. Member Bar Council Quality Mark Steering Group.
Personal: Married, three children. Skiing. Italy. Music. Football.

ELIAS, Gerard QC
Farrar's Building (John Leighton Williams QC), London
(020) 7583 9241
Recommended in Crime
Specialisation: Crime and public inquiries. Leading counsel to the North Wales Child Abuse Tribunal inquiry, 1996-8; Bloody Sunday inquiry 2000-.
Career: Exeter (LLB); called to the Bar 1968; took silk 1984; Recorder 1984 -; Deputy High Court Judge 1996 -; Master of the Bench, Inner Temple; Former leader of Wales v Chester Circuit (1992-95).
Personal: Chairman of Glamorgan County Cricket Club; Chairman of Disciplinary Committee England & Wales Cricket Board (ECB).

ELLERAY, Anthony QC
Exchange Chambers (David Turner QC & Bill Braithwaite QC & Henry Globe QC), Manchester
(0161) 833 2722
ellerayqc@exchangechambers.co.uk
Recommended in Commercial (Litigation)
Specialisation: Chancery and General Commercial Litigation; Professional Negligence; Landlord and Tenant. Recent cases in C.A. include Walker v Turpin (1994) (payment in); Jervis v Harris (1996) (Landlord and Tenant repairs and 1938 Act); Bass v Latham Crossley and Davies (1996) (partnership/holding out); Shaikh v Bolton MBC (1996) (statutory interest on compulsory purchase). Pearce Deceased (1998) (Inheritance Act). Lynch [2000] laches. Lloyd v Dugdale (2001); In H.L, Wibberley v Insley (1999).
Prof. Memberships: Chancery Bar Association; Northern Chancery Bar Association; Professional Negligence Bar Association.
Career: Called to the Bar 1977; took Silk 1993.

ELLIOTT, Margot
Regency Chambers, Peterborough
(01733) 315215 (Peterborough)
(01223) 301517 (Cambridge)
margot.elliott@virgin.net
Recommended in Family
Specialisation: All aspects of family law especially public law children work.
Prof. Memberships: Family Law Bar Association.
Career: Educated at Wakefield Girl's High School and University of Newcastle Upon Tyne (LL.B 1987). Called to the Bar in 1989; member of current chambers since 1991.
Personal: Born 29 July 1966. Lives in Cambridgeshire with husband and three children.

ELLIOTT, Rupert
1 Brick Court (Richard Rampton QC), London
(020) 7353 8845
Recommended in Defamation
Specialisation: Defamation and media-related law; confidence and privacy; pre-publication work; reporting restrictions; contempt.
Career: Called 1988; joined Chambers 1989.
Personal: Harrow School; Jesus College, Cambridge.

ELLIOTT, Timothy QC
Keating Chambers, London
(020) 7544 2600
telliott@keatingchambers.com
Recommended in Arbitration, Construction, Professional Negligence
Specialisation: Building and civil engineering and related professional negligence including valuation; bonds and guarantees. High Court litigation, arbitration, adjudication and mediation in UK, Hong Kong and elsewhere overseas. Clients include national and international contractors and developers; architects, engineers, surveyors and other professionals; insurers; national and local government. Also acts as arbitrator, adjudicator and mediator (CEDR accredited).
Career: Qualified 1975. Middle Temple (Astbury Law Scholar). QC 1992.
Personal: Marlborough College and Trinity College, Oxford (Lit.Hum. Exhibitioner. 1973 MA). Born 1950; married, two children, resides London.

LEADERS AT THE BAR

ELLIS, Diana QC
3 Gray's Inn Square (Rock Tansey QC), London
(020) 7520 5600
Recommended in Crime
Specialisation: Specialises in defence crime. Wide range of work including murder, fraud, child abuse and sexual abuse, drugs, human rights. On United Nations list of counsel assigned to represent accused at ICTR, appointed counsel at International Criminal Tribunal for Rwanda.
Prof. Memberships: Criminal Bar Association. Liberty. South Eastern Circuit.
Career: LLB Hons London; Diploma in Social Admin, LSE. Called to the Bar in July 1978 – Inner Temple. Worked for several years as a teacher. Recorder, 1998.

ELLIS, Morag
2-3 Gray's Inn Square (Anthony Porten QC & Anthony Scrivener QC), London
(020) 7242 4986
Recommended in Planning
Specialisation: Planning and local government. Extensive experience of public inquiries including planning appeals on retail, housing, windfarms and local plan inquiries, CPO and footpaths, for developers, authorities and other statutory bodies. Recently promoted Bracknell Forest, Wycombe District Local Plan and Bridgend UDP, including major housing, town centre and brown field redevelopment proposals. Town and Village Green inquiries. Court experience includes judicial review and statutory appeals. On editorial panel of Halsbury's laws (Public Health). Lecturer on planning for RTPI.
Prof. Memberships: Planning and Environment Bar Association (Committee Member and Local Plans Sub-Committee). Ecclesiastical Law Society; Society of Advanced Legal Studies Planning Law Reform Group (Town and Village Greens Sub-Group).
Career: Called to the Bar 1984, (Gray's Inn).
Personal: Educated Penrhos College, Colwyn Bay, and St Catharine's College, Cambridge (MA). Married with three children. Member of Bach Choir and Cambridge Taverner Choir.

ELLISON, Mark
Hollis Whiteman Chambers (QEB) (Julian Bevan QC & Peter Whiteman QC), London
(020) 7583 5766
Recommended in Crime, Fraud
Specialisation: Criminal practice specialising in commercial fraud and Treasury Counsel work.
Career: Called 1979. Appointed Junior Treasury Counsel to the Crown at the Central Criminal Court 1994. Senior Treasury Counsel 2000. Recorder.
Personal: Educated at Pocklington School, Skinners School and the University of Wales.

ELVIN, David QC
4 Breams Buildings (Christopher Lockhart-Mummery QC), London
(020) 7430 1221
djelvinqc@aol.com
Recommended in Environment, Local Government, Planning
Specialisation: Judicial review, compulsory purchase, compensation, planning, environmental law (including nature conservation), nuisance, highways, local government, education, real property, landlord and tenant, agriculture, trespass and professional negligence.
Career: Called to the Bar by the Middle Temple in 1983 and is Member of the Administrative Law Bar Association, Chancery Bar Association and the Planning and Environmental Bar Association. Took silk in 2000. Educated at the A.J. Dawson Grammar School, Co. Durham and at Hertford College, Oxford obtaining a BA (First Class Honours) in Jurisprudence and a BCL. In 1983 he won the Bar Association for Finance Commerce and Industry Prize. Was one of the Junior Counsel to the Crown ('A' Panel) until he took silk, having served as a Supplementary Panellist from 1991-95. He was made a Recorder in 2002. Is an Assistant Commissioner with the Boundary Commission
Publications: Co-author of 'Unlawful Interference with Land' (2002) and a number of articles in 'Judicial Review' and the 'Journal of Planning Law'.

ELWICK, Martin
No.1 High Pavement (John B Milmo QC), Nottingham
(0115) 941 8218
Recommended in Crime

EMMERSON, Ben QC
Matrix Chambers, London
(020) 7404 3447
Recommended in Crime, Human Rights
Specialisation: Civil liberties and international human rights law, including representation of applicants before the European Court of Justice in Luxembourg and the European Court of Human Rights in Strasbourg; civil actions against police and public law, particularly prisoners' rights. Also criminal law, especially serious fraud, political offences and cases involving police malpractice; Commonwealth capital appeals, extradition, deportation and international enforcement of asset confiscation. Human rights Editor of Archbold Criminal Pleading, Evidence and Practice. Author 'Butterworth's Guide to the Police Act 1997'. Co-author 'Human Rights and Criminal Justice' (2001) (Sweet & Maxwell).
Career: Called to the Bar 1986. Silk 3 May 2000.
Personal: Bristol University 1982-85. Born 30 August 1963.

ENGLAND, William
2-4 Tudor Street (Richard Ferguson QC), London
(020) 7797 7111
Recommended in Crime

ENGLEHART, Robert QC
Blackstone Chambers (Presiley Baxendale QC & Charles Flint QC), London
(020) 7583 1770
robertenglehart@blackstonechambers.com
Recommended in Media & Entertainment
Specialisation: Both commercial and copyright aspects of music business and media, especially broadcasting, disputes; also practices in general commercial law, including commercial judicial review, and intellectual property.
Career: Called 1969, QC 1986, Recorder and Deputy High Court Judge.

EPSTEIN, Paul
Cloisters (Laura Cox QC), London
(020) 7827 4000
Recommended in Employment

ESCOTT-COX, Brian QC
36 Bedford Row (Michael Pert QC), London
(020) 7421 8000
Recommended in Crime

ESPLEY, Susan
Fenners Chambers (Paul Hollow), Cambridge
(01223) 368761
Recommended in Family
Specialisation: Children cases, both public and private law. Representing Guardian ad litem, Local Authorities and parents.
Prof. Memberships: FLBA. Part-time Chairman: Mental Health Review Tribunals.
Personal: Antiques, music, theatre.

ETHERINGTON, David QC
18 Red Lion Court (Anthony Arlidge QC), London
(020) 7520 6000
etheremail@aol.com
Recommended in Crime, Fraud
Specialisation: Criminal practitioner. Experienced in wide range of criminal work including commercial fraud, VAT, drugs and serious professional crime. Also experienced in civil jury actions such as malicious prosecution. Advisor to television companies on documentary and dramatic work including 'Kavanagh QC', and 'Judge John Deed'.
Prof. Memberships: Appointed member of the Criminal Bar Association Committee and Vice Chairman of the Professional Conduct Committee. Chambers 18 Red Lion Court (Anthony Arlidge QC).
Career: Call 1979 (Middle Temple), Recorder of the Crown Court 2000, Queen's Counsel 1998.

EVANS, Catrin
1 Brick Court (Richard Rampton QC), London
(020) 7353 8845
clerks@1brickcourt.co.uk
Recommended in Defamation
Specialisation: Defamation and trade libel in traditional and electronic media; breach of confidence/privacy and data protection, passing off; media reporting restrictions, obscenity. European human rights law in media context and media related law generally. Does work for the Treasury Solicitor. Interesting cases: Libel – Gregson v Channel 4 TV [2002] EWCACiv 941, Steedman v BBC, 2001, Sugar v Associated Newspapers Ltd (2001), £100,000 jury award; Gregson v Channel 4, Times, 11 August 2000, CA; Taylor v SFO [1998] 4 AER 801, HL; McNab v Associated Newspapers Ltd (1996), CA. Breach of confidence – Amanda Holden v Express Newspapers, 2001, Beckhams v Niblett &Ors (2000), CH.D; British Biotech plc v Millar (1999); Duchess of York v Starkie & Ors. Reporting restrictions – R v Great Grimsby Crown Court ex p. Littlewood, CA (Crim.Div), 2002.
Career: Called to the Bar 1994.
Publications: Author 'Confidence and Data Protection' title, Atkins Court Forms.

EVANS, D Anthony QC
9-12 Bell Yard (D Anthony Evans QC), London
(020) 7400 1800
Recommended in Crime

EVANS, David
1 Crown Office Row (Robert Seabrook QC), London
(020) 7797 7500
Recommended in Clinical Negligence

EVANS, David QC
Hollis Whiteman Chambers (QEB) (Julian Bevan QC & Peter Whiteman QC), London
(020) 7583 5766
Recommended in Fraud
Specialisation: Principal area of specialisation within criminal law is criminal fraud. Before taking silk in 1991 appeared in several high profile cases as Junior. Acted for Ian Posgate in the Howden trial, for Morgan Grenfel in the Guinness enquiry, and for UBS Phillips & Drew in the Blue Arrow trial. Since 1991 has appeared both for the prosecution and defence in a series of major fraud trials including defendants in the BCCI enquiry, the collapse of the Swithland motor group, the Aveling Barford pension fund fraud and several high profile mortgage frauds including acting for the solicitor defendant in the Harrovian case. Has prosecuted for the SFO and the Fraud Investigation Group.
Prof. Memberships: Criminal Bar Association
Career: Educated at the London School of Economics BSc. Econ, MSc 1962-67, Wadham College Oxford BA Oxon 1968-70. QC 1991.

EVANS, Elwen Mair QC
Iscoed Chambers (Elwen Mair Evans QC), Swansea
(01792) 652988/9
Recommended in Crime

EVANS, Gareth QC
No5 Chambers (Gareth Evans QC), Birmingham
(0121) 606 0500
Recommended in Personal Injury

LEADERS AT THE BAR

EVANS, Jill
Doughty Street Chambers (Geoffrey Robertson QC), London
(020) 7404 1313
j.evans@doughtystreet.co.uk
Recommended in Crime
Specialisation: Specialises in defence crime: extensive practice both in fraud and confiscation and also cases involving children and Young Persons both as defendants and victims of crime. Increasingly instructed in Leading Junior work.
Prof. Memberships: Criminal Bar Association, Legal Action Group and Haldane Society.
Career: Former Solicitor, Partner *Saunders & Co* W9. Called to Bar in 1986.

EVANS, John
1 Fountain Court (Melbourne Inman QC), Birmingham
(0121) 236 5721
Recommended in Crime

EVANS, Mark QC
Temple Chambers (David J M Aubrey QC), Cardiff
(029) 2039 7364
mevansqc@aol.com
Recommended in Family
Specialisation: Family, high value ancillary relief, crime, PI.
Career: Called to the Bar after career in industry in engineering/accounting. Junior practice in PI and ancillary relief. In silk much high profile crime as well.
Personal: Music; vintage and racing cars.

EVANS, Michael
No.1 High Pavement (John B Milmo QC), Nottingham
(0115) 941 8218
Recommended in Crime
Specialisation: All areas of crime. Last year, dealt with a number of high profile drugs trials and serious matters of sex and violence.

EVANS, Susan
Pump Court Chambers (Christopher Harvey Clark QC), Winchester
(01962) 868161
Recommended in Crime

EVERALL, Mark QC
1 Hare Court (Bruce Blair QC), London
(020) 7797 7070
clerks@1hc.com
Recommended in Family
Specialisation: Work includes matrimonial finance, public and private law children cases, international child abduction, adoption, parentage, surrogacy and assisted conception and cases with an international aspect or involving human rights.
Prof. Memberships: Family Law Bar Association; Bar European Group; International Academy of Matrimonial Lawyers; Administrative Law Bar Association; Inter-country Adoption Lawyers Association.
Career: QC 1994; Recorder 1996; Deputy High Court Judge 1996.
Publications: Editor, Rayden & Jackson on 'Divorce & Family Matters'.

EVERARD, William
King Charles House Chambers (William Everard), Nottingham
(0115) 941 8851
Recommended in Crime

EWART, David
Pump Court Tax Chambers, London
(020) 7414 8080
Recommended in Tax
Specialisation: Revenue, trusts, professional negligence, Billingham v Cooper (2001), Garner v Pounds (2000), Keeping Newcastle Warm v CCE (2000) ex p Lorimer (2000) ex p Newfields (2001), Dr Beynon v CCE (2002). Junior Counsel to the Inland Revenue (Chancery).
Prof. Memberships: Revenue Bar Association.
Career: Hamilton Grammar School; Trinity College, Oxford.
Personal: Bridge, golf.

EYRE, Stephen
1 Fountain Court (Melbourne Inman QC), Birmingham
(0121) 236 5721
Recommended in Commercial (Litigation)

FALKENSTEIN, John
Plowden Buildings (William Lowe QC), Newcastle upon Tyne
(020) 7583 0808
falkenstein@blueyonder.co
Recommended in Employment
Specialisation: Employment and discrimination law. Regularly instructed on behalf of employers and employee organisations throughout England and Wales, with a particular interest in police and local government work. Appears frequently in the EAT.
Prof. Memberships: Employment Law Bar Association.
Career: Worked in local government for several years as a policy and employment law advisor before being called to the Bar in 1996.
Publications: Author of 'Disability Discrimination Act 1995' journal of local government law (Sweet and Maxwell).
Personal: Born 4 August 1959.

FANCOURT, Timothy
Falcon Chambers (Jonathan Gaunt QC & Kim Lewison QC), London
(020) 7353 2484
fancourt@falcon-chambers.com
Recommended in Agriculture, Property Litigation
Specialisation: Principal area of practice is real property based chancery work (litigation). This includes commercial property, landlord and tenant, surveyors' and solicitors' professional negligence, conveyancing, building contracts, mortgages, easements and restrictive covenants, equity and trusts and insolvency. Other main area is commercial contracts.
Prof. Memberships: Lincoln's Inn; member of Chancery Bar Association and LCLCBA and committee member, Property Bar Association. Member of Bar Council (1996-2001).
Career: Called to the Bar in 1987 and joined Falcon Chambers in 1989.
Publications: General editor of Megarry's 'The Rent Acts' and Megarry's 'Assured Tenancies' (1999); author of 'Enforceability of Landlord and Tenant Covenants' (1997).
Personal: Educated at Whitgift School 1974-82 and Gonville & Caius College, Cambridge 1983-86. Born 30 August 1964.

FARBEY, Judith
Tooks Court Chambers (Michael Mansfield QC), London
(020) 7405 8828
Judith.Farbey@tooks.law.co.uk
Recommended in Immigration
Specialisation: Immigration; public and administrative law.
Prof. Memberships: ILPA, EC member and co-convenor of Access to Justice Sub-committee; member ALBA.
Career: Member of Advisory Panel of the Immigration Services Commissioner; immigration consultant for Public Law Project's research on judicial review; annual lecturer since 1996 on refugee law at Tavistock Clinic's refugee studies programme; JUSTICE Council member 1992-99; winner, Bar Council Award for Outstanding Commitment to Pro Bono Work, 1997.
Publications: Co-author of immigration law chapter in 'Making Rights Real: Using the Human Rights Act to Challenge Racism and Racial Discrimination' (2002; forthcoming); author of immigration law chapter in 'Working with Refugees' (2002; forthcoming); article 'Who is a Refugee? A Legal Perspective' (2001) in mental health journal 'Context'.

FARQUHAR, Stuart A
St. Mary's Chambers Family Law Chambers (Nigel B Page), Nottingham
(0115) 950 3503
Recommended in Family

FARRELL, Simon
3 Raymond Buildings (Clive Nicholls QC), London
(020) 7400 6400
chambers@3raymondbuildings.com
Recommended in Crime, Fraud
Specialisation: Serious and complex criminal commercial fraud with particular experience defending in major prosecutions conducted by the SFO and Customs and Excise. Cases undertaken include banking fraud, money laundering, illegal share dealing, illegal deposit taking, conspiracies to cheat the public revenue, VAT and income tax fraud, duty diversion, drawback and smuggling, corruption, companies in debt (Phoenix Trading), fine art forgeries and fakes, advance fee fraud, telephone fraud (cloning, auto dialling, callselling), mortgage fraud (solicitors and brokers), and offences contrary to European law triable in the UK section 71 of the Criminal Justice Act 1993. Other areas of specialisation include the law relating to criminal and civil confiscation, major drugs offences, judicial review, civil actions against the police and the law relating to endangered species. Regularly undertakes work as Leading Junior Counsel. Most notable cases include: R v Maidstone Crown Court ex parte Harrow BC 1999 3ALLER 542; R v Henry Sissen 2001 1 WLR 902 (smuggling endangered species); R v John Drewe 2001 Southwark CC and CA (fake fine art); R v Bimal Pattni and others Southwark CC 2001 (massive alleged VAT fraud involving gold trade); R v Massingham and others Luton CC 2000 (SFO commercial fraud); and R v Brett and others Southwark CC 2000 (Phoenix company fraud).
Career: Gonville and Caius College, Cambridge. B.A (hons), M.A. Diploma Law (City University). Hardwicke Scholar, Lincolns Inn. Call 1983.
Publications: Regular contributor to Legal Action. Article in 'Criminal Law Review on Voluntary Bills', September 1998. Drafted Criminal Bar's response to government proposals for civil seizure of criminal assets in the High Court included in Proceeds of Crime Bill 2001. Drafted Liberty submissions on right of silence to the Royal Commission on Criminal Justice and drafted Liberty's response to government proposals for Community Safety Orders.

FARRER, David QC
7 Bedford Row (David Farrer QC), London
(020) 7242 3555
Recommended in Crime
Specialisation: All areas of serious crime including murder and commercial fraud, both prosecution and defence, often with an international dimension. Clients include SFO, DTI, CPS, (HQ and regionally on SE and Midlands and Oxford Circuits), as well as range of large and medium firms. Variety of non-criminal work in QBD and Chancery Divisions involving fraud, undue influence and accounting issues including partnership and insolvency. Civil clients include former England football coach Martin Johnson (England and Lions rugby captain) and boxing promoter Don King. Prosecuted John Palmer and others (£40m timeshare fraud), SFO 'Blackspur' and 'Norton' cases and R v Morgan (Celine Figard murder). Defended first 'DNA profiling' murder (R v Pitchfork). Regularly trains and organises seminars for accountants on investigation, reporting and giving evidence in court. NITA qualified advocacy trainer.
Prof. Memberships: European Bar Group; Criminal Bar Association.
Career: Teaching modern languages 1965-67. Called to Bar in 1967. Appointed Recorder 1983. Took Silk 1986. Member of Bar Council 1987-93. Chairman Bar services committee 1989-92. Edited current Bar action pack (Good practice guide). Educated at Queen Elizabeth's Grammar School,

Barnet and Downing College Cambridge. Took LLB in Public and Private International Law.
Personal: Leisure pursuits include tennis, rugby (watching only), local history, after dinner speaking and cabaret, music and cricket (playing and watching). Fluent French and German, working Italian.

FARRER, Paul
1 Fountain Court (Melbourne Inman QC), Birmingham
(0121) 236 5721
Recommended in Crime

FAULKS, Edward QC
No. 1 Serjeants' Inn (Edward Faulks QC), London
(020) 7415 6666
clerks@no1serjeantsinn.com
Recommended in Clinical Negligence, Personal Injury
Specialisation: Principal areas of practice: professional and clinical negligence; personal injury (including child abuse); education and liability in negligence of public authorities. He is instructed on behalf of NHS Trusts, local authorities, police authorities, insurance companies and individual claimants. He has been or is involved in group litigation arising out of radiotherapy treatment, cardiac surgery errors, cervical cancer screening errors and child abuse. Recent cases include Bradford-Smart v West Sussex County Council [2002] CA; Chittock v Woodbridge School [2002] CA; Peter McConnell v Congregation of Christian Brothers [2001] CA; Fairchild v Glenhaven Funeral Services [2001] CA; Johnson v Unisys (HL) [2001]; Phelps v Hillingdon LBC (HL) [2000]; G v Bromley LBC (HL) [2000]; Anderton v Clwyd (HL) [2000]; W v Essex CC (HL) [2000]; Penney v East Kent Health Authority (CA) [1999]; Kent v Griffiths and London Ambulance Service (CA) [1998]; Capital and Counties v Hampshire CC [1997]; X v Bedfordshire CC (HL) [1995].
Prof. Memberships: Fellow of Chartered Institute of Arbitrators, London Common Law & Commercial Bar Association, Professional Negligence Bar Association (Chairman).
Career: Called to the Bar 1973. Silk in 1996. Recorder. Head of Chambers 1998.
Publications: Contributing editor of 'Local Authority Liabilities' (Jordans).
Personal: Educated at Wellington College and Jesus College, Oxford. Former literary agent. Leisure pursuits include cricket. Lives in London.

FEATHERBY, William
12 King's Bench Walk (Richard Methuen QC), London
(020) 7583 0811
Recommended in Personal Injury

FEDER, Ami
Lamb Building (Ami Feder), London
(020) 7797 7788
clerks@lambbldg.co.uk
Recommended in Crime

Specialisation: Principal area of practice is fraud work in both the criminal and civil fields and general commercial and international work. Also practices at 9 Malchei Israel Square, Tel-Aviv 64163. Tel: 03-5243381, Fax: 03-5243387, email:mozingel@zahav.net.il.
Prof. Memberships: Criminal Bar Association; Common Law and Commercial Bar Association; European Bar Association; European Criminal Bar Association.
Career: Called to the Bar 1965; member of the Israel Bar.
Personal: Educated in Israel (Hebrew University of Jerusalem, the branch in Tel Aviv) and in England (London LSE).

FEINBERG, Peter QC
2-4 Tudor Street (Richard Ferguson QC), London
(020) 7797 7111
Recommended in Crime
Specialisation: Criminal law. R v Powell & Daniels –House of Lords; R v Burstow – House of Lords.
Career: Recorder. President, Mental Health Tribunal. Chairman, Liaison Committee.

FENTON, Adam
7 King's Bench Walk (Gavin Kealey QC & Julian Flaux QC), London
(020) 7910 8300
Recommended in Insurance
Specialisation: Insurance, reinsurance, shipping. Recent cases include AIG v QBE 2001 [2] Lloyd's Rep 268 (incorporation of jurisdiction clause); Imperio v CE Heath 2000 [1] WLR 268 (limitation period for breach of fiduciary duty) The 'ABT Rasha' 2000 1 Lloyds Rep. 8 (recoverability of GA liability from insurers); Kirkaldy v Walker [1999] Lloyd's Rep IR 571 (construction of warranty); North Atlantic v Bishopsgate [1998] 1 Lloyd's Rep. 459 (Basis on which excess to be applied); Johnston v Leslie & Godwin [1995] LRLR 472 (Duty of broker to retain documentation/collect claims).
Career: Called to the Bar, 1984.
Personal: Born 1961.

FENWICK, Justin QC
Four New Square (Justin Fenwick QC), London
(020) 7822 2000
barristers@4newsquare.com
Recommended in Construction, Product Liability, Professional Negligence
Specialisation: Commercial and insurance litigation, professional negligence and construction; product liability.
Prof. Memberships: Combar; PNBA; LCLBA; Tecbar; PEBA.
Career: MA (Cantab) 1971 (Modern Languages and Architectural History). Grenadier Guards 1968-81; called to the Bar November 1980. Lamb Building - July 81 - July 89. 2 Crown Office Row (now 4 New Square) July 1989 - present. (Head of Chambers 2000-) QC 1993. Recorder 1999; Chairman Bar Mutual Indemnity Fund 1999-.

FERGUSON, Richard QC
2-4 Tudor Street (Richard Ferguson QC), London
(020) 7797 7111
Recommended in Crime, Health & Safety
Specialisation: All forms of jury advocacy and in particular: commercial fraud; health and safety; criminal defence; libel; food and drugs. Important cases include: Peter Buck (REM) air rage; Ramsgate Ferry disaster [for Lloyds Register]; Severn Bridge [for consulting engineers]; New Zealand butter importation [for Anchor Butter]; Guiness Trial [for Earnest Saunders]; Hong Kong corruption [for local solicitor]; Solicitor Green form fraud [Liverpool Crown Court]; Cyprus Spy Trial; Terry Marsh; Brighton Bombing; Birmingham 6; allegation of police perversion of justice [Melvin & Dingle]; allegation of murder by police shooting [for the officer]; Ronnie Knight; Taylor Sisters; Rosemary West; Branson v Snowden [Libel]; acted in Ireland for Sunday Times and News International; environmental law; [for United Biscuits, food misdescription]; M.O.D. v Green; House of Lords, Brophy [voir dire]; Asiz [good character direction] in re M suit against magistrate; Clegg [shooting by soldier]; Privy Council; judicial review; extradition.
Career: QC [Northern Ireland] 1973; SC [Republic of Ireland] 1982; QC [England and Wales] 1986; practice in Hong Kong, Cayman, Bermuda; Bencher Gray's Inn; former Chairman, Criminal Bar Association; Bar Council.

FERNYHOUGH, Richard QC
Keating Chambers, London
(020) 7544 2600
clerks@keatingchambers.com
Recommended in Arbitration, Construction
Specialisation: Construction and engineering law; arbitration both international and domestic; arbitrator, domestic and international including I.C.C.
Career: Qualified 1970; Middle Temple; QC 1986; FCI Arb 1992; Recorder of the Crown Court 1986.
Personal: Merchant Taylors School; University College, London (1966 LLB Hons). Born 1943; resides London. Tennis, flying, opera. Languages: French.

FERRIER, Susan
9 Park Place (Ian Murphy QC), Cardiff
(029) 2038 2731
Recommended in Crime

FETHERSTONHAUGH, Guy
Falcon Chambers (Jonathan Gaunt QC & Kim Lewison QC), London
(020) 7353 2484
clerks@falcon-chambers.co.uk
Recommended in Property Litigation
Specialisation: Landlord and tenant litigation (commercial and residential) and advisory work particularly in rent review. Other aspects of real property, including easements, restrictive covenants, conveyancing and mortgages. Property-related aspects of professional negligence and insolvency.

Prof. Memberships: Chancery Bar Association; LCLBA; Property Bar Association.
Career: Specialist Standing Counsel to the Rent Assessment Panel; Supplementary Panel of Counsel to do property law work.
Publications: 'Handbook of Rent Review' (co-author); 'The Litigation Practice' (contributing editor).

FINCH, Nadine
Two Garden Court (Owen Davies QC & Courtenay Griffiths QC), London
(020) 7353 1633
Recommended in Immigration
Specialisation: Predominantly civil liberties practice, specialising in all areas of immigration law. Particular experience of cases involving asylum, the interaction between immigration and family law, applications by gay and lesbian appellants, the use of European Convention on Human Rights and European law, and procedures to be employed when an appellant or applicant is suffering from mental illness. Has recently represented a number of appellants who have been detained in prison, pending deportation, at the conclusion of prison sentences, despite conditions in their country having changed since the order was originally made. In June 2001, she was a member of an international workshop in Washington DC, which discussed the situation of refugee children and children who had been trafficked. Was recently the legal advisor for a BBC investigatory programme on the trafficking of women. Presently assisting a number of NGOs to draft amendments and lobby in relation to the Nationality, Immigration and Asylum Bill 2002. Cases include R v Secretary of State for the Home Department ex parte Meftah Zighem [1996] Imm AR 194, R v Secretary of State for the Home Department ex parte Toprak [1996] Imm AR 332, and R v SSHD ex p Lucy Ouma [1997] Imm AR 606, Yasin Sepet & Erdem Bulbul v SSHD [2001] Imm AR 187, R v Special Adjudicator ex p T [2001] Imm AR 187.
Prof. Memberships: Executive Member of Immigration Law Practitioners Association, member of Stonewall Immigration Group, Administrative Law Bar Association, Family Law Bar Association.
Career: Called to the Bar 1991. Joined present chambers in 2000. Previously practiced at Doughty Street Chambers. Prior to 1989 employed in legal research and community work.
Publications: Contributor to Macdonald's 'Immigration Law and Practice', 'Human Rights Practice' (Sweet & Maxwell) and 'Cohabitation: Law and Precedents' (Sweet & Maxwell), and 'Halsbury's Laws of England', Nationality and Immigration Section. One of the authors of 'Putting Children First: A Guide for Immigration Practitioners' (LAG).

LEADERS AT THE BAR

FINDLAY, James
2-3 Gray's Inn Square (Anthony Porten QC & Anthony Scrivener QC), London
(020) 7242 4986
Recommended in Local Government
Specialisation: Principal area of practice includes local government, planning and environment and administrative law. Extensive experience both in Judicial Review (e.g. R v Durham CC & Others, ex parte Huddlestone, R v West Dorset D.C. ex p. Searle, R v Brighton & Hove B.C. ex p. Nacion, Warsame v Hounslow L.B.C, Hughes v Kingston Upon Hull DC, Birmingham CC v Oakley, R v Newcastle Under Lyme Magistrates, ex p. Massey) and Inquiry work (planning and other, both for and against local authorities). Regular lecturer on such matters, including impact of Human Rights Act.
Prof. Memberships: PEBA; ALBA.
Career: Called: 1984.
Personal: Born 1961. Educated at Glenalmond and Magdalene College, Cambridge.

FISH, David QC
Deans Court Chambers (Stephen Grime QC), Manchester
(0161) 214 6000
Recommended in Crime
Specialisation: Fraud, serious drugs cases, licensing.
Prof. Memberships: Criminal Bar Association.
Career: Called 1973, QC 1997, Recorder 1994.
Personal: Ashton-Under-Lyne Grammar School, London School of Economics.

FISHER, David QC
6 King's Bench Walk (Roy Amlot QC), London
(020) 7583 0410
clerks@6kbw.com
Recommended in Crime
Specialisation: Criminal law specialist, including drugs, sexual allegations and fraud.
Prof. Memberships: General Council of the Bar 1997-99. Deputy Chairman of the Law Reform Committee 1999-2001. Advocacy Studies Board 1997-2001. Criminal Bar Association. South Eastern Circuit.
Career: Called to the Bar in 1973. Tenant of current chambers since 1974. Recorder since 1991. QC since 1996.

FITTON, Michael
Albion Chambers (Neil Ford QC), Bristol
(0117) 927 2144
Recommended in Crime
Specialisation: Crime; mental health.
Career: Crown Court Recorder. Formerly a solicitor for 10 years.
Publications: 'The Advocate's Sentencing Guide' (Law Society).

FITZGERALD, Edward QC
Doughty Street Chambers (Geoffrey Robertson QC), London
(020) 7404 1313
Recommended in Administrative & Public Law, Crime, Human Rights

FITZGERALD, Susanna QC
One Essex Court (Lord Grabiner QC), London
(020) 7583 2000
Recommended in Licensing

FLAUX, Julian QC
7 King's Bench Walk (Gavin Kealey QC & Julian Flaux QC), London
(020) 7910 8300
clerks@7kbw.law.co.uk
Recommended in Commercial (Litigation), Insurance, Shipping
Specialisation: Specialises in all aspects of commercial law including insurance and reinsurance, shipping, professional negligence, international sale of goods, banking and international arbitration.
Prof. Memberships: Chairman: Supporting Members Liaison Committee of London Maritime Arbitrators Association; Commercial Bar Association; LCIA; ACI.
Career: BCL; M.A. (Oxon: First Class Honours in Jurisprudence); Called to the Bar 1978. Member of present Chambers from 1979; took silk 1994; appointed Recorder 2000. Authorised to sit as a Deputy High Court Judge of the Queen's Bench Division, Commercial Court.
Personal: Born 1955; Married, three sons. Interests: Cricket; opera.

FLENLEY, William
4 Paper Buildings (Jean Ritchie QC), London
(020) 7643 5000
William.flenley@dial.pipex.com
Recommended in Professional Negligence
Specialisation: Professional negligence, insurance, real property, freezing orders. Appeared in the Nationwide managed litigation against 400 firms of Solicitors (Nationwide v Balmer Radmore (1999) PNLR 606), and was involved in the large-scale mediation between Halifax Plc and the Solicitors' Indemnity Fund. Cases include: Ruparel v Awan (2001) Lloyd's Rep PN 258, Solicitors' undertakings; Jenmain v Steed & Steed (2000) PNLR 616, CA, professional negligence - loss of profit; Matlock Green v Potter (2000) Lloyd's Rep PN 935, damages for loss of business tenancy; Mahoney v Purnell (1996) 3 All ER 61, undue influence: solicitors' duties.
Prof. Memberships: PNBA, Society for Computers and Law.
Career: Exeter College, Oxford (BA, BCL); Cornell University, USA (LLM). Called in 1988.
Publications: Flenley & Leech – 'Solicitors' Negligence' (1999); an editor of 'Cordery on Solicitors'; contributor to chapters 1 and 2 (general principles of liability and damages) of 'Professional Negligence and Liability' (2000); Assistant General Editor, Lloyd's law Reports: Professional Negligence; co-author, 'The Mareva Injunction and Anton Piller Order' (1993).

FLESCH, Michael QC
Gray's Inn Tax Chambers (Milton Grundy), London
(020) 242 2642
mf@taxbar.com
Recommended in Tax
Specialisation: Advises on all aspects of revenue law, and appears before the Commissioners, High Court, Court of Appeal, House of Lords, Privy Council and also in Hong Kong in revenue cases. Regular lecturer on tax-related topics.
Prof. Memberships: Revenue Bar Association, past chairman. Fellow, Chartered Institute of Taxation.
Career: Called to the Bar 1963. Teaching Fellow, University of Chicago 1963-64. Part-time lecturer in Revenue law, University College London 1964-82. Joined present chambers 1965. Took Silk 1983. Bencher of Gray's Inn 1993.
Personal: Educated at Gordonstoun School 1953-58 and University College, London 1959-62 (LLB Class 1, Hons). Governor of Gordonstoun School 1976-96. Leisure pursuits include all forms of sport. Keen Arsenal and Middlesex supporter, member of MCC, Twickenham and Wimbledon debenture holder. Born 11 March 1940. Lives in London.

FLETCHER, Andrew
3 Verulam Buildings (Christopher Symons QC & John Jarvis QC), London
(020) 7831 8441
afletcher@3vb.com
Recommended in Commercial (Litigation)
Specialisation: Particular experience in share purchase agreements (especially misrepresentation and breach of warranty claims); insurance and reinsurance (including involvement in arbitrations relating to the 1993 PA LMX spiral); banking (including disputes as to foreign exchange and margin trading); corporate governance issues; disputes between telecoms carriers and service providers; company and insolvency issues arising out of or inter-relating with commercial disputes; professional negligence, primarily in a financial context; and investigations and inquiries. Recent cases include: Larussa-Chigi v C S First Boston Limited [1998] CLC 227, QBD (Comm Ct) (whether foreign exchange margin trading was subject to SFA Conduct of Business Rules); Thornton Springer v NEM Insurance [2000] 2 All ER 489 (dispute as to policy coverage in respect of the costs of an insured's successful defence of claims brought against it; construction of accountant's minimum wording professional indemnity policy); Rosedale (JW) Investments Ltd and ors v British Steel plc (CA, 15 November 2000) New Law Online 200120603 (construction of provisions in share purchase agreement); Rosedale Investments Ltd and ors v British Steel plc (Comm Ct, 6 December 2000) New Law Online (liability under tax indemnity in share purchase agreement); Elton John and others v Price Waterhouse and anr, ChD (11 April 2001) New Law Online 201047201 (Construction of management agreement; rectification; estoppel by convention; effect of settlement; director's duties; negligence; limitation).

FLINT, Charles QC
Blackstone Chambers (Presiley Baxendale QC & Charles Flint QC), London
(020) 7583 1770
clerks@blackstonechambers.com
Recommended in Administrative & Public Law, Commercial (Litigation), Financial Services, Fraud, Sport
Specialisation: Charles Flint QC practises in commercial and public law, specialising in financial services, commercial fraud and sports law. He has been involved in many of the major regulatory cases which have arisen in the last 10 years, as well as some of the largest civil fraud claims to come to court. In 1999 he was retained as leading counsel for the Singapore Stock Exchange in its dispute with the Malaysian authorities over the freezing of the offshore market in Malaysian listed securities. In 2000 he acted for the defendant in the action brought by the State of Brunei against HRH Prince Jefri Bolkiah, and in 2001 was retained in the case brought by the State of Nigeria against the Abacha family.
Prof. Memberships: He is a member of the Lawyers Consultative Working Group established by the Financial Services Authority to advise on issues arising from the Financial Services and Markets Act 2000. Fellow of the Chartered Institute of Arbitrators and a CEDR accredited mediator. Member of the Commercial Bar Association, Administrative Law Bar Association, British Association for Sport and Law.
Career: Called to the Bar in 1975, and became a Junior Counsel to the Crown in 1990, responsible for advising and acting for government departments in the commercial field. He became a QC in 1995 and was appointed joint Head of Blackstone Chambers in 1998.

FLOYD, Christopher QC
11 South Square (Christopher Floyd QC), London
(020) 7405 1222
Recommended in Intellectual Property
Specialisation: Intellectual property including patents, trademarks, copyright and designs, breach of confidence and related EU law. Major cases include Mentor v Hollister [1993] RPC 7 (CA insufficiency principles); Molnlycke v Procter & Gamble [1994] RPC 7 (CA obviousness principles); Gerber v Lectra [1995] RPC 383, [1997] RPC 443 (law damages for patent infringement); Merrell Dow Pharmaceuticals v HN Norton [1996] RPC 76 (HL novelty of a pro-drug); Pearce v Ove Arup [2000] Ch 403 (CA Brussels Convention: infringement of foreign IP rights). Important cases in last year Dyson v Hoover [2001] RPC 473, 544, Rohm & Haas v Collag [2001] FSR 426 (declaration of non-infringement);

LEADERS AT THE BAR

Texas Iron Works' Patent [2000] RPC 207 (added matter); Cairnstores v Hassle (right to apply for revocation by straw man); Amersham v Amicon (construction, chromatography valves), Asahi v Macopharma (obviousness, blood systems).
Prof. Memberships: IP Bar Association, Chancery Bar Association, Irish Bar.
Career: Called 1975, Inner Temple, QC 1992; Head of IP Chambers at 11 South Square; Deputy Chairman Copyright Tribunal 1995-; Assistant Recorder 1994; Recorder 2000-; Deputy High Court Judge 1998-; Bar Council Professional Conduct Committee 1998-; Chairman IP Bar Association 1999-; Bar Council Member 1999-; Bencher Inner Temple 2001-.
Personal: Educated: Westminster School, Trinity College, Cambridge (BA Natural Sciences and Law 1974). Interests: Austin Sevens, cricket (watching), skiing, walking. Married, one son, two daughters.

FLYNN, James
Brick Court Chambers (Christopher Clarke QC), London
(020) 7379 3550
flynn@brickcourt.co.uk
Recommended in Competition/European Law
Specialisation: European Community/Competition Law. Reported cases include: (English courts): R v Customs & Excise ex p Lunn Poly (High Court and CA); Sockel GmbH v Body Shop International (High Court); Trent Taverns v Sykes (CA); Scottish & Newcastle v Dixon (High Court); Whitbread plc v Falla (High Court); (in the European Court of Justice): British Aerospace v Commission; BP Chemicals v Commission No 1; Gencor v Commission; Compagnie Maritime Belge v Commission; BP Chemicals v Commission (No 2); Steel beams cartel; Euroalliages v Commission; (in the Competition Commission Appeal Tribunal;) IIB v DGFT; BetterCare v DGFT.
Prof. Memberships: Competition Law Association (Committee Member); UIA EC Section (Committee Member); JUSTICE EU Expert Panel; Bar European Group; Law Society's European Group; European Circuit; EC Advisory Board; British Institute of International and Comparative Law.
Career: Legal Secretary, European Court of Justice (1986-89); Partner, *Linklaters & Paines*, Brussels (1993-96); Tenant Brick Court Chambers, 1996 to date.
Publications: Co-author 'Competition: Understanding the 1998 Act' and many articles and contributions to books on EC and competition law topics. Co-editing forthcoming volume of articles on EC state aid law.
Personal: Fluent French (written and spoken).

FLYNN, Vernon
Essex Court Chambers (Gordon Pollock QC), London
(020) 7813 8000
vflynn@essexcourt.net
Recommended in Commercial (Litigation), Media & Entertainment
Specialisation: Broad-based practice in international and commercial law. In particular media and entertainment, commercial, arbitration, banking and finance and shipping. A full CV is available for viewing at www.essexcourt.net.
Career: Trinity College, Cambridge: Law (1st Class Hons). Called to the Bar 1991.

FORD, Michael
Old Square Chambers (John Hendy QC), London
(020) 7269 0300
Recommended in Health & Safety
Specialisation: Principal areas of practice are employment law, public law, civil liberties, health and safety and data protection.
Prof. Memberships: Member of the Industrial Law Society, Institute for Employment Rights, Justice.
Career: University of Bristol, LLB 1st Class; MA (Distinction). Qualified as solicitor (1989). Lecturer in Law at University of Manchester (1990-92). Called to Bar 1992. Recent cases include Steel, Lush and others v UK (ECHR) (1999) 28 EHRR 603; Vider v Unison [1999] ICR 746; Allen v AMCO (ECJ) [2000] IRLR 119; Southwark v Whillier [2001] ICR 142 (EAT) [2001] ICR 1016 (CA); R v Mallet ex p Stunt [2001] ICR 989, CA; Beckmann v Dynamco Whicheloe, ECJ, 4.6.02. Counsel for the bereaved and injured at Southall and Ladbroke Grove Railway Accident Public Inquiries (1999-2000). Visiting fellow at LSE.
Publications: Co-author of 'Redgrave's Health and Safety' and 'Munkman on Employers' Liability' and author of 'Privacy and Surveillance at Work'. Numerous other publications, especially on employment law.
Personal: Keen cyclist.

FORD, Neil QC
Albion Chambers (Neil Ford QC), Bristol
(0117) 927 2144
Recommended in Crime

FORDHAM, Michael
Blackstone Chambers (Presiley Baxendale QC & Charles Flint QC), London
(020) 75831770
michaelfordham@blackstonechambers.com
Recommended in Administrative & Public Law, Environment, Sport
Specialisation: Specialist in public and administrative law, and particularly judicial review. Member of Attorney-General's Supplementary Panel. Cases include Pinochet [2000] 1AC 61 & 147 (extradition of former head of state), Diane Blood [1999] Fam 151 (posthumous use of sperm), Fayed [1998] 1 All ER 93 (review of Parliamentary Commissioner for Standards), Walker [2000] 1 WLR 806 (UN peacekeeper) and Baby Products [2000] LGR 171. Also environmental law, human rights and sports law. Author of 'Judicial Review Handbook'. Editor of journal 'Judicial Review'. Lectures in administrative law at Hertford College, Oxford. Advisory Board Member, British Institute of International and Comparative Law. Called to the Bar 1990.
Personal: Educated at Spalding Grammar School, Hertford College, Oxford (BA & BCL), and University of Virginia (LLM). Oxford Hockey Blue (1986). Awarded Karmel, Mould and Prince of Wales Scholarships at Gray's Inn. Lives in St Albans.

FORLIN, Gerard
2-3 Gray's Inn Square (Anthony Porten QC & Anthony Scrivener QC), London
(020) 7242 4986
gforlin@2-3graysinnsquare.co.uk
Recommended in Health & Safety
Specialisation: Crime (specialising in health and safety and corporate and gross negligence manslaughter); disaster litigation; aviation; railways; shipping safety; driving; oil and gas; environmental crime; regulatory offences; fraud; disciplinary offences; human rights; public inquiries; inquests. Recent major cases: R v Factory Covers Limited (corporate manslaughter); R v Preston and others (manslaughter and corporate manslaughter); Faversham M2 coach crash; Watford train crash (manslaughter); Southall train crash (manslaughter and public inquiry); Paddington train crash (public inquiry); Mayoress of Croydon (corporate manslaughter); the Belle Tout lighthouse case (manslaughter); Hatfield train crash; Notting Hill Carnival; Earls Court (Spice Girls Concert Fatality); DVT and international airline crashes. Numerous other cases involving doctors, nurses, directors, individuals and companies charged with manslaughter and health and safety cases and other regulatory offences. He also acts for Government Departments in Crown Censure cases. He undertakes numerous inquests including acting recently for the FBU in the Manchester fireman case. He also prosecutes health and safety cases. He chairs and lectures for IBC, CLT, IIR, Lawtel, IATA, TEN, ROSPA, Iosh and numerous universities, law firms and institutions worldwide. He appears regularly on TV and radio as an expert and is a script advisor for various TV companies. He is a lecturer and facilitator for the Bar Council on the HRA.
Prof. Memberships: CBA; Bar pro bono unit; current member of the Attorney General's Panel of Counsel.
Career: Called Lincoln's Inn 1984 - previously Senior Crown Counsel, Hong Kong.
Publications: Numerous articles published, joint author of corporate manslaughter practical research paper (Sweet & Maxwell) - general editor of a major loose-leaf work to be published by Butterworths early in 2002 on corporate manslaughter and a further book on health and safety also due out in early 2002 for Informa. Contributor to Tolleys' 'Manual on Disaster Management'.
Personal: Educated London School of Economics LLB (Hons); LLM; Trinity Hall; Cambridge M.Phil; Diploma in Air and Space Law. Leisure - travel, walking, sub-aqua.

FORSYTH, Julie
Chavasse Court Chambers (Theresa Pepper), Liverpool
(0151) 707 1191
Recommended in Crime

FORTSON, Rudi
3 Gray's Inn Square (Rock Tansey QC), London
(020) 7520 5600
Recommended in Crime
Specialisation: Extensive criminal law experience, with specialist knowledge on law relating to misuse of drugs, drug-trafficking offences, money-laundering and fraud. Author of 'The Criminal Justice Act 1993' and 'Law on the Misuse of Drugs and Drug Trafficking Offences'. Annotator for 'Current Law Statutes' on Criminal Justice Acts 1991 and 1993, Police and Magistrates Courts Act 1994 and Drug Trafficking Act 1994. Member of the Police Foundation Independent Inquiry (2000) into the Misuse of Drugs Act 1971. Former contributing editor of Archbold Criminal Pleading, Evidence and Practice'. Addresses conferences and seminars.
Prof. Memberships: Criminal Bar Association, International Bar Association, American Bar Association, Forensic Science Society.
Career: Called to the Bar 1976 (pupillage at 1 Crown Office Row) and joined current chambers in 1978.
Personal: Educated at University College, London 1972-75 (LLB Hons). Leisure pursuits include yachting, chess and cooking. Born 2 March 1952.

FOSKETT, David QC
1 Crown Office Row (Robert Seabrook QC), London
(020) 7797 7500
david.foskett@1cor.com
Recommended in Clinical Negligence, Personal Injury
Specialisation: All fields of common law advocacy and advice including clinical and other professional negligence, personal injury, medical and dental disciplinary tribunals, contract and general domestic commercial work and product liability. He also has experience in judicial review, administrative law and civil and criminal fraud cases. Recent cases include Langford v Hebran, Makepeace v Evans Bros, Jimenez v Lambeth Borough Council (personal injury); O'Brien v Solomon, Temple v South Manchester HA (clinical negligence); Nwabueze v GMC (appeal to Privy Council in doctor's disciplinary

LEADERS AT THE BAR

case); Morris v Wentworth-Stanley (commercial); R v Secretary of State for Health, ex p. Eastside Cheese Co (judicial review).
Prof. Memberships: Fellow of the Chartered Institute of Arbitrators; member London Common Law and Commercial Bar Association; Administrative Law Bar Association; Family Law Bar Association and Midland Circuit; member of the Civil Procedure Rules Committee 1997-2001.
Career: Called to the Bar (Gray's Inn) 1972. Bencher 1999. Queen's Counsel 1991. Assistant Recorder 1992-95; Recorder 1995-; Deputy High Court Judge 1997-.
Publications: He is the author of 'The Law and Practice of Compromise' (Sweet & Maxwell), (5th edition, 2002). He has contributed articles to 'The Times' and has lectured extensively on the subject of the settlement of litigation.
Personal: Educated at Warwick School and King's College London (LLB, President of the Union). Interests include cricket, golf, reading poetry and birdwatching. Lives in London and Gloucestershire.

FOSTER, Catherine
Plowden Buildings (William Lowe QC), Newcastle upon Tyne
(020) 7583 0808
catherine-foster@lineone.net
Recommended in Personal Injury
Specialisation: Occupational diseases, medical negligence, general personal injury litigation.
Prof. Memberships: PIBA.

FOSTER, Charles
6 Pump Court (Kieran Coonan QC), London
(020) 7583 6013
Recommended in Clinical Negligence
Specialisation: Medical and other professional negligence. Reported cases include Calver v Westwood Group [2001] Lloyd's Rep Med 20, In re D (mental patient: Habeas Corpus) [2001] 1 FLR 218, Briggs v Pitt-Payne [1999] Lloyd's LR: Med 1, Drake v Pontefract HA [1998] Lloyd's LR: Med 425, Reed v Sunderland HA, The Times, 16 October 1998, Fallows v Randle [1997] 8 Med LR 160, Bancroft v Harrogate HA [1997] 8 Med LR 398, Hind v York HA [1997] 8 Med LR 377, Ogden v Airedale HA [1996] 7 Med LR 153, Kahl v Freistaat Bayern [1995] PIQR P401.
Prof. Memberships: PNBA, Medico-Legal Society.
Career: Educated at Shrewsbury School & St John's College, Cambridge (MA, Vet MB, MRCVS). Research in wild animal anaesthesia in Saudi Arabia and comparative anatomy at RCS, Research Fellow at Hebrew University, Jerusalem. Also a member of the Irish Bar. Numerous publications.

FOWLER, Richard QC
Monckton Chambers (Kenneth Parker QC & Paul Lasok QC), London
(020) 7405 7211
rfowler@monckton.co.uk
Recommended in Competition/European Law
Specialisation: EC and UK competition law.
Prof. Memberships: Chairman of Performing Right Society Appeal Panel; Committee Member COMBAR; Member Competition Law Association; Member Legal Services Committee and Professional Conduct & Complaints Committee of Bar Council.
Career: Specialised since 1973 (including working from 1977 to 1984 on Case No IV/29.479 - IBM) in the preparation, drafting and presentation of submissions on behalf of clients to the European Commission (also OFT and Competition Commission) and in High Court and European Court proceedings, and advising a wide range of national and international clients on competition law matters and in related areas, particularly utility regulation. Recent cases include appearing for the Hong Kong administration in the HK Legislative Council in relation to the HK Telecommunications Bill; Tate & Lyle v the EC Commission; JCB v the EC Commission; Competition Commission mobile phones inquiry; OFT investigation of credit card interchange fees; ABTA v DGFT re GISC in the CCAT.

FOXTON, David
Essex Court Chambers (Gordon Pollock QC), London
(020) 7813 8000
Recommended in Commercial (Litigation), Insurance, Shipping
Specialisation: Commercial practice, in particular international insurance and reinsurance; shipping and the international carriage of goods; professional negligence; Lloyd's litigation. Banking, sale of goods, company sales, share warranty claims and professional negligence actions. Has appeared on numerous occasions in commercial arbitration.
Career: Magdalen College, Oxford 1983-86 BA (1st Class Hons) in Jurisprudence, 1986. Bachelor of Civil Law (1st Class Hons). Called to the Bar 1989. PhD (London) 2001.
Publications: Scrutton on Charterparties and Bill of Lading.
Personal: Born 1965.

FOY, John QC
9 Gough Square (John Foy QC), London
020 7832 0500
clerks@9goughsq.co.uk
Recommended in Personal Injury
Specialisation: Practice encompasses plaintiff and defendant personal injury and clinical negligence work. Appeared in Mountenay v. Bernard Matthews [1994]; Mughal v. Reuters Ltd [1993]; Hunt v. Douglas Roofing [1990] and Arnold v. CEGB [1988]; British Coal Respiration Disease Litigation [1998]; Alexander v. Midland Bank plc [1999]; Wadey v. Surrey County Council [2000]. Clients include all major trade unions. Frequently chairs and addresses conferences and seminars, and has appeared on BBC TV and radio.
Prof. Memberships: Association of Personal Injury Lawyers; Personal Injury Bar Association; Professional Negligence Bar Association.
Career: Called to the Bar and joined 9 Gough Square in 1969; Recorder (2000).
Personal: LLB (Hons) Birmingham University, 1967. Leisure pursuits include sports. Born 1st June 1946. Lives in Suffolk.

FRANCIS, Nicholas QC
29 Bedford Row Chambers (Nicholas Francis QC), London
(020) 7404 1044
nfrancis@29bedfordrow.co.uk
Recommended in Family
Specialisation: Principal area of practice is matrimonial ancillary relief work, with a particular interest in pension issues and foreign asset cases. Other main areas within practice are professional negligence; and residence, contact, education and child abduction cases. Major cases include Re P (A Minor) [1992] (Education); Re D (minors) [1993] (conciliation: Privilege); C v C [1994] (wasted costs order); S v S (reserved costs order) [1995] B v Miller & Co [1996] and H v H [1997]. Several articles on ancillary relief for Family Law with particular emphasis on the issue of costs and discovery. Regular lecturer on costs and discovery and on international aspects of family proceedings; and contributor to Legal Network T.V.
Prof. Memberships: Family Law Bar Association (former committee member). Member for three years of Bar Council Professional Conduct and Complaints Committee.
Personal: Educated at Radley College 1971-76 and Downing College, Cambridge 1977-80 (BA Law 1980, MA 1984). Leisure pursuits include racing dinghies. Born 1958. Lives in London.

FRANCIS, Robert QC
3 Serjeants' Inn (Robert Francis QC & John Grace QC), London
(020) 7427 5000
Recommended in Clinical Negligence
Specialisation: Principal area of practice is medical law, including medical negligence actions for plaintiffs and defendants, ethical cases concerning treatment of patients, and disciplinary proceedings (General Medical Council, General Dental Council etc). Leading cases include: Re F (Mental Patient: Sterilisation); Airedale NHS Trust v Bland; Roy v Kensington etc FPC; T (Wardship: Medical Treatment); MB; GMC v Roylance; Miss B: Healthcare Worker v Associated Newspaper: Royal Liverpool Children's Inquiry. Other areas of practice include administrative law, employment, crime, public inquiries.
Prof. Memberships: Professional Negligence Bar Association, LCLCBA, CBA.
Career: Called to the Bar 1973; Queen's Counsel 1992. Recorder.
Personal: Uppingham School, Exeter University. Born 4 April 1950.

FRANSMAN, Laurie QC
Two Garden Court (Owen Davies QC & Courtenay Griffiths QC), London
(020) 7353 1633
Recommended in Immigration
Specialisation: Advice, strategic planning and advocacy in all aspects of immigration and nationality, particularly concerning employment, self-employment and corporate work, the music and entertainment industry, national security and other sensitive cases and complex nationality issues; with an emphasis throughout on European Community law and international and human rights laws.
Prof. Memberships: Administrative Law Bar Association; Bar European Group; Immigration Law Practitioners' Association (co-founder, executive committee member 1993-98, 1999-).
Career: Member of the editorial boards of 'Immigration and Nationality Law and Practice' (Tolleys), and 'Immigration and International Employment Law' (Eclipse). Nationality law consultant to Halsbury's 'Laws of England' (4th ed., 1991 issue). Books: 'British Nationality Law and the 1981 Act' (1982); 'Tribunals Practice and Procedure' (jointly 1985); 'Immigration Emergency Procedures' (jointly, 1986); 'Fransman's British Nationality Law' (1989); 'The Constitution of the United Kingdom' (contrib., 1991); 'Strangers and Citizens' (contrib., 1994); 'Citizenship and Nationality Status in the New Europe' (contrib., 1998); 'Fransman's British Nationality Law' (1998), 2nd ed; 'Immigration, Nationality and Asylum under the Human Rights Act 1998' (contrib. and co-editor, 1999); Macdonald's 'Immigration Law and Practice in the United Kingdom' (contrib., 2001); 5th ed., Jackson & Warr's 'Immigration Law and Practice' looseleaf (contrib., 2001); Halsbury's 'Laws of England', 4th ed., title on British Nationality, Immigration and Asylum (contrib. and co-editor, anticipated 2002).

FRASER, Peter D
Atkin Chambers (Robert Akenhead QC), London
(020) 7404 0102
Recommended in Construction
Specialisation: Construction and engineering disputes; multi-party contractual disputes and commercial litigation. Insurance litigation, professional negligence of architects, surveyors and engineers. Arbitration proceedings including international arbitrations. Cases involving following projects: ICC arbitrations concerning the Bokaa Dam, Botswana; the National Dam, Cyprus; the Xiaolangdi water project in the People's Republic of China; MTR in Hong Kong.

International arbitration and litigation concerning car factories (both in UK and in Europe); manufacturing process plants; oil exploitation in Chile; Euro Disney; and other major civil engineering projects worldwide. Domestic projects include construction works at Harbour exchange, Canary Wharf and Canary Wharf Riverside in the London Docklands; West Yorkshire Playhouse in Leeds; Metro extension in Sunderland's jubilee line extension works. Numerous cases concerning professional negligence of architects, engineers, surveyors and multi-disciplinary partnerships.
Career: Called to Bar by Middle Temple 1989. Editor of the Building Law Reports since 1991 to date. Author of 'How to Pass Law Exams' (HLT Publications 1991).
Publications: Editor of the Building Law Reports 1991 to date. Author of 'How to Pass Law Exams' HLT Publications 1991. Past legal columnist of 'Building' magazine.
Personal: Born 1963. Educated Harrogate Grammar School and St John's College Cambridge. LLM Cambridge University; MA in Law, Cambridge University. Open exhibitioner and MacMahon Law Scholar of St. John's College, Cambridge. Astbury Scholar of the Middle Temple.

FRASER, Vincent QC
40 King St, Manchester
(0161) 832 9082
vfraser@40kingstreet.co.uk
Recommended in Planning
Specialisation: Town and Country Planning, environment, compulsory purchase, land tribunals, local government finance law, administrative law and judicial review. Particular interests in highways and related aspects of civil liability, environmental protection and data protection laws. Co-author of 'Planning Decisions Digest'. Recent reported cases include: R (Application of Barry) v Liverpool CC (Times 27/3/01); Enterprise Inns plc v SSETR [2000] 4 PLR 52.
Prof. Memberships: Planning and Environment Bar Association. Member of Northern Circuit. Administrative Law Bar Association, UK Environmental Law Association.
Career: Called 1981 (Gray's Inn) (Holker entrance award, Reid Scholar, Band prize); Oxford (MA); QC 2001; Recorder 2002.

FREEDMAN, Clive QC
Littleton Chambers (Michel Kallipetis QC), London
(020) 7797 8600
Recommended in Commercial (Litigation)

FREEDMAN, Clive
3 Verulam Buildings (Christopher Symons QC & John Jarvis QC), London
(020) 7831 8441
cfreedman@3vb.com
Recommended in Information Technology
Specialisation: General commercial litigation with emphasis on information technology; also banking, professional negligence and construction.
Prof. Memberships: COMBAR; TECBAR; Society for Computers and Law; Society for Construction Law; Franco-British Lawyers Society; CEDR Solve Mediator.
Career: Called to the Bar in 1975. Member of Bar Council IT Panel since 1990. Mediated a number of IT disputes as a CEDR mediator. Developed and maintained the Chambers web site, and was closely involved in setting up and administering the Chambers computer network. Trustee of BAILII, and wrote software for adding judgments to the BAILII web site.
Publications: Contributor to 'Banking Litigation' (1999), 'Bullen & Leake's Precedents of Pleadings' (section on IT disputes, 2001) and 'Expert Determination' (Kendall, 2001).
Personal: Educated at Harrow School and Trinity College, Cambridge. Interests include computer programming, home automation and bridge.

FREEDMAN, Jeremy
Plowden Buildings (William Lowe QC), Newcastle upon Tyne
(020) 7583 0808
jeremy.freedman@btinternet.com
Recommended in Clinical Negligence, Personal Injury
Specialisation: Practises exclusively in personal injury work and clinical negligence. Instructed equally on behalf of defendants and claimants, working for NHS trusts, major insurance companies and trade unions. Recent notable cases include Re: M (Child requiring heart transplant) and Ballantine v Newalls Insulation Co Ltd (2000) PIQR, Q57.
Prof. Memberships: North Eastern Circuit, Professional Negligence Bar Association and Personal Injury Bar Association. Recorder.
Career: Called to the Bar, 1982. Joined present set of Chambers in 1999.
Personal: Educated at Oundle, Manchester University and City University of London. Born 1959. Married, two children.

FRENCH, Paul
Guildhall Chambers (Adrian Palmer QC), Bristol
(0117) 930 9000
paul.french@guildhallchambers.co.uk
Recommended in Insolvency
Specialisation: Insolvency (all aspects of corporate, personal and partnership insolvency, including directors disqualification); bank recovery (including mortgages, receiverships, guarantees and indemnities); company law and partnership (including shareholder and partnership disputes and fiduciary duties). Recently reported cases: ReX (a company) Times 5 June 2001 (interim injunction in company unfair prejudice petition to prevent irredeemable prejudice); Boorer v Trustee in Bankruptcy of Boorer [2002] BPIR 12 (bankruptcy – review of consent orders – duties of trustee bankruptcy, rule in ex p James.
Prof. Memberships: Chancery Bar Association; Bristol and Cardiff Chancery Bar Association; Association of Business Recovery Professionals; Insolvency Lawyer's Association; Bar Sports Law Group; Society for Computers and Law.
Career: Called 1989.

FRIEDMAN, Daniel
Matrix Chambers, London
(020) 7404 3447
dannyfridman@matrixchambers.co.uk
Recommended in Human Rights
Specialisation: Criminal practice includes defence and appellate representation focusing in particular on due process and ECHR in all areas of serious crime. Civil and public law practice specialises in actions against state organisations that violate the rights of marginalised individuals and groups. Recent cases include Keenan v UK 33 EHRR 38; R v Offen [2001] 1 WLR 253; R v Rezvi and Benjafield [2002] 2 WLR 235; Attorney General's Reference No 3 of 2000; R v Loseley [2001] 1 WLR 2060; R v Sargeant [2001] 3 WLR 992; R v G (conspiracy to cheat) [2002] 1 WLR 200 and R (Wright and Bennett) v SSHD [2002] EHRLR 1.
Prof. Memberships: Inquest Lawyer's Group.
Career: Called 1996.
Publications: Co-authored 'Butterworths Guide to the Police Act' (1998) and 'Inquests: A Practitioners Guide' (forthcoming LAG, 2002) and has published numerous articles (most recently), Defending the Essence of the Right: Judicial Discretion and the Human Rights Act 1998, Archbold News, Issue 4, May 15 2001; The Human Rights Act and the Inquest Process, Legal Action, November and December 2001; From Due Deference to Due Process: Human Rights Litigation in the Criminal Law [2002] EHRLR Issue 2, 218.
Personal: BA (Hons) in Modern History: Wadham College 1992; LLM: London School of Economics 1995.

FRIEDMAN, David QC
4 Pump Court, London
(020) 7842 5555
dfriedman@4pumpcourt.com
Recommended in Construction
Specialisation: Principal area of practice covers all stages and all aspects of construction and engineering litigation and arbitration, both domestic and international. Also deals with professional negligence, particularly in relation to claims relating to professionals in the construction field.
Prof. Memberships: Technology and Construction Bar Association (former Chairman).
Career: Called to the Bar 1968. Tenant at 3 Paper Buildings 1970-92. Took Silk 1990. Joined Pump Court 1992. Appointed Recorder 1998. Appointed to act as Deputy Judge of TCC 2000. CEDR Accredited Mediator 1999. Acts as Arbitrator.
Personal: Educated at Tiffin Boys' School, Kingston-upon-Thames and Lincoln College, Oxford 1963-67 (MA, BCL). Born 1 June 1944.

FRIEL, John
Hardwicke Building (Nicholas Stewart QC), London
(020) 7242 2523
Recommended in Education
Specialisation: Administrative law, human rights in particular education, children with special needs, community care, SEN tribunal work, professional negligence.
Prof. Memberships: Education Law Association, Administrative Law Bar Association, Advisory Board of Education, Public Law & Individual, Author 'Children with Special Needs Assessment Law & Practice', 'Special Educational Needs of the Law'.
Career: LLB Hons UC London, In Practice since 1975, at 2 Kings Bench Walk 10 years plus.

FULFORD, Adrian QC
Tooks Court Chambers (Michael Mansfield QC), London
(020) 7405 8828
Recommended in Crime

FURBER, John QC
Wilberforce Chambers (Edward Nugee QC), London
(020) 7306 0102
jfurber@wilberforce.co.uk
Recommended in Property Litigation
Specialisation: Principally law of landlord and tenant but also covers property litigation, planning and compulsory purchase of land.
Prof. Memberships: Member of Chancery Bar Association, Property Bar Association and Planning and Environmental Bar Association.
Publications: Contributor to 'Halsbury's Laws of England', 'Landlord and Tenant' (1981 edn) and 'Compulsory Acquisition'. Contributor to and now general editor of Hill and Redman's 'Law of Landlord and Tenant'. Joint editor of 'Butterworths New Law Guide to the Commonhold and Leasehold Reform Act 2002'.
Personal: Called to Bar in 1973, took silk in 1995.

FURNESS, Jonathan
30 Park Place (John Jenkins QC), Cardiff
(029) 2039 8421
Recommended in Family

FURNESS, Michael QC
Wilberforce Chambers (Edward Nugee QC), London
(020) 7306 0102
Recommended in Pensions, Tax
Specialisation: Trusts, both private and commercial, especially pensions (advisory work, ombudsman appeals

LEADERS AT THE BAR

and other litigation) and charities (particularly in relation to the making of charitable schemes). Has wide experience of conducting tax litigation at all levels.
Prof. Memberships: Chancery Bar Association, Revenue Bar Association, Association of Pension Lawyers.
Career: Called 1982; Formerly First Standing Junior Counsel to the Inland Revenue in Chancery Matters; QC 2000.
Personal: Secretary, Bar Theatrical Society.

FURST, Stephen QC
Keating Chambers, London
(020) 7544 2600
sfurst@keatingchambers.com
Recommended in Arbitration, Construction
Specialisation: Building and civil engineering; professional negligence including valuation; computers including software; important cases include Darlington v Wiltshire; Bank of East Asia v SDA; Tesco Stores Ltd v Ward Investments; Strachan & Henshaw v Stein Industrial; Macob v Morrison; Henry Boot v Alstom; Bouygues v Dahl-Jensen.
Career: Qualified 1975, Bencher of the Middle Temple; QC 1991; Recorder; editor of 'Construction Law Yearbook' and 'Keating on Building Contracts'; arbitrator; mediator.
Personal: The Edinburgh Academy, St Edmund Hall, Oxford, Leeds University (1972 BA Hons, 1974 LLB Hons). Born 1951; resides London.

FURZE, Caroline
Wilberforce Chambers (Edward Nugee QC), London
(020) 7306 0102
Recommended in Chancery, Pensions
Specialisation: Practice covers most aspects of chancery/commercial litigation and advice, including landlord and tenant, professional negligence, insolvency, pension funds, partnership, contentious probate and the administration of estates. Interest in ecclesiastical law and cases under the School Sites Acts.
Prof. Memberships: Member of Chancery Bar Association.
Career: BA (Cantab): 1st class honours in Natural Sciences (Chemistry). Called to the Bar 1992.
Publications: Contributor to the titles 'Real Property and 'Custom Usage' in Halsburys Laws and to 'Butterworths' Civil Court Precedents' and 'Atkins' Court Forms'.

GAISMAN, Jonathan QC
7 King's Bench Walk (Gavin Kealey QC & Julian Flaux QC), London
(020) 7910 8300
Recommended in Insurance, Shipping

GAITSKELL, Robert QC
Keating Chambers, London
(020) 7544 2600
rgaitskell@keatingchambers.com
Recommended in ADR
Specialisation: Over 40 commercial, construction and intellectual property mediations. Construction law, including in particular electrical, mechanical, and process engineering; instructed in numerous international and UK manor engineering/building disputes, both litigation and arbitration (including frequent appointments as an arbitrator [including as chairman of ICC tribunal] and mediator) concerning, inter alia, complex engineering projects (especially power stations), defence, computer facilities, chemical processing, food and drink production, oil and gas rigs, hospitals, motorways, bridges, tunnels, dredging, water treatment, airports, abattoirs, nuclear fuel processing and commercial property. Cases include University of Glasgow v Whitefield; ICI v Bovis; Lamacrest v Case; Cameron v Mowlem; Surrey Heath v Lovell.
Career: Qualified 1978; Gray's Inn; QC 1994; practising Queen's Counsel; arbitrator, mediator and adjudicator; Recorder; Vice President of the IEE (1998-2001); Senator of the Engineering Council (1997-2002), practised in UK and abroad as professional electrical engineer, lectures widely in UK and abroad on legal and engineering matters, particularly international construction contracts; lecturer; King's College, London; MSc in Construction Law under Far Eastern Legal Systems; Chairman of IEE/IMechE Model Form Contracts committee; IEE Arbitration & Adjudication Panel, former examiner in contract law, RICS; regular columnist 'Engineering Management Journal'; numerous publications on legal and engineering topics, contributor to 'Construction Law Yearbook'.
Personal: BSC Eng. PhD (King's College, London), FIEE, C Eng, FI Mech E, FCI Arb. Born 1948; Worshipful Company of Engineers, Past Chairman IEE Professional Group on Engineering and Law.

GAL, Sonia
28 St John St, Manchester
(0161) 834 8418
Recommended in Family

GALBRAITH-MARTEN, Jason
Cloisters (Laura Cox QC), London
(020) 7827 4000
jgm@cloisters.com
Recommended in Employment
Specialisation: Employment, public and human rights law. Reported cases: Jenvey v Australian Broadcasting Corporation [2002] EWHC 927; Henry v London General Transport Services Ltd. [2001] IRLR 132; Barber v RJB Mining [1999] ICR 679; Beynon v Scaddon [1999] IRLR 700; West Kent College v Richardson [1999] ICR 511; Gregory v Wallace [1998] IRLR 387; R v North Derbyshire HA ex p Fisher [1998] 10 Admin LR 27; R v Secretary of State ex p. Unison [1996] IRLR 438; and R v Cleveland CC ex p Cleveland Care Homes Association [1994] COD 221. Noteworthy cases: Steve Jackson v Kiss FM (race discrimination); Roycroft v Lennox Lewis/Panix Promotions (sex discrimination) and Soloman v MSF ('whistleblowing').
Prof. Memberships: Employment Law Bar Association, Employment Lawyers Association and Industrial Law Society.
Career: Lecturer for the Bar Council, ELA, IRS, CLT, the specialist employment unit of the LawNet group of solicitors and for Justice. Member of the subscriber panel for Legal Network Television. Advocacy trainer for the Middle Temple. EOC and CRE panel advocate. Legal advisor to the Andrea Adams Trust, an anti-bullying organisation.
Publications: Bullen & Leake & Jacobs's 'Precedents of Pleadings' and of Butterworths 'Employment Law Guide'. Contributor to Butterworths online XpertHR service.

GALLAFENT, Kate
Blackstone Chambers (Presiley Baxendale QC & Charles Flint QC), London
(020) 7583 1770
kategallafent@blackstonechambers.com
Recommended in Employment
Specialisation: Employment, public, human rights, entertainment/media, sports.
Prof. Memberships: ELA, ALBA, Combar, ELBA, BEG.
Career: Called 1997. Previously worked as a fast-stream civil servant.
Publications: Contributing editor to Lester and Pannick 'Human Rights Law and Practice'.

GAMMIE, Malcolm QC
One Essex Court (Lord Grabiner QC), London
(020) 7583 2000
mgammie@compuserve.com/www.malcolmgammie.com
Recommended in Tax
Specialisation: All commercial taxation and related administrative law, including international and European taxation, corporate and employee taxation, property taxation and value added tax. Director of Research of Tax Law Review Committee; 1998 Unilever Professor of International Business Law at Leiden University, The Netherlands. Visiting professor of tax law, LSE.
Prof. Memberships: Chartered Institute of Taxation (president 1993-94); Association of Taxation Technicians, International Fiscal Association (member, Permanent Scientific Committee), European Bar Group, Revenue Bar Association.
Career: Sidney Sussex College, Cambridge; qualified 1975 as solicitor with *Linklaters & Paines*, subsequently with CBI and as Director of National Tax Services at KMG Thomson McLintock (now KPMG); tax partner at *Linklaters & Paines* 1987-97; called to the Bar 1997.
Publications: 'Land Taxation', 'Tax on Company Reorgansiations', consultant editor of 'Butterworths Tax Handbooks'.
Personal: Married with 4 children. Interests include music and church architecture.

GARDEN, Ian
Derby Square Chambers (Simon Newton), Liverpool
(0151) 709 4222
Recommended in Church

GARDINER, John QC
11 New Square (John Gardiner QC), London
(020) 7242 4017
taxlaw@11newsquare.com
Recommended in Tax
Specialisation: Revenue law. Involved in the two Woolwich cases, Pattison v Marine Midland, Ensign Tankers (Leasing) v Stokes, International Commercial Bank v Willingale, Glaxo Group Ltd v IRC and Nuclear Electric v Bradley.
Prof. Memberships: Revenue Bar Association.
Career: Called to the Bar 1968 and joined New Square in 1970. Took Silk 1982. Treasurer of Senate of Inns of Court and Bar Council, 1985-86; Bencher, Middle Temple.
Personal: Educated at Bancroft's School, Woodford 1957-63 and Fitzwilliam College, Cambridge 1964-68 (MA, LLM) Born 28 February 1946. Lives in London.

GARDINER, Nicholas
187 Fleet Street (Andrew Trollope QC), London
(020) 7430 7430
Recommended in Crime

GARNETT, Kevin QC
Hogarth Chambers (Jonathan Rayner James QC & Christopher Morcom QC), London
(020) 7404 0404
Recommended in Media & Entertainment
Specialisation: Practises extensively in the field of media and entertainment with a particular leaning to music, film, broadcasting and publishing work. Also practises widely in the intellectual property field. Is Senior Editor of 'Copinger and Skone James on Copyright'. Other main area of practice is general Chancery litigation.
Prof. Memberships: Chancery Bar Association; Intellectual Property Bar Association.

GARNHAM, Neil QC
1 Crown Office Row (Robert Seabrook QC), London
(020) 7797 7500
neil.garnham@1cor.com
Recommended in Administrative & Public Law, Health & Safety
Specialisation: Principal areas of practice are Administrative and Public Law, Human Rights, Professional Negligence including Medical Negligence, Personal Injury and Health and Safety. Public Law work includes health law, extradition, education, immigration and asylum. Cases include Thomas v Bunn [1991] (HL - interest in PI cases); Racz v Home Office [1994] (HL - misfeasance in public office); Re K [1994] (CA - adoption of foreign

national); ex p McQuillan [1995] (Exclusion orders); Ex parte Onibiyo [1996] (CA - fresh claims for political asylum); T v Home Office [1996] (HL - political offences in asylum law); Gregory v UK [1994] (ECHR - bias in jury trials); D v UK [1997] (ECHR - Article 3); TI v UK [2000] (ECHR Articles 2 and 3); R v SSND ex p Salem [1999] (social security benefits and asylum); Re K (a child) [2001] (secure accommodation orders) 5 ECHR; R v W&B [2001] (care order) 688 ECHR.
Prof. Memberships: ALBA, PNBA, PIBA.
Career: Called 1982; Junior Counsel to the Crown 1995-2001. Silk 2001. Junior Counsel Ladbroke Grove Rail Inquiry (2000); Counsel to Victoria Climbie Inquiry (2001).
Personal: Educated Ipswich School and Peterhouse Cambridge.

GARRETT, Annalissa
6 Pump Court (Kieran Coonan QC), London
(020) 7583 6013
Recommended in Clinical Negligence

GARSIDE, Charles QC
9 St. John Street (John Hand QC), Manchester
(0161) 955 9000
clerks@9stjohnstreet.co.uk
Recommended in Crime
Specialisation: Also at 9 Bedford Row (Anthony Berry QC) (020) 7489 2727. Specialises in crime, including fraud; judicial review; other Crown office work.
Prof. Memberships: Criminal Bar Association.
Career: Called 1971. QC 1993.

GATT, Ian QC
Littleton Chambers (Michel Kallipetis QC), London
(020) 7797 8600
ian@gatt.co.uk
Recommended in Employment, Professional Negligence
Specialisation: Professional negligence (principally solicitors and surveyors). Nationwide managed litigation (1997-1999), Birmingham Midshires v David Parry, Nationwide v Various Solicitors (managed litigation costs). Employment: unfair and wrongful dismissal (Duffield v Jupiter International; Clark v Nomura [2000], IRLR 766 (city bonuses)), sex, race and disability discrimination and restraint of trade. Commercial fraud: Guinness Trial 1990, numerous SFO prosecutions; Commercial. Partco v Wragg and Scott (2002) (directors' liability in public offer).
Prof. Memberships: COMBAR; Professional Negligence Bar Association; Employment Law Bar Association; Criminal Bar Association.
Career: Hutton GS, Preston (1974-81); Hertford College, Oxford (1981-84) BA Jurisprudence (1st). Called to the Bar 1985. Joined 2 Crown Office Row (now Littleton Chambers) 1986. CEDR Accredited Mediator. Appointed Recorder, 2000.
Publications: Co-author 'Arlidge and Parry on Fraud' (2nd ed). Bowers and Gatt, 'Procedure in Courts and Tribunals' (2nd ed).
Personal: Married with three children. Interests: rugby, cars, wine. Lives Winchester, Hampshire.

GAUNT, Jonathan QC
Falcon Chambers (Jonathan Gaunt QC & Kim Lewison QC), London
(020) 7353 2484
Recommended in Agriculture, Property Litigation

GEE, Anthony QC
28 St John St, Manchester
(0161) 834 8418
Recommended in Crime

GEE, Steven QC
Stone Chambers (Steven Gee QC), London
(020) 7440 6900
steven.gee@stonechambers.com
Recommended in Arbitration
Specialisation: Commercial law and litigation, insurance/reinsurance, contracts, banking, fraud cases, tracing and equitable remedies, arbitration, shipping, aviation, computer law. Author: 'Mareva Injunctions and Anton Piller Relief' (4th ed, 1998, Sweet & Maxwell).
Prof. Memberships: COMBAR; Supporting member of the London Maritime Arbitrators Association.
Career: Head of Chambers (1999); QC (1993); formerly standing junior Counsel to DTI (ECGD). Foreign Jurisdictions: New York (admitted to State Courts and Federal Courts); Antigua.

GEERING, Ian QC
3 Verulam Buildings (Christopher Symons QC & John Jarvis QC), London
(020) 7831 8441
chambers@3vb.com
Recommended in Commercial (Litigation), Fraud
Specialisation: Commercial law, specialising in civil claims based on international and domestic commercial fraud and claims for restitution.
Prof. Memberships: COMBAR, London Common Law and Commercial Association.
Career: Queen's Counsel 1991. Further details are on chambers' web site: www.3vb.com

GEORGE, Charles QC
2 Harcourt Buildings (Robin Purchas QC), London
(020) 7353 8415
clerks@2hb.law.co.uk
Recommended in Church, Environment, Local Government, Planning
Specialisation: Principal area of practice is public law especially planning and environmental law, local government and parliamentary matters. Has advised and represented applicants and local planning authorities in relation to major development schemes, particularly those involving public infrastructure provision, housing, minerals, listed buildings and local government finance. Involved in promoting the King's Cross Railways Bill and Transport and Works Orders for extensions to the Manchester and Leeds Light Rail systems. Counsel in, inter alia, Pioneer Aggregates (UK) Ltd v Secretary of State for the Environment 1985; Save Britain's Heritage v Number 1 Poultry Ltd (1991); R v Parliamentary Commissioner for Administration ex p Balchin Nos 1 and 2 (1996 and 1999); Millington v Secretary of State for the Environment [1999]; South Buckinghamshire District Council v Porter (2001). Clients include Railtrack; Transco plc; Transport for London; Manchester City Council; Greater Manchester, West Yorkshire and Merseyside Passenger Transport Executives; Laing Homes Ltd. Has frequently represented applicants (many publicly funded) in judicial review proceedings involving public law challenges, particularly in relation to planning and environmental law challenges. Other main area of practice is ecclesiastical law and commons.
Prof. Memberships: Inner Temple; King's Inns, Dublin.
Career: Called to the Bar 1974 and joined 2 Harcourt Buildings in 1975. Conducted independent inquiry into planning decisions in the London Borough of Brent 1991. Took Silk 1992. Called to the Irish Bar 1995. Appointed Recorder 1997. Appointed Chancellor of the Diocese of Southwark 1996. Bencher at Inner Temple 2001.
Personal: Educated at Bradfield College 1958-63, Magdalen College, Oxford 1963-66 (1st Class Hons Modern History) and Corpus Christi, Cambridge 1966-67. Author of 'The Stuarts: A Century of Experiment' (1973). Leisure pursuits include tennis, architecture and travel. Born 8 June 1945. Lives in Sevenoaks, Kent.

GEORGE, Sarah
St Philips Chambers (John Randall QC), Birmingham
(0121) 246 7000
Recommended in Employment

GHOSH, Julian
Pump Court Tax Chambers, London
(020) 7414 8080
clerks@pumptax.com
Recommended in Tax
Specialisation: Mergers and acquisitions, structured finance, loan relationships, foreign exchange, financial instruments EC tax, VAT. Recent cases: Memec v IRC; Trinidad Oilwell Service Ltd v Board of Inland Revenue (PC); Nationwide Acess Ltd; PPP Ltd v CEC; Cadbury Schweppes plc v Williams; Royal Bank of Scotland Group plc v CEC.
Prof. Memberships: Revenue Bar Association; Bar European Group; Share Scheme Lawyers' Group. Also a member of the Faculty of Advocates, Edinburgh.
Publications: Co-author: 'Taxation of Law Relationships, Financial Instruments and Foreign Exchange' (Butterworths).

GIBBS, Patrick
2 Harcourt Buildings, Atkinson Bevan Chambers (Nicholas Atkinson QC & John Bevan QC), London
(020) 7353 2112
clerks@2hb.co.uk
Recommended in Crime
Specialisation: Defence advice and advocacy in the following fields: crime; 'quasi-crime'; regulatory proceedings; judicial review; disciplinary proceedings; confiscation proceedings; public inquiries. Most recently engaged in defending allegations surrounding 'Misconduct in Public Office' and in the Victoria Climbie Inquiry. Within conventional crime principally engaged over the last ten years in cases involving professional fraud, sexual offences and homicide. Experienced in the cross-examination of vulnerable witnesses.
Prof. Memberships: Criminal Bar Association.
Career: Called 1986.

GIBNEY, Malcolm T P
17 Carlton Crescent (Jeremy S Gibbons QC), Southampton
(023) 8032 0320/2003
Recommended in Consumer Law

GIBSON, Charles QC
2 Harcourt Buildings (Roger Henderson QC), London
(020) 7583 9020
clerks@harcourt.co.uk
Recommended in Product Liability
Specialisation: Common law/commercial with an emphasis on product liability (in particular group actions), professional negligence, personal injury, health and safety, insurance. Notable cases include Connelly v RTZ; Lubbe v Cape plc; Hodgson v Imperial Tobacco (the tobacco litigation); Bass Britvic v Terra; the Opren litigation; the Benzodiazepine litigation; Garland v West Wiltshire District Council; The Norplant litigation; the MMR litigation; group actions involving Prozac, Lariam, Minocin, Shiley heart valve, breast implants, drink contamination; the organo-phosphate litigation; the interest rate swap litigation; asbestos claims, Mine Radiation Injury claims; other product liability cases for various manufacturers including product liability litigation; the King's Cross and Clapham Inquiries for the London Fire Brigade; the Severn Tunnel Inquiry.
Prof. Memberships: PNBA. Common Law and Commercial Bar Association.
Career: Educated Wellington College; BA Hons Durham; Dip Law. Called to the Bar 1984. Author: 'Group Actions - Product Liability Law and Insurance'. CEDR Accredited Mediator. Recorder.
Personal: Born 1960. Married with four children.

LEADERS AT THE BAR

GIBSON, Christopher QC
Four New Square (Justin Fenwick QC), London
(020) 7822 2000
barristers@4newsquare.com
Recommended in Clinical Negligence
Specialisation: Professional negligence (lawyers, medical practitioners, accountants, valuers and building professionals); general commercial law, insurance, and building and construction. Cases include Mortgage Express v Bowerman, the consolidated appeal in the BBL litigation, Abbey National v Key Surveyors (Court appointed expert), and Thorman v New Hampshire (professional indemnity insurance).
Prof. Memberships: COMBAR, Professional Negligence Bar Association, Fellow of the Chartered Institute of Arbitrators.
Career: Educated at St Paul's School, and Brasenose College, Oxford; called to the Bar Middle Temple 1976; silk in 1995. FCI Arb 1992.
Personal: Married with 2 daughters; interests include Whitstable and motor-cycles.

GIFFIN, Nigel
11 King's Bench Walk Chambers (Eldred Tabachnik QC & James Goudie QC), London
(020) 7632 8500
clerksroom@11kbw.com
Recommended in Administrative & Public Law, Education, Employment, Local Government
Specialisation: Specialises principally in public and administrative law including Human Rights Act, commercial judicial review, education, local authority powers, local government finance, environment, housing, social services, travellers, elections and public procurement. Practice also covers employment law and general commercial law. Important cases include Beeson v Dorset CC (ECHR article 6); Hazell v Hammersmith & Fulham LBC (local authority interest rate swaps); Palmer v ABP (personal contracts and union membership); R v A.B.P. ex p Plymouth CC (judicial review of animal exports); R v Institute of Chartered Accountants ex p Brindle (stay of disciplinary proceedings pending litigation); Wandsworth LBC v A (access to school premises); R v Hammersmith & Fulham LBC ex p M (asylum seeker's rights under National Assistance Act); Hillsdown Holdings plc v Pensions Ombudsman (use of pension fund surplus); London Underground v RMT (industrial action); P v NASUWT (school exclusions).
Prof. Memberships: Administrative Law Bar Association, Education Law Association, Planning and Environmental Bar Association, Employment Law Bar Association, Member of A Panel of Treasury Counsel.
Career: Called to the Bar 1986.
Publications: Contributor of Administrative Court chapter to 'Foskett's Law and Practice of Compromise (5th Edition).
Personal: Educated at Worcester College, Oxford (BA Hons 1st class).

GILBART, Andrew QC
40 King St, Manchester
(0161) 832 9082
agilbart@40kingstreet.co.uk
Recommended in Planning
Specialisation: Town planning, compulsory purchase, highways, environment law and judicial review. Particularly experienced in major development projects involving airport expansion, retail and commercial development, roads, incineration, waste disposal, landfill, minerals, housing and motorway services. Represented a consortium of northern airports at the Doncaster Finningley Airport Inquiry in 2001-02 and will be promoting a number of motorway service areas in 2002. Contributor of articles to 'Journal of Planning and Environment Law'.
Prof. Memberships: Northern Circuit, Planning and Environment Bar Association, Administrative Law Bar Association, American Bar Association (international associate), UK Environmental Law Association.
Career: Called 1972, Queens Counsel 1991; Recorder 1996; Bencher of Middle Temple.
Personal: Read Law at Trinity Hall, Cambridge. Enjoys tramping in the hills of the Peak District when time permits.

GILEAD, Beryl
St. Mary's Chambers Family Law Chambers (Nigel B Page), Nottingham
(0115) 950 3503
Recommended in Family

GILL, Manjit Singh QC
6 King's Bench Walk (Sibghat Kadri QC), London
(020) 7583 0695
Recommended in Immigration

GILL, Tess
Old Square Chambers (John Hendy QC), London
(020) 7269 0300
gill@oldsquarechambers.co.uk
Recommended in Employment
Specialisation: Specialises in employment and human rights law, particularly discrimination and equal pay and industrial and trade union law. She has considerable experience of EC and human rights law and was for many years a member of the EC Network of experts on the equality directives. She has recently appeared in the following significant employment cases: Miriki v General Counsel of the Bar [2001] EWCA civ 1973 [2002] ICR505 (race discrimination and EAT procedure), O'Donohue v Redcar Cleveland Borough Council [2001] EWCA civ 701 [2001] IRLR 615 (compensation for unfair dismissal and discrimination), IGE Medical Systems Ltd v Halfpenny, HL [2001] IRLR 96 (maternity and sex discrimination); Allonby v Accrington & Rossendale College, Court of Appeal [2001] IRLR 364, CA (an agency lecturer claiming indirect discrimination, equal pay and access to the teachers pension scheme); Localbail (UK) v Bayfield Properties Ltd [2000] IRLR 96, CA (leading case on what constitutes bias by the court); Coyne v Home Office [2000] ICR 1443, CA (sex discrimination); Carmichael and Leese v National Power [1999] ICR 1226, HL (employment status of casual workers); Banks and Tesco Stores [1999] ICR 1141 (challenge to the exclusion of low paid women from statutory maternity pay); Strathclyde Regional Council v Wallace [1998] ICR 205, HL (the role of the material factor defence in equal pay); Grant v South West Trains [1998] IRLR 188, HC (contractual status of equal opportunities policy in context of discrimination on grounds of sexual orientation).
Prof. Memberships: Member of Lawyers for Liberty, Employment Law Bar Association, Personal Injury Bar Association, Industrial Law Society, Discrimination Law Association.
Career: Practised as a solicitor until 1990 when she transferred to the Bar. Has experience in private practice and as the GMB legal officer. She has been a part-time chairman of the employment tribunals since 1995. She is on the advisory panel of the Equal Opportunities Review and a member of the Equal Pay Task Force which made recommendations to reform the Equal Pay Act 1970 in February 2001. She was on the management committee of the Public Law Project until July 2000, and has previously been a management committee member of the National Council of Civil Liberties and Child Poverty Action Group. She is a founder member of Workplace Mediation project, a scheme for mediation of sexual or racial harassment or bullying in the workplace, and is a CEDR trained mediator.
Publications: Author of chapter on discrimination in 'Human Rights at Work' (Institute of Employment Rights, 2000) and the chapter on workers rights in 'Your Rights', the Liberty Guide to Human Rights (Pluto Press, 2000).

GILLESPIE, James
Renaissance Chambers (Brian Patrick Jubb & Henry Setright QC), London
(020) 7404 1111
Recommended in Immigration

GILLYON, Philip
Erskine Chambers (Robin Potts QC), London
(020) 7242 5532
pgillyon@erskine-chambers.co.uk
Recommended in Company
Specialisation: Company law, corporate insolvency, financial services. Cases include Re BSB Holdings Ltd [1996] 1 BCLC 155; Possfund Custodian Trustee Ltd v Diamond [1996] 1 WLR 1351; Re Exchange Travel (Holdings) Ltd [1996] 2 BCLC 524; Guinness Peat Group plc v British Land Company plc [1999] 2 BCLC 243; Banco Nacional de Cuba v Cosmos Trading Corporation [2000] 1 BCLC 813; Jarvis plc v PricewaterhouseCoopers [2000] 2 BCLC 368; Re Leyland Daf Ltd [2001] 1 BCLC 419; Banca Carige v Banco Nacional de Cuba [2001] 2 BCLC 604; Winpar Holdings Ltd v Joseph Holt Group plc [2001] 2 BCLC 604. Represents the Secretary of State for Trade and Industry in company director disqualification proceedings in relation to Queens Moat Houses plc.
Prof. Memberships: Commercial Bar Association; Chancery Bar Association; Middle Temple.
Career: Hymers College, (1974-84); Downing College, Cambridge (1984-87). Called 1988. Joined Erskine Chambers 1989.
Personal: Born 1965. Lives in London.

GILMAN, Jonathan QC
Essex Court Chambers (Gordon Pollock QC), London
(020) 7813 8000
Recommended in Shipping
Specialisation: Insurance, reinsurance and shipping cases. Appears as counsel in very many London arbitrations. Regularly acts as umpire or arbitrator in London arbitrations. Has been retained as expert witness on English law in foreign proceedings on many occasions (mostly insurance or reinsurance cases).
Career: Called to the Bar 1965. Silk 1990.
Personal: Born 1942.

GILROY, Paul
9 St. John Street (John Hand QC), Manchester
(0161) 955 9000
pgilroy@9stjohnstreet.co.uk
Recommended in Employment
Specialisation: Paul Gilroy has extensive experience of all aspects of employment law, ranging from the traditional areas of practice such as non-contentious advisory work, and Employment Tribunal/High Court/County Court litigation, to internal inquiries in the NHS, police and professional sports bodies. He acts for and against local and public authorities, trade unions and plcs. He is approved by the Commission for Racial Equality, the Equal Opportunities Commission and the Disability Rights Commission to act in discrimination cases. He has developed a special interest in public inquiries, having acted in the Inquiry into the Personality Disorder Unit at Ashworth High Security Hospital, and is currently retained on behalf of the relatives of the deceased in the Shipman Inquiry. He contributes to professional publications, annotates employment legislation for Current Law Statutes and is a frequent speaker on employment law.
Prof. Memberships: Employment Lawyers Association; Employment Law Bar Association; NCFRAS.
Career: Called 1985 (Gray's Inn). Door Tenant: Farrar's Building, Temple,

London EC4Y 7BD. Part-time Chairman of Employment Tribunals (2000). Treasury Counsel (2000).

GIRET, Jane QC
11 Stone Buildings (Murray Rosen QC), London
(020) 7831 6381
giret@11stonebuildings.com
Recommended in Chancery, Company, Insolvency

Specialisation: Head of 11 Stone Buildings' Company and Insolvency Group and a specialist in company, corporate and personal insolvency and partnership law. Her practice also includes general Chancery and commercial litigation. Much of her work focuses on company directors and their conduct, including directors' fraud and disqualification proceedings. An experienced and forceful advocate, her expertise includes shareholder disputes, complex receiverships and administrations. She also has a full non-contentious corporate advisory practice encompassing reconstruction, amalgamation and management.

GIROLAMI, Paul QC
Maitland Chambers (Michael Lyndon-Stanford QC & Charles Aldous QC), London
(020) 7406 1200
clerks@maitlandchambers.com
Recommended in Chancery, Company, Insolvency

Specialisation: Practice principally concerns Chancery matters of the commercial type, with an emphasis on litigation, including matters involving company, insolvency (corporate and personal), landlord and tenant, property, equitable remedies and trust questions.
Prof. Memberships: Chancery Bar Association and COMBAR.
Career: Called to the Bar, 1983. Junior Counsel to the Crown (Chancery) 1991-2000.
Personal: Born 5 December 1959. Educated St Paul's School London and Corpus Christi College, Cambridge. Lives in London.

GLANCY, Robert QC
Devereux Chambers (Colin Edelman QC), London
(020) 7353 7534
Recommended in Personal Injury

Specialisation: Principal areas of practice are personal injury and medical negligence cases, professional negligence generally (architects, engineers, surveyors and solicitors), construction law and employment law. Considerable experience of industrial disease cases such as repetitive strain injury, asbestos related conditions and welder's fume cases. Appeared in case of D and F. Estates v Church Commisioners for England and whether builder is liable for sub-contractor. Also appeared in a number of medical negligence cases such as Newell v Goldenberg concerned with warnings and sterilisation operations. Other cases include: Groom v Selby on damages for wrongful birth of disabled child; Robson v Liverpool County Council on damages for handicap on open labour market; Larby v Thurgood on employment consultants and their right to interview claimants; Sutherland v Hatton on damages for psychiatric illness caused by stress at work. One of the joint authors of the 'P.I.B.A. Personal Injury Handbook'.
Prof. Memberships: Personal Injury Bar Association.
Career: Called to the Bar 1972. Assistant Recorder 1993. Recorder 1998. Queen's Counsel 1997.
Personal: Educated at Manchester Grammar School and St. John's College, Cambridge. Lives in London.

GLASGOW, Edwin QC
39 Essex Street (Nigel Pleming QC), London
(020) 7832 1111
Recommended in Commercial (Litigation), Personal Injury

Specialisation: All areas of commercial and common law litigation including insurance, professional negligence and major personal injury cases. Has been involved in most of the public inquiries and litigation associated with disasters over the past 10 years. Has extensive experience of litigation, arbitration and human rights work overseas including USA; Australia; Hong Kong; Singapore; France and Africa. Recent cases include: Svenska Bank v Sun Alliance; Trafalgar House v Davy Offshore; Capital and Counties v Planned Maintenance; BBL; Sun Valley Poultry; Kuwait Investment Office; Bloody Sunday Inquiry.
Prof. Memberships: London Common Law and Commercial Bar Association.
Career: LLB (Hons); Called to the Bar 1969; Silk 1987. Chairman Financial Reporting Review Panel 1992-98. CBE 1999.

GLASS, Anthony QC
Hollis Whiteman Chambers (QEB) (Julian Bevan QC & Peter Whiteman QC), London
(020) 7583 5766
barristers@holliswhiteman.co.uk
Recommended in Crime, Fraud

Specialisation: Principal area of specialisation is in cases of white collar fraud although his practice covers all aspects of criminal law. Has prosecuted and defended in many high profile cases where diversion fraud, money laundering and VAT evasion have been alleged. Since taking Silk has defended many cases involving allegations of perverting the course of justice, causing death in custody, murder and has advised in cases before the General Medical Council.
Prof. Memberships: Criminal Bar Association, South Eastern Circuit.
Career: Called to the Bar 1965 and joined current chambers in 1982. Appointed Recorder 1985. Took Silk 1986. Bencher of Inner Temple.
Personal: Educated at Royal Masonic Schools 1948-58 and Lincoln College, Oxford 1960-63. Born 6 June 1940. Lives in London.

GLASSON, Jonathan
Doughty Street Chambers (Geoffrey Robertson QC), London
(020) 7404 1313
j.glasson@doughtystreet.co.uk
Recommended in Clinical Negligence, Product Liability

Specialisation: Clinical negligence, product liability, personal injury, Inquests and health-related public law. Generic first junior counsel for claimants in the Creutzfeldt-Jakob Disease/Human Growth Hormone Litigation (1996-98) and for the families at the BSE Inquiry before Lord Phillips. Briefed in a number of multi-party pharmaceutical product liability actions, including Roacuttane, Lariam and Minocin. Instructed by the Government in the PTSD Litigation brought by soldiers from Falklands, Northern Ireland, the Gulf and Bosnia. Other cases include Briody v St Helen's & Knowsley AHA (damages for surrogacy), Infantino v Maclean; Clunis v Camden & Islington Health Authority; R v HM Coroner for Lincoln ex p Hay.
Prof. Memberships: AVMA, APIL, PNBA, INQUEST, PIBA.
Career: Junior Counsel to the Crown (B Panel) – January 2002. Former Solicitor (Honours) and public health manager for a Regional Health Authority.
Personal: Maidstone GS and New College, Oxford.

GLEDHILL, Andreas
3-4 South Square (Michael Crystal QC & Lord Alexander of Weedon QC), London
(020) 7696 9900
andreasgledhill@southsquare.com
Recommended in Insolvency

Specialisation: Insolvency, fraud and tracing claims, banking law, company law and related areas of professional negligence.
Prof. Memberships: COMBAR; Chancery Bar Association; Insolvency Lawyers' Association.
Publications: 'Gore-Browne on Companies', 44th edn (contributing chapter 31 on Administrations, Voluntary Arrangements and Administrative Receiverships) and 'Muir Hunter on Personal Insolvency' (junior author).
Personal: Educated Westminster School and Christ's College Cambridge (1st class Hons, 1988).

GLEN, Ian QC
Guildhall Chambers (Adrian Palmer QC), Bristol
(0117) 930 9000
ian.glen@guildhallchambers.co.uk
Recommended in Crime, Licensing

Specialisation: Criminal work from homicide to serious fraud (including SFO work) with particular experience of drugs importations and health and safety (see R v Gateway Foodmarkets [1997] 3 ALL ER 78). All aspects of liquor, betting, gaming and public entertainment licensing including criminal defence (see Westminster City Council v Blenheim Leisure Ltd, The Times February 24, 1999). Broad judicial review practice complements crime and licensing (see R v Hereford Magistrates' Court ex p Rowlands [1998] QB 110).
Career: King's College, London 1972. Called in 1973 began practice in 1979. Silk 1996 (Hon) Research Fellow, Bristol University. Recent Lecturing: 'Judicial Review in Licensing Cases' (IBC annual conference) 'Confiscation of Criminal Proceeds' (National Fraud Forum Bramshill) 'False Memory Syndrome' (annual conference of UK Council for Psychotherapy). 'HWSA Criminal Liability of Companies and Company Directors' (for *Eversheds*). 'Human Rights Act' (for Bar Council and Western Circuit).

GLENNIE, Angus QC
20 Essex Street (Iain Milligan QC), London
(020) 7842 1200
clerks@20essexst.com
Recommended in Shipping

Specialisation: Principal areas of practice are shipping, insurance, reinsurance and arbitration. Recent cases include Stocznia Gdanska SA v Latvian Shipping company & others [2001] 1 Lloyd's Rep 537; LG Caltex Ltd v China Petroleum Corp All ER 2001 Vol 4 (C of A); BP Exploration Operating Co Ltd v Chevron Shipping Co [2002] 1 Lloyd's Rep 77; Baker v Black Sea Baltic General Insurance [1998] 1 WLR 974.
Career: MA (Cantab), Trinity Hall. Called 1974, QC 1991. Also practising member of Scots Bar (QC 1998). Member of Gibraltar Bar.

GLICK, Ian QC
One Essex Court (Lord Grabiner QC), London
(020) 7583 2000
Recommended in Arbitration, Commercial (Litigation), Energy, Tax

Specialisation: Principal areas of practice are arbitration (both as arbitrator and counsel), banking, commercial law, energy law, financial services, insurance and revenue litigation. Important cases include PCW litigation; Tin Council litigation; Woolwich BS v CIR (restitution); Smith New Court v Citibank (measure of damages in fraud); Gallagher v Jones (application of accepted principles of commercial accountancy to computation of profits for tax purposes), Shah v Bank of England (banking regulation); Deeny v Gooda Walker (taxability of damages recovered in Lloyds' litigation); R v CIR ex p Warburgs (judicial review of Revenue decisions); Northern Ireland Electricity v Director General of Electricity Supply (electricity price regulation) and Fuji Finance v Aetna (nature of a contract of

LEADERS AT THE BAR

insurance).
Prof. Memberships: Chairman, Commercial Bar Association, 1997-99; vice-chairman, Education and Training Committee of the Bar Council, 1999-2000.
Career: Called to the Bar in 1970. At Lamb Building 1970-80. Joined 1 Essex Court in 1980. Junior Counsel to the Crown, Common Law 1985-87. Standing Counsel to the DTI in export credit cases 1985-87. Took Silk in 1987, FCIArb.
Personal: Educated at Bradford Grammar School and Balliol College, Oxford. Born 18 July 1948. Lives in London.

GLOBE, Henry QC
Exchange Chambers (David Turner QC & Bill Braithwaite QC & Henry Globe QC), Liverpool
(0151) 236 7747
Recommended in Crime, Health & Safety

GLOSTER, Elizabeth QC
One Essex Court (Lord Grabiner QC), London
(020) 7583 2000
egloster@oeclaw.co.uk
Recommended in Chancery, Commercial (Litigation), Company, Energy, Fraud, Insolvency
Specialisation: Principal areas of expertise are company law, banking, insurance and insolvency. Also covers commercial fraud, financial services, media and telecommunications, energy and professional negligence. Recent major cases include: acting for the Equitable Life in the House of Lords to determine the rights of policyholders (2000); acting for the liquidators of Manhattan Investment Fund (2000); appearing in the House of Lords for defendants in Canada Trust v Stolzenburg (jurisdiction under the Lugano Convention) (2000); acting for BF&M Ltd in the action brought by the liquidators of Bermuda Fire & Marine Insurance Company (1999); acting for the DTI in the disqualification proceedings arising out of the collapse of Barings (1998); acting for EMLICO and its liquidators in the litigation arising out of EMLICO's redomestication to Bermuda (1996-98); acting for Charterhouse Development (France) in its action against Lloyd's underwriters (1996); acting for the administrators of Barings in the action against ING (1996); acting for the banks in the interest rate swaps litigation; representing the liquidators of Barlow Clowes in litigation against various directors and third party professionals (1992-2001); acting for banks/administrators of Olympia & York, Canary Wharf (1993-94); acting for the Society of Lloyd's in a case involving the question of priority between the Society and various Names (1993); representing recently-appointed trustees of Maxwell Pension Funds in relation to the Maxwell collapse (1992-95); acting for the D.T.I in the case of Sher v The Policy Holders Protection Board (1993); Hazell v Hammersmith & Fulham Borough Council (1992) (House of Lords); prosecuting in the criminal trials arising out of the Guinness bid for Distillers (1990) and (1991). Called to the Bars of Bermuda, Gibraltar and the Isle of Man for specific cases. Working knowledge of French.
Prof. Memberships: Chancery Bar Association, COMBAR, Insolvency Lawyers' Association, INSOL.
Career: Called to the Bar in 1971. Member of the panel of junior counsel representing the DTI in company matters 1982-89. Took Silk in 1989. Bencher of the Inner Temple and Deputy High Court Judge of the Chancery Division in 1992, Judge of the Courts of Appeal of Jersey & Guernsey (part-time) in 1994 and Recorder 1995.
Personal: Educated at Roedean School 1962-67 and Girton College, Cambridge 1967-70. Born 5 June 1949.

GLOVER, Richard
2 Mitre Court Buildings (Guy Roots QC), London
(020) 7583 1380
Recommended in Planning
Specialisation: Specialises in all areas of planning and local government law.
Prof. Memberships: Member of the Planning and Environment Bar Association and The Parliamentary Bar.
Career: Called in 1984. Has acted in a wide range of inquiries including the new HQ for Mclaren Racing near Woking, the Manchester Free Trade Hall, the Genome Campus extension for the Wellcome Trust and the proposals for 2500 houses south of Reading and many retail, housing and other inquiries. Parliamentary Bills include Channel Tunnel, Dartford River Crossing and Heathrow Express. Recent rating cases include Mosanto Chemical works, Port Talbot Steelworks, Shall Haven Oil refinery, Anston Properties, Coventry & Solihull Waste Disposal (in the House of Lords) and BT. Recent High Court work includes Corus v Clement on fairness and discrimination and BT v Gloucester CC on environmental impact assessment. Editor of 'Ryde on Rating and the Council Tax' and Butterworths' 'Local Government Law'.
Personal: Educated at Harrow and Cambridge.

GLOVER, Stephen J
37 Park Square (Stephen J Glover & Paul Kirtley), Leeds
(0113) 243 9422
chambers@no37.co.uk
Recommended in Family
Specialisation: Substantial asset matrimonial finance, professional negligence, personal injury, medical law.
Prof. Memberships: PNBA, PIBA. Association of Northern Mediators.
Career: 1978 call.

GODDARD, Andrew
Atkin Chambers (Robert Akenhead QC), London
(020) 7400 8501
clerks@atkinschambers.law.co.uk
Recommended in Construction
Specialisation: Specialises in construction and engineering and the law of commercial obligations. This has involved advocacy and advisory work in respect of major commercial developments, including PFI projects, hospitals, hotels, motorways, stations and railways, power stations, process plants, wet and dry docks as well as ship conversion, offshore and submarine structures and oil and gas exploration and exploitation. Clients include employers (both public and private), contractors, sub-contractors and professionals. He has advised on amendments to the standard forms of building and engineering contracts as well as drafted bespoke contracts. He has regularly advised and acted in connection with substantial claims for damages, loss and expense and extensions of time as well as claims in respect of professional negligence including solicitors' negligence. He also has extensive experience of information technology disputes involving software development, microelectronics and telecommunications. Although based in London, he has acted on behalf of many international clients, including foreign governments, and has a keen interest in projects with an international element. He has acted in many international arbitrations under the auspices of both the ICC and the LCIA. Related areas of law in which he has detailed experience include performance bonds, guarantees and insurance.
Prof. Memberships: TECBAR.
Career: Called to the Bar 1985.
Personal: Independent Schools Association Whitbread Memorial Trophy; BA Hons Law (First Class) Sussex 1984; Inner Temple Queen Elizabeth II Scholarship 1985; Poland Prize 1985.

GODDARD, Christopher
Devereux Chambers (Colin Edelman QC), London
(020) 7353 7534
goddard@devchambers.co.uk
Recommended in Personal Injury
Specialisation: Principal area of practice is claimant and defendant personal injury with a special interest in occupational disease. Also medical and legal professional negligence. Regularly speaks at conferences and seminars in these fields. Co-author 'Health and Safety: The New Legal Framework', Butterworths and contributor to Butterworths 'Personal Injury Handbook'. Executive editor of the 'Personal Injury Handbook', Gee Publishing.
Prof. Memberships: Personal Injury Bar Association.
Career: Manchester University 1969-72. Called to Bar in 1973.

GODFREY, Howard QC
2 Bedford Row (William Clegg QC), London
(020) 7440 8888
Recommended in Fraud
Specialisation: Serious crime especially fraud, both corporate and personal, and money laundering, including some work in USA and elsewhere overseas. Experienced in VAT and tax frauds, insider dealing, Stock Exchange, banking, accounting, insurance, corruption and extradition. Practice also includes general crime especially drugs cases and civil fraud.
Prof. Memberships: South Eastern Circuit, Criminal Bar Association. Member of Bar of Turks and Caicos Islands, 1996.
Career: Called 1970. Took Silk in 1991. Recorder 1992.
Personal: Born 17 August 1946. Educated University of London – London School of Economics (LLB). Lives in Berkshire.

GOLDBERG, David QC
Gray's Inn Tax Chambers (Milton Grundy), London
(020) 7242 2642
Recommended in Tax
Specialisation: Practice concentrates on revenue law and commercial litigation with a tax or financial aspect. Clients include solicitors, accountants and corporations. Co-author of 'Introduction to Company Law' (1971, 3rd edn 1987) and 'The Law of Partnership Taxation' (1976, 2nd edn 1979). Author of various articles and notes for legal periodicals, mainly concerning tax and company law.
Prof. Memberships: Revenue Bar Association; Chancery Bar Association.
Career: Called to the Bar and joined current chambers in 1971. Took Silk 1987. Bencher of Lincoln's Inn 1997.
Personal: Educated at Plymouth College and London School of Economics 1966-70 (LLB, LLM). Chairman of Trustees of the Skills Workshop for Anatomical Techniques. Leisure pursuits include reading, writing letters and thinking. Born 12 August 1947. Lives in London.

GOLDBERG, Jonathan QC
3 Temple Gardens (Jonathan Goldberg QC), London
(020) 7353 5446
jongold@talk21.com
Recommended in Crime
Specialisation: Has defended in many of the most notable jury trials at the Old Bailey and elsewhere over the past three decades. These include Roger Levitt (white collar fraud); Brinksmat; R v Rosenthal (The Stamford Hill child sex abuse case involving Orthodox Jews); R v Laming (The Sonic Binoculars horse nobbling case); R v Charlie Kray and many others. He is qualified at the New York Bar and has worked in Malaysia, Singapore and Gibraltar. He has had successes in libel and commercial civil and chancery cases requiring strong cross-examination, and is by no means limited to crime. Has defended solicitors, accountants and police officers.
Career: Called in 1971; appointed a QC in 1989; a Recorder in 1992.

Personal: Educated at Manchester Grammar and Trinity Hall Cambridge. A member of the International Presidency of the International Association of Jewish Lawyers and Jurists.

GOLDREIN, Iain QC
7 Harrington Street Chambers (David Steer QC & Robert Fordham QC & Iain Goldrein QC), Liverpool
Mobile (07831) 703 156
goldhaas@netcomuk.co.uk
Recommended in Clinical Negligence
Specialisation: Complex Professional (including Clinical) Negligence (with particular expertise in brain damage at birth and spinal cord injury); catastrophic injury claims; genetics together with human fertilisation and embryology; general commercial including insurance coverage; pre-emptive commercial relief; judicial review and human rights; product liability; complex crime with particular reference to medical/genetic issues. Cases of Interest: James v Preseli Pembrokeshire District Council (tripping accidents); Crozier v Crozier (retrospective legislation); Sion v Hampstead Health Authority (nervous shock); Fong Moi Yin v Suhali (Privy Council Appeal from Brunei on inferences to be drawn when a man is dead); Hill v West Lancashire Health Authority (cerebral palsy claims and causation); Lec (Liverpool) Ltd v Glover (insurance coverage dispute involving policy wording); Hallatt v North West Anglia Health Authority (gestational diabetes); Rayeware v TGWU; Rossiter v Dr Tilsley and other.
Prof. Memberships: Professional Negligence Bar Association; Personal Injury Bar Association; London Common Law & Commercial Bar Association. Companion of the Academy of Experts; Fellow of the Royal Society of Arts; Associate of the Chartered Institute of Arbitrators; Nominated Counsel: Environmental Law Foundation; Mediator, registered with the Academy of Experts. Awards: University of Cambridge Squire Scholarship for Law; Exhibitioner and Ziegler Prize, Pembroke College Cambridge; Inner Temple Duke of Edinburgh Scholarship.
Career: Appointments: Queen's Counsel; Recorder; Visiting Professor (The Sir Jack Jacob Chair in Litigation) Nottingham Law School; Member of the Mental Health Review Tribunal.
Publications: 'Property Distribution on Divorce' [FT Law and Tax] [1st and 2nd editions with Margaret de Haas QC]; 'Personal Injury Litigation: Practice and Precedents' [Butterworths]; 'Ship Sale and Purchase, Law and Technique' [Lloyds of London Press] with *Clifford Chance*; 'Commercial Litigation: Pre-emptive Remedies' [Sweet and Maxwell] with Judges Wilkinson and Kershaw QC; 'Butterworths Personal Injury Litigation Service' with Margaret de Haas QC; 'Bullen and Leake and Jacob's Precedents of Pleadings' [Sweet and Maxwell], with Sir Jack Jacob; 'Pleadings, Principles and Practice' [Sweet and Maxwell], with Sir Jack Jacob; 'Structured Settlements' [Butterworths], Editor-in-Chief with Margaret de Haas QC [1st Edition 1993. 2nd Edition May 1997]; 'Medical Negligence: Cost Effective Case Management' [Butterworths] with Margaret de Haas QC, [May, 1997]; Editor 'Civil Court Practice' 1999 to date; 'Insurance Disputes' [Lloyd's of London Press], Co-editor in Chief with Lord Justice Mance and Professor Merkin; 'Personal Injury Major Claims Handling: Cost Effective Case Management'; [Butterworths], Author and Editor with Margaret Haas QC and John Frenkel; 'Genetics Law Monitor 2000-2002', Editor; 'Human Rights and Judicial Review: Case Studies in Context' [Butterworths 2001], Editor with Lord Clyde, Sir Patrick Elias, Timothy Straker QC; 'Practical Civil Court Precedents' [Sweet and Maxwell], Consulting Editor.
Personal: New ideas, Classical Hebrew, English legal history and classic motor vehicles. Educated at Merchant Taylors' School, Crosby (Harrison Scholar), Hebrew University, Jerusalem (1971), Pembroke College, Cambridge (1971-74).

GOLDRING, Jeremy
3-4 South Square (Michael Crystal QC & Lord Alexander of Weedon QC), London
(020) 7696 9900
jeremygoldring@southsquare.com
Recommended in Insolvency
Specialisation: Insolvency, banking, professional negligence. Recent cases: Cleaver v Delta Re. [2001] AC 328; advising and acting for the English Liquidators of HIH Group.
Prof. Memberships: Combar, Chancery Bar Association.
Career: Called to Bar, 1996; called to Bar and Cayman Islands, 1998; called to Bar and British Virgin Islands, 2000.
Publications: Contributor to 'Rowlatt on Principal and Surety'; 'Professional Negligence and Liability' (ed. Simpson).
Personal: BA (Oxon), MA (Yale).

GOLDSTONE, David
4 Essex Court (Nigel Teare QC), London
(020) 7653 5653
Recommended in Shipping
Specialisation: Shipping (wet and dry), international trade, insurance and reinsurance, banking, commodities, arbitration.
Prof. Memberships: COMBAR, LMAA (supporting member).
Career: Called to the Bar 1986, tenant since 1989, appointed First Standing Counsel to the Government in shipping matters (Admiralty Junior) 1999.
Personal: Educated at Haberdashers' Aske's School 1973-80; Emmanuel College, Cambridge 1981-84 (BA) (double first in law); 1985-87 New College Oxford (BCL). Married with two daughters. Lives in Islington. Interests include science and technology, chess, skiing, tropical plants.

GOLDSTONE, L Clement QC
28 St John St, Manchester
(0161) 834 8418
Recommended in Crime

GOODE, Sir Roy QC
Blackstone Chambers (Presiley Baxendale QC & Charles Flint QC), London
(020) 7583 1770
roygoode@blackstonechambers.com
Recommended in Consumer Law
Specialisation: Commercial law; banking; credit and security; international trade law; consumer credit. Author of 'Commercial Law' (2nd edn. 1995) and other leading textbooks in the above fields which are widely cited in the courts.
Prof. Memberships: Emeritus Professor of Law in the University of Oxford, Emeritus Fellow of St John's College, Oxford. Former Chairman of Executive Committee of JUSTICE. Panel Chairman of appeal under Consumer Credit Act 1974. Member of Board of London Court of International Arbitration. Former Chairman of the Commission on International Commercial Practice of the International Chamber of Commerce.
Career: Admitted as solicitor 1955; partner, *Victor Mishcon & Co.*, solicitors, 1963-1971. Appointed Professor of Law, Queen Mary College, University of London 1971, and Crowther Professor of Credit and Commercial Law 1973. Founder and first Director of Centre for Commercial Law Studies, QMC. Transferred to Bar 1988. Took silk 1990. Hon. Bencher, Inner Temple, 1992. Appointed Norton Rose Professor of English Law. University of Oxford, 1990. Member of Department of Trade and Industry Advisory Committee on Arbitration 1985-. Chairman of Pension Law Review Committee 1992-93. LLB (Lond.) 1954; LLD (Lond.) 1976; OBE 1972, CBE 1994; Hon. DSc Econ (Lond.) 1996; elected Fellow of the British Academy 1988; Fellow of the Royal Society of Arts 1990. Knighted 2000.

GOODE, Rowena
28 St John St, Manchester
(0161) 834 8418
Recommended in Crime

GOODHART, Lord QC
Gough Square Chambers (Fred Philpott), London
(020) 7353 0924
Recommended in Consumer Law
Specialisation: Principal area of practice is Chancery work, encompassing pension funds, trusts and estates, property, consumer credit and personal taxation. Other main area of work is company law and insolvency. Recent cases include Director General of Fair Trading v First National Bank plc [2000] AER 371, Davis v Richards & Wallington Industries [1990] 1WLR 1511 (pensions) and Hambro v Duke of Marlborough [1994] ch. 158 (trusts).
Prof. Memberships: Chancery Bar Association, International Commission of Jurists, Institute for Fiscal Studies, Tax Law Review Committee, Trust Law Committee.
Career: Called to the Bar 1957. In practice at the Chancery Bar since 1960 (QC 1979). Knighted 1989. Member Committee on Standards in Public Life since 1997.
Publications: 'Specific Performance' (with Prof Gareth Jones QC), 2nd edn 1996 (leading modern authority on subject). Section in 'Halsbury's Laws of England', 4th edn re-issue 198, on Corporations.
Personal: Educated at Eton College 1946-51; Trinity College, Cambridge 1953-57 (BA, MA) and Harvard Law School 1957-58 (LL.M). Chairman, Court of Discipline of Cambridge University since 1993. Life Peer, 1997. Born 18 January 1933.

GOODISON, Adam
3-4 South Square (Michael Crystal QC & Lord Alexander of Weedon QC), London
(020) 7696 9900
adamgoodison@southsquare.com
Recommended in Insolvency
Specialisation: Commercial law including insolvency, contract, banking, company, directors disqualification. Cases include acting for the liquidators of BCCI (Re Bank of Credit and Commerce International SA (No4) [1995] BCC 453 (Scott V-C); BCCI v Haque (Lightman J & CA); BCCI v Shoaib (Evans Lombe J); BCCI v Makhan Jan (Jonathan Parker J). Also Re Thirty Eight Building Ltd (In Liquidation) [1999] BCC 260 & [2000] BCLC 201 (Hazell Williamson QC) (preferences); Straume v Bradlor Developments, [2000] BCC 333 (leave in administration proceedings); Holder v Supperstone, Independent, December 1999 (costs of proceedings re charging orders).
Prof. Memberships: Chancery Bar Association, Combar, ILA.
Career: Called 1990. Elected member Bar Council 1995-98.
Publications: Chapter on retention of title 'The Law of Receivers', (Lightman & Moss); chapter on company voluntary arrangements 'Insolvency' (Totty & Moss); contributor to 'Rowlatt on Principal and Surety' (5th edn); 'Distress and Distraint' for R3; voluntary arrangements legal update for R3; various solicitor programme lectures (including *Linklaters, Sidley & Austin, Frere Cholmeley, Wragge & Co*).

GORDON, Richard QC
Brick Court Chambers (Christopher Clarke QC), London
(020) 7379 3550
gordon@brickcourt.co.uk
Recommended in Administrative & Public Law, Environment, Human Rights
Specialisation: Specialist in public, administrative law and human rights

LEADERS AT THE BAR

law. Acts for both respondents and applicants in judicial review, especially in the areas of commercial, environmental, local authority, civil liberties and human rights, health and social services. Visiting Professor of Law, University College, London.
Prof. Memberships: Administrative Law Bar Association.
Career: Called to the Bar 1972. Took Silk 1994.
Publications: Author of 'Judicial Review and the Human Rights Act', 'Judicial Review: Law and Procedure', 'Judicial Review and Crown Office Practice', 'Local Authority Powers' 'Human Rights in the United Kingdom'; 'The Human Rights Act 1988 and Judicial Review'. Co-editor of 'Local Authority Law'; editor in chief 'Crown Office Digest'. Consultant editor 'Human Rights Law Reports - UK Cases'.
Personal: Educated at Oxford University (Open Scholar).

GORE, Allan
12 King's Bench Walk (Richard Methuen QC), London
(020) 7583 0811
Recommended in Personal Injury
Specialisation: Professional negligence, encompassing medical, dental and legal cases both contentious and non-contentious. Personal injury work. Special interest and experience in transport mass accidents and disasters, and industrial disease, particularly concerning asbestos cases.
Prof. Memberships: Treasurer of Association of Personal Injury Lawyers and Personal Injury Bar Association. Professional Negligence Bar Association, AVMA, ATLA, APLA. Fellow, College of Personal Injury Litigation.
Career: Called 1977. Joined current chambers 1991. Recorder 2000.
Publications: Contributing author to 'Butterworths County Court Precedents and Pleadings: Divisions P on Professional Negligence and Q on Personal Injury', 'Cordery on Solicitors: Division J on Negligence', Butterworths 'Personal Injury Litigation Service' Division VIII on Pleadings, 'Personal Injury Handbook' (2nd ed) and 'Curran on Personal Injury Pleadings' (2nd ed). Regular conference and seminar speaker.
Personal: Educated Purley Grammar School, Croydon 1962-69; Trinity Hall, Cambridge 1970-74. Born 25 August 1951. Lives in London.

GOSLING, Jonathan
4 Fountain Court (John Saunders QC), Birmingham
(0121) 236 3476
Recommended in Licensing

GOUDIE, James QC
11 King's Bench Walk Chambers (Eldred Tabachnik QC & James Goudie QC), London
(020) 7632 8500
goudie@11kbw.com
Recommended in Administrative & Public Law, Education, Employment, Local Government
Specialisation: Specialises in all aspects of employment law, with particular emphasis on TUPE, restrictive covenants and European law relating to employment matters. Other main areas of practice include public law and commercial law.
Career: Solicitor 1966-70. Called to the Bar Inner Temple 1970. Bencher; Recorder; Deputy Chairman National Security Panel of Information Tribunal; Deputy High Court Judge, Queen's Bench and Chancery Divisions; past Chairman Law Reform Committee; General Council of the Bar; past Chairman Administrative Law Bar Association; past Chairman Society of Labour Lawyers; Chairman Bar European Group.
Personal: Educated at Dean Close School, Cheltenham and LSE (LLB Hons). FCI Arb. Governor of LSE.

GOULDING, Jonathan
Gough Square Chambers (Fred Philpott), London
(020) 7353 0924
Recommended in Consumer Law
Specialisation: Consumer law – prosecuting and defending regulatory prosecutions especially food safety, misleading prices, trade descriptions and weights and measures. Clients include banks, food producers and local authorities.
Prof. Memberships: Food Law Group.
Career: Called to the Bar 1984.

GOULDING, Paul QC
Blackstone Chambers (Presiley Baxendale QC & Charles Flint QC), London
(020) 7583 1770
clerks@blackstonechambers.com
Recommended in Employment, Sport
Specialisation: Specialist in employment and sports law. Employment: Chairman (1998-2000) and Vice-President (2000-), Employment Lawyers Association. Particular interests – restraint of trade, transfers of undertakings, Europe, discrimination. Recent cases – Neary v Dean of Westminster; Reed v Stedman; Bahl v Law Society. Sport: recent cases – Modahl v BAF; Korda v ITF; Hendry v World Snooker; Jones v Southampton FC; Formula 1, rugby union and league cases. Member of British Association for Sport and Law. SDRP Arbitrator.
Career: St Edmund Hall, Oxford (MA, BCL, Tutor). Call 1984. Silk 2000.
Publications: 'European Employment Law and the UK' (2001).

GOURIET, Gerald
3 Raymond Buildings (Clive Nicholls QC), London
(020) 74006400
chambers@3raymondbuildings.com
Recommended in Licensing
Specialisation: Specialist preparation and advice relating to all aspects of liquor, betting and gaming licensing, including advice on all forms of internet gambling. Advice on lotteries and other related activities. All levels of representation from local committees to Divisional Court and Court of Appeal.
Career: Called to the Bar 1974.

GOWER, Peter
6 Pump Court (Stephen Hockman QC), London
(020) 7797 8400
petergower@6pumpcourt.co.uk
Recommended in Crime
Specialisation: Both prosecuting and defending; commercial crime; Customs Excise offences; breaches of health and safety; planning and other regulatory legislation.
Prof. Memberships: Criminal Bar Association.
Career: Educated at Christ Church, Oxford (Classics scholar) (MA Oxon); called Lincoln's Inn 1985; appointed standing counsel for Department of Trade and Industry in 1991.

GOY, David QC
Gray's Inn Tax Chambers (Milton Grundy), London
(020) 7242 2642
Recommended in Tax
Specialisation: Specialist in all aspects of revenue law. Has particular expertise in the tax aspects of real property transactions, and in all types of tax litigation. Important cases include Lubbock Fine v HM Customs & Excise [1994] (VAT on the surrender of tenancies); LASMO (TNS) Ltd v IRC [1994] (oil taxation); IRC v Willoughby [1997] (taxation under s739 ICTA); CE v First National Bank of Chicago [1998] (VAT and foreign exchange transactions); Bestway (Holdings) Ltd v Luff [1998] (industrial buildings allowances); United Friendly Insurance PLC v IRC [1998] (life assurance taxation); Beneficiary v IRC [1999] (Taxation under S.740); Carr v Fielden & Ashworth Ltd [2000] (relief for ACT); CE v Cantor Fitzgerald 2001 (VAT on reverse premiums); ABC Ltd v M 2001 (capital allowances). Publications include 'Whiteman on Income Tax', co-editor 3rd edn 1988, 'VAT on Property' (co-author) (Sweet & Maxwell 2nd Edition 1993), and Butterworths 'Tax Planning' (consultant editor). Regular speaker on the subject of revenue law.
Prof. Memberships: Revenue Bar Association.
Career: Called to the Bar 1973. Joined present chambers 1974. Took Silk 1991.
Personal: Educated at Haberdashers' Askes School and King's College, London. Born 11 May 1949. Lives in Guildford.

GRABINER, Lord QC
One Essex Court (Lord Grabiner QC), London
(020) 7583 2000
Recommended in Arbitration, Banking & Finance, Commercial (Litigation), Energy, Fraud

GRACE, John QC
3 Serjeants' Inn (Robert Francis QC & John Grace QC), London
(020) 7427 5000
Recommended in Clinical Negligence

GRAY, Gilbert QC
3 Raymond Buildings (Clive Nicholls QC), London
(020) 7400 6400
Recommended in Licensing

GRAY, Richard QC
39 Essex Street (Nigel Pleming QC), London
(020) 7832 1111
Recommended in Construction
Specialisation: Principal area of practice is construction and engineering litigation or arbitration in UK and abroad. Acts as arbitrator in such disputes, both domestic and international, and as mediator or conciliator.
Prof. Memberships: TecBar (Technology and Construction Bar Association).
Career: Called to the Bar in 1970. Took silk in 1993.

GREEN, Brian QC
Wilberforce Chambers (Edward Nugee QC), London
(020) 7306 0102
Recommended in Chancery, Pensions
Specialisation: Pensions and private client specialist having wide ranging experience of contentious and non-contentious general Chancery work. Has acted for the sponsoring companies or the trustees of major pension schemes, and for the trustees and/or the beneficiaries of the largest trusts (private and commercial).
Prof. Memberships: APL, Revenue Bar Association, STEP, Chancery Bar Association.
Career: Called to the Bar 1980. Member of Revenue Law Committee of the Law Society since 1994. (1978-85 tenured lectureship in Law at LSE).
Personal: Educated at Ilford County High School and St Edmund Hall Oxford (BA, BCL: double first).

GREEN, Michael
Fountain Court (Anthony Boswood QC), London
(020) 7583 3335
Recommended in Company
Specialisation: Principal areas of work are company, insolvency, civil fraud and professional negligence including large scale commercial actions, having been involved for three years in Maxwell litigation (acting for Lehman Brothers), and then Lloyds litigation (acting on behalf of auditors). Noteworthy cases include Derby v Weldon (civil fraud), Macmillan Inc v Bishopsgate Investment Trust Plc (Maxwell recovery actions), numerous public interest winding up petitions acting for the DTI including illegal lotteries and investment schemes; a large number of directors' disqualification cases including Barings, Barlow Clowes, Kaytech International Plc (in Court of Appeal), Secretary of State v Deverell (leading CA authority on shadow directors), Aurum Marketing (CA, cost against third parties), SIB v

FIMBRA (financial services); Wolverhampton Wanderers v Stones (professional negligence); Shalson v Russo (civil fraud); Inmassat v APR (expert's jurisdiction).
Prof. Memberships: COMBAR, Chancery Bar Association.
Career: Called to the Bar in 1987. Joined *7 Stone Buildings* in 1988. Joined present chambers in 1998. Appointed Junior Counsel to the Crown (A Panel) in 1997 and a DTI Inspector in 1997.
Personal: Educated at University College School 1971-82 and Jesus College, Cambridge 1983-86.

GREEN, Nicholas QC
Brick Court Chambers (Christopher Clarke QC), London
(020) 7379 3550
green@brickcourt.co.uk
Recommended in Competition/European Law, Sport
Specialisation: Litigation, advisory and representational work in relation to the EC and United Kingdom competition law, aspects of mergers and takeovers; intellectual property licensing; sports law; media law and broadcasting; telecommunications; environmental law; public procurement; conflicts of laws; public law. Has been instructed in over 60 cases before the European Court of Justice and Court of First Instance. Recent cases include Factortame, Coloroll, Francovich II, Sunag (shipping conferences), Eurotunnel; Parma Ham and designations of origin, trademarks; matters re the beef ban; acting for pharmaceutical companies in disputes over licenses and consents and use of confidential data; acting for sporting unions in disputes with clubs with regulators and competitors; intellectual property cases involving EU law; merger cases.
Career: Called to Bar 1986; appointed Queen's Counsel in 1998; Barrister of the Inner Temple, Brick Court Chambers both in London and Brussels. 1981-85: Lecturer in Law, University of Southampton. Visiting Professor in Law, University of Durham 2000 -; Chairman Bar European Group, 1999-2001; Vice Chairman, International Relations Committee; Bar Council 2002-; Member of General Management Committee of the Bar Council 2002-.
Publications: Over 60 articles in publications worldwide and a major textbook in UK and EC competition law. Two principal publications are 'Commercial Agreements and Competition law: Practice and Procedure in the UK and EEC' (1997) (second edition); and 'Legal Foundations of the Single European Market' (1991).
Personal: Born 15 October 1958. LLB (1980), LLM (1981), PhD (1985).

GREENBERG, Joanna QC
3 Temple Gardens
(Jonathan Goldberg QC), London
(020) 7583 1155
clerks@3templegardens.co.uk
Recommended in Crime
Specialisation: Defending in all types of serious criminal cases.
Prof. Memberships: Bar Council, Criminal Bar Association, Justice, Liberty.
Career: Called to the Bar 1972, took Silk 1994, Assistant Recorder 1992, Recorder 1995, Chairman of Police Discipline Appeals Tribunals 1997.
Personal: Educated University of London, King's College. Lives in London.

GREENWOOD, Christopher QC
Essex Court Chambers
(Gordon Pollock QC), London
(020) 7813 8000
Recommended in Public International Law
Specialisation: Public international law before English and public international courts (as counsel) and before foreign courts (as expert witnesses). Recently appeared in: ex p Pinochet [2000] 1 AC 147, Kuwait Airways [2001] 3 WLR 1117 (CA) and [2002] UKHL 19 (HL), Holland v Lampen-Wolfe [2000] 1 WLR 1573 (HL), Bankovic v NATO States (ECtHR 2001), Kingsley v UK (ECtHR 2002), Lockerbie and Kosovo cases (ICJ), Loewen v USA (ICSID. Recent international arbitration experience.
Career: Barrister 1978, QC 1999. Professor of International Law LSE since 1996. Formerly Fellow of Magdalene College, Cambridge (1978-96).
Publications: Editor 'International law Reports'; author of 50 articles in various law journals.
Personal: Born 12 May 1955; educated at Wellingborough School and Magdalene College, Cambridge (First class honours). Married with two daughters.

GREGORY, James
Lincoln House Chambers (Mukhtar Hussain QC), Manchester
(0161) 832 5701
Recommended in Crime

GREGORY, Philip
No.6 Fountain Court (Roger Smith QC), Birmingham
(0121) 233 3282
Recommended in Clinical Negligence

GREY, Robin QC
Hollis Whiteman Chambers (QEB)
(Julian Bevan QC & Peter Whiteman QC), London
(020) 7583 5766
barristers@holliswhiteman.co.uk
Recommended in Crime
Specialisation: Criminal law. Defends and prosecutes in all areas of criminal law, with a particular emphasis on large-scale fraud in recent years. Has also defended in over 30 high-profile murder cases during the course of his career. Successfully defended in the Richardson Gang case of 1970s, in the 'Nasty Tales' case at the time of the Oz trial, in the 'King Squealer' robberies in the late 1970s and in the Brinks Matt case in the early 1990s. Fraud trials include a successful defence in the Eagle Trust case (1993). In the past 10 years has defended solicitors, accountants and bank managers in relation to white collar offences. Has considerable experience lecturing on professional conduct, jury trials and criminal procedure. Has also written articles for the Centre for Policy Studies and the Criminal Bar Association newsletter. Practice also includes civil matters arising out of criminal cases.
Prof. Memberships: Bar Council, Society of Forensic Medicine, Criminal Bar Association, European Criminal Bar Association, International Bar Association, Eastern Europe Forum and the Council of Russian and UK Cooperation.
Career: Called to the Bar 1957 and worked as Crown Counsel in Aden 1959-63, before joining present chambers in 1963. Took Silk in 1979 and was appointed Recorder in the same year. Chairman of Police Appeals Tribunals 1988. Advisor to the Foreign Office in Russian Federation jury trials in 1993-97. Legal Assessor to General Medical Council, 1995.

GRIEVE, Dominic
1 Temple Gardens (Geoffrey Nice QC), London
(020) 7583 1315
Recommended in Health & Safety
Specialisation: Health and safety at work and pollution cases (criminal and civil). Junior prosecution counsel in: R v Nuclear Electric Plc (Mold September 1995 incident at Wylfa Power Station); R v Coalite Ltd (Leicester February 1996 Pollution by Dioxins); R v Port Ramsgate, Old Bailey January - March 1997; R v J Sainsbury Plc, Winchester - November 1998 (operation and maintenance of fork lift trucks). Personal injury. Insurance/negligence work. Local government (enforcement work). Counsel in R v Railcare (derailment of high speed train through wheel failure), Luton Crown Court. London Underground Ltd v HSE (appeal against prohibition notice in relation to the checking of trains before they are reversed in sidings), July 2000. Prosecution counsel R v Homebase (scope of undertaking in relation to accident in service yard), Bristol 2001.
Prof. Memberships: Common Law Bar Association and Criminal Bar Association.
Career: Hon Degree Modern History Oxford 1978. Called to Bar 1980. 1982-90 Chambers of Anthony Cripps QC: 1, Harcourt Buildings (General Common Law). 1990-date: 1 Temple Gardens.

GRIEVE, Michael QC
Doughty Street Chambers (Geoffrey Robertson QC), London
(020) 7404 1313
Recommended in Crime, Fraud

GRIFFITHS, Alan
One Essex Court
(Lord Grabiner QC), London
(020) 7583 2000
Recommended in Administrative & Public Law, Energy
Specialisation: Administrative and public law (especially commercial judicial review), general commercial law (including insurance, company law, complex contracts, conflict of laws jurisdiction), energy (including oil and gas), utility regulation and environmental law. Most recently: 20 weeks Commercial Court trial on driving services contract. For Milk Marque defeating the JR challenge to the reorganisation of the UK milk industry. For Lloyd's defeating the JR challenge to Lloyd's reconstruction and renewal. For Scottish Power in the successful JR challenge to OFFER's price control decisions. For pharmaceutical, agrochemical, TV and radio, and telecommunications companies in judicial reviews of licensing and planning decisions. For EMLICO (General Electric's main insurer) in insolvency and JR actions in Bermuda. For the ABI in the Policyholders Protection Board litigation (insurance). For Orion in Sphere Drake v Orion (1998) (insurance). Advises major insurance companies on the restructuring of life funds and on legal accounting issues. For the banks in the Hammersmith & Fulham interest rate swaps litigation, and in subsequent restitution cases. In the environmental field, clients include British Nuclear Fuels, National Grid, NORWEB and Powergen. For BNFL defeating the Greenpeace JR challenges to the Sellafield THORP plant.
Prof. Memberships: Administrative Law Bar Association, Commercial Bar Association (Committee).
Career: Called 1981 (Called to Bermuda Bar for EMLICO litigation).
Personal: Born 1953. Educated Jesus College, Oxford (MA, BCL). Formerly Fellow and Tutor in Law, Exeter College, Oxford.

GRIFFITHS, Courtenay QC
Two Garden Court (Owen Davies QC & Courtenay Griffiths QC), London
(020) 7353 1633
Recommended in Crime
Specialisation: Criminal Law: mainly leading work in murders (most alleged to be result of 'organised crime'). Major drug importations, frauds and sexual offences. Civil actions against the police. Has lectured in law in the UK and the USA. Has been Junior Counsel in R v Silcott and Or5 (Broadwater Farm riot). Major IRA cases including Canary Wharf & Harrods Bombing. Risley remand centre riot trial. Past holder of the record for the highest jury award against the police in a civil action £302,000 Goswell v MP/C (1996) Appeal Johnson, Davis & Rowe. Damilola Taylor Trial.
Prof. Memberships: Member of the South Eastern Circuit, Criminal Bar Association. Bar Race Relations Committee. Member of Gray's Inn. Chair Bar Relations and Public Affairs Committee.
Career: Recorder.

LEADERS AT THE BAR

Personal: Married to Angela with whom two children, Marcus (12) and Adam (nine). Four children in all. Interested in music (reggae), cricket, football (Liverpool) and reading.

GRIFFITH-JONES, David QC
Devereux Chambers
(Colin Edelman QC), London
(020) 7353 7534
griffith-jones@devchambers.co.uk
Recommended in Employment, Sport
Specialisation: General common lawyer. Specialist in employment (including dismissal, discrimination, TUPE, industrial disputes, restraint of trade and injunctions) and sport (including personal injury, discipline and regulation and the commercial exploitation of sport).
Prof. Memberships: London Common Law and Commercial Bar Association; Employment Lawyers' Association; Employment Law Bar Association; British Association of Sport and the Law; Bar Sports Law Group (Committee Member).
Career: Called to the Bar 1975. FCIArb 1991. Recorder 1997. Silk 2000. Sports Dispute Resolution Panel 2000. Assistant Boundary Commissioner 2000.
Publications: 'Law and the Business of Sport' (Butterworths, 1997).

GRIFFITHS, Martin
Essex Court Chambers
(Gordon Pollock QC), London
(020) 7813 8000
Recommended in Employment
Specialisation: Appears as an advocate in Courts and tribunals including domestic arbitrations, all divisions of the High Court (including Mercantile Courts), the Court of Appeal and the Privy Council. Employment and human rights law practice including domestic disciplinary tribunals, the Employment Tribunal, the Employment Appeal Tribunal, all divisions of the High Court, the Court of Appeal and the Privy Council.
Prof. Memberships: Member of COMBAR; member of ELBA; member of the Bar European Group.
Career: New College, Oxford: BA (1st Class Hons with Distinction) 1984; MA 1988; City University, London: Postgraduate Diploma in Law 1985. Called to the Bar 1986.
Personal: Born 1962.

GRIFFITHS, Peter
4 Stone Buildings (Philip Heslop QC), London
(020) 7242 5524
clerks@4stonebuildings.com
Recommended in Chancery, Company, Insolvency
Specialisation: Principal area of practice is company law, focusing on insolvency and minority shareholder disputes. Other main areas of work include partnership, civil fraud, bankruptcy and professional negligence.
Prof. Memberships: Chancery Bar Association, Insolvency Lawyers' Association and COMBAR.
Career: Called to the Bar in 1977 and joined present chambers in 1978.
Publications: Contributor to 'Atkins Court Forms' Vol 10 (Companies Winding Up) 1988, 'Encyclopaedia of Forms and Precedents' 5th Ed Vol 11 (Companies) 1992, and Butterworths 'Practical Insolvency' 1999.
Personal: Educated at Repton, 1966-71 and St Catharine's College, Cambridge, 1972-75.

GRIME, Stephen QC
Deans Court Chambers (Stephen Grime QC), Manchester
(0161) 214 6000
grime@deanscourt.co.uk
Recommended in Clinical Negligence
Specialisation: Personal injury including disease litigation; insurance-related litigation; construction; clinical negligence; professional negligence - other than clinical; commercial; arbitration. Significant reported cases: J (a child) v Wilkins [2001] PIQR P 179; JD Williams & Co Ltd v Michael Hyde [2001] BLR 99; Jenkins v Grocott [2000] PIQR Q17; Bence Graphics International v Fasson [1998] QB 87; R v CICB (Ex parte C) [1997] PIQR P128; Thomas v Plaistow [1997] PIQR P540; Wisniewski v Central Manchester HA [1996] 7 Med LR 248; Cruden Construction v Commission for the New Towns [1995] 2 Lloyd's Rep 387; Crocker v British Coal Corporation [1995] 29 BMLR 159; Fairhurst v St Helens & Knowsley HA [1995] PIQR Q1; Khan v Armaguard [1994] 3 All ER 545; Wood v Gahlings [1993] PIQR P76; Family Housing Association (Manchester) Ltd v Michael Hyde [1993] 1 WLR 354; Bradley v Eagle Star Insurance Co Ltd [1989] 1 AC 957; Wilkinson v Ancliff (BLT) Ltd [1986] 3 All ER 427, [1986] 1 WLR 1352; Gandolfo v Gandolfo [1981] QB 359.
Prof. Memberships: Past Chairman Northern Circuit Medical Law Association; Past Chairman of Northern Arbitration Association; Fellow – Chartered Institute of Arbitrators. Member – Northern Circuit Commercial Bar Association; Society for Computers and Law; United Kingdom Environmental Law Association; Professional Negligence Bar Association; Personal Injury Bar Association.
Career: Trinity College, Oxford (Scholar). Called (Middle Temple) - 1970. Queen's Counsel - 1987. Recorder - 1990. Technology and Construction Recorder - 1996. Fellow - Chartered Institute of Arbitrators - 1996. Bencher of Middle Temple - 1997. Head of Chambers 2000.

GROVES, Hugo
Enterprise Chambers (Anthony Mann QC), Leeds
(0113) 246 0391
hgroves@dial.pipex.com
Recommended in Commercial (Litigation), Insolvency
Specialisation: Insolvency, company, partnership.
Prof. Memberships: Attorney New York State.
Publications: Butterworths 'Corporate Insolvency - Law and Practice' (2001).

GRUDER, Jeffrey QC
Essex Court Chambers
(Gordon Pollock QC), London
(020) 7813 8000
Recommended in Arbitration, Commercial (Litigation), Shipping
Specialisation: Principal areas of practice are commercial disputes, insurance and reinsurance, banking, oil and gas disputes. Other areas of practice are shipping and transport, financial services and commodity disputes. Recently appeared in United Assurance v UNISYS, Standard Chartered Bank v PNSC; RZB v Five Star; XL v Owens Corning; Czech Ocean v Van Ommeren; Investors Compensation Scheme v West Bromwich Building Society; Vitol Energy v Pisco; Indian Grace (No 2) (1997); Chevron v Total (1996); Autocar v Motemtronic (1996); British Gas v Eastern Electricity (1996). Has appeared frequently in arbitrations and acted as arbitrator. Clients include major banks, insurance companies and corporations. Supervisor at Cambridge University 1977-79. Previously part-time lecturer at Central London Polytechnic on International Trade.
Prof. Memberships: COMBAR (Secretary).
Career: Called to the Bar in 1977. QC 1997. At 4 Essex Court (now Essex Court Chambers) 1978-93. 1 Essex Court 1993-2000. Rejoined Essex Court Chambers February 2000.
Personal: Educated at City of London School 1966-72 and Trinity Hall, Cambridge 1973-76. Born 18 September 1954. Interests include tennis, theatre, cinema and reading. Lives in Radlett.

GRUNDY, Nigel
9 St. John Street (John Hand QC), Manchester
(0161) 955 9000
Recommended in Employment
Specialisation: Recent cases: Parkinson v March Consulting Ltd CA 1997 IRLR 519; Boys and Girls Welfare Society v McDonald 1996 IRLR 129; Mennell v Newell and Wright (Transport Contractors) Ltd 1996 ICR 607. Specialises in employment, discrimination and trade union law.
Prof. Memberships: Employment Law Bar Association, Professional Negligence Bar Association, Northern Circuit Commercial Bar Association.
Career: MA (Hons) Oxon Jurisprudence. Recorder.
Personal: Golf, tennis.

HACKER, Richard QC
3-4 South Square (Michael Crystal QC & Lord Alexander of Weedon QC), London
(020) 7696 9900
richardhacker@southsquare.com
Recommended in Banking & Finance, Insolvency
Specialisation: A mixed litigation/advisory commercial law practice including contentious and non-contentious insolvency work, banking law, professional negligence, asset tracing and general commercial litigation. Clients have included the major international accountancy firms, major UK banks and a variety of overseas banks and governments. Heavily involved in all major collapses of the last 20 years including Laker, Banco Ambrosiano, Mentor Insurance, Maxwell, BCCI, Rafidain, KWELM, NEMGIA and Barings. Has appeared and given expert evidence in a variety of overseas courts including New York and Bermuda. Recent significant UK trial appearances include the Grupo Torras litigation in which he appeared for the Kuwait Investment Authority.
Career: Called 1977. QC 1998.

HACKETT, Philip QC
2 Bedford Row (William Clegg QC), London
(020) 7440 8888
phackett@2bedrowrow.co.uk
Recommended in Crime, Fraud
Specialisation: Practice is principally in the area of commercial fraud, general crime and related issues such as restraint, confiscation, money laundering and directors disqualification. He also has experience in a broad range of commercial work including banking, insurance and insolvency. Other areas of specialisation include health and safety, manslaughter by gross negligence and the application of human rights law to criminal, regulatory and disciplinary matters. He has acted in a number of well known cases including Maxwell, three BCCI trials (including Gokal), Gooda Walker and the recent trial arising from the discovery of accounting irregularities at Wickes plc.

HACON, Richard
11 South Square (Christopher Floyd QC), London
(020) 7405 1222
Recommended in Intellectual Property

HADDON-CAVE, Charles QC
4 Essex Court (Nigel Teare QC), London
(020) 7653 5653
chaddon-cave@4sx.com
Recommended in Arbitration, Aviation
Specialisation: Has a broad commercial practice and is a specialist in air law. Has been instructed in many of the major aviation disasters of recent times including the Virgin Airbus A-340 crash-landing at Heathrow, the Knight Air crash at Dunkeswick, the Aeroflot crash in Siberia, the Thai Air crash at Kathmandu, the British Midland air crash at Kegworth and the British Airtours disaster at Manchester. Has acted on behalf of Virgin Atlantic in CAA routing applications, including London-Shanghai and London-Capetown. Represented insurers in the House of Lords in Morris v KLM

RoyalDutch Airlines on the meaning of 'bodily injury' under Article 17 of the Amended Warsaw Convention. Represented insurers in Giambrone v JMC on the proportionality of claimants' GLO costs. Regularly appears as an advocate in the High Court in London, Cayman Islands and Hong Kong as well as international arbitration.
Prof. Memberships: Vice-Chairman of the Royal Aeronautical Society Air Law Committee, Member of COMBAR, Member of PIBA and one of the only members of the English Bar called generally to the Hong Kong Bar.

HAGGAN, Nicholas Somerset
17 Carlton Crescent
(Jeremy S Gibbons QC), Southampton
(023) 8032 0320
Recommended in Consumer Law

HAJIMITSIS, Anthony
Zenith Chambers (Andrew Campbell QC & John Collins), Leeds
(0113) 245 5438
Recommended in Family

HALL, Andrew QC
Doughty Street Chambers (Geoffrey Robertson QC), London
(020) 7404 1313
Recommended in Crime
Specialisation: Practice predominantly crime. Substantial experience of homicide and other serious violence, firearms, explosives, and large drug conspiracies. Growing fraud practice including VAT, mortgage and insolvent trading cases. Has regularly written, lectured and broadcast on a wide range of issues within the criminal justice sphere.
Prof. Memberships: Criminal Bar Association, Bar Overseas Advocacy Committee, South Eastern Circuit.
Career: Educated at Marist College, University of Birmingham (LL.B 1974), University of Sheffield (MA [Criminology] 1976). Admitted as solicitor 1980. Partner and Head of Criminal Law Department, *Hodge Jones & Allen* London before transfer to the Bar in 1991. Former Director of Legal Action Group. Member of Editorial Board of 'International Journal of Evidence and Proof'. Member of General Council of Bar and Human Rights Committee of the Bar of England and Wales.

HALL, Joanna
14 Gray's Inn Square
(Joanna Dodson QC), London
(020) 7242 0858
Recommended in Family

HALLIWELL, Mark
40 King St, Manchester
(0161) 832 9082
mhalliwell@40kingstreet.co.uk
Recommended in Chancery
Specialisation: General chancery and commercial law including contentious and non-contentious real property, landlord and tenant law, corporate and individual insolvency, partnerships, charities, trusts and the administration of estates, professional negligence, housing and markets, fairs and commercial arbitration. Is the sole author of 'Distribution on Intestacy'. Recent reported cases include: Re Broadbent deceased (The Times 27/6/01) (wills and trusts); Inco Europe v FirstChoice Distribution [2000] 1 WLR 586 (statutory construction and arbitration); Bradford & Bingley BS v Seddon [1999] 1WLR 1482 (abuse of process).
Prof. Memberships: Chancery Bar Association, Northern Chancery Bar Association, Junior Counsel to the Treasury on Charity Matters. Provincial Panel of Treasury Council.
Career: Called 1985 (Lincoln's Inn) (Hardwicke Scholar).
Publications: Distribution of Intestacy [FT Law and Tax, 1996].
Personal: University London School of Economics, BSc (Econ).

HALPERN, David
Four New Square (Justin Fenwick QC), London
(020) 7822 2000
barristers@4newsquare.com
Recommended in Professional Negligence
Specialisation: Professional negligence and property litigation.
Career: Educated at St Paul's School; won Open Exhibition to Magdalen College, Oxford. Practised from Chancery Chambers for 20 years before moving to 4 New Square in 2000. Practises in professional negligence and in all areas of commercial chancery work (emphasis on property litigation). Cases include: Barclays Bank v Weeks Legg Dean [1999] QB 309 (solicitor's undertaking to bank); Portman Building Society v Hamlyn Taylor Neck [1998] 4 All ER 202 (whether lender may bring restitutionary claim against solicitor reporting on title); Raja v Rubin [2000] Ch. 274 (power to vary IVA informally). Co-author of chapter on Accountants and Auditors for fifth edition of Jackson & Powell on 'Professional Negligence'.

HAM, Robert QC
Wilberforce Chambers
(Edward Nugee QC), London
(020) 7306 0102
rham@wilberforce.co.uk
Recommended in Chancery
Specialisation: Practice largely in the fields of trusts and tax law, including offshore trusts and pension schemes, but extends to other areas of property law and associated professional negligence. Special expertise in disputes involving civil law/forced heirship as a result of the Thyssen-Bornemisza case.
Prof. Memberships: Association of Pension Lawyers. Chancery Bar Association, Revenue Bar Association, Society of Trust and Estate Practioners, Wales and Chester Circuit.
Career: BA and BCL (Oxon). Called to the Bar 1973; QC 1994.

HAMBLEN, Nicholas QC
20 Essex Street (Iain Milligan QC), London
(020) 7842 1200
clerks@20essexst.com
Recommended in Shipping
Specialisation: Principal areas of practice are shipping, international sale of goods, commodities, insurance and re-insurance, conflicts of laws and arbitration. Acts as arbitrator in maritime, insurance and international commercial arbitrations. ICC, LCIA, LAS and ACI arbitrator. Recent cases include: 'Grecia Express' Strive Shipping v Hellenic Mutual [2002] EWHC 203; 'Hill Harmony' [2000] 3 WLR 1954; Jan de Nul v NV Royal Belge [2000] 2 Lloyds Rep 700.
Career: Called to the Bar 1981. Took Silk 1997. Sits as Recorder.
Personal: Educated at St John's College, Oxford (MA) and Harvard Law School (LLM). Born 1957.

HAMER, George
8 New Square (Mark Platts-Mills QC), London
(020) 7405 4321
george.hamer@8newsquare.co.uk
Recommended in Intellectual Property
Specialisation: Barrister specialising in all aspects of intellectual property and media law, including patents, copyright, passing off, trademarks, service marks and confidential information. Cases include: Ordnancey Survey v Automobile Assoc. (copyright); Catnic Components v Hill & Smith (patents); SKM v Wagner Hsiung's Patent (patents); Rolls Royce v Dodd (trade marks/passing off); Neutrogena v Golden (trade marks/passing off); Sillitoe v McGraw Hill (copyright); Goodyear tyre treads (registered designs); Amper S.A ; Estate of Bob Marley (PC); expert witness in Israel (LEGO) and for proceedings in the United States (Apple Computer). For comprehensive CV and list of recent cases, visit chambers' website at www.8newsquare.co.uk.
Prof. Memberships: Intellectual Patent Bar Association (IPBA); The Intellectual Property Lawyers Organisation (TIPLO).
Career: Called to the Bar 1974.
Personal: Born 1949. Educated at Sedbergh School; Imperial College, London University (1971), BSc Chemistry and ARCS.

HAMILTON, Eben QC
New Square Chambers
(Charles Purle QC), London
(020) 7419 8000
Recommended in Insolvency

HAMILTON, Eleanor QC
No.6 Barristers Chambers (Jennifer Kershaw QC), Leeds
(0113) 245 9763
Recommended in Family

HAND, John QC
Old Square Chambers (John Hendy QC), London
(020) 7269 0300
hand@oldsquarechambers.co.uk
9 St. John Street (John Hand QC), Manchester
(020) 7269 0300
hand@oldsquarechambers.co.uk
Recommended in Employment, Environment
Specialisation: Is experienced in most areas of common law litigation, concentrates on employment law, personal injury and environmental law with emphasis on health and safety litigation and is familiar with EC law principles. In employment law he deals with all aspects of individual and collective disputes including equal opportunity work. Recent cases have been Martin/Bernadone v Pall Mall (TUPE), Khan v West Yorkshire Police (race discrimination), LUL v RMT (industrial action), MSF v Refuge Assurance (consultation). In environment/health and safety he has appeared both in the Crown Court and the Magistrates Court in cases of explosions, airborne pollution and radiation. Cases include R v Hickson and Welch (the Castleford explosion), R v Associated Octel (No. 2)(the Ellesmere port Explosion), R v Coalite (Dioxin emissions), R v University of Cambridge (loss of radioactive source) and Clifton v Powergen (Airbourne Pollution).
Prof. Memberships: ELA, ELBA, PIBA, PNBA, UKELA, BEG and Society for Computer and Law.
Career: Called 1972; Bencher 1996 (Gray's Inn); Queen's Counsel 1988; Recorder 1991.

HANDYSIDE, Richard
Fountain Court (Anthony Boswood QC), London
(020) 7583 3335
richardhandyside@fountaincourt.co.uk
Recommended in Banking & Finance
Specialisation: Commercial litigation, including banking, insurance/reinsurance, civil fraud, conflicts of laws, restitution, international trade and professional negligence. Notable cases include: United Pan-Europe Communications v Deutsche Bank (injunction/confidential information/investment bank - customer relationship); Morgan Grenfell v SACE (export credit insurance/due diligence by lending banks); Steamship Mutual v Feasey (insurable interest/Life Assurance Act 1774); Arab Bank v Zurich Insurance (composite professional indemnity policy/attribution of knowledge); Scottish Equitable Plc v Derby (recovery of payments made by mistake/defences of estoppel and change of position); the Camdex v Bank of Zambia litigation (assignment/champerty; Mareva injunction over unissued bank notes; enforcement of foreign public law); Bates v Robert Barrow (insurance contracts and illegality). Also acted for defendant auditors in the First Tokyo Index Trust litigation (Maxwell related) and in the KWELM litigation.

LEADERS AT THE BAR

Prof. Memberships: COMBAR.
Career: Called 1993.
Publications: Contributing Editor to 'Commercial Court Procedure' (Sweet & Maxwell, 2001).
Personal: Educated Marlborough College, Bristol University (LLB Hons 1st Class) and Brasenose College, Oxford (BCL 1st Class). Born 1968.

HANNAFORD, Sarah
Keating Chambers, London
(020) 7544 2600
shannaford@keatingchambers.com
Recommended in Construction
Specialisation: Construction and engineering law, (including delay, loss and expense claims, energy, party wall and professional negligence. Litigation, arbitration, mediation and adjudication. Advising, drafting and appearing in adjudication and enforcement proceedings.
Career: Qualified 1989, Middle Temple.
Personal: Lincoln College, Oxford (MA Oxon 1986 BA). Born 1965.

HAPGOOD, Mark QC
Brick Court Chambers
(Christopher Clarke QC), London
(020) 7379 3550
Recommended in Banking & Finance, Commercial (Litigation), Company

HARDING, Cherry
Renaissance Chambers (Brian Patrick Jubb & Henry Setright QC), London
(020) 7404 1111
Recommended in Family
Specialisation: Family: children, abduction, adoption, private/public law. Matrimonial (all aspects), education. Mental health.
Prof. Memberships: Family Law Bar Association, Bar European Group, Justice, Legal Action Group, Inter Country Adoption Association.
Career: LLB (Hons) Kings College, London. Called to the Bar 1978, Gray's Inn, Inner Temple. Married, three children.

HARGREAVES, Simon
Keating Chambers, London
(020) 7544 2600
shargreaves@keatingchambers.com
Recommended in Construction, Professional Negligence
Specialisation: All aspects of litigation and arbitration concerning general construction, engineering, power and utilities contracts (both domestic and international). All related negligence and professional negligence claims. ICC Arbitrations. Adjudication and mediation. Appointed Junior Counsel to the Crown (B Panel) 2002. Cases include: Davies Middleton & Davies Ltd v Toyo engineering Corporation [1997] 85 BLR 59 [CA]; Lobb Partnership Ltd v Aintree Racecourse Company Ltd [2000] BLR 65 [QBD, Comm Ct]; Fastrack Contractors v Morrison [2000] BLR 168 [QBD, TCC]; Rainsford House Ltd (in administrative receivership) v Cadogan Ltd [2001] CILL 1709 [QBD, TCC]; JA Payne Ltd v GAJ Construction Ltd (presently unreported) 16 March 2001; Fence Gate Ltd v NEL Construction Ltd [2002] CILL 1817.
Career: Called to Bar, October 1991 (called to the Bar of Gibraltar, May 1997). Researcher for 'Keating on Building Contracts' (7th Edition).
Personal: Shrewsbury School (scholar); Worcester College, Oxford (1989 BA Law 2(1)). Born 1968. Resides London. Hobbies: diving.

HARMAN, Sarah
4 Stone Buildings (Philip Heslop QC), London
(020) 7242 5524
Recommended in Company

HARPER, Mark
40 King St, Manchester
(0161) 832 9082
mharper@40kingstreet.co.uk
Recommended in Chancery, Commercial (Litigation)
Specialisation: Banking and finance litigation; professional negligence; directors disqualification; personal and corporate insolvency, contracted disputes.
Prof. Memberships: Chancery Bar Association; Northern Chancery Bar Association; Northern Circuit Commercial Bar Association.
Career: Called to the Bar by Lincoln's Inn in 1993. Pupillage with existing chambers.
Personal: Arnold Hill Comprehensive School, Nottingham. Downing College, Cambridge. Interested in all sports especially football, cricket and hill walking. Married to Julie and father of Jessie.

HARRIS, Paul
Monckton Chambers (Kenneth Parker QC & Paul Lasok QC), London
(020) 7405 7211
Recommended in Sport
Specialisation: All aspects of sports law including commercial, employment and tort, but particularly European and domestic competition issues, broadcasting and free movement, including TV Danmark [2001] 1 WLR 1604 (HL).
Prof. Memberships: British Association of Sport and Law, COMBAR Bar Sports Law Group, Bar European Group.
Career: Called 1994. Trinity Hall, Cambridge (1st class). LLM (Berkeley). Also legal practitioner of New South Wales.
Publications: Co-author 'Transfers' and 'Relationships in Sport', Butterworths 'Sport: Law and Practice' (forthcoming). Frequent contributor to 'BASL Journal' (including salary caps, ECJ jurisprudence). Abusive Sports Governing Bodies 2002 'Competition Law Journal'
Personal: Manchester City fan.

HARRIS, Russell
Eldon Chambers (Patrick Clarkson QC & William Hicks QC), London
(020) 7583 1355
clerks@eldonchambers.com
Recommended in Environment, Planning
Specialisation: Public law aspects of environmental law including public inquiry advocacy, judicial review, injunctions, integrated pollution control, town and country planning and environmental crime.
Prof. Memberships: Committee Member of PEBA, Member of UKELA, IPC Working Party.
Personal: Co-author of 'Environmental Law and Practice O.U.P.' (in progress).

HARRISON, Christopher
4 Stone Buildings (Philip Heslop QC), London
(020) 7242 5524
clerks@4stonebuildings.com
Recommended in Chancery
Specialisation: Company law, corporate fraud and asset recovery, corporate insolvency, shareholder disputes, financial services and regulatory law, banking, public law, professional negligence, commercial litigation. Recent reported cases include: Morris v Bank of America [2000] 1 All ER 954 (section 213); Sasea Finance Ltd (in liquidation) v KPMG [2000] 1 All ER 676 (auditors, professional negligence); Secretary of State for Industry v Layton Houses Trustees Ltd [2000] 2 BCCC 808 (public interest petition); Sasea Finance Ltd (in liquidation) v KPMG [1998] BCC 216 (section 236 Insolvency Act 1986); SIB v Scandex Capital Management A/S [1998] 1 WLR 712 (financial services).
Career: Called to the Bar 1988. Junior Counsel to the Crown (B panel). DTI Inspector (1996). Called to the Bar of the Turks & Caicos Islands and Cayman Islands for specific cases.
Personal: Trinity Hall, Cambridge.

HARRISON, Keith
24A St. John Street (Paul Chambers), Manchester
(0161) 833 9628
Recommended in Crime

HARRISON, Michael QC
Park Court Chambers
(Robert Smith QC), Leeds
(0113) 243 3277
Recommended in Crime

HARRISON, Richard
One King's Bench Walk (Anthony Hacking QC), London
(020) 7936 1500
rharrison@1kbw.co.uk
Recommended in Family
Specialisation: All areas of family law including matrimonial finance, international forum disputes, international child abduction, private and public law children, wardship, TOLATA 1996 disputes. Recent cases of interest include: Mubarak [2001] 1 FLR 698 (judgment summons); Mubarak [2001] 1 FLR 673 (piercing corporate veil in ancillary relief); TB v JB (Abduction: Grave risk of Harm) [2001] 1 FLR 515; Re X and Y (Leave to remove) [2001] 2 FLR 118; Re M and J (Abduction: International Judicial Collaboration) [2000] 1 FLR 803; Dawson v Wearmouth [1999] 2 AC 308 (name change); Re C (Abduction: Grave risk of Physical and Psychological Harm) [1999] 2 FLR 478.
Prof. Memberships: SE Circuit, Family Law Bar Association, Lawyers for Liberty, Criminal Bar Association.
Career: Called to the Bar 1993.
Personal: Educated at Cranleigh School, Emmanuel College Cambridge, City University. Fluent Spanish, proficient French.

HARRISON, Robert
30 Park Place (John Jenkins QC), Cardiff
(029) 2039 8421
Recommended in Personal Injury

HARRISON, Sally
28 St John St, Manchester
(0161) 834 8418
Recommended in Family

HARRISON, Stephanie
Two Garden Court (Owen Davies QC & Courtenay Griffiths QC), London
(020) 7353 1633
Recommended in Administrative & Public Law, Immigration

HARROD, Henry
5 Stone Buildings (Henry Harrod), London
(020) 7242 6201
Recommended in Chancery
Specialisation: Specialises in all areas of Chancery work.
Prof. Memberships: Chancery Bar Association; Society of Trust and Estate Practitioners. Association of Contentious Trust and Probate Specialists.
Career: Called to the Bar 1963. Tenant at 46 Grainger Street, Newcastle-upon-Tyne 1964-68 before joining 4 Paper Buildings in 1968. Member of present chambers since 1969 and Head since 1990. Conveyancing Counsel of the Court 1991. Bencher of Lincoln's Inn 1991. Appointed Recorder 1993.

HARRY, Timothy
9 Old Square (Michael Driscoll QC), London
(020) 7405 4682
Recommended in Property Litigation
Specialisation: Property litigation, professional negligence and Chancery work.
Prof. Memberships: PNBA, Chancery Bar Association, Property Bar Association.
Career: Called 1983. Lecturer, Hertford College, Oxford, 1983-88. Called to the Bar 1983, Hong Kong 1992.
Publications: An editor Hill & Redman's 'Landlord & Tenant'. Contributor to 'Lloyds Professional Negligence Law Reports'.
Personal: Educated Monmouth School; MA, BCL (Oxford).

HART, David
1 Crown Office Row
(Robert Seabrook QC), London
(020) 7797 7500
david.hart@1cor.com
Recommended in Environment

Specialisation: Has conducted much public and private environmental litigation, including water (Cambridge Water, Bowden on enforceability of EC Directives, Falmouth on abatement notices), particulate emissions (Coalite and Orimulsion), methane (Loscoe), waste (Castle) and claims against environmental consultants re-contaminated land (Mott) and assessment of methane risks. Involved in the recent environmental human rights case of McKenna. Frequently instructed in professional negligence cases (particularly clinical, solicitors and engineers) and arbitrations (construction, engineering and general contract), as well as flood and fire claims. Currently instructed in Group Litigation involving the Alder Hey Hospital and also on multi-party claims in respect of a landfill site.
Prof. Memberships: Member of UKELA and ALBA.
Career: Called 1982.
Publications: Articles on environmental issues in JEL, JPEL and NLJ. Chapter on environmental human rights issues in 'Introduction to Human Rights and Common Law' (2000) and Garner bulletin on same subject.

HART, William
Albion Chambers (Neil Ford QC), Bristol
(0117) 927 2144
Recommended in Crime
Specialisation: Practice is exclusively criminal, divided roughly equally between prosecuting and defending. Grade 4 Prosecutor. Particular experience of homicide, drug trafficking and sexual offences, especially against children. Recent cases of particular interest: Hewson (MOD corruption); Operation Panorama (homosexual paedophile ring); Redding (the Michael Fry murder, where DNA advances led to detection of the killer four years on); Dunnett (murder where conviction upheld after appeal to Court of Appeal on causation); Johnson and Wake (random attack murder involving autrefois acquit); Benfield (serial armed robber – extensive ECHR arguments re legality of PACE powers); O'Neill (multimillion pound computer company liquidation fraud); Operations Farm and Rowel (large scale car fringing).
Prof. Memberships: Criminal Bar Association. Western circuit.
Career: LLB (Hons) Exon. Call 1979. Joined present chambers 1982. Assistant Recorder 1999. Recorder 2000.
Personal: Married, two children.

HARVEY, Colin
St. Paul's Chambers
(Nigel Sangster QC), Leeds
(0113) 245 5866
Recommended in Crime
Specialisation: Criminal specialist with successful practice for both prosecution and defence. R v Geddes (murder); R v Saunders (deception, prison officer); R v Petrie (fraud); R v Elliott tors (drugs importation).
Prof. Memberships: Criminal Bar Association.
Career: Called to Bar 1975. Founder member of St Pauls Chambers in 1982.
Personal: LLB (Hons) (London External).

HARVEY, Michael QC
Crown Office Chambers (Michael Spencer QC & Christopher Purchas QC), London
(020) 7797 8100
harvey@crownofficechambers.com
Recommended in Professional Negligence
Specialisation: Predominantly civil and commercial matters, including but not limited to: commercial and contractual disputes, professional negligence, international arbitration, construction and engineering contracts, insurance and reinsurance law, conflict of laws, sale of goods, carriage of goods, agency, product liability. Sits as arbitrator.
Prof. Memberships: Legal Services Committee of Bar Council 1994-99; COMBAR; LCCLBA; TECBAR.
Career: Called 1966. QC 1982. Recorder 1986. Authorised to sit as a Deputy High Court Judge and Deputy Official Referee. Bencher, Gray's Inn 1991. Review Board, Council of Legal Education 1993-94; speaker at conferences; joint author of title 'Damages' in Halsbury's Laws of England.
Personal: Born 22 May 1943. Educated at St. John's School, Leatherhead and Christ's College, Cambridge. Married with two children.

HAVERS, Philip QC
1 Crown Office Row
(Robert Seabrook QC), London
(020) 7797 7500
philip.havers@1cor.com
Recommended in Administrative & Public Law, Clinical Negligence, Environment, Human Rights
Specialisation: Principal areas of practice are public and administrative law, clinical negligence, environmental law and human rights law (including cases at the European Court of Human Rights), health law and breach of confidence. Recent reported cases include: Pretty v DPP (2002) (right to die); Hunter v Canary Wharf (1997) (nuisance); R v Falmouth PHA ex p SWW (watercourse pollution); Thomas v Brighton Health Authority (1998) (multipliers); Findlay v UK (2000) (1996) (fair trial); AG v Blake (2000) (fiduciary duties of a spy); R v Collins, ex parte S (rights of fetus); Heil v Rankin (test cases on level of general damages). Other important cases include: Clapham Railway Inquiry Disaster Inquiry, Southall Rail Inquiry and Ladbroke Grove Rail Inquiry, R v Hull University, ex parte Page (university law), Benzodiazepine litigation and Spycatcher. Regularly addresses seminars on clinical negligence and human rights.
Prof. Memberships: South Eastern Circuit, Administrative Law Bar Association, Bar European Group, London Common Law, Commercial Bar Association and Bar European Circuit.
Career: Called to the Bar 1974 and joined current Chambers 1975. Took Silk 1995. Deputy High Court Judge.
Publications: 'An Introduction to Human Rights and the Common Law', Hart, 2000.
Personal: Educated at Eton College 1963-68 and Corpus Christi College, Cambridge 1969-73. Leisure pursuits include tennis, music, gardening, wine and travel. Born 16 June 1950. Lives in London.

HAY, Deborah
Hardwicke Building
(Nicholas Stewart QC), London
(020) 7242 2523
Recommended in Education

HAYES, Josephine
Gough Square Chambers (Fred Philpott), London
(020) 7353 0924
Recommended in Chancery
Specialisation: Pension schemes; property litigation; mortgages and securities; timeshare; banking; general chancery; insolvency; company. Reported cases include: Bank of Scotland v Wright; Springette v Defoe; Penn v Bristol & West BS; Hambros Bank v BHBT; Miller v Stapleton; Miller v Scorey; Seifert v Pensions Ombudsman; Lloyds Bank v Carrick; Buckley v Hudson Forge Ltd; First National Bank v Walker; Steele v Steele; Rowe v Sanders; Watts v Eden.
Prof. Memberships: Chancery Bar Association; Association of Women Barristers (Chairwoman 1996-98; Vice-president 1998-date); Association of Pension Lawyers.
Career: MA (Oxon), 1st Class Hons in Greats. Called 1980. Alumni Fellow, Yale Law School; LLM (Yale).

HAYWARD SMITH, Rodger QC
One King's Bench Walk (Anthony Hacking QC), London
(020) 7936 1500
Recommended in Family
Specialisation: Specialises in family law and criminal law.
Prof. Memberships: South Eastern Circuit, Family Law Bar Association, Criminal Bar Association.
Career: Called to the Bar in 1967 and joined 1 King's Bench Walk in 1968. Appointed Recorder in 1986. Took Silk 1988. Deputy High Court Judge Family Division since 1990. Legal Assessor General Medical Council since 2000.
Publications: Co-writer of Jackson's 'Matrimonial Finance and Taxation' (5th, 6th and 7th eds) and formerly Child Law Bulletin in 'Solicitors' Journal'.
Personal: Educated at Brentwood School and St. Edmund Hall, Oxford.

HEALY, Alexandra
9-12 Bell Yard (D Anthony Evans QC), London
(020) 7400 1800
Recommended in Fraud
Specialisation: General common law, specialising in crime. Practice encompasses a wide range of criminal work including murder, drugs, organised crime and local authority and health and safety proceedings. Particularly specialises in commercial fraud. Recent cases include R v Palmer & Others, R v Latif.
Career: Call 1992.
Personal: MA Cantab – Trinity Hall.

HEATON, David
18 St John Street (Jonathan Foster QC), Manchester
(0161) 278 1800
davidmichaelheaton@btopenworld.com
Recommended in Clinical Negligence, Personal Injury
Specialisation: Clinical negligence. Personal injury.
Prof. Memberships: PIBA, PNBA, NCMLA.
Career: Educated at William Hulme's Grammar School, Manchester and Corpus Christi College, Cambridge. MA (Cantab). Avory Studentship.
Personal: Enjoys walking, reading, music, good food and wine. Married, four children.

HEATON, Frances
Deans Court Chambers (Stephen Grime QC), Manchester
(0161) 214 6000
heaton@deanscourt.co.uk
Recommended in Family
Specialisation: Practises exclusively in Family Law. Public Law: care disputes relating to children adoption proceedings, representing local authorities, parents and children. Private law: matrimonial finance.
Prof. Memberships: FLBA (committee member), child concern.
Career: Sheffield University.

HEDWORTH, Toby QC
Trinity Chambers (Toby Hedworth QC), Newcastle upon Tyne
(0191) 232 1927
info@trinitychambers.co.uk
Recommended in Crime
Specialisation: Crime, particularly homicide, major professional crime (conspiracies to rob, murder and the importation and distribution of controlled drugs) and terrorism, together with white collar crime. Substantial contested caseload has recently included conduct of the first ever prosecution for membership of proscribed organisation, successful defence of multiple murder and gangland murders, historical sex abuse, dentist accused of major fraud on NHS, and successful prosecution of multimillion pound armed robbery and drugs importation/supply conspiracies. Appreciates importance of early consultation to assist with case

LEADERS AT THE BAR

preparation.
Prof. Memberships: CBA; Justice.
Career: Called to the Bar 1975. Pupillage then membership of Trinity Chambers since 1976. Head of chambers since 1999. Assistant Recorder 1991. Recorder 1995. QC 1996.
Personal: Born 1952. Educated at Kings School Tynemouth, Royal Grammar School, Newcastle upon Tyne and St Catherine's College, Cambridge. Married with two daughters. Interests away from the Bar: the Lake District, the built environment and Newcastle United.

HEGARTY, Kevin
St Philips Chambers (John Randall QC), Birmingham
(0121) 246 7000
Recommended in Crime

HEILBRON, Hilary QC
Brick Court Chambers (Christopher Clarke QC), London
(020) 7379 3550
heilbron@brickcourt.co.uk
Recommended in Arbitration
Specialisation: General commercial law, including financial services; corporate law; insurance; banking; conflict of laws; shipping; international trade and commerce; e-mail and internet law; sale of goods; mediation; commercial and international arbitration (including sitting as arbitrator); consumer law including consumer credit; administrative law and some common law including professional negligence and defamation law.
Prof. Memberships: Director of The City Disputes Panel Limited. Member of the Advisory Council of CEDR 1996. Member of Civil Justice Council (1998-2002).
Career: Called to the Bar 1971. Silk 1987. Bencher of Gray's Inn (July 1995). Senior Counsel Bar of NSW, Australia, Nov 1997. Deputy High Court Judge. CEDR accredited mediator.
Personal: MA (Oxon).

HENDERSON, Launcelot QC
5 Stone Buildings (Henry Harrod), London
(020) 7242 6201
lhenderson@5-stonebuildings.law.co.uk
Recommended in Chancery, Tax
Specialisation: General Chancery, mainly concentrating on trusts, private client work, pensions, charities, Court of Protection, and all aspects of direct taxation. Reported cases include: Deeny v Gooda Walker (taxation of damages); IRC v Willoughby and McGuckian v IRC (tax avoidance); Bricom Holdings v IRC (controlled foreign companies); Memec Plc v IRC (double tax treaties); LM Tenancies 1 Plc v IRC (stamp duty and the contingency principle); EMI v Coldicott (taxation of payments in lieu of notice); Garner v Pounds (CGT and options); NMB Holdings v Secretary of State for Social Security (national insurance contributions and the Ramsay principle); IRC v Trustees of Sema Group Pension Scheme (Share buy-backs); Harries v Church Commissioners (ethical investment of church funds); Spooner v BT (interaction of BT and Civil Service pension schemes); and numerous other cases appearing for the Inland Revenue at all levels. Has appeared for the Commissioner of Estate Duty in the Court of Final Appeal in Hong Kong, and in major international trust litigation in the Cayman Islands.
Prof. Memberships: Chancery Bar Association; Revenue Bar Association; STEP.
Career: Called 1977; standing Junior Counsel to the Inland Revenue (Chancery) 1987-91; standing Junior Counsel to the Inland Revenue 1991-95. Took Silk 1995. Appointed Deputy High Court Judge 2001.
Personal: Born 1951. Educated at Westminster School and Balliol College, Oxford. Fellow of All Souls College, Oxford, 1974-81 and 1982-89. Married with three young children.

HENDERSON, Mark
Doughty Street Chambers (Geoffrey Robertson QC), London
(020) 7404 1313
m.henderson@doughtystreet.co.uk
Recommended in Immigration
Specialisation: Asylum, immigration, human rights, public law, social welfare. Areas of interest include administrative detention; benefits and support for asylum seekers; European law; confidentiality, privacy and reporting restrictions in asylum cases; public funding and regulatory issues (including representing solicitors in LSC appeals). Reported cases include: Adan and Aitsegeur [2001] 2 AC 477 (France and Germany as unsafe third countries); Turgut [2001] 1 All ER 719 (standard of review in article 3 cases); Revenko [2001] QB 601 (statelessness); Husain [2002] ACD 10 (withdrawal of asylum support violating article 3 and applicability of article 6 to asylum support cases); Senkoy [2001] Imm AR 399 (definition of fresh claim for asylum); Bensaid v UK [2001] INLR 325 (applicability of articles 3 and 8 to expulsion of mentally ill person); M [1999] Imm AR 548 (expulsion of person with AIDS); Demirkaya [1999] Imm AR 498 (relevance of past persecution); B [1998] INLR 315 (damages for false imprisonment where administrative detention unlawful on public law grounds); Bostanci [1999] Imm AR 411 (challenging exclusion of legal interpreter from asylum interview); and Sarbjit Singh [1999] Imm AR 445 (definition of torture).
Prof. Memberships: Member of Executive of ILPA and Convenor of ILPA Refugee Sub-Committee; member of ALBA, Liberty.
Career: Called to the Bar 1994. Expert Consultant to the Immigration Services Commissioner. Training conducted for ILPA, Justice, EIN and IAS.
Publications: 'Best Practice Guide to Human Rights and Asylum Appeals' (2nd ed 2002, published jointly by the ILPA, the Law Society, and RLG).

HENDERSON, Roger QC
2 Harcourt Buildings
(Roger Henderson QC), London
(020) 7583 9020
clerks@harcourt.co.uk
Recommended in Local Government
Specialisation: Specialises in local government, common law, public law, public transport and telecommunications. Work covers professional negligence, product liability, contract, personal injuries, judicial review, parliamentary and finance, especially local government finance. Counsel for British Rail at the Clapham Rail Crash Inquiry, counsel to the Kings Cross Fire Inquiry and counsel for Railtrack at the Southall and Ladbroke Grove Rail Crash Inquiries. Has acted for British Rail, Railtrack, GMC, British Telecom, London Regional Transport, Stock Exchange and many local authorities. Promoted numerous Parliamentary Bills. Promoted London Money Bills for GLC. Appeared for International Stock Exchange at numerous Inquiries. Chaired Accountants' Joint Disciplinary Scheme tribunals. Appeared for ABP at Southampton Harbour Inquiry. Involved in three Lloyds' names' actions. Represented the GMC in the 'Turkish Kidneys for Sale' and Bristol Paediatric Heart Surgery cases. Reported cases include: Roylance v General Medical Council 1999, The Times 27 January, Privy Council; R v Brent London Borough Council ex p Awua [1996] AC 55; Canterbury City Council v Colley [1993] AC 401; R v International Stock Exchange of the United Kingdom and the Republic of Ireland Limited ex p Else (1982) Limited [1993] QB 534 (CA); R v London Boroughs Transport Committee ex p Freight Transport Association [1991] 1 WLR 828 (HL); R v Secretary of State for the Environment ex p Hammersmith and Fulham London Borough Council and Others [1991] 1 AC 521; R v Secretary of State for Social Services ex p Association of Metropolitan Authorities [1986] 1 WLR 1; R v Secretary of State for Transport ex p GLC [1986] QB 556; In re Westminster City Council [1986] AC 668; Pickwell v Camden London Borough Council [1983] QB 962; R v London Transport Executive ex p GLC [1983] QB 485; R v Secretary of State for the Environment ex p Hackney London Borough Council [1983] 1 WLR 534; R v Secretary of State for the Environment ex p Hackney London Borough Council [1983] 1 WLR 534; R v Secretary of State for the Environment ex p Brent London Borough Council [1982] QB 593.
Prof. Memberships: Bencher of Inner Temple 1985. Member of St Kitts and Nevis Bar.
Career: Called to the bar in 1964. Joined 2 Harcourt Buildings in 1966. Took silk in 1980. Recorder from 1983, Deputy High Court Judge from 1987. Chairman of Civil Service Arbitration Tribunal 1994-date. Chairman of Association of Regulatory and Disciplinary Lawyers 2002-date.
Personal: Educated at Radley College 1956-61. 1st Class Hons in Law at St Catharine's College, Cambridge. Positions held include Chairman Council of Governors of London Hospital Medical College, former president of British Academy of Forensic Sciences. Leisure pursuits include fly fishing, gardening, shooting and travel. Born 21 April 1943.

HENDY, John QC
Old Square Chambers (John Hendy QC), London
(020) 7269 0300
hendyqc@oldsquarechambers.co.uk
Recommended in Employment, Health & Safety, Personal Injury
Specialisation: Primarily trade union and industrial relations law and has appeared in most of the leading cases over the last 20 years. Also deals with employment law more generally. Extensive practice also in PI and clinical negligence. Standing counsel to CWU, NUM, NUJ and POA.
Prof. Memberships: ILS; ELA; ELBA, Vice-Chair 2001-date; APIL; PIBA; ATLA; CLBA; ABA; SE Circuit; W Circuit; Chair Institute of Employment Rights 1989-date. Visiting Professor of Law, King's College London, 1999-date.
Career: Called 1972 Gray's; director, Newham Rights Centre 1973-76; practice 1977-date; Silk 1987; bencher of Gray's Inn 1995.
Publications: Co-author of: 'Redgrave's Health and Safety', 'Munkman's Employer's Liability' and 'Personal Injury Practice'. Member of editorial board of 'Encyclopaedia of Employment Law'; 'The Litigator'.
Personal: LLB London (external); LLM (Queens, Belfast).

HENKE, Ruth
30 Park Place (John Jenkins QC), Cardiff
(029) 2039 8421
r.henke@virgin.net
Recommended in Family
Specialisation: Family law with an emphasis on public law both in the family courts, before educational tribunals and the administrative courts.
Prof. Memberships: FLBA.
Career: Tenant at 30 Park Place, Cardiff. Member of the Provincial Panel of Counsel to the Crown (Civil). Member of the Panel of Counsel to the National Assembly for Wales.

HENRY, Annette
10 King's Bench Walk
(David Nathan QC), London
(020) 7353 2501
annettehenry@10kbw.co.uk
Recommended in Crime

1414

Specialisation: Regularly appears in substantial criminal cases including drugs, fraud, murder and other serious sexual and physical assaults. High profile cases include R v Jacques, a one million pound antiquarian book fraud involving the theft, disguise and onward sale of rare and valuable items through various auction houses. Defended in the Munch-Peterson trial, a highly publicised case of multiple deaths caused by 'dangerous driving' and which provoked a serious debate on the legal definition of 'dangerous driving'. Has consistently been recognised as a highly recommended junior at the London Criminal Bar. Special interest in mental health law and has represented many psychiatrically disordered defendants. A former Mental Health Act Commissioner and author of the 'Mental Health Law Referencer' (Sweet and Maxwell).
Prof. Memberships: Recently appointed as a legal member of the Mental Health Review Tribunal.

HERBERG, Javan
Blackstone Chambers (Presiley Baxendale QC & Charles Flint QC), London
(020) 7583 1770
javanherberg@blackstonechambers.com
Recommended in Administrative & Public Law
Specialisation: Specialist in commercial law (in particular financial services and civil fraud), public and administrative law and human rights. Interesting cases include (in commercial field): conducting regulatory proceedings for FSA, SIB, PIA and IMRO (Morgan Grenfell/Peter Young unit trusts affair) and for and against SFA (SBC Warburg REC derivatives; SFA v Crisanti 'Flaming Ferraris'); British Steel v Customs & Excise [1997] 2 All ER 366 (CA) (restitution of overpaid duties); Brunei v Prince Jefri (acting for Prince Jefri in US$30 bn asset recovery claim). In public law field, R v HEFC ex p Institute of Dental Surgery [1994] 1 WLR 242 (right to reasons); Ming Pao Newspapers v AG of Hong Kong [1996] AC 907, PC (freedom of expression); R v Legal Aid Board ex p Eccleston [1998] 1 WLR 1279 (legal expenses); R v Manchester Magistrate ex parte Granada Television [2000] 1 A.C.300 (HL) (enforceability of Scottish warrant); Cable & Wireless (Dominica) v Marpin [2001] 1 WLR 1123 (PC) (telecommunications); R (Morgan Grenfell) v Special Commissioners [2002] 3 All E R 1 (HL).
Prof. Memberships: Administrative Law Bar Assn (Hon Sec), COMBAR.
Career: Called 1992.
Publications: Publications include 'Principles of Public Law' (Cavendish, 2000, 2nd ed, co-author); de Smith Woolf and Jowell, 'Judicial Review of Administrative Action' (assistant editor, 5th ed supplement, 1998); case notes in 'Public Law' and in 'Judicial Review'.
Personal: Educated at University College School, University College London (LL.B), and Merton College, Oxford (BCL).

HERBERT, Douglas
Ropewalk Chambers (Ian McLaren QC), Nottingham
(0115) 947 2581
clerks@ropewalk.co.uk
Recommended in Personal Injury
Specialisation: Personal injury and clinical negligence. Professional negligence. Notable cases include: Heer v Tutton and Others [1995] 1 W.L.R 1336 C.A (County Court Order 17 rule 11); Whybro v Seymour [1998] P.I.Q.R 130 C.A. (striking out); McCauley v Vine [1999] 1 W.L.R 1977 C.A (Order 14); Shakoor v Situ [2000] 2 A.E.R. 181 (negligence - practitioner of alternative medicine); Darby v The National Trust [2001] CA (duty of care).
Prof. Memberships: Professional Negligence Bar Association.
Career: Called 1973. Assistant Recorder 1996. Recorder 2000.
Personal: Family, golf and rugby.

HERBERT, Mark QC
5 Stone Buildings (Henry Harrod), London
(020) 7242 6201
mherbert@5-stonebuildings.law.co.uk
Recommended in Chancery, Charities
Specialisation: Principal area of practice is general chancery work including trusts, capital taxation, taxation of trusts, probate, family provision, charities and offshore trusts. Also handles pensions work, both advisory and litigation. Important cases include: Mettoy Pension Trustees v Evans [1990]; Re Christy Hunt Pension Fund [1991]; Fitzwilliam v IRC [1993]. Hamar v Pensions Ombudsman, R v Opra ex p Littlewoods (1997); Edge v Pensions Ombudsman (1999); Espinosa v Burke (1999). Co-editor of 'Whiteman on Capital Gains Tax'. Other publications include 'The Drafting and Variation of Wills'.
Prof. Memberships: Chancery Bar Association; Revenue Bar Association; Association of Pension Lawyers.
Career: Called to the Bar 1974. Tenant at 17 Old Buildings 1975-77 before joining Queen Elizabeth Building in 1977. At present chambers since 1991. Took Silk 1995.
Personal: Educated at Lancing College 1962-66 and King's College, London 1967-70. Born 12 November 1948. Lives in London.

HERMAN, Ray
India Buildings Chambers (Ray Herman), Liverpool
(0151) 243 6000
Recommended in Crime

HERMER, Richard
Doughty Street Chambers (Geoffrey Robertson QC), London
(020) 7404 1313
Recommended in Clinical Negligence, Product Liability

HERSHMAN, David QC
St Philips Chambers (John Randall QC), Birmingham
(0121) 246 7000
hershman@st-philips.co.uk
Recommended in Family
Specialisation: Family Law. Particular expertise in the law relating to children, international child abduction and adoption. Also criminal cases concerning child abuse and Registered Homes Tribunal work.
Prof. Memberships: Family Law Bar Association, The British Agencies for Adoption and Fostering, the Intercountry Adoption Lawyers' Association and the Association of Lawyers for Children. Public and administrative law concerning children.
Career: Called to the Bar in 1981. Appointed part-time chairman of the Registered Homes Tribunal in 1995. Recorder 2001. Lecturer for the Law Society Children Panel and accredited course provider for the Law Society. Lecturer for Judicial Conferences and Justices Family Panel Training.
Publications: Co-author of 'Children: Law and Practice', contributor to 'Family Court Practice and Child Protection Training and Resource Pack' (National Childrens Bureau).
Personal: Educated at The Kings School, Worcester; Kings College, London. Married with four daughters. Lives near Worcester.

HESLOP, Martin S QC
2 Hare Court (Stephen Kramer QC), London
(020) 7353 5324
Recommended in Crime
Specialisation: Serious crime (both prosecution and defence), commercial fraud, gaming, licensing generally, health and safety, food and drugs.
Career: Called 1972 (Lincoln's Inn), Junior Treasury Counsel 1987, First Junior Treasury Counsel 1991, Senior Treasury Counsel 1992, Queen's Counsel 1995 - Recorder of the Crown Court.
Personal: Sailing, travel, photography, wine and good food.

HESLOP, Philip QC
4 Stone Buildings (Philip Heslop QC), London
(020) 7242 5524
Recommended in Chancery, Company, Financial Services, Insolvency

HIBBERT, William
Gough Square Chambers (Fred Philpott), London
(020) 7353 0924
william.hibbert@goughsq.co.uk
Recommended in Consumer Law
Specialisation: Consumer law – in particular consumer credit licensing (particulary Minded to Revoke Notices), advising on credit and loan agreements, defending regulatory prosecutions, and acting in civil litigation. Clients include finance houses, product manufacturers, timeshare companies, food producers and multiple retailers. Other main areas of practice include corporate, commercial, insolvency and fraud matters.
Prof. Memberships: Food Law Group and London Common and Commercial Bar Association.
Career: Called to the Bar 1979.
Personal: Charterhouse and Worcester College, Oxford. Lives in London.

HICKS, Michael
19 Old Buildings (Alastair Wilson QC), London
(020) 7405 2001
mch@19oldbuildings.com
Recommended in Intellectual Property
Specialisation: All aspects of intellectual property including patents, designs, copyrights, trademarks and confidential information. Computer hardware, software and electronics disputes including disputes concerning software licences and software development contracts. Other commercial cases with a scientific or technical subject matter. For fuller CV and list of cases see www.19oldbuildings.com
Prof. Memberships: Inner Temple, Intellectual Property Bar Association, Society for Computers & Law, Chancery Bar Association.
Career: Educated Brighton College school and Trinity College, Cambridge (Natural Sciences degree with emphasis on theoretical physics). Called 1976. Joined present chambers in 1980.
Personal: Races dinghies and small keel boats.

HICKS, William QC
Eldon Chambers (Patrick Clarkson QC & William Hicks QC), London
(020) 7583 1355
Recommended in Planning
Specialisation: A wide range of planning and related work. Some particular areas of expertise are retail, highways and transportation, energy, environment and listed buildings.
Prof. Memberships: Planning and Environmental Bar Association, Committee Parliamentary Bar Mess, Administrative Law Bar Association, Committee Joint Oxford Planning Conference.
Career: Magdalene College Cambridge MA (Economics). Called to the Bar 1975. Joined present chambers in 1976. Took silk in 1995. Called to the Bar in Northern Ireland 2000.

HILDYARD, Robert QC
4 Stone Buildings (Philip Heslop QC), London
(020) 7242 5524
clerks@4stonebuildings.com
Recommended in Chancery, Company, Energy, Financial Services, Insurance
Specialisation: Principally, company law, financial services, company/commercial litigation and corporate insolvency. Specialist in insurance company transfer schemes. Other specialist work areas include insurance/reinsurance litigation and oil and gas litigation. Recent court cases

LEADERS AT THE BAR

include: Macmillan v BIT (Maxwell litigation/conflicts of laws), NRG Victory (insurance company transfer scheme), AXA Sun Life plc (insurance company orphan state), LDDC v Regalian (restitution), Kurz v Stella Musical (choice of jurisdiction clause), Phillips Petroleum v Enron (take or pay gas sales agreement), Market Wizard Systems (UK) Ltd (public interest winding up), Hall v Bank of England (misfeasance in public office; rule in Foss v Harbottle), Charter Re ('pay to be paid' reinsurance clause), Cleaver v Delta (Privy Council).
Prof. Memberships: Chancery Bar Association, Insolvency Lawyers' Association, Commercial Bar Association (COMBAR).
Career: Called to the Bar in 1977, Junior Counsel to the Crown (Chancery) 1992-94, appointed Queen's Counsel 1994. Called to the Bar of Bermuda, Bahamas, Cayman Islands, Turks, Caicos Islands, and Hong Kong for specific cases.
Publications: Contributor: Butterworth's 'Encyclopaedia of Forms and Precedents' (company volume); Tolley's 'Company Law'.
Personal: Educated at Eton College; Christ Church, Oxford. Languages: Spanish.

HILL, Mark
Pump Court Chambers (Christopher Harvey Clark QC), London
(020) 7363 0711
mh@3pumpcourt.com
Recommended in Church
Specialisation: Ecclesiastical law, personal injury, professional and clinical negligence. Leading cases include: NEM v Jones [1990] 1 AC 24 (HL); Pacific Associates v Baxter [1990] 1 QB 993 (CA); Tribe v Tribe [1996] Ch 107 (CA); Re St Peter's Oundle [1997] 4 Ecc LJ 163; Re Durrington Cemetery [2001] Fam 33; Re Blagdon Cemetery (ct of Arches).
Prof. Memberships: PNBA; PIBA; Ecclesiastical Law Society.
Career: Chancellor of the Diocese of Chichester; Editor, 'Ecclesiastical Law Journal'; Visiting Fellow, Emmanuel College, Cambridge [1998]; Research Fellow, Centre for Law of Religion, Cardiff University [1999-2001]; Member of Legal Advisory Commission (General Synod).
Publications: 'English Canon Law' (1998); 'Ecclesiastical Law' (2nd edn, 2001); 'Clergy Discipline in Anglican and Roman Catholic Canon Law' (2001); 'Religious Liberty and Human Rights' (2002).

HILL, Michael QC
23 Essex Street (Michael Lawson QC), London
(020) 7413 0353
michaelhill@23essexstreet.com
Recommended in Crime, Fraud
Specialisation: Principal areas of practice are commercial fraud, international crime, homicide and professional crime.
Prof. Memberships: Criminal Bar Association (Chairman 1982-86); International Society for the Reform of Criminal Law; President (1999-date), Board of Directors (1988-date); Chairman, Management Committee (1992-95); Inns of Court Advocacy Training Committee (Chairman, 1994-2000); Bar Mutual Indemnity Fund Ltd (Director 1989-2001; Chairman, Investment Committee 1992-2001).
Career: Treasury Counsel (Inner London Sessions/Crown Court), 1969-74; Counsel Central Criminal Court 1974-79; Queen's Counsel 1979; Queen's Counsel (NSW) 1991; Recorder 1977-97; called, Gray's Inn, 1958; Bencher, Gray's Inn, 1986.

HILL, Richard G
4 Stone Buildings (Philip Heslop QC), London
(020) 7242 5524
clerks@4stonebuildings.com
Recommended in Chancery, Commercial (Litigation)
Specialisation: Specialist in company and commercial litigation; corporate insolvency litigation and advice (including bondholder disputes); financial services; commercial fraud; banking. Emphasis on city disputes and substantial experience in acting for and against regulatory and government bodies. Leading recent cases: Re BCCI SA (Morris v Bank of America); Re Barings Plc; Philip Morris v BAT; Express Newspapers v Telegraph Group Plc; Re Westminster Properties Management Ltd (Official Receiver v Stern); Re Market Wizard Systems (UK) Ltd; Dawnay Day & Co Ltd v D'Alphen; Ispahani v Bank Melli Iran.
Prof. Memberships: Member of Attorney General's 'B' Panel Counsel for government work; COMBAR; CBA.
Career: 1993 Call. Educated at Gonville & Caius College, Cambridge (BA Hons - 1st class); Prince of Wales Scholar of Gray's Inn.
Publications: Contributor to Butterworths 'Practical Insolvency'.

HILL, Thomas
4-5 Gray's Inn Square (Elizabeth Appleby QC), London
(020) 7404 5252
clerks@4-5graysinnsquare.co.uk
Recommended in Environment, Planning
Specialisation: Principal area of practice is planning and environmental law, in particular public inquiry work involving detailed investigation of environmental and other impacts. Recent instructions have involved proposals for major retail, housing and business development, works to listed buildings, minerals, waste and airport-related development (including successfully promoting Manchester Airport's Second Runway). Also judicial review and advisory work involving the interpretation and application of the Town and Country Planning Act 1990, the Environmental Protection Act 1990 and subordinate legislation, and prosecutions under EPA. Has also appeared in parliament for promoters of private legislation with environmental implications.
Prof. Memberships: Planning and Environmental Bar Association (committee member 1990-95); Administrative Law Bar Association.
Career: Called to the Bar 1988.

HILL, Timothy
Stone Chambers (Steven Gee QC), London
(020) 7440 6900
timothy.hill@stonechambers.com
Recommended in Shipping
Specialisation: Commercial litigation, shipping, international trade and commodities, admiralty, arbitration (practice and procedure), insurance and banking.
Career: Union Trans-Pacific Co Ltd v Orient Shipping Rotterdam BV ('Dan Xia Shan') [2002] EWHC 1451 (Comm); Handelsbanken ASA v Dandridge & ors ('Aliza Glacial') [2002] EWCA Civ 577 (CA); The Torepo [2002] EWHC 1481 (Admlty); Fortune Hong Kong Trading Ltd v Cosco-Feasco (Singapore) Pte Ltd [2002] EWHC 79 (Comm); The Seaflower [2001] 1 Lloyds Rep 341 (CA), [2000] 2 Lloyds Rep 37; The Goodpal [2000] 1 Lloyds Rep 638; The Ambor [2000] 1 ALL ER; Whitbread Plc v UCB Corporate Services Ltd The Times June 22, 2000 (CA); The Jalagoui [2000] 1 Lloyds Rep 515 (CA), [1999] 1 Lloyds Rep 903; The Sea Empress (unreported); The Sea Maas [1999] 2 Lloyds Rep 281; Bawjem v MC Fabrications ('Hull No 1029A') [1999] 1 ALL ER (Comm) 377 (CA).
Publications: Contributing to various insurance and law publications such as the 'International Insurance Law Review'.

HILLIARD, Lexa
3-4 South Square (Michael Crystal QC & Lord Alexander of Weedon QC), London
(020) 7696 9900
clerks@southsquare.com
Recommended in Insolvency
Specialisation: Insolvency, civil fraud, professional negligence, banking, human rights.
Prof. Memberships: Bar member of Insolvency Law Sub-Committee of Law Society. CEDR Accredited Mediator.
Career: Lecturer in Law, Durham University 1984-87. Lloyds Bank Legal Department 1988. 3-4 South Square 1990 to date.
Publications: Contributor to 'Totty & Moss on Insolvency' (Sweet & Maxwell) and 'Halsbury's Laws'.

HILLIARD, Nicholas
6 King's Bench Walk (Roy Amlot QC), London
(020) 7583 0410
Recommended in Crime
Specialisation: Criminal law.
Career: Senior Treasury Counsel at the Central Criminal Court. Contributing editor to 'Archbold'.

HILLIER, Andrew QC
11 King's Bench Walk Chambers (Eldred Tabachnik QC & James Goudie QC), London
(020) 7632 8500
hillier@11kbw.com
Recommended in Employment
Specialisation: Principal area of practice is employment law including all types of contractual disputes, employer/employee disputes (wrongful/unfair dismissal); protection of confidential information; non-solicitation of customers; board-room disputes; partnership disputes; strikes and collective disputes; trade union law and race, sex and disabilities discrimination. Particular emphasis on local government and health service law. Other main areas of work are public law, mental health law, including psychiatric damage and medical negligence cases and disciplinary tribunals.

HILLIER, Nicolas
9 Gough Square (John Foy QC), London
(020) 7832 0500
nhillier@9goughsq.co.uk
Recommended in Personal Injury
Specialisation: Principal areas of practice are personal injury and professional (clinical and legal) negligence litigation. Personal injury work includes both accident claims and occupational disease, particularly asbestos-related diseases and noise induced deafness.
Prof. Memberships: Personal Injury Bar Association; Association of Personal Injury Lawyers.
Career: Called to the Bar in 1982. Joined present Chambers in 1983.
Personal: LLB (Hons) Southampton University, 1977. Leisure pursuits: a young and extremely energetic family. Lives in London. General interest in most sports – now a retired rugby player, a struggling golfer and an organiser of a junior football club.

HIMSWORTH, Emma
One Essex Court (Lord Grabiner QC), London
(020) 7583 2000
Recommended in Intellectual Property
Specialisation: All aspects of intellectual property law.
Prof. Memberships: The Intellectual Property Lawyers Organisation, the Intellectual Property Bar Association, the Chancery Bar Association and the Commercial Bar Association.
Career: Called 1993.
Personal: BSc in Biological Sciences with Honours in Biochemistry, Dip Law (City), Dip EC Law (Kings).

HINCHLIFF, Benjamin
1 Brick Court (Richard Rampton QC), London
(020) 7353 8845
Recommended in Defamation

HINCHLIFFE, Nicholas QC
9 St. John Street (John Hand QC), Manchester
(0161) 955 9000
clerks@9stjohnstreet.co.uk

LEADERS AT THE BAR

Recommended in Personal Injury
Specialisation: Personal injury, industrial disease, catastrophe injury claims, clinical negligence.
Prof. Memberships: PIBA.
Career: LLB. Manchester, Middle Temple 1980. Recorder 1998. QC 1999.
Personal: Championship rifle shooting.

HINKS, Frank QC
Serle Court (Lord Neill of Bladen QC), London
(020) 7242 6105
clerks@serlecourt.co.uk
Recommended in Chancery, Partnership
Specialisation: Domestic and international trusts, including expert evidence in relation to offshore jurisdictions: Re Ojjeh Trusts [1993] (Cayman Islands); Re Hampstead Trusts [1995] (Cayman Islands); Re 18 Aug. 1995 trust [1995] (Jersey); Re 1995 and 1996 Trusts [1998] Washington State; Wight v Olswang [1999] (trustee exemption clauses); Flemmer v HRO [2000] Colorado. Partnership law: Kerr v Morris [1987]. Real property, including landlord and tenant and commons: Mid-Glamorgan CC v Ogwr BC [1995] (commons); Dugan - Chapman v Grosvenor Estate Belgravia [1997] (leasehold enfranchisement); National Trust v Ashbrook [1997] (commons). Inspector and counsel in town and village green inquiries. Chancery and commercial litigation: Finers v Miro [1991] (constructive trust); BCCI v Gokal (constructive trust/undue influence); Azaz v Self-realisation Healing Centre (undue influence). Professional negligence and regulation.
Prof. Memberships: Chancery Bar Association, Association of Contentious Trust and Probate Specialists, Association of Partnership Practitioners, Property Bar Association.
Career: Called to Bar in 1973. Joined present chambers in 1974.
Personal: Educated at Bromley Grammar School 1961-67; St Catherine's College, Oxford 1968-72. BA 1st Class Hons; BCL 1st Class Hons.

HIORNS, Roger
9 Gough Square (John Foy QC), London
020 7832 0500
rhiorns@9goughsq.co.uk
Recommended in Personal Injury
Specialisation: Occupational diseases, particularly work related upper limb disorders on which he lectures nationally. Appeared in Mountenay v Bernard Matthews and Alexander v Midland Bank.
Prof. Memberships: APIL; PIBA.
Career: Has practised for 19 years in all areas of personal injury litigation since completing pupillage in chambers.
Personal: Active DIY enthusiast, passive sports enthusiast and lover of all good music.

HIRST, Jonathan QC
Brick Court Chambers (Christopher Clarke QC), London
(020) 7379 3550
hirst@brickcourt.co.uk
Recommended in Commercial (Litigation)
Specialisation: General commercial law, including shipping, insurance, reinsurance, banking and professional negligence and entertainment. Recent important cases: Sphere Drake Personal Accident litigation (2001-02); Heaton v Axa (HL) [2002] 2 WLR 1081; Mercandian Continent (CA) [2001] Lloyd's Reps 563; Groupama Navigation et Transports v Catatumbo CA Seguros (CA) [2001] Lloyd's Rep IR 141; Credit Lyonnais Bank Nederland v ECGD [1999] 1 Lloyd's Reps 563 (HL); JH Rayner v Cafenorte SA Importadara a Exportara SA [1999] 2 Lloyd's Reps 750; Brown v GIO Insurance Ltd. (CA) [1998] Lloyd's Reps IR 201.
Prof. Memberships: QC 1990, Recorder 1997; Chairman of the Bar of England and Wales 2000.
Career: Called to Bar 1975, Inner Temple, Bencher 1994.
Publications: Contributor, 'Paget on Banking' (11th edn), chapter on Money Laundering.
Personal: Born 2 July 1953, London. Educated at Eton College and Trinity College, Cambridge (MA Law).

HITCHCOCK, Richard G
35 Essex Street (Christopher Wilson-Smith QC), London
(020) 7353 6381
Recommended in Pensions

HITCHING, Isabel
No5 Chambers (Gareth Evans QC), Birmingham
(0121) 606 0500
Recommended in Commercial (Litigation)

HITCHMOUGH, Andrew
Pump Court Tax Chambers, London
(020) 7414 8080
clerks@pumptax.com
Recommended in Tax
Specialisation: Practices in all areas of revenue law, including VAT and customs duties, both advisory and litigation. Recent cases include Wiggett Construction v CCE and Wardhaugh v Penrith RUFC.
Prof. Memberships: Revenue Bar Association; VAT Practitioners Group; Law Society VAT and Duties Sub-Committee. Publications: co-editor of 'Potter Monroe's Tax Planning'; 'Ray's Practical Inheritance Tax Planning'. Managing Editor, 'Personal Tax Planning Review'.

HOBBS, Geoffrey QC
One Essex Court (Lord Grabiner QC), London
(020) 7583 2000
Recommended in Intellectual Property

HOBSON, John QC
4-5 Gray's Inn Square (Elizabeth Appleby QC), London
(020) 7404 5252
Recommended in Local Government, Planning
Specialisation: Public law, local government, planning and environmental law.
Prof. Memberships: Admininstrative Law Bar Association; Planning and Environmental Bar Association.
Career: Former solicitor, called to Bar 1980. 1995-96 Specialist Advisor to the Northern Ireland Affairs Committee of the House of Commons for its enquiry into the planning system in Northern Ireland. 1992-2000: Supplementary Panel of Treasury Counsel. 1997-2000: Standing Counsel to the Rent Assessment Panel. Assistant Recorder 1999. Queen's Counsel 2000. Recorder 2000.
Personal: LLM (St John's College, Cambridge).

HOCHBERG, Daniel
Wilberforce Chambers (Edward Nugee QC), London
(020) 7306 0102
Recommended in Chancery
Specialisation: Commercial chancery and a wide range of general chancery litigation including offshore trust litigation, real property, business agreements, professional negligence, succession, securities and loans, insolvency and landlord and tenant. Reported cases include: West v Lazards (Jersey breach of trust), Blampied v Ram (Jersey trust; disclosure), Midland Bank v Federated Pension Services (breach of trust and exemption clauses), Co-Operative v Tesco (restrictive covenants), Hammersmith & Fulham v Tops Shop Centre (relief from forfeiture), Wates v Citygate Properties (section 25 notice); Greenhaven Motors Ltd (insolvency); Prestwich v Royal Bank of Canada (Jersey) (offshore trusts, tax indemnities), Corbett v Bond Pearce (solicitors negligence), Abacus (CI) Ltd v Al-Sabah and Grupo Torras v Al-Sabah (offshore trusts, fraud).
Prof. Memberships: Chancery Bar Association; Association of Contentious Trust and Probate Specialists; Property Bar Association.

HOCHHAUSER, Andrew QC
Essex Court Chambers (Gordon Pollock QC), London
(020) 7813 8000
Recommended in Commercial (Litigation), Employment
Specialisation: Areas of practice include arbitration, banking, breach of contract, company law, commercial fraud, entertainment cases, employment, partnership disputes, professional negligence, sports law cases, takeovers, mergers and share sale disputes.
Prof. Memberships: Fellow of the Chartered Institute of Arbitrators; member of Gibraltan Bar.
Career: University of Bristol (LLB), University of London (LLM). Called to the English Bar 1977. Harmsworth Scholar of Middle Temple. Queen's Counsel 1997. Bencher 2000.
Personal: Born 1955.

HOCKMAN, Stephen QC
6 Pump Court (Stephen Hockman QC), London
(020) 7797 8400
StephenHockmanQC@6PumpCourt.co.uk
Recommended in Environment
Specialisation: Principal area of practice is environmental, planning and administrative law. Led the challenge in the High Court, and subsequently in the House of Lords, based on the European Convention on Human Rights, against the role of the Secretary of State for the Environment, Transport and the Regions in determining planning cases. Recently appeared for the successful claimant in a leading case on environmental nuisance, Marcic v Thames Water (CA). Regularly instructed by national and local government bodies in environmental matters. Chair of the Environmental Law Foundation and a member of the Council of English Nature.
Prof. Memberships: Planning and Environment Bar Association, Administrative Law Bar Association.
Career: Called to the Bar in 1970 and joined Pump Court in 1971. Appointed Recorder 1987. Took Silk 1990. Elected Leader, SE Circuit, January 2001.
Personal: Educated at Eltham College, London (1955-65) and Jesus College, Cambridge (1966-69). Born 4 January 1947. Lives in London and Peterborough.

HOCKTON, Andrew
6 Pump Court (Kieran Coonan QC), London
(020) 7583 6013
Recommended in Clinical Negligence

HODGE, David QC
9 Old Square (Michael Driscoll QC), London
(020) 7405 4682
Recommended in Professional Negligence, Property Litigation
Specialisation: Principal areas of practice are general Chancery and property litigation and related professional negligence, particularly solicitors, barristers and valuers. Notable reported cases include: Graham v Philcox [1984] (easements); TCB v Gray [1986-88] (guarantees); Sharma v Knight [1986] (landlord and tenant); Bank of Baroda v Shah [1988] (undue influence); Sen v Headley [1991] (equity); Mortgage Corporation v Nationwide Credit [1994] (registered land); Ridehalgh v Horsefield [1994] (wasted costs); Allied Maples v *Simmons & Simmons* [1995] (professional negligence); Garston v Scottish Widows [1996-98] (landlord and tenant); Railtrack v Gojra [1998] (landlord and tenant); Lemmerbell v Britannia LAS Direct [1998] (landlord and tenant); Bristol & West v Bhadresa [1999] (costs); Shirley v Caswell [2000] (professional negligence); Nationwide BS v James Beauchamp [2001] (easements); Ramnarace v Lutchman [2001] (limitation); Hart Investments v Burton Hotel [2002] (landlord and tenant); Spring House v Mount Cook Land

LEADERS AT THE BAR

[2002] (landlord and tenant); Robinson Webster v Agombar [2002] (highways).
Prof. Memberships: Chancery Bar Association. Professional Negligence Bar Association. Property Bar Association.
Career: Called to bar in 1979. Joined 9 Old Square in 1980. QC 1997. Assistant Recorder 1998. Recorder 2000. Bencher Lincoln's Inn 2000.
Publications: Contributed chapter on Chancery Matters to the 4th and 5th editions of 'The Law and Practice of Compromise' by David Foskett QC. Author of 'Secret Trusts: The Fraud Theory Revisited' (1980), Conveyancer.
Personal: Born 1956. Educated at University College, Oxford 1974-78 (BA, BCL). Chairman, Lincoln's Inn Bar Representation Committee 1997-98.

HODGSON, Margaret
St. Ive's Chambers (Julia Macur QC), Birmingham
(0121) 236 0863
stives.chambers@btinternet.com
Recommended in Family
Specialisation: Private matrimonial: residence/contact; adoption. Public family law: child care; freeing; adoption. Representation of parents, local authorities and children's guardians. Cases: G and others (minors) and R (A minor) ex parte, R v Birmingham Juvenile Court [1989] CA 2 FLR 454. Re P (Minors) (Breakdown of Adoption Placement) F.D. (1996) 3 FCR 657.
Prof. Memberships: Family Law Bar Association.
Career: Warwick University LLB (Hons).

HOFMEYR, Stephen QC
7 King's Bench Walk (Gavin Kealey QC & Julian Flaux QC), London
(020) 7910 8300
shofmeyr@7kbw.law.co.uk
Recommended in Shipping
Specialisation: Practice encompasses insurance and reinsurance (both marine and non-marine) and shipping and maritime law. Most recent cases include: Kiriacoulis Lines SA v Camat (marine insurance); Bergen Industries v Dalmore Product (ship finance); Seashore Marine v Phoenix Assurance (marine insurance); Petrotrade Inc. v Smith (Port agency dispute); Shell UK Ltd. v CLM Engineering (Marine Insurance); the Metro litigation (oil fraud); Raiffeisen Zentralbank Osterreich AG and others v Crosseas Shipping and Others (Bank guarantee); Royal Boskalis v Mountain; Manifest Shipping v Uni-Polaris Insurance (the 'Starsea') (both marine insurance); Glencore v Bank of China (letters of credit); L'Alsacienne v Unistorebrand (reinsurance); Brown v KMR (Lloyd's litigation). Other specialisations include all aspects of commercial law (arbitration, aviation, banking, oil and gas, and professional negligence). His combination of legal and accounting qualifications makes him particularly suited to these areas of the law.
Prof. Memberships: COMBAR.

Career: A Rhodes Scholar from Cape Town, commenced practice at the Bar in 1987, having previously practised as an attorney and conveyancer in South Africa. Also an advocate of the Supreme Court of South Africa.
Personal: Educated at Diocesan College, Rondebosch, Cape Town, University of Cape Town (B. Com 1974-76, LLB 1977-78) and University College, Oxford (MA, Jurisprudence, 1979-81). Leisure pursuits include walking, birdwatching, tennis and skiing. Born 10 February 1956. Lives in Guildford.

HOGGETT, John QC
40 King St, Manchester
(0161) 832 9082
jhoggett@40kingstreet.co.uk
Recommended in Planning
Specialisation: Town and country planning, compulsory purchase, highways, retail developments, airports, minerals, waste disposal, motorways, environment law, local authorities and judicial review. Has appeared in many major public inquiries into a wide range of planning and environmental issues.
Prof. Memberships: Northern Circuit; Planning & Environment Bar Association; Editorial Board, Environmental Law Reports; Advisory Council to the Rural Buildings Preservation Trust; General Medical Council Legal Assessor.
Career: Called 1969, Queen's Counsel 1986, Recorder of the Crown Court 1988.
Personal: University: Clare College, Cambridge.

HOLGATE, David QC
4 Breams Buildings (Christopher Lockhart-Mummery QC), London
(020) 7353 5835
clerks@4breams.co.uk
Recommended in Environment, Local Government, Planning
Specialisation: Judicial review, planning, compulsory purchase, rating, local government, environment law and property law. Reported cases covering a wide field include: Bushell v Secretary of State, Shimizu v Westminster City Council, Coventry and Solihull Waste Disposal Co v Russell, Surrey Free Inns v Gosport BC, Regina v Hillingdon London Borough ex parte London Regional Transport, R v Secretary of State for Social Services ex p. AMA, R v Somerset CC ex p. Fewings, and Chesterfield Properties v Secretary of State, and, in the Lands Tribunal, Glasshouse Properties v DTp and Fennessy v London City Airport. Has appeared for government bodies, local authorities, developers and local objectors in a broad range of public inquiries including Sizewell B, Canvey Island, Piper Alpha, and Point of Ayr Gas Terminal.
Prof. Memberships: PEBA and ALBA.
Career: Called to Bar in 1978. Formerly a member of the panel of Junior Counsel to the Crown (1986-97) and Junior Counsel to the Inland Revenue in Rating and Valuation matters (1990-97). Queen's Counsel (1997). Called to the Hong Kong Bar (2000) and appeared in the Court of Final Appeal (2001).
Personal: Graduated in Law from Exeter College, Oxford.

HOLLAND, Charles
Trinity Chambers (Toby Hedworth QC), Newcastle upon Tyne
(0191) 232 1927
info@trinitychambers.co.uk
Recommended in Licensing
Specialisation: Commercial and licensing. Commercial work includes contract, company and partnership, director's disqualification, landlord and tenant, and professional negligence. Liquor, gaming, public entertainment, sex establishment and taxi licensing matters, advising and representing applicants and objectors at all levels of tribunal.
Prof. Memberships: North Eastern Circuit, Association of Licensing Practitioners.
Career: Called to the Bar in 1994. Practised at Trinity Chambers since 1996. Junior Counsel to the Crown (Provincial Panel) 2000-.
Personal: Born Harrogate, 1969. Educated Oundle School, University of Nottingham (LLB Law).

HOLLAND, Katharine
9 Old Square (Michael Driscoll QC), London
(020) 7405 4682
Recommended in Property Litigation
Specialisation: All aspects of property litigation, including commercial and residential property disputes, surveyors' and solicitors' professional negligence, mortgages, landlord and tenant, leasehold enfranchisement, conveyancing, easements, restrictive covenants, property rights, insolvency and commercial contracts. Reported cases include: Wentworth v Wiltshire (highways), Millman v Ellis (easements), Charville v Unipart Group (forfeiture/surrender), Titanic Investments v *Macfarlanes* (solicitors' negligence), Gregory v Shepherds (solicitors' negligence), Kaiser v Jones (rectification), Lloyds Bank v Burd Pearce (solicitors' negligence), Lloyds Bank v Parker Bullen (solicitors' negligence), Carroll v Manek and Bank of India (mortgages/ adverse possession), Law Society v Southall (gifts and transactions defrauding creditors).
Prof. Memberships: Chancery Bar Association and Professional Negligence Bar Association.
Career: Called to the Bar in 1989 and joined 9 Old Square in 1990.
Personal: Educated at Lady Manners School, Bakewell and Hertford College, Oxford (BA, BCL).

HOLLANDER, Charles QC
Brick Court Chambers (Christopher Clarke QC), London
(020) 7379 3550
Recommended in Commercial (Litigation),
Sport
Specialisation: Commercial litigation, especially city litigation and energy, and sport and media. Recent commercial cases: Railtrack, Three Rivers, Barings, Prince Jefri Bolkiah, J-Block North Sea litigation, TGU Energy v Drax, Marconi. Sport: Don King v Frank Warren, IAAF v Linford Christie, 'Go Racing', FA v Arsene Wenger, Wimbledon FC v FL, Sunderland FC v Uruguay Montevideo FC. Most recent reported cases: Black v Sumitomo Times 2002 1 WLR 1562, Interbrew SA v Financial Times Times 21.03.02, RS Residuals v Regent Chemicals Times, 22.5.02.
Career: Became Queen's Counsel in 1999.
Publications: 'Conflicts of interest and Chinese Walls', Documentary Evidence (7th ed), 'Phipson on Evidence' (15th ed).

HOLLINGTON, Robin QC
New Square Chambers (Charles Purle QC), London
(020) 7419 8000
robin.hollington@newsquarechambers.co.uk
Recommended in Company, Insolvency
Specialisation: Principal areas of work are company law, insolvency and chancery litigation.
Prof. Memberships: Chancery Bar Association; Lincoln's Inn (Cassell Scholar).
Career: MA (Oxon) Jurisprudence 1977; LLM (University of Pennsylvania) 1978; called to the Bar 1979; QC 1999.
Publications: Author of 'Minority Shareholders' Rights' (Sweet & Maxwell, 3rd ed 1999) with supplement on New Square chambers website www.newsquarechambers.co.uk/minoritysharesindex.htm
Personal: Married with one son. Principal leisure interests: tennis and golf.

HOLROYDE, Tim QC
Exchange Chambers (David Turner QC & Bill Braithwaite QC & Henry Globe QC), Liverpool
(0151) 236 7747
holroyde@exchangechambers.co.uk
Recommended in Crime
Specialisation: Crime. Personal injuries.
Prof. Memberships: Criminal Bar Association. Personal Injuries Bar Association.
Career: Called 1977. QC 1996. Recorder 1997. Educated Bristol GS; Wadham College, Oxford.

HOLWILL, Derek
4 Paper Buildings (Jean Ritchie QC), London
(020) 7643 5000
Recommended in Professional Negligence
Specialisation: Professional negligence including clinical negligence cases. Acts both for defendant insurance companies, Solicitors Indemnity Fund and health authorities, and for claimants including mortgage lenders. Also handles commercial litigation, insurance litigation and general common law work, including personal injury cases. Reported cases include: Landall v Dennis

Faulkner and Alsop; Saddington v Colleys Professional Services; Halifax Plc v Gould & Swayne; TSB Plc v Robert Irving and Burns; John A Pike v Independent Insurance Co; Estill v Cowling Swift & Kitchen.
Prof. Memberships: Professional Negligence Bar Association.
Career: Called to the Bar 1982.
Personal: Leisure pursuits include Lindy Hop, scuba diving and travel.

HOPKINS, Adrian
3 Serjeants' Inn (Robert Francis QC & John Grace QC), London
(020) 7427 5000
Recommended in Clinical Negligence
Specialisation: Deals with all aspects of medical law, including medical negligence, professional ethics and discipline. Recent cases include: Re F (A mental patient – sterilisation); Re C (refusal of medical treatment); Re G and Re S (PVS cases) and Ratcliffe v Plymouth & Torbay HA (res ipsa).
Prof. Memberships: Western Circuit, PNBA.
Career: Called to the Bar and joined 3 Serjeants' Inn in 1984. Appointed to supplementary panel of Treasury Counsel, Common Law, in 1995 and London B Panel for The Crown's Civil Litigation, in 1999. Contributing editor to Lloyd's 'Medical Law Reports'.
Personal: Educated at Warwick School and St. Peter's College, Oxford. Born 1961. Lives in London.

HOPKINS, Philippa
Essex Court Chambers (Gordon Pollock QC), London
(020) 7813 8000
phopkins@essexcourt-chambers.co.uk
Recommended in Shipping
Specialisation: Commercial practice in line with chambers profile. In particular: aviation; banking; carriage of goods; commercial arbitration; commercial shipping (dry work); commodity and international arbitration; finance of international trade; general commercial and contract (including sale of goods); insurance and reinsurance; international trade; professional negligence; public and private international law.
Career: BA, BCL, Merton College, Oxford. Called to the Bar in 1994.
Publications: Colman, Lyon & Hopkins – 'Practice and Procedure of the Commercial Court' (5th edn 2000).
Personal: Born 1971.

HORLOCK, Timothy QC
9 St. John Street (John Hand QC), Manchester
(0161) 955 9000
clerks@9stjohnstreet.co.uk
Recommended in Health & Safety, Personal Injury
Specialisation: Personal injury, industrial disease, clinical negligence.
Prof. Memberships: PIBA.
Career: Called 1981, Silk 1997. Manchester Grammar School and St John's College, Cambridge. Recorder 1997.
Personal: Football, tennis, cricket, golf. Married, four sons.

HORNE, Michael
3 Serjeants' Inn (Robert Francis QC & John Grace QC), London
(020) 7427 5000
mhorne@3serjeantsinn.com
Recommended in Clinical Negligence
Specialisation: Deals with all aspects of medical and dental law. Considerable experience acting for claimants and defendants in all aspects of High Court and County Court clinical negligence cases, including birth injury claims. Medical and Dental Disciplinary cases. Reported cases include: Ms B v An NHS Hospital Trust [2002] EWHC 429 Fam (capacity of adult to refuse medical treatment), Smith v Leicestershire Health Authority (1998) Lloyd's Rep Med 77 (limitation, constructive knowledge), Rhodes v West Surrey & North East Hampshire Health Authority (1998) Lloyd's Rep Med 246 (duties of experts) and Smith v Ealing, Hammersmith and Hounslow Health Authority [1997] 8 Med LR 290 (medical examinations; stay of proceeedings)
Prof. Memberships: Professional Negligence Bar Association, London Common Law and Commercial Bar Association.
Career: Royal Grammar School, Newcastle-upon-Tyne (1977-87); Trinity Hall, Cambridge University (1988-91), Law Degree, MA. Called to the Bar, October 1992 (Gray's Inn).
Publications: Contributing Editor, Lloyds Law Reports, Medical.
Personal: Leisure interests: rugby, football, skiing, scuba diving and walking. Born 24 November 1969.

HOROWITZ, Michael QC
1 Hare Court (Bruce Blair QC), London
(020) 7797 7070
horowitz@1hc.com
Recommended in Family
Specialisation: Family law, including ancillary relief, childcare and child abduction. Contributing Editor Rayden & Jackson on Divorce 17th edition and 'Essential Family Practice 2002'.
Prof. Memberships: Director Bar Mutual Indemnity Fund Ltd; FLBA.
Personal: Married with one daughter. Lives in London.

HORROCKS, Peter
One Garden Court Family Law Chambers (Eleanor F Platt QC & Alison Ball QC), London
(020) 7797 7900
p.horrocks@onegardencourt.co.uk
Recommended in Family
Specialisation: Principal area of practice is child law, both public and private, including disputes as to residence and contact, care proceedings, wardship, adoption and abduction cases under the Hague and European Conventions. Frequently advises and represents local authorities and childrens' guardians as well as private clients. Other areas of work include child-related criminal cases, probate, boundaries and easements.
Prof. Memberships: Family Law Bar Association.
Career: Called to the Bar in 1977. Joined present chambers in 1996.
Personal: Educated at Winchester 1968-72; Trinity Hall, Cambridge 1973-76; College of Law 1976-77. Leisure pursuits include real tennis, cricket and opera. Born 31 January 1955. Lives in Surrey.

HORTON, Mark
Colleton Chambers (Martin Meeke QC), Exeter
(01392) 274898
Recommended in Family
Specialisation: Public and private law childcare and ancillary relief.
Prof. Memberships: Family Law Bar Association.
Career: Family specialist since 1990.

HORTON, Mark
St John's Chambers (Christopher Sharp QC), Bristol
(0117) 921 3456
Recommended in Crime

HORTON, Matthew QC
2 Mitre Court Buildings (Guy Roots QC), London
(020) 7583 1380
Recommended in Planning
Specialisation: A genuine all rounder within the fields of parliamentary, public and administrative law, local government, environmental, town and country planning, compensation, rating, landlord and tenant and related areas of European law, property law and professional negligence.
Prof. Memberships: Administrative Law Bar Association. Planning and Environmental Bar Association. Elected Member of Parliamentary Bar. Former Committee Member of Joint Planning Law Conference.
Career: Called 1969, took Silk 1989. A standing counsel to the Department of the Environment on Land Commission matters (1973).
Personal: Educated at Sevenoaks School and Trinity Hall, Cambridge, MA (Law 1st Class Hons) and LLM (English and Private International Law); Open Exhibitioner and Foundation Scholar (Trinity Hall), Squire Law Scholar (University of Cambridge), Astbury Scholar (Middle Temple). Fluent in French, some Russian. Organic farmer. Keen skier. Born 23 September 1946.

HORWELL, Richard
Hollis Whiteman Chambers (QEB) (Julian Bevan QC & Peter Whiteman QC), London
(020) 7583 5766
Recommended in Crime
Specialisation: Practice encompasses all aspects of the criminal law, with particular experience in commercial fraud, drug importations, terrorism and murder trials. Also tribunal work including GMC and RAC Motorsport. Involved in Postgate and Grob; Guinness; MTM and many other high profile criminal cases.
Career: Called in 1976. Treasury Counsel 1991. Senior Treasury Counsel 1996. First Senior Treasury Counsel 2002.

HOSKINS, Mark
Brick Court Chambers (Christopher Clarke QC), London
(020) 7379 3550
hoskins@brickcourt.co.uk
Recommended in Competition/European Law, Sport
Specialisation: Principal areas of practice are EC law, competition law, judicial review, human rights and sports. Has acted in over 50 cases before ECJ/CFI including Case C-321/95P Greenpeace [1998] ECR I-1651, Case C-37/98 First Corporate Shipping The Times 16.11.00, Case C-1/00 Commission v France The Times 19.12.01. Cases before domestic courts and tribunals include: ex p Fayed [2001] Imm AR 134, ex p Camelot The Times 12.10.00, Gough v Chief Constable of Derbyshire [2001] 3 WLR 1392, Aberdeen Journals v DGFT [2002] CompAR 1.
Prof. Memberships: Bar European Group, Administrative Law Bar Association, COMBAR.
Career: Called in 1991. Legal Secretary, European Court of Justice, 1994-95. Member of B Panel to the Crown. Visiting Fellow, Durham University.
Publications: 'Remedies in EC Law' (2nd ed, Sweet & Maxwell).

HOULDER, Bruce QC
6 King's Bench Walk (Roy Amlot QC), London
(020) 7583 0410
Recommended in Crime

HOWARD, Charles QC
One King's Bench Walk (Anthony Hacking QC), London
(020) 7936 1500
Recommended in Family
Specialisation: Family law, not only conventional areas but also related matters including Inheritance Act and Probate disputes, constructive trust issues, family-oriented judicial review and solicitor's negligence in relation to family work.
Prof. Memberships: FLBA.
Career: Called to the Bar in 1975. In full-time practice since 1976. QC 1999.
Publications: Wildblood and Eaton 'Encyclopaedia of Family Provision in Family Matters' (contributor); 'Ancillary Relief Applications and Insolvency' (Sweet and Maxwell Practical Research Papers); speaker at 1999 Expert Witness Institute conference on 'Experts in the New Legal World' which was subsequently published as a booklet for the institute.
Personal: Education: St John's College, Cambridge 1969-72 and St Antony's College, Oxford 1972-73.

LEADERS AT THE BAR

HOWARD, M N QC
4 Essex Court (Nigel Teare QC), London
(020) 7653 5653
mnh@4sx.co.uk
Recommended in Arbitration
Specialisation: Principal areas of practice are international commercial and shipping law, including insurance, international trade and sale of goods. Extensive experience of arbitrations both as counsel and as arbitrator in many international arbitrations connected with international trade, shipping or insurance. Acts for shipowners, charterers, insurers, P&I clubs and salvage companies.
Prof. Memberships: COMBAR, London Common Law and Commercial Bar Association.
Career: Called to the Bar, Gray's Inn 1971 (Bencher 1995). Tenant at Queen Elizabeth Building 1972-89. Took Silk 1986. Member of the Panel of Salvage Arbitrators appointed by the Committee of Lloyd's since 1989. Joined 4 Essex Court in 1990. Appointed Recorder 1993. Leader of the Admiralty Bar 2000.
Publications: General editor, 'Phipson on Evidence' (15th Ed 2000), contributor of 'Frustration and Shipping Law' in 'Frustration and Force Majeure' (ed McKendrick, 2nd edn 1995), 'Foreign Currency Judgments in Contract Claims' in 'Consensus Ad Idem: Essays for Guenter Treitel' (ed Rose, 1996) Halsbury, Laws of England, title, 'Damages' and author of articles in legal periodicals.
Personal: Educated at Clifton College, 1960-64 and Magdalen College, Oxford 1965-70 (MA BCL). Leisure pursuits include books, music and sport. Born 10 June 1947. Lives in London. Other: Visiting Professor of Law, Essex University 1987-92; Visiting Professor of Maritime Law, University College, London 1996-99. Member, Editorial Board, Lloyd's Maritime Commercial Law Quarterly.

HOWARD, Mark QC
Brick Court Chambers
(Christopher Clarke QC), London
(020) 7379 3550
howard@brickcourt.co.uk
Recommended in Banking & Finance, Commercial (Litigation), Energy, Insurance, Professional Negligence
Specialisation: All areas of commercial law, particularly major contract disputes, City disputes and takeovers, insurance and reinsurance, banking, energy oil and gas, professional negligence, commercial fraud, international disciplinary arbitration, DTI and similar investigations.
Prof. Memberships: Combar, LCLCBA.
Career: Called to Bar in 1980, took Silk in 1996. Recent important cases in which involved include: Barings v Coopers and Lybrand; BHP v Dalmine; Elton John v Price Waterhouse; Fyffes Group v Templeman; R v Secretary of State for Department of Health ex parte Source Informatics; Messier Dowty v Sabena; Wurttembergische; Camdex v Bank of Zambia; Banco Santander v Banque Paribas; CATS v TGTL; Sphere Drake v Orion; Deepak v ICI; East European Shipping (market wide X/L reinsurance dispute); WSTC v Coopers & Lybrand; Axa v Field; CU v Mander; Henderson v Merrett and Ernst & Whinney; Denny and Walker v Willis Corroon and others; CNW v Girozentrale; Kuwait Airways Corporation v Kuwait Insurance Company; B&C v Samuel Montagu v BZW; Sudwestdeutsche Landesbank v Bank of Tokyo; Jones v Sherwood; AMF v Hashim; Channel Tunnel Group v Balfour Beatty. He has advised and acted for various parties in relation to a number of DTI and similar inquiries. Currently retained for insurers/reinsurers in relation to film finance litigation and for claimant banks in relation to solo litigation.
Personal: Born 1 April 1958. Educated at University of London – QMC and LSE (LL.B, 1978; LL.M,1979).

HOWE, Martin QC
8 New Square (Mark Platts-Mills QC), London
(020) 7405 4321
clerks@8newsquare.co.uk
Recommended in Information Technology, Intellectual Property
Specialisation: Specialist in all aspects of intellectual property, (patents, trade marks, copyrights, designs, confidential information etc) and European Community law relating both to IP and other fields. Many high technology cases, with particular emphasis on computing, information technology and internet field; also extensive experience in biotechnology/genetic engineering cases. Regular appearances in the ECJ, Luxembourg, and the European Patent Office, Munich. For comprehensive CV and list of recent cases, visit chambers' website at www.8newsquare.co.uk.
Prof. Memberships: Intellectual Property Bar Association (IPBA); The Intellectual Property Lawyers Organisation (TIPLO).
Career: Called 1978. QC 1996. Worked for IBM (UK), computer and engineering contract programmer 1976-78.
Publications: Halsbury's Laws on Trade Marks, 'Trade Names and Designs'; 'Europe and the Constitution after Maastricht' Nelson & Pollard, Oxford; editor 'Russell-Clarke on Industrial Design' (6th edn).
Personal: Born 1955. Educated at Winchester College; Trinity Hall, Cambridge (1977 BA Engineering and Law, 1979 MA).

HOWE, Robert
Blackstone Chambers (Presiley Baxendale QC & Charles Flint QC), London
(020) 7583 1770
roberthowe@blackstonechambers.com
Recommended in Commercial (Litigation), Media & Entertainment, Sport
Specialisation: Principal areas of practice are general domestic and international commercial law; entertainment/media and copyright; sport law; employment /disciplinary law. Handles a range of cases within these fields, including disputes involving conflicts of law, copyright/media, sale of goods and international trade, financial services, commercial fraud. Examples of interesting cases: Re London United Investments [1992] Ch 578 (CA - DTI Inquiry/privilege); Sundt Wrigley v Wrigley (marevas & legal costs/ financial services/ foreign exchange trading/ investment mandates); Baldock v Addison [1995] 1 WLR 158 (copyright/ discovery), 'The Jam' litigation (partnership/ copyright); 'The Smiths' litigation (partnership); Chief Rabbi v Jewish Chronicle (confidentiality/copyright); Edwards v The International Amateur Athletic Federation, The Times, 30th June 1997 (restraint of trade/ EU law -Arts.59/ 60); AG for Gibraltar v May [1999] 1 WLR 598 (CA - discovery & privilege); Memory Corporation v Sidhu, The Times, 3rd November 1999 (freezing orders/cross examination on assets); Virgin Retail Limited v Phonographic Performance Limited [1999] EMLR (Copyright Tribunal); Donohue v Armco Inc [2000] AER (Comm.) 641 (CA - conflicts of laws/anti-suit injunction).
Prof. Memberships: COMBAR, Employment Lawyers Association, Employment Law Bar Association.
Career: Called to the Bar 1988. Joined present chambers 1990.
Personal: Educated at Trinity Hall, Cambridge 1983-86 (MA) and at St. Edmunds Hall, Oxford 1988-89 (BCL). Middle Temple Fox Scholar 1988-89 (one year fellowship in the litigation department of a Canadian commercial law firm, *Frazer & Beatty*, Toronto). Born 10 June 1964.

HOWE, Timothy
Fountain Court (Anthony Boswood QC), London
(020) 7583 3335
Recommended in Banking & Finance, Insurance
Specialisation: Civil and commercial litigation (domestic and international), including banking, financial services, insurance, reinsurance, international trade, professional negligence, mergers and acquisitions, energy law and commercial arbitration. Cases include: Pensions mis-selling PI coverage litigation, film finance insurance litigation; Mannesmann A.G. v Goldman Sachs; Morgan Grenfell v SACE; JP Morgan Securities v MNI; Lloyd's Names Litigation; British Commonwealth v Atlantic Computers; Polly Peck International v StoyHayward; BBL v Eagle Star and US$2 billion Thyssen litigation in Bermuda. Clients include major investment and merchant banks, leading insurers and reinsurers, FTSE 100 companies, City law and accountancy firms.
Prof. Memberships: Executive Committee Member, COMBAR.
Career: Called 1987. Bermudian Bar 1998. Queen Mother's, Harmsworth and Astbury Scholarships, Middle Temple.
Publications: Co-author, 'Law of Bank Payments' (Longmans). Co-editor 'Commercial Court Procedure' (Sweet & Maxwell).
Personal: St. Paul's School, Magdalen College, Oxford (MA 1st Class Hons 1985).

HOWELL, John QC
Blackstone Chambers (Presiley Baxendale QC & Charles Flint QC), London
(020) 7583 1770
johnhowell@blackstonechambers.com
Recommended in Administrative & Public Law, Environment, Local Government, Planning
Specialisation: Public law, human rights, tortious liability and public bodies, local government law including local government powers, decision making and finance, planning, highways, compulsory purchase and compensation, education, social services, social security, housing, environment law, immigration and asylum, public utilities and procurement and European law.
Prof. Memberships: Committee member of the Administrative Law Bar Association and a member of the Planning and Environment Bar Association.
Career: Queen's College, Oxford. Called 1979, Queen's Counsel (1993).

HOWELL WILLIAMS, Craig
2 Harcourt Buildings
(Robin Purchas QC), London
(020) 7353 8415
Recommended in Planning
Specialisation: Town and country planning and environment law. Public inquiries: Heathrow Teminal 5 (on behalf of a consortium of 10 local authorities); Alconbury Developments Limited v Huntingdonshire District Council; Laing Homes v St Albans DC (key worker homes and private finance). Court cases include: R v Bristol City Council ex p Anderson [2000] 79 P&CR 358 (planning conditions and certainty) Court of Appeal; R (Alconbury Developments Limited) v SSE [2001] 2 WLR 1389 (planning and human rights) House of Lords; R v Environment Agency ex p Turnbull [2000] 8 Env LR 715 (judicial review and waste management licensing) High Court; R (Adlard) v SSE [2002] EWTTC Admin 7 (call in, human rights, reasons) High Court.
Prof. Memberships: Planning and Environment Bar Association; Parliamentary Bar.
Career: Called to the Bar in 1983. Junior Counsel to the Crown ('B' Panel) (1993-99); PEBA Secretary (1994-96).
Personal: Chairman of the London Luton Airport Consultative Committee.

LEADERS AT THE BAR

HOWELLS, James
Atkin Chambers (Robert Akenhead QC),
London
(020) 7404 0102
clerks@atkinchambers.law.co.uk
Recommended in Construction
Specialisation: Construction and engineering disputes both domestic and international with experience of litigation, arbitration and other terms of dispute resolution. Experience in engineering disputes has included a number of energy-related cases involving, amongst other things, oil and gas production platforms and rigs, FPSO's, gas storage caverns, combined power and desalination plant, power station/dams. Other work includes building and engineering disputes in Hong Kong, Indonesia, Australia, UAE, South Africa, Jersey, India and Tanzania. In the past year involved in seven month commercial court case regarding a North Sea drilling contract.
Prof. Memberships: TECBAR, LCLCBA.
Publications: One time editor of 'Building Law Reports' and of 'Technology and Construction Law Reports'.
Personal: MA (Cantab), BCL (Oxon).

HUBBLE, Ben
Four New Square (Justin Fenwick QC),
London
(020) 7822 2000
Recommended in Professional Negligence
Specialisation: Professional liability claims involving lawyers, accountants and auditors, insurance brokers and agents, construction professionals and healthcare as well as general commercial litigation, particularly banking and insurance. Junior Counsel for both the Law Society and the solicitor appellants in Etridge [2001] 3 WLR 1021 HL, the leading authority on undue influence and surety transactions, in which the House of Lords both allowed the solicitors' appeal and laid down the scheme for all future personal surety transactions.
Prof. Memberships: Professional Negligence Bar Association, COMBAR.
Career: Called to the Bar 1992.
Publications: Chapter on insurance brokers in 'Jackson & Powell: Professional Liability Precedents' (Sweet & Maxwell).
Personal: BA Hons (Oxon). Leisure interests: family and football.

HUDSON, Rachel
Trinity Chambers (Toby Hedworth QC),
Newcastle upon Tyne
(0191) 232 1927
info@trinitychambers.co.uk
Recommended in Family
Specialisation: All aspects of family law, with particular emphasis on care work (acting for local authorities, parents and guardians) and ancillary relief. In recent years has been involved in a large number of significant High Court cases. During the past year these have included issues of consent to medical treatment, fabricated illness and allegations of unlawful killing. Head of the Trinity Chambers' Family Group and the Bar representative on the Newcastle upon Tyne Family Court Business Committee. Trinity Chambers' pupillage and equal opportunities representative.
Prof. Memberships: FLBA, BAAF, North Eastern Circuit.
Career: Called to the Bar in 1985. Practised at Trinity Chambers since 1986.
Personal: Born in 1963. Educated at Newcastle upon Tyne Church High School and Queen Elizabeth Grammar School, Hexham. London School of Economics (LLB Law). Away from the Bar enjoys spending time with her family, music, sport and eating out.

HUGHES, Adrian
4 Pump Court, London
(020) 7842 5555
ahughes@4pumpcourt.com
Recommended in Construction
Specialisation: Broad commercial practice which includes insurance and reinsurance, shipping, commodities, construction and engineering and environmental law work. He has a particular interest in international arbitration and public international law.
Prof. Memberships: Recorder; Court Examiner; Lloyd's Arbitrator; CEDR Accredited Mediator; Panel member of the China International Economic and Trade Arbitration Commission; Chairman China Law Council; Bar Council International Relations Committee (Chairman of Far East Sub-Committee), COMBAR, TECBAR.
Career: Royal Naval Officer (1977-84). Called to the Bar 1984; practising from 4 Pump Court.
Personal: Educated at Warwick School and Wadham College, Oxford.

HUGHES, Simon
Keating Chambers, London
(020) 7544 2600
shughes@keatingchambers.com
Recommended in Construction
Specialisation: Construction and engineering litigation and arbitration and related commercial work.
Prof. Memberships: TECHBAR; COMBAR.
Publications: 'Chitty on Contracts' (specialist editor).
Personal: Magdalen College, Oxford (Scholar, Double First Class). Running. Resides in Camberwell. Fluent German.

HUMPHREYS, Richard
4-5 Gray's Inn Square (Elizabeth Appleby QC), London
(020) 7404 5252
Recommended in Planning

HUMPHRIES, Michael
2 Mitre Court Buildings (Guy Roots QC), London
(020) 7583 1380
Recommended in Planning
Specialisation: Practices principally in the areas of Town and Country Planning, and Compulsory Purchase and Compensation. Has appeared for major clients at many high profile planning inquiries including BAA plc at the Heathrow Terminal 5 inquiry, Capital Shopping Centres plc at the inquiry into the extension of the Westgate Centre (Oxford), the Walton Group plc at the Chavasse Park (Liverpool) retail inquiry and the Commission for Architecture and the Build Environment (CABE) at the Heron Tower inquiry. Recent Compulsory Purchase and Compensation clients include Union Rail Property, Eurotunnel, British Waterways Board and Prudential Assurance.
Prof. Memberships: Committee member of the Planning and Environmental Bar Association. Committee member of the Joint Planning Law Conference, Oxford. Member of the Anglo-American Real Property Institute.
Career: Called to the Bar in 1982 and joined current chambers in 1983.
Publications: Senior editor of Butterworths 'Compulsory Purchase and Compensation Service'. Lectured extensively on compulsory purchase and compensation issues.
Personal: Born 1959. Studied law at the University of Leicester. Married with three children. Leisure pursuits include reading, music and travel with family.

HUNJAN, Satinder QC
No5 Chambers (Gareth Evans QC), Birmingham
(0121) 606 0500
Recommended in Clinical Negligence

HUNT, Murray
Matrix Chambers, London
(020) 7404 3447
murrayhunt@matrixlaw.co.uk
Recommended in Administrative & Public Law, Education, Human Rights
Specialisation: Human rights and public law, including judicial review in all areas, especially economic, social and cultural rights, eg education, community care, health, mental health, rights of minorities. Recent representative cases include: Chapman v UK (right of Gypsies to traditional way of life); Edwards v UK (death in custody); Kansal (retrospectivity of HRA); Porter (Gypsies and planning); Lyons (enforceability of Strasbourg judgments); S v Brent (school exclusions); Carson (pensions discrimination); Colley (civil procedure); S v Plymouth (access to social services files); Holmes v GMC (professional discipline). He enjoys working as part of a relatively informal team with clients and those instructing him. He is particularly interested in the use of international standards in domestic courts, and the enforcement of public law standards in private contexts.
Career: BA, BCL (Oxford), LLM (Harvard). Barrister since 1992.
Publications: He is the author of 'Using Human Rights Law in English Courts' (1997) and writes and lectures frequently on human rights and public law.

HUNTER, Andrew
Blackstone Chambers (Presiley Baxendale QC & Charles Flint QC), London
(020) 7583 1770
andrewhunter@blackstonechambers.com
Recommended in Commercial (Litigation)
Specialisation: Commercial law (reinsurance, civil fraud, financial services); sport and music; public law.
Prof. Memberships: COMBAR.
Career: Called to the Bar 1993; practice at Blackstone Chambers 1994-present.
Personal: School: Royal Belfast Academical Institution. University: St Edmund Hall, Oxford (BA Hons in Jurisprudence; BLL).

HUNTER, Ian QC
Essex Court Chambers (Gordon Pollock QC), London
(020) 7813 8000
Recommended in Arbitration, Aviation, Insurance
Specialisation: Broad-based commercial practice. More particularly arbitration, aviation, banking, conflict of laws, European law, financial services, insurance and reinsurance, international commercial fraud, professional negligence and shipping.
Career: Pembroke College, Cambridge MA (Law; double first) 1966; LLB 1967; Harvard Law School, Cambridge, USA LLM 1968. Called to the English Bar 1967. Called to the Bar of New South Wales 1993. Queen's Counsel 1980. Bencher 1986. Recorder 1986. Deputy High Court Judge 1993.
Personal: Born 1944. Fluent French.

HUSAIN, Raza
Matrix Chambers, London
(020) 7404 3447
Recommended in Human Rights, Immigration
Specialisation: Practises mainly in public law with emphasis on immigration and human rights. Co-author with Nicholas Blake QC of 'Immigration and the Human Rights Act 1998'. Important cases include: Radiom and Shingara (ECJ), Kaur (ECJ intervenor), Adan, (HL), Lamey (PC), Farrakhan (CA), Robinson (CA), Chahal (CA), Waite (CA), Saad (the 'Oakington' case) (CA intervenor), Adimi (QBD), Quaquah (QBD), Cakmak and Uluyol (QBD), Mills and Poole (QBD).
Prof. Memberships: Council Member of JUSTICE, Liberty Human Rights Panel, Administrative Law Bar Association.
Career: Exeter College, Oxford (1987-90). Called 1993. 2 Garden Court 1994-2000; founder member of present chambers.

HUSSEY, Ann
1 Hare Court (Bruce Blair QC), London
(020) 7797 7070
Recommended in Family
Specialisation: All areas of ancillary relief with extensive experience in both

LEADERS AT THE BAR

middle income and complex big money cases. Lectures extensively on matrimonial finance.
Prof. Memberships: FLBA.
Career: Middle Temple. Called to the Bar 1981.
Personal: Born 1959. Educated St Albans Girls' Grammar School and University of Kent. Married with four children.

HUTTON, Caroline
Enterprise Chambers (Anthony Mann QC), London
(020) 7405 9471
carolinehutton@enterprisechambers.com
Recommended in Agriculture, Property Litigation
Specialisation: Practice covers all aspects of real property law, principally landlord and tenant (commercial, agricultural and residential) and including conveyancing, boundaries, easements, equitable rights and trusts of land, mortgages and professional negligence, insolvency and fraud matters related to major property. Major cases included Saunders v Edwards, Coastplace Ltd v Hartley, Sutton (Hastoe) H.A. v Williams, Midland Bank v Chart Enterprises, Culworth Estates v Licensed Victuallers, Aspen Properties v Ratcliffe, Ponderosa v Pengap, Adams v Michael Batt, Hertsmere Borough Council v Brent Walker Group, Nationwide BS v James Beauchamp and Well Barn Shooting Ltd v G. Shackleton & Others. Clients include property companies, retailers and banks as well as many private clients. Contributed to many commercial conferences on property law and landlord and tenant. Directly instructed by numerous valuers and surveyors.
Prof. Memberships: Justice, Association of Women Barristers, Bar European Group, Secretary of Property Bar Association.
Career: Called to the Bar 1979 and joined Enterprise Chambers 1981 after pupillage with Kirk Reynolds QC. Chairman, Disciplinary and Appeals Tribunal for Licenced Conveyancing 1988-93. Fellow of chartered Institute of Arbitrators.
Publications: Co-editor of 'Commercial Property Disputes' (Sweet & Maxwell, 1999).
Personal: Educated at Clare College, Cambridge 1975-78. Leisure pursuits include embroidery, reading, walking, theatre and art history. Born 25 March 1956. Lives in London with MP husband and two sons.

HYAMS, Oliver
5 Paper Buildings (Richard King), London
(020) 7815 3200
oliverhyams@5paper.com
Recommended in Education
Specialisation: Education; related public law; employment; discrimination. Recent reported cases include Hagen v ICI chemicals & Polymers Ltd [2002] IRCR 31; S v Brent London Borough Council [2002] The Times, 4 June.
Prof. Memberships: Administrative Law Bar Association; Employment Law Bar Association; Education Law Association; Employment Lawyers Association.
Career: Called 1989.
Publications: 'Law of Education' (1998, Sweet & Maxwell); 'Employment in Schools – A Legal Guide' (2000, Jordans); annotations for 'Current Law Statutes'; for all Education Acts since 1998 and Employment Act 2002.

HYDE, Charles
Albion Chambers (Neil Ford QC), Bristol
(0117) 927 2144
Recommended in Family

HYLAND, J Graham K QC
Broadway House
(J Graham K Hyland QC), Bradford
(01274) 722560
Recommended in Crime
Specialisation: Crime.
Prof. Memberships: Criminal Bar Association.
Career: Call 1978 (Inner Temple). Recorder 1992. QC 1998.

IFE, Linden
Enterprise Chambers (Anthony Mann QC), London
(020) 7405 9471
Recommended in Company, Insolvency
Specialisation: Principal area of practice is commercial chancery, including insolvency, company, property, professional negligence, banking and securities and financial services. Recent reported cases include: Sterling Estates v Pickard [1997] (lease disclaimer by liquidator); TSB v Platts [1997] (cross-claims in bankruptcy); Re Double S Printers Limited [1998] (fixed and floating charges); SJB Stephenson v Mandy [1999] (third party costs orders); Michael Gerson v Wilkinson [2001] (title of competing finance companies to goods); Dexter v Harley [2001] (Brussels Convention and constructive trust claims). Member of the Association of Business Recovery Professionals.

INGLIS-JONES, Nigel J QC
35 Essex Street (Christopher Wilson-Smith QC), London
(020) 7353 6381
Recommended in Pensions
Specialisation: Specialist with over 40 years experience in occupational pension schemes; also deals with other trusts, contract and tort. During past 15 years he has fought many of the major cases concerning occupational pension schemes. These include: Re Imperial Foods' Pension Scheme, Re Courage Group's Pension Scheme (1987), Mettoy Pension Trustees v Evans (1990), LRT Pension Fund Trustee Company v Hatt (1993), British Coal corporation v British Coal Staff Superannuation Scheme (1994), Century Life plc v Pension Ombudsman (1997), Hillsdown Holdings v Pension Ombudsman (1997), Legal and General Assurance Society v Pension Ombudsman (1999), Coloroll Pension Trustees v Sedgwick Noble Lowndes (1999), Re National Grid plc and others v Laws and Mayes (1998, 1999, 2001), Re The National Provident Institute Pension Scheme (2000), The Merchant Navy Ratings Pension scheme (2000), and The British Airways Pension Scheme (2001 and 2002) and Re: The Hoover (1987) Pension Scheme (2002). Author of 'The Law of Occupational Pension Schemes' (Sweet and Maxwell); has spoken at and chaired many conferences.
Prof. Memberships: Chancery Bar Association, Association of Pensions Lawyers, Western Circuit. Bencher of the Inner Temple since 1982.
Career: National Service with the Grenadier Guards (subaltern) 1953-55. Called to the Bar in 1959 and joined chambers at Essex Street in 1960. Took Silk in 1982. Recorder 1978-93. Deputy Social Security Commissioner 1993-2002.
Personal: Educated at Eton College 1948-53 and Trinity College, Oxford 1955-58. Leisure pursuits include fishing, collecting English drinking glass and English miniature glass, gardening and travelling. A member of the congregation of St Mary's Church, Bryanston Square. Born 7 May 1935. Lives in London.

INGRAM, Nigel
2 Bedford Row (William Clegg QC), London
(020) 7440 8888
Recommended in Fraud

INMAN, Melbourne QC
1 Fountain Court
(Melbourne Inman QC), Birmingham
(0121) 236 5721
Recommended in Crime

IRWIN, Stephen QC
Doughty Street Chambers
(Geoffrey Robertson QC), London
(020) 7404 1313
Recommended in Clinical Negligence, Personal Injury, Product Liability
Specialisation: Principal area of practice is clinical negligence covering a broad range of serious medical accidents including cerebral palsy, surgical and other medical cases. Other main areas of work are major personal injury cases, legal negligence arising out of public law cases with a medical or health content. Major cases include the Human Growth Hormone/Creutzfeldt-Jacob disease, BSE-linked CJD litigation, PTSD for servicemen and organophosphate sheepdip group action, Gulf War Syndrome, Clunis v Camden & Islington HA Alder Hay body parts case; Birmingham Orthopaedic Hospital Bone Tumour Service; and the Clapham Rail disaster enquiry. Author of 'Practitioner's Guide to Medical Negligence' (Legal Action Group, 1995). Regularly lectures and writes on medico-legal issues. Chairman, Remuneration Committee of Bar Council.
Prof. Memberships: Professional Negligence Bar Association, Association of Personal Injury Lawyers, Action for the Victims of Medical Accidents, Personal Injury Bar Association, Justice.
Career: Called to the Bar 1976 and tenant of No.1 Dr. Johnson's Buildings, founder member of Doughty Street Chambers. Called to the Bar of Northern Ireland 1997. QC 1997.
Personal: Educated at Methodist College, Belfast 1961-71 and Jesus College, Cambridge 1972-75. Leisure pursuits include reading prose and verse, Irish history and hillwalking. Born 5 February 1953. Lives in Radlett, Herts.

ISAACS, Barry
3-4 South Square (Michael Crystal QC & Lord Alexander of Weedon QC), London
(020) 7696 9900
barryisaacs@southsquare.com
Recommended in Insolvency
Specialisation: Commercial, insolvency, company, professional negligence, insurance. Recently appeared or advised in the following cases: BCCI v Bank of England (claim for misfeasance in public office); Equitable Life (scheme of arrangement); Bermuda Fire & Marine (eight-month trial in Bermuda); Global TeleSystems (scheme of arrangement); Lloyd's of London v names; and in relation to the following insolvencies: Enron; HIH Insurance; MCC; Arrows; Ferranti; Nemgia; CA Pacific (Hong Kong). Recent reported cases include: Munns v Perkins [2002] BPIR 120; Three Rivers DC v Bank of England (HL) [2001] 2 All ER 513; Society of Lloyd's v Waters [2001] BPIR 698; Re Mathew [2001] BPIR 531.
Prof. Memberships: Associate of the Society of Actuaries.
Career: 1994-present, practising barrister; 1991-93, investment manager, venture capital, Societe Generale; 1987-91, strategy consultant, Bain & Company. MA (Harvard), MA (Oxon).
Personal: Tennis, karate (black belt).

ISAACS, Paul
Mercury Chambers
(Benjamin Nolan QC), Leeds
(0113) 234 2265
Recommended in Family
Specialisation: Highly regarded specialist in matrimonial property work. The counsel of choice of the leading firms of solicitors in cases involving substantial assets and complex accountancy/valuation evidence. Recent cases have involved assets of £10-40 million.
Personal: Read Law at Trinity College, Cambridge (Lizette Bentwich prize winner). Called to the Bar in 1974. Recorder of the Crown Court approved to try family cases.

ISAACS, Stuart QC
3-4 South Square (Michael Crystal QC & Lord Alexander of Weedon QC), London

LEADERS AT THE BAR

(020) 7696 9900
clerks@southsquare.com
Recommended in Commercial (Litigation)
Specialisation: Principal areas of practice are commercial law, including arbitration, banking, insurance/reinsurance and shipping and all aspects of EU law. Clients include major banks and other financial institutions, insurers/reinsurers, government and other public bodies, trade organisations and multinational corporate clients. LCIA, ICC and SIAC Arbitrator. Author, 'EC Banking Law' (2nd Ed, 1994); Consultant Editor, Butterworths' EC Case Citator; Co-editor, 'The EC Regulations on Insolvency Proceedings' (OUP, 2002). Has addressed many seminars on commercial and EU law topics both in the UK and Singapore.
Prof. Memberships: COMBAR, Chancery Bar Association, Member of the New York Bar.
Career: Called to the Bar 1975. Took silk 1991. Appointed Recorder 1997.
Personal: Educated at The Haberdashers' Aske's School, Elstree 1963-70; Downing College, Cambridge 1971-74 (MA Law, Double First); and Universite Libre de Bruxelles 1975-76 (Licence Special en Droit Europeen: Grande Distinction). Speaks French, German and Spanish. Leisure pursuits include travel and languages. Born 8 April 1952. Lives in London. Married with one son.

IVIMY, Cecilia
11 King's Bench Walk Chambers (Eldred Tabachnik QC & James Goudie QC), London
(020) 7632 8500
ivimy@11kbw.com
Recommended in Employment
Specialisation: Judicial review, human rights, local government, employment and discrimination law.
Prof. Memberships: Employment Law Bar Association; Administrative Law Bar Association.
Career: Called to the Bar 1995.
Publications: Contributor to: Halsbury's Laws 'Administrative Law' (2001 reissue), Tolleys 'Employment Law Handbook', Butterworths 'Local Government Law', 'Local Authorities and the Human Rights Act' (Butterworths).
Personal: Merton College, Oxford BA (1st class); City University Dip Law (distinction).

IVORY, Thomas QC
One Essex Court (Lord Grabiner QC), London
(020) 7583 2000
Recommended in Commercial (Litigation)
Specialisation: Principal areas of practice include banking, general commercial disputes, jurisdiction disputes, share sales, oil and gas, telecommunications, professional negligence, pensions.
Prof. Memberships: COMBAR; Chancery Bar Association.

JACKLIN, Susan
St John's Chambers (Christopher Sharp QC), Bristol
(0117) 921 3456
clerks@stjohnschambers.co.uk
Recommended in Family
Specialisation: Matrimonial finance, cohabitation disputes, Inheritance Act claims, professional negligence in ancillary relief context. Children cases, particularly care applications involving allegations of physical and sexual abuse.
Prof. Memberships: Family Law Bar Associations, Criminal Bar Association.
Career: Durham University (BA). Called to the Bar 1980. Assistant Recorder 1998. Recorder 2000.

JACKSON, Andrew
3 Fountain Court (Robert Juckes QC), Birmingham
(0121) 236 5854
clerks@3fc.co.uk
Recommended in Crime
Specialisation: Crime: Prosecution and Defence work.
Prof. Memberships: Criminal Bar Association.
Career: Manchester University: [1981-84] BA (Hons). The City University: (1984-85). Diploma in law.

JACKSON, Judith QC
9 Old Square (Michael Driscoll QC), London
(020) 7405 4682
judith.jackson@9oldsquare.co.uk
Recommended in Property Litigation
Specialisation: Commercial and residential property litigation, particularly landlord and tenant and restrictive covenants, chancery and professional negligence. Cases include: Prudential Assurance Co Ltd v Newman Industries Ltd (minority shareholders' rights), Re Bond Worth (retention of title), Abbey National v Moss (trusts for sale), UCB Bank plc v Beasley (s70 (1)(g), Locabail UK Ltd v Bayfield Properties (conjoined appeals on Judicial bias), Scott v National Trust (Judicial Review of Charity), Malekshad v Howard de Walden Estates Ltd (whether house and mews house were together a house).
Prof. Memberships: Chancery Bar Association; Professional Negligence Bar Association; Property Bar Association.
Career: Queen Mary College, London (1970-73) (LLB); (1973-74) (LLM). Called to Bar in 1975. Took Silk in 1994. Bencher of Lincoln's Inn 2001. Director of Bar Mutual Indemnity Fund Ltd (1999).
Publications: Contributor to Megarry's Rent Acts (11th edn).

JACKSON, Peter QC
4 Paper Buildings (Lionel Swift QC), London
(020) 7583 0816
pj@4pb.com
Recommended in Family
Specialisation: Children (private and public law); adoption; medical treatment.
Career: Called 1978 and joined chambers 1979. Recorder 1998. Silk 2000. Cases include: B (Adult: Refusal of Treatment) [2002] EWHC 429 (Fam); B (Interim Care Order) [2002] ECWA Civ 25; R (Judicial Intervention) EWCA Civ 1880; F v Lambeth Borough Council [2002] 1 FLR 217; O (Paternity, Blood Tests) [2000] 2 WLR 1284; R (Inter-County Adoption) [1999] 1 WLR 1324; K (Adoption) [1997] 2 FLR 221; C (Refusal of Medical Treatment) [1994] 1 WLR 290.
Personal: Born 9 December 1955. Educated at Marlborough College 1969-73; Brasenose College, Oxford 1974-77.

JACKSON, Simon
Park Court Chambers (Robert Smith QC), Leeds
(0113) 243 3277
Recommended in Personal Injury
Specialisation: Clinical negligence/personal injury: clinical negligence, disciplinary proceedings, GMC proceedings. Inquests: specialising in cases involving police, local authorities and hospitals. Criminal Law: homicide, sexual offences, fraud and regulatory offences. Attorney General's List for HMCE and HSE. Instructions also received from MDOs. Recent cases include: R v Hull Coroner for East Riding of Yorkshire and Kingston upon Hull, ex parte Dawson and others (2001), Administrative court; R v Hayward, 1998 CA (excise duty/VAT/fraud); R v Dallagher, 2002 CA (admissibility of ear print evidence).
Prof. Memberships: PNBA, PIBA, CBA.
Career: LLB (Hons), Leeds University. Called 1982.

JACOBS, Nigel
4 Essex Court (Nigel Teare QC), London
(020) 7653 5653
njacobs@4sx.com
Recommended in Shipping
Specialisation: Practice encompasses shipping, insurance, admiralty and general commercial work. Nigel was the successful counsel for the cargo interests in the 'Starsin' (both at first instance and in the Court of Appeal). He was junior counsel to the Marchioness Action Group at the Public Inquiry. Other recent cases include the 'Happy Ranger' (construction of Hague/Hague-Visby Rules); Aoun v Bahri (security for costs) and 'Pride of Donegal' (unseaworthiness/marine insurance). He sits as a mediator and maritime arbitrator.
Prof. Memberships: Bar Council, COMBAR.
Career: Called to the Bar 1983 and joined 4 Essex Court in 1986.
Personal: Educated at Pembroke College, Cambridge 1979-82 (MA) and Trinity College, Cambridge 1983-84 (LLM). Leisure pursuits include gym, tennis, cycling, theatre and cinema. Born 31 May 1960. Lives in London.

JACOBS, Richard QC
Essex Court Chambers (Gordon Pollock QC), London
(020) 7813 8000
rjacobs@essexoourt.net
Recommended in Commercial (Litigation), Insurance, Shipping
Specialisation: All types of commercial work – shipping, insurance, reinsurance, professional negligence, commodities, banking.
Career: Pembroke College, Cambridge MA (1st Class Hons), 1978. Called to the Bar, 1979.
Personal: Born 1956.

JAFFA, Ronald
3 Gray's Inn Square (Rock Tansey QC), London
(020) 7520 5600
Recommended in Crime
Specialisation: Long-term experience of defending those charged with serious crime including murder, robbery, rape, drugs trafficking, importation and serious assaults. Often instructed in cases where the defendant is difficult, has psychiatric problems or where the allegation revolves around sexual abuse of children. Has conducted many fraud cases involving companies, company VAT, charities, local authority employees, advanced fee and mortgages.
Prof. Memberships: Criminal Bar Association, European Criminal Bar Association.
Career: LLB Nottingham University. One of the founder members who set up the Bar Pro Bono Unit. A member of the management committee solely responsible for considering all applications relating to criminal work.
Personal: Married with two children. An elected trustee of the Rett Syndrome Association UK, a national charity helping families, carers and sufferers of this neurological disorder which only affects females.

JAFFERJEE, Aftab
2 Harcourt Buildings, Atkinson Bevan Chambers (Nicholas Atkinson QC & John Bevan QC), London
(020) 7353 2112
clerks@2hb.co.uk
Recommended in Crime
Specialisation: Senior Treasury Counsel to the Crown at the Central Criminal Court since 2001; Junior Treasury Counsel 1997-2001. Recent cases include prosecution of The Greek Embassy siege, the Afghan Airlines hijack and the NATO Secrets trial. Specialises in criminal medical negligence.
Prof. Memberships: Criminal Bar Association.
Career: Past member of the Committee of the Criminal Bar Association. Past member of the Professional Conduct Committee of the Bar.

JAMES, Alun
3 Temple Gardens Tax Chambers (Richard Bramwell QC), London
(020) 7853 7884
clerks@taxcounsel.co.uk
Recommended in Tax

LEADERS AT THE BAR

Specialisation: Tax and VAT. Litigation: appeals to the General and Special Commissioners, the VAT and Duties Tribunal and the higher courts, and tax-related professional negligence. Appears both for and against HM Customs & Excise being a member of the Crown's Provincial Panel. Revenue (SCO) enquiries and C&E investigations: advice on handling the enquiry/investigation and representation on appeal. Tax advice generally: particularly corporate tax issues including reorganisations.
Prof. Memberships: Revenue Bar Association.
Career: Called to the Bar 1986 and joined 3 Temple Gardens 1988. Also a member of Exchange Chambers (William Waldron QC), Liverpool.
Publications: Co-author of 'Taxation of Companies and Company Reconstructions' (Sweet & Maxwell, 6th-8th edn).
Personal: Scholar of St John's College, Oxford (BA, Hons 1st Class, Jurisprudence, BCL). Born 13 May 1964.

JAMES, Christopher
No5 Chambers (Gareth Evans QC), Birmingham
(0121) 606 0500
Recommended in Family

JAMES, Ian
Octagon House Chambers (Guy Ayers & Andrew Lindquist), Norwich
(01603) 623186
Recommended in Crime

JAMES, Michael
Enterprise Chambers (Anthony Mann QC), Leeds
(0113) 246 0391
michaeljames@enterprisechambers.com
Recommended in Commercial (Litigation)
Specialisation: Commercial and chancery litigation, with particular expertise in disputes with an international aspect. Wide experience of employment law and directors' disqualification cases.
Prof. Memberships: Chancery Bar Association. Chartered Institute of Arbitrators. Association of Northern Mediators.
Career: Open Scholar at Christ Church, Oxford. Solicitor 1983-93.
Personal: Born 17 May 1953. Married, two children.

JAMESON, Rodney
No.6 Barristers Chambers (Jennifer Kershaw QC), Leeds
(0113) 245 9763
Recommended in Crime

JANNER, Daniel QC
23 Essex Street (Michael Lawson QC), London
(020) 7413 0353
danieljanner@23essexstreet.co.uk
Recommended in Crime
Specialisation: Crime (general); police law.
Prof. Memberships: 23 Essex Street.
Career: Called to Bar in 1980 (Jules Thorn Scholar, Middle Temple).
Publications: Editor 'Criminal Appeal Reports' since 1994.
Personal: President Cambridge Union Society (1978).

JARMAN, Milwyn QC
9 Park Place (Ian Murphy QC), Cardiff
(029) 2038 2731
milwyn@aol.com
Recommended in Chancery
Specialisation: Chancery, planning and local government, personal injury. Reported cases include R v Port Talbot Borough Council ex p Jones [1988] 2 ALL ER 207 (judicial review: housing); R v Dairy Produce Quota Tribunal for England and Wales ex p Davies [1987] 2 EGLR 7 (judicial review: agriculture); R v West Glamorgan County Council ex p Morris and Hood-Williams [1992] JPL 374 (judicial review planning), Huish v Ellis [1995] BCC 462 (professional negligence); Harris v Welsh Development Agency [1999] 3 EGLR 207 (compulsory purchase compensation); Bolwell v Radcliffe Homes Ltd [1999] PIQR P243 (personal injury); Jones v Morgan [2001] Lloyd's Rep Bank 323 (mortgages).
Prof. Memberships: Chancery Bar Association, Bristol and Cardiff Chancery Bar Association, Wales Commercial Law Association, Wales Public Law and Human Rights Association.
Career: Called 1980. QC 2001. Recorder 2002.
Personal: Born 1957. LLB (Wales) 1st Class. LLM (Cantab).

JARVIS, John QC
3 Verulam Buildings (Christopher Symons QC & John Jarvis QC), London
(020) 7831 8441
chambers@3vb.com
Recommended in Arbitration, Banking & Finance, Commercial (Litigation), Fraud
Specialisation: Principal areas of practice are banking (both litigation and transactional work) and commercial law. Specialist experience in banking and financing work, insolvency and professional negligence. Practice covers law and practice of international finance, project development and finance, trade disputes, professional liability, insolvency, constructive trusts and arbitration. Has drafted all the major security documentation for a new bank and appeared in a number of the leading banking cases such as, Tai Hing Cotton Ltd v Lin Chong Bank Ltd [1986] AC 80 in the Privy Council and the Etridge appeals in the House of Lords, 2001. Has also appeared in Dubai Aluminium (2001), Suomitomo (2000), Polly Peck (1998), Grupo Torras (1998) and for Ian Maxwell before the Select Committee. Other reported cases include: Barclays Bank v Goff (2001); PIC v Kantupan (2001); Barclays Bank v O'Brien [1993] (priority in equity of wife's interest against creditor); Deposit Protection Board y Dalia [1993] (validity of equitable assignments to enable claim on fund); Wadha Bank v Arab Bank [1993] (legality of performance bonds and counter guarantees); Re Arrows Ltd Nos 1-4 [1992-93]; Brink Mat Ltd v Noye [1991] (bank as constructive trustee) and Barclays Bank Plc v Taylor, TSB v Taylor [1989] (extent of bank's duty of confidentiality). International Editor of the 'Journal of Banking and Finance Law and Practice'. Author of a number of articles in banking law. Co-author of 'Lender Liability' (1993), and contributing author to 'Banks; Liability and Risk'(1995).
Prof. Memberships: COMBAR (Chairman 1995-97), London Common Law and Commercial Bar Association.
Career: Called to the Bar and joined present Chambers 1970. Took Silk 1989. Appointed Recorder 1992. Sits as a Deputy High Court Judge.
Personal: Educated at King's College School, Wimbledon 1955-65. Open Exhibitioner and Senior Scholar of Emmanuel College (and Cambridge University Scholar) 1966-69 (MA Hons). Governor of King's College School. Leisure pursuits include riding, tennis, sailing, skiing, cycling, collecting modern British paintings, opera and gardening. Born 20 November 1947.

JAY, Robert QC
39 Essex Street (Nigel Pleming QC), London
(020) 7832 1111
rj@39essex.co.uk
Recommended in Administrative & Public Law
Specialisation: Extensive practice in public law, judicial review and general common law, having been Junior Council to the Crown (Common Law) between 1989 and 1998.
Prof. Memberships: Chairman of the Administrative Law Bar Association.
Career: QC (1998).
Personal: Interests: cooking, classical music and languages.

JEANS, Christopher QC
11 King's Bench Walk Chambers (Eldred Tabachnik QC & James Goudie QC), London
(020) 7632 8500
clerksroom@11kbw.com
Recommended in Employment
Specialisation: Specialises in employment law.
Prof. Memberships: Employment Lawyers Association, Employment Law Bar Association.
Career: 1974-77: LLB degree at King's College, London. 1977-79: BCL degree at St John's College, Oxford. 1980: called to the Bar (Gray's Inn). Since 1983 has practised full time at the Bar, specialising in employment law, at chambers of Lord Irvine QC (now chambers of Eldred Tabachnik QC and James Goudie QC).
Personal: Main interests: sport (especially football and cricket), travel, theatre, cinema.

JEARY, Stephen
Temple Chambers (David J M Aubrey QC), Cardiff
(029) 2039 7364
Recommended in Crime

JEFFORD, Nerys
Keating Chambers, London
(020) 7544 2600
njefford@keatingchambers.com
Recommended in Construction
Specialisation: Construction and engineering; domestic and international arbitration; professional negligence.
Career: Qualified 1986; Gray's Inn; member of editorial team 'Keating on Building Contracts'.
Personal: Lady Margaret Hall, Oxford (1984, MA); University of Virginia (1985, LLM, Fulbright Scholar). London Welsh Chorale.

JEFFREYS, Alan QC
Farrar's Building (John Leighton Williams QC), London
(020) 7583 9241
Recommended in Personal Injury
Specialisation: Principal area of practice is personal injury litigation, both claimant and defendant. Work includes motor, employment and public liability claims. Other main areas of practice are clinical and solicitors negligence, general insurance, and health and safety.
Prof. Memberships: PIBA; CLCBA.
Career: Called to the Bar in 1970 (Gray's Inn) and joined Farrar's Building in 1971. Recorder since 1993. Took Silk April 1996. Member of the CICAP 1999-2002.
Personal: Born 27 September 1947. Lives in London.

JELF, Simon
48 Bedford Row (Roderick I'Anson Banks), London
(020) 7430 2005
sjelf@partnershipcounsel.co.uk
Recommended in Partnership
Specialisation: Exclusively partnership law. Deals with a wide variety of partnership matters, including the drafting and construction of agreements, and is known for taking a hands-on commercial approach in providing advice and representation in partnership disputes. Acts for professional and trading partnerships, including accountants, doctors and solicitors.
Prof. Memberships: Association of Partnership Practitioners.
Career: Called to the Bar (Gray's Inn) 1996. Law Commission 1996-98, principally involved with the review of partnership law. Joined 48 Bedford Row (chambers of Roderick I'Anson Banks) in 1999.
Publications: Assists in editing the 'Encyclopedia of Professional Partnerships'.
Personal: Educated at John Taylor High School, Burton-upon-Trent and University of East Anglia. Leisure pursuits include property renovation and golf. Born 21 February 1973. Lives in London.

JENKINS, T Alun QC
Queen Square Chambers (Don Tait & T Alun Jenkins QC), Bristol
(01179) 211966
crime@qs-c.co.uk
Recommended in Crime

Specialisation: Criminal and commercial fraud, diversion frauds, money laundering and large scale importation of drugs. Prosecuted: Op Barlow – Customs & Excise diversion fraud; Op Rhythm and Op Jaegar C and E importation of drugs; Op Sirrocco, diversion fraud. Defended: Large scale distribution of drugs, passing-off fraud, long firm fraud, computer frauds, Mareva and Anton Piller injunctions. Defended 'Op Mamba' mobile telephone VAT fraud [2001].
Career: Recorder.

JENNINGS, Anthony QC
Matrix Chambers, London
(020) 7404 3447
Recommended in Crime
Specialisation: Involved in major Crown Court criminal cases including terrorism, animal rights, drugs, prison disturbances, armed robbery, murder and fraud. Cases include disturbances at Risley Remand Centre (1990), Dartmoor Prison (1991), Manchester United supporters riot on ferry, dolphin interference case; IRA cases: MacFlhoinn; Hayes and Taylor; Gallagher Sehan (largest ever police seizure of heroin); Ronnie Lee (animal rights bombing); Whitemoor prison egress, North Wales sex abuse inquiry; Brownbill v M.P.C. (£150,000 damages against the police); Michael Smith v Police (largest damages in W. Midlands); Keith Birchall (murder conviction quashed on appeal). Arms from Serbia/W. Midlands Police Corruption (1999). Condron v UK and Beckler v UK.
Prof. Memberships: Criminal Bar Association.
Career: Called to the Bar 1983 and Northern Ireland Bar in 1987, joined current chambers in 2000. CBA lecture November 1999 and 2000, and Human Rights lecturer for Bar Council & CBA 2000. Recorder (2000).
Publications: Editor of 'Justice under Fire: The Abuse of Civil Liberties in Northern Ireland' (1990). Written articles on criminal justice for 'The Times', 'Independent', 'Guardian', 'Archbold News' and 'The New Law Journal'. Contributing editor of 'Archbold'. Contributor to Simor and Emmerson, 'Human Rights Practice' and Starmer, Strange and Whittaker, 'Criminal Justice, Police Powers & Human Rights'.
Personal: Educated at St Patrick's College, Belfast 1971-78, Warwick University 1978-81 and Inns of Court School of Law 1981-82. Leisure pursuits include theatre, Italy, Liverpool FC and Irish literature. Born 11 May 1960. Lives in London.

JOFFE, Victor QC
Serle Court (Lord Neill of Bladen QC), London
(020) 7242 6105
Recommended in Chancery, Insolvency

JOHNS, Alan
9 Old Square (Michael Driscoll QC), London
(020) 7405 4682
Recommended in Property Litigation
Specialisation: Main expertise is in property litigation, including landlord and tenant, mortgages, real property and professional negligence, but is experienced in a broad range of modern Chancery work. Recent cases include: Upton v Taylor & Colley (1999) (Divisional Court) and Inntrepeneur Pub cv (IPC) Ltd v Deans (1999).
Career: Called to the bar in 1994. Part-time tutor at Magdalen College, Oxford during 1996 and 1997.
Personal: Helston School, Cornwall. Magdalen College, Oxford. Member of Philosophy Football Football Club.

JOHNSON, Christine
14 Castle Street (Andrew Edis QC), Liverpool
(0151) 236 4421
Recommended in Family
Specialisation: Children and financial relief. Crime.
Prof. Memberships: FBLA. RCN (Royal College of Nursing). CBA. Bar Race Relationships Committee.
Career: Registerer Nurse, Registerer Sick Childrens Nurse, Registerer Midwife.

JOHNSON, Edwin
9 Old Square (Michael Driscoll QC), London
(020) 7405 4682
Recommended in Property Litigation
Specialisation: Property, chancery and commercial litigation and advisory work. In particular commercial and property disputes, professional negligence, mortgages, general landlord and tenant (including leasehold enfranchisement), conveyancing, easements, restrictive covenants, property rights, insolvency and commercial contracts, building and construction work and insurance work. Cases of interest include: Church Commissioners v Ibrahim [1997] 1 EGLR 13 (right to indemnity costs in leases); Gardner v Marsh & Parsons [1997] 1 WLR 489 (mitigation of damages for professional negligence); Rothschild v Bell [2000] QB 33 (bankruptcy and termination of long residential tenancy); UCB Corporate Services Ltd v Halifax (SW) Ltd [2000] 1 EGLR 87 (duty of valuer in mortgage valuation); Wallis Fashion Group Ltd v CGU Life Assurance Ltd [2000] 2 EGLR 49 (right to require authorised guarantee agreement on assignment of lease); Rosen v Trustees of the Campden Charities [2001] 3 WLR 1470 (disregard of improvements on leasehold enfranchisement); Hurstwood v Motor and General and Aldersley Insurance Services [2002] PNLR 250 (meaning of same damage under Civil Liability (Contribution) Act 1978); John Lyon's Charity v Shalson [2002] 2 EG 185 (disregard of improvements on leasehold enfranchisement).
Prof. Memberships: Chancery Bar Association. Professional Negligence Bar Association.
Career: Called to the Bar in 1987 and joined 9 Old Square in 1988. Educated at Lancing College and Christ Church College, Oxford (BA). Appointed Standing Counsel to the Rent Assessment Panel 2000.

JOHNSON, Michael
9 St. John Street (John Hand QC), Manchester
(0161) 955 9000
clerks@9stjohnstreet.co.uk
Recommended in Chancery
Specialisation: General Chancery, with emphasis on traditional chancery fields, and on revenue matters, professional negligence and High Court Litigation.
Prof. Memberships: Chancery Bar Association, Northern Chancery Bar Association (past Chairman) Professional Negligence Bar Association.
Career: Chancery Practitioner since 1972; Recorder (Civil and Crime); part-time Chairman, VAT and Duties Tribunals; part-time Special Commissioner of Taxes.
Personal: Fluent in Spanish, good knowledge of French, educated in North and South America, and at Trinity College, Cambridge University.

JOHNSTON, Christopher
3 Serjeants' Inn (Robert Francis QC & John Grace QC), London
(020) 7427 5000
Recommended in Clinical Negligence
Specialisation: Principal areas of practice: clinical negligence, medical ethics and police law. Considerable experience acting for both claimant and defendant in all aspects of medico-legal work including high value claims (brain damage, blindness, serious physical injury). Experience in medical ethics work (M & H: permanent vegetative state: whether Bland compatible with ECHR; B v Croydon: forcefeeding of mental patient). Co-author 'Medical Treatment: Decisions and the Law' (Butterworths, 2001). Acted for defendant in first dental negligence class action (Appleton v Garrett). Professional medical, dental and police disciplinary work. Experience acting in police civil actions, police pension and employment cases. Employment experience also comprises unfair dismissal, race and sex discrimination. Judicial review cases include Tucker v National Crime Squad (reasons for return to force). Presented seminars on human rights including 'Learning from the US experience', 'Containment' and 'Contract Killing' at Europol in the Hague (2002).
Prof. Memberships: Professional Negligence Bar Association. LCLCBA .
Career: Called to the Bar in 1990. Joined Serjeants' Inn in 1991. Junior Counsel to the Crown (B Panel).
Personal: Ballymena Academy; Trinity Hall, Cambridge (Law, 1st class). Interests: cinema and history.

JONES, Alun QC
3 Raymond Buildings (Clive Nicholls QC), London
(020) 7400 6400
chambers@3raymondbuildings.com
Recommended in Crime, Fraud
Specialisation: Principal areas of practice are commercial crime and extradition. Acts in cases of serious and complex fraud, both trials and advisory work, primarily for the defence. Undertakes extradition and advisory work for foreign governments and fugitives. Appears frequently on appeal or review in criminal cases and associated matters such as coroners' cases. Notable cases include the Alexander Howden reinsurance trials (appearing for Kenneth Grob in the first SFO trial, 1989-90); the Blue Arrow Trial 1990-91 (defending Stephen Clark); the defence of Andrew Kent in an alleged fraud against The Securities Association (1993) and the Maxwell Criminal Trial (defending Kevin Maxwell, 1995-96); Westminster Council v Dame Shirley Porter & Others 1997; Senator Pinochet 1998-99; Lord Hardwicke 1999; Frank Warren 2000; private prosecution for the Hillsborough Family Support Group 1996-2000. Involved in 14 full House of Lords appeals in extradition cases, acting in 10 of them for foreign governments, including Pinochet in Spain. Author of 'Jones on Extradition' (Sweet & Maxwell 2001); second edition.
Prof. Memberships: Bar Council, Criminal Bar Association.
Career: Called to the Bar in 1972 and joined current chambers in 1973. Took silk 1989. Appointed Recorder 1992.
Personal: Educated at Oldershaw Grammar School, Wallasey 1960-67 and Bristol University 1967-70. Leisure pursuits include bridge, cricket, gardening and writing (currently working on book concerning the law of conspiracy). Born 19 March 1949. Lives in Greenwich, London.

JONES, Charlotte
Crown Office Chambers (Michael Spencer QC & Christopher Purchas QC), London
(020) 7797 8100
Recommended in Clinical Negligence

JONES, Elizabeth QC
Serle Court (Lord Neill of Bladen QC), London
(020) 7242 6105
clerks@serlecourt.co.uk
Recommended in Commercial (Litigation)
Specialisation: Wide ranging litigation practice, both in the chancery fields of company, insolvency, property and trusts, and in a wide range of commercial disputes, such as fraud, sale of goods, banking, railway industry, and contractual disputes in many different business areas. Also regulatory work in the City and in relation to solicitors.
Prof. Memberships: Chancery Bar Association, COMBAR, ACTAPS.
Career: Called to the Bar 1984. Silk 2000.

LEADERS AT THE BAR

JONES, Gregory
2 Harcourt Buildings
(Robin Purchas QC), London
(020) 7353 8415
Recommended in Environment

JONES, Jennifer
No5 Chambers (Gareth Evans QC), Birmingham
(0121) 606 0500
Recommended in Employment
Specialisation: All aspects of individual and collective employment law, with a specialist interest in sex, race and disability discrimination claims, acting for a good balance of Applicant and Respondent clients. Respondent clients include a number of large public bodies as well as high profile members of the international business community. Applicant clients include trade unions and individual employees from the shop floor to senior managers and directors.
Prof. Memberships: Employment Lawyers Association. Bar Council Human Rights Committee. Chair of Disciplinary Panel for the Methodist Church.
Career: Called to the Bar in 1991. Deputy Head of Chambers Employment Group, 2002.
Personal: Interests include music and theatre; West African food and culture; international politics and human rights.

JONES, Philip
Serle Court (Lord Neill of Bladen QC), London
(020) 7242 6105
clerks@serlecourt.co.uk
Recommended in Chancery
Specialisation: Company and Insolvency; financial sevices; Chancery and Commercial litigation; European law; judicial review and professional negligence in relation to the foregoing.
Prof. Memberships: Chancery Bar Association, COMBAR.
Career: Junior Counsel to the Crown (Chancery) 1994, Junior Counsel to the Crown (A Panel) 1999.
Publications: 'The Practice and Procedure of the Companies Court' (1997).

JONES, Seán
11 King's Bench Walk Chambers (Eldred Tabachnik QC & James Goudie QC), London
(020) 7632 8500
sjones@11kbw.com
Recommended in Employment
Specialisation: Seán specialises in employment law. His practice is broad. He has acted for individuals, trade unions, employers' federations, international banks, airlines, public and private utilities, hospitals, universities, firms of solicitors, television and other media companies, local authorities, technology and computer companies, and charities. He advises upon and litigates claims across the full range of employment issues including unfair and wrongful dismissal, race, sex and disability discrimination, equal pay, transfer of undertakings and pensions.

JORY, Hugh
Enterprise Chambers (Anthony Mann QC), Leeds
(0113) 246 0391
Recommended in Commercial (Litigation), Insolvency

JOSEPH, David
Essex Court Chambers (Gordon Pollock QC), London
(020) 7813 8000
Recommended in Aviation, Commercial (Litigation), Shipping
Specialisation: Experienced in arbitration. Advocate in many ad hoc arbitrations in London involving a wide variety of commercial disputes particularly charterparty, aviation, insurance, reinsurance and commodities. Many of these disputes are governed by foreign law. Litigation experience: all types of commercial work including insurance, reinsurance, aviation, shipping, sale of goods, letters of credit, commercial fraud.
Career: Law Society Finals 1983. Called to Bar – 1984; began practice – 1985, in commercial chambers at Essex Court.
Personal: Born 22 April 1961. Educated at Pembroke College, Cambridge, BA Law, 2nd Class Hons. Good working French and basic Italian.

JOURDAN, Stephen
Falcon Chambers (Jonathan Gaunt QC & Kim Lewison QC), London
(020) 7353 2484
Recommended in Agriculture, Property Litigation
Specialisation: Commercial, agricultural and residential landlord and tenant, conveyancing, mortgages, solicitors' and surveyors' professional negligence, real property, insolvency aspects of real property.
Prof. Memberships: Professional Negligence Bar Association, Chancery Bar Association.
Career: Formerly a practising solicitor. Contributor to 'Halsbury's Laws' (4th Edition), volume 27 (Landlord and Tenant).
Publications: Writing a book on Adverse Possession.

JOYCE, Michael
9 Gough Square (John Foy QC), London
020 7832 0500
Recommended in Crime
Specialisation: Criminal practice.
Prof. Memberships: Criminal Bar Association; Midland Circuit.

JOYCE, Peter QC
No.1 High Pavement (John B Milmo QC), Nottingham
(0115) 941 8218
Recommended in Crime
Specialisation: Serious crime – including corruption, serious sexual offences, homicide. In the past two years cases involving senior police officer and doctors.
Prof. Memberships: Criminal Bar Association.
Career: Called to the Bar 1968. Recorder 1986. Queens Counsel 1991.

JUBB, Brian Patrick
Renaissance Chambers (Brian Patrick Jubb & Henry Setright QC), London
(020) 7404 1111
brian.jubb@btopenworld.com
Recommended in Family
Specialisation: Family, children, abduction, adoption, private/public law. Matrimonial (all aspects). Education and mental health. Local Government.
Prof. Memberships: FLBA, ALBA.
Career: Called November 1971 (Gray's Inn); Head of Chambers 1994.

JUDD, Frances
Harcourt Chambers (June Rodgers), Oxford
(01865) 791559
fjudd@harcourtchambers.law.co.uk
Recommended in Family
Specialisation: Family law, particularly children's cases – public/private law and adoption. Matrimonial finance.
Prof. Memberships: FLBA, Association of Lawyers for Children, Midland Circuit.
Career: Called to the Bar 1984; Member of Harcourt Chambers since 1985; based in Oxford since 1993.
Personal: New Hall, Cambridge, 1979-82. Born 1961. Married with two children.

KALLIPETIS, Michel QC
Littleton Chambers (Michel Kallipetis QC), London
(020) 7797 8600
michel@kallipetis.com
Recommended in ADR
Specialisation: Professional negligence, employment law, entertainment and media law, building and construction, general commercial and business law. Other areas of practice include health and safety. Regularly mediates with considerable experience in a variety of commercial disputes in excess of £30 million, professional negligence, employment including discrimination, pensions, building and construction and general contractual disputes.
Prof. Memberships: Professional Negligence Bar Association, COMBAR, Employment Law Bar Association, TECBA, accredited CEDR Mediator, Chartered Arbitrator.
Career: Called 1968 Gray's Inn; QC 1989; Recorder 1989, Deputy High Court Judge, Judge of Technological and Construction Court.
Personal: Cardinal Vaughan School. University College London. Exchequer and Audit Department (now National Audit Office) 1960-68. Languages: German (fluent), French (working knowledge).

KAMLISH, Stephen
Tooks Court Chambers (Michael Mansfield QC), London
(020) 7405 8828
Recommended in Crime
Specialisation: Principal area of practice is criminal defence work in particular murder, Prevention of Terrorism Act cases, serious fraud, large scale importation of Class A drugs, armed robbery (flying squad and regional crime squad cases), defence of alleged major 'target' criminals, and extradition in UK and Europe. Acts as leading Junior Counsel in the Central Criminal Court, London Crown Courts, High Court, Court of Appeal and House of Lords. Has made several media appearances.
Prof. Memberships: Criminal Bar Association, Lesbian and Gay Lawyers Association.
Personal: BA (Hons) 1978. Labour Party member. Leisure pursuits include gliding, cookery, badminton and go-karting.

KARAS, Jonathan
Wilberforce Chambers (Edward Nugee QC), London
(020) 7306 0102
Recommended in Property Litigation
Specialisation: Practises in the fields of real property and planning (with a particular emphasis on landlord and tenant).
Prof. Memberships: Planning and Environment Bar Association, Chancery Bar Association.
Career: Member of A Panel of Junior Counsel to the Crown.
Publications: Co-author of 'Unlawful Interference with Land' (1996, new edition due 2002) and a contributing editor to the 'Compulsory Purchase' title of Halsbury's Laws of England (1996) and to Hill and Redman's 'Law of Landlord and Tenant'. Editor of the re-issue of the 'Distress' title of Halsbury's Laws (2000).

KARK, Tom
Hollis Whiteman Chambers (QEB) (Julian Bevan QC & Peter Whiteman QC), London
(020) 7583 5766
Recommended in Fraud
Specialisation: Practice principally involves cases of commercial fraud including: fraudulent trading; VAT fraud; duty diversion; mortgage fraud; bankruptcy offences. Has also been involved in cases of alleged insider dealing, prosecuting for the DTI and defending. Also defends and prosecutes cases concerning money laundering, computer misuse and data protection (see DPP v Brown – House of Lords). Landmark cases have included defending as junior several SFO and Special Casework prosecutions (eg second defendant in the Levitt case; Terry Ramsden; Swithland Motors). Criminal Law (General): prosecutes and defends in all areas of criminal law. Member of 'Justice'.
Career: Called to the Bar 1982, appointed assistant recorder 1999, Recorder 2000. Appointed Standing Counsel to HM Customs & Excise 2002.
Personal: Born 12 December 1960. Educated at Eton, Buckingham University and Ronnie Scotts.

KATKOWSKI, Christopher QC
4 Breams Buildings (Christopher Lockhart-Mummery QC), London

(020) 7430 1221
Recommended in Administrative & Public Law, Environment, Local Government, Planning
Specialisation: Specialises in planning. Bulk of work consists of appearing at, and preparing form, planning inquiries. Has developed a particular expertise in retail cases. Nearly all clients are private and corporate. Significant proportion of work comes from Direct Professional Access instructions. Regularly appears at planning appeal and call-in inquiries, local plan and UDP inquiries, and enforcement notice appeal inquiries. Also works in related fields such as compulsory purchase and highways. Also appears regularly in Court cases; most of these related to planning, for example when planning appeal decisions or local plans are challenged in the High Court. Also, a fair amount of Court work is judicial review. Due to the fact that held the appointment of Junior Counsel to the Crown (Common Law) 1992-99, he was a member of the Attorney-General's Panel and before that (1988-92) was on the Supplementary Panel, has often appeared for (as was then) the Secretary of State for the Environment and occasionally for other ministers. Other leading planning court cases include: Bolton (House of Lords, on the nature of the duty to give reasons for appeal decisions); Tesco Witney (House of Lords, on planning gain); Mitchell (Court of Appeal, on affordable housing); Hambletone (High Court, on the interpretation of PPG6 concerning need). Since taking Silk in 1999, has appeared at 49 planning inquiries of which 18 concerned retail development; 14 residential; 17 a variety of different types of development eg offices, industry, waste; three were major projects including the Heron Tower (proposal for the tallest building in the City of London), Chester (an extensive guided busway scheme and Otterburn (new training facilities for the Army in a National Park). Appeared for the developer/promoter at 48 of these 49 inquiries. Appeared in 37 court cases related to planning issues of which 29 were in the High Court and eight in the Court of Appeal. Current major projects include Shellhaven (a new container port), New Tyne Crossing, Newcastle and Kings Cross Central (a large residential and commercial regeneration scheme). In addition has been advising Islington LBC on Arsenal FC's proposals for a new stadium.

KAUFMANN, Phillippa
Doughty Street Chambers (Geoffrey Robertson QC), London
(020) 7404 1313
Recommended in Human Rights
Specialisation: Public and human rights law particularly prisoners rights, mental health and crime-related judicial review. Appellate crime for life sentence prisoners, extradition and Commonwealth capital appeals. Civil actions against the police and Home Office. Recent cases include: R v Offen; R (Daly) v SSHD; R (Wilkinson) v Broadmoor Hospital Authority; R v SSHD ex p Anderson and Taylor; R v Pyrah and Lichniak.
Prof. Memberships: Executive Committee ALBA; Council Member, Justice; Member Lawyers For Liberty.
Career: Called 1991.
Publications: Contributor to 'Prison Law' (OUP, 2nd edn, 2000); co-editor Halsbury's Laws Vol 36 (2) 'Prisons and Prisoners'.

KAY, R Jervis QC
Stone Chambers (Steven Gee QC), London
(020) 7440 6900
JervisKayQC@stonechambers.com
Recommended in Shipping
Specialisation: All areas of shipping and commercial law, including international trade, arbitration, marine insurance, carriage of goods, salvage, collision, marine pollution, towage, personal injury and professional negligence. Also sports law particularly related to yachting.
Prof. Memberships: London Maritime Arbitration Association (supporting member), London Common Law and Commercial Bar Association (Committee), COMBAR, British Maritime Law Association, Bar Sports Law Group.
Career: Called to Bar 1972. Called to Bar of New South Wales 1984. Called to Bar of Antigua and Barbuda 1998. Took Silk 1996.
Personal: Educated Wellington College and Nottingham University (LL.B). Editor Atkins Court Forms – vol 3 'Admiralty.'

KAY, Steven QC
3 Gray's Inn Square (Rock Tansey QC), London
(020) 7520 5600
goodnightvienna@quista.net
Recommended in Crime
Specialisation: Wide experience in all areas of UK and international criminal law. Work in association with Professor Mischa Wladimiroff at Jan Van Nassaustraat 113, 2596 BS Den Haag, Netherlands in joint conduct of international work. Defence counsel for Tadic, the first defendant before the UN War Crimes Tribunal for Yugoslavia and the first International Criminal Trial since the Nuremberg and Tokyo trials. Represented Musema a defendant before the UN International Criminal Tribunal for Rwanda. First UN Defence Counsel to enter Rwanda. Appointed amicus curiae in the trial of Slobodan Milosevic before the UN War Crimes Tribunal in The Hague, September 2001. Expertise in cases of complex factual background. Lectures at universities and conferences throughout the world on subjects ranging from war crimes to the Financial Services & Markets Act 2000.
Prof. Memberships: Criminal Bar Association, European Criminal Bar Association, International Bar Association, Forensic Science Society, Society for the Reform of Criminal Law.
Career: Called to the Bar 1977, QC 1997, Secretary CBA 1993-96.
Publications: Contributor to 'Commentary on The Rome Statute of the International Criminal Court', OUP 2002.
Personal: Born 4 August 1954, lives in Surrey.

KAYE, Roger QC
24 Old Buildings (Martin Mann QC & Alan Steinfeld QC), London
(020) 7404 0946
Recommended in Chancery, Church, Insolvency

KEALEY, Gavin QC
7 King's Bench Walk (Gavin Kealey QC & Julian Flaux QC), London
(020) 7910 8300
clerks@7kbw.law.co.uk
Recommended in Arbitration, Commercial (Litigation), Insurance, Shipping
Specialisation: Specialises in all aspects of commercial law for mainly international clients. Particular emphasis on commercial litigation and international arbitration, insurance, reinsurance, banking, financial services, professional negligence, shipping and contracts of all kinds. Also has experience appearing before foreign courts as both advocate and expert. Speaks very good French. Considerable experience of international arbitration in England and abroad. Recent reported cases include: Kingscroft and Walbrook v Nissan [1999] LRLR 603, (Reinsurance Pool/quota share/ excess of loss/retention/utmost good faith); Rothschild Assurance v Collyear [1999] 1 LRLR Rep 6, (Pensions mis-selling); Denby v Marchant & Yasuda v Lloyds's Underwriters [1998] 1 LRLR 343. CA. (Aggregate Extension Clauses); Den Danske A/S, Normura Bank and others v Kleinwort Benson, Skipton BS and Economic Insurance (Dec. 1997, Thomas J, Loan Portfolio Transfers, lending criteria, insurance construction); Sumitomo Bank Ltd, Sanwa Bank Ltd & Arab Bank Ltd v Banque Bruxelles Lambert [1997] 1 Lloyd's Rep 487 (bank syndication issues), Tharros Shipping v Bias Shipping [1997] 1 Lloyd's Rep 246 and Pendennis Shipyard v Magrathea [1998] 1 Lloyd's Rep 315 (costs payable by a non-party); Glencore v Portman [1997] 1 Lloyd's Rep 225 (insurance, non-disclosure, waiver); Excess Insurance v Mander [1997] 2 Lloyd's Rep 119 (reinsurance, incorporation, arbitration clause). Recent international arbitrations (2001-02) include three month Bermudian/English arbitration concerning the illegal application of pesticides on cereal products in the USA; equity share swaps and options in relation to French supermarket chains (France); and company merger/valuation disputes between car/truck manufacturers (Paris/Amsterdam).
Career: Called to the Bar 1977; Joined present chambers 1978; Took Silk 1994. Recorder 2000. Authorised to sit as a Deputy High Court Judge of the Queen's Bench Division, Commercial Court.
Personal: Educated at University College, Oxford (BA Hons Jurisprudence 1st class). Lecturer in law, King's College, London 1976-77.

KEEHAN, Michael QC
St. Ive's Chambers (Julia Macur QC), Birmingham
(0121) 236 0863
Recommended in Family
Specialisation: Specialises in family law, dealing with children's cases, both public and private law, ancillary relief and personal injury.
Prof. Memberships: Family Law Bar Association; Personal Injury Bar Association; BAAF.
Career: Birmingham University LLB (Hons); Called to the Bar 1982; QC 2001; Recorder 2001.

KEFFORD, Anthony
East Anglian Chambers (Roderick Newton), Norwich
(01603) 617351
Recommended in Family

KELLY, Andrew QC
2 Harcourt Buildings (Robin Purchas QC), London
(020) 7353 8415
clerks@2hb.law.co.uk
Recommended in Planning
Specialisation: Town and country planning, local government, environment, Heathrow Terminal 5 Public Inquiry (British Airways), retail, housing, minerals, local plan inquiries.
Prof. Memberships: PEBA, ALBA.
Career: Called 1978 (Northern Ireland 1982). Chambers 1981. Silk 2000.
Personal: Education: Bangor Grammar (Northern Ireland), Christ Church, Oxford. MA (Oxon), Lincoln's Inn. Leisure: sport, arts, gardening, travel.

KELLY, Matthias QC
Old Square Chambers (John Hendy QC), London
(020) 7269 0300
kellyqc@oldsquarechambers.co.uk
Recommended in Personal Injury
Specialisation: Personal injuries, professional negligence, health and safety, employment, consumer protection. Has dealt with all types of cases for both claimants and defendants. Particular specialisation in catastrophic injuries including brain injuries. Experienced in complicated litigation including radioactive pollution: Merlin v BNFL (1990) 3 WLR 383. Other cases: H v MOD (1991) 2 QB 103; Rastin v British Steel (1994) 1 WLR 732; Wells v Wells, Thomas v Brighton Health Authority; Page v Sheeness Steel (1998) 3WLR 329; Firth v Geo Ackroyd Ltd (2000) Lloyds LR (medical) 312; R v Broxtowe Borough Council, ex p

LEADERS AT THE BAR

Bradford (2000) IRLR 329; Rozario v Post Office (1997) PIQR P15; R v HM Coroner for Portsmouth, ex p Keane (1989) 153 JP65; Perry v Post Office (High Court London) 18/10/2001 - MS caused by trauma; Dalton v Wright Hassell (High Court London 10/11/00 - psychiatric damage following solicitors negligence; Hooper v Young (1998) Lloyds Medical Law Reports 60; Kampitchler v Moore and Blatch (High Court, Winchester, 18/4/02).
Prof. Memberships: Chairman, Personal Injury Bar Association (2001-02).
Career: Called to the Bar 1979. QC 1999. Member Irish Bar (Belfast and Dublin). Member New York State Bar and US Federal Bar. Former consultant to the European Commission on UK health and safety law. Editor, Sweet & Maxwell 'Personal Injuries Manual'. Fellow of Royal Society of Medicine. Member Bar Council 1998-date. Member General Management Committee, Bar Council 1999-date. Chairman Policy Committee, Bar Council 2000-01. Member Ogden Tables Working Party (3rd and 4th edns). Chairman Public Affairs Committee Bar Council 2001. Vice-Chairman Bar Council (2002-date).
Publications: Editor and contributor 'Personal Injury Handbook' (Sweet & Maxwell, 2000). Contributor, Munkman 'Employers' Liability' (13th edn).

KELSEY-FRY, John QC
Hollis Whiteman Chambers (QEB) (Julian Bevan QC & Peter Whiteman QC), London
(020) 7583 5766
barristers@holliswhiteman.co.uk
Recommended in Crime, Fraud
Specialisation: Practice divided between high profile prosecution and defence but now predominantly defence, especially white-collar crime, eg Co-op corruption case, Jubilee line extension case etc. Notable cases: Serafinowicz (war crimes); Donald & Cressey (largest police corruption case since 1960s); Charlie Kray, Sawoniuk (war crimes); Mohammed Fayed (deposit box); Jane Andrews (Duchess of York's dresser charged with murder). Currently involved in Roger Cook (The Cook Report series) libel case.
Career: Former Senior Treasury Counsel.

KEMPSTER, Toby
Old Square Chambers (John Hendy QC), Bristol
(0117) 9277 1111
kempster@oldsquarechambers.co.uk
Recommended in Employment
Specialisation: Concentrates primarily on employment law and personal injury law. His employment practice covers both individual and collective rights, dealing with contractual and statutory remedies. His personal injury practice is mainly work or industry-related, but he has been involved in multi-plaintiff product liability, disease and 'disaster' cases. His involvement in both personal injury and employment law has resulted in regular involvement both in DDA and stress at work claims. Notable cases Alexander v STC; Isle of Scilly v Brintel; Johnson v British Midland Airways.
Prof. Memberships: ILS, ELA and PIBA.
Career: Member of chambers since 1982.
Publications: Contributor to 'EU Employee Consultation 2000', Sweet & Maxwell.
Personal: Sailing, walking, theatre.

KENDRICK, Dominic QC
7 King's Bench Walk (Gavin Kealey QC & Julian Flaux QC), London
(020) 7910 8300
Recommended in Insurance

KENNEDY, Andrew
6 Pump Court (Kieran Coonan QC), London
(020) 7583 6013
Recommended in Clinical Negligence
Specialisation: All areas of Healthcare Law: clinical negligence; inquests; professional disciplinary tribunals (particularly GMC and GDC). Professional Negligence (particularly solicitors). Personal Injury.
Prof. Memberships: PNBA and PIBA.
Career: Called to the Bar 1989.

KENNEDY, Helena QC
Doughty Street Chambers (Geoffrey Robertson QC), London
(020) 7404 1313
Recommended in Crime
Specialisation: Practises predominantly in the criminal law; she also undertakes judicial review, public inquiries and sex discrimination work. She has acted in many prominent cases including the Brighton Bombing Trial and Guilford Four Appeal, the bombing of the Israeli Embassy, the abduction of Baby Abbie Humphries and a number of key domestic violence cases.
Prof. Memberships: British Council (Chair), Human Genetics Commission (Chair), World Bank Institute (Advisory Council). A Life Peer since 1997, a member of the IBAS task force on international terrorism and a Bencher of Gray's Inn.
Publications: 'Eve was Framed' (1992). Seminal report in further education, 'Learning Works' (1997).
Personal: Honorary Doctorates from 18 British Universities. Honorary Fellow of the City and Guilds Institute and the Royal Society of Arts.

KENNEDY, Michael
India Buildings Chambers (Ray Herman), Liverpool
(0151) 243 6000
Recommended in Family

KENNERLEY, Ian
Broad Chare Chambers (Patrick Cosgrove QC), Newcastle upon Tyne
(0191) 232 0541
Recommended in Family

KENTRIDGE, Sir Sydney QC
Brick Court Chambers (Christopher Clarke QC), London
(020) 7379 3550
moyler@brickcourt.co.uk
Recommended in Administrative & Public Law, Commercial (Litigation), Insurance
Specialisation: General commercial and common law, constitutional law and law relating to newspapers.
Career: Called to Bar 1977, Lincoln's Inn. Practising barrister, England, 1977 to date. Silk 1984. Admitted as Advocate of the Supreme Court of South Africa, 1949. Appointed Senior Counsel, South Africa 1965. Former Judge of the Courts of Appeal of Jersey and Guernsey and Constitutional Court of South Africa. Cases of note include: R v Foreign & Commonwealth Office – ex p Bancoult - Caledonia North Sea Ltd v British Telecom (Piper Alpha Insurance Claims - House of Lords), Hamilton v Al Fayed (Court of Appeal re Costs).
Personal: Born Johannesburg, South Africa, 1922. Educated University of Witwatersrand (BA 1941) and Oxford University (BA Hons in Jurisprudence, 1948; MA 1955).

KERR, Tim QC
11 King's Bench Walk Chambers (Eldred Tabachnik QC & James Goudie QC), London
(020) 7632 8500
kerr@11kbw.com
Recommended in Administrative & Public Law, Education, Sport
Specialisation: Judicial review, sports law, education law, local government, employment law, professional negligence, disciplinary tribunals, defamation, European, human rights and commercial. Sports law clients include: Nicholas Anelka, Tottenham Hotspur FC (gaining readmission to FA Cup and six restored points); Chelsea FC; Middlesbrough FC; Ipswich Town FC; Ipswich Town FC; AEK Athens FC (gaining readmission to UEFA Cup); Slavia Prague FC; the Football Association; the Football League (Stevenage FC v Football League, CA, 1996); the Rugby Football League; the Rugby Football Union; several rugby union Premiership clubs; the Welsh Rugby Union; the R&A Golf Club of St Andrews; the Amateur Boxing Association of England; Lennox Lewis (Lewis v Bruno and WBC, 1995); the athlete Mark Richardson; the jockeys Adrian Maguire and Mick Fitzgerald. Co-author of 'Sports Law' 1999. Judicial reviews include Bart's hospital closure cases (including R v Health Secretary ex p Hackney LBC, CA, 1995); challenges to disciplinary investigations into audits of Maxwell and Polly Peck companies (including R v Chance ex p Smith, DC, 1995); and Camelot's challenge to the 'Big Three' bookmakers' competing product (R v DPP ex p Camelot Group plc, DC, 1997). Education cases include: X v Bedfordshire CC (HL, 1995), Christmas v Hampshire County Council (1997), Richardson v Solihull MBC (CA, 1998), R v East Sussex ex p Tandy (1998, HL), Phelps v Hillingdon LBC/Jarvis v Hampshire CC (2000 HL), R (w) v Governors of B School, CA, 2001 and R (Hounslow LBC) v Hounslow School Admission Appeals Panel, CA, 2002. Employment cases include: Doughty v Rolls-Royce (1992: CA); Duffy v Yeomans & Partners (1995, CA) and Preston v Wolverhampton MBC (HL, 1998 ECJ, 2000).
Prof. Memberships: Administrative Law Bar Association; Employment Law Bar Association; Secretary of the Bar Sports Law Group.
Career: Appointed Silk April 2001. Part-time Chairman of Employment Tribunals; member of the panel of arbitrators of the Sports Dispute Resolution Panel.
Personal: Runner of four marathons and keen Chelsea supporter. Married with three children. Fluent in French; working knowledge of German and Spanish.

KER-REID, John
Pump Court Chambers (Christopher Harvey Clark QC), Winchester
(020) 7353 0711
jkr@ker-law.co.uk
Recommended in Family
Specialisation: Family law – ancillary relief. Children – public and private law. Hague and European Convention. Medical issues and the inherent jurisdiction. International and domestic law adoptions. White v White [1999] 2 WLR 1213 [CA]; REL, v, m, h (contact: Domestic violence) 2000 2 FLR 334; REX 1998 2 FLR 1124 (adult sterilisations).
Prof. Memberships: FLBA.
Personal: MA (Cantab), Trinity College, Cambridge.

KERSHAW, Jennifer QC
No.6 Barristers Chambers (Jennifer Kershaw QC), Leeds
(0113) 245 9763
Recommended in Crime

KERSHEN, Lawrence QC
Tooks Court Chambers (Michael Mansfield QC), London
(020) 7405 8828
kershen@london.com
Recommended in ADR
Specialisation: Experienced in mediating commercial disputes in many sectors, from high value to apparently low. They include professional negligence (eg architects, accountants), insurance (international bank), partnership (aviation co), shareholders (media group), defamation (premier league football club), intellectual property (university). Range of non-commercial mediations includes police complaints (discipline), human rights (Caribbean government and 14 Death Row prisoners) Community consensus-building (350 participants). Currently advisor on introduction of ADR to civil justice system in Slovakia. Litigation experience includes commercial contract, also professional negligence, personal injury and defamation. Also practised in complex and large-scale

criminal cases, including corporate fraud and tax.
Prof. Memberships: CEDR, Mediation UK, Restorative Justice Consortium.
Career: Called 1967. Crown Court Recorder 1991. Queens Counsel 1992. CEDR accredited and Training Faculty member since 1994. NLP Trainer 1998.
Personal: Effective in mediation by combining practical experience with legal and facilitation skills. Married, 2 children. Speaks French, working Italian and basic German.

KESSLER, James
24 Old Buildings (Rex Bretten QC), London
(020) 7242 2744
kessler@kessler.co.uk
Recommended in Charities
Specialisation: Revenue law, more particularly CGT, IHT, and what is loosely described as 'private client' work; offshore trusts; foreign domiciliaries; also taxation of charities and Inland Revenue prosecutions in tax avoidance cases. Has a particular fondness for trust drafting (having written the leading textbook on the subject). Founder of the Trusts Discussion Forum.
Career: Called to the Bar 1984.

KEYSER, Andrew
9 Park Place (Ian Murphy QC), Cardiff
(029) 2038 2731
clerks@9parkplace.co.uk
Recommended in Chancery
Specialisation: Contract litigation; banking; professional negligence; partnership; companies.
Prof. Memberships: Chancery Bar Association. Wales Commercial Law Association.
Career: Education: Cardiff High School; Balliol College, Oxford; MA (1st Class Hons). Called to Bar 1986. Recorder. Member of Panel of Counsel (General) for the National Assembly for Wales. Part-time tutor in company law on the Bar Vocational Course, Cardiff Law School, since 1999.

KHALIL, Karim S
1 Paper Buildings (Roger N Titheridge QC), London
(020) 7353 3728
karimkhalil@lex.tv
Recommended in Crime
Specialisation: Defence and prosecution with particular experience in serious fraud (including Inland Revenue and Customs), drug trafficking violence (including murder) and sexual offence. Represented the principal appellant in The Cambridge Two (misuse of Drugs Act), and the principal masochist in R v Brown and others (sado-masochism/human rights). Prosecuted in R v Jacques (theft of over £1.1m worth of rare antiquarian books and pamphlets belonging to Cambridge University and London libraries). Significant amount of confiscation work for defence and crown arising mainly out of fraud and drug trafficking. Criminal and civil litigation relating to company fraud (Hannan v DTI, Company Directors Disqualification Act). Civil claims against the police and the prison service. Representations to the Discretionary Lifer Panel on behalf of those serving life sentences.
Prof. Memberships: SE Circuit; SE Circuit Liaison Committee (Chairman); Criminal Bar Association; Norwich Bar Mess; Cambridge Bar Mess (Vice Chairman); three years on the Professional Conduct and Complaints Committee; Bar Disciplinary Tribunal member.
Career: Cheadle Hulme School (Manchester); Queen's College (Cambridge); called to the Bar 1984; assistant recorder 1984; recorder 2000.
Personal: Married with two sons. Member of Hawks Club; member of Okeford Duck Golf Society; alto sac in The Eye (soul and R&B band); lacrosse player now turned to tennis and golf.

KHANGURE, Avtar
St Philips Chambers (John Randall QC), Birmingham
(0121) 246 7000
Recommended in Commercial (Litigation), Insolvency
Specialisation: Company Law; General Commercial Law Insolvency.
Prof. Memberships: Midland Chancery and Commercial Association.
Career: BA, LLM University of Cambridge. Called to the Bar 1985. Recorder.

KIBLING, Thomas
Cloisters (Laura Cox QC), London
(020) 7827 4000
thomaskibling@cloisters.org.uk
Recommended in Employment
Specialisation: Employment law with a particular emphasis on discrimination law. In recent years he has been involved in a number of leading appeal cases including: Jones v 3M (HL) (post termination disability discrimination); Anyanwu and Ebuzoeme v South Bank University (HL) (aiding unlawful acts); Delaney v Staples HL (unauthorised deductions and notice pay); Jones v Tower Boots CA (liability of employers in respect of discrimination claims); Smith v Gardner Merchant CA (gays bringing claims for unlawful discrimination); Khan v The General Medical Council CA (claims against the GMC for unlawful discrimination); Cowley v Manson Timbers CA (re-employment orders); Aparau v Iceland Frozen Foods CA (scope of employment tribunal powers); Dr Shawkat v Nottingham City Council CA (the definition of redundancy); Jones v The Governors of Burdett Cootes School CA (raising new points of law on appeal); Owusu v London Fire and Civil Defence Authority EAT (continuing acts of discrimination); WA Goold (Pearmak) Ltd v McConnell EAT (implied term concerning the operation of grievance procedures); Coote v Granada Hospitality (victimisation post termination); P v S (transsexuals bringing claims for unlawful discrimination). Sits on the Editorial Board of the 'Encyclopaedia of Employment Law,' founder member of the Employment Lawyers Association and is a member of the Employment Bar Association.
Career: Called to the Bar 1990. Joined present chambers 1991.
Publications: Lectures widely on all aspects of employment law and publications include 'The Employment Law Handbook' (LAG).
Personal: Born 19 August 1957.

KILLALEA, Stephen
Devereux Chambers (Colin Edelman QC), London
(020) 7353 7534
killalea@devchambers.co.uk
Recommended in Health & Safety, Personal Injury
Specialisation: Principal areas of practice are personal injury and health and safety. Predominantly plaintiff but some defence work. Emphasis on accidents in industry and accidents involving death, brain damage and spinal injury. Also specialised crime, including a substantial health and safety practice.
Prof. Memberships: Personal Injuries Bar Association; Association of Personal Injury Lawyers.
Career: Called to the Bar in 1981.
Personal: Born 25 January 1959. LL.B (Hons) Sheffield. Lives in Sussex.

KILVINGTON, Simon
18 St John Street (Jonathan Foster QC), Manchester
(0161) 278 1800
clerks@18stjohn.co.uk
Recommended in Personal Injury
Specialisation: Personal injury.
Prof. Memberships: PIBA.
Career: Hertford College, Oxford. Called 1995.

KIMBLIN, Richard
3 Fountain Court (Robert Juckes QC), Birmingham
(0121) 236 5854
richard.kimblin@3fc.co.uk
Recommended in Environment
Specialisation: Environmental, planning and regulatory criminal law.
Prof. Memberships: The Planning and Environmental Bar Association; United Kingdom Environmental Law Association; ALBA.
Career: BSc (Dunelm); PhD; Royal Society Western European Fellowship. Prior to his call to the Bar, he was Associate Director of a firm of consultants, advising and negotiating on environmental and planning matters. Waste, water, pollution, minerals and associated criminal cases.
Publications: He has published widely in both academic and practitioner journals, including most recently 'Judicial Review of the Grant of Planning Permission' [22 October 1999]; 'Solicitors Journal', Risk, Jurisprudence and the Environment' [April 2000], JPL 359; 'The New Contaminated Land Regime' [19 May 2000], 'Solicitors Journal'.

KING, Neil QC
2 Mitre Court Buildings (Guy Roots QC), London
(020) 7583 1380
neil.king@2mcb.co.uk
Recommended in Environment, Planning
Specialisation: Practice encompasses town and country planning, compulsory purchase and compensation, rating, local government, environmental and public and administrative law.
Prof. Memberships: Planning and Environment Bar Association.
Career: Called to the Bar 1980 and joined current chambers 1982. Silk 2000.
Publications: Joint editor 'Ryde on Rating and the Council Tax'.
Personal: Born 14 November 1956. Educated at Harrow School 1970-74 and New College, Oxford 1975-78. Married with four children. Leisure pursuits include music, golf and real tennis. Lives in Whitchurch-on-Thames.

KING, Simon
7 Bedford Row (David Farrer QC), London
(020) 7242 3555
Recommended in Personal Injury
Specialisation: Personal injury and professional negligence practice acting for both plaintiffs and defendants but with an emphasis on defence work. Regular clients are principally insurers and corporate bodies, including professional indemnity insurers for solicitors, architects and surveyors. Experience includes professional and insurance fraud cases.
Prof. Memberships: Professional Negligence Bar Association, Fellow of the Chartered Institute of Arbitrators (FCIArb).
Career: Called to the Bar in 1987, joined current chambers in 1988. Early practice in crime and general common law; subsequent specialisation as above.

KINGSLAND, The Rt. Hon Lord QC
2 Harcourt Buildings (Robin Purchas QC), London
(020) 7353 8415
clerks@2hblaw.co.uk
Recommended in Environment
Specialisation: Waste and waste disposal; contaminated land; integrated pollution control; water resources; pollution and planning; European Community environmental law; planning; judicial review.
Prof. Memberships: PEBA; UKELA; Bar European Group.
Career: Call to the Bar, 1972; Queen's Counsel, 1988; Member of the European Parliament 1979-94; Privy Counsellor 1994; Bencher of the Middle Temple since 1996; Recorder of the Crown Court, since 1997.
Publications: Contributor to Halsbury's Laws on Compulsory Acquisition and

LEADERS AT THE BAR

on the European Communities and to the Bar Council's 'Practitioners Handbook of EC Law on Environmental Law'.

KINGSTON, Martin R QC
No5 Chambers (Gareth Evans QC), Birmingham
(0121) 606 0500
Recommended in Planning

KIRK, Anthony QC
One King's Bench Walk (Anthony Hacking QC), London
(020) 7936 1500
Recommended in Family
Specialisation: Family (including divorce and children), child care, international child abduction.
Prof. Memberships: Committee member of the General Council of the Bar 1996-99. Secretary of the Family Law Bar Association. Member of Family Mediators Association.
Career: Recent cases include: Re B (Wardship: Abortion) 1991 2 FLR 426; Re H (A Minor) (Role of Official Solicitor) 1993 2 FLR 552; Essex County Council v B (Education Supervision Order) 1993 1 FLR 866; Re B (Child Sex Abuse: Standard of Proof) 1995 1 FLR 904; Re C (Adoption: Parties) 1995 2 FLR 483; Re B (Contempt Evidence) 1996 1 FLR 239. Re W (Minor) (Unmarried Father: Child Abduction), Re B (A Minor) (Unmarried father: Child Abduction) 1998 2 FLR 146; Re K (supervision orders) 1999 2 FLR 303. Re C (HIV test) 1999 2 FLR 1004; TB v JB (abduction: grave risk of harm) 2001 2 FLR 515.
Personal: Ipswich School and King Edward VII School, Lytham; Kings College London (LLB Hons AKC).

KITCHIN, David QC
8 New Square (Mark Platts-Mills QC), London
(020) 7405 4321
clerks@8newsquare.co.uk
Recommended in Intellectual Property
Specialisation: All areas of intellectual property including patents, trademarks, passing off, copyright, designs, malicious falsehood, confidential information, media and entertainment law, computer law and EC and other competition law with an intellectual property element. For comprehensive CV and list of recent cases, visit chambers' website at www.8newsquare.co.uk
Prof. Memberships: Chancery Bar Association; Intellectual Property Bar Association (IPBA); The Intellectual Property Lawyers Organisation (TIPLO).
Career: Took Silk 1994. Deputy High Court Judge, 2001. Appointed person to hear Trade Mark Appeals, 2001.
Publications: 'Kerly's Law of Trade Marks and Trade Names' (Sweet & Maxwell); 'The Trade Marks Act 1994' Sweet & Maxwell.
Personal: Educated at Oundle School 1968-72, Cambridge University (Natural Sciences and Law).

KNAFLER, Stephen
Two Garden Court (Owen Davies QC & Courtenay Griffiths QC), London
(020) 7353 1633
Recommended in Administrative & Public Law
Specialisation: Community care and NHS care, mental health, immigration, disability, race and religious discrimination, asylum support, housing, education, local government, travellers, benefits, planning, criminal judicial review, professional negligence, real property and landlord and tenant: over 50 reported cases in all areas.
Prof. Memberships: Legal Action Group, Housing Law Practitioners Group, Administrative Law Bar Association, Immigration Law Practitioners Association, Community Care Practitioners Group.
Career: Solicitor 1998-93, barrister from 1993.
Publications: Editor of the 'Community Care Law Reports', author of 'Remedies for Disrepair and other Building Defects' (Sweet & Maxwell, 1996), co-author of 'Disrepair: Tenants' Rights' (Legal Action, 1999), 'Support for Asylum Seekers' (Legal Action, 2001), contributor to 'De Smith, Woolf & Jowell's Judicial Review of Administrative Action' (Sweet & Maxwell, 1996).

KNOWLES, Julian
Matrix Chambers, London
(020) 7404 3447
julianknowles@matrixlaw.co.uk
Recommended in Human Rights
Specialisation: International human rights, public and constitutional law, extradition, white collar crime including mutual assistance and money laundering. Many reported and unreported cases in these fields. Recent particularly important cases: Ex p Pinochet Ugarte (Nos 1, 2 and 3) (1998-99); Re Ismail (1998) (extradition); Taylor v Director of the SFO (1998) (libel/prosecutorial immunity); R v English (1997) (murder/joint enterprise); Mohammed v State (1998) (evidence/death row); ex p Fininvest (1996) (mutual assistance); Logan v The Queen (1996) (Privy Council's capital jurisdiction); Thomas v Baptiste (1999) (human rights/death row); Briggs v Baptiste (international law/death row); Lewis v Attorney General (2000) (judicial review/prerogative of mercy); Cedeno v Logan (2001)(reasons/due process).
Prof. Memberships: CBA.
Career: Balliol College, Oxford (BA, 1990). Called 1994. Tenant *3 Raymond Buildings* 1996-2000. Founder Member, Matrix Chambers, 2000.
Publications: 'Extradition and Mutual Assistance' (2001). 'Capital Punishment: Strategies for Abolition' (2001). Sweet & Maxwell, 'Human Rights Practice' (Contributor).

KNOWLES, Robin QC
3-4 South Square (Michael Crystal QC & Lord Alexander of Weedon QC), London
(020) 7696 9900
clerks@southsquare.com
Recommended in Banking & Finance, Company, Insolvency
Specialisation: Practice covers a wide aspect of general commercial, business and financial litigation, and legal advice, including banking and financial services, professional negligence, regulation, commercial fraud, corporate insolvency and reconstruction, corporate and partnership disputes, insurance and reinsurance. Range of contentious work illustrated by: Consignia v Hays (New Law Online 11 December 2001) (statutory interpretation); O'Donnell v HSBC [2001] EWCA Civ. 2108 (construction of a bank security documentation); Bermuda International Securities v KPMG [2001] Lloyd's Rep PN 392 (pre-action disclosure in professional negligence cases); Re Drake Insurance plc [2001] Lloyd's Rep IR 643 (refund of premium in insurance); Clark v Nomura International plc [2000] IRLR 766 (proprietary trading and performance bonuses in City-based employment); Hillsbridge Investments Ltd v Moresfield Ltd [2000] 2 BCLC 241 (expert determination clauses; disposals of companies); Grupo Torras SA v Sheikh Fahad Mohammed Al-Sabah [1999] CLC 1469 (commercial fraud and conflict of laws); Moscow Bank v Amadeus Trading [1997] TLR (bills of exchange; company winding up); Re Schuppan [1996] 2 All ER 664 (solicitors and conflicts of interest); Socomex Ltd v Banque Bruxelles Lambert SA [1996] 1 Lloyd's Rep 156 (banking and commodity trading). Alternative Dispute Resolution experience includes mediation advocacy in more than 15 mediations.
Prof. Memberships: Commercial Bar Association (Executive, Committee and Chairman, North American Committee); Chancery Bar Association; Bar Pro Bono Unit (Trustee and Management Committee); Bar in the Community (Trustee); Solicitors Pro Bono Group (Trustee); Royal Courts of Justice CAB (Management Committee): Member of other Bar Council and Bar committees. Advocacy trainer for Middle Temple, Gray's Inn and South Eastern Circuit. Middle Temple (Education Committee); Gray's Inn; South Eastern Circuit (Committee, co-opted).
Career: Called to the Bar in 1982; Queen's Counsel 1999; Recorder.

KNOX, Christopher John
Trinity Chambers (Toby Hedworth QC), Newcastle upon Tyne
(0191) 232 1927
info@trinitychambers.co.uk
Recommended in Family
Specialisation: High value matrimonial property (and cohabitation) cases (not children or public law). Particularly with fiscal, company, pension funds and missing money problems and sometimes trust problems. Keen on resolution of cases without court system. Has heavyweight criminal practice as well as matrimonial property.
Prof. Memberships: FLBA, CLBA, APIL.
Career: Kings School, Tynemouth. Durham University. Recorder 1996.
Personal: Interests include crime and France. Likes to be regarded as numerate and financially literate. Independent school governor.

KOLINSKY, Daniel
4 Breams Buildings (Christopher Lockhart-Mummery QC), London
(020) 7430 1221
clerks@breams.co.uk
Recommended in Planning
Specialisation: Administrative and public law, local government, human rights, planning and environment. Recent cases include R (Friends Provident) v SSETR, R (Barker) v Waverley BC and JS Bloor v Swindon BC. Acted for Arsenal FC (challenge to stadium relocation) and Bridgnorth DC (challenge to Secretary of State's recovery of overpaid housing benefit subsidy). Practice involves wide range of public law work including social security, education and local government as well as High Court planning cases and inquiries.
Career: Called to the Bar 1998. Completed training contract with *Anthony Gold* solicitors before coming to the Bar. Former judicial assistant to the Court of Appeal.
Publications: Regular contributor to the journal 'Judicial Review'.
Personal: Educated at Wadham College, Oxford (1st class degree in law). Lectured in contract law at Mansfield, Oxford and Queen Mary and Westfield, London.

KORN, Anthony
199 Strand (David Phillips QC), London
(020) 7520 4000
akorn@chambers2.demon.co.uk
Recommended in Employment
Specialisation: Specialises in all aspects of employment law, including sex, race, and disability discrimination, equal pay, TUPE, contracts of employment, restrictive covenants, unlawful deductions, redundancy and unfair dismissal. Appeared for the Respondent in Kellaway v Thames Valley Police (2000) IRLR 170, Mingo v Kent County Council (2000) IRLR 90 and Rossiter v Pendragon plc (2001) IRLR 256. Sits as an ACAS arbitrator.
Prof. Memberships: Employment Lawyers Association: member of management committee. Member of Employment Law Bar Association.
Career: Magdalen College, Oxford. Called to the Bar 1978.

KORNER, Joanna QC
6 King's Bench Walk (Roy Amlot QC),

London
(020) 7583 0410
Recommended in Crime

KOSMIN, Leslie QC
Erskine Chambers (Robin Potts QC), London
(020) 7242 5532
lkosmin@erskine-chambers.co.uk
Recommended in Company, Insolvency
Specialisation: Practice encompasses company law and corporate insolvency; especially litigation involving directors' duties, shareholders rights and remedies, internal company disputes and claims of professional negligence against Accountants and Solicitors.
Prof. Memberships: COMBAR, Chancery Bar Association.
Career: Called to the Bar 1976 and joined Erskine Chambers 1977. Took Silk: 1994. Deputy High Court Judge 2001.
Personal: MA, LL.M (Cantab), LL.M Harvard Law School. Born 12 August 1952. Lives in London.

KOVATS, Steven
39 Essex Street (Nigel Pleming QC), London
(020) 7832 1111
Recommended in Administrative & Public Law, Immigration
Specialisation: Public law, immigration, prisons, social security, mental health, human rights.
Prof. Memberships: ALBA, BEG.
Career: Call 1989.
Publications: Chapters on judicial review and habeas corpus in 'Civil Court Service'; chapters on judicial review and immigration in Bullen and Leake and Jacob.
Personal: Fluent French.

KRAMER, Stephen QC
2 Hare Court (Stephen Kramer QC), London
(020) 7353 5324
stephenkramer@2harecourt.com
Recommended in Crime
Specialisation: Criminal law specialist.
Prof. Memberships: Criminal Bar Association: Vice-Chairman 1999-2000. Chairman 2000-01.
Career: Called to the Bar in 1970. Joined 1 Hare Court, (now 2 Hare Court), Temple in 1988 from 10 King's Bench Walk. Assistant Recorder 1987-91. Recorder since 1991. Standing Counsel (Criminal Law) to Customs & Excise 1989-95. Appointed QC 1995. Head of Chambers 1996 -. President, Mental Health Review Tribunal.
Personal: Educated at Keble College, Oxford and the University of Nancy (France). Born 12 September 1947.

KVERNDAL, Simon QC
4 Essex Court (Nigel Teare QC), London
(020) 7653 5653
skverndal@4sx.co.uk
Recommended in Shipping
Specialisation: Time and voyage charters; carriage of liquid bulk cargoes; collision; salvage.
Prof. Memberships: LMAA (supporting member), COMBAR, LCLCBA
Career: Called to the Bar in 1982 (Middle Temple, Astbury Scholar).
Personal: Educated at Haileybury; Sidney Sussex College, Cambridge (Open Scholar, MA).

KYRIAKIDES, Tina
11 Stone Buildings (Murray Rosen QC), London
(020) 7831 6381
kyriakides@11stonebuildings.com
Recommended in Insolvency
Specialisation: Practises in commercial and Chancery litigation and advisory work, including contract, company law, corporate and personal insolvency, sale of goods, banking, guarantees and other securities, commercial fraud, credit and leasing transactions. Was appointed as an inspector for the Department of Trade and Industry to investigate insider dealing. An extremely effective advocate, she also has an excellent reputation for drafting and advising on company and commercial documentation.
Personal: Interests outside the law include the theatre and enjoying her Scottish art collection.

KYTE, Peter QC
Hollis Whiteman Chambers (QEB) (Julian Bevan QC & Peter Whiteman QC), London
(020) 7583 5766
Recommended in Fraud
Specialisation: All aspects of crime, particularly commercial fraud, though recent practice has included murders, robberies and major drugs cases.
Prof. Memberships: Criminal Bar Association.
Career: Five years in mining finance and investment banking before practising at Bar. Called 1970, Recorder 1992, Silk 1996. Legal assessor for GMC.
Personal: Trinity Hall Cambridge (MA Law). Ex-member NY Stock Exchange and Chicago Board of Trade. Married. Two children.

LAIDLAW, Jonathan
2 Hare Court (Stephen Kramer QC), London
(020) 7353 5324
jonathanlaidlaw@2harecourt.com
Recommended in Crime
Specialisation: Criminal law specialist. Prosecution work includes Mardi Gra commercial blackmail campaign, Canary Wharf bombing, Hungerford Bridge murder, Jill Dando murder, David Shayler and Jeremy Bamber (on appeal) cases. Recent defence work includes representing Ford, Texaco, B.O.C, B.H.P and Landrover in HSE and other regulatory authority prosecutions and investigations.
Career: Called to the Bar 1982. Junior Treasury Counsel 1995-2001. Senior Treasury Counsel 2001-. Recorder 1998-.
Personal: Educated Hull University. Date of Birth: 28 February 1960.

LAMBERT, Christina
6 Pump Court (Kieran Coonan QC), London
(020) 7583 6013
Recommended in Clinical Negligence

LAMBERT, Julian
Albion Chambers (Neil Ford QC), Bristol
(0117) 927 2144
lambert@albionchambers.freeserve.co.uk
Recommended in Crime, Health & Safety
Specialisation: Organised crime, corporate, commercial and regulatory offences, homicide and fraud. Disciplinary tribunals. Notable cases include: R v Canaan (1991) 92 Cr. App. R 16 (joinder with murder); R v Smith (1994) 15 Cr. App. R (S) 106 (contamination of goods); R v Sallis & Others (1994) 15 Cr. App. R (S) 281 (prison riots); R v Hampshire [1995] 2 Cr. App. R 219 (childrens' evidence); Attorney General's Reference No.s 25-27 of 1995 [1996] 2 Cr. App. R (S) 290 (racially aggravated GBH); R v Broad [1997] Crim. LR 666 (conspiracy to produce drugs); R v Sweeting and Thomas [1999] Crim. L.R. 75 (treatment statements section 23 CJA 1988); R v Taylor-Sabori [1999] 1 Cr. App. R 437 (interception of communications); R v GWTC - The Times, 3 July 1999 (corporate manslaughter, health and safety at work).
Prof. Memberships: Criminal Bar Association, Western Circuit.
Career: London School of Economics, call 1983. Recorder.

LANDAU, Toby
Essex Court Chambers (Gordon Pollock QC), London
(020) 7813 8000
Recommended in Arbitration
Specialisation: International and commercial arbitration. All aspects of international and commercial litigation.
Prof. Memberships: New York Bar Association; COMBAR; London Court of International Arbitration; Swiss Arbitration Association; Chartered Institute of Arbitrators (MCIArb); Co-Founder of the Young International Arbitration Group (LCIA); Editorial Board of the 'International Arbitration Law Review'.
Career: Merton College, Oxford: BA (Law) – First Class Hons (1990); MA (1994); Bachelor of Civil Law (BCL) – First Class Hons (1991); Eldon Scholarship (1991); Harvard Law School: LL.M (1993); Kennedy Scholarship & Lewis Fellowship; called to the Bar in 1993 (Middle Temple Queen Mother Scholarship & Harmsworth Exhibition); admitted as an Attorney-at-Law by the state of New York in 1994; called to the Bar of Northern Ireland in 2000. Retained by the DTI to advise on and assist in the drafting of the Arbitration Act 1996 (with Lord Saville). Advised on the arbitration provisions of the Contract (Rights of Third Parties) Act 1999 and drafted the ACAS Employment arbitration scheme. Member of the Lord Chancellor's Department Committee on the Hague Judgments Convention. Member of the UK delegation to UNCITRAL (since 2000). Annual visiting lecturer on arbitration law at the Asser Instituut in The Hague. Legal consultant to the Ministry of Justice of Thailand (Arbitration Office): 1993. Director of the London Court of International Arbitration.
Publications: Publications include 'The English Arbitration Act 1996: Text and Notes' (with Martin Hunter), Kluwer 1998.
Personal: Born 1967.

LANDSBURY, Alan
6 Gray's Inn Square (Michael Boardman), London
(020) 7242 1052
Recommended in Crime

LANG, Beverley QC
Blackstone Chambers (Presiley Baxendale QC & Charles Flint QC), London
(020) 7583 1770
Recommended in Administrative & Public Law, Education
Specialisation: Public law, education, human rights, employment and discrimination law. Interesting cases include DPP v Hutchinson (Greenham Common Byelaws held unlawful by the House of Lords.); Lloyd v McMahon (surcharged Liverpool Labour Councillors); Thomas v NUM (right of striking miners to picket); Halford v Sharples (acted for Assistant Chief Constable Alison Halford in her sex discrimination claim against Merseyside Police); Christmas v Hampshire County Council (House of Lords held duty of care owed by teachers to children with special education needs); ex parte S (admission to mental hospital and Caesarean section against patient's wishes); R v Secretary of State ex parte Owen Oysten (prisoners' rights). Publications include articles for the 'Modern Law Review', 'Industrial Law Journal' and 'Legal Action' and co-author of Public Law Project's 'Applicant's Guide to Judicial Review'.
Career: Called to the Bar 1978. Part-time chairman of Industrial Tribunal 1995-2001. Former lecturer in law at the University of East Anglia.
Personal: Born 13 October 1955.

LANGDALE, Timothy QC
Hollis Whiteman Chambers (QEB) (Julian Bevan QC & Peter Whiteman QC), London
(020) 7583 5766
barristers@holliswhiteman.co.uk
Recommended in Crime, Fraud
Specialisation: Principal area of practice is all aspects of criminal law with an emphasis on high profile, serious crime cases and commercial fraud. Practice involves both prosecution and defence work in these areas. Particular past cases include Alexander Howden, BCCI, Birmingham Six (final appeal), Judith Ward, Hillier (Swindon Town FC fraud), Darius Guppy, MTM, Landhurst

LEADERS AT THE BAR

Leasing, Derek Goldsmith, Stephen Hinchliffe, and prosecuting in the Sarah Payne case.
Prof. Memberships: Criminal Bar Association.
Career: Called to the Bar 1966. Treasury Counsel (Junior and Senior) 1979-92. QC 1992.

LANGDON, Andrew
Guildhall Chambers
(Adrian Palmer QC), Bristol
(0117) 930 9000
andrew.langdon@guildhallchambers.co.uk
Recommended in Crime, Health & Safety
Specialisation: Health and safety, serious fraud, confiscation and money laundering, drugs importation.
Prof. Memberships: CBA.
Career: Bristol University, call 1986.

LANGSTAFF, Brian QC
Cloisters (Laura Cox QC), London
(020) 7827 4000
bl@cloisters.com
Recommended in Clinical Negligence, Employment, Personal Injury, Product Liability
Specialisation: Principal area of practice is personal injury, employment and Trade Union cases. Has been instructed in most major industrial disputes (eg ambulancemen's strike, coal strike, Wapping) since the early 1980s and many important collective employment and Trade Union cases, although majority of practice has been in cases of serious personal injury (usually caused at work). Other area of practice is medical negligence and product liability, including actions against drug producers. Important cases include: Fairchild (asbestos causation); Page v Hull University (employment); Walker v Northumberland CC (personal injury: stress at work); Reay & Hope v BNFL (The 'Sellafield' case); Peach v Metropolitan Police (fatal assault by police/discovery issues); Ratcliffe v North Yorkshire CC (Equal Pay); Lawrence v Regent Office Care; News International v SOGAT (picketing: the 'Wapping' dispute); Clarke & Others v NUM (Miners' strike); Milligan & Securicor (TUPE; employment); R v Employment Secretary ex p Unison (Judicial Review, employment); Adams v Lancs CC (Transfers of Undertaking); Clark v BET (wrongful dismissal); Carmichael v National Power (contracts of employment); Jesuthasan v Hammersmith (discrimination); MOD v Wheeler (compensation); Barber v RJB Mining (working time); Quinn v MOD (mesothelioma); Jolley v Sutton (personal injury); RCO v Unison and Humphreys v Oxford (TUPE) and the 'tobacco' cases. Appointed Counsel to Inquiry into Bristol Heart Babies deaths. Major lay clients include most Trade Unions and their members as well as legally aided victims of accidents (both factory and medical). Professional clients include Trade Union solicitors (in private practice and in-house), law centres, medical and environmental practices and the Medical Defence Union. Former senior lecturer in law. Conference speaker on equal pay and employment issues, and employers' liability for work-related illnesses.
Prof. Memberships: Chairman of PIBA (1999-2001); Judge of EAT (since 2000); LCLCBA; ELBA; ALBA; ILS (Committee Member).
Career: Called to the Bar in 1971. Lecturer in law 1971-75. Joined present chambers in 1977. Appointed Assistant Recorder in 1991, Recorder 1995. Member of Northern Ireland Bar. Took Silk in 1994. Bencher (MT) 2001; Chair of Master of Rolls' working party on structured settlements, 2001 to date.
Publications: Consulting editor 'Bullen & Leake' and 'Personal Injury Handbook' (2001); contributor to Munkman; author of 'Health & Safety at Work' in Vol 20 of Halsbury's Laws (4th edn); 'Personal Injury Schedules: Calculating Damages' (2002) and of various articles in journals.
Personal: Educated at George Heriot's School, Edinburgh 1953-66 and St. Catharine's College, Cambridge 1967-70. Governor of local primary school. Enjoys sport, theatre and TV, politics, mowing the lawn, his family and travel.

LAPRELL, Mark
18 St John Street (Jonathan Foster QC), Manchester
(0161) 278 1800
Recommended in Personal Injury
Specialisation: Personal injury, clinical negligence, catastrophic injuries and heavy goods vehicle road transport law. Junior for claimant in Gorringe v Calderdale MBC in Court of Appeal - Times May 2002. Vehicle Inspectorate v Nuttall -H/C 1999 WLR G29. Vehicle Inspectorate v Bruce Cook 2000 RTR 90. Yorkshire Traction v V.1 2001 RTR J18.
Prof. Memberships: Northern circuit. FLBA.
Career: Pupillage 1979-80 with Rodney Klevan. Assistant Recorder 1997. Recorder 2000.
Personal: Born 1956. Bradford Grammar School 1966-74; Magdalen College, Oxford 1975-78. Married 1984; two children.

LASOK, Paul QC
Monckton Chambers (Kenneth Parker QC & Paul Lasok QC), London
(020) 7405 7211
Recommended in Competition/European Law, Tax
Specialisation: Specialist in all aspects of European Community law. Main areas of work include agriculture, competition, trade law and VAT. Cases include: Intel v VIA, 2002, competition/IPR; Broomco v CCE, 2002, customs duties; Marks & Spencers v CCE (2002, ECJ VAT capping); Three Rivers District Council v Bank of England (2000 HL, liability of banking regulator). Halifax v CCE (VAT avoidance).
Prof. Memberships: Bar European Group; European Circuit; Northern Ireland Bar.
Career: Called to the Bar 1977. Legal secretary (law clerk) to advocate-general JP Warner and advocate-general Sir Gordon Slynn, Court of Justice of the European Communities 1980-84. Private practice in Brussels, specialising in European Community law 1985-87.
Publications: Publications include 'The European Court of Justice: Practice and Procedure' (Butterworths 2nd edn 1994). 'Law and Institutions of the European Union' (Butterworths 2001). European editor of 'Weinberg & Blank on Take-Overs and Mergers' (Sweet & Maxwell). Joint editor of the Common Market Law Reports and CMLR Antitrust Reports.
Personal: Educated at Jesus College, Cambridge 1972-75 (MA) and at Exeter University 1975-77 (LLM). PhD Exeter University 1986.

LATHAM, Richard QC
7 Bedford Row (David Farrer QC), London
(020) 7242 3555
rlatham@7br.co.uk
Recommended in Fraud
Specialisation: Head of the Criminal Team at 7 Bedford Row specialising in prosecuting and defending commercial fraud and other serious crime. Clients include the SFO, CPS Central Casework, the DTI, C & E, Bank of England, the CPS and major solicitors in London and on Circuit. Standing counsel to the Inland Revenue, 1987-91. Sits at the Central Criminal Court. Authorised to try rape and other serious sexual offences. Prosecuted Aveling Barford Pension Fraud; Deutsche Morgan Grenfell fraud, British Bus corruption case, Operation Cornwall; defended R v Lawler tax fraud, R v Bryant mortgage fraud, R v Etchells corruption case. Prosecuted and defended circa 60 homicide cases.
Career: Called 1971, Midland Circuit, Recorder 1987, Queen's Counsel 1991.
Personal: Sailing, opera, photography. Advocacy trainer for Gray's Inn and Nottingham Trent University.

LATIMER, Andrew
40 King St, Manchester
(0161) 832 9082
alatimer@40kingstreet.co.uk
Recommended in Commercial (Litigation)
Specialisation: Commercial litigation, recoveries by office holders, directors duties, shareholders remedies, quasi-partnership and partnership, convenors in restraint of trade, passing off, winding up and administration. Reported cases: The Anglo-Eastern Trust Ltd v Kermanshahchi [2002] EWCA 198, South Coast Investments Ltd v Axisa [2002] All ER (D) 123, Lunnun v Singh [1999] All ER (D) 718, R v CLE ex p Nightingale, Latimer and Toms, Times 5.5.94.
Prof. Memberships: Chancery Bar Association, Northern Circuit Commercial Bar Association, Northern Chancery Bar Association.
Career: BA (Oxon), BCL. 1st Class in Law (1993). Joint winner of Oxford University Land Law Prize (1993), Bachelor of Civil Law (1994). Holt Award, Gray's Inn (1995). Appointed to Attorney-General's Panel for Civil Litigation (Provinces) in 2000.
Personal: Educated: St Mary's RC School, Newcastle upon Tyne and Hertford College, Oxford.

LAURENCE, George QC
New Square Chambers
(Charles Purle QC), London
(020) 7419 8000
clerks@newsquarechambers.co.uk
Recommended in Chancery
Specialisation: Practice encompasses property litigation (including landlord and tenant, planning and judicial review), parliamentary and countryside law (rights of way, town and village greens). Has appeared frequently as counsel before opposed Bill Committees in both Houses of Parliament (Channel Tunnel, Crossrail etc). Promoted Wye Navigation Order for Environment Agency under TWA 1992 [1997]. Acted in numerous reported cases, many on rights of way, including Celsteel [1986]; ex p Rubinstein [1990], Burrows [1991], O'Keefe [1993, 1996], Cowell [1993, CA], Bagshaw [1994], Emery [1997, CA], Billson [1998], White v Minnis [2000 CA], Sunningwell [2000 HL], Masters [2000, CA], Trevelyan [2001, CA].
Career: Called to the Bar 1972. Joined 9 Old Square 1973; current chambers January 1991. Silk 1991.
Personal: Educated at University of Cape Town 1966-68 (BA) and University College, Oxford 1969-71 (MA). Rhodes Scholar. Leisure pursuits include sport and theatre. Born 15 January 1947. Lives in London.

LAUTERPACHT, Sir Elihu QC
20 Essex Street (Iain Milligan QC), London
(020) 7842 1200
clerks@20essexst.com
Recommended in Public International Law
Specialisation: Specialist in international law, international arbitration and oil.
Prof. Memberships: London Court of International Arbitration.
Career: Called to Gray's Inn 1950; QC 1970.
Personal: Harrow; Trinity College, Cambridge (1948 BA; 1950 LLB).

LAWRENCE, Heather
11 South Square
(Christopher Floyd QC), London
(020) 7405 1222
hlawrence@11southsquare.com
Recommended in Information Technology, Intellectual Property
Specialisation: All aspects of intellectual property: patents, trademarks, copyright, registered and unregistered design right, passing off and breach of confidence; other matters with a technical content such as computer

contract disputes, and data protection.
Prof. Memberships: Intellectual Property Bar Association (formerly Patent Bar Association); (Hon. Sec, 1992-97) Royal Society of Chemistry (Associate Member); Institute of TM Attorneys (Associate Member).
Career: BA Hons (1st Class) Oxon (Chemistry). MA, DPHIL Oxon (Chemistry). Called to the Bar October 1991 (Middle Temple).

LAWRENCE, Nigel
7 Harrington Street Chambers (David Steer QC & Robert Fordham QC & Iain Goldrein QC), Liverpool
(0151) 242 0707
john@7harringtonstreet.co.uk
Recommended in Health & Safety
Specialisation: Health and safety and personal injury litigation. Considerable experience in all forms of health and safety work, and in particular in major and complex health and safety prosecutions in the Crown Court, and also in all forms of personal injury litigation (including large value injury claims and fatal accidents).
Career: Called to the Bar in 1988 (Lincoln's Inn). Member of Northern Circuit.
Personal: Educated at Rydal School, North Wales 1979-84. University of Leicester 1984-87 (LLB Honours). Inns of Court School of Law 1987-88. Interests include travel and sport (in particular football, rugby, cricket and golf). Married with four children (three daughters and one son).

LAWRENCE, Patrick QC
4 Paper Buildings (Jean Ritchie QC), London
(020) 7643 5000
patrick.lawrence@4paperbuildings.com
Recommended in Professional Negligence
Specialisation: Professional negligence, particularly that of solicitors, barristers surveyors and accountants. In addition, has extensive experience in insurance and commercial contracts. Cases include: Penn v Brill [1997] 1 WLR 1356 (solicitors; breach of warranty of authority); Bristol & West Building Society v Fancy & Jackson [1997] 4 All ER 582 (solicitors' liability to residential lenders); Platform Home Loans v Oyston Shipways Ltd [1998] 3 WLR 94 (Saamco and contributory negligence); Cave v Robinson Jarvis & Rolfe [2001] Lloyds Rep Pn 290 (solicitors; deliberate concealment).
Career: BA (Oxon) 1st class; called 1985; Silk 2002.

LAWSON, Edmund QC
9-12 Bell Yard (D Anthony Evans QC), London
(020) 7400 1800
Recommended in Crime, Fraud

LAWSON, Michael QC
23 Essex Street (Michael Lawson QC), London
(020) 7413 0353
michaellawson@23essexstreet.co.uk
Recommended in Crime
Specialisation: Criminal law specialist. Practice covers general crime, serious organised crime, drugs, child sexual abuse, commercial fraud, police-related actions. Contributor to the 'Inns of Court School of Law Manual of Professional Conduct' and author of 'Refocus on Child Abuse' (1994). Experience of advocacy teaching. Governing Committee IATC.
Prof. Memberships: Criminal Bar Association.
Career: Called to the Bar in 1969 and joined present chambers in 1971. Appointed Assistant Recorder in 1983 and Recorder in 1987. Took Silk in 1991. Leader of the South Eastern Circuit, Nov 1997-2000. Boundary Commissioner 2000.
Personal: Educated at Monkton Combe School 1959-64 and London University 1966-69. Born 3 February 1946.

LAWSON, Robert
4 Essex Court (Nigel Teare QC), London
(020) 7653 5653
rlawson@4sx.co.uk
Recommended in Aviation
Specialisation: All aspects of aviation litigation, arbitration and advisory work. In particular: aviation insurance; liability of carriers, manufacturers, maintainers and tour operators; regulatory issues; aircraft leases and finance; and arrest of aircraft. Cases include: Morris v KLM Royal Dutch Airlines [2002] 2 WLR 578; Disley v Levine [2002] 1 WLR 785; Rolls Royce Plc v Heavylift-Volga Dnepr Ltd [2000] 1 Lloyd's Rep 653; The Post Office v British World Airlines Ltd [2000] 1 Lloyd's Rep 378; Monarch Airlines Ltd v London Luton Airport Ltd [1998] 1 Lloyd's Rep 403; Deaville v Aeroflot Russian International Airlines [1997] 2 Lloyd's Rep 67; Milor SRL v British Airways Plc [1996] QB 702; and Gurtner v Beaton [1993] 2 Lloyd's Rep 369.
Prof. Memberships: COMBAR, MRAES.
Career: BA (Oxon). Dip Law (City). Called 1989.

LE GRICE, Valentine QC
1 Hare Court (Bruce Blair QC), London
(020) 7797 7070
legrice@1hc.com
Recommended in Family
Specialisation: Ancillary relief.
Prof. Memberships: FLBA; PNBA.
Career: Called to the Bar in 1977. QC 2002.
Personal: BA (Dunelm).

LEAVER, Peter QC
One Essex Court (Lord Grabiner QC), London
(020) 7583 2000
Recommended in Sport
Specialisation: Main areas of practice are commercial law, insurance, banking and financial services and arbitration. Involved in Tin Council and Mirror Pension Fund litigation, the Ford Europe case in the ECJ and major arbitrations including a large scale arbitration about the validity of the termination of a management contract governed by Middle Eastern law. Contributor to 'Pre-Trial and Pre-Hearing Procedures Worldwide' (Graham & Trotman and IBA, 1990). Deputy High Court Judge. Recently has appeared in a case that was heard in the House of Lords concerning anti-trust injunctions, and in a lengthy international commercial arbitration in Singapore. Was a member of the Court of Arbitration for Sport ad hoc division for the Winter Olympics at Salt Lake City.
Prof. Memberships: COMBAR, IBA, Bar European Group, Midland and Oxford Circuit, London Common Law and Commercial Bar Association, Society of Commonwealth Lawyers, Society of Public Teachers of Law. Member of the Chartered Institute of Arbitrators. Member of Court of Arbitration of Sport.
Career: Called to the Bar in 1967. At Paper Buildings 1968-72, and joined current chambers in 1973. Took silk in 1987. Member of General Council of the Bar 1987-90 (Chairman of the Bar Committee, 1989). Appointed Recorder and Director of IMRO in 1994. Bencher of Lincoln's Inn 1995.
Personal: Educated at Aldenham School and Trinity College, Dublin. Leisure pursuits include being a football referee, sport, wine, opera and theatre. Born 28 November 1944.

LEDERMAN, David QC
18 Red Lion Court (Anthony Arlidge QC), London
(020) 7520 6000
david.lederman@18rlc.co.uk
Recommended in Crime
Specialisation: Crime in all its aspects from fraud to robbery to murder to Brinks Gold Bullion Robbery.
Prof. Memberships: Criminal Bar Association.
Career: Cambridge MA.
Personal: Eating, drinking, sport, theatre, cinema, opera, history, reading.

LEECH, Stewart
Queen Elizabeth Building (Florence Baron QC), London
(020) 7797 7837
Recommended in Family

LEECH, Thomas
9 Old Square (Michael Driscoll QC), London
(020) 7405 4682
Recommended in Chancery
Specialisation: Modern Chancery practitioner with particular experience in commercial Chancery litigation (including equitable remedies, fiduciary duties, financial services, offshore trusts, share disputes, telecommunications and warranty claims), professional negligence (including auditors, barristers, investigating accountants, solicitors, surveyors, valuers and US attorneys) and property litigation (including commercial landlord and tenant, leasehold valuation and real property). Junior counsel for the plaintiff in the Nationwide managed litigation and junior counsel for a number of the defendants in Thyssen-Bornemisza v Thyssen-Bornemisa in Bermuda. Notable cases include: Target Holdings Ltd v Redferns (1996) AC 421 (breach of trust); Mannai Investments Ltd v Eagle Star (1997) 1 BCLC 390 (share warranty, rectification); Electra Private Equity Partners v KPMG Peat Marwick (1998) PNLR 137 (auditors' duty of care); Nationwide BS v Balmer Radmore (1999) Lloyd's Rep (PN) 241 (solicitors' negligence, managed litigation).
Prof. Memberships: Chancery Bar Association, Professional Negligence Bar Association.
Career: Educated at Lancaster Royal Grammar School and Wadham College, Oxford (MA, BCL), called in 1988 (Harmsworth Major Scholar of the Middle Temple, winner of the Astbury Prize).
Publications: 'Flenley & Leech, Solicitors' Negligence' (Butterworths, 1999), contributor to the Lloyds' Law Reports (PN), co-editor of 'Spencer Bower on Estoppel by Representation' (2002).

LEEMING, Ian QC
St. James's Chambers (Robert Sterling & Ian Leeming QC), Manchester
(0161) 834 7000
Recommended in Chancery
Specialisation: Chancery and commercial litigation; building and construction work (technology and construction court/arbitrations). Insolvency, contentious company work, banking, professional negligence and civil fraud are emphasised. Reported cases include: Williams v Burlington (1977) (Company Charges), Brady v Brady (1988) (Financial assistance for purchase of shares). Re: Abbey Leisure (1990) (Unfair prejudice petitions) P&C&R&T Ltd (1991) (Administrators and Section 11 of Insolvency Act 1986). Sen v Headly (1991) (death-bed gifts of land). Connaught Restaurants (1992) (Indemnity costs in forfeiture proceedings). Morse v Barratt (1993) (exception to Murphy v Brentwood principles). Re Jennings (1994) (Family provisions claims). Kershaw v Whelan (1996) (Discovery and waiver of Professional Privilege). Kershaw v Whelan (No. 2) (1997) (Fiduciary duties). Hurst v Bryk (1999) (solicitors partnership dispute). For more information see website www.ianleemingqc.com
Prof. Memberships: Chancery Bar Association; Northern Chancery Bar Association; TECBAR; Professional Negligence Bar Association; Society of Construction Law.
Career: Called 1970. Silk 1988. Recorder of the Crown Court 1989. Practised at Northern Chancery and Commercial Bar until taking silk. Since has divided

LEADERS AT THE BAR

time between London and Manchester. Joined Lamb Chambers 1992. Deputy Deemster 1998.
Personal: Born 10 April 1948. Manchester University LLB (1970). Sometime lecturer in Law, Manchester University. Fellow of the Society for Advanced Legal Studies. Interests: the family; gourmet food; sports cars.

LEES, Andrew
St. Paul's Chambers
(Nigel Sangster QC), Leeds
(0113) 245 5866
Recommended in Crime

LEGGATT, George QC
Brick Court Chambers (Christopher Clarke QC), London
(020) 7379 3550
leggatt@brickcourt.co.uk
Recommended in Commercial (Litigation), Insurance
Specialisation: Commercial law: including insurance and reinsurance, professional negligence (involving accountants, actuaries, insurance brokers, solicitors and barristers), commercial fraud, computer systems litigation, shipping, company acquisitions, sale of goods and international trade. Other areas of practice include product liability law and media law/defamation.
Career: Called 1983; QC 1997. Cases of note: Westdeutsche Landesbank v Islington; NRG v Bacon & Woodrow; Hill v M&G; Guiness Mahon v Kensington & Chelsea; Commercial Union v NRG Victory; Dubai Aluminium v Salaam; South West Water v ICL; Re Medicaments.

LEGGE, Henry
5 Stone Buildings (Henry Harrod), London
(020) 7242 6201
Recommended in Chancery
Specialisation: Chancery practitioner with particular emphasis on onshore and offshore trusts with related taxation issues and on pensions and professional negligence. Recent cases include Adam International Trustees v Theodore Goddard (2000) (professional negligence relating to failed export of trust), Meegan v Commercial Vehicle Spares (enforcement of determination of the Pensions Ombudsman) (1998) and Evans v Westcombe (1999) (missing beneficiary indemnity policies and relief from breach of trust). Particular experience of disputes arising out of venture capital acquisitions. Has contributed a number of articles to 'Trusts and Estates Law Journal' and to 'Private Client Business'.
Career: Called in 1993.
Personal: Educated Eton College and Worcester College, Oxford.

LEIGHTON WILLIAMS, John QC
Farrar's Building (John Leighton Williams QC), London
(020) 7583 9241
Recommended in Personal Injury
Specialisation: General common law, with emphasis on personal injuries and clinical negligence work.
Prof. Memberships: LCBA; PIBA; SE Circuit.
Career: Called to the Bar 1964. Appointed Recorder 1985. Took silk 1986. Member of the Criminal Injuries Compensation Board 1987-2002. Master of the Bench, Gray's Inn 1994, Deputy High Court Judge 1995.

LEIPER, Richard
11 King's Bench Walk Chambers (Eldred Tabachnik QC & James Goudie QC), London
(020) 7632 8500
leiper@11kbw.com
Recommended in Employment
Specialisation: All aspects of employment law in both courts and tribunals, including discrimination, TUPE, industrial action, restraint of trade and confidential information. Other practice areas include commercial litigation and public law. Cases include: BG plc v O'Brien, CA (EAT[2001] IRLR 496) (scope of trust and confidence term); Clark v Nomura International plc [2000] IRLR 766 (discretionary bonus for proprietary trader); R (BMA) v Specialist Training Authority [1999] EdCR 661 (implementation of subordinate legislation).
Prof. Memberships: Employment Lawyers Association.
Career: Called 1996.
Publications: Contributor to Tolley's 'Employment Handbook' and 'Halsbury's Laws on Administrative Law'.
Personal: Birmingham University (LLB); Keble College, Oxford (MJur).

LEIST, Ian
2 Hare Court (Stephen Kramer QC), London
(020) 7353 5324
Recommended in Crime
Specialisation: Criminal Law and Public Law.
Prof. Memberships: Criminal Bar Association and Administrative Law Bar Association.
Career: Called 1981; currently instructed in the Bloody Sunday Inquiry.
Personal: Film, music, reading, sport and travel.

LEMON, Jane
Keating Chambers, London
(020) 7544 2600
jlemon@keatingchambers.com
Recommended in Construction
Specialisation: Barrister specialising in building and civil engineering; architects', engineers' and quantity surveyors' professional liability; arbitrations in UK and Far East; Technical and Construction Court.
Career: Qualified 1993; Inner Temple.
Publications: 'Professional Negligence and Liability LLP' – Chapter Seven.
Personal: King Edward V1 High School for Girls; Jesus College, Oxford (BA Hons).

LEONARD, Anthony QC
6 King's Bench Walk (Roy Amlot QC), London
(020) 7583 0410
worsley@6kbw.freeserve.co.uk
Recommended in Crime
Specialisation: General criminal practice with a concentration on fraud.
Prof. Memberships: Inner Temple, South Eastern Circuit, Criminal Bar Association.
Career: Called to the Bar in 1978 and joined current chambers in 1979. Standing Counsel to the Inland Revenue, South Eastern Circuit 1993-99. Took Silk 1996.
Personal: Leisure interests include music and theatre. Born 21 April 1956. Lives in London.

LESLIE, Stephen QC
Furnival Chambers
(Andrew Mitchell QC), London
(020) 7405 3232
Recommended in Crime
Specialisation: General and commercial/white collar crime in particular S.F.O Inland Revenue, major custom fraud and other complex fraud (including overseas) criminal taxation appeals. Privy Council Commonwealth Appeals.
Prof. Memberships: Criminal Bar Association. South Eastern practise on other circuits.
Career: Call 1971. Silk 1993.
Publications: Articles in the 'Times Newspaper Legal Magazine' on disclosure in child cases and on legal and criminal taxations.

LORD LESTER OF HERNE HILL QC
Blackstone Chambers (Presiley Baxendale QC & Charles Flint QC), London
(020) 7583 1770
clerks@blackstonechambers.com
Recommended in Administrative & Public Law, Human Rights
Specialisation: Specialises in public law, employment, media and European law. Was called to the English Bar in 1963, appointed QC in 1975 and a Bencher of Lincoln's Inn in 1985. Became a Life Peer in 1993. Is a former Recorder and Deputy High Court Judge, and was Special Advisor to the Home Secretary (Roy Jenkins) 1974-76 on anti-discrimination legislation. Campaigned for 30 years for a Human Rights Act, and is President of INTERIGHTS and a Council member of JUSTICE. Co-editor of Butterworths 'Human Rights Law and Practice' (1999), and Honorary Professor of Public Law at University College London. Has argued many leading public law cases in England, in other Commonwealth countries and before both European Courts.
Personal: Married to a Special Immigration and Asylum Adjudicator and they have a son and a daughter.

LETT, Brian
South Western Chambers (Brian Lett), Taunton
(01823) 331919
Recommended in Crime

LEVER, Sir Jeremy QC
Monckton Chambers (Kenneth Parker QC & Paul Lasok QC), London
(020) 7405 7211
chambers@monckton.co.uk
Recommended in Competition/European Law
Specialisation: Administrative law, competition law, European Community law, international and comparative law, utilities regulation. R v Secretary of State for Trade and Industry, ex p Isle of Wight Council, 7 April 2000 (judicial review, EC Law).
Prof. Memberships: Council of Management and Executive Committee, British Institute of International and Comparative Law.
Career: Fellow (1957-) and Senior Dean (1988-), All Souls College, Oxford. Director (non-ex), Dunlop Holdings Ltd. 1973-80; Wellcome plc 1983-94; Member, Arbitral Tribunal, US/UK Arbitration concerning Heathrow Airport User Charges 1989-94. Visiting Fellow Wiessenschaftszentrum Berlin für Sozialforschung, 1999.
Publications: 'Butterworths Competition Law' (consulting editor); 'Common Law of Europe', 'Tort Law' (comparative casebooks); Bellamy & Child, 'Common Market Law of Competition', 1st-3rd eds. (consulting editor).
Personal: Educated: Bradfield College, Berks; University College, Oxford and Nuffield College, Oxford. Interests include classical music and porcelain.

LEVY, Allan QC
17 Bedford Row (Allan Levy QC), London
(020) 7831 7314
allanlevyqc@compuserve.com
Recommended in Family
Specialisation: Expertise in child law, medical law and human rights law. Appeared in numerous leading cases in House of Lords, Court of Appeal and European Court of Human Rights including Re F (sterilisation), Re M (Children Act, Re H (Children Act), Barratt v L.B. of Enfield (negligence), W v Essex CC (negligence), In re S and In re W (human rights and care orders) and A v UK (Art 3 ECHR). Frequent broadcaster and lecturer. Chairman, Staffordshire Pindown Inquiry 1990-91.
Prof. Memberships: Fellow, Royal Society of Medicine; honorary legal advisor National Children's Bureau; Council of Justice; Fellow, Society for Advanced Legal Studies.
Career: Called to the Bar 1969. Silk 1989. Recorder 1993.
Publications: Author and editor of books on child law and child abuse.
Personal: Educated Bury Grammar School 1953-61 and Hull University 1961-64. Senior Visiting Fellow, Southampton University.

LEVY, Jacob
9 Gough Square (John Foy QC), London

(020) 7832 0500
Recommended in Personal Injury
Specialisation: All aspects of clincal negligence and personal injury work, particularly cases involving dental, gynaecological and orthopaedic problems. Has a particular interest in industrial disease work, principally deafness but also work-related upper limb disorders. Bulk of personal injury work comprises slippers, trippers, snippers, lifters, and rear-end shunters.
Career: LLB (Hons) London (LSE) 1984. Called July 1986 and joined 9 Gough Square following pupillage there with John Foy and John Reddihough.
Personal: Young family prevents anything much other than supporting failing football team (as well as playing in one) and watching late night TV whilst eating pizza. Otherwise fanatical film and music buff. Byline: 'Eat football, sleep football - practice PI'.

LEVY, Michael
2 Bedford Row (William Clegg QC), London
(020) 7440 8888
mlevy@2bedfordrow.co.uk
Recommended in Crime
Specialisation: Wholly criminal practice, mostly defence but not exclusively; general crime and fraud; regular leading work. Fraud cases include: R v McMakin (diversion fraud centering on Fort Patrick and involving London City Bond); R v Kerry (VAT fraud); R v Khaliq & Others (Nigerian advance fee fraud). Serious crime cases include: R v Serafinowicz (the first ever prosecution under the War Crimes Act); R v Jelesic (war crimes case at the International Criminal Tribunal for the former Yugoslavia); R v Murphy & Others (importation of £125,000,000 of cocaine); R v Uddin (murder) [1999] 2 All ER 744; R v Jeans (drug importation) (reported as Van Bokkum and Ors) [2000] 6 Archbold News 2, CA. Represented a number of sporting personalities. Instructed a number of police disciplinary cases. Inquests. Instructed by *Henry Milner & Co* (Henry Milner); *Burton Copeland* (Mark Haslam and Rachael Hubbard); *Nelsons* (Catherine Parsons); *Russell Jones & Walker* (Scott Ingram); *McCormacks* (Leslie Cuthbert); *Magrath & Co* (Kevin Roberts).
Prof. Memberships: SE Circuit; Criminal Bar Association; British Academy of Forensic Science; International Criminal Law Association.
Career: Called to Bar 1979.

LEVY, Neil
St John's Chambers (Christopher Sharp QC), Bristol
(0117) 921 3456
clerks@stjohnschambers.co.uk
Recommended in Commercial (Litigation)
Specialisation: Banking. Cases of note: Jarrett v Barclays Bank [1999] QB 1; Natwest Bank v Story, The Times 14 May 1999; Woolwich Plc v Gomm, [2000], 79 P & CR 61.

Prof. Memberships: Chancery Bar Association.
Career: Called to the Bar 1986. In-house lawyer, Lloyds Bank 1987. Joined St John's Chambers 1992.
Personal: Contributor to 'Paget's Law of Banking', 11th edn (1996) and to 'Law and Practice of Domestic Banking' (Penn & Wadsley), 2nd edn (2000).

LEWIS, Adam
Blackstone Chambers (Presiley Baxendale QC & Charles Flint QC), London
(020) 7583 1770
Recommended in Administrative & Public Law, Sport
Specialisation: European Community law within a public, commercial, competition and sports law practice.
Career: Call 1985. Professional experience with *Wilmer Cutler & Pickering* in Washington DC and London and *McCutcheon Doyle Brown & Enersen* in San Francisco between 1985-88, and in the Cabinet of Sir Leon Brittan, European Commissioner responsible for competition and financial institutions, in Brussels in 1991-1992.
Personal: Fluent in French and a working knowledge of German and Norwegian.

LEWIS, Clive
11 King's Bench Walk Chambers (Eldred Tabachnik QC & James Goudie QC), London
(020) 7682 8500
lewis@11kbw.com
Recommended in Administrative & Public Law, Education
Specialisation: Main areas of practice are public law and judicial review, EC law, education, local government, discrimination and environmental law. Interesting cases include: R v Secretary for Trade and Industry ex p. BT3G (state aids and mobile phone auction); R v Head Teacher of Alperton Community School ex p. B (Article 6 and school expulsions); R v Secretary of State for the Environment ex p. Eurotunnel (imposition of security measures on Channel Tunnel); Preston v Wolverhampton NHS Trust (1998) (compatibility of time limits for equal pay claims with European law); Barry v Midland Bank plc (1999) (sex discrimination in calculation of redundancy payments); R v Powys Council ex p. Hambidge (1998) (power to charge for provision of community care services).
Prof. Memberships: Administrative Law Bar Association; Bar European Group.
Career: Fellow, Selwyn College, Cambridge 1986-93, Lecturer in Law, University of Cambridge 1989-93. Called to the Bar 1987. Joined present chambers in 2000.

LEWIS, James QC
3 Raymond Buildings (Clive Nicholls QC), London
(020) 7400 6400

chambers@3raymondbuildings.com
Recommended in Crime
Specialisation: Extradition; fraud: judicial review of criminal matters and especially review of warrants; case stated; restraint orders; election work. Recent notable cases: R v Bow Street Magistrate ex parte Pinochet (No. 1) [1998] 3 WLR 1456, (No. 2) [1999] 2 WLR 272, (No.3) [1999] 2 WLR 287; R v Governor of Brixton Prison ex parte Levin [1997] AC 741; R v Secretary of State for the Home Department ex parte Launder HL [1997] 1 WLR 839 (HL); R v Secretary of State for the Home Department ex parte Gilmore [1997] 2 Cr App R 374. R v Bow Street Magistrates Court [1998] 2 WLR 498; R v Staines Magistrates Court ex parte Westfallen [1998] 1 WLR 652; Government of Switzerland v Rey [1998] 3 WLRI (PC). R v Governor of Belmarsh Prison ex parte Gilligan (No 2) [1998] COD 195. Private prosecution for the Hillsborough Family Support Group 1996-2000.
Career: BSc (Hons). Call 1987. Recorder of the Crown Court 2000. Attorney General's List 2000.

LEWIS, Marian
30 Park Place (John Jenkins QC), Cardiff
(020) 2939 8421
Recommended in Crime
Specialisation: All forms of serious sexual cases particularly involving the examination and cross-examination of children of all ages and young persons. Serious fraud and serious violence. First language Welsh and able to conduct cases of whatever complexity in that language.
Prof. Memberships: Criminal Bar Association.
Career: Called 1977.
Personal: LLB at University College, London. Married with two children. Involved with advocacy training on Circuit. Outside interests include opera and music, Pembrokeshire. Parent Governor, Ysgol Gyfun Gymraeg Glantaf, Caerdydd.

LEWIS, Paul QC
30 Park Place (John Jenkins QC), Cardiff
(02920) 398421
clerk@30.parkplace.law.co.uk
Recommended in Crime
Specialisation: Crime: commercial fraud; customs and excise cases. Both prosecutes and defends.
Prof. Memberships: Criminal Bar Association.
Career: Called 1981; Silk 2001; Recorder, Wales and Chester Circuit.
Personal: Leisure pursuits include sport, travel and music. Educated: Pontypridd Boys' Grammar School; University of Leicester (LLB Hons).

LEWIS, Ralph QC
No5 Chambers (Gareth Evans QC), Birmingham
(0121) 606 0500
rl@5fountaincourt.law.co.uk

LEADERS AT THE BAR

Recommended in Clinical Negligence, Personal Injury
Specialisation: Catastrophic injury claims; industrial diseases; HSE prosecutions; clinical negligence; professional negligence.
Prof. Memberships: Personal Injury Bar Association; Professional Negligence Bar Association.
Career: Jesus College, Oxford MA (Oxon). Called to Bar 1978. Middle Temple. Assistant Recorder 1996. Recorder of the Crown Court 2000. Bar Council Elected Member 1999-2002; Silk 1999. Reported cases include: Thomas v Bunn [1991] 1 A.C. 362 H.L. (interest on judgments); Langley v Dray [1998] PIQR P314 C.App. (liability of fleeing driver to pursuing policeman); Daniels v Walker [2000] 1 WLR 1382 C.App. (use of joint experts); Larner v Solihull MBC [2001] PIQR P248 C.App. (liability of local authority for road safety improvements); Sutherland v Hatton [2002] PIQR P241 C.App. (work place stress).
Personal: Born 29 June 1956. Married with three children. Shooting, skiing and family.

LEWIS, Rhodri Price QC
Eldon Chambers (Patrick Clarkson QC & William Hicks QC), London
(020) 7583 1355
Recommended in Environment, Planning
Specialisation: Principal area of practice is town and country planning and environmental law including judicial review, public inquiries and statutory appeals to the High Court. Clients include development and waste disposal companies, waste regulation authorities and county and district councils. Author of article on Waste Management in 'Journal of Planning and Environmental Law' 1993. Co-author 'Environmental Law' OUP 2000.
Prof. Memberships: Local Government Planning and Environmental Bar Association, Wales and Chester Circuit, Midland and Oxford Circuit, UK Environmental Law Association 1999.
Career: Called to the Bar 1975. Appointed Recorder 1998. Appointed QC 2001. Assistant Parliamentary Boundary Commissioner 2001.
Publications: 'Environmental Law' (OUP 2000).
Personal: MA Oxon 1970-73, Dip Crim (Cantab) 1973-74. Born 7 June 1952.

LEWIS, Robert
11 New Square (Sonia Proudman QC), London
(020) 7831 0081
Recommended in Environment

LEWISON, Kim QC
Falcon Chambers (Jonathan Gaunt QC & Kim Lewison QC), London
(020) 7353 2484
Recommended in Property Litigation
Specialisation: Specialises in Chancery and real property law. Practice covers landlord and tenant, rent review, interpretation of contracts, agricultural

LEADERS AT THE BAR

holdings, conveyancing, easements, restrictive covenants, compulsory acquisitions, suretyship and professional negligence in connection with real property. Recent reported cases include Pye v Graham (adverse possession); Southwark LBC v Mills (quiet enjoyment); Bruton v London and Quadrant (licence or tenancy); Jervis v Harris (entry to repair); Curtis v London Rent Assessment Committee (fair rent). In 1988 appointed by the Department of the Environment as a member of the Study Team investigating professional negligence and insurance against professional liability. Blundell lecturer three times.
Prof. Memberships: COMBAR; London Common Law & Commercial Bar Association; Chancery Bar Association. Governor of Anglo-American Real Property Institute 1995-99, Chairman 2002, Chairman Property Bar Association.
Career: Called to the Bar in 1975. Member of Falcon Chambers since 1976. Took Silk 1991. Appointed Assistant Recorder in 1993. Recorder 1997. Deputy High Court Judge 2000 Bencher Lincoln's Inn.
Publications: Publications include 'Woodfall on Landlord and Tenant' (General Editor since 1990); 'The Interpretation of Contracts' (1997); 'Lease or Licence' (1985); 'Development Land Tax' (1976); 'Drafting Business Leases' (2001). Consultant editor of Property & Compensation Reports since 1990.
Personal: Educated at St Paul's School 1965-70 and Downing College, Cambridge (1st Class Hons in English Tripos) 1970-73. Fluent French speaker. Council member of the Liberal Jewish Synagogue 1989-95; council member Leo Baeck College (1996-2001). Trustee Centre for Jewish Education (1999-2001).

LIEVEN, Nathalie
4 Breams Buildings (Christopher Lockhart-Mummery QC), London
(020) 7430 1221
Recommended in Administrative & Public Law, Education, Local Government, Planning
Specialisation: Planning, public and administrative law including local government, social security, education, mental health and community care. Has promoted a number of Parliamentary Bills. Recent cases include Nessa v Chief Adjudication Officer; R v Leominster DC ex p Pothecary; White v Special Educational Needs Tribunal.
Career: Called to the Bar in 1989. Appointed to the Supplementary Panel of Junior Counsel to the Crown (Common Law) in 1995. Member of the Planning and Environmental Bar Association and the Administrative Law Bar Association.
Personal: Educated at Godolphin and Latymer School and Trinity Hall, Cambridge. Awarded Karmel, Reid and Prince of Wales Scholarships at Grays Inn.

LIGHTMAN, Daniel
Serle Court (Lord Neill of Bladen QC), London
(020) 7242 6105
dlightman@serlecourt.co.uk
Recommended in Chancery
Specialisation: General chancery and commercial litigation. Recent cases include: Gil v Baygreen Properties Ltd, The Times, 17th July 2002 (possession order); Jeeves v Official Receiver [2002] BCC 453 (insolvency); Murphy v McGlynn & anr [2002] WTLR 231 (probate); Re Assico Engineering Ltd [2002] BPIR 15 (bankruptcy); Mamidoil-Jetoil Greek Petroleum Co SA v Okta Crude Oil Refinery AD [2001] 2 All ER (Comm) 193 (commercial contract); Verjee v CIBC Bank and Trust Co (Channel Islands) Ltd [2001] Lloyd's Law Rep (Banking) 279 (banking); In re the Estate of Phyllis Mary Bliss (Deceased) [2001] 1 WLR 1973 (will); Peskin v Anderson [2001] 1 BCLC 372 (fiduciary duties); Re Duke Group Ltd (in liquidation) [2001] BPIR 459 (cross-border insolvency); Re Lummus Agricultural Services Limited [2001] 1 BCLC 137 (insolvency); The University of Nottingham v Dr Simon Fishel, [2000] IRLR 471 (fiduciary duties); Re a Company No. 007356/98 [2000] BCC 214 (insolvency); Secretary of State for Trade and Industry v North West Holdings Limited and North West Holdings Plc [1999] 1 BCLC 425 (insolvency); Mealey Horgan plc v Timothy Horgan, The Times, 6 July 1999 (fiduciary duties).
Prof. Memberships: Chancery Bar Association, COMBAR.
Career: Called to the Bar 1995.
Publications: Co-authored Chapters 2 and 7 of Lightman & Moss, 'The Law of Receivers and Administrators of Companies' (3rd Ed, 2000). 'Appointment of Representatives under the Civil Procedure Rules' ([2001] 'Private Client Business', Sept/Oct, p 311). 'Testamentary Options: all are the options clear?' ('Trusts and Estates Law Journal', July/August 2001). 'Lord Chancellor and Master of the Multifarious Roles' ('The Times', 27 February 2001), 'The Bailiffs of Jersey and Guernsey, the Lord Chancellor and the Separation of Powers' [1999] JR 54, and 'The Jersey and Guernsey Bailiffs and the Lord Chancellor Revisited' [2000] JR 111.
Personal: BA Lit. Hum. (First Class), Magdalen College, Oxford; Dip. Law (Distinction) City University, London. Hardwicke, Mansfield and Denning Scholar of Lincoln's Inn.

LIGHTWING, Stuart
Counsel's Chambers (Stuart Lightwing), Middlesbrough
(01642) 315000
Recommended in Family
Specialisation: Family/matrimonial finance, employment, medical and other professional negligence, personal injury and partnership.
Prof. Memberships: Professional Negligence and the Family Law Bar Associations.
Career: LLB, FCIS, FRSA, MCMI, FCIArb. Called 1972 (M.T). Harmsworth Law Scholar. Also barrister in NSW, Australia. Chairman of Appeal Tribunals.

LIMB, Patrick
Ropewalk Chambers (Ian McLaren QC), Nottingham
(0115) 947 2581
clerks@ropewalk.co.uk
Recommended in Personal Injury
Specialisation: Psychiatric harm and industrial diseases litigation: Hicks v Chief Constable of South Yorkshire Police [1992] 2 AER 63; Alcock v Chief Constable of South Yorkshire Police [1992] 1 AC 310; Barnsley v Prest [1996] ICR 85; Frost v Chief Constable of South Yorkshire Police [1997] 3 WLR 1195; Bannister v SGB plc [1997] 4 AER 129; VSEL v Cape [1998] PIQR 207; Tranmore v Scudder (CAT April 28, 1998); King v RCO [2001] PIQR 206; Green v Yorkshire Traction [2001] EWCA Civ 1925.
Prof. Memberships: Personal Injuries Bar Association; Nottinghamshire Medico-Legal Society.
Career: The Edinburgh Academy; Pembroke College, Cambridge.

LINDBLOM, Keith QC
2 Harcourt Buildings (Robin Purchas QC), London
(020) 7353 8415
Recommended in Planning
Specialisation: Planning, local government, parliamentary, compulsory purchase and compensation law. Works for both private and public sector clients.
Prof. Memberships: Planning and Environment Bar Association; Parliamentary Bar Mess.
Career: Called to the Bar 1980. Joined 2 Harcourt Buildings (Gerard Ryan QC) in 1981. QC 1996.

LINDEN, Thomas
Matrix Chambers, London
(020) 7404 3447
Recommended in Employment
Specialisation: Employment law, discrimination law, public law, human rights and sports law. His employment law work tends to be cases which overlap with commercial law (restraint of trade, breach of contract, executive terminations), appellate work, cases with a European dimension (transfer of undertakings, equal pay, working time) and collective labour law (industrial action, recognition, etc). His discrimination law work covers race, sex and disability discrimination in a range of legal contexts. His public sector work is focused mainly on health and education. His sports cases include disputes between sportsmen and clubs or agents, and cases concerning doping in sport.
Prof. Memberships: The Employment Lawyers Association, Administrative Law Bar Association.
Career: BA Jurisprudence (First Class) and BCL at Keble College, Oxford 1984-89; called to the Bar 1989. Awarded Council of Legal Educational Studentship, and Prince of Wales, Atkin and Karmel Scholarships at Gray's Inn. Appointed Junior Counsel to the Crown (B Panel) in 1999.

LISSACK, Richard QC
35 Essex Street (Christopher Wilson-Smith QC), London
(020) 7353 6381
www.ralqc.com
Recommended in Crime, Fraud, Health & Safety, Personal Injury
Specialisation: Public inquiries; public law including human rights; professional negligence including clinical negligence; personal injury; commercial fraud; corporate manslaughter by negligence. He brings to his work his undoubted skill as an advocate, his ability to grasp issues of real difficulty, his appetite for detail and his ability to cross-examine expert and lay witnesses alike. This is all underpinned by the ability to strike up an excellent rapport with all manner of clients - corporate or personal, law enforcement agencies, and claimants and defendants. A team player, Richard Lissack is always open minded and receptive to group preparation whilst not abrogating his position at the head of the legal team. He has recently gained unequalled experience in the field of gross negligence manslaughter, as well as appearing in almost every significant public inquiry of recent times. Each of these areas has embraced health and safety law in all its forms. Recent Inquiries: Shipman Inquiry, Bristol Royal Infirmary Inquiry, Re Ladbroke Grove Rail Inquiry, Southall Rail Inquiry, Burns Inquiry, Neale Inquiry, Leicester Epilepsy Inquiry, Royal College of Pathologists Seminar, Chair of multi-disciplinary meeting re organ retention, National Seminar on Organ Retention, Royal Brompton Hospital Inquiry. Internal Inquiry, re Lawrence Dallaglio RFU Disciplinary Proceedings, re Coral Cove Internal Inquiry. Recent Criminal Cases: Manslaughter by Gross Negligence - prosecuting: A-G Reference Corporate liability in Crime, CPS Policy Directorate Generic Advice re Manslaughter by gross negligence, re Hatfield Train Crash, re Ladbroke Grove Train Crash, R v Litchfield (Maria Asumpta), R v Great Western Trains Ltd. (Southall Rail Crash), re Imperial War Museum, re Paloma I, re Army Cadet Force, re Exmouth Diving Centre. Manslaughter by Gross Negligence - defending: R v Stoddart and Kite and OLL Ltd, (Lyme Bay Canoe Disaster), R v Ayres O'Connor and Guideday Ltd (Pescado), R v Jessey (Lone Signature), re Imco Plastics Ltd, re Millenium and Copthorne plc, re Norton. Serious Fraud for SFO: Maxwell, Operation Holbein £400 million fraud on the NHS Balfron

LEADERS AT THE BAR

Group, Gidney Securities; Serious Fraud for Defence: R v Malik (Pharmaceutical), R v Oza (Pharmaceutical), R v Dean (Millenium Champagne). Recent Civil Cases: R v Secretary of State for Defra (re Foot and Mouth), R v Secretary of State for Health ex p Wright-Hogeland (Neale case), Microsoft Europe (Advising on confidential issue), Re Hunting with Dogs (Advising re English and European legal challenge to Hunting Bill), Gregory v Portsmouth City Council (House of Lords/European Court - scope of the tort of malicious prosecution), London Borough of Richmond, London Borough of Harrow, Manchester City Council and Redcar and Cleveland Council (Court of Appeal and House of Lords test case re cost of care in the community), Nationwide Multi-party action re Organ Retention (Multi Claimant series of linked group and representative actions for thousands of claimants), Ratcliff v Harper Adams College (Court of Appeal - Occupiers Liability Act -What is the duty owed to an adult trespasser?), Mirage Inks v Rexam Limited (Court of Appeal/ Mercantile Court case - technical issues re Ink Manufacture), Wyke v Lloyds Bank (Court of Appeal - Extent of duties of Mortgages in possession), Diocese of Honk Kong and Macao v China (High Court, Hong Kong - Change in Education in Hong Kong), Sorsky Defries v C&E (Claim for damages for unlawful C&E raid on firm of accountants - large claim settled), Beverly Allitt litigation (QBD - Clinical Negligence - Including £2m action - infant who survived attack by nurse), re Princess Madawi (Chancery Division - Solicitors negligence Action for Crown Princess and Saudi Arabian Embassy), re Wheelwash Limited (Patents Court), re Hyder plc (Patents Court), Re Home Equity Release Schemes (QBD Multi Claimant series of linked group and representative actions for 11,000+ Claimants).
Career: Called 1978, QC 1994 aged 37, Recorder 1993 onwards.
Publications: For details see www.ralqc.com.

LISTER, Caroline
One King's Bench Walk (Anthony Hacking QC), London
(020) 7936 1500
Recommended in Family
Specialisation: Child abduction, public law and private law cases involving children and their families, representing parents, local authorities, guardians and the official solicitor. Ancillary relief and other financial matters.
Prof. Memberships: FLBA.
Career: BSc London University in Comparative Physiology and Microbiology.
Personal: Two children. Endurance riding, renovating ancient cottage.

LITHMAN, Nigel QC
2 Bedford Row (William Clegg QC), London
(020) 7440 8888
nlithman@2bedfordrow.co.uk
Recommended in Crime
Specialisation: Serious fraud and serious crime: cases include high profile and 'sensitive' murders: R v Pearce and R v Tien Lai (murder by 16 year olds); R v Ngai (murder by mother of four children); R v Paton (murder by battered wife of husband); 2001 R v Tsang (murder by father of daughter); 2002, R v Smith (manslaughter of child). Instructed in first high publicity carjacking/murder case. Death in custody: R v Linford. General crime: R v David Courtney CCC (perverting the course of justice). Substantial white collar crime: R v Walker and others ('The Ostrich Farm' SFO case); R v Kaye (fraud on Balfour Beatty); R v Massingham, lead defendant in massive SFO case; 2002 R v Kelsall and others 4 month financing fraud; 2002 R v Hashash Carousel/£14 million VAT fraud. Confiscation and restraint: R v Rassool 2001 claim by Customs of £16 million; Operation Uproar. Extradition work Customs & Excise. Briefs in Michael Michael supergrass case. 2002 R v Palmer London City Bond Case. Inland revenue fraud: R v Litanzios and Edwards. Health and safety: R v Morris explosion/manslaughter case; R v Wheeler, involuntary manslaughter. Tribunal and judicial review work. Major police inquiry cases: R v Stimpson and Bird 'Operation Apache' Essex Police; 2002 'Operation Lancet' Teeside Police; 2001 R v O'Brien, public malfeasance trial for high ranking officer involved in 'Zero Tolerance' policing. Road traffic - for many years specialised in death by dangerous driving cases: R v Douglas Taylor (Sentencing authority) 2000. Private prosecutions and representing the campaign against drunken driving. National television appearances. Has appeared in British Indian Ocean territories. Recorder of South East Circuit; CBA and Chairman of the Essex Bar Mess.

LITTLE, Ian
9 St. John Street (John Hand QC), Manchester
(0161) 955 9000
Recommended in Personal Injury

LIVESEY, Bernard QC
Four New Square (Justin Fenwick QC), London
(020) 7822 2000
barristers@4newsquare.com
Recommended in Personal Injury, Professional Negligence
Specialisation: Principal specialisation is litigation in the following fields: general common and commercial law, personal injuries, professional negligence (architects, accountants, doctors, engineers, solicitors, surveyors and valuers) and insurance. Leading cases include Rahman v Arearose (contribution between tortfeasors); Pearson v Sanders Witherspoon (damages for loss of a chance); Kapur v JW Francis & Co (liability of insurance broker); Spring v Guardian Assurance (negligent references); Ancell v Chief Constable of Bedfordshire (liability of police); Halford v Brookes (limitation); Kumar v AGF Insurance Ltd (construction of insurance contract); Wood v Bentall Simplex Ltd (Fatal Accidents Act damages).
Prof. Memberships: COMBAR, Bar European Group; Personal Injuries Bar Association, Professional Negligence Bar Association.
Career: Called to the Bar 1969. Recorder 1987. Silk in 1990. Fellow of International Academy of Trial Lawyers. Deputy High Court Judge. Bencher of Lincoln's Inn.
Personal: Educated at Peterhouse, Cambridge (MA, LLB).

LLOYD, Heather
Chavasse Court Chambers (Theresa Pepper), Liverpool
(0151) 707 1191
Recommended in Crime
Specialisation: Crime, particularly allegations of sexual abuse.
Prof. Memberships: Criminal Bar Association.
Career: Liverpool University 2:1 LLB 1979.
Personal: Married, two children.

LLOYD, Huw
3 Serjeants' Inn (Robert Francis QC & John Grace QC), London
(020) 7427 5000
hlloyd@3serjeantsinn.com
Recommended in Clinical Negligence
Specialisation: Specialises in medical law, medical negligence and medical ethics work. Recent interesting cases include Re J (A minor) (1992) 3 WLR 5c7; Re S [1993] Fam 123; R v Mid Glamorgan FHSA, South Glamorgan H.A. ex p. Martin; Re S (1995) 1 WLR 110; Secretary of State for Home Dept. v Robb (1995) 2 WLR 722; Re S (hospital patient: court's jurisdiction) (1995) 2 WLR 38; Re J (hospital patient: foreign curator) [1995] 3 WLR 596; Re CH [1996] 1 FLR; Re R (adult: medical treatment) [1996] 2 FLR 99; Re C (adult patient: publicity) [1996] 2 FLR 25; Re T (wardship: medical treatment) [1997] 1 FLR 502; Re D (Medical Treatment) [1998] 1 FLR 411; Re D (medical treatment, mentally disabled patient) [1988] 2 FLR 22; Re JT (adult, refusal of medical treatment) [1998] 1 FLR 48; Re A (children) (conjoined twins: surgical separation) [2000] 4 All ER 961.
Prof. Memberships: London Common Law and Commercial Bar Association. Professional Negligence Bar Association.
Career: Called to the Bar 1975. Middle Temple, Blackstone Entrance Exhibition and Benefactors Senior Law Scholar.
Personal: Educated at City of London School and Leicester University (LLB). Born 10 May 1952.

LLOYD JONES, David QC
Brick Court Chambers (Christopher Clarke QC), London
(020) 7379 3550
lloydjones@brickcourt.co.uk
Recommended in Competition/European Law
Specialisation: EU law, public and private international law, public law, commercial law. Recent cases include Al Adsani v UK; Fogarty v UK; McElhinney v UK (State Immunity); Hamilton v Al Fayed (third party costs); Muvunyi v Secretary of State; Lilly v Novo Nordisk; Ex p Pinochet (No 1) & (No 3) (HL); Locabail v Bayfield (CA); R v Lord Saville ex p A (CA); R (Widgery A) v Lord Saville (CA); P v P (Diplomatic Immunity) (CA); Philip Brothers v Republic of X (CA); A Ltd v B Bank (Act of State); Westland Helicopters v Arab Organisation for Industrialisation. Brussels Convention cases in Luxembourg include Webb v Webb; Kleinwort Benson v City of Glasgow; Cinnamond v Von Horn; Mietz v Gesselschaft Yachting; Société Group Josi v UGIC; Ganter v Basch. Competition Cases in Luxembourg include LdPE; PVC I; PVC II; TetraPak v Commission; Blue Circle v Commission; British Cement Association v Commission; Banks v British Coal Corporation; Hopkins v National Power; NALOO v Commission I and II; Banks v Coal Authority. EU cases before English Courts include R v MAFF ex p RSPCA; R v Dover Harbour Board ex p Gilder; Richard Cound Ltd v BMW (CA); First County Garages v Fiat Auto; R v Comptroller of Patents ex p Lenzing.
Career: Fellow of Downing College, Cambridge 1975-91. Junior Crown Counsel, Common Law 1997-99; QC 1999; Recorder 1994; Deputy High Court Judge 2001.

LLOYD-ELEY, Andrew
2 Hare Court (Stephen Kramer QC), London
(020) 7353 5324
andrewlloyd-eley@2harecourt.com
Recommended in Crime
Specialisation: General crime with particular emphasis on serious fraud. Involved in a number of the big diversion fraud cases (Hare Wines, Operation Galleon, Ellis Martin) often for the main defendant. Appeared for the main defendant in the biggest smuggling (duty goods) trial so far, R v Amsbury. Also involved in large VAT and other commercial frauds including EEC subsidy frauds. Defended in the largest murder investigation Hampshire police had undertaken, R v Rai (the body in the field).
Prof. Memberships: Criminal Bar Association.
Career: Called 1979.

LOCKEY, John
Essex Court Chambers (Gordon Pollock QC), London
(020) 7813 8000
jlockey@essexcourt.net

LEADERS AT THE BAR

Recommended in Commercial (Litigation), Insurance
Specialisation: Insurance and reinsurance. International trade. Shipping law. Professional Negligence.
Prof. Memberships: Committee Member, British Insurance Law Association.
Career: Downing College, Cambridge BA (Law) 1985. Harvard Law School LLM 1986. Called to the Bar 1987.
Personal: Born 1963.

LOCKHART, Andrew
St Philips Chambers (John Randall QC), Birmingham
(0121) 246 7000
Recommended in Crime
Specialisation: Experience in all aspects of serious criminal work including complex PII applications. Specialisation in Trading Standards prosecutions including Trade Marks work.
Prof. Memberships: Criminal Bar Association.
Career: Regular Commissioner in the Army 1984-90.

LOCKHART-MUMMERY, Christopher QC
4 Breams Buildings (Christopher Lockhart-Mummery QC), London
(020) 7430 1221
Recommended in Local Government, Planning
Specialisation: Advises and appears for developers and local authorities at public inquiries and in the High Court. Planning inquiries include the Channel Tunnel Terminal (Waterloo), National Gallery Extension, and Mansion House Square Development. Planning cases in the House of Lords include Westminster City Council v British Waterways Board, Westminster City Council v Great Portland Estates, Tesco Stores Ltd v Secretary of State for the Environment.
Career: Called to the Bar July 1971. Took Silk 1986; Bencher Inner Temple 1993; Head of Chambers April 1993; Recorder May 1994; Deputy High Court Judge 1995; Assistant Boundary Commissioner 2000.
Personal: Born 7 August 1947. Educated at Stowe School and Trinity College, Cambridge (BA Hons).

LODDER, Peter QC
2 Bedford Row (William Clegg QC), London
(020) 7440 8888
pnlodder@2bedfordrow.co.uk
Recommended in Crime
Specialisation: Heavy defence workload in fraud, money laundering and general crime. Substantial experience as a prosecutor for the Serious Fraud Office and Customs & Excise ('A' list). Recent cases include: corporate manslaughter proceedings; murder; Inland Revenue Fraud; solicitors' client account fraud and alleged fraud by solicitors on Legal Aid Fund. Court of Appeal on the relevant confiscation regime where offending straddles amendments to 1988 legislation R v Aarons (part of Martin & Ors - 2002 Crim LR 228).
Prof. Memberships: Committee member of Criminal Bar Association, elected member of the General Council of the Bar since 1994.
Career: QC since 2001, Recorder of the Crown Court 2000, Jules Thorn (Major) scholarship Middle Temple 1982. Called to Bar 1981.

LOFTHOUSE, Simon
Atkin Chambers (Robert Akenhead QC), London
(020) 7404 0120
Recommended in Construction
Specialisation: Domestic and international construction, civil engineering, energy oil and gas projects. Professional negligence (architects, surveyors, engineers and quantity surveyors). Contentious (litigation, arbitration and adjudication), non-contentious, mediation and adjudication. Practice includes large engineering projects, onshore and offshore, Treasury advisory and litigation, commercial and residential developments, airport terminals, hospitals and computer installations. Cases include J Jarvis and Sons Ltd v Castle Wharf Developments Ltd [2001] Lloyds PN 308 (CA); Dal Sterling v Kenchington Ford [2001] CILL 1779; ABB v Zedal [2001] BLR 66; Amec Civil Engineering Ltd and Alfred McAlpine Construction Ltd v Cheshire County Council [1999] BLR 303; King v McKenna [1991] 2 QB 480; Humber Oil Terminals Trustees v Harbour and General 59 BLR 1 (CA); Crittal Windows TJ Evers 54 Con LR 66; Cadmus v Amec 51 Con LR 105; Vickery v Modern Securities [1988] 1 BCLC 428 (CA).
Prof. Memberships: TECBAR. Common Law and Commercial Bar Association. TECBAR accredited Adjudicator.
Career: LLB (Hons) (Lond); called 1988. Articles Editor for Current Law 1990-95. Member of Bar Council.
Personal: Married. Main leisure interests: squash, theatre.

LOMAS, Mark H
Littleton Chambers (Michel Kallipetis QC), London
(020) 7797 8600
Recommended in Professional Negligence
Specialisation: Professional negligence, instructed particularly by insurers of solicitors, barristers and accountants, but also acts for surveyors, engineers, insurance brokers, financial advisors and patent and trademark agents. Appears regularly for professionals before their professional disciplinary bodies. Particular expertise in wasted costs claims, having conducted numerous cases at first instance for solicitors and barristers and having acted for barristers in two recent cases in the Court of Appeal where indemnity costs were ordered against the claimants - Wall v Lefever and Fryer v RICS. Member of the SIF dishonesty panel, examining solicitors on issues of dishonesty and advising whether cover should be withdrawn. Regularly appointed as arbitrator in disputes between firms of solicitors or between SIF and its insured. Recently successfully defended a firm of solicitors against a claim of racial discrimination brought by a member of the Bar.
Prof. Memberships: Combar; Professional Negligence Bar Association.
Career: Called to the Bar in 1977; three years in mixed common law/criminal chambers in 2 Pump Court; joined present chambers in 1982, then situated at 2 Crown Office Row, moving to present address in 1995.
Personal: Educated at Oundle School and Trinity Hall, Cambridge. Lives in London and Rutland.

LOMNICKA, Prof. Eva
Four New Square (Justin Fenwick QC), London
(020) 7822 2000
barristers@4newsquare.com
Recommended in Financial Services
Specialisation: Advisory work on Consumer Credit Act 1974, securities regulation and financial services, reflecting publications: (1) 'Encyclopedia of Consumer Credit Law'; (2) 'Lomnicka and Powell, Encyclopedia of Financial Services Law'; (3) articles and papers in various national and international publications. (4) 'Palmer's Company Law' (Part 11); (5) 'Ellinger and Lomnicka, Modern Banking Law'. Advisor to UK delegation to UNCITRAL convention on receivables financing (1997-2001 Vienna and New York).
Career: Professor of Law, King's College London. Called to the Bar 1974.
Personal: Born 17 May 1951; 1969-73 Girton College, Cambridge (MA, LLB, Chancellor's Medal). Married with three children.

LONG, Andrew
Peel Court Chambers (Michael Shorrock QC), Manchester
(0161) 832 3791
Recommended in Crime

LONGMAN, Michael
St John's Chambers (Christopher Sharp QC), Bristol
(0117) 921 3456
Recommended in Crime

LORD, Richard QC
Brick Court Chambers (Christopher Clarke QC), London
(020) 7379 3550
Recommended in Commercial (Litigation), Shipping
Specialisation: General commercial law, including shipping, insurance and reinsurance, and professional negligence. Selected cases: 'HOUDA'; 'ADITYA VAIBHAV'; 'SUBRO VALOUR'; NRG V Bacon & Woodrow; 'APOSTOLIS'; IMP v Cape & Dagleish; 'EVER SUCCESS'; Groupama Navigation v Catatumbo; 'SLETREAL'; 'ASTERI'; Bacardi v THP; 'HAPPY RANGER'.
Prof. Memberships: Heilbron Committee (Joint Working Party of the Civil Courts).
Career: Called to Bar 24 November 1981, Inner Temple; QC 2002.
Personal: Born 2 January 1959 in Leamington. Educated at Stowe School and Cambridge - MA 1 year Scholarship at Cambridge (1979-80). Publication: 'Guide to the Arbitration Act 1996' (with Simon Salzedo) (Cavendish 1996).

LORD, Tim
2 Temple Gardens (Dermod O'Brien QC), London
(020) 7822 1200
tlord@2templegardens.co.uk
Recommended in Personal Injury
Specialisation: Recent cases include: Nanglegan v Royal Free Hampstead NHS Trust (2002) 1 WLR 1043, CA.; Dunnett v Railtrack Plc; The Times 3.4.02, CA.
Prof. Memberships: Secretary of LCLCBA. Member of COMBAR, PIBA, Western Circuit.
Career: Called by Inner Temple 1992.
Personal: Educated at Bedford Modern School and Christ's College Cambridge (First in law). Married and lives in London. Hobbies: cricket, golf, sailing.

LOVELL-PANK, Dorian QC
6 King's Bench Walk (Roy Amlot QC), London
(020) 7583 0410
clerks@6kbw.com
Recommended in Crime
Specialisation: General crime including commercial fraud.
Prof. Memberships: Committee Criminal Bar Association 1989-; General Council of the Bar 1989-92 and 1998-; International Bar Association 1993-; Panel of Chairmen Police Discipline Appeals 1991-; Human Rights Institute 1996-. American Bar Association (Associate) 1997-.
Career: QC 1993; Recorder since 1989; called 1971.

LOWE, (Nicholas) Mark QC
2-3 Gray's Inn Square (Anthony Porten QC & Anthony Scrivener QC), London
(020) 7242 4986
Recommended in Administrative & Public Law, Local Government, Planning
Specialisation: Town and country planning (all areas, with particular experience of shopping; housing; employment; leisure; listed buildings and major energy; waste and incineration projects). Local government and administrative law (particularly local authority powers and finance, including PFI and major projects) environmental and property related litigation and all tribunal work including Lands Tribunal. Judicial Review - planning, local government and housing.
Prof. Memberships: PEBA, ALBA.
Career: Called to Bar 1972. Same Chambers since 1973. QC 1996.

LEADERS AT THE BAR

LOWE, Vaughan
Essex Court Chambers (Gordon Pollock QC), London
(020) 7813 8000
Recommended in Public International Law
Specialisation: Public international law. Reported cases, as counsel, include: 'Case concerning passage Through the Great Belt', International Court of Justice, 1991-92 (for Finland); Southern Bluefin Tuna case, UNCLOS ad hoc arbitral tribunal, 2000 (for Japan); Lauder v Czech Repucli, CME v Czech Republic, UNCITRAL arbitrations, 2001- (for Czech Republic); case concerning the MOX plant, ITLOS and UNCLOS ad hoc tribunal, 2001- (for Ireland).
Prof. Memberships: American Society of International law; British Institute of International & Comparative Law; International Bar Association; International Law Association.
Career: Chichele Professor of Public International Law in the University of Oxford; Fellow of All Souls College, Oxford. Previously Lecturer in law, University of Wales, Cardiff, 1973-79; Lecturer in Law, 1979-86, then Senior Lecturer in Law, University of Manchester, 1986-88; University Lecturer in Law, then Reader in International Law, University of Cambridge and Fellow of Corpus Christi College 1988-99. Visiting Professor, Duke Law School, Fall 1990; Tulane Law School, Summer 2000.
Publications: Books include 'Extraterritorial Jurisdiction' (1983); Churchill & Lowe, 'The Law of the Sea' (3rd edition, 1999); Collier & Lowe, 'The Settlement of International Disputes' (1999). Many articles and chapters in books. Joint editor (with JR Crawford) 'British Year Book of International Law', (1999 to date). Editorial boards: 'Marine Policy'; 'International Journal of Marine and Coastal Law'; 'European Journal of International Law'; 'International Arbitration Law Review'; 'Law and Practice of International Courts and Tribunals'; 'A Practitioners Journal'.
Personal: LLB (Wales) 1973; Maxwell Prize, 1973. LLM (Wales) 1978. PhD (Wales) 1980. MA (Cambridge) 1991. MA (Oxford) 1999. Barrister (Gray's Inn), 1993.

LUBA, Jan QC
Two Garden Court (Owen Davies QC & Courtenay Griffiths QC), London
(020) 7353 1633
Recommended in Administrative & Public Law, Local Government

LUCAS, Noel
187 Fleet Street (Andrew Trollope QC), London
(020) 7430 7430
chambers@187fleetstreet.com
Recommended in Crime, Fraud
Specialisation: Crime, fraud.
Prof. Memberships: Criminal Bar Association.
Career: Standing Counsel to HM Customs & Excise for the South Eastern Circuit. Recorder.

LYDIARD, Andrew
Brick Court Chambers (Christopher Clarke QC), London
(020) 7379 3550
lydiard@brickcourt.co.uk
Recommended in Aviation, Commercial (Litigation), Product Liability
Specialisation: Commercial litigation, product liability, insurance, reinsurance and aviation.
Career: BA (Oxon) LLM (Harvard).

LYNCH, Adrian QC
11 King's Bench Walk Chambers (Eldred Tabachnik QC & James Goudie QC), London
(020) 7632 8500
clerksroom@11kbw.com
Recommended in Employment
Specialisation: Principal area of practice is employment law, covering the full gamut of that specialism including unfair and wrongful dismissal, sex, race and disability discrimination, trade union law and restrictive covenants. Has appeared in the European Court of Justice in Luxembourg as well as before the Commission and Court of Human Rights in Strasbourg. Other areas of practice are commercial and public law.
Prof. Memberships: Gray's Inn.
Career: Called to the Bar in 1983 and joined present chambers in 1984. Took Silk in 2000, prior to which he was a member of the Attorney General's Panel of Junior Counsel (Supplementary Panel).
Publications: As an academic teaching at King's College London between 1971-84, published a number of articles and book reviews, including publications in the 'Law Quarterly Review'. Author of the chapter on settlements in employment law in David Foskett QC's work 'The Law and Practice of Compromise' in the most recent edition of that work.
Personal: Jelf Medallist 1971 at King's College, London. .

LYNCH, Jerome QC
Charter Chambers (Stephen Solley QC), London
(020) 7832 0300
Recommended in Fraud

LYNCH, Patricia QC
18 Red Lion Court (Anthony Arlidge QC), London
(020) 7520 6000
Recommended in Crime
Specialisation: Crime, prosecution and defence, covering the most serious sexual offences/murder etc, plus hijacking. In the past year, cases successfully prosecuted, defended, have included numerous murder cases and also defence before the General Medical Council.
Career: Recorder. Silk 1998.

LYNDON-STANFORD, Michael QC
Maitland Chambers (Michael Lyndon-Stanford QC & Charles Aldous QC), London
(020) 7406 1200
Recommended in Company
Specialisation: Principal fields of practice consist of company and commercial litigation, including minority shareholders proceedings, insolvency, business law, commercial fraud, professional negligence, equity, insurance, reinsurance and property. Recent cases include Shaker v Bedrawi & Others concerning application of the Prudential v Newman principle and Senate Electrical Wholesalers Ltd v Alcatel Submarine Networks Ltd. (Court of Appeal) concerning share purchase agreements.
Prof. Memberships: Chancery Bar Association, Commercial Bar Association.
Career: QC 1979. Has practised in foreign jurisdictions and has been called (ad hoc) for cases in Hong Kong, Singapore and the Isle of Man.
Personal: MA (Cantab). Bencher of the Inner Temple and Member of Lincoln's Inn.

LYNESS, Scott
Eldon Chambers (Patrick Clarkson QC & William Hicks QC), London
(020) 7583 1355
Recommended in Planning

MABB, David QC
Erskine Chambers (Robin Potts QC), London
(020) 7242 5532
Recommended in Company

MACDONALD, Charles QC
4 Essex Court (Nigel Teare QC), London
(020) 7653 5653
cmacdonald@4sx.co.uk
Recommended in Shipping
Specialisation: Admiralty and commercial shipping; carriage of goods; international trade; commercial and international arbitration; insurance; private international law; marine/environmental law; transport. Has extensive experience of all types of marine litigation including upwards of 140 salvage arbitration disputes. Among his recent cases concerning road transport, collision, arrest, sovereign immunity; statutory inquiries, carriage by sea and limitation of liability by tonnage are: Spectra v Hayesoak [1997] 1LLR 153, CA; The Giuseppe Di Vittorio [1998] 1LLR 136, CA; Northern Shipping v Deutsche Seereederei and others [2000] 2 LLR 255, CA; The ENIF [1997] 1LLR 643, Admiralty Court; The Sitarem & Spirit [2001] 2LLR 107, Admiralty Court; The Zim Piraeus [2001] 2 LLR 291, CA. Formal Investigations: The Derbyshire (2000); Bowbelle/Marchioness (2000). Also regularly appears in City of London commercial arbitrations.
Prof. Memberships: Member of the Panel of Lloyd's Salvage Arbitrators 2000.
Career: Glasgow Academy, New College Oxford (MA Hons Jurisprudence 1971). Called to Bar, Lincoln's Inn, 1972. Appointments: Queen's Counsel, 1992. Assistant Recorder of the Crown Court, 1996. Recorder of the Crown Court 1999. Lloyd's Salvage Arbitrator 2000. Recorder of the County Court 2002.
Publications: Editorial Board, 'International Maritime Law' (Lawtext Publishing Limited).
Personal: DOB 31.8.49, Glasgow. Married with three daughters and lives in East Sussex.

MACDONALD, Ian QC
Two Garden Court (Owen Davies QC & Courtenay Griffiths QC), London
(020) 7353 1633
Recommended in Crime, Immigration

MACDONALD, Ken QC
Matrix Chambers, London
(020) 7404 3447
Recommended in Crime, Fraud
Specialisation: A criminal law specialist. Complex frauds (including SFO work, deposit-taking frauds, advance fee frauds, solicitor frauds etc). Sanctions-busting cases (all aspects, including the illegal export of arms and weapons-making equipment, computers, high technology, pharmaceuticals etc. Clients in this area include major foreign defence corporations). Political violence (Irish, Sikh, Palestinian and Algerian). Bombings, murders and possession of arms and explosives. Major drugs conspiracies (importation, manufacture and supply). Murders (including multiple murders and child killings). Cases include Matrix Churchill; The Ordtech Appeal; R v McKane (an IRA trial involving bombings and multiple murders); R v Kinsella (the Warrington bombing case); R v Sakaria (a Sikh separatist case involving explosives and conspiracies to murder); R v Zekra (the car-bombing of the Israeli Embassy in London).
Prof. Memberships: Member Treasury Counsel Selection Committee (CCC); Vice Chair, Criminal Bar Association.

MACHELL, John
Serle Court (Lord Neill of Bladen QC), London
(020) 7242 6105
clerks@serlecourt.co.uk
Recommended in Partnership
Specialisation: General commercial/chancery dispute resolution and advisory work, particularly partnership, company, insolvency, property, wills, trusts and probate.
Prof. Memberships: Association of Partnership Practitioners, COMBAR.
Career: University of Southampton 1988-92 LLB (1st Class). Serle Court (formerly 13 Old Square) 1994 to date.
Publications: 'Limited Liability Partnerships: The New Law', Jordans.
Personal: Married with two children.

MACHELL, Raymond QC
Byrom Street Chambers, Manchester
(0161) 829 2100
Recommended in Personal Injury

LEADERS AT THE BAR

MACLEAN, Alan
Brick Court Chambers (Christopher Clarke QC), London
(020) 7379 3550
maclean@brickcourt.co.uk
Recommended in Administrative & Public Law
Specialisation: Administrative law specialism within wide-ranging commercial practice. Particular emphasis on commercial judicial review and related regulatory, EU and human rights issues. Also has experience of the fields of environment, health, funding entitlement, local government and sporting bodies. Has appeared without a leader in public law cases in the ECJ, House of Lords and Court of Appeal. Recent cases include In re Northern Ireland Human Rights Commission [2002] UKHL 25 [2002] All ER (D) 140 Jun; BT3G Ltd v Secretary of State (challenge to legality of 3G Mobile Phones auction); Hamilton v Al Fayed (resisting costs application against funders of libel action); Heather v Leonard Cheshire (whether private sector body 'public authority'); Transport for London v London Regional Transport (challenge to PPP tube financing plans). Reported cases include Smith v Bridgend County Borough Council [2002] 1 AC 333 HL (powers of company administrator); Legal Aid Board ex p Coe [2000] 1 WLR 1909 CA (circumstances in which the Legal Aid Board could amend a certificate); Gloucestershire ex p Barry [1997] AC 584 (whether local authority entitled to take account of resources when assessing need); Porter v Magill (1997) 96 LGR 157 DC (Westminster 'Homes for Votes' appeal); Cosslett Contractors Ltd [1998] Ch 495 C.A. (equitable charges); Wandsworth ex p Beckwith [1996] 1 WLR 60 (contracting out of local authority services); Secretary of State ex p Richmond [1996] 4 All ER 93 (night flights policy).
Prof. Memberships: Administrative Law Bar Association.
Career: Called 1993. First in year at Bar School. Karmel, Bacon, Prince of Wales and Macaskie Awards from Gray's Inn. Scarman Scholar of Inns of Court School of Law. Appointed to Treasury C Panel 1999, B Panel in 2002. Junior Counsel to the Bristol Royal Infirmary Public Inquiry.
Publications: Contributor to 'Halsbury's Laws' (local authority powers, Vol 44(2) reissue), Richard Gordon QC 'Judicial Review Law and Procedure' (2nd ed) (Sweet & Maxwell, 1995).
Personal: Educated University College, Oxford (double First in PPE), Harvard University (Kennedy Scholarship) and City University (CPE: distinction).

MACLENNAN, Alison
11 Old Square (Grant Crawford & Jonathan Simpkiss), London
(020) 7430 0341
clerks@11oldsquare.co.uk
Recommended in Charities
Specialisation: Detailed experience acting for charities in a litigious and advisory capacity, with additional expertise in property litigation, general commercial and contractual disputes, fraud and insolvency issues in particular where these touch upon the interests of charities and other societies. Also welcomes instructions to act for non-charitable corporations and individuals in property and general commercial disputes.
Prof. Memberships: The Charity Law Association; Chancery Bar Association.
Career: Called 1996; Tutor in Law at Reading University and the College of Law. Joined present chambers in 2001.
Personal: Educated at Christ's Hospital and Reading University (LLB).

MACRORY, Richard
Brick Court Chambers (Christopher Clarke QC), London
(020) 7379 3550
Recommended in Environment

MACUR, Julia QC
St. Ive's Chambers (Julia Macur QC), Birmingham
(0121) 236 0863
Recommended in Family

MAHER, Martha
Guildhall Chambers (Adrian Palmer QC), Bristol
(0117) 927 3366
martha.maher@guildhallchambers.co.uk
Recommended in Chancery, Commercial (Litigation), Insolvency
Specialisation: Company, especially shareholder actions; insolvency (company and individual); partnership disputes especially involving professional partnerships; banking; director disqualifications; professional negligence involving accountants, vets; commercial contracts and fraud; equestrian work. Recent cases include Bristol and West Building Society v Back and Melinek and Secretary of State for Trade and Industry v Griffiths (RE West Mid Packaging Services Limited) (CA).
Prof. Memberships: Chancery Bar Association, Society of Practitioners in Insolvency.
Career: BCL, LLB (Cork) LLM (Cantab). Call 1987 Inner Temple. Cork Examiner Scholarship, Inner Temple Major Scholarship. Member of Irish Bar and New South Wales Bar.
Personal: Very keen on all equestrian sports, gardening, tennis.

MAIDMENT, Kieran
Doughty Street Chambers (Geoffrey Robertson QC), London
(020) 7404 1313
Recommended in Crime
Specialisation: Specialist in criminal law. Civil practice covers defamation, including libel advice to various diverse publications and actions against the police.
Career: Called to the Bar 1989.
Personal: Education: LLB (LSE), MA (KCL). Born 1963.

MALCOLM, Helen
3 Raymond Buildings (Clive Nicholls QC), London
(020) 7400 6400
Recommended in Crime, Fraud

MALE, John QC
4 Breams Buildings (Christopher Lockhart-Mummery QC), London
(020) 7430 1221
Recommended in Property Litigation
Specialisation: Landlord and tenant, town and country planning, compulsory purchase and compensation.
Prof. Memberships: Called to the Bar by Lincolns Inn in 1976 and is a member of the Property Bar Association, the Chancery Bar Association and the Planning and Environment Bar Association.
Career: Educated at Minchenden Grammar School, London and Sidney Sussex College, Cambridge obtaining a BA in law. One of the contributors to 'Halsbury's Laws on Town and Country Planning'. An editor of 'Hill & Redman's Law of Landlord and Tenant'.

MALEK, Ali QC
3 Verulam Buildings (Christopher Symons QC & John Jarvis QC), London
(020) 7831 8441
amalek@3vb.com
Recommended in Arbitration, Banking & Finance, Commercial (Litigation), Fraud
Specialisation: All aspects of commercial law with emphasis on banking. International arbitration and domestic arbitration. Professional negligence, fraud, oil and gas, and conflict of laws. Cases include Cryne v Barclays (1987) (bank's repayment rights); A v B (1993) (Banking Act). Barclays v Khaira (1992) (securities). Re Rafidain (1992) (bank accounts/sovereign immunity). Tudorgrange v Citibank (1992) (releases and UCTA 1977). EDF Mann v Haryanto (1991) (anti-suit injunctions). Natwest v Daniel (1993) (summary judgment). Robertson v CICB (1994) (confidentiality). Glencore v Bank of China (1996) (ICC 500) National Provincial Building Society v Lloyd (1996) (suspended possession orders). Barclays Bank v Thomson (1997) (undue influence). BCCI v PW (1998) (Banking Act). Bank Melli v Ispahani (1998) (illegality/conflict of laws). Box v Barclays (1998) (constructive trusts). Bolkiah v Prince Jefri (1998) (chinese walls). Yorkshire Bank v Lloyds (1999) (collecting bank's duties). Turner v RBS (1999) (confidentiality). Young v Robson Rhodes (1999) (chinese walls). Halewood v *Addleshaw Booth & Co* (1999) (chinese Walls), Sepoong v Formula One (2000) (contract): Dubai Aluminium v Salaam (2000) (constructive trusts/fraud); Portman v Dussangh (2000) (unconscionable bargain). Alliance and Leicester v Slayford (2000) (mortgagees rights); Montrod v Grundkotter (2001) (letter of credit and fraud); Casson v Ostley (2001) (fire insurance and exclusion clauses); Paragon Finance v Staunton (2001) (consumer credit and implied terms); Lloyds TSB Bank v Hayward (2002) (guarantees); Yukos Oil v Dardana (2002) (arbitration). Frequent speaker on these topics at seminars. 'Banks, Fraud and Crime' published in 'Cross-Border Fraudulent Activity' (Pub Lloyd's of London Press, 2nd Edition, 2000). Jack, Malek and Quest; 'Documentary Credits' (3rd edn) (2001).
Prof. Memberships: IBA, COMBAR.
Career: Called to the Bar 1980. QC 1996. Recorder 1998.
Personal: Bedford School, Keble College, Oxford. BA (1978), BCL (Oxon) (first class). Leisure pursuits and family life. Born 1956.

MALEK, Hodge M QC
4-5 Gray's Inn Square (Elizabeth Appleby QC), London
(020) 7404 5252
hmalek@4-5graysinnsquare.co.uk
Recommended in Banking & Finance
Specialisation: Specialises in commercial law, including accountancy, banking, company, financial services, fraud, insurance, securities, professional negligence and shipping. Instructed in complex commercial litigation in the commercial court and in arbitrations, including Banque Financiere v Westgate [1990] (banking and insurance fraud), Johnson Matthey v Arthur Young (collapse of Johnson Matthey Bank), Ocean v Bimeh Iran Insurance Company [1990] (reinsurance), Trafalgar Tours v Henry (jurisdiction), Gucci v Gucci [1991] (passing-off), Lombard Finance v Brookplain [1991] (banking), Westdeutsche Landesbank v Islington [1994] (interest rate swaps), NPRT v *Allen, Allen and Hemsley* [1996] (banking), R v Secretary of State ex p Greenpeace [2000] (judicial review), AEI v PPL [1998] (copyright); Richmond Oil [1999 and 2001] (stock exchange/fraud), Baghbadrani v Commercial Union [2000] (insurance), Co-op [2002]. Instructed in fraud cases by Serious Fraud Office. Acted for SROs in disciplinary proceedings and judicial review. Acts in French proceedings, including Tribunal de Commerce (2001) and investigation into Alma crash [1998]. Counsel for Customs & Excise (European) and on Supplemental Panel for Treasury (1995-99). Lectures on civil procedure.
Prof. Memberships: COMBAR, ALBA, PEBA, Franco-British Lawyers Society, Bar Sports Group. Member, Bar Disciplinary Tribunal (2000-).
Publications: Joint author of 'Disclosure' (Sweet & Maxwell, 2001).
Personal: Educated at Bedford School 1968-77, University of the Sorbonne, 1978 and Keble College, Oxford 1978-82 (MA, BCL).

MALES, Stephen QC
20 Essex Street (Iain Milligan QC), London

LEADERS AT THE BAR

(020) 7842 1200
clerks@20essexst.com
Recommended in Energy, Shipping
Specialisation: International trade and commercial law; shipping; sale of goods and commodity trading; banking and letters of credit; arbitration; energy law; insurance; conflict of laws; breach of confidence. Acts as arbitrator. Recent cases: The Selda [1999] 1 Lloyd's Rep 729; Cargill v Bangladesh Sugar [1998] 1 WLR 461; Czarnikow-Rionda v Standard Bank [1999] 2 Lloyd's Rep. 187; CAI v Muslim Commercial Bank [2000] 1 Lloyd's Rep.275; Chailease v CAI [2000] 1 Lloyd's Rep.348; Molins v GD [2000] 1 WLR 1741; The Spiros C [2000] 2 Lloyd's Rep 319; Zenziper v Bulk [2001] 1 Lloyd's Rep 357; Factortame (No 7) [2001] 1 WLR 942; CAI v CSFB [2001] 1 ALLER 1088.
Prof. Memberships: Member of Commercial Court Committee.
Career: St John's College, Cambridge 1974-77. Called 1978. Queens Counsel 1998. Assistant Recorder 1999. Recorder 2000.
Publications: Confidence in arbitration [1998] LMCLQ 245; Comity and anti-suit injunctions [1998] LMCLQ 543.

MALLALIEU, Ann QC
6 King's Bench Walk (Roy Amlot QC), London
(020) 7583 0410
Recommended in Crime

MANGAT, Tejina
6 Pump Court (Kieran Coonan QC), London
(020) 7583 6013
Recommended in Clinical Negligence

MANN, Anthony QC
Enterprise Chambers (Anthony Mann QC), London
(020) 7405 9471
Recommended in Chancery, Commercial (Litigation), Company, Insolvency, Professional Negligence
Specialisation: Broad commercial chancery practice with an emphasis on insolvency and professional negligence. Recent reported cases include Berkeley v Applegate [1989] (liquidator's remuneration); Re MC Bacon [1990] (insolvency, transaction at undervalue); Re David Meek Plant Ltd [1993] (Proceedings for recovery of leased equipment); National Westminster Bank v Skelton [1993] (cross-claims in mortgage possession actions) Smith New Court v Citibank [1996] (damages for fraud); Kleinwort Benson v South Tyneside [1993] and South Tyneside v Svenska [1994] (local authority swaps; ultra vires transactions; interest; Re Secure & Provide Plc [1992] (public interest winding-up petitions); Nestle v National Westminster Bank [1993] (principles for assessing losses arising from breach of trust) and Target Holdings v Redfern [1995] (solicitors' negligence and breach of trust); Barclays Bank v Eustice [1995] (discovery; privilege; transactions at an undervalue); Barrow v Bankside Agency Ltd [1996] (issue estoppel; Lloyds litigation); Fitch v Official Receiver [1996] (bankruptcy - rescinding bankruptcy order); Gold Coin Joailliers v UBK [1996] (duty of care in bank references); London Borough of Sutton v Wellesley Housing Assoc [1996] (Local authority ultra vires); Richbell Information Systems, The Times (1998) (winding up foreign company; set-off); Locabail v Emmanuel [1999] (lender and wife's interest); Locabail v Emmanuel No.2 [1999] (judicial bias); Lowsley v Forbes [1998] (limitations - House of Lords); MMI v London Stock Exchange [2002] - insolvency - British Eagle Principle.

MANN, Paul QC
No.1 High Pavement (John B Milmo QC), Nottingham
(0115) 941 8218
Recommended in Crime
Specialisation: Crime: murder, sexual offences, drugs, criminal malpractice of doctors/nurses, police officers and political office holders, and health and safety gross negligence manslaughters.
Prof. Memberships: Criminal Bar Association, Assistant Treasurer of the Midland Circuit (1999-).
Career: Called Gray's Inn 1980. Assistant Recorder 1999, Recorder 2001. Queen's Counsel 2002.

MANNING, Colin
Littleton Chambers (Michel Kallipetis QC), London
(020) 7797 8600
Recommended in ADR
Specialisation: Principal areas of practice are general commercial and business law specialising in commercial contract disputes including computer litigation (involving the supply and implementation of computer systems, networking and associated intellectual property rights) and also professional negligence (primarily solicitors and valuers).
Prof. Memberships: COMBAR London Common Law and Commercial Bar Association. CEDR Accredited Mediator. Fellow of the Chartered Institute of Arbitrators.
Career: Called, Gray's Inn, 1970. Recorder, 2000.
Personal: Educated at University College London.

MANSFIELD, Guy QC
1 Crown Office Row (Robert Seabrook QC), London
(020) 7797 7500
guy.mansfield@1cor.com
Recommended in Professional Negligence
Specialisation: Covers professional negligence with a particular interest in legal and clinical negligence and personal injuries. Cases include: Brown v Bennett [2002] (successfully resisted application for wasted costs); Corbett v Bond Pearce [2001] (solicitors' negligence in formalities of fresh will created no liability under the former will); Kuddus v Chief Constable of Leicestershire [2001] (exemplary damages not available for misfeasance); Fryer v RICS [2000] (wasted costs); Thrul v Ray [2000] (quantum; claimant was already severely mentally handicapped and receiving care); Green v Collyer-Bristow [1999] (negligence of solicitors, not cause of loss); Marriott v West Midlands AHA and Patel [1999] (successful claimant; no logical basis for defendant's expert's opinion); Carr-Glynn v Frearsons [1998] (duty owed to beneficiary of will to sever joint tenancy); Young v Purdy [1997] (solicitor's breach did not cause loss nor was loss foreseeable); Nelson v Nelson [1997] (solicitor ignorant of client's bankruptcy incurred no liability for costs); Tolstoy v Aldington [1996] (solicitors acting pro bono was not basis for a personal costs order); Ridehalgh v Horsefield [1994] (acted for Law Society and solicitors in test cases on wasted costs' jurisdiction).
Prof. Memberships: London Common Law & Commercial Bar Association; Professional Negligence Bar Association; Personal Injury Bar Association.
Career: Called to the Bar 1972 (Middle Temple, Bencher 2000). Recorder of the Crown Court 1993. QC 1994. Bar Council (Chairman, Remuneration Committee 1998, 1999; Chairman, Legal Services Committee 2000, 2001, 2002; Member, General Management Committee 1998-2002). Publications: Financial Provision in Family Matters, chapter, 'Ancillary Relief and Professional Negligence', Sweet & Maxwell, 1999 to date; Human Rights and Common Law, chapter 'Costs, Conditional Fees and Legal Aid', Hart Publishing, 2000; 'Personal Injury Handbook' - chapters on Costs & Wasted Costs, Sweet & Maxwell, 1998, 2000.
Personal: Education: Harrow; Oriel College, Oxford (MA).

MANSFIELD, Michael QC
Tooks Court Chambers (Michael Mansfield QC), London
(020) 7405 8828
Recommended in Crime, Human Rights
Specialisation: Criminal-Civil Rights work particularly in Appeal and Privy Council plus Inquests and Inquiries.
Prof. Memberships: CBA; President of National Civil Rights Movement and Amicus, providing assistance for Death Row cases in USA.
Career: Called 1967, established own set of chambers 1984, Silk 1989, Professor of Law, University of Westminster, Fellow, University of Kent.

MANSOORI, Sara
5 Raymond Buildings (Patrick Milmo QC), London
(020) 7242 2902
saramansoori@5rb.co.uk
Recommended in Defamation
Specialisation: All aspects of media law, including defamation, privacy, confidence, copyright, contempt of court, judicial review and human rights. Recent cases include Lillie and Reed v Newcastle City Council and others, Rupert Allason v Random House UK Limited, Berezovsky v Forbes (CA) and A v B and C (No 1) (Mackay J).
Prof. Memberships: Bar Human Rights Committee, member of the Executive.
Career: LLB (1st Class) University of Leeds. Called to Bar, 1997 (Lincoln's Inn). Libel reader for 'The Observer' and 'Sunday Telegraph'. Languages: French and conversational Farsi.
Publications: Contributor to 'The Law of Privacy and the Media' (2002, OUP).

MARKS, David
3-4 South Square (Michael Crystal QC & Lord Alexander of Weedon QC), London
(020) 7696 9900
clerks@southsquare.com
Recommended in Insolvency
Specialisation: Insolvency, company, commercial. 1998-2002 cases include: John Dee Group v WMH; Re A & C Supplies Ltd; Re Datadeck Ltd; BCCI v Akindele; Winchester Commodities v Black; Re Brabon; Ashurst v Pollard; Solomons v Williams; Re Factortame; Re TTR Ltd; Europhone v Frontel.
Prof. Memberships: Chancery Bar Association. Insolvency Lawyers Association. Society of Practitioners of Insolvency (legal member). Insol. International Bar Association. Justice.
Career: Oxford University: MA, BCL. Member, Illinois and Federal Bars, United States. Deputy Registrar in Bankruptcy. Data Appeal and Information Tribunal, Chairman.
Publications: Joint Editor: 'Rowlatt on Principal and Surety'. General Editor: 'Tolley's Insolvency Service'. Editor: 'Encyclopaedia of Forms and Precedents' (Guarantees). Contributor to Lightman & Moss: 'Law of Receivers of Companies' and Totty & Moss: 'Insolvency' and forthcoming Oxford University Press Publication on European Insolvency Regulation.

MARKS, Lewis QC
Queen Elizabeth Building (Florence Baron QC), London
(020) 7797 7837
lxm@hplace.fsnet.co.uk
Recommended in Family
Prof. Memberships: Family Law Bar Association; DPA Accepted.
Career: Recent cases include: Cornick v Cornick (No 3) [2001] 2 FLR 1240; White v White [2000] 3 WLR 1571 [2000] 2 FLR 981 H/L; Kellman v Kellman [2000] 1 FLR 785; F v F (Ancillary Relief: Substantial Assets) [1995] 2 FLR 45. Dart v Dart [1996] 2 FLR 286 C/A; H v H (Child Abduction: Acquiescence) [1997] 1 FLR 872 H/L; S v S (Child Abduction: Non-Convention Country) [1994] 2 FLR 681.
Personal: Born 1961. Called 1984. Silk 2002. Educated Oxford University (BA Juris).

LEADERS AT THE BAR

MARKS, Richard QC
Peel Court Chambers (Michael Shorrock QC), Manchester
(0161) 832 3791
Recommended in Crime

MARKUS, Kate
Doughty Street Chambers (Geoffrey Robertson QC), London
(020) 7404 1313
Recommended in Administrative & Public Law, Human Rights

MARQUAND, Charles
4 Stone Buildings (Philip Heslop QC), London
(020) 7242 5524
clerks@4stonebuildings.com
Recommended in Financial Services
Specialisation: Financial services (including insurance and banking) UK and EU, disciplinary tribunals, arbitrations. Instructed in Needler Financial Services v Taber (pensions reviews test case). Also company/commercial. Instructed in Tequila Cuervo v Diageo plc (English company law issues arising in Texas litigation). Engaged to advise various ex-Soviet governments on financial services legislation.
Prof. Memberships: Chancery Bar Association; COMBAR; Bar European Group; Association of Regulatory and Disciplinary Lawyers; fellow Chartered Institute of Arbitrators; Bar of Northern Ireland.
Career: Called 1987. Practised at chambers of JJ Rowe QC. 1993-96: legal advisor at HM Treasury dealing with wide range of financial services issues and related areas (company/ commercial), drafting legislation (closely involved *inter alia* with Public Offers of Securities Regulations, investment advertisement exemptions, CREST), negotiating EU directives. 1996: returned to the Bar.
Publications: Author of articles on financial services topics; Halsbury's Laws: 'Corporations', 'Money'. Lectures on financial services to universities, solicitors, conferences.
Personal: MA (Oxon), MA Law (City).

MARRIN, John QC
Keating Chambers, London
(020) 7544 2600
jmarrin@keatingchambers.com
Recommended in Construction
Specialisation: Barrister practising also as arbitrator, mediator, adjudicator and lecturer in the field of building and civil engineering; professional negligence; contaminated land; bonds and guarantees; computer software disputes; clients include national and international contractors, professionals, and national and local government.
Career: Qualified 1974; Inner Temple; QC 1990; CEDR accredited mediator 1993; recorder 1997; Chartered Arbitrator; FCI Arb 1998.
Personal: Sherborne School and Magdalene College, Cambridge (1973 MA Cantab). Born 1951; resides London.

MARSHALL, Philip
One King's Bench Walk (Anthony Hacking QC), London
(020) 7936 1500
Recommended in Family
Specialisation: Principally matrimonial finance. Junior counsel in the House of Lords in White v White (2000). Related private law children cases and international child abduction.
Prof. Memberships: Family Law Bar Association (FLBA).
Career: Called 1989.
Publications: Regular speaker at London and national regional seminars on matrimonial finance for Jordans Publishing (Family Law) and at FLBA Annual Conference.
Personal: Merchant Taylors School, Liverpool University (LLB).

MARSHALL, Philip
Serle Court (Lord Neill of Bladen QC), London
(020) 7242 6105
clerks@serlecourt.co.uk
Recommended in Chancery, Company, Insolvency
Specialisation: Commercial fraud (Cala Cristal v Al-Borno; Canada Trust v Stolzenberg; Berry Trade Ltd v Moussavi); insolvency (BIM v Maxwell; Re: Murjani; Haig v Aitken; Rooney v Cardona); banking (Wahda Bank v Arab Bank); company (Tech Textiles v Vane); commercial litigation (Shanshal v Al-kishtaini); professional negligence (Brown v GRE; Peach Publishing v Slater; David Lee v *Coward Chance*; Goose v Wilson Sandford).
Prof. Memberships: Chancery Bar Association, Insolvency Lawyers Association.
Career: Queens' Cambridge; Harvard Law School. Former fellow of Queens' Cambridge.
Publications: Joint editor of 'The Practice and Procedure of the Companies Court'.

MARSON, Geoffrey C QC
Sovereign Chambers (Geoffrey C Marson QC), Leeds
(0113) 245 1841
Recommended in Crime

MARTEN, Hedley
11 New Square (Sonia Proudman QC), London
(020) 7405 5577
law@threenewsquare.co.uk
Recommended in Chancery
Specialisation: Specialist in a broad area of Chancery work including company law, (particularly minority shareholders' disputes and directors' disqualification proceedings), contract, insolvency, landlord and tenant, trusts and contested probate; judicial review. Also acts for solicitors in proceedings brought by the Law Society under the Solicitors Act 1974. Important cases include Re Packaging Direct Ltd [1993] (Directors' Disqualification); Re: a Solicitor [1996] (judicial review); Re Bheekun [1999] F.L.379 (domicile); Mander v Evans [2001] WLR (fraud and bankruptcy).
Career: Called to the Bar 1966. Chancery Bar representative on the Bar Council 1989-95.
Personal: Born 1943. Educated at Winchester College and Magdalene College, Cambridge (MA 1966). Lives in London. Three children.

MARTIN, John QC
Wilberforce Chambers (Edward Nugee QC), London
(020) 7306 0102
Recommended in Chancery, Property Litigation

MARTIN-SPERRY, David
Charter Chambers (Stephen Solley QC), London
(020) 7832 0300
Recommended in Crime

MARZEC, Alexandra
5 Raymond Buildings (Patrick Milmo QC), London
(020) 7242 2902
Recommended in Defamation

MASKREY, Simeon QC
7 Bedford Row (David Farrer QC), London
(020) 7242 3555
Recommended in Clinical Negligence, Personal Injury, Product Liability
Specialisation: Principal area of practice is professional negligence with an emphasis on clinical negligence. Also involved in disciplinary cases and all forms of litigation with a clinical element (including public law childcare proceedings). Past member of the education faculty of the Royal College of Surgeons. Regular contributor to AVMA conferences. Leading counsel in R v Dixon (1995), Poynter v Hillingdon Health Authority (1997), Spargo v Essex Health Authority (1998), Fleming v Lincolnshire Police (1998), In Re D (child assessment) (1999), North Wales child abuse cases (2000), Interlink Mod v Night Trunkers Ltd (2001). Currently instructed in major product liability cases.
Prof. Memberships: Professional Negligence Bar Association. Member of the Midland and Oxford Circuit. Member of AVMA Bar group.
Career: Called to the Bar in 1977. Appointed Recorder in 1997. Appointed Deputy High Court Judge in 2000. Took silk in 1995.
Personal: Educated at King's School, Grantham and Leicester University. Born 17 May 1955. Married. Lives in London.

MASON, Alexandra
3 Stone Buildings (Geoffrey Vos QC), London
(020) 7242 4937
amason@3sb.law.co.uk
Recommended in Chancery
Specialisation: Private client litigation and advisory work centred on wills and probate, the administration of estates, settlements and the administration of trusts but including related taxation and professional negligence and also Court of Protection matters. Recent litigation has included the construction of wills and trust documents; applications under the Inheritance (Provision for Family and Dependants) Act 1975; contentious probate actions; claims to beneficial interests in property; the rectification of trust documents; the removal of executors and trustees; actions concerning breaches of duty on the part of trustees/executors; applications for statutory wills and settlements for patients; negligence claims in respect of the drafting of wills and trust documents and advice on the administration of estates.
Prof. Memberships: Chancery Bar Association, Revenue Bar Association, STEP.
Career: BA Hons, History, UCL 1979. Diploma in Law, City University 1980. Joint Author of 7th edn 'Spencer Maurice's Family Provision on Death'.

MATTHEWS, Dennis
Crown Office Chambers (Michael Spencer QC & Christopher Purchas QC), London
(020) 7797 8100
Recommended in Clinical Negligence, Personal Injury

MATTHEWS, Duncan QC
20 Essex Street (Iain Milligan QC), London
(020) 7842 1200
clerks@20essexst.com
Recommended in Shipping
Specialisation: Principal areas of work include international and domestic commercial disputes including in particular international trade and carriage of goods, oil and gas, construction, conflict of laws, insurance and reinsurance, banking, financial services, professional negligence. Advocacy: Counsel appearing before the High Court, Court of Appeal and House of Lords in England and a variety of legal and commercial arbitration tribunals both in England and abroad including international bodies such as UNCITRAL and ICC and other domestic organisations such as the LMAA. Have also been appointed and sat as arbitrator and mediator. Major reported cases include House of Lords - 'The Maria D' [1992] 1 AC 21; 'The Naxos' [1990] 1 WLR 1337. Privy Council - 'The Mahkutai' [1996] AC 650. Court of Appeal AIG v Ethniki [2000] W Rep IR 343 'The Berge Sund' [1993] 2 Ll Rep 453; Soules v Intertradex [1991] 1 Ll Rep 378; Dole Dried Fruit v Trustin Kerwood [1990] 1 Ll Rep 309; Medway v Meurer [1990] 2 Ll Rep 112. 1st Instance; KBC Bank v Industrial Steels (UK) Ltd [2001] 1 LI Rep 370; Sinochem v Fortune oil [2000] 1 W Rep 682; Doce nav v Bosco [2000] 2 4 Rep 1; Minmetals v Ferco Steel; Glencore v Shell [1999] 2 4 Rep 692; 'The Visvliet' [1997] 2 4 Rep 456, 476; Toepfer v Molino Boschi [1996] 1 Ll Rep 510; Aratra v *Taylor Joynson Garrett* [1995] 4 AER 695; Swiss

Bank Corporation v Premier League The Times 9 February 1995; Kaufmann v Credit Lyonnais Bank The Times 1 February 1995; The Sophie J [2001] 1 LLR 763.
Prof. Memberships: COMBAR; LCLCBA. Supporting member LMAA; Franco British Lawyers Society; British Italian Law Association; British German Jurists Association.
Career: Westminster School. Magdalen College, Oxford. BA (Hons) Oxon 1984. MA 1996. Called 1986, Gray's Inn. Silk 2002.

MATTHEWS, Richard
2 Bedford Row (William Clegg QC), London
(020) 7440 8888
rmatthews@2bedfordrow.co.uk
Recommended in Crime, Fraud, Health & Safety

Specialisation: Criminal law specialist including fraud, health and safety (crime) Inland Revenue/VAT, trading standards and confiscation/asset forfeiture. Cases include: R v Turner (extra-jurisdictional murder trial involving Japanese victim killed in Venezuela); R v Carlton (series of kidnaps of bank managers and manager of Tescos; R v Trevelyan & others (corruption trial of senior civil servant in MOD and wife); R v Walker (allegation of copyright theft and corruption by consultant retained by Min of Agriculture, MOD and CPS. High Court asset restraint under Criminal Justice Act); R v Morris (manslaughter case against gas fitter) R v Wheeler (manslaughter case against landlord following tenant death through CO poisoning); Travel v HM Customs and Excise Commissioners (judicial review of Customs powers of seizure under s.141 C.E.M.A. 1979). R v Ketchell, Walker et al (S.F.O prosecution of £22 million fraud - Ostrich Farms). R v Polycarpou & Langley (Inland Revenue/ Customs; PAYE, VAT & Corporation tax prosecution concerning eight years 'phoenix' operation); R v Barrett & others (£multimillion excise/VAT diversion fraud); R v John Palmer & others (prosecution alleging £30 million mis-selling of timeshare in Tenerife); HEALTH AND SAFETY CASES: HSE v Edmund Nuttall Ltd: (fatality involving breaches of Health and Safety at Work etc. Act 1974); HSE v Keltbray Plc [2001] 1 Cr.App.R.(S) 39 (double fatality on demolition site. HSWA 1974 and Construction (health, safety and welfare) Regulations 1996); HSE v Lambeth Borough Council (gas explosion in boiler room of occupied tower block. HSWA 1974 and Gas Safety (installation and use) Regulations 1994/8); Environmental Agency v Babtie Group Ltd (watercourse pollution case alleged against contract supervisors); Environmental Agency v Pharmacos Ltd and Brown (prosecution of company and director concerning mercury nitrate processing); HSE v FC Ltd (Construction (Design and Management) Regulations prosecution of planning supervisor); HSE v Thames Water Products Ltd (prosecution of subsidiary of Thames Water Plc); HSE v Bison Concrete Products Ltd and Fitzpatrick Contractors Ltd\ Construction fatality (lifting operations and lifting equipment regulations 1998 and construction (design and management) regulations 1994 ; HSE v SDC Builders Ltd (HSWA 1974 prosecution resulting from off-site construction death); HSE v Tarmac Heavy Building Materials Ltd (HSWA 1974 prosecution resulting from death of road worker); HWM (Traffic Management) Ltd v H M Inspector (Prohibition notice appeal to Employment Tribunal).
Prof. Memberships: Criminal Bar Association SE Circuit.
Career: Principal Legal Advisor Parliamentary War Crimes Group 1988-89. Called to the Bar 1989. Joined chambers 1989.
Publications: 'Corporate Governance: Health and Safety at Work/Corporate and Directors' Criminal Liability' (Finance & Investment Research Ltd).
Personal: Born 5 April 1966. Educated at Girton College, Cambridge University. (MA Cantab).

MAURICI, James
4 Breams Buildings (Christopher Lockhart-Mummery QC), London
(020) 7430 1221
jmaurici@4breams.co.uk
Recommended in Administrative & Public Law

Specialisation: Administrative and public law, environment, human rights, local government, planning. Recent cases include: R (on the application of Adlard) v Secretary of State for the Environment, Transport and the Regions [2002] EWCA Civ 614 (CA) (Article 6 and right to an oral hearing in planning cases) and Berkeley v Secretary of State for the Environment, Transport and the Regions (No. 2) [2001] 3 C.M.L.R 11 (HC and CA) (Environmental impact assessments, EC law, transposition of Directive into national law).
Prof. Memberships: ALBA, BEG and PEBA.
Career: Called to the Bar 1996. Appointed to the Attorney-General's London 'C' Panel of Junior Counsel to the Crown in April 2000.
Publications: Editor and regular contributor of journal 'Judicial Review'. Also published recent articles in 'JPL'.
Personal: Educated at Hertford College, Oxford 1991-95 (BA and BCL First Class). Lectured in EC Law at Hertford College 1997-2000.

MAXWELL, Richard QC
Ropewalk Chambers (Ian McLaren QC), Nottingham
(0115) 947 2581
clerks@ropewalk.co.uk
Recommended in Personal Injury

Specialisation: Principal areas of practice are personal injury (including insidious disease and health and safety), clinical and professional negligence. Particular emphasis on group and multi-party actions including advising and appearing as Senior Lead Counsel in the Prescription Pricing Authority litigation (repetitive strain injury); Metro-Cammell litigation (asbestosis); British Coal vibration white finger litigation; 'Frank Beck' litigation (physical and sexual abuse in children's homes); North West child abuse cases, Cambridgeshire child abuse cases; Scotforth House litigation (autistic children group action); Hillsborough disaster inquest and inquiry and the leading case regarding vicarious liability - Lister v Hesley Hall Limited [2001] UKHL [2001] 2WLR 1311.
Prof. Memberships: Personal Injuries Bar Association; Nottinghamshire Medico-Legal Society.
Career: Called to the Bar 1968. Queen's Counsel 1988. Recorder and Deputy High Court Judge. Head of Ropewalk Chambers 1994-2000.

MAY, Charlotte
8 New Square (Mark Platts-Mills QC), London
(020) 7405 4321
clerks@8newsquare.co.uk
Recommended in Intellectual Property

Specialisation: Barrister specialising in all areas of intellectual property law and scientific commercial law, including patents, biotechnology, trademarks, copyrights and database rights, passing off, registered design, design right and confidential information. Cases include Oxford Gene Technology v Affymetrix (biotech patent - revocation-infringement); Monsanto and Others v Merck (biotech patent-infringement-validity); Zino Davidoff SA v A & G Imports Ltd (trademark infringement and passing off). For comprehensive CV and list of recent cases, visit the set's website at www.8newsquare.co.uk.
Prof. Memberships: Intellectual Property Bar Association (IPBA); The Intellectual Property Lawyers Organisation (TIPLO)
Career: Called 1995.
Personal: Born 1971. Educated at The Abbey School; Brasenose College, Oxford (1993 Biochemistry); City University (1994 Dip Law); Inns of Court School of Law.

MAYNARD-CONNOR, Giles
Exchange Chambers (David Turner QC & Bill Braithwaite QC & Henry Globe QC), Liverpool
(0161) 833 2722
maynardconnor@exchangechambers.co.uk
Recommended in Insolvency

Specialisation: General Chancery with emphasis on insolvency (corporate and personal), company, professional negligence and banking. Cammell Laird Group and Enron (corporate insolvencies).
Prof. Memberships: Chancery Bar Association, Northern Chancery Bar Association, Bar Pro Bono Unit.
Career: Called to Bar 24 November 1992.
Personal: University of Lancaster. Leisure interests: football, motor racing, rugby union, travel, film and dining.

MCALLISTER, Ann
Serle Court (Lord Neill of Bladen QC), London
(020) 7242 6105
clerks@serlecourt.co.uk
Recommended in Agriculture, Property Litigation

Specialisation: Principal area of practice is landlord and tenant, property law and agricultural tenancies, although practice also includes all aspects of general chancery law (mortgages, partnerships, guarantees, insolvency) and professional negligence work.
Prof. Memberships: Committee member of the Property Bar Association.
Career: Called to the Bar in 1982.
Personal: Read law and languages at Newnham College, Cambridge. After graduating in 1975 went to LSE and gained an LLM in law. Taught law for three years at the University of London (School of Oriental and African Studies).

MCCAFFERTY, Jane
11 King's Bench Walk Chambers (Eldred Tabachnik QC & James Goudie QC), London
(020) 7632 8500
mccafferty@11kbw.com
Recommended in Employment

Specialisation: Employment law, commercial law and public law including education.
Prof. Memberships: Employment Law Bar Association; Administrative Law Bar Association.
Career: Called to the Bar in 1998.
Publications: Tolley's 'Employment Handbook', Halsburys 'Laws of England's Administrative Law'.
Personal: Educated at Foyle and Londonderry College and Newnham College Cambridge (BA Hons in Law, LLM).

MCCALL, Christopher QC
Maitland Chambers (Michael Lyndon-Stanford QC & Charles Aldous QC), London
(020) 7406 1200
cmccall@maitlandchambers.com
Recommended in Chancery, Charities, Tax

Specialisation: Specialises in trust, revenue and charity law. Has appeared in numerous appeals in the House of Lords, Privy Council and Court of Appeal: has regularly addressed specialist associations and seminars and written in legal journals.
Prof. Memberships: STEP, ACTAPS, Chancery Bar Association, Revenue Bar Association.
Career: Called to Bar Lincolns Inn, November 1966. Took silk, April 1987. Bencher 1993. 2nd Junior Counsel to the

LEADERS AT THE BAR

Inland Revenue in Chancery Matters 1977-87. Junior Counsel to the Attorney-General in Charity Matters 1981-87. Practised at 7 New Square Lincolns Inn 1967-94, subsequently 13 Old Square (now Maitland Chambers). Member of Bar Council 1973-76.
Personal: Born 3 March 1944. Married 1981, no children. Educated Winchester College (Scholar), Magdalen College, Oxford (Demy): 1st class, Mathematical Moderations 1962 and Finals 1964. Eldon Law Scholarship: 1966. Trustee of British Museum 1999-.

MCCALL, Duncan
4 Pump Court, London
(020) 7842 5555
dmccall@4pumpcourt.com
Recommended in Information Technology
Specialisation: Commercial and technical disputes involving a variety of applications including financial and accounting packages, ERP, logistics software, e-sales and internet. Recent reported cases include Pegler v Wang [2000] BLR 218. Also specialises in other TCC disputes including construction and civil engineering disputes.
Prof. Memberships: TECBAR, Society for Computers & Law.
Personal: BA (Hons) Oxon.

MCCAUGHRAN, John
One Essex Court (Lord Grabiner QC), London
(020) 7583 2000
Recommended in Banking & Finance, Commercial (Litigation), Fraud
Specialisation: Principal area of practice is commercial litigation.
Prof. Memberships: Commercial Bar Association
Career: Called to the Bar in 1982.
Personal: Educated at Methodist College, Belfast 1969-76 and Trinity Hall, Cambridge 1977-80. Born 24 April 1958. Lives in London.

MCCRACKEN, Robert
2 Harcourt Buildings (Robin Purchas QC), London
(020) 7353 8415
clerks@2hb.law.co.uk
Recommended in Environment
Specialisation: Environmental law especially at land use and planning inquiries. Acts for a wide range of clients from multinational corporations and regulatory authorities to small entrepreneurs and groups of active citizens. Promoted Windermere Speed Limit for Lake District NPA, East London Overhead Power Line for National Grid. Represented consortium of oil companies at Heathrow Terminal 5 Inquiry. Acted for successful appellants in Berkeley v SSETR (House of Lords) [2001] 2 AC 603; R v Durham CC ex p Huddlestone (Court of Appeal) [2000] 1 WLR 1484; R v Flintshire CC ex p Armstong Braun (Court of Appeal) ('Times' 8 March 2001); Hewlings v McLeans (Divisional Court) [2001] Env LR 323; R v St Edmundsbury ex p Walton (High Court) [1999] Env LR 879; R v Cornwall CC ex p hardy (High Court) [2001] ENv LR 473; Porter v South Bucks [2002] 1 AE 425; Burkett v LBHF [2002] UKHL.
Prof. Memberships: Planning and Environmental Bar Association (secretary 1992-94); UK Environmental Law Association (chairman 1995-97).
Career: Called to the Bar 1973. Honorary Standing Counsel to Council for National Parks since 1999.
Publications: Many and various for legal journals. Co-author of Butterworths 'Statutory Nuisance' 2001.
Personal: Worcester College, Oxford, MA 1973. Former educational missionary in East Africa. Leisure pursuits include fell walking, natural science and painting.

MCCULLOUGH, Angus
1 Crown Office Row (Robert Seabrook QC), London
(020) 7797 7500
Recommended in Clinical Negligence

MCDERMOTT, John
Chavasse Court Chambers (Theresa Pepper), Liverpool
(0151) 707 1191
Recommended in Crime

MCDONNELL, Conrad
Gray's Inn Tax Chambers (Milton Grundy), London
(020) 7242 2642
cm@taxbar.com
Recommended in Tax
Specialisation: Revenue law, VAT, and tax issues in EC law. Work covers all areas of tax, but specifically taxation of companies and their shareholders, partnerships, employees, pension schemes, UK and offshore trusts. Also special interest in tax issues arising in commercial litigation. Recent cases: GIL Insurance v C&EC (EC: State Aids; VAT avoidance); United Utilities v C&EC (VAT); Venables v Hornby (pension scheme); Walker v Centaur Clothes Group (corporation tax and ACT); Hostgilt v Megahart (commercial property); EMI v Coldicott (employee taxation: PILONs).
Career: Called to the Bar 1994, joined present chambers 1996.
Publications: Co-author (tax) of: 'Partnership' (Blackett-Ord) (Butterworths, 1997); 'The Laws of the Internet' (Gringras) (Butterworths, 1997); 'Offshore Business Centres' (Grundy) (Sweet & Maxwell); 'The Law of the European Communities' (Vaughan) (forthcoming).
Personal: Son of John McDonnell QC.

MCDONNELL, John QC
New Square Chambers (Charles Purle QC), London
(020) 7419 8000
Recommended in Chancery
Specialisation: Practice has a strong bias towards litigation. Regularly instructed in trials both in the Chancery Division and in the Queen's Bench Division. Matters include securities for borrowing, company or insolvency matters, judicial review, human rights, questions concerning trusts (especially charities) or constructive trusts, commercial fraud, professional negligence, copyright and intellectual property, real property, landlord and tenant and partnership. Has regularly advised two of the clearing banks on banking and security matters. Frequently involved in cases with an international element. Has appeared often in the Supreme Court of Hong Kong, the High Court of the Isle of Man and the Grand Court of the Cayman Islands.
Prof. Memberships: Governor of the Inns of Court School of Law.
Career: Called to the Bar, 1968. Took Silk 1984. Elected a Bencher of Lincoln's Inn, 1993. Before commencing practice at the Bar had worked in the United States Congress, Conservative Research Dept, H.M. Diplomatic Service (as Assistant Private Secretary to the Foreign Secretary). Sits as a Deputy High Court Judge attached to the Chancery Division.

MCFARLAND, Denise
Three New Square (David Young QC), London
(020) 7405 1111
clerks@3newsquare.co.uk
Recommended in Intellectual Property
Specialisation: Barrister specialising in all aspects of individual property; recent Court of Appeal cases include: Shirin Guild v Eskandar Nabavi (haute couture, design right, 'commonplace'); Pensher Security Doors v Sunderland City Council (authorisation); Ray v Classic FM (copyright); Cinpres v Melea (patent CA); PLG v Ardon (patent); Cala v McAlpine (copyright); Bell Atlantic v Bell (trademarks and summary judgment); as well as numerous decisions from the European Patent Office, UK Trade Marks and Patent Registry, and Copyright Tribunal.
Prof. Memberships: Hon Fellow Institute of Trade Mark Attorneys; member Chartered Institute of Patent Attorneys Professional Disciplinary Panel; member Royal Institution of Great Britain; British Council member of AIPPI; member of T.I.P.L.O Executive Committee; Women's Bar Assn; Intellectual Property Bar Assn; Chancery Bar Assn; former examiner for Chartered Institute of Trade Mark Attorneys professional examination. Appointed expert for settlement of Nominet UK Dispute Resolution Procedures. Nominated as examiner for International IPR disputes deposition hearings.
Career: Cambridge University (MA).
Personal: Riding and all country pursuits, music and theatre.

MCFARLANE, Andrew QC
One King's Bench Walk (Anthony Hacking QC), London
(020) 7936 1500
Recommended in Family
Specialisation: Principal area of practice is family law. Handles all aspects with particular expertise in the law relating to children (both public and private law), international child abduction and adoption. Has appeared before the House of Lords and before the European Court of Human Rights. Regular lecturer at nationally organised conferences and seminars.
Prof. Memberships: Midlands Circuit, Chairman (2001-04) Family Law Bar Association, Bar Council General Management Committee, Association of Lawyers for Children, British Agencies for Adoption and Fostering.
Career: Called to the Bar in 1977. At Priory Chambers, Birmingham 1978-93 and remains a door tenant at St Philip's Chambers, Birmingham. Joined 1 King's Bench Walk in 1993. Appointed Recorder in 1999. QC 1998. Deputy High Court Judge in 2000.
Publications: Co-author with David Hershman of 'Children: Law & Practice' (Family Law 1991) and contributor to 'Family Court Practice' (Family Law 2001).
Personal: Educated at Shrewsbury School 1968-72, Durham University 1972-76, University of Wales (LLM (Canon Law)) 1994-98. Trustee: Young Minds. Leisure interests include theatre, conjuring, walking and his children. Born 20 June 1954. Lives in Herefordshire.

MCGHEE, John
9 Old Square (Michael Driscoll QC), London
(020) 7405 4682
Recommended in Property Litigation
Specialisation: John McGhee has wide experience in a broad range of property, Chancery and commercial litigation incuding banking, commercial fraud, landlord and tenant, professional negligence and property disputes. Recent cases include: Barrett v Morgan [2000] 2 AC 264 (notice to quit); Grupo Torras v Al Sabah Litigation [1999] CLC 1469 (civil fraud); Mobil Oil Co Ltd v Birmingham City Council [2001] EWCA Civ 1608 (rent review; rights of way); Action Strength v International Glass Engineering [2002] 1 WCR 566 (guarantees; estoppel; Pennington v Waine [2002] WTLR 387 (gift of shares). Supplemental panel member for Treasury Solicitor.
Career: University College Oxford 1980-83 (MA).
Publications: Editor of Snell's 'Equity' 30th edn.

MCGRATH, Paul
Essex Court Chambers (Gordon Pollock QC), London
(020) 7813 8000
Recommended in Commercial (Litigation), Shipping
Specialisation: Banking law (including the Cayman Islands jurisdiction); conflict of laws; equity in a commercial context (eg constructive trusts, bribes, civil fraud); pre-emptive remedies (domestic and worldwide Mareva injunctions, tracing orders, Norwich Pharmacal relief); insolvency (advising

liquidators on all aspects thereof, including schemes of arrangement, payment of dividend and the general conduct of liquidations as well as potential claims against directors of insolvent companies); all aspects of restitution, joint ventures, financial services, shipbuilding contracts and general commercial practice involving court and arbitration work.
Career: BA, BCL, University College, Oxford. Called to the Bar in 1994.
Personal: Born 1970.

MCGREGOR, Alistair J QC
11 King's Bench Walk Chambers (Eldred Tabachnik QC & James Goudie QC), London
(020) 7632 8500
mcgregor@11kbw.com
Recommended in Employment
Specialisation: Principal areas of practice are trade secrets, confidential information (particularly in relation to employment contracts and commercial transactions), restraint of trade (in all areas of application but especially employment law), wrongful dismissal. Other main areas are commercial law including sale of goods, entertainment contracts, agency, partnership and commercial fraud (especially of directors). Lecturer for London University External LLB (1974-77) and for solicitors and accountant's professional examinations. Has written journal articles.
Prof. Memberships: COMBAR, ELBA.
Career: Called to the Bar in 1974. At Crown Office Row from 1975 until joining present chambers in 1981.
Personal: Educated at Haberdasher's Aske's School, Elstree 1963-70 and Queen Mary College, London University (LLB Hons, 1973). Leisure interests include orchestral music. Professional musician (trombone) and teacher (1970-78). Born 11 March 1950. Lives in Stamford, Lincs.

MCKAY, Hugh
Gray's Inn Tax Chambers (Milton Grundy), London
(020) 7242 2642
hm@taxbar.com
Recommended in Tax
Specialisation: Revenue law especially tax litigation, commercial/corporate tax issues and VAT.
Prof. Memberships: Secretary, Revenue Bar Association 1996-2000, Member - Chancery Bar Association, Chartered Institute of Taxation, VAT Practitioners Group, Law Society VAT and Duties Sub-committee (co-opted), 1994-98, Institute of Indirect Taxation, Bar Council 1999-2000.
Career: Called to the Bar 1990, joined present chambers 1991. Visiting fellow (tax), London School of Economics 1993-97, Attorney General's 'B' Panel of Junior Counsel since 2001.
Personal: Born 26 June 1966. Lives in Marylebone. Educated at King's College, London (LLM Tax) and Leeds University (MA), FTII, AIIT.

MCKENDRICK, John
Goldsmith Building (Christopher Llewellyn-Jones QC), London
(020) 7353 7881
Recommended in Education

MCLAREN, Ian QC
Ropewalk Chambers (Ian McLaren QC), Nottingham
(0115) 947 2581
Recommended in Personal Injury
Specialisation: Personal injury, common law and local government. Three cases in House of Lords in recent years; Longden v British Coal [1988] A.C. 653; Jameson v CEGB [1999] 2WLR 141; and Dimond v Lovell [2000] 2 WLR 1121.
Prof. Memberships: Personal Injury Bar Association; European Bar Association; Planning and Environment Bar Association.
Career: Called 1962; Bar finals prize, Macaskie Scholar, Gray's Inn plus three other scholarships. Law Tutor, University of Nottingham. Silk 1993; Recorder 1996.
Publications: Various articles in 'New Law Journal'.
Personal: Sandbach School, Blackpool Grammar School, Nottingham University (LLB). Interests: travel, wine and photography. Married, three children. President Nottinghamshire Medico-Legal Society 1997-98.

MCLAUGHLIN, Andrew
St John's Chambers (Christopher Sharp QC), Bristol
(0117) 921 3456
clerks@stjohnschambers.co.uk
Recommended in Personal Injury
Specialisation: Personal injury and clinical negligence.
Prof. Memberships: Personal Injury Bar Association.
Career: BA (Hons) York 1991. Called 1993. Lecturer to MASS.
Personal: Married, two dogs.

MCLOUGHLIN, Timothy
East Anglian Chambers (Roderick Newton), Norwich
(01603) 617351
Recommended in Family

MCMANUS, Richard QC
4-5 Gray's Inn Square (Elizabeth Appleby QC), London
(020) 7404 5252
Recommended in Aviation, Education

MCMEEKIN, Ian
Kingsgate Chambers (Beverley Lunt), Manchester
(0161) 831 7477
Recommended in Crime

MCMULLAN, Manus
Atkin Chambers (Robert Akenhead QC), London
(020) 7404 0102
clerks@atkinchambers.law.co.uk
Recommended in Construction
Specialisation: Construction, arbitration, professional negligence, energy, utilities and general commercial litigation. Recent cases include: CRS v Taylor Young (House of Lords), damage by fire - insurance - contribution between parties; Reliance Industries Ltd v Enron [2002] 1 All ER (Comm) 59 International commercial arbitration - foreign law - whether appeal possible; Woods Hardwick Ltd v Chiltern Air Conditioning [2001] BLR 23 Adjudication - enforcement - natural justice; Imperial Square Developments (Hoxton) Ltd v Aegon Insurance Co (UK) Ltd (1999) 62 Con LR 59, on demand bond - whether enforceable.
Prof. Memberships: TECBAR.
Career: Called 1994.
Publications: Editor: 'Technology and Construction Law Reports' (Sweet & Maxwell).
Personal: BA Oxon (1st Class).

MCNEILL, Jane QC
Old Square Chambers (John Hendy QC), London
(020) 7269 0300
mcneill@oldsquarechambers.co.uk
Recommended in Employment
Specialisation: Employment including discrimination under domestic and European law; wrongful and unfair dismissal; redundancy; restraint of trade. Cases include Kapur v Barclays; Preston v Wolverhampton Healthcare NHS Trustee; Fletcher v Midland Bank plc; Hallam v Avery; British Airways (European Operations at Gatwick) Ltd v Moore. Also personal injury and medical negligence.
Prof. Memberships: Employment Law Bar Association; PIBA.
Personal: BA Hons (Oxon); Dip Law (City University). Fluent Italian and French. Called 1982.

MCPHERSON, Graeme
Four New Square (Justin Fenwick QC), London
(020) 7822 2000
Recommended in Professional Negligence
Specialisation: Principal areas of practice are professional negligence (in particular claims involving accountants and auditors, solicitors and barristers, company directors, financial service professionals, sports agents, insurance brokers and construction professionals), commercial and insurance litigation, financial services and bloodstock. Important cases include Coulthard v Neville Russell [1998] (auditors' duty of care toward directors); Barex Brokers Ltd v Morris Dean [1999] (valuer's duty of care to assignee of a loan); Flannery v Halifax Estate Agency Ltd [2000] (duties of a judge to give reasons); Eric Alston (appeal under Jockey Club Rules of Racing).
Prof. Memberships: PNBA, COMBAR. Member of the Bar Council's PCC summary procedure panel.
Career: MA (Cantab). Called to Bar (Gray's) 1993. Joined Four New Square (formerly 2 Crown Office Row) in 1994.
Publications: Editor of 'Jackson & Powell on Professional Negligence' (5th edition).

Personal: Educated at Canford School, Wimborne and Emmanuel College, Cambridge. Leisure interests: horse riding and racing.

MCQUATER, Ewan
3 Verulam Buildings (Christopher Symons QC & John Jarvis QC), London
(020) 7831 8441
chambers@3vb.com
Recommended in Banking & Finance, Commercial (Litigation), Fraud, Insolvency
Specialisation: Commercial work specialising in banking, commercial fraud, insolvency and more general finance related work. Also has considerable experience in professional negligence work. Important cases include: the Libyan asset freeze litigation (US freeze on Libyan asset worldwide), the expropriation of the National Bank of Brunei, the collapse of the Maxwell group, the Arrows liquidation (series of important insolvency decisions), BBL (measure of damages in professional negligence cases), the BCCI liquidation, the collapse of the Barings group, Grupo Torras and Prince Jefri of Brunei (defence of claim by State of Brunei and Brunei Investment Agency). Assistant Editor of the 'Encyclopaedia of Banking Law'.
Prof. Memberships: COMBAR.
Career: Called to the Bar 1985 and joined current Chambers 1986. Admitted to the Bar of the Cayman Islands on a series of individual cases.
Personal: Educated at Merchiston Castle School, Edinburgh (1975-80) and Cambridge University 1981-84 (MA Hons in Law, First Class). Born 30 October 1962. Lives in London.

MEAD, Philip
Old Square Chambers (John Hendy QC), London
(020) 7269 0300
mead@oldsquarechambers.co.uk
Recommended in Environment
Specialisation: Environmental law (in particular common law and statutory nuisance), personal injury law and health and safety law including foreign accidents, toxic torts and product liability, employment and discrimination law. Has particular knowledge of the application of European law and conflicts of law to the above areas. Acts for both claimants/applicants and defendants/respondents, appearing in both the civil and criminal courts. Consultant to the European Commission on Health and Safety.
Prof. Memberships: Association of Personal Injury Lawyers, Personal Injuries Bar Association, Employment Law Bar Association and Bar European Group.
Career: Called to the Bar 1989; member Western Circuit, and practises from chambers' annexe in Bristol.
Publications: Litigation manual for the Environmental Law Foundation on European Environmental Law; co-author of Tort and Product Liability in

LEADERS AT THE BAR

'Practitioners' Handbook of EC Law'; co-editor and author of 'Personal Injury Handbook' and contributor to Munkman on 'Employers' Liability'.

MEADE, Richard
8 New Square (Mark Platts-Mills QC), London
(020) 7405 4321
clerks@8newsquare.co.uk
Recommended in Information Technology, Intellectual Property
Specialisation: Barrister specialising in all aspects of intellectual property, with particular experience in biotechnology and electronics patent litigation; trademark litigation including comparative advertising cases; music copyright; euro defences and jurisdiction under the Brussels Convention. For comprehensive CV and list of recent cases, visit the set's website at www.8newsquare.co.uk.
Prof. Memberships: Intellectual Property Bar Association (IPBA); The Intellectual Property Lawyers Organisation (TIPLO).
Career: Called 1991.
Publications: Kerly's 'Law of Trade Marks' (co-author).
Personal: Born 1966. Educated at William Ellis School; University College, Oxford (BA Law).

MEADOWCROFT, Stephen
Peel Court Chambers (Michael Shorrock QC), Manchester
(0161) 832 3791
Recommended in Crime

MEADWAY, Susannah
10 Old Square (Leolin Price CBE QC), London
(020) 7242 5002
susannahmeadway@10oldsquare.ndo.co.uk
Recommended in Chancery
Specialisation: Advisory, drafting and litigation work in the fields of trusts and associated taxation, pensions, wills, probate and the administration of estates, family provision Court of Protection matters and charities and professional negligence in those fields. A contributor to Foster's Inheritance Tax and 'Atkin's Court Forms: Probate & Family Provision', co-editor of 'Williams on Wills', co-editor of 'Halsbury's Laws of England: Wills' and 'Halsbury's Laws of England: Executors & Administrators', co-author of Contentious Trust and Probate (Tolley). Counsel in Re Segelman [1996] Ch 171 and Henley v Brown [2002] 19 EG 147 (CS)
Prof. Memberships: STEP (Society of Trust and Estate Practitioners). Chancery Bar Association.

MEEKE, Martin QC
Colleton Chambers (Martin Meeke QC), Exeter
(01392) 274898
Recommended in Crime
Specialisation: Prosecutes and defends in all serious crime, including murder, manslaughter, drugs, fraud and sexual offences. Prosecutes and defends in environmental consumer and food law cases. Also ancillary relief.
Career: Called 1973. Recorder 1999. Silk 2000
Personal: Born 1950. Bristol University LLB (Hons). Married with two children.

MEESON, Nigel QC
4 Essex Court (Nigel Teare QC), London
(020) 7653 5653
Recommended in Shipping
Specialisation: Commercial litigation, international trade and transport including aviation, banking carriage of goods, commodities, commercial fraud, conflict of laws, insurance and reinsurance, professional negligence, railways, road haulage, sale of goods, shipping. Sits as arbitrator and mediator.
Prof. Memberships: MCIArb. LMAA (supporting member), COMAR, BMLA, ABA, Forum on Air & Space Law.
Career: Called 1982, Silk 2002. California Bar 1990. Accredited mediator CEDR 1993. Visiting lecturer at University College London since 1994. Supplementary Panel of Treasury Counsel 1997-2002. CIArb/BMIF and ACI panels of mediators and arbitrators.
Publications: 'Admiralty Jurisdiction and Practice' (1993, 2nd Edn 2000), 'Ship and Aircraft Mortgages' (1989), 'Ship Sale & Purchase' (contributor 2nd Edn 1993, 3rd Edn 1998).
Personal: Magdalen College, Oxford (First Class Hons Jurisprudence).

MEHIGAN, Simon QC
5 Paper Buildings (Godfrey Carey QC & Jonathan Caplan QC), London
(020) 7583 6117
Recommended in Licensing

MELLOR, James
8 New Square (Mark Platts-Mills QC), London
(020) 7405 4321
james.mellor@8newsquare.co.uk
Recommended in Intellectual Property, Media & Entertainment
Specialisation: Barrister with wide ranging intellectual property practice in patents (electronic/chemical/mechanical devises/biotech), copyright and designs (engineering drawings/databases/computer software/literary works), trademarks and passing off and confidential information (chemical formulae/business information). Further experience in arbitrations with intellectual property or technical elements and in the Copyright tribunal. For comprehensive CV and list of recent cases, visit the set's website at www.8newsquare.co.uk.
Prof. Memberships: Intellectual Property Bar Association (IPBA). Member of the Disability Panel of the Bar Council. Chancery Bar Association (committee member 1998-99, speaker at two seminars).
Career: Called 1986. Prior work experience in a variety of engineering disciplines in the UK, France, Germany, Somalia, the Congo and Iraq.
Publications: Co-author of 'Kerly on Trade Marks' 13th edn, 'The Trade Marks Act 1994 - Text and Commentary', editor of 'Patents - Atkin's Court Forms', co-editor of Intellectual Property section of Bullen, Leake & Jacob's 'Precedents of Pleadings' 14th edn, former editor of 'Computers - Atkin's Court Forms'.
Personal: Born 1961. Educated at Rugby School; Kings College, Cambridge (1983 BA, MA Engineering and Production Engineering, 1985 Law (1st Class).

MELTON, Christopher QC
Byrom Street Chambers, Manchester
(0161) 829 2100
Recommended in Clinical Negligence

MENDELSON, Maurice QC
Blackstone Chambers (Presiley Baxendale QC & Charles Flint QC), London
(020) 7583 1770
clerks@blackstonechambers.com
Recommended in Public International Law
Specialisation: Public International Law (all aspects).
Prof. Memberships: International Law Association; American Law Institute; International Bar Association; Fellow, Royal Geographical Society; Royal Institute of International Affairs; American Society of International Law; Bencher of Lincoln's Inn.
Career: QC (practising) 1992. Emeritus Professor of International Law in the University of London.
Personal: Fluent French, Working knowledge: Spanish, Italian.

MERCER, Geoffrey QC
Walnut House (Paul Dunkels QC), Exeter
(01392) 279751
Recommended in Crime

MERCER, Hugh
Essex Court Chambers (Gordon Pollock QC), London
(020) 7813 8000
Recommended in Agriculture
Specialisation: Specialist in EU and commercial law. Recent practice includes application of the Rome Convention by the Court of Appeal; Brussels Convention jurisdictional arguments in the House of Lords; Articles 81/82 in the context of milk distribution and liner shipping; judicial review on EU grounds of decisions to use new food safety legislation, to refuse subsidies to the Isle of Wight, to order a contiguous cull on foot and mouth grounds; right to a hearing for agricultural IACS forms before the European Court of Justice; state aid, competition, public procurement and pharmaceutical product authorisation before the European Commission; proceedings before the High Court and the UK Competition Commission in the context of gas and water regulatory issues.
Prof. Memberships: European Circuit (Circuit Junior); Union Internationale Des Avocats, Agriculture Law Association.
Career: Called to the Bar 1985.
Personal: Downing College, Cambridge 1981-84; Université Libre de Bruxelles 1985-86. Fluent in French, German, good Spanish and Italian. Leisure pursuits include squash, mountain walking, and photography.

MEREDITH, George
King's Bench Chambers, Plymouth
(01752) 221551
Recommended in Family

MERRIMAN, Nicholas QC
3 Verulam Buildings (Christopher Symons QC & John Jarvis QC), London
(020) 7831 8441
chambers@3vb.com
Recommended in Media & Entertainment
Specialisation: Barrister specialising in commercial work; banking; insurance; international trade, financial services, shipping and related aspects of company and insolvency work. Maritime, commodity and international arbitration. Intellectual property, entertainment law and gaming, and professional negligence. Cases: The Beatles v Lingasong Music 1998; Ritz Casino v Adnan Khashoggi 1998; Creation Records v News Group 1997; Macmillan v Bishopsgate Investment Trust 1995; Re: Paramount Holdings 1993; Barclays Bank v Homan 1993: Baytur V Finagro Holdings 1992; Crockfords v Mehta 1992.
Career: Qualified 1969; QC 1988; recorder; Master of the Bench, Inner Temple

METHUEN, Richard QC
12 King's Bench Walk (Richard Methuen QC), London
(020) 7583 0811
methuen@12kbw.co.uk
Recommended in Personal Injury
Specialisation: Personal injury and professional negligence.
Prof. Memberships: PIBA and PNBA.
Career: Called 1972. QC 1997.
Personal: Born 22 August 1950.

MEYER, Lorna
No5 Chambers (Gareth Evans QC), Birmingham
(0121) 606 0500
Recommended in Family

MICHAELS, Amanda
Hogarth Chambers (Jonathan Rayner James QC & Christopher Morcom QC), London
(020) 7404 0404
amichaels@hogarthchambers.com
Recommended in Media & Entertainment
Specialisation: Intellectual property, with an emphasis on copyright and design right, trademarks (registration and litigation) and passing off. Entertainment and media law, including music industry, performing rights, publishing, advertising, film and television disputes. Breach of confidence and all other aspects of intellectual property. General Chancery and commercial litigation.
Career: Call: 1981.
Personal: BA in law from Durham, MA

in Advanced European Studies from College of Europe, Bruges. Fluent French. Author of 'A Practical Guide to Trade Mark Law' (3rd edn 2001) Sweet & Maxwell.

MIFFLIN, Helen
30 Park Place (John Jenkins QC), Cardiff
(029) 2039 8421
Recommended in Family
Specialisation: Family, Care Proceedings, Ancillary Relief, Education.
Prof. Memberships: Family Bar Association.
Career: LLB (Hons) Leicester. Recorder, Wales and Chester Circuit.

MILES, Robert QC
4 Stone Buildings (Philip Heslop QC), London
(020) 7242 5524
clerks@4stonebuildings.law.co.uk
Recommended in Banking & Finance, Chancery, Company, Energy, Insolvency
Specialisation: Company and Commercial Litigation, Corporate Insolvency; Oil and gas; Amongst reported cases are: Derby v Weldon (worldwide Marevas); Re Atlantic Computers (corporate insolvency); acting for the liquidators of the pension fund trustee company in the Maxwell affair; BCCI (corporate insolvency) Phillips v Euron (oil and gas); Bermuda Fire & Marine litigation in Bermuda.
Prof. Memberships: Committee of the Chancery Bar Association; COMBAR.
Career: Called to the Bar 1987. Called to the Bars of Bermuda and the Isle of Man for specific cases.
Personal: BA (Hons) in PPE (1st Class) Christ Church, Oxford. 1985 Diploma in Law (with distinction) City University, London. 1986 Bar Finals (Denning Prize; Megarry Prize). 1987 BCL (1st Class) Christ Church, Oxford.

MILL, Ian QC
Blackstone Chambers (Presiley Baxendale QC & Charles Flint QC), London
(020) 7583 1770
ianmill@blackstonechambers.com
Recommended in Commercial (Litigation), Media & Entertainment, Sport
Specialisation: Principal areas of practice are commercial law (including financial services and commercial fraud) and intellectual property (copyright, passing off and confidential information) with specialist knowledge and experience in the music industry and other entertainment fields, and in sports law. Major cases include Panayiotou v Sony Music (the George Michael case) and Hadley v Kemp (the Spandau Ballet case). Clients have included all the major record and music publishing companies, film production companies, television and radio broadcasters, recording artists and songwriters, and leading sports organisations and figures.
Prof. Memberships: Recently appointed chairman of UK Athletics Disciplinary Committee, and of the Sports Dispute Resolution Panel.
Career: Called to the Bar 1981 and joined current chambers 1982. Appointed QC in 1999.
Publications: Editorial board member for 'The International Sports Law Review'
Personal: Educated at Epsom College 1971-75 and Trinity Hall, Cambridge 1976-80 (MA in Classics and Law). Leisure pursuits include golf, cricket, theatre and opera. Born 9 April 1958. Lives in London.

MILLER, Celia
East Anglian Chambers (Roderick Newton), Ipswich
(01473) 214481
Recommended in Family

MILLER, Nicholas
Guildhall Chambers (Adrian Palmer QC), Bristol
(0117) 930 9000
Recommended in Family

MILLER, Richard QC
Three New Square (David Young QC), London
(020) 7405 1111
3newsquareip@lineone.net
Recommended in Intellectual Property
Specialisation: Specialist in patents, copyright, design rights, trademarks, passing off, breach of confidence, restrictive covenants and all other aspects of intellectual property, including EU law relating to IP. Also appears at the European Patent Office in Munich on behalf of applicants and opponents for European Patents. Co-editor of 'TERRELL on the Law of Patents'.
Prof. Memberships: Intellectual Property Bar Association, Chancery Bar Association, Bar European Group, International Association for the Protection of Industrial Property (AIPPI).
Career: Called to the Bar 1976 (Middle Temple). Appointed QC 1995.
Personal: Educated: Charterhouse 1966-70; University of Sussex 1971-74, BSc (Chemical Physics).

MILLER, Stephen QC
1 Crown Office Row (Robert Seabrook QC), London
(020) 7797 7500
stephen.miller@1cor.com
Recommended in Clinical Negligence
Specialisation: Professional negligence, particularly medical negligence and medically related disciplinary and Inquiry work. Interesting cases include: Wilsher v Essex Health Authority; Gold v Haringey Health Authority; Aboul Hosn v The Trustees of the Italian Hospital; AB v Wyeth and others (Benzodiazepine litigation); Rage (Breast Radiation Injury Group Action); Bristol Royal Infirmary Inquiry; OCP (oral contraceptive pill) Group Action; Johnstone v Camden & Islington Heath Authority; Hallat v North West Anglia Health Authority, Robertson v Nottingham Health authority; Saeed v Royal Wolverhampton NHS Trust, Galli-Atkinson v Seghal, Walters v North Glamorgan NHS Trust. Al-Kandari v J R Brown & Co; Talbot v Berkshire County Council; Al Fayed and Others v Commissioner of Police of the Metropolitan Police and Others; Zeebrugge Ferry Inquiry and criminal proceedings. Publications include a chapter in 'Medical Negligence' (contributor) Powers & Harris (Butterworths 2000 3rd Edition). 'Personal Injury Handbook' (Editors Brennan & Curran) Second Edition 2000 'Professional Negligence and Liability' (LLP Ltd 2000). Regular speaker at conferences and seminars on the subject of medical negligence and damages.
Prof. Memberships: Professional Negligence Bar Association; London Common Law & Commercial Bar Association; Personal Injury Bar Association.
Career: Called to the Bar 1971; Silk 1990. Appointed Recorder of the Crown Court 1993.
Personal: Educated at Oxford University (BA).

MILLETT, Kenneth
2 Hare Court (Stephen Kramer QC), London
(020) 7353 5324
Kennerf@lineone.net
Recommended in Crime
Specialisation: Criminal defence; civil liberties; civil actions against the police.

MILLETT, Richard
Essex Court Chambers (Gordon Pollock QC), London
(020) 7813 8000
Recommended in Arbitration, Banking & Finance, Commercial (Litigation), Insolvency, Media & Entertainment
Specialisation: Main areas of practice cover banking, insolvency, commercial litigation, reinsurance, company law, and media and entertainment. Major litigation includes the Maxwell, Polly Peck, Barings, BCCI and Bermuda Fire and Marine cases. Regularly addresses conferences and seminars. Junior Counsel to the Crown, London A Panel.
Prof. Memberships: Commercial Bar Association, Chancery Bar Association.
Career: Called to the Bar 1985. Joined present chambers 1990.
Publications: Co-author of 'The Law of Guarantees' (3rd edn, Sweet & Maxwell 2000).

MILLIGAN, Iain QC
20 Essex Street (Iain Milligan QC), London
(020) 7842 1200
clerks@20essexst.com
Recommended in Arbitration, Banking & Finance, Commercial (Litigation), Shipping
Specialisation: Arbitration, aviation, banking, carriage of goods, commodities, conflict, energy, financial services, insurance and reinsurance, shipping. Recent cases have included advice and litigation concerning banking, numerous derivatives disputes, bond issues, financial services, corporate mergers, demergers and acquisitions, the consequences of change of control and related regulatory matters, auditors' negligence in the context of takeovers and insolvency, pension mis-selling, assignment and set-off, participation in the exploitation of oil and gas fields, insurance and reinsurance, aviation (including franchising, ticketing, operational charges, aircraft leading and carriage by air), shipping, carriage by land, the financing and construction of power stations and chemical plants, the construction of oil rigs and ships, joint ventures in respect of ships, dispositions of land as part of a corporate transaction, land development in Hong Kong, EC regulation of competition (including in respect of patents) and public interest immunity. Appointed as arbitrator by the ICC and LCIA and under the rules of the LMAA. Report cases include: Deepak Fertilisers & Petrochemicals Corp and ICI Chemicals [Court of Appeal - 29.5.2002 - not yet reported]; Partco Group Ltd and another v Wragg and another [Court of Appeal - 12.2.2002] (10.5.2002 - Times Law Reports); Clark v Ardington Electrical Services [Helphire] - [2002] A11ER (D) 155, [2002] ewca Civ 510; Glencore v Metro Trading [Injunction - Court of Appeal - 19.2.2002 - not yet reported]; 'Happy Ranger' Parsons Corporation v CVS [Shipping - Court of Appeal - 30.4.2002]; Reliance Industries Ltd v Enron Oil & Gas (India) Ltd [2002] 1 Lloyd's Rep 645; ABCI v Banque Franco-Tunisienne [2002] 1 Lloyd's Rep 511; Shanning International Ltd v Lloyd's TSB Bank [2001] 1 WLR 1462; Ace Insurance SA NV v Zurich Insurance Co [2001] Lloyd's Rep 618; Petroleo Brasiliero SA v Mellittus Shipping Inc [2001] 1 A11ER (Com) 993; JP Morgan Securities v MNI [2001] 2 Lloyd's Rep 41; The Berge Sisar Borealis A/B v Stargas Ltd [2001] 2 WLR 1118; The Kapitan Sakharov Northern Shipping Co v Deutsche Seereederi [2002] 2 Lloyd's Rep 255; UBS AG v OMNI Holding AG [in liquidation] [2000] 1 WLR 916; Australia New Zealand Banking Group Ltd v Societe Generale [200] A11ER (D) 203; Sandvik AB v Pfiffner (UK) Ltd [1999] 1 A11ER 372; Sinochem International Oil (London) Co Ltd v Mobil Sales and Supply Corporation [1999] 2 Lloyd's Rep 769; Glencore Grain Ltd v Agros Trading Co Ltd [1999] 2 Lloyd's Rep 410; Credit Suisse First Boston (Europe) Ltd v MLC (Bermuda) Ltd [1999] 1 Lloyd's Rep 767; Credit Suisse First Boston (Europe) Ltd v Seagate Trading Co Ltd [1999] 1 Lloyd's Rep 784.
Prof. Memberships: Commercial Bar Association; London and Common Law Bar Association.
Career: Cambridge (1st) 1972; called to Bar 1973; Queen's Counsel 1991.

LEADERS AT THE BAR

MILLIKEN-SMITH, Mark
2 Bedford Row (William Clegg QC), London
(020) 7440 8888
mmilliken-smith@2bedfordrow.co.uk
Recommended in Crime
Specialisation: Defence advocacy, with considerable experience of all areas of heavyweight criminal work, from homicide to serious fraud and appellate work. Regularly instructed as a leading junior.
Prof. Memberships: South Eastern Circuit, Criminal Bar Association.
Career: Called to the Bar in 1986.
Personal: Married with two children. Educated at Wellington College and Bristol University. Interests include sport (whenever possible), particularly cricket, rugby and football.

MILMO, Patrick QC
5 Raymond Buildings (Patrick Milmo QC), London
(020) 7242 2902
Recommended in Defamation
Specialisation: Defamation, copyright, breach of confidence (privacy) and all other areas of law concerned with the media; judicial review; sporting regulations, especially horseracing (acts for the Jockey Club). Recent cases. R v Disciplinary Committee of Jockey Club. Exp Aga Khan [1993] I WLR 909 (judicial review); Time Warner v Channel 4 TV [1994] EMLR 1. [Copyright - film]; McDonald's Corporation v Steel [1995] 3 ALLER 615 [defamation]; Godfrey v Lees [1995] EMLR 307 (copyright - musical work); Broxton v McClelland [1997] EMLR 157; Ramsden v MGN [1998]; Emaco & Electrolux v Dyson TLR 4 Feb 1999 [trade libel and trademark infringement]; Druck v Associated Newspapers [2000] EMLR 284 (defamation by photograph); Alexander v Arts Council of Wales [2001] 1 WLR 1840; Carlton Communication v News Group Newspapers [2002] EMLR 299.
Career: Trinity College, Cambridge. Called 1962. QC 1985. Bencher Middle Temple 1994.
Publications: Publication: joint editor of 'Gatley on Libel & Slander' (9th edn).

MILNE, David QC
Pump Court Tax Chambers, London
(020) 7414 8080
clerks@pumptax.com
Recommended in Tax
Specialisation: Specialist in revenue law, especially tax litigation and dispute resolution.
Prof. Memberships: Institute of Chartered Accountants in England and Wales. Former Chairman of the Revenue Bar Association.
Career: Accountant, articled to *Whinney Murray & Co* 1966-69. Called to the Bar 1970 and joined current chambers in 1972. Took Silk 1987. Appointed Recorder 1989. Bencher of Lincoln's Inn 1996.
Personal: Read law at Jesus College, Oxford 1963-66. Born 22 September 1945. Lives in London.

MISKIN, Charles QC
23 Essex Street (Michael Lawson QC), London
(020) 7413 0353
Recommended in Fraud

MITCHELL, Andrew
Fountain Court (Anthony Boswood QC), London
(020) 7583 3335
Recommended in Banking & Finance
Specialisation: Practises in commercial litigation and arbitration, with particular experience of international and domestic banking, civil fraud, professional negligence (particularly solicitors), insurance/reinsurance and employment. Recent cases have included acting for the new Nigerian Government in its claims against the former regime; Bank Leumi v Miloubar (bills of exchange); Ebert v Midland Bank [1999] 3 WLR 670, a leading authority on the power of the Court to control vexatious litigation.
Prof. Memberships: COMBAR.
Career: Called 1992.
Publications: Contributing Editor to 'Commercial Court Procedure' (Sweet & Maxwell, 2000).
Personal: Educated at Cambridge University (1987-90 (MA)) and Oxford University (1990-91), BCL. Harmsworth Scholar of Middle Temple. Born 1968.

MITCHELL, Andrew QC
Furnival Chambers (Andrew Mitchell QC), London
(020) 7405 3232
arm@furnivallaw.co.uk
Recommended in Crime, Fraud
Specialisation: Financial crime: white collar fraud - advance fee, mortgage, computer and letter of credit, handling the transfer of serious and complex fraud, drafting statements of evidence and case statements for both the defence and prosecution. Money laundering - advised on practice and procedures in relation to money laundering regulations and legislation. Acted in both prosecutions and defence of money laundering offences. Asset forfeiture and confiscation - advised, represented prosecuting authorities, defendants, receivers and third parties in House of Lords, Court of Appeal (Civil and Criminal), High Court and Crown Court on all matters affecting the restraint, management receivers and confiscation of property. General crime: defended and represented the prosecution in significant drug cases. Priority interests: asset forfeiture, confiscation, white collar fraud, money laundering, drugs. International work: advised governments of Trinidad and Tobago, Turks and Caicos Islands, Cayman Islands, Canada, USA, Abu Dhabi, Pakistan. Acted in civil and criminal litigation in Trinidad and Tobago, Turks and Caicos Islands and Gibraltar, Cayman Islands.
Career: Called to Bar 1976, Gray's Inn, Ireland, Gibraltar, Trinidad, and the Turks and Caicos Islands. Assistant Recorder 1995. Queens Counsel 1998. Recorder 1999. Has been a principal speaker at training programmes organised by the UN for prosecutors and investigators in the Caribbean as well as at judicial symposiums in Trinidad, Jamaica and the Bahamas. Regular lecturer on matters affecting restraint, confiscation and money laundering for United Nations, National Crime Squad, Criminal Bar Association (England and Wales) and Temple Lectures. Consultant to Caribbean anti-money laundering programme.
Publications: Author - 'A Concise Guide to the Criminal Procedure and Investigations Act', 1996. Co-author - 'Confiscation and the Proceeds of Crime', 3rd edn (the leading textbook on asset forfeiture and confiscation, published by Sweet & Maxwell). Articles published in the 'New Law Journal' and the 'Journal of Criminal Law'.
Personal: Born 6 August 1954.

MITCHELL, Janet
4 Brick Court (David Medhurst), London
(020) 7797 8910
Recommended in Family
Specialisation: Childcare law, public law cases, family law and litigation. Provided procedure guidelines to local authorities on setting up Care in the Community Programme. Particular areas include: child sexual abuse, child protection issues, female and male paedophiles, public interest immunity. Recently five week case representing a local authority in respect of incest, child sexual abuse, sexual abuse by mother, father, stepfather and inter-sibling abuse. Abuse in which question of 13 year old under represented was raised. Also numerous cases involving unexplained injuries/cot deaths.
Prof. Memberships: Family Law Bar Association. Lawyers for children.
Career: Called to the Bar in 1979. Lecturing on advocacy, litigation and public law cases particularly in the area of child sexual and physical abuse.
Personal: Travel, reading, swimming, tennis, crosswords. Widow - two daughters. Husband, also a Barrister, died in 1989.

MITCHESON, Thomas
Three New Square (David Young QC), London
(020) 7405 1111
tom@mitcheson.com
Recommended in Intellectual Property
Specialisation: All aspects of intellectual property law. Recent cases include Norowzian v Arks (Copyright in television advertisement, CA); Kimberly-Clark v Procter & Gamble (Patent Amendment, CA); 3M v ATI Atlas (patent infringement); Hewlett Packard v Waters (patent infringement, CA); Arsenal v Reed (trademark - ECJ reference).
Prof. Memberships: Member of IP Pre-Action Protocol Committee.
Career: Internship at Cold Spring Harbor Laboratory, USA 1990-91. Trinity College, Cambridge, 1991-94 - First Class Hons Natural Sciences. City University (Dip-Law), 1995 (Distinction). Called to the Bar 1996.
Publications: 'Two Genes in Saccharomyces Cerevisiae Encode a Membrane Bound Form of Casein Kinase-1' Wang, Vancura, Mitcheson & Kuret (1992). Contributor to 'Terrell on Patents' (15th edition).

MOGER, Christopher QC
4 Pump Court, London
(020) 7842 5555
cmoger@4pumpcourt.com
Recommended in Licensing, Professional Negligence
Specialisation: General commercial and common law, especially insurance, construction matters; professional negligence, and regulatory and disciplinary proceedings.
Prof. Memberships: TECBAR; LCLBA; COMBAR; PNBA; Barristers' Overseas Advocacy Committee.
Career: Called 1972; joined 4 Pump Court 1973; Assistant Recorder 1990; Silk 1992; Recorder 1993; FCIA 1997. Deputy Judge of High Court 1999. Trained mediator and member of ADR Chambers, London. Member of Panel of Chairmen of Lloyds Disciplinary Tribunal 2001.
Personal: Educated Sherborne School 1963-68 and Bristol University 1969-71 (LLB Hons).

MOLONEY, Patrick QC
1 Brick Court (Richard Rampton QC), London
(020) 7353 8845
pm@1brickcourt.co.uk
Recommended in Defamation
Specialisation: Media law, (libel, slander, malicious falsehood, passing off, breach of confidence, contempt of court, reporting restrictions). Recent cases: GKR Karate v Yorkshire Post (CA) (Reynolds privilege); Al Fagih v Saudi research (Reynolds privilege, neutral reportage); Totalise v Motley Fool (disclosure of internet source); Gregson v Ch.4 (CA) (mode of trial).
Prof. Memberships: Northern Irish Bar.
Career: BA BCL (Oxon); Asst. Prof. Univ. of British Columbia (1974-75); 1 Brick Court (1978 to present). QC (1998). Recorder (2000).
Publications: Co-author 'Libel and Slander' Halsbury's Laws of England.

MOLYNEUX, Brenton
29 Bedford Row Chambers (Nicholas Francis QC), London
(020) 7404 1044
bmolyneux@29bedfordrow.co.uk
Recommended in Family
Specialisation: All aspects of family law but with a particular emphasis on matrimonial finance and private law children work.
Prof. Memberships: Family Law Bar Association.
Career: Called to the Bar, February 1994.
Personal: Born 31 December 1968.

Educated at Birkenhead School, Christ Church, Oxford (BA) and City University (Dip Law). Married. Lives in London.

MONKCOM, Stephen
Tanfield Chambers (Peter Hughes QC), London
(020) 7353 9942
monkcom@dial.pipex.com
Recommended in Licensing
Specialisation: Specialises in all aspects of licensing with particular emphasis on betting, gaming and lotteries and allied sales promotions. Has advised extensively on the application of internet technologies in this field. Practice also includes commercial and public law work.
Prof. Memberships: Member of Administrative Law Bar Association.
Career: Called 1974. Joined present Chambers 1976.
Publications: Include 'Smith & Monkcom: The Law of Betting, Gaming and Lotteries' (Butterworths 2001 - 2nd edition). Contributor to 'Halsbury's Laws of England' Vol 4(1) (Re-issue), title 'Betting' (new edition in preparation). Joint editor 'Encyclopaedia of Forms and Precedents' 5th Edition Re-issue, title 'Gaming, Betting and Lotteries'. Consulting Editor of 'Licensing Review'.
Personal: Born 9 June 1949.

MONTGOMERY, Clare QC
Matrix Chambers, London
(020) 7404 3447
Recommended in Crime, Fraud, Human Rights

MOODY, Neil
2 Temple Gardens (Dermod O'Brien QC), London
(020) 7822 1229
nmoody@2templegardens.co.uk
Recommended in Professional Negligence
Specialisation: Professional negligence. Widespread experience of claims for and against solicitors, surveyors, insurance brokers, accountants and architects. Also specialises in flooding and fire cases, insurance and serious personal injury claims. Recent cases include: Stevens v Gullis [2000] All ER (CA) (architects: duties of experts) and Bybrook Barn v Kent County Council [2001] All ER (CA) (nuisance, flooding).
Prof. Memberships: LCCLBA, PNBA, PIBA.
Career: Tenant 2 Temple Gardens 1990.
Personal: Married: three children, sailing.

MOODY-STUART, Thomas
8 New Square (Mark Platts-Mills QC), London
(020) 7405 4321
tom.moodystuart@8newsquare.co.uk
Recommended in Intellectual Property
Specialisation: Barrister specialising in all areas of intellectual property including patents, copyright, registered/unregistered design, trademarks, passing off, biotechnology, comparative advertising, broadcasting and breach of confidence. For comprehensive CV and list of recent cases, visit the set's website at www.8newsquare.co.uk.
Prof. Memberships: Intellectual Property Bar Association (IPBA); The Intellectual Property Lawyers Organisation.
Career: Called 1995, Middle Temple; conservation research assistant: US Government Captive Breeding Centre 1989.
Personal: Called 1970. Educated at Shrewsbury School; Gonville & Caius College, Cambridge (1993 MA Hons Natural Science); College of Law; Inns of Court School of Law.

MOON, Angus
3 Serjeants' Inn (Robert Francis QC & John Grace QC), London
(020) 7427 5000
Recommended in Clinical Negligence
Specialisation: Specialist in medical negligence and medically related litigation. Particular interest in judicial review in the medical context and medical ethical decisions. Instructed by both Plaintiffs and Defendants in medical negligence actions and for parties involved in medical disciplinary tribunals and inquests. Additional areas of practice include commercial contract and employment law. Major reported cases in the medical field include Gregory v Ferro (GB) Ltd and ors [1995] 6 Med LR 321 (Court of Appeal); Mahmood v Siggins [1996] 7 Med LR 76; R v Milling (Medical Referee), ex p West Yorkshire Police Authority [1997] 8 Med LR 392; Re C (A Minor) (Medical Treatment) [1998] 1 Lloyd's Rep Med 1; Palmer v Tees Health Authority [1998] Lloyd's Rep Med 447; Davis v Jacobs & Camden & Islington Health Authority & Novartis [1999] Lloyd's Rep Med 72; Bordin v St Mary's NHS Trust [2000] Lloyd's Rep Med 287; Reynolds v The Health First Medical Group [2000] Lloyd's Rep Med 240. Editor of the Lloyd's Law Reports 'Medical' (formerly the 'Medical Law Reports'). Member of the Committee of the London Common Law and Commercial Bar Association. Member of the Bar Council.
Career: Called to the Bar 1986.
Personal: Christ's College, Cambridge (MA Law).

MOONEY, Stephen
Albion Chambers (Neil Ford QC), Bristol
(0117) 927 2144
Recommended in Crime

MOOR, Philip QC
1 Hare Court (Bruce Blair QC), London
(020) 7797 7070
moor@1hc.com
Recommended in Family
Specialisation: Family law, with particular emphasis on the financial aspects of marital breakdown. Regular lecturer and contributor (with Nicholas Mostyn QC as co-author) to 'Family Law' magazine.
Prof. Memberships: Family Law Bar Association (Committee member since 1987; Head of Education & Training 1993-2000; Acting Treasurer 2000-01; Vice Chairman 2002-).
Career: Called to the Bar in 1982 and joined Mitre Court Buildings in 1983. QC 2001. Member of General Council of the Bar 1987-89. Council of Legal Education 1988-91 (Board of Examiners 1989-92). Phillips Committee on Financing Pupillage (1989). Professional Standards Committee of the Bar 2002.
Personal: Educated at Canford School 1972-77 and Pembroke College, Oxford 1978-81. Leisure pursuits include cricket, football and rugby union. Lives in Bromley.

MOOR, Sarah
Old Square Chambers (John Hendy QC), London
(020) 7269 0300
moor@oldsquarechambers.co.uk
Recommended in Employment
Specialisation: Principal area of practice is employment law including sex, race and disability discrimination, equal pay, restrictive covenant and industrial action. Cases include Kenny v Hampshire Constabulary and Edwards v Mid Suffolk District Council.
Prof. Memberships: Employment Law Bar Association, Industrial Law Society and Employment Lawyers Association.
Career: Queen's College, Cambridge BA Law (1989), Kennedy Memorial Scholar at Harvard Law School (1990), Council of Legal Education (1991). Called 1991. Joined Old Square Chambers 1992.
Publications: Contributor to 'Employment Precedents and Company Documents' (FT Law and Tax).

MOORE, Katherine
Octagon House Chambers (Guy Ayers & Andrew Lindquist), Norwich
(01603) 623186
Recommended in Crime

MOORE, Martin QC
Erskine Chambers (Robin Potts QC), London
(020) 7242 5532
clerks@erskine-chambers.co.uk
Recommended in Company
Specialisation: Litigation and advice on all aspects of company law, corporate insolvency and corporate reorganisation, including Schemes of Arrangement, and Schemes for transfer of insurance and banking business. Recent cases: Re BSB Holdings Ltd (1996) 1 BCLC 155; Possfund Custodian Trustee Ltd v Diamond (1996) 1 WLR 1351, Bermuda Fire and Marine Insurance Company and others v BF&M Limited and others heard in the Supreme Court of Bermuda, and Axa Equity & Law Life Assurance Security plc and Axa Sun Life plc 2001 2 BCLC447. The Equitable Life Assurance Society (November 2001-February 2002).
Career: BA (Oxon). Year qualified: 1982. Lincoln's Inn.
Personal: Born: 1960.

MOORE, Miranda
5 Paper Buildings (Godfrey Carey QC & Jonathan Caplan QC), London
(020) 7583 6117
Recommended in Crime

MORAN, Andrew G QC
Byrom Street Chambers, Manchester
(0161) 829 2100
Recommended in Clinical Negligence

MORCOM, Christopher QC
Hogarth Chambers (Jonathan Rayner James QC & Christopher Morcom QC), London
(020) 7404 0404
cmorcom@hogarthchambers.com
Recommended in Intellectual Property
Specialisation: Intellectual property including in particular trademarks; also copyright; designs; patents; confidential information.
Prof. Memberships: Member of SACIP; council member and vice-president of AIPPI (British Group). Associate member of ITMA, CIPA, INTA, past president of LIDC; honorary president (2000-date); chairman of Competition Law Association (1985-99); director of the Intellectual Property Institute; member of Board of International Trademark Association (INTA) (1998-2000).
Career: Called to the Bar 1963 (Middle Temple); Bencher (1996); Certificate of Honour; Astbury Scholarship. Took Silk 1991.
Publications: Author (with Roughton & Graham) of 'The Modern Law of Trade Marks' (Butterworths, 2000).
Personal: Interests include music and walking.

MORGAN, Lynne
Temple Chambers (David J M Aubrey QC), Cardiff
(029) 2039 7364
Recommended in Family

MORGAN, Paul QC
Falcon Chambers (Jonathan Gaunt QC & Kim Lewison QC), London
(020) 7353 2484
morgan@falcon-chambers.com
Recommended in Agriculture, Property Litigation
Specialisation: All aspects of real property, commercial property litigation and agricultural holdings.
Prof. Memberships: Chancery Bar Association, London Commercial and Common Law Bar Association, Agricultural Law Association.
Career: Called to the Bar in 1975, Silk 1992. Deputy chairman, Agricultural Land Tribunal; Assistant Boundary Commissioner, Deputy High Court Judge.
Publications: Joint editor 'Woodfall on Landlord and Tenant', loose leaf edition. Joint editor 'Gale on Easements', 16th edn.

MORGAN, Simon
St John's Chambers (Christopher Sharp QC), Bristol
(0117) 921 3456
Recommended in Crime

LEADERS AT THE BAR

MORGAN, Stephen
Eldon Chambers (Patrick Clarkson QC & William Hicks QC), London
(020) 7583 1355
clerks@eldonchambers.com
Recommended in Planning
Specialisation: Local Government; Town and Country Planning; Environmental Law and Public Law. Compulsory purchase and compensation; highways; advertisements.
Prof. Memberships: PEBA
Career: Law degree, followed by MA in Town and Country Planning. Always been in local government Chambers.
Personal: Family; walking; bird watching; football

MORGANS, John
Octagon House Chambers (Guy Ayers & Andrew Lindquist), Norwich
(01603) 623186
Recommended in Crime

MORRIS, Anthony QC
Peel Court Chambers (Michael Shorrock QC), Manchester
(0161) 832 3791
Recommended in Crime

MORRIS, Fenella
39 Essex Street (Nigel Pleming QC), London
(020) 7832 1111
Recommended in Administrative & Public Law
Specialisation: Administrative and public law, human rights, discrimination and incapacity. Particular interests include health, mental health, education and community care, professional regulation and discipline, local government and environmental law. Notable cases include Pretty v UK (Suicide Act 1961 compatible with ECHR), R (A) v Partnerships in Care Ltd (private hospital is a public authority under the HRA), R v LB Richmond ex p Watson (charging for after-care services), R (A) v Ashworth Hospital Authority (guidelines to doctors and public bodies that disagree with a decision of the MHRT to discharge a patient), R (Munjaz) v Merseycare NHS Trust (abuse of process in judicial review), Re F (Adult Patient) sub nom Re F (Adult: Court's Jurisdiction) and A v A Health Authority (extent of jurisdiction in judicial review and declaratory relief proceedings in the Family Division).
Prof. Memberships: ALBA, ELBA, Liberty and MIND legal network.
Career: Called to the Bar in 1990 and joined present chambers in 1998.
Personal: Educated at Wadham College, Oxford, BA (Hons) Politics, Philosophy and Economics and City University, Dip Law.

MORRIS, Stephen QC
20 Essex Street (Iain Milligan QC), London
(020) 7842 1200
smorris@20essexst.com
Recommended in Competition/European Law
Specialisation: All aspects of EC and UK competition law; other EC law, in particular free movement of goods, intellectual property, air transport, customs, sanctions; commercial and international trade, in particular conflict of laws, insurance and arbitration. Recent competition/EC cases include R v IRC ex p Professional Contractors Group (CA); Morgan Stanley v Visa (Comm Ct); Shanning v Lloyds TSB (HL); R v Secretary of State for Trade ex p Thomson Holidays (CA); Sandvik v Pfiffner (CA); Mid Kent Holdings v General Utilities (Ch D); Airtours/First Choice (EC Comm); Mid Kent Holdings (MMC); Foreign Package Holidays (MMC); AIUFFASS v Commission (ECJ); Potato Marketing Board v Hampden Smith (CA); Commercial cases include Maxwell Communication Corporation v New Hampshire Insurance (CA); PASF v Bamberger (CA); Akai v PIC (Comm Ct); Toepfer v Cargill (CA). Further information at www.20essexst.com.
Prof. Memberships: COMBAR, Bar European Group.
Career: Called 1981. At 4 Raymond Buildings, Gray's Inn 1983-91. Joined present chambers in 1992. Junior Counsel to the Crown (A Panel) 1999-2002. QC 2002. Recorder.
Publications: Bellamy and Child, 'European Community Law of Competition' (5th edn 2001 - chapter on enforcement in member states); contributor to Plender, 'European Courts Practice and Precedent'; Bar Council's 'Practitioners Handbook of EC law'.
Personal: Educated at Bradford Grammar School and Christ's College, Cambridge.

MORRISON, Howard QC
36 Bedford Row (Michael Pert QC), London
(020) 7421 8000
chambers@bedfordrow.co.uk
Recommended in Crime
Specialisation: Crime generally, including murder, fraud and drugs cases, particularly international criminal law (war crimes, crimes against humanity and genocide; laws of war and military law particularly issues of command responsibility). Recent high profile cases include the trial and appeal of Zdravko Mucic and the trial of Dragan Nikolic at the Yugoslav tribunal in The Hague and the trial of the former Rwandan cabinet minister Justin Mugenzi for genocide at the Rwanda tribunal in Tanzania.
Prof. Memberships: Criminal Bar Association, European CBA, International Bar Association, Commonwealth Judges and Magistrates Association, International Criminal Defence Attorneys Association, International Society for Military Law, Equal Opportunities Committee of the Bar Council, Judicial Practice Committee ICTY, ICTY and ICTR Counsel Associations, Justice, Member of Fijian and Eastern Caribbean Bars.
Career: LLB [Lond]. Experience of voluntary work in Ghana, Zambia and Malawi. Former infantry officer, regular, TAVR and RARO. Called to Bar, Grays Inn 1977. QC 2001. Practice on the Midland Circuit and International UN Tribunals. Former Chief Magistrate of Fiji and Senior Magistrate of Tuvalu, sometime Attorney General of Anguilla. Assistant Recorder/Recorder of Crown Court since 1993 [criminal, civil and family] OBE Diplomatic List 1988. Fellow of the Royal Geographical Society. Advocacy teacher/trainer Grays Inn. Various publications, mainly international criminal law, conference and seminar lecturing in Europe and USA.

MORSHEAD, Timothy
4 Breams Buildings (Christopher Lockhart-Mummery QC), London
(020) 7353 5835
tmorshead@4breams.co.uk
Recommended in Property Litigation
Specialisation: All aspects of property law including landlord and tenant law and planning. Also accepts work in certain public law matters. Member of C Panel of Junior Counsel to the Crown.
Prof. Memberships: Chancery Bar Association, Property Bar Association, Planning and Environment Bar Association.

MORT, Justin
2 Temple Gardens (Dermod O'Brien QC), London
(020) 7822 1230
jmort@2templegardens.co.uk
Recommended in Construction
Specialisation: Construction disputes. Recent cases have arisen out of a wide range of building and refurbishment projects, as well as process and civil engineering works, both in the UK and in the Far East. He has particular experience of resisting substantial adjudication claims, acting on behalf of the main contractors, private individuals, developers, local authorities and other public bodies. He has also acted in a number of construction related professional negligence disputes, including claims for defective design and negligent contract administration. Represented the employer in David McLean Contractors Ltd v Swansea Housing Association Ltd.
Prof. Memberships: Society of Construction Law, Adjudication Society, King's College Construction Law Association and TECBAR.
Career: Called to the Bar in 1994. Tenant of 2 Temple Gardens since 1995.
Personal: Born 1970. MSc in Construction Law and Arbitration, King's College, London. Dissertation; 'Claims for contribution under the Civil Liability (Contribution) Act 1978'. Jules Thorn Scholar (Middle Temple).

MORTIMORE, Simon QC
3-4 South Square (Michael Crystal QC & Lord Alexander of Weedon QC), London
(020) 7696 9900
simonmortimore@southsquare.com
Recommended in Insolvency
Specialisation: Business and financial law, particularly insolvency. Recent work: acting for the liquidators of Barings, for US investors in $180 million fraud claim, and in many of the recent telecom failures. Substantial involvement in the major insolvencies of the 1990s: BCCI, Olympia & York, Maxwell, Polly Peck, Metro, Ferranti. More than 50 reported cases including: AD Little v Abelco (2002) charge on shares in subsidiary; Barings (2001) removal of liquidators and sanction of compromise; Omega v Kozeny (2001) injunction to restrain USC 1782 proceedings; Adbury Park Estate (2001) attempted disqualification of liquidators; Triffit v Salads Etc (2000) effect of termination of agency on rights to debts; Glencore v Metro (1999) forum issues under Brussels Convention; Richbell Information Services, TSB v Platts (1998) effect of cross-claims on petitions; Cosslett Contractors (1997) charge in building contract; BCCI (no 10) (1997) cross-border set-off issues; Leeds United (1996) dispute takeover; Macmillan v Bishopsgate (1995) priorities over shares in foreign company.
Prof. Memberships: ILA, R3, INSOL, Chancery Bar Association, COMBAR.
Career: Called to the Bar (Inner Temple) 1972; QC 1991. Called to BVI Bar 1991; admitted for specific cases to Bermuda and Cayman Island Bars. Accredited CEDR mediator 1997.

MORTON, Keith
1 Temple Gardens (Geoffrey Nice QC), London
(020) 7583 1315
clerks@1templegardens.co.uk
Recommended in Health & Safety
Specialisation: Health and safety law, in which he regularly advises and represents both prosecution and defendants (eg junior prosecution counsel in R v Balfour Beatty and Geoconsult GmBH - (1999); arising out of collapse of tunnels at Heathrow Airport). Employment law, administrative law, personal injury, coroners (including judicial review) and public inquiries (eg Ladbroke Grove Rail Inquiry).
Prof. Memberships: South Eastern Circuit, Employment Lawyers Association, Justice.
Career: Called to the Bar Lincoln's Inn 1990; Treasury Counsel (common law) B Panel (since 1997).
Personal: University of Hull, City University. Interests include theatre, art, music, architecture, cycling.

MOSS, Gabriel QC
3-4 South Square (Michael Crystal QC & Lord Alexander of Weedon QC), London
(020) 7696 9900
clerks@southsquare.com

LEADERS AT THE BAR

Recommended in Chancery, Insolvency
Specialisation: Mainly in business and financial law with a special emphasis on insolvency and restructuring. Recent cases include Railtrack, Enron, Federal Mogul, ITV Digital, Energis and Global Crossing.
Prof. Memberships: Chancery Bar Association, Commercial Bar Association, Insol Europe, Fellow of the Society for Advanced Legal Studies, Bencher of Lincoln's Inn, Honorary Member of the Association of Fellows and Legal Scholars of the Centre for International Legal Studies, Member of Insolvency Lawyers Association.
Career: 1st Class Hons Law Degree at Oxford University (BA), Post Graduate Law Degree from Oxford University (BLC); Lecturer in Law at the University of Connecticut, part-time lecturer/tutor at Oxford University; Eldon Scholar (Oxford); Bar Exams: Appointed QC (1989); Authorised to sit as Deputy High Court Judge (2001).
Publications: Co-editor of Rowlatt on 'Principal and Surety'; Co-author of Lightman & Moss on the 'Law of Receivers of Companies'; Joint Consultant Editor of Totty & Moss on 'Insolvency'.

MOSS, Joanne R
Falcon Chambers (Jonathan Gaunt QC & Kim Lewison QC), London
(020) 7353 2484
Recommended in Agriculture

MOSTYN, Nicholas QC
1 Hare Court (Bruce Blair QC), London
(020) 7797 7070
Recommended in Family

MOULD, Timothy
4 Breams Buildings (Christopher Lockhart-Mummery QC), London
(020) 7430 1221
Recommended in Local Government, Planning
Specialisation: Specialises in local government and planning law and related areas of public law. Currently on the A Panel of Junior Counsel to the Crown, Junior Counsel to the Inland Revenue on Rating and Valuation matters, and contributor to Halsbury's Laws of England, 'Town and Country Planning' and the 'Encyclopaedia of Rating and Local Taxation'.
Prof. Memberships: Member of the Planning and Environment Bar Association and the Administrative Law Bar Association.

MOUNTFIELD, Helen
Matrix Chambers, London
(020) 7404 3447
helenmountfield@matrixlaw.co.uk
Recommended in Administrative & Public Law, Education, Employment, Human Rights
Specialisation: Specialises in administrative public law, human rights, discrimination, employment, and EC law. She practises in English, European and Commonwealth courts acting for private individuals, commercial organisations, NGOs and public authorities. She is an editor of the 'European Human Rights Law Review', the 'Education Law Reports' and co-author of the 'Blackstone Guide to the Human Rights Act 1998', and has lectured for the Judicial Studies Board and elsewhere. Junior Counsel to the Crown (B panel). Notable cases include R v Secretary of State for the Environment ex p Friends of the Earth (drinking water standards litigation), Meade-Hill v British Council (indirect discrimination), Snares v CAO (free movement of persons, ECJ), R v Secretary of State for Health ex p Source Informatics (confidentiality and data protection), Faulkner v UK (Article 6 ECHR) and representing the government of Belgium in Pinochet.
Career: Called to the Bar 1991.
Personal: Educated at Magdalen College Oxford (BA (Hons) Modern History (1st Class), City University 1989-90 (Dip Law), King's College London 1994 (Dip European Law).

MOVERLEY SMITH, Stephen QC
24 Old Buildings (Martin Mann QC & Alan Steinfeld QC), London
(020) 7404 0946
Recommended in Insolvency

MOWBRAY, John QC
New Square Chambers (Charles Purle QC), London
(020) 7419 8000
clerks@newsquarechambers.co.uk
Recommended in Chancery
Specialisation: Litigation, with some advisory work, mediating and arbitrating, mainly in the following fields: Trusts, including related taxes, pension funds and Caribbean and other offshore trusts; Contract disputes, mainly international; Conflict of laws in connection with the above and generally; Property, including landlord and tenant, mortgages and insolvency aspects. Representative reported cases include: Arlen Bahamas Management v Trust Corporation of Bahamas (1971-6) 1 Law Reports of Bahamas 456 (power of modification of trust instrument); Security Trust v Royal Bank [1976] A.C. 503 P.C. (priority of charges on Bahamian land); Tito v Waddell [1977] Ch. 106 (governmental trusts); Borden U.K. v Scottish Timber Products [1981] Ch. 25 C.A. (retention of title clause); Official Custodian v Parway Estates [1985] Ch. 151 C.A. (insolvency of tenant-equitable relief from forfeiture-mortgagee's rights - and see the next case in the volume); News Group v SOGAT [1986] I.C.R. 716 C.A. (trust of trade union branch funds - sequestration); Basingstoke and Deane BC v Host Group [1988] 1 W.L.R. 348 C.A. (rent review clause); Alghussein v Eton College [1988] 1 W.L.R. 587 H.L. (breach of contract - not profiting from one's own wrong); Australian Commercial Research and Development v ANZ [1989] 3 All E.R. 65 (plaintiff with same action in two jurisdictions); Dubai Bank v Galadari [1990] Ch. 98 C.A. (privilege for copy documents); Imperial Group Pension Trust v Imperial Tobacco [1991] 1 W.L.R. 589 (employment principles applied to pension fund trusts); Lemos v Coutts & Co. (Cayman) 1992-93 CILR 460 Cayman Islands C.A. (cross-border trust litigation - discovery and Mareva orders against trustees); Inverugie Investments v Hackett [1995] 1 W.L.R. 713 P.C. (assessment of damages for trespass in letting property); Re T.C. Pagarani (1998/99) 2 O.F.L.R. 1 British Virgin Islands C.A (incompletely constituted trust); Re Z Trust 1997 CILR 248 (conflicts of interest on amending trusts under a power). Michaels v Harley House (Marylebone) Ltd [2000]Ch. 104 C.A. (enfranchisement of flats - constructive trust arising on the sale of shares); Michaels v Taylor Woodrow [2001] 2 WLR 224 (conspiracy to injure by unlawful means not separately actionable).
Prof. Memberships: Chancery Bar Association; Centre for Dispute Resolution (Accredited Mediator); STEP International Committee; ACTAPS.
Career: Former Chairman Chancery Bar Association, Member of Bar Council and Deputy High Court Judge. A permanent member of the Bars of The Bahamas (1971) and of The Eastern Caribbean (1992) and appears in the Cayman Islands. Senior Editor of Lewin on Trusts 17th edn.

MOWSCHENSON, Terence QC
Wilberforce Chambers (Edward Nugee QC), London
(020) 7306 0102
Recommended in Chancery, Commercial (Litigation), Company
Specialisation: Principal areas of practice: company/commercial matters including matters involving the law relating to banking (including bills of exchange, letters of credit, syndicated loan agreements); breach of trust; conflict of laws; contract (including conditions of sale, share and business sale agreements, licensing and franchising, restraint of trade, retention of title, and sale of goods); companies (including shareholder disputes, shareholder agreements, technical aspects of company law, takeovers, Stock Exchange regulations, broking and dealing); equitable remedies; financial services (including matters relating to the various self regulatory organisations); insolvency; insurance; partnership; professional negligence. Reported cases including Derby v Weldon; Sharneyford Supplies v Edge; Elliss v BP Oil Northern Ireland Refinery Ltd; Re Westock Realisations Ltd; Dept of Environment v Bates; Investment and Pensions Services v Gray; Acatos v Watson Crimpfil Ltd v Barclays Bank plc; Eastglen Ltd v Grafton; Metalloy (Supplies) Limited v MA (UK) Limited (CA); Wake v Renault (UK) Ltd; BCCI v Prince Fahd Bin Salman Al Saud; Arbuthnot Latham Bank v Trafalgar Holdings; Board of Governors of National Heart and Chest Hospital v Chettle; HSBC Life (UK) (and others) v Stubbs, Re AXA Equity and Laws Life Assurance Society plc and Deepak Fertilisers and Petrochemicals Ltd v Davy McKee.
Prof. Memberships: Chancery and Commercial Bar Associations.
Career: Called to the Bar in 1977. Queen's Counsel 1995. Recorder 2000. Chairman, Financial Services and Markets Act Tribunal (2001).
Personal: Educated at Eagle School and Peterhouse. London University, LLB (Hons) and Oxford BCL (Hons). FCIArb 1989.

MOXON-BROWNE, Robert QC
2 Temple Gardens (Dermod O'Brien QC), London
(020) 7822 1200
Recommended in Professional Negligence
Specialisation: A well known advocate who heads the Professional Negligence Group at 2 Temple Gardens. His work includes cases involving accountants, solicitors and surveyors as well as construction industry professionals, especially where disputes arise as to allocation of responsibility within multidisciplinary teams. He is also very experienced in all matters relating to insurance law and practice including subrogated recoveries in cases involving fire, flood and other catastrophic events, policy construction questions and repudiation for fraud. He is a specialist in the law affecting the valuation of loss of change. Recent reported Court of Appeal cases include Withers v Ambic Equipment CA 2002 (need for judicial reasoning), Sharif v Garrett 2001 CA (solicitors' negligence, loss of a chance); Beckett v Midland Electricity 2001 1 WLR 281 (catastrophic fire, statutory interpretation); Fennelly v Connex SE (vicarious liability); Habib Bank v Abbeypearl CA 2001 (banking fraud); Ball v Banner & Ors CA 2000 L1 L Rep PN 1 (relative responsibility of solicitors and surveyors for investment prospectus); MacAreary v Coal Authority CA 2000 (statutory interpretation); Burns v Shuttleworth (1999) 1 WLR 1449 (insurance law, statutory interpretation); Housing Loan Corporation v Win Browne (1999) L1L Rep PN 185 (relative responsibility of surveyors, solicitors and bankers for loan fraud); Routestone v Minories Finance 1997 BCLC 97 (relative duties of receivers and surveyors to those interested in equity of redemption); Sainsburys v Broadway Malyan 61 Con Law Rep 31 (relative duties of architects and engineers for firewall; loss of chance); Allied Maples v *Simmons & Simmons* (1995) 1 WLR 1602 (solicitors' duty in takeover negotiations; loss of a chance).
Prof. Memberships: ORBA, Professional Negligence Bar Association, CLBA, COMBAR.
Career: Called to the Bar 1969, QC 1990,

LEADERS AT THE BAR

Recorder 1992. Deputy Judge of the Technology and Construction Court 1993. Deputy Judge of the High Court 1999.
Personal: Born 1946. Educated Gordonstoun School, University College Oxford (BA).

MOYLAN, Andrew QC
Queen Elizabeth Building (Florence Baron QC), London
(020) 7797 7837
Recommended in Family
Specialisation: Ancillary relief; other aspects of family law including child residence/contact; Inheritance Act claims; professional negligence (matrimonial).
Prof. Memberships: Family Law Bar Association.
Career: Counsel to the Queen's Proctor (1997-2000).

MUIR, Andrew
3 Raymond Buildings (Clive Nicholls QC), London
(020) 7400 6400
chambers@3raymondbuildings.com
Recommended in Licensing
Specialisation: Extensive experience of licensing work encompassing liquor, gaming, betting, lotteries and public entertainment. Represented General Medical Council at disciplinary tribunal hearings. Appointed Department of Trade and Industry Inspector for insider share dealing enquiries. Represents London Cab Office in hackney carriage appeals. Also practises in Environmental Protection and Health & Safety law.
Prof. Memberships: South Eastern Circuit.
Career: Called to the Bar 1975, and joined 3 Raymond Buildings in 1976. BA (Hons).
Personal: Educated at Stonyhurst College 1965-70, Ealing Technical College 1970-73 and Council of Legal Education 1974-75. Leisure pursuits include horse racing, cricket and rugby. Born 25 December 1951. Lives in Lodsworth.

MULCAHY, Jane
Blackstone Chambers (Presiley Baxendale QC & Charles Flint QC), London
(020) 7583 1770
janemulcahy@blackstonechambers.com
Recommended in Employment
Specialisation: Employment, human rights, public, entertainment and media, and sports.
Prof. Memberships: Employment Law Association, Administrative Law Bar Association.
Career: Called 1995. Previously worked as a journalist.
Publications: Joint author of conflicts chapter in 'European Employment Law and the UK'; contributor to ELA Briefing; joint author of chapter on employment relationships in sport, in forthcoming 'Sport Law and Practice'.

MULLIS, Roger
11 New Square (Sonia Proudman QC), London
(020) 7831 0081
clerks@11newsquare.co.uk
Recommended in Chancery
Specialisation: Landlord and tenant; real property; probate and administration of estates; professional negligence. Reported cases include Hurley v Hurley [1998] 1FLR 213; Plant v Plant [1998]1BCLC 38; Rees-Davies v Westminster City Council [1998] R V R 219; Borman v LEL [2002] WTLR 237.
Prof. Memberships: Chancery Bar Association; Professional Negligence Bar Association.
Career: Called 1987.
Personal: Educated at Portsmouth Grammar School and Christ Church, Oxford (BA, BCL). Interests include music, especially singing (lay clerk at St Albans Cathedral). Trustee of Holy Cross Centre Trust.

MUNDAY, Andrew QC
2 Bedford Row (William Clegg QC), London
(020) 7440 8888
amunday@2bedfordrow.co.uk
Recommended in Crime
Specialisation: All areas of criminal law but particularly large scale drug trafficking, VAT fraud, commercial, financial services, accountancy and mortgage fraud.
Prof. Memberships: Criminal Bar Association.
Career: Called 1973 and joined current set in 1975. Standing Counsel to HM Customs and Excise 1995. Took silk in 1996. Recorder.

MUNRO, Sarah QC
Walnut House (Paul Dunkels QC), Exeter
(01392) 279751
clerks@walnuthouse.co.uk
Recommended in Crime
Specialisation: Serious crime including all sexual offences, drugs, fraud and violence/murder. Prosecution and defence.
Prof. Memberships: Western Circuit. CBA. Criminal Justice Strategy Committee.
Career: Call 1984.
Personal: Cricket.

MURFITT, Catriona
1 Hare Court (Bruce Blair QC), London
(020) 7797 7070
Recommended in Family
Specialisation: Family Law: Child Care (Public and Private Law) and Hague Convention Child Abduction Proceedings; Matrimonial Finance (and financial proceedings under The Children Act and Inheritance Acts)
Prof. Memberships: Family Law Bar Association; Grays Inn. FLBA committee member.
Career: St. Mary's Ascot 1968-76. Leicester Polytechnic School of Law 1977-80. Called to the Bar 1981. From 1981 in Practice at 1 Mitre Court. Assistant recorder 1998, recorder 2000.
Personal: Art and architecture, travel, skiing, gardening and sacred choral music.

MURPHY, Ian QC
9 Park Place (Ian Murphy QC), Cardiff
(029) 2038 2731
clerks@9parkplace.co.uk
Recommended in Crime, Personal Injury
Specialisation: Queen's Bench Division work, in particular personal injury litigation. Clinical negligence, criminal law, Children Act, public and private law.
Prof. Memberships: Personal Injury Bar Association.
Career: St.Illtyd's College Cardiff. L.S.E. (LLB), Baltic Exchange. Called 1972. Recorder 1990. QC 1992. Bencher Middle Temple 2001.
Personal: Married Penelope 1974. Two daughters - Anna 3/4/82 and Charlotte 3/12/84. Golf, cricket, skiing.

MURPHY, Peter QC
30 Park Place (John Jenkins QC), Cardiff
(029) 2039 8421
Recommended in Crime

MYERS, Benjamin J
Young Street Chambers (John Jackson & David Hernandez), Manchester
(0161) 833 0489
Recommended in Crime

MYERSON, Simon
Park Court Chambers (Robert Smith QC), Leeds
(0113) 243 3277
simon.myerson@netserv.net
Recommended in Crime
Specialisation: All areas of commercial law and regulatory especially corporate fraud (civil and criminal). Working knowledge of Jewish (Talmudic) law. Clinical negligence.
Prof. Memberships: CBA, PIBA.
Career: Downing College, Cambridge (MA).
Personal: Married, four children. Interests - reading, sailing, walking, securing a moment for himself.

MYLNE, Nigel QC
2 Harcourt Buildings, Atkinson Bevan Chambers (Nicholas Atkinson QC & John Bevan QC), London
(020) 7353 2112
nmylneswalker@aol.com
Recommended in Crime
Specialisation: Criminal law specialist. In particular, specialises in serious commercial and professional frauds. Prosecutes and defends in all aspects of serious crime, including murder, sexual offences and drugs.
Prof. Memberships: Special adjudicator on asylum appeals and immigration appeals. President in Mental Health Review Tribunals.
Career: Practises in London and on the Western Circuit. Took silk in 1984. Appointed Recorder in 1983.

MYNORS, Charles
2 Harcourt Buildings (Robin Purchas QC), London
(020) 7353 8415
clerks@2hb.law.co.uk
Recommended in Church
Specialisation: Specialises in planning, ecclesiastical and environmental law, compulsory purchase and commons; particular expertise in listed buildings, trees and village greens. Appears in the courts and at planning inquiries for and against planning authorities (including a number of significant cases for English Heritage), at consistory court hearings, and in the Lands Tribunal. Sits as inspector at non-statutory inquiries. Member, Society of Advanced Legal Studies Planning and Environment Law Reform Group.
Prof. Memberships: Member of committee, Planning and Environment Bar Association; fellow, Royal Town Planning Institute; member, Royal Institution of Chartered Surveyors; member, Institute of Historic Building Conservation.
Career: Local authority planning officer 1977-86; called to the Bar 1988; chancellor, Diocese of Worcester, 1998.
Publications: Author of 'Planning Applications and Appeals', 'Planning Control and the Display of Advertisements', 'Listed Buildings, Conservation Areas and Monuments' (3rd edn, 1999) and 'Law of Trees, Forests and Hedgerows' (1st edn, 2002); member, Editorial Board, 'Journal of Planning and Environment Law'.
Personal: Degrees in architecture (Cambridge) and town planning (Sheffield).

NAISH, Christopher
Southernhay Chambers (Anthony Ward), Exeter
(01392) 255777
southernhay.chambers@lineone.net
Recommended in Family
Specialisation: Family Law. All aspects of the law relating to children (acting for Local Authorities, guardians and family members); ancillary relief. Family mediator. Personal injuries. Acting mainly for plaintiffs but also for defendants' insurers.
Prof. Memberships: Family Law Bar Association. Personal Injuries Bar Association.
Career: Call 1980. Joined chambers in 1981. Deputy DJ 2001.
Personal: Born 21 December 1957. Married with three children.

NAPIER, Brian
Fountain Court (Anthony Boswood QC), London
(020) 7583 3335
Recommended in Employment
Specialisation: Transfer of Undertakings - Meade and Baxendale v British Fuels [1998] House of Lords; Discrimination (sex, race, disability) and equal pay; General employment law, statutory and common law.
Prof. Memberships: Member, Faculty of Advocates, Edinburgh (Clerk: Susan Hastie); Member ACAS Panel of arbitrators.
Career: Academic lawyer 1975-94.

Practising barrister/advocate, 1994-. Joint editor: (1) 'Harvey on Industrial Relations' (chapters on European law, equal opportunities, equal pay); (2) 'Transfer of Undertakings' (Sweet & Maxwell, 1998-). Standing Junior to the Scottish Executive, 2001-. QC (Scotland), 2002.

NASH, Jonathan
3 Verulam Buildings (Christopher Symons QC & John Jarvis QC), London
(020) 7831 8441
chambers@3vb.com
Recommended in Banking & Finance
Specialisation: Principal areas of work are banking, corporate insolvency, professional negligence (particularly accountants and solicitors), and general commercial work including arbitration. Recent cases include KBC Bank v Industrial Steels (UK) Ltd (non-conforming documents and deceit under letter of credit), Credit Agricole Indosuez v Muslim Commercial Bank (compliance of documents under letter of credit); ANZ Banking v Societe Generale (construction of ISDA Master agreement after close-out of Russian market NDF transaction); Credit Suisse First Boston v MLC (anti-suit injunction in Russian derivatives transaction); J Rothschild v Collyear (notification obligations under professional indemnity insurance in respect of pensions misselling.)
Prof. Memberships: COMBAR; European Society for Banking and Financial Law.
Career: Called to the Bar in 1986 and joined 3 Verulam Buildings in 1987.
Personal: BA (Oxon).

NATHAN, David QC
10 King's Bench Walk (David Nathan QC), London
(020) 7353 2501
clerks@10kbw.co.uk
Recommended in Crime
Specialisation: Criminal defence: all areas including fraud, corruption, drugs, robbery and serious violence.

NATHAN, Peter
One Garden Court Family Law Chambers (Eleanor F Platt QC & Alison Ball QC), London
(020) 7797 7900
p.nathan@onegardencourt.co.uk
Recommended in Family
Specialisation: Family.
Prof. Memberships: FLBA.
Career: Called 1973. Spent 15 months as solicitor. Deputy District Judge since 1993. Mediator (trained 1996). Appointed Recorder, 2000.
Personal: Married, three children.

NAUGHTON, Philip QC
3 Serjeants' Inn (Robert Francis QC & John Grace QC), London
(020) 7427 5000
Recommended in ADR
Specialisation: Specialist in construction and engineering law, including domestic and international contract disputes, often of a highly technical nature. Commercial and manufacturing contracts. Professional negligence, particularly in relation to surveyors, engineers, architects and lawyers. A recognised expert in the field of Alternative Dispute Resolution. (Experienced and accredited).
Prof. Memberships: Fellow Chartered Institute of Arbitrators, member of LCLCBA, ORBA, COMBAR, IBA, LCIA.
Career: Held various positions in the chemical and chemical engineering industry 1964-71. Called to the Bar 1970. Joined present chambers 1973. Took Silk 1988. Bencher Gray's Inn (1997).
Personal: Educated at Nottingham University (LLB) 1961-64.

NAWAZ, Amjad
Coleridge Chambers (Simon Brand), Birmingham
(0121) 233 8500
Recommended in Crime

NEALE, Fiona
3 Serjeants' Inn (Robert Francis QC & John Grace QC), London
(020) 7427 5000
fneale@3serjeantsinn.com
Recommended in Clinical Negligence
Specialisation: Practice is divided between medical disciplinary work (presenting and defending) and clinical negligence, keeping a balance between claimant and defendant.
Prof. Memberships: PNBA, PIBA, CLCBA, Western Circuit.
Career: Called to the Bar 1981.

NEAMAN, Sam
Littleton Chambers (Michel Kallipetis QC), London
(020) 7797 8600
samneaman@aol.com
Recommended in Employment
Specialisation: Employment, principally discrimination, transfer of undertakings, restraint of trade and large scale redundancy issues, primarily in the banking, finance and computer industries. Other main areas of work are banking and securities, consumer credit and sport-related matters. Principal client base consists of banks, major national and multinational companies, and sports bodies, clubs and players. He is a legal advisor to the Amateur Boxing Association of England. Reported cases include: Johnson v Unisys Ltd (House of Lords), Kapadia v London Borough of Lambeth, Wilson v Post Office, Jarrett and Ors v Barclays Bank and Ors, First Sport Ltd v Barclays Bank, and Winchester Cigarette Co Ltd v Payne (No's 1 and 2) (Court of Appeal)>
Prof. Memberships: Employment Lawyers' Association, British Association for Sport and the Law, Industrial Law Society, Employment Bar Association.
Career: Called to the Bar 1988.
Personal: Educated at Oxford University 1983-86 (MA Hons) and City University 1986-87 (Dip Law). Leisure pursuits include boxing (former boxer: Oxford University double blue and member of Angel ABC since 1981) and playing drums in jazz and rhythm and blues bands. Former drummer with top UK r&b band, the Burke Brothers. Married with two children. Lives in London.

NEISH, Andrew
4 Pump Court, London
(020) 7842 5555
aneish@4pumpcourt.com
Recommended in Professional Negligence
Specialisation: General commercial law. Principal areas of practice are insurance and reinsurance and professional negligence (especially brokers, lawyers and accountants).
Prof. Memberships: COMBAR, London Common Law and Commercial Bar Association.
Career: Called 1988.
Personal: MA (St Andrews), Dip Law (City). Admitted in the BVI.

NELSON, Vincent QC
39 Essex Street (Nigel Pleming QC), London
(020) 7832 1111
Recommended in Media & Entertainment
Specialisation: Media and entertainment.
Career: Author of 'Law of Entertainment & Broadcasting' (Publishers: Sweet & Maxwell).

NEWEY, Guy QC
Maitland Chambers (Michael Lyndon-Stanford QC & Charles Aldous QC), London
(020) 7406 1200
gnewey@maitlandchambers.com
Recommended in Chancery, Charities, Company, Insolvency
Specialisation: Chancery practice includes charities, company, financial regulation, insolvency, property, professional negligence and trusts.
Prof. Memberships: Chancery Bar Association, Charity Law Association, COMBAR and Insolvency Lawyers' Association.
Career: Called to the Bar 1982. Junior Counsel to the Crown (Chancery) and Junior Counsel to the Crown ('A' Panel) 1990-2001. Junior Counsel to the Charity Commissioners 1991-2001. DTI Inspector in 1998-99. QC 2001. Recent cases include Britannia [2001] 2 BCLC 63 (directors' disqualification), Walker v Stones [2001] QB 902 (trusts/company), Baldwin [2001] WTLR 137 (charity), Adam & Partners [2001] 1 BCLC 222 (CVA), Woodland v IRC [2001] 73 TC 516 (malicious presentation of bankruptcy petition), Shaker v Bedrawi [2001] WL 825485 (trusts/company), IRC v Fry [2001] STC 1715 (contract), P&B v Woolley [2002] 1 All ER (Comm) 577 (insurance/illegality), Whale v Viasystems [2002] EWCA Civ 480 (land/insolvency).
Publications: Contributor to 'Mithani: Directors Disqualification' and 'Civil Court Service'.
Personal: Educated at Queens' College, Cambridge (MA 1st class, LLM 1st class). Bar Exams 1st class. Born 21 January 1959.

NEWMAN, Catherine QC
Maitland Chambers (Michael Lyndon-Stanford QC & Charles Aldous QC), London
(020) 406 1200
cnewman@maitlandchambers.com
Recommended in Chancery, Company, Insolvency
Specialisation: Principal area of work encompasses business and commercial chancery work, including corporate insolvency, business agreements and breach of contract, loans and security, partnership and professional negligence. Involved in large insolvencies: Maxwell, BCCI. Leading Counsel to the DTI Inspectors who investigated the 1991 flotation of Mirror Group Newspapers. Other main area of work is equity and contentious trusts; see for example Satnam Investments v Dunlop Heywood & Co Ltd [1999] 3 All ER652 CA. Acted (for the London Borough of Hammersmith and Fulham) at all stages of the swaps litigation: capacity, restitution and successive claims.
Prof. Memberships: Chancery Bar Association, COMBAR; Bar Sports Law Group.
Career: Called to the Bar 1979 and joined present chambers in 1980. Took Silk in 1995. Assistant Recorder 1998. Recorder 2000. Lieutenant-Bailiff of the Royal Courts of Guernsey 2001. Acts as an arbitrator.
Personal: Educated at Convent of the Sacred Heart High School 1965-72 and University College, London. (LLB 1st Class Hons 1978). Harmsworth Scholar of the Middle Temple 1979-80. Born 7 February 1954. Lives in London.

NEWMAN, Paul
Wilberforce Chambers (Edward Nugee QC), London
(020) 7306 0102
Recommended in Pensions, Professional Negligence
Specialisation: Specialises in personal and occupational pension schemes, with a particular interest in the pensions aspects of corporate and personal insolvency. Acts for trustees, beneficiaries and employers across the spectrum of pensions litigation and advisory work and acts both for and against the Pensions Ombudsman in appeals against his determinations. General chancery/commercial matters (with an emphasis on litigation), disputes relating to the provision of financial services, and professional negligence involving solicitor, actuaries and accountants. Major pensions cases include Melton Medes; Belling; Simpson Curtis Pension Trustee Ltd v Readson; Cocking v Prudential Insurance, SWT v Wightman and Elliot v Pensions Ombudsman National Grid, British Airways, Kemble v Nicks. Contributor to 'Ellison on Pensions Law and Practice' and to Lightman & Moss, 'Law of Corporate Receivers'.

LEADERS AT THE BAR

Prof. Memberships: Association of Pension Lawyers. Member of Chancery Bar Association.
Career: MA (Cantab); LLM (Harvard Law School); Called to the Bar in 1991.

NEWSOM, George
Guildhall Chambers (Adrian Palmer QC), Bristol
(0117) 930 9000
GeorgeNewsom@guildhallchambers.co.uk
Recommended in Church
Specialisation: Restrictive Covenants; title; easements; agricultural holdings; farming partnerships; wills; trusts; charities; churches and burial grounds.
Prof. Memberships: Fellow of the Chartered Institute of Arbitrators; Chancery Bar Association; Bristol & Cardiff Chancery Bar Association.
Career: Called to the Bar in 1973, Chairman of the Agricultural Land Tribunal for the South West Area since 1988.
Publications: Current publications: Preston & Newsom's 'Covenants affecting Freehold Land', Newsom's 'Faculty Jurisdiction of the Church of England'.
Personal: Born 1948, MA (Oxon: Eng & Econ).

NEWTON, Clive QC
One King's Bench Walk (Anthony Hacking QC), London
(020) 7936 1500
Recommended in Family
Specialisation: General common law, family (including divorce and children), childcare, matrimonial finance and property. Frequently represents local authorities, guardians and parents in substantial public law cases and frequently appears in private law child and finance cases. On the common law side, recent cases include FNCB v Humberts (1995) 2 AER 673 (important CA decision on limitation in professional negligence cases).
Personal: Born 1944. Call 1968 Middle Temple. Oxford University MA (Oxon) Jurisprudence (1st Class Honours), B.C.L. (Oxon); Lecturer in Law, Oriel College, Oxford; Co-editor of 'Jackson's Matrimonial Finance and Taxation,' 6th edn; Co-author of the 'Child Law Bulletin' for the 'Solicitors' Journal'.

NEWTON, Roderick
East Anglian Chambers (Roderick Newton), Ipswich
(01473) 214481
Recommended in Family

NICE, Geoffrey QC
1 Temple Gardens (Geoffrey Nice QC), London
(020) 7583 1315
gnice@1templegardens.co.uk
Recommended in Health & Safety
Specialisation: Principal areas of practice are general common law, including personal injury, HSE (including Channel Tunnel and Heathrow Express cases), clinical and professional negligence, major crime, commercial and administrative law (eg Ex P: Doody, prisoners rights; Callery v Gray, conditional fees, costs etc).
Prof. Memberships: South Eastern Circuit.
Career: Called to the Bar (Inner Temple) and joined Farrar's Building in 1971. Moved to 1 Temple Gardens in 2001. Appointed Recorder of the Crown Court in 1987. Took Silk in 1990. Member CICB 1995-2002. Senior Trial Attorney at ICTY (Yugoslav War Crimes Tribunal) 1998-2000. Principal Trial Attorney at ICTY (Milosevic case) 2002.

NICHOLLS, Benjamin
1 Fountain Court (Melbourne Inman QC), Birmingham
(0121) 236 5721
Recommended in Crime

NICHOLLS, Clive QC
3 Raymond Buildings (Clive Nicholls QC), London
(020) 7400 6400
chambers@3raymondbuildings.com
Recommended in Crime, Fraud
Specialisation: Principal area of practice is extradition, which he practises worldwide, being a member of the Bar of the Australian Capital Territories and having been specially called and admitted to the Bars of Hong Kong, The Bahamas, Cayman Islands, Malaysia, Ireland and Fiji. The factual complex of his extradition practice includes commercial crime, as well as terrorism and drug trafficking. He is particularly experienced (with teams drawn from his own chambers) in preparing and presenting extradition requests for foreign governments, both in the UK and abroad. These have included the Bank Bumiputra fraud (the Osman case) in which he represented the Attorney General of Hong Kong in the UK, Hong Kong and Malaysia and the Werner Rey case (corporate fraud) in which he represented the Government of Switzerland in the Bahamas. He has advised and represented many countries and prominent fugitives including Senator Augusto Pinochet Ugarte and appeared in most of the leading extradition cases in England, including 16 in the House of Lords and Privy Council. Much of his practice is outside the UK, including currently advising in cases in Asia, the Middle East, USA, South America and Australia, and includes mutual assistance, money laundering, confiscation and human rights.
Prof. Memberships: Member of the International Law Association Committee on Mutual Assistance. Member of the British Institute of International and Comparative Law, Bar European Group, Criminal Bar Association, European Criminal Bar Association, Franco British Lawyers Society. Co-founder and Chairman of the International Criminal Law Association 2000-02.
Career: Educated at Brighton College, Trinity College Dublin, Sidney Sussex College Cambridge, MA LLM. Call 1957. QC 1982. Head of Chambers since 1994.
Publications: Co-author 'The Law of Extradition and Mutual Assistance - International Criminal Law: Practice and Procedure' (April 2002).

NICHOLLS, Colin QC
3 Raymond Buildings (Clive Nicholls QC), London
(020) 7400 6400
chambers@3raymondbuildings.com
Recommended in Fraud
Specialisation: Principal areas of practice are complex commercial crime, extradition, criminal mutual assistance and human rights. Specialises in cases having an international element. Notable trials include 'Guinness' 1990 (defending the stockbroker, Anthony Parnes); 'Brent Walker' 1994 (defending George Walker), and 'BCCI' 1997 (defending the shipping magnate, Abbas Gokal). Significant reported cases include the 'Soering Case', 1989 in the European Court of Human Rights (death row in the US); and R v Horseferry Road Magistrate, ex parte Bennett 1994 (disguised extradition and abuse of power), Gilligan v Governor of HM Prison Belmarsh 1999 (Irish backing of Warrants with the United Kingdom). Advised in the Bhopal, Marcos litigations and in the *mani puliti* trials in Italy.
Prof. Memberships: Admitted ad hoc to the Bar of Hong Kong. Commonwealth Lawyers Association, Vice-President (1985-96), Hon. Treasurer (1997), Secretary (1999), Bar European Group, British Institute of International and Comparative Law, Criminal Bar Association. Fellow of the Society of Advanced Legal Studies.
Career: Called to the Bar 1957, QC in 1981 and elected a Bencher of Gray's Inn in 1990. Recorder of Crown Courts 1983-98.
Personal: MA, LLB, Dublin.

NICHOLLS, John
Maitland Chambers (Michael Lyndon-Stanford QC & Charles Aldous QC), London
(020) 7406 1200
Recommended in Chancery

NICHOLLS, Michael
1 Hare Court (Bruce Blair QC), London
(020) 7797 7070
nicholls@1hc.com
Recommended in Family
Specialisation: International and domestic family law and medical ethics, including jurisdiction, conflicts of laws, child abduction, private children's cases, families and the media (freedom of expression and press injunctions) and disputes about medical treatment. Recent cases include Re TB v JB (abduction: grave risk of harm) [2001] 2 FLR 515; CA Re N (abduction: habitual residence) [2000] 2 FLR 899; Re W; ReB (child abduction: unmarried father) [1998] 2 FLR 146 (a review of the rights of unmarried fathers under the Hague Child Abduction Convention); Re J (specific issue orders: Muslim upbringing and circumcision) [1999] 2 FLR 678; [2000] 1 FLR 571 (CA) and Nottingham CC v October Films Ltd [1999] 2 FLR 347 (an attempt by a local authority to stop the filming of children living on the streets).
Prof. Memberships: Family Law Bar Association.
Career: Called 1975 (solicitor 1980). Family lawyer in the Official Solicitor's Office and head of Lord Chancellor's Child Abduction Unit 1983-98; consultant to the Council of Europe's Family Law Committee; member of the President's International Family Law Committee; Chairman of Appeals Panels of the Specialist Training Authority of the Medical Royal Colleges 1997-2001; member of the BMA's Children's Consent to Medical Treatment Steering Group.
Publications: Recent publications include 'The Human Rights Act 1998 - A Special Bulletin for Family Lawyers' (with Michael Horowitz QC and Geoffrey Kingscote), 'Children and Brussels II', May [2000] Family Law 368 and a contribution to 'Consent, Rights and Choices in Healthcare for Children and Young People', BMA, 2001.

NICHOLLS, Paul
11 King's Bench Walk Chambers (Eldred Tabachnik QC & James Goudie QC), London
(020) 7632 8500
Recommended in Employment

NICHOLSON, Jeremy QC
4 Pump Court, London
(020) 7842 5555
jnicholson@4pumpcourt.com
Recommended in Construction
Specialisation: Construction and professional negligence work, covering all aspects of litigation, arbitration and advisory matters. Also general commercial and contract law work. Clients include insurers, contractors, employers, engineers, architects, surveyors and other professionals. He has acted in a number of international arbitrations, and in mediations. He has given various lectures and seminar papers.
Prof. Memberships: TECBAR, Professional Negligence Bar Association, COMBAR, London Common Law and Commercial Bar Association.
Career: Called to the Bar 1977. Joined 4 Pump Court 1978. Appointed QC 2000. TECBAR Adjudicator.
Personal: Educated at Rugby School 1968-73, Trinity Hall, Cambridge 1973-76 (MA) and College of Law 1976-77 (Harmsworth Scholar). Born 21 March 1955.

NICKLIN, Matthew
5 Raymond Buildings (Patrick Milmo QC), London
(020) 7242 2902
matthewnicklin@5rb.co.uk
Recommended in Defamation

Specialisation: All aspects of media law including defamation, malicious falsehood, breach of confidence, privacy, copyright (and related rights), passing-off, media contempt and reporting restrictions, judicial review and human rights. Gregson v Channel 4 [21 Jun 2002]; English v Hastie [31 Jan 2002]; Carlton v News Group Newspapers [2002] EMLR 299 (CA); Best v Charter Medical [2002] EMLR 335; The Times, 19 Nov 2001 (CA); Berezovsky v Forbes (No.2) [2001] EMLR 1030 (CA); Monty Norman v Times [April 2001]; Sean McPhilemy v Times [1999] 3 All ER 775; [1999] EMLR 751; The Times 26 May 1999 (CA); (No.2) [2000] 1 WLR 1732; The Times 7 June 2000 (CA); (No.3) [2001] EMLR 832; The Times 19 June 2001 (CA); (No.4) [2001] 4 All ER 861; [2001] EMLR 858; The Times 3 July 2001 (CA); Re Gracie Attard [15 June 2001]; Trinity Mirror v Punch [19 July 2000]; Thomas v News Group Newspapers [2002] EMLR 78; The Times 25 July 2001 (CA); R v Secretary of State for Health ex p Associated Newspapers & Others [2001] 1 WLR 292; [2000] HRLR 646; The Times 31 August 2000; Independent 30 October 2000 (DC); and Ex parte News Group Newspapers [2002] EMLR 160; The Times 21 May 1999 (CA). For up to date information visit www.5rb.co.uk/cvs/nicklin.html.
Career: LLB (1st class) University of Newcastle upon Tyne. Called to the Bar, 1993 (Lincoln's Inn). Pegasus Scholar to Sydney, Australia, 1998. (*Mallesons Stephen Jaques*).
Publications: Contributing Author of 'The Law of Privacy and the Media' published by OUP in July 2002. Regular contributor on media law to BBC Radio 4's Law in Action programme.

NICOL, Andrew QC
Doughty Street Chambers (Geoffrey Robertson QC), London
(020) 7404 1313
a.nicol@doughtystreet.co.uk
Recommended in Administrative & Public Law, Defamation, Human Rights, Immigration
Specialisation: Media law in all its aspects including defamation, confidence, copyright, contempt, restrictions on court reporting, publicity injunctions and rights of access to information. Administrative law especially immigration and nationality but extending to all situations where decisions of public bodies are subject to judicial review. Human rights and civil liberties especially concerning freedom of expression and privacy. Diverse range of other civil work including (non-medical) professional negligence, race and sex discrimination, contract and tort. Appellate crime including Divisional Court, Court of Appeal and Privy Council.
Prof. Memberships: Chair of Immigration Law Practitioners' Association 1997-2000. Member of Council of Europe delegations to advise on media law to Croatia, Albania, Slovakia, Belarus, Moldova, Serbia and Georgia. Presented papers to international conferences on National Security and Freedom of Expression (Article 19, Johannesburg 1995). Libel (LRDC London 1998+2000), security of residence in Europe (Nijmegen 1999). Media Law (Beijing 2001) and presented seminars to ILPA, Solicitors, university groups.
Career: Called to the Bar in 1978. QC 1995. Asst. Recorder 1998. Recorder 2000. Taught law at London School of Economics for 10 years.
Publications: 'Media Law and Human Rights' (2001), 'Media Law' (2002), 'Subjects, Citizens, Aliens and Others' (1990) and contributed to an annual survey on Reporting Restrictions to OUP's 'Yearbook of Copyright and Media Law'.
Personal: Born 1951. Degrees: BA 1st Class; LLB 1st Class, LLM (Harvard), Harkness Fellow 1973-76.

NICOL, Andrew R
Four New Square (Justin Fenwick QC), London
(020) 7822 2000
a.nicol@4newsquare.com
Recommended in Professional Negligence
Specialisation: Professional negligence, insurance, general commercial, employment. Important cases in last year include Direct Line v Khan CA [2002] Lloyds Rep IR 364 (insurance); Khan v Falvey & Co CA; Daly v Hubner (barristers/wasted costs) [2002] EWCA Civ 400 (solicitors/limitation); Preferred Mortgages v Bradford & Bingley [2002] EWCA Civ 336 (valuers/causation); Meredith v Co Lleys [2001] EWCA Civ 1456 (valuers, experts, procedure).
Prof. Memberships: PNBA, TECBAR, COMBAR, LCCLBA.
Personal: Born 6 October 1967, Aberdeen Scotland. MA (Cantab). Interests: skiing, mountaineering, salmon fishing.

NISSEN, Alexander
Keating Chambers, London
(020) 7544 2600
anissen@keatingchambers.com
Recommended in Construction
Specialisation: Construction and civil engineering law including professional negligence, arbitration, mediation and adjudication (both substantive and enforcement). Reported cases include Darlington Borough Council v Wiltshier, Royal Brompton Hospital v Hammond (No 1), Baxall v Sheard Walshaw Partnership, ABB v Northwest Holst, John Mowlem v Hydra-Tight, Gibson Lea v Makro Self Service Ltd and Discain v Opecprime Development (No-2).
Career: Qualified 1985; Middle Temple; member of editorial team for 'Keating on Building Contracts' (5th to 7th edition) and 'Construction Law Yearbook'; FCI Arb; TECBAR Adjudicator; member of TECBAR, Society of Construction Law and COMBAR.
Personal: Mill Hill School; Manchester University (1984 LLB Hons). Born 1963; resides London.

NOCK, Reginald
24 Old Buildings (Rex Bretten QC), London
(020) 7242 2744
Recommended in Tax

NOLAN, Dominic
Ropewalk Chambers (Ian McLaren QC), Nottingham
(0115) 947 2581
clerks@ropewalk.co.uk
Recommended in Personal Injury
Specialisation: Large personal injury and medical negligence claims including claims for birth injury and catastrophic injury. Defence of health and safety prosecutions. Recent reported case: Bates v Leicestershire HA (1998) Lloyds Med 93. Advised Grantham Hospital in claims arising from crimes of Beverley Allitt. Chairman of Statutory Inquiry into homicide by a former mental patient.
Prof. Memberships: Professional Negligence Bar Association.
Career: Graduate of Nottingham University; Buchanan Prizeman Lincoln's Inn.
Personal: Family, friends, sport, music.

NORRIS, William QC
Farrar's Building (John Leighton Williams QC), London
(020) 7583 9241
Recommended in Personal Injury
Specialisation: Defamation: Morelli & Coyle v Times Newspapers (first conditional fee case in libel). Personal injury: Allen v BREL (negligent/non-negligent harm); Scutts v Keyse (duty of emergency driver); Hadden v Smith (£4 million award to brain injury/tetraplegic); Contract: Albright & Wilson v Biacheim (2 contracts, one explosion). Sports and competition law and licensing: Jones & Ebbw Vale v WRU (private law challenge to disciplinary process of WRU); Cardiff RFC v WRU (restraint of trade/EU competition law); O'Callaghan v Coral (illegality of gaming contracts/arbitration). Costs: Claim Direct Test Cases. Public inquiries: BSE Inquiry.
Prof. Memberships: PIBA - Personal Injury Bar Association; Executive Committee.
Career: Benefactors Scholarship, Middle Temple, QC 1997.
Personal: Lecturer to Judicial Studies Board (Damages). Advocacy Teaching UK & USA.

NSUGBE, Oba QC
Pump Court Chambers (Christopher Harvey Clark QC), Winchester
(020) 7353 0711
oba.nsugbe@virgin.net
Recommended in Health & Safety
Specialisation: Regulatory: health and safety and environmental law. Insolvency and directors disqualification, serious fraud. Cases: R v F Howe & Son Ltd, CA [1999] 2 ALL ER 249 (leading case on sentencing in health and safety cases); R v Hampshire CA [1995] 2 ALL ER 1019; R v Rachel, 15 Cr App R (S) 265; Krumpa & Anor v DPP [1989] Crim LR 295. Highlight 2002: Hse v Moeuer Holding Ltd, reverse burden of proof in health and safety cases.
Prof. Memberships: Member of the Criminal Committee of the Judicial Studies Board, Member of the Bar Council Professional Conduct Committee and Bar Council Pupillage Committee.
Career: Recorder: Jan 2000. Silk: March 2002.
Personal: St Edward's School, Oxford, Hull University LLB (Hons). Married with two children. Interests: jazz, art in particular contemporary African art, travel, squash.

NUGEE, Christopher QC
Wilberforce Chambers (Edward Nugee QC), London
(020) 7306 0102
Recommended in Chancery, Pensions, Property Litigation
Specialisation: Chancery and commercial litigation including property, landlord and tenant, professional negligence, pensions and trusts. Recent cases include Phillips v British Gas (sale of North Sea Gas); Republic of Panama v Noriega (tracing assets); Central London Commercial Estates v Kato Kagaku (adverse possession of registered leasehold land); SWT v Wightman (Railway Pension Scheme); Department of Health v Moss (index linking of public sector pensions); International Power v Healy (Electricity Pension Scheme); Silven v Royal Bank of Scotland (receivership).
Prof. Memberships: Member of COMBAR; Association of Pension Lawyers; Chancery Bar Association.
Career: Called 1983. QC 1998.

NUGEE, Edward QC
Wilberforce Chambers (Edward Nugee QC), London
(020) 7306 0102
Recommended in Chancery, Charities, Pensions
Specialisation: Mainstream Chancery practice, with emphasis on trusts, occupational pension schemes, revenue law, landlord and tenant and property law generally. Has appeared in a substantial number of landlord and tenant, revenue and other appeals in the House of Lords, and in many of the leading cases on trusts, land law and pension schemes.
Prof. Memberships: Member of Chancery Bar Association; Association of Pension Lawyers; Trust Law Committee.
Career: Called 1955, Inner Temple (Bencher 1976, Treasurer 1996); QC 1977.
Personal: Educated Radley College;

LEADERS AT THE BAR

Worcester College, Oxford (Eldon Law Scholar). T.D. 1964. QC Church Commissioner 1990-2001. Legal Advisory Commission of the Church of England.

NUTTING, Sir John QC
3 Raymond Buildings (Clive Nicholls QC), London
(020) 7400 6400
chambers@3raymondbuildings.com
Recommended in Crime
Specialisation: Extensive experience in criminal law: Many IRA trials, Jonathan Aitken (perjury), R v Bailey & Others (child murders), Michael Smith (the GEC Spy) the Taylor Sisters murder trial, Seymon Serafimovich and Anthony Sawoniuk (War Crimes), the Rachel Nickell murder, Donald & Cressey (police corruption), Colin Ireland (multiple murder of homosexuals), Harry Greenway MP (Parliamentary corruption), Lord Blandford (drugs), Sydney Cooke (grave sexual abuse of children). Also specialises in Commercial crime, Disciplinary tribunals, Inquests and Inquiries (the Falkland Islands War Crimes Inquiry).
Prof. Memberships: Member of the Bar Council (1976-80, 1986-87). Chairman of the Young Bar (1978-79). Vice Chairman of the Criminal Bar Association (1995-97). Member of the Lord Chancellor's Advisory Committee on Legal Education and Conduct (1997).
Career: Called 1968. Recorder of the Crown Court (1986-). Bencher of the Middle Temple (1991-). Treasury Counsel at the Central Criminal (1987-95) (First Junior Treasury Counsel 1987-88; First Senior Treasury Counsel 1993-95) QC 1995-. A Judge of the Courts of Appeal of Jersey and Guernsey (1995-). Deputy High Court Judge attached to the Queen's Bench and Chancery Divisions (1998-).
Personal: Educated at Eton and McGill University BA 1964.

O'BRIEN, Dermod QC
2 Temple Gardens (Dermod O'Brien QC), London
(020) 7822 1200
Recommended in Personal Injury
Specialisation: Insurance claims, policy issues (particularly involving compulsory motor insurance), fires, floods, explosions. Electrical and mechanical engineering. Personal injury. Restitution. Local authority liabilities. Major reported cases include: White v White and MIB [2001] Evans v SSETR and MIB [2001], Wake v Wylie (SMP Motor Policies) [2001]. Heil v Rankin [2000], Makepeice v Evans and McAlpine [2000], Mighell v Reading and MIB [1998], Hurst v Hampshire CC [1997], Silverton v Goodall [1997], Evans v MIB [1997], Vernon v Bosley [1997], Hippolyte v Bexley LB [1995], Costellow v Somerset CC [1993], Talbot v Berkshire CC [1993], Lipkin Gorman v Karpnale (Playboy Club) [1991], Legal Aid Board v Russell [1991], Wharf v Eric Cumine Associates [1991 HK], Surtees v Kingston upon Thames BC [1991], Rigby v Chief Constable of Northamptonshire [1985], Russell v Barnet LB [1984], Hobbs v Marlowe [1978], Taylor v Hepworths [1977], Heath v Drown [1972].
Prof. Memberships: London Common Law Bar Association. Western Circuit.
Career: Oxford BA (Law) 1961 MA. Called: Inner Temple 1962. Crown Court Recorder 1978 (and TCC business). QC 1983. Bencher Inner Temple 1993.
Personal: Farming, forestry.

O'BYRNE, Andrew
Peel Court Chambers (Michael Shorrock QC), Manchester
(0161) 832 3791
Recommended in Crime

O'CONNOR, Patrick QC
Doughty Street Chambers (Geoffrey Robertson QC), London
(020) 7404 1313
Recommended in Crime, Human Rights

O'DEMPSEY, Declan
Cloisters (Laura Cox QC), London
(020) 7827 4000
dod@cloisters.com
Recommended in Employment
Specialisation: His areas of practice are employment, immigration, administrative law and professional negligence. His practice deals with discrimination (disability, race, equal pay and sex), immigration, asylum, human rights cases. He was instructed in the Inquiry into the Personality Disorder Unit, Ashworth Special Hospital (Fallon Inquiry) 1997-98 and has a particular interest in mental disorders. Cases include: Stevens v Bexley HA [1989] ICR 224; ex p Ghebretatios [1993] Imm AR 585; ex p Sarwar & Getachew [1996] COD 87; Mugford v Midland Bank plc [1997] ICR 399; Ikhlaq [1997] Imm AR 404; Horst v High Table [1998] ICR 409; Goodwin v Patent Office [1999] IRLR 4; Ashton v Chief Constable of West Mercia [2001] ICR 67; Shawkat v Nottingham City Hospital NHS Trust [2002] ICR 7.
Prof. Memberships: Immigration Law Practitioners Association, Administrative Law Bar Association, Employment Law Bar Association.
Career: Called to the Bar in 1987, first full-time employment law caseworker for the Free Representation Unit 1987-88. Active in the ELAAS scheme.
Publications: 'Supperstone & O'Dempsey on Immigration and Asylum' (4th edition Sweet & Maxwell 1996, with Michael Supperstone QC); Unfair Dismissal I and III in 'Tolley's Emploment Law'; 'Disability Discrimination: The Law and Practice' (1st edition, Sweet & Maxwell). 'Employment Law and the Human Rights Act 1998' (Jordans 2000).

ODITAH, Fidelis
3-4 South Square (Michael Crystal QC & Lord Alexander of Weedon QC), London
(020) 7696 9900
Recommended in Insolvency

O'FARRELL, Finola QC
Keating Chambers, London
(020) 7544 2600
fofarrell@keatingchambers.com
Recommended in Construction
Specialisation: Construction law in general, including IT disputes, professional negligence, insurance, loss and expense claims (lectures regularly on various aspects); energy disputes, shipbuilding and dredging litigation.
Prof. Memberships: Member Bar/IBC Committee; Joint Editor of 'Construction Law Yearbook'; member of Official Referees Bar Association.
Career: Qualified 1983; Inner Temple; QC 2002; Council of Legal Education 1983.
Personal: St Philomena's School; Durham University (1982 BA Hons Dunelm).

OKOYA, William
Arden Chambers (Andrew Arden QC), London
(020) 7242 4244
william.okoya@ardenchambers.com
Recommended in Local Government
Specialisation: Housing; local government (including human rights); landlord and tenant (residential and commercial); property; public law and judicial review. He advises and represents both public and private sector clients, including local authorities, RSLs, leaseholders, tenants and the homeless. He also speaks at and conducts training courses and seminars on housing and local government law topics for local authorities, RSL's, voluntary organisations and private practice lawyers. Recent advisory work includes RSL rent increases and local authority procedures and compliance with Human Rights Act 1998.
Prof. Memberships: Housing Law Practitioners' Association and Property Bar Association.
Career: Called to the Bar in 1989. He joined Arden Chambers in September 1997. He was formerly employed in-house as a senior legal officer for a local authority and legal and estates manager for a large-scale voluntary transfer.
Publications: An author of 'Local Government Act 2000' (Current Law annotations) and of 'RSL Finance and Rents', 2000. An editor of the 'Encyclopaedia of Local Government Law', 1999 to date; and formerly an editor of 'Encyclopaedia of Housing Law and Practice', 1998-99; Housing Law Reports, 1998-99; and Local Government Law Reports, 1999-2000.
Personal: Currently board member Cricklewood Homeless Concern and Harding Housing Association Ltd.

OLDHAM, Peter
11 King's Bench Walk Chambers (Eldred Tabachnik QC & James Goudie QC), London
(020) 7632 8500
oldham@11kbw.com
Recommended in Education
Specialisation: Public law and employment law. Recent cases in CA/HL: Hounslow v Hounslow Admission Panel (exclusions); S v Brent and Dunraven School (exclusions); Catchpole (SENs); Nagarajan v LT (victimisation); Clark v Novacold (DDA).
Career: 1990 call. Very wide experience in employment, education and administrative law, advising and appearing in courts, tribunals and domestic panels.
Personal: Born 1963.

OLIVER, Andrew
Octagon House Chambers (Guy Ayers & Andrew Lindquist), Norwich
(01603) 623186
Recommended in Crime

OLIVER, David QC
Erskine Chambers (Robin Potts QC), London
(020) 7242 5532
Recommended in Banking & Finance, Chancery, Company, Insolvency
Specialisation: Principally commercial/Chancery, with some insolvency.
Career: Called to the Bar 1972. Took silk 1986. (Lincoln's Inn: Hardwick Scholar) Standing junior counsel to the director general of fair trading. Acted for Guinness in connection with the aftermath of the distillers takeover, Price Waterhouse in claims arising after the collapse of BCCI, Macmillan Inc. and Swiss Bank with claims arising out of the collapse of Robert Maxwell's corporate empire, Granada plc in connection with the financing of BSB and subsequently BSkyB, and Victor Chandler International in connection with the establishment of offshore credit betting.
Personal: Born 4 June 1949. Educated Westminster School; Trinity Hall Cambridge; Institut d'Etudes Europeenes, Brussels. BA Cantab (2:1), Licence Special en droit Europeen. Fluent Spanish and working knowledge of French.

OMAMBALA, Ijeoma
Old Square Chambers (John Hendy QC), London
(020) 7269 0300
omambala@oldsquarechambers.co.uk
Recommended in Employment
Specialisation: Specialises in employment and discrimination law. Experience includes advocacy, drafting, advisory, policy and strategic work. Client base includes individuals, trade unions, private, voluntary and public sector organisations. Practice includes all aspects of individual and collective employment law together with related contractual disputes including restraint of trade and wrongful dismissal. Has a particular interest in all aspects of discrimination law. Instructed by all three statutory commissions: (EOC, CRE and DRC). Has particular

experience of dealing with complex, high profile and high value claims. In addition, her practice includes a significant amount of equal pay work. Currently instructed in a number of multi-claimant equal value cases in the public and private sectors. Has experience of drafting, pleading, litigating and advising in respect of such claims. Reported cases include Okuda v Photostatic Copiers v Okuda [1995] IRLR 11 EAT; Orlando v Didcot Power Station Social Club [1996] IRLR 262 EAT; Cleveland NHS Trust v Blane [1997] ICR 851 EAT; Chan v LB Hackney [1997] ICR EAT; CC Lincolnshire v Stubbs [1999] ICR 547 EAT; Parmar v Ford Motor Co Ltd [1999] ET; Brooks v CMP & ors [2002] CA; CC Bedfordshire v Liversidge [2002] IRLR EAT.
Prof. Memberships: Justice, ELBA, DLA, PIBA.

ONIONS, Jeffery QC
One Essex Court (Lord Grabiner QC), London
(020) 7583 2000
Recommended in Commercial (Litigation), Energy
Specialisation: Undertakes a wide range of complex commercial work. He has a particular experience in arbitration, banking, insolvency, insurance and reinsurance, oil and gas contracts and media related cases.
Prof. Memberships: London Common Law and Commercial Bar Association, Administrative Law Bar Association.

ONSLOW, Andrew QC
3 Verulam Buildings (Christopher Symons QC & John Jarvis QC), London
(020) 7831 8441
chambers@3vb.com
Recommended in Banking & Finance, Commercial (Litigation)
Specialisation: Banking and finance; financial services; commercial fraud; solicitors', auditors' and valuers' negligence. Major recent cases include Wallace Smith Trust Co. v Deloittes Haskins and Sells, London Underground Ltd v Kenchington Ford, regulatory proceeding arising from Sumitomo/Hamanaka Affair.
Prof. Memberships: COMBAR.
Career: 1970-74 Lancing College. 1975-79 Corpus Christi College, Oxford. BA Hons Literae Humaniores (1st Class).
Personal: Married. Five children.

OPPENHEIM, Robin
Doughty Street Chambers (Geoffrey Robertson QC), London
(020) 7404 1313
Recommended in Clinical Negligence, Product Liability
Specialisation: Specialist in the areas of medico-legal work, personal injury and multi-party actions. Personal injury and medico-legal practice includes clinical negligence and serious personal injury (particularly cerebral palsy, spinal and head injuries claims); group actions; medical inquests; mental health law and

Human Rights Act 1998/health related public law. He is currently generic counsel in the contraceptive pill litigation and the Alder Hey litigation. Recent reported cases: Afrika and others v Cape Plc (costs in group actions); Heil v Rankin (general damages appeal); Warren v Northern General Hospital NHS Trust (multipliers); Rahman v Arearose Ltd (successive torts and several liability); Hope v CC of Greater Manchester (discrimination); Hutton v East Dyfed HA (clinical negligence); Hodgson v Imperial Tobacco (liability of lawyers under conditional fee agreements).
Prof. Memberships: Action for Victims of Medical Accidents; Association of Personal Injury Lawyers; Administrative Law Bar Association; Professional Negligence Bar Association; Personal Injury Bar Association.
Career: Called to the Bar 1988.
Publications: Contributing author of 'Personal Injury Manual' and Bullen and Leake, 'Precedents of Pleadings' (Sweet & Maxwell 2000) and forthcoming books on clinical negligence and quantum. Regular lecturer to solicitors.

ORNSBY, Suzanne
2 Harcourt Buildings (Robin Purchas QC), London
(020) 7353 8415
clerks@2hblaw.co.uk
Recommended in Planning
Specialisation: Specialist fields are planning and environmental law (civil and criminal jurisdictions) for both the private and public sector.
Prof. Memberships: Member of the Planning and Environment Bar Association; member of the United Kingdom Environmental Law Association and Administrative Law Bar Association.
Career: Called to the Bar in 1986. Joined present chambers in 1990, previously practised at the Criminal Bar and employed in the electricity supply industry.
Personal: Educated at St Georges College, Weybridge and University College London (LLB Hons 1985).

O'ROURKE, Mary
3 Serjeants' Inn (Robert Francis QC & John Grace QC), London
(020) 7427 5000
Recommended in Clinical Negligence

ORR, Craig
Fountain Court (Anthony Boswood QC), London
(020) 7583 3335
Recommended in Commercial (Litigation)
Specialisation: Practice covers all areas of commercial law, including city related litigation, especially merchant banking, accountants' negligence, commercial fraud (civil actions) and insurance. Important cases include British & Commonwealth v Quadrex, Caparo v Dickman [1990]; Eagle Trust v Cowan de Groot [1992]; Society of Lloyd's v Mason and Clementson [1995]; AMF v Hashim [1996]; Domicrest v SBC [1998]; Peskin v Anderson [2000] and Barings plc v Coopers & Lybrand [2001].
Prof. Memberships: COMBAR.
Career: Called to the Bar in 1986 and joined Fountain Court in 1988.
Personal: Educated at Cambridge University 1981-84 (MA) and Oxford University (BCL, Vinerian Scholar). Born 8 January 1962.

ORR, Nicholas
14 Castle Street (Andrew Edis QC), Liverpool
(0151) 236 6757
nickorr@14castlestreet.co.uk
Recommended in Chancery
Specialisation: General chancery, particularly property litigation, family provision, landlord and tenant and partnerships. Also commercial litigation and drafting and professional negligence.
Prof. Memberships: Northern Circuit, Chancery Bar Association, Northern Chancery Bar Association, Northern circuit Commercial Bar Association.

OWEN, Gail
India Buildings Chambers (Ray Herman), Liverpool
(0151) 243 6000
Recommended in Family

OWEN, Robert QC
Ropewalk Chambers (Ian McLaren QC), Nottingham
(0115) 947 2581
clerks@ropewalk.co.uk
Recommended in Personal Injury
Specialisation: Principal areas of practice are personal injury and clinical negligence claims. Insidious disease litigation includes The Metro-Cammell litigation; North East Shipyard Asbestos litigation (against T & N plc); North West Shipyard Asbestos litigation (against Cape plc.); Gnitrow v Cape plc. (Isle of Wight asbestos litigation); Armstrong & Ors v B.C.C. (V.W.F.); British Steel Deafness litigation; Parr & Ors v Sunderland Shipbuilders (welders lung). Child abuse group actions include the Leicestershire County Council/Beck litigation and the North Wales Childrens' Homes litigation (including Coxon & Others v Flintshire County Council and Rowlands and Others v Bryn Alyn Community Limited). Duty of care cases include Larner v Solihull MBC.
Prof. Memberships: PNBA, PIBA.
Career: Prestatyn High School. Polytechnic of Central London (University of London Ext.). Called 1977. Queen's Counsel 1996. Assistant Recorder 1997. Recorder 2000.
Publications: 'New Law Journal', July 2000, Causation and Apportionment.
Personal: Family, friends, sport.

OWEN, Tim QC
Matrix Chambers, London
(020) 7404 3447
timowen@matrixlaw.co.uk
Recommended in Administrative & Public Law, Crime, Human Rights

Specialisation: Public law (especially criminal, prison, mental health, police and inquest law). Criminal law, especially political offences, confiscation, money laundering and mutual assistance, public order and appellate work. Civil actions involving abuse of power (especially police and prison actions) and international human rights law. Commonwealth capital appeals and constitutional motions, extradition and deportation.
Prof. Memberships: ALBA, Criminal Bar Association, INQUEST Lawyers' Group.
Career: Called 1983. Silk 2000.
Publications: Co-author 'Prison Law' (OUP, 2nd edn, 2000), co-editor Halsbury's Laws vol 36(2) 'Prisons and Prisoners', co-author 'Criminal Justice, police powers and human rights', Blackstone 2001.
Personal: Educated at Atlantic College and LSE. Lives in London.

OWEN, Tudor
9-12 Bell Yard (D Anthony Evans QC), London
(020) 7400 1800
Recommended in Aviation, Crime

OWEN-JONES, David Roderic
3 Temple Gardens (Jonathan Goldberg QC), London
(020) 7583 1155
Recommended in Crime
Specialisation: Drugs and fraud cases - prosecution and defence. Environmental law cases - practice on South Eastern Circuit and Midland Circuit. Recorder of the Crown Court. Member Wales and Chester Circuit.
Prof. Memberships: CBA.
Career: University of London LLB LLM. Council of Europe, Commission of Human Rights.

PAGE, Adrienne QC
5 Raymond Buildings (Patrick Milmo QC), London
(020) 7242 2902
Recommended in Defamation
Specialisation: In practice as a defamation specialist from 5 Raymond Buildings since 1975. During the first half of 2002, appeared as leading counsel for the claimant: in the trial of Reed & Lillie v Newcastle City Council & Others (79 days before Judge alone) and, in June 2001, as leading counsel for the claimants in Elite Model Agency v BBC, which settled on the eve of trial. Recently reported cases in the Court of Appeal include Al-Fagih v HH Saudi Research & Marketing [2002] EMLR 215; Skrine & Co v Euromoney Publications Plc [2002] EMLR 278.
Prof. Memberships: Fellow of the Society for Advanced Legal Studies.
Career: Called to the Bar, Middle Temple 1974. Appointed Silk 1999. Recorder, SE Circuit.

LEADERS AT THE BAR

PAGE, Nigel B
St. Mary's Chambers Family Law Chambers (Nigel B Page), Nottingham
(0115) 950 3503
Recommended in Family

PAINES, Nicholas QC
Monckton Chambers (Kenneth Parker QC & Paul Lasok QC), London
(020) 7405 7211
npaines@monckton.co.uk
Recommended in Competition/European Law
Specialisation: Administrative, public, competition EC and human rights law. All areas of administrative and public law, challenges to central and local government and other administrative decision-making, particularly but not exclusively on EC law grounds. Areas of practice include agriculture, anti-dumping, competition, customs, employment, free movement of goods, free movement of persons, human rights, public procurement, sex discrimination, social security, state aid, VAT. UK and EC competition law. Has appeared in a number of reported competition cases, and in monopoly and merger references. Numerous ECJ appearances include: The Sunday Trading cases; Coloroll and the subsequent cases on pensions; R v Secretary of State for Employment ex p Seymour-Smith; Card Protection Plan v Cmmrs of Customs & Excise (VAT); R v Secretary of State ex p Imperial Tobacco (tobacco advertising directive).
Prof. Memberships: Administrative Law Bar Association; Bar European Group (former chairman); Competition Law Association, UK Association for European Law; Bars and Law Societies Joint Working Party on Competition Law.
Career: Called to the Bar 1978. QC 1997.
Publications: Former contributor to Bellamy & Child 'Common Market Law of Competition'; 'Halsbury's Laws of England'; Vaughan 'Law of the European Communities'. Joint editor (with Paul Lasok QC) 'Common Market Law Reports'.
Personal: Educated at Oxford University 1973-76 (MA, jurisprudence) and Université libre de Bruxelles (Licence spéciale en droit Européen).

PALMER, Adrian QC
Guildhall Chambers (Adrian Palmer QC), Bristol
(0117) 930 9000
adrian.palmer@guildhallchambers.co.uk
Recommended in Commercial (Litigation)
Specialisation: Professional negligence (especially financial services and lawyers); mercantile (especially contract disputes); personal injuries (major injury cases).
Prof. Memberships: PNBA, PIBA (Executive Committee Member).
Career: Recorder, 1992; Silk 1992; Deputy High Court Judge, 1999; Head of chambers.
Publications: Various articles in professional journals.
Personal: MA Cantab (mathematics and law). Personal interests include gardens, walking, tennis, sheep.

PALMER, Patrick J S
Sovereign Chambers (Geoffrey C Marson QC), Leeds
(0113) 245 1841
Recommended in Crime

PANNICK, David QC
Blackstone Chambers (Presiley Baxendale QC & Charles Flint QC), London
(020) 7583 1770
clerks@blackstonechambers.com
Recommended in Administrative & Public Law, Employment, Human Rights, Immigration, Sport
Specialisation: Practises mainly in the fields of public and administrative law, employment law, human rights law, immigration law, European law and sports law. He has appeared in more than 40 cases in the House of Lords, over 20 cases in the European Court of Justice, and over a dozen cases in the European Court of Human Rights. He is a Fellow of All Souls College, Oxford, and a member of the Editorial Committee of 'Public Law'. He writes a fortnightly column on the law for 'The Times'. His recent cases include ex p Myra Hindley, Camelot v National Lottery Commission, Lustig-Prean v UK, Thompson and Venables v UK, and R v DPP ex p Kebilene.

PARKER, Judith QC
One King's Bench Walk (Anthony Hacking QC), London
(020) 7936 1500
Recommended in Family
Specialisation: All aspects of family law, including medico-legal issues, childcare and adoption, divorce and matrimonial finance, international aspects of family law (including intercountry adoption and child abduction), parentage, surrogacy and assisted conception.
Prof. Memberships: Family Law Bar Association. International Academy of Matrimonial Lawyers. Chairman of Inter-Country Adoption Lawyers Association. Association of Lawyers for Children.
Career: Called to the Bar in 1973. Took Silk in 1991.
Publications: Consulting editor of 'Butterworths Essential Family Practice'. Contributor to Wildblood & Eaton: 'Financial Provision in Family Matters'.

PARKER, Kenneth QC
Monckton Chambers (Kenneth Parker QC & Paul Lasok QC), London
(020) 7405 7211
Recommended in Competition/European Law, Tax

PARKIN, Fiona
Atkin Chambers (Robert Akenhead QC), London
(020) 7404 0102
Recommended in Construction
Specialisation: Construction and Engineering disputes which involves advising and representing employers and contractors on all aspects of disputes arising out of the design, construction and commissioning of large scale construction and engineering projects. Counsel in Whites Properties Ltd v Birse Construction Ltd. Arbitration Adjudication ADR - advising and appearing in domestic and international arbitrations and arbitration appeals. Has been engaged to draft submissions for adjudication proceedings and to advise on the enforcement of adjudicators' decisions. Public Procurement - advising major public bodies on the application of the EU Procurement regulations and remedies for breach. Counsel in Harman v Corporate Officer of the House of Commons. Professional Negligence - advising and acting for and against all professionals connected to the construction industry. Chesham Properties v Bucknell Austin PMC. Technology - Advises in connection with disputes concerning bespoke software contractors and telecommunications systems. Oil and Gas - Counsel in BPAmoco v British American Offshore Limited.
Prof. Memberships: Tec bar; London Common Law and Commercial Barristers.
Career: Called 1993.
Personal: LLB (Hons) first class, Exeter; LLM (Hons), Sidney Sussex, Cambridge.

PARNELL, Graham
East Anglian Chambers (Roderick Newton), Ipswich
(01473) 214481
Recommended in Family

PARSONS, Luke
4 Essex Court (Nigel Teare QC), London
(020) 7653 5653
iparsons@4sx.co.uk
Recommended in Shipping
Specialisation: Luke Parsons is a highly regarded and well known commercial and admiralty junior. His broad practice encompasses insurance/reinsurance, international trade, sale of goods, banking, commercial contracts and shipping. Much of his work combines complex legal and factual analysis, often requiring the co-ordination of a range of expert specialisms. He believes in combining a friendly, down to earth approach with tenacious and well prepared presentation of his clients' case.
Career: LLB (Bristol). Called 1985, Inner Temple.
Publications: Editor of 'Steel & Parsons on Forms & Precedents' (2nd Ed).

PARTRIDGE, Richard
3 Serjeants' Inn (Robert Francis QC & John Grace QC), London
(020) 7427 5000
Recommended in Clinical Negligence

PASCOE, Martin QC
3-4 South Square (Michael Crystal QC & Lord Alexander of Weedon QC), London
(020) 7696 9900
clerks@southsquare.com
Recommended in Chancery, Insolvency
Specialisation: Practice includes a broad range of commercial and financial law with particular emphasis on corporate insolvency, often with substantial international elements. Currently acting for the English Administrators of Enron and the provisional liquidators of Swissair. Recently has been lead counsel for the Government of Brunei and the Brunei Investment Agency in worldwide proceedings against HRH Prince Jefri and some 70 other defendants seeking to trace and recover substantial sums of misappropriated public monies. Acted for the English administrators of the Olympia & York group, and has since 1991 acted for the English liquidators of BCCI SA and the Cayman Island liquidators of BCCI Overseas. Some recent reported cases are: Re N T Gallagher [2002] EWCA Civ 404 (CVAs and Trusts); Latreefers Inc [1999] BCLC 271 (English court's jurisdiction to wind up foreign companies); Torvale Group [1999] 2 BCLC 591 (scope of ss35A, 322A CA 1985); Re BCCI SA (No11) [1997] 1 BCLC 80 (English ancillary liquidations and cross-border set-off issues); Hughes v Hannover Re [1997] 1 BCLC 497 (the first Court of Appeal case on cross-border co-operation between insolvency courts). Has had substantial experience of insurance insolvencies, including acting for US-based reinsurers of EMLICO in the winding-up proceedings before the Supreme Court of Bermuda and in judicial review proceedings in the Supreme Court, Court of Appeal for Bermuda and Privy Council seeking the quashing of decisions permitting EMLICO's redomestication to Bermuda; Kemper Re v Minister of Finance (Bermuda) [1998] 3 WLR 630 (PC).
Prof. Memberships: Chancery Bar Association, Commercial Bar Association.
Career: BA, BCL (Oxon). Called to the Bar 1977. QC 2002.

PASCOE, Nigel QC
Pump Court Chambers (Christopher Harvey Clark QC), Winchester
(01962) 868161
clerks@3pumpcourt.com
Recommended in Crime
Specialisation: Serious crime, including fraud. Also defamation and Courts Martial work.
Prof. Memberships: Former Leader of the Western Circuit.
Career: Called in 1966, joining 3 Pump Court. Recorder: 1979. Silk: 1988. Co-author of 'Successful Advocacy' (cassette).
Personal: Presents 'The Trial of Penn & Mead'.

PATON, Ewan
Guildhall Chambers (Adrian Palmer QC), Bristol
(0117) 927 3366
ewan.paton@guildhallchambers.co.uk
Recommended in Commercial (Litigation)
Specialisation: Property law, including commercial and residential real property disputes; commercial and residential

landlord/tenant; wills and estates; property aspects of insolvency; some general commercial litigation.
Prof. Memberships: Chancery Bar Association; Property Bar Association; Western Circuit.
Career: Called 1996 (Inner Temple), Inner Temple Major Scholar. Formerly: lecturer in law, University of Nottingham; tutor in law, Bristol and London Universities; Research Assistant, Law Commission.
Publications: Various articles in legal journals, including (1999) Conv. 535; (1995) OJLS 225; Editor, 'Guildhall Chambers Property Newsletter'.
Personal: Education: MA, BCL, New College, Oxford. Interests: reading, music, sport. Married, one son.

PATTERSON, Frances QC
40 King St, Manchester
(0161) 832 9082
fpatterson@40kingstreet.co.uk
Recommended in Environment, Planning
Specialisation: Specialist in town planning, compulsory purchase, highways, environmental law and judicial review.
Prof. Memberships: Member of Planning and Environment Bar Association; member of Administrative Law Bar Association; member of Northern Circuit; Committee Member Law Reform Working Group on Planning and Environment Law.
Career: Called 1977. Appointed Queen's Counsel 1998. Assistant Boundary Commissioner 2000. Recorder 2000.

PAUFFLEY, Anna QC
4 Paper Buildings (Lionel Swift QC), London
(020) 7583 0816
ap@4pb.com
Recommended in Family
Career: BA (London); called 1979; QC 1995; Recorder 1998.

PEACOCK, Jonathan QC
11 New Square (John Gardiner QC), London
(020) 7242 4017
taxlaw@11newsquare.com
Recommended in Tax
Specialisation: Revenue law. Work encompasses advice on all aspects of UK tax, including VAT, Customs and Excise duties and EC levies; tax litigation in all tribunals (including tax-related aspects of commercial disputes, judicial review and professional negligence. Recent cases include Amerada Hess v IRC (High Court); Halifax et al v HMCE (VAT Tribunal); Halifax plc v Davidson (SC); NMB Holdings v DSS (High Court).
Prof. Memberships: Revenue Bar Association, Chancery Bar Association, VAT Practitioners Group.
Career: Called to the Bar 1987; joined current chambers 1988.
Publications: 'Taxation for Employment Specialists', Butterworths 2000.
Personal: Educated at King's School, Macclesfield 1975-79, Nunthorpe Grammar School, York 1979-82 and Corpus Christi College, Oxford 1983-86 (1st Class Degree in Jurisprudence). Born 21 April 1964.

PEARCE, Ivan
Furnival Chambers (Andrew Mitchell QC), London
(020) 7405 3232
Recommended in Crime

PEARCE, Robert
11 New Square (Sonia Proudman QC), London
(020) 7831 0081
clerks@11newsquare.co.uk
Recommended in Charities
Specialisation: Principal areas of practice are property law; trusts; probate and administration of estates; contract and commercial law; charities; professional negligence. Recent reported cases include Varsani v Jesani [1999] Ch 219 (charity); Wells and Bournemouth Borough Council (Lands Tribunal 2000, compensation); Re W (Enduring Powers of Attorney) [2000] Ch 372 (court of protection); Rodway v Landy [2001] EWCA Civ 471; [2001] Ch 703 (property trusts); Barton v Tod [2002] EWHC 264 (Ch); (administration of estates, conflict of laws).
Prof. Memberships: Chancery Bar Association; Association of Contentious Trust and Probate Specialists.
Career: Called to the bar 1977. Standing Counsel to the Charity Commission 2001-.
Publications: Contributing editor to Butterworths 'Civil Court Practice' and Butterworths 'Civil Court Precedents', and various articles.
Personal: Education: Whitgift School (1963-71), Christ Church, Oxford (BA 1st class honours; BCL; 1972-76).

PEART, Icah QC
Two Garden Court (Owen Davies QC & Courtenay Griffiths QC), London
(020) 7353 1633
Recommended in Crime
Specialisation: All major criminal work. Areas of particular expertise include public order offences, armed robbery, conspiracy to defraud, terrorism, murder and large-scale drugs conspiracy/importation.
Prof. Memberships: SE Circuit; CBA; LSE Lawyers Group.
Career: 9 Stone Buildings 1978-82; 76B Chancery Lane 1982-87; 2 Garden Court, Temple, 1987-date. Assistant Recorder 1997; Recorder 2000-date.
Personal: Interests include sports, cinema, reading, music and my children (not necessarily in that order!).

PEDDIE, Ian QC
One Garden Court Family Law Chambers (Eleanor F Platt QC & Alison Ball QC), London
(020) 7797 7900
i.peddieqc@onegardencourt.co.uk
Recommended in Family
Specialisation: Childcare law: regularly appears in serious Children Act proceedings for parents, local authorities and Guardians eg physical and sexual abuse; 'Munchhausen' allegations; mental health issues. Many reported cases including recent HL Human Rights case of Re S; RE W 2002 1 FLR 815 and Re M (Contact: Parental Responsibility) 2001 2 FLR 342. Especially criminal cases where there are children who are victims or witnesses eg murder, attempted murder, (eg R v Owen [Maidstone Crown Court] - revenge attack on lorry driver who caused son's death by dangerous driving and R v Campbell - man who went beserk with a machete in a Wolverhampton Primary School attacking children and nursery teacher, Lisa Potts, who was subsequently given the GC); Munchausen cases, (eg R v Flannery, [Stafford Crown Court] - poisoning son with paracetamol, caffeine and warfarin); paedophile rings, (eg R v Davis and Others - the six month South Wales paedophile case). In addition, has often appeared for the defence in other serious and lengthy criminal cases not involving children eg fraud, drug importation, rape.
Prof. Memberships: Committee Member. FLBA since 1990.
Career: Gordonstoun School, LLB (Hons) University College London. Called to the Bar in 1971; QC in 1991; Assistant Recorder 1993; Recorder of Crown Court 1996.

PEEL, Robert
29 Bedford Row Chambers (Nicholas Francis QC), London
(020) 7404 1044
rpeel@29bedfordrow.co.uk
Recommended in Family
Specialisation: Principal areas of practice are ancillary relief, child abduction, children law and professional negligence.
Career: Oxford University (BA Hons). City University (DIP Law). Called to the Bar 1990.
Personal: Fluent in French and Spanish.

PENNICOTT, Ian
Keating Chambers, London
(020) 7544 2600
ipennicott@keatingchambers.com
Recommended in Construction
Specialisation: Building and engineering contracts.
Career: Qualified 1982; Middle Temple. Member of Hong Kong Bar.
Personal: Born 1958. Leisure, Golf.

PERETZ, George
Monckton Chambers (Kenneth Parker QC & Paul Lasok QC), London
(020) 7405 7211
gperetz@monckton.co.uk
Recommended in Competition/European Law
Specialisation: Competition law: mergers (IMS/PMSI, WJE/Pointing and Icopal/IKO, before Competition Commission; SCA/AMP, BEAP/Keesing and others before OFT); High Court litigation under Competition Act (Claritas v Post Office [2001] UKCLR2, Synstar v ICL [2001] UKCLR 585 (CLD), [2001] UKCLR 902 (OFT)); advice to major companies on UK/EC competition law and telecommunications issues; State aids: Scott v Commission (CFI, Case T-366/00) acted for complainants in State aid cases in High Court and advised government departments on State aid issues; EC law: Optident v DTI [2001] UKHL32 (meaning of EC directives on cosmetics and medical devices).
Prof. Memberships: Bar European Group, Administrative Law Bar Association.
Career: Legal Advisor, OFT, 1992-97, since then tenant at Monckton Chambers.
Publications: Contributor to: Bellamy and Child, 'Common Market Law of Competition'; 'Copinger & Skone James on Copyright'; 'PLC Competition Manual'.

PERRY, David
6 King's Bench Walk (Roy Amlot QC), London
(020) 7583 0410
Recommended in Crime, Fraud

PERRY, John QC
3 Gray's Inn Square (Rock Tansey QC), London
(020) 7520 5600
Recommended in Crime

PERSEY, Lionel QC
4 Essex Court (Nigel Teare QC), London
(020) 7653 5653
Recommended in Shipping
Specialisation: Commercial litigation, arbitration and mediation, with particular emphasis upon shipping and maritime law, aviation, insurance, international trade, commodities, product liability, construction, oil and gas and conflict of laws. Sits as arbitrator and mediator in commercial disputes.
Prof. Memberships: COMBAR, LCLCBA, LMAA (supporting member). Fellow of Institute of Advanced Legal Studies.
Career: Called to the Bar in 1981, took silk in 1997. Supplementary Panel of Treasury Counsel 1992-97. Member of the Gibraltar Bar.
Personal: Born 1958. Educated at Haberdashers' Aske's School, Birmingham University 1976-80 (LLB) and Université de Limoges 1978-79.

PETCHEY, Philip
2 Harcourt Buildings (Robin Purchas QC), London
(020) 7353 8415
Recommended in Church

PHILIPPS, Guy QC
Fountain Court (Anthony Boswood QC), London
(020) 7583 3335
Recommended in Professional Negligence
Specialisation: All areas of commercial litigation (including arbitration), particularly insurance and reinsurance, banking and financial services, and professional negligence.
Career: Called 1986. QC 2002. Member

LEADERS AT THE BAR

of California Bar. Admitted to Bahamas and British Virgin Island Bars.
Personal: Born 1961. Educated Magdalen College, Oxford and City University.

PHILLIPS, Jane
1 Brick Court (Richard Rampton QC), London
(020) 353 0845
jrp@1brickcourt.co.uk
Recommended in Defamation
Specialisation: Libel and slander (including e-libels), malicious falsehood, contempt, passing-off, breach of confidence, privacy, reporting restrictions and all forms of media law, including pre-publication advice. Cases include: Walker v Central Television; Adams v Associated Newspapers (CA); Allason v BBC; Ashby v Times Newspapers; C v MGN (CA); Lloyd v Express Newspapers (CA); Marks and Spencer v Granada; Upjohn v BBC; Williamson v Commissioner of Police (CA); Little v George; Mori v BBC; McCahill v Royal Sun Alliance; Khalili v Associated Newspapers (CA); Blackstone v MGN; Sir Alex Ferguson v Associated Newspapers; Bonnick v The Greater (Privy Council).
Career: Called to the Bar in July 1989, Inner Temple Scholar.
Publications: Co-author of the section on 'Libel and Slander, Malicious Falsehood' in Bullen & Leake, 'Precedents & Pleadings'.
Personal: Educated at St. Paul's Girls' School and Worcester College, Oxford.

PHILLIPS, Mark QC
3-4 South Square (Michael Crystal QC & Lord Alexander of Weedon QC), London
(020) 7696 9900
clerks@southsquare.com
Recommended in Banking & Finance, Company, Insolvency
Specialisation: Area of practice: insolvency - administration, insurance, banking - regulatory work for the Bank of England. Commercial work arising out of insolvencies and football related work. Notable cases: Re Toshoku Finance UK plc (HL) [2002] 1 WLR 671; Three Rivers District Council + Ors v The Governor and Company of the Bank of England (HL) [2000] 3 WLR 1220; Somji v Cadbury Schweppes plc [2001] 1BCLC 498; Re Galileo Group Ltd, Elles v Hambros bank (Bank of England intervening) (Ch D) [1999] Ch 100; Barings Plc v Cooper & Lybrand [2000] 3 AER 910.
Career: Education: LLB LLM (commercial) Bristol University. Appointed Assistant Recorder July 1998. Recorder April 2000. QC 1999.
Publications: Butterworths 'Insolvency Law Handbook' (editor); 'Paget's Law of Banking' (contributor).
Personal: Motorsport enthusiast.

PHILLIPS, Richard QC
2 Harcourt Buildings (Robin Purchas QC), London
(020) 7353 8415
Recommended in Planning
Specialisation: Principal areas of practice are planning and local government work. Also handles licensing cases.
Prof. Memberships: Planning & Environment Bar Association. Member of South Eastern Circuit.
Career: Called to the Bar 1970 and joined Harcourt Buildings in 1971. Assistant Parliamentary Boundary Commissioner. Took silk in 1990.
Personal: Educated at Kings School, Ely and Sidney Sussex College, Cambridge 1966-69. Born 8 August 1947.

PHILLIPS, Rory QC
3 Verulam Buildings (Christopher Symons QC & John Jarvis QC), London
(020) 7831 8441
chambers@3vb.com
Recommended in Insurance, Professional Negligence
Specialisation: Principal areas of practice are insurance and reinsurance and professional negligence.
Career: Called 1984. Junior Counsel to the Crown (A Panel) 1999-2002. QC 2002.

PHILLIPS, Stephen QC
3 Verulam Buildings (Christopher Symons QC & John Jarvis QC), London
(020) 7831 8441
chambers@3vb.com
Recommended in Banking & Finance
Specialisation: Principal area of practice is commercial and business law. Work includes general contractual disputes, banking and finance, company law and insolvency, international and domestic trade, commercial fraud, professional negligence and gaming contracts. Clients include banks and other financial institutions, insurance companies and funds and casinos.
Prof. Memberships: Wales and Chester Circuit, COMBAR, London Common Law and Commercial Bar Association.
Career: Called to the Bar 1984 and joined present chambers 1985. Recorder.
Personal: Educated at King's School, Chester 1973-80 and University College, Oxford 1980-83. Born 10 October 1961.

PHILPOTT, Fred
Gough Square Chambers (Fred Philpott), London
(020) 7353 0924
fred.philpott@goughsq.com
Recommended in Consumer Law
Specialisation: Consumer Law - consumer credit (drafting of regulated credit and hire agreements), credit hire, advising on consumer credit advertising, consumer credit licensing, acting in civil litigation eg extortionate credit bargains - Ketley v Scott [1981] ICR 241 and connected lender claims - (Jarrett v Barclays Bank [1997] 2 All ER 484) and in criminal prosecutions (eg Carrington Carr v Leicester [1993] Crim LR 938), food safety (criminal proceedings), pollution (Empress Car Co (Abertillery) Ltd v National Rivers Authority [1998] 1 All ER 481, misleading prices (eg R v Warwickshire CC [1993] AC 583), trade descriptions, weights and measures, Fair Trading Act, Trading Schemes Act. Unfair Terms Regulations (OFT v FNB [2000] 1 WLR 1353). Clients include banks, finance houses, food producers and supermarkets.
Prof. Memberships: Food Law Group.
Career: Called 1974.

PICARDA, Hubert QC
Hubert Picarda - Sole Practitioner (Hubert Picarda QC), London
(020) 7405 5577
h.picarda@aol.com
Recommended in Charities
Specialisation: Chancery law generally but particular expertise in all aspects of law relating to charities, banking, corporate insolvency and derivative trading. Important cases include Wellcome Plc v Glaxo Holdings (disputed takeover); Oldham BC v AG (sale of recreation ground); R v Lord President of Council (judicial review of university visitor); Bridge Trust Ld v AG of Caymans; Jyske Bank (Gibraltar) Ltd v Spjeldnaes (banking, fraud and tracing). Clients include: Wellcome Trust, RNLI, British Heart Foundation, Nuffield Homes, Various Oxford Colleges, Great Ormond Street Hospital, Garfield Weston, Wolfson and Clore Foundations, General Medical Council, housing associations, universities and local authorities. Advisory work and appearances in receiverships of Gomba Holdings, BCCI and Royal Masonic Hospital. Advisory work in Singapore, Hong Kong (2002) Secretary of Justice and Caymans.
Prof. Memberships: Chancery Bar Association, Insolvency Lawyers Association, Charity Law Association (President).
Career: Called 1962. QC 1992. Visiting lecturer in banking and derivative trading law 1995-96; 2000-01: Malaysia, Singapore. WA Lee Equity Lecture (2001) Brisbane. Editorial Board: 'Journal of International Banking and Finance Law', 'Trust Law International'.
Publications: 'Picarda Law relating to Receivers Managers Administrators' (3rd ed 2000), 'Picarda Law and practice relating to Charities' (3rd ed 1999). Halsbury Title on 'Receivers' (1998) and on 'Charities' (2001).

PICKUP, James QC
Lincoln House Chambers (Mukhtar Hussain QC), Manchester
(0161) 832 5701
Recommended in Crime

PICTON, Martin
Albion Chambers (Neil Ford QC), Bristol
(0117) 927 2144
martin.picton@virgin.net
Recommended in Crime
Specialisation: Fraud (including commercial); organised crime; homicide; computer and internet crime; health and safety; Customs prosecutions; disciplinary tribunals. Notable cases include defence counsel for Fred West; R v Billington, Locked and Ryder - defending in SFO prosecution; R v Martens, Tuegel and Saia - defence counsel in international banking fraud prosecuted by SFO; defence counsel in both Phase I and II of R v Robinson and Others - legal aid fraud prosecuted by SFO; prosecution counsel in R v Chepstow Plant Hire and Bazley Plant Hire - accident involving multiple deaths prosecuted by CPS under Health and Safety at Work Act; defence counsel in R v Paul Brooks and Others - alleged abuse by carer in South Wales children's home; defence counsel in R v Tully and Others - abuse of mentally disordered adults by carers; prosecution counsel in R v De Vey and Others - manslaughter/HSE ACT offences arising from fairground fatality.
Prof. Memberships: Criminal Bar Association (Western Circuit Rep.), Western Circuit.

PIPE, Gregory
Chancery House Chambers (Adrian Dent), Leeds
(0113) 244 6691
gregory.pipe@chanceryhouse.co.uk
Recommended in Commercial (Litigation)
Specialisation: Commercial contract and finance disputes; construction and engineering litigation and associated professional negligence issues; sale and supply of goods; agency; contractual construction; business sales; restraint of trade.
Career: Graduated in 1987 and taught law, latterly at the University of Leeds, until moving to the Bar to undertake commercial and construction work.
Publications: Numerous articles in periodicals on contractual and remedies issues. Some early work on computers and the law.
Personal: MA, Oxford University; LLM Cambridge University; formerly a keen oarsman; now rowing rather less frequently but still playing tennis (badly). Grew up with a strongly scientific/engineering background and entered University with entrance papers in that area; to a greater extent, that has influenced and made accessible the nature of the subject matter of much of the work now undertaken.

PIRANI, Rohan
Old Square Chambers (John Hendy QC), Bristol
(020) 7269 0300
pirani@oldsquarechambers.co.uk
Recommended in Employment
Specialisation: Principal areas of practice are employment law and personal injury.
Career: University of Oxford (MA, BCL), University of Toronto (LLM). Formerly Management Consultant. Called to Bar 1995. Recent cases include: Lewisham and Guys Mental Health Trust v Andrews 1999 ICR 774, McNicol v Balfour Beatty IRLR 2001 664, Ladbroke Grove Rail Inquiry and Bristol Royal Infirmary Inquiry.

PITT-PAYNE, Timothy
11 King's Bench Walk Chambers (Eldred Tabachnik QC & James Goudie QC), London
(020) 7632 8500
Recommended in Employment
Specialisation: Principal areas of practice are employment law (especially race and sex discrimination, wrongful and unfair dismissal, transfer of undertakings and industrial action) and public and local government law (including education law). Also handles commercial law matters including professional negligence, sale of goods and general contractual disputes. Contributor to 'Supperstone and Goudie on Judicial Review' (Butterworths, 1992). Co-author of 'Pitt-Payne and Supperstone on the Freedom of Information Act' (Butterworths, 2002).
Prof. Memberships: Employment Law Bar Association.
Career: Lecturer in Law, University of Melbourne 1986-87. Lecturer in Law, University of Auckland 1988. Called to the Bar in 1989 and joined present chambers in 1990. Member of the Attorney General's Supplementary Panel of Counsel (later the B Panel) 1994-2001.
Personal: Educated at St. Augustine's College, Westgate-on-Sea, Kent 1976-82 and Worcester College, Oxford 1982-86 (BA (Hons) Jurisprudence 1985, BCL 1986). Born 18 November 1964. Lives in London.

PLANTEROSE, Rowan
Littman Chambers (Mark Littman QC), London
(020) 7404 4866
rowanplanterose@littmanchambers.com
Recommended in Arbitration, Construction
Specialisation: Principal areas of practice as counsel are building and engineering contract litigation, arbitration (domestic and international), adjudication and mediation. Also acts as arbitrator and adjudicator, and advises arbitrators and adjudicators under direct access rules. Has experience in most areas of engineering including structural, civil, mechanical and electrical, marine, power generation, hazardous waste disposal, oil (refining, FPSO conversion, on-share drilling and storage), chemicals, food processing, railways and train building, roads, telephones and computing.
Prof. Memberships: TECBAR (Committee Member); COMBAR; Chartered Institute of Arbitrators, LCIA.
Career: Called to the Bar 1978.
Personal: Educated at Eastbourne College and Downing College, Cambridge. Lives in Surrey.

PLATT, Eleanor F QC
One Garden Court Family Law Chambers (Eleanor F Platt QC & Alison Ball QC), London
(020) 7797 7900
e.plattqc@onegardencourt.co.uk
Recommended in Family
Specialisation: All aspects of family law with particular emphasis upon children and cases involving medical issues. Has been involved in sterilisation/surrogacy matters. Instructed on behalf of the Northern Region in the Cleveland Enquiry. Special interest in Jewish family law.
Prof. Memberships: Family Law Bar Association; SE circuit; President Medico-Legal Society 2002-; Legal Assessor General Medical/Dental Councils. Called to the Bar 1960, Recorder 1982, Silk 1982. Deputy Judge, High Court Family Division since 1987.
Personal: LLB London. Married with two children. Many interests including music, travel and skiing.

PLATTS-MILLS, Mark QC
8 New Square (Mark Platts-Mills QC), London
(020) 7405 4321
clerks@8newsquare.co.uk
Recommended in Intellectual Property
Specialisation: Barrister specialising in all aspects of intellectual property, including patents, trademarks, passing off, registered designs, copyright and design right; also handles commercial work with a technical content. For comprehensive CV and list of recent cases, visit the set's website at www.8newsquare.co.uk.
Prof. Memberships: Intellectual Property Bar Association (IPBA); The Intellectual Property Lawyers Organisation (TIPLO); Chancery Bar Association.
Career: Called 1974; QC 1995.
Personal: Born 1951. Educated at Bryanston School; Balliol College, Oxford (1972 BA Engineering Science and Economics).

PLEMING, Nigel QC
39 Essex Street (Nigel Pleming QC), London
(020) 7832 1111
nigel.pleming@39essex.com
Recommended in Administrative & Public Law, Environment, Human Rights
Specialisation: Administrative and public law; human rights; environmental law and related regulatory work; local government law; and employment/discrimination law.
Career: Called 1971, Junior Counsel to the Crown (Common Law) - 1985-92, Queen's Counsel - 1992. Deputy Judge of the High Court. Bencher of the Inner Temple.

PLENDER, Richard QC
20 Essex Street (Iain Milligan QC), London
(020) 7842 1200
rplender@20essexst.com
Recommended in Competition/European Law, Public International Law
Specialisation: European Community, public and private international law and administrative law.
Career: Dulwich College, LCC scholar, 1957-64; Queens' College Cambridge, open exhibitioner, BA 1967, LLB 1968 (Rebecca Squire Prize) LLD 1993; University of Illinois, LLM 1970 (summa cum laude), JSD 1971 (College of Law Prize). Called to the Bar 1972 (Berridale Keith Prize); Legal Advisor, UNHCR, 1974-76; Référendaire Court of Justice of the European Communities, 1980-83; QC 1989; Bencher Inner Temple 1996; Recorder 1998; member various WTO panels. Principal publications: International Migration Law, 1972, 2nd edn, 1988; Cases and Materials on the Law of the European Communities, with JA Usher, 1979, 2nd ed 1988, 3rd edn 1993; The European Contracts Convention: The Rome Convention on the Choice of Law for Contracts, 1991, 2nd edn 2001; European Courts Practice and Precedents, 1996; loose-leaf edition 'European Courts Procedure' since 2000. Contributions to encyclopaedias, periodicals and books in English, French and German. International Tribunal for the Law of the Sea - Ireland v UK, 'The Mox Plant Case', 3 December 2001; House of Lords and Court of Appeal - Horvath v Secretary of State [2001] 1 AC 489 (HL); Cantabrica Coaches v Vehicle Inspectorate [2001] 1 WLR 2288 (HL); Professional Contractors' Group v Commissioners of Inland Revenue [2002] 1 CMLR 46 (CA); North Range Shipping v Seatrans [2002] EWCA 405 (CA); Evans v Secretary of State for the Environment [2001] EWCA Civ 32 (CA). For further reported cases, chambers' website: www.20essexst.com.
Personal: Born 1945.

PLIMMER, Melanie
Garden Court North (Chambers of Ian MacDonald QC) (Ian MacDonald QC), Manchester
(0161) 236 1840
Recommended in Immigration

POCOCK, Christopher
One King's Bench Walk (Anthony Hacking QC), London
(020) 7936 1500
cpocock@1kbw.co.uk
Recommended in Family
Specialisation: Family (including divorce and children), matrimonial finance and property. Financial disputes between unmarried couples, inheritance and family provision.
Prof. Memberships: S.E. Circuit; Family Law Bar Association.
Personal: Born 1960. Call 1984 Inner Temple. Education, St Dunstan's College; Pembroke College Oxford (BA Juris). Working knowledge of French; DPA Accepted.

POINTER, Martin QC
1 Hare Court (Bruce Blair QC), London
(020) 7797 7070
Recommended in Family
Specialisation: Handles all types of family law, but principally financial relief claims. Pioneer of pension-splitting in ancillary relief.
Prof. Memberships: Family Law Association, International Academy of Matrimonial Lawyers.
Career: Called to the Bar in 1976 and joined Mitre Court Buildings in 1978. Silk 1996.
Personal: Educated at The King's School, Grantham 1964-71 and the University of Leicester 1972-75. Born 17 July 1953. Lives in London.

POLLOCK, Gordon QC
Essex Court Chambers (Gordon Pollock QC), London
(020) 7813 8000
Recommended in Arbitration, Banking & Finance, Commercial (Litigation), Energy, Fraud, Insurance, Media & Entertainment, Shipping
Specialisation: Broad-based commercial lawyer with a substantial court and advisory practice dealing with the major commercial issues of the day. He has been instructed in most of the major commercial litigation of recent years. Areas of practice include arbitration; banking; commodity disputes; conflict of laws; employment law; entertainment and sports law; financial services; insurance and reinsurance; judicial review; monopolies and mergers; oil and gas cases; professional negligence; shipping; takeovers.
Career: Trinity College, Cambridge: MA, LLB. Called to the Bar 1968. Queen's Counsel 1979. Bencher: Gray's Inn. Sits as Deputy High Court Judge of the Chancery and Queen's Bench Divisions.
Personal: Born 1943.

POOLES, Michael QC
4 Paper Buildings (Jean Ritchie QC), London
(020) 7643 5000
michael.poole@4paperbuildings.com
Recommended in Professional Negligence
Specialisation: Principal area of practice is professional negligence, particularly concerning solicitors. Also acts for and against members of the Bar, accountants, surveyors, architects, engineers, veterinary surgeons and doctors. Other main areas of practice are personal injury and general insurance matters, on behalf of claimants as well a large number of insurance companies.
Prof. Memberships: Professional Negligence Bar Association.
Career: Called to the Bar 1978 and joined present chambers in 1980. Silk 1999. Recorder 2000.
Personal: Educated at Perse School, Cambridge, 1967-74 and University of London 1974-77. Born 14 December 1955. Lives in Cambridge.

POPAT, Prashant
2 Harcourt Buildings (Roger Henderson QC), London
(020) 7583 9020
Recommended in Health & Safety, Product Liability
Specialisation: Product Liability. Has been retained in a number of product liability cases, including product liability group actions such as: Benzodiazapene

LEADERS AT THE BAR

litigation, Norplant litigation, Breast implant litigation, MMR/MR litigation, Anti-epilepsy medication. Has also been instructed in individual product liability cases involving both civil and criminal actions under Consumer Protection Act 1987 and the General Product Safety Regulations 1994 as well as advising companies, including companies involved in the supply of mobile phones, on compliance with their obligations under consumer protection legislation. His reported cases in this field include recent Court of Appeal decisions in the MMR Litigation on the substitution of parties after the expiry of the ten year long stop (Re: Horne Roberts) and the seminal costs sharing appeal (Sayers v Smith Kline Beecham). Health and Safety: has extensive experience of health and safety law, particularly in relation to the railways. Has been instructed by Railtrack in: the Southall rail inquiry, the Joint Inquiry into train protection systems, Ladbroke Grove rail inquiries Part 1 and Part 2. Has also been instructed by Railtrack following the incidents at Hatfield and Selby and represented Railtrack following a fatal incident at Slade Lane which led to a prosecution for corporate manslaughter and offences under the HSWA 1974. Was retained during the privatisation process as a member of a team drafting and revising safety standards and has advised railway authorities in Northern Ireland on safety cases and standards setting. Has represented the British Railways Board and Railtrack at numerous inquests into fatalities on the railway and regularly acts for them in personal injury actions. In addition to his experience of health and safety in relation to the railways represents many large organisations in different industries in actions involving accidents or deaths at work. His clinical negligence practice extends to both Claimant and NHSLA work.
Career: MA (Oxon) First Class Honours. University Scholar. Baker and McKenzie International Scholar. Gray's Inn Scholar. Judicial Assistant to the Court of Appeal. Judicial Assistant to Lord Woolf MR (as he then was).

POPLE, Alison
2 Bedford Row (William Clegg QC), London
(020) 7440 8888
apople@2bedfordrow.co.uk
Recommended in Fraud
Specialisation: Has defended and prosecuted as junior counsel in a number of substantial fraud cases. Cases include defending in Regina v Clews & Others (Bute Mining, SFO prosecution); defending in Regina v Leckie & Others (United Mizrahi Bank, SFO prosecution) and prosecuting in Regina v Pattni & Others (Gold VAT fraud, HM Customs & Excise prosecution). Currently instructed on behalf of a defendant in the Jubilee Line Extension case. Included in the list of approved counsel to prosecute for the Serious Fraud Office.
Prof. Memberships: Criminal Bar Association, South Eastern Circuit.
Career: Called to Bar 1993. Fox Scholar (Middle Temple) 1993-94. Joined present chambers in 1995.

POPPLEWELL, Andrew QC
Brick Court Chambers (Christopher Clarke QC), London
(020) 7379 3550
popplewell@brickcourt.co.uk
Recommended in Commercial (Litigation), Fraud, Insurance
Specialisation: General commercial, including shipping, banking, insurance and reinsurance, international trade, financial services, arbitration, professional disciplinary, civil fraud and some employment and defamation.
Prof. Memberships: Queens Council 1997. Member of the Bar of the Cayman Islands and Seychelles. Has been appointed as arbitrator in LMAA, ICC and LCIA arbitrations.
Career: Called to Bar of England and Wales 1981. Cases of note: Grupo Torras v Sheikh Fahad, The 'BERGE SISAR', Hill v Mercantile & General, Vitol v Norelf.
Personal: Born 14 January 1959. Educated at Radley College and Downing College, Cambridge (BA Hons (Cantab) in Law, Class: First).

PORTEN, Anthony QC
2-3 Gray's Inn Square (Anthony Porten QC & Anthony Scrivener QC), London
(020) 7242 4986
aporten@2-3graysinnsquare.co.uk
Recommended in Local Government, Planning
Specialisation: Planning and Local Government work; compulsory purchase; public inquiries, tribunals and related litigation; judicial review. Recent leading cases include Reprotech v East Sussex County Council (House of Lords), London Borough of Wandsworth v Railtrack, Waters v Welsh Development Agency (Court of Appeal).
Prof. Memberships: PEBA, ALBA, UKELA.
Career: Called 1969; Silk 1988; Recorder 1993-2001; Assistant Boundary Commissioner 2000; Head of Chambers July 2001.
Personal: Epsom College 1959-64; Emmanuel College, Cambridge 1965-68; FSALS 1999.

PORTER, Martin
2 Temple Gardens (Dermod O'Brien QC), London
(020) 7822 1200
Recommended in Personal Injury
Specialisation: Common law (principally personal injury and professional negligence claims), judicial review (especially liabilities of local authorities exercising statutory functions), commercial (particularly insurance-related work). Reported cases include Elmes v Hygrade [2001] EWCA Civ 121, Kamenou v Dodson [1999] 2 AHER 764; Young v Church, Times 1.5.97 (Liability for psychiatric injury); ex p Steed [1996] 71P + CR 463; Thompson v Wickens [1996] 1 WLR 561; Vasey v Surrey Free Inns [1996] PIQR P373; Yates v Thakenham Tiles [1995] PIQR P135; Oliver v Monk [1995] PIQR P465.
Prof. Memberships: Inner Temple, Western Circuit, LCCBA, PIBA.
Career: Born 1962. Call 1986. Educated St John's College, Cambridge: MA (Law) LLM (Public Law).
Personal: Married, two daughters. PPL (1989); skiing; cycling.

POSNANSKY, Jeremy QC
1 Hare Court (Bruce Blair QC), London
(020) 7797 7070
jeremy@posnansky.net
Recommended in Family
Specialisation: Family law. Practice covers all areas of family law: ancillary relief and the law relating to children. Appeared in many reported cases, including M v M (pre-nuptial agreement) 2002; Wells v Wells (lump sum, appeal) 2002; X v X (enforcement of agreement) 2002; Cornick v Cornick No. 3 (capitalisation of maintenance principles) 2001; A-M v A-M (divorce, jurisdiction, validity of marriage) 2001; A v A (interim maintenance to include sums for legal fees) 2001; Re L and others (Court of Appeal guidelines in contact cases involving domestic violence: amicus curiae) 2000; W v W (refusal of decree absolute) 1998; S v S (forum non conveniens and pre-nuptial agreement) 1997; Baker v Baker (standard of proof in ancillary relief applications) 1995; Cornick v Cornick, Nos. 1 and 2 (leave to appeal out of time and variation of maintenance principles) 1995. Articles in International Family Law and Family Law. Practice includes advising on and settling pre-nuptial agreements.
Prof. Memberships: Family Law Bar Association; Fellow of International Academy of Matrimonial Lawyers.
Career: Call 1972; Silk 1994. Deputy High Court Judge 1997. Admitted to the Bar of Antigua.
Personal: Born 8 March 1951. Married with two daughters. Lives in London. Enjoys travel, scuba diving and computers.

POTTS, Richard
Octagon House Chambers (Guy Ayers & Andrew Lindquist), Norwich
(01603) 623186
Recommended in Crime

POTTS, Robin QC
Erskine Chambers (Robin Potts QC), London
(020) 7242 5532
Recommended in Banking & Finance, Company, Financial Services, Insolvency
Specialisation: Specialist in all aspects of company law and corporate insolvency including related commercial matters, banking and financing transactions, share and bond issues and takeover bids; both advisory work and litigation; recent cases include Re: Astec (BSR plc [1998] 2 BCLC 556; Soden v British Commonwealth Holdings [1997] 2 WLR 206 (CA), [1997] 3 WLR 840 (HL); also cases in Bermuda, Cayman, Hong Kong, Gibraltar, Bahamas, British Virgin Islands and Isle of Man.
Prof. Memberships: Chancery Bar Association; COMBAR.
Career: Called to the Bar 1968. Took silk 1982. Bencher, Gray's Inn.
Publications: Consultant editor 'Gore Browne on Companies'.
Personal: Educated at Wolstanton Grammar School, Newcastle-under-Lyme, and at Magdalen College, Oxford (BA and BCL) 1963-67. Bigelow Fellow, University of Chicago Law School 1967-68. Leisure pursuits include history, gardening, travel and wine. Born 2 July 1944. Lives in London.

POWELL, John L QC
Four New Square (Justin Fenwick QC), London
(020) 7822 2000
barristers@4newsquare.com
Recommended in Financial Services, Professional Negligence
Specialisation: Commercial practice centred on professional liability, financial services and securities regulation (UK, EU and international), fraud recovery and related insurance. Practice reflects his publications. Many cases involving accountants, actuaries, investment and pension sellers, banks and other financial institutions (including IPO and M&A claims), regulators, insurers and insurance brokers, valuers, internet providers as well as lawyers and construction industry professionals. Cases in the Gulf, Hong Kong, Jersey, USA and West Indies. Advises extensively on regulatory aspects of financial products and schemes (including collective investment schemes) and internet promotion. Recent reported cases have related to accountants, barristers and wasted costs (Brown v Bennett) (BCCI v Price Waterhouse (No 2 and No 4)); insolvency practitioners (Mond v DTI); patent agents (Arbiter v Gill Jennings Every); public bodies (Swinney v Chief Constable of Northumbria) and a financial regulatory context (Kaufman v Credit Lyonnais). Past cases have related to Barlow Clowes, Maxwell, Lloyd's, lease back transactions and misselling of home income plans, pensions and endowment policies and several in a construction and engineering context. Wide experience of arbitration (as advocate and arbitrator) in the UK and overseas.
Prof. Memberships: COMBAR (Executive Committee 1999-2000); PNBA; Bar European Group; Society of Construction Law (President 1991-93); Society for Advanced Legal Studies (Advisory Council member).
Career: Called 1974. Silk 1990. Recorder. Bencher, Middle Temple. Head of Chambers 1997-99. Bar Council

member 1999 - (Chairman Bar Law Reform Committee (1997-98)).
Publications: 'Jackson and Powell on Professional Negligence'; 'Encyclopaedia of Financial Services Law' (with Prof Eva Lomnicka). 'Palmer's Company Law' (specialist editor 24th ed); 'Issues and Offers of Company Securities'; various papers in national and international legal publications.
Personal: Born 1950. Trinity Hall, Cambridge (MA, LLB).

POWNALL, Orlando QC
2 Hare Court (Stephen Kramer QC), London
(020) 7353 5324
Recommended in Crime

PRATT, Camden QC
One King's Bench Walk (Anthony Hacking QC), London
(020) 7936 1500
Recommended in Family
Specialisation: Cross-examination of lying witnesses, matrimonial finance and property, family (including divorce and children), childcare, crime, commercial fraud (criminal), commercial fraud (civil), clinical negligence/disciplinary, medical law, environment, general common law, personal injuries. Interesting cases: Southern Water Authority v Nature Conservancy Council [1992] 3 AER 481, HL (environmental damage/The Wildlife & Countryside Act); Cutter v Eagle Star Insurance 1998 4 AER 417 (HL) (definition of 'road': motor insurance); Re C (deceased) [1995] 2 FLR 24 (Inheritance Act - financial provision for illegitimate daughter); Re P [1995] 1 FLR 831 (international child abduction); Wicks v Wicks (C.A) [1998] 1 FLR 470 (matrimonial financial relief: interim lump sum and transfer of property orders); Ikimi v Ikimi [2002] Fam. 72 (Court of Appeal) (concurrent habitual residence: divorce); re X and Y 2001 FLR (leave to remove children from the jurisdiction and s1(5) of the Children Act; R v Curtis Howard (the Gatwick Airport 'Body in Boot case'); prosecution counsel case of Regina v Sion Jenkins (the murder of 'Billie Jo') [1998]; R v Ron Brown (case of the MP's mistress's knickers).
Prof. Memberships: South Eastern Circuit (Committee Member); Chairman, Sussex Sessions Bar Mess; Chairman, Sussex Courts Liaison Committee 1993; Member Area Criminal Justice Liaison Committee 16.
Career: Call 1970, Silk 1992. Recorder 1993. Deputy High Court Judge 1993, Family Division. Bencher of Gray's Inn 2001.
Personal: Educated at Lincoln College, Oxford (MA Juris).

PRATT, Duncan
6 Pump Court (Kieran Coonan QC), London
(020) 7583 6013
duncan.pratt@6pumpcourt.com
Recommended in Clinical Negligence
Specialisation: Principally practises in clinical negligence and substantial personal injury claims. Considerable experience of claims involving birth and brain injuries of the utmost severity and has conducted clinical negligence claims involving most medical and surgical specialities. Lectures on topics related to medical law. Other areas of practice: solicitors' negligence, product liability, employment-related claims, and claims arising out of failures to diagnose and manage dyslexia.
Prof. Memberships: Professional Negligence Bar Association, AVMA, APIL, Medico-Legal Society.
Career: Called to the Bar 1971. Joined present chambers 2000. Part-time Chairman Family Health Services Appeals Authority.
Personal: Educated RGS Newcastle and University College, Oxford. Lives in London. Leisure pursuits include choral singing, local amenity societies, theatre, concert and opera.

PRENTICE, Dan
Erskine Chambers (Robin Potts QC), London
(020) 7242 5532
clerks@erskine-chambers.co.uk
Recommended in Company
Specialisation: Company law, corporate insolvency, financial services. Recent reported case: Soden v British & Commonwealth Holdings plc [1997] 2 BCLC 501.
Prof. Memberships: Member of the Law Society's Committee on Company Law; Member of the Law Society's Committee on Insolvency Law; COMBAR; Chancery Bar Association.
Career: Called to *Lincoln's Inn* 1982. Professor of Corporate Law, University of Oxford.
Publications: Joint General Editor with Dame Mary Arden of 'Buckley on the Companies Acts'. Assistant editor of the 'Law Quarterly Review'. Contributor to 'Chitty on Contracts' (27th edn). Contributor to 'Gower, Company Law' (5th edn).

PRESCOTT, Peter QC
8 New Square (Mark Platts-Mills QC), London
(020) 7405 4321
clerks@8newsquare.co.uk
Recommended in Intellectual Property, Media & Entertainment
Specialisation: A specialist in all aspects of intellectual property law; has been involved in numerous reported cases. Recent examples include: British Horseracing Board v William Hill; Cantor Fitzgerald v Tradition. For comprehensive CV and list of recent cases, visit the set's website at www.8newsquare.co.uk.
Prof. Memberships: Intellectual Property Bar Association (IPBA); The Intellectual Property Lawyers Organisation (TIPLO).
Career: Called 1970; QC 1990; deputy high court judge.
Publications: 'Modern Law of Copyright' 2000 and 'Data Processing and the Law' 1984. Contributions to 'European Intellectual Property Review' include Towards a small claims patent court 10 EIPR 246.
Personal: Born 1943. Educated at Dulwich College; University College, London (BSc Physics); Queen Mary College (MSc Nuclear Engineering).

PREVEZER, Susan QC
Essex Court Chambers (Gordon Pollock QC), London
(020) 7813 8000
sprevezer@essexcourt-chambers.co.uk
Recommended in Insolvency
Specialisation: Main area of practice covers insolvency, commercial litigation, commercial chancery and property, company law. Major litigation includes BCCI. Millwall FC, Levitt, Emlico, KWELM, District.com, Atlantic Telecom Group plc; Ioanica plc; Bank of China v UBS; Twinsectra v Yardley.
Prof. Memberships: Commercial Bar Association. Chancery Bar Association.
Career: Called to Bar 1983. Seven years at Michael Crystal QC's Chambers. Joined present chambers 1997 (December). Appointed as Recorder (April 2000); QC (April 2000).

PRICE, James QC
5 Raymond Buildings (Patrick Milmo QC), London
(020) 7242 2902
Recommended in Defamation
Specialisation: Defamation, breach of confidence, contempt, media-related human rights, publishing, media copyrights, general commercial and common law. Recent libel cases include Reynolds v Times Newspapers; Aitken v Guardian and Granada; Hamilton v Fayed; Gaddafi v Telegraph Group; Marco Pierre White v Anthony Allan; Monty Norman v Times Newspapers; McPhilemy v Times Newspapers; Branson v Bower. McManus v Victoria Beckham. Breach of confidence: John Bryan v Mirror Group (photographs of Duchess of York); Service Corporation International v Channel Four (covert film inside funeral home).
Prof. Memberships: Inner Temple.
Career: Call 1974. QC 1995.
Personal: Born 1948.

PRICE, Nicholas QC
3 Raymond Buildings (Clive Nicholls QC), London
(020) 7400 6400
chambers@3raymondbuilding.com
Recommended in Crime
Specialisation: Criminal law, particularly murder, corporate manslaughter (Herald of Free Enterprise), rape, blackmail, armed robbery; commercial crime-fraud: corporate, leasing mortgage; public corruption cases; public enquiries (the Guildford and Woolwich Enquiry by Sir John May).
Prof. Memberships: Bencher, Gray's Inn 2000-; Member of the Professional Standards Committee.
Career: Called to the Bar in November 1968. Took silk in 1992. Recorder of the Crown Court since 1983. Chairman of Gray's Inn Continuing Education/ Advocacy Training Committee. Facilitator for the Bar Human Rights Course.

PRICE, Roderick
Tooks Court Chambers (Michael Mansfield QC), London
(020) 7405 8828
Recommended in Crime
Specialisation: Specialises in criminal defence work with particular emphasis on fraud, drug trafficking and murder cases. Consistently appears in leading reported cases which have established important principles in complex areas of the criminal law. Some recent cases include R v Black and Others [2002] (conspiracy: importation of Class A and B drugs); R v Pearson and Others [2000] (conspiracy to defraud) R v Ball and Others [1999] (fraudulent trading); R v Cajee [1999] (murder); R v Elias [1998] (conspiracy to defraud); R v Harding [1998] (armed robber received six mandatory life terms - leave to appeal granted specifically to test recommended tariffs in respect of mandatory life sentences); R v Avis [1997] (sentencing guidelines in firearms cases); R v Jones and Barham [1997] (conditional admissability rule in conspiracy and joint enterprise cases); R v Gray and Liggins [1995] (insider dealing); R v Preston [1994] (interception of telecommunications).
Prof. Memberships: Criminal Bar Association.
Career: Called to the Bar 1971, Inner Temple.
Personal: Interests include sailing, badminton, tennis and cricket.

PRICE OBE, Richard QC
Littleton Chambers (Michel Kallipetis QC), London
(020) 7797 8600
rmp@priceqc.co.uk
Recommended in Media & Entertainment
Specialisation: Principal areas of entertainment and media law experience include film, video and music rights and financing disputes, copyright infringement and piracy, the 'fair dealing' provisions of copyright law (BBC v British Sky Broadcasting Ltd. 1991 re: World Cup Football broadcasts), Anton Piller and Mareva injunctions, and corporate/partnership disputes within the entertainment industry. Clients have included major film and music production and distribution companies and broadcasters, and leading artists, directors and producers. Also specialises in election and administrative law, professional negligence and commercial contract work and mediation.
Prof. Memberships: COMBAR, London Common Law and Commercial Bar Association, PNBA.
Career: Called to the Bar in 1969. Joined present Chambers in 1987, having

LEADERS AT THE BAR

previously been a member of Chambers of the late Lewis Hawser QC. Appointed QC 1996. Accredited CEDR mediator 1997.
Personal: Educated at King Edward VII School, Sheffield, and King's College London.

PRIDAY, Charles
7 King's Bench Walk (Gavin Kealey QC & Julian Flaux QC), London
(020) 7910 8300
clerks@7kbw.law.co.uk
Recommended in Shipping
Specialisation: Principal areas of practice are shipping, banking, insurance and general commercial work, acting for shipowners, charterers, oil traders, other commodity traders, banks, insurance companies and brokers. Reported shipping cases of note include: charterparty dispute, the Nour (1999), the Anangel Express (1996), the Ulyanovsk (1990); laytime, the Petr Shmidt (1998), the Agamemnon (1998), the Kyzicos (1989); jurisdiction, the Maciej Rataj (1995), the Deichland (1990), fire on a car carrier, the Eurasian Dream (2002).
Prof. Memberships: London Maritime Arbitration Association.
Career: Called to the Bar and joined Seven King's Bench Walk in 1982.

PRINCE, Christopher
New Court Chambers (John Evans), Newcastle upon Tyne
(0191) 232 1980
Recommended in Crime

PRITCHARD, Sarah
40 King St, Manchester
(0161) 832 9082
spritchard@40kingstreet.co.uk
Recommended in Clinical Negligence
Specialisation: All aspects of clinical negligence (including birth damage, orthopaedic, obstetric, gynaecological, intensive care, anaesthetics) and personal injury with emphasis on employers' and public liability.
Prof. Memberships: Personal Injuries Bar Association, Committee Member Northern Circuit Medical Law Association.
Career: Called 1993 (Gray's Inn) Junior Scholarship.
Personal: University: Manchester, LLB (Hons). Interests include amateur dramatics and theatre.

PROSSER, Kevin QC
Pump Court Tax Chambers, London
(020) 7414 8080
Recommended in Tax
Specialisation: Principal area of practice is Revenue law, including litigation. Co-author of Potter and Prosser, 'Tax Appeals' (Sweet & Maxwell).
Career: Called to the Bar 1982 and joined present chambers in 1983. Took Silk in 1996. Became Recorder in 2000.
Personal: Was once expelled from Tanzania for spying.

PROUDMAN, Sonia QC
11 New Square (Sonia Proudman QC), London
(020) 7831 0081
Recommended in Chancery, Charities
Specialisation: Area of work: general chancery litigation and advice, with particular emphasis on trusts, charities, bankers' securities and all aspects of property law. Considerable experience in pursuing and in defending breach of trust claims, involving private, charitable and commercial trusts. Also professional negligence.
Prof. Memberships: Chancery Bar Association, STEP, Charity Law Association.
Career: Called to the Bar (Lincoln's Inn) 1972. (Kennedy Scholar, Buchanan Prize). Joined Chambers at 11 New Square in 1974. Took silk in 1994. Bencher 1996. Assistant Recorder 1996. Recorder 2000.
Personal: Born 1949; married 1987, one daughter. Educated at St Paul's Girls' School and Lady Margaret Hall Oxford. BA 1st Class Hons 1971, Eldon Law Scholar 1973, MA 1973. Member Oxford University Law Faculty Advisory Panel 2000.

PRYNNE, Andrew QC
2 Harcourt Buildings (Roger Henderson QC), London
(020) 7583 9020
clerks@harcourt.co.uk
Recommended in Product Liability
Specialisation: General common and commercial law practice with an emphasis on product liability (principally pharmaceutical and tobacco), insurance disputes, clinical negligence, personal injury, railway law and employment matters. Notable cases include the MMR litigation for Merck (1999-2002); the Benzine litigation for Terra Nitrogen Ltd; the tobacco lung cancer litigation for Imperial Tobacco (1999), the Lariam litigation for Roche Products (1999), the Opren litigation for Eli Lilly from 1986, the Clapham Accident Inquiry for British Railways Board (BRB) (1989), the Benzodiazepine litigation for Roche Products Ltd (1990-92), the Severn Tunnel Accident Enquiry for BRB 1992 and Crizzle v Board of Governors of St. Matthias School (EAT, 1993 - race discrimination). Advised BRB and Railtrack on safety implications and legal duties arising from privatisation. Member of the Lord Chancellor's Working Group on Multi-Party Actions. CEDR Accredited Mediator. Assistant Boundary Commissioner.
Prof. Memberships: South Eastern Circuit.
Career: Called to the Bar 1975 and tenant at King's Bench Walk 1976-78 and then joined current chambers.
Personal: Educated at Marlborough College and Southampton University (LLB, Hons). Born 28 May 1953. Interests: sailing, shooting and skiing.

PRYOR, Michael
9 Old Square (Michael Driscoll QC), London
(020) 7405 4682
Recommended in Professional Negligence
Specialisation: Barrister specialising in property and general commercial Chancery litigation, including real property disputes, landlord and tenant, professional negligence, mortgages and other securities, contentious probate. Cases include the Nationwide Managed Litigation, reported in part as Nationwide v Balmer Radmore [1999] Lloyds Rep PN 241, the Paragon Finance plc Managed Litigation against various solicitors and surveyors during 2000, Edwin Shirley Production Limited v Workspace plc [2001] 23 EG 158, Aubergine Enterprises Ltd v Lakewood International Ltd [2002] EWCA Civ 177.
Career: Qualified 1992.
Personal: University of Newcastle upon Tyne (LLB). Born 1969.

PUGH, Charles
Old Square Chambers (John Hendy QC), London
(020) 7269 0300
read@oldsquarechambers.co.uk
Recommended in Environment, Health & Safety
Specialisation: Representing both claimants and defendants, principal areas of practice are pollution/nuisance claims, accident claims (rail, aviation, work place) and statutory crime in health and safety/environmental fields. Recently reported cases include Wadey v Surrey CC, HL, 2000 (interest on damages); Hunter v Canary Wharf, HL, 1998 (leading case on nuisance); Underwood v British Midland, CA, 1996 (injury damages, principles of assessment). Current litigation includes multi-party 'dust nuisance' action (for major plc); statutory appeal against variation of consents (for numerous companies); multi-party toxic occupational exposure; numerous carbon monoxide poisoning claims; advising plc's being prosecuted for health and safety and/or environmental offences; multi-party pharmaceutical product liability. Co-author of 'Toxic Torts' (2nd edn 1995).

PUGH, Vernon QC
2-3 Gray's Inn Square (Anthony Porten QC & Anthony Scrivener QC), London
(020) 7242 4986
Recommended in Planning
Specialisation: Town and country planning; local government law; environmental law; common law - professional negligence and personal injury; international law/extradition.
Prof. Memberships: Local Government and Planning Bar.
Career: LLB (UCW); LLM (Cantab); University Lecturer in Property, Commercial and Planning; Hardwicke Scholar; Sir Thomas Moore Bursary; Bencher Lincoln's Inn; Crown Court Recorder.
Personal: Married, three daughters. Chairman, International Rugby Football Board and Rugby World Cup. IOC Federation Member.

PUGH-SMITH, John
39 Essex Street (Nigel Pleming QC), London
(020) 7832 1111
clerks@39essex.com
Recommended in Environment
Specialisation: Planning, environmental, local government and parliamentary matters.
Prof. Memberships: Planning and Environment Bar Association (Former Committee Member), United Kingdom Environmental Law Association, Environmental Law Foundation, Fellow of Society of Antiquaries of London.
Career: Called to the Bar 1977. Joined current Chambers in April 2002 with four other colleagues from Chambers of Lionel Read QC.
Publications: Publications for Sweet & Maxwell include 'Neighbours and the Law' (1st to 3rd Editions: 1988 to 2002), 'Archaeology at Law' (1996). Joint Editorial Advisor for 'Property and Compensation Reports' and 'Planning Law Case Reports'. General Editor 'Environmental Law' (Oxford University Press) (2000).
Personal: Born 1954. Lives mainly in Norfolk.

PULMAN, George F QC
Hardwicke Building (Nicholas Stewart QC), London
(020) 7242 2523
Recommended in Personal Injury
Specialisation: Personal injuries: esp. multi-party actions, radiation-induced injuries (cancers), Myalgic Encephalomyelitis (post viral fatigue syndrome). Related professional negligence: solicitors and doctors. Amicus Curiae in Opren; Ldg Col. for MAFF in L.S.A. litigation; Molinari v Min. of Defence; Sellafield & Dounreay Radiation cancers; Kegworth 'Kings Cross' and 'Herald of Free Enterprise' disasters. 'McDonnell' costs order (plaintiff's payment into court).
Prof. Memberships: Legal action group - author of paper on multi-party actions (Book published 1995). Public Law: Judicial Review (esp. Repts) Dairy produce quotas, transport, roads and vehicles.
Career: Junior Counsel to crown (common law) 1982-89. QC: 1989. Recorder: 1996. Lecturer: Judicial Studies Board. Formerly member: Legal Aid Board (Chairman of Multi-Party Action Committee). Deputy Chancellor: Diocese of Peterborough. Member: Lord Chancellor's Advisory Committee on Legal Education and Conduct (ACLEC). Fellow of Royal Society of Medicine.

PURCHAS, Christopher QC
Crown Office Chambers (Michael Spencer QC & Christopher Purchas QC), London
(020) 7797 8600
purchas@crownofficechambers.com
Recommended in Personal Injury
Specialisation: Personal injury, professional and clinical negligence, general insurance law, fire claims, sports

injury, highway authority claims, product liability. Recent cases include: Wells v Wells; Page v Sheerness Steel; Heil v Rankin; Griffin v Kingsmill; Doyle v Wallace; Mighell v Reading & MBI; Carroll v Dunlop; Fitzgerald v Ford.
Prof. Memberships: LCLCBA, PIBA.
Career: Called to the Bar 1966. Appointed Recorder 1986. Silk 1990. Deputy High Court Judge 1999.
Personal: Marlborough College 1957-61, Trinity College Cambridge 1962-65. Leisure pursuits: golf tennis and shooting. Born 20 June 1943. Lives in Surrey.

PURCHAS, Robin QC
2 Harcourt Buildings (Robin Purchas QC), London
(020) 7353 8415
Recommended in Local Government, Planning
Specialisation: Principal areas of practice are parliamentary, planning and public law, compulsory purchase and compensation, human rights and community law and environmental and utilities law. Recent cases include: in the House of Lords, Burkett v LB Hammersmith and Fulham 2002; Fletcher v SSE 2000; Bolton MBC v SSE 1995 and Forbes 1999; in the Court of Appeal Staffordshire CC v Pepper Street Developments, Motor Crown Petroleum Ltd; R v Newbury DC ex p Chieveley PC; English Properties v Kingston LBC; Pye v Kingswood BC; Wards v Barclays Bank; Prudential v Waterloo Real Estate; Pickering v Kettering DC and Batchelor v Kent CC. Major promotions include the West Coast Route Modernisation, the Channel Tunnel Rail Link and the Channel Tunnel.
Prof. Memberships: Parliamentary Bar Mess (Leader); Bar European Group, Planning and Environment Bar Association, Vice Chairman; Administrative Law Bar Association; South Eastern and the Bar European Circuit.
Career: Called to the Bar in 1968 and joined Harcourt Buildings in 1969. Took silk in 1987. Appointed Recorder in 1989; Deputy High Court Judge 1994; Master of Bench Inner Temple 1996; Bar Council 2000. Chairman, Education and Training Committee 2001.
Personal: Educated at Marlborough College and Trinity College, Cambridge (Senior Exhibitioner). Born 12 June 1946.

PURLE, Charles QC
New Square Chambers (Charles Purle QC), London
(020) 7419 8000
charles.purle@newsquarechambers.co.uk
Recommended in Chancery, Company, Fraud
Specialisation: Leading litigator in cases covering a wide sphere, from computers through breach of trust to VAT. Recent cases have had the emphasis on fraud, including a fraudulent trading and misrepresentation appeal in Hong Kong and important decisions on constructive trusts, fraudulent breach of trust, directors' duties and vicarious liability of partners for fraud.
Prof. Memberships: Gray's Inn, Lincoln's Inn.
Career: LLB (Nottingham), BCL (Oxon). FICPD.
Personal: Married twice, with six children. Opera, music, horseracing, fine wine and food help to relax.

PURNELL, Nicholas QC
23 Essex Street (Michael Lawson QC), London
(020) 7413 0353
nicholaspurnell@23essexstreet.co.uk
Recommended in Crime, Fraud
Specialisation: Principal area of practice is criminal law, particularly commercial fraud. Work includes financial regulatory and professional disciplinary tribunals. Member of the Lord Chancellor's Advisory Committee on Legal Education and Conduct 1991-97. Member of the Criminal Committee Judicial Studies Board 1991-96.
Prof. Memberships: South Eastern Circuit. Fellow, Society for Advanced Legal Studies; Fellow, Institute of Continuing Professional Development.
Career: Called to the Bar 1968. Prosecuting Counsel, Inland Revenue 1977-79. Treasury Counsel 1979-85. Took Silk in 1985. Recorder since 1986. Bencher of the Middle Temple since 1990.
Personal: Educated at the Oratory School 1958-62 and King's College, Cambridge 1963-66 (MA). Governor of the Oratory School. Born 29 January 1944.

PURVIS, Iain
11 South Square (Christopher Floyd QC), London
(020) 7405 1222
Recommended in Intellectual Property
Specialisation: All aspects of intellectual property. Reported cases include Gerber v Lectra (patent damages); United Biscuits v ASDA (Penguin/Puffin 'own brand' dispute); Mark Wilkinson v Woodcraft (design right - furniture); Designers Guild v Russell Williams (Copyright - fabric designs); VISX v Nidek (patent infringement - eye surgery); Fylde Microsystems v Key Radio (copyright - computer software); Altecnic v Reliance (trademarks - relevance of classification).
Prof. Memberships: IPBA member.
Career: MA Cantab; BCL Oxon. 16 years practice in this field.
Publications: Co-editor of 'Working with Technology'.
Personal: Married. Three children. Skiing, sailing, watching football and exploring prehistoric monuments.

PYE, M Jayne
Sovereign Chambers (Geoffrey C Marson QC), Leeds
(0113) 245 1841
Recommended in Family

PYMONT, Christopher QC
Maitland Chambers (Michael Lyndon-Stanford QC & Charles Aldous QC), London
(020) 7406 1200
cpymont@maitlandchambers.com
Recommended in Chancery, Professional Negligence
Specialisation: Practice encompasses company, landlord and tenant, banking, commercial chancery and insolvency matters.
Prof. Memberships: Chancery Bar Association, COMBAR.
Career: Called to the Bar 1979 and joined 13 Old Square in 1980 (now merged in Maitland Chambers). Appointed QC 1996.
Personal: Educated at Marlborough College and Christ Church, Oxford (MA). Born 16 March 1956.

QUINT, Francesca
11 Old Square (Grant Crawford & Jonathan Simpkiss), London
(020) 7430 0341
f.quint@11oldsquare.co.uk
Recommended in Charities
Specialisation: Principal area of practice is chancery, with a focus on charities. Work includes advice on setting up charities, amending constitutions, negotiating with Charity Commission, schemes, arrangements with other charities or trading companies and dispute resolution. Other main areas of practice are trusts, land, probate and capital taxation. Recent cases include Gunning v Buckfast Abbey Trustees (dispute between parents and charity school); Henrietta Barnett School Governors v Hampstead Garden Suburb Institute (dispute between voluntary school and landlord charity), Gray v Taylor CA (status of almshouse resident), Fuller v Evans (private settlement) and RSPCA v Attorney General (charity membership).
Prof. Memberships: Clarity, Chancery Bar Association, Charity Law Association (executive committee member), Statute Law Society (council member).
Career: Called to the Bar 1970. Law Reporter, 1970-71. Charity Commission 1972-89. Independent practice since 1990. Qualified Mediator (1997).
Publications: Publications include 'Running a Charity' (Jordans); 'Charities: The Law & Practice' (Sweet & Maxwell, co-author); Butterworth's 'Encyclopaedia of Forms and Precedents - Charities and Charitable Giving'; Charity Law Association model governing documents for charities.
Personal: Educated at St Paul's Girls' School and King's College, London (LLB, AKC). Trustee/advisor to various charities.

QURESHI, Khawar
Serle Court (Lord Neill of Bladen QC), London
(020) 7242 6105
kmqureshi@aol.com
Recommended in Public International Law
Specialisation: The areas of law in which extensive advice has been given and court appearances made are commercial, public international law, adminstrative and public law.
Prof. Memberships: ALBA, BIICL, COMBAR, Bar Council International Relations Committee, PIL Sub-committee Chairman.
Career: LLB, LLM (Cantab). Queen Mother's Scholar 1990 (Middle Temple). (1990 call). Guest lecturer/supervisor Cambridge University (1990-93). Visiting lecturer in international law, King's College, London (1994-). Legal advisor to Bosnian Government in Dayton peace talks (November 1995). Has advised several foreign governments on constitutional and international matters. Appeared for and advised foreign governments extensively. Junior Counsel to the Crown since 1999.

RABINOWITZ, Laurence QC
One Essex Court (Lord Grabiner QC), London
(020) 7583 2000
Recommended in Banking & Finance, Commercial (Litigation), Company, Energy, Fraud
Specialisation: Banking, insurance, professional negligence, railway industry disputes, financial services, energy, computer, and other commercial disputes. Recent cases include: Alcock and ors v Phildrew Nominees Ltd & UBS; Shell and Esso v Enterprise; BP v Corby Power Limited, Amoco (UK) Exploration Co v TGTL; Total Gas Marketing Ltd v ARCO; B & C v Atlantic Computers; Evans v Gov. of Brockhill Prison; Marsh & McLennan Companies UK Ltd v Pensions Ombudsman & Anor; Turner v Grovit & Ors; Kuwait Shipping v UBS; Lloyds Bank and Abbey National v Lee and Ors; Decaril and Ors v Prudential Bache International Bank Ltd; NM Rothschild v Equitable Life; Equitable Life v Bowley & Ors.
Prof. Memberships: Member of Middle Temple.
Career: One Essex Court 1987. Junior counsel for the crown, Chancery (1995), Queen's Counsel 2002.
Personal: BA LLB (Wits). BA BCL (Oxon). Rhodes Scholar (1983, South Africa).

RADEVSKY, Anthony
Falcon Chambers (Jonathan Gaunt QC & Kim Lewison QC), London
(020) 7353 2484
radevsky@falcon-chambers.com
Recommended in Property Litigation
Specialisation: Landlord and tenant law relating to commercial and residential property, leasehold enfranchisement, rent review, dilapidations and service charges. Also handles mortgages, specific performance of contracts for the sale of land, restrictive covenants and professional negligence claims against solicitors and surveyors.
Prof. Memberships: Chancery Bar Association, Property Bar Association.
Career: Called to the Bar 1978 and joined Falcon Chambers in 1998.
Publications: 'Service of Documents'

LEADERS AT THE BAR

(Longman, 2nd edn, 1989); 'Drafting Pleadings' (Tolley, 2nd edn 1995); 'Hague on Leasehold Enfranchisement' (Sweet & Maxwell, 3rd edn 1999); 'Tenants' Right of First Refusal' (Butterworths, 2001).
Personal: Educated at Alleyn's School, Dulwich 1966-73 and Southampton University 1974-77 (LLB, Hons). Born 22 August 1955.

RAESIDE, Mark QC
Atkin Chambers (Robert Akenhead QC), London
(020) 7404 0102
Recommended in Construction, Professional Negligence
Specialisation: English High Court and both international ICC; LCIA and domestic arbitrations (mediations adjudications); FIDIC, ICE and JCT contracts in most European countries, Africa, Middle and Far East. Cases including hotels, shopping centres, dams, river and road projects, bridges, power stations, car factory and other developments under English, French, Swiss, Spanish, Swedish, German, Italian, Polish, Egyptian, Turkish, Chinese and Tansanian law. Claims include defects, loss and expense and all related construction issues, professional negligence and fraud together with computer cases.
Career: Called to Middle Temple 1982.
Personal: B.A., M.Phil, (Cantab.).

RAGGATT, Timothy QC
4 King's Bench Walk (Timothy Raggatt QC), London
(020) 7822 7000
Recommended in Crime
Specialisation: Undertakes crime and fraud. Regina v Bartlet: defence of the managing director of computer leasing company in £30 million fraud 1995/6. The client was granted bail as the largest surety ever fixed by an English Court. R v Canon (murder of Shirley Banks). Regina v Richards: 54 day bank fraud defence. Dartmoor Prison Riots, "Sleepwalker" murder in Stafford. Prosecuted R v Myles and others: the largest murder trial in the West Midlands since the Birmingham bombings. Prosecuted R v Cotter & Ors: the bogus race conspiracy case surrounding Ashia Hansen and other athletes. R v Trigwell: the 'Black Widow'.
Career: Called to the Bar, 1972. Took silk 1993. Member of 3 Fountain Court Chambers Birmingham until 1994 (still door tenant) now member of 4 King's Bench Walk (Head of Chambers) London EC4. Criminal Bar Association. Midlands and Oxford Circuit. Bencher Inner Temple, 1999.
Personal: Golf. Scuba Diving.

RAILTON, David QC
Fountain Court (Anthony Boswood QC), London
(020) 7583 3335
Recommended in Banking & Finance, Commercial (Litigation), Insurance
Specialisation: Commercial disputes, in particular banking, insurance and reinsurance. Cases include Banque Bruxelles Lambert v Eagle Star [1995] 1 IRLR 17, Assitalia v Overseas Union Insurance [1995] 1 IRLR 76, Bates v Barrow [1995] 1 LLR 680, O'Brien v Hughes Gibbs [1995] 1 IRLR 90, CTI v Oceanus [1984] 1 LLR 476, RPPC v Bank Leumi [1992] 1 LLR 513, Sumitomo Bank v BBL [1997] 1 LLR 487, Federal Republic of Nigeria v Abacha [2001], Gan v Tai Ping [2001].
Career: Balliol College, Oxford (BA Jurisprudence, first class). Called Gray's Inn 1979; QC, 1996; tenant Fountain Court since 1980. Recorder 2000.
Personal: Born 1957; resides London.

RAINEY, Simon QC
4 Essex Court (Nigel Teare QC), London
(020) 7653 5653
strainey@4sx.co.uk
Recommended in Shipping
Specialisation: Simon Rainey's practice centres on shipping and international commerce and he practises almost exclusively in the Commercial and Admiralty Courts as well as in maritime commercial arbitration in London and in commodity trade arbitrations before the major trade associations. He has been consistently singled out over the past five years in the specialist directories as one of the leading shipping practitioners.
Prof. Memberships: Member of COMBAR; supporting member of LMAA.
Career: Called to the Bar in 1982; took silk 2000; appointed Recorder of the Crown Court 2001.

RAMPTON, Richard QC
1 Brick Court (Richard Rampton QC), London
(020) 7353 8845
clerks@1brickcourt.co.uk
Recommended in Defamation
Specialisation: Defamation, confidence, contempt of court and media related law generally. Cases include: Lucas-Box v Associated Newspapers; Atkinson v Fitzwalter; Control Risks v New English Library; Telnikoff v Matusevich; Shah v Standard Chartered Bank; Aldington v Tolstoy; McDonald's Corp v Steel and Morris; Irving v Lipstadt and Penguin Books; Sugar v News Group; Sugar v Associated Newspapers.
Career: Educated at Bryanston and The Queen's College, Oxford. Called to the Bar in 1965, took Silk in 1987.
Publications: 'Duncan & Neill on Defamation' ed, with Sir Brian Neill; 2nd edn (1983); 3rd edn (imminent).
Personal: Speaks French, some Italian and German.

RAMSEY, Vivian QC
Keating Chambers, London
(020) 7544 2600
clerks@keatingchambers.com
Recommended in Arbitration, Construction
Specialisation: Building and construction law; professional negligence; arbitration, including international arbitration; energy.
Career: Qualified 1979; Middle Temple Bencher 2002; QC 1992; Assistant Recorder 1998; Recorder 2000; chartered engineer; member of Institution of Civil Engineers 1976; graduate engineer Ove Arup & Partners, London Middle East 1972-1977. Arbitrator (domestic and international, including ICC) 1988 to date; special professor, department of Civil Engineering, University of Nottingham 1990 to date.
Publications: Joint editor 'Construction Law Journal'; joint author 'Keating on Building Contracts' (7th Edition) 2000.
Personal: Harley School, Rochester, USA; Abingdon School; Oriel College Oxford; City University (1972 MA, 1978 Dip Law, C Eng MICE). Born 1950; resides Swanley Village.

RANDALL, John QC
St Philips Chambers (John Randall QC), Birmingham
(0121) 246 7000
clerks@st-philips.co.uk
Recommended in Chancery, Commercial (Litigation), Insolvency
Specialisation: Principal areas of practice are chancery and commercial law, companies, corporate insolvency, judicial review, professional negligence, real property.
Prof. Memberships: Midland Circuit; International Bar Association; Chancery Bar Association; COMBAR; Midland Chancery and Commercial Bar Association.
Career: Called Lincoln's Inn 1978; Bar of New South Wales 1979; Silk 1995; Assistant Recorder 1995; Deputy Head of Chambers 1998. Recorder 1999. Deputy High Court Judge 2000. Member, Legal Services Consultative Panel 2000. Head of Chambers 2001. Barrister and Solicitor of Western Australia 2001. London Chambers: Maitland Chambers Charles Aldous QC and Michael Lyndon-Stanford QC, 7 Stone Buildings, Lincolns Inn (020 7406 1200).
Personal: Born 1956. Educated at Rugby School, Loomis Institute, Conn. USA and Jesus College, Cambridge (MA).

RANDALL, Louise
Keating Chambers, London
(020) 7544 2600
lrandall@keatingchambers.com
Recommended in Construction
Specialisation: Construction, engineering and professional negligence.
Career: Qualified 1988; Middle Temple.
Personal: Keele University (BA Hons). Born 1964; resides London.

RANDALL, Nicholas
Devereux Chambers
(Colin Edelman QC), London
(020) 7353 7534
randall@devchambers.co.uk
Recommended in Employment
Specialisation: Broad range of employment and pensions work undertaken for both employers and trade unions. Has appeared at all levels from tribunals up to the House of Lords. Reported cases include Wilson v St. Helens MBC [1998] ICR 114; Credit Suisse v Lister [1998] IRLR 700; ADI (UK) Ltd v Willer [2001] IRLR 542; Knowles v FBU [1997] ICR 595; TSC v Massey [1999] IRLR 22 and Wild v The Pensions Ombudsman [1996] OPLR 129. Also practices in the fields of VAT and general commercial work.
Prof. Memberships: Employment Law Bar Association. Association of Pension Lawyers.
Career: Part-time lecturer in labour law at LSE (1990-93).
Publications: A contributing editor of 'Harvey on Industrial Relations and Employment Law' and author of 'Halsbury's Laws Pensions Volume'.
Personal: Football, cricket and jazz.

RANKIN, James
3 Raymond Buildings
(Clive Nicholls QC), London
(020) 7400 6400
chambers@3raymondbuildings.com
Recommended in Licensing
Specialisation: All aspects of licensing law including liquor, public entertainment, betting and gaming and bingo. Regularly appears on behalf of applicants and objectors (including police and local authorities) at Magistrates' Courts, Crown Courts and Town Halls throughout the UK. Advises in lotteries and competitions.
Career: Called to the Bar 1983. Joined Raymond Buildings (Formerly Queen Elizabeth Building) in 1984.
Personal: Educated at Eton and Buckingham University LLB (Hons) 1982.

RAWLEY, Dominique
Atkin Chambers (Robert Akenhead QC), London
(020) 7404 0102
clerks@atkinchambers.law.co.uk
Recommended in Construction
Specialisation: All areas of construction and civil engineering disputes in arbitration and litigation. Contractual disputes regarding the design and supply of computer networks. General commercial disputes. Private International Law aspects of contractual disputes. Professional Negligence.
Career: Called 1991.

RAWLINGS, Clive
Goldsmith Building (Christopher Llewellyn-Jones QC), London
(020) 7353 7881
Recommended in Education

RAYNER JAMES, Jonathan QC
Hogarth Chambers (Jonathan Rayner James QC & Christopher Morcom QC), London
(020) 7464 0404
barristers@hogarthchambers.com
Recommended in Media & Entertainment
Specialisation: Principal areas of practice are media and entertainment law and intellectual property law, in particular contract, licensing, confidence, copyright, design rights,

performers' rights, trademarks and passing off. Advisory and litigation. Specialisation in EC aspects.
Prof. Memberships: Member of the Chancery Bar Association, Intellectual Property Bar Association and the International Association of Entertainment Lawyers.
Career: Commenced practice in 1975, having been called to the Bar in 1971. Appointed Silk in 1988. Recorder since 1998.
Publications: Co-editor of 'Copinger and Skone James' on copyright since 1980. Joint Consulting Editor for 'The Encyclopaedia of Forms and Precedents' (entertainment). Member of Editorial Board of 'Entertainment Law Review'.
Personal: Born 26th July 1950. Educated at King's College School, Wimbledon 1961-68, Christ's College, Cambridge 1968-72 (MA, LLM) and Brussels University 1972-73 (Lic. spéc. Droit Européen). Fluent in French. Lives in London.

READ, Graham
Devereux Chambers
(Colin Edelman QC), London
(020) 7353 7534
read@devchambers.co.uk
Recommended in Environment
Specialisation: Commercial (including TCC work), telecommunications, environmental law. Example of cases include Pickering v Liverpool Daily Echo [1990] 1 All ER 335; Reay v British Nuclear Fuels [1994] 1 MLR 1; Agrafax Public Relations v USS Inc, [1995] CLC 862; R v Secretary of State for Trade and Industry v ex p Duddridge, Times 26th October 1995; Ngcombo v Thor Chemical Holdings, Times 10th November 1995; R v Greenwich London Borough Council ex p Williams, Times 29th December 1995; Connelly v RTZ, Times 12th July 1996 and [1998] AC 854; Sonardyne Limited v Firth & Co [1997] EGCS 84; Lubbe v Cape [1998] CLC 155; Sithole v Thor, Times 15th February 1999; Africa v Cape [2000] 1 Lloyds Law Report 139 and [2001] 1 WLR 1545.
Prof. Memberships: Combar; Professional Negligence Bar Association.
Career: MA Trinity Hall, Cambridge; Arden Scholar Gray's Inn; called 1981.

READ, Lionel QC
Eldon Chambers (Patrick Clarkson QC & William Hicks QC), London
(020) 7583 1355
clerks@eldonchambers.com
Recommended in Environment, Local Government, Planning
Specialisation: M40 inquiry 1973. Stanstead/T5 inquiry for BAA 1981-83. Lakeside Regional shopping centre inquiry for Capital and Counties 1984. Runnymede shopping centre inquiry for applicants 1988. Cambridge sub-regional shopping centre inquiry for Capital and Counties 1990. Various superstore inquiries for Tesco and Sainsbury. Rock characterisation facility inquiry 1995 for NIREX. Cement inquiry for Blue Circle 1999. Bracknell Town Centre Shopping Inquiry 1999.
Prof. Memberships: Planning and Environmental Bar Association. Administrative Law Bar Association.
Career: Smith v Skinner 1986 for Camden Councellors.

READE, Kevin
7 Harrington Street Chambers (David Steer QC & Robert Fordham QC & Iain Goldrein QC), Liverpool
(0151) 242 0707
Recommended in Family

READHEAD, Simon
No. 1 Serjeants' Inn
(Edward Faulks QC), London
(020) 7415 6666
clerks@no1serjeantsinn.com
Recommended in Clinical Negligence
Specialisation: Principal areas of practice: clinical negligence (including dental negligence) for both claimants and defendants; professional negligence work (especially solicitors' and barristers' negligence in the areas of clinical negligence and personal injury); a wide range of personal injury work including industrial accidents and occupational diseases; health and safety work; public and administrative law including judicial review. Instructed in the last 12 months on behalf of claimants and defendants in a number of clinical negligence and personal injury cases involving very substantial claims. Expertise of and special interest in catastrophic injury claims including birth trauma, cerebral palsy, head injuries and spinal injuries. Regular speaker at seminars and conferences.
Prof. Memberships: Administrative Law Bar Association; Professional Negligence Bar Association; Personal Injury Bar Association, London Common Law and Commercial Bar Association, AVMA. Trained in mediation by ALARM. Member of the General Council of the Bar's Wasted Costs Panel.
Career: Called to the Bar in 1979. Appointed Recorder in 1995.
Personal: Educated Lincoln College, Oxford. BCL, MA. Lives in Richmond, Surrey.

REDFERN, Michael QC
28 St John St, Manchester
(0161) 834 8418
clerk@28stjohnst.co.uk
Recommended in Clinical Negligence, Personal Injury
Specialisation: Clinical negligence (in particular cerebral palsy), brain injuries, spinal injuries (utmost severity), employers' liability, road traffic accidents.
Prof. Memberships: Personal Injury Bar Association, Northern Circuit Medical Law Association.
Career: Call 1970. Silk 1993. Recorder, Chairman Royal Liverpool Children's Enquiry December 1999 to January 2001.
Publications: Recent cases include: Wisniewski v Central Manchester Health Authority (1998) Lloyds Rep Med 223, (1996) 7 Medical LR 248; Stark v Post Office, (2000) PIQR 105, TLR 29 March 2000; Pickford v ICI (1998) 1 WLR 1189; Brown v Lewisham and North Southwark Health Authority (1999) 4 Lloyds Rep Med 110; Stephens v Doncaster Health Authority, Kemp Vol 3 para A4-107, (1996) 7 Medical LR 357.
Personal: Married to Her Honour Judge Eaglestone. All female household! Active rather than passive sports.

REED, Piers
3 Temple Gardens (John Coffey QC), London
(020) 7353 3102
Recommended in Crime
Specialisation: Consumer/regulatory work (e.g) trading standards, food safety, health and safety at work, defended Birse Construction Re fatal accident prosecution; defended SAPPI (UK) Ltd Re: environmental pollution prosecution; general defence work for MARS (UK) Ltd. Defence work generally from murder to fraud.
Prof. Memberships: Criminal Bar Association. Assistant Junior Herts & Beds Bar Mess. Bar Liason Member St Albans TIG Group.
Career: Called 1974. Member Lincoln's Inn and Northern Ireland Inns of Court. Approved Tutor for Lincoln's Inn continuing education programme.
Personal: Married with two daughters. Fanatic sports follower.

REES, Edward QC
Doughty Street Chambers
(Geoffrey Robertson QC), London
(020) 7404 1313
Recommended in Crime
Specialisation: Was appointed Silk in 1998. He is well known both for defending in criminal trials with civil libertarian implications and for his particular experience in homicide, dangerous drugs, public order and serious fraud and confiscation cases. With Andrew Hall he is publishing 'A Guide to the Proceeds of Crime Act', Oxford University Press/ Blackstones. Notable cases in which he has appeared in the last 12 months include: R v Jama: whether Asperger's Syndrome (a form of autism) is a basis for diminished responsibility. R v Allan (CA): the meaning of private/public communications system (prison intercepts) within the Interception of Telecommunications Act 1985. In Re P (CA) The necessity for an independent and impartial tribunal in wasted costs hearings. R v Hakala (CA) a CCRC referral involving ESDA evidence and legal argument as to the subjective or jury impact tests in appeals. Earlier notable cases: the trial and appeals of Winston Silcott for the murder of PC Blakelock (he has also drafted the representations to both the Home Office and the CCRC in respect of Mr Silcott's outstanding conviction); the appeal of Sharon Roberts in which the Court of Appeal quashed an 8 year old murder conviction on the basis of an unrecognised battered woman syndrome: the Whitemoor Prison breakout trial, the M25 prison escape trial; the Orgreave Miners trial; the St Paul's, Bristol riot trial; the 'Bradford Twelve' trial; the trial of Ron Brown MP; the Rettendon Murders (3 men shot dead in a Range Rover in Essex); the trial and appeals of Patricia Bass - twice convicted of the same murder and twice quashed by the Court of Appeal; R v Aziz a serious VAT fraud; R v Howes a 10 month gold fraud.

REES, Gareth
Hollis Whiteman Chambers (QEB) (Julian Bevan QC & Peter Whiteman QC), London
(020) 7583 5766
grees@holliswhiteman.co.uk
Recommended in Crime, Fraud
Specialisation: Practice increasingly concerned with company and commercial fraud including cases involving market abuse, fraudulent trading, company director offences (including allegations connected to collapse of Johnson Matthey Bank and corruption). In the last year has been involved in Customs diversion frauds and money laundering allegations as a leading junior. In 2003 will appear for the defence in the Jubilee Line Extension Fraud. Has represented defendants charged with offences by the Occupational Pensions Regulatory Authority. Has advised city solicitor's corporate clients on privilege, self-incrimination and third-party witness summons. Advised Linklaters acting for Wickes in the criminal fraud allegations. Has also presented seminars to accountants, bankers and solicitors on money laundering, expert evidence and the criminal powers of the FSA. In general crime has continued to represent defendants charged with serious offences such as murder and crimes. Represented three police sergeants in the Victoria Climbie Public Inquiry. Has appeared in the General Medical Council.
Career: Worked for Canadian law firm and as journalist before beginning practice in 1981.

REES, John Charles QC
33 Park Place (Neil Bidder QC), Cardiff
(029) 2023 3313
Recommended in Crime, Personal Injury
Specialisation: Crime, including commercial fraud and breach of copyright; personal injury; and general common law. Has appeared in many high profile murder cases both as a Junior and a Silk.
Prof. Memberships: Criminal Bar Association, Personal Injury Bar Association.
Career: Educated at St Illtyd's College, Cardiff; Jesus College, Cambridge (BA Law (1st class LL.B International Law (1st class) MA LL.M Russell Vick Prize); McNair scholar.
Personal: Boxing Blue (Cambridge).

LEADERS AT THE BAR

Played football for University. Chairman Welsh Area Council of the British Boxing Board of Control. Governor and Trustee of St John's College, Cardiff. Married with four children.

REES, Paul QC
1 Crown Office Row (Robert Seabrook QC), London
(020) 7797 7500
Recommended in Clinical Negligence

REES, Philip
9 Park Place (Ian Murphy QC), Cardiff
(029) 2038 2731
clerks@9parkplace.co.uk
Recommended in Personal Injury
Specialisation: Personal injury. Clinical negligence. Trusts. Commercial. Landlord and tenant.
Career: LL.B. (Hons) Bristol. Called 1965 (Middle Temple). Recorder of the Crown Court since 1983. Assistant Boundary Commissioner.
Personal: Music, sport.

REESE, Colin QC
Atkin Chambers (Robert Akenhead QC), London
(020) 7404 0102
Recommended in Arbitration

REID, Paul Campbell QC
Lincoln House Chambers (Mukhtar Hussain QC), Manchester
(0161) 832 5701
paul.reid@lincolnhse.co.uk
Recommended in Crime
Prof. Memberships: Criminal Bar Association.
Career: M.A. (Cantab.) (Engineering). Called to Bar 1973. Recorder 1993. Queen's Counsel 2001.
Personal: Born 27 March 1949. Educated at Merchant Taylors School, Crosby and Christ's College Cambridge (1968-72). Married with 2 children. Leisure interests include tennis, acoustic guitar and amateur dramatics.

REILLY, John
Tooks Court Chambers (Michael Mansfield QC), London
(020) 7405 8828
Recommended in Crime

REYNOLDS, Adrian
No.1 High Pavement (John B Milmo QC), Nottingham
(0115) 941 8218
Recommended in Crime
Specialisation: Exclusively criminal practice provided fairly evenly between prosecution and defence work. Has been involved in Customs & Excise cases (drugs and cigarette importation and VAT evasion) and health and safety cases. Many years experience of sexual cases especially child abuse. Some fraud work, for example money laundering.
Career: Called 1982. Recorder 2000

REYNOLDS, Kirk QC
Falcon Chambers (Jonathan Gaunt QC & Kim Lewison QC), London
(020) 7353 2484
Recommended in Property Litigation
Specialisation: Called to the Bar 1974. Queen's Counsel 1993. Full-time practice as property law specialist at Falcon Chambers since 1975. Co-author 'The Handbook of Rent Review', 'The Renewal of Business Tenancies' and 'Dilapidations: the Modern Law and Practice'. Blundell memorial lecturer 1982, 1987, 1993 and 2002. Advisor to Royal Institution of Chartered Surveyors on arbitration practice and course tutor on official RICS training courses for arbitrators.
Prof. Memberships: Member of RICS Committee producing and revising official Guidance Notes for Arbitrators and Independent Experts. Appointed on a number of occasions by president of RICS and president of Law Society as arbitrator, and by arbitrators as legal assessor. Elected an honorary member of RICS in 1997.

RICH, Barbara
5 Stone Buildings (Henry Harrod), London
(020) 7242 6201
brich@5-stonebuildings.law.co.uk
Recommended in Chancery, Pensions
Specialisation: Pensions, trusts, contentious probate and other succession disputes, administration of estates, Inheritance Act, Court of Protection. Recent cases: Pensions: Stevens v Bell [2001] PLR 99; Bestrustees v Stuart [2001] PLR 283. Trusts: Iliffe v Trafford and FitzGerald [2002] NPC 3. Succession: Fuller v Strum [2001] WLTR 677; Gandhi v Patel [2002] 1 FLR 603; Jennings v Rice [2001] WLTR 871, [2002] WLTR 367; Singer v Isaac [2001] WLTR 1045. Real property and conveyancing: Braymist v Wise Finance Co Ltd [2002] 2 All ER 333.
Prof. Memberships: Chancery Bar Association; Association of Pension Lawyers.
Career: 1991-date, practising at 5 Stone Buildings.
Publications: Contributor to 13th edition of 'Heywood & Massey: Court of Protection Practice'.
Personal: Education: St Paul's Girls' School, London; Emmanuel College Cambridge (BA, MA); Polytechnic of Central London (Dip Law). Leisure interests: music, history, literature.

RICHARDS, David QC
Erskine Chambers (Robin Potts QC), London
(020) 7242 5532
Recommended in Banking & Finance, Company, Financial Services, Insolvency
Specialisation: Company, corporate finance, insolvency and commercial. Recent contentious work includes Re Duckwari plc [1998] 3 WLR 913 (directors' liability), UMB v Doherty [1998] 1 WLR 435 (freezing orders), OR v Vass [1999] BCC 516, DTI v Stephen Hinchliffe and O.R. v William Stern (directors' disqualification) Re Benfield Greig Group [2000] 2BCLC 488 and Re BAT Industries plc and Re Allied Domecq plc (opposed schemes of arrangement), Re Sedgefield Steeplechase Ltd [2000] 2 BCLC 211, Jarvis plc v PcW [2000] 2 BCLC 368, Re Nottingham Forest plc, Queens Moat houses plc v Bairstow [2001] 2BCLC 531, Re AXA Equity and Law [2001] 2 BCLC 447. Other recent work includes the Equitable Life scheme of arrangement, the demutualisations of the AA, Friends Provident and Scottish Life, Granada/Compass merger, Cable & Wireless HKT/Pacific Cyberworks merger (in Hong Kong), Allied Zurich plc reconstruction and Williams plc demerger.
Prof. Memberships: Chancery Bar Association, Commercial Bar Association.
Career: Trinity College, Cambridge (BA 1973, MA 1980).

RICHARDS, Jennifer
39 Essex Street (Nigel Pleming QC), London
(020) 7832 1111
clerks@39essex.co.uk
Recommended in Administrative & Public Law
Specialisation: Specialises in all aspects of public and administrative law, including local government, mental health, community care, health services, education, prisons, and human rights. Regularly acts for claimants, central government, local government and NHS bodies. Recent cases include: R v Broadmoor ex p Wilkinson (compulsory psychiatric treatment and human rights) and R (Noorkoiv) v Parole Board (compliance of Parole Board system with Article 5(4)). Co-author of the Social Services title of 'Halsbury's Laws of England' and contributor to R Gordon's 'Judicial Review: Practice and Procedure'. Co-author of forthcoming book on 'Health Law and Public Law'. Appointed to the Treasury B Panel in 1999; appointment renewed in 2002.
Prof. Memberships: Administrative Law Bar Association, London Commercial and Common Law Bar Association, Community Care Practitioners Group.
Career: Called to the Bar 1991 and joined present chambers in 1992.
Personal: Educated at Clare College, Cambridge (BA (Hons) Law, 1st Class) and at University of Toronto (Masters in Laws, specialist thesis on Canadian Charter of Rights and Freedoms).

RICHARDS, Jeremy
Octagon House Chambers (Guy Ayers & Andrew Lindquist), Norwich
(01603) 623186
Recommended in Family

RICHARDSON, James
Trinity Chambers (Toby Hedworth QC), Newcastle upon Tyne
(0191) 232 1927
info@trinitychambers.co.uk
Recommended in Family
Specialisation: General commercial; ancillary relief; employment.
Career: Called 1982. Appointed Deputy District Judge 2001.

RIDDLE, Nicholas
14 Castle Street (Andrew Edis QC), Liverpool
(0151) 236 8240
nickriddle@14castlestreet.co.uk
Recommended in Chancery
Specialisation: General Chancery, recent cases: Halliwell v Cuozzo (1999, unreported), concerning the duties of a football pools collector; Webb v Chief Constable of Merseyside Police [2000] 2 W.L.R. 546, concerning application of proceeds of drug trafficking; Hardy & Co v Sorrentino (2000, unreported), concerning accountants' negligence. R v P.I.A.O.B and Goss (judicial review of Ombudsman; decision about construction of policy).
Prof. Memberships: Chancery Bar Association. Northern Chancery Bar Association. Society for Computers and Law.
Career: Educated at The King's School, Canterbury; Gonville and Caius College. Practice in Liverpool Chancery Chambers, from 1972. Head of chambers from 1977, until merger with present chambers in 1996.
Personal: Leisure interests: reading, music, food, wine, travel.

RILEY-SMITH, Toby
2 Harcourt Buildings (Roger Henderson QC), London
(020) 7583 9020
clerks@harcourt.co.uk
Recommended in Product Liability
Specialisation: Principal areas of practice: product liability including group actions; personal injury including health and safety at work, occupiers' liability and road traffic accidents; professional negligence, particularly surveyors' and valuers'; consumer credit including hire purchase. Other areas of practice: landlord and tenant (particularly for local authorities); employment; general commercial and common law. He has a commercial and common law practice and is one of the members of chambers who successfully defended Imperial Tobacco Limited in the recent UK tobacco multi-party litigation. He is now involved in another group action, the MMR/MR vaccine litigation. He undertakes a broad range of civil work predominantly for insurer clients, local authorities and other bodies. He has lectured on the CPR. Reported cases include: Hobin v Douglas (1998 The Times, 3 December): costs - personal injury - civil procedure - appeal on causation with offer of global figure for damages; Hodgson and Others v Imperial Tobacco Limited and Others (1998 1 WLR 1056 1998 2 All ER 673): costs - conditional fees - order for costs - publication of proceedings in chambers.
Prof. Memberships: Member of the Personal Injury Bar Association; chambersí human rights team.
Career: Called 1995. Jules Thorn Scholar, Middle Temple, 1994. CEDR accredited mediator.
Publications: Contributor to 'Volume

9(1) of Halsbury's Laws - Consumer Credit' (1998).
Personal: Born 1969. MA (Cantab).

RIORDAN, Kevin
Iscoed Chambers
(Elwen Mair Evans QC), Swansea
(01792) 652988
Recommended in Crime

RIORDAN, Stephen QC
25-27 Castle Street (Stephen Riordan QC),
Liverpool
(0151) 236 5072
Recommended in Crime

RITCHIE, Andrew
9 Gough Square (John Foy QC), London
(020) 7832 0500
aritchie@9goughsq.co.uk
Recommended in Personal Injury
Specialisation: Personal injury covering employers liability and industrial diseases and other accidents. Clinical negligence specialising in back injury claims. Recent cases include Thomas v King [2001], back injury, acceleration of symptoms by fall at work; Donaldsun v Brighton DC [2001], pelvic injury due to defective equipment; Smee v Adaye [1999], hip and leg injury, pension loss and future risk of retirement; Fletcher v Thames Valley Police [2000], arthritis of hip; Wells v Watford NHS Trust [2000], liability trial, manual handling in the delivery suite of NHS hospitals; Drage v Grassrouts [2000], strict liability for surface of floor; Re Jones [2000], policeman who suffered an attempt on his life, head injuries, serious scarring and likelihood of being cast from the force; Re Nichols [1996], head injury award, child abuse; Various v Tesco [1997], 40+ RSI cases against Tesco for checkout cashiers; The needlestick doctor [1998], phobia of needles after needlestick injury.
Prof. Memberships: AVMA, PIBA, PNBA (elected to Executive Committee 1996-99), APIL.
Career: Called 1985.
Publications: General Editor 'The Journal of Personal Injury Law' 5/2000 - continuing; 'MIB Claims' Jordans 2001; Co-Editor 'The Professional Negligence and Liability Reports' Sweet & Maxwell; 'Medical Evidence in Whiplash Cases' 1998 Sweet & Maxwell.

RITCHIE, Jean QC
4 Paper Buildings (Jean Ritchie QC), London
(020) 7643 5000
Recommended in Clinical Negligence
Specialisation: All aspects of clinical negligence, medical work, and personal injury work. Acts for claimants, trusts and authorities. Cases include Re F [1990]; De Martell v Merton and Sutton Health Authority [1993] and [1995]; Joyce v Merton, Sutton and Wandsworth Health Authority [1995] and [1996]; Corley v North West Hertfordshire Health Authority [1997]; Mirza v Birmingham Health Authority [2001] Med Lit. Cases 0412. Contributor to 'Safe Practice in Obstetrics and Gynaecology' (Ed. Clements) 1994.
Prof. Memberships: Professional Negligence Bar Association.
Career: Called to the Bar 1970. Silk 1992. Recorder 1993. Member of Supreme Court Rules Committee 1993-1997. Chairman of Inquiry into care of Christopher Clunis 1993-94. Member of Judicial Studies Board 1998-2001. Chairman of inquiry into quality and practice in the NHS, arising from actions of Rodney Ledward, 2000.
Personal: Kings College London (LL.B) and McGill University, Montreal (LL.M).

RITCHIE, Richard
24 Old Buildings (Martin Mann QC & Alan Steinfeld QC), London
(020) 7404 0946
Recommended in Company, Insolvency

ROBERTS, Catherine
Erskine Chambers (Robin Potts QC), London
(020) 7242 5532
croberts@erskine-chambers.co.uk
Recommended in Company
Specialisation: Specialist in Company law and in commercial litigation involving issues of Company law and corporate insolvency, shareholder and partnership disputes and professional negligence; advisory work in the same fields.
Prof. Memberships: COMBAR. Chancery Bar Association.
Career: Churchill College Cambridge M.A. LL.M. Called to Lincoln's Inn 1986.

ROBERTS, James
One King's Bench Walk
(Anthony Hacking QC), London
(020) 7936 1500
clerks@1kbw.co.uk
Recommended in Family
Specialisation: Ancillary relief.
Prof. Memberships: FLBA (Committee member); Bar Council (Remuneration Committee); SE Circuit (Committee member); Joint Inns Disciplinary Tribunal.
Publications: Wildblood & Eaton (Enforcement Chapter).
Personal: Born 21 September 1969. Oriel College, Oxford (Jurisprudence).

ROBERTS, Jennifer
Queen Elizabeth Building
(Florence Baron QC), London
(020) 7797 7837
Recommended in Family

ROBERTS, Lisa
Lincoln House Chambers
(Mukhtar Hussain QC), Manchester
(0161) 832 5701
Recommended in Crime

ROBERTSON, Aidan
Brick Court Chambers
(Christopher Clarke QC), London
(020) 7379 3550
robertson@brickcourt.co.uk
Recommended in Competition/European Law
Specialisation: Competition law, European Community law and public and administrative law. Important cases include Case C-27/00 R v Secretary of State ex p Omega Air Ltd, European Court of Justice, 12th March 2002; Land Rover v UPF (in administrative receivership), High Court, 25th January 2002; Case C-390/98 HJ Banks & Co v Coal Authority & Secretary of State for Trade and Industry [2001] ECR I-6117; IIB & ABTA v Director General of Fair Trading and GISC [2001] Comp AR 62; R v Competition Commission and Secretary of State for Trade and Industry ex p Interbrew [2001] UKCLR 954; Ordnance Survey v AA [2001] EuLR 80, High Court; C-344/98 Masterfoods [2000] ECR I-11369; C-380/98 R v HM Treasury ex p University of Cambridge [2000] ECR I-8035; Case C-3/99 Cidrerie Ruwet SA v Cidre Stassen SA & HP Bulmer Ltd [2000] ECR I-8749; Supermarket Prices (Competition Commission, October 2000, Cm 4842); New Motor Vehicles (Competition Commission, April 2000, Cm 4660); R v Customs & Excise ex p Lunn Poly [1999] STC 350, Court of Appeal; Crehan v Courage [1999] EuLR 834, Court of Appeal; Passmore v Morland [1999] EuLR 501; Attorney General v Blake [1998] Ch 439, Court of Appeal; R v OFTEL ex p Cellcom [1998] The Times, 7 December, High Court.
Prof. Memberships: Committee Member of the Bar European Group. Also Member of Solicitors European Group, Administrative Law Bar Association, COMBAR, the Bar Pro Bono Unit, the Society of Legal Scholars and the Association of Law Teachers.
Career: Called to Bar 1995. Solicitor of the Supreme Court of England and Wales 1988-1995. Fellow and Tutor in Law, Wadham College, Oxford 1990-99. University Lecturer at Oxford University 1990-96. 1981-84 BA Hons, Law, Jesus College, Cambridge (1st Class); 1984-85 LLM, Jesus College, Cambridge (1st Class); Member of the Treasury B Panel (2002-).
Publications: Co-author with Nicholas Green QC of second edition of 'Commercial Agreements and Competition Law' (1997, publisher Kluwer Law International). Co-author with Nicholas Green QC of 'The Europeanisation of UK Competition Law' (1999, publisher Hart Publishing). Numerous articles in academic and professional journals. Member of editorial boards of the European Competition Law Review, European Law Reports and UK Competition Law Reports.

ROBERTSON, Geoffrey QC
Doughty Street Chambers
(Geoffrey Robertson QC), London
(020) 7404 1313
g.robertson@doughtystreet.co.uk
Recommended in Crime, Defamation, Human Rights
Specialisation: Has appeared in many landmark cases involving public, media and criminal law, both at trial and on appeal, and has argued human rights cases in Commonwealth Courts, the Privy Council and the European Court in Strasbourg. His memoir, 'The Justice Game', was published in 1998, and 'Crimes Against Humanity - The Struggle for Global Justice' was published in 2000 (2nd ed, 2002).
Career: Called to Bar 1973; Silk 1988. Recorder and Master of the Middle Temple.
Personal: Born 1946. BA, LLB, BCL, Rhodes Scholar. Author of current textbooks, 'Freedom, the Individual and the Law', and 'Media Law' (4th ed, 2002). Visiting Professor in Human Rights at Birkbeck College. His play, 'The Trials of Oz', won a BAFTA 'Best Play' nomination for 1991, and he was the recipient of a 1993 Freedom of Information Award. Has conducted a number of missions on behalf of Amnesty International to South Africa and Vietnam, and led the 1992 Bar Council/ Law Society Human Rights Mission to Malawi. In 1990 he served as counsel to the Royal Commission investigating trafficking in arms and mercenaries to the Colombian drugs cartels; and in 2000 was counsel to Lord MacKay's Commission on the administration of Justice in Trinidad.

ROBERTSON, Patricia
Fountain Court (Anthony Boswood QC), London
(020) 7583 3335
Recommended in Professional Negligence
Specialisation: Civil and commercial: including professional negligence, banking, electronic commerce, civil claims arising out of commercial fraud, employment, (including discrimination and restrictive covenants), disputes over jurisdiction and aspects of European law. Cases include Unilever Superannuation Trustees v Mercury Asset Management, NRG v Bacon and Woodrow and others (professional negligence) and Kapur v Barclays Bank (racial discrimination). Contributor to 'The Law of Bank Payments', editors Brindle and Cox, Sweet and Maxwell 1999, on plastic money and on internet payments.
Prof. Memberships: COMBAR, London Common Law and Commercial Bar Association, Bar European Group. ICC United Kingdom Electronic Commerce Group.
Career: Called to the Bar in 1988. Joined Fountain Court 1989. Stage in Brussels 1991.
Personal: Educated at St. George's, Edinburgh and Balliol College, Oxford (Brackenbury Scholar; BA 1986). Duke of Edinburgh Scholarship, Inner Temple, 1988. Born 1964.

ROBINSON, Vivian QC
Hollis Whiteman Chambers (QEB)
(Julian Bevan QC & Peter Whiteman QC), London
(020) 7583 5766
Recommended in Fraud
Specialisation: All aspects of crime,

LEADERS AT THE BAR

particularly commercial fraud. Was involved for the Defence in the Blue Arrow trial and the Blackspur Leasing trial and has prosecuted cases on behalf of the Serious Fraud Office. In 1998 defended in a substantial fraud trial in Hong Kong.
Prof. Memberships: Criminal Bar Association.
Career: Educated at Queen Elizabeth Grammar School, Wakefield. The Leys School, Cambridge and Sidney Sussex College, Cambridge. Called to the Bar in 1967. Took Silk 1986. A Recorder of the Crown Court since 1986.
Personal: Married with three children. Lives in Oxfordshire.

RODGER, Martin
Falcon Chambers (Jonathan Gaunt QC & Kim Lewison QC), London
(020) 7353 2484
rodger@falcon-chambers.com
Recommended in Agriculture, Property Litigation
Specialisation: Handles all aspects of commercial and agricultural property litigation, including landlord and tenant, rent review, milk quota, agricultural holdings, licensed premises and real property. Important cases include Courage v Crehan (Court of Appeal, 1999 - beer tie litigation), Attwood v Bovis (Chancery Division, 2000 - easements) and Zubaida v Hargreaves (Court of Appeal, 1995 - negligence of expert).
Prof. Memberships: Chancery Bar Association, Agricultural Law Association, Professional Negligence Bar Association.
Career: Called to the Bar and joined Falcon Chambers in 1986.
Publications: Editor of 'Woodfall on Landlord & Tenant'.
Personal: Educated at St Aloysius College, Glasgow 1973-79 and University College, Oxford 1979-83. Born 1962. Lives in Kent.

RODGERS, June
Harcourt Chambers (June Rodgers), London
(020) 7353 6961
jrodgers@harcourtchambers.law.co.uk
Recommended in Church
Specialisation: Fax (020) 7353 6968 Oxford (01865) 791559 Fax (01865) 791585 Family and ecclesiastical.
Prof. Memberships: Family Law Bar Association. Ecclesiastical Law Society.
Career: MA Trinity College Dublin. MA Lady Margaret Hall Oxford. Called: 1971: Middle Temple. Midland and Oxford Circuit. Chancellor of the Diocese of Gloucester. Recorder.
Personal: Architectural history.

RODWAY, Susan QC
12 King's Bench Walk
(Richard Methuen QC), London
(020) 7583 0811
rodway@12kbw.co.uk
Recommended in Personal Injury
Specialisation: Clinical negligence and medical law; complex medical and scientific issues, cerebral palsy, birth or genetic injuries, brain damage, failures to diagnose and serious spinal injuries. Education (including educational negligence) specialist expertise in novel arena of professional negligence of teachers and failures to educate. Acted for one of defendants in leading House of Lords case of Phelps v Hillingdon and others. Sports law: established equine specialist in all aspects of equine law: insurance policy disputes, contractual disputes, misrepresentation, disputes on membership and rules of riding and racing and riding injuries. Group litigation: acted for defendants in recent LSD group litigation and in litigation arising out of medical, pharmaceutical or personal injury issues. All aspects of personal injury, for claimants and defendants.
Prof. Memberships: Committee PNBA. Member Clinical Standards Committee, Guys and St Thomas's NHS Trust.
Career: Called to the Bar, 1981. Silk 2002. Committee member PNBA; PIBA. LCLCBA; Lay Member Clinical Standards Committee, Guys and St Thomas's NHS Trust [1998-2001]; Accredited Mediator 1999; Deputy Chairman of the NHS Tribunal [2000-01]; past Secretary of Pegasus Club [Bar Point to Point].
Publications: 'Clinical Applications of Artificial Neural Networks,' 2001; 'Clinical Litigation,' Palladian 2003; 'Equine Law' [in preparation].
Personal: Keen rider and motorcyclist.

ROGERS, Beverly-Ann
Serle Court (Lord Neill of Bladen QC), London
(020) 7242 6105
clerks@serlecourt.co.uk
Recommended in ADR, Chancery
Specialisation: Chancery and commercial litigation and advice. All aspects of property litigation and advice. Professional negligence. Contentious trusts and probate, charities, partnerships.
Prof. Memberships: Chancery Bar. Association of Contentious Trust and Probate Specialists.
Career: Called to Bar in 1978. Joined Serle Court in 1980. CEDR registered mediator.

ROGERS, Heather
Matrix Chambers, London
(020) 7404 3447
Recommended in Defamation

ROGERS, Mark N
St. Mary's Chambers Family Law Chambers (Nigel B Page), Nottingham
(0115) 950 3503
Recommended in Family

ROMNEY, Daphne
Cloisters (Laura Cox QC), London
(020) 7827 4000
Recommended in Employment
Specialisation: Employment law, discrimination, civil liberties and human rights and media law. Handles employment work for a large number of organisations, including health authorities, electronic communication companies, merchant banks, insurance companies, building societies, and advertising agencies, as well as for applicants. This work includes unfair and wrongful dismissal, sex, race and disability discrimination, equal pay claims in employment tribunals and the Employment Appeal Tribunal, and restrictive covenant work in the High Court. Defamation work, includes acting for newspapers (including Head of 'The Observer' libel readers team), broadcasters and individuals, together with Civil Liberties and Human Rights. Cases include: Sykes v J.P.Morgan (EAT: direct and indirect discrimination relating to working mothers), Colt Group Ltd v Couchman (Disability discrimination and the 'small employer' exemption), National Federation of Self-Employed and Small Businesses v Philpott [1997] ICR 518 (Applicability of the SDA to the relationship between the Federation and its Members), Re S (Hospital Patient: Foreign Curator: appearance for the Norwegian guardian of an elderly Norwegian citizen in an adult 'tug of love' between his wife and his mistress).
Prof. Memberships: ELBA (Secretary).
Career: Called to the Bar 1979. Joined Cloisters 2001.
Personal: Member of the Almeida Theatre Capital committee. Arsenal season ticket holder.

ROOK, Peter QC
18 Red Lion Court (Anthony Arlidge QC), London
(020) 7520 6000
peter.rook@18rlc.co.uk
Recommended in Fraud
Specialisation: Commercial and tax fraud. Sex cases. Major cases include Lester Pigott, Barlow Clowes, Nissan, Maxwell, Africar, R v A (re Previous Sexual History, House of Lords, March 2001).
Prof. Memberships: Chairman, Criminal Bar Association, July 2002. QC 1991.
Publications: Rook and Ward on 'Sexual Offences', 2nd ed. 1997, Sweet & Maxwell. Lecturer. Conference - 'Criminal Law in the Divisional Court', Sweet & Maxwell [2002].

ROOTS, Guy QC
2 Mitre Court Buildings (Guy Roots QC), London
(020) 7583 1380
Recommended in Planning
Specialisation: Main areas of practice are town and country planning, environmental law, compulsory purchase and compensation, rating, local government, parliamentary and administrative law. Has been involved in many leading cases acting for a wide cross section of clients in the public and private sectors. Has spoken at and chaired numerous conferences and seminars. General Editor of 'Ryde on Rating and the Council Tax'. General Editor of 'Butterworths Compulsory Purchase Law Service'.
Prof. Memberships: Chairman Planning and Environment Bar Association, Administrative Law Bar Association.
Career: Called to the Bar in 1969. Joined 2 Mitre Court Buildings in 1972. Took Silk in 1989.
Personal: Educated at Winchester College and Brasenose College, Oxford (MA in Jurisprudence).

ROSE, Dinah
Blackstone Chambers (Presiley Baxendale QC & Charles Flint QC), London
(020) 7583 1770
clerks@blackstonechambers.com
Recommended in Administrative & Public Law, Employment, Human Rights
Specialisation: Administrative and public law, human rights, discrimination, employment, European law, sports law. Particular interests include equal pay, maternity rights, financial services, City regulation and the Human Rights Act 1998, European social policy, pharmaceuticals, telecommunications, broadcasting, prisoners rights.
Prof. Memberships: ALBA, ELBA, member Council of JUSTICE.
Career: Called to Bar 1989. Member of Treasury A Panel.
Publications: Co-editor Halsbury's Laws 4th edn re-issue, 'Race Relations'; contributor to Halsbury's Laws 4th edn re-issue, 'Constitutional Law and Human Rights'; contributor to Lester & Pannick 'Human Rights Law and Practice' (Butterworths 1999).

ROSE, Jonathan
St. Paul's Chambers
(Nigel Sangster QC), Leeds
(0113) 245 5866
Recommended in Crime

ROSE, Paul QC
Old Square Chambers (John Hendy QC), London
(020) 7269 0300
rose@oldsquarechambers.co.uk
Recommended in Employment
Specialisation: Discrimination, unfair dismissal, wrongful dismissal and restraint of trade. Personal injury.
Prof. Memberships: ELA, Employment Law Bar Association, Personal Injury Bar Association, APIL.
Career: Called to Bar 1981. In employment law acted in leading cases in discrimination, unfair dismissal, Transfer of Undertakings regulations. Undertaken injunctive work in field of restraint of trade and wrongful dismissal litigation, also instructed regularly in collective redundancy litigation. In personal injury acted on behalf of the plaintiffs in Opren litigation, Benzodiazepine litigation, British Midland air crash, Camelford Water Pollution, Mull of Kyntyre helicopter crash. Acted in a substantial number of catastrophic injury claims particularly involving servicemen in claims against

Ministry of Defence. Recent reported cases include: Liversidge v Chief Constable of Bedfordshire Police [2002] IRLR 15; Kerry Foods v Creber [2000] IRLR 10; Leicester University v A [1999] IRLR 352; Crosville Wales v Tracey [1998] AC167.

ROSEN, Murray QC
11 Stone Buildings (Murray Rosen QC), London
(020) 7831 6381
rosen@11stonebuildings.com
Recommended in Chancery, Commercial (Litigation), Fraud, Sport
Specialisation: Head of Chambers at 11 Stone Buildings. An incisive and creative tactitian and advocate. Is experienced as a leader or team-member in a wide range of international commercial cases, especially involving asset tracing, and in sports, media and entertainment disputes. Has guided and executed many cases in the fields of fraud and insolvency and lawyers' and accountants' negligence, whether acting for banks, insurers and enforcement agencies, or for corporate, professional and individual defendants. Consistently features in Chambers Directory as a leading silk in the areas of sport and commercial law and was founding chairman of the Bar Sports Law Group. He is also a Fellow of the Chartered Institute of Arbitrators.

ROSENBLATT, Jeremy
4 Paper Buildings (Lionel Swift QC), London
(020) 7583 0816
jr@4pb.com
Recommended in Family
Specialisation: Children, international child law and matrimonial finance. 35 reported cases include Glaser v UK [European Court of Human Rights] [2001] 1 FLR 153; B v UK [European Court of Human Rights] [2000] 1 FLR 1; Re L (Abduction: European Convention: Access) [1999] 2 FLR 1089. Represented the American father in the internet twins case.
Prof. Memberships: FLBA; IBA; chair: Bar Committee on the rights of the child.
Career: Barrister, called 1985, LLB, Therapist (systemic and psychodynamic).
Publications: 'International Child Abduction' (Sweet & Maxwell); 'International Adoption' (Sweet & Maxwell); 'International Conventions Affecting Children' (Jordan); 'Children and Immigration' (Cavendish).
Personal: TV, radio and newspaper contributor. Education: London School of Economics, Asser Institute of International Law, the Hague, London Centre for Psychotherapy.

ROTH, Peter M QC
Monckton Chambers (Kenneth Parker QC & Paul Lasok QC), London
(020) 7405 7211
chambers@monckton.com
Recommended in Competition/European Law
Specialisation: Public law (eg R v Chief Constable of Sussex ex p International Trader's Ferry [1998] (HL: export of livestock)). Competition law (eg Napp Pharmaceuticals v Director General of Fair Trading (2002) (Competition Act). MD Foods v Baines [1997] (HL: RTPA). EC law (eg White v White (HL: insurance directives). Case C-219/98 Anastasiou. Agriculture (eg Case C-304/00 Strawson v Gagg). Commercial litigation and ADR. Professional negligence (eg Hemmens v Wilson Browne).
Career: Publications: General Editor, 'Bellamy & Child's European Community Law of Competition' (5th ed.).
Personal: MA (Oxon), LLM. Called to the Bar, 1976. QC, 1997. Recorder, 2000. Harmsworth Scholar, Middle Temple. Visiting associate professor, University of Pennsylvania Law School, 1987. Vice-Chairman, Competition Law Association.

ROWE, Judith
One Garden Court Family Law Chambers (Eleanor F Platt QC & Alison Ball QC), London
(020) 7797 7900
jrowe@onegardencourt.co.uk
Recommended in Family
Specialisation: The law relating to children. This includes public and private law aspects of the Children Act, adoption, child abduction and children cases with an international element; related human rights issues.
Prof. Memberships: FLBA.
Career: Called to the Bar in 1979. Moved to One Garden Court in 1996 to specialise wholly in family law. Appointed Assistant Recorder, 1999. Recorder 2000. Elected to the Bar Council 1999 and again in 2002 where presently member of the Law Reform Committee and Policy Advisory Group.
Personal: Born 7 August 1957. Educated at Rednock School, Gloucestershire. University College London (LLB Hons 1978). Lives in London. Married with two young children.

ROWELL, David
9 Stone Buildings (Michael Ashe QC), London
(020) 7404 5055
clerks@9stonebuildings.com
Recommended in Chancery
Specialisation: Chancery and personal taxation, especially capital taxes, trusts, land law, charities and landlord and tenant. Cases include Hambro v Duke of Marlborough (the management of Blenheim Palace); Challock Parish Council v Shirley (land valuation); Rabin v Gerson Berger (Trusts); Re Box Hill Common (common land); Re Evans deceased (claims against estates).
Prof. Memberships: Chancery Bar Association. Charity Law Association.
Career: Called 1972. Practised at 3 New Square, Lincoln's Inn 1973-2001. Joined 9 Stone Buildings in October 2001.
Publications: Law Pack's 'Last Will and Testament'.
Personal: New College Oxford BA (First Class Honours).

ROWLAND, John QC
4 Pump Court, London
(020) 7842 5555
jrowland@4pumpcourt.com
Recommended in Insurance
Specialisation: Principal areas of practice are insurance and reinsurance disputes, professional negligence and general advisory work related to the insurance industry. Work has included close involvement in Lloyd's names litigation, policy disputes, broker's negligence and regulatory work. Other areas of practice include general commercial disputes including complex engineering projects and a number of major ICC Arbitrations, professional negligence involving claims against lawyers, accountants and brokers; gaming and casino licensing work and the provision of commercial law advice direct to overseas lawyers. Sits as an arbitrator.
Prof. Memberships: COMBAR.
Career: Called to the Bar in 1979 and joined 4 Pump Court in 1980. Took Silk in 1996. Admitted to practice in New South Wales and Victoria.

ROWLAND, Robin
No5 Chambers (Gareth Evans QC), Birmingham
(0121) 606 0500
Recommended in Family

ROWLANDS, Marc
Keating Chambers, London
(020) 7544 2600
mrowlands@keatingchambers.com
Recommended in Construction
Specialisation: Technology and construction cases, arbitration law and practice.
Prof. Memberships: ORBA, COMBAR.
Career: Magdalen, Oxford (Law).

ROWLANDS, Peter
18 Red Lion Court (Anthony Arlidge QC), London
(020) 7520 6000
peter.rowlands@18rlc.co.uk
Recommended in Crime
Specialisation: Major drugs and fraud cases, murder and serious crime. Specialises in criminal defence work.
Prof. Memberships: CBA, Justice.
Career: Solicitor 1984-89. Barrister 1990 to date. Moved to 18 Red Lion Court in 1999.

ROWLEY, James
28 St John St, Manchester
(0161) 834 8418
clerk@28stjohnst.co.uk
Recommended in Clinical Negligence, Personal Injury
Specialisation: Personal injuries and clinical negligence together with Inquiries involving a medical content. Cases of maximum severity: Brain injury (Jebson v MOD [2000] 1 WLR 2055; Cargill v PR Excavations, apil vol 10 issue two, May 2000, QBD). Spinal injury (Craven v John Riches et al and Knockhill Racing Circuit, CA Transcript and Lawtel 5 March 2001). Amputee cases at all levels (McFarlane v Clifford Smith and Buchanan, current law May 2000 189, QBD). Psychiatric injury including PTSD (Monk Wearmouth mining disaster; British Airways wind shield blow-out; Veterans' Groups 1 and 2 v MOD - ongoing). Obstetric and neonatal mismanagement (Swift v South Manchester Health Authority - QBD 9.2000 unrep.) Experienced in cases involving: delay in diagnosis of cancers (especially breast and colon), meningitis, subarachnoid haemorrhage, aortic aneurysm, ectopic pregnancy and slipped femoral epiphysis. Cardiac disease. Minimally-invasive surgery; ERCP including torn oesophagus. Gastro-enterological and colo-rectal disease; acute pancreatitis; hepatobiliary tract disease. Radiation enteritis.
Prof. Memberships: Co-opted member of Bar Council CFA Panel and Personal Injuries' Bar Association Executive Committee.
Career: MA (Classics) Cantab; Dip. Law. Stonyhurst and Emmanuel. Hardwicke Scholar of Lincoln's Inn. Called 1987. Regional Treasury Counsel. Counsel to the Royal Liverpool Children's Inquiry (Redfern Report into organ retention at Alder Hey Hospital). Lectured widely in PI.
Personal: Married with three children. Armchair sportsman, gardener and cook.

ROYCE, John QC
Guildhall Chambers (Adrian Palmer QC), Bristol
(0117) 930 9000
Recommended in Crime
Specialisation: Serious crime; commercial fraud; personal injuries. Cryptosporidiosis litigation against Thames Water and Yorkshire Water. Lead contaminated cattle feed group action for NFU. Public inquiries. Counsel to inquiry into Ashworth High Security Hospital.
Prof. Memberships: Criminal Bar Association; Personal Injury Bar Association; Sports Law Bar Association.
Career: QC 1987; Recorder 1986; Deputy High Court Judge QBD 1993.
Personal: Austrian qualified ski instructor.

RUBIN, Stephen QC
Fountain Court (Anthony Boswood QC), London
(020) 7583 3335
sr@fountaincourt.co.uk
Recommended in Commercial (Litigation)
Specialisation: General commercial litigation particularly civil fraud, banker/customer disputes, foreign exchange, business disputes and professional negligence. Recent reported cases: First American v Sheikh Zayad Al Nahayan [1999] 1 WLR 1154, Den Norske Bank v Antonatos [1999] QB 271, Pharaon v BCCI [1998] 4 All ER 455, BOC plc v Centeon Inc [1991] 1 All

LEADERS AT THE BAR

ER (Comm) 970, Finance for Mortgage v Farley & Co [1998] 2 PNLR 145. Vangelis v Sealart Ltd [2002]; IPC v Middlesborough F.C. [2002]; Sequin v UBS A.G. [2002].
Prof. Memberships: London Common Law and Commercial Bar Association (Committee); Professional Negligence Bar Association.
Career: Called to Bar 1977; QC 2000; Professional Conduct and Complaints Committee of Bar 1995-99.
Personal: Merchant Taylor's School, Northwood; Exhibition Brasenose College, Oxford - MA Jurisprudence; Married with four children.

RUCK, Mary
Peel Court Chambers (Michael Shorrock QC), Manchester
(0161) 832 3791
clerks@peelcourt.co.uk
Recommended in Clinical Negligence
Specialisation: Medical law including clinical negligence; disease claims and heath and safety at work claims; personal injuries; mental health. She has experience of severe brain injury claims, birth injuries and claims involving injuries of maximum severity.
Prof. Memberships: PIBA; APIL; AVMA; PNBA; Northern Circuit Medical Law Association.
Career: BA (Hons) (Wales); MA (London) Medical Law and Ethics. Called to the Bar 1993 (Gray's Inn).
Publications: Editor, Fatal Accidents Section of Butterworths 'Personal Injury Litigation Service'.

RUMFITT, Nigel QC
7 Bedford Row (David Farrer QC), London
(020) 7242 3555
Recommended in Crime
Specialisation: Crime of all types, prosecuting and defending. Extensive experience of medical issues (Junior, Beverley Allitt case). R v Manning - murder/child neglect of Anna Climbie - CCC (Galbraith Branley). R v Sutherland - Conspiracy to murder - Execute. Leading case re police cells being bugged (Bird & Co.). R v Dias (CCA) - Leading authority on death by administering drugs (F Jones & Harley). Since taking Silk has done a number of high profile cases. Successfully defended Ruth Neave, helped expose police/Home Office malpractice in R v Robinson & Ors at Leicester (Yardie case). Prosecuted Bedford Hotel murder and Celia Beckett (child poisoner).
Career: Educated at Leeds Modern School; Pembroke College, Oxford; Northwestern University School of Law, Chicago Illinois. MA (Oxon) in Jurisprudence; BCL (Oxon); 2:2 in Bar Finals; Harmsworth Law Scholar (Middle Temple). Called to Bar (Middle Temple) 1974. Assistant Recorder 1991, Recorder 1995. Chambers of D. Draycott QC, 1 Essex Court 1975-88. Present chambers 1988 to date. QC 1994.
Personal: Born 6 March 1950, Leeds. Married. Interests include skiing,

windsurfing and sailing. Speaks fluent French and has studied French law, holds consultations in French without interpreter.

RUSHBROOKE, Justin
5 Raymond Buildings (Patrick Milmo QC), London
(020) 7242 2902
clerks@5rb.co.uk
Recommended in Defamation
Specialisation: Defamation including Internet libel; entertainment and media law, including copyright, passing off, trademarks, data protection, privacy and confidence, contempt; general chancery and commercial litigation. Recent cases include: McManus v Beckham (July 2002) (CA) - acting for Mrs Beckham in slander action brought by shopowner; Appleton v Elle (July 2002) - acted for Nicole Appleton and Liam Gallagher in privacy claim against magazine; Burstein v Times Newspapers Ltd. [2001] 1WLR 579 (CA); Berezovsky v Forbes [2000] 1WLR 1004 (HL); Takenaka v Frankl Oct. 2000 (QB) - first ever 'anonymous' email libel trial; Beckham v Niblett etc 2000/2001 (Ch.D.) - privacy claim for Beckhams against former bodyguard; Godfrey v Demon [2001] 1QB 201; Loveless v Earl [1999] EMLR 53; Aitken v Pressdram [1997] EMLR 415 (CA); Botham v Khan, The Times, 15 July 1996 (CA); Attorney General v Newspaper Publishing [1997] 1 WLR 926 (CCA); Re: Austintel [1997] 1WLR 616 (CA).
Career: MA (Oxon). Worked for Morgan Grenfell & Co Ltd, 1986-88.

RUSSELL, Christina
9-12 Bell Yard (D Anthony Evans QC), London
(020) 7400 1800
Recommended in Fraud

RUSSELL, Christopher
2 Temple Gardens
(Dermod O'Brien QC), London
(020) 7822 1200
crussell@2templegardens.co.uk
Recommended in Personal Injury, Professional Negligence
Specialisation: Professional negligence with an emphasis on valuers', surveyors' and clinical negligence. Personal injury, in particular industrial diseases and stress and other claims for psychiatric injury. Health and safety. General insurance, common law and procedural matters. Cases include Wentworth v Wiltshire CC [1993], BBL v Eagle Star [1993], Lancashire CC v Municipal Mutual [1997], Burns v General Accident [1999], Farrell v Avon HA [2001].
Career: LLB (Exeter). Called 1982. PNBA; LCLCBA; PIBA.

RUSSELL, Jeremy QC
4 Essex Court (Nigel Teare QC), London
(020) 7653 5653
jjr@4sx.co.uk
Recommended in Arbitration, Shipping
Specialisation: Specialist in shipping law and international trade. Practice covers shipping, admiralty, insurance

(marine and non-marine), sale and carriage of goods (domestic and international). Also handles commercial arbitrations both as advocate and occasionally as arbitrator. Has addressed a number of conferences in London and Singapore on shipping matters.
Prof. Memberships: COMBAR; London Common Law and Commercial Bar Association; London Maritime Arbitrators Association (supporting member); LCIA (member); FSALS.
Career: Called to the Bar 1975. Joined present chambers 1977. Took Silk 1994. Appointed to panel of Lloyd's Salvage Arbitrators 2000. CEDR accredited mediator.

RUSSEN, Jonathan
Maitland Chambers (Michael Lyndon-Stanford QC & Charles Aldous QC), London
(020) 7406 1200
jrussen@maitlandchambers.com
Recommended in Chancery
Specialisation: Commercial litigation; contractual disputes; insolvency (corporate and personal); bankruptcy; directors' disqualification; shareholders' disputes; partnership and property.
Prof. Memberships: Chancery Bar Association. COMBAR.
Career: University of Wales LLB (1st Class Hons.) 1984. University of Cambridge LLM 1985. Called to Bar (Lincoln's Inn) 1986.
Publications: Contributor to Butterworth's 'Practical Insolvency'.
Personal: Married with 2 children.

RUTTLE, Stephen QC
Brick Court Chambers (Christopher Clarke QC), London
(020) 7379 3550
ruttle@brickcourt.co.uk
Recommended in ADR, Insurance
Specialisation: (i) ADR Specialist Commercial Mediator. CEDR accredited and registered mediator 1998. Has acted as mediator in over 80 commercial disputes since February 1999. Most disputes initially from fields in (ii) below; but range of mediation work now increasingly varied. (ii) Reinsurance, insurance and Lloyds. Also shipping, commodities, general commercial and professional negligence. Co-author of Insurance Brokers section in 'Professional Negligence and Liability', LLP 12/2000 publication date. Member of CEDR, Mediation UK (Community mediation); on the mediation panels of various mediation service providers; involved in insurance and reinsurance market initiatives.
Prof. Memberships: Member: British Insurance Law Association: LMAA; Lloyds Arbitrator Tier 1 and Tier 2.
Career: Called to Bar 1976, Gray's Inn. Pupillage with Sir Nicholas Lyell QC MP. Practised at Brick Court Chambers since 1976. Queen's Counsel 1997.
Personal: Educated Westminster School (Queen's Scholar) and Queens' College, Cambridge (Exhibitioner). BA Honours Degree in English/Law. Lecturer at

numerous insurance and reinsurance seminars.

RYDER, John QC
6 King's Bench Walk (Roy Amlot QC), London
(020) 7583 0410
Recommended in Crime

RYDER, Matthew
Matrix Chambers, London
(020) 7404 3447
Recommended in Crime, Human Rights
Specialisation: All areas of serious criminal work including fraud and political crime, and the interface between civil and criminal work such as judicial review, civil actions against the police, human rights, regulatory work, forfeiture and confiscation. Regular contributor to several publications involving police and the law. Notable cases include Lynch v DPP (human rights challenge to reverse burdens in criminal cases); R v Regan and others (defence of SFO prosecution of alleged bribes); R v Macdonald and others (alleged offences under the Terrorism Act 2000 in foreign jurisdictions; Abraham v Commissioner of Police for the Metropolis (whether acceptance of police is a bar to civil proceedings); R (Farrakhan) v Secretary of State for the Home Department (human rights challenge to exclusion order as a bar to free speech); DPP v Todd (judicial review of prosecution or roads protestors); R v CPS ex p Hitchens (judicial review of decision not to prosecute after inquest); Lawrence v Commissioner of Police for the Metropolis (civil claim by parents of murdered teenager, Stephen Lawrence).
Career: Called to Bar 1992. Recently conducted extensive research into human rights at Columbia University, New York. Called to New York Bar 1999.
Personal: Graduated from Emmanuel College, Cambridge, 1989.

RYDER TD, Ernest QC
Deans Court Chambers (Stephen Grime QC), Manchester
(0161) 214 6000
ryder@deanscourt.co.uk
Recommended in Family
Specialisation: Family, public and administrative law; providing a specialist service in matrimonial finance and all disputes relating to children, public authorities, health care, professional negligence and ethics. Private and public tribunal work.
Prof. Memberships: Chairman: Manchester region. FLBA. PIBA. Child Concern. NYAS (Professional Advisory Group). ALC.
Career: MA (Cantab). Call 1981 Gray's Inn. Assistant Recorder 1996. QC 1997. Counsel to the Tribunal (North Wales) 1996-98. Recorder 2000. Deputy High Court Judge 2001.
Publications: Editor: Clarke Hall and Morrison on Children (Butterworths).
Personal: TA Commission 1982. TD 1996.

LEADERS AT THE BAR

SADIQ, Tariq
9 St. John Street (John Hand QC), Manchester
(0161) 955 9000
clerks@9stjohnstreet.co.uk
Recommended in Employment
Specialisation: Employment law and discrimination law. Junior Counsel to the Crown (Provincial Panel) and regularly instructed in cases for Ministry of Defence, the Lord Chancellor's Department and the Prison Service. Approved by the Commission for Racial Equality, the Equal Opportunities Commission and the Disability Rights Commission to act in discrimination cases. His employment law work includes unfair dismissal, redundancy (individual and collective), transfer of undertakings and restraint of trade. He has a substantial practice in all areas of discrimination law, with particular expertise in complex discrimination cases. Acts for both applicants and respondents.
Prof. Memberships: Employment Lawyers Association, Employment Law Bar Association (Committee Member), Race Relations Committee of the Bar Council (Committee Member), Industrial Law Society, NCFRAS.
Career: Called to the Bar in 1993 (Gray's Inn). Awarded Gray's Inn Scholarship. Appointed Junior Counsel to the Crown (Provincial Panel) in 1999.
Personal: Enjoys cricket, football and walking.

SAGGERSON, Alan
No. 1 Serjeants' Inn
(Edward Faulks QC), London
(020) 7415 6666
clerks@no1serjeantsinn.com
Recommended in Consumer Law
Specialisation: Main areas of practice: all aspects of travel and personal injury litigation - with particular emphasis in the package travel industry, foreign accidents (including health and food safety) and international travel conventions. Highlights of the last year include several group actions arising out of travel and natural disasters, food poisoning; swimming pool and leisure facility safety.
Significant cases in the last year have included: Mawdsley v Cosmosair plc [May 2002, CA - causation of injury in breach of holiday contract]; Horan v Neilson Holidays Ltd [aircraft seat pitches and tour operator's liability]; Donoghue v Folkstone Properties Ltd [QBD, occupier's liability for underwater hazards]; and Watson v First Choice Holidays and Aparta Hotels Caledonia SA [The Jurisdiction Regulation - European Court of Justice]. Other important recent cases include: Hulse v Chambers and Hamill v Hamill [Private International Law Act1995]; Hone v Going Places Leisure Travel [QBD]; Logue v First Choice Holidays Ltd [Package Travel Regulations 1992]; Codd v Thomson Tour Operators Ltd Brannan v Airtours Holidays Limited and Williams v Travel Promotions [CA - Package Travel Regulations 1992]; Brannan v Airtours Holidays Limited and Williams v Travel Promotions [CA - tour operators' contractual liability for compliance with local standards]. Regular speaker on travel law to consumers and the industry and various accredited training providers.
Prof. Memberships: Chairman of the Travel and tourism Lawyers Association. Member of PIBA and PNBA. Lincoln's Inn continuing education teams in advocacy and ethics.
Career: Called to the Bar in 1981.
Publications: Author: Travel Law & Litigation (2nd Edition 2000 CLT Professional Publishing). Editor: 'Personal Injury Quarterly' (1996 to date).
Personal: Educated: Hertford College, Oxford (MA Jurisprudence; BCL). Born 1956. Resides, London.

SAINI, Pushpinder
Blackstone Chambers (Presiley Baxendale QC & Charles Flint QC), London
(020) 7583 1770
clerks@blackstonechambers.com
Recommended in Administrative & Public Law, Media & Entertainment
Specialisation: Commercial law (including copyright and entertainment law) public law (including human rights). Cases include George Michael v Sony; A&M Records v VCI Ltd; ZYX Music v King; Wailer v Island Records; R v Radio Authority ex p Guardian Media Group; Tony Bland, Banks v CBS; R v Secretary of State ex p O'Dhiuibir; A-G v Blake; Lisa Stansfield v Sovereign; R v Secretary of State ex p RP Scherer; R v Secretary of State ex p Monsanto; Reynolds v Times newspapers; Walmsley v Acid Jazz; R v DG Telecoms ex p Mercury; Ludlow Music v Robbie Williams; Charlotte Church v Shalit.
Prof. Memberships: JUSTICE, ELA, ALBA, BEG
Career: Called to the Bar 1991.
Publications: Co-author, 'Halsbury's Laws, European Convention on Human Rights' and Lester & Pannick, 'Human Rights Law and Practice'.
Personal: Educated at Corpus Christi College, Oxford (BA and BCL, both 1st Class) Atkin Scholar of Gray's Inn.
Languages: Punjabi, Hindi, French, Urdu.

SALLON, Christopher QC
Doughty Street Chambers (Geoffrey Robertson QC), London
(020) 7404 1313
Recommended in Crime

SALTER, Richard QC
3 Verulam Buildings (Christopher Symons QC & John Jarvis QC), London
(020) 7831 8441
chambers@3vb.com
Recommended in Banking & Finance
Specialisation: Principal areas of practice are banking, commercial law, financial services, insolvency, insurance, professional negligence and building. Clients include most major UK and international banks.
Prof. Memberships: London Common Law and Commercial Bar Association, COMBAR, TECBAR, Chartered Institute of Arbitrators.
Career: Called to the Bar 1975. Tenant at Hare Court, 1977-82, then joined current chambers. Bencher of the Inner Temple 1991. Member of the Council of Legal Education 1990-96. Chairman of the Board of Examiners, Bar Vocational Course, 1992-93. Governor of the Inns of Court School of Law 1996-. Took Silk in 1995. Recorder 2000- (Assistant Recorder 1997-2000).
Publications: Contributor to 'Banks - Liability and Risk' (3rd ed 2001) and 'Banks and Remedies' (2nd ed 1999) for Lloyd's of London Press; and to Vol. 20 'Halsbury's Laws' (4th ed 1993 - Re-issue 'Guarantees'). Consulting editor, All England Commercial Cases 1999-. Legislation editor, Encyclopedia of Insurance Law 1999-. Editor, 'Legal Decisions Affecting Bankers', vols 12-4 (2001).
Lectures frequently on banking and other commercial law topics.
Personal: Educated at Harrow County School for Boys 1963-70, Balliol College, Oxford 1970-73 and Inns of Court School of Law 1973-75. Chairman, Shoscombe Village Cricket Club.

SALZEDO, Simon
Brick Court Chambers (Christopher Clarke QC), London
(020) 7379 3550
salzedo@brickcourt.co.uk
Recommended in Commercial (Litigation)
Specialisation: Commercial litigation (Zockoll v Mercury [1998] FSR 354); professional negligence (Matrix Securities v Theodore Goddard [1998] PNLR 290, Perry v Moysey [1998] PNLR 657, George Barkes v LFC [2000] PNLR 21, Stewart v Engel & BDO Stoy Hayward [2000] 1 WLR 2268); financial services (Equitable Life v Hyman [2000] 3 WLR 529); insurance and reinsurance (The Travel Insurance Litigation [2002] CLC 41); banking, shipping (The Zeus V [1999] 1 Lloyd's Rep 703), arbitration.
Prof. Memberships: Institute of Chartered Accountants of England and Wales; Junior Counsel to the Crown (C Panel).
Career: 1990 BA (Oxon) (top PPE first in year); 1990-93 Price Waterhouse; 1994 DipLaw (City); 1995 Eldon Scholarship; 1996 Brick Court Chambers.
Publications: 'Conflicts of Interest and Chinese Walls', Sweet & Maxwell, 2000; 'Guide to the Arbitration Act 1996', Cavendish Publishing, 1996; 'Briefcase on Contract Law', Cavendish Publishing, 3rd ed. 1999.

SANDER, Andrew
Oriel Chambers (Andrew Sander), Liverpool
(0151) 236 7191/ 236 4321
Recommended in Family

SANDERS, Neil
29 Bedford Row Chambers (Nicholas Francis QC), London
(020) 7404 1044
nsanders@29bedfordrow.co.uk
Recommended in Family
Specialisation: Principal area of practice encompasses all areas of matrimonial finance and the law relating to children including child abduction cases. Other main areas of practice cover work relating to the Inheritance (Provision for Family and Dependents) Act 1975.
Prof. Memberships: Family Law Bar Association.
Career: Called to the Bar 1975 and joined present chambers in 1976.
Personal: Educated at Fettes College, Edinburgh 1966-71, Pembroke College, Cambridge 1971-74 and the College of Law 1974-75. Leisure pursuits include tennis, sailing, skiing, music and theatre. Born 17th April 1953. Lives in London.

SANDS, Philippe
Matrix Chambers, London
(020) 7404 3447
Recommended in Environment, Public International Law
Specialisation: Barrister specialising in litigation and advisory work for governments, international organisations, corporations and individuals on public international law (including ICJ and Arbitration), EU law, environmental law. Cases include R v Secretary of State ex p (High Court) Hungary/Slovakia (International Court of Justice); Greenpeace and others v European Commission (ECJ); Tradex v Republic of Albania (International Centre for the Settlement of Investment Disputes - arbitration); Ireland v UK (International Tribunal for the Law of the Sea); Swissbourgh Diamond Mines v World Bank (World Bank Inspection Panel); numerous intergovernmental negotiations and consultancies (UN, EC, World Bank, Asia Development Bank).
Career: Qualified 1985, Professor of international law at the University of London (SOAS); global professor of law. New York University.

SAUNDERS, John QC
4 Fountain Court (John Saunders QC), Birmingham
(0121) 236 3476
Recommended in Crime, Licensing

SAUNDERS, Neil
3 Raymond Buildings (Clive Nicholls QC), London
(020) 7400 6400
chambers@3raymondbuildings.com
Recommended in Crime
Specialisation: General crime - prosecuting and defending in all criminal courts. Leading and junior work includes murder, manslaughter (R v Hardy - defence for rugby player), robbery, serious assault, sexual offences including children and video evidence, drugs cases and confiscation hearings, police corruption (Donald & Cressey). Appeared in Divisional Court in cases

LEADERS AT THE BAR

involving drink driving legislation and custody time limits. Serious fraud and commercial crime (including defence of His Honour Judge Gee). Instructed by defence in SFO case involving directors of Wickes. Police Disciplinary Tribunals. Licensing appearances involving liquor, public entertainment, betting and gaming at first instance and on appeal.
Prof. Memberships: Bar Council, Criminal Bar Association.
Career: BA (Hons) Law 1982; called to the Bar 1983. Govenor ICSL 1999-.

SAUNDERS, Nicholas
199 Strand (David Phillips QC), London
(020) 7520 4000
nicholasjsaunders@hotmail.com
Recommended in Shipping
Specialisation: Shipping law: practice covers all aspects of wet and dry work. Aviation law: practice covers all aspects, including air accidents, pilot/aircrew negligence, aviation insurance, carriage of goods by air, and licensing. General commercial work also undertaken, including international trade and insurance.
Prof. Memberships: COMBAR.
Career: Former RAF pilot. Joined present Chambers 2001.
Personal: Educated at Radley College 1967-72, Hull University LL.B (1987) and Cambridge University LL.M (1988). Governor of Woodleigh Preparatory School, Malton, N.Yorks. Leisure pursuits include shooting, fly fishing and golf. Born 20 July 1954. Lives in Cambridgeshire.

SAUVAIN, Stephen QC
40 King St, Manchester
(0161) 832 9082
ssauvain@40kingstreet.co.uk
Recommended in Planning
Specialisation: Town planning, compulsory purchase and compensation, highways, housing and commercial development, local government and finance, education law, rating, judicial review, minerals, landfill. Recent reported cases include: R v Secretary of State for the Environment, Transport and the Regions ex p, Trustees of the Friends of the Lake District 17 April 2001 TLR.
Prof. Memberships: Northern Circuit, Planning and Environment Bar Association, UKELA, European Bar Group.
Career: Called 1977. Queen's Counsel 1995. Appointed Assistant Boundary Commissioner 2000.
Publications: Editor 'Encyclopedia of Highway Law and Practice'. Author of Sauvain's 'Highway Law'.

SAVILL, Mark
Deans Court Chambers (Stephen Grime QC), Manchester
(0161) 214 6000
savill@deanscourt.co.uk
Recommended in Crime
Specialisation: Specialises in all areas of criminal law.

Prof. Memberships: Criminal Bar Association.
Career: Called to the Bar - November 1993 (Inner Temple).
Personal: Born 17 May 1969. Educated at Eton College and Durham University BA (Hons). Interests include sport and cooking.

SAYER, Peter
Gough Square Chambers (Fred Philpott), London
(020) 7353 0924
Recommended in Consumer Law
Specialisation: Consumer Law - consumer credit, credit and charge cards, trades descriptions and fair trading. Also Financial Services Act work and fraud (criminal and civil). Clients include banks, finance houses, card issuers and retailers. Has written 'Credit Cards and the Law' (Fourmat) and articles in legal journals.
Career: Called to the Bar 1975. Formerly in-house Counsel to Access, the Joint Credit Card Company Ltd and American Express Europe Ltd. Part-time Legal Panel Member of the Appeals Service.
Personal: Christ's College, Cambridge. Lives in London and Cornwall.

SAYERS, Michael QC
2 King's Bench Walk, London
(020) 7353 1746
Recommended in Crime

SCANNELL, Rick
Two Garden Court (Owen Davies QC & Courtenay Griffiths QC), London
(020) 7353 1633
Recommended in Immigration
Specialisation: All immigration, refugee and related human rights work at all levels. In 1998 he was appointed a special advocate by the Attorney General representing the interests of appellants in national security cases before the Special Immigration Appeals Commission. In the last three years he has taken work as a 'leading' junior. Major cases include: M v Home Office [1994] (HL) (Home Secretary in contempt); T v Secretary of State for the Home Department [1996] (HL) (exclusion); SSHD v Savchenkov [1996] (CA) (particular social group); Jain v SSHD [2000] (CA) (leading) (homosexuals as particular social group); TI v United Kingdom [2000] (ECHR) (Article 3 ECHR); Sepet and Bulbul v SSHD [2001] Imm AR (CA) (conscientious objection); Saad, Diriye and Osorio v SSHD [2002] (CA) (leading) (scope of refugee appeals) and challenges to detention of asylum seekers at 'Oakington Reception Centre' (leading in Administrative Court and Court of Appeal) (Saadi and others v SSHD) [2001 and 2002] (Article 5 ECHR).
Prof. Memberships: ILPA (Chair since 2000); ALBA.
Publications: Editor Butterworth's Immigration Law Service; co-author 'Immigration - recent developments in Legal Action' (since 1985); contributor 'Macdonald's Immigration Law and Practice' (2001).

SCHAFF, Alistair QC
7 King's Bench Walk (Gavin Kealey QC & Julian Flaux QC), London
(020) 7910 8300
clerks@7kbw.law.co.uk
Recommended in Arbitration, Insurance, Shipping
Specialisation: All aspects of international commercial law: specifically, conflict of laws/ jurisdiction disputes, shipping, insurance (marine and non-marine), reinsurance, banking, international sale of goods, oil disputes, professional and commercial negligence. Leading cases: "The Maciej Rataj" [1999] 2 WLR 181 (ECJ; Art.21&22 of Brussels Convention); Effort v Linden [1998] AC 605 (HL; dangerous goods); Royal Boskalis v Mountain [1999] QB. 674 (CA; illegality and marine insurance); MacFarlane / Hegarty v Caledonia [1994] 1 LLR 16; [1997] 2 LLR 259 (CA; Piper Alpha/negligence); Huyton v Peter Cremer [1999] 1 LLR 620 (sale of goods/economic duress); Kingscroft v Nissan [1999] LRLR 603 (reinsurance of Weaver pool); Glencore v Metro [2001] 1 LLR 283 (conflicts of laws and title to oil in M East); Jan de Nul v Royale Belge [2002] 1 LLR 583 (liability insurance).
Career: Called to the Bar 1983; Queen's Counsel 1999.
Personal: Born 1959. MA (Cantab).

SCHOLZ, Karl
Nicholas Street Chambers (Robert Trevor-Jones), Chester
(01244) 323886
Recommended in Consumer Law

SCOBIE, James
Two Garden Court (Owen Davies QC & Courtenay Griffiths QC), London
(020) 7353 1633
Recommended in Crime
Specialisation: Specialist in all areas of criminal law. Exclusively defence work. Acted in high profile cases including offences of murder, attempted murder, sexual offences and cases involving the supplying and/ or importation of drugs on a large scale. Leading Junior in large scale armed robbery conspiracies, multi-million diversion fraud, VAT fraud involving 'outsourcing', multi-handed conspiracy to supply class A drugs and a trial involving the systematic torture of a mentally vulnerable family by a number of youths in a tower block flat.
Career: Educated at Eton College 1974-78. Exeter University 1979-81. Dip Law City University 1982. Called 1984.
Personal: Secretary Old Etonian Football Club. Interested in playing and watching all sports, especially football and cricket. MCC member since 1979.

SCOLDING, Fiona
Hardwicke Building (Nicholas Stewart QC), London
(020) 7242 2523
Recommended in Education

SCOTT, Ian
Old Square Chambers (John Hendy QC), London
(020) 7269 0329
scott@oldsquarechambers.co.uk
Recommended in Employment
Specialisation: Discrimination, in particular disability discrimination and whistleblowing. Also specialising in labour law including recognition. Further interest in local government employment issues. Recent cases: Post Office v Howell [2000] IRLR 224; [2000] ICR 913 Employment Appeal Tribunal; Care First Partnership Ltd v Roffey [2001] IRLR 65; [2001] ICR 87 Court of Appeal (November 2000).
Prof. Memberships: Employment Law Bar Association; Industrial Law Society; Employment Lawyers Association.
Career: Prior to being called to the Bar in October 1991, had been employed by a major trade union as a research and press officer and negotiator. Also held position of elected councillor in a London Borough.
Personal: BA Hons Economics, Newcastle-upon-Tyne University; MSC Industrial Relations, London School of Economics. Enjoys sport. Member of Wimbledon Squash Club.

SCOTT, Timothy QC
29 Bedford Row Chambers (Nicholas Francis QC), London
(020) 7404 1044
tscott@29bedfordrow.co.uk
Recommended in Family
Specialisation: Principal area of practice is family law. Works in all areas, including ancillary relief, child abduction, private and public law children's cases. Involved in a large amount of international work including jurisdictional disputes, recognition of foreign decrees and transnational enforcement. Other main area of practice is solicitors' negligence, both arising out of family law matters and generally. Clients include leading Family Law solicitors firms in and outside London. Contributor of articles to Family Law magazine and of chapter on matrimonial law in 'International Tracing of Assets' (FT Law & Tax 1997). Regular speaker at seminars on various family law topics.
Prof. Memberships: Family Law Bar Association; Professional Negligence Bar Association.
Career: Called to the Bar in 1975 and joined present Chambers in 1976. Appointed QC and Assistant Recorder in 1995. Appointed recorder in 1999.
Personal: Queen's Scholar, Westminster School 1962-66, Open Exhibitioner New College, Oxford 1967-70. Born 19 July 1949. Lives in London.

SCOTT-MANDERSON, Marcus
4 Paper Buildings (Lionel Swift QC), London
(020) 7583 0816
clerks@4pb.com
Recommended in Family
Specialisation: International child

abduction, International child law, human rights - child cases. Important cases: Venables v News Group Newspapers Ltd [2001] 1 WLR 1038; Re M&J (abduction: International Judicial Collaboration) [2000] FLR 803; Re P (a child) (mirror orders) [2000] 1 FLR 350; Re JS (Private International Adoption) [2000] 2 FLR 638; Re H (abduction: acquiescence) [1998] AC 72 (HL).
Prof. Memberships: Trustee for REUNITE, International Child Abduction Centre, member of its Legal Working Group; member of British Academy of Forensic Sciences; Family Law Bar Association
Career: Harrow School (1969-74); Christ Church Oxford (1975-79), Boulter Exhibition in Law, BCL, MA; Hague Academy of International Law in the Netherlands, Dana Fellowship (1980); Glasgow University (Dept of Forensic Medicine); Inns of Court School of Law; Ver Heyden de Lancey Prize in Forensic Medicine; called Lincoln's Inn 1980, Hardwicke Scholarship, Droop Scholarship.
Publications: Contributor to Butterworths 'Essential Family Practice' 2002.
Personal: Born 1956. Town of residence: London. Clubs: Lansdowne Club.

SCRIVENER, Anthony QC
2-3 Gray's Inn Square (Anthony Porten QC & Anthony Scrivener QC), London
(020) 7242 4986
chambers@2-3graysinnsquare.co.uk
Recommended in Consumer Law, Crime, Health & Safety
Specialisation: Administrative and public law, consumer law, health and safety, crime, serious fraud, civil liberties, environmental law, personal injury, local government and City regulatory, monopolies work and food law. Also specialises in appeal work (over 30 appearances in house of Lords). Has appeared in courts in Hong Kong, Malaysia, Singapore, Australia, Trinidad, Jamaica, British Virgin Islands as well as European Court of Justice. Also called to Bar in Jamaica and Tasmania.
Career: Practice 1961. Took Silk 1975. Chairman of the Bar 1991. Bencher of Lincoln's Inn. President of EFLA.
Personal: Leisure: walking, opera, chess.

SEABROOK, Robert QC
1 Crown Office Row
(Robert Seabrook QC), London
(020) 7797 7500
robert.seabrook@1cor.com
Recommended in Crime, Family
Specialisation: Extensive experience includes notably professional negligence (clinical, solicitors, surveyors, accountants), civil jury actions, matrimonial finance and property, commercial fraud and major crimes. Cases include Al Kandari v Brown [1987]; Smith v Bush [1990]; Baker v Kaye (1997); Kapkunde v Abbey National Building Society (1998); Professor Nicolaides (GMC) (1998) John Studd (GMC) 1996; Rodney Ledward (GMC); (1999) John Rogers (GMC) (2001); Lady Foster v H M Customs and Excise [1993]; Silcott v Metropolitan Police Commissioner [1996]; Waters v Metropolitan Police Commissioner (2000); Farah v Metropolitan Police Commissioner (1998); Henderson v Chief Constable of Cleveland (2001); Duane Brooks v Metropolitan Police Commissioner (2002); Grey v Roman Catholic Archbishop of Birmingham (2002); HRH The Prince of Wales (Royal Divorce) (1996); Tombolis [1991]; Flick [re-appeal 1995]; the Charing Cross Lynn Rogers murder case [1992].
Career: Called to Bar in 1964. Took silk in 1983. Recorder since 1985. Deputy High Court Judge since 1991. Leader of the South Eastern Circuit since 1989-92. Chairman of the Bar, 1994. Member of the Investigatory Powers Tribunal since 2000.
Personal: Educated at St Georges's College, Harare, Zimbabwe and University College, London (LLB). Member of the court of the University of Sussex 1988-93. Chairman of the Governors of Brighton College since 1998. Interests include travel, listening to music and wine. Lives in London and Brighton.

SEARS, David
4 Pump Court, London
(020) 7842 5555
dsears@4pumpcourt.com
Recommended in Construction
Specialisation: Building/civil engineering disputes and professional negligence - the latter including not only building professionals (engineers, quantity surveyors and architects) but also solicitors, accountants and surveyors.
Prof. Memberships: TECBAR, Professional Negligence Bar Association, London Common Law and Commercial Bar Association, COMBAR.
Career: 1979-83: Civil Servant - Ministry of Defence; 1984 to date in practice at Bar.
Personal: Education: Trinity College, Oxford (MA Oxon). Leisure interests: sailing, flying, motorcycling, travelling and being at home in the country. Family: married with two children.

SEDDON, Duran
Two Garden Court (Owen Davies QC & Courtenay Griffiths QC), London
(020) 7353 1633
Recommended in Immigration

SEED, Nigel QC
3 Paper Buildings (Michael Parroy QC), London
(020) 7583 8055
Recommended in Church

SEGAL, Oliver
Old Square Chambers (John Hendy QC), London
(020) 7269 0300
segal@oldsquarechambers.co.uk
Recommended in Employment
Specialisation: Employment; commercial agency; commercial sale of goods. Cases: RMT v LUL [1998] 1RLR 636, CA; BBC v Farnworth [1998] ICR 1116 EAT; Moore v Piretta PTA Ltd [1999] 1 ALL ER 174, H Ct; Newbold & Smith v Leicester City Council; [1999] ICR 1182, CA; Barrett McKenzie v Escada UK Ltd, 'The Times', May 15, 2001, H Ct.
Prof. Memberships: ELBA.
Career: Corpus Christi College, Oxford (1981-85). School Oriental & African Studies, University. London (1985-86). Called 1992, Middle Temple.
Personal: Expert bridge player and writer.

SEITLER, Jonathan
Wilberforce Chambers (Edward Nugee QC), London
(020) 7306 0102
Recommended in Professional Negligence, Property Litigation
Specialisation: Property litigation and associated professional negligence including landlord and tenant, bank securitisation and negligence claims against solicitors and valuers. Acts for both landlords and tenants, banks and their customers and, in professional negligence actions, plaintiffs and insurers.
Prof. Memberships: Professional Negligence Bar Association, COMBAR, Chancery Bar Association.
Career: Called to the Bar 1985
Publications: Co-author of 'Property Finance Negligence: Claims Against Solicitors and Valuers' (Sweet & Maxwell) and the looseleaf 'Commercial Property Disputes' (Sweet & Maxwell). Lectures widely both at conferences and in-house.
Personal: Educated Pembroke College, Oxford, City University (Dip. Law).

SELVARATNAM, Vasanti QC
Stone Chambers (Steven Gee QC), London
(020) 7440 6900
vasanti.selvaratnam@stonechambers.com
Recommended in Shipping
Specialisation: All aspects of international commercial and shipping law, including admiralty. Clients include the major P & I clubs, shipowners, charterers and salvors.
Prof. Memberships: COMBAR; European Bar Association; LMAA; BMLA.
Career: Called to the Bar 1983: joined current chambers (formerly located at Queen Elizabeth Building) in 1985. Recorder 2000. Queen's Counsel 2001.
Personal: Born 9 April 1961. Educated at St. Augustine's Priory, Ealing and King's College, London LL.B (Hons.) 1982, LL.M (1st) 1984.

SENDALL, Antony
Littleton Chambers (Michel Kallipetis QC), London
(020) 7797 8600
antony@sendall.co.uk
Recommended in Employment
Specialisation: Principal areas of practice are employment, all areas including wrongful/unfair dismissal, redundancy, transfer of undertakings, discrimination, equal pay, working time, restraint of trade, industrial disputes; sports law, mostly employment and disciplinary issues; professional indemnity; mostly solicitors and surveyors; commercial; all forms of commercial disputes, including interim injunctions and arbitrations.
Prof. Memberships: Employment Law Bar Association, Employment Lawyers Association, Industrial Law Society, Bar Sports Law Group, Professional Negligence Bar Association, London Commercial and Common Law Bar Association, chambers member of COMBAR.
Career: Called to the Bar 1984.
Personal: Born 1 July 1961. Educated: Cambridge University (Law: 1st Class Hons). Interests: photography, cooking, amateur dramatics, running.

SEPHTON, Craig QC
Deans Court Chambers (Stephen Grime QC), Manchester
(0161) 214 6000
sephton@deanscourt.co.uk
Recommended in Personal Injury
Specialisation: Personal injury (particularly catastrophic injuries and diseases); professional negligence (especially Solicitors' and Surveyors' negligence); technology and construction; commercial.
Prof. Memberships: Personal Injuries Bar Association (Treasurer); Professional Negligence Bar Association; Northern Circuit Commercial Bar Association.
Career: The Ecclesbourne School, Duffield; Lincoln College Oxford; Deans Court Chambers 1981-; Queens Counsel 2001; Recorder 2002.

SETRIGHT, Henry QC
Renaissance Chambers (Brian Patrick Jubb & Henry Setright QC), London
(020) 7404 1111
Recommended in Family

SEYS LLEWELLYN, Anthony
Farrar's Building (John Leighton Williams QC), London
(020) 7583 9241
asllewellyn@farrarsbuilding.co.uk
Recommended in Personal Injury
Specialisation: Practice in personal injury, clinical and professional negligence and inquiries. Also general common law and insurance. Not restricted to but predominantly engaged in heavy cases of severe injury or disability, for both claimants and insurers/authorities. Recent cases include Heil v Rankin 2000 (CA general increase in damages for personal injuries) and Ladbroke Grove Rail Inquiry 2000 (leading counsel for Thames Trains a principal party).
Prof. Memberships: PIBA; APIL; LCLCB.
Career: Called 1972. Joined chambers 1974. Appointed Recorder 1990.

LEADERS AT THE BAR

Personal: King's School, Chester 1957-67; Jesus College, Oxford 1967-71 (MA and BCL). Fluent in French; working knowledge of German. Assistant Boundary Commissioner. Leisure pursuits include music, sport and art. Born 24 April 1949. Lives in Buckinghamshire.

SHAH, Akhil
Fountain Court (Anthony Boswood QC), London
(020) 7583 3335
Recommended in Aviation
Specialisation: General commercial work specialising in: carriage by air of goods and passengers; aircraft insurance disputes; air disasters - product liability; aviation finance and operating lease disputes; conditions of carriage; jurisdiction; regulatory work - operators' licences. Counsel in Airbus Industrie G.I.E v Patel [1999] 1 AC 119: (Product liability; Jurisdiction; anti-suit injunction) House of Lords. Counsel in Western Digital v British Airways [2001] QB733; (Warsaw Convention : Article 18 : right of owner to sue for loss of goods). Counsel in First Security National Bank v Air Gabon [1999] 2 Lloyds 380 (Aircraft lease, delivery of aircraft); Counsel in Messier Dowty Ltd v Airbus Industrie G.I.E and another [2000] 1 All ER (comm) 101 (stay of proceedings; product design).
Prof. Memberships: COMBAR.

SHANT, Nirmal
No.1 High Pavement (John B Milmo QC), Nottingham
(0115) 941 8218
Recommended in Crime
Specialisation: Specialises in criminal law. Most cases are of considerable gravity. Deals with offences of serious violence including murder and manslaughter, sexual offences and drugs matters. Her practice also includes some fraud cases.
Prof. Memberships: Member of the Criminal Justice Strategy Committee, Bar Human Rights Committee and part of the Bar disciplinary panel.
Career: Called in 1984. Has specialised in criminal law for over a decade. Has recently been appointed Recorder.
Personal: Leicester University graduate. Hobbies include reading, swimming and playing squash.

SHARLAND, Andrew
4-5 Gray's Inn Square (Elizabeth Appleby QC), London
(020) 7404 5252
asharland@4-5graysinnsquare.co.uk
Recommended in Education
Specialisation: Specialises in public law, human rights, employment and media law. He practises in English and European courts acting for private individuals, public authorities, commercial organisations and NGOs. Junior Counsel for the Crown (C Panel). He regularly lectures on public law and human rights in the UK and Europe. Notable case include: Washington First v UK (Freedom of Expression, in ECHR) R v Sec of State for Health, ex p SW (Privacy , HC). R v East Sussex CC, ex p Tandy (Education, HL) R v Sefton MBC, ex p Help the Aged (Community Care, CA).
Prof. Memberships: Administrative Law Bar Association.
Career: Called to the Bar in 1996.
Publications: Co-author of 'Blackstone's Guide to Media Law and Human Rights'. Contributing editor to 'Human Rights and Judicial Review: Case Studies in Context' (Butterworths). Contributor to 'Freedom of Information' (Sweet & Maxwell) (forthcoming)

SHARP, Christopher QC
St John's Chambers (Christopher Sharp QC), Bristol
(0117) 921 3456
clerks@stjohnschambers.co.uk
Recommended in Family, Personal Injury
Specialisation: Matrimonial finance. Personal injury. Professional negligence in these fields. Recent reported cases include Fearon v Dunlop (1999) - CA, product liability; Giblett v Murray (1999) - CA, psychiatric injury; Sheargold v Smith (2001) - QBD, multiple injuries, quantum; Mutch v Allan (2001) - CA, CPR, expert evidence; Mirvahedy v Henley (2001) - CA, Animals Act 1971; Irwin v Stevenson (2002) - CA, RTA, negligence.
Prof. Memberships: FLBA. PIBA.
Career: MA Oxon. Called to the Bar 1975; Silk 1999. Head of Chambers.
Publications: Articles in the legal press.
Personal: Born 17 September 1952; educated at Worcester College, Oxford. Married, two children. Interests: travel, real tennis, theatre.

SHARP, Victoria QC
1 Brick Court (Richard Rampton QC), London
(020) 7353 8845
clerks@1brickcourt.co.uk
Recommended in Defamation
Specialisation: Defamation, confidence, contempt of court and media related law generally. Cases include David Irving v Guardian Newspapers Ltd, Marks & Spencer v Granada, Branson v Snowden and GTECH, Bennett v Guardian Newspapers Ltd, Sugar v Venables, Hamilton/Greer v Guardian Newspapers Ltd, Souness v MGN, HRH Princess of Wales v MGN, Angelsea v HTV, Rt Hon Michael Foot v Times Newspapers, Maxwell v Bower, Lord Aldington v Tolstoy, Marco Pierre White v Anthony Allan, A v B & C sub nom Gary Flitcroft.
Prof. Memberships: London Commercial and Common Bar Association.
Career: North London Collegiate School, University of Bristol (1978). Called to the Bar 1979. Member of the Supreme Court Committee on Defamation (the Neill Committee). Recorder (South Eastern Circuit).

SHARPE, Thomas QC
One Essex Court (Lord Grabiner QC), London
(020) 7583 2000
Recommended in Competition/European Law
Specialisation: Principal areas of practice are European Community and UK competition law (Competition Commission/ OFT, EC Commission and European Court). Cases representing British Gas, British Telecom, British Sugar, Eurostar. Extensive telecommunications practice in UK and Hong Kong. Wide range of Art 81, 82 in High Court and general EC law cases in the European Court of Justice. Also judicial review. Leading cases include Eurostar (in European Court), Clear Communications Ltd v New Zealand Telecommunications (in Privy Council) on interconnection; Shearson Lehman v Maclaine Watson; An Bord Bainne v. Milk Marketing Board; R v MAFF exp. Fedesa; Hopkins v National Power; Contributor to Halsbury (European Community Law) and author of monographs and articles on UK and EEC competition law and utility regulation in Law Quarterly Review, European Law Review etc. Formerly Fellow in Law, Nuffield College, Oxford.
Career: Called to the Bar in 1976. Of counsel to Gibson, Dunn & Crutcher (US law firm) 1984-88; on board of NERA, 1982-88 and executive director, Institute for Fiscal Studies, 1981-87. Commenced practise in 1987. Took silk in 1994.
Personal: Educated at Trinity Hall, Cambridge. Degrees in Economics and in Law.

SHARPLES, John
St John's Chambers (Christopher Sharp QC), Bristol
(0117) 921 3456
clerks@stjohnschambers.co.uk
Recommended in Chancery
Specialisation: Commercial landlord and tenant; real property; equity and trusts; residential landlord and tenant.
Prof. Memberships: Property Bar Association; Chancery Bar Association; Bristol and Cardiff Chancery Bar Association.
Career: Oxford University BA (1st class) 1986; Cambridge University LLM 1987; University of Pennsylvania LLM 1988; Thouron Scholar 1987-88; Attorney-at-Law New York 1991; Associate, Davis Polk and Wardwell, New York 1989-91; Middle Temple 1991; Queen Mother's Fund Scholar (Middle Temple) 1991; Sachs Prize and Campbell Foster Prize (Middle Temple) 1992; St John's Chambers Bristol 1993.
Personal: Rugby league, sailing and raising daughter.

SHARPSTON, Eleanor QC
4 Paper Buildings (Jean Ritchie QC), London
(020) 7643 5000
Recommended in Competition/European Law
Specialisation: All areas of EU law, from competition, equal treatment and immigration to agriculture, free movement of goods and intellectual property; also ECHR work.
Prof. Memberships: UKAEL, BEG, COMBAR; member of Irish Bar; member of Bar of Gibraltar; Fellow, King's College Cambridge; Senior Fellow, Centre for European Legal Studies (CELS), Cambridge.
Career: Undergraduate degree at King's College, Cambridge (economics and law); research at Corpus Christi College, Oxford. Private practice in Brussels chambers 1981-87. Référendaire (legal secretary) at Court of Justice of the EC 1987-90. Since 1990, in practice at the Bar concurrently with academic appointments at UCL (1990-92) and Cambridge (1992-).
Publications: 'Interim and Substantive Relief in Claims under Community Law'; 'Practitioners' Handbook of EC Law' 1998 (contributor), various academic articles.
Personal: Main off-duty interests: classical music, theatre and European literature; rowing, scuba diving and sailing square-riggers.

SHAW, Antony QC
18 Red Lion Court (Anthony Arlidge QC), London
(020) 7520 6000
antony.shaw@18rlc.co.uk
Recommended in Crime, Fraud
Specialisation: General crime and fraud, including SFO, VAT, corporate, mortgage, ECGD, tax, charity and other frauds. Major SFO cases include Guinness, Polly Peck, Eagle Trust, BCCI, Butte Mining, Alpine, Alliance.
Prof. Memberships: Criminal Bar Association.
Career: Major History Scholar, Trinity College, Oxford: 1967-1970. Astbury Scholar, Middle Temple: 1976. QC: 1994. Assistant Recorder: 1998; Recorder, 2000.
Publications: Co-editor, Archbold, 'Criminal Pleadings and Practice': 1991 to date.
Personal: Governor, International Students House.

SHAW, Geoffrey QC
1 Brick Court (Richard Rampton QC), London
(020) 7353 8845
Recommended in Defamation
Specialisation: Defamation.
Prof. Memberships: Gray's Inn.
Career: BA, BCL (Oxon). Called to the Bar 1968. Took Silk, 1991. Trials include: unification church case, Gee v BBC, Archer v Star, Rantzen v People, Upjohn v Oswald; Ashby v Sunday Times. Reported cases include: Lucas-Box 1986 1 WLR 147; Khashoggi 1986 1 WLR 1412; Bobolas 1987 1 WLR 1101; Al-Fayed 1988 1 WLR 1412; Tebbitt 1989 1 WLR 640; Sutcliffe 1991 1 QB 153; Kingshott 1991 1 QB 88; Rantzen 1994 QB 670; Condliffe 1996 1 WLR 753; Evans 1996 EMLR 429; Geenty 1998 EMLR 524; Newham 1998 EMLR 583; Awwad 2001 QB 570.

SHAW, Howard
29 Bedford Row Chambers (Nicholas Francis QC), London

(020) 7404 1044
hshaw@29bedfordrow.co.uk
Recommended in Family
Specialisation: All aspects of family law. Professional negligence (particularly clinical negligence). Major cases include: C v C (Financial Provision: Personal Damages) (1995), Pereira v Keleman (1995), R v R (Divorce: Stay of Proceedings) (1994), London Borough of Sutton v Davis (Costs) (No 2) (1994) C v C (Wasted Costs Order) (1994), London Borough of Sutton v Davies (1994), L v L (Minors) (Separate Representation), Edmonds v Edmonds (1990), Newton v Newton (1990), B v B (Financial Provision) (1987), Barder v Barder (Caluori Intervening) (1987), RE M (Minors) (confidential documents), (1987), Singer (Formerly Sharegin) v Sharegin (1984). Brava v Spring (1994) 5MR120. Duties of a G.P. Dobbie v Medway Health Auth. (1992). Rawlinson v North Essex Health Authority (1999). 2001 achieved highest award (including IHT provision) under Schedule One Children Act 1989. Chapman v Estate of Dr Moll Deceased (2001) limitation period. Chinchin v University Hospital of Wales (2002) informal consent.
Prof. Memberships: Professional Negligence Bar Association, Personal Injury Bar Association, Family Law Bar Association.
Career: Head of chambers 3 Dr Johnsons Buildings 1989. Joined present chambers 1995. Member Irish Bar 1998.
Personal: Married with two children. Lives in London. Leisure pursuits: Sport and walking the dogs. Theatre.

SHAW, Malcolm QC
Essex Court Chambers (Gordon Pollock QC), London
(020) 7813 8000
Recommended in Public International Law
Specialisation: Clients have included the Governments of Chad (Chad v Libya, ICJ, 1990-93); Cameroons (Cameroon v Nigeria, ICJ 1994-2002); Cyprus (ECHR, 1995-01); Quebec, 1992, 1995, 1997-8 and 2001-2; Treasury Solicitor 1995, 1998 and 1999; Westland Helicopters Ltd (Westland v AOI, 1994); Crown Prosecution Service/Government of Spain, (Re Pinochet, 1998); Crown Prosecution Service (Re Operation January, 2001). A full CV is available on request.
Prof. Memberships: Visiting Fellow, Lauterpacht Research Centre for International Law, University of Cambridge (2000-2001). Fellow of the Royal Geographical Society, Fellow of the Royal Society for the Arts, Member of the American Society of International Law, Member of the British Institute of International and Comparative Law.
Career: Called to the Bar at Gray's Inn (1988), QC in 2002. PhD, Keele University (1979); LLM, Hebrew University of Jerusalem, Israel (1971); LLB Hons, Liverpool University (1968).
Publications: 'International Law' (4th edn) 1997, Groltius, Cambridge University Press; Title to Territory in Africa, 'International Legal Issues' 1986 Oxford University Press; 'External Debt', Hague Academy of International Law 1995. Numerous other contributions to books and articles.

SHAW, Mark QC
Blackstone Chambers (Presiley Baxendale QC & Charles Flint QC), London
(020) 7583 1770
markshaw@blackstonechambers.com
Recommended in Administrative & Public Law
Specialisation: Principal area of practice is administrative/public law, with emphasis on judicial review, human rights, immigration and nationality, local government, regulatory/disciplinary proceedings, environment, prisons, social security, health, social services and EU law. Notable Cases include: R v SSHD ex parte Thompson and Venables [1998] AC 407 (HL) and T and V v UK [2000] 30 EHRR 121 (ECtHR); R v SSHD ex parte Myra Hindley [2001] 1 AC 410; R v SSHD, ex parte Al-Fayed [1998] 1 WLR 763 (CA); Reeves v Metropolitan Police Commissioner [1999] 3 WLR 363 (HL); R v DPP, ex parte Duckenfield [2000] 1 WLR 55 (DC); R v SSHD, ex parte Robinson [1998] QB 929 (CA); R v SSHD, ex parte Rahman [1998] QB 136 (CA); R v SSHD, ex parte Mbanja [1999] Imm AR 63 (QBD) and 508 (CA); Adan v SSHD [1999] 1 AC 293; Laskey, Jaggard and Brown v UK [1997] 24 EHRR 39 (ECtHR); A v UK [1999] 27 EHRR 611 (ECtHR); Condron v UK [2001] 31 EHRR 1 (ECtHR); Pyrah & Lichniak v SSHD, [2001] 3 WLR 933 (CA); R (Anderson & Taylor) v SSHD [2002] 2 WLR 1143 (CA); B v SSHD [2000] EuLR 687 (CA); Jain v SSHD [2000] Imm AR 76 (CA); Mark Wilkinson Furniture Ltd v CITB, Times, 10th October 2000 (QBD); R v GMC, ex parte Richards [2001] Lloyds Medical Law Reports 47 (QBD); Kingsley v UK, Times, 9th January 2001 and 28th May 2002 (ECtHR); R (Bulger) v Lord Chief Justice & SSHD 16th February 2001 (DC); V & T v News Group Newspapers Ltd [2001] 2 WLR 1038 (Fam Div); R v GMC ex parte Toth [2000] 1 WLR 2209 (QBD); Sepet and Bulbul v SSHD [2001] Imm AR 452 (CA); R (Gupta) v GMC, Times 16 October 2001 (DC) and 9 January 2002 (PC); CG v UK, Times 4 January 2002 (ECtHR); R (Profile Alliance) v BBC 14 March 2002 (CA); Stafford v UK, 28 May 2002 (ECtHR).
Prof. Memberships: Administrative Law Bar Association, Bar Golfing Society (Honorary Secretary).
Career: Member of Borough Solicitor's Department, Bournemouth Borough Council 1985-87. Stagiaire at the European Parliament (Human Rights Unit) 1986. Called to the Bar 1987 and joined current chambers in 1988. Pegasus scholarship to Melbourne law firm 1991. Junior Counsel to the Crown (Common Law) (the 'A' list) since 1995. Member of the Attorney General's panel of counsel appointed to act for the Government and as a Special Advocate before the Special Immigration Appeals Commission and the Proscribed Organisations Appeal Commission (dealing with national security cases). Took Silk in 2002.
Publications: Publications include 'Halsbury's Laws of England' (4th Edn) volume on Immigration and Nationality (Butterworths, 1992), and 'Human Rights Law and Practice', contributor, (Butterworths, 1999 and 2000). Member of the Advisory Board of, and contributor to, 'JR'.
Personal: Educated at Durham University (BA) and Cambridge University (LLM). Born 6 June 1962.

SHEA, Caroline
Falcon Chambers (Jonathan Gaunt QC & Kim Lewison QC), London
(020) 7353 2484
shea@falcon-chambers.com
Recommended in Agriculture, Property Litigation
Specialisation: Landlord and tenant, commercial, residential, agricultural, property litigation.
Prof. Memberships: Chancery Bar Association. LCLCBA. Property Bar Association.
Career: MA Cantab. Diploma in Law (City University). Called to Bar 1994. Joined Falcon Chambers 1995. Previously a management consultant. Diplock Scholar.
Publications: Editor of 'PLC Property Service'.
Personal: Born 1961. Lives in London. Married with three children.

SHEKERDEMIAN, Marcia
11 Stone Buildings (Murray Rosen QC), London
(020) 7831 6381
shekerdemian@11stonebuildings.com
Recommended in Company, Insolvency
Specialisation: Specialises in company law and all aspects of personal and corporate insolvency, including administrations, receiverships, voluntary arrangements, shareholders' disputes, wrongful trading, misfeasance and disqualification of directors. Was one of the counsel instructed in the Carecraft case. Her practice also includes other areas of commercial litigation, including contractual disputes, partnerships and banking.

SHELDON, Clive
11 King's Bench Walk Chambers (Eldred Tabachnik QC & James Goudie QC), London
(020) 7632 8500
sheldon@11kbw.com
Recommended in Education
Specialisation: Education, employment and public law. Recent cases include N v Head Teacher of X School [2002] E.L.R. 187 (school exclusion and bias); H v Gloucestershire CC [2000] E.L.R. 357 (SENT and natural justice); A and S School, ex p T [2000] E.L.R. 274 (admissions and SEN); Denson [2002] 1 F.C.R. 460 (child support and HRA); Hopper (The Times, 17/6/02: registration officers and unfair dismissal).
Prof. Memberships: ALBA.
Career: Called 1991; New York Bar (Oct 1992); 'C' panel of Treasury Counsel (Feb 1999).
Publications: Contributor to 'Tolley's Employment Handbook' and 'Tolley's Employment Law'.
Personal: BA (Cantab) (First Class); LLM (University of Pennsylvania). Governor of Akiva School, London.

SHELDON, Richard QC
3-4 South Square (Michael Crystal QC & Lord Alexander of Weedon QC), London
(020) 7696 9900
clerks@southsquare.com
Recommended in Insolvency
Specialisation: Banking, bank securities, bankruptcy and insolvency. Corporate insolvency, general commercial and fraud (civil), company law, mergers, acquisitions and disposal of companies, financial services, international trade, finance of international trade, mortgages, partnership, solicitors' negligence, accountants' negligence. Recent cases: Three Rivers DC v Bank of England (HL) [2001] 2 All ER 513; Re BCCI, Banque Arabe Internationale d'Investissement SA v Morris [2001] 1 BCLC 263; Banco Nacional de Cuba v Cosmos Trading Corp (CA) [2000] 1 BCLC 813; Morris v Bank of America National Trust (CA) [2000] 1 All ER 954; Bank of Credit and Commerce International (Overseas) Ltd v Akindele (CA) [2000] 3 WLR 1423.
Prof. Memberships: Chancery Bar Association, Commercial Bar Association.
Career: Called to the Bar 1979. Queen's Counsel 1996. Cambridge MA.
Publications: Contributed to Halsbury's Laws (4th ed vol 7).

SHELTON, Gordon
Broadway House (J Graham K Hyland QC), Bradford
(01274) 722560
Recommended in Family

SHEPHERD, Nigel
2 Paper Buildings (Desmond de Silva QC), London
(020) 7556 5500
shepherd@dial.pipex.com
Recommended in Crime
Specialisation: Crime; commercial fraud; money-laundering; drugs; VAT fraud; mortgage fraud; bond laundering; advance fee fraud; computer fraud. R v Edwards CA 11/5/99; Drug Trafficking hearing period cannot be extended retrospectively. R v Deroda CA 24/5/99; Archbold News. S.23 unavailable witness requirements clarified. R v Tomas Honz [1998] 2 Cr.App.R(S) 283 - importation: sentence 24 years reduced to 16.
Prof. Memberships: Criminal Bar Association; SE Circuit.

LEADERS AT THE BAR

Career: Inner Temple, Lincolns Inn; called 1973. Receiving leading briefs since 1991.
Publications: 1973 Criminal Law Review: 'When is a Court not a Court?'
Personal: Two sons. Leisure interests: high altitude sport, leasehold reform, comparative penology, annoying normative people.

SHEPHERD, Philip
24 Old Buildings (Martin Mann QC & Alan Steinfeld QC), London
(020) 7404 0946
Recommended in Aviation

SHER, Jules QC
Wilberforce Chambers (Edward Nugee QC), London
(020) 7306 0102
Recommended in Chancery, Energy, Pensions

Specialisation: Chancery and commercial litigation and advice. Covers the wide range of work comprised in a modern commercial chancery practice including Lloyd's litigation and advice; North Sea Oil and Gas tract participation disputes (acting for British Gas and major oil companies in litigation in the Commercial Court and Chancery Division); trust litigation in the UK and abroad (Singapore, Cayman Islands, Bahamas, Hong Kong); trust aspects of takeovers (acted in Glaxo takeover of Wellcome and Granada takeover of Forte and Wolverhampton and Dudley take over of Mansfield Brewery); professional negligence (accountants, solicitors); pensions litigation (Imperial Group v Imperial Tobacco, London Regional Transport Pension Fund Trustee Co Ltd v Hatt, MacDonald v Horn and the BT Pension Schemes Trust); restitution: 2002, defended Singapore Telecommunications Ltd against large claim by regulator; undue influence: 2001, the Royal Bank of Scotland v Etridge, House of Lords.
Career: B Comm, LLB (Rand), BCL (Oxon). Called to the Bar of England and Wales in 1968. Took silk 1981. Recorder. Advocate of the Supreme Court of South Africa; Deputy High Court Judge (Commercial Court and Chancery Division); member of the Commercial Bar Association and Chancery Bar Association.

SHERBORNE, David
5 Raymond Buildings
(Patrick Milmo QC), London
(020) 7242 2902
Recommended in Defamation

SHERIDAN, Maurice
Matrix Chambers, London
(020) 7404 3447
Recommended in Environment

Specialisation: EC environmental, especially regarding direct effect of Directives; domestic environmental, including nuisance and negligence, waste management, water legislation and utilities regulatory active professional negligence and commercial.
Prof. Memberships: Bar European Group; British Italian Law Association; British Bulgarian Law Association; COMBAR.
Career: Sorbonne 1980; Stage with EC Commission 1985; LLB Bristol 1983; LLM (International law) Cantab 1985-96; assisting in approximation programmes regarding EC environmental Acquis in Central and Eastern Europe - 1992 to 1999.
Personal: Travelling, theatre, cinema, contemporary dance.

SHIELDS, Thomas QC
1 Brick Court (Richard Rampton QC), London
(020) 7353 8845
Recommended in Defamation
Specialisation: Defamation and media related law generally.

SHIPLEY, Graham
19 Old Buildings (Alastair Wilson QC), London
(020) 7405 2001
Recommended in Information Technology
Specialisation: Principal area of practice encompasses intellectual property and technology work, including electronic and computer cases and EC aspects. Regular seminar speaker, and has appeared on radio and television ('Science Now') broadcasts.
Prof. Memberships: Intellectual Property Bar Association, Chancery Bar Association.
Career: Called to the Bar 1973 and joined present chambers in 1975, when located at Pump Court.
Personal: Educated at King's School, Chester 1959-66, Trinity College, Cambridge 1966-71 (BA Mathematics 1969, Diploma in Computer Science, Distinction 1970) and Inns of Court School of Law 1971-73. Former Director of 'Trinity 69 Foundation' charity. Leisure pursuits include electronics, house restoring, woodwork, Japanese cookery and motor cycle riding. Born 10 January 1948. Lives in London.

SHIPWRIGHT, Adrian J
Pump Court Tax Chambers, London
(020) 7414 8080
Recommended in Tax
Specialisation: All tax related matters including dispute resolution and litigation particularly corporate matters such as reorganisations, financings and share purchases and sales including takeovers, trust matters, land development, indirect taxation and the taxation of intellectual property.
Prof. Memberships: Lincoln's Inn; Chartered Institute of Taxation; Institute of Indirect Taxation; VAT Practitioners Group; STEP [FRSA]. Member of the Trust Law Committee chaired by Sir John Vinelott.
Career: Admitted as a solicitor 1976, called to the Bar 1993. Visiting Professor, King's College London 1996-. Professor of Business Law and director of the Tax Research Unit, King's College, London 1992-96. Tax partner *SJ Berwin & Co* 1987-92 (consultant till 1993). Tax partner *Denton Hall* 1982-87. Official student (fellow) and tutor in Law, Christ Church, Oxford and lecturer in law (CUF), Oxford University 1977-82. Member of the tax department and articles *Linklaters & Paines* 1974-77. 2002, Deputy Special Commissioner and part-time VAT Tribunal Chairman.
Publications: Publications include 'Trusts and UK Tax' (Key Haven); 'UK Taxation Intellectual Property' (Sweet & Maxwell); 'Tax Avoidance and the Law' (editor for SPTL); 'Tax Planning and UK Land Development' (Key Haven); textbook on Revenue Law. Member of the editorial boards of 'The Tax Journal', Tolley 'Trust Law International' and 'The Personal Tax Planning Review'.
Personal: Education: BA (1972), BCL (1973), MA (1977), Christ Church, Oxford. King Edward VI School, Southampton (governor till 1995).

SHORROCK, Michael QC
Peel Court Chambers (Michael Shorrock QC), Manchester
(0161) 832 3791
Recommended in Crime
Specialisation: Crime, commercial fraud, clinical negligence. Reported cases include R v Doheny Adams CA (leading case on DNA) and R v Winston Brown HL Disclosure.
Prof. Memberships: C.B.A.
Career: Clifton College. Pembroke, Cambridge. Northern Circuit, Junior of Circuit. Secretary Executive Committee Members of C.I.C.B. & C.I.C.A.P., Bencher Inner Temple.
Personal: Married with two daughters. Gardening, walking, opera, cinema, conversation.

SIBERRY, Richard QC
Essex Court Chambers
(Gordon Pollock QC), London
(020) 7813 8000
Recommended in Energy
Specialisation: Shipping and carriage of goods, international trade and finance, insurance and reinsurance, banking and financial services, commodities, oil and gas, and other complex contractual disputes, Brussels Convention and other jurisdictional disputes.
Prof. Memberships: Member of the Executive of the Commercial Bar Association (COMBAR).
Career: Pembroke College, Cambridge BA (Law) (First Class Hons with distinction); LL.B (First Class Hons, with distinction); MA. Law Fellow, Pembroke College, 1973-75. Called to the Bar 1974. Queen's Counsel 1989.
Personal: Born 1950.

SILVERLEAF, Michael QC
11 South Square
(Christopher Floyd QC), London
(020) 7405 1222
Recommended in Information Technology, Intellectual Property

SIMLER, Ingrid
Devereux Chambers (Colin Edelman QC), London
(020) 7353 7534
simler@devchambers.co.uk
Recommended in Employment
Specialisation: Principal area of practice is employment, encompassing all areas of individual and collective employment law, including discrimination, restraint of trade and business transfers. Also handles general commercial work, professional negligence, revenue and public law. Member of A Panel - Junior Counsel to the Crown. Recorder.
Prof. Memberships: Employment Law Bar Association, Employment Lawyers Association, Commercial Law Bar Association, Administrative Law Bar Association, Vice-Chair Bar Council's Sex Discrimination Committee.
Career: Called to the Bar 1987.
Publications: Contributor to 'Tolleys' Employment Law'. Co-author of Butterworths 'Discrimination Law' (published Autumn 1999), Halsbury's Laws 'Discrimination' volume.
Personal: Educated at Cambridge University 1982-85 (MA) and University of Amsterdam 1985-86 (Diploma in European law).

SIMMONDS, Andrew QC
5 Stone Buildings (Henry Harrod), London
(020) 7242 6201
Recommended in Chancery, Pensions, Professional Negligence
Specialisation: Specialises in professional negligence litigation (other than medical) and contentious pensions work. In the former field, has particular experience of claims against solicitors, barristers and accountants but has also acted in claims against actuaries, insurance brokers, fund managers and others. Pensions experience covers all manner of disputes involving employers, trustees and members, claims against pensions professionals, complaints to the Pensions Ombudsman and the jurisdiction of OPRA. Recent cases include Wakelin v Read [2000] PLR 319; University of Nottingham v Eyett (Nos 1 and 2) [1999] 2 AER 437, 445; Spooner v BT [2000] PLR 65; Barclays Bank v Holmes [2000] PLR 339; Walker v Stones [2000] 4 AER 412; Liverpool v Goldberg [2001] 1 AER 182; AMP v Barker [2001] PLR 77; International Power v Healy [2001] PLR 121; Hagen v ICI [2002] PLR 1.
Prof. Memberships: Member of the Association of Pension Lawyers, the Professional Negligence Bar Association and the Pension Litigation Court Users' committee chaired by Lloyd J.
Career: Called 1980. Silk 1999.

SIMPSON, Mark
4 Paper Buildings (Jean Ritchie QC), London
(020) 7643 5000
marksimpson@zen.co.uk
Recommended in Professional Negligence
Specialisation: Specialises in all aspects of professional negligence and general insurance, including professional indemnity insurance. Recent cases include: Farley v Skinner [2001] 3 WLR

LEADERS AT THE BAR

899 (HL); Green v Hancocks [2001] Lloyd's Rep PN 212 (CA); Raiss v Palmano [2001] Lloyd's Rep PN 341 (QBD); Hall v Simons [2000] 3 WLR 543 (HL); UCB v Halifax (SW) - Times, 23/12/99 (CA); Brick v Colleys [1999] Lloyd's Rep PN 309 (CA); Mortgage Corporation v Halifax [1999] Lloyd's Rep PN 159 (QBD); Brophy v Dunphys [1998] EGCS 37 (CA); S v M [1998] 3 FCR 665 (ChD).
Prof. Memberships: Professional Negligence Bar Association. London Common Law and Commercial Bar Association. Bar European Group.
Career: Called to Bar 1992. Educated at King's School Canterbury, Oriel College Oxford (MA Classics 1986), Hughes Hall Cambridge (PCGE 1987), City University (Dip Law 1991), ICSL (Bar Finals 1992), King's College London (Dip European Law 1994). Taught classics at St Paul's School, Barnes (1987-90).
Publications: General Editor, 'Professional Negligence and Liability' (LLP 2000); 'Lloyd's Law Reports: Professional Negligence'. Associate Editor: 'Tolley's Professional Negligence'. Regular contributor to 'Solicitors' Journal'.
Personal: Born 5 January 1963. Lives in London. Working knowledge of French.

SINCLAIR, Fiona
Four New Square (Justin Fenwick QC), London
(020) 7822 2000
f.sinclair@4newsquare.com
Recommended in Professional Negligence
Specialisation: Practice: professional negligence in relation to construction (architects, engineers, quantity surveyors), finance (accountants, solicitors, insurance brokers, financial advisers) and property (solicitors and surveyors); insurance and reinsurance contracts; construction law; financial services law. Editor of 'Jackson and Powell on Professional Negligence' (Chapter 8 Construction Professionals and Chapter 6(2) Expert Evidence). Cases include Koetter Kim Associates v Tryg Baltica [2001] (insurance); Worcester CC v HT (UK) Ltd [2001] (construction; contractual limitation clauses); Jarvis v Castle Wharf Development Ltd [2000] (architects negligence: planning); Republic International Trust Co v Fletcher Ramos [2000] (structural surveyors' negligence) Ministry of Defence v Scott Wilson Kirkpatrick [1997] (structural engineers' negligence); Capital & Counties v Laing [1997] (architects' negligence: fire); Kelly v Bastible [1997] (insurance); HIV/Haemophiliacs Litigation [1996]; Banque Bruxelles Lambert v Eagle Star Insurance [1995] (valuers' negligence); Nash v Eli Lilly [1991] (limitation).
Prof. Memberships: Professional Negligence Bar Association, Technology and Construction Court Bar Association (Committee Member), Society of Construction Law.
Career: Called 1989.
Personal: Born 1963. Educated at Jesus College, Cambridge (BA in Philosophy and Law, 1983-87; LLM, 1987-88). Interests: mountaineering, skiing, flying.

SINGH, Kuldip QC
5 Paper Buildings (Godfrey Carey QC & Jonathan Caplan QC), London
(020) 7583 6117
Recommended in Fraud, Sport

SINGH, Rabinder QC
Matrix Chambers, London
(020) 7404 3447
rabindersingh@matrixlaw.co.uk
Recommended in Administrative & Public Law, Human Rights, Local Government, Planning
Specialisation: All aspects of public law, employment law and European Community and human rights law.
Prof. Memberships: Administrative Law Bar Association (Treasurer), Planning and Environment Bar Association, Employment Law Bar Association; Bar European Group.
Career: Called: 1989. Appointed to A Panel of Junior Counsel to the Crown: 2000. Additional Junior Counsel to the Inland Revenue: 1997. Silk: 2002.
Personal: BA (Law) 1985: Trinity College, Cambridge LLM. 1986: University of California, Berkeley. Visiting fellow, Queen Mary and Westfield College, London since 1995.

SINGLETON, Barry QC
One King's Bench Walk (Anthony Hacking QC), London
(020) 7936 1500
Recommended in Family

SINGLETON, Sarah
28 St John St, Manchester
(0161) 834 8418
Recommended in Family

SLADE, Elizabeth QC
11 King's Bench Walk Chambers (Eldred Tabachnik QC & James Goudie QC), London
(020) 7632 8500
slade@11kbw.com
Recommended in Employment
Specialisation: Specialises in all aspects of employment law with particular emphasis on European aspects of employment law, transfer of undertakings, sex and race discrimination, equal pay, employment aspects of pensions. Leading cases include Westminster City Council v Pensions Ombudsman and Haywood, Halfpenny v IGE Medical Systems Ltd, London Regional Transport v Nagarajan, Foster & Others v British Gas, Reed Executive plc v Sommers, Newns v British Airways plc, R v Mallett ex p, Transport and General Workers Union and another v Middlesborough Council.
Prof. Memberships: Employment Law Bar Association; Employment Lawyers' Association; ALBA; Bar European Group.
Career: Called to the Bar in 1972; Recorder 1998; Deputy High Court Judge 1998-; part-time Judge of the Employment Appeal Tribunal 2000-; 1990 Bencher of the Inner Temple; 1992 Appointed QC; 1994-98 Master of the Staff, Inner Temple; Chair of Employment Law Bar Association 1995-97; Hon Vice-President 1998-; Chairman Sex Discrimination Committee, Bar Council 2000-; Trustee, Free Representation Unit; 1998-2002 Member of the Administrative Tribunal of the Bank for International Settlements.
Publications: Original author of 'Tolleys Employment Handbook' and editor or co-editor of 2nd to 7th edns.
Personal: Education: Lady Margaret Hall, Oxford. Exhibitioner, 1971 MA.

SLATER, John QC
Crown Office Chambers (Michael Spencer QC & Christopher Purchas QC), London
(020) 7797 8100
jslaterqc@crownofficechambers.com
Recommended in Construction, Professional Negligence
Specialisation: Construction and civil engineering; professional negligence (architects, engineers, surveyors, accountants, barristers, solicitors and trademark agents); insurance/reinsurance; product liability. Recent cases include Arab Bank v John D Wood; Capital & Counties v Hampshire County Council (first leader for claimants); Alzal v Ford, Wessex Regional Health Authority v HLM; Alliance & Leicester v Edgestop; Team Services v Kier Management; Kier Construction v Royal Insurance. Mainly briefed by insurers and major corporations. Much used for lengthy complex trials with large volumes of paper. Reputation as an effective cross examiner. Also much used in interrelated insurance policy and project disputes eg in fire, flood, building collapse, product failure cases. Enjoys court and arbitration work of all types.
Career: Called to the Bar 1969, QC 1987 (Aged 40), sits as domestic and international arbitrator (LCIA, ICC UNCITRAL).
Personal: Born 1946. Educated Sedbergh School, University College, Oxford. Lives in Highgate with wife and three offspring.

SLOAN, Paul QC
Trinity Chambers (Toby Hedworth QC), Newcastle upon Tyne
(0191) 232 1927
info@trinitychambers.co.uk
Recommended in Licensing
Specialisation: Crime (prosecution and defence), licensing (liquor and public entertainment), firearms and shotguns (all aspects), police disciplinary tribunals (presenting cases for and against police officers and acting as legal advisor to Chief Constables).
Prof. Memberships: Inner Temple. North Eastern Circuit. Criminal Bar Association. Bar representative on Area Criminal Justice Strategy Committee. North Eastern Bar Press Office spokesman.
Career: LL.B (Lond.) Call 1981. Recorder 2000. Queens Counsel 2001.

SLOMNICKA, Barbara
14 Gray's Inn Square (Joanna Dodson QC), London
(020) 7242 0858
Recommended in Family

SMALLWOOD, Anne E
No5 Chambers (Gareth Evans QC), Birmingham
(0121) 606 0500
Recommended in Family

SMITH, Emma
Old Square Chambers (John Hendy QC), London
(020) 7269 0300
smith@oldsquarechambers.co.uk
Recommended in Employment
Specialisation: All aspects of employment law, including unfair and wrongful dismissal, discrimination, equal pay, redundancy and collective disputes.
Personal injury and clinical law.
Prof. Memberships: Industrial Law Society; Employment Law Bar Association; Employment Lawyers' Association; Personal Injury Bar Association; Association of Personal Injury Lawyers.
Career: LLB (Hons), University of Leicester (1993); MA Medical Ethics and Law, Kings College, London (1994); called to the Bar 1995.
Publications: Co-author 'Discrimination: Remedies and Quantum' (Sweet & Maxwell); contributor 'UK and EU Employee Consultation' (Sweet & Maxwell).
Personal: Born 1971.

SMITH, Jamie
Four New Square (Justin Fenwick QC), London
(020) 7822 2000
j.smith@4newsquare.com
Recommended in Professional Negligence
Specialisation: Principal areas of practice are professional negligence and insurance litigation. Specialisms within professional negligence: auditors and accountants, construction professionals, lawyers, insurance brokers, clinical, surveyors and valuers. Important cases include Swinney v Northumbria Police [1999] (police's duty of care to keep information confidential); Shade v Compton Partnership [2000] (limitation); Hagirhan v Allied Dunbar [2001] (construction of insurance contract); Smith v NHSLA [2001] and Harrild v Hunt NHS Trust [2001] (clinical negligence).
Prof. Memberships: PNBA, COMBAR.
Career: MA (Cantab). Called to Bar 1995. Joined Four New Square 1996.

SMITH, Julia
Gough Square Chambers (Fred Philpott), London
(020) 7353 0924
Recommended in Consumer Law
Specialisation: Consumer Law - in

LEADERS AT THE BAR

particular consumer credit and mortgage actions (eg First National Bank v Syed [1991] 2 All ER 250, Jarrett v Barclays Bank [1997] 2 All ER 484 and Kenyon-Brown v Desmond Banks [2000] Lloyd's Rep. Banks) including consumer credit drafting, extortionate credit bargains, and licensing. Clients include banks, finance houses, leasing companies and retailers.
Prof. Memberships: London Common Law and Commercial Bar Association.
Career: Called to the Bar 1988
Personal: Cheltenham Ladies College and Liverpool University.

SMITH, Nicholas G
Queen Square Chambers (Don Tait & T Alun Jenkins QC), Bristol
(0117) 921 1966
ngs@qs-c.co.uk
Recommended in Employment
Specialisation: Practising exclusively in employment law, including sporting contracts. Clients include Professional Sporting Associations, large corporations, individuals, trade unions, the police and central and local government. Extensive experience in tribunal litigation at first instance and on appeal. Increasingly involved in arbitration of employment/sporting disputes and advisor to the BBC, independent radio and press regarding threatened strike action by members of The Professional Footballers Association. Lectured ELA at expert level and regular provider of seminars and training. CPD accredited.
Prof. Memberships: Member of Employment Lawyers Association, Lincolns Inn
Career: Called 1990.
Publications: ELA Bulletin.
Personal: Born 1965. Married with three young children. Interests include rugby union, motorsport, sailing.

SMITH, Richard QC
Guildhall Chambers
(Adrian Palmer QC), Bristol
(0117) 930 9000
richard.smith@guildhallchambers.co.uk
Recommended in Crime
Specialisation: Crime, sports disciplinary law.
Prof. Memberships: CBA.
Career: University of London, King's College. Call 1986. Silk 2001.

SMITH, Robert QC
Park Court Chambers
(Robert Smith QC), Leeds
(0113) 203 5501
robert.smithqc@btinternet.com
Recommended in Crime, Health & Safety
Specialisation: A balanced practice involving prosecution and defence work (principally homicide, commercial fraud and specialist issues such as corporate and medical manslaughter, data protection, health and safety, environmental pollution, etc). Defence instructions include a large proportion of professional defendants such as medical practitioners, accountants and police officers. Has a particular interest in medico-legal matters and scientific evidence. Recent cases of importance: Attorney General's Reference (No 3 of 1994), criminal liability for pre-natal injuries, House of Lords [1998] AC 245; R v Beedie, Court of Appeal Criminal Division - the double jeopardy rule in criminal proceedings [1997] 2 Cr.App.R. 167; R v Woolin - foresight of consequences as proof of intent in murder, House of Lords [1999] AC 82; R v Kerr, Court of Appeal - unfitness to plead and the implications of Article 6 of the Convention [2002] 1 Cr.App.R. 25 (application to the European Court pending).
Prof. Memberships: Member of the International Bar Association, Personal Injuries Bar Association, Bar European Group and Criminal Bar Association.
Career: Common law practitioner specialising in criminal and civil litigation (principally personal injury and medical and professional negligence) from commencing practice in Leeds in 1971. Appointed Queen's Counsel and a Recorder in 1986. Served for three years as a Member of the Criminal Injuries Compensation Board. Joined London chambers at 3 Serjeants' Inn [Adrian Whitfield QC] as a door tenant in 1994.

SMITH, Roger QC
No.6 Fountain Court (Roger Smith QC), Birmingham
(0121) 233 3282
Recommended in Crime

SMITH, Sally QC
1 Crown Office Row
(Robert Seabrook QC), London
(020) 7797 7500
Recommended in Clinical Negligence
Specialisation: Medical law including clinical negligence and disciplinary work. Special interest in group litigation.
Prof. Memberships: Nine year membership of St Thomas' Ethics Committee (ending 2002). Member of the Royal College of Physicians Ethics Committee.
Career: General common law experience for first 10 years of practice. Specialist in medical law for last 15 years. Extensive experience in group litigation; benzodiazepine litigation; RAGE (breast radiation) litigation; currently representing defendants in Liverpool and nationwide organ retention litigation.
Publications: Published articles in medical journals and legal textbook.

SMITH, Shaun
No.1 High Pavement
(John B Milmo QC), Nottingham
(0115) 941 8218
Recommended in Crime
Specialisation: All criminal defence work, particularly rape and sexual abuse cases. Serious violence and drugs cases.
Prof. Memberships: Criminal Bar Association.
Career: Practitioner on North Eastern Circuit 1981-90 and thereafter on Oxford and Midland circuit to date. Lecturer on advanced criminal procedure on Bar Vocational Course (practical). Pupil Master - Recorder.
Personal: Sheffield University, CLE (London). Cinema, theatre, music, football.

SMITH, Stephen QC
New Square Chambers (Charles Purle QC), London
(020) 7419 8000
stephen.smith@newsquarechambers.co.uk
Recommended in Chancery, Commercial (Litigation), Company, Fraud
Specialisation: Complex and heavy commercial litigation, often with a Chancery or jurisdictional element (especially issues arising under the Brussels/ Lugano Convention) and involving restraints on disposals of assets; also professional negligence, civil fraud, insurance, property disputes and insolvency. Conducted numerous witness examinations, including several in the USA and in New Zealand. Called to the Bar of the Eastern Caribbean States Supreme Court and conducted several hearings on Tortola BVI at first instance (including at trial) and on appeal to the Court of Appeal of the Eastern Caribbean, and appeared on a further appeal to the Privy Council. Heavily involved in the legal issues arising out of the 2001 epidemic of foot-and-mouth disease. Previous cases: Derby v Weldon (acted for Salomon Inc); DSQ Property Company (formerly DeLorean Motor Company) v Lotus Cars (acted for John Z. DeLorean); Morris v Mahfouz BCCI (acted for Khalid Bin Mahfouz and others); FTIT Ltd v Morgan Stanley and Coopers & Lybrand (acted for liquidators (Deloitte Touche) appointed by Swiss Bank Corporation); Senate Electrical Wholesalers v Alcatel Submarines Networks (acted for Northern Telecom); Village Cay Marina v Acland (Privy Council decision about share registration and receivership in the BVI); Trustor v Moyne, Trustor v Smallbone; Trustor v Barclays (acted for Trustor); Pagarani v T Choithram International SA (Privy Council decision); W v H (restraint orders in the Family Division); R (Persey) v DEFRA (refusal at public inquiry into fmd epidemic); RGB Resources Plc v Rastogi (Freezing orders in provisional liquidation).
Prof. Memberships: Middle Temple (Jules Thorn Scholar).
Career: Scholar, University College Oxford 1979-1982. First Class Hons degree in Jurisprudence, Oxford University 1982 (Wronker and Jurisprudence Prizes winner). Called to the Bar in England and Wales, August 1983. QC 2000.
Personal: Married to Lorraine, five children. Principal leisure interests: family, alpaca farming.

SMOUHA, Joe
Essex Court Chambers (Gordon Pollock QC), London
(020) 7813 8000
Recommended in Arbitration, Banking & Finance, Commercial (Litigation), Fraud, Shipping, Tax
Specialisation: Litigation involving appearances in arbitration, the Commercial Court, Court of Appeal, the House of Lords and other courts hearing civil claims. All aspects of commercial law including shipping, banking, insurance and reinsurance, international sale of goods, oil and gas, public international law and other related areas. Art litigation including title, dealer commission, purchasing syndicate disputes. VAT: includes both substantial High Court and tribunal work and general advisory work on non-contentious matters, schemes etc.
Career: Magdalene College, Cambridge, BA Law (Hons) 1984. MA 1988. New York University School of Law, 1984-85: LLM in International Trade Law. Called to the Bar 1986 (Middle Temple).
Personal: Born 1963.

SNOWDEN, Richard
Erskine Chambers (Robin Potts QC), London
(020) 242 5532
rsnowden@erskine-chambers.co.uk
Recommended in Company, Financial Services, Insolvency
Specialisation: Company law, corporate insolvency, financial services and related commercial litigation. Currently, about 75% of cases are contentious matters, with the remainder being non-contentious advisory work. Notable cases include acting for the successful employees in Paramount Airways (Powdrill v Watson); for the bondholders in the hearings to approve the sale of Barings to ING; for Lloyds of London in litigation in Bermuda relating to the insolvency of EMLICO; for the English and Luxembourg liquidators of BCCI in various cases in England including BCCI No 10 and Mahomed v Morris; for the SPI in relation to multiple searches of court records; for the successful majority shareholder in Re Astec (BSR) plc; for the company in Re Osiris Insurance Limited; for the successful majority shareholders in Arrow Nominees v Blackledge; for the administrative receivers of Transtec plc in a dispute with various motor manufacturers; for the OFT in proceedings concerning estate agents and misleading advertisements; for the company in the restructuring of Garuda; for the Financial Services Authority in relation to Equitable Life; and for the liquidators of Leyland Daf Limited concerning the priority of liquidation expenses.
Prof. Memberships: Chancery Bar Association, COMBAR, R3, The British Association for Sport and Law.
Career: Called to the Bar in 1986; appointed Junior Counsel to the Crown

(A Panel) in 1999.
Publications: Joint Editor of Lightman and Moss, 'The Law of Receivers and Administrators of Companies' and 'Company Directors: Law and Liability' (both Sweet and Maxwell). Regularly speaks and lectures at conferences.
Personal: Educated at Downing College, Cambridge 1981-84 (MA, 1st Class Hons; Harvard Law School 1984-85 (LLM). Leisure pursuits include golf, cricket, rugby and music. Born 22nd March 1962. Lives in East Sussex.

SOLLEY, Stephen QC
Charter Chambers (Stephen Solley QC), London
(020) 7832 0300
Recommended in Crime, Fraud

SOMERVILLE, Bryce
No.6 Fountain Court (Roger Smith QC), Birmingham
(0121) 233 3282
Recommended in Family

SOORJOO, Martin
Tooks Court Chambers (Michael Mansfield QC), London
(020) 7405 8828
Recommended in Immigration
Specialisation: Public law with emphasis on immigration, asylum, prison and human rights challenges. Cases of significance include Saad (CA) entitlement of persons with ELR to asylum appeal, Bidar (ECJ reference concerning entitlement of EU students to student loans), Amin (CA) scope of duty on state under Article 2 ECHR to investigate death in custody, Ullah, (entitlement under Article 9 ECHR to manifest religion), Francois (HL) and Evans and Reid (DC) calculation of remand time. Also represented family of Stephen Lawrence throughout their various legal proceedings up to and including the Public Inquiry. Former member of ILPA executive and regular course trainer for various organisations including ILPA and JCWI.
Prof. Memberships: Immigration Law Practitioners Association, Bar European Group and Administrative Law Bar Association.
Career: Called to the Bar in 1990.
Publications: Co-author of ILPA's 'Asylum Best Practice Guide' (2002).

SOUTHERN, Richard
7 King's Bench Walk (Gavin Kealey QC & Julian Flaux QC), London
(020) 7910 8300
Recommended in Shipping
Specialisation: Main areas of practice are shipping and maritime, insurance and reinsurance, professional negligence, and commercial fraud, as well as general commercial litigation and arbitration. Recent cases include Aneco Reinsurance Underwriting Ltd v Johnson & Higgins [2002] 1 Lloyd's Rep 157 (HL); Glencore International v Metro Trading [2001] 1 Lloyd's Rep 284; Lloyd v Popely [2000] 1 BCLC 19; Jordan Grand Prix Ltd v Baltic Insurance Group [1999] 2 AC 127 (HL); Dubai Aluminium Co Ltd v Salaam [1999] 1 Lloyd's Rep 415.
Prof. Memberships: The Commercial Bar Association.
Career: Called 1987.

SOUTHEY, David Hugh
Tooks Court Chambers (Michael Mansfield QC), London
(020) 7405 8828
Recommended in Human Rights, Immigration
Specialisation: Human Rights Act 1998, prisoners rights, mental health, immigration and asylum, crime, community care, privacy, education and other public law. Cases include Svazas v SSHD (2002) The Times, 26 February; R (Carroll and others) v SSHD [2002] 1WLR 545; Ivanauskiene v A Special Adjudicator (2001) The Times, 18 September; R (P and Q) v SSHD [2001] 1 WLR 2002; R (Akhtar) v SSHD (2001) The Times, 23 February; Gomez v SSHD (2000) INLR 549; Zaitz v SSHD (2000) INLR 346
Prof. Memberships: ILPA, Prisoners Advice Service.
Publications: Joint editor of 'United Kingdom Human Rights Reports' and 'Human Rights' and joint author of 'A Criminal Practitioners Guide to Judicial Review and Case Stated'.

SPARKS, Paula
Doughty Street Chambers (Geoffrey Robertson QC), London
(020) 7404 1313
p.sparks@doughtystreet.co.uk
Recommended in Clinical Negligence
Specialisation: Specialist in the areas of medico-legal work, including clinical negligence, inquests and CICA tribunals. Major cases include Rahman v (1) Arearose Ltd & anor (2) University College London NHS Trust, CA (2000) and written submission together with Stephen Irwin QC on behalf of the Association of Personal Injury Lawyers (APIL) in Callery v Gray [Conditional Fee Agreements]. Reported settlements in AVMA Medical & Legal Journal (Clinical Risk) and Personal Injury Medical Law Letter (PMILL). She has also lectured on human rights related aspects of medical law and provides training in the area of inquests.
Prof. Memberships: Inquest Lawyers Group; Action for Victims of Medical Accidents' Association of Personal Injury Lawyers; Professional Negligence Bar Association.
Career: Called to the Bar in 1994.
Publications: Contributor to the 'The Medical Accidents Handbook: A Practical Guide for Patients and their Advisers' Wileys; National Council for Civil Liberties 'Your Rights on-line' (chapter, 'The Rights of the Bereaved').

SPEAIGHT, Anthony QC
4 Pump Court, London
(020) 7842 5555
aspeaight@4pumpcourt.com
Recommended in Construction
Specialisation: Construction contracts, professional negligence (especially architects, surveyors and engineers), other commercial contracts and financial services, other property-related work, public law. Cases include Linden Gardens v Lenesta Sludge [1994] 1 AC 85 (assignment of cause of action between successive owners of property); Gable House Estates v Halpern [1995] CILL 1072 (architects' negligence); Kelly v Norwich Union [1990] 1 WLR 139 (subsidence claim); R v Wicks [1998] AC 92 (planning enforcement); Thornton Springer v NEM Insurance [2000] 2 All ER 489 (meaning of professional indemnity insurance policy wording); R (Fleurose) v Securities and Futures Authority 'The Times' 15 May 2001 (European Convention of Human Rights and financial services regulation).
Prof. Memberships: TECBAR, COMBAR, PNBA, PIBA, ALBA.
Career: Barrister in practice in the Temple since 1973. Silk 1995.
Publications: Co-editor of 'Butterworths Professional Negligence Service'.
Personal: Chairman of Bar Council working party on Modernising Civil Justice (2001).

SPEARMAN, Richard QC
4-5 Gray's Inn Square (Elizabeth Appleby QC), London
(020) 7404 5252
Recommended in Defamation, Sport
Specialisation: General commercial and common law, including: commercial fraud, media and entertainment (contracts, copyright, breach of confidence, defamation, arbitration), music industry (contracts, copyright, Copyright Tribunal), sports law (including disciplinary proceedings, arbitration), insurance and reinsurance, sale of goods, restraint of trade, professional negligence. Reported cases concerning restraint of trade, freezing injunctions, letters of credit, civil fraud, tracing, judicial review, discovery, insurance, defamation, copyright and confidence, including: Warren v Mendy (boxing); Istel v Tully (privilege against self-incrimination); R v Jockey Club ex p Aga Khan (Jockey Club/judicial review); AIRC v PPL (Copyright Tribunal/licensing scheme); Formica v ECGD (discovery/privilege/ ECGD guarantee); Brinks v Abu Saleh (tracing); Kazakstan Wool Producers v NCM (insurance/construction of contract); Hyde Park Residence v Yelland and Ashdown v Telegraph (copyright/public interest/fair dealing); Grobbelaar v News Group (defamation/qualified privilege/perverse jury verdict); Loutchansky v Times (defamation/qualified privilege/after-acquired information/test for duty to publish); Mills v News Group, Theakston v MGN, A v B (confidence/privacy/injunction); Athletic Union of Constantinople v NBA (basketball/arbitration/award/jurisdiction).
Prof. Memberships: COMBAR, Bar Sports Law Group.
Career: Called 1977; QC 1996; Assistant Recorder 1998; Recorder 2000.
Personal: Born 1953. Educated Bedales; King's College, Cambridge.

SPECK, Adrian
8 New Square (Mark Platts-Mills QC), London
(020) 7405 4321
clerks@8newsquare.co.uk
Recommended in Information Technology, Intellectual Property
Specialisation: Barrister specialising in all aspects of intellectual property, including patents trade marks and passing off, confidential information, designs, copyright and performers' rights; also specialises in jurisdiction disputes under the CJJA 1982/Brussels Convention and entertainment litigation. For comprehensive CV and list of recent cases, visit our website at www.8newsquare.co.uk.
Prof. Memberships: Patent Bar Association (PBA); Chancery Bar Association; The Intellectual Property Lawyers Organisation (TIPLO).
Career: Called 1993.
Publications: 'Modern Law of Copyright', 3rd edn.
Personal: Born 1969. Educated at Seaford Head Comprehensive; Kings College, Cambridge (1992 BA Physics and Theoretical Physics - 1st Class); College of Law 1991 (Common Professional Exam with distinction); ICSL 1993 (Bar Vocational Course).

SPENCER, Martin
4 Paper Buildings (Jean Ritchie QC), London
(020) 7643 5000
Recommended in Clinical Negligence
Specialisation: Clinical negligence, professional negligence and personal injury. Recent cases include Farley v Skinner (HL), Daniels v Walker, Swain v LAS, Forbes v Wandsworth HA.
Prof. Memberships: Professional Negligence Bar Association (Executive Committee member), Personal Injury Bar Association.
Career: MA (Oxon), BCL (Oxon), called to Bar 1979. Danish Government Scholar in 1979/80. Pupil at Fountain Court 1980-81, Recorder 2001. Director, Bar Services Company Limited.
Publications: 'The Civil Procedure Rules in Action' (2000) with Ian Grainger and Michael Feeley; 'The Danish Criminal Code' (1999) with Gitte Hoyer and Vagn Greve; 'The Danish System of Criminal Justice with Vagn Greve and others.
Personal: Married with three children. Languages: Danish. Interests: music, sport and bridge. School Governor.

SPENCER, Michael QC
Crown Office Chambers (Michael Spencer QC & Christopher Purchas QC), London
(020) 7797 8100
Recommended in Clinical Negligence, Personal Injury, Product Liability

LEADERS AT THE BAR

SPINK, Andrew JM
35 Essex Street (Christopher Wilson-Smith QC), London
(020) 7353 6381
Recommended in Clinical Negligence

SQUIRES, Dan
Matrix Chambers, London
(020) 7404 3447
Recommended in Education
Specialisation: Public and employment law, in particular education, community care, social welfare and discrimination.
Prof. Memberships: Administrative Law Bar Association and Employment Law Bar Association.
Career: BA (Law) 1995; Christ's College, Cambridge; LLM 1997, Harvard Law School; called to Bar 1998.

STADLEN, Nicholas QC
Fountain Court (Anthony Boswood QC), London
(020) 7583 3335
Recommended in Banking & Finance, Commercial (Litigation), Fraud
Specialisation: 1) General commercial law including banking, insurance, city takeovers and professional negligence and 2) libel. Recent cases include acting for Bank of England on BCCI in House of Lords (twice) for Marconi plc before the FSA, for Prince Mohamad against Said Ayas, for British Commonwealth against Atlantic Computers, BZW, NM Rothschild and Spicer and Oppenheim in ADR leading to £150 million settlement, for Milk Marketing Board in EU law dispute, for the Guardian, Sunday Times and BBC in libel actions brought by Keith Schellenberg, for Daily Mail and News International in libel actions brought by Sir Alan Sugar, for Glaxo Wellcome against Inland Revenue and for Belling Pension Fund in professional negligence action against Hereward Phillips. Previously acted for British Airways against Virgin, British & Commonwealth against Samuel Montagu & Quadrex, ACLI against M&R, Savoy against THF, CE Heath against Gooda Walker Syndicates. Pro Bono: Privy Council Capital Punishment Appeal from Jamaica; appeal by President of Oxford Union against dismissal from office.
Prof. Memberships: Chairman, Bar Caribbean Pro Bono Committee; Former member, Combar North American Committee; Bar Council Public Affairs Committee. Recorder, South Eastern Circuit.
Career: Classical Scholar at St. Paul's and Trinity College, Cambridge. English Speaking Union Scholar, Hackley School, New York. President Cambridge Union Society. BA Hons in Classics and History, Cambridge University. Winner Observer Mace Debating Championship. 1st in Order of Merit, Part 1 Bar Exams.

STAFFORD, Andrew QC
Littleton Chambers
(Michel Kallipetis QC), London
(020) 7797 8600

Recommended in Employment
Specialisation: Employment law, professional negligence and general commercial. Reported cases include: Malik v BCCI, Hagen v ICI, Symbian v Christensen, University of Nottingham v Eytt, Rock Refrigeration v Jones, Byrne Brother v Baird, Gerrard Ltd v Read, Whitewater Leisure v Barnes, SBJ Stephenson v Mandy, Brostoff and Hornsby v CKL, Greenland Houchen v Bennett, Beswarick v Ripman.
Career: RGS Newcastle-upon-Tyne; Trinity Hall, Cambridge; called to the Bar 1980; QC 2000; appointed part-time Employment Tribunal Chairman 2000.
Publications: Author of 'Dishonest Assistance in a Breach of Trust' ('Trusts Estates Journal') and 'Solicitors Liability for Dishonest Assistance in a Breach of Trust' (PNLR).

STAFFORD-MICHAEL, Simon
4 King's Bench Walk
(Robert Rhodes QC), London
(020) 7822 8822
Recommended in Fraud
Specialisation: Fraud, insurance and reinsurance. Fraud: Regulation, compliance and money laundering; serious fraud investigations conducted by the SFO, CPS, Inland Revenue, C&E, DTI and SIB; and criminal and commercial litigation. Major trials include: Jyske Bank, Guinness, Arrows and Wallace Duncan Smith. Notable recent matters include R v W & Another (Court of Appeal), R v EPA ex p Green Environmental Industries. Insurance and Reinsurance: Marine and Non-marine; Regulation and Insolvency; London Market/ Lloyd's of London law and practice; construction of complex policy language; Equitas; international litigation and arbitration; long tail-environmental/ mass tort/ product's liability; CAT claims; professional indemnity claims; D&O claims; settlement counsel and mediator. Notable recent matters include: Lasmo plc v London Market Insurers et al (Court of Appeal) and settlement counsel retained on behalf of US corporate assureds to advise on settlement of certain environmental claims brought against London Market Insurers.
Prof. Memberships: Criminal Bar Association, American Bar Association, International Bar Association and Federation of Insurance and Corporate Counsel.
Career: West Bridgeford Comprehensive School, University of Bristol and Gray's Inn. Co-Chair of the International Insurance Coverage Litigation Committee of the ABA 1995-99. Journal of Money Laundering, Advisory Board 1998-date.

STALLWORTHY, Nicolas
35 Essex Street (Christopher Wilson-Smith QC), London
(020) 7353 6381
clerks@35essexstreet.com
Recommended in Pensions

Specialisation: Specialises in pensions law (particularly in relation to occupational pension schemes). Acted in Stevens v Bell & Others (for members re: the construction of a British Airways pension scheme; CA, 2002); Hoover Ltd v Hetherington & Others (for trustee re: construction of the early retirement provisions of the Hoover (1987) Pension Scheme; ChD, 2002); Bradstock Group Pension Scheme Trustees Ltd v Bradstock Group Plc (for members re: compromise of employer's debts under section 75 of the Pensions Act 1995; ChD, 2002); Trustee Corporation v Asil Nadir & Others (for contingent beneficiaries re: vesting of pension entitlements in trustee in bankruptcy; ChD, 2002); Abbey National Independent Trustee Ltd v Woodhead & Lewis (for trustee alleging wilful default by previous trustees; ChD and oral hearing before Pensions Ombudsman, 2000); and Southernhay Pension Trustees Ltd v Orris & Neep (for beneficiaries resisting hostile Beddoes application; ChD, 2000). Involved in National Grid Co Plc v Laws; HL, 2000. Cases have concerned maladministration and breaches of trust/fiduciary duty by trustees; tracing/restitution of trust property; the distribution of surpluses; applications for Beddoes relief; pensions mis-selling; pensions and insolvency; appeals from and complaints to the Pensions Ombudsman; submissions to OPRA re: civil and criminal proceedings against former trustees; and submissions to the PIA Ombudsman re: pensions mis-selling. Also practices in general chancery work (contractual/property litigation) and professional negligence (particularly relating to solicitors).
Prof. Memberships: Association of Pension Lawyers; Chancery Bar Association; Professional Negligence Bar Association.
Career: Called to the Bar in 1993; completed pupillage 1994; post-graduate degree 1995; joined 35 Essex Street in 1996.
Personal: Born 10 June 1970; educated Radley College 1983-88; Christ Church, Oxford 1989-92 (BA, Jurisprudence) & 1994-95 (Bachelor of Civil Law).

STANISTREET, Penelope
Paradise Chambers
(Gary Burrell QC), Sheffield
(0115) 255 9144
booth@paradise-sq.co.uk
Recommended in Crime
Specialisation: Crime, prosecuting and defending. Youth specialist in Youth Court and Crown Court, often dealing with young and vulnerable witnesses and defendants. Also family work, private and public.
Prof. Memberships: Criminal Bar Association, FLBA.
Career: Having graduated in Classical Civilisation from Nottingham University, undertook the CPE at City University, then ICSL, being called in 1993 by Lincoln's Inn. Took a career break to have son returning to Nottingham for pupillage and has been practising at the Bar in Leicester for three years, recently moving to Sheffield.
Personal: Interested in classical history, fine art and photography, also keeping fit and keeping one step ahead of young family.

STANLEY, Paul
Essex Court Chambers
(Gordon Pollock QC), London
(020) 7813 8000
Recommended in Commercial (Litigation)
Specialisation: Commercial litigation and advisory work (especially international commercial litigation and arbitration, insurance and reinsurance, commercial fraud); EC litigation and advisory work.
Prof. Memberships: COMBAR; British Maritime Law Association European Committee.
Career: Downing College, Cambridge: BA 1991 (Law); Harvard Law School: LLM 1992. Called to Bar 1993. Treasury Panel (C List).
Publications: Current Law Statutes annotations to Human Rights Act 1998 (with Peter Duffy QC).
Personal: Born 1970.

STARMER, Keir QC
Doughty Street Chambers (Geoffrey Robertson QC), London
(020) 7404 1313
Recommended in Administrative & Public Law, Crime, Human Rights

STARTE, Harvey
1 Brick Court (Richard Rampton QC), London
(020) 7353 8845
Recommended in Defamation

STEAD, Richard
St John's Chambers
(Christopher Sharp QC), Bristol
(0117) 921 3456
clerks@stjohnschambers.co.uk
Recommended in Commercial (Litigation), Personal Injury
Specialisation: Specialist in construction law, personal injury and professional negligence.
Prof. Memberships: Personal Injury Bar Association - Society at Construction Law - Chartered Institute of Arbitrators.
Career: Called to the Bar in 1979. Recorder 1996.

STEEL, John QC
4-5 Gray's Inn Square
(Elizabeth Appleby QC), London
(020) 7404 5252
clerks@4-5graysinnsquare.co.uk
Recommended in Local Government, Planning
Specialisation: Has worked for many national and international clients in both the public and private sectors at the highest level in public, administrative, planning and environmental law. Practices in judicial review and public inquiry work. Specialities include retail, leisure, sports (especially football stadiums), housing, minerals, waste

disposal, highways, aviation, compulsory purchase and licensing. Particularly experienced in cases involving scientific, engineering and technically complex issues.
Prof. Memberships: Planning and Environment Bar Association; Administrative Law Bar Association. Fellow Royal Geographical Society; Vice Chairman Durham University Institute.
Career: Called to the Bar 1978. Silk 1993. Recorder.
Personal: Educated: Harrow School 1967-72; Durham University (BSc Hons chemistry) 1973-76; President Durham University Athletic Union 1975; Gray's Inn Moots Prize 1978, Member Attorney General's panel junior counsel (planning etc) 1979-93.

STEER, David QC
7 Harrington Street Chambers (David Steer QC & Robert Fordham QC & Iain Goldrein QC), Liverpool
(0151) 242 0707
Recommended in Crime

STEINFELD, Alan QC
24 Old Buildings (Martin Mann QC & Alan Steinfeld QC), London
(020) 7404 0946
Recommended in Chancery, Company, Insolvency, Partnership, Pensions

STEPHENS, John L
35 Essex Street (Christopher Wilson-Smith QC), London
(020) 7353 6381
Recommended in Pensions
Specialisation: Principal area of practice is pensions, covering all aspects of UK and international occupational pension schemes and claims associated therewith (eg professional negligence, executive severance etc). Subsidiary areas of practice include offshore trusts, shipping finance and claims to ownership of antiquities (ie claims by nations, museums, temples, etc to ownership of ancient works of art). Frequently addresses both commercial and legal conferences.
Prof. Memberships: Association of Pensions Lawyers, Chancery Bar Association, IPEBLA.
Career: Called to the Bar in 1975. Joined present chambers in 1977.
Personal: Educated at Oxford University (BA, 1974). Born 30 March 1953. Leisure pursuits include travel. Lives in London.

STEPHENSON, Geoffrey
2-3 Gray's Inn Square (Anthony Porten QC & Anthony Scrivener QC), London
(020) 7242 4986
Recommended in Consumer Law, Planning
Specialisation: Local government and public law with particular emphasis on planning local government finance and administration, housing and consumer and environmental law.
Prof. Memberships: Planning and Environment Bar Association. Administrative Law Bar Association. Parliamentary Bar Association. Fellow of the Chartered Insurance Institute. Member of the Bar of Texas.

STERLING, Robert
St. James's Chambers (Robert Sterling & Ian Leeming QC), Manchester
(0161) 834 7000
Recommended in Chancery, Insolvency
Specialisation: Chancery with emphasis on commercial litigation, corporate and personal insolvency and professional negligence. Recently reported cases: White v Richards (1993) 68 P & CR 105; Griffiths v Yorkshire Bank plc (1994) 2W.L.R. 1427; Alsop Wilkinson v Neary (1996) 1W.L.R. 1220; Ross v Telford (1998) 1 BCLC 82; Provincial North West plc v Bennett, 'The Times' February 12 1999 CA; Naidoo v Naidu and Brown Turner Crompton Carr ('The Times' November 1st 2000); Transco plc (British Gas plc) v Stockport MBC 2001 EGCS27CA.
Prof. Memberships: Chancery Bar Association, Northern Chancery Bar Association, Professional Negligence Bar Association, Northern Circuit Commercial Bar Association.
Career: Head of chambers, chairman of Northern Chancery Bar Association 1994-97. Acts as arbitrator in commercial disputes.

STERN, Ian
Hollis Whiteman Chambers (QEB) (Julian Bevan QC & Peter Whiteman QC), London
(020) 7583 5766
Recommended in Fraud
Specialisation: Disciplinary Tribunals: regular appearances at a number of professional bodies - including the General Medical Council, the General Optical Council, the General Dental Council and the General Osteopathic Council. Fraud: involved in a number of large fraud cases.
Prof. Memberships: One of the founders of the Association of Regulatory and Disciplinary Lawyers. Member of the Criminal Bar Association, South East Circuit and a number of local Bar Messes. Called to the New South Wales Bar, Australia in 1989.
Personal: Married to a GP and has three daughters. Runs on a fairly regular basis and completed the London Marathon in 1992 and 2000.

STERNBERG, Michael
4 Paper Buildings (Lionel Swift QC), London
(020) 7583 0816
mvs@4pb.com
Recommended in Family
Specialisation: All aspects of family and family-related law including matrimonial finance; Inheritance Act claims, and child law with specific reference to sexual abuse and contested adoptions. Matrimonial finance work includes investigation of overseas trusts and companies. Recent cases include Re: M (Sexual abuse allegations Interviewing Techniques) 1999 2FLR G2; Re: AMR (Adoption procedure) 1999 2FLR 801; Re J (adoption procedure Isle of Man) 2000 2FLR 633; Re: AGN (Adoption: Foreign adoption) 2000 2FLR 431 and B v P (adoption of one natural parent to exclusion of another) 2001 1FLR 589 CA; Re: M (Petition to European Commission of Human Rights) [1997] IFLR 755; S v. S [1997] 1WLR 1621, financial relief - inference of tax evasion by husband, Inland Revenue receiving copy of judgement - confidential information - breach of confidence, public interest; Re: F (a minor: paternity test) [1993] 3 WLR 369 (C.A.). Description: evidence - blood test -application blood test for DNA profiling by claimant for paternity; H v. H (financial provision: capital allowance) [1993] 2FLR 335; R v. Plymouth Justices ex parte W, [1993] 2FLR 777. Family proceedings - judicial review; H v. H (Residence order leave to remove from jurisdiction) [1995] 1FLR 529 (C.A.); Re: M (child's upbringing) [1996] 2FLR 441 (C.A.); DI v UK Government admissible complaint in ECHR on rights of post/operative gender reassigned individuals.
Prof. Memberships: Family Law Bar Association. Assistant Secretary Family Law Bar Association 1986-1988.
Career: Called to the Bar 1975 and joined 3 Dr. Johnson's Buildings, Temple. Moved to 4 Paper Buildings EC4, Temple, in 1994.
Personal: Educated at Carmel College, Wallingford 1962-70, Queens College, Cambridge 1970-74. (MA, LL.M). Governor of North London Collegiate School, Trustee of Sternberg Charitable Settlement. Freeman of the City of London and Member of the Worshipful Company of Horners. Member of Reform Club. Born 12th September 1951. Decoration: Medaglia D'Argento di Benemerenza of sacred military Constantinian Order of St. George (1990).

STEVENSON, William QC
Crown Office Chambers (Michael Spencer QC & Christopher Purchas QC), London
(020) 7797 8100
wsqc@crownofficechambers.com
Recommended in Personal Injury
Specialisation: Principal area of practice involves health and safety, product, public and employers' liability, occupation-related diseases and disorders including legionella pneumophilia, asthmas, asbestos-related diseases and disorders, cancers and noise induced hearing loss. Has acted in WRULD claims by ceramic, banking and electronics industry employees and toxic shock syndrome claims against sanitary protection manufacturers. Experienced in assessment of damages for severe and catastrophic personal injuries and in multi-party litigation. Has chaired and addressed conferences and seminars on occupational diseases.
Prof. Memberships: London Common Law and Commercial Bar Association.
Career: Called to the Bar 1968 and joined present chambers in 1969. Recorder 1992, Queen's Counsel 1996.
Personal: Admitted Lincoln's Inn 1962 - Hardwicke and Droop Scholarships, Bencher 2001.

STEWART, Roger QC
Four New Square (Justin Fenwick QC), London
(020) 7822 2000
barristers@4newsquare.com
Recommended in Construction, Professional Negligence
Specialisation: Sorting wheat from chaff.
Prof. Memberships: TECBAR, PNBA, COMBAR, LCLCBA.
Career: MA LLM, General Editor 'Jackson and Powell on Professional Negligence'.

STEWART SMITH, Rodney
New Square Chambers (Charles Purle QC), London
(020) 7419 8000
rodney.stewartsmith@newsquarechambers.co.uk
Recommended in Chancery
Specialisation: General chancery, especially commercial and residential property, easements, partnership, wills, trusts and court of protection matters, professional negligence.
Prof. Memberships: Chancery Bar Association.
Career: Called to the Bar 1964. Practised since then at 1 New Square and New Square Chambers, Lincoln's Inn. Assistant Recorder 1990-94. Recorder 1994 to date. Member of Land Registration Rules Committee since 1991. General Tax Commissioner since 1991.
Publications: 'Butterworths Land Development Encyclopaedia' (1976).
Personal: Winchester College and Trinity Hall, Cambridge (BA 1963, LLB 1964). Leisure interests: watching cricket and hill walking.

STEYN, Karen
11 King's Bench Walk Chambers (Eldred Tabachnik QC & James Goudie QC), London
(020) 7632 8500
steyn@11kbw.com
Recommended in Education
Specialisation: Principal areas of practice are public law and human rights law, including local government, education, prisoners, mental health, community care, immigration and asylum, social security, housing, tax, financial services and regulation, planning and licensing. Practice also covers employment law and European Community law. Cases include R v East Sussex CC ex p Reprotech [2002] UKHL 8 (estoppel in planning law); Oxfordshire CC v GB [2002] ELR 8 (costs of special educational needs placement); Phelps v LB of Hillingdon [2001] 2 AC 619 (negligence in education); R (Pearson) v SSHD [2001] HRLR 39 (prisoners' right to vote); Williams v SSHD [2002] EWCA Civ 498

LEADERS AT THE BAR

(security categorisation of prisoners); Abadeh v BT [2001] ICR 156 (disability discrimination); Selvanathan v GMC [2001] Lloyd's Rep Med 1 (reasons); Hitch v Stone [2001] STC 214 (sham transaction); R v SSE ex p Bandtock [2001] ELR 333 (school closure); R v Governors of W School ex p H [2001] ELR 192 (school exclusion and industrial action); R v Midlands Police Authority ex p LM [2000] UKHRR 143 (unlawful disclosure of allegations of paedophilia); Bath and NE Somerset DC v Warman [1999] ELR 81 (prosecution for child's non-attendance at school).
Prof. Memberships: Constitutional and Administrative Law Bar Association; Bar European Group.
Career: Called: 1995. Appointed to C panel of junior counsel to the Crown: 2001.
Publications: Contributor to Local Government title of Halsbury's Laws; various articles on public law and human rights in [2001] JR 244, [1999] EHRLR 614, [1997] JR 22, [1997] JR 33 and [1996] JR 17.

STILITZ, Daniel
11 King's Bench Walk Chambers (Eldred Tabachnik QC & James Goudie QC), London
(020) 7632 8500
stilitz@11kbw.com
Recommended in Employment
Specialisation: Employment law, public law and commercial law.
Prof. Memberships: Employment Law Bar Association; Administrative Law Bar Association; COMBAR; CEDR accredited mediator (1997).
Career: Called to the Bar in 1992. Junior Counsel to the Crown (Panel B).
Personal: New College Oxford, BA (1st Class Hons). City University, MA. Born 1 August 1968.

STOBART, John
King Charles House Chambers (William Everard), Nottingham
(0115) 941 8851
Recommended in Crime

STOCKDALE, David QC
Deans Court Chambers (Stephen Grime QC), Manchester
(0161) 214 6000
Recommended in Personal Injury
Specialisation: Personal injury: all aspects, including accident, industrial disease, catastrophic injuries and multi-claimant litigation; employer's liability; health and safety; professional negligence (in particular, medical and solicitors). Also associated with 7 Bedford Row, London WC1R 4BU Tel: (020) 7242 3555 and Chancery House Chambers, 7 Lisbon Square, Leeds LS1 4LY Tel: (0113) 244 6691.
Prof. Memberships: Northern Circuit, Personal Injuries Bar Association, Professional Negligence Bar Association.
Career: Called 1975. Assistant Recorder 1990. Recorder 1993. Queen's Counsel 1995.
Personal: Educated at Giggleswick School and Pembroke College, Oxford.

STOCKDALE BT, Thomas
Erskine Chambers (Robin Potts QC), London
(020) 7242 5532
Recommended in Company, Insolvency
Specialisation: Corporate reorganisation and reconstructions including reduction of capital and schemes of arrangement. Takeovers and mergers. Schemes of arrangement in insolvency, including insolvent insurance companies.
Prof. Memberships: COMBAR. Chancery Bar Association. Law Society's Company Law Committee.
Career: Worcester College, Oxford MA. Bencher, Lincoln's Inn.
Publications: Contributor to 'Buckley on the Companies Act' (15th edition).

STOCKILL, David
No5 Chambers (Gareth Evans QC), Birmingham
(0121) 606 0500
Recommended in Chancery

STOKES, Mary
Erskine Chambers (Robin Potts QC), London
(020) 7242 5532
Recommended in Company
Specialisation: Principal area of practice is company law including corporate insolvency, commercial law with a company element and financial services both advisory and litigation. Recent cases include British Commonwealth Holdings plc v Barclays de Zoete Wedd Ltd [1999] 1 BCLC 86; North Holdings Ltd. v Southern Tropics Ltd [1999] 2 BCLC 625; New Hampshire Insurance v Rush & Tompkins [1998] 2 BCLC 47.
Prof. Memberships: Chancery Bar Association, COMBAR.
Career: BA, BCL (Oxon), LL.M (Harvard). Former fellow and Tutor in Law, Brasenose College. Called to the Bar in 1989, in practice at Erskine Chambers since 1990.
Publications: Consultant editor of 'Butterworths Company Law Cases'. Contributed chapter on Reductions of Capital to 'Butterworths Corporate Law Service'.

STONE, Lucy QC
Queen Elizabeth Building (Florence Baron QC), London
(020) 7797 7837
l.stone@qeb.co.uk
Recommended in Family
Specialisation: Specialises in family law, principally 'big money' ancillary relief cases. Has acted on behalf of numerous high-profile media clients.
Prof. Memberships: Member of Bar Council Law Reform committee 1994-97; Family Law Bar Association committee 1998-96; F v F [1996] 1 FLR 833; Clark v Clark [1999] 2 FLR 498.
Career: MA Cantab; called to the Bar in 1983; Silk 2001.
Personal: Born 1959. Married with one child. Lives in London.

STONEFROST, Hilary
3-4 South Square (Michael Crystal QC & Lord Alexander of Weedon QC), London
(020) 7696 9900
hilarystonefrost@southsquare.com
Recommended in Insolvency
Specialisation: Insolvency, company law and banking law. General commercial work arising out of insolvencies. Minority shareholders' petitions. Directors' disqualifications.
Career: Called to the Bar (Middle Temple) in 1991. Economist, Bank of England 1979-89.
Publications: Contributor to the 'Law of Receivers of Companies' Lightman and Moss.
Personal: MSc London School of Economics 1978. Diploma in law, City University 1990.

STONER, Christopher
Serle Court (Lord Neill of Bladen QC), London
(020) 7242 6105
cstoner@serlecourt.co.uk
Recommended in Sport
Specialisation: All aspects of sports law with a particular emphasis on litigation, drafting and enforcement of rules and regulations. Member of editorial board: 'Sports Law Administration and Practice'. Recent cases include: Wilander & Anor v Tobin & Anor; Korda v ITF Limited. Bingham v British Boxing Board of Control; Premier League disciplinary hearing against Liverpool FC and Christian Ziege. Clients include The International Tennis Federation; The International Cricket Council; The British Boxing Board of Control, The FA Premier League and The Football Association. All aspects of property litigation, particularly landlord and tenant. Recent cases include McDonalds Property Co Ltd v HSBC plc; Ipswich Borough Council v Duke & Moore.
Prof. Memberships: Chancery Bar Association. Bar Sports Law Group (committee member).
Career: Called to the Bar in 1991.
Personal: Educated at Shoreham College and the University of East Anglia.

STOREY, Jeremy QC
4 Pump Court, London
(020) 7842 5555
jstorey@4pumpcourt.com
Recommended in Information Technology
Specialisation: Information technology, construction and commercial work.
Prof. Memberships: Chartered Institute of Arbitrators, ADR Chambers (UK) Limited, Society for Computers and Law, TECBAR.
Career: Called to the Bar 1974, Assistant Recorder 1990, QC 1994, Recorder and Deputy Judge of TCC 1995, acting Deemster of the Isle of Man Courts 1999, Assistant Boundary Commissioner, England and Wales 2000; qualified Mediator and Arbitrator, ACI Panel of Arbitrators (IT), ACI Panel of Mediators (IT), World Intellectual Property Organization of Arbitration and Mediation Center (Geneva) Panel of Neutrals (IT).
Personal: Cambridge University (Scholar, BA Law 1st Class) 1970-73. Born 1952.

STOREY, Paul QC
29 Bedford Row Chambers (Nicholas Francis QC), London
(020) 7404 1044
Recommended in Family
Specialisation: Family law: public law/adoption (eg 1999 - appeared for applicants for adoption in Re Jade & Hannah Bennett); private law (re B [1998] 1 FLR 368, Re W [1999] 1 FLR 869); cases with a European element (eg U v W [1997] 2 FLR 282); matrimonial and cohabitee finance (eg Roy v Roy [1996] 1 FLR 541).
Prof. Memberships: FLBA
Career: Called Lincoln's Inn Trinity 1982. Chambers: 7 Stone Buildings 1983-85; Goldsmith Building 1985-91; 29 Bedford Row 1992 - . Tutor professional ethics at CLE 1989-97. Chairman Nagalro annual conference 1996. Appears in legal network tv training videos. Articles in Family Law (12/95, 4/96, 10/96, 3/97). Speaker at Law Society Local Government Child Care Group annual conference 1998. Regular speaker at national and local conferences/training days. Recorder.
Personal: Married, four children. Cycling, rugby, football, motor racing, golf.

STOUT, Roger
18 St John Street (Jonathan Foster QC), Manchester
(0161) 278 1800
Recommended in Crime

STRAKER, Timothy QC
4-5 Gray's Inn Square (Elizabeth Appleby QC), London
(020) 7404 5252
tstraker@4-5graysinnsquare.co.uk
Recommended in Local Government, Planning
Specialisation: Principal areas of practice are local government, public law and town and country planning. Has acted in many leading public law cases concerning, inter alia, environmental assessments, compulsory purchase, planning, housing and housing benefits, Sunday trading, caravan sites and 'new age travellers', free speech, professional advertising, discrimination and professional conduct. Appeared in many Privy Council Appeals. Represented the returning officers in the first challenge to a European election result and in the first challenge to a Parliamentary result for 70 years. Acts for many local authorities and regulatory bodies. Consultant editor of the Registration of Political Parties Act 1998, contributor to the Rights of Way Law Review and to Judicial Review. Advisory editor Public Health and Environmental Protection (Halsbury's Laws of England) and Local Government (Halsbury's Laws of England). Editor Civil Court Practice, also author, 'Markets' (Halsbury's Laws

of England).
Prof. Memberships: Administrative Law Bar Association, Planning Bar Association, Administrative Court Users' Committee.
Career: Called to the Bar 1977. Silk 1996. Assistant Recorder 1998, Recorder 2000.
Personal: Educated at Malvern College and Downing College, Cambridge (1st Class Hons). Senior Harris Scholar, Downing College Prize for Law, Holt Scholar of Gray's Inn, awarded Lord Justice Holker Senior Award. Admitted (2001), for the purposes of planning and election cases, to the Bars of Northern Ireland and Trinidad and Tobago.

STRATFORD, Jemima
Brick Court Chambers (Christopher Clarke QC), London
(020) 7379 3550
stratford@brickcourt.co.uk
Recommended in Competition/European Law
Specialisation: Principal areas of practice are European law including competition law, judicial review and human rights. Important cases include: R (Smeaton) v Secretary of State for Health, The Times 18.4.02; R v Secretary of State for Trade and Industry, ex p Imperial Tobacco, The Times (29.10.99 Div. Ct: 17.12.99 CA; 10.10.00 ECJ; 20.12.00 HL) [2001] 1 WLR 127; R v Dept of Health, ex p Source Informatics [2000] 2 WLR 940; Tamarind v Eastern Natural Gas, The Times 12.6.00; Z v UK and TP&KM v UK, The Times 31.5.01, (2002) 34 EHRR 3; Kingsley v UK, The Times 9.1.01.
Prof. Memberships: Bar European Group; ALBA; COMBAR; Executive Board of JUSTICE.
Career: Called in 1993; Junior Counsel to the Crown (2002, B-Panel; 1999, C-Panel).
Publications: 'Competition: Understanding the 1998 Act' (Palladian, 1999).

STREATFEILD-JAMES, David QC
Atkin Chambers (Robert Akenhead QC), London
(020) 7404 0102/
Emergency Tel: (020) 7242 4703
Recommended in Construction, Information Technology
Specialisation: Building and civil engineering. Experience of all the main standard forms of contract and subcontracts, together with contracts for the petrochemical industry, process engineering, the utilities (water and electricity), power stations, telecommunications and computer software supply and development. In addition, general commercial related matters - financing arrangements, guarantees and bonds, sale of goods, service agreements and commercial leases. Professional negligence. engineers, architects, quantity surveyors and surveyors and valuers. International commercial arbitration.
Career: BA (Oxon). Called 1986.

STRUDWICK, Linda
Hollis Whiteman Chambers (QEB) (Julian Bevan QC & Peter Whiteman QC), London
(020) 7583 5766
Recommended in Crime
Specialisation: Specialises in defence work but also handles prosecution. 25 years covering all areas of serious crime including murder, manslaughter, fraud, sexual offences, drug offences and disciplinary tribunal work.
Career: Called 1973.
Personal: Educated Manchester University.

STUART-SMITH, Jeremy QC
2 Temple Gardens (Dermod O'Brien QC), London
(020) 7822 1253
jstuart-smith@2templegardens.co.uk
Recommended in Personal Injury, Product Liability, Professional Negligence
Specialisation: Insurance and insurance related disputes; product liability; professional negligence; general commercial and common law.
Prof. Memberships: LCLCBA, PIBA.
Career: MA Cantab. QC 1997, Recorder 1999.
Publications: 'Recovery of Damages After Misrepresentation', 2000 MLJ 865.
Personal: Playing the french horn, skiing, history, keeping sheep.

STUBBS, Andrew
St. Paul's Chambers (Nigel Sangster QC), Leeds
(0113) 245 5866
Recommended in Crime

STUBBS, Rebecca
Maitland Chambers (Michael Lyndon-Stanford QC & Charles Aldous QC), London
(020) 7406 1200
rstubbs@maitlandchambers.com
Recommended in Chancery, Company
Specialisation: Company and commercial chancery litigation with particular emphasis on insolvency, civil fraud, restitution and conflicts of law. Reported cases include Grand Metropolitan plc v The William Hill Group Ltd [1997] (rectification); Jordan Grand Prix Limited v Baltic Insurance Group [1999] (Brussels Convention), Piccadilly Property Management Limited v Commissioners of Inland Revenue [1999] (corporate insolvency), Gehe v NBTY Inc [1999] (corporation tax, rectification) and Re Cedarwood Productions Ltd [2001] (directors disqualification).
Prof. Memberships: Chancery Bar Association, COMBAR, Insolvency Court Users' Committee.
Career: Called to the Bar 1994. Appointed Junior Counsel to the Crown (B Panel) 2001.
Publications: Contributor to Butterworths 'Practical Insolvency'.
Personal: Educated at Darton High School and Downing College Cambridge (1st class hons 1993). Former Queen Mother Scholar of the Middle Temple.

STURMAN, Jim QC
2 Bedford Row (William Clegg QC), London
(020) 7440 8888
jsturman@2bedfordrow.co.uk
Recommended in Crime, Fraud
Specialisation: Specialist criminal defence advocate instructed in many major cases. Particular expertise in fraud, regulatory work and advisory work to banks on criminal matters and in 'quasi criminal' tribunals. Acted for Primrose Shipman before The Shipman Inquiry. Regularly instructed in asset confiscation and DTA work. Extensive experience in The Court of Appeal Criminal Division, particularly in cases where he did not act in the lower court. Example, R v Lummes, December 2000, convictions for murder quashed and no evidence offered at the re-trial. Extensive experience of FA disciplinary tribunal work, has acted for Chelsea FC, Dennis Wise, Celestine Babayaro, Graeme Le Saux, Jimmy Floyd Hasselbaink and Mauricio Tarrico. Major cases in general crime include R v Stagg (Wimbledon common murder). Sivalingham, alleged Tamil Tiger murders in London. Ian Kay, 'Woolworths' murder. R v Gould and Charles Kray. R v Machin 'sex on an aeroplane case'. R v Kelly, first appeal on 'two strikes' life sentence, subsequently acted pro bono and persuaded the CCRC to refer the case back to the Court of Appeal where the life sentence was quashed. A European Court challenge to the original sentence is still pending. R v Reilly, disclosure. R v Callan on the DTA. Woodward - effect of drink in reckless driving. Griffiths - abuse of process. Acted in 2 'Operation Care' cases in Liverpool. Highly experienced in drugs cases. Extradition cases include USA v Sukharno, USA v Newton (Part of the Howard Marks case) and USA v Kleasen - the 'Texas band saw massacre'. Fraud cases include the successful appeal for Michael Villiers in the LCB diversion case. R v Bonner, a part of 'Hare Wines', extensive experience of all serious crime and complex fraud, including mortgage, revenue, VAT and diversion frauds.
Prof. Memberships: Member of Gibraltar Bar, CBA, IBA, BAFS.
Career: Called 1982, joined chambers 1983, Silk 2002.
Personal: Cricket, football, music and chasing his three young children around the house.

SUCKLING, Alan QC
Hollis Whiteman Chambers (QEB) (Julian Bevan QC & Peter Whiteman QC), London
(020) 7583 5766
Recommended in Fraud
Specialisation: Crime and Fraud. Clowes. Maxwell. Warren. Shivpuri 1987 AC 1, Howe & Others 1987 AC 417.
Prof. Memberships: Middle Temple, Bencher. CBA.
Career: Queens' College, Cambridge MA, LLM Harmsworth Law Scholar, Middle Temple.
Personal: Born Hong Kong 1938.

SUMPTION, Jonathan QC
Brick Court Chambers (Christopher Clarke QC), London
(020) 7379 3550
Recommended in Administrative & Public Law, Banking & Finance, Commercial (Litigation), Energy, Financial Services, Fraud, Insurance, Professional Negligence

SUPPERSTONE, Michael QC
11 King's Bench Walk Chambers (Eldred Tabachnik QC & James Goudie QC), London
(020) 7632 8500
clerksroom@11kbw.com
Recommended in Administrative & Public Law, Local Government
Specialisation: All aspects of administrative and public law and local government law. Other main areas of practice include employment law.
Career: Called to the Bar in 1973. Bencher, Middle Temple. Appointed Queen's Counsel 1991. Recorder 1996; Deputy High Court Judge 1998; past Chairman of Administrative Law Bar Association; Principal editor of latest edition of the Administrative Law title of 'Halsbury's Laws of England'; contributor to the latest edition of the Extradition Law title of 'Halsbury's Laws of England'; co-editor of 'Supperstone and Goudie on Judicial Review'; co-author of Supperstone, Goudie and Coppel on 'Local Authorities and the Human Rights Act 1998'; contributor to Butterworth's 'Local Government Law'; consulting editor of 'Supperstone and O'Dempsey on Immigration and Asylum'. Member of editorial committee of 'Public Law'.
Personal: Educated at St. Paul's School and Lincoln College, Oxford (MA; BCL).

SUTCLIFFE, Andrew QC
3 Verulam Buildings (Christopher Symons QC & John Jarvis QC), London
(020) 7831 8441
asutcliffe@3vb.com
Recommended in Media & Entertainment
Specialisation: Principal area of practice is commercial and business law, with emphasis on entertainment law, intellectual property (copyright, breach of confidence), banking and finance, professional negligence (especially in commercial transactions), fraud, company law/insolvency and conflict of laws. Cases include: Elton John v Dick James (1991); Holly Johnson v ZTT Records (1993); Gabrielle v Trim (1996); MCA Records v Charly Records (2001); Hadley v Kemp (1999); Spice Girls v Aprilia (2002); Dexter Ltd v Harley (2001); Saab v Saudi American Bank (1998); Wallace v RBS (1999); Chapman v Barclays Bank (1997); Barclays Bank v Sumner (1996); Investors Compensation Scheme v Various Solicitors (Home Income Plan litigation) (1999); West Bromwich BS v Mander Hadley (1998); First City Insurance v Orchard (2002). Acts as arbitrator in commercial and IP matters; CEDR mediator.

LEADERS AT THE BAR

Prof. Memberships: COMBAR, LCLCBA; PNBA.
Career: Call 1983; Recorder 2000; QC 2001.
Personal: Born September 1960. Educated at Winchester College and Worcester College Oxford. Lives in London and Yorkshire.

SUTHERLAND, Paul
Four New Square (Justin Fenwick QC), London
(020) 7822 2000
p.sutherland@4newsquare.com
Recommended in Professional Negligence
Specialisation: Principal areas of practice are professional negligence (including information technology professionals), construction (particularly construction professionals and complex technical/engineering cases) and insurance, including insurance fraud. Litigation and arbitration. Important cases include: Alfred McAlpine Construction Ltd v Panatown Ltd [2001] 1 AC 518 (the "no loss" case); Bovis Lend Lease Ltd v Saillard Fuller & Partners (2001) 77 Con LR 134 (contribution claim by contractor against architect and M & E engineer; proper construction of the Contribution Act 1978); The London Borough of Barking and Hackney v Terrapin Construction Limited [2000] BLR 279 (construction of final account clause in JCT 1981 Standard Form); Skipton Building Society v Lea Hough [2000] PNLR 545 (valuers' negligence; successful "100% contributory negligence" defence against lender claim); Morley v Carden & Godfrey, TCC, June 1999 (high profile architect's negligence); Carrs Bury St. Edmunds Ltd v Whitworth Partnership and The Barnes Group (1996) 84 BLR 117 (effects of separate payments into court by contractor and architect co-defendants); The Lowry Centre v Christiani & Nielsen, TCC [2000] (engineer's negligence, contract formation and jurisdiction in adjudication).
Prof. Memberships: Professional Negligence Bar Association; Technology and Construction Bar Association; Western Circuit (advocacy trainer); licensed to practice in Isle of Man; Editor of 'Jackson & Powell on Professional Negligence' and 'Jackson & Powell: Professional Liability Precedents'.
Career: Called to Bar 1992 and joined 4 New Square (formerly 2 Office Row) in 1993; Lecturer in Law (King's College London) 1990-93; Naval Officer 1984-88.
Personal: MA (Oxon) Mathematics (1988), MA (Cantab) Law (1990). Interests: Sailing, skiing. Good French.

SUTTLE, Stephen
1 Brick Court (Richard Rampton QC), London
(020) 7353 8845
ss@1brickcourt.co.uk
Recommended in Defamation
Specialisation: Defamation, malicious falsehood, contempt of court, reporting restrictions, confidence and media related law generally. Cases include Jameson v BBC, Bobolas v Economist, Papandreou v Time, Bookbinder v Tebbitt, Skuse v Granada, Taylforth v News Group and Police, Bottomley v Express, Botham v Imran Khan, Bennett v Guardian, Al Fayed v Conde Nast, Bleakley v Granada, Frost Group v RMIF, Venables & Thompson v News Group (identification ban), Att-Gen. v MGN (contempt), Att-Gen. v MEN (contempt), Chase v Newsgroup.
Personal: Chorister Westminster Abbey, Westminster School, Christ Church Oxford (graduated in Classics 1972), taught Classics 1973-8, City University (Law Diploma 1979). Called to Bar 1980). Interests include music, cricket, Greece.

SUTTON, Richard QC
18 Red Lion Court (Anthony Arlidge QC), London
(020) 7520 6000
Recommended in Crime
Specialisation: Crime, prosecution and defence. Fraud (revenue and commercial); drug trafficking; offences against the person; sexual offences; extradition; money laundering.
Prof. Memberships: Criminal Bar Association, South Eastern Circuit.
Career: Recorder; Silk 1993.
Personal: Educated: Culford School, Wadham College, Oxford. Married, two children.

SWAIN, Jon
Furnival Chambers (Andrew Mitchell QC), London
(020) 7405 3232
Recommended in Crime

SWAINSTON, Michael QC
Brick Court Chambers (Christopher Clarke QC), London
(020) 7379 3550
Swainston@Brickcourt.co.uk
Recommended in Commercial (Litigation), Insurance, Professional Negligence
Specialisation: Michael Swainston is a commercial litigator and advisor with a broad practice covering insurance and reinsurance, banking, financial services (litigation and disciplinary tribunals), commercial fraud, professional negligence, international trade, shipping, energy and competition law. His cases of note generally include the Lloyd's litigation (Cox v Bankside, Napier and Ettrick v Kershaw, Axa v Field, Brown v GIO), the Maxwell litigation and the defence of claims by Qatar against the former Emir. In the past year they include: Peregrine Fixed Income Limited v Robinson Department Store plc on the ISDA master swaps agreement, the Solitaire arbitration and related hearings in the Commercial Court, Guild (Claims) Ltd v Eversheds (a firm) (successful defence of claims arising from the takeover of Sunsail plc), a record FSA prosecution and related human rights proceedings, Mann and another v Lexington Insurance Co, (CA) [2001] Lloyd's Rep 1 (reinsurance dispute in relation to the number of 'events' involved in Indonesian riots), Shaker v MBC (claims arising out of the acquisition of television and radio companies in America)' Islamic Investment Company of the Gulf (Bahamas) Ltd v Symphony Gems NV (February 2002 - leading case on enforceability of Morabaha agreements. Presently engaged on a $200m arbitration over termination of a distributorship agreement.
Prof. Memberships: Called in 1985. Called to the California Bar in 1988 (inactive). Member of COMBAR, North American Committee of COMBAR, ABA, Insurance Litigation Committee, Law Reform Committee of the Bar Council, International Relations Committee of the Bar Council (responsible for North America).
Publications: 'Commercial Regulation and Judicial Review (Court Procedures and Remedies)' Hart 1998; 'White Book, European Jurisdiction'; 'Retrospectivity of the Human Rights Act: New Law Journal'.

SWEENEY, Nigel QC
6 King's Bench Walk (Roy Amlot QC), London
(020) 7583 0410
Recommended in Crime

SWEENEY, Seamus
Plowden Buildings (William Lowe QC), Newcastle upon Tyne
(020) 7583 0808
Recommended in Employment
Specialisation: Specialises exclusively in all aspects of employment law acting for private individuals, commercial organisations and local authorities.
Career: Called to the Bar in 1989 and practised in London until 1996. In 1996 he joined the Newcastle office of Eversheds and their specialist employment team. He returned to private practice at the Bar in September 1999.
Personal: Born 14 February 1966 in Derry City. Main interests are his family, reading and football. He is also known as James.

SWIFT, Caroline QC
Byrom Street Chambers, Manchester
(0161) 829 2100
cs@byromstreet.com
Recommended in Clinical Negligence, Personal Injury
Specialisation: Personal injury; clinical negligence; industrial disease.
Prof. Memberships: PIBA.
Career: Called to the Bar 1977. Appointed Silk 1993. Assistant Recorder 1992-95. Recorder 1995-date. Deputy High Court Judge 2000-date. Governing Bencher of the Temple, 1997-date.

SWIFT, John QC
Monckton Chambers (Kenneth Parker QC & Paul Lasok QC), London
(020) 7405 7211
jswift@monckton.co.uk
Recommended in Competition/European Law
Specialisation: John Swift QC returned to the Bar as head of Monckton Chambers in January 1999, having completed a five year appointment as the first Rail Regulator, a public office established under the Railways Act 1993. Since his return he has been engaged on a series of major cases in the area of UK and European Communities competition law, including the British Airways/City Flyer, IMS/PMSI, Universal Foods Corporation/Pointing, NTL/Cable & Wireless merger references, the Director General of Fair Trading's reference of the supply of medicaments to the Restrictive Practices Court, the Airtours/First Choice merger on appeal to the CFI, Luxembourg and Competition Commission inquiries into supermarkets, banking services and mobile phones.
Prof. Memberships: Member of the Competition Law Association and fellow of the Chartered Institute of Transport.

SWIFT, Jonathan
11 King's Bench Walk Chambers (Eldred Tabachnik QC & James Goudie QC), London
(020) 7632 8500
swift@11kbw.com
Recommended in Employment
Specialisation: Specialises in all aspects of employment and trade union law including dismissal, discrimination, collective disputes and European law advising and appearing for both employees and employers. Employment practice also includes restraint of trade, protection of confidential information and interim injunctions. Other practice areas include public and administrative law and all aspects of local government law and the law of education. Appointed to the Attorney General's B Panel in July 1999.
Prof. Memberships: Employment Law Bar Association; Employment Lawyers Association; Industrial Law Society; Discrimination Law Association; COMBAR; Administrative Law Bar Association.
Career: Called to the Bar in 1989; joined present chambers in the same year.
Publications: Contributor to 'Judicial Review' (eds Supperstone & Goudie) Butterworths 1997; contributing editor Butterworths 'Local Government Law' 1999; contributor to Halsbury's Laws of England: 'Administrative Law' 2001.
Personal: Educated at New College, Oxford (BA (Hons) Jurisprudence) and Emmanuel College, Cambridge (LLM). Born 11 September 1964. Lives in London.

SWIFT, Malcolm QC
Park Court Chambers (Robert Smith QC), Leeds
(0113) 243 3277
Recommended in Crime

SYMONS, Christopher QC
3 Verulam Buildings (Christopher Symons QC & John Jarvis QC), London
(020) 7831 8441
csymons@3vb.com

Recommended in Commercial (Litigation), Insurance, Professional Negligence
Specialisation: Commercial work particularly insurance/reinsurance and professional negligence. Appeared in many commercial court cases and arbitrations for and against insurance companies, reinsurers, Lloyd's syndicates, brokers, solicitors, accountants and other professionals. Recent cases include acting for insurers in Credit Hire litigation Clark v Ardington 2002 (CA); Smith v Henniker Major 2002 (solicitors' negligence in CA); Somatra v *Sinclair Roche & Temperley* 2001 (solicitors' negligence - commercial court); Britvic v Messer 2001 (product liability - commercial court); *Hammond Suddards* v Agrichem 2001 (solicitors' negligence); London Borough of Redbridge v Municipal Mutual 2000 (insurance - commercial court); J Rothschild v Collier (insurance claim arising from pension mis-selling - commercial court); BBL v Eagle Star and John D Wood for insurers of valuers JDW. Construction, particularly engineers and architects. Aviation. Arbitration: sits as arbitrator and acts as counsel. Mediation: acts as mediator.
Career: Called to the Bar 1972; Junior Counsel to the Crown (Common Law) 1985-89; Silk 1989; Recorder 1993; Deputy High Court Judge 1998; Bencher Middle Temple 1998. Member, Bars of Ireland, Northern Ireland, Gibraltar and Brunei.

TABACHNIK, Eldred QC
11 King's Bench Walk Chambers (Eldred Tabachnik QC & James Goudie QC), London
(020) 7632 8500
clerksroom@11kbw.com
Recommended in Employment, Local Government
Specialisation: Principal area of practice is employment law. Has appeared in numerous matters for individuals, trade unions, multinational businesses, local authorities and employer's federations in the areas of unfair dismissal, wrongful dismissal, discrimination, collective disputes, restraint of trade and European law relating to employment.
Prof. Memberships: ALBA; London Common Law and Commercial Bar Association.
Career: Called to the Bar 1970; appointed Queen's Counsel 1982; Assistant Recorder 1995; Master of the Bench, Inner Temple 1988; Recorder 2000.
Publications: 'Anticipatory Breach of Contract' (Current Legal Problems 1971).
Personal: Educated at University of Cape Town (BA, LLB) and London University (LLM).

TABOR, James QC
Albion Chambers (Neil Ford QC), Bristol
(0117) 927 2144
Recommended in Crime

TACKABERRY, John QC
Arbitration Chambers (John Tackaberry QC), London
(020) 7267 2137
Recommended in Arbitration

TAGGART, Nicholas
4 Breams Buildings (Christopher Lockhart-Mummery QC), London
(020) 7430 1221
Recommended in Property Litigation
Specialisation: All aspects of property law, including landlord and tenant, conveyancing and property related professional negligence matters.
Prof. Memberships: Member of Chancery Bar Association, Property Bar Association.
Career: Called to the Bar 1991.
Publications: Specialist Editor of Hill and Redman's 'Law of Landlord and Tenant

TAGHAVI, Shahram
Doughty Street Chambers (Geoffrey Robertson QC), London
(020) 7404 1313
s.taghavi@doughtystreet.co.uk
Recommended in Immigration
Specialisation: Specialises in administrative, immigration and nationality, human rights, european union and education law, with experience at all levels including the House of Lords, European Court of Human Rights and European Court of Justice. Reported cases include: Horvath v Secretary of State for the Home Department [2001] 1 AC 489, HL (definition of 'persecution' and interrelation with State protection); R v Secretary of State for the Home Department, ex parte S [1998] Imm AR 252, QBD (vires of subordinate legislation denying oral hearings in asylum appeals); R v Secretary of State for the Home Department, ex parte Kaur [2001] ECR I - 1237, ECJ (European Union citizenship and British nationality). Other notable cases include: R v Secretary of State for the Home Department ex parte Badami (legality of Secretary of State's Standard Acknowledgment Letter policy); The Queen on the application of Karaoglan v Secretary of State for the Home Department (legality of Secretary of State's Statement of Evidence Form policy); The Queen on the Application of Sedrati, Buitrago-Lopez & Anaghatu v Secretary of State for the Home Department (ECHR compatibility of the Secretary of State's detention policy).
Prof. Memberships: Member of Administrative Law Bar Association, Bar European Group, Education Law Association, Immigration Law Practitioners Association, International Bar Association (Human Rights Section) and an Executive Committee member of the Joint Council for the Welfare of Immigrants.
Career: Called to the Bar in 1994 (*Gray's Inn*). Teaches Administrative and Constitutional law at the School of Oriental and African Studies, University of London.
Publications: Immigration and Nationality Law Reports (joint editor), The Human Rights Act 1998 (contributing author).

TALBOT, Patrick QC
Serle Court (Lord Neill of Bladen QC), London
(020) 7242 6105
Recommended in Chancery

TAM, Robin B-K
1 Temple Gardens (Geoffrey Nice QC), London
(020) 7583 1315
clerks@1templegardens.co.uk
Recommended in Administrative & Public Law
Specialisation: Administrative and public law/judicial review, immigration/asylum, nationality, human rights. Personal injuries. General common law. Major reported cases: Bugg v DPP [1993] QB 473; M v Home Secretary [1996] 1 WLR 507; Percy v Hall [1997] QB 924; ex parte Flood [1998] 1 WLR 156; Harris v Evans [1998] 1 WLR 1285; Defence Secretary v Percy [1999] 1 All ER 732; ex parte Jeyeanthan [2000] 1 WLR 354; Horvath v Home Secretary [2001] 1 AC 489; R (Montana) v Home Secretary [2001] 1 WLR 552; R (Balbo B and C) v Home Secretary [2001] 1 WLR 1556; R (Home Secretary) v Immigration Appeal Tribunal [2001] QB 1224; Rehman v Home Secretary [2001] 3 WLR 877; Svazas v Home Secretary [2002] 1 WLR 1891.
Prof. Memberships: Administrative Law Bar Association. Personal Injuries Bar Association. South Eastern Circuit. Hong Kong Bar. New South Wales Bar.
Career: Called 1986. Junior counsel to the Crown (A Panel). Standing Prosecuting Junior counsel to Inland Revenue (South Eastern Circuit).

TAMLYN, Lloyd
3-4 South Square (Michael Crystal QC & Lord Alexander of Weedon QC), London
(020) 7696 9900
lloydtamlyn@compuserve.com
Recommended in Insolvency
Specialisation: Insolvency; company; professional negligence; instructed in Re Leigh Estates (UK) Limited [1994] BCC 292 (Disputed winding-up petition based on liability order for unpaid rates; Re Kingscroft Insurance Company Limited [1994] 2 BCLC 80 (Continuation of orders under section 236 of IA 1986 when provisional liquidators discharged from office); Re Dollar Land (Feltham) Limited [1995] 2 BCLC 370 (Court's power to review winding-up orders); Mytre Investments Limited v Reynolds & Others (No 2) [1996] BPIR 464 (Time limits for IVAs); Tam Wing Chuen & Anor v Bank of Credit and Commerce Hong Kong Limited [1996] 2 BCLC 69 (Privy Council: Charge backs); Mutual Reinsurance Co Limited v Peat Marwick Mitchell & Co [1997] 1 BCLC 1 (Court of Appeal: entitlement of auditors to rely on indemnity granted in Articles of Association of a Bermudian company); Aspinalls Club Limited v Halabi [1998] BPIR 322 (Jurisdiction to amend bankruptcy petition); Re Structures and Computers Limited [1998] 1 BCLC 283 (Exercise of Court's discretion to make an administration order where major creditor is opposed); Kempe v Ambassador Insurance Company [1998] 1 WLR 271 (Privy Council: power of Court to extend time limits under Scheme of Arrangement); Alf Vaughan & Co Limited v Royscot Trust Plc [1999] 1 All ER (Commercial) 856 (Hire purchase agreements with 'equity' at date of receivership; extent of remedy for relief from forfeiture); Commissioners of Inland Revenue v Robinson [1999] BPIR 329 (Extent of the Court's jurisdiction to review the making of a bankruptcy order); Re J N Taylor Finance Pty Limited [1999] 2 BCLC 256 (Extent of Court's jurisdiction under section 426 of IA 1986 re letters of request from foreign courts); Morgans (A Firm) v Needham (Court of Appeal: The Times, 5th November 1999) (Power to strike out for failure to comply with ambiguous unless orders); Re Bank of Credit and Commerce International SA & Anor; Morris & Ors v State Bank of India [1999] BCC 943 (Striking out of pleading of claim for transaction defrauding creditors); Re Deadduck Limited [2000] 1 BCLC 148 (Disqualification of director); Smith v UIC Insurance Co Limited [2001] BCC 11, Commercial Court) (Status of provisional liquidators of insolvent insurance company; power to award security for costs against company in provisional liquidation); Re Dianoor Jewels Limited [2001] BCLC 450 (interaction of Administration procedure with family law); Frans Maas UK Ltd. v Habib Bank Zurich AG (3/8/00, unreported; demand guarantees and illegality); O'Donnell & Sons (Huddersfield) Limited v Midland Bank Plc (2/4/01 and CA; scope of bank debenture over 'other debts'); Re Boorer [2002] BPIR 21 (jurisdiction of Court to vary consent orders); Cartwright v Cartwright [2002] EWCA Civ. 931 (CA; provability of foreign maintenance orders).
Publications: Contributor to Halsbury's 'Laws of England' (4th ed 1996 reissue) volumes 7(2) and 7(3); 'The Law of Receivers of Companies' (2nd ed and forthcoming 3rd ed), Sir Gavin Lightman and Gabriel Moss QC, Chapters 11 (Receivers and Winding-Up) and 17 (Receivers and Unsecured Creditors: Execution, Distress, Marevas and Trusts); 'Insolvency of Banks: Managing the Risks' (ed Oditah) (1996) Chapter 4, Choice and Initiation of Insolvency Procedure, with Mark Phillips QC.

TANNEY, Anthony
Falcon Chambers (Jonathan Gaunt QC & Kim Lewison QC), London
(020) 7353 2484

LEADERS AT THE BAR

tanney@falcon-chambers.com
Recommended in Property Litigation
Specialisation: All aspects of the law of real property including litigation and advisory work, with an emphasis on landlord and tenant.
Prof. Memberships: Chancery Bar Association; Property Bar Association.
Career: Called 1994; (Lincoln's Inn); member Falcon Chambers 1995-date.
Publications: 'Distress for Rent', A Tanney & I Travers (Jordans 2000); Fisher and Lightwood: 'Law of Morgage' (Butterworths 2001) 11th edn.

TANSEY, Rock QC
3 Gray's Inn Square (Rock Tansey QC), London
(020) 7520 5600
Recommended in Crime
Specialisation: Specialist Criminal Defence Silk with considerable expertise and experience in the conduct of the gravest cases in particular human rights, terrorism, espionage, murder, serious fraud, drug trafficking and organised crime. Most notable cases include the attempted assassination of the Israeli Ambassador; the Tottenham Riots which concerned the murder of PC Blakelock; the Blackmail of Heinz Plc; a conspiracy to post incendiary devices; numerous terrorist cases including the bombing of the Israeli Embassy (also the Brighton and Warrington 'Bombings'); uniquely the trading of state secrets by a KGB Spy. Accomplishments in the sphere of human rights comprise inter alia; representation Council of Europe at a conference in St Petersburg, Russia 1994; the formation, chairmanship and organisation of conferences in Europe for the European Criminal Bar Association in order to advance major legal issues of mutual concern among European Defence Lawyers.
Prof. Memberships: South Eastern Circuit, Criminal Bar Association (Committee member 1990-96, 2000-02), IBA, Chairman of the European Criminal Bar Association 1997-2002.
Career: Called to the Bar 1966 and head of chambers 1988.
Personal: Educated at Bristol University - LLB and Diploma in Social Studies

TAPPIN, Michael
8 New Square (Mark Platts-Mills QC), London
(020) 7405 4321
michael.tappin@8newsquare.co.uk
Recommended in Intellectual Property
Specialisation: Barrister specialising in all aspects of intellectual property law, but with a particular interest in chemical, pharmaceutical and biotechnological work. For comprehensive CV and list of recent cases, visit our website at www.8newsquare.co.uk.
Prof. Memberships: Intellectual Property Bar Association (IPBA)
Career: Called 1991.
Personal: Born 1964. Educated at Cheltenham Grammar School; St John's College, Oxford (1986 BA Hons Chemistry); Merton College, Oxford (1989 DPhil Biochemistry).

TASKIS, Catherine
Falcon Chambers (Jonathan Gaunt QC & Kim Lewison QC), London
(020) 7353 2484
Recommended in Property Litigation
Specialisation: Residential, commercial, agricultural, landlord & tenant and real property litigation.
Prof. Memberships: Chancery Bar Association.
Career: MA, BCL, Oxon. Called to the Bar 1995. Joined Falcon Chambers 1997. Assistant editor, 'Muir Watt & Moss on Agricultural Holdings'. Contributor of legal articles to Landlord and Tenant Review. Contributor to Woodfall CD updates service and New Law Journal.

TATTERSALL, Geoffrey QC
Byrom Street Chambers, Manchester
(0161) 829 2100
Recommended in Personal Injury
Specialisation: Principal areas of practice are personal injury claims involving severe and permanent disablement and professional negligence. Other areas include commercial litigation, insurance, administrative law and judicial review, civil claims against the police and general common law.
Prof. Memberships: Personal Injury Bar Association.
Career: Recorder 1989. Queen's Counsel 1992. Senior Counsel New South Wales 1995. Bencher of Lincoln's Inn 1997. The Judge of Appeal of the Isle of Man 1997.
Personal: Born 1947. Educated Manchester Grammar School and Christ Church Oxford.

TATTERSALL, Simon
Fenners Chambers (Paul Hollow), Cambridge
(01223) 368761
Recommended in Family

TAUBE, Simon QC
10 Old Square (Leolin Price CBE QC), London
(020) 7405 0758
Recommended in Chancery
Specialisation: Specialising in Chancery work (both litigation and advisory work) with special expertise in the fields of trusts, estates and tax, professional negligence, charity, real property, Inheritance Act claims, partnership; important cases include Berill v IRC (1981), Moore v IRC (1985), Re: Bunning (1984), Sinclair v Lee (1993), Re: Hobley (1997), Re: Ingram (1998), Re: Hoicrest (1999) X v A (1999), Public Trustee v Cooper.
Prof. Memberships: Member Chancery Bar Association, STEP and Working Party Trust Law Committee.
Career: Westminster School; Merton College, Oxford (1978 Modern History 1st class), Called 1980, Middle Temple and Lincoln's Inn, QC 2000.
Personal: Singing, tennis.

TAUSSIG, Anthony
Wilberforce Chambers (Edward Nugee QC), London
(020) 7306 0102
Recommended in Chancery
Specialisation: Equity and trusts, land/conveyancing, revenue, pensions, financial services, charities, housing associations.
Career: Called to the Bar 1966. Conveyancing Counsel of the Court since 1991. Publication: 'Housing associations and their committees'. A guide to the legal framework. 1992.
Personal: Educated at Winchester College and Magdalen College, Oxford.

TAVERNER, Marcus QC
Keating Chambers, London
(020) 7544 2600
mtaverner@KEATINGCHAMBERS.COM
Recommended in Arbitration, Construction, Professional Negligence
Specialisation: Construction and engineering; professional negligence: Arbitrator in domestic and international disputes.
Career: Qualified 1981; Gray's Inn.
Personal: Monmouth School; Leicester University; King's College, London (1979 LLB Hons, 1980 LLM). Interests: music, drama, literature, sport, trees. Born 1958; resides Benington, Herts.

TAYLER, James
Devereux Chambers (Colin Edelman QC), London
(020) 7353 7534
tayler@devchambers.co.uk
Recommended in Employment
Specialisation: Employment; discrimination; administrative and local government. Cases of interest include ABP v T&G [2001] EWCA CIV 2032 (industrial action); Hayes v Security and Facilities Executive [2001] IRLR 81 CA. ECM v Cox; [1999] ICR 1162, CA (transfer of undertakings); Noorani v Merseyside Tec [1999] IRLR 184 CA (procedure); Thompson v Walon and BRS Automotive [1997] IRLR 343 EAT; BSG Property Services v Tuck [1996] IRLR 134 EAT (transfer of undertakings).
Prof. Memberships: ELBA (Committee member); ILS; ELA; ALBA.
Career: Wadham College Oxford; BA (Hons) Biology (1983-86): PCL (1987-88); CPE: ICSL Bar Finals (1988-89). [Queen Mother Scholarship; CLE Studentship]; part-time Chairman of Employment Tribunals.
Publications: Editor 'Butterworths Discrimination Law'. Contributor Halsbury's Laws (Equal Pay)'.

TAYLOR, Debbie
29 Bedford Row Chambers (Nicholas Francis QC), London
(020) 7404 1044
dtaylor@29bedfordrow.co.uk
Recommended in Family
Specialisation: International family law disputes including child abduction, relocation applications, divorce and the cross-jurisdiction enforcement of financial orders. Expert evidence in Australian family law matters, particular interest and experience in Indian and Middle Eastern family law cases. Mental health related private and public law applications and child protection.
Career: Called 1984. Solicitor and Barrister Western Australia 1990. Legal member, Mental Health Review Tribunals 1994.

TAYLOR, Gregg QC
9 Park Place (Ian Murphy QC), Cardiff
(029) 2038 2731
Recommended in Crime
Specialisation: All aspects of criminal law.
Prof. Memberships: CBA.
Career: Called 1974 (Middle Temple). Keele University.
Personal: Rock and roll. Fluent in Welsh.

TAYLOR, Martin
2-4 Tudor Street (Richard Ferguson QC), London
(020) 7797 7111
Recommended in Crime

TAYLOR, Simon W
Cloisters (Laura Cox QC), London
(020) 7827 4000
simontaylor@cloisters.com
Recommended in Clinical Negligence
Specialisation: Specialises in medical law, including clinical negligence, medical disciplinary cases, mental health cases, health service administrative law, inquests and defamation and criminal cases involving medical disputes. Interesting cases include Peet v Mid Kent Healthcare NHS Trust [2002] 1 WLR 210 (access to joint experts), R (Touche) v Inner North London Coroner [2001] 3 WLR 148 (duty to hold inquest), Re A (children) (Conjoined Twins: Surgical Separation) [2001] 2 WLR 480 (case of Jodie and Mary), Re L [1998] 2 FLR 810 (blood transfusion - Jehovah's Witness), Hooper v Young [1998] Lloyd's Rep Med 61 (hysterectomy - ureteric damage - res ipsa loccuitur), Williamson v East London Health Authority [1998] Lloyd's Rep Med 6 (silicone breast implants - mastectomy), Crouchman v Burke and Others 40 BMLR 163, (sterilisation - existing pregnancy - warnings), Taylor v West Kent Health Authority [1997] 8 Med LR 251 (breast cancer - effect of delay in diagnosis), GMC v Dr Eagles and Others (October 1995) (confidentiality - case reports in medical literature), R v Canterbury & Thanet DHA, ex parte F & W [1994] 5 Med LR 132 (complaints procedure where litigation is pending), Silverman v Singer & Others (1992 and ff) (bowel damage at laparoscopic operation).
Prof. Memberships: Professional Negligence Bar Association; British Academy of Forensic Sciences; Society of Doctors In Law; British Medical Association.
Career: Qualified doctor. Called to the Bar 1984. Joined present chambers 1998.
Personal: Educated at Cambridge (BA

Hons) 1983. MB BChir 1987. Born 4 July 1962.

TEARE, Nigel QC
4 Essex Court (Nigel Teare QC), London
(020) 7653 5653
nteare@4sx.co.uk
Recommended in Arbitration, Shipping
Specialisation: Commercial and admiralty matters, in Court and in arbitration. His practice has covered many areas of commercial law but in particular the law associated with the shipping industry, eg charterparties and international trade, marine insurance, jurisdiction disputes and conflicts of laws, shipbuilding, collisions at sea, pilotage and the law relating to ports.
Prof. Memberships: COMBAR.
Career: Junior Counsel to Treasury in Admiralty Matters 1989-91; Queen's Counsel 1991; Assistant Recorder 1993-97, Recorder 1997-; Lloyd's Salvage Arbitrator 1994-2000; Lloyd's Salvage Appeal Arbitrator 2000-; acting Deemster in the Isle of Man High Court 1998-; Deputy High Court Judge 2001.
Personal: Educated: King William's College, Isle of Man and St. Peter's College, Oxford.

TEDD, Rex QC
St Philips Chambers (John Randall QC), Birmingham
(0121) 246 7000
Recommended in Crime

TEMPLE, Anthony QC
4 Pump Court, London
(020) 7842 5555
Recommended in Commercial (Litigation), Professional Negligence

TEMPLE, Victor QC
6 King's Bench Walk (Roy Amlot QC), London
(020) 7583 0410
Recommended in Crime

TEMPLEMAN, Mark
Essex Court Chambers (Gordon Pollock QC), London
(020) 7813 8000
Recommended in Insurance
Specialisation: Insurance and reinsurance, shipping, international sale of goods and international trade finance, in the context of both domestic and international litigation and arbitration. Also general commercial litigation of all types.
Career: Keble College, Oxford MA (Jurisprudence); BCL (1980). Inns of Court, 1979. Called to the Bar 1981.
Personal: Born 1958.

TENNET, Michael
Wilberforce Chambers (Edward Nugee QC), London
(020) 7306 0102
Recommended in Pensions
Specialisation: Undertakes a broad range of commercial/chancery litigation specialising in the areas of occupational pension schemes, financial services and professional negligence. Has appeared in a number of important cases concerning the rights of members of occupation pension schemes, including SWT v Wightman (1998) PLR 114, Lansing Linde v Albe & Others [2000] PLR 15; AMP v Baker [2000] PLR 77 and BEST v Harrod [1999] 2 ALL ER 993. In the area of professional negligence work centres around the work of solicitors, actuaries and accountants. Considerable experience in general chancery/commercial litigation, reported cases include Ashley Guarantee v Zacaria (CA) (1993) 1 ALL ER 254 (principle and surety/mortgages). Yale v Newman (1990) FSR 320 (competition law).
Career: Called to the Bar 1985. First Class degree in Law at New College, Oxford. Contributor to Ellison on Pensions Law and Practice, Professional Negligence and Liability (LLP) and International Trust Laws (Jordan).

TER HAAR, Roger QC
Crown Office Chambers (Michael Spencer QC & Christopher Purchas QC), London
(020) 7797 8100
terhaar@crownofficechambers.com
Recommended in Construction, Professional Negligence
Specialisation: Practice encompasses professional negligence, construction law and insurance and reinsurance work.
Prof. Memberships: Official Referee's Bar Association, Administrative Law Bar Association, London and Commercial Bar Association, COMBAR.
Career: Called to the Bar and joined Crown Office Row 1974. Took Silk 1992. Bencher of the Inner Temple.
Personal: Educated at Magdalen College, Oxford 1970-73. Born 14th June 1952.

TERRY, Jeffrey
8 King St (Gerard McDermott QC), Manchester
(0161) 834 9560
jeffreyterry@genie.co.uk
Recommended in Chancery, Commercial (Litigation)
Specialisation: Commercial and Chancery. Recent reported cases include Universities Superannuation Scheme v Royal Insurance (2000) 1 All ER (Comm) 266; Unchained Growth v Granby Village (2000) 1 WLR 739; Re Hancock (1998) 2 FLR 346; Co-Operative Bank plc v Tipper (1996) 4 All ER 366; Transthene v Royal Insurance (1996) LRLR 32; Bank of Baroda v Reyarel (1995) 2 FLR 376; Jones v Roberts (1995) 2 FLR 422.
Prof. Memberships: Northern Circuit Commercial Bar Association; COMBAR; Northern Chancery Bar Association; American Bar Association; Professional Negligence Bar Association; Union Internationale des Avocats; Bar European Group.
Career: LLB (Lond) 1975. Called 1976. MA (Business Law) with Distinction 1981. Fellow of the Chartered Institute of Arbitrators, President's Prize, 1996. CEDR Accredited Mediator 1999.
Publications: Various papers and publications in England, USA and Canada.
Personal: Married, two children (born 1983, 1987). Interests: theology and church affairs. Smallholding husbandry.

TETHER, Melanie
Old Square Chambers (John Hendy QC), London
(020) 7269 0300
tether@oldsquarechambers.co.uk
Recommended in Employment
Specialisation: Formerly a partner in *Norton Rose*, transferred to the Bar in 1995. Deals with all aspects of employment law, including unfair and wrongful dismissal, transfer of undertakings, collective disputes, restraint of trade and all areas of discrimination law. Leading cases in which she has been involved include Kerry Foods Ltd v Creber and others [2000] IRLR 10; Unicorn Consultancy Services Ltd v Westbrook and others [2000] IRLR 80; Everson and another v Secretary of State for Trade and Industry and Bell Lines Limited (in liquidation) Case C - 198/98 [2000] IRLR 202; Chief Constable of West Yorkshire Police v Khan [2000] IRLR 324; Preston and others v Wolverhampton NHS Trust and others Case C - 78/98 [2000] IRLR 236; Jones v Post Office [2001] IRLR 384; Ralton v Havering College [2001] IRLR 738.
Prof. Memberships: Former Chair and current Vice-President of the Industrial Law Society.
Publications: Writes the Equal Pay section of 'Tolley's Employment Law' and contributes to the Employment Law section of 'Butterworth's Education Law'.

THANKI, Bankim
Fountain Court (Anthony Boswood QC), London
(020) 7583 3335
Recommended in Aviation, Banking & Finance, Commercial (Litigation), Fraud, Professional Negligence, Sport
Specialisation: Commercial and civil including general commercial litigation, banking, aviation, professional negligence, civil fraud, arbitration, insurance, and sports law. Noteworthy cases include acting for Barclays Bank in Deposit Protection Board v Barclays Bank and Dalia (banking), for the Bank of England in Three Rivers DC v Bank of England (BCCI) (banking), for BAE in connection with the termination of its Regional Aircraft business (commercial aviation), for Quantas in the Deep Vein Thrombosis Group Litigation (aviation), for Swiss Bank Corporation in NRG v Bacon & Woodrow & others (reinsurance/professional negligence), Codelco v Metallgesellschaft (civil fraud), for Wembley National Stadium Ltd and The Football Association in connection with the Wembly Stadium project (sport), in disciplinary proceedings for the Football Association against Leicester City players over the 1999 Worthington Cup Final and against Tottenham Hotspur FC over players' contractual terms (sport), Nuova Safim v Sakura Bank (banking/swap agreements), Eastgate Group Ltd v Lindsey Morden Group Inc (contribution), Nat West v Utrecht America Finance (conflicts); Federal Republic of Germany v Sotheby's (conflicts), Dowles Manor Properties v Bank of Namibia (unless orders); Hall v Bank of England (banking), Caribjet v Air India (aviation/arbitration), Gurtner v Beaton (aviation/agency), Conchita Martinez v Ellesse International (sport), Gotha City v Sotheby's (privilege), Paragon Finance v *Freshfields* (professional negligence), Minories Finance v Afribank Nigeria (documentary credits/bills & exchange), Leeds Rugby League Club v Craig Innes (sport), BCCI v Price Waterhouse (discovery, Banking Act 1987, auditor's negligence), Southampton CC v Academy Cleaning (local authority/contract tenders), Re a firm of solicitors (solicitors/conflicts), Kecskemeti v Rubens Rabin (professional negligence), HIV haemophilia litigation. Involved in civil and disciplinary aspects of the Barlow Clowes, CKL/Nicholas Young and Polly Peck affairs. Joint editor of 'Commercial Court Procedure' (Sweet & Maxwell) and co-author of Fountain Court on 'Carriage by Air' (Butterworths).
Prof. Memberships: Commercial Bar Association.
Career: Called to the Bar 1988.
Personal: Educated at Balliol College, Oxford (MA, 1st Class Hons 1986). Harmsworth Scholar, Middle Temple 1988.

THOM, James
New Square Chambers (Charles Purle QC), London
(020) 7419 8000
Recommended in Property Litigation

THOMAS, Christopher QC
Keating Chambers, London
(020) 7544 2600
clerks@keatingchambers.com
Recommended in Arbitration, Construction
Specialisation: Construction and engineering; professional negligence; bonds and guarantees; oil, power and transport projects in UK and overseas; arbitration and mediation - domestic and international; Arbitrator under ICC and other rules; cases include Croudace Ltd v Lambeth BC; Int'l Press Centre v Norwich Union Life Insurance Society; McAlpine Humberoak v McDermott Int'l; VHE Construction v RBSTB Trust.
Career: Qualified 1973; Lincoln's Inn, Queen's Counsel 1989, admitted to the Bar of Gibraltar 1990; Recorder; lecturer; Fellow of the Chartered Institute of Arbitrators.
Personal: University of Kent, Canterbury (BA Law 1st class); Faculté Internationale de Droit Compare (Diplôme de Droit Comparé avec merite); King's College, London (PhD. Law). Arbitrator CEDR accredited

LEADERS AT THE BAR

mediator. Born 1950; resides London.

THOMAS, David QC
2 Temple Gardens (Dermod O'Brien QC), London
(020) 7822 1200
Recommended in Construction
Specialisation: Construction, engineering and other technical contracts. Associated professional liability, litigation and UK and international arbitration. Recent reported cases: Matalan v Tokenspire, Cook v Shimizu, Weldon v CNT, Davy Offshore v Emerald Field Contracting, GPT Realisations v Panatown. Soundcraft v Padmanor, Balfour Beatty v DLR, Chesham Properties v Bucknall Austin.
Prof. Memberships: TECBAR, PNBA.
Career: Oxford: 1st Class Honours in Law 1981. Called to Bar 1982; Called to Bar of Gibraltar 1996.

THOMAS, Keith
9 Park Place (Ian Murphy QC), Cardiff
(029) 2038 2731
Recommended in Crime

THOMAS, Leslie
Two Garden Court (Owen Davies QC & Courtenay Griffiths QC), London
(020) 7353 1633
leslie@global.force9.net
Recommended in Human Rights
Specialisation: Civil actions against the police and prisons. Inquests (deaths in custody and fatal shootings). Judicial review of Police Complaints Authority, Coroners, Magistrates. Human Rights specialist.
Prof. Memberships: Lawyers for liberty; Inquest Lawyers; Member of Civil Liberties Trustees; APIL.
Publications: Numerous articles and case notes on Inquests for various legal journals and media.

THOMAS, Michael QC
Essex Court Chambers (Gordon Pollock QC), London
(020) 7813 8000
Recommended in Arbitration
Specialisation: Maritime, International Trade, Construction, Sale and Purchase. Recent arbitrations: Oil Rig Charterparty dispute, sale of high speed vessel, shipbuilding dispute.
Prof. Memberships: Member of Hong Kong Bar.
Career: Practice at the English Bar since 1959, Treasury Junior (MOD) 1966, Queen's Counsel 1973.
Publications: Temperley: 'Merchant Shipping Act'.

THOMAS, Nigel
Maitland Chambers (Michael Lyndon-Stanford QC & Charles Aldous QC), London
(020) 7406 1200
nthomas@maitlandchambers.com
Recommended in Agriculture
Specialisation: Agricultural Law: Davies v H & R Eckroyd Ltd (1996) EGCS 77; Law of Commons and Village Green: R v Suffolk CC ex Parte Steed (1995) 2EGLR 232, Lord Dynevor v Richardson [1995] ChD 173.

Prof. Memberships: Chancery Bar Association, Bristol and Cardiff Chancery Bar Association Wales and Chester Circuit.
Career: Called to the Bar 1976 (Gray's Inn). Sometime lecturer in Agricultural Law, Central Law Training. Chairman Agricultural Land Tribunal (Midland Area), Recorder.

THOMAS, Paul Huw
Iscoed Chambers (Elwen Mair Evans QC), Swansea
(01792) 652988/9
Recommended in Crime
Specialisation: Prosecuted and defended all major categories. Junior Counsel in Pembrokeshire paedophile case (1993-94) for Crown.
Prof. Memberships: Criminal Bar Association.
Career: MA (Cantab). Recorder.
Personal: Theatre, reading, travel. Sport especially Rugby (Committee member Swansea R.F.C.). Married with two children. Passably proficient in Welsh.

THOMAS, R Neville QC
3 Verulam Buildings (Christopher Symons QC & John Jarvis QC), London
(020) 7831 8441
chambers@3vb.com
Recommended in Banking & Finance
Specialisation: Principal area of practice encompasses all aspects of commercial contracts, especially for banks, shipping companies, trading companies, commodity dealers and property companies.
Prof. Memberships: Commercial Bar Association, London Common Law Bar Association.
Career: Called to the Bar and joined present chambers 1962. Took Silk 1975. Recorder 1975-81. Master of the Bench, Inner Temple 1985.
Personal: Educated at Oxford University (MA 1960, BCL 1961). Born 31 March 1936. Lives in London and Wales.

THOMAS, Roger QC
9 Park Place (Ian Murphy QC), Cardiff
(029) 2038 2731
clerks@9parkplace.co.uk
Recommended in Crime
Specialisation: Criminal law of all types including Revenue and Excise fraud.
Prof. Memberships: CBA.
Career: Recorder 1987, Silk 1994.
Personal: LLB (Wales.)

THOMAS, Roger
Pump Court Tax Chambers, London
(020) 7414 8080
clerks@pumptax.com
Recommended in Tax
Specialisation: Indirect and corporate tax, stamp duty and tax litigation of all kinds. Cases of note: LM Tendancies v IRC, Labour Party v courts, Wellcome Trust v courts, Faroe Seafood v courts, Yarburgh Children's Trust v courts, Pattison v Marine Midland, Ensign Tankers v Stokes, Victoria and Albert Museum v courts.
Prof. Memberships: VAT Practitioners Group.

Career: Qualified 1979, Lincoln's Inn.
Publications: Halsbury's Laws of England: (1) VAT (2) Customs Duties. De Voil Law of Indirect Taxation.
Personal: Portsmouth Grammar School; St Johns College Oxford, MA BCL.

THOMAS, Sybil
3 Fountain Court (Robert Juckes QC), Birmingham
(0121) 236 5854
clerks@3fc.co.uk
Recommended in Crime, Family
Specialisation: All aspects of criminal and family law, with a particular interest in cases involving the disabled and mentally ill.
Prof. Memberships: Midland Circuit, Family Law Bar Association (Chairman, Birmingham branch), Criminal Bar Association.
Career: LLB (Hons) (Bristol) Called to the Bar 1976. Recorder.

THOMPSON, Andrew
Erskine Chambers (Robin Potts QC), London
(020) 7242 5532
Recommended in Company
Specialisation: Specialist in commercial litigation, particularly involving issues of company law, corporate insolvency, partnership disputes and professional negligence; advisory work in the same fields; cases include Re BSB Holdings Ltd (No 2) (1996 1 BCLC 155), Re H & K (Medway) Ltd (1997 1 WLR 1422), Re Sentinel Securities plc (1996 1 WLR 316), Re SH & Co (Realizations) 1990 Ltd (1993 BCC 60), Re CSTC Ltd (1995 BCC 173), Banque Financière de la Cité v Parc (Battersea) Ltd (1999 1 AC 221), New Hampshire Insurance v Rush & Tompkins (1998 2 BCLC 471), Re Holiday Promotions (1996 BCC 671), Re Lummus Agricultural Services (1999 BCC 953), Re Kaytech (1999) 2 BCLC 351, Gwembe Valley Development Company v Koshy (No 2) [2000] 2 BCLC 705, Re Sedgefield Staplechase Co [2000] 2 BCLC 211; DEG v Koshy [2001] 3 All ER 878; Konamaneni v Rolls-Royce [2002] 1BCLC 336; DEG v Koshy (No 2) [2002] 1 BCLC 478.
Career: Merchant Taylors' School; St Catharine's College, Cambridge (1989 BA; 1990 LLM; 1992 MA); Called to Inner Temple 1991.
Personal: Leisure: family, gardening, hill walking, birding.

THOMPSON, Rhodri QC
Matrix Chambers, London
(020) 7404 3447
rhodrithompson@matrixlaw.co.uk
Recommended in Competition/European Law
Specialisation: European Community law including administrative law, human rights and competition. Cases include Gough and Smith v Chief Constable of Derby (free movement rights and football banning orders); Roth v Home Office (penalties for importation of clandestine entrants; R v ITC ex p TV Danmark (cross-border broadcasts of 'listed events'); BCCI et al v Bank of England (misfeasance in public office); R v Chief Constable of Sussex ex p ITF (exports of livestock); acted for BBC in RPC reference of Premier League TV contract. Contributor to 'Bellamy & Child, Common Market Law of Competition', (5th edn); Vaughan Law of the European Communities Service, 'Rights of Establishment and Freedom to Provide Services' (looseleaf); 'Human Rights Practice', ed Emerson and Simor (looseleaf) (freedom of assembly); author of 'The Single Market for Pharmaceuticals' (1994). Regular speaker at conferences/in-house seminars on EC and ECHR law.

THORLEY, Simon QC
Three New Square (David Young QC), London
(020) 7405 1111
3newsquareip@lineone.net
Recommended in Intellectual Property
Specialisation: Extensive intellectual property practice particularly in field of Chemical and Biotechnical Patents and expanding to passing off, trademarks, copyright, designs and breach of confidence. Advises on EC law relating to IP. Experience in arbitrations. Recent Cases: Biogen v Medeva, Biotech Patents, House of Lords; Canon v Green Cartridge, patent/copyright, Hong Kong Privy Council; Chocosuisse v Cadburys - passing off; Phillips v Remington - trade marks; Pfizer v Lilly (Viagra) - patents. Arsenal v Reed (trademark - ECJ Reference).
Prof. Memberships: Chairman Intellectual Property Bar Assn (1995-99); Member Chancery Bar Assn; AIPPI; Member of Bar Council (1995-99).
Career: Rugby School, 1963-67. Keble College, Oxford, MA Jurisprudence, 1968-71. Called to Bar 1972. Q.C.1989. Appointed person to hear Trade Mark Appeals, 1996. Deputy High Court Judge, 1998. Deputy Chairman Copyright Tribunal, 1998.

THORNHILL, Andrew QC
Pump Court Tax Chambers, London
(020) 7414 8080
Recommended in Tax
Specialisation: Principal area of practice is revenue law, both advisory and litigation. Specialisations include Schedule E, share schemes and private companies.
Prof. Memberships: Revenue Bar Association.
Career: Called to the Bar 1969. Took Silk 1985. Currently Head of Chambers.
Personal: Born 4 August 1943.

THORNTON, Peter QC
Doughty Street Chambers (Geoffrey Robertson QC), London
(020) 7404 1313
Recommended in Crime, Human Rights
Specialisation: Principal area of practice is criminal defence work including commercial fraud; appellate work, notably Privy Council appeals (Caribbean, Mauritius, New Zealand)

often in capital cases; and all forms of serious crime including murder, terrorism, Official Secrets Act, corruption and drugs cases. Other main area of work is civil rights cases including actions against the police or government, suspects' and prisoners' rights and international human rights. Recent reported cases include R v Christou [1992] (undercover police); Walker v R [1994] (Privy Council jurisdiction: appeal against death sentence); R v Basford and Lawless (witness too ill to continue); R v Aroyewumi [1994] (sentencing in Class A drugs cases); Freemantle v R [1994] (the proviso in identification cases), Re W [1994] (rights of children), Lobban [1995] (editing co-defendant's statement) and R v Kelly and Lindsay [1998] (stealing body parts), R v Smith (Morgan) [1999] (provocation and the reasonable man). Author of 'Public Order Law' (Blackstone Press 1987) and 'Decade of Decline: Civil Liberties in the Thatcher Years' (Liberty 1989). Editor of the Penguin Civil Liberty Guide (1989); currently contributing editor to Archbold and member of editorial board of the Criminal Law Review. Regular broadcaster on legal and civil liberty topics. Teaches human rights, advocacy and criminal evidence to solicitors and barristers. Has lectured and chaired seminars, on trial by jury, PACE, police powers, the CPS, evidence, white collar crime, emergency powers, miscarriages of justice, and the right of silence.
Prof. Memberships: Midland and Oxford Circuit, Criminal Bar Association, Administrative Law Bar Association, formerly chairman of the National Council for Civil Liberties and of the Civil Liberties Trust.
Career: Called to the Bar 1969. Also called to the Bars of Trinidad, Northern Ireland, Isle of Man. Tenant at 1 King's Bench Walk 1971-78 and at 1 Dr Johnson's Buildings 1978-90. Founder member of Doughty Street Chambers in 1990 and currently deputy head of chambers. Took Silk 1992. Recorder of the Crown Court 1997. Benches of the Middle Temple.

THORNTON, Rebecca
Zenith Chambers (Andrew Campbell QC & John Collins), Leeds
(0113) 245 5439
clerks@zenithchambers.co.uk
Recommended in Family
Specialisation: Called to the Bar in 1976. A well thought of family practitioner, Rebecca Thornton acts in all kinds of children cases. She represents parents, guardians and local authorities in care proceedings involving every kind of allegation of child abuse and often detailed expert evidence of a medical, psychiatric or psychological nature. Also acts in adoption, private law residence, contact and leave to remove from jurisdiction. Instructed in the 'Cleveland' litigation and numerous reported cases.

Prof. Memberships: Family Law Bar Association.

THOROGOOD, Bernard
No5 Chambers (Gareth Evans QC), Birmingham
(0121) 606 0500
Recommended in Crime
Specialisation: Criminal Law - all areas covered but very extensive experience of the most serious categories of offences, including commercial fraud. Very significant experience of Video-Link and Appellate work. Particular interest in matters involving claims of public interest immunity and matters involving expert evidence. Trading Standards, Health and Safety, Road Traffic, Customs Work.
Prof. Memberships: Criminal Bar Association. Forensic Science Society.
Career: 1981-85 Short Service Commission (Army). 1986 Called to the Bar.
Personal: Married, three children.

THOROLD, Oliver
Doughty Street Chambers (Geoffrey Robertson QC), London
(020) 7404 1313
Recommended in Product Liability
Specialisation: Specialist in medico-legal and mental health law with extensive experience in handling negligence claims arising from both medical treatment and the use of pharmacutical products. Frequently involved in inquests, professional conduct hearings, Mental Health Review Tribunals and Residential Homes Tribunals that stem from decisions taken under mental health legislation. Experience includes many applications to the European Commission and Court of Human Rights concerning British mental health law and treatment. Has lectured widely to mental health professionals.
Career: Called to the Bar 1971. In-house lawyer for MIND 1978-81.

THORP, Simon
Park Lane Chambers (Stuart Brown QC), Leeds
(0113) 228 5000
sthorp@parklanechambers.co.uk
Recommended in Personal Injury
Specialisation: Practises almost exclusively in the fields of personal injury and clinical negligence along with associated areas of law (professional negligence; insurance; health and safety at work). Acts on behalf of both claimants and defendants. Has long experience in all areas of personal injury law including claims of maximum severity; industrial disease; employers liability; public liability; fatal accident claims. Substantial expertise in the quantification of damages in large claims.
Prof. Memberships: PIBA, AVMA.
Career: Called 1988. Provincial Treasury Council. Recorder.

THWAITES, Ronald QC
Ely Place Chambers (Ronald Thwaites QC), London
(020) 7400 9600
rthwaites@elyplace.com
Recommended in Defamation
Specialisation: Substantial and varied court and advisory practice dealing with defamation, public inquiries, inquests and advising chief officers of police on civil disputes, health and safety matters and policy issues. Other civil work also undertaken. His background is in high profile criminal cases and he also does the occasional criminal case. Recent libel cases include Blackstone v Mirror Group Newspapers; Frank Warren v BBC and Naseem Hamed; Foulds v Mirror Group Newspapers; Dr Rahamin v Channel 4; Condliffe v Ian Hislop and Pressdram Ltd (Private Eye); David Soul v Mirror Group Newspapers.
Prof. Memberships: Gray's Inn and Inner Temple.
Career: Call 1970. QC 1987.
Personal: Born 1946.

TIDBURY, Andrew
Queen Elizabeth Building (Florence Baron QC), London
(020) 7797 7837
Recommended in Family

TIDMARSH, Christopher QC
5 Stone Buildings (Henry Harrod), London
(020) 7242 6201
Recommended in Chancery, Pensions, Tax
Specialisation: Chancery practitioner, with a particular emphasis on trusts and associated taxes, pension schemes and professional negligence, principally solicitors and accountants. Important cases include AG of Cayman Islands v Wahr Hansen (charities) [2001]; British Coal v British Coal Staff Superannuation Scheme Trustees [1994]; Stannard v Fisons [1991]; Royal Masonic Hospital v PO [2001] (all pensions); The Pointwest litigation (solicitors negligence); IRC v Lloyds Private Banking, IRC v Botner (1999), Cooper v Billingham (2001) (all tax).
Prof. Memberships: Chancery Bar Association, STEP.
Career: Called 1985; silk 2002. Junior counsel to Inland Revenue 1995-2002.
Personal: Educated at Merton College, Oxford (BA) 1980-83.

TILLYARD, James QC
30 Park Place (John Jenkins QC), Cardiff
(029) 2039 8421
Recommended in Family

TIPPLES, Amanda
Maitland Chambers (Michael Lyndon-Stanford QC & Charles Aldous QC), London
(020) 7406 1200
atipples@maitlandchambers.com
Recommended in Property Litigation
Specialisation: Practice covers business and commercial chancery work, (litigation emphasis), including corporate and personal insolvency, partnership, landlord and tenant and property law generally.
Prof. Memberships: Chancery Bar Association, COMBAR, Property Bar Association.
Career: Called to the Bar in 1991 and joined 13 Old Square in 1992.
Personal: Educated at Roedean School and Gonville and Caius College, Cambridge (1986-90). Lives in London.

TODD, Michael QC
Erskine Chambers (Robin Potts QC), London
(020) 7242 5532
Recommended in Company
Specialisation: Company law, corporate finance and corporate insolvency; work involves all advisory and litigation aspects with an emphasis on litigation both in the UK and abroad and covers areas such as mergers, acquisitions and disposals of companies, shareholder disputes, board meetings, bank securities, financial services and related commercial and professional negligence (accountants and solicitors). Recent reported cases include North Holdings Ltd. v Southern Tropics Ltd. [1999] BCLC 625; Re Rotadata Ltd. [2000] 1 BCLC 122; Re: Allied Domecq plc [2000] BCLC 134; Re Sedgefield Steeplechase Co (1927) Ltd. [2000] 2 BCLC 211; [2002] BCC 889; Re Prudential Enterprise Ltd [2001] 2 HKC 686.
Prof. Memberships: COMBAR, Chancery Bar Association.
Career: Called to the Bar in 1977 and joined Erskine Chambers. QC year 1997.
Personal: Educated at Keele University (BA). Born 16 February 1953.

TOLANEY, Sonia
3 Verulam Buildings (Christopher Symons QC & John Jarvis QC), London
(020) 7831 8441
chambers@3vb.com
Recommended in Banking & Finance
Specialisation: Commercial litigation, arbitration and mediation. Advisory work. Specialist areas: domestic and international banking (including bills of exchange, letters of credit, bonds, guarantees, standbys and flawed asset arrangements); domestic and international commercial fraud and asset tracing; corporate and personal insolvency, insurance and reinsurance, contractual disputes, professional negligence. Recent cases include Libra Bank v Financiera de la Republica (2002) (assignment of secondary market debt), Smith v Lloyds CA (2000) (conversion, fraudulent alteration of a cheque, s64 Bills of Exchange Act); Lloyds Bank v Voller, CA (2000) (Bank's right to charge interest on unauthorised overdraft); Casson & anr v Ostley PJ Ltd & Ors, CA (2001) (construction of an exclusion clause in an insurance policy); Anglian Water Services v Crawshaw Robbins (2000) (contract, construction of an indemnity clause, nuisance, negligence, breach of statutory duty);

LEADERS AT THE BAR

Crest Holmes (South East) v Browne (1999) (application of s284, Insolvency Act 1986 to trust property).
Prof. Memberships: COMBAR; Membership Secretary of the LCLCBA (2002).
Career: MA (Oxon), Jurisprudence. Called to the Bar in 1995, Middle Temple. Tenant at 3 Verulam Buildings from October 1996 to date. CEDR Accredited Mediator (2000).
Publications: Chapter on Financing International Sales (emphasis on letters of credit, bonds and standbys) in 'McKendrick on Sale of Goods' (Dec 2000).
Personal: Education: Bolton School, Girls' Division. Lady Margaret Hall, Oxford.

TOLEDANO, Daniel
One Essex Court (Lord Grabiner QC), London
(020) 7583 2000
Recommended in Commercial (Litigation), Energy
Specialisation: Broad commercial practice including energy and utilities, financial services, insurance, sale of goods, company/insolvency and arbitration. Recent work includes BP Amoco v British American Offshore (oil and gas), Armco v Donohue (jurisdiction/anti-suit injunctions) and Sumitomo Corporation v Credit Lyonnais Rouse (options and futures trading).
Prof. Memberships: COMBAR.
Career: Called to the Bar 1993 (Inner Temple). Junior Counsel to the Crown (C Panel).
Personal: Born 1969. MA, Jesus College, Cambridge.

TOMLINSON, Hugh QC
Matrix Chambers, London
(020) 7404 3447
Recommended in Defamation
Specialisation: A leading commercial and common law practitioner, who has particular expertise in defamation, professional negligence, travel and public law. He has been involved in a number of high profile cases, including the Virgin and British Airways litigation.
Career: Called to the Bar 1983, Gray's Inn. Silk 2002.
Personal: Balliol College Oxford (BA), Sussex University (MA), Paris University; City University (Dip Law). Born 20 January 1954.

TOPHAM, Geoffrey J
3 Stone Buildings (Geoffrey Vos QC), London
(020) 7242 4937
Recommended in Chancery, Pensions
Specialisation: Main field of practice is occupational pension schemes, acting both in litigation and advisory work for members, pensioners, trustees and employers (cases include Imperial Tobacco, Courage, Brooks v Brooks, Lloyds Bank, National Grid). Other main areas are trusts and estates, and capital taxes.
Prof. Memberships: Chancery Bar Association, Association of Pensions Lawyers, Associate of Pensions Management Institute, Revenue Bar Association.
Career: Called June, 1964. Member of Lincoln's Inn. Joined Stone Buildings in 1965.
Personal: Educated at Haileybury and Trinity Hall, Cambridge.

TOUBE, Felicity
3-4 South Square (Michael Crystal QC & Lord Alexander of Weedon QC), London
(020) 7969 9900
felicitytoube@southsquare.com
Recommended in Insolvency
Specialisation: Insolvency, company, general commercial, banking, restitution. Cases: Secretary of State v Anderson [1999] BCC 121; Continental Assurance [1999] 1 BCLC 751; BCCI v Bank of America; Douai School [2000] 1 WLR 502; Toshoku Finance UK [2002] 1 WLR 671; Ross [2000] BPIR 636; Horne v Dacorum BC [2000] 4 All ER 550; UCT (UK) Limited [2001] 1 WLR 436; Hawk Insurance Co [2002] BCC 301; Liberty Mutual v HSBC; Cover Europe (New Law Online, 26 February 2002).
Prof. Memberships: COMBAR, Chancery Bar Association.
Publications: Rose (ed) 'Failure of Contracts' and 'Restitution and Banking Law'; 'Insolvency Intelligence' board member; cases editor (Totty & Moss, Sweet & Maxwell Complete Insolvency Service CD ROM); Lightman & Moss on Receivers, Rowlatt, Halsbury's Laws, Totty & Moss; 'Recovery' case summaries; EU Regulation on Insolvency Proceedings.

TOZZI, Nigel QC
4 Pump Court, London
(020) 7842 5555
Recommended in Commercial (Litigation), Insurance, Professional Negligence
Specialisation: General commercial and common law practice, specialising in commercial litigation, professional negligence (especially solicitors, accountants, financial advisors, surveyors, valuers, brokers and barristers), insurance and reinsurance, fire claims, media and entertainment, financial and banking disputes and gaming. He also has experience in aviation, employment, agency, advertising, construction work and professional disciplinary hearings.
Prof. Memberships: COMBAR, Professional Negligence Bar Association, London Common Law and Commercial Bar Association, British Insurance Law Association.
Career: Called to the Bar 1980, took Silk 2001.
Personal: Educated at Exeter University (LLB Hons first class) 1976-79. Bar Finals 1980 (first class). Leisure pursuits include sport (especially hockey), theatre and cinema. Born 31 August 1957.

TRACE, Anthony QC
Maitland Chambers (Michael Lyndon-Stanford QC & Charles Aldous QC), London
(020) 7406 1200
clerks@maitlandchambers.com
Recommended in Chancery, Professional Negligence
Specialisation: Principal area of practice encompasses insolvency, property, trusts, chancery and general commercial work, including a number of cases outside the UK. Recent cases include: Re Jeffrey S. Levitt Ltd [1992] (privilege against self-incrimination); Re Mirror Group (Holdings) Ltd [1993] (liability of assignees on liquidation); Gomba Holdings (UK) Ltd v Minories Finance Ltd (No.2) [1993] (mortgagee's costs); Lotteryking Ltd v AMEC Properties Ltd [1995] (set-off against assignees); Re BCCI SA (No.10) [1996] (insolvency set-off); Slough Estates Plc v Welwyn Hatfield DC [1996] (measure of damages for fraudulent misrepresentation); Grand Metropolitan plc v The William Hill Group Ltd [1997] (rectification); Bogg v Raper [1998] (will drafting and exclusion clauses); Plant v Plant [1998] (individual voluntary arrangements); Jordan Grand Prix Ltd v Baltic Insurance Group [1999] (Brussels Convention); Landare Investments Ltd v Welsh Development Agency [2000] (misfeasance in public office); Shalson v Russo [2001] (committal). Has sat as an Arbitrator. Vice-Chairman, Chancery Bar Association.
Prof. Memberships: Chancery Bar Association; COMBAR; Bar Sports Law Group; ACTAPS (Association of Contentious Trust and Probate Specialists).
Career: Called to the Bar 1981.
Publications: Contributor to 'Butterworths European Law Service' (company law) and 'Butterworths Practical Insolvency'. Deputy Managing Editor: 'Receivers, Administrators and Liquidators Quarterly'. Member, International Editorial Board, Briefings in Real Estate Finance.
Personal: Educated at Magdalene College, Cambridge (MA, 1st Class Honours).

TRACY FORSTER, Jane
4 Paper Buildings (Jean Ritchie QC), London
(020) 7643 5000
clerks@13kbw.co.uk
Recommended in Clinical Negligence
Specialisation: Clinical negligence of all descriptions. Recent Cases: Miles v West Kent Health Authority 1997 Med LR 191; Smith v Leicester Health Authority 1998 Lloyds Rep. (Med) 77; Thurman v Bath and Wiltshire Health Authority 1997 P.I.Q.R. Q115.
Prof. Memberships: Professional Negligence Bar Association; Personal Injury Bar Association; Employment Law Bar Association.
Career: LLB (Hons) Liverpool University 1974; Called July 1975 (Inner Temple); Sept 1975 - May 1986 Peel House Chambers, Liverpool. From May 1986 to May 2002 - 13 King's Bench Walk. August 2002 - 4 Paper Buildings.
Personal: Married with one son. Lives in London.

TRAVERS, David
6 Pump Court (Stephen Hockman QC), London
(020) 7797 8400
clerks@6pumpcourt.co.uk
Recommended in Consumer Law, Environment, Health & Safety
Specialisation: Practice made up of all aspects of regulatory work; including health and safety trading standards and consumer protection as well as environmental protection, waste management and planning, and public law. Experienced in appellate work and cases with a strong technical or scientific component. Clients include well known high street names (as well as small traders), local authorities and regulatory bodies. Cases include: R v Coffey [1987] Crim LR 498, CA; A v Wigan MBC [1986] FLR 608, DC; Birmingham CC v H [1994] 2AC212; Farrand v Tse (1992) Times 10 December, DC (meaning of 'application' for emergency prohibition order - Food Safety Act); Dudley MBC v Firman BTCL (1992) Independent 26 October DC ('due diligence' - sufficiency of sampling); Janbo Trading v Dudley MBC [1993] 157 JPN 256, DC ('due diligence'); Gale v Dixons Stores Group (1994) 158 JPN 256, DC (extent of trade description); T&S Stores Ltd v Hereford & Worcester CC [1995] Tr LR 337 (under age sales - 'due diligence'); Edwards v CPS [1881] 155 JP 746, DC (licensing); Lazarus v Coventry CC (1998) 160JP 188 (consumer credit advertisement -meaning of 'information' - 'due diligence'); North Yorkshire CC v Entergold Guardian 8.2.95 (breach of site licence and planning control at waste transfer station); Meston Technical Services v Warwickshire CC [1995] Env LR 380 (breach of site licence - meaning of 'waste'); Taw & Torridge Fisheries Byelaw Inquiry, Daily Telegraph 31.1.97; Hilliers Ltd v Sefton MBC [1997] CLY 2566 (delegation of powers within Food authority); Inspirations East Ltd v Dudley MBC [1998] 162 JP 800 (misdescription in holiday brochure); R v Snaresbrook Crown Court, ex p Input Management [1999] Times 29 April (duty to give reasons). HSE Harvestime Bakeries and others new item Times 12 June 2001 (double fatality in commercial bakery oven), Monks v E Northamptonshire DC Times 15 March 2002 (prosecution by council in its own name), Farrand v Lazarus [2002] 166 JP 227 (trade description - validity of disclaimer on odometer), R v Killian & Lang [2002] 166 JP 169 (whether trade description or indication as to price), waste management licensing appeals and numerous public inquiries, particularly involving waste

management facilities.
Prof. Memberships: Food Law Group, Planning and Environment Bar Association, Administrative Law Bar Association, UKELA. Midland Circuit.
Career: Called Middle Temple 1981, Kings College London 1975-1980 (LLB, LLM, AKC). Editor 'Kings Counsel' the KCL Law Journal 1978. President Kings College London Union of Students 1979, elected Honorary Life Member 1981. Harmsworth Scholar 1982. Member of the Bar Council 1995 - Member of Law Reform and IT Committees 1996-1998. Sometime Occasional Lecturer School of Management Sciences University of Manchester Institute of Science and Technology. Sometime Royal Institution Australian Science Scholar. Accredited mediator. Also at 3 Fountain Court Birmingham.
Personal: Married with children. Interests language, music, running and family life.

TREACY, Colman QC
3 Fountain Court (Robert Juckes QC), Birmingham
(0121) 236 5854
clerks@3fc.co.uk
Recommended in Consumer Law, Crime
Specialisation: Criminal Law. All types of serious crime cases including commercial fraud and miscarriage of justice cases. Equal split between prosecution and defence work. Recent reported cases: Fellows (computer pornography); Callender (res gestae); Kendrick & Hopkins (theft and gifts inter vivos); Ryan James (successful vet murder appeal); Jeremy Bamber appeal (forthcoming). Regulatory law of all types, representing businesses and local authorities; Popeley (Timeshare Act), Nottinghamshire CC v BT (Streetworks Act).
Career: Jesus College Cambridge (open scholar): Call 1971: Silk 1990: Recorder. Bencher Middle Temple. Mental Health Review Tribunal. Assistant Boundary Commissioner.

TREHARNE, Jennet
33 Park Place (Neil Bidder QC), Cardiff
(029) 2023 3313
Recommended in Crime

TREVETT, Peter QC
11 New Square (John Gardiner QC), London
(020) 7242 4017
taxlaw@11newsquare.com
Recommended in Tax
Specialisation: Revenue law. Practice covers all aspects of commercial, private client and trust taxation in the UK, including stamp duty, VAT, unit trusts, insurance company taxation and offshore trusts. Hong Kong profits tax, stamp duty and estate duty planning. Regular lecturer on revenue law.
Prof. Memberships: Revenue Bar Association, Society of Trust and Estate Practitioners. Fellow of the Society for Advanced Legal Studies.
Career: Called to Bar 1971. Joined present chambers 1973. Took Silk 1992.
Personal: Educated Kingston Grammar School. Queens' College, Cambridge (1966-71) (MA LLM). Born 25 November 1947.

TRITTON, Guy
Hogarth Chambers (Jonathan Rayner James QC & Christopher Morcom QC), London
(020) 7404 0404
guytritton@hogarthchambers.com
Recommended in Intellectual Property
Specialisation: Intellectual property. Experienced in both soft IP (trademarks, copyright and passing off) and hard IP (patents and technical design). A number of reported cases including Springsteen v Flute and Ors (big media copyright dispute); WILD CHILD TM (leading trademark case); Fylde Microsystems v Key Radio (joint authorship in computer programmes); Hodgkinson & Corby v Wards (passing off in functional items); Hazelgrove Superleague v Business Machines (right to modify patented articles); Chiron v Organon (biotechnological patent infringement action). Also substantial practices in franchise and IT disputes; Dyno Rod v Reeve (enforceability of post-termination restraint of trade covenants in franchise).
Prof. Memberships: Intellectual Property Bar Association, Bar European Group, Chancery Bar Association, Institute of Trade Mark Agents.
Career: Eton College; Durham University BSc Natural Sciences (applied physics, computing, psychology and mathematics). Inner Temple Pegasus scholar. Author of a number of computer programmes including a chambers fee billing package, a legal discovery programme and a designer and programmer of chambers own website.
Publications: Author of 'Intellectual Property in Europe' (2nd Edition), Sweet & Maxwell, 1050 pp 2002. This has become a university textbook in several universities including University of Maastricht.
Personal: Married. Three children. Piano, computers and windsurfing.

TROLLOPE, Andrew QC
187 Fleet Street (Andrew Trollope QC), London
(020) 7430 7430
chambers@187fleetstreet.com
Recommended in Crime, Fraud
Specialisation: Wide experience of fraud and serious or organised crime cases. Practice has predominantly consisted of City, commercial, tax and other fraud cases over nearly 20 years. Other categories include money laundering, confiscation and drug-trafficking. Cases include R v Relton [Brinks Mat], R Viccei [Knightsbridge Safe Deposit], R v Cohen [Blue Arrow], R v T Ward [Guinness], R v Masterson [Caird plc], R v M Ward [European Leisure], R v Johnston [Harrovian Properties/Leisure], R v Keyes [McNicholas], R v Myles [Richmond Oil and Gas plc].
Prof. Memberships: Committee member of Criminal Bar Association 1990-2001, Bar Council International Relations Committee, Council of Management British Institute of International and Comparative Law, Fellow of the Institute of Advanced Legal Studies.
Career: Head of Chambers specialising in criminal law. Appointed Assistant Recorder 1984, Recorder 1989.

TROMANS, Stephen
39 Essex Street (Nigel Pleming QC), London
(020) 7832 1111
stephen.tromans@39essex.com
Recommended in Environment
Specialisation: All aspects of environmental and planning law, and associated areas of international, EC, human rights, commercial, public and property law and dispute resolution.
Prof. Memberships: UKELA (Council Member and former Chairman); PEBA, ALBA, Bar European Group; Research Professor, Nottingham Law School.
Career: Former solicitor (admitted 1981). University lecturer at Cambridge 1981-87. Partner and Head of Environmental Law at *Simmons & Simmons* 1990-99. Called to the Bar 1999.
Publications: 'Encyclopedia of Environmental Law'; 'Planning Law, Practice & Precedents'; textbooks on contaminated land, nuclear installations, commercial leases. Contributor to 'Butterworths Local Government Law and to Human Rights and Judicial Review'.

TROWER, William QC
3-4 South Square (Michael Crystal QC & Lord Alexander of Weedon QC), London
(020) 7696 9900
williamtrower@southsquare.com
Recommended in Chancery, Insolvency, Professional Negligence
Specialisation: Business law especially corporate and international insolvency banking, company law and professional negligence.
Prof. Memberships: COMBAR, Chancery Bar Association, CEDR accredited mediator.
Career: Called 1983. Acted in many of the major insolvencies of the 1990s (BCCI, Polly Peck, Maxwell and Barings). Particular interest in insurance insolvency, and professional negligence claims arising out of insolvency.
Publications: Fletcher Higham and Trower: 'Law and Practice of Corporate Administrations' (1994).

TRUSTED, Harry
35 Essex Street (Christopher Wilson-Smith QC), London
(020) 7353 6381
Recommended in Personal Injury
Specialisation: Personal Injury, Clinical Negligence, Contract.
Prof. Memberships: APIL.
Career: Called to the Bar 1985. Wide variety of substantial accident and professional negligence claims.
Publications: Editor 'Facts and Figures'.
Personal: Married, two children.

TUCKER, Katherine
St Philips Chambers (John Randall QC), Birmingham
(0121) 246 7000
Recommended in Employment
Specialisation: Employment law, European law and commercial law.
Prof. Memberships: Employment Lawyers Association; Bar European Group; Employment Law Bar Association; Midland Chancery and Commercial Bar Association.
Career: Hardwicke, Mansfield and J.P. Warner Scholar, Lincoln's Inn. Sometime Stagière to Advocate General Jacobs, European Court of Justice. Visiting lecturer at Birmingham University. Particular interest in European and discrimination law. Speaks fluent French.
Publications: Author of the contractual restraints section for online Sweet & Maxwell/New Law Employment Law Service and regular contributor to Sweet & Maxwell 'Employment Lawyer'; and Butterwoth Tolley's employment seminars.

TUCKER, Lynton
New Square Chambers (Charles Purle QC), London
(020) 7419 8000
Recommended in Chancery

TUCKER, Paul
40 King St, Manchester
(0161) 832 9082
ptucker@40kingstreet.co.uk
Recommended in Planning
Specialisation: Planning, Local Government, Environmental Law, Highways, Compulsory Purchase, Local Authority Licensing. Acts for public and private sectors including a wide range of private sector developers including major retail proposals, mineral and landfill proposals, large housing sites. Has acted as counsel for local authorities in over a dozen development plan inquiries. Also undertakes supervisory work of students on a pro bono basis for the Manchester University Law Department's Legal Advice Centre.
Prof. Memberships: PEBA, UKELA, ALBA.
Career: Called 1990 (Gray's Inn).
Personal: University: Cambridge (Selwyn College).

TUDOR-EVANS, Quintin
199 Strand (David Phillips QC), London
(020) 7520 4000
qte@btinternet.com
Recommended in Personal Injury
Specialisation: Specialises in personal injury litigation. Undertakes work for claimants and for insurers, handling cases arising from accidents at work, including employers liability, public liability and serious road traffic

LEADERS AT THE BAR

accidents. Has a particular interest in cases involving technical engineering and electrical evidence and in psychiatric illnesses. He also has a detailed practical knowledge of the road transport industry and its licensing. He has extensive experience of cases for local authorities, and is instructed by the NHSLA and by insurers direct. In addition to personal injury litigation, he deals with non-accident insurance cases, for example fire damage claims and product liability matters.
Career: Called to the Bar 1977.

TUGENDHAT, Michael QC
5 Raymond Buildings (Patrick Milmo QC), London
(020) 7242 2902
Recommended in Commercial (Litigation), Defamation
Specialisation: Defamation, media law and contempt of court. Wide range of domestic and international commercial law -including experience as an arbitrator.
Prof. Memberships: Member of the Bar Council 1992-94. Member of Commercial Bar Association - member of Executive 1992-94. Member of the London Court of International Arbitration. Fellow of the Institute of Advanced Legal Studies.
Career: Born 21 October 1944. 1963-67 Gonville & Caius College Cambridge, Scholar and MA; 1967-68 Yale University, Henry Fellowship; 1969 called to the Bar, Inner Temple; 1986 Queen's Counsel; 1988 Bencher of the Inner Temple. Judge of the Courts of Appeal of Jersey and Guernsey. Recorder of the Crown Court, Deputy Judge of the High Court, trained as a mediator with World Intellectual Property Organisation, Geneva. Publications: contributions to 'Restitution and Banking Law' ed Francis Rose Mansfield Press 1998; co-editor 'The Law of Privacy and The Media' (OUP) 2002.

TURNER, David
2 Temple Gardens (Dermod O'Brien QC), London
(020) 7822 1200
dbt@2tg.co.uk
Recommended in Product Liability, Professional Negligence
Specialisation: Non-marine commercial insurance (policy response and interpretation). Professional negligence (particularly accountants (including tax), solicitors, brokers). Commercial product liability. Cases include McCarroll v Statham Gill Davies (Oasis recording contract), GNER v Avon Insurance plc, Daly v Hubner, Llambias v Baker Tilly, Flynn v Robin Thompson, Blaenau Gwent v Robinson Jones, Sun Valley fire, Digital/Capital & Counties fire, Heathrow fire, South Mimms fire.
Prof. Memberships: COMBAR, TECBAR.
Career: MA Cantab. Called 1982.
Publications: 'Rewriting Limitation?', 2001 'NLJ' 574.
Personal: Skiing, diving.

TURNER, David QC
Exchange Chambers (David Turner QC & Bill Braithwaite QC & Henry Globe QC), Liverpool
(0151) 236 7747
Recommended in Crime
Specialisation: Criminal advocacy and licensing. Leading counsel for Robert Thompson in the James Bulger case.
Prof. Memberships: Northern Circuit. Criminal Bar Association.
Career: King George V Grammar School, Southport. MA, LLM, Queens' College, Cambridge. Called 1971. Recorder since 1990. Appointed QC 1991.

TURNER, James QC
One King's Bench Walk (Anthony Hacking QC), London
(020) 7936 1500
jturner@1kbw.co.uk
Recommended in Family
Specialisation: Principal areas of practice encompass all areas of criminal law, family law and administrative law. Many reported cases in each of these fields. Criminal work includes both prosecution and defence and regular instructions to represent medical practitioners in connection with both criminal and disciplinary matters. Considerable knowledge and experience of technical and procedural points of law. Within family law, has particular expertise in financial ancillary relief and international child abduction work and has appeared in finance cases in the Grand Court of the Cayman Islands. Speaker at criminal and family law conferences. Administrative law includes work for the Treasury Solicitor and extradition work in England and abroad.
Prof. Memberships: Criminal Bar Association, Family Law Bar Association and Administrative Law Bar Association.
Career: Called to the Bar and joined current chambers, 1976. Appointed Queen's Counsel 1998.
Publications: Archbold, 'Criminal Pleading, Evidence and Practice' - an editor.
Personal: Educated at Robertsbridge Secondary Modern School, Bexhill Grammar School and the University of Hull (LLB (Hons) 1975). Born 23 November 1952. Lives in London.

TURNER, Jon
Monckton Chambers (Kenneth Parker QC & Paul Lasok QC), London
(020) 7405 7211
jturner@monckton.co.uk
Recommended in Competition/European Law
Specialisation: Specialisms include EC law of all kinds, competition law at both national and EC levels, judicial review, and environmental and energy law. Practice also includes utility regulation work in the water, electricity and telecoms sectors (9 months working as legal advisor in the DTI), and general commercial litigation. Recent competition law litigation include the Napp Pharmaceuticals and Bettercare cases in the Competition Commission Appeals Tribunal (2002); Intel Corporation v VIA Technologies in the Patents Court (2002); Suretrack Rail Services Ltd v Infraco JNP in the Chancery Division (injunction application, 2002); In re Medicaments (2001) and In Re Premier League Football (2000) in the Restrictive Practices Court and Court of Appeal. Recent European Court of Justice cases include Case C-94/00, Roquette Freres (2001). Recent environmental and judicial review cases include R v Secretary of State for the Environment on the appl. of Greenpeace (Court of Appeal, 2002); R v Environment Agency ex p. Levy (2002).
Prof. Memberships: Member of the New York Bar.
Career: Standing Counsel to the Director General of Fair Trading. Appointed to Crown 'A' Panel for public litigation in 2002.
Publications: Contributor to Bellamy & Child, 'The Common Market Law of Competition', 5th edn.
Personal: LLM (Harvard).

TURNER, Jonathan
6 King's Bench Walk (Roy Amlot QC), London
(020) 7583 0410
jonathan.turner@6kbw.com
Recommended in Crime
Specialisation: All and any criminal matters.
Prof. Memberships: CBA.
Career: Hindley & Abram Grammar School. University College, London.
Personal: Golf, cricket, rugby league.

TURNER, Justin
Three New Square (David Young QC), London
(020) 7405 1111
clerks@3newsquare.co.uk
Recommended in Intellectual Property
Specialisation: Intellectual Property especially those areas relating to Biotechnology, Pharmacology and medicine. Leading cases include: Biogen v Medeva (House of Lords); SKB v Norton and LEK (Clavulanic Acid); Bristol Myers v Baker Norton (Taxol); Coflexip v Stolt Comex; VISX v NIDEK (PRK); Monsanto v Merck (cox - 2 inhibitors); DSM v Novo; BASF v SKB (paroxetine). Appears in European Patent office in Munich.
Prof. Memberships: Intellectual Property Bar Assn; Chancery Bar Assn; Royal College of Veterinary Surgeons.
Career: Royal Veterinary College, London University (1981-86). Emmanual College, Cambridge - PhD on immunology/virology. Called to the Bar in 1991. Contributor to Terrell on Law of Patents (14th Edn).

TURNER, Mark QC
Deans Court Chambers (Stephen Grime QC), Manchester
(0161) 214 6000
turner@deanscourt.co.uk
Recommended in Personal Injury
Specialisation: Industrial disease litigation; group actions; insurance law; professional negligence.
Prof. Memberships: Personal Injury Bar Association; Northern Commercial Bar Association.
Career: Sedbergh School 1972-77. The Queen's College, Oxford 1977-80. Dean's Court Chambers 1981. Assistant Recorder 1997-. Queens Counsel 1998. Recorder 2000.

TURNER, Michael QC
Tooks Court Chambers (Michael Mansfield QC), London
(020) 7405 8828
Recommended in Crime

TWOMLOW, Richard
9 Park Place (Ian Murphy QC), Cardiff
(029) 2038 2731
clerks@9parkplace.co.uk
Recommended in Crime
Specialisation: Criminal work of all types, prosecution and defence.
Prof. Memberships: Criminal Bar Association.
Career: Called (Gray's) 1976; Recorder (1997).
Personal: BA (Cantab). Married. Sport, literature, music, languages, travel.

UFF CBE, John QC
Keating Chambers, London
(020) 7544 2600
juff@keatingchambers.com
Recommended in Arbitration, Construction
Specialisation: Construction and engineering; international arbitration; appointed arbitrator in many substantial disputes in most parts of the world.
Career: Qualified 1970. Gray's Inn; Assistant Engineer 1966-70; Barrister in construction chambers 1970; Arbitrator in various disputes 1977; QC 1983; Recorder 1998; Professor of Engineering Law, King's College, London 1991; Chairman of Commission of Inquiry into Yorkshire Water (1996); Chairman of Public Enquiry into rail accident at Southall (1997) and joint Chairman of Public Inquiry into rail safety (2000); FICE, FCI Arb, Fellow Royal Academy of Engineering.
Publications: 'Construction Law'; Construction Industry Model Arbitration Rules; contributor to 'Keating on Building Contracts'; and 'Chitty on Contracts'.
Personal: King's College, London (BSc Engineering, PhD).

ULLSTEIN, Augustus QC
29 Bedford Row Chambers (Nicholas Francis QC), London
(020) 7404 1044
Recommended in Product Liability

UNDERHILL, Nicholas QC
Fountain Court (Anthony Boswood QC), London
(020) 7583 3335
nunderhill@fountaincourt.co.uk
Recommended in Employment, Product Liability
Specialisation: Specialist in commercial and employment law and in medical/pharmaceutical product

LEADERS AT THE BAR

liability. Recent cases include: Arklow v Maclean (PC: fiduciary duties of merchant bank); Kleinwort Benson v Lincoln (HL: restitution/mistake of law); MSF v Refuge (EAT: redundancy consultation); RCO v UNISON (CA: TUPE); Barber v RJB Mining (working time regs); Meade v British Fuels (HL: TUPE); Grant v South West Trains (ECJ: sexual orientation discrimination); Associated Newspapers v Wilson (HL: union derecognition); A v National Blood Authority (product liability - hepatitis C); 3rd generation oral contraceptive litigation.
Prof. Memberships: COMBAR; Employment Lawyers Association; Employment Law Bar Association; Industrial Law Society.
Career: Called to the Bar 1976. Joined present chambers 1977. Took silk 1992. Recorder 1994. Deputy High Court Judge 1998. Appointed Attorney-General to Prince of Wales 1998. Judge (part-time) of Employment Appeal Tribunal 2000.
Personal: Born 12 May 1952.

UPTON, William
6 Pump Court (Stephen Hockman QC), London
(020) 7797 8400
williamupton@6pumpcourt.co.uk
Recommended in Environment
Specialisation: Main area of practice is environmental, planning and local government law. Clients include local authorities, developers and local amenity groups. Experienced lecturer.
Prof. Memberships: Planning and Environment Bar Association. Administration Law Bar Association
Career: Called to the Bar in 1990.
Publications: General Editor, Environmental Law (OUP 2000); contributing editor, 'Encyclopaedia of Forms and Precedents' (Butterworths Environment Volume 2000 Reissue); 'Contaminated Land' (CLT 2001); 'Neighbours and the Law' (Sweet & Maxwell, 3rd edition, 2001).
Personal: Educated at Trinity College, Cambridge 1985-89 (MA & LLM). Fellow of the Royal Society of Arts. UKELA council member.

VAJDA, Christopher QC
Monckton Chambers (Kenneth Parker QC & Paul Lasok QC), London
(020) 7405 7211
cvajda@monckton.co.uk
Recommended in Competition/European Law
Specialisation: All aspects of EC law, competition law, judicial review and VAT.
Career: Has appeared in over 50 cases before the Court of Justice of the European Communities and Court of First Instance acting for companies, private individuals and the UK government. Cases include Ford v Commission (1982 and 1984), Bulk Oil (1986), Sharp v Council (1988), the Factortame cases, Saeger v Dennemeyer (1991), Air France v Commission (1994), Alpine Investments (1995), the Ladbroke cases, Cartonboard (1998) and ICI (1998). Domestic EC reported cases include Garden Cottage Foods v Milk Marketing Board, (HL), Factortame (HL), Optident (HL), Thorn (HL), Mann (HL), ABTA (RPC), Bourgoin v MAFF (CA), Optident (CA) Shearson Lehman Hutton v Maclaine Watson & Co (Commercial Ct), Apple Corps Ltd v Apple Computer (Ch. D). R v OFTEL ex p BT (QBD) and R v Secretary of State for Health ex p Imperial Tobacco (CA) and BUPA Hospitals (VAT Trib). Numerous publications including the state aid chapter in Bellamy & Child, 'Common Market Law of Competition' 5th edn.

VANHEGAN, Mark
11 South Square (Christopher Floyd QC), London
(020) 7405 1222
clerks@southsquare.com
Recommended in Information Technology, Intellectual Property
Specialisation: All areas of intellectual property: Dyson v Hoover [2002] RPC 22; NLA v Marks & Spencer Plc [2002] RPC 225; Wheatley v Drillsafe [2001] RPC 133; Springsteen v Masquerade Music [2001] EMLR 25; DaimlerChrysler v Alavi [2001] RPC 42; Mars v Teknowledge [2000] FSR 138; Pro Seiben v Carlton TV [1999] FSR 610; Gerber v Lectra [1997] RPC 443.
Prof. Memberships: IP Bar Association; Chancery Bar Association.
Career: Called to Bar (Lincolns Inn) 1990; Tenant, 11 South Square 1991.
Personal: Abingdon School; Trinity College, Cambridge (Natural Sciences and Law). Married; two daughters.

VAUGHAN CBE, David QC
Brick Court Chambers (Christopher Clarke QC), London
(020) 7379 3550
vaughan@brickcourt.co.uk
Recommended in Competition/European Law
Specialisation: EC law generally, EC-related public law cases and competition law.
Prof. Memberships: Honorary vice-president of the Bar European Group.
Career: QC (1981) QC (NI) 1981. Judge of the County Appeals of Jersey and Guernsey, Deputy High Court Judge. Leader of the European Circuit. Appeared in over 90 cases in the European Court of Justice since 1975 in a wide range of cases and in major EC-related public law cases, in particular Factortame I, II, III, IV; Stoke City Council v B&Q; Anastasiou I, II and III; Kesko; the Petrochemical Cartel cases (PP, PVC I and II, LDPE); the Soda Ash cases; the Coal Cases (Banks I and II, Hopkins. NALOO I and II); BT3G; Courage v Crehan; GIL Insurance; 3 pending OFT Investigations (as at May 2002).

VEEDER, V V QC
Essex Court Chambers (Gordon Pollock QC), London
(020) 7813 8000
Recommended in Arbitration, Insurance
Specialisation: Practised at the Commercial Bar to date, principally as advocate and arbitrator in the field of international trade and dispute resolution.
Prof. Memberships: Chairman of ARIAS (UK). Member of the United Kingdom's Department of Trade and Industry Advisory Committee on the Law of Arbitration 1990-96. Editor 'Arbitration International'. Member of FIA FI
Career: Jesus College, Cambridge MA 1970 (Modern Languages & Law). Called to the English Bar 1971. Queen's Counsel 1986.
Personal: Born 1948.

VENMORE, John
30 Park Place (John Jenkins QC), Cardiff
(029) 2039 8421
Recommended in Personal Injury
Specialisation: Personal injury including industrial disease litigation. Some clinical negligence. Professional negligence claims arising out of the conduct of personal injury and clinical accident litigation.
Prof. Memberships: Wales and Chester Circuit. PIBA. Wales Personal Injury Lawyers Association.
Career: Called 1971 after a short success in the Merchant Navy and in the Maritime Branch of the Army. He retains an interest in nautical matters and cases.

VILLAGE, Peter QC
4-5 Gray's Inn Square (Elizabeth Appleby QC), London
(020) 7404 5252
Recommended in Planning
Specialisation: All aspects of planning, compulsory purchase and environmental law, including High Court challenges to the grant of planning permission (statutory and judicial review) and local plans. Recent cases include acting for Guinness in its Lands Tribunal litigation against Railtrack (instructed by *Herbert Smith*), for Hammerson and Birmingham City Council in promoting the Bull Ring CPO (*Herbert Smith*), for Wereldahave in promoting the Folkestone Town Centre CPO (*Masons*), for University College Hospital NHS Trust in promoting the new UCL/Middlesex Hospital CPO (*Herbert Smith & Linklaters*) for Peel Investments in promoting the new Doncaster Finningley Airport (*Berwin Leighton Paisner*). Undertakes a substantial amount of planning inquiry work for national volume housebuilders, most notably George Wimpey plc. Recently promoted the proposed new Canterbury College (*Stephenson Harwood*). Notable cases include: The Rose Theatre case [1990] 2 WLR 186 (*Theodore Goddard*); Ex parte Sister Frost [1997] 73 P&CR 186 on behalf of the owners of Canary Wharf (*Clifford Chance*); the Costco litigation (for Safeway, instructed by *Clifford Chance*) [1993] 3 PLR 114; British Railways Board v Slough BC [1993] 2 PLR 42 (quashing a planning permission).
Prof. Memberships: Planning and Environmental Bar Association; Administrative Bar Association. Member, Steering Committee of the Compulsory Purchase Association.
Career: Educated: Repton, Leeds University. Called 1983. Called to Bar of Northern Ireland 1997. QC 2002.
Personal: Governor Repton School since 1998; Leisure pursuits: fly fishing.

VINE, James
Hardwicke Building (Nicholas Stewart QC), London
(020) 7242 2523
james.vine@hardwicke.co.uk
Recommended in Crime
Specialisation: Both prosecution and defence of: drugs importation, VAT and Inland Revenue fraud, confiscation proceedings and computer fraud. Customs & Excise list 'A' and Inland Revenue approved list. Extensive experience of PII proceedings. Appears regularly as a leading junior. Recently successfully prosecuted a 20 defendant excise fraud. Current practice includes Inland Revenue Phoenix fraud, Railtrack fraud, World Wide American Express fraud and an ongoing SFO investigation. Successful prosecution and defence of large scale VAT frauds.
Prof. Memberships: SE Circuit. CBA Kent & Inner London Bar Messes.
Career: He has developed and used a computer database program which has been used successfully in the preparation and presentation of numerous cases.
Personal: Travels when possible, and speaks a few foreign languages badly.

VIRGO, John
Guildhall Chambers (Adrian Palmer QC), Bristol
(0117) 930 9031
john.virgo@guildhallchambers.co.uk
Recommended in Commercial (Litigation)
Specialisation: Professional negligence of surveyors, solicitors, and financial advisors.
Prof. Memberships: Bristol and Cardiff Chancery Bar Association; Professional Negligence Bar Association.
Career: Reported cases include Bell v McCubbin 1990 1 A11 ER.54 (CA); Rhone v Stevens 1994 2 WLR 429 (HL); Crocker v British Coal 1995-29-BMLR 159; Cocking v Prudential 1996 CCH 692; May v Woollcombe Beer Watts 1999 PNLR 283; Hale v Guildarch 1999 PNLR 44; Searles v Cann & Hallett 1999 PNLR 494; Truk (UK) Ltd. v Tokmakidis GmbH 2000 1 Lloyds Law Rep.543; Loosemore v Financial Concepts 2001 Lloyds Law Rep. PN 235; Devine v Jefferies 2001 Lloyds Law Rep. PN301; National Westminster Bank v Somer International (UK) Ltd [2002] 1 AER 198.
Publications: 'Surveyors' Liability, Law

LEADERS AT THE BAR

and Practice' (Jordans 1998); 'Financial Advice and Financial Products' (Oxford University Press 2001).

VITORIA, Mary QC
8 New Square (Mark Platts-Mills QC), London
(020) 7405 4321
clerks@8newsquare.co.uk
Recommended in Intellectual Property, Media & Entertainment
Specialisation: Barrister specialising in intellectual property law and media law, covering patents, copyright, trademarks, passing off, performers' rights, design rights, confidential information and contracts relating to the above. For comprehensive CV and list of recent cases, visit our website at www.8newsquare.co.uk.
Prof. Memberships: Intellectual Property Bar Association (IPBA).
Career: Called 1975; QC 1997; patent examiner - chemical patents; lecturer in law - Polytechnic of North London and Queen Mary College, University of London (1975 - 1978).
Publications: Co-author 'Modern Law of Copyright & Designs'; co-editor 'European Intellectual Property Review'; editor 'Fleet Street Reports' and 'Reports of Patent Design & Trade Mark Cases'. Author of sections on copyright and patents in 'Halsbury's Laws.'
Personal: University of London, BSc Chemistry, PhD Chemistry, LLB.

VOS, Geoffrey QC
3 Stone Buildings (Geoffrey Vos QC), London
(020) 7242 4937
Recommended in Chancery, Commercial (Litigation), Company, Insolvency
Specialisation: Principal area of practice is chancery and commercial litigation, including particularly company, insurance and reinsurance, financial services, media and pensions. Acted in Estate of Francis Bacon; Bermuda Fire & Marine Insurance Co Ltd; Director General of Fair Trading v Premier League; Investors Compensation Scheme v West Bromwich Building Society; Deeny v Gooda Walker; Global Container Lines v Bonyal Shipping Co; Cox v Bankside; LDC Trustees Ltd v Barings plc; MGN Pension Trustees Limited v Credit Suisse; Scher v Policyholder Protection Board; Re MC Bacon Limited amongst others.
Prof. Memberships: Chancery Bar Association. Bencher of Lincoln's Inn.
Career: Called to the Bar 1977 and joined current chambers in 1979. Took Silk in 1993. Chairman of Chancery Bar Association 1999-2001.
Personal: Educated at University College School, and Gonville and Caius College, Cambridge.

WADSLEY, Peter
St John's Chambers (Christopher Sharp QC), Bristol
(0117) 921 3456
Recommended in Licensing

WAIN, Peter
East Anglian Chambers (Roderick Newton), Ipswich
(01473) 214481
Recommended in Family

WAITE, Jonathan QC
Crown Office Chambers (Michael Spencer QC & Christopher Purchas QC), London
(020) 7797 8100
Recommended in Health & Safety, Product Liability
Specialisation: Product liability, personal injury, health and safety, professional negligence. Important cases: Bourne v Colodense [1985] ICR 291 (costs in relation to Trade Union backed plaintiff); McFarlane v EE Caledonia (No 2) [1995] IWLR 366 (costs - maintenance/champerty); Hegarty v EE Caledonia [1996] 1 LIR 413 (Piper Alpha – psychiatric injury); R v Trustees of Science Museum [1993] 3 AER 853 (legionnaires disease - s.3 Health & Safety at Work Act 1974); Carroll v Fearon & Dunlop Limited [1998] PIQR P416 (manufacture of defective tyre). Instructed in Organophosphate Sheep Dip litigation, MMR/MR litigation and Oral Contraceptive litigation: all group actions.
Prof. Memberships: Personal Injury Bar Association; London Common Law and Commercial Bar Association.
Career: Sherborne, Trinity College, Cambridge. Called to the Bar 1978. QC 2002.
Personal: Golf, skiing, bridge.

WAKERLEY, Richard QC
4 Fountain Court (John Saunders QC), Birmingham
(0121) 236 3476
Recommended in Crime

WAKSMAN, David QC
Fountain Court (Anthony Boswood QC), London
(020) 7583 3335
dwaksmon@fountaincourt.co.uk
Recommended in Banking & Finance, Commercial (Litigation), Media & Entertainment
Specialisation: Commercial litigation. Main areas of practice are banking, civil fraud, commercial litigation, copyright, entertainment law (advisory and contentious) and professional negligence. Clients include clearing and international banks, and other financial institutions and substantial corporations. Also major record and publishing companies, artistes, managers and producers. Recent cases: Definitely Maybe v Lieberberg [2001] 1 WLR 1745 (proper law of pop festival performance contract), MCA v Mushroom Records (2001) (performance and recording copyright issues concerning the band 'Garbage'), Mitco v Cannon 2001 (major international commercial fraud), Murray v YFM (CA) [1998] 1 WLR 951 (confidential information in management buyout context), Morgan v Lloyds Bank (CA) [1998] Lloyd's Rep. Banking 73 (duties of bank concerning sale of mortgaged property), Girobank v Clarke (CA) [1998] 1 WLR 942 (tax treatment of Girobank data-processing centre), News International v Clinger (Chd) 1998 (major international commercial fraud), Next Room v FX Music (Chd) Times 8 July 1999 (trust claim relating to recording royalties). Has lectured extensively on commercial law topics and is a contributor to 'The Law of Bank Payments' (Sweet & Maxwell), 'Banks and Remedies' (Lloyd's of London Press) 'Commercial Court Procedure' (Sweet & Maxwell) and Bullen & Leake & Jacobs (Professional Negligence) (Sweet & Maxwell).
Prof. Memberships: Commercial Bar Association. Chancery Bar Association.
Career: Called to the Bar 1982. Recorder of the Crown Court, 2001. Silk 2002.
Personal: Born 28 August 1957 LLB (Manchester) BCL (Oxon). Leisure pursuits include running, fell walking, music, sailing. Married. Lives in London.

WALKER, Andrew P D
9 Old Square (Michael Driscoll QC), London
(020) 7405 4682
Recommended in Property Litigation
Specialisation: Property and commercial Chancery litigation, with the main emphasis on landlord and tenant, commercial and residential property and development disputes, mortgages, commercial disputes, professional negligence, property and commercial fields, trust litigation, partnerships, company and insolvency. Most recent reported cases include BHP Petroleum GB Ltd v Chesterfield Properties Ltd [2002] 2 WLR 672 (CA); Melbury Road Properties 1995 Ltd v Kreidi [1999] 43 EG 157 (CC); Courage Ltd v Crehan, Walker Cain Ltd v McCaughey [1999] 2 EGLR 145 (CA); Platform Home Loans Ltd v Oyston Shipways Ltd [2000] 2 AC 190 (HL); Electricity Supply Nominees Ltd v The National Magazine Company Ltd [1999] 1 EGLR 130 (TCC).
Prof. Memberships: Chancery Bar Association, Professional Negligence Bar Association.
Career: Haberdashers' Aske's School, Elstree; Trinity College, Cambridge (MA); called Lincoln's Inn (1991).
Personal: Born Chester.

WALKER, Jane
28 St John St, Manchester
(0161) 834 8418
Recommended in Family

WALKER, Ronald QC
12 King's Bench Walk (Richard Methuen QC), London
(020) 7583 0811
Recommended in Personal Injury

WALL, Mark
4 Fountain Court (John Saunders QC), Birmingham
(0121) 236 3476
Recommended in Crime

WALLINGTON, Peter
11 King's Bench Walk Chambers (Eldred Tabachnik QC & James Goudie QC), London
(020) 7632 8500
wallington@11kbw.com
Recommended in Employment
Specialisation: Principal area of practice is employment law. Deals with all types of work in Employment Tribunals and Employment Appeal Tribunal, High Court and County Court litigation on all aspects of employment disputes including injunctions, wrongful dismissal, discrimination, and European social legislation. Advises and lectures on all these areas. Also has extensive industrial consultancy experience. Other main area of practice is public law, especially in relation to local authorities and education.
Prof. Memberships: Employment Lawyers Association, Employment Law Bar Association, Industrial Law Society.
Career: Fellow of Trinity Hall, Cambridge, and University Lecturer in Law 1973-79. Professor of Law, Lancaster University 1979-88, Brunel University 1988-91. Called to the Bar in 1987 and joined present chambers in 1990.
Publications: Editor 'Butterworths Employment Law Handbook'; advisory editor, 'Harvey on Industrial Relations and Employment Law'; contributor to 'Supperstone and Goudie on Judicial Review'; 'Tolley's Employment Law Handbook'.
Personal: Educated Hemel Hempstead Grammar School 1957-64 and Trinity Hall, Cambridge 1965-69 (MA and LLM, both 1st Class Hons). Past area chairman NACAB. Enjoys hill walking, music and reading. Born 25 March 1947. Lives in Wadhurst, E Sussex.

WALLINGTON, Richard
10 Old Square (Leolin Price CBE QC), London
(020) 7405 0758
richard.wallington@virgin.net
Recommended in Chancery
Specialisation: Wills, trusts, probate, inheritance tax, capital gains tax.
Prof. Memberships: Chancery Bar Association; Revenue Bar Association; STEP.
Career: Called to the Bar 1972. In practice at the Chancery Bar from 1974.
Publications: 'Williams on Wills' (co-editor); Halsbury's Laws of England, 'Wills' and 'Executors and Administrators' titles (co-editor); Foster's Inheritance Tax (general editor).
Personal: Educated at Dulwich College and Gonville and Caius College, Cambridge.

WALLWORK, Bernard
28 St John St, Manchester
(0161) 834 8418
Recommended in Family

WALSH, John
Doughty Street Chambers (Geoffrey Robertson QC), London
(020) 7404 1313

Recommended in Immigration
Specialisation: He is a specialist practitioner in the fields of immigration and education law. He has appeared before numerous tribunals and courts including the EU Court of Justice. His reported cases include: Savas [2000] All ER (EC) 627 on standstill clause in EC-Turkey Agreement; M v SSHD [1996] 1 All ER 870, CA; Kurumoorthy [1998] Imm AR 410, DC; Yennin [1995] Imm AR 93 on free movement of persons within the EC; Carpenter [2002] ECR 000 on freedom of movement to provide services within the EC; A v London Borough of Lambeth [2002] ELR 231 on strike out in SEN tribunal tribunals.
Prof. Memberships: He is a member of ALBA (Administrative Law Bar Association), BEG (Bar European Group), ELAS (Education Law Association), EPG (Education Practitioners Group), ILPA (Immigration Law Practitioners Association).
Career: Called to the Bar in 1993 after a career as teacher and headmaster. He received his third level education at University College Dublin (BA and MA) and University of London (LLB).

WALSH, Martin
Peel Court Chambers (Michael Shorrock QC), Manchester
(0161) 832 3791
Recommended in Licensing

WALSH, Stephen
3 Raymond Buildings (Clive Nicholls QC), London
(020) 7400 6400
chambers@threeraymond.demon.co.uk
Recommended in Licensing
Specialisation: All aspects of licensing. Advising on liquor and public entertainment licensing issues affecting a wide range of clients and establishments, from small independent operators seeking to maintain or expand existing licensed outlets to major new leisure developments by public companies. Appearing on behalf of applicants and objectors before local authorities and courts including case stated and judicial review hearings in the High Court. Representing and advising clients on criminal prosecutions and health and safety matters affecting the licensed trade. Advising on betting, gaming and lotteries.

WALTERS, Graham
33 Park Place (Neil Bidder QC), Cardiff
(029) 2023 3313
clerks@33parkplace.co.uk
Recommended in Licensing, Local Government
Specialisation: Most aspects of local government work, in particular highways, compulsory purchase and planning. Property and housing disputes. Judicial review of public authority functions generally, for example, education, police powers/procedures. Liquor licensing.
Prof. Memberships: Wales Commercial Law Association (Committee Member).
Career: Called to the Bar 1986. Appointed to the panel of Counsel to the National Assembly for Wales for planning and judicial review.
Personal: Queen Mary's Grammar School, Walsall. Wadham College, Oxford MA (Jurisprudence). Former solicitor and clerk to licensing committee.

WALTERS, Jill Mary
30 Park Place (John Jenkins QC), Cardiff
(029) 2039 8421
Recommended in Family

WALTERS, Jonathan
33 Park Place (Neil Bidder QC), Cardiff
(029) 2023 3313
Recommended in Licensing
Specialisation: Employment, personal injury and licensing.
Prof. Memberships: Employment Lawyers Association.
Career: University College Cardiff; part-time Chair of Employment Tribunal 09/01; part-time tutor at Bar Vocational College in Cardiff.

WALTON, Alastair
Maitland Chambers (Michael Lyndon-Stanford QC & Charles Aldous QC), London
(020) 7406 1200
awalton@maitlandchambers.com
Recommended in Chancery
Specialisation: General Chancery practice including company, insolvency, property, professional negligence, trusts, and contract and commercial disputes. Cases include Alstom v British Airways; Prince Jefri v Manoukian and others; TBV Power v Elm Energy; Re H and others; McDonald v Horn; Re Little Olympian Each Ways Limited; Re BSB Holdings Limited; Lonrho v Fayed.
Prof. Memberships: Chancery Bar Association; COMBAR.
Career: Called 1977.
Personal: Born 26 August 1954. Educated at Winchester and Balliol College, Oxford (BA 1976). Married with four children. Lives in London.

WARBY, Mark QC
5 Raymond Buildings (Patrick Milmo QC), London
(020) 7242 2902
markwarby@5rb.co.uk
Recommended in Defamation
Specialisation: Media and entertainment, principally defamation, privacy, breach of confidence and contempt of court. Also contractual disputes, literary and artistic copyright, sports disciplinary and related matters. Cases in 2002 include Naomi Campbell v MGN (privacy), Jockey Club v Buffham (confidence claim against former head of security), Attorney General v MGN (contempt re Leeds footballer trial), R (Persey) v SoS for DEFRA (media consortium seeking public inquiry into FMD). Other recent cases are Monty Norman v Times [2001] (James Bond Theme libel dispute), O'Shea v MGN [2001] (Article 10 overriding common law of libel), Imutran v Uncaged Campaigns [2001] (interpretation of s12 HRA), the libel cases of Michael Ashcroft v Times [1999], Mickey Duff v MGN [1999] and Jessye Norman v Future Publishing, CA [1998], and Bunn v BBC [1998] (confidentiality re police statements of Robert Maxwell finance director). Newspaper night lawyer 1981-86. For fuller career details see www.5rb.co.uk.
Prof. Memberships: Gray's Inn.
Career: Called to the Bar 1981 and joined current chambers 1983.
Publications: 'The Law of Privacy and the Media' (OUP) 2002 (contributor); 'A Life after Reynolds' (privilege in defamation), Farrers Media Bulletin, Autumn 2000; Confidentiality and the Media, CLT conferences 1999 & 2000.
Personal: Educated at Bristol Grammar School and St John's College, Oxford. Born 1958.

WARDELL, John QC
Wilberforce Chambers (Edward Nugee QC), London
(020) 7306 0102
Recommended in Professional Negligence
Specialisation: Wide-ranging commercial/chancery litigation practice covering all aspects of commercial life including banking, financial services, sale of goods, shareholders disputes and civil fraud. Strong emphasis on professional negligence acting for and against, valuers, accountants, solicitors and barristers. Recent cases include Arab Bank v John D Wood (mortgage indemnity policy), Langley v Coal Authority (right to elect to repair), Prettys v Carter (limitation/CPR Part 24), Hamilton v Fayed (costs against third parties), Jordan v One2One (construction of share purchase agreement), Healey v Mercedes-Benz (negligent misstatement), UCB v Hepherd Winstanley & Pugh (causation of loss/contributory negligence) and Ogilvy & Mather Ltd v Rubinstein Callingham Polden & Gale (loss of a chance).
Prof. Memberships: Professional Negligence Bar Association; COMBAR; Chancery Bar Association.
Career: LLB (Hons). MPhil (Cantab). Called to the Bar in 1979; QC 2002.

WARNOCK-SMITH, Shân QC
5 Stone Buildings (Henry Harrod), London
(020) 7242 6201
swarnocksmith@5-stonebuildings.law.co.uk
Recommended in Chancery
Specialisation: Practice encompasses all aspects of trusts, estates, charities and associated taxation. Handles both advisory and contentious work in the UK and offshore in connection with trusts and estates, variations of trusts, construction and rectification of settlements and wills; probate actions; Court of Protection applications; professional negligence in those areas. Lecturer, writer and broadcaster on trust and estate matters.
Prof. Memberships: Society of Trust and Estate Practitioners, Chancery Bar Association and the Association of Contentious Trust and Probate Specialists.
Career: Called to the Bar 1971 and has practised at the Chancery Bar since 1980 following an academic career. Took Silk 2002.

WARREN, Nicholas QC
Wilberforce Chambers (Edward Nugee QC), London
(020) 7306 0102
Recommended in Chancery, Pensions
Specialisation: Main areas of practice are in the fields of pensions and private client business, both advisory and litigation. Has appeared in many of the leading pensions cases including Imperial Foods, Courage, Thrells, LRT, Coloroll, Chloride, National Grid/National Power and South West Trains. Also has wide experience of revenue litigation having formerly been standing junior counsel to the Inland Revenue in Chancery matters.
Prof. Memberships: Association of Pensions Lawyers; STEP; Revenue Bar Association; Chancery Bar Association (Chairman).
Career: BA (Oxon) 1970. Called to the Bar in 1972; QC 1993. Recorder; Deputy High Court Judge.
Personal: Chairman, London Musici.

WARREN, Rupert
2 Mitre Court Buildings (Guy Roots QC), London
(020) 7583 1380
rupert.warren@2MCB.co.uk
Recommended in Planning
Specialisation: Planning, compulsory purchase, rating, environment and public law.
Prof. Memberships: Committee member of PEBA.
Career: Joined 2 MCB in 1995 after pupillage at Blackstone Chambers. Appointed to the Attorney General's Panel (C) in 2000.
Publications: Contributor to 'Halsbury's Laws' (Rating), Butterworths 'Local Government Law', and DETR's 'Compulsory Purchase Manual', (TSO).
Personal: Born London 1969. Educated at Whitgift School and Christ Church Oxford (First Class Honours Degree). Lives in London.

WASS, Sasha QC
6 King's Bench Walk (Roy Amlot QC), London
(020) 7583 0410
Recommended in Crime
Specialisation: Criminal law. Defence and prosecution practice. Serious fraud: professional (eg lawyer's), commercial (eg gambling industry), and financial cases (City, eg defence of Roger Levitt). Environmental law: specialist expertise on criminal aspects of oil spillage etc (eg Sea Empress 1996). Serious crime: murder, rape, police corruption, drug

LEADERS AT THE BAR

importation, money laundering, sexual abuse of children and specialist expertise in complex medical, scientific and identification cases (eg Rosemary West, Popat I & II) and criminal misconduct of the medical profession.
Prof. Memberships: Elected member of the Committee of the Criminal Bar Association: 1992-95; 1995-98; 2000- and the South Eastern Circuit Committee: 1989-92; 1993-96; Treasurer of the CBA 1997-99.
Career: Called 1981; Assistant Recorder 1997; Recorder 2000; Queen's Counsel 2000.

WATERS, David QC
2 Hare Court (Stephen Kramer QC), London
(020) 7353 5324
davidwaters@2harecourt.com
Recommended in Crime
Specialisation: High profile serious criminal cases. They include: R v Kinsella & ors (Warrington bombing); R v Davis, Johnson & Rowe; R v Jonathan Aitken; R v Delroy Denton; R v Jeffrey Archer & anor; R v Pendleton (H. of Ls).
Career: Called 1973. Treasury Counsel: 1989-99. Recorder: 1990. Appointed QC: 1999. President, Mental Health Review Tribunal 1999.

WATERS, Malcolm QC
11 Old Square (Grant Crawford & Jonathan Simpkiss), London
(020) 7430 0341
clerks@11oldsquare.co.uk
Recommended in Banking & Finance, Charities, Consumer Law
Specialisation: Principal specialist areas are mortgage lending, consumer credit, savings products, building societies and charities. Also covers other areas of general chancery practice, including land law, trusts and professional negligence. Acted in Director General of Fair Trading v First National Bank (unfair terms in common contracts), C&G v B.S.C. and B.S.C. v Halifax B.S. and Leeds P.B.S. (building society conversions), C&G v Norgan and Woolwich v Gomm (mortgages), Harwood-Smart v Caws (pensions) and Peggs v Lamb (charities). Drafts standard form mortgage, investment and consumer credit documentation for banks and building societies. Regularly advises on constitutional issues affecting mutual organisations and charities. Member of working parties involved in drafting Standard Conditions of Sale and the Standard Commercial Property Conditions.
Prof. Memberships: Chancery Bar Association, Charity Law Association, Professional Negligence Bar Association.
Career: Called to Bar 1977. Joined 11 Old Square 1978. Took silk 1997.
Publications: Joint editor of 'Wurtzburg & Mills - Building Society Law', and 'Current Law Commentary on the Building Societies Act 1986'.
Personal: Educated at Whitgift School 1963-71 and St. Catherine's College Oxford 1972-76 (BA and BCL).

WATSON, Antony QC
Three New Square (David Young QC), London
(020) 7405 1111
Recommended in Intellectual Property

WATSON, David
14 Castle Street (Andrew Edis QC), Liverpool
(0151) 236 4421
Recommended in Crime

WATSON, James QC
3 Serjeants' Inn (Robert Francis QC & John Grace QC), London
(020) 7427 5000
Recommended in Clinical Negligence

WATTS, Sir Arthur QC
20 Essex Street (Iain Milligan QC), London
(020) 7842 1200
clerks@20essexst.com
Recommended in Public International Law
Specialisation: Specialist in public international law.
Prof. Memberships: Institut du Droit Internationale; President, British Branch of the International Law Association (1992-98).
Career: Called to Gray's Inn 1957, Silk 1988; Legal Advisor, Foreign and Commonwealth Office 1987-91; Legal Adviser, UK Permanent Representative to the EC 1973-77; International Mediator for Succession Issues (former Yugoslavia) 1996 to date.
Personal: Born 1931. Royal Military Academy, Sandhurst; Downing College, Cambridge; Hague Academy of International Law.

WAUGH, Andrew QC
Three New Square (David Young QC), London
(020) 7405 1111
3newsquareip@lineone.net
Recommended in Intellectual Property
Specialisation: All aspects of intellectual property with particular emphasis on chemical, pharmaceutical and biotechnical/generic engineering matters. Appears regularly at European Patent Office in Munich for clients which have included Eli Lilly, Amgen and Biogen. Notable UK cases have included: Eli Lilly v Genentech (recombinant growth hormone and insulin); Bonzel v Intervention (cardiac catheters); Optical Recording v Hayden Labs (compact discs); Biogen v Medeva (recombinant Hepatitis B vaccine); Amgen v Boehringher Mannheim (erythropoietin); SKB v Norton (augmentin); Merrell Dow v Norton (terfenadine); Chrion v Medera (pertactin); Optical Sciences v Aspect Vision Care (contact lenses); Hoechst v BP (purification of acetic acid); UCC v BP (polyethylene production); Palmaz v Boston Scientific (cardiac stents); HFC Bank plc v Midland Bank plc (trade name); Lilly Icos v Pfizer (Viagra); GlaxoSmithKline v Generics (paroxetine).
Prof. Memberships: Intellectual Property Bar Assn; Chancery Bar Assn; AIPPI.

Career: City University First Class Hons in Chemical and Administrative Studies; 1981 Dip-Law; 1982 Called to the Bar. QC 1998, six month pupillage at Chambers of Kenneth Rokison QC. 1983 joined Chambers of William Aldous QC at 6 Pump Court (now that of David Young QC at 3 New Square).

WEBB, Geraint
2 Harcourt Buildings (Roger Henderson QC), London
(020) 7583 9020
clarks@harcourt.co.uk
Recommended in Product Liability
Specialisation: Product liability (including Consumer Protection Act and product recall claims), multi-party and group actions; personal injury; property damage (including subsidence claims); health and safety; professional negligence; information technology; general common and commercial law; employment law. Main area of specialisation is product liability, having acted in numerous individual product liability matters and several multi-party actions. Is currently retained as junior counsel for the manufacturer in the multi party Benzene litigation. Recent reported cases include Britvic Soft Drinks Ltd & Others v Messer UK Ltd & Others [2002] 1 Lloyd's Rep 20 and on appeal [2002] EWCA Civ 548 and Bacardi-Martini Beverages Ltd v Thomas Hardy Packaging Ltd & Others [2002] 1 Lloyd's Rep 62 and on appeal [2002] EWCA Civ 548. Has also acted as junior counsel to The Boots Company plc in multi-party asbestos proceedings, and has been involved in the MMR/MR litigation. Undertakes a wide range of common law and commercial matters. In particular, he regularly undertakes Technology and Construction Court claims, including subsidence claims, software disputes, construction and public procurement. Lectures on product liability and group action claims.
Prof. Memberships: Personal Injury Bar Association, Employment Law Bar Association.
Career: Called 1995, Inner Temple Scholarship (1993), Princess Royal Scholarship (1994), CEDR accredited mediator (2000).
Publications: Contributor to 'The Practitioner's Guide to the Human Rights Act 1998' and to 'Halsbury's Laws' (Vol. 37).
Personal: BA (Oxon) First Class Honours (1992), Exhibitioner of Christ Church, Oxford.

WEBBER, Frances
Two Garden Court (Owen Davies QC & Courtenay Griffiths QC), London
(020) 7415 6265
fran.webber@mcr1.poptel.org.uk
Recommended in Immigration
Specialisation: All aspects of immigration, particularly refugee law, human rights, family and same sex cases, European Community law, deportation, work, detention. Judicial review, habeas corpus, statutory appeals. Criminal work with immigration angle. Recent reported cases include: R v Uxbridge MC ex Adimi; R v SSHD ex p Popatia; R v SSHD ex p Khatib; R (Mahmood) v SSHD.
Prof. Memberships: ILPA.
Career: BSc (social science), has written extensively on immigration and refugee issues for lay audience (eg. 'Crimes of Arrival' 1996; 'Inside Racist Europe' 1994), regular contributor to 'Race & Class', 'Statewatch'. Teaches courses for ILPA, LAG and Liberty.
Publications: Co-editor of MacDonald's 'Immigration Law and Practice' (5th edition, July 2001).

WEDDERSPOON, Rachel
9 St. John Street (John Hand QC), Manchester
(0161) 455 4000
clerks@9stjohnstreet.co.uk
Recommended in Employment
Specialisation: Principal area of practice is employment law. She specialises in race, disability and sex discrimination, unfair and wrongful dismissal before the Employment Tribunal and at appeal.
Prof. Memberships: The Employment Lawyers Association and the Professional Negligence Bar Association.
Career: LLB (Manchester). Called to the Bar in 1993.

WEIR, Robert
Devereux Chambers (Colin Edelman QC), London
(020) 7353 7534
Recommended in Personal Injury
Specialisation: Personal injury, clinical negligence, health and safety and human rights, particularly as it affects these areas. Recent reported cases include: Matthews v MoD, Roerig v Valiant Trawlers Ltd, Walters v North Glamorgan NHS Trust, Koonjul v Thameslink NHS Trust.
Prof. Memberships: PIBA, PNBA, Fellow of RSM.
Career: Called in 1992. Visiting tutor, Oxford (1994-95). MA in Medical Law and Ethics (1997-99).
Publications: Regular contributor to 'All England Legal Opinion'. Also written articles for 'Journal of Personal Injury Litigation', 'Solicitors Journal', 'New Law Journal'.
Personal: Educated at Downside School and Christ's College, Cambridge (1st Class degree). Enjoys skiing, golf and chess.

WEITZMAN, Tom
3 Verulam Buildings (Christopher Symons QC & John Jarvis QC), London
(020) 7831 8441
chambers@3vb.com
Recommended in Commercial (Litigation), Professional Negligence
Specialisation: General commercial practice specialising in insurance and reinsurance work. He also does a substantial amount of professional negligence work. In recent years, his practice has also included some product liability work. He has experience of both

commercial arbitration and ADR. Clients have included major UK insurers, various Lloyd's syndicates, major UK brokers, major UK plcs, the trustees of the Maxwell Pension Funds, international accountancy firms (professional negligence claims), a major UK tobacco manufacturer (product liability claims) and directors of insolvent insurance company (misfeasance/wrongful trading claim).
Prof. Memberships: COMBAR.
Career: BA (Oxon), 1984 Call, Gray's Inn.
Publications: Bullen & Leake & Jacob's 'Precedents and Pleadings' (insurance section).

WEST, Lawrence
2 Harcourt Buildings (Roger Henderson QC), London
(020) 7583 9020
clerks@harcourt.co.uk
Recommended in Environment
Specialisation: Regularly instructed in environmental cases on behalf of the chemical, petrochemical and agrochemical industries, local authorities, statutory water undertakers, general industry and private individuals. Other areas of practice: personal injury, including clinical negligence; product liability; commercial; local authority and governmental agency law; professional negligence of all kinds and insurance.
Career: Called to Bar in Ontario in 1973. Practised in Toronto as an advocate with the leading Canadian law firm, *McCarthy, Tetrault*, where he was involved in substantial commercial and medical negligence litigation. Called to Bar by Gray's Inn 1979. Since then has practised from 2 Harcourt Buildings. Reported cases include Cambridge Water Co v Eastern Counties Leather Plc (1994 – environmental pollution), Stubbings v Webb (1993 – limitation in personal injury action) and Thake v Maurice (1985 – public policy aspects of claims for damages following conception after vasectomy). Also, junior counsel for Paul McKenna in the hypnotherapy/schizophrenia case brought against him.
Personal: Toronto, 1946. LLM (London); LLB, BA (Toronto).

WESTON, Amanda
Garden Court North (Chambers of Ian MacDonald QC), Manchester
(0161) 236 1840
Recommended in Immigration

WHIPPLE, Philippa
1 Crown Office Row (Robert Seabrook QC), London
(020) 7797 7500
philippa.whipple@1cor.com
Recommended in Clinical Negligence
Specialisation: Clinical negligence, medical law, public law.
Prof. Memberships: London Commercial and Common Law Bar Association; Personal Injuries Bar Association; Bar European Group.
Career: Formerly a solicitor (1989-93).

Called in 1994 (Middle Temple). Junior Counsel to the Crown (B Panel).
Publications: Contributor to 'An Introduction to Human Rights and the Common Law'; English and Havers, Hart Publishing 2000.
Personal: MA (Oxford) in Law. Married, two children.

WHITE, Andrew QC
Atkin Chambers (Robert Akenhead QC), London
(020) 7404 0102
Recommended in Arbitration, Construction
Specialisation: Principal areas of expertise are domestic and international civil engineering, building, shipbuilding and ship repair disputes, and energy law. Also covers professional negligence and general commercial law. Has extensive experience of arbitration conducted under the ICC, LCIA, LMAA and UNCITRAL rules. Significant cases include: Harman CFM Facades v Corporate Officer of the House of Commons (UK procurement law); ABB Lummus Global Ltd v Keppel Fels Ltd (arbitration, curial law); BICC v Parkman (jurisdiction under Civil Liability Contribution Act), Channel Tunnel Group Ltd v Balfour Beatty Construction (jurisdiction of English Court to grant injunctions in foreign arbitration), Murphy v Brentwood (negligence).
Prof. Memberships: TECBAR, COMBAR, Western Circuit.
Career: Called to the Bar 1980, QC (1997).
Publications: Contributor: 'Atkins Forms and Precedents: Building Contracts'.
Personal: Educated University College Cardiff, LLB (Hons), 1975-1979. Megarry Scholar and Hardwicke Scholar of Lincoln's Inn. Born 25th January 1958. Lives London and Dorset. Interests include music, horses, farming and gardening.

WHITE, Sasha
Eldon Chambers (Patrick Clarkson QC & William Hicks QC), London
(020) 7583 1355
Recommended in Planning

WHITEHALL, Mark
Colleton Chambers (Martin Meeke QC), Exeter
(01392) 274898
Recommended in Crime

WHITEHOUSE, David QC
3 Raymond Buildings (Clive Nicholls QC), London
(020) 74006400
chambers@3raymondbuildings.com
Recommended in Crime, Fraud
Specialisation: Principal specialist areas are crime, including The Dome Robbery, Mafia and Colombian cartel drugs importing trials and the murder of Lennie 'The Gov'ner' McLean; fraud including Timeshare Fraud (R v John 'Goldfinger' Palmer), City fraud (Barlow Clowes - Investment fraud, Landhurst Leasing Plc - leasing fraud and corruption, Abbey National plc - corruption and Norton Plc - rights issue); local authority fraud (West Wiltshire privatisation case, Brent housing); mortgage fraud (R v Annen and others), Insolvency fraud (Baron Group of Companies), Legal Aid fraud (O'Malley), licensing – liquor, casino and bingo. Also specialises in disciplinary tribunals and has appeared before the Institute of Chartered Accountants, Securities and Futures Authority, LIFFE, General Medical Council, Institute of Chartered Engineers, British Boxing Board of Control.
Prof. Memberships: Criminal Bar Association, International Bar Association.
Career: Called to the Bar 1969 and joined current chambers in 1970 after pupillage in defamation chambers. Libel read The Sun 1969-75. Appointed Recorder 1987. Took silk 1990.
Personal: Educated at Trinity College, Cambridge 1964-67 (MA).

WHITFIELD, Adrian QC
3 Serjeants' Inn (Robert Francis QC & John Grace QC), London
(020) 7427 5000
Recommended in Clinical Negligence
Specialisation: Principal area of practice is medical negligence and other medical law, including treatment decisions. Cases include Sidaway, Hotson, in Re F (sterilisation), de Martell and conjoined twins. Has extensive GMC and other tribunal experience. Acts for claimants and defendants. Writes and lectures regularly on medico-legal subjects.
Prof. Memberships: London Common Law and Commercial Bar Association, Personal Injury Bar Association. Professional Negligence Bar Association, Medico-Legal Society.
Career: Call 1964: Queen's Counsel 1983: Chairman of NHS Tribunal 1993.
Personal: Educated Ampleforth College and Magdalen College Oxford: Demy (Open Scholar). Lives in London.

WHITTAKER, John
Serle Court (Lord Neill of Bladen QC), London
(020) 7242 6105
clerks@serlecourt.co.uk
Recommended in Partnership
Specialisation: Principal area of practice is chancery including related commerce and property. Partnership law is a specialist area of practice.
Prof. Memberships: Association of Partnership Practitioners.
Career: Called 1969, joined Serle Court in 1970.
Publications: Co-author of Whittaker and Machell 'Limited Liability Partnerships: The New Law', Jordans 2001; and co-editor of 'Limited Liability Partnership Legislation Handbook', Jordans 2001.
Personal: Magdalen College, Oxford (MA, BCL).

WHITTAM, Richard
Furnival Chambers (Andrew Mitchell QC), London
(020) 7405 3232
Recommended in Crime
Specialisation: First Junior Treasury Counsel to the Crown at the Central Criminal Court. Specialist Criminal practitioner with considerable experience in complex cases. Serious fraud experience in advance fee, leasing, Certificate of Deposit, mortgage and DSS frauds. Defended in substantial Customs and Excise cases. Public Interest Immunity. Information Technology.
Prof. Memberships: Criminal Bar Association; S E Circuit.
Personal: Educated at Marple Hall School and University College London. Formerly active in sport, now golf and occasional cricket.

WHITTLE, Henry
11 South Square (Christopher Floyd QC), London
(020) 7405 1222
Recommended in Intellectual Property

WILDBLOOD, Stephen QC
Albion Chambers (Neil Ford QC), Bristol
(0117) 927 2144
Recommended in Family

WILLIAMS, David H
Chavasse Court Chambers (Theresa Pepper), Liverpool
(0151) 707 1191
Recommended in Crime

WILLIAMS, Heather
Doughty Street Chambers (Geoffrey Robertson QC), London
(020) 7404 1313
h.williams@doughtystreet.co.uk
Recommended in Human Rights
Specialisation: Civil liberties and human rights, particularly actions against the police and related judicial review work and all aspects of discrimination law. Recent reported cases include: Farah v Commr. of Metropolitan Police [1998] QB 65 C.A. (liability of police - Race Relations Act), Percy v A.S. Hall [1997] QB 924 C.A. (false imprisonment), N v Agrawal (1999) PNLR 939 C.A. (duty of care - F.M.E.), Rovenska v G.M.C. [1998] ICR 85 C.A. (race discrimination), Cast v Croydon College [1998] ICR 500 C.A. (sex discrimination), Derby Specialist Fabrications Ltd. v Burton [2001] 2 All ER 840 EAT (race discrimination), Murray v Newham CAB [2001] ICR 708 EAT (disability discrimination). Acted for applicant in Bower v Schroders (record £1.5million sex discrimination compensation award).
Prof. Memberships: Discrimination Law Association, Police Actions Lawyers Group, ALBA & Liberty.
Career: Called to Bar in 1985; in practice since 1987.
Publications: Contributor to 'Making Rights Real (Using the Human Rights Act to Challenge Racism & Race Discrimination)'; various articles and

LEADERS AT THE BAR

lectures on areas of specialisation.
Personal: Married with two children. Born 1963. LLB, King's College London 1981-84; Scarman Scholarship for Bar Finals 1985.

WILLIAMS, John Melville QC
Old Square Chambers (John Hendy QC), London
(020) 7269 0300
jmwq@dial.pipex.com
Recommended in Environment
Specialisation: Environmental toxic torts; agricultural environmental damages claims; waste-incineration; environmental insurance; some planning; particular interest in scientific aspects of environmental issues. Notable cases: Graham v Rechem; Camelford Water Claims, organophosphate sheep dip cases.
Prof. Memberships: Environmental Law Foundation - Member of Advisory Council; Association of Personal Injury Lawyers (1st president 1990-94); Association of Trial Lawyers of America (Chair International Practice Section 1992); Personal Injury Bar Association.
Career: Called 1955; QC 1977; Recorder 1985-93; legal assessor to the General Medical Council and General Dental Council 1984-date. Member CICB 1998-2000; Member of CICAP 2000-date. Chairman Y2K Lawyers Association. Member of editorial board JPIL.
Publications: Various articles.
Personal: Hill walking.

WILLIAMS, Lloyd
30 Park Place (John Jenkins QC), Cardiff
(029) 2039 8421
Recommended in Personal Injury

WILLIAMS, Rhodri
30 Park Place (John Jenkins QC), Cardiff
(029) 2039 8421
rjw@30parkplace.law.co.uk
Recommended in Local Government
Specialisation: Local Government and administrative law; EC law. Cases include: R v HM Treasury ex parte University of Cambridge (2000) AER(EC) 920 ECJ; Stagecoach Finland v City of Helsinki (2002) ECR I ECJ.
Prof. Memberships: Bar European Group; Association for Regulated Procurement; Wales Public Law & Human Rights Association.
Career: Qualified 1987; Gray's Inn; tenant 30 Park Place since 1997; tenant 2 Harcourt Buildings since 1999; appointed to Attorney General's list of approved Counsel (provincial panel) 2000; appointed to list of Counsel General to the National Assembly for Wales 2000.
Publications: Public Procurement Law Review, Butterworths Expert Guide to the European Union (Internal Market).
Personal: Educated Cardiff High School and Exeter College, Oxford. BA Modern Languages 1985; Dip Law 1986.

WILLIAMSON, Adrian QC
Keating Chambers, London
(020) 7544 2600
awilliamson@keatingchambers.com
Recommended in Construction
Specialisation: Construction and engineering law; professional negligence; disputes concerning substantial commercial and technical projects; international commercial arbitration; cases include Aughton v Kent; Damond Lock v Laing Investments; Barclays Bank v Fairclough Building Ltd; West Faulkner Associates v LB Newham; Birse v Haiste; Hytec v Coventry CC; Bernhards Rugby Landscapes Ltd v Stockley Park; Royal Brompton Hospital v Hammond & Others.
Career: Qualified 1983; Middle Temple; tenant in chambers of John Loyd QC 2 Crown Office Row 1985-1989; tenant at Keating Chambers 1989 to date QC 2002.
Publications: Wrote chapters on JCT and NSC Forms of Contract for 'Keating on Building Contracts' (5th 1991, 6th 1995 and 7th 2001editions); joint editor Halsbury's 'Laws of England' volume 4(2) 'Building Contracts etc.' to be published 2002.
Personal: Highgate School, Trinity Hall, Cambridge (1982 BA 1st Class Hons 1985 MA). Born 1959. Married with 3 children.

WILLIAMSON, Hazel QC
Maitland Chambers (Michael Lyndon-Stanford QC & Charles Aldous QC), London
(020) 7406 1200
hwilliamson@maitlandchambers.com
Recommended in Partnership, Property Litigation
Specialisation: Chancery litigation including property, company and insolvency, commercial contract, partnership and related negligence aspects. Particular emphasis on commercial property including acquisition, financing and development and landlord and tenant aspects. Also, leasehold enfranchisement, markets and fairs, Court of Protection. Cases include National Westminster Bank v Arthur Young (1986-93) series of cases on rent review, arbitration procedure and appeals; BCCI v Aboody (1988); Banco Exterior v Thomas (1997); Barclays Bank v Coleman (1999) undue influence and bank mortgages; Crown Estate Commissioners v Signet Ltd (1997); Moss Bros Group v CSC Properties (1999): refusal of consent to leasehold assignment; Lumsden Ltd v Holdsworth (Isle of Man 1998 and 1999 on appeal): failed timeshare, dishonest assistance in breach of trust, partnership, solicitors' negligence; Re: Forester & Lamego Ltd (1997) public interest winding up; Re Brian D Pierson (Contractors) Ltd 1999: decision on wrongful trading and misfeasance, Re: Thirty Eight Building Ltd 1999: decision on undue preferences; Locabail (UK) Ltd v Bayfield Properties Ltd and anor (1999): judicial bias/proprietary estoppel, undue influence, overriding interests in land registration, scope of bank mortgagee's right or subrogation; Coventry and Solihull Waste Disposal v Russell (VO) (1999) HL: rating: Re C (2000): Enduring Powers of Attorney.
Career: Qualified 1972, Gray's and Lincoln's Inn. Silk 1988. Recorder 1996. Deputy High Court Judge 1994. Acting Deemster of the Isle of Man 1999. Chairman of the Chancery Bar Association 1994-97. Member of the DETR, Property Advisory Group.
Publications: 'Law and Valuation of Leisure Property' (Estates Gazette), joint editor and contributor. Mediator (ADR chambers) 2000.
Personal: Educated Wimbledon High School and St Hilda's College, Oxford. BA 1969, MA 1982, FCIArb 1992.

WILLS-GOLDINGHAM, Claire
Albion Chambers (Neil Ford QC), Bristol
(0117) 927 2144
Recommended in Family
Specialisation: Childcare/ancillary relief.
Career: Called 1988. Western Circuit; GLO5 CCUP 1998 3 FCR 114.
Publications: Contributor Butterworth 'Essential Family Practice' (Finance Volume); joint editor Butterworths 'Encyclopedia Forms & Precedents'; jointly rewritten Atkins 'Court Forms (infants)'.
Personal: LLB (Hons); Side saddle Panel Judge and Competitor.

WILMOT-SMITH, Richard QC
39 Essex Street (Nigel Pleming QC), London
(020) 7832 1111
richard.wilmot-smith@39essex.com
Recommended in Construction
Specialisation: A specialist in all aspects of construction and engineering, process engineering, oil and gas, mining and other energy litigation and arbitration. His experience includes disputes involving performance bonds, guarantees, insolvency and related professional negligence claims against architects, engineers and surveyors and insolvency. He has acted in litigation and arbitration concerned with major projects in the United Kingdom, the United States, Tanzania, Egypt, India, Singapore, Hong Kong, Canada, Iran, Iraq, Dubai, Qatar, Pakistan, Bangladesh, Malaysia and Saudi Arabia. These projects include major tunnels, roads, bridges and other structures including ports and drydocks, housing estates and universities, factories, power stations and other energy systems, food processing plants, oil platforms and refineries. John Mowlem & Co plc v Eagle Star Insurance Co Ltd and others 44 Con LR 134 (CA); Trafalgar House v General Surety [1996] AC 119 (HL); In re Cosslett (Contractors) Ltd [1998] Ch 495 (CA); Scottish Power plc v Britoil (Exploration) Ltd and Others, 141 SJ LB 246 (CA); Bedford County Council v Fitzpatrick (1998) CILL 1440 (QB); Pozzolanic Lytag Ltd v Bryan Hobson Associates (1998) CILL 1450 (QB); Deepak Fertilizers and Petrochemicals Ltd v Davy McKee (London) Limited [1999] 1 Lloyds LR 387 69 (CA); Smith v Bridgend (2000) AC 336 (HL).
Prof. Memberships: ORBA, London Common Law and Commercial Bar Association.
Career: Called to Bar in 1978, took silk 1994.

WILSON, Adam
No.6 Barristers Chambers (Jennifer Kershaw QC), Leeds
(0113) 245 9763
Recommended in Family

WILSON, Alastair QC
19 Old Buildings (Alastair Wilson QC), London
(020) 7405 2001
alw@19oldbuildings.com
Recommended in Information Technology, Intellectual Property
Specialisation: Principal areas of practice are intellectual property (including privacy and EC aspects); information technology and other cases requiring technological expertise. Other areas of work include lotteries and gaming. Cases of importance include A v B plc and C, H v Associated Newspapers, DaimlerChrysler v Alavi, Designers Guide v Russell Williams, Marks & Spencers v One in a Million, Chelsea Man v Chelsea Girl, PLG (Netlon) v Ardon, Stephens v Avery and BL v Armstrong. Clients have included British Railways Board, Ford Motor Company, Associated Newspapers, Irish Dairy Board and Netlon. Has presented numerous seminars on intellectual property and computer law. Recently involved in a video on privacy for Legal Network Television.
Prof. Memberships: Middle Temple Society for Computers and Law, Intellectual Property Bar Association, Chancery Bar Association.
Career: Called to the Bar 1968 and joined current chambers when located at 3 Pump Court in 1970. Took Silk in 1987. Appointed Recorder in 1996.
Personal: Educated at Wellington College and Pembroke College. Leisure pursuits include gardening and building. Born 26 May 1946. Lives near Norwich.

WINBERG, Stephen
2-4 Tudor Street (Richard Ferguson QC), London
(020) 7797 7111
Recommended in Crime, Fraud

WINDSOR, Emily
Falcon Chambers (Jonathan Gaunt QC & Kim Lewison QC), London
(020) 7353 2484
windsor@falcon-chambers.com
Recommended in Agriculture
Specialisation: Real property based litigation and advisory work, including commercial property, landlord and tenant, agriculture, easements,

restrictive covenants, mortgages and professional negligence. Also related insolvency and European law. Recent cases include Yenula Properties Ltd v Naidu [2002] EWCA Civ 719; State Bank of New South Wales v Harrison [2002] EWCA Civ 363 and Blackburn v David Alston (Suffolk) Ltd [2001] PLSCS 263.
Prof. Memberships: Chancery Bar Association, London Common Law and Commercial Bar Association, Property Bar Association, Agricultural Law Association (member of ALA Committee 1997-99) and Bar European Group. Elected member of the Bar Council and Chairman of the Young Barristers' Committee of the Bar Council 2002.
Career: Worcester College, Oxford (MA). Paris II University (DSU). Called in 1995.
Publications: Contributing editor of Bullen & Leake & Jacob's 'Precedents of Pleadings' (14th edn). Contributing editor of 'Woodfall Property Update Service'.

WINGATE-SAUL, Giles QC
Byrom Street Chambers, Manchester
(0161) 829 2100
gws@byromstreet.com
Recommended in Clinical Negligence, Commercial (Litigation), Personal Injury
Specialisation: Catastrophic injury, mercantile/commercial law, contract, tort, insurance, building and construction.
Prof. Memberships: Northern Circuit Commercial Bar Association, Society of Construction Law, Technology and Construction Court Bar Association, Professional Negligence Bar Association, Personal Injury Bar Association, Bar European Group.
Career: Winchester College, Southampton University (LLB Hons). Called to the Bar 1967. QC 1983. Deputy High Court Judge, Deputy Judge of Technology & Construction Court, Governing Bencher of Inner Temple, Chairman Northern Circuit Commercial Bar Association, The European Circuit.
Personal: Church affairs and sport.

WINTER, Ian
Hollis Whiteman Chambers (QEB) (Julian Bevan QC & Peter Whiteman QC), London
(020) 7583 5766
Recommended in Fraud
Specialisation: Specialist in criminal law with a particular emphasis on fraud and white collar crime. Acted for the defence in the Lady Aberdour and Swindon Town FC frauds. More recently represented Langaker, a defendant in the Morgan Grenfell Managment Fraud. Practice also covers police powers and civil liberties law. Even split between prosecution and defence work. Represented Dr Shipman.
Prof. Memberships: Bar Council Legal Services Committee.
Career: Called to the Bar in 1988. Joined present chambers in 1990.
Personal: Educated at Bristol UWE 1984-87. Leisure pursuits include international rally driving and playing the saxophone and piano. Born 25 March 1966. Lives in Fulham.

WISE, Ian
Doughty Street Chambers (Geoffrey Robertson QC), London
(020) 7404 1313
Recommended in Education, Human Rights
Specialisation: All areas of public law and human rights law with particular emphasis on public law aspects of criminal, education, prisoners, social welfare, health and children's law.
Prof. Memberships: Administrative Law Bar Association; Chair Howard League Youth Justice Committee.
Career: BA (Open) Dip Law, Dip EC Law, called to the Bar 1992. Formerly worked in industry.
Publications: 'Enforcement of Local Taxation'.
Personal: Born 1959.

WOLANSKI, Adam
5 Raymond Buildings (Patrick Milmo QC), London
(020) 7242 2902
adamwolanski@5rb.co.uk
Recommended in Defamation
Specialisation: Media law, including defamation, breach of confidence/privacy and reporting restrictions. Regularly instructed by national newspapers and broadcasters, including (in 2001-02) Times Newspapers, Mirror Group Newspapers, Associated Newspapers and News Group Newspapers. Recent cases include Campbell v News Group Newspapers, Benjamin Pell v John Mappin, Safeway v Tate [2001] QB 1120, Venables and Thompson v News Group Newspapers and Others [2001] 2 WLR 1038. Recent work for claimants include libel action brought by ex editor of The Cook Report against News Group Newspapers and Times Newspapers. Frequently provides pre-publication advice to newspaper, book and magazine publishers.
Career: MA (Cantab), Lincoln's Inn CPE Scholarship, called 1995.
Publications: Co-author of 'Privacy and The Media' (OUP 2002).

WOLFE, David
Matrix Chambers, London
(020) 7404 3447
davidwolfe@matrixlaw.co.uk
Recommended in Administrative & Public Law, Education, Environment
Specialisation: Public law, especially local government law and environmental law, including: Environment law: JRs of planning and regulatory decisions particularly including EC law. Has PhD in Engineering, and is regularly involved in cases involving complex technical evidence. Education law: Statutory appeals and JRs (including relating to special educational needs, exclusions, admissions and school reorganisations). David is an editor of Butterworths' 'Law of Education' (aka The Education Encyclopaedia). Community Care/Health Law: JRs including: on care planning, rationing, mental health, charging, complaints procedures, health care and benefit entitlements. Is happy to discuss matters ahead of formal instruction where appropriate. Enjoys working as part of a relatively informal team with clients and those instructing him.
Prof. Memberships: Administrative Law Bar Association, Planning and Environmental Bar Association, UK Environmental Law Association, Education Law Practitioners Association
Career: BSc MEng (Manchester) 1987, PhD (Engineering, Cambridge) 1991, Barrister since 1992.

WOLFSON, David
One Essex Court (Lord Grabiner QC), London
(020) 7583 2000
dwolfson@oeclaw.co.uk
Recommended in Banking & Finance, Commercial (Litigation)
Specialisation: Practice encompasses all areas of commercial law, specialising in banking, finance and insolvency law, professional negligence, domestic and international sale of goods, arbitration (domestic and international) and entertainment law. General commercial work incorporates major banking and commercial cases and ICC arbitrations. Recent and reported cases include: Enron [2002] - involved in a number of disputes arising out of the collapse of Enron; Unilever Superannuation Trustees v Mercury Asset Management [Comm Ct 2001] - major negligence claim against City fund managers; Royal Bank of Scotland v Etridge [HL 2001] - undue influence and enforcement of security; Definitely Maybe (Touring) v Marek Liebererg Konzertagentur [Comm Ct 2001] contractual and conflict of laws dispute between Oasis and a German concert promoter; Harvey Jones v Woolwich [CA 2001] - materially altered bills of exchange; Investors Compensation Scheme v West Bromwich Building Society [ChD 1998] - Home Income Plan litigation; Ghana Commercial Bank v C [QBD 1997] - tracing proceeds of fraud and freezing orders.
Prof. Memberships: COMBAR.
Career: MA (Cantab); Exhibitioner and Scholar of Selwyn College. Stuart of Rannoch award. Squire scholarship. Inner Temple Major scholarship. CLE scholarship. Called 1992.
Publications: Contributing author to 'Bank Liability and Risk' (1995, Lloyds) and 'Banking Litigation' (1999, Sweet & Maxwell). Writes regularly for 'All England Litigation Review'.

WOLKIND, Michael QC
2 Bedford Row (William Clegg QC), London
(020) 7440 8888
Recommended in Crime
Specialisation: Has led in more than 120 murder cases, with specialities of psychiatric and medical causation defences. Regularly acts for the very top target criminals and has appeared in many notorious gangland trials (Patrick Adams, Tommy Adams, Tony White, George Polemos. Has also acted in the largest drug matters and in substantial frauds. Cases include a dismemberment 'nagging wife' provocation (Boyce), paedophile killing of 6 year old (Morss), killing of a brother where a jury refused to convict even after a change of plea to Guilty (Jennings), 10 year old girl accused of 3 murders (Lynch), killing of 4 family members (Aderdour) middle aged professional man accused of road rage killing (Janjirker), teenager charged with murder of abusive stepfather (Keaveney), the London Nailbomber (David Copeland), the successful Appeal of the Norfolk farmer convicted of murdering a burglar (Tony Martin). Has acted in Turkish and Libyan terrorist cases and he advised in the Lockerbie Bombing. Has appeared in Privy Council Capital cases and in fraud has acted for lawyers, accountants and bankers. Has been described in the independent Chambers Directory as 'the distilled essence of the great Jury advocate' and is widely considered as one of the best cross-examiners at the Criminal Bar.

WOLTON, Harry QC
2-3 Gray's Inn Square (Anthony Porten QC & Anthony Scrivener QC), London
(020) 7242 4986
harry@wolton.com
Recommended in Planning
Specialisation: Town and Country Planning in all respects.
Prof. Memberships: Planning & Environment Bar Association.
Career: Called 1969. Silk 1982. Recorder 1985. Authorised to sit as Deputy High Court Judge 1990.
Personal: Director, Bar Mutual Insurance Fund. Cattle breeding & dendrology.

WONNACOTT, Mark
Maitland Chambers (Michael Lyndon-Stanford QC & Charles Aldous QC), London
(020) 7406 1200
Recommended in Property Litigation

WOOD, Christopher
1 Hare Court (Bruce Blair QC), London
(020) 7797 7070
wood@lmcb.com
Recommended in Family
Specialisation: Principally ancillary relief.
Prof. Memberships: FLBA.
Career: Oxford University (MA). Université d'Aix-Marseilles III (Diplôme d'Etudes Supérieures d'Université). Called 1986; occasional lecturer.
Personal: Married with a daughter. Interests: history, politics, Norway, France.

WOOD, Derek QC
Falcon Chambers (Jonathan Gaunt QC & Kim Lewison QC), London
(020) 7353 2484

LEADERS AT THE BAR

wood@falcon-chambers.com
Recommended in Agriculture
Specialisation: Specialises in all aspects of property law, including commercial and agricultural landlord and tenant disputes, rent review, housing, easements and boundaries, compulsory purchase, tax and planning, building and engineering disputes, joint development agreements and professional negligence in connection with real property. Experienced in the conduct of cases in the courts, before public inquiries and tribunals, and also in arbitrations. Has made numerous appearances as advocate before arbitrators in England and Hong Kong, including two engineering disputes as leading counsel for the Government of Hong Kong. Many appointments as both arbitrator in England (mostly as sole arbitrator) and independent expert across a whole range of property related matters. Consulting Editor (with Bernstein, Marriott and Tackaberry) and contributor to 3rd Edition of the 'Handbook of Arbitration Practice' 1998 (Sweet & Maxwell and Chartered Institute of Arbitrators). Public appointments include Property Advisory Group 1975-94; Chairman of Expert Committees on the Rating of Plant and Machinery 1991-92 & 1997-98 (both Department of the Environment); Chairman of Standing Advisory Committee on Trunk Road Assessment (SACTRA) (Department of Transport). 1986-94. Chaired working party which produced Code of Practice on Commercial Leases in England and Wales 1995.
Prof. Memberships: Honorary Fellow of Central Association of Agricultural Valuers (FAAV) 1988; Honorary Member of Royal Institute of Chartered Surveyors (Hon RICS) 1991; Fellow of Chartered Institute of Arbitrators (FCIArb) by examination 1993.
Career: Called to the Bar 1964. Took Silk 1978. Recorder to the Crown Court 1985. Bencher of the Middle Temple 1986. Deputy Official Referee and Deputy High Court Judge.
Personal: Educated at the University of Oxford (MA, BCL). Principal of St Hugh's College, Oxford (since 1991). Awarded CBE in New Year's Honours List 1995 for services to property law. Born 14th October 1937.

WOOD, Graham QC
Exchange Chambers (David Turner QC & Bill Braithwaite QC & Henry Globe QC), Liverpool
(0151) 236 7747
graham.wood@rapid.co.uk
Recommended in Personal Injury
Specialisation: Personal injury, including health and safety and industrial disease, medical and other professional negligence. Commercial and construction disputes. Crime and commercial fraud. Administrative law, especially education and local government cases. Recent work has involved test litigation for 85 dBA liability against Fords and other major industrial deafness cases and solicitor negligence in handling large scale scheme settlements for industrial disease. Particular interest in catastrophic injury. Ecclesiastical law.
Prof. Memberships: PIBA PNBA.
Career: Recorder 2000. Co-founder Northern Circuit Free Representation and Advice Scheme. Deputy chancellor, Diocese of Liverpool.
Publications: 'Binghams Negligence Cases'.
Personal: Sailing. Married with three children.

WOOD, James QC
Doughty Street Chambers (Geoffrey Robertson QC), London
(020) 7404 1313
j.wood@doughtystreet.co.uk
Recommended in Crime
Specialisation: He specialises in human rights and criminal appellate work, and he prioritises cases raising political and policing issues. Appellate work includes numerous celebrated miscarriage of justice cases, such as the Birmingham Six, the Carl Bridgewater case, cases arising from the West Midlands Serious Crime Squad, and numerous other reported cases. He appears regularly in the Privy Council in death sentence cases from the Caribbean. His civil work includes actions against the police, inquests and prisoners rights.
Career: Silk 1999, Assistant Recorder 1998. Recorder 2000.
Publications: Author of 'Right to Silence: Case for Retention' (1991), and various Sweet and Maxwell Practical research Papers.

WOOD, Martin
Broadway House (J Graham K Hyland QC), Bradford
(01274) 722560
Recommended in Family
Specialisation: Family law, specialising in high value ancillary relief cases.
Prof. Memberships: FLBA.
Career: King James' Grammar School, Almondbury; Christ's College, CANTAB; call 1973.

WOOD, Nicholas
5 Paper Buildings (Richard King), London
(020) 7815 3217
nw5pb@aol.com
Recommended in Health & Safety
Specialisation: Other regulatory matters (trading standards, weights and measures, consumer protection), professional negligence (lawyers, valuers, engineers), personal injury (including clinical negligence).
Prof. Memberships: ACI Arb.

WOOD, Simon
Plowden Buildings (William Lowe QC), Newcastle upon Tyne
(020) 7583 0808
simonwood@clara.co.uk
Recommended in Personal Injury
Specialisation: All aspects of personal injury law acting for claimants and defendants alike, including clinical negligence. Professional negligence claims involving solicitors arising out of personal injury claims. Stark v The Post Office [2000] PIQR P105, CA.
Career: Called in 1981, Harmsworth Scholar. Practised continuously in North of England, from Plowden Buildings since 1999. Recorder 2000.
Publications: Member editorial team, 'Charlesworth & Percy on Negligence' (10th edn, published Autumn 2001).
Personal: Born 1958. Choristers' School, Durham; Royal Grammar School, Newcastle upon Tyne (governor, 1999); University of Newcastle upon Tyne. Married with four sons. Music.

WOOD, William QC
Brick Court Chambers (Christopher Clarke QC), London
(020) 7379 3550
wood@brickcourt.co.uk
Recommended in Aviation, Insurance
Specialisation: Commercial, insurance and reinsurance, aviation, competition and mediation.
Prof. Memberships: Member of Combar, Bar European Group and Competition Law Association.
Career: BA (1st class) Oxford, BCL (1st class) Oxford, LLM (Harvard Law School). Called 1980, silk 1998, CEDR Accredited Mediator 1999, Member of the Bar of Tonga, 2000.

WOODWARD, William QC
Ropewalk Chambers (Ian McLaren QC), Nottingham
(0115) 947 2581
clerks@ropewalk.co.uk
Recommended in Personal Injury
Specialisation: Embraces common law, personal injury, employer's liability, insurance, disaster, insidious disease, poisoning, clinical, professional and other negligence throughout the land. Involvement in consequences of Markham mine, Flixborough, Hillsborough disasters and in asbestos, noise induced hearing loss, white finger, bladder and other cancer, mucous membrane, fire and explosion litigation for example.
Prof. Memberships: Bar European Group. Founder member Nottinghamshire Medico-Legal Society and East Midlands Business and Property Bar Association. Special Professor Nottingham University Law Department.
Career: St. John's College Oxford. Called 1964, Inner Temple. Queen's Counsel 1985. Head of Ropewalk Chambers 1985-94. Recorder. Deputy High Court Judge. President Mental Health Review Tribunal.
Personal: Married, three children. Ponds. Fungi. Serendipity.

WOODWARK, Jane
Plowden Buildings (William Lowe QC), Newcastle upon Tyne
(020) 7583 0808
jewoodwark@aol.com
Recommended in Employment
Specialisation: Almost exclusively employment and discrimination law, acting for both employers and employees. Background in local government.
Prof. Memberships: Employment Law Bar Association; Industrial Law Society.
Career: Master's degree in Industrial Relations, London School of Economics 1983. Called 1995. Prior to the Bar, worked for a national employers' organisation advising on employment law, particularly equalities issues and transfers of undertakings. Advised employers during three national industrial disputes in 1986, 1989 and 1992.

WORDSWORTH, Sam
Essex Court Chambers (Gordon Pollock QC), London
(020) 813 8000
Recommended in Public International Law
Specialisation: Public international law, international and commercial arbitration, general commercial litigation. Cases include: Hungary v Slovakia, Guinea v Congo (both International Court of Justice), Ireland v United Kingdom (International Law of the Sea Tribunal and two arbitrations), the Kuwait Airways v Iraq and Iraqi Airways litigation (in the English courts and before the United Nations Compensation Commission).
Career: Practised in Paris 1991-1997 (*Frere Cholmeley Bischoff*); called to Bar in 1997. Treasury Panel (C List). Avocat à la cour (Paris Bar).

WORTHINGTON, Stephen
12 King's Bench Walk (Richard Methuen QC), London
(020) 7581 0811
worthington@12kbw.co.uk
Recommended in Personal Injury
Specialisation: Professional negligence, personal injury, environmental law. Blue Circle v Ministry of Defence, Nuclear Pollution, [1998] 3 All ER 385. Heil v Rankin (2001) QB 272. Martin v Lancashire County Council (2000) 3 All ER 54 (TUPE). Watson v British Boxing Board of Control (2001) QB 1134.
Prof. Memberships: PIBA, LCLCBA, TECBAR, PNBA.
Career: Trinity College, Cambridge.
Publications: Contributor to Butterworths 'Professional Negligence' and 'Structured Settlements: A Practical Guide'.

WRIGHT, Peter QC
Lincoln House Chambers (Mukhtar Hussain QC), Manchester
(0161) 832 5701
Recommended in Crime

WYAND, Roger QC
Hogarth Chambers (Jonathan Rayner James QC & Christopher Morcom QC), London
(020) 7404 0404
rwyand@hogarthchambers.fsnet.co.uk
Recommended in Intellectual Property
Specialisation: All aspects of intellectual property law including the effect of EU competition law. Important cases:

LEADERS AT THE BAR

Assidoman v Mead Nokia Mobile Phones Limited's Application, Biotrading and Financing v Biohit, Ladney's Application, Philips v Remington. Oren v Red Box, Cantor Fitzgerald v Tradition, Citymax v Cristal, PPL v South Tyneside, BMS v Baker Norton, GlaxoSmithkline and BASF, Hewlett Packard v Waters, REEF TM.
Prof. Memberships: Bar European Group, Intellectual Property Bar Association Vice-Chairman, Chancery Bar Association.
Career: MA (Natural Sciences) Downing College, Cambridge. Assistant Recorder, Patents County Court 1994. QC 1997. Recorder 2000.

WYNTER, Colin
Devereux Chambers (Colin Edelman QC), London
(020) 7353 7534
Recommended in Insurance
Specialisation: Insurance and reinsurance, general commercial, professional negligence.
Prof. Memberships: COMBAR.
Career: All aspects of insurance and reinsurance: Cases include: Scott v Copenhagen [2002] Commercial Court (to be reported), Gan Insurance Co. Ltd v Tai Ping Insurance Co Ltd (No.1) [1999] LRIR, 229, and (CA) [1999] LRIR 472, (No.2) [2001] LRIR, 291 and (No.3) [2001] LRIR 670 and (CA) [2001] LRIR 682, Mabey & Johnson v Ecclesiastical & Ors [2001] LRIR 369, Baker & Ors v McCall International [2001] LRIR 149, Trygg Hansa v Equitas [1998] 2 Lloyd's Rep 439, Pacific & General Insurance v Baltica Insurance [1996] LRIR 8, Equitas v Sirius (1999, Commercial Court), Home Insurance Co. v ME Rutty [1996] LRIR 415, Colonial v Chung, (Privy Council) (to be reported 2001 Lloyd's Rep), Pride Valley v The Independent Insurance Co. (1997) and (CA) (1999), Caudle v Sharp (arbitration only). Also various Lloyd's Names Insurance actions: Stockwell v Outhwaite (1990-1992), Agnew v Wellington (1994-1996). Other Commercial: Sale and carriage of goods, and general commercial disputes: Cases include Stephenson v Rogers (CA) [1999] 2 WLR 1064, [1999] 1 All ER 613, Cicatiello v Anglo European [1994] 1 LLR 678, Governor of Bank of Scotland v Butcher (CA) (1998), Barnard Marcus v Ashraf (CA) [1988] 1 EGLR 7, Lambert v West Devon Borough Council, [1997] JPL 735. Employment: Unfair and wrongful dismissals, race and sex discrimination (not equal pay, equal value or part time workers), injunctive relief. Cases include Schultz v Esso Petroleum (CA) [1999] 3 All ER 338, [1999] ICR 1202, and Virdee v National Grid Co. Plc [1992] IRLR 555.
Publications: Author of Insurance Chapter in 'Law and the Business of Sport', by Griffith-Jones (Butterworths, 1997). Has appeared on legal education videos to discuss certain of the above and other cases. Lectures frequently on insurance and reinsurance matters.
Personal: LLB (1st Class) (London), M.Phil (Cantab); fluent in French. Interests: sports and music.

WYVILL, Alistair
St Philips Chambers (John Randall QC), Birmingham
(0121) 246 7000
awyvill@st-philips.co.uk
Recommended in Commercial (Litigation)
Specialisation: General commercial litigation, including intellectual property (particularly in information technology), insolvency, commercial fraud, construction law and human rights in commercial law.
Prof. Memberships: Chancery Bar Association, Midland Chancery and Commercial Bar Association.
Career: B.Econ.; LLB (Hons) (Qld), LLM (Distinction)(Lond.) Admitted as a solicitor in Australia in 1984. Called to the Bar in Australia in 1986. Practised in Australia as a barrister in commercial and company law for 12 years. Also admitted in Papua New Guinea. Called to the Bar in England and Wales in 1998.
Publications: 'Enrichment, Restitution and the Collapsed Negotiations Cases' (1993-94)' 11 Aust Bar Review 93. With D Fitzpatrick, 'Business Bankruptcy Law Reform in Vietnam' (1996) 5 Asia Pacific Law Review 37. 'The Law of Fraudulent Conveyances as the Basis of Mareva Jurisdiction' (1998) 73, Australian Law Journal 672.

YOUNG, David QC
Three New Square (David Young QC), London
(020) 7405 1111
3newsquareip@lineone.net
Recommended in Intellectual Property
Specialisation: All aspects of intellectual property, patent (especially chemical patent cases), and passing off, trademarks, copyright, franchising, restrictive practices, designs, breach of confidence and computer law. Appears in Hong Kong and Singapore. Notable cases include: American Cyanamid v Ethicon (interloc. injunction); 3M v Rennicks (patent); Windsurfing International v Tabur Marine (GB) Ltd (patent); Willemijn v Madge Networks (patent/computers); Germinal Holdings (plant variety); Allied Signal v Sundstrand (Patent County Court - electronics); Glaverbel v British Coal; Hoechst v BP (patent, account of profits) Improver Corpn. v Remington Consumer Products (patent, infringement) Lubrizol Corpn. v Exxon; Monsanto v Merck (patent infringement, pharmaceuticals); Scandecor Development v Scandecor Marketing (passing off and trademark); Collag Corpn. v Merck & Co. (confidential information); Pfizer & Eli Lilly/ICOS (Patent- Viagra).
Prof. Memberships: Intellectual Property Bar Association; Chancery Bar Association.
Career: Monckton Combe School, Hertford College Oxford - MA. Called to Bar 1966, appointed QC 1980. Bencher of Lincolns Inn; Recorder of Crown Court (1987-2000); Chairman Plant Seeds and Varieties Tribunal (1987-); Deputy High Court Judge Chancery Division (1993-); Deputy Judge of Patent County Court (1993-).
Publications: Co-author 'Terrell on Law of Patents' (12th-14th ed); 'Young on Passing Off', 1985; 1994.
Personal: Tennis, skiing, country pursuits.

YOUNG, Timothy QC
20 Essex Street (Iain Milligan QC), London
(020) 7842 1200
clerks@20essexst.com
Recommended in Shipping
Specialisation: Main areas of practice are commercial law and international trade and related areas including arbitration and judicial review. Sometime lecturer in law at St. Edmund Hall, Oxford. Significant recent reported cases: Glencore Grain Rotterdam v Lorico [1997] 2 Lloyd's Rep 386 (FOB Sale Letter of credit waiver) CA; The Kriti Rex [1996] 2 Lloyd's Rep 171 (COA, unseaworthiness, damages); AG of New Zealand v Anderson [1995] 2 Lloyd's Rep 264 (due diligence); Gill & Duffus v Rionda Futures [1994] 2 Lloyd's Rep 67 (sale of goods, demurrage, counter guarantee); The Island Archon [1994] 2 Lloyd's Rep 227 (implied indemnities); Standard Chartered Bank v PNSC/Mehra [2000] 1 LLR 218/[2000] 2 LLR 511; Hill Harmony 2001 [AC] 638.
Prof. Memberships: COMBAR, London Common Law & Commercial Bar Association.
Career: Called to the Bar in 1977 and joined present chambers in 1978. Took Silk 1996.
Publications: Voyage Charters (LLP).
Personal: Supporting member of the London Maritime Arbitrators Association and panel member of Securities and Futures Authority arbitrators. Educated at Malvern College 1967-71 and Magdalen College, Oxford 1972-76 (BA, BCL). Born 1 December 1953. Lives in London.

ZACAROLI, Antony
3-4 South Square (Michael Crystal QC & Lord Alexander of Weedon QC), London
(020) 7696 9900
clerks@southsquare.com
Recommended in Chancery, Insolvency
Specialisation: Practice covers a wide area of business and commercial law, including all aspects of corporate and personal insolvency, restructuring, litigation relating to property, commercial fraud, constructive trusts, banking, securities, insurance, pensions and professional negligence. Recent cases include Re NT Gallagher, Court of Appeal, 2002; Bank of Scotland v Henry Dutcher [2001] 2 ALLER (comm) 691; Grupo Torras SA v Al Sabah [1999] CLC 1469; Re Cosslett (Contractors) Limited [1998] Ch 495.
Career: Called to the Bar (Middle Temple) November 1987. Lecturer in Law at Pembroke College, Oxford, from 1987-91.
Publications: Contributor to Lightman & Moss: 'The Law of Receivers of Companies'; Totty & Moss: 'Insolvency'; Gore-Browne on Companies.

ZELIN, Geoffrey
Enterprise Chambers (Anthony Mann QC), London
(020) 7405 9471
Recommended in Company
Specialisation: London (020) 7405 9471 Newcastle (0191) 222 3344 Leeds (0113) 246 0391. Practises in all areas of company and partnership law including shareholder and partnership disputes, insolvency, enforcement of directors' duties and disqualification. Apart from company law his practice encompasses all areas of commercial Chancery work including property disputes and professional negligence.
Prof. Memberships: Chancery Bar Association, Property Bar Association.
Career: Called to the Bar 1984. Practising in these chambers since December 1986.
Personal: Interests include skiing, cricket.

THE BAR A-Z

London page 1506
Regions 1617

LONDON

Arbitration Chambers (John Tackaberry QC) — Set No.1

22 Willes Road, London, NW5 3DS
Tel (020) 7267 2137 **Fax** (020) 7482 1018 **DX** 46454 LDN/Kentish Town
Email jatqc@atack.demon.co.uk

Head of Chambers	John Tackaberry QC
Tenants	1

Members
John Tackaberry QC (1967) (QC-1982)

The Chambers John Tackaberry is a specialist practitioner whose principal area of expertise is international and domestic construction disputes and related areas. He offers advocacy, both in litigation and arbitration, arbitration as arbitrator with particular experience of ICC arbitration and Mediation Adjudication and DRB services. He is a Registered Arbitrator admitted to various panels of arbitrators in this country, and has been a Recorder since 1988. He is also a Fellow of the Chartered Institute of Arbitrators and the Faculty of Building. He is admitted to practice at the Bars of California and the Irish Republic and as a QC in New South Wales. He is ex-chairman of C.I.Arb, ex-president of Society of Construction Law & European Society of Construction Law. Appointed as an arbitrator on Panel of China International Economic and Trade Arbitration Commission. Appointed a Commissioner to Chair a panel constituted under the auspices of the United Nations Compensation Commission. He is, or has been, a member of and/or on the arbitration panels of the Chartered Institute of Arbitrators (Past Chairman); European Society of Construction Law (Past President); Faculty of Building (Fellow); UK Society of Construction Law (Past President); Inst. of Civil Engineers; Royal Inst. of British Architects; Los Angeles Center for Commercial Arbitration; American Arbitration Association; Association of Arbitrators in South Africa; Indian Council of Arbitration; Singapore International Arbitration Council; Mauritius Chamber of Commerce and Industry. A full CV is available on request.

Arden Chambers (Andrew Arden QC) — Set No.2

Arden Chambers, 2 John Street, London, WC1N 2ES
Tel (020) 7242 4244 **Fax** (020) 7242 3224 **DX** 29 Chancery Lane
Email clerks@ardenchambers.com **Website** www.ardenchambers.com

Head of Chambers	Andrew Arden QC
Senior Clerk	Christopher James
Tenants	29

Members

Andrew Arden QC (1974) (QC-1991)
David Carter (1971)
John Robson (1974)
Timothy Jones (1975)
Linda Hayton (1975)
Ian Mason (1978)
Christopher Baker (1984)
Christopher Balogh (1984)
Caroline Hunter (1985)
Jonathan Manning (1989)
Iain Colville (1989)
William Okoya (1989)
Jacqueline Ann Rubens (1989)
Josephine Henderson (1990)
Andrew Dymond (1991)
Samuel Waritay (1993)
Stanley Gallagher (1994)
Scott Collins (1994)
Annette Cafferkey (1994)
Dominic Preston (1995)
Jonathon Rushton (1997)
Alastair Redpath-Stevens (1998)
Jim Shepherd (1998)
Sonia Rai (1998)
Sarah McKeown (1998)
Rebecca Cattermole (1999)
John McCafferty (2000)
Jane Hodgson (2000)
Simon Strelitz (2000)
Prof. Martin Partington (1984) *
Siobhan McGrath (1982) *
Gareth Thomas MP (1977) *
Ceilidh Halloran (1992) *
Emma Saunders (1994) *
Sarah Pengelly (1996) *

* Door Tenant

The Chambers Arden Chambers is founded on the concept of the specialist barrister, providing clients with the benefits of particular expertise in chosen areas. Chambers' profile was originally derived from housing and local government law, but today extends also to a broad range of property and planning work. The changing needs of clients are met by a forward-thinking, imaginative and adaptable approach. In addition to offering a comprehensive service for legal advocacy, advice and drafting at all levels, clients are offered up-to-the-minute general legal information by email, assembled by in-house legal information associates. Clients can also take advantage of bespoke training and in-house seminars, the expertise for which is supported by the large volume of publications for which the set is responsible (see below). Instructions are accepted not only from solicitors, but also via direct professional access and BarDIRECT sources. Clients include individuals (tenants, owners, homeless persons, applicants, service users) as well as public authorities, commercial and social bodies, Ombudsmen and regulatory authorities, across the country and in other jurisdictions. The set operates its own pro bono scheme, and work is undertaken for the Bar Pro Bono Unit. Current news and information are available on the website.

Continued overleaf

BAR A-Z

Work Undertaken Specialism and expertise are provided in all aspects of housing, local government, property and planning work, embracing both public and private law. Particular areas include landlord and tenant (residential and commercial), home ownership, enfranchisement, right to buy, mortgages, homelessness and housing allocation, public and administrative law, human rights, local government powers and finance, procurement, local government prosecutions and enforcement proceedings, regulation and administration of registered social landlords, housing administration and intervention, anti-social behaviour, environmental health, food safety, health and safety, community care, development and planning, compulsory purchase, highways, licensing, trading standards, housing grants, benefits and social security.

Publications Members of chambers and the in-house legal information associates are involved in a very wide range of leading publications, closely linked with the areas of practice. Legal writing is considered to be an important means of professional and practice development, and members are frequently invited to address professional conferences around the country. Full details of publications, including copies of recent articles, are available on the website.

Recruitment Chambers has an active recruitment policy. Current information about pupillage applications, awards and recruitment is available on the website.

Atkin Chambers (Robert Akenhead QC)   Set No.3

1 Atkin Building, Gray's Inn, London, WC1R 5AT
Tel (020) 7404 0102   **Emergency Tel** (020) 7242 4703   **Fax** (020) 7405 7456
DX 1033
Email clerks@atkinchambers.law.co.uk   **Website** www.atkinchambers.com

Head of Chambers	Robert Akenhead QC
Senior Clerks	Stuart Goldsmith
	David Barnes
Tenants	31

Members

Peter D Fraser (1989)
Ian N D Wallace QC (1948) (QC-1973)
John Blackburn QC (1969) (QC-1984)
Colin Reese QC (1973) (QC-1987)
Robert Akenhead QC (1972) (QC-1989)
Nicholas Dennys QC (1975) (QC-1991)
Jonathan Acton Davis QC (1977) (QC-1996)
Andrew White QC (1980) (QC-1997)

Nicholas Baatz QC (1978) (QC-1998)
Martin Bowdery QC (1980) (QC-2000)
Stephen Dennison QC (1985) (QC-2001)
David Streatfeild-James QC (1986) (QC-2001)
Mark Raeside QC (1982) (QC-2002)
Donald Valentine (1956)
Darryl Royce (1976)
Andrew Burr (1981)
Delia Dumaresq (1984)
Andrew Goddard (1985)

Stephanie Barwise (1988)
Simon Lofthouse (1988)
Robert Clay (1989)
Dominique Rawley (1991)
Chantal-Aimée Doerries (1992)
Steven Walker (1993)
Fiona Parkin (1993)
Manus McMullan (1994)
James Howells (1995)
Nicholas Collings (1997)
Patrick Clarke (1997)
Christopher Lewis (1998)
Serena Cheng (2000)

The Chambers Atkin Chambers is known particularly for its expertise in litigation and advice on the law relating to domestic and international construction and engineering projects. Within this wide area of practice chambers have developed particular experience in the following areas: arbitration, insurance, energy, professional negligence and information technology. The set was the first to specialise in the law relating to domestic and international construction and engineering projects. Chambers have steadily expanded in size and have developed their expertise in the many aspects of construction and engineering projects and also in the area of information technology. There are now 31 members including 12 QCs. Members have wide experience of courts and tribunals ranging from the House of Lords, Privy Council, international and domestic arbitrations, public enquiries, adjudications and all forms of ADR. Members also have experience dealing with litigation and advice in many offshore jurisdictions including China, Australia, Hong Kong, Singapore, Malaysia, Indonesia, Jersey and Greece. Some members are qualified as mediators, some sit as arbitrators both in domestic and in offshore jurisdictions and as adjudicators. All members undertake direct professional access instructions in appropriate cases. Since 1959 the leading standard textbook, *Hudson's Building and Engineering Contracts*, has been edited in chambers. The editors of both the *Building Law Reports* and the *Technology and Construction Law Reports* are also members of chambers. Members are available to act as mediators, adjudicators and arbitrators.

Specialist Areas Construction; energy and natural resources; information technology; professional negligence; shipping - dry shipping; arbitration (international/domestic); Alternative Dispute Resolution.

Work Undertaken

Construction & Engineering This is the core specialism of chambers. Within this very broad area members provide representation and advice on a wide range of legal issues in a domestic and an international context. Projects in relation to which members' services are sought include house construction, road building, power plants, tunnels, bridges, office construction, airports, telecommunication projects, railway construction and rolling stock disputes, hydrocarbon and chemical pipelines, offshore and submarine structures, shipbuilding and ship repair projects. The legal aspects of such projects are varied and so are the legal services which members are called upon to provide. These services range from advice in connection with the drafting of contracts for their procurement, advice on claims and representation in court or in domestic or international arbitrations and representation in mediations and adjudications.

Energy Members act in connection with large scale national and international projects for the exploration and exploitation of oil and gas, often involving joint ventures. Advice is given on differing aspects of the oil and gas world including long-term natural gas contracts, tariff agreements, oil and gas transportation, pipeline installation and the design and construction of offshore structures including platforms and FPSOs. Members frequently act in connection with contracts and disputes concerning the design, construction and commissioning of power stations (coal, gas, combined cycle and nuclear) and related funding and development agreements.

Information Technology In 1998 the Official Referee's Court was replaced by the Technology and Construction Court. This was a recognition of the close similarity between the legal and technical skills which are required for construction and engineering disputes and those which are required in the field of information technology disputes. Members offer advice on hardware and software agreements, including IT procurement, management and internet contracts and they represent parties involved in related disputes.

Professional Negligence Members provide advice and representation in the field of professional negligence concerning architects, engineers, surveyors, quantity surveyors, project managers, valuers and solicitors.

Commercial Law Members have developed expertise on a wide range of commercial matters both as an adjunct to construction, energy and IT matters but also independently of them. Services are provided in connection with banking, performance bonds and guarantees, insurance, PFI matters and the financing and structuring of large multi-party commercial projects.

2 Bedford Row (William Clegg QC)   Set No.4

2 Bedford Row, London, WC1R 4BU
Tel (020) 7440 8888 **Fax** (020) 7242 1738 **DX** 17
Email (initialsurname)@2bedfordrow.co.uk **Website** www.2bedfordrow.co.uk

Head of Chambers	William Clegg QC
Senior Clerk	John Grimmer
Tenants	53

Members

William Clegg QC (1972) (QC-1991) +
The Rt Hon Lord Morris of Aberavon QC (1954) (QC-1973) +
Michael Lewis QC (1956) (QC-1975) +
Howard Godfrey QC (1970) (QC-1991) +
Peter Griffiths QC (1970) (QC-1995) +
Andrew Munday QC (1973) (QC-1996) +
T Alun Jenkins QC (1972) (QC-1996) * +
Nigel Lithman QC (1976) (QC-1997) +
Michael Wolkind QC (1976) (QC-1999)
Philip Hackett QC (1978) (QC-1999)
Maura McGowan QC (1980) (QC-2001) +
Trevor Burke QC (1981) (QC-2001)
Peter Lodder QC (1981) (QC-2001) +

Jim Sturman QC (1982) (QC-2002)
David Thomas QC (1992) (QC-1996) *
Robert Flach (1950)
Charles Conway (1969)
Deborah Champion (1970) +
Nigel Ingram (1974) †
Mark Halsey (1974)
Robert Neill (1975)
John Caudle (1976) +
Anthony Abell (1977)
Barry Gilbert (1978)
John Dodd (1979) + ‡
Margaret Dodd (1979) *
Michael Levy (1979)
John Livingston (1980)
Brian Altman (1981)
Keith Mitchell (1981)
Tracy Ayling (1983) ‡
Gelaga King (1985) +
Timothy Kendal (1985)
Mark Milliken-Smith (1986)

Christopher Campbell-Clyne (1988) †
Richard Matthews (1989)
Jonathan Ashley-Norman (1989)
Tayo Adebayo (1989)
Thomas Derbyshire (1989)
Craig Rush (1989)
James Ageros (1990)
Christine Agnew (1992)
Adam Budworth (1992)
Michael Epstein (1992)
Valerie Charbit (1992)
John Hurlock (1993)
Alison Pople (1993)
Christine Henson (1994)
Kieran Galvin (1996)
Maria Dineen (1997)
Navaz Daruwalla (1997)
Andrew McGee (1999)
Emma King (1999)
Jacqueline Carey (1999)
Rod Dixon (2000)
Quentin Hunt (2000)

* Door Tenant + Recorder † Standing Counsel to the Department of Trade & Industry ‡ Standing Counsel to Customs & Excise   Senior Treasury Counsel at CCC

Continued overleaf

BAR A-Z

The Chambers 2 Bedford Row is well established as a leading Chambers specialising in criminal law and related areas of practice. After many years in the Temple, the set moved to its own freehold premises at 2 Bedford Row in January 2000. Chambers have continued the tradition of both defending and prosecuting in all types of criminal work, and have developed to meet the demands of modern practice by providing a complete range of experience in general criminal matters as well as in a number of specialist areas (see below). Chambers presently consist of 15 Queen's Counsel and 41 juniors. Members include the former Attorney-General, Treasury Counsel at the Central Criminal Court and Standing Counsel to the Department of Trade and Industry and Customs & Excise. Additionally, a number of members of chambers hold office as Recorders and as Deputy District Judges. For further information please visit the chambers website which includes profiles for individual members.

Work Undertaken In general criminal practice, the size and varied experience of chambers enables them to offer practitioners at all levels and for all types of cases. Members of chambers appear before all tribunals from the Magistrates' Court to the House of Lords and also before foreign courts and the International War Crimes Tribunal at The Hague. Specialist areas include fraud (including computer fraud), money laundering, restraint and confiscation proceedings, health and safety, environmental law and trading standards. Individual members of chambers are experienced in judicial review, extradition, immigration and local authority prosecutions. Human rights law and practice now plays a major part in the work of chambers. There is particular experience in investigations and prosecutions brought by the Serious Fraud Office and in advising parties from the commencement of the investigation, including issues arising from international judicial assistance. A growth area relates to regulatory and disciplinary work, especially in connection with financial services and the disciplinary tribunals of professional and professional sporting bodies. Members have also represented both Premiership clubs and players before the Football Association. Members of chambers have appeared in many leading cases including:
Serious Crime Colin Stagg; Fashanu, Grobbelaar and Ors; David Copeland; Colin Ireland; Michael Stone; Corporal Lee Clegg; R v Sawoniuk; R v Duffy & Mulcahy
Fraud Maxwell & Ors, BCCI, Polly Peck, Levitt and Ors, Resort Hotels, Bute Mining, Richmond Oil and Gas, Alliance Resources, Cairns and Ors, Leckie & Ors and Alpine Double Glazing.

International Work is handled in Arabic, Dutch, French, German, Hebrew, Italian, Krio (Sierra Leone) and Serbo-Croat.

7 Bedford Row (David Farrer QC) — Set No.5

7 Bedford Row, London, WC1R 4BU
Tel (020) 7242 3555 **Fax** (020) 7242 2511 **DX** 347 (Ch.Ln.)
Email clerks@7br.co.uk **Website** www.7br.co.uk

Head of Chambers	David Farrer QC
Tenants	60

Members

David Farrer QC (1967) (QC-1986)
Martin Wilson QC (1963) (QC-1982)
Stephen Coward QC (1964) (QC-1984)
Timothy Barnes QC (1968) (QC-1986)
Nigel Baker QC (1969) (QC-1988)
Richard Latham QC (1971) (QC-1991)
Christopher Hotten QC (1972) (QC-1994)
William Coker QC (1973) (QC-1994)
Nigel Rumfitt QC (1974) (QC-1994)
Simeon Maskrey QC (1977) (QC-1995)
Philip P Shears QC (1972) (QC-1996)
Collingwood Thompson QC (1975) (QC-1998)
Joan Butler QC (1977) (QC-1998)

Kate Thirlwall QC (1982) (QC-1999)
Yvonne A Coen QC (1982) (QC-2000)
Nigel G Godsmark QC (1979) (QC-2001)
Timothy Spencer QC (1982) (QC-2001)
Derek Sweeting QC (1983) (QC-2001)
Witold Pawlak (1970)
David H Christie (1973)
J Philip T Head (1976)
Julian D Matthews (1979)
Simon Wheatley (1979)
Jeremy Pendlebury (1980)
John Pini (1981)
Nicholas Dean (1982)
Ebraham Mooncey (1983)
Farooq Ahmed (1983)
Susan C Reed (1984)
Maureen Baker (1984)

Adam Clemens (1985)
Barbara Connolly (1986)
Louise Varty (1986)
David Matthew (1987)
Rupert Mayo (1987)
Simon King (1987)
Andrew Wheeler (1988)
Gordon Aspden (1988)
Brendan Roche (1989)
Stephen Baker (1989)
Rachel Langdale (1990)
Cathryn McGahey (1990)
Steven Ford (1992)
Adam Korn (1992)
Maryam Syed (1993)
Adam Weitzman (1993)
Vanessa Marshall (1994)
Hugh Preston (1994)
Matthew Jowitt (1994)
Bilal Rawat (1995)
William Redgrave (1995)
Anwar Nashashibi (1995)

SEVEN BEDFORD ROW

Susannah Johnson (1996)	Louise Bass (1999)	Steven Gray (2000)
Simon Thomas (1995)	Jenny Carter-Manning (1999)	David O'Mahony (2000)
David Allan (1998)	Gareth Weetman (1999)	

The Chambers Chambers is a leading general common law set, founded more than 50 years ago, with an emphasis on clinical and professional negligence, personal injury, local authority liability, insurance disputes, contract and tort, children law, fraud and white collar crime. In 1995 chambers moved from 2 Crown Office Row to 9 Bedford Row and then to substantially larger premises at 7 Bedford Row in 2000 to accommodate organic growth. In 2000 chambers became the seventh set in the country to be awarded Barmark, an assurance of high quality services and client care. Most members began their careers working on Circuit, widely recognised as an ideal training ground for advocacy. Three members sit as deputy High Court Judges, 21 as Recorders, one as Deputy Judge Advocate, two on the Mental Health Review Tribunal and one as a fellow of the Chartered Institute of Arbitrators.

Work Undertaken

Civil Litigation Civil expertise includes education, employment, environment law, financial services, fraud, clinical and professional negligence including claims against local authorities and the Police, personal injury, product liability and sports law. Some members have a commercial bias and offer on all aspects of company law, insolvency and intellectual property.

Criminal Law Members have a great deal of experience in criminal cases at all levels and in all areas, including regulatory work, both prosecuting and defending. A specialist team acts as advocates and advisors in complex commercial fraud and money laundering, both in the UK and overseas.

Child Law Members undertake work for public and private child care cases, with particular expertise in non-accidental injury, including brain injury, poisoning, suffocation and factitious illness. The local authority liability team undertakes work relating to sexual and emotional abuse and neglect.

International Instructions are welcomed from overseas lawyers directly.

17 Bedford Row (Allan Levy QC) — Set No.6

17 Bedford Row, London, WC1R 4EB
Tel (020) 7831 7314 **Fax** (020) 7831 0061 **DX** 370 Ldn/Ch
Email IBoard7314@aol.com

Head of Chambers	Allan Levy QC
Senior Clerk	Ian Boardman
Tenants	25

Members

Allan Levy QC (1969) (QC-1989)	Richard Anthony Southall (1983)	Max Thorowgood (1995)
Michael Gettleson (1952)	John Critchley (1985)	Carolyn Hamilton (1996)
Nigel Jennings (1967)	Miles Croally (1987)	Michael Joy (1997)
Jane Gill (1973)	Julian Date (1988)	Jonathan Pennington Legh (2000)
Susan Garnett (1973)	Mark Twomey (1990)	Angela Ward (2000)
John McLinden (1991)	Bernard Lo (1991)	Neville Maryon Green (1963) *
Dennis Sharpe (1976)	Barry McAlinden (1993)	James Chapman (1987) *
Brian Huyton (1977)	Christopher Stirling (1993)	Hugh Bevan (1959) *
Graham Campbell (1979)	Christina Michalos (1994)	
Hashim Reza (1981)	John Crosfil (1995)	

* Door Tenant

The Chambers Members are instructed by solicitors' firms throughout the country and by or on behalf of government departments, local authorities and financial institutions. Chambers were founded in the Temple over 50 years ago by Leonard Caplan QC. Former members include Lord Justice Farquharson and Sir Laurence Verney, the Recorder of London. Mobile telephone number is (07831) 234 861.

Work Undertaken Particular areas of work in which individuals specialise are asset recovery and preservation, including tracing, banking, and building society and insurance law; criminal law commercial work; entertainment and media, including defamation, music business, copyright and other intellectual property; medical law; human rights; family, children and divorce; landlord and tenant and property law; personal injury; professional negligence; direct professional access work.

International Work is handled in French, German and Italian. For overseas bars in New Zealand, contact John McLinden. France: has strong connections with foreign jurisdictions; contact Neville Maryon Green (Paris). Western Australia: contact Allan Levy QC.

BAR A-Z

29 Bedford Row Chambers (Nicholas Francis QC)

Set No.7

29 Bedford Row Chambers, London, WC1R 4HE
Tel (020) 7404 1044 **Fax** (020) 7831 0626 **DX** 1044
Email clerks@29bedfordrow.co.uk **Website** www.29br.com

Head of Chambers	Nicholas Francis QC
Senior Clerk	Martin Poulter
Tenants	47

Members

Peter Ralls QC (1972) (QC-1997)
Evan Stone QC (1954) (QC-1979)
Augustus Ullstein QC (1970) (QC-1992)
Timothy Scott QC (1975) (QC-1995)
Ajmalul Hossain QC (1976) (QC-1998)
Paul Storey QC (1982) (QC-2001)
Philip Cayford QC (1975) (QC-2002)
Nicholas Francis QC (1981) (QC-2002)
Peter Duckworth (1971)
John Zieger (1962)
Clare Renton (1972)
Howard Shaw (1973)
John Tonna (1974)
Mark Warwick (1974)
Neil Sanders (1975)
Charles Atkins (1975)
Geoffrey Ames (1976)
Simon Gill (1977)
Simon Edwards (1978)
Jonathan Ferris (1979)
John Wilson (1981)
Timothy Walker (1984)
Nicholas Bowen (1984)
David Holland (1986)
Stephen Reynolds (1987)
Smair Singh Soor (1988)
Nicholas Chapman (1990)
Robert Peel (1990)
Alexis Campbell (1990)
Annabel Wentworth (1990)
Alexa Storey-Rea (1990)
Jonathan Southgate (1992)
Stuart Hornett (1992)
Craig Barlow (1992)
Patrick Chamberlayne (1992)
Victoria Domenge (1993)
Brenton Molyneux (1994)
Duncan Kynoch (1994)
Nicholas Allen (1995)
Peter Mitchell (1996)
Gary Pryce (1997)
Laura Heaton (1998)
Galina Ward (2000)
Anne Hudd (2000)
Michael Keane (1979) *
Nicholas Tse (1995) *
Prof. Robert Upex *

* Door Tenant

The Chambers Bedford Row Chambers is a progressive and growing set committed to providing its clients with an effective and efficient legal service. It operates from one of the Bar's largest and contemporary offices, having added a further 50% to its office space by taking over its neighbouring premises. Bedford Row Chambers resides in two Grade II listed buildings, completely modernised and wired for the latest technology and with room to expand.

Work Undertaken The work of chambers is primarily in commercial, property, family, personal injury and general common law, and extends to a wide range of litigation, advisory and drafting work.
Chancery Breach of trust, Court of Protection, partnership, trusts, wills and probate.
Commercial Arbitration, building and construction, commercial, companies, consumer credit, contract, economic torts, guarantees, licensing, misrepresentation, and sale of goods.
Common Law Injunctions, employment, libel and slander, nuisance and property-related torts, personal injuries, tort, professional negligence.
Family: Family law and family provision.
Intellectual Property Confidential information, intellectual property, copyright and passing off, trademarks and trade names.
Insolvency Bankruptcy, insolvency, liquidations and administrations and receivership.
Property Conveyancing, housing, land law, landlord and tenant, mortgages and securities, planning, rent reviews.
Public & Administrative Law Judicial review, statutory appeals and tribunal work, particularly education, special educational needs, community care and mental health work.

BAR A-Z

33 Bedford Row (David Barnard) — Set No.8

33 Bedford Row, London, WC1R 4JH
Tel (020) 7242 6476 **Fax** (020) 7831 6065 **DX** 75
Email clerks@33bedfordrow.co.uk **Website** www.33bedfordrow.co.uk

Head of Chambers	David Barnard
Senior Clerk	Michael Lieberman
Tenants	25

Members

David Barnard (1967) +
Barry Kogan (1973) +
Nigel May (1974) +
Constance Whippman (1978)
Richard Bendall (1979)
Marc Galberg (1982)
Michael Burke (1985)
Christopher Spratt (1986)
Susan Castle (1986)
Timothy Thorne (1987)
Joanne Oxlade (1988)
David Lonsdale (1988)
Jean-Paul Sinclair (1989)
Rhys Jones (1990)
Mukhtiar Otwal (1991)
Philip Brown (1991)
Thomas Cleeve (1993)
Ronnie Bergenthal (1993)
Stuart Armstrong (1995)
Frida Hussain (1995)
John Law (1996)
Piers Harrison (1997)
Daniel Dovar (1997)
Mark Stanger (1998)
Joanne Cobb (1999)
Gary Webber (1979)*
Robert Carrow (1981)*

+ Recorder * Door Tenant

The Chambers Chambers undertake work in property, criminal law, family law and commercial and civil litigation. Members regularly publish and lecture. David Barnard is Standing Counsel to HM Customs and Excise, and Nigel May and Timothy Thorne are part-time Judge Advocates.

Publications These include *Residential Possession Proceedings* (Webber), *Possession of Business Premises* (Webber and Dovar), and *The Woolf Reforms: A Practitioner's Guide* (Barnard, Galberg & Lonsdale).

36 Bedford Row (Michael Pert QC) — Set No.9

36 Bedford Row, London, WC1R 4JH **Tel** (020) 7421 8000 **Fax** (020) 7421 8080 **DX** LDE 360 Chancery Lane

48 Bedford Row (Roderick I'Anson Banks) — Set No.10

48 Bedford Row, London, WC1R 4LR
Tel (020) 7430 2005 **Fax** (020) 7831 4885 **DX** 284 LDE
Email sarah@partnershipcounsel.co.uk **Website** www.partnershipcounsel.co.uk

Head of Chambers	Roderick I'Anson Banks
Practice Manager	Sarah Vaughan
Tenants	2

Members

Roderick I'Anson Banks (1974) LLB (London)
Simon Jelf (1996) LLB (Eur)

The Chambers Specialise exclusively in partnership law and provide solicitors and other professional and trading partnerships with a full range of legal services, from the drafting of new agreements and the review of existing agreements to advice and representation in partnership disputes, arbitrations and mediations. Chambers' aim, where possible, is to assist clients with the process of resolving disputes, without recourse to litigation and provide ongoing support from the embryonic stages of a developing dispute, right through to the conclusion of any litigation or until a negotiated settlement is reached. Direct Professional Access work is undertaken. Out of hours number (0775) 102 2914.

Publications Roderick I'Anson Banks is the editor of *Lindley & Banks on Partnership*, the authoritative guide to partnership law, and the author and editor of the *Encyclopedia of Professional Partnerships*.

BAR A-Z

9-12 Bell Yard (D Anthony Evans QC)

Set No.11

9-12 Bell Yard, London, WC2A 2JR
Tel (020) 7400 1800 **Fax** (020) 7404 1405 **DX** 390
Email clerks@bellyard.co.uk

Head of Chambers	D Anthony Evans QC
Senior Clerk	Gary Reed
Tenants	64

Members

D Anthony Evans QC (1965) (QC-1983) BA (Cantab)
Edmund Lawson QC (1971) (QC-1988) BA (Cantab)
Lord Carlile of Berriew QC (1970) (QC-1984) LLB (AKC)
Michael Birnbaum QC (1969) (QC-1992) BA (Oxon)
Jeremy Carter-Manning QC (1975) (QC-1993)
Patrick Curran QC (1972) (QC-1995) MA (Oxon)
Sonia Woodley QC (1968) (QC-1996)
Peter Rouch QC (1972) (QC-1996) LLB (Wales)
Robin Spencer QC (1978) (QC-1999) MA (Cantab)
Philip Katz QC (1976) (QC-2000) MA (Oxon)
John McGuinness QC (1980) (QC-2001) BA (Lond)
Mukul Chawla QC (1983) (QC-2001) LLB (Lond)
Herbert Kerrigan QC (1970) (QC-1992)
Richard Cherrill (1967) MA (Cantab) LLB
Martin Field (1966)
Bernard Phelvin (1971) BA (Cantab)
Richard Merz (1972) LLB (Soton)
Alison Barker (1973) LLB (Hons)
John Greaves (1973) LLB (Lond)
Anthony Heaton-Armstrong (1973) LLB
Tudor Owen (1974) LLB (Lond)

Alexander Cranbrook (1975) BA (Hons)
Stephen John (1975) MA (Oxon)
John Harwood-Stevenson (1975) MA (Oxon)
Timothy Spencer (1976)
Peter Moss (1976)
Keith Hadrill (1977)
Simon Wild (1977) BA (Lond)
Michael Orsulik (1978) BA LLM (Lond)
Dianne Chan (1979) LLB (Bris)
John Alban Williams (1979)
Michael Egan (1981)
Jonathan Davies (1981) LLB (Lond)
Sean Enright (1982) LLB (Nott)
Graham Brown (1982) BA
Constance Briscoe (1983) LLB (Newcastle)
Christine Laing (1984) LLB
Mohammed Khamisa (1985) BA (Hons) (Lond)
Philippa McAtasney (1986) LLB (Lond)
Mark Bryant-Heron (1986) MA (Cantab)
William Hughes (1989) BSc (Leic)
Sarah Ellis (1989) LLB (Wales)
Adrian Chaplin (1990) BA (Cantab)
Alexandra Healy (1992) MA (Cantab)
Mark Seymour (1992) MA (Hons)

Richard Jory (1993) BA (Hons) (Reading)
Warwick Tatford (1993) BA (Hons) (Oxon)
Tina Davey (1993) LLB (Hons) (Cardiff)
Jonathan S Kinnear (1994) LLB
Christina Russell (1994) MA (Cantab)
Jessica Gavron (1995) BA (Cantab)
Michelle Denton (1996) LLB (Soton)
Neil Griffin (1996) LLB (Hons) (Lond)
Anita Saran (1996) LLB (Lond)
Michael Goodwin (1996) BSc (Hons)
Kristian Mills (1998) LLB (Hons) (Wales)
Neerja Sharma (1998) BA (Hons)
Ryan Richter (1998) BA (Hons)
David McDowell (1999) BA (Oxon)
Nicholas Dunham (1999) BA (Hons) Dunelm
Henrietta Paget (1999) BA (Oxon)
Stuart Biggs (1999) BA (Hons) (Cantab)
Xanthe Craddock (2000) BA (Hons) (Oxon)
Paul Sharkey (2000) LLB (Hons) (Warwick) MSc (London)

The Chambers A leading criminal set which can also provide general common law expertise.

Work Undertaken Members have been involved in some of the most widely reported cases, involving such well-known names as Blue Arrow, Maxwell, BCCI, the Marchioness disaster, the Dome robbery and Palmer & Others (largest ever timeshare fraud). Members of chambers regularly appear in notable public inquiries such as the Stephen Lawrence, 'Bloody Sunday' and Climbie. Tribunal work and judicial review are well established areas of practice.

Additional Specialisations Other areas of practice include arbitration, criminal injuries compensation, inquests, licensing, planning, professional disciplinary, public inquiries, self-regulatory tribunals and trading standards. For further information on individual specialisations and chambers' news please visit the website on www.bellyard.co.uk

Blackstone Chambers (Presiley Baxendale QC & Charles Flint QC)

Set No.12

Blackstone House, Temple, London, EC4Y 9BW
Tel (020) 7583 1770   Fax (020) 7822 7350   DX 281
Email clerks@blackstonechambers.com   Website www.blackstonechambers.com

Head of Chambers	Presiley Baxendale QC
	Charles Flint QC
Senior Clerk	Martin Smith
Practice Manager	Julia Hornor
Tenants	61

Members

Presiley Baxendale QC (1974) (QC-1992)
Charles Flint QC (1975) (QC-1995)
Colin Ross-Munro QC (1951) (QC-1972)
Stanley Brodie QC (1954) (QC-1975)
Lord Lester of Herne Hill QC (1963) (QC-1975)
Sir Ian Sinclair QC (1952) (QC-1979)
Ian Brownlie QC (1958) (QC-1979)
Michael Beloff QC (1967) (QC-1981)
David Donaldson QC (1968) (QC-1984)
Robert Englehart QC (1969) (QC-1986)
David Hunt QC (1969) (QC-1987)
Barbara Dohmann QC (1971) (QC-1987)
Andrew Pugh QC (1961) (QC-1988)
Sir Roy Goode QC (1988) (QC-1990)
Maurice Mendelson QC (1965) (QC-1992)
Jonathan Harvie QC (1973) (QC-1992)
David Pannick QC (1979) (QC-1992)
Jeffrey Jowell QC (1965) (QC-1993)
Stephen Nathan QC (1969) (QC-1993)
John Howell QC (1979) (QC-1993)
Bob Hepple QC (1966) (QC-1996)
Ian Mill QC (1981) (QC-1999)
Beverley Lang QC (1978) (QC-2000)
Paul Goulding QC (1984) (QC-2000)
Thomas Beazley QC (1979) (QC-2001)
Monica Carss-Frisk QC (1985) (QC-2001)
Hugo Page QC (1977) (QC-2002)
Mark Shaw QC (1987) (QC-2002)
Dawn Oliver (1965)
Guy Goodwin-Gill (1971)
Alastair Sutton (1972)
Judith Beale (1978)
Nicholas Khan (1983)
Anthony Peto (1985)
Gerard Clarke (1986)
Adam Lewis (1985)
Robert Anderson (1986)
Andrew Green (1988)
Robert Howe (1988)
Adrian Briggs (1989)
Dinah Rose (1989)
Michael Fordham (1990)
Pushpinder Saini (1991)
Thomas Croxford (1992)
Javan Herberg (1992)
Joanna Pollard (1993)
Andrew Hunter (1993)
Gemma White (1994)
Jane Collier (1994)
Thomas de la Mare (1995)
Tom Weisselberg (1995)
Jane Mulcahy (1995)
Julia Ellins (1994)
Andrew George (1997)
Kate Gallafent (1997)
Claire Weir (1998)
Ben Jaffey (1999)
Brian Kennelly (1999)
Catherine Callaghan (1999)
Stephanie Palmer (2000)
Nicholas De Marco (2001)
David Pievsky (2001)
Shaheed Fatima (2001)
Victoria Windle (2001)

The Chambers Blackstone Chambers is a long established set, combining formidable strengths in commercial, public law and human rights and employment law, with state of the art facilities and a friendly and open approach to client service.

Work Undertaken Chambers' practice breaks down into the following practice areas:
Commercial Within this area, members' established skills and specialisations include international trade; banking; insurance and reinsurance; carriage of goods; conflict of laws; corporate fraud; financial services; regulatory tribunals; shipping; defamation; intellectual property; media, entertainment and sports law.
Public Law & Human Rights Work includes judicial review, both for and against public bodies and regulatory authorities, arising from decisions and areas such as: freedom of expression; equality of treatment; immigration; education; social security; housing; planning; local government. The combined expertise of members of chambers in commercial and public law proves particularly valuable in City regulation and financial services cases. Advice in the human rights arena is also available, with particular reference to the impact of the Human Rights Act 1998 in all its aspects.
Employment Law Within this area, members of chambers have extensive expertise in all aspects of employment law, ranging from pure contract work to sex, race and disability discrimination.
Mediation Chambers recognises the increasingly important role which mediation has to play in dispute resolution. Two members are CEDR accredited mediators.

Publications These are many in number and include: *Legal Problems of Credit and Security*; *Hire Purchase Law and Practice*; *Principles of Corporate and Insolvency Law*; *Consumer Credit Legislation*; *Halsbury on Arbitration*; *Dicey & Morris* (13th ed); *Principles of Public International Law*; *The Vienna Convention on the Law of Treaties and International Law Commission*; De Smith Woolf and Jowell: *Judicial Review of Administrative Action*; *Judicial Review Handbook*; *Halsbury on Aliens*; *Halsbury on the European Convention of Human Rights*; *Butterworths Human Rights - Law and Practice*, *Constitutional Law & Human Rights*; *European Employment*
Continued overleaf

LONDON
BAR A-Z

Law and the UK; Basic Documents on Human Rights.

International European law with its ever growing impact on national law is an integral part of Chambers' practice in all areas of specialism. One member of Chambers is a former member of the Legal Service of the European Commission and one other member of Chambers practises full-time in European Community law from offices in Brussels. Chambers also have a strong tradition of practice in the specialised field of public international law. Several members of Chambers are highly experienced in advising in litigation in public international law disputes arising before national and international courts and tribunals. A current member was formerly the legal advisor to the Foreign and Commonwealth Office. Members of Chambers have a wide-ranging experience of advocacy before English, European and Commonwealth courts and tribunals, and frequently appear before the European Courts of Justice and the European Court of Human Rights. Languages spoken include Finnish, French, German, Hindi, Italian, Punjabi, Spanish, Swedish and Urdu.

Recruitment Blackstone Chambers is a member of OLPAS. A first or upper second class degree is usually required, although not necessarily in law. Pupillage awards of up to £30,000 are available. Mini-pupillages for a week in the year preceding pupillage are required for potential pupils of chambers. Further information, either about chambers generally or about pupillage in particular, is available from chambers' website www.blackstonechambers.com

4 Breams Buildings (Christopher Lockhart-Mummery QC) — Set No.13

4 Breams Buildings, London, EC4A 1AQ
Tel (020) 7430 1221   **Fax** (020) 7421 1399   **DX** 1042 LDE
Email clerks@4breams.co.uk   **Website** www.4breams.co.uk

Head of Chambers	Christopher Lockhart-Mummery QC
Senior Clerk	Stephen Graham
1st Junior Clerk	Jay Fullilove
Director of Marketing & Administration	Vicky Thompson
Tenants	33

Members

Christopher Lockhart-Mummery QC (1971) (QC-1986)
John Cherryman QC (1955) (QC-1982)
Joseph Harper QC (1970) (QC-1992)
Richard Drabble QC (1975) (QC-1995)
David Holgate QC (1978) (QC-1997)
Christopher Katkowski QC (1982) (QC-1999)
John Male QC (1976) (QC-2000)
David Elvin QC (1983) (QC-2000)
Colin Sydenham (1963)
Stephen Bickford-Smith (1972)
Eian Caws (1974)
Robert Bailey-King (1975)
Anne Seifert (1975)
Christopher Lewsley (1976)
David Smith (1980)
Anne Williams (1980)
Thomas Jefferies (1981)
Alice Robinson (1983)
Timothy Mould (1987)
Nathalie Lieven (1989)
John Litton (1989)
Nicholas Taggart (1991)
Karen McHugh (1992)
David Forsdick (1993)
Timothy Morshead (1995)
Graeme Keen (1995)
Camilla Lamont (1995)
James Maurici (1996)
Daniel Kolinsky (1998)
Myriam Stacey (1998)
Katherine Olley (1999)
Carine Patry (1999)
Charlotte Kilroy (2001)

The Chambers 4 Breams Buildings is a well established leading set of chambers in public law, local government, planning, environmental law and property. Chambers advise, and appear regularly for all types of client, including individuals, pressure groups, landlords (including institutional landlords), developers, regulators, local authorities and central government. Chambers offer a high quality, efficient and friendly service which meets their clients' requirements. Direct Professional Access is welcomed.

Work Undertaken

Public & Administrative Law Including Human Rights Members have considerable experience in judicial review and statutory applications and appeals. They frequently advise and appear both for public bodies and those who wish to challenge their decisions. Several junior members are on a Treasury Panel. Particular subject areas in which chambers specialise include local government, education, health, housing, mental health, community care and social services, social security, utility and other regulators, public procurement and the tortious liability of public authorities.

Planning & Environmental Law All aspects. Chambers include 24 members of the Planning and Environmental Bar Association. Their clients include individuals; pressure groups; amenity and local residents groups; developers (such as large retailers, housebuilders and mineral undertakers); a large number of local authorities; the Environment Agency and the Secretary of State for the Environment Transport and the Regions. Members of chambers have been involved, for example, in recent cases on the impact of European law and human rights in this area.

Other All aspects of landlord and tenant and property (including vendor and purchaser, covenants, easements, mortgages and party walls). There are related specialisms in mining, rating, property related torts (including trespass and nuisance) and professional negligence. Around these main areas of work chambers also offer a specialist service in European law, compulsory purchase and compensation (the volume on which for Halsbury's Laws was edited entirely by members of chambers), Parliamentary work and Transport and Works Act inquiries, and building contracts.

Publications Chambers' publications include *Hill's Law of Town and Country Planning (4th edn)*; *Town Planning Law Handbook and Case Book*; *Atkins Court Forms - Town and Country Planning*; *Hill and Redmond's Law of Landlord and Tenant*; *Halsbury's Laws - Town and Country Planning*; *Halsbury's Laws - Compulsory Acquisition*; *Halsbury's Laws - Mortgages*; *Atkin's Court Forms - Rating and Community Charge*; *Journal of Planning Law*; *Judicial Review*; *Corfield and Carnwath's Compulsory Acquisition and Compensation*; *Emden's Building Contracts and Practice*; *Unlawful Interference with Land*; *Party Walls - the New Law*.

Recruitment Pupillage applications are accepted via the OLPAS scheme. Up to three funded pupillages are awarded annually each of £21,000 for 12 months. Applications for mini-pupillages are encouraged and should be made in writing with full CV. All pupillage enquiries to be addressed to Nathalie Lieven. All mini-pupillage applications to be addressed to the Administrator Ann Day.

Brick Court Chambers (Christopher Clarke QC) Set No.14

7-8 Essex Street, London, WC2R 3LD
Tel (020) 7379 3550   **Fax** (020) 7379 3558   **DX** 302
Email [surname]@brickcourt.co.uk   **Website** www.brickcourt.co.uk

Head of Chambers	Christopher Clarke QC
Senior Clerks	Julian Hawes
	Ian Moyler
Tenants	61

Members

Christopher Clarke QC (1969) (QC-1984)
Sir Sydney Kentridge QC (1977) (QC-1984)
David Vaughan CBE QC (1962) (QC-1981)
Jonathan Sumption QC (1975) (QC-1986)
Hilary Heilbron QC (1971) (QC-1987)
Mark Cran QC (1973) (QC-1988)
Jonathan Hirst QC (1975) (QC-1990)
Gerald Barling QC (1972) (QC-1991)
Peregrine Simon QC (1973) (QC-1991)
Timothy Charlton QC (1974) (QC-1993)
Richard Gordon QC (1972) (QC-1994)
Mark Hapgood QC (1979) (QC-1994)
Mark Howard QC (1980) (QC-1996)
Stephen Ruttle QC (1976) (QC-1997)
Andrew Popplewell QC (1981) (QC-1997)
George Leggatt QC (1983) (QC-1997)

William Wood QC (1980) (QC-1998)
Nicholas Green QC (1986) (QC-1998)
David Lloyd Jones QC (1975) (QC-1999)
Charles Hollander QC (1978) (QC-1999)
Paul Walker QC (1979) (QC-1999)
David Anderson QC (1985) (QC-1999)
Catharine Otton-Goulder QC (1983) (QC-2000)
Richard Lord QC (1981) (QC-2002)
Mark Brealey QC (1984) (QC-2002)
Michael Swainston QC (1985) (QC-2002)
Peter Irvin (1972)
Peter Brunner (1971)
James Flynn (1978)
Andrew Lydiard (1980)
Fergus Randolph (1985)
Conor Quigley (1985)
David Garland (1986)
Neil Calver (1987)
Richard Slade (1987)
Harry Matovu (1988)
Cyril Kinsky (1988)

Paul Wright (1990)
Sarah Lee (1990)
Helen Davies (1990)
Tom Adam (1991)
Mark Hoskins (1991)
Michael Rollason (1992)
Alan Roxburgh (1992)
Alan Maclean (1993)
Jemima Stratford (1993)
Alec Haydon (1993)
Michael Bools (1991)
Roger Masefield (1994)
Aidan Robertson (1995)
Simon Salzedo (1995)
Marie Demetriou (1995)
Jasbir Dhillon (1996)
Andrew Thomas (1996)
Martin Chamberlain (1997)
Margaret Gray (1998)
Simon Birt (1998)
Kelyn Bacon (1998)
Colin West (1999)
Andrew Henshaw (2000)
Maya Lester (2001)
Derrick Wyatt QC (1972) (QC-1993) *
Richard Macrory (1974) *
Andrew Le Sueur (1987) *
Jan Woloniecki (1983) *

* Door Tenant

The Chambers A leading set in the fields of commercial, European and public law. The core of our work includes all aspects of international trade, finance and commerce. For further information on chambers expertise please visit the website www.brickcourt.co.uk

BAR A-Z

1 Brick Court (Richard Rampton QC)

Set No.15

1 Brick Court, Temple, London, EC4Y 9BY
Tel (020) 7353 8845 **Fax** (020) 7583 9144 **DX** 468
Email clerks@1brickcourt.co.uk

Head of Chambers	Richard Rampton QC
Senior Clerk	David Mace
Tenants	21

Members

Richard Rampton QC (1965) (QC-1987)
Richard Hartley QC (1956) (QC-1976)
Geoffrey Shaw QC (1968) (QC-1991)
Harry Boggis-Rolfe (1969)
Thomas Shields QC (1973) (QC-1993)
Andrew Caldecott QC (1975) (QC-1994)
Edward Garnier QC (1976) (QC-1995)
Patrick Moloney QC (1976) (QC-1998)
Stephen Suttle (1980)
Victoria Sharp QC (1979) (QC-2001)
Harvey Starte (1985)
Manuel Barca (1986)
Timothy Atkinson (1988)
Rupert Elliott (1988)
Jane Phillips (1989)
Caroline Addy (1991)
Benjamin Hinchliff (1992)
Catrin Evans (1994)
Joanne Cash (1994)
Lorna Skinner (1997)
Sarah Palin (1999)

The Chambers 1 Brick Court is a long established and leading set specialising in the law as it affects the media and all claims based on the publication of false or damaging information. Chambers offers a wealth of experience and expertise across junior and QC ranks in defamation, privacy, breach of confidence, malicious falsehood, media reporting restrictions (in criminal and civil proceedings), data protection, passing off and all claims involving a tension between rights to reputation and privacy and freedom of expression; all other related human rights law, including in judicial review applications. Members of chambers act for corporate, media and individual claimants and defendants, as well as government departments, local authorities and trade unions. Members appear in all divisions of the High Court, as well as the Court of Appeal and the House of Lords, and regularly receive instructions from solicitors worldwide, including solicitors from Malaysia, Hong Kong and Singapore. Members of chambers also provide advice and representation in cases before the media regulatory bodies, including the Broadcasting Standards Commission and Press Complaints Commission. 1 Brick Court is also experienced in the pre-publication review of newspapers, books, radio and television programmes, video and all other electronic media. Chambers prides itself on being a modern and friendly set with an approachable and highly efficient clerking team. It has excellent IT and library facilities and is happy to receive instructions and send out written work via e-mail.

Publications Members of chambers have written and contributed to many of the leading works on defamation, including *Duncan & Neill on Defamation*, *Carter-Ruck on Libel and Slander*, *Halsbury's Laws of England*, *Bullen & Leake Precedents of Pleadings* and *Atkin's Court Forms* titles on defamation and confidence, privacy and data protection.

Recruitment Chambers accept up to two pupils annually for a first six months or 12 month pupilage with a substantial award. It has an excellent record of recruiting tenants from among its pupils.

4 Brick Court (David Medhurst)

Set No.16

4 Brick Court, Temple, London, EC4Y 9AD
Tel (020) 7797 8910 **Fax** (020) 7797 8929 **DX** 491
Email clerks@4bc.co.uk

Head of Chambers	David Medhurst
Senior Clerk	Michael Corrigan
Tenants	36

Members

David Medhurst (1969)
Mira Chatterjee (1973)
David Burgess (1975)
Robert Colover (1975)
Marianna Hildyard QC (1977) (QC-2002)
Janet Mitchell (1979)
Michael Haynes (1979)
Roma Whelan (1981)
Richard St Clair-Gainer (1983)
Susan Quinn (1983)
Roderick Jones (1983)
Marc Roberts (1984)
Peter Lynch (1985)
Anthony Bell (1985)
Simon Molyneux (1986)
Finola Moore (1988)
Abigail Sheppard (1990)
Peter Marshall (1991)
Isabelle Watson (1991)
Edward Knapp (1992)
Jacqui Gilliatt (1992)
Levi Peter (1993)
Caroline Sumeray (1993)
Sue Piyadasa (1994)
Teresa Pritchard (1994)
Lisa Smith (1994)
Sarah Morris (1996)
Sarah Elliott (1996)
Ian Griffin (1997)
Maria Gallagher (1997)

Yasmeen Jamil (1998) Laura Bayley (1999)
Nairn Purss (1999)   Sarah Malik (1999)

The Chambers A progressive set of chambers consisting of 36 barristers who provide a comprehensive service to solicitors and local government authorities.

Bridewell Chambers (Colin Challenger) — Set No.17

Bridewell Chambers, 2 Bridewell Place, London, EC4V 6AP
Tel (020) 7797 8800 **Fax** (020) 7797 8801 **DX** 383
Email HughesGage@bridewell.law.co.uk **Website** www.bridewell.law.co.uk

Head of Chambers	Colin Challenger
Senior Clerk	Lee Hughes-Gage
Tenants	35

Members

Colin Challenger (1970)
Baroness Scotland of Asthal QC (1977) (QC-1991) †
Jo Boothby (1972)
Gordon Pringle (1973)
Juliet Oliver (1974)
Ernest James (1977)
Roger Davey (1978)
Adrienne Knight (1981)
Elizabeth Goodchild (1981)
Peter Gray (1983)
Ian Lawrie (1985)

David Josse (1985)
Adam Clemens (1985)
James Doyle (1985)
Pieter Briegel (1986)
Simon Walsh (1987)
Sally Atherton (1987) †
Alan Walmsley (1991)
Brian Cummins (1992)
Andrew Slaughter (1993)
Lloyd Sefton-Smith (1993)
Paul Walker (1993)
Stuart Nicol (1994)

Nathan Palmer (1994)
Maria Scotland (1995)
Christopher Pearson (1995)
Jason Bartfeld (1995)
Victoria Maude (1995)
Stephen Morley (1996)
Elaine Banton (1996)
Karen Dempsey (1996)
Parosha Chandran (1997)
Charles Woodhouse (1997)
Guy Coleman (1998)
Polly Higgins (1998)

† Associate member

The Chambers Chambers cover most significant areas of criminal, civil and family law. Specialist teams deal with serious crime, housing, landlord and tenant, family and children, personal injury and cases for and against police forces. Individual tenants specialise in commercial law, judicial review, licensing, wills and probate, human rights, professional negligence, Official Referee work, marine accidents and family law. A detailed guide to the full services provided, including the Bridewell Conditional Fee Agreement, can be found on the chambers' website at www.bridewell.law.co.uk or by contacting the clerks.

International Work is handled in French and German.

Recruitment Pupillage applications to OLPAS. Tenancy applications may be sent to Ian Lawrie.

Charter Chambers (Stephen Solley QC) — Set No.18

Two Dr Johnson's Buildings, Temple, London, EC4Y 7AY
Tel (020) 7832 0300 **Fax** (020) 7334 0242 **DX** 429 Ch.Ln
Email clerks@charterchambers.com **Website** www.charterchambers.com

Head of Chambers	Stephen Solley QC
Senior Clerk	Patrick Duane
Consultant	Michael Martin
Clerks	Kevin Crawley
	Rod McGurk
	Claire Wright
	Ashley Baum
	Nils Howard
Administration (Fees)	Chris Blake
Administration	John Brewster
	Jean Brown
Tenants	60

Members

Stephen Solley QC (1969) (QC-1989) +
Jerome Lynch QC (1983) (QC-2000)
Jonathan Durham Hall QC (1975) (QC-1995) +
Richard Marks QC (1975) (QC-1999) +
Brian Forster QC (1977) (QC-1999) +
Peter Kelson QC (1981) (QC-2001) +
David Batcup (1974) +
Alan Bayliss (1966) +
Anthony Fogg (1970)

Graham Davies (1971)
David Martin-Sperry (1971)
David Wurtzel (1974)
Peter Higginson (1975)
Robert Sherman (1977)
Ian Wheatly (1977)
Ivor Frank (1979)
Stephen Mejzner (1978)
Susan Williams (1978)
Mark Paltenghi (1979)
Nicholas Rhodes (1981)
Mark Tomassi (1981)
Timothy Horgan (1982)
Thomas Buxton (1983)

Tyrone Belger (1984)
Bernard Tetlow (1984)
David Taylor (1986)
Jonathan Rose (1986)
Anna Hamilton-Shield (1989)
Neil Hawes (1989)
Alan Fraser (1990)
Michael Lavers (1990)
Paul Phillips (1991)
Mary-Teresa Deignan (1991)
Claire Robinson (1991)
Jennifer Edwards (1992)
John RWD Jones (1992)
Robert Benzynie (1992)

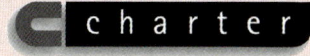

Continued overleaf

BAR A-Z

Julia Flanagan (1993)
Gary Morton (1993)
Siobhan Grey (1994)
Daniel Jones (1994)
Tarquin McCalla (1994)
Zafar Ali (1994)
Paul Raudnitz (1994)
Andrew Bodnar (1995)

Philip Norman (1995)
Dominic Alexander (1995)
Martin Goudie (1996)
Adam Morgan (1996)
Alison Slater (1996)
Jonathan Lennon (1997)
Rachel Darby (1997)
Stephen Bentley (1997)

Dominic Thomas (1998)
Susan Doris (1998)
Roshnee Shah (1998)
Roderick James (1999)
Alexander Dos Santos (1999)
Mellisa Tollman (1999)
Irfan Butt (2000)

+ Recorder

The Chambers Charter Chambers is a busy criminal and common law set offering expertise in a variety of fields at all levels of seniority.

Work Undertaken
Criminal Law Criminal practitioners accept instructions in both prosecution and defence work. Members of chambers are regularly involved in substantial fraud and drugs cases as well as confiscation hearings and cases involving serious sexual offences.
Civil Litigation Chambers provides civil practitioners who specialise in the areas of employment law, personal injury, landlord and tenant and other property litigation, construction law, general commercial and contractual litigation and actions against the police.
Family Law Chambers can offer practitioners who are experienced in all aspects of family law, including divorce, ancillary relief, Children's Act applications and domestic violence cases. Chambers also provide expertise in Social Security Law and Child Support Agency matters.
Administrative Law Chambers also offers an administrative law team with particular focus on the fields of immigration, trading standards, planning and education.

International French, German, Italian, Spanish, Urdu, Punjabi, Hindi, Gujerati, Malay and Indonesian are spoken.

Clarendon Chambers
Set No.19

7 Stone Buildings, Lincoln's Inn, London, WC2A 3SZ
Tel (020) 7681 7681 **Fax** (020) 7681 7684 **DX** LDE 0022 Chancery Lane
Email clerks@clarendonchambers.com

Senior Clerk	Russell Burton
Tenants	40

Members

Gay Martin (1970)
John Bishop (1970)
Julian Lynch (1976)
Robert Anthony (1979)
Simon Birks (1981)
Stephen Crouch (1982)
Adrian Jenkala (1984)
Juliann Manson (1985)
Susan Pyle (1985)
Geoffrey Porter (1988)
Adam Swirsky (1989)
Stuart Yeung (1989)
Mark Gordon (1990)
Terry Burns (1990)

Simon Livingstone (1990)
Allison Fordham (1990)
Stephen Murch (1991)
Andrew Bullock (1992)
Lucinda Benner (1992)
Richard Carron (1992)
Simon Gerrish (1993)
Michael Ellis (1993)
Richard Holloway (1993)
Catherine Le Quesne (1993)
Anna Mathias (1994)
Peter Linstead (1994)
Nicola Smith (1994)
Ben Gow (1994)

Matthew Rudd (1994)
Jonathan Ellis (1995)
David Willans (1995)
Mugni Islam-Choudhury (1996)
Alexander McGregor (1996)
Sarah Porter (1996)
Richard Harris (1997)
Laureen Husain (1997)
Steven Evans (1997)
Penny Van Spall (1998)
Joanne Wardale (1998)
Sylvia Johnson (1999)

The Chambers Clarendon Chambers is a large common law set with the members of Chambers practising in specialist teams in the fields of crime, family, civil and commercial, landlord and tenant, personal injury, employment, licensing and immigration. Chambers have a strong client base in London and the South East and in the East Midlands where Chambers have an annexe in Northampton. All enquiries in respect of the services Chambers offer should be referred to the Senior Clerk. Business Hours: 8.30am-6.30pm Out of Hours Tel: (07971) 285796. Annexe at: Clarendon Chambers, 5 St Giles Terrace, Northampton, NN1 2BN Tel: (01604) 637245 Fax: (01604) 633167 DX: 12404 Northampton.

■ BAR A-Z

LONDON

Cloisters (Laura Cox QC)   Set No.20

Cloisters, 1 Pump Court, Temple, London, EC4Y 7AA
Tel (020) 7827 4000   **Fax** (020) 7827 4100   **DX** LDE 452
Email clerks@cloisters.com   **Website** www.cloisters.com

Head of Chambers	Laura Cox QC
Practice Director	Gerald Newman
Senior Clerk	Glenn Hudson
Clerks	Michelle Hughton
	Kaye Brooks
	Mark Skipp
Senior Fees Clerk	Stephen Herbert
Junior Fees Clerk	Alberta Sharpe
Chambers Administrator	Christine Brown
Tenants	41

Members

Laura Cox QC (1975) (QC-1994)
Arthur Davidson QC (1953) (QC-1976)
Brian Langstaff QC (1971) (QC-1994)
Robin Allen QC (1974) (QC-1995)
Jonathan Crystal (1972)
Philip Engelman (1979)
Daphne Romney (1979)
Jacques Algazy (1980)
Andrew Buchan (1981)
Martin Kurrein (1981)
Simon W Taylor (1984)
Pauline Hendy (1985)

Simon Dyer (1987)
Declan O'Dempsey (1987)
Anthony Bradley (1989)
Patricia Hitchcock (1988)
Paul Epstein (1988)
Paul Spencer (1988)
Graham Brodie (1989)
Thomas Kibling (1990)
Joel Donovan (1991)
Jason Galbraith-Marten (1991)
Yvette Genn (1991)
Paul Michell (1991)
Christopher Quinn (1992)
Caspar Glyn (1992)
John Horan (1993)
Louise Brooks (1994)

Rachel Crasnow (1994)
Damian McCarthy (1994)
Sally Robertson (1995)
William Latimer-Sayer (1995)
Thomas Coghlin (1998)
Adam Solomon (1998)
Jonathan Cohen (1999)
Schona Jolly (1999)
David Massarella (1999)
Akua Reindorf (1999)
Claire McCann (2000)
Thomas Brown (2000)
Peter J Pimm (1991) †
John Whitmore (1976) †
Amir Majid †

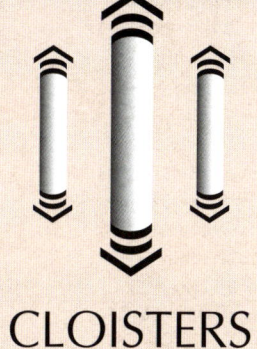

† Associate member

The Chambers User-friendly expertise: practical and approachable, Cloisters' top-rated silks and juniors frequently appear in leading edge cases that define the law. Full CVs are on the set's website.

Work Undertaken

Employment & Discrimination Regularly in the House of Lords, ECHR, and ECJ, Cloisters' 30 employment specialists often have an advisory role too, on HR policies, TUPE and anti-discrimination compliance for example. Members contribute substantial sections to *Halsbury's Laws*, Bullen Leake & Jacob, Sweet & Maxwell's *Employment Law Encyclopaedia* and others. The EOC, CRE and now the DRC instruct members, as do trades unions, individuals, PLCs, local authorities, financial institutions, NHS trusts, and City law firms.

Personal Injury at Work Chambers' combined employment and PI expertise is unique. It handles many industrial accident or disease cases, including many of the leading stress and bullying at work cases.

Clinical Negligence, Medical Law & Personal Injury The conjoined twins and the Bristol Royal Infirmary inquiry are two recent high profile matters that the set has been involved with. Members frequently handle catastrophic injury, product liability, accident cases, inquests and major clinical negligence trials.

Administrative & Public Law Many local authorities and other public sector bodies instruct chambers. Human rights law informs every area of its practice, and its specialisms include immigration, education law, local government law, social security, mental health and registered homes. Publications include *Employment Law and Human Rights*, O'Dempsey and Supperstone on *Immigration and Asylum*, and Bradley and Ewing's *Constitutional and Administrative Law*.

Commercial The set undertakes commercial fraud, search, seizure, freezing orders, agency, contract law and professional negligence. It has specialist EU expertise. Publications include *Commercial Judicial Review*.

Media & Sports Law Cloisters is one of the few chambers to focus on sports law, with an array of household name clients. It also acts in defamation, IP and media cases.

LONDON — BAR A-Z

Coram Chambers (Roger McCarthy QC) — Set No.21

4 Brick Court, Temple, London, EC4Y 9AD
Tel (020) 7797 7766 **Fax** (020) 7797 7700 **DX** 404 (Chancery Lane)
Email mail@coramchambers.co.uk **Website** www.coramchambers.co.uk

Head of Chambers	Roger McCarthy QC
Senior Clerk	Paul Sampson
Administration Manager	Martin Dyke
Tenants	50

Members

Roger McCarthy QC (1975) (QC-1996)
Shelagh Farror (1970)
Jane Drew (1976)
Catherine Nicholes (1977)
Aditya Kumar Sen (1977)
Laura Harris (1977)
David Boyd (1977)
Vera Mayer (1978)
Martha Cover (1979)
Anne Spratling (1980)
Kate Hudson (1981)
Meena Gill (1982)
Nicola Simpson (1982)
Fiona Gibb (1983)
Christina Morris (1983)
Carol Atkinson (1985)
Nicholas O'Brien (1985)
Anne Gibberd (1985)
Divya Bhatia (1986)
Debora Price (1987)
Michelle Corbett (1987)
Jane Probyn (1988)
Kate Purkiss (1988)
Mark Mullins (1988)
Elpha LeCointe (1988)
Jennifer Driscoll (1989)
Susan Belgrave (1989)
Neil Bullock (1989)
Frances Orchover (1989)
Alan Inglis (1989)
Andrew Short (1990)
Jillian Brown (1991)
Anthony Ross (1991)
Neil Fry (1992)
Sharon Sawyerr (1992)
David Vavrecka (1992)
Sima Kothari (1992)
Michael Horton (1993)
Susan Gore (1993)
Dermot Casey (1994)
Alison Easton (1994)
Andrew Allen (1995)
Gerald Browne (1995)
Timothy Parker (1995)
Sarah Marley (1995)
Jerry Fitzpatrick (1996)
Mai-Ling Savage (1998)
Daisy Hughes (1999)
Anne-Marie Glover (2000)
Mark de Souza (2000)

The Chambers Chambers undertake a wide range of work, which falls into two main fields: family and civil.

Work Undertaken

Family Including divorce; matrimonial finance; public and private Children Act proceedings; child abduction; domestic violence; adoption; wardship; inheritance and cohabitees.
Civil Employment (including trade union law), discrimination, landlord and tenant, local government, social services, community care, mental health, education, judicial review, human rights, housing and registered homes.

International Work is handled in Bengali, French, Hebrew, Hindi, Italian, Punjabi and Spanish.

Crown Office Chambers (Michael Spencer QC & Christopher Purchas QC) — Set No.22

1 Paper Buildings, Temple, London, EC4Y 7EP
Tel (020) 7797 8100 **Fax** (020) 7797 8101 **DX** 80 LONDON/CHANCERY LANE
Email mail@crownofficechambers.com **Website** www.crownofficechambers.com

Head of Chambers	Michael Spencer QC
	Christopher Purchas QC
Senior Clerks	Julian Campbell
	David Newcomb
Tenants	73

Members

Michael Spencer QC (1970) (QC-1989)
Christopher Purchas QC (1966) (QC-1990)
John Crowley QC (1962) (QC-1982)
Michael Harvey QC (1966) (QC-1982)
John Slater QC (1969) (QC-1987)
Nigel Wilkinson QC (1972) (QC-1990)
Antony Edwards-Stuart QC (1976) (QC-1991)
Roger ter Haar QC (1974) (QC-1992)
Andrew Bartlett QC (1974) (QC-1993)
Simon Brown QC (1976) (QC-1995)
William Stevenson QC (1968) (QC-1996)
Richard Lynagh QC (1975) (QC-1996)
Michael Kent QC (1975) (QC-1996)
Richard Hone QC (1970) (QC-1997)
Anna Guggenheim QC (1982) (QC-2001)
Jonathan Waite QC (1978) (QC-2002)
Jonathan Woods (1965)
Martyn Berkin (1966)
Margaret Bickford-Smith (1973)
Colin Nixon (1973)
David Tucker (1973)
Dennis Matthews (1973)
Thomas Saunt (1974)
John Powles (1975)
John Stevenson (1975)
Nicholas Davies (1975)
James Holdsworth (1977)
Andrew Phillips (1978)
John Greenbourne (1978)
Gordon Catford (1980)

Julian Field (1980)	William Vandyck (1988)	James Maxwell-Scott (1995)
Jane Davies (1981)	Marion Egan (1988)	Robert Stokell (1995)
Michael Curtis (1982)	Steven Snowden (1989)	Suzanne Chalmers (1995)
Paul Dean (1982)	Ian Wright (1989)	Andrew O'Connor (1996)
Charlotte Jones (1982)	Erica Power (1990)	Andrew Davis (1996)
Deborah Taylor (1983)	Jason Evans-Tovey (1990)	Muhammed Haque (1997)
Steven Coles (1983)	Benedict Newman (1991)	Susan Lindsey (1997)
Kim Franklin (1984)	Simon Howarth (1991)	Ben Quiney (1998)
James Medd (1985)	Toby Gee (1992)	Victoria Woodbridge (1998)
Ian Swan (1985)	Andrew Rigney (1992)	Jack Ferro (1998)
Shaun Ferris (1985)	Clive Weston (1993)	Julian Horne (1998)
David Platt (1987)	Patrick Blakesley (1993)	Sarah McNally (1999)
Jane DeCamp (1987)	Alexander Antelme (1993)	Daniel Shapiro (1999)
Raymond Ng (1987)	Claire Toogood (1995)	

The Chambers Crown Office Chambers was founded in 2000 and brought together the two long-established common law sets of chambers, One Paper Buildings and Two Crown Office Row. It is the largest civil common law set in London and has currently 71 members of chambers. Operating from both buildings, it has its administrative and reception facilities at 1 Paper Buildings. Chambers offer a modern, flexible and friendly service. They operate block agreements and protocols for the return of paperwork and for court appearances. They are able to provide first class reception and conference facilities. The size of the merged chambers has also permitted the development of a new centre for alternative dispute resolution, and Crown Office Chambers offers a fully administered ADR service.

Work Undertaken Crown Office Chambers specialises in professional and clinical negligence, product liability, personal injury, insurance and reinsurance, commercial, contract and construction work. Within these areas it is able to offer depth and breadth of experience at all levels of call, and is widely recognised as a market leader.

Professional Negligence Chambers undertake all forms of professional negligence, and in particular clinical negligence. They also specialise in construction-related claims (architects, engineers, valuers, residential, commercial and quantity surveyors); legal negligence (barristers and solicitors); claims against other professionals (accountants and insurance brokers).

Product Liability Product liability is a leading component of chambers' work. They have participated in most of the major multi-party claims which have so far been brought, including the tobacco, benzodiazepine, organo-phosphate, MMR and the oral contraceptive litigation.

Personal Injury/Health & Safety Personal Injury and Health and Safety are an important part of Crown Office Chambers. Industrial accident, occupational disease, disaster claims, road traffic litigation, aviation/marine claims and local authority based disputes are all undertaken. Chambers act for both claimants and defendants, although they are widely acknowledged for their established connections with insurance-funded litigation.

Insurance & Reinsurance Insurance and reinsurance work is a major element of chambers' business. Crown Office Chambers has strong links with the insurance market, and many of its clients are major insurers, underwriting syndicates and brokers. All forms of contentious and advisory work are undertaken, including work in the Commercial Court and in arbitration.

Commercial Contract Members conduct general commercial litigation and arbitration including ICC arbitrations. These involve contractual claims of all kinds.

Construction Construction and engineering disputes form a significant part of the workload of chambers. Members have substantial experience in the Technology and Construction Courts, acting for employers, contractors, construction professionals, insurers and developers.

Other Members of chambers have particular expertise in other areas of law. Such specialities include administrative law and judicial review, public enquiries, planning and environmental work, employment law, commercial fraud and banking. Chambers also undertake all forms of residual negligence and nuisance claims. Direct access, conditional fee work and instructions in all forms of alternative dispute resolution are accepted.

Publications Members of chambers contribute to *Medical Negligence* and *Emden's Construction Law* (general editor, Andrew Bartlett QC).

BAR A-Z

1 Crown Office Row (Robert Seabrook QC)   Set No.23

Temple, London, EC4Y 7HH
Tel (020) 7797 7500   **Fax** (020) 7797 7550   **DX** LDE1020
Email mail@1cor.com   **Website** www.1cor.com

Head of Chambers	Robert Seabrook QC
Chambers Director	Bob Wilson
Senior Clerk	Matthew Phipps
Tenants	44

Members

Robert Seabrook QC (1964) (QC-1983)
James Badenoch QC (1968) (QC-1989)
Stephen Miller QC (1971) (QC-1990)
David Foskett QC (1972) (QC-1991)
Terence Coghlan QC (1968) (QC-1993)
Guy Mansfield QC (1972) (QC-1994)
Philip Havers QC (1974) (QC-1995)
Sally Smith QC (1977) (QC-1997)
Paul Rees QC (1980) (QC-2000)
Margaret Bowron QC (1978) (QC-2001)
Neil Garnham QC (1982) (QC-2001)

David Balcombe QC (1980) (QC-2002)
Gregory Chambers (1973)
Anthony Niblett (1976) †
James King-Smith (1980) †
David Hart (1982)
Martin Forde (1984)
William Edis (1985)
John Gimlette (1986)
David Evans (1988)
Amanda Grant (1988)
Paul Rogers (1989) †
Angus McCullough (1990)
Keeley Bishop (1990) †
John Whitting (1991)
Martin Downs (1990) †
Jeremy Cave (1992) †
Richard Booth (1993)

Philippa Whipple (1994)
Giles Colin (1994)
Sydney Chawatama (1994)
Sarah Lambert (1994)
Owain Thomas (1995)
Jeremy Hyam (1995)
Ben Collins (1996)
Shaheen Rahman (1996)
Zoe Taylor (1998)
Neil Sheldon (1998)
Caroline Neenan (1998)
Richard Smith (1999)
Christopher Mellor (1999)
Jennifer Johnston (1999)
Robert Kellar (1999)
Matthew Barnes (2000)

ONE CROWN OFFICE ROW

† Mainly practice from Brighton

The Chambers Long established as a leading civil set providing the full range of advisory and advocacy services, with an emphasis on professional negligence, public law, and human rights. With a modern and friendly commitment to client service, chambers welcome direct instructions from fellow professionals such as accountants, architects and engineers. A number of members (†) practise mainly from their Brighton Annexe at the recently expanded and modernised premises at Blenheim House, 120 Church Street, Brighton BN1 1WH, Tel: (01273) 625625, which is available for local conferences. To celebrate nearly 50 years at 1 Crown Office Row, chambers have now acquired and refurbished all five floors at this building, providing four conference rooms and the latest IT systems.

Work Undertaken Professional negligence, in particular clinical and solicitors' negligence; multi-party actions and group litigation; personal injury; health law; domestic commercial contract; administrative law and judicial review; technology; construction and environmental law; planning and local government; representation at public inquiries and before professional disciplinary tribunals; human rights and civil liberties; employment and discrimination; matrimonial finance; sports law, immigration and VAT. Chambers are informally grouped into teams in these specialist areas in which they have in depth expertise at both senior and junior level. Criminal work is also undertaken, in particular fraud and other serious crime. Full details of chambers' services are available at www.1cor.com or in the chambers brochure on request. Building on the set's recognised expertise on the Human Rights Act, on which members regularly lecture and write, chambers are re-launching their unique Human Rights Act Up-Date service at www.1cor.com containing commentaries on all significant cases up-dated weekly with an archive back to 1998.

Publications Members are authors of or contributors to a number of textbooks including *The Law and Practice of Compromise* (5th Edition, 2002) and *Settlement under the Civil Procedure Rules* (both by David Foskett QC); four contributors to *Clinical Negligence* (Editors Powers & Harris); five contributors to *Personal Injury Handbook* (Editors Brennan & Curran); four contributors to *Professional Negligence and Liability*; 14 contributors to *Human Rights and the Common Law* (edited by Rosalind English and Philip Havers QC).

Recruitment Up to three pupils are taken annually for 12 months. An award of £20,000 is offered, split between the first six months and a guaranteed level of earnings for the second six. A first or upper second class degree is required. The set is a member of the OLPAS scheme. Applications for a third six month pupillage are invited from July for selection in September. In 2001 chambers launched an annual £10,000 scholarship in Lord Woolf's name to support a deserving student through the Bar Vocational Course (details at www.1cor.com).

Devereux Chambers (Colin Edelman QC)

Set No. 24

Devereux Chambers, Devereux Court, London, WC2R 3JH
Tel (020) 7353 7534 **Fax** (020) 7353 1724 **DX** 349 (Ch.Ln.)
Email mailbox@devchambers.co.uk **Website** www.devchambers.co.uk

Head of Chambers	Colin Edelman QC
Senior Clerk	Elton Maryon
Practice Managers	Clifford Holland
	Andrew Frankland
Practice Development Manager	Laura Colin
Tenants	44

Members

Colin Edelman QC (1977) (QC-1995)
Diana Cotton QC (1964) (QC-1983)
Jeffrey Burke QC (1964) (QC-1984)
Alan Pardoe QC (1971) (QC-1988)
Robert Glancy QC (1972) (QC-1997)
David Griffith-Jones QC (1975) (QC-2000)
Timothy Brennan QC (1981) (QC-2001)
Roy Lemon (1970)
Peter Wulwik (1972)
Ian Smith (1972)
Gerald Rabie (1973)
Christopher Goddard (1973)
Ian Lee (1973)
Richard Greening (1975)
Ruth Downing (1978)
Nicholas Bard (1979)
Stephen Killalea (1981)
Graham Read (1981)
Bruce Silvester (1983)
Colin Mendoza (1983)
Colin Wynter (1984)
Bruce Carr (1986)
Ingrid Simler (1987)
Joanna Heal (1988)
Philip Thornton (1988)
James Tayler (1989)
Nicholas Randall (1990)
Keith Bryant (1991)
Richard Harrison (1991)
Natasha Joffe (1992)
Alison Padfield (1992)
Robert Weir (1992)
Andrew Burns (1993)
Katharine Gollop (1993)
Suzanne McKie (1991)
Peter Edwards (1992)
Dijen Basu (1994)
Anna Thomas (1995)
David Craig (1997)
Lydia Seymour (1997)
Ben Adamson (1999)
Akash Nawbatt (1999)
Shaen Catherwood (2000)
Diya Sen Gupta (2000)

The Chambers Devereux Chambers offers a comprehensive interdisciplinary service to its clients. Areas of special expertise include administrative and local government law; commercial litigation; employment law; insurance and reinsurance; professional negligence; personal injury and clinical negligence. There is a strong emphasis on advocacy. Devereux Chambers is a thriving and well established set of chambers with a wide client base, ranging from public companies, underwriters and brokers to local authorities, government departments, trade unions and individual litigants. A number of senior members of chambers are deputy High Court judges and recorders. Members of chambers sit on the Criminal Injuries Compensation Appeals Panel, Mental Health Independent Review Tribunal, Rent Assessment Panel and the Boundary Commission; they also chair tribunals and inquiries. Members of chambers hold or have held various government appointments including junior counsel to the Inland Revenue, Common Law and membership of the A,B&C Panels of Treasury Counsel, Common Law. Members of chambers play a prominent role in the Bar's professional bodies and associations and chambers includes members of the Bar Council Professional Conduct Committee. Members of chambers are available to give lectures and seminars in their specialist fields both externally and as part of chambers' own Law Society accredited seminar programme.

Work Undertaken The major areas of practice are commercial and common law, especially administrative and local government; commercial; construction; consumer and business credit; discrimination; education; employment; environment; Europe; health and safety; human rights; industrial injury and disease; insurance and reinsurance; judicial review; landlord and tenant; pensions; personal injury and clinical negligence; police complaints and civil liberties; product liability; professional negligence; property; public interest immunity; sport; revenue; telecommunications; tribunals and inquiries; VAT/Customs & Excise. In addition, individual members of chambers offer expertise in the following areas of law: community care; contempt; crime (including white-collar crime); defamation; electoral and parliamentary; family; and housing.

Publications Members of chambers regularly appear in leading cases and have written or co-written prominent text and practitioner's books in their specialist fields. Professor Ian Smith co-wrote *Smith and Wood on Industrial Law* and is the author of the Employment Law and Social Security titles in *Halsbury's Laws*. He and Nicholas Randall are editors of *Harvey on Industrial Relations and Employment Law* of which Timothy Brennan QC is also a co-editor. David Griffith-Jones QC is the author of *Law & the Business of Sport (Butterworths 1998)* to which Timothy Brennan QC and Colin Wynter are also contributors. Bruce Carr is a contributing author to *FT Law & Tax, Litigation Practice (Emergency Procedures)*. Ingrid Simler is a contributing author to *Tolley's Employment Law* (1994). James Tayler is a contributor to *Dix on Employment Law (Butterworths)*, and Nicholas Randall is the author of the *Pensions* title in *Halsbury's Laws* and a contributor to *Butterworths' Employment Law Guide*. Alison Padfield is the co-author of the *Contempt of Court* title in *Halsbury's Laws*. Nicholas Randall and Ian Smith are co-authors of *Butterworths' Guide to Employment Relations Act 1999*. James Tayler, Ingrid Simler, Natasha Joffe and Andrew Burns co-wrote *Butterworths' Discrimination Law 1999* (with assistance from Lydia Seymour, David Craig and Richard Greening). James Tayler is the

Continued overleaf

BAR A-Z

co-author of the Equal Pay section of *Halsbury's Laws* and he, Andrew Burns, Ingrid Simler, Keith Byrant and Natasha Joffe co-wrote the Discrimination section of *Halsbury's Laws*. Three members of chambers, Professor Ian Smith, Christopher Goddard and Nicholas Randall, co-wrote *Health and Safety - The New Legal Framework* published by Butterworths. Stephen Killalea is a co-author of the 2001 edition. Nicholas Randall and Professor Ian Smith are co-authors of *Butterworths' Contract Actions in Modern Employment Law - Development & Issues* (expected publishing date October 2002). Alison Padfield is the author of *Butterworths' Insurance Claims* (due late 2002) and has been a contributing author for *Butterworths' Civil Court Practice* 2002. Members of chambers are also contributors to *Personal Injury Factbook* (*Sweet & Maxwell*).

Recruitment Great emphasis is placed on the calibre of pupils received to ensure that the high standards are maintained and generous pupillage awards are offered.

Doughty Street Chambers (Geoffrey Robertson QC) — Set No.25

Doughty Street Chambers, 10-11 Doughty Street, London, WC1N 2PL
Tel (020) 7404 1313 **Fax** (020) 7404 2283 **DX** 223 Chancery Lane
Email enquiries@doughtystreet.co.uk **Website** www.doughtystreet.co.uk

Head of Chambers	Geoffrey Robertson QC
Practice Manager	Christine Kings
Senior Clerk	Michelle Simpson
Crime Clerks	Paul Venables
	Elly Foster
Civil Clerks	Richard Bayliss
	Paul Friend
	Melanie Stephenson
	Jason Savage
Junior Clerks	Ciaran O'Fathaigh
	Iqbal Hussein
Tenants	73

Members

Geoffrey Robertson QC (1973) (QC-1988)
Louis Blom-Cooper QC (1952) (QC-1983)
Richard Maxwell QC (1968) (QC-1988)
Peter Thornton QC (1969) (QC-1992)
Helena Kennedy QC (1972) (QC-1991)
Patrick O'Connor QC (1970) (QC-1993)
Christopher Sallon QC (1973) (QC-1993)
Andrew Nicol QC (1978) (QC-1995)
Edward Fitzgerald QC (1978) (QC-1995)
Stephen Irwin QC (1976) (QC-1997)
Edward Rees QC (1973) (QC-1998)
Michael Grieve QC (1975) (QC-1998)
Frank Panford QC (1972) (QC-1999)
James Wood QC (1975) (QC-1999)
Gavin Millar QC (1981) (QC-2000)
Keir Starmer QC (1987) (QC-2002)
Andrew Hall QC (1991) (QC-2002)
Oliver Thorold (1971)
Robert Latham (1976)
David Hislop (1989) (NZ Bar 1979)

Nicolas Paul (1980)
Jill Evans (1986)(Solicitor 1980)
Kate Markus (1981)
Christopher Hough (1981)
Isabella Forshall (1982)
Jeannie Mackie (1995) (Solicitor 1982)
Paul Bogan (1983)
David Bentley (1984)
Tracey Bloom (1984)
Heather Williams (1985)
Martin Westgate (1985)
Aswini Weereratne (1986)
Gerwyn Samuel (1986)
Francis FitzGibbon (1986)
Anthony Metzer (1987)
Sally Hatfield (1988)
Robin Oppenheim (1988)
Michelle Strange (1989)
Kieran Maidment (1989)
Paul Taylor (1989)
Hugh Barton (1989)
Paul Brooks (1989)
Sadakat Kadri (1989)
Phillippa Kaufmann (1991)
Quincy Whitaker (1991)
Stephen Reeder (1991)
Ian Wise (1992)
Simon Cox (1992)
Lucy Moorman (1992)
Richard Hermer (1993)
Paul Bowen (1993)
John Walsh (1993)
Timothy Pullen (1993)

Mark Henderson (1994)
Paula Sparks (1994)
Siza Agha (1994)
Shahram Taghavi (1994)
Richard Fisher (1994)
Althea Brown (1995)
Rebecca Trowler (1995)
Jonathan Glasson (1996)
Anthony Hudson (1996)
Stephen Cragg (1996)
Nick Toms (1996)
Joseph Middleton (1997)
Ulele Burnham (1997)
Henrietta Hill (1997)
Steven Powles (1997)
Peter Lownds (1998)
Neil McInnes (1999)
Jamie Burton (1999)
Peter Morris (2000)
Philip Haywood (2001)
Ismail Mahommed (1956) Justice *
Guy Ollivry QC (1957) (QC-1987) *
Fenton Ramsahoye (1953) SC *
Adrian Hardiman (1988) SC *
Kevin Boyle (1992) Prof. *
Christine Booker (1977) *
Julian Fulbrook (1977) *
Geraldine Van Bueren (1980) *
Gilbert Marcus (1999) SC *
Jill Peay (1991) *
Jonathan Cooper (1992) *

* Door Tenant

The Chambers Emphasis is on civil liberties and human rights with specialists in criminal law; media law and defamation; public law; prisoners rights and cases involving issues of mental health; discrimination; immigration; employment; housing; personal injury and clinical negligence. Former winner of Chambers of the Year award, Bar Pro Bono award, Bronze winner of Law Firm Management award and accredited in Investor in People 2000.

■ BAR A-Z

2 Dyers Buildings (Nadine Radford QC) — Set No.26

2 Dyers Buildings, Holborn, London, EC1N 2JT
Tel (020) 7404 1881   **Fax** (020) 7404 1991   **DX** 175 London Chancery Lane
Email admin@2dyersbuildings.com   **Website** www.2dyersbuildings.com

Head of Chambers	Nadine Radford QC
Clerks	Graham Islin (07956) 985 929
	David Scothern (07931) 776 630
	Ryan Bartlett (07870) 866 048
Administration	Lisa Young
	Victoria Clark
Tenants	29

Members

Nadine Radford QC (1974) (QC-1995) +
Michael Gledhill QC (1976) (QC-2001) +
Raymond Lewis (1971)
Andrew Campbell-Tiech (1978) +
Sanderson Munro (1981)
Ian Jobling (1982)
Daniel Flahive (1982)
Julia Postill (1982)

Charles Burton (1983)
Adam Davis (1985)
Terence Boulter (1986)
Harriette Black (1986)
Lauren Soertsz (1987)
Michael Magarian (1988)
Simon Kitchen (1988)
Sam Stein (1988)
Tobias Long (1988)
Andrew Jefferies (1990)
Dominic Bell (1992)

Robert Tolhurst (1992)
Jonathan Green (1993)
Timothy Forte (1994)
Peter Caldwell (1995)
Gavin Irwin (1996)
Gregory Fishwick (1996)
Trilby Millet (1996)
Zarif Khan (1996)
Emma Goodall (1996)
Ben Cooper (1999)
Ian Way (1988) *

* Door Tenant + Recorder

The Chambers Chambers specialise in criminal law and associated matters. Members of chambers regularly represent clients charged with the most serious of offences, from fraud, money laundering and drugs to computer crime and murder. In addition chambers have a particular specialisation in High Court restraint and confiscation matters. Chambers' service includes the provision of counsel for overnight, week-end and bank holiday cases. Clerks may be contacted anytime.

Continuing Education Chambers see continuing education as vital to their ongoing expansion. Lectures are held on a regular basis - both in house and for professional clients.

Work Undertaken Members of chambers are increasingly instructed in other niche areas, including extradition, mental health tribunals, environmental law and matters relating to health and safety at work. In addition, members of chambers appear before coroner's inquests and a variety of regulatory and disciplinary tribunals.

Human Rights Pro bono work is undertaken for the Free Representation Unit and Bar Pro Bono Unit. Members of chambers have advised Amnesty International and a number of foreign bar associations with regards to the incorporation of human rights legalisation in foreign jurisdictions. Chambers' regularly undertakes Privy Council 'death row' cases.

International Languages spoken include French, German, Italian, Punjabi and Urdu.

Recruitment Pupillage contact: Gavin Irwin. Training and Lectures: Andrew Jefferies.

Eldon Chambers (Patrick Clarkson QC & William Hicks QC) — Set No.27

Falcon Court, 30-32 Fleet Street, London, EC4Y 1AA
Tel (020) 7583 1355   **Fax** (020) 7583 1672   **DX** 440 LDE
Email clerks@eldonchambers.com

Head of Chambers	Patrick Clarkson QC
	William Hicks QC
Senior Clerk	William King
Tenants	19

Members

Lionel Read QC (1954) (QC-1973) MA (Cantab)
David Woolley QC (1962) (QC-1980) MA (Cantab)
Patrick Clarkson QC (1972) (QC-1991)
Christopher Whybrow QC (1965) (QC-1992) LLB (London)
William Hicks QC (1975) (QC-1995) MA (Cantab)

Rhodri Price Lewis QC (1975) (QC-2001) MA (Oxon) DipCrim (Cantab)
Roy Martin (1990) (QC-Scotland), LLB (Glasgow)
Martin Wood (1972) LLB (London)
Simon Pickles (1978) MA (Cantab)

John Dagg (1980) BSc, LLB MRTPI
Neil Cameron (1982) BA (Dunelm)
Stephen Morgan (1983) LLB (Warw), MA (Nott)
Richard Langham (1986) BA (Oxon)

Continued overleaf

BAR A-Z

Russell Harris (1986) MA (Cantab)
Megan Thomas (1987) BA (Sheff)
Sasha White (1991) MA (Cantab)
Matthew Reed (1995) MA (Cantab) MA (City)
Scott Lyness (1996) LLB (Hull)
Edmund Robb (1998) MA (Oxon)

The Chambers A specialist planning, local government, environmental and public law set. Members undertake both advocacy and advisory work and accept Direct Professional Access.

Work Undertaken Town and country planning; environment; integrated pollution control; waste disposal; contaminated land; compulsory purchase and compensation; highways; public health; local government; statutory undertakers; administrative law and judicial review; parliamentary work; landlord and tenant; rating; related human rights.

International Members of chambers also practise in Scotland, Northern Ireland and the Isle of Man.

Recruitment Pupillage applications to chambers. Chambers offer up to two first six-months' and up to two second six-months' pupillages each year. Chambers may offer a 12-months' pupillage. Awards of up to £9,000 are available.

Ely Place Chambers (Ronald Thwaites QC)   Set No.28

30 Ely Place, London, EC1N 6TD
Tel (020) 7400 9600 **Fax** (020) 7400 9630 **DX** 291 Chancery Lane
Email admin@elyplace.com

Head of Chambers	Ronald Thwaites QC
Senior Clerk	Christopher Drury
Administration	Richard Sheehan
Tenants	11

Members

Ronald Thwaites QC (1970) (QC-1987)
William McCormick (1985)
Simon Cheetham (1991)
Russell Stone (1992)
Iain Daniels (1992)
Hefin Rees (1992)
Garry Herbert MBE (1995)
Simon Butler (1996)
Johnathan Payne (1997)
Charles Barker (1997)
Scott Pearman (1999)

The Chambers The barristers of Ely Place Chambers are specialist advocates who advise on civil and commercial litigation with a particular emphasis on media/defamation, civil actions involving the police and employment law. Full consideration is given to the application of human rights within chambers' specialist areas. Headed by Ronald Thwaites QC, chambers pride themselves on their accessibility to both professional and lay clients. Chambers have an ethos of vigorous representation and sound pragmatic advice. Every effort is made to ensure dedicated and efficient client care. Chambers operate from 30 Ely Place, Holborn Circus, which is a renovated Georgian building purchased when the set was founded in 2000. The premises contain an extensive and adaptable seminar and conference facility from which chambers present a series of seminars given by barristers and invited speakers. The facility is ideal for arbitrations and can accommodate up to 90 people. The team of clerks is committed to assisting clients and ensuring that chambers provide a first class service. The fully integrated computer network allows a speedy response from both barristers and the clerking team. The clerks and barristers are sensitive to the particular needs and requirements of professional clients. Chambers have been involved in a number of recent high profile trials including the successful defences of Private Eye Magazine (Condliffe v Private Eye) and the Mirror Newspaper (Foulds v MGN); the 'Metric Martyrs' case; the House of Lords decision on confiscation (HM Customs & Excise v Norris); the defence of Jonathan King. Chambers are regularly instructed by the police and local authorities in relation to civil litigation and represent them at public inquiries and inquests (Marchioness, Climbie and Telford Inquest).

Work Undertaken Chambers operate practice teams in the following areas: commercial (including contract, corporate recovery and sports law); employment; media/defamation (including privacy); personal injury; police actions; professional/clinical negligence; property (including commercial property, landlord and tenant and housing); public law (including public inquiries, inquests and administrative law).

Recruitment Chambers maintain a policy of gradual expansion and welcome applications from energetic, able individuals with good application who wish to contribute towards a set with a distinct identity and a building of its own. Currently chambers provide for one funded pupillage per year.

Enterprise Chambers (Anthony Mann QC) — Set No.29

9 Old Square, Lincoln's Inn, London, WC2A 3SR
Tel (020) 7405 9471 **Fax** (020) 7242 1447 **DX** LDE 301
Email enterprise.london@dial.pipex.com **Website** www.enterprisechambers.com

Head of Chambers	Anthony Mann QC
Senior Clerk	Antony Armstrong
Practice Development Clerk	Barry Clayton
Clerks	Dylan Wendleken
	Mark Belford
	Robert McGill
Tenants	26

Members

Anthony Mann QC (1974) (QC-1992)
Bernard Weatherill QC (1974) (QC-1996)
Charles Morgan (1978)
Caroline Hutton (1979)
Michael James (1976) †
Linden Ife (1982)
Peter Arden (1983)
Geoffrey Zelin (1984)
Nigel Gerald (1985)
Jonathan Holmes (1985)
James Barker (1984)
Adrian Jack (1986)
Hugo Groves (1980) †
Zia Bhaloo (1990)
James Pickering (1991)
Soraya McKinnell (1991)
Hugh Jory (1992)
Bridget Williamson (1993) †
Jonathan Klein (1992)
Sarah Richardson (1993)
Edward Francis (1995)
Shanti Mauger (1996)
Shaiba Ilyas (1998)
Timothy Calland (1999)
Jonathan Rodger (1999)
Niall McCulloch (2000)

† Practised as a solicitor before joining chambers.

The Chambers Enterprise Chambers is a leading commercial Chancery set, specialising in company and commercial law, insolvency, landlord and tenant and property, professional negligence and general Chancery work. Chambers have qualified arbitrators and members use alternative dispute resolution procedures in appropriate cases. Chambers have branches in Leeds and Newcastle that affords them the unique advantage of providing a high quality service to clients from two major legal centres in the North East as well as from London. As part of their service, chambers offer cost-effective video conferencing facilities to clients with the ability of linking all chambers sites with each other. Enterprise Chambers aims to combine an excellent quality of service and to anticipate clients' needs with a progressive and flexible approach to practice at the Bar. Members of chambers recognise the importance of working as a team and being approachable and accessible to solicitors and clients. Chambers know that clients often find it useful to be given fee estimates and their clerks are happy to provide hourly rates or give overall estimates for items of work. Members regularly speak at seminars and chambers are authorised by the Law Society as a course provider.

Erskine Chambers (Robin Potts QC) — Set No.30

Erskine Chambers, 30 Lincoln's Inn Fields, London, WC2A 3PD
Tel (020) 7242 5532 **Fax** (020) 7831 0125 **DX** 308 Lon Ch'ry Lane
Email clerks@erskine-chambers.co.uk

Head of Chambers	Robin Potts QC
Senior Clerk	Mike Hannibal
Tenants	22

Members

Robin Potts QC (1968) (QC-1982) BA, BCL (Oxon)
Thomas Stockdale Bt (1966) MA (Oxon)
David Oliver QC (1972) (QC-1986) BA (Cantab)
David Richards QC (1974) (QC-1992) MA (Cantab)
John Cone (1975) LLB
Leslie Kosmin QC (1976) (QC-1994) MA, LLM (Cantab), LLM (Harvard)
Michael Todd QC (1977) (QC-1997) BA (Keele)
David Mabb QC (1979) (QC-2001) MA (Cantab)
Martin Moore QC (1982) (QC-2002) BA (Oxon)
David Chivers QC (1983) (QC-2002) BA (Cantab)
Ceri Bryant (1984) MA, LLM (Cantab)
Richard Snowden (1986) MA (Cantab), LLM (Harvard)
Catherine Roberts (1986) MA, LLM (Cantab)
Philip Gillyon (1988) BA (Cantab)
Mary Stokes (1989) MA (Oxon), LLM (Harvard)
Andrew Thompson (1991) MA, LLM (Cantab)
Dan Prentice (1982) LLB (Belfast) JD (Chicago), MA (Oxon)
Nigel Dougherty (1993) BA, LLM (Cantab)
Leon Kuschke (1993) BCOM, LLB
James Potts (1994) BA (Oxon)
Andrew Thornton (1994) LLB (Hull)
Edward Davies (1998) BA (Cantab), BCh (Oxon)
Richard Nolan (1999) BA, MA (Cantab) *

* Door Tenant

The Chambers Erskine Chambers has a long-established reputation as a company law set. It covers all aspects of company law; corporate finance; corporate insolvency; financial services and related commercial and professional negligence matters. Alongside its reputation in company law, the set is known for its commercial litigation experience over a range of practice areas and business sectors. There are 23 members of chambers including eight QCs. The practices of the majority of the individual members of chambers are lit-

Continued overleaf

BAR A-Z

igation-based, although they also continue to maintain their strength in advisory and drafting matters. It is chambers' aim to provide a professional service in a personal and approachable manner and the clerks are always available to discuss the practices of individual members. The office is open Monday to Friday 8.30am to 7.00pm and at other times an answerphone message provides numbers to contact.

Work Undertaken In the company law field, chambers cover a full range of litigation, advisory work and drafting. Members of chambers deal with all areas where company law issues may arise, including directors' duties; shareholders' disputes; takeovers; mergers and acquisitions; corporate reconstructions; loan capital and banking securities; schemes of arrangement; reductions of capital; insurance schemes. Erskine Chambers' standing in the corporate insolvency field is demonstrated by their involvement in the largest and most high-profile insolvencies of recent years. The set has traditionally attracted substantial litigation work and members advise on, and appear in, a considerable number of general commercial and professional negligence disputes. Direct Professional Access is accepted from members of recognised professional institutions.

International There is a strong international dimension to Erskine Chambers' work - the type of business on which the set advises and the clients for whom they act inevitably raise issues or involve disputes in other parts of the world. Members of chambers are frequently engaged as experts, or advocates, in other jurisdictions.

Recruitment All applications for pupillage in 2003/4 should be made directly using Chambers' application form.

Essex Court Chambers (Gordon Pollock QC)   Set No.31

24 Lincoln's Inn Fields, London, WC2A 3EG
Tel (020) 7813 8000 **Fax** (020) 7813 8080 **DX** 320
Email clerksroom@essexcourt.net **Website** www.essexcourt.net

Head of Chambers	Gordon Pollock QC
Senior Clerk	David Grief
Clerks	Joe Ferrigno
	Nigel Jones
	Sam Biggerstaff
Office Manager	Jean Muircroft
Tenants	65

Members

Gordon Pollock QC (1968) (QC-1979)
Michael Thomas QC (1955) (QC-1973)
Ian Hunter QC (1967) (QC-1980)
Stewart Boyd QC (1967) (QC-1981)
V V Veeder QC (1971) (QC-1986)
Michael Collins QC (1971) (QC-1988)
Richard Siberry QC (1974) (QC-1989)
Jonathan Gilman QC (1965) (QC-1990)
Bernard Eder QC (1975) (QC-1990)
Roderick Cordara QC (1975) (QC-1994)
Simon Crookenden QC (1975) (QC-1996)
Jeffrey Gruder QC (1977) (QC-1997)
Andrew Hochhauser QC (1977) (QC-1997)
Jack Beatson QC (1973) (QC-1998)
Richard Jacobs QC (1979) (QC-1998)
Christopher Greenwood QC (1978) (QC-1999)

David Mildon QC (1980) (QC-2000)
Susan Prevezer QC (1983) (QC-2000)
Geraldine Andrews QC (1981) (QC-2001)
Graham Dunning QC (1982) (QC-2001)
Victor Lyon QC (1980) (QC-2002)
Steven Berry QC (1984) (QC-2002)
Anthony Dicks QC (1961) (QC-1994)
Franklin Berman QC (1966) (QC-1992)
Mark Smith (1981)
Mark Templeman (1981)
David Joseph (1984)
Richard Millett (1985)
Huw Davies (1985)
Joe Smouha (1986)
Philippa Watson (1988)
Hugh Mercer (1985)
Martin Griffiths (1986)
Karen Troy-Davies (1981)
John Lockey (1987)
Simon Bryan (1988)
David Foxton (1989)
Christopher Smith (1989)

Malcolm Shaw QC (1988) (QC-2002)
Sara Cockerill (1990)
John Snider (1982)
Vernon Flynn (1991)
Brian Dye (1991)
Nigel Eaton (1991)
Charles Ciumei (1991)
Claire Blanchard (1992)
Perdita Cargill-Thompson (1993)
Vaughan Lowe (1993)
Toby Landau (1993)
Paul Stanley (1993)
Martin Hunter (1994)
Philippa Hopkins (1994)
Paul McGrath (1994)
James Collins (1995)
Tim Eicke (1993)
Stephen Houseman (1995)
Paul Key (1997)
Martin Lau (1996)
David Scorey (1997)
Sam Wordsworth (1997)
Nathan Pillow (1997)
Salim Moollan (1998)
Ricky Diwan (1998)
Neil Hart (1998)
Edmund King (1999)
Dominic O'Sullivan (2001)

The Chambers Consistently acknowledged as one of London's leading full-service commercial sets, Essex Court Chambers has an enviable track record of quality and high profile work and both its silks and juniors are much sought-after. Members advise across the whole spectrum of international, commercial and European law, and act as advocates in litigation and commercial arbitration worldwide. Clients range from major institutions and multinational corporations to private companies and individuals.

The Set Essex Court Chambers was established in 1961. The founding members were Michael Kerr (later Lord Justice Kerr), Robert MacCrindle, Michael Mustill (now Lord Mustill), Anthony Evans (later Lord Justice Evans), and Anthony Diamond (later Judge Diamond). Chambers grew rapidly, developing a reputation as one of the leading commercial sets and attracting a number of prominent legal figures: Mark Saville (now Lord Saville), Johan Steyn (now Lord Steyn), Anthony Colman (now Mr Justice Colman) and John Thomas (now Mr Justice Thomas). Under the leadership of Gordon Pollock since 1992, the set comprises 65 members and now occupies five adjacent buildings in Lincoln's Inn Fields. Essex Court Chambers is not a 'firm' or a 'partnership' but a collection of individuals who have developed personal reputations which are complemented by the solid profile and recognised sound management of the set to which they have chosen to be members. David Grief and his clerks have acquired a reputation for responsiveness and integrity and there is a modern approach to client care and commercial requirements.

Work Undertaken Essex Court Chambers has been particularly recognised as a leading set in alternative dispute resolution; arbitration; aviation; banking; commercial litigation; energy and natural resources; insurance; media and entertainment; and shipping. The set has also a strong reputation in commodities, employment; international trade; public international law; professional negligence; tax and VAT. Members continue to develop expertise in: administrative law and judicial review; agriculture and farming; Australian trade practices law; Chinese law; computer law; company law, construction and engineering; customs duty; European law; Hong Kong law; human rights; immigration and nationality law; industrial relations; injunctions and arrests; insolvency; intellectual property; international commercial fraud; Irish law, public law; rail disputes; sale of goods and product liability; South Asian law; sports law; and tribunals and inquiries. Members also act as arbitrators and mediators in domestic and international arbitrations.

International The strong international nature of the set differentiates it from other practices. It has barristers qualified to practise in non-UK jurisdictions and a wide range of commercial language skills. Members have appeared as advocates in the European Commission, European Court of Justice, European Court of Human Rights and International Court of Justice; in the courts of Hong Kong, Malaysia, Australia, Belfast, Dublin, Gibraltar, St Vincent, Brunei, Kenya and the Cayman Islands; and in arbitrations in places such as Paris, Geneva, Singapore, New Orleans and Beijing.

Recruitment Up to four funded 12 month pupillages are offered each year for an October start through OLPAS (summer season). Mini pupillages: Chambers offers up to 30 mini-pupillages during the months of June and July.

One Essex Court (Lord Grabiner QC) Set No.32

One Essex Court, Temple, London, EC4Y 9AR
Tel (020) 7583 2000 **Fax** (020) 7583 0118 **DX** 430 (Ch.Ln.)
Email clerks@oeclaw.co.uk **Website** www.oeclaw.co.uk

Head of Chambers	Lord Grabiner QC
Clerks	Robert Ralphs
	Paul Shrubsall MBE
Tenants	56

Members

Lord Grabiner QC (1968) (QC-1981)
Gerald Butler QC (1955) (QC-1975)
Christopher Carr QC (1968) (QC-1983)
Nicholas Strauss QC (1965) (QC-1984)
Peter Leaver QC (1967) (QC-1987)
Ian Glick QC (1970) (QC-1987)
Elizabeth Gloster QC (1971) (QC-1989)
Geoffrey Hobbs QC (1977) (QC-1991)
Mark Barnes QC (1974) (QC-1992)
Sir Sydney Lipworth QC (1991) (QC-1993)(HON.)
Alastair MacGregor QC (1974) (QC-1994)

Thomas Sharpe QC (1976) (QC-1994)
Thomas Ivory QC (1978) (QC-1998)
Jeffery Onions QC (1981) (QC-1998)
Susanna FitzGerald QC (1973) (QC-1999)
Rhodri Davies QC (1979) (QC-1999)
Stephen Auld QC (1979) (QC-1999)
Kenneth MacLean QC (1985) (QC-2002)
Laurence Rabinowitz QC (1987) (QC-2002)
Malcolm Gammie QC (1997) (QC-2002)
Alan Redfern (1995)
Michael Malone (1975)
Ian Grainger (1978)

Alan Griffiths (1981)
Clare Reffin (1981)
John McCaughran (1982)
Richard Gillis (1982)
Andrew Lenon (1982)
Michael Sullivan (1983)
Siobhan Ward (1984)
Charles Graham (1986)
Anthony de Garr Robinson (1987)
Neil Kitchener (1991)
Alain Choo Choy (1991)
Hannah Brown (1992)
David Wolfson (1992)
David Cavender (1993)
Daniel Toledano (1993)
Zoe O'Sullivan (1993)
Emma Himsworth (1993)
Lisa Lake (1994)

Continued overleaf

BAR A-Z

Edmund Nourse (1994)
Graeme Halkerston (1994)
Sa'ad Hossain (1995)
Daniel Jowell (1995)
Camilla Bingham (1996)

Philip Roberts (1996)
Michael Fealy (1997)
Orlando Gledhill (1998)
Simon Colton (1999)
Piu Das Gupta (1999)

Matthew Cook (1999)
Steven Elliott (2001)
Guy Hollingworth (2001)
Ben Strong (2001)
Derek Spitz (2001)

Work Undertaken The range of work carried out embraces every aspect of domestic and international commerce and finance. The principal areas of practice are arbitration; commercial law; company and insolvency; European Union law; intellectual property and revenue law.

Recruitment Chambers offer four 12 month pupillages each year. Chambers operate an award scheme which offers to each pupil the sum of £37,500 in his or her year of pupillage. Part of the award may, at the discretion of chambers, be advanced during a prospective pupil's year of vocational training. Applicants for pupillage should (save in exceptional circumstances) have at least an upper second class degree. Chambers participate in OLPAS, and all applications for pupillage should be made through OLPAS.

4 Essex Court (Nigel Teare QC)   Set No.33

4 Essex Court, Temple, London, EC4Y 9AJ
Tel (020) 7653 5653   **Fax** (020) 7653 5654   **DX** 292 London (Chancery Lane)
Email pupillage@4sx.co.uk   **Website** www.4sx.co.uk

Head of Chambers	Nigel Teare QC
Senior Clerk	Gordon Armstrong
Tenants	41

Members

Nigel Teare QC (1974) (QC-1991)
M N Howard QC (1971) (QC-1986)
Belinda Bucknall QC (1974) (QC-1988)
Charles Macdonald QC (1972) (QC-1992)
Jeremy Russell QC (1975) (QC-1994)
Lionel Persey QC (1981) (QC-1997)
Charles Haddon-Cave QC (1978) (QC-1999)
Simon Rainey QC (1982) (QC-2000)
Simon Kverndal QC (1982) (QC-2002)
Nigel Meeson QC (1982) (QC-2002)
John Suttner SC (1979)
George Economou (1965)

Simon Gault (1970)
Michael Nolan (1981)
Marion Smith (1981)
Nigel Jacobs (1983)
Michael McParland (1983)
Luke Parsons (1985)
Simon Croall (1986)
David Goldstone (1986)
Nigel Cooper (1987)
Matthew Reeve (1987)
Chirag V Karia (1988)
Poonam Melwani (1989)
Robert Lawson (1989)
James Turner (1990)
Michael Davey (1990)
Robert Thomas (1992)
Nevil Phillips (1992)
John Russell (1993)
Thomas Macey-Dare (1994)

John Kimbell (1995)
Nichola Warrender (1995)
Jonathan Chambers (1996)
Stewart Buckingham (1996)
Guy Blackwood (1997)
Peter Ferrer (1998)
Nicholas Craig (1998)
Nathan Tamblyn (1999)
Jo Cunningham (2000)
Christopher M Smith (1999)
His Honour Harvey Crush *
Nicholas Gaskell (1976) *
Paul Griffin (1979) *
Francis D Rose (1983) *
Richard Gardiner (1969) *
Harold Caplan (1955) *
Asif Qureshi (1978) *
Ian Kott

* Door Tenant

The Chambers 4, Essex Court concentrates on international trade litigation and arbitration in all areas of commercial law. From its basis as a leading set of shipping and aviation specialists, this committed and forward-thinking Chambers have expanded considerably in recent years and now provide litigation, arbitration, mediation and advisory services across the breadth of the commercial field. 4, Essex Court is renowned for the approachability of its members and staff. Members provide rigorous and vigorous solution-orientated advice. Members and staff are wholly attentive to the commercial concerns and interests of clients. Well over half the work carried out by chambers is for international clients or involves international commercial law. Many of the barristers at 4, Essex Court have membership of overseas bars including those of America (New York and California), Cyprus, Hong Kong, New South Wales, Germany and Greece and South Africa. Members of chambers edit and contribute to many leading textbooks and legal publications. A number of members of chambers sit on the editorial board of *International Maritime Law* magazine. Chambers have a modern and flexible attitude to structuring fees.

Work Undertaken Chambers provide first class advocacy and advice across the whole spectrum of commercial law. Members of chambers advise on domestic, commercial and international litigation and act as advocates in court, arbitration and inquiries in England and abroad. Members of chambers also act as arbitrators, mediators and expert witnesses. Principal areas of work include international trade and transport, commercial agreements, banking, insurance and reinsurance, arbitration, commodities, oil, aviation, admiralty and maritime law generally. In addition, members of chambers practise in media law, construction law, multi-party disaster litigation and judicial review. All members of chambers pride themselves on combining first-class legal advocacy skills with integrity and a friendly, down-to-earth approach. This is reflected in the supportive and unstuffy atmosphere within the Chambers' Practice Management teams. Chambers intend to maintain their policy of expansion and diversification whilst retaining and enhancing their standing in their core practice fields of maritime and aviation law.

5 Essex Court (Christopher Moss QC) — Set No.34

5 Essex Court, Temple, London, EC4Y 9AH
Tel (020) 7410 2000 **Fax** (020) 7410 2010 **DX** 1048
Email barristers@5essexcourt.co.uk **Website** www.5essexcourt.co.uk

Head of Chambers	Christopher Moss QC
Chambers Director	Daniel Clark
Senior Clerk	Mark Waller
Tenants	35

Members

Christopher Moss QC (1972) (QC-1994)
Jeremy Gompertz QC (1962) (QC-1988)
Simon Freeland QC (1978) (QC-2002)
Nicholas Ainley (1973)
John Bassett (1975)
Nicholas Wilcox (1977)
Gerard Pounder (1980)
Charles Apthorp (1983)
John Butcher (1984)
Gareth Hughes (1985)
Fiona Barton (1986)
Stephanie Farrimond (1987)
Andrew Waters (1987)
Kate Davey (1988)
Christopher Kerr (1988)
Rosalyne Mandil-Wade (1988)
Anne Studd (1988)
Georgina Kent (1989)
Lyn Hayhow (1990)
Giles Powell (1990)
Jason Beer (1992)
Stephen Akinsanya (1993)
Samantha Leek (1993)
Amanda Rippon (1993)
Jeremy Johnson (1994)
Stephen Rose (1995)
Lindsey Thompson (1995)
Prabhjot Virdi (1995)
Nadeem Ahmad (1996)
Mandy McLean (1996)
Lawrence Selby (1997)
Mathew Holdcroft (1998)
Barnabas Branston (1999)
Russell Fortt (1999)
Sherry Dalesandro (2000)

The Chambers 5 Essex Court is a long established common law set with a very strong reputation for providing high quality advocacy and advice. The set prides itself on giving a professional service in an approachable, flexible and utterly dependable manner, with the client's needs its priority. 5 Essex Court is acknowledged to be among the leading sets in the field of civil police law, and also has a very strong and thriving crime practice. Members also have considerable expertise in the fields of personal injury and employment. The strength in depth, expertise and experience within the main practice groups is such that clients are afforded a wholly reliable and comprehensive service in an effective, efficient and professional matter. Work is undertaken for the Treasury Solicitor, the Serious Fraud Office, HM Customs and Excise and the Home Office. In specialist areas of law, members have been involved in landmark cases both in the domestic and European courts. Chambers are accredited by the Law Society for the provision of continuing education and training, and members of the police team in particular are regularly invited to speak at lectures and seminars.

Work Undertaken The police actions practice group acts for many of the country's police forces. At all levels of seniority, members of the police group are instructed in the full range of police work including civil jury actions involving civil liberties and human rights issues such as trespass, malicious prosecution and false imprisonment; judicial reviews; inquests; employment; police disciplinary matters; pensions; and personal injuries. Members are also instructed to give legal advice on operational issues and sensitive issues of police policy. Members of the crime group undertake both prosecution and defence work in all aspects and levels of criminal work, including the full range of serious crime. The strength in depth of the criminal team throughout the set is such that a truly comprehensive service can be offered to clients. No matter how small, or complicated, or high profile a case, the expertise available enables chambers to provide the appropriate level of counsel, from the most junior tenant to the highly experienced Queen's Counsel. Work is predominantly undertaken in London and on the South Eastern Circuit. Within the areas of personal injuries and employment law, members regularly act for both claimants/applicants and defendants/respondents. The range of call and experience of practitioners means that whatever the scale and complexities of such cases, they can be covered in an efficient, proactive and sensitive manner. Individual members also have successful practices in other disciplines, including family, professional negligence, landlord and tenant, contract and sale of goods, consumer credit, company and partnership law, and commercial litigation (including EU competition.)

20 Essex Street (Iain Milligan QC)

Set No.35

20 Essex Street, London, WC2R 3AL
Tel (020) 7583 9294 **Fax** (020) 7583 1341 **DX** 0009 (Ch.Ln.)
Email clerks@20essexst.com **Website** www.20essexst.com

Head of Chambers	Iain Milligan QC
Chambers Manager	Janet Newton (020) 8533 3789
	Mobile (07374) 274841
Clerks	Neil Palmer (020) 8660 2633
	Mobile (07775) 713925
	Brian Lee (020) 8642 5865
	Mobile (0797) 759 0220
	Mathew Kesbey (01634) 388922
	Mobile (0794) 169 3666
Tenants	45

Members

Iain Milligan QC (1973) (QC-1991)
Sir Elihu Lauterpacht QC (1950) (QC-1970)
Sir Arthur Watts QC (1957) (QC-1988)
Sir Peter North QC (1992) (QC-1993) CBE
David Johnson QC (1967) (QC-1978)
Murray Pickering QC (1963) (QC-1985)
Nicholas Legh-Jones QC (1968) (QC-1987)
Richard Plender QC (1972) (QC-1989)
Angus Glennie QC (1974) (QC-1991)
Alexander Layton QC (1976) (QC-1995)
Timothy Young QC (1977) (QC-1996)
Nicholas Hamblen QC (1981) (QC-1997)
Stephen Males QC (1978) (QC-1998)
Christopher Hancock QC (1983) (QC-2000)
Stephen Morris QC (1981) (QC-2002)
Duncan Matthews QC (1986) (QC-2002)
Julian Cooke (1965)
Richard Wood (1975)
Michael Tselentis SC (1995) (SC - South Africa - 1989)
Edmund Broadbent (1980)
David Owen (1983)
William Godwin (1986)
Andrew Baker (1988)
Daniel Bethlehem (1988)
Michael Coburn (1990)
Timothy Otty (1990)
Lawrence Akka (1991)
Clare Ambrose (1992)
Karen Maxwell (1992)
Graham Charkham (1993)(CEDR Accredited)
Guy Morpuss (1991)
Sara Masters (1993)
Philip Edey (1994)
Charles Kimmins (1994)
Michael Collett (1995)
Michael Ashcroft (1997)
Sudhanshu Swaroop (1997)
Julian Kenny (1997)
Malcolm Jarvis (1998)
David Lewis (1999)
Susannah Jones (1999)
Thomas Raphael (1999)
Sean Snook (2000)
Henry Byam-Cook (2000)
Michael Lee (2001)
David St John Sutton (2001)

The Chambers This long established, progressive set of chambers is one of the leading sets in commercial law. Members advise on all aspects of international trade, commerce and finance with specialist expertise in banking, shipping, insurance, public international law and European Community law. Although much of chambers' work is in the Commercial Court, the practice and clientele are international. Chambers aim to combine an outstanding standard of work with a friendly and approachable attitude to clients, lay and professional. Notable recent events include Stephen Morris and Duncan Matthews successfully applying for silk and Tim Otty joining chambers to further expand its insurance and human rights expertise. Chambers already pre-eminent panel of full time arbitrators and foreign lawyers has been further enhanced with the addition of J. William Rowley QC of *McMillan Binch* based in Toronto, Canada. The Honourable Charles N Brower (formerly *White & Case*, Washington), Michael Lee (formerly *Norton Rose*) and David St John Sutton (formerly *Allen & Overy*). Office Hours: 8.15am-6.45pm.

Work Undertaken

Commercial Members advise on a range of commercial matters including the following: admiralty; agency; arbitration; aviation; bailment; banking and financial services; carriage by land, sea and air; commodities and futures; company law and partnership; conflicts of laws; construction; disciplinary proceedings; entertainment law; insurance and reinsurance; international sales and commodity trading; IT; oil and gas; professional negligence; sale of goods; shipping; all types of domestic and international commercial agreements.
European Union A number of members are specialists in European Community law and are regularly engaged to provide advice and representation to Community institutions, member states and other litigants on such issues as agriculture, the free movement of goods, those relating to individuals, services and capital, competition and state aids.
Domestic & International Arbitration & Mediation All senior members, together with Lord Donaldson, Lord Bridge, Lord Griffiths (CEDR accredited), Sir Brian Neill, Sir Philip Otton (CEDR registered), Sir Christopher Staughton and Kenneth Rokison QC (CEDR accredited), Malcolm Holmes QC (QC Australia NSW) and J William Rowley QC (Canada) accept appointment as arbitrators under a variety of auspices, including, ICC, LCIA, Stockholm Chamber of Commerce, WTO and ICSID, as well as in accordance with LMAA terms or UNCITRAL rules. Mediations and inquiries are conducted through recognised appropriate bodies as well as ad hoc.

Publications A number of members are authors and editors of leading publications and journals full details of which are available on chambers' website, address given above.

International Work is handled in French, German, Italian, Spanish, Dutch and Hindi. Members of chambers engaged in this field appear before the International Court of Justice and other international tribunals. Some members specialise in public international law, dealing with such matters as boundaries, interpretation of treaties, state immunity, international investment and human rights. Those practising in these areas appear as advocates in the International Court of Justice; the European Court of Human Rights; Dispute Settlement Panels of the World Trade Organisation; the International Tribunal on the Law of the Sea and comparable tribunals. Members also practise in private international law, including the Brussels and Lugano Conventions on Jurisdiction and the Enforcement of Judgements and the Rome Convention on the Law Applicable to Contractual Obligations. Some have experience of conducting litigation before the Court of Justice of the European Communities on the Brussels Convention. Members will accept instructions to appear in courts abroad including Hong Kong, Singapore, Malaysia and other jurisdictions subject to admission rules, whilst some members have been called to the local bars of Australia, Gibraltar and South Africa.

23 Essex Street (Michael Lawson QC) — Set No.36

23 Essex Street, London, WC2R 3AA
Tel (020) 7413 0353 **Fax** (020) 7413 0374 **DX** 148 (LDE) Chancery Lane
Email clerks@23essexstreet.co.uk **Website** www.23essexstreet.co.uk

Head of Chambers	Michael Lawson QC
Practice Manager	Nicholas Hopgood
Deputy Practice Manager	Daren Milton
Tenants	65

Members

Michael Lawson QC (1969) (QC-1991) +
Michael Hill QC (1958) (QC-1979)
Nicholas Purnell QC (1968) (QC-1985) +
Michael Austin-Smith QC (1969) (QC-1990) +
Susan Edwards QC (1972) (QC-1993) +
Stuart Lawson Rogers QC (1969) (QC-1994) +
Charles Miskin QC (1975) (QC-1998) +
Nigel Sangster QC (1976) (QC-1998) * + †
Michael Wood QC (1976) (QC-1999) +
Christopher Kinch QC (1976) (QC-1999) +
Daniel Janner QC (1980) (QC-2002)
Joanna Glynn QC (1983) (QC-2002) +
James Richardson (1975)
Brendan Finucane (1976) +
Simon Davis (1978) +
John Causer (1979)
Robin Johnson (1979)
Simon Russell Flint (1980) +
John Price (1982)
Oscar Del Fabbro (1982)
Graham Cooke (1983)
Sally Howes (1983)
Elroy Claxton (1983) +
Rupert Pardoe (1984)
Jane Calnan (1984)
James Lloyd (1985)
Philip St. John-Stevens (1985) +
Dafydd Enoch (1985)
Alan Kent (1986)
Johannah Cutts (1986)
Wayne Cranston-Morris (1986)
Paul Ozin (1987)
Karen Holt (1987)
Cairns Nelson (1987)
Heather Norton (1988)
Iain Morley (1988)
William Carter (1989)
Hugh Forgan (1989)
Isobel Ascherson (1990)
Lynn Griffin (1991)
Ian Acheson (1992)
Mark Fenhalls (1992)
Andrew Hurst (1992)
Richard Milne (1992)
Fiona Horlick (1992)
Giles Curtis-Raleigh (1992)
Andrew Rodger (1993)
Eloise Marshall (1994)
Hannah Swain (1994)
Rufus Stilgoe (1994)
Alexia Durran (1995)
Clare Strickland (1995)
Alan May (1995)
Ian Hope (1996)
Marcus Thompson (1996)
Gareth Branston (1996)
Sarah Campbell (1997)
Katherine Hunter (1997)
Tetteh Turkson (1998)
Toyin Salako (1998)
Daniel Fugallo (1999)
Oliver Dunkin (1999)
Lesley Bates (1999)
David Povall (2000)
Laura McQuitty (2000)
Alison Jones (1988) *
Simon Medland (1991) *

* Door Tenant + Recorder † Practising principally in Leeds

The Chambers A leading mainstream criminal set, with 65 tenants including 12 QCs. Members have provided chairmen of the Criminal Bar Association, a leader of the South Eastern Circuit, a member of the Lord Chancellor's Advisory Committee, and the president of the International Society for the Reform of Criminal Law. Chambers offer dedicated conference rooms and a lecture room.

Work Undertaken

Criminal The entire range of criminal law, for defence and prosecution, across London and the South Eastern Circuit. Specialisations include money laundering, commercial fraud, customs and revenue offences; also sexual offences and other cases involving vulnerable witnesses.
Other Disciplinary tribunals (police, general medical and dental), City regulatory work, courts martial, civil actions arising from criminal investigations, licensing. Members have experience in major public inquiries.

Continued overleaf

BAR A-Z

Publications James Richardson is editor of *Archbold and Criminal Law Week*. Joanna Glynn QC and William Carter are contributing editors for *Archbold*. Daniel Janner QC is one of the two editors of the *Criminal Appeal Reports*.

Recruitment Tenancy applications to Michael Wood QC.
Pupillage Chambers offer three 12 month funded pupillages. Travel allowances are available. The set is a member of OLPAS. Full details are published in the Bar Council's *Chambers Pupillages and Awards Handbook*. Applications to Simon Russell Flint.
Mini-pupillages A limited number are available. Applications to Cairns Nelson.
Training Chambers have developed teams in specialist areas, which provide regular in-house training to tenants. Leading members of the teams also provide external lecturing to professional bodies and other lawyers. There is an internal continuing education programme for pupils.

35 Essex Street (Christopher Wilson-Smith QC) — Set No.37

35 Essex Street, Temple, London, WC2R 3AR
Tel (020) 7353 6381 **Fax** (020) 7583 1786 **DX** 351 London
Email derekjenkins@35essexstreet.com **Website** www.35essexstreet.com

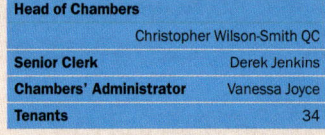

Head of Chambers	Christopher Wilson-Smith QC
Senior Clerk	Derek Jenkins
Chambers' Administrator	Vanessa Joyce
Tenants	34

Members

Christopher Wilson-Smith QC (1965) (QC-1986)
Nigel J Inglis-Jones QC (1959) (QC-1982)
David C Calcutt QC (1955) (QC-1972)
Alan D Rawley QC (1958) (QC-1977)
Philip C Mott QC (1970) (QC-1991)
Linda E Sullivan QC (1973) (QC-1994)
Richard Lissack QC (1978) (QC-1994)
Paul Garlick QC (1974) (QC-1996)

Robin S Tolson QC (1980) (QC-2001)
Hywel I Jenkins (1974)
John L Stephens (1975)
Richard M Mawhinney (1977)
William L Coley (1980)
Stephen Climie (1982)
David G Westcott (1982)
Christopher M Kemp (1984)
Harry Trusted (1985)
Andrew JM Spink (1985)
Alison McCormick (1988)
Susan C Freeborn (1989)
Richard G Hitchcock (1989)

Jonathan ES Hand (1990)
Thomas RG Leeper (1991)
Nathan W Tavares (1992)
Grace Malden (1993)
Matthew J Phillips (1993)
Nicolas Stallworthy (1993)
Abhijeet Mukherjee (1995)
Robert-Jan Temmink (1996)
Peter Skelton (1997)
Harriet Jerram (1998)
David Grant (1999)
Cara Guthrie (2000)
Samantha Presland (2001)

The Chambers 35 Essex Street is a thriving, well-established and progressive set which successfully combines the levels of expertise and specialisations expected of the leading sets with an accessible and open to all approach. Chambers have developed significantly over the years to meet successfully the demands of both lay and professional clients across all their common and commercial law practices. With proven high quality barristers, strength in depth and experience at all levels of call, chambers are renowned for providing a genuinely first-class service tailored specifically to the needs of each individual client. Approachable, receptive and flexible in its handling of casework, the set has shown itself adept at responding to the fast changing requirements of the legal world. The set is acknowledged to be among the leading chambers in the fields of pensions, clinical negligence, personal injury and corporate crime, and members of chambers also undertake work relating to child care, professional negligence, employment and extradition. Members of 35 Essex Street have considerable experience of arbitration and are also increasingly recognized for their expanding involvement in Public Inquiry work, having been involved in almost every major inquiry in the last five years.

Work Undertaken Members of 35 Essex Street appear regularly in high profile cases covering the complete spectrum of work undertaken in chambers. In addition to appearing as advocates in the English Appellate Courts, the High Court, the County Courts and a wide variety of tribunals and arbitration work, chambers place particular emphasis on providing focused and practical advice both on paper and in conference on litigious and non-litigious matters. Work is also undertaken in foreign jurisdictions. Members of chambers regularly work for the Bar pro bono unit and have also conducted litigation on a pro bono basis until funding has been made available. Chambers also have wide experience and a successful record of undertaking work on a conditional fee basis in many of their areas of specialisation, and of assisting solicitors in the initial risk assessment process.

Pensions & Employment Chambers are among the leading sets in respect of occupational pension schemes and trusts. Nigel Inglis-Jones QC is the author of a leading pensions textbook and is recognised as one of the experts in this field of law. Several of the leading juniors in this field are members of chambers. The pension team has been involved in all the recent major cases, including British Airways, National Grid, NPI, Merchant Navy, National Bus, Bradstock & Hoover.

Personal Injury & Clinical Negligence A large group within chambers has extensive experience in both these fields, acting on behalf of both claimants and defendants in cases covering the full spectrum of work within these specialisations, including major group actions (Cape Litigation, Nationwide Organ Retention, Corby Limb Disorders and Devon Breast Screening) and related Public Inquiry work (Bristol Royal Infirmary and Shipman; Bangladesh Arsenic Poisoning; and the Fairchild House of Lords appeal).

Professional Negligence Members of chambers specialise in most areas of professional negligence, including surveyors', actuaries', accountants' and lawyers' negligence. 35 Essex Street is also among the leading sets covering all areas in which corporations and their directors are called to account, including cases relating to corporate killing, directors' responsibilities, regulatory provisions, governance, civil liability and professional negligence.

Corporate Crime, Commercial Fraud & Criminal Negligence Chambers' considerable experience in this area of law extends to involvement in the Maxwell, Blue Arrow and Guinness fraud cases. Members of chambers are instructed in a number of large cases for the SFO. Chambers are established at the forefront of criminal negligence work, having been involved in major prosecutions arising out of the sea-borne disasters of Lyme Bay, Pescado, Maria Asumpta and Lone Signature, as well as the three recent rail crashes at Southall, Ladbroke Grove and Hatfield. In addition, chambers are involved in dozens of similar, if less high profile cases.

Childcare & Child Abuse Litigation An experienced team of barristers within chambers specialises in childcare law, acting in particular for local authorities, guardians and the Official Solicitor (now CAFCASS). It instructed in the recent case of Re: W & B and Re: W (House of Lords), which will effect substantial changes in practice required for all professionals in this field. Chambers are instructed on civil actions on behalf of children arising out of abuse sustained in care and/or inadequate educational provision.

Extradition Chambers are steadily building a reputation for successful advocacy in this specialised area of law.

Public Inquiries Increasingly, members of chambers are being instructed in major public inquiry work including the Southall and Ladbroke Grove train inquiries, the BRI Inquiry, Alder Hey Inquiry, The Organ Retention Commission and the Shipman Inquiry.

International Languages spoken include: French, German, Russian, Bengali, Hindi.

39 Essex Street (Nigel Pleming QC) — Set No.38

39 Essex Street, London, WC2R 3AT
Tel (020) 7832 1111 **Fax** (020) 7353 3978 **DX** 298 London/Chancery Lane
Email clerks@39essex.com **Website** www.39essex.com

Head of Chambers	Nigel Pleming QC
Chambers Director	Michael Meeson
Tenants	55

Members

Nigel Pleming QC (1971) (QC-1992)
Simon Goldblatt QC (1953) (QC-1972)
Edwin Glasgow QC (1969) (QC-1987)
Wyn Williams QC (1974) (QC-1992)
Richard Gray QC (1970) (QC-1993)
Richard Davies QC (1973) (QC-1994)
Richard Wilmot-Smith QC (1978) (QC-1994)
Michael Tillett QC (1965) (QC-1996)
Robert Jay QC (1981) (QC-1998)
Vincent Nelson QC (1980) (QC-2001)
David Melville QC (1975) (QC-2002)
Richard Clayton QC (1977) (QC-2002)
Neil Block QC (1980) (QC-2002)
Alison Foster QC (1984) (QC-2002)

Stuart Catchpole QC (1987) (QC-2002)
Alan Cooper (1969)
Charles Brown (1976)
Roderick Noble (1977)
John Pugh-Smith (1977)
Colin McCaul (1978)
Geoffrey Brown (1981)
Christian Du Cann (1982)
Charles Cory-Wright (1984)
Jonathan Bellamy (1986)
David Bradly (1987)
Charles Manzoni (1988)
Steven Kovats (1989)
Jeremy Morgan (1989)
Eleanor Grey (1990)
Fenella Morris (1990)
Bernard Doherty (1990)
Sean Wilken (1991)
Jennifer Richards (1991)
Rohan Pershad (1991)
Daniel Oudkerk (1992)
Bruce Brodie (1993)

Richard Harwood (1993)
Matthew Seligman (1994)
Adam Robb (1995)
Gordon Nardell (1995)
Martin Edwards (1995)
Sam Grodzinski (1996)
Parishil Patel (1996)
Kristina Stern (1996)
Christiaan Zwart (1997)
Judith Ayling (1998)
Kate Grange (1998)
Caroline Truscott (1998)
Vikram Sachdeva (1998)
Colin Thomann (1999)
Nicola Greaney (1999)
Katie Scott (1999)
Stephen Tromans (1999)
Jess Connors (2000)
Ashwin Maini (2001)
Archibald Findlay (1967) (SC (South Africa) – 1981) *
Sharise Weiner (1978) (SC (South Africa) – 1998) *

39 ESSEX STREET
LONDON WC2R 3AT

* Door Tenant

Continued overleaf

BAR A-Z

The Chambers 39 Essex Street is a long established barristers' set whose members offer substantial expertise in almost every aspect of commercial, public and common law. Members of chambers have wide experience of all courts and tribunals including the House of Lords, Privy Council, Court of Appeal, the European Court of Human Rights and the European Court of Justice and Mental Health, Employment and VAT Tribunals. Members have participated in many significant investigations before Parliamentary Select Committees and several members are on the Treasury Panels of Counsel instructed on behalf of the Crown. Members also undertake pro bono work for public interest organisations.

Work Undertaken Chambers' particular expertise lies in the fields of commercial law, administrative and public law, employment, personal injury and clinical negligence, construction and engineering, entertainment and sports law and European law. Within this broad range, members of chambers have developed specialisms in the following areas:

Personal Injury & Clinical Negligence The full range of personal injury litigation, especially sea, air and crowd disasters, group actions, industrial disease, sports injuries, injuries of maximum severity, pharmaceuticals, product liability and high profile and complex matters, ranging from sensitive consent-to-treatment cases to those involving serious disability and death.

Construction & Engineering All categories of construction and engineering litigation and related claims, including professional negligence and indemnity work; from major international ventures to smaller domestic contracts, acting for employers, contractors, subcontractors and professional advisors. Members act as advocates, mediators and arbitrators in the United Kingdom, the EU and worldwide.

Commercial Insurance and reinsurance, commodities and derivatives, funding disputes, banking, mergers and acquisitions, sale and carriage of goods, insolvency, company law, financial services law, professional negligence and professional indemnity work for auditors and legal advisors and international commercial arbitration.

Entertainment & Sports Law All entertainment and media-related work including performers' contracts, passing-off, breach of confidence, film and management agreements and broadcasting regulation. Sports-related work includes public liability of sports clubs for acts of their players, employer's liability, disciplinary tribunals, disputes concerning control of clubs, transfer fee disputes, EU free movement and other employment issues.

Employment All aspects of employment work for employers and employees, local authorities and central government. Particular emphasis is on public law related work, discrimination, restrictive covenants, wrongful dismissal and breach of fiduciary duties.

Administrative & Public Law All aspects of judicial review and public law, including civil liberties and human rights, commercial and environmental law, planning, education, local authorities, health trusts, mental health, community care, housing and housing associations, immigration, VAT and Customs & Excise.

European Law All areas of EU law before domestic and EU courts, including competition, discrimination and equality law, public procurement, free movement, state aids and milk quotas.

Human Rights 39 Essex Street has a long established commitment to human rights cases. Members of chambers regularly appear in domestic Human Rights Act cases and also have extensive experience as advocates before the European Court of Human Rights and in courts overseas. Members have appeared in leading cases with a human rights dimension in diverse fields including civil liberties, commercial law, health care, housing, immigration, local government, mental health and community care, planning, police and prisoners. Members of chambers regularly write and lecture on human rights topics.

Public Inquiries Members of chambers have been instructed in most of the major public inquiries over the past 10 years, including Hillsborough, BSE, the King's Cross fire and most recently, the Bristol Royal Infirmary Inquiry and the Saville Inquiry.

Publications Numerous, including *The Law of Human Rights* (Clayton); *The Law of Entertainment and Broadcasting* (Nelson); *Waiver, Variation and Estoppel* (Wilken).

International Languages spoken include French, German, Italian, Spanish and Gujarati. Many members of chambers also act as advocates in overseas jurisdictions including Hong Kong, Singapore, India, Malaysia, Australia, Bermuda and the USA.

Recruitment The set is a member of OLPAS. It offers up to three pupillages each year, with scholarship awards of £25,000. The decision as to offers of pupillage depends in particular upon: academic record (a first or upper second class degree is usually required), performance at interview, performance in any mini-pupillages and references.

---

46 Essex Street (Geoffrey Hawker)
46 Essex Street, London, WC2R 3GH **Tel** (020) 7583 8899 **Fax** (020) 7583 8800
DX: 1014 London/Chancery Lane

Set No.39

■ BAR A-Z

Falcon Chambers (Jonathan Gaunt QC & Kim Lewison QC) — Set No.40

Falcon Court, London, EC4Y 1AA
Tel (020) 7353 2484   **Fax** (020) 7353 1261   **DX** 408
Email clerks@falcon-chambers.com   **Website** www.falcon-chambers.com

Head of Chambers	Jonathan Gaunt QC
	Kim Lewison QC
Chambers Director	Edith A Robertson
Senior Clerk	Steven Francis
Tenants	31

Members

Derek Wood QC (1964) (QC-1978) MA, BCL
Jonathan Gaunt QC (1972) (QC-1991) BA
Kim Lewison QC (1975) (QC-1991) MA
Paul Morgan QC (1975) (QC-1992) MA
Kirk Reynolds QC (1974) (QC-1993) MA
Jonathan Brock QC (1977) (QC-1997) MA
Nicholas Dowding QC (1979) (QC-1997) MA
Edwin Prince (1955) BA

Paul de la Piquerie (1966) LLB
Joanne R Moss (1976) MA LLM (EC Law)
Anthony Radevsky (1978) LLB
Edward Cole (1980) MA
Wayne Clark (1982) LLB, BCL
Guy Fetherstonhaugh (1983) BSc
Martin Rodger (1986) BA
Timothy Fancourt (1987) MA
Barry Denyer-Green (1972) LLM, PhD
Stephen Jourdan (1989) MA
Gary Cowen (1990) LLB
Jonathan Small (1990) BA

Janet Bignell (1992) MA, BCL
Martin Dray (1992) LLB
Caroline Shea (1994) MA
Anthony Tanney (1994) BA M. Jur
Catherine Taskis (1995) BA BCL
Emily Windsor (1995) BA DSU (EC Law)
Mark Sefton (1996) MA
Siri Cope (1997) BSc
Edward Peters (1998) BA
Adam Rosenthal (1999) BA
Charles Harpum (1976) MA

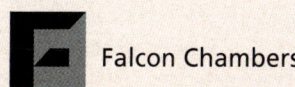 Falcon Chambers

The Chambers A set of 31 barristers, including seven QCs, all of whom specialise in litigation and property law. Members are the authors or editors of leading textbooks such as Woodfall, Megarry & Wade's *Law of Real Property*, Gale, Muir Watt and Moss, Fisher & Lightwood's *Law of Mortgage*, Bernstein and Reynolds and Hague. Chambers enjoy strong links with the RICS and the CIArb, and organise the annual Blundell Lectures. All are members of the Chancery Bar Association, the Property Bar Association and LCLCBA.

Work Undertaken Falcon Chambers is generally recognised as the leading set for landlord and tenant (commercial, residential and agricultural); property litigation, including all aspects of general property law (easements, restrictive covenants, mortgages, options); property-related areas, such as insolvency and solicitors' and surveyors' professional negligence. Chambers have particular expertise in contract and arbitration law. Some members specialise in agricultural production controls, competition law, compulsory purchase, planning and building disputes. Litigation is the core of chambers' work, but much advisory and drafting work is also carried out. Direct Professional Access is welcomed, and members often sit as arbitrators, experts and legal assessors.

Farrar's Building (John Leighton Williams QC) — Set No.41

Farrar's Building, Temple, London, EC4Y 7BD
Tel (020) 7583 9241   **Fax** (020) 7583 0090   **DX** 406
Email chambers@farrarsbuilding.co.uk   **Website** www.farrarsbuilding.co.uk

Head of Chambers	John Leighton Williams QC
Senior Clerk/Practice Manager	Alan Kilbey
Chambers Manager	Janet Eades
Tenants	33

Members

John Leighton Williams QC (1964) (QC-1986) +
Gerard Elias QC (1968) (QC-1984) +
Douglas Day QC (1967) (QC-1989) +
Patrick Harrington QC (1973) (QC-1993) +
Leighton Davies QC (1975) (QC-1994) +
Alan Jeffreys QC (1970) (QC-1996) +
William Norris QC (1974) (QC-1997) +
Stephen Hopkins QC (1973) (QC-2000) +

Christopher Vosper QC (1977) (QC-2000) +
Richard Nussey (1971)
Anthony Seys Llewellyn (1972) +
Ian Ridd (1975)
Gregory Treverton-Jones QC (1977) (QC-2002) +
Tom McDermott (1980)
Gillian Keene (1980)
Simon Peter Buchanan Browne (1982)
Nigel Spencer Ley (1985)
Jonathan Watt-Pringle (1987)
Andrew Peebles (1987)
David Wicks (1989)

Georgina Middleton (1989)
Shabbir Lakha (1989)
James Todd (1990)
Helen Hobhouse (1990)
Peter Freeman (1992)
Melissa Pack (1995)
Sally Cowen (1995)
Lee Evans (1996)
Huw Davies (1998)
James Pretsell (1998)
Sarah Tozzi (1998)
Senay Rodgers (1999)
Elizabeth Connor (2000)

+ Recorder

Continued overleaf

LONDON — BAR A-Z

The Chambers Farrar's Building is a long established set of common law chambers with an excellent reputation built up over many years.

Work Undertaken Areas of practice fall under general common law but members of chambers have particular specialities in: administrative and public law; contract and commercial litigation; criminal law; defamation and media law; disciplinary tribunals; employment; environmental and agricultural law; health and safety; insurance litigation; landlord and tenant; licensing; medical law; personal injury; police actions and civil liberties; product liability; public inquiries and tribunals; professional negligence; solicitors' costs and taxation; sports law; competition law.

■ Field Court Chambers (Melanie Spencer) — Set No.42

Field Court Chambers, 2nd Floor, 3 Field Court, Grays Inn, London, WC1R 5EP
Tel (020) 7404 7474 **Fax** (020) 7404 7475 **DX** 136 (Ch.Ln.)
Email enquiries@fieldcourtchambers.com **Website** www.fieldcourtchambers.com

Head of Chambers	Melanie Spencer
Senior Clerk	Paul Mellor
Tenants	6

A civil set practising in the following areas: commercial, employment, environmental, family, immigration, landlord and tenant, local authority, personal injury and professional negligence.

■ 187 Fleet Street (Andrew Trollope QC) — Set No.43

187 Fleet Street, Temple, London, EC4A 2AT
Tel (020) 7430 7430 **Fax** (020) 7430 7431 **DX** 464
Email chambers@187fleetstreet.com **Website** www.187fleetstreet.com

Head of Chambers	Andrew Trollope QC
Senior Clerk	John Pyne
Tenants	51

Members

Andrew Trollope QC (1971) (QC-1991)
Paul Purnell QC (1962) (QC-1982)
Roger Backhouse QC (1965) (QC-1984)
Michael Borrelli QC (1977) (QC-2000)
Philip King QC (1974) (QC-2002)
Nicholas Gardiner (1967)
Graham Arran (1969)
Tony Docking (1969)
Colin Dines (1970)
Jonathan Davies (1971)
Brian Argyle (1972)
Andrew Campbell (1972)
Gopal Hooper (1973)
Brian Reece (1974)
Phillip Matthews (1974)

John Plumstead (1975)
Bernard Eaton (1978)
Noel Lucas (1979)
Kaly Kaul (1983)
Christopher Amor (1984)
Simon Mayo (1985)
Mark Rainsford (1985)
Andrew Marshall (1986)
Richard Butcher (1985)
Gary Summers (1985)
James Lachkovic (1987)
Harry Bowyer (1989)
Anthony Korda (1988)
Andrew Newton (1989)
Avirup Chaudhuri (1990)
Rachel Bright (1991)
Richard Beynon (1990)
Mark Graffius (1990)

Nicholas Barraclough (1990)
Kirsty Brimelow (1991)
Philomena Murphy (1992)
Natasha Wong (1993)
Robert Jones (1993)
Sarah Clarke (1994)
Warwick Aleeson (1994)
Gideon Cammerman (1996)
Sharon Leene (1996)
Tara McCarthy (1997)
John Madden (1997)
Katharine Blackburn (1998)
Timothy Grey (1999)
Leon Kazakos (1999)
Emma Kurzner (1999)
James Rouse (2000)
Fiona Rutherford (2000)
Neelam Sharma (2000)

BSI No: FS55575

The Chambers Chambers were established in December 1976 by Mr Ronald Grey QC, and since then have flourished, growing both in size and in the quality and range of work undertaken. Members practise mainly in London, the South East and the Home Counties, but have accepted cases all over the country. Most members belong to the Criminal Bar Association, and several serve on various committees connected with criminal law. In addition, two members are on the Immigration Panel for the Home Office. 10 members are recorders. One member is standing counsel to HM Customs & Excise. At the beginning of 2002 chambers relocated from 1 Middle Temple Lane to new, completely refurbished premises at 187 Fleet Street, and Colin Dines who had been head and joint head for 16 years, took the opportunity to step down in favour of his joint head Andrew Trollope QC. Outside office hours, the senior clerk can be contacted on: mobile (07976) 281902.

Work Undertaken

Criminal For both prosecution and defence, with an increasing amount of serious white-collar crime. Members have recently acted in major VAT, company and mortgage fraud cases. The whole range of crime is handled from war crimes, murder, drugs and sexual offences to motoring offences and juvenile crime.
Additional Areas Courts martial; employment law; immigration, for applicants and the government; licensing; extradition.

International Bengali, French and German are spoken.

Recruitment Tenancy and pupillage applications to the appropriate committee. Chambers usually have between seven and 10 pupils and applications are welcome at any time. Pupillage awards and mini-pupillages are available at chambers' discretion.

Fountain Court (Anthony Boswood QC) Set No.44

Fountain Court, Temple, London, EC4Y 9DH
Tel (020) 7583 3335 **Fax** (020) 7353 0329 **DX** LDE 5
Email chambers@fountaincourt.co.uk **Website** www.fountaincourt.co.uk

Head of Chambers	Anthony Boswood QC
Senior Clerks	Mark Watson
	Michael Couling
Chambers Administrator	Prue Woodbridge
Tenants	54

Members

Conrad Dehn QC (1952) (QC-1968)
Christopher Bathurst QC (1959) (QC-1978)
Anthony Boswood QC (1970) (QC-1986)
Lord Goldsmith QC (1972) (QC-1987) †
Michael Lerego QC (1972) (QC-1995)
Michael Brindle QC (1975) (QC-1992)
Michael Crane QC (1975) (QC-1994)
Nicholas Underhill QC (1976) (QC-1992)
Nicholas Stadlen QC (1976) (QC-1991)
David Railton QC (1979) (QC-1996)
Timothy Dutton QC (1979) (QC-1998)
Brian Doctor QC (1991) (QC-1999)
Stephen Moriarty QC (1986) (QC-1999)

Stephen Rubin QC (1977) (QC-2000)
Michael McLaren QC (1981) (QC-2002)
Philip Brook Smith QC (1982) (QC-2002)
Raymond Cox QC (1982) (QC-2002)
David Waksman QC (1982) (QC-2002)
Guy Philipps QC (1986) (QC-2002)
Timothy Wormington (1977)
Anthony Martino (1982)
Thomas Keith (1983)
Craig Orr (1986)
Michael Green (1987)
Timothy Howe (1987)
Bankim Thanki (1988)
Patricia Robertson (1988)
Jeffrey Chapman (1989)
Bridget Lucas (1989)
Brian Napier (1990)
Derrick Dale (1990)

Akhil Shah (1990)
Marcus Smith (1991)
Paul Gott (1991)
Veronique Buehrlen (1991)
Andrew Mitchell (1992)
Richard Handyside (1993)
John Taylor (1993)
Richard Coleman (1994)
Adam Tolley (1994)
Louise Merrett (1995)
Philippa Hamilton (1996)
Paul Sinclair (1997)
Patrick Goodall (1998)
Deepak Nambisan (1998)
Giles Wheeler (1998)
Henry King (1998)
Rosalind Phelps (1998)
Edward Levey (1999)
Natalie Stopps (2000)
James Cutress (2000)
Nik Yeo (2000)
Adam Zellick (2000)
Chloe Carpenter (2001)

Neil Andrews (1981) (Fellow, Clare College, Cambridge) *; Peter Carter QC (1947) (QC-1990) (Emeritus Fellow, Wadham College, Oxford) *†; Gladys Li (SC) (Resides in Hong Kong) *; Peter Scott QC (1960) (QC-1978) (Accepts appointments through chambers as an arbitrator) *†; Izzet Sinan (Resident in Brussels) *; Andrew Burrows (Norton Rose Professor, Commercial and Financial Law, Oxford) *; William Swadling (Fellow and Tutor in law at Brasenose College, Oxford and Lecturer at University of Oxford) ‡; Jane Stapleton (Professor of Law at the Australian National University, Canberra) ‡.
*Door Tenant † Non- practising ‡Academic Associate

The Chambers Fountain Court is a leading commercial set of chambers with 54 barristers, of whom 19 are silks. The core of its work is commercial, and members advise and represent clients over the entire range of business problems. The set offers a high quality and efficient service which meets the practical requirements of commercial clients. Members of chambers appear in courts and tribunals of all levels from complex high-value commercial disputes to more straightforward County Court and tribunal work. The size of chambers, and the range of experience of its members, enables Fountain Court to assemble balanced teams of counsel to suit the requirements of individual cases. Prominent former members include Lord Bingham of Cornhill and many other current and former Lords of Appeal and High Court Judges. Hours: 8.00am to 9.00pm Monday to Friday and from 9.00am to 1.00pm on Saturdays. After hours (0786) 780 3335.

Work Undertaken Members of Fountain Court are recognised leaders in the fields of commercial litigation, banking, financial services, insurance and reinsurance, professional negligence, aviation and employment. Fountain Court also retains a strong 'generalist' tradition and is notable for the wide range of other civil work

Continued overleaf

BAR A-Z

undertaken, including oil and gas, entertainment and media, intellectual property, company, insolvency, product liability, human rights, administrative, civil fraud, sports, international trade, shipping and telecommunications law. Several members of chambers have experience of sitting as arbitrators in commercial and other disputes, and of mediation and alternative dispute resolution.

Publications Many members of chambers have written or contributed to legal textbooks and other articles. *Carriage By Air*, an aviation textbook by a number of members of chambers, was published by Butterworths in 2001. A second edition of *The Law of Bank Payments* by Michael Brindle QC and Raymond Cox QC, with contributions by other members of Chambers, was published in 1999. Brian Napier is an editor of *Harvey on Employment and Industrial Relations Law* and has published widely on employment law. Chambers provides the editorial team under Stephen Moriarty QC and Raymond Cox QC as general editors of the *Commercial Court Procedure* published by Sweet & Maxwell as a part of the White Book series. Many members of chambers have contributed to the 14th edition of *Bullen & Leake & Jacob's Precedents of Pleadings* published in 2001.

International There are members of chambers who are fluent in Afrikaans, French, German, Italian and Modern Hebrew; others have a working knowledge of Spanish and Greek. Members regularly work abroad, not only in international arbitrations but also as advocates in overseas jurisdictions, including Hong Kong and Singapore and in the European Court of Justice. Members of chambers are also members of the bars of California, New York and Gibraltar and of the Faculty of Advocates in Scotland.

Furnival Chambers (Andrew Mitchell QC) — Set No.45

32 Furnival Street, London, EC4A 1JQ
Tel (020) 7405 3232   **Fax** (020) 7405 3322   **DX** 72
Email clerks@furnivallaw.co.uk   **Website** www.furnivallaw.co.uk

Head of Chambers	Andrew Mitchell QC
Clerks	John Gutteridge
	Stephen Ball
Tenants	54

Members

Andrew Mitchell QC (1976) (QC-1998)
Oliver Blunt QC (1974) (QC-1994)
Peter Collier QC (1970) (QC-1992)
Stephen Leslie QC (1971) (QC-1993)
Sally O'Neill QC (1976) (QC-1997)
Michel G A Massih QC (1979) (QC-1999)
Kim Hollis QC (1979) (QC-2002)
Hugh Griffiths (1972)
Christopher Baur (1972)
Gino Connor (1974)
Lisa Matthews (1974)
Michael Latham (1975)
Stephen Holt (1978)
Vincent Coughlin (1980)
Francis Sheridan (1980)
Paul Mytton (1982)
Richard Whittam (1983)

Nicola Merrick (1983)
Jon Swain (1983)
Sherrie Caddle (1983)
Roy Headlam (1983)
John Carmichael (1984)
Kennedy Talbot (1984)
David Brock (1984)
Carolyn Blore (1985)
Charles Sherrard (1986)
Allison Hunter (1986)
Philip Romans (1982)
Kathryn Hirst (1986)
Linda Saunt (1986)
Barry Gregory (1987)
Patricia Lees (1988)
Nicolas Gerasimidis (1988)
Stephen Earnshaw (1990)
Tim Forster (1990)
Tanya Woolls (1991)
Sandip Patel (1991)
Andrew Henley (1992)
Alexia Power (1992)
Fiona Henderson (1993)

Ivan Pearce (1994)
Gerard McEvilly (1994)
John Kearney (1994)
Julian Winship (1995)
Giles Cockings (1996)
Christopher Convey (1994)
Mark Summers (1996)
Laban Leake (1996)
Fer Chinner (1998)
Fiona Jackson (1998)
Sally Fudge (1998)
Andrew Mazibrada (1999)
Gary Venturi (1996)
Caroline Haughey (1999)
Graham Henson (1976) *
Linda Candler (1977) *
Elizabeth Coughlin (1989) *
Simon Reevell (1990) *
Leon de Costa (1992) *
Lefi Panayioti (1992) *
Mark Giuliani (1993) *
Kate Mulkerrins (1998) *

* Door Tenant

The Chambers A set of specialist criminal practitioners, housed in fully computerised modern offices with dedicated conference facilities and a comprehensively equipped library.

Work Undertaken

Criminal Law Service Furnival Chambers was formed in 1985 as a specialist criminal set and has continued to provide both a comprehensive and specialist criminal law service to professional and lay clients. The set comprises leading and junior counsel of considerable and varied experience, enabling them to deal expertly with the entire range of criminal cases from the most serious and complicated cases down to the relatively straightforward. There is particular expertise throughout chambers in white collar fraud and cases involving very serious violence and abuse. Chambers are well placed to deal competently with the rapidly increasing use of technology to both investigate cases and present the evidence in court. Chambers are particularly concerned to ensure that high standards are maintained by their pupils and junior tenants and have their own advocacy training scheme.

Asset Forfeiture & Money Laundering Furnival Chambers has a specialist team which deals with confiscation, asset forfeiture and money laundering. Members of the team have appeared in most of the leading cases in the High Court, Court of Appeal and House of Lords as well as both advising and appearing in cases in Trinidad, the Turks and Caicos Islands and Cayman Islands and advising in Pakistan and Antigua.

International French, German, Arabic, Hindi, Russian and Spanish are spoken.

Recruitment Furnival Chambers takes four 12 month pupillages, terminable at the end of the first six months by either chambers or the pupil. Selection is made from OLPAS applications by two-stage interviews. Financial assistance is available for the first six months. Contact chambers for further detail.

One Garden Court Family Law Chambers (Eleanor F Platt QC & Alison Ball QC) — Set No.46

One Garden Court, Temple, London, EC4Y 9BJ
Tel (020) 7797 7900 **Fax** (020) 7797 7929 **DX** 1034 (Ch.Ln.)
Email clerks@onegardencourt.co.uk **Website** www.onegardencourt.co.uk

Head of Chambers	Eleanor F Platt QC
	Alison Ball QC
Chief Executive	Claire Wilford-Smith
Senior Clerk	Howard Rayner
First Junior Clerk	Chris Ferrison
Fees Clerk	Dennis Davies
Tenants	46

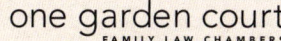

Members

Eleanor F Platt QC (1960) (QC-1982)
Alison Ball QC (1972) (QC-1995)
Ian Peddie QC (1971) (QC-1992)
Jane Crowley QC (1976) (QC-1998) †
Caroline Willbourne (1970)
Bruce Coleman (1972)
Peter Nathan (1973)
Suzanne H Shenton (1973)
Elizabeth Szwed (1974)
Peter Horrocks (1977)
Martin O'Dwyer (1978)
Ann Marie Wicherek (1978)
Richard Scarratt (1979)

Judith Rowe (1979)
Kay Halkyard (1980)
Janet Bazley (1980)
Susan Shackleford (1980)
Kay Firth-Butterfield (1980)
Susannah Walker (1985)
Stephen Cobb (1985)
John Stocker (1985)
Charles Geekie (1985)
Gary Crawley (1988)
Gillian Cleave (1988)
Sarah Morgan (1988)
Andrew Bagchi (1989)
Michael Liebrecht (1989)
David Burles (1985)
Malcolm Chisholm (1989)
Ariff Rozhan (1990)

Catherine Jenkins (1990)
Claire Heppenstall (1990)
Ian Robbins (1991)
Doushka Krish (1991)
Andrew Norton (1992)
Emma Hudson (1995)
Gillian C Downham (1993)
Susan Budaly (1994)
Sally Stone (1994)
Alexander Chandler (1995)
Nicola Fox (1996)
Sassa-Ann Amaouche (1996)
Marcus Lazarides (1999)
Anthony Geadah (2000)
Sharon Segal (2000)
Ellen Saunders (2000)

† Practises mainly from 30 Park Place, Cardiff

The Chambers One Garden Court is the largest chambers where all members specialise in family law. Work includes ancillary relief, local authorities, human rights, child abduction, care and adoption and mediation.

LONDON — BAR A-Z

Two Garden Court (Owen Davies QC & Courtenay Griffiths QC)   Set No.47

1st Floor, 2 Garden Court, Temple, London, EC4Y 9BL
Tel (020) 7353 1633 **Fax** (020) 7353 4621 **DX** 34 Chancery Lane
Email barristers@2gardenct.law.co.uk **Website** www.2gardenct.law.co.uk

Head of Chambers	Owen Davies QC
	Courtenay Griffiths QC
Senior Clerk	Colin Cook
Clerks	Lesley Perrott
	Bob Archer
	Amanda Boylen
	Caroline Mitchell
	Emma McCreight
	Keith Poynter
	Joseph Fisher
	Matthew Archer
	Matthew Butchard
Tenants	74

Members

Owen Davies QC (1973) (QC-1999)
Courtenay Griffiths QC (1980) (QC-1998)
Ian Macdonald QC (1963) (QC-1988)
Laurie Fransman QC (1979) (QC-2000)
Jan Luba QC (1980) (QC-2000)
David Watkinson (1972)
Marguerite Russell (1972)
Michael House (1972)
Terry Munyard (1972)
Mark George (1976)
Frances Webber (1978)
Henry Blaxland QC (1978) (QC-2002)
Icah Peart QC (1978) (QC-2002)
Lalith De Kauwe (1978)
Kathryn Cronin (1980)
Anne Jessup (1981)
Celia Graves (1981)
Markanza Cudby (1983)
Michael Hall (1983)
Ravinder Rahal (1983)
Nerida Harford-Bell (1984)
Stephen Cottle (1984)
James Scobie (1984)
Beatrice Prevatt (1985)
Debra Gold (1985)
Peter Jorro (1986)
Mary McKeone (1986)
Rick Scannell (1986)
Elizabeth Veats (1986)
Stephen Knafler (1993)
Dexter Dias (1988)
Adrian Eissa (1988)
Leslie Thomas (1988)
Judy Khan (1989)
Alexander Taylor-Camara (1989)
Alison Grief (1990)
Bethan Harris (1990)
Colin Hutchinson (1990)
Liz Davies (1994)
Maggie Jones (1990)
Michael Baker (1990)
Joanne Harris (1991)
Jon Holbrook (1991)
Stephanie Harrison (1991)
Malek Wan Daud (1991)
Sonali Naik (1991)
Nadine Finch (1991)
Catrin Lewis (1991)
Stephen Simblet (1991)
Alastair Edie (1992)
Helen Curtis (1992)
Peter Weatherby (1992)
Valerie Easty (1992)
Julia Krish (1992)
Rajiv Menon (1993)
Robert Littlewood (1993)
Kieran Vaughan (1993)
Rajeev Thacker (1993)
David Jones (1994)
Duran Seddon (1994)
Keir Monteith (1994)
Sam Momtaz (1995)
Shereener Browne (1996)
Judith Trustman (1996)
Anya Lewis (1997)
Maya Sikand (1997)
Patrick Lewis (1997)
Louise Hooper (1997)
Adrian Marshall Williams (1998)
Josephene Uzuegbunam (1998)
Rachael Rowley-Fox (1998)
Emma Favata (1999)
Ronan Toal (1999)
Catherine O'Donnell (2000)

The Chambers The set's work reflects the progressive aspirations it has to develop the law to make a difference to people's lives and enhance the causes of social justice and human rights for which the set has always stood. Chambers' historical commitment to fostering a multidisciplinary set continues to produce cases on the cutting edge of the 'law'. Chambers' motto continues to be 'Do Right, Fear No-one'.

Work Undertaken Criminal; family; housing; immigration; public law and judicial review; extradition; actions against the police; discrimination and employment; environmental law; community care; mental health; personal injury; education.

Goldsmith Building (Christopher Llewellyn-Jones QC)   Set No.48

Goldsmith Building, Temple, London, EC4Y 7BL **Tel** (020) 7353 7881 **Fax** (020) 7353 5319 **DX** 435

■ BAR A-Z

LONDON

Gough Square Chambers (Fred Philpott) — Set No.49

6-7 Gough Square, London, EC4A 3DE
Tel (020) 7353 0924 **Fax** (020) 7353 2221 **DX** 476
Email gsc@goughsq.co.uk **Website** www.goughsq.co.uk

Head of Chambers	Fred Philpott
Senior Clerk	Bob Weekes
Practice Manager	Richard Bayliss
Chambers Administrator	Elizabeth Owen-Ward
Tenants	15

Members

Fred Philpott (1974)
Lord Goodhart QC (1957) (QC-1979)
Peter Sayer (1975)
Claire Andrews (1979)
William Hibbert (1979)
Josephine Hayes (1980)
Barry Stancombe (1983)
Jonathan Goulding (1984)
Stephen Neville (1986)
Julia Smith (1988)
Julian Gun Cuninghame (1989)
Anthony Vines (1993)
Iain MacDonald (1996)
Sandra McCalla (1999)
Simon Popplewell (2000)

The Chambers Gough Square Chambers is a commercial set with a particular specialisation in both the civil and criminal aspects of consumer law. Chambers aims to provide an efficient, friendly and flexible service at competitive rates. Outside normal working hours, the Senior Clerk can be contacted on (07860) 219162.

Work Undertaken

Consumer Law Consumer credit (agreements, licensing and advertising); trade descriptions and trademarks; food safety; pricing; weights and measures; consumer contracts; mortgages; trading schemes; timeshare; sale and supply contracts; product safety; package travel. Chambers are instructed in this specialist area by in-house lawyers and solicitors acting for high street lenders, manufacturers, food producers, distributors and retailers. Members of chambers also prosecute on behalf of the consumer protection departments of local authorities.

Business & Commercial Law Banking; secured lending; pension schemes; company and partnership; insolvency; employment; commercial contracts; professional negligence; taxation; criminal and civil fraud.

Publications Chambers publish a free quarterly *Trading Law Bulletin* which charts the recent developments in this area of law. Please contact the senior clerk to join the mailing list.

9 Gough Square (John Foy QC) — Set No.50

9 Gough Square, London, EC4A 3DG
Tel (020) 7832 0500 **Fax** (020) 7353 1344 **DX** 439
Email clerks@9goughsq.co.uk **Website** www.9goughsq.co.uk

Head of Chambers	John Foy QC
Chief Executive	Joanna Poulton MBA LLB
Tenants	50

Members

John Foy QC (1969) (QC-1998) +
Gary Burrell QC (1977) (QC-1996) Deputy High Ct Judge +
Andrew Baillie QC (1970) (QC-2001) +
Giles Eyre (1974)
Michael Joyce (1976)
Trevor Davies (1978)
Frederick Ferguson (1978)
Grahame Aldous (1979) +
Philip I Henry (1979)
Duncan Macleod (1980)
Christopher Wilson (1980)
Graham Robinson (1981)
Nicolas Hillier (1982)
Roger Hiorns (1983)
Simon Carr (1984)

Gaurang Naik (1985)
Andrew Ritchie (1985)
Vincent Williams (1985)
Martin Hurst (1985)
Jacob Levy (1986)
Jonathan Loades (1986)
Alexander Verdan (1987)
Edwin Buckett (1988)
James Shaw (1988)
Susan Baldock (1988)
Mark Whalan (1988)
Rosina Cottage (1988)
Leslie Keegan (1989)
Sally Bradley (1989)
Susan Belgrave (1989)
Stephen Glynn (1990)
Philip Jones (1990)
Clare Padley (1991)

John Tughan (1991)
Jeremy Crowther (1991)
Aileen Downey (1991)
Laura Begley (1993)
Adrian Maxwell (1993)
Christopher Stephenson (1994)
Daniel Lawson (1994)
Rajeev Shetty (1996)
Tara Vindis (1996)
Laura Elfield (1996)
Tom Little (1997)
Perrin Gibbons (1998)
Busola Johnson (1998)
Oliver Jones (1998)
Will Noble (2000)
Cleo Perry (2000)
Shahram Sharghy (2000)

+ Recorder

Continued overleaf

BAR A-Z

The Chambers A well established common law set specialising in personal injury; clinical and professional negligence; serious fraud; crime; family; employment; landlord and tenant; civil actions against the police. Chambers pride themselves on their friendly yet commercial approach which they believe enhances their ability to provide realistic advice to their clients. Focused around specialist teams, Chambers draws upon its considerable depth of knowledge and expertise through regular team meetings. Facilities are modern and up to date including disabled facilities, large dedicated conference rooms and full computerisation. They are professionally managed by a qualified Chief Executive who is happy to discuss any aspect of their service and in particular to recommend suitable counsel. A brochure is available on request or visit the website at www.9goughsq.co.uk

Work Undertaken

Personal Injury Representing either claimants or defendants, chambers can offer experts on complex multi-party actions; industrial disease; RSI; deafness; lifting; marine accidents; PTSD; RTA; accidents at work. Special payment terms are negotiable for union or insurance-backed claims. All members of chambers have agreed to accept conditional fee work and where appropriate single agreements covering individual firms can be negotiated.

Clinical & Professional Negligence Chambers can offer experts who are sensitive to the issues in these cases, while remaining tenacious advocates and negotiators. Areas of experience, for both claimants and defendants, in clinical negligence includes brain injuries; birth defects; failed sterilisations; surgical and non-surgical maltreatment. Members of chambers' professional negligence team regularly advise on, and appear in, cases involving all aspects of professional negligence, but particularly actions involving solicitors, accountants, insurance brokers and surveyors.

Serious Fraud Chambers have some of the country's leading fraud practitioners. Members of chambers regularly prosecute for the SFO, the CPS and other regulatory bodies. They have also defended some of the most complex fraud cases and can provide experts in all areas of fraud including all aspects of financial crime such as money laundering and confiscation of assets.

General Crime The crime team has established a reputation for both prosecuting and defending high profile crime. Members of chambers regularly appear in the major London Crown Courts as well as the Crown Courts throughout the UK.

Family Chambers' specialist family team undertake a full range of family law work but is particularly known for its experience in care proceedings, adoption, residence and contact applications and ancillary relief. Chambers have also represented parties at major Public Inquiries.

Civil Actions Against the Police Chambers have extensive experience of appearing in these difficult 'hybrid' cases. Clients include police constabularies throughout the UK as well as individuals seeking personal redress.

Landlord & Tenant Chambers provide advice and representation on all aspects of commercial or residential disputes and are happy to act for either landlords or tenants. Chambers edit the Sweet & Maxwell Landlord and Tenant Law Reports.

Employment The employment group is able to provide advice and representation both before and once litigation has commenced. Members of chambers regularly undertake cases involving claims for sexual, race and disability discrimination, equal pay, restraint of trade, TUPE, national minimum wage, unfair dismissal and redundancy. The group can provide expert advice swiftly on the telephone to minimise unnecessary litigation.

2 Gray's Inn Square Chambers (Jane Rayson) — Set No.51

2 Gray's Inn Square, London, WC1R 5AA
Tel (020) 7440 8450 **Fax** (020) 7440 8452 **DX** 43 London Chancery Lane
Email clerks@2gis.co.uk **Website** www.2gis.co.uk

Head of Chambers	Jane Rayson
Senior Clerk	Perry Allen
First Junior Clerk	Sue Reding
Senior Junior Clerk	Julie Kempston
Tenants	35

Members

Jane Rayson (1982)
Peter Leighton (1966)
Keith Knight (1969)
Edward Cross (1975)
John Parker (1975)
Richard Robinson (1977)
Peter Fortune (1978)
Christopher McConnell (1979)
David Hughes (1980)
Nergis-Anne Matthew (1981) †
Milan Dulovic (1982)
Jacqueline Marks (1984)

Gabrielle Jan Posner (1984)
John Church (1984)
Fawzia King (1985)
Francis Collaco Moraes (1985)
Surinder Bhakar (1986)
Sorrel Dixon (1987)
Terence Woods (1989)
James Holmes-Milner (1989)
Myles Watkins (1990) †
Christopher Rice (1991)
Chima Umezuruike (1991)
Delyth Evans (1991)

Christopher Wagstaffe (1992)
Henry Drayton (1993)
Daniel Barnett (1993)
Neelima Mehendale (1993)
Paul Hepher (1994)
Philip McCormack (1994)
Tony Badenoch (1996)
Piers Martin (1997)
Elizabeth Conaghan (1999)
Justin Slater (1999)
Philip Thompson (2000)

† Associate Member

The Chambers Chambers provide an efficient service in all areas of common law practice. Specialisation is achieved through the use of practice groups, which enable members to pool their specialist knowledge and expertise. Comprehensive details of chambers' fee structures are available from the Senior Clerk. Chambers also operate a Law Society accredited seminar programme offering CPD credit.

Work Undertaken

Family Members' practices encompass all areas of family law. Matters covered include residence and contact cases, care proceedings, adoption, wardship and child abduction (in public law children proceedings, members act for local authorities, parents and children's guardians). Members undertake all aspects of matrimonial and related proceedings, including ancillary relief and other property and financial disputes and disputes between co-habitants.

Criminal Members practise in all areas of crime, receiving instructions on behalf of the defence. Members have particular experience in areas of fraud, child abuse, drug trafficking, sexual offences, public order, licensing and actions against the police.

Personal Injury & Clinical Negligence Members act for individuals, trade unions and insurance company clients, for both claimant and defendant, in claims arising from accidents at work, clinical negligence, road traffic accidents, occupiers' liability and defective products. Conditional Fee Agreements are undertaken.

Employment Chambers undertake advisory and advocacy work in Employment Tribunals, EAT, High Court and internal disciplinary hearings. Specific areas of expertise are unfair dismissal, redundancy, discrimination and the provision of advice to employers prior to the dismissal of employees and directors.

Property Chambers offer representation and advice on all property matters including public and private sector housing, business tenancies and all aspects of landlord and tenant law, trusts, claims to possession of land, easement and mortgage disputes, conveyancing and disputes involving joint owners and co-habitants.

Contract & Commercial Areas of law covered include contract and tort, partnership disputes, professional negligence, sale of goods, agency, bills of exchange, banking, insolvency, building and engineering contracts, consumer credit, insurance, guarantee and suretyship and disqualification of directors.

Publications Gabrielle Jan Posner is author of *The Teenager's Guide to The Law* (Cavendish 1995). Jane Rayson is co-author of *How to Make Applications in the Family Proceeding Court* and Blackstone's *Guide to the Family Law Act 1996*. Jane Rayson and Gabrielle Jan Posner are contributors to the Sweet & Maxwell *Practical Research Papers* and are respectively the authors of *Defending Divorce* and *The Welfare Officer*. Daniel Barnett is the author of *Avoiding Unfair Dismissal Claims*, a guide for employers and advisors on how to dismiss employees (John Wiley 1999).

International French, Serbo-Croat, Malay and Punjabi are spoken.

Recruitment Pupillage applications through OLPAS. Mini-pupillages are available.

LONDON — BAR A-Z

2-3 Gray's Inn Square (Anthony Porten QC & Anthony Scrivener QC)   Set No.52

2-3 Gray's Inn Square, Gray's Inn, London, WC1R 5JH
Tel (020) 7242 4986   **Fax** (020) 7405 1166   **DX** 316 (Ch.Ln.)
Email chambers@2-3graysinnsquare.co.uk   **Website** www.2-3graysinnsquare.co.uk

Head of Chambers	Anthony Porten QC
	Anthony Scrivener QC
Chambers Director	Lindsay Scott
Senior Clerk	Martin Hart
Tenants	40

Members

Anthony Porten QC (1969) (QC-1988)
Anthony Scrivener QC (1958) (QC-1975)
Malcolm Spence QC (1958) (QC-1979)
Patrick Ground QC (1960) (QC-1981)
Harry Wolton QC (1969) (QC-1982)
Christopher Cochrane QC (1965) (QC-1988)
Anthony Dinkin QC (1968) (QC-1991)
Vernon Pugh QC (1969) (QC-1986)
(Nicholas) Mark Lowe QC (1972) (QC-1996)

John Haines (1967)
Geoffrey Stephenson (1971)
David Lamming (1972)
Adrian Trevelyan Thomas (1974)
Nicholas Nardecchia (1974)
Graham Stoker (1977)
David Matthias (1980)
Ian Albutt (1981)
Steven Gasztowicz (1981)
Mary Cook (1982)
Morag Ellis (1984)
James Findlay (1984)
Gerard Forlin (1984)
Katie Astaniotis (1985)
Michael Bedford (1985)
Philip Kolvin (1985)

Simon Bird (1987)
Ranjit Bhose (1989)
Jonathan Clay (1990)
Celina Colquhoun (1990)
Robin Green (1992)
Harriet Murray (1992)
Peter Miller (1993)
Thomas Cosgrove (1994)
Richard Ground (1994)
David Lintott (1995)
Jonathon Easton (1995)
Wayne Beglan (1995)
Rory Clarke (1996)
Katy Skerrett (1999)
Johanna Boyd (1999)

The Chambers Established in the late 19th century, 2-3 Gray's Inn Square is recognised as one of the leading local government sets with highly-rated expertise in nine specialist areas. Former members of chambers include Sir Edward Marshall Hall KC, Lord Birkett, Lord Chief Justice Widgery, Lord Bridge of Harwich, Mr Justice Hidden, and Mr Justice Penry-Davey. Current members of chambers include Anthony Scrivener QC, a former chairman of the Bar, and Malcolm Spence QC, the erstwhile chairman of the Planning and Environment Bar Association. Over the last 40 years, and with increasing size, chambers have widened their original common law base to develop substantial practices in administrative law, local government law and town and country planning law. They have, however, retained a strong common law practice, covering both general and large commercial disputes, and they continue to enjoy a solid criminal practice.

Work Undertaken First-class representation is provided in all the principal areas of work undertaken by chambers, and details of the specialities of each member are available on request from the senior clerk. Counsel are available at any level of experience required. The junior tenants are available at short notice for all Magistrates' Court, County Court and tribunal hearings as well as for any procedural applications. Members of chambers will work in any part of England, Wales, Scotland (planning matters only) and Ireland. Chambers' administration has been upgraded to meet the demands of a modern business environment.

Town & Country Planning, Administrative & Local Government Law Including judicial review, housing law and social security, public and local government finance, compulsory purchase, education, rating, highway and environmental law.
Common Law Including personal injuries; professional negligence including medical, accountants and solicitors; employment law, including industrial tribunal work.
Consumer Law Including sale of goods, trade descriptions, trading law, food safety and data protection.
Criminal Law Including white collar crime, serious fraud and capital cases.
Property Law Including landlord and tenant, mortgages and housing associations.

International French, German, Greek and Italian are spoken. Various members also practice or are admitted in other jurisdictions including Hong Kong, Singapore, Malaysia, Jamaica, Trinidad, the Cayman Islands, the British Virgin Islands and certain Australian jurisdictions.

Recruitment Pupils are received each year; pupillage funds are available.

BAR A-Z

3 Gray's Inn Square (Rock Tansey QC)

Set No.53

3 Gray's Inn Square, Gray's Inn, London, WC1R 5AH
Tel (020) 7520 5600 **Fax** (020) 7520 5607 **DX** 1043 (Ch.Ln.)
Email clerks@3gis.co.uk **Website** www.3gis.co.uk

Head of Chambers	Rock Tansey QC
Senior Clerk	Guy Williams
Clerks	Marc King
	Stephen Lucas
Tenants	45

Members

Rock Tansey QC (1966) (QC-1990)
John Perry QC (1975) (QC-1989)
Steven Kay QC (1977) (QC-1997)
George Carter-Stephenson QC (1975) (QC-1998)
William Taylor QC (1990) (QC-1998)
Diana Ellis QC (1978) (QC-2001)
David Hooper (1971)
Colin Allan (1971)
David Farrington (1972)
Ronald Jaffa (1974)
Brendan Keany (1974)
Jonathan Mitchell (1974)
Philip Statman (1975)
Rudi Fortson (1976)
Roger Offenbach (1978)
Chester Beyts (1978)
Charles Bott (1979)
Paul Keleher (1980)
Paul Mendelle (1981)
Penelope Barrett (1982)
Jeremy Dein (1982)
Simon Pentol (1982)
Bill Maley (1982)
Leroy Redhead (1982)
John Cooper (1983)
Colin Wells (1987)
Paul Hynes (1987)
Alison Levitt (1988)
Adrian Kayne (1989)
Jonathan Mann (1989)
Helen Valley (1990)
Arlette Piercy (1990)
Emma Akuwudike (1992)
Sylvia de Bertodano (1993)
Ali Naseem Bajwa (1993)
Harry Potter (1993)
Navjot Sidhu (1993)
Richard Furlong (1994)
Tyrone Smith (1994)
Aisling Byrnes (1994)
Nicola Howard (1995)
Sebastian Gardiner (1997)
Lindsey Rose (1996)
Gillian Higgins (1997)
Beth O'Reilly (1999)

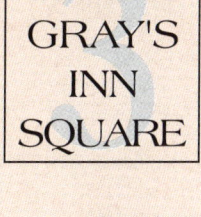

The Chambers Established in 1975, 3 Gray's Inn Square is a specialist criminal defence set which aims to ensure that everyone has equal access to the best representation. The set has earned a reputation as a leader in its field by maintaining the highest standards of professionalism, integrity, commitment and both accessibility and approachability. Services for the set include: conference rooms, video conferences, e-mail, disks accepted, voice mail for all members of chambers. A 24-hour clerking service for emergencies and overnight cases is provided. Chambers are fully computerised as is their Crown Court list checking system. In December 1999, the set became the first chambers to be awarded the Bar Mark, the Bar Council's kite mark for quality assurance.

Work Undertaken First-class representation is provided at every level of seniority by practitioners who appear regularly in high-profile cases and who offer experience in the conduct of all categories of criminal case including European human rights, international criminal tribunal, (international) terrorism and war crimes, murder, serious fraud, organised crime, international drugs trafficking/allied money laundering and offences of extreme/sexual violence. Within this framework there is a positive commitment to legally-aided clients and, where appropriate, pro bono work is undertaken. Particular expertise is provided in all aspects of appellate work, including judicial review and Privy Council. Further, there is experience in the conduct of civil cases, especially actions against the police and allied issues and mental health review tribunals. Chambers present lectures to solicitors and practitioners generally, concerning the effect of significant changes in criminal legislation. Some members also lecture nationally and internationally to and on behalf of legal/human rights organisations on drug trafficking and international war crimes.

Publications Rudi Fortson: *Law on the Misuse of Drugs*. Several members are regular contributors to legal publications, including *The Solicitors Journal* and *The Lawyer*.

International Rock Tansey QC & Steven Kay QC founded the European Criminal Bar Association in order to advance issues of mutual concern for European criminal defence lawyers. Rock Tansey QC is the chairman of the ECBA and organised its inaugural conference at the European Commission for Human Rights. Steven Kay QC, Defence Counsel in the first International Criminal tribunal for the former Yugoslavia undertakes European Human Rights cases. John Perry QC also practises in Bermuda and is a member of the West Indian Bar.

BAR A-Z

4-5 Gray's Inn Square (Elizabeth Appleby QC)

Set No.54

4-5 Gray's Inn Square, Gray's Inn, London, WC1R 5AH
Tel (020) 7404 5252 **Fax** (020) 7242 7803 **DX** 1029
Email clerks@4-5graysinnsquare.co.uk **Website** www.4-5graysinnsquare.co.uk

Head of Chambers	Elizabeth Appleby QC
Head Clerk	Michael Kaplan
Clerks	Mark Regan
	Daniel Perry
	Elliot Langdorf
Chambers Manager	Tracey Jones
Tenants	47

Members

Elizabeth Appleby QC (1965) (QC-1979)
William Wade QC (1946) (QC-1968)
Gary Flather QC (1962) (QC-1984)
Reg Weir QC (1970) (QC-1985) QC (NI)
Brian Ash QC (1975) (QC-1990)
W Robert Griffiths QC (1974) (QC-1993)
John Steel QC (1978) (QC-1993)
Richard Spearman QC (1977) (QC-1996)
Timothy Straker QC (1977) (QC-1996)
Frances Patterson QC (1977) (QC-1998)
Richard McManus QC (1982) (QC-1999)

Hodge M Malek QC (1983) (QC-1999)
Stuart Isaacs QC (1975) (QC-1991)
John Hobson QC (1980) (QC-2000)
Timothy Corner QC (1981) (QC-2002)
Peter Village QC (1983) (QC-2002)
Sam Aaron (1986) SC (SA)
Robin Campbell (1969)
Nicholas Huskinson (1971)
Toby Davey (1977)
Prof. Ingrid Detter (1977)
Julian Chichester (1977)
Andrew Carnes (1984)
Murray Shanks (1984)
Paul Stinchcombe (1985) MP
Richard Humphreys (1986)
Garrett Byrne (1986)

James Ramsden (1987)
Philip Coppel (1994)
Thomas Hill (1988)
Geraldine Clark (1988)
Gillian Carrington (1990)
Paul Brown (1991)
Andrew Tabachnik (1991)
Andrew Fraser-Urquhart (1993)
Robert White (1993)
Dr Ami Barav (1993)
Sarah-Jane Davies (1996)
Jonathan Moffett (1996)
Andrew Sharland (1996)
James Strachan (1996)
Robert Palmer (1998)
Prof. Malcolm Grant (1998)
Caroline Bolton (1998)
Clare Lockhart (1999)
Paul Greatorex (1999)
Jonathan Auburn (1999)
Lisa Busch (2000)

The Chambers 4-5 Gray's Inn Square is regarded as one of the leading chambers in London, and its pre-eminence has been recognised for many years in various independent legal publications. Members of chambers possess expertise and experience of the highest quality in the fields of public law and judicial review, planning and environmental law, commercial law, EU law, human rights, employment law and sports law. The intersection of these specialisations within chambers allows collaboration between members on complex litigation. Many members hold part time judicial appointments in England, as well as overseas. The Head of Chambers Elizabeth Appleby QC was the first woman to head a leading set of chambers. Several of the present juniors are on the Treasury Panels of Counsel instructed on behalf of the Crown. The chambers have been the first set to appoint an academic panel as a research and advisory facility. Its members are Professor Craig (administrative), Professor M Grant (local government and planning), Professor P Davies (Employment), Professor J Usher (EU), Professor E Barendt (media, human rights, welfare), Professor A Arnull (Birmingham), Professor D Harris (Nottingham - international law and human rights).

Former Members The Right Honourable Lord Justice Schiemann; The Right Honourable Lord Justice Keene; The Honourable Mr Justice Collins; The Honourable Mr Justice Moses; The Honourable Mr Justice Sullivan; The Honourable Mr Justice Ouseley; Sir Douglas Frank QC, former President of the Lands Tribunal; His Honour Judge Marder QC, former President of the Lands Tribunal; His Honour Judge Barratt QC, Victor Wellings QC, former President of the Lands Tribunal, His Honour Judge Gregory Stone QC, His Honour Judge David Mole QC.

Door Tenants Professor G H Treitel QC; Professor E P Ellinger; Lord Borrie QC; Sir John Freeland QC (1952)(QC-1987); Professor Sir D G T Williams; Narinder Hargun (Bermuda); Brian Harris QC; Jeremy Gauntlett (SC) (South Africa); John Sacker QC (NSW); Mansoor Jamal Malik (Oman); Professor M Grant (Cantab); William Orbinson, Ian Dove.

Work Undertaken

Public Law/Judicial Review Members of chambers have considerable experience in the fields of public law and judicial review. Members appear frequently in court on behalf of individual applicants and companies whose rights may be affected by the decisions of public bodies and on behalf of local authorities, central government departments and other public bodies such as regulatory authorities. Chambers are especially well placed to advise on all matters relating to the Human Rights Act 1998 which will inevitably impact on all areas of UK law.

Planning & Environmental Law 4-5 Gray's Inn Square is one of the leading sets in both planning and environmental law, providing advice or advocacy to developers, government departments, local authorities and objectors in all aspects of these and related fields. Members of chambers regularly appear in public inquiries held under planning and related legislation and in the High Court in statutory appeals and applications for judicial review.

Commercial Law The core of the set's commercial work relates to domestic and international banking (including securities), insurance and reinsurance and the sale of goods and international trade. A wide range of other contract-related work is also done. There is considerable experience in dealing with conflict of law problems and jurisdictional disputes, including under the Brussels Convention and its successors, and in financial regulation work which intersects with judicial review.

European Law This is one of the leading sets in both European Union Law and the European Convention on Human Rights. Members of chambers have appeared in Luxembourg and in Strasbourg. Chambers is in pole position to advise clients on the implications of the Human Rights Act 1998.

Employment Law The work includes commercial (restraint of trade; wrongful dismissal), European (transfer of undertakings; equal pay), collective (trade unions; industrial action) and individual (sex, race and disability discrimination; unfair dismissal).

Other Areas Defamation, media law, sports law, breach of confidence, professional negligence.

Publications All members of chambers have either written or contributed to leading legal publications, ranging from Halsbury's *Laws of England* to text books on human rights and the *Encyclopedia of Planning*.

International Members of chambers have appeared in the Privy Council, the European Court of Justice and of Human Rights, international arbitration tribunals and other courts worldwide, including the Far East, the Caribbean, Gibraltar, Belfast, Bermuda, Anguilla and Trinidad. One member is a former Judge of the Court of Appeal in Swaziland and a current Judge of the Court of Appeal in Lesotho.

---

6 Gray's Inn Square (Michael Boardman)   Set No.55

6 Gray's Inn Square, Gray's Inn, London, WC1R 5AZ   **Tel** (020) 7242 1052   **Fax** (020) 7405 4934   **DX** 224

---

14 Gray's Inn Square (Joanna Dodson QC)   Set No.56

14 Gray's Inn Square, Gray's Inn, London, WC1R 5JP
Tel (020) 7242 0858   **Fax** (020) 7242 5434   **DX** 399 (Ch.Ln.)
Email clerks@14graysinnsquare.co.uk

Head of Chambers	Joanna Dodson QC
Senior Clerk	Geoffrey Carr
First Junior Clerk	Jonathan Cue
Second Junior Clerk	Kenny Martin
Third Junior Clerk	Joseph Bernard
Fees Clerk	Peter Hoskins
Tenants	32

Members

Joanna Dodson QC (1971) (QC-1993)
Louise Godfrey QC (1974) (QC-1992) *
David Turner QC (1976) (QC-2000)
Joanna Hall (1973)
Mhairi McNab (1974)
Barbara Slomnicka (1976)
Sarah Forster (1976)
Gillian Brasse (1977)
Brenda Morris (1978)
Gillian Marks (1981)
Karen McLaughlin (1982)
Caroline Reid (1982)
Monica Ford (1984)
Sylvester McIlwain (1985)
Mark Emanuel (1985)
Pamela Warner (1985)
Richard Buswell (1985)
Karoline Sutton (1986)
Patricia Roberts (1987)
Rebecca Brown (1989)
Mark Jarman (1989)
Richard Alomo (1990)
Samantha King (1990)
Jonathan Tod (1990)
David Bedingfield (1991)
Marcia Hyde (1992)
Alison Moore (1994)
Dominic Brazil (1995)
Samantha Whittam (1995)
Ronan O'Donovan (1995)
Michael Glaser (1998)
Christopher Miller (1998)
Rebecca Mitchell (2000)

* Door Tenant

The Chambers A family and civil set with particular expertise in children's cases and financial matters, with a strong general common law side. Members of chambers belong to the Family Law Bar Association. Chambers are both Barmark and ISO 9002 accredited.

Work Undertaken Family and matrimonial, including wardship, adoption, care, children and ancillary relief; personal injury, including running-down accidents; employment and labour law; landlord and tenant; housing; licensing work; building and construction; contract cases.
Additional Areas of Work Civil liberties; crime; company; discrimination; ecclesiastical; judicial review; police cases; product liability; professional negligence; sale of goods; welfare; immigration/asylum.

Clientele Individuals, companies, local authorities, guardians ad litem, the Official Solicitor.

International One member is a member of the Georgia Bar.

Recruitment Tenancy applications should be sent to Joanna Dodson QC; pupillage applications to Ronan

Continued overleaf

BAR A-Z

O'Donovan. Two first six and one second six months pupils are taken each year. Awards of £4,000 are offered for the first six months of pupillage and minimum earnings are guaranteed at that level for the second six. Mini-pupillages are available.

Gray's Inn Tax Chambers (Milton Grundy) — Set No.57

Third Floor, Gray's Inn Chambers, Gray's Inn, London, WC1R 5JA
Tel (020) 7242 2642 **Fax** (020) 7831 9017 **DX** 352 London Chancery Lane
Email clerks@taxbar.com **Website** www.taxbar.com

Head of Chambers	Milton Grundy
Senior Clerk	Chris Broom
Tenants	16

Members

Milton Grundy (1954)
Michael Flesch QC (1963) (QC-1983)
David Goldberg QC (1971) (QC-1987)
David Goy QC (1973) (QC-1991)
John Walters QC (1977) (QC-1997)

Philip Baker QC (1979) (QC-2002)
Patrick Soares (1983)
Felicity Cullen (1985)
Barrie Akin (1976)
Patrick Way (1994)
Hugh McKay (1990)
Aparna Nathan (1994)

Conrad McDonnell (1994)
Nicola Shaw (1995)
Claire Simpson (1999)
Michael Thomas (2000)
Graham Wilson (1975) *
Brian Cleave QC (1999) (QC-1999) *

* Door Tenant

The Chambers Gray's Inn Tax Chambers is a leading set of specialist tax practitioners. Its members deal with all aspects of UK revenue law and cover all areas of work dealt with by tax practitioners, from accumulation and maintenance settlements to zero-coupon bonds. They have established expertise in litigation before the Special Commissioners, General Commissioners, the VAT and Duties Tribunals, the Supreme Court, the House of Lords, the Privy Council, the European Court of Justice and the courts of certain colonies, Commonwealth and foreign jurisdictions. Chambers are fully computerised and maintain a popular website, which offers a rapid reporting of tax cases. The address is www.taxbar.com.

Appointments & Memberships All members of chambers belong to the Revenue Bar Association of which Michael Flesch QC is a former chairman and Hugh McKay is a former secretary. Milton Grundy is president of the International Tax Planning Association and a fellow of the Chartered Institute of Taxation; he is the draftsman of the Trusts Law of the Cayman Islands and (with Philip Baker QC) of the IBC Act and the Trusts Act of Belize. John Walters QC and Barrie Akin are chartered accountants. Philip Baker QC is a visiting professor, and Aparna Nathan a visiting lecturer, at London University. Hugh McKay and Nicola Shaw are members of the Attorney General's Panel of Junior Counsel and appear frequently in Court for the Inland Revenue and Customs and Excise.

Work Undertaken Members give advice to taxpayers who are in dispute with the Inland Revenue or Customs and advise clients on the planning of their business and personal affairs. They advise on corporate tax planning including acquisitions, mergers, takeovers and methods of financing, property transactions, international business, cross-border transactions, offshore and domestic trusts estate planning and all the direct and indirect taxes, including VAT. Work is accepted from (amongst others) local authorities, companies, charities and private clients. Direct Professional Access is accepted from members of the appropriate professional bodies.

Publications Members have written, contributed to, or edited: *Whiteman on Income Tax*; *VAT and Property*; *British Tax Review*; *Asset Protection Trusts*; *Double Taxation Conventions and International Tax Law*; *Value Added Tax Encyclopedia*; *Offshore Business Centres*; *The Law of Partnership Taxation*; *Copinger and Skone James on Copyright*; *The Laws of the Internet*; *The International Trust and Estate Law Reports and International Law Reports*; various articles on domestic and international tax developments.

International Languages spoken include Chinese (Mandarin and some Cantonese), French, German, Hebrew, Hindi, Italian and Tamil. Members of chambers advise clients from Hong Kong, Singapore, Australia, New Zealand, the USA and Mauritius. Chambers also advise the revenue departments of Commonwealth countries and ex-colonies on the interpretation and drafting of their statutes.

100E Great Portland Street (Robert Banks) — Set No.58

100E Great Portland Street, London, W1W 6PB **Tel** (020) 7636 6323 **Fax** (020) 7436 3544 **DX** 94252 Marylebone

■ BAR A-Z

LONDON

2 Harcourt Buildings, Atkinson Bevan Chambers (Nicholas Atkinson QC & John Bevan QC) Set No.59

2 Harcourt Buildings, Temple, London, EC4Y 9DB
Tel (020) 7353 2112   Fax (020) 7353 8339   DX 489 Chancery Lane
Email clerks@2hb.co.uk   Website www.2hb.co.uk

Head of Chambers	Nicholas Atkinson QC
	John Bevan QC
Senior Clerk	Hadyn Robson
Tenants	34

Members

Nigel Mylne QC (1963) (QC-1984) +
John Bevan QC (1970) (QC-1997) +
Nicholas Atkinson QC (1971) (QC-1991) +
Jeffrey Pegden QC (1973) (QC-1996) +
John Williams (1973) +
Stephen Smyth (1974) +
Stephen Clayton (1973)
William Adlard (1978) *
Philip Shorrock (1978) +
Robin Leach (1979)

Mark Gadsden (1980)
Aftab Jafferjee (1980)
Timothy Probert-Wood (1983)
Jane Carpenter (1984)
Ian Darling (1985)
Lucia Whittle-Martin (1985)
Patrick Gibbs (1986)
Jonathan Rees (1987)
Matthew Farmer (1987)
Peter Clement (1988)
Stewart Hamblin (1990)
Toby Fitzgerald (1993)
Thomas Wilkins (1993)

James Dawes (1993)
Lisa Wilding (1993)
Sally Halkerston (1994)
Sally Thompson (1994)
Benedict Kelleher (1994)
William Emlyn Jones (1996)
Jennifer Knight (1996)
Kevin Baumber (1998)
Quinn Hawkins (1999)
Christopher Stimpson (1999)
Sarah Giddens (1999)
Leila Gaskin (2000)

* Door Tenant + Recorder

The Chambers With four QCs and one Senior Treasury Counsel, Atkinson Bevan Chambers is a specialist criminal set practising predominantly in London and on the South Eastern and Western Circuits. The set has been continuously represented on the Treasury Counsel team since 1953.

Work Undertaken Members of chambers both defend and prosecute the full spectrum of criminal cases, ranging from high profile and sensitive matters requiring specialist expertise such as terrorism, murder, corruption and serious fraud, to the more routine offences found everyday in the Magistrates and Crown Courts. Chambers also undertake work in other practice areas including confiscation, sports law, regulatory work, health and safety, food and drugs, trades descriptions, police and medical disciplinary tribunals, coroners' inquests, extradition, data protection, courts martial and ecclesiastical matters.

Clientele Chambers receive instructions from individual private and public clients including government departments (SFO, CPS), local authorities, corporate bodies and sporting clients.

Recruitment Applications to Lisa Wilding or Sue Watt. The set is a member of OLPAS. Chambers take two pupils completing six and 12 month pupillages at any one time. Discretionary funding is available.

2 Harcourt Buildings (Roger Henderson QC) Set No.60

2 Harcourt Buildings (Ground Floor), Temple, London, EC4Y 9DB
Tel (020) 7583 9020   Fax (020) 7583 2686   DX LDE 1039
Email clerks@harcourt.co.uk   Website www.harcourt.co.uk

Head of Chambers	Roger Henderson QC
Senior Clerk	John White
Tenants	42

Members

Roger Henderson QC (1964) (QC-1980) +
Richard Mawrey QC (1964) (QC-1986) +
Adrian Brunner QC (1968) (QC-1994) +
Stephen Powles QC (1972) (QC-1995) +
Andrew Prynne QC (1975) (QC-1995)
Peter Susman QC (1966) (QC-1997)

Charles Gibson QC (1984) (QC-2001)
Alan Dashwood (1969)
Adrian Cooper (1970) +
Bernard O'Sullivan (1971)
Gavin Gore-Andrews (1972)
Jonathan Harvey (1974)
Kenneth Hamer (1975) +
Lawrence West (1979) +
Mark Piercy (1976)
Roger Eastman (1978)
Barbara Cameron (1979) +

James Palmer (1983)
George Alliott (1981)
Terence Bergin (1985)
Conrad Griffiths (1986)
Jonathan Steinert (1986)
Marina Wheeler (1987)
Rhodri Williams (1987)
Andrew Davies (1988)
David Brook (1988)
Wendy Outhwaite (1990)
Patrick Green (1990)
Charles Bourne (1991)

Continued overleaf

BAR A-Z

Prashant Popat (1992)
Oliver Campbell (1992)
Isabella Zornoza (1993)
Malcolm Sheehan (1993)
Felicia Fenston (1994)
Geraint Webb (1995)
Toby Riley-Smith (1995)

Julianna Mitchell (1994)
Andrew Kinnier (1996)
James Martin-Jenkins (1997)
Tamara Trefusis (1999)
Adam Heppinstall (1999)
Annabel Walker (2001)
Adrian Garner (1985) *

Lance Ashworth (1987) *
Frank Schoneveld (1992) *
Debra Holland (1996) *
Heather Tibbo (1989) *
Melissa Cacciotti (1997) *
John Ratliff (1990) *

Door Tenant + Recorder

Work Undertaken Commercial and common law, particularly product liability; personal injury; medical and other professional negligence; insurance; local government; public procurement; public law; judicial review; environmental law; health and safety; railways; telecommunications; information technology; intellectual property; education; food; sport; employment and discrimination; human rights; construction and engineering; consumer credit; financial services; EU law; competition; property litigation; land; housing; landlord and tenant; family and inheritance.

International Members of chambers also practise at the above address in association with the English barristers of the firm of Stanbrook & Hooper, 2 Rue de Taciturne, B-1000 Brussels under the name Stanbrook and Henderson.

2 Harcourt Buildings (Robin Purchas QC)   Set No.61

2 Harcourt Buildings, Temple, London, EC4Y 9DB
Tel (020) 7353 8415   **Fax** (020) 7353 7622   **DX** 402 LDE
Email clerks@2hblaw.co.uk

Head of Chambers	Robin Purchas QC
Senior Clerk	Allen Collier
First Junior Clerk	Paul Munday
Second Junior Clerk	Andrew Briton
Tenants	24

Members

Robin Purchas QC (1968) (QC-1987)
The Rt. Hon Lord Kingsland QC (1972) (QC-1988)
Richard Phillips QC (1970) (QC-1990)
Charles George QC (1974) (QC-1992)
Clive Newberry QC (1978) (QC-1993)

Keith Lindblom QC (1980) (QC-1996)
Andrew Kelly QC (1978) (QC-2000)
Robert McCracken (1973)
Philip Petchey (1976)
Jonathan Milner (1977)
Timothy Comyn (1980)
Andrew Tait (1981)
Craig Howell Williams (1983)
Suzanne Ornsby (1986)

Meyric Lewis (1986)
Andrew Newcombe (1987)
Charles Mynors (1988)
Gregory Jones (1991)
Douglas Edwards (1992)
Paul Hardy (1992)
Joanna Clayton (1995)
James Pereira (1996)
Hereward Phillpot (1997)
Alexander Booth (2000)

The Chambers A specialist Chambers for over half a century with particular expertise in planning, environmental, administrative and local government law. A leading set in these fields at all levels of call, providing a high quality service to a wide range of commercial and public sector clients, interest groups and private individuals. All members of Chambers belong to the Planning and Environment Bar Association, of which Robin Purchas QC is the vice-chairman and Douglas Edwards the secretary. Chambers is administered by a friendly, efficient and dedicated team of clerks and support staff. The quality of Chambers' practice management has recently been recognised by the award of BarMark. For further information on Chambers and individual members, visit our website at www.2hblaw.co.uk.

Former Members Roy Vandermeer QC, the Inspector at the Heathrow Terminal Five inquiry; Peter Boydell QC, former Leader of the Parliamentary Bar and first Chairman of what is now the Planning and Environment Bar Association; Michael Harrison QC, now Mr Justice Harrison; Michael Mann QC, later Lord Justice Mann; Sir John Drinkwater QC; Gerard Ryan QC, former head of Chambers; Sheila Cameron QC, Dean of the Arches.

Work Undertaken Public law, planning, environmental (including regulatory offences), contaminated land, compulsory purchase, administrative, local government, public procurement, parliamentary, transport and works, energy, utilities, education, highways, licensing, housing, human rights (European Convention) and EU Law.

Additional areas Ecclesiastical law; landlord and tenant; the law of commons and that relating to easements, agricultural tenancies, rating and restrictive covenants.

Publications *Journal of Planning and Environment Law* (editorial board), *Journal of Architectural Conservation* (editorial board), *Planning and Environmental Law Bulletin* (joint editor), Charles Mynors is the author of *Planning Applications and Appeals* (1987), *Planning Control and the Display of Advertisements* (1992), *Listed Buildings and Conservation Areas* (1998), *The Law of Trees and Forestry* (2002); Robert McCracken, Gregory Jones and James Pereira are co-authors of *Statutory Nuisance - Law and Practice* (2001).

International Chambers include members called to the Dublin and Northern Ireland Bars.

Harcourt Chambers (June Rodgers) — Set No.62

2 Harcourt Buildings, Temple, London, EC4Y 9DB
Tel (020) 7353 6961 **Fax** (020) 7353 6968 **DX** 373
Email clerks@harcourtchambers.law.co.uk **Website** www.harcourtchambers.law.co.uk

Head of Chambers	June Rodgers
Senior Clerk	Brian Wheeler
Tenants	27

Members

June Rodgers (1971)
Roger Evans (1970)
Benedict Sefi (1972)
John Dixon (1975)
Gavyn Arthur (1975)
Stephen Barstow (1976)
Jonathan Baker QC (1978) (QC-2001)
Alicia Collinson (1982)
Christopher Frazer (1983)
Frances Judd (1984)
Edward Hess (1985)
Matthew Brett (1987)
Sarah Gibbons (1987)
Fiona Hay (1989)
Piers Pressdee (1991)
Sara Granshaw (1991)
Sally Max (1991)
Rohan Auld (1992)
Louise Potter (1993)
John Vater (1995)
Nicholas Goodwin (1995)
Aidan Vine (1995)
Jonathan Sampson (1997)
Oliver Wright (1998)
Andrew Leong (1998)
Edward Kirkwood (1999)
Helen Little (1999)

The Chambers Based in London and Oxford, Harcourt Chambers provides a friendly and efficient advisory and advocacy service within five specialist practice groups: family, business, property, local government and personal injury. Individual members of chambers have additional areas of personal specialisation, particularly in election law, judicial review, planning, media, criminal and ecclesiastical law.

Hardwicke Building (Nicholas Stewart QC) — Set No.63

Hardwicke Building, New Square, Lincoln's Inn, London, WC2A 3SB
Tel (020) 7242 2523 **Fax** (020) 7691 1234 **DX** LDE393
Email clerks@hardwicke.co.uk **Website** www.hardwicke.co.uk

Head of Chambers	Nicholas Stewart QC
Clerks	Kevin Mitchell
	Danny O'Brien
	Gary Brown
	Hudson Brewer
Tenants	93

Members:

Nicholas Stewart QC (1971) (QC-1987)
Walter Aylen QC (1962) (QC-1983)
George F Pulman QC (1971) (QC-1989)
Patrick Upward QC (1972) (QC-1996)
Nigel Jones QC (1976) (QC-1999)
Robert Willer (1970)
Kenneth Aylett (1972)
Lindsay Burn (1972)
Michael Hopmeier (1974)
James Pavry (1974)
John Gallagher (1974)
John Friel (1974)
Kenneth Craig (1975)
Charles Calvert (1975)
Stephen Lennard (1976)
Stephen Warner (1976)
Robert Leonard (1976)
Michael Oliver (1977)
James Vine (1977)
Steven Weddle (1977)
Philip Wakeham (1978)
Peter Walsh (1978)
Wendy Parker (1978)
Nicholas Baker (1980)
Rory Field (1980)
David Aaronberg (1981)
Ian Brook (1983)
Timothy Banks (1983)
John Greenan (1984)
Charles Briefel (1984)
Jonathan Whitfield (1985)
Lindsey MacDonald (1985)
Karl King (1985)
Richard Buswell (1985)
Christopher Baylis (1986)
Michelle Stevens-Hoare (1986)
Tom Nicholson Pratt (1986)
James Mulholland (1986)
Helen McCormack (1986)
Francis Lloyd (1987)
Paul Reed (1988)
Peter Kirby (1989)
Ann Mulligan (1989)
Steven Woolf (1989)
Caroline Hallissey (1990)
Eithne Ryan (1990)
Ian Clarke (1990)
Sara Benbow (1990)
Kyriakos Argyropoulos (1991)
Kevin McCartney (1991)
Deborah Hay (1991)
Ingrid Newman (1992)
Colm Nugent (1992)

Continued overleaf

BAR A-Z

Kerry Bretherton (1992)
Arthur Moore (1992)
John Passmore (1992)
Roshi Amiraftabi (1993)
Sabuhi Chaudhry (1993)
Emily Formby (1993)
David Preston (1993)
Niki Langridge (1993)
Brian St. Louis (1994)
Alexander Goold (1994)
Deanna Heer (1994)
Clive Rawlings (1994)
Dr Margaret Bloom (1994)
Bart Casella (1995)
Jamie Clarke (1995)
Lynn Freeston (1996)
Sarah Wood (1996)
Philip Grey (1996)
Edward Rowntree (1996)
David Pliener (1996)
Fiona Scolding (1996)
Brendan Mullee (1996)
Christopher Camp (1996)
Charles Bagot (1997)
Stephen Vullo (1997)
David Lewis (1997)
Tianne Goolo (1998)
Nicola Muir (1998)
Peter Roberts (1998)
Stephen Coyle (1998)
Romilly Cummerson (1998)
Simon Calhaem (1999)
Andrew Lane (1999)
Charlotte Hadfield (1999)
Sophie Shotton (1999)
Angela Ayo-Ojo (1999)
John McKendrick (1999)
Henry Slack (1999)
Rupert Jones (2000)
Katrina McAteer (2001)
Sa'id Mosteshar (1975) *
Jennet Treharne (1975) *
Stephen Joelson (1980) *
Pauline Gray (1980) *
Julia Jarzabkowski (1993) *

* Door Tenant

The Chambers This modern, progressive set is large enough to contain strong teams specialising in civil and commercial law, crime and family law. Above all, it is dedicated to providing a high quality client-focused service to all its solicitors. For the latest and fullest information about Hardwicke Building, its teams and individual barristers, you are invited to visit their website.

1 Hare Court (Bruce Blair QC)   Set No.64

1 Hare Court, Temple, London, EC4Y 7BE
Tel (020) 7797 7070   **Fax** (020) 7797 7435   **DX** LDE 342 Chancery Lane
Email clerks@1hc.com   **Website** www.1hc.com

Head of Chambers	Bruce Blair QC
Senior Clerk	Steve McCrone
Tenants	34

Members

Bruce Blair QC (1969) (QC-1989)
Michael Horowitz QC (1968) (QC-1990)
Jeremy Posnansky QC (1972) (QC-1994)
Mark Everall QC (1975) (QC-1994)
Martin Pointer QC (1976) (QC-1996)
Nicholas Mostyn QC (1980) (QC-1997)
Philip Moor QC (1982) (QC-2001)
Valentine Le Grice QC (1977) (QC-2002)
John Elvidge (1968)
Michael Nicholls (1975)
Robin Spon-Smith (1976)
Heather Pope (1977)
Deborah Bangay (1981)
Nicholas Carden (1981)
Ann Hussey (1981)
Catriona Murfitt (1981)
Gavin Smith (1981)
Nigel Dyer (1982)
Charles Todd (1983)
Christopher Wood (1986)
Nicholas Cusworth (1986)
Katharine Davidson (1987)
Richard Todd (1988)
Rachel Platts (1989)
Elisabeth Todd (1990)
Nicola Gray (1991)
Timothy Bishop (1991)
Geoffrey Kingscote (1993)
Stephen Trowell (1995)
Justin Warshaw (1995)
Nicholas Yates (1996)
Simon Webster (1997)
Rebecca Wood (1999)
Emma Sumner (1999)

The Chambers 1 Hare Court (previously at 1 Mitre Court Buildings) is the longest established set practising exclusively in the area of family law. The set offers advocacy, advisory and drafting expertise over the entire range of family and matrimonial law, whether child or finance oriented, and undertakes work at all levels of court. Together with its service to privately paying clients, 1 Hare Court has a commitment to and involvement in publicly funded family work. The set is instructed by CAFCASS and local authorities, as well as on behalf of individual clients. 1 Hare Court frequently handles cases with an international dimension. All members of chambers belong to the Family Law Bar Association.

■ BAR A-Z

2 Hare Court (Stephen Kramer QC) Set No.65

2 Hare Court, Temple, London, EC4Y 7BH
Tel (020) 7353 5324 **Fax** (020) 7353 0667 **DX** 444 (Ch.Ln.)
Email clerks@2harecourt.com **Website** www.2harecourt.com

Head of Chambers	Stephen Kramer QC
Senior Clerk	Richard Fowler
Chambers Director	Barbara-Ann Tweedie
Tenants	44

Members

Stephen Kramer QC (1970) (QC-1995)
Sir Allan Green QC (1959) (QC-1987)
Paul Worsley QC (1970) (QC-1990)
Anthony Morris QC (1970) (QC-1991)
Martin S Heslop QC (1972) (QC-1995)
Charles Salmon QC (1972) (QC-1996)
David Waters QC (1973) (QC-1999)
Andrew Radcliffe QC (1975) (QC-2000)
Jeremy Benson QC (1978) (QC-2001)
Orlando Pownall QC (1975) (QC-2002)
David Howker QC (1982) (QC-2002)
Brian Warner (1969)
Jacqueline Samuel (1971)
John Jones (1972)
Louise Kamill (1974)
Martin Hicks (1977)
Andrew Lloyd-Eley (1979)
Andrew Colman (1980)
Ian Leist (1981)
Jonathan Laidlaw (1982)
James Dawson (1984)
Sallie Bennett-Jenkins (1984)
Michael Holland (1984)
Shani Barnes (1986)
Brian O'Neill (1987)
Kenneth Millett (1988)
Michael Logsdon (1988)
Brendan Kelly (1988)
Parmjit-Kaur Cheema (1989)
Marios P Lambis (1989)
Christopher Hehir (1990)
Alex Lewis (1990)
Craig Ferguson (1992)
Kate Bex (1992)
Karim Khan (1992)
Nina Grahame (1993)
Christopher Foulkes (1994)
Stephen Brassington (1994)
Oliver Glasgow (1995)
Riel Karmy-Jones (1995)
Emma Lowe (1996)
Christopher Coltart (1998)
Angus Bunyan (1999)
Miranda Bevan (2000)

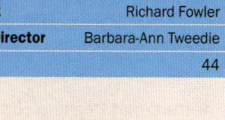

The Chambers Chambers specialise in criminal law. Prosecution and defence work is undertaken at all levels of seriousness in London and throughout England and Wales. Chambers offer particular expertise, both prosecution and defence, in cases involving serious fraud and corruption. Other specialisations include extradition work (on behalf of both individuals and foreign governments), courts martial, coroners inquests, licensing and cases involving trades description and food and drugs legislation. Members of chambers include Treasury Counsel at the Central Criminal Court and many Recorders of the Crown Court. More information can be found on chambers' website and a brochure is available on request.

3 Hare Court (James Guthrie QC) Set No.66

3 Hare Court, Temple, London, EC4Y 7BJ
Tel (020) 7415 7800 **Fax** (020) 7415 7811 **DX** 212 London
Email clerks@3harecourt.com **Website** www.3harecourt.com

Head of Chambers	James Guthrie QC
Senior Clerk	James Donovan
Marketing Director	Liz Heathfield
Tenants	24

Members

James Guthrie QC (1975) (QC-1993)
Sir Godfray Le Quesne QC (1947) (QC-1962)
Mark Strachan QC (1969) (QC-1987)
Richard Jones QC (1972) (QC-1996)
James Dingemans QC (1987) (QC-2002)
Michael Irvine (1964)
Iain McLeod (1969)
Terence Walker (1973)
Sebastian Neville-Clarke (1973)
Andrew Young (1977)
Pierre Janusz (1979)
Peter Knox (1983)
Simon Davenport (1987)
Joseph O'Neill (1987)
Howard Stevens (1990)
Paul Marshall (1991)
Aidan Casey (1992)
Marcus Dignum (1994)
Ian Rogers (1995)
Thomas Roe (1995)
Katherine Deal (1997)
Katherine Awadalla (1998)
Sarah Crowther (1999)
Dan Saxby (2000)

The Chambers 3 Hare Court is a long-established and highly regarded common law and commercial set, providing a wide range of advisory and advocacy services. It has always had a strong connection with the work of the Privy Council. The move to current premises from 1 Crown Office Row enables chambers to offer efficient, client-centred services which meet modern business needs. Senior members of chambers sit in the High Court, as Deputy High Court Judge, as Recorders, and as legal assessors to professional disciplinary tribunals. Chambers has facilities for the conduct of mediation proceedings and members of chambers are available to conduct commercial arbitrations.

Continued overleaf

BAR A-Z

Work Undertaken Chambers' work covers commercial and business law; common law, including personal injury and clinical and professional negligence; administrative law; police civil work; employment, and landlord and tenant. Appeals to the Privy Council, in constitutional, civil and also criminal cases, are an important part of chambers' work. Other specialist areas include financial services, commercial fraud and insolvency, and the set has experience in the application of the Human Rights Act in English litigation. Expertise is available in each practice area at both senior and junior level.

International Chambers has numerous connections abroad, not only through its work in the Privy Council, and particularly in Hong Kong. Languages spoken include Dutch, French, German, Italian and Spanish.

Recruitment The set is a member of the OLPAS scheme.

Hogarth Chambers (Jonathan Rayner James QC & Christopher Morcom QC)   Set No.67

5 New Square, Lincoln's Inn, London, WC2A 3RJ
Tel (020) 7404 0404   **Fax** (020) 7404 0505   **DX** 16 London
Email barristers@hogarthchambers.com   **Website** www.hogarthchambers.com

Head of Chambers Jonathan Rayner James QC
Christopher Morcom QC
Clerks Susan Harding
Clive Nicholls
Spencer Davis
Matthew Morley
Tenants 25

Members

Jonathan Rayner James QC (1971) (QC-1988)
Christopher Morcom QC (1963) (QC-1991) MA (Cantab)
Kevin Garnett QC (1975) (QC-1991)
Roger Wyand QC (1973) (QC-1997) MA (Cantab)
James Sunnucks (1950)
Ernest Scamell (1949)
Sir Patrick Sinclair (1961)

John Ross Martyn (1969) FCIArb
David Micklethwait (1970) MA (Cantab)
Alexander Stewart (1975)
Edward Bragiel (1977)
Paul Dickens (1978) ARCO
Amanda Michaels (1981)
Julia Clark (1984)
John Adams (1984) LLB (Dunelm)
Nicholas Caddick (1986)

Guy Tritton (1987) BSc (Dunelm)
Gwilym Harbottle (1987)
Ashley Roughton (1992) BSc (Lond) PhD (Cantab)
Michael Edenborough (1992) MA (Cantab) DPhil (Oxon)
Richard Davis (1992)
Andrew Norris (1995)
Simon Malynicz (1997)
George Hayman (1998)
Alexander Learmonth (2000)

The Chambers Members specialise in three core areas: intellectual property, media and entertainment, and chancery/commercial and insolvency work. Chambers aim to provide a cost-effective service to clients by offering a wide range of counsel at all levels of seniority. Chambers accept instructions from solicitors, in-house lawyers, patent attorneys, trademark attorneys and other approved bodies. Members of chambers have experience of appearing as advocates before all relevant forums in London and the provinces, including the High Court, Court of Appeal, House of Lords, Patents County Court, European and UK Patent Offices, European Court of Justice, Court of First Instance, OHIM, Trademarks and Designs Registry, Copyright Tribunal and Lands Tribunal. Its clerking team is available to discuss all aspects of the comprehensive service chambers provides and would be happy to assist with any enquiries.

Work Undertaken

Intellectual Property All aspects including patents (UK and European); trademarks; passing off; registered designs; unregistered design right; plant varieties; rights in databases; copyright; copyright tribunal; related EC aspects. Chambers are also involved in computer litigation and internet matters; IP insurance; character merchandising; franchising; criminal proceedings connected with IP rights; data protection issues; commercial matters requiring technical competence; UK European competition disputes.

Media & Entertainment Including publishing agreements; recording contracts; management agreements; merchandising rights; performers' rights; moral rights; confidential information and privacy; criminal remedies; related EC aspects.

Chancery/Commercial & Insolvency General commercial including e-commerce, company law; partnership; banking and securities; commercial contracts; professional negligence; corporate and personal insolvency; land law and conveyancing; landlord and tenant; charities; trusts and fiduciaries; wills and the administration of estates; applications under the Inheritance Act.

Hollis Whiteman Chambers (QEB) (Julian Bevan QC & Peter Whiteman QC)

Set No.68

Queen Elizabeth Building, Temple, London, EC4Y 9BS
Tel (020) 7583 5766 **Fax** (020) 7353 0339 **DX** 482 London/Chancery Lane
Email barristers@holliswhiteman.co.uk **Website** www.holliswhiteman.co.uk

Head of Chambers	Julian Bevan QC
	Peter Whiteman QC
Senior Clerk	Will Whitford
Tenants	52

Members

Julian Bevan QC (1962) (QC-1991)
Peter Whiteman QC (1967) (QC-1977)
Robin Grey QC (1957) (QC-1979)
Alan Suckling QC (1963) (QC-1983)
Anthony Glass QC (1965) (QC-1986)
Vivian Robinson QC (1967) (QC-1986)
John Hilton QC (1964) (QC-1990)
David Evans QC (1972) (QC-1991)
Timothy Langdale QC (1966) (QC-1992)
David Bate QC (1969) (QC-1994)
Rebecca Poulet QC (1975) (QC-1995)
Peter Kyte QC (1970) (QC-1996)
Peter Clarke QC (1973) (QC-1997)
John Kelsey-Fry QC (1978) (QC-2000)
William Boyce QC (1976) (QC-2001)
Peter Doyle QC (1975) (QC-2002) MA (Oxon)
Anthony Wilcken (1966)
Christopher Mitchell (1968)
Linda Strudwick (1973)
Ian Paton (1975)
Richard Horwell (1976)
David Jeremy (1977)
Jeremy Donne (1978)
Mark Ellison (1979)
Peter Finnigan (1979)
Nick Wood (1980)
Gareth Rees (1981)
Tom Kark (1982)
Edward Brown (1983)
Ian Stern (1983)
Jane Sullivan (1984)
Phillip Bennetts (1986)
Sean Larkin (1987)
Jocelyn Sparks (1987)
Edward Henry (1988)
Sarah Plaschkes (1988)
Ian Winter (1988)
Zoe Johnson (1990)
Emma Lowry (1991)
Lydia Barnfather (1992)
Victoria Coward (1992)
Selva Ramasamy (1992)
Adrian Darbishire (1993)
Benjamin Summers (1994)
Mark Aldred (1996)
Jonathan Barnard (1997)
Julian Evans (1997)
Rebecca Harris (1997)
Clare Sibson (1997)
Natasha Tahta (1998)
Jocelyn Ledward (1999)
Ben Fitzgerald (2000)

The Chambers A large criminal set with 16 silks undertaking all areas of criminal law with a particular emphasis on corporate and financial fraud. In recent years chambers have developed their practice in regulatory and disciplinary tribunals. Peter Whiteman QC, a deputy High Court judge, provides specialist advice, particularly on corporate and international tax law, and representation at both national and international levels.

Work Undertaken

Criminal Law Members are frequently involved in high profile cases most recently the Sarah Payne murder trial, the Dome Robbery and the Jonathan King Child Abuse Case. The work is both prosecution and defence from magistrates courts to the House of Lords.

Commercial, Corporate & Financial Crime The set has particular expertise in this field and has been one of the leading sets in these areas in *Chambers Guide to the Legal Profession* for some time. Some recent cases are the Cooperative Fraud, the Jubilee Line Extension fraud and Versailles fraud. Members are involved in all areas in this field from advisory work to representation of parties in the trial process. Members of chambers have experience in new areas of prosecution in this field such as money laundering and the international rules and procedures on evidence.

General Fraud Work in this field covers Customs & Excise fraud to Inland Revenue investigations as well as more general fraud such as the Robinsons Solicitor Legal Aid fraud.

Professional Tribunals Hollis Whiteman Chambers is now one of the leading sets in this field with an emphasis on medical tribunals where it has developed a group of specialists at all levels who regularly appear before such bodies as the General Medical Council, the General Dental Council and the General Optical Council. In addition members have appeared before a wide range of tribunals covering different fields including all levels of Police Disciplinary Tribunals.

Public Inquiries Members have experience of large-scale public inquiries including the Bloody Sunday Inquiry, the Victoria Climbie Inquiry and the Stephen Lawrence Inquiry.

Health & Safety, Environment, Trading Standards, Licensing & Food Law Members have experience at all levels of work in these fields.

Keating Chambers

Set No.69

15 Essex Street, London, WC2R 3AU
Tel (020) 7544 2600 **Fax** (020) 7240 7722 **DX:** 1045
Email clerks@keatingchambers.com **Website** www.keatingchambers.com

Senior Clerk	Barry Bridgman
Tenants	38

Members

Richard Fernyhough QC (1970) (QC-1986)
John Uff CBE QC (1970) (QC-1983)
Martin Collins QC (1952) (QC-1972)
Christopher Thomas QC (1973) (QC-1989)
John Marrin QC (1974) (QC-1990)
Stephen Furst QC (1975) (QC-1991)
Timothy Elliott QC (1975) (QC-1992)
Vivian Ramsey QC (1979) (QC-1992)
Robert Gaitskell QC (1978) (QC-1994)

Philip Boulding QC (1979) (QC-1996)
Paul Darling QC (1983) (QC-1999)
Marcus Taverner QC (1981) (QC-2000)
Peter Coulson QC (1982) (QC-2001)
Finola O'Farrell QC (1983) (QC-2002)
Adrian Williamson QC (1983) (QC-2002)
Alan Steynor (1975)
Rosemary Jackson (1981)
Ian Pennicott (1982)
Alexander Nissen (1985)
Nerys Jefford (1986)
Louise Randall (1988)

Robert Evans (1989)
Sarah Hannaford (1989)
Simon Hargreaves (1991)
Vincent Moran (1991)
Marc Rowlands (1991)
Richard Harding (1992)
Jane Lemon (1993)
Piers Stansfield (1993)
Jonathan Lee (1993)
Simon Hughes (1995)
Abdul-Lateef Jinadu (1995)
Richard Coplin (1997)
Gaynor Chambers (1998)
Gideon Scott-Holland (1999)
Samuel Townend (1999)
Jonathan Selby (1999)
Robert Williams (2000)

The Chambers Keating Chambers specialises in all aspects of construction and engineering matters in the UK and abroad, and in the associated areas of professional negligence, IT and other property-related matters.

Work Undertaken Chambers work covers the whole spectrum of disputes and advisory work from the very small to the exceptionally large. Members of chambers undertake advisory work and act in litigation and arbitration both in the UK and abroad. Senior members of chambers are also often appointed as arbitrators and legal assessors. Members of chambers are active in all forms of alternative dispute resolution (some being accredited mediators) and in all aspects of adjudication, both acting for the parties and as adjudicators.

Main areas Construction and all kinds of engineering matters (including civil, mechanical, electrical and chemical engineering projects, major infrastucture projects, process plants, power plants, oil, coal and gas recovery); development contracts; contractual claims; claims in respect of defective buildings and other structures; the professional negligence of architects, surveyors, valuers, engineers and other consultants concerned with buildings and engineering projects; local authority work (including building control work); IT; European law, particularly public procurement and competition law as it affects building, engineering and IT projects.

Additional Areas Performance bonds and warranties; most types of commercial and insurance contracts; freezing and other types of injunctions. Some members of chambers also have experience in environmental law, aviation law, landlord and tenant and other property-related areas.

Clientele Building contractors (both main and sub-contractors); property owners and developers; government departments and agencies; local authorities; architects; engineers; quantity surveyors; surveyors; insurance companies; and professional indemnity insurers. Members of chambers accept work by Direct Professional Access.

International Many members of chambers advise or act in international litigation or arbitration, whether based in the UK or abroad. Members of chambers act in and are appointed as arbitrators particularly in ICC, LCIA, FIDIC and Hong Kong arbitrations.

Recruitment Both six- and twelve-month pupillages are offered. Awards of up to £27,500 over a 12 month period are available to pupils, with an additional £7,500 to cover the BVC year available.

■ BAR A-Z

One King's Bench Walk (Anthony Hacking QC)   Set No.70

1 King's Bench Walk, Temple, London, EC4Y 7DB
Tel (020) 7936 1500   Fax (020) 7936 1590   DX LDE 20
Email ddear@1kbw.co.uk   Website www.1kbw.co.uk

Head of Chambers	Anthony Hacking QC
Senior Clerk	David Dear
Practice Manager	Lisa Pavlovsky
Tenants	45

Members

Anthony Hacking QC (1965) (QC-1983)
Rodger Hayward Smith QC (1967) (QC-1988)
James Townend QC (1962) (QC-1978)
Barry Singleton QC (1968) (QC-1989)
Judith Parker QC (1973) (QC-1991)
Camden Pratt QC (1970) (QC-1992)
Pamela Scriven QC (1970) (QC-1992)
Richard Anelay QC (1970) (QC-1993)
Stephen Bellamy QC (1974) (QC-1996)
Michael Gale QC (1957) (QC-1979)
James Turner QC (1976) (QC-1998)
Andrew McFarlane QC (1977) (QC-1998)

Charles Howard QC (1975) (QC-1999)
Anthony Kirk QC (1981) (QC-2001)
Clive Newton QC (1968) (QC-2002)
Michael Warren (1971)
John Reddish (1973)
Gordon Jackson (1989) (1979 QC 1990 Scot.)
Caroline Budden (1977)
Sarah Staite (1979)
Caroline Lister (1980)
Julian Woodbridge (1981)
Christopher Pocock (1984)
Stephen Shay (1984)
Deborah Eaton (1985)
Janet Waddicor (1985)
Sarah O'Connor (1986)
Deiniol Cellan-Jones (1988)
Neil Mercer (1988)
Philip Marshall (1989)

Elizabeth Selman (1989)
Richard Barton (1990)
Marcus Fletcher (1990)
Caroline Gibson (1990)
Joanna Grice (1991)
James Roberts (1993)
Richard Harrison (1993)
Ian Cook (1994)
Graham Crosthwaite (1995)
Shaun Esprit (1996)
Alan Gardner (1997)
Nicholas Anderson (1995)
Richard Castle (1998)
Harry Oliver (1999)
Fiona Shannon (2000)
Stephen Wildblood QC (1981) (QC-1999) *
Heather Swindells QC (1974) (QC-1995) *
Susan R Maidment (1968) *
Benedick Rayment (1996) *

One King's Bench Walk
The Chambers of Anthony Hacking QC

* Door Tenant

The Chambers One King's Bench Walk is a large, long established set, specialising in family, criminal and civil law. It has strength at all levels of seniority and teams of counsel can be provided for more protracted and complex cases. The work of chambers is principally in London and on the South Eastern Circuit but work is also undertaken throughout the country. Also at One King's Bench Walk at Lewes, 174 High Street, Lewes, BN7 1YE. Tel: (01273) 402600; Fax: (01273) 402609

Work Undertaken Chambers have specialist groups of members for the three main areas of work who meet regularly holding internal and external lectures and drawing upon their members' expertise and experience.
Family Chambers have considerable depth of expertise in all aspects of family law including the related areas of probate and trusts, Inheritance Act, Human Rights Act, judicial review and solicitors negligence work. The family law group is subdivided into child law and matrimonial finance in order to allow for greater emphasis to be placed upon each of these distinct areas.
Criminal Chambers have an established criminal law practice in London and the South East representing both prosecution and defence and including serious fraud work.
Civil Members of chambers have expertise in personal injury, professional and clinical negligence, medical disciplinary, employment, judicial review, landlord and tenant, contracts (including sale of goods), police cases, and cases for the European Court of Human Rights. Individual members of chambers are willing to accept Conditional Fee and Direct Professional Access instructions.

Publications R. Hayward Smith QC and Clive Newton are the editors of Jackson's *Matrimonial Finance & Taxation*. James Turner QC and Stephen Shay are editors of *Archbold: Criminal Pleading Evidence & Practice*. Andrew McFarlane QC is co-author of *Hershman and McFarlane: Children Law and Practice*. Stephen Wildblood QC and Deborah Eaton are authors of *The Encyclopaedia of Family Provision in Family Matters*, Deborah Eaton is an author of *Essential Family Practice*.

■ 2 King's Bench Walk   Set No.71

2 King's Bench Walk, Temple, London, EC4Y 7DE   Tel (020) 7353 1746   Fax (020) 7583 2051   DX 1032

LONDON — BAR A-Z

2 King's Bench Walk (Philip Rueff) — Set No.72

2 King's Bench Walk, Temple, London, EC4Y 7DE
Tel (020) 7353 9276 **Fax** (020) 7353 9949 **DX** 477 Chancery Lane
Email chambers@2kbw.co.uk

Head of Chambers	Philip Rueff
Senior Administrator	Brenda Anderson
Clerk	Alex Mark
Tenants	27

Members

David Mendes da Costa (1976)
Philip Rueff (1969)
Arnold Cooper (1969)
Anthony Dalgleish (1971)
Alun Evans (1971)
René Yee Lock Wong (1973)
Ian Slack (1974)
Patricia Lloyd (1979)
George Papageorgis (1981)
James Shrimpton (1981)
Sheila Gaylord (1983)
Deepak Kapur (1984)
Steven Perian (1987)
Anthony Montgomery (1987)
Nan Alban-Lloyd (1988)
Brian Kennedy (1992)
Tanya Callman (1993)
Janice Johnson (1994)
Anne Donelon (1995)
Andrew Frymann (1995)
Philippa Daniels (1995)
Michael Hall (1996)
Hugh Blake-James (1998)
Mark Stephens (1998)
Emma Messenger (1999)
Deborah Baljit (1999)
Jonathan Foy (2000)
David Owen Thomas QC (1952) (QC-1972) *
Julia Livesay *
Robert Baker *
Osmond Lam *
Keith Oderberg *
Zahid Yaqub *
Simon Watters (1992) *
Karen Phillips *

2
Kings Bench Walk Chambers
(Lord Campbell of Alloway)
Temple
London EC4Y 7DE

* Door Tenant

The Chambers These chambers are located on the first and second floors of one of the oldest buildings in the Temple, built by Christopher Wren. A wide range of work is undertaken in the field of general common law as well as criminal law, family law, administrative law, work before tribunals, education law, employment law and human rights. Constant review is kept on the changing needs of solicitors and the public, while at the same time the Bar's traditional values are maintained and fostered by members who present a welcoming attitude to lay and professional clients.

4 King's Bench Walk (Timothy Raggatt QC) — Set No.73

2nd floor, 4 King's Bench Walk, Temple, London, EC4Y 7DL
Tel (020) 7822 7000 **Fax** (020) 7822 7022 **DX** 1050 London (Chancery Lane)
Email clerks@4kbw.co.uk **Website** www.4kbw.co.uk

Head of Chambers	Timothy Raggatt QC
Principal Clerk	Lee Cook
Senior Clerks	Philip Burnell
	Graeme Logan
Tenants	40

Members

Timothy Raggatt QC (1972) (QC-1993)
Stephen Williamson QC (1964) (QC-1981)
Nicholas Jarman QC (1965) (QC-1985)
Basil Hillman (1968)
Robert Spencer Bernard (1969)
Christopher Cousins (1969)
John Denniss (1974)
Moira Pooley (1974)
Kate Mallison (1974)
Barnaby Evans (1978)
John Riley (1983)
Reginald Arkhurst (1984)
Jane Alt (1984)
Philip Goddard (1985)
Peter Nightingale (1986)
Andrew Granville Stafford (1987)
Claire Jacobs (1989)
John Metcalf (1990)
Paul Wakerley (1990)
Kate Mather (1990)
Michael Skelley (1991)
Kim Preston (1991)
Timothy Ashmole (1992)
Jillian Hurworth (1993)
Sanjay Lal (1993)
Iain Burnett (1993)
Brendan Davis (1994)
Benn Maguire (1994)
Sarah Phillimore (1994)
Tamala McGee (1995)
Susan Monaghan (1995)
Amanda Millmore (1996)
Nadia Chbat (1996)
Alan Blake (1997)
Cameron Brown (1998)
Kirsten Allan (1998)
Nigel Povoas (1998)
Gavin Holme (1999)
Elizabeth Morton (1999)
Victoria Constable (2000)

The Chambers Areas of practice include contract, crime, education, employment, family, immigration, landlord and tenant, media and defamation, personal injury, probate, professional negligence, public and administrative, real property and tort.

4 King's Bench Walk (Robert Rhodes QC)

Set No.74

4 King's Bench Walk, Temple, London, EC4Y 7DL
Tel (020) 7822 8822   **Fax** (020) 7822 8844   **DX** 422
Email clerks@4kbwchambers.co.uk   **Website** www.barristersatlaw.com

Head of Chambers	Robert Rhodes QC
Consultant	Ian Lee
Tenants	28

Members

Robert Rhodes QC (1968) (QC-1989)
Raymond Walker QC (1966) (QC-1988)
John Toogood (1957)
Simon Buckhaven (1970)
Anthony Clover (1971)
Greville Davis (1976)
Clive Anderson (1976)
Bruce Stuart (1977)
Chris Van Hagen (1980)
John Evan Jones (1982)
Simon Stafford-Michael (1982)

David Harounoff (1984)
Samuel Jarman (1989)
Michael Fullerton (1990)
Graham Huston (1991)
Michael Nelson (1992)
Nigel Hood (1993)
Emma Edhem (1993)
Simon Taylor (1993)
Derek Kerr (1994)
Nicola Murphy (1995)
Lawrence Power (1995)
Clare Evans (1995)
Samantha Riggs (1996)

Kimberly Farmer (1997)
Francesca Levett (1997)
Christopher Rodwell (1997)
Andrew Ramsubhag (2000)
HHJ Heppel QC *
Walter Rudeloff (1990) *
Jim Wilson (1994) *
Kathleen Anderson (1997) *
Michael Horton (1993) *
Katherine Dunn (1993) *
Katherine Toogood (1998) *
Edward Morgan (1989) *

* Door Tenant

The Chambers Common law set specialising in commercial and criminal fraud, financial services, heavy crime, commercial litigation, environmental law and insurance and reinsurance. In association with King's Bench Chambers, 175 Holdenhurst Road, Bournemouth, BN8 8DQ.

6 King's Bench Walk (Roy Amlot QC)

Set No.75

6 King's Bench Walk, Temple, London, EC4Y 7DR
Tel (020) 7583 0410   **Fax** (020) 7353 8791   **DX** 26 (Ch.Ln.)
Email clerks@6kbw.co.uk

Head of Chambers	Roy Amlot QC
Senior Clerk	David Garstang
Tenants	48

Members

Michael Worsley QC (1955) (QC-1985)
Ann Curnow QC (1957) (QC-1985)
Roy Amlot QC (1963) (QC-1989)
Ann Mallalieu QC (1970) (QC-1988)
James Curtis QC (1970) (QC-1993)
Victor Temple QC (1971) (QC-1993)
Dorian Lovell-Pank QC (1971) (QC-1993)
Joanna Korner QC (1974) (QC-1993)
Bruce Houlder QC (1969) (QC-1994)
David Spens QC (1973) (QC-1995)
David Fisher QC (1973) (QC-1996)
Wendy Joseph QC (1975) (QC-1998)

Anthony Leonard QC (1978) (QC-1999)
Nigel Sweeney QC (1976) (QC-2000)
John Ryder QC (1980) (QC-2000)
Sasha Wass QC (1981) (QC-2001)
Howard Vagg (1974)
Jonathan Turner (1974)
Mark Dennis (1977)
Philippa Jessel (1978)
Marks Moore (1979)
David Perry (1980)
Nicholas Hilliard (1981)
Martyn Bowyer (1984)
Simon Denison (1984)
Emma Broadbent (1986)
Irena Ray-Crosby (1990)
Dean Armstrong (1985)
Peter Grieves-Smith (1989)
Timothy Cray (1989)
Duncan Penny (1992)

Jason Dunn-Shaw (1992)
Isabel Dakyns (1992)
Annabel Darlow (1993)
Sarah Whitehouse (1993)
Gareth Patterson (1995)
Duncan Atkinson (1995)
Annabel Pilling (1996)
Jacob Hallam (1996)
Adina Ezekiel (1997)
Alison Foulkes (1997)
Louis Mably (1997)
Kate Wilkinson (1999)
Miranda Hill (1999)
Mark Weekes (1999)
Robin McCoubrey (2000)
Esther Schutzer-Weissmann (2000)
Alison Morgan (2000)
Prof. Di Birch *
David Turner QC (1971) (QC-1991) *
Andrew Oldland (1990) *
Simon Laws (1991) *

* Door Tenant

The Chambers A specialist criminal set with 16 QCs, three Senior and one Junior Treasury Counsel. Cham-

Continued overleaf

BAR A-Z

bers have particular experience in advocacy in the higher courts. Members also handle civil work with individual specialisations. 20 members of chambers are recorders and one is a DTI Inspector. Additionally, members of chambers belong to the committees of the Bar Council and the Criminal Bar Association. Bruce Houlder QC is Chairman of the Criminal Bar Association.

Work Undertaken
Criminal For both prosecution and defence, mainly in London and the South Eastern Circuit, specialising in commercial crime, fraud, VAT cases and regulatory work.
Other Individual members also appear in defamation, libel, licensing and trades descriptions cases. Members appear at Mental Health Tribunals, City Tribunals, Employment Tribunals, Police Disciplinary Tribunals, before Coroners' Courts and for defendants in Courts Martial. Members also undertake all aspects of human rights cases.

International Languages spoken include French, German, Italian and Spanish.

Recruitment Applications for tenancy should be sent to the head of chambers, those for pupillage to Sarah Whitehouse. There are 10 pupils in chambers at any one time. Awards and mini-pupillages are available.

---

6 King's Bench Walk (Sibghat Kadri QC) — Set No. 76
6 King's Bench Walk, Temple, London, EC4Y 7DR **Tel** (020) 7583 0695 **Fax** (020) 7353 1726 **DX** 471 (Ch.Ln.)

---

7 King's Bench Walk (Gavin Kealey QC & Julian Flaux QC) — Set No. 77
7 King's Bench Walk, Temple, London, EC4Y 7DS
Tel (020) 7910 8300 **Fax** (020) 7910 8400 **DX** LDE 239
Email clerks@7kbw.law.co.uk **Website** www.7kbw.co.uk

Head of Chambers	Gavin Kealey QC
	Julian Flaux QC
Administration Director	Lawrence Wiliiams
Senior Clerk	Bernie Hyatt
Clerks	Greg Leyden
	Eddie Johns
	Gary Rose
Arbitrators	Lord Goff
	Adrian Hamilton
	John Willmer
Tenants	36

Members
Gavin Kealey QC (1977) (QC-1994)
Julian Flaux QC (1978) (QC-1994)
Timothy Saloman QC (1975) (QC-1993)
Francis Reynolds (Hon) QC (1960) (QC-1993)
Jonathan Gaisman QC (1979) (QC-1995)
Dominic Kendrick QC (1981) (QC-1997)
Timothy Brenton QC (1981) (QC-1998)
Alistair Schaff QC (1983) (QC-1999)
Stephen Hofmeyr QC (1982) (QC-2000)
Christopher Butcher QC (1986) (QC-2001)
Charles Priday (1982)
Adam Fenton (1984)
Stephen Kenny (1987)
Richard Southern (1987)
Robert Bright (1987)
Gavin Geary (1989)
David Bailey (1989)
David Edwards (1989)
David Allen (1990)
Simon Picken (1989)
Andrew Wales (1992)
Siobán Healy (1993)
S J Phillips (1993)
Rebecca Sabben-Clare (1993)
Jawdat Khurshid (1994)
Richard Waller (1994)
Timothy Kenefick (1996)
John Bignall (1996)
Charles Holroyd (1997)
Simon Kerr (1997)
James Drake (1998)
Peter MacDonald Eggers (1999)
James Brocklebank (1999)
Michael Holmes (1999)
Caroline Laband (2000)
Benjamin Parker (2000)

KING'S BENCH WALK

The Chambers 7KBW has an established reputation for excellence and intellectual rigour in all fields of commercial law. This is combined with a practical and commercial approach to advice and litigation. The importance of a modern and flexible approach to meeting the needs of solicitors and commercial clients is well understood. Members of chambers turn work around quickly and efficiently and are ready to give urgent advice whenever the circumstances require it.

Work Undertaken All members of chambers specialise in all aspects of commercial law, in particular insurance and reinsurance and shipping law. As advocates, they accept instructions to appear in any court, tribunal or enquiry in England and Wales, but the majority of their work is in the Commercial Court and in commercial arbitrations in London. They also appear in those other jurisdictions where members of the Bar are permitted to practise, such as Hong Kong, Singapore, Bermuda and the Cayman Islands. Members undertake advisory work and drafting of legal documents both in connection with litigation or prospective litigation and in non-contentious matters. They will readily settle or draft documents whether as a statement of case, as submissions in a dispute, or for use in business. Senior members of chambers regularly sit as arbitrators and/or mediators.

International The general character of chambers' work is of an international flavour and members of chambers regularly deal with foreign clients, foreign lawyers and foreign law. In appropriate circumstances, members are able to accept instructions directly from overseas clients and foreign lawyers.

Recruitment Chambers attracts pupils of only the highest quality and pursues a policy of only taking new tenants of such quality either from those starting their careers in law, or from those in mid-career who have elected to change from another part of the profession. The emphasis of quality has meant a steady but selective growth in the overall number of tenants over the past years. For further information on 7KBW please visit the chambers' website at www.7kbw.co.uk.

9 King's Bench Walk (Ali Mohammed Azhar) — Set No.78

9 King's Bench Walk, Temple, London, EC4Y 7DX
Tel (020) 7353 9564　**Fax** (020) 7353 7943　**DX** 118 Chancery Lane

The range of work covers crime, family law, landlord and tenant, personal injury, immigration, clinical and professional negligence, arbitration, commercial and construction law, employment, banking law, corporate insolvency and individual bankruptcy. Experts in Islamic and Hindu law. Languages: Urdu, Punjabi, Bengali, and Sinhalese.

Head of Chambers	Ali Mohammed Azhar
Senior Clerk	Barry Henderson
Tenants	20

10 King's Bench Walk (David Nathan QC) — Set No.79

10 King's Bench Walk, Temple, London, EC4Y 7EB
Tel (020) 7353 2501　**Fax** (020) 7353 0658　**DX** 294 Chancery Lane
Email clerks@10kbw.co.uk　**Website** www.10kbw.co.uk

Head of Chambers	David Nathan QC
Senior Clerk	Michael Price
Tenants	39

Members

David Nathan QC (1971) (QC-2002)
Alper Riza QC (1973) (QC-1991)
Richard Akinjide (1956)
Jonathan Lurie (1972)
Peter Prideaux-Brune (1972)
Sheilagh Davies (1974)
Timothy Sewell (1976)
Robin Miric (1978)
Jonathan Woodcock (1981)
Jollyon Robertson (1983)
Nicholas Doherty (1983)
Annette Henry (1984)
Allan Goh (1984)
Michael Lee (1987)
Andrew Jackson (1987)
Miles Trigg (1987)
Trevor Berriman (1988)
Nigel Daniel (1988)
Dina Karallis (1989)
Susan Rodham (1989)
Bosmath Sheffi (1991)
Andrew Copeland (1992)
M Ayaz Qazi (1993)
Mary Ruck (1993)
Karl Volz (1993)
Glenn Harris (1994)
James Kirby (1994)
Phillip Lucas (1995)
Francesca Wiley (1996)
Melanie Winter (1996)
Christopher Surtees-Jones (1997)
Scott Ivill (1997)
Pauline Thompson (1997)
David Miller (1998)
Rupert Gregory (1998)
Robert Garson (1999)
Jai Patel (1999)
Michael Roques (2000)
Michael Salter (2000)

The Chambers A powerful, long-established leading set which has offered strong representation in common law matters over many years. Members of chambers appear in criminal courts at every level. Chambers have an acknowledged reputation in commercial white collar fraud. Chambers offer spacious conference rooms and a computerised administration centre. Practitioners are able to offer written work in a wide variety of formats for the convenience of clients.

Work Undertaken

Criminal Work embraces all aspects of crime, especially commercial crime, serious fraud, drugs and DTOA confiscation orders, money laundering, computer crime, licensing and firearms. Many members defend in major trials and undertake cases on behalf of the prosecuting authorities.
Family All aspects of matrimonial law, including wardship and local authority work. Immigration work

Recruitment Chambers are a member of the OLPAS pupillage scheme administered by the Bar Council. Awards are available. No third six-month pupils or squatters are taken. 10 King's Bench Walk is an equal opportunities organisation.

LONDON — BAR A-Z

11 King's Bench Walk (FJ Muller QC)
Set No.80

11 King's Bench Walk, Temple, London, EC4Y 7EQ
Tel (020) 7353 3337 Fax (020) 7583 2190 DX DX 389 CHANCERY LANE
Email clerks@11kbw.co.uk Website www.11kbw.co.uk

Head of Chambers	FJ Muller QC
Senior Clerk	Jo Pickersgill
Clerks	Jayne Turner
	Deborah Pain
	James McDonald
	Lee Baines
Administration/Fees	Amanda Kershaw
Tenants	27

Members

FJ Muller QC (1961) (QC-1978)
Andrew Robertson QC (1975) (QC-1996)
Roger Thorn QC (1970) (QC-1990)
Nicholas Campbell QC (1979) (QC-2000)
Jeremy Richardson QC (1980) (QC-2000)
Francis Radcliffe (1962)
Matthew Caswell (1968)
Richard Barlow (1970)
Michael O'Neill (1979)
Christopher Attwooll (1980)
Toby Wynn (1982)
Rebecca Caswell (1983)
Graham Reeds (1984)
Simon Mallett (1986)
Peter Johnson (1986)
Adrian Waterman (1988)
Sarah Mallett (1988)
David Brooke (1990)
Robert Toone (1993)
Ian Skelt (1994)
Tom Mitchell (1995)
Sarah Margree (1996)
Tina Dempster (1997)
Matthew Bean (1997)
Shabbir Merali (1998)
Martina Connolly (1999)
Emma Farnsworth (2000)

The Chambers 11 King's Bench Walk is a long-established common law London set with an extensive North East Circuit practice. Chambers have criminal and civil teams, each offering expertise and experience at all levels.

Work Undertaken The principal areas of practice are crime; commercial fraud, immigration, health and safety; clinical negligence; personal injury; professional negligence; commercial litigation including contractual, tort, taxation and copyright disputes; companies and partnership disputes; probate; employment. **Additional Specialisations** Include civil actions against the police. Chambers have a reputation for high quality plaintiff and defendant work in every force area on the North Eastern Circuit. Individual members offer expertise in VAT and Customs & Excise law.

11 King's Bench Walk Chambers (Eldred Tabachnik QC & James Goudie QC)
Set No.81

11 King's Bench Walk, Temple, London, EC4Y 7EQ
Tel (020) 7632 8500 Fax (020) 7583 9123/3690 DX 368 (Ch.Ln.)
Email clerksroom@11kbw.com Website www.11kbw.com

Head of Chambers	Eldred Tabachnik QC
	James Goudie QC
Senior Clerk	Philip Monham
Tenants	41

Members

Eldred Tabachnik QC (1970) (QC-1982)
James Goudie QC (1970) (QC-1984)
Michael Supperstone QC (1973) (QC-1991)
Elizabeth Slade QC (1972) (QC-1992)
Alistair J McGregor QC (1974) (QC-1997)
Christopher Jeans QC (1980) (QC-1997)
Adrian Lynch QC (1983) (QC-2000)
Tim Kerr QC (1983) (QC-2001)
John Cavanagh QC (1985) (QC-2001)
Andrew Hillier QC (1972) (QC-2002)
Philip Sales (1985) First Junior Counsel to the Treasury, Common Law
Elisabeth Laing (1980)
Jane Oldham (1985)
Nigel Giffin (1986)
Charles Béar (1986)
Peter Wallington (1987)
Clive Lewis (1987)
Simon Devonshire (1988)
Jonathan Swift (1989)
Timothy Pitt-Payne (1989)
Peter Oldham (1990)
Sarah Moore (1990)
Seán Jones (1991)
Akhlaq Choudhury (1992)
Paul Nicholls (1992)
Daniel Stilitz (1992)
Clive Sheldon (1991)
Nigel Porter (1994)
Jason Coppel (1994)
Cecilia Ivimy (1995)
Tom Restrick (1995)
Karen Steyn (1995)
Richard Leiper (1996)
Julian Wilson (1997)
Anya Proops (1998)
Deok-Joo Rhee (1998)
Jane McCafferty (1998)
Harini Iyengar (1999)
Julian Milford (2000)
Andrew Blake (2000)
Ben Hooper (2000)

11 KING'S BENCH WALK
CHAMBERS

The Chambers This modern set, founded in 1981, provides a very high quality legal service. Members of chambers are friendly and approachable; they expect to work closely with their clients, operating as part of a team.

BAR A-Z

Work Undertaken

Employment Law 11 King's Bench Walk Chambers is widely regarded as the leading set in employment law. Members act on behalf of employers, employees and trade unions in areas including unfair dismissal; redundancy; race, sex and disability discrimination; restrictive covenant and springboard claims; wrongful dismissal; pension and share schemes; disciplinary hearings; employment-related aspects of EU law; drafting contracts of employment.

Public & Administrative Law Judicial review and practices of public bodies of all kinds; local government finance; the scope of the powers of public bodies; education; social services; public procurement; environmental law, and employment in the civil service and by public authorities. Members also advise on matters such as the regulation of financial services, the control of broadcasting and the organisation of the health service.

Contract & Commercial Law Areas of expertise include agency, asset recovery, competition, confidential information, copyright, economic torts, financial regulation, minority shareholder protection, professional negligence, share options, technology and software licensing, trade secrets, unlawful competition, warranty claims, and all forms of interim injunctions including search and seizure and freezing orders.

EU & Human Rights Law The whole span of European work is covered, including free movement of persons and goods, competition and state aids, environment, aviation, agriculture, procurement and discrimination. Members also have experience in sports law, entertainment, health and safety at work, immigration, and planning.

Other Details Office hours: Monday - Friday 8:00am - 7:00pm. Out of office hours: 07831 304714 (mobile).

Publications Members of chambers have written or contributed to numerous works including *Halsbury's Laws* (Administrative Law and Extradition Titles); *Supperstone & Goudie on Judicial Review*; *Harvey on Industrial Relations and Employment Law*; *Butterworths Employment Law Handbook*; *Tolley's Employment Handbook*; *Immigration Law and Practice*; *Butterworths Local Government Law*; *Supperstone, Goudie & Coppel Local Authorities and the Human Rights Act*; *Butterworths Local Government Reports*; *Supperstone & O'Dempsey on Immigration and Asylum*; *Audit Commission Act 1998*; *Human Rights and Judicial Review: Case Studies in Context*; *Foskett: The Law and Practice of Compromise*; *Supperstone and Pitt-Payne: Freedom of Information Act 2000*; *Sports Law*; *Tolley's Employment Law*; *Butterworths Education Law Manual*; *The Human Rights Act 1998: Enforcing the European Convention in the Domestic Courts*; *Judicial Remedies in Public Law*; *Supreme Court Practice*.

12 King's Bench Walk (Richard Methuen QC)   Set No.82

12 King's Bench Walk, Temple, London, EC4Y 7EL
Tel (020) 7583 0811 **Fax** (020) 7583 7228 **DX** 1037 (Ch.Ln.)
Email chambers@12kbw.co.uk **Website** www.12kbw.co.uk

Head of Chambers	Richard Methuen QC
Senior Clerk	John Cooper
Practice Manager	Roderick Marshall
Tenants	40

Members

Richard Methuen QC (1972) (QC-1997)
Ronald Walker QC (1962) (QC-1983)
Anthony Goldstaub QC (1972) (QC-1992)
Frank Burton QC (1982) (QC-1998)
Toby Hooper QC (1973) (QC-2000)
Susan Rodway QC (1981) (QC-2002)
Neville Spencer-Lewis (1970)
John King (1973)
Andrew Hogarth (1974)
Brian Gallagher (1975)
Stephen Worthington (1976)
Nicholas Heathcote Williams (1976)
Allan Gore (1977)
Simon Levene (1977)
Lincoln Crawford (1977) OBE
William Featherby (1978)
Stephen Archer (1979)
Paul Russell (1984)
David Sanderson (1985)
Nigel Lewers (1986)
Freya Newbery (1986)
Henry Charles (1987)
Andrew Pickering (1987)
Hugh Hamill (1988)
Adam Chambers (1989)
Catherine Brown (1990)
Patrick Vincent (1992)
Willliam Audland (1992)
Stephanie Jackson (1992)
Joel Kendall (1993)
Richard Viney (1994)
Carolyn D'Souza (1994)
Catherine Peck (1995)
Timothy Petts (1996)
Harry Steinberg (1997)
Joanna Droop (1998)
Kweku Aggrey-Orleans (1998)
David White (1999)
Lisa Stephenson (1999)
Jane Rankin (2000)

The Chambers 12 King's Bench Walk is widely recognised as being one of the three leading sets specialising in personal injury. Chambers are also known for the particular expertise of their specialist groups of barristers in clinical negligence, professional negligence, construction, insurance and employment law. One of the longest established sets in the Temple, chambers have the reputation of being friendly and approachable. Considerable expansion during the past ten years has enabled chambers to invest in staff development and

Continued overleaf

the latest computer technology, ensuring that work is dealt with quickly and efficiently. Members are fully conversant with the requirements of recent human rights legislation and its implications for the work undertaken by chambers.
Video Conferencing: (020) 7583 4190.

Work Undertaken
Personal Injury Includes all industrial disease claims, particularly asbestos, RSI and VWF; brain damage; spinal injuries; all other employers', public and product liability claims; all road traffic related work.
Clinical Negligence Includes injuries at birth; catastrophic brain damage; injuries from pharmaceutical products; all other cases involving complex medical and scientific issues.
Professional Negligence Includes solicitors' and barristers' negligence; architects', engineers', surveyors' and valuers' negligence; accountants' and bankers' negligence; insurance brokers' and IFAs' negligence; auctioneers' negligence; veterinary negligence; IT professionals' negligence.
Construction & Technology Includes contractual claims arising out of the JCT, ICE and other standard forms of construction contract and subcontracts; engineering and mining contracts; computer contracts.
Insurance & Reinsurance Includes policy wording issues and drafting of policy wording amendments; acting for insurance clients in professional indemnity, employers' liability, motor policy and public liability claims.
Employment Includes race relations; equal opportunity; trade union work; restrictive covenants; transfers of undertakings; wrongful and unfair dismissal; equal pay; bonus and pension schemes; expertise in all aspects of EU employment law. In addition to the above work undertaken by chambers' specialist teams, individual members can offer expertise in the following areas:
Property Law Includes commercial and residential landlord and tenant; Housing Association; local authority disrepair work.
Environmental Includes pollution of land by chemicals and nuclear matter; pollution related criminal charges; advising clients on obtaining site licences.
Equine Law Includes insurance policy disputes; contractual disputes; misrepresentation and misdescription; disputes concerning membership and rules of riding and racing organisations; disciplinary proceedings; riding accidents.
Other Information Chambers are fully computer networked and all members have email facilities. Meetings, conferences and interviews can be arranged through chambers' video conferencing facilities. Brochures and individual member details are available on request. Details of chambers' seminar and lecture programme can be found on the website. Chambers accept Direct Professional Access instructions and Conditional Fee work, by prior arrangement with the clerks. They also offer qualified and experienced mediators and arbitration services.

Publications Up-to-date details of publications which members of chambers have written, edited or contributed to can be found on the 12 King's Bench Walk website at www.12kbw.co.uk. The website also gives details and analysis of important cases involving members of chambers.

Recruitment Chambers are a member of PACH to which all applications for pupillage should be made. Pupils are offered 12 month pupillage with a comprehensive training package and a guaranteed income of £20,000.

■ BAR A-Z

13 KING'S BENCH WALK (Roger Ellis QC)

Set No.83

13 King's Bench Walk, Temple, London, EC4Y 7EN
Tel: (020) 7353 7204 **Fax:** (020) 7583 0252 **DX:** 359 London
Email: clerks@13kbw.co.uk **Website:** www.13kbw.co.uk

Head of Chambers	Roger Ellis QC
Senior Clerk	Kevin Kelly
Chambers Director	Stephen Rogers
Chambers Administrator	Penny Macfall
Tenants	45

Members

Roger Ellis QC (1962) (QC-1996)LLB BSc (Lond)
Graeme Williams QC (1959) (QC-1983)MA (Oxon)
Julian Baughan QC (1967) (QC-1990)BA (Oxon)
David Ashton (1962)MA (Oxon)
Alexander Dawson (1969)MA (Oxon)
Anthony McGeorge (1969)MA (Cantab)
Robert Lamb (1973)MA (Cantab)
Deirdre Goodwin (1974)LLB (Lond)
Simon Hughes MP (1974)BA (Cantab)
Paul W Reid (1975)MA (Cantab)
David Bright (1976)
Simon Draycott QC (1977) (QC-2002)
Nigel Daly (1979)LLB (London)
Nicholas Syfret (1979)MA (Cantab)

Andrew Glennie (1982)MA (Oxon)
Andrew Pote (1983)LLB (East Anglia)
Jonathan Coode (1984)BA (East Anglia)
Neil Vickery (1985)MA (Cantab)
Neil Moore (1986)LLB (Nottingham)
Mark Maitland-Jones (1986)MA (Edinburgh)
Sarah Gibbons (1987)BA (Birmingham)
Arthur Blake (1988)LLB (Lond)
Sinclair Cramsie (1988)LLB (Leeds)
Fiona Hay (1989)BSc BA (Exeter)
Adrian Higgins (1990)MA (Oxon)
Edmund Walters (1991)BA (Bristol)
Vivian Walters (1991)BA (Leic)
Hugh Williams (1992)
Deshpal Singh Panesar (1993)LLB (Lond)

Peter Coombe (1993)BA (Oxon)
Gabriel Buttimore (1993)LLB (East Anglia)
Susan Chan (1994)BA (Oxon)
Paul Mitchell (1994)BA (York)
Rachel Drake (1995)LLB (Hons) (Brunel)
Lucy Owens (1997)LLB (Hons) (Kingston)
Louise McCabe (1997)
Thomas Payne (1998)BA (Oxon) LLM (research) (Birmingham)
Christopher Mann (1998)BA (Oxon)
Clare Harrington (1998)LLM (LSE)
Julie Hopkins (1999)BA (Oxon)
Sarah Keogh (1999)
John Simmons (2000)LLB (Oxon)
Peter Ross (2000)PhB (Pontifical Gregorian University)
Sophie Eloquin (2000)
Matthew Walsh (2000)

The Chambers These are an established chambers with some 40 members in premises in the Inner Temple in London and Beaumont Street in Oxford. They cover a wide spectrum of common law and chancery matters, have an expanding family practice, and provide a comprehensive service in criminal law on the Midland and Oxford circuit. They like to take a commercial approach by combining prompt action with practical advice. Chambers are proud of their client service, and are now preparing for Barmark Quality assessment.

Work Undertaken Chambers have nine practice areas as follows: Administrative and public law, which includes immigration and civil liberties, environmental and consumer law; clinical negligence; company and commercial, including banking, commercial litigation, insolvency, insurance, partnerships and professional negligence; construction; crime, including criminal fraud; employment; family; personal injury; property and chancery, which includes real property, landlord and tenant, chancery remedies and other related matters.

LONDON — BAR A-Z

Lamb Building (Ami Feder)   Set No.84

Lamb Building, Ground Floor, Temple, London, EC4Y 7AS
Tel (020) 7797 7788 **Fax** (020) 7353 0535 **DX** 1038 (Ch.Ln.)
Email clerks@lambbldg.co.uk **Website** www.lambbldg.co.uk

Head of Chambers	Ami Feder
Senior Clerk	Gary Goodger
	Mobile (07721) 339232
Tenants	40

Members

Ami Feder (1965)
Anna Worrall QC (1959) (QC-1989) +
Ivan Krolick (1966)
David Edlin (1971)
John Fox (1973)
Anthony Edie (1974)
Jeremy Gordon (1974)
Alan Barton (1975)
Spenser Hilliard (1975)
Jacqueline Perry (1975)
Angela Hodes (1979)
Michael Phillips (1980)
J David Cook (1982)

Richard Roberts (1983)
John King (1983)
Julie O'Malley (1983)
Deborah Sawhney (1987)
Susannah Cotterill (1988)
Bernard Richmond (1988) +
M Jane Terry (1988)
Maureen O'Connor (1988)
Jonathan de Rohan (1989)
Jeremy Haughty (1989) *
David Brounger (1990)
Lewis Power (1990)
JM Seamus Kearney (1992)
Paul Crampin (1992)

Anita Geser (1992)
Pippa Alderson (1993)
Dafna Spiro (1994)
Joy Dykers (1995)
Anne Faul (1996)
Geri Peterson (1997) *
Andreas Pretzell (1997)
Nicola Shannon (1997)
Zoe Lane-Smith (1997)
A Mark Tempest (1997)
Andrew Alexander (1999)
Dale Sullivan (1999)
Michael Newport (1999)

* Door Tenant + Recorder

Work Undertaken The work of chambers covers all aspects of English common law and some general chancery, predominantly on the South Eastern and Western Circuits. The principal areas of practice are civil and criminal commercial fraud; professional and particularly medical negligence; personal injury; family and childcare including wardship and property; landlord and tenant and housing law; insolvency and bankruptcy; contractual disputes including partnership and sale of goods; all criminal law; disciplinary hearings and the armed forces; consumer credit, hiring, and leasing transaction; building law; licensing; employment, immigration specialists.
Additional Specialisations Individual members offer expertise in actions against the police, prisoners' rights, food and drugs, mental health, fine arts, computer law, and Israeli law (Ami Feder is qualified as an advocate in Israel). One member belongs to the Chartered Institute of Arbitrators. A brochure is available on request.

Littleton Chambers (Michel Kallipetis QC)   Set No.85

3 King's Bench Walk North, Temple, London, EC4Y 7HR
Tel (020) 7797 8600 **Fax** (020) 7797 8699/8697 **DX** 1047
Email clerks@littletonchambers.co.uk

Head of Chambers	Michel Kallipetis QC
Chief Executive	David Douglas
Clerks	Alistair Coyne
	Tim Tarring
	Jason Drakeford
A/Cs Receivable Manager	Nita Johnston
Tenants	39

Members

Michel Kallipetis QC (1968) (QC-1989)
Julian Malins QC (1972) (QC-1991)
Ian Mayes QC (1974) (QC-1993)
Richard Price OBE QC (1969) (QC-1996)
Clive Freedman QC (1978) (QC-1997)
Andrew Clarke QC (1980) (QC-1997)
John Bowers QC (1979) (QC-1998)
Andrew Stafford QC (1980) (QC-2000)
Selwyn Bloch QC (1982) (QC-2000)

Ian Gatt QC (1985) (QC-2002)
Colin Manning (1970)
Richard Perkoff (1971)
Philip Bartle (1976)
Mark H Lomas (1977)
Timothy Higginson (1977)
Caroline Harry Thomas (1981)
John Davies (1981)
Shirley Bothroyd (1982)
David Reade (1983)
Martin Fodder (1983)
Antony Sendall (1984)
Michael Duggan (1984)
Peter Trepte (1987)
Raoul Downey (1988)

Sam Neaman (1988)
Martyn Barklem (1989)
Charles Samek (1989)
Jeffrey Bacon (1989)
Jeremy Lewis (1992)
Naomi Ellenbogen (1992)
Gavin Mansfield (1992)
Daniel Tatton-Brown (1994)
Stuart Ritchie (1995)
Carol Davis (1996)
Dale Martin (1997)
Niran de Silva (1997)
Lucy Bone (1999)
Matthew Sheridan (2000)
Marianna Patané (1999)
Eleena Misra (2001)

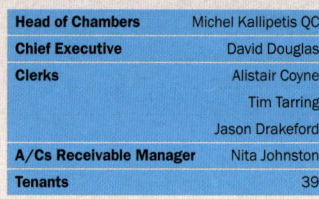

BAR A-Z

Donald Harris QC (1958) (QC-2001) †
The Lord Hacking (1963) †
Neil MacCormick QC (1971) (QC-1999) †

Jean Yves de Cara †
Robert M Smith †
Klaus Reichert †
Matthieu de Boisséson †
Pierre A Karrer †

Wolfgang Peter †
Mauro Rubino-Sammartano (1961) †
Eugen Salpius †
Hans van Houtte †

† Associate Tenant

Work Undertaken A set practising in civil and commercial law with a wide spread of work including all aspects of business, contract and employment law, professional negligence and human rights. Chambers are members of COMBAR. Chambers provide mediation services via a dedicated company Littleton Dispute Resolution Services Ltd and have recently formed an International Arbitration Group.

Main areas There are four main specialities in chambers: employment law; professional negligence, including medical negligence; ADR and arbitration; commercial law incorporating banking, financial services and insurance, entertainment and media, construction, commercial fraud, public and European and insolvency.

Additional areas Carriage of goods; company law; consumer credit law; corporate finance; insolvency; international trade; letters of request; competition law; computer law; EU; environment; family; pharmaceuticals; telecommunications; transport; sale of goods; administrative law; civil liberties; charities; discrimination; education; election law; housing; judicial review; landlord and tenant; local government; mental health; parliamentary; planning; construction; sports and entertainment law; matrimonial finance and children; and pensions. Members of chambers provide lectures on a wide range of subjects and chambers are accredited by the Law Society and Bar Council.

International Languages spoken include Cantonese, French, German, Italian and Spanish plus numerous others by the international arbitration group.

Recruitment Members of chambers fund two pupils per year. Chambers are not members of OLPAS.

Littman Chambers (Mark Littman QC)

Set No.86

12 Gray's Inn Square, Gray's Inn, London, WC1R 5JP
Tel (020) 7404 4866 **Fax** (020) 7404 4812 **DX** 0055 (Ch.Ln.)
Email admin@littmanchambers.com **Website** www.littmanchambers.com

Head of Chambers	Mark Littman QC
Senior Clerk	Andrew Moore
Tenants	22

Members

Mark Littman QC (1947) (QC-1961)
John Tackaberry QC (1967) (QC-1982) †
Michael Stimpson (1969)
Robert Kirk (1972)
Brian McClure (1976)
Graham Cunningham (1976)
Rowan Planterose (1978)

Andrzej Kolodziej (1978)
Jonathan Tecks (1978)
Barbara Hewson (1985)
Monique Allan (1986)
Seán Naidoo (1990)
Martin Gibson (1990)
Rupert Higgins (1991)
Niamh McCarthy (1991)
Julie Anderson (1993) †

Damian Falkowski (1994)
Richard Holden (1996)
Richard Clegg (1999)
Karim Lahham (1999)
Deborah Tompkinson (1984)
Gary Lidington (2000)
Philip Lewis (1958)
John Finnis (1970)

LITTMAN CHAMBERS
BARRISTERS

12
GRAY'S INN SQUARE

GRAY'S INN
LONDON WC1R 5JP

† Standing Counsel to the Crown.

The Chambers Members of chambers offer specialist advocacy, advisory, drafting, arbitration and mediation services to solicitors and to those with direct access to the Bar. Main areas of work: construction, commercial litigation, ADR, judicial review, property and European Union law.

Maitland Chambers (Michael Lyndon-Stanford QC & Charles Aldous QC)

Set No.87

7 Stone Buildings, Lincoln's Inn, London, WC2A 3SZ
Tel (020) 7406 1200 **Fax** (020) 7406 1300 **DX** LDE 326
Email clerks@maitlandchambers.com **Website** www.maitlandchambers.com

Head of Chambers	
	Michael Lyndon-Stanford QC
	Charles Aldous QC
Chief Executive	Peter Bennett FCCA MCIM
Clerks	Jim Bisland
	Martin Colley
	Andy Flanagan
	Lee Cutler
Fees Clerk	John Rugg
Tenants	42

Members

Michael Lyndon-Stanford QC (1962) (QC-1979)
Charles Aldous QC (1967) (QC-1985)
Christopher McCall QC (1966) (QC-1987)
Hazel Williamson QC (1972) (QC-1988)
Catherine Newman QC (1979) (QC-1995)
Christopher Pymont QC (1979) (QC-1996)
Anthony Trace QC (1981) (QC-1998)
Mark Cunningham QC (1980) (QC-2001)
Guy Newey QC (1982) (QC-2001)

Paul Girolami QC (1983) (QC-2002)
Michael Nield (1969)
Nigel Thomas (1976)
Alastair Walton (1977)
Timothy Evans (1979)
Simon Barker (1979)
Lindsey Stewart (1983)
Christopher Parker (1984)
James Clifford (1984)
Matthew Collings (1985)
Philomena Harrison (1985)
John Nicholls (1986)
Carolyn Walton (1980)
Jonathan Russen (1986)
Dominic Chambers (1987)
Richard Morgan (1988)

Nicholas Peacock (1989)
Gregory Banner (1989)
Mark Wonnacott (1989)
David Brownbill (1989)
Edmund Cullen (1991)
Amanda Tipples (1991)
Patricia Carswell (1993)
Michael Gibbon (1993)
Rebecca Stubbs (1994)
James Aldridge (1994)
Andrew Westwood (1994)
Siward Atkins (1995)
Andrew Ayres (1996)
Catherine Addy (1998)
Louise Hutton (1998)
Oliver Mitchell (1999)
David Mumford (2000)

maitland
CHAMBERS

The Chambers Maitland Chambers was formed in January 2001 by the merger of two long established chancery sets - 13 Old Square (Michael Lyndon Stanford QC) and 7 Stone Buildings (Charles Aldous QC). It is pre-eminent in the field of commercial chancery litigation. All barristers are members of the Chancery Bar Association and the Commercial Bar Association. All members can receive instructions by email to their desks.

Work Undertaken Chambers and Partners recommended members of Maitland as leaders in their field in the following areas - commercial chancery, company, charities, insolvency, media and entertainment, traditional chancery, property litigation, partnership, pensions, banking, energy, tax, agriculture and professional negligence. Expertise is available in all areas of chancery and commercial law.

Clientele Instructions are received from most of the top 100 solicitors in the UK, and also from a very wide range of firms, whose instructions are very valued. Many members are or have been junior counsel to the Crown. Chambers welcome instructions under Direct Professional Access and Bar Direct rules and regularly receive them from accountants, local authorities and others. Members are regularly instructed by international firms for work in the UK and in many offshore jurisdictions.

Recruitment Three, £30,000, 12 month pupillages are offered each year. Full details are available on the website. Chambers do not currently participate in OLPAS. Mini-pupillages are encouraged.

■ BAR A-Z

LONDON

Matrix Chambers
Set No.88

7 Stone Buildings, Lincoln's Inn, London, WC2A 3SZ
Griffin Building, Gray's Inn, London, WC1R 5LN
Tel (020) 7404 3447   **Fax** (020) 7404 3448   **DX** 400 Chancery Lane
Email matrix@matrixlaw.co.uk   **Website** www.matrixlaw.co.uk

Chief Executive	Nicholas Martin
Practice Managers	Amanda Campbell
	Paul Robinson
Administrator	Kevin Hooper
Practice Assistants	Andy Hall
	Carla Owen
	Zoe Osmotherly
Legal Information Manager	Anna Edmundson
Tenants	39

Members

Lord Brennan QC (1967) (QC-1985)
Nicholas Blake QC (1974) (QC-1994)
David Bean QC (1976) (QC-1997)
Cherie Booth QC (1976) (QC-1995)
Andrew Clapham (1985)
James Crawford SC (1999) (NSW-1987) (SC-1997)
Ben Emmerson QC (1986) (QC-2000)
Daniel Friedman (1996)
Conor Gearty (1995)
Murray Hunt (1992)
Raza Husain (1993)
Anthony Jennings QC (1983) (QC-2001)

Julian Knowles (1994)
Thomas Linden (1990)
Ken Macdonald QC (1978) (QC-1997)
Jonathan Marks (1992)
Clare Montgomery QC (1980) (QC-1996)
Helen Mountfield (1991)
Tim Owen QC (1983) (QC-2000)
Heather Rogers (1983) LLB
Matthew Ryder (1992)
Philippe Sands (1985)
Maurice Sheridan (1984)
Jessica Simor (1992)
Rabinder Singh QC (1989) (QC-2002)
Dan Squires (1998)

Rhodri Thompson QC (1989) (QC-2002)
Hugh Tomlinson QC (1983) (QC-2002)
Antony White QC (1983) (QC-2001)
David Wolfe (1992)
Mark Afeeva (1997)
Kate Cook (1991)
Janet Kentridge (1999)
Karon Monaghan (1989)
Gillian Morris (1997)
James Laddie (1995)
Arnondo Chakrabarti (2000)
Alison MacDonald (2000)
Aileen McColgan (2001)

The Chambers Matrix was formed in May 2000 by 26 barristers from a wide range of legal disciplines who recognised that common principles of constitutional, European, and international law increasingly influence their areas of expertise. They saw that these developments, new legislation, and changes in the funding of legal services provided major challenges to lawyers practising at the Bar. Together they were agreed on the need for a new organisation to meet these challenges - an organisation committed to excellence in all areas of service delivery, to innovation in responding to change, and to working in new ways to meet the needs of clients. Since Matrix opened for business it has been joined by other established practitioners and by barristers starting out in practice. Matrix uses paralegals and legal researchers to provide case and research support to members and clients. Matrix has associates in Europe and Australia. Matrix is founded on 'core values' including the independence of its practitioners, and a commitment to quality services, innovation, equality of opportunity, and the provision of training opportunities. Matrix has some of the leading lawyers in all of the practice areas listed, but is unique in being able to combine experts in different areas of the law into teams of advisors and advocates. Matrix is committed to new ways of delivering legal services where these are of real value to clients. Expertise in a wide range of disciplines means that Matrix can put together teams of lawyers for particular cases or legal assignments.

2 Mitre Court Buildings (Guy Roots QC)
Set No.89

2 Mitre Court Buildings, Temple, London, EC4Y 7BX
Tel (020) 7583 1380   **Fax** (020) 7353 7772   **DX** 0032 Chancery Lane
Email clerks@2mcb.co.uk

Head of Chambers	Guy Roots QC
Senior Clerk	Robert Woods
Clerks	Frances Kaliszewska
	Kirstie Durrant
	Tom Rook
Clerk (Administrator)	Joan Matthewson
Tenants	18

Members

Guy Roots QC (1969) (QC-1989)
Matthew Horton QC (1969) (QC-1989)
Stephen Sauvain QC (1977) (QC-1995)
Neil King QC (1980) (QC-2000)

Alun Alesbury (1974)
Robert Fookes (1975)
Michael Humphries (1982)
Richard Glover (1984)
Mary Macpherson (1984)
Paul Shadarevian (1984)
Michael Druce (1988)

Reuben Taylor (1990)
Rupert Warren (1994)
Christopher Boyle (1994)
Richard Wald (1997)
Robert Walton (1999)
Jenny Wigley (2000)
Guy Williams (2000)

2MCB

The Chambers A long-established and well known set currently comprising 18 members of whom four

Continued overleaf

www.ChambersandPartners.com

1573

are QCs. All members specialise in planning and local government law.

Work Undertaken The main specialist area practised by all members comprises planning and local government which includes town and country planning, environmental law, compulsory purchase and compensation, rating and council tax, utilities and infrastructure, local government, public and administrative law, parliamentary bills and transport and works act orders. All members appear at public inquiries, the Lands Tribunal and the courts.

Clientele A wide range including companies, corporations, public and private utilities, local authorities, government departments and foreign governments, individuals and residents associations. Instructions are accepted by direct professional access and BarDirect.

International Members have appeared or advised in relation to a number of jurisdictions including Hong Kong, Singapore, Jersey and Bermuda.

Recruitment Applications for tenancy should be addressed to the chair of the executive committee. Applications for pupillage should be addressed to the administrator. Chambers have two to three pupils at any one time and substantial awards are available for pupils; details will be provided on application. Mini-pupillages are also available.

Monckton Chambers (Kenneth Parker QC & Paul Lasok QC)

Set No. 90

4 Raymond Buildings, Gray's Inn, London, WC1R 5BP
Tel (020) 7405 7211 **Fax** (020) 7405 2084 **DX** 257
Email chambers@monckton.co.uk **Website** www.monckton.co.uk

Head of Chambers	Kenneth Parker QC
	Paul Lasok QC
Senior Clerk	David Hockney
Tenants	29

Members

Kenneth Parker QC (1975) (QC-1992)
Paul Lasok QC (1977) (QC-1994)
Sir Jeremy Lever QC (1957) (QC-1972)
Nicholas Lyell QC (1965) (QC-1980)
John Swift QC (1965) (QC-1981)
Richard Fowler QC (1969) (QC-1989)
Peter M Roth QC (1976) (QC-1997)

Nicholas Paines QC (1978) (QC-1997)
Christopher Vajda QC (1979) (QC-1997)
Melanie Hall QC (1982) (QC-2002)
Rupert Anderson (1981)
Michael Patchett-Joyce (1981)
Michael Bowsher (1985)
Andrew Macnab (1986)
Jon Turner (1988)
Peter Mantle (1989)
George Peretz (1990)

Jennifer Skilbeck (1991)
Raymond Hill (1992)
Paul Harris (1994)
Rebecca Haynes (1994)
Tim Ward (1994)
Kassie Smith (1995)
Daniel Beard (1996)
Ian Hutton (1998)
Meredith Pickford (1999)
Piers Gardner (2000)
Mario Angiolini (2001)
Valentina Sloane (2001)

The Chambers Monckton Chambers has a long tradition of specialist advocacy and advice dating back to the 1930s. The set is one of the English Bar's leading commercial practices and has earned a reputation as a leader in competition law, EC law, commercial law, public and human rights law, VAT and customs law. Members have an exceptional understanding of the interplay between UK and EC law, which is combined with sound commercial judgement and a practical approach. Monckton Chambers prides itself on providing its clients with an efficient and cost-effective service from an approachable and enthusiastic team. Office hours are between 8am-7pm, Monday-Friday. Out of hours you can contact chambers on (07973) 757979.

Work Undertaken

European Law Members of chambers are recognised as leading practitioners in all areas of EC law, acting as advisors and advocates for private sector clients, the UK Government, local authorities and the Community Institutions. Monckton Chambers is particularly renowned for its expertise in, agriculture; anti-dumping; customs and commercial policy; equal pay, employment, transfer of undertakings; environmental; financial services; free movement of goods, persons, capital, and services; pensions; public procurement; rights of establishment; social policy; sports and media; state aids; transport. Recent cases include: Case C-137/00 R v Monopolies and Mergers Commission and Secretary of State, ex parte Milk Marque; KB v NHS Pension Agency & SS; Capespan; PR Strawson; R (British American Tobacco) v Secretary of State for Health.

Competition Law Members of chambers regularly act in competition and regulatory matters before the OFT and sectoral regulators. They also regularly act in merger, monopoly and utility licensing references before the Competition Commission, representing a wide range of UK and overseas clients. Members also advise and represent clients in competition and state aid matters before the European Commission, Court of First

Instance and European court of Justice. They frequently act as advocates in High Court litigation on competition and state aid matters. Most of the early cases involving the Competition Act 1998, both before the High Court and the Competition Commission Appeals Tribunal, have involved members of chambers. Chambers also has significant expertise in utilities and utilities regulation and regularly acts for regulated companies, regulators and other interested parties, providing advice, drafting submissions and appearing at hearings. Recent cases include: Airtours v EC Commission; Bettercare; NAPP Pharmaceutical Holdings Ltd v DGFT; Intel v VIA (Lawrence Collins J); Crehan v Courage; Institute of Independent Insurance Brokers v DGFT.

Commercial Law Monckton Chambers was one of the founding members of the Commercial Bar Association, reflecting its long-standing role as a supplier of specialist advocacy and advisory services in relation to domestic and international commercial disputes. All members of the commercial team are experienced litigators. Members regularly appear in commercial arbitrations as well as in the Commercial Court specialising in the following areas: commercial agency, construction and engineering, freezing orders and injunctions, international arbitration, professional negligence, sale of goods and securities litigation. Recent cases include: Valuable Resources Ltd v Goyal; Saranabu SA v Lombard Commodities Ltd; JME v Miller Construction; NMTV Jobserve; Factortame Damages.

Public & Human Rights Law A number of members of chambers are Crown Panel members and appear regularly on behalf of the government and other public bodies. They also continue to appear for claimants. Monckton Chambers is one of the leading Judicial Review Chambers, in particular in the areas of: agriculture; broadcasting; competition and mergers; customs; employment; environment; fisheries; health and pharmaceuticals. An important aspect of Monckton Chambers' work, the Human Rights Act and the European Convention on Human Rights, has broad implications and crosses into other of chambers' core areas, in particular commercial law. Members have leading expertise in this area and write and edit leading human rights journals and publications. Recent cases include: R v DEFRA ex parte Persey and Jackson and Associated Newspapers; R (Smeaton) v Secretary of State for Health; R v Kansal; International Transport Roth v Secretary of State for Home Dept; Han and Yau v Customs and Excise; R (Quintaville) v Secretary of State for Health.

VAT & Customs Law Monckton Chambers has a large team of experienced advocates with extensive knowledge of VAT and customs law. As a leader in EC law, human rights and judicial review, it is able to deal effectively with the most complex tax litigation. Members have represented taxpayers and the government in the VAT and Duties Tribunal, High Court, Court of Appeal, House of Lords and the ECJ in many leading cases. Recent cases include: Plantifor; Halifax and others v Commissioners of Customs and Excise [2002] STC 402; Bupa Hospitals; Case C-62/00 Marks & Spencer Plc v Commisisioners of Customs and Excise; EDS [CA]; Capital One.

Publications Members of chambers have produced and contributed to a number of leading publications in their fields including: *Atkin's Court Forms on European Court Procedure*, co-authored by Paul Lasok QC and Ian Hutton; *Bellamy & Child: European Community Law of Competition*, edited by Peter Roth QC (including substantial chapters by nine members of chambers); *Common Market Law Reports*, co-edited by Paul Lasok QC and Nicholas Paines QC; *Comparative Law Case Book on Tort*, co-edited by Jeremy Lever QC; *Competition Law Journal*, co-edited by Daniel Beard; *Copinger & James on Copyright (Competition Law)*, specialist editor Rupert Anderson; *Human Rights Law Reports*, general editor Tim Ward; *Law and Institutions of the European Union*, written by Paul Lasok QC; *The Strasbourg Caselaw*, co-editor Tim Ward.

Recruitment Monckton Chambers is a modern and friendly chambers looking for intelligent and ambitious pupils to join it through its funded pupillage scheme. All applications should be made through the OLPAS system. Visit www.monckton.co.uk for more details.

Three New Square (David Young QC) — Set No.91

3 New Square, Lincoln's Inn, London, WC2A 3RS
Tel (020) 7405 1111 **Fax** (020) 7405 7800 **DX** 454
Email clerks@3newsquare.co.uk **Website** www.3newsquare.co.uk

Head of Chambers	David Young QC
Senior Clerk	Ian Bowie
Tenants	14

Members

David Young QC (1966) (QC-1980)
Antony Watson QC (1968) (QC-1986)
Simon Thorley QC (1972) (QC-1989)
Richard Miller QC (1976) (QC-1995)
Guy Burkill QC (1981) (QC-2002)
Andrew Waugh QC (1982) (QC-1998)
Denise McFarland (1987)
Colin Birss (1990)
Justin Turner (1992)
Douglas James Campbell (1993)
Thomas Mitcheson (1996)
Thomas Hinchliffe (1997)
Geoffrey Pritchard (1998)
Helyn Mensah (1998)

Continued overleaf

BAR A-Z

The Chambers A specialist intellectual property set. Members belong to the Intellectual Property and Chancery Bar Associations. David Young is the author of *Passing Off*, chairman of the Plant Seeds Varieties Tribunal and Deputy Judge of the Patent County Court. David Young and Simon Thorley are Deputy High Court Judges in Chancery and Queens' Bench Division. Simon Thorley is a part-time chairman of the Copyright Tribunal and is also an appointed person to hear appeals from the Trade Mark Registry. In addition, for many years, members have edited *Terrell on the Law of Patents*.

Work Undertaken
Intellectual Property Particularly science, technology, biotechnology, entertainment and media. Including patents (UK and European), copyright, designs (registered and unregistered), service marks, plantbreeders rights, trademarks (registered and unregistered), passing off, trade libel and malicious falsehood, confidential information, franchising and licensing (including licences of right and product licensing) and IT. Members also handle related aspects of competition law and general litigation with a significant technical content. Direct Professional Access is accepted.
Additional Areas Arbitration and professional negligence.

International Languages include French, German and Japanese. Chambers' QCs have appeared in Singapore and Hong Kong.

Recruitment Tenancy and pupillage applications should be made via the OLPAS scheme. Awards of £9000 per six months are available. Mini-pupillages are offered throughout the year. A science degree is preferred.

Four New Square

Set No.92

4 New Square, Lincoln's Inn, London, WC2A 3RJ
Tel (020) 7822 2000 **Fax** (020) 7822 2001 **DX** 1041 L.D.E.
Email barristers@4newsquare.com **Website** www.4newsquare.com

Head of Chambers	Justin Fenwick QC
Senior Clerk	Lizzy Wiseman
Tenants	45

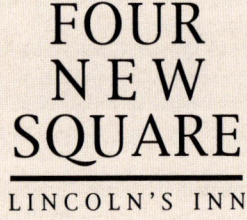

FOUR NEW SQUARE
LINCOLN'S INN

Members

Justin Fenwick QC (1980) (QC-1993)
John L Powell QC (1974) (QC-1990)
Bernard Livesey QC (1969) (QC-1990)
Nicholas Davidson QC (1974) (QC-1993)
Michael Brooke QC (1969) (QC-1994)
Christopher Gibson QC (1976) (QC-1995)
Roger Stewart QC (1986) (QC-2001)
Michael Soole QC (1977) (QC-2002)
Prof. Eva Lomnicka (1974)
Simon Russen (1976)
Charles Douthwaite (1977)

Glen Tyrell (1977)
David Halpern (1978)
Gavin Hamilton (1979)
Simon Monty (1982)
Graeme Mew (1982)
Mark Cannon (1985)
Ian Holtum (1985)
Paul Parker (1986)
Ben Patten (1986)
Sue Carr (1987)
Hugh Evans (1987)
Jalil Asif (1988)
Fiona Sinclair (1989)
Nicholas Brown (1989)
Andrew R Nicol (1991)
Ben Hubble (1992)
Charles Phipps (1992)
Paul Sutherland (1992)

Graeme McPherson (1993)
Aisha Bijlani (1993)
Leigh-Ann Mulcahy (1993)
Nicola Shaldon (1994)
Nicole Sandells (1994)
Jamie Smith (1995)
Anneliese Day (1996)
Ben Elkington (1996)
Seânin Gilmore (1996)
Alex Hall Taylor (1996)
Siân Mirchandani (1997)
Graham Chapman (1998)
Richard Liddell (1999)
Amanda Savage (1999)
Stephen Innes (2000)
Scott Allen (2000)

The Chambers Four New Square is a commercial and civil set with a particular reputation for claims involving professionals and other service providers. It also has a strong construction, financial services, insurance, commercial, commercial chancery and employment practice. Based for over 50 years in the Temple (most recently at 2 Crown Office Row), the set moved to new, larger premises in 1999 in Lincoln's Inn. This has allowed chambers to introduce a modern IT network and to acquire enlarged conference facilities (including video-conferencing) as part of its continuing commitment to providing all its clients with the highest level of service, both as advocates and as advisors.

Work Undertaken Chambers have particular expertise in the field of professional liability and cover the full range of claims against professionals, including claims for fraud, breach of fiduciary duty and trust, negligence and breach of contract and regulatory and disciplinary proceedings. The main professions covered are accountants and auditors, actuaries, architects and engineers, solicitors and barristers, bankers, financial intermediaries and institutions, insurance intermediaries, Lloyd's agents, surveyors and valuers and medical practitioners. *Jackson & Powell on Professional Negligence* is edited by current members of chambers. Other major areas of practice include construction and engineering; commercial litigation including chancery; banking and financial services (including UK, EU and international securities regulation); consumer credit; insurance and reinsurance; employment; IT and computer contracts; product liability and personal injury. Chambers have considerable experience of multi-party litigation in the context of product liability, professional negligence, fraud recovery and disaster claims.

Publications Apart from *Jackson & Powell on Professional Negligence* (General editors John L Powell QC and Roger Stewart QC; editors Christopher Gibson QC, David Halpern, Mark Cannon, Hugh Evans, Fiona Sinclair, Paul Sutherland, Graeme McPherson, Ben Elkington and Leigh-Ann Mulcahy assisted by other members of chambers), publications include *Lawyer's Liabilities* (Hugh Evans), *Confidentiality* (Charles Phipps with Toulson J.), and *The Encyclopaedia of Financial Services Law* (Professor Eva Lomnicka and John L Powell QC). The companion work to *Jackson & Powell*, *Professional Liability Precedents* is written and edited by Sue Carr, Simon Russen, Simon Monty, Paul Parker, Jalil Asif, Ben Hubble, Charles Phipps, Paul Sutherland and Ben Elkington. *Encyclopaedia of Consumer Credit and Modern Banking Law* is written by Professor Eva Lomnicka. Leigh-Ann Mulcahy is general editor of *Human Rights & Civil Practice* to which Anneliese Day, Alex Hall Taylor and Scott Allen contributed.

International Members of chambers appear in court and arbitration proceedings in Hong Kong, Singapore, Paris and the West Indies. Michael Brooke QC is an Avocat à la Cour d'Appel de Paris.

7 New Square (Bernard Pearl) — Set No.93

7 New Square, Lincoln's Inn, London, WC2A 3QS
Tel (020) 7430 1660 **Fax** (020) 7430 1531 **DX** 106 (Ch.Ln.)
Email clerks@7nsq.com

Head of Chambers	Bernard Pearl
Tenants	18

Members

Bernard Pearl (1970)
Margaret Puxon QC (1954) (QC-1982)
Philip Proghoulis (1963)
Paul Taylor (1981)
Andrew Gifford (1988)
Simon Airey (1989)

Linda Goldman (1990)
Francis Navaratne (1990)
Dr Catherine MacKenzie (1995)
Marianne Perkins (1997)
Melvyn Harris (1997)
Alastair B Hodge (1997)

Leon Taylor (1997)
Cecilia Hulse (1998)
Barry Harwood (1998)
Paula Rhone-Adrien (1998)
Peter Feldschreiber (2000)
Fiona Beach (2001)

Work Undertaken Civil/commercial, especially employment; professional negligence (members include two dentists and a doctor); commercial and residential property; construction; insolvency; local authority; immigration; judicial review. Seminars and lectures are available.

International Languages spoken include French, German and Italian.

7 New Square Intellectual Property (John Fitzgerald) — Set No.94

7 New Square, Lincoln's Inn, London, WC2A 3QS
Tel (020) 7404 5484 **Fax** (020) 7404 5369 **DX** 420 (CH LN)
Email clerks@7newsquare.com **Website** www.7newsquare.com

Head of Chambers	John Fitzgerald
Senior Clerk	Simon Coomber
Tenants	7

Members

John Fitzgerald (1971)
Alison Firth (1980)
Matthew Kime (1988)

Mark Engelman (1987)
Gary Fern (1992)
Christy Rogers (1999)

Ian Silcock (1997)

The Chambers A progressive set specialising in all aspects of the law of intellectual property. Many members of chambers have prior relevant experience including work in Scientific Research Media and in-house IP management. A detailed brochure is available. Up-to-date information is available on their website.

Work Undertaken Primarily, members practice in the areas of patents, copyright, design rights, trademarks and passing off, trade secrets and confidentiality, computer and information technology. Members of chambers also assist in other areas of concern often closely associated with general intellectual property practice such as technical contract, e-commerce, internet, criminal IP liability, EU competition law, entertainment, trade libel, defamation and other media orientated work and general contractual or tortuous problems in appropriate contexts.

LONDON — BAR A-Z

8 New Square (Mark Platts-Mills QC) — Set No.95

8 New Square, Lincoln's Inn, London, WC2A 3QP
Tel (020) 7405 4321 **Fax** (020) 7405 9955 **DX** 379 (Ch.Ln)
Email clerks@8newsquare.co.uk **Website** www.8newsquare.co.uk

Head of Chambers	Mauh Platts–Mills QC
Senior Clerk	John Call
Deputy Senior Clerk	Tony Liddon
Principal Clerks	Nicholas Wise
	Martin Williams
Assistant Clerks	Martin Kilbey
	Andrew Clayton
Tenants	23

Members

Peter Prescott QC (1970) (QC-1990)
John Baldwin QC (1977) (QC-1991)
David Kitchin QC (1977) (QC-1994)
Mark Platts-Mills QC (1974) (QC-1995)
Martin Howe QC (1978) (QC-1996)
Mary Vitoria QC (1975) (QC-1997)
George Hamer (1974)
Fiona Clark (1982)
James Mellor (1986)
Daniel Alexander (1988)
Robert Onslow (1991)
Michael Tappin (1991)
Richard Meade (1991)
Adrian Speck (1993)
James St. Ville (1995)
Charlotte May (1995)
Thomas Moody-Stuart (1995)
Lindsay Lane (1996)
James Abrahams (1997)
Iona Berkeley (1999)
Mark Chacksfield (1999)
Henry Ward (2000)
Jonathan Hill (2000)

The Chambers The set specialises in intellectual property law of all kinds, and is the largest set in the country practising in this area. Many members of chambers are authors of, or contributors to, the leading books and encyclopaedias on intellectual property law. All are members of the Intellectual Property Bar and Chancery Bar Associations. A brochure giving further information and individual biographies of all members of chambers is available upon request. Biographies may also be viewed on 8 New Square's website along with current news. The senior clerks have been with chambers for over 20 years and have considerable experience of the work undertaken by chambers. They will be happy to assist in choice of Counsel.

Work Undertaken Intellectual property, including patents; copyright; passing off; trade and service marks; designs and registered designs; counterfeiting; data protection; franchising; publishing; telecommunications; internet domain names; trade libel; trade descriptions; trade secrets and confidential information; hallmarks; plant breeders' rights. Members also specialise in European law, competition and restrictive trade practices, entertainment and media law, advertising law, computer law, licensing and administrative law (principally where these are ancillary to intellectual property cases). Commercial, environmental and other work with a significant scientific or technical content are also handled.

International French, German, Spanish and Italian. Several members of chambers conduct cases in the Far East, West Indies and Ireland.

Recruitment Up to two pupillages are offered each year, usually for twelve months. Pupils with scientific or technical backgrounds are strongly encouraged, although others will be considered in exceptional circumstances. Awards of £20,000 are offered. Chambers are members of OLPAS (Online Pupillage Application System).

11 New Square (John Gardiner QC) — Set No.96

11 New Square, Lincoln's Inn, London, WC2A 3QB
Tel (020) 7242 4017 **Fax** (020) 7831 2391 **DX** 315
Email taxlaw@11newsquare.com **Website** www.11newsquare.com

Head of Chambers	John Gardiner QC
Senior Clerk	John Moore
Tenants	8

Members

John Gardiner QC (1968) (QC-1982)
Barry Pinson QC (1949) (QC-1973)
Peter Rees QC (1953) (QC-1969)
Peter Trevett QC (1971) (QC-1992)
Jonathan Peacock QC (1987) (QC-2001)
Francis Fitzpatrick (1990)
Grania Lyster (1992)
Jolyon Maugham (1997)

The Chambers This is the oldest established set to specialise exclusively in revenue law. Members advise in the UK and abroad on all aspects of tax law including all personal and corporate taxes, VAT, customs and excise and stamp duties. Tax planning and advocacy services are provided for clients ranging from large multinational corporations to private individuals, including those of modest means. The set also advises in relation to professional negligence actions. Chambers offer a considerable range of experience in litigation before tribunals of first instance including the Commissioners of Inland Revenue and VAT Tribunals, through the High Court to the House of Lords, the European Court of Human Rights and the Courts of certain colonies and Commonwealth jurisdictions. Chambers can accommodate electronic file transfer with or without secure encryption. Worldwide video conferences can be arranged. Chambers have a website displaying information about chambers, including tax law articles.

International Languages spoken include French and Luxembourgeoise.

11 New Square (Sonia Proudman QC)   Set No.97

11 New Square, Lincoln's Inn, London, WC2A 3QB
Tel (020) 7831 0081   **Fax** (020) 7405 0798/2560   **DX** 319 LONDON/CHANCERY LANE
Email clerks@11newsquare.co.uk   **Website** www.11newsquare.co.uk

Head of Chambers	Sonia Proudman QC
Practice Director	John Lister
Senior Clerk	Graham Lister
Tenants	28

Members

Sonia Proudman QC (1972) (QC-1994)
Peter Crampin QC (1976) (QC-1993)
Hedley Marten (1966)
Roger Horne (1967)
Peter Castle (1970)
Stephen Lloyd (1971)
Jill Gibson (1972)
Michael Heywood (1975)
Michael Jefferis (1976)
Mark Studer (1976)
Robert Lewis (1996) Admitted as a solicitor (1977)
Robert Pearce (1977)
Andrew Francis (1977)
Thomas Dumont (1979)
Simon Randle (1982)
Alistair Craig (1983)
Ulick Staunton (1984)
Piers Feltham (1985)
Howard Smith (1986)
Roger Mullis (1987)
Clive Moys (1998) Admitted as a solicitor (1988)
Adam Deacock (1991)
Peter Smith (1993)
Marie-Claire Bleasdale (1993)
Justin Holmes (1994)
Dov Ohrenstein (1995)
Catherine Finely (1999)
Nathan Wells (2000)

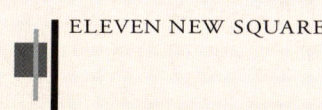

The Chambers Chambers is one of the largest specialist chancery sets. It has notable expertise in commercial and property law, professional indemnity, and trusts and charities work. 11 New Square is a leading and progressive chambers specialising in chancery work. Its members, two silks and 26 juniors, possess notable expertise in both traditional and evolving areas of chancery practice. The aims of chambers are: to provide first class advocacy, advice and drafting in the areas of members' expertise; to develop constructive and lasting working relationships between members and their clients; to be approachable and responsive to the needs of clients. Chambers offer teams of practitioners of varying levels of seniority, specialising in each of the principal areas of the practice covered by chambers. Members have gained experience through involvement in significant recent cases or transactions in all the principal areas of practice covered by chambers. Two members, Robert Lewis and Clive Moys, previously qualified as solicitors in 1977 and 1988 before joining the Bar. A strong and efficient clerking and administration team which is dedicated to ensuring that the service provided by chambers is tailored as closely as possible to the needs and resources of clients.

Work Undertaken

Charities & Pensions Chambers contain groups of members with particular expertise in both these areas.
Commercial Law Particularly in areas such as banking and security, partnerships and joint ventures.
Company Law & Corporate & Individual Insolvency In the corporate field, members have particular experience in areas such as minority shareholders' rights and directors' conduct, winding up, administration and receivership.
Planning & Local Government Work Including inquiries, enforcement, compulsory purchase, environmental, highways, housing, public health, corporate controls and governance, regulatory, contracts and procurement and capital finance.
Professional Negligence Members of chambers at all levels have wide experience in the conduct and defence of claims for professional negligence, particularly of solicitors, accountants and surveyors.
Property All aspects of land law and conveyancing, and landlord and tenant work, chambers contain specialists in restrictive covenants; easements (including rights of light) and mines and minerals.
Public Law Judicial review, especially for and against local authorities, statutory appeals and boundary commission inquiries.
Trusts & Estates All aspects of the administration of trusts and estates, including probate and family provision litigation. Members offer specialist expertise in the field of taxation of trusts.
Additional Specialisations Individual members of chambers have developed particular expertise in intellectual property, court of protection work, and the taxation of costs. Members of chambers regularly lecture and conduct seminars on topics arising in their field of practice. Three members of chambers are currently writing or editing legal textbooks and others have contributed to a variety of legal publications. Members of chambers are members of the Chancery Bar Association, the Professional Negligence Bar Association, PEBA, STEP, the Charity Law Association, ACTAPS, COMBAR, ABA, ABI, IBA and ALBA.

BAR A-Z

New Square Chambers (Charles Purle QC)
Set No.98

12 New Square, Lincoln's Inn, London, WC2A 3SW
Tel (020) 7419 8000 **Fax** (020) 7419 8050 **DX** 1056 London/Chancery Lane
Email clerks@newsquarechambers.co.uk **Website** www.newsquarechambers.co.uk

Head of Chambers	Charles Purle QC
Senior Clerk	Clive Petchey
Tenants	44

Members

John Mowbray QC (1953) (QC-1974)
Eben Hamilton QC (1962) (QC-1981)
John Macdonald QC (1955) (QC-1976)
John McDonnell QC (1968) (QC-1984)
Charles Purle QC (1970) (QC-1989)
George Laurence QC (1972) (QC-1991)
Robin Mathew QC (1974) (QC-1992)
Robin Hollington QC (1979) (QC-1999)
Stephen Smith QC (1983) (QC-2000)
Rodney Stewart Smith (1964)
Michael Kennedy (1967)
Lynton Tucker (1971)
Colin Braham (1971)
Christopher Russell (1971)
Kenneth Munro (1973)
Gordon Bennett (1974)
James Thom (1974)
Nicholas Le Poidevin (1975)
Malcolm Chapple (1975)
Christopher Semken (1977)
Michael Roberts (1978)
Alexander Hill-Smith (1978)
Clive Jones (1981)
Leigh Sagar (1983)
David Eaton Turner (1984)
Claire Staddon (1985)
Thomas Graham (1985)
Ross Crail (1986)
Stephen Schaw Miller (1988)
Robert Levy (1988)
Colette Wilkins (1989)
Ian Peacock (1990)
Gerard van Tonder (1990)
Edwin Simpson (1990)
Mark Hubbard (1991)
Simon Adamyk (1991)
John Eidinow (1992)
Jane Evans-Gordon (1992)
Sebastian Prentis (1996)
David Warner (1996)
Adrian Pay (1999)
James Bailey (1999)
James Brightwell (1999)
Professor Richard Buckley (1969)

NEW SQUARE CHAMBERS

The Chambers New Square Chambers was formed in October 2000 by the merger of two leading chancery sets, 1 New Square and 12 New Square.

Work Undertaken New Square Chambers undertakes litigation and advisory work both in the UK and internationally, including Direct Professional Access and Legal Aid. The work done by members of chambers covers three broad areas: company and commercial (including individual and corporate insolvency, receivership, partnership, freezing injunctions, search orders and fraud); property (including landlord and tenant, mortgages, intellectual property, construction and conveyancing; taxes, trusts and wills (including probate, pension schemes and both revenue and capital taxation. Members also cover public/administrative law including parliamentary law, public inquiries, local government and planning law, judicial review and constitutional law. Members cover professional negligence related to the above fields. A brochure, containing a more detailed profile of chambers, is available on request, or via chambers website.

International Languages spoken include French and German. Members are regularly instructed to appear in overseas jurisdictions, including Antigua, the Bahamas, Bermuda, the British Virgin Islands, the Caymans, the Channel Islands, Gibraltar, Hong Kong and Singapore and before the Privy Council.

Recruitment Applications for pupillage via OLPAS.

No5 Chambers (Gareth Evans QC)
Set No.99

4th Floor, 199 Strand, London, WC2R 1DR **Tel** (020) 7836 5500
Fax (020) 7240 9458 **DX** DX 449 Chancery Lane
Email info@no5.com **Website** www.no5.com

Head of Chambers:	Gareth Evans QC
Tenants:	119

No5 Chambers London office opened in July 2002. An extension of the Birmingham Office, the new premises offer excellent conference facilities for all 119 tenants and their clients. Members of No5 Chambers practice within six specialist groups - for further information and a list of tenants please see the Birmingham listing.

BAR A-Z
LONDON

19 Old Buildings (Alastair Wilson QC)

Set No.100

19 Old Buildings, Lincoln's Inn, London, WC2A 3UP
Tel (020) 7405 2001 **Fax** (020) 7405 0001 **DX** 397 (Ch.Ln.)
Email clerks@19oldbuildings.com **Website** www.19oldbuildings.com

Head of Chambers	Alastair Wilson QC
Senior Clerk	Barbara Harris
Tenants	7

Members

Alastair Wilson QC (1968) (QC-1987) MA (Cantab)
Brian Reid (1971) MA (Cantab), LLM (Lond)
Graham Shipley (1973) MA (Cantab), Dip Comp Sci (Cantab)
Michael Hicks (1976) BA (Cantab)
Peter McLean Colley (1989) BSc (Lond), PhD (Lond), LLB (Lond)
Cedric Puckrin (1990) BA, LLB (Cape Town)
Jeremy Reed (1997) MA (Cantab)

The Chambers This set, founded by Sir Duncan Kerly, has specialised for over a century in intellectual property law. Chambers also offer expertise in cases relating to computers (and other technical subject-matter), competition, media and entertainment. Direct Professional Access work is undertaken. A chambers brochure is available on request.

Work Undertaken

Intellectual Property Patents; copyright; designs; trademarks; passing off; plant varieties; confidential information (including ex-employee cases).
Science & Technology Work requiring understanding of scientific and technical issues.
Computers and IT All aspects of litigation involving computers and information technology including data protection and internet disputes.
Media & Entertainment Public performance, film, recording and performers' rights; merchandising; broadcasting; cable and satellite distribution.
Competition Law UK and EU monopolies and restrictive practices law, in particular relating to R&D, licensing, distribution and franchising.
Additional areas Pharmaceutical registration.

Publications Publications written, or contributed to, by members of chambers include: *European Patent Office Reports*, *The Future of Legal Protection for Industrial Design*, *The CIPA Black Book*, *Melville's Forms and Agreements on Intellectual Property and International Licensing*.

International Work is handled in French.

22 Old Buildings (Benet Hytner QC)

Set No.101

22 Old Buildings, Lincoln's Inn, London, WC2A 3UP
Tel (020) 7831 0222 **Fax** (020) 7831 2239 **DX** 201 London Chancery Lane
Email clerks@22oldbuildings.law.co.uk

Head of Chambers	Benet Hytner QC
Senior Clerk	Alan Brewer
Clerks	Maxine Rogers
	James Stammers
Chambers Administrator	Tony Charlick
Fees Clerk	Terry Sullivan
Tenants	56

Members

Benet Hytner QC (1952) (QC-1970)
John Price QC (1961) (QC-1980)
John Rowe QC (1960) (QC-1982)
Giles Wingate-Saul QC (1967) (QC-1983)
Rodney Scholes QC (1968) (QC-1987)
Raymond Machell QC (1973) (QC-1988)
Timothy King QC (1973) (QC-1991)
Geoffrey Tattersall QC (1970) (QC-1992)
Caroline Swift QC (1977) (QC-1993)
Andrew G Moran QC (1976) (QC-1994)
David Allan QC (1974) (QC-1995)
Stephen Stewart QC (1975) (QC-1996)
Winston Hunter QC (1985) (QC-2000)
Christopher Melton QC (1982) (QC-2001)
Patrick Hamlin (1970)
Mark Batchelor (1971)
Susan Cooper (1976)
Michael Daiches (1977)
Philip Newman (1977)
Charles Utley (1979)
Jane Hill (1980)
Howard Lederman (1982)
Rehna Azim (1984)
David Dabbs (1984)
Jonathan Bennett (1985)
Garfield Braithwaite (1987)
Tina Cook (1988)
Frank Feehan (1988)
Gemma Taylor (1988)
Nicholas Berry (1988)
Ronald Coster (1989)
Anthony Jerman (1989)
Desmond Kilcoyne (1990)
Richard Furniss (1991)
Mary Lazarus (1991)
Paul Lonergan (1991)
Carolyn Rothwell (1991)

Continued overleaf

22 Old Buildings

BAR A-Z

Benjamin Uduje (1992)
Matthew Hutchings (1993)
Naomi Hawkes (1994)
Tina Villarosa (1995)
Damian Woodward-Carlton (1995)
Angus Withington (1995)
Fareha Choudhury (1995)
Matthew Feldman (1995)
Henry Pitchers (1996)
Scott Matthewson (1996)
Toby Watkin (1996)
Jude Shepherd (1996)
Aysha Ahmad (1996)
Gareth Compton (1997)
Eilidh Gardner (1997)
Rebecca Thomas (1999)
Sebastian Naughton (1999)
Richard Gregory (2000)
Shomik Datta (2000)

The Chambers Areas of specialisation: Clinical negligence, personal injury, contract/commercial, employment, family and social services, planning and local government, professional negligence, property and construction. Also at Byrom Street Chambers, 12 Byrom Street, Manchester M3 4PP. Telephone: (0161) 829 2100 Fax: (0161) 829 2101.

24 Old Buildings (Rex Bretten QC)   Set No.102
24 Old Buildings (First Floor), Lincoln's Inn, London, WC2A 3UP **Tel:** (020) 7242 2744 **Fax:** (020) 7831 8095 **DX:** 386

24 Old Buildings (Martin Mann QC & Alan Steinfeld QC)   Set No.103
24 Old Buildings, Lincoln's Inn, London, WC2A 3UP
Tel (020) 7404 0946 **Fax** (020) 7405 1360 **DX** 307 Chancery Lane
Email clerks@xxiv.co.uk   **Website** www.xxiv.co.uk

Head of Chambers	Martin Mann QC
	Alan Steinfeld QC
Practice Director	Nicholas Luckman
Practice Managers	Jeremy Hopkins
	Daniel Wilson
	Chris Lane
Tenants	30

Members

Martin Mann QC (1968) (QC-1983)
Alan Steinfeld QC (1968) (QC-1987)
Roger Kaye QC (1970) (QC-1989)
Lawrence Cohen QC (1974) (QC-1993)
Stephen Moverley Smith QC (1985) (QC-2002)
Thomas Baxendale (1962)
Michael King (1971)
Philip Shepherd (1975)
Paul Teverson (1976)
Richard Ritchie (1978)
Francis Tregear (1980)
Daniel Gerrans (1981)
Michael Gadd (1981)
Elizabeth Weaver (1982)
Helen Galley (1987)
Adrian Francis (1988)
Amanda Harington (1989)
Elspeth Talbot Rice (1990)
Nicholas Cherryman (1991)
Christopher Young (1988)
Arshad Ghaffar (1991)
Marcus Staff (1994) Geneva
Clare Stanley (1994)
Stuart Adair (1995)
Alexander Pelling (1995)
Bajul Shah (1996)
Steven Thompson (1996)
Jessica Chappell (1997)
Lyndsey Mein (1999)
Edward Knight (1999)
Graham Virgo *

XXIV
TWENTY FOUR OLD BUILDINGS

* Door Tenant

The Chambers Twenty Four Old Buildings is a leading London barristers' chambers, which has continuously adapted to meet the changing needs of modern business. Chambers' experience and reputation is in business litigation and international trust law. Instructions are taken from UK firms, in-house legal departments, recognised institutions under Direct Professional Access and Bar Direct, international law firms and foreign clients. Barristers and staff are well known for their friendly, efficient and practical approach, and their commitment to the highest standards of professional service. Cases in recent years have included Atlantic Computers, Gruppo Torras Litigation, Maxwell, Baring and BCCI; Pan Am in the Lockerbie air disaster, and ABTA on passenger service charges. Twenty Four Old Buildings' strength lies in its ability to handle complex cases involving more than one aspect of the law, offering both breadth and depth of expertise.
Office Hours 8am to 7pm, Monday to Friday. Please call the Clerks or visit the website for further information. Chambers provides 24-hour cover for urgent cases - Nicholas Luckman at (07774) 240112.

Work Undertaken Key areas of expertise are company law; insolvency and corporate rescue; bankruptcy; civil fraud; asset tracing and recovery; international trusts; insurance; property; partnership; professional negligence. Growth areas are arbitration and mediation, e-commerce and IT litigation. Some members have niche specialisms in banking; aviation and travel; pensions; financial services; probate; EU law; charities and church law.

Clientele Multinational corporations, private companies and partnerships, financial institutions, trustees and trust companies, insolvency practitioners, accountants, overseas lawyers, property developers, government departments, industry associations, and private individuals.

International Chambers have a permanent office in Geneva. Members regularly advise and appear as advocates in other jurisdictions including the Isle of Man and Channel Islands; Bahamas, Bermuda, British Virgin Islands; Cayman; the Far East and Europe. Chambers have particular expertise in multijurisdictional disputes, ICC and UNCITRAL arbitrations, and the European Convention on Human Rights. Chambers have a strong association with a leading Swiss law firm.

Old Square Chambers (John Hendy QC) — Set No.104

1 Verulam Buildings, Gray's Inn, London, WC1R 5LQ
Tel (020) 7269 0300 **Fax** (020) 7405 1387 **DX** 1046 Chancery Lane/London
Email clerks@oldsquarechambers.co.uk **Website** www.oldsquarechambers.co.uk

Head of Chambers	John Hendy QC
Senior Clerk	John Taylor
Tenants	51

Members

John Hendy QC (1972) (QC-1987)
John Melville Williams QC (1955) (QC-1977)
Frederic Reynold QC (1960) (QC-1982)
John Hand QC (1972) (QC-1988)
Lord Wedderburn QC (1953) (QC-1990)
Ian Truscott QC (1995) (QC-1997)
David Wilby QC (1974) (QC-1998)
Matthias Kelly QC (1979) (QC-1999)
Nigel Cooksley QC (1975) (QC-2002)
Paul Rose QC (1981) (QC-2002)
Jane McNeill QC (1982) (QC-2002)

Charles Lewis (1963)
Christopher Carling (1969)
William Birtles (1970)
Diana Brahams (1972)
John H Bates (1973)
Christopher Makey (1975)
Charles Pugh (1975)
Toby Kempster (1980)
Alan Smith (1981)
Mark Sutton (1982)
Barry Cotter (1985)
Louise Chudleigh (1987)
Ijeoma Omambala (1989)
Jennifer Eady (1989)
Philip Mead (1989)
Damian Brown (1989)
Tess Gill (1990)
Jonathan Clarke (1990)
Christopher Walker (1990)
Nicholas Booth (1991)

Sarah Moor (1991)
Ian Scott (1991)
Oliver Segal (1992)
Michael Ford (1992)
Helen Gower (1992)
Roy Lewis (1992)
Elizabeth Melville (1994)
Mark Whitcombe (1994)
Melanie Tether (1995)
Emma Smith (1995)
Rohan Pirani (1995)
Rebecca Tuck (1998)
Hilary Winstone (1998)
Steven Langton (1998)
Stuart Brittenden (1999)
Anya Palmer (1999)
Katharine Newton (1999)
Daniel Bennett (2000)
Bella Morris (2000)
Ben Cooper (2000)

OLD SQUARE CHAMBERS

The Chambers Chambers have an annexe at 3 Orchard Court, Orchard Lane, Bristol, BS1 5WS
DX 78229 Tel (0117) 930 5100 Fax (0117) 927 3478

Work Undertaken

Employment Law Chambers boast several of the UK's leading specialists at the Bar and they frequently appear in landmark cases. Six members of the seven QCs and 30 junior team are part-time Employment Tribunal chairmen.

Personal Injury Dealt with at all levels of seniority, chambers cover the entire range of claims including Package Holiday Regulations and Forum Non Conveniens. Disaster litigation is an area where chambers have particular expertise, as well as complex multi-party actions. Members are active in all relevant associations and they regularly write and speak on topical cases.

Clinical Law The group covers not only clinical negligence work but - perhaps uniquely - is able to offer representation at both professional body and internal NHS disciplinary proceedings, as well as expertise in the handling of waste material from hospitals and public inquiries arising out of accidents in hospitals. David Wilby QC, who joined chambers in January 2001, is the head of the group.

Environmental Chambers' expertise incorporates major toxic tort litigation, work on behalf of regulatory bodies and a wide variety of prosecutions for statutory nuisance. The highly respected group has been instructed in some of the most notable cases.

Product Liability & Regulatory Compliance Group The product liability work has expanded to incorporate health and safety compliance. Chambers are former consultants to the EC on the implementation of European Health and Safety Directives in the UK. Members have appeared in the Southall and the Ladbroke Grove Train Inquiries. Their expertise in product liability lies in advising and appearing for companies, local authorities, individuals and specialist associations with regard to all aspects of civil and criminal liability in respect of defective and unsafe products.

Sports Law Members have represented various clubs and individual sporting personalities in breaches of contract, injuries and appeals to governing bodies.

Continued overleaf

BAR A-Z

Public Inquiries Chambers have been instructed in numerous high profile inquiries over the last decade, ranging from rail, fire, prisons, hospitals and children's homes.

9 Old Square (Michael Driscoll QC)   Set No.105

9 Old Square, Lincoln's Inn, London, WC2A 3SR
Tel (020) 7405 4682 **Fax** (020) 7831 7107 **DX** 305 LONDON/CHANCERY LANE
Email chambers@9oldsquare.co.uk **Website** www.9oldsquare.co.uk

Head of Chambers	Michael Driscoll QC
Tenants	21

Members

Michael Driscoll QC (1970) (QC-1992)
Judith Jackson QC (1975) (QC-1994)
Simon Berry QC (1977) (QC-1990)
David Hodge QC (1979) (QC-1997)
Michael Booth QC (1981) (QC-1999)

John Dagnall QC (1983) (QC-1999)
John McGhee (1984)
Timothy Harry (1983)
Edwin Johnson (1987)
Thomas Leech (1988)
Katharine Holland (1989)
Andrew P D Walker (1991)
Simon Burrell (1988)
Michael Pryor (1992)

Thomas Grant (1993)
Alan Johns (1994)
Daniel Margolin (1995)
Stephanie Tozer (1996)
William V W Norris (1997)
Paul Clarke (1997)
Charles Courtenay (1999)
Adam Smith (2001)

The Chambers 9 Old Square is a long-established and leading set of commercial chancery chambers. It has an established reputation for all aspects of property and modern chancery litigation. Particular fields of expertise for all members include landlord and tenant, conveyancing, contract, professional negligence, trusts, banking, company, and partnership law and for some members, also, the fields of insolvency, mining, judicial review, and sports law. Former members include Sir Robert Megarry, Lord Hoffmann and Sir Nicholas Patton. There are presently five QCs and 17 junior members of chambers. Many members of chambers are listed in professional publications (such as this one) as leaders in their fields and such is the breadth of experience and years of call within the members of chambers that all cases from the largest to the smallest can be catered for. Members of chambers sit as arbitrators and as legal assessors. Direct Professional Access is available. The rates charged by members are intended to be competitive and flexible, and the aim of chambers is to provide clients with a professional and efficient but approachable service. A brochure is available on request and the Senior Clerk, Christopher McSweeney, can be contacted for further information on the experience of and rates charged by individual members.

Work Undertaken

Real Property & Landlord & Tenant Members advise on, and appear as advocates in disputes relating to, all aspects of landlord and tenant law, all types of land and buildings, and all manner of dispute viz claims for possession, rent reviews, 1954 Act renewals, leasehold enfranchisement claims, dilapidations claims, breaches of alienation and other covenants, service charge disputes, environmental protection etc. Also in relation to all other real property work viz contracts and conveyancing, development agreements and options, restrictive covenants, easements, overriding interests, mortgages, subrogation, liens, removal of cautions etc.

Professional Negligence Members have appeared in many of the leading cases against solicitors, valuers, barristers and accountants in relation to all types of claim from property finance to company acquisitions, flotations to domestic conveyancing.

Other Commercial & Chancery Areas of Work: Chambers regularly undertake not only the modern commercial chancery work based upon contractual interpretation and litigation but also the more traditional work of the Chancery Bar, trusts and wills, though nowadays this latter work involves more often than not disputes relating to offshore trusts, constructive trusts and tracing remedies. Some members also practise in the fields of company and partnership law, particularly in relation to share valuations, and disputes between shareholders and partners.

Publications 9 Old Square has continued the tradition of contributing to leading textbooks and publications within their fields of expertise. Publications in which present members of chambers have participated and papers which they have presented include: Michael Driscoll QC, *Halsbury's Laws: Law of Family Arrangement*, Blundell Memorial Lecture 2002; Judith Jackson QC, contributor to *Megarry's Rent Acts* (Sweet & Maxwell); consultant editor on *Enforcement of Money Judgments* (Butterworths); Simon Berry QC, *1995 Blundell Memorial Lecture*; David Hodge QC, *Foskett on Compromise (Chancery Matters)*; *Secret Trusts: The Fraud Theory Revisited*; *Encyclopaedia of Forms & Precedents*; Tim Harry, *Hill and Redman's Law of Landlord and Tenant*, and case editor of LLP *Professional Negligence Law Reports*; John McGhee, editor of *Snell on Equity*; Tom Leech, co-author *Solicitor's Negligence* (Butterworths), case editor of LLP *Professional Negligence*

Law Reports. Members are also invited regularly to give lectures and seminars for the Bar, solicitors and other professionals.

International Members appear as advocates in all courts and tribunals in England & Wales, and in Jersey, Hong Kong, Bermuda, the Far East, the Bahamas, and Brunei. They also act as arbitrators, legal assessors, legal experts and advocates in arbitrations and expert determinations.

10 Old Square (Leolin Price CBE QC) — Set No.106

10 Old Square, Lincoln's Inn, London, WC2A 3SU
Tel (020) 7405 0758   **Fax** (020) 7831 8237   **DX** 306
Email clerks@tenoldsquare.com   **Website** www.tenoldsquare.com

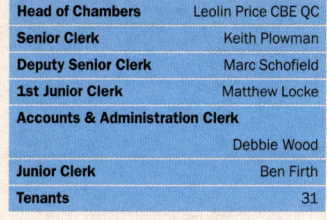

Head of Chambers	Leolin Price CBE QC
Senior Clerk	Keith Plowman
Deputy Senior Clerk	Marc Schofield
1st Junior Clerk	Matthew Locke
Accounts & Administration Clerk	Debbie Wood
Junior Clerk	Ben Firth
Tenants	31

Members

Leolin Price CBE QC (1949) (QC-1968)
James Bonney QC (1975) (QC-1995)
Simon Taube QC (1980) (QC-2000)
Michael Mello (QC Bermuda)
David Ainger (1961)
Francis Barlow (1965)
David Ritchie (1970)
Frances Burton (1972)
Gregory Hill (1972)
Richard Wallington (1972)
Rt Hon James Arbuthnot MP (1975)
Andrew Walker (1975)
David Schmitz (1976)
Owen Rhys (1976)
Geraint Thomas (1976)
Andrew De La Rosa (1981)
Michael Michell (1984)
Paul Stafford (1987)
David Partington (1987)
Julian Roberts (1987)
Susannah Meadway (1988)
Eason Rajah (1989)
Rupert D'Cruz (1989)
Jeremy Callman (1991)
Jonathan Gavaghan (1992)
Samuel Laughton (1993)
Kevin Farrelly (1993)
Michael Waterworth (1994)
Luke Norbury (1995)
Robert Arnfield (1996)
Evan Price (1997)
Richard Dew (1999)

10 OLD SQUARE

The Chambers 10 Old Square has an excellent reputation for traditional chancery matters and litigious chancery work. Each member of 10 Old Square has developed a unique and often highly specialised practice. The set's instructions come from a myriad of diverse sources such as solicitors in the UK, Hong Kong, Singapore and the Channel Islands as well as from other foreign and Commonwealth jurisdictions. Three Queen's Counsel and 24 junior barristers are supported by four experienced clerks. Leolin Price CBE QC is the Head of Chambers and is one of the most senior chancery silks practising at the English Bar. James Bonney QC has a formidable reputation in real property matters and Simon Taube QC enjoys unparalleled standing for his private client, trusts and administration of estates work. Keith Plowman leads the clerks room and, with his colleagues Marc Schofield and Matthew Locke, provides administrative support to the barristers and more importantly, is able to advise clients on the suitability, availability and cost of the instructing appropriate counsel. The website provides further information about the set.

Work Undertaken The set specialises in real property; partnership; pensions; tax; private client including trusts and settlements; professional negligence; equitable remedies; company law; wills; insolvency; charities; commercial contracts; probate; administration of estates. In addition the set will provide qualified arbitrators and lecturers on request. Some members hold judicial posts and many are involved in editing and producing leading legal textbooks. Chambers are accredited by the Law Society to provide CPD training to solicitors and chambers accept work under the DPA and Conditional Fee regulations.

BAR A-Z

11 Old Square (Grant Crawford & Jonathan Simpkiss) — Set No.107

11 Old Square, Lincoln's Inn, London, WC2A 3TS
Tel (020) 7430 0341 **Fax** (020) 7831 2469 **DX** 1031
Email clerks@11oldsquare.co.uk **Website** www.11oldsquare.co.uk

Head of Chambers	Grant Crawford
	Jonathan Simpkiss
Senior Clerk	Keith Nagle
Tenants	24

Members

Edward Davidson QC (1966) (QC-1994)
Francesca Quint (1970)
Gordon Nurse (1973)
Grant Crawford (1974)
Jonathan Simpkiss (1975) FCI Arb
Peter Smith QC (1975) (QC-1992)
Reziya Harrison (1975) FCI Arb †

Malcolm Waters QC (1977) (QC-1997)
Stephen Acton (1977)
Elizabeth Ovey (1978)
Keith Rowley QC (1979) (QC-2001)
Siân Thomas (1981)
Glenn Campbell (1985)
Mark West (1987)
Katherine McQuail (1989)

Nigel Burroughs (1991)
Peter Dodge (1992)
Tony Oakley (1994)
Kate Selway (1995)
Alison Maclennan (1996)
Michael Bowmer (1997)
Myriam Stacey (1998)
William Moffett (2000)
Iqbal Moollan (1998) (Mauritius Bar) *

* Door Tenant † Accredited Mediator

The Chambers IT:Chambers word processing system is Microsoft Word, IBM compatible and floppy disks. Please speak to the clerks if you wish to deliver or receive text on disk or by electronic communication.

Work Undertaken The work undertaken by members of chambers is primarily in the chancery and commercial fields, and extends to a wide range of litigation, advisory and drafting work.
Business Agency, commercial litigation, consumer credit, intellectual property, freezing and other injunctions, partnerships, sale of goods, supply of services, securities and guarantees.
Charities and Associations Charities, clubs, friendly societies, industrial and provident societies and unincorporated associations.
Company and Insolvency Acquisition; amalgamation; dissolution and disposal of companies; corporate governance; directors' duties and disqualification; shareholder and boardroom disputes; tracing and recovery of corporate assets; company insolvency; administrations; liquidations; receiverships and voluntary arrangements; insolvent partnerships and all aspects of personal insolvency.
Financial Banking; building societies; consumer credit; financial services and regulation; insurance; mortgages; pensions; securities and guarantees; standard form documentation for commercial and residential lending transactions; trustee and fiduciary duties; unfair terms in consumer contracts.
Private Client Administration of estates, Court of Protection, family provision, probate, taxation, trusts and trustees and wills.
Professional Negligence Includes accountants; barristers; financial advisors; solicitors; surveyors and valuers; disciplinary proceedings.
Property Agricultural holdings, commercial property, conveyancing, landlord and tenant, mineral rights, mortgages and property litigation.

Clientele Chambers accept instructions from BarDIRECT clients. Instructions are also accepted from lawyers abroad, in particular the Bahamas, but also from jurisdictions in Europe and elsewhere.

Publications 'Swaps and Local Authorities: A Mistake?' in *Swaps and Off-Exchange Derivatives Trading: Law and Regulation*, Mark West (co-author); *Good Faith in Sales*, Reziya Harrison; *Wurtzburg and Mills on Building Society Law,* eds. Malcolm Waters QC, Elizabeth Ovey, Kate Selway; *Barnsley, Conveyancing Law and Practice,* Peter Smith QC; *Constructive Trusts,* Parker & Mellows, *The Modern Law of Trusts,* and *McGarry's Manual of the Law of Real Property,* Tony Oakley; 'Charities and Charitable Giving' in *Butterworth's Encyclopaedia*; *Charities: The Law & Practice* (co-editor), *Running a Charity,* Francesca Quint; *Insolvency in Corporate Governance: The Practical Guide for Directors,* eds. Stephen Acton and Peter Dodge.

International Languages spoken include French, German and Spanish.

---

1 Paper Buildings (Roger N Titheridge QC) — Set No.108

1 Paper Buildings (1st Floor), Temple, London, EC4Y 7EP **Tel** (020) 7353 3728 **Fax** (020) 7353 2911 **DX** 332

2 Paper Buildings (Mark Love) — Set No.109

2 Paper Buildings, Temple, London, EC4Y 7ET
Tel (020) 7936 2613 **Fax** (020) 7353 9439 **DX** 210 (Ch.Ln.)
Email post@2paper.co.uk **Website** www.2paper.co.uk

Head of Chambers	Mark Love
Senior Clerk	Stephen Lavell
First Junior	Marc Newson
Second Junior	Jamie Thornton
Tenants	27

Members

Mark Love (1979)	Jamal Sapsard (1987)	Silas Reid (1995)
Robin Griffiths (1970)	Alison Robins (1987)	Peter Dahlsen (1996)
Charlotte Buckhaven (1969)	Polly-Anne Comfort (1988)	Simone Start (1994)
Richard Hayden (1964)	John Talbot-Bagnall (1988)	Michael McAlinden (1996)
Peta Gee (1973)	Kevin Dent (1991)	David Jones
Wendy Fisher-Gordon (1983)	Simon Tolkien (1994)	Mark Braid
Neil Petersen (1983)	Sandra Folkes (1989)	Ben Smitten
Andrew Evans (1984)	Pankaj Pathak (1992)	Jason Reed
James Dennison (1986)	Jane Keysall (1992)	Richard Craven
Mark Stern (1988)	Jason Elliott (1993)	Nanta Bahra
Sandra Briggs-Watson (1985)	Fay Baker (1994)	Poonam Bhairi

The Chambers An established common law set offering a wide range of services with particular emphasis upon all aspects of criminal law and family law.

Work Undertaken Criminal law; family law; personal injury; judicial review; landlord and tenant; courts martial; mental health; licensing; immigration; education.

International Certain members of chambers are fluent in foreign languages such as French, German, Hindi, Punjabi and Urdu.

Recruitment Four pupillages will be offered: two first six pupillages (to commence in October 2001) and two second six pupillages to commence in April 2002. Two of these will be funded.

2 Paper Buildings (Desmond de Silva QC) — Set No.110

First and Second Floors, 2 Paper Buildings, London, EC4Y 7ET **Tel** (020) 7556 5500 **Fax** (020) 7583 3423 **DX** LDE 494

3 Paper Buildings (Michael Parroy QC) — Set No.111

3 Paper Buildings, Temple, London, EC4Y 7EU **Tel** (020) 7583 8055 **Fax** (020) 7353 6271 (Two lines) **DX** 102

BAR A-Z

4 Paper Buildings (Jean Ritchie QC)

4 Paper Buildings (Ground Floor), Temple, London, EC4Y 7EX
Tel (020) 7643 5000   **Fax** (020) 7353 5778   **DX** 1036 London/Chancery Lane
Email clerks@4paperbuildings.com   **Website** www.4paperbuildings.com

Set No.112

Head of Chambers	Jean Ritchie QC
Senior Clerk	Stephen Smith
Tenants	35

Members

Jean Ritchie QC (1970) (QC-1992)
Harvey McGregor QC (1955) (QC-1978)
Harold Burnett QC (1962) (QC-1982)
Antonio Bueno QC (1964) (QC-1989)
Douglas Hogg QC (1968) (QC-1990)
Michael J Powers QC (1979) (QC-1995)
Michael Pooles QC (1978) (QC-1999)
Eleanor Sharpston QC (1980) (QC-1999)

LJ West-Knights QC (1977) (QC-2000)
Patrick Lawrence QC (1985) (QC-2002)
Michael Keane (1963)
Anthony De Freitas (1971)
Jane Mishcon (1979)
Martin Spencer (1979)
Derek Holwill (1982)
Prof. Peter Kunzlik (1983)
Matthew Jackson (1986)
Julian Picton (1988)
Francis Bacon (1988)
William Flenley (1988)
Clare Price (1988)

Alison Gulliver (1989)
Evelyn Pollock (1991)
Mark Simpson (1992)
Philip Moser (1992)
Simon Wilton (1993)
Sarah Christie-Brown (1994)
Spike Charlwood (1994)
Kieron Beal (1995)
Catherine Ewins (1995)
Katrine Sawyer (1996)
Eva Ferguson (1999)
Paul Mitchell (1999)
Eleni Mitrophanous (1999)
Prof. Takis Tridimas (2000)

The Chambers This is a long-established set whose members practise civil and commercial law, principally in professional and clinical negligence. Chambers aim to provide a service of excellence, adopting a flexible, practical and commercial approach to litigation which is driven by the needs and convenience of its clients.

Work Undertaken The set specialises in professional negligence and clinical negligence, commercial contract matters, European and human rights law and personal injury claims. Members of chambers act for both claimants and defendants. In the field of professional negligence they appear in cases concerning all the various professions, but particularly solicitors, barristers, accountants, surveyors and insurance brokers. In the area of clinical negligence members represent patients, NHS trusts and doctors. The European and human rights group undertake judicial review and civil actions involving European Union law, the Brussels Convention and the Human Rights Act.
Additional areas Chambers also have considerable expertise in IT law, civil litigation relating to commercial fraud and money laundering, landlord and tenant, and professional disciplinary work.

Publications Significant legal publications produced or contributed to by members of chambers include *McGregor on Damages; Cordery on Solicitors, Powers and Harris - Clinical Negligence; Simpson - Professional Negligence and liability; Flenley and Leech - Solicitors' Negligence; Lloyd's Reports: Professional Negligence; A Practitioner's Handbook of EC Law; General Principles of EC Law; Jordan's Civil Procedure; Butterworths' Personal Injury Litigation Service.*

■ BAR A-Z

4 Paper Buildings (Lionel Swift QC) Set No.113

4 Paper Buildings, Temple, London, EC4Y 7EX
Tel (020) 7583 0816   **Fax** (020) 7353 4979   **DX** 1035
Email clerks@4pb.com   **Website** www.4pb.com

Head of Chambers	Lionel Swift QC
Senior Clerk	Michael Reeves
Chambers Manager	Hilary Rollings
Tenants	38

Members

Lionel Swift QC (1959) (QC-1975)
Gordon Murdoch QC (1970) (QC-1995)
Anna Pauffley QC (1979) (QC-1995)
Jonathan Cohen QC (1974) (QC-1997)
Peter Jackson QC (1978) (QC-2000)
Harry Turcan (1965)
Roger Smith (1968)
Amanda Barrington-Smyth (1972)
Rozanna Malcolm (1974)
Robin Barda (1975)
Michael Sternberg (1975)
Christopher Coney (1979)
Marcus Scott-Manderson (1980)
Charles Joseph (1980)
Michael Stern (1983)
Mark Johnstone (1984)
Elizabeth Coleman (1985)
Catherine Wood (1985)
Jeremy Rosenblatt (1985)
Christopher Hames (1987)
Adrienne Morgan (1988)
Barbara Mills (1990)
Joy Brereton (1990)
David Williams (1990)
Joanne Brown (1990)
Cyrus Larizadeh (1992)
William Hansen (1992)
Charles Hale (1992)
Michael Simon (1992)
Christopher McCourt (1993)
Justin Ageros (1993)
Judith Murray (1994)
Cliona Papazian (1994)
Sarah Lowe (1995)
Justine Johnston (1997)
James Copley (1997)
Kiril Waite (1997)
Lucy Cheetham (1999)

The Chambers A leading family law set with a strong civil side.

Work Undertaken

Family Law Adoption; care proceedings (for local authorities, families and children's guardians); child abduction; Children Act cases; cohabitees; divorce; inheritance and family provision; judicial review; matrimonial finance and wardship.
Civil Arbitration; banking and securities; construction; contract (commercial and general); employment and industrial tribunals; judicial review; landlord and tenant; personal injury; professional negligence; sale of goods; consumer credit; tort.

Recruitment Chambers is a member of OLPAS.

5 Paper Buildings (Godfrey Carey QC & Jonathan Caplan QC) Set No.114

5 Paper Buildings, Temple, London, EC4Y 7HB
Tel (020) 7583 6117   **Fax** (020) 7353 0075   **DX** 365
Email clerks@5-paperbuildings.law.co.uk

Head of Chambers	Godfrey Carey QC
	Jonathan Caplan QC
Senior Clerk	Stuart Bryant
Tenants	39

Members

Michael Corkery QC (1949) (QC-1981)
Timothy Cassel QC (1965) (QC-1988)
Godfrey Carey QC (1969) (QC-1991)
Jonathan Caplan QC (1973) (QC-1991)
Kuldip Singh QC (1975) (QC-1993)
Oliver Sells QC (1972) (QC-1995)
Simon Mehigan QC (1980) (QC-1998)
Edward Jenkins QC (1977) (QC-2000)
Stanley Hughes (1971)
Michael Brompton (1973)
Ian Wade (1977)
Graham Trembath (1978)
Nicholas Fooks (1978)
Penelope Rector (1980)
Charles Judge (1981)
Maurice Aston (1982)
Miranda Moore (1983)
Mark Wyeth (1983)
Amanda Pinto (1983)
Miles Bennett (1986)
David Groome (1987)
Robert O'Sullivan (1988)
Julian Christopher (1988)
Martin Evans (1989)
Anuja Dhir (1989)
Justin Cole (1991)
Nicholas Griffin (1992)
Emma Deacon (1993)
Janet Weeks (1993)
Tom Allen (1994)
Michael Hick (1995)
Alex Bailin (1995)
Denis Barry (1996)
Tom Quinton (1997)
Gaby Bonham Carter (1997)
Catherine Purnell (1999)
James Norman (2000)
Jonathan Rees (2000)
Dominic Lewis (2000)

Continued overleaf

BAR A-Z

The Chambers For more than a century these chambers have been recognised as one of the leading sets of criminal advocates. Chambers expertise has led in recent years to a broadening of their areas of practice extending to environmental and trading law, media law, disciplinary tribunals of all kinds, and specialist areas of civil law.

Work Undertaken
Criminal Law This set deals with all aspects of criminal law, including commercial fraud. Members regularly appear in all levels of criminal courts, including capital appeals in the Privy Council. Work is regularly undertaken in Singapore, Hong Kong and the West Indies. Chambers both prosecute and defend.
Licensing Considerable experience in both liquor and gaming licensing.
Consumer Protection & Trading Law Including environmental law, food and drugs, health and safety, trade descriptions and copyright theft.
Tribunals: Disciplinary and Regulatory proceedings, public inquiries (e.g. Southall Bloody Sunday).
Civil Law Commercial litigation (including fraud), defamation, contempt, sports law.

Publications Simon Mehigan QC is an editor of *Patersons Licensing Acts and Mehigan and Griffiths on Restraint of Trade*. Forthcoming publications: *Martin Evans and Amand Pinto on Corporate Criminal Liability*.

5 Paper Buildings (Richard King) Set No.115

5 Paper Buildings, Temple, London, EC4Y 7HB
Tel (020) 7815 3200 **Fax** (020) 7815 3201 **DX** 415
Email clerks@5paper.com **Website** www.5paper.com

Head of Chambers	Richard King
Senior Clerk	Alan Stammers
Tenants	35

Members

Richard King (1978)
Paul Norris (1963)
Angus Nicol (1963)
Steven Walsh (1965)
Robert Denman (1970)
Nicholas Wood (1970)
Graham Platford (1970)
Donald Broatch (1971)
Robert Percival (1971)
Roger Bull (1974)
Adrian Iles (1980)
Paul Infield (1980)

Mark Lyne (1981)
Norman Joss (1982)
Ian Wright (1983)
Lawrence Jacobson (1985)
Alison Rowley (1987)
Oliver Hyams (1989)
Jonathan Rich (1989)
Peter John (1989)
Stuart Nichols (1989)
Satinder Gill (1991)
Nicholas Grundy (1993)
Nicola Rushton (1993)

Richard Evans (1993)
Paul Pavlou (1993)
Simon Mills (1994)
Cyril Adjei (1995)
Rachel Sleeman (1996)
Joanna Brownhill (1997)
Jake Davies (1997)
Robert Harrap (1997)
Ben Maltz (1998)
Sara Beecham (1999)
Angela Hall (2000)

5 PAPER BUILDINGS

The Chambers 5 Paper Buildings is committed to exceptional standards of expertise and service. It aims to provide true expertise through a range of specialist practice teams. Each team maintains a continuing programme of development through meetings, writing and seminars, designed to ensure that members are at the forefront of the specialist Bar. Individual members are able to offer specific expertise within the teams in which they practise. Chambers are Barmark accredited. The set's commitment to excellence is underwritten in the guide: *Standards of Professional Service*. Chambers' facilities include conference rooms, email, voicemail, lectures and seminars. Chambers' opening times are 8.00am to 6.30pm. Out of hours telephone number: 07930 463737.

Work Undertaken Specialisations include commercial, property, ancillary relief, employment, personal injury, public law and any inclusionary issues of human rights and professional negligence.
Commercial All aspects of domestic and international commercial litigation, arbitration and mediation, including freezing and search orders, tracing and asset-recovery, sale of goods, partnership, agency and factoring. Domestic and international banking, including syndicated lending, lender's liability, documentary credits, negotiable instruments, guarantees and other securities. Personal and corporate insolvency, including liquidation, voluntary arrangements, administration, receivership and related property matters. Construction and consumer credit.
Property Commercial and residential landlord and tenant, including renewal of business tenancies, rent review, service charge disputes and leasehold enfranchisement. Recovery of possession, disrepair, right to buy, succession and management and similar orders. Easements, restrictive covenants, boundary disputes and adverse possession, mortgages, options and rights of pre-emption, and conveyancing. Construction and validity of wills, administration of estates and claims under the Inheritance (Provision for Family and Dependants) Act 1975.

Ancillary Relief Dispositions of property and finance on domestic and foreign divorce, disputes between cohabitees, and protective and pre-emptive remedies.
Employment Contracts of employment, wrongful and unfair dismissal, redundancy, discrimination and equal opportunities, industrial disputes, restrictive covenants, trade secrets and confidential information.
Personal Injury Claims for fatalities and injuries of all degrees of severity arising out of all types of accident and clinical negligence.
Public Law Health and safety, food safety, trading standards and similar regulatory matters. Admissions and exclusions in educational matters. Special educational needs, further and higher education. Local Authority allocations in housing matters, homelessness. Business, asylum and family rights in immigration matters.
Recent Cases Barry v Heathcote Ball [2001] 1 All ER 94; Cohort Construction Ltd v Julius Melchior [2001] CP Rep 23; D v D [2001] 1FLR 633; DPP v Ara [2001] 4 All ER 559; Evans v Secretary of State for the Environment and Transport [2001] PIQR 37; Levy v Legal Aid Board [2001] 1 All ER 895; Print Concept GmbH v GEW (EC) Ltd [2001] EWCA Civ 352; Re B and T (Care Proceedings: Legal representation) [2001] 1 FLR 485; Royal Bank of Scotland v Etridge & Others [2001] 4 All ER 449; Southwark London Borough Council v Mills [2001] 1 AC 1; Standard Chartered Bank v Pakistan National Shipping Corporation (No 4) [2001] QB 167; Stirling v Leadenhall Residential Ltd [2001] 3 All ER 645; Standard Chartered Bank v Pakistan National Shipping Corporation (No 2) [2000] 1 Lloyd's Rep 218; Jacobs v Coster [2000] CLL Rev 3 (Sep); R v Stockton-on-Tees Borough Council, ex parte W [2000] ELR 93; R v London Borough of Brent and Vassie, ex parte F [2000] ELR 550; Burrells Wharf Freeholds Ltd v Galliard Homes Ltd [2000] C.P.Rep. 4.

Publications These include *Employment in Schools - A Legal Guide,* Jordans, 2000, Oliver Hyams; *Law of Education,* Sweet & Maxwell, 1998, Oliver Hyams; *The Law of Harassment & Stalking,* Butterworths, 2000, Graham Platford and Paul Infield; Gulteridge & Megrah's *Law of Bankers' Commercial Credits,* 8th edn, 2001, editor Richard King; *Essential Law for Marketers,* Ardi Kolah, 2002, contributors Richard King and Angela Hall; *Stalking and Psychosexual Obsession,* John Wiley & Son, 2002, Paul Infield and Graham Platford.

International Work is handled in English, French, German, Italian, Punjabi and Spanish.

Recruitment Pupillage application forms available from Mr Stuart Nichols. Awards are available of £17,500 per pupil per year. Mini-pupillage applications to Mr Robert Harrap. Chambers operate an equal opportunities policy.

Plowden Buildings (William Lowe QC)

Set No.116

2 Plowden Buildings, Temple, London, EC4Y 9BU
Tel (020) 7583 0808 **Fax** (020) 7583 5106 **DX** 0020 (Ch.Ln.)
Email bar@plowdenbuildings.co.uk

Head of Chambers	William Lowe QC
Senior Clerk	Paul Hurst
Tenants	30

Members

William Lowe QC (1972) (QC-1997) +
Catherine MacKenzie Smith (1968)
Elizabeth Hindmarsh (1974)
Christopher Williams (1981) + †
Simon Wood (1981) +
Jeremy Freedman (1982) + †
Philip Kramer (1982) ‡
Lawrence McNulty (1985)
Catherine Foster (1986)
Peter Morton (1988)

Roger Cooper (1988)
Hari Menon (1989)
Michael James (1989)
Seamus Sweeney (1989)
Martin Haukeland (1988)
Kerry Cox (1990)
Andrew Crouch (1990)
Mark Watson-Gandy (1990) †
Claire Lindsay (1991)
Elizabeth Hodgson (1993)
Jayne Atkinson (1994)
Jane Woodwark (1995)

Edward Broome (1996)
John Falkenstein (1996)
Monica Whyte (1996)
Dominic Bayne (1997)
Samuel Faulks (1997)
Holly Pelham (1999)
Mark Armitage (1999)
Claire Guppy (2001)
John Lowe (1976) *
David Brook (1988) *
Ian West (1985) *

* Door Tenant + Recorder † Junior Counsel to the Crown ‡ Junior Counsel to the Crown/Deputy District Judge

The Chambers Plowden Buildings is amongst the leading personal injury sets both in London and in the North of England. Founded in 1980, chambers have expanded to 30 members who divide their time between court centres in the north such as Newcastle upon Tyne and the South East. Many members live on the North Eastern Circuit. Although chambers core business is personal injury litigation for both claimants and defendants, members have significant specialisms in clinical and professional negligence, together with employment, commercial work and insolvency. Plowden Buildings is clerked exclusively from its Middle Temple

Continued overleaf

premises but maintains fully staffed premises in Newcastle upon Tyne, directly under the famous Tyne Bridge. Four members of chambers are Recorders, and one is a Deputy District Judge. Plowden Buildings prides itself upon its excellent record of client care and its dynamic clerking team is always willing to discuss matters such as turn-around times for paperwork and of course, fees. All members are computer literate and instructions are accepted on disk and by email. Plowden Buildings relishes the opportunities provided by the fast-changing legal marketplace and further expansion is anticipated.

Work Undertaken Personal injury, clinical negligence, professional negligence, employment, commercial, insolvency and crime (general) are handled.

Publications Members of chambers include editors of *Charlesworth & Percy on Negligence* 10th edition, *European Current Law*, the *Thomson Tax Guide* and the author of *Watson-Gandy on The Law of Accountants*.

2 Pump Court (Philip Singer QC) Set No.117
2 Pump Court, Temple, London, EC4Y 7AH **Tel** (020) 7353 5597 **Fax** (020) 7583 2122 **DX** 290 (Ch.Ln.)

4 Pump Court Set No.118
4 Pump Court, Temple, London, EC4Y 7AN
Tel (020) 7842 5555   **Fax** (020) 7583 2036   **DX** 303 LDE
Email chambers@4pumpcourt.com   **Website** www.4pumpcourt.com

Senior Clerk	Carolyn McCombe
Tenants	44

Members

David Friedman QC (1968) (QC-1990)
Christopher Moger QC (1972) (QC-1992)
Anthony Temple QC (1968) (QC-1986)
Bruce Mauleverer QC (1969) (QC-1985)
David Blunt QC (1967) (QC-1991)
Jeremy Storey QC (1974) QC-1994)
Jonathan Marks QC (1975) (QC-1995)
Anthony Speaight QC (1973) (QC-1995)
John Rowland QC (1979) (QC-1996)
Michael Douglas QC (1974) (QC-1997)

Lindsay Boswell QC (1982) (QC-1997)
Jeremy Nicholson QC (1977) (QC-2000)
Laurence Marsh (1975)
Allen Dyer (1976)
Oliver Ticciati (1979)
Nigel Tozzi QC (1980) (QC-2001)
Peter Hamilton (1968)
Alex Charlton (1983)
David Sears (1984)
Adrian Hughes (1984)
James Cross (1985)
Duncan McCall (1988)
Aidan Christie (1988)
Andrew Neish (1988)
Nicholas Vineall (1988)
Kirsten Houghton (1989)
Simon Henderson (1993)

Michael Davie (1993)
Alexander Gunning (1994)
Sean Brannigan (1994)
Kate Vaughan-Neil (1994)
Richard Cartwright (1994)
Rachel Ansell (1995)
Alexander Hickey (1995)
Claire Packman (1996)
Sean O'Sullivan (1997)
Benjamin Pilling (1997)
Lynne McCafferty (1997)
Michael Taylor (1996)
Yash Kulkarni (1998)
James Purchas (1997)
James Leabeater (1999)
Jennie Gillies (2000)
Alex Potts (2000)

The Chambers 4 Pump Court's main focus is on litigation. It aims to provide, at every level, experienced advisors and strong and effective advocates. It is an expanding set which welcomes the opportunities that the relaxation of the ways in which the Bar can offer its services has provided. It is always ready, in the interests of clients, to consider new ideas for improving the way business is done.

Work Undertaken The work of chambers covers a wide spectrum of commercial and common law with the following specialist areas:
Professional Negligence Members of chambers have expertise acting for both plaintiffs and insurers and dealing with a wide range of claims against all professionals, including solicitors and barristers, architects, engineers, surveyors and valuers, accountants, auditors and actuaries, brokers, consultants, agents and IT professionals, bankers and financial intermediaries and advisors, doctors and other medical practitioners. Members of chambers regularly advise on policy interpretation and indemnity questions.
Construction A substantial number of silks and juniors specialise in construction and civil engineering work and are recognised as leading practitioners in the field. They have acted in numerous major disputes arising out of onshore and offshore projects both in the UK and overseas, acting variously for employers, contractors and sub-contractors, and professional advisors. Adjudication, mediation and arbitration are other areas in which the team is similarly skilled and expert.

Insurance & Reinsurance Members of chambers have been involved in most of the significant events in the London insurance market over the last decade, including the Longtail claims in the USA arising from problems such as asbestosis, pollution and more recently with pensions and other investment product compensation claims against life insurers and claims arising from US workers' compensation rules. Work with Lloyd's and other insurance markets includes litigation and arbitration of both insurance and reinsurance disputes between syndicates and with outside insurers, litigation between names and agents, disciplinary hearings and regulatory control.

Commercial Members of chambers deal with a range of matters including commercial fraud, insurance and reinsurance, banking, sale and carriage of goods, aviation, shipping, the purchase and sale of commodities, the construction and performance of mercantile contracts and media and entertainment.

Information Technology Members of chambers include experts in computer law (including in law relating to the internet and e-commerce) and disputes arising out of computer contracts and consultancy. Such expertise involves a detailed understanding of complex technical matters as well as the legal and commercial issues. Members of chambers were retained in the early landmark case of Salvage Association v CAP Financial Services Limited and have been instructed in a large number of high-profile cases since that decision.

Licensing, Gaming & Lotteries Expertise in this field has been built up over many years of acting for and advising the regulator of the gaming industry and many of its major operators.

Financial Services The work of members of chambers spans investment business, including life assurance and personal pensions and the rules of various regulatory bodies.

Additional areas Members of chambers undertake mainstream common law work of all types, including personal injury, contractual disputes and property and employment law. Some members of chambers have particular expertise in matrimonial finance.

6 Pump Court (Kieran Coonan QC) — Set No.119

6 Pump Court, Ground and Lower Ground, London, EC4Y 7AR
Tel (020) 7583 6013 **Fax** (020) 7353 0464 **DX** 409
Email clerks@6pumpcourt.com **Website** www.6pumpcourt.com

Head of Chambers	Kieran Coonan QC
Senior Clerk	Adrian Barrow
Tenants	25

Members

Kieran Coonan QC (1971) (QC-1990)
Michael Curwen (1966)
Duncan Pratt (1971)
David Morris (1976)
Richard Craven (1976)
Siobhan Goodrich (1980)
Anthony Haycroft (1982)
Richard Power (1983)
Andrew Hockton (1984)
Alan Jenkins (1984)
Susan Burden (1985)
Christina Lambert (1988)
Charles Foster (1988)
Andrew Post (1988)
Andrew Kennedy (1989)
Tejina Mangat (1990)
Annalissa Garrett (1991)
Alexander Hutton (1992)
Nicholas Peacock (1992)
Alice Robertson (1996)
Natalia Jeremiah (1997)
Mark Friston (1997)
Roger Mallalieu (1998)
Jamie Carpenter (2000)
Robert Sowersby (2000)

The Chambers These chambers have enjoyed a reputation over the past 30 years for providing specialist advice and advocacy on behalf of claimants and defendants in the field of healthcare law.

Work Undertaken Most members of chambers specialise in the major areas of clinical negligence, mental health law and the regulation of the conduct of care professionals. Individuals also undertake criminal cases which frequently incorporate medico-legal issues. Personal injury and professional negligence work are strongly represented in chambers. A small group practises in the developing and specialist area of the law relating to costs.

BAR A-Z

6 Pump Court (Stephen Hockman QC) — Set No.120

6 Pump Court, Temple, London, EC4Y 7AR
Tel (020) 7797 8400 **Fax** (020) 7797 8401 **DX** 293 Chancery Lane, London
Email clerks@6pumpcourt.co.uk **Website** www.6pumpcourt.co.uk

Head of Chambers	Stephen Hockman QC
Senior Clerk	Richard Constable
Tenants	27

Members

Stephen Hockman QC (1970) (QC-1990)
Neville Willard (1976)
Grant Armstrong (1978)
Richard Barraclough (1980)
David Travers (1981)
Nicholas Baldock (1983)
Caroline Topping (1984)
David Walden-Smith (1985)
Peter Gower (1985)
Kevin Leigh (1986)
Peter Harrison (1987)
Eleanor Laws (1990)
Peter Forbes (1990)
William Upton (1990)
Oliver Saxby (1992)
Paul Mee (1992)
Judith Butler (1993)
Mark Watson (1994)
Edward Grant (1994)
Nina Ellin (1994)
Clare Wright (1995)
Peter Alcock (1995)
Mark Beard (1996)
Deborah Charles (1996)
Tanya Robinson (1997)
Richard Banwell (1998)
Gordon Menzies (1998)
Lee Bennett (1998)

The Chambers This set of Chambers was established in the 1920's and operates primarily in London and the South East. Building from a general common law base, Chambers now comprises four specialist teams. The Head of Chambers, Stephen Hockman QC, is currently the Leader of the South Eastern Circuit.

Work Undertaken

Public, Planning & Environmental Members appear for and against regulators and public authorities. The proceedings include judicial review, public inquiries and regulatory criminal proceedings. The team has established a particular niche in relation to work on the interface between environmental, planning and human rights law. Recent significant cases include 'Alconbury' and 'Marcic v Thames Water'.

Civil/Commercial Commercial disputes, clinical and other professional negligence, personal injury and landlord and tenant work. The work is split between claimants and defendants and undertaken, inter alia, on behalf of a range of substantial insurers, public companies, local authorities and government departments.

Crime The team undertake the whole range of criminal work (including homicide, complex commercial fraud and drugs and revenue offences) on behalf of defendants; and on behalf of the CPS and other prosecutors, particularly HM Customs & Excise and the DTI.

Family Members of the family team advise and appear in the private and public law arenas, in child abuse and child care cases. The expertise in matrimonial finance extends particularly to corporate, agricultural and high value matters.

International Languages spoken include French, German, Russian and Japanese.

Pump Court Chambers (Christopher Harvey Clark QC) — Set No.121

3 Pump Court, Temple, London, EC4Y 7AJ
Tel (020) 7353 0711 **Fax** (020) 7353 3319 **DX** 362
Email clerks@3pumpcourt.com **Website** www.3pumpcourt.com

Head of Chambers	Christopher Harvey Clark QC
Senior Clerk	David Barber
Deputy Senior Clerk	Danny Fantham
Tenants	60

Member

Christopher Harvey Clark QC (1969) (QC-1984)
Nigel Pascoe QC (1966) (QC-1988)
Guy Boney QC (1968) (QC-1990)
Peter Birts QC (1968) (QC-1990)
Jane Miller QC (1979) (QC-2000)
Oba Nsugbe QC (1985) (QC-2002)
Geoffrey Still (1966)
Stewart Patterson (1967)
Adam Pearson (1969)
Frank Moat (1970)
Giles Harrap (1971)
Frank Abbott (1972)
Charles Parry (1973)
Michael Butt (1974)
John Ker-Reid (1974)
Charles Gabb (1975)
Andrew Barnett (1977)
Michael Dineen (1977)
Jonathan Swift (1977)
Julie MacKenzie (1978)
Stephen Jones (1978)
Timothy O'Flynn (1979)
Robert Hill (1980)
Miranda Allardice (1982)
Damien Lochrane (1983)
Sandra Stanfield (1984)
Matthew Scott (1985)
Desmond Bloom-Davies (1986)
Mark Hill (1987)
Anne Waddington (1988)
Hugh Travers (1988)
Philip Warren (1988)
Leslie Samuels (1989)
Edward Boydell (1989)

Justin Gau (1989)
Anthony Akiwumi (1989)
Helen Khan (1990)
Penelope Howe (1991)
Geoffrey Kelly (1992)
James Newton-Price (1992)
Patricia Poyer-Sleeman (1992)
Mark Ruffell (1992)
Elizabeth Gunther (1993)
Oliver Peirson (1993)
Marcus Tregilgas-Davey (1993)
Helen Fields (1993)
Luke Blackburn (1993)
Mark Ashley (1993)
Roderick Moore (1993)
Jonathan Simpson (1993)
Richard Ferry-Swainson (1994)
Robert Pawson (1994)
Arabella Grundy (1995)
Mark Dubbery (1996)
Ruth Arlow (1997)
Andrew Grime (1997)
Anne Ward (1997)
Lorna Sproston (1998)
Louise de Rozarieux (1999)
Richard Tutt (2000)

The Chambers An established set undertaking a wide variety of work, with members working in specialist teams. DPA and Bar Direct work accepted.
Associated Chambers 31 Southgate Street, Winchester; Temple Street, Swindon.

Work Undertaken
Main areas Family, employment, inheritance, property, PI, crime.
Specialisations Childcare; matrimonial finance; all areas of crime; professional and clinical negligence; contract; ecclesiastical law; Inheritance Act; courts martial; environment; landlord and tenant; taxation appeals.

International Oba Nsugbe is also a barrister and solicitor of the Supreme Court of Nigeria.

Recruitment Tenancy applications should be sent to Head of the Tenancy Committee. Pupillage applications should be made via OLPAS.

Pump Court Tax Chambers
Set No.122

16 Bedford Row, London, WC1R 4EF
Tel (020) 7414 8080 **Fax** (020) 7414 8099 **DX** London 312
Email clerks@pumptax.com **Website** www.pumptax.com

Senior Clerk	Geraldine O'Sullivan
Tenants	23

Members

Andrew Thornhill QC (1969) (QC-1985)
Graham Aaronson QC (1966) (QC-1982)
David Milne QC (1970) (QC-1987)
William Massey QC (1977) (QC-1996)
Kevin Prosser QC (1982) (QC-1996)
John Tallon QC (1975) (QC-2000)
Michael Conlon QC (1974) (QC-2002)
Ian Richards (1971)
Janek Matthews (1972)
Roger Thomas (1979)
Penelope Hamilton (1972)
Jeremy White (1976)
Giles W J Goodfellow (1983)
David Ewart (1987)
Jeremy Woolf (1986)
Andrew Hitchmough (1991)
Adrian J Shipwright (1993)
Rupert Baldry (1987)
Julian Ghosh (1993)
Elizabeth Wilson (1995)
Richard Vallat (1997)
James Henderson (1997)
Sarah Dunn (1998)

Work Undertaken Pump Court Tax Chambers is the largest specialist tax set. Chambers undertake litigation and advisory work on all aspects of tax law, corporate and personal.

Queen Elizabeth Building (Florence Baron QC)   Set No.123

Queen Elizabeth Building, Temple, London, EC4Y 9BS
Tel (020) 7797 7837   **Fax** (020) 7353 5422   **DX** 339 London/Chancery Lane
Email clerks@qeb.co.uk   **Website** www.qeb.co.uk

Head of Chambers	Florence Baron QC
Senior Clerk	Ivor Treherne
Tenants	26

Members

Florence Baron QC (1976) (QC-1995)
Andrew Moylan QC (1978) (QC-2000)
Lucy Stone QC (1983) (QC-2001)
Lewis Marks QC (1984) (QC-2002)
Lord Phillimore (1972)
Peter Wright (1974)
Michael Hosford-Tanner (1974)

Andrew Tidbury (1976)
Thomas Brudenell (1977)
Roderick Blyth (1981)
Oliver Wise (1981)
Tim Amos (1987)
Jennifer Roberts (1988)
Sarah Edwards (1990)
Matthew Firth (1991)
Elizabeth Clarke (1991)
Stewart Leech (1992)

Alexander Thorpe (1995)
Catherine Cowton (1995)
James Ewins (1996)
Antonia Lyon (1997)
Sarah Phipps (1997)
Rachael Young (1997)
Mark Saunders (1999)
Duncan Brooks (2001)
Daniel Bentham (2001)

Work Undertaken A set specialising in family law and undertaking general and common law work including disciplinary tribunals; employment law; equine and animal law; judicial review; landlord and tenant; medical negligence; personal injury; professional negligence; and sports law.

International Members are fluent in French, German and Italian.

3 Raymond Buildings (Clive Nicholls QC)   Set No.124

3 Raymond Buildings, Gray's Inn, London, WC1R 5BH
Tel (020) 7400 6400   **Fax** (020) 7400 6464   **DX** 237 London
Email chambers@3raymondbuildings.com   **Website** www.3raymondbuildings.com

Head of Chambers	Clive Nicholls QC
Senior Clerk	Ian Collins
Tenants	37

Members

Clive Nicholls QC (1957) (QC-1982)
Colin Nicholls QC (1957) (QC-1981)
Gilbert Gray QC (1953) (QC-1971)
Richard Beckett QC (1965) (QC-1987)
Sir John Nutting QC (1968) (QC-1995)
Stephen Batten QC (1968) (QC-1989)
Alun Jones QC (1972) (QC-1989)
David Whitehouse QC (1969) (QC-1990)
Nicholas Price QC (1968) (QC-1992)

Kevin de Haan QC (1976) (QC-2000)
Michael Bromley-Martin QC (1979) (QC-2002)
James Lewis QC (1987) (QC-2002)
John Blair-Gould (1970)
Gerald Gouriet (1974)
Andrew Muir (1975)
Richard Atchley (1977)
Mark Harris (1980)
James Hines (1982)
James Rankin (1983)
Jane Humphryes (1983)
Neil Saunders (1983)
Stephen Walsh (1983)

Simon Farrell (1983)
Crispin Aylett (1985)
Alexander Cameron (1986)
Helen Malcolm (1986)
John Hardy (1988)
Hugo Keith (1989)
Hugh Davies (1990)
Campaspe Lloyd-Jacob (1990)
Richard Wormald (1993)
Alisdair Williamson (1994)
Saba Naqshbandi (1996)
Edmund Gritt (1997)
Ailsa Williamson (1997)
Clair Dobbin (1999)
Guy Ladenburg (2000)

The Chambers A multi-disciplined set with a national and international reputation.

Work Undertaken

Crime Criminal law lies at the heart of these chambers, with members defending and prosecuting at all levels in this country. Substantial experience of international criminal law and of advocacy abroad. Commercial crime: serious frauds and financial regulatory offences, again with expertise in international aspects. Major cases in which members have been involved include Kevin Maxwell (pension fraud), BCCI (bank fraud, Jonathan Aitken (perjury), Lord Hardwicke (drugs offences), Judge Gee (mortgage fraud), Kenneth Noye (the M25 road rage murder), John 'Goldfinger' Palmer and others (timeshare fraud), Roy Whiting (the Sarah Payne murder).

Extradition/Mutual Assistance A worldwide reputation for expertise which includes commercial crime as well as terrorism and drug trafficking. Members have appeared in almost every significant extradition case in England, including the Pinochet litigation, and represented over 40 foreign and commonwealth governments in extradition proceedings. Expertise includes bringing judicial reviews proceedings in connection with mutual assistance matters and advising in connection with restraint orders and the other financial aspects.

Licensing Chambers are recognised as having an incomparable team specialising exclusively in every facet of licensing law including liquor, public entertainment and taxi licensing. Members provide advice and representation to solicitors and other professional clients on licensing matters and appear throughout England and Wales on behalf of applicants and objectors in relation to betting office licences, bookmakers' permits, gaming licences and bingo licences. Expertise in internet gambling has risen to a level of international recognition.

Money Laundering & Confiscation Members have special expertise in dealing with complex and difficult confiscation proceedings in the criminal Courts under the existing legislation (Criminal Justice Acts and the Drug Trafficking Acts). Members of chambers have also been involved in the consultation process for the Proceeds of Crime Bill 2001 which consolidates and amends the existing legislation covering criminal confiscation.

Public & Administrative Law Members appear regularly in the High Court on all types of applications for judicial review. Expertise includes judicial review of Ministers, Magistrates' Courts, Local Authorities, the Police, the Prison Service, the Armed Forces, Courts Martial, Coroners' Courts and the Criminal Injuries Compensation Authority. Substantive areas include extradition, search warrants, warrants for commitment or distress, prison conditions, the environment, public health and criminal injuries compensation. There are members of chambers appointed to the Common Law Treasury Panel who appear regularly for the Crown on judicial review.

Environmental & Health & Safety Chambers have specialist expertise in all areas of environmental law, with advisory work and cases regularly undertaken for both the Environment Agency and corporate and individual clients. The areas in which work is most frequently undertaken include waste licensing and management, water quality and radioactive substances. Health and safety work covers a similarly broad area and client base, with work being undertaken on behalf of the Health and Safety Executive and other clients in equal measure. Particular experience in advising and representing companies in the construction and retail industries.

5 Raymond Buildings (Patrick Milmo QC)   Set No.125

5 Raymond Buildings, Gray's Inn, London, WC1R 5BP
Tel (020) 7242 2902 **Fax** (020) 7831 2686 **DX** 1054 LDE
Email clerks@5rb.co.uk **Website** www.5rb.co.uk

Head of Chambers	Patrick Milmo QC
Senior Clerk	Kim Janes
Tenants	24

Members

Patrick Milmo QC (1962) (QC-1985) MA (Cantab)
Gordon Bishop (1968) MA (Cantab)
Michael Tugendhat QC (1969) (QC-1986) MA (Cantab)
Desmond Browne QC (1969) (QC-1990) BA (Oxon)
Adrienne Page QC (1974) (QC-1999) BA (Kent)
James Price QC (1974) (QC-1995) BA (Oxon)
Richard Parkes (1977) MA (Cantab)
Mark Warby QC (1981) (QC-2002) MA (Oxon)

Stephen Bate (1981) MA (Cantab) Dip Law
Andrew Monson (1983) BA (Oxon)
Iain Christie (1989) BA (Dunelm)
Alexandra Marzec (1990) LLB (Warw)
David Sherborne (1992) BA(Oxon)
Justin Rushbrooke (1992) MA (Oxon)
Matthew Nicklin (1993) LLB (Newcastle)
Jonathan Barnes (1999) BA (Hons) (Oxon) †

Godwin Busuttil (1994) MA, MPhil (Cantab)
Adam Wolanski (1995) MA (Cantab)
William Bennett (1994) BA (Liverpool)
Jacob Dean (1995) BA (Oxon)
Anna Coppola (1996) BA (London) Dip Law
Sara Mansoori (1997) LLB (Leeds)
Adam Speker (1999) BA (Bristol)
Sapna Jethani (1999) BA (Oxon)

† Formerly a solicitor (admitted 1993)

The Chambers An established set specialising in all areas of the law that affect the media, the communications industry and world of entertainment, with particular emphasis on defamation, confidentiality and intellectual property and aspects of Human Rights laws relating to privacy and freedom of expression. Chambers also undertake work in a broad range of commercial matters. Though chiefly practising in the High Court, members represent clients before professional and sporting tribunals and in arbitrations, conduct cases before the ECHR, and advise on, and appear in, overseas litigation.

Work Undertaken All matters concerning all forms of publishing (including pre-publication advice), news dissemination, broadcasting and IT communication or arising from disputes in the entertainment world. The areas of law particularly engaged in these fields include defamation, breach of confidence, trade libel,

Continued overleaf

BAR A-Z

passing off, contempt, statutory restrictions on reporting and PACE applications, the rights and restrictions on publication arising under Human Rights legislation, and in relation to children and family law cases, copyright and contractual disputes of all kinds (in relation to books, music, film, video and television), Copyright Tribunal applications; restraint of trade disputes (in sport and pop), data protection and freedom of information.

18 Red Lion Court (Anthony Arlidge QC) — Set No.126

18 Red Lion Court, London, EC4A 3EB
Tel (020) 7520 6000 **Fax** (020) 7520 6248/9 **DX** 478 LDE
Email chambers@18rlc.co.uk

Head of Chambers	Anthony Arlidge QC
Senior Clerk	Kenneth Darvill
First Junior	Mark Bennett
Tenants	71

Members

Anthony Arlidge QC (1962) (QC-1981)
Derek Spencer QC (1961) (QC-1980)
David Cocks QC (1961) (QC-1982)
James Stewart QC (1966) (QC-1982)
Henry Green QC (1962) (QC-1988)
David Lederman QC (1966) (QC-1990)
Graham Parkins QC (1972) (QC-1990)
Peter Rook QC (1973) (QC-1991)
Richard Sutton QC (1969) (QC-1993)
Antony Shaw QC (1975) (QC-1994)
Peter Carter QC (1947) (QC-1990)
Rosamund Horwood-Smart QC (1974) (QC-1996)
James Goss QC (1975) (QC-1997)
Nigel Peters QC (1976) (QC-1997)
John Black QC (1975) (QC-1998)
Patricia Lynch QC (1979) (QC-1998)

David Etherington QC (1979) (QC-1998)
Linda Dobbs QC (1981) (QC-1998)
David Green QC (1979) (QC-2000)
David Radcliffe (1966)
Carey Johnston (1977)
Martyn Levett (1978)
Peter Fenn (1979)
Stephen Harvey (1979)
Jonathan Fisher (1980)
Alexander Milne (1981)
Kim Jenkins (1982)
Janine Sheff (1983)
Richard Kovalevsky (1983)
Mark Lucraft (1984)
Angela Morris (1984)
Rupert Overbury (1984)
David Marshall (1985)
Brendan Morris (1985)
Simon Spence (1985)
Robert Boyle (1985)
Robin du Preez (1985)
Jane Bewsey (1986)
John Lyons (1986)
Steven Dyble (1986)
Max Hill (1987)
David Walbank (1987)
Shane Collery (1988)

Sally-Ann Hales (1988)
David Huw Williams (1988)
John Anderson (1989)
Peter Rowlands (1990)
Candida Hill (1990)
Sara Lawson (1990)
David Holborn (1991)
Sean Hammond (1991)
Allison Clare (1992)
Matthew Gowen (1992)
Rufus D'Cruz (1993)
Tom Forster (1993)
Barnaby Jameson (1993)
Jennifer Dempster (1993)
Claudia Mortimore (1994)
Michelle Nelson (1994)
Jacqueline Hall (1994)
Adam Wiseman (1994)
Noel Casey (1995)
Samantha Leigh (1995)
Elizabeth Webster (1995)
Gillian Jones (1996)
Stephen Requena (1997)
Nicholas Medcroft (1998)
Louis-Peter Moll (1998)
Rebecca Chalkley (1999)
Ella Schulster (1999)
Lydia Jonson (2000)

The Chambers The main areas of practice are criminal and common law. The criminal work is divided between prosecution and defence and most members of Chambers do a mixture of both. The South East Circuit is served by our annexe in Chelmsford. Chambers have standing counsel to the Inland Revenue and Customs and Excise.

Work Undertaken There is particular expertise in the fields of: serious fraud, Inland Revenue and VAT offences, drugs and the problems arising from the Drug Trafficking Offences Act, extradition, child abuse, obscene publications, road traffic, cases involving forensic experts, licensing, judicial review and human rights. Representation is also provided at a wide variety of disciplinary tribunals, inquiries and commissions. Pro bono work in the Privy Council is undertaken by silks and work for Free Representation Unit by juniors.

Clientele Individuals, public and private companies, HM Customs and Excise, local authorities, Serious Fraud Office and CPS government departments.

Publications Arlidge and Parry on *Fraud*; Arlidge and Eady on *Contempt*; *Journal of International Banking Law* (UK Correspondent); Dobbs and Lucraft, *Road Traffic Law and Practice* (Sweet & Maxwell 1994); Rook and Ward, *Sexual Offences* (Waterlows 1990); Carter and Harrison *Offences of Violence* (Waterlows 1991); Fisher and Merrills *Pharmacy Law and Practices* (Blackwells 1995); Fisher and Bewsey, *The Law of Investor*

Protection, Mortimore on Immigration and Adoption (Hammicks 1994).

International Nigel Peters is a member of the Northern Ireland Bar and Barbados Bar. David Marshall is a member of the Hong Kong Bar and the New York Bar.

Recruitment Applications for tenancy should be sent to the Head of Chambers; pupillage applications to Rebecca Chalkley. There are usually 4 pupils who undertake a full 12 month pupillage in Chambers. They receive an award for their first 6 months and equivalent earnings in their second 6 months are guaranteed. Additional pupillages are offered at the discretion of Chambers.

■ Renaissance Chambers (Brian Jubb & Henry Setright QC) — Set No.127

5th Floor, Gray's Inn Chambers, Gray's Inn, London, WC1R 5JA **Tel** (020) 7404 1111 **Fax** (020) 7430 1522 **DX** 0074 (Ch.Ln.)

Selbourne Chambers (Romie Tager QC) — Set No.128

10 Essex Street, London, WC2R 3AA
Tel (020) 7420 9500 **Fax** (020) 7420 9555 **DX** DX 185 London Chancery Lane
Email clerks@selbornechambers.co.uk **Website** www.selbornechambers.co.uk

Head of Chambers	Romie Tager QC
Senior Clerk	Greg Piner
Tenants	11

Members

Romie Tager QC (1970) (QC-1995)
Ajmalul Hossain QC (1976) (QC-1998)
Mark Warwick (1974)
Philip Kremen (1975)
Stephen Boyd (1977)
Jonathan Ferris (1979)
Hugh Jackson (1981)
Neil Mendoza (1982)
William Bojczuk (1983)
Ian Clarke (1990)
Justin Kitson (2000)

The Chambers Selborne Chambers was established in 2002, to serve the commercial and property bar. It was founded by barristers from two different chambers, working closely to form standards of professional excellence and a common vision. Members of chambers undertake work in the following areas: commercial, property, chancery, international arbitration, finance, financial services and regulatory work, stock market-related issues, professional negligence, fraud and asset recovery, sports law. Members are not only experts at practising the law (as advisors and advocates) but are able to assimilate specialised and complex information essential to the overall effective management of any case.

No. 1 Serjeants' Inn (Edward Faulks QC) — Set No.129

No.1 Serjeants' Inn, Fleet Street, London, EC4Y 1LH
Tel (020) 7415 6666 **Fax** (020) 7583 2033 **DX** 364 London
Email clerks@no1serjeantsinn.com **Website** www.no1serjeantsinn.co.uk

Head of Chambers	Edward Faulks QC
Senior Clerk	Clark Chessis
Practice Development Manager	
	Rosemary Thorpe
Tenants	34

Members

Edward Faulks QC (1973) (QC-1996) +
Adrian Redgrave QC (1968) (QC-1992) +
David Pittaway QC (1977) (QC-2000) +
John Ross QC (1971) (QC-2001) +
William Andreae-Jones QC (1965) (QC-1984) + †
Jonathan Foster QC (1970) (QC-1989) + †
Brian Leech (1967) +
William Hunter (1972)
John Bryant (1976)
Veronica Hammerton (1977) +
Andrew Goodman (1978)
Simon Readhead (1979) +
Nicholas Yell (1979)
John Norman (1979)
Alan Saggerson (1981)
Alastair Hammerton (1983)
Timothy Dutton (1985)
Edward Bishop (1985)
Sarah Paneth (1985) +
Julian Waters (1986)
Marc Rivalland (1987)
Justin Althaus (1988)
Angus Piper (1991)
Andrew Warnock (1993)
Paul Stagg (1994)
David Thomson (1994)
Matthew Chapman (1994)
Ivor Collett (1995)
Sophie Mortimer (1996)
Zachary Bredemear (1996)
Mohinderpal Sethi (1996)
David Bridgman (1997)
Ian Miller (1999)
Simon Trigger (2000)

NO.1 SERJEANTS' INN

+ Recorder † Associate member

Continued overleaf

LONDON

BAR A-Z

The Chambers No. 1 Serjeants' Inn is an established common law set which is known particularly for its handling of professional and clinical negligence claims, personal injury actions, property litigation, claims against public authorities and employment law.

Work Undertaken

Professional Negligence Members of chambers represent claimants and defendants in all aspects of professional negligence litigation, but particularly in actions involving surveyors, accountants, solicitors, financial advisors and insurance brokers.

Clinical Negligence This is a leading specialism in chambers and covers cervical screening errors, negligence leading to cerebral palsy, serious brain damage or paralysis and claims for failed sterilisation, negligently performed spinal surgery, failed plastic surgery and late diagnosis.

Personal Injury Expertise in personal injury matters includes disaster litigation, industrial injuries and asbestos related diseases, road traffic claims, stress related illnesses, multi-party claims involving allegations of sexual abuse and complex issues on assessment of damages and implementation of structured settlements. A specialist team handles claims involving holiday accidents and all issues arising from travel and tourism.

Property Litigation The property team is well known for its landlord and tenant and commercial property work. It also deals with real property matters, including land registration, as well as matters relating to agricultural holdings and housing.

Commercial Commercial law matters dealt with include insurance law and policy disputes; undue influence claims against commercial lenders; contractual claims; sale of goods and partnership law. A specialist employment team handles cases involving claims for racial, sexual and disability discrimination as well as the full spectrum of employment law matters.

Public Authorities Claims against public authorities, including the police, constitute a major area of chambers' expertise. Educational negligence by local authorities and breaches of duties of care in the public sector have led to numerous high profile cases. Other administrative law matters dealt with include judicial review, social welfare and housing law, community care and health and safety.

3 Serjeants' Inn (Robert Francis QC & John Grace QC)

Set No.130

3 Serjeants' Inn, London, EC4Y 1BQ
Tel (020) 7427 5000   **Fax** (020) 7353 0425   **DX** 421
Email clerks@3serjeantsinn.com   **Website** www.3serjeantsinn.com

Head of Chambers	Robert Francis QC
	John Grace QC
Senior Clerk	Nick Salt
Junior Clerks	Lee Johnson
	Tracy Barker
Administrator	Julia Davis
Tenants	36

Members

Robert Francis QC (1973) (QC-1992)
John Grace QC (1973) (QC-1994)
Adrian Whitfield QC (1964) (QC-1983)
Philip Naughton QC (1970) (QC-1988)
Nicola Davies QC (1976) (QC-1992)
James Watson QC (1979) (QC-2000)
Philip Gaisford (1969)
Malcolm Fortune (1972)
Geoffrey D Conlin (1973)

Huw Lloyd (1975)
Andrew Grubb (1980)
Fiona Neale (1981)
Mary O'Rourke (1981)
George Hugh-Jones (1983)
Adrian Hopkins (1984)
Angus Moon (1986)
John Beggs (1989)
Michael Mylonas (1988)
Jonathan Holl-Allen (1990)
Christopher Johnston (1990)
Michael Horne (1992)
Fionnuala McCredie (1992)
Gerard Boyle (1992)

Richard Partridge (1994)
Mark Ley-Morgan (1994)
Anthony Jackson (1995)
Debra Powell (1995)
George Thomas (1995)
Clodagh Bradley (1996)
Ranald Davidson (1996)
Bridget Dolan (1997)
Sharon Flockhart (1997)
Abigail Johnson (1998)
Simon Cridland (1999)
Briony Ballard (2000)
Neil Davy (2000)

The Chambers Three Serjeants' Inn is consistently recognised as one of the leading chambers specialising in all aspects of law relating to medicine, and is renowned also for its strong civil police team and its expertise in commercial construction and engineering law. Chambers occupy recently modernised and extended accommodation, and have a modern IT infrastructure, including video conferencing facilities. The set has facilities for ADR, in which a number of its members are trained. It has full disabled access and facilities, including parking (by prior arrangement) for the disabled. It has air-conditioned conference rooms, but members are willing to attend conferences elsewhere if convenient. The clerking team is efficient, friendly and helpful. Chambers are happy to carry out work on a BarDIRECT, as well as Direct Professional Access basis. Clients' needs are the chambers' priority.

Work Undertaken
Medical & Related Areas of Law Members of chambers act in clinical negligence cases for claimants, NHS bod-

ies, private hospitals and their insurers, and all the medical defence organisations. They have appeared in many of the leading cases such as Sidaway, Hotson and Kent v London Ambulance Service, multi-party cases such as the breast radiation litigation, and in cases of maximum damage; members of all levels of seniority do this work. Members also use their extensive scientific and medical expertise in pharmaceutical product liability claims. They have unrivalled experience in medical ethics cases, having appeared in most of the leading cases in this sensitive and often urgent area of work, for example Bland, Re F (sterilisation), B v Croydon HA, Re MB (caesarean section, and the first PVS cases since the coming into affect of the Human Rights Act (NHS Trust A v Mrs M). Members also have particular expertise and experience in mental health cases, and judicial review and human rights related to medical issues, for example Bournewood, Clunis and ex p Fisher. They regularly appear in professional disciplinary tribunals and inquiries, such as the General Medical Council, General Dental Council and the UKCC, as well as internal hospital disciplinary proceedings. Examples are the Bristol paediatric cardiac surgery inquiry and GMC proceedings. Members are also instructed in criminal cases related to medicine, most significantly in the recent case of Dr Harold Shipman.

Civil Police Law Three Serjeants' Inn is one of the leading police law chambers, and acts for some 30 police forces, including three metropolitan forces. 12 members of chambers of all levels of seniority are part of the police team and cover the entire spectrum of police work, including civil jury trials, human rights, police discipline, police pensions, employment, public enquiries, judicial review, and operational advice. Recent noted cases conducted by members include ex p Harman (s. 40 PACE reviews), Lamothe v MPS (PII), Orange v West Yorks (police liability for prisoner's suicide), Yates and Stewart (pensions), and the Marchioness inquiry. The police team has a strong reputation for providing risk management and training seminars for police forces.

Building & Engineering Members of the construction team advise and act for employers, local authorities, contractors, insurers, and construction professionals in a wide variety of construction, engineering and other technical disputes. Areas covered include building and engineering, industrial processes and nuclear plants, mechanical and electrical engineering, dredging, temporary works, and cases concerning the liability of construction professionals and Health and Safety matters. Both domestic and overseas matters are dealt with, in the context of court-based litigation, arbitrations and ADR.

Additional Areas of Work

Employment Members act for both employers and employees, particularly in the specialist areas of the health and police services, in employment and internal tribunals, with a particular emphasis on discrimination cases.

Professional Negligence Architects, surveyors, engineers, valuers, accountants and lawyers.

Personal Injuries: A wide range of cases, from major brain damage cases to road traffic and factory accidents, is undertaken.

Commercial Contract & Sale of Goods

Recruitment Chambers offer two or three funded (£17,500 p.a.) pupillages starting each October. A chambers brochure and profiles of individual members are available from the senior clerk, Nick Salt.

Serle Court (Lord Neill of Bladen QC)

Set No.131

6 New Square, Lincoln's Inn, London, WC2A 3QS
Tel (020) 7242 6105 **Fax** (020) 7405 4004 **DX** LDE 1025
Email clerks@serlecourt.co.uk **Website** www.serlecourt.co.uk

Head of Chambers	Lord Neill of Bladen QC
Senior Clerks	Terry Buck
	Steven Whitaker
	Barry Ellis
	Paul Ballard
Chief Executive	Helena Miles
Tenants	44

Members

Lord Neill of Bladen QC (1951) (QC-1966)
Richard Southwell QC (1959) (QC-1977)
Howard Page QC (1967) (QC-1987)
Patrick Talbot QC (1969) (QC-1990)
Alan Boyle QC (1972) (QC-1991)
Nicholas Padfield QC (1972) (QC-1991)
Frank Hinks QC (1973) (QC-2000)
Victor Joffe QC (1975) (QC-2001)
Michael Briggs QC (1978) (QC-1994)
Simon Browne-Wilkinson QC (1981) (QC-1998)
Elizabeth Jones QC (1984) (QC-2000)
Dominic Dowley QC (1983) (QC-2002)
Nicholas Asprey (1969)
John Whittaker (1969)
William Ballantyne (1977)
Beverly-Ann Rogers (1978)
William Henderson (1978)
James Behrens (1979)
Peter McMaster (1981)
Ann McAllister (1982)
James Eadie (1984)
Richard Walford (1984)
Philip Jones (1985)
Philip Marshall (1987)
Nicholas Harrison (1988)
Andrew Moran (1989)
Nicholas Lavender (1989)
Khawar Qureshi (1990)
Clare Hoffmann (1990)
Kathryn Purkis (1991)
Christopher Stoner (1991)
Douglas Close (1991)
David Blayney (1992)
Andrew Bruce (1992)
John Machell (1993)
David Drake (1994)
Justin Higgo (1995)
Daniel Lightman (1995)
Hugh Norbury (1995)
Timothy Collingwood (1996)
Jonathan Adkin (1997)
Giles Richardson (1997)
Thomas Braithwaite (1998)
Simon Hattan (1999)

serle court

The Chambers The merger in February 2000 of One Hare Court and Serle Court Chambers was the first between leading sets from the Temple and Lincoln's Inn. The merger is a tangible manifestation of Serle Court's forward-looking approach to business and commitment to excellence. The merger has provided a unique product: a set of chambers which transcends the outmoded division between 'commercial' and 'Chancery commercial' work. The full range of business law expertise is now available under one roof. Serle Court contains individuals at all levels who are recognised in the principal directories as leading practitioners in their fields. Chambers' commitment is to intellectual and forensic excellence delivered in an approachable and efficient way. Chambers is housed in extensive and newly refurbished premises in Lincoln's Inn. It prides itself on high standards of administration and is backed by an experienced clerking team, which its clients can rely on and trust.

Work Undertaken Chambers covers a broad range of business-related litigation, arbitration and legal advice, both in the UK and internationally. The main areas of work are administrative and public law, arbitration, banking, civil fraud, commercial litigation, company, financial services, human rights, insolvency, partnership, professional negligence, property, regulatory and disciplinary matters, trusts and probate. Chambers can provide a first-class team at all levels of call in each of these areas. Members are equally happy working as part of a team with those who instruct it. Individual members of chambers have particular expertise in the following additional areas: Arab laws, charities, public international law, sports law and telecoms law.

International A significant proportion of Chambers' work originates overseas. Members of chambers appear in proceedings in Europe, the British Virgin Islands, Cayman Islands, Bermuda, the Channel Islands, the United States of America, Hong Kong and Singapore.

BAR A-Z

LONDON

Settlement Counsel (David Stern)
Set No.132

The Lloyd's Building, 12 Leadenhall Street, London, EC3V 1LP
Tel (020) 7816 3600   Fax (020) 7816 7430
Email dstern@settlementcounsel.com   Website www.settlementcounsel.com

Head of Chambers	David Stern
Practice Manager	Nicholas Brand
Tenants	8

Members

Gerald Godfrey QC (1954) (QC-1971) †
David Stern (1989)

Michael Beckman QC (1954) (QC-1976) †
Margaret Howard (1977)
Graham Todd (1999)

Anthony van Hagen (1974)
Stephen Mason †
Lisa Hatch (1995) †

† Associate member

The Chambers Settlement Counsel is an international commercial practice with significant experience in the resolution of major national and international disputes. Members provide an advisory and dispute resolution service, specialising in areas affecting global commerce and industry. Members are instructed by solicitors, international companies and foreign law firms under the IPR. Chambers have associate offices in Paris and New York.

Work Undertaken Members specialise primarily in the fields of insurance, environmental protection, maritime law, corporate financial services and fraud, European Community law and in the resolution of other cross-border disputes.

3-4 South Square (Michael Crystal QC & Lord Alexander of Weedon QC)
Set No.133

3-4 South Square, Gray's Inn, London, WC1R 5HP
Tel (020) 7696 9900   Fax (020) 7696 9911   DX 338 (Ch.Ln.)
Email clerks@southsquare.com   Website www.southsquare.com

Head of Chambers	Michael Crystal QC
	Lord Alexander of Weedon QC
Senior Practice Manager	Paul Cooklin
Practice Managers	Michael Killick
	Jim Costa
	Dylan Playfoot
	Nicola Skinner
Administration Manager	Lesley Mortimer
Tenants	42

Members

Michael Crystal QC (1970) (QC-1984) LLB (Lond), BCL (Oxon)
Lord Alexander of Weedon QC (1961) (QC-1973) MA (Cantab)
Christopher Brougham QC (1969) (QC-1988) BA (Oxon)
Gabriel Moss QC (1974) (QC-1989) MA, BCL (Oxon)
Simon Mortimore QC (1972) (QC-1991) LLB (Exon)
Stuart Isaacs QC (1975) (QC-1991) MA (Cantab) Lic Sp Dr Eur (Bruxelles)
Marion Simmons QC (1970) (QC-1994) LLB, LLM (Lond)
Richard Adkins QC (1982) (QC-1995) MA (Oxon)
Richard Sheldon QC (1979) (QC-1996) MA (Cantab)
Richard Hacker QC (1977) QC-1998) MA (Cantab) Lic Sp Dr Eur (Bruxelles)
Robin Knowles QC (1982) (QC-1999) MA (Cantab)
Mark Phillips QC (1984) (QC-1999) LLB, LLM (Bristol)
Robin Dicker QC (1986) (QC-2000) BA, BCL (Oxon)
William Trower QC (1983) (QC-2001) MA (Oxon)
Martin Pascoe QC (1977) (QC-2002) BA, BCL (Oxon)

Prof. Ian Fletcher (1971) MA, LLM, Phd, LLD, (Cantab), MCL (Tulane)
Colin Bamford (2002) MA (Cantab)
John Briggs (1973) LLB, (Lond) Ex, Du D d'U (Nancy)
David Marks (1974) MA, BCL (Oxon)
David Alexander (1987) MA (Cantab)
Antony Zacaroli (1987) BA, BCL (Oxon)
Mark Arnold (1988) MA (Cantab)
Lexa Hilliard (1987) LLB, (Lond)
Stephen Atherton (1989) LLB,(Lancaster) LLM (Cantab)
Sandra Bristoll (1989) MA (Cantab)
Adam Goodison (1990) BA (Dunelm)
Hilary Stonefrost (1991) MSC (Lond)
Lloyd Tamlyn (1991) BA (Cantab)
Glen Davis (1992) MA (Oxon)
Andreas Gledhill (1992) MA (Cantab)
Fidelis Oditah (1992) MA BCL D Phil (Oxon)
Roxanne Ismail (1993) LLB (Lond)

Barry Isaacs (1994) BA (Oxon) MA (HARV) ASA
Ben Valentin (1995) BA BCL (Oxon) LLM (Cornell)
Felicity Toube (1995) BA BCL (Oxon)
Jeremy Goldring (1996) BA (Oxon) MA (Yale)
Samantha Knights (1996) BA (Oxon)
Lucy Frazer (1996) MA (Cantab)
David Allison (1998) MA (Cantab)
Daniel Bayfield (1998) MA (Cantab)
Thomas Smith (1999) BA LLM (Cantab)
Richard Fisher (2000) LLB (Lond) BCL (Oxon)
Muir Hunter QC (1938) (QC-1965) MA (Oxon) †
Clive Cohen (1989)(SC 1975) BA, LLB (Witwatersrand) †
Barry Mortimer QC (1956) (QC-1971) MA (Cantab) †
Issac Shapiro LLB (Columbia Law School) †
Prof. Peter Ellinger M.Jur (Jerusalem) D. Phil (Oxon) †
Andrew Martin (1983) LLB †

Continued overleaf

www.ChambersandPartners.com

1603

BAR A-Z

† Associate member

The Chambers A commercial and business law set with a pre-eminent reputation in insolvency and reconstruction law and specialist expertise in banking; financial services; company law; professional negligence; domestic and international arbitration; mediation; European Union law; insurance, reinsurance and general commercial litigation. 3-4 South Square has 42 practising barristers, including 15 Queen's Counsel. Chambers aims to provide the most effective professional services to clients and has developed a modern administration system which is supported by advanced information technology. Members of chambers adopt a business-like and commercial approach to their practice and are capable of reacting swiftly (individually or as members of a team) to urgent problems as the need may arise. 3-4 South Square is accustomed to dealing with matters at all levels of complexity often at very short notice. In the course of their work, members see similar problems from many different angles and keep abreast of recent developments in business, financial and commercial law. The Practice Managers are available 24 hours per day, seven days a week to deal with all enquiries.

Work Undertaken

Insolvency 3-4 South Square is well-known for its insolvency work. Work undertaken includes contentious and non-contentious problems arising out of domestic and international corporate and personal insolvencies. This work is not just limited to the technical issues that arise in receiverships, administrations, liquidations and personal bankruptcies. It also includes analysis and problem-solving in the diverse areas that arise in the rescue and reconstruction of failed and failing businesses. Many important issues of banking and business law only ever arise for determination in the context of an insolvency. It follows that members of 3-4 South Square have considerable experience of those issues. They arise in the many different types of litigation in which officeholders are seeking to recover assets on behalf of an insolvent estate.

Other 3-4 South Square's expertise is by no means limited to work related to or arising out of insolvency. Members of chambers are frequently instructed in banking, insurance and other commercial disputes, dealing with every kind of contentious problem such as the civil aspects of commercial fraud and the obtaining of evidence for foreign proceedings. These problems can arise in many different situations in which a good general understanding of commercial law is required. Members of chambers also have much experience of professional negligence proceedings (primarily in cases against accountants and solicitors) and in disciplinary proceedings.

Publications The members of 3-4 South Square have written, edited and contributed to numerous books and articles on corporate and personal insolvency, company law and banking.

International Several members of chambers are fluent in or have a good working knowledge of foreign languages including French, German, Italian, Spanish, Russian, Hungarian and Chinese (Mandarin). The barristers at 3-4 South Square are regularly instructed to appear in courts and tribunals overseas. These jurisdictions include Bermuda, the Cayman Islands, the British Virgin Islands, Channel Islands, Singapore, Hong Kong and the USA. They are also retained as expert witnesses to appear before both arbitrators and courts in these and other overseas jurisdictions. Several members sit as both arbitrators and mediators in domestic and international disputes.

---

11 South Square (Christopher Floyd QC)

Set No.134

11 South Square (2nd Floor), Gray's Inn, London, WC1R 5EY
Tel (020) 7405 1222　**Fax** (020) 7242 4282　**DX** 433
Email clerks@11southsquare.com　**Website** www.11southsquare.com

Head of Chambers	Christopher Floyd QC
Senior Clerks	Martyn Nicholls
	Rochelle Haring
First Junior Clerk	Ashley Carr
Tenants	15

Members

Christopher Floyd QC (1975) (QC-1992)
Henry Whittle (1975)
Michael Silverleaf QC (1980) (QC-1996)
Henry Carr QC (1982) (QC-1998)
Richard Hacon (1979)
Richard Arnold QC (1985) (QC-2000)
Iain Purvis (1986)
Heather Lawrence (1990)
Mark Vanhegan (1990)
Jacqueline Reid (1992)
Piers Acland (1993)
Hugo Cuddigan (1995)
Giles Fernando (1998)
Benet Brandreth (1999)
Brian Nicholson (2000)

The Chambers 11 South Square is a leading set of barristers' chambers specialising in the law of intellectual property. The set is additionally well known for its information technology and media and entertainment work. Former Heads of Chambers include Sir Stafford Cripps KC, who was Solicitor General in the 1930s and went on to become Chancellor of the Exchequer. Later Sir Lionel Heald QC became Head, as well as becoming Attorney-General in his time. Many members of chambers have gone on to hold judicial office. Most recently, Sir Nicholas Pumfrey was appointed in 1997 to the Chancery Division of the High Court. The

Head of Chambers is now Christopher Floyd QC, who is Chairman of the Intellectual Property Bar Association.

Work Undertaken Patents; copyright and designs; trademarks and passing off; confidential information and privacy; computer law and other technical litigation; data protection and freedom of information; entertainment and media law and performers' rights; and European Community law.

Stanbrook & Henderson (Clive Stanbrook QC & Roger Henderson QC) Set No.135

2 Harcourt Buildings, Temple, London, EC4Y 9DB
Tel (020) 7353 0101 **Fax** (020) 7583 2686 **DX** LDE 1039
Email clerks@harcourt.co.uk **Website** www.harcourt.co.uk

Head of Chambers	Clive Stanbrook QC
	Roger Henderson QC
Chief Clerk	John White
Senior Clerk	Simon Boutwood
Tenants	44

The Chambers Stanbrook & Henderson is an association between the chambers of Roger Henderson QC at 2 Harcourt Buildings (see other reference for a full list) and the members of the European law firm of Stanbrook & Hooper in Brussels who are also members of the English bar, namely Clive Stanbrook OBE QC (1972) (QC-1989), Philip Bentley QC (1970) (QC-1991). The association was initiated in 1991 to satisfy clients' growing requirement for combined expertise in European and domestic law by providing a single port of call for solicitors and other professionals requiring advice and advocacy and by taking advantage of Stanbrook & Hooper's link with legal practices throughout mainland Europe. The work undertaken reflects chambers' detailed knowledge of EU institutions and the way in which they work, knowledge which is essential for anyone affected by EU action or legislation. The Brussels-based barristers have a close link with daily developments in the European Commission, the Council and the Parliament Secretariat, with the result that a complete legal monitoring and information service can be offered.

Work Undertaken Areas covered include the law relating to competition; merger control; trade; financial services; insurance; offshore investment; fiscal policy; local government and the public sector; the environment; product liability; agriculture and food; health and safety; employment and discrimination; human rights; immigration and freedom of movement; intellectual property; sport; and general EU regulatory policy.

3 Stone Buildings (Geoffrey Vos QC) Set No.136

3 Stone Buildings, Lincoln's Inn, London, WC2A 3XL
Tel (020) 7242 4937 **Fax** (020) 7405 3896 **DX** 317
Email clerks@3sb.law.co.uk **Website** www.3stonebuildings.com

Head of Chambers	Geoffrey Vos QC
Senior Clerk	Andrew Palmer
Tenants	19

Members

Geoffrey Vos QC (1977) (QC-1993) MA (Cantab)
Edward Alexander Bannister QC (1974) (QC-1991) BA (Oxon)
Sarah J Asplin QC (1984) (QC-2002) MA (Cantab), BCL (Oxon)
David R Stanford (1951) LLB, MA (Cantab)
Geoffrey J Topham (1964) MA (Cantab)
Andrew J Cosedge (1972) LLB (Exon)

James Gibbons (1974)
Alan M Tunkel (1976) BA (Oxon)
David da Silva (1978) MA (Oxon)
Alexandra Mason (1981) BA (Hons) (London)
Robert A Hantusch (1982) MA (Cantab)
Teresa Rosen Peacock (1982) MA BA (Mich)
Gilead Cooper (1983) MA (Oxon) Dip Law
David W Lord (1987) LLB (Bristol)

Asaf Kayani (1991) LLB (Leeds), BCL (Oxon)
Andrew M Twigger (1994) BA (Oxon)
Fenner Moeran (1996) BSc (Bristol)
Andrew J Child (1997) BA (Cantab)
Kerry Bornman (1999) LLB (Reading)
Charlotte Downes (1996) BA (Cantab) LLB, LLM, ALA

The Chambers 3 Stone Buildings is a thriving set of chancery and commercial chambers. Its main practice areas are commercial and chancery litigation, pensions, company and insolvency, property and trusts, and insurance and reinsurance. In addition, 3 Stone Buildings offers specialists in media entertainment and sports, partnership, professional negligence and banking and financial services. Members of chambers undertake litigation drafting and advice in all these areas. Direct instructions are accepted from accountants, and other professional, and under the BarDirect scheme.

4 Stone Buildings (Philip Heslop QC)

Set No.137

4 Stone Buildings, Lincoln's Inn, London, WC2A 3XT
Tel (020) 7242 5524 **Fax** (020) 7831 7907 **DX** 385
Email clerks@4stonebuildings.com **Website** www.4stonebuildings.com

Head of Chambers	Philip Heslop QC
Senior Clerk	David Goddard
Tenants	26

Members

Philip Heslop QC (1970) (QC-1985)
Peter Curry QC (1953) (QC-1973)
Stephen Hunt (1968)
Anthony George Bompas QC (1975) (QC-1994)
Robert Hildyard QC (1977) (QC-1994)
Peter Griffiths (1977)
John Brisby QC (1978) (QC-1996)
Jonathan Crow (1981)
John Scott (1982) (QC Hong Kong 1996)
Malcolm Davis-White (1984)
Robert Miles QC (1987) (QC-2002)
Rosalind Nicholson (1987)
Sarah Harman (1987)
Christopher Harrison (1988)
Jonathan Brettler (1988)
Paul Greenwood (1991)
Andrew Clutterbuck (1992)
Nicholas Cox (1992)
Richard G Hill (1993)
Orlando Fraser (1994)
Charles Marquand (1987)
Anna Markham (1996)
Hermann Boeddinghaus (1996)
Andrew de Mestre (1998)
Vina Shukla (1992)
Gregory Denton-Cox (2000)

The Chambers 4 Stone Buildings specialise in company law, corporate insolvency, financial services and regulatory work and commercial law. Chambers currently consist of 26 members including 6 silks and 1 Hong Kong silk. Jonathan Crow is the First Treasury Junior (Chancery) ('the Treasury Devil') and 7 other members are currently on one of the Treasury panels. Chambers belong to the Commercial Bar Association, Insolvency Lawyers Association and Chancery Bar Association.

Work Undertaken Work undertaken includes company law, corporate insolvency, financial services and regulatory, shareholder disputes, commercial law, corporate banking and public law. Further information about chambers and the work undertaken is contained in the chambers' brochure, which is available on request and on the website www.4stonebuildings.com. The clerks' room is staffed from 8 a.m. to 8 p.m. Monday to Friday and chambers can be contacted out of hours on the number given on the chambers' answering machine and in the brochure and website.

Publications Members of chambers have contributed to numerous publications in their specialist fields including *Tolley's Company Law, Butterworth's Practical Insolvency, Butterworth's Encyclopaedia of Forms and Precedents* (Companies Volume), *Atkin Court Forms* 2nd ed., (volumes on companies, winding up and equitable remedies), *Halsbury's Laws of Hong Kong* (arbitration volume), *Halsbury's Laws of England* 4th ed. (volumes on corporations and money) and *Clayton & Tomlinson* on *Law of Human Rights* (OUP). Malcolm Davis-White is the co-author of *Directors Disqualification: Law and Practice (Sweet & Maxwell 1999)*, Rosalind Nicholson is the author of *Table A Articles of Association (Sweet & Maxwell, 1997)* and Vina Shukla is the co-author of *Interpreting Convention Rights (Butterworths)*.

International Chambers undertake a substantial amount of work for overseas clients and members travel frequently to the United States, Europe and the Far East to advise. In recent years, members have appeared in Court in Hong Kong, Bermuda, the Cayman Islands, Bahamas, Gibraltar, Anguilla, British Virgin Islands, the Turks and Caicos Islands, Malaysia, Singapore and Trinidad. Various members of chambers have been called to these Bars for specific cases. In addition certain members are full members of the New York State Bar, the Cayman Islands Bar and the Bahamian Bar.

Recruitment 4 Stone Buildings' policy is to seek to recruit one new member each year from among its pupils. Prospective applicants for pupillage will find further information including details of chambers' awards in the Pupillage Pack which is available on request. Mini-pupillages are strongly encouraged.

■ BAR A-Z

5 Stone Buildings (Henry Harrod)   Set No.138

5 Stone Buildings, Lincoln's Inn, London, WC2A 3XT
Tel (020) 7242 6201   **Fax** (020) 7831 8102   **DX** 304 London/Chancery Lane
Email clerks@5-stonebuildings.law.co.uk   **Website** www.5-stonebuildings.law.co.uk

Head of Chambers	Henry Harrod
Senior Clerk	Paul Jennings
Tenants	23

Members

Henry Harrod (1963) +
Shân Warnock-Smith QC (1971) (QC-2002)
Christopher Whitehouse (1972)
Mark Herbert QC (1974) (QC-1995)
Mark Blackett-Ord (1974)
Barry McCutcheon (1975)
Martin Farber (1976)
Launcelot Henderson QC (1977) (QC-1995)

Andrew Simmonds QC (1980) (QC-1999)
Penelope Reed (1983)
Christopher Tidmarsh QC (1985) (QC-2002)
Michael O'Sullivan (1986)
Emma Chamberlain (1998)(former solicitor since 1986)
Patrick Rolfe (1987)
Barbara Rich (1990)

Karen Walden-Smith (1990)
Tracey Angus (1991)
Henry Legge (1993)
David Rees (1994)
Anna Clarke (1994)
Leon Sartin (1997)
Sarah Haren (1999)
Thomas Entwistle (2001)

+ Recorder

The Chambers 5 Stone Buildings is one of the outstanding sets of chancery chambers. Chambers have expertise at all levels in the fields of private client, estate planning, probate disputes, partnership, property litigation, professional negligence, pensions and all chancery related commercial matters. Chambers have an extensive team experienced in the field of advice, drafting and litigation relating to trusts, wills and associated taxation both in the UK and overseas. Chambers aim to provide a fast, efficient modern service of the highest standard.

8 Stone Buildings (John M Cherry QC)   Set No.139

8 Stone Buildings, Lincoln's Inn, London, WC2A 3TA
Tel (020) 7831 9881   **Fax** (020) 7831 9392   **DX** 216 Chancery Lane
Email clerks@8stonebuildings.co.uk

Head of Chambers	John M Cherry QC
Senior Clerk	Alan Luff
	Mobile (0790) 3180116
Junior Clerk	Paul Eeles
Tenants	10

Members

John M Cherry QC (1961) (QC-1988)
Timothy J Briden (1976)
Kieran May (1971)

Martin Seaward (1978)
Richard Menzies (1993)
Marcus Baldwin (1994)
Martyn McLeish (1997)

Mark King (1997)
Camilla Church (1998)
Victoria Ling (1998)

Work Undertaken Members of chambers practise principally in the areas of personal injury and professional negligence. Individual specialisations include ecclesiastical law; health and safety; Inheritance Act claims; insurance; asbestos related diseases; industrial deafness; employment law; clinical negligence; occupational pensions; administrative law.

■ 9 Stone Buildings (Michael Ashe QC)   Set No.140

9 Stone Buildings, Lincoln's Inn, London, WC2A 3NN   **Tel** (020) 7404 5055   **Fax** (020) 7405 1551   **DX** 314 Chancery Lane

www.ChambersandPartners.com

1607

BAR A-Z — LONDON

11 Stone Buildings (Murray Rosen QC)   Set No.141

11 Stone Buildings, Lincoln's Inn, London, WC2A 3TG
Tel (020) 7831 6381   **Fax** (020) 7831 2575   **DX** 1022 Chancery Lane WC2
Email clerks@11stonebuildings.com   **Website** www.11stonebuildings.com

Head of Chambers	Murray Rosen QC
Senior Clerk	Christopher Berry
Clerks	Gareth Davies
	Caron Levy
	Matthew Curness
Listing	Will Shrubsall
Tenants	44

Members

Murray Rosen QC (1976) (QC-1993)
Gerald Godfrey QC (1954) (QC-1971) †
Michael Beckman QC (1954) (QC-1976)
Peter Sheridan QC (1956) (QC-1977)
Iain Goldrein QC (1975) (QC-1997) †
Margaret de Haas QC (1977) (QC-1998) †
Jane Giret QC (1981) (QC-2001)
Edward Cousins (1971)
Edward Cohen (1972)
Alan Bishop (1973)
Adrian Salter (1973)
Donald McCue (1974)
John Phillips (1975) †
Nigel Meares (1975)
Robert Deacon (1976)
Jonathan Arkush (1977)
Sidney Ross (1983)
Roland Higgs (1984)
Marc Dight (1984)
Alan Gourgey (1984)
Tina Kyriakides (1984)
Raquel Agnello (1986)
Marcia Shekerdemian (1987)
Charles Holbech (1988)
Tim Penny (1988)
Sally Barber (1988)
Marilyn Kennedy-McGregor (1989)
David Stern (1989) †
Jonathan Middleburgh (1990)
Birgitta Meyer (1992)
Christopher Wilkins (1993)
Max Mallin (1993)
James Barnard (1993)
Nick Parfitt (1993)
Timothy Cowen (1993)
Jonathan Lopian (1994)
Denis Daly (1995)
Christopher Boardman (1995)
Tom Weekes (1995)
Jamie Riley (1995)
Alaric Watson (1997)
Douglas Keel (1997) †
Stephen Tudway (1998)
Iain Pester (1999)

† Associate member

Murray Rosen QC

The Chambers The barristers at 11 Stone Buildings practise in commercial litigation with specialist groups for all types of contract, commercial, company, insolvency and property disputes. The set has won awards for Barristers' Chambers of the year and has been praised in the press for its responsiveness, flexibility in working practices and approach to fee levels. There are 44 barristers working for law firms across the country and internationally as well as with in-house legal departments and direct access clients. They are particularly well known for their expertise in the specialist bar categories listed below.

Emergency Overnight & Weekend Service Contact Matthew Curness on (020) 8300 9634 (home) or 07776 235 906 (mobile), or Gareth Davies on (020) 8542 1211 (home) or 07767 443 519 (mobile), or Christopher Berry on (020) 8241 7903 (home) or 07836 566 251 (mobile).

Work Undertaken

Commercial Chancery Profiled in the major directories as a leading set in commercial chancery, with Murray Rosen QC, Jane Giret QC, Edward Cohen and Alan Gourgey all leaders in their field.

Contract & Commercial The largest group dealing with all aspects of business and banking litigation and commercial drafting.

Company Jane Giret QC and Marcia Sherkerdemian are profiled as leaders in the company field.

Insolvency Consistently featured in the major directories as a leading set with Jane Giret QC, Tina Kyriakides, Raquel Agnello, Marcia Sherkerdemian Birgitta Meyer, and Chris Boardman particularly recommended. Recent cases of interest include Re Lomax Leisure Ltd, Re Floor Fourteen Ltd (Lewis v HM Inland Revenue), Re Levey v Legal Services Commission.

Fraud The specialist groups deal in all aspects of civil fraud such as commercial fraud; fraudulent trading; property fraud; professional misconduct and VAT fraud. Murray Rosen QC is a leader in the field of fraud. Michael Beckman QC deals with both civil and criminal fraud and all aspects of serious crime.

Intellectual Property A major area of work for the set, their experience includes a wide variety of copyright, trademark, design rights and non-technical patent work, internet and e-commerce disputes.

Media & Entertainment Chambers deal with a significant amount of work in the media and music industry including defamation, press freedom, publishing and film and music contracts.

Sports Law Chambers has a well developed sports law practice with a history of representing high profile clubs, organisations and individuals in a variety of sports. Murray Rosen QC is highly recommended as a leading silk in this area of law. He was the founding chairman of the Bar Sports Law Group. Tim penny is also a leading junior.

Property & Land 10 property lawyers dealing with all aspects of property litigation and advice. Jonathan Arkush is recommended as a leading junior.

Tribunals: The work in this area relates mainly to disciplinary, employment, regulatory, sports and VAT.

Succession & Trusts Members of this group are experts in trust drafting and advisory work and are experienced in friendly and hostile litigation. They offer expertise in the Court of Protection.

Tax Specialists including Douglas Keel formerly an international tax partner at Pricewaterhouse dealing with all aspects of tax law from estate tax planning to international tax.

Professional Negligence Using the experience of all the specialist groups, chambers deal with a substantial amount of lawyers', accountants', architects', medical and surveyors' negligence.

Ancillary Relief The set has a small team at silk and senior junior level dealing with high-asset divorce settlement.

Alternative Disputes Resolution 11 Stone Buildings has a fully equipped ADR/Arbitration facility available for commercial use and each of the chambers specialist groups has accredited barristers available for dispute resolution.

Fees Levels are carefully monitored and a flexible approach is maintained, as chambers believe that each case has its own special requirements. This flexibility allows lay clients greater access to experienced lawyers. Conditional fee work is being continually developed and the chambers will respond to government and other initiatives as they arise. As an aid to efficient and cost effective legal services chambers has a team of lawyers for fast/multi-track cases available on a fixed fee basis. For a copy of the chambers' specialist brochures or legal bulletins contact the clerks or alternatively visit their website www.11stonebuildings.com.

Publications John Phillips is author of the *Modern Contract of Guarantee and Protecting Designs: Law and Litigation*; Edward Cousins is the author of *Cousins on Mortgages and Pease and Chitty's Law of Markets and Fairs*; Sidney Ross is the author of *Inheritance Act Claims, Law and Practice*. Iain Goldrein QC and Margaret de Haas QC are the authors of many publications. For further details visit www.11stonebuildings.com. Iain Goldrein QC is currently working on *Commercial Litigation Pre-emptive Remedies* (4th Edition).

Stone Chambers (Steven Gee QC)

Set No.142

4 Field Court, Gray's Inn, London, WC1R 5EF
Tel (020) 7440 6900 **Fax** (020) 7242 0197 **DX** 483 London/Chancery Lane
Email clerks@stonechambers.com **Website** www.stonechambers.com

Head of Chambers	Steven Gee QC
Clerks	Paul Coveney
	Jean-Pierre Schulz
Tenants	17

Members

Steven Gee QC (1975) (QC-1993)
Richard Stone QC (1952) (QC-1968)
John Reeder QC (1971) (QC-1989)
R Jervis Kay QC (1972) (QC-1996)

Elizabeth Blackburn QC (1978) (QC-1998)
Vasanti Selvaratnam QC (1983) (QC-2001)
Allan Myers (1988) (QC Aus)
Sarah Miller (1971)
Jonathan D C Turner (1982)
Colin Wright (1987)

Timothy Hill (1990)
Charles Davies (1995)
Madeleine Heal (1996)
Rachel Toney (1998)
Ishfaq Ahmed (1999)
Mary Gibbons (1999)
Mark Jones (2000)

The Chambers A specialist commercial set recently established under the direction of leading silk Steven Gee QC. Stone Chambers provides advocacy, advisory and arbitral services in all aspects of contentious and non-contentious international and domestic commercial shipping, and intellectual property work. Combining a dynamic, friendly and innovative approach with a comprehensive and client-focused service, members of Stone Chambers provide a leading expertise, ranging from the very urgent applications for relief, such as freezing and search orders and other interim applications, through to trial and beyond. Recent significant cases include the leading commercial/competition case Arkin v Borchard Lines, the pending appeal to the House of Lords in The Starsin, the pending appeal to the Court of Appeal in Compagnie Noga v the Abacha Defendants, and a leading intellectual property decision of the House of Lords, Designers Guild. Members are all specialist advocates and appear in all courts and tribunals in England and Wales. Senior members also act as arbitrators, mediators and expert witnesses. Members are also entitled and regularly appear in all European jurisdictions, including the European Court of Justice and the European Court of Human Rights. Much of the work of Stone Chambers is international and several members hold practising certificates in some US States, Australia, New Zealand, Hong Kong and a number of jurisdictions in the West Indies. Languages spoken by members include: French, German, Italian, Persian, Spanish, Urdu, Hindi and Arabic. Members write or contribute to numerous publications, including *Mareva Injunctions & Anton Piller Relief* (Steven Gee QC), *The Maritime Law of Salvage* (John Reeder QC) and *Law of the European Communities* (Jonathan DC Turner, EC Competition Law).

Work Undertaken Stone Chambers offers expertise in a wide range of commercial law and arbitration including the following key areas:
COMMERCIAL
Sale of Goods & Commodities International and domestic contracts as well as related transactions (letters of credit, bills of exchange and insurance).

Continued overleaf

BAR A-Z

Insurance All aspects of marine and non-marine insurance and reinsurance law.

Banking & Finance International and domestic banking and finance, freezing orders, asset tracing, leases, loans, securitisation, bills of exchange, promissory notes and documentary credits.

Construction & Engineering Construction and engineering projects, both on land and offshore in all relevant tribunals.

Road Rail & Air Transport Carriage of goods and passengers, including terms of carriage, arrangements with freight forwarders/other transport intermediaries, regulatory/competition issues, environmental matters and safety.

SHIPPING Charterparty and bill of lading disputes; contracts of affreightment and containerisation contracts (inc. connecting carrier and slot chartering agreements); ship sale and purchase; shipbuilding contracts; offshore and shipping activities including oil and gas, environmental, fisheries and conservation matters; admiralty including collisions, salvage and general average.

INTELLECTUAL PROPERTY & COMPETITION LAW

Intellectual Property (IP) Litigation, arbitration and advice relating to patents, trademarks, designs, copyright, domain names, trade secrets and related areas in the Patents Court, Patents County Court, Chancery Division of the High Court, UK and European Patents and Trade Marks Offices.

Competition (Anti-trust) & Free Trade UK, EC and US, often in relation to international transport, IP and IT/telecoms.

IT & Electronic Commerce Contracts and disputes relating to supply of computer systems, internet/electronic transactions, defamation, privacy, data protection and regulatory issues.

199 Strand (David Phillips QC)   Set No.143

199 Strand, London, WC2R 1DR
Tel (020) 7379 9779 **Fax** (020) 7379 9481 **DX** 322 Ch.Ln.
Email chambers@199strand.co.uk **Website** www.199strand.co.uk

Head of Chambers	David Phillips QC
Chief Executive	Nick Quarrelle
Business Development Director	Martin Griffiths
Senior Clerk	Graham Johnson
Tenants	36

Members

David Phillips QC (1976) (QC-1997) +
Peter Andrews QC (1970) (QC-1991) +
Robin de Wilde QC (1971) (QC-1993) +
Elizabeth-Anne Gumbel QC (1974) (QC-1999)
Malcolm Stitcher (1971)
Keith Walmsley (1973)
Quintin Tudor-Evans (1977)
Anthony Korn (1978)
Robert Bourne (1978)
Sara Hargreaves (1979)
Francis Treasure (1980)
Jacqueline Beech (1981)

Kevin Haven (1982)
Patrick Sadd (1984)
David Fisher (1985)
Martin Hutchings (1986)
Michael Harrison (1986)
James Aldridge (1987)
Henry Witcomb (1989)
Nicholas Saunders (1989)
Sophie Garner (1990)
Timothy Nesbitt (1991)
Amanda Eilledge (1991)
Rachel Vickers (1992)
Anthony Cheshire (1992)
Robert Duddridge (1992)
Eliot Woolf (1993)

Nick Isaac (1993)
Louise Thomson (1996)
Jeremy Ford (1996)
Toby Vanhegan (1996)
Stuart McKechnie (1997)
Simon Brindle (1998)
Farrah Mauladad (1999)
Adam Dawson (2000)
Emma Parker (2000)
Prof. Stephen Guest (1980) *
Leslie Blohm (1982) *
Richard Serlin (1987) *
Nicholas Price (1987) *
Roger Harper (1994) *

* Door Tenant + Recorder

The Chambers 199 Strand is a long-established set specialising in civil work and undertakes instructions for clients in London, throughout the country and abroad.

Work Undertaken The principal areas of work undertaken, in which specialist groups are offered, are personal injury, clinical negligence, property, professional negligence, general commercial litigation, employment law and road transport law. Their website at www.199strand.co.uk provides full details of the work undertaken by chambers as well as detailed profiles of the members. A comprehensive brochure is also available on request from the clerks. Chambers accept instructions under the Direct Professional Access and the Bar DIRECT rules and also accept cases under Conditional Fee Agreements.

International Members are fluent in French, German, Hebrew, Japanese, Mandarin and Chinese.

Tanfield Chambers (Peter Hughes QC)

Set No.144

Francis Taylor Building (2nd Floor), Temple, London, EC4Y 7BY
Tel (020) 7353 9942 **Fax** (020) 7353 9924 **DX** 46 London Chancery Lane
Email clerks@tanfieldchambers.co.uk **Website** www.tanfieldchambers.co.uk

Head of Chambers	Peter Hughes QC
Chambers Director	Paul A Green
Senior Clerk	Kevin Moore
Administrator	Kate Thornton
Tenants	62

Members

Peter Hughes QC (1971) (QC-1993)
Alan Tyrrell QC (1956) (QC-1976) FCI Arb
John Hall QC (1948) (QC-1967) FCI Arb
David Berkley QC (1979) (QC-1999)
Edward Raw (1963)
Gavin Merrylees (1964)
Andrew E C Thompson (1969)
Timothy Shuttleworth (1971)
David Guy (1972) FCI Arb
Philip Conrath (1972)
Stephen Monkcom (1974)
D A Pears (1975)
Paul Staddon (1976)
Mark Dencer (1978)
Mark Hoyle (1978) FCI Arb
David Daly (1979)
Kerstin Boyd (1979)
Simon Cheves (1980)
William Holland (1982)
Sebastian Reid (1982)
Marc Brittain (1983)
Michael Shrimpton (1983)
Richard Colbey (1984)
Mark Kelly (1985)
Robin Howard (1986)
Mark Loveday (1986)
Brian Riley (1986)
Philip Dixon (1986)
David Sharp (1986)
Michael Bailey (1986)
Robin Howat (1986)
Simon Livesey (1987)
Christopher Bamford (1987)
John Buck (1987)
Michael Buckpitt (1988)
Sarah Dines (1988)
Sheila Phil-Ebosie (1988)
Gerald Wilson (1989)
Carole Murray (1989)
Philip Rainey (1990) MCI Arb
James Candlin (1991)
Gwen Bankole-Jones (1991)
Stephen Heath (1992)
Lisa Sinclair (1993)
Catriona MacLaren (1993)
Andrew Butler (1993)
Daniel Tobin (1994)
Michelle Marnham (1994)
Christopher Heather (1995)
Robert Bowker (1995)
Mark Walsh (1996)
David Holloway (1996)
Catherine Aherne (1997)
Timothy Polli (1997)
James Fieldsend (1997)
Martina Murphy (1998)
Alejandra Hormaeche (1998)
Anna Laney (1998)
Marc Glover (1999)
Ellodie Gibbons (1999)
Charlotte Jewell (1999)
Adrian Carr (1999)

The Chambers 2001 was the most significant year to date in the development of chambers with the merger of Tanfield Chambers and the chambers of DA Pears. Chambers now boast 62 full tenants divided into specialist teams, supported by a dedicated clerking and administrative team of 11. The expansion means that chambers can now offer as comprehensive a service as any chambers. The set has a tremendous breadth of expertise with several top flight practitioners in each field. Chambers have large dedicated conference rooms and a fully networked computer system. French, German, Hebrew, Italian, Mandarin, Portuguese, Russian and Spanish are spoken.

Work Undertaken Work handled includes commercial, arbitration and European law; employment and discrimination including restraint of trade, transfer of undertakings and restrictive covenants; family, both children and property; personal injury and professional negligence; property. Direct Private Access and Conditional Fee work accepted.

Publications Members of chambers have written or contribute to a number of legal textbooks and articles. These include the following: Andrew Thompson is joint editor of both *Harvey on Industrial Relations & Employment Law* and *Butterworths Education Law Manual*; Stephen Monkcom is the editor of and contributes to *The Law of Betting, Gaming and Lotteries* of which Christopher Bamford is a contributor and co-editor. Carole Murray is a co-author of *Schmittoff's Export Trade; The Law and Practice of International Trade*.

LONDON
BAR A-Z

1 Temple Gardens (Geoffrey Nice QC)

Set No.145

1 Temple Gardens, Temple, London, EC4Y 9BB
Tel (020) 7583 1315 **Fax** (020) 7353 3969 **DX** 382 London
Email clerks@1templegardens.co.uk **Website** www.1templegardens.co.uk

Head of Chambers	Geoffrey Nice QC
Senior Clerk	Dean Norton
Tenants	43

Members

Geoffrey Nice QC (1971) (QC-1990)
Lord Mayhew of Twysden QC (1955) (QC-1972)
Norman Miscampbell QC (1952) (QC-1974)
Hugh Carlisle QC (1961) (QC-1978)
Ian Burnett QC (1980) (QC-1998)
John Bate-Williams (1976)
Ian Ashford-Thom (1977)
Angus Macpherson (1977)
William Hoskins (1980)
Dominic Grieve (1980)
Mark Bishop (1981)
Alison Hewitt (1984)

Alastair McFarlane (1985)
Robin B-K Tam (1986)
Paul Kilcoyne (1985)
James Bell (1987)
Mark James (1987)
Simon Brown (1988)
Philip Astor (1989)
Keith Morton (1990)
James Laughland (1991)
Charles Curtis (1992)
Richard Wilkinson (1992)
Nicholas Bacon (1992)
James Arney (1992)
Marcus Grant (1993)
David Barr (1993)
Alexandra Issa (1993)

Benjamin Williams (1994)
Robert Marven (1994)
Alexander Glassbrook (1995)
Nicholas Moss (1995)
Timothy Kevan (1996)
Emma-Jane Hobbs (1996)
Jonathan Hough (1997)
Paul McGrath (1997)
Dominic Adamson (1997)
Anna Kotzeva (1998)
Sacha Ackland (1998)
Stephen Cottrell (1998)
Angus Edwards (1999)
Benjamin Casey (2000)
Pamela Morrison (2000)

Work Undertaken General common law, including personal injury, professional negligence and product liability claims and claims in nuisance and other torts; insurance and other contractual disputes; consumer credit; public and administrative law and judicial review; immigration law; employment law; public inquiries and inquests; health and safety; fraud both civil and criminal; the law relating to costs.

International Members are fluent in Bulgarian, French, German, Russian and Spanish.

2 Temple Gardens (Dermod O'Brien QC)

Set No.146

2 Temple Gardens, London, EC4Y 9AY
Tel (020) 7822 1200 **Fax** (020) 7822 1300 **DX** 134 (Ch.Ln.)
Email clerks@2templegardens.co.uk **Website** www.2templegardens.co.uk

Head of Chambers	Dermod O'Brien QC
Senior Clerk	Christopher Willans
Tenants	49

Members

Dermod O'Brien QC (1962) (QC-1983)
Michael de Navarro QC (1968) (QC-1990)
Robert Moxon-Browne QC (1969) (QC-1990)
Andrew Collender QC (1969) (QC-1991)
Michael Black QC (1978) (QC-1995)
Benjamin Browne QC (1976) (QC-1996)
Jeremy Stuart-Smith QC (1978) (QC-1997)
Daniel Pearce-Higgins QC (1973) (QC-1998)
Howard Palmer QC (1977) (QC-1999)
Geraint Jones QC (1976) (QC-2001)
David Thomas QC (1982) (QC-2002)

Graham Eklund QC (1984) (QC-2002)
Henry de Lotbiniere (1968)
Rosalind Foster (1969)
Roger Hetherington (1973)
Alison Green (1974)
Monya Anyadike-Danes (1980)
John McDonald (1981)
Christopher Russell (1982)
Sarah Vaughan-Jones (1983)
Daniel Matovu (1985)
Martin Porter (1986)
Katharine Gordon (1988)
Andrew Miller (1989)
Neil Moody (1989)
Bradley Martin (1990)
Daniel Crowley (1990)
John Snell (1991)
Paul Downes (1991)
Christopher Lundie (1991)

Tim Lord (1992)
Rupert Reece (1993)
David Turner (1993)
Clare Brown (1993)
Dore Green (1994)
Lucy Wyles (1994)
Justin Mort (1994)
Bruce Gardiner (1994)
Nina Goolamali (1995)
Adam Constable (1995)
Neil Hext (1995)
Roger Harris (1996)
Krista Lee (1996)
Charles Dougherty (1997)
Peter de Verneuil Smith (1998)
Niazi Fetto (1999)
Darren Eales (2000)
Brent McDonald (2000)
Leona Powell (2000)

Work Undertaken Common and commercial law including personal injuries (including catastrophic injury, health and safety and occupational diseases); construction, technology and engineering; accountancy and banking; employment; fraud; insurance and reinsurance; professional negligence; clinical negligence; landlord and tenant; disaster litigation; pharmaceutical product liability, fires and floods, nuisance; conflicts of law, jurisdiction and EU problems. Members are experienced arbitrators and mediators. Instructions are accepted under the Bar Council's direct access rules.

International Members are fluent in French, German, Italian, Spanish and Swedish. Extensive experience in Asia, Africa and The Americas.

Recruitment Mini-pupillages by arrangement with Pupillage Administrator; pupils are recruited through OLPAS. Applications are welcomed from experienced practitioners: please write to the Chambers Director.

3 Temple Gardens (John Coffey QC)   Set No.147

3 Temple Gardens, Temple, London, EC4Y 9AU
Tel (020) 7353 3102 **Fax** (020) 7353 0960 **DX** 485
Email clerks@3tg.co.uk

Head of Chambers	John Coffey QC
Senior Clerk	Kevin Aldridge
Tenants	37

Members

John Coffey QC (1970) (QC-1996)
Jeffrey Pegden QC (1973) (QC-1996)
Ann Cotcher QC (1979) (QC-2000)
Geoffrey Birch (1972)
Richard Crabtree (1974)
Piers Reed (1974)
Jayne Gilbert (1976)
Robert Whittaker (1977)
David Stanton (1979)
William Saunders (1980)
Simon Connolly (1981)

Simon Smith (1981)
Alasdair Smith (1981)
Brian Stork (1981)
David Barnes (1981)
Kim Halsall (1982)
Dee Connolly (1982)
Martin Lahiffe (1984)
Wayne Cleaver (1986)
Gordon Ross (1986)
Benjamin Aina (1987)
Nicholas Bleaney (1988)
Frances McKeever (1988)
Martin Rutherford (1990)

Sibby Salter (1991)
Clemency Firth (1992)
Nicholas Corsellis (1993)
Alexander Williams (1995)
Amanda Hamilton (1995)
Caroline Carberry (1995)
Matthew Lawson (1995)
Nicola Cafferkey (1998)
Ruby Selva (1999)
Simon Shannon (1999)
Graham Smith (1999)
Mark Humphries (2000)
Maria Karaiskos (2000)

The Chambers Chambers of John Coffey are a well-established set providing a high level of advocacy and advice to an extensive range of clients. Chambers have widespread expertise and experience at every level and advise across the whole spectrum of criminal law. In addition, some members practise in the field of family law. Accreditation to Barmark in October 2000 ensures that chambers are committed to providing an excellent quality of service and meeting clients' needs in a rapidly changing profession. Members appear in the Magistrates Court, Crown Court, High Court, Queen's Bench, Divisional Court, the Court of Appeal and the House of Lords. Other tribunals include Professional tribunals, Mental Health tribunals, Industrial tribunals, inquests and other judicial inquiries. Some members are able to provide qualified training, accredited by Inner Temple and Lincoln's Inn, under the criminal advocacy module of the Professional Skills Course.

Recruitment Training and pupillage applications should be sent to Ruby Selva, including a detailed CV and references. Chambers currently offer pupillage awards.

3 Temple Gardens Tax Chambers (Richard Bramwell QC)

Set No.148

3 Temple Gardens, Temple, London, EC4Y 9AU
Tel (020) 7353 7884   **Fax** (020) 7583 2044
Email clerks@taxcounsel.co.uk   **Website** www.taxcounsel.co.uk

Head of Chambers	Richard Bramwell QC
Senior Clerk	Anne de Rose
Tenants	9

Members

Richard Bramwell QC (1967) (QC-1989)
John Dick (1974)
Michael Sherry (1978)
Alun James (1986)
Eamon McNicholas (1994)
David Southern (1982)
Jonathan Schwarz (1998) (SA 1977, Can 1981)
Peter Harris (1980)
Louise Rippon (2000)

Work Undertaken Specialist tax practitioners offering comprehensive tax planning. Advice on domestic and international tax investigations, disputes and appeals before all Courts. Professional liability involving tax. Current positions held by members of chambers include Chairman of the Tax Faculty of the ICAEW; Secretary of the Revenue Bar Association; visiting Professor at Queen Mary & Westfield College, London University; memberships of the CIOT Corporation Tax Technical Sub-committee, the International Tax Sub-Committee, the Working Party on Reform of Intellectual Property Taxation, the Inland Revenue E-commerce Forum; Editorial Board Taxation. Details on individual members are to be found at www.tax-counsel.co.uk

Publications Members have written, contributed to or edited: *Taxation of Companies and Company Reconstructions; Whiteman on Income Tax; Tolley's Taxation of Corporate Debt and Financial Instruments; Simon's Taxes; De Voil on VAT; Taxation; the Tax Journal; British Tax Review; Bulletin for International Fiscal Documentation; the Financial Times; CCH British International Tax Agreements.*

International Members have specific experience in relation to Canada, France, South Africa, the United States, Germany and Latvia. Members are fluent in French and German.

---

3 Temple Gardens (Jonathan Goldberg QC)

Set No.149

Three Temple Gardens, Temple, London, EC4Y 9AU   **Tel** (020) 7583 1155   **Fax:** (020) 7353 5446   **DX** 0064

Tooks Court Chambers (Michael Mansfield QC)

Set No.150

14 Tooks Court, Cursitor St, London, EC4A 1LB   **Tel:** (020) 7405 8828   **Fax** (020) 7405 6680   **DX** 68 (Ch.Ln.)

2-4 Tudor Street (Richard Ferguson QC)

Set No.151

2-4 Tudor Street, London, EC4Y 0AA   **Tel** (020) 7797 7111   **Fax** (020) 7797 7120   **DX** 226

■ BAR A-Z

LONDON

3 Verulam Buildings (Christopher Symons QC & John Jarvis QC)

Set No.152

3 Verulam Buildings, Gray's Inn, London, WC1R 5NT
Tel (020) 7831 8441   **Fax** (020) 7831 8479   **DX** LDE 331
Email chambers@3vb.com   **Website** www.3vb.com

Head of Chambers	Christopher Symons QC
	John Jarvis QC
Senior Practice Manager	Nicholas Hill
Tenants	51

Members

Christopher Symons QC (1972) (QC-1989)
John Jarvis QC (1970) (QC-1989)
R Neville Thomas QC (1962) (QC-1975)
Nicholas Merriman QC (1969) (QC-1988)
Ian Geering QC (1974) (QC-1991)
William Blair QC (1972) (QC-1994)
Nicholas Elliott QC (1972) (QC-1995)
Richard Salter QC (1975) (QC-1995)
Ali Malek QC (1980) (QC-1996)
Gregory Mitchell QC (1979) (QC-1997)
Ross Cranston MP QC (1976) (QC-1998)
Richard de Lacy QC (1976) (QC-2000)

Andrew Sutcliffe QC (1983) (QC-2001)
Michael Kay QC (1981) (QC-2002)
Andrew Onslow QC (1982) (QC-2002)
Stephen Phillips QC (1984) (QC-2002)
Rory Phillips QC (1984) (QC-2002)
Michael Blair QC (1965) (QC-1996) (Hon Causa)
Clive Freedman (1975)
Elizabeth Birch (1978)
Mark Pelling (1979)
Andrew Fletcher (1980)
Peter Cranfield (1982)
Tom Weitzman (1984)
Ewan McQuater (1985)
Jonathan Nash (1986)
Michael Lazarus (1987)
Juliet May (1988)
Angharad Start (1988)
Paul Lowenstein (1988)

Adrian Beltrami (1989)
Amanda Green (1990)
John Odgers (1990)
Jonathan Mark Phillips (1991)
James Evans (1991)
David Quest (1993)
Richard Edwards (1993)
Jonathan Davies-Jones (1994)
Matthew Hardwick (1994)
Richard Brent (1995)
Sonia Tolaney (1995)
Ian Wilson (1995)
Natalie Baylis (1996)
Catherine Gibaud (1996)
Matthew Parker (1997)
David Head (1997)
Ewan McKendrick (1998)
Peter Ratcliffe (1998)
Sophie Mallinckrodt (1999)
Lara Jabbour (2000)
Henry Knox (2000)

The Chambers 3 Verulam Buildings is a leading set of chambers specialising in commercial work. Members accept instructions and briefs to advise and represent clients in court, arbitration and other tribunals in England, Wales and internationally.

Work Undertaken All members of chambers are specialist advocates in various aspects of commercial work. Among them are acknowledged experts in the fields of banking; insurance and reinsurance; professional negligence; insolvency; entertainment and media; commercial fraud; public international and environmental law. The set also has an established reputation in international and domestic arbitration. Chambers include a number of individuals who have been involved in EU cases in the national courts and the European Court of Justice. Expertise is also offered in an extremely wide range of other matters, including agency, agriculture, building and construction, commodities trading, all aspects of company law, competition law, IT, telecoms and computer legislation, employment, financial services, gaming, intellectual property, judicial review, landlord and tenant matters, pensions, restraint of trade, and sale of goods. The diversity of experience available enables 3 Verulam Buildings to offer advice and representation to clients in the huge variety of business contexts in which legal issues arise. Barristers work individually or in teams to carry out all the preparatory and interlocutory work necessary to bring a case to trial or to settle a case by way of ADR. They also undertake non-contentious legal work, for example, drafting standard terms and conditions in contracts both for financial institutions and commercial clients. Additionally, members advise clients on the effects of new law. Chambers are managed by a friendly and efficient team of practice managers and support staff. In appropriate circumstances, chambers will carry out work on a conditional fee basis. The practice managers would be pleased to discuss this further and a draft agreement is available on request.

Recruitment Chambers offer three or four pupillages of 12 months, each with an award of not less than £32,000. Candidates should have a first class or 2.1 degree (which need not be in law). Applications must be made through the OLPAS scheme operated by the Bar Council.

Wilberforce Chambers (Edward Nugee QC)

Set No.153

8 New Square, Lincoln's Inn, London, WC2A 3QP
Tel (020) 7306 0102 Fax (020) 7306 0095 DX 311 London Chancery Lane
Email chambers@wilberforce.co.uk Website www.wilberforce.co.uk

Head of Chambers	Edward Nugee QC
Senior Clerk	Declan Redmond
Chambers Director	Gareth Mason
Clerks	Danny Smillie
	Tanya Tong
Tenants	37

Members

Edward Nugee QC (1955) (QC-1977)
Jules Sher QC (1968) (QC-1981)
Michael Barnes QC (1965) (QC-1981)
David Lowe QC (1965) (QC-1984)
John Martin QC (1972) (QC-1991)
Nicholas Warren QC (1972) (QC-1993)
Ian Croxford QC (1976) (QC-1993)
Robert Ham QC (1973) (QC-1994)
John Furber QC (1973)(QC-1995)
Terence Mowschenson QC (1977) (QC-1995)
Brian Green QC (1980) (QC-1997)
Michael Bloch QC (1979) (QC-1998)
Christopher Nugee QC (1983) (QC-1998)
Michael Furness QC (1982) (QC-2000)
John Wardell QC (1979) (QC-2002)
Anthony Taussig (1966)
John Child (1966)
Thomas Seymour (1975)
Gabriel Hughes (1978)
Daniel Hochberg (1982)
Michael Tennet (1985)
Jonathan Seitler (1985)
Thomas Lowe (1985)
Jonathan Karas (1986)
James Ayliffe (1987)
Judith Bryant (1987)
Joanna Smith (1990)
Joanne Wicks (1990)
Paul Newman (1991)
Gabriel Fadipe (1991)
Caroline Furze (1992)
Jonathan Evans (1994)
Emily Campbell (1995)
Rupert Reed (1996)
Julian Greenhill (1997)
Tiffany Scott (1998)
Nikki Singla (2000)

The Chambers The set is widely recognised as one of the leading chambers in its core specialist areas of commercial and financial services, pensions, private client and trusts, property and professional negligence. With 37 barristers (14 QCs), the set is able to offer specialist barristers at all levels of seniority and across the spectrum of commercial and chancery work. It has individuals who possess excellent reputations for their specialist capabilities in the additional fields of arbitration and dispute resolution, company, banking, insolvency, oil and gas law, intellectual property, sports and media law, planning, employment and charities. With its strength and depth of expertise, members of chambers undertake many of the most complex and important cases. They work hard to build and maintain strong long term relationships with their clients, who include the leading UK and international law firms. Clients value the modern quality of chambers' clerking and organisational management and the approachable service provided by barristers and clerks. Details of each individual member's practice, including selected report cases, can be found on the set's website listed above.

Work Undertaken The set's aim is always to provide practical and effective advice and to settle disputes in its clients' favour by the most effective means available.

Commercial & Other Contracts Commercial contracts, banking, insurance loans and security, guarantees, Lloyds' drafting and litigation, economic torts, breach of confidence, oil and gas law.

Financial Services & Regulatory Work Pensions, unit trusts, property enterprise trusts and collective investment schemes; regulatory work including investigations and disciplinary proceedings under the Financial Services Act 1986, Financial Services and Markets Act 2000, subordinate legislation and rules of conduct.

Property All matters relating to land, commercial property transactions, landlord and tenant, property finance negligence and fraud, mortgages and other securities.

Professional Negligence Accountants, actuaries, auditors, barristers, solicitors, surveyors and trustees and construction related professional negligence.

Pensions Occupational and personal pension schemes.

Trusts Drafting, advice on administration and construction and contentious and non-contentious litigation.

Tax & Estate Planning Including offshore tax planning and a wide range of tax litigation.

Company Law & Insolvency Including shareholder disputes, directors' disqualification proceedings, mergers and acquisitions, partnerships and joint ventures, corporate and personal insolvency.

Arbitration & Dispute Resolution Advice and representation at arbitrations, or acting as Arbitrator, in a wide range of commercial disputes in the UK and internationally.

Intellectual Property, Sports & Media Law Representing individuals, group and company interests in contract negotiations and disputes, advertising and intellectual property rights.

Equitable Remedies Injunctions, search orders, freezing injunctions, tracing, constructive trusts and proprietary estoppel.

Wills & Probate Contentious and non-contentious, administration of estates, intestacy and family provision.

Charities, Partnerships & Associations Housing associations, clubs, societies and the law as it relates to other associations.

International Members of chambers frequently advise and appear in jurisdictions outside the UK including Bahamas, Bermuda, the Cayman Islands, Jersey, Gibraltar, Hong Kong and Singapore.

THE REGIONS

▼BIRMINGHAM

■ Coleridge Chambers (Simon Brand) — Set No.154
Coleridge Chambers, 190 Corporation Street, Birmingham, B4 6QD **Tel:** (0121) 233 8500 **Fax** (0121) 233 8501 **DX** 23503

1 Fountain Court (Melbourne Inman QC) — Set No.155
1 Fountain Court, Steelhouse Lane, Birmingham, B4 6DR
Tel (0121) 236 5721 **Fax** (0121) 236 3639 **DX** 16077
Email clerks@fountaincourt.com **Website** www.fountaincourt.com

Head of Chambers	Melbourne Inman QC
Senior Clerk	Paul McNab
Tenants	39

Members

David Crigman QC (1969) (QC-1989)
Melbourne Inman QC (1979) (QC-1998)
Malcolm Morse (1967)
Robert Hodgkinson (1968)
Michael Dudley (1972)
Thomas Busby (1975)
Christopher Millington QC (1976) (QC-2001)
Giles Harrison-Hall (1977)
Benjamin Nicholls (1978)
Michael Conry (1979)
Stephen Eyre (1981)
Thomas Dillon (1983)
John Evans (1983)
Neal Williams (1984)
Mohammed Latif (1985)
Simon Ward (1986)
Blondel Thompson (1987)
Jonathan Salmon (1987)
Sarah Buxton (1988)
Paul Farrer (1988)
Gerard Quirke (1988)
Richard Atkins (1989)
James Puzey (1990)
William Baker (1991)
Anthony Johnston (1993)
Mark Garside (1993)
Nicholas Smith (1994)
Thomas Williams (1995)
Stuart Baker (1995)
Carolyn Jones (1995)
Simon Phillips (1996)
Huma Ali (1997)
Andrew Smith (1997)
Emma Kelly (1997)
Elizabeth Muir (1998)
Lucianne Allen (1998)
Leisha Bond (1999)
Jonathan Derrington (2000)
Nigel Gowling (2000)

The Chambers Broadly-based chambers practising in all aspects of criminal, civil, commercial and family law.

■ 3 Fountain Court (Robert Juckes QC) — Set No.156
3 Fountain Court, Steelhouse Lane, Birmingham, B4 6DR **Tel** (0121) 236 5854 **Fax** (0121) 236 7008 **DX** 16079

■ 4 Fountain Court (John Saunders QC) — Set No.157
4 Fountain Court, Steelhouse Lane, Birmingham, B4 6DR **Tel** (0121) 236 3476 **Fax** (0121) 200 1214 **DX** 16074

■ No.6 Fountain Court (Roger Smith QC) — Set No.158
6 Fountain Court, Steelhouse Lane, Birmingham, B4 6DR **Tel** (0121) 233 3282 **Fax** (0121) 236 3600 **DX** 16076

BAR A-Z ■ BIRMINGHAM

No 5 Chambers (Gareth Evans QC) — Set No.159

5 Fountain Court, Steelhouse Lane, Birmingham, B4 6DR
Tel (0121) 606 0500 **Fax** (0121) 606 1501 **DX** 16075 Birmingham Fountain Court
Email info@no5.com **Website** www.no5.com

Head of Chambers	Gareth Evans QC
Deputy	Ralph Lewis QC
Practice Director	Tony McDaid
Tenants	119

Members:

Gareth Evans QC (1973) (QC-1994)
Ralph Lewis QC (1978) (QC-1999)
Anthony Barker QC (1966) (QC-1985)
David H Stembridge QC (1955) (QC-1990)
Martin R Kingston QC (1972) (QC-1992)
Richard Jones QC (1972) (QC-1996) †
William Wood QC (1970) (QC-1997)
Paul Bleasdale QC (1978) (QC-2001)
Jeremy Cahill QC (1975) (QC-2002)
Satinder Hunjan QC (1984) (QC-2002)
John West (1965)
Roger Smith (1968)
Stephen Whitaker (1970)
Allan Dooley (1991)
John Harvey (1973)
Roger S Giles (1976)
Walter Bealby (1976)
Graham Henson (1976)
Anne E Smallwood (1977)
Robin Rowland (1977)
Christopher James (1977)
David Iles (1977)
Kevin J O'Donovan (1978)
Rosalind Bush (1978)
Simon Michael (1978)
Alasdair Brough (1979)
Jean Draycott (1980)
Timothy Newman (1981)
Stephanie Brown (1982)
Neil Thompson (1982)
Steven B Clifford (1982)
Michael Stephens (1983)
Andrew McGrath (1983)

David Stockill (1985)
Richard Lee (1985)
Richard Moat (1985)
Ian Dove (1986)
Lorna Meyer (1986)
Bernard Thorogood (1986)
Mark Heywood (1986)
Simon Drew (1987)
Anthony Crean (1987)
Sally Hickman (1987)
Eugene Hickey (1988)
Caroline Baker (1988)
Joanna Chadwick (1988)
Ekwall Singh Tiwana (1988)
Ian Bridge (1988)
Sara Williams (1989)
Malcolm Duthie (1989)
Martin Liddiard (1989)
Becket Bedford (1989)
Gary Bell (1989)
Moira Phillips (1989)
Michael Anning (1990)
Melanie McDonald (1990)
Ashley Wynne (1990)
Mary Bennett (1990)
Andrew Baker (1990)
Douglas Armstrong
Mark Radburn (1991)
Michele Friel (1991)
Jennifer Jones (1991)
Marion Wilson (1991)
Howard Reid (1991)
Gary Thornett (1991)
Sarah Buckingham (1991)
Hugh O'Brien-Quinn (1992)
David Park (1992)
Peter Goatley (1992)
Nicholas Xydias (1992)
Marc Wilkinson (1992)
Nicola Preston (1992)
Hugh Richards (1992)
Isabel Hitching (1992)
William Hansen (1992)

Nigel Brockley (1992)
David Taylor (1993)
Sarah Clover (1993)
Nageena Khalique (1994)
Rachael Price (1994)
Robert Smallwood (1994)
Rachel Cotter (1994)
Joanne Duffy (1994)
Anthony Potter (1994)
Victoria Green (1994)
Peter Collie (1994)
Satnam Choongh (1994)
Anna Diamond (1995)
David Mitchell (1995)
Patricia Hawthorne (1995)
Tim Sheppard (1995)
Jeremy Wright (1996)
Emma Hogan (1996)
Michael Walsh (1996)
Talbir Singh (1996)
Sally Hancox (1996)
Cheryl Jones (1996)
Tim Mayer (1997)
Karl Hirst (1997)
Christopher Young (1997)
Richard Hadley (1997)
Joanne Wallbanks (1997)
Harbinder Singh Lally (1997)
Tarlowchan Dubb (1997)
Matthew Brunning (1997)
Beth Coll (1997)
Alexander Stein (1998)
Jamie Gamble (1999)
Louisa Denning (1999)
Teresa Hargreaves (1999)
Charles Crow (1999)
Jonathan Barclay (1999)
Raza Mithani (2000)
Glenn Willetts (2000)
Heather Dardis (2000)
Param K Bains (2001)
Simon Worlock (2001)
Jas Mann (2001)

† Associate Tenant

The Chambers Chambers have six specialist practice groups, each with its own membership, group identity and Head of Group. This enables them to offer genuine expertise in all main areas of work. The younger tenants usually gain experience from several disciplines until their particular field of expertise is ascertained, at which point they will join one of the established specialist groups. The six specialist groups are: personal injury and clinical negligence; crime and licensing; commercial and chancery; planning and environment; family; and employment. No 5 Chambers offers unrivalled facilities for its clients, including 11 purpose-built dedicated conference rooms; a video-conference studio capable of providing both national and international video conference links; a large arbitration room; and a seminar suite, capable of seating 40 delegates.

BIRMINGHAM — BAR A-Z

No 5 Chambers has also recently opened a London office which offers excellent conference facilities to tenants and their clients.

St. Ive's Chambers (Julia Macur QC) — Set No.160

St. Ive's Chambers, Whittall Street, Birmingham, B4 6DH **Tel** (0121) 236 0863 **Fax** (0121) 236 6961 **DX** 16072 Birmingham

St Philips Chambers (John Randall QC) — Set No.161

55 Temple Row, Birmingham, B2 5LS
Tel (0121) 246 7000 **Fax** (0121) 246 7001 **DX** 723240 BIRMINGHAM 56
Email clerks@st-philips.co.uk **Website** www.st-philips.co.uk

Head of Chambers	John Randall QC
Chief Executive	Paul Wilson
Chief Clerks	Matthew Fleming
	Joe Wilson
Senior Clerks	David Partridge
	Jenny Culligan
Clerks	Su Gilbert
	Marguerite Lawrence
	Claire Meyrick
	Philip Jones
	Ramesh Chauhan
	Abigail Kirk
Tenants	95

Members

John Randall QC (1978) (QC-1995) + †
Rex Tedd QC (1970) (QC-1993) +
Heather Swindells QC (1974) (QC-1995) + †
William Davis QC (1975) (QC-1998) +
James Corbett QC (1975) (QC-1999) +
Jeremy Cousins QC (1977) (QC-1999) +
David Hershman QC (1981) (QC-2002) +
Michael Garrett (1967)
Brian Healy (1967)
John Price (1969) +
Douglas Readings (1972) +
Graham Cliff (1973) +
James Quirke (1974)
Timothy Jones (1975)
Guy Spollon (1976)
Andrew Neaves (1977)
William Pusey (1977)
Morris Cooper (1979)
James Burbidge (1979) +
Simon Clegg (1980)
Martine Kushner (1980) +
Stephen Thomas (1980) +
Roger Dyer (1980)
David Worster (1980) +
Makhan Shoker (1981)
Nergis-Anne Matthew (1981)
Barry Berlin (1981)
Stephen Campbell (1982) +
Kevin Hegarty (1982)
John Edwards (1983) +
Peter Haynes (1983)
Lawrence Messling (1983) ‡
Petar Starcevic (1983)

Thomas Rochford (1984)
Avtar Khangure (1985) +
Samantha Powis (1985)
Mohammed Zaman (1985)
Christopher Adams (1986)
Nicolas Cartwright (1986)
Gareth Walters (1986)
Lorna Findlay (1987)
Lance Ashworth (1987)
Elizabeth McGrath (1987)
Alastair Smail (1987)
Aubrey Craig (1987)
Tracey Lloyd-Nesling (1988)
Conrad Rumney (1988)
Lawrence Watts (1988)
Andrew Maguire (1988)
Alison Cook (1989)
Ailsa Cox (1989)
Edward Pepperall (1989)
Amarjit Rai (1989)
Mark Knowles (1989)
Simon Davis (1990)
John Robotham (1990)
Edmund Beever (1990)
Philip Capon (1990)
Vanessa Meachin (1990)
Sophie Garner (1990)
Sarah George (1991)
Robert Grierson (1991)
Robin Lewis (1991)
Andrew Lockhart (1991)
Glyn Samuel (1991)
John de Waal (1992)
Julie Moseley (1992)
Katherine Tucker (1993)
Anthony Verduyn (1993)
David Maxwell (1994)
Angus Burden (1994)
Elizabeth Walker (1994)

Rosalyn Carter (1994)
Andrew Charman (1994) ‡
Brian Dean (1994)
Simon Fox (1994)
David Tyack (1994)
Patrick Wainwright (1994)
Alistair MacDonald (1995)
Darron Whitehead (1995)
Brian Mahon (1996)
James Morgan (1996)
Claire Cunningham (1996)
Huw Jones (1997)
Alastair Young (1997)
Vinesh Mandalia (1997)
Alistair Wyvill (1998)
Elizabeth Hodgetts (1998)
Barbara Caulfield (1999) ‡
Shakhil Najib (1999)
Jane Sarginson (2000)
Jennifer Josephs (2000)
Edmund Williams (2000)
Jonathan Nosworthy (2000)
David Munro (2001)
Andrew McFarlane QC (1977) (QC-1998) *
Howard Morrison QC (1977) (QC-2000) *
Gerard Martin QC (1978) (QC-2000) *
Anthony Connerty (1974) *
Alan Turner (1984) *
Anna-Rose Landes (1986) *
Claire Starkie (1991) *
Esther Clarke ◊
Rebecca Franklin ◊
David Griffiths ◊
Ben Mills ◊
Paul Dean ◊
Paul Burton ◊
Jeremy Richmond ◊

* Door Tenant   + Recorder   † Deputy High Court Judge   ‡ Formerly a practising solicitor   ◊ Pupil

The Chambers This regional set received the 'Chambers of the Year' award from two leading legal publications in both 1999 and 2000. The set has also attained BarMark (the Bar council's quality award audited by the British Standards Institution). The client's professional needs are met by an individually tailored service, which is rooted in traditional practices, but wedded to modern approaches. The premises provide multi-

Continued overleaf

BAR A-Z ■ BIRMINGHAM/BRADFORD

media presentation, a video conferencing suite for up to 100 people, extensive conferencing and seminar facilities, large arbitration rooms and a first class library.

Work Undertaken Specialist teams have been established in: chancery and commercial; criminal law; employment and discrimination law; family law; immigration; personal injury and clinical negligence; public and administrative law.

Victoria Chambers (Lee Masters) — Set No.162

Victoria Chambers, 177 Corporation St, Birmingham, B4 6RG
Tel (0121) 236 9900 or 236 7863 **Fax** (0121) 233 0675 **DX** 23520 Birmingham 3
Email clerks@victoriachambers.co.uk **Website** www.victoriachambers.co.uk

Head of Chambers	Lee Masters
Senior Clerk	Lisa Clarke
Assistant Clerk	Patricia Venables
Tenants	17

Members

- Lee Masters (1984)
- Stephen Migdal (1974)
- David Pearson (1983)
- Andrew Dickens (1983)
- Julie Slater (1988)
- Gary Cook (1989)
- John Smart (1989)
- Dorothy Thomas (1991)
- Catherine Rowlands (1992)
- Tracy Lakin (1993)
- Alistair Redford (1995)
- Oliver Woolhouse (1996)
- Sara Pratt (1996)
- Nicola Beese (1998)
- Harjinder Johal (1998)
- Saleema Mahmood (1999)
- Victoria Richards (2000)

The Chambers An established common law set handling all areas of criminal and civil litigation. Specialist teams deal with family; crime; personal injury; employment/immigration; civil litigation and housing law before all tribunals. Chambers promise a 14 day turnaround for paperwork. Chambers have new premises available for conferences, lectures and training. Members of chambers are always willing to travel to meet lay or professional clients.

Work Undertaken Crime; family; civil litigation; housing; judicial review; personal injury and professional negligence; chancery.

▼ BRADFORD

Broadway House (J Graham K Hyland QC) — Set No.163

Broadway House, 9 Bank St, Bradford, BD1 1TW
Tel (01274) 722560 **Fax** (01274) 370708 **DX** 11746
Email clerks@broadwayhouse.co.uk **Website** www.broadwayhouse.co.uk

Head of Chambers	J Graham K Hyland QC
Practice & Finance Manager	Matthew Clarke
Tenants	34

Members

- J Graham K Hyland QC (1978) (QC-1998)
- Roger Thomas QC (1976) (QC-2000)
- Martin Wood (1973)
- John Topham (1970)
- Ian Newbon (1977)
- David Kelly (1980)
- Gordon Shelton (1981)
- Jonathan Gibson (1982)
- David McGonigal (1982)
- David Jones (1985)
- Peter Birkby (1987)
- Ian Howard (1987)
- Simon Myers (1987)
- Nicholas Askins (1989)
- Sophie Drake (1990)
- Mark Fletton (1990)
- Stephen Wood (1991)
- Tahir Khan (1986)
- J Ben Crosland (1992)
- Gerald Hendron (1992)
- Michelle Colborne (1993)
- Julia Nelson (1993)
- Jayne Chaplain (1995)
- Nicola Peers (1996)
- Camille Morland (1996)
- Robert Blantern (1996)
- Simon Anderson (1997)
- Ian Brown (1971)
- Shufqat M Khan (1996)
- Tasaddat Hussain (1998)
- Ian Miller (1999)
- Joanna E Moody (1998)
- Giles Bridge (2000)
- Ken Green (2001)
- Jonathan Cannan (1989) *
- Aisha Jamil (1995) *

* Door Tenant

The Chambers Broadway House Chambers is a long established set within 200 yards of the city's Combined Court Centre. Chambers also have fully staffed premises at 31 Park Square, Leeds.

Work Undertaken General common law; commercial; chancery; family and crime. Civil work includes contract, commercial, personal injuries, professional negligence, matrimonial property and finance, employment, immigration, landlord and tenant, real property, income and capital taxation and environmental.

Criminal work includes all aspects of prosecution and defence work mostly on the North East circuit.

International French, German, Hindi, Punjabi and Urdu.

▼ BRIGHTON

Crown Office Row Chambers (Robert Seabrook QC)   Set No.164

Blenheim House, 119-120 Church Street, Brighton, BN1 1WH
Tel (01273) 625625   **Fax** (01273) 698888   **DX** 36670 Brighton 2
Email clerks@1cor.com   **Website** www.1cor.com

Head of Chambers	Robert Seabrook QC
Chambers Director	Bob Wilson
Senior Clerk	Matthew Phipps
Clerk (Brighton)	Jenny Lewis
Tenants	23

Members

Robert Seabrook QC (1964) (QC-1983)
Anthony Niblett (1976)
James King-Smith (1980)
Paul Ashwell (1977)
Christopher Smyth (1972)
Roger Booth (1966)
Jacqueline Ross (1985)
Adam Smith (1987)
Timothy Bergin (1987)
Paul Rogers (1989)
Keeley Bishop (1990)
Martin Downs (1990)
Jeremy Cave (1992)
Ian Bugg (1992)
Darren Howe (1992)
Simon Sinnatt (1993)
Rachael Claridge (1996)
Richard Balchin (1997)
Robert Hall (1997)
Pegah Sharghy (1998)
Camilla Wells (1998)
Jane Peckham (1999)
Iain O'Donnell (2000)

The Chambers Chambers have been in Brighton for 30 years as an annexe of 1 Crown Office Row, a long established common law set in the Temple which has maintained strong Sussex connections for nearly half a century. Members practise from centrally located modern premises which doubled in size in 2001 to accommodate the set's rapid growth. Chambers are equipped with modern computer technology and direct telephone and computer links to 1 Crown Office Row. Conference and seminar facilities are excellent. The Brighton County and Magistrates' Courts are a few minutes walk away.

Work Undertaken Chambers undertake all types of general common law work - civil, criminal and family. Particular expertise can be offered in all types of family proceedings, prosecuting and defending crime, professional negligence, personal injury, landlord and tenant, building, employment and licensing.

Recruitment Please apply to Miss Keeley Bishop for pupillages in Brighton.

▼ BRISTOL

Albion Chambers (Neil Ford QC)   Set No.165

Albion Chambers, Broad St, Bristol, BS1 1DR
Tel (0117) 927 2144   **Fax** (0117) 926 2569   **DX** 7822

Head of Chambers	Neil Ford QC
Director of Client Services	D H Milsom
Senior Clerk (Criminal)	Bonnie Colbeck
Senior Clerk (Civil/Family)	Michael Harding
Junior Clerk (Criminal)	Nicholas Jeanes
Junior Clerk (Civil/Family)	Paul Taylor
Fees Clerks	Lesley Carpenter
	Rosemarie Blanshard
Tenants	45

Members

James Tabor QC (1974) (QC-1995)
Neil Ford QC (1976) (QC-1997)
Stephen Wildblood QC (1981) (QC-1999)
Christopher Jervis (1966)
Timothy Hills (1968)
Nicholas O'Brien (1968)
David Spens (1972)
Nicholas Fridd (1975)
Martin Steen (1976)
William Hart (1979)
John Geraint Norris (1980)
Martin Picton (1981)
Tacey Cronin (1982)
Julian Lambert (1983)
Caroline Wright (1983)
Ignatius Hughes (1986)
Stephen Mooney (1987)
Charles Hyde (1988)
Deborah Dinan-Hayward (1988)
Claire Wills-Goldingham (1988)
Myles Watkins (1990)
John Livesey (1990)
Caroline Ralph (1990)
Alexander Ralton (1990)
Virginia Cornwall (1990)
Nkumbe Ekaney (1990)
Claire Rowsell (1991)
Michael Cullum (1991)
Michael Fitton (1991)
Fiona Elder (1991)
Nicholas Sproull (1992)
Simon Burns (1992)
Paul Cook (1992)
Allan Fuller (1993)
Jason Taylor (1995)
Richard English (1996)
Daniel Leafe (1996)

Continued overleaf

BAR A-Z ■ BRISTOL

Kirsty Real (1996)
Archna Dawar (1996)
Kate Brunner (1997)
James Wilson-Smith (1999)

Charlotte Pitts (1999)
Samuel Butterfield (1999)
Kate Bramall (1999)
Sarah Regan (2000)

Christopher Wilson-Smith QC (1965) (QC-1986) *
Paul Dunkels QC (1972) (QC-1993) *

* Door Tenant

The Chambers A large and still expanding set, the members of which handle a wide variety of specialist legal areas.

Guildhall Chambers (Adrian Palmer QC)   Set No.166

Guildhall Chambers, Broad Street, Bristol, BS1 2HG
Tel (0117) 930 9000   **Fax** (0117) 930 3800   **DX** 7823 Bristol
Email info@guildhallchambers.co.uk

Head of Chambers	Adrian Palmer QC
Head Clerk	Paul Fletcher
Chambers Director (Non-practising Barrister)	Robert Thomas
Tenants	54

Members

John Royce QC (1970) (QC-1987)
Adrian Palmer QC (1972) (QC-1992)
Ian Glen QC (1973) (QC-1996)
Stephen Davies QC (1983) (QC-2000)
Richard Smith QC (1986) (QC-2001)
George Newsom (1973)
Adam Chippindall (1975)
Peter Barrie (1976)
Ian Charles Fenny (1978)
Brian Watson (1978)
Ian Pringle (1979)
Malcolm Warner (1979)
James Townsend (1980)
Ralph Wynne-Griffiths (1981)
William Batstone (1982)

John Virgo (1983)
Peter Blair (1983)
Andrew Langdon (1986)
Raj Sahonte (1986)
Martha Maher (1987)
Ray Tully (1988)
James Patrick (1989)
Jeremy Bamford (1989)
Paul French (1989)
Robert Davies (1990)
Stephen Dent (1991)
Kerry Barker (1972)
Anthony Reddiford (1991)
Louise Price (1972)
Euan Ambrose (1992)
Christopher Quinlan (1992)
Gerard McMeel (1993) †
Nicholas Miller (1994)
Mark Worsley (1994)
Matthew Wales (1994)

Gabriel Farmer (1994)
Victoria Hufford (1994)
Nicholas Briggs (1994)
Andrew Macfarlane (1995)
Richard Ascroft (1995)
James Hassall (1995)
Rosaleen Collins (1996)
Anna Vigars (1996)
Ramin Pakrooh (1996)
Rhys Taylor (1996)
Ewan Paton (1997)
Zira Hussain (1998)
Tabitha Macfarlane (1998)
Hugh Sims (1999)
Matthew Porter-Bryant (1999)
Katherine Gibb (1999)
Abigail Bond (1999)
Jennifer Tallentire (2000)
Timothy Walsh (2000)

† Associate member

The Chambers An established set with a modern outlook. Work undertaken includes insolvency/company; professional negligence; commercial/bank recovery; personal injury; property; crime and family.

Old Square Chambers (John Hendy QC)   Set No.167

3 Orchard Court, Orchard Lane, Bristol, BS1 5WS
Tel (0117) 930 5100   **Fax** (0117) 927 3478   **DX** 78229 Bristol
Email clerks@oldsquarechambers.co.uk   **Website** www.oldsquarechambers.co.uk

Head of Chambers	John Hendy QC
Senior Clerk	John Taylor
Tenants	51

Members

John Hendy QC (1972) (QC-1987)
John Melville Williams QC (1955) (QC-1977)
Frederic Reynold QC (1960) (QC-1982)
John Hand QC (1972) (QC-1988)

Lord Wedderburn QC (1953) (QC-1990)
Ian Truscott QC (1995) (QC-1997)
David Wilby QC (1974) (QC-1998)
Matthias Kelly QC (1979) (QC-1999)
Nigel Cooksley QC (1975) (QC-2002)

Paul Rose QC (1981) (QC-2002)
Jane McNeill QC (1982) (QC-2002)
Charles Lewis (1963)
Christopher Carling (1969)
William Birtles (1970)
Diana Brahams (1972)
John H Bates (1973)

BRISTOL ■ BAR A-Z

Christopher Makey (1975)
Charles Pugh (1975)
Toby Kempster (1980)
Alan Smith (1981)
Mark Sutton (1982)
Barry Cotter (1985)
Louise Chudleigh (1987)
Ijeoma Omambala (1989)
Jennifer Eady (1989)
Philip Mead (1989)
Damian Brown (1989)
Tess Gill (1990)
Jonathan Clarke (1990)
Christopher Walker (1990)
Nicholas Booth (1991)
Sarah Moor (1991)
Ian Scott (1991)
Oliver Segal (1992)
Michael Ford (1992)
Helen Gower (1992)
Roy Lewis (1992)
Elizabeth Melville (1994)
Mark Whitcombe (1994)
Melanie Tether (1995)
Emma Smith (1995)
Rohan Pirani (1995)
Rebecca Tuck (1998)
Hilary Winstone (1998)
Steven Langton (1998)
Stuart Brittenden (1999)
Anya Palmer (1999)
Katharine Newton (1999)
Daniel Bennett (2000)
Bella Morris (2000)
Ben Cooper (2000)

The Chambers Also at: 1 Verulam Buildings, Gray's Inn, London, WC1R 5LQ DX 1046 Chancery Lane/London Tel (020) 7269 0300 Fax (020) 7405 1387.

Work Undertaken Employment law, personal injury, clinical negligence, product liability and health and safety compliance law, environmental law and sports law (see London entry for more details).

International There are door tenants practising at the Hong Kong, Bermuda and Jersey Bars. Tenants are also members of the Scottish and Northern Irish Bars. John Hendy QC is a member of the NSW and Australian Bar.

Queen Square Chambers (Don Tait & T Alun Jenkins QC)   Set No.168
Queen Square Chambers, 56 Queen Square, Bristol, BS1 4PR **Tel** (0117) 921 1966 **Fax** (0117) 927 6493 **DX** 7870 Bristol

St John's Chambers (Christopher Sharp QC)   Set No.169
Civil Department, St John's Chambers, Small St, Bristol, BS1 1DW
Tel (0117) 921 3456 **Fax** (0117) 929 4821 **DX** 78138
Email clerks@stjohnschambers.co.uk   **Website** www.stjohnschambers.co.uk

Head of Chambers	Christopher Sharp QC
Chief Executive	Kate Blackburn
Senior Clerk (Civil)	Dick Hyde
Senior Clerk (Family/Civil)	Maureen Rowe
Senior Clerk (Crime)	Annette Moles
Tenants	56

Members
Christopher Sharp QC (1975) (QC-1999)
Nigel Hamilton QC (1965) (QC-1981)
Martin Mann QC (1968) (QC-1983)
Roger Kaye QC (1970) (QC-1989)
David Fletcher (1971)
George Threlfall (1972)
Paul Grumbar (1974)
Ian Bullock (1975)
Nicholas Marston (1975)
Timothy Grice (1975)
Sheelagh Corfield (1975)
Mark Horton (1976)
John Blackmore (1983)
Michael Longman (1978)
Richard Stead (1979)
Robert Duval (1979)
Susan Jacklin (1980)
Charles Auld (1980)
Peter Wadsley (1984)
Ian Dixey (1984)
Catriona Duthie (1981)
Richard Bromilow (1977)
Leslie Blohm (1982)
Susan Hunter (1985)
Glyn Edwards (1987)
Graham Howard (1987)
Lynne Matthews (1987)
Simon Morgan (1988)
Louise O'Neill (1989)
Neil Levy (1986)
Guy Adams (1989)
Andrew Marsden (1994)
Kamala Das (1975)
Derek O'Sullivan (1990)
John Sharples (1992)
Dianne Martin (1992)
Prof. Roy Light (1992)
Edward Burgess (1993)
Kathryn Skellorn (1993)
David Maunder (1993)
Andrew McLaughlin (1993)
Jacqueline Humphreys (1994)
David Regan (1994)
John Dickinson (1995)
Giles Nelson (1995)
Judi Evans (1996)
Simon Goodman (1996)
Matthew White (1997)
Rupert Lowe (1998)
Kambiz Moradifar (1998)
Emma Zeb (1998)
Alex Troup (1998)
Vanessa McKinlay (2000)
Prof. Nigel Lowe (1972) †
Jean Corston MP (1991) †
Alexander Dawson (1969) *

* Door Tenant † Associate Member

The Chambers Chambers offer a specialised and expert service on a departmental basis: chancery commercial, personal injury, family and crime with additional expertise in insolvency, revenue law, banking, local government work, professional negligence, construction, planning, licensing, environmental and employment matters. Chambers' criminal department is located at St Bartholomew's Court, Bristol, BS1 5BT Tel (0117) 910 0700 Fax (0117) 910 0701.

BAR A-Z ■ BRISTOL/CAMBRIDGE

Unity Street Chambers (John Isherwood)   Set No.170

5 Unity Street, College Green, Bristol, BS1 5HH
Tel (0117) 906 9789 **Fax** (0117) 906 9799
Website www.unitystreetchambers.com

Head of Chambers	John Isherwood
Senior Clerk	Clair Wadden
Tenants	13

Members:

John Isherwood (1978)
Christopher Ferguson (1979)
David Curwen (1982)
Iain Wightwick (1985)
Peter Langlois (1991)
Toby Halliwell (1992)
Judy Dawson (1993)
Jonathan Stanniland (1993)
Fergus Currie (1997)
Sarah Boyd (1998)
Toby Huggins (1998)
Rosalind Cameron-Mowat (2000)
Sarah-Jane Hurrion (2000)

The Chambers Unity Street Chambers is a recently established set, committed to an efficient and cost-effective service. Instructions are accepted/returned by email or on disc as well as in the more traditional manner, with paperwork being turned around within seven working days. Chambers is a forward-looking and friendly set, to whom working in partnership with its instructing solicitors is important. Situated in the centre of Bristol, with full conference facilities and convenient parking, chambers undertake cases throughout the country.

Work Undertaken Teams within chambers specialise in personal injury, landlord and tenant, criminal, employment, family, chancery and commercial law.

▼CAMBRIDGE

Fenners Chambers (Paul Hollow)   Set No.171

Fenners Chambers, 3 Madingley Road, Cambridge, CB3 0EE
Tel (01223) 368761 **Fax** (01223) 313007 **DX** 5809 Cambridge 1
Email clerks@fennerschambers.co.uk   **Website** www.fennerschambers.co.uk

Head of Chambers	Paul Hollow
Tenants	34

Members

Paul Hollow (1981) (Deputy D.J.)
Oliver Sells QC (1972) (QC-1995)*
Geraint Jones (1972)
Andrew Gore (1973)
Lindsay Davies (1975) +
Susan Espley (1976)
Simon Tattersall (1977) (Deputy D.J.)
Paul Leigh-Morgan (1978)
T.C.E. Brown (1980)
Andrew Gordon-Saker (1981)(Deputy Costs Judge)

Jane Bennington (1981)
Martin Collier (1982)
Liza Gordon-Saker (1982)
Meryl Hughes (1987)
George Foxwell (1987)
Robin Chaudhuri (1988) (Deputy D.J.)
Alasdair Wilson (1988)
Clive Pithers (1989)
Jeffrey Deegan (1989)
Sally Hobson (1991)
Caroline Horton (1993)
Michael Proctor (1993)
Katharine Ferguson (1995)

William Josling (1995)
Daniel Pitt (1995)
Terence Vaughan (1996)
Giles Surman (1997) *
Mike Magee (1997)
Roderick Spinks (1997)
George Keightley (1997)
Alasdair Foster (1998)
Stuart Lockhart (1998)
Martin Kingerley (1999)
Daniel Owen (1999)
Beth Cook (2000)
Guy Sims (2000)

* Door Tenant + Recorder

The Chambers An established East of England set, occupying extensive premises with on-site parking and full disabled access. See also Chambers entry for Peterborough.

Work Undertaken Chambers operate through six specialist teams: business; crime; employment; family; personal injury; property and environment.

CANTERBURY/CARDIFF ■ BAR A-Z

▼CANTERBURY

Becket Chambers   Set No.172

17 New Dover Road, Canterbury, CT1 3AS
Tel (01227) 786331   **Fax** (01227) 786329   **DX** 5330 Canterbury
Email clerks@becket-chambers.co.uk   **Website** www.becket-chambers.co.uk

Senior Clerk	Meagan Wilson
Tenants	11

Members

Philip Newton (1984)
Ronald Edginton (1984)
Kevin Jackson (1984)
Christopher Wall (1987)
Corey Mills (1987)
Jeremy Hall (1988)
Clive Styles (1990)
Paul Tapsell (1991)
Louisa Adamson (1994)
Nicholas Fairbank (1996)
Julia Agnini (1999)
Lionel Swift QC (1959)
(QC-1975) *
John Bishop (1970) *

* Door Tenant

The Chambers Becket Chambers is located only a few minutes drive from the local courts and the city centre. There is a dedicated conference facility and a large private car park.

Work Undertaken Chambers undertake all aspects of general common law and criminal work. Members specialise in the following areas: children and family proceedings; matrimonial finance and family provision; medical and professional negligence; personal injury; bankruptcy and insolvency; employment; sale of goods; consumer credit; housing; landlord and tenant; local government; and crime. The senior clerk will be happy to provide further details on any aspect upon request.

International Work is also handled in French.

▼CARDIFF

9 Park Place (Ian Murphy QC)   Set No.173

9 Park Place, Cardiff, CF10 3DP
Tel (029) 2038 2731   **Fax** (029) 2022 2542   **DX** 50751 Cardiff 2
Email clerks@9parkplace.co.uk

Head of Chambers	Ian Murphy QC
Senior Clerk	James Williams
Clerks	Nigel East
	Lesley Haikney
	Lisa Atwood
Tenants	41

Members

Ian Murphy QC (1972) (QC-1992)
Roger Thomas QC (1969) (QC-1994)
Nicholas Cooke QC (1977) (QC-1998)
Gregg Taylor QC (1974) (QC-2001)
Geraint Jones QC (1976) (QC-2001) †
Milwyn Jarman QC (1980) (QC-2001)
Philip Rees (1965) †
Martyn Kelly (1972)
Richard Francis (1974)
David Essex Williams (1975)
Richard Twomlow (1976)
Keith Thomas (1977)
Isabel Parry (1979)
Ieuan Morris (1979)
Karl Williams (1982)
Janet McDonald (1985)
Owen Prys Lewis (1985)
Susan Ferrier (1985)
Andrew Keyser (1986)
Peter Brooks (1986)
Ieuan Bennett (1989)
Paul Hopkins (1989)
Emily Davies (1989)
Julian Reed (1991)
Michelle Withers (1991)
Steven Donoghue (1992)
Hugh Wallace (1993)
Richard Kember (1993)
David Elias (1994)
Owen Thomas (1994)
Siân Parry (1994)
Gwydion Hughes (1994)
Peter Davies (1996)
Heath Edwards (1996)
Christopher Felstead (1998)
Lisa Thomas (1998)
Matthew Cobbe (1998)
Nuhu Gobir (1998)
Emyr Jones (1999)
Elizabeth Pearson (1999)
Owen Williams (2000)

† Associate Member

The Chambers A long established, leading set providing expert, client-friendly service on a specialised team basis. Former members include a Lord Justice of Appeal and several circuit judges. Several members of chambers are fluent in Welsh.

Work Undertaken Specialisations include chancery and commercial, administrative, local government, professional negligence, personal injury, planning, construction, employment, family and crime.

www.ChambersandPartners.com

1625

BAR A-Z ■ CARDIFF/CHELMSFORD

30 Park Place (John Jenkins QC) — Set No.174
30 Park Place, Cardiff, CF1 3BA **Tel** (029) 2039 8421 **Fax** (029) 2039 8725 **DX** 50756 Cardiff 2

33 Park Place (Neil Bidder QC) — Set No.175
33 Park Place, Cardiff, CF10 3TN
Tel (029) 2023 3313 **Fax** (029) 2022 8294 **DX** 50755 Cardiff 2
Email clerks@33parkplace.co.uk **Website** www.33parkplace.co.uk

Head of Chambers	Neil Bidder QC
Chief Executive	Alan Davies
Clerks	Stephen Price
	Elizabeth Champion
Process & Performance Co-ordinator	
	Julie Batten
Tenants	32

Members

Neil Bidder QC (1976) (QC-1998)
Mary Parry Evans (1953)
Roger Garfield (1965)
Richard Jones (1969)
Nicholas Gareth Jones (1970)
Jennet Treharne (1975)
Bryan Thomas (1979)
Jonathan Walters (1984)
Timothy Evans (1984)
Jeremy Jenkins (1984)
Andrew Taylor (1984)
Theodore Huckle (1985)
Graham Walters (1986)
Nicholas David Jones (1987)

Alan Troy (1990)
Gareth Jones (1991)
Lucy Higginson (1992)
Nicola Harris (1992)
Daniel Williams (1992)
Nigel Osborne (1993)
Andrew Arentsen (1995)
Sara Owen (1995)
Christopher Rees (1996)
Joan Campbell (1996)
Lucy Murray (1997)
Simon John (1998)
David Callow (1998)
Joanne Williams (2001)
Nick Gedge (2001)

Linda Duenas (2001)
Vernon Pugh QC (1969) (QC-1986) *
Wyn Williams QC (1974) (QC-1992) *
Rhodri Price Lewis QC (1975) (QC-2001) *
Cenydd Howells (1964) *
Russell Harris (1986) *
John Charles Rees QC (1972) (QC-1991) †
Heather Pope (1977) †
Colin Davies (1973) †
Charles Cook (1966) †
Angharad Ellis Owen ‡
Richard Cole ‡

* Door Tenant † Associate Member ‡ Pupil

The Chambers A leading set of many years' standing. Accommodation is substantial and well furbished and includes a well stocked library, conference rooms (including a disabled conference room) and all other necessary facilities. It is fully equipped with the most up-to-date technology. A chambers brochure is available on request. Several members of chambers are fluent in Welsh.

Work Undertaken Members of chambers practise across a broad range of legal areas including commercial and company law; criminal law, employment law, family law; judicial review; landlord and tenant; local government; Official Referee's business; personal injury; planning; professional negligence; property; tribunal work; trusts, wills and probate. Particular expertise can be offered in the following areas:
Crime All areas of criminal work including fraud.
Personal Injury (inc. Clinical Negligence) A well deserved reputation has been acquired over many years. A dedicated Conditional Fees team has been set up.
Family The family team has recently been strengthened by the addition of established practitioners.
Public Law A team has been put in place to deal with this rapidly growing area of work.

Temple Chambers (David J M Aubrey QC) — Set No.176
32 Park Place, Cardiff, CF1 3BA **Tel** (029) 2039 7364 **Fax** (029) 2023 8423 **DX** 50769 Cardiff 2

▼CHELMSFORD

Thornwood House (annexe of 18 Red Lion Court) (Anthony Arlidge) — Set No.177
Thornwood House, 102 New London Road, Chelmsford, CM2 0RG
Tel (01245) 280880 **Fax** (01245) 280882 **DX** 139165 Chelmsford 11
Email chelmsford@18rlc.co.uk

Head of Chambers	Anthony Arlidge
Senior Clerk	Ken Darvill
Tenants	9

Chambers specialise in a wide variety of criminal and common law work. For full details see the entry under 18 RED LION COURT.

CHESTER/CHICHESTER — BAR A-Z

▼CHESTER

■ Nicholas Street Chambers (Robert Trevor-Jones)   Set No.178
22 Nicholas Street, Chester, CH1 2NX **Tel** (01244) 323886 **Fax** (01244) 347732 **DX** 22154

Sedan House (Geoffrey Little)   Set No.179
Sedan House, Stanley Place, Chester, CH1 2LU
Tel (01244) 348282 **Fax** (01244) 342336 **DX** 19984

Head of Chambers	Geoffrey Little
Senior Clerk	Gavin James Reeves
Practice Manager	Angela Malcolmson LLB (Hons)
Tenants	25

Members

Lord Thomas of Gresford QC (1967) (QC-1979) *
Lord Carlile of Berriew QC (1970) (QC-1984) *
Robin Spencer QC (1978) (QC-1999) *
Geoffrey Little (1973)
Meirion Lewis-Jones (1971)
Wyn Lloyd Jones (1979)
Michael Chambers (1980)
Rhys Rowlands (1986)
Steven Everett (1989)
Andrew Thomas (1989)
Robert Hornby (1990)
Shân Morris (1991)
Gaynor Lloyd (1992)
Owen Edwards (1992)
John Wyn Williams (1992)
Linda Knowles (1993) *
Carolyn Stanton (1993)
Huw Roberts (1993)
Richard Mullan (1994)
Nicholas Williams (1994)
Andrew Clarke (1996)
Elfyn Llwyd MP (1997)
Bethan Japheth (1997)
Helen Waller (1997)
Benjamin Collins (1998)
Sion ap Mihangel (1998)
Matthew Corbett-Jones (1999)
Heledd Llwyd Williams (1999)

* Door Tenant

The Chambers Sedan House is a long established set which covers a wide range of work and is committed to a high quality service. Its reputation derives from both advocacy and advisory work.

Work Undertaken All aspects of criminal law including complex fraud, serious sexual offences and homicide; personal injury; clinical/professional negligence; licensing; employment; police claims; landlord and tenant; judicial review; property; probate; Inheritance Act claims; family law both public and private; ancillary relief; town and country planning, environment and local government law.

▼CHICHESTER

Chichester Chambers (Michael Beckman QC)   Set No.180
12 North Pallant, Chichester, PO19 1TQ
Tel (01243) 784538 **Fax** (01243) 780861 **DX** 30303 Chichester
Email clerks@chichesterchambers.law.co.uk

Head of Chambers	Michael Beckman QC
Senior Clerk	Alister Williams
Tenants	29

Members

Michael Beckman QC (1954) (QC-1976)
Bernard Weatherill QC (1974) (QC-1996) †
Charles Taylor (1974) LLB Hons
Lucinda Davis (1981) LLB Hons
Wendy Rowlinson (1981) BA Hons
Orlando Gibbons (1982) †
Roger Mullis (1987) BA (Oxon) BCL †
Henry Charles (1987) LLB LLM †
Clifford Darton (1988) BA (Oxon)
Colin Morgan (1989) BA (Oxon)
Adam Deacock (1991) BA (Oxon) †
Mary Loosemore (1992) BSc Hons ‡
William Emerson (1992) LLB (Hons)
Portia Spears (1992) BA (Oxon)
Simon Hamilton (1992) BA (Oxon)
Christine Bateman (1992) LLB Hons
Rosein Magee (1994) BA Hons
Emma Burgess (1995) LLB Hons
Kevin Pain (1995) BA (Oxon)
Beverley Cherrill (1996) LLB Hons
Raj Kothari (1996) BA Hons
Charles Barker (1997) BA Hons †
Nerys Wyn Rees (1997) LLB Hons
Andrew Selby (1997) BA Hons
Claire Sparrow (1997) MA Hons
Sarah Earley (1998) LLB Hons
Yasmin Kauser (1999) MA Hons
Barbara Down (1999) LLB Hons
Rachel Beckett (1999) LLB Hons

† Associate Tenant ‡ Former Solicitor

Continued overleaf

BAR A-Z ■ COLCHESTER/EXETER

The Chambers Chichester Chambers continues to expand its provision of specialist advocates to the south of England in its three core areas of family, civil and crime.

Work Undertaken

Family The set's eight specialist practitioners cover all aspects of family law, particularly care proceedings and ancillary relief. Chambers are regularly instructed by local authorities and guardian ad litems in both High Court and County Court cases.

Civil Employment, personal injury, chancery and probate, property, landlord and tenant, insolvency, company, building and contractual disputes.

Crime Defence and prosecution work undertaken, with specialists in trading standards, health and safety and environment law.

▼COLCHESTER

East Anglian Chambers (Roderick Newton) — Set No.181

52 North Hill, Colchester, CO1 1PY
Tel (01206) 572756 Fax (01206) 562447 DX 3611
Email colchesterchambers@ealaw.co.uk Website www.ealaw.co.uk

Head of Chambers	Roderick Newton
Senior Clerk	Fraser McLaren
Administrator	Carol Bull (01473) 254559
Tenants	53

Members

- Roderick Newton (1982)
- John Akast (1968)
- John Wardlow (1971)
- Peter Wain (1972)
- Stephen Franklin (1974)
- Andrew Marsden (1975)
- Caroline Bryant (1976)
- Celia Miller (1978)
- David Pugh (1978)
- Timothy McLoughlin (1978)
- Graham Sinclair (1979)
- John Hamey (1979)
- Anthony Kefford (1980)
- John Brooke-Smith (1981)
- Simon Redmayne (1982)
- Graham Parnell (1982)
- Michael Lane (1983)
- Hugh Vass (1983)
- Jane Davies (1983)
- Lindsay Cox (1984)
- Janet Bettle (1985)
- Anthony Bate (1987)
- Nicholas Elcombe (1987)
- Jonathan Seely (1987)
- Ray Smith (1991)
- Katharine Bundell (1991)
- Marika Bell (1991)
- Jeremy Dugdale (1992)
- Carole Parry-Jones (1992)
- Dominic Barratt (1992)
- Helen Gilbertson (1993)
- Patricia Walsh (1993)
- Jacqui Hanlon (1994)
- Richard Kelly (1994)
- Jude Durr (1995)
- Sally Freeman (1995)
- Alan Wheetman (1995)
- David Wilson (1996)
- Fiona Baruah (1996)
- Ashley Thain (1996)
- Saqib Rauf (1996)
- Marc Cannatella (1997)
- David Sunman (1997)
- Stephen Goodfellow (1997)
- Alison Underhill (1997)
- Andrew Shaw (1998)
- Joanne Bradbury (1999)
- Neil Ashley (1999)
- Rebekah Korniej (1999)
- Ian Dyble (2000)
- Christopher Pigram (2000)
- Luke Brown (2000)
- Richard O'Sullivan (2000)

The Chambers For further information, please see full entry under East Anglian Chambers, Ipswich.

▼EXETER

■ Colleton Chambers (Martin Meeke QC) — Set No.182

Colleton Crescent, Exeter, EX2 4DG Tel (01392) 274898 Fax (01392) 412368 DX 8330 Exeter

EXETER/GRIMSBY ■ BAR A-Z

Walnut House (Paul Dunkels QC) Set No.183

Walnut House, 63 St. David's Hill, Exeter, EX4 4DW
Tel (01392) 279751 **Fax** (01392) 412080 **DX** 115582 Exeter St. Davids
Email clerks@walnuthouse.co.uk **Website** www.walnuthouse.co.uk

Head of Chambers	Paul Dunkels QC
Senior Clerk	Chris Doe
Tenants	21

Members

Paul Dunkels QC (1972) (QC-1993)
Geoffrey Mercer QC (1975) (QC-2002)
Sarah Munro QC (1984) (QC-2002)
Jonathan Barnes (1970)
Iain Leadbetter (1975)
Shane Lyon (1976)
Corinne Searle (1982)
Martin Edmunds (1983)
Michael Melville-Shreeve (1986)
Mark Treneer (1987)
Andrew Eaton Hart (1989)
Elizabeth Ingham (1989)
Robert MacRae (1990)
Andrew Oldland (1990)
Sean Brunton (1990)
Simon Laws (1991)
Mary McCarthy (1994)
David Evans (1996)
Adam Vaitilingam (1987)
Hannah Marshall (1998)
Lara Spencer (2000)

The Chambers Established in 1972, the chambers now have 21 members, including five who sit as recorders. The work of chambers covers the full range of civil and criminal matters in the South West. Brochures are available on request detailing the areas of expertise of members in chambers.

Work Undertaken Includes courts martial; criminal law; discrimination; employment; family; children; general common law; general Chancery; housing; judicial review; landlord and tenant; licensing; matrimonial; mental health; personal injury; planning; police cases; professional negligence; sale of goods; trusts and wills.

Southernhay Chambers (Anthony Ward) Set No.184

33 Southernhay East, Exeter, EX1 1NX
Tel (01392) 255777 **Fax** (01392) 412021 **DX** 8353 Exeter
Email southernhay.chambers@lineone.net

Head of Chambers	Anthony Ward
Senior Clerk	Joy Daniell
Tenants	13

Members

Anthony Ward (1971)
Robert Alford (1970)
Michael Templeman (1973)
Christopher Naish (1980)
Susan Campbell (1986)
Nicholas Berry (1988)
Rebecca Ogle (1989)
Jacqueline Ahmed (1988)
Deborah Archer (1989)
Emma Crawforth (1992)
Benjamin Winzer (1997)
Heather Burwin (1983)
Stephen Ball (1995)
Juliet Williams (1998)
Richard Owen-Thomas (2000)

* Door Tenant

The Chambers Established in 1975, chambers have 14 members. The set's strategy has been one of carefully planned expansion, and it has grown to become one of the leading specialist family/civil sets on the Western Circuit. Brochure and further information on request.

Work Undertaken Family/Civil. Children Act (public and private law); matrimonial finance; family provision; chancery; equity trusts and wills; landlord & tenant; personal injury; professional negligence; commercial. Conditional Fee Agreements accepted in all civil cases.

▼GRIMSBY

■ Wilberforce Chambers (Bernard Gateshill) Set No.185

2 Abbey Walk, Grimsby, DN31 1NQ **Tel** (01472) 355567
Annexe and conference rooms. See entry for Wilberforce Chambers, Hull.

Head of Chambers	Bernard Gateshill
Tenants	2

BAR A-Z ■ HULL/IPSWICH

▼HULL

Wilberforce Chambers (Bernard Gateshill)   Set No.186

Wilberforce Chambers, 7 Bishop Lane, Hull, HU1 1PA
Tel (01482) 323264   **Fax** (01482) 325533   **DX** 11940
Email clerks@hullbar.demon.co.uk   **Website** www.hullbar.demon.co.uk

Head of Chambers	Bernard Gateshill
Senior Clerk	Frances Sheard
Practice Manager	Phillip Paxton
Tenants	21

Members

Bernard Gateshill (1972)	David Tremberg (1985)	Simon Hirst (1993)
Lorna Cole (1950)	Mark Bury (1986)	John Thackray (1994)
Tony Stevenson (1972)	Neil Cameron (1984)	Simon Pickering (1996)
Paul Miller (1974)	Anil Murray (1989)	Stephen Robinson (1999)
Paul Genney (1976)	Elizabeth Shaw (1986)	Nigel Clive (1998)
John Godfrey (1985) †	Andrew Comaish (1989)	Sarah Fearon (2000)
James Sampson (1985)	Carol Trimmer (1993) ‡	Charlotte Baines (2000)

† Former solicitor (admitted 1976)   ‡ Former solicitor (admitted 1979)

The Chambers Established in Hull in 1957 and now occupying modern premises within the Old Town conservation area together with an annexe in Grimsby.

Work Undertaken Members practise from specialist groups in crime; family; personal injury; property, commercial and employment; licensing; immigration.

▼IPSWICH

East Anglian Chambers (Roderick Newton)   Set No.187

5 Museum St, Ipswich, IP1 1HQ
Tel (01473) 214481   **Fax** (01473) 218466   **DX** 3227
Email ipswichchambers@ealaw.co.uk   **Website** www.ealaw.co.uk

Head of Chambers	Roderick Newton
Senior Clerk	Peter Hall
Administrator	Carol Bull (01473) 254559
Tenants	53

Members

Roderick Newton (1982)	Jane Davies (1983)	Alan Wheetman (1995)
John Akast (1968)	Lindsay Cox (1984)	David Wilson (1996)
John Wardlow (1971)	Janet Bettle (1985)	Fiona Baruah (1996)
Peter Wain (1972)	Anthony Bate (1987)	Ashley Thain (1996)
Stephen Franklin (1974)	Nicholas Elcombe (1987)	Saqib Rauf (1996)
Andrew Marsden (1975)	Jonathan Seely (1987)	Marc Cannatella (1997)
Caroline Bryant (1976)	Ray Smith (1991)	David Sunman (1997)
Celia Miller (1978)	Katharine Bundell (1991)	Stephen Goodfellow (1997)
David Pugh (1978)	Marika Bell (1991)	Alison Underhill (1997)
Timothy McLoughlin (1978)	Jeremy Dugdale (1992)	Andrew Shaw (1998)
Graham Sinclair (1979)	Carole Parry-Jones (1992)	Joanne Bradbury (1999)
John Hamey (1979)	Dominic Barratt (1992)	Neil Ashley (1999)
Anthony Kefford (1980)	Helen Gilbertson (1993)	Rebekah Korniej (1999)
John Brooke-Smith (1981)	Patricia Walsh (1993)	Ian Dyble (2000)
Simon Redmayne (1982)	Jacqui Hanlon (1994)	Christopher Pigram (2000)
Graham Parnell (1982)	Richard Kelly (1994)	Luke Brown (2000)
Michael Lane (1983)	Jude Durr (1995)	Richard O'Sullivan (2000)
Hugh Vass (1983)	Sally Freeman (1995)	

The Chambers East Anglian Chambers was founded in 1947 as a provincial common law set of chambers, and has developed over the years, retaining its broad common law base. It is now able to offer teams of specialists in commercial, chancery, construction, crime, family, land, personal injury and planning. Many members of East Anglian Chambers are active members of professional groups and associations within their field of practice, have contributed to, edited and written textbooks, and sit as Recorders, Stipendiary Magistrates and Deputy District Judges. East Anglian Chambers is instructed by most firms of solicitors in East Anglia, as well as many from further afield. In addition, it receives work in all fields of practice from local authorities, and does an increasing amount of DPA work. Chambers are actively involved in the Community Legal Services in East Anglia. They prosecute for the CPS, HM Customs & Excise and government departments throughout the region. Chambers have also achieved Bar Mark and ISO 9002 quality standards.

Recruitment East Anglian Chambers operates from three centres in Norwich, Ipswich and Colchester. 12 month pupillages are offered each year, with pupils being expected to divide their time between the three centres. In addition, from time to time, working pupillages are offered. Procedures and timetables for applications can be obtained by contacting the Chambers Administrator and logging onto the website.

▼LEEDS

Chancery House Chambers (Adrian Dent)   Set No.188

7 Lisbon Square, Leeds, LS1 4LY
Tel (0113) 244 6691 **Fax** (0113) 244 6766 **DX** 26421 Leeds
Email colin.hedley@chanceryhouse.co.uk **Website** www.chanceryhouse.co.uk

Head of Chambers	Adrian Dent
Senior Clerk	Colin Hedley
Tenants	13

Members

Adrian Dent (1974)	William Hanbury (1985)	Bruce Walker (1994)
Harry Wolton QC (1969)	Mark Walker (1986)	Gregory Pipe (1995)
(QC-1982) *	David Partington (1987)	Lisa Linklater (1995)
David Stockdale QC (1975)	Aubrey Craig (1987) †	Jonathan French (1997)
(QC-1995) *	Stephen Howd (1989)	Richard Wilson (1996) *
Richard Carpenter (1981)	Paul Creaner (1990)	Paul Lakin (2000)

* Door Tenant   † Member of the New York Bar

The Chambers Formed in 1996 as a breakaway group from a large, general set of chambers to create a northern-based set of specialist chancery/commercial barristers. Chambers offer relaxed and informal access to specialist barristers with experienced clerking. Chambers are committed to quality and pride themselves on papers being dealt with in a timely matter and by the date promised. Further information in relation to chambers can be obtained from Colin Hedley or from the website.

Work Undertaken Commercial litigation; commercial property; construction; company and commercial; chancery; banking; bankruptcy; insolvency; intellectual property; trademarks; planning/environmental; competition law; insurance/re-insurance; consumer credit; sale and carriage of goods; international trade; professional negligence; partnership; equity, wills and trusts; employment/discrimination.

Enterprise Chambers (Anthony Mann QC)   Set No.189

38 Park Square, Leeds, LS1 2PA
Tel (0113) 246 0391 **Fax** (0113) 242 4802 **DX** 26448 (Leeds Park Square)
Email enterprise.leeds@dial.pipex.com **Website** www.enterprisechambers.com

Head of Chambers	Anthony Mann QC
Senior Clerk (London)	Antony Armstrong
Practice Development Clerk	Barry Clayton
Clerk	Joanne Glew
Tenants	26

The Chambers For a full list of members please see the London entry. For further information about the set please visit the chambers' website.

BAR A-Z ■ LEEDS

■ 11 King's Bench Walk (FJ Muller QC)   Set No.190
3 Park Court, Park Cross Street, Leeds, LS1 2QH
Tel (0113) 297 1200 **Fax** (0113) 297 1201 **DX** 26433
Email clerks@11kbw.co.uk **Website** www.11kbw.co.uk

London common law set with extensive North East Circuit practice. 3 Park Court is the Leeds annexe for 11 King's Bench Walk, London. See London entry for details of practice and members.

Head of Chambers	FJ Muller QC
Senior Clerk	Jo Pickersgill
Clerks	Jayne Turner, Deborah Pain
	James McDonald, Lee Baines
Administration/Fees	Amanda Kershaw
Tenants	27

■ 5 Park Place   Set No.191
5 Park Place, Leeds, LS1 2RU
Tel (0113) 242 1123 **Fax** (0113) 242 1124 **DX** 713113 (LEEDS PKSQ)
Email clerks@40kingstreet.co.uk **Website** www.40kingstreet.co.uk

Chief Executive	Colin Wardale
Senior Clerk	William Brown
Bar Management Services	William Brown
	Colin Griffin
	Michael Stubbs
Assistant Clerks	Lisa Williams
	Paul Clarke
Tenants	56

Members

Andrew Gilbart QC (1972) (QC-1991)
John Hoggett QC (1969) (QC-1986)
Stephen Sauvain QC (1977) (QC-1995)
Frances Patterson QC (1977) (QC-1998) †
Michael Booth QC (1981) (QC-1999)
Nicholas Braslavsky QC (1983) (QC-1999)
Vincent Fraser QC (1981) (QC-2001)
Paul Chaisty QC (1982) (QC-2001)
Reverend Eric Owen (1969)
Harold Halliday (1972)
Shokat Khan (1979)
David Manley (1981)
John Barrett (1982)
Alan Evans (1978)
Neil Berragan (1982)

Mark Halliwell (1985)
John Cooper (1985)
Simon Hilton (1987)
Katherine Dunn (1987)
Nigel Clayton (1987)
Ruth Stockley (1988)
Fiona Ashworth (1988)
Paul Tucker (1990)
Geoffrey Pass (1975)
Andrew Singer (1990)
Stephen Pritchett (1990)
Lesley Anderson (1989)
Matthew Smith (1991)
Andrew Grantham (1991)
Martin Carter (1992)
Wilson Horne (1992)
Lucy Powis (1992)
Mark Harper (1993)
Sarah Pritchard (1993)
Richard Lander (1993)
Ian Ponter (1993)
Simon Antrobus (1995)

Andrew Latimer (1995)
Louis Doyle (1996)
Elizabeth Berridge (1996)
Colin Crawford (1997)
Nicholas Siddall (1997)
Giles Cannock (1998)
Mark Cooper (1998)
Andrew McGee (1998)
Simon Young (1998)
Matthew Hall (1999)
Helen Mulholland (1999)
Catherine Brown (1999)
Tina Rañales-Cotos (1999)
Eleanor Temple (2000)
Matthew Copeland (2000)
John Tackaberry QC (1967) (QC-1982) †
John Campbell (1981)(QC Scotland 1999) †
Julian Ghosh (1993) †
James Henderson (1997) †

40 KING STREET MANCHESTER

5 PARK PLACE LEEDS

† Associate Member

The Chambers Also at: 40 King St, Manchester, M2 6BA Tel (0161) 832 9082 Fax (0161) 835 2139 DX 718188 Mch 3

5 Park Place, the Leeds address of 40 King St Chambers, is one of the leading sets outside London. The set is dedicated to providing clients with specialist, practical and commercial legal advice from barristers with the highest reputation for advocacy, knowledge and professional standards. Chambers are regularly involved in the full range of courts in which their members are characterised by a reputation for strong and incisive advocacy backed by tough negotiating skills. Chambers are also regularly and increasingly involved in arbitration and mediation. Chambers' clients are individual and corporate, national and multinational, plc and private. Chambers work for all the leading firms of solicitors in the North and North East and for many in the City of London and elsewhere. Chambers welcome instructions by direct access when permitted. They have a strong and wide base of clients across the whole spectrum of industries including banks (including clearing and secondary), developers, retailers, manufacturers, services, professional bodies and local authorities. Chambers also now regularly represent many emerging companies in the newer information technology, e-commerce and leisure markets.

Work Undertaken Chambers believe that their clients' interests are best served by increasing specialisation, strength in depth and above all in uncompromising attitudes to quality and client service. As such they are now a large specialist set with a national reputation practising from Manchester and Leeds in the following specific areas: chancery and commercial including chancery, commercial, insolvency and banking, property and construction and professional negligence; planning, environment and public law; common law including personal injury, clinical negligence, employment and regulatory.

International Languages include French, German, Punjabi, Urdu, Russian, Welsh and Spanish.

LEEDS ■ BAR A-Z

■ **Mercury Chambers** (Benjamin Nolan QC) — Set No.192
Mercury House, 33-35 Clarendon Road, Leeds, LS2 9NZ **Tel** (0113) 234 2265 **Fax** (0113) 244 4243 **DX** 713115 LEEDS PARK SQUARE

■ **No.6 Barristers Chambers** (Jennifer Kershaw QC) — Set No.193
6 Park Square, Leeds, LS1 2LW **Tel** (0113) 245 9763 **Fax** (0113) 242 4395 **DX** 26402

Park Court Chambers (Robert Smith QC) — Set No.194

16 Park Place, Leeds, LS1 2SJ
Tel (0113) 243 3277 **Fax** (0113) 242 1285 **DX** 26401
Email clerks@parkcourtchambers.co.uk **Website** www.parkcourtchambers.co.uk

Head of Chambers	Robert Smith QC
Senior Clerk	Terry Creathorn
Tenants	42

Members

Robert Smith QC (1971) (QC-1986)
Michael Harrison QC (1969) (QC-1987)
Malcolm Swift QC (1970) (QC-1988)
Anton Lodge QC (1966) (QC-1989)
Paul Worsley QC (1970) (QC-1990)
Simon Bourne-Arton QC (1975) (QC-1994)
David Hatton QC (1976) (QC-1996)
Alistair MacDonald QC (1983) (QC-2000)
Henry Prosser (1969)
John Muir (1969)
Timothy Hartley (1970)
Tom Bayliss (1977)
Jonathan Devlin (1978)
Bryan Cox (1979)

Adrian Robinson (1981)
John Lodge (1980)
Michael Taylor (1980)
Simon Jackson (1982)
Caroline Wigin (1984)
Simon Phillips (1985)
Sharon Beattie (1986)
Simon Myerson (1986)
Nadim Bashir (1988)
Taryn Turner (1990)
Christopher Tehrani (1990)
Elyas Patel (1991)
Ashley Tucker (1990)
Joanna Cross (1992)
Paul Greaney (1993)
Nicholas Johnson (1994)
Jenny Kent (1993)
Jason Pitter (1994)
Ceri Widdett (1994)
Uthra Sethupathi (1998)
Valerie Sterling (1981)

Alan Taylor (1986)
Samuel Green (1998)
Alexander Offer (1998)
Elizabeth Darlington (1998)
Franklyn Zakers (1999)
Nicola Twine (1999)
Alex Taylor (2000)
Gilbert Gray QC (1953) (QC-1971) *
James Chadwin QC (1958) (QC-1976) *
Andrew Thornhill QC (1969) (QC-1985) *
Peter Feinberg QC (1972) (QC-1992) *
Joanna Dodson QC (1971) (QC-1993) *
Roger Thomas (1979) *
Jeremy Woolf (1986) *
Peter Carter QC (1974) (QC-1995) *

* Door Tenant

The Chambers Park Court Chambers is one of the largest sets of chambers outside London. It is a long-established but modern and expanding set based in the thriving commercial centre of Leeds. It offers a wide range of services.

Work Undertaken Crime, corporate fraud, personal injury, general commercial, family, landlord and tenant, licensing, medical negligence and tax are undertaken.

BAR A-Z — LEEDS

Park Lane Chambers (Stuart Brown QC)

Set No.195

Park Lane House, 19 Westgate, Leeds, LS1 2RD
Tel (0113) 228 5000 **Fax** (0113) 228 1500 **DX** 26404 Leeds Park Square
Email clerks@parklanechambers.co.uk **Website** www.parklanechambers.co.uk

Head of Chambers	Stuart Brown QC
Chambers Director	Mike Sayers
Senior Team Clerks	John Payne
	Andy Gray
Tenants	33

Members

Martin Bethel QC (1965) (QC-1983)
Stuart Brown QC (1974) (QC-1991)
Christopher Storey QC (1979) (QC-1995)
David Wilby QC (1974) (QC-1998)
Alaric Dalziel (1967)
Tim Hirst (1970)
Howard Elgot (1974)
Sally Cahill (1978)
Elizabeth O'Hare (1980)
Lindy Armitage (1985)
Simon Thorp (1988)
Joanne Astbury (1989)
Craig Moore (1989)
Richard Copnall (1990)
Alexander Foster (1990)
Jonathan Godfrey (1990)
Kaiser Nazir (1991)
Guy Swiffen (1991)
Andrew Axon (1992)
James Murphy (1993)
Corin Furness (1994)
Steven Turner (1993)
Dornier Whittaker (1994)
Sara Anning (1995)
Stephen Friday (1996)
Alan Weir (1996)
Simon Plaut (1997)
Helen Waddington (1998)
Jonathan Ashworth (1998)
Simon Stevenson (1999)
Tom Nossiter (1999)
Richard Beddoe (1999)
Alison Jole (2001) †

† Former solicitor

The Chambers This set of chambers has a strong reputation in civil litigation with particular emphasis on personal injury, clinical and professional negligence and commercial work. Members of chambers belong to specialist bodies including the Personal Injuries Bar Association, the Association of Personal Injury Lawyers, Action for Victims of Medical Negligence (AVMA), the Professional Negligence Bar Association, the Family Bar Association, the Chancery Bar Association and the Criminal Bar Association. Martin Bethel QC and Stuart Brown QC are both Deputy High Court judges.

Work Undertaken

Personal Injury There is a long history of clinical negligence and employers' liability work within chambers. Major litigation cases have involved industrial deafness; pharmaceuticals; British Coal respiratory disease. 'Credit hire' litigation has expanded following the reported case of Dimond v Lovell (HL). Members have long-standing relationships with major institutional clients, unions and insurers. Other specialisms include sports injuries, holiday claims, RSI and stress at work.
Family The team has extensive experience in public law childcare and adoption, private proceedings involving children, divorce and ancillary relief (including high value claims), cohabitees' property disputes, trusts and inheritance disputes and applications for committal and injunctions.
Chancery & Commercial A growing team deals with construction; landlord and tenant; general chancery; insolvency; company and partnership law; insurance law; direct and indirect taxation including VAT.
Crime Members, and in particular the four silks, undertake criminal work including fraud, health and safety prosecutions for claimants and defendants and trading standards prosecutions.

30 Park Square (Peter Collier QC)

Set No.196

30 Park Square, Leeds, LS1 2PF
Tel (0113) 243 6388 **Fax** (0113) 242 3510 **DX** 26411
Email clerks@30parksquare.co.uk **Website** www.30parksquare.co.uk

Head of Chambers	Peter Collier QC
Senior Clerk	Jennifer Thompson
Tenants	30

Members

Peter Collier QC (1970) (QC-1992) +
JW Mellor (1953)
A Kershaw (1975) +
M Haigh (1970) †
SN Haring (1982)
MS Rodger (1983)
RML Hallam (1984) +
K Buckingham (1986) +
CL Hill (1988)
M Pearson (1984)
A Granville-Fall (1990)
J Hargan (1990)
N Frith (1992)
M Teeman (1993) †
Joanna Geddes (1992)
Tim White (1993)
I Shiels (1992)
N Barker (1994)
P Williams (1994)
John Edwards (1994)
E Auckland (1995)
W Tyler (1996)
Steven Pidcock (1996)
Diane Nixon (1997)
A Stewart (1997)
A Rhys-Davies (1998)
Glenn Parsons (1999)
Claire Murden (1999)
Karamjit Singh (2000)
Andrew Stranex (2000)

+ Recorder † Formerly a solicitor

LEEDS ■ BAR A-Z

The Chambers Specialists in criminal and family law. Also undertakes work (including non-contentious and advisory) in a wide range of common law subjects. Advocates with experience in all courts, tribunals and inquiries.

Work Undertaken All aspects of family law; divorce; childcare; injunctions; criminal defence and prosecution. Common law expertise in personal injury; contract; property disputes; professional negligence; licensing; insolvency; planning; employment law.

37 Park Square (Stephen J Glover & Paul Kirtley) — Set No.197

37 Park Square, Leeds, LS1 2NY
Tel (0113) 243 9422 **Fax** (0113) 242 4229 **DX** 26405 Leeds
Email chambers@no37.co.uk **Website** www.no37.co.uk

Head of Chambers	Stephen J Glover
	Paul Kirtley
Senior Clerk	Ann Fothergill
Criminal Clerk	Ian Spencer
Civil Clerk	Donna Mullen
Tenants	29

Members

Stephen J Glover (1978)
Paul Kirtley (1982)
Douglas Hogg QC (1968) (QC-1990)
Robert Marshall-Andrews QC (1967) (QC-1989)
John Sleightholme (1982)
Rodney Ferm (1972)
John Dunning (1973)
Anthony Korn (1978)
Paul Fleming (1983)

Freddy Apfel (1986)
Jeremy Lindsay (1986)
Amanda Ginsburg (1985)
Dawn Tighe (1989)
Linda Cains (1990)
Steven Crossley (1992)
Piers Hill (1987)
Caroline Ford (1993)
Mark Gore (1994)
David Taylor (1995)

Joanne Holroyd (1994)
Stuart Roberts (1994)
Taryn Lee (1992)
Michael Burdon (1993)
Kama Melly (1997)
Michael Collins (1998)
Claire Thompson (1998)
Amanda Howard (1994)
Hugh Milburn (1997)
Richard Butters (2001)

Work Undertaken General common law including criminal law, licensing, family law, personal injury, contract, employment law, company and commercial, landlord and tenant, real property disputes, planning and local government law.

■ 39 Park Square (Tim Bubb) — Set No.198

39 Park Square, Leeds, LS1 2NU **Tel** (0113) 245 6633 **Fax** (0113) 242 1567 **DX** 26407

St. Paul's Chambers (Nigel Sangster QC) — Set No.199

5th Floor, St. Paul's House, 23 Park Square South, Leeds, LS1 2ND
Tel (0113) 245 5866 **Fax** (0113) 245 5807 **DX** 26410 Leeds (Park Square)
Email clerks@stpaulschambers.com **Website** www.stpaulschambers.com

Head of Chambers	Nigel Sangster QC
Senior Clerk	Catherine Grimshaw
Tenants	29

Members

Nigel Sangster QC (1976) (QC-1998) +
Guy Kearl QC (1982) (QC-2002) +
Colin Harvey (1975)
Jeremy Barnett (1980) +
Philip Standfast (1980)
Jonathan Rose (1981) +
Mushtaq Khokhar (1982)
Andrew Lees (1984) +
Derek Duffy (1997)

Fiona Dix-Dyer (1986)
Howard Crowson (1987)
David de Jehan (1988)
Andrew Stubbs (1988)
Simon Bickler (1988)
Christopher Batty (1989)
Jason MacAdam (1990)
Andrew Haslam (1991)
Robin Mairs (1992)
Jonathan Sandiford (1992)

Nicola Saxton (1992)
John Harrison (1994)
Alexander Bates (1994)
Kirstie Watson (1994)
Ann Marie Gregory (1994)
Nigel Edwards (1995)
Nick Dry (1996)
Rukhshanda Hussain (1998)
Oliver Longstaff (1999)
Denise Breen-Lawton (2000)

+ Recorder

The Chambers Founded in 1982, St. Paul's Chambers has 29 practitioners. Members have complementary areas of expertise, with the specific intention of providing a service in most areas of legal work. Nigel Sangster QC and Jeremy Barnett are elected members of the Bar Council. Members of chambers belong to the Family Law Bar Association and the Criminal Bar Association.

Continued overleaf

BAR A-Z ■ LEEDS/LEICESTER

Work Undertaken
Criminal Work includes the traditional areas of crime, with members acting for both prosecution and defence. In addition, there are specialists in fraud and corporate crime, asset seizure, money laundering, serious crime (including violence and sexual offences), breathalyser cases, licensing, Firearms Act offences.

Civil Chambers have particular expertise in personal injury claims; employment; landlord and tenant; Trading Standards cases; Directors' Disqualification cases; family and childcare work; matrimonial; professional negligence; police disciplinary cases; immigration work.

■ Sovereign Chambers (Geoffrey C Marson QC) — Set No.200
25 Park Square, Leeds, LS1 2PW **Tel** (0113) 245 1841 **Fax** (0113) 242 0194 **DX** 26408 Leeds Park Square

■ Zenith Chambers (Andrew Campbell QC & John Collins) — Set No.201
10 Park Square, Leeds, LS1 2LH **Tel** (0113) 245 5438 **Fax** (0113) 242 3515 **DX** 26412

▼ LEICESTER

New Walk Chambers (John Snell) — Set No.202
27 New Walk, Leicester, LE1 6TE
Tel (0116) 255 9144 **Fax** (0116) 255 9084 **DX** 723940 Leicester 22
Email clerks@newwalkchambers.law.co.uk **Website** www.newwalkchambers.co.uk

Head of Chambers	John Snell
Practice Manager	Michael Ryan
Tenants	29

Members

- John Snell (1973)
- Jonathan Durham Hall QC (1975) (QC-1995)
- Patrick Thomas QC (1973) (QC-1999) *
- Jeremy Cousins QC (1977) (QC-1999) *
- Nicholas Leigh-Smith (1976)
- John Ginns (1977)
- Paul Atkinson (1978)
- Robert Rees (1978)
- Peter Bates (1978)
- Simon Liddy (1979)
- Rebecca Fitton Brown (1981)
- Nicholas George (1983)
- Nala Lawrence (1987)
- Robin Chaudhuri (1988)
- Sean McGovern (1990)
- Timothy Cockrill (1991)
- Steven Taylor (1992)
- Penelope Stanistreet (1993)
- Simon Parsons (1993)
- Craig Lowe (1994)
- Richard Nicholls (1994)
- Janet Ruscoe (1995)
- Harinder Kaur (1995)
- John Ryan (1997)
- Semon Piper (1997)
- Emma Cutts (1998)
- Sasha Watkinson (1998)
- Simon Reed (1998)
- Kirstie Danton (1999)
- Jeremy Robson (1999)
- Ben Norman (2000)

* Door Tenant

The Chambers New Walk Chambers is a long established set situated in a large Georgian property close to the Crown Court, County Court and Industrial Tribunal building.

LIVERPOOL

14 Castle Street (Andrew Edis QC) — Set No.203

14 Castle Street, Liverpool, L2 ONE
Tel (0151) 236 4421 **Fax** (0151) 236 1559 **DX** 14176 Liverpool
Email clerks@14castlestreet.co.uk **Website** www.14castlestreet.co.uk

Head of Chambers	Andrew Edis QC
Clerks	Stuart Jones
	Gary Quinn
	Neil Grisdale
	David Blunsden
Tenants	46

Members

- Andrew Edis QC (1980) (QC-1997)
- John Benson QC (1978) (QC-2001)
- Eric Goldrein (1961)
- Nicholas Riddle (1970)
- Nicholas Orr (1970)
- Scott Donovan (1975)
- Ian Haselhurst (1976)
- Robert Warnock (1977)
- Thomas Eaton (1976)
- Nigel Ginniff (1978)
- David Dennis (1979)
- Michael Sellars (1980)
- Arthur Gibson (1980)
- Ian Johnson (1982)
- John Corless (1984)
- Ivan Woolfenden (1985)
- Nicholas Ryan (1984)
- Simon Booth (1985)
- Andrew Pickering (1987)
- Stuart Driver (1988)
- Simon Gorton (1988)
- Celia Lund (1988)
- Malcolm Sharpe (1988)
- Robert Golinski (1990)
- Graham Sellers (1990)
- David Watson (1990)
- Christine Johnson (1991)
- Richard Hall (1991)
- Nicholas Jackson (1992)
- Timothy Grace (1993)
- Anne Whyte (1993)
- David Green (1993)
- Michelle Davey (1993)
- Rachael Banks (1993)
- Gwynneth Knowles (1993)
- Andrew Williams (1994)
- Andrew Banks (1994)
- Liam Grundy (1995)
- Charles Prior (1995)
- John de Bono (1995)
- Kenderik Horne (1996)
- Mark Rawcliffe (1996)
- Neil Downey (1997)
- Sophie Smith (1999)
- Alison Miller (1999)
- Lee Bonner (2000)

The Chambers The result of two mergers involving three sets, two specialist chancery sets and one common law. Now divided into departments offering specialist advice and advocacy in five broad areas. A Conditional Fee scheme is in place which covers all areas of work where this is permitted. The departments are as follows:

Crime Prosecuting and defending at all levels from the Magistrates' Court upwards. Serious fraud, murder, sexual offences are covered by experienced practitioners, but less serious work is given equal attention. The availability of commercial expertise in chambers and the library and IT facilities which they have, means that they are particularly capable of dealing with large and complex cases involving fraud or other similar offences.

Chancery & Commercial A large group (16) offering all levels of experience and considerable specialist expertise. The group includes a specialist tax and pensions lawyer, and covers probate, property, tax and trust work as well as contractual and professional negligence disputes. Contentious and non-contentious work is covered.

Civil Litigation This includes clinical negligence, personal injury, police and human rights law, and other professional negligence cases. Chambers cover Judicial Review cases, and other local authority work. They have lawyers who deal with civil litigation who also have experience in areas such as childcare and education law for cases which may require dual experience. Chambers act for claimants and defendants.

Family A highly experienced group dealing with public and private law childcare work and financial aspects of divorce. The group acts for individuals and local authorities. The presence of the chancery group enables chambers to deal with all aspects of family finance and property under one roof.

Employment This is a specialism of these chambers. John Benson QC is an employment expert and leads a substantial group of experienced employment lawyers who act for claimants and respondents. The respondents include local authorities, police forces, and major national companies. The claimants are treated with equal respect.

Recruitment Chambers recruit through OLPAS. Chambers will seek and fund pupils who will be able to choose which areas or work they wish to pursue and will train appropriately.

25-27 Castle Street (Stephen Riordan QC) — Set No.204

25-27 Castle Street, 1st Floor, Liverpool, L2 4TA **Tel** (0151) 236 5072 **Fax** (0151) 236 4054 **DX** 14224

Chavasse Court Chambers (Theresa Pepper) — Set No.205

2nd Floor, Chavasse Court, 24 Lord Street, Liverpool, L2 1TA **Tel** (0151) 707 1191 **Fax** (0151) 707 1189 **DX** 14223 Liverpool

BAR A-Z ■ LIVERPOOL

THE REGIONS

Derby Square Chambers (Simon Newton) — Set No.206

Merchants Court, Derby Square, Liverpool, L2 1TS Tel (0151) 709 4222 Fax (0151) 708 6311 DX 14213 Liverpool 1

Exchange Chambers (David Turner QC & Bill Braithwaite QC & Henry Globe QC) — Set No.207

Pearl Assurance House, Derby Square, Liverpool, L2 9XX
Tel (0151) 236 7747 Fax (0151) 236 3433 DX 14207 Liverpool
Email info@exchangechambers.co.uk Website www.exchangechambers.co.uk

Head of Chambers	David Turner QC
	Bill Braithwaite QC
	Henry Globe QC
Practice Manager	Tom Handley
Senior Clerk	Roy Finney
Tenants	63

Members

William Waldron QC (1970) (QC-1982)
David Turner QC (1971) (QC-1991)
Bill Braithwaite QC (1970) (QC-1992)
Charles Chruszcz QC (1973) (QC-1992)
Anthony Elleray QC (1977) (QC-1993)
Henry Globe QC (1972) (QC-1994)
Graham Morrow QC (1974) (QC-1996)
Tim Holroyde QC (1977) (QC-1996)
Edward Bartley Jones, QC (1975) (QC-1997)
Gerard Martin QC (1978) (QC-2000)
Mark Cawson QC (1982) (QC-2001)
John Richard Jones QC (1981) (QC-2002)
Graham Wood QC (1979) (QC-2002)
Francis Nance (1970)
Simon Earlam (1975)
Christopher Cornwall (1975)
Eric Lamb (1975)
James Rae (1976)
Judith Fordham (1991)
Gordon Cole (1979)
Ian Harris (1990)
Tania Griffiths (1982)
Roger Hillman (1983)
Neil Cadwallader (1984)
Karen Gregory (1985)
Dennis Talbot (1985)
Paul Clark (1994)
Paul Taylor (1991)
Simon Berkson (1986)
Alun James (1986)
William F Waldron (1986)
Guy Vickers (1986)
Mark Mulrooney (1988)
Brian Cummings (1988)
John J McCarroll (1988)
Louis Browne (1988)
Ian Foster (1988)
Rebecca Clark (1989)
Catherine Howells (1989)
Michael Wood (1989)
Jonathan Cannan (1989)
Christopher Stables (1990)
Julie Case (1990)
John Philpotts (1990)
Christopher Cook (1990)
Amanda Yip (1991)
Paul Timothy Evans (1992)
David Casement (1992)
Ian Unsworth (1992)
Giles Maynard-Connor (1992)
Charlotte Kenny (1993)
Robert Dudley (1993)
Simon Fox (1994)
Kelly Pennifer (1994)
Rachel Silverbeck (1996)
Kevin Slack (1997)
Claire Gourley (1996)
Louise Metcalf (1997)
Nancy Dooher (1997)
Paul Burns (1998)
Sarah O'Brien (1998)
Daniel Travers (1999)
Jonathan Clarke (1999)
David Mohyuddin (1999)
Martine Snowdon (2000)
Jonathan Rogers (2000)
Andrew Vinson (2000)
Nicola Daley (2001)

The Chambers Chambers also at 4 Ralli Courts, West Riverside, Manchester, M3 5FT Tel (0161) 833 2722 Fax (0161) 833 2789 DX 14330 Manchester.

7 Harrington Street Chambers (David Steer QC & Robert Fordham QC & Iain Goldrein QC) — Set No.208

7 Harrington Street, Liverpool, L2 9YH
Tel (0151) 242 0707 Fax (0151) 236 2800 DX 14221 Liverpool 1
Website www.7harringtonst.co.uk

Head of Chambers	David Steer QC
	Robert Fordham QC
	Iain Goldrein QC
Practice Director	John Kilgallon
Tenants	68

Members

David Steer QC (1974) (QC-1993)
Robert Fordham QC (1967) (QC-1993)
Iain Goldrein QC (1975) (QC-1997)
David Aubrey QC (1974) (QC-1998)
Margaret de Haas QC (1977) (QC-1998)
David Geey (1970)
David Kerr (1971)
Andrew McDonald (1971)
Jack Cowan (1971)
Gordon Bellis (1972)
Antonis Georges (1972)
Rodney Halligan (1972)
Mary Compton-Rickett (1972)
Michael J Pickavance (1974)
Kevin Grice (1977)
Michael Davies (1979)
Richard Pratt (1980)
Neil Flewitt (1981)
Henry Riding (1981)
Grant Lazarus (1981)
Andrew Menary (1982)
Peter Gregory (1982)
James McKeon (1982)
Andrew Loveridge (1983)
Mark Chatterton (1983)
Deirdre McGuire (1983)
Donal McGuire (1983)
Philip J O'Neill (1983)
Kevin Reade (1983)
Simon J Killeen (1984)

LIVERPOOL ■ BAR A-Z

Sarah Leigh (1984)
Jamil Khan (1986)
Stephen Knapp (1986)
David Knifton (1986)
Peter Davies (1986)
Peter Kidd (1987)
Janet Reaney (1987)
Steven Parker (1987)
Keith Sutton (1988)
Nigel Lawrence (1988)
Andrew Downie (1990)
Kate Symms (1990)
Christine Bispham (1991)
Deborah Shield (1991)
Timothy Grover (1991)
Stephen Seed (1991)
Jonathan Dale (1991)
Trevor Parry-Jones (1992)
Gregory Hoare (1992)
Robert Altham (1993)
David Edwards (1994)
Helen Wrenn (1994)
Clive Baker (1995)
Andrew Carney (1995)
Malcolm Dutchman-Smith (1995)
Jeremy Greenfield (1995)
Brendon Burke (1995)
Stuart Clare (1997)
Andrew Ford (1997)
Daniel Rogers (1997)
Mark Beesley (1998)
Martin Knight (1998)
Lloyd Morgan (1999)
Nicola Miles (1999)
Rachel Spearing (2001)
William Ralston (2001)
Lee Jenkinson (2001)
Mark Roberts (2001)

The Chambers These chambers have their work base in the North but have established contacts in Cheshire and North Wales. The size of chambers has enabled a broad base of specialisations to be developed particularly in the following fields: crime, family law, personal injuries, professional negligence (in particular clinical, legal and surveyors), all forms of local government work and general common law work. In addition there are specialists available in the following fields: employment, mental health, commercial work, licensing, housing and welfare law. Some members of chambers write for legal publications and lecture whilst several retain working links with London chambers.

India Buildings Chambers (Ray Herman) — Set No.209

India Buildings, Water Street, Liverpool, L2 0XG
Tel (0151) 243 6000   **Fax** (0151) 243 6040   **DX** 14227
Email clerks@indiabuildings.co.uk

Head of Chambers	Ray Herman
Practice Manager/Senior Clerk	J Robert Moss
Assistant Senior Clerk	Mark Shannon
Clerks	Helen Southworth
	Alastair Webster
	Gail Curran
	Greg Brooker
	Claire Labio
	Elisa Roberts
Tenants	41

Members

Ray Herman (1972) +
Graham Wood QC (1979) (QC 2002) +
Michael Wolff (1964)
Michael Byrne (1971) +
Stephen Bedford (1974) +
Geoffrey Lowe (1975) +
Ross Duggan (1978) +
Gail Owen (1980) +
Gareth Jones (1984)
Michael Kennedy (1985)
Jacqueline Wall (1986)
Jean France-Hayhurst (1987)
Charles Davey (1989)
Damian Sanders (1988)
Simon Holder (1989)
Deborah Gould (1990)
Zia Chaudhry (1991)
Jonathan Taylor (1991)
Patricia Pratt (1991)
Steven Swift (1991)
Jonathan Butler (1992)
John Gibson (1993)
Ben Jones (1993)
David Flood (1993)
Leona Harrison (1993)
David Polglase (1993)
Sara Mann (1994)
Michael Scholes (1996)
John Dixon (1995)
John Chukwuemeka (1994)
Emma Barron-Eaves (1998)
Katharine Titchmarsh (1998)
Kate Burnell (1998)
Helen Conway (1999)
David Watson (1963) (Deputy District Judge)
Matthew Stockwell (1998)
Christopher Barnes (2000)
Philip Astbury (1999)
Michael Humphreys (2001)
David Taylor (1998)
Dean O'Leary (1999)

+ Recorder

The Chambers There are currently 41 members of chambers.

Work Undertaken

Main Areas Chambers practise in the following fields: crime, both prosecution and defence, including fraud work; all aspects of family work, including disputes about children and ancillary relief claims; personal injury litigation; commercial disputes; professional negligence claims; employment law; general common law.
Additional Areas Certain members of chambers have experience in building disputes; administrative law; insurance disputes; landlord and tenant; licensing; financial services; company law; partnership disputes; contract law.

Recruitment Normally one pupillage each year. Financial support on merit and subject to negotiation. All pupils stand a good chance of tenancy.

BAR A-Z ■ LIVERPOOL/MAIDSTONE

Oriel Chambers (Andrew Sander) — Set No.210

Oriel Chambers, 14 Water Street, Liverpool, L2 8TD
Tel (0151) 236 7191/236 4321 **Fax** (0151) 227 5909/236 3332 **DX** 14106 Liverpool
Email clerks@oriel-chambers.co.uk **Website** www.oriel-chambers.co.uk

Head of Chambers	Andrew Sander
Chambers Director	Sarah Cavanagh
Chambers Manager	Paul Thompson
Clerks	Michael Gray
	Andrew Hampton
	Ian Pitt
	John Newsham
Accounts	Wendy O'Donnell
	Jenny Connor
Tenants	38

Members

Andrew Sander (1970) +
M Bennett (1969)
C Alldis (1970) +
A Edwards (1972) +
W Rankin (1972)
A Murray (1974) +
NA Wright (1974) +
R Bradley (1978)
T Somerville (1979)
P Cowan (1980) +
T Gibson (1981)
P Fogarty (1982)
G Bundred (1982)
S Evans (1985)
A Fox (1986)
P Goodbody (1986)
J Nicholls (1989)
J Baldwin (1990)
J Lewthwaite (1990)
Yaqub Rahman (1991)
J Gruffydd (1992) †
H Belbin (1992)
RS Mills (1992)
P Foster (1992)
P Brant (1993)
H Brandon (1993)
J Dawson (1994)
F Somerset-Jones (1994)
WK Rankin (1994)
L Whaites (1994)
R Hughes (1995)
M Cottrell (1996)
AM Frodsham (1996)
J Sawyer (1978) ‡
S Clarke (1996)
J Close (1997)
M Stephenson (1997)
L Clarke (1999)

+ Recorder † Former Solicitor ‡ Previously CPS

▼MAIDSTONE

Maidstone Chambers (Alison Ginn & Richard Travers) — Set No.211

33 Earl St, Maidstone, ME14 1PF
Tel (01622) 688592 **Fax** (01622) 683305 **DX** 51982 Maidstone 2
Email clerks@maidstonechambers.co.uk

Head of Chambers	Alison Ginn
	Richard Travers
Senior Clerk	Neil Calver
Tenants	13

Members

Alison Ginn (1980)
Richard Travers (1985)
Aviva Le Prevost (1990)
Mary Jacobson (1992)
Paul Greene (1994)
Thomas Stern (1995)
Philip Sinclair (1995)
Richard Samuel (1996)
Thomas Allen (1995)
Simon Wickens (1998)
Alex Wilson (1998)
John Fitzgerald (1998)
Tom Dunn (1998)

The Chambers Maidstone Chambers is a general common law set established in 1994, prior to which it was the annexe to a London chambers from 1987. A broad range of civil and criminal work is undertaken at all levels in London, Kent and throughout the South East circuit. Individual members also specialise in various areas of law including crime, licensing, employment, planning, contract, tort (including professional negligence and personal injury), commercial and general civil work. Conferences can be held in chambers or at the instructing solicitor's office.

MAIDSTONE/MANCHESTER ■ BAR A-Z

6-8 Mill Street (Stephen Hockman QC)   Set No.212

6-8 Mill Street, Maidstone, ME15 6XH
Tel (01622) 688094/688095   **Fax** (01622) 688096   **DX** 51967 Maidstone 2
Email annexe@6pumpcourt.co.uk   **Website** www.6pumpcourt.co.uk

Head of Chambers	Stephen Hockman QC
Senior Clerk	Richard Constable
Tenants	29

Members

Stephen Hockman QC (1970) (QC-1990)
Neville Willard (1976)
Grant Armstrong (1978)
Richard Barraclough (1980)
David Travers (1981)
Nicholas Baldock (1983)
Caroline Topping (1984)
David Walden-Smith (1985)
Peter Gower (1985)
Kevin Leigh (1986)
Peter Harrison (1987)
Eleanor Laws (1990)
Peter Forbes (1990)
William Upton (1990)
Oliver Saxby (1992)
Paul Mee (1992)
Judith Butler (1993)
Mark Watson (1994)
Edward Grant (1994)
Nina Ellin (1994)
Clare Wright (1995)
Peter Alcock (1995)
Mark Beard (1996)
Deborah Charles (1996)
Tanya Robinson (1997)
Richard Banwell (1998)
Gordon Menzies (1998)
Lee Bennett (1998)
Linsey Knowles (2000)

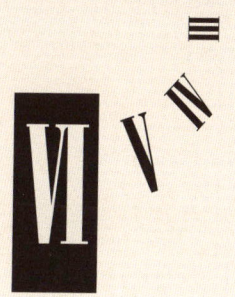

The Chambers The Maidstone annexe provides comfortable and well-appointed facilities for meetings and conferences, and enables chambers to meet the needs of clients throughout the county of Kent in an efficient, cost-effective and responsive manner.

Work Undertaken The work of chambers includes a wide range of common law work in London and on the South Eastern Circuit. The set has specialists in criminal law, personal injury, planning, environmental, local government and administrative and family law.

▼MANCHESTER

■ Byrom Street Chambers   Set No.213

12 Byrom St, Manchester, M3 4PP   **Tel** (0161) 829 2100   **Fax** (0161) 829 2101

Central Chambers   Set No.214

89 Princess Street, Manchester, M1 4HT
Tel (0161) 236 1133   **Fax** (0161) 236 1177   **DX** 14467 Manchester 2

Senior Clerk	Jayne Lever
Clerk	Neil Vickers
Tenants	16

Members

Stella Massey (1990)
Vincent Deane (1976)
Anthony J Morris (1986)
Tonia Grace (1992)
Nazmun Nisha Ismail (1992)
Steven Wild (1994)
Tony Thorndike (1994)
James Collins (1997)
Wayne Nathan Goldstein (1999)(New South Wales 1992)
Katherine Hodson (2000)
Caroline Patrick (1999)
Penelope Maudsley (1998)
Steven Levine (1989)
Christine Hendrickson (1982)
Prof Rebecca Wallace (1999)*
Abid Mahmood (1992) *

* Door Tenant

The Chambers Established 1996. A modern, approachable, progressive set of chambers with a particular emphasis on civil liberties and human rights. Individual practitioners specialise in administrative law, criminal law, housing, family law, welfare rights, human rights, personal injury, clinical negligence, immigration, judicial review, mental health, care in the community law, employment, prison law and civil actions against the police.

Out of Hours Tel (07973) 744906

■ Garden Court North (Chambers of Ian MacDonald QC) (Ian MacDonald QC)   Set No.215

Waldorf House, 5 Cooper Street, Manchester, M2 2FW   **Tel** (0161) 236 1840   **Fax** (0161) 236 0929   **DX** 715637 Manchester-2

BAR A-Z ■ MANCHESTER

Cobden House Chambers (Roger Farley QC)
Set No.216

19 Quay Street, Manchester, M3 3HN
Tel (0161) 833 6000   Fax (0161) 833 6001   DX 14327 Manchester 3
Email clerks@cobden.co.uk   Website www.cobden.co.uk

Head of Chambers	Roger Farley QC
Senior Clerk	Trevor Doyle
Junior Clerk	David Hewitt
Assistant Clerks	Daniel Monaghan
	Gary Douglas
Administrator	Jackie Morton
Tenants	44

Members

Roger Farley QC (1974) (QC-1993)
Jonathan Goldberg QC (1971) (QC-1989)
Howard Baisden (1972)
Peter Keenan (1962)
Harry Narayan (1970) +
John Broadley (1973)
Charles Machin (1973)
Carolyn Johnson (1974)
Nigel Fieldhouse (1976)
Stuart Neale (1976)
Michael Goldwater (1977)
Richard Oughton (1978)
Paula Fallows (1981)
Colin Green (1982)
Louise Blackwell (1985)
Ian Metcalfe (1985)

Richard Hartley (1985) +
Mark Monaghan (1987)
Deanna Hymanson (1988)
Joanne Woodward (1989)
Timothy Willitts (1989)
Martin Littler (1989)
Sarah Harrison (1989)
Jonathan Gregg (1990)
Sean Kelly (1990)
Marc Willems (1990)
Yasmin Wright (1990)
Alison Kilpatrick (1991)
Rajen Dalal (1991)
Jonathan Smith (1991)
Simon Nichol (1994)
Richard Littler (1994)
Susan Gilmour (1994)

David Maddison (1995)
Julian Orr (1995)
Chris Oakes (1996)
Hilary Manley (1996)
Martin Callery (1997)
Adrian Farrow (1997)
Michael Jones (1998)
Louise Kitchin (1998)
Richard Goddard (1999)
Rebecca Pearson (1999)
Michael J Knowles (2000)
John Duncan (1971) *
Michael Heywood (1975) *
James Morris *
Matthew Kime (1988) *
Richard Gee (1993) *

* Door Tenant + Recorder

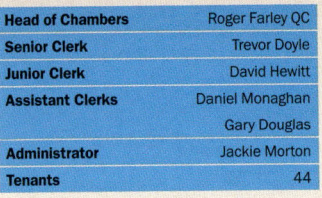

The Chambers Cobden House Chambers is able to offer a wide range of expertise by means of specialist departments in the area of Chancery, commercial law, crime, employment law, family, housing and personal injury. Individual members are able to offer additional specialisms and full details can be obtained from the clerk. Chambers provide a fast and efficient service and a timetable for the completion of instructions can be given on delivery. In addition, chambers provide services for alternative dispute resolution and mediation and video conferences. The senior clerk will be happy to discuss fee levels and tailor quotations to meet most budgets. Further details can be found on the website and in chambers' brochure which can be obtained on request.

Deans Court Chambers (Stephen Grime QC)
Set No.217

Deans Court Chambers, 24 St John Street, Manchester, M3 4DF
Tel (0161) 214 6000   Fax (0161) 214 6001   DX 718155 Manchester 3
Email clerks@deanscourt.co.uk   Website www.deanscourt.co.uk

Head of Chambers	Stephen Grime QC
Clerk to Chambers	Clive Witcomb
Tenants	50

Members

Stephen Grime QC (1970) (QC-1987)
Keith Goddard QC (1959)(QC-1979)
David Stockdale QC (1975) (QC-1995)
David Fish QC (1973) (QC-1997)
Ernest Ryder TD QC (1981) (QC-1997)
Mark Turner QC (1981)(QC-1998)
Patrick Field QC (1981) (QC-2000)
Craig Sephton QC (1981)(QC-2001)
John Bromley-Davenport QC (1972) (QC-2002)
Kevin Talbot (1970)
John Gregory (1972)
Peter Atherton (1975)
Alan Booth (1978)
Ruth Trippier (1978)

Philip Butler (1979)
Peter Main (1981)
Stuart Denney (1982)
Timothy Smith (1982)
Timothy Trotman (1983)
Russell Davies (1983)
Wayne Jackson (1984)
Louise Bancroft (1985)
Frances Heaton (1985)
Paul Humphries (1986)
Karen Brody (1986)
Christopher Hudson (1987)
Nicholas Grimshaw (1988)
Jonathan Grace (1989)
Robin Kitching (1989)
Julia Cheetham (1990)
Seamus Andrew (1991)
Janet Ironfield (1992)

Andrew Alty (1992)
Timothy Edge (1992)
Alison Woodward (1992)
Peter Burns (1993)
Mark Savill (1993)
Hannah Spencer (1993)
Michael Hayton (1993)
Lisa Judge (1993)
Sebastian Clegg (1994)
David Boyle (1996)
Simon McCann (1996)
Elizabeth Dudley-Jones (1997)
Sophie Cartwright (1999)
Richard Whitehall (1999)
Ross Olson (1999)
Howard Cohen (1999)
Pascale Hicks (1999)
Joseph Hart (2000)

The Chambers Deans Court Chambers is a progressive set with a reputation for the highest standards of professionalism, service and response to clients' needs. It offers specialist advocacy and drafting expertise at every level of seniority. Chambers' purpose-designed premises at 24 St John Street provide a wide range of services to clients. A new seminar suite enables them to deliver lectures and seminars on current topics of interest; video-conferencing has been installed; facilities for arbitration, mediation and alternative dispute resolution are also available.

Work Undertaken
Civil Litigation Personal injury (including injuries of the utmost severity, class actions, industrial disease, factory accidents, road traffic and credit hire); professional negligence, particularly clinical, lawyers, architects and surveyors; insurance (including coverage, Road Traffic Act and Motor Insurers' Bureau); contractual disputes; sale of goods; consumer credit; product liability; technology and construction; human rights; false imprisonment.
Commercial & Chancery Including arbitration; banking; carriage of goods; civil fraud and tracing of assets; corporate and personal insolvency; company law; credit and leasing; financial services; injunctions and equitable remedies; insurance and reinsurance; intellectual property; landlord and tenant; 'old' chancery; partnerships; pensions; sale of goods.
Family Including matrimonial finance; children; incapacity and competence; public and administration; education and special educational needs; Inheritance Act claims; professional negligence; mediation.
Criminal Including prosecution and defence work in all fields at every level, including homicide; offences of serious violence and sexual offences; commercial fraud; conspiracy; drug importation and supply; excise and revenue offences; health and safety.

Exchange Chambers (David Turner QC & Bill Braithwaite QC & Henry Globe QC)   Set No.218

4 Ralli Courts, West Riverside, Manchester, M3 5FT
Tel (0161) 833 2722   **Fax** (0161) 833 2789   **DX** 14330 Manchester
Email info@exchangechambers.co.uk   **Website** www.exchangechambers.co.uk

Head of Chambers	David Turner QC
	Bill Braithwaite QC
	Henry Globe QC
Practice Manager	Tom Handley
Senior Clerk	Roy Finney
Tenants	68

Members:

William Waldron QC (1970) (QC-1982)
David Turner QC (1971) (QC-1991)
Bill Braithwaite QC (1970) (QC-1992)
Charles Chruszcz QC (1973) (QC-1992)
Anthony Elleray QC (1977) (QC-1993)
Henry Globe QC (1972) (QC-1994)
Graham Morrow QC (1974) (QC-1996)
Tim Holroyde QC (1977) (QC-1996)
Edward Bartley Jones, QC (1975) (QC-1997)
Gerard Martin QC (1978) (QC-2000)
Mark Cawson QC (1982) (QC-2001)
John R Jones QC (1981) (QC-2002)
Graham Wood QC (1979) (QC-2002)
Francis Nance (1970)
Simon Earlam (1975)
Christopher Cornwall (1975)

Eric Lamb (1975)
James Rae (1976)
Judith Fordham (1991)
Gordon Cole (1979)
Ian Harris (1990)
Tania Griffiths (1982)
Roger Hillman (1983)
Neil Cadwallader (1984)
Karen Gregory (1985)
Dennis Talbot (1985)
Paul Taylor (1991)
Paul Clark (1994)
Simon Berkson (1986)
Alun James (1986)
William F Waldron (1986)
Guy Vickers (1986)
Mark Mulrooney (1988)
Brian Cummings (1988)
John J McCarroll (1988)
Louis Browne (1988)
Ian Foster (1988)
Rebecca Clark (1989)
Catherine Howells (1989)
Michael Wood (1989)
Jonathan Cannan (1989)
Christopher Stables (1990)

Julie Case (1990)
John Philpotts (1990)
Christopher Cook (1990)
Amanda Yip (1991)
Paul Timothy Evans (1992)
David Casement (1992)
Ian Unsworth (1992)
Giles Maynard-Connor (1992)
Charlotte Kenny (1993)
Robert Dudley (1993)
Simon Fox (1994)
Kelly Pennifer (1994)
Rachel Silverbeck (1996)
Kevin Slack (1997)
Claire Gourley (1996)
Louise Metcalf (1997)
Nancy Dooher (1997)
Paul Burns (1998)
Sarah O'Brien (1998)
Daniel Travers (1999)
Jonathan Clarke (1999)
David Mohyuddin (1999)
Martine Snowdon (2000)
Jonathan Rogers (2000)
Andrew Vinson (2000)
Nicola Daley (2001)

The Chambers Chambers also at: Pearl Assurance House, Derby Square, Liverpool, L2 9XX
Tel: (0151) 236 7747, Fax: (0151) 236 3433, DX: 14207 Liverpool.

BAR A-Z ■ MANCHESTER

Kenworthy's Chambers (Frank Burns) *Set No.219*

Kenworthy's Chambers, 83 Bridge St, Manchester, M3 2RF
Tel (0161) 832 4036   **Fax** (0161) 832 0370   **DX** 718200
Email clerks@kenworthys.co.uk

Head of Chambers	Frank Burns
Practice Manager	Maria Rushworth
Listing Clerk	Paul Mander
Fee Clerk	Zishan Ellahi
Administrator	Sue Barlow
Tenants	18

Members

Frank Burns (1971)
Richard Heap (1963)
Deborah Lambert (1977)
Barry Grennan (1977)
Patrick Cassidy (1982)
Gita Patel (1988)
Kathryn Korol (1996)
Andrew Marrs (1995)
Mark Smith (1997)
Janet Ruscoe (1995)
Imran Shafi (1996)
Geoff Whelan (1996)
Vanessa Thomson (1998)
Sharon Amesu (1998)
Erica Carleton (2000)
Alison Mather (1997)
Rachel White (2000)
Mark Schwenk (2001)

KENWORTHY'S CHAMBERS

The Chambers The hallmark of Kenworthy's Chambers is its approachability, blended with a commitment to the highest professional standards.

Work Undertaken The strengths of chambers lie in criminal law, family law and immigration matters. The criminal team divides into a defence team and a prosecution team of varying experience. A particular strength is the quality of chambers' defence work, which regularly involves cases of murder, gang violence, fraud and drug trafficking. The family team is hugely experienced in representing children's cases, working with guardians and local authorities including matters of the utmost gravity with links to criminal proceedings. Complex ancillary relief matters are a particular forte of the team. Chambers offer a comprehensive nationwide service on all apsects of immigration law and judicial review. Members of chambers also undertake personal injury work on a conditional fee and contract arrangements.

International Languages spoken include Gujarati, Hindi, Punjabi and Urdu.

Recruitment Chambers have an established training programme and are accredited by the Law Society, ILEX and the Bar Council as a training provider.

■ Kingsgate Chambers (Beverley Lunt) *Set No.220*

First Floor, Kingsgate House, 51-53 South King St, Manchester, M2 6DE   **Tel** (0161) 831 7477   **Fax** (0161) 832 5645

8 King St (Gerard McDermott QC) *Set No.221*

8 King St, Manchester, M2 6AQ
Tel (0161) 834 9560   **Fax** (0161) 834 2733   **DX** 14354 Manchester 1
Email clerks@8ks.co.uk   **Website** www.8ks.co.uk

Head of Chambers	Gerard McDermott QC
Senior Clerk	Peter Whitman
Practice Manager & Clerk	David Lea
Clerks	David Haslam
	Martin Leech
	Christina Brindley
Research & Marketing Manager	
	Catherine Healy LLM
Academic Consultant	Geraint Howells
Tenants	39

Members

Gerard McDermott QC (1978) (QC-1999) LLB
Clive Freedman QC (1978) (QC-1997) MA (Cantab)
Elizabeth Rylands (1973) LLB
David Eccles (1976) MA (Cantab)
Jeffrey Terry (1976) LLB, MA, FCIArb
Digby C Jess (1978) PhD, BSc, LLM, FCIArb
Philip Holmes (1980) MA (Cantab)
Glyn Williams (1981) BA
Kim Frances Foudy (1982) LLB
Farooq Ahmed (1983) LLB
Stephen Davies (1985) MA(Cantab)
Conor Quigley (1983) LLB, MA, Dip Eur Int
Michael Smith (1989) MA, BCL (Oxon)
Mark Forte (1989) LLB
Simon Vaughan (1989) LLB, LLM
Ian Wood (1990) BA
Jonathan Thompson (1990) LLM, MA (Cantab)
Christopher Scorah (1991) MA (Oxon)
Timothy Hodgson (1991) BA, D.Phil (Oxon)
Alistair Bower (1986) LLB
Joanne Connolly (1992) LLB
Kevin Naylor (1992) MB ChB, MRCGP, LLB, LLM
Karim Sabry (1992) BA
Kirsten Barry (1993) LLB
John Parr (1989) LLB
Rachael Hamilton-Hague (1993) BA
Graham Bailey (1993) LLB
James Boyd (1994) LLB, LLM
Andrew Clark (1994) MA (Oxon)
David Sandiford (1995) BA (Oxon)
Paul Higgins (1996) BA (Oxon)
David Hoffman (1997) MA, BCL (Oxon)
Anna Short (1997) MA (Cantab)
Lee Nowland (1997) LLB
Nigel Edwards (1998) MA (Cantab)
Jane Bresnahan (1998) LLB
Matthew Haisley (1999) LLB
Zoë Allen (1999) LLB
Andrew Ward (2000) BA, BCL (Oxon)

KING STREET CHAMBERS

MANCHESTER ■ BAR A-Z

The Chambers A leading Manchester set offering specialist expertise in civil and commercial matters.

Work Undertaken General common law; commercial and chancery; personal injury; clinical and professional negligence; employment (including race and sex discrimination); commercial fraud; matrimonial and child law; landlord and tenant; contract (including building); administrative law; European law; human rights; immigration; insurance law; arbitration; environmental law; company law; licensing; construction; sale of goods; consumer credit; Anglo-American disputes. Video conferencing facilities available.

40 King St   Set No.222

40 King St, Manchester, M2 6BA
Tel (0161) 832 9082   **Fax** (0161) 835 2139   **DX** 718188 Mch 3
Email clerks@40kingstreet.co.uk   **Website** www.40kingstreet.co.uk

Chief Executive	Colin Wardale
Senior Clerk	William Brown
Bar Management Services	William Brown
	Colin Griffin
	Michael Stubbs
Assistant Clerks	Lisa Williams
	Paul Clark
Tenants	56

Members

Andrew Gilbart QC (1972) (QC-1991)
John Hoggett QC (1969)(QC-1986)
Stephen Sauvain QC (1977) (QC-1995)
Frances Patterson QC (1977) (QC-1998) †
Michael Booth QC (1981) (QC-1999)
Nicholas Braslavsky QC(1983) (QC-1999)
Vincent Fraser QC (1981) (QC-2001)
Paul Chaisty QC (1982) (QC-2001)
Reverend Eric Owen (1969)
Harold Halliday (1972)
Shokat Khan (1979)
David Manley (1981)
John Barrett (1982)
Alan Evans (1978)
Neil Berragan (1982)

Mark Halliwell (1985)
John Cooper (1985)
Simon Hilton (1987)
Katherine Dunn (1987)
Nigel Clayton (1987)
Ruth Stockley (1988)
Fiona Ashworth (1988)
Paul Tucker (1990)
Geoffrey Pass (1975)
Andrew Singer (1990)
Stephen Pritchett (1990)
Lesley Anderson (1989)
Matthew Smith (1991)
Andrew Grantham (1991)
Martin Carter (1992)
Wilson Horne (1992)
Lucy Powis (1992)
Mark Harper (1993)
Sarah Pritchard (1993)
Richard Lander (1993)
Ian Ponter (1993)

Simon Antrobus (1995)
Andrew Latimer (1995)
Louis Doyle (1996)
Elizabeth Berridge (1996)
Colin Crawford (1997)
Nicholas Siddall (1997)
Giles Cannock (1998)
Mark Cooper (1998)
Andrew McGee (1998)
Simon Young (1998)
Matthew Hall (1999)
Helen Mulholland (1999)
Catherine Brown (1999)
Tina Rañales-Cotos (1999)
Eleanor Temple (2000)
Matthew Copeland (2000)
John Tackaberry QC (1967) (QC-1982) †
John Campbell (1981)(QC Scotland 1999) †
Julian Ghosh (1993) †
James Henderson (1997) †

40 KING STREET
MANCHESTER

40

5 PARK PLACE
LEEDS

† Associate Member

The Chambers Also at: 5 Park Place, Leeds, LS1 2RH Tel (0113) 242 1123   Fax (0113) 242 1124   DX 713113 (Leeds PKSQ)

40 King Street Chambers is one of the leading sets outside London. The set is dedicated to providing clients with specialist, practical and commercial legal advice from barristers with the highest reputation for advocacy, knowledge and professional standards. Chambers are regularly involved in the full range of courts in which their members are characterised by a reputation for strong and incisive advocacy backed by tough negotiating skills. Chambers are also regularly and increasingly involved in arbitration and mediation. Chambers' clients are individual and corporate, national and multinational, plc and private. Chambers work for all the leading firms of solicitors in the North and North East and for many in the City of London and elsewhere. Chambers welcome instructions by direct access when permitted. They have a strong and wide base of clients across the whole spectrum of industries including banks (including clearing and secondary), developers, retailers, manufacturers, services, professional bodies and local authorities. Chambers also now regularly represent many emerging companies in the newer information technology, e-commerce and leisure markets.

Work Undertaken Chambers believe that their clients' interests are best served by increasing specialisation, strength in depth and above all in uncompromising attitudes to quality and client service. As such they are now a large specialist set with a national reputation practising from Manchester and Leeds in the following specific areas: chancery and commercial including chancery, commercial, insolvency and banking; property and construction and professional negligence; planning, environment and public law; common law including personal injury, clinical negligence, employment and regulatory.

International Languages include French, German, Punjabi, Urdu, Russian, Welsh and Spanish.

BAR A-Z ■ MANCHESTER

■ **Lincoln House Chambers** (Mukhtar Hussain QC) Set No.223
5th Floor Lincoln House, 1 Brazennose Street, Manchester, M2 5EL **Tel** (0161) 832 5701 **Fax** (0161) 832 0839 **DX** 14338 Manchester 1

■ **Manchester House Chambers** (J D S Wishart) Set No.224
Manchester House Chambers, 18-22 Bridge St, Manchester, M3 3BZ **Tel** (0161) 834 7007 **Fax** (0161) 834 3462 **DX** 718153 Manchester 3

Merchant Chambers (David Berkley QC) Set No.225

Number One, North Parade, Parsonage Gardens, Manchester, M3 2NH
Tel (0161) 839 7070 **Fax** (0161) 839 7111 **DX** 710280 Manchester 3
Email inquiries@merchantchambers.com **Website** www.merchantchambers.com

Head of Chambers	David Berkley QC
Senior Clerk	Alastair Campbell
Tenants	11

Members

David Berkley QC (1979) (QC-1999)
David Uff (1981)
Stephen Cogley (1984)
Catherine Fisher (1990)
Richard Carter (1990)
Andrew Noble (1992) FRICS FCIArb
Jonathan Rule (1993)
Stefan Brochwicz-Lewinski (1995)
Ghazan Mahmood (1997)
Susanne Muth (1998)
Martin Budworth (1999)

The Chambers Merchant Chambers was founded in 1996 by established practitioners in order to provide a high quality service to the banking and business community in the north west region and beyond. Since its launch the chambers have attracted other specialists to become a leading commercial set on the Northern Circuit. The approach of the set is to offer effective advocacy at all levels and efficient and cost effective return of papers and advice. The set prides itself on delivering its services in a relaxed unstuffy and down to earth manner. The work of chambers includes banking, insolvency, partnership and general commercial work. Full details can be found in the chambers information booklet available on request. In addition to its core services, Merchant Chambers provides training and offers seminars to solicitors.

Peel Court Chambers (Michael Shorrock QC) Set No.226

Peel Court Chambers, 45 Hardman Street, Manchester, M3 3PL
Tel (0161) 832 3791 **Fax** (0161) 835 3054 **DX** 14320
Email clerks@peelct.co.uk

Head of Chambers	Michael Shorrock QC
Clerks	Shell Edmonds
	David Haley
	Stuart Howard-Cofield
	Sean Henry
Tenants	39

Members

Michael Shorrock QC (1966) (QC-1988)
Anthony Morris QC (1970) (QC-1991)
David Lane QC (1968) (QC-1991)
Howard Bentham QC (1970) (QC-1996)
Stephen Meadowcroft (1973)
Anthony Russell QC (1974) (QC-1999)
Richard Marks QC (1975)(QC-1999)
Andrew O'Byrne (1978)
Andrew Long (1981)
Fiorella Brereton (1979)
David Pickup (1984)
Steven Johnson (1984)
Paul Sheridan (1984)
Richard Pearce (1985)
Julian Taylor (1986)
Jeremy Grout-Smith (1986)
Tina Landale (1988)
Neil Fryman (1989)
Mark Rhind (1989)
Martin Walsh (1990)
Rachel Smith (1990)
Graham Knowles (1990)
Simon Burrows (1990)
David Toal (1990)
Michael Lavery (1990)
William Baker (1991)
Mark Ainsworth (1992)
Henry Blackshaw (1993)
Richard Orme (1993)
Claire Evans (1994)
Rebecca Lloyd-Smith (1994)
June Morris (1995)
Mary Ruck (1993)
Darryl Allen (1995)
Gavin McBride (1996)
Anthony Mazzag (1996)
Alexandra Simmonds (1998)
Maisie Burke (1999)
David Temkin (2000)

The Chambers A large general common law set including six QCs.

Work Undertaken A wide range of common law work is covered, with particular emphasis on crime; clinical negligence and medical law; licensing (gaming and liquor); commercial fraud; personal injury; professional negligence; family law including childcare and matrimonial finance. Chambers also provide expertise in consumer credit and commercial law; landlord and tenant; health and safety law; EC and revenue law.

International Languages spoken include French, German and Mandarin.

MANCHESTER ■ BAR A-Z

St. James's Chambers (Robert Sterling & Ian Leeming QC)

Set No.227

St. James's Chambers, 68 Quay St, Manchester, M3 3EJ
Tel (0161) 834 7000   **Fax** (0161) 834 2341   **DX** 14350 Manchester 1
Email clerks@stjameschambers.co.uk

Head of Chambers	Robert Sterling
	Ian Leeming QC
Senior Clerk	Stephen J Diggles
Tenants	19

Members

Ian Leeming QC (1970) (QC-1988) +
Robert Sterling (1970)
Percy Wood (1961)
Barrie Searle (1975) +
David Porter (1980)
Timothy Lyons (1980)
Michael Mulholland (1976)

David Binns (1983)
Lucy Wilson-Barnes (1989)
Sarah Wheeldon (1990)
Ruth Tankel (1990)
James Hurd (1994)
David Calvert (1995)
Christopher Taft (1997)

Fayaz Hammond (1999)
Richard Moore (1992)
Paul Tindall (1999)
Alisan Bilsland (2000)
Haroon Rashid (1999)
Anthony Rubin (1960) *
Joseph Jaconelli (1972) *

* Door Tenant + Recorder

The Chambers A long established Chancery and Commercial set of Chambers.

Work Undertaken

Chancery Personal and company insolvency, company including shareholders disputes, director disqualification, tax, partnership, charities, contentious probate, pensions, wills, settlements and trusts, family provision, equitable remedies, intellectual property, mortgages, agricultural holdings, commercial and residential landlord and tenant, all aspects of property law including advising on conveyancing and developments, commons, restrictive covenants, easements including rights of light and party walls.

Commercial Professional negligence, banking, construction and building, all aspects of contract law, consumer credit, sale of goods, confidential information, restraint of trade. All aspects of civil litigation with specialist teams for the following work: personal injury, including health and safety at work; employment law, including unfair dismissal, discrimination, TUPE and breach of contract; family: divorce, matrimonial finance; civil liberties: police disciplinary hearings, human rights and immigration.

Publications Ian Leeming QC is the author of Equity and Trusts division in Butterworths *Law of Limitation and Service Issues*. Timothy Lyons has written works on inheritance tax and insolvency, and sits on the editorial board of the *Law and Tax Review*.

International French, Italian, Urdu.

9 St. John Street (John Hand QC)

Set No.228

9 St. John Street, Manchester, M3 4DN
Tel (0161) 955 9000   **Fax** (0161) 955 9001   **DX** 14326
Email clerks@9stjohnstreet.co.uk   **Website** www.9stjohnstreet.co.uk

Head of Chambers	John Hand QC
Chambers Administrator	Jo Kelly
Senior Clerk (Crime)	Graham Livesey
Senior Clerk (Civil)	Tony Morrissey
Senior Clerk (Family)	Paul Morecroft
Assistant Civil Clerk	Jane Slingsby
Assistant Criminal Clerk	Andrew Leech
Tenants	43

Members

John Hand QC (1972) (QC-1988) +
Roderick Carus QC (1971) (QC-1990) +
Charles Garside QC (1971) (QC-1993) +
Timothy Horlock QC (1981) (QC-1997) +
Nicholas Hinchliffe QC (1980) (QC-1999) +
Terence Rigby (1971) +
Michael Johnson (1971) +
Christine Riley (1974)
Peter Cadwallader (1973)
Simon Temple (1977)
Paul McDonald (1975)
Michael Murray (1979) +

Nicholas Clarke (1981) +
Nigel Grundy (1983) +
Michael Leeming (1983) +
Gillian Irving (1984)
Paul Gilroy (1985)
Carlo Breen (1987)
Nicola Gatto (1987)
David Gilchrist (1987)
Simon James (1988)
David Friesner (1988)
Thomas Fitzpatrick (1988)
Ian Little (1989)
Christopher L P Kennedy (1989)
Nigel Bird (1991)
Anthony Howard (1992)
Rachel Wedderspoon (1993)
Jaime Hamilton (1993)

Tariq Sadiq (1993)
Alaric Bassano (1993)
James Fryer-Spedding (1994)
Michael Lemmy (1994)
Robert Darbyshire (1995)
Brian McCluggage (1995)
Katie Nowell (1996)
Gary Woodhall (1997)
Kate Hollyoak (1997)
Rachael Heppenstall (1997)
Helen Redmond (1999)
Lucinda Leeming (1999)
Louise Dobson (2000)
Katherine Mallory (1998)
Rebecca Eeley (2001) †
Alison Hayworth (2001) †
Matthew Snarr (2001) †

Continued overleaf

BAR A-Z ■ MANCHESTER

+ Recorder † Pupil

The Chambers In order to meet the increasing demand for specialisation, members of chambers have formed themselves into the following five special interest groups: employment, criminal, commercial and property, personal injury and family. They are therefore able to offer specialised advice and advocacy in the following areas: employment; industrial relations and discrimination; human/civil rights; personal injury; clinical negligence; environmental law; commercial and property with general chancery; crime; trading standards work; family and mental health. Chambers also have an association with chambers at 42 Castle Street, Liverpool.

18 St John Street (Jonathan Foster QC) — Set No.229

18 St. John Street, Manchester, M3 4EA
Tel (0161) 278 1800 **Fax** (0161) 835 2051 **DX** 728854 Manchester 4
Email clerks@18stjohn.co.uk **Website** www.eighteen-stjohn.co.uk

Head of Chambers	Jonathan Foster QC
Senior Clerks	John Hammond
	William Sheldon
Chambers Administrator	Pippa Jessop
Tenants	39

Members

Jonathan Foster QC (1970) (QC-1989)
Peter Birkett QC (1972) (QC-1989)
Raymond Wigglesworth QC (1974) (QC-1999)
Roger Hedgeland (1972)
Alastair Forrest (1972)
Paul Dockery (1973)
Jennifer Caldwell (1973)
Paul O'Brien (1974)
Christopher Diamond (1975)
Roger Stout (1976)
Malcolm McEwan (1976)

Nicholas Fewtrell (1977)
Mark Laprell (1979)
David Heaton (1983)
Richard Vardon (1985)
Brian Williams (1986)
Yvonne Healing (1988)
Toby Sasse (1988)
Samantha Birtles (1989)
Nigel Poole (1989)
Elisabeth Tythcott (1989)
Edward Morgan (1989)
Mark Benson (1992)
Susan Harrison (1993)
Raquel Simpson (1990)

Simon Csoka (1991)
Rachel Shenton (1993)
Chris Daw (1993)
Sarah Williams (1995)
Simon Kilvington (1995)
Andrew Moore (1996)
Saul Brody (1996)
Rachel Faux (1997)
Richard Chapman (1998)
N Jonathan Grierson (1999)
Darren Dunn (1999)
Kalsoom Maqsood (1998)
Leonie Caplan (2001)
Nell Goodwin (2000)

The Chambers A general common law chambers with distinct civil, family and criminal departments, together with four chancery practitioners and expertise at all levels.

■ 24A St. John Street (Paul Chambers) — Set No.230

24A St. John Street, Manchester, M3 4DF **Tel** (0161) 833 9628 **Fax** (0161) 834 0243 **DX** 710301 (Manchester 3)

MANCHESTER ■ BAR A-Z

28 St John St

Set No.231

28 St John St, Manchester, M3 4DJ
Tel (0161) 834 8418 **Fax** (0161) 835 3929 **DX** 728861 Manchester 4
Email clerk@28stjohn.co.uk

Chief Executive	Mike Fry
Senior Clerk	Christopher Ronan
Tenants	46

Members

L Clement Goldstone QC (1971) (QC-1993)
Anthony Rumbelow QC (1967) (QC-1990)
Anthony Gee QC (1972) (QC-1990)
Michael Redfern QC (1970) (QC-1993)
Anthony Hayden QC (1987) (QC-2002)
Philip Cattan (1970)
Richard Humphry (1972)
Rowena Goode (1974)
Bernard Wallwork (1976)
Graham Platts (1978)
Philip Grundy (1980)
Sonia Gal (1982)
Maurice Greene (1982)
Sarah Singleton (1983)
Richard Gray (1986)
James Rowley (1987)
Jane Walker (1987)
Timothy Brennand (1987)
Charles Eastwood (1988)
Jeffrey Samuels (1986)
David Humphries (1988)
Bunty Batra (1986)
Clare Grundy (1989)
Sally-Ann Ross (1990)
Andrew Fox (1990)
Michael Rawlinson (1991)
Alastair Wright (1991)
Matthew Mawdsley (1991)
Richard Norton (1992)
Magdalen Case (1992)
Sally Harrison (1992)
Richard Tyrrell (1993)
Guy Mathieson (1993)
Alexander Kloss (1993)
Annette Gumbs (1994)
Darrel Crilley (1996)
Sarah Spear (1997)
Jeremy Roussak (1996)
Pauline McHugh (1995)
Siân Jones (1998)
Susan Machin (2000)
John Ratledge (2000)
Lorraine Cavanagh (2001)
Michael Horowitz QC (1968) (QC-1990) †
Julian Nutter (1979) †
Diana Kloss (1986) †

† Associate Tenant

The Chambers 28 St John Street has a strong professional reputation as one of Manchester's leading common law sets. Members are organised into practice groups and counsel at all levels can be provided. In addition to achieving a high number of judicial and silk appointments the set is active in the activities of the circuit, the specialist bar associations and various tribunals. A number of members sit as Recorders and Appeal Tribunal Chairmen. The set benefits from a highly rated support team that was one of the first in the country to achieve both Barmark and ISO9002 accreditation. 28 St John Street is accredited by the Law Society for continuing professional development and regularly holds seminars on major and topical issues. Video conferencing facilities are available. Wheelchair access and disabled facilities are available.

Work Undertaken

Criminal Group Members appear in courts and tribunals at all levels for both prosecution and defence. Counsel cover the full range of criminal offences from minor theft and public order to murder. Specialist interests include road traffic, trading standards, Customs & Excise, licensing, fraud, sexual abuse, cases involving children, regulatory matters and white collar crime.

Family Group Members comprise the largest family group in the North and provide a service covering every aspect of family work. Specialist interests include local authority children's work, financial provision, medical intervention, Hague convention cases, private law applications for residence, contact, etc, conflict of law cases involving other jurisdictions, Inheritance Act and professional negligence arising from matrimonial cases.

Employment Group The employment team provides advisory and advocacy services in employment law and related areas for employers and employees in both Employment Tribunals and Civil Courts. The team deals with all aspects of employment law including unfair dismissal, wrongful dismissal, unlawful deductions from wages, other contract disputes, redundancy, transfer of undertakings, race, sex and disability discrimination, equal pay, maternity and parental leave issues, stress at work claims, protective disclosures. The team has particular expertise in personal injury and health and safety work.

Civil Group All forms of personal injury work are undertaken. These include industrial disease claims, brain damage and spinal injury cases, employer and public liability claims together with road traffic related work. Clinical negligence work includes injuries at birth, major head injury and all other associated clinical professional negligence claims.

Other Areas Members undertake Mental Health Tribunal work and associated public law matters. In addition a fast growing specialism concerns professional regulation notably medical tribunals.

Recruitment Tenancy and mini-pupillage applications to chambers' Chief Executive. Pupillage applications should be made through OLPAS.

■ **Young Street Chambers** (John Jackson & David Hernandez)   Set No.232
38 Young Street, Manchester, M3 3FT **Tel** (0161) 833 0489 **Fax** (0161) 835 3938 **DX** 25583 M5

BAR A-Z ■ MIDDLESBOROUGH/NEWCASTLE

▼MIDDLESBOROUGH

■ **Counsel's Chambers** (Stuart Lightwing) Set No.233
Tudor House, Church Lane, Nunthorpe, Middlesbrough, TS7 0PD **Tel** (01642) 315000 **Fax** (01642) 315500 **DX** 60524 (Middlesbrough)

▼NEWCASTLE

Broad Chare Chambers (Patrick Cosgrove QC) Set No.234

Broad Chare Chambers, 33 Broad Chare, Newcastle upon Tyne, NE1 3DQ
Tel (0191) 232 0541 **Fax** (0191) 261 0043 **DX** 61001
Email clerks@broadcharechambers.co.uk
Website www.broadcharechambers.law.co.uk

Head of Chambers	Patrick Cosgrove QC
Senior Clerk	Brian Bell
Tenants	42

Members

Patrick Cosgrove QC (1976) (QC-1994)
James Chadwin QC (1958) (QC-1976)
Paul Batty QC (1975) (QC-1995)
James Harper (1957)
Giles Bavidge (1968)
Ian Dawson (1971)
Euan Duff (1973)
Christine Harmer (1973)
J Ronald Mitchell (1973)
Robin Horner (1975)
Roger Elsey (1977)
Christopher Dorman O'Gowan (1979)
Thomas Finch (1981)
Brian Mark (1981)
Kester Armstrong (1982)
Lesley McKenzie (1983)
Ian Kennerley (1983)
Pauline Moulder (1983)
John O'Sullivan (1984)
Richard Selwyn-Sharpe (1985)
Anne Richardson (1986)
Anthony Davis (1986)
David Rowlands (1988)
Mark Styles (1988)
Joseph O'Brien (1989)
James Brown (1990)
Jonathan Carr (1990)
Stephanie Jarron (1990)
Julie Clemitson (1991)
Claire Middleton (1991)
Nicola Shaw (1992)
Michelle Temple (1992)
Rachel Smith (1992)
S Anderson (1993)
Mark Giuliani (1993)
Elizabeth Lugg (1994)
Sara Robinson (1994)
Nicholas Peacock (1996)
Kirti Jeram (1997)
Donald MacFaul (1998)
Andrew Walker (1998)
Andrew Christopher Holmes (2000)
Bruce Blair QC (1969) (QC-1989) *
Michael Horowitz QC (1968) (QC-1990) *
Pamela Scriven QC (1970) (QC-1992) *
David Harte (1967) *
Michael Nicholls (1975) *
Richard Merritt (1981) *
David Richards (1981) *

* Door Tenant

The Chambers A large and long-established set, with an increasing range of specialists. Four members of chambers are Recorders.

Work Undertaken
Criminal Work All aspects.
Family Law Including all aspects of child law, financial disputes, divorce, Inheritance Act cases and emergency protection.
Civil Work Including personal injury, professional negligence, general contract, building disputes, employment law, licensing, planning and some commercial.
Chancery Work Most aspects.

■ Enterprise Chambers (Anthony Mann QC) Set No.235

65 Quayside, Newcastle upon Tyne, NE1 3DS
Tel (0191) 222 3344 **Fax** (0191) 222 3340 **DX** 61134 Newcastle upon Tyne 1
Email enterprise.newcastle@dial.pipex.com **Website** www.enterprisechambers.com

Head of Chambers	Anthony Mann QC
Senior Clerk	Antony Armstrong (London)
Practice Development Clerk	Barry Clayton
Clerk	Dylan Wendleken
Tenants	26

The Chambers For a full list of members please see the London entry. For further information about the set please visit the chambers' website.

NEWCASTLE ■ BAR A-Z

■ Milburn House Chambers (Paul Cape) Set No.236

E Floor, Milburn House, Dean Street, Newcastle upon Tyne, NE1 1LE
Tel (0191) 230 5511   **Fax** (0191) 230 5544   **DX** 716640 Newcastle 20
Email admin@milburnhousechambers.co.uk
Website www.milburnhousechambers.co.uk

Head of Chambers:	Paul Cape
Clerk/Admin:	Kelly Walton
Tenants:	2

Milburn House Chambers was founded in 1998 as a set specialising in employment and discrimination work, including dismissal, sex, race and disability discrimination and post-termination restraints. Chambers have a strong following amongst public sector employers. Paul Cape is a part-time Chairman of the Employment Tribunal.

■ New Court Chambers (John Evans) Set No.237

3 Broad Chare, Newcastle upon Tyne, NE1 3DQ   **Tel** (0191) 232 1980   **Fax** (0191) 232 3730   **DX** 61012

Plowden Buildings (William Lowe QC) Set No.238

Lombard House, Lombard Street, Newcastle upon Tyne, NE1 1AE
Tel (020) 7583 0808   **Fax** (020) 7583 5106   **DX** 0020 Chancery Lane

Head of Chambers	William Lowe QC
Tenants	30

Members

William Lowe QC (1972) (QC-1997) +
Catherine MacKenzie Smith (1968)
Elizabeth Hindmarsh (1974)
Christopher Williams (1981) +
Simon Wood (1981) +
Jeremy Freedman (1982) + †
Philip Kramer (1982) ‡
Lawrence McNulty (1985)
Catherine Foster (1986)
Peter Morton (1988)

Roger Cooper (1988)
Hari Menon (1989)
Michael James (1989)
Seamus Sweeney (1989)
Martin Haukeland (1988)
Kerry Cox (1990)
Andrew Crouch (1990)
Mark Watson-Gandy (1990) †
Claire Lindsay (1991)
Elizabeth Hodgson (1993)
Jayne Atkinson (1994)
Jane Woodwark (1995)

Edward Broome (1996)
John Falkenstein (1996)
Monica Whyte (1996)
Dominic Bayne (1997)
Samuel Faulks (1997)
Holly Pelham (1999)
Mark Armitage (1999)
Claire Guppy (2001)
John Lowe (1976) *
David Brook (1988) *
Ian West (1985) *

* Door Tenant + Recorder † Junior Counsel to the Crown ‡ Junior Counsel to the Crown/Deputy District Judge

The Chambers Plowden Buildings is amongst the leading personal injury sets both in London and in the North of England. Founded in 1980, chambers have expanded to 30 members who divide their time between court centres in the North such as Newcastle upon Tyne and the South East. Many members live on the North Eastern Circuit. Although chambers' core business is personal injury litigation for both claimants and defendants, members have significant specialisms in clinical and professional negligence, together with employment, commercial work and insolvency. Plowden Buildings is clerked exclusively from its Middle Temple premises but maintains fully staffed premises in Newcastle upon Tyne, directly under the famous Tyne Bridge. Four members of chambers are Recorders, and one is a Deputy District Judge. Plowden Buildings prides itself upon its excellent record of client care and its dynamic clerking team is always willing to discuss matters such as turn-around times for paperwork and of course, fees. All members are computer literate and instructions are accepted on disk and by email. Plowden Buildings relishes the opportunities provided by the fast-changing legal marketplace and further expansion is anticipated.

Work Undertaken Personal injury, clinical negligence, professional negligence, employment, commercial, insolvency and crime (general) are handled.

Publications Members of chambers include editors of *Charlesworth & Percy on Negligence* 10th edition, *European Current Law*, the *Thomson Tax Guide* and the author of *Watson-Gandy on The Law of Accountants*.

BAR A-Z ■ NEWCASTLE/NORTHAMPTON

Trinity Chambers (Toby Hedworth QC)

Set No.239

Trinity Chambers, 9-12 Trinity Chare, Quayside, Newcastle upon Tyne, NE1 3DF
Tel (0191) 232 1927 **Fax** (0191) 232 7975 **DX** 61185 (Newcastle)
Email info@trinitychambers.co.uk **Website** www.trinitychambers.co.uk

Head of Chambers	Toby Hedworth QC
Practice Director	Simon Stewart
Criminal Clerks	Sharon Robson
	Colin Hands
	Alisa Charlton
Civil and Family Clerks	Clare Thomas
	David Craigen
Tenants	38

Members

Toby Hedworth QC (1975) (QC-1996)
Brian Forster QC (1977) (QC-1999)
Paul Sloan QC (1981) (QC-2001)
Charles Kelly (1965)
Stephen Duffield (1969)
Christopher John Knox (1974)
Graham Duff (1976)
Christopher Vane (1976)
John Lowe (1976)
David Callan (1979)
John Wilkinson (1979)
Jacqueline Smart (1981)
James Richardson (1982)
Peter Walsh (1982)
Tim Spain (1983)
Rachel Hudson (1985)
Fiona McCrae (1987)
Paul Richardson (1986)
Caroline Goodwin (1988)
Shaun Routledge (1988)
Tim Gittins (1990)
Robert Adams (1993)
Michael Ditchfield (1993)
Katherine Dunn (1993)
Justin Gray (1993)
Rosalind Scott Bell (1993)
Nicholas Stonor (1993)
Jane Gilbert (1994)
Charles Holland (1994)
Sarah Woolrich (1994)
Gavin Doig (1995)
Paul Caulfield (1996)
Fiona Parkin (1998)
Michael Graham (1999)
Simon Goldberg (1999)
Rachel Hedworth (1999)
Angela Giovannini (2000)
Paul Currer (2000)

INVESTOR IN PEOPLE

The Chambers Trinity Chambers is a leading and progressive common law set in the North of England that has completed a major review of its services, procedures and client care standards. This determination to modernise has resulted in the award of the Bar Mark in April 2000, the Bar Council's kitemark of quality assurance. Trinity Chambers was the first set north of London and the fourth in the country to receive this acknowledgement of quality assurance and attention to client care. All members and staff of chambers believe in the importance of the Bar Mark accreditation and welcome feedback from clients as well as guidance on how services may be improved. Trinity Chambers was also awarded the Investors in People in 2000 which, for a profession that deals with people, is singularly appropriate. The barristers of Trinity Chambers are members of one or more of the seven practice groups: criminal law (three QCs and 19 Juniors); common law (one QC and 10 Juniors); family law (one QC and 11 Juniors); chancery and commercial (six Juniors); employment law (six Juniors); licensing law (one QC and 4 Juniors) and immigration (2 Juniors). Chambers have two specialist clerking teams (criminal law, civil and family law). Each practice group has a member who is prepared to discuss areas of work, specialisations and notable abilities. Fees are negotiated through the clerks from the outset. Chambers have an open charging policy. Urgent work receives special handling. As part of the determination to provide a high quality service, Trinity Chambers has made a significant investment in the provision of support facilities. Chambers have disabled access, video and audio conferencing facilities and the on-going seminar programme. Practice groups regularly give seminars, with the Law Society's CPD accreditation, that are free to clients; in 2001 they gave seminars in Newcastle and Middlesbrough at which over 400 solicitors attended. The set has its own Equality Policy, copies of which are available on request. Trinity Chambers understands the importance of being approachable and so welcomes inquires, of a general nature to the Practice Director, or of aspects of the barristers' work through the appropriate specialist clerks. Chambers brochure is also available on request.

▼NORTHAMPTON

■ Chartlands Chambers (Jane Page & Joy Pinkham)

Set No.240

3 St Giles Terrace, Northampton, NN1 2BN
Tel (01604) 603322 **Fax** (01604) 603388 **DX** 12408 Northampton

Head of Chambers	Jane Page
	Joy Pinkham
Senior Clerk	Andrew Davies
Tenants	12

Family and general common law service including matrimonial finance; cohabitation disputes; children; domestic violence; personal injury; employment; tort; contract; criminal law.

■ Clarendon Chambers

Set No.241

5 St. Giles Terrace, Northampton, NN1 2BN **Tel** (01604) 637245
Fax (01604) 633167 **DX** 12404 Northampton

Senior Clerk	Russell Burton
Tenants	41

Annexe of Clarendon Chambers, 7 Stone Buildings, Lincoln's Inn, London, WC2A 3SZ **Tel** (020) 7681 7681.
Out of Hours Tel (07971) 285796. All enquiries to London.

NORTHAMPTON/NORWICH ■ BAR A-Z

Northampton Chambers at 22 Albion Place (Maria Savvides)   Set No.242

22 Albion Place, Northampton, NN1 1UD
Tel (01604) 636271 **Fax** (01604) 232931 **DX** 12464
Email clerks@northamptonchambers.co.uk
Website www.northhamptonchambers.co.uk

Head of Chambers	Maria Savvides
Senior Clerk	James Edmonds
Tenants	9

Members

Maria Savvides (1986)	Terry Lynch (1989)	Sarah Briden (1999)
Pearl Willis (1986)	Peter Hollingworth (1993)	Michelle Christie (1999)
Clive Sutton (1987)	Barbara Williams (1995)	Moira Walsh (2000)

The Chambers Northampton Chambers is an established common law set with members specialising in the following areas: family; child care; ancillary relief; criminal litigation; personal injury; contract and tort; employment; landlord and tenant. For further information please contact the senior clerk or visit the set's website.

▼NORWICH

East Anglian Chambers (Roderick Newton)   Set No.243

East Anglian Chambers, 15 The Close, Norwich, NR1 4DZ
Tel (01603) 617351 **Fax** (01603) 751400 **DX** 5213
Email norwichchambers@ealaw.co.uk **Website** www.ealaw.co.uk

Head of Chambers	Roderick Newton
Senior Clerk	Stephen Collis
Administrator	Carol Bull (01473 254559)
Tenants	53

Members

Roderick Newton (1982)	Jane Davies (1983)	Alan Wheetman (1995)
John Akast (1968)	Lindsay Cox (1984)	David Wilson (1996)
John Wardlow (1971)	Janet Bettle (1985)	Fiona Baruah (1996)
Peter Wain (1972)	Anthony Bate (1987)	Ashley Thain (1996)
Stephen Franklin (1974)	Nicholas Elcombe (1987)	Saqib Rauf (1996)
Andrew Marsden (1975)	Jonathan Seely (1987)	Marc Cannatella (1997)
Caroline Bryant (1976)	Ray Smith (1991)	David Sunman (1997)
Celia Miller (1978)	Katharine Bundell (1991)	Stephen Goodfellow (1997)
David Pugh (1978)	Marika Bell (1991)	Alison Underhill (1997)
Timothy McLoughlin (1978)	Jeremy Dugdale (1992)	Andrew Shaw (1998)
Graham Sinclair (1979)	Carole Parry-Jones (1992)	Joanne Bradbury (1999)
John Hamey (1979)	Dominic Barratt (1992)	Neil Ashley (1999)
Anthony Kefford (1980)	Helen Gilbertson (1993)	Rebekah Korniej (1999)
John Brooke-Smith (1981)	Patricia Walsh (1993)	Ian Dyble (2000)
Simon Redmayne (1982)	Jacqui Hanlon (1994)	Christopher Pigram (2000)
Graham Parnell (1982)	Richard Kelly (1994)	Luke Brown (2000)
Michael Lane (1983)	Jude Durr (1995)	Richard O'Sullivan (2000)
Hugh Vass (1983)	Sally Freeman (1995)	

The Chambers For further information, please see full entry under East Anglian Chambers, Ipswich.

■ Octagon House Chambers (Guy Ayers & Andrew Lindquist)   Set No.244

Octagon House Chambers, 19 Colegate, Norwich, NR3 1AT **Tel** (01603) 623186 **Fax** (01603) 760519 **DX** 5249 Norwich-1

BAR A-Z ■ NOTTINGHAM

▼NOTTINGHAM

No. 1 High Pavement (John B Milmo QC) — Set No.245

No. 1 High Pavement, Nottingham, NG1 1HF
Tel (0115) 941 8218   Fax (0115) 941 8240   DX 10168 Nottingham
Website www.1highpavement.co.uk

Head of Chambers	John B Milmo QC
Clerk	David Duric
Tenants	41

Members

John B Milmo QC (1966) (QC-1984)
Peter Joyce QC (1968) (QC-1991)
John Warren QC (1968) (QC-1994)
Paul Mann QC (1980) (QC-2002)
Gregory Dickinson QC (1981) (QC-2002)
Peter Walmsley (1964)
Stuart Rafferty (1975)
Justin Wigoder (1977)
John Burgess (1978)
Guy Napthine (1979)
Robert Brown (1979)

Duncan Smith (1979)
Shaun Smith (1981)
Martin Elwick (1981)
Balraj Bhatia (1982)
Timothy Palmer (1982)
Adrian Reynolds (1982)
Nirmal Shant (1984)
Godfrey Napthine (1983)
Errol Ballentyne (1983)
Martin Hurst (1985)
Clive Stockwell (1988)
Robert Egbuna (1988)
Christopher Geeson (1989)
Richard Thatcher (1989)
James McNamara (1990)

Michael Evans (1988)
Michael Auty (1990)
Andrew Easteal (1990)
Avik Mukherjee (1990)
Paul King (1992)
Kate Hargreaves (1991)
Dawn Pritchard (1992)
Sarah Munro (1990)
Steven Coupland (1993)
Steven Gosnell (1995)
Sonal Ahya (1995)
Mark Achurch (1996)
Julia King (1998)
Abigail Joyce (1998)
Catherine McKeever (2000)

The Chambers Chambers specialise in crime to the exclusion of all other work. All members do a mixture of both prosecution and defence. The clerking team can assist with the specialism of individual members.

■ King Charles House Chambers (William Everard) — Set No.246

King Charles House, Standard Hill, Nottingham, NG1 6FX   Tel (0115) 941 8851   Fax (0115) 941 4169   DX 10042

Ropewalk Chambers (Ian McLaren QC) — Set No.247

24 The Ropewalk, Nottingham, NG1 5EF
Tel (0115) 947 2581   Fax (0115) 947 6532   DX 10060 Nottingham 17
Email clerks@ropewalk.co.uk   Website www.ropewalk.co.uk

Head of Chambers	Ian McLaren QC
Senior Clerk	David Austin
Clerk	Tony Hill
Tenants	37

Members

Ian McLaren QC (1962) (QC-1993)
William Woodward QC (1964) (QC-1985)
Richard Maxwell QC (1968) (QC-1988)
Anthony Goldstaub QC (1972) (QC-1992)
Robert Owen QC (1977) (QC-1996)
G M Jarand (1965)
Graham Machin (1965)
Richard Burns (1967)
Richard Swain (1969)
Antony Berrisford (1972)

Douglas Herbert (1973)
Stephen Beresford (1976)
Simon Gash (1977)
Alison Hampton (1977)
Simon Beard (1980)
Jayne Adams (1982)
Rosalind Coe (1983)
Richard Hedley (1983)
Soofi Din (1984)
Dominic Nolan (1985)
Bryony Clark (1985)
Andrew Prestwich (1986)
Patrick Limb (1987)
Richard Seabrook (1987)

Philip Turton (1989)
Toby Stewart (1989)
Jinder Boora (1990)
Andrew McNamara (1992)
Jonathan Mitchell (1992)
Jason Cox (1992)
Deborah Davies (1993)
Richard Gregory (1993)
Andrew Hogan (1996)
Mark Diggle (1996)
Judith Butler (1997)
Nick Blake (1997)
Shilpa Shah (1998)

The Chambers A long established set which has grown to become one of the largest purely civil sets outside London. Chambers undertake a broad range of general common law, commercial, planning and environmental, employment and human rights cases. Enhanced by a competitive pricing policy, punctual return of paperwork and the utilisation of current information technology, members of chambers offer a specialist independent advisory and advocacy referral service. Chambers are strategically positioned, both regionally and nationally, to offer the services of individuals or teams with expertise of the highest calibre.

Work Undertaken

Personal Injury & Clinical Negligence The personal injury and clinical negligence specialist group covers all areas including industrial and insidious disease (asbestos-induced, asthma, cancer, dermatitis, poisoning, radiation, repetitive strain injury, stress at work, vibration white finger amongst others); every aspect of clinical negligence litigation; disaster; employers' liability; product liability; road traffic; sports injuries; health and safety at work and Compensation Recovery Unit appeals to the Medical Appeal Tribunal.

Business & Property Work undertaken by the business and property group includes commercial (banking, competition, consumer credit and protection, corporate finance and sale of goods); professional negligence (legal, financial and negligence within the building, engineering and surveying professions); chancery (boundaries, conveyancing, easements, inheritance, probate, wills and trusts); building and construction; company; engineering; intellectual property; landlord and tenant (commercial, residential, agricultural and housing) and partnership.

Planning & Environment The planning and environment group offers advice and representation in the following areas: administrative; compulsory purchase; heritage; judicial review; lands tribunal; local government; nature conservation; pollution; rating and planning enquiries.

Employment The work of the employment practice group covers cases involving wrongful and unfair dismissal; D.D.A; discrimination; European related matters; human rights; restrictive covenants; trade secrets; trade unions and TUPE.

■ St. Mary's Chambers Family Law Chambers (Nigel B Page)   Set No.248
50 High Pavement, Nottingham, NG1 1HW   **Tel** (0115) 950 3503   **Fax** (0115) 958 3060   **DX** 10036

▼OXFORD

Harcourt Chambers (June Rodgers)   Set No.249

Churchill House, 3 St. Aldates Courtyard, St. Aldates, Oxford, OX1 1BA
Tel (01865) 791559   **Fax** (01865) 791585   **DX** 96453 Oxford 4
Email clerks@harcourtchambers.law.co.uk
Website www.harcourtchambers.law.co.uk

Head of Chambers	June Rodgers
Senior Clerk	Brian Wheeler
Tenants	27

Members

June Rodgers (1971)
Roger Evans (1970)
Benedict Sefi (1972)
John Dixon (1975)
Gavyn Arthur (1975)
Stephen Barstow (1976)
Jonathan Baker QC (1978) (QC-2001)
Alicia Collinson (1982)
Christopher Frazer (1983)
Frances Judd (1984)
Edward Hess (1985)
Matthew Brett (1987)
Sarah Gibbons (1987)
Fiona Hay (1989)
Piers Pressdee (1991)
Sara Granshaw (1991)
Sally Max (1991)
Rohan Auld (1992)
Louise Potter (1993)
John Vater (1995)
Nicholas Goodwin (1995)
Aidan Vine (1995)
Jonathan Sampson (1997)
Oliver Wright (1998)
Andrew Leong (1998)
Edward Kirkwood (1999)
Helen Little (1999)

HARCOURT CHAMBERS
LONDON OXFORD

The Chambers Based in London and Oxford, Harcourt Chambers provides a friendly and efficient advisory and advocacy service within five specialist practice groups: family, business, property, local government and personal injury. Individual members of chambers have additional areas of personal specialisation, particularly in election law, judicial review, planning, media, criminal and ecclesiastical law.

BAR A-Z ■ OXFORD/PETERBOROUGH

King's Bench Chambers (Roger Ellis QC)

Set No.250

King's Bench Chambers, 32 Beaumont St., Oxford, OX1 2NP
Tel (01865) 311066 **Fax** (01865) 311077 **DX** 4318 Oxford
Email clerks@13kbw.co.uk **Website** www.13kbw.co.uk

Head of Chambers	Roger Ellis QC
Senior Clerk	Kevin Kelly
Chambers Director	Stephen Rogers
Chambers Adminstrator	Penny McFall
Tenants	45

13 KBW

Members

Roger Ellis QC (1962) (QC-1996)
Graeme Williams QC (1959) (QC-1983)
Julian Baughan QC (1967) (QC-1990)
David Ashton (1962)
Alexander Dawson (1969)
Anthony McGeorge (1969)
Robert Lamb (1973)
David Richardson (1973)
Deirdre Goodwin (1974)
Simon Hughes MP (1974)
Paul W Reid (1975)
David Bright (1976)
Simon Draycott QC (1977) (QC-2002)
Nigel Daly (1979)
Nicholas Syfret (1979)
Andrew Glennie (1982)

Andrew Pote (1983)
Jonathan Coode (1984)
Neil Vickery (1985)
Neil Moore (1986)
Mark Maitland-Jones (1986) MA (Edinburgh)
Arthur Blake (1988)
Sinclair Cramsie (1988)
Adrian Higgins (1990)
Edmund Walters (1991)
Vivian Walters (1991)
Hugh Williams (1992)
Deshpal Singh Panesar (1993)
Peter Coombe (1993) BA (Oxon)
Gabriel Buttimore (1993) LLB (East Anglia)
Paul Mitchell (1994) BA (York)
Susan Chan (1994)
Rachel Drake (1995)

Lucy Owens (1997) LLB (Kingston)
Matthew White (1997)
Louise McCabe (1997)
Thomas Payne (1998) BA (Oxon) LLM (research) (Birmingham)
Clare Harrington (1998) LLM (LSE)
Christopher Mann (1998) BA (Oxon)
Julie Hopkins (1999) BA (Oxon)
Sarah Keogh (1999)
Sophie Eloquin (2000)
Peter Ross (2000) PhD (Pontifical Gregorian University)
John Simmons (2000) LLB (Oxon)
Matthew Walsh (2000)

See 13 King's Bench Walk, Temple, London EC4Y 7EN for a full listing of chambers.

▼PETERBOROUGH

Fenners Chambers (Paul Hollow)

Set No.251

Fenners Chambers, 8-12 Priestgate, Peterborough, PE1 1JA
Tel (01733) 562030 **Fax** (01733) 343660 **DX** 12314 Peterborough 1
Email clerks@fennerschambers.co.uk **Website** www.fennerschambers.co.uk

Head of Chambers	Paul Hollow
Tenants	34

Members

Paul Hollow (1981)(Deputy D.J.)
Oliver Sells QC (1972) (QC-1995) *
Geraint Jones (1972)
Andrew Gore (1973)
Lindsay Davies (1975) +
Susan Espley (1976)
Simon Tattersall (1977) (Deputy D.J.)
Paul Leigh-Morgan (1978)
T.C.E. Brown (1980)
Andrew Gordon-Saker (1981)(Deputy Costs Judge)
Jane Bennington (1981)

Martin Collier (1982)
Liza Gordon-Saker (1982)
Meryl Hughes (1987)
George Foxwell (1987)
Robin Chaudhuri (1988) (Deputy D.J.)
Alasdair Wilson (1988)
Clive Pithers (1989)
Jeffrey Deegan (1989)
Sally Hobson (1991)
Caroline Horton (1993)
Michael Proctor (1993)
Katharine Ferguson (1995)

William Josling (1995)
Daniel Pitt (1995)
Terence Vaughan (1996)
Giles Surman (1997) *
Mike Magee (1997)
Roderick Spinks (1997)
George Keightley (1997)
Alasdair Foster (1998)
Stuart Lockhart (1998)
Martin Kingerley (1999)
Daniel Owen (1999)
Beth Cook (2000)
Guy Sims (2000)

* Door Tenant + Recorder

The Chambers Please refer to the main entry under Cambridge.

Regency Chambers — Set No.252
Cathedral Square, Peterborough, PE1 1XW **Tel** (01733) 315215 **Fax** (01733) 315851 **DX** 12349 Peterborough 1

King's Bench Chambers — Set No.253
King's Bench Chambers, 115 North Hill, Plymouth, PL4 8JY **Tel** (01752) 221551 **Fax** (01752) 664379

▼PORTSMOUTH

Guildhall Chambers Portsmouth (Lee Young) — Set No.254
Prudential Buildings, 16 Guildhall Walk, Portsmouth, PO1 2DE
Tel (023) 9275 2400 **Fax** (023) 9275 3100 **DX** 2225 Portsmouth 1

Head of Chambers	Lee Young
Senior Clerk	Tristan Thwaites (02392) 752400
Junior Clerk	Jodi McGuire (02392) 752400
Tenants	16

Members

Lee Young (1991)
Peter Griffith (1964)
Peter Fortune (1978)
John Sabine (1979)
Richard Colbey (1984)
Stuart Ellacott (1989)
Sheila Taurah (1991)
Lisa England (1992)
Lincoln Brookes (1992)
Yasmin Hall (1993)
Tim Concannon (1993)
Martyn Booth (1996)
James Britton (1996)
Richard Withey (1996)
Robyn Day (1997)
John Atwill (1997) *
Roderick Jones (1983) *
Edo de Vries (Ret.) (1969) †

* Door Tenant † Associate Member

The Chambers An established common law set of chambers handling a wide range of law including landlord and tenant, personal injury, professional negligence, family and crime.

Portsmouth Barristers' Chambers (Andrew Parsons) — Set No.255
Victory House, 7 Bellevue Terrace, Portsmouth, PO5 3AT
Tel (023) 9283 1292 **Fax** (023) 9229 1262 **DX** 2239 Portsmouth
Email clerks@portsmouthbar.com **Website** www.portsmouthbar.com

Head of Chambers	Andrew Parsons
Senior Clerk	Jackie Morrison
Tenants	6

The Chambers Chambers undertake predominantly civil work and aim to provide a modern, high quality, fast, friendly and efficient service. A brochure is available on request.

Work Undertaken

Business & Commerce Arbitration, carriage of goods, contract, company, construction and partnership.
Family & Matrimonial Ancillary relief.
Negligence Especially professional negligence.
Property & Finance Banking, consumer credit, financial services, insolvency, land law, mortgages, pensions, tax and trusts.

BAR A-Z ■ PRESTON/SOUTHAMPTON

▼PRESTON

15 Winckley Square (R Stephen Dodds) — Set No.256

15 Winckley Square, Preston, PR1 3JJ
Tel (01772) 252828 **Fax** (01772) 258520 **DX** 17110 Preston 1
Email clerks@15winckleysq.co.uk **Website** www.15winckleysq.co.uk

Head of Chambers	R Stephen Dodds
Senior Clerk	Michael Jones
Tenants	36

Members

- R Stephen Dodds (1976)
- Roger M Baldwin (1969)
- Simon Newell (1973)
- Kenneth Hind (1973)
- Robert Crawford (1976)
- P Nicholas D Kennedy (1977)
- Timothy G White (1978)
- Richard A Haworth (1978)
- David J Kenny (1982)
- Jane E Cross (1982)
- Anthony Cross (1982)
- Paul Hart (1982)
- Charles Brown (1982)
- Paul Hague (1983)
- John Woodward (1984)
- Richard M Hunt (1985)
- D Mark Stuart (1985)
- Richard J Bennett (1986)
- Bruce Henry (1988)
- Peter J Anderson (1988)
- Kathryn Johnson (1989)
- Samantha Bowcock (1990)
- Michael Whyatt (1992)
- Louise Harvey (1991)
- Julie Taylor (1992)
- Fraser Livesey (1992)
- Jonathan Buchan (1994)
- Martin Hackett (1994)
- Lee Blakey (1995)
- Paul Davis (1996)
- Jacob Dyer (1995)
- Paul Gillott (1996)
- Zabeda Maqsood (1996)
- Prudence Beever (2000)
- Saima Bhat (1999)
- Huw Dixon (1999)

The Chambers A medium-sized set, seeking to provide a comprehensive service to solicitor clients both in private and institutional practice throughout the town, the county and beyond into Cumbria, Manchester and Merseyside. Several tenants are members of the Family Law Bar Association.

Work Undertaken All common law work, with particular emphasis and experience in all areas of family work; crime; contract; personal and industrial injury; licensing; planning; landlord and tenant; employment law. Work on a Direct Access basis is accepted. Expanding chancery and associated case types.

▼SOUTHAMPTON

■ 17 Carlton Crescent (Jeremy S Gibbons QC) — Set No.257

17 Carlton Crescent, Southampton, SO15 2XR **Tel** (023) 8032 0320/2003 **Fax** (023) 8032 0321 **DX** 96875 Southampton 10

Eighteen Carlton Crescent (Martin Blount) — Set No.258

Eighteen Carlton Crescent, Southampton, SO15 2ET
Tel (023) 8063 9001 **Fax** (023) 8033 9625 **DX** 96877 Southampton
Email clerks@18carltoncrescent.co.uk **Website** www.18carltoncrescent.co.uk

Head of Chambers	Martin Blount
Senior Clerk	Lynda Knight
	Paul Cooke
Tenants	22

Members

- Andrew Massey (1969)
- Ashley Ailes (1975)
- Gary Fawcett (1975)
- Charles Cochand (1978)
- Angus Robertson (1978)
- Simon Lillington (1980)
- Richard Egleton (1981)
- Martin Blount (1982)
- Elizabeth Manuel (1987)
- Andrew Houston (1989)
- Omar Malik (1990)
- Roderick Blain (1991)
- Christine Munks (1991)
- Imogen Robins (1991)
- Peter Glenser (1993)
- Sally Carter (1994)
- Richard Hall (1995)
- Peter Asteris (1996)
- Timothy Dracass (1998)
- Rachel Robertson (1998)
- Keely Harvey (1999)
- Rachael Goodall (2000)
- Guy Boney QC (1968) (QC-1990) *
- Helene Pines Richman (1992) *

* Door Tenant

Work Undertaken General common law, including personal injury; criminal law; family and matrimonial law, including child care law, wardship and matrimonial property; landlord and tenant; planning; employment; commercial law; licensing; professional negligence; Chancery.

College Chambers (Robin Belben)

Set No.259

College Chambers, 19 Carlton Crescent, Southampton, SO1 2ET
Tel (023) 8023 0338 **Fax** (023) 8023 0376 **DX** 38533 (Southampton 3)

Head of Chambers	Robin Belben
Senior Clerk	Wayne Effeny
Tenants	19

Members

Robin Belben (1969)
Kenneth Pain (1969)
Derek Marshall (1980)
Douglas Taylor (1981)
Mark Courtney Stewart (1989)
Anthony Hand (1989)
Jessica Habel (1991)
Gary Self (1991)
Catherine Breslin (1990)
Daniel Nother (1994)
Carol Davies (1995)
Andrew Lorie (1996)
Baljinder Bath (1996)
Graeme Harrison (1997)
Amanda Gillett (1998)
Anil Patil (1999)
Andrew Bond (1999)
Katherine Huyton (1999)
Stuart McGhee (2000)

Work Undertaken General common law including family and matrimonial, childcare law, wardship, matrimonial property and cohabitee disputes; personal injury; contract; tort; landlord and tenant; employment; immigration; licensing; professional and medical negligence; commercial law; chancery; land law (including boundary disputes); criminal law. Instructing solicitors are always welcome to have an informal discussion with the clerks.

▼SWANSEA

Iscoed Chambers (Elwen Mair Evans QC)

Set No.260

Iscoed Chambers, 86 St Helen's Rd, Swansea, SA1 4BQ **Tel** (01792) 652988/9 **Fax** (01792) 458089 **DX** 39554 Swansea

Pendragon Chambers (Wayne Beard)

Set No.261

124 Walter Road, Swansea, SA1 5RG
Tel (01792) 411188 **Fax** (01792) 411189 **DX** 39572 Swansea
Email clerks@pendragonchambers.fsnet.co.uk

Head of Chambers	Wayne Beard
Senior Clerk	Gwyn Davies
Junior Clerk	Nolan Goodman
Tenants	11

Members

Wayne Beard (1991)
Huw Rees Davies (1982)
Gerard Heap (1985)
Andrew David (1986)
John Brooks (1990)
Sara Rudman (1992)
Gareth Thomas (1993)
Rebecca Mann (1995)
Kathryn McConnochie (1997)
Susan Jenkins (1998)
Christopher Howells (1999)
Nicholas Bourne (1976) *
Donald Anderson MP (1964) *

* Door Tenant

The Chambers Progressive set established in 1996. Predominantly civil and family chambers.

Work Undertaken Employment, personal injury, medical negligence, landlord and tenant, local authority, environmental, planning, agricultural holdings, general chancery, revenue, family and crime.

Publications Members have published articles for various periodicals including *Taxation*, the *Tax Journal*, and *Financial Advisor*. Kathryn McConnochie is extensively published in medical journals and other medical publications.

Recruitment Tenancy and pupillage applications to Head of Chambers with detailed CV.

BAR A-Z — SWINDON/TAUNTON/WINCHESTER

▼SWINDON

■ Pump Court Chambers (Christopher Harvey Clark QC) — Set No.262
5 Temple Chambers, Temple Street, Swindon, SN1 1SQ
Tel (01793) 539899 **Fax** (01793) 539866 **DX** 38639 Swindon 2
Email clerks@3pumpcourt.com **Website** www.3pumpcourt.com

Head of Chambers	Christopher Harvey Clark QC
Senior Clerk	David Barber
Swindon Clerk	Dot Hewitt
Tenants	60

An established set undertaking a wide variety of work. Members practise within specialist teams, for civil, family and all aspects of criminal law. Chambers are also at London and Winchester.

▼TAUNTON

■ 2HG Chambers (Jonathan Dingle & Harry Hodgkin) — Set No.263
2 Heron Gate, Taunton Riverside, Taunton, TA1 2LR **Tel** (0845) 083 3000 **Fax** (01823) 083 3001 **DX** 97188 Taunton Blackbrook

■ South Western Chambers (Brian Lett) — Set No.264
12 Middle Street, Taunton, TA1 1SH **Tel** (01823) 331919 **Fax** (01823) 330553 **DX** 32146 (Taunton)

▼WINCHESTER

■ Pump Court Chambers (Christopher Harvey Clark QC) — Set No.265
31 Southgate Street, Winchester, SO23 9EB
Tel (01962) 868161 **Fax** (01962) 867645 **DX** 2514
Email clerks@3pumpcourt.com **Website** www.3pumpcourt.com

Head of Chambers	Christopher Harvey Clark QC
Senior Clerk	David Barber
Tenants	60

Members

- Christopher Harvey Clark QC (1969) (QC-1989)
- Nigel Pascoe QC (1966) (QC-1988)
- Guy Boney QC (1968) (QC-1990)
- Peter Birts QC (1968) (QC-1990)
- Jane Miller QC (1979) (QC-2000)
- Oba Nsugbe QC (1985) (QC-2002)
- Geoffrey Still (1966)
- Stewart Patterson (1967)
- Adam Pearson (1969)
- Frank Moat (1970)
- Giles Harrap (1971)
- Frank Abbott (1972)
- Charles Parry (1973)
- Michael Butt (1974)
- John Ker-Reid (1974)
- Charles Gabb (1975)
- Andrew Barnett (1977)
- Michael Dineen (1977)
- Jonathan Swift (1977)
- Julie MacKenzie (1978)
- Stephen Jones (1978)
- Timothy O'Flynn (1979)
- Robert Hill (1980)
- Miranda Allardice (1982)
- Damien Lochrane (1983)
- Sandra Stanfield (1984)
- Matthew Scott (1985)
- Desmond Bloom-Davies (1986)
- Mark Hill (1987)
- Anne Waddington (1988)
- Hugh Travers (1988)
- Philip Warren (1988)
- Leslie Samuels (1989)
- Edward Boydell (1989)
- Justin Gau (1989)
- Anthony Akiwumi (1989)
- Susan Evans (1989)
- Helen Khan (1990)
- Penelope Howe (1991)
- Geoffrey Kelly (1992)
- James Newton-Price (1992)
- Patricia Poyer-Sleeman (1992)
- Mark Ruffell (1992)
- Elizabeth Gunther (1993)
- Oliver Peirson (1993)
- Marcus Tregilgas-Davey (1993)
- Helen Fields (1993)
- Luke Blackburn (1993)
- Mark Ashley (1993)
- Roderick Moore (1993)
- Jonathan Simpson (1993)
- Richard Ferry-Swainson (1994)
- Robert Pawson (1994)
- Arabella Grundy (1995)
- Mark Dubbery (1996)
- Ruth Arlow (1997)
- Andrew Grime (1997)
- Anne Ward (1997)
- Louise de Rozarieux (1999)
- Richard Tutt (2000)

The Chambers An established set undertaking a wide variety of work, with members working in specialist teams. DPA and Bar Direct work accepted.
Associated Chambers 3 Pump Court, London; Temple Street, Swindon.

Work Undertaken
Main Areas Family; employment; inheritance; property; PI; crime.

Specialisations Childcare; matrimonial finance; all areas of crime; professional and clinical negligence; contract; ecclesiastical law; Inheritance Act; courts martial; environment; landlord and tenant; taxation appeals.

Recruitment Tenancy applications should be sent to Head of the Tenancy Committee. Pupillage applications should be made via OLPAS.

▼YORK

■ York Chambers (Aidan Marron QC) — Set No.266
14 Toft Green, York, YO1 6JT **Tel** (01904) 620048 **Fax** (01904) 610056 **DX** 65517 York 7

INDEX OF PRACTISING BARRISTERS

CHAMBERS UK 2002–2003

BARRISTERS ■ INDEX

Aaron, Sam (1986) Set 54
Aaronberg, David (1981) Set 63
Aaronson, Graham (1966) (QC-1982) Set 122 Profile p.1355
Abberley, Stephen (2000) Set 248
Abberton, David (1994) Set 178
Abbott, Frank (1972) Sets 121, 262, 265
Abell, Anthony (1977) Set 4 Profile p.1355
Aberavon, The Rt Hon Lord Morris of (1954) (QC-1973) Set 4
Abrahams, James (1997) Set 95
Ace, Richard (1993) Set 157
Acheson, Ian (1992) Set 36
Achurch, Mark (1996) Set 245
Ackland, Sacha (1998) Set 145
Acland, Piers (1993) Set 134 Profile p.1355
Acton, J (1995) Set 220
Acton, Stephen (1977) Set 107
Acton Davis, Jonathan (1977) (QC-1996) Set 3 Profile p.1355
Adair, Stuart (1995) Set 103
Adam, Tom (1991) Set 14
Adams, Christopher (1986) Set 161
Adams, Guy (1989) Set 169
Adams, Jamie (1978) Set 237
Adams, Jayne (1982) Set 247 Profile p.1355
Adams, John (1984) Set 67
Adams, Richard (1999) Set 158
Adams, Robert (1993) Set 239
Adamson, Ben (1999) Set 24
Adamson, Dominic (1997) Set 145
Adamson, Louisa (1994) Set 172
Adamyk, Simon (1991) Set 98
Addezio, Mario (1971) Set 55
Addison, Paul (1987) Set 149
Addy, Caroline (1991) Set 15 Profile p.1355
Addy, Catherine (1998) Set 87
Adebayo, Tayo (1989) Set 4
Adedeji, Yinka (1997) Set 78
Adewale, R A S (1996) Set 78
Adjei, Cyril (1995) Set 115
Adkin, James (1992) Set 237
Adkin, Jonathan (1997) Set 131
Adkin, Tana (1992) Set 149
Adkins, Richard (1982) (QC-1995) Set 133 Profile p.1355
Adlard, William (1978) Set 59
Aeberli, Peter (1990) Set 39 Profile p.1355
Afeeva, Mark (1997) Set 88
Agbamu, Alexander (1988) Set 117
Ageros, James (1990) Set 4 Profile p.1355
Ageros, Justin (1993) Set 113
Aggrey-Orleans, Kweku (1998) Set 82
Agha, Siza (1994) Set 25
Agnello, Raquel (1986) Set 141 Profile p.1355
Agnew, Christine (1992) Set 4
Agnini, Julia (1999) Set 172
Aherne, Catherine (1997) Set 144
Ahluwalia, Navi (2001) Set 150
Ahmad, Aysha (1996) Set 101
Ahmad, Nadeem (1996) Set 34
Ahmad, Zubair (1995) Set 108
Ahmed, Amina (1996) Set 127
Ahmed, Farooq (1983) Sets 5, 221
Ahmed, Ishfaq (1999) Set 142
Ahmed, Jacqueline (1988) Set 184
Ahya, Sonal (1995) Set 245
Ailes, Ashley (1975) Set 258
Aina, Benjamin (1987) Set 147

Ainger, David (1961) Set 106 Profile p.1355
Ainley, Nicholas (1973) Set 34
Ainsworth, Mark (1992) Set 226
Airey, Simon (1989) Set 93
Aitken, John Russell (1984) Set 237
Akast, John (1968) Sets 181, 187, 243
Akenhead, Robert (1972) (QC-1989) Set 3 Profile p.1355
Akin, Barrie (1976) Set 57
Akinjide, Richard (1956) Set 79
Akinsanya, Stephen (1993) Set 34
Akiwumi, Anthony (1989) Sets 121, 262, 265
Akka, Lawrence (1991) Set 35
Akuwudike, Emma (1992) Set 53
Alban-Lloyd, Nan (1988) Set 72
Albutt, Ian (1981) Set 52 Profile p.1355
Alcock, Peter (1995) Sets 120, 212
Alderson, Pippa (1993) Set 84
Aldous, Charles (1967) (QC-1985) Set 87 Profile p.1356
Aldous, Grahame (1979) Set 50
Aldous, Robert (1985) Set 244
Aldred, Mark (1996) Set 68
Aldridge, James (1987) Set 143
Aldridge, James (1994) Set 87
Aleeson, Warwick (1994) Set 43
Alesbury, Alun (1974) Set 89
Alexander, Andrew (1999) Set 84
Alexander, Daniel (1988) Set 95 Profile p.1356
Alexander, David (1987) Set 133
Alexander, Dominic (1995) Set 18
Alford, Robert (1970) Set 184
Algazy, Jacques (1980) Set 20
Al'Hassan, Khadim (1993) Set 193
Ali, Huma (1997) Set 155
Ali, Ishtiyaq (1996) Set 240
Ali, Zafar (1994) Set 18
Aliker, Phillip (1990) Set 117
Allan, Colin (1971) Set 53
Allan, David (1998) Set 5
Allan, David (1974) (QC-1995) Sets 101, 213 Profile p.1356
Allan, Kirsten (1998) Set 73
Allan, Monique (1986) Set 86
Allardice, Miranda (1982) Sets 121, 262, 265 Profile p.1356
Alldis, C (1970) Set 210
Allen, Andrew (1995) Set 21
Allen, Darryl (1995) Set 226
Allen, David (1977) Set 77
Allen, James H (1973) (QC-1995) Set 193 Profile p.1356
Allen, Lucianne (1998) Set 155
Allen, Mark (1981) Set 174 Profile p.1356
Allen, Neil (1999) Set 232
Allen, Nicholas (1995) Set 7
Allen, Robin (1974) (QC-1995) Set 20 Profile p.1356
Allen, Scott (2000) Set 92
Allen, Thomas (1995) Set 211
Allen, Tom (1994) Set 114
Allen, Zoĺ (1999) Set 221
Alliott, George (1981) Sets 60, 135
Allison, David (1998) Set 133
Allman, Marisa (1998) Set 193
Allsop, Julian (1999) Set 168
Alomo, Richard (1990) Set 56
Al-Qasem, Anis (1959) Set 110
Alt, Jane (1984) Set 73
Altaras, David (1969) Set 9
Altham, Robert (1993) Set 208
Althaus, Justin (1988) Set 129

Altman, Brian (1981) Set 4 Profile p.1356
Alty, Andrew (1992) Set 217
Amakye, Grace (1983) Set 149
Amaouche, Sassa-Ann (1996) Set 46
Ambrose, Clare (1992) Set 35
Ambrose, Euan (1992) Set 166
Ames, Geoffrey (1976) Set 7
Amesu, Sharon (1998) Set 219
Amiraftabi, Roshi (1993) Set 63
Amis, Christopher (1991) Set 71
Amlot, Roy (1963) (QC-1989) Set 75 Profile p.1356
Amor, Christopher (1984) Set 43
Amos, Tim (1987) Set 123 Profile p.1356
Ancliffe, Shiva (1991) Set 127
Anderson, Brendan (1985) Set 178
Anderson, Clive (1976) Set 74
Anderson, Colin J D (1973) Set 9
Anderson, David (1985) (QC-1999) Set 14 Profile p.1356
Anderson, John (1989) Set 126
Anderson, Julie (1993) Set 86
Anderson, Kathleen (1997) Set 74
Anderson, Lesley (1989) Sets 191, 222 Profile p.1357
Anderson, Mark (1983) Set 156 Profile p.1357
Anderson, Nicholas (1995) Set 70
Anderson, Peter J (1988) Set 256
Anderson, Robert (1986) Set 12 Profile p.1357
Anderson, Rupert (1981) Set 90 Profile p.1357
Anderson, S (1993) Set 234
Anderson, Simon (1997) Set 163
Anderson MP, Donald (1964) Set 261
Andreae-Jones, William (1965) (QC-1984) Sets 129, 154
Andrew, Seamus (1991) Set 217
Andrews, Claire (1979) Set 49 Profile p.1357
Andrews, Geraldine (1981) (QC-2001) Set 31 Profile p.1357
Andrews, Peter (1970) (QC-1991) Sets 143, 156
Andrews, Philip (1977) Set 232 Profile p.1357
Andrews, Samuel (1991) Set 198
Anelay, Richard (1970) (QC-1993) Set 70 Profile p.1357
Angiolini, Mario (2000) Set 90
Angus, Tracey (1991) Set 138
Anning, Michael (1990) Set 159
Anning, Sara (1995) Set 195
Ansell, Rachel (1995) Set 118
Antelme, Alexander (1993) Set 22
Anthony, Peter (1981) Set 160
Anthony, Robert (1979) Set 19
Antrobus, Simon (1995) Sets 190, 191, 222 Profile p.1357
Anyadike-Danes, Monya (1980) Set 146
ap Mihangel, Sion (1998) Set 179
Apfel, Freddy (1986) Set 197
Appleby, Elizabeth (1965) (QC-1979) Set 54
Apthorp, Charles (1983) Set 34
Arbuthnot MP, Rt Hon James (1975) Set 106
Archer, Christopher (1996) Set 127
Archer, Deborah (1989) Set 184
Archer, Stephen (1979) Set 82 Profile p.1357
Arden, Andrew (1974) (QC-1991) Set 2 Profile p.1357
Arden, Peter (1983) Sets 29, 189, 235 Profile p.1358
Arentsen, Andrew (1995) Set 175
Argles, Robert (1965) Set 102

Argyle, Brian (1972) Set 43
Argyropoulos, Kyriakos (1991) Set 63
Aris, Jason (1998) Set 157
Arkhurst, Reginald (1984) Set 73
Arkush, Jonathan (1977) Set 141
Arlidge, Anthony (1962) (QC-1981) Set 126 Profile p.1358
Arlow, Ruth (1997) Sets 121, 262, 265
Armitage, Lindy (1985) Set 195
Armitage, Mark (1999) Sets 116, 238
Armstrong, Dean (1985) Set 75 Profile p.1358
Armstrong, Douglas (1990) Set 159
Armstrong, Grant (1978) Set 120
Armstrong, Grant (1978) Set 212
Armstrong, Kester (1982) Set 234 Profile p.1358
Armstrong, Nicholas (2001) Set 150
Armstrong, Stuart (1995) Set 8
Arney, James (1992) Set 145
Arnfield, Robert (1996) Set 106
Arnold, Mark (1989) Set 133 Profile p.1358
Arnold, Peter (1972) Set 156
Arnold, Richard (1985) (QC-2000) Sets 134, 134 Profile p.1358
Arran, Graham (1969) Set 43
Arthur, Gavyn (1975) Sets 62, 249
Ascherson, Isobel (1990) Set 36
Ascroft, Richard (1995) Set 166 Profile p.1358
Ash, Brian (1975) (QC-1990) Set 54 Profile p.1358
Ash, Simon (1999) Set 9
Ashcroft, Michael (1997) Set 35
Ashe, Michael (1971) (QC-1994) Set 140
Ashford-Thom, Ian (1977) Set 145
Ashley, Mark (1993) Sets 121, 262, 265
Ashley, Neil (1999) Sets 181, 187, 243
Ashley-Norman, Jonathan (1989) Set 4 Profile p.1358
Ashman, Peter M (1985) Set 182
Ashmole, Timothy (1992) Set 73
Ashton, David (1962) Sets 83, 250
Ashwell, Paul (1977) Set 164
Ashworth, Fiona (1988) Sets 191, 222 Profile p.1358
Ashworth, Jonathan (1998) Set 195
Ashworth, Lance (1987) Sets 60, 161 Profile p.1358
Ashworth, Piers (1956) (QC-1973) Set 135
Asif, Jalil (1988) Set 92 Profile p.1359
Askham, Nigel (1973) Set 264
Askins, Nicholas (1989) Set 163
Aspden, Gordon (1988) Set 5
Aspinall, John (1975) (QC-1995) Set 111
Asplin, Sarah J (1984) (QC-2002) Set 136 Profile p.1359
Asprey, Nicholas (1969) Set 131
Astaniotis, Katie (1985) Set 52
Astbury, Joanne (1989) Set 195
Astbury, Philip (1999) Set 209
Asteris, Peter (1996) Set 258
Aston, Maurice (1982) Set 114
Astor, Philip (1989) Set 145
Atchley, Richard (1977) Set 124
Atherton, Peter (1975) Set 217
Atherton, Sally (1987) Set 17
Atherton, Stephen (1989) Set 133 Profile p.1359
Atkins, Charles (1975) Set 7

Atkins, Richard (1989) Set 155
Atkins, Siward (1995) Set 87
Atkins, Victoria (1998) Set 149
Atkinson, Carol (1985) Set 21
Atkinson, Duncan (1990) Set 75
Atkinson, Jayne (1994) Sets 116, 238
Atkinson, Nicholas (1971) (QC-1991) Set 59 Profile p.1359
Atkinson, Paul (1978) Set 202
Atkinson, Timothy (1988) Set 15
Atreya, Navita (1999) Set 127
Attwood, John (1989) Set 158
Attwooll, Christopher (1980) Sets 80, 190
Atwill, John (1997) Sets 254, 255
Aubrey, David (1974) (QC-1998) Set 208
Aubrey, David J M (1976) (QC-1996) Set 176 Profile p.1359
Auburn, Jonathan (1999) Set 54
Auckland, E (1995) Set 196
Audland, Willliam (1992) Set 82
Auld, Charles (1980) Set 169
Auld, Rohan (1992) Sets 62, 249
Auld, Stephen (1979) (QC-1999) Set 32
Austin, Jonathan (1991) Set 174
Austin-Smith, James (1999) Set 71
Austin-Smith, Michael (1969) (QC-1990) Set 36 Profile p.1359
Auty, Michael (1990) Set 245
Awadalla, Katherine (1998) Set 66
Axon, Andrew (1992) Set 195
Ayers, Guy (1979) Set 244 Profile p.1359
Aylen, Walter (1962) (QC-1983) Set 63
Aylett, Crispin (1985) Set 124
Aylett, Kenneth (1972) Set 63
Ayliffe, James (1987) Set 153 Profile p.1359
Ayling, Judith (1998) Set 38
Ayling, Tracy (1983) Set 4
Aylwin, Christopher (1970) Set 111
Ayo-Ojo, Angela (1999) Set 63
Ayres, Andrew (1996) Set 87
Azhar, Ali Mohammed (1962) Set 78
Azhar, S (1995) Set 78
Azim, Rehna (1984) Set 101
Aziz, Shahzad (1996) Set 160
Baatz, Nicholas (1978) (QC-1998) Set 3 Profile p.1359
Backhouse, Roger (1965) (QC-1984) Set 43
Bacon, Francis (1988) Set 112 Profile p.1359
Bacon, Jane (1999) Set 240
Bacon, Jeffrey (1989) Set 85
Bacon, Kelyn (1998) Set 14
Bacon, Nicholas (1992) Set 145
Badenoch, James (1968) (QC-1989) Set 23 Profile p.1359
Badenoch, Tony (1996) Set 51
Badley, Pamela (1974) Set 204
Bagchi, Andrew (1989) Set 46
Bagley, Michael (1984) Set 205
Bagnall, Mathew (1993) Set 39
Bagot, Charles (1997) Set 63
Bahia, Sharonjit (2000) Set 176
Bailey, Anthony R (1972) Set 71
Bailey, David (1989) Set 77
Bailey, Edward (1990) Sets 71, 253
Bailey, Graham (1993) Sets 221, 224
Bailey, James (1999) Set 98
Bailey, Michael (1986) Set 144
Bailey, Russell (1985) Set 111
Bailey, Steven (1992) Set 156
Bailey-King, Robert (1975) Set 13

INDEX ■ BARRISTERS

Bailin, Alex (1995) Set 114
Baillie, Andrew (1970) (QC-2001) Set 50
Bainbridge, Laura (1997) Set 117
Baines, Charlotte (2000) Set 186
Bains, Param K (2001) Set 159
Baird, Vera (1975) (QC-2000) Set 150
Baisden, Howard (1972) Set 216
Bajwa, Ali Naseem (1993) Set 53
Baker, Andrew (1988) Set 35 Profile p.1359
Baker, Andrew (1990) Set 159
Baker, Caroline (1988) Set 159
Baker, Christopher (1984) Set 2 Profile p.1360
Baker, Clive (1995) Set 208
Baker, Fay (1994) Set 109
Baker, Harry (1992) Set 174
Baker, Jacqueline (1985) Sets 189, 235
Baker, Jonathan (1978) (QC-2001) Sets 62, 249 Profile p.1360
Baker, Maureen (1984) Set 5
Baker, Michael (1990) Set 47
Baker, Nicholas (1980) Set 63
Baker, Nigel (1969) (QC-1988) Set 5
Baker, Philip (1979) (QC-2002) Set 57 Profile p.1360
Baker, Stephen (1989) Set 5
Baker, Stuart (1995) Set 155
Baker, William (1991) Sets 155, 226
Balchin, Richard (1997) Set 164
Balcombe, David (1980) (QC-2002) Set 23 Profile p.1360
Baldock, Nicholas (1983) Sets 120, 212
Baldock, Susan (1988) Set 50
Baldry, Rupert (1987) Set 122 Profile p.1360
Baldry MP, Tony (1975) Set 110
Baldwin, J (1990) Set 210
Baldwin, John (1977) (QC-1991) Set 95 Profile p.1360
Baldwin, Marcus (1994) Set 139
Baldwin, Roger M (1969) Set 256
Baljit, Deborah (1999) Set 72
Ball, Alison (1972) (QC-1995) Set 46 Profile p.1360
Ball, Ian (1992) Set 158
Ball, Stephen (1995) Set 184
Ball, Steven (1996) Set 205
Ballantyne, William (1977) Set 131
Ballard, Briony (2000) Set 130
Ballentyne, Errol (1983) Set 245
Balogh, Christopher (1984) Set 5
Baltaian, Anna (1995) Set 192
Balysz, Mark A (1995) Set 257
Bamford, Christopher (1987) Set 144
Bamford, Colin (2002) Set 133
Bamford, Jeremy (1989) Set 166 Profile p.1360
Bancroft, Louise (1985) Set 217 Profile p.1360
Bangay, Deborah (1981) Set 64 Profile p.1360
Bankole-Jones, Gwen (1991) Set 144
Banks, Andrew (1994) Set 203
Banks, Rachael (1993) Set 203
Banks, Robert (1978) Set 58 Profile p.1361
Banks, Roderick I'Anson (1974) Set 10 Profile p.1361
Banks, Timothy (1983) Set 63
Banner, Gregory (1989) Set 87
Bannister, Edward Alexander (1974) (QC-1991) Set 136 Profile p.1361
Banton, Elaine (1996) Set 17

Banwell, Richard (1998) Sets 120, 212
Barav, Dr Ami (1993) Set 54
Barber, Abigail (1997) Set 117
Barber, Sally (1988) Set 141
Barber, Stuart (1979) Set 200
Barca, Manuel (1986) Set 15 Profile p.1361
Barclay, Jonathan (1999) Set 159
Barclay, Robin (1999) Set 55
Bard, Nicholas (1979) Set 24
Barda, Robin (1975) Set 113 Profile p.1361
Barker, Alison (1973) Set 11
Barker, Anthony (1966) (QC-1985) Set 159 Profile p.1361
Barker, Charles (1997) Sets 28, 180
Barker, James (1984) Sets 29, 189, 235
Barker, John (1982) Set 55
Barker, Kerry (1972) Set 166 Profile p.1361
Barker, N (1994) Set 196
Barker, Simon (1979) Set 87 Profile p.1361
Barklem, Martyn (1989) Set 85
Barling, Gerald (1972) (QC-1991) Set 14 Profile p.1361
Barlow, Craig (1992) Set 7
Barlow, Francis (1965) Set 106 Profile p.1362
Barlow, Mark (1992) Set 215
Barlow, Melissa (1991) Set 168
Barlow, Richard (1970) Sets 80, 190 Profile p.1362
Barnard, David (1967) Set 8
Barnard, James (1993) Set 141
Barnard, Jonathan (1997) Set 68
Barnes, Christopher (2000) Set 209
Barnes, David (1981) Set 147
Barnes, Jonathan (1970) Set 183
Barnes, Jonathan (1999) Set 125
Barnes, Mark (1974) (QC-1992) Set 32 Profile p.1362
Barnes, Matthew (1992) Set 156
Barnes, Matthew (2000) Set 23
Barnes, Michael (1965) (QC-1981) Set 153 Profile p.1362
Barnes, Shani (1986) Set 65
Barnes, Timothy (1968) (QC-1986) Set 5 Profile p.1362
Barnett, Andrew (1977) Sets 121, 262, 265
Barnett, Daniel (1993) Set 51
Barnett, Jeremy (1980) Set 199 Profile p.1362
Barnett, Joanne (1989) Set 174
Barnfather, Lydia (1992) Set 68
Baron, Florence (1976) (QC-1995) Set 123 Profile p.1362
Barr, David (1993) Set 145
Barr, Peter (1998) Set 108
Barraclough, Anthony (1978) Set 204
Barraclough, Nicholas (1990) Set 43
Barraclough, Richard (1980) Sets 120, 212
Barratt, Dominic (1992) Sets 181, 187, 243
Barrett, Cecilia (1998) Set 117
Barrett, John (1982) Sets 191, 222 Profile p.1362
Barrett, Penelope (1982) Set 53 Profile p.1362
Barrett, Robert (1978) Set 117
Barrie, Peter (1976) Set 166 Profile p.1362
Barrington-Smyth, Amanda (1972) Set 113
Barron-Eaves, Emma (1998) Set 209
Barry, Denis (1996) Set 114

Barry, Kevin (1997) Set 9
Barry, Kirsten (1993) Set 221
Barstow, Stephen (1976) Sets 62, 249
Bartfeld, Jason (1995) Set 17
Bartle, Philip (1976) Set 85
Bartlett, Andrew (1974) (QC-1993) Set 22 Profile p.1362
Bartlett, David (1975) Set 111
Bartley Jones,, Edward (1975) (QC-1997) Sets 207, 218 Profile p.1362
Barton, Alan (1975) Set 84
Barton, Fiona (1986) Set 34
Barton, Hugh (1989) Sets 25, 223
Barton, Richard (1990) Set 70
Baruah, Fiona (1996) Sets 181, 187, 243
Barwise, Stephanie (1988) Set 3 Profile p.1362
Bashir, Nadim (1988) Set 194
Bass, Louise (1999) Set 5
Bassano, Alaric (1993) Set 228
Bassett, John (1975) Set 34
Bassra, Sukhbir (1993) Set 193
Basu, Dijen (1994) Set 24
Batchelor, Mark (1971) Set 101
Batcup, David (1974) Set 18
Bate, Anthony (1987) Sets 181, 187, 243
Bate, David (1969) (QC-1994) Set 68 Profile p.1363
Bate, Stephen (1981) Set 125 Profile p.1363
Bateman, Christine (1992) Set 180
Bates, Alexander (1994) Set 199
Bates, John H (1973) Sets 104, 167 Profile p.1363
Bates, Lesley (1999) Set 36
Bates, Pascal (1994) Set 149
Bates, Peter (1978) Set 202
Bate-Williams, John (1976) Set 145
Bath, Baljinder (1996) Set 259
Bathurst, Christopher (1959) (QC-1978) Set 44
Batiste, Simon (1994) Set 193
Batra, Bunty (1986) Set 231
Batstone, William (1982) Set 166
Battcock, Benjamin (1987) Set 135
Batten, Stephen (1968) (QC-1989) Set 124 Profile p.1363
Batts, Gillian (1999) Set 198
Batty, Christopher (1989) Set 199 Profile p.1363
Batty, Paul (1975) (QC-1995) Set 234
Baughan, Julian (1967) (QC-1990) Sets 83, 250
Baumber, Kevin (1998) Set 59
Baur, Christopher (1972) Set 45
Bavidge, Giles (1968) Set 234
Baxendale, Presiley (1974) (QC-1992) Set 12 Profile p.1363
Baxendale, Thomas (1962) Set 103
Baxter, Bernadette (1987) Set 223
Baxter, Gerald (1971) Set 204
Baxter, Sharon (1987) Set 110
Bayati, Charlotte (1997) Set 127
Bayfield, Daniel (1998) Set 133
Bayley, Laura (1999) Set 16
Baylis, Christopher (1986) Set 63
Baylis, Natalie (1996) Set 152
Bayliss, Alan (1966) Set 18
Bayliss, Tom (1977) Set 194
Bayne, Dominic (1997) Sets 116, 238
Bazini, Daniel (1994) Set 76
Bazley, Janet (1980) Set 46
Beach, Fiona (2001) Set 93
Beach, Peter (1970) Set 151
Beal, Jason (1995) Set 71

Beal, Jason (1993) Set 253
Beal, Kieron (1995) Set 112
Bealby, Walter (1976) Set 159
Beale, Judith (1978) Set 12
Bean, David (1976) (QC-1997) Set 88 Profile p.1363
Bean, Matthew (1997) Set 80
BEar, Charles (1986) Set 81 Profile p.1363
Beard, Daniel (1996) Set 90 Profile p.1363
Beard, Mark (1996) Sets 120, 212
Beard, Simon (1980) Set 247
Beard, Wayne (1991) Set 261
Beatson, Jack (1973) (QC-1998) Set 31
Beattie, Ann (1989) Set 206
Beattie, Sharon (1986) Set 194
Beaumont, Andrew (1998) Set 246
Beazley, Thomas (1979) (QC-2001) Set 12 Profile p.1363
Bebb, Gordon M (1975) (QC-2002) Set 71
Beck, James (1989) Set 151 Profile p.1364
Becker, Paul A (1990) Set 205
Beckett, Rachel (1999) Set 180
Beckett, Richard (1965) (QC-1987) Set 124 Profile p.1364
Beckman, Michael (1954) (QC-1976) Sets 132, 141, 180
Beddoe, Martin (1979) Set 9
Beddoe, Richard (1991) Set 195
Bedeau, Stephen (1980) Set 200
Bedford, Becket (1989) Set 159
Bedford, Michael (1985) Set 52
Bedford, Stephen (1974) Set 209
Bedingfield, David (1991) Set 56
Beech, Jacqueline (1981) Set 143
Beecham, Sara (1995) Set 115
Beer, Jason (1992) Set 34
Beese, Nicola (1998) Set 162
Beesley, Mark (1986) Set 208
Beever, Edmund (1990) Set 161
Beever, Prudence (2000) Set 256
Beggs, John (1989) Set 130
Beglan, Wayne (1995) Set 52
Begley, Laura (1993) Set 50
Behrens, James (1979) Set 131 Profile p.1364
Behrens, James (1979) Set 201
Belben, Robin (1969) Set 259
Belbin, H (1992) Set 210
Belford, Dora (1977) Set 150
Belger, Tyrone (1984) Set 18
Belgrave, Susan (1989) Sets 21, 50
Bell, Alphege (1995) Set 151
Bell, Anthony (1985) Set 16
Bell, Dominic (1992) Set 26
Bell, Gary (1989) Set 159
Bell, James (1987) Set 145
Bell, Jillian (2000) Set 201
Bell, Marika (1991) Sets 181, 187, 243
Bellamy, Jonathan (1986) Set 38
Bellamy, Stephen (1974) (QC-1996) Set 70
Bellis, Gordon (1972) Set 208
Beloff, Michael (1967) (QC-1981) Set 12 Profile p.1364
Beltrami, Adrian (1989) Set 152 Profile p.1364
Benbow, Sara (1990) Set 63
Bendall, Richard (1979) Set 8
Bennathan, Joel (1985) Set 150
Benner, Lucinda (1992) Set 19
Bennett, Daniel (2000) Set 104
Bennett, Daniel (2000) Set 167
Bennett, Gordon (1974) Set 98
Bennett, Ieuan (1989) Set 173
Bennett, Jonathan (1985) Set 101
Bennett, Lee (1998) Set 120
Bennett, Lee (1998) Set 212

Bennett, M (1969) Set 210 Profile p.1364
Bennett, Mary (1990) Set 159
Bennett, Miles (1986) Set 114
Bennett, Richard J (1986) Set 256
Bennett, William (1994) Set 125
Bennett-Jenkins, Sallie (1984) Set 65 Profile p.1364
Bennetts, Phillip (1986) Set 68
Bennington, Jane (1981) Sets 171, 251
Benson, Charles (1990) Set 110
Benson, James (1995) Set 206
Benson, Jeremy (1978) (QC-2001) Set 65 Profile p.1364
Benson, John (1978) (QC-2001) Set 203 Profile p.1364
Benson, Mark (1992) Set 229
Benson, Richard (1974) (QC-1995) Set 9
Bentham, Daniel (2001) Set 123
Bentham, Howard (1970) (QC-1996) Set 226 Profile p.1365
Bentley, David (1984) Set 25
Bentley, David (1998) Set 230
Bentley, Philip (1970) (QC-1991) Set 135
Bentley, Stephen (1997) Set 18
Bentwood, Richard (1994) Set 39
Benzynie, Robert (1992) Set 18
Beresford, Stephen (1976) Set 247
Bergenthal, Ronnie (1993) Set 8
Bergin, Terence (1985) Set 60
Bergin, Timothy (1987) Set 164
Berkeley, Iona (1999) Set 95
Berkin, Martyn (1966) Set 22
Berkley, David (1979) (QC-1999) Sets 144, 225
Berkson, Simon (1986) Sets 207, 218 Profile p.1365
Berlin, Barry (1981) Set 161 Profile p.1365
Berman, Franklin (1966) (QC-1992) Set 31 Profile p.1365
Bernard, Robert Spencer (1969) Set 73
Berragan, Neil (1982) Sets 191, 222 Profile p.1365
Berrick, Steven (1986) Set 110
Berridge, Elizabeth (1996) Sets 191, 222
Berriman, Trevor (1988) Set 79
Berrisford, Antony (1972) Set 247
Berry, Adrian (1998) Set 76
Berry, Nicholas (1988) Sets 101, 184
Berry, Simon (1977) (QC-1990) Set 105 Profile p.1365
Berry, Steven (1984) (QC-2002) Set 31 Profile p.1365
Bethel, Martin (1965) (QC-1983) Set 195
Bethlehem, Daniel (1988) Set 35 Profile p.1365
Bettle, Janet (1985) Sets 181, 187, 243
Bevan, Hugh (1959) Set 6
Bevan, John (1970) (QC-1997) Set 59 Profile p.1365
Bevan, Julian (1962) (QC-1991) Set 68 Profile p.1365
Bevan, Miranda (2000) Set 65
Beveridge, Jody (1998) Set 266
Bewsey, Jane (1986) Set 126
Bex, Kate (1992) Set 65
Beynon, Richard (1990) Set 43
Beyts, Chester (1978) Set 53
Bhakar, Surinder (1986) Set 51
Bhalla, Bitu (1978) Set 110
Bhaloo, Zia (1990) Sets 29, 189, 235
Bhat, Saima (1999) Set 256
Bhatia, Balraj (1982) Set 245
Bhatia, Divya (1986) Set 21

1666 — INDEX TO ALL BARRISTERS IN CHAMBERS WHO ARE LISTED IN THIS GUIDE. **BOLD** TYPE INDICATES PROFILES – SEE PAGE 1353

BARRISTERS ■ INDEX

Bhose, Ranjit (1989) Set 52 Profile p.1365
Bickerdike, Roger (1986) Set 201 Profile p.1365
Bickerstaff, Jane (1989) Set 55
Bickford-Smith, Margaret (1973) Set 22
Bickford-Smith, Stephen (1972) Set 13
Bickler, Simon (1988) Set 199
Bidder, Neil (1976) (QC-1998) Set 175 Profile p.1365
Biddle, Neville (1974) Set 204
Biggs, Stuart (1999) Set 11
Bignall, John (1996) Set 77
Bignell, Janet (1992) Set 40
Bijlani, Aisha (1993) Set 92
Billington, Moira (1988) Set 178
Bilsland, Alisan (2000) Set 227
Binder, Peter (1991) Set 151
Bindloss, Edward (1993) Set 201
Bingham, Anthony (1992) Set 111
Bingham, Camilla (1996) Set 32
Binns, David (1983) Set 227
Birch, Elizabeth (1978) Set 152 Profile p.1365
Birch, Geoffrey (1972) Set 147
Birch, Roger A (1979) Set 200
Bird, Nigel (1991) Set 228
Bird, Simon (1987) Set 52 Profile p.1366
Birk, Dewinder (1988) Set 248
Birkby, Peter (1987) Sets 163, 190
Birkett, Peter (1972) (QC-1989) Set 229 Profile p.1366
Birks, Simon (1981) Set 19
Birnbaum, Michael (1969) (QC-1992) Set 11
Birss, Colin (1990) Set 91 Profile p.1366
Birt, Simon (1998) Set 14
Birtles, Samantha (1989) Set 229
Birtles, William (1970) Sets 104, 167 Profile p.1366
Birts, Peter (1968) (QC-1990) Sets 121, 265
Bisarya, Neil (1998) Set 204
Bishop, Alan (1973) Set 141
Bishop, Edward (1985) Set 129
Bishop, Gordon (1968) Set 125
Bishop, John (1970) Sets 19, 172
Bishop, Keeley (1990) Sets 23, 164
Bishop, Malcolm (1968) (QC-1993) Sets 110, 174 Profile p.1366
Bishop, Mark (1981) Set 145
Bishop, Timothy (1991) Set 64 Profile p.1366
Bispham, Christine (1991) Set 208
Biswas, Nisha (1996) Set 205
Black, Harriette (1986) Set 26
Black, John (1975) (QC-1998) Set 126
Black, Michael (1978) (QC-1995) Set 146 Profile p.1366
Blackband, Laura (1997) Set 55
Blackburn, Elizabeth (1978) (QC-1998) Set 142
Blackburn, John (1969) (QC-1984) Set 3 Profile p.1366
Blackburn, Katharine (1998) Set 43
Blackburn, Luke (1993) Sets 121, 262, 265
Blackett-Ord, Mark (1974) Set 138 Profile p.1367
Blackford, R (1988) Set 78
Blackmore, John (1983) Set 169
Blackshaw, Henry (1993) Set 226
Blackwell, Kate (1992) Set 223 Profile p.1367
Blackwell, Louise (1985) Set 216
Blackwood, Guy (1997) Set 33

Blain, Roderick (1991) Set 258
Blair, Bruce (1969) (QC-1989) Sets 64, 234 Profile p.1367
Blair, Michael (1965) (QC-1996) Set 152 Profile p.1367
Blair, Peter (1983) Set 166
Blair, William (1972) (QC-1994) Set 152 Profile p.1367
Blair-Gould, John (1970) Set 124
Blake, Alan (1997) Set 73
Blake, Andrew (2000) Set 81
Blake, Arthur (1988) Sets 83, 250
Blake, Nicholas (1974) (QC-1994) Set 88 Profile p.1367
Blake, Nick (1997) Set 247
Blake-James, Hugh (1998) Set 72
Blakesley, Patrick (1993) Set 22
Blakey, Lee (1995) Set 256
Blakey, Michael (1989) Set 232
Blanchard, Claire (1992) Set 31 Profile p.1367
Bland, Carolyn (1995) Set 232
Blantern, Robert (1996) Set 163
Blaxland, Henry (1978) (QC-2002) Set 47 Profile p.1367
Blayney, David (1992) Set 131
Bleaney, Nicholas (1988) Set 147
Bleasdale, Marie-Claire (1993) Set 97
Bleasdale, Paul (1978) (QC-2001) Set 159 Profile p.1367
Bloch, Michael (1979) (QC-1998) Set 153
Bloch, Selwyn (1982) (QC-2000) Set 85 Profile p.1367
Block, Neil (1980) (QC-2002) Set 38 Profile p.1367
Blohm, Leslie (1982) Sets 143, 169 Profile p.1367
Blom-Cooper, Louis (1952) (QC-1983) Set 25
Bloom, Dr Margaret (1994) Sets 48, 63
Bloom, Tracey (1984) Set 25
Bloom-Davies, Desmond (1986) Sets 121, 262, 265
Bloomer, Charles (1985) Set 223
Bloomfield, Richard (1984) Set 266
Blore, Carolyn (1985) Set 45
Blount, Martin (1982) Set 258
Blunt, David (1967) (QC-1991) Set 118
Blunt, Oliver (1974) (QC-1994) Set 45 Profile p.1367
Blyth, Roderick (1981) Set 123
Boardman, Christopher (1995) Set 141 Profile p.1368
Boardman, Michael (1979) Set 55
Bodnar, Andrew (1995) Set 18
Boeddinghaus, Hermann (1996) Set 137
Bogan, Paul (1983) Set 25 Profile p.1368
Boggis-Rolfe, Harry (1969) Set 15
Bojarski, Andrzej (1995) Set 9
Bojczuk, William (1983) Set 128
Bolton, Caroline (1998) Set 54
Bolton, Richard (1987) Set 71
Bolton, Sally Ann (1997) Set 178
Bompas, Anthony George (1975) (QC-1994) Set 137 Profile p.1368
Bond, Abigail (1999) Set 166
Bond, Andrew (1999) Set 259
Bond, Leisha (1999) Set 155
Bond, Richard I W (1988) Set 154
Bone, Lucy (1999) Set 85
Boney, Guy (1968) (QC-1990) Sets 121, 258, 262, 265
Bonham Carter, Gaby (1997) Set 114
Bonner, Lee (2000) Set 203

Bonney, James (1975) (QC-1995) Set 106
Booker, Christine (1977) Set 25
Bools, Michael (1991) Set 14
Boora, Jinder (1990) Set 247
Booth, Alan (1978) Set 217 Profile p.1368
Booth, Alexander (2000) Set 61
Booth, Cherie (1976) (QC-1995) Set 88 Profile p.1368
Booth, Martyn (1996) Sets 254, 255
Booth, Michael (1981) (QC-1999) Sets 105, 191, 222 Profile p.1368
Booth, Nicholas (1991) Sets 104, 167
Booth, Nigel (1994) Set 230
Booth, Richard (1993) Set 23
Booth, Roger (1966) Set 164
Booth, Simon (1985) Set 203
Boothby, Jo (1972) Set 17
Boothroyd, Susan (1990) Set 266
Bornman, Kerry (1999) Set 136
Borrelli, Michael (1977) (QC-2000) Set 43 Profile p.1368
Borthwick, Lorna (1997) Set 158
Bosomworth, M (1979) Set 198
Boswell, Lindsay (1982) (QC-1997) Set 118
Boswood, Anthony (1970) (QC-1986) Set 44 Profile p.1368
Bothroyd, Shirley (1982) Set 85 Profile p.1368
Bott, Charles (1979) Set 53
Bould, Duncan (1984) Set 178
Boulding, Philip (1979) (QC-1996) Set 69 Profile p.1368
Boulter, Terence (1986) Set 26
Bourne, Charles (1991) Sets 60, 135 Profile p.1369
Bourne, Colin (1997) Set 266
Bourne, Ian (1977) Set 149 Profile p.1369
Bourne, Nicholas (1976) Set 261
Bourne, Robert (1978) Set 143
Bourne-Arton, Simon (1975) (QC-1994) Set 194 Profile p.1369
Bovey, Mungo (2000) Set 150
Bowcock, Samantha (1990) Set 256
Bowdery, Martin (1980) (QC-2000) Set 3 Profile p.1369
Bowen, James (1979) Set 76
Bowen, Nicholas (1984) Set 7 Profile p.1369
Bowen, Paul (1993) Set 25 Profile p.1369
Bower, Alistair (1986) Set 221
Bowerman, Michael (1970) Set 266
Bowers, John (1979) (QC-1998) Set 85 Profile p.1369
Bowes, Michael (1980) (QC-2001) Set 71 Profile p.1369
Bowker, Robert (1995) Set 144
Bowley, Ivan (1990) Set 223
Bowley, Martin (1962) (QC-1981) Set 9
Bowling, James (1999) Set 110
Bowmer, Michael (1997) Set 107
Bown, Philip (1974) Set 158
Bowron, Margaret (1978) (QC-2001) Set 23 Profile p.1369
Bowsher, Michael (1985) Set 90 Profile p.1369
Bowyer, Harry (1989) Set 43
Bowyer, Martyn (1984) Set 75
Boyce, William (1976) (QC-2001) Set 68 Profile p.1369
Boyd, David (1977) Set 21
Boyd, James (1994) Set 221
Boyd, Joe (1993) Set 223
Boyd, Johanna (1999) Set 52

Boyd, Kerstin (1979) Set 144
Boyd, Sarah (1998) Set 170
Boyd, Stephen (1977) Set 128
Boyd, Stewart (1967) (QC-1981) Set 31 Profile p.1369
Boydell, Edward (1989) Sets 121, 262, 265 Profile p.1370
Boye-Anawoma, Margo (1989) Set 150
Boyle, Alan (1972) (QC-1991) Set 131 Profile p.1370
Boyle, Christopher (1994) Set 89 Profile p.1370
Boyle, David (1996) Set 217
Boyle, Gerard (1992) Set 130
Boyle, Karen (2000) Set 223
Boyle, Kevin (1992) Set 25
Boyle, Robert (1985) Set 126
Brabin, Michael (1976) Set 182
Brace, Michael (1991) Set 174
Bradberry, Rebecca (1996) Set 264
Bradbury, Joanne (1999) Sets 181, 187, 243
Bradbury, Timothy (1989) Set 111
Bradley, Anthony (1989) Set 20 Profile p.1370
Bradley, Caroline (1985) Set 246
Bradley, Clodagh (1996) Set 130
Bradley, Phillip (1993) Set 156
Bradley, R (1978) Set 210 Profile p.1370
Bradley, Sally (1978) (QC-1999) Set 266 Profile p.1370
Bradley, Sally (1989) Set 50
Bradly, David (1987) Set 38
Bradnock, Thomas (1997) Set 182
Bradshaw, David (1975) Set 201
Brady, M A (1992) Set 220
Braganza, Nicola (1992) Set 76
Bragiel, Edward (1977) Set 67
Braham, Colin (1971) Sets 98, 200
Brahams, Diana (1972) Sets 104, 167
Braithwaite, Bill (1970) (QC-1992) Sets 207, 218 Profile p.1370
Braithwaite, Garfield (1987) Set 101
Braithwaite, Thomas (1998) Set 131
Bramall, Kate (1999) Set 165
Bramwell, Christopher (1996) Set 252
Bramwell, Richard (1967) (QC-1989) Set 148 Profile p.1370
Branchflower, George (1997) Set 201
Brand, Rachel (1981) (QC-2000) Set 154
Brand, Simon (1973) Set 154 Profile p.1370
Brandon, H (1993) Set 210
Brandon, Stephen (1978) (QC-1996) Set 102
Brandreth, Benet (1999) Set 134
Branigan, Kate (1984) Set 111
Brann, Elisabeth (1970) Set 127
Brannigan, Sean (1994) Set 118 Profile p.1370
Branston, Barnabas (1999) Set 34
Branston, Gareth (1996) Set 36
Brant, P (1993) Set 210
Braslavsky, Nicholas (1983) (QC-1999) Sets 111, 191, 222 Profile p.1370
Brasse, Gillian (1977) Set 56 Profile p.1370
Brassington, Stephen (1994) Set 65
Brazil, Dominic (1995) Set 56

Brealey, Mark (1984) (QC-2002) Set 14 Profile p.1370
Bredemear, Zachary (1996) Set 129
Breen, Carlo (1987) Set 228 Profile p.1371
Breen-Lawton, Denise (2000) Set 199
Breheny, Mark (1986) Set 178
Brennan, Janice (1980) Set 71
Brennan, John (1996) Set 157
Brennan, Lord (1967) (QC-1985) Set 88 Profile p.1371
Brennan, Timothy (1981) (QC-2001) Set 24 Profile p.1371
Brennand, Timothy (1987) Sets 224, 231 Profile p.1371
Brent, Richard (1995) Set 152
Brenton, Timothy (1981) (QC-1998) Set 77 Profile p.1371
Brereton, Fiorella (1979) Set 226
Brereton, Joy (1990) Set 113
Breslin, Catherine (1990) Set 259
Bresnahan, Jane (1998) Set 221
Bretherton, Kerry (1992) Set 63
Brett, Matthew (1987) Sets 62, 249
Bretten, Rex (1965) (QC-1980) Set 102 Profile p.1371
Brettler, Jonathan (1988) Set 137
Brickman, Laura (1976) Set 151
Briden, Sarah (1999) Set 242
Briden, Timothy J (1976) Set 139 Profile p.1371
Bridge, Giles (2000) Set 163
Bridge, Ian (1988) Set 159
Bridgman, David (1997) Set 129
Briefel, Charles (1984) Set 63
Briegel, Pieter (1986) Set 17
Briggs, Adrian (1989) Set 12
Briggs, John (1973) Set 133 Profile p.1371
Briggs, Michael (1978) (QC-1994) Set 131 Profile p.1371
Briggs, Nicholas (1994) Set 166 Profile p.1371
Briggs-Watson, Sandra (1985) Set 109
Bright, Christopher (1985) Set 156 Profile p.1372
Bright, David (1976) Sets 83, 250
Bright, Rachel (1991) Set 43
Bright, Robert (1987) Set 77 Profile p.1372
Brightwell, James (1999) Set 98
Brimelow, Kirsty (1991) Set 43
Brindle, Michael (1975) (QC-1992) Set 44 Profile p.1372
Brindle, Simon (1998) Set 143
Brisby, John (1978) (QC-1996) Set 137 Profile p.1372
Briscoe, Constance (1983) Set 11 Profile p.1372
Bristoll, Sandra (1989) Set 133
Brittain, Marc (1983) Set 144
Brittain, Richard (1971) Set 206
Brittenden, Stuart (1999) Set 104
Brittenden, Stuart (1999) Set 167
Britton, James (1996) Sets 254, 255
Broadbent, Edmund (1980) Set 35
Broadbent, Emma (1986) Set 75
Broadley, John (1973) Set 216
Broatch, Donald (1971) Set 115
Brochwicz-Lewinski, Stefan (1995) Set 225
Brock, David (1984) Set 45
Brock, Jonathan (1977) (QC-1997) Set 40 Profile p.1372
Brocklebank, James (1999) Set 77
Brockley, Nigel (1992) Set 159
Brodie, Bruce (1993) Set 38 Profile p.1372
Brodie, Graham (1989) Set 20

INDEX ■ BARRISTERS

Brodie, Stanley (1954) (QC-1975) Set 12
Brodrick, William (1991) Set 237
Brodwell, John (1998) Set 201
Brody, Karen (1986) Set 217
Brody, Saul (1996) Set 229
Brogan, M (1990) Set 224
Brogan, Shaun (1990) Set 204
Bromilow, Daniel (1996) Set 140
Bromilow, Richard (1977) Set 169 Profile p.1372
Bromley-Davenport, John (1972) (QC-2002) Set 217
Bromley-Martin, Michael (1979) (QC-2002) Set 124 Profile p.1372
Brompton, Michael (1973) Set 114
Brook, David (1988) Sets 60, 116, 238
Brook, Ian (1983) Set 63
Brook, Matthew (1999) Set 156
Brook, Paul (1986) Set 201
Brook Smith, Philip (1982) (QC-2002) Set 44 Profile p.1372
Brooke, David (1990) Sets 80, 190
Brooke, Michael (1969) (QC-1994) Set 92 Profile p.1372
Brookes, Lincoln (1992) Sets 254, 255
Brooke-Smith, John (1981) Sets 181, 187, 243
Brooks, Duncan (2001) Set 123
Brooks, John (1990) Set 261
Brooks, Louise (1994) Set 20
Brooks, Paul (1989) Set 25
Brooks, Peter (1986) Set 173
Broome, Edward (1996) Sets 116, 238
Brotherton, John P (1994) Set 160
Brough, Alasdair (1979) Set 159
Brougham, Christopher (1969) (QC-1988) Set 133 Profile p.1373
Brounger, David (1990) Set 84
Brown, Althea (1995) Set 25
Brown, Cameron (1998) Set 73
Brown, Catherine (1990) Set 82
Brown, Catherine (1999) Set 191
Brown, Catherine (1999) Set 222
Brown, Charles (1982) Set 256
Brown, Charles (1976) Set 38 Profile p.1373
Brown, Clare (1993) Set 146
Brown, Damian (1989) Sets 104, 167 Profile p.1373
Brown, Edward (1983) Set 68
Brown, Geoffrey (1981) Set 38 Profile p.1373
Brown, Grace (1995) Set 76
Brown, Graham (1982) Set 11
Brown, Hannah (1992) Set 32
Brown, Ian (1971) Set 163
Brown, James (1990) Set 234
Brown, Jillian (1991) Set 21
Brown, Joanne (1990) Set 113
Brown, Kristina (1998) Set 160
Brown, Luke (2000) Sets 181, 187, 243
Brown, Nicholas (1989) Set 92
Brown, Nicola (1998) Set 232
Brown, Paul (1991) Set 54 Profile p.1373
Brown, Philip (1991) Set 8
Brown, Rebecca (1989) Set 56
Brown, Richard (1996) Set 71
Brown, Robert (1979) Set 245
Brown, Roger (1976) Set 232
Brown, Simon (1988) Set 145
Brown, Simon (1976) (QC-1995) Set 22
Brown, Stephanie (1982) Set 159 Profile p.1373

Brown, Stuart (1974) (QC-1991) Set 195
Brown, Susan (1989) Set 140
Brown, T C E (1980) Sets 171, 251
Brown, Thomas (2000) Set 20
Brownbill, David (1989) Set 87
Browne, Benjamin (1976) (QC-1996) Set 146 Profile p.1373
Browne, Desmond (1969) (QC-1990) Set 125 Profile p.1373
Browne, Gerald (1995) Set 21
Browne, Julie (1989) Set 48
Browne, Louis (1988) Sets 207, 218
Browne, Nicholas (1971) (QC-1995) Set 9
Browne, Shereener (1996) Set 47
Browne, Simon Peter Buchanan (1982) Set 41
Browne-Wilkinson, Simon (1981) (QC-1998) Set 131 Profile p.1373
Brownhill, Joanna (1997) Set 115
Brownlie, Ian (1958) (QC-1979) Set 12 Profile p.1373
Bruce, Andrew (1992) Set 131
Bruce, David (1982) Set 230
Bruce, Gaenor (1997) Set 150
Brudenell, Thomas (1977) Set 123 Profile p.1373
Brunnen, David (1976) Set 206
Brunner, Adrian (1968) (QC-1994) Sets 60, 135
Brunner, Kate (1997) Sets 9, 165
Brunner, Peter (1971) Set 14
Brunning, Matthew (1997) Set 159
Brunton, Sean (1990) Sets 183, 262
Bryan, Robert (1992) Set 108
Bryan, Simon (1988) Set 31
Bryant, Caroline (1976) Sets 181, 187, 243
Bryant, Ceri (1984) Set 30
Bryant, John (1976) Set 129
Bryant, Judith (1987) Set 153 Profile p.1373
Bryant, Keith (1991) Set 24
Bryant-Heron, Mark (1986) Set 11 Profile p.1374
Bubb, Tim (1970) Set 198 Profile p.1374
Buchan, Andrew (1981) Set 20 Profile p.1374
Buchan, Jonathan (1994) Set 256
Buchanan, Vivien (1981) Set 248 Profile p.1374
Buck, John (1987) Set 144
Buckett, Edwin (1988) Set 50
Buckhaven, Charlotte (1969) Set 109
Buckhaven, Simon (1970) Set 74
Buckingham, K (1986) Set 196
Buckingham, Sarah (1991) Set 159
Buckingham, Stewart (1996) Set 33
Buckland, Matthew (1997) Set 108
Buckland, Robert James (1991) Set 174
Buckle, Jonathan (1990) Set 252
Buckley, Professor Richard (1969) Set 98
Buckley, Sophie (1999) Set 266
Buckley-Clarke, Amanda (1991) Set 111
Bucknall, Belinda (1974) (QC-1988) Set 33 Profile p.1374
Buckpitt, Michael (1988) Set 144
Budaly, Susan (1994) Set 46
Budden, Caroline (1977) Set 70 Profile p.1374
Budworth, Adam (1992) Set 4

Budworth, Martin (1999) Set 225
Buehrlen, Veronique (1991) Set 44
Bueno, Antonio (1964) (QC-1989) Set 112
Bugeja, Eve (1997) Set 158
Bugg, Ian (1992) Set 164
Bull, Gregory (1976) Set 174 Profile p.1374
Bull, Roger (1974) Set 115
Bull, Simon (1984) Set 9
Bullen, James E (1966) Set 108
Bullock, Andrew (1992) Set 19
Bullock, Ian (1975) Set 169 Profile p.1374
Bullock, Neil (1989) Set 21
Bundell, Katharine (1991) Sets 181, 187, 243
Bundred, G (1982) Set 210
Bunyan, Angus (1999) Set 65
Burbidge, James (1979) Set 161 Profile p.1374
Burden, Angus (1994) Set 161
Burden, Emma L V (1994) Set 200
Burden, Susan (1985) Set 119
Burdon, Michael (1993) Set 197
Burgess, David (1975) Set 16
Burgess, Edward (1993) Set 169
Burgess, Emma (1995) Set 180
Burgess, John (1978) Set 245
Burke, Brendon (1995) Set 208
Burke, Jeffrey (1964) (QC-1984) Set 24 Profile p.1374
Burke, Maisie (1999) Set 226
Burke, Michael (1985) Set 8
Burke, Trevor (1981) (QC-2001) Set 4 Profile p.1374
Burke-Gaffney, Rupert D C J (1988) Set 108
Burkill, Guy (1981) (QC-2002) Set 91 Profile p.1374
Burles, David (1985) Set 46
Burn, Lindsay (1972) Set 63
Burnell, Kate (1998) Set 209
Burnett, Harold (1962) (QC-1982) Set 112
Burnett, Iain (1993) Set 73
Burnett, Ian (1980) (QC-1998) Set 145 Profile p.1374
Burnham, Ulele (1997) Set 25
Burns, Alec (1987) Set 237
Burns, Andrew (1993) Set 24
Burns, Frank (1971) Set 219
Burns, Jeremy (1996) Set 257
Burns, Paul (1998) Sets 207, 218
Burns, Peter (1993) Set 217
Burns, Richard (1967) Set 247
Burns, Simon (1992) Set 165
Burns, Terry (1990) Set 19
Burr, Andrew (1981) Set 3 Profile p.1374
Burrell, Gary (1977) (QC-1996) Set 50
Burrell, Simon (1988) Set 105
Burrett, Catherine (1992) Set 257
Burrington, Richard (1993) Set 117
Burroughs, Nigel (1991) Set 107
Burrow, John (1980) Set 110
Burrows, Michael (1979) Set 156
Burrows, Simon (1990) Set 226
Burton, Charles (1983) Set 26
Burton, Frances (1972) Set 106
Burton, Frank (1982) (QC-1998) Set 82 Profile p.1375
Burton, Jamie (1999) Set 25
Burwin, Heather (1983) Set 184
Bury, Mark (1986) Set 186
Busby, Thomas (1975) Set 155
Busch, Lisa (2000) Set 54
Bush, Rosalind (1978) Set 159 Profile p.1375
Busuttil, Godwin (1994) Set 125 Profile p.1375

Buswell, Richard (1985) Sets 56, 63
Butcher, Christopher (1986) (QC-2001) Set 77 Profile p.1375
Butcher, John (1984) Set 34
Butcher, Richard (1985) Set 43
Butler, Andrew (1993) Set 144
Butler, Christopher M (1972) Set 248 Profile p.1375
Butler, Gerald (1955) (QC-1975) Set 32
Butler, Joan (1977) (QC-1998) Set 5
Butler, Jonathan (1992) Set 209
Butler, Judith (1997) Set 247
Butler, Judith (1993) Sets 120, 212
Butler, Philip (1979) Set 217
Butler, Simon (1996) Set 28
Butt, Irfan (2000) Set 18
Butt, Michael (1974) Sets 121, 262, 265
Butterfield, John (1995) Set 156
Butterfield, Samuel (1999) Set 165
Butters, Richard (2001) Set 197
Butterworth, Martin (1985) Set 154
Butterworth, Paul (1982) Set 244
Buttimore, Gabriel (1993) Sets 83, 250
Buxton, Sarah (1988) Set 155
Buxton, Thomas (1983) Set 18
Byam-Cook, Henry (2000) Set 35
Byrne, Garrett (1986) Set 54 Profile p.1375
Byrne, James (1983) Set 206
Byrne, Michael (1971) Set 209
Byrnes, Aisling (1994) Set 53
Cacciotti, Melissa (1997) Set 60
Caddick, Nicholas (1986) Set 67
Caddle, Sherrie (1983) Set 45
Cadney, Paul (1984) Set 168
Cadwaladr, Stephen (1992) Set 158
Cadwallader, Neil (1984) Sets 207, 218
Cadwallader, Peter (1973) Set 228
Cafferkey, Annette (1994) Set 2
Cafferkey, Nicola (1998) Set 147
Cahill, Jeremy (1975) (QC-2002) Set 159 Profile p.1375
Cahill, Patrick (1979) Set 110
Cahill, Sally (1978) Set 195 Profile p.1375
Cains, Linda (1990) Set 197
Cairnes, Paul (1980) Set 111
Calcutt, David C (1955) (QC-1972) Set 37
Caldecott, Andrew (1975) (QC-1994) Set 15 Profile p.1375
Caldwell, Jennifer (1973) Set 229
Caldwell, Peter (1995) Set 26
Calhaem, Simon (1999) Set 63
Callaghan, Catherine (1999) Set 12
Callaghan, Elizabeth M (1998) Set 266
Callan, David (1979) Set 239
Calland, Timothy (1999) Sets 29, 189, 235
Callaway, Anthony Leonard (1978) Sets 117, 198
Callery, Martin (1997) Set 216
Callman, Jeremy (1991) Set 106
Callman, Tanya (1993) Set 72 Profile p.1375
Callow, David (1998) Set 175
Calnan, Jane (1984) Set 36
Calver, Neil (1987) Set 14 Profile p.1375
Calvert, Charles (1975) Sets 48, 63
Calvert, David (1995) Set 227

Cameron, Alexander (1986) Set 124 Profile p.1375
Cameron, Barbara (1979) Sets 60, 135
Cameron, Neil (1984) Set 186 Profile p.1376
Cameron, Neil (1982) Set 27 Profile p.1376
Cameron-Mowat, Rosalind (2000) Set 170
Cammerman, Gideon (1996) Set 43
Camp, Christopher (1996) Sets 48, 63
Campbell, Alasdair (1999) Set 198
Campbell, Alexis (1990) Set 7
Campbell, Andrew (1972) (QC-1994) Set 201
Campbell, Andrew (1972) Set 43
Campbell, Diane (1995) Set 266
Campbell, Douglas James (1993) Set 91 Profile p.1376
Campbell, Emily (1995) Set 153 Profile p.1376
Campbell, Gayle (1997) Set 178
Campbell, Glenn (1985) Set 107
Campbell, Graham (1979) Set 6
Campbell, Graham J (1982) Set 230
Campbell, Joan (1996) Set 175
Campbell, John (1981) Sets 191, 222
Campbell, Nicholas (1979) (QC-2000) Sets 80, 190
Campbell, Oliver (1992) Sets 60, 135
Campbell, Robin (1969) Set 54
Campbell, Sarah (1997) Set 36
Campbell, Stephen (1982) Set 161 Profile p.1376
Campbell, Susan (1986) Set 184 Profile p.1376
Campbell-Clyne, Christopher (1988) Set 4
Campbell-Tiech, Andrew (1978) Set 26
Canavan, Sandy (1987) Set 151
Candler, Linda (1977) Set 45
Candlin, James (1991) Set 144
Cannan, Jonathan (1989) Sets 163, 207, 218
Cannatella, Marc (1997) Sets 181, 187, 243
Cannock, Giles (1998) Sets 191, 222
Cannon, Mark (1985) Set 92 Profile p.1376
Cant, Christopher I (1973) Set 140
Cape, Paul (1990) Set 236 Profile p.1376
Caplan, Harold (1955) Set 33
Caplan, Jonathan (1973) (QC-1991) Set 114 Profile p.1376
Caplan, Leonie (2001) Set 229
Capon, Philip (1990) Set 161
Capstick, Timothy (1986) Set 193
Carberry, Caroline (1995) Set 147
Carden, Nicholas (1981) Set 64
Carey, Godfrey (1969) (QC-1991) Set 114
Carey, Jacqueline (1999) Set 4
Cargill-Thompson, Perdita (1993) Set 31 Profile p.1376
Carleton, Erica (2000) Set 219
Carlile of Berriew, Lord (1970) (QC-1984) Sets 11, 179
Carling, Christopher (1969) Sets 104, 167
Carlisle, Hugh (1961) (QC-1978) Set 145 Profile p.1376
Carmichael, John (1984) Set 45
Carnes, Andrew (1984) Set 54
Carney, Andrew (1995) Set 208

BARRISTERS ■ INDEX

Carpenter, Chloe (2001) Set 44
Carpenter, Jamie (2000) Set 119
Carpenter, Jane (1984) Set 59
Carpenter, Richard (1981) Set 188
Carr, Adrian (1999) Set 144
Carr, Bruce (1986) Set 24 Profile p.1377
Carr, Christopher (1968) (QC-1983) Set 32 Profile p.1377
Carr, Henry (1982) (QC-1998) Set 134 Profile p.1377
Carr, Jonathan (1990) Set 234
Carr, Peter (1976) Set 160 Profile p.1377
Carr, Simon (1984) Set 50
Carr, Sue (1987) Set 92 Profile p.1377
Carrington, Gillian (1990) Set 54
Carroll, Jonathan (1994) Set 201
Carron, Richard (1992) Set 19
Carrott, Sylvester (1980) Set 76
Carrow, Robert (1981) Set 8
Carss-Frisk, Monica (1985) (QC-2001) Set 12 Profile p.1377
Carswell, Patricia (1993) Set 87
Carter, David (1971) Set 2
Carter, Lesley (1990) Set 204
Carter, Martin (1992) Sets 191, 222
Carter, Peter (1947) (QC-1990) Set 126 Profile p.1377
Carter, Peter (1974) (QC-1995) Set 194
Carter, Richard (1990) Set 225
Carter, Rosalyn (1994) Set 161
Carter, Sally (1994) Set 258
Carter, William (1989) Set 36
Carter-Manning, Jenny (1999) Set 5
Carter-Manning, Jeremy (1975) (QC-1993) Set 11
Carter-Stephenson, George (1975) (QC-1998) Set 53 Profile p.1377
Cartmell, Nicholas (1990) Set 237
Cartwright, Ivan (1993) Set 206
Cartwright, Nicolas (1986) Set 161
Cartwright, Richard (1994) Set 118
Cartwright, Sophie (1999) Set 217
Carus, Roderick (1971) (QC-1990) Set 228 Profile p.1377
Carville, Brendan (1980) Set 204
Case, Julie (1990) Sets 207, 218
Case, Magdalen (1992) Set 231
Case, Richard (1996) Set 111
Casella, Bart (1995) Set 63
Casement, David (1992) Sets 207, 218 Profile p.1377
Casey, Aidan (1992) Set 66
Casey, Benjamin (2000) Set 145
Casey, Dermot (1994) Set 21
Casey, Mairin (1989) Set 248 Profile p.1378
Casey, Noel (1995) Set 126
Cash, Joanne (1994) Set 15
Cassel, Timothy (1965) (QC-1988) Set 114 Profile p.1378
Cassidy, Patrick (1982) Set 219
Castle, Peter (1970) Set 97
Castle, Richard (1984) Set 70
Castle, Susan (1986) Set 8
Caswell, Benjamin (1993) Set 193
Caswell, Matthew (1968) Sets 80, 190
Caswell, Matthew (1968) Set 190
Caswell, Rebecca (1983) Sets 80, 190
Catchpole, Stuart (1987) (QC-2002) Set 38 Profile p.1378
Catford, Gordon (1980) Set 22
Catherwood, Shaen (2000) Set 24

Cattan, Philip (1970) Set 231 Profile p.1378
Cattermole, Rebecca (1999) Set 2
Caudle, John (1976) Set 4 Profile p.1378
Caulfield, Barbara (1999) Set 161
Caulfield, Paul (1996) Set 239
Causer, John (1979) Set 36 Profile p.1378
Cavanagh, John (1985) (QC-2001) Set 81 Profile p.1378
Cavanagh, Lorraine (2001) Set 231
Cave, Jeremy (1992) Sets 23, 164
Cavender, David (1993) Set 32 Profile p.1378
Caws, Eian (1974) Set 13
Cawson, Mark (1982) (QC-2001) Sets 207, 218 Profile p.1378
Cayford, Philip (1975) (QC-2002) Set 7 Profile p.1378
Cellan-Jones, Deiniol (1988) Set 70
Chacksfield, Mark (1999) Set 95
Chadwick, Joanna (1988) Set 159
Chadwin, James (1958) (QC-1976) Sets 55, 194, 234
Chaisty, Paul (1982) (QC-2001) Sets 191, 222 Profile p.1378
Chakrabarti, Arnondo (2000) Set 88
Chalkley, Rebecca (1999) Set 126
Challenger, Colin (1970) Set 17
Challinor, Jonathan (1998) Set 158
Challinor, Michael (1974) Set 156
Chalmers, Suzanne (1995) Set 22
Chamberlain, Emma (1998) Set 138
Chamberlain, Francis (1985) Set 111
Chamberlain, Martin (1997) Set 14
Chamberlain CMG, Kevin (1965) Set 266
Chamberlayne, Patrick (1992) Set 7
Chambers, Dominic (1987) Set 87 Profile p.1378
Chambers, Gaynor (1998) Set 69
Chambers, Gregory (1973) Set 23
Chambers, Jonathan (1996) Set 33
Chambers, Michael (1980) Set 179
Chambers, Paul (1973) Set 230
Champion, Deborah (1970) Set 4
Chan, Dianne (1979) Set 11
Chan, Susan (1994) Sets 83, 250
Chandarana, Yogain (1997) Set 110
Chandler, Alexander (1995) Set 46
Chandran, Parosha (1997) Set 17
Chaplain, Jayne (1995) Set 163
Chaplin, Adrian (1990) Set 11
Chaplin, John (1986) Set 230
Chapman, Graham (1998) Set 92
Chapman, James (1987) Set 6
Chapman, Jeffrey (1989) Set 44
Chapman, Matthew (1994) Set 129
Chapman, Nicholas (1990) Set 7
Chapman, Peter (1991) Set 39
Chapman, Rebecca (1990) Set 150
Chapman, Richard (1998) Set 229
Chapman, Vivian R (1970) Set 140 Profile p.1378
Chappell, Jessica (1997) Set 103
Chapple, Malcolm (1975) Set 98
Charbit, Valerie (1992) Set 4
Charkham, Graham (1993) Set 35

Charles, Deborah (1996) Sets 120, 212
Charles, Henry (1987) Set 180
Charles, Henry (1987) Set 82
Charlton, Alex (1983) Set 118 Profile p.1378
Charlton, Timothy (1974) (QC-1993) Set 14
Charlwood, Spike (1994) Set 112 Profile p.1378
Charman, Andrew (1994) Set 161 Profile p.1379
Chatterjee, Adreeja (1997) Set 156
Chatterjee, Mira (1973) Set 16
Chatterton, Mark (1983) Set 208
Chaudhry, Sabuhi (1993) Set 63
Chaudhry, Zia (1991) Set 209
Chaudhuri, Avirup (1990) Set 43
Chaudhuri, Robin (1988) Sets 171, 202, 251
Chavasse, Ann (1971) Set 156
Chawatama, Sydney (1994) Set 23
Chawla, Mukul (1983) (QC-2001) Set 11 Profile p.1379
Chbat, Nadia (1996) Set 73
Cheah, Albert (1989) Set 39
Cheema, Parmjit-Kaur (1989) Set 65
Cheetham, Julia (1990) Set 217
Cheetham, Lucy (1999) Set 113
Cheetham, Simon (1991) Set 28
Cheng, Serena (2000) Set 3
Cherrill, Beverley (1996) Set 180
Cherrill, Richard (1967) Set 11
Cherry, John M (1961) (QC-1988) Set 139
Cherryman, John (1955) (QC-1982) Set 13 Profile p.1379
Cherryman, Nicholas (1991) Set 103
Cheshire, Anthony (1992) Set 143
Cheves, Simon (1980) Set 144
Chichester, Julian (1977) Set 54
Child, Andrew J (1997) Set 136
Child, John (1966) Set 153 Profile p.1379
Chinner, Fer (1998) Set 45
Chippindall, Adam (1975) Set 166 Profile p.1379
Chisholm, Malcolm (1989) Set 46
Chivers, David (1983) (QC-2002) Set 30 Profile p.1379
Choo Choy, Alain (1991) Set 32 Profile p.1379
Choongh, Satnam (1994) Set 159
Choudhury, Akhlaq (1992) Set 81 Profile p.1379
Choudhury, Fareha (1995) Set 101
Choudhury, Nafeesa (1990) Set 237
Chowdhary, I (1982) Set 78
Christie, Aidan (1988) Set 118
Christie, David H (1973) Set 5
Christie, Iain (1989) Set 125
Christie, Michelle (1999) Set 242
Christie, Richard (1986) Set 117 Profile p.1379
Christie, Ronald D (1974) Set 176
Christie, Simon (1988) Set 205
Christie-Brown, Sarah (1994) Set 112
Christopher, Julian (1988) Set 114
Chruszcz, Charles (1973) (QC-1992) Sets 207, 218 Profile p.1380
Chudleigh, Louise (1987) Sets 104, 167 Profile p.1380
Chukwuemeka, John (1994) Set 209
Church, Camilla (1998) Set 139
Church, John (1984) Set 51
Chute, Andrea (1995) Set 150

Ciumei, Charles (1991) Set 31 Profile p.1380
Clapham, Andrew (1985) Set 88
Clappison MP, James (1981) Set 201
Clare, Allison (1992) Set 126
Clare, Michael (1986) Set 244 Profile p.1380
Clare, Stuart (1997) Set 208
Clargo, John (1994) Set 111
Claridge, Rachael (1996) Set 164
Clark, A (1994) Set 224
Clark, Andrew (1994) Set 221 Profile p.1380
Clark, Bryony (1985) Set 247
Clark, Christopher Harvey (1969) (QC-1989) Sets 121, 262, 265 Profile p.1380
Clark, Fiona (1982) Set 95 Profile p.1380
Clark, Geraldine (1988) Set 54
Clark, Julia (1984) Set 67
Clark, Neil (1987) Set 193
Clark, Paul (1994) Sets 207, 218
Clark, Peter (1988) Set 151
Clark, Rebecca (1989) Sets 207, 218
Clark, Wayne (1982) Set 40 Profile p.1380
Clarke, Andrew (1996) Set 179
Clarke, Andrew (1980) (QC-1997) Set 85 Profile p.1380
Clarke, Anna (1994) Set 138
Clarke, Christopher (1969) (QC-1984) Set 14
Clarke, Elizabeth (1991) Set 123 Profile p.1380
Clarke, Gerard (1986) Set 12 Profile p.1380
Clarke, Helen (1988) Set 76
Clarke, Ian (1990) Sets 63, 128
Clarke, Ivan (1973) Set 39
Clarke, Jamie (1995) Set 63
Clarke, Jonathan (1990) Sets 104, 167
Clarke, Jonathan (1999) Sets 207, 218
Clarke, L (1999) Set 210
Clarke, Malcolm (1994) Set 253
Clarke, Michelle (1988) Set 108
Clarke, Nicholas (1981) Set 228 Profile p.1380
Clarke, Patrick (1997) Set 3
Clarke, Paul (1997) Set 105
Clarke, Peter (1973) (QC-1997) Set 68
Clarke, Peter (1970) Set 249
Clarke, Rory (1996) Set 52
Clarke, S (1996) Set 210
Clarke, Sarah (1994) Set 43
Clarkson, Patrick (1972) (QC-1991) Set 27 Profile p.1380
Clarkson, Stuart (1987) Set 160
Claxton, Elroy (1983) Set 36
Claxton, Judith (1991) Set 248
Clay, Jonathan (1990) Set 52
Clay, Robert (1989) Set 3
Clayden, Sally (1999) Set 200
Clayton, Joanna (1995) Set 61
Clayton, Nigel (1987) Sets 191, 222
Clayton, Peter (1977) Set 140
Clayton, Richard (1977) (QC-2002) Set 38 Profile p.1381
Clayton, Stephen (1973) Set 59
Cleasby, Paul (1994) Set 198
Cleave, Brian (1999) (QC-1999) Set 57
Cleave, Gillian (1988) Set 46
Cleaver, Wayne (1986) Set 147
Cleeve, Thomas (1993) Set 8
Clegg, Richard (1999) Set 86
Clegg, Sebastian (1994) Set 217
Clegg, Simon (1980) Set 161

Clegg, William (1972) (QC-1991) Set 4 Profile p.1381
Clemens, Adam (1985) Sets 5, 17
Clement, Peter (1988) Set 59
Clemitson, Julie (1991) Set 234
Clews, Richard (1986) Set 193
Cliff, Elizabeth (1975) Set 205
Cliff, Graham (1973) Set 161
Clifford, James (1984) Set 87 Profile p.1381
Clifford, Steven B (1982) Set 159
Climie, Stephen (1982) Set 37 Profile p.1381
Clive, Nigel (1998) Set 186
Close, Douglas (1991) Set 131 Profile p.1381
Close, J (1997) Set 210
Clough, Geoffrey (1961) Set 154
Clough, Richard (1971) Set 127
Clover, Anthony (1971) Set 74
Clover, Sarah (1993) Set 159
Clutterbuck, Andrew (1992) Set 137
Cobb, Joanna (1999) Set 8
Cobb, Stephen (1985) Set 46 Profile p.1381
Cobbe, Matthew (1998) Set 173
Coburn, Michael (1990) Set 35 Profile p.1381
Cochand, Charles (1978) Set 258
Cochrane, Christopher (1965) (QC-1988) Set 52
Cockerill, Sara (1990) Set 31
Cockings, Giles (1996) Set 45
Cockrill, Timothy (1991) Set 202
Cocks, David (1961) (QC-1982) Set 126
Coe, Rosalind (1983) Set 247 Profile p.1382
Coen, Yvonne A (1982) (QC-2000) Set 5
Coffey, John (1970) (QC-1996) Set 147
Cogan, Michael (1986) Set 76
Coghlan, Terence (1968) (QC-1993) Set 23 Profile p.1382
Coghlin, Thomas (1998) Set 20
Cogley, Stephen (1984) Set 225 Profile p.1382
Cohen, Andrew (1982) Set 150
Cohen, Clive (1989) Set 133
Cohen, Edward (1972) Set 141 Profile p.1382
Cohen, Howard (1999) Set 217
Cohen, Jonathan (1974) (QC-1997) Set 113 Profile p.1382
Cohen, Jonathan (1999) Set 20
Cohen, Lawrence (1974) (QC-1993) Set 103 Profile p.1382
Cohen, Raphael (1981) Set 192 Profile p.1382
Coke, Edward (1976) Set 160
Coker, William (1973) (QC-1994) Set 5
Colbey, Richard (1984) Set 254
Colbey, Richard (1984) Set 144
Colborne, Michelle (1993) Set 163
Cole, Edward (1980) Set 40 Profile p.1382
Cole, Gordon (1979) Sets 207, 218
Cole, Justin (1991) Set 114
Cole, Lorna (1950) Set 186
Cole, Nicholas (1993) Set 160
Cole, Robert (1991) Set 192
Coleman, Anthony (1973) Set 111
Coleman, Bruce (1972) Set 46
Coleman, Elizabeth (1985) Set 113
Coleman, Guy (1998) Set 17
Coleman, Richard (1994) Set 44
Coles, Steven (1983) Set 22
Coley, William L (1980) Set 37

www.ChambersandPartners.com

1669

INDEX ■ BARRISTERS

Colin, Giles (1994) Set 23
Coll, Beth (1997) Set 159
Collaco Moraes, Francis (1985) Set 51
Collender, Andrew (1969) (QC-1991) Set 146 Profile p.1382
Collery, Shane (1988) Set 126
Collett, Ivor (1995) Set 129
Collett, Michael (1995) Set 35
Colley, Christine (1992) Set 193
Colley, Peter McLean (1989) Set 100
Collie, Peter (1994) Set 159
Collier, Jane (1994) Set 12
Collier, Martin (1982) Sets 171, 251
Collier, Peter (1970) (QC-1992) Sets 45, 196 Profile p.1382
Collings, Matthew (1985) Set 87 Profile p.1382
Collings, Nicholas (1997) Set 3
Collingwood, Timothy (1996) Set 131
Collins, Ben (1996) Set 23
Collins, Benjamin (1998) Set 179
Collins, James (1997) Set 214
Collins, James (1995) Set 31
Collins, John (1956) Set 201
Collins, Martin (1952) (QC-1972) Set 69
Collins, Michael (1998) Set 197
Collins, Michael (1971) (QC-1988) Set 31 Profile p.1382
Collins, Robert (1978) Set 201
Collins, Rosaleen (1996) Set 166
Collins, Scott (1994) Set 2
Collinson, Alicia (1982) Sets 62, 249
Colman, Andrew (1980) Set 65
Colover, Robert (1975) Set 16
Colquhoun, Celina (1990) Set 52
Coltart, Christopher (1998) Set 65
Colton, Simon (1999) Set 32
Colville, Iain (1989) Set 2
Comaish, Andrew (1989) Set 186
Comfort, Polly-Anne (1988) Set 109
Compton, Gareth (1997) Set 101
Compton, Timothy (1984) Set 127
Compton-Rickett, Mary (1972) Set 208
Compton-Welstead, Benjamin (1979) Set 71
Comyn, Timothy (1980) Set 61
Conaghan, Elizabeth (1999) Set 51
Concannon, Tim (1993) Set 254
Cone, John (1975) Set 30 Profile p.1383
Coney, Christopher (1979) Set 113
Conlin, Geoffrey D (1973) Set 130
Conlon, Michael (1974) (QC-2002) Set 122 Profile p.1383
Connerty, Anthony (1974) Sets 161, 201
Connolly, Barbara (1986) Set 5
Connolly, Dee (1982) Set 147
Connolly, Joanne (1992) Set 221 Profile p.1383
Connolly, Martina (1999) Set 80
Connolly, Oliver (1997) Set 9
Connolly, Simon (1981) Set 147
Connor, Elizabeth (2000) Set 41
Connor, Gino (1974) Set 45
Connors, Jess (2000) Set 38
Conrad, Alan (1976) (QC-1999) Set 223
Conrath, Philip (1972) Set 144
Conry, Michael (1979) Set 155
Constable, Adam (1995) Set 146 Profile p.1383

Constable, Victoria (2000) Set 73
Convey, Christopher (1994) Set 45
Conway, Charles (1969) Set 4 Profile p.1383
Conway, Helen (1999) Set 209
Conway, Robert (1978) Set 117
Coode, Jonathan (1984) Sets 83, 250
Cook, Alison (1989) Set 161
Cook, Beth (2000) Sets 171, 251
Cook, Charles (1966) Set 175
Cook, Christopher (1990) Sets 207, 218
Cook, Gary (1989) Set 162
Cook, Ian (1994) Set 70 Profile p.1383
Cook, J David (1982) Set 84
Cook, Kate (1991) Set 88
Cook, Mary (1982) Set 52 Profile p.1383
Cook, Matthew (1999) Set 32
Cook, Paul (1992) Set 165
Cook, Tina (1988) Set 111
Cook, Wendy (1997) Set 39
Cooke, Graham (1983) Set 36
Cooke, Julian (1965) Set 35
Cooke, Nicholas (1977) (QC-1998) Set 173 Profile p.1383
Cooke, Peter (1985) Set 158
Cooksley, Nigel (1975) (QC-2002) Sets 104, 167 Profile p.1383
Coombe, Peter (1993) Sets 83, 250
Coombes, Timothy (1980) Set 111
Coombes-Davies, Mair (1988) Set 174
Coonan, Kieran (1971) (QC-1990) Set 119 Profile p.1383
Cooper, Adrian (1970) Sets 60, 135
Cooper, Alan (1969) Set 38
Cooper, Arnold (1969) Set 72
Cooper, Ben (1999) Set 26
Cooper, Ben (2000) Sets 104, 167
Cooper, Danielle (1999) Set 150
Cooper, Gilead (1983) Set 136
Cooper, John (1985) Sets 190, 191, 222 Profile p.1383
Cooper, John (1983) Set 53 Profile p.1383
Cooper, Jonathan (1992) Set 25
Cooper, Mark (1998) Sets 191, 222 Profile p.1384
Cooper, Morris (1979) Set 161
Cooper, Nigel (1987) Set 33
Cooper, Peter (1996) Set 160
Cooper, Roger (1988) Sets 116, 238
Cooper, Susan (1976) Set 101
Cope, Siri (1997) Set 40
Copeland, Andrew (1992) Set 79
Copeland, Matthew (2000) Sets 191, 222
Copley, James (1997) Set 113
Coplin, Richard (1997) Set 69
Copnall, Richard (1990) Set 195
Coppel, Jason (1994) Set 81
Coppel, Philip (1994) Set 54
Coppel, Yvonne R (1976) Set 230
Coppola, Anna (1996) Set 125
Corbett, James (1975) (QC-1999) Sets 161, 201, 246 Profile p.1384
Corbett, Michelle (1987) Set 21
Corbett-Jones, Matthew (1999) Set 179
Cordara, Roderick (1975) (QC-1994) Set 31 Profile p.1384
Cordey, Daniel (1997) Set 266
Corfield, Sheelagh (1975) Set 169 Profile p.1384

Corkery, Michael (1949) (QC-1981) Set 114
Corless, John (1984) Set 203
Corner, Timothy (1981) (QC-2002) Set 54 Profile p.1384
Cornwall, Christopher (1975) Sets 207, 218
Cornwall, Virginia (1990) Set 165
Corrigan, Peter A (1972) Set 151 Profile p.1384
Corsellis, Nicholas (1993) Set 147
Corston MP, Jean (1991) Set 169
Cory-Wright, Charles (1984) Set 38 Profile p.1384
Cosedge, Andrew J (1972) Set 136
Cosgrove, Patrick (1976) (QC-1994) Set 234 Profile p.1384
Cosgrove, Thomas (1994) Set 52
Coster, Ronald (1989) Set 101
Cotcher, Ann (1979) (QC-2000) Set 147
Cottage, Rosina (1988) Set 50
Cotter, Barry (1985) Sets 104, 167 Profile p.1384
Cotter, Rachel (1994) Set 159
Cotterill, Susannah (1988) Set 84
Cottle, Stephen (1984) Set 47
Cotton, Diana (1964) (QC-1983) Set 24
Cottrell, M (1996) Set 210
Cottrell, Stephen (1998) Set 145
Coughlin, Elizabeth (1989) Set 45
Coughlin, Vincent (1980) Set 45
Coughtrie, Scott (2000) Set 160
Coulson, Peter (1982) (QC-2001) Set 69 Profile p.1384
Coulter, Barry (1985) Set 48
Counsell, Edward (1990) Set 264
Counsell, James (1984) Set 71
Counsell, Lynne M (1986) Set 140
Coupland, Steven (1993) Set 245
Courtenay, Charles (1999) Set 105
Cousens, Michael (1973) Set 151
Cousins, Christopher (1969) Set 73
Cousins, Edward (1971) Set 141
Cousins, Jeremy (1977) (QC-1999) Sets 161, 202 Profile p.1384
Cover, Martha (1979) Set 21
Cowan, Jack (1971) Set 208
Cowan, P (1980) Set 210
Coward, Stephen (1964) (QC-1984) Set 5 Profile p.1385
Coward, Victoria (1992) Set 68
Cowen, Gary (1990) Set 40
Cowen, Jonathan (1983) Set 127
Cowen, Jonathan (1983) Set 240
Cowen, Sally (1995) Set 41
Cowen, Timothy (1993) Set 141
Cowton, Catherine (1995) Set 123 Profile p.1385
Cox, Ailsa (1989) Set 161
Cox, Bryan (1979) Set 194
Cox, Buster (1993) Set 127 Profile p.1385
Cox, Jason (1992) Set 247
Cox, Kerrie (1998) Set 264
Cox, Kerry (1990) Sets 116, 238
Cox, Kharin (1982) Set 127
Cox, Laura (1975) (QC-1994) Set 20 Profile p.1385
Cox, Lindsay (1984) Sets 108, 181, 187, 243
Cox, Nicholas (1992) Set 137
Cox, Nigel (1986) Set 127
Cox, Raymond (1982) (QC-2002) Set 44 Profile p.1385
Cox, Simon (1992) Set 25 Profile p.1385
Coyle, Stephen (1998) Set 63
Crabb, Richard (1975) Set 182

Crabb, Samantha (1996) Set 157
Crabtree, Richard (1974) Set 147
Crabtree, Simon J G (1988) Set 230
Craddock, Xanthe (2000) Set 11
Cragg, Stephen (1996) Set 25 Profile p.1385
Craig, Alistair (1983) Set 97
Craig, Aubrey (1987) Sets 161, 188
Craig, David (1997) Set 24
Craig, Kenneth (1975) Set 63
Craig, Nicholas (1998) Set 33
Crail, Ross (1986) Sets 98, 200
Crampin, Paul (1992) Set 84
Crampin, Peter (1976) (QC-1993) Set 97 Profile p.1386
Cramsie, Sinclair (1988) Sets 83, 250
Cran, Mark (1973) (QC-1988) Set 14
Cranbrook, Alexander (1975) Set 11
Crane, Michael (1975) (QC-1994) Set 44 Profile p.1386
Crane, Rebecca (1998) Set 9
Cranfield, Peter (1982) Set 152
Cranmer-Brown, Michael (1986) Sets 9, 246
Cranston MP, Ross (1976) (QC-1998) Set 152
Cranston-Morris, Wayne (1986) Set 36
Crasnow, Rachel (1994) Set 20 Profile p.1386
Craven, Richard (1976) Set 119
Craven, Robert Michael (1979) Set 260
Crawford, Colin (1997) Sets 191, 222
Crawford, Grant (1974) Set 107
Crawford, Lincoln (1977) Set 82
Crawford, Robert (1976) Set 256
Crawford SC, James (1999) Set 88 Profile p.1386
Crawforth, Emma (1992) Set 184
Crawley, Gary (1988) Set 46
Cray, Timothy (1989) Set 75
Crean, Anthony (1987) Set 159 Profile p.1386
Crean, Catherine (1982) Set 252
Creaner, Paul (1990) Set 188
Cridland, Simon (1999) Set 130
Crigman, David (1969) (QC-1989) Set 155 Profile p.1386
Crilley, Darrel (1996) Set 231
Critchley, John (1985) Set 6
Critelli, N (1991) Set 140
Croall, Simon (1986) Set 33
Croally, Miles (1987) Set 6
Cronin, Kathryn (1980) Set 47
Cronin, Tacey (1982) Set 165
Cronshaw, Michael (1994) Set 117
Crook, Adam (1994) Set 55
Crookenden, Simon (1975) (QC-1996) Set 31 Profile p.1386
Crosbie, Susan (1988) Set 193
Crosfil, John (1995) Set 6
Crosland, J Ben (1992) Set 163
Cross, Anthony (1982) Set 256
Cross, Edward (1975) Set 51
Cross, James (1985) Set 118 Profile p.1386
Cross, Jane E (1982) Set 256
Cross, Joanna (1992) Set 194
Cross, Paul (1981) Set 237
Crossley, Justin (1993) Set 201
Crossley, Steven (1992) Set 197
Crosthwaite, Graham (1995) Set 70
Crouch, Andrew (1990) Sets 116, 238
Crouch, Stephen (1982) Set 19
Crow, Charles (1999) Set 159

Crow, Jonathan (1981) Set 137 Profile p.1386
Crowley, Daniel (1990) Set 146
Crowley, Jane (1976) (QC-1998) Sets 46, 174, 232 Profile p.1386
Crowley, John (1962) (QC-1982) Set 22
Crowson, Howard (1987) Set 199
Crowther, Jeremy (1991) Set 50
Crowther, Lucy (1999) Set 176
Crowther, Sarah (1999) Set 66
Crowther, Tom (1994) Set 176
Croxford, Ian (1976) (QC-1993) Set 153 Profile p.1386
Croxford, Thomas (1992) Set 12 Profile p.1386
Croxon, Raymond (1960) (QC-1983) Set 252
Crozier, Rawdon (1984) Sets 71, 253
Crystal, Jonathan (1972) Set 20 Profile p.1386
Crystal, Michael (1970) (QC-1984) Set 133 Profile p.1386
Csoka, Simon (1991) Set 229
Cudby, Markanza (1983) Set 47
Cuddigan, Hugo (1995) Set 134 Profile p.1386
Cullen, Edmund (1991) Set 87 Profile p.1387
Cullen, Felicity (1985) Set 57 Profile p.1387
Cullum, Michael (1991) Set 165 Profile p.1387
Culver, Thomas (1976) Set 150
Cummerson, Romilly (1998) Set 63
Cummings, Brian (1988) Sets 207, 218
Cummins, Brian (1992) Set 17
Cuninghame, Julian Gun (1989) Set 49
Cunningham, Claire (1996) Set 161
Cunningham, Graham (1976) Set 86
Cunningham, Jo (2000) Set 33
Cunningham, Mark (1980) (QC-2001) Set 87 Profile p.1387
Curnow, Ann (1957) (QC-1985) Set 75
Curran, Leo (1972) Set 111
Curran, Patrick (1972) (QC-1995) Sets 11, 174
Curran, Philip (1979) Set 223
Currer, Paul (2000) Set 239
Currie, Fergus (1997) Set 170
Curry, Peter (1953) (QC-1973) Set 137
Curtis, Charles (1992) Set 145
Curtis, Helen (1992) Set 47
Curtis, James (1970) (QC-1993) Set 75
Curtis, Michael (1982) Set 22
Curtis, Nicole D (1992) Set 108
Curtis-Raleigh, Giles (1992) Set 36
Curwen, David (1982) Set 170
Curwen, Michael (1966) Set 119
Cusworth, Nicholas (1986) Set 64 Profile p.1387
Cutress, James (2000) Set 44
Cutts, Emma (1998) Sets 202, 246
Cutts, Johannah (1986) Set 51
da Silva, David (1978) Set 136
Dabbs, David (1984) Set 101
Dagg, John (1980) Set 27
Dagnall, John (1983) (QC-1999) Set 105 Profile p.1387
Dahlsen, Peter (1996) Set 109
Daiches, Michael (1977) Set 101
Dakyns, Isabel (1992) Set 75
Dalal, Rajen (1991) Set 216
Dale, Derrick (1990) Set 44
Dale, Jonathan (1991) Set 208

BARRISTERS ■ INDEX

Dalesandro, Sherry (2000) Set 34
Daley, Nicola (2001) Sets 207, 218
Dalgleish, Anthony (1971) Set 72
Dallas, Andrew (1978) Set 193
Daly, David (1979) Set 144
Daly, Denis (1995) Set 141
Daly, Nigel (1979) Sets 83, 250
Dalziel, Alaric (1967) Set 195
Daniel, Nigel (1988) Set 79
Daniels, Iain (1992) Set 28
Daniels, Philippa (1995) Set 72
Danton, Kirstie (1999) Set 202
Darbishire, Adrian (1993) Set 68
Darby, Patrick (1978) Set 156
Darby, Rachel (1997) Set 18
Darbyshire, Robert (1995) Set 228
Dardis, Heather (2000) Set 159
Darian, Ann (1974) Set 168
Darling, Ian (1985) Set 59
Darling, Paul (1983) (QC-1999) Set 69 Profile p.1387
Darlington, Elizabeth (1998) Set 194
Darlow, Annabel (1993) Set 75
Darton, Clifford (1988) Set 180
Daruwalla, Navaz (1997) Set 4
Das, Kamala (1975) Set 169
Dashwood, Alan (1969) Set 60
Dashwood, Professor Alan (1969) Set 135
Date, Julian (1988) Set 6
Datta, Shomik (2000) Set 101
Davenport, Simon (1987) Set 66
Davey, Charles (1989) Set 209
Davey, Helen (1984) Set 117
Davey, Kate (1988) Set 34
Davey, Michael (1990) Set 33 Profile p.1387
Davey, Michelle (1993) Set 203
Davey, N (1978) (QC-2001) Set 198
Davey, Roger (1978) Set 17
Davey, Tina (1993) Set 11
Davey, Toby (1977) Set 54
David, Andrew (1986) Set 261
Davidson, Arthur (1953) (QC-1976) Set 20
Davidson, Edward (1966) (QC-1994) Set 107
Davidson, Katharine (1987) Set 64
Davidson, Nicholas (1974) (QC-1993) Set 92 Profile p.1387
Davidson, Ranald (1996) Set 130
Davie, Michael (1993) Set 118
Davies, Andrew (1988) Set 60
Davies, Anthony M (1971) (QC-1999) Set 108
Davies, Ben (1999) Set 174
Davies, Carol (1995) Set 259
Davies, Charles (1995) Set 142
Davies, Colin (1973) Set 175
Davies, Deborah (1993) Set 247
Davies, Edward (1998) Set 30
Davies, Eleanor (1998) Set 111
Davies, Emily (1989) Set 173
Davies, Felicity A (1980) Set 200
Davies, Graham (1971) Set 18
Davies, Helen (1990) Set 14 Profile p.1387
Davies, Hugh (1982) Set 223
Davies, Hugh (1990) Set 124
Davies, Huw (1998) Set 41
Davies, Huw (1985) Set 31
Davies, Huw (1978) (QC-2001) Set 174 Profile p.1387
Davies, Huw Rees (1982) Set 261
Davies, Iwan (1995) Set 260
Davies, J Meirion (1975) Set 176
Davies, Jake (1997) Set 115
Davies, Jane (1983) Sets 181, 187, 243
Davies, Jane (1981) Set 22 Profile p.1387

Davies, John (1981) Set 85
Davies, Jonathan (1981) Set 11
Davies, Jonathan (1971) Set 43
Davies, Leighton (1975) (QC-1994) Set 41
Davies, Lindsay (1975) Sets 171, 251 Profile p.1387
Davies, Liz (1994) Set 47
Davies, Michael (1979) Set 208
Davies, Nicholas (1975) Set 22
Davies, Nicola (1976) (QC-1992) Set 130 Profile p.1387
Davies, Owen (1973) (QC-1999) Set 47 Profile p.1387
Davies, Peter (1986) Set 208
Davies, Peter (1996) Set 173
Davies, Rhodri (1979) (QC-1999) Set 32 Profile p.1387
Davies, Richard (1973) (QC-1994) Set 38 Profile p.1387
Davies, Robert (1990) Set 166
Davies, Russell (1983) Set 217
Davies, Sarah-Jane (1996) Set 54
Davies, Sheilagh (1974) Set 79
Davies, Stephen (1985) Set 221 Profile p.1388
Davies, Stephen (1983) (QC-2000) Set 166 Profile p.1388
Davies, Trefor (1972) Set 260 Profile p.1388
Davies, Trevor (1978) Set 50
Davies-Jones, Jonathan (1994) Set 152 Profile p.1388
Davis, Adam (1985) Set 26
Davis, Andrew (1996) Set 22
Davis, Anthony (1986) Set 234
Davis, Brendan (1994) Set 73
Davis, Carol (1996) Set 85
Davis, Glen (1992) Set 133 Profile p.1388
Davis, Greville (1976) Set 74
Davis, Jonathan (1983) Set 158
Davis, Louise (1995) Set 200
Davis, Lucinda (1981) Set 180
Davis, Paul (1996) Set 256
Davis, Richard (1992) Set 67
Davis, Simon (1990) Set 161
Davis, Simon (1978) Set 36
Davis, William (1975) (QC-1998) Set 161
Davis-White, Malcolm (1984) Set 137 Profile p.1388
Davitt, Paula A (1988) Set 230
Davy, Neil (2000) Set 130
Daw, Chris (1993) Set 229
Dawar, Archna (1996) Set 165
Dawes, James (1993) Set 59
Dawes, Simon (1990) Set 206
Dawson, Adam (2000) Set 143
Dawson, Alexander (1969) Sets 83, 169, 250
Dawson, Ian (1971) Set 234
Dawson, J (1994) Set 210
Dawson, James (1984) Set 65
Dawson, Judy (1993) Set 170
Day, Anneliese (1996) Set 92 Profile p.1388
Day, Douglas (1967) (QC-1989) Set 41
Day, Robyn (1997) Set 254
D'Cruz, Rufus (1993) Set 126
D'Cruz, Rupert (1989) Set 106
de Bertodano, Sylvia (1993) Set 53
de Bono, John (1995) Set 203
De Burgos, Jamie (1973) Set 9
de Costa, Leon (1992) Set 45
De Freitas, Anthony (1971) Set 112 Profile p.1388
De Freitas, Melanie (1995) Set 111
de Garr Robinson, Anthony (1987) Set 32 Profile p.1388
de Haan, Kevin (1976) (QC-2000) Set 124 Profile p.1388

de Haas, Margaret (1977) (QC-1998) Sets 141, 208 Profile p.1389
de Jehan, David (1988) Set 199
De Kauwe, Lalith (1978) Set 47
de la Mare, Thomas (1995) Set 12 Profile p.1389
de la Piquere, Paul (1966) Set 40
De La Rosa, Andrew (1981) Set 106
de Lacy, Richard (1976) (QC-2000) Set 152 Profile p.1389
de Lotbiniere, Henry (1968) Set 146
De Marco, Nicholas (2001) Set 12
De Mello, Rambert (1983) Set 76 Profile p.1389
de Mestre, Andrew (1998) Set 137
de Navarro, Michael (1968) (QC-1990) Set 146 Profile p.1389
de Rohan, Jonathan (1989) Set 84
de Rozarieux, Louise (1999) Sets 121, 265
de Silva, Desmond (1964) (QC-1984) Set 110 Profile p.1389
de Silva, Harendra (1970) (QC-1995) Set 110
de Silva, Niran (1997) Set 85
de Souza, Mark (2000) Set 21
de Verneuil Smith, Peter (1998) Set 146
de Vries (Ret), Edo (1969) Set 254
de Waal, John (1992) Set 161
de Wilde, Robin (1971) (QC-1993) Set 143
Deacock, Adam (1991) Set 97
Deacock, Adam (1991) Set 180
Deacon, Emma (1993) Set 114
Deacon, Robert (1976) Set 141
Deal, Katherine (1997) Set 66
Dean, Brian (1994) Set 161
Dean, Jacob (1995) Set 125
Dean, Nicholas (1982) Set 5
Dean, Paul (1982) Set 22
Dean, Peter (1987) Set 9
Dean, Rosa (1993) Set 9
Deane, Vincent (1976) Set 214
Deans, Jacqueline (1998) Set 205
Dear, Ian (1999) Set 39
DeCamp, Jane (1987) Set 22
Dee, Jonathon (1989) Set 246
Deegan, Jeffrey (1989) Sets 171, 251
Dehn, Conrad (1952) (QC-1968) Set 44
Deignan, Mary-Teresa (1991) Set 18
Dein, Jeremy (1982) Set 53 Profile p.1389
Del Fabbro, Oscar (1982) Set 36
Del Mese, Francesca (1998) Set 76
Delahunty, Jo (1986) Set 150
Delaney, Kenneth (1996) Set 206
Demetriou, Marie (1995) Set 14
Dempsey, Karen (1996) Set 17
Dempster, Jennifer (1993) Set 126
Dempster, Tina (1997) Sets 80, 190
Den Brinker, Melanie (1984) Set 127
Dencer, Mark (1978) Set 144
Denehan, Edward (1981) Set 140
Denison, Simon (1984) Set 75
Denman, Robert (1970) Set 115
Dennett, Angelina (1980) Set 230
Denney, Stuart (1982) Set 217 Profile p.1389
Denning, Louisa (1999) Set 159
Dennis, David (1979) Set 203
Dennis, Mark (1977) Set 75 Profile p.1389
Dennis, Rebecca (1994) Set 168
Dennison, James (1986) Set 109

Dennison, Stephen (1985) (QC-2001) Set 3 Profile p.1389
Denniss, John (1974) Set 73
Denny, R H A (1969) Set 237
Dennys, Nicholas (1975) (QC-1991) Set 3 Profile p.1389
Dent, Adrian (1974) Set 188
Dent, Kevin (1991) Set 109
Dent, Stephen (1991) Set 166
Denton, Michelle (1996) Set 11
Denton-Cox, Gregory (2000) Set 137
Denyer-Green, Barry (1972) Set 40 Profile p.1389
Derbyshire, Thomas (1989) Set 4
Derrington, Jonathan (2000) Set 155
Desmond, Denis (1974) Set 158
Detter, Ingrid (1977) Set 54
Devlin, Jonathan (1978) Set 194
Devlin, Tim (1985) Set 117
Devonshire, Simon (1988) Set 81 Profile p.1390
Dew, Richard (1999) Set 106
Dewsbery, Richard (1992) Set 160
Dhadli, Pami (1984) Set 246
Dhillon, Jasbir (1996) Set 14
Dhir, Anuja (1989) Set 114
Diamond, Anna (1995) Set 159
Diamond, Christopher (1975) Set 229
Dias, Dexter (1988) Set 47
Dick, John (1974) Set 148
Dick, Julia (1988) Set 150
Dickens, Andrew (1983) Set 162
Dickens, Paul (1978) Set 67 Profile p.1390
Dicker, Robin (1986) (QC-2000) Set 133 Profile p.1390
Dickinson, Gregory (1981) (QC-2002) Set 245
Dickinson, J D (1986) Set 220
Dickinson, John (1995) Set 169
Dicks, Anthony (1961) (QC-1994) Set 31
Digby, Charles (1982) Set 117
Diggle, Mark (1996) Set 247
Dight, Marc (1984) Set 141
Dignum, Marcus (1994) Set 66
Dillon, Thomas (1983) Set 155
Din, Soofi (1984) Set 247
Dinan-Hayward, Deborah (1988) Set 165 Profile p.1390
Dineen, Maria (1997) Set 4
Dineen, Michael (1977) Sets 121, 168, 262, 265
Dines, Colin (1970) Set 43
Dines, Sarah (1988) Set 144
Dingemans, James (1987) (QC-2002) Set 66
Dinkin, Anthony (1968) (QC-1991) Set 52 Profile p.1390
Dismorr, Edward (1983) Set 160
Ditchfield, Michael (1993) Set 239
Diwan, Ricky (1998) Set 31
Dix-Dyer, Fiona (1986) Sets 193, 199
Dixey, Ian (1984) Set 169 Profile p.1390
Dixon, David S (1992) Set 200
Dixon, Huw (1999) Set 256
Dixon, John (1995) Set 209
Dixon, John (1975) Sets 62, 249
Dixon, Philip (1986) Set 144
Dixon, Ralph (1980) Set 263 Profile p.1390
Dixon, Rod (2000) Set 4
Dixon, Sorrel (1987) Set 51
Dobbin, Clair (1999) Set 124
Dobbs, Linda (1981) (QC-1998) Set 126
Dobson, Louise (2000) Set 228
Dockery, Paul (1973) Set 229
Docking, Tony (1969) Set 43

Doctor, Brian (1991) (QC-1999) Set 44
Dodd, Christopher (1984) Set 201
Dodd, John (1979) Set 4
Dodd, Margaret (1979) Set 4
Dodd, S (1987) Set 220
Dodds, R Stephen (1976) Set 256 Profile p.1390
Dodge, Peter (1992) Set 107
Dodson, Joanna (1971) (QC-1993) Sets 56, 194 Profile p.1390
Doerries, Chantal-Aimée (1992) Set 3 Profile p.1390
Doherty, Bernard (1990) Set 38
Doherty, Nicholas (1983) Set 79
Doherty, Patrizia (2000) Set 200
Dohmann, Barbara (1971) (QC-1987) Set 12 Profile p.1390
Doig, Gavin (1995) Set 239
Dolan, Bridget (1997) Set 130
Domenge, Victoria (1993) Set 7
Donaldson, David (1968) (QC-1984) Set 12
Donelon, Anne (1995) Set 72
Donne, Anthony (1973) (QC-1988) Sets 71, 168
Donne, Jeremy (1978) Set 68
Donnellan, Christopher (1981) Set 9
Donnelly, Kevin (1991) Set 223
Donoghue, Steven (1992) Set 173
Donovan, Joll (1991) Set 20
Donovan, Scott (1975) Set 203
Dooher, Nancy (1997) Sets 207, 218
Dooley, Allan (1991) Set 159
Dooley, Christine (1980) Set 117
Doran, Gerard (1993) Set 151
Doris, Susan (1998) Set 18
Dorman O'Gowan, Christopher (1979) Set 234
Dos Santos, Alexander (1999) Set 18
Dougherty, Charles (1997) Set 146
Dougherty, Nigel (1993) Set 30
Doughty, Peter (1988) Set 257
Douglas, Colin (1998) Set 176
Douglas, Michael (1974) (QC-1997) Set 118
Douglas, Stephen (1994) Set 230
Douthwaite, Charles (1977) Set 92
Dovar, Daniel (1997) Set 8
Dove, Ian (1986) Set 159 Profile p.1390
Dowding, Nicholas (1979) (QC-1997) Set 40 Profile p.1390
Dowley, Dominic (1983) (QC-2002) Set 131 Profile p.1390
Down, Barbara (1999) Set 180
Down, Jonathan (1993) Set 157
Downes, Paul (1991) Set 146
Downey, Aileen (1991) Set 50
Downey, Neil (1997) Set 203
Downey, Raoul (1988) Set 85
Downham, Gillian C (1993) Set 46
Downie, Andrew (1990) Set 208
Downing, Ruth (1978) Set 24
Downs, Martin (1990) Sets 23, 164
Doyle, James (1985) Set 17
Doyle, Louis (1996) Sets 191, 222 Profile p.1390
Doyle, Peter (1975) (QC-2002) Set 68
Drabble, Richard (1975) (QC-1995) Set 13 Profile p.1391
Dracass, Timothy (1998) Set 258 Profile p.1391
Drake, David (1994) Set 131
Drake, James (1998) Set 77

www.ChambersandPartners.com 1671

INDEX ■ BARRISTERS

Drake, Rachel (1995) Sets 83, 250
Drake, Sophie (1990) Set 163
Dray, Martin (1992) Set 40
Draycott, Jean (1980) Set 159
Draycott, Simon (1977) (QC-2002) Sets 83, 250
Drayton, Henry (1993) Set 51
Drew, Jane (1976) Set 21 Profile p.1391
Drew, Sandhya (1993) Set 150
Drew, Simon (1987) Set 159
Drinkwater, Philip (1995) Set 182
Driscoll, Jennifer (1989) Set 21
Driscoll, Lynn (1981) Set 193
Driscoll, Michael (1970) (QC-1992) Set 105 Profile p.1391
Driver, Emily (1988) Set 76
Driver, Simon (1991) Set 204
Driver, Stuart (1988) Set 203
Droop, Joanna (1998) Set 82
Druce, Michael (1988) Set 89 Profile p.1391
Drummond, Bruce (1992) Set 178
Dry, Nick (1996) Set 199
D'Souza, Carolyn (1994) Set 82
D'Souza, Dominic (1991) Set 110
Du Cann, Christian (1982) Set 38 Profile p.1391
du Preez, Robin (1985) Set 126
Dubb, Tarlowchan (1997) Set 159
Dubbery, Mark (1996) Sets 121, 262, 265
Duck, Michael (1988) Set 156 Profile p.1391
Duckworth, Peter (1971) Set 7
Duddridge, Robert (1992) Set 143
Dudley, Michael (1972) Set 155
Dudley, Robert (1993) Sets 207, 218
Dudley-Jones, Elizabeth (1997) Set 217
Duenas, Linda (2001) Set 175
Duff, Euan (1973) Set 234
Duff, Graham (1976) Set 239
Duffield, Stephen (1969) Set 239
Duffy, Derek (1997) Set 199
Duffy, Joanne (1994) Set 159 Profile p.1391
Dugdale, Jeremy (1992) Sets 181, 187, 243
Dugdale, Paul (1990) Set 71
Duggan, Michael (1984) Set 85 Profile p.1391
Duggan, Ross (1978) Set 209 Profile p.1391
Dulovic, Milan (1982) Set 51
Dumaresq, Delia (1984) Set 3 Profile p.1391
Dumont, Thomas (1979) Set 97 Profile p.1391
Duncan, John (1971) Set 216
Dunford, Matthew (1997) Set 178
Dunham, Nicholas (1999) Set 11
Dunkels, Paul (1972) (QC-1993) Sets 165, 183 Profile p.1391
Dunkin, Oliver (1999) Set 36
Dunn, Christopher (1996) Set 200
Dunn, Darren (1999) Set 229
Dunn, Katherine (1993) Sets 74, 239
Dunn, Katherine (1987) Sets 191, 222 Profile p.1392
Dunn, Sarah (1998) Set 122
Dunn, Tom (1998) Set 211
Dunne, Jonathan (1986) Set 149
Dunning, Graham (1982) (QC-2001) Set 31 Profile p.1392
Dunning, John (1973) Set 197
Dunn-Shaw, Jason (1992) Set 75 Profile p.1392
Dunstan, James (1995) Set 158
Durance, Alex (1997) Set 215

Durham Hall, Jonathan (1975) (QC-1995) Sets 18, 202
Durose, David W (1996) Set 110
Durr, Jude (1995) Sets 181, 187, 243
Durran, Alexia (1995) Set 36
Dutchman-Smith, Malcolm (1995) Set 208
Duthie, Catriona (1981) Set 169 Profile p.1392
Duthie, Malcolm (1989) Set 159
Dutton, Timothy (1979) (QC-1998) Set 44
Dutton, Timothy (1985) Set 129 Profile p.1392
Duval, Robert (1979) Set 169 Profile p.1392
Dyble, Ian (2000) Sets 181, 187, 243
Dyble, Steven (1986) Set 126
Dye, Brian (1991) Set 31
Dyer, Allen (1976) Set 118
Dyer, Jacob (1991) Set 256
Dyer, Nigel (1982) Set 64 Profile p.1392
Dyer, Roger (1980) Set 161
Dyer, Simon (1987) Set 20
Dykers, Joy (1995) Set 84
Dymond, Andrew (1991) Set 2 Profile p.1392
Eadie, James (1984) Set 131
Eady, Jennifer (1989) Sets 104, 167 Profile p.1392
Eales, Darren (2000) Set 146
Earlam, Simon (1975) Sets 207, 218
Earle, Judy (1994) Set 111
Earley, Sarah (1998) Set 180
Earnshaw, Stephen (1990) Set 45
Easteal, Andrew (1990) Set 245 Profile p.1392
Eastman, Roger (1978) Sets 60, 135 Profile p.1392
Easton, Alison (1994) Set 21
Easton, Jonathon (1995) Set 52
Eastwood, Charles (1988) Set 231
Easty, Valerie (1992) Set 47
Eaton, Bernard (1978) Set 43
Eaton, Deborah (1985) Set 70 Profile p.1392
Eaton, Nigel (1991) Set 31
Eaton, Thomas (1976) Set 203
Eaton Hart, Andrew (1989) Set 183
Eaton Turner, David (1984) Set 98
Eccles, David (1976) Set 221 Profile p.1393
Eckersley, Simon (1995) Set 246
Ecob, Joanne (1985) Set 9
Economou, George (1965) Set 33
Edelman, Colin (1977) (QC-1995) Set 24 Profile p.1393
Edenborough, Michael (1992) Set 67
Eder, Bernard (1975) (QC-1990) Set 31 Profile p.1393
Edey, Philip (1994) Set 35 Profile p.1393
Edge, Ian (1981) Set 111
Edge, Timothy (1992) Set 217 Profile p.1393
Edginton, Ronald (1984) Set 172
Edhem, Emma (1993) Set 74
Edie, Alastair (1992) Set 47 Profile p.1393
Edie, Anthony (1974) Set 84
Edis, Andrew (1980) (QC-1997) Set 203 Profile p.1393
Edis, William (1985) Set 23 Profile p.1393
Edlin, David (1971) Set 84
Edmondson, Harriet (1997) Set 174
Edmunds, Martin (1983) Set 183

Eduesi, Francis (1989) Set 215
Edwards, A (1972) Set 210
Edwards, Angus (1999) Set 145
Edwards, Daniel (1993) Set 266
Edwards, David (1994) Set 208
Edwards, David (1989) Set 77 Profile p.1393
Edwards, Douglas (1992) Set 61
Edwards, Glyn (1987) Set 169 Profile p.1393
Edwards, Heath (1996) Set 173
Edwards, Jennifer (1992) Set 18
Edwards, John (1994) Set 196
Edwards, John (1983) Set 161
Edwards, Martin (1995) Set 38
Edwards, Nigel (1989) Set 221
Edwards, Nigel (1995) Set 199
Edwards, Owen (1992) Set 179
Edwards, Peter (1992) Set 24
Edwards, Richard (1993) Set 152
Edwards, Sarah (1990) Set 123
Edwards, Simon (1987) Set 108
Edwards, Simon (1978) Set 7
Edwards, Susan (1972) (QC-1993) Set 36 Profile p.1393
Edwards, Susan (1998) Set 206
Edwards-Stuart, Antony (1976) (QC-1991) Set 22 Profile p.1393
Eeley, Rebecca (2001) Set 228
Egan, Caroline (1993) Set 158
Egan, Eugene (1993) Set 174
Egan, Marion (1988) Set 22
Egan, Michael (1981) Set 11 Profile p.1394
Egbuna, Robert (1988) Set 245
Egerton, C (1992) Set 198
Egleton, Richard (1981) Set 258
Eicke, Tim (1993) Set 31 Profile p.1394
Eidinow, John (1992) Set 98
Eilledge, Amanda (1991) Set 143
Eissa, Adrian (1988) Set 47 Profile p.1394
Ekaney, Nkumbe (1990) Set 165
Ekins, Charles W (1980) Set 200
Eklund, Graham (1984) (QC-2002) Set 146 Profile p.1394
Elcombe, Nicholas (1987) Sets 181, 187, 243
Elder, Fiona (1991) Set 165
Elfield, Laura (1996) Set 50
Elgot, Howard (1974) Set 195 Profile p.1394
Elias, David (1994) Set 173
Elias, Gerard (1968) (QC-1984) Set 41 Profile p.1394
Elias, Robert (1979) Set 223
Elkington, Ben (1996) Set 92
Ellacott, Stuart (1989) Set 254
Ellenbogen, Naomi (1992) Set 85
Elleray, Anthony (1977) (QC-1993) Sets 207, 218 Profile p.1394
Ellin, Nina (1994) Sets 120, 212
Ellins, Julia (1994) Set 12
Elliott, Christopher (1974) Set 232
Elliott, Eric (1974) Set 266
Elliott, Jason (1993) Set 109
Elliott, Margot (1989) Set 252 Profile p.1394
Elliott, Nicholas (1972) (QC-1995) Set 152
Elliott, Rupert (1988) Set 15 Profile p.1394
Elliott, Sarah (1996) Set 16
Elliott, Simon (2001) Set 32
Elliott, Timothy (1975) (QC-1992) Set 69 Profile p.1394
Ellis, Catherine (1987) Set 206
Ellis, Christopher (1991) Set 252
Ellis, Diana (1978) (QC-2001) Set 53 Profile p.1395
Ellis, Jonathan (1995) Set 19

Ellis, Michael (1993) Set 19
Ellis, Morag (1984) Set 52 Profile p.1395
Ellis, Roger (1962) (QC-1996) Sets 83, 250
Ellis, Sarah (1989) Set 11
Ellison, Mark (1979) Set 68 Profile p.1395
Eloquin, Sophie (2000) Sets 83, 250
Elsey, Roger (1977) Set 234
Elvidge, John (1988) Sets 64, 266
Elvin, David (1983) (QC-2000) Set 13 Profile p.1395
Elwick, Martin (1981) Set 245 Profile p.1395
Emanuel, Mark (1985) Set 56
Emerson, William (1992) Set 180
Emlyn Jones, William (1996) Set 59
Emmerson, Ben (1986) (QC-2000) Set 88 Profile p.1395
Engel, Anthony (1965) Set 156
Engelman, Mark (1987) Set 94
Engelman, Philip (1979) Set 20
England, Lisa (1992) Set 254
England, William (1991) Set 151 Profile p.1395
Englehart, Robert (1969) (QC-1986) Set 12 Profile p.1395
English, Richard (1996) Set 165
Enoch, Dafydd (1985) Set 36
Enright, Sean (1982) Set 11
Entwistle, Thomas (2001) Set 138
Ephgrave, Amy (1997) Set 168
Epstein, Michael (1992) Set 4
Epstein, Paul (1988) Set 20 Profile p.1395
Escott-Cox, Brian (1954) (QC-1974) Set 9 Profile p.1395
Espley, Susan (1976) Sets 171, 251 Profile p.1395
Esprit, Shaun (1996) Set 70
Etherington, David (1979) (QC-1998) Set 126 Profile p.1395
Evans, Alan (1978) Sets 191, 222
Evans, Alun (1971) Set 72
Evans, Andrew (1984) Set 109
Evans, Ann (1983) Set 55
Evans, Barnaby (1978) Set 73
Evans, Catrin (1994) Set 15 Profile p.1395
Evans, Claire (1994) Set 226
Evans, Clare (1995) Set 74
Evans, D Anthony (1965) (QC-1983) Set 11 Profile p.1395
Evans, David (1996) Set 183
Evans, David (1988) Set 23 Profile p.1395
Evans, David (1972) (QC-1991) Set 68 Profile p.1395
Evans, Delyth (1991) Set 51
Evans, Elwen Mair (1980) (QC-2002) Set 260 Profile p.1395
Evans, Gareth (1973) (QC-1994) Sets 99, 159 Profile p.1395
Evans, Hugh (1987) Set 92
Evans, Huw (1985) Set 176
Evans, James (1991) Set 152
Evans, Jane L (1971) Set 176
Evans, Jill (1986) Set 25 Profile p.1396
Evans, Joanna (1998) Set 150
Evans, John (1983) Set 155 Profile p.1396
Evans, John (1973) Set 237
Evans, Jonathan (1994) Set 153
Evans, Judi (1996) Set 169
Evans, Julian (1997) Set 68
Evans, Lee (1996) Set 41
Evans, Mark (1971) (QC-1995) Set 176 Profile p.1396
Evans, Martin (1989) Set 114
Evans, Michael (1988) Set 245 Profile p.1396

Evans, Paul Timothy (1992) Sets 207, 218
Evans, Philip (1995) Set 55
Evans, Richard (1993) Set 115
Evans, Robert (1989) Set 69
Evans, Roger (1970) Sets 62, 249
Evans, S (1985) Set 210
Evans, Simeon (1997) Set 232
Evans, Steven (1997) Set 19
Evans, Susan (1989) Set 265 Profile p.1396
Evans, T Gareth (1996) Set 182
Evans, Timothy (1984) Set 175
Evans, Timothy (1979) Set 87
Evans-Gordon, Jane (1992) Sets 98, 200
Evans-Tovey, Jason (1990) Set 22
Everall, Mark (1975) (QC-1994) Set 64 Profile p.1396
Everard, William (1973) Set 246 Profile p.1396
Everett, Steven (1989) Set 179
Ewart, David (1987) Set 122 Profile p.1396
Ewing, Hal (1997) Set 246
Ewins, Catherine (1995) Set 112
Ewins, James (1996) Set 123
Exall, Gordon (1991) Set 201
Exall, Rosemary (2000) Set 201
Eyre, Giles (1974) Set 50
Eyre, Stephen (1981) Set 155 Profile p.1396
Eyres, Anthony (1994) Set 230
Ezekiel, Adina (1997) Set 75
Faber, Trevor (1970) Set 156
Facenna, Gerry (2001) Set 90
Fadipe, Gabriel (1991) Set 153
Fairbairn, Rebecca (2000) Set 39
Fairbank, Nicholas (1996) Set 172
Falkenstein, John (1996) Sets 116, 238 Profile p.1396
Falkowski, Damian (1994) Set 86
Fallows, Paula (1981) Set 216
Fancourt, Timothy (1987) Set 40 Profile p.1396
Fane, Angela (1992) Set 48
Farber, Martin (1976) Set 138
Farbey, Judith (1992) Set 150 Profile p.1396
Farley, Roger (1974) (QC-1993) Set 111
Farley, Roger (1974) (QC-1993) Set 216
Farmer, Gabriel (1994) Set 166
Farmer, John M H (1970) Set 108
Farmer, Kimberly (1997) Set 74
Farmer, Matthew (1987) Set 59
Farmer, Michael (1972) (QC-1995) Set 48
Farnsworth, Emma (2000) Set 80
Farquhar, Stuart A (1985) Set 248 Profile p.1396
Farquharson, Jonathan (1988) Set 182
Farrell, David (1978) (QC-2000) Set 9
Farrell, Edmund (1981) Set 9
Farrell, Simon (1983) Set 124 Profile p.1396
Farrelly, Kevin (1993) Set 106
Farrer, Adam (1992) Set 157
Farrer, David (1967) (QC-1986) Set 5 Profile p.1396
Farrer, Paul (1988) Set 155 Profile p.1397
Farrimond, Stephanie (1987) Set 34
Farrington, David (1972) Set 53
Farror, Shelagh (1970) Set 21
Farrow, Adrian (1997) Set 216
Fatima, Shaheed (2001) Set 12
Faul, Anne (1996) Set 84
Faulks, Edward (1973) (QC-1996) Set 129 Profile p.1397

BARRISTERS ■ INDEX

Faulks, Samuel (1997) Sets 116, 238
Faux, Rachel (1997) Set 229
Favata, Emma (1999) Set 47
Fawcett, Gary (1975) Set 258
Fealy, Michael (1997) Set 32
Fearon, Sarah (2000) Set 186
Featherby, William (1978) Set 82 Profile p.1397
Feder, Ami (1965) Set 84 Profile p.1397
Feehan, Frank (1988) Set 101
Feest, Adam (1994) Set 71
Feinberg, Peter (1972) (QC-1992) Sets 151, 194 Profile p.1397
Feldman, Matthew (1995) Set 101
Feldschreiber, Peter (2000) Set 93
Felix, Alexandra (1999) Set 55
Fell, Alistair (1994) Set 149
Felstead, Christopher (1998) Set 173
Feltham, Piers (1985) Set 97
Femi-Ola, John (1985) Set 151
Fender, Carl (1994) Set 252
Fenhalls, Mark (1992) Set 36
Fenn, Peter (1979) Sets 126, 177
Fenny, Ian Charles (1978) Set 166
Fenston, Felicia (1994) Sets 60, 135
Fenton, Adam (1984) Set 77 Profile p.1397
Fenwick, Justin (1980) (QC-1993) Set 92 Profile p.1397
Ferguson, Christopher (1979) Set 170
Ferguson, Craig (1992) Set 65
Ferguson, Eva (1999) Set 112
Ferguson, Frederick (1978) Set 50
Ferguson, Gregor (1995) Set 127
Ferguson, Katharine (1995) Sets 171, 251
Ferguson, Niall (1996) Set 9
Ferguson, Richard (1956) (QC-1973) Set 151 Profile p.1397
Ferguson, Stephen M (1991) Set 108
Ferm, Rodney (1972) Set 197
Fern, Gary (1992) Set 94
Fernando, Giles (1998) Set 134
Fernyhough, Richard (1970) (QC-1986) Set 69 Profile p.1397
Ferrer, Peter (1998) Set 33
Ferrier, Susan (1985) Set 173 Profile p.1397
Ferris, Jonathan (1979) Sets 7, 128
Ferris, Shaun (1985) Set 22
Ferro, Jack (1998) Set 22
Ferry-Swainson, Richard (1994) Sets 121, 265
Fetherstonhaugh, Guy (1983) Set 40 Profile p.1397
Fetto, Niazi (1999) Set 146
Fewtrell, Nicholas (1977) Set 229
Field, Julian (1980) Set 22
Field, Martin (1966) Set 11
Field, Patrick (1981) (QC-2000) Set 217
Field, Rory (1980) Set 63
Fielden, Christa (1982) Set 76
Field-Fisher, Thomas (1942) (QC-1967) Sets 71, 168
Fieldhouse, Nigel (1976) Set 216
Fielding, Janick (1997) Set 110
Fields, Helen (1993) Sets 121, 262, 265
Fieldsend, James (1997) Set 144
Finch, Nadine (1991) Set 47 Profile p.1397
Finch, Thomas (1981) Set 234
Findlay, Archibald (1967) Set 38
Findlay, James (1984) Set 52 Profile p.1398
Findlay, Lorna (1987) Set 161

Finely, Catherine (1999) Set 97
Finlay, A S (1993) Set 237
Finlay, Darren (1994) Set 200
Finnigan, Peter (1979) Set 68
Finnis, John (1970) Set 86
Finucane, Brendan (1976) Set 36
Fireman, Mark (1986) Sets 224, 230
Firth, Alison (1980) Set 94
Firth, Clemency (1992) Set 147
Firth, Georgina (1995) Set 215
Firth, Matthew (1991) Set 123
Firth-Butterfield, Kay (1980) Set 46
Fish, David (1973) (QC-1997) Set 217 Profile p.1398
Fisher, Andrew (1980) Set 154
Fisher, Catherine (1990) Set 225
Fisher, David (1973) (QC-1996) Set 75 Profile p.1398
Fisher, David (1985) Set 143
Fisher, Jonathan (1980) Set 126
Fisher, Richard (1994) Set 25
Fisher, Richard (2000) Set 133
Fisher, Sandra (1993) Set 127
Fisher-Gordon, Wendy (1983) Set 109
Fishwick, Gregory (1996) Set 26
Fitton, Michael (1991) Set 165 Profile p.1398
Fitton Brown, Rebecca (1981) Set 202
Fitzgerald, Ben (2000) Set 68
Fitzgerald, Edward (1978) (QC-1995) Set 25 Profile p.1398
Fitzgerald, John (1971) Set 94
Fitzgerald, John (1998) Set 211
FitzGerald, Susanna (1973) (QC-1999) Set 32 Profile p.1398
Fitzgerald, Toby (1993) Set 59
FitzGibbon, Francis (1986) Set 25
Fitzgibbon, Neil (1989) Set 151
Fitzharris, Ginnette (1993) Set 111
Fitzpatrick, Francis (1990) Set 96
Fitzpatrick, Jerry (1996) Set 21
Fitzpatrick, Thomas (1988) Set 228
Flach, Robert (1950) Set 4
Flahive, Daniel (1982) Set 26
Flanagan, Julia (1993) Set 18
Flather, Gary (1962) (QC-1984) Set 54
Flaux, Julian (1978) (QC-1994) Set 77 Profile p.1398
Flax, Maya (1999) Set 149
Fleischmann, Laureen (1978) Set 117
Fleming, Adrian (1991) Set 71
Fleming, Paul (1983) Set 197
Flenley, William (1988) Set 112 Profile p.1398
Flesch, Michael (1963) (QC-1983) Set 57 Profile p.1398
Fletcher, Andrew (1980) Set 152 Profile p.1398
Fletcher, Christopher (1984) Set 244
Fletcher, David (1971) Set 169
Fletcher, Marcus (1990) Set 70
Fletcher, Prof Ian (1971) Set 133
Fletton, Mark (1997) Set 163
Flewitt, Neil (1981) Set 208
Flint, Charles (1975) (QC-1995) Set 12 Profile p.1398
Flockhart, Sharon (1997) Set 130
Flood, David (1993) Set 209
Flower, Philip (1979) Set 140
Floyd, Christopher (1975) (QC-1992) Set 134 Profile p.1398
Flynn, James (1978) Set 14 Profile p.1399
Flynn, Vernon (1991) Set 31 Profile p.1399
Fodder, Martin (1983) Set 85

Fogarty, P (1982) Set 210
Fogg, Anthony (1970) Set 18
Foley, Sheila (1988) Set 140
Folkes, Sandra (1989) Set 109
Fookes, Robert (1975) Set 89
Fooks, Nicholas (1978) Set 114
Forbes, Peter (1990) Sets 120, 212
Ford, Andrew (1997) Set 208
Ford, Caroline (1993) Set 197
Ford, Jeremy (1996) Set 143
Ford, Margo (1991) Set 246
Ford, Mark S (1991) Set 232
Ford, Michael (1992) Sets 104, 167 Profile p.1399
Ford, Monica (1984) Set 56
Ford, Neil (1976) (QC-1997) Set 165 Profile p.1399
Ford, Steven (1992) Set 5
Forde, Martin (1984) Set 23
Fordham, Allison (1990) Set 19
Fordham, Judith (1991) Sets 207, 218
Fordham, Michael (1990) Set 12 Profile p.1399
Fordham, Robert (1967) (QC-1993) Set 208
Forgan, Hugh (1989) Set 36
Forlin, Gerard (1984) Set 52 Profile p.1399
Formby, Emily (1993) Set 63
Forrest, Alastair (1972) Set 229
Forsdick, David (1993) Set 13
Forshall, Isabella (1982) Set 25
Forster, Brian (1977) (QC-1999) Sets 18, 239
Forster, Michael W (1984) Set 257
Forster, Sarah (1976) Set 56
Forster, Tim (1990) Set 45
Forster, Tom (1993) Set 126
Forsyth, Julie (1983) Set 205 Profile p.1399
Forsyth, Samantha (1988) Set 154
Forte, Mark (1989) Set 221
Forte, Timothy (1994) Set 26
Fortson, Rudi (1976) Set 53 Profile p.1399
Fortt, Russell (1999) Set 34
Fortune, Malcolm (1972) Set 130
Fortune, Peter (1978) Sets 51, 254
Foskett, David (1972) (QC-1991) Set 23 Profile p.1399
Foster, Alasdair (1998) Sets 171, 251
Foster, Alexander (1990) Set 195
Foster, Alison (1984) (QC-2002) Set 38
Foster, Catherine (1986) Sets 116, 238 Profile p.1400
Foster, Charles (1988) Set 119 Profile p.1400
Foster, Ian (1988) Sets 207, 218
Foster, Jonathan (1970) (QC-1989) Set 129
Foster, Jonathan (1970) (QC-1989) Set 229
Foster, P (1992) Set 210
Foster, Rosalind (1969) Set 146
Foster, Simon (1982) Set 71
Foudy, Kim Frances (1982) Set 221
Foulkes, Alison (1997) Set 75
Foulkes, Christopher (1994) Set 65
Foulser, Jane (1994) Set 176
Fowler, Michael (1974) Set 9
Fowler, Richard (1969) (QC-1989) Set 90 Profile p.1400
Fox, A (1986) Set 210
Fox, Andrew (1990) Set 231
Fox, John (1973) Set 84
Fox, Nicola (1996) Set 46
Fox, Simon (1994) Sets 161, 207, 218

Foxton, David (1989) Set 31 Profile p.1400
Foxwell, George (1987) Sets 171, 251
Foy, John (1969) (QC-1998) Set 50 Profile p.1400
Foy, Jonathan (2000) Set 72
France-Hayhurst, Jean (1987) Set 209
Francis, Adrian (1988) Set 103
Francis, Andrew (1977) Set 97
Francis, Edward (1995) Sets 29, 189, 235
Francis, Nicholas (1981) (QC-2002) Set 7 Profile p.1400
Francis, Richard (1974) Set 173
Francis, Robert (1973) (QC-1992) Set 130 Profile p.1400
Frank, Ivor (1979) Set 18
Franklin, Kim (1984) Set 22
Franklin, Stephen (1974) Sets 181, 187, 243
Fransman, Laurie (1979) (QC-2000) Set 47 Profile p.1400
Fraser, Alan (1990) Set 18
Fraser, Orlando (1994) Set 137
Fraser, Peter D (1989) Set 3 Profile p.1400
Fraser, Vincent (1981) (QC-2001) Sets 191, 222 Profile p.1401
Fraser-Urquhart, Andrew (1993) Set 54
Frazer, Alison (1999) Set 168
Frazer, Christopher (1983) Sets 62, 249
Frazer, Lucy (1996) Set 133
Freeborn, Susan C (1989) Set 37
Freedman, Clive (1978) (QC-1997) Set 85 Profile p.1401
Freedman, Clive (1975) Set 152 Profile p.1401
Freedman, Clive (1978) (QC-1997) Set 221
Freedman, Jeremy (1982) Sets 116, 238 Profile p.1401
Freeland, Simon (1978) (QC-2002) Set 34
Freeman, Marilyn (1986) Set 127
Freeman, Peter (1992) Set 41
Freeman, Sally (1995) Sets 181, 187, 243
Freeston, Lynn (1996) Set 63
French, Jonathan (1997) Set 188
French, Paul (1989) Set 166 Profile p.1401
Friday, Stephen (1996) Set 195
Fridd, Nicholas (1975) Set 165
Friedman, Charlotte (1982) Set 9
Friedman, Daniel (1996) Set 88 Profile p.1401
Friedman, David (1968) (QC-1990) Set 118 Profile p.1401
Friel, John (1974) Sets 48, 63 Profile p.1401
Friel, Michele (1991) Set 159
Friesner, David (1988) Set 228
Frieze, Daniel (1994) Set 230
Frieze, Robin (1985) Set 193
Friston, Mark (1997) Set 119
Frith, N (1992) Set 196
Frodsham, AM (1996) Set 210
Fry, Neil (1992) Set 21
Fryer-Spedding, James (1994) Set 228
Fryman, Neil (1989) Set 226
Frymann, Andrew (1995) Set 72
Fudge, Sally (1998) Set 45
Fugallo, Daniel (1999) Set 36
Fulbrook, Julian (1977) Set 25
Fulford, Adrian (1978) (QC-1994) Set 150 Profile p.1401
Fuller, Allan (1993) Set 165
Fuller, Jonathan (1977) (QC-2002) Set 71

Fullerton, Michael (1990) Set 74
Fullwood, Adam (1996) Set 215
Fulthorpe, Jonathan M (1970) Set 257
Furber, John (1973) (QC-1995) Set 153 Profile p.1401
Furlong, Richard (1994) Set 53
Furness, Corin (1994) Set 195
Furness, Jonathan (1979) Set 174 Profile p.1401
Furness, Michael (1982) (QC-2000) Set 153 Profile p.1401
Furniss, Richard (1991) Set 101
Furst, Stephen (1975) (QC-1991) Set 69 Profile p.1402
Furze, Caroline (1992) Set 153 Profile p.1402
Gabb, Charles (1975) Sets 121, 262, 265
Gadd, Michael (1981) Set 103
Gadd, Ronald (1971) Set 176
Gadsden, Mark (1980) Set 59
Gaisford, Philip (1969) Set 130
Gaisman, Jonathan (1979) (QC-1995) Set 77 Profile p.1402
Gaitskell, Robert (1978) (QC-1994) Set 69 Profile p.1402
Gal, Sonia (1982) Set 231 Profile p.1402
Galberg, Marc (1982) Set 8
Galbraith-Marten, Jason (1991) Set 20 Profile p.1402
Gale, Michael (1957) (QC-1979) Set 70
Gallafent, Kate (1997) Set 12 Profile p.1402
Gallagher, Brian (1975) Set 82
Gallagher, John (1974) Sets 48, 63
Gallagher, Maria (1997) Set 16
Gallagher, Stanley (1994) Set 2
Galley, Helen (1987) Set 103
Galley, Robert (1993) Set 198
Gallivan, Terence (1981) Set 76
Galloway, Malcolm (1992) Set 264
Galvin, Kieran (1996) Set 4
Gamble, Jamie (1999) Set 159
Gammie, Malcolm (1997) (QC-2002) Set 32 Profile p.1402
Ganner, Joseph (1983) Set 178
Garcia-Miller, Laura (1989) Sets 189, 235
Garden, Ian (1989) Set 206 Profile p.1402
Gardiner, Bruce (1994) Set 146
Gardiner, John (1968) (QC-1982) Set 96 Profile p.1402
Gardiner, Nicholas (1967) Set 43 Profile p.1402
Gardiner, Richard (1969) Set 33
Gardiner, Sebastian (1997) Set 53
Gardner, Alan (1997) Set 70
Gardner, Eilidh (1997) Set 101
Gardner, Piers (2000) Set 90
Garfield, Roger (1965) Set 175
Gargan, Catherine (1978) Set 9
Gargan, Mark (1983) Set 193
Garland, David (1986) Set 14
Garlick, Paul (1974) (QC-1996) Sets 37, 262
Garner, Adrian (1985) Set 60
Garner, Sophie (1990) Sets 143, 161
Garnett, Kevin (1975) (QC-1991) Set 67 Profile p.1402
Garnett, Susan (1973) Set 6
Garnham, Neil (1982) (QC-2001) Set 23 Profile p.1402
Garnier, Edward (1976) (QC-1995) Set 15
Garrett, Annalissa (1991) Set 119 Profile p.1403
Garrett, Michael (1967) Set 161
Garrido, Damian (1994) Set 117

INDEX ■ BARRISTERS

Garside, Charles (1971) (QC-1993) Set 228 Profile p.1403
Garside, Mark (1993) Set 155
Garson, Robert (1999) Set 79
Garth, Steven D (1983) Set 200
Gash, Simon (1977) Set 247
Gaskell, Nicholas (1976) Set 33
Gaskin, Leila (2000) Set 59
Gasztowicz, Steven (1981) Set 52
Gatenby, James M (1994) Set 205
Gateshill, Bernard (1972) Set 186
Gateshill, Bernard (1972) Set 185
Gatland, Glenn (1972) Set 237
Gatt, Ian (1985) (QC-2002) Set 85 Profile p.1403
Gatto, Nicola (1987) Set 228
Gau, Justin (1989) Sets 121, 262, 265
Gault, Simon (1970) Set 33
Gaunt, Jonathan (1972) (QC-1991) Set 40 Profile p.1403
Gaunt, Sarah (1992) Set 9
Gavaghan, Jonathan (1992) Set 106
Gavron, Jessica (1995) Set 11
Gaylord, Sheila (1983) Set 72
Geadah, Anthony (2000) Set 46
Gearty, Conor (1995) Set 88
Geary, Gavin (1989) Set 77
Geddes, Joanna (1992) Set 196
Gedge, Nick (2001) Set 175
Gee, Anthony (1972) (QC-1990) Set 231 Profile p.1403
Gee, Peta (1973) Set 109
Gee, Richard (1993) Set 216
Gee, Steven (1975) (QC-1993) Set 142 Profile p.1403
Gee, Toby (1992) Set 22
Geekie, Charles (1985) Set 46
Geering, Ian (1974) (QC-1991) Set 152 Profile p.1403
Geeson, Christopher (1989) Set 245
Geey, David (1970) Set 208
Geldart, William (1975) Set 76
Genn, Yvette (1991) Set 20
Genney, Paul (1976) Set 186
George, Andrew (1997) Set 12
George, Anna (1999) Set 160
George, Charles (1974) (QC-1992) Set 61 Profile p.1403
George, Mark (1976) Sets 47, 215
George, Nicholas (1983) Set 202
George, Sarah (1991) Set 161 Profile p.1403
Georges, Antonis (1972) Set 208
Gerald, Nigel (1985) Sets 29, 235
Gerasimidis, Nicolas (1988) Set 45
Gerrans, Daniel (1981) Set 103
Gerrard, L J (1996) Set 78
Gerrish, Simon (1993) Set 19
Geser, Anita (1992) Set 84
Gettleson, Michael (1952) Set 6
Ghaffar, Arshad (1991) Set 103
Ghosh, Julian (1993) Sets 122, 191, 222 Profile p.1403
Gibaud, Catherine (1996) Set 152
Gibb, Fiona (1983) Set 21
Gibb, Katherine (1999) Set 166
Gibberd, Anne (1985) Set 21
Gibbon, Juliet (1994) Set 176
Gibbon, Michael (1993) Set 87
Gibbons, Ellodie (1999) Set 144
Gibbons, James (1974) Set 136
Gibbons, Jeremy S (1973) (QC-1995) Set 257
Gibbons, Mary (1999) Set 142
Gibbons, Orlando (1982) Set 180
Gibbons, Perrin (1998) Set 50
Gibbons, Sarah (1987) Sets 62, 83, 249
Gibbs, Patrick (1986) Set 59 Profile p.1403

Gibney, Malcolm T P (1981) Set 257 Profile p.1403
Gibson, Arthur (1980) Set 203
Gibson, Caroline (1990) Set 70
Gibson, Charles (1984) (QC-2001) Sets 60, 135 Profile p.1403
Gibson, Christopher (1976) (QC-1995) Set 92 Profile p.1404
Gibson, Jill (1972) Set 97
Gibson, John (1991) Set 9
Gibson, John (1993) Set 209
Gibson, Jonathan (1982) Set 163
Gibson, Martin (1990) Set 86
Gibson, T (1981) Set 210
Giddens, Sarah (1999) Set 59
Gidney, Jonathan (1991) Set 160
Giffin, Nigel (1986) Set 81 Profile p.1404
Gifford, Andrew (1988) Set 93
Gilbart, Andrew (1972) (QC-1991) Sets 191, 222 Profile p.1404
Gilbert, Barry (1978) Set 4
Gilbert, Jane (1994) Set 239
Gilbert, Jayne (1976) Set 147
Gilbertson, Helen (1993) Sets 181, 187, 243
Gilchrist, David (1987) Set 228
Gilead, Beryl (1989) Set 248 Profile p.1404
Giles, Roger S (1976) Set 159
Gill, Jane (1973) Set 6
Gill, Manjit Singh (1982) (QC-2000) Set 76 Profile p.1404
Gill, Meena (1982) Set 21
Gill, Satinder (1991) Set 115
Gill, Simon (1977) Set 7
Gill, Tess (1990) Sets 104, 167 Profile p.1404
Gillard, Isabelle (1980) Set 151
Gillespie, Christopher (1991) Set 149
Gillespie, James (1991) Set 127 Profile p.1404
Gillett, Amanda (1998) Set 259
Gilliatt, Jacqui (1992) Set 16
Gillibrand, Philip (1975) Set 262
Gillies, Jennie (2000) Set 118
Gilling, Denise (1992) Set 150
Gillis, Richard (1982) Set 32
Gillott, Paul (1996) Set 256
Gillyon, Philip (1988) Set 30 Profile p.1404
Gilman, Jonathan (1965) (QC-1990) Set 31 Profile p.1404
Gilmore, Se-nin (1996) Set 92
Gilmour, Susan (1994) Set 216
Gilroy, Paul (1985) Set 228 Profile p.1404
Gimlette, John (1986) Set 23
Gingell, Melanie (1988) Set 150
Ginn, Alison (1980) Set 211
Ginniff, Nigel (1978) Set 203
Ginns, John (1977) Set 202
Ginsburg, Amanda (1985) Set 197
Gioserano, Richard (1992) Set 193
Giovannini, Angela (2000) Set 239
Giovene, Laurence (1962) Set 117
Giret, Jane (1981) (QC-2001) Set 141 Profile p.1405
Giret, Joseph (1985) Set 151
Girolami, Paul (1983) (QC-2002) Set 87 Profile p.1405
Gittins, Tim (1990) Set 239
Giuliani, Mark (1993) Sets 45, 234
Giz, Alev (1988) Set 76
Glancy, Robert (1972) (QC-1997) Set 24 Profile p.1405
Glaser, Michael (1998) Set 56

Glasgow, Edwin (1969) (QC-1987) Set 38 Profile p.1405
Glasgow, Oliver (1995) Set 65
Glass, Anthony (1965) (QC-1986) Set 68 Profile p.1405
Glassbrook, Alexander (1995) Set 145
Glasson, Jonathan (1996) Set 25 Profile p.1405
Gledhill, Andreas (1992) Set 133 Profile p.1405
Gledhill, Michael (1976) (QC-2001) Set 26
Gledhill, Orlando (1998) Set 32
Glen, Ian (1973) (QC-1996) Set 166 Profile p.1405
Glen, Philip A (1983) Set 257
Glenn, Paul (1983) Set 157
Glennie, Andrew (1982) Sets 83, 250
Glennie, Angus (1974) (QC-1991) Set 35 Profile p.1405
Glenser, Peter (1993) Set 258
Glick, Ian (1970) (QC-1987) Set 32 Profile p.1405
Globe, Henry (1972) (QC-1994) Sets 207, 218 Profile p.1406
Gloster, Elizabeth (1971) (QC-1989) Set 32 Profile p.1406
Glover, Anne-Marie (2000) Set 21
Glover, Marc (1999) Set 144
Glover, Richard (1984) Set 89 Profile p.1406
Glover, Stephen J (1978) Set 197 Profile p.1406
Glyn, Caspar (1992) Set 20
Glynn, Joanna (1983) (QC-2002) Set 36
Glynn, Stephen (1990) Set 50
Goatley, Peter (1992) Set 159
Gobir, Nuhu (1998) Set 173
Goddard, Andrew (1985) Set 3 Profile p.1406
Goddard, Christopher (1973) Set 24 Profile p.1406
Goddard, Keith (1959) (QC-1979) Set 217
Goddard, Philip (1985) Set 73
Goddard, Richard (1999) Set 216
Goddard, Suzanne (1986) Set 223
Godfrey, Gerald (1954) (QC-1971) Sets 132, 141
Godfrey, Howard (1970) (QC-1991) Set 4 Profile p.1406
Godfrey, John (1985) Set 186
Godfrey, Jonathan (1990) Set 195
Godfrey, Louise (1974) (QC-1992) Set 56
Godfrey, Timothy (1997) Set 149
Godsmark, Nigel G (1979) (QC-2001) Set 5
Godwin, William (1986) Set 35
Goff, Anthony (1978) Set 204
Goh, Allan (1984) Set 79
Gold, Debra (1985) Set 47
Goldberg, David (1971) (QC-1987) Set 57 Profile p.1406
Goldberg, Jonathan (1971) (QC-1989) Sets 149, 216 Profile p.1406
Goldberg, Simon (1999) Set 239
Goldblatt, Simon (1953) (QC-1972) Set 38
Goldman, Linda (1990) Set 93
Goldrein, Eric (1961) Set 203
Goldrein, Iain (1975) (QC-1997) Sets 141, 208 Profile p.1407
Goldring, Jeremy (1996) Set 133 Profile p.1407
Goldsmith, Lord (1972) (QC-1987) Set 44
Goldstaub, Anthony (1972) (QC-1992) Sets 82, 247
Goldstein, Wayne Nathan (1999) Set 214

Goldstone, David (1986) Set 33 Profile p.1407
Goldstone, L Clement (1971) (QC-1993) Set 231 Profile p.1407
Goldwater, Michael (1977) Set 216
Golinski, Robert (1990) Set 203
Gollop, Katharine (1993) Set 24
Gompertz, Jeremy (1962) (QC-1988) Set 34
Goodall, Charles (1986) Set 168
Goodall, Emma (1996) Set 26
Goodall, Patrick (1998) Set 44
Goodall, Rachael (2000) Set 258
Goodbody, P (1986) Set 210
Goodchild, Elizabeth (1981) Set 17
Goode, Sir Roy (1988) (QC-1990) Set 12 Profile p.1407
Goode, Rowena (1974) Set 231 Profile p.1407
Goodfellow, Giles W J (1983) Set 122
Goodfellow, Stephen (1997) Sets 181, 187, 243
Goodhart, Lord (1957) (QC-1979) Set 49 Profile p.1407
Goodison, Adam (1990) Set 133 Profile p.1407
Goodman, Andrew (1978) Set 129
Goodman, Bernadette (1983) Set 206
Goodman, Simon (1996) Set 169
Goodrich, Siobhan (1980) Set 119
Goodwin, Caroline (1988) Set 239
Goodwin, Deirdre (1974) Sets 83, 250
Goodwin, Michael (1996) Set 11
Goodwin, Nell (2000) Set 229
Goodwin, Nicholas (1995) Sets 62, 249
Goodwin-Gill, Guy (1971) Set 12
Goolamali, Nina (1995) Set 146
Goold, Alexander (1994) Set 63
Goolo, Tianne (1998) Set 63
Goose, Julian (1984) (QC-2002) Set 201
Gordon, Christina (1997) Set 150
Gordon, David M (1984) Set 200
Gordon, Jeremy (1974) Set 84
Gordon, Katharine (1988) Set 146
Gordon, Mark (1990) Set 19
Gordon, Richard (1972) (QC-1994) Set 14 Profile p.1407
Gordon-Saker, Andrew (1981) Sets 171, 251
Gordon-Saker, Liza (1982) Sets 171, 251
Gore, Allan (1977) Set 82 Profile p.1408
Gore, Andrew (1973) Sets 171, 251
Gore, Mark (1994) Set 197
Gore, Susan (1993) Set 21
Gore-Andrews, Gavin (1972) Sets 60, 135
Gorton, C (1999) Set 220
Gorton, Simon (1988) Set 203
Gosling, Jonathan (1980) Set 157 Profile p.1408
Gosnell, Steven (1995) Set 245
Goss, James (1975) (QC-1997) Sets 126, 193
Gott, Paul (1991) Set 44
Goudie, James (1970) (QC-1984) Set 81 Profile p.1408
Goudie, Martin (1996) Set 18
Gould, Deborah (1990) Set 209
Goulding, Jonathan (1984) Set 49 Profile p.1408

Goulding, Paul (1984) (QC-2000) Set 12 Profile p.1408
Gourgey, Alan (1984) Set 141
Gouriet, Gerald (1974) Set 124 Profile p.1408
Gourley, Claire (1996) Sets 207, 218
Gow, Ben (1994) Set 19
Gow, Elizabeth (1995) Set 260
Gowen, Matthew (1992) Set 126
Gowen, Matthew (1992) Set 177
Gower, Helen (1992) Sets 104, 167
Gower, Peter (1985) Sets 120, 212 Profile p.1408
Gowling, Nigel (2000) Set 155
Goy, David (1973) (QC-1991) Set 57 Profile p.1408
Gozem, Guy (1972) (QC-1997) Set 223
Grabiner, Lord (1968) (QC-1981) Set 32 Profile p.1408
Grace, John (1973) (QC-1994) Set 130 Profile p.1408
Grace, Jonathan (1989) Set 217
Grace, Timothy (1993) Set 203
Grace, Tonia (1992) Set 214
Graffius, Mark (1990) Set 43
Graham, Charles (1986) Set 32
Graham, Ian (1978) Set 237
Graham, Michael (1999) Set 239
Graham, Stuart (1996) Set 237
Graham, Thomas (1985) Set 98
Grahame, Nina (1993) Set 65
Grainger, Ian (1978) Set 32
Grange, Kate (1998) Set 38
Granshaw, Sara (1991) Sets 62, 249
Grant, Amanda (1988) Set 23
Grant, David (1999) Set 37
Grant, Edward (1994) Sets 120, 212
Grant, Gary (1995) Set 149
Grant, Gary A (1985) Set 257
Grant, Kenneth (1998) Set 204
Grant, Malcolm (1986) Set 54
Grant, Marcus (1993) Set 145
Grant, Thomas (1993) Set 105
Grantham, Andrew (1991) Sets 191, 222
Granville-Fall, A (1990) Set 196
Graves, Celia (1981) Set 47
Gray, Gilbert (1953) (QC-1971) Sets 124, 194 Profile p.1408
Gray, Justin (1993) Sets 127, 239
Gray, Margaret (1998) Set 14
Gray, Nicola (1991) Set 64
Gray, Pauline (1980) Set 63
Gray, Peter (1983) Set 17
Gray, Richard (1970) (QC-1993) Set 38 Profile p.1408
Gray, Richard (1986) Sets 230, 231
Gray, Steven (2000) Set 5
Greaney, Nicola (1999) Set 38
Greaney, Paul (1993) Set 194
Greatorex, Helen (1997) Set 201
Greatorex, Paul (1999) Set 54
Greaves, John (1973) Set 11
Greaves, Michael (1976) Set 9
Green, Alison (1974) Set 146
Green, Amanda (1990) Set 152
Green, Andrew (1988) Set 12
Green, Andrew (1974) Set 174
Green, Brian (1980) (QC-1997) Set 153 Profile p.1408
Green, Colin (1982) Set 216
Green, David (1993) Set 203
Green, David (1979) (QC-2000) Set 126
Green, Dore (1994) Set 146
Green, Henry (1962) (QC-1988) Sets 126, 177
Green, Jonathan (1993) Set 26
Green, Ken (2001) Set 163

BARRISTERS ■ INDEX

Green, Michael (1987) Set 44 Profile p.1408
Green, Nicholas (1986) (QC-1998) Set 14 Profile p.1409
Green, Patrick (1990) Sets 60, 135
Green, Robin (1992) Set 52
Green, Samuel (1998) Set 194
Green, Sir Allan (1959) (QC-1987) Set 65
Green, Tim (1995) Set 156
Green, Victoria (1994) Set 159
Greenan, John (1984) Set 63
Greenan, Sarah (1987) Set 201
Greenberg, Joanna (1972) (QC-1994) Set 149 Profile p.1409
Greenbourne, John (1978) Set 22
Greene, Maurice (1982) Set 231
Greene, Paul (1994) Set 211
Greenfield, Jeremy (1995) Set 208
Greenhill, Julian (1997) Set 153
Greening, Richard (1975) Set 24
Greenwood, Alexander (2002) Set 176
Greenwood, Celestine (1991) Set 205
Greenwood, Christopher (1978) (QC-1999) Set 31 Profile p.1409
Greenwood, Paul (1991) Set 137
Gregg, Jonathan (1990) Set 216
Gregory, Ann Marie (1994) Set 199
Gregory, Barry (1987) Set 45
Gregory, James (1970) Set 223 Profile p.1409
Gregory, John (1972) Set 217
Gregory, Julian (2001) Set 90
Gregory, Karen (1985) Sets 207, 218
Gregory, Peter (1982) Set 208
Gregory, Philip (1975) Set 158 Profile p.1409
Gregory, Richard (1993) Set 247
Gregory, Richard (2000) Set 101
Gregory, Rupert (1998) Set 79
Grenfell, Jeremy Gibson (1969) (QC-1994) Set 117
Grennan, Barry (1977) Set 219
Grenyer, Mark (1969) Set 266
Gresford, Lord Thomas of (1967) (QC-1979) Set 179
Gresty, Denise L (1990) Set 200
Grewal, Harjit (1980) Set 76
Grey, Eleanor (1990) Set 38
Grey, Michael (1975) Set 154
Grey, Philip (1996) Set 63
Grey, Robert (1979) Set 111
Grey, Robin (1957) (QC-1979) Set 68 Profile p.1409
Grey, Siobhan (1994) Set 18
Grey, Timothy (1999) Set 43
Grice, Joanna (1991) Set 70
Grice, Kevin (1977) Set 208
Grice, Peter (1984) Set 160
Grice, Timothy (1975) Set 169
Grief, Alison (1990) Set 47
Grierson, N Jonathan (1999) Set 229
Grierson, Robert (1991) Set 161
Grieve, Dominic (1980) Set 145 Profile p.1409
Grieve, Michael (1975) (QC-1998) Set 25 Profile p.1409
Grieves-Smith, Peter (1989) Set 75
Griffin, Ian (1997) Set 16
Griffin, Lynn (1991) Set 36
Griffin, Neil (1996) Set 11
Griffin, Nicholas (1992) Set 114
Griffin, Paul (1979) Set 33
Griffith, Peter (1964) Set 254
Griffith-Jones, David (1975) (QC-2000) Set 24 Profile p.1410
Griffiths, Alan (1981) Set 32 Profile p.1409

Griffiths, Conrad (1986) Sets 60, 135
Griffiths, Courtenay (1980) (QC-1998) Set 47 Profile p.1409
Griffiths, Emma (1998) Set 111
Griffiths, Hayley (1990) Set 257
Griffiths, Hugh (1972) Set 45
Griffiths, Martin (1986) Set 31 Profile p.1410
Griffiths, Patrick Thomas John (1973) Set 260
Griffiths, Peter (1970) (QC-1995) Sets 4, 174
Griffiths, Peter (1977) Set 137 Profile p.1410
Griffiths, Robert (1988) Set 257
Griffiths, Robin (1970) Set 109
Griffiths, Roger (1983) Set 176
Griffiths, Tania (1982) Sets 207, 218
Griffiths, W Robert (1974) (QC-1993) Set 54
Grime, Andrew (1997) Sets 121, 262, 265
Grime, Stephen (1970) (QC-1987) Set 217 Profile p.1410
Grimshaw, Libby (1993) Set 246
Grimshaw, Nicholas (1988) Set 217
Gritt, Edmund (1997) Set 124
Grodzinski, Sam (1996) Set 38
Groome, David (1987) Set 114
Ground, Patrick (1960) (QC-1981) Set 52
Ground, Richard (1994) Set 52
Grout-Smith, Jeremy (1986) Set 226
Grover, Timothy (1991) Set 208
Groves, Hugo (1980) Sets 29, 189, 235 Profile p.1410
Grubb, Andrew (1980) Set 130
Gruchy, Simon (1993) Set 151
Gruder, Jeffrey (1977) (QC-1997) Set 31 Profile p.1410
Gruffydd, J (1992) Set 210
Grumbar, Paul (1974) Set 169
Grundy, Arabella (1995) Sets 121, 265
Grundy, Clare (1989) Set 231
Grundy, Liam (1995) Set 203
Grundy, Madeleine (1999) Set 117
Grundy, Milton (1954) Set 57
Grundy, Nicholas (1993) Set 115
Grundy, Nigel (1983) Set 228 Profile p.1410
Grundy, Philip (1980) Sets 151, 231
Grunwald, Henry C (1972) (QC-1999) Set 151
Guest, Helen (1996) Set 149
Guest, Neil (1989) Set 149
Guest, Peter (1975) Set 150
Guest, Prof Stephen (1980) Set 143
Guggenheim, Anna (1982) (QC-2001) Set 22
Guha, Anita (1999) Set 127
Gulliver, Alison (1989) Set 112
Gumbel, Elizabeth-Anne (1974) (QC-1999) Set 143
Gumbiti-Zimuto, Andrew (1983) Set 76
Gumbs, Annette (1994) Set 231
Gumpert, Benjamin (1987) Set 9
Gumsley, Carl (1989) Set 237
Gunning, Alexander (1994) Set 118
Gunther, Elizabeth (1993) Sets 121, 262, 265
Guppy, Claire (2001) Sets 116, 238
Gupta, Diya Sen (2000) Set 24
Gupta, Piu Das (1999) Set 32
Gupta, Teertha (1990) Set 127

Gupta, Usha (1984) Set 110
Gursoy, Ramiz (1991) Set 110
Guthrie, Cara (2000) Set 37
Guthrie, James (1975) (QC-1993) Set 66
Guthrie, Mark J (1984) Set 150
Guy, David (1972) Set 144
Guy, Richard (1970) Set 127
Habel, Jessica (1991) Set 259
Hacker, Richard (1977) (QC-1998) Set 133 Profile p.1410
Hackett, Martin (1994) Set 256
Hackett, Philip (1978) (QC-1999) Set 4 Profile p.1410
Hacking, Anthony (1965) (QC-1983) Set 70
Hacking, The Lord (1963) Set 85
Hacon, Richard (1979) Set 134 Profile p.1410
Haddon-Cave, Charles (1978) (QC-1999) Set 33 Profile p.1410
Hadfield, Charlotte (1999) Set 63
Hadley, Richard (1997) Set 159
Hadrill, Keith (1977) Set 11
Haeems, David (1996) Set 151
Haggan, Nicholas Somerset (1977) Set 257 Profile p.1411
Hague, Paul (1983) Set 256
Haigh, M (1970) Set 196
Haines, John (1967) Set 52
Haisley, Matthew (1999) Set 221
Hajimitsis, Anthony (1984) Set 201 Profile p.1411
Halden, Angus (1999) Set 168
Hale, Charles (1992) Set 113
Hale, Grace (1998) Set 246
Hale, Sean (1988) Set 246
Hales, Sally-Ann (1988) Set 126
Halkerston, Graeme (1994) Set 32
Halkerston, Sally (1994) Set 59
Halkyard, Kay (1980) Set 46
Hall, Andrew (1991) (QC-2002) Set 25 Profile p.1411
Hall, Angela (2000) Set 115
Hall, David (1980) Set 201
Hall, Jacqueline (1994) Set 126
Hall, Jeremy (1988) Set 172
Hall, Joanna (1973) Set 56 Profile p.1411
Hall, John (1948) (QC-1967) Set 144
Hall, Matthew (1999) Sets 191, 222
Hall, Melanie (1982) (QC-2002) Set 90
Hall, Michael (1996) Set 72
Hall, Michael (1983) Set 47
Hall, Philip J (1973) Set 205
Hall, Richard (1995) Set 258
Hall, Richard (1991) Set 203
Hall, Robert (1997) Set 164
Hall, Yasmin (1993) Set 254
Hall Taylor, Alex (1996) Set 92
Hallam, Jacob (1996) Set 75
Hallam, RML (1984) Set 196
Halliday, Harold (1972) Sets 191, 222
Halliday, Ian (1989) Set 168
Halliday-Davis, Lee (1999) Set 151
Halligan, Brendan (1998) Set 76
Halligan, Rodney (1972) Set 208
Hallissey, Caroline (1990) Set 63
Halliwell, Mark (1985) Sets 191, 222 Profile p.1411
Halliwell, Toby (1992) Set 170
Halloran, Cathy (1997) Set 150
Halloran, Ceilidh (1992) Set 2
Hall-Smith, Martin (1972) Set 48
Halpern, David (1978) Set 92 Profile p.1411
Halsall, Kim (1982) Set 147
Halsey, Mark (1974) Set 4
Halstead, Robin (1996) Set 110

Ham, Robert (1973) (QC-1994) Set 153 Profile p.1411
Hamblen, Nicholas (1981) (QC-1997) Set 35 Profile p.1411
Hamblin, Stewart (1990) Set 59
Hamer, George (1974) Set 95 Profile p.1411
Hamer, Keneth (1975) Set 135
Hamer, Kenneth (1975) Set 60
Hames, Christopher (1987) Set 113
Hamey, John (1979) Sets 181, 187, 243
Hamill, Hugh (1988) Set 82
Hamilton, Amanda (1995) Set 147
Hamilton, Carolyn (1996) Set 6
Hamilton, Eben (1962) (QC-1981) Set 98 Profile p.1411
Hamilton, Eleanor (1979) (QC-1999) Set 193 Profile p.1411
Hamilton, Gavin (1979) Set 92
Hamilton, Jaime (1993) Set 228
Hamilton, Nigel (1965) (QC-1981) Set 169
Hamilton, Penelope (1972) Set 122
Hamilton, Peter (1968) Set 118
Hamilton, Philippa (1996) Set 44
Hamilton, Simon (1992) Set 180
Hamilton-Hague, Rachael (1993) Set 221
Hamilton-Shield, Anna (1989) Set 18
Hamlin, Patrick (1970) Set 101
Hammerton, Alastair (1983) Set 129
Hammerton, Veronica (1977) Set 129
Hammond, Fayaz (1999) Set 227
Hammond, Sean (1991) Set 126
Hampton, Alison (1977) Set 247
Hanbury, William (1985) Set 188
Hancock, Christopher (1983) (QC-2000) Set 35
Hancox, Sally (1996) Set 159
Hand, Anthony (1989) Set 259
Hand, John (1972) (QC-1988) Sets 104, 167, 228 Profile p.1411
Hand, Jonathan ES (1990) Set 37
Handyside, Richard (1993) Set 44 Profile p.1411
Hanham, James (1996) Set 140
Hankin, Jonas (1994) Set 154
Hanlon, Jacqui (1994) Sets 181, 187, 243
Hannaford, Sarah (1989) Set 69 Profile p.1412
Hannam, Timothy (1995) Set 157
Hansen, William (1992) Sets 113, 159
Hantusch, Robert A (1982) Set 136
Hapgood, Mark (1979) (QC-1994) Set 14 Profile p.1412
Haque, Muhammed (1997) Set 22
Harbage, William (1983) Set 9
Harbottle, Gwilym (1987) Set 67
Hardiman, Adrian (1988) Set 25
Harding, Cherry (1978) Set 127 Profile p.1412
Harding, Richard (1992) Set 69
Harding-Roberts, Peter (1981) Set 176
Hardwick, Matthew (1994) Set 152
Hardy, Amanda (1993) Set 102
Hardy, John (1988) Set 124
Hardy, Paul (1992) Set 61
Haren, Sarah (1999) Set 138
Harford-Bell, Nerida (1984) Set 47
Hargan, J (1990) Set 196

Hargreaves, Benjamin (1989) Set 151
Hargreaves, Kate (1991) Set 245
Hargreaves, Sara (1979) Sets 143, 200
Hargreaves, Simon (1991) Set 69 Profile p.1412
Hargreaves, Teresa (1999) Set 159
Haring, SN (1982) Set 196
Harington, Amanda (1989) Set 103
Harman, Sarah (1987) Set 137 Profile p.1412
Harmer, Christine (1973) Set 234
Harounoff, David (1984) Set 74
Harper, James (1957) Set 234
Harper, Joseph (1970) (QC-1992) Set 13
Harper, Mark (1993) Sets 191, 222 Profile p.1412
Harper, Roger (1994) Sets 143, 168
Harpum, Charles (1976) Set 40
Harpwood, Vivienne (1969) Set 174
Harrap, Giles (1971) Sets 121, 262, 265
Harrap, Robert (1997) Set 115
Harries, Mark (1995) Set 151
Harrington, Clare (1998) Sets 83, 250
Harrington, Patrick (1973) (QC-1993) Sets 41, 174
Harrington, Timothy (1997) Set 154
Harris, Bethan (1990) Set 47
Harris, David Andrew (1990) Set 260
Harris, David J (1979) Set 176
Harris, Donald (1958) (QC-2001) Set 85
Harris, Glenn (1994) Set 79
Harris, Ian (1990) Sets 204, 207, 218
Harris, Joanne (1991) Set 47
Harris, Laura (1977) Set 21
Harris, Mark (1980) Set 124
Harris, Melvyn (1997) Set 93
Harris, Nicola (1992) Set 175
Harris, Paul (1994) Set 90 Profile p.1412
Harris, Peter (1980) Set 148
Harris, Rebecca (1997) Set 68
Harris, Richard (1997) Set 19
Harris, Roger (1996) Set 146
Harris, Russell (1986) Sets 27, 175 Profile p.1412
Harrison, Averil (1990) Set 135
Harrison, Carl (1997) Set 257
Harrison, Christopher (1988) Set 137 Profile p.1412
Harrison, Graeme (1997) Set 259
Harrison, John (1994) Set 199
Harrison, Keith (1983) Set 230 Profile p.1412
Harrison, Leona (1993) Set 209
Harrison, Michael (1986) Set 143
Harrison, Michael (1969) (QC-1987) Set 194 Profile p.1412
Harrison, Nicholas (1988) Set 131
Harrison, Peter (1987) Sets 120, 212
Harrison, Peter (1983) Set 230
Harrison, Philomena (1985) Set 87
Harrison, Piers (1997) Set 8
Harrison, Reziya (1975) Set 107
Harrison, Richard (1993) Set 70 Profile p.1412
Harrison, Richard (1991) Set 24
Harrison, Robert (1988) Set 174 Profile p.1412
Harrison, Roger D (1970) Set 108

INDEX ■ BARRISTERS

Harrison, Sally (1992) Set 231 Profile p.1412
Harrison, Sarah (1989) Set 216
Harrison, Stephanie (1991) Set 47 Profile p.1412
Harrison, Susan (1993) Set 229
Harrison-Hall, Giles (1977) Set 155
Harrod, Henry (1963) Set 138 Profile p.1412
Harry, Timothy (1983) Set 105 Profile p.1412
Hart, David (1982) Set 23 Profile p.1412
Hart, Joseph (2000) Set 217
Hart, Neil (1998) Set 31
Hart, Paul (1982) Set 256
Hart, William (1979) Set 165 Profile p.1413
Harte, David (1967) Set 234
Hartley, Richard (1956) (QC-1976) Set 15
Hartley, Richard (1985) Set 216
Hartley, Timothy (1970) Set 194
Hartley-Davies, Paul (1977) Set 174
Harvey, Colin (1975) Set 199 Profile p.1413
Harvey, John (1973) Set 159
Harvey, Jonathan (1974) Sets 60, 135
Harvey, Keely (1999) Set 258
Harvey, Louise (1991) Set 256
Harvey, Michael (1966) (QC-1982) Set 22 Profile p.1413
Harvey, Richard (1971) Set 150
Harvey, Simon (1995) Set 156
Harvey, Stephen (1979) Sets 126, 177
Harvie, Jonathan (1973) (QC-1992) Set 12
Harwood, Barry (1998) Set 93
Harwood, Richard (1993) Set 38
Harwood-Stevenson, John (1975) Set 11
Haselhurst, Ian (1976) Set 203
Haslam, Andrew (1991) Sets 199, 200
Hassall, Craig (1999) Set 200
Hassall, James (1995) Set 166
Hatch, Lisa (1995) Set 132
Hatfield, Sally (1988) Set 25
Hattan, Simon (1999) Set 131
Hatton, Andrew (1987) Set 193
Hatton, David (1976) (QC-1996) Set 194
Haughey, Caroline (1999) Set 45
Haughty, Jeremy (1989) Set 84
Haukeland, Martin (1988) Sets 116, 238
Haven, Kevin (1982) Set 143
Havers, Philip (1974) (QC-1995) Set 23 Profile p.1413
Hawes, Neil (1989) Set 18
Hawker, Geoffrey (1970) Set 39
Hawkes, Naomi (1994) Set 101
Hawkins, Lucy (1994) Set 160
Hawkins, Quinn (1999) Set 59
Hawkins, Robert (1998) Set 176
Hawks, Anthony (1975) Set 237
Hawley, Carol (1990) Set 150
Haworth, Richard A (1978) Set 256
Hawthorne, Patricia (1995) Set 177
Hay, Deborah (1991) Sets 48, 63 Profile p.1413
Hay, Fiona (1989) Sets 62, 83, 249
Hay, Robin (1964) Set 48
Haycroft, Anthony (1982) Set 119
Hayden, Anthony (1987) (QC-2002) Set 7
Hayden, Richard (1964) Set 109
Haydon, Alec (1993) Set 14
Hayes, Jerry (1977) Set 110

Hayes, John (1992) Set 201
Hayes, Josephine (1980) Set 49 Profile p.1413
Haygarth, Edmund (1988) Set 204
Hayhow, Lyn (1990) Set 34
Hayman, George (1998) Set 67
Haynes, John (1968) Set 111
Haynes, Matthew (1991) Set 160
Haynes, Michael (1979) Set 16
Haynes, Peter (1983) Set 161
Haynes, Rebecca (1994) Set 90
Hayton, Linda (1975) Set 2
Hayton, Michael (1993) Set 217
Hayton, Virginia (1999) Set 178
Hayward, James (1985) Set 182
Hayward Smith, Rodger (1967) (QC-1988) Set 70 Profile p.1413
Haywood, Janette (1977) Set 127
Haywood, Jennifer (2001) Set 131
Haywood, Philip (2001) Set 25
Hayworth, Alison (2001) Set 228
Head, David (1997) Set 152
Head, J Philip T (1976) Set 5
Headlam, Roy (1983) Set 45
Heal, Joanna (1988) Set 24
Heal, Madeleine (1996) Set 142
Healing, Yvonne (1988) Set 229
Healy, Alexandra (1992) Set 11 Profile p.1413
Healy, Brian (1967) Set 161
Healy, Sam (1999) Set 266
Healy, Siob·n (1993) Set 77
Heap, Gerard (1985) Sets 192, 261
Heap, Richard (1963) Set 219
Heath, Stephen (1992) Set 144
Heather, Christopher (1995) Set 144
Heaton, Clive (1992) Set 201
Heaton, David (1983) Set 229 Profile p.1413
Heaton, Frances (1985) Set 217 Profile p.1413
Heaton, Laura (1998) Set 7
Heaton-Armstrong, Anthony (1973) Set 11
Heavey, Ciara (1992) Set 110
Hedgeland, Roger (1972) Set 229
Hedley, Richard (1983) Set 247
Hedworth, Rachel (1999) Set 239
Hedworth, Toby (1975) (QC-1996) Set 239 Profile p.1413
Heer, Deanna (1994) Set 63
Hegarty, Kevin (1982) Set 161 Profile p.1414
Hehir, Christopher (1990) Set 65
Heilbron, Hilary (1971) (QC-1987) Set 14 Profile p.1414
Heimler, George (1978) Set 55
Henderson, Fiona (1993) Set 45
Henderson, James (1997) Sets 122, 191, 222
Henderson, Josephine (1990) Set 2
Henderson, Launcelot (1977) (QC-1995) Set 138 Profile p.1414
Henderson, Mark (1994) Set 25 Profile p.1414
Henderson, Roderick (1978) Set 160
Henderson, Roger (1964) (QC-1980) Sets 60, 135 Profile p.1414
Henderson, Simon (1993) Set 118
Henderson, Sophie (1990) Set 150
Henderson, William (1978) Set 131
Hendrickson, Christine (1982) Set 214
Hendron, Gerald (1992) Set 163

Hendy, John (1972) (QC-1987) Sets 104, 167 Profile p.1414
Hendy, Pauline (1985) Set 20
Henke, Ruth (1987) Set 174 Profile p.1414
Henley, Andrew (1992) Set 45
Henley, Christopher (1989) Set 151
Henley, Mark (1994) Set 201
Hennessy, Shirley (1997) Set 206
Henry, Annette (1984) Set 79 Profile p.1414
Henry, Bruce (1988) Set 256
Henry, Edward (1988) Set 68
Henry, Peter (1977) Set 111
Henry, Philip I (1979) Set 50
Henshaw, Andrew (2000) Set 14
Henson, Christine (1994) Set 4
Henson, Graham (1976) Set 45
Henson, Graham (1976) Set 159
Heppenstall, Claire (1990) Set 46
Heppenstall, Rachael (1997) Set 228
Heppinstall, Adam (1999) Set 60
Hepple, Bob (1966) (QC-1996) Set 12
Heraghty, David (1995) Set 150
Herberg, Javan (1992) Set 12 Profile p.1415
Herbert, D Peter (1982) Set 150
Herbert, Douglas (1973) Set 247 Profile p.1415
Herbert, Mark (1974) (QC-1995) Set 138 Profile p.1415
Herbert MBE, Garry (1995) Set 28
Herman, Ray (1972) Set 209 Profile p.1415
Hermer, Richard (1993) Sets 25, 174 Profile p.1415
Hernandez, David (1976) Set 232
Hershman, David (1981) (QC-2002) Set 161 Profile p.1415
Heslop, Martin S (1972) (QC-1995) Set 65 Profile p.1415
Heslop, Philip (1970) (QC-1985) Set 137 Profile p.1415
Hess, Edward (1985) Sets 62, 249
Hester, Paul (1989) Set 111
Hetherington, Roger (1973) Set 146
Hett, James (1991) Set 246
Hewitt, Alexandra (1995) Set 178
Hewitt, Alison (1984) Set 145
Hewson, Barbara (1985) Set 86
Hext, Neil (1995) Set 146
Heywood, Mark (1986) Set 159
Heywood, Michael (1975) Sets 97, 216
Heywood, Peter (1988) Set 174
Heyworth, Catherine Louise (1991) Set 260
Heyworth, Catherine Louise (1991) Set 174
Hibbert, William (1979) Set 49 Profile p.1415
Hick, Michael (1995) Set 114
Hickey, Alexander (1995) Set 118
Hickey, Eugene (1988) Set 159
Hickey, Simon (1985) Set 201
Hickland, Margaret (1988) Set 232
Hickling, Sally (1993) Set 108
Hickman, Sally (1987) Sets 157, 159
Hickmet, Richard (1974) Set 264
Hicks, Martin (1977) Set 65
Hicks, Michael (1976) Set 100 Profile p.1415
Hicks, Pascale (1999) Set 217
Hicks, William (1975) (QC-1995) Set 27 Profile p.1415
Hiddleston, Adam (1990) Set 257
Higgins, Adrian (1990) Sets 83, 250

Higgins, Anthony (1978) Set 48
Higgins, Gillian (1997) Set 53
Higgins, Paul (1996) Set 221
Higgins, Polly (1998) Set 17
Higgins, Rupert (1991) Set 86
Higginson, Lucy (1992) Set 175
Higginson, Peter (1975) Set 18
Higginson, Timothy (1977) Set 85
Higgo, Justin (1995) Set 131
Higgs, Roland (1984) Set 141
Hikmet, Berin (2000) Set 110
Hilder, Carolyn (1991) Set 156
Hildyard, Marianna (1977) (QC-2002) Set 16
Hildyard, Robert (1977) (QC-1994) Set 137 Profile p.1415
Hill, Candida (1990) Set 126
Hill, CL (1988) Set 196
Hill, Gregory (1972) Set 106
Hill, Henrietta (1997) Set 25
Hill, Jane (1980) Set 101
Hill, Jonathan (2000) Set 95
Hill, Mark (1987) Sets 121, 262, 265 Profile p.1416
Hill, Max (1987) Set 126
Hill, Michael (1958) (QC-1979) Set 36 Profile p.1416
Hill, Miranda (1999) Set 75
Hill, Nicholas (1993) Set 193
Hill, Piers (1987) Set 197
Hill, Raymond (1992) Set 90
Hill, Richard G (1993) Set 137 Profile p.1416
Hill, Robert (1980) Sets 121, 262, 265
Hill, Thomas (1988) Set 54 Profile p.1416
Hill, Timothy (1990) Set 142 Profile p.1416
Hill-Baker, Jeremy (1983) Set 193
Hilliard, Lexa (1987) Set 133 Profile p.1416
Hilliard, Nicholas (1981) Set 75 Profile p.1416
Hilliard, Spenser (1975) Set 84
Hillier, Andrew (1972) (QC-2002) Set 81 Profile p.1416
Hillier, Nicolas (1982) Set 50 Profile p.1416
Hillman, Basil (1968) Set 73
Hillman, Roger (1983) Sets 207, 218
Hills, Timothy (1968) Set 165
Hill-Smith, Alexander (1978) Set 98
Hilton, John (1964) (QC-1990) Set 68
Hilton, Simon (1987) Sets 191, 222
Himsworth, Emma (1993) Set 32 Profile p.1416
Hinchliff, Benjamin (1992) Set 15 Profile p.1416
Hinchliffe, Doreen (1953) Set 127
Hinchliffe, Nicholas (1980) (QC-1999) Set 228 Profile p.1416
Hinchliffe, Thomas (1997) Set 91
Hind, Kenneth (1973) Set 256
Hind CBE, Kenneth (1973) Set 149
Hindmarsh, Elizabeth (1974) Sets 116, 238
Hines, James (1982) Set 124
Hinks, Frank (1973) (QC-2000) Set 131 Profile p.1417
Hiorns, Roger (1983) Set 50 Profile p.1417
Hipkin, John (1989) Set 260
Hirst, Jonathan (1975) (QC-1990) Set 14 Profile p.1417
Hirst, Karl (1997) Set 159
Hirst, Kathryn (1986) Set 45
Hirst, Simon (1993) Set 186
Hirst, Tim (1970) Set 195

Hislop, David (1989) Set 25
Hitchcock, Patricia (1988) Set 20
Hitchcock, Richard G (1989) Set 37 Profile p.1417
Hitchen, John (1961) Set 193
Hitching, Isabel (1992) Set 159 Profile p.1417
Hitchmough, Andrew (1991) Set 122 Profile p.1417
Hoare, Gregory (1992) Set 208
Hobbs, Emma-Jane (1996) Set 145
Hobbs, Geoffrey (1977) (QC-1991) Set 32 Profile p.1417
Hobhouse, Helen (1990) Set 41
Hobson, John (1980) (QC-2000) Set 54 Profile p.1417
Hobson, John (1999) Set 215
Hobson, Sally (1991) Sets 171, 251
Hochberg, Daniel (1982) Set 153 Profile p.1417
Hochhauser, Andrew (1977) (QC-1997) Set 31 Profile p.1417
Hockman, Stephen (1970) (QC-1990) Sets 120, 212, 252 Profile p.1417
Hockton, Andrew (1984) Set 119 Profile p.1417
Hodes, Angela (1979) Set 84
Hodge, Alastair B (1997) Set 93
Hodge, David (1979) (QC-1997) Set 105 Profile p.1417
Hodge, David (1979) (QC-1997) Set 201
Hodges, Victoria (1980) Set 248
Hodgetts, Elizabeth (1998) Set 161
Hodgetts, Glen (1995) Set 150
Hodgkinson, Robert (1968) Set 155
Hodgson, Elizabeth (1993) Sets 116, 238
Hodgson, Jane (2000) Set 2
Hodgson, Margaret (1975) Set 160 Profile p.1418
Hodgson, Timothy (1991) Set 221
Hodson, Katherine (2000) Set 214
Hodson, Michael (1977) Set 237
Hodson, Peter (1994) Set 215
Hoffman, David (1975) Set 221
Hoffman, Simon (1997) Set 260
Hoffmann, Clare (1990) Set 131
Hofmeyr, Stephen (1982) (QC-2000) Set 77 Profile p.1418
Hogan, Andrew (1996) Set 247
Hogan, Emma (1996) Set 159
Hogarth, Andrew (1974) Set 82
Hogg, Douglas (1968) (QC-1990) Sets 112, 197
Hoggett, John (1969) (QC-1986) Sets 191, 222 Profile p.1418
Holbech, Charles (1988) Set 141
Holborn, David (1991) Sets 126, 177
Holbrook, Jon (1991) Set 47
Holdcroft, Mathew (1998) Set 34
Holden, Richard (1996) Set 86
Holder, Simon (1989) Set 209
Holder, Terence (1984) Set 182
Holdsworth, James (1977) Set 22
Holgate, David (1978) (QC-1997) Set 13 Profile p.1418
Holl-Allen, Jonathan (1990) Set 130
Holland, C (1996) Set 223
Holland, Charles (1994) Set 239 Profile p.1418
Holland, David (1986) Set 7
Holland, Debra (1996) Set 60
Holland, Katharine (1989) Set 105 Profile p.1418
Holland, Michael (1984) Set 65

1676   INDEX TO ALL BARRISTERS IN CHAMBERS WHO ARE LISTED IN THIS GUIDE. **BOLD** TYPE INDICATES PROFILES – SEE PAGE 1353

BARRISTERS ■ INDEX

Holland, Roberta (1989) Set 257
Holland, William (1982) Set 144
Hollander, Charles (1978) (QC-1999) Set 14 Profile p.1418
Hollard, Rick (1994) Set 223
Hollier, Mark (1994) Set 168
Hollington, Robin (1979) (QC-1999) Set 98 Profile p.1418
Hollingworth, Guy (2001) Set 32
Hollingworth, Peter (1993) Set 242
Hollis, Kim (1979) (QC-2002) Set 45
Holloran, Fiona A (1989) Set 220
Hollow, Paul (1981) Sets 171, 251
Holloway, David (1996) Set 144
Holloway, Richard (1993) Set 19
Holloway, Timothy (1991) Set 206
Hollyoak, Kate (1997) Set 228
Holme, Gavin (1999) Set 73
Holmes, Andrew Christopher (2000) Set 234
Holmes, Helen (2000) Set 193
Holmes, Jon (1999) Set 174
Holmes, Jonathan (1985) Sets 29, 189, 235
Holmes, Justin (1994) Set 97
Holmes, Michael (1999) Set 77
Holmes, Philip (1980) Set 221
Holmes, Susan (1989) Set 71
Holmes-Milner, James (1989) Set 51
Holroyd, Charles (1997) Set 77
Holroyd, Joanne (1994) Set 197
Holroyd, John (1989) Set 201
Holroyde, Tim (1977) (QC-1996) Sets 207, 218 Profile p.1418
Holt, Abigail (1993) Set 223
Holt, Karen (1987) Set 36
Holt, Stephen (1978) Set 45
Holtum, Ian (1985) Set 92
Holwill, Derek (1982) Set 112 Profile p.1418
Hone, Richard (1970) (QC-1997) Set 22
Hood, Nigel (1993) Set 74
Hookway, Aelred (1990) Set 201
Hoon, Notu (1975) Set 110
Hooper, Ben (2000) Set 81
Hooper, David (1971) Set 53
Hooper, Gopal (1973) Set 43
Hooper, Louise (1997) Set 47
Hooper, Toby (1973) (QC-2000) Set 82
Hope, Derwin (1970) Set 111
Hope, Ian (1996) Set 36
Hopkins, Adrian (1984) Set 130 Profile p.1419
Hopkins, Julie (1999) Sets 83, 250
Hopkins, Paul (1989) Set 173
Hopkins, Philippa (1994) Set 31 Profile p.1419
Hopkins, Stephen (1973) (QC-2000) Sets 41, 176
Hopmeier, Michael (1974) Set 63
Horan, John (1993) Set 20
Horgan, Timothy (1982) Set 18
Horlick, Fiona (1992) Set 36
Horlock, Timothy (1981) (QC-1997) Set 228 Profile p.1419
Hormaeche, Alejandra (1998) Set 144
Hornby, Robert (1990) Set 179
Horne, Julian (1998) Set 22
Horne, Kenderik (1996) Set 203
Horne, Michael (1992) Set 130 Profile p.1419
Horne, Roger (1967) Set 97
Horne, Wilson (1992) Sets 191, 222
Horner, Robin (1975) Set 234
Hornett, Stuart (1992) Set 7

Horowitz, Michael (1968) (QC-1990) Sets 64, 192, 231, 234 Profile p.1419
Horrocks, Peter (1977) Set 46 Profile p.1419
Horsley, Nick (1999) Set 127
Horton, Caroline (1993) Sets 171, 251
Horton, Mark (1981) Set 182 Profile p.1419
Horton, Mark (1976) Set 169 Profile p.1419
Horton, Matthew (1969) (QC-1989) Set 89 Profile p.1419
Horton, Michael (1993) Sets 21, 74
Horwell, Richard (1976) Set 68 Profile p.1419
Horwood, Anya (1991) Set 204
Horwood-Smart, Rosamund (1974) (QC-1996) Set 126
Hosford-Tanner, Michael (1974) Set 123
Hoskins, Mark (1991) Set 14 Profile p.1419
Hoskins, William (1980) Set 145
Hossain, Ajmalul (1976) (QC-1998) Sets 7, 128
Hossain, Sa'ad (1995) Set 32
Hotten, Christopher (1972) (QC-1994) Set 5
Hotten, Keith (1990) Set 246
Hough, Christopher (1981) Set 25
Hough, Jonathan (1997) Set 145
Houghton, Kirsten (1989) Set 118
Houghton, L J (1994) Set 220
Houlder, Bruce (1969) (QC-1994) Set 75 Profile p.1419
House, Michael (1972) Set 47
Houseman, Stephen (1995) Set 31
Houston, Andrew (1989) Set 258
Houston, David (1976) Set 127
Howard, Amanda (1994) Set 197
Howard, Anthony (1992) Set 228
Howard, Charles (1975) (QC-1999) Set 70 Profile p.1419
Howard, Graham (1987) Set 169
Howard, Ian (1987) Set 163
Howard, M N (1971) (QC-1986) Set 33 Profile p.1420
Howard, Margaret (1977) Set 132
Howard, Mark (1980) (QC-1996) Set 14 Profile p.1420
Howard, Nicola (1995) Set 53
Howard, Robin (1986) Set 144
Howard, Timothy D (1981) Set 257
Howarth, Andrew (1988) Set 9
Howarth, Simon (1991) Set 22
Howat, Robin (1986) Set 144
Howd, Stephen (1989) Set 188
Howe, Darren (1992) Set 164
Howe, Martin (1978) (QC-1996) Set 95 Profile p.1420
Howe, Penelope (1991) Sets 121, 262, 265
Howe, Robert (1988) Set 12 Profile p.1420
Howe, Ruth (1983) Set 206
Howe, Timothy (1987) Set 44 Profile p.1420
Howell, John (1979) (QC-1993) Set 12 Profile p.1420
Howell Williams, Craig (1983) Set 61 Profile p.1420
Howell-Jones, Nicholas (2000) Set 160
Howells, Catherine (1989) Sets 207, 218
Howells, Cenydd (1964) Sets 140, 175
Howells, Christopher (1999) Set 261

Howells, James (1995) Set 3 Profile p.1421
Howes, Sally (1983) Set 36
Howker, David (1982) (QC-2002) Set 65
Howlett, James (1980) Set 246
Hoyle, Mark (1978) Set 144
Hubbard, Mark (1991) Set 98
Hubbard, Michael J (1967) (QC-1989) Set 108
Hubble, Ben (1992) Set 92 Profile p.1421
Huckle, Theodore (1985) Set 175
Hudd, Anne (2000) Set 7
Hudson, Anthony (1996) Set 25
Hudson, Christopher (1987) Set 217
Hudson, Elisabeth (1987) Set 111
Hudson, Emma (1995) Set 46
Hudson, Kate (1981) Set 21
Hudson, Rachel (1985) Set 239 Profile p.1421
Huffer, Ian (1979) Set 232
Hufford, Victoria (1994) Set 166
Huggins, Toby (1998) Set 170
Hughes, Adrian (1984) Set 118 Profile p.1421
Hughes, Daisy (1999) Set 21
Hughes, Gabriel (1978) Set 153
Hughes, Gareth (1985) Set 34
Hughes, Gwydion (1994) Set 173
Hughes, Hywel (1995) Set 174
Hughes, Ignatius (1986) Set 165
Hughes, Kate (1992) Set 260
Hughes, Kate (1992) Set 174
Hughes, Leighton (1989) Set 176
Hughes, Merfyn (1971) (QC-1994) Set 48
Hughes, Meryl (1987) Sets 171, 251
Hughes, Peter (1971) Set 178
Hughes , Peter (1971) (QC-1993) Set 144
Hughes, R (1995) Set 210
Hughes, Simon (1995) Set 69 Profile p.1421
Hughes, Stanley (1971) Set 114
Hughes, William (1989) Set 11
Hughes M P, Simon (1974) Sets 83, 250
Hugh-Jones, George (1983) Set 130
Hulse, Cecilia (1998) Set 93
Humpage, Heather (1996) Set 201
Humphreys, Jacqueline (1994) Set 169
Humphreys, Michael (2001) Set 209
Humphreys, Richard (1986) Set 54 Profile p.1421
Humphries, David (1988) Set 231
Humphries, Mark (2000) Set 127
Humphries, Michael (1982) Set 89 Profile p.1421
Humphries, Paul (1986) Set 217
Humphry, Richard (1972) Set 231
Humphryes, Jane (1983) Set 124
Hunjan, Satinder (1984) (QC-2002) Set 159 Profile p.1421
Hunt, Alison (1986) Set 193
Hunt, David (1969) (QC-1987) Set 12
Hunt, James (1968) (QC-1987) Sets 9, 246
Hunt, Murray (1992) Set 88 Profile p.1421
Hunt, Quentin (2000) Set 4
Hunt, Richard M (1985) Set 256
Hunt, Stephen (1968) Set 137
Hunter, Allison (1986) Set 45
Hunter, Andrew (1993) Set 12 Profile p.1421
Hunter, Caroline (1985) Set 2
Hunter, Geoffrey (1979) Set 266

Hunter, Ian (1967) (QC-1980) Set 31 Profile p.1421
Hunter, Katherine (1997) Set 36
Hunter, Martin (1994) Set 31
Hunter, Muir (1938) (QC-1965) Set 133
Hunter, Robert (1979) Set 151
Hunter, Susan (1985) Set 169
Hunter, William (1972) Set 129
Hunter, Win (1990) Set 55
Hunter, Winston (1985) (QC-2000) Sets 101, 213
Hurd, James (1994) Set 227
Hurlock, John (1993) Set 4
Hurrion, Sarah-Jane (2000) Set 170
Hurst, Andrew (1992) Set 36
Hurst, Brian (1983) Set 198
Hurst, Martin (1985) Sets 50, 245
Hurworth, Jillian (1993) Set 73
Husain, Laureen (1997) Set 19
Husain, Raza (1993) Set 88 Profile p.1421
Huseyin, Martin (1988) Set 150
Huskinson, Nicholas (1971) Set 54
Hussain, Frida (1995) Set 8
Hussain, Mukhtar (1971) (QC-1992) Set 223
Hussain, Nawaz Mahboob (2000) Set 246
Hussain, Rukhshanda (1998) Set 199
Hussain, Tasaddat (1998) Set 163
Hussain, Zira (1998) Set 166
Hussey, Ann (1981) Set 64 Profile p.1421
Huston, Graham (1991) Set 74
Hutchings, Martin (1986) Set 143
Hutchings, Matthew (1993) Set 101
Hutchinson, Colin (1990) Set 47
Hutt, Michael (1968) Set 158
Hutton, Alexander (1992) Set 119
Hutton, Caroline (1979) Sets 29, 189 Profile p.1422
Hutton, Ian (1998) Set 90
Hutton, Louise (1984) Set 87
Huyton, Brian (1977) Set 6
Huyton, Katherine (1999) Set 259
Hyam, Jeremy (1995) Set 23
Hyams, Oliver (1989) Set 115 Profile p.1422
Hyde, Charles (1988) Set 165 Profile p.1422
Hyde, Marcia (1992) Set 56
Hyland, J Graham K (1978) (QC-1998) Sets 110, 163 Profile p.1422
Hymanson, Deanna (1988) Set 216
Hynes, Paul (1987) Set 53
Hytner, Benet (1952) (QC-1970) Sets 101, 213
Ibqal, Abdul (1994) Set 201
Ife, Linden (1982) Sets 29, 189, 235 Profile p.1422
Iles, Adrian (1980) Set 115
Iles, David (1977) Set 159
Ilyas, Shaiba (1998) Sets 29, 189, 235
Infield, Paul (1980) Set 115
Ingham, Elizabeth (1989) Sets 9, 183
Ingham, R Lee (1994) Set 176
Inglis, Alan (1989) Set 21
Inglis-Jones, Nigel J (1959) (QC-1982) Set 37 Profile p.1422
Ingram, Nigel (1974) Set 4 Profile p.1422
Inman, Melbourne (1979) (QC-1998) Set 155 Profile p.1422
Innes, Stephen (2000) Set 92
Ironfield, Janet (1992) Set 217
Irvin, Peter (1972) Set 14

Irvine, Michael (1964) Set 66
Irving, Gillian (1984) Set 228
Irwin, Gavin (1996) Set 26
Irwin, Stephen (1976) (QC-1997) Set 25 Profile p.1422
Isaac, Nick (1993) Set 143
Isaacs, Barry (1994) Set 133 Profile p.1422
Isaacs, Elizabeth (1998) Set 156
Isaacs, Paul (1974) Set 192 Profile p.1422
Isaacs, Stuart (1975) (QC-1991) Sets 54, 133 Profile p.1422
Isherwood, John (1978) Set 170
Islam-Choudhury, Mugni (1996) Set 19
Ismail, Roxanne (1993) Set 133
Issa, Alexandra (1993) Set 145
Ivill, Scott (1997) Set 79
Ivimy, Cecilia (1995) Set 81 Profile p.1423
Ivory, Thomas (1978) (QC-1998) Set 32 Profile p.1423
Iwi, Quintin (1956) Set 135
Iyengar, Harini (1999) Set 81
Iyer, Sunil (1988) Set 246
Jabbour, Lara (2000) Set 152
Jack, Adrian (1986) Sets 29, 189, 235
Jack, Simon (1974) Set 201
Jacklin, Susan (1980) Set 169 Profile p.1423
Jackson, Andrew (1987) Set 79
Jackson, Andrew (1986) Set 156 Profile p.1423
Jackson, Anthony (1995) Set 130
Jackson, David (1986) Set 160
Jackson, Fiona (1998) Set 45
Jackson, Gordon (1989) Set 70
Jackson, Hugh (1981) Set 128
Jackson, John (1970) Set 232
Jackson, Judith (1975) (QC-1994) Set 105 Profile p.1423
Jackson, Kevin (1984) Set 172
Jackson, Mark (1997) Set 55
Jackson, Matthew (1986) Set 112
Jackson, Nicholas (1992) Set 203
Jackson, Peter (1978) (QC-2000) Set 113 Profile p.1423
Jackson, Rosemary (1981) Set 69
Jackson, Simon (1982) Set 194 Profile p.1423
Jackson, Stephanie (1992) Set 82
Jackson, Wayne (1984) Set 217
Jacob, Isaac (1963) Set 140
Jacobs, Alexander (1997) Set 160
Jacobs, Claire (1989) Set 73
Jacobs, Nigel (1983) Set 33 Profile p.1423
Jacobs, Richard (1979) (QC-1998) Set 31 Profile p.1423
Jacobson, Lawrence (1985) Set 115
Jacobson, Mary (1992) Set 211
Jaconelli, Joseph (1972) Set 227
Jaffa, Ronald (1974) Set 53 Profile p.1423
Jafferjee, Aftab (1980) Set 59 Profile p.1423
Jaffey, Ben (1999) Set 12
James, Alun (1986) Sets 148, 207, 218 Profile p.1423
James, Christopher (1977) Set 159 Profile p.1424
James, David (1998) Set 232
James, Emily (2000) Set 71
James, Ernest (1977) Set 17
James, Grahame (1989) Set 151
James, Ian (1981) Set 244 Profile p.1424
James, Mark (1987) Set 145
James, Michael (1989) Sets 116, 238
James, Michael (1976) Sets 29, 189, 235 Profile p.1424

INDEX ■ BARRISTERS

K

James, Roderick (1999) Set 18
James, Simon (1988) Set 228
Jameson, Barnaby (1993) Set 126
Jameson, Rodney (1976) Set 193 Profile p.1424
Jamieson, Anthony (1974) Set 178
Jamil, Aisha (1995) Set 163
Jamil, Yasmeen (1998) Set 16
Janes, Jeremy (1992) Set 246
Janner, Daniel (1980) (QC-2002) Set 36 Profile p.1424
Janusz, Pierre (1979) Set 66
Japheth, Bethan (1997) Set 179
Jarand, G M (1997) Set 247
Jarman, Mark (1989) Set 56
Jarman, Milwyn (1980) (QC-2001) Set 173 Profile p.1424
Jarman, Nicholas (1965) (QC-1985) Set 73
Jarman, Samuel (1989) Set 74
Jarron, Stephanie (1990) Set 234
Jarvis, John (1970) (QC-1989) Set 152 Profile p.1424
Jarvis, Malcolm (1998) Set 35
Jarvis, Oliver (1992) Set 178
Jarzabkowski, Julia (1993) Set 63
Jay, Grenville R (1975) Set 232
Jay, Robert (1981) (QC-1998) Set 38 Profile p.1424
Jayanathan, Shamini (1996) Set 117
Jeans, Christopher (1980) (QC-1997) Set 81 Profile p.1424
Jeary, Stephen (1987) Set 176 Profile p.1424
Jebb, Andrew (1993) Set 178
Jefferies, Andrew (1990) Set 26
Jefferies, Thomas (1981) Set 13
Jefferis, Michael (1976) Set 97
Jefford, Nerys (1986) Set 69 Profile p.1424
Jeffreys, Alan (1970) (QC-1996) Set 41 Profile p.1424
Jegarajah, Shivani (1993) Set 127
Jelf, Simon (1996) Set 10 Profile p.1424
Jenkala, Adrian (1984) Set 19
Jenkins, Alan (1984) Set 119
Jenkins, Catherine (1990) Set 46
Jenkins, David (1967) Set 71
Jenkins, Edward (1977) (QC-2000) Set 114
Jenkins, Hywel I (1974) Set 37
Jenkins, James John (1974) Set 260
Jenkins, Jeremy (1984) Set 175
Jenkins, John (1970) (QC-1990) Set 174
Jenkins, Kim (1982) Set 126
Jenkins, Martin (1994) Set 154
Jenkins, Susan (1998) Set 261
Jenkins, T Alun (1972) (QC-1996) Sets 4, 168 Profile p.1424
Jenkinson, Lee (2001) Set 208
Jennings, Anthony (1983) (QC-2001) Set 88 Profile p.1425
Jennings, Nigel (1967) Set 6
Jennings, Peter (1972) Set 111
Jennings, Timothy (1962) Sets 189, 235
Jeram, Kirti (1997) Set 234
Jeremiah, Natalia (1997) Set 119
Jeremy, David (1977) Set 68
Jerman, Anthony (1989) Set 101
Jerram, Harriet (1998) Set 37
Jervis, Christopher (1966) Set 165
Jess, Digby C (1978) Set 221
Jessel, Philippa (1978) Set 75
Jessup, Anne (1981) Set 47
Jesudason, Premila (1993) Set 178
Jethani, Sapna (1999) Set 125
Jewell, Charlotte (1999) Set 144
Jewell, Matthew (1989) Set 108

Jinadu, Abdul-Lateef (1995) Set 69
Jobling, Ian (1982) Set 26
Joelson, Stephen (1980) Set 63
Joffe, Natasha (1992) Set 24
Joffe, Victor (1975) (QC-2001) Set 131 Profile p.1425
Johal, Harjinder (1998) Set 162
Johal, Sukhjinder (1991) Set 76
John, Catrin (1992) Set 174
John, Peter (1989) Set 115
John, Simon (1998) Set 175
John, Stephen (1975) Set 11
Johns, Alan (1994) Set 105 Profile p.1425
Johnson, Abigail (1998) Set 130
Johnson, Amanda (1992) Set 232
Johnson, Amanda (1990) Set 9
Johnson, Busola (1998) Set 50
Johnson, Carolyn (1974) Set 216
Johnson, Christine (1991) Set 203 Profile p.1425
Johnson, David (1967) (QC-1978) Set 35
Johnson, Edwin (1987) Set 105 Profile p.1425
Johnson, Greg (1998) Set 151
Johnson, Ian (1982) Set 203
Johnson, Janice (1994) Set 72
Johnson, Jeremy (1994) Set 34
Johnson, Kathryn (1989) Set 256
Johnson, Michael (1971) Set 228 Profile p.1425
Johnson, Nicholas (1994) Set 194
Johnson, Nicholas (1987) Set 204
Johnson, Peter (1986) Sets 80, 190
Johnson, Robin (1979) Set 36
Johnson, Roderick (1975) Set 110
Johnson, Steven (1984) Set 226
Johnson, Susannah (1996) Set 5
Johnson, Sylvia (1999) Set 19
Johnson, Zoe (1990) Set 68
Johnston, Anne (1990) Set 108
Johnston, Anthony (1993) Set 155
Johnston, Carey (1977) Set 126
Johnston, Christopher (1990) Set 130 Profile p.1425
Johnston, Jennifer (1999) Set 23
Johnston, Justine (1997) Set 113
Johnston, Karen (1994) Set 9
Johnstone, Mark (1984) Set 113
Jole, Alison (2001) Set 195
Jolly, Schona (1999) Set 20
Jonathan-Jones, Gareth (1991) Set 124
Jones, Alison (1988) Set 36
Jones, Alun (1972) (QC-1989) Set 124 Profile p.1425
Jones, Andrew (1996) Set 174
Jones, B (1994) Set 224
Jones, Ben (1993) Set 209
Jones, Carolyn (1995) Set 155
Jones, Carwyn (1989) Set 176
Jones, Charlotte (1982) Set 22 Profile p.1425
Jones, Cheryl (1996) Set 159
Jones, Claire (1999) Set 205
Jones, Clive (1981) Set 98
Jones, Daniel (1994) Set 18
Jones, David (1985) Set 163
Jones, David (1967) Set 156
Jones, David (1994) Set 47
Jones, Elisabeth (1995) Set 71
Jones, Elizabeth (1984) (QC-2000) Set 131 Profile p.1425
Jones, Emyr (1999) Set 173
Jones, Francis (1980) Set 260
Jones, Gareth (1984) Set 209
Jones, Gareth (1991) Set 175
Jones, Geraint (1972) Sets 171, 251
Jones, Geraint (1976) (QC-2001) Sets 146, 173
Jones, Gillian (1996) Set 126

Jones, Gregory (1991) Set 61 Profile p.1426
Jones, Guy Howel (1975) Set 176
Jones, Howard (1992) Set 151
Jones, Huw (1997) Set 161
Jones, Jennifer (1991) Set 159 Profile p.1426
Jones, John (1972) Set 65
Jones, John Evan (1982) Set 74
Jones, John Richard (1981) (QC-2002) Sets 151, 207, 218
Jones, John RWD (1992) Set 18
Jones, Jonathan (1995) Set 156
Jones, Laurence (1994) Set 176
Jones, Maggie (1990) Set 47
Jones, Mark (2000) Set 142
Jones, Michael (1999) Set 204
Jones, Michael (1998) Set 216
Jones, Michael (1995) Set 174
Jones, Nicholas David (1987) Set 175
Jones, Nicholas Gareth (1970) Set 175
Jones, Nicola (1996) Set 154
Jones, Nigel (1976) (QC-1999) Set 63
Jones, Oliver (1998) Set 50
Jones, Philip (1990) Set 50
Jones, Philip (1985) Set 131 Profile p.1426
Jones, Rhys (1990) Set 8
Jones, Richard (1979) Set 168
Jones, Richard (1991) Set 246
Jones, Richard (1984) (QC-1996) Set 159
Jones, Richard (1969) Set 175
Jones, Richard (1972) (QC-1996) Sets 66, 159
Jones, Robert (1993) Set 43
Jones, Roderick (1983) Sets 16, 254
Jones, Rupert (2000) Set 63
Jones, Sarah (1989) Set 71
Jones, Se·n (1991) Set 81 Profile p.1426
Jones, Si,n (1998) Set 231
Jones, Stephen (1978) Sets 121, 262, 265
Jones, Stewart (1972) (QC-1994) Set 111
Jones, Susannah (1997) Set 244
Jones, Susannah (1999) Set 35
Jones, Timothy (1975) Sets 2, 161
Jones, Wyn Lloyd (1979) Set 179
Jonson, Lydia (2000) Set 126
Jordan, Andrew (1974) Set 135
Jordan, Ruth (2001) Set 131
Jordash, Wayne (1995) Set 150
Jorro, Peter (1986) Set 47
Jory, Hugh (1992) Sets 29, 189, 235 Profile p.1426
Jory, Richard (1993) Set 11
Jose, Calder (1971) Set 246
Joseph, Charles (1980) Set 113
Joseph, David (1984) Set 31 Profile p.1426
Joseph, Wendy (1975) (QC-1998) Set 75
Josephs, Jennifer (2000) Set 161
Josling, William (1995) Sets 171, 251
Joss, Norman (1982) Set 115
Josse, David (1985) Set 17
Jourdan, Stephen (1989) Set 40 Profile p.1426
Jowell, Daniel (1995) Set 32
Jowell, Jeffrey (1965) (QC-1993) Set 12
Jowitt, Matthew (1994) Set 5
Joy, Michael (1997) Set 6
Joyce, Abigail (1998) Set 245
Joyce, Michael (1976) Set 50 Profile p.1426
Joyce, Peter (1968) (QC-1991) Sets 9, 245 Profile p.1426

Jubb, Brian Patrick (1971) Set 127 Profile p.1426
Juckes, Robert (1974) (QC-1999) Set 156
Judd, Frances (1984) Sets 62, 249 Profile p.1426
Judge, Charles (1981) Set 114
Judge, Lisa (1993) Set 217
Jupp, Jeffrey (1994) Set 9
Juss, Satvinder (1989) Set 76
Kadri, Sadakat (1989) Set 25
Kadri, Sibghat (1969) (QC-1989) Set 76
Kallipetis, Michel (1968) (QC-1989) Set 85 Profile p.1426
Kamill, Louise (1974) Set 65
Kamlish, Stephen (1979) Set 150 Profile p.1426
Kang, Birinder (1996) Set 150
Kapur, Deepak (1984) Set 72
Karaiskos, Maria (2000) Set 147
Karallis, Dina (1989) Set 79
Karas, Jonathan (1986) Set 153 Profile p.1426
Karia, Chirag V (1988) Set 33
Kark, Tom (1982) Set 68 Profile p.1426
Karmy-Jones, Riel (1995) Set 65
Karu, Lee (1985) Set 110
Katkowski, Christopher (1982) (QC-1999) Set 13 Profile p.1426
Katrak, Cyrus (1991) Set 111
Katyar, Arun (1993) Set 111
Katz, Philip (1976) (QC-2000) Set 11
Kaufmann, Phillippa (1991) Set 25 Profile p.1427
Kaul, Kaly (1983) Set 43
Kaur, Harinder (1995) Set 202
Kaur, Rani (1993) Set 215
Kauser, Yasmin (1999) Set 180
Kay, Dominic (1997) Set 111
Kay, Michael (1981) (QC-2002) Set 152
Kay, R Jervis (1972) (QC-1996) Set 142 Profile p.1427
Kay, Steven (1977) (QC-1997) Set 53 Profile p.1427
Kayani, Asaf (1991) Set 136
Kayne, Adrian (1989) Set 53
Kazakos, Leon (1999) Set 43
Kealey, Gavin (1977) (QC-1994) Set 77 Profile p.1427
Kealey, Simon (1991) Set 201
Kealy, Brian (1965) Set 201
Keane, Michael (1963) Set 112
Keane, Michael (1979) Set 7
Keany, Brendan (1974) Set 53
Kearl, Guy (1982) (QC-2002) Set 199
Kearney, JM Seamus (1992) Set 84
Kearney, John (1994) Set 45
Kearney, Robert (1996) Set 230
Keegan, Leslie (1989) Set 50
Keehan, Michael (1982) (QC-2001) Set 160 Profile p.1427
Keel, Douglas (1997) Set 141
Keeley, James F (1993) Set 200
Keeling, Adrian (1990) Set 156
Keen, Graeme (1995) Set 13
Keenan, Peter (1962) Set 216
Keene, Gillian (1980) Set 41
Kefford, Anthony (1980) Sets 181, 187, 243 Profile p.1427
Keightley, George (1997) Sets 171, 251
Keith, Hugo (1989) Set 124
Keith, Thomas (1983) Set 44
Kelbrick, Anthony (1992) Set 193
Keleher, Paul (1980) Set 53
Kellar, Robert (1999) Set 23

Kelleher, Benedict (1994) Set 59
Kellett, J Charles (1971) Set 108
Kelly, Andrew (1978) (QC-2000) Set 61 Profile p.1427
Kelly, Brendan (1988) Set 65
Kelly, Charles (1965) Set 239
Kelly, David (1980) Set 163
Kelly, Emma (1997) Set 155
Kelly, Geoffrey (1992) Sets 121, 262, 265
Kelly, Geraldine (1996) Set 201
Kelly, Mark (1985) Set 144
Kelly, Martyn (1972) Set 173
Kelly, Matthias (1979) (QC-1999) Sets 104, 167 Profile p.1427
Kelly, Patricia (1988) Set 111
Kelly, Richard (1994) Sets 181, 187, 243
Kelly, Sean (1990) Set 216
Kelsey-Fry, John (1978) (QC-2000) Set 68 Profile p.1428
Kelson, Peter (1981) (QC-2001) Set 18
Kember, Richard (1993) Set 173
Kemp, Christopher M (1984) Set 37
Kempster, Toby (1980) Sets 104, 167 Profile p.1428
Kendal, Timothy (1985) Set 4
Kendall, Joel (1993) Set 82
Kendrick, Dominic (1981) (QC-1997) Set 77 Profile p.1428
Kenefick, Timothy (1996) Set 77
Kennedy, Andrew (1989) Set 119 Profile p.1428
Kennedy, Brian (1992) Set 72
Kennedy, Christopher L P (1989) Set 228
Kennedy, Helena (1972) (QC-1991) Set 25 Profile p.1428
Kennedy, Michael (1985) Set 209 Profile p.1428
Kennedy, Michael (1967) Set 98
Kennedy, P Nicholas D (1977) Set 256
Kennedy-McGregor, Marilyn (1989) Set 141
Kennedy-Morrison, Caroline (1990) Set 149
Kennelly, Brian (1999) Set 12
Kennerley, Ian (1983) Set 234 Profile p.1428
Kenning, Thomas (1989) Set 157
Kenny, Charlotte (1993) Sets 207, 218
Kenny, David J (1982) Set 256
Kenny, Julian (1997) Set 35
Kenny, Stephen (1987) Set 77
Kent, Alan (1986) Set 36
Kent, Georgina (1989) Set 34
Kent, Jenny (1993) Set 194
Kent, Michael (1975) (QC-1996) Set 22
Kent, Peter (1978) Set 111
Kentridge, Janet (1999) Set 88
Kentridge, Sir Sydney (1977) (QC-1984) Set 14 Profile p.1428
Kenward, Tim (1987) Set 204
Keogh, Sarah (1999) Sets 83, 250
Kerr, Christopher (1988) Set 34
Kerr, David (1971) Set 208
Kerr, Derek (1994) Set 74
Kerr, Simon (1997) Set 77
Kerr, Tim (1983) (QC-2001) Set 81 Profile p.1428
Ker-Reid, John (1974) Sets 121, 262, 265 Profile p.1428
Kerrigan, Herbert (1970) (QC-1992) Set 11
Kershaw, A (1975) Set 196
Kershaw, Jennifer (1974) (QC-1998) Set 193 Profile p.1428
Kershen, Lawrence (1967) (QC-1992) Set 150 Profile p.1428

1678 INDEX TO ALL BARRISTERS IN CHAMBERS WHO ARE LISTED IN THIS GUIDE. **BOLD** TYPE INDICATES PROFILES – SEE PAGE 1353

BARRISTERS ■ INDEX

Kessler, James (1984) Set 102 Profile p.1429
Kevan, Timothy (1996) Set 145
Key, Paul (1997) Set 31
Keysall, Jane (1992) Set 109
Keyser, Andrew (1986) Set 173 Profile p.1429
Khalil, Karim S (1984) Set 108 Profile p.1429
Khalique, Nageena (1994) Set 159
Khamisa, Mohammed (1985) Set 11
Khan, Helen (1990) Sets 121, 262, 265
Khan, Jamil (1986) Set 208
Khan, Judy (1989) Set 47
Khan, Karim (1992) Set 65
Khan, M W (1969) Set 78
Khan, Nicholas (1983) Set 12
Khan, Shokat (1979) Sets 191, 222
Khan, Shufqat M (1996) Set 163
Khan, Tahir (1986) Set 163
Khan, Zarif (1996) Set 26
Khangure, Avtar (1985) Set 161 Profile p.1429
Khawar, Aftab (1983) Set 230
Khodagoda, F (1993) Set 78
Khokhar, Mushtaq (1982) Sets 199, 200
Khubber, Ranjiv (1994) Set 76
Khurshid, Jawdat (1994) Set 77
Kibling, Thomas (1990) Set 20 Profile p.1429
Kidd, J (1995) Set 198
Kidd, Peter (1987) Set 208
Kilcoyne, Desmond (1990) Set 101
Kilcoyne, Paul (1985) Set 145
Killalea, Stephen (1981) Set 24 Profile p.1429
Killeen, Simon J (1984) Set 208
Killen, Geoffrey (1990) Set 111
Kilpatrick, Alison (1991) Set 216
Kilpatrick, Jean (1990) Set 111
Kilroy, Charlotte (2001) Set 13
Kilvington, Sarah (1999) Set 232
Kilvington, Simon (1995) Set 229 Profile p.1429
Kimbell, John (1995) Set 33
Kimblin, Richard (1997) Set 156 Profile p.1429
Kime, Matthew (1988) Sets 94, 216
Kimmins, Charles (1994) Set 35
Kincade, Julie-Anne (1991) Set 151
Kinch, Christopher (1976) (QC-1999) Set 36
King, Edmund (1999) Set 31
King, Emma (1999) Set 4
King, Fawzia (1985) Set 51
King, Gelaga (1985) Set 4
King, Henry (1998) Set 44
King, John (1983) Set 84
King, John (1973) Set 82
King, Julia (1998) Set 245
King, Karl (1985) Set 63
King, Mark (1997) Set 139
King, Michael (1971) Set 103
King, Neil (1980) (QC-2000) Set 89 Profile p.1429
King, Paul (1992) Set 245
King, Philip (1974) (QC-2002) Set 43
King, Richard (1978) Set 115
King, Samantha (1990) Set 56
King, Simon (1987) Set 5 Profile p.1429
King, Timothy (1973) (QC-1991) Sets 101, 213
Kingerley, Martin (1999) Sets 171, 251
Kingscote, Geoffrey (1993) Set 64

Kingsland, Lord (1972) (QC-1988) Set 61 Profile p.1429
King-Smith, James (1980) Sets 23, 164
Kingston, Martin R (1972) (QC-1992) Set 159 Profile p.1430
Kinnear, Jonathan S (1994) Set 11
Kinnier, Andrew (1996) Sets 60, 135
Kinsky, Cyril (1988) Set 14
Kirby, James (1994) Set 79
Kirby, Peter (1989) Set 63
Kirk, Anthony (1981) (QC-2001) Set 70 Profile p.1430
Kirk, Jonathan (1995) Set 9
Kirk, Robert (1972) Set 86
Kirkpatrick, Krystyna (1992) Set 111
Kirkwood, Edward (1999) Sets 62, 249
Kirsten, Adrian (1962) Set 224
Kirtley, Paul (1982) Set 197
Kirwin, Tracey (1995) Set 246
Kitchen, Simon (1988) Set 26
Kitchener, Neil (1991) Set 32
Kitchin, David (1977) (QC-1994) Set 95 Profile p.1430
Kitchin, Louise (1998) Set 216
Kitching, Robin (1989) Set 217
Kitson, Justin (2000) Set 128
Klein, Jonathan (1975) Sets 29, 189, 235
Klonin, S J (1970) Set 220
Kloss, Alexander (1993) Set 231
Kloss, Diana (1986) Set 231
Knafler, Stephen (1993) Set 47 Profile p.1430
Knapp, Edward (1992) Set 16
Knapp, Stephen (1986) Set 208
Knifton, David (1986) Set 208
Knight, Adrienne (1981) Set 17
Knight, Christopher (1994) Set 240
Knight, Edward (1999) Set 103
Knight, Jennifer (1996) Set 59
Knight, Keith (1969) Set 51
Knight, Martin (1998) Set 208
Knight, Rachel (2000) Set 174
Knight, Sarah (1996) Set 246
Knights, Samantha (1996) Set 133
Knotts, Carol (1996) Set 154
Knowles, Graham (1990) Set 226
Knowles, Gwynneth (1993) Set 203
Knowles, Julian (1994) Set 88 Profile p.1430
Knowles, Linda (1993) Sets 48, 179
Knowles, Linsey (2000) Set 212
Knowles, Mark (1989) Set 161
Knowles, Michael J (2000) Set 216
Knowles, Robin (1982) (QC-1999) Set 133 Profile p.1430
Knox, Christopher John (1974) Set 239 Profile p.1430
Knox, Henry (2000) Set 152
Knox, Peter (1983) Set 66
Kogan, Barry (1973) Set 8
Kolinsky, Daniel (1998) Set 13 Profile p.1430
Kolodynski, Stefan (1993) Set 160
Kolodziej, Andrzej (1978) Set 86
Kolvin, Philip (1985) Set 52
Kopieczek, Louis (1983) Set 55
Korda, Anthony (1988) Set 43
Korn, Adam (1992) Set 5
Korn, Anthony (1978) Sets 143, 197 Profile p.1430
Korner, Joanna (1974) (QC-1993) Set 75 Profile p.1430
Korniej, Rebekah (1999) Sets 181, 187, 243
Korol, Kathryn (1996) Set 219

Kosmin, Leslie (1976) (QC-1994) Set 30 Profile p.1431
Kothari, Raj (1996) Set 180
Kothari, Sima (1992) Set 21
Kothari, Vasant (1960) Set 110
Kotzeva, Anna (1998) Set 145
Kovalevsky, Richard (1983) Set 126
Kovats, Steven (1989) Set 38 Profile p.1431
Kramer, Philip (1982) Sets 116, 238
Kramer, Stephen (1970) (QC-1995) Set 65 Profile p.1431
Krawczyk, M (1998) Set 220
Kremen, Philip (1975) Set 128
Krish, Doushka (1991) Set 46
Krish, Julia (1992) Set 47
Krolick, Ivan (1966) Set 84
Kubik, Heidi (1993) Set 156
Kulkarni, Yash (1998) Set 118
Kumar Sen, Aditya (1977) Set 21
Kunzlik, Peter (1983) Set 112
Kurrein, Martin (1981) Set 20
Kurzner, Emma (1999) Set 43
Kuschke, Leon (1993) Set 30
Kushner, Martine (1980) Set 161
Kverndal, Simon (1982) (QC-2002) Set 33 Profile p.1431
Kynoch, Duncan (1994) Set 7
Kyriakides, Tina (1984) Set 141 Profile p.1431
Kyte, Peter (1970) (QC-1996) Set 68 Profile p.1431
Laband, Caroline (2000) Set 77
Lachkovic, James (1987) Set 43
Laddie, James (1995) Set 88
Ladenburg, Guy (2000) Set 124
Lahham, Karim (1999) Set 86
Lahiffe, Martin (1984) Set 147
Laidlaw, Jonathan (1982) Set 65 Profile p.1431
Laing, Christine (1984) Set 11
Laing, Elisabeth (1980) Set 81
Laird, Francis (1986) Set 156
Lake, Lisa (1994) Set 32
Lakha, Shabbir (1989) Set 41
Lakin, Gordon (1972) Set 193
Lakin, Paul (2000) Set 188
Lakin, Tracy (1993) Set 162
Lal, Sanjay (1993) Set 73
Lally, Harbinder Singh (1997) Set 159
Lamb, David (1987) Set 266
Lamb, Eric (1975) Sets 207, 218
Lamb, Maria J (1984) Set 108
Lamb, Robert (1973) Sets 83, 250
Lamb, Timothy (1974) (QC-1995) Set 111
Lambert, Christina (1988) Set 119 Profile p.1431
Lambert, Deborah (1977) Set 219
Lambert, Julian (1983) Set 165 Profile p.1431
Lambert, Nigel (1974) (QC-1999) Set 151
Lambert, Sarah (1994) Set 23
Lambis, Marios P (1989) Set 65
Lamming, David (1972) Set 52
Lamont, Camilla (1995) Set 13
Lancaster, P (1982) Set 198
Landale, Tina (1988) Set 226
Landau, Toby (1993) Set 31 Profile p.1431
Lander, Charles (1993) Set 204
Lander, Richard (1993) Sets 191, 222
Landes, Anna-Rose (1986) Set 161
Landsbury, Alan (1975) Set 55 Profile p.1431
Lane, Andrew (1999) Set 63
Lane, David (1968) (QC-1991) Sets 168, 226
Lane, Lindsay (1996) Set 95

Lane, Michael (1983) Sets 181, 187, 243
Lane-Smith, Zoe (1997) Set 84
Laney, Anna (1998) Set 144
Lang, Beverley (1978) (QC-2000) Set 12 Profile p.1431
Langdale, Rachel (1990) Set 5
Langdale, Timothy (1966) (QC-1992) Set 68 Profile p.1431
Langdon, Andrew (1986) Set 166 Profile p.1432
Langham, Richard (1986) Set 27
Langley, Charles (1999) Set 110
Langlois, Peter (1991) Set 170
Langridge, Niki (1993) Set 63
Langstaff, Brian (1971) (QC-1994) Set 20 Profile p.1432
Langton, Steven (1998) Sets 104, 167
Laprell, Mark (1979) Set 229 Profile p.1432
Large, Alan (1988) Set 264
Larizadeh, Cyrus (1992) Set 113
Larkin, Sean (1987) Set 68
Lasker, Jeremy (1976) Set 223
Lasok, Paul (1977) (QC-1994) Set 90 Profile p.1432
Latham, Michael (1975) Set 45
Latham, Richard (1971) (QC-1991) Set 5 Profile p.1432
Latham, Robert (1976) Set 25
Latif, Mohammed (1985) Set 155
Latimer, Andrew (1995) Sets 191, 222 Profile p.1432
Latimer-Sayer, William (1995) Set 20
Lattimer, Justine (1991) Set 156
Lau, Martin (1996) Set 31
Laughland, James (1991) Set 145
Laughton, Samuel (1993) Set 106
Laurence, George (1972) (QC-1991) Set 98 Profile p.1432
Laurence, George S (1972) Set 200
Lauterpacht, Sir Elihu (1950) (QC-1970) Set 35 Profile p.1432
Lavender, Nicholas (1989) Set 131
Lavers, Michael (1990) Set 18
Lavery, Michael (1990) Set 226
Law, John (1996) Set 8
Lawrence, Heather (1990) Set 134 Profile p.1432
Lawrence, Ivan (1962) (QC-1981) Set 110
Lawrence, Nala (1987) Set 202
Lawrence, Nigel (1988) Set 208 Profile p.1433
Lawrence, Patrick (1985) (QC-2002) Set 112 Profile p.1433
Lawrence, Rachel (1992) Set 110
Lawrie, Ian (1985) Set 17
Laws, Eleanor (1990) Sets 120, 212
Laws, Simon (1991) Sets 75, 183
Lawson, Andrew (1995) Set 230
Lawson, Daniel (1994) Set 48
Lawson, Daniel (1994) Set 50
Lawson, Edmund (1971) (QC-1988) Set 11 Profile p.1433
Lawson, Matthew (1995) Sets 147, 151
Lawson, Michael (1969) (QC-1991) Set 36 Profile p.1433
Lawson, Robert (1989) Set 33 Profile p.1433
Lawson, Sara (1990) Set 126
Lawson Rogers, Stuart (1969) (QC-1994) Set 36
Lawton, Paul A (1987) Set 223
Layton, Alexander (1976) (QC-1995) Set 35
Lazarides, Marcus (1999) Set 46
Lazarus, Grant (1981) Set 208
Lazarus, Mary (1991) Set 101

Lazarus, Michael (1987) Set 152
Le Brocq, Mark (1982) Set 178
Le Grice, Valentine (1977) (QC-2002) Set 64 Profile p.1433
Le Poidevin, Nicholas (1975) Sets 98, 200
Le Prevost, Aviva (1990) Set 211
Le Quesne, Catherine (1993) Set 19
Le Quesne, Sir Godfray (1947) (QC-1962) Set 66
Le Sueur, Andrew (1987) Set 14
Lea, Jeremy H C (1978) Set 9
Leabeater, James (1999) Set 118
Leach, Robin (1979) Set 59
Leadbetter, Iain (1975) Set 183
Leafe, Daniel (1996) Set 165
Leake, Laban (1996) Set 45
Learmonth, Alexander (2000) Set 67
Leaver, Peter (1967) (QC-1987) Set 32 Profile p.1433
LeCointe, Elpha (1988) Set 21
Lederman, David (1966) (QC-1990) Set 126 Profile p.1433
Lederman, Howard (1982) Set 101
Ledward, Jocelyn (1999) Set 68
Lee, David (1973) Set 9
Lee, Ian (1973) Set 24
Lee, Jonathan (1993) Set 69
Lee, Krista (1996) Set 146
Lee, Michael (1987) Set 79
Lee, Michael (2001) Set 35
Lee, Richard (1985) Set 159
Lee, Rosslyn (1978) Set 266
Lee, Sarah (1990) Set 14
Lee, Taryn (1992) Set 197
Leech, Ben (1997) Set 111
Leech, Brian (1967) Set 129
Leech, Stewart (1992) Set 123 Profile p.1433
Leech, Thomas (1988) Set 105 Profile p.1433
Leek, Samantha (1993) Set 34
Leeming, Ian (1970) (QC-1988) Set 227 Profile p.1433
Leeming, Lucinda (1999) Set 228
Leeming, Michael (1983) Set 228
Leene, Sharon (1996) Set 43
Leeper, Thomas RG (1991) Set 37
Lees, Andrew (1984) Set 199 Profile p.1434
Lees, Patricia (1988) Set 45
Legard, Edward (1996) Set 266
Leggatt, George (1983) (QC-1997) Set 14 Profile p.1434
Legge, Henry (1993) Set 138 Profile p.1434
Legh-Jones, Nicholas (1968) (QC-1987) Set 35
Leigh, Kevin (1986) Sets 120, 212, 252
Leigh, Leonard (1994) Set 117
Leigh, Samantha (1995) Set 126
Leigh, Sarah (1984) Set 208
Leigh-Morgan, Paul (1978) Sets 171, 251
Leigh-Smith, Nicholas (1976) Set 202
Leighton, Peter (1966) Set 51
Leighton Williams, John (1964) (QC-1986) Set 41 Profile p.1434
Leiper, Richard (1996) Set 81 Profile p.1434
Leist, Ian (1981) Set 65 Profile p.1434
Lemmy, Michael (1994) Set 228
Lemon, Jane (1993) Set 69 Profile p.1434
Lemon, Roy (1970) Set 24
Lennard, Stephen (1976) Set 63
Lennon, Desmond (1986) Set 204
Lennon, Jonathan (1997) Set 18

L

INDEX ■ BARRISTERS

Lenon, Andrew (1982) Set 32
Leonard, Anthony (1978) (QC-1999) Set 75 Profile p.1434
Leonard, Edna (1992) Set 246
Leonard, James (1989) Set 71
Leonard, Robert (1976) Sets 48, 63
Leong, Andrew (1998) Sets 62, 249
Lerego, Michael (1972) (QC-1995) Set 44
Leslie, Stephen (1971) (QC-1993) Set 45 Profile p.1434
Lester, Maya (2001) Set 14
Lester of Herne Hill, Lord (1963) (QC-1975) Set 12 Profile p.1434
Letman, Paul (1987) Set 111
Lett, Brian (1971) Set 264 Profile p.1434
Levene, Simon (1977) Set 82
Lever, John (1978) Set 178
Lever, Sir Jeremy (1957) (QC-1972) Set 90 Profile p.1434
Levett, Francesca (1997) Set 74
Levett, Martyn (1978) Set 126
Levey, Edward (1999) Set 44
Levine, Steven (1989) Set 214
Leviseur, Nicholas (1979) Set 111
Levitt, Alison (1988) Set 53
Levy, Allan (1969) (QC-1989) Set 6 Profile p.1434
Levy, Jacob (1986) Set 50 Profile p.1434
Levy, Michael (1979) Set 4 Profile p.1435
Levy, Neil (1986) Set 169 Profile p.1435
Levy, Philip G (1968) Set 149
Levy, Robert (1988) Set 98
Levy (Gibraltar), James (1972) Set 140
Lewers, Nigel (1986) Set 82
Lewin, Nicholas (1989) Sets 71, 253
Lewis, Adam (1985) Set 12 Profile p.1435
Lewis, Alex (1990) Set 65
Lewis, Andrew W (1985) Set 200
Lewis, Anya (1997) Set 47
Lewis, Catrin (1991) Set 47
Lewis, Charles (1977) Set 9
Lewis, Charles (1963) Sets 104, 167
Lewis, Christopher (1998) Set 3
Lewis, Clive (1987) Set 81 Profile p.1435
Lewis, David (1997) Sets 48, 63
Lewis, Dominic (2000) Set 114
Lewis, Ian (1989) Set 127
Lewis, James (1987) (QC-2002) Set 124 Profile p.1435
Lewis, Jeremy (1992) Set 85
Lewis, Jonathan (1996) Set 140
Lewis, Marian (1977) Set 174 Profile p.1435
Lewis, Matthew (2000) Set 174
Lewis, Meyric (1986) Set 61
Lewis, Michael (1956) (QC-1975) Set 4
Lewis, Owen Prys (1985) Set 173
Lewis, Patrick (1997) Set 47
Lewis, Paul (1981) (QC-2001) Set 174 Profile p.1435
Lewis, Philip (1958) Set 86
Lewis, Ralph (1978) (QC-1999) Set 159 Profile p.1435
Lewis, Ray (1994) Set 176
Lewis, Raymond (1971) Set 26
Lewis, Rhodri Price (1975) (QC-2001) Sets 27, 175 Profile p.1435
Lewis, Robert (1996) Set 97
Lewis, Robin (1991) Set 161

Lewis, Roy (1992) Sets 104, 167
Lewis-Jones, Meirion (1971) Set 179
Lewison, Kim (1975) (QC-1991) Set 40 Profile p.1435
Lewsley, Christopher (1976) Set 13
Lewthwaite, J (1990) Set 210
Ley, Nigel Spencer (1985) Set 41
Ley-Morgan, Mark (1994) Set 130
Lickert, Martin (1986) Set 117
Lickley, Nigel (1983) Set 111
Liddell, Richard (1999) Set 92
Liddiard, Martin (1989) Set 159
Liddy, Simon (1979) Set 202
Lidington, Gary (2000) Set 86
Liebrecht, Michael (1989) Set 46
Lieven, Nathalie (1989) Set 13 Profile p.1436
Light, Roy (1992) Set 169
Lightman, Daniel (1995) Set 131 Profile p.1436
Lightwing, Stuart (1972) Set 233 Profile p.1436
Lillington, Simon (1980) Sets 127, 258
Limb, Christopher (1975) Set 232
Limb, Patrick (1987) Set 247 Profile p.1436
Limont, Anthony (1964) Set 205
Lindblom, Keith (1980) (QC-1996) Set 61 Profile p.1436
Linden, Thomas (1990) Set 88 Profile p.1436
Lindquist, Andrew (1968) Set 244
Lindsay, Claire (1991) Sets 116, 238
Lindsay, Jeremy (1986) Set 197
Lindsey, Susan (1997) Set 22
Linehan, Stephen (1970) (QC-1993) Set 156
Ling, Victoria (1998) Set 139
Linklater, Lisa (1995) Set 188
Linnemann, Bernard (1980) Set 156
Linstead, Peter (1994) Set 19
Lintott, David (1995) Set 52
Lipworth, Sir Sydney (1991) (QC-1993) Set 32
Lissack, Richard (1978) (QC-1994) Set 37 Profile p.1436
Lister, Caroline (1980) Set 70 Profile p.1437
Litchfield, Linda (1974) Set 111
Lithman, Nigel (1976) (QC-1997) Set 4 Profile p.1437
Little, Geoffrey (1973) Set 179
Little, Helen (1999) Sets 62, 249
Little, Ian (1989) Set 228 Profile p.1437
Little, Tom (1997) Set 50
Littler, Martin (1989) Set 216
Littler, Richard (1994) Set 216
Littlewood, Robert (1993) Set 47
Littman, Mark (1947) (QC-1961) Set 86
Litton, John (1989) Set 13
Livesey, Bernard (1969) (QC-1990) Set 92 Profile p.1437
Livesey, Fraser (1992) Set 256
Livesey, John (1990) Set 165
Livesey, Simon (1987) Set 144
Livingston, John (1980) Set 4
Livingstone, Simon (1994) Set 19
Llewellyn-Jones, Christopher (1965) (QC-1990) Set 48
Lloyd, Francis (1987) Set 63
Lloyd, Gaynor (1992) Set 179
Lloyd, Heather (1979) Set 205 Profile p.1437
Lloyd, Huw (1975) Set 130 Profile p.1437
Lloyd, James (1985) Set 36
Lloyd, Patricia (1979) Set 72
Lloyd, Stephen (1971) Set 97

Lloyd, Wendy-Jane (1983) Set 204
Lloyd Jones, David (1975) (QC-1999) Set 14 Profile p.1437
Lloyd-Eley, Andrew (1979) Set 65 Profile p.1437
Lloyd-Jacob, Campaspe (1990) Set 124
Lloyd-Jones, John (1993) Set 9
Lloyd-Nesling, Tracey (1988) Set 161
Lloyd-Smith, Rebecca (1994) Set 226
Llwyd MP, Elfyn (1997) Set 179
Llwyd Williams, Heledd (1999) Set 179
Lo, Bernard (1991) Set 6
Loades, Jonathan (1986) Set 50
Lobbenberg, Nicholas (1987) Set 55
Lochrane, Damien (1983) Sets 121, 262, 265
Lockey, John (1987) Set 31 Profile p.1437
Lockhart, Andrew (1991) Set 161 Profile p.1438
Lockhart, Clare (1999) Set 54
Lockhart, Stuart (1998) Sets 171, 251
Lockhart-Mummery, Christopher (1971) (QC-1986) Set 13 Profile p.1438
Lodder, Peter (1981) (QC-2001) Set 4 Profile p.1438
Lodge, A R (1996) Set 220
Lodge, Anton (1966) (QC-1989) Set 194
Lodge, Hugo (1999) Set 110
Lodge, John (1980) Set 194
Lody, Stuart (1992) Set 246
Lofthouse, John (1979) Set 71
Lofthouse, Simon (1988) Set 3 Profile p.1438
Loftus, Teresa (1995) Set 204
Logsdon, Michael (1988) Set 65
Lomas, Mark H (1977) Set 85 Profile p.1438
Lomas, Mark S (1983) Set 111
Lomnicka, Prof Eva (1974) Set 92 Profile p.1438
Lonergan, Paul (1991) Set 101
Long, Andrew (1981) Set 226 Profile p.1438
Long, Tobias (1988) Set 26
Longman, Michael (1978) Set 169 Profile p.1438
Longstaff, Oliver (1999) Set 199
Longworth, Anthony (1978) Set 230
Lonsdale, David (1988) Set 8
Lonsdale, Marion (1984) Set 39
Loosemore, Mary (1992) Set 180
Lopez, Paul (1982) Set 160
Lopian, Jonathan (1994) Set 141
Lord, David W (1987) Set 136
Lord, Richard (1981) (QC-2002) Set 4 Profile p.1438
Lord, Tim (1992) Set 146 Profile p.1438
Lorie, Andrew (1996) Set 259
Love, Mark (1979) Set 109
Loveday, Mark (1986) Set 144
Lovelady, John (1998) Set 178
Lovell-Pank, Dorian (1971) (QC-1993) Set 75 Profile p.1438
Loveridge, Andrew (1983) Set 208
Lowe, (Nicholas) Mark (1972) (QC-1996) Set 52 Profile p.1438
Lowe, Anthony (1976) Set 158
Lowe, Craig (1994) Set 202
Lowe, David (1965) (QC-1984) Set 153
Lowe, Emma (1996) Set 65
Lowe, Geoffrey (1975) Set 209

Lowe, John (1976) Sets 116, 238, 239
Lowe, Matthew (1991) Set 9
Lowe, Nigel (1972) Set 169
Lowe, Rupert (1998) Set 169
Lowe, Sarah (1995) Set 113
Lowe, Thomas (1985) Set 153
Lowe, Vaughan (1993) Set 31 Profile p.1439
Lowe, William (1972) (QC-1997) Sets 116, 238
Lowenstein, Paul (1988) Set 152
Lownds, Peter (1998) Set 25
Lowne, Stephen (1981) Set 246
Lowry, Emma (1991) Set 68
Lowry, Stephen (1960) Set 182
Luba, Jan (1980) (QC-2000) Set 47 Profile p.1439
Lucas, Bridget (1989) Set 44
Lucas, Edward (1991) Set 168
Lucas, Felicie (1999) Set 176
Lucas, Noel (1979) Set 43 Profile p.1439
Lucas, Phillip (1995) Set 79
Lucie, Gary (1994) Set 257
Lucraft, Mark (1984) Set 126
Lugg, Elizabeth (1994) Set 234
Lumley, Gerald (1972) Set 201
Lumley, Nicholas J H (1992) Set 200
Lumsden, K (1994) Set 71
Lund, Celia (1988) Set 203
Lundie, Christopher (1991) Set 146
Lunt, Beverley (1977) Set 220
Lunt, Steven (1991) Set 201
Lurie, Jonathan (1972) Set 79
Lydiard, Andrew (1980) Set 14 Profile p.1439
Lyell, Nicholas (1965) (QC-1980) Set 90
Lynagh, Richard (1975) (QC-1996) Set 22
Lynch, Adrian (1983) (QC-2000) Set 81 Profile p.1439
Lynch, Jerome (1983) (QC-2000) Set 18 Profile p.1439
Lynch, Julian (1976) Set 19
Lynch, Patricia (1979) (QC-1998) Sets 126, 177 Profile p.1439
Lynch, Peter (1985) Set 16
Lynch, Terry (1989) Set 242
Lyndon-Stanford, Michael (1962) (QC-1979) Set 87 Profile p.1439
Lyne, Mark (1981) Set 115
Lyness, Scott (1996) Set 27 Profile p.1439
Lynn, Jeremy (1983) Set 151
Lyon, Antonia (1997) Set 123
Lyon, Shane (1976) Set 183
Lyon, Victor (1980) (QC-2002) Set 31
Lyons, Graham (1972) Set 117
Lyons, John (1986) Set 126
Lyons, Timothy (1980) Sets 102, 227
Lyster, Grania (1992) Set 96
Mabb, David (1979) (QC-2001) Set 30 Profile p.1439
Mably, Louis (1997) Set 75
MacAdam, Jason (1990) Sets 199, 200
Maccabe, Irvine (1983) Set 111
MacCormick, Neil (1971) (QC-1999) Set 85
MacDonald, Ailsa (2000) Set 237
MacDonald, Alison (2000) Set 88
MacDonald, Alistair (1995) Set 161
MacDonald, Alistair (1983) (QC-2000) Set 194
Macdonald, Charles (1972) (QC-1992) Set 33 Profile p.1439
MacDonald, Iain (1996) Set 49

MacDonald, Ian (1963) (QC-1988) Set 215
Macdonald, Ian (1963) (QC-1988) Set 47 Profile p.1439
MacDonald , John (1955) Set 200
Macdonald, John (1955) (QC-1976) Set 98
Macdonald, Ken (1978) (QC-1997) Set 88 Profile p.1439
MacDonald, Lindsey (1985) Set 63
Macdonald, Sheila (1993) Set 246
MacDonald Eggers, Peter (1999) Set 77
Macey-Dare, Thomas (1994) Set 33
Macfarlane, Andrew (1995) Set 166
Macfarlane, Tabitha (1998) Set 166
MacFaul, Donald (1998) Set 234
MacGregor, Alastair (1974) (QC-1994) Set 32
MacGregor, Heather (1982) Set 127
Machell, John (1993) Set 131 Profile p.1439
Machell, Raymond (1973) (QC-1988) Sets 101, 213 Profile p.1439
Machin, Charles (1973) Set 216
Machin, Graham (1965) Set 247
Machin, Susan (2000) Set 231
MacKenzie, Dr Catherine (1995) Set 93
MacKenzie, Julie (1978) Sets 121, 262, 265
MacKenzie Smith, Catherine (1968) Sets 116, 238
Mackie, Jeannie (1995) Set 25
MacLaren, Catriona (1993) Set 144
Maclean, Alan (1993) Set 14 Profile p.1440
MacLean , Kenneth (1985) (QC-2002) Set 32
Maclennan, Alison (1996) Set 107 Profile p.1440
Macleod, Duncan (1980) Set 50
Macnab, Andrew (1986) Set 90
Macpherson, Angus (1977) Set 145
Macpherson, Mary (1984) Set 89
MacRae, Robert (1990) Set 183
Macrory, Richard (1974) Set 14 Profile p.1440
Macur, Julia (1979) (QC-1998) Set 160 Profile p.1440
Madan, Pankaj (1997) Set 201
Madden, John (1997) Set 43
Maddick, Bruce (1970) Set 71
Maddison, David (1995) Set 216
Maddox, Peter (1994) Set 260
Magarian, Michael (1988) Set 26
Magee, Mike (1997) Sets 171, 251
Magee, Rosein (1994) Set 180
Maguire, Andrew (1988) Set 161
Maguire, Benn (1994) Set 73
Maguire, Michael (1949) (QC-1967) Set 48
Maher, Martha (1987) Set 166 Profile p.1440
Mahmood, Abid (1992) Set 214
Mahmood, Ghazan (1997) Set 225
Mahmood, Saleema (1999) Set 162
Mahommed, Ismail (1956) Set 25
Mahon, Brian (1996) Set 161
Mahoney, Constance (2000) Set 140
Maidment, Kieran (1989) Set 25 Profile p.1440
Maidment, Susan R (1968) Set 70
Main, Peter (1981) Set 217

BARRISTERS — INDEX

M

Main Thompson, Dermot (1977) Set 127
Mainds, A G (Sam) (1977) Set 9
Maini, Ashwin (2001) Set 38
Mairs, Robin (1992) Set 199
Maitland, Andrew (1970) Sets 71, 253
Maitland-Jones, Mark (1986) Sets 48, 83, 250
Makepeace, Peter (1988) Set 266
Makey, Christopher (1975) Sets 104, 167
Malcolm, Alastair R (1971) (QC-1996) Set 108
Malcolm, Helen (1986) Set 124 Profile p.1440
Malcolm, Rosalind (1979) Set 42
Malcolm, Rozanna (1974) Set 113
Malden, Grace (1993) Set 37
Male, John (1976) (QC-2000) Set 13 Profile p.1440
Malek, Ali (1980) (QC-1996) Set 152 Profile p.1440
Malek, Hodge M (1983) (QC-1999) Set 54 Profile p.1440
Males, Stephen (1978) (QC-1998) Set 35 Profile p.1440
Maley, Bill (1982) Set 53
Malik, Amjad (1987) Set 9
Malik, Omar (1990) Set 258
Malik, Sarah (1999) Set 16
Malins, Julian (1972) (QC-1991) Set 85
Mallalieu, Ann (1970) (QC-1988) Set 75 Profile p.1441
Mallalieu, Roger (1998) Set 119
Mallender, Paul Nigel (1974) Set 117
Mallett, Sarah (1988) Set 80
Mallett, Simon (1986) Sets 80, 190
Mallin, Max (1993) Set 141
Mallinckrodt, Sophie (1999) Set 152
Mallison, Kate (1974) Set 73
Mallon, Joanna (1996) Set 206
Mallory, Katherine (1998) Set 228
Malone, Michael (1975) Set 32
Maltz, Ben (1998) Set 115
Malynicz, Simon (1997) Set 67
Manasse, Paul (1995) Set 232
Mandalia, Vinesh (1997) Set 161
Mandil-Wade, Rosalyne (1988) Set 34
Mangat, Tejina (1990) Set 119 Profile p.1441
Manley, David (1981) Sets 191, 222
Manley, Hilary (1996) Set 216
Mann, Anthony (1974) (QC-1992) Sets 29, 189, 235 Profile p.1441
Mann, Christopher (1998) Sets 83, 250
Mann, Jas (2001) Set 159
Mann, Jonathan (1989) Set 53
Mann, Martin (1968) (QC-1983) Sets 103, 169
Mann, Paul (1980) (QC-2002) Set 245 Profile p.1441
Mann, Rebecca (1995) Set 261
Mann, Sara (1994) Set 209
Manning, Colin (1970) Set 85 Profile p.1441
Manning, Jonathan (1989) Set 2
Mansell, Richard (1991) Set 193
Mansfield, Gavin (1992) Set 85
Mansfield, Guy (1972) (QC-1994) Set 23 Profile p.1441
Mansfield, Michael (1967) (QC-1989) Set 150 Profile p.1441
Manson, Juliann (1985) Set 19
Mansoori, Sara (1997) Set 125 Profile p.1441
Mantle, Peter (1989) Set 90

Manuel, Elizabeth (1987) Set 258
Manzoni, Charles (1988) Set 38
Maqsood, Kalsoom (1998) Set 229
Maqsood, Zabeda (1996) Set 256
Marcus, Gilbert (1999) Set 25
Margolin, Daniel (1995) Set 105
Margree, Sarah (1996) Sets 80, 190
Mark, Brian (1981) Set 234
Markham, Anna (1996) Set 137
Marklew, Lee (1992) Set 156
Marks, David (1974) Set 133 Profile p.1441
Marks, Gillian (1981) Set 56
Marks, Jacqueline (1984) Set 51
Marks, Jonathan (1992) Set 88
Marks, Jonathan (1975) (QC-1995) Set 118
Marks, Lewis (1984) (QC-2002) Set 123 Profile p.1441
Marks, Medina (1992) Set 39
Marks, Richard (1975) (QC-1999) Sets 18, 226 Profile p.1442
Markus, Kate (1981) Set 25 Profile p.1442
Marley, Sarah (1995) Set 21
Marlow, Claire (1983) Set 168
Marnham, Michelle (1994) Set 144
Marquand, Charles (1987) Set 137 Profile p.1442
Marrin, John (1974) (QC-1990) Set 69 Profile p.1442
Marron, Aidan (1973) (QC-1993) Set 266
Marrs, Andrew (1995) Set 219
Marsden, Andrew (1994) Set 169
Marsden, Andrew (1975) Sets 181, 187, 243
Marsh, Laurence (1975) Set 118
Marshall, Andrew (1986) Set 43
Marshall, David (1985) Set 126
Marshall, David (1981) Set 111
Marshall, Derek (1980) Set 259
Marshall, Eloise (1994) Set 36
Marshall, Hannah (1998) Set 183
Marshall, Paul (1991) Set 66
Marshall, Peter (1991) Set 16
Marshall, Philip (1989) Set 70 Profile p.1442
Marshall, Philip (1987) Set 131 Profile p.1442
Marshall, Philip Derek (1975) Set 260
Marshall, Vanessa (1994) Set 5
Marshall Williams, Adrian (1998) Set 47
Marshall-Andrews, Robert (1967) (QC-1989) Sets 151, 197
Marson, Geoffrey C (1975) (QC-1997) Set 200 Profile p.1442
Marten, Hedley (1966) Set 97 Profile p.1442
Martignetti, Ian (1990) Set 252
Martin, Andrew (1983) Set 133
Martin, Bradley (1990) Set 146
Martin, Dale (1997) Set 85
Martin, David (1969) Set 168
Martin, Dianne (1992) Set 169
Martin, Gay (1970) Set 19
Martin, Gerard (1978) (QC-2000) Sets 161, 207, 218
Martin, John (1972) (QC-1991) Set 153 Profile p.1442
Martin, Peter (1969) Set 151
Martin, Piers (1997) Set 51
Martin, Roy (1990) Set 27
Martineau, Harry (1966) Set 48
Martin-Jenkins, James (1997) Set 60
Martino, Anthony (1982) Set 44
Martin-Sperry, David (1971) Set 18 Profile p.1442

Marven, Robert (1994) Set 145
Maryon Green, Neville (1963) Set 6
Marzec, Alexandra (1990) Set 125 Profile p.1442
Masefield, Roger (1994) Set 14
Mashembo, Carol (1999) Sets 71, 253
Maskrey, Simeon (1977) (QC-1995) Set 5 Profile p.1442
Mason, Alexandra (1981) Set 136 Profile p.1442
Mason, David (1986) Set 156
Mason, David (1984) Set 236
Mason, Ian (1978) Set 2
Mason, John (1971) Set 158
Mason, Nicholas (1984) Set 178
Mason, Patrick (1997) Set 264
Massarella, David (1999) Set 20
Massey, Andrew (1969) Set 258
Massey, Stella (1990) Set 214
Massey, William (1977) (QC-1996) Set 122
Massih, Michel G A (1979) (QC-1999) Set 45
Masters, Lee (1984) Set 162
Masters, Sara (1993) Set 35
Mather, Alison (1997) Set 219
Mather, Kate (1990) Set 73
Mather-Lees, Michael (1981) Set 174
Mathew, Robin (1974) (QC-1992) Set 98
Mathews, Deni (1996) Set 157
Mathias, Anna (1994) Set 19
Mathieson, Guy (1993) Set 231
Matovu, Daniel (1985) Set 146
Matovu, Harry (1988) Set 14
Matthew, David (1987) Set 5
Matthew, Nergis-Anne (1981) Sets 51, 161
Matthews, Claire (1998) Set 108
Matthews, Dennis (1973) Set 22 Profile p.1442
Matthews, Duncan (1986) (QC-2002) Set 35 Profile p.1442
Matthews, Gillian (1985) Set 266
Matthews, Janek (1972) Set 122
Matthews, Julian D (1979) Set 5
Matthews, Lisa (1994) Set 45
Matthews, Lynne (1987) Set 169
Matthews, Phillip (1974) Set 43
Matthews, Richard (1989) Set 4 Profile p.1443
Matthewson, Scott (1996) Set 101
Matthews-Stroud, Jackie (1984) Set 9
Matthias, David (1980) Set 52
Matuk, Helen (1990) Set 220
Maude, Victoria (1995) Set 17
Maudslay, Diana (1997) Set 200
Maudsley, Penelope (1998) Set 214
Mauger, Shanti (1996) Sets 29, 189, 235
Maughan, Jolyon (1997) Set 96
Mauladad, Farrah (1999) Set 143
Mauleverer, Bruce (1969) (QC-1985) Set 118
Maunder, David (1993) Set 169
Maurici, James (1996) Set 13 Profile p.1443
Mawdsley, Matthew (1991) Sets 224, 251
Mawhinney, Richard M (1977) Set 37
Mawrey, Richard (1964) (QC-1986) Sets 60, 135
Max, Sally (1991) Sets 62, 249
Maxwell, Adrian (1993) Set 50
Maxwell, David (1985) Set 161
Maxwell, John (1985) Set 232
Maxwell, John (1965) Set 157
Maxwell, Karen (1992) Set 35

Maxwell, Richard (1968) (QC-1988) Sets 25, 247 Profile p.1443
Maxwell-Scott, James (1995) Set 22
May, Alan (1995) Set 36
May, Charlotte (1995) Set 95 Profile p.1443
May, Juliet (1988) Set 152
May, Kieran (1971) Set 139
May, Nigel (1974) Set 8
Maycock, Elizabeth (1996) Set 248
Mayer, Tim (1997) Set 159
Mayer, Vera (1978) Set 21
Mayes, Ian (1974) (QC-1993) Set 85
Mayhew, Jerome (1995) Set 48
Mayhew of Twysden, Lord (1955) (QC-1972) Set 145
Maynard-Connor, Giles (1992) Sets 207, 218 Profile p.1443
Mayo, Rupert (1987) Set 5
Mayo, Simon (1985) Set 43
Mazibrada, Andrew (1999) Set 45
Mazzag, Anthony (1996) Set 226
McAlinden, Barry (1993) Set 6
McAlinden, Michael (1996) Set 109
McAllister, Ann (1982) Set 131 Profile p.1443
McAllister, Elmear (1992) Set 201
McAtasney, Philippa (1986) Set 11
McAteer, Katrina (2001) Set 63
McAulay, Mark (1993) Set 55
McBride, Gavin (1996) Set 226
McCabe, Louise (1997) Sets 83, 250
McCabe, Margaret (1981) Set 200
McCafferty, Jane (1998) Set 81 Profile p.1443
McCafferty, John (2000) Set 2
McCafferty, Lynne (1997) Set 118
McCall, Christopher (1966) (QC-1987) Set 87 Profile p.1443
McCall, Duncan (1988) Set 118 Profile p.1444
McCalla, Sandra (1999) Set 49
McCalla, Tarquin (1994) Set 18
McCallum, Louise (1999) Set 201
McCann, Claire (2000) Set 20
McCann, Simon (1996) Set 217
McCarroll, John J (1988) Sets 207, 218
McCarthy, Damian (1994) Set 20
McCarthy, Mary (1994) Set 183
McCarthy, Niamh (1991) Set 86
McCarthy, Roger (1975) (QC-1996) Set 21
McCarthy, Tara (1997) Set 43
McCarthy, William (1996) Set 200
McCartney, Kevin (1991) Set 63
McCartney, Peter (1983) Set 157
McCaughran, John (1982) Set 32 Profile p.1444
McCaul, Colin (1978) Set 38
McCavish, Kevin (1998) Set 9
McCluggage, Brian (1995) Set 228
McClure, Brian (1976) Set 86
McClure, John P (1975) Set 230
McColgan, Aileen (2001) Set 88
McConnell, Christopher (1979) Set 51
McConnochie, Kathryn (1997) Set 261
McConville, Donald (1963) Set 156
McCormack, Helen (1986) Set 63
McCormack, Philip (1994) Set 51
McCormick, Alison (1988) Set 37
McCormick, William (1985) Set 28

McCoubrey, Robin (2000) Set 75
McCourt, Christopher (1993) Set 113
McCoy, Gerard (1986) Set 110
McCracken, James (1998) Set 158
McCracken, Robert (1973) Set 61 Profile p.1444
McCrae, Fiona (1987) Set 239
McCredie, Fionnuala (1992) Set 130
McCue, Donald (1974) Set 141
McCulloch, Niall (2000) Set 29
McCullough, Angus (1990) Set 23 Profile p.1444
McCutcheon, Barry (1975) Set 138
McDermott, Gerard (1978) (QC-1999) Set 221
McDermott, John (1976) Set 205 Profile p.1444
McDermott, Tom (1980) Set 41
McDonald, Andrew (1971) Set 208
McDonald, Brent (2000) Set 146
McDonald, Janet (1985) Set 173
McDonald, John (1981) Set 146
McDonald, Melanie (1990) Set 159
McDonald, Paul (1975) Set 228
McDonnell, Conrad (1994) Set 57 Profile p.1444
McDonnell, John (1968) (QC-1984) Set 140 Profile p.1444
McDowell, David (1999) Set 11
McEvilly, Gerard (1994) Set 45
McEwan, Malcolm (1976) Set 229
McFarland, Denise (1987) Set 91 Profile p.1444
McFarlane, Alastair (1985) Set 145
McFarlane, Andrew (1977) (QC-1998) Sets 70, 161 Profile p.1444
McGahey, Cathryn (1990) Set 5
McGahey, Elizabeth (1994) Set 174
McGee, Andrew (1998) Set 191
McGee, Andrew (1998) Set 222
McGee, Andrew (1999) Set 4
McGee, Tamala (1995) Set 73
McGeorge, Anthony (1969) Sets 83, 250
McGhee, John (1984) Set 105 Profile p.1444
McGhee, Stuart (2000) Set 259
McGinn, Dominic (1990) Set 149
McGinty, Robert (1994) Set 230
McGonigal, David (1982) Set 163
McGovern, Sean (1990) Set 202
McGowan, Maura (1980) (QC-2001) Set 4
McGrail, Peter (1977) Set 151
McGrath, Andrew (1983) Set 159
McGrath, David (1993) Set 151
McGrath, Elizabeth (1987) Set 161
McGrath, Paul (1997) Set 145
McGrath, Paul (1994) Set 31 Profile p.1444
McGrath, Siobhan (1982) Set 2
McGregor, Alexander (1996) Set 19
McGregor, Alistair J (1974) (QC-1997) Set 81 Profile p.1445
McGregor, Harvey (1955) (QC-1978) Set 112
McGuinness, John (1980) (QC-2001) Set 11
McGuire, Deirdre (1983) Set 208
McGuire, Donal (1983) Set 208
McHugh, Karen (1992) Set 13
McHugh, Pauline (1995) Set 231
McIlroy, David (1995) Set 111
McIlwain, Sylvester (1985) Set 56
McInnes, Neil (1999) Set 25

1681

INDEX ■ BARRISTERS

McIvor, Helen (1992) Set 232
McKay, Christopher (1976) Set 176
McKay, Hugh (1990) Set 57 Profile p.1445
McKechnie, Stuart (1997) Set 143
McKee, Hugh (1983) Sets 224, 230
McKeever, Catherine (2000) Set 245
McKeever, Frances (1988) Set 147
McKendrick, Ewan (1998) Set 152
McKendrick, John (1999) Sets 48, 63 Profile p.1445
McKenna, Brian (1983) Sets 224, 230
McKenzie, Lesley (1983) Set 234
McKeon, James (1982) Set 208
McKeone, Mary (1986) Sets 47, 215
McKeown, Sarah (1998) Set 2
McKie, Suzanne (1991) Set 24
McKinlay, Vanessa (2000) Set 169
McKinnell, Soraya (1991) Sets 29, 189, 235
McKone, Mark D (1988) Set 200
McLachlan, David (1996) Set 204
McLaren, Ian (1962) (QC-1993) Set 247 Profile p.1445
McLaren, Michael (1981) (QC-2002) Set 44
McLaughlin, Andrew (1993) Set 169 Profile p.1445
McLaughlin, Elaine (1993) Set 201
McLaughlin, Karen (1982) Set 56
McLean, Mandy (1996) Set 34
McLeese, Stuart (2000) Set 174
McLeish, Martyn (1997) Set 139
McLeod, Iain (1969) Set 66
McLinden, John (1991) Set 6
McLoughlin, Timothy (1978) Sets 181, 187, 243 Profile p.1445
McManus, Richard (1982) (QC-1999) Set 54 Profile p.1445
McMaster, Peter (1981) Set 131
McMeekin, Ian (1987) Set 220 Profile p.1445
McMeel, Gerard (1993) Set 166
McMullan, Manus (1994) Set 3 Profile p.1445
McNab, Mhairi (1974) Set 56
McNally, Sarah (1999) Set 22
McNamara, Andrew (1992) Sets 9, 247
McNamara, James (1990) Set 245
McNeilis, Sharron (1990) Set 246
McNeill, Fiona (1992) Set 205
McNeill, Jane (1982) (QC-2002) Sets 104, 167 Profile p.1445
McNeill, John (1974) Set 230
McNicholas, Eamon (1994) Set 148
McNulty, Lawrence (1985) Sets 116, 238
McParland, Michael (1983) Set 33
McPherson, Graeme (1993) Set 92 Profile p.1445
McQuail, Katherine (1989) Set 107
McQuater, Ewan (1985) Set 152 Profile p.1445
McQuitty, Laura (2000) Set 36
Meachin, Vanessa (1990) Set 161
Mead, Philip (1989) Sets 104, 167 Profile p.1445
Meade, Richard (1991) Set 95 Profile p.1446
Meadowcroft, Stephen (1973) Set 226 Profile p.1446
Meadway, Susannah (1988) Set 106 Profile p.1446
Meares, Nigel (1975) Set 141
Medcroft, Nicholas (1998) Set 126

Medd, James (1985) Set 22
Medhurst, David (1969) Set 16
Medland, Simon (1991) Sets 36, 178
Mee, Paul (1992) Sets 120, 212
Meek, Susan (1997) Set 110
Meeke, Martin (1973) (QC-2000) Set 182 Profile p.1446
Meeson, Nigel (1982) (QC-2002) Set 33 Profile p.1446
Megyery, Ayshea (1997) Set 193
Mehendale, Neelima (1993) Set 51
Mehigan, Simon (1980) (QC-1998) Set 114 Profile p.1446
Mein, Lyndsey (1999) Set 103
Mejzner, Stephen (1978) Set 18
Mellor, Christopher (1999) Set 23
Mellor, James (1986) Set 95 Profile p.1446
Mellor, JW (1953) Set 196
Melly, Kama (1997) Set 197
Melton, Christopher (1982) (QC-2001) Set 213 Profile p.1446
Melton, Christopher (1982) (QC-2001) Set 101
Melville, David (1975) (QC-2002) Set 38
Melville, Elizabeth (1994) Sets 104, 167
Melville-Shreeve, Michael (1986) Set 183
Melwani, Poonam (1989) Set 33
Menary, Andrew (1982) Set 208
Mendelle, Paul (1981) Set 53
Mendelson, Maurice (1965) (QC-1992) Set 12 Profile p.1446
Mendes da Costa, David (1976) Set 72
Mendoza, Colin (1983) Set 24
Mendoza, Neil (1982) Set 128
Menon, Hari (1989) Sets 116, 238
Menon, Rajiv (1993) Set 47
Mensah, Helyn (1998) Set 91
Menzies, Gordon (1998) Sets 120, 212
Menzies, Richard (1993) Set 139
Merali, Shabbir (1998) Sets 80, 190
Mercer, Geoffrey (1975) (QC-2002) Set 183 Profile p.1446
Mercer, Hugh (1985) Set 31 Profile p.1446
Mercer, Neil (1988) Set 70
Meredith, George (1969) Set 253 Profile p.1446
Meredith-Hardy, John (1989) Set 71
Merrett, Louise (1995) Set 44
Merrick, Nicola (1983) Set 45
Merriman, Nicholas (1969) (QC-1988) Set 152 Profile p.1446
Merritt, Richard (1981) Set 234
Merry, Hugh (1979) Set 257
Merrylees, Gavin (1964) Set 144
Merz, Richard (1972) Set 11
Messenger, Emma (1999) Set 72
Messling, Lawrence (1983) Set 161
Metaxa, William (1997) Set 127
Metcalf, Christopher (1972) Set 9
Metcalf, John (1990) Set 73
Metcalf, Louise (1997) Sets 207, 218
Metcalfe, Ian (1985) Set 216
Methuen, Richard (1972) (QC-1997) Set 82 Profile p.1446
Metzer, Anthony (1987) Set 25
Mew, Graeme (1982) Set 92
Meyer, Birgitta (1992) Set 141
Meyer, Lorna (1986) Set 159 Profile p.1446
Miah, Zacharias (1990) Set 151
Michael, Simon (1978) Set 159

Michaels, Amanda (1981) Set 67 Profile p.1446
Michalos, Christina (1994) Set 6
Michell, Michael (1984) Set 106
Michell, Paul (1991) Set 20
Micklethwait, David (1970) Set 67
Middleburgh, Jonathan (1990) Set 141
Middleton, Claire (1991) Set 234
Middleton, Georgina (1989) Set 41
Middleton, Joseph (1997) Set 25
Mifflin, Helen (1982) Set 174 Profile p.1447
Migdal, Stephen (1974) Set 162
Milburn, Hugh (1997) Set 197
Mildon, David (1980) (QC-2000) Set 31
Miles, Nicola (1999) Set 208
Miles, Richard (1997) Set 110
Miles, Robert (1987) (QC-2002) Set 137 Profile p.1447
Milford, Julian (2000) Set 81
Mill, Ian (1981) (QC-1999) Set 12 Profile p.1447
Millar, Gavin (1981) (QC-2000) Set 25
Miller, Alison (1999) Set 203
Miller, Andrew (1989) Set 146
Miller, Celia (1978) Sets 181, 187, 243 Profile p.1447
Miller, Christopher (1998) Set 56
Miller, David (1998) Set 79
Miller, Ian (1999) Set 129
Miller, Ian (1999) Set 163
Miller, Jane (1979) (QC-2000) Sets 121, 262, 265
Miller, Jonathan (1996) Set 110
Miller, Nicholas (1994) Set 166 Profile p.1447
Miller, Paul (1974) Set 186
Miller, Peter (1993) Set 52
Miller, Richard (1991) Set 176
Miller, Richard (1976) (QC-1995) Set 91 Profile p.1447
Miller, Robin (1960) Sets 71, 253
Miller, Sarah (1971) Set 142
Miller, Simon (1996) Set 111
Miller, Stephen (1971) (QC-1990) Set 23 Profile p.1447
Millet, Trilby (1996) Set 26
Millett, Kenneth (1988) Set 65 Profile p.1447
Millett, Richard (1985) Set 31 Profile p.1447
Milligan, Iain (1973) (QC-1991) Set 35 Profile p.1447
Milliken-Smith, Mark (1986) Set 4 Profile p.1448
Millington, Christopher (1976) (QC-2001) Set 155
Millmore, Amanda (1996) Set 73
Mills, Barbara (1990) Set 113
Mills, Corey (1987) Set 172
Mills, Kristian (1998) Set 11
Mills, RS (1992) Set 210
Mills, Simon (1994) Set 115
Milmo, John B (1966) (QC-1984) Set 245
Milmo, Patrick (1962) (QC-1985) Set 125 Profile p.1448
Milne, Alexander (1981) Set 126
Milne, David (1970) (QC-1987) Set 122 Profile p.1448
Milne, Michael (1987) Set 39
Milne, Richard (1992) Set 36
Milner, Jonathan (1977) Set 61
Milsom, Catherine (1994) Set 110
Minihan, Sean (1988) Set 55
Mintz, Simon (1996) Set 205
Mirchandani, Si,n (1997) Set 92
Miric, Robin (1978) Set 79
Miscampbell, Norman (1952) (QC-1974) Set 145

Mishcon, Jane (1979) Set 112
Miskin, Charles (1975) (QC-1998) Set 36 Profile p.1448
Misner, Philip (1984) Set 55
Misra, Eleena (2001) Set 85
Mitchell, Andrew (1992) Set 44 Profile p.1448
Mitchell, Andrew (1991) Set 193
Mitchell, Andrew (1976) (QC-1998) Set 45 Profile p.1448
Mitchell, Christopher (1968) Set 68
Mitchell, David (1995) Set 159
Mitchell, Gregory (1979) (QC-1997) Set 152
Mitchell, J Ronald (1973) Set 234
Mitchell, Jack (1994) Set 111
Mitchell, Janet (1979) Set 16 Profile p.1448
Mitchell, Jonathan (1992) Set 247
Mitchell, Jonathan (1974) Set 53
Mitchell, Julianna (1994) Sets 60, 135
Mitchell, Keith (1981) Set 4
Mitchell, Nigel (1978) Set 111
Mitchell, Oliver (1999) Set 87
Mitchell, Paul (1994) Sets 83, 250
Mitchell, Paul (1999) Set 112
Mitchell, Peter (1996) Set 7
Mitchell, Rebecca (2000) Set 56
Mitchell, Tom (1995) Sets 80, 190
Mitcheson, Thomas (1996) Set 91 Profile p.1448
Mithani, Raza (2000) Set 159
Mitrophanous, Eleni (1999) Set 112
Mitropoulos, Chris (1997) Set 39
Mitropoulos, Georgia (1989) Set 39
Moat, Frank (1970) Sets 121, 262, 265
Moat, Richard (1985) Set 159
Modgil, Sangita (1990) Set 151
Moeran, Fenner (1996) Set 136
Moffat, Russell (1998) Set 178
Moffett, Jonathan (1996) Set 54
Moffett, William (2000) Set 107
Moger, Christopher (1972) (QC-1992) Set 118 Profile p.1448
Mohabir, Gerald (1996) Set 151
Mohyuddin, David (1999) Sets 207, 218
Moll, Louis-Peter (1998) Set 126
Moloney, Patrick (1976) (QC-1998) Set 15 Profile p.1448
Moloney, Tim (1993) Set 150
Molyneux, Brenton (1994) Set 7 Profile p.1448
Molyneux, Simon (1986) Set 16
Momtaz, Sam (1995) Set 47
Monaghan, Karon (1989) Set 88
Monaghan, Mark (1987) Set 216
Monaghan, Susan (1995) Set 73
Monkcom, Stephen (1974) Set 144 Profile p.1449
Monson, Andrew (1983) Set 125
Monteith, Keir (1994) Set 47
Montgomery, Anthony (1987) Set 72
Montgomery, Clare (1980) (QC-1996) Set 88 Profile p.1449
Montgomery, James (1989) Set 151
Montgomery, Kristina (1993) Set 156
Montrose, Stuart (1972) Set 150
Monty, Simon (1992) Set 92
Moody, Joanna E (1998) Set 163
Moody, Neil (1989) Set 146 Profile p.1449
Moody-Stuart, Thomas (1995) Set 95 Profile p.1449
Moollan, Iqbal (1998) Set 107
Moollan, Salim (1998) Set 31

Moon, Angus (1986) Set 130 Profile p.1449
Mooncey, Ebraham (1983) Set 5
Mooney, Giles (1998) Set 160
Mooney, Stephen (1987) Set 165 Profile p.1449
Moor, Philip (1982) (QC-2001) Set 64 Profile p.1449
Moor, Sarah (1991) Sets 104, 167 Profile p.1449
Moore, Alison (1994) Set 56
Moore, Andrew (1996) Set 229
Moore, Arthur (1992) Set 63
Moore, Craig (1989) Set 195
Moore, Finola (1988) Set 16
Moore, Katherine (1995) Set 244 Profile p.1449
Moore, Marks (1979) Set 75
Moore, Martin (1982) (QC-2002) Set 30 Profile p.1449
Moore, Miranda (1983) Set 114 Profile p.1449
Moore, Neil (1986) Sets 83, 250
Moore, Richard (1992) Set 227
Moore, Roderick (1993) Sets 121, 265
Moore, Roger (1969) Set 237
Moore, Sarah (1990) Set 81
Moores, Timothy K (1987) Set 257
Moorman, Lucy (1992) Set 25
Moradifar, Kambiz (1998) Set 169
Moran, Andrew (1989) Set 131
Moran, Andrew G (1976) (QC-1994) Sets 101, 213 Profile p.1449
Moran, Thomas (1996) Set 237
Moran, Vincent (1991) Set 69
Morcom, Christopher (1963) (QC-1991) Set 67 Profile p.1449
Moreland, Penelope (1986) Set 237
Morgan, Adam (1996) Set 18
Morgan, Adrienne (1988) Set 113
Morgan, Alison (2000) Set 75
Morgan, Charles (1978) Sets 29, 189, 235
Morgan, Christopher (1987) Set 108
Morgan, Colin (1989) Set 180
Morgan, Dylan R (1986) Set 257
Morgan, Edward (1989) Set 74
Morgan, Edward (1989) Set 229
Morgan, Helen (1993) Set 127
Morgan, James (1996) Set 161
Morgan, Jeremy (1989) Set 38
Morgan, Lloyd (1999) Set 208
Morgan, Lynne (1984) Set 176 Profile p.1449
Morgan, Paul (1975) (QC-1992) Set 40 Profile p.1449
Morgan, Richard (1988) Set 87
Morgan, Sarah (1988) Set 46
Morgan, Simon (1988) Set 169 Profile p.1449
Morgan, Stephen (1983) Set 27 Profile p.1450
Morgan-Jenkins, D (1990) Set 176
Morgans, John (1996) Set 244 Profile p.1450
Moriarty, Stephen (1986) (QC-1999) Set 44
Morland, Camille (1996) Set 163
Morley, Iain (1988) Set 36
Morley, Stephen (1996) Set 17
Morpuss, Guy (1991) Set 35
Morris, Angela (1984) Set 126
Morris, Anthony (1970) (QC-1991) Sets 65, 226 Profile p.1450
Morris, Anthony J (1986) Set 214
Morris, Bella (2000) Sets 104, 167
Morris, Ben (1996) Set 204

BARRISTERS ■ INDEX

Morris, Brenda (1978) Set 56
Morris, Brendan (1985) Set 126
Morris, Christina (1983) Set 21
Morris, David (1976) Set 119
Morris, Fenella (1990) Set 38 Profile p.1450
Morris, Gillian (1997) Set 88
Morris, Ieuan (1975) Set 173
Morris, Jane (1991) Set 246
Morris, June (1995) Set 226
Morris, Paul Howard (1986) Set 266
Morris, Peter (2000) Set 25
Morris, Sarah (1996) Set 16
Morris, Sean (1983) Set 193
Morris, Sh,n (1991) Set 179
Morris, Stephen (1981) (QC-2002) Set 35 Profile p.1450
Morris-Coole, Christopher (1974) Set 48
Morrison, Howard (1977) (QC-2000) Sets 9, 161 Profile p.1450
Morrison, Pamela (2000) Set 145
Morrissey, Joanna (1999) Set 71
Morrow, Graham (1974) (QC-1996) Sets 207, 218
Morse, Malcolm (1967) Set 155
Morshead, Timothy (1995) Set 13 Profile p.1450
Mort, Justin (1994) Set 146 Profile p.1450
Mortimer, Barry (1956) (QC-1971) Set 133
Mortimer, Sophie (1996) Set 129
Mortimore, Claudia (1994) Set 126
Mortimore, Simon (1972) (QC-1991) Set 133 Profile p.1450
Morton, Elizabeth (1999) Set 73
Morton, Gary (1993) Set 18
Morton, Keith (1990) Set 145 Profile p.1450
Morton, Peter (1988) Sets 116, 238
Morwood, Boyd (1996) Set 232
Moseley, Julie (1992) Set 161
Moser, Philip (1992) Set 112
Moss, Christopher (1972) (QC-1994) Set 34
Moss, Gabriel (1974) (QC-1989) Set 133 Profile p.1450
Moss, Joanne R (1976) Set 40 Profile p.1451
Moss, Nicholas (1995) Set 145
Moss, Peter (1976) Set 11
Mosteshar, Sa'id (1975) Set 63
Mostyn, Nicholas (1980) (QC-1997) Set 64 Profile p.1451
Mostyn, Piers (1989) Set 150
Mott, Geoffrey (1982) Set 127
Mott, Philip C (1970) (QC-1991) Set 37
Mould, Timothy (1987) Set 13 Profile p.1451
Moulder, Pauline (1983) Set 234
Moulson, Peter (1991) Set 193
Mountfield, Helen (1991) Set 88 Profile p.1451
Mousley, Timothy (1979) Set 71
Mousley, William (1986) Set 71
Moverley Smith, Stephen (1985) (QC-2002) Set 103 Profile p.1451
Mowbray, John (1953) Set 200
Mowbray, John (1953) (QC-1974) Set 98 Profile p.1451
Mowschenson, Terence (1977) (QC-1995) Set 153 Profile p.1451
Moxon-Browne, Robert (1969) (QC-1990) Set 146 Profile p.1451
Moylan, Andrew (1978) (QC-2000) Set 123 Profile p.1452
Moys, Clive (1998) Set 97

Muir, Andrew (1975) Set 124 Profile p.1452
Muir, Elizabeth (1998) Set 155
Muir, John (1969) Set 194
Muir, Nicola (1998) Set 63
Mukherjee, Abhijeet (1995) Set 37
Mukherjee, Avik (1990) Set 245
Mukherjee, Tublu (1996) Set 127
Mulcahy, Jane (1995) Set 12 Profile p.1452
Mulcahy, Leigh-Ann (1993) Set 92
Mulholland, Helen (1999) Set 191
Mulholland, Helen (1999) Set 222
Mulholland, James (1986) Set 63
Mulholland, Michael (1976) Set 227
Mulkerrins, Kate (1998) Set 45
Mullan, Richard (1994) Set 179
Mullan, Rory (2000) Set 102
Mullee, Brendan (1996) Set 63
Mullen, Jayne (1989) Set 160
Mullen, Patrick (1967) Set 110
Muller, Anthonie (1990) Set 157
Muller, FJ (1961) (QC-1978) Sets 80, 190
Mulligan, Ann (1989) Set 63
Mullins, Mark (1988) Set 21
Mullis, Roger (1987) Sets 97, 180 Profile p.1452
Mulrennan, Maria (1990) Set 248
Mulrooney, Mark (1988) Sets 207, 218
Mumford, David (2000) Set 87
Munday, Andrew (1973) (QC-1996) Set 4 Profile p.1452
Munday, Anne (1994) Set 200
Munks, Christine (1991) Set 258
Munro, David (2001) Set 161
Munro, Kenneth (1973) Set 98
Munro, Sanderson (1981) Set 26
Munro, Sarah (1990) Set 245
Munro, Sarah (1984) (QC-2002) Set 183 Profile p.1452
Munroe, Allison (1992) Set 150
Munt, Alastair (1989) Set 246
Munyard, Terry (1972) Set 47
Murch, Stephen (1991) Set 19
Murden, Claire (1999) Set 196
Murdin, Liam (1998) Set 206
Murdoch, Gordon (1970) (QC-1995) Set 113
Murfitt, Catriona (1981) Set 64 Profile p.1452
Murphy, Ian (1972) (QC-1992) Set 173 Profile p.1452
Murphy, James (1993) Set 195
Murphy, Martina (1998) Set 144
Murphy, Nicola (1995) Set 74
Murphy, Peter (1980) (QC-2002) Set 174 Profile p.1452
Murphy, Philomena (1992) Set 43
Murray, A (1974) Set 210
Murray, Anil (1989) Set 186
Murray, Carole (1984) Set 144
Murray, Harriet (1992) Set 52
Murray, Judith (1994) Set 113
Murray, Lucy (1997) Set 175
Murray, Michael (1979) Set 228
Murray, Stephen (1986) Set 157
Muth, Susanne (1998) Set 225
Myatt, Charles (1993) Set 108
Myers, Allan (1988) Set 142
Myers, Benjamin J (1994) Set 232 Profile p.1452
Myers, Simon (1987) Set 163
Myerson, Simon (1986) Set 194 Profile p.1452
Mylne, Nigel (1963) (QC-1984) Set 59 Profile p.1452
Mylonas, Michael (1988) Set 130
Mylvaganam, Paul (1993) Set 110
Mynors, Charles (1988) Set 61 Profile p.1452

Mytton, Paul (1982) Set 45
Nadim, Ahmed (1982) Set 232
Naidoo, Se·n (1990) Set 86
Naik, Gaurang (1985) Set 50
Naik, Sonali (1991) Set 47
Naish, Christopher (1980) Set 184 Profile p.1452
Najib, Shakhil (1999) Set 161
Nambisan, Deepak (1998) Set 44
Nance, Francis (1970) Sets 207, 218
Napier, Brian (1990) Set 44 Profile p.1452
Napthine, Godfrey (1983) Set 245
Napthine, Guy (1979) Set 245
Naqshbandi, Saba (1996) Set 124
Narayan, Harry (1970) Set 216
Nardecchia, Nicholas (1974) Set 52
Nardell, Gordon (1995) Set 38
Nash, Jonathan (1986) Set 152 Profile p.1453
Nashashibi, Anwar (1995) Set 5
Nathan, Aparna (1994) Set 57
Nathan, David (1971) (QC-2002) Set 79 Profile p.1453
Nathan, Peter (1973) Set 46 Profile p.1453
Nathan, Stephen (1969) (QC-1993) Set 12
Naughton, Philip (1970) (QC-1988) Set 130 Profile p.1453
Naughton, Sebastian (1999) Set 101
Navaratne, Francis (1990) Sets 78, 93
Nawaz, Amjad (1983) Set 154 Profile p.1453
Nawaz, Mohammed (1995) Set 223
Nawbatt, Akash (1999) Set 24
Naylor, Kevin (1992) Set 221
Nazareth, Melanie (1984) Set 127
Nazir, Kaiser (1991) Set 195
Neale, Fiona (1981) Set 130 Profile p.1453
Neale, Stuart (1976) Set 216
Neaman, Sam (1988) Set 85 Profile p.1453
Neathey, Rona (1990) Set 76
Neaves, Andrew (1977) Set 161
Neenan, Caroline (1998) Set 23
Neill, Robert (1975) Set 4
Neill of Bladen, Lord (1951) (QC-1966) Set 11
Neish, Andrew (1988) Set 118 Profile p.1453
Nelson, Cairns (1987) Set 36
Nelson, Giles (1995) Set 169
Nelson, Julia (1993) Set 163
Nelson, Michael (1992) Set 74
Nelson, Michelle (1994) Set 126
Nelson, Vincent (1980) (QC-2001) Set 38 Profile p.1453
Nesbitt, Timothy (1991) Set 143
Neville, Stephen (1986) Set 49
Neville-Clarke, Sebastian (1973) Set 66
Newberry, Clive (1978) (QC-1993) Set 61
Newbery, Freya (1986) Set 82
Newbon, Ian (1977) Set 163
Newbury, Richard L (1976) Set 200
Newcombe, Andrew (1987) Set 61
Newell, Simon (1973) Set 256
Newey, Guy (1982) (QC-2001) Set 87 Profile p.1453
Newman, Alan (1968) (QC-1989) Set 150
Newman, Austin (1987) Set 201
Newman, Benedict (1991) Set 22
Newman, Catherine (1979) (QC-1995) Set 87 Profile p.1453

Newman, Ingrid (1992) Set 63
Newman, James (2000) Set 39
Newman, Janet (1990) Set 160
Newman, Paul (1991) Set 153 Profile p.1453
Newman, Philip (1977) Set 101
Newman, Timothy (1981) Set 159
Newport, Michael (1999) Set 84
Newsom, George (1973) Set 166 Profile p.1454
Newton, Andrew (1989) Set 43
Newton, Claire (1992) Set 48
Newton, Clive (1968) (QC-2002) Set 70 Profile p.1454
Newton, Katharine (1999) Sets 104, 167
Newton, Philip (1984) Set 172
Newton, Roderick (1982) Sets 181, 187, 243 Profile p.1454
Newton, Simon (1970) Set 206
Newton-Price, James (1992) Sets 121, 262, 262, 265
Ng, Raymond (1987) Set 22
Niblett, Anthony (1976) Sets 23, 164
Nice, Geoffrey (1971) (QC-1990) Set 145 Profile p.1454
Nichol, Simon (1994) Set 216
Nicholes, Catherine (1977) Set 21
Nicholls, Benjamin (1978) Set 155 Profile p.1454
Nicholls, Clive (1957) (QC-1982) Set 124 Profile p.1454
Nicholls, Colin (1957) (QC-1981) Set 124 Profile p.1454
Nicholls, Elizabeth (1984) Set 223
Nicholls, J (1989) Set 210
Nicholls, John (1986) Set 87 Profile p.1454
Nicholls, Michael (1975) Sets 64, 234 Profile p.1454
Nicholls, Paul (1992) Set 81 Profile p.1454
Nicholls, Richard (1994) Set 202
Nichols, Stuart (1989) Set 115
Nicholson, Brian (2000) Set 134
Nicholson, Jeremy (1977) (QC-2000) Set 118 Profile p.1454
Nicholson, Rosalind (1987) Sets 137, 201
Nicholson Pratt, Tom (1986) Set 63
Nicklin, Matthew (1993) Set 125 Profile p.1454
Nicol, Andrew (1978) (QC-1995) Set 25 Profile p.1455
Nicol, Andrew R (1991) Set 92 Profile p.1455
Nicol, Angus (1963) Set 115
Nicol, Stuart (1994) Set 17
Nield, Michael (1969) Set 87
Nield, Zoe (1998) Set 223
Nightingale, Peter (1986) Set 73
Nilsen, Wendy (1998) Set 232
Nisha Ismail, Nazmun (1992) Set 214
Nissen, Alexander (1985) Set 69 Profile p.1455
Nixon, Colin (1973) Set 22
Nixon, Diane (1997) Set 196
Noble, Andrew (1992) Set 225
Noble, Arthur (1965) Set 205
Noble, Roderick (1977) Set 38
Noble, Will (2000) Set 50
Nock, Reginald (1968) Set 102 Profile p.1455
Nolan, Benjamin (1971) (QC-1992) Set 192
Nolan, Damian (1994) Set 204
Nolan, Dominic (1985) Set 247 Profile p.1455
Nolan, Michael (1981) Set 33
Nolan, Richard (1999) Set 30
Norbury, Hugh (1995) Set 131
Norbury, Luke (1995) Set 106

Norman, Ben (2000) Set 202
Norman, Charity (1988) Set 266
Norman, James (2000) Set 114
Norman, John (1979) Set 129
Norman, Mark A (1989) Set 108
Norman, Michael (1971) Set 111
Norman, Philip (1995) Set 18
Norris, Andrew (1995) Set 67
Norris, John Geraint (1980) Set 165
Norris, Paul (1963) Set 115
Norris, William (1974) (QC-1997) Set 41 Profile p.1455
Norris, William V W (1997) Set 105
North, Sir Peter (1992) (QC-1993) Set 35
Norton, Andrew (1992) Set 46
Norton, Heather (1988) Set 36
Norton, Richard (1992) Set 231
Nossiter, Tom (1999) Set 195
Nosworthy, Jonathan (2000) Set 161
Nother, Daniel (1994) Set 259
Nourse, Edmund (1994) Set 32
Nowell, Katie (1996) Set 228
Nowland, Lee (1997) Set 221
Nsugbe, Oba (1985) (QC-2002) Sets 121, 262, 265 Profile p.1455
Nugee, Christopher (1983) (QC-1998) Set 153 Profile p.1455
Nugee, Edward (1955) (QC-1977) Set 153 Profile p.1455
Nugent, Colm (1992) Set 63
Nurse, Gordon (1973) Set 107
Nusrat, A (1977) Set 78
Nussey, Richard (1971) Set 41
Nuttall, Andrew (1978) Set 223
Nutter, Julian (1979) Set 231
Nutting, Sir John (1968) (QC-1995) Set 124 Profile p.1456
Nuvoloni, Stefano (1994) Set 160
Oakes, Chris (1996) Set 216
Oakley, Paul (1995) Set 110
Oakley, Tony (1994) Set 107
O'Brien, Dermod (1962) (QC-1983) Set 146 Profile p.1456
O'Brien, Haylee (1984) Set 117
O'Brien, Joseph (1989) Set 234
O'Brien, Nicholas (1985) Set 21
O'Brien, Nicholas (1968) Set 165
O'Brien, Paul (1974) Set 229
O'Brien, Sarah (1998) Sets 207, 218
O'Brien-Quinn, Hugh (1992) Set 159
O'Byrne, Andrew (1978) Set 226 Profile p.1456
O'Connor, Andrew (1996) Set 22
O'Connor, Gerard (1993) Set 48
O'Connor, Maureen (1988) Set 84
O'Connor, Patrick (1970) (QC-1993) Set 25 Profile p.1456
O'Connor, Sarah (1986) Set 70
O'Dempsey, Declan (1987) Set 20 Profile p.1456
Odgers, John (1990) Set 152
Oditah, Fidelis (1992) Set 133 Profile p.1456
O'Donnell, Catherine (2000) Set 47
O'Donnell, Duncan (1992) Set 108
O'Donnell, Iain (2000) Set 164
O'Donohoe, Anthony (1983) Set 205
O'Donovan, Kevin J (1978) Set 159
O'Donovan, Paul G (1975) Set 110
O'Donovan, Ronan (1995) Set 56

INDEX ■ BARRISTERS

O'Dwyer, Martin (1978) Set 46
of Asthal, Baroness Scotland (1977) (QC-1991) Set 17
of Weedon, Lord Alexander (1961) (QC-1973) Set 133
O'Farrell, Finola (1983) (QC-2002) Set 69 Profile p.1456
Offenbach, Roger (1978) Set 53
Offer, Alexander (1998) Set 194
Offoh, J I (1972) Set 78
O'Flynn, Timothy (1979) Sets 121, 262, 265
Ogle, Rebecca (1989) Set 184
O'Gorman, Christopher (1987) Set 158
O'Hara, Sarah (1984) Set 111
O'Hare, Elizabeth (1980) Set 195
Ohrenstein, Dov (1995) Set 97
O'Keeffe, Darren (1984) Set 206
Okoya, William (1989) Set 2 Profile p.1456
Oldham, Frances (1977) (QC-1994) Set 9
Oldham, Jane (1985) Set 81
Oldham, Peter (1990) Set 81 Profile p.1456
Oldland, Andrew (1990) Sets 75, 183
O'Leary, Dean (1999) Set 209
O'Leary, Robert (1990) Set 174
Oliver, Andrew (1993) Set 244 Profile p.1456
Oliver, Crispin (1990) Set 266
Oliver, David (1972) (QC-1986) Set 30 Profile p.1456
Oliver, Dawn (1965) Set 12
Oliver, Harry (1999) Set 70
Oliver, Juliet (1974) Set 17
Oliver, Michael (1977) Set 63
Olley, Katherine (1999) Set 13
Ollivry, Guy (1957) (QC-1987) Set 25
Olson, Ross (1999) Set 217
O'Mahony, David (2000) Set 5
O'Malley, Julie (1983) Set 84
Omambala, Ijeoma (1989) Sets 104, 167 Profile p.1456
Omere, Femi (1999) Set 150
O'Neill, Brian (1987) Set 65
O'Neill, Joseph (1987) Set 66
O'Neill, Louise (1989) Set 169
O'Neill, Michael (1979) Set 80
O'Neill, Philip J (1983) Set 208
O'Neill, Sally (1976) (QC-1997) Set 45
Ong, Grace (1985) Set 110
Onions, Jeffery (1981) (QC-1998) Set 32 Profile p.1457
Onslow, Andrew (1982) (QC-2002) Set 152 Profile p.1457
Onslow, Richard (2000) Set 71
Onslow, Robert (1991) Set 95
Oon, Pamela (1982) Set 151
Oppenheim, Robin (1988) Set 25 Profile p.1457
Opperman, Guy (1989) Set 111
Orchard, Anthony (1991) Set 151
Orchover, Frances (1989) Set 21
O'Reilly, Beth (1999) Set 53
Orme, Richard (1993) Set 226
Ornsby, Suzanne (1986) Set 61 Profile p.1457
O'Rourke, Mary (1981) Set 130 Profile p.1457
Orr, Craig (1986) Set 44 Profile p.1457
Orr, Julian (1995) Set 216
Orr, Nicholas (1970) Set 203 Profile p.1457
Orriss, Sarah (1999) Set 127
Orsulik, Michael (1978) Set 11
Osborne, David (1974) Set 264
Osborne, Nigel (1993) Set 175
O'Shea, J A (1983) Set 220
Osman, Osman (1995) Set 151

O'Sullivan, Bernard (1971) Sets 60, 135
O'Sullivan, Derek (1990) Set 169
O'Sullivan, Dominic (2001) Set 31
O'Sullivan, John (1984) Set 234
O'Sullivan, Michael (1986) Set 138
O'Sullivan, Richard (2000) Sets 181, 187, 243
O'Sullivan, Robert (1988) Set 114
O'Sullivan, Sean (1997) Set 118
O'Sullivan, Zoe (1993) Set 32
O'Toole, Anthony (1993) Set 178
Otton-Goulder, Catharine (1983) (QC-2000) Set 14
Otty, Timothy (1990) Set 35
Otwal, Mukhtiar (1991) Set 8
Oudkerk, Daniel (1992) Set 38
Oughton, Richard (1978) Set 216
Oulton, Richard (1995) Set 71
Oultram, J (1998) Set 220
Outhwaite, Wendy (1990) Sets 60, 135
Overbury, Rupert (1984) Sets 126, 177
Ovey, Elizabeth (1978) Set 107
Owen, Daniel (1999) Sets 171, 251
Owen, David (1983) Set 35
Owen, David (1981) Set 204
Owen, Gail (1980) Set 209 Profile p.1457
Owen, Reverend Eric (1969) Sets 191, 222
Owen, Robert (1977) (QC-1996) Set 247 Profile p.1457
Owen, Sara (1995) Set 175
Owen, Tim (1983) (QC-2000) Set 88 Profile p.1457
Owen, Tudor (1974) Set 11 Profile p.1457
Owen-Jones, David Roderic (1972) Set 149 Profile p.1457
Owens, Lucy (1997) Sets 83, 250
Owen-Thomas, Richard (2000) Set 184
Oxlade, Joanne (1988) Set 8
Ozin, Paul (1987) Set 36
Pack, Melissa (1995) Set 41
Packman, Claire (1996) Set 118
Padfield, Alison (1992) Set 24
Padfield, Nicholas (1972) (QC-1991) Set 131
Padley, Clare (1991) Set 50
Page, Adrienne (1974) (QC-1999) Set 125 Profile p.1457
Page, David (1984) Set 71
Page, Howard (1967) (QC-1987) Set 131
Page, Hugo (1977) (QC-2002) Set 12
Page, Jane (1982) Set 240
Page, Jonathan (1996) Set 151
Page, Nigel B (1976) Set 248 Profile p.1458
Paget, Henrietta (1999) Set 11
Paige, Richard (1997) Set 200
Pain, Kenneth (1969) Set 259
Pain, Kevin (1995) Set 180
Paines, Nicholas (1978) (QC-1997) Set 90 Profile p.1458
Pakrooh, Ramin (1996) Set 166
Palin, Sarah (1999) Set 15
Palmer, Adrian (1972) (QC-1992) Set 166 Profile p.1458
Palmer, Anthony (1962) (QC-1979) Set 156
Palmer, Anya (1999) Set 104
Palmer, Anya (1999) Set 167
Palmer, Howard (1977) (QC-1999) Set 146
Palmer, James (1983) Sets 60, 135
Palmer, Nathan (1994) Set 17

Palmer, Norman E (1973) Set 266
Palmer, Patrick J S (1978) Set 200 Profile p.1458
Palmer, Robert (1998) Set 54
Palmer, Stephanie (2000) Set 12
Palmer, Suzanne (1995) Set 42
Palmer, Timothy (1982) Set 245
Paltenghi, Mark (1979) Set 18
Panayi, Pavlos (1995) Set 151
Panayioti, Lefi (1992) Set 45
Panesar, Deshpal Singh (1993) Sets 83, 250
Panesar, Manjit Singh (1989) Set 76
Paneth, Sarah (1985) Set 129
Panford, Frank (1972) (QC-1999) Set 25
Pannick, David (1979) (QC-1992) Set 12 Profile p.1458
Papageorgis, George (1981) Set 72
Papazian, Cliona (1994) Set 113
Pardoe, Alan (1971) (QC-1988) Set 24
Pardoe, Rupert (1984) Set 36
Parfitt, Nick (1993) Set 141
Parish, Stephen (1965) Set 71
Park, David (1992) Set 159
Parker, Alan (1995) Set 154
Parker, Benjamin (2000) Set 77
Parker, Christopher (1986) Set 111
Parker, Christopher (1984) Set 87
Parker, Emma (2000) Set 143
Parker, Hugh (1973) Sets 71, 253
Parker, John (1975) Set 51
Parker, Judith (1973) (QC-1991) Set 70 Profile p.1458
Parker, Kenneth (1975) (QC-1992) Set 90 Profile p.1458
Parker, Matthew (1997) Set 152
Parker, Paul (1986) Set 92
Parker, Philip (1976) (QC-2000) Set 156
Parker, Steven (1987) Set 208
Parker, Timothy (1995) Set 21
Parker, Wendy (1978) Sets 48, 63
Parkes, Malcolm (1984) Set 157
Parkes, Richard (1977) Set 125
Parkin, Fiona (1998) Set 239
Parkin, Fiona (1993) Set 3 Profile p.1458
Parkin, Timothy (1971) Set 237
Parkins, Graham (1972) (QC-1990) Sets 126, 177
Parnell, Graham (1982) Sets 181, 187, 243 Profile p.1458
Parr, John (1989) Set 221
Parrish, Samuel (1962) Set 111
Parroy, Michael (1969) (QC-1991) Set 111
Parry, Charles (1973) Sets 121, 262, 265
Parry, Des (1995) Set 178
Parry, Gwyn (1993) Set 176
Parry, Isabel (1979) Set 173
Parry, Si,n (1994) Set 173
Parry Evans, Mary (1953) Set 175
Parry-Jones, Carole (1992) Sets 181, 187, 243
Parry-Jones, Trevor (1992) Set 208
Parsley, Charles (1973) Set 174
Parsons, Andrew (1985) Set 255
Parsons, Glenn (1999) Set 196
Parsons, Luke (1985) Set 33 Profile p.1458
Parsons, Simon (1993) Set 202
Partington, David (1987) Set 188
Partington, David (1987) Set 106
Partington, Lisa S (1989) Set 230
Partington, Martin (1984) Set 2
Partridge, Ian (1979) Set 111

Partridge, Richard (1994) Set 130 Profile p.1458
Pascoe, Martin (1977) (QC-2002) Set 133 Profile p.1458
Pascoe, Nigel (1966) (QC-1988) Sets 121, 168, 262, 265 Profile p.1458
Pasiuk, Janina (1983) Sets 110, 219
Pass, Geoffrey (1975) Sets 191, 222
Passmore, John (1992) Set 63
PatanÈ, Marianna (1999) Set 85
Patchett-Joyce, Michael (1981) Set 90
Patel, Elyas (1991) Set 194
Patel, Gita (1988) Set 219
Patel, Jai (1999) Set 79
Patel, Parishil (1996) Set 38
Patel, Sandip (1991) Set 45
Pathak, Pankaj (1992) Set 109
Patil, Anil (1999) Set 259
Paton, Ewan (1997) Set 166 Profile p.1458
Paton, Ian (1975) Set 68
Patrick, Caroline (1999) Set 214
Patrick, James (1989) Set 166
Patry, Carine (1999) Set 13
Patten, Ben (1986) Set 92
Patterson, Frances (1977) (QC-1998) Sets 54, 191, 222 Profile p.1459
Patterson, Gareth (1995) Set 75
Patterson, Stewart (1967) Sets 121, 262, 265
Patton, Robin (1983) Set 237
Pauffley, Anna (1979) (QC-1995) Set 113 Profile p.1459
Paul, Daniel (1998) Set 206
Paul, Nicolas (1980) Set 25
Pavlou, Paul (1993) Set 115
Pavry, James (1974) Set 63
Pawlak, Witold (1970) Set 5
Pawson, Robert (1994) Sets 121, 262, 265
Paxton, Christopher (1991) Set 117
Pay, Adrian (1999) Set 98
Payne, Johnathan (1997) Set 28
Payne, Richard (1964) Set 9
Payne, Thomas (1998) Sets 83, 250
Peacock, Ian (1990) Sets 98, 200
Peacock, Jonathan (1987) (QC-2001) Set 96 Profile p.1459
Peacock, Nicholas (1996) Set 234
Peacock, Nicholas (1992) Set 119
Peacock, Nicholas (1989) Set 87
Pearce, Ivan (1994) Set 45 Profile p.1459
Pearce, Linda (1982) Set 76
Pearce, Richard (1985) Set 226
Pearce, Robert (1977) Set 97 Profile p.1459
Pearce-Higgins, Daniel (1973) (QC-1998) Set 146
Pearl, Bernard (1970) Set 93
Pearman, Scott (1999) Set 28
Pears, DA (1975) Set 144
Pearse Wheatley, Robin (1971) Set 110
Pearson, Adam (1969) Sets 121, 262, 265
Pearson, Christopher (1995) Set 17
Pearson, David (1983) Set 162
Pearson, Elizabeth (1999) Set 173
Pearson, M (1984) Set 196
Pearson, Rebecca (1999) Set 216
Peart, Icah (1978) (QC-2002) Set 47 Profile p.1459
Peay, Jill (1991) Set 25
Peck, Catherine (1995) Set 82
Peckham, Jane (1999) Set 164

Peddie, Ian (1971) (QC-1992) Set 46 Profile p.1459
Peebles, Andrew (1987) Set 41
Peel, Robert (1990) Set 7 Profile p.1459
Peers, Nicola (1996) Set 163
Pegden, Jeffrey (1973) (QC-1996) Sets 59, 147
Peirson, Oliver (1993) Sets 121, 262, 265
Pelham, Holly (1999) Sets 116, 238
Pelling, Alexander (1995) Set 103
Pelling, Mark (1979) Set 152
Pema, Anesh (1994) Set 201
Pendlebury, Jeremy (1980) Set 5
Pengelly, Sarah (1996) Set 2
Pennicott, Ian (1982) Set 69 Profile p.1459
Pennifer, Kelly (1994) Sets 207, 218
Pennington Legh, Jonathan (2000) Set 6
Penny, Duncan (1992) Set 75
Penny, Tim (1988) Set 141
Pentol, Simon (1982) Set 53
Pepper, Theresa (1973) Set 205
Pepperall, Edward (1989) Set 161
Percival, Robert (1971) Set 115
Pereira, James (1996) Set 61
Peretz, George (1990) Set 90 Profile p.1459
Perez, Rachel (1992) Set 201
Perian, Steven (1987) Set 72
Perkins, Alistair (1986) Set 127
Perkins, Marianne (1997) Set 93
Perkins, Simon (1999) Set 201
Perkoff, Richard (1971) Set 85
Perks, Richard (1977) Set 156
Perrins, Gregory (1997) Set 108
Perry, Cleo (2000) Set 50
Perry, David (1980) Set 75 Profile p.1459
Perry, Jacqueline (1975) Set 84
Perry, John (1975) (QC-1989) Set 53 Profile p.1459
Persey, Lionel (1981) (QC-1997) Set 33 Profile p.1459
Pershad, Rohan (1991) Set 38
Pert, Michael (1970) (QC-1992) Set 9
Pester, Iain (1999) Set 141
Petchey, Philip (1976) Set 61 Profile p.1459
Peter, Levi (1993) Set 16
Peters, Edward (1998) Set 40
Peters, Nigel (1976) (QC-1997) Set 126
Peters, William (1992) Set 260
Petersen, Neil (1983) Set 109
Peterson, Geri (1997) Set 84
Peto, Anthony (1985) Set 12
Pettit, Sean (1997) Set 76
Petts, Timothy (1996) Set 82
Phelan, Margaret (1993) Set 127
Phelan, Sarah (1999) Set 205
Phelps, Rosalind (1998) Set 44
Phelvin, Bernard (1971) Set 11
Phil-Ebosie, Sheila (1988) Set 144
Phillipps, Guy (1986) (QC-2002) Set 44 Profile p.1459
Phillimore, Lord (1972) Set 123
Phillimore, Sarah (1994) Set 73
Phillips, Andrew (1978) Set 22
Phillips, David (1976) (QC-1997) Sets 143, 174
Phillips, Frank (1972) Set 260
Phillips, Jane (1989) Set 15 Profile p.1460
Phillips, John (1975) Set 141
Phillips, Jonathan Mark (1991) Set 152
Phillips, Mark (1984) (QC-1999) Set 133 Profile p.1460
Phillips, Matthew J (1993) Set 37

1684 INDEX TO ALL BARRISTERS IN CHAMBERS WHO ARE LISTED IN THIS GUIDE. **BOLD** TYPE INDICATES PROFILES – SEE PAGE 1353

BARRISTERS ■ INDEX

Phillips, Michael (1980) Set 84
Phillips, Moira (1989) Set 159
Phillips, Nevil (1992) Set 33
Phillips, Paul (1991) Set 18
Phillips, Richard (1970) (QC-1990) Set 61 Profile p.1460
Phillips, Rory (1984) (QC-2002) Set 152 Profile p.1460
Phillips, S J (1993) Set 77
Phillips, Simon (1996) Set 155
Phillips, Simon (1985) Set 194
Phillips, Stephen (1984) (QC-2002) Set 152 Profile p.1460
Phillipson, Nicola (1999) Set 201
Phillpot, Hereward (1997) Set 61
Philo, Noel (1975) Set 246
Philpott, Fred (1974) Set 49 Profile p.1460
Philpotts, John (1990) Sets 207, 218
Phipps, Charles (1992) Set 92
Phipps, Sarah (1997) Set 123
Pickavance, Graham (1973) Set 205
Pickavance, Michael J (1974) Set 208
Picken, Simon (1989) Sets 77, 174
Pickering, Andrew (1987) Sets 82, 203
Pickering, James (1991) Sets 29, 189, 235
Pickering, Murray (1963) (QC-1985) Set 35
Pickering, Simon (1996) Set 186
Pickford, Meredith (1999) Set 90
Pickles, Simon (1978) Set 27
Pickthall, Claire (1999) Set 176
Pickup, David (1984) Set 226
Pickup, James (1976) (QC-2000) Set 223 Profile p.1460
Picton, Julian (1988) Set 112
Picton, Martin (1981) Set 165 Profile p.1460
Pidcock, Steven (1996) Set 196
Piercy, Arlette (1990) Set 53
Piercy, Mark (1976) Set 60
Pierpoint, Katherine (1998) Set 223
Pievsky, David (2001) Set 12
Pigot, Diana (1978) Set 117
Pigram, Christopher (2000) Sets 181, 187, 243
Pilkington, Mavis (1990) Set 201
Pilling, Annabel (1996) Set 75
Pilling, Benjamin (1997) Set 118
Pillow, Nathan (1997) Set 31
Pimm, Peter J (1991) Set 20
Pine-Coffin, Margaret Ann (1981) Set 257
Pines Richman, Helene (1992) Sets 140, 258
Pini, John (1981) Set 5
Pinkham, Joy (1993) Set 240
Pinson, Barry (1949) (QC-1973) Set 96
Pinto, Amanda (1983) Set 114
Pipe, Gregory (1995) Set 188 Profile p.1460
Piper, Angus (1991) Set 129
Piper, Semon (1997) Set 202
Pirani, Rohan (1995) Sets 104, 167 Profile p.1460
Pitchers, Henry (1996) Set 101
Pithers, Clive (1989) Sets 171, 251
Pitt, Daniel (1995) Sets 171, 251
Pittaway, Amanda (1980) Set 158
Pittaway, David (1977) (QC-2000) Set 129
Pitter, Jason (1994) Set 194
Pitt-Lewis, Janet (1976) Set 158
Pitt-Payne, Timothy (1989) Set 81 Profile p.1461
Pitts, Charlotte (1999) Set 165
Pitts, Emily (2000) Set 182
Piyadasa, Sue (1994) Set 16

Plange, Janet (1981) Set 150
Planterose, Rowan (1978) Set 86 Profile p.1461
Plaschkes, Sarah (1988) Set 68
Platford, Graham (1970) Set 115
Platt, David (1987) Set 22
Platt, Eleanor F (1960) (QC-1982) Set 46 Profile p.1461
Platts, Graham (1978) Set 231
Platts, Rachel (1989) Set 64
Platts, Robert (1973) Set 223
Platts-Mills, Mark (1974) (QC-1995) Set 95 Profile p.1461
Plaut, Simon (1997) Set 195
Playford, Jonathan (1962) (QC-1982) Set 135
Pleming, Nigel (1971) (QC-1992) Set 38 Profile p.1461
Plender, Richard (1972) (QC-1989) Set 35 Profile p.1461
Plienter, David (1996) Set 63
Plimmer, Melanie (1996) Set 215 Profile p.1461
Plumstead, John (1975) Set 43
Plunkett, Christopher (1983) Set 9
Pocock, Christopher (1984) Set 70 Profile p.1461
Pointer, Martin (1976) (QC-1996) Set 64 Profile p.1461
Pointing, John (1992) Set 42
Polglase, David (1983) Set 209
Pollard, Joanna (1993) Set 12
Polli, Timothy (1997) Set 144
Pollock, Evelyn (1991) Set 112
Pollock, Gordon (1968) (QC-1979) Set 31 Profile p.1461
Ponter, Ian (1993) Sets 191, 222
Poole, Nigel (1989) Set 229
Pooles, Michael (1978) (QC-1999) Set 112 Profile p.1461
Pooley, Moira (1974) Set 73
Poots, Carolyn (1995) Set 168
Popat, Prashant (1992) Sets 60, 135 Profile p.1461
Pope, Heather (1977) Sets 64, 175
Pople, Alison (1993) Set 4 Profile p.1462
Popplewell, Andrew (1981) (QC-1997) Set 14 Profile p.1462
Popplewell, Simon (2000) Set 49
Porten, Anthony (1969) (QC-1988) Set 52 Profile p.1462
Porter, David (1980) Set 227
Porter, Geoffrey (1988) Set 19
Porter, Martin (1986) Set 146 Profile p.1462
Porter, Nigel (1994) Set 81
Porter, Sarah (1996) Set 19
Porter-Bryant, Matthew (1999) Set 166
Posnansky, Jeremy (1972) (QC-1994) Set 64 Profile p.1462
Posner, Gabrielle Jan (1984) Set 51
Post, Andrew (1988) Set 119
Posta, Adrian (1996) Set 264
Postill, Julia (1982) Set 26
Pote, Andrew (1983) Sets 83, 250
Potter, Anthony (1994) Set 159
Potter, Harry (1993) Set 53
Potter, Louise (1993) Sets 62, 249
Potts, Alex (2000) Set 118
Potts, James (1994) Set 30
Potts, Richard (1991) Set 244 Profile p.1462
Potts, Robin (1968) (QC-1982) Set 30 Profile p.1462
Poulet, Rebecca (1975) (QC-1995) Set 68
Pounder, Gerard (1980) Set 34
Povall, David (2000) Set 36
Povoas, Nigel (1998) Set 73
Povoas, Simon (1996) Set 205
Powell, Bernard (1991) Set 176

Powell, Debra (1995) Set 130
Powell, Giles (1990) Set 34
Powell, John L (1974) (QC-1990) Set 92 Profile p.1462
Powell, Leona (2000) Set 146
Powell, William (1971) Set 252
Power, Alexia (1992) Set 45
Power, Erica (1990) Set 22
Power, Lawrence (1995) Set 74
Power, Lewis (1990) Set 84
Power, Nigel (1992) Set 204
Power, Richard (1983) Set 119
Powers, Michael J (1979) (QC-1995) Set 112
Powis, Lucy (1992) Sets 191, 222
Powis, Samantha (1985) Set 161
Powles, John (1975) Set 22
Powles, Stephen (1972) (QC-1995) Sets 60, 135
Powles, Steven (1997) Set 25
Pownall, Orlando (1975) (QC-2002) Set 65 Profile p.1463
Poyer-Sleeman, Patricia (1992) Sets 121, 262, 265
Pratt, Camden (1970) (QC-1992) Set 70 Profile p.1463
Pratt, Duncan (1971) Set 119 Profile p.1463
Pratt, Patricia (1991) Set 209
Pratt, Richard (1980) Set 208
Pratt, Sara (1996) Set 162
Preen, Catherine (1988) Set 160
Prentice, Dan (1982) Set 30 Profile p.1463
Prentis, Sebastian (1996) Set 98
Prescott, Peter (1970) (QC-1990) Set 95 Profile p.1463
Presland, Samantha (2001) Set 37
Pressdee, Piers (1991) Sets 62, 249
Preston, Darren (1991) Set 220
Preston, David (1993) Set 63
Preston, Dominic (1995) Set 2
Preston, Hugh (1994) Set 5
Preston, Kim (1991) Set 73
Preston, Nicola (1992) Set 159
Prestwich, Andrew (1986) Set 247
Pretsell, James (1998) Set 41
Pretzell, Andreas (1997) Set 84
Prevatt, Beatrice (1985) Set 47
Prevezer, Susan (1983) (QC-2000) Set 31 Profile p.1463
Price, Anna (1996) Set 178
Price, Clare (1988) Set 112
Price, Debora (1987) Set 21
Price, Evan (1997) Set 106
Price, James (1974) (QC-1995) Set 125 Profile p.1463
Price, John (1982) Set 36
Price, John (1961) (QC-1980) Sets 101, 213
Price, John (1969) Set 161
Price, John (1990) Set 240
Price, Louise (1972) Set 166
Price, Nicholas (1987) Sets 143, 266
Price, Nicholas (1968) (QC-1992) Set 124 Profile p.1463
Price, Rachael (1994) Set 159
Price, Robert (1990) Set 158
Price, Roderick (1971) Set 150 Profile p.1463
Price, Tom (1985) Set 55
Price, Wayne (1982) Set 176
Price CBE, Leolin (1949) (QC-1968) Set 106
Price OBE, Richard (1969) (QC-1996) Set 85 Profile p.1463
Priday, Charles (1982) Set 77 Profile p.1464
Prideaux-Brune, Peter (1972) Set 79
Priestley, Roderick (1996) Set 223
Prince, Christopher (1981) Set 237 Profile p.1464
Prince, Edwin (1955) Set 40

Pringle, Gordon (1973) Set 17
Pringle, Ian (1979) Set 166
Prinn, Helen (1993) Set 244
Prior, Charles (1995) Set 203
Pritchard, Dawn (1992) Set 245
Pritchard, Geoffrey (1998) Set 91
Pritchard, Sarah (1997) Set 160
Pritchard, Sarah (1993) Sets 191, 222 Profile p.1464
Pritchard, Teresa (1994) Set 16
Pritchett, Stephen (1990) Sets 191, 222
Privett, Simon K (1976) Set 108
Probert-Wood, Timothy (1983) Set 59
Probyn, Jane (1988) Set 21
Proctor, Michael (1993) Sets 171, 251
Proghoulis, Philip (1963) Set 93
Proops, Anya (1998) Set 81
Proops, Helen (1986) Set 266
Prosser, Henry (1969) Set 194
Prosser, Kevin (1982) (QC-1996) Set 122 Profile p.1464
Proudman, Sonia (1972) (QC-1994) Set 97 Profile p.1464
Provasoli (Gibraltar), Anthony (1976) Set 140
Pryce, Gary (1997) Set 7
Pryce, Greg (1988) Set 9
Prynne, Andrew (1975) (QC-1995) Sets 60, 135 Profile p.1464
Pryor, Michael (1992) Set 105 Profile p.1464
Puckrin, Cedric (1990) Set 100
Pugh, Andrew (1961) (QC-1988) Set 12
Pugh, Charles (1975) Sets 104, 167 Profile p.1464
Pugh, David (1978) Sets 181, 187, 243
Pugh, Vernon (1969) (QC-1986) Sets 52, 175 Profile p.1464
Pugh-Smith, John (1977) Set 38 Profile p.1464
Pullen, Timothy (1993) Set 25
Pulling, Dean (1993) Set 260
Pulman, George F (1971) (QC-1989) Set 63 Profile p.1464
Purcell, Deirdre (2000) Set 206
Purchas, Christopher (1966) (QC-1990) Set 22 Profile p.1464
Purchas, James (1997) Set 118
Purchas, Robin (1968) (QC-1987) Set 61 Profile p.1465
Purdy, Catherine (1997) Set 111
Purkis, Kathryn (1991) Set 131
Purkiss, Kate (1988) Set 21
Purle , Charles (1970) Set 200
Purle, Charles (1970) (QC-1989) Set 98 Profile p.1465
Purnell, Catherine (1999) Set 114
Purnell, Nicholas (1968) (QC-1985) Set 36 Profile p.1465
Purnell, Paul (1962) (QC-1982) Set 43
Purss, Nairn (1999) Set 16
Purvis, Iain (1986) Set 134 Profile p.1465
Pusey, William (1977) Set 161
Puxon, Margaret (1954) (QC-1982) Set 93
Puzey, James (1990) Set 155
Pye, M Jayne (1995) Set 200 Profile p.1465
Pyle, Susan (1985) Set 19
Pymont, Christopher (1979) (QC-1996) Set 87 Profile p.1465
Pyne, Russell (1991) Set 71
Qazi, M Ayaz (1993) Set 79
Quest, David (1993) Set 152
Quigley, Conor (1985) Set 14

Quigley, Conor (1983) Set 221
Quiney, Ben (1998) Set 22
Quinlan, Christopher (1992) Set 166
Quinn, Christopher (1992) Set 20
Quinn, Susan (1983) Set 16
Quint, Francesca (1970) Set 107 Profile p.1465
Quinton, Tom (1997) Set 114
Quirke, Gerard (1988) Set 155
Quirke, James (1974) Set 161
Qureshi, Asif (1978) Set 33
Qureshi, Khawar (1990) Set 131 Profile p.1465
Qureshi, Shamim (1982) Set 168
Rabie, Gerald (1973) Set 24
Rabinowitz , Laurence (1987) (QC-2002) Set 32 Profile p.1465
Radburn, Mark (1991) Set 159
Radcliffe, Andrew (1975) (QC-2000) Set 65
Radcliffe, David (1966) Set 126
Radcliffe, Francis (1962) Sets 80, 190
Radevsky, Anthony (1978) Set 40 Profile p.1465
Radford, Nadine (1974) (QC-1995) Set 26
Rae, James (1976) Sets 207, 218
Raeside, Mark (1982) (QC-2002) Set 3 Profile p.1466
Rafati, Ali R (1993) Sets 71, 253
Rafferty, Angela (1995) Set 108
Rafferty, Stuart (1975) Set 245
Raggatt, Timothy (1972) (QC-1993) Set 73 Profile p.1466
Rahal, Ravinder (1983) Set 47
Rahman, Shaheen (1996) Set 23
Rahman, Yaqub (1991) Set 210
Rai, Amarjit (1989) Set 161
Rai, Sonia (1998) Set 2
Railton, David (1979) (QC-1996) Set 44 Profile p.1466
Rainey, Philip (1990) Set 144
Rainey, Simon (1982) (QC-2000) Set 33 Profile p.1466
Rainsford, Mark (1985) Set 43
Rajah, Eason (1989) Set 106
Ralls, Peter (1972) (QC-1997) Set 7
Ralph, Caroline (1990) Set 165
Ralston, William (2001) Set 208
Ralton, Alexander (1990) Set 165
Ramasamy, Selva (1992) Set 68
Rampton, Richard (1965) (QC-1987) Set 15 Profile p.1466
Ramsahoye, Fenton (1953) Set 25
Ramsden, James (1987) Set 54
Ramsey, Vivian (1979) (QC-1992) Set 69 Profile p.1466
Ramsubhag, Andrew (2000) Set 74
RaÔales-Cotos, Tina (1999) Sets 191, 222
Randall, John (1978) (QC-1995) Set 161 Profile p.1466
Randall, Louise (1988) Set 69 Profile p.1466
Randall, Nicholas (1990) Set 24 Profile p.1466
Randhawa, Ravinder (1995) Set 266
Randle, Simon (1982) Set 97
Randolph, Fergus (1985) Set 14
Rankin, C (1983) Set 220
Rankin, James (1983) Set 124 Profile p.1466
Rankin, Jane (2000) Set 82
Rankin, W (1972) Set 210
Rankin, WK (1994) Set 210
Raphael, Thomas (1999) Set 35
Rashid, Haroon (1999) Set 227
Rashid, M A (1991) Sets 76, 78
Ratcliffe, Peter (1998) Set 152

INDEX ■ BARRISTERS

Ratledge, John (2000) Set 231
Ratliff, John (1980) Set 135
Ratliff, John (1990) Set 60
Raudnitz, Paul (1994) Set 18
Rauf, Saqib (1996) Sets 181, 187, 243
Raw, Edward (1963) Set 144
Rawat, Bilal (1995) Set 5
Rawcliffe, Mark (1996) Set 203
Rawley, Alan D (1958) (QC-1977) Set 37
Rawley, Dominique (1991) Set 3 Profile p.1466
Rawlings, Clive (1994) Sets 48, 63 Profile p.1466
Rawlinson, Michael (1991) Set 231
Ray-Crosby, Irena (1990) Set 75
Rayment, Benedick (1996) Set 70
Rayner, Catherine (1989) Set 150
Rayner James, Jonathan (1971) (QC-1988) Set 67 Profile p.1466
Raynor, Philip (1973) (QC-1994) Set 111
Rayson, Jane (1982) Set 51
Rea, Karen (1980) Set 168
Read, Graham (1981) Set 24 Profile p.1467
Read, Lionel (1954) (QC-1973) Set 27 Profile p.1467
Read, Simon (1989) Set 201
Reade, David (1983) Set 85
Reade, Kevin (1983) Set 208 Profile p.1467
Readhead, Simon (1979) Set 129 Profile p.1467
Readings, Douglas (1972) Set 161
Real, Kirsty (1996) Set 165
Reaney, Janet (1987) Set 208
Rector, Penelope (1980) Set 114
Reddiford, Anthony (1991) Set 166
Reddish, John (1973) Set 70
Redfern, Alan (1995) Set 32
Redfern, Michael (1970) (QC-1993) Set 231 Profile p.1467
Redford, Alistair (1995) Set 162
Redgrave, Adrian (1968) (QC-1992) Set 129
Redgrave, Diane (1977) Set 127
Redgrave, William (1995) Set 5
Redhead, Leroy (1982) Set 53
Redmayne, Simon (1982) Sets 181, 187, 243
Redmond, Helen (1999) Set 228
Redmond, Steven (1975) Set 157
Redpath-Stevens, Alastair (1998) Set 2
Reece, Brian (1974) Set 43
Reece, Jason (2000) Set 248
Reece, Rupert (1993) Set 146
Reed, Jeremy (1997) Set 100
Reed, Julian (1991) Set 173
Reed, Matthew (1995) Set 27
Reed, Paul (1988) Set 63
Reed, Penelope (1983) Set 138
Reed, Piers (1974) Set 147 Profile p.1467
Reed, Rupert (1996) Set 153
Reed, Simon (1998) Set 202
Reed, Susan C (1984) Set 5
Reeder, John (1971) (QC-1989) Set 142
Reeder, Stephen (1991) Set 25
Reeds, Graham (1984) Sets 80, 190
Reeds, Madeleine (1988) Set 193
Rees, Caroline (1994) Set 174
Rees, Christopher (1996) Set 175
Rees, David (1994) Set 138
Rees, Edward (1973) (QC-1998) Set 25 Profile p.1467
Rees, Gareth (1981) Set 68 Profile p.1467

Rees, Hefin (1992) Set 28
Rees, Ieuan (1982) Set 174
Rees, James (1994) Sets 71, 253
Rees, John Charles (1972) (QC-1991) Sets 110, 175 Profile p.1467
Rees, Jonathan (1987) Set 59
Rees, Jonathan (2000) Set 114
Rees, Mathew (1996) Set 260
Rees, Owen Huw (1983) Set 260
Rees, Paul (1980) (QC-2000) Set 23 Profile p.1468
Rees, Peter (1953) (QC-1969) Set 96
Rees, Philip (1965) Set 173 Profile p.1468
Rees, Robert (1978) Set 202
Rees, Stephen Robert Tristram (1979) Set 260
Rees, William (1973) Set 174
Reese, Colin (1973) (QC-1987) Set 3 Profile p.1468
Reeve, Matthew (1987) Set 33
Reevell, Simon (1990) Sets 45, 198
Reffin, Clare (1981) Set 32
Regan, David (1994) Set 169
Regan, Sarah (2000) Set 165
Reid, Brian (1971) Set 100
Reid, Caroline (1982) Set 56
Reid, David (1994) Set 111
Reid, Howard (1991) Set 159
Reid, Jacqueline (1992) Set 134
Reid, Paul Campbell (1973) (QC-2001) Set 223 Profile p.1468
Reid, Paul W (1975) Sets 83, 250
Reid, Sebastian (1982) Set 144
Reid, Silas (1995) Set 109
Reilly, John (1972) Set 150 Profile p.1468
Reindorf, Akua (1999) Set 20
Relan, Vershal (1997) Set 111
Renouf, Gerard (1977) Set 117
Renton, Clare (1972) Set 7
Requena, Stephen (1997) Set 126
Restrick, Tom (1995) Set 81
Reynold, Frederic (1960) (QC-1982) Sets 104, 167
Reynolds, Adrian (1982) Set 245 Profile p.1468
Reynolds, G (1994) Set 224
Reynolds, Gary (1994) Set 230
Reynolds, Kirk (1974) (QC-1993) Set 40 Profile p.1468
Reynolds, Stella (1983) Set 151
Reynolds, Stephen (1987) Set 7
Reynolds (Hon), Francis (1960) (QC-1993) Set 77
Reza, Hashim (1981) Set 6
Rhee, Deok-Joo (1998) Set 81
Rhind, Mark (1989) Set 226
Rhodes, Nicholas (1981) Set 18
Rhodes, Robert (1968) (QC-1989) Set 74
Rhone-Adrien, Paula (1998) Set 93
Rhys, Owen (1976) Set 106
Rhys-Davies, A (1998) Set 196
Rice, Christopher (1991) Set 51
Rich, Barbara (1990) Set 138 Profile p.1468
Rich, Jonathan (1989) Set 115
Richard, Lord (1955) (QC-1971) Set 110
Richards, David (1989) Set 257
Richards, David (1974) (QC-1992) Set 30 Profile p.1468
Richards, David (1981) Set 234
Richards, Hugh (1992) Set 159
Richards, Ian (1971) Set 122
Richards, Jennifer (1991) Set 38 Profile p.1468
Richards, Jeremy (1981) Set 244 Profile p.1468
Richards, Jonathan (1996) Set 157

Richards, Stephan (1993) Set 168
Richards, Victoria (2000) Set 162
Richardson, Anne (1986) Set 234
Richardson, David (1973) Set 250
Richardson, Garth (1975) Set 111
Richardson, Giles (1997) Set 131
Richardson, James (1982) Set 239 Profile p.1468
Richardson, James (1975) Set 36
Richardson, Jeremy (1980) (QC-2000) Sets 80, 190
Richardson, Paul (1986) Set 239
Richardson, Sarah (1993) Sets 29, 189, 235
Richmond, Bernard (1988) Set 84
Richter, Ryan (1998) Set 11
Rickarby, William (1975) Set 158
Ridd, Ian (1975) Set 41
Riddle, Nicholas (1970) Set 203 Profile p.1468
Riding, Henry (1981) Set 208
Rigby, Charity E (1993) Set 200
Rigby, Terence (1971) Set 228
Riggs, Samantha (1996) Set 74
Rigney, Andrew (1992) Set 22
Riley, Brian (1986) Set 144
Riley, Christine (1974) Set 228
Riley, Jamie (1995) Set 141
Riley, John (1983) Set 73
Riley-Smith, Toby (1995) Sets 60, 135 Profile p.1468
Riordan, Kevin (1972) Set 260
Riordan, Kevin (1972) Set 260 Profile p.1469
Riordan, Stephen (1972) (QC-1992) Set 204 Profile p.1469
Rippon, Amanda (1993) Set 34
Rippon, Louise (2000) Set 148
Ritchie, Andrew (1985) Set 50 Profile p.1469
Ritchie, David (1970) Set 106
Ritchie, Jean (1970) (QC-1992) Set 112 Profile p.1469
Ritchie, Richard (1978) Set 103 Profile p.1469
Ritchie, Stuart (1995) Set 85
Rivalland, Marc (1987) Set 129
Riza, Alper (1973) (QC-1991) Set 79
Robb, Adam (1995) Set 38
Robb, Edmund (1998) Set 27
Robbins, Ian (1991) Set 46
Roberts, Catherine (1986) Set 30 Profile p.1469
Roberts, Gareth (1999) Set 178
Roberts, Hilary (1978) Set 176
Roberts, Huw (1993) Set 179
Roberts, James (1993) Set 70 Profile p.1469
Roberts, Jennifer (1988) Set 123 Profile p.1469
Roberts, Julian (1987) Set 106
Roberts, Lisa (1993) Set 223 Profile p.1469
Roberts, Marc (1984) Set 16
Roberts, Mark (2001) Set 208
Roberts, Michael (1978) Set 98
Roberts, Patricia (1987) Set 56
Roberts, Peter (1998) Set 63
Roberts, Philip (1996) Set 32
Roberts, Richard (1983) Set 84
Roberts, Samuel (1973) Set 252
Roberts, Stuart (1994) Set 197
Robertshaw, M (1977) Set 198
Robertshaw, Miranda (1985) Sets 71, 253
Robertson, Aidan (1995) Set 14 Profile p.1469
Robertson, Alice (1996) Set 119
Robertson, Andrew (1975) (QC-1996) Sets 80, 190
Robertson, Angus (1978) Set 258
Robertson, Geoffrey (1973) (QC-1988) Set 25 Profile p.1469
Robertson, Jollyon (1983) Set 79

Robertson, Patricia (1988) Set 44 Profile p.1469
Robertson, Rachel (1998) Set 258
Robertson, Sally (1995) Set 20
Robins, Alison (1987) Set 109
Robins, Imogen (1991) Set 258
Robinson, Adrian (1981) Set 194
Robinson, Alice (1983) Set 13
Robinson, Claire (1991) Set 18
Robinson, Graham (1981) Set 50
Robinson, James (1992) Set 266
Robinson, Matthew (1994) Set 240
Robinson, Richard (1977) Set 51
Robinson, Sara (1994) Set 234
Robinson, Simon (1991) Set 215
Robinson, Stephen (1999) Set 186
Robinson, Tanya (1997) Sets 120, 212
Robinson, Vivian (1967) (QC-1986) Set 68 Profile p.1469
Robotham, John (1990) Set 161
Robson, David (1965) (QC-1980) Set 237
Robson, Jeremy (1999) Set 202
Robson, John (1974) Set 2
Roche, Brendan (1989) Set 5
Roche, Patrick (1977) Set 150
Rochford, Thomas (1984) Set 161
Roderick, Arwel (2001) Set 176
Rodger, Andrew (1993) Set 36
Rodger, Caroline (1968) Set 17
Rodger, Jonathan (1999) Sets 29, 189, 235
Rodger, Martin (1986) Set 40 Profile p.1470
Rodger, MS (1983) Set 196
Rodgers, June (1971) Sets 62, 249 Profile p.1470
Rodgers, Senay (1999) Set 41
Rodham, Susan (1989) Set 79
Rodikis, Joanna (1993) Set 230
Rodway, Susan (1981) (QC-2002) Set 82 Profile p.1470
Rodwell, Christopher (1997) Set 74
Roe, Thomas (1993) Set 48
Roe, Thomas (1995) Set 66
Rogers, Beverly-Ann (1978) Set 131 Profile p.1470
Rogers, Christy (1999) Set 94
Rogers, Daniel (1997) Set 208
Rogers, Gregory (1992) Set 160
Rogers, Heather (1983) Set 88 Profile p.1470
Rogers, Ian (1995) Set 66
Rogers, Jonathan (2000) Sets 207, 218
Rogers, Mark N (1980) Set 248 Profile p.1470
Rogers, Paul (1989) Sets 23, 164
Rogers, Shona (1998) Set 246
Rolfe, Patrick (1987) Set 138
Rollason, Michael (1992) Set 14
Romans, Philip (1982) Set 45
Romney, Daphne (1979) Set 20 Profile p.1470
Rook, Peter (1973) (QC-1991) Set 126 Profile p.1470
Roots, Guy (1969) (QC-1989) Set 89 Profile p.1470
Roques, Michael (2000) Set 79
Rose, Anthony (1978) Set 205
Rose, Christopher (1999) Set 237
Rose, David (1977) Set 193
Rose, Dinah (1989) Set 12 Profile p.1470
Rose, Francis D (1983) Set 33
Rose, Jonathan (1981) Set 199 Profile p.1470
Rose, Jonathan (1986) Set 18
Rose, Lindsey (1996) Set 53
Rose, Paul (1981) (QC-2002) Sets 104, 167 Profile p.1470
Rose, Stephen (1995) Set 34

Rosen, Murray (1976) (QC-1993) Set 141 Profile p.1471
Rosen Peacock, Teresa (1982) Set 136
Rosenblatt, Jeremy (1985) Set 113 Profile p.1471
Rosenthal, Adam (1999) Set 40
Ross, Anthony (1991) Set 21
Ross, Gordon (1986) Set 147
Ross, Iain (1991) Set 111
Ross, Jacqueline (1985) Set 164
Ross, John (1971) (QC-2001) Set 129
Ross, Peter (2000) Sets 83, 250
Ross, Sally-Ann (1990) Set 231
Ross, Sidney (1983) Set 141
Ross Martyn, John (1969) Set 67
Ross-Munro, Colin (1951) (QC-1972) Set 12
Roth, Peter M (1976) (QC-1997) Set 90 Profile p.1471
Rothwell, Carolyn (1991) Set 101
Rothwell, Joanne (1993) Set 76
Rouch, Peter (1972) (QC-1996) Sets 11, 260
Rouch, Robin (1999) Set 260
Rought-Brooks, Hannah (1999) Set 150
Roughton, Ashley (1992) Set 67
Rouse, James (2000) Set 43
Rouse, Philip (1993) Set 232
Roussak, Jeremy (1996) Set 231
Routledge, Shaun (1988) Set 239
Routley, Patrick (1979) Set 48
Row, Charles (1993) Set 168
Rowe, John (1960) (QC-1982) Sets 101, 213
Rowe, Judith (1979) Set 46 Profile p.1471
Rowell, David (1972) Set 140 Profile p.1471
Rowland, John (1979) (QC-1996) Set 118 Profile p.1471
Rowland, Nicholas (1988) Set 111
Rowland, Robin (1977) Set 159 Profile p.1471
Rowlands, Catherine (1992) Set 162
Rowlands, David (1988) Set 234
Rowlands, Gwynn Price (1985) Set 204
Rowlands, Marc (1991) Set 69 Profile p.1471
Rowlands, Peter (1990) Set 126 Profile p.1471
Rowlands, Rhys (1986) Set 179
Rowley, Alison (1987) Set 115
Rowley, James (1987) Set 231 Profile p.1471
Rowley, Karl (1994) Set 232
Rowley, Keith (1979) (QC-2001) Set 107
Rowley, L L Jane (1988) Set 176
Rowley, Rachel (1997) Set 248
Rowley-Fox, Rachael (1998) Set 47
Rowlinson, Wendy (1981) Set 180
Rowntree, Edward (1996) Set 63
Rowsell, Claire (1991) Set 165
Rowsell, Paul John (1971) Sets 71, 253
Roxborough, Adam (1998) Set 230
Roxburgh, Alan (1992) Set 14
Royce, Darryl (1976) Set 3
Royce, John (1970) (QC-1987) Set 166 Profile p.1471
Rozhan, Ariff (1990) Set 46
Rubens, Jacqueline Ann (1989) Set 2
Rubin, Anthony (1960) Set 227
Rubin, Stephen (1977) (QC-2000) Set 44 Profile p.1471
Rubino-Sammartano, Mauro (1961) Set 85

BARRISTERS ■ INDEX

Ruck, Mary (1993) Sets 79, 226 Profile p.1472
Rudd, Matthew (1994) Set 19
Rudeloff, Walter (1990) Set 74
Rudland, Martin (1977) Set 193
Rudman, Sara (1992) Set 261
Rueff, Philip (1969) Set 72
Ruffell, Mark (1992) Sets 121, 262, 265
Rule, Jonathan (1993) Set 225
Rumbelow, Anthony (1967) (QC-1990) Set 231
Rumfitt, Nigel (1974) (QC-1994) Set 5 Profile p.1472
Rumney, Conrad (1988) Set 161
Ruscoe, Janet (1995) Sets 202, 219
Rush, Craig (1989) Set 4
Rushbrooke, Justin (1992) Set 125 Profile p.1472
Rushton, Jonathon (1997) Set 2
Rushton, Nicola (1993) Set 115
Russell, Anthony (1974) (QC-1999) Set 226
Russell, Christina (1994) Set 11 Profile p.1472
Russell, Christopher (1982) Set 146 Profile p.1472
Russell, Christopher (1971) Sets 98, 200
Russell, Fearn (1994) Set 71
Russell, Jeremy (1975) (QC-1994) Set 33 Profile p.1472
Russell, Jeremy (1973) Set 117
Russell, John (1993) Set 33
Russell, Marguerite (1972) Set 47
Russell, Paul (1984) Set 82
Russell Flint, Simon (1980) Set 36
Russen, Jonathan (1986) Set 87 Profile p.1472
Russen, Simon (1976) Set 92
Rutherford, Fiona (2000) Set 43
Rutherford, Martin (1990) Set 147
Rutter, Andrew (1990) Set 149
Ruttle, Stephen (1976) (QC-1997) Set 14 Profile p.1472
Ryan, David (1985) Set 39
Ryan, Eithne (1990) Set 63
Ryan, John (1997) Sets 176, 202
Ryan, Nicholas (1984) Set 203
Ryder, John (1980) (QC-2000) Set 75 Profile p.1472
Ryder, Matthew (1992) Set 88 Profile p.1472
Ryder TD, Ernest (1981) (QC-1997) Set 217 Profile p.1472
Rylands, Elizabeth (1973) Set 221
Sabben-Clare, Rebecca (1993) Set 77
Sabine, John (1979) Set 254
Sabry, Karim (1992) Sets 221, 224
Sachdeva, Vikram (1998) Set 38
Sadd, Patrick (1984) Set 143
Sadiq, Tariq (1993) Set 228 Profile p.1473
Sagar, Leigh (1983) Sets 98, 200
Saggerson, Alan (1981) Set 129 Profile p.1473
Sahonte, Raj (1986) Set 166
Saini, Pushpinder (1991) Set 12 Profile p.1473
Salako, Toyin (1998) Set 36
Sales, Philip (1985) Set 81
Sallon, Christopher (1973) (QC-1993) Set 25 Profile p.1473
Salmon, Charles (1972) (QC-1996) Set 65
Salmon, Jonathan (1987) Set 155
Salmon, Kevin (1984) Set 248
Saloman, Timothy (1975) (QC-1993) Set 77
Salter, Adrian (1973) Set 141
Salter, Michael (2000) Set 79
Salter, Richard (1975) (QC-1995) Set 152 Profile p.1473

Salter, Sibby (1991) Set 147
Salts, Nigel T (1961) (QC-1983) Set 110
Salzedo, Simon (1995) Set 14 Profile p.1473
Samat, Daren (1992) Set 110
Samek, Charles (1989) Set 85
Sammon, Sarah (1991) Set 178
Sampson, James (1985) Set 186
Sampson, Jonathan (1997) Sets 62, 249
Samuel, Gerwyn (1986) Set 25
Samuel, Glyn (1991) Set 161
Samuel, Jacqueline (1971) Set 65
Samuel, Richard (1996) Set 211
Samuels, Jeffrey (1986) Set 231
Samuels, Leslie (1989) Sets 121, 262, 265
Sandbrook-Hughes, Stewart Karl Anthony (1980) Set 260
Sandells, Nicole (1994) Set 92
Sander, Andrew (1970) Set 210 Profile p.1473
Sandercock, Natalie (2000) Set 174
Sanders, Damian (1988) Set 209
Sanders, Neil (1975) Set 7 Profile p.1473
Sanderson, David (1985) Set 82
Sandiford, David (1995) Set 221
Sandiford, Jonathan (1992) Set 199
Sands, Philippe (1985) Set 88 Profile p.1473
Sangster, Nigel (1976) (QC-1998) Sets 36, 199
Sapiecha, David (1990) Set 182
Sapsard, Jamal (1997) Set 109
Sapwell, Timothy (1997) Set 158
Saran, Anita (1996) Set 11
Sarginson, Jane (2000) Set 161
Sartin, Leon (1997) Set 138
Sasse, Toby (1988) Set 229
Sastry, Bob (1996) Set 232
Saudek, Katya (1999) Set 9
Saunders, Ellen (2000) Set 46
Saunders, Emma (1994) Set 2
Saunders, John (1972) (QC-1991) Set 157 Profile p.1473
Saunders, Mark (1999) Set 123
Saunders, Neil (1983) Set 124 Profile p.1473
Saunders, Nicholas (1989) Set 143 Profile p.1474
Saunders, William (1980) Set 147
Saunt, Linda (1986) Set 45
Saunt, Thomas (1974) Set 22
Sauvain, Stephen (1977) (QC-1995) Sets 89, 191, 222 Profile p.1474
Savage, Amanda (1999) Set 92
Savage, Mai-Ling (1998) Set 21
Savill, Mark (1993) Set 217 Profile p.1474
Savill, Peter (1995) Set 257
Savvides, Maria (1986) Set 242
Sawhney, Deborah (1987) Set 84
Sawyer, J (1978) Set 210
Sawyer, Katrine (1996) Set 112
Sawyerr, Sharon (1992) Set 21
Saxby, Dan (2000) Set 66
Saxby, Oliver (1992) Sets 120, 212
Saxton, Nicola (1992) Set 199
Sayer, Peter (1975) Set 49 Profile p.1474
Sayers, Michael (1970) (QC-1988) Set 71 Profile p.1474
Scally, J (1984) Set 224
Scamell, Ernest (1949) Set 67
Scannell, Rick (1986) Set 47 Profile p.1474
Scarratt, Richard (1979) Set 46
Schaff, Alistair (1983) (QC-1999) Set 77 Profile p.1474

Schaw Miller, Stephen (1988) Set 98
Schmitz, David (1976) Set 106
Schofield, Peter (1982) Set 237
Scholes, Michael (1996) Set 209
Scholes, Rodney (1968) (QC-1987) Sets 101, 213
Scholz, Karl (1973) Set 178 Profile p.1474
Schoneveld, Frank (1992) Set 60
Schulster, Ella (1999) Set 126
Schutzer-Weissmann, Esther (2000) Set 75
Schwarz, Jonathan (1998) Set 148
Schwenk, Mark (2001) Set 219
Scobie, James (1984) Set 47 Profile p.1474
Scolding, Fiona (1996) Sets 48, 63 Profile p.1474
Scorah, Christopher (1991) Set 221
Scorey, David (1997) Set 31
Scotland, Maria (1995) Set 17
Scott, Ian (1991) Sets 104, 167 Profile p.1474
Scott, John (1982) Set 137
Scott, Katie (1999) Set 38
Scott, Matthew (1985) Sets 121, 262, 265
Scott, Richard (1992) Set 266
Scott, Tiffany (1998) Set 153
Scott, Timothy (1975) (QC-1995) Set 7 Profile p.1474
Scott Bell, Rosalind (1993) Set 239
Scott-Holland, Gideon (1999) Set 69
Scott-Manderson, Marcus (1980) Set 113 Profile p.1474
Scriven, Pamela (1970) (QC-1992) Sets 70, 234
Scrivener, Anthony (1958) (QC-1975) Set 52 Profile p.1475
Seabrook, Richard (1987) Set 247
Seabrook, Robert (1964) (QC-1983) Set 23 Profile p.1475
Seabrook, Robert (1964) (QC-1983) Set 164
Seal, Kevin (1998) Set 176
Searle, Barrie (1975) Set 227
Searle, Corinne (1982) Set 183
Sears, David (1984) Set 118 Profile p.1475
Seaward, Martin (1978) Set 139
Sechiari, H (1991) Set 224
Seconde, David (1968) Set 154
Seddon, Dorothy (1974) Set 158
Seddon, Duran (1994) Set 47 Profile p.1475
Seed, Nigel (1978) (QC-2000) Set 111 Profile p.1475
Seed, Stephen (1991) Set 208
Seely, Jonathan (1987) Sets 181, 187, 243
Sefi, Benedict (1972) Sets 62, 249
Sefton, Mark (1996) Set 40
Sefton-Smith, Lloyd (1993) Set 17
Segal, Oliver (1992) Sets 104, 167 Profile p.1475
Segal, Sharon (2000) Set 46
Seifert, Anne (1975) Set 13
Seitler, Jonathan (1985) Set 153 Profile p.1475
Selby, Andrew (1997) Set 180
Selby, Jonathan (1999) Set 69
Selby, Lawrence (1997) Set 34
Self, Gary (1991) Set 259
Selfe, Michael (1965) Set 71
Seligman, Matthew (1994) Set 38
Sellars, Michael (1980) Set 203
Sellers, Graham (1990) Set 203
Sellick, Llewellyn (1973) Sets 71, 253
Sells, Oliver (1972) (QC-1995) Sets 114, 171, 251

Selman, Elizabeth (1989) Set 70
Selva, Ruby (1999) Set 147
Selvaratnam, Vasanti (1983) (QC-2001) Set 142 Profile p.1475
Selway, Kate (1995) Set 107
Selwyn-Sharpe, Richard (1985) Set 234
Semken, Christopher (1977) Set 98
Semple, Andrew B (1993) Set 200
Sendall, Antony (1984) Set 85 Profile p.1475
Sephton, Craig (1981) (QC-2001) Set 217 Profile p.1475
Serlin, Richard (1987) Set 143
Serr, Ashley (1996) Set 192
Sethi, Mohinderpal (1996) Set 129
Sethi, Rita (2000) Set 150
Sethupathi, Uthra (1998) Set 194
Setright, Henry (1979) (QC-2001) Set 127 Profile p.1475
Sewell, Timothy (1976) Set 79
Seymour, Lydia (1997) Set 24
Seymour, Mark (1992) Set 11
Seymour, Thomas (1975) Set 153
Seys Llewellyn, Anthony (1972) Set 41 Profile p.1475
Shackleford, Susan (1980) Set 46
Shadarevian, Paul (1984) Set 89
Shafi, Imran (1996) Set 219
Shah, Akhil (1990) Set 44 Profile p.1476
Shah, Bajul (1996) Set 103
Shah, Roshnee (1998) Set 18
Shah, Shilpa (1998) Set 247
Shaikh, M R (1969) Set 78
Shakoor, Tariq Bin (1992) Set 158
Shaldon, Nicola (1994) Set 92
Shamash, Anne (1986) Set 150
Shanks, Murray (1984) Set 54
Shannon, Fiona (2000) Set 70
Shannon, Nicola (1997) Set 84
Shannon, Simon (1999) Set 147
Shant, Nirmal (1984) Set 245 Profile p.1476
Shapiro, Daniel (1999) Set 22
Sharghy, Pegah (1998) Set 164
Sharghy, Shahram (2000) Set 50
Sharkey, Paul (2000) Set 11
Sharland, Andrew (1996) Set 54 Profile p.1476
Sharma, Neelam (2000) Set 43
Sharma, Neerja (1998) Set 11
Sharp, Christopher (1975) (QC-1999) Set 169 Profile p.1476
Sharp, David (1986) Set 144
Sharp, Jonathan (1987) Set 71
Sharp, Victoria (1979) (QC-2001) Set 15 Profile p.1476
Sharpe, Dennis (1976) Set 6
Sharpe, Malcolm (1988) Set 203
Sharpe, Martin (1989) Sets 151, 215
Sharpe, Thomas (1976) (QC-1994) Set 32 Profile p.1476
Sharples, John (1992) Set 169 Profile p.1476
Sharpston, Eleanor (1980) (QC-1999) Set 112 Profile p.1476
Shaw, Andrew (1998) Sets 181, 187, 243
Shaw, Antony (1975) (QC-1994) Set 126 Profile p.1476
Shaw, Barnaby (1996) Set 108
Shaw, Elizabeth (1986) Set 186
Shaw, Geoffrey (1968) (QC-1991) Set 15 Profile p.1476
Shaw, Howard (1973) Set 7 Profile p.1476
Shaw, James (1988) Set 50
Shaw, Malcolm (1988) (QC-2002) Set 31 Profile p.1477
Shaw, Mark (1987) (QC-2002)

Set 12 Profile p.1477
Shaw, Michael (1994) Set 151
Shaw, Nicola (1995) Set 57
Shaw, Nicola (1992) Set 234
Shaw, Peter (1992) Set 150
Shaw, Peter (1995) Set 140
Shay, Stephen (1984) Set 70
Shea, Caroline (1994) Set 40 Profile p.1477
Sheard, Hilary (2000) Set 150
Shears, Philip P (1972) (QC-1996) Set 5
Sheehan, Malcolm (1993) Sets 60, 135
Sheff, Janine (1983) Set 126
Sheffi, Bosmath (1991) Set 79
Shekerdemian, Marcia (1987) Set 141 Profile p.1477
Sheldon, Clive (1991) Set 81 Profile p.1477
Sheldon, Neil (1998) Set 23
Sheldon, Richard (1979) (QC-1996) Set 133 Profile p.1477
Shellard, Robin (1992) Set 168
Shelton, Gordon (1981) Set 163 Profile p.1477
Shenton, Rachel (1993) Set 229
Shenton, Suzanne H (1973) Set 46
Shepherd, Jim (1998) Set 2
Shepherd, Jude (1996) Set 101
Shepherd, Nigel (1973) Set 110 Profile p.1477
Shepherd, Philip (1975) Set 103 Profile p.1478
Sheppard, Abigail (1990) Set 16
Sheppard, Tim (1995) Set 159
Sher, Jules (1968) (QC-1981) Set 153 Profile p.1478
Sherborne, David (1992) Set 125 Profile p.1478
Sheridan, Francis (1980) Set 45
Sheridan, Matthew (2000) Set 85
Sheridan, Maurice (1984) Set 88 Profile p.1478
Sheridan, Paul (1984) Sets 224, 226
Sheridan, Peter (1956) (QC-1977) Set 141
Sherman, Robert (1977) Set 18
Sherman, Susan (1993) Set 205
Sherrard, Charles (1986) Set 45
Sherry, Eamonn M (1990) Set 151
Sherry, Michael (1978) Set 148
Shetty, Rajeev (1996) Set 50
Shield, Deborah (1991) Set 208
Shields, Sonja (1977) Set 151
Shields, Thomas (1973) (QC-1993) Set 15 Profile p.1478
Shiels, I (1992) Set 196
Shiner, Brendan (1955) Set 168
Shipley, Graham (1973) Set 100 Profile p.1478
Shipwright, Adrian J (1993) Set 122 Profile p.1478
Shoker, Makhan (1981) Set 161
Sholicar, Ann (2000) Set 206
Shorrock, Michael (1966) (QC-1988) Set 226 Profile p.1478
Shorrock, Philip (1978) Set 59
Short, Andrew (1990) Set 21
Short, Anna (1997) Set 221
Shotton, Sophie (1999) Set 63
Shrimpton, James (1981) Set 72
Shrimpton, Michael (1983) Set 144
Shukla, Vina (1992) Set 137
Shuttleworth, Timothy (1971) Set 144
Siberry, Richard (1974) (QC-1989) Set 31 Profile p.1478
Sibson, Clare (1997) Set 68
Siddall, Nicholas (1997) Sets 191, 222

www.ChambersandPartners.com
1687

INDEX ■ BARRISTERS

Sidhu, Navjot (1993) Set 53
Sidhu, Sukhwant (1996) Set 110
Sidhu-Brar, Sean (1991) Set 157
Sikand, Maya (1997) Set 47
Silcock, Ian (1997) Set 94
Silverbeck, Rachel (1996) Sets 207, 218
Silverleaf, Michael (1980) (QC-1996) Set 134 Profile p.1478
Silvester, Bruce (1983) Set 24
Simblet, Stephen (1991) Set 47
Simkin, Iain (1995) Set 232
Simler, Ingrid (1987) Set 24 Profile p.1478
Simmonds, Alexandra (1998) Set 226
Simmonds, Andrew (1980) (QC-1999) Set 138 Profile p.1478
Simmons, John (2000) Sets 83, 250
Simmons, Marion (1970) (QC-1994) Set 133
Simms, Alan (1976) Set 205
Simon, Michael (1992) Set 113
Simon, Peregrine (1973) (QC-1991) Set 14
Simons, Richard (1991) Set 223
Simor, Jessica (1992) Set 88
Simpkiss, Jonathan (1975) Set 107
Simpson, Claire (1999) Set 57
Simpson, Edwin (1990) Set 98
Simpson, Graeme (1994) Set 158
Simpson, Jonathan (1993) Sets 121, 265
Simpson, Mark (1992) Set 112 Profile p.1478
Simpson, Melanie (1998) Set 150
Simpson, Nicola (1982) Set 21
Simpson, Raquel (1990) Set 229
Sims, Guy (2000) Sets 171, 251
Sims, Hugh (1999) Set 166
Sims, Paul (1990) Set 55
Sinclair, Fiona (1989) Set 92 Profile p.1479
Sinclair, Graham (1979) Sets 181, 187, 243
Sinclair, Jean-Paul (1989) Set 8
Sinclair, Lisa (1993) Set 144
Sinclair, Paul (1997) Set 44
Sinclair, Philip (1995) Set 211
Sinclair, Sir Ian (1952) (QC-1979) Set 12
Sinclair, Sir Patrick (1961) Set 67
Sinclair-Morris, Charles (1966) Set 201
Singer, Andrew (1990) Sets 191, 222
Singer, Philip (1964) (QC-1994) Set 117
Singh, Gurdial (1989) Set 151
Singh, Karamjit (2000) Set 196
Singh, Kuldip (1975) (QC-1993) Set 114 Profile p.1479
Singh, Rabinder (1989) (QC-2002) Set 88 Profile p.1479
Singh, Talbir (1996) Set 159
Singh-Hayer, B (1988) Set 220
Singla, Nikki (2000) Set 153
Singleton, Barry (1968) (QC-1989) Set 70 Profile p.1479
Singleton, Michael (1987) Set 160
Singleton, Sarah (1983) Set 231 Profile p.1479
Sinnatt, Simon (1993) Set 164
Sisley, Timothy (1989) Set 140
Sj'lin, Catarina (1998) Set 9
Skelley, Michael (1991) Set 73
Skellorn, Kathryn (1993) Set 169
Skelly, Andrew (1994) Set 110
Skelt, Ian (1994) Sets 80, 190
Skelton, Peter (1997) Set 37
Skerrett, Katy (1999) Set 52
Skilbeck, Jennifer (1991) Set 90
Skilbeck, Rupert (1996) Set 9

Skinner, Lorna (1997) Set 15
Slack, Henry (1999) Set 63
Slack, Ian (1974) Set 72
Slack, Kevin (1997) Sets 207, 218
Slade, Elizabeth (1972) (QC-1992) Set 81 Profile p.1479
Slade, Richard (1987) Set 14
Slade Jones, Robin (1993) Set 240
Slater, Alison (1996) Set 18
Slater, John (1969) (QC-1987) Set 22 Profile p.1479
Slater, Julie (1988) Set 162
Slater, Justin (1999) Set 51
Slaughter, Andrew (1993) Set 17
Sleeman, Rachel (1996) Set 115
Sleight, Nigel (1998) Set 252
Sleightholme, John (1982) Set 197
Slevin, F (1985) Set 78
Sliwinski, Robert (1990) Set 39
Sloan, Paul (1981) (QC-2001) Set 239 Profile p.1479
Sloane, Valentina (2000) Set 90
Slomnicka, Barbara (1976) Set 56 Profile p.1479
Smail, Alastair (1987) Set 161
Smales, Suzanne (1990) Set 193
Small, Arlene (1999) Set 127
Small, Gina (1991) Sets 71, 71, 253
Small, Jonathan (1990) Set 40
Smallwood, Anne E (1977) Set 159 Profile p.1479
Smallwood, Robert (1994) Set 159
Smart, David (1977) Set 246
Smart, Jacqueline (1981) Set 239
Smart, John (1989) Sets 140, 162
Smith, Abigail (1990) Set 257
Smith, Adam (1987) Set 164
Smith, Adam (2001) Set 105
Smith, Alan (1981) Sets 104, 167
Smith, Alasdair (1981) Set 147
Smith, Andrew (1996) Set 230
Smith, Andrew (1997) Set 155
smith, anna (1995) Set 262
Smith, Christopher (1989) Set 31
Smith, Christopher M (1999) Set 33
Smith, David (1980) Set 13
Smith, Duncan (1979) Set 245
Smith, Emma (1995) Sets 104, 167 Profile p.1479
Smith, Gavin (1981) Set 64
Smith, Graham (1999) Set 147
Smith, Helen (1990) Set 55
Smith, Howard (1986) Set 97
Smith, Ian (1972) Set 24
Smith, Jamie (1995) Set 92 Profile p.1479
Smith, Jason (1989) Set 204
Smith, Joanna (1990) Set 153
smith, joe (1992) Set 262
Smith, Jonathan (1991) Set 216
Smith, Julia (1988) Set 49 Profile p.1479
Smith, Julian (1991) Set 237
Smith, Kassie (1995) Set 90
Smith, Lisa (1994) Set 16
Smith, Marcus (1991) Set 44
Smith, Marion (1981) Set 33
Smith, Mark (1997) Set 219
Smith, Mark (1981) Set 31
Smith, Matthew (1991) Sets 191, 222
Smith, Matthew R (1996) Set 200
Smith, Michael (1980) Set 193
Smith, Michael (1989) Set 221
Smith, Nicholas (1994) Set 155
Smith, Nicholas G (1990) Set 168 Profile p.1480
Smith, Nicola (1994) Set 19
Smith, Peter (1993) Set 97
Smith, Peter (1975) (QC-1992) Set 107

Smith, Peter R (1988) Set 230
Smith, Rachel (1992) Set 234
Smith, Rachel (1990) Set 226
Smith, Ray (1991) Sets 181, 187, 243
Smith, Richard (1986) (QC-2001) Set 166 Profile p.1480
Smith, Richard (1999) Set 23
Smith, Robert (1995) Set 192
Smith, Robert (1971) (QC-1986) Set 194 Profile p.1480
Smith, Roger (1972) (QC-1992) Set 158 Profile p.1480
Smith, Roger (1968) Sets 113, 159
Smith, Ruth E A (1987) Set 176
Smith, Sally (1977) (QC-1997) Set 23 Profile p.1480
Smith, Shaun (1981) Set 245 Profile p.1480
Smith, Simon (1981) Set 147
Smith, Sophie (1999) Set 203
Smith, Stephen (1983) (QC-2000) Set 98 Profile p.1480
Smith, Stephen J (1983) Set 200
Smith, Thomas (1999) Set 133
Smith, Timothy (1982) Set 217
Smith, Tyrone (1994) Set 53
Smoker, Kathleen (1974) Set 168
Smouha, Joe (1986) Set 31 Profile p.1480
Smoult-Hawtree, Karen (2000) Set 266
Smyth, Christopher (1972) Set 164
Smyth, Stephen (1974) Set 59
Snarr, Matthew (2001) Set 228
Snell, John (1991) Set 146
Snell, John (1973) Set 202
Snelus, James (1999) Set 248
Snider, John (1982) Set 31
Snook, Sean (2000) Set 35
Snowden, Richard (1986) Set 30 Profile p.1480
Snowden, Steven (1989) Set 22
Snowdon, Martine (2000) Sets 207, 218
Soares, Patrick (1983) Set 57
Soertsz, Lauren (1987) Set 26
Sokol, C J F (1975) Set 102
Solicitor, Virtual (2002) Set 241
Solley, Stephen (1969) (QC-1989) Set 18 Profile p.1481
Solomon, Adam (1998) Set 20
Solomon, Susan (1967) Set 111
Solomons, Geoffrey (1974) Set 9
Somerset Jones, Eric (1952) (QC-1978) Set 48
Somerset-Jones, F (1994) Set 210
Somerville, Bryce (1980) Set 158 Profile p.1481
Somerville, T (1979) Set 210
Soole, Michael (1977) (QC-2002) Set 92
Soor, Smair Singh (1988) Set 7
Soorjoo, Martin (1990) Set 150 Profile p.1481
Soubry, Anna (1995) Set 246
Southall, Richard Anthony (1983) Set 6
Southern, David (1982) Set 148
Southern, Richard (1987) Set 77 Profile p.1481
Southey, David Hugh (1996) Set 150 Profile p.1481
Southgate, Jonathan (1992) Set 7
Southgate, Marie (1997) Set 252
Southwell, Richard (1959) (QC-1977) Set 131
Sowersby, Robert (2000) Set 119
Spackman, Mark (1986) Set 260
Spain, Tim (1983) Set 239
Sparks, Jocelyn (1987) Set 68
Sparks, Paula (1994) Set 25 Profile p.1481
Sparrow, Claire (1997) Set 180

Sparrow, Julie (1992) Sets 157, 158
Speaight, Anthony (1973) (QC-1995) Set 118 Profile p.1481
Spear, Sarah (1997) Set 231
Spearing, Rachel (2001) Set 208
Spearman, Richard (1977) (QC-1996) Set 54 Profile p.1481
Spears, Portia (1992) Set 180
Speck, Adrian (1993) Set 95 Profile p.1481
Speker, Adam (1999) Set 125
Spence, Malcolm (1958) (QC-1979) Set 52
Spence, Simon (1985) Sets 126, 177
Spence, Stephen N (1983) Set 108
Spencer, Derek (1961) (QC-1980) Set 126
Spencer, Hannah (1993) Set 217
Spencer, Lara (2000) Set 183
Spencer, Martin (1979) Set 112 Profile p.1481
Spencer, Melanie (1986) Set 42
Spencer, Michael (1970) (QC-1989) Set 22 Profile p.1481
Spencer, Paul (1988) Set 20
Spencer, Robin (1978) (QC-1999) Sets 11, 179
Spencer, Timothy (1982) (QC-2001) Set 5
Spencer, Timothy (1976) Set 11
Spencer-Lewis, Neville (1970) Set 82
Spens, David (1972) Set 165
Spens, David (1973) (QC-1995) Set 75
Spicer, Jonathan (1995) Set 9
Spink, Andrew JM (1985) Set 37 Profile p.1482
Spink, Peter (1979) Set 257
Spinks, Roderick (1997) Sets 171, 251
Spiro, Dafna (1994) Set 84
Spitz, Derek (2001) Set 32
Spollon, Guy (1976) Set 161
Spon-Smith, Robin (1976) Set 64
Spooner, Judith (1987) Set 51
Spratling, Anne (1980) Set 21
Spratt, Christopher (1986) Set 8
Sproston, Lorna (1998) Set 262
Sproull, Nicholas (1992) Set 165
Squires, Dan (1998) Set 88 Profile p.1482
St John-Stevens, Philip (1985) Set 36
St Louis, Brian (1994) Set 63
St Ville, James (1995) Set 95
St Clair-Gainer, Richard (1987) Set 16
St John Sutton, David (2001) Set 35
Stables, Christopher (1990) Sets 207, 218
Stacey, Myriam (1998) Sets 13, 107
Staddon, Claire (1985) Sets 98, 200
Staddon, Paul (1976) Set 144
Stadlen, Nicholas (1976) (QC-1991) Set 44 Profile p.1482
Staff, Marcus (1994) Set 103
Stafford, Andrew (1987) (QC-2000) Set 85 Profile p.1482
Stafford, Andrew Granville (1987) Set 73
Stafford, Paul (1987) Set 106
Stafford-Michael, Simon (1982) Set 74 Profile p.1482
Stage, Peter (1971) Set 151
Stagg, Paul (1994) Set 129
Staite, Sarah (1979) Set 70
Stallworthy, Nicolas (1993) Set 37 Profile p.1482

Stamford, Susan (1997) Set 76
Stanage, Nick (1997) Set 215
Stanbrook, Clive (1972) (QC-1989) Set 135
Stancombe, Barry (1983) Set 49
Standfast, Philip (1980) Set 199
Stanfield, Sandra (1984) Sets 121, 265
Stanford, David R (1951) Set 136
Stanger, Mark (1998) Set 8
Stanistreet, Penelope (1993) Set 202 Profile p.1482
Stanley, Clare (1994) Set 103
Stanley, Paul (1993) Set 31 Profile p.1482
Stanniland, Jonathan (1993) Set 170
Stansby, Alexandra (1985) Set 232
Stansfield, Piers (1993) Set 69
Stanton, Carolyn (1993) Set 179
Stanton, David (1979) Set 147
Starcevic, Petar (1983) Set 161
Stark, James (1998) Set 215
Starkie, Claire (1991) Set 161
Starks, Nicholas (1989) Set 160
Starmer, Keir (1987) (QC-2002) Set 25 Profile p.1482
Start, Angharad (1988) Set 152
Start, Simone (1994) Set 109
Start, Victoria (1995) Set 71
Starte, Harvey (1985) Set 15 Profile p.1482
Statman, Philip (1975) Set 53
Staunton, Ulick (1984) Set 97
Staunton, W J (1986) Set 220
Stavros, Eve (1997) Set 110
Stead, Richard (1979) Set 169 Profile p.1482
Stead, Timothy H (1979) Set 193
Steel, John (1978) (QC-1993) Set 54 Profile p.1482
Steen, Martin (1976) Set 165
Steenson, David (1991) Set 111
Steer, David (1974) (QC-1993) Set 208 Profile p.1483
Stein, Alexander (1998) Set 159
Stein, Sam (1988) Set 26
Steinberg, Harry (1997) Set 82
Steinert, Jonathan (1986) Set 60
Steinfeld, Alan (1968) (QC-1987) Set 103 Profile p.1483
Stelling, Nigel (1987) Set 154
Stembridge, David H (1955) (QC-1990) Set 159
Stenhouse, John (1986) Sets 158, 158
Stent, Caroline (1993) Set 176
Stephens, John L (1975) Set 37 Profile p.1483
Stephens, Mark (1998) Set 72
Stephens, Michael (1983) Set 159
Stephenson, Ben (1973) Set 111
Stephenson, Christopher (1994) Set 50
Stephenson, Geoffrey (1971) Set 52 Profile p.1483
Stephenson, Lisa (1999) Set 82
Stephenson, M (1997) Set 210
Sterling, Robert (1970) Set 227
Sterling, Valerie (1981) Set 194
Stern, David (1989) Sets 132, 141
Stern, Ian (1983) Set 68 Profile p.1483
Stern, Kristina (1996) Set 38
Stern, Mark (1988) Set 109
Stern, Michael (1983) Set 113
Stern, Thomas (1995) Set 211
Sternberg, Michael (1975) Set 113 Profile p.1483
Stevens, Howard (1990) Set 66
Stevens, Susannah (1997) Set 149
Stevens-Hoare, Michelle (1986) Set 63
Stevenson, Brett (1998) Set 157
Stevenson, John (1975) Set 22

BARRISTERS ■ INDEX

Stevenson, Simon (1999) Set 195
Stevenson, Tony (1972) Set 186
Stevenson, William (1968) (QC-1996) Set 22 Profile p.1483
Stewart, A (1997) Set 196
Stewart, Alexander (1975) Set 67
Stewart, James (1966) (QC-1982) Set 126
Stewart, Lindsey (1983) Set 87
Stewart, Mark Courtney (1989) Set 259
Stewart, Nicholas (1971) (QC-1987) Set 63
Stewart, Roger (1986) (QC-2001) Set 92 Profile p.1483
Stewart, Stephen (1975) (QC-1996) Sets 101, 213
Stewart, Toby (1989) Set 247
Stewart Smith, Rodney (1964) Set 98 Profile p.1483
Steyn, Karen (1995) Set 81 Profile p.1483
Steynor, Alan (1975) Set 69
Stiles, John (1986) Set 192
Stilgoe, Rufus (1994) Set 36
Stilitz, Daniel (1992) Set 81 Profile p.1484
Still, Geoffrey (1966) Sets 121, 262, 265
Stimpson, Christopher (1999) Set 59
Stimpson, Michael (1969) Set 86
Stinchcombe, Paul (1985) Set 54
Stirling, Christopher (1993) Set 6
Stitcher, Malcolm (1971) Set 143
Stobart, John (1974) Set 246 Profile p.1484
Stockdale, David (1975) (QC-1995) Sets 188, 217 Profile p.1484
Stockdale Bt, Thomas (1966) Set 30 Profile p.1484
Stocker, John (1985) Set 46
Stockill, David (1985) Set 159 Profile p.1484
Stockley, Ruth (1988) Sets 191, 222
Stockwell, Clive (1988) Set 245
Stockwell, Matthew (1998) Set 209
Stokell, Robert (1995) Set 22
Stoker, Graham (1977) Set 52
Stokes, Mary (1989) Set 30 Profile p.1484
Stokes, Michael (1971) (QC-1994) Set 9
Stone, Evan (1954) (QC-1979) Set 7
Stone, Lucy (1983) (QC-2001) Set 123 Profile p.1484
Stone, Richard (1952) (QC-1968) Set 142
Stone, Russell (1992) Set 28
Stone, Sally (1994) Set 46
Stonefrost, Hilary (1991) Set 133 Profile p.1484
Stoner, Christopher (1991) Set 131 Profile p.1484
Stonor, Nicholas (1993) Sets 127, 239
Stopa, Christopher (1976) Set 71
Stopps, Natalie (2000) Set 44
Storey, Christopher (1979) (QC-1995) Set 195
Storey, Jeremy (1974) (QC-1994) Set 118 Profile p.1484
Storey, Paul (1982) (QC-2001) Set 7 Profile p.1484
Storey, Tom (1993) Set 201
Storey-Rea, Alexa (1990) Set 7
Stork, Brian (1981) Set 147
Storr, Philip (1990) Set 39
Storrie, Tim (1993) Set 223
Stout, Roger (1976) Set 229 Profile p.1484

Strachan, Christopher (1975) Set 110
Strachan, Elaine (1995) Set 111
Strachan, James (1996) Set 54
Strachan, Mark (1969) (QC-1987) Set 66
Straker, Timothy (1977) (QC-1996) Set 54 Profile p.1484
Stranex, Andrew (2000) Set 196
Strange, Michelle (1989) Set 25
Stratford, Jemima (1993) Set 14 Profile p.1485
Strauss, Nicholas (1965) (QC-1984) Set 32
Straw, Jonathan (1992) Set 246
Streatfeild-James, David (1986) (QC-2001) Set 3 Profile p.1485
Strelitz, Simon (2000) Set 2
Strickland, Clare (1995) Set 36
Strong, Ben (2001) Set 32
Strudwick, Linda (1973) Set 68 Profile p.1485
Strutt, Martin (1981) Set 111
Stuart, Bruce (1977) Set 74
Stuart, D Mark (1985) Set 256
Stuart-Smith, Jeremy (1978) (QC-1997) Set 146 Profile p.1485
Stubbs, Andrew (1988) Set 199 Profile p.1485
Stubbs, Rebecca (1994) Set 87 Profile p.1485
Studd, Anne (1988) Set 34
Studer, Mark (1976) Set 97
Sturman, Jim (1982) (QC-2002) Set 4 Profile p.1485
Stuttard, Arthur (1967) Set 224
Styles, Clive (1990) Set 172
Styles, Mark (1988) Set 234
Suckling, Alan (1963) (QC-1983) Set 68 Profile p.1485
Sugar, Simon (1990) Set 9
Sugarman, Jason (1995) Set 117
Sullivan, Dale (1999) Set 84
Sullivan, Jane (1984) Set 68
Sullivan, Linda E (1973) (QC-1994) Sets 37, 257
Sullivan, Mark (1997) Set 111
Sullivan, Michael (1983) Set 32
Sumeray, Caroline (1993) Set 16
Summers, Benjamin (1994) Set 68
Summers, Gary (1985) Set 43
Summers, Mark (1996) Set 45
Sumner, Emma (1999) Set 64
Sumption, Jonathan (1975) (QC-1986) Set 14 Profile p.1485
Sunman, David (1997) Sets 181, 187, 243
Sunnucks, James (1950) Set 67
Supperstone, Michael (1973) (QC-1991) Set 81 Profile p.1485
Surman, Giles (1997) Sets 171, 251
Surtees-Jones, Christopher (1997) Set 79
Susman, Peter (1966) (QC-1997) Set 60
Sutcliffe, Andrew (1983) (QC-2001) Set 152 Profile p.1485
Sutherland, Paul (1992) Set 92 Profile p.1486
Sutherland Williams, Mark (1995) Set 111
Suttle, Stephen (1980) Set 15 Profile p.1486
Suttner SC, John (1979) Set 33
Sutton, Alastair (1972) Set 12
Sutton, Clive (1987) Set 242
Sutton, Karoline (1986) Set 56
Sutton, Keith (1988) Set 208
Sutton, Mark (1982) Sets 104, 167
Sutton, Richard (1969) (QC-1993) Set 126 Profile p.1486

Sutton, Ruth (1994) Set 230
Sutton-Mattocks, Christopher (1975) Set 110
Swain, Fiona P (1983) Set 190
Swain, Hannah (1994) Set 36
Swain, Jon (1983) Set 45 Profile p.1486
Swain, Richard (1969) Set 247
Swainston, Michael (1985) (QC-2002) Set 14 Profile p.1486
Swallow, Jodie (1989) Set 178
Swan, Ian (1985) Set 22
Swan, Timothy (1983) Set 108
Swaroop, Sudhanshu (1997) Set 35
Sweeney, Christian (1992) Set 111
Sweeney, Linda (1999) Set 230
Sweeney, Nigel (1976) (QC-2000) Set 75 Profile p.1486
Sweeney, Seamus (1989) Sets 116, 238 Profile p.1486
Sweet, Louise (1994) Set 151
Sweeting, Derek (1983) (QC-2001) Set 5
Sweeting, Margaret (1996) Set 237
Swiffen, Guy (1991) Set 195
Swift, Caroline (1977) (QC-1993) Sets 101, 213 Profile p.1486
Swift, John (1965) (QC-1981) Set 90 Profile p.1486
Swift, Jonathan (1989) Set 81 Profile p.1486
Swift, Jonathan (1977) Sets 121, 262, 265
Swift, Lionel (1959) (QC-1975) Sets 113, 172
Swift, Malcolm (1970) (QC-1988) Sets 55, 194 Profile p.1486
Swift, Steven (1991) Set 209
Swindells, Heather (1974) (QC-1995) Sets 70, 161, 246
Swindells, Heather (1974) (QC-1995) Set 201
Swinnerton, David (1995) Set 158
Swinstead, David (1970) Set 111
Swirsky, Adam (1989) Set 19
Sydenham, Colin (1963) Set 13
Syed, Maryam (1993) Set 5
Syfret, Nicholas (1979) Sets 83, 250
Symms, Kate (1990) Set 208
Symons, Christopher (1972) (QC-1989) Set 152 Profile p.1486
Szwed, Elizabeth (1974) Set 46
Tabachnik, Andrew (1991) Set 54
Tabachnik, Eldred (1970) (QC-1982) Set 81 Profile p.1487
Tabor, James (1974) (QC-1995) Set 165 Profile p.1487
Tackaberry, John (1967) (QC-1982) Sets 1, 86, 191, 222 Profile p.1487
Taft, Christopher (1997) Set 227
Tager, Romie (1970) (QC-1995) Set 128
Taggart, Nicholas (1991) Set 13 Profile p.1487
Taghavi, Shahram (1994) Set 25 Profile p.1487
Tagliavini, Lorna (1989) Set 76
Tahta, Natasha (1998) Set 68
Tait, Andrew (1981) Set 61
Tait, Campbell (1979) Set 223
Tait, Don (1987) Set 168
Talbot, Dennis (1985) Sets 207, 218
Talbot, Kennedy (1984) Set 45
Talbot, Kevin (1970) Set 217
Talbot, Patrick (1969) (QC-1990) Set 131 Profile p.1487
Talbot Rice, Elspeth (1990) Set 103

Talbot-Bagnall, John (1988) Set 109
Tallentire, Jennifer (2000) Set 166
Tallon, John (1975) (QC-2000) Set 122
Tam, Robin B-K (1986) Set 145 Profile p.1487
Tamblyn, Nathan (1999) Set 33
Tamlyn, Lloyd (1991) Set 133 Profile p.1487
Tankel, Ruth (1990) Set 227
Tanney, Anthony (1994) Set 40 Profile p.1487
Tansey, Rock (1966) (QC-1990) Set 53 Profile p.1488
Tapper, Paul (1991) Set 240
Tappin, Michael (1991) Set 95 Profile p.1488
Tapsell, Paul (1991) Set 172
Tarbitt, Nicholas (1988) Set 158
Tarr, Beverly (1995) Set 117
Taskis, Catherine (1995) Set 40 Profile p.1488
Tatford, Warwick (1993) Set 11
Tatlow, Nicholas (1996) Set 157
Tattersall, Geoffrey (1970) (QC-1992) Sets 101, 213 Profile p.1488
Tattersall, Simon (1977) Sets 171, 251 Profile p.1488
Tatton-Brown, Daniel (1994) Set 85
Taube, Simon (1980) (QC-2000) Set 106 Profile p.1488
Taurah, Sheila (1991) Set 254
Taussig, Anthony (1966) Set 153 Profile p.1488
Tavares, Nathan W (1992) Set 37
Taverner, Marcus (1981) (QC-2000) Set 69 Profile p.1488
Tayler, James (1989) Set 24 Profile p.1488
Taylor, Alan (1986) Set 194
Taylor, Alex (2000) Set 194
Taylor, Andrew (1989) Set 246
Taylor, Andrew (1984) Set 175
Taylor, Araba (1984) Set 140
Taylor, Charles (1974) Set 180
Taylor, Christopher (1982) Set 168
Taylor, David (1995) Set 197
Taylor, David (1993) Set 159
Taylor, David (1986) Set 18
Taylor, David (1998) Set 209
Taylor, Debbie (1984) Set 7 Profile p.1488
Taylor, Deborah (1983) Set 22
Taylor, Douglas (1981) Set 259
Taylor, Gemma (1988) Set 101
Taylor, Gregg (1974) (QC-2001) Set 173 Profile p.1488
Taylor, Jason (1995) Set 165
Taylor, John (1993) Set 44
Taylor, Jonathan (1987) Set 149
Taylor, Jonathan (1991) Set 209
Taylor, Julian (1986) Set 226
Taylor, Julie (1992) Set 256
Taylor, Leon (1997) Set 93
Taylor, Martin (1988) Set 151 Profile p.1488
Taylor, Michael (1980) Set 194
Taylor, Michael (1996) Set 118
Taylor, Paul (1991) Sets 207, 218
Taylor, Paul (1989) Set 25
Taylor, Paul (1981) Set 93
Taylor, Reuben (1990) Set 89
Taylor, Rhys (1996) Set 166
Taylor, Rufus (1999) Set 71
Taylor, Simon (1993) Set 74
Taylor, Simon (1997) Set 149
Taylor, Simon W (1984) Set 20 Profile p.1488
Taylor, Steven (1992) Set 202
Taylor, Susan (1987) Set 266

Taylor, William (1990) (QC-1998) Set 53
Taylor, Zoe (1998) Set 23
Taylor-Camara, Alexander (1989) Set 47
Tayo, Ann (1991) Set 151
Tayton, Lynn (1981) Set 9
Teague, Thomas (1977) (QC-2000) Set 178
Teare, Nigel (1974) (QC-1991) Set 33 Profile p.1489
Tecks, Jonathan (1978) Set 86
Tedd, Rex (1970) (QC-1993) Set 161 Profile p.1489
Teeman, M (1993) Set 196
Tehrani, Christopher (1990) Set 194
Temkin, David (2000) Set 226
Temmink, Robert-Jan (1996) Set 37
Tempest, A Mark (1997) Set 84
Temple, Anthony (1968) (QC-1986) Set 118 Profile p.1489
Temple, Eleanor (2000) Sets 191, 222
Temple, Michelle (1992) Set 234
Temple, Simon (1977) Set 228
Temple, Victor (1971) (QC-1993) Set 75 Profile p.1489
Temple-Bone, Gillian (1978) Set 9
Templeman, Mark (1981) Set 31 Profile p.1489
Templeman, Michael (1973) Set 184
Tennet, Michael (1985) Set 153 Profile p.1489
ter Haar, Roger (1974) (QC-1992) Set 22 Profile p.1489
Terry, Jeffrey (1976) Set 221 Profile p.1489
Terry, M Jane (1988) Set 84
Terry, Robert (1986) Set 266
Tether, Melanie (1995) Sets 104, 167 Profile p.1489
Tetlow, Bernard (1984) Set 18
Tettenborn, Andrew (1988) Set 252
Teverson, Paul (1976) Set 103
Thacker, Rajeev (1993) Set 47
Thackray, John (1994) Set 186
Thain, Ashley (1996) Sets 181, 187, 243
Thanki, Bankim (1988) Set 44 Profile p.1489
Thatcher, Richard (1989) Set 245
Thind, Anita (1988) Set 252
Thirlwall, Kate (1982) (QC-1999) Set 5
Thom, James (1974) Set 98 Profile p.1489
Thomann, Colin (1999) Set 38
Thomas, Andrew (1996) Set 14
Thomas, Andrew (1989) Set 179
Thomas, Anna (1995) Set 24
Thomas, Bryan (1979) Set 175
Thomas, Caroline Harry (1981) Set 85
Thomas, Charles A M (1990) Set 108
Thomas, Christopher (1973) (QC-1989) Set 69 Profile p.1489
Thomas, David (1992) (QC-1996) Set 4
Thomas, David (1982) (QC-2002) Set 146 Profile p.1490
Thomas, David (1975) Set 176
Thomas, David Owen (1952) (QC-1972) Set 72
Thomas, Dominic (1998) Set 18
Thomas, Dorothy (1991) Set 162
Thomas, Gareth (1993) Set 261
Thomas, George (1995) Set 130
Thomas, Geraint (1976) Set 106
Thomas, Ian (1993) Set 160

INDEX ■ BARRISTERS

Thomas, Keith (1977) Set 173 Profile p.1490
Thomas, Leslie (1988) Set 47 Profile p.1490
Thomas, Lisa (1998) Set 173
Thomas, Megan (1987) Set 27
Thomas, Michael (1955) (QC-1973) Set 31 Profile p.1490
Thomas, Michael (2000) Set 57
Thomas, Nigel (1976) Set 87 Profile p.1490
Thomas, Owain (1995) Set 23
Thomas, Owen (1994) Set 173
Thomas, Patrick (1973) (QC-1999) Sets 157, 202
Thomas, Paul Huw (1979) Set 260 Profile p.1490
Thomas, R Neville (1962) (QC-1975) Set 152 Profile p.1490
Thomas, Rebecca (1999) Set 101
Thomas, Robert (1992) Set 33
Thomas, Roger (1969) (QC-1994) Set 173 Profile p.1490
Thomas, Roger (1976) (QC-2000) Set 163
Thomas, Roger (1979) Sets 122, 194 Profile p.1490
Thomas, Si,n (1981) Set 107
Thomas, Simon (1995) Set 5
Thomas, Stephen (1980) Set 161
Thomas, Steven (1993) Set 176
Thomas, Sybil (1976) Set 156 Profile p.1490
Thomas MP, Gareth (1977) Set 2
Thompson, Andrew (1991) Set 30 Profile p.1490
Thompson, Andrew E C (1969) Set 144
Thompson, Blondel (1987) Set 155
Thompson, Claire (1998) Set 197
Thompson, Collingwood (1975) (QC-1998) Set 5
Thompson, Jonathan (1990) Set 221
Thompson, Lindsey (1995) Set 34
Thompson, Marcus (1996) Set 36
Thompson, Neil (1982) Set 159
Thompson, Pauline (1997) Set 79
Thompson, Philip (2000) Set 51
Thompson, Rhodri (1989) (QC-2002) Set 88 Profile p.1490
Thompson, Sally (1994) Set 59
Thompson, Steven (1996) Set 103
Thomson, David (1994) Set 129
Thomson, Louise (1996) Set 143
Thomson, Vanessa (1998) Set 219
Thorley, Simon (1972) (QC-1989) Set 91 Profile p.1490
Thorn, Roger (1970) (QC-1990) Sets 80, 190, 237
Thornberry, Emily (1983) Set 150
Thorndike, Tony (1994) Set 214
Thorne, Timothy (1987) Set 8
Thornett, Gary (1991) Set 159
Thornhill, Andrew (1969) (QC-1985) Sets 122, 194 Profile p.1490
Thornton, Andrew (1994) Set 30
Thornton, Delia (1999) Set 168
Thornton, Peter (1976) (QC-1992) Set 25 Profile p.1490
Thornton, Philip (1988) Set 24
Thornton, Rebecca (1976) Set 201 Profile p.1491
Thorogood, Bernard (1986) Set 159 Profile p.1491
Thorold, Oliver (1971) Set 25 Profile p.1491
Thorowgood, Max (1995) Set 6
Thorp, Simon (1988) Set 195 Profile p.1491
Thorpe, Alexander (1995) Set 123
Threlfall, George (1972) Set 169

Thwaites, Ronald (1970) (QC-1987) Set 28 Profile p.1491
Tibbo, Heather (1989) Set 60
Ticciati, Oliver (1979) Set 118
Tidbury, Andrew (1976) Set 123 Profile p.1491
Tidmarsh, Christopher (1985) (QC-2002) Set 138 Profile p.1491
Tighe, Dawn (1989) Set 197
Tilbury, James (1996) Set 110
Tillett, Michael (1965) (QC-1996) Set 38
Tillyard, James (1978) (QC-2002) Set 174 Profile p.1491
Timpson, Edward (1998) Set 178
Tindall, Paul (1999) Set 227
Tipples, Amanda (1991) Set 87 Profile p.1491
Titchmarsh, Katharine (1998) Set 209
Titheridge, Roger N (1954) (QC-1975) Set 108
Tiwana, Ekwall Singh (1988) Set 159
Tiwana, Pardeep (1993) Set 157
Toal, David (1990) Set 226
Toal, Ronan (1999) Set 47
Tobin, Daniel (1994) Set 144
Tod, Jonathan (1990) Set 56
Todd, Charles (1983) Set 64
Todd, Elisabeth (1990) Set 64
Todd, Graham (1999) Set 132
Todd, James (1990) Set 41
Todd, Martin (1991) Set 266
Todd, Michael (1977) (QC-1997) Set 30 Profile p.1491
Todd, Richard (1988) Set 64
Todd, Susan (1991) Set 156
Tolaney, Sonia (1995) Set 152 Profile p.1491
Toledano, Daniel (1993) Set 32 Profile p.1492
Tolhurst, Robert (1992) Set 26
Tolkien, Simon (1990) Set 109
Tolley, Adam (1994) Set 44
Tollman, Mellisa (1999) Set 18
Tolson, Robin S (1980) (QC-2001) Set 37
Tomassi, Mark (1981) Set 18
Tomlinson, Hugh (1983) (QC-2002) Set 88 Profile p.1492
Tompkinson, Deborah (1984) Set 86
Toms, Nick (1996) Set 25
Toney, Rachel (1998) Set 142
Tonna, Ken (1974) Set 7
Toogood, Claire (1995) Set 22
Toogood, John (1957) Set 74
Toogood, Katherine (1998) Set 74
Toone, Robert (1993) Sets 80, 190
Topham, Geoffrey J (1964) Set 136 Profile p.1492
Topham, John (1970) Set 163
Topliss, Megan (1994) Set 108
Topolski, Michael (1986) (QC-2001) Set 150
Topping, Caroline (1984) Sets 120, 212
Toube, Felicity (1995) Set 133 Profile p.1492
Towler, Peter J H (1974) Set 257
Townend, James (1962) (QC-1978) Set 70
Townend, Samuel (1999) Set 69
Townsend, James (1980) Set 166
Townshend, Timothy (1972) Set 244
Tozer, Stephanie (1996) Set 105
Tozzi, Nigel (1980) (QC-2001) Set 118 Profile p.1492
Tozzi, Sarah (1998) Set 41
Trace, Anthony (1981) (QC-1998) Set 87 Profile p.1492

Tracy Forster, Jane (1975) Set 112 Profile p.1492
Trafford, Mark (1992) Set 71
Travers, Daniel (1999) Sets 207, 218
Travers, David (1981) Sets 120, 156 Profile p.1492
Travers, David (1981) Set 212
Travers, Hugh (1988) Sets 121, 262, 265
Travers, Richard (1985) Set 211
Treacy, Colman (1971) (QC-1990) Sets 9, 156 Profile p.1493
Treasure, Francis (1980) Set 143
Treble, P J (1994) Set 220
Trefusis, Tamara (1999) Set 60
Tregear, Francis (1980) Set 103
Tregilgas-Davey, Marcus (1993) Sets 262, 265
Tregilgas-Davey, Marcus (1993) Set 121
Treharne, Jennet (1975) Sets 63, 175 Profile p.1493
Trembath, Graham (1978) Set 114
Tremberg, David (1985) Set 186
Treneer, Mark (1987) Set 183
Trepte, Peter (1987) Set 85
Trevelyan Thomas, Adrian (1974) Set 52
Treverton-Jones, Gregory (1977) (QC-2002) Set 41
Trevethan, Susan (1967) Set 111
Trevett, Peter (1971) (QC-1992) Set 96 Profile p.1493
Trevor-Jones, Robert (1977) Set 178
Tridimas, Takis (2000) Set 112
Trigg, Miles (1987) Set 79
Trigger, Simon (2000) Set 129
Trimmer, Carol (1993) Set 186
Trimmer, Stuart (1977) Set 55
Trippier, Ruth (1978) Set 217
Tritton, Guy (1987) Set 67 Profile p.1493
Trollope, Andrew (1971) (QC-1991) Set 43 Profile p.1493
Tromans, Stephen (1999) Set 38 Profile p.1493
Trotman, Timothy (1983) Set 217
Troup, Alex (1998) Set 169
Trowell, Stephen (1995) Set 64
Trower, William (1983) (QC-2001) Set 133 Profile p.1493
Trowler, Rebecca (1995) Set 25
Troy, Alan (1990) Set 175
Troy, Jill (1986) Set 193
Troy-Davies, Karen (1981) Set 31
Truscott, Caroline (1998) Set 38
Truscott, Ian (1995) (QC-1997) Sets 104, 167
Trusted, Harry (1985) Set 37 Profile p.1493
Trustman, Judith (1996) Set 47
Tse, Nicholas (1995) Set 7
Tselentis SC, Michael (1995) Set 35
Tuck, Rebecca (1998) Sets 104, 167
Tucker, Andrew (1977) Set 158
Tucker, Ashley (1990) Set 194
Tucker, David (1973) Set 22
Tucker, Katherine (1993) Set 161 Profile p.1493
Tucker, Lynton (1971) Sets 98, 200 Profile p.1493
Tucker, Paul (1990) Sets 191, 222 Profile p.1493
Tudor-Evans, Quintin (1977) Set 143 Profile p.1493
Tudway, Stephen (1998) Set 141
Tugendhat, Michael (1969) (QC-1986) Set 125 Profile p.1494
Tughan, John (1991) Set 50
Tully, Ray (1988) Set 166

Tunkel, Alan M (1976) Set 136
Turcan, Harry (1965) Set 113
Turkson, Tetteh (1998) Set 36
Turner, David (1993) Set 146 Profile p.1494
Turner, David (1971) (QC-1991) Sets 75, 207, 218 Profile p.1494
Turner, David (1976) (QC-2000) Set 56
Turner, James (1990) Set 33
Turner, James (1976) (QC-1998) Set 70 Profile p.1494
Turner, Jon (1988) Set 90 Profile p.1494
Turner, Jonathan (1974) Set 75 Profile p.1494
Turner, Jonathan D C (1982) Set 142
Turner, Justin (1992) Set 91 Profile p.1494
Turner, Mark (1981) (QC-1998) Set 217 Profile p.1494
Turner, Michael (1981) (QC-2002) Set 150 Profile p.1494
Turner, Steven (1993) Set 195
Turner, Taryn (1990) Set 194
Turton, Andrew (1977) Set 151
Turton, Philip (1989) Set 247
Tutt, Richard (2000) Sets 121, 265
Twigger, Andrew M (1994) Set 136
Twine, Nicola (1999) Set 194
Twist, Stephen (1979) Set 266
Twomey, Mark (1990) Set 6
Twomlow, Richard (1976) Set 173 Profile p.1494
Tyack, David (1994) Set 161
Tyler, Paula M (1997) Set 232
Tyler, W (1996) Set 196
Tyrell, Glen (1977) Set 92
Tyrrell, Alan (1956) (QC-1976) Set 144
Tyrrell, Richard (1993) Set 231
Tyson, Richard (1975) Set 111
Tythcott, Elisabeth (1989) Set 229
Uduje, Benjamin (1992) Set 101
Uff, David (1981) Set 225
Uff CBE, John (1970) (QC-1983) Set 69 Profile p.1494
Ullstein, Augustus (1970) (QC-1992) Set 7 Profile p.1494
Umezuruike, Chima (1991) Set 51
Underhill, Alison (1997) Sets 181, 187, 243
Underhill, Nicholas (1976) (QC-1992) Set 44 Profile p.1494
Underwood, Robert (1986) Set 9
Unsworth, Ian (1992) Sets 207, 218
Upton, William (1990) Sets 120, 212 Profile p.1495
Upward, Patrick (1972) (QC-1996) Sets 63, 192
Urquhart, Andrew (1963) Set 9
Usher, Neil (1993) Set 223
Utley, Charles (1979) Set 101
Uzuegbunam, Josephene (1998) Set 47
Vagg, Howard (1974) Set 75
Vaitilingam, Adam (1987) Set 183
Vajda, Christopher (1979) (QC-1997) Set 90 Profile p.1495
Valentin, Ben (1995) Set 133
Valentine, Donald (1956) Set 3
Valentine, Justin (1999) Set 206
Vallat, Richard (1997) Set 122
ValleJo, Jacqueline (1997) Set 55
Valley, Helen (1990) Set 53
Valli, Yunus (1994) Set 193
Van Besouw, Eufron (1988) Set 240
Van Bueren, Geraldine (1980) Set 25

Van der Zwart, Mark (1988) Set 246
van Hagen, Anthony (1974) Set 132
Van Hagen, Chris (1980) Set 74
Van Spall, Penny (1998) Set 19
Van Stone, Grant (1988) Set 55
van Tonder, Gerard (1990) Set 98
Vandyck, William (1988) Set 22
Vane, Christopher (1976) Set 239
Vanhegan, Mark (1990) Set 134 Profile p.1495
Vanhegan, Toby (1996) Set 143
Vardon, Richard (1985) Set 229
Varty, Louise (1986) Set 5
Vass, Hugh (1983) Sets 181, 187, 243
Vater, John (1995) Sets 62, 249
Vaughan, Kieran (1993) Set 47
Vaughan, Simon (1989) Sets 221, 224
Vaughan, Terence (1996) Sets 171, 251
Vaughan CBE, David (1962) (QC-1981) Set 14 Profile p.1495
Vaughan-Jones, Sarah (1983) Set 146
Vaughan-Neil, Kate (1994) Set 118
Vavrecka, David (1992) Set 21
Veats, Elizabeth (1986) Set 47
Veeder, V V (1971) (QC-1986) Set 31 Profile p.1495
Venables, Robert (1973) (QC-1990) Set 102
Venmore, John (1971) Set 174 Profile p.1495
Ventham, Anthony (1991) Set 151
Venturi, Gary (1996) Set 45
Verdan, Alexander (1987) Set 50
Verduyn, Anthony (1993) Set 161
Vere-Hodge, Michael J D (1970) (QC-1993) Set 71
Vickers, Guy (1986) Sets 207, 218
Vickers, Rachel (1992) Set 143
Vickery, Neil (1985) Sets 83, 250
Vigars, Anna (1996) Set 166
Village, Peter (1983) (QC-2002) Set 54 Profile p.1495
Villarosa, Tina (1995) Set 101
Vincent, Patrick (1992) Set 82
Vincent, Ruth (1995) Set 182
Vindis, Tara (1996) Set 50
Vine, Aidan (1995) Sets 62, 249
Vine, James (1977) Set 63 Profile p.1495
Vineall, Nicholas (1988) Set 118
Vines, Anthony (1993) Set 49
Viney, Richard (1994) Set 82
Vinson, Andrew (2000) Sets 207, 218
Virdi, Prabhjot (1995) Set 34
Virgo, John (1983) Set 166 Profile p.1495
Vitoria, Mary (1975) (QC-1997) Set 95 Profile p.1496
Vollenweider, Amiot (2000) Set 205
Volz, Karl (1993) Set 79
Vos, Geoffrey (1977) (QC-1993) Set 136 Profile p.1496
Vosper, Christopher (1977) (QC-2000) Set 41
Vout, Andrew (1995) Set 117
Vullo, Stephen (1997) Set 63
Waddicor, Janet (1985) Set 70
Waddington, Anne (1988) Sets 121, 262, 265
Waddington, Helen (1998) Set 195
Waddington, James (1983) Set 117
Wade, Clare (1990) Set 150
Wade, Ian (1977) Set 114

BARRISTERS ■ INDEX

Wade, William (1946) (QC-1968) Set 54
Wadge, Richard (1997) Set 237
Wadling, Anthony (1977) Set 151
Wadsley, Peter (1984) Set 169 Profile p.1496
Wagstaffe, Christopher (1992) Set 51
Wain, Peter (1972) Sets 181, 187, 243 Profile p.1496
Waine, Stephen (1969) Set 9
Wainwright, Patrick (1994) Set 161
Waite, John-Paul (1995) Set 42
Waite, Jonathan (1978) (QC-2002) Set 22 Profile p.1496
Waite, Kiril (1997) Set 113
Wakeham, Philip (1978) Set 63
Wakerley, Paul (1990) Set 73
Wakerley, Richard (1965) (QC-1982) Set 157 Profile p.1496
Waksman, David (1982) (QC-2002) Set 44 Profile p.1496
Walbank, David (1987) Set 126
Wald, Richard (1997) Set 89
Walden-Smith, David (1985) Sets 120, 212
Walden-Smith, Karen (1990) Set 138
Waldron, William (1970) (QC-1982) Sets 207, 218
Waldron, William F (1986) Sets 207, 218
Wales, Andrew (1992) Set 77
Wales, Matthew (1994) Set 166
Waley, Simon (1988) Set 201
Walford, Richard (1984) Set 131
Walker, Andrew (1998) Set 234
Walker, Andrew (1975) Set 106
Walker, Andrew P D (1991) Set 105 Profile p.1496
Walker, Annabel (1976) (QC-1997) Set 9
Walker, Annabel (2001) Set 60
Walker, Bruce (1994) Set 188
Walker, Christopher (1990) Sets 104, 167
Walker, Elizabeth (1994) Set 161
Walker, James (1994) Set 151
Walker, Jane (1974) Set 158
Walker, Jane (1987) Set 231 Profile p.1496
Walker, Mark (1986) Set 188
Walker, Nick (1998) Set 178
Walker, Paul (1979) (QC-1999) Set 14
Walker, Paul (1993) Set 17
Walker, Raymond (1966) (QC-1988) Sets 74, 266
Walker, Ronald (1962) (QC-1983) Set 82 Profile p.1496
Walker, Steven (1993) Set 3
Walker, Susannah (1985) Set 46
Walker, Terence (1973) Set 66
Walker, Timothy (1984) Set 7
Wall, Christopher (1987) Set 172
Wall, Jacqueline (1994) Set 209
Wall, Mark (1985) Set 157 Profile p.1496
Wall, William (1985) Set 156
Wallace, Andrew (1988) Set 156
Wallace, Hugh (1993) Set 173
Wallace, Ian N D (1948) (QC-1973) Set 3
Wallace, Prof Rebecca (1999) Set 214
Wallbanks, Joanne (1997) Set 159
Waller, Helen (1997) Set 179
Waller, Richard (1994) Set 77
Wallington, Peter (1987) Set 81 Profile p.1496
Wallington, Richard (1972) Set 106 Profile p.1496
Wallwork, Bernard (1976) Set 231 Profile p.1496

Walmsley, Alan (1991) Set 17
Walmsley, Keith (1973) Sets 143, 266
Walmsley, Peter (1964) Set 245
Walsh, John (1993) Set 25 Profile p.1496
Walsh, Mark (1996) Set 144
Walsh, Martin (1990) Set 226 Profile p.1497
Walsh, Matthew (2000) Sets 83, 250
Walsh, Michael (1996) Set 159
Walsh, Moira (2000) Set 242
Walsh, Pat (1999) Set 215
Walsh, Patricia (1993) Sets 181, 187, 243
Walsh, Peter (1982) Set 239
Walsh, Peter (1978) Set 63
Walsh, Simon (1987) Set 17
Walsh, Stephen (1983) Set 124 Profile p.1497
Walsh, Steven (1965) Set 115
Walsh, Timothy (2000) Set 166
Walter, Francesca (1994) Set 111
Walters, Edmund (1991) Sets 83, 250
Walters, Gareth (1986) Set 161
Walters, Graham (1986) Set 175 Profile p.1497
Walters, Jill Mary (1979) Set 174 Profile p.1497
Walters, John (1977) (QC-1997) Set 57
Walters, Jonathan (1984) Set 175 Profile p.1497
Walters, Terence (1993) Set 246
Walters, Vivian (1991) Sets 83, 250
Walton, Alastair (1977) Set 87 Profile p.1497
Walton, Carolyn (1980) Set 87
Walton, Robert (1999) Set 89
Wan Daud, Malek (1991) Set 47
Warburton, Julie (1993) Set 246
Warby, Mark (1981) (QC-2002) Set 125 Profile p.1497
Ward, Andrew (2000) Set 221
Ward, Angela (2000) Set 6
Ward, Anne (1997) Sets 121, 262, 265
Ward, Anthony (1971) Set 184
Ward, Galina (2000) Set 7
Ward, Henry (2000) Set 95
Ward, Simon (1986) Set 155
Ward, Simon K (1984) Set 110
Ward, Siobhan (1984) Set 32
Ward, Tim (1994) Set 90
Ward, Trevor (1991) Set 257
Ward, Vincent (1998) Set 237
Wardale, Joanne (1998) Set 19
Wardell, John (1979) (QC-2002) Set 153 Profile p.1497
Ward-Jackson, Charles (1985) Set 151
Wardlow, John (1971) Sets 181, 187, 243
Ward-Prowse, John (1997) Set 71
Waritary, Samuel (1993) Set 2
Warne, Peter (1993) Set 223
Warner, Anthony (1979) Set 156
Warner, Brian (1969) Set 65
Warner, David (1996) Set 98
Warner, Malcolm (1979) Set 166
Warner, Pamela (1985) Set 56
Warner, Stephen (1976) Set 63
Warnock, Andrew (1993) Set 129
Warnock, Robert (1977) Set 203
Warnock-Smith, Sh,n (1971) (QC-2002) Set 138 Profile p.1497
Warren, John (1968) (QC-1994) Set 245
Warren, Michael (1971) Set 70
Warren, Nicholas (1972) (QC-1993) Set 153 Profile p.1497

Warren, Philip (1988) Sets 121, 262, 265
Warren, Rupert (1994) Set 89 Profile p.1497
Warrender, Nichola (1995) Set 33
Warshaw, Justin (1995) Set 64
Warwick, Mark (1974) Sets 7, 128
Wass, Sasha (1981) (QC-2001) Set 75 Profile p.1497
Waterman, Adrian (1988) Sets 80, 190
Waters, Andrew (1987) Set 34
Waters, David (1973) (QC-1999) Set 65 Profile p.1498
Waters, Julian (1986) Set 129
Waters, Malcolm (1977) (QC-1997) Set 107 Profile p.1498
Waters, Sarah (1999) Set 174
Waterworth, Michael (1994) Set 106
Watkin, Toby (1996) Set 101
Watkins, Myles (1990) Sets 51, 165
Watkins, Rachel (1998) Set 240
Watkinson, David (1972) Set 47
Watkinson, Sasha (1998) Set 202
Watson, Alaric (1997) Set 141
Watson, Andrew (1966) Set 157
Watson, Antony (1968) (QC-1986) Set 91 Profile p.1498
Watson, Brian (1978) Set 166
Watson, David (1963) Set 209
Watson, David (1990) Set 203 Profile p.1498
Watson, David (1994) Set 158
Watson, Dennis (1985) Set 223
Watson, Hilary (1979) Set 248
Watson, Isabelle (1991) Set 16
Watson, James (1979) (QC-2000) Set 130 Profile p.1498
Watson, Kirstie (1994) Set 199
Watson, Mark (1994) Sets 120, 212
Watson, Philippa (1988) Set 31
Watson, Robert (1963) Set 149
Watson, Tom (1990) Set 205
Watson-Gandy, Mark (1990) Sets 116, 238
Watters, Simon (1992) Set 72
Watt-Pringle, Jonathan (1987) Set 41
Watts, Lawrence (1988) Set 161
Watts, Martin (1995) Set 151
Watts, Sir Arthur (1957) (QC-1988) Set 35 Profile p.1498
Waugh, Andrew (1982) (QC-1998) Set 91 Profile p.1498
Waugh, Jane (1992) Set 237
Way, Ian (1988) Sets 26, 246
Way, Patrick (1994) Set 57
Weatherby, Pete (1992) Set 215
Weatherby, Peter (1992) Set 47
Weatherill, Bernard (1974) (QC-1996) Sets 29, 180
Weaver, Elizabeth (1982) Set 103
Webb, Geraint (1995) Sets 60, 135 Profile p.1498
Webb, Nicholas (1972) Set 157
Webber, Frances (1978) Set 47 Profile p.1498
Webber, Gary (1979) Set 8
Webster, Alistair (1976) (QC-1995) Set 223
Webster, David (1993) Set 176
Webster, Elizabeth (1995) Set 126
Webster, Leonard (1984) Set 230
Webster, Simon (1997) Set 64
Webster, William H (1975) Set 257
Weddell, Geoffrey (1990) Set 71
Wedderburn, Lord (1953) (QC-1990) Sets 104, 167
Wedderspoon, Rachel (1993) Set 228 Profile p.1498
Weddle, Steven (1977) Set 63

Weekes, Anesta (1981) (QC-1999) Set 9
Weekes, Mark (1999) Set 75
Weekes, Tom (1995) Set 141
Weeks, Janet (1993) Set 114
Weereratne, Aswini (1986) Set 25
Weetman, Gareth (1999) Set 5
Weiner, Sharise (1978) Set 38
Weiniger, Noah (1984) Set 127
Weir, Alan (1996) Set 195
Weir, Claire (1998) Set 12
Weir, Reg (1970) (QC-1985) Set 54
Weir, Robert (1992) Set 24 Profile p.1498
Weisselberg, Tom (1995) Set 12
Weitzman, Adam (1993) Set 5
Weitzman, Tom (1984) Set 152 Profile p.1498
Wells, Camilla (1998) Set 164
Wells, Colin (1987) Set 53
Wells, Graham (1982) Set 206
Wells, Justin (1998) Set 151
Wells, Nathan (2000) Set 97
Welsh, Paschal (1971) Set 110
Wentworth, Annabel (1990) Set 7
West, Colin (1999) Set 14
West, Ian (1985) Sets 116, 238
West, John (1965) Set 159
West, Lawrence (1979) Sets 60, 135 Profile p.1499
West, Mark (1987) Set 107
Westcott, David G (1982) Set 37
Western, Adam (1997) Set 154
Westgate, Martin (1985) Set 25
West-Knights, LJ (1977) (QC-2000) Set 112
Weston, Amanda (1995) Set 215 Profile p.1499
Weston, Clive (1993) Set 22
Weston, Jeremy (1991) Set 160
Westwood, Andrew (1994) Set 87
Whaites, L (1994) Set 210
Whalan, Mark (1988) Set 50
Wheatley, Simon (1979) Set 5
Wheatly, Ian (1977) Set 18
Wheeldon, Sarah (1990) Set 227
Wheeler, Andrew (1988) Set 5
Wheeler, Giles (1998) Set 44
Wheeler, Marina (1987) Sets 60, 135
Wheetman, Alan (1995) Sets 181, 187, 243
Whelan, Geoff (1996) Set 219
Whelan, Roma (1981) Set 16
Whipple, Philippa (1994) Set 23 Profile p.1499
Whippman, Constance (1978) Set 8
Whitaker, Quincy (1991) Set 25
Whitaker, Stephen (1970) Set 159
Whitcombe, Mark (1994) Sets 104, 167
White, Abigail (2000) Set 39
White, Andrew (1980) (QC-1997) Set 3 Profile p.1499
White, Antony (1983) (QC-2001) Set 88
White, David (1999) Set 82
White, Gemma (1994) Set 12
White, Jeremy (1976) Set 122
White, Matthew (1997) Sets 169, 250
White, Rachel (2000) Set 219
White, Robert (1993) Set 54
White, Robin (1995) Set 42
White, Sasha (1991) Set 27 Profile p.1499
White, Tim (1993) Sets 196, 266
White, Timothy G (1978) Set 256
Whitehall, Mark (1983) Set 182 Profile p.1499
Whitehall, Richard (1999) Set 217
Whitehead, Darron (1995) Set 161

Whitehouse, Christopher (1972) Set 138
Whitehouse, David (1969) (QC-1990) Set 124 Profile p.1499
Whitehouse, Sarah (1993) Set 75
Whiteman, Peter (1967) (QC-1977) Set 68
Whitfield, Adrian (1964) (QC-1983) Set 130 Profile p.1499
Whitfield, Jonathan (1985) Set 63
Whitmore, John (1976) Set 20
Whittaker, Dornier (1994) Set 195
Whittaker, John (1969) Set 131 Profile p.1499
Whittaker, Robert (1977) Set 147
Whittam, Richard (1983) Set 45 Profile p.1499
Whittam, Samantha (1995) Set 56
Whitting, John (1991) Set 23
Whittle, Henry (1975) Set 134 Profile p.1499
Whittle-Martin, Lucia (1985) Set 59
Whittlestone, Kim (1995) Set 149
Whyatt, Michael (1992) Set 256
Whybrow, Christopher (1965) (QC-1992) Set 27
Whyte, Anne (1993) Set 203
Whyte, Monica (1996) Sets 116, 238
Wicherek, Ann Marie (1978) Set 46
Wickens, Simon (1998) Set 211
Wicks, David (1989) Set 41
Wicks, Joanne (1990) Set 153
Widdett, Ceri (1994) Set 194
Wigglesworth, Raymond (1974) (QC-1999) Set 229
Wightwick, Iain (1985) Set 170
Wigin, Caroline (1984) Set 194
Wigley, Jenny (2000) Set 89
Wignall, Gordon (1987) Set 9
Wigoder, Justin (1977) Set 245
Wilby, David (1974) (QC-1998) Sets 104, 195
Wilby, David (1974) (QC-1998) Set 167
Wilcken, Anthony (1966) Set 68
Wilcock, Peter (1988) Set 150
Wilcox, Lawrence (1996) Set 264
Wilcox, Nicholas (1977) Set 34
Wild, Simon (1977) Set 11
Wild, Steven (1994) Set 214
Wildblood, Stephen (1981) (QC-1999) Sets 70, 165 Profile p.1499
Wilding, Lisa (1993) Set 59
Wiley, Francesca (1996) Set 79
Wilken, Sean (1991) Set 38
Wilkins, Christopher (1993) Set 141
Wilkins, Colette (1989) Set 98
Wilkins, Thomas (1993) Set 59
Wilkinson, John (1979) Set 239
Wilkinson, Kate (1999) Set 75
Wilkinson, Marc (1992) Set 159
Wilkinson, Nigel (1972) (QC-1990) Set 22
Wilkinson, Richard (1992) Set 145
Willams, Mark (1996) Set 110
Willans, David (1995) Set 19
Willard, Neville (1976) Sets 120, 212
Willbourne, Caroline (1970) Set 46
Willems, Marc (1990) Set 216
Willer, Robert (1970) Set 63
Willetts, Glenn (2000) Set 159
Williams, Alexander (1995) Set 147
Williams, Andrew (1994) Set 203
Williams, Anne (1980) Set 13
Williams, Barbara (1995) Set 242

www.ChambersandPartners.com 1691

INDEX ■ BARRISTERS

Williams, Benjamin (1994) Set 145
Williams, Brian (1986) Set 229
Williams, Cheryl (1982) Set 193
Williams, Chris (1988) Set 150
Williams, Christopher (1981) Sets 116, 238
Williams, Christopher M (1972) Set 176
Williams, Daniel (1992) Set 175
Williams, David (1990) Set 113
Williams, David Essex (1975) Set 173
Williams, David H (1990) Set 205 Profile p.1499
Williams, David Huw (1988) Set 126
Williams, Edmund (2000) Set 161
Williams, Glyn (1981) Set 221
Williams, Graeme (1959) (QC-1983) Sets 83, 250
Williams, Guy (2000) Set 89
Williams, Heather (1985) Set 25 Profile p.1499
Williams, Helen (2002) Set 192
Williams, Hugh (1992) Sets 83, 250
Williams, Jeanette (1985) Set 154
Williams, Joanne (2001) Set 175
Williams, John (1973) Set 59
Williams, John Alban (1979) Set 11
Williams, John Melville (1955) (QC-1977) Sets 104, 167 Profile p.1500
Williams, John Wyn (1992) Set 179
Williams, Juliet (1998) Set 264
Williams, Juliet (1998) Set 184
Williams, Karl (1982) Set 173
Williams, Lloyd (1981) Set 174 Profile p.1500
Williams, Mark (1998) Set 168
Williams, Neal (1984) Set 155
Williams, Nicholas (1994) Set 179
Williams, Nicholas Heathcote (1976) Set 82
Williams, Owen (2000) Set 173
Williams, P (1994) Set 196
Williams, Rhodri (1987) Sets 60, 174 Profile p.1500
Williams, Richard (1992) Set 168
Williams, Robert (2000) Set 69
Williams, Sara (1989) Set 159
Williams, Sarah (1995) Set 229
Williams, Susan (1978) Set 18
Williams, Thomas (1996) Set 174
Williams, Thomas (1995) Set 155
Williams, Vincent (1985) Set 50
Williams, Wyn (1974) (QC-1992) Sets 38, 175
Williamson, Adrian (1983) (QC-2002) Set 69 Profile p.1500
Williamson, Ailsa (1997) Set 124
Williamson, Alisdair (1994) Set 124
Williamson, Bridget (1993) Sets 29, 189, 235
Williamson, Hazel (1972) (QC-1988) Set 87 Profile p.1500

Williamson, Melanie J (1990) Set 193
Williamson, Stephen (1964) (QC-1981) Sets 73, 193
Willis, Pearl (1986) Set 242
Willitts, Timothy (1989) Set 216
Wills, Janice (1991) Set 232
Wills-Goldingham, Claire (1988) Set 165 Profile p.1500
Wilmot-Smith, Richard (1978) (QC-1994) Set 38 Profile p.1500
Wilson, Adam (1994) Set 193 Profile p.1500
Wilson, Alasdair (1988) Sets 171, 251
Wilson, Alastair (1968) (QC-1987) Set 100 Profile p.1500
Wilson, Alex (1998) Set 211
Wilson, Andrew (1995) Set 201
Wilson, Christopher (1980) Set 50
Wilson, David (1996) Sets 181, 187, 243
Wilson, Elizabeth (1995) Set 122
Wilson, Elizabeth (1989) Set 110
Wilson, Gerald (1989) Set 144
Wilson, Graham (1975) Set 57
Wilson, Ian (1995) Set 152
Wilson, Jim (1994) Set 74
Wilson, John (1981) Set 7
Wilson, John Barker (1988) Set 230
Wilson, Julian (1997) Set 81
Wilson, Marion (1991) Set 159
Wilson, Martin (1963) (QC-1982) Set 5
Wilson, Penny (1979) Set 168
Wilson, Peter J (1995) Set 200
Wilson, Rebekah (1998) Set 150
Wilson, Richard (1996) Set 188
Wilson, Richard (1996) Set 140
Wilson, Richard (1981) Set 9
Wilson-Barnes, Lucy (1989) Set 227
Wilson-Smith, Christopher (1965) (QC-1986) Sets 37, 165
Wilson-Smith, James (1999) Set 165
Wilton, Simon (1993) Set 112
Winberg, Stephen (1974) Set 151 Profile p.1500
Windle, Victoria (2001) Set 12
Windsor, Emily (1995) Set 40 Profile p.1500
Wing, Christopher (1985) Set 108
Wingate-Saul, Giles (1967) (QC-1983) Sets 101, 213 Profile p.1501
Winship, Julian (1995) Set 45
Winstone, Hilary (1998) Sets 104, 167
Winteler, John (1969) Set 193
Winter, Ian (1988) Set 68 Profile p.1501
Winter, Melanie (1996) Set 79
Winzer, Benjamin (1997) Set 184
Wise, Ian (1992) Set 25 Profile p.1501
Wise, Oliver (1981) Set 123

Wiseman, Adam (1994) Set 126
Wishart, J D S (1974) Set 224
Witcomb, Henry (1989) Set 143
Withers, Michelle (1991) Set 173
Withey, Richard (1996) Set 254
Withington, Angus (1995) Set 101
Withyman, James (1999) Set 266
Wolanski, Adam (1995) Set 125 Profile p.1501
Wolff, Michael (1964) Set 209
Wolfson, David (1992) Set 32 Profile p.1501
Wolkind, Michael (1976) (QC-1999) Set 4 Profile p.1501
Woloniecki, Jan (1983) Set 14
Wolstenholme, Alan (1989) Set 230
Wolton, Harry (1969) (QC-1982) Sets 52, 188 Profile p.1501
Wong, Natasha (1993) Set 43
Wonnacott, Mark (1989) Set 87 Profile p.1501
Wood, Catherine (1985) Set 113
Wood, Christopher (1986) Set 64 Profile p.1501
Wood, Derek (1964) (QC-1978) Set 40 Profile p.1501
Wood, Graeme C (1968) Set 140
Wood, Graham (1979) (QC-2002) Sets 207, 209, 218 Profile p.1502
Wood, Ian (1990) Set 221
Wood, James (1975) (QC-1999) Set 25 Profile p.1502
Wood, James (1989) Set 158
Wood, Lana (1993) Set 140
Wood, Martin (1973) Set 163 Profile p.1502
Wood, Martin (1972) Set 27
Wood, Michael (1989) Sets 207, 218
Wood, Michael (1976) (QC-1999) Set 36
Wood, Nicholas (1970) Set 115 Profile p.1502
Wood, Nick (1980) Set 68
Wood, Penelope (1999) Set 9
Wood, Percy (1961) Set 227
Wood, Rebecca (1999) Set 64
Wood, Richard (1975) Set 35
Wood, Sarah (1996) Set 63
Wood, Simon (1981) Sets 116, 238 Profile p.1502
Wood, Stephen (1991) Set 163
Wood, William (1980) (QC-1998) Set 14 Profile p.1502
Wood, William (1970) (QC-1997) Set 159
Woodall, Peter (1983) Set 151
Woodbridge, Julian (1981) Set 70
Woodbridge, Victoria (1998) Set 22
Woodcock, Jonathan (1981) Set 79
Woodcock, Robert (1978) Set 237
Woodcraft, Elizabeth (1980) Set 150
Woodhall, Gary (1997) Set 228

Woodhouse, Charles (1997) Set 17
Woodley, Sonia (1968) (QC-1996) Set 11
Woodruff, Sarah (1996) Set 39
Woods, Jonathan (1965) Set 22
Woods, R (1992) Set 224
Woods, Terence (1989) Set 51
Woodward, Alison (1992) Set 217
Woodward, Joanne (1989) Set 216
Woodward, John (1984) Set 256
Woodward, William (1964) (QC-1985) Set 247 Profile p.1502
Woodward-Carlton, Damian (1995) Set 101
Woodwark, Jane (1995) Sets 116, 238 Profile p.1502
Woolf, Eliot (1993) Set 143
Woolf, Jeremy (1986) Sets 122, 194
Woolf, Steven (1989) Set 63
Woolfenden, Ivan (1985) Set 203
Woolgar, Dermot (1988) Set 111
Woolhouse, Oliver (1996) Set 162
Woolley, David (1962) (QC-1980) Set 27
Woolls, Tanya (1991) Set 45
Woolman, Andrew (1973) Set 201
Woolrich, Sarah (1994) Set 239
Wordsworth, Philippa (1995) Set 201
Wordsworth, Sam (1997) Set 31 Profile p.1502
Worlock, Simon (2001) Set 159
Wormald, Richard (1993) Set 124
Wormington, Timothy (1977) Set 44
Worrall, Anna (1959) (QC-1989) Set 84
Worrall, John (1984) Set 201
Worsley, Daniel (1971) Set 135
Worsley, Mark (1994) Set 166
Worsley, Michael (1955) (QC-1985) Set 75
Worsley, Nicholas (1998) Set 201
Worsley, Paul (1970) (QC-1990) Sets 65, 194
Worster, David (1980) Set 161
Worthington, Stephen (1976) Set 82 Profile p.1502
Wortley, Natalie (1999) Set 237
Wrack, Nick (1997) Set 150
Wray, Nigel (1986) Set 266
Wrenn, Helen (1994) Set 208
Wright, Alastair (1991) Set 231
Wright, Caroline (1983) Set 165
Wright, Clare (1995) Sets 120, 212
Wright, Colin (1987) Set 142
Wright, Ian (1994) Set 260
Wright, Ian (1989) Set 22
Wright, Ian (1983) Set 115
Wright, Jeremy (1996) Set 159
Wright, Jeremy J (1970) Set 71
Wright, NA (1974) Set 210
Wright, Oliver (1998) Sets 62, 249
Wright, Paul (1990) Set 14
Wright, Peter (1981) (QC-1999) Set 223 Profile p.1502

Wright, Peter (1974) Set 123
Wright, Richard (1998) Set 193
Wright, Sadie (1994) Set 48
Wright, Yasmin (1990) Set 216
Wulwik, Peter (1972) Set 24
Wurtzel, David (1974) Set 18
Wyand, Roger (1973) (QC-1997) Set 67 Profile p.1502
Wyatt, Derrick (1972) (QC-1993) Set 14
Wyeth, Mark (1983) Set 114
Wyles, Lucy (1994) Set 146
Wylie, Neil (1996) Set 246
Wyn Rees, Nerys (1997) Set 180
Wynn, Toby (1982) Sets 80, 190
Wynne, Ashley (1990) Set 159
Wynne-Griffiths, Ralph (1981) Set 166
Wynter, Colin (1984) Set 24 Profile p.1503
Wyvill, Alistair (1998) Set 161 Profile p.1503
Xydias, Nicholas (1992) Set 159
Yajnik, Ram (1965) Set 55
Yates, Nicholas (1996) Set 64
Yates, Sean (1996) Set 201
Yee Lock Wong, RenÈ (1973) Set 72
Yell, Nicholas (1979) Set 129
Yeo, Nik (2000) Set 44
Yeung, Stuart (1989) Set 19
Yip, Amanda (1991) Sets 207, 218
Young, Alastair (1997) Set 161
Young, Andrew (1977) Set 66
Young, Christopher (1997) Set 159
Young, Christopher (1988) Set 103
Young, David (1966) (QC-1980) Set 91 Profile p.1503
Young, Gudrun (2001) Set 110
Young, Lee (1991) Set 254
Young, Martin (1984) Set 140
Young, Rachael (1997) Set 123
Young, Rebecca (1993) Set 198
Young, Simon (1998) Sets 191, 222
Young, Timothy (1977) (QC-1996) Set 35 Profile p.1503
Zacaroli, Antony (1987) Set 133 Profile p.1503
Zakers, Franklyn (1999) Set 194
Zaman, Mohammed (1985) Set 161
Zeb, Emma (1998) Set 169
Zelin, Geoffrey (1984) Sets 29, 189, 235 Profile p.1503
Zellick, Adam (2000) Set 44
Zentar, Remy (1997) Set 230
Zieger, John (1962) Set 7
Zimbler, Alexia (1993) Set 71
Zoest, Jacqueline (1995) Set 151
Zorbas, Panos C (1964) Set 110
Zornoza, Isabella (1993) Sets 60, 135
Zwart, Christiaan (1997) Set 38

INDEX TO THE LEADING LAWYERS

CHAMBERS
UK
2002–2003

INDEX TO THE LEADING LAWYERS

A

Aarons, Elaine
Employment Band 1 — 298

Abbess, Lynne
Partnership Band 1 — 599

Abell, Mark
Franchising Band 1 — 391

Abraham, Henry
Environment Band 2 — 351
Planning Band 2 — 642

Abrahamson, Elkan
Human Rights Band 3 — 412

Abrams, Charles
Financial Services Band 1 — 386

Abramson, John
ADR Band 5 — 66

Abramson, Lawrence
Media & Entertainment Band 4 — 584

Acock, Roger
Corporate Finance Band 4 — 218

Acomb, Nick
Trusts & Personal Tax Band 2 — 815

Acton, Joseph
Social Housing Band 2 — 757

Adams, Elizabeth
Employment Band 3 — 298

Adamson, Derek
Personal Injury Band 1 — 624

Adlington, Jonathan
Social Housing Band 1 — 753

Agar, Nick
Insolvency Band 4 — 447

Agnew, Phyllis
Real Estate Band 2 — 724

Agnew, Seamus
Personal Injury Band 1 — 629

Ainscoe, Raymond
Pensions Band 1 — 609

Ainsworth, Lesley
Competition/Anti-trust Band 3 — 164

Airs, Graham
Tax Band 2 — 776

Aitchison, Karen
Environment Up and coming — 356

Aitman, David
Competition/Anti-trust Band 1 — 164

Akitt, Ian
Banking & Finance Band 3 — 100

Alderson, Richard
Sport Band 1 — 769

Alderton, John Charles
Insolvency Up and coming — 451

Aldred, Hilary
Employment One to watch — 310

Alexander, Ann
Clinical Negligence Band 2 — 146

Alexander, Ewan
Real Estate Up and coming — 723

Alexander, Miles
Product Liability Band 5 — 665

Alexander, Roger
Advertising & Marketing Band 1 — 51

Alexiou, Douglas
Family Band 1 — 365

Alfandary, Peter
Immigration Band 2 — 416

Allan, Bill
Competition/Anti-trust Band 1 — 164

Allan, David
Corporate Finance Band 3 — 229

Allan, David
Personal Injury Band 1 — 627

Allan, Derek
Professional Negligence Band 2 — 679

Allan, Michael
Transport Band 5 — 798

Allan, Robert
Media & Entertainment Band 3 — 584

Allen, Amanda
Corporate Finance Band 4 — 220

Allen, Anthony
ADR Band 2 — 66

Allen, Barbara
Employee Share Schemes Band 4 — 292

Allen, Elizabeth
Family Band 3 — 368

Allen, Heather
ADR Band 5 — 66

Allen, Jeremy
Licensing Band 1 — 507

Allen, Martin
Litigation Band 1 — 547

Allen, Maurice
Banking & Finance Band 2 — 92

Allen, Patrick
Personal Injury Band 2 — 617

Allen, Simon
Personal Injury Band 1 — 626

Allen, Tony
Environment Band 2 — 351
Planning Band 2 — 642

Allen, Tony
Shipping Band 6 — 741

Allinson LIP, Stephen
Insolvency Band 3 — 447

Allison, Margaret
Pensions Band 3 — 609

Allton, Ashley
Banking & Finance Band 3 — 98

Al-Nuaimi, Omar
Banking & Finance Band 2 — 96

Alston, Suzanne
Trusts & Personal Tax Band 3 — 819

Alton, Philip
Banking & Finance Band 3 — 98

Amner, Neil
Environment Band 4 — 356

Amsden, Mark
Litigation Band 3 — 530

Anderson, Alastair H
Agriculture Band 4 — 59

Anderson, David
Travel Band 1 — 808

Anderson, Frances
Media & Entertainment Band 1 — 586

Anderson, Hamish
Insolvency Band 2 — 441

Anderson, Harry
Litigation Band 1 — 518

Anderson, Joanne
Projects/PFI Up and coming — 690

Anderson, John
Insolvency Band 1 — 452

Anderson, Keith T
Corporate Finance Band 3 — 229

Anderson, Peter
Aviation Band 1 — 87
Litigation Band 1 — 534
Personal Injury Band 1 — 629
Professional Negligence Band 1 — 679

Anderson, Robert
Intellectual Property Band 3 — 479

Anderson, Tom
Real Estate Band 1 — 723

Andonian, Bernard
Immigration Band 4 — 416

Andrea, Costas
Travel Band 2 — 806

Andress, Stephen
Personal Injury Band 1 — 629

Andrewartha, Jane
ADR Band 1 — 66
Aviation Band 3 — 86

Andrews, Mark
Insolvency Band 1 — 441

Andrews, Sue
Pensions Band 3 — 604

Angel, Peter
Corporate Finance Band 1 — 216

Annandale, Richard
Healthcare Band 1 — 405

Anson, Peter
Personal Injury Band 1 — 627

Anthony, Rachel
Insolvency Up and coming — 441

Antoniades, Reno
Media & Entertainment Band 2 — 580

Appleby, John
Family Band 2 — 370

Archer, David
Insolvency Band 3 — 446
Pensions Band 1 — 607

Archer, Nick
Litigation: Banking Band 1 — 538
Litigation: General Band 5 — 518

Archer, Quentin
Information Technology Band 3 — 428

Arden, Roger
Church Band 1 — 137

Arkell, Catherine
Personal Injury Band 2 — 624

Armitage, David W K
Corporate Finance Band 3 — 226

Armitage, Richard
Projects/PFI Band 5 — 690

Armstrong, Nicholas
Defamation Band 5 — 268

Armstrong, Ruth
Employment Band 5 — 309

Armstrong, Stuart
Transport Band 4 — 796

Arnold, Michael R
Information Technology Band 2 — 432

Arnot, Richard
Licensing Band 2 — 510

Arnott, David
Construction Band 3 — 190

Arrowsmith-Brown, Matthew
Agriculture Band 2 — 57

Arthur, David
Professional Negligence Band 1 — 675

Arthur, Hugh
Pensions Band 2 — 604

Ashdown, Tim
Intellectual Property Band 2 — 481

Ashford, Mark
Crime Band 2 — 251

Ashley, Jacqueline
Family Band 1 — 368

Ashley Taylor, Andrew M
Pensions Band 2 — 608

Ashtiany, Sue
Employment Band 3 — 298

Ashworth, Chris
Corporate Finance Band 3 — 203

Ashworth, Peter
Real Estate Band 3 — 718

Ashworth, Stephen
Planning Band 1 — 640

Askew, Martin
Insolvency Band 2 — 447

Askin, David
Real Estate Band 3 — 715

Aslan, Susan
Defamation Band 1 — 268

Aspinall, Mark
Commodities Band 5 — 158
Shipping Band 6 — 741

Aspinall, Tim
Litigation Band 1 — 523

Assim, Gary
Intellectual Property Band 2 — 483

Astleford, Peter
Investment Funds Band 3 — 498

Atack, Iain F
Employment Band 3 — 316

Athanas, Chris
Financial Services Band 1 — 389
Investment Funds Band 1 — 500

Atkinson, Carole
Family Band 2 — 371

Atkinson, Joe
Shipping Band 5 — 741

Atkinson, Mark
Litigation Band 3 — 543
Pensions Band 3 — 604

Attle, Gary
Education Band 1 — 286

Aubrey, Michael J
Agriculture Band 3 — 57

Audley, Max
Corporate Finance Band 1 — 212

www.ChambersandPartners.com

1695

INDEX ■ LEADING LAWYERS

B

Auerbach, Simon	Employment Band 1	298
Austin, Ian	Litigation Band 3	530
Austin, James	Corporate Finance Up and coming	223
Austwick, Malcolm	Projects/PFI Band 5	690
Ayre, Carole	Clinical Negligence Band 1	145
Ayre, Paul	Real Estate Band 3	720
Ayrton, Lyn	Family Band 3	372
Azim-Khan, Rafi	E-commerce Band 4	277

B

Backhouse, James A	Transport Band 1	798
Bacon, Alistair	Insolvency Band 3	446
Bacon, Gavin	Litigation Band 5	518
Baggallay, Roger	Litigation Band 2	538
Bagge, James	Litigation: Civil Fraud Band 1	541
	Litigation: Banking Band 3	538
Bailes, Tony	E-commerce Band 1	279
	Information Technology Band 2	430
Bailey, Jeffrey	Real Estate Band 3	702
Bailey, Michael	Real Estate Band 3	708
Baillie, Kirstene	Investment Funds Band 4	498
Baily, Tim	Real Estate Band 1	708
Baines, Richard	Insolvency Band 6	441
Baird, Derek	Private Equity Band 4	657
Baird, James	Private Equity Band 1	657
Baird, Ken	Insolvency Band 4	441
Baker, Andrew	Corporate Finance Band 3	212
Baker, Andrew	Offshore: Corporate Band 3	832
Baker, Huw	Construction Band 2	186
	Projects/PFI Band 3	692
Baker, Ian	Banking & Finance Band 1	98
	Insolvency Band 1	449
Baker, Miranda	Family Band 4	365
Baker, Neil	Environment Band 1	351
Bakes, Martin	Insurance Band 1	466
Balcomb, Anne	Immigration Band 4	416
Baldock, Anne	Projects/PFI Star	690
Baldwin, Mark	Tax: Indirect Band 1	776
	Tax: Corporate Band 2	776
Balen, Paul	Clinical Negligence Band 1	144
	Personal Injury Band 2	623
	Product Liability Band 1	667
Balfour, Andrew	Banking & Finance Band 2	92
Balfour, John	Aviation Band 1	85
Ball, Anne	Clinical Negligence Band 2	146
Ball, Susan	Tax Band 3	776
Ballantine, Tom	Family Band 2	373
Ballard, Andy	Social Housing Band 3	758
Ballard, Richard	Tax Band 2	776
Ballard, Tony	Media & Entertainment Band 3	581
	Telecommunications Band 2	792
Ballingall, James	Projects/PFI Band 4	690
Ballmann, William	Insolvency Band 2	450
Bamber, Andrew	Banking & Finance Band 6	92
	Private Equity Band 4	659
Bamber, Roger	Family Band 2	370
Bambury, Derek	Professional Negligence Band 3	677
Band, Christa	Litigation: Banking Band 2	538
	Litigation: Civil Fraud Band 3	541
	Litigation: General Band 4	518
Bandurka, Andrew	Insurance Band 2	468
Bankier, David	Real Estate Band 2	723
Banks, Sandra	Planning Band 3	640
Bannister, Richard	Clinical Negligence Band 2	144
Baranski, Karl	Insolvency Band 2	448
Barber, Janice	Healthcare Band 4	404
Barber, Paul	Clinical Negligence Band 1	145
	Healthcare Band 1	405
Barbor, Cynthia	Travel Band 1	805
Barcan, Richard A	Clinical Negligence Band 1	143
Barclay, Jonathan	Trusts & Personal Tax Band 2	819
Barclay, Marcus	Litigation Band 4	545
Bardot, Andrew	Shipping Band 2	741
Barker, Alan	Insurance Band 3	469
Barker, Bridget	Private Equity Band 2	661
Barker, Christine	Family Band 3	371
Barker, Matthew	Insolvency Band 3	445
Barker, Richard	Agriculture Band 2	57
Barker, Sheila	Family Band 3	373
Barker, William	Intellectual Property Band 2	483
Barley, Mark	Litigation Up and coming	548
Barlow, James	Investment Funds Band 5	498
Barlow, Richard	Environment Band 3	353
Barnard, Stephen	Corporate Finance Band 4	203
Barnes, Ged	Insolvency Band 4	450
Barnes, James	Real Estate Band 2	702
Barnes, Jeremy	Professional Negligence Band 2	677
Barnes, Oliver	Corporate Finance Band 2	208
Barnett, Ian	Agriculture Band 2	56
Barnett, Nigel	Insolvency Band 3	441
Barnfather, Anthony	Fraud Band 3	395
Barr, Alan	Corporate Finance Band 2	218
Barr, Alan	Tax Band 2	783
Barr, William	Agriculture Band 1	57
Barratt, Jeffery	Projects Band 1	686
Barratt, Richard	Sport Band 5	767
Barrett, David	Information Technology Band 3	428
Barrett, Elizabeth	Litigation Band 3	541
Barrett, Geoff	Professional Negligence Band 3	675
Barrett, Kevin	Construction Band 2	184
Barrie, Sidney	Corporate Finance Band 3	229
Barron, David	Intellectual Property Band 2	483
Barron, Michael	Private Equity Band 2	659
Barr-Smith, Adrian	Sport Band 1	767
Barry, Robert	Intellectual Property Band 6	479
Barter, Charles	Private Equity Band 3	657
Barth, Philip	Immigration Band 3	416
Barton, Grainne	Clinical Negligence Band 1	140
Bartram, Peter	Immigration Band 3	418
Bastow, Gillian	Social Housing Band 1	753
Bastow, Martin	Litigation Band 3	548
Batchelor, Claire	Clinical Negligence Band 2	146
	Healthcare Band 1	406
Bates, Anton	Franchising Band 2	391
Bates, Chris	Capital Markets Band 4	116
	Financial Services Band 2	386
Bates, Michael	Banking & Finance Up and coming	92
Bates, Stephanie	Corporate Finance Band 4	208
Bateson, James	Insurance Band 2	469
Batten, Elizabeth	Clinical Negligence Band 2	140
Batters, John A	Licensing Band 1	511
Battiscombe, David	Real Estate Band 4	702
Baxter, Richard	Corporate Finance Band 2	215
Baylis, Craig	Licensing Band 1	504
	Product Liability Band 2	669
Baylis, Simon	Construction Band 1	184
Bays, Kevin	Defamation Band 2	268
Beach, Steven	Real Estate Band 3	717
Beale, Robert	Personal Injury Band 1	622
Beardsley, Alison	Corporate Finance Band 5	203
Beare, Tony	Tax Band 2	776
Beasley, Adrian	Asset Finance One to watch	79
Beastall, Jonathan	Corporate Finance Up and coming	203
Beck, Andrew	Litigation Band 1	551
Beckett, Roy	Real Estate Band 1	718
Beckett, Sam	Construction Band 1	191
	Litigation Band 1	536
Beckford, Trevor	Crime Band 1	253

1696

LEADING LAWYERS ■ INDEX

Beckitt, Jonathan	Projects/PFI Band 5	690
Beddow, Simon	Private Equity Band 3	657
Bedford, Paul	Capital Markets Band 2	114
Bedford, Richard	Litigation Band 2	548
Beechey, John	Arbitration Band 1	74
Beesley, Chris	Shipping Band 5	741
Beesley, PF	Church Band 1	134
	Education Band 2	282
Belchak, Hilary	Immigration Band 1	416
Belcher, Penny	Litigation Band 1	551
Belderbos, Mark	Church Band 2	137
Bell, Alasdair	Sport Band 3	767
Bell, Christopher	Corporate Finance Band 1	208
Bell, Emma	Employment Band 3	316
Bell, Stuart	Environment Band 2	355
Bellew, Derek	Corporate Finance Band 5	218
	Partnership: Medical Band 1	599
	Partnership Band 2	598
Bellhouse, John	Projects Band 5	686
Bellis, Nigel	Corporate Finance Band 1	227
Bellis, Tim	Corporate Finance Band 5	203
Beltrami, Joseph	Crime Band 2	255
Bennett, Graham	Real Estate Band 2	708
Bennett, Jennifer	Social Housing Band 1	756
Bennett, John	Corporate Finance Band 2	208
Bennett, Nigel	Media & Entertainment Band 4	580
Bennett, Philip	Pensions Band 1	604
Benney, Belinda	Pensions Band 3	604
Benson, Edward	Employment Band 3	309
Benson, Justin	Asset Finance Band 6	79
Benson, Nick	Employment Band 3	307
Benson, Stephen	Real Estate Band 2	718
Bentham, Paul	Intellectual Property Band 2	484
Bentley, Bruce	Construction Band 1	188
Benton, David	Capital Markets Band 1	116
Benzecry, Edward	Real Estate Band 3	702
Beresford, Amanda	Environment Band 2	355
	Planning Band 4	646
Berger, Jonathan	Media & Entertainment Band 2	580
Berkeley, Christopher	Pensions Band 4	604
Berry, Christopher	Insolvency Band 6	441
Berry, Paul	Real Estate Band 3	708
Berry, Roger John	Real Estate Band 1	714
Berry, Stephen	Corporate Finance Band 3	219
Berry, Timothy	Church Band 2	135
Berwick, Guy	Construction Band 3	184
Bessy, James	Construction Band 3	184
Best, David	Commodities Band 4	158
Beswick, David	Employment Band 1	309
Bevan, Jonathan	Transport Band 4	799
Bevan, Peter	Financial Services One to watch	386
Beven, Raymond	Transport Band 3	799
Bhatt, Raju	Human Rights Band 1	410
Bickerstaff, Roger	Information Technology Band 3	428
Bickerton, David	Capital Markets Band 4	111
	Projects/PFI Band 1	690
Biggar, John	Trusts & Personal Tax Band 1	821
Billing, Petra	Litigation One to watch	551
Billingham, Nick	Social Housing Band 3	753
Billings, Martin J	Real Estate Band 3	710
Bindman, Geoffrey	Defamation Band 4	268
	Human Rights Band 1	410
Binks, Nigel	Trusts & Personal Tax Band 2	820
Binning, Peter	Fraud Band 2	393
Birch, John	Construction Band 3	183
Birchall, David	Energy Band 3	337
Birchall, Roger	Corporate Finance Band 4	220
Bird, Christina	Construction One to watch	184
Bird, David	Trusts & Personal Tax Band 2	817
Bird, Steven	Crime Band 3	251
Birkby, Gillian	Construction Band 3	177
Birt, Tim	Advertising & Marketing Band 2	51
	Corporate Finance Band 2	208
Birtwistle, Colin	Social Housing Band 2	760
Bishop, David	Trusts & Personal Tax Band 2	820
Bishop, Gillian	Family Band 4	365
Bishop, John	ADR Band 4	66
	Construction Band 1	177
Bissell, Helen	Transport Band 3	799
Bitel, Nicholas	Sport Band 2	767
Black, Alan	Projects Band 1	686
Black, Ian	Real Estate Band 5	718
Black, Richard	Pensions Band 2	607
Black, Richard	Commodities Band 2	158
Blackler, Tony	Construction Band 1	177
Blackwell, Hilary	Healthcare Band 4	404
Blackwell, Nigel	Corporate Finance Band 3	222
Blain, John	Sport Band 5	767
Blair, J Michael G	Agriculture Band 2	59
Blair, Jonathan	Insolvency Band 2	452
Blair, Jonathan	Media Up and coming	580
Blake, Carey	Real Estate Band 1	708
Blake, Jonathan	Investment Funds Band 3	498
	Private Equity Band 1	661
Blake, Peter	Litigation Band 2	529
Blake, Peter	Energy: Electricity Band 1	337
	Energy: Oil & Gas Band 3	336
	Projects Band 2	686
Blakemore, Craig	Litigation Band 4	530
Blake-Roberts, Philippa	Trusts & Personal Tax Band 4	813
Blaney, Trevor	Planning Band 4	640
Bliss, Nick	Projects/PFI Band 1	690
Bloom, Martin	Employment Band 4	310
Bloom, Robin	Employment Band 2	315
Blore, Siân	Family Band 2	367
Blower, Geoffrey	Corporate Finance Band 3	225
Bloxham, Peter	Insolvency Band 5	441
Blyth, Mark	Litigation Band 1	543
Blythe, Deborah	Clinical Negligence Band 3	140
Boaden, Jon H	Shipping Band 3	745
Boag-Thomson, Joanna	E-commerce Band 1	279
	Information Technology Band 3	433
Boardman, John	Education Band 1	286
Boardman, Nigel	Corporate Finance Star	203
Bochenski, Tony	Asset Finance Band 1	80
Bode, Adrian	Social Housing Band 3	759
Body, David	Clinical Negligence Band 1	147
	Product Liability Band 2	667
Bon, Gordon	Insolvency Band 3	447
Bonar, Mary	Transport Band 2	799
Bond, Richard	Corporate Finance Band 4	203
	Energy Band 2	336
Bonner, Margaret	Family Band 1	368
Boobier, Nigel	Insolvency Band 2	447
Booth, Christopher	Employment Band 1	313
Booy, Anna	Intellectual Property Band 1	481
Bordell, Keith	Insolvency Band 5	441
Borkowski, Andrew	Corporate Finance Band 3	222
Born, Gary	Arbitration Band 1	74
Borrows, Jane	Capital Markets Band 5	114
Borthwick, Trevor	Banking & Finance Band 4	92
Boswall, Julian	Environment Band 1	352
	Planning Band 1	644
Bosworth, John	Planning Band 2	643
Bothamley, Michael	Real Estate Band 1	712
Bott, Adrian	Corporate Finance Band 3	208
Boumphrey, Patrick	Insolvency Band 4	447

www.ChambersandPartners.com 1697

INDEX ■ LEADING LAWYERS

B

Name	Detail	Page
Bound, Andrew	Corporate Finance Band 2	219
Bourgeois, Christopher	Construction Band 6	177
Bourne, Tim	Travel Band 2	808
Bowden, Jeremy	Insolvency Band 3	449
Bowden, Paul	Administrative & Public Law Band 3	43
	Environment Band 1	347
	Product Liability Band 3	665
Bowden, Ronnie	Personal Injury Band 1	630
Bowman, Marcus	Shipping Band 5	741
Bown, Christopher	Private Equity Band 3	657
Bowyer, Russell	Information Technology Band 3	430
Box, Linda M	Church Band 2	137
Boyd, Robert	Education Band 2	284
Brabner, Michael	Corporate Finance Band 4	225
Bracken, Jonathan	Parliamentary Band 2	594
Bradbeer, Ronald	ADR Band 2	67
Bradford, Katie	Litigation Star	545
Bradley, David	Employment Band 2	313
Bradley, David	Trusts & Personal Tax Band 3	819
Bradley, Deborah	Personal Injury Band 1	622
Bradley, Graeme	Construction Band 3	184
Bradley, Nicholas	Insurance Band 2	468
Bradshaw, David	Personal Injury Band 2	627
Brady, Peter	Planning Band 1	645
Brady, Yvonne	Insolvency Band 1	454
Brafman, Guilherme	Advertising & Marketing Band 3	51
Braham, Edward	Corporate Finance Band 2	203
Braithwaite, Andrew	Intellectual Property Band 1	482
	Sport Band 2	769
Braithwaite, Anne	Family Band 3	372
Braithwaite, Neil	Real Estate Band 1	721
Braithwaite, Stephen	Corporate Finance Band 4	220
Brannan, Guy C H	Tax Band 3	776
Branson, Christopher	Insolvency Band 1	446

Name	Detail	Page
Braun, Simon	Social Housing Band 1	756
Bray, Richard	Media & Entertainment Band 2	584
Brearley, Kate	Employment Band 3	298
Breen, Helga	Employment Band 5	298
Brennan, Paul	Energy Band 2	339
Brennan, Sharon	Tax Up and coming	782
Bresslaw, James	Capital Markets Band 4	114
Bretherton, Philip	Real Estate Band 1	702
Brett, Adam	Employment Band 2	318
Brett, Alan	Real Estate Band 2	717
Bretton, Linda	Energy Band 4	336
Bretton, Richard	Health & Safety Band 1	401
Briam, Tony	Real Estate Band 2	702
Bridge, John	Personal Injury Band 2	626
Bridges, Mark	Trusts & Personal Tax Band 2	813
Bridges Webb, Crispin	Corporate Finance Band 3	222
Bridgewater, Martin	Construction Band 5	177
Brierley, Chris	Banking & Finance Band 3	98
Brierley, Ian	Litigation Band 3	545
Briffa, Margaret	Intellectual Property Band 5	479
Briggs, Graham	Insolvency Band 2	451
Briggs, Leona	Litigation Band 1	548
Bright, Christopher	Competition/Anti-trust Band 1	164
Brimelow, Russell	Employment Band 5	298
Bristol, Jeremy	Real Estate Band 1	717
Broadfield, Alice	Banking & Finance Band 2	98
Broadhurst, Marisa	Healthcare Band 4	404
Broadie, Charles	Professional Negligence Band 2	676
Brock, Adrienne	Employment Band 2	318
Brock, David	Environment Band 3	354
	Planning Band 1	645
Brockbank, Anthony	Corporate Finance Band 3	212
Brockman, Christopher	Insolvency Band 1	445

Name	Detail	Page
Brook, Nigel	Insurance Band 2	468
Brooker, Suzanne	Insolvency Band 2	446
Brookes, Mike	Media & Entertainment Band 4	584
Brooks, Egan	Insolvency Star	450
Brooks, Ken	Charities Band 1	125
Brooks, Roger	Personal Injury Band 1	626
Brookshaw, Oliver	Corporate Finance Band 3	222
Brothwood, Graham	Real Estate Band 3	712
Broudie, Robert	Crime Band 2	254
Brough, Gordon	Investment Funds Band 3	498
Browell, Philip	Personal Injury Band 1	627
Brown, Anthony	Shipping Band 6	741
Brown, Chris	Projects/PFI Band 4	690
Brown, Claude	Capital Markets Band 3	116
Brown, David	Intellectual Property Band 4	479
Brown, Duncan	Social Housing Band 3	753
Brown, Fiona	Family Up and coming	365
Brown, Graham	Trusts & Personal Tax Band 5	813
Brown, Henry	ADR Band 2	66
Brown, Hugh	Shipping Band 5	741
Brown, Jacqueline	Media Up and coming	584
Brown, Jane	Capital Markets Band 4	111
Brown, Jeffrey	Construction Band 3	184
Brown, Jeremy	Intellectual Property Band 2	479
Brown, Mitch	Social Housing Band 1	760
Brown, Nicholas	Real Estate Band 3	702
Brown, Nicholas	Parliamentary Band 3	593
Brown, Nicola	Employment Band 3	310
Brown, Robert	Insolvency Band 2	451
Brown, Sandra	Trusts & Personal Tax Band 3	817
Brown, Simon	Trusts & Personal Tax Band 2	815
Brown, Steven	Projects/PFI Band 3	693

Name	Detail	Page
Brown, Susan	Clinical Negligence Band 2	142
Brown, Timothy	Professional Negligence Band 4	675
Brown, Victoria	Franchising Band 5	391
Brown, Vincent	Environment Band 2	356
Browne, Ben	Shipping Band 4	741
Browning, Lesley	Pensions Band 4	604
Browning, Stephen	Insurance Band 3	469
Bruce, Roderick	Corporate Finance Band 2	229
Bruce, Simon	Family Band 4	365
Bruce Lockhart, Karen	Family Band 2	373
Bruce-Smith, Keith	Trusts & Personal Tax Band 5	813
Bruffell, Martin	Personal Injury Band 1	620
Brumby, Frank	Insolvency Up and coming	449
Brumwell, Mark	Environment Band 4	347
Bryce, Andrew John	Environment Band 2	354
Brymer, Stewart	Education Band 1	287
	Real Estate Band 4	723
Brymer, Tim	Aviation Band 2	86
Brynes, Joanna	Licensing Band 4	511
Brynmor Thomas, David	Arbitration Band 3	74
Buchan, Gordon	Corporate Finance Band 4	229
Buchanan, Andrew	Insolvency Band 3	450
Buckley, Liam	Real Estate Band 2	718
Buckworth, Nicholas	Projects Band 3	686
Budd, Elizabeth	Investment Funds Up and coming	498
Bugg, Tony	Insolvency Band 2	441
Bull, Rod	Planning Band 1	644
Bunch, Anthony	Construction Band 2	177
Bundey, Ruth	Human Rights Band 1	412
	Immigration Band 1	421
Bundy, Claire	Insolvency Up and coming	447
Burch, Simon	Construction Band 4	177
Burchfield, Jonathan	Charities Band 2	123

1698

LEADING LAWYERS ■ INDEX

Burd, Michael — Employment **Band 2** — 298
Burdon-Cooper, Alan — Sport **Band 5** — 767
Burgess, David — Administrative & Public Law **Band 2** — 41; Immigration **Band 1** — 418
Burgess, James — Real Estate **Band 2** — 710
Burgess, Mark — Tax **Band 2** — 781
Burn, Lachlan — Capital Markets **Band 2** — 111
Burnett, Rachel — Information Technology **Band 5** — 428
Burnley, Paul — Health & Safety **Band 1** — 402
Burns, John — Real Estate **Band 3** — 715
Burnside, David M — Employment **Band 2** — 316
Burnside, Graham — Banking & Finance **Band 3** — 102
Burrow, Robert — Corporate Finance **Band 2** — 208
Burrows, Lesley — Fraud **Band 1** — 395
Burton, Anthony — Crime **Band 3** — 251
Burton, Carl — Real Estate **Band 3** — 708
Burton, Ian — Fraud **Star** — 393
Bush, Jane — Capital Markets **Band 4** — 116
Butcher, Christopher — Church **Band 2** — 135
Butcher, Trevor — Construction **Band 2** — 177
Butler, Alan — Real Estate **Band 4** — 702
Butler, Kay — Tax **Band 5** — 776
Butler, Michael — Crime **Band 1** — 252
Butler-Gallie, Stuart — Corporate Finance **Band 1** — 215
Butterfield, Christopher — Transport **Band 5** — 798
Buxton, James — Agriculture **Band 1** — 55
Buxton, Richard — Administrative & Public Law **Band 1** — 46; Environment **Band 1** — 354
Buzzoni, Mark — Trusts & Personal Tax **Band 5** — 813
Bye, Eileen — Immigration **Band 3** — 418
Byrne, Chris — Offshore: Corporate **Band 1** — 832
Byrne, David — Fraud **Band 2** — 393; Litigation **Band 4** — 541
Byrne, Peter — Offshore: Corporate **Band 3** — 832
Byrne, Richard — Health & Safety **Band 2** — 401
Byrt, Sarah — Advertising & Marketing **Band 4** — 51

C

Cahill, John — Personal Injury **Band 2** — 617
Cahill, Julia — Clinical Negligence **Band 2** — 140
Cairns, Elizabeth — Charities **Band 1** — 124
Caldwell, Anne I M — Family **Band 1** — 374
Calladine, Paul — Energy **Band 2** — 339
Callaghan, Edward — Litigation **Band 1** — 529
Calow, Duncan — E-commerce **Band 4** — 277
Cameron, Gillian — Information Technology **Band 2** — 433
Campbell, Alan — Projects/PFI **Band 3** — 693
Campbell, Marcus — Professional Negligence **Band 2** — 677
Campbell, Mark — Banking & Finance **Band 1** — 92; Private Equity **Band 3** — 659
Campbell, Morag — Asset Finance **Band 2** — 80
Campion, Hilary — Employment **Band 4** — 309
Canavan, Kerry — Corporate Finance **Band 3** — 231
Canby, Michael — Capital Markets **Band 1** — 111
Canham, Stephanie — Construction **Band 6** — 177
Canning, Clare — Professional Negligence **Band 4** — 675
Cannon, Lista — Litigation: General **Band 3** — 518; Litigation: Banking **Band 4** — 538
Cant, Michael — Tax **Band 2** — 776
Capel, Stuart — Agriculture **Band 1** — 54
Caplan QC, Michael — Fraud **Band 2** — 393
Capper, Phillip — Arbitration **Band 2** — 74; Construction **Band 1** — 177
Capstick, Charlotte — Education **Band 3** — 282
Carboni, Anna — Intellectual Property **Band 4** — 479
Care, Tim — Projects/PFI **Band 3** — 692
Carew-Jones, Owen — Education **Band 2** — 282
Carey, Nigel — Offshore: Corporate **Band 1** — 831
Carless, Michael Joseph — Transport **Band 4** — 798
Carlisle, Kenneth — Family **Band 2** — 373
Carlton, Roderick — Competition **Up and coming** — 164
Carmedy, Russell — Corporate Finance **Band 3** — 208
Carmichael, Graeme — Family **Band 1** — 370
Carnegie, Andrew — Travel **Band 1** — 807
Carnell, Bernard — Fraud **Band 3** — 393
Carolina, Robert — Information Technology **Band 5** — 428
Carpanini, Fabrizio — Private Equity **Band 4** — 657
Carpenter, Clive — Asset Finance **Band 2** — 79
Carr, Robert — Clinical Negligence **Band 1** — 148; Personal Injury **Band 2** — 628
Carr, Kenneth — Crime **Band 2** — 253
Carriage, Rebecca — Environment **Band 3** — 354
Carruthers, Alex — Family **Band 3** — 365
Carruthers, Andrew — Litigation **Band 2** — 543
Carslake, Hugh — Church **Band 2** — 136; Trusts & Personal Tax **Band 1** — 818
Carslaw, Debbie — Banking & Finance **Band 6** — 92
Carson, Peter — Personal Injury **Band 1** — 626
Carson, Rosemary — Real Estate **Band 3** — 724
Carstensen, Laura — Competition/Anti-trust **Band 1** — 164
Carter, Adrian — Social Housing **Band 2** — 755
Carter, Barbara — Family **Band 2** — 370
Carter, Stephen — Insurance **Band 3** — 468
Cartmell, Timothy H — Agriculture **Band 1** — 57
Carty, Gillian — Insolvency **Up and coming** — 454
Carver CBE, Jeremy — Energy **Band 4** — 336
Cary, Tim — Immigration **Band 1** — 420
Casely-Hayford, Margaret — Planning **Band 2** — 640
Cassel, Richard — Employment **Band 3** — 310
Cassidy, Fiona — Employment **Band 2** — 318
Cater, Sheila — Employment **Band 2** — 306
Catto, Joan — Family **Band 2** — 373
Cauldwell, Helen — Corporate Finance **One to watch** — 226
Cavalier, Stephen — Employment **Band 4** — 298
Cave, Tim — Litigation **Band 3** — 538
Cetta, Maria — Aviation **Band 4** — 86
Chadwick, Peter — Trusts & Personal Tax **Band 2** — 820
Chalcraft, Stephen — Real Estate **Band 5** — 718
Challands, Richard — Professional Negligence **Band 1** — 677
Challoner, John — Tax **Band 5** — 776
Chamberlain, Andrew — Employment **Band 1** — 312
Chamberlain, Colin — Employee Share Schemes **Band 1** — 292
Chamberlain, Jonathan — Employment **Band 2** — 309
Chamberlain, Margaret — Financial Services **Band 2** — 386
Chamberlain, Simon — Travel **Band 2** — 805
Chambers, John — Franchising **Band 5** — 391
Chandler, Nick — Asset Finance **Band 6** — 79
Chandler, Pauline — Personal Injury **Band 2** — 625
Chandler, Stephen — Intellectual Property **Band 1** — 485
Chaplin, Clive — Offshore: Corporate **Band 3** — 832
Chapman, John — Clinical Negligence **Band 1** — 145
Chapman, Richard — Information Tech **Up and coming** — 428
Chapman, Stuart — Litigation **Band 3** — 532
Chappatte, Philippe — Aviation **Band 3** — 85; Competition/Anti-trust **Band 2** — 164
Charalambous, Louis — Human Rights **Band 3** — 410
Charlton, Bob — Asset Finance **Band 1** — 79; Transport **Band 1** — 799
Charnley, William — Corporate Finance **Band 5** — 203
Chater, Stephen — Employee Share Schemes **Band 3** — 292
Chatfield, Christopher — Transport **Up and coming** — 796
Chatfield, James — Corporate Finance **Band 3** — 215
Cheal, Jonathan — Agriculture **Band 3** — 55
Cheetham, David — Church **Band 2** — 136

www.ChambersandPartners.com

1699

INDEX ■ LEADING LAWYERS

Cheffings, Nicholas
Litigation Band 1 — 545

Cherry, Anthony
Personal Injury Band 1 — 622

Cherry, Peter
Litigation Band 3 — 530

Cherry, Robert
Corporate Finance Band 3 — 219

Chester, Mark
Real Estate Up and coming — 715

Chester, Martin
Corporate Finance Band 2 — 208

Chesterman, James
Banking & Finance Band 4 — 92

Cheyne, David
Corporate Finance Star — 203

Child, Tony
Administrative & Public Law Band 1 — 41
Local Government Band 1 — 572

Childs, Christopher
Licensing Band 2 — 507

Childs, David
Corporate Finance Band 4 — 203

Chinn, David
Construction Band 2 — 186

Chism, Debbie
Family Up and coming — 365

Chissick, Michael
E-commerce Band 2 — 277
Information Technology Band 3 — 428

Chitty, Martin
Employment Band 1 — 309

Christian, John
Tax Band 1 — 782

Christian, Louise
Human Rights Band 2 — 410

Cirell, Stephen
Administrative & Public Law Band 1 — 46
Local Government Band 1 — 575
Projects/PFI Band 3 — 692

Claricoat, John
Charities Band 3 — 123

Clark, Adrian
Corporate Finance Band 3 — 203

Clark, Charles
Capital Markets Band 3 — 111

Clark, David
Pensions Band 1 — 607

Clark, David
Aviation Band 3 — 86

Clark, Ian
Aviation Band 3 — 86

Clark, John
Investment Funds Up and coming — 498

Clark, Paul
Real Estate Band 4 — 702

Clark, Richard
Aviation Band 1 — 87

Clark, Simon
Real Estate Band 2 — 702
Tax Band 2 — 776

Clark, Tim
Litigation Band 1 — 525

Clark, Tim
Corporate Finance Band 4 — 203

Clarke, Claire
Banking & Finance Up and coming — 99

Clarke, Dominic
Investment Funds Band 5 — 498

Clarke, G Timothy H
Corporate Finance Band 2 — 203

Clarke, John
Education Band 3 — 284

Clarke, Mary
Employment Band 3 — 312

Clarke, Michael
Employment Band 3 — 308

Clarke, Ray
Environment Band 1 — 355

Clarke, Richard
Personal Injury Band 2 — 628

Clavell-Bate, Michael
Litigation Band 1 — 530

Clay, Andrew J
Intellectual Property Band 3 — 485

Claydon, Laura
Competition/Anti-trust Band 1 — 166

Clayson, Murray
Tax Band 5 — 776

Cleal, Adam
Real Estate Band 4 — 702

Cleland, John
Banking & Finance Band 2 — 100

Clement-Jones, Tim
Parliamentary Band 2 — 594

Clifton, David
Licensing Band 1 — 504

Clinton, Robert
Defamation Band 1 — 268

Clist, Angela H
Capital Markets Band 4 — 114

Close, Chris
Pensions Band 4 — 604

Clough, Adrian
Energy Band 3 — 337

Clough, Peter
Litigation Band 2 — 525

Clover, Sarah
Professional Negligence Band 4 — 675

Clutton, Owen
Trusts & Personal Tax Band 4 — 813

Coates, Katherine
Insurance Band 2 — 469

Coates, Philip
Insolvency Band 4 — 450

Cochrane, Charles
Banking & Finance One to watch — 92

Cochrane, Scott
Investment Funds One to watch — 498

Cockburn, Alistair
Employment Band 2 — 316

Cockburn, David
Planning Band 2 — 648

Cockerill, Vivien
Pensions Band 1 — 607

Cockram, Richard
Construction Band 2 — 188
Projects/PFI Band 2 — 692

Codrington, Eddie
Employee Share Schemes Band 2 — 292

Cody, Nick
Product Liability Band 3 — 669

Coffell, Howard
Energy Band 4 — 336

Cohen, Adrian
Insolvency Band 3 — 441

Cohen, David
Employee Share Schemes Band 1 — 292

Cohen, Howard
Asset Finance Band 3 — 81

Cohen, John
Media & Entertainment Band 1 — 585

Cohen, Larry J
Intellectual Property Band 3 — 479

Cohen, Ralph
Competition/Anti-trust Band 5 — 164

Cohen, Raymond
Partnership Up and coming — 596

Cohen, Roger
Litigation Band 2 — 545

Coker, Jane
Immigration Band 1 — 418

Colacicchi, Clare
Trusts & Personal Tax Band 1 — 818

Colacicchi, William
Trusts & Personal Tax Band 2 — 818

Colbridge, Christopher
Arbitration Band 4 — 74

Cole, Alun
Administrative & Public Law Band 1 — 45
Local Government Band 2 — 574

Cole, Jeremy
Litigation Band 4 — 541

Cole, Margaret R
Litigation Band 6 — 518

Cole, Michael
Crime Band 1 — 253

Coleclough, Stephen
Tax Band 2 — 776

Coleman, Brenda
Tax Band 5 — 776

Coleman, Martin
Competition/Anti-trust Band 5 — 164

Coll, Harry
Employment Band 2 — 318

Collar, Neil
Planning Band 1 — 648

Collingwood, Mark
Construction Band 3 — 183

Collins, Andrew
Asset Finance Band 5 — 79

Collins, Anthony
Licensing Band 1 — 507

Collins, Dale
Health & Safety Band 3 — 401

Collins, Peter
Agriculture Band 1 — 57

Collinson, Adam G
Competition/Anti-trust Band 1 — 167

Collinson, Ian
Litigation Band 1 — 533

Collis, Pamela
Family Band 2 — 365

Combe, Jonathan
Real Estate Band 2 — 721

Compagnoni, Marco
Private Equity Band 2 — 657

Concagh, Anthony
Shipping Up and coming — 741

Concannon, Simon
Tax Band 2 — 782

Conlan, Sue
Immigration Band 1 — 420

Connal QC, Craig
Litigation Band 1 — 534
Planning Band 2 — 648

Connell, Douglas
Charities Band 1 — 129
Trusts & Personal Tax Band 2 — 821

Connolly, Sean
Insurance Band 3 — 466
Professional Negligence Band 2 — 675

Connor, Michael
Personal Injury Band 3 — 625

Connor, Vincent
Construction Band 1 — 190

Conrathe, Paul
Education Band 2 — 283
Human Rights Band 3 — 410

Conroy, Paul
Real Estate Band 4 — 718

Conway, Keith
Litigation Band 3 — 545

Conway, Philip
Defamation Band 3 — 268

Cook, John
Travel Band 3 — 805

Cook, Mark
Local Government Band 3 — 574

Cook, Nigel
Insolvency Band 3 — 445

Cook, Patrick
Insolvency Band 3 — 447

Cook, Trevor
Intellectual Property Band 1 — 479

Cooke, Adam
Intellectual Property Band 5 — 479

Cooke, Darryl
Corporate Finance Band 3 — 225

Cooke, Ken
Projects/PFI Band 3 — 692

Cooke, Stephen
Trusts & Personal Tax Band 2 — 813

Cooke, Stephen
Corporate Finance Band 1 — 203

Coombs, Monica
Litigation Band 2 — 543

Coombs, Richard
Corporate Finance Band 3 — 218

Cooper, Edward
Employment Band 5 — 298

Cooper, Ian
Fraud Band 2 — 395

Cooper, Janet
Employee Share Schemes Band 1 — 292

Cooper, Jon
Health & Safety Band 1 — 401

Cooper, Paul
Corporate Finance Band 1 — 218

1700

LEADING LAWYERS ■ INDEX

Coppen, Simon
Competition/Anti-trust **Band 1** — 166
Transport **Band 2** — 799

Coppin, Jonathan
Corporate Finance **Band 5** — 203

Coppinger, Vincent
Aviation **Up and coming** — 86

Copson, James
Family **Band 3** — 365

Corbett, Edward
Construction **Band 4** — 182

Corke, Andrew
Partnership **Band 1** — 597

Corker, David
Fraud **Band 1** — 393

Corlett, Andrew
Offshore: Corporate **Band 1** — 832

Cornes, David
ADR **Band 3** — 66
Construction **Band 3** — 177

Cornick, Timothy
Investment Funds **Band 2** — 498

Cornish, Sarah
Professional Negligence **Band 1** — 677

Cornthwaite, Richard
Fraud **Band 3** — 393

Cornwell, John
Family **Band 2** — 365

Cottis, Matthew
Banking & Finance **Band 3** — 92
Private Equity **Band 2** — 659

Cottrell, Patricia
Family **Band 2** — 371

Couchman, Nicholas
Sport **Band 5** — 767

Coulson, Edward W H
Professional Negligence **Band 2** — 678

Coulter, David
Projects/PFI **Band 4** — 690

Courtenay-Stamp, Bronwen
Travel **Band 2** — 806

Courtenay-Stamp, Jeremy
Advertising & Marketing **Band 3** — 51

Cowan, Andrew
Social Housing **Band 2** — 755

Cowan, Andrew
Social Housing **Band 2** — 760

Cowan, Matthew
E-commerce **Band 4** — 277

Cowell, Adam
Fraud **Band 2** — 393

Cowell, Martin
Licensing **Band 2** — 510

Cowen, Léonie
Local Government **Band 1** — 572

Cowie, Pauline
Franchising **Band 5** — 391

Cowper, Tony
Real Estate **Band 1** — 717

Cox, David
Litigation **Band 3** — 545

Cox, Helen
Pensions **Band 3** — 604

Cox, Ian
Real Estate **Up and coming** — 702

Cox, Simon F T
Investment Funds **Band 5** — 498

Cox, Tim
Pensions **Band 1** — 604

Cradick, Simon
Personal Injury **Band 1** — 623

Craft, Max
Employment **Band 3** — 304

Craig, Alec
Corporate Finance **Band 2** — 225

Craig, Nigel
Insolvency **Band 3** — 445

Craig, Seán
Construction **Band 1** — 191

Crane, David
Projects **Band 3** — 686

Cranfield, Richard
Corporate Finance **Band 4** — 203

Cranston, Peter
Insolvency **Band 1** — 451

Craven, Diana
Real Estate **Band 3** — 718

Crawford, Adrian
Employment **Band 2** — 304

Crawford, Allan
Personal Injury **Band 2** — 629

Crawford, Sandra
Litigation **Band 2** — 536

Crawford, Susan
Tax **Band 4** — 776

Creed, Angus
Banking & Finance **Band 1** — 103

Creighton, Simon
Human Rights **Band 3** — 410

Crier, Phil
Licensing **Band 1** — 505

Cripps, James
Investment Funds **Band 3** — 498

Critchlow, Julian
Construction **Band 3** — 177

Croall, Philip
Arbitration **Band 3** — 74

Crocker, Nic
Real Estate **Band 3** — 720

Croft, Anne
Employee Share Schemes **Band 2** — 292

Croker, Richard
Tax **Band 3** — 776

Croly, Colin
Insurance **Band 1** — 468

Crombie, June
Pensions **Band 2** — 610

Crook, Christopher
Personal Injury **Band 1** — 625

Crookes, Alan
Asset Finance **Band 6** — 79

Croome, Andrew
Banking & Finance **Band 1** — 99
Corporate Finance **Band 3** — 223

Cross, James
Licensing **Band 2** — 506

Cross, Jeremy
Banking & Finance **Band 3** — 96

Cross, John
Personal Injury **Band 1** — 630

Cross, Siobhan
Litigation **Band 3** — 545

Cross, Stefan
Employment **Band 1** — 315

Crossley, Peter
Litigation **Band 2** — 532

Croucher, Yvette
Insolvency **Band 5** — 441

Crown, Giles
Advertising **Up and coming** — 51

Crozier, John
Information Tech **Up and coming** — 428

Cruddace, Martin
Defamation **Band 5** — 268

Crump, Richard
Shipping **Band 1** — 741

Cuckson, David
Environment **Band 4** — 347

Cullen, Iain
Investment Funds **Band 2** — 498

Cullen, Joyce
Employment **Band 2** — 316
Litigation **Band 2** — 534

Cullinane, Lee
Banking & Finance **Band 5** — 92

Cumming, Donald
Energy **Band 1** — 341

Cumming, Kenny
Litigation **Band 1** — 551

Cummings, Gavin
Corporate Finance **Band 3** — 222

Cummins, Caroline
Construction **Band 4** — 177

Cummins, Jack
Licensing **Band 1** — 511

Cunliffe, Michael
Planning **Band 1** — 640

Cunningham, Kevin
Corporate Finance **Band 3** — 226

Cunningham, Neil
Corporate Finance **Band 3** — 229

Curnow, Tony
Local Government **Band 2** — 572
Planning **Band 2** — 640

Curran, Angela
Clinical Negligence **Band 2** — 147

Curry, Adam
Litigation **Band 3** — 536

Curtis, Anthony G
Licensing **Band 1** — 507

Curtis, Stephen
Capital Markets **Up and coming** — 114

Curtis, Tim
Media & Entertainment **Band 4** — 580

Curtis, Tony
ADR **Band 3** — 66

Cuthbert, Michael
Energy **Band 2** — 337

Cuthbertson, Ian
Insolvency **Band 1** — 454

Cutting, Michael
Competition/Anti-trust **Band 5** — 164

Cuttle, Barry M
Crime **Band 2** — 254

Cutts, Dan
Personal Injury **Band 3** — 624

D

Da Costa, Alastair
Corporate Finance **Band 1** — 226

Dabbs, Louise
Employment **Band 1** — 304

Dace, Nigel
Personal Injury **Band 2** — 624

Dadak, Roderick
Defamation **Band 5** — 268

Dakeyne, Mark
Real Estate **Band 1** — 715

Dale, Michael
Shipping **Band 1** — 745

Dale, Nigel A
Banking & Finance **Band 1** — 99

Dale, Stephanie
Employment **Band 3** — 298

Dalgarno, David
Employment **Band 4** — 298

Dalgarno, Leslie
Real Estate **Band 3** — 723

Dalgleish, Andrew
Trusts & Personal Tax **Band 2** — 821

Dalgleish, Douglas S
Licensing **Band 2** — 511

Dallas, James
Energy **Band 3** — 336

Dalrymple, Hew
Agriculture **Band 2** — 59

Daly, James
Asset Finance **Up and coming** — 80

Damms, Martin
Planning **Band 2** — 644

Dandridge, Nicola
Employment **Up and coming** — 298

Daniels, Paul
Employment **Band 5** — 298

Danilunas, Marija
Intellectual Property **Band 6** — 479

Dann, Adam
Energy **Band 4** — 336

D'Arcy, Adrienne
Clinical Negligence **Band 2** — 147

Darley, Mark
Projects **Band 5** — 686

Darlington, Michael C
Church **Band 1** — 137

Darwin, Andrew
Corporate Finance **Band 1** — 226

Davey, Catherine
Environment **Band 2** — 351

Davey, Henry
Energy: Electricity **Band 2** — 337
Energy: Oil & Gas **Band 3** — 336

Davey, Jonathan
Competition/Anti-trust **Band 2** — 167

Davidson, David
Family **Band 2** — 365

Davidson, John
Corporate Finance **Band 5** — 203
Insurance **Band 3** — 469

1701

www.ChambersandPartners.com

INDEX ■ LEADING LAWYERS

Davies, Andrew
Clinical Negligence **Band 2** — 144

Davies, Andrew
Real Estate **Band 1** — 710

Davies, Clive
Information Technology **Band 4** — 428

Davies, Edward
Construction **Band 1** — 186

Davies, Gwendoline
Litigation **Band 3** — 532

Davies, Ian
Pensions **Band 1** — 607

Davies, Isabel
Intellectual Property **Band 2** — 479

Davies, James
Employment **Band 1** — 298

Davies, Joanne
Employment **Band 4** — 308

Davies, Julie
Employment **Up and coming** — 307

Davies, Matthew
Immigration **Band 2** — 418

Davies, Mike
ADR **Band 3** — 67

Davies, Murray
Family **Band 1** — 370

Davies, Neil
Family **Band 3** — 367

Davies, Nicola
Offshore: Corporate **Band 3** — 832

Davies, Paul
Environment **Up and coming** — 347

Davies, Peter
Construction **Band 3** — 184
Litigation **Band 3** — 528

Davies, Rowland
Real Estate **Band 1** — 714

Davies, Suzanne
Licensing **Band 2** — 504

Davies, Tim
Licensing **Band 1** — 506

Davies, Valerie E M
Litigation: General **Band 1** — 518
Litigation: Banking **Band 3** — 538

Davis, Dai
Information Technology **Band 3** — 432

Davis, Elizabeth
Charities **Band 1** — 124

Davis, James
Corporate Finance **Band 5** — 203

Davis, Michael
Arbitration **Band 4** — 74
Construction **Band 2** — 177

Davis, Nigel R
Agriculture **Band 1** — 56

Davis, Richard
Pensions **Band 3** — 607

Davis, Sandra
Family **Band 2** — 365

Davis, Simon
Litigation: Banking **Band 4** — 538
Litigation: General **Band 5** — 518

Davis, Steven
Private Equity **Band 3** — 657

Davison, Andrew J
Corporate Finance **Band 2** — 227

Davison, Peter
Construction **Band 2** — 191

Dawes, Edward
Corporate Finance **Band 4** — 220

Dawson, William
Employment **Band 2** — 298

Day, Martyn
Administrative & Public Law **Band 3** — 41
Environment **Band 2** — 347
Personal Injury **Band 2** — 617
Product Liability **Band 1** — 667

Day, Philip J
Licensing **Band 2** — 505

Day, Sarah
Banking & Finance **Band 1** — 100

Dean, Kevin
Corporate Finance **Band 3** — 212

Dean, Michael
Competition/Anti-trust **Band 1** — 168

Dean, Veronica
Employment **Band 2** — 309

Deanesly, Clare
Environment **Band 3** — 347

Dearle, Marcus
Family **Band 3** — 365

Dearsley, Ken
Media & Entertainment **Band 2** — 580

De'Ath, Gary
Charities **Band 2** — 125

Dedman, Richard
Professional Negligence **Band 2** — 675

Deeny, Brian
Defamation **Band 2** — 270

Deering, Bob
Shipping **Band 2** — 741

Deighton, Jane
Human Rights **Band 3** — 410

Delahunty, Louise
Fraud **Band 2** — 393

de la Rue, Colin
Shipping **Band 4** — 741

Delemore, Ceri
Information Technology **Band 1** — 431
Intellectual Property **Band 1** — 482

Delves, Simon
Construction **Band 6** — 181

Dennis, Jeanette
Agriculture **Band 3** — 57

de Pury, Chris
Real Estate **Band 3** — 702

Desmond, Adrian
Clinical Negligence **Band 1** — 142
Personal Injury **Band 2** — 621

Devereux, Mark
Media & Entertainment **Band 2** — 580

Devine, Laura
Immigration **Band 2** — 416

Devitt, Paul
Corporate Finance **Band 2** — 225

Devlin, Michael
Family **Band 1** — 371

de Walden, Ludovic
Litigation **Band 5** — 518

Dewar, Kate
Social Housing **Band 2** — 760

De Wit, Elisa
Environment **One to watch** — 347

Diamond, W Maurice
Personal Injury **Band 1** — 629

Dias, James
Personal Injury **Band 1** — 628

Dick, Anne
Family **Band 1** — 373

Dickie, Paul
Shipping **Band 2** — 745

Dickinson, Alexander
Trusts & Personal Tax **Band 2** — 820

Dickinson, Graham
Personal Injury **Band 1** — 619

Dickinson, Malcolm
Education **Band 3** — 284

Dickinson, Nick
Licensing **Band 3** — 509

Dickinson, Peter
Telecommunications **Band 4** — 792

Dickson, Alastair
Private Equity **Band 1** — 657

Dickson, Ian
Corporate Finance **Band 3** — 229
Energy **Band 1** — 341

Dierden, Kenneth
Pensions **Band 2** — 604

Dillarstone, Robert
Employment **Band 3** — 310

Dillon, Paula
Real Estate **Band 2** — 720

Dimmick, Simon
Planning **Band 1** — 643

Dimsdale Gill, Angela
Litigation **Band 1** — 543

Dineley, Rachel
Employment **Band 5** — 298

Dingwall, Christian
Clinical Negligence **Band 2** — 141

Dingwall, Francis
Professional Negligence **Band 1** — 676

Dinsdale, Danelle
Information Technology **Band 5** — 428

d'Inverno, Isobel
Tax **Band 1** — 783

Diss, Paul
Banking & Finance **Band 6** — 92

Dix, John
Corporate Finance **Band 2** — 223

Dixon, Marian
Immigration **Band 3** — 416

Dobias, Michael
Insurance **Band 3** — 468

Dobie, James
Real Estate **Band 3** — 723

Dobson, Julian
Insolvency **Band 1** — 445

Dobson, Nicholas
Administrative & Public Law **Band 2** — 46
Local Government **Band 2** — 575

Docking, Peter
Pensions **Band 3** — 604

Dodd, Andrew
Family **Band 3** — 368

Dodds-Smith, Ian
Product Liability **Band 1** — 665

Dodgson, Robert
Real Estate **Up and coming** — 708

Dodson, Charles
ADR **Band 3** — 66

Doley, Cameron
Defamation **Up and coming** — 268

Dollimore, Jean
Charities **Band 3** — 123

Dolman, Robert
Trusts & Personal Tax **Band 4** — 813

Dolphin, Huw
Insolvency **Band 3** — 449

Don, Andrew
Family **Band 1** — 367

Donald, Hugh
Aviation **Band 1** — 87
Clinical Negligence **Band 1** — 148
Litigation **Band 3** — 534
Professional Negligence **Band 2** — 679

Donkersley, John
Immigration **Band 2** — 421

Donovan, Terry
Clinical Negligence **Band 3** — 140

Doolittle, Ian
Environment **Band 4** — 347
Local Government **Band 3** — 572
Social Housing **Band 2** — 753

Dorai-Raj, Dinesh
Shipping **One to watch** — 745

Doran, Frank
Financial Services **Band 2** — 389
Investment Funds **Band 3** — 500

Doran, Gill
Family **Band 1** — 365

Doran, Iain
Real Estate **Band 2** — 723

Doran, Nigel
Tax **Band 4** — 776

Dougherty, Paul
Offshore: Corporate **Band 3** — 832

Douglas, Alasdair
Tax **Band 4** — 776

Dowen, Denise
Environment **Band 2** — 355

Dowling, Susan
Licensing **Band 2** — 505

Downie, Gordon
Competition/Anti-trust **Band 2** — 168

Downing, Ian
Family **Band 2** — 368

Downing, Robbie
E-commerce **Band 3** — 277

Downs, William N
Corporate Finance **Band 4** — 225

Doyle, David
Offshore: Corporate **Band 1** — 832

Drake, Michael
Family **Band 2** — 365

Drake, Ronald
Employment **Band 4** — 313

Draycott, Shaun
Crime **Band 2** — 254

1702

LEADING LAWYERS ■ INDEX

Dresden, Brinsley
Advertising & Marketing **Band 2** — 51

Drew, Dean
Corporate Finance **Band 3** — 216

Drew, Jeff
Insolvency **Band 1** — 449

Drewe, David
Personal Injury **Band 2** — 628

Driscoll, Helen
Intellectual Property **Band 3** — 483

Drukarz, Daniel
Planning **Band 1** — 643

Drummond, Caroline
Real Estate **Up and coming** — 723

Drysdale, James
Agriculture **Band 3** — 59

Dudley, Andrew
Social Housing **Band 3** — 758

Du-Feu, Viv
Employment **Band 1** — 308

Duff, Alistair
Sport **Band 2** — 770

Duff, Alistair
Crime **Band 2** — 255

Duff, John
Insurance **Band 1** — 468

Dufficy, Frank
Projects/PFI **Band 2** — 690

Dukes, Rodney
Banking & Finance **Band 6** — 92

Duncan, Michael G
Banking & Finance **Band 2** — 92

Duncan, Michelle
Litigation **Up and coming** — 538

Duncan, Nikki
Employment **Band 1** — 307

Duncan, Susan
Tax **Band 4** — 776

Dunlop, Stewart
Capital Markets **Band 4** — 111

Dunn, Chris
Shipping **Band 5** — 741
Transport **Band 2** — 796

Dunn, Ian
Real Estate **Band 3** — 712

Dunn, John
Real Estate **Band 2** — 712

Dunne, Frank
Shipping **Band 2** — 743

Dunnigan, David
Capital Markets **Band 2** — 111

Dunsire, David
Investment Funds **Band 3** — 500

Durkin, Joseph
Parliamentary **Band 1** — 593

Dutton, Paul
Insolvency **Band 4** — 452

Dwyer, Maurice
Corporate Finance **Band 1** — 220

Dyer, Carl
Planning **Band 2** — 640

Dyer, Nick
Social Housing **Band 2** — 757

Dyson, Henry
Clinical Negligence **Band 3** — 140

E

Eardley, Kathryn
Licensing **Band 2** — 506

Earle, Rupert
Advertising & Marketing **Band 3** — 51

East, Lindsay
Shipping **Band 3** — 741

Eastgate, Andrew
Corporate Finance **Band 2** — 220

Easton, Ewan
Litigation: Real Estate **Band 1** — 551
Litigation: General **Band 2** — 534

Eastwell, Nicholas W
Capital Markets **Band 1** — 111

Eaton, John
Trusts & Personal Tax **Band 2** — 820

Eatough, David
Capital Markets **Band 5** — 111

Eddy, Alison
Clinical Negligence **Band 3** — 140

Eddy, Catherine
Family **Band 1** — 367

Edgar, Andrew
Product Liability **Band 5** — 665

Edge, Mike
Real Estate **Band 5** — 718

Edge, Steve
Tax **Star** — 776

Edlmann, Stephen
Capital Markets **Band 2** — 111

Edmond, John
Planning **Band 3** — 644

Edmonds, Steven
Product Liability **Band 3** — 669

Edney, Robert
Licensing **Band 2** — 504

Edwards, Anthony
Crime **Band 2** — 251

Edwards, Jeremy
Asset Finance **Band 3** — 79

Edwards, John
Telecommunications **Band 3** — 792

Edwards, Jonathan
Banking & Finance **Band 3** — 99

Edwards, Julia
Employment **Band 4** — 309

Edwards, Martin
Employment **Band 2** — 312

Edwards, Martin
Litigation **Up and coming** — 549

Edwards, Peter
Healthcare **Band 2** — 406

Edwards, Robert
Family **Band 2** — 369

Edwards, Stephen
Media & Entertainment **Band 2** — 581

Egan, Sean
Media & Entertainment **Band 2** — 585

Elborne, Mark
Insurance **Band 2** — 468
Professional Negligence **Band 2** — 675

Elder, Ian
Energy: Electricity **Band 1** — 337
Energy: Oil & Gas **Band 3** — 336

Eldergill, Anselm
Healthcare **Band 1** — 406

Ellacott, Sara
Information Technology **Band 2** — 430

Ellard, John
Corporate Finance **Band 5** — 203
Transport **Band 1** — 799

Ellerman, Paul
Employee Share Schemes **Band 4** — 292

Elliker, Michael
Health & Safety **Band 1** — 402

Elliott, Laurence
Insolvency **Up and coming** — 441

Elliott, Martin
Real Estate **Band 1** — 702

Elliott, Penelope
Agriculture **Band 3** — 53

Elliott, Peter
Tax **Band 4** — 776

Elliott, Robert
Banking & Finance **Band 5** — 92
Insolvency **Band 1** — 441

Elliott, Robert
Litigation **Band 1** — 533

Ellis, Jon
Projects/PFI **Band 3** — 690

Ellis, Michael
Real Estate **Band 3** — 708

Ellis, Peter
Intellectual Property **Band 2** — 483

Elman, Jonathan
Tax **Band 2** — 776

Elphicke, Natalie
Social Housing **One to watch** — 755

Elsey, Mark
Projects/PFI **Band 1** — 690

Elvy, Mark
Product Liability **Band 4** — 665

Emmerson, John
Trusts & Personal Tax **Band 2** — 817

Emmerson, Tim
Corporate Finance **Band 2** — 203

Emmett, Paul
Corporate Finance **Band 2** — 226

Emmott, Jeremy
Employment **Band 3** — 313

Engert, Nick
Planning **Band 1** — 643

England, Richard
Clinical Negligence **Band 2** — 143

Enock, Roger
Insurance **Band 3** — 468

Enright, Joanna
Environment **One to watch** — 347

Enser, John
E-commerce **Band 1** — 277

Ereira, David
Banking & Finance **Band 1** — 92

Erskine, Sarah
Family **Band 2** — 373

Etchells, Simon
Real Estate **Band 4** — 723

Ettinger, Colin
Personal Injury **Band 1** — 617

Evagora, Kyri
Commodities **Band 3** — 158

Evans, Chris
Social Housing **Band 3** — 753

Evans, Della
Agriculture **Band 2** — 55

Evans, Douglas
Planning **Band 3** — 640

Evans, Edward
Banking & Finance **Band 3** — 92

Evans, Eric
Administrative & Public Law **Band 1** — 45
Local Government **Band 1** — 574
Planning **Band 1** — 644
Projects/PFI **Band 2** — 691
Real Estate **Band 3** — 714

Evans, Jacqueline
Private Equity **Up and coming** — 659

Evans, John
Shipping **Band 2** — 741

Evans, John
Product Liability **Band 5** — 665

Evans, Katherine
Planning **Band 2** — 643

Evans, Martin
Planning **Band 3** — 640

Evans, Michael
Trusts & Personal Tax **Band 2** — 817

Evans, Rod
Personal Injury **Band 1** — 620

Evans, Simon
Employee Share Schemes **Band 2** — 292

Evans, Stephen
Clinical Negligence **Band 2** — 147

Evans, Stuart
Corporate Finance **Band 5** — 203

Evason, John
Employment **Up and coming** — 298

Evenett, Hilary
Insurance **Band 2** — 469

Everson, Ingrid
Pensions **Band 3** — 607

Ewart, Peter
Trusts & Personal Tax **Band 3** — 819

Ewing, Mark
Social Housing **Band 2** — 760

F

Fabian, Mark
Real Estate **Band 3** — 712

Fagan, Neil
Litigation: Banking **Band 2** — 518
Litigation: General **Band 2** — 538

Fagelson, Ian
Corporate Finance **Band 3** — 212

Fairclough, Neville
Church **Band 3** — 137

Fairley, Ross
Environment **Band 1** — 347

Falk, Sarah
Tax **Band 2** — 776

Falkner, James
Litigation **Band 1** — 549

INDEX ■ LEADING LAWYERS

Falkus, Bryony
Corporate Finance Band 3 — 223

Fallon, Liz
Pensions Band 2 — 607

Fanson, David
Crime Band 1 — 252

Faris, Neil
Administrative & Public Law Band 1 — 48
Environment Band 1 — 357
Real Estate Band 3 — 724

Farquharson-Black, Elaine
Planning Band 4 — 648

Farr, John
Employment Band 2 — 298

Farr, Nigel
Investment Funds Band 1 — 498

Farrant, Patrick
Intellectual Property Band 1 — 484

Farrell, Patrick
Aviation: Regulatory Band 2 — 85
Aviation: Insurance Band 4 — 86
Travel Band 3 — 805

Farren, Miles
Agriculture Band 3 — 55

Farthing, Peter
Insurance Band 3 — 466

Faulds, Ann
Planning Band 1 — 648

Fawke, Derek
Banking & Finance One to watch — 99

Fazan, Claire
Clinical Negligence Band 1 — 140

Fea, Michael
Charities Band 2 — 126

Fear, Jeremy
Transport Band 3 — 798

Feeny, Mark
Trusts & Personal Tax Band 2 — 820

Feinstein, Naomi
Employment Band 4 — 298

Fellingham, Michael
Agriculture Band 1 — 54
Trusts & Personal Tax Band 2 — 815

Fellows, Alison
Projects/PFI Band 2 — 692

Fenn, Jonathan
Employee Share Schemes Band 2 — 292
Pensions Band 4 — 604

Fenton, Jonathan
Pensions Band 3 — 604

Ferguson, Gerry M
Clinical Negligence Band 2 — 143

Ferguson, Ian
Telecommunications Band 3 — 792

Fergusson, Richard
Insolvency Up and coming — 451

Fernandez Lewis, Jon
Corporate Finance Band 4 — 219

Ferrie, Audrey
Licensing Band 3 — 511

Field, Christopher
Real Estate Band 2 — 702

Field, Ian
Insolvency Band 5 — 441

Field, Rena
Clinical Negligence Band 2 — 141

Field, Sally
Intellectual Property Band 1 — 479

Fife, Peter R G
Family Band 3 — 370

Fife, Robert
Personal Injury Band 2 — 629

Finbow, Roger
Competition/Anti-trust Band 3 — 164

Finch, Margaret
Immigration Band 1 — 420

Finch, Paul
Planning Band 1 — 647

Finch, Robert
Real Estate Band 1 — 702

Finch, Stephen
Asset Finance Band 2 — 81

Fincham, Anthony
ADR Band 2 — 66

Findlay, Richard
Media & Entertainment Band 1 — 586

Findley, Christopher
Agriculture Band 2 — 53

Finkler, Deborah
Litigation: Banking Band 3 — 541
Litigation: Civil Fraud Band 3 — 538
Litigation: General Band 5 — 518

Finlay, Peter
Projects Band 3 — 686

Finney, Robert
Commodities Band 1 — 159

Finnigan, Kevin
Personal Injury Band 1 — 626

Firth, Beverley
Planning Band 2 — 645

Firth, Simon
Capital Markets Band 1 — 116
Commodities Band 2 — 159

Fischl, Nicolas
Corporate Finance Band 1 — 223

Fisher, Ian
Crime Band 1 — 253

Fisher, Jeremy
Family Band 2 — 365

Fisher, Michael
Crime Band 2 — 251

Fisher, Nicholas
Shipping Band 3 — 741

Fitton, Roger
Social Housing Band 3 — 753

Fitzgerald, Peter R
Agriculture Band 3 — 55
Trusts & Personal Tax Band 1 — 817

Fitzmaurice, Anthony
Real Estate Band 4 — 718

Fitzpatrick, Nick
Sport Band 4 — 767

Fitzpatrick, Stuart
Shipping Band 6 — 741

Fitzsimmons, Anthony
Aviation Band 4 — 86

Flanagan, Tom
Employment Band 4 — 298

Fleck, Richard
Competition/Anti-trust Band 5 — 164

Fleet, Terry
Construction Band 3 — 177

Fleming, Andrew
Pensions Band 1 — 610

Fletcher, Alistair G
Social Housing Band 3 — 759

Fletcher, Ian
Insolvency Band 4 — 441

Fletcher, Kevin
Employment Band 3 — 315

Fletcher, Phillip
Projects Band 3 — 686

Fletcher, Rod
Fraud Band 2 — 393

Fletcher, Simon
Shipping Band 6 — 741

Flint, David
Information Technology Band 1 — 433
Insolvency Band 2 — 454
Intellectual Property Band 2 — 486

Flint, Peter
Family Band 2 — 370

Flounders, Andrew
Real Estate Band 2 — 720

Flynn, John
Corporate Finance Band 2 — 227

Fogleman, Valerie
Environment Band 2 — 347

Follett, Martin
Church Band 2 — 135

Follis, Richard
Clinical Negligence Band 1 — 144

Fongenie, Wesley
Planning Band 4 — 640

Foord, Roland
Litigation Band 4 — 538

Forbes, Sandra
Banking & Finance Band 1 — 96

Ford, John
Education Band 3 — 283

Ford, Lindsay
Family Band 3 — 369

Ford, Peter
Pensions Band 2 — 604

Fordham, John
Litigation: Civil Fraud Band 2 — 541
Litigation: General Band 2 — 518
Litigation: Banking Band 3 — 538

Forge, Anna
Local Government Band 2 — 572

Forrest, Ian
Pensions Band 1 — 607

Forryan, Andrew
Capital Markets Band 3 — 114

Forster, Malcolm
Environment Band 2 — 347

Fortnam, Jonathan
Litigation Up and coming — 528

Foster, Stephen
Family Band 1 — 367

Foster, Stephen
Insolvency Band 2 — 441

Fotheringham, John M
Family Band 3 — 373

Fowler, Pauline
Family Band 2 — 365

Fox, Alasdair
Agriculture Band 1 — 59

Fox, Brendan
Construction Band 2 — 191
Litigation Band 2 — 536

Fox, Jason
Projects Band 2 — 686
Projects/PFI Band 4 — 690

Fox, Julie
Charities Band 2 — 126

Fox, Paul
Defamation Band 5 — 268

Fox, Ronnie
Employment Band 4 — 298
Partnership Band 1 — 596

Fox, Ruth
Financial Services Band 3 — 386

Fox, Stephen
Fraud Band 2 — 395

Fox-Edwards, Jane
Litigation Band 3 — 545

Francies, Michael
Corporate Finance Band 1 — 208

Francis, Barry
Healthcare Band 3 — 404
Projects/PFI Band 4 — 690

Francis, Penelope
Litigation Band 2 — 545

Francis, Vanessa
Crime Band 1 — 252

Frank, David
Capital Markets Band 3 — 111

Frankland, Matthew
Fraud Band 3 — 393

Franklin, Mark
Aviation Band 3 — 86

Franks, David
Media & Entertainment Band 2 — 585

Fraser, David
Arbitration Band 5 — 74
Litigation Band 6 — 518

Fraser, Jane
Employment Up and coming — 316

Fraser, Moira
Planning Band 4 — 640

Fraser, Ross
Tax Band 3 — 776

Free, Dominic
Media & Entertainment Band 2 — 584

Freedman, Len
Social Housing Band 1 — 760

Freeland, Rowan
Intellectual Property Band 2 — 479

Freeman, Adam
Banking & Finance Up and coming — 92
Private Equity Up and coming — 659

Freeman, Bill
Licensing Band 1 — 507

Freeman, Keith Michael
Licensing Band 2 — 510

Freeman, Mark
Asset Finance Band 6 — 79

Freeman, Nicholas
Crime Band 2 — 254

1704

LEADING LAWYERS — INDEX

Freeman, Peter — Competition/Anti-trust Band 1 — 164
Freeman, Rod — Product Liability Up and coming — 665
French, Douglas — Tax Band 1 — 776
French, Matthew — Insolvency Band 2 — 441
Freyne, Michele — Litigation Band 2 — 545
Friedman, Paul — Litigation Band 6 — 518
Friel, Daniel — Tax Band 5 — 776
Friend, Mark — Competition/Anti-trust Band 3 — 164
Frier, George — Corporate Finance Band 4 — 229
Frieze, Steven — Insolvency Band 2 — 451
Frith, Stuart — Insolvency Band 2 — 451
Frome, Nicholas P — Insolvency Band 1 — 441
Frost, Peter — Employment Band 1 — 298
Frydenson, Henry — Trusts & Personal Tax Band 5 — 813
Fuller, Geoff — Capital Markets Band 3 — 114
Fullerlove, Michael — Trusts & Personal Tax Band 2 — 817
Fulton, Richard — Corporate Finance Band 1 — 231
Fulton, Robin — Trusts & Personal Tax Band 2 — 821
Furber, James — Agriculture Band 2 — 53
Furman, Mark — Banking & Finance Band 5 — 92
Furnivall, Peter — Trusts & Personal Tax Band 2 — 819
Fynn, Lionel — Licensing Band 1 — 505

G

Gadsby, Gillian — Clinical Negligence Band 2 — 145
Gaines, Alison — Asset Finance Band 3 — 81
Gaines, Keith — Insolvency Band 4 — 441; Litigation Band 2 — 541
Gaines, Peter — Projects Band 4 — 686
Gale, Stephen — Insolvency Band 2 — 441
Gallagher, Yvonne — Employment Band 5 — 298
Gallimore, Michael — Planning Band 1 — 640
Galloway, Diane — Commodities Band 1 — 158

Garbutt, John — Environment Band 3 — 347
Garcia, Dario — Tax Band 2 — 776
Gardner, Ceris — Trusts & Personal Tax Band 4 — 813
Gardner, Nick — Information Technology Band 3 — 428
Gardner, Paul — Information Technology Band 5 — 428
Gare, Stephen — Intellectual Property Band 6 — 479
Garner, Clive — Travel Band 3 — 806
Garnett, Chris J — Corporate Finance Band 3 — 220
Garnham, Caroline — Trusts & Personal Tax Band 4 — 813
Garrett, Graeme — Personal Injury Band 2 — 628
Garrett, Robin — Real Estate Band 1 — 723
Garrett, Susan — Litigation Up and coming — 532
Garston, Clive R — Corporate Finance Band 3 — 225
Garthwaite, Helen — Construction Band 6 — 177
Garvie, Carl — Litigation Band 1 — 528
Gaskell, Mike — Social Housing Band 1 — 759
Gaskill, Shelagh — Information Technology Band 4 — 428
Gatenby, John — ADR Band 2 — 67; Litigation Band 2 — 530
Gates, Ellen — Projects/PFI Band 5 — 690
Gates, Kathryn — Real Estate Band 3 — 714
Gates, Sean — Aviation Band 1 — 86
Gaul, Patrick — Professional Negligence Band 2 — 678
Gault, Ian — Pensions Band 3 — 604
Gaunt, John R T — Licensing Band 2 — 510
Gawade, Jeremy — Media & Entertainment Band 4 — 580
Gay, Mark — Sport Band 1 — 767
Gee, Tim — Corporate Finance Band 4 — 208
Geen, Jonathan — Real Estate Band 2 — 714
Geffen, Charles — Private Equity Band 1 — 657
Gemmill, Thomas — Defamation Band 2 — 270
Gentle, Stephen — Fraud Up and coming — 393
George, Jane — Transport Band 5 — 798

Gerrard, Neil — Litigation Band 2 — 541
Gervasio, James — Financial Services Band 1 — 388
Gerwat, Richard — Offshore: Corporate Band 2 — 832
Gething, Heather — Tax Band 3 — 776
Ghee, Tony — Media & Entertainment Band 1 — 581
Gherson, Roger — Immigration Band 4 — 416
Ghirardani, Paolo — Shipping Band 4 — 741
Gibb, Andrew — Family Band 2 — 373
Gibb, Jeremy — Asset Finance Band 3 — 79; Shipping Band 1 — 743
Gibb, Stephen — Corporate Finance Band 3 — 229
Gibbons, Anthony — Clinical Negligence Band 1 — 146
Gibbs, Kevin — Environment Band 1 — 351; Planning Band 2 — 643
Gibbs, Robert — Real Estate Band 2 — 717
Gibbs, Ronald — Asset Finance Band 3 — 79
Gibson, David — Insolvency Band 3 — 454
Gibson, Michael — Construction Band 4 — 177
Gibson, Michael — Personal Injury Band 1 — 630
Gibson, Robert — Employment Band 2 — 315
Gibson, Simon — Professional Negligence Band 4 — 675
Gibson-Bolton, Elaine — Competition Up and coming — 164
Gidney, David — Real Estate Band 2 — 712
Gieve, Katherine — Family Band 2 — 365
Gilbert, Ian — Corporate Finance Band 2 — 226
Gilbert, Ralph — Litigation Band 3 — 532
Gilbertson, Kathryn — Product Liability Band 3 — 669
Gilbey, Iain — Planning Band 3 — 644
Gilfedder, Brian — Crime Band 2 — 255
Gill, Jaswinder — Education Band 3 — 283
Gill, Judith A E — Arbitration Band 2 — 74; Litigation Band 6 — 518
Gill, Julian — Insolvency Band 3 — 452

Gill, Mark — Insolvency Band 4 — 441; Litigation Band 3 — 538
Gillery, Bryan — Real Estate Band 1 — 717
Gilles, June — Planning Band 4 — 648
Gillespie, Michael — Employment Band 3 — 309
Gillespie, Stephen — Banking & Finance Band 1 — 92; Private Equity Band 1 — 659; Projects Band 2 — 686
Gillibrand, Martin — Agriculture Band 1 — 57
Gillingham, Adam — Agriculture Band 4 — 59
Gilmore, Laurence — Media & Entertainment Band 2 — 584
Gilmour, Moira — Telecommunications Band 4 — 792
Gilthorpe, Ian — Corporate Finance Band 3 — 227
Gimblett, Richard — Aviation: Regulatory Band 2 — 85; Aviation: Insurance Band 3 — 86; Travel Band 2 — 805
Ginsberg, Roy — Shipping Band 2 — 741
Gittings, Simon — Agriculture Band 2 — 58
Gizzi, Julian — Education Band 1 — 282
Glaister, Anthony — ADR Band 2 — 67
Glaister, William — Asset Finance Band 5 — 79
Glass, Jane — Fraud Up and coming — 393
Glazebrook, Peter — Licensing Band 1 — 504
Glazier, Barry — Trusts & Personal Tax Band 2 — 815
Gleeson, Simon — Financial Services Up and coming — 386
Glen, Marian — Corporate Finance Band 3 — 229
Glendinning, David — Family Band 2 — 373
Glick, David — Media & Entertainment Band 2 — 584
Glover, Jason — Private Equity Band 2 — 661
Glynn, Andrew — Real Estate Band 3 — 712
Gniadkowski, Stan — Projects/PFI Band 2 — 690; Real Estate Band 2 — 702
Goalen, Iain — Private Equity Band 4 — 659
Goddard, John — Litigation Band 4 — 538
Godden, Richard — Corporate Finance Band 2 — 203; Partnership Band 1 — 596

www.ChambersandPartners.com

1705

INDEX ■ LEADING LAWYERS

Godfrey, Christopher
Corporate Finance Band 1 — 218
Investment Funds Band 1 — 499

Godfrey, Patricia
Insolvency Band 4 — 441

Goff, Tony
Personal Injury Band 1 — 620

Gold, Antony
Intellectual Property Band 2 — 484

Gold, David
Litigation Star — 518
Partnership Band 2 — 596

Gold, Josyane
Private Equity Band 3 — 661

Gold, Richard
Education Band 1 — 284

Goldberg, Mel
Sport Band 3 — 767

Goldberg, Simon
Media & Entertainment Band 4 — 580

Goldburn, Tim
Clinical Negligence Band 2 — 143

Golden, Jeffrey
Capital Markets Band 1 — 116

Goldie, Ian
Projects/PFI Band 5 — 690

Goldman, Ruth
Pensions Band 1 — 604

Goldspink, Robert
Insurance Band 3 — 468
Litigation Band 3 — 518

Good, Diana
Litigation: Banking Band 3 — 518
Litigation: General Band 3 — 538

Good, Natasha
Telecommunications Up and coming — 792

Goodall, Caroline
Corporate Finance Band 5 — 203

Goode, Naomi
Social Housing Band 3 — 753

Goodger, Ben
Information Technology Band 3 — 430

Goodman, David
Planning Band 3 — 646

Goodman, Dawn
Trusts & Personal Tax Band 5 — 813

Goodman, Nick
Insolvency Band 4 — 450

Goodman, Stephen
Real Estate Band 1 — 718

Goodrham, Stephen
Litigation Band 4 — 528

Goodwill, Christopher
Employment Up and coming — 298

Goodwill, Peter
Personal Injury Band 2 — 627

Goodwin, Peter
Trusts & Personal Tax Band 4 — 813

Gordon, Ian
Pensions Band 1 — 610
Tax Band 1 — 783

Gordon, John Gerard
Insolvency Band 1 — 454

Gordon-Saker, Paul
Insolvency Band 6 — 441

Gorlov, Alison
Parliamentary & Public Aff Band 2 — 593

Gornall-King, William
Information Technology Band 2 — 430

Gorrie, Euan
Banking & Finance Band 5 — 92
Private Equity Band 2 — 659

Gosling, James
Shipping Band 1 — 741

Gosling, John
Litigation Band 2 — 530

Gosnay, Andrew
Banking & Finance Band 3 — 99

Gossling, Margaret
Projects Band 4 — 686

Gostyn, Antony
Media & Entertainment Band 3 — 580

Gotelee, Michael
Transport Band 3 — 798

Goulborn, Caroline
Crime Band 1 — 253

Gould, Jean
Administrative & Public Law Band 1 — 45

Gould, Nicholas
Construction Band 3 — 177

Gould, Terry
Corporate Finance Band 1 — 223

Goulding, Jane
Personal Injury Band 2 — 623

Gowan, Daniel
Construction Band 5 — 177

Gowans, Andrew
Corporate Finance Band 1 — 216

Gowar, Martyn
Trusts & Personal Tax Band 1 — 813

Goyder, Bill
ADR Band 2 — 67

Grabiner, Martin
Real Estate Band 3 — 720

Grafton Green, Paddy
Media & Entertainment Band 1 — 584

Graham, Caroline J M
Family Band 2 — 373

Graham, Drysdale
Projects/PFI Band 3 — 693

Graham, Ian
Social Housing Band 1 — 753

Graham, Ronald
Pensions Band 2 — 608

Graham, Rory
Information Technology Band 3 — 428

Grandison, Richard
Litigation: Banking Band 3 — 538
Litigation: General Band 6 — 518

Grant, Alison
Professional Negligence Band 2 — 679

Grant, Gregor
Intellectual Property Band 1 — 479

Grant, James
Environment Band 3 — 356
Planning Band 4 — 648

Grant, Mark
Pensions Band 4 — 604

Grant, Mike
Professional Negligence Band 2 — 678

Grant, Rachel
Insolvency Band 3 — 454

Grassie, Gill
Intellectual Property Band 2 — 486

Graves, Patrick
Corporate Finance Band 2 — 218

Gravill, Robert
Pensions Band 3 — 607

Gray, Amanda
Banking & Finance Up and coming — 99

Gray, Colin
Corporate Finance Band 2 — 229

Gray, David
Litigation Band 4 — 530

Gray, David
Insolvency Up and coming — 450

Gray, David
Immigration Band 1 — 421

Gray, David J
Employment Band 3 — 318

Gray, Edward
Shipping Band 5 — 741

Gray, Nick
Litigation Band 6 — 518

Gray, Richard
Corporate Finance Band 2 — 231

Gray, Tim
Family Band 1 — 373

Grayston, Clare
Corporate Finance Band 2 — 212

Greaves, Adam
Private Equity Band 5 — 657

Greaves, Judith
Employee Share Schemes Band 1 — 293
Tax Band 2 — 782

Green, Andy
Real Estate Band 5 — 718

Green, David
Employment Band 3 — 298

Green, Gilbert
Real Estate Band 3 — 708

Green, Guy
Corporate Finance Band 3 — 220

Green, Lawrence
Employee Share Schemes Band 2 — 293

Green, Martin
Trusts & Personal Tax Band 2 — 818

Green, Michael
Family Band 2 — 371

Greenbank, Ashley
Tax Band 4 — 776

Greene, Edward
Capital Markets Band 4 — 111

Greenfield, G N Ian
Corporate Finance Band 3 — 226

Greenlees, Mark
Pensions Band 1 — 604

Greenley, Simon
Insurance Band 1 — 466
Professional Negligence Band 1 — 675

Greeno, Ted
Energy Band 3 — 336
Litigation Band 1 — 518

Greensmith, Nicholas
Shipping Band 4 — 741

Greenstreet, Ian Alexander
Pensions Band 4 — 604

Greenwood, Brian
Environment Band 4 — 347
Planning Band 1 — 640

Greenwood, Duncan
Professional Negligence Band 1 — 678

Gregan, Paddy
Partnership Band 1 — 599

Gregg, Andrew
Licensing Band 2 — 506
Product Liability Band 3 — 669

Gregory, Andrew
Insolvency Band 3 — 450

Gregory, Deborah
Insolvency Band 3 — 441

Gregory, Keith
Tax Up and coming — 776

Gregory, Lesley
Corporate Finance Band 1 — 212

Gregory, Tony
Personal Injury Band 2 — 627

Gregory-Jones, Rosemary
Family Band 2 — 369

Grew, Chris
E-commerce Up and coming — 277

Grey, Rupert
Defamation Band 3 — 268

Grice, Helen
Health & Safety Up and coming — 402

Grier, Ian Stephen
Insolvency Band 5 — 441

Grierson, Christopher
Insolvency Band 4 — 441
Litigation Band 3 — 518

Griffin, Paul
Energy: Oil & Gas Band 1 — 336
Energy: Electricity Band 3 — 337

Griffiths, David
Pensions Band 2 — 608

Griffiths, David
E-commerce Band 3 — 277
Information Technology Band 2 — 428

Griffiths, John
Clinical Negligence Band 1 — 148
Employment Band 3 — 316

Griffiths, Marian
Planning Band 4 — 646

Griffiths, Paul
Shipping Band 5 — 741

Griffiths, Trevor
Administrative & Public Law Band 3 — 41
Local Government Band 2 — 572

Grisewood, Rebecca
Corporate Finance Band 4 — 225

Grogan, Peter
Crime Band 1 — 254

Gronow, Simon
Corporate Finance Band 3 — 220

Groom, Stephen
Advertising & Marketing Band 1 — 51

Grosz, Stephen
Administrative & Public Law Band 1 — 41
Human Rights Band 1 — 410

Gryk, Wesley
Immigration Band 1 — 418

1706

LEADING LAWYERS — INDEX

Guedalla, Vicky
Immigration **Band 1** — 418

Guest, Jonathan
Asset Finance **Band 2** — 81

Guild, Elspeth
Immigration **Band 1** — 416

Gummers, Eric
Travel **Band 2** — 808

Gunn, David
Real Estate **Band 1** — 712

Gunn, Sheila
Employment **Band 2** — 316

Guppy, W Nicholas
Construction **Band 3** — 183

Gwilliam, Michael
Travel **Band 3** — 805

Gwynne, Richard
Litigation **Band 4** — 538

Gwynne, Simon
Transport **Band 3** — 799

H

Haddock, Simon A
Capital Markets **Band 1** — 116

Haftke, Mark
E-commerce **Band 2** — 277

Haggett, Paul
Litigation **Band 1** — 525

Hale, Chris
Private Equity **Band 2** — 657

Hale, Paul
Tax **Band 2** — 776

Hall, Antony
Clinical Negligence **Band 1** — 144

Hall, Brendan JC
Trusts & Personal Tax **Band 5** — 813

Hall, Brian
Planning **Band 2** — 640

Hall, Daniel
Corporate Finance **Band 2** — 225

Hall, Gareth
Social Housing **Band 3** — 753

Hall, Gordon
Asset Finance **Band 5** — 79

Hall, Graham
Offshore: Corporate **Band 1** — 831

Hall, James
Church **Band 3** — 136

Hall, John
Insurance **Band 2** — 468

Hall, John
Education **Star** — 282

Hall, Peter
Projects **Band 5** — 686

Hall, Priscilla
Construction **Band 3** — 183

Hall, Simon
Asset Finance **Band 1** — 79

Hall, Stuart
Professional Negligence **Band 2** — 675

Hallam, Catherine
Family **Band 1** — 368

Hallam, Murray
Trusts & Personal Tax **Band 4** — 813

Hallam, Richard
Crime **Band 3** — 251

Hallam, Robin
Asset Finance **Band 3** — 79

Hallatt, Diane
Healthcare **Band 1** — 406

Halliwell, Tilly
Licensing **Band 2** — 504

Hall-Smith, Vanessa
Advertising & Marketing **Band 2** — 51

Hallsworth, Chris
Transport **Band 4** — 798

Hally, Paul
Insolvency **Band 2** — 454

Halpin, Peter
Corporate Finance **Band 3** — 225

Ham, Brian
Real Estate **Band 3** — 724

Ham, Neil
Litigation **Band 2** — 548

Hambleton, Jonathan
Corporate Finance **Band 3** — 216

Hamblin, Julian
Information Technology **Band 1** — 430

Hamer, Melanie
Family **Band 3** — 369

Hamill, Robert
Corporate Finance **Band 4** — 208

Hamilton, Dan
Insolvency **Band 4** — 441

Hamilton, Keith
Real Estate **Band 2** — 717

Hamilton, Sophie
Real Estate **Band 1** — 702

Hamlett, David
Energy **Band 1** — 339

Hand, Catherine
Local Government **Band 3** — 572
Social Housing **Band 2** — 753

Handley, Richard
Real Estate **Band 3** — 712

Handling, Erica
Capital Markets **Band 3** — 114

Handy, David
Banking & Finance **Up and coming** — 100

Haniford, Paul
Real Estate **Band 1** — 723

Hanley, Christine
Construction **Band 3** — 183

Hanley, Michael
Immigration **Band 2** — 418

Hannam, Andrew
Clinical Negligence **Band 2** — 143

Hansell, Matthew
Trusts & Personal Tax **Band 1** — 818

Hanslip Ward, Matthew
Transport **Band 4** — 799

Hanson, Christopher
Media & Entertainment **Band 4** — 580

Hanson, Marc
Construction **Up and coming** — 177

Hantom, Charles
Employment **Band 1** — 312

Hanton, Bruce
Private Equity **Band 2** — 657

Haque, Tony
Immigration **Band 2** — 416

Harbottle, James
Agriculture **Band 3** — 57

Harcombe, Laura
Travel **Up and coming** — 805

Harcus, James
Family **Band 2** — 365

Hardie, David
Corporate Finance **Band 3** — 229

Harding, Andrew
Personal Injury **Band 1** — 622

Harding, John
Fraud **Band 3** — 393

Harding, Mark
Commodities **Band 1** — 159
Financial Services **Band 5** — 386

Harding, Nicola
Church **Band 2** — 137

Hardingham, Adrian
Transport **Band 1** — 796

Hardwick, Michael J
Tax **Band 3** — 776

Hardy, Tim
Insurance **Band 3** — 466

Hargreave, R Hume M
Agriculture **Band 1** — 58

Hargreaves, Colin
Tax **Band 5** — 776

Harker, Chris
Banking & Finance **Band 1** — 101
Corporate Finance **Band 3** — 227

Harkness, David
Tax **Band 5** — 776

Harling, Marcus
Construction **Band 1** — 183

Harman, James
Media & Entertainment **Band 2** — 584

Harman, Martin
Construction **Band 2** — 177

Harper, David
Employment **Band 3** — 298

Harper, Mark
Family **Band 2** — 365

Harrington, Alison
Information Technology **Band 1** — 430
Intellectual Property **Band 2** — 481

Harrington, Dan
Sport **Band 5** — 767

Harris, Adam
Construction **Band 2** — 183

Harris, Andrew
Litigation **Band 1** — 530

Harris, Anne
Transport **Band 2** — 799

Harris, Anthony
Insolvency **Band 4** — 447

Harris, Clare
Insolvency **Band 4** — 447

Harris, David
Product Liability **Band 2** — 667

Harris, Edward
Agriculture **Band 1** — 55

Harris, Gordon
Franchising **Band 4** — 391
Intellectual Property **Band 1** — 483

Harris, Graham
Shipping **Band 5** — 741

Harris, Jacqueline
Planning **Band 4** — 648

Harris, Jeremy
Pensions **Band 3** — 608

Harris, Julian
Licensing **Band 2** — 504

Harris, Paul
Investment Funds **Band 2** — 498

Harris, Paul
Intellectual Property **Band 5** — 479

Harrison, Brian
Projects **Band 3** — 686

Harrison, Christopher
Real Estate **Band 2** — 702

Harrison, Frances
Clinical Negligence **Band 1** — 146
Healthcare **Band 1** — 406

Harrison, Julie
Banking & Finance **Band 2** — 101

Harrison, Lawrence
Media & Entertainment **Band 2** — 585

Harrison, Richard
Professional Negligence **Band 4** — 675

Harrison, Wendy
Corporate Finance **Band 3** — 226

Harriss, David
Intellectual Property **Band 4** — 479

Harrold, Neil
Insolvency **Band 3** — 452

Hart, Andrew R
Litigation **Band 4** — 538

Hart, Michael
Information Technology **Band 4** — 428
Intellectual Property **Band 5** — 479

Hart, Nicola
Education **Band 1** — 285

Hartley, Keith
Construction **Band 4** — 188

Hartley, Liz
Defamation **Band 2** — 268

Hartley, Simon
Asset Finance **Band 6** — 79
Shipping **Band 1** — 743

Hartwell, Roger
Licensing **Band 2** — 505

Harvey, Guy
Litigation **Band 1** — 533

Harvey, Jennifer
Immigration **Band 1** — 419

Harvey, Margaret
Information Tech **Up and coming** — 432

Harvey, Mark
Personal Injury **Band 1** — 622
Product Liability **Band 3** — 667

Harvey, Richard
Shipping **Band 6** — 741

Harwood, Peter
Offshore: Corporate **Band 2** — 831

Harwood, Ros
Charities **Band 1** — 128

1707

INDEX ■ LEADING LAWYERS

Haslam, Mark
Crime Band 1 — 251

Hatchard, Michael
Corporate Finance Band 4 — 203

Hattersley, Charles
Shipping Band 1 — 744

Hattrell, Martin
Corporate Finance Band 2 — 203

Havard, Robin
Health & Safety Band 1 — 401

Havard-Williams, Vanessa
Environment Band 2 — 347

Hawes, Roger
Corporate Finance Band 3 — 218

Hawkes, Ian
Shipping Band 6 — 741

Hawkins, David
Planning Band 3 — 640

Hawkins, James
Social Housing Band 3 — 753

Hay, David Leslie
Licensing Band 1 — 505

Hay, Katie
Clinical Negligence Band 3 — 141

Hayden, Tim
Environment Band 2 — 351
Licensing Band 2 — 506

Hayes, Michael
Trusts & Personal Tax Band 1 — 813

Hayes, Richard
Employee Share Schemes Band 2 — 293

Hayes, Sarah
Social Housing Band 3 — 755

Haymes, Duncan
Insolvency Band 1 — 450

Hayward, Paul
Corporate Finance Band 3 — 220

Haywood, Brent
Litigation Band 3 — 534

Haywood, Richard
Corporate Finance Band 3 — 220

Head-Rapson, Niall
Intellectual Property Band 3 — 485

Heal, Jeremy
Agriculture Band 2 — 57
Trusts & Personal Tax Band 2 — 819

Heaps, John
Litigation Band 2 — 532

Hearn, Andrew
Litigation Band 5 — 518

Hearn, Keith
Employment Band 4 — 313

Heath, Kevin
Asset Finance Band 2 — 80

Heath, Philip
Social Housing Band 2 — 758

Heathcock, Andrew
Corporate Finance Band 3 — 215

Heaton, John Graham
Transport Band 3 — 798

Hegarty, Simon
Professional Negligence Band 1 — 677

Hellier, Tim
Planning Band 1 — 640

Helps, Dominic
Construction Band 3 — 181

Hemingway, Ray
Church Band 3 — 136

Hemming, Dan
Planning Band 2 — 644

Hemming, Julian
Employment Band 1 — 307

Hemmings, Richard
Employment Band 2 — 310

Henchie, Nicholas
Construction One to watch — 177

Henderson, Brian
Banking & Finance Band 1 — 103
Real Estate Band 2 — 724

Henderson, Colin
Trusts & Personal Tax Band 2 — 821

Henderson, David
Projects/PFI Band 3 — 693

Henderson, Guy
Litigation Band 3 — 518

Henderson, Nick
Construction Up and coming — 189

Henderson, Stuart
Personal Injury Band 1 — 623
Travel Band 2 — 806

Hennessy, Tony
Tax Band 3 — 782

Henney, Colin
Employment Band 2 — 306

Henry, Graeme
Insolvency Band 3 — 454
Sport Band 2 — 770

Henson, John S
Family Band 2 — 370

Henson, Michaela
Real Estate Band 3 — 717

Hepburn, Daniel
Employee Share Up and coming — 292

Hepher, Christopher
Licensing Band 3 — 504

Hepworth, Allan
Insurance Band 3 — 468

Herbert, Alan
Litigation Band 1 — 551

Herbert, Andrew
Personal Injury Band 1 — 621

Herbert, Mary
Construction Band 1 — 184

Herbert, Tim
Offshore: Corporate Band 2 — 832

Herbertson, Lesley
Clinical Negligence Up and coming — 146

Herring, Andrew
Transport Up and coming — 799

Herring, John
Charities Band 1 — 127

Herring, Paul
Shipping Band 2 — 741

Herrington, Tim
Financial Services Band 1 — 386
Investment Funds Band 1 — 498

Hertz, Philip
Insolvency Up and coming — 441

Hesselberth, David
Employment Band 3 — 315

Hetherington, David
Product Liability Band 3 — 669

Hewes, Simon
Corporate Finance Band 3 — 218

Hewetson, Charles
Litigation Band 6 — 518

Hewison, John
Sport Band 2 — 770

Hewitt, Christopher
Agriculture Band 2 — 58

Hewitt, Stephen
Crime Band 3 — 251

Hewitt, V Alan
Real Estate Band 2 — 724
Trusts & Personal Tax Band 1 — 822

Hewson, Carol
Litigation Band 3 — 545

Hibbs, Michael
Employment Band 4 — 309

Hick, Mark
Professional Negligence Band 2 — 677

Hickey, Denys
Commodities Band 4 — 158

Hickman, Jane
Crime Band 2 — 251

Hiester, Elizabeth
Telecommunications Band 1 — 792

Higginbottom, Louise
Tax Band 5 — 776

Higgins, David
Insurance Band 2 — 466

Higginson, Antony
Energy Band 3 — 336

Higgs, Rachel
Litigation Band 1 — 529

Higham, John QC
Insolvency Band 6 — 441

Higham, Nicholas
Information Technology Band 4 — 428
Telecommunications Band 3 — 792

Highmore, Robert
Litigation Band 3 — 545

Hignett, Andrew
Planning Band 3 — 642

Higton, Jonathan
Sport Band 5 — 767

Hill, Alistair
Pensions Up and coming — 610

Hill, David
Employment Band 3 — 313

Hill, Jeremy
Insurance Band 2 — 469

Hill, Jeremy
Real Estate Band 3 — 724

Hill, Judith
Charities Band 1 — 123

Hill, Martin
Shipping Band 3 — 745
Transport Band 2 — 796

Hillebron, Richard
Planning Band 2 — 640

Hilton, Chris
Shipping Band 1 — 745

Hilton, Mark W
Construction Band 2 — 188

Hinchliffe, David
Insolvency Band 2 — 451

Hindle, Andrew
Litigation Band 4 — 545

Hine, Andrew
Trusts & Personal Tax Band 4 — 813

Hingley, Gerald
Pensions Band 2 — 607

Hitchcock, Teresa
Environment Band 1 — 355

Hoath, Helen
Litigation Band 2 — 550

Hobbs, Jane
Transport Band 3 — 796

Hobday, Natasha
Telecommunications Up and coming — 792

Hobley, Anthony
Environment Band 4 — 347

Hodge, Andrew
Employment Band 5 — 309

Hodges, Christopher
Product Liability Band 1 — 665

Hodges, Paula
Litigation Band 6 — 518

Hodgetts, Tim
Clinical Negligence One to watch — 145

Hodgkinson, Milly
Tax Band 4 — 776

Hodgson, Derek
Shipping Band 4 — 741

Hodgson, Gary
Transport Band 2 — 798

Hodgson, Guy
Professional Negligence Band 1 — 678

Hodgson, Mark
Intellectual Property Band 1 — 479

Hodson, Christopher
Church Band 3 — 136

Hogan, Ronald
Litigation Band 4 — 545

Hogg, Derek
Social Housing Band 2 — 760

Hoggett, Jonathan
Real Estate Band 3 — 712

Holderness, Andrew
Insurance Band 2 — 469

Holehouse, Andrew
Pensions Band 1 — 610

Holland, Barry
Licensing Band 1 — 509
Product Liability Band 1 — 669

Holland, Jeanette
Pensions Up and coming — 604

Holland, Jon
Litigation Up and coming — 538

Hollerin, Gordon
Insolvency Band 2 — 454

Hollingworth, Sara
Transport Band 3 — 799

Holloway, Julian
ADR Band 5 — 66
Construction Band 5 — 177

1708

LEADING LAWYERS — INDEX

Holmes, John
Clinical Negligence Band 1 — 141
Healthcare Band 2 — 404

Holmes, John
Planning Band 3 — 646

Holmes, Katherine
Competition/Anti-trust Band 3 — 164

Holmes, Leigh
Pensions Band 2 — 609

Holmes, Patrick
Construction Band 6 — 177

Holmes, Sarah
Environment Band 1 — 351

Holmes, Simon
Competition/Anti-trust Band 5 — 164
Parliamentary Band 3 — 594

Holmes, Susan
Church Band 3 — 137

Holroyd, Andrew
Immigration Band 3 — 421

Holt, Andrew
Corporate Finance Band 1 — 225

Holt, David
Personal Injury Band 1 — 626

Holt, Jeremy
Information Technology Band 2 — 430

Holy, Julian
Real Estate Band 5 — 702

Hood, Brian
Church Band 3 — 136

Hooper, David
Defamation Band 2 — 268

Hooper, John
Clinical Negligence Band 2 — 142

Hopkins, Ian
Personal Injury Band 1 — 622

Hopkins, Martin
Employment Band 3 — 309

Hopkins, Paul
Litigation Band 1 — 527

Hopkins, Stephen Martyn
Corporate Finance Band 3 — 226

Hopkins, Wendy
Family Band 3 — 369

Hornby, John
Agriculture Band 2 — 53

Horne, Anthony
Licensing Band 3 — 509

Hornsby, Stephen
Sport Band 4 — 767

Horsfall, Robert
Media & Entertainment Band 3 — 584

Horton, Naomi
Transport Band 3 — 799

Horton, Nicholas
Shipping Band 2 — 744

Horwood-Smart, Adrian
Agriculture Band 2 — 57
Trusts & Personal Tax Band 3 — 819

Hosie, Jonathan
Construction Band 3 — 177

Hoskins, Julian
Employment Band 3 — 307

Hough, Christopher
Construction Band 6 — 177

Houghton, John
Insolvency Band 3 — 441

Houghton, Paul
ADR Band 3 — 67

Hougie, Andrew
Investment Funds Band 3 — 498

Houldsworth, David
Agriculture Band 3 — 59

House, Tim
Litigation Band 1 — 538
Litigation Band 2 — 518

Houston, James
Real Estate Band 3 — 724

Houston, Paul
Travel Band 3 — 807

Hovell, Mark
Sport Band 4 — 770

Howard, Amanda
Real Estate Band 3 — 702

Howard, BK
Media & Entertainment Band 1 — 584

Howard, Clive
Employment Band 5 — 298

Howard, Jenni
Family Band 2 — 367

Howard, Karen
Planning Band 4 — 640

Howard, Paul
Litigation Band 1 — 528

Howard, Simon
Offshore: Corporate Band 2 — 832

Howard, Susan
Private Equity Band 5 — 657

Howarth, Mark
Real Estate Band 2 — 708

Howe, Martin
Construction Band 3 — 183

Howell, Paul
Trusts & Personal Tax Band 2 — 820

Howell-Richardson, Phillip
ADR Star — 67

Howes, Colin
Aviation Band 3 — 85

Howles, Kate
Corporate Finance Up and coming — 203

Hoyle, Andrew
Corporate Finance Band 3 — 227

Hoyle, Stephen
Tax Band 5 — 776

Hoyle, Susan
Tax Band 2 — 783

Hoyle, Thomas
Church Band 2 — 137

Huber, Bernard
Crime Band 3 — 251

Hudd, David
Capital Markets Band 5 — 114

Huddleston, David
Social Housing Band 2 — 758

Huddleston, Ian
Real Estate Band 3 — 724

Hudson, James
Construction Band 3 — 177

Hughes, David
Corporate Finance Band 4 — 220

Hughes, Frances
Family Band 1 — 365

Hughes, Kathryn L
Family Band 2 — 371

Hughes, Michael
Insolvency Band 3 — 454

Hughes, Nicholas
Aviation Band 2 — 86

Hughes, Norna
Planning Band 3 — 640

Hughes, Richard
Capital Markets Band 3 — 114

Hughes, Stephen
Projects/PFI Band 1 — 691

Hughes-Williams, Clare
Professional Negligence Band 1 — 677

Hull, David
Corporate Finance Band 3 — 220

Hulls, Martin
Corporate Finance Band 1 — 227

Humphrey, Ann L
Tax Band 1 — 776

Humphrey, Tony
Banking & Finance Band 2 — 92
Projects Band 2 — 686

Humphreys, Robert
Intellectual Property Band 2 — 482

Humphries, Mark
Litigation Band 4 — 518

Hunjan, Ranbir
Projects Up and coming — 686

Hunt, Matthew
Insolvency Band 2 — 448

Hunter, Alison
Immigration Band 3 — 418

Hunter, Ian
Employment Band 5 — 298

Hunter, James
Corporate Finance Band 2 — 223

Hunter, Jason
Litigation Band 4 — 545

Hunter, Robert
Litigation Band 1 — 541

Huntley, Graham
Litigation Band 4 — 518

Hurst, Andrew
Social Housing Band 2 — 760

Hurst, Philip
Energy Band 1 — 337

Hurt, Jacqueline
Media & Entertainment Band 3 — 580

Hussain, Belayeth
Immigration Band 3 — 418

Hutchings, Michael
Competition/Anti-trust Band 5 — 164

Hutchinson, John
Corporate Finance Band 2 — 216

Hutchinson, Lucy
Litigation Band 2 — 545

Hutchinson, Michael
Environment Band 5 — 347

Hutchinson, Anne-Marie
Family Band 2 — 365

Hutton, Robert
Real Estate Band 3 — 717

Hutton, Stuart
Crime Band 1 — 252

Hyde, Ian
Tax Band 1 — 781

Hyde, Mark
Insolvency Band 1 — 441

I

Iley, Malcolm
Administrative & Public Law Band 3 — 41
Local Government Band 1 — 572

Iliff, Catherine
Family Band 3 — 370

Illston, Tim
Pensions Band 1 — 606

Imperato, Michael
Education Band 1 — 285

Ingle, Michael
Employee Share Schemes Band 4 — 292

Ingleby, Claire
Travel Band 3 — 806

Inglis, Alan
Banking & Finance Band 4 — 92
Private Equity Band 4 — 659

Inglis, Andrew
Intellectual Property Band 4 — 479

Ingram, Kevin
Capital Markets Band 1 — 114

Innes, Colin
Planning Band 2 — 648

Innes, Richard
Real Estate Band 1 — 720

Irons, Ashley
Healthcare Band 3 — 406

Irvine, James
Intellectual Property Band 6 — 479

Irvine, John
Corporate Finance Band 1 — 231
Partnership Band 1 — 599

Irving, Paul
Parliamentary Band 2 — 593

Isaacs, Jeffrey
Commodities Band 1 — 158

Israel, Jennifer
Litigation Band 4 — 545

Isted, Jonathan
Environment Band 4 — 347

Ito, Stephen
Pensions Band 3 — 604

Ive, David
Investment Funds Band 4 — 498

Ivison, Andrew
Projects/PFI Band 2 — 690

J

Jackaman, Jake
Capital Markets Up and coming — 111

Jackman, Angela
Education Up and coming — 283

Jacks, David
Employment Band 4 — 312

Jackson, Andrew
Agriculture Band 3 — 53
Planning Band 4 — 640

1709

INDEX ■ LEADING LAWYERS

Jackson, Carol — Personal Injury Band 1	625
Jackson, Karl — Real Estate Band 5	718
Jackson, Mark — Insolvency Band 2	451
Jackson, Peter — Shipping Band 2	745
Transport Band 2	796
Jackson, Ray — Planning Band 1	640
Jackson, Stuart — Intellectual Property Band 3	485
Jackson-Stops, Mark — ADR Band 1	68
Jacob, Nicholas — Trusts & Personal Tax Band 4	813
Jacobs, Charles — Corporate Finance Up and coming	203
Jacobs, Howard — Employment Band 2	298
Pensions Band 4	604
Jacobs, Laurence — Information Technology Band 2	428
Jacobs, Michael — Employee Share Schemes Band 4	292
Trusts & Personal Tax Band 5	813
Jacobs, Russel — Tax Band 4	776
Jacomb, Brian — Real Estate Band 3	712
Jacovides, Mario — Asset Finance Band 4	79
Jaffa, Tony — Defamation Band 1	269
Jagusch, Stephen — Arbitration Up and coming	74
James, Benedict — Banking & Finance Up and coming	92
James, Charles — Immigration Band 2	421
James, Glen — Corporate Finance Band 5	203
Insurance Band 2	469
James, Ian — Offshore: Corporate Band 1	832
James, Jim — Insolvency Band 4	452
James, Robert — Real Estate Band 2	714
James, Sean — Media & Entertainment Band 1	581
James, Stuart — Pensions Band 2	604
Jameson, Robert — Planning Band 1	643
Jamieson, Andrew P — Employment Band 5	309
Jamison, David — Corporate Finance Band 1	231
Jansen, Karl — Corporate Finance Band 2	222
Jarman, Chris — Trusts & Personal Tax Band 3	813

Jarvis, Timothy — Tax Up and coming	782
Jeeps, Barry — Planning Band 3	640
Jefferies, Michael — Litigation Band 2	527
Jeffers, Raymond — Employment Band 3	298
Jefferson, Ian — Personal Injury Band 2	630
Jeffreys, Peter — Charities Band 1	125
Jeffreys, Simon — Employment Band 1	298
Jeffries, Graham — Banking & Finance Band 1	96
Corporate Finance Band 2	215
Insolvency Band 2	445
Jeffries, Jonathan — Insolvency Band 2	451
Jenkins, Edmund — Tax Band 1	782
Jenkins, Jane — Construction Band 6	177
Jenkins, Keith — Social Housing Band 1	753
Jenkins, Martin — Pensions Band 2	609
Jennings, Steven — Litigation Band 1	550
Jervis, David — Tax Band 2	782
Jessel, Christopher — Agriculture Band 1	53
Jewkes, Penny — Environment Band 4	354
Johansen, Lynn — Commodities Band 1	159
John, Alan — Environment Band 1	351
John, Simon — Clinical Negligence Band 1	145
Personal Injury Band 1	624
Johns, Michael — Corporate Finance Band 2	212
Johnson, Andrew — Shipping Band 3	741
Johnson, Andrew — Church Band 3	135
Johnson, Angus — Shipping Up and coming	741
Johnson, Ben — Corporate Finance Band 4	220
Johnson, Christopher R — Licensing Band 3	509
Johnson, David — Corporate Finance Up and coming	203
Johnson, Digby — Crime Band 2	253
Johnson, Ian — Tax Band 5	776
Johnson, James — Banking & Finance Band 1	92
Private Equity Band 1	659

Johnson, Jennifer — Real Estate Band 2	723
Johnson, Jonathan — Shipping Band 1	744
Johnson, M Clare — Licensing Band 2	510
Johnson, Paul — Litigation Band 4	530
Johnson, Robin — Corporate Finance Band 2	226
Johnson, Tim — Media & Entertainment Band 2	580
Johnston, Bruce — Projects Band 5	686
Johnston, David — Shipping Band 5	741
Johnston, Keith — Corporate Finance Band 2	225
Johnston, Michael — Corporate Finance Band 1	231
Johnston, Tom — Licensing Band 3	511
Johnstone, Frank — Asset Finance Band 1	81
Johnstone, Pat — Banking & Finance Band 1	98
Jolliffe, Peter — Asset Finance Band 1	79
Jones, Alan — Employment Band 3	309
Jones, Beverley — Employment Band 1	318
Jones, Bill — Information Technology Band 1	432
Jones, Calum — Insolvency Up and coming	454
Jones, Catherine — Family Band 1	371
Jones, Chris — Real Estate Band 3	714
Jones, David — Construction Band 3	177
Jones, David — Clinical Negligence Band 2	145
Personal Injury Band 1	624
Jones, Eddie — Clinical Negligence Band 3	146
Jones, Elizabeth — Real Estate Band 2	717
Jones, Gareth — Energy Band 4	336
Jones, Gareth — Intellectual Property Band 1	482
Jones, Geoffrey — Transport Band 4	798
Jones, Gwyn — Crime Band 2	252
Jones, Howard — Media & Entertainment Band 3	584
Jones, Hugh — Corporate Finance Band 2	216
Jones, Jonathan — Corporate Finance Band 3	226
Jones, Linda — Employment Band 4	309

Jones, Martyn — Tax Band 1	783
Jones, Medwyn — Media & Entertainment Band 3	580
Jones, Michael — Corporate Finance Band 3	218
Jones, Michael — Real Estate Band 5	718
Jones, Michael — Litigation Band 2	527
Jones, Michael — Real Estate Band 2	714
Jones, Nefydd — Real Estate Band 3	714
Jones, Pamela — Real Estate Band 1	718
Jones, Patricia — Intellectual Property Band 2	484
Jones, Peter — Family Band 2	372
Jones, Peter Watkin — Litigation Band 1	527
Jones, Robert — Tax Band 2	781
Jones, Siân — Litigation Band 1	548
Jones, Simon — Licensing Band 2	509
Jones, Stephen — Clinical Negligence Band 1	146
Jones, Stephen — Intellectual Property Band 4	479
Jordan, Geoffrey — Real Estate Band 3	712
Joyce, Andrew — Asset Finance Band 4	79
Joyce, John — Insolvency Band 2	450
Judge, Ian — Intellectual Property Band 2	479
Julyan, Alan — Employment Band 3	298
Jump, Graeme — Partnership Band 2	598
Partnership Band 2	599
Jupe, Erika — Tax Up and coming	780
Jurkiw, Andrij — Competition/Anti-trust Band 2	167
Jury, Susan — Family Band 3	368

K

Kahn, Gregory — Asset Finance Band 3	79
Kalderon, Mark — Financial Services Band 5	386
Kamstra, Gerry — Intellectual Property Band 6	479
Kamstra, Simon — Litigation Band 1	532
Kane, Hilary — Corporate Finance Band 4	229

LEADING LAWYERS ■ INDEX

Karet, Ian	Intellectual Property Band 4	479
Kavanagh, Giles	Aviation Band 2	86
Kaye, Laurence	E-commerce Band 2	277
	Media & Entertainment Band 3	582
Keal, Anthony	Banking & Finance Band 1	92
	Private Equity Band 3	659
Kean, Caroline	Defamation Band 5	269
Kearney, Mary Frances	Insolvency Band 3	454
Keck, Colleen	Information Tech Up and coming	428
Keddie, Joanne	Agriculture Band 3	53
Keeble, Ed	Environment Band 2	347
Keeble, Jeffrey	Clinical Negligence Band 1	148
Keeble, Sarah	Employment Up and coming	298
Keele, Helen	Environment Up and coming	347
Keenan, Andrew	Crime Band 3	251
Kefford, Alan	Licensing Band 1	508
Keir, Jane	Family Band 3	365
Keith-Lucas, Peter	Administrative & Public Law Band 1	45
	Local Government Band 1	574
Keitley, Nicholas	Insolvency Band 1	445
Keliher, James	Corporate Finance Band 5	218
Kellaway, Rosalind	Competition/Anti-trust Band 5	164
Kelleher, John	Product Liability Band 3	665
Kelly, Christopher	Energy Up and coming	337
Kelly, Don	Tax Band 5	776
Kelly, Jacky	Capital Markets Band 3	114
Kelly, Jill	Employment Band 1	306
Kelly, Jonathan	Litigation: Banking Band 2	538
	Litigation: General Band 3	518
	Litigation: Civil Fraud Band 4	541
Kelly, Neil J	Construction Band 2	190
Kelly, Philip	Crime Band 2	253
Kelly, Russell	Shipping Band 2	744
Kelly, Susan	Banking & Finance Band 1	102
Kelly, Susan	Insolvency Up and coming	450
Kemp, Jonathan	Shipping Band 3	745
Kemp, Lesley	Immigration Band 3	416
Kemp, Richard	E-commerce Band 1	277
	Information Technology Band 2	428
Kemp, Sandy	Employment Band 2	316
	Personal Injury Band 1	628
Kempner, Richard	Intellectual Property Band 1	485
Kendall, David	Insurance Band 1	468
	Insurance Band 3	466
Kendall, John	ADR Band 3	67
Kennedy, A J Spencer	Professional Negligence Band 2	679
Kennedy, John	Trusts & Personal Tax Band 5	813
Kennedy, Patrick	Pensions Band 2	608
Kenny, Stephen	Projects/PFI Band 3	691
Kensell, Stephen	Banking & Finance Band 4	92
Kent, Michael	Financial Services Band 5	386
Kent, Paul	Litigation Band 2	549
Kenyon, Andrew	Fraud Band 3	395
Kenyon, Michael	Fraud Band 1	395
Kerr, David	Telecommunications Band 2	792
Kerr, Drummond	Trusts & Personal Tax Band 2	818
Kerr, John	Sport Band 1	770
Kerr, Steven	Real Estate Band 4	723
Kerry, David G	Clinical Negligence Band 3	145
Kershaw, Anne	Litigation Band 3	530
	Partnership Band 1	598
Kershaw, Nick	Offshore: Corporate Band 2	832
Keuls, Peter	Social Housing Band 1	757
Keyden, Gordon	Personal Injury Band 1	629
Khan, Charles	Litigation Band 3	530
Khan, Imran	Human Rights Band 3	410
Khan, Sadiq	Human Rights Band 2	410
Kidby, Robert	Real Estate Band 1	702
Kidd, Philip	Family Band 2	368
Kilduff, David	Local Government Band 2	575
Kilner, John	Investment Funds Band 6	498
Kilner, Peter	Banking & Finance Band 6	92
Kim, Suyong	Competition/Anti-trust Band 5	164
King, Michael	Charities Star	125
	Church Band 1	135
	Education Band 3	284
King, Peter	Corporate Finance Band 5	203
King, Richard	Church Band 1	135
King, Ronnie	Arbitration Band 4	74
	Energy Band 4	336
	Litigation Band 3	518
King, Vicky	Human Rights Up and coming	410
King, Vivien	Litigation Band 1	545
Kingdon, Danielle	Employment Band 2	306
King-Jones, Amanda	Trusts & Personal Tax Band 2	815
Kinnersley, Tom	Asset Finance Band 1	79
Kinsey, Julian	Banking & Finance Band 1	96
Kirby, Richard	Trusts & Personal Tax Band 5	813
Kirk, David	Fraud Band 2	393
Kirk, Graeme	Immigration Band 1	420
Kirk, Ian	Offshore: Corporate Band 1	831
Kirkbright, Stephen	Transport Band 1	798
Kirkman, Trevor	Church Band 3	136
Kirkup, Simon	Agriculture Band 2	58
Kirtley, Deborah	Banking & Finance Band 2	101
Kissack, Nigel	Litigation Band 2	532
Kitchingman, John	Clinical Negligence Band 1	146
Kitson, Paul	Personal Injury Band 2	617
Kitson, Tony	Planning Band 1	640
Kitts, Stephen	Banking & Finance Band 3	98
	Corporate Finance Band 1	222
Knight, Matthew	Administrative & Public Law Band 1	44
	Agriculture Band 1	54
Knight, Tim	Transport Band 1	796
Knox, James	Real Estate Band 4	702
Knox, Louisa	Pensions Band 2	610
Knox, Martin	Local Government Band 3	574
	Social Housing Band 1	758
Koffman, Brian	Crime Band 3	254
Kon, Stephen	Competition/Anti-trust Band 1	164
Konynenburg, Frederick	Commodities One to watch	158
Kordan, Joel	Real Estate Band 2	715
Korman, Andy	Sport Band 4	767
Kowalik, Mark	Pensions Band 3	604
Kramer, Martin	Defamation Band 2	268
Kratz, Philip	Planning Band 2	645
Krischer, David	Capital Markets Band 1	114
Kustow, David	Real Estate Band 3	702
Kyrke, Richard	Agriculture Band 1	54

L

La Follette, Maryly	Family Band 3	365
Laight, Simon	Pensions Band 3	607
Laing, Robert J	Banking & Finance Band 3	102
Laing, Sue	Trusts & Personal Tax Band 1	816
Lake, Tim	Real Estate Band 5	702
Lambert, Robert	Arbitration Band 3	74
Lambert, Tracy	Family Band 3	368
Lambie, Christian	Capital Markets Up and coming	114
Lamont, Duncan	Defamation Band 5	268
Lamont, Sarah	Employment Band 2	307
Lancaster, Roger	Planning Band 1	646
Landsman, David	Media & Entertainment Band 4	584
Lane, Andrew	Agriculture Band 1	53
Lane, Mark	Construction Band 4	177
	Energy Band 3	337
Lane, Robert	Energy Band 2	337
Langley, Dale	Employment Band 5	298
Langley, Robert	Construction Band 1	189

www.ChambersandPartners.com

1711

INDEX ■ LEADING LAWYERS

Langlois, John
Offshore: Corporate **Band 2** — 831

Lavery, James
Corporate Finance **Band 3** — 220

Lawes, William
Corporate Finance **Band 1** — 203

Lawrence, Daniel
Environment **Band 5** — 347

Lawson, Hamish K
Licensing **Band 1** — 509

Lawson, Peter J
Licensing **Band 2** — 511

Lawton, F A (Tony)
Charities **Band 3** — 128
Church **Band 1** — 137

Lawton Smith, Andrew
Corporate Finance **Band 4** — 220

Lax, Michael
Shipping **Band 2** — 741

Lax, Peter
Litigation **Band 4** — 528

Laycock, Andrew
Insolvency **Band 3** — 451

Layton, Matthew
Private Equity **Band 1** — 657

Lea, Alison
Planning **Band 3** — 640

Leach, Ben
Commodities **Band 3** — 158

Le Bas, Malcolm
Insolvency **Band 2** — 445

Lee, David P
Projects/PFI **Up and coming** — 690

Lee, Paul
Corporate Finance **Band 3** — 225

Lee, Richard
Corporate Finance **Band 2** — 225

Lee, Richard
Corporate Finance **Band 2** — 216

Lee, Robert
Banking & Finance **Band 6** — 92

Lee, Robert
Media & Entertainment **Band 2** — 584

Lee, Terry
Clinical Negligence **Band 3** — 140
Personal Injury **Band 1** — 617

Lee, Trevor
Licensing **Band 4** — 507

Leech, Catherine
Personal Injury **Band 1** — 625

Leek, Robert
Trusts & Personal Tax **Band 1** — 818

Leeming, Richard
Banking & Finance **Band 2** — 96

Leigh, Bertie
Clinical Negligence **Band 1** — 141
Healthcare **Band 1** — 404

Leigh, Guy
Competition/Anti-trust **Band 5** — 164

Leigh, Robert
Transport **Band 4** — 799

Leitch, David A
Real Estate **Band 2** — 724

Leney, Simon
Trusts & Personal Tax **Band 1** — 815

Lennox, Lionel
Church **Band 1** — 137

Leonard, Paul
Insurance **Band 3** — 466
Litigation **Band 2** — 518

Leonard, Tessa
Real Estate **Band 3** — 718

Le Pard, Geoffrey
Real Estate **Band 2** — 702

Leseberg, Petra
Commodities **Up and coming** — 158

Leskin, Nigel
Immigration **Band 3** — 418

Leslie, Alex
Healthcare **Band 4** — 404

Leth, Mary
Corporate Finance **Band 5** — 203

Leverton, David
Family **Band 3** — 365

Levine, Marshall
Construction **Band 2** — 177

Levine, Simon
Intellectual Property **Band 6** — 479

Levinson, Jan
Litigation **Band 2** — 550

Levinson, Stephen
Employment **Band 5** — 298

Levison, Jeremy I
Family **Band 1** — 365

Levy, David N
Travel **Band 1** — 807

Levy, Graeme
Corporate Finance **Band 3** — 208

Levy, Robert
Corporate Finance **Band 4** — 225

Levy, Russell
Clinical Negligence **Band 1** — 140

Lew, Simon
Asset Finance **Band 5** — 79

Lew QC, Julian
Arbitration **Band 1** — 74

Lewin, Olive
Clinical Negligence **Band 3** — 140

Lewis, Alastair
Parliamentary **Band 1** — 593

Lewis, David E
Tax: Indirect **Band 2** — 776
Tax: Corporate **Band 3** — 776

Lewis, Emyr
Media & Entertainment **Band 2** — 586

Lewis, Harold
Litigation **Band 3** — 543

Lewis, Mark
Corporate Finance **Band 4** — 218

Lewis, Mark
Defamation **Band 2** — 269

Lewis, Michael
Trusts & Personal Tax **Band 5** — 813

Lewis, Roger
Pensions **Band 3** — 604

Lewis, Simon
Construction **Band 2** — 189

Lewis, Stephen
Insurance **Band 3** — 468

Lewis, Susan
Corporate Finance **Band 2** — 220

Leydecker, Sonya
Litigation **Band 4** — 541

Leyshon, Greg
Corporate Finance **Band 3** — 216

Lidbetter, Andrew
Administrative & Public Law **Band 1** — 43

Lilley, Andrew
Employment **Band 5** — 298

Lindrup, Garth
Competition/Anti-trust **Band 2** — 167

Lindsay, Alistair
Competition/Anti-trust **Band 5** — 164

Lindsey, Michael
Intellectual Property **Band 2** — 482

Lindsley, Fiona
Immigration **Band 2** — 418

Ling, Timothy
Tax **Band 3** — 776

Linsell, Richard
Partnership **Band 1** — 596

Lintott, Tim
Asset Finance **Band 2** — 79

Lippell, Sean
Corporate Finance **Band 2** — 226

Lister, Richard
Information Technology **Band 3** — 428

Liston, Stephanie
Telecommunications **Band 3** — 792

Little, Andrew
Travel **Band 2** — 807

Little, Tamasin
Financial Services **Band 3** — 386

Littlejohns, Andrew
Asset Finance **Band 2** — 79
Transport **Band 4** — 799

Livingston, Dorothy
Competition/Anti-trust **Band 1** — 164

Livingston, Michael
Corporate Finance **Band 4** — 229
Financial Services **Band 2** — 389

Livingstone, Alisdair
Corporate Finance **Band 4** — 218

Livingstone, Hugh
Shipping **Band 2** — 741

Llewellyn, Paul
Product Liability **Band 1** — 667

Llewelyn, David
Intellectual Property **Band 4** — 479

Llewelyn Evans, Adrian
Partnership **Band 1** — 598

Lloyd, Deborah
Environment **Band 4** — 347

Lloyd, Stephen
Charities **Band 1** — 123

Lloyd Holt, Suzanne
Litigation **Band 1** — 549

Lloyd Jones, David
Construction **Band 2** — 184

Lloyd-Jones, Jonathan
ADR **Band 1** — 67

Loake, Jonathan
Corporate Finance **Band 3** — 216

Lochner, Ludi
Intellectual Property **Band 1** — 481

Lockley, Andrew
Human Rights **Band 3** — 412

Lodder, David
Agriculture **Band 1** — 56

Logan, Niall
Energy **Band 1** — 339

Lom, Nicholas
Media & Entertainment **Band 4** — 580

Lomas, Owen
Environment **Band 1** — 347

Lomas, Paul
Litigation **Band 4** — 518

Lombardi, Michael
Offshore: Corporate **Band 2** — 832

Long, Andrew
Professional Negligence **Band 2** — 677

Long, Colin
Telecommunications **Band 1** — 792

Long, David
Trusts & Personal Tax **Band 5** — 813

Long, Julian
Corporate Finance **Band 3** — 203

Long, Peter
Banking & Finance **Band 6** — 92

Longrigg, William
Family **Band 2** — 365

Loose, Helen
Environment **Band 2** — 347

Loudon, Alasdair
Family **Band 1** — 373

Loudon, John
Licensing **Band 1** — 511

Lougher, Guy
Competition/Anti-trust **Band 1** — 167

Loughlin, Grahame
Personal Injury **Band 2** — 630

Louveaux, Bertrand
Competition/Anti-trust **Band 5** — 164

Love, Alison
Employment **Band 4** — 308

Love, James
Intellectual Property **Band 2** — 485

Love, Robert
Education **Band 1** — 284

Lovel, John
Clinical Negligence **Band 1** — 147

Lovitt, Arthur
Projects/PFI **Band 2** — 692

Lowdon, Jane
Church **Band 3** — 137

Lowe, James
Shipping **Band 1** — 746

Lowe, Kevin
Tax **Band 1** — 781

Lowe, Paul
Corporate Finance **Band 2** — 219

Lowe, Rita
Insolvency **Band 5** — 441

Loweth, Craig
Litigation **One to watch** — 528

Lowless, Peter
Real Estate **Band 3** — 712

1712

LEADING LAWYERS ■ INDEX

Lowson, Greg
Litigation Band 4 — 528

Loxley, Martin
Family Band 2 — 372

Loy, Simon
Employment Band 2 — 315

Lubbock, Mark
Information Technology Band 5 — 428

Lucas, David
Commodities Band 1 — 158

Lucas, David
Licensing Band 2 — 507

Lucas, Richard
Projects/PFI Up and coming — 690

Luckman, Michael
Intellectual Property Band 2 — 483

Luder, Sara
Tax Band 4 — 776

Lumsden, Christopher
Asset Finance Band 2 — 80

Lumsden, Ian G
Corporate Finance Band 2 — 229

Lumsden, Lawrence
Personal Injury Band 2 — 628

Luqmani, Jawaid
Immigration Band 2 — 418

Lust, Graham
Real Estate Band 3 — 702

Lyall, George
Trusts & Personal Tax Band 1 — 820

Lynch, Malcolm
Charities Band 1 — 128
Energy Band 1 — 339
Financial Services Band 1 — 388

Lynch, Michael
Litigation Band 1 — 536

Lynchehan, Martin
Tax: Corporate Band 3 — 776
Tax: Indirect Band 3 — 776

Lyne, Amanda
Employment Band 3 — 310

M

Macara, J D Murray
Crime Band 2 — 255

Macaulay, Anthony
Corporate Finance Band 2 — 203

Macaulay, Iain
Banking & Finance Band 4 — 102
Projects/PFI Band 3 — 693

MacCarthy, Rory
Asset Finance Band 6 — 79

Macdonald, Morag
Intellectual Property Band 1 — 479

Macdonald-Brown, Charters
Intellectual Property Band 5 — 479

Macfadyen, Michael R
Trusts & Personal Tax Band 5 — 813

Macfarlane, John
Insolvency Band 2 — 454

Macfarlane, Nicholas
Intellectual Property Band 2 — 479

MacGregor, Ewen
Licensing Up and coming — 506

MacGregor, Robert
Real Estate Band 1 — 702

MacGregor, Stephen
Social Housing Band 2 — 760

Machover, Daniel
Human Rights Band 2 — 410

Macintosh, Duncan
Corporate Finance Band 1 — 219

Maciver, Archibald D
Licensing Band 1 — 511

Mackay, Malcolm
Employment Band 1 — 316

Mackay, Philip
Financial Services Band 1 — 389
Investment Funds Band 2 — 500

Mackenzie, Marcus
Capital Markets Band 3 — 114

Mackey, Michael
Crime Band 2 — 254

Mackie, Chris
Private Equity Band 5 — 657

Mackie, Francis
Insurance Band 2 — 468

Mackie, Karl
ADR Band 2 — 66

Mackie QC, David L
Litigation Band 1 — 518

Mackin, Stephen
Shipping Band 1 — 745

Mackinlay, Hannah
Environment Band 2 — 353

Mackintosh, Nicola
Administrative & Public Law Band 2 — 41
Healthcare Band 2 — 406

Mackintosh, Simon
Charities Band 1 — 129
Trusts & Personal Tax Band 1 — 821

MacLean, Duncan
Shipping Band 1 — 746

Macleod, Colin
Litigation Band 1 — 534
Professional Negligence Band 1 — 679

MacLeod, Euan
Employment Band 2 — 316

MacLeod, Ewan
Planning One to watch — 648

Macniven, Iain
Real Estate Band 4 — 723

Macpherson, Shonaig
Information Technology Band 2 — 433
Intellectual Property Band 1 — 486

MacRae, Keith
Shipping Band 1 — 746

MacRitchie, Kenneth
Projects Band 1 — 686

MacRobert, David
Trusts & Personal Tax Band 1 — 821

MacVicar, Robert
Capital Markets Band 4 — 111

MacWilkinson, Jeffrey
Personal Injury Band 2 — 623

Madden, Andrew
Banking & Finance Band 1 — 98

Madden, Michael
Litigation Band 1 — 545

Maddock, Geoffrey
Insurance Band 2 — 469

Magnin, John
Litigation Band 5 — 518

Magrath, Chris
Immigration Band 2 — 416

Maguire, Frank
Personal Injury Band 2 — 628

Maher, Frank
Professional Negligence Band 1 — 678

Maher, Paul
Corporate Finance Band 2 — 208

Mahood, W Laurence
Real Estate Band 1 — 724

Maidment, Allan
Crime Band 1 — 254

Main, Douglas
Crime Band 2 — 255

Mainprice, Hugh
Tax Band 2 — 776

Mair, Leonard
Family Band 2 — 373

Mair, Logan
Projects/PFI Up and coming — 690

Mallon, Christopher
Insolvency Band 4 — 441

Malone, Michael
Employment Band 3 — 312

Maloney, Tim
Litigation Band 6 — 518

Manley, Mark
Defamation Band 2 — 269
Litigation Band 2 — 530

Mann, Jane
Employment Band 3 — 298
Immigration Band 4 — 416

Manning, Peter
Insolvency Band 4 — 441

Manning, Richard
Family Band 3 — 372

Manning Cox, Andrew
Litigation Band 3 — 528

Mansell, Mark
Employment Band 1 — 298

Mansfield (nÈe Ford), Rachel
Financial Services Band 5 — 386

Manson, Stephen
Planning Band 1 — 644

Marchant, Simon
Corporate Finance Band 5 — 203

Marco, Alan
Family Band 3 — 365

Mardle, David
Corporate Finance Band 3 — 223

Margrave-Jones, Clive
Agriculture Band 1 — 55
Trusts & Personal Tax Band 1 — 818

Marks, Geoffrey
Real Estate Band 3 — 718

Marks, Lisa
Asset Finance Band 6 — 79

Marriott QC, Arthur
Arbitration Band 1 — 74

Marron, Peter
Planning Band 1 — 644

Marsden, Tim
Investment Funds Band 2 — 498

Marsh, David
Corporate Finance Band 5 — 218
Partnership Band 2 — 598

Marsh, William
ADR Band 2 — 66

Marshall, Anna
Environment Band 5 — 347

Marshall, David
Personal Injury Band 2 — 617

Marshall, Ian
Employment Band 3 — 309

Marshall, J Richard
Insolvency Band 4 — 451

Marshall, James
Intellectual Property Band 6 — 479

Marshall, Jane
Pensions Band 2 — 604

Marshall, John
Corporate Finance Band 4 — 231

Marshall, Julia
Transport Band 1 — 796

Marsland, Vanessa
Intellectual Property Band 4 — 479

Martin, Bonnie
Litigation Band 2 — 548

Martin, Charles
Corporate Finance Band 5 — 203
Private Equity Band 2 — 657

Martin, Matthew T
Charities Band 2 — 127

Martin, Patricia
Commodities Band 2 — 158

Martin, Stefan
Employment Up and coming — 298

Martin, Stuart
Investment Funds Up and coming — 498

Martin Alegi, Lynda
Competition/Anti-trust Band 2 — 164

Martindale, Avril
Information Technology Band 5 — 428
Intellectual Property Band 3 — 479

Martinez, Liz
Clinical Negligence Band 3 — 140

Maskill, Andrew
Asset Finance Band 1 — 80

Mason, Carol
Trusts & Personal Tax Band 3 — 820

Mason, David
Clinical Negligence Band 1 — 141
Healthcare Band 2 — 404

Mason, Helen
Employment Band 5 — 309

Mason, Stephen
Travel Band 1 — 806

Massarano Salt, Vikki
Pensions Band 2 — 609

Massey, William
Family Band 3 — 365

Masters, David
Litigation Band 4 — 545

Masters, Peter
Crime Band 2 — 253

1713

INDEX ■ LEADING LAWYERS

M

Masters, Richard	Corporate Finance Band 4	229
Matheou, Michael	Projects/PFI Band 1	690
Mather, B J	Crime Band 2	253
Mather, Ian Philip	Employment Band 4	310
Mathieson, Keith	Defamation Band 4	268
Matthew, Stephen	Local Government Band 2	574
	Projects/PFI Band 1	691
Matthews, Carol	Social Housing Band 3	758
Matthews, Paul	Litigation Band 1	529
Mattison, Mark	Litigation Band 2	530
Maughan, Alistair	Information Technology Band 2	428
Maughan, Peter J	Clinical Negligence Band 1	147
Maurice, Clare M	Trusts & Personal Tax Band 3	813
Mawhood, John	Information Technology Band 5	428
Max, Richard	Planning Band 1	640
Maxtone-Smith, Michael	Media & Entertainment Band 3	580
Maxwell, Elaine	Education Band 1	287
May, Caroline	Environment Band 2	347
May, Philip	Insolvency Band 4	447
	Litigation Band 1	525
	Partnership Band 1	598
May, Sara	Personal Injury Band 3	624
Mayer, Stephen	Partnership Band 3	596
Mayhew, Lisa	Employment Up and coming	298
Maynard, Robert	Construction Band 6	177
McAllester, Alan K	Church Band 2	137
McArthur, Colin	Partnership Band 4	596
McAuley, Michael	Projects/PFI Band 2	693
McBride, Paul	Corporate Finance Band 3	231
McCallough, Robert	Information Technology Band 3	428
McCammon, Avril	Banking & Finance One to watch	103
McCann, Martin	Projects/PFI Band 4	690
McCarthy, Frances	Personal Injury Band 2	617
McCarthy, Michael	Insolvency Band 6	441
McCarthy, Paul	Employee Share Schemes Band 4	292
McCaw, Elma	Trusts & Personal Tax Band 2	822
McChlery, Frances	Planning Band 3	648
McClea, Nigel	Real Estate Band 1	720
McClure, Alison	Clinical Negligence Band 1	142
McCool, Geraldine	Personal Injury Band 2	625
	Product Liability Band 3	667
McCormack, Carol	Projects/PFI Band 3	690
McCormick, Roger	Projects Band 4	686
McCormick, Peter	Media & Entertainment Band 2	586
	Sport Band 1	770
McCreath, Rob	Education Band 2	282
McCue, Jason	Defamation Band 4	268
McCulloch, Ian	Parliamentary Band 3	593
McDermott, Jennifer	Administrative & Public Law Band 2	43
	Defamation Band 5	268
McDonald, Kevan	Corporate Finance Band 2	229
McDonald, Roberta	Family Band 2	370
McDonnell, Paul	Defamation Up and coming	270
McDonnell, Phil	Competition/Anti-trust Band 4	167
McDougall, Arundel	Product Liability Band 4	665
McEvoy, Eamonn	Personal Injury Band 1	629
McEwan, Alastair	Projects/PFI Band 3	693
McFadyen, Laurence	Shipping Band 6	741
McFadzean, Christopher	Capital Markets Band 5	111
McGee-Osborne, Christopher	Transport Band 1	799
McGeever, Brendan	Insolvency Band 2	449
McGilchrist, Neil	Aviation Band 3	86
McGinn, James	Corporate Finance Band 4	229
McGowan, Michael T	Tax Band 4	776
McGowan, Paul	Employment One to watch	315
McGrath, Matthew	Clinical Negligence Band 1	142
McGrath, Roisin	Licensing Band 1	511
McGurk, Anthony	Insolvency Band 1	449
McHale, Colin	Banking & Finance Band 1	102
McHardy, Iain	Real Estate Band 4	723
McHugh, Peter	Corporate Finance Band 3	220
McInerney, Peter	Media & Entertainment Band 4	580
McInnes, John	Crime Band 2	255
McIntosh, Ian	Corporate Finance Band 2	226
McKay, Anna	Intellectual Property Band 6	479
McKay, Colin	Banking & Finance Band 2	102
McKay, Maura	Licensing Band 1	511
McKeand, James	Capital Markets Band 5	114
McKenna, Catherine M P	Pensions Band 1	609
McKenna, Ian	Insurance Band 2	468
McKenzie, Rod	Employment Band 3	316
	Sport Band 2	770
McKie, Alastair	Planning Band 4	648
McKnight, Elizabeth	Competition/Anti-trust Band 1	164
	Energy Band 3	337
McLachlan, Campbell	Litigation Band 1	518
McLean, Alistair	Construction Band 2	190
McLean, James	Competition/Anti-trust Band 3	168
McLean, Neil	Real Estate Band 1	720
McLoughlin, Kevin	Health & Safety Up and coming	402
McMullen, John	Employment Band 3	313
McNabb, Heather	Intellectual Property Band 2	482
McNair, Martin	Private Equity Up and coming	657
McNeil, Paul	Clinical Negligence Band 1	140
McNeill, Morag	Corporate Finance Band 1	229
McNeive, Liam	E-commerce Band 1	277
McNicol, Stephen	Banking & Finance Band 3	101
	Insolvency Band 4	452
McNiven, Alan	Insolvency Band 3	454
McNulty, Stephen	Real Estate Band 2	712
	Social Housing Band 1	757
McPake, Ian	Projects/PFI Band 3	693
McPherson, Lyn	Health & Safety Up and coming	402
McQuater, Gavin	Projects Band 4	686
McQuay, Elizabeth	Family Band 2	367
McRobb, Liz	Information Technology Band 3	433
McVeigh, Kevin	Corporate Finance Up and coming	231
McWhirter, Anthony	Investment Funds Band 5	498
Meadon, Simon	Media & Entertainment Band 2	585
Meakin, Robert	Charities Band 4	123
Mears, Patrick	Tax Band 1	776
Meek, Charles	Private Equity Band 3	657
Meeks, Alastair	Pensions Band 4	604
Meeran, Richard	Personal Injury Band 3	617
	Product Liability Band 2	667
Meggitt, Edward	Litigation Up and coming	548
Mehmet, G lay	Immigration Band 2	416
Mehta, Nikhil	Tax Band 4	776
Meiklejohn, Iain	Corporate Finance Band 4	229
Meisel, Mari	Family Band 2	370
Melbourne, William	Transport Band 4	796
Melrose, Jonathan	Commodities Band 2	159
Meltzer, John	Product Liability Band 2	665
Melville-Brown, Amber	Defamation Up and coming	268
Mendelowitz, Michael	Insurance Band 3	468
Mercer, Edward	Telecommunications Band 2	792
Meredith, Alan	Real Estate Band 3	714
Merriam, Joy	Crime Band 3	251
Messenger, Mercy	Family Band 2	370
Messent, Andrew	Transport Band 1	796
Messent, Michael	Licensing Band 1	505
Metcalfe, Ian	Corporate Finance Band 1	220
Metcalfe, Rob	Corporate Finance Band 1	222
Metcalfe, Stephen	Litigation Band 2	525
Metliss, Jonathan	Sport Band 4	767

1714

LEADING LAWYERS — INDEX

Metliss, Michael — Litigation Band 4 — 545
Micklem, Barney — Professional Negligence Band 1 — 675
Micklethwaite, Neil — Litigation Band 3 — 518
Middleditch, Matthew — Corporate Finance Band 1 — 203; Insurance Band 2 — 469; Investment Funds Band 2 — 498
Middlemiss, Susie — Intellectual Property Up and coming — 479
Middleton, Fiona — Charities Band 2 — 123
Middleton-Smith, Charles — ADR Band 4 — 66
Mifsud, Mark — Private Equity Band 3 — 661
Milburn, Paula — Family Band 2 — 371
Miles, Adrian — Asset Finance Band 2 — 79
Miles, Anthony — Crime Band 1 — 252
Miles, David — ADR Band 2 — 66
Miles, Helen — Pensions Band 3 — 607
Miles, Stephen — Banking & Finance Band 1 — 98
Millar, Stephen — Energy Up and coming — 340
Millard, Christopher — E-commerce Band 1 — 277; Information Technology Band 1 — 428
Miller, Adrian — Trusts & Personal Tax Band 2 — 817
Miller, Colin — Competition/Anti-trust Band 2 — 168
Miller, Stephen — Employment Band 2 — 316; Sport Band 2 — 770
Miller, Stephen M — Capital Markets Band 2 — 111
Millichip, Peter — Sport Band 4 — 767
Millington, Jeremy — Corporate Finance Band 2 — 220
Mills, Guy B — Shipping Band 1 — 745
Mills, Stephen — Shipping Band 1 — 745
Milner, Henry — Crime Band 2 — 251
Milton, Kevin — Pensions Band 3 — 607
Minogue, Ann — Construction Band 1 — 177
Minter, Melanie — Clinical Negligence Band 2 — 142
Minto, Bruce — Corporate Finance Band 1 — 229; Financial Services Band 1 — 389; Investment Funds Band 2 — 500
Mireskandari, Razi — Defamation Band 3 — 268

Miscampbell, Andrew — Partnership Band 1 — 597
Mitchard, Paul — Arbitration Band 3 — 74
Mitchell, Andrew — Investment Funds Band 5 — 498
Mitchell, Bob — Sport Band 5 — 767
Mitchell, James — Real Estate Band 2 — 708
Mitchell, Jane — Family Band 1 — 367
Mitchell, Jocelyn — Employee Share Schemes Band 2 — 292
Mitchell, John — Fraud Band 1 — 394
Mitchell, Martin — Trusts & Personal Tax Band 1 — 817
Mitchell, Patrick — Banking & Finance Band 1 — 100
Mitchell, Paul — Media & Entertainment Band 2 — 582
Moakes, Jonathan — Information Technology Band 2 — 432; Intellectual Property Band 1 — 484
Mobley, Samantha — Competition Up and coming — 164
Moffat, Douglas — Real Estate Band 4 — 723
Molloy, Susan — Banking & Finance Band 2 — 99
Molyneux, Anne — Litigation Band 3 — 545
Monaghan, Iain — Information Technology Band 5 — 428
Moncreiffe, Mark — Telecommunications Band 4 — 792
Money-Kyrie, Rebecca — Administrative & Public One to watch — 43
Monro, Pat — Family Band 3 — 365
Montgomery, Nigel — Clinical Negligence Band 1 — 144
Montgomery, Nigel — Insolvency Band 2 — 441
Monty, Craig — Litigation Band 2 — 543
Moodie, Bill — Intellectual Property Band 4 — 479
Moody, John — Real Estate Band 5 — 718
Mooney, Kevin — Intellectual Property Band 1 — 479
Moore, Austin — Corporate Finance Band 2 — 222
Moore, Charles — Media & Entertainment Band 3 — 580
Moore, David — Offshore: Corporate Band 2 — 831
Moore, George — Personal Injury Band 1 — 629
Moore, Gideon — Banking & Finance Band 4 — 92
Moore, John — Agriculture Band 2 — 53

Moore, Louise — Environment Band 5 — 347
Moore, Nigel — Pensions Band 2 — 604
Mordsley, Barry — Employment Band 4 — 298
More, George — Crime Band 2 — 255
Morgan, Claire — Real Estate Band 2 — 721
Morgan, Glyn — Information Technology Band 4 — 428
Morgan, Leon — Media & Entertainment Band 2 — 580
Morgan, Matthew — Banking & Finance Up and coming — 99
Morgan, Meryl — Banking & Finance Band 2 — 97
Morgan, Neil Christopher — Litigation Band 1 — 548
Morgan, Roy — Fraud Band 2 — 394
Morgan, Simon — Corporate Finance Band 3 — 208
Moritz, John — Planning Band 2 — 646
Morley, David — Banking & Finance Star — 92
Morley, Trevor — Social Housing Band 2 — 753
Morpeth, Iain — Real Estate Band 1 — 702
Morris, Andrew — Corporate Finance Band 2 — 219
Morris, Antony — Litigation Band 1 — 525
Morris, Christopher — Real Estate Band 3 — 702
Morris, Gregory — Tax Band 1 — 781
Morris, Howard — Insolvency Band 3 — 441
Morris, Paul — Church Band 1 — 134
Morris, Peter — Litigation Band 1 — 525
Morris, Simon — Financial Services Band 2 — 386
Morris, Tim — Capital Markets Up and coming — 111
Morrison, Alastair — Construction Band 1 — 190
Morrison, Alastair — Agriculture Band 2 — 55
Morrison, Michael — Sport Band 4 — 770
Morse, John — Licensing Band 2 — 507
Morse, Stephen — Corporate Finance Band 3 — 218
Morshead, Ros — Litigation Band 4 — 545
Mortimer, Ken — Social Housing Band 2 — 757

Morton, David — Banking & Finance Band 4 — 102
Morton, Guy — Financial Services Band 1 — 386
Morton, Robin J M — Licensing Band 4 — 511
Mosey, David — Construction Band 4 — 177
Moss, David J — Construction Band 2 — 186
Moss, Gary — Intellectual Property Band 4 — 479
Moss, Nicholas — Partnership Band 2 — 598
Moss, Peter — Immigration Band 3 — 416
Moss, Philip G S — Tax Band 1 — 780
Most, Lionel — Real Estate Band 2 — 723
Motani, Habib — Capital Markets Band 1 — 116
Moule, Jos — Partnership Band 2 — 598
Mowat, Allan — Clinical Negligence Band 2 — 146; Healthcare Band 1 — 406
Moxon, Richard — Media & Entertainment Band 4 — 580
Moylan, Adrian — Shipping Band 5 — 741
Moyle, Andrew — Information Technology Band 5 — 428
Moyse, Richard — Trusts & Personal Tax Band 2 — 813
Mudd, Philip — Insolvency Band 1 — 451
Mullen, Chris — Pensions Band 2 — 604
Mulligan, Claire — Travel Band 3 — 805
Mullock, James — E-commerce Up and coming — 277
Mumford, Nicola — Insolvency Up and coming — 449; Litigation Band 3 — 528
Munday, Nicholas — Insurance Band 3 — 468
Munday, Peter — Corporate Finance Band 3 — 215
Munro, Rick — Insolvency Band 2 — 445
Murdie, Alastair — Trusts & Personal Tax Band 5 — 813
Murfitt, Stephen — Litigation Band 1 — 523
Murphy, Fiona — Human Rights Band 2 — 410
Murphy, Frances — Corporate Finance Band 4 — 203
Murphy, Michael — Projects/PFI Band 1 — 693
Murphy, Niall — Tax Band 1 — 780

M

INDEX ■ LEADING LAWYERS

Murphy, Robert
Asset Finance **Band 6** — 79

Murphy, Shaun
Crime **Band 3** — 251

Murphy, Tony
Human Rights **Up and coming** — 410

Murray, Andrew
Social Housing **Band 1** — 753

Murray, Christopher
Fraud **Band 1** — 393

Murray, Clare
Partnership **Band 4** — 596

Murray, David
Banking & Finance **Band 6** — 92

Murray, Duncan
Banking & Finance **Band 3** — 98

Murray, Lynne
Social Housing **Band 1** — 753

Murray, Neil
Banking & Finance **Band 5** — 92

Murray-Jones, Allan
Private Equity **Band 3** — 657

Musgrave, Tim
Clinical Negligence **Band 1** — 144

Musters, Patrick
Crime **Band 2** — 253

Myers, Andrew
Media **Up and coming** — 584

Myers, John
Family **Band 3** — 372

Myers, Miranda
Church **Band 2** — 137

Myers, Sidney A
Litigation **Band 2** — 541

Mylrea, Kathy
Environment **Band 2** — 347

N

Naccarato, J
Banking & Finance **Up and coming** — 92

Nairn, Karyl
Arbitration **Band 4** — 74

Napper, Isabel
Intellectual Property **Band 1** — 484

Nash, David
Projects/PFI **Band 2** — 693

Nash, Mike
Environment **Band 3** — 347

Naylor, Lynne
Family **Band 3** — 369

Needham, Andrew
Corporate Finance **Band 4** — 225

Neil, Don
Real Estate **Band 3** — 708

Neill, Bryan
Personal Injury **Band 3** — 619

Neill, Robert
ADR **Band 4** — 66

Nellist, Peter
Trusts & Personal Tax **Band 3** — 817

Nelson, Paul
Financial Services **Band 1** — 386

Nelson, Richard
Fraud **Band 1** — 395

Nelson-Jones, Rodney
Personal Injury **Band 1** — 617

Nesbitt, Sean
Employment **Up and coming** — 298

Neville, William
Agriculture **Band 1** — 55

Newbury, Andrew
Family **Up and coming** — 371

Newcombe, Mark
Real Estate **Band 3** — 715

Newman, Helen
Intellectual Property **Band 3** — 479

Newman, Iain
Corporate Finance **Band 4** — 208

Newman, Paul
Construction **Band 1** — 184

Newmark, Chris
ADR **Band 3** — 66

Newstead, Jackie
Real Estate **Up and coming** — 702

Newton, Alison
Real Estate **Band 3** — 723

Newton, Jeremy
Information Technology **Band 3** — 430

Nias, Peter
Tax **Band 3** — 776

Nice, Anna
Family **Up and coming** — 365

Nichol, James
Crime **Band 1** — 251
Human Rights **Band 2** — 410

Nicholas, Paul
Professional Negligence **Band 1** — 675

Nicholl, Victoria
Employee Share Schemes **Band 3** — 292

Nicholls, Simon
Crime **Band 1** — 253
Licensing **Band 2** — 508

Nicholson, Brinsley
Litigation **Band 3** — 518

Nicholson, Graham
Corporate Finance **Band 5** — 203

Nicholson, John
Family **Up and coming** — 365

Nicholson, Jonathan
Charities **Band 2** — 125
Trusts & Personal Tax **Band 2** — 817

Nicholson, Kim
E-commerce **Band 2** — 277
Information Technology **Band 5** — 428
Telecommunications **Band 4** — 792

Nicholson, Malcolm
Competition/Anti-trust **Star** — 164

Nicholson, Mark
Insolvency **Band 2** — 449

Nickson, Sue
Employment **Band 1** — 312

Nicol, Diane
Employment **Band 3** — 316

Nicol, Frazer
Family **Band 1** — 369

Nicoll, Richard
Travel **Band 3** — 807

Nicolson, Fiona
Information Technology **Band 2** — 433
Intellectual Property **Band 1** — 486

Niekirk, Malcolm
Insolvency **Band 1** — 445

Nisse, Ian
Real Estate **Band 2** — 702

Noble, Nicholas
Tax **Band 3** — 776

Noble, Perry
Projects/PFI **Band 2** — 690

Nodder, Edward
Intellectual Property **Band 2** — 479

Nolan, Brandon
Construction **Band 2** — 190

Norbury, Peter
Employment **Band 1** — 312

Norfolk, Christopher
Tax **Band 1** — 776

Norley, Lyndon
Insolvency **Up and coming** — 441

Norman, Guy T D
Corporate Finance **Band 5** — 203

Norton, Philip
Charities **Band 2** — 127

Norwood, Andrew
Tax **Band 4** — 776

Nott, Christopher
Employment **Band 4** — 308
Litigation **Band 2** — 527

Nott, Colin
Crime **Band 2** — 251

Nowlan, Howard
Tax **Band 1** — 776

Nunn, Stephen
Crime **Band 1** — 252

Nurney, Simon
Construction **Band 6** — 177

Nurse-Marsh, Isabel
Litigation **Band 3** — 543

Nurse-Marsh, Tony
Professional Negligence **Band 1** — 676

Nuttall, Graeme
Employee Share Schemes **Band 4** — 292

Nyman, Bernard
Media & Entertainment **Band 2** — 582

O

Oakley, Chris
Capital Markets **Band 2** — 114

Oats, Simon
Construction **Band 1** — 186

Obank, Richard
Insolvency **Band 3** — 451

O'Brien, Barry
Corporate Finance **Band 1** — 203

O'Brien, Christine
Employment **Band 3** — 298

O'Brien, Gary
Litigation **Band 2** — 549

O'Connell, Clive
Insurance **Band 3** — 468

O'Connor, Mark
Corporate Finance **Band 4** — 225

O'Connor, Mike
Projects/PFI **Band 1** — 692

O'Conor, John
Litigation **Band 4** — 538

O'Donnell, Caroline
Family **Band 3** — 370

O'Donovan, Hugh
Aviation **Band 1** — 85

O'Driscoll, Pat
Litigation **Band 2** — 536

O'Farrell, Vincent
Litigation **Band 2** — 550

Ogilvie, Graham
Trusts & Personal Tax **Band 5** — 813

O'Hanlon, Liam
Construction **Band 6** — 177

Ohlsson, Alex
Offshore: Corporate **Band 2** — 832

O'Keeffe, Jacqui
Environment **Band 2** — 347

Oldfield, Alison
Litigation **Up and coming** — 551

O'Leary, Marcus
E-commerce **Band 1** — 279
Information Technology **Band 1** — 430

Oliver, David
Insolvency **Band 1** — 445

Oliver, Keith
Fraud **Band 1** — 393
Litigation **Band 3** — 541

Oliver, Timothy
Personal Injury **Band 3** — 619

Olmer, Philip
Real Estate **Band 5** — 702

O'Loughlin, Philip
Litigation **Band 1** — 551

O'May, Neil
Crime **Band 2** — 251

O'Meara, Anne
Real Estate **Band 3** — 715

On, Nicholas
Banking & Finance **Band 2** — 101

O'Neill, Orlagh
Employment **Up and coming** — 318

O'Neill, Terry
Insurance **Band 2** — 468

Onslow-Cole, Julia
Immigration **Band 1** — 416

Orchison, Graeme
Intellectual Property **Band 2** — 484

O'Regan, Tim
Family **Band 2** — 370

Organ, CD
Media & Entertainment **Band 2** — 584

Orr, Alistair C
Information Technology **Band 3** — 433

Orton, Giles
Litigation **Band 1** — 543

Osborne, David
Asset Finance **Band 3** — 79

Osborne, John
Competition/Anti-trust **Band 5** — 164

Osborne, Tom
Clinical Negligence **Band 2** — 142
Personal Injury **Band 1** — 621

Osman, Chris
Employment **Band 2** — 298

1716

LEADING LAWYERS — INDEX

O'Toole, Eliza — Planning Up and coming	640
Ovenden, F Simon — Capital Markets Band 5	111
Over, Christopher — Clinical Negligence Band 3	143
Transport Band 2	798
Overs, John — Tax Band 5	776
Owen, Mark — Licensing Band 2	509
Owen, Robert — Parliamentary Band 2	593
Owen, Simon — Banking & Finance Up and coming	100

P

Padfield, Brendan — Personal Injury Band 1	625
Pagan, Bill — Trusts & Personal Tax Band 2	821
Paines, Alison — Charities Band 1	123
Paisner, Martin — Charities Band 3	123
Palca, Julia — Defamation Band 5	268
Pallett, Julian — Banking & Finance Band 1	98
Insolvency Band 1	449
Pallister, Stephen — Trusts & Personal Tax Band 2	818
Palmer, James — Corporate Finance Band 2	203
Palmer, Nigel — Media & Entertainment Band 1	580
Palmer, Simon — Construction Band 2	188
Pantelia, Despina — Social Housing Band 1	755
Papworth, Richard — Banking & Finance Band 1	100
Social Housing Band 2	755
Parford, Simon — Clinical Negligence Band 3	143
Parish, Philip — Litigation: Banking Up and coming	541
Litigation: Civil Fraud Up and coming	538
Parkash, Raj — Information Technology Band 5	428
Parker, Adrian — Healthcare Band 1	406
Parker, Alison — Personal Injury Band 3	617
Parker, Andrew — Personal Injury Band 3	619
Parker, Diana — Family Band 1	365
Parker, Raj — Insurance Band 3	466
Litigation Band 1	518
Sport Band 3	767
Parkinson, Helen — Employment Band 3	312

Parnell, Catherine — Employment Band 3	304
Parr, Nigel — Competition/Anti-trust Band 2	164
Parrington, Simon — Health & Safety Band 1	402
Parrott, Michael — Licensing Band 1	506
Parry, Richard — Family Band 2	365
Parson, Robert — Commodities Band 2	158
Parsons, Andrew — Healthcare Band 2	406
Parton, Nicholas — Shipping Band 4	741
Partridge, Malcolm — Licensing Band 1	508
Paskell, F C — Real Estate Band 3	717
Pass, Jamie — Corporate Finance Band 2	227
Pasterfield, Stephen — Planning Band 1	643
Patel, Anjan — Education Band 2	283
Paterson, Ian J C — Real Estate Band 4	723
Patience, Iain — Family Band 2	373
Paton, Andrew — ADR Star	67
Professional Negligence Band 1	677
Patrick, Bruce — Corporate Finance Band 3	229
Patrick, Hamish — Banking & Finance Band 3	102
Patterson, Anthony — Real Estate Band 5	702
Patterson, Frank — Personal Injury Band 1	625
Patterson, Lindy A — Construction Band 1	190
Pattison, Mark — Real Estate Band 3	718
Paul, Alan — Corporate Finance Band 1	203
Private Equity Band 2	657
Paul, Sarah — Real Estate Band 3	710
Pawlik, Andrew — Environment Band 2	351
Pay, Alex — Insolvency Band 3	448
Payne, Abigail — Media & Entertainment Band 4	580
Payne, Kate — Pensions Band 2	609
Payne, Peter — Family Band 3	368
Payton, Michael — Insurance: General Band 1	466
Insurance: Reinsurance Band 3	468
Peacock, Ian — Professional Negligence Band 1	677

Peak, Chris — Church Band 3	135
Pearce, John — Licensing Band 3	507
Pearl, Simon — Product Liability Band 2	665
Pears, Melanie — Travel Band 2	806
Pearson, Chris — Corporate Finance Band 4	203
Pearson, David — Corporate Finance Band 3	203
Private Equity Band 5	657
Pearson, Hilary — Information Technology Band 4	428
Pearson, Jeffrey — Corporate Finance Band 3	219
Pearson, John — Pensions Band 4	604
Pearson, Nick — Litigation: General Band 2	518
Litigation: Civil Fraud Band 4	541
Pearson, Philippa — Family Band 3	365
Peck, Andrew — Corporate Finance Band 2	203
Peerless, Bart — Trusts & Personal Tax Band 5	813
Peet, Carole — Litigation Band 2	545
Peeters, Michael — Information Technology Band 2	432
Peirce, Gareth — Crime Band 1	251
Human Rights Band 1	410
Peirce, Jacqueline — Immigration Band 3	418
Pembridge, Eileen — Family Band 4	365
Penn, Graham — Capital Markets Band 4	114
Penney, Andrew — Trusts & Personal Tax Band 5	813
Pennie, John — Insolvency Band 2	452
Pennington, John — Crime Band 3	252
Penrose, Martin — Immigration Band 3	418
Pepper, Alasdair — Defamation Band 3	268
Peppiatt, Stephen — Projects Band 5	686
Perkins, David — Intellectual Property Band 3	479
Perkins, Jonathan — Investment Funds Band 4	498
Perrott, Brian — Commodities Band 4	158
Perrott, Edward — Litigation Band 2	529
Perry, Bill — Insurance Band 3	466
Perry, Timothy — Personal Injury Band 2	624

Pescod, Peter — Personal Injury Band 1	628
Pester, David — Corporate Finance Band 2	218
Peter, Charles — Crime Band 3	254
Petheram, Claire — Pensions Band 4	604
Peto, Monica — Parliamentary Band 3	593
Pett, David — Employee Share Schemes Star	293
Pharaoh, Paul Grenville — Education Band 1	285
Pheasant, John — Competition/Anti-trust Band 4	164
Pheasant, Louise — Insolvency Band 1	449
Phelops, Warren — Sport Band 3	767
Philipps, Richard — Media & Entertainment Band 1	580
Philipps, Susan — Family Band 3	365
Phillips, Andrew — Charities Band 2	123
Phillips, Ann — Charities Band 2	123
Phillips, Hilary — Charities Band 4	123
Phillips, Jeremy — Licensing Star	506
Phillips, Mark — E-commerce Band 4	277
Phillips, Mark — Human Rights Band 1	411
Immigration Band 1	420
Phillips, Paul — Financial Services Band 4	386
Phillips, Rachel — Travel Band 2	807
Phillips, Richard — Transport Band 1	799
Phillips, Robert — Projects Band 5	686
Phillips, Robert — Corporate Finance Band 2	227
Phillips, Stephen — Banking & Finance Band 4	102
Phippard, Simon — Aviation Band 4	86
Phipps, Matthew — Licensing Band 2	506
Piatt, Andrew — Planning Band 2	646
Pickering, John — Clinical Negligence Band 1	147
Personal Injury Band 1	626
Product Liability Band 2	667
Pickering, John — Personal Injury Band 1	625
Pickston, John — Litigation Band 2	545

www.ChambersandPartners.com

1717

INDEX ■ LEADING LAWYERS

Pickup, Bryan
Real Estate **Band 4** — 702
Travel **Band 1** — 807

Pickup, Raith
Healthcare **Band 1** — 405
Projects/PFI **Band 2** — 691

Picton-Turbervill, Geoffrey
Energy: Oil & Gas **Band 2** — 336
Energy: Electricity **Band 3** — 337

Pierce, Sean
Banking & Finance **Band 3** — 92

Pigott, Ashley
Construction **Band 3** — 184

Pigott, Simon
Family **Band 2** — 365

Pike, John
Environment **Band 2** — 355
Real Estate **Band 1** — 720

Pike, Julian
Defamation **Band 5** — 268

Pike, Malcolm
Employment **Band 1** — 312

Pike, Nicholas
Insolvency **Band 5** — 441

Pillman, Joe
Corporate Finance **Band 3** — 216

Pink, Stephen
Shipping **Band 5** — 741

Pinsent, Jim
Construction **Band 3** — 186

Pinson, Mike
Offshore: Corporate **Band 3** — 832

Pintus, Matthew
Trusts & Personal Tax **Band 4** — 813

Piper, Anne-Marie
Charities **Band 1** — 123

Pitkin, Jeremy
Capital Markets **Band 3** — 111

Pittaway, Ian
Pensions **Band 2** — 604

Pizzey, Simon
Litigation **Band 1** — 525

Plant, Charles
Litigation **Band 2** — 518

Plant, Patrick
Real Estate **Band 2** — 702
Travel **Band 2** — 807

Plascow, Ronald H
Construction **Band 1** — 186

Plews, Tim
Commodities **Band 1** — 159

Plummer, Alan J
Agriculture **Band 2** — 57

Polglase, Timothy
Banking & Finance **Band 3** — 92
Private Equity **Band 2** — 659

Polito, Simon
Competition/Anti-trust **Band 1** — 164

Pollack, Craig
Litigation **Band 4** — 518

Pollard, David
Pensions **Band 1** — 604

Pollard, Stephen
Fraud **Band 1** — 393
Litigation **Band 2** — 541

Polson, Michael
Investment Funds **Band 3** — 500

Poole, Kevin
Employee Share Schemes **Band 3** — 293

Poore, Alasdair
Intellectual Property **Band 1** — 484

Pope, Caroline
Construction **Band 6** — 177

Pope, Caron
Immigration **Band 3** — 416

Poppleston, Susanna
Licensing **Band 2** — 507

Popplewell, Nigel
Tax **Band 1** — 780

Porter, Sue
Tax **Band 4** — 776

Porteus, Stephen
Personal Injury **Band 1** — 627

Portlock, Richard
Professional Negligence **Band 2** — 676

Portrait, Judith
Charities **Band 3** — 123

Postlethwaite, Robert
Employee Share Schemes **Band 4** — 292

Potter, Bruce
Insolvency **Band 3** — 446

Potter, David
Employment **Band 4** — 309

Potter, Hugh
Personal Injury **Band 2** — 625

Potter, Selina
Media **Up and coming** — 581

Potts, Andrew
Licensing **Band 2** — 507

Potts, Christopher
Commodities **Band 2** — 158

Potts, John
Litigation **Band 3** — 541

Poulter, Alan
Charities **Band 1** — 125

Pound, Toby
Agriculture **Band 3** — 57

Powell, Andrew M
Pensions **Band 4** — 604

Powell, Greg
Crime **Band 3** — 251

Powell, Mark
Family **Band 1** — 369

Powell, Nicholas R D
Trusts & Personal Tax **Band 2** — 813

Powell, Ted
Tax **Band 2** — 781

Poynton, Ian
Insurance **Band 3** — 469

Prain, David
Personal Injury **Band 2** — 623

Pratt, John
Franchising **Band 3** — 391

Preece, Andrew
Projects **Band 5** — 686
Transport **Band 4** — 799

Preiskel, Daniel
Telecommunications **Band 4** — 792

Prentice, Alexander
Crime **Band 1** — 255

Preston, Christopher
Tax: Indirect **Band 3** — 776
Tax: Corporate **Band 4** — 776

Preston, Dermot
Insolvency **Band 3** — 450

Preston, Edward
Crime **Band 2** — 251

Preston, Miles
Family **Band 1** — 365

Price, David
Defamation **Band 2** — 266

Price, Hugh
Personal Injury **Band 2** — 623

Price, Richard
Human Rights **Up and coming** — 412

Price, Richard
Intellectual Property **Band 5** — 479

Pridmore, Nigel
Capital Markets **Band 4** — 111

Prince, Michael
Corporate Finance **Band 1** — 225

Pring, Simon
Agriculture **Band 2** — 53

Prinsley, Mark
Information Technology **Band 5** — 428

Prior, Barry A
Transport **Band 3** — 798

Prior, Judith
Commodities **Band 4** — 158

Pritchard, Nicholas
Real Estate **Band 2** — 712

Proctor, Jane
Family **Band 2** — 370

Protani, Moira
Charities **Band 2** — 123

Proudler, Geraldine
Defamation **Band 1** — 268

Prowel, Martyn
Crime **Band 1** — 252
Fraud **Band 1** — 394

Pryke, Oliver
Employment **Band 3** — 310

Pryor, Nicholas
ADR **Band 1** — 66

Prytherch, Rosalie
Employment **Band 3** — 318

Psyllides, Milton
Corporate Finance **Band 1** — 220

Puddicombe, Nigel
Litigation: General **Band 1** — 525
Litigation: Real Estate **Band 3** — 548

Pugh, Chris
Energy **Band 3** — 336

Pugh, Keith
Employment **Band 4** — 313

Pugh, Tim
Planning **Band 2** — 640

Puleston Jones, Haydn
Banking & Finance **Band 1** — 92

Pullen, David
Commodities **Star** — 158

Purcell, Michael
Crime **Band 2** — 253

Pysden, Edward
Corporate Finance **Star** — 225

Pysden, Kay
Transport **Band 2** — 796

Q

Qualtrough, John
Planning **Band 4** — 640

Quarrell, John
Pensions **Band 2** — 604

Quayle, Sophie
Planning **Band 2** — 640

Quicke, Martin
Real Estate **Band 3** — 702

Quigley, Ian
Real Estate **Band 3** — 723

Quinlan, Andrew
Real Estate **Band 3** — 720

Quinn, JS
Agriculture **Band 2** — 56

Qureshi, Ashar
Capital Markets **Band 5** — 111

R

Rabinowicz, Jack
Administrative & Public Law **Band 2** — 41
Education **Band 1** — 283

Race, David
Construction **Band 5** — 177

Radcliffe, Malcolm
Licensing **Band 4** — 507

Rae, Maggie
Family **Band 2** — 365

Rae, Scott
Trusts & Personal Tax **Band 1** — 821

Rafferty, John
Corporate Finance **Band 2** — 229

Raines, Marke
Capital Markets **Band 3** — 114

Rajani, Shashi
Insolvency **Band 6** — 441

Ralph, Nick
Employment **Band 5** — 298

Ramshaw, Simon
Pensions **Band 2** — 607

Randall, Christopher
Immigration **Band 1** — 418

Randall, Helen
Local Government **Band 3** — 572

Randall, Paul
Employee Share Schemes **Band 3** — 292

Randall, Simon
Local Government **Band 2** — 572
Social Housing **Band 3** — 753

Randell, Charles
Corporate Finance **Band 3** — 203

Randle, Anthony
Projects/PFI **Band 1** — 691

Rands, Harvey
Litigation **Band 5** — 518

Rankin, Alastair
Trusts & Personal Tax **Band 1** — 822

Ransome, Clive
Projects **Band 3** — 686

Ranson, Lee
Litigation **Band 1** — 550

Raphael, Monty
Fraud **Star** — 393
Litigation **Band 3** — 541

1718

LEADING LAWYERS ■ INDEX

Rawding, Nigel
Arbitration Band 2 — 74

Rawkins, Jason
Intellectual Property Band 6 — 479

Rawle, Claire
Licensing Band 1 — 507

Rawlinson, David
Litigation Band 4 — 530

Rawlinson, Mark
Corporate Finance Band 1 — 203

Rawnsley, Rachel
Pensions Band 1 — 609

Rawstron, Chris
Corporate Finance Band 3 — 220

Ray, Peggy
Family Band 2 — 365

Rayfield, Richard
Shipping Band 3 — 745

Rayman, Alice
Advertising Up and coming — 51

Raymont, Mary
Family Band 3 — 367

Rayner, David
Environment Band 2 — 351

Read, Anthony
Projects/PFI Band 3 — 693

Readett, Helen
Insolvency Band 2 — 449

Readhead, Siobhan
Family Band 4 — 365

Rearden, Shaun
Banking & Finance Band 2 — 99

Redfern, Paul
Professional Negligence Band 2 — 677

Redman, Michael
Environment Band 4 — 347

Redmond, John
Construction Band 1 — 183

Rees, Anthony
Employment Band 2 — 308

Rees, Bleddyn
Insolvency Band 3 — 448

Rees, Chris
E-commerce Band 3 — 277
Information Technology Band 2 — 428

Rees, John
Charities Band 1 — 125
Church Band 1 — 136

Rees, Jonathan
Energy Band 3 — 336

Rees, Kate
Competition/Anti-trust Band 1 — 167

Rees, Peter
Construction Band 3 — 177

Reeve, Felicity
Sport Band 4 — 767

Reeves, Tony
Energy Band 2 — 339

Reevey, Michael
Real Estate Band 3 — 720

Regan, Michael
Construction Band 3 — 177
Professional Negligence Band 4 — 675

Reid, David
Real Estate Band 3 — 723

Reid, Fraser
Sport Band 4 — 767

Reid, Nigel
Trusts & Personal Tax Band 3 — 813

Reid, Ron
Health & Safety Band 1 — 401
Product Liability Band 2 — 669

Reid, Sandy
Real Estate Band 3 — 723

Reilly, Alan
Real Estate Band 1 — 724

Reith, David
Charities Band 3 — 129

Rendell, Simon
E-commerce Band 4 — 277
Information Technology Band 4 — 428

Renger, Mike
Energy Band 1 — 339
Environment Band 1 — 355

Rennie, Brenda
Charities Band 2 — 129

Rennie, Richard
Real Estate Up and coming — 723

Rennie, Donald G
Agriculture Band 2 — 59

Renouf, Terence
Personal Injury Band 2 — 619

Reston, Vincent
Employment Band 3 — 312

Reynell, Daniel Humphrey
Projects Band 5 — 686

Reynolds, Carmen
Financial Services Up and coming — 386

Reynolds, John
Litigation Band 2 — 518

Reynolds, Justin
Transport Band 4 — 796

Rhatigan, Michael
Social Housing Band 3 — 759

Rhodes, John
Trusts & Personal Tax Band 1 — 813

Rhys-Jones, Mark
Litigation Band 2 — 527

Riccio, Maria
Pensions Up and coming — 606

Rice, Dermot
Real Estate Band 4 — 702

Rice, Jim
Capital Markets Band 3 — 114

Rice, Paul
Environment Band 2 — 347

Rich, Andrew
Intellectual Property Band 5 — 479

Richards, Geraint
Crime Band 3 — 252

Richardson, Joe
Trusts & Personal Tax Band 5 — 813

Richbell, David
ADR Band 1 — 68

Richens, NJ
Church Band 1 — 134

Riches, John
Trusts & Personal Tax Band 3 — 813

Richomme, Jacqueline
Offshore: Corporate Band 1 — 832

Rickard, Jennifer
Litigation Band 1 — 545

Ricketts, Robert
Aviation Band 3 — 85

Ricketts, Simon
Planning Band 1 — 640

Ridgwell, Robert
Professional Negligence Band 1 — 677

Ridler, Graham
Insolvency Band 3 — 451

Ridler, Mark
Pensions Band 3 — 609

Ridley, Michael
Media & Entertainment Band 2 — 581

Rimell, Katherine
Defamation Band 5 — 268

Rimmer, John
Offshore: Corporate Band 3 — 832

Rintoul, David
Construction Band 1 — 182

Ripley, Fiona
Immigration Band 2 — 418

Ripman, Justin
Trusts & Personal Tax Band 1 — 819

Ritchie, Angela
Administrative & Public Law Band 1 — 48

Rivers, Elizabeth
ADR Band 4 — 66

Roach, Andrew
Personal Injury Band 2 — 624

Robb, Sophia
Media Up and coming — 584

Robert, Gavin
Competition/Anti-trust Band 4 — 164

Robert, Louis
Social Housing Band 1 — 753

Roberts, David
Real Estate Band 3 — 714

Roberts, David
Real Estate Band 4 — 702

Roberts, Gavin
Personal Injury Band 1 — 621

Roberts, Ian
Social Housing Band 3 — 755

Roberts, Martin
Construction Band 3 — 177

Roberts, Simon C
Banking & Finance Up and coming — 92

Roberts, Stephen
Employment Band 3 — 307

Robertson, Andrew
Social Housing Band 3 — 760

Robertson, Jonathan
Agriculture Band 2 — 59

Robertson, Nicholas
Employment Band 2 — 298

Robertson, Ranald
Information Technology Band 5 — 428

Robertson, Rhory
Defamation Band 4 — 268

Robertson, Stuart
Employment Band 4 — 313

Robinson, Clare
Litigation Band 2 — 525

Robinson, David
Trusts & Personal Tax Band 4 — 813

Robinson, Herbert
Real Estate Band 2 — 717

Robinson, Kevin
Fraud Band 3 — 393

Robinson, Michael
Litigation Band 1 — 525

Robinson, Patrick
Planning Band 2 — 640
Real Estate Band 4 — 702

Robinson, Patrick
Planning Band 1 — 643

Robinson, Stephen
Investment Funds Band 6 — 498

Robinson, Tim
Travel Band 2 — 805

Robson, Nigel R
Construction Band 3 — 188

Roche, Paddy
Licensing Band 1 — 505

Rodgers, Christopher
Agriculture Band 2 — 55

Rodgers, Hilary
Family Band 4 — 365

Roe, Mark
Construction Band 2 — 177

Roe, Sally
Construction Band 2 — 177

Roessler, Max
Litigation Band 1 — 529

Rogan, Peter
Insurance Band 1 — 468

Rogers, Anna
Pensions Band 2 — 604

Rogers, Jane
Litigation Up and coming — 548

Rogers, Nick
Personal Injury Band 1 — 620

Rogerson, Gary
Trusts & Personal Tax Band 1 — 815

Rohde, Kate
Clinical Negligence Band 3 — 140

Rolfe, Andrew
Projects/PFI Band 5 — 690

Rollason, Nicolas
Immigration Band 2 — 416

Ronaldson, Cheryl
Insurance Band 2 — 469

Roome, James
Insolvency Band 2 — 441

Rooney, Phillip
Real Estate Band 4 — 718

Rooth, Tony
Shipping Band 4 — 741

Roper, Robert
Litigation Band 2 — 530

Roscoe, James
Real Estate Band 4 — 723

Roscoe, Robert
Crime Band 3 — 251

Rose, David
Intellectual Property Up and coming — 479

Rose, Digby H
Litigation Band 2 — 528

www.ChambersandPartners.com

INDEX ■ LEADING LAWYERS

Rose, Kenneth — Corporate Finance Band 4	229
Rose, Simon — Tax Band 2	776
Rose, Stephen — Competition/Anti-trust Band 5	164
Rose, Timothy — Crime Band 1	252
Rosenberg, Daniel — Corporate Finance Band 4	208
Rosenthal, Dennis — Asset Finance Band 1	81
Roskill, Julian — Employment Band 2	298
Ross, Alexander — Insolvency Band 2	454
Ross, David — Energy Band 1	341
Ross, Hilary — Product Liability Band 1	669
Ross, Kenneth — Real Estate Band 4	723
Ross, Kenneth — Environment Band 2	356
Ross, Lex — Banking & Finance Band 2	103
Rosser, Mari — Clinical Negligence Band 2	144
Rothera, Ian — Transport Band 1	798
Rothwell, Charles — Litigation Band 4	532
Rous, Simon — Corporate Finance Band 2	218
Rout, Peter — Construction Band 3 / Projects/PFI Band 3	186 / 692
Rowe, Bernard — Personal Injury Band 1	621
Rowe, Claire — Litigation Band 1	525
Rowe, Heather — Information Technology Band 3	428
Rowe, Tim — Real Estate Band 4	715
Rowey, Kent — Energy Band 3 / Projects Band 3	337 / 686
Rowland, Simon — Construction Band 2	189
Rowlands-Hempel, Graham — Employee Share Schemes Band 3	292
Rowley, Robert — Corporate Finance Band 3	222
Rowson, Stuart — Projects/PFI Up and coming	690
Roxburgh, Bruce — Corporate Finance Band 2	218
Roxburgh, Roy — Insolvency Band 1	454
Royle, Charles — Fraud Band 2	395
Rubinstein, John — Media & Entertainment Band 3	582
Ruddiman, Robert — Energy Band 1	340
Rudin, Simeon — Capital Markets Band 3	116
Rudolf, Peter — Real Estate Band 3	702
Ruebain, David — Administrative & Public Law Band 2 / Education Band 1	41 / 283
Rundall, Francis R S — Corporate Finance Band 4	218
Rupal, Yash — Tax Band 3	776
Rushton, John Michael — Construction Band 1	177
Rushworth, Jonathan — Insolvency Band 3	441
Russ, Tim — Agriculture Band 2	55
Russell, AD — Media & Entertainment Band 1	584
Russell, George — Charities Band 1	129
Russell, Mark — Shipping Band 2	743
Russell, Patrick — Sport Band 3	767
Russell, Stuart — Corporate Finance Band 4	229
Russell, Timothy — Employment Band 5	298
Russell, Victoria E — Construction Band 3	177
Rustemeyer, Alistair — Shipping Band 2	744
Rutherford, Lyn — Family Band 1	373
Rutter, Geoffrey — Family Band 2	365
Ryan, Geraldine — Litigation Band 4	530
Ryan, Ian — Crime Band 3	251
Ryde, Andy — Corporate Finance Band 4	203
Ryden, Nick — Real Estate Band 1	723
Ryden, Peter — Charities Band 3	129
Ryland, David — Real Estate Band 1 / Travel Band 1	702 / 807
Ryland, Glyn — Pensions Band 1	607

S

Sacker, Tony — Partnership Band 2	596
Sackman, Simon — Corporate Finance Band 3	203
Sadka, Tim — Corporate Finance Band 3	215
Saeedi, Terry — Pensions Band 3	609
Saffer, Laurence — Immigration Band 3	421
Saleh, David — Tax Up and coming	776
Sales, Martin — Environment Band 4 / Planning Band 3	356 / 648
Salmon, John — E-commerce Band 1	279
Salmon, Ken — Construction Band 1	186
Salomonsen, Erik — Professional Negligence Band 1	677
Salt, Julia — Asset Finance Band 2	79
Salt, Stuart — Energy: Oil & Gas Band 1 / Energy: Electricity Band 2 / Projects: Band 1	336 / 337 / 686
Salter, David — Family Band 1	372
Salter, Ian — Environment Band 1	351
Saltissi, Sally — Tax Band 3	776
Saluja, Sean — Employment Band 2	316
Sampson, Ian — Information Technology Band 1	432
Samson, John — Real Estate Band 3	702
Samsworth, Jane — Pensions Band 2	604
Sandelson, Daniel — E-commerce Up and coming / Media & Entertainment Band 2	277 / 581
Sandelson, Jeremy — Litigation: General Band 1 / Litigation: Banking Band 2 / Litigation: Civil Fraud Band 3	518 / 538 / 541
Sanders, Andrew — Real Estate Band 3	702
Sanders, Shona — Banking & Finance Band 4	102
Sanders, Tim — Tax Band 4	776
Sanderson, Gordon — Insolvency Band 1	452
Sandilands, Keith — Asset Finance Up and coming	79
Sandison, Francis — Tax Band 2	776
Sandison, Hamish — Information Technology Band 3	428
Sasse, Sarah — Information Technology Band 2	432
Saunders, Carolyn — Pensions Band 3	604
Saunders, James — Energy Band 1	341
Saunders, James — Crime Band 2	251
Saunders, Joss — Charities Band 1	125
Saunders, Mark — Energy Band 3	336
Saunders, William — Investment Funds Band 5	498
Savill, Lisbeth — Media & Entertainment Band 2	580
Sax, Richard — Family Band 1	365
Sayer, Nick — Employment Band 1	310
Sayers, Shane — Product Liability Band 4	665
Scanlan, Margaret — Family Band 2	373
Scates, Olivia — Clinical Negligence Band 2	146
Schaffer, Daniel — Pensions Band 2	604
Schaffer, Danny — Insolvency Band 4	441
Schilling, Keith — Defamation Band 1	268
Schofield, Belinda — Insurance Band 1 / Professional Negligence Band 2	466 / 675
Scholefield, Stephen — Pensions Band 3	608
Scholes, Jeremy — Competition/Anti-trust Band 4	167
Schulz, Peter F — Banking & Finance Band 4	92
Schwartz, Peter — Insurance Band 3	468
Schwarz, Michael — Human Rights Band 3	410
Schwarz, Tim — Telecommunications Band 2	792
Schwer, Chris — Real Estate Up and coming	717
Scofield, Ian — Family Band 2	368
Scoggins, Mark — Health & Safety Band 1	400
Scorer, Tim — Aviation Band 3	86
Scott, Christopher — Banking & Finance Band 4	102
Scott, Gordon — Litigation Band 2	549
Scott, Harry — Pensions Band 1	608
Scott, Jonathan — Competition/Anti-trust Band 2	164
Scott, Martin — Construction Band 4	188
Scott, Michael — Charities Band 4	123
Scott, Peter — Real Estate Band 2	712
Scott, Peter — Environment Band 2	351
Scott, Toby — Personal Injury Band 2	628
Scott, Tom — Tax Band 5	776
Scott-Moncrieff, Lucy — Healthcare Band 1	406

LEADING LAWYERS ■ INDEX

Scoular, Gillie Employment Band 4	310
Scriven, John Energy Band 3	337
Scrivenger, Mark Clinical Negligence Band 3	145
Scully, Dermot Aviation Band 3	85
Seabrook, Michael Corporate Finance Band 4	220
Seabrook, Vicki Clinical Negligence Band 3	145
Seager, Nicola Litigation Band 3	548
Searle, Helen Media & Entertainment Band 4	584
Sears, Trevor Travel Band 2	805
Seary, Peter Corporate Finance Band 3	222
Seaton, Christopher Employment Band 2	307
Seaward, Charlie Real Estate Band 3	710
Seed, Sarah Banking & Finance One to watch	99
Segal, Nicholas A Insolvency Band 1	441
Seligman, George Insolvency Band 5	441
Seres, Jonathan Pensions Band 2	604
Serrelli, Roseanne Local Government Band 3	572
Seward, Karen Employment Band 3	298
Seymour, Michael Professional Negligence Band 4	675
Shackleton, Fiona Family Band 1	365
Shackleton, Stewart Arbitration Band 4	74
Shadbolt, Richard Construction Band 1	177
Shakespear, Felicity Family Band 1	368
Shand, Kenneth Corporate Finance Band 4	229
Shandro, Sandy Insolvency Band 2	441
Shapiro, David ADR Band 1	66
Sharkey, Lisa Licensing Band 4	507
Sharland, Andrew Media & Entertainment Band 1	584
Sharland, John Local Government Up and coming	572
Sharp, Cate Environment Band 5	347
Sharp, Roland Transport Band 4	796
Sharples, Deborah Transport Up and coming	798

Shaw, Barry Media & Entertainment Band 1	585
Shaw, Deborah Licensing Band 2	507
Shaw, Kate Administrative & Public Law Band 1	47
Local Government Band 1	576
Shaw, Martin Corporate Finance Band 2	226
Shaw, Michael Investment Funds Band 6	498
Shaw, Murray Construction Band 2	190
Insolvency Band 2	454
Shaw, Patrick Shipping Band 4	741
Shaw, Peter Construction Band 4	177
Sheach, Andrew Private Equity Band 4	657
Shearer, Roy Agriculture Band 2	59
Sheath, John Clinical Negligence Band 1	142
Healthcare Band 1	405
Shebson, Jeremy Aviation Band 4	86
Sheehan, Wendy Family Band 2	373
Sheldon, Jeremy Private Equity Band 3	661
Shelley, Daniel Pensions Band 2	607
Shelton, Erica Family Band 3	365
Shelton, John H Shipping Band 1	743
Shepherd, Claire Banking & Finance Band 3	99
Shepherd, Elizabeth Environment Band 1	354
Shepherd, Michael Environment Band 1	354
Health & Safety Band 4	402
Shepherd, Stuart Commodities Band 4	158
Sheppard, Audley W Arbitration Band 2	74
Sheppard, Claire Environment Band 4	347
Shergold, Stephen Environment Up and coming	347
Sheridan, Paul Environment Band 2	347
Sherman, Henry Construction Band 4	177
Sherrard, Harry Employment Band 1	304
Sherrington, Patrick Litigation Band 4	518
Product Liability Band 4	665
Sherwin, Nick Pensions Band 3	604
Shillito, Mark Intellectual Property Band 5	479

Shillito, Richard Defamation Band 2	268
Shimmin, Kathryn Corporate Finance Band 3	215
Shindler, Geoffrey A Trusts & Personal Tax Band 1	820
Shiner, Philip Administrative & Public Law Band 1	45
Environment Band 1	353
Shipton, Tim Investment Funds Band 1	498
Shore, Larry Arbitration Band 5	74
Short, David Personal Injury Band 1	628
Short, David Environment One to watch	347
Short, John Corporate Finance Band 1	223
Insolvency Band 1	449
Short, Michael Employment Band 1	315
Short, Stephen Banking & Finance Band 5	92
Shrimpton, Julie Family Band 3	368
Shrives, Mark Employment Band 1	313
Shurman, Daniel J Capital Markets Band 5	111
Sibbald, Graham I Media & Entertainment Band 2	586
Sibley, Edward ADR Band 3	66
Sibree, William Competition/Anti-trust Band 3	164
Signy, Adam Corporate Finance Band 2	203
Silas, Douglas Education Band 3	283
Silk, Ken Transport Band 3	796
Silva, David Real Estate Band 3	710
Silver, Raphael Family Band 2	370
Simm, Peter Immigration Band 1	421
Simmons, Michael Partnership Band 3	596
Simmons, William Corporate Finance Band 4	229
Projects/PFI Band 3	693
Simpson, Barbara Family Band 1	367
Simpson, Danny Human Rights Band 2	412
Simpson, Jane Family Band 1	365
Simpson, Mark Tax Band 1	782
Simpson, William Offshore: Corporate Band 1	831
Sinclair, Franklin Crime Band 1	254

Sinclair, Jonathan Litigation Band 1	532
Sinfield, Greg Tax Star	776
Singh, Jit Corporate Finance Band 3	222
Singh, Parmjit Real Estate Band 3	715
Singleton, Bernard Litigation Band 3	528
Singleton, Susan Information Technology Band 4	428
Sinnott, Mark Media & Entertainment Band 4	584
Sinyor, Alan Tax Up and coming	776
Sippitt, Michael Employment Band 1	306
Sisson, David Family Band 3	370
Skeens, Julian Licensing Band 3	504
Skrein, Michael Defamation Band 5	268
Litigation Band 6	518
Skuse, Ian Travel Band 3	805
Skuter, John Capital Markets One to watch	114
Slater, Richard Financial Services Band 4	386
Investment Funds Band 2	498
Slater, Richard Banking & Finance Band 3	92
Sleigh, Andrew Corporate Finance Band 3	229
Insolvency Band 2	454
Sport Band 2	770
Sleigh, Russell Litigation Band 3	518
Sless, Tania Personal Injury Band 3	619
Sloan, Derek Pensions Band 1	604
Sloan, Graeme Corporate Finance Band 3	229
Slowe, Richard Litigation Band 5	518
Small, Graham Litigation Band 4	530
Small, Harry E-commerce Band 2	277
Information Technology Band 1	428
Smart, Peter Corporate Finance Band 3	226
Smellie, David Employment Band 5	298
Smith, Antony Professional Negligence Band 3	675
Smith, Barry Media & Entertainment Band 4	580
Smith, Blaise Personal Injury Band 2	626
Smith, Bruce Planning Band 2	648

INDEX ■ LEADING LAWYERS

Smith, Campbell Corporate Finance **Band 4**	229
Smith, Caroline Family **Band 2**	373
Smith, Catriona Intellectual Property **Band 3**	479
Smith, Charles Environment **Band 1**	356
Smith, Chris Social Housing **Band 3**	753
Smith, Christian Capital Markets **Band 5**	114
Smith, Christopher Capital Markets **Band 4**	114
Smith, David Asset Finance **Band 6** Shipping **Band 2**	79 743
Smith, David Real Estate **Band 1**	723
Smith, David Immigration **Band 1**	420
Smith, David Licensing **Band 1**	505
Smith, Gillian Insolvency **Band 4**	447
Smith, Graham E-commerce **Band 1** Information Technology **Band 2**	277 428
Smith, Graham Asset Finance **Band 4**	79
Smith, Graham C H Agriculture **Band 1**	57
Smith, Hugh Litigation **Band 4** Product Liability **Band 3**	532 669
Smith, Ian Sport **Band 1**	769
Smith, Isla Tax **Band 4**	776
Smith, Janice Clinical Negligence **Band 2** Healthcare **Band 4**	141 404
Smith, Jason Sport **Band 3**	770
Smith, Mark Banking & Finance **Band 2**	100
Smith, Martin Competition/Anti-trust **Band 2**	164
Smith, Martin B Defamation **Band 1**	270
Smith, Michael Family **Band 1**	373
Smith, Michael J Shipping **Band 3**	745
Smith, Paul Environment **Star**	355
Smith, Phillip Insolvency **Band 3**	446
Smith, Quentin ADR **Band 2**	67
Smith, Robert Banking & Finance **Band 6**	92
Smith, Rod Insurance **Band 2**	466

Smith, Rosamund Charities **Band 4**	123
Smith, Sarah Capital Markets **Band 5**	114
Smith, Sarah Licensing **Band 3**	510
Smith, Shona Family **Band 3**	373
Smith, Sid Personal Injury **Band 1**	628
Smith, Stephanie Pensions **Band 3**	604
Smith, Tim Planning **Band 4**	640
Smith, Tim Employment **Band 2**	315
Smithers, Tim Energy **Band 1** Real Estate **Band 2**	338 712
Smyth, Michael Administrative & Public Law **Band 1** Defamation **Band 4**	43 268
Smyth, Richard Fraud **Band 1**	395
Smyth, Robert Real Estate **Band 3**	712
Solly, Gillian Clinical Negligence **Band 3** Personal Injury **Band 1**	143 621
Soloman, Martin Litigation **Band 2**	533
Solomon, Jonathan Real Estate **Band 2**	702
Solomon, Nicola Media & Entertainment **Band 3**	582
Somekh, Peter Insolvency **Band 4**	450
Soppitt, Alan Banking & Finance **Band 4**	102
Sorrell, Kit Litigation **Band 1**	530
Sorrell, Stephen Real Estate **Band 1**	718
Southern, Steve Pensions **Band 3**	608
Southorn, Elizabeth Licensing **Band 1**	504
Sparrow, Edward Litigation **Band 2** Litigation **Band 4**	518 538
Spearing, Nicholas Competition/Anti-trust **Band 2**	164
Speirs, Simon Real Estate **Band 3**	712
Speirs, William Employment **Band 3**	316
Speker, Barry Clinical Negligence **Band 1** Family **Band 2**	147 373
Spencer, Robin Insolvency **Band 1**	441
Spencer, Shân Insolvency **Band 3**	450
Spetch, Mike Corporate Finance **Band 3**	227

Spink, Richard Corporate Finance **Band 4**	218
Spiro, Brian Fraud **Band 2**	393
Spitz, Louise Family **Band 4**	365
Spooner, Andrew Litigation **Band 3**	528
Spring, Paul Defamation **Band 1** Litigation **Band 2** Product Liability **Band 1**	270 536 668
Stacey, Paul Energy **Band 2**	337
Stafford, Peter Corporate Finance **Up and coming**	231
Stakes, John Anthony Family **Band 2**	372
Stancombe, Michael Real Estate **Band 2**	702
Stanczyk, Julia Family **Band 4**	365
Stanfield, Glynne Corporate Finance **Band 2** Education **Band 1**	223 286
Stanford-Tuck, Michael Trusts & Personal Tax **Band 2**	813
Stanger, Michael Energy **Band 2**	336
Staniforth, Alison J Construction **Band 4**	188
Stanley, Alison Immigration **Band 1**	418
Stanley, Ed Insurance **Band 3**	468
Stannard, Paul Pensions **Band 1**	604
Staple, George Litigation **Band 2**	541
Staples, Martin Personal Injury **Band 2**	619
Stapleton, Mark Tax **Band 3**	776
Stark, Jamie Corporate Finance **Band 4**	229
Starks, Brian Partnership **Band 2**	598
Starr, Ian Intellectual Property **Band 3**	479
Steadman, Tim Construction **Band 2** Projects/PFI **Band 1**	177 690
Stedman, Graham Corporate Finance **Band 3**	208
Steel, David A Real Estate **Band 1**	723
Steel, John Agriculture **Band 1**	54
Steel, Philip Professional Negligence **Band 3**	677
Stein, Richard Administrative & Public Law **Band 1**	41
Steinberg, David Insolvency **Band 1**	441

Steiner, Michael Insolvency **Band 3**	441
Steinfeld, Michael Corporate Finance **Band 3**	208
Stella, Keith G Corporate Finance **Band 2**	208
Stephens, Hugo Local Government **Band 2** Social Housing **Band 1**	574 758
Stephens, Jonathan Agriculture **Band 2**	55
Stephens, Lindy Family **One to watch**	368
Stephens, Mark Defamation **Band 5**	268
Stephenson, Andrew Defamation **Band 3**	268
Stephenson, Barbara Corporate Finance **Band 4**	203
Stern, Robert Corporate Finance **Band 5**	203
Stevenson, David Personal Injury **Band 2**	628
Stewart, Brian J C Product Liability **Band 1**	668
Stewart, Gordon Insolvency **Band 1**	441
Stewart, James Family **Up and coming**	365
Stewart, Mark Banking & Finance **Band 2** Private Equity **Band 2**	92 659
Stewart, Peter Travel **Band 1**	805
Stewart, Suzy Banking & Finance **Up and coming**	92
Stibbard, Paul Trusts & Personal Tax **Band 3**	813
Stillwell, Kevin Partnership **Band 2**	599
Stilton, Andrew Corporate Finance **Band 2**	220
Stimpson, Maria Pensions **Up and coming**	604
Stinson, Philip Sport **Band 5**	767
Stobart, Guy Insolvency **Band 3**	447
Stoker, Robert Intellectual Property **Band 2**	484
Stone, David J Real Estate **Band 2**	720
Stone, James Agriculture **Band 1**	58
Stone, Paul Litigation **Band 2**	532
Stone, Peter Defamation **Band 2** Litigation **Band 1**	269 550
Stoneham, Michael Banking & Finance **Band 2**	102
Stones, Richard Financial Services **Band 3** Investment Funds **Band 3**	386 498

LEADING LAWYERS — INDEX

Stopford, Philip
Projects Band 4 — 686

Storar, Michael
Corporate Finance Band 2 — 212

Storer, Robert
Media & Entertainment Band 3 — 580

Stowe, Marilyn J
Family Band 2 — 372

Strachan, Dale
Real Estate Band 3 — 723

Strachan, Russell
Pensions Band 3 — 604

Strang Steel, Malcolm
Agriculture Band 1 — 59

Stratton, Richard
Tax Band 4 — 776

Street, Robert
Corporate Finance Band 3 — 225

Strivens, Peter
Telecommunications Band 2 — 792

Stubbs, Ian
Partnership Band 1 — 599
Trusts & Personal Tax Band 1 — 821

Studdert, Mark
Crime Band 3 — 251

Sturrock, David
Agriculture Band 2 — 59

Sturtivant, Karen
Immigration Band 2 — 416

Style, Christopher
Arbitration: Band 2 — 74
Litigation: General Star — 518
Litigation: Banking Band 1 — 538

Sugaré, Anthony
Crime Band 1 — 254

Sugden, Paul
Offshore: Corporate Band 3 — 832

Sullivan, Michael
Corporate Finance Band 5 — 203

Sumerling, Robert
Healthcare Band 4 — 404

Summerfield, Spencer
Corporate Finance Band 1 — 208

Sutch, Andrew
Investment Funds Band 3 — 498

Suttie, Frank
Projects/PFI Band 3 — 692

Sutton, Robert
Corporate Finance Band 4 — 203

Svensson, Zara
Crime Band 1 — 252

Swaffer, Patrick
Media & Entertainment Band 3 — 581

Swan, Charles
Advertising & Marketing Band 2 — 51

Swanney, Robert
Personal Injury Band 2 — 628

Swanson, Alayne
Litigation Band 2 — 534

Swanson, Magnus
Corporate Finance Band 1 — 229

Swanton, Vicki
Clinical Negligence Band 3 — 141

Swart, Chris
Commodities Band 5 — 158

Sweet, Jon
Corporate Finance Band 3 — 212

Sweeting, Malcom
Banking & Finance Band 1 — 92
Private Equity Band 3 — 659

Swift, Robert
Agriculture Band 2 — 55

Swinburn, Richard
Commodities Band 1 — 158

Swycher, Nigel
Information Technology Band 3 — 428
Intellectual Property Band 4 — 479

Syed, Catriona
Charities Band 4 — 123
Trusts & Personal Tax Band 3 — 813

Sykes, Annabel
Financial Services Band 2 — 386

Sykes, John
Intellectual Property Band 3 — 485

Symington, Anita
Agriculture Band 3 — 53

Syson, Keith
Corporate Finance Band 3 — 215

T

Tabakin, Roger
ADR Band 1 — 68

Tait, Fiona
Family Band 2 — 373

Tait, Nigel
Defamation Band 2 — 268

Talman, Iain
Pensions Band 1 — 610

Tata, Rustom
Employment Band 2 — 304

Tatton-Brown, Sam
Media Up and coming — 580

Taube, Martin
Crime Band 3 — 251

Tavener, Chris
Real Estate Band 5 — 702

Taylor, Alan
Corporate Finance Up and coming — 231

Taylor, Andrew
Shipping Band 3 — 741

Taylor, Andrew
Insolvency Band 1 — 445

Taylor, Anne
Pensions Band 3 — 609

Taylor, Carolyn
Crime Band 3 — 251

Taylor, Catherine
Employment Band 5 — 298

Taylor, David
Tax Band 1 — 776

Taylor, David
Real Estate Band 2 — 702

Taylor, Douglas
Environment Band 4 — 356

Taylor, Elisabeth
Professional Negligence Band 1 — 678

Taylor, Elizabeth
Insolvency Band 2 — 446

Taylor, Glyn
Corporate Finance Band 3 — 216

Taylor, Ian
Litigation: Banking Band 1 — 538
Litigation: Civil Fraud Band 2 — 541

Taylor, Isaac
Tax One to watch — 776

Taylor, James Sinclair
Charities Band 2 — 123

Taylor, Jonathan
Sport Band 2 — 767

Taylor, Kevin
Construction Up and coming — 190

Taylor, Michael
Banking & Finance Band 3 — 100

Taylor, Norman
Family Band 2 — 372

Taylor, Paul
Fraud Band 2 — 395

Taylor, Peter
Planning Band 2 — 644

Taylor, Peter D
Intellectual Property Band 5 — 479

Taylor, Philip Greig
Trusts & Personal Tax Band 3 — 820

Taylor, Silas
Shipping Band 2 — 745

Taylor, Stephen
Tax Band 5 — 776

Taylor, Tim
Litigation Band 2 — 518

Taylor, Timothy
Shipping Band 2 — 741

Teague, Gavin
Projects/PFI Band 5 — 690

Temperley, William
Licensing Band 1 — 510

Temperton, Ellen
Employment Up and coming — 298

Temple, Euan
ADR Band 3 — 67

Temple, Richard
Energy Band 2 — 337

Templeton-Knight, Jane
Projects Band 5 — 686

Tench, Dan
Defamation One to watch — 268

Tester, Stephen
ADR Band 5 — 66
Professional Negligence Band 1 — 675

Tettmar, Victor
Insolvency Band 1 — 447

Thaine, Colin
Asset Finance Band 5 — 79

Thanki, Girish
Crime Band 2 — 251

Thatcher, Michael
Education Band 2 — 282

Thomas, Alun
Employment Band 3 — 316

Thomas, David
Employment Up and coming — 307

Thomas, Keith
Clinical Negligence Band 2 — 144

Thomas, Margaret A M
Health & Safety Band 2 — 400

Thomas, Martin
Litigation Band 3 — 545

Thomas, Michelle
Corporate Finance Band 4 — 219

Thomas, Nick
Construction Band 6 — 177
Professional Negligence Band 4 — 675

Thomas, Patricia
Planning Band 1 — 640

Thomas, Richard
Advertising & Marketing Band 3 — 51
Parliamentary Band 1 — 594

Thomas, Richard
Offshore: Corporate Band 1 — 832

Thomas, Tony
Shipping Band 5 — 741
Transport Band 4 — 796

Thomas-Green, Susan
Pensions Band 3 — 609

Thompsell, Nicholas
Transport Band 3 — 799

Thompson, Alison
Social Housing Band 3 — 760

Thompson, Andrew
Media & Entertainment Band 3 — 584

Thompson, Blair
Investment Funds Up and coming — 498

Thompson, David
Personal Injury Band 2 — 627

Thompson, Kevin
Employee Share Schemes Band 4 — 292

Thompson, Mark
Personal Injury Band 1 — 621

Thompson, Michael
Employment Band 3 — 312

Thompson, Michael
Tax Band 4 — 776

Thompson, Pamela
Investment Funds Band 2 — 498

Thompson, Paul
Parliamentary Band 1 — 593

Thompson, Romaine
Charities Band 1 — 126

Thompson, Sally
Immigration Band 3 — 418

Thompson, Tony
Trusts & Personal Tax Band 4 — 813

Thompson, Tony
Employment Band 4 — 298

Thompson, Wenna
Trusts & Personal Tax Band 1 — 818

Thomson, Alan
Employment Band 3 — 316

Thomson, Chris J
Corporate Finance Band 3 — 223

Thomson, Clive
Litigation Band 1 — 523

Thomson, Keith
Capital Markets Band 3 — 111

Thomson, Mark
Defamation Band 5 — 268

Thomson, Michael
Agriculture Band 1 — 56

1723

INDEX ■ LEADING LAWYERS

Thomson, Morag Planning Band 1	644
Thorne, Clive Intellectual Property Band 4	479
Thorne, Peter Asset Finance Band 1	79
Thorne, Peter Real Estate Band 3	715
Thornely, Richard Trusts & Personal Tax Band 2	815
Thorneycroft, John Church Band 3	136
Thorneycroft, Max Corporate Finance Band 3	208
Thorneycroft, Phil Family Band 1	368
Thorp, Clive Shipping Band 3	741
Thurston, Martyn Trusts & Personal Tax Band 2	815
Thurston, Michael Fraud Band 1	395
Thurston Smith, Martin Financial Services Band 1	389
Investment Funds Band 3	500
Pensions Band 3	610
Tier, Sarah Pensions Band 3	604
Tighe, David Information Technology Band 2	430
Timmins, Jacqueline Pensions Band 2	609
Tinman, Mark Real Estate Band 2	724
Tisdall, Miles Church Band 1	135
Todd, Andrew Investment Funds Band 3	500
Tolvas-Vincent, Christina Employment Band 2	304
Tomlinson, Geoffrey Agriculture Band 2	57
Tomlinson, Kevin Crime Band 2	253
Toon, John Tax Band 2	782
Tooth, Ray Family Band 1	365
Tosh, Nial Tax Band 3	783
Tott, Nick Asset Finance Band 5	79
Projects/PFI Band 3	690
Tout, Liz Litigation Band 5	518
Towers, Lennox Asset Finance Band 2	81
Towner, Chris Energy One to watch	337
Townsend, Matthew Environment Band 5	347
Townsend, Peter Tax Band 3	782
Tozer, Roy Product Liability Band 3	669

Tranter, Ian Employment Band 3	312
Trapp, Deirdre Competition/Anti-trust Band 1	164
Trask, Michael Tax Band 5	776
Travers, Harry Fraud Band 1	393
Travers, Iain Litigation Band 2	545
Trayhurn, Neil Professional Negligence Band 1	676
Tredgett, Richard P Capital Markets Up and coming	116
Tregear, Steven Media & Entertainment Band 3	584
Trehearne, Ian Planning Band 2	640
Tremaine, Robin Employee Share Schemes Band 2	292
Triggs, Jeff Partnership Band 1	596
Trinick, Marcus Energy Band 1	338
Environment Band 1	351
Planning Band 1	642
Trott, David Capital Markets Band 2	114
Trott, Philip Immigration Band 2	416
Trotter, Andrew Corporate Finance Band 1	215
Trotter, John Litigation Band 4	518
Professional Negligence Band 3	675
Trotter, John Administrative & Public Law Band 3	41
Trotter, Peter Employee Share Schemes Band 1	293
Pensions Band 2	610
Troup, Edward Tax Band 3	776
True, Justin Planning Band 4	640
Truex, David Family Band 3	365
Tsiattalou, Bambos Crime Band 3	251
Tucker, Andrew Personal Injury Band 1	626
Product Liability Band 1	667
Tucker, John C Banking & Finance Band 2	92
Tucker, Julian A Capital Markets Band 3	114
Tudway, Robert Energy Band 3	337
Tuffnell, Kevin Private Equity Band 4	657
Tugwell, Andrew Litigation Band 4	545
Tulley, Christopher Intellectual Property Band 2	485
Tunnard, Chris Church Band 3	137

Turcan, Robert Agriculture Band 3	59
Turing, Dermot Commodities Band 3	159
Turley, Brendan Employee Share Sch Up and coming	293
Turnbull, Andrew Pensions Band 2	609
Turnbull, Craig Construction Band 3	190
Turnbull, John Litigation: General Band 3	518
Litigation: Banking Band 4	538
Turnbull, Robert Corporate Finance Band 4	225
Turner, Catrin Intellectual Property Band 6	479
Turner, Graham Social Housing Band 2	759
Turner, John Environment Band 1	353
Turner, Mark E-commerce Band 4	277
Information Technology Band 3	428
Turner, Paul Commodities Band 2	158
Turner, Paul Shipping Band 2	743
Turnor, Richard Partnership Band 1	596
Trusts & Personal Tax Band 3	813
Turpin, Philip Immigration Band 1	419
Turtle, Brian Employment Band 3	318
Litigation Band 1	536
Professional Negligence Band 1	679
Turtle, Trevor Energy Band 1	337
Turton, Julian Media & Entertainment Band 2	584
Tweed, Paul Defamation Band 1	270
Personal Injury Band 1	630
Tweedie, Colin Employment Band 3	313
Twemlow, Tony Insolvency Band 4	450
Partnership Band 1	598
Twentyman, Jeff Corporate Finance Band 4	203
Twineham, Andrew Employment Up and coming	315
Tyler, Alfred Clinical Negligence Band 1	148
Litigation Band 3	534
Personal Injury Band 1	628
Tyler, Hilary A G Church Band 2	135
Tyler, Mark Health & Safety Band 1	400
Product Liability Band 3	665
Tyndall, Timothy Employment Band 3	310
Tyrell, Vivien Insolvency Band 3	441

U

Underhill, William Corporate Finance Band 1	203
Underwood, Kerry Employment Band 2	306
Upton, Neil Energy Band 1	339
Usher, Tom Competition/Anti-trust Band 5	164

V

Valentine, Richard Planning Band 1	643
Vallance, Philip Environment Band 4	347
Vallance, Richard Clinical Negligence Band 1	140
Vanderplank, Richard Offshore: Corporate Band 2	832
Vasey, John Construction Band 2	183
Vaswani, Mona Litigation Up and coming	541
Vaughan, David Corporate Finance Band 3	220
Vaughan, Philip Banking & Finance Band 1	97
Insolvency Band 1	448
Vaughan, Philip Litigation Band 5	518
Venters, June Crime Band 3	251
Vernon, Philip Projects/PFI Up and coming	690
Verrill, John Energy Band 4	336
Insolvency Band 3	441
Vick, Laurence Clinical Negligence Band 3	143
Vickers, Cathryn Projects/PFI Band 3	691
Vickers, Mark Banking & Finance Band 3	92
Private Equity Band 2	659
Vinter, Graham Projects Band 1	686
Vivian, Jon Real Estate Band 3	702
Vlasto, Tony Shipping Band 1	741
Vleck, Karena Sport Band 2	767
Voge, Julian Franchising Band 4	391
Voisey, Peter G Capital Markets Band 3	114
Voisin, Maria Clinical Negligence Band 3	143
Voisin, Michael Capital Markets Band 5	114
von Bismarck, Nilufer Corporate Finance Band 5	203
Voremberg, Rhoderick Trusts & Personal Tax Band 3	817

LEADING LAWYERS ■ INDEX

Vos, Robin
Trusts & Personal Tax Band 4 — 813

W

Wade-Smith, Richard
Planning Band 2 — 646

Waghorn, Mark
Banking & Finance Band 6 — 92

Wagland, Nigel
Shipping Band 5 — 741

Waine, Ian
Corporate Finance Band 3 — 223
Insolvency Band 1 — 449

Waite, Andrew
Environment Band 2 — 347

Wake, Brian
Energy Band 1 — 339
Environment Band 2 — 354

Wakeford, Carol
Litigation Band 1 — 547

Waldie, Roderick
Real Estate Band 5 — 718

Walker, Alan
Litigation Band 2 — 550

Walker, Andrew
Litigation Band 3 — 545

Walker, David James
Employment Band 3 — 316

Walker, Deirdre
Litigation Band 3 — 541

Walker, Gary
Banking & Finance Up and coming — 98

Walker, Ian
Personal Injury Band 2 — 617

Walker, John
Capital Markets Band 5 — 114

Walker, Mark
Energy Band 3 — 337

Walkey, Justin
Sport Band 2 — 767

Walkling, Kim
Asset Finance Band 4 — 79

Wallace, Alastair
Administrative & Public Law Band 2 — 45

Wallace, Patrick
Energy Band 3 — 337

Waller, Simon
Insolvency Band 3 — 450

Walley, Ray
Trusts & Personal Tax Band 2 — 815

Wallis, Guy
Real Estate Band 4 — 718

Wallis, Robert
Shipping Band 4 — 741

Walls, Alan
Litigation Band 2 — 541

Walser, Nicholas
Commodities Band 5 — 158

Walsh, Brian
Charities Band 4 — 123

Walsh, Christopher
Trusts & Personal Tax Band 5 — 813

Walsh, Jeremy
Insolvency Band 4 — 441

Walsh, Jonathan
Capital Markets Band 5 — 114

Walsh, Paul
Intellectual Property Band 2 — 479

Walsom, Roger
Investment Funds Band 4 — 498

Walters, Kathryn
Banking & Finance Up and coming — 100

Waltham, Anne
Litigation Band 2 — 545

Walton, Miles
Tax Band 3 — 776

Ward, Anthony
Banking & Finance Band 4 — 92
Private Equity Band 1 — 659

Ward, Conor
Information Technology Band 2 — 428

Ward, Dominic
Transport Band 3 — 796

Ward, Helen
Family Band 1 — 365

Ward, Ian
Real Estate Band 2 — 721

Ward, John
Professional Negligence Band 2 — 675

Ward, Michael
Corporate Finance Band 4 — 220

Ward, Nigel
Banking & Finance Band 4 — 92
Private Equity Band 3 — 659

Ward, Trevor
Clinical Negligence Band 3 — 146

Ware, Anne
Product Liability Band 2 — 665

Ware, James
Media & Entertainment Band 4 — 584

Warna-kula-suriya, Sanjev
Capital Markets Band 2 — 116

Warne, David
Litigation Band 3 — 538

Warne, Jonathan
Litigation Band 3 — 543

Warne, Penelope
Energy Band 1 — 340

Warnock, Owen
Employment Band 1 — 310
Product Liability Band 3 — 669

Warren, Jennifer
Charities Band 1 — 127
Real Estate Band 3 — 717

Warren, Martin
Employment Band 1 — 308

Warriner, Neil
Tax Band 2 — 776

Warwick, Neil
Competition/Anti-trust Band 3 — 167

Watchman, Paul
Environment Band 1 — 347

Watkins, David
Planning Band 4 — 640

Watkins, David
Real Estate Band 3 — 714

Watkins, Gareth
Health & Safety Band 1 — 402

Watkins, Maurice
Sport Star — 770

Watling, John
Shipping Band 6 — 741

Watson, Adrian
Real Estate Band 2 — 715

Watson, Andrew
Clinical Negligence Band 1 — 142

Watson, Chris
Telecommunications Band 2 — 792

Watson, Gary
Real Estate Band 3 — 702

Watson, John
Tax Band 2 — 776

Watson, Judith
Employment Band 2 — 312

Watson, Martin
Shipping Band 2 — 743

Watson, Michael
Banking & Finance Up and coming — 102
Projects/PFI Up and coming — 693

Watson, Peter
Administrative & Public Law Band 3 — 43
Litigation: Banking Band 2 — 538
Litigation: General Band 3 — 518

Watson, Peter
Defamation Band 1 — 270
Litigation Band 3 — 534
Media & Entertainment Band 2 — 586

Watson, Sean
Corporate Finance Band 2 — 208

Watson, Simon
Employment Band 3 — 298

Watters, James
Asset Finance Band 4 — 79

Watterson, Mark
Investment Funds Band 4 — 498

Wattie, Ian
Real Estate Band 2 — 723

Watts, Alan
Sport Band 5 — 767

Watts, Clive
Corporate Finance Band 5 — 218

Watts, Sylvie
Employee Share Schemes Band 4 — 292

Way, Philip
Family Band 2 — 372

Wayte, Peter
Corporate Finance Band 3 — 208

Weatherburn, David
Clinical Negligence Band 1 — 148

Webb, David John
Immigration Band 4 — 416

Webb, Sarah
Defamation Band 5 — 268

Webb, Tim
Real Estate Band 2 — 715

Webber, Lesley
Litigation Band 2 — 545

Weber, David
Projects Band 5 — 686

Webster, John
Personal Injury Band 1 — 621

Webster, Michael
Information Technology Band 4 — 428

Webster, Sheila
Litigation Band 2 — 551

Wedderburn-Day, Roger
Capital Markets Band 3 — 111

Wegenek, Robert
Advertising & Marketing Band 4 — 51

Weightman, Anita
Real Estate Band 3 — 718

Weil, Simon
Charities Band 4 — 123

Weitzman, Polly
Competition/Anti-trust Band 3 — 164

Wellman, Derek
Church Band 2 — 136

Wells, Boyan
Capital Markets Band 1 — 111

Wells, Harriet
Licensing Band 2 — 508

Wells, Martin
Planning Band 4 — 640

Welsh, John
Construction Band 3 — 190
Professional Negligence Band 1 — 679

Wentzel, Peter
Offshore: Corporate Band 3 — 832

West, David E
Corporate Finance Band 3 — 222

West, Nick
Media & Entertainment Band 3 — 581

West, Robert
Pensions Band 1 — 604

Western, Mark
Asset Finance Band 6 — 79

Westhead, Tim
Real Estate Band 4 — 702

Westmacott, Philip
Information Technology Band 3 — 428

Weston, John
Shipping Band 1 — 745
Transport Band 4 — 796

Wetherfield, Alison
Employment Up and coming — 298

Whaite, Robin
Intellectual Property Band 4 — 479

Whatnall, John
Banking & Finance Band 1 — 99
Corporate Finance Band 3 — 225

Wheadon, Tom
Telecommunications Band 2 — 792

Wheatley, Jamie
Insolvency Band 1 — 449

Wheeler, Richard
Church Band 3 — 135

Whincup, David
Employment Band 3 — 298

Whish, Richard
Competition/Anti-trust Star — 164

Whitaker, Neil
Energy Band 1 — 339

White, Andrew
Pensions Band 2 — 604

White, Bruce
Projects/PFI Star — 690

White, Denis
Family Band 3 — 370

INDEX ■ LEADING LAWYERS

White, Geoffrey	Asset Finance Band 1	79
White, Giles	Banking & Finance Band 4	92
White, Graham	Real Estate Band 2	702
White, Graham	Private Equity Band 3	657
White, Iain	Family Band 3	370
White, John	Insolvency Band 2	441
White, Martin	Administrative & Public Law Band 2	45
	Planning Band 1	644
White, Neil	Construction Band 5	177
White, Peter	Church Band 1	135
White, Rowan	Real Estate Band 3	724
White, Stephen	Real Estate Band 4	718
White, Stuart	Professional Negligence Band 3	675
Whiteford, Michael G	Transport Band 1	798
Whitehead, Andrew	Energy Band 1	339
Whitehead, Peter	Personal Injury Band 2	626
Whitehouse, Michael	Transport Band 4	799
Whitemore, Sarah	Employment Band 2	304
Whitewright, Louise	Employee Share Schemes Band 3	292
Whitfield, Ann	Trusts & Personal Tax Band 4	813
Whitfield, Stuart	Projects/PFI Band 2	691
Whittell, Mark	Litigation Band 3	530
Whitty, Oonagh	Tax Band 4	776
Whur, Paddy	Licensing Band 3	507
Whybrow, Annette	Corporate Finance Band 3	223
Wicks, Roger	Clinical Negligence Band 2	145
Wignall, Douglas	Travel Band 3	807
Wilbraham, Peter	Planning Band 1	646
Wilcock, Christopher	Construction Band 3	184
Wild, David	Corporate Finance Band 3	222
Wilder, Gay	Healthcare Band 4	404
Wildish, Nigel	Information Technology Band 4	428
Wilford, Nick	Real Estate Band 3	720
Wilkes, Chris	Product Liability Band 5	665
Wilkin, Ashley	Trusts & Personal Tax Band 1	816
Wilkins, Beth	Family Band 1	371
Wilkins, Patricia	Education Band 2	283
Wilkinson, Andrew	Insolvency Band 2	441
	Insolvency Band 3	441
Wilkinson, Charles	Investment Funds Band 6	498
Will, James	Corporate Finance Band 2	229
Willcox, David	Aviation Band 3	86
Willetts, Jayne	Litigation Band 4	528
Williams, Alan	E-commerce Band 4	277
	Media & Entertainment Band 1	582
Williams, Alun C	Personal Injury Band 2	628
Williams, Audrey	Employment Band 2	308
Williams, Charles	Commodities Band 5	158
Williams, Christine	Corporate Finance Band 2	212
	Partnership Band 2	596
Williams, Elaine	Family Band 4	365
Williams, Frances	Family Band 1	369
Williams, Gail	Family Band 3	369
Williams, Gareth	Litigation Band 2	527
	Personal Injury Band 1	623
Williams, Gordon	Media & Entertainment Band 4	584
Williams, Huw	Administrative & Public Law Band 1	45
	Local Government Band 2	574
	Planning Band 1	644
Williams, Ian	Crime Band 3	252
	Family Band 2	369
Williams, Jane R	Family Band 1	369
Williams, M H	Real Estate Band 2	714
Williams, Nigel	Corporate Finance Band 3	227
Williams, Paul	Shipping Band 5	741
Williams, Peter Rhys	Agriculture Band 1	55
Williams, Rhys	Telecommunications Band 3	792
Williams, Robin	Personal Injury Band 1	622
Williams, Sian	Trusts & Personal Tax Band 3	818
Williams, Sian	Crime Band 3	251
Williamson, Andrew	Planning Band 2	646
Williamson, David	Litigation Band 1	534
	Professional Negligence Band 2	679
Williamson, Raymond	Employment Band 1	316
Willis, David	Trusts & Personal Tax Band 2	813
Willis, John-George	Corporate Finance Band 4	231
Willis, Tony	ADR Star	66
Willis-Stewart, Marcia	Human Rights Band 3	410
Willoughby, Tony	Intellectual Property Band 1	479
Willson, Stephen	Real Estate Band 3	702
Wilson, Alistair	Real Estate Band 4	723
Wilson, Allan	Litigation Band 2	527
Wilson, Bruce	Family Band 1	370
Wilson, Dave	Banking & Finance Band 6	92
Wilson, James	Shipping Band 2	741
Wilson, Keith	Asset Finance Band 6	79
Wilson, Mark	Fraud Band 1	395
Wilson, Michael	Professional Negligence Band 4	675
Wilson, Michael	Insolvency Band 3	454
	Litigation Band 1	536
	Product Liability Band 1	668
Wilson, Robert	Shipping Band 3	741
Wilson, Robin	Licensing Band 3	507
Wilson, Scott	Banking & Finance Band 3	102
Wilson, Timothy	Personal Injury Band 3	619
Wiltshire, Peter	Banking & Finance Band 3	96
	Insolvency Band 3	447
Winkworth-Smith, John	ADR Band 2	67
Winrow, Janet	Social Housing Band 3	759
Winter, Glenn	Shipping Band 1	741
Winter, Hilary	Corporate Finance Band 4	208
Winter, Jeremy	Arbitration Band 4	74
	Construction Band 3	177
Winter, Paul	Planning Band 1	646
Winterburn, Anthony	Litigation Band 2	530
Winton, Ashley	E-commerce Band 1	279
Winyard, Anne	Clinical Negligence Band 1	140
Wippell, Mark	Corporate Finance Band 4	203
Wiseman, Andrew	Environment Band 3	347
Wisking, Stephen	Competition Up and coming	164
Wistow, Michael John	Tax Band 4	776
Wistrich, Harriet	Human Rights Band 3	410
Withyman, Tom	Insolvency Up and coming	441
Woffenden, Sara	Employment Band 3	309
Wollen, Nigel	Trusts & Personal Tax Band 2	817
Womersley, Mark	Employee Share Schemes Band 3	293
	Pensions Band 2	606
Wong, Etienne	Tax Band 1	776
Wood, Alan	Intellectual Property Band 2	482
Wood, Bruce	Asset Finance Band 1	80
Wood, Charles	Energy Band 1	336
Wood, David	Health & Safety Band 3	401
	Planning Band 2	643
Wood, Ian	Intellectual Property Band 6	479
Wood, Jonathan	Litigation Band 6	518
Wood, Martin	Construction Band 1	186
Wood, Michael	Personal Injury Band 2	629
Woodcock, Tony	Litigation Band 3	541
Woodgate, Neil	Tax Band 5	776
Woodhall, John	Capital Markets Band 3	114
Woodhouse, Sarah	Immigration Band 2	418
Woodrow, Cameron	Projects/PFI Band 3	691
Woods, Andrew	Licensing Band 1	510
Woods, Paul	Family Band 2	368
Woods, Philip	Intellectual Property Band 1	484
Woodward, David	Family Band 1	368
Woodward, Mark	Charities Band 1	125

W

1726

LEADING LAWYERS ■ INDEX

Woolcock, Brian
Banking & Finance **Band 2** 98

Woolf, Fiona
Energy **Band 1** 337

Woolf, Geoffrey
Insolvency **Band 5** 441

Woolfall, Andrew
Transport **Band 4** 798

Woolich, Richard
Tax **Band 2** 776

Woolley, Linda
Fraud **Band 3** 393

Woolley, Simon
Banking & Finance **Star** 99

Wootton, David
Corporate Finance **Band 3** 203

Wormald, Chris
Franchising **Band 4** 391

Worrall, Simon
Real Estate **Up and coming** 718

Worthy, John
Information Technology **Band 5** 428

Worwood, Lucy
Trusts & Personal Tax **One to watch** 818

Wotton, John
Competition/Anti-trust **Band 4** 164

Wright, Barbara
Family **Band 2** 367

Wright, Cherry
Trusts & Personal Tax **Band 2** 818

Wright, David
Pensions **Band 1** 608

Wright, David
Real Estate **Band 2** 702

Wright, John
Construction **Band 5** 177

Wright, Nicholas
Partnership **Band 4** 596

Wright, Sean
Corporate Finance **Band 2** 215

Wrighton, Ralph
Construction **Band 1** 189

Wrigley, Matthew
Charities **Band 2** 128
Trusts & Personal Tax **Band 1** 820

Wrigley, Richard
Corporate Finance **Band 4** 220

Wurzal, Jason
Banking & Finance **Up and coming** 100

Wyld, Charles
Charities **Band 2** 125
Trusts & Personal Tax **Band 1** 817

Wyles, David
Projects/PFI **Up and coming** 690

Wylie, Amanda
Transport **Band 5** 798

Wyllie, Gordon
Charities **Band 2** 129

Wyman, Chris
Projects **Band 4** 686

Wyman, Michael
Pensions **Band 4** 604

Wyn Davies, Cerys
Intellectual Property **Band 2** 483

Wynn-Evans, Charles
Employment **Band 2** 298

Y

Yates, Andrew
Real Estate **Band 4** 715

Yates, John
Information Technology **Band 1** 432

Yates, Tracy
Employment **Band 4** 310

Yeaman, Anthony
Healthcare **Band 1** 405

York, Stephen
Arbitration **Band 5** 74
Litigation **Band 3** 518

Yorke, Jon
Insolvency **Band 2** 441

Young, Andrew
Trusts & Personal Tax **Band 5** 813

Young, David
Agriculture **Band 1** 57

Young, David A
Licensing **Band 4** 507
Product Liability **Band 1** 669

Young, Ian
Family **Band 2** 370

Young, Jim
Employment **Band 3** 316

Young, John
Insurance **Band 1** 469

Young, Magi
Clinical Negligence **Band 2** 143

Younghusband, Victoria
Investment Funds **Band 6** 498

Younson, Fraser
Employment **Band 1** 298

Yule, Ian
Construction **Band 3** 184

Z

Zeffman, David
Media & Entertainment **Band 1** 581
Sport **Band 4** 767

Zindani, Jeffry
Personal Injury **Band 2** 623